THE
Mennonite Encyclopedia

A Comprehensive Reference Work
on the
Anabaptist-Mennonite Movement

VOLUME IV

O–Z

Supplement

Mennonite Publishing House, Scottdale, Pennsylvania
Mennonite Publication Office, Newton, Kansas
Mennonite Brethren Publishing House, Hillsboro, Kansas

1959

EDITORIAL COUNCIL

PREFACE

It is in place to say a few words now that the fourth volume of the corrected reprint edition of the *Mennonite Encyclopedia*, begun in 1969, is being submitted to the publishers. When the editors and publishers, at the end of World War II, projected a four-volume encyclopedia they found a wealth of information and inspiration in the *Mennonitisches Lexikon* and its editors. Two volumes had appeared prior to World War II. The two remaining volumes of the *Lexikon* were completed by 1969. The American *Mennonite Encyclopedia* begun in 1955 was completed in 1959. The editors of the last volume of the *Lexikon* benefited from the use of the completed *Encyclopedia*. There was always a close cooperation between the editors of the two encyclopedias in the exchange of information and materials.

It must be said, however, that the two encyclopedias devoted to the same subject matter differ not only in language and publishers and editors but also in scope, approach, and content. The scholar and interested layman will often benefit by consulting both. At the end of the *Encyclopedia* articles frequent references are made to the same or related articles in the *Lexikon (ML)*.

The editors of the completed reprint edition of the *Mennonite Encyclopedia* gratefully acknowledge the help generously offered in regard to factual and typographical errors submitted by many readers. All have been absorbed as far as the limitations of a reprint permitted. Major additions and changes will be possible in the projected revised new edition. The editors have been charged with the responsibility of making plans for the revision of the *Encyclopedia*. Suggestions are solicited in regard to new articles that should be included, articles that should be enlarged or revised, and typographical and factual errors regardless of how insignificant they may appear to be.

Melvin Gingerich
Goshen College
Goshen, Indiana 46526

Cornelius Krahn
Bethel College
North Newton, Kansas 67117

KEY TO SYMBOLS AND ABBREVIATIONS

A. Symbols Used for the North American Mennonite Bodies

Church of God in Christ, Mennonite	(CGC)	Krimmer Mennonite Brethren	(KMB)
Conservative (Amish) Mennonite	(CAM)	Mennonite Brethren Church	(MB)
Evangelical Mennonite Brethren	(EMB)	Mennonite Brethren in Christ	(MBC)
Evangelical Mennonite Church	(EMC)	Mennonite Church	(MC)
Evangelical Mennonite Church (Kleine		Old Order Amish Mennonite Church	(OOA)
Gemeinde)	(EMC, KG)	Old Order Mennonite Church	(OOM)
General Conference Mennonite		United Missionary Church	(UMC)
Church	(GCM)		

B. Geographical Abbreviations

States of the United States of America

Cal.	California	N.D.	North Dakota
Col.	Colorado	N.Y.	New York
Ill.	Illinois	Okla.	Oklahoma
Ind.	Indiana	Ore.	Oregon
Kan.	Kansas	Pa.	Pennsylvania
Minn.	Minnesota	S.D.	South Dakota
Mo.	Missouri	Va.	Virginia
Neb.	Nebraska		

Countries

Can.	Canada
Ger.	Germany
Neth.	Netherlands
Par.	Paraguay
P.R.	Puerto Rico
Sw.	Switzerland
U.S.	United States

Provinces of Canada

Alta.	Alberta
B.C.	British Columbia
Man.	Manitoba
Ont.	Ontario
Sask.	Saskatchewan

Other

Co.	County
N.A.	North America
Twp.	Township

C. Bibliographical Symbols

ADB *Allgemeine Deutsche Biographie* 56v. (Leipzig, 1875-1912)

Beck, Geschichts-Bücher Josef Beck, *Die Geschichts-Bücher der Wiedertäufer in Oesterreich-Ungarn* (Vienna, 1883)

Bender, Two Centuries H. S. Bender, *Two Centuries of American Mennonite Literature, A Bibliography of Mennonitica Americana 1727-1928* (Goshen, 1929)

Bibliographie des Martyrologes F. Vander Haeghen, Th. Arnold, and R. Vanden Berghe, *Bibliographie des Martyrologes Protestants Néerlandais. II. Receuils* (The Hague, 1890)

Biogr. Wb. H. Visscher and L. A. van Langeraad, *Biographisch Woordenboek van Protestantsche Godgeleerden in Nederland,* A-L (I, Utrecht), later by J. P. de Bie and J. Loosjes (II, III, IV, V, and installment #29, The Hague) 1903-

Blaupot t. C., Friesland Steven Blaupot ten Cate, *Geschiedenis der Doopsgezinden in Friesland* (Leeuwarden, 1839)

Blaupot t. C., Groningen . . . *Groningen, Overijssel en Oost-Friesland,* 2v. (Leeuwarden, 1842)

Blaupot t. C., Holland . . . *Holland, Zeeland, Utrecht en Gelderland,* 2v. (Amsterdam, 1847)

BRN S. Cramer and F. Pijper, *Bibliotheca Reformatoria Neerlandica,* 10v. (The Hague, 1903-14)

Catalogus Amst. *Catalogus der werken over de Doopsgezinden en hunne geschiedenis aanwezig in de bibliothuek der Vereenigde Doopsgezinde Gemeente te Amsterdam* (Amst., 1919)

DB *Doopsgezinde Bijdragen* (Amsterdam, 1861-1919)

DJ *Doopsgezind Jaarboekje* vv. 1-48 (Assen, et al., 1901-43, 1949-)

Dirks, Statistik Heinrich Dirks, *Statistik der Mennonitengemeinden in Russland Ende 1905 (Anhang zum Mennonitischen Jahrbuche 1904/05). Gesammelt von Heinrich Dirks, Prediger der Gnadenfelder Gemeinde* (Gnadenfeld, 1906).

Friesen, Brüderschaft P. M. Friesen, *Die Alt-Evangelische Mennonitische Brüderschaft in Russland (1789-1910) im Rahmen der mennonitischen Gesamtgeschichte* (Halbstadt, 1911)

Gbl. *Gemeindeblatt der Mennoniten* vv. 1-85 (Sinsheim, later Karlsruhe, 1870-)

Gem.-Kal. *Mennonitischer Gemeinde-Kalender* (formerly *Christlicher Gemeinde-Kalender*) (various places, chiefly Kaiserslautern, Weierhof, Karlsruhe, 1892-)

Gesch.-Bl. *Mennonitische Geschichtsblätter. Herausgegeben vom Mennonitischen Geschichtsverein* (Frankfurt, later Karlsruhe, 1936-40, 1951-)

Grosheide, Bijdrage Greta Grosheide, *Bijdrage tot de geschiedenis der Anabaptisten in Amsterdam* (Hilversum, 1938)

Grosheide, Verhooren . . . *Verhooren en Vonissen der Wederdoopers, betrokken bij de aanslagen op Amsterdam in 1534 en 1535,* in *Bijdragen en Mededeelingen van het Historisch Genootschap,* Vol. XLI (Amsterdam, 1920)

HRE Herzog-Hauck, *Realencyclopädie für Protestantische Theologie und Kirche,* 24v. (3.ed., Leipzig, 1896-1913)

Inv. Arch. Amst. J. G. de Hoop Scheffer, *Inventaris der Archiefstukken berustende bij de Vereenigde Doopsgezinde Gemeente te Amsterdam,* 2v. (Amsterdam, 1883-84)

Kühler, Geschiedenis I W. J. Kühler, *Geschiedenis der Nederlandsche Doopsgezinden in de Zestiende Eeuw* (Haarlem, 1932)

Kühler, Geschiedenis II,1 *Idem, Geschiedenis van de Doopsgezinden in Nederland II. 1600-1735 Eerste Helft* (Haarlem, 1940)

Kühler, Geschiedenis II,2 *Idem, Geschiedenis van de Doopsgezinden in Nederland: Gemeentelijk Leven 1650-1735* (Haarlem, 1950)

Lietboecxken *Een Lietboecxken, tracterende van den Offer des Heeren,* contained in *Het Offer des Heeren* (see *Offer*)

Loserth, Anabaptismus Johann Loserth, *Der Anabaptismus in Tirol* (Vienna, 1892)

Loserth, Communismus *Idem, Der Communismus der mährischen Wiedertäufer im 16. und 17. Jahrhundert: Beiträge zu ihrer Lehre, Geschichte und Verfassung (Archiv für österreichische Geschichte,* Vol. LXXXI, 1, 1895)

Mart. Mir. D(utch) Tileman Jansz van Braght, *Het Bloedigh Tooneel of Martelaers Spiegel der Doops-gesinde of Weereloose Christenen, Die om 't getuygenis van Jesus haren Salighmaker geleden hebben ende gedood zijn van Christi tijd af tot desen tijd toe. Den Tweeden Druk* (Amsterdam, 1685), Part II

Mart. Mir. E(nglish) *Idem, The Bloody Theatre or Martyrs' Mirror of the Defenseless Christians Who Baptized Only upon Confession of Faith and Who Suffered and Died for the Testimony of Jesus Their Saviour . . . to the Year A.D. 1660* (Scottdale, Pa., 1951)

ME *Mennonite Encyclopedia* (I, 1955; II, 1956; III, 1957; IV, 1959)

Mellink, Wederdopers A. F. Mellink, *De Wederdopers in de noordelijke Nederlanden 1531-1544* (Groningen, 1954)

Menn. Bl. *Mennonitische Blätter* vv. 1-88 (1854-1941), published variously at Danzig, Hamburg-Altona, and Elbing (W. Prussia)

MHB *Mennonite Historical Bulletin* (Scottdale, Pa.; 1940-)

Menn. Life *Mennonite Life* (North Newton, Kan., 1946-)

ML Christian Hege and Christian Neff, *Mennonitisches Lexikon,* 3v., A-R (Frankfurt and Weierhof, I, 1913; II, 1937; III, #31-36, 1938-42; #37-42 at Karlsruhe, 1951-58) *et seq.*

Menno Simons, Opera *Opera Omnia Theologica, of alle de Godtgeleerde wercken van Menno Simons* (Amsterdam, 1681)

Menno Simons, Writings *The Complete Writings of Menno Simons c. 1496-1561. Translated from the Dutch by Leonard Verduin* (Scottdale, 1956)

MQR *Mennonite Quarterly Review* (Goshen, Ind., 1927-)

Müller, Berner Täufer Ernst Müller, *Geschichte der Bernischen Täufer* (Frauenfeld, 1895)

Naamlijst *Naamlijst der tegenwoordig in dienst zijnde predikanten der Mennoniten in de vereenigde Nederlanden* (Amsterdam, 1731, 1743, 1755, 1757, 1766, 1769, 1775, 1780, 1782, 1784, 1786, 1787, 1789, 1791, 1793, 1802, 1804, 1806, 1808, 1810, 1815, 1829)

N.N.B.Wb. P. C. Molhuysen and P. J. Blok, *Nieuw Nederlandsch Biografisch Woordenboek* vv. 1-10 (Leiden, 1911-37)

Offer *Dit Boec wort genoemt: Het Offer des Heeren, om het inhout van sommighe opgheofferde kinderen Godts . . .* (n.p., 1562, 1567, 1570, 1578, 1580, Amsterdam, 1590, n.p., 1591, Amsterdam, 1595, Harlingen, 1599). The 1570 edition is cited as reproduced in *BRN* II, 51-486, including *Een Lietboecxken, tracterende van den Offer des Heeren* (pp. 499-617)

Reimer, Familiennamen Gustav E. Reimer, *Die Familiennamen der westpreussischen Mennoniten* (Weierhof, 1940)

Rembert, Wiedertäufer Karl Rembert, *Die "Wiedertäufer" im Herzogtum Jülich* (Berlin, 1899)

RGG *Die Religion in Geschichte und Gegenwart* (2.ed., 5v., Tübingen, 1927-32)

Schijn-Maatschoen, Geschiedenis I Hermanus Schijn, *Geschiedenis dier Christenen, welke in de Vereenigde Nederlanden onder de Protestanten Mennoniten genaamd worden . . . Tweede Druk op nieuws uit het Latyn vertaald, en vermeerdert door Gerardus Maatschoen* (Amsterdam, 1743)

Schijn-Maatschoen, Geschiedenis II, which is volume II of the preceding work, entitled *Uitvoeriger Verhandeling van de Geschiedenisse der Mennoniten* (Amsterdam, 1744)

Schijn-Maatschoen, Geschiedenis III, which is volume III of the preceding work, entitled *Aanhangzel Dienende tot den Vervolg of Derde Deel van de Geschiedenis der Mennoniten . . . in het welke noch Negentien Leeraars der Mennoniten . . .*, by Maatschoen alone (Amsterdam, 1745)

TA Baden-Pfalz M. Krebs, *Quellen zur Geschichte der Täufer. IV. Band, Baden und Pfalz* (Gütersloh, 1951)

TA Bayern I Karl Schornbaum, *Quellen zur Geschichte der Wiedertäufer II. Band, Markgraftum Brandenburg (Bayern I. Abteilung)* (Leipzig, 1934)

TA Bayern II *Idem, Quellen zur Geschichte der Täufer, V. Band (Bayern, II. Abteilung)* (Gütersloh, 1951)

TA Hessen G. Franz, *Urkundliche Quellen zur hessischen Reformationsgeschichte. Vierter Band, Wiedertäuferakten 1527-1626* (Marburg, 1951)

TA Württemberg G. Bossert, *Quellen zur Geschichte der Täufer I. Band, Herzogtum Württemberg* (Leipzig, 1930)

TA Zürich L. von Muralt und W. Schmid, *Quellen zur Geschichte der Täufer in der Schweiz. Erster Band Zürich* (Zürich, 1952)

Unruh, Hintergründe B. H. Unruh, *Die niederländisch-niederdeutschen Hintergründe der mennonitischen Ostwanderungen im 16., 18. und 19. Jahrhundert* (Karlsruhe-Rüppurr, 1955)

Verheyden, Brugge A. L. E. Verheyden, *Het Brugsche Martyrologium (12 October 1527-7 Augustus 1573)* (Brussels, n.d., [1944])

Verheyden, Courtrai *Idem, Le Martyrologe Courtraisien et la Martyrologe Bruxellois* (Vilvorde, 1950)

Verheyden, Gent *Idem, Het Gentsche Martyrologium (1530-1595)* (Brugge, 1946)

Vos, Antwerpen Karel Vos, *De Doopsgezinden te Antwerpen in de zestiende eeuw* (reprint from *Bulletin de la Commission Royale de Belgique* LXXXIV, Brussels, 1920)

Vos, Menno Simons . . . *Menno Simons, 1496-1561, zijn leven en werken en zijne reformatorische denkbeelden* (Leiden, 1914)

Wackernagel, Kirchenlied Philipp Wackernagel, *Das deutsche Kirchenlied von der ältesten Zeit bis zu Anfang des XVII. Jahrhunderts,* 5v. (Leipzig, 1864-77)

Wackernagel, Lieder *Idem, Lieder der niederländischen Reformierten aus der Zeit der Verfolgung im 16. Jahrhundert* (Frankfurt, 1867)

Wappler, Thüringen Paul Wappler, *Die Täuferbewegung in Thüringen von 1526-1584* (Jena, 1913)

Wiswedel, Bilder W. Wiswedel, *Bilder und Führergestalten aus dem Täufertum,* 3v. (Kassel, I, 1928; II, 1930; III, 1952)

Wolkan, Geschicht-Buch Rudolf Wolkan, *Geschicht-Buch der Hutterischen Brüder* (Macleod, Alta., and Vienna, 1923)

Wolkan, Lieder *Idem, Die Lieder der Wiedertäufer* (Berlin, 1903)

Zieglschmid, Chronik A. J. F. Zieglschmid, *Die älteste Chronik der Hutterischen Brüder: Ein Sprachdenkmal aus frühneuhochdeutscher Zeit* (Ithaca, 1943)

Zieglschmid, Klein-Geschichtsbuch *Idem, Das Klein-Geschichtsbuch der Hutterischen Brüder* (Philadelphia, 1947)

D. Other Symbols and Abbreviations

A.D.S. Algemene Doopsgezinde Societeit. **MCC** Mennonite Central Committee

Vereinigung Vereinigung der Deutschen Mennonitengemeinden

Verband Verband badisch-württembergisch-bayrischer Mennonitengemeinden e. V.

CPS Civilian Public Service. **KfK** Kommission für kirchliche Angelegenheiten (or Kirchenangelegenheiten). **CO** Conscientious objector to military service.

q.v. "quod vide," "which see," is a cross-reference indicating that an article on the subject is to be found in the regular alphabetical order.

* signifies deceased. **†** indicates that an illustration will be found in the pictorial section at the end of the volume.

AML Amsterdam Mennonite Library

BeCL Bethel College Historical Library; **GCL** Goshen College Mennonite Historical Library

MAPS AND ILLUSTRATIONS

The maps listed below will generally be found close to the articles they serve. Illustrations are grouped at the end of each volume. This final list of maps differs slightly from the lists published in the first three volumes. For a complete list of illustrations in Volume IV, see the **Illustration** section at the end of the volume, pp. 1 f.

ALPHABETICAL INDEX OF MAPS, VOLUMES I—IV

Abrahams, David, *Headingly, Man.*	D.Ab.	Dahlenberg, Paul, *Bridgewater, S.D.*	P.Da.
Adrian, J. S., *Swift Current, Sask.*	J.S.Ad.	Decker, David, *Olivet, S.D.*	D.D.
Alwine, David C., *Johnstown, Pa.*	D.C.A.	*Dedic, Paul, *Graz, Austria*	P.De.
Andres, F. J., *St. Catharines, Ont.*	F.J.A.	Detweiler, Richard C., *Perkasie, Pa.*	R.C.D.
Andres, H. J., *North Newton, Kan.*	H.J.A.	DeWind, Henry A., *Whitewater, Wis.*	DeWind
Arnold, E. C. H., *Farmington, Pa.*	E.C.H.A.	Dick, A. A., *Mountain Lake, Minn.*	A.A.D.
Aschliman, Freeman, *Toledo, O.*	F.W.A.	Dick, H. H., *Mountain Lake, Minn.*	H.H.Di.
Augsburger, Myron S., *Harrisonburg, Va.*	M.S.A.	Dick, Karl, *Wolf Point, Mont.*	K.D.
Badertscher, Ivan L., *Orrville, O.*	I.L.B.	Diener, Charles, *Canton, Kan.*	C.D.
Baer, Joseph F., *Sarasota, Fla.*	J.F.B.	Diener, Harry A., *Hutchinson, Kan.*	H.A.D.
Baer, Paul E., *Royersford, Pa.*	P.E.B.	Dirks, Albert, *Scott City, Kan.*	A.Di.
Bainton, Roland H., *New Haven, Conn.*	R.H.B.	Dirks, David J., *Sun Valley, Cal.*	D.J.D.
Barkman, J. F., *Steinbach, Man.*	J.F.Ba.	*Driver, Joseph R., *Waynesboro, Va.*	J.R.D.
Bartel, John, *Shafter, Cal.*	J.Ba.	Duerksen, A. R., *Bluffton, O.*	A.R.D.
*Basinger, Elmer, *Mt. Pleasant, Iowa*	E.B.	Duerksen, Jacob A., *Washington, D.C.*	J.A.D.
Bauman, Harold E., *Goshen, Ind.*	H.B.	Duerksen, John W., *Premont, Tex.*	J.W.D.
Beachy, Claude R., *Grantsville, Md.*	C.R.B.	Dyck, Cornelius J., *Elkhart, Ind.*	C.J.D.
Becker, Alvin G., *Woodburn, Ind.*	A.G.B.	Dyck, H. H., *Mountain Lake, Minn.*	H.H.D.
Becker, Eduard, *Darmstadt, Ger.*	Ed.B.	Dyck, Peter J., *Frankfurt, Ger.*	P.J.D.
Bender, Allen, *Baden, Ont.*	A.Be.	*Dyck, Peter P., *Rosemary, Alta.*	P.P.D.
Bender, Elizabeth Horsch, *Goshen, Ind.*	E.H.B.	Dyck, Walter J., *Richfield, Pa.*	W.J.D.
Bender, Ezra C., *Martinsburg, Pa.*	E.C.B.	Eash, Samuel T., *Middlebury, Ind.*	S.T.E.
Bender, Harold S., *Goshen, Ind.*	H.S.B.	Ebersole, Myron, *Newton, Kan.*	M.Eb.
Bender, Ross T., *Kitchener, Ont.*	R.T.B.	Ediger, Elmer, *N. Newton, Kan.*	E.Ed.
*Berg, P. H., *Hillsboro, Kan.*	P.H.B.	Eicher, William R., *Milford, Neb.*	W.R.E.
Bittinger, Elmer E., *Springs, Pa.*	E.E.B.	Enns, J. H., *Winnipeg, Man.*	J.H.En.
Blanke, Fritz, *Zürich, Sw.*	F.Bl.	Enns, William H., *Springstein, Man.*	W.H.E.
Block, John A., *Waldheim, Sask.*	J.A.Bl.	Ensz, H. A., *Inman, Kan.*	H.A.E.
*Block, Theodor, *Oberursel, Ger.*	T.B.	Epp, August, *Newton, Kan.*	Au.E.
Boese, Curt D., *Walton, Kans.*	C.D.B.	Epp, A. W., *Fairview, Okla.*	A.W.E.
Bontrager, John M., *Centerville, Mich.*	J.M.B.	*Epp, David H., *Chortitza, Russia*	D.H.E.
Bontrager, J. P., *Winton, Cal.*	J.P.Bo.	Epp, Frank H., *Altona, Man.*	F.H.E.
*Bontreger, Eli J., *Shipshewana, Ind.*	E.J.B.	Epp, G. G., *Rosthern, Sask.*	G.G.E.
Bontreger, Manasseh E., *Calico Rock, Ark.*	M.E.B.	Epp, H. F., *Mountain Lake, Minn.*	H.F.E.
Borntrager, Lillie, *Bloomfield, Mont.*	L.B.	Epp, Hans P., *Colonia Volendam, Paraguay*	H.P.E.
Bos, C. A. W., *Rotterdam, Neth.*	C.A.W.B.	Epp, Henry P., *Waterloo, Ont.*	H.P.Ep.
*Bossert, Gustav, Jr., *Stuttgart, Ger.*	G.Bos.	Epp, J. H., *Hepburn, Sask.*	J.H.E.
Bowman, H. E., *Springfield, O.*	H.E.Bo.	Erb, Paul, *Scottdale, Pa.*	P.E.
Braun, Abraham, *Nierstein, Ger.*	A.B.	Esau, John T., *Crooked Creek, Alta.*	J.T.E.
Brenneman, T. H., *Sarasota, Fla.*	T.H.B.	Esch, Ben, *Tiskilwa, Ill.*	B.Es.
Bricker, Samuel L., *Chambersburg, Pa.*	S.L.B.	Esh, Glenn, *Akron, Pa.*	G.Es.
Brown, Peter, *Winkler, Man.*	P.Br.	Esh, Jacob D., *Glendale, Ariz.*	J.D.E.
Buckwalter, Earl, *Hesston, Kan.*	E.Bu.	Falk, William H., *Altona, Man.*	W.H.F.
Buckwalter, Harry R., *Hannibal, Mo.*	H.R.Bu.	Farmwald, Andrew D., *Plain City, O.*	A.D.F.
Buckwalter, Ira J., *New Holland, Pa.*	I.J.B.	Fisher, John B., *Mechanicsville, Md.*	J.B.F.
Buller, Joe, *Goltry, Okla.*	J.Bu.	Flaming, John H., *Ulysses, Kan.*	J.H.Fl.
Burkhard, Sarah Schiffler, *Roseland, Neb.*	S.S.B.	Flickinger, W. J., *Bluffton, O.*	W.J.F.
Burkholder, Harold D., *Dallas, Ore.*	H.D.B.	Fox, Sam, *Okeene, Okla.*	S.F.
*Burkholder, Oscar, *Breslau, Ont.*	O.B.	Frank, Walter H., *Allentown, Pa.*	W.H.Fr.
Burkholder, Paul H., *Markham, Ont.*	P.H.Bu.	Franz, John M., *Dallas, Ore.*	J.M.F.
Byler, J. N., *Akron, Pa.*	J.N.B.	Friedmann, Robert, *Kalamazoo, Mich.*	R.F.
Carper, Mrs. Reuben, *Denbigh, Va.*	E.W.C.	Gering, William, *Newton, Kan.*	W.Ge.
Castillo, Mrs. David, *La Junta, Col.*	E.S.C.	Gingerich, Andrew, *Mannsville, N.Y.*	A.Gi.
Claassen, Willard, *Newton, Kan.*	W.Cl.	Gingerich, LeRoy, *Versailles, Mo.*	L.G.
Classen, Johann Peter, *Winnipeg, Man.*	J.P.C.	Gingerich, Melvin, *Goshen, Ind.*	M.G.
Classen, Mrs. Jonas, *West Liberty, O.*	M.B.C.	Gingerich, Orland, *Baden, Ont.*	O.G.
Clemens, James R., *Goshen, Ind.*	J.R.C.	Goerz, Heinrich, *Vancouver, B.C.*	H.G.
Clemens, Paul R., *Lansdale, Pa.*	P.R.C.	Good, A. C., *Sterling, Ill.*	A.C.G.
Coblentz, J. Simon, *Norfolk, Va.*	S.J.C.	Graber, Daniel J., *Goshen, Ind.*	D.J.G.
Coffman, Vinetta, *Shipshewana, Ind.*	V.C.	Graber, Ellis, *Souderton, Pa.*	E.Gr.
Conrad, Lloyd, *Wakarusa, Ind.*	L.D.C.	Graber, Harvey, *Goshen, Ind.*	H.Gr.
*Cornies, Johann, *Molotschna, Russia*	J.C.	Graber, Mrs. O'Ray, *Buhler, Kan.*	E.C.G.
Crous, Ernst, *Göttingen, Ger.*	E.C.	Graeff, Arthur D., *Philadelphia, Pa.*	A.D.G.
Culp, Elmer I., *Tiskilwa, Ill.*	E.I.C.	Gratz, Delbert L., *Bluffton, O.*	D.L.G.

Greiman, Mrs. Loyd, *Intake, Mont.*	L.B.G.	Keener, Oliver M., *Harrisonburg, Va.*	O.M.K.
Groff, Llewellyn, *Ogema, Minn.*	L.Gr.	Keim, Leander S., *Haven, Kan.*	L.S.K.
Groh, Harold D., *Kitchener, Ont.*	H.D.G.	Keim, Noah A., *Uniontown, O.*	N.A.K.
Grunau, J. C., *Hillsboro, Kan.*	J.C.Gr.	Kenagy, Mrs. Edward, *Silverton, Ore.*	E.G.Ken.
Guengerich, Paul T., *Parnell, Iowa*	P.T.G.	Kennel, P. R., *Shickley, Neb.*	P.R.K.
*Habegger, Alfred, *Lame Deer, Mont.*	A.H.	Kennel, Vernon, *Atglen, Pa.*	V.K.
Habegger, Loris A., *Wayland, Iowa*	L.A.H.	King, Donald E., *Pigeon, Mich.*	D.E.K.
*Hallman, E. S., *Akron, Pa.*	E.S.H.	King, Sanford E., *Hutchinson, Kan.*	S.E.K.
Hallman, William E., *Pehuajó, Argentina*	W.E.Ha.	Klassen, George H., *O'Neal, Ark.*	G.H.K.
Hamm, H. H., *Altona, Man.*	H.H.H.	Klassen, Herbert C., *Abbotsford, B.C.*	H.C.Kl.
*Harder, Franz, *Germany*	F.H.	Klassen, J. H., *Inman, Kan.*	J.H.K.
Harder, J. A., *Yarrow, B.C.*	J.A.Har.	Klassen, Jacob J., *Coaldale, Alta.*	Ja.Kl.
Harder, Leland, *Elkhart, Ind.*	L.Ha.	Klassen, Johann Peter, *Winnipeg, Man.*	J.P.Kl.
Harms, J. A.	J.A.Ha.	Klassen, John J., *Clearbrook, B.C.*	J.J.Kl.
Harms, Orlando, *Hillsboro, Kan.*	O.H., OHa.	Klassen, Peter, *St. Catharines, Ont.*	P.K.
Hartzler, John D., *Eureka, Ill.*	J.D.H.	Klassen, William, *Elkhart, Ind.*	W.Kl.
Haury, Helmut, *Weierhof, Ger.*	H.Ha.	Kleinsasser, Samuel, *Headingly, Man.*	S.K.
Heatwole, Nelson J., *Harrisonburg, Va.*	N.J.H.	Klügel, Maria, *Göttingen, Ger.*	M.K.
Heffner, W. F., *York, Pa.*	W.F.H.	Koch, Roy S., *West Liberty, O.*	R.S.K.
*Hege, Christian, *Frankfurt, Ger.*	Hege	Koehn, John A., *Livingston, Cal.*	J.A.K.
Hege, Henry, *Geary, Okla.*	H.H.	Koehn, John J., *Galva, Kan.*	J.J.Ko.
Hege, Ulrich, *Reihen, Ger.*	U.H.	Koehn, Noah, *Winton, Cal.*	N.K.
Heidebrecht, David A., *Tofield, Alta.*	D.A.H.	Koehn, Reuben J., *Lahoma, Okla.*	R.J.K.
Hein, Gerhard, *Berlin, Ger.*	G.H.	Kolb, Elmer G., *Pottstown, Pa.*	E.G.Ko.
Helmick, Chester M., *Elkhart, Ind.*	C.M.H.	Krabill, Murray, *Fredericktown, O.*	M.Kr.
Hershberger, Guy F., *Goshen, Ind.*	G.F.H.	Krahn, Cornelius, *N. Newton, Kan.*	C.K.
Hershey, Paul, *Gulfport, Miss.*	P.H.	Kratz, Mrs. Warren A., *Harrisonburg, Va.*	M.W.K.
*Hershey, T. K., *Goshen, Ind.*	T.K.H.	Kraus, C. Norman, *Durham, N.C.*	C.N.K.
Hertzler, Frank N., *Elizabethtown, Pa.*	F.N.H.	Krebs, Manfred, *Karlsruhe, Ger.*	M.K.
Hess, John H., *Toronto, Ont.*	J.H.H.	Kreider, Mrs. Leonard, *Wadsworth, O.*	R.W.K.
Hiebert, H. H., *Hillsboro, Kan.*	H.H.Hie.	Kreider, M. Lena, *Palmyra, Mo.*	M.L.K.
Hiebert, Jacob N., *Langham, Sask.*	J.N.H.	Kroeker, M. A., *Hillsboro, Kan.*	M.A.K.
Hiebert, Lando, *Hillsboro, Kan.*	L.Hi.	Kurtz, Christian J., *Elverson, Pa.*	C.J.K.
Hiebert, P. G., *Atmore, Ala.*	P.G.H.	Kurtz, J. A., *Oley, Pa.*	J.A.Ku.
Hiebert, P. N., *Bakersfield, Cal.*	P.N.H.	Kurtz, Omar A., *Oley, Pa.*	O.A.Ku.
Histand, Nelson, *Pryor, Okla.*	N.H.	Landes, Emanuel, *Ingolstadt, Ger.*	E.L.
Histand, Paul W., *Trevose, Pa.*	P.W.H.	Landis, Ira D., *Bareville, Pa.*	I.D.L.
Hofer, Clarence E., *Dinuba, Cal.*	C.E.H.	Langenwalter, J. H., *N. Newton, Kan.*	J.H.La.
Hofer, Jacob N., *Langham, Sask.*	J.M.H.	*Lapp, George J., *Goshen, Ind.*	G.J.L.
Hofer, John J., *Arden, Man.*	J.J.Ho.	Lapp, John E., *Lansdale, Pa.*	J.E.L.
Holsinger, Justus G., *Hesston, Kan.*	J.G.H.	Leatherman, John D., *Upland, Cal.*	J.D.L.
Horst, John L., *Harrisonburg, Va.*	J.L.H.	Lehman, Chester K., *Harrisonburg, Va.*	C.K.L.
Horst, Moses K., *Maugansville, Md.*	M.K.H.	Lehman, J. Irvin, *Harrisonburg, Va.*	J.I.L.
Hostetler, David E., *Apple Creek, O.*	D.E.H.	Lehman, Walter H., *Chambersburg, Pa.*	W.H.L.
Hostetler, Guy M., *Upland, Cal.*	G.M.H.	Leisy, A. J., *Wisner, Neb.*	A.J.L.
Hostetler, J. J., *Peoria, Ill.*	J.J.H.	Lind, N. A., *Sweet Home, Ore.*	N.A.L.
Hostetler, John A., *Scottdale, Pa.*	J.A.H.	Linscheid, Willis, *Butterfield, Minn.*	W.L.
Hostetler, Lester, *Sugarcreek, O.*	L.Ho.	Litwiller, Nelson, *Montevideo, Uruguay*	N.L.
Hostetler, S. Jay, *Accra, Ghana*	S.J.Ho.	Loewen, Mrs. Henry R., *Wichita, Kan.*	E.C.L.
Hovens Greve, K., *Amsterdam, Neth.*	K.Ho.	Loewen, S. L., *Hillsboro, Kan.*	S.L.L.
Huebert, G. D., *Winnipeg, Man.*	G.D.H.	Lohrenz, Gerhard, *Winnipeg, Man.*	G.L.
Huffman, J. A., *Winona Lake, Ind.*	J.A.Hu.	Lohrenz, J. H., *Hughestown, India*	J.H.L.
Isaac, John P., *Glendale, Cal.*	J.P.I.	Long, C. Warren, *Tiskilwa, Ill.*	C.W.L.
Jaehde, Mrs. William, Jr., *Ransom, Kan.*	M.J.	McCrory, Mrs. J. D., *Pueblo, Col.*	M.McC.
Jantz, Jesse H., *Neodesha, Kan.*	J.J.	McDowell, Emerson L., *Toronto, Ont.*	E.L.M.
Jantzen, G. H., *Dallas, Ore.*	G.H.J.	Martin, Daniel L., *Sheldon, Wis.*	D.L.M.
Janz, B. B., *Coaldale, Alta.*	B.B.J.	Martin, Jesse B., *Waterloo, Ont.*	J.B.M.
Janzen, A. E., *Hillsboro, Kan.*	A.E.J.	Martin, Loyal J., *Hillsboro, Kan.*	L.J.M.
Janzen, David, *Winnipeg, Man.*	D.Ja.	Martin, Simon B., *Kitchener, Ont.*	S.B.M.
Janzen, H. H., *Basel, Sw.*	H.H.J.	Massanari, Karl, *Goshen, Ind.*	K.L.M.
Jeltes, H. F. W., *The Hague, Neth.*	H.F.W.J.	Mast, Russell L., *N. Newton, Kan.*	R.L.M.
Jost, Arthur, *Reedley, Cal.*	A.J.	Matthijssen, Jan, *Pati, Java*	J.M.
Kauffman, A. H., *Goshen, Ind.*	A.H.K.	Maust, Earl J., *Bay Port, Mich.*	E.J.M.
Kauffman, Floyd, *Minot, N.D.*	F.E.K.	Mecenseffy, Grete, *Vienna, Austria*	G.Me.
Kaufman, Abram, *Plain City, O.*	Ab.K.	Menzel, Gustav, *Germany*	G.M.
*Kaufman, Ammon, *Davidsville, Pa.*	A.Ka.	Metz, Abram G., *Bergey, Pa.*	A.G.M.

Metzler, Edgar, *Kitchener, Ont.*	E.Me.	Raber, Chester A., *Louisville, Ken.*	C.A.R.
Meyer, Mrs. J. C., *Cleveland, O.*	E.S.M.	Rahn, Ben, *Inman, Kan.*	B.R.
Miller, Amon M., *Fairview, Neb.*	A.M.M.	Ramge, Karl, *Germany*	K.Ra.
Miller, D. Paul, *Mankato, Minn.*	D.P.M.	Redekop, H. H., *Winkler, Man.*	H.H.R.
Miller, D. Walter, *Orrville, O.*	D.W.M.	Redekop, J. F., *N. Clearbrook, B.C.*	J.F.R.
Miller, Daniel E., *McMinnville, Ore.*	D.E.M.	Reese, Goldie S., *Pittsburgh, Pa.*	G.S.R.
Miller, Edward J., *Gulfport, Miss.*	Ed.J.M.	Regehr, Ernst, *El Ombu, Uruguay*	E.Re.
Miller, George S., *Wellman, Iowa*	G.S.M.	Regehr, J. I., *Main Centre, Sask.*	J.I.R.
Miller, H. E., *Elkhart, Ind.*	H.E.M.	*Regier, C. H., *Elbing, Kan.*	C.H.R.
Miller, Ira E., *Harrisonburg, Va.*	I.E.M.	Regier, Daniel G., *Alsen, N.D.*	D.G.R.
Miller, Ivan J., *Grantsville, Md.*	I.J.M.	Regier, Otto, *Bad Segeberg, Ger.*	O.R.
Miller, Jacob J., *Bowling Green, Mo.*	J.J.Mi.	Regier, P. K., *N. Newton, Kan.*	P.K.R.
Miller, Jonathan M., *Kalona, Iowa*	J.M.M.	Reichenbach, R. C., *Shamokin, Pa.*	R.C.Re.
Miller, Mary, *Hesston, Kan.*	M.M.	Reimer, B. D., *Steinbach, Man.*	B.D.R.
Miller, Myrtle, *High River, Alta.*	M.Mi.	Reimer, David P., *Giroux, Man.*	D.P.R.
Miller, Omar G., *Hubbard, Ore.*	O.G.M.	Reimer, Gustav E., *Nova Witmarsum, Brazil*	G.R.
Miller, Paul R., *Walnut Creek, O.*	P.R.M.	Reimer, Peter J., *Rosenort, Man.*	P.J.R.
Miller, Mrs. William S. *Hutchinson, Kan.*	C.Y.M.	Reist, H. F., *Premont, Tex.*	H.F.R.
*Mininger, H. J., *Ithica, Mich.*	H.J.Mi.	Rempel, Alexander, *Göttingen, Ger.*	A.R.
Mishler, Raymond, *Sheridan, Ore.*	R.M.	Rempel, Hans, *Kiel, Ger.*	H.R., F.R.
Moyer, Ernest K., *Quakertown, Pa.*	E.K.M.	Rempel, Jacob, *Saskatoon, Sask.*	J.R.
Moyer, Jacob M., *Souderton, Pa.*	J.M.Mo.	Rempel, J. G., *Saskatoon, Sask.*	J.G.R.
Muffley, John Wesley, *Bowmansville, Pa.*	J.W.M.	Risler, Walter, *Crefeld, Ger.*	W.R.
Nafziger, Valentine, *Milverton, Ont.*	V.N.	*Risser, John D., *Hagerstown, Md.*	J.D.R.
Near, Richard, *Shelby, Mich.*	R.N.	Rocke, Emanuel M., *Woodburn, Ind.*	E.M.R.
*Neff, Christian, *Weierhof, Ger.*	Neff	Ropp, Herman E., *Wellman, Iowa*	H.E.R.
Neufeld, G. G., *Manitou, Man.*	G.G.N.	Rosenberger, Arthur S., *Quakertown, Pa.*	A.S.R.
Neufeld, Herman, *Vancouver, B.C.*	H.Ne.	Roszhart, Herbert, *Aurora, Neb.*	H.Ro.
Neufeld, Heinrich T., *Enid, Okla.*	H.T.N.	Rotermund, Hans-Martin, *Göttingen, Ger.*	H-M.R.
Neufeld, I. G., *Fresno, Cal.*	I.G.N.	Roth, Roy D., *Hesston, Kan.*	R.D.R.
Neufeld, Vernon H., *N. Newton, Kan.*	V.H.N.	Roth, Ruth C., *Goshen, Ind.*	R.C.R.
Neufeld, William, *San Jose, Cal.*	W.Ne.	Rupp, E. E., *Archbold, O.*	E.E.R.
*Newman, A. H., *Macon, Ga.*	A.H.N.	Ruth, Marvin D., *Lansdale, Pa.*	M.D.R.
Nickel, Arnold, *Freeman, S.D.*	A.N.	Ruth, Melvin L., *Phoenix, Ariz.*	M.L.R.
Nickel, H. H., *Abbotsford, B.C.*	H.H.N.	Sawatzky, John J., *Calgary, Alta.*	J.J.Sa.
Nickel, J. D., *Rosemary, Alta.*	J.D.N.	Schantz, Albert, *Fronberg, Ger.*	A.S.
Nickel, J. W., *N. Newton, Kan.*	J.W.N.	Schellenberg, Bernhard J., *Winnipeg, Man.*	B.J.S.
Niepoth, Wilhelm, *Crefeld, Ger.*	W.N.	Schellenberg, Theo. R., *Washington, D.C.*	T.R.Sc.
Nyce, Howard G., *Newton, Kan.*	H.G.N.	Schertz, Dale, *Remington, Ind.*	D.S.
Odlozilik, Otakar, *Philadelphia, Pa.*	O.O.	Schertz, Mrs. J. J., *Flanagan, Ill.*	Mrs. J.J.S.
Ortman, Arthur F., *Warroad, Minn.*	A.F.O.	Schmidt, August, *Canton, Okla.*	A.Sch.
Ortmann, Anna F., *Marion, S.D.*	A.F.Or.	Schmidt, Edwin T., *Waldheim, Sask.*	E.T.S.
Ortmann, Hellmuth F., *Munich, N.D.*	H.F.O.	Schmidt, Mrs. Herbert B., *Newton, Kan.*	M.P.S.
Oswald, Samuel, *Beemer, Neb.*	S.O.	Schmidt, H. U., *Meno, Okla.*	H.U.S.
Paetkau, David, *Coaldale, Alta.*	D.Pa.	Schmidt, John F., *N. Newton, Kan.*	J.F.S.
Pannabecker, S. F., *Elkhart, Ind.*	S.F.P.	Schmidt, John R., *Asunción, Paraguay*	J.R.Sc.
Pauls, D. C., *Inman, Kan.*	D.C.P.	Schmidt, P. U., *Goessel, Kan.*	P.U.S.
Peachey, Paul, *Tokyo, Japan*	P.P.	Schmidt, Rudolf, *Newport, Wash.*	R.Sc.
Pelsy, René, *Sarrebourg, Alsace*	R.P.	Schowalter, Paul, *Weierhof, Ger.*	P.S.
Penner, Archie, *Steinbach, Man.*	A.P.	Schrag, Martin H., *Grantham, Pa.*	M.H.S.
Penner, G. H., *Plum Coulee, Man.*	G.H.P.	Schroeter, August A., *Reedley, Cal.*	A.A.S.
Penner, Horst, *Weierhof, Ger.*	H.P.	Schrock, Leroy E., *Glen Flora, Wis.*	L.E.S.
Penner, John D., *Morris, Man.*	J.D.P.	Schweitzer, Charles, *Moscow, Kan.*	C.Sc.
Penner, John P., *Vineland, Ont.*	J.P.Pe.	Schweizer, Albert, *Sterling, Kan.*	A.Sc.
Persijn, J. H., *Netherlands*	J.H.P.	Shank, Mrs. Charles S., *Goshen Ind.*	L.S.S.
Peters, Francis, *Walnut Hill, Fla.*	F.P.	Shank, Clarence, *Marion, Pa.*	C.S.
Peters, Frank C., *Winnipeg, Man.*	F.C.P.	Shank, Harvey E., *Chambersburg, Pa.*	H.E.S.
Peters, G. W., *Fresno, Cal.*	G.W.P.	*Shank, John R., *Versailles, Mo.*	J.R.S.
Peters, John, *Yarrow, B.C.*	J.Pe.	Shank, Lester C., *Harrisonburg, Va.*	L.C.S.
Peters, William J., *Gruenthal, Man.*	W.J.Pe.	Shantz, Merle, *Hespeler, Ont.*	Me.S.
Pletscher, Werner, *Germany*	W.Pl.	Shellenberg, Menno A., *Winton, Cal.*	M.A.S.
Plett, C. F., *Doland, S.D.*	C.F.P.	Shelly, Maynard, *N. Newton, Kan.*	M.Sh.
Prieb, Wesley J., *Hillsboro, Kan.*	W.J.P.	Shelly, Paul R., *Bluffton, O.*	P.R.S.
Quiring, Horst, *Korntal, Ger.*	H.Q.	Shelly, Wilmer S., *Frederick, Pa.*	W.S.S.
*Quiring, Jakob, *New York, N.Y.*	J.Q.	Sherk, J. Harold, *Washington, D.C.*	J.Ha.S.
Quiring, Walter, *Rosthern, Sask.*	W.Q.	Short, Reuben, *Archbold, O.*	R.Sho.

Showalter, Richard L., *Reedley, Cal.*	R.L.S.	Unruh, John, *Warden, Wash.*	J.U.
*Showalter, Timothy, *Broadway, Va.*	T.S.	Unruh, P. D., *Colfax, Wash.*	P.D.U.
Siemens, Ernest, *Shafter, Cal.*	E.Si.	Unruh, William F., *Newton, Kan.*	W.F.U.
Slagell, John, *Hydro, Okla.*	J.S.	*Vos, Karel, *Middelstum, Neth.*	K.V.
*Smith, C. Henry, *Bluffton, O.*	C.H.S.	Voth, Abraham, *Morden, Man.*	A.V.
Smith, Lena Mae, *Newton, Kan.*	L.M.S.	Waldner, Friedrich, *Poplar Point, Man.*	F.W.
Smith, Tilman R., *Eureka, Ill.*	T.R.S.	Waldner, Joseph A., *Mitchell, S.D.*	J.A.Wa.
Smith, Willard H., *Goshen, Ind.*	W.H.S.	Wall, P. F., *Downey, Cal.*	P.F.W.
Smucker, Herman J., *Iowa City, Iowa*	H. J. Sm.	Walter, Jacob, *Macleod, Alta.*	J.Wa.
Smucker, Silas J., *Rensselaer, Ind.*	S.J.S.	Walter, Solomon F., *Mount Pleasant, Iowa*	S.F.W.
Snyder, Earle S., *Guelph, Ont.*	E.S.S.	Waltner, Erland, *Elkhart, Ind.*	E.W.
Snyder, Elvin V., *La Plata, Puerto Rico*	E.V.S.	Waltner, Harris, *Moundridge, Kan.*	H.Wal.
Snyder, Harvey E., *Kitchener, Ont.*	H.E.Sn.	Warkentin, Henry, *Yarrow, B.C.*	H.Wa.
Snyder, William T., *Akron, Pa.*	W.T.S.	Warkentin, Melvin L., *Hillsboro, Kan.*	M.L.W.
Springer, N. P., *Goshen, Ind.*	N.P.S.	*Warns, Johannes, *Wiedenest, Ger.*	J.Wa.
Sprunger, Eva F., *Berne, Ind.*	E.F.S.	Weaver, Ivan K., *Petoskey, Mich.*	I.K.W.
Sprunger, Samuel F., *Coopersburg, Pa.*	S.F.S.	Weaver, William B., *Bloomington, Ill.*	W.B.W.
*Stauffer, Ezra, *Tofield, Alta.*	E.S.	Wedel, J., *Steinbach, Man.*	J.We.
Stauffer, William H., *Sugarcreek, O.*	W.H.St.	Wenger, John C., *Goshen, Ind.*	J.C.W.
Steiner, James A., *Wadsworth, O.*	J.A.S.	Wenger, Linden M., *Harrisonburg, Va.*	L.M.W.
Steiner, John S., *Goshen, Ind.*	J.S.S.	Whitmer, Paul E., *Bluffton, O.*	P.E.W.
Stoll, Abraham J., *Wheatland, N.D.*	A.J.S.	Wichert, John J., *Vineland, Ont.*	J.J.W.
Stoll, Henry J., *Rensselaer, Ind.*	H.J.St.	Widmer, Joseph, *Modenheim, Alsace, France*	J.Wid.
Stoltzfus, Grant M., *Harrisonburg, Va.*	G.M.S.	Wiebe, Alfred, *Seiling, Okla.*	A.Wi.
Stoneback, George S., *Wichita, Kan.*	G.S.S.	Wiebe, David V., *Hillsboro, Kan.*	D.V.W.
Stucky, Harley J., *N. Newton, Kan.*	H.J.S.	*Wiebe, Herbert, *Gross-Falkenau, West Prussia*	
Studer, Gerald C., *Smithville, O.*	G.C.S.		H.Wi.
Stutzman, Harry J., *Berlin, O.*	Ha.S.	Wiebe, Herman J., *Madison, Sask.*	H.J.W.
Stutzman, Milo D., *Kingman, Alta.*	M.D.S.	Wiebe, Jacob Z., *Marion, Kan.*	J.Z.W.
Suderman, John P., *Pandora, O.*	J.P.S.	Wiebe, Johannes, *Golzwarden, Ger.*	J.Wi.
Swarr, Harry C., *E. Petersburg, Pa.*	H.C.S.	Wiebe, John A., *Mountain Lake, Minn.*	J.A.W.
Swartz, Mrs. Alvin, *Talbert, Ken.*	E.R.Sw.	Wiebe, Orlando H., *Omaha, Neb.*	O.H.W.
Swartzendruber, A. Lloyd, *Kalona, Iowa*	A.L.S.	Wiebe, Pete V., *Hillsboro, Kan.*	P.V.W.
Swartzendruber, Elmer G., *Wellman, Iowa*	E.G.S.	Wiebe, Willard W., *Mountain Lake, Minn.*	W.W.W.
Swartzendruber, Victor E., *Bloomfield, Iowa*	V.E.S.	Wiens, Frank, *Asunción, Paraguay*	Fr.W.
Swartzentruber, Amos, *Tres Lomas, Argentina*		Wiens, Henry A., *Langham, Sask.*	H.A.W.
	A.Sw.	Wiens, H. E., *Mountain Lake, Minn.*	H.E.W.
Swartzentruber, Clayton, *Dalton, O.*	C.Sw.	Wiens, Henry J., *Swift Current, Sask.*	He.J.W.
Swope, Wilmer D., *Leetonia, O.*	W.D.S.	Wipf, Daniel S., *Alexandria, S.D.*	D.S.W.
*Teufel, Eberhard, *Stuttgart-Fellbach, Ger.*	E.T.	Wipf, Joseph, *Frankfort, S.D.*	Jo.W.
Thiesen, Daniel S., *Newton, Kan.*	D.S.T.	Wiswedel, Wilhelm, *Bayreuth, Ger.*	W.W.
Thiessen, D. J., *Vauxhall, Alta.*	D.J.Th.	Wolf, N. H., *Harrisburg, Pa.*	N.H.W.
Thiessen, Gerhardt T., *Orange Grove, Cal.*	G.T.T.	Wood, J. S., *Yale, Mich.*	J.S.W.
Thiessen, J. F., *Newton, Kan.*	J.F.T.	Wurz, John M., *Beiseker, Alta.*	J.M.W.
Thiessen, J. J., *Saskatoon, Sask.*	J.J.Th.	Yeackley, Earl, *Thurman, Col.*	E.Ye.
*Tilitzky, C. G., *Abbotsford, B.C.*	C.G.T.	*Yntema, J., *Haarlem, Neth.*	J.Y.
Toews, A. A., *N. Clearbrook, B.C.*	A.A.T.	Yoder, Edwin, *Parnell, Iowa*	E.Yo.
Toews, Isaac J., *Linden, Alta.*	I.J.T.	Yoder, Edwin J., *Topeka, Ind.*	E.J.Y.
Toews, Jacob C., *Leamington, Ont.*	J.C.T.	Yoder, Gideon G., *Hesston, Kan.*	G.G.Y.
Toews, Jacob J., *Kitchener, Ont.*	J.J.T.	Yoder, Jacob P., *Reedsville, Pa.*	J.P.Y.
Troyer, Mrs. Clarence, *Engadine, Mich.*	W.I.T.	Yoder, John Howard, *Goshen, Ind.*	J.H.Y.
*Troyer, Levi S., *Mio, Mich.*	L.S.T.	Yoder, John L., *West Liberty, O.*	J.L.Y.
Troyer, Menno M., *Conway, Kan.*	M.M.T.	Yoder, Ray F., *Nappanee, Ind.*	R.F.Y.
Troyer, Reuben, *Conway Springs, Kan.*	R.Tr.	Yoder, S. C., *Goshen, Ind.*	S.C.Y.
Tschetter, David W., *Bridgewater, Kan.*	D.W.T.	Yoder, Walter E., *Goshen, Ind.*	W.E.Y.
Tschetter, Mrs. P. A., *Fort Macleod, Alta.*		Yost, A. L., *Moundridge, Kan.*	A.L.Y.
	Mrs. P.A.T.	Yost, Burton G., *Zionsville, Pa.*	B.G.Y.
Tschetter, P. A., *Estuary, Sask.*	P.A.T.	Zacharias, John L., *Waldheim, Sask.*	J.L.Z.
Ulrich, Wilfred, *Kitchener, Ont.*	W.U.	Zacharias, Werner, *Swift Current, Sask.*	W.Z.
Umble, John S., *Goshen, Ind.*	J.S.U.	*Zehr, Edmund P., *Beatrice, Neb.*	E.Z.
Unruh, A. H., *Winnipeg, Man.*	A.H.U.	Zehr, Harold A., *Roanoke, Ill.*	H.A.Z.
Unruh, Abe J., *Montezuma, Kan.*	A.J.U.	Zijpp, N. van der, *Rotterdam, Neth.*	vdZ.
*Unruh, B. H., *Karlsruhe-Rüppurr, Ger.*	B.H.U.	Zimmerman, E. E., *Peoria, Ill.*	E.E.Z.
*Unruh, Edward, *Chickasha, Okla.*	E.U.	Zook, Le Roy A., *Wooster, Ohio*	L.A.Z.
Unruh, J. D., *Freeman, S.D.*	J.D.U.	Zook, Ruby, *Garden City, Mo.*	R.Z.

THE
MENNONITE ENCYCLOPEDIA

O

Oak Dale Mennonite Church (CM), near Salisbury, Somerset Co., Pa., is one of the three meetinghouses of the Casselman River (*q.v.*) congregation of the Conservative Mennonite Conference. Services are held every two weeks, simultaneously with Cherry Glade in the southern part of the district. On alternate Sundays and for communion or special meetings the whole congregation meets at Maple Glen near Grantsville, Md. The Oak Dale church, a frame structure built in 1896, was remodeled and enlarged in 1931. Present seating capacity is 350.   I.J.M.

Oak Grove Mennonite Church (MC), located about five miles west and one-half mile south of Adair, Mayes Co., Okla., had its beginning as a mission station about 1927, when Monroe Hostetler of Hesston, Kan., located in the community and conducted a Sunday school in the schoolhouse. Later preaching services were also arranged for and a mission was organized under the South Central Conference. Richard Birky served as the resident pastor 1942-47. In 1944 a house was remodeled as a church. In the spring of 1957 a new concrete block building was finished and dedicated; this building is located five miles west of Adair on Highway 28. In 1956 the membership was 21, with Richard Birky as pastor again 1954- , now a bishop.   N.H.

Oak Grove Beachy Amish Church, near Centreville, Mich., was established *c*1954. In 1957 it had 32 members with Clarence Miller and Moses Yoder serving as ministers.   H.S.B.

Oak Grove Mennonite Church (MC) located in Champaign County, Ohio, was organized in 1845-50 by Amish settlers from Fairfield County, Ohio, and Mifflin County, Pa. The first center of the settlement lay several miles southeast of the present Oak Grove church built in 1875. The earlier meetinghouse, built soon after 1855, was located on the plot known as the Hooley cemetery, the present burying place of the congregation. Until the beginning of the present century, baptismal services still were conducted in near-by Kings Creek south of the cemetery. Early ministers were Jacob Hartzler, bishop (1854), Jonas Troyer, later of Clinton Frame (*q.v.*), Elkhart Co., Ind., and John P. King, bishop-deacon (*völliger Armendiener*), who later moved to Logan County, Ohio. John Werrey (later Warye), an immigrant from Hesse-Darmstadt, Germany, ordained preacher in 1855 and bishop in 1862, led his congregation from a strict Old Order Amish to a more liberal Amish Mennonite discipline, but thereafter resisted any change. He and David Plank (*q.v.*), the latter at Walnut Grove in Logan County, could not agree with John P. King's stricter discipline which still required hooks and

eyes and, for unmarried men, topless buggies. Another cause of friction was Warye's contention that King's ordination as bishop-deacon did not entitle him to take his regular turn with the other ministers in the Sunday morning preaching service. The Oak Grove congregation under the leadership of David Plank organized a Sunday school in 1865. Virile lay leadership through the Sunday school built up a strong congregation. It has benefited from contacts with local Methodist and Quaker religious movements. But in 1880 the congregation suffered loss of membership through the unskillful handling of a disciplinary problem involving the use of a musical instrument in a home in the Walnut Grove congregation. The result was the withdrawal of important sections of both congregations and the founding of the Indiana or Miller congregation (now extinct), so called because it was organized by Eli Miller, bishop at the Clinton Frame (Indiana) congregation. During the present century the leading figures in the congregation were Samuel E. Allgyer (*q.v.*), minister and bishop; and Samuel L. Warye and Jonathan J. Warye, deacon and preacher, respectively, the sons of John Warye. The Mennonite Church (MC) has drawn heavily on the congregation for educational and missionary personnel. However, the group has also suffered its full share of loss of membership to other religious bodies. The membership in 1957 was 239, with Nelson Kanagy as pastor.   J.S.U.

John Umble, "Early Sunday Schools at West Liberty, Ohio," *MQR* IV (1930) 6-50.

Oak Grove Mennonite Church (MC) located 2 miles west of Grantsville, Md., on top of Negro Mountain, a member of the Allegheny Conference, was started as a Sunday school in a log schoolhouse. The first members were received in 1888. The first meetinghouse was built in 1900 and remodeled in 1954. The church membership reached 45 in 1920 and then gradually declined. Since 1950 the work has been revived and in 1957 there were 30 members, with A. C. Walls as pastor.   C.R.B.

Oak Grove Mennonite Church, unaffiliated, located near Smithville, Wayne Co., Ohio, is probably the oldest Mennonite congregation of Amish background in the state. The first settlers came to the area about 1817 from Somerset and Mifflin counties, Pa., and organized a congregation in 1818, meeting in homes for worship. Other families of Swiss Mennonite background came directly from Switzerland and Alsace-Lorraine. Early bishops were David Zook, Christian Schantz, Jacob Yoder, assisted by ministers Christian Brandt, Christian Naftzinger, Peter Blough, Solomon Zook, and deacons Jacob King and Jacob Troyer.

The first meetinghouse (frame) was built in 1862, and a second (Pleasant Hill) in 1881 to accommodate members in the northern part of the district. In 1905 the Oak Grove meetinghouse was replaced by the large frame structure used by the present congregation.

The early congregation was a member of the Amish General Conference and Eastern A.M. Conference, and until 1947 of the Ohio and Eastern A.M. Conference. Since 1947 Pleasant Hill has been a separate congregation, still under the Ohio and Eastern Conference, while Oak Grove continued independent. Under able and progressive leadership the varied background of the Oak Grove congregation led to a fused polity, highly active congregational interest and participation in higher education, missions, and the broader program of the church at large. Though a rural church, less than half the members (numbering 400 in January 1958) are actively employed in agriculture. The bishop, now retired, is Jacob S. Gerig, with Virgil M. Gerig minister with full pastoral authority in the local congregation.

Other leaders serving earlier in addition to the above were John K. Yoder and Benjamin Gerig (bishops), C. K. Yoder, Jonathan Smucker, Christian Kureth (Conrad), John Smiley, Isaac Miller, D. Z. Yoder, S. K. Plank, David Hostetler, Stephen Miller, C. Z. Yoder, Peter Conrad, Albert Hartzler, P. R. Lantz, Peter Baumgartner, J. N. Smucker, Wm. G. Detweiler, Elmer Meyer (ministers and deacons).   V.M.GE.

J. Umble, *Ohio Mennonite Sunday Schools* (Goshen, 1941) 209-31; *ML* III, 282.

Oak Grove Old Order Mennonite Church, Dayton, Va., one of the two O.O.M. congregations in Virginia. The meetinghouse was built in 1921, 1½ miles south of Dayton. It is one of two meetinghouses shared by the two factions of the O.O.M. in Virginia (*q.v.*).   H.S.B.

Oak Shade Mennonite Church, located in the Baptist Chapel, Kirkwood, Route 1, Lancaster Co., Pa., was opened by the Mennonites (MC) in 1923, with Abram L. Huber in charge. The results among the Scotch-Irish here were somewhat disappointing and the work closed in late 1930. But when more Mennonites moved into southern Lancaster County it was reopened on May 14, 1933. In 1957 the membership was 35. It is the southern end of the Jacob L. Harnish Bishop District. Ray S. Yost and Mervin A. Good are the ministers.   I.D.L.

Oak Terrace Mennonite (MC) Church, Blountstown, Fla., under the Indiana-Michigan Conference, was begun in 1953 by a number of families moving in chiefly from near Kouts, Ind. In 1957 the membership was 41, with Kore Zook as pastor. H.S.B.

Oakhill Amish Mennonite Church (now extinct) was located about 11 miles west of Eugene, Lane Co., Ore. (See **Eugene** Mennonite Church.) M.G.

Oakwood Mennonite Church (MC), Conowingo, Md., a mission church under the Lancaster Confer-

ence, was started in 1950. In 1957 it had 44 members, with Paul G. Leaman as pastor. The meetinghouse is 1½ miles north of the Conowingo Dam, and 6 miles west of Rising Sun, Md.   H.S.B.

Oath. The oath is the strongest possible confirmation of the truth of a statement by calling upon God to witness. The most familiar and most common explanation is that the oath is the calling upon the holy and omniscient God as witness and protector of the truth and as judge and avenger of untruth and lying.

Among the Jews, who had a living faith in a personal God, the oath had a deeper religious meaning than among the pagans. With the Jews the prescribed oath before a tribunal was very rare. It was used only as a sort of oath of purification in case of injury or theft of some entrusted or found property. Ex. 22:6 ff.; Lev. 5:23; Prov. 29:24. But it was very frequent in their civil and business life. In the Old Testament the oath was required. The basic passage is designated as Gen. 21:28-31, where Abimelech, the king of the Philistines, demanded of Abraham an oath that he would not deal falsely with him or his descendants but show mercy as Abimelech had shown Abraham. Abraham rendered the oath and as a testimony of the oath gave the king seven lambs. This is the origin of the Hebrew word for swearing, which means to affirm with seven sacrifices. The simplest form of the oath was the elevation of the right hand or both hands. Gen. 14:22; Deut. 32:40; Dan. 12:7. It appears to have been generally customary, so that the expression "to lift the hand" is equivalent to swearing (Hebrew and German of Ex. 6:8; Num. 14:30).

A presupposition of a proper oath in the Old Covenant is faith in the living God. Only the oath by Him is expressly commanded. Ex. 22:10. It is considered a sign of faithful attachment to God. Deut. 6:13; 10:20; Jer. 12:16; Isa. 48:1. A special blessing of God is promised for it. Ps. 24:4; Isa. 65:16. Only the oath by false gods is prohibited. Ex. 20:7; Lev. 19:12; Josh. 23:7. God swears by Himself (Isa. 45:23), by His soul (Amos 6:8), by His eternal life (Deut. 32:40), by His all-power (Isa. 62:8), or by His holiness (Amos 4:2; Ps. 89:36). Man swears by God and His name. Ex. 22:10. The most common formula for the oath was "As the Lord liveth" (Judg. 8:19; I Sam. 14:39). Less usual was the assertion, "The Lord be (watch) between me and thee" (Gen. 31:50; I Sam. 20:42; Jer. 42:5). Curses upon others and upon oneself are frequent with the formula, "The Lord do so to me" (I Sam. 3:17; 14:44), "Let the Lord even require it" (I Sam. 20:16), "The Lord shall return thy wickedness upon thine own head" (I Kings 2:44; see also Num. 21). The Israelites also swore by the king and his life. Gen. 42:15; II Sam. 11:11. Not unusual is the oath by the life of the one addressed, "As thou livest" (I Sam. 1:26; 17:55; also I Sam. 20:3; 25:26; II Kings 2:2; 4:6; 4:30). Later the practice of swearing by calling curses upon oneself increased among the Jews. Their hesitancy to speak the name of God also led to their swearing oaths by things that had some relation to Him, as by heaven, by Jerusalem, by the angels, by the earth, by the temple, by the altar, and by the sacrifice. Against this increasing abuse of the oath earnest voices of urgent warning were raised. Eccl. 9:2; Sir. 23:9-17.

The N.T. position on the oath is on a higher plane than that of the Old; it adopts an actually opposite position. Whereas in the O.T. the oath was commanded as a religious duty, in the N.T. it is expressly forbidden. This is taught unequivocally and clearly by the words of Jesus in the Sermon on the Mount (Matt. 5:33-37): "Again, ye have heard that it hath been said by them of old time, Thou shalt not forswear thyself, but shalt perform unto the Lord thine oaths: but I say unto you, Swear not at all." Jesus here definitely opposes the O.T. custom with something new and essentially different. If the oath was permitted and even commanded to those of "old times," which means the members of the Old Covenant, it is now abrogated for His disciples. For them is meant the strict command of the Lord, the "I say unto you," that they must not only refrain from swearing falsely, but that they must not in any case or under any circumstance whatever swear an oath. Jesus mentions several kinds of oaths, formulas for the oath that were especially popular in that day, i.e., by heaven, by earth, by Jerusalem, and by one's head. It is possible that He is here opposing the casuistry of the Pharisees, which distinguished between such oaths and an oath by God, declaring the former less binding than the latter.

It is therefore completely erroneous to say that Jesus made an exception of the oath by God in His prohibition. Much more the conclusion from the lesser to the greater is correct here. If even the oath by heaven, by earth, by Jerusalem, and by one's head are forbidden because and in so far as they are in a relationship with God, so much the more is the oath by God prohibited. To this strict and rigorous prohibition of the oath Jesus adds the definite command that His disciples in their assurances restrict themselves to a simple yes or no and avoid all that goes beyond them by way of strengthening a statement because it is of evil. Whether this is interpreted to mean the evil one (devil) or abstract evil makes little difference. Jesus means that the oath has its basis in a corrupt and sinful condition and that it leads to such a condition, both of which the Christian is to avoid and put away.

An express repetition of the prohibition of the oath by Jesus is found in James 5:12: "But above all things, my brethren, swear not, neither by heaven, neither by the earth, neither by any other oath: but let your yea be yea; and your nay, nay; lest ye fall into condemnation." The closing words, which constitute the only difference between these words and those of Jesus in the Sermon on the Mount, suggest that the oath is punishable; it is a wrong toward God and is thus subject to His punishment.

There are therefore religious and moral concerns which underlie the prohibition of the oath. A deep reverence for God must restrain man from using the absolutely holy God as a witness to his statements. Even if one is ever so sure of telling the truth, it is very easy to be in error and thereby sin, and thus by an oath involve God in his sin. It is presumptuous for a man to assert in extreme form his trust in his own ability to be truthful and to call down upon himself the judgment of God. The Christian should rather so live before God that His presence sanctifies heart and mouth; consequently he does not willingly sin against God's commandments and always has God for a witness wherever he is and whatever he does. Hence the Christian does not make a special attempt to be truthful before courts and in extraordinary considerations but always seeks to live in the highest truth. The oath dulls this sense of absolute commitment and hence has a demoralizing rather than morally elevating effect. Jesus' prohibition of the oath is therefore not a literalistic, legalistic command but is grounded on a deep and solid religious and ethical foundation. The rejection of the oath binds one to absolute obedience to Jesus in full discipleship and always to live and testify in complete truthfulness.

The leading Church Fathers, such as Origen, Gregory of Nazianzus, Tertullian, and Chrysostom, rejected the oath most vigorously. It was only after the state church was set up and Christianity became a state religion that the oath returned to use among Christians. It was the state's interest that called for the oath, and the church as the willing servant of the state supported and sanctioned its demand. Augustine gave the theological foundation for the oath. He was quite aware of the objections to the oath and hence called for its use only in urgent matters. But he nevertheless held that the oath contributed to the glory of God and was useful to the state and the neighbor. This remained the basic position of the Catholic Church. Councils and popes, especially Innocent III, constantly increased the emphasis upon the oath as a matter of divine law.

The Reformers and the Protestant churches adopted the position of the Catholic Church on the oath. Luther interpreted the passage in Matthew 5 as forbidding the swearing of an oath on one's own initiative or out of custom, but taught that the command of the state to render an oath must be obeyed. His *Greater Catechism* says, "The oath is a right good work, by which God is praised, the truth and the right are confirmed, lies are stopped, people are brought to peace, obedience is done, and strife is overcome, since God Himself enters in to separate right from wrong and good from evil." The *Heidelberg Catechism* answers thus the question whether one may piously swear an oath with the name of God: "Yes, if it is required by the authorities or in case of need to maintain and promote loyalty and truth to the honor of God and the welfare of one's neighbor. For such swearing is grounded in the Word of God and therefore was rightly used by the saints of the Old and New Testaments." This is the general Protestant understanding and teaching concerning the oath down to the present time. It is claimed that the oath is necessary even in Christian society because of the all too common unreliability of ordinary statements and the general distrust of people toward each other, in short because of the imperfection of human society. Says Martenson, "Lying and mutual distrust are with us, and so from ancient times the oath has been used as a guarantee for truthfulness." Such a position fails to recognize and properly evaluate Jesus' strict prohibition of the oath.

But alongside of the church's position there has always been another position which rejects the oath completely in obedience to the command of Jesus and of James. This has been the position of the medieval sects (though not uniformly), the Cathari, Albigenses, Waldenses, Beguines, and Beghards, also the Wiclifites, Hussites, and Bohemian Brethren.

The Anabaptists rejected and opposed the oath from the beginning in strict obedience to the express prohibition of Jesus. Andreas Castelberger requested the Zürich Council in 1526 to excuse him from the oath (*Urfehde*) when he was to be exiled. Georg Blaurock refused to swear the oath when he was expelled on Jan. 5, 1527. The seventh article of the Schleitheim Confession of Feb. 24, 1527, expressly refers to the prohibition of Christ "who taught the perfection of the law and forbids Christians all swearing." Our speech is to be simply yes and no. This was the general rule among the Anabaptists as is frequently attested in the trials, disputations, and confessions extracted by torture, although Hubmaier and Denk did not take such a strong position. (See the disputations of Zofingen in 1532 and Frankenthal in 1571, also the discussion with Hans Pfistermeyer in 1531.) Felix Manz, swore the Urfehde, as did Blaurock shortly after Jan. 5, 1527.

The case was slightly different among the Anabaptists in Holland. At first Menno Simons was not so strict on the oath as he was later. Hoekstra says that at first, on the ground of Jesus' use of "verily" and Paul's use of several strong asseverations, Menno thought that the prohibition of the oath in the N.T. referred only to temporal matters, such as flesh and blood and money and property, whereas one was allowed to use only yes and no in affirming divine truth to the honor of God and the welfare of one's neighbor. Later he declared that the asseverations of the N.T. had nothing to do with the swearing of an oath. Peter Tasch (*q.v.*), an Anabaptist leader in Hesse, wrote a tract *Vom Eid*, which has apparently been lost.

Menno dealt with the oath in only two of his writings. The first was his booklet of 1552 entitled *A Fundamental and Clear Confession*, in which he earnestly admonishes: "Worthy Reader, are you one who fears the Lord and you are pressed to take an oath—stand by the Word of the Lord, which forbids you so clearly to swear, and let your yea be yea and your nay be nay, as He has commanded, whether it means life or death to you, so that you may by your valiance and steadfast truthfulness so admonish and rebuke the worthless, unfruitful, vain world, which respects nothing less than the Word of the Lord, that by your yea and nay it may be brought in its faithlessness and falsity to righteousness, so that perchance someone may be converted from his unrighteousness and thereby led to deeper thought and be saved."

Menno's second writing dealing with the oath was his *Epistle to Martin Micron* of 1556 written in reply to Micron's *A Clear and Scriptural Instruction on the Oath*. Most skillfully Menno points his opponent to the "bright and clear words of the Son of God whose word is truth and whose commandment is eternal life," and deplores that they "are falsified for the sake of human authorities."

Among the martyrs in *Offer des Heeren* who expressly rejected the oath were Elizabeth (1549), Frans van Bolsward (1545), Joos Kind (1553), Leenaert Plovier (1559), and Hans van der Maes (1559).

All the Mennonite confessions of faith without exception have included a prohibition of the oath. The Concept of Cologne (1591) says: "According to the teaching of Christ and James one is not to swear, rather all words and deeds are to be confirmed by a truthful yes or no, and nothing added thereto, and this is to be kept just like a sworn oath." The Confession of Hans de Ries and Lubbert Gerrits of 1610 declares briefly and laconically, "Jesus Christ, king and lawgiver (Matt. 28:20; Gal. 6:2) of the N.T., has forbidden the Christian all swearing of the oath (Matt. 5:33, 37; Jas. 5:12), wherefore the N.T. believer is not permitted to swear an oath." The Dordrecht Confession of 1632 concludes emphatically from the prohibition of Christ "that all high and low oaths are forbidden us," and calls upon us to keep all promises, sayings, and testimonies as faithfully "as if we had sworn with a high oath." The prohibition of swearing is most thoroughly defended in the Cornelis Ris Confession of 1766.

The Hutterites also had a high regard for the prohibition of the oath. Peter Riedemann discusses the oath extensively in his *Rechenschaft* (1545). He bases the difference between the Old and New Testaments in the fact that the O.T. has the shadow (Col. 2:17) of the truth while the N.T. has the full brightness, the O.T. has the spirit of the slave while the N.T. has the spirit of sonship, hence the shadow "must give way to the spirit of truth which operates in us."

Since the oath has always been held to be essential to the existence of the state it was inevitable that the refusal of Mennonites to use it would bring them into conflict with government. It was only gradually and after long and serious attempts to suppress them that those countries in which Mennonites settled became willing to grant them the special privilege of substituting the simple affirmation (*Handgelübde*) for the oath. This was especially true in Switzerland, for the authorities felt that the rejection of the oath meant the undermining of all authority; hence they fought the Anabaptists as a sect dangerous to the very existence of the state. Stubbornly they insisted on the oath (*Urfehde*) whenever an Anabaptist was expelled from their territory, and the loyalty oath if they granted toleration. Not until late in the 17th century did Zürich, for instance, finally authorize the affirmation in place of the oath for expellees and even then the exception was simply allowed in practice without putting it into the legal regulations. Similarly in Bern as late as 1813 a decree was issued denying to the Mennonites all civil and voting rights because they refused the loyalty oath. A regulation of Nov. 22, 1820, specified that instead of the loyalty oath an affirmation which had the same consequences as the oath could be rendered in the official residence of the judge (*Oberamtmann*). With the adoption of the new federal constitution of 1874 Mennonites have been permitted to substitute the affirmation for the normal oath.

In Holland the Mennonites early received special consideration for their position on the oath through the good will of Prince William of Orange. He granted the request of the Mennonites of Antwerp (Sept. 23, 1566) for release from the requirement of the oath. Likewise his intervention secured to the Mennonites of Middelburg in 1577 and 1578 exemption from the civil oath. Four years later the state of Zeeland attempted without success to impose a law requiring all Mennonites to perform the oath. In 1585 the Dutch States General decided to exempt the Mennonites from the oath, and a law of March 28, 1588, specified the wording of the substitute formula. Friesland, on the other hand, issued a decree on March 8, 1597, denying those who refused the oath the privilege of living in the country, and not until March 19, 1659, was the requirement of the oath canceled for Mennonites; on July 10, 1700, a substitute formula was provided. The city of Groningen passed a decree on April 25, 1616, exempting Mennonites from the oath.

Louis XVI of France rejected the request of the Alsatian Mennonites in 1766 for exemption from the oath. Jacob Frey of Dürrenzen, who refused to swear an oath, was sentenced on Sept. 7, 1769, to lifelong exile from France and a fine of 10 pounds and court costs. But the Mennonites of France refused to yield and finally won their release when the Court of Cassation in 1810 decreed that "Anabaptists and Quakers" need not render an oath, and since 1812 it has been the general practice in France to permit members of recognized religious bodies to substitute an affirmation for the oath.

In Austria Mennonites were freed from taking an oath by a royal decree of Jan. 10, 1816.

The *Privilegium* (*q.v.*) granted by Paul I of Russia on Sept. 6, 1800, guaranteed "for all time" to the Mennonites the right to substitute a simple yes and no for an oath before the courts.

In Germany the practice in regard to the oath has been variable. On Oct. 13, 1768, the imperial high court decreed that the Mennonite affirmation was to be accepted as a substitute for the oath; but only a few states in the empire, e.g., Hesse-Nassau, observed this decree. Almost everywhere Mennonites had to fight for exemption. In Prussia it took the Mennonites a long time to secure toleration. The rulers repeatedly ordered expulsion of the Mennonites, but their decrees were not executed because of the economic advantages accruing from Mennonite settlement, and the Mennonites were quietly allowed the religious freedom which the laws did not openly grant. Those settlements living under Polish rule, however, were granted special privileges of freedom by the Polish kings, which evidently included exemption from the oath. In Elbing they were allowed to substitute the simple yes and no but required to place the hand on the breast. The first express grant by a Prussian king of substitution of affirmation for the oath was by Frederick II on June 14, 1773, in response to a Mennonite petition of June 7. The affirmation was fully legalized by a law of May 11, 1827. In East Friesland a decree of Aug. 30, 1631, governing leasing of land authorized the substitution of the "Mennonite oath." But Mennonites still had much trouble before the courts and in spite of repeated petitions did not acquire full exemption until the decree of June 2, 1701. In Friedrichstadt the *Privilegium* of Feb. 13, 1623, granted Mennonites exemption. In Altona the grant was made as early as 1601 and reconfirmed on June 6, 1641.

The earlier Mennonite practice of settling all disputes without going to law long kept the oath question from becoming a serious issue in Germany. But after the 18th century, with settlement in the city and entering business life, involvement in legal matters was almost inevitable. Trouble arose on this account in Crefeld and in Mannheim. In the latter city a legal action was broken off because two Mennonites refused to swear the required oath. An appeal to the ruler resulted in a decree that Mennonites were to be granted the privilege of affirmation "according to previous practice." By 1893 Mennonites were exempt from the oath in practically all the German states (ten Doornkaat-Koolman). In the absence of a general uniform law for all Germany, however, Mennonite conference petitions were directed to securing such a law; e.g., the Vereinigung (*q.v.*) presented such a request to the Prussian authorities on Dec. 22, 1892, and again in 1910, and in 1910 to the federal authorities. The 1919 constitution of the German Republic instituted the secular oath (all reference to God omitted), but since Mennonites did not want to swear in any form they requested exemption.

In the United States and Canada the Mennonite immigrants coming from Europe at various times 1683-1880 received full recognition for their position on the oath. In this they were greatly aided by the prior arrival of the Quakers who had an identical position, the Quaker Colony of Pennsylvania being the only place of direct Mennonite settlement up to 1815. Recognition of the affirmation instead of the oath on grounds of conscience is not provided in the federal constitution, but the guarantee of religious freedom which it contains is understood to include this and has been so interpreted by the courts. However, many state constitutions include express provisions for the use of the affirmation in place of the oath, and there has never been any serious trouble on this point in the United States or Canada. The modern spirit of toleration in most countries makes it relatively easy to secure recognition of conscience in such matters almost anywhere, even in the absence of specific constitutional or legal guarantees.

It is noteworthy that the principle of nonswearing of oaths has been and still is upheld by all Mennonite groups of whatever country, conference, or theological position, the one historic Anabaptist-Mennonite principle of which this can be said. Individual exceptions of course have taken place, and there are no doubt Mennonites today who are careless in applying this principle in all legal matters. Some Mennonites, for example, who are notaries, follow the inconsistent practice of administering the oath to others; and others sign legal forms on which the oath is printed without substituting the word "affirm" for "swear," as they may legally do. To some this may seem to be a minor technicality, but where it is ignored the deeper meaning of the rejection of the oath has been obscured or lost.

(Details of the history and practice in Germany regarding the Mennonite objection to the oath are given in the exhaustive treatment by Neff in the article **Eid**, *ML* I, 542-46, which carried the account up to 1920, which article has been reproduced in somewhat condensed form above. The following supplementary section by William Klassen adds material chiefly on the attitude of the 16th-century South German Anabaptists toward the oath.)

NEFF, H.S.B.

In the major disputations between the Anabaptists and the Reformers the question of the oath had an important place. Hans Hillerbrand has correctly noted, "Contrary to the question of nonparticipation in war, where due to the absence of universal conscription in the sixteenth century the Anabaptist position remained largely a theoretical one, the problem of the oath was real and pertinent."

The earliest confession, drafted at Schleitheim in February 1527, makes it clear that the Anabaptist stand against oaths was absolute. The oath is there defined as a confirmation among those who promise or are in disagreement with each other. It has been commanded in the law, but Christ who is the fulfillment of the law teaches that under no circumstances should His disciples swear an oath. The reason for this is that we cannot make a hair on our head white or black. Since we may not be able to accomplish the content of the oath due to the contingencies of human existence, the oath is forbidden.

After this definition of the oath and the exposition of Christ's teaching, the writers deal with certain objections to this interpretation. (1) To the objection implying that since God swore an oath to Abraham, man can do so also, Sattler, the editor if not author of the Schleitheim articles, replies that God is able to accomplish His promise, whereas human beings cannot. (2) The objection insisting that Christ forbade only the swearing by certain things, such as temple, heaven, or the head, is answered with a reference to Christ's question: "You blind fools, what is greater, the throne, or he that sits upon it?" (3) To the argument asserting that swearing must be right, since Peter and Paul swore, the reply is that the apostles in calling God to witness were actually only testifying to what God will do, and not themselves promising what they will do; swearing and testifying are two different things. Testifying refers to the present, while swearing refers to the future. Even the statement by Simeon to Mary is here called a testimony, even though it clearly refers to the future. The final (4) argument for the rejection of the oath is the word of Christ, Let your word be Yes, Yes, and No, No, and whatever is above that is from the evil one. For it is clear that Christ did not permit the oath. All those who simply seek Christ will follow His clear word and understand it.

The Confession of Schleitheim (*q.v.*) exerted a profound influence, not only among Anabaptists, but also evoked a reply from Zwingli and Calvin.

The standard objections to this Anabaptist position on the oath, found in both of these Reformers, are to a large extent anticipated in the Schleitheim Confession. A large number of Anabaptists followed this interpretation of the oath and refused to swear under any circumstances. At Strasbourg those who refused to take the oath were identified as Anabaptists. Also the only Anabaptist treatise devoted exclusively to the oath was written at Strasbourg by Fridolin Meyer (*q.v.*, Meiger) in 1528 in which the various Scripture passages on the oath were set side by side. This manuscript leaflet of four pages found with the record of his cross-examination indicates that the Strasbourg Anabaptists were discussing this issue.

Already before the convocation at Schleitheim Hans Denk had formulated a position on the oath which he discussed in his treatise *Von der wahren Liebe* (January 1527). He argues that since man is unable to keep his vows or covenants, whatever appears as right should be performed without a promise or commitment. Where a man makes a vow concerning something over which he has no power, there is either a presumption without understanding, or else hypocrisy with understanding. He deals also with the argument that God's swearing justifies ours, since we are to become perfect as our Father in heaven is perfect! Denk rejects this because we do not have the power to accomplish our oath, and insists that we must follow the example of Christ.

Nor should anyone be too hasty in saying yes or no simply because it is allowed, for whoever assures someone with an affirmation, has already sworn, because he anticipates the will of God and might become a perjurer. This is not the case if one deals correctly as Paul did when it was impossible for him to carry out his plans with the Corinthians.

With respect to matters which have taken place in the past, Denk says that whoever would testify to them should do so with as few words as possible, yes or no, for whatever is above that must be settled with God. If someone has God as a witness to the truth of his statement, he may appeal to this fact, as Paul also did, only let him be careful not to take the name of God in vain, for this is forbidden in the law, as also the N.T. forbids swearing. In his "Recantation," Denk devotes the last section (X) to the oath. He begins again, as he did earlier, with the assertion that swearing, judging, etc., are not wrong in themselves, but forbidden so that no occasion be given to the flesh. The abuse of the oath, seen everywhere, is that it is assumed certain that what is sworn will take place. "Whoever has the mind and spirit of the Lord, promises, vows, and swears nothing, except that which he may do with a good conscience, namely, that which he is obligated to do out of the teaching of Christ, such as not to steal, not to kill, not to commit adultery, not to avenge oneself, and the like. And yet he will promise nothing, except on the grace of God, not what he will do, but rather what he would like to do, so that he is not guilty of presumptuousness.

"Summa, whatever one can say by the truth, that he may also testify to by God, even more by creatures, such as raising the hand and the like, . . .

whether one call it swearing or not, it has not been the meaning of Christ at any time to forbid such. Paul says: I call upon God as witness to my soul, as if to say, God shall repay my soul if I do not speak the truth. That is no different than the way a man swears today: This or that I will or desire to do, so help me God, i.e., if my will is not this, God will not help me, etc."

Denk is here cited at some length because he indicates a difference from the position of Schleitheim in some important respects, and it may be that it is due to him that a number of important South German Anabaptists diverged from the statement of Schleitheim on the subject of the oath.

Hans Hut, in his testimony of 1527 (October), asserts that the oath in community, civic, and state affairs is not forbidden by God and that the authority of government in this area can only be questioned when it demands an oath which is against God (see **Hut** in *ML*, but not in *ME*). Hut surely knew of Schleitheim, and there are indications that he had had discussions with the Kürschner (Jacob Gross?) and others about the oath. The lack of uniformity in the traditions surrounding Hut calls for caution in evaluating this evidence, but on the surface it would seem to agree with the position which is later seen in the Marpeck brotherhood.

Pilgram Marpeck himself was accused by Bucer of teaching the Strasbourg Anabaptists that swearing and resisting are wrong, but he never discusses the oath at any length in any of his writings. The only possible exception is an epistle in the *Kunstbuch* attributed by Heinold Fast to Marpeck, directed to the Swiss Brethren (No. 8), dated 1543. The reference to the oath there is as follows: "Concerning the oath, we cannot captivate or bind anyone's conscience to your understanding of it (which we have abundantly and earnestly understood from you), nor can we bind a cord on anyone's neck, nor can we subjugate our conscience to your understanding. . . ." Unfortunately at this point a page is torn out, leaving the statement on the oath incomplete without proof of authorship. But the epistle shows that the South Germans had discussions with the Swiss about the oath, and that there was disagreement on it.

Jörg Rothenfelder (*q.v.*), the editor of the *Kunstbuch,* wrote a one-page discussion of the oath (fol. 157). But since this folio is without signature, it is possible that the page mentioned above as missing at the end of the Marpeck epistle is simply displaced to here. The position reflected in this statement deviates from the absolute rejection of the oath by Schleitheim by equating calling God as witness with swearing an oath, and making it legitimate since Paul and Peter did this. Rothenfelder gave as one of the reasons why he left St. Gall earlier the differences between him and the Swiss Brethren, and one of the issues was the oath. So it is clear that there is a difference on this point between the Swiss Brethren and at least some of the South German Anabaptists.

How can one account for this difference? A comparison of Schleitheim and Denk would reveal first of all that Denk was more interested in meeting abstract theological arguments than in legislating for a congregation. Schleitheim, on the other hand, set out to demarcate clearly the differences between them and the false brethren. As a result it appears to be more legalistic than do the writings of Denk. A greater difference, however, is seen in their approach to the Scriptures. The method of Sattler is to take the face value of the words of Scriptures and attempt to fulfill them, whereas Denk and others after him attempted to grapple with the meaning of the Scripture.

On the question of the oath this difference becomes most apparent in connection with the pamphlet written by Wolfgang Musculus (*q.v.*) entitled *Ain frydsams vnnd Christlichs Gesprech, ains Euangelischen, auff ainer, vnd ains Widertauffers, auff der andern seyten, so sy des Aydschwurs halben mitainander thund* (Augsburg, 1533) (in GCL). Musculus knew the Anabaptists well, having served as Bucer's secretary in Strasbourg, and having left Strasbourg shortly before Pilgram Marpeck. In Augsburg in the later years he had discussions with Marpeck. Musculus was an acute exegete and a temperate polemicist against the Anabaptists, believing that they could be won through convincing arguments. The tone of his pamphlet is very gentle, and his effort to understand their position is apparent. Rothenfelder and perhaps Marpeck were convinced by his statement on the oath, mainly no doubt, because Musculus began with the Bible and allowed it to speak to the matter of the oath, trying to show that the Anabaptist interpretation actually did violence to the intent of Scripture. He begins his refutation with the definition of an oath, making it so broad that it includes not only the asseverations of Paul and the apostles, but also the "Verily, verily" of Jesus Himself, and then appeals to the principle of *imitatio Christi* as an argument for the oath. Musculus also discusses the assertion of the Anabaptists that the future is uncertain, hence human beings cannot commit themselves by means of an oath, saying that this interpretation would rule out all commitments and all vows, including the marriage vow. His position is that the oath is acceptable because it assures the hearer that the one who takes an oath has searched his heart and promises that, God giving him strength, he will fulfill his obligations. For the past, the oath has the effect of calling on God to witness that what he is saying is indeed true.

Musculus' treatment of the oath is a distinctly different approach to the subject. The main basis of his argument is not the Old Testament, but the New, but in the New he shows exegetical skill and an amazing knowledge of Jewish traditions that must have impressed any Anabaptist who read his pamphlet.

Through Martin Micron's translation into Dutch in 1535 the book by Musculus became an important element in the discussions between Menno and Micron in 1556. Micron defended the position of Musculus, while Menno said that the plain word of Scripture is "lamentably falsified and plastered over with the vile dung of satanic glosses, merely to suit the rulers" by both Musculus and Micron. Menno does more than simply discard their interpretations; he grapples with their views in several respects.

By bringing in the temporal and eternal categories Menno sought to invalidate Musculus' argument by stating that Paul and Christ's asseverations were only in the sphere of eternal matters, and that in temporal matters they did not use them. In doing so he tacitly granted the equating of the oath with calling God to witness, thus departing from Schleitheim on this point. He also admits that in a sense a vow is the same as an oath, but is valid and necessary in the area of eternal truth which does not relate to temporal matters. Marriage vows and baptismal vows would come under this category. For his position he claims the support of men like Jerome, Erasmus, Philip Melanchthon, Haymo, and Origen. The yea and the nay of the Anabaptist has the force of an oath because he does not lie, and so the rulers should not fear his refusal to swear. In Menno's writings on the oath the desire to fulfill the words of Christ literally comes strongly to the fore, and the faith is clearly stated that God will not decive us with His doctrine. The aspect of promise for the future in an oath does not appear as strongly as it does among the Swiss and the South Germans.

The Anabaptists lived their lives in the immediacy of the divine Spirit, and a life thus lived refuses to be held by an oath. Thus when a group of Anabaptists were asked to swear an oath (*Urfehde*) never to return to Strasbourg in 1532, they refused to do so, stating that this would be trying to ascertain where the Spirit would next lead them. Logically, of course, while there is a strong element of Biblical truth here, this freedom rules out any long-term contract or commitment.

Widmoser has suggested that Marpeck distinguished between the secular and religious oath in much the same way Menno did, only he reversed the tables and made the secular oath permissible (e.g., to serve the city faithfully as an engineer) but ruled out any oath which might restrict his religious life. Support for this view is utterly lacking in the sources, and it is perhaps still more accurate to state that the Anabaptists did not differentiate between the secular and the religious realms in the way that Luther did in his two-kingdom view.

For the contemporary problem it is obvious that the oath has little place in a secularized society, whose God if it believes in one is totally irrelevant. The oath in that context is either a legal tool to make punishment for perjury possible, or else simply a remnant of a civilization once supposedly based on a Deity. Otto Bauernfeind has ably demonstrated the dilemma in which the oath has placed Protestant Christianity, and has shown that when the security of a society is threatened, recourse is taken to an oath (Nazis, loyalty oaths in America, Reformation time). This pathological trait of society creates difficulties for the church which has no policy on the oath, because in war, for instance, "the good and acceptable and perfect will of God is always affirmatively related to preparations for war, while for the establishment of peace it is always comfortably neutral." In a context like modern society the oath becomes utterly absurd, but a mere mechanical abstention from it does little to change the situation. As Bauernfeind shows, the oath was not a part of early Christianity, where the simple formula was yes, yes, and no, no. The principles involved in the oath go far beyond any slavish literal obedience to the letter of Scripture.   W.KL.

Beatrice Jenny, *Das Schleitheimer Täuferbekenntnis 1527* (Thayngen, 1951) 16 f., 75 f.; Walter Fellmann, ed., *Hans Denck Schriften* II (Gütersloh, 1956) 84, 110; Menno Simons, *Writings*, 517-21, 922-27; Peter Rideman, *Account of Our Religion, Doctrine and Faith* (n.p., 1950, Engl. tr. of the *Rechenschaft* of 1545, printed 1565) 114-18; S. Hoekstra Bz., *Beginselen en leer der oude Doopsgezinden* (Amsterdam, 1863) 268; W. Mannhardt, *Die Wehrfreiheit der Altpreussischen Mennoniten* (Marienburg, 1863); Joh. Dyserinck, *De vrijstelling van den eed voor de Doopsgezinden, eene historische Studie* (Haarlem, 1883, enlarged reprint from *De Gids*, 1882, No. 10); idem, *Het Recht der Waarheid tegenover den Staat (Bijdrage tot de eedvraag)* (Amsterdam, 1902); J. ten Doornkaat-Koolman, *Die Verpflichtung der Mennoniten an Eidesstatt* (Berlin, 1893); Philipp Kieferndorf, *Der Eid* (Worms, 1892); K. Vos, "Bastiaan vaan Weenigem en het eedvraagstuk," in *Nederl. Archief voor Kerkgeschiedenis*, 1908; "Was heisst Mennonit" (extensive discussion of the oath), *Monatsblätter der Mennonitengemeinde Krefeld* (1905); *Ein Christenlich gespräch gehallten zuo Bern zwüschen den Predicanten und Hansen Pfyster Mayer von Aarouw den Widertouff, Eyd, Oberkeyt, und andere Widertoufferische Artikel betreffende* (n.p., n.d.—Bern, 1531); Joh. Oecolampadius, *Underrichtung von den Widertauff, von der Oberkeit und von dem Eyd, auff Carlins N. Widertouffer Artickel* (Basel, 1527); Wolfgang Meüszlin, *Ain frydsams unnd christlichs Gesprech ains Evengelischenn, auff ainer, und ains Widerteuffers, auff der andern seyten, so sy des Aydschwurs halben mitainander thund* (n.p., 1533); Johann Faber, *Von dem Ayd schwören. Auch von der Widertauffer Marter* ... (n.p., 1550); Klaas Toornburg, *Schriftuurlijke verhandelingh tegens het eedzweren, en voor de wraak en weerloose lydsaemheyt en volmaeckt liefde, die de christen moeten oeffenen, aen en omtrent de boose en vyanden* ... (Alkmaar, 1688) (all the above titles are in GCL); *DB* 1863, 61; 1868, 27, 53 f.; 1875, 93 ff.; 1876, 75; 1881, 43; 1883, 19; 1899, 181; 1904, 233; 1907, 162; 1908, 33-41; 1909, 83, 113; *Menn. Bl.*, repeated references 1876-1921 (see *ML* I, 546 for specifics); B. Bauer, *Der Eid, Eine Studie* (Heidelberg, 1854); Brandt, *Der Eid in den Reichsprozessordnungen* (Kassel, 1895); Otto Proksch, "Das Eidesverbot Jesu Christi," *Thüringer Kirchliches Jahrbuch* XIII (1907) 21 f.; Johannes Pedersen, *Der Eid bei den Semiten* (1924); Otto Bauernfeind, *Eid und Friede* (Stuttgart, 1956); Hans J. Hillerbrand, "The Anabaptist View of the State," *MQR* XXX (1958) 105-7; Daniel Kauffman, *Doctrines of the Bible* (Scottdale, 1929, 2nd ed. 1949) 517-21; George R. Brunk, *Ready Scriptural Reasons* (Scottdale, 1926) 189-91; John C. Wenger, *Separated Unto God* (Scottdale, 1951) 104-8; Gerhard Roosen, "On the Swearing of Oaths," *Christian Conversation on Saving Faith* (Scottdale, 1941, Engl. tr. of *Christliches Gemüthsgespräch*, first ed. 1702 at Ratzeburg?); *Das von den Gliedern der Mennonitengemeinde im Grossherzogthum Baden an Eidesstatt abzuleistende Handgelübde* (Heilbronn, 1862, 2nd ed. Sinsheim, 1890); J. Dyserinck.

Ob Mission, a Mennonite mission along the Ob River in Siberia, Russia, opened by the Mennonites when World War I and the Russian Revolution cut them off from their work in foreign fields. As early as 1889 F. W. Baedeker (*q.v.*) and J. G. Kargel (*q.v.*), well-known leaders of the evangelical movement in Russia, preached in the prisons of Siberia. Here, in the Omsk district on the Ob River, they especially noticed the native Ostyaks (Khants), who lived under conditions similar to those of the Eskimos. During the Russo-Japanese War Karl Benzien (*q.v.*), a German Baptist and associated with Mennonite Brethren of Chortitza, engaged in evangelistic work and distribution of Bibles in this area, and during these five years among the German and Russian population he became acquainted with the Ostyaks. Upon his return to European Russia he advocated the cause of missions among them, especially in the Mennonite circles.

In 1918, during the Revolution, a group consisting of Johann Peters, his wife, his sister Helena, and Johann Kehler, all Mennonites, and Paul Beer and his wife, undertook the trip to Northern Siberia to begin mission work. They had no special preparation or any idea where they would find a field of labor nor any congregational backing. They settled on the territory along the Ob River from Tomsk to Narym, up to Khante Mansiysk, where the Irtish River joins the Ob. They first contacted all evangelical Christians, usually Baptists, who had migrated or had been banished to this place. The natives of the territory are, besides the Ostyaks (Khants), the Voguls (Mans) and further north the Samoyeds (Nents). Small outposts were established from which the missionaries undertook preaching trips. Johann Peters and his group worked for five years around Narym. Karl Benzien and Johann Peters undertook a trip to the Mennonite settlements in Siberia to create interest in their work. In 1924 they were joined by six families and a few individuals. More stations were opened, some as far north as Obdorsk, covering at times an area extending some 750 miles north and south. In 1925 Johann Peters returned to his home settlement in Orenburg and also reported to the Mennonite General Conference (Bundeskonferenz) in Moscow, on the success in the work and the need for more workers and support. Enthusiastically he wrote in 1926: "Brethren, for nine years we have now had religious freedom in our country. Why do so many go to America and so very few come to the northern mission field where we can proclaim the Gospel without interference?" As a result interest in this work increased. Reports were published in Unser Blatt, contributions were made, and new workers arrived. Some of the workers preached in Russian, while others learned the native tongues of the various tribes. Special interest was shown by the Mennonites, especially the Mennonite Brethren, of the settlements in Siberia, Samara, and Orenburg, some of whose leaders even visited the mission stations.

A complete history of the efforts of Mennonites and other evangelical Christians to bring the Gospel to the exiled and imprisoned Russians and the natives of this area has not been written, nor is it known how long this work was continued. C.K.

Unser Blatt I, 24, 216, 242, 309; II, 271, 374; III, 16, 188; J. G. Kargel, *Zwischen den Enden der Erde* (Wernigerode, 1928); R. S. Latimer, *Ein Bote des Königs, Dr. F. W. Baedeker's Leben und Wirken.*

Obbe (Ubbo) **Philips(z)** (Filips) (c1500-68), a leader of the Anabaptists in the Netherlands, the (probably older) brother of the well-known Dirk Philips (q.v.), was the illegitimate son of a Catholic priest at Leeuwarden. The father gave the son a careful education. Whereas the gifted Dirk devoted himself to the study of theology, the likewise talented brother applied himself to the study of medicine. According to the custom of the time he practiced his profession as a barber rather than a physician,

though the surgical services were the most important part of the barber's profession. About 1530 he married and set up shop in Leeuwarden.

Considering his intellectual interests it is not surprising to find that Obbe was drawn into the movements that began to stir the town. The idea of the Reformation came to the city early. Gellius Faber (q.v.) in the neighboring Jelsum was a zealous exponent of the new teaching. In the city itself Obbe made contacts with learned men who had studied at the University of Wittenberg and had there become acquainted with the leaders of the Reformation. Thus he soon began to question the correctness of Catholic doctrine. It is probable that he witnessed the first execution of an Anabaptist, Sicke Freerks (q.v.), which took place in his home town on March 20, 1531. The evangelicals of Leeuwarden at this time formed a circle that practiced a sort of mystic individualistic piety that attracted Obbe. They wished to "worship God quietly in the manner of the fathers and the patriarchs," so that "each one could seek God from his heart, and serve and follow Him without a preacher, teacher, or any other outward meeting" (Bekentenisse, 122).

His further religious development he described in his only extant writing, the "Confession" which, although written before 1560, was published after his death from the original manuscript by Cornelis Claesz in Amsterdam in 1584. The full title reads *Bekentenisse Obbe Philipsz, waermede hy verclaert, sijn Predick-ampt sonder wettelicke beroeping gebruyckt te hebben, beclaecht hem dies, en waerschuwet einen yeders, wt sijnen eygen Boeck, met eyghener Handt gheschreuen, ghecopieert.* It soon went through a second edition (without date), was translated into French by Charles de Nielles (Leiden, 1595) and republished in Dutch by Willem Jansz Stam in 1609. (Copies of all editions in AML, and of the 1609 edition in GCL.)

Soon afterward Obbe became acquainted with the Anabaptists, who were under the influence of Melchior Hofmann (q.v.). The feverish excitement stirred up in wide circles by his prophecies made a deep impression on Obbe. When Bartholomeus (Boeckbinder) van Halle (q.v.) and Dirck Cuper (q.v.), emissaries of Jan Matthijsz of Haarlem (q.v.), arrived in Leeuwarden, Obbe did not hesitate, emerged from his seclusion and was baptized with many others by these emissaries. This happened in November or December 1533. These men must have considered him to be the best suited person to spread their ideas, for on the next day he and a friend Hans Scheerder (q.v.) were ordained to preach, to baptize, and to lead the brotherhood (Bekentenisse, 129).

Filled with zeal Obbe left the city at once after his ordination, to preach and baptize with his brethren and to promote the new doctrine. Meanwhile, however, the authorities had become aware of the movement, especially when in Obbe's absence another prophet, Peter de Houtzager (q.v.), had appeared in Leeuwarden and continued the preaching of "the imminent destruction of all tyrants." Thus when Obbe returned after some time, he found the city gates closed at midday, and managed only with difficulty to enter. The authorities were looking for the leaders of the movement; finally when his name appeared on a bulletin of the Stadholder (Feb. 23, 1534) as one of the "seducers and deceivers who wander about the country, who rebaptize people and teach bad and dangerous errors and sects," he realized that he could no longer stay in the city.

Obbe then went to Amsterdam and made contacts with the very numerous brethren there, who called themselves Bondgenoten (*q.v.*, comrades of the covenant). There were already two wings, representing diametrically opposed ideas. The majority had preserved their sobriety and leaned toward the quiet ideas of Jacob of Campen (*q.v.*). Obbe was attracted to this group. But the other party was already under the dubious influence of Jan Matthijsz, who wanted to bring about by violent means the imminent coming of the kingdom of God which he proclaimed. Obbe did not stay in Amsterdam. He was no longer secure anywhere. In the late fall of 1534 he came to Delft, where he ordained David Joris (*q.v.*) as elder. He had already ordained his brother Dirk Philips at Appingedam, and he also ordained Menno Simons later in Groningen (about 1537, after he had baptized Menno probably at the end of 1535 or in January 1536).

In the time before and after the Münster catastrophe it was difficult to find the right course to follow. The men who had really drawn him to the Anabaptist movement he saw in the camp of the revolutionaries. He needed all his strength to resist the enticing ideas of this group. "But God knows that Dirk and I could not find it in our hearts that such attacks were right, and also diligently preached against them, but nothing did any good, for the great majority were of that mind. . . . Sometimes some of us were saddened to death and our hearts became chilled in our bodies, and we did not know whither to go or what we ought to do: the whole world was persecuting us for the sake of our faith with fire, water, sword, and bloody tyranny, the prophets deceived us on every hand and the letter of Scripture took us captive, the false brethren whom we reproved and opposed swore to kill us, and the love of so many hearts aroused our pity to such a degree, as God knows, that my soul was often saddened to death" (*Bekentenisse*, 135). The assertion by Mellink (*Wederdopers*, 367 f., 381, 394) that in 1534-35 Obbe had much contact with revolutionary Anabaptists is at the least very questionable. The fact that many persons baptized by him soon after belonged to the revolutionary wing is no proof, and Mellink himself admits (*op. cit.*, 390 and especially 267) that Obbe in 1535 remained aloof from the revolutionary plans.

Until Menno Simons became the leader of the peaceful Anabaptists, all that were averse to violence and fanatical enthusiasm looked up to Obbe as their leader. For this reason the early Dutch Anabaptists of this period were often called Obbites or Obbenites. After Münster, when no distinction was made by the public anywhere between the violent and the peaceful Anabaptists, though the radical difference had just been very clearly demonstrated, Obbe apparently went to Germany. Nearly all trace of him is lost. He appeared about 1539 in the region of Rostock, after he had found some followers in Schwerin. This is gathered from a letter written by Joachim Kükenbieter, the Lutheran preacher of Schwerin, to Johann Gartze, his colleague in Hamburg, warning him of the Obbenites; he gave them the surprising testimony that they "to some extent honored the government and were not revolutionaries" (*DB* 1884, 16).

By 1540 Obbe's activity seems to have come to an end. A list of elders of the early period contains for 1540 the note that Obbe Philips had "fallen away." He was no longer working with Menno Simons. In his writing against Gellius Faber, Menno said, "That Obbe has become a Demas and Adam Pastor has left us I could not prevent; the same thing happened also during the time of the apostles. May God restore them according to His will. They have received their dismissal and are no longer (as long as they are not converted) reckoned among us" (*Complete Writings*, 761). It is more difficult to determine to whom Obbe then attached himself. For his "falling away" he gives only one important reason: the illegitimacy of his office, which made him feel that his ordaining others was also a great wrong. That is the reason for his writing the confession. It begins and ends with this. Some have concluded from it that he returned to the Catholic Church, which alone offers a guarantee for the legality of a church office by the apostolic succession. But de Hoop Scheffer is right in calling attention to the fact that his utterances concerning the papacy as "a Sodom of Babylon, Egypt, and an abominataion of desolation" (*Bekentenisse*, 122) refute this supposition. Other suppositions, viz., that he became an unbeliever (Herman Schijn), or joined the "House of Love" as a follower of Hendrik Niclaes (*q.v.*), are not very tenable. The attempt of W. J. Kühler to present him as typical of the individualistic-spiritualistic Anabaptist wing of Sebastian Franck (*q.v.*) merits consideration (*Geschiedenis* I, 1932, 230 ff.). Indeed, there is some similarity between his ideas and those of Franck. In his confession he cited Franck's *Chronica* (*Bekentenisse*, 122). Like the latter he repudiated all existing churches, believing that the true church of God is invisible, and any attempt to establish it in a visible form is wrong, unless there were a direct commission of God. Obbe received his commission from Jan Matthijsz, and this call was "illegitimate." He therefore considered himself as one who has been deceived and has deceived others.

Nevertheless Obbe spoke with deep respect of baptism on confession of faith even after his defection, and was on the whole not far removed from the principles of the peaceful Anabaptists. He spoke sharp words only against those who had been revealed as false prophets and revolutionaries, not against Menno and his followers.

Even if the shadows concealing the last year of his life until his death in 1568 can never be entirely lifted, it can be asserted, in the light of known facts, that Kühler's verdict is not unjustified, "that in Obbe the brotherhood certainly lost its most appealing leader" (*Geschiedenis* I, 232). P.S., vDZ.

Kühler, *Geschiedenis* I; J. G. de Hoop Scheffer, "De bevestiger van Menno Simons," *DB* 1884, 1-24, German translation in *Menn. Bl.*, 1884, 77 ff. (somewhat shortened); *Bekentenisse Obbe Philipsz* (*BRN* VII, 121-38), with critical introduction by Samuel Cramer, 91-120; J. C. Burgmann, *Commentatio Historio - ecclesiastica. De Ubbone Philippi et Ubbonitis* (n.p.-Rostock, 1773); K. Vos, "Obbe Philips," *DB* 1917, 124-38; 1876, 20; 1906, 29 f.; *Groningsche Volksalmanak* 1909, 161; 1916, 131; Mellink, *Wederdopers, passim; ML* III, 369-71.

Obbe Philipsz Bekentenisse: see Bekentenisse.

Obbenites, the name given to the followers of Obbe Philips 1533 ff.

Obbes(z), Nittert (*c*1581-*c*1636), a Mennonite preacher, a native of Pilsum, East Friesland, Germany, came to Amsterdam as a tailor in 1598. In 1614 he was called to preach for the Waterlander congregation in the Groote Spijker, as a colleague of Reynier Wybrands, Cornelis Claesz Anslo (*q.v.*), and Pieter Andriesz Hesseling (*q.v.*). The choice was unfortunate. Nittert came under the influence of Socinianism and brought it to the pulpit, though in concealed form. Called to account by the fellow ministers and by Hans de Ries (*q.v.*), the Waterlander elder, Nittert promised to refrain from preaching this doctrine. Nittert then drew up in writing a number of points in which he accused de Ries as well as the other Amsterdam preachers of fanaticism; they taught two different Words of God, i.e., besides the written Word also an unwritten Word. De Ries denied the charge. The fact is that whereas Nittert held determinedly that the written Word is a dead letter, being therein a disciple of Socinus, de Ries and his following made a distinction but not a separation, between the Scripture and Jesus Christ, the inner Word. The charge that de Ries suppressed the written Word in favor of the inner Word he vigorously denied.

It was Jan Theunisz (*q.v.*), a friend and follower of Nittert Obbesz, who in 1625 published without Nittert's knowledge a book written by Nittert, and gave it the insulting title *Raegh-besem, seer bequaem om sommige Mennonijtsche schuren te reynigen van de onnutte spinnewebbens, sotte grollen en ydelheden eeniger Gheest-drijveren, Swinck-veldianen ende des selfs voorstanderen, die op hun bysondere drijvingen ende inspraken steunen tot verminderingh van 't beschreven woordt Godts.*

De Ries defended himself in a pamphlet *Ontdekkinge der dwalingen* (1627); the Amsterdam preachers wrote their *Apologia* in 1626. Jan Theunisz tried to defend his friend. The poet Joost van den Vondel (*q.v.*), at that time a member of the Waterlander congregation, intervened in Nittert's favor and wrote his malicious *Antidotum* (*q.v.*). He apparently did not grasp the core of the quarrel and completely misunderstood the Amsterdam preachers. A large number of pamphlets dealt with the quarrel; e.g., *Dialogus ofte T'samen-sprekinge tusschen een Waerheydt-soeckende Neutralist ghenaemt Vrederick ende een Waterlandsch Broeder* (Amsterdam, 1626). Nittert himself wrote *Eenighe Vragen met een brief aen Hans de Rys* and *Oprechtigheyd van Reynier Wybrandsz, Pieter Andriesz en Cornelis Claesz . . .*, both of 1626.

When Nittert found followers in other places, especially in Rotterdam (Eduard Nabels, *q.v.*), North Holland (Jan Willemsz of De Rijp, *q.v.*), and even in Franeker, an attempt was made to mediate the difficulty. Rippert Eenkes and other neutral preachers drew up a confession of faith on Sept. 5, 1626, which agreed with de Ries and repudiated Socinianism. Nittert yielded his views and signed the document on Sept. 9, 1626. He was suspended from preaching and not reinstated. His following continued the dispute for a time. Jan Theunisz submitted in 1634. vDZ.

Inv. Arch. Amst. I, No. 548; II, Nos. 1180, 1204-31, 1366; Kühler, *Geschiedenis* II, 143-75; H. F. Wijnman, "Jan Theunisz," in *Jaarboek Amstelodamum* XXV (1928), paricularly pp. 78-100; *DB* 1865, 51, 57-72; *ML* III, 282.

Obbites or **Obbenites** (Dutch, *Obbi(e)ten* or *Obbeniten*), a wing of the Dutch Anabaptists named for Obbe Philips (*q.v.*).

Obelecker, Tele, an Anabaptist martyr of Mühlhausen, Thuringia, Germany, baptized by Heinz Kraut (*q.v.*), was drowned in the Unstrut between Mühlhausen and Ammern with nine brethren on Nov. 8, 1537. In the cross-examinations held on Oct. 19 and 22, 1537, she confessed her faith, rejecting infant baptism and the oath, but promising obedience to the government. (Wappler, *Thüringen,* 158 ff.; *ML* III, 283.) NEFF.

Oberbayern: see Bavaria.

Oberbiegelhof: see Büchelhof.

Oberecker (Overacker, Overakker), **Hans,** an Anabaptist martyr of Affers in the Adige Valley of Tirol, Austria (now Italy), was sent with Hieronymus Käls (*q.v.*) and Michael Seifensieder (*q.v.*) to Tirol as a missionary of the Hutterian Brethren. They were seized in Vienna. Hans was burned at the stake on March 31, 1536. In prison the two men wrote an important *Rechenschaft und Bekenntnis* besides several epistles to the brotherhood in Moravia and their relatives. Three times, wrote Hans Oberecker, the day of the Lord had appeared to him, so that he "prayed that God would let him incur this wrath, which is so great and dreadful upon wickedness." NEFF.

Wolkan, *Geschicht-Buch,* 119-22; Beck, *Geschichts-Bücher,* 127-29; Zieglschmid, *Chronik,* 158; L. Müller, *Glaubenszeugnisse oberdeutscher Taufgesinnten* (Leipzig, 1938) 205-10, contains their Confession; Wolkan, *Lieder,* 170; *Mart. Mir.* D 39, E 445; *ML* III, 283.

Oberflörsheim, a village between Alzey and Monsheim, Rhenish Hesse, Germany. As early as 1664 the Mennonite lists in the Karlsruhe archives name four Mennonite families in this village, and in 1685 the families of Peter Weber, Peter Mundorf, Peter Dahlem, Johann Dahlem, Johann Horbach, and Dietrich Schwarz are listed with 42 persons. In 1738 the families of Arnold Kramer, Johann Hahn, and Johannes Schmidt were added. In 1732 the congregation numbered 13 families; the preacher was Christian Weber, the deacons Johann Dahlem and Heinrich Rupp; the latter lived in Gundersheim. Members of the congregation also lived in Monzernheim and Dahlsheim. Here the families of Jakob Heer, Johann Geber, Abraham Müller, Johannes Nold, and Abraham Kolb are named in 1743.

The Dutch *Naamlijst* names Christian Weber as a preacher here from 1725 and elder 1728-c75. Other ministers were Jacob Dalman (Dahlem), elder 1740-?, Wilhelm Kramer (Krämer) 1748-c80, Johann Schörger, Heinrich Müller 1759-?, Henrich Strohm, Peter Müller, Jacob Hahn, Jilles (?) Hahn 1772, Wilhelm Weber 1775, Peter Krämer 1775. In 1766 the *Naamlijst* calls this congregation Oberflörsheim-Spiesheim-Griesheim, in 1769-82 Oberflörsheim and Guntersheim, and from 1784 Oberflörsheim. In 1769 the Oberflörsheim-Spiessheim congregation had about 100 members. The list of 1752 gives particulars concerning the families and financial resources of the Mennonites of Oberflörsheim. It lists six families: Jakob Dahlem with six children, Jakob Hahn with seven, Wilhelm Krämer with four, Johannes Schmitt with five, Christian Weber with four, and Peter Weber with four children, a total of 42 persons, with a total capital of 12,000 florins.

In 1737 the following incident of religious intolerance is recorded: Dietrich Weber married a Catholic servant girl; the children were brought up in the Mennonite faith. The oldest was baptized as an adult. Then the Catholic clergy compelled the children to become Catholic. The father was compelled to join one of the three recognized churches. All pleas and petitions of the father and the congregation were in vain. The father finally joined the Reformed Church.

The Danzig *Namensverzeichnis* of 1805 lists Johann Galle as the elder of the congregation from 1766 until his death in 1838 (he had left Monzernheim in 1803), Philip Weber and Peter Krämer as leaders from 1775. The Danzig *Namensverzeichnis* of 1857 names only Jakob Krämer as leader. It states further that preaching services were alternately conducted by Löwenberg of the Weierhof and Molenaar of Monsheim; the latter soon took charge alone until 1866, when the congregation was dissolved. The inhabitants of the village joined the Monsheim congregation. The cemetery was sold. In 1957 there were four Mennonite families and four part families living in the village, and the burgomaster was a Mennonite named Stauffer.   NEFF, VDZ.

Inv. Arch. Amst. I, No. 1472; Müller, *Berner Täufer*, 211; *Namensverzeichnis*; *Naamlijst*; *Der Mennonit* IX (1956) No. 11, p. 170; *ML* III, 283 f.

Obergum, a village in the Dutch province of Groningen, formerly the seat of a small Mennonite congregation, which had a meetinghouse here, remodeled in 1806, but soon after abandoned. The congregation was also known as Winsum and Obergum, or only Winsum (a neighboring village). It belonged to the Flemish branch, not to the Old Flemish as most congregations in this province did, and was a member of the "Humsterlandsche Sociëteit" (*q.v.*). In the 18th century the following preachers served here: Eltje Hans, resigned 1754, Andreas Huizinga 1740-c55, Jan Syrts 1740-c55, Jan Pieters Reckers 1754-c65, Johannes Adema 1766-c87. Then the pulpit became vacant. In 1816 the Mennonites at Obergum and Winsum joined the newly founded congregation of Mensingeweer (*q.v.*), which arose from the merger of a number of small congregations in this area. About 1670 a sec-

ond Mennonite congregation, belonging to the Ukowallist (*q.v.*) group, built a meetinghouse at Obergum. About this congregation no further information was available. Probably it soon died or merged with another congregation.   VDZ.

Inv. Arch. Amst. II, Nos. 2175 f.; *Naamlijst* 1815, 107; 1829, 65; *DB* 1906, 46; G. A. Wumkes, *De Gereformeerde Kerk in de Ommelanden* . . . (Groningen, 1904) 39.

Oberholtzer (Overholtzer, Overholser, Overholt), a Mennonite family name, probably of Swiss origin. One of the immigrants bearing this family name was a Martin Oberholtzer (1709-44) of Germany who settled in the Deep Run (*q.v.*) area of Bucks County, Pa. A Jacob Oberholtzer was living in Franconia Township, Montgomery Co., Pa., in 1719. The settlers of 1710 in what is now Lancaster County, Pa., included two Oberholtzers, Martin and Michael. Descendants of the family in Lancaster County included two deacons, a preacher (MC), and Bishop Jacob Oberholtzer (c1826-88) of Bowmansville (GCM). The Franconia Conference Oberholtzers included at least six preachers, three deacons, and a bishop, Isaac Oberholtzer (1815-87) of the Blooming Glen congregation. The Ontario Conference (MC) included a deacon and a preacher bearing the name. By far the most prominent representative of the family was John H. Oberholtzer (*q.v.*, 1809-95), a preacher from 1842 in the Franconia Conference, founder of what is now the Eastern District Conference of the General Conference Mennonite Church in 1847, a bishop from 1847 (GCM), schoolteacher, locksmith, publisher, and author. He played a major role in the formation of the General Conference (GCM). In Westmoreland County, Pa., one of the pillars in what is now the Scottdale church (MC) was John D. Overholt (1797-1878), ordained preacher in 1830 and bishop in 1833. His uncle Abraham Overholt (1785-1870) was a successful distiller from 1810 (Old Overholt Whiskey) and a member (trustee at times) in the church (MC). This Overholt family descends from the above Martin Oberholtzer. A preacher Jacob Oberholtzer of Bucks County, Pa., moved to Mahoning County, Ohio, in 1806, and became the first ordained Mennonite minister in Ohio, organizing the congregation there.   J.C.W.

E. S. Loomis, *Some Account of Jacob Oberholtzer who settled about 1719, in Franconia Township, Montgomery County, Pennsylvania* (Cleveland, 1931); A. J. Fretz, *A Genealogical Record of the Descendants of Martin Oberholtzer* (Milton, N.J., 1903).

Oberholtzer, Jacob (1767-1847), a Mennonite (MC) minister, who (according to tradition) lived in Bucks County, Pa., and moved to what is now Mahoning County, Ohio, in 1806. He was the first ordained Mennonite minister to take up residence in Ohio. He organized the congregation in Mahoning County in 1815, and in 1833 he contributed land for church, cemetery, and school.

The Mennonites of Beaver Township supported a church school. In 1828, when legislation was enacted by the state whereby taxes could be levied to establish public schools, dissension arose within the congregation on the question of private or public schools. A group, led by Jacob Oberholtzer, favored church schools in order to preserve the German language. When the issue was decided in favor of public schools in 1834, Jacob Oberholtzer moved to Ashland County, Ohio, and served the congregations there until his death. He was a forceful speaker. He was married twice. His first wife was Catherine Baughman (d. 1806), to whom were born seven children, and his second Elisabeth Mellinger, of Mahoning County, to whom were born thirteen children. W.D.S.

Oberholtzer, John H. (1809-95), one of the founders and outstanding leaders of the General Conference Mennonite Church, was born on a farm near Clayton, Berks Co., Pa., on Jan. 10, 1809, the second child of Abraham and Susanna Hunsberger Oberholtzer and the fourth generation from immigrant Jacob Oberholtzer, who landed at Philadelphia in 1732. At the age of 16 he began teaching in local schools. Later learning the trade of a locksmith, he established himself in a shop near Milford Square, Bucks County. He became very skillful as a locksmith and his German locks are still to be found in the community. He supported himself by this trade during his later ministry when his ministerial labors and printing enterprises were causes of expense to him. His aggressive spirit did not rest with these accomplishments, for he continued to educate himself in spare moments. He became an able writer and fluent speaker. In 1842, at the age of 33 years, the Swamp Mennonite Church (Franconia Conference, MC) called him as a preacher. He became a fluent and fascinating speaker and preached in neighboring churches of other denominations, an unheard-of innovation among Mennonites of the day. From the beginning of his ministry he organized children's Bible classes which he called "Kinderlehre." He started using a European Mennonite catechism and later developed these Sunday afternoon classes into one of the early Mennonite Sunday schools in America at West Swamp in 1857.

Following his call into the ministry in 1842 Oberholtzer found himself dissatisfied with many customs and methods of the Mennonite church of his day. He did not at first wear the ministerial straight-collar coat as required by the conference, though later he was willing to do so. Perhaps the greatest cause of distress was the lack of a written constitution and minutes in the conference. Questions of discipline and polity from pioneer days had always been decided by the conference without any definite written standards. In 1847 Oberholtzer proposed such a written constitution to the Franconia Conference. This proposed innovation, coupled with a growing ill-will against him engendered by other things, such as the temporary refusal to wear the prescribed coat, occasioned the unfortunate conference division of October 1847. On Oct. 28, 1847, Oberholtzer took the lead in organizing a new Mennonite conference with other older and younger ministers and leaders dissatisfied with the old conference. This division, perhaps the most far-reaching of all schisms in the American Mennonite Church, brought forth much controversy during the past century. Without maligning or defending John Oberholtzer, or aligning him with later errors

of his group, it is fair to state that from his own writings and actions it is clear he was not interested in changing the basic doctrines of the church. It was his desire rather to introduce new ways of propagating the old Gospel, such as Christian education through ministerial training and Sunday schools, missionary work, and publication work. He was ahead of his time. The Mennonite Church (MC) for the most part was not ready to accept the new ways of working.

Oberholtzer pioneered in other "firsts." In 1844 he drew up a constitution for the Swamp Mennonite congregation, probably the first congregational constitution among American Mennonites. In 1850, through his leadership, West Swamp adopted a plan for "the poor and suffering members of the Christian community," an early mutual aid plan. Probably the most important of all was his periodical, the *Religiöser Botschafter,* started in 1852, the first successful Mennonite periodical in America. He purchased a hand printing press for his locksmith shop, learned to set type, and became the editor, printer, and agent for this enterprise. He was one of the leaders who founded the General Conference of the Mennonite Church in Iowa in 1860. He was a staunch supporter of its early mission work among the American Indians, and was a mission board member until 1881. He was one of the first to encourage a trained and supported ministry and was a leader in supporting the Mennonite seminary operated at Wadsworth, Ohio, 1867-78.

In 1872 Oberholtzer resigned as chairman of the Eastern District Conference, a position he had held from the beginning in 1848. From then until his death he continued to preach and serve, but not as a conference leader. The work had passed into other hands. But he still attended conferences and took a vital interest in the ongoing work of the General Conference Mennonite Church. He preached until October 1894. He died Feb. 15, 1895, at the age of 86.† J.H.F.

"Life of John H. Oberholtzer," *The Mennonite,* March 1895, p. 44; "Obituary of J. H. Oberholtzer," *Mennonite Yearbook and Almanac for 1896,* p. 28; "A Pennsylvania Mennonite Church," *Menn. Life* II (October 1947) 33; J. C. Wenger, *History of the Mennonites of the Franconia Conference* (Telford, 1937); J. H. Oberholtzer, *Der Wahre Character von J. H. Oberholtzer* (Milford Square, 1860); Bender, *Two Centuries,* 90-93; *ML* III, **284.**

Oberholtzer Mennonite Church (MC), built in Beaver Twp., Mahoning Co., Ohio, in 1825. The land was donated by Jacob Oberholtzer (*q.v.*), a minister of the congregation. The building committee for this log church, 30 x 36 ft., was George Baughman and Jonathan Oberholtzer. In 1871 this log church was replaced by a brick church, 40 x 50 ft., begun in 1869 located a short distance to the southwest. The building committee for this brick church was Jacob Yoder, Daniel Ziegler, and Melchior Mellinger. The erection of this new church precipitated an Old Order (Wisler) (*q.v.*) schism in the Columbiana-Mahoning congregation in 1872, which followed Bishop Jacob Wisler from the main body in Indiana. In 1898 the building was enlarged. This church was known as Oberholtzer's until 1898, when it was called the Middle Church. About 1900 Allen

Rickert, a minister, suggested, "Let's call it Midway." David Lehman was the first to use the name in making announcements from the pulpit. The name Midway (q.v.) Mennonite Church continues to the present. In August 1957 a marker of Georgia granite was placed on the site of the original log church.   W.D.S.

Oberländer: see **Overlanders.**

Oberlehen and **Oberpenning** (Oberpanning), villages in the Tirolean districts of Kitzbühel and Hopfgarten, Austria. Upon the request of the clerk Hans Finsterwalder the imperial government at Innsbruck sent him detailed instructions on April 2, 1528, on how to deal with penitent Anabaptists and those who reported to the authorities. The instructions were as follows: Leaders and baptizers should be put to death. Special efforts should be made to apprehend the preacher Pauls and his successor Hans Rat, who had been so brazen as to hold meetings at Münichau (q.v.), the castle of the suspect Helene von Freyberg (q.v.), for which she was to be called to account by the Innsbruck authorities. The possessions of 30 fugitive Anabaptists were to be confiscated. The houses in which Anabaptist meetings were held in Oberpanning, Taurer, Seebach, Oberlehen, Bühel, and Pfaffenberg, and Schussling at Münichau should be burned or torn down, unless they were in such a location that other houses would be threatened thereby, to set an example, as had already been done in the Rattenberg district. If it should not be possible to destroy them, they should be confiscated and held for further instruction.   P.DE.

Kopialbuch Causa Domini im Tiroler Land, Regierungsarchiv II, 204 ff.; Loserth, *Anabaptismus; ML* III, 284 f.

Oberlen (Oberli), **Christian,** an Anabaptist martyr, put to death at Bern, Switzerland, on Sept. 17, 1543. Particulars are lacking. This martyr is not listed in the Dutch editions of 1660 and 1685 of van Braght's *Martyrs' Mirror,* but is found with some other Bernese martyrs in the German edition published at Ephrata in 1748. A Peter Oberley (Oberli) is named in a letter dated June 13, 1711, by the Dutch ambassador Runckel (q.v.). He was an Amish elder in Switzerland; in 1762 he made a tour of the congregations in the Palatinate, Germany.   vdZ.

Mart. Mir. E 1130; Müller, *Berner Täufer,* 211; Delbert L. Gratz, *Bernese Anabaptists* (Scottdale, 1953) 24, No. 37; *Inv. Arch. Amst.* I, No. 1334.

Obernessau, one of the oldest Mennonite congregations in West Prussia, Germany, formerly called Nischefke (Nieschewski, q.v.), founded in the middle of the 16th century below the town of Thorn, apparently by Dutch settlers; the congregation belonged to the Waterlander (also called Frisian) branch. Some of the members lived on the Korzeniecer Kämpe (q.v.), an island in the Vistula. In Obernessau a church was built in 1778, which was burned by lightning on June 11, 1889, but was rebuilt with the aid of other congregations and dedicated on Nov. 2, 1890, by Elder Hans Foth. The substantial tower on this church was an exception

in Mennonite church architecture. The Dutch *Naamlijst* names a number of ministers who served here: Jacob Adriaen, Jacob Adriaen de Jonge, Hans Flemming (Flaming, Vlaming) 1737, Hendrik Bartels, Cornelis Jantzen, Jacob Eck about 1760-80, Peter Bartels 1764, Hans Nikkel, preacher 1766, elder 1779-after 1810, Zacharias Bartel 1773, Jakob Bartel 1779-82, Abraham Eck 1780, Zacharias Bartel 1796, Cornelius Baltzer 1801.

About 1775 a number of members left Obernessau and moved to Deutsch-Kazun (q.v.) near Warsaw, Poland; among these emigrants was their preacher Hans Flaming. The reason for this migration was apparently economic, farming having become very difficult in Obernessau because of repeated floods and high taxes. After the serious flood of 1736 the Dutch Mennonites gave considerable relief, as they did again in 1888.

In the 19th century emigration to Russia and to America reduced the congregation; living conditions had changed. When they settled on the island the Vistula flooded their land, to be sure, but the sediment left on the fields produced good crops. But the dams built for the railroads narrowed the channel of the river to such an extent that the river washed away the good soil and destroyed crops. The dams built by the people offered little protection. Great damage was caused by the flood of 1855, followed by others, usually just before the harvest, in 1871, 1879, 1883, 1888, 1891, 1896, and 1903. At the beginning of the 20th century the farmers on the Korzeniecer Kämpe had to leave when a harbor was built there. Two Mennonite families, Dirks and Foth, moved to Thorn in 1906.

In 1815 twenty families belonged to this congregation; in 1852 the baptized membership was 64 (besides 28 children), in 1888 it was 61 (besides 27 children); in 1905 the membership numbered 43, and in 1933 only 12, including children. The last ministers were David Dirks, elder from 1878, and Heinrich Foth, preacher from 1875, later elder, died c1909. The *Gemeinde-Kalender* of 1941 lists the congregation as having 12 members, four of them with the right to vote.   HEGE.

W. Kerber, "Die Kirche zu Nessau," *Gem.-Kal.,* 1906, 107-14 with pictures; "Die Gemeinde zu Obernessau bei Thorn," *Menn. Bl.,* 1905, 29; *Gesch.-Bl.,* 1937, 73; 1939, 34; Mannhardt, *Jahrbuch,* 1883, 17, 19; 1888, 15 f.; *Inv. Arch. Amst.* I, Nos. 1640, 1642, 1647 f.; *DB* 1910, 189; *ML* III, 285.

Oberösterreich: see **Austria.**

Oberpfalz: see **Bavaria.**

Oberschulze (German for mayor or executive official) was the highest officer of the district or county (German, *Gebietsamt, q.v.;* Russian *volost*) in the Mennonite settlements in Russia, Manitoba, Mexico, and South America. Each village had a mayor (*Schulze*) and all the villages of a single Mennonite settlement were administered by the Gebietsamt, of which the Oberschulze was the head. The position of the Oberschulze in civic matters was parallel to that of the elder in the spiritual realm (see also **Government of Mennonites in Russia**).

The Oberschulzen of Chortitza were Peter Siemens, 1801-5; Nikolai Krahn and Peter Siemens,

1808-23; Isaak Töws, Jacob Penner, Peter Löwen, and Jacob Bartsch, 1832-38; Jakob von Kampen and Jacob Bartsch, 1841-54; Johann Siemens, Jacob Dyck, Jakob Hamm, and Heinrich Martens, 1869-72; Jakob Braun, Isaak Lehn, Peter Andres, and Johann Hildebrand, 1881-87; Franz Thiessen, Peter Dyck, Heinrich Fröse, Kornelius Martens, Peter Koop, and Jacob Wiebe, 1905-8; Johann Hübert and Jakob Wiebe, 1909.

Molotschna Oberschulzen were Klaas Wiens, 1804-6; Johann Klassen, 1806-9; Gerhard Reimer and Johann Klassen, 1812-15; Peter Töws, Gerhard Enns, Johann Klassen (Orloff), Johann Klassen (Tiegerweide), and Johann Regehr, 1833-42; Abraham Töws, 1842-48; David Friesen, 1848-65; Franz Dyck, 1865-67; Abraham Driedger and Kornelius Töws, 1868-73; Abraham Wiebe, 1873-79; Peter Dück and Klaas Enns, 1882-85; Johann Enns, 1885-89; Klaas Enns and Peter Neufeld, 1889-99; Franz Nickel, 1899-1906; Dietrich Dyck, 1906-10.

In 1870 a new district was organized known as "Gnadenfeld," where the following served as Oberschulze: Wilhelm Ewert, 1870-71; Franz Penner, 1871; Peter Ewert, Gerhard Fast, and David Unruh, 1878-87; Gerhard Dürksen, 1887-1904; Jacob Dürksen, 1904-10. (Friesen, *Brüderschaft,* 678 ff.)

C.K.

Obersülzen, a village near Grünstadt in the Palatinate, Germany, in which there was a comparatively large Anabaptist congregation in 1568 with preachers and deacons. After the Thirty Years' War the congregation was united with Gerolsheim (*q.v.*) and Heppenheim a.d. Wiese (*q.v.*). Regular church services were held in rotation in the three villages. The congregation was originally called Gerolsheim; Müller states that Dirmstein (*q.v.*) and Offstein (*q.v.*) belonged to the total congregation. In 1732 it numbered 40 families; the preachers were Hans and Christian Borckholder, the deacons were Christian Stauffer of Obersülzen and Johannes Hirschler of Gerolsheim; in 1769 the congregation had 69 baptized members. Beginning in 1783 the congregation was called Heppenheim. It is listed thus in the resolutions of Ibersheim (*q.v.*), which were signed for the congregation by Gerhard Hüthwohl of Heppenheim. Several years later the center of gravity shifted to Obersülzen, which has remained the seat of the congregation. Since the middle of the 19th century it has been merged with Monsheim.

In 1671 a number of Swiss Mennonite emigrants settled near Obersülzen. Jacob Everlin (Eberlinck), probably a minister of the Obersülzen congregation, corresponded with the Lamist Mennonite congregation at Amsterdam, sending a list of the names of these Swiss Brethren. Thereupon four delegates of the Amsterdam congregation visited Obersülzen in 1672 and supported the immigrants with a considerable amount of money. Everlin also reports concerning doctrinal differences between the Swiss Brethren and his own congregation. Abstracts of letters written by the Dutch delegates in 1671-72 and sent from Obersülzen are found in van Braght's *Martyrs' Mirror,* E 1125-27.

On May 5, 1682, the Alzey district officials demanded a report on a funeral of the Anabaptists in Obersülzen, at which a large meeting of the same took place, and on their Sunday service, at which preachers coming from other localities functioned. The reply was that after the preacher who had lived among them for twenty years had died, they had been holding a meeting every three or four weeks in a home or in a barn, attended by 50-100 Anabaptists from the surrounding villages. The present preacher (*Vermahner*) lived at Gerolsheim, and occasionally one came from Rodenbach and Mannheim. Thus the funeral had been attended by many Mennonites from the vicinity. Thereupon all meetings of the Mennonites were prohibited in Obersülzen and at Heppenheim. Then the Mennonites in the Alzey district presented a joint petition to the elector on Sept. 7, 1682, to be permitted to conduct their services according to the concession they had received. The petition was granted. On March 5, 1688, a conference was held at Obersülzen, at which the Strasbourg Articles of 1568 and 1607 with directions and advice for preachers and elders were augmented. The Dutch *Naamlijst* names the following ministers in the 18th century: Ulrich Burckholder, preacher 1742-c80, Jacob Hirschler, preacher 1756, elder 1761-81, Martin Blühm 1760, Gerhard Hutwohl 1769, Johann Burckholder 1784, Johann Lehman, elder 1782. Heinrich Fried (d. 1761), preacher, is named in letters sent from Obersülzen to Amsterdam.

The last lay preachers chosen from the members were Johann Burkholder of Gerolsheim from 1838, Heinrich Herstein of Obersülzen from 1845 (also elder), and Daniel Hirschler of Heppenheim from 1853. On Sept. 25, 1859, Johannes Molenaar, pastor of the Monsheim congregation, preached his funeral sermon and assumed the duties of minister in the congregation, which dedicated a new chapel in 1866. From 1862 the Obersülzen congregation was officially a branch of the Monsheim congregation. In 1890 the Mennonite residents of Battenburg, who had belonged to the Altleiningen congregation, joined Obersülzen. There were in Obersülzen in 1802 33 Mennonites, including children, and 66 in 1834. In 1869 it numbered 68 baptized members, in 1888 120, children included, in 1941 about 100, in 1957 94 baptized members. Formerly the congregation had two meetinghouses; in addition to the one at Obersülzen, which was built in 1806, there was also one in Heppenheim, built in 1783. Now only the one in Obersülzen is used.   NEFF.

Miller, *Berner Täufer,* 52, 211; *Menn. Bl.,* 1855, 54; 1861, 34 f.; *Inv. Arch. Amst.* I, Nos. 1248 f., 1405, 1407, 1417; *Mart. Mir.* D 827-30, E 1125 f.; *ML* III, 288.

Obihiro Mennonite Church, Obihiro, Hokkaido, Japan, was started in 1951. In 1957 it had 14 members with missionary Carl Beck as pastor. The congregation meets in the basement of the Beck home.

H.S.B.

Ochino, Bernardino (1487-1567), a Protestant clergyman of Siena, Italy, early entered the Franciscan order and later the Capuchin, whose vicar general he became, and preached with superior success. In 1541 he became acquainted with Waldensian doctrines and in the following year he fled from Italy to Augsburg via Constance, Zürich, Geneva, where he stayed three years, and Basel. In Augsburg he was appointed pastor of the Italian congregation. After the defeat of the Schmalkaldian League he again had to flee. By way of Zürich and Basel his path went to London, whither Archbishop Cranmer called him in 1547. For six years he worked here with great blessing. When Edward VI died and Mary Stuart came to the throne, he fled. By way of Strasbourg and Basel he went to Geneva, arriving there on the day of the execution of Michael Servetus (Oct. 27, 1553), and won disfavor by expressing his disapproval of the execution. In 1555 he took charge of the newly created Protestant Italian congregation in Zürich. For ten years he served with unwavering faithfulness in addition to great literary activity. In 1563 the council expelled him from the city on the absolutely false charge that he had sponsored polygamy in his book, *Die 30 Dialoge*. This book was translated into Latin by Sebastian Castellio (*q.v.*). Without a home, Bernardino Ochino wandered from country to country. When he was expelled from Cracow in Poland, he turned to Moravia, and at Austerlitz in a Hutterite house he died on Jan. 21, 1567. His books *Tragödie, Labyrinthe,* and especially his *Catechism* show some noteworthy echoes of Anabaptist doctrine. Ochino, however, differs from the Mennonites in his anti-Trinitarianism. His unitarian views made him sincerely welcome among a group of anti-Trinitarian Italian scholars like Biandrata (Blandrata) and Gentile. (*HRE* XIV, 256 ff.; *Menn. Bl.*, 1893, 27, 47, 58; *ML* III, 290.)   **NEFF.**

Ochsenbach, a town in the Güglingen district of Württemberg, Germany. Not far from the mother community of Ochsenbach and the daughter community of Spielberg, the Anabaptists found a good hiding place at Bromberg. The local pastor reported in 1574 that the Anabaptist Simon Kress (*q.v.*) had come frequently from Moravia to Ochsenbach as a deceiver and was lodged by his cousin Klaus Eysenbrei. The latter had a son and a daughter in Moravia, and had also kept the pastor's little daughter without the father's knowledge for two weeks and led her astray, though he must have "felt and heard my displeasure in my diligent seeking and inquiring." The "leading astray" of the parson's daughter obviously consisted in keeping her concealed and indoctrinating her in Anabaptist teaching, while the worried father missed his child for two weeks—certainly an unusual, but reliably recorded incident. In 1575 a case of an inheritance came up before the church council in Stuttgart which had its roots in Ochsenbach; a member of the community wished to acquire several vineyards which were left by Anabaptist relatives who emigrated to Moravia. The council wished to sell the vineyards to the relatives, but the proceeds of the sale were to go into the church treasury on account of the heavy expense of keeping the Anabaptists imprisoned. This is surprising, for it was generally known that the Anabaptists had to pay for their detention in prison by working, or if they were released, by payment of cash. It is known that Duke Frederick appropriated the Anabaptist properties, and that after his death (1608) the guardian of these

properties was held accountable for them (*TA Württemberg,* p. XIII).

In 1577 the dean of the region reported to Stuttgart that the miller of the Schöppen Mill, which was part of the Ochsenbach parish, had refused to render the customary oath of submission, and that his three children, the oldest of whom was nine years old, were not yet baptized. In the same year it was reported that the Baron of Bromberg employed Anabaptists in the Schöppen Mill as servants —not an isolated instance among the nobility, and a testimonial for the diligence and faithfulness of these workers in the house and the fields. In 1583 two thirds of an Anabaptist home near the church was given to the Ochsenbach community free of charge to be used as a school; the third they were to buy of the owner with community funds and have it repaired. In January 1589 an order was issued from Stuttgart to the magistrate of Güglingen to bring Friedrich, the Schöppen miller, who had been arrested, to Stuttgart under custody and to report where his unbaptized ten-year-old child was. In August 1589 the magistrate was informed that the Anabaptist Friedrich Miller of the Ochsenbach parish had promised to leave the principality, and had moved away. Eberhard of Weitershausen had put another into the mill, by the name of Dionysius Reitboldt, who was even worse than the former miller. For when the pastor of Ochsenbach summoned him to give an account of his faith, he uttered terrible and frightening blasphemies against "our" religion with defiance. The magistrate was to arrest the blasphemous Anabaptist (was he really an Anabaptist?) Dionysius and bring him to Stuttgart. The two weeks' concealment of the pastor's little daughter in 1574 had some consequences after all. In 1604 it is reported: "At Ochsenbach two little children of the former pastor Stephan Schultheiss (in Ochsenbach 1558-78), Anna 28 years ago, and Timotheus 12 years ago have left the country and become Anabaptists, leaving an estate of 700 gilders, welcome to the treasurer." In 1610 there was a case of illegal confiscation of alleged Anabaptist property by the procurator in favor of the duke, who was in need of money. The government recognized the claim for repayment; 255 gilders had to be paid the heirs, not by the duke, but from the income of the Anabaptist property in the Güglingen district. In 1616 the pastor, mayor, and judge of Ochsenbach asked to keep two estates of the inheritance of the two daughters of Veit Schuhmacher who had gone to Moravia, to be given the manager of the church treasury, to pay 10 Talers to the schoolmaster and sexton, and repair the tower clock, the bell, and windows in the very dilapidated little church. Numerous cases are known of the application of funds confiscated from Anabaptists to the erection and repair of Lutheran churches and schools, which is of course better than for personal enrichment. The government did not give away the property in question, but sold it for a small price to the community.   E.T.

TA Württemberg, p. XIII, 1181, under "Ochsenbach"; on page 912 also the literature on the management of Anabaptist property in Württemberg; E. Teufel, "Die Beschlagnahme und Verwaltung des Täufergutes durch den Fiscus im Herzogtum Württemberg ...," *Theol. Ztscht* VIII (1952) 296-304; *ML* III, 290 f.

Ochsentreiber(in), Urschl (Ursula), an Anabaptist martyr of the Tirol, Austria. In 1528-29 the Anabaptists had won a strong following in Hall near Innsbruck. When the government of Tirol interfered, they moved to a meadow near Mils. At the head of this group was Peter Egger, the baker, the baker of Hall, who is described in the placard issued against him as a "man with a long red beard," with his young son, and also a cloth shearer of Hall, "the real leader, a stately, brave person with a short, thick red beard."

On Aug. 15, 1529, the judge of Hertenberg in a raid caught about 20 brethren and sisters, but those named above managed to escape. The government ordered the authorities of that region to search for them, so that they would not succeed in reaching the Ziller Valley. The mayor and council of Hall were commanded to guard Egger's house at night in order to catch him if he came to see his family. Meanwhile Erhard Haller had seized three women, Dorothea (Anna) Malerin (*q.v.*), Ursula Ochsentreiberin, and Katharina Braunin, who had taken part in the meetings, as the cross-examinations revealed. None would comply with the demand to name other participants in Hall. Nevertheless some other arrests were made. On Sept. 14 the Tirol government ordered the Hall authorities to bring Malerin before the criminal court as a backslider for breaking her pledge of loyalty (*Urfehde*), but first to torture her "in a manner suitable for a woman." At the same time the magistrate was censured because the prisoners were lodged together, so that they "with much singing, as they are accustomed to sing in their sect, make themselves heard, which is also listened to publicly by the common man, from which nothing good can come." Furthermore, this merely strengthened and consoled them, for which reason they were to be separated at once and placed in solitary confinement. Anna Malerin was drowned soon afterward.

Braunin seems to have been "converted," since an order of government of October describes the manner of her pardon. Ursula remained steadfast; therefore a mandate of Nov. 27 commanded the authorities of Hall to bring her also before the criminal court. Of her and Anna the *Geschicht-Buch* boasts that they "armed their feminine spirit with manliness and valor in God, so that many marveled at their steadfastness." She was also drowned in the Inn.

The chronicle of Hall reports for 1528-29 that many Anabaptists, young and old, men and women, were under cross-examination, some of whom let themselves be converted by the town parson; "two women were condemned to death and drowned, who would not leave the sect." This figure agrees with the list of martyrs in the Hutterite chronicles. The fate of the two became the theme of the song, preserved in the Pressburg Codex, "An unsern Frauen Tag geschah."   P.DE.

Wolkan, *Lieder*, 16 f.; Beck, *Geschichts-Bücher*; Loesche, *Tirolensia*; Loserth, *Anabaptismus*; Wolkan, *Geschicht-Buch*; Mart. Mir. D 28, E 437; *ML* III, 291 f.

Ockenfuss, Hans: see **Oggenfuss, Hans.**

Odenbach, Johann, pastor at Moscheln, below Landsberg, which is the old name of the town of Obermoschel in the Palatinate, Germany, between Kreuznach and Kaiserslautern. The ruins of the Landsberg fortress still dominate the handsome little town. This was the scene of Johann Odenbach's preaching during the Reformation. His was a tolerant soul, extraordinarily rare at the time. This is shown in the letter he wrote in 1528 to the judges of Alzey (*q.v.*), when they were deciding on the life or death of several Anabaptists imprisoned there. The letter is titled, "Ein Sendbrief und Ratschlag an verordnete Richter über die armen Gefangenen in Alzey, so man nennet Wiedertäufer."

Odenbach opened the letter by reminding the judges that they must hold just judgment, citing Deut. 1:15-17 and chapter 17; they were inexperienced in the divine Scripture and had not learned responsibility for faith, therefore they could not conduct nor fathom this legal matter. The case must be conducted by instruction from the Word of God. "If one wanted to punish the error of faith of their heresy which is not founded on the Word of God, then priests, monks, Junkers, pope, and cardinals would be much more liable to punishment who have earned a thousandfold greater punishment before God than these poor Anabaptists, although I do not praise them either. One should provide better, more pious, upright, learned and good preachers, then all great and small errors would soon be removed. These poor Anabaptists have not committed such a great sin against God through their Anabaptism that He would condemn their souls for it, nor had they so wantonly disobeyed the government, that they had forfeited their lives. Neither true baptism or Anabaptism possesses such power that it can save or damn a man; for that pertains not to a man or to a symbol, but to God alone." "Therefore do not become guilty of presumptuous sin, that the wrath of God may not come upon you, greater than upon the Sodomites and all the evildoers upon earth. You have seen many thieves, murderers, and rogues treated more mercifully in prison than these poor people who have not stolen, murdered, robbed, burned, betrayed, or committed any shameful misdeed, but have only to the honor of God and to nobody's injury, but in good simplicity of intention and out of a slight error let themselves be baptized and have promised to desist from it if they could be shown from the Bible a better course. And how can you in your heart and conscience find a basis to say or to confess that they should be therefore beheaded or condemned? If you would deal with them as is fitting for Christian judges and if you knew how to instruct them from the Bible, no executioner would be needed; they would without doubt give place to the truth and would be severely enough punished with imprisonment." In conclusion Odenbach offered to come for a public examination, if he would be promised safe conduct, so that judgment would be passed not with fire and sword, but with instruction from God's Word.

Unfortunately this warm appeal was not heeded. The voice of the pastor of Obermoschel remained an isolated phenomenon in the general murdering and raging against the Anabaptists. Odenbach was arrested upon a complaint of Elector Louis V of the Palatinate, "because of some writings," but was soon released, for they were convinced of his "honesty and innocent teaching and life." But it was impressed upon him that he must publish nothing more without government permission.   NEFF.

Chr. Hege, *Die Täufer in der Kurpfalz* (Frankfurt, 1908) 53; Fr. Jung, *Johannes Schwebel, der Reformator von Zweibrücken* (Kaiserslautern, 1910) 199; *Menn. Bl.,* 1876, 76 ff.; *ML* III, 292.

Odenkirchen, a village on the Niers near Düsseldorf, Germany, under the dominion of the Elector of Cologne (now belongs to Rheydt), was since the middle of the 16th century the seat of an Anabaptist congregation, in which Adam Pastor (*q.v.*) was preacher for a time. William III of Flodorf, Baron of Odenkirchen and Grevenbicht, favored the Anabaptists. In 1533 an Anabaptist on his way to Münster stopped in Odenkirchen in "Driesschen's house by the castle." Since there was until 1549 a chaplain Hermann Drieschen in Odenkirchen, he became suspect of leaning toward Anabaptism. In 1534 two merchant apprentices journeyed from Dremmen to Maastricht and Odenkirchen, to proclaim the miracles of the Anabaptist prophets and to summon people to come to Münster, the "New Zion." The one who came to Odenkirchen was Peter Schumacher, the son of the Dremmen magistrate. For a long time thereafter there were Anabaptist traces in Odenkirchen; especially since after the removal of the Münsterite bogey the lord of Odenkirchen offered the persecuted refugees protection and shelter. Theunis van Hastenrath (*q.v.*) baptized four persons here about 1550. The pastor of Odenkirchen 1540-*c*49 was "Herr" Wolter, who cried out in the church at Crefeld on March 25, 1545, while lifting the sacrament: "Alas, how blinded you poor people are! What you see here is nothing but simple bread." After his departure from Odenkirchen the pastors of Hüls, Anrath, and Kempen complained in 1550 that Anabaptist doctrine was on the increase. There was in Hüls a preacher, "a vagabond by the name of Wolter, with a long white beard, a resident of Crefeld, previously pastor of Odenkirchen and there had been a follower of Anabaptists." For 80 years the Anabaptists were tolerated in Odenkirchen. Odelia von Flodorf, who protected Calvinism in Odenkirchen, left the Mennonites in peace. A congregation was organized, for the Concept of Cologne (1591) was signed by Wolter of Wetschenwel as representative of the Odenkirchen Mennonites. But in 1628, when the Archbishop of Cologne restored his authority in and over Odenkirchen and took the church from the Reformed, the Mennonites could no longer stay here. The church records of the Reformed Church at Rheydt show several transfers of membership to that church. Other Mennonites presumably emigrated. Peter Davids, a Mennonite wheelwright, moved to Nijmegen, Holland, in 1655. A congregation was no longer possible here. By 1700 there were no Mennonites left in Odenkirchen.   W.N.

DB 1890, 59; 1909, 109, 122, 125; Rembert, *Wiedertäufer,* 59, 437; K. Vos, *Menno Simons* (Leiden, 1914) 105, 107; P. C. Guyot, *Bijdragen tot de Geschiedenis der Doopsgezinden te Nijmegen* (Nijmegen, 1846) 62; *ML* III, 292 f.

Odessa, a city located 25 miles northeast of the mouth of the Dniester River on Odessa Bay and the shore of the Black Sea, Ukraine, USSR, had a population of 604,000 in 1948. Odessa was founded by a Tatar chief, was later held by the Poles and Turks, and became Russian in 1789, the year during which the first Mennonites moved to the Ukraine. The first German colonies in the region of Odessa were established in 1803 primarily by immigrants coming from South Germany, among whom were many Pietists. At the beginning of the 20th century Odessa had a German population of 12,000 and a number of German organizations, schools, and churches. In the immediate vicinity of Odessa were the German settlements of Bessarabia and Liebental. Odessa became a German cultural center far beyond the immediate German settlements. Here Louis Nietzsche founded the *Odessaer Zeitung* in 1863 and the *Neuer Haus- und Landwirtschafts-Kalender* in 1865, which were read all over the Ukraine and in other parts of Russia. There were a number of other publishing and printing enterprises in Odessa. The Mennonites had several books and publications printed here. Odessa was also a very significant export and import and trading center not only for the German population of Russia but also for Russia in general.

The "Fürsorge-Komitee" (*q.v.,* Guardians' Committee) of the foreign colonists in southern regions of Russia was located in Odessa from 1821 to 1871, when it dissolved (see also **Government of Mennonites in Russia**). This was one of the chief attractions for Mennonites to visit Odessa, although their settlements were located some distance from the city. Starting around 1900 Mennonites frequently attended the University of Odessa. Under Communism the German cultural enterprises of Odessa suffered severely and were to a large extent discontinued. During World War II the German population of Odessa was evacuated.   C.K.

Handbuch des Deutschtums im Auslande (Berlin, 1906) 183 ff.; *Neuer Haus- und Landwirtschafts-Kalender* (1913) 137.

Odon (Ind.) Beachy Amish Church was begun in 1948. In 1957 it had 165 members, with Jacob D. Gingerich, William Yoder, and Ben S. Wagler as ministers.   H.S.B.

Oecolampadius, Johannes (1482-1531), reformer of Basel, Switzerland. He studied law at the University of Bologna, Italy, then theology at the University of Heidelberg, Germany, accepted a pastorate in Weinsberg in order to continue his studies at the University of Tübingen, where he became the good friend of Melanchthon. Then he went to Stuttgart, studied Greek under Reuchlin, and then to Heidelberg, where he became acquainted with Capito and Brenz. In 1515 he became cathedral preacher at Basel, was won by Erasmus as a collaborator in his publication of the New Testament, lived a while in Weinsberg, returned to Basel in August 1518, then became preacher in Augsburg, where he entered the monastery of St. Bridgett for a year. After a brief sojourn on the Ebernburg, from April to November 1522, he returned to Basel and became an outstanding Reformer. He soon came into contact with the Swiss Brethren there. When Hans Denk came to Basel in 1523 he attached himself closely to Oecolampadius and attended his lectures on Isaiah, thus coming indirectly under the influence of Erasmian Bible interpretation. To a letter of recommendation from Oecolampadius to Willibald Pirkheimer Denk owed his appointment to the rectorship of the school of St. Sebaldus in Nürnberg. After Denk's expulsion from the city in 1525 Oecolampadius wrote Pirkheimer that he had been deceived in Denk. In November 1527 Oecolampadius again met Denk, who was mortally ill, hoping to win him to his views. He thought he had accomplished this when Denk, at Oecolampadius' insistence, shortly before his death presented to him a confession of faith; Oecolampadius had it published under the title, *Hans Denken Widerruf* (see **Hans Denk**).

Toward the close of 1524 or early in 1525 Thomas Müntzer made a brief visit to Basel. Oecolampadius received him kindly. In the presence of Hugwald they discussed infant baptism. Müntzer said that he was still practicing infant baptism, though not immediately after birth, but at longer intervals for a number of children, so that the ceremony would become more solemn, a procedure approved by Oecolampadius.

On Jan. 16, 1525, Oecolampadius received a letter from Balthasar Hubmaier (*q.v.*) requesting his view on infant baptism; he had abolished the practice and substituted the consecration of the children before the assembled congregation. Oecolampadius replied that he was holding to infant baptism, since the kingdom of heaven was closed to unbaptized infants on account of original sin. The faith of their parents would be reckoned in their favor.

Oecolampadius sent an excerpt from Hubmaier's letter to Zwingli. Evidently under Zwingli's influence Oecolampadius wrote a second letter to Hubmaier, definitely defending infant baptism, which, though not commanded in the Bible, was not forbidden. Even in the case of adults one could not see whether they had faith. Therefore the faith of the parents and godparents was sufficient.

In August 1525 Oecolampadius had a debate with the Anabaptists in his home (Loserth gives the date erroneously as June 5, in the church of St. Mary). He published an account of it, *Gespräch etlicher Prädikanten zu Basel gehalten mit etlichen Bekennern des Wiedertaufs*. The Anabaptists defended their position on the basis of the Great Commission, which sets teaching before baptism, and on the example of the chamberlain whom Philip baptized; baptism must not be equated with circumcision. They denied that they were introducing a second baptism, since in their eyes infant baptism was not baptism at all. Oecolampadius reminded them that they were founding a new sect which would end in separation and mob spirit, so that they could not be of one spirit. No agreement was reached in the

debate. The Swiss Brethren felt themselves strengthened in their views. On Oct. 10 another disputation was to be held in the church of St. Martin, concerning which there is no definite information. The opposing views were more sharply in conflict, the struggle grew more and more bitter.

In two writings Oecolampadius presented his position on infant baptism: *Unterrichtung von dem Wiedertauf, von der Obrigkeit und vom Eid auf Karlins N. Wiedertäufers Artikel*, and *Balthasar Hubmaiers Büchlein wider der Predikanten Gespräch zu Basel von dem Kindertauf* (August 1527). The former booklet is an attack on Karlin (*q.v.*), who had stated the articles of his faith in writing and had planned to defend them against Oecolampadius and the Catholic clergy before the council. When this was not permitted, Oecolampadius composed the booklet mentioned, in which he attacked the Swiss Brethren with an unusual acerbity. He calls them Katabaptists (drowners); "for you murder the noble souls and good consciences in your baptism." In the second booklet he defended infant baptism against Hubmaier on the above grounds, while he attacked adult baptism on the ground that it offended faith and love. Nonetheless his position is gentler than Zwingli's. The difference between the two was that "Zwingli proved that the infants must be baptized, Oecolampadius that infants may be baptized."

On March 14, 1528, a sharp mandate was issued by Basel against the Swiss Brethren, threatening them with loss of property and life. On July 1, 1528, Oecolampadius wrote to Zwingli, "Recently there were over 100 together in the neighborhood, of whom several were brought to prison here, who had already been driven out from this place and that with rods."

Late in the summer of 1528 Oecolampadius instituted a church inspection which revealed the increase of the Anabaptist movement in the rural areas. Thereupon he issued the Shepherd's Epistle to the thirteen pastors of the canton and four of the Bishopric of Basel, in which he had Anabaptism uppermost in mind.

On Jan. 12, 1530, the Anabaptist Hans Ludi (*q.v.*) was drowned. The execution created a deep impression. This comes to light in a letter Oecolampadius wrote to Zwingli in that month: "Therein that they (the Swiss Brethren) die so steadfastly and pretend innocence, is a new danger; some namely, who are not founded on solid ground, are beginning to waver; for they regard the steadfastness more than the reason for it, and the cross more than the reason for it, as if faith were confirmed only by suffering." Other executions followed. The movement was violently suppressed. On May 29, 1531, Oecolampadius wrote to Konrad Sohm (Sam) in Ulm: "Hardly a place of refuge remains for the Anabaptists, the church is again respected, gradually all resistance is removed." But this rejoicing was premature, as the Reformer was to learn on a tour of church inspection for the city council in May 1531, when he was preaching in Läufelfingen in the church and an Anabaptist interrupted him, whereupon a tumult resulted. The representative of the council and the mercenaries accompanying him freed him from threatening danger. A few months later he died. NEFF.

* * *

Ernst Stähelin wrote an outstanding biography of Oecolampadius (see bibliography below), which presents the disputes with the Anabaptists. Besides this biography Stähelin published the equally valuable volumes of letters and records concerning Oecolampadius. On the basis of these recently available sources Eberhard Teufel urged (*Theologische Rundschau*) a closer investigation of the influence of Oecolampadius' lectures on Isaiah upon the translation of the prophets by Denk and Haetzer in Worms (1527) than had hitherto been possible. As an expositor of the Bible, Oecolampadius was a student of Erasmus, and only in the second place of Luther. His Erasmian zeal as a translator of the Bible he transferred to his Basel auditors, including Haetzer and Denk. In so far as these Anabaptist leaders were versed in the Biblical languages, they also acquired more from Erasmus via Oecolampadius than from Luther. Erasmus is the instigating influence in the scholarly study of the Bible by the Swiss Brethren through the lectures of Oecolampadius. E.T.

J. Loserth, *Balthasar Hubmaier* (Brno, 1893); Paul Burckhart, *Die Basler Täufer* (Basel, 1898) 38; E. Stähelin, *Das theologische Lebenswerk Johannes Oekolampads* ("Quellen und Forschungen zur Reformationsgeschichte" XXI, 1939) pp. xxiv and 652; *idem, Briefe und Akten zum Leben Oekolampads* (*op. cit.,* X and XIV) I (*1499-1526*) 1927; II (*1527-93*) 1934; *Theologische Rundschau* XV, Nos. 1-3, pp. 60 f.; *ML* III, 296 f.

Oede Willemsdochter, the wife of Pieter Aelbrechtsz, an Anabaptist martyr of Hattem, Dutch province of Overijssel, was baptized in 1534 at Brielle, South Holland, in the house of Adriaen Jansz. She belonged to the revolutionary Anabaptists. In 1541 she was arrested at Utrecht, and on the charge of lodging Anabaptists she was sentenced at Utrecht and executed there by drowning on July 18, 1541. (*Inv. Arch. Amst.* I, No. 243; Mellink, *Wederdopers,* 228.) vDZ.

Oedekerk, a former Dutch Mennonite family, which may have immigrated from Odenkirchen (*q.v.*) on the Niers near Düsseldorf, Germany. In the 17th century members of this family were living in the province of Overijssel, particularly at Enschedé. Pieter Oedekerk was a preacher of the Mennonite congregation of Kampen, Overijssel, in the first half of the 18th century. Whether this family is the same as the Oudekerk family found at Haarlem in the 18th century could not be ascertained. vDZ.

Oeder, Marx: see **Eder, Marx.**

Oelbronn, Maulbronn district, Württemberg, Germany, a village parish, located on the border of Baden. It was, like the entire vicinity of Maulbronn, a point on the route of many Anabaptists. Crossing the border also offered escape from persecution. Hans, a peasant of Oelbronn, who was baptized in Moravia, was found in a cross-examination at Strasbourg. In 1537 Elsa Messner, who had emigrated to Moravia with her husband, returned to Oelbronn and was imprisoned in Maulbronn. At her release she refused to render the oath, giving instead a simple affirmation promising not to return to the duchy for the rest of her life. "In case of return she forfeits her life and property." In 1574 the parson and mayor of Oelbronn reported to the abbot of Maulbronn that Oelbronn residents had taken part in the "nocturnal chatter-preaching of the Anabaptists in the forest between Bretten (*q.v.*) and Derdingen on Wednesday, July 30, 1574, who attended partly from curiosity, partly because they wanted to leave with them." Eight persons were named and given the severest sentence possible. Two wanted to emigrate, not because of religion, but because of the "fleshpots of Egypt." In 1583 the daughter of the sexton, Anna, in spite of the arrest she had suffered in punishment, did not come to communion in the state church.

In 1590-95 there are records of the legacy left by Dorothea, the widow of Bernhard Greglich of Oelbronn, a total of 1,336 guilders. Of the eight children, two sons with their families moved to Moravia. One son returned in 1594 to stay, and asked for his mother's portion, which he finally received. In 1597 there was again a case of inheritance, and at least the interest on the estate, which was in the hands of the state, was granted the petitioner. In these two cases the decision was reasonable; in others very harsh.

In a letter of 1602 an anonymous member of the Oelbronn parish complained to the pastor Georg Heinrich Bürcklin about some participants in an Anabaptist meeting in the Schilling forest, and gave some names, though the charge is not clear. The writer of the letter hoped that the matter would not pass unpunished and that the false prophets would be dispersed, so that no false guidance might ensue. If in this instance a single member of a parish takes sides against the Anabaptists without revealing his identity, there are numerous instances of the open sympathy and intercession of entire communities for the persecuted. (*TA Württemberg; ML* III, 298.) E.T.

Oeschelbronn, Maulbronn district, Württemberg, Germany. The Anabaptist M. Zorlin, who came to Oeschelbronn from Moravia in 1577, had with him letters to various persons in the town. They were taken from him. About 38 persons of the parish attended Anabaptist preaching in 1577 and were cross-examined by the prelate and the magistrate of Maulbronn. Those liable to punishment were Jörg Kisselbronner and Claus Riebssam. They had lodged the Anabaptist Simon Kress. In 1592 the pastor of Oeschelbronn complained about the large number of Anabaptists in neighboring Baden. In 1598 a consultation was held concerning the request of Konrad Werts, who had emigrated to Moravia, for the inheritance of his parents. In 1606 Martin Bayer returned from Moravia in dissatisfaction, and was permitted to remain on probation. In 1616 Michael Nöstler requested the payment of his inheritance. In 1627 there was a similar case. (*TA Württemberg,* 1181; *ML* III, 312.) E.T.

Oet(h)enbach, a tower at Zürich (*q.v.*), Switzerland, which served as a prison for many Swiss Brethren, particularly about 1640. Hans Landis was executed here in 1614. Another Hans Landis and his daughter Margaretha were imprisoned here for 60 weeks in 1638-39, Hans Müller for two years, Adelheyd Egli, the wife of Felix Landis, for four years. Rudolf Bachmann was imprisoned in the Oetenbach tower from 1640 to the end of his life. Some others died there during imprisonment.

vᴅZ.

Oetisheim, Maulbronn district, Württemberg (today belonging to Baden), Germany. Like Oelbronn and Oeschelbronn, situated on the border between Württemberg and Baden, Oetisheim was once on the route taken by many Anabaptists. In 1576 the Protestant abbot of Maulbronn, the prelate Mogirus, received instructions to examine and indoctrinate Hans Weisser, a tailor of Oetisheim, suspected of Anabaptist beliefs, in the presence of the local parson. In 1577 the tailor was again in the audience at an Anabaptist preaching service. Many of the attendants at this sermon had moved away from Oetisheim; some had returned. The latter were to be questioned about their reasons. Many of the members of the parish rarely went to church, to communion not at all; they were to be summoned and punished. In 1578 several had come back from Moravia in disappointment and had publicly recanted at Easter and communed. The frequently mentioned tailor was to be arrested when he came back from Moravia for a possible attempt to take his family.

In 1583 the old schoolteacher was replaced by his son, who had returned from Moravia, and was probably filling the children with heresy. The teacher was to hire a suitable substitute; his son was not to go to church if he wanted to live in Oetisheim. In 1596 Matthias Kappel, who had gone to Moravia sixteen years before, had without permission slipped into Oetisheim, stayed there and in the vicinity, found shelter with his father and brought letters from Moravia, finally held a meeting in the woods on Pentecost evening, and took some young people away with him to Moravia.

The supreme council in Stuttgart decreed the following penalties: a severe reproof to the father of Matthias; a fine of three pounds to the gatekeeper and to those who lodged the Anabaptist; the same fine and a twenty-four-hour arrest to those who had attended the preaching service in the woods.

About 1619 ff. the matter of the inheritance of the Anabaptist Franz Walter of Oetisheim came up. Walter was chosen preacher of his Anabaptist brotherhood in 1597 and died in 1621. Another lawsuit developed in 1629 on the legacy of the Anabaptist Katherine Fessler of Oetisheim.

A church inspection record of 1592 relates of Oetisheim: "Many children are hired out to the neighboring Palatinate where Calvinism is practiced; the children may be infected by this poison. But the Anabaptists are more dangerous."   E.T.

The involved lawsuit regarding Franz Walter's inheritance is found in *TA Württemberg,* 89 ff.; also in Beck, *Geschichts-Bücher,* Wolkan, *Geschicht-Buch,* and Zieglschmid, *Chronik;* the Fessler lawsuit is found in *TA Württemberg,* 906; *ML* III, 326.

Oetting (today Altötting), a town in Upper Bavaria, Germany, a famous pilgrimage resort. In 1555 the Anabaptist Hans Mändl (*q.v.*), who was executed

on June 10, 1561, at Innsbruck with Eustachius Kotter (*q.v.*) and Jörg Rack (*q.v.*), was working in this region.

During the period of persecution many Anabaptist refugees fleeing on the Inn River from Tirol to Moravia were arrested here. In 1578 Andree Schlosser and Adam Schneider were thus imprisoned; after they had been racked and remained constant, they were mocked with the comment that they were not like the apostles, or God would free them from prison. The guard, wishing to make an escape impossible, placed on his feet the heavier lock, which Andree had hitherto worn on his hands and which he could not open without the use of both hands, and placed on his hands the lighter lock, which he could open with one hand. The heavier lock, now on Andree's feet, the keeper attached to a chain which he drew through an opening in the door into the anteroom, the better to secure Andree. After a prayer Andree found a nail and succeeded in opening both locks, and after another prayer he was also able to release Adam Schneider from his bonds, since the keeper had forgotten to lock the heavy door between them. With praise and thanks for God's assistance they escaped over the city wall during a thunderstorm.

The Anabaptist prisoners who refused to return to the Catholic Church were executed. According to a compilation of the Hutterian Brethren of 1581 seven Anabaptists died a martyr's death in Oetting.

HEGE.

Beck, *Geschichts-Bücher,* 227; Wolkan, *Geschicht-Buch,* 182, 389-91; Zieglschmid, *Chronik,* 233, 503-5; their confession is found in *Archiv für Ref.-Gesch.* XXVI (1929) 161-66; *ML* III, 326 f.

Oever, Den: see **Wieringen.**

Offenthal Conference, a meeting of representatives of the Amish congregations on May 20 and 21, 1867, in Offenthal near St. Goarshausen (until 1945 in Hesse-Nassau), Germany, dealing with a partial adaptation of the Amish to the other Mennonites in Germany. Seventeen representatives of the six Amish Mennonite congregations in the Palatinate, Hesse-Nassau, Oberhesse, and Neuwied were present. An agreement was reached on the basis of ten articles, which were unanimously signed. The most important were articles 5, 7, 8, and 9.

Article five deals with footwashing (*q.v.*) and says, "It shall be left to each congregation, whether it is to be literally carried out or whether it shall be spiritually interpreted as a sign of remembrance and as such impressed upon the communion guests." "But it shall not be the basis of a future division among us."

Article seven deals with nonresistance (*q.v.*) and designates: "How each congregation and each young man will preserve this ancient Mennonite principle to do justice first to his own conscience and then also to the government, we leave to the careful consideration of each one."

Article eight deals with mixed marriages (*q.v.*) and declares: "In accord with the express word of the Apostle Paul (I Cor. 7:14) we believe that such marriages as are called mixed because one part belongs to our brotherhood and the other to some other Christian body can be blessed; therefore we no longer feel authorized to maintain the church discipline to which mixed marriages have hitherto been subject."

Article nine limits the application of church discipline to exclusion from communion.

Though this beginning of a union with the Mennonites had promising prospects, the course of events did not correspond. The chief obstacle to unification was the objection by the congregations not represented in the conference to the attitude on mixed marriages. A conference of the French Mennonites at Einville near Lunéville on June 2, 1867, stated that they put a different interpretation on the quotation from Paul, namely, that such a mixed marriage is not permissible. The congregations in West Prussia and Baden were also sharply in disagreement with the decision on mixed marriages. Most of the congregations participating in the Offenthal Conference died out at the end of the 19th century. (*Menn. Bl.,* 1867, 38-40; 1868, 28-31; *ML* II, 293.)

NEFF.

Offer des Heeren, Het, a compilation of reports on the martyrs, which, as far as known, appeared in 1562. The full title reads as follows: *Dit Boec wort genoemt: Het Offer des Heeren, om het inhout van sommighe opgheofferde kinderen Godts: De welcke voortgebracht hebben wt den goeden schat haers herten, Belijdingen, Sendtbrieven, ende Testamentcn, de welcke sy metten monde beleden ende metten bloede bezegelt hebben, Tot troost ende versterckinghe der Slachschaepkens Christi, die totter doot geschict zijn, Tot lof, prijs ende eere des geens diet al in allen vermach, wiens macht duert van eewicheyt tot eewicheyt, Amen.* This book contains descriptions of the sufferings of Dutch Anabaptists who were imprisoned, their letters to their next of kin and brethren, reports of eyewitnesses, and also hymns which were in part written by them in prison and in part written by others to describe their death. These contemporary reports give the book especial value. They offer important source material for the history of the persecution of the Mennonites in the Netherlands in 1527-92. The letters of their brethren offer the prisoners courage and comfort in their suffering, while the letters from the prisoners breathe a deep, earnest spirit, with the admonition to faithful endurance in a Christian walk amid all persecution. In all editions the *Offer des Heeren* is followed by a hymnal entitled *Een Lietboecxken* (*q.v.*), *tracterende van den Offer des Heeren, int welke oude ende nieuwe Liedekens, wt verscheyden Copien vergadert zijn, om by het Offerboeck ghevoecht te worden.* . . . Eleven songs from this *Lietboecxken,* translated into German, are found in the *Ausbund* (*q.v.*).

The book does not, however, report all the Dutch Mennonite martyrs, but only some of those who lived in the province of Holland, in Flanders, in Antwerp, and in Friesland. The first edition of the *Offer* contains accounts on 21 Dutch Anabaptist martyrs, while the last edition of 1599 includes 33 martyrs. Besides this the *Lietboecxken* mentions in the first edition 135 martyrs, the last edition 179. Of the German martyrs, the cross-examination of

Michael Sattler (*q.v.*), who was burned at the stake in Rottenburg on the Neckar in 1527, is presented in excerpts, as was ascertained by G. Kawerau, who published the omitted text in the *Göttingische Gelehrten-Anzeigen* (1905, 493-96), having found in the library at Wolfenbüttel a copy not accessible to Cramer of *Ain newes wunderbarlichs geschicht von Michel Sattler,* by an anonymous eyewitness.

The *Offer des Heeren* was widely read by the Mennonites of the time and went through eleven editions: 1562 (the *Lietboecxken* of this edition being signed 1563), n.p.; 1566, n.p.; 1567, 1570, n.p.; two editions of 1578, both n.p.; 1580, n.p.; 1590, n.p.; 1592, n.p.; 1595, published by Willem Jansz Buys at Amsterdam; and 1599, published by Peter Sebastiaenszoon at Harlingen. There may have been other editions. Each edition amplifies the preceding one by adding informaton on the executions occurring in the meantime, especially under Alba's reign of terror.

In the literature on church history this martyr-book, in spite of its powerful examples of strong faith and courage, is scarcely mentioned. The letters with their expression of devotion to the Lord are reminiscent of the days of the early persecution of Christians under heathen governments. The Dutch authorities sought to suppress the distribution of this great source book, for the publication of such testimonies, in sharp contradiction to the suspicions of their enemies and the content of the numerous mandates, brought a stream of new converts to the Mennonites.

In spite of many reprints, also in the period of tolerance in Holland, only a few copies have been preserved. The Amsterdam Mennonite Library has a copy of the editions of 1562, 1567, 1570, 1578a, 1580, 1590, 1592, 1595, 1599. In the library of the University of Gent are found a copy each of the 1566 and the 1578b editions; a copy of the 1578a edition is found in the Royal Library in The Hague and the Utrecht University Library; the 1578b edition is also found in the Library of the University of Utrecht. The Goshen College Library has the editions of 1570, 1578, 1580, and 1595. For a long time this great book had disappeared entirely, and only in 1875 was a copy of the first edition found. In view of its significance in the evaluation of the Anabaptist movement in the 16th century S. Cramer (*q.v.*) published a new edition as the second volume of the *BRN* (The Hague, 1910, XII and 683 pages), based on the edition of 1570, and in his introduction called attention to the most important differences between the various editions and added information gleaned from old court records.

The *Offer des Heeren* was the foundation of the later Dutch Mennonite martyrbooks, including van Braght's *Martyrs' Mirror.* HEGE, vDZ.

DB 1870, 54-58; 1906, 53-92; *Bibliographie des Martyrologes* (The Hague, 1890) II, 441-99; *ML* III, 293 f.

Offerings. Information is lacking about offerings for church needs among the 16th-century Anabaptists in Switzerland and South Germany. Most likely the only funds needed, those for the poor and needy, were secured privately by the deacon as need arose. Money for church buildings and janitor service was not needed until the late 18th century or early 19th in the Palatinate and Alsace, and not until the late 19th century in Switzerland. Both there and in America the first method of "collecting" for church purposes was by placing the contributions in offering boxes placed at the exits of the meetinghouse. In a few congregations in the Franconia Conference (MC) in Eastern Pennsylvania this practice was continued until recently, and it is still standard practice among the Old Order Mennonites of Lancaster County who broke off from the main body in 1893, also among the Old Order Mennonites in other areas, such as Ontario.

In many American Mennonite churches funds are raised for regular expenses by assessments on an annual basis, sometimes per capita, sometimes on a property or income basis.

The taking of offerings during the church service by having the deacons, or most commonly ushers, send collection plates through the pews probably came in connection with offerings for special purposes such as missions, although the custom of taking offerings in Sunday school for expenses of that work was established at the very beginning of Sunday-school effort. In the Mennonite Church (MC) the mission offerings were first established on a monthly basis; only recently have weekly Sunday morning offerings become a regular practice.
                                                    H.S.B.

In the Netherlands, the Mennonites from the start contributed to their congregations, in particular for the support of the poor. This was done by two methods: (*a*) By collections at the religious services. In the early days the members gave their gifts to the deacons (*armendienaren*) before the beginning of the service; but after 1600 boxes (*bossen*) were placed at the exit to receive the offering. This method remained in use in conservative groups like the Groningen Old Flemish, in some of the churches until the present. Among the more progressive Lamists (*q.v.*) the Reformed way of taking collections was adopted about 1675; i.e., during the service, usually while the congregation was singing, a collection-bag attached to a long stick was passed. The method is still used in certain Dutch Mennonite congregations. In Leiden (*q.v.*) the latter method was introduced in 1674, because the "bossen" raised so little. At present the gift of charity is usually received by two deacons at the door after the benediction. Open offering plates are little used. (*b*) The second method is to receive the gifts at the homes of the members. In former centuries the deacons of a congregation visited the members, especially those in better financial circumstances, and encouraged them to make large donations, usually in the fall, and sometimes before Christmas. At present annual contributions are requested of the members and are sent in a modern businesslike way. Although these contributions are entirely voluntary, it is a common practice in many congregations that the members give one or one and a half per cent of their income.

As the expenses of the congregation increased, especially since *c*1820 when a salaried ministry became general, larger offerings have been asked of the members.   voZ.

Office Holding: see **State.**

Offrus Greysinger, an Anabaptist martyr: see **Griesinger, Onophrius.**

Offstein, a village near Worms in Rhenish Hesse, Germany, once the seat of a Mennonite congregation, which was founded by Swiss refugees who settled here soon after the Thirty Years' War (1618-48). The lists of Mennonites in the Karlsruhe archives name three families in 1664; one of them was Peter Dahlem, and another was the preacher Heinrich Schneider. By 1685 the number of families had increased to seven. In March 1688 a conference of elders and preachers of the South German congregations was held in Offstein, and resolutions were passed on the attitude to be taken by preachers and elders toward transgressors. Only four families survived the French War.

The Amsterdam Mennonite Archives contain several letters written by Jonas, preacher of the Offstein congregation (from before 1670 until after 1714), which give information about the Mennonite refugees expelled from Switzerland in 1710, who had settled in Alsace and the Palatinate and who asked for financial aid from the Dutch Mennonites; this aid was given.

In 1742 the Johannes Dahlem and Jonas Schnebele families moved away from Offstein. Johannes Schneider joined the Reformed Church. In 1768 a Nikolaus Kägy family is mentioned. At the beginning of the 19th century the number of Mennonites in the village must have been larger.

On May 1, 1828, the Mennonites of Offstein presented a petition to the government at Mainz for the release of their children from obligatory attendance at religious instruction in the community school, "since we have our children learn in their youth what belongs to their religion." They objected to the books which were prescribed for instruction, and declared it to be a violation of religious liberty to compel their children to use these books.

On Nov. 13, 1835, representatives of the stricter wing of the Mennonites in Hesse and the Palatinate met in conference in Offstein and declared that the new catechism and also the hymnal of 1832 were not acceptable to them, and that they would not deviate a hair's breadth from the faith of their fathers.

For a long time the Mennonites of Offstein and Dirmstein (*q.v.*) belonged to the circuit Heppenheim-Obersülzen-Gerolsheim (*q.v.*), and later to the Kriegsheim (*q.v.*) congregation, as is recorded (about 1820) in the Kriegsheim city church building record.

In 1942 there were two Mennonites living in Offstein, members of the Monsheim congregation; in 1957 there were four Mennonite families and two part families.   NEFF, voZ.

Mathias Pohl, "Geschichtliche Beiträge aus den Mennonitengemeinden," *Gem.-Kal.* 1906, 135-43; *Inv. Arch. Amst.* I, Nos. 1257, 1435-37; II, No. 2849; *ML* III, 294.

Ogemaw County (Mich.) Amish settlement, now extinct, was a small group of Old Order Amish living near West Branch, Ogemaw County, Mich., in 1908-30. Most of the early settlers moved there from Nobles County, Minn., including the Joseph N. Gerber, Daniel B. Gerber, and a number of Jantzi families. They were followed by Miller, Eash, Swartz, Kropf, and Bender families from Oscoda County, Mich., and by a few Miller families from Elkhart County, Ind. The bishop in charge was Joseph N. Gerber, succeeded by Jacob Gascho. Other ministers were John B. Gerber, Klaus Jantzi, Jacob Swartz, and Solomon Jantzi. The group at its largest consisted of about twenty families. In 1925-28 the Amish families began to move away, most of them going to Ontario; by 1933 the congregation had died out.   C.R.G.

Oggenfuss (Ockenfuss), **Hans,** a tailor of Stadelhofen near Zürich, Switzerland, who was in the Grebel (*q.v.*) group as early as 1524; Oggenfuss was one of the signatories of the letter of this group to Thomas Müntzer (Sept. 5, 1524). On Jan. 22, 1525, he was present at the first baptism which Brötli (*q.v.*) performed at Zollikon (*q.v.*) near Zürich. Soon after that he joined the Anabaptist congregation and was active in preaching and baptizing. He was imprisoned several times because of his activity, but released on his promise not to preach and baptize, which promise he did not keep. His name is found in the records of the Zürich city council for the last time in January 1528. Then he disappeared from history. Like all the other Anabaptists of the Zollikon group he may have given up Anabaptism.   vDZ.

TA Zürich, passim; Fritz Blanke, *Brüder in Christo* (Zürich, n.d.-1955) 16, 22, 25, 50, 57 f., 61, 65.

Ohain, Belgium, the location of the Home of Hope, a children's home established in 1952 by the Belgium Mennonite Mission (MC). It serves some 25 abandoned children.   H.S.B.

Ohio, bounded on the north by Lake Erie, on the south by the Ohio River, on the east by Pennsylvania, and on the west by Indiana, was the first state carved out of the Northwest Territory. It is part of the mid-continent area first settled by the French, who came up the Mississippi and explored its tributaries, and ceded by them in 1763 to the English. They in turn transferred it to the United Colonies in 1783. The Indians relinquished their claim to the Ohio lands by the Treaty of Greenville in 1795. But, encouraged by the English, they continued to make trouble for the early settlers until the end of the War of 1812.

The first Mennonite settlers to found a congregation within the state came to Fairfield and Perry counties from Lancaster County, Pa., and Rockingham County, Va., by way of southwestern Pennsylvania in 1799. Mennonites from Bucks County, Pa., settled in Mahoning County in 1806 and a group from Lancaster County and Rockingham County arrived in Stark County in 1811. Amish from Somerset County, Pa., settled in Tuscarawas County in 1808 and others from Somerset and Mifflin counties a little farther west in Holmes County two years later. But until the close of the War of 1812 made the Ohio frontier comparatively safe from molestation by the Indians, Amish and Mennonite settlements made slow growth. A short-lived settlement was begun in Trumbull County (*q.v.*) 1804-10.

The two decades following the end of hostilities witnessed the founding of most of the present large flourishing congregations of Amish and Mennonites in the state, and a few now extinct:

Date of Founding	Location	Origin
1817	Oak Grove, Wayne Co. (Amish)	Somerset and Mifflin Co., Pa.
1817	Leetonia, Columbiana Co. (Mennonite)	Bucks Co., Pa.
1819	Butler County (Amish)	Alsace and Hesse-Darmstadt
1819	Sonnenberg (Mennonite)	Jura, Switzerland
1823	Beech (Amish)	Jura, Switzerland
1824	Martins Creek (Amish)	Lancaster Co., Pa.
1825	Crown Hill (Swiss Mennonite)	Switzerland and Upper Alsace
1825	Kolbs (Mennonite)	Bucks Co., Pa.
1825–30	Longenecker (Mennonite)	Bucks Co., Pa.
1827	North Lima (Mennonite)	Bucks Co., Pa.
1829	Guilford (Mennonite)	Ontario, Maryland, and Bucks, Lancaster, and Lehigh Counties, Pa.
1831	Salem in Allen County (Mennonite)	Fairfield Co., Ohio
1832	Blanchard (Mennonite)	Maryland
1834	Central in Fulton County (Amish)	Alsace and Montbéliard
1834	Martins (Mennonite)	Lancaster Co., Pa.
1835	Putnam County (Swiss Mennonite)	the canton of Bern

Amish settlers began arriving in Logan County from Wayne County, Ohio, and Mifflin County, Pa., in 1840, and 8 or 10 miles southeast in Champaign County from Wayne and Fairfield counties, Ohio, and Mifflin County, Pa., in 1846. These two in the course of a few decades developed into the strong South Union and Oak Grove congregations.

Early Mennonite leaders in the state were Henry Stemen of Fairfield (later of Allen), Jacob Oberholtzer in Mahoning, Jacob Nold in Columbiana, Hans Lehman and Ulrich Gerber at Sonnenberg, Peter and Daniel Steiner at Crown Hill, William Westheffer at Martins, Jacob Koppes, William Overholt, and Martin Leatherman at Guilford in Medina

County. Their Amish contemporaries were Christian Brandt and David Zook in Wayne County (Zook later in Fairfield), Moses Beachy in Holmes, John Schloneger in Stark, Benedicht King and Joseph Goldschmidt in Butler County, Frederick Hagi (Hege?) at Martins Creek, and Christian Beck and Christian Rupp in Fulton County.

Mennonite leaders during the middle and later years of the 19th century were John Thut, John M. and George Brenneman, and John M. Shenk of Allen County, Adam Kornhaus at Martins, Peter Imhoff in Ashland, Abraham Rohrer in Medina, and among the Swiss Mennonites, Christian Sommer at Sonnenberg and John Moser at Bluffton. Amish Mennonite leaders during the same period were Jacob and John K. Yoder, cousins, and Hannes Yoder of Wayne County, John Warye in Champaign, Jacob C. Kenagy, David Plank, and John P. King of Logan, and Eli and Jacob Frey of Fulton.

Coming from such varied backgrounds, it is not surprising that differences existed. These differences actually were not so great because all Amish and Mennonites spoke German, dressed in a plain modest garb, and practiced the simple life. But their small differences were at times magnified out of all proportion to their importance. On at least one occasion Mennonites and Amish refused to cross the Atlantic on the same vessel. And a congregation in Wayne County divided on whether it was necessary for a Mennonite who wished to unite with the Amish congregation to be rebaptized by an Amish bishop. One frequent cause of difficulty was that differences in congregational practice developed almost imperceptibly as the years passed. Few Amish and Mennonite settlers came to Ohio directly from Europe. The most striking exceptions were the entire colony of Swiss Mennonites who came to Wayne, Putnam, and Allen counties 1819-50; the Alsatian Amish families who came to Wayne and Stark counties and were assimilated by the Oak Grove and Beech congregations, the Alsatians who founded the Fulton County Amish congregation, and the Alsatians and Hessians who settled in Butler County in the southwestern corner of the state. Most of the Mennonite settlers in Ohio came from Pennsylvania settlements established 75-125 years earlier in Bucks and Lancaster counties, and most of the Amish from well-established congregations in Lancaster, Mifflin, and Somerset counties in the same state. These settlers sought farms or larger holdings in the newer lands in America's great western wilderness. A few later immigrants from Europe, both Amish and Mennonites, remained in the Pennsylvania counties only long enough to repay the passage money advanced for their transportation across the Atlantic, and then joined the general westward movement. Mennonite families established a line of settlements extending from east of Pittsburgh, Pa., westward to South Bend., Ind., many of them now extinct. The Amish, on the other hand, made fewer settlements, but with two notable exceptions, Knox and Fairfield counties, their Ohio congregations remain permanent. As their congregations developed in Ohio, their history becomes confusing and complicated. Satisfactory generalizations become well-nigh impossible.

One difference between Amish and Mennonite in cultural practice related to the plain garb seems to have affected the relative permanence of their congregations. Among the Mennonites the marks of "separation from the world" were put on by the individual on application for church membership which was frequently delayed until marriage. Then the young man laid aside his worldly clothes for the plain Mennonite garb, and the young woman made a radical change when she adopted the simple dress of the church. Especially in the small Mennonite churches of the Ohio frontier such a change set young people off into so small a group that satisfactory social fellowship was almost impossible. Few young people could bring themselves to such a radical change while their friends in their German-speaking social circle united with the Lutheran, Reformed, United Brethren, or Evangelical churches, all of whom conducted their services in German, but, in addition, provided for the religious and social life of their young people. Many small Mennonite congregations on the Ohio frontier consequently endured little longer than a generation or two. Amish children, on the other hand, wore the garb of their parents from early childhood. This costume was no barrier when they united with the church in their middle or late teens. Amish were more reluctant, too, to settle in a neighborhood that gave little promise of building a congregation strong enough to guarantee adequate intra-congregational social life. The Knox and Fairfield County Amish congregations, for example, did not die out through the loss of their young people to other denominations, but when it became evident that land values were already too high to attract Amish settlers the entire congregation moved to other growing Amish congregations.

Mennonite Settlements in Ohio. The Mennonites who settled in Fairfield and Perry counties at the beginning of the 19th century chose a hilly section because it was well drained. After the canal system several miles west opened level land more suitable for cultivation and more accessible to good markets, the group became dissatisfied and founded congregations in Franklin, Logan, and Allen counties. With them went some of their ablest leaders: John M. Brenneman (*q.v.*), first to Franklin and later to Allen; his brother George to Putnam, and two younger brothers, Henry and Daniel Brenneman (*q.v.*), to Elkhart County, Ind. The Logan County group moved on west after a few decades and founded the now extinct congregation in Clay and Owen counties (*q.v.*), Ind. The Fairfield County congregations, which had built two meetinghouses, Pleasant Hill and Turkey Run (*q.v.*), suffered further decline during the Civil War through the loss of whole families to the German Evangelicals ("Albrechtsleut") and by the end of the century were nearing the point of extinction. Recent attempts to revive the congregation have been only moderately successful. The Allen County settlement of 125 years ago, now three congregations: Salem, Pike, and Central under the Ohio and Eastern Mennonite Conference, has survived serious internal difficulties and the loss of many individuals, even whole families, to neighboring non-Mennonite groups.

KEY TO MAP OF
Ohio
• Mennonite Churches
▲ Mennonite Institutions
▨ Old Order Amish Settle-
   ment Areas
▢ See also detailed maps for:
   Allen-Putnam Counties,
Holmes County, & Wayne County.

Scale of Miles
0 5 10 15 20 25 30 35 40 45

Congregation	Address
Mennonite Church	
1. Beech	Louisville
2. Bethel	Wadsworth
3. Bethel	West Liberty
4. Burton	Burton
5. Central	Archbold
6. Dillonvale	Dillonvale
7. Fairpoint	Fairpoint
8. First	Canton
8a. Flatridge	Newcomerstown
9. Friendship	Bedford
10. Gilead	Mt. Gilead
11. Gladstone Mission	Cleveland
12. Hartville	Hartville
13. Hillside Chapel	Jackson
14. Huber	Medway
14a. Lee Heights	Cleveland
15. Leetonia	Leetonia
16. Lockport	Stryker
17. Lost Creek	Hicksville
18. Lower Owl Creek	Beaver
19. Midway	Columbiana
20. North Clinton	Wauseon
21. North Lima	North Lima
22. Oak Grove	West Liberty
23. Pine Grove	Stryker
24. Pine Grove	Vinton
25. Plain View	Aurora
26. Pleasant View	North Lawrence
27. Sharon	Plain City
28. South Union	West Liberty

29. Springfield Twp. Chapel	Holland
29a. Stoner Heights	Louisville
30. Tedrow	Tedrow
31. Turkey Run	Bremen
31a. Warneke Chapel	Pedro
32. Bancroft	Toledo
33. West Clinton	Pettisville
34. Rockview	Youngstown
35. Zion	Archbold
35a. Mexican Mission	Archbold
35b. Hi-Way Chapel	East Greenville
35c. Kennedy Avenue	Dayton
Conservative Mennonite	
36. Akron	Akron
37. Johnsville	Johnsville
38. Maple Grove	Hartville
39. Maple View	Middlefield
40. Marlboro	Marlboro
41. United Bethel	Plain City
41a. Sharon	Ragersville
41b. New Franklin (non-conf.)	New Franklin
Beachy Amish Mennonite Church	
42. Canaan	Plain City
42a. Bunker Hill	Holmesville
43. Pleasant View	Hartville
General Conference Mennonite	
44. Apostolic	Trenton
45. First	Wadsworth
45a. First	Sugarcreek

Church of God in Christ, Mennonite	
46. Pettisville	Pettisville
Evangelical Mennonite Church	
47. Archbold	Archbold
48. Pioneer	Pioneer
49. Wauseon	Wauseon
Old Order (Wisler) Mennonite	
50. Lower	Wadsworth
51. Pleasant View	Mahoning Co.
Old Order Amish Mennonite	
52. Walnut Grove (King Amish)	Hartville
Church districts	
Reformed Mennonite Church	
52a. Lauber Hill	Archbold
Institutions	
53. Adriel School (MC)	West Liberty

[Churches and institutions not listed here are
named on county maps in volumes I, II, and IV.]

The Mahoning-Columbiana settlement in the earlier years was entirely agricultural, but with the growth of heavy industry and the great increase of population in near-by industrial centers Mennonites are turning to truck gardening and poultry raising. The three congregations, Midway, Leetonia, and North Lima, long considered as one congregation, are now independent, each with its own organization and its own bishop. Under the conservatively progressive leadership of its aged bishop, A. J. Steiner, now retired, the congregation has maintained a high degree of stability. During the 1872 Wisler controversy in Indiana a considerable number of members left the main body and founded the Pleasant View (q.v.) Old Order Mennonite congregation.

The Wayne County Mennonite congregation, which founded the Martins (q.v.) church southeast of Orrville, also lost a number of members to the Wisler group in 1872. The Wayne County Wisler congregation is the largest Old Order Mennonite church in the United States. Some members of the Martins church who lived near Orrville united with the Salem congregation (q.v.) when it was organized by disaffected members of the Oak Grove Amish Mennonite Church (q.v.) in 1892. It has lost members also to the Orrville Mennonite Church (q.v.), founded by members of the Oak Grove congregation who engaged in business in this thriving railroad center.

The Medina County Mennonite group built the Guilford meetinghouse near Wadsworth and followed their bishop, Abraham Rohrer, into the Wisler branch in 1872, leaving a bare half-dozen members in the Ohio Conference. After a severe struggle for survival, aided by John F. Funk and others, the congregation began to grow and is now the Bethel congregation (MC, q.v.). Medina County also is the home of the Wadsworth First Mennonite Church (GCM), founded in 1852 by "Oberholtzer" (GCM) families from Bucks County, Pa., led by Ephraim Hunsberger. The Huber Mennonite Church (q.v.), also known as Medway, founded soon after 1830 in Clark County near Dayton, has suffered throughout its 125-year history the precarious existence of other small Mennonite congregations in the state. Torn by dissension, losing members to the Reformed Mennonite branch, and led sometimes by an unprogressive leadership or served by nonresident ministers supplied by Conference, it has several times been in danger of extinction.

The saddest picture of the original Mennonite settlements in Ohio is the number of extinct congregations. Each has left its neglected cemetery, the site of a small church building and many Mennonite names, some no longer on any church roll. Beginning with Pleasant Hill in Fairfield County and Canal Winchester and Stemens in Franklin County, the list includes a congregation in Trumbull County, Kolbs in Holmes County, Brubachers, Pleasant View, and Salemskirche in Ashland County, one in Richland and Crawford counties, and one each in Seneca, Wood, and Williams counties. This line continues westward with extinct congregations in Bronson County, Mich., and DeKalb, Lagrange,

Elkhart, and St. Joseph counties in Indiana. Most of these followed Jacob Wisler in the O.O.M. movement in the 1870's and for reasons already mentioned lost their young people. From all of the extinct Ohio congregations, however, some of the more progressive members moved westward, many to the western part of Elkhart County, Ind., where their descendants are members of the Olive, Yellow Creek, Clinton Brick, or Old Order Mennonite congregations. A few moved farther west to Illinois, Kansas, or Iowa, where their descendants are making an appreciated contribution to the religious and institutional life of Mennonite congregations, both M.C. and G.C.M. The only one of the above-mentioned extinct Ohio Mennonite congregations to become G.C.M. was the Salemskirche (Salem Mennonite Church), whose last pastor was the German immigrant, Carl Justus van der Smissen (1879-90), retired theological teacher of the Wadsworth Mennonite School. His son had been pastor both of Salem and of the G.C.M. church in Cleveland. After Van der Smissen's death most of the remaining members together with a few members of the Pleasant View Church (MC) united with the thriving Stone Lutheran Church near the former site of Salem. Most of the Lutheran members of the congregation were descendants of Lutheran families who had come to the neighborhood with the Palatine Mennonites in the 1830's.

Amish Settlements in Ohio. In 1808-12, about a decade after the Mennonites settled in Fairfield County, Amish from Mifflin and Somerset counties, Pa., began to arrive in Tuscarawas and Holmes counties and a few years later in Wayne. The change from Amish to Amish Mennonite in 1840-60 affected both Holmes and Wayne counties. In Wayne County (q.v.), however, so small a number clung to the old order discipline and practices that the Amish wing disappeared entirely before 1870. The congregation, then numbering about 300, built the Oak Grove meetinghouse in 1862 and Pleasant Hill in 1881. Joined by Alsatian families in 1850-70, the congregation early became one of the most progressive in the state. A small group seceded in 1869 and later founded the Sterling (Ohio) Mennonite church (GCM, q.v.). By 1880 the congregation had a membership of 401. In 1947 when the Ohio and Eastern A.M. Conference adopted a new constitution the members at Oak Grove refused to accept it because they felt that it abridged their traditional congregational autonomy. The group at Pleasant Hill accepted the new constitution and is now a member of the Ohio and Eastern Mennonite Conference. Oak Grove is an independent congregation without conference affiliation but a large majority of the members support the educational and missionary organizations of the Ohio and Eastern Mennonite Conference and the Mennonite Church (MC) in general. Its present membership is 401. The membership of Pleasant Hill is 190.

Soon after 1830 the first Wayne County Amish bishop, David Zook, moved to Bern Township, Fairfield County, with a number of his friends and relatives from Wayne County and Mifflin County, Pa., and founded a congregation which became extinct after a few decades when the members moved to

Champaign County, Ohio, and to Topeka, Ind. A small Amish settlement founded near Martinsburg, Knox Co., Ohio, c1840 organized a congregation and ordained Isaac Schmucker preacher but moved as a group to Champaign County, Ohio, and Noble County, Ind., before the end of the decade.

About 1840 Amish from Mifflin County, Pa., and Wayne County began settling in Union Township, Logan County, Ohio, where they founded what is now the South Union church (MC). A few years later settlers from Fairfield and Wayne counties, including Jacob Hertzler, the bishop in Fairfield, founded the Champaign County congregation eight or ten miles southeast of the Logan County congregation. They were joined a few years later by John Warye, of Hesse-Cassel, Germany, ordained preacher in 1855, bishop in 1862 for what is now the Oak Grove church (q.v.) in Champaign County. For the first few years the two congregations met in each other's services on alternate Sundays as the North and South "districts" of the same congregation, a practice still followed by Old Order Amish congregations. Difficulties developed when Jacob Hertzler allowed certain deviations from the strict Amish requirements. When a considerable number of the members of the Logan County district advocated the same progressive measures, they withdrew and worshiped on alternate Sundays with the Champaign County district. They held their Logan County meetings in non-Mennonite meetinghouses on the intervening Sunday. In 1875 the Champaign district built the Oak Grove church and their friends in Logan County the Walnut Grove church (q.v.). The original Logan County congregation built a new church in 1876, South Union (q.v.). The two groups, Walnut Grove-Oak Grove and South Union, refused each other full fellowship until 1895 when a new bishop was to be ordained to serve the Logan County churches. South Union and Walnut Grove then agreed to place both of their leading ministers in the lot and to accept whichever one should be chosen, as bishop of the two congregations. David Plank (q.v.) of Walnut Grove was chosen and ordained. Under his beneficent administration the two groups drew together and at his death A. I. Yoder (q.v.), a son of the preacher who had served the South Union congregation for many years, was ordained bishop for the two congregations. After a few years the Walnut Grove church building was closed and sold.

The years have brought other experiences to the Logan and Champaign congregations, some good, some sad. In 1880 a small group seceded from Oak Grove and Walnut Grove over the issue of English preaching and the use of musical instruments in the homes. Locally they were known as the "Miller Church" because an Indiana Amish Mennonite bishop, Eli Miller, had organized the congregation. They were members of the Indiana A.M. Conference. The movement died out at Oak Grove in less than a dozen years but lasted a few years more at Walnut Grove. A Church of God camp meeting in the early 1890's raised emotions to a high pitch and drew away several members from Oak Grove and from the Miller church and resulted in the organization of the Church of God congregation in West

Liberty. In 1890 a revival meeting held at the South Union church by John F. Funk and D. J. Johns of Elkhart County, Ind., led to the founding of the Bethel Mennonite Church (q.v.) in West Liberty in 1895. In the course of the next few years the English church and Sunday-school services at Bethel attracted a considerable number of young Amish Mennonites who otherwise might have been lost to the church. During the 1890's a stirring revival meeting at the Mt. Tabor M.E. Church led to the conversion of S. E. Allgyer (q.v.) and his wife in their home and profoundly affected his life and service in the Mennonite Church. At that time he was Sunday-school superintendent at Oak Grove. Later he was ordained preacher and bishop. After the death of A. I. Yoder, Allgyer served the three churches, Oak Grove, Bethel, and South Union, as bishop. The three congregations now have a combined membership of 682. These congregations, especially Bethel, have contributed an unusually large number of workers to the institutions of the church, especially in the areas of education and missions.

Old Order Amish Survival of Early Amish Settlements. Although the last "no-meetinghouse Amish" disappeared from the Green Township, Wayne County, Amish settlement before the end of the third quarter of the 19th century, the quiet remoteness of the Holmes County hills was particularly conducive to the persistence of the time-honored Amish social and religious practices. And, although a progressive Amish group under the leadership of their bishop, Elias L. Frey, built a meetinghouse (Walnut Creek) in 1862 (the same date as the first such building of the Wayne County Amish), at least an equal number held firmly to the old customs. Beginning with this Holmes County nucleus, the state of Ohio, with 6,500 of the 17,000 baptized members of the Old Order Amish congregations in America, now has 71 congregations in 13 counties in the state, making Ohio the leading state in the Union from the standpoint of its Amish population. Major areas of concentration are located in the following groups of counties: (1) Holmes, Wayne, Stark, Tuscarawas, and Coshocton; (2) Geauga, Trumbull, and Ashtabula; (3) Madison and Union. Amish from Holmes County settled in Geauga County southeast of Cleveland in 1886 and in Madison County west of Columbus in 1896. After a number of Amish from Geauga County had united with the Plainview congregation (MC) in Portage County about 1930, the Ohio and Eastern Mennonite Conference organized the Burton congregation (MC) in 1948, present membership 74. In 1926 after several members of the Amish congregation in Madison County had united with the Oak Grove congregation (MC) near West Liberty and had been expelled by the Amish for leaving their congregation, Oak Grove members organized a Sunday school at Resaca, and in 1933 the Ohio and Eastern Mennonite Conference organized the Sharon Mennonite congregation (q.v.) near Plain City, which had 163 members in 1957. The first preacher ordained for this church has been ordained bishop and is serving as bishop also at Bethel and Oak Grove near West Liberty. In 1939 the Beachy Amish organized a congregation, Canaan, near Plain

City, membership 60, and in 1944 the Conservative Mennonite Conference organized the United Bethel congregation near the same place, membership 164. This active organization has established two mission points, one in Columbus, the other at Blue Creek. In spite of losing members or even an occasional congregation to one of the more progressive groups, the number of Old Order Amish in Ohio is constantly increasing. This is not due to missionary effort, but to the natural increase in population and the ability of the group to hold the interest of its young people.

The Swiss Mennonites. Two Swiss Mennonites from the Jura Mountain area in Switzerland arrived in Green Township, Wayne County, and united with the Oak Grove Amish congregation in 1818, but in the next year a number of their friends arrived and after a brief period of prospecting decided to settle in the rolling hills of Paint Township several miles farther south. Here during the next few years they were joined by friends from the Jura and founded the strong Sonnenberg congregation (*q.v.*). In 1825 others from the same region in Switzerland founded another settlement several miles farther north. For some time the two settlements were considered parts of the same congregation. Each built its own meetinghouse and the northern group (Crown Hill, *q.v.*) eventually joined the Ohio Conference (MC). The Sonnenberg congregation, long independent and without conference affiliation, owes its present conservative attitude to the firm but beneficent administration of its bishop, Christian Sommer (1811-91). As early as 1879 he severed all connection with the other Swiss Mennonite congregations in western Ohio and eastern Indiana because, he asserted, they had left their early pattern of simple life and faith. In 1886 a few members withdrew under the influence of the Wadsworth Mennonite School group to found the Salem Mennonite Church (*q.v.*) near by. In 1893-94 the "Russellite" heresy led several members away from Sonnenberg. During World War I when several young men who had been attending Bluffton College enlisted for military service with the support of the Salem congregation, the pastor and a group of supporters left Salem and founded the Kidron Tabernacle congregation. After 1926 the ministers of the Sonnenberg group worked more and more with the Ohio and Eastern A.M. Conference. The transition from German to English was not begun until the third decade of the 20th century and then only after a severe struggle. In 1936 more than three fifths of the 500 members of the Sonnenberg congregation withdrew to found the Kidron Mennonite Church (MC), 1957 membership 484. The original Sonnenberg congregation was admitted to the Virginia Mennonite Conference (MC) a few years ago, membership 174. About 40 members withdrew from the Sonnenberg congregation to found the independent Bethel congregation at Apple Creek, present membership 49.

Beginning in 1833 friends of the Sonnenberg group began a Swiss Mennonite settlement in Putnam and Allen counties, Ohio. Located in a rich agricultural region, the original Swiss settlement now consists of four congregations: Ebenezer, St.

Johns, Grace in Pandora, and the First Mennonite Church in Bluffton. Under the able, progressive administration of their bishop, John Moser, during the latter half of the 19th century, these congregations have made phenomenal growth. Their present combined membership is 1,670. Extremely plain in their general cultural pattern, they came under the influence of the Wadsworth Mennonite School during the 1870's and laid aside many of the marks of their earlier Swiss culture, but were able to do so without serious internal difficulty. In 1848 a former Swiss Mennonite, John Thut, who had been ordained to the ministry in the Kolbs congregation in Holmes County, settled in the neighborhood. But because this congregation did not practice footwashing he withdrew from them and founded the Riley Creek congregation (later Zion, MC). After his death one of the ministers with more than half of the congregation withdrew to found a Defenseless Mennonite (now Evangelical Mennonite) congregation, present membership 62. After a difficult period of rehabilitation the Zion congregation became a vital force in the educational, missionary, and charitable organizations of the Mennonite Church (MC). It was the home of Menno S. and Albert J. Steiner. Some of its members helped to organize the congregation at New Stark in adjoining Hancock County, the home of John Blosser, first president of the Mennonite Board of Education. The Zion congregation was reabsorbed by the First Mennonite Church of Bluffton in 1925 and the church building razed.

The Alsatian Amish in Fulton and Williams Counties. Beginning in 1834 an entirely new immigration of Amish direct from Europe founded what has now become a veritable cluster of churches (MC) in Fulton and Williams counties in northwestern Ohio, one of the most prosperous agricultural sections of the state. Coming from Alsace and Montbéliard many of them spoke and wrote both French and German. Of a different cultural background from the older Amish congregations in the state and of sufficient numerical strength to be self-dependent, they avoided close organizational ties with their American brethren but co-operated with them in a general way in conference activities. Until well into the present century the groups worshiping at their three meetinghouses—Central, Lockport, and West Clinton—were considered as one congregation with Elias L. Frey as their bishop and his brother, Jacob Frey, deacon. The rather large number of ministers preached at the different meetinghouses in rotation. The three congregations are now separate organizations each with its own bishop and church organization. In addition to these three there are now five other congregations: Lost Creek, Pine Grove, Tedrow, Zion, and North Clinton, each with its own church building and pastor, besides four mission outposts with a combined membership of 72. The total membership of the 8 congregations and their 4 mission stations is over 1900. These congregations are members of the Ohio and Eastern Mennonite Conference (MC). The original Amish congregations in this general area lost members to two other Mennonite conferences. The Reformed Mennonite Church (*q.v.*) established a congregation near Archbold in 1852, erected the

Lauber Hill meetinghouse in 1864, and now has a membership of 71. The Evangelical Mennonite Church (*q.v.*), formerly known as the Egli Amish and later as the Defenseless Mennonites, organized a congregation in Archbold in 1870 and now maintains two thriving congregations at Archbold and at Wauseon with a combined membership of 650.

Ohio Mennonites have developed the following institutions: Bluffton College (GCM, known as Central Mennonite College 1898-1913); Orphans' Home (MC, 1896) at West Liberty, since 1957 called Adriel School; Home for the Aged (MC, 1901) near Rittman; Mennonite Memorial Home (GCM, 1945) near Bluffton; Camp Luz (MC, 1953) near Orrville.   J.S.U.

STATISTICAL SUMMARY OF MENNONITE AND AMISH CONGREGATIONS IN OHIO BY CONFERENCES

Body or Conference	Congregations	Members
Mennonite Church (MC)	74	9808
Ohio and Eastern*	61	8111
Conservative Mennonite	9†	1037
Virginia Conference	2	212
Unaffiliated	2	448
Old Order Amish	71‡	6586
General Conference Mennonite	9	2591
Evangelical Mennonite	4	853
Old Order (Wisler) Mennonite	6	341
Beachy Amish Mennonite	3	225
Reformed Mennonite	6	150
Church of God in Christ, Menn.	2	58
Total		20,612

* Of the 65 organized and 37 unorganized congregations in the Conference, 70 are in Ohio.

† Also 5 mission stations.

‡ Districts rather than congregations.

Ohio and Canada West Mennonite Conference (GCM) was organized in 1855 under the leadership of Daniel Hoch (*q.v.*), of Jordan, Ont., under the formal name, "Conference Council of the United Mennonite Community of Canada West and Ohio." No list of member congregations is available, but in Ohio the only one apparently was the newly organized Wadsworth congregation, formed from families who came from the Oberholtzer Conference in Eastern Pennsylvania. The Canadians were small dissident groups from a number of congregations in Waterloo County and Lincoln County, possibly also in the Markham district north of Toronto. The chief purpose of the conference, which met annually at first, was the promotion of home missions and evangelism, and by September 1859, the conference had a fully organized "Home and Foreign Missionary Society of the Mennonites." Daniel Hoch was appointed traveling minister (*Reiseprediger*) at an early date. The conference joined with the Oberholtzer group in Eastern Pennsylvania and a small group in Iowa to organize the General Conference of the Mennonite Church of North America in 1860.

The Canada-Ohio Conference continued until about 1869. The group in Ontario disintegrated, most of the members ultimately joining the Mennonite Brethren in Christ (*q.v.*), a new schismatic movement which started in 1874. The Ohio church-es ultimately joined the newly formed Middle District Conference.   H.S.B.

H. P. Krehbiel, *The History of the General Conference . . .* (n.p., 1898).

Ohio and Eastern Mennonite Conference (MC), first known as the Ohio Mennonite and Eastern Amish Mennonite Joint Conference, was formed in 1927 by a merger of the Ohio Mennonite Conference (*q.v.*) and the Eastern Amish Mennonite Conference (*q.v.*). The new conference held its first full session in 1928. In 1955 it dropped the last vestige of the age-old separation by adopting as its official title the present name. At that time the annual report showed a total of 11,109 members, 78 congregations, 26 bishops, 109 ministers, and 96 deacons. The membership as reported in the 1958 *Mennonite Yearbook* is 65 organized congregations and 37 unorganized congregations or mission stations with a total of 10,893 baptized members. The apparent decrease is due to the withdrawal of several eastern congregations to unite with their nearer conference, the Southwestern Pennsylvania (*q.v.*), now known as the Allegheny Conference: Maple Grove at Belleville in 1944 and the following in 1957: Allensville, Otelia, Rockville, and Mattawana. The present combined membership of these congregations is 594. There are still 22 congregations in the conference east of Ohio, with some 2,400 members (mostly in Eastern Pennsylvania and Maryland), sufficient to warrant the name Ohio and Eastern.   J.S.U.

Ohio Conference of the United Missionary Church was a part of the United Evangelical Mennonite denomination, which was organized in 1879. It was listed as a part of the Indiana-Michigan-Ohio Conference. In 1883 the union of the United Evangelical Mennonites and the Brethren in Christ created the Mennonite Brethren in Christ Church (which changed its name to United Missionary Church in 1947). Several churches of the Swankite Branch of the Brethren in Christ located in Clark County, Ohio, and in Westmoreland and Armstrong counties in Western Pennsylvania were added and formed a nucleus from which the district was localized in several areas. On Oct. 27, 1942, the General Conference Executive Committee granted the request for separation.

On April 11, 1944, the Ohio Conference met in its first annual session at Hubert Avenue Church in Springfield.

The Ohio Conference has conducted an annual camp meeting at Ludlow Falls for 35 consecutive years. Foreign missionary work is one of the primary objectives and the conference is represented by five missionaries at present.

The twelfth annual session, in 1956, reported 18 ministers, 1,268 members, and a total offering for the twelve-month period of $166,101. The estimated value of the property is $439,850.   H.E.Bo.

Ohio Mennonite Christian Workers Conference, successor to the Ohio Sunday School Conference (known also for a number of years as the Ohio Sunday School and Young People's Bible Meeting Conference), served both Mennonites and Amish Mennonites as an outlet for united Sunday school, missionary, and young people's Christian activities, before and after the merger of the Ohio Mennonite and Ohio and Eastern Amish Mennonite conferences. Its first meeting was held at the Salem Mennonite Church near Wooster, Ohio, in 1895. It was probably the first conference to meet in a large tent, because of the large attendance, and owns a tent for use in its annual meetings.

The conference was from the beginning an excellent combination of lay and ministerial interest and activity and was autonomous in organization. Early efforts of some leaders of the Indiana Mennonite and Ohio Mennonite conferences to supervise and control the activities of the Ohio Sunday School Conference were ineffective for several reasons: (1) some of the most active early Sunday-school workers in the state were Amish Mennonites, such as David Plank (q.v.), D. S. Yoder, S. E. Allgyer (q.v.), C. Z. Yoder (q.v.), Jerome Smucker, S. H. Miller, and younger men, e.g., I. W. Royer, C. K. Hostetler, and E. J. Zook; (2) on one occasion when the Sunday School Conference was held in a Mennonite church and directed by the Ohio Mennonite Conference attendance was small and interest at a low ebb; (3) on a subsequent occasion after the Ohio Mennonite Conference had prescribed certain limits to the work of the Sunday School Conference, Sunday-school leaders in the state announced that the next conference was to be held at the Amish Mennonite Church in Logan County (Walnut Creek) and appointed David Plank corresponding secretary to arrange for the conference. This conference session was attended by so large a number of Sunday-school workers from both branches of the church and such a fine spirit of fellowship and cooperation was in evidence that the concept of an autonomous Sunday-school conference organization received added impetus. The constitution adopted in 1914 provided for an executive secretary, an executive committee, and a delegate body. The delegate body consists of all ordained men in the state and lay delegates elected by each Sunday school.

Soon after the constitution was adopted, I. W. Royer was elected executive secretary and served for more than a third of a century. His industry, tact, and co-operative spirit made the conference a vital force in promoting Bible study and teaching, missionary spirit, spiritual Christian activity among the young people, and unity among the brotherhood. Months before the annual conference he met with the executive committee and spent days arranging the conference program, then took it to the local ministry for their advice and counsel. Wherever local conditions were favorable, the program provided for special vocal music by young people's groups as an added inspirational feature. The conference has proved a powerful cohesive force in Ohio Mennonitism. It has regularly raised funds to support home and foreign missions, and recently established a fund to aid young men from the Ohio area preparing for the ministry by attending seminary.

The Ohio conference is the outstanding conference of its kind in the Mennonite Church (MC)

and has made a major contribution to the life of that church in the 20th century.   J.S.U.

John Umble, *Ohio Mennonite Sunday Schools* (Goshen, 1941), written at the request of the Ohio Mennonite Sunday School Conference and subsidized by it, though published by the Mennonite Historical Society at Goshen College.

Ohio Evangel, the 7¾ x 10½ in. 16-page bimonthly organ of the Ohio Mennonite Mission Board, first called *Ohio Mission News Bulletin* (1947), then *Ohio Mission Evangel* (1949-52), *Ohio Evangel* (1953-   ), with an earlier subtitle and motto, "A Mission Outpost for Every Congregation." Editors have been Stanford Mumaw (1947-48), Harold Bauman (1949-53), David Hostetler (1953-55), and Edward Stoltzfus (1955-   ).   H.S.B.

Ohio Mennonite Conference. Mennonite historians, following the lead of C. Henry Smith, have agreed on 1834 as the date of the organization of this conference, meeting annually in late spring at the Mahoning County or Oberholser Church (now Midway, q.v.) and later alternating with the Martins Church (q.v.) in Wayne County (q.v.). (Since, however, Mennonite ministers were holding conferences both in eastern Pennsylvania as early as 1750 and in Canada soon after 1800, and since at least 10 congregations were established in eastern Ohio and western Pennsylvania before 1830, it seems unlikely that no Ohio conference was held before 1843.) According to John F. Funk the early Ohio conferences had no regular agenda, passed no formal motions, kept no written minutes, but reached decisions by general oral agreement after informal discussion. This was true for several decades, even after Funk began to print the annual reports in the *Herald of Truth*. After a number of congregations had been organized in Indiana, ministers from that state attended the Ohio conference sessions. Later (by 1854 at least) an annual fall conference was held at the Yellow Creek Mennonite Church in Elkhart County, Ind., but it did little more than agree to the informal decisions expressed at the spring conference in Ohio. The Indiana meeting had by 1864 become an independent Indiana-Michigan Conference. Toward the end of the century Mennonite ministers began to attend the annual conferences of their Amish Mennonite brethren and to labor for an organic union of the Amish Mennonite and Mennonite conferences. John F. Funk (q.v.), John S. Coffman (q.v.), and Menno S. Steiner (q.v.) were tactful but persistent leaders in the movement for unification.

Meanwhile the American Amish wing of the Swiss Brethren-Anabaptist movement continued the traditional practice of holding formal conferences, adopting rules and policies and keeping minutes of the proceedings. From manuscript copies of some of these minutes material has been printed in the *Mennonite Quarterly Review* (see bibliography). Without the slightest intention of uniting with the Mennonites the Amish gradually took several steps that led in that direction. Even before 1850 some Amish congregations on the Ohio frontier departed from some of their traditional practices and began to adopt the name Amish Mennonite. A Wayne County Amish congregation even ventured so far as to accept a Mennonite as a member without requiring him first to be rebaptized by an Amish bishop. The same congregation fellowshiped with later Hessian, Alsatian, and Palatine Amish immigrants, whose gradual acculturation in Europe had led them away from some of the earlier cultural practices. Toward the end of the 19 century Amish Mennonites and Mennonites gradually became acquainted and drew closer together, first through the columns of the *Herald of Truth,* then through using the same Sunday-school "Lesson Helps," 1889; meeting in a church-wide general Sunday-school conference (*q.v.*), 1892; engaging in a co-operative educational project (Elkhart Institute, *q.v.*), 1895; and finally organizing a general conference of Amish Mennonites and Mennonites in the United States and Canada, 1897. In 1904 the Ohio and Eastern A.M. Conference voted to unite with the Ohio Mennonite Conference "in establishing a mission post" in Canton. Even before that date the members of each conference attended the sessions of the other. At this 1904 Ohio and Eastern A.M. Conference six of the sixteen bishops in attendance were Mennonites, as were ten of the twenty-two ministers and one of the five deacons. Even then, however, some of the Amish Mennonites were unfriendly toward too close collaboration with the Mennonites. They preferred their own type of congregational government. It was not until 1926 that each conference appointed a "merger committee" to work out a plan for an organic union of the two conferences. Each conference held a final separate session in 1927. Under the name Ohio Mennonite and Eastern A.M. Joint Conference, the merged conferences held their first meeting in 1928.

The Ohio Mennonite Conference reported the following congregations at the time of the merger in 1927: Midway, North Lima, East Lewistown, and Leetonia, together 390 members; Salem 32; Turkey Run 25; Martins 125; Kolbs, Longenecker, and Union Hill, together 40; Marion 12; Bethel and Guilford 100; Central 82; Pike and Salem, together 225; Mt. Pleasant 40; Medway 34; Bethel (West Liberty) 110; Lima 20; Crown Hill 126; Canton 75; Pleasant View 90; a total of 16 congregations with 23 meeting places and a membership of 1,526. At the time of the merger two of the congregations of this conference were in charge of bishops in the Ohio and Eastern Amish Mennonite Conference: Central at Elida and Bethel at West Liberty.

J.S.U.

H. S. Bender, "Some Early American Amish Mennonite Disciplines," *MQR* VII (1934) 90-98; XI (April 1937) 163-80; see also *MQR* XX (1946) 232-40, and XXII (1948) 94-115.

Ohio Mennonite Mission Board (MC) was organized in 1920 and held its first annual meeting in that year. The first president of the board was A. J. Steiner. Other officers were J. S. Gerig, S. E. Allgyer, Eli D. Yoder, and E. B. Stoltzfus. The Orrville Mennonite Church (*q.v.*) is the outgrowth of the first full-time mission project under the Ohio board. The *Ohio Evangel* (*q.v.*), which it publishes bimonthly, reports the activities of the organiza-

tion as well as news from its mission congregations. In 1957 the Ohio Mennonite Mission Board had the following eight missions: Fairpoint (at Fairpoint), Hillside Chapel (Jackson), Kennedy Avenue (Dayton), Lower Owl Creek (Lucasville), Pine Grove (Vinton), Rockview (Youngstown), St. John's Chapel (Logan), and Warneke Chapel (Pedro). Outside of the jurisdiction of the board were 24 outposts of congregations which were members of the board. The Mennonite Board of Missions and Charities operated five additional missions in Ohio.

M.G.

Ohm or **Onkel** (German), **Oom** (Dutch), i.e., Uncle, is used by certain Mennonites as a title of affectionate regard or honor. The early Dutch Mennonites used the title "Oom" for ministers and other persons to be honored. This practice was transplanted by the Mennonites settling in Danzig and Russia, where it was "Ohm" in Low German and "Onkel" in High German. The latter was also used in South Germany although "Vetter" (cousin) is also common.

C.K.

Ohnenheim, a village in Alsace (*q.v.*), district of Schlettstadt (Sélestat), where the Dordrecht Confession (*q.v.*) of April 1632 was signed on Feb. 4, 1660, in a conference of the Mennonite preachers of Alsace-Lorraine. Ohnenheim was the meeting place of the Mennonites who lived in the Bishopric of Strasbourg (see **Colmar**). (*ML* III, 295 f.)

NEFF.

Ohrloff: see also **Orloff.**

Ohrloff Mennonite Hospital, located in the Molotschna Mennonite settlement, Russia, was established by the heirs of H. H. Reimer in 1910. The first doctors were Fink (Dorpat University), Gerhard D. Dürksen (Odessa University), and J. J. Isaak (Medical School at St. Petersburg). The manager was H. D. Günther. The report for the year 1912 lists the following doctors in service: O. Pinker, P. Dück, and Gerhard G. Dürksen. During that year, 467 patients were treated and the average number of patients in the hospital at one time was 17. Some of the nurses received their training at Morija (*q.v.*). After the Revolution, the hospital was nationalized. (Friesen, *Brüderschaft,* 58; Dirks, *Jahrbuch 1913,* 172.)

C.K.

Ohrloff Mennonitische Zentralschule was the first secondary school established among the Mennonites in Russia. It was founded in 1820 by an educational society (*Schulverein*) headed by Johann Cornies (*q.v.*), the great Mennonite organizer and colonizer. The first site of the school, which at that time had only one classroom, was between the villages of Ohrloff and Tiege in the Molotschna settlement in the Ukraine. In 1847 the school building burned down, the following year J. Cornies died, and the school remained closed till 1860, when it was reopened in a new building at Ohrloff.

Like all other Zentralschulen in the Molotschna and its daughter settlements, the Ohrloff school had a three-year course of study, in contrast to this type of schools in the Chortitza settlement, where the course of study was four years. The first teacher was Tobias Voth, whom Cornies invited to come from Prussia. Because he could teach only in the German language and was not strict enough in his school discipline, Cornies dismissed him after seven years of service. He was followed by Heinrich Heese, another pioneer of education among the Russian Mennonites, who also came from Prussia. He had studied Russian for several years and now at the wish of Cornies this language was introduced into the curriculum of the school. Heese taught for 15 years, then also disagreed with Cornies, left the school, and went to Chortitza, where he founded the Chortitza Zentralschule. After its reopening in 1860 the Ohrloff Zentralschule had three classrooms with three teachers. Its curriculum supplied a very substantial higher elementary education. Some prominent teachers of the school were Hermann Janzen, P. H. Ediger, P. J. Wiens, J. Janzen, and especially Cornelius Unruh and Johann Bräul, two of the most prominent schoolmen among the Russian Mennonites.

In 1912 the school was moved into its new beautiful modern building. But soon, with the advent of World War I and after it the Russian Revolution, the Communist regime took over the school and it ceased to be a center of Mennonite education. (Friesen, *Brüderschaft*.)   H.G.

Ohrlofferfelde: see **Orlofferfelde.**

Ohrloff-Petershagen Mennonite Church: see **Orloff Mennonite Church.**

Ojo de lad Yegua, a Mennonite settlement (north settlement) near Cuauhtemoc, Chihuahua, Mexico, was established by landless Old Colony Mennonite families in 1946 northeast of the Manitoba Mennonite settlement. The Buena Vista ranch, formerly occupied by J. E. Enns, is located in this settlement. The beginning of this daughter colony of the Manitoba and Swift Current settlement was a difficult one. In 1953 it had a population of 3,594.   C.K.

Okeene Mennonite Brethren Church, also sometimes called the Ebenfeld Church, located at Okeene, Okla., was organized on April 20, 1903, with Adam Fischer as the first leader. Heinrich Rusch, an ordained minister, served the church 1903-32. The following have served as pastors: R. C. Seibel 1932-35, H. H. Hiebert 1935-37, Waldo Wiebe 1937, Dan Friesen 1939-44, Arthur Willems 1944-48, Henry Heinrichs 1948-52, E. C. Ollenburger 1952- . The membership in 1954 was 91, with J. C. Neufeld as leader.   S.F.

Oklahoma, a southwestern state, bounded on the north by Colorado and Kansas, on the east by Missouri and Arkansas, on the south by Texas, and on the west by Texas and New Mexico, has an area of 69,919 miles, and a population 2,189,000 (1956). Originally Oklahoma formed a part of the Louisiana Purchase from France in 1803 and existed as an unorganized Indian Territory in 1820-40, reserved for Indians exclusively. A part was opened to general settlement in 1889 and the western part organized as Oklahoma Territory in 1890. The rest was gradually opened to settlement, and then by

the Enabling Act of 1906 the Indian Territory and the Oklahoma Territory were merged and admitted into the Union as a state on Nov. 16, 1907.

Mennonite settlement in Oklahoma began as soon as the Indian Territory was opened for white settlement on April 22, 1892. The Mennonites who came to this territory were primarily those who had settled in the Great Plains of Kansas and Nebraska two decades before the opening of Oklahoma. Many of them did not have enough land for their children, or were lured by the prospect of vast unoccupied space in this area. However, the first Mennonites who came to Oklahoma did not do so for economic reasons. The General Conference Mennonite Church, which had been organized as a conference in 1860, and had been looking for an appropriate mission field, was attracted to the Indian Territory (Oklahoma) and opened a mission there.

Missions. In 1875 S. S. Haury was ordained as a missionary and the following year he was sent to the Indian Territory to look for a field. He became acquainted with the Cheyenne and Arapaho Indians. Through the help of the Indian agent Miles, a Quaker stationed at Darlington, the General Conference Mennonite Church began its first mission work among the Arapaho Indians in 1880. A frame mission school building was established at Darlington (*q.v.*), northwest of the present city of El Reno, to accommodate twenty-five Indian children and the missionary family. S. S. Haury (*q.v.*) was the first Mennonite missionary to do work among the Indians of Oklahoma and possibly also the first Mennonite to enter the Indian territory. Later the mission work was extended to Cantonment (*q.v.*) (now Canton) and the Cheyennes (*q.v.*). Other stations were added.

The Mennonite Brethren began the Post Oak mission a few miles northeast of the present city of Indiahoma in 1894, when Henry Kohfeld (*q.v.*) started his work among the Comanche Indians. A. J. Becker, who came here in 1901, spent his whole life among the Comanches.

The first actual Mennonite settlement to be established in Oklahoma resulted from the establishment of the Darlington Mission. In 1891 some people who had settled between the present towns of Okarche and El Reno, Canadian County, established the Mennoville Mennonite Church (*q.v.*), the first Mennonite church in Oklahoma. On April 19, 1892, three million acres of land in the Cheyenne and Arapaho territories were opened to white settlement. Among the earliest homesteaders in the western part of the Oklahoma territory were numerous Mennonites, primarily from Kansas and Nebraska. Their settlements extended into the counties later called Blaine, Custer, and Washita. One group homesteaded near the present site of Geary, another in the vicinity of Watonga, and a third in the vicinity of Okeene. In 1893 the Cooper Mennonite Brethren Church was organized. In 1902 this settlement was disbanded. The first Old Order Amish settled in the Thomas community in 1893.

Through a study it has been estimated that some 100,000 people joined in the race to establish claims in the Oklahoma Territory; many Mennonites were among them, coming from Kansas, Nebraska,

4

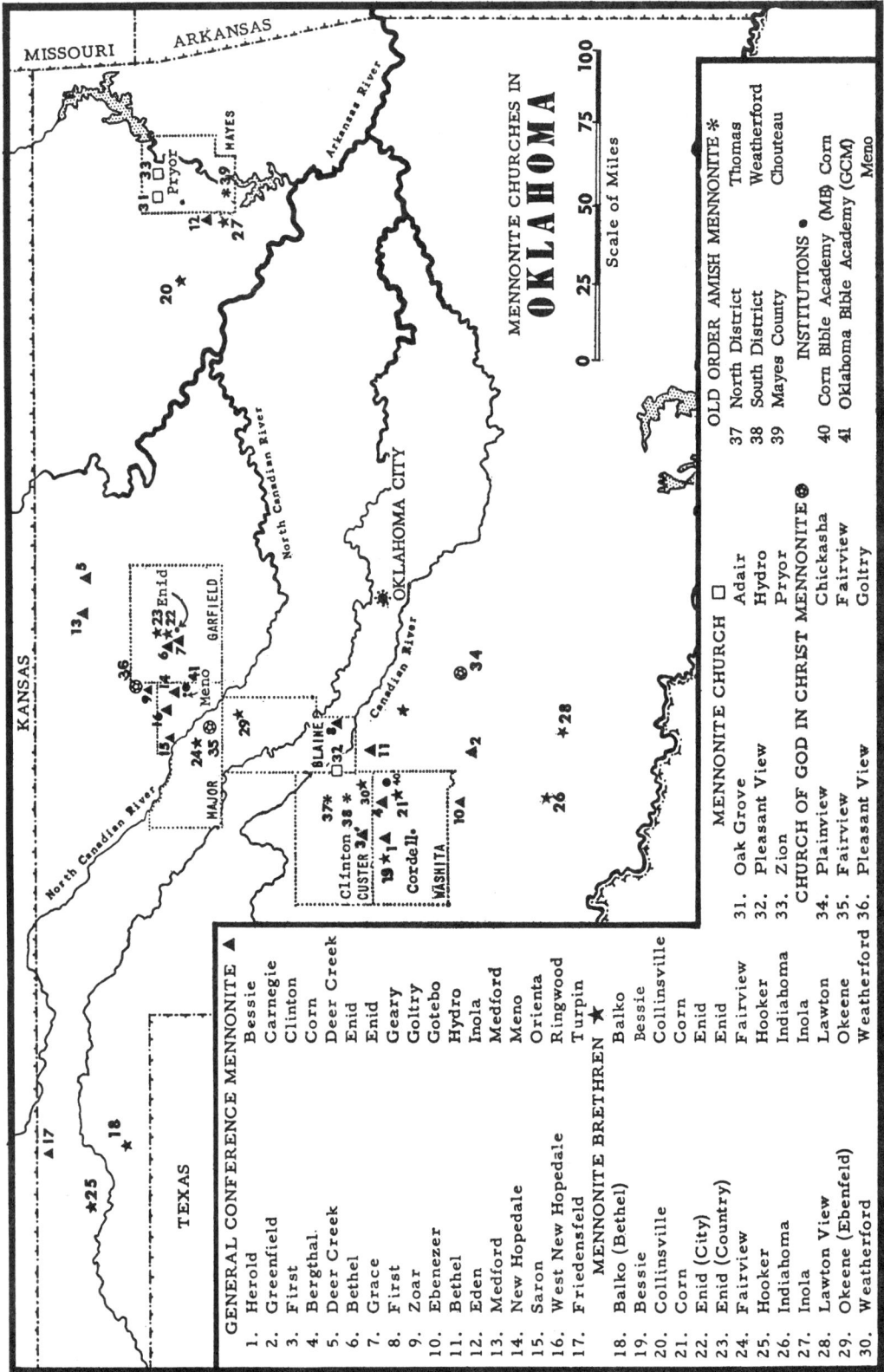

MENNONITE CHURCHES IN OKLAHOMA

Scale of Miles
0   25   50   75   100

MISSOURI   ARKANSAS   KANSAS   TEXAS

OKLAHOMA CITY

Arkansas River   North Canadian River   Canadian River

MAYES   GARFIELD   BLAINE   MAJOR   CUSTER   WASHITA

Pryor   Enid   Meno   Clinton   Cordell

GENERAL CONFERENCE MENNONITE ▲

1. Herold — Bessie
2. Greenfield — Carnegie
3. First — Clinton
4. Bergthal — Corn
5. Deer Creek — Deer Creek
6. Bethel — Enid
7. Grace — Enid
8. First — Geary
9. Zoar — Goltry
10. Ebenezer — Gotebo
11. Bethel — Hydro
12. Eden — Inola
13. Medford — Medford
14. New Hopedale — Meno
15. Saron — Orienta
16. West New Hopedale — Ringwood
17. Friedensfeld — Turpin

MENNONITE BRETHREN ★

18. Balko (Bethel) — Balko
19. Bessie — Bessie
20. Collinsville — Collinsville
21. Corn — Corn
22. Enid (City) — Enid
23. Enid (Country) — Enid
24. Fairview — Fairview
25. Hooker — Hooker
26. Indiahoma — Indiahoma
27. Inola — Inola
28. Lawton View — Lawton
29. Okeene (Ebenfeld) — Okeene
30. Weatherford — Weatherford

MENNONITE CHURCH □

31. Oak Grove — Adair
32. Pleasant View — Hydro
33. Zion — Pryor

CHURCH OF GOD IN CHRIST MENNONITE ⊕

34. Plainview — Chickasha
35. Fairview — Fairview
36. Pleasant View — Goltry

OLD ORDER AMISH MENNONITE ✳

37. North District — Thomas
38. South District — Weatherford
39. Mayes County — Chouteau

INSTITUTIONS ●

40. Corn Bible Academy (MB) — Corn
41. Oklahoma Bible Academy (GCM) — Meno

Iowa, and Missouri. They were the founders of the communities of Meno, Medford, Deer Creek, Orienta, Fairview, Lahoma, Kremlin, North Enid, Enid, etc. The first Mennonite (GCM) church founded in 1894 as a result of this "run" was located in the Fairview community. The North and South Hoffnungsfeld Mennonite Brethren congregations were established here.

Mennonite (GCM) families from McPherson and Marion counties, Kan., organized the present Meno community on June 13, 1895. They established the New Hopedale Mennonite Church (*q.v.*) and the Ringwood West New Hopedale Mennonite Church (*q.v.*). The village of Meno (Menno) was founded in 1902. The Mennonite Brethren Church of Medford (*q.v.*) was organized on Feb. 4, 1897. J. F. Harms was the minister there and the editor and printer of the *Zionsbote*. The town of Deer Creek (*q.v.*) was founded in 1898 adjacent to a Mennonite settlement of persons primarily of South German background who organized a congregation in 1899.

Mennonites of the M.C. group settled in Alfalfa County and organized the Milan Valley Church. Other settlements were established near Manchester and Newkirk. A few families of the Church of God in Christ, Mennonite, settled near Fairview. The Church of God (*Apostolische Brüdergemein-*

de), followers of Herman Peters (*q.v.*), established a small group (see **Fairview** Church of God). Mennonites also settled in Kiowa, Beaver, Texas, and Caddo counties in 1901-7. Two General Conference congregations and one Mennonite Brethren in the Gotebo vicinity were established shortly after 1901. In the Oklahoma Panhandle, Mennonites settled in Beaver County near Turpin and Balko, and in Texas County near Hooker.

Pioneer life on the Oklahoma plains was difficult, intensified by poverty and drought conditions. Pioneers lived in sod houses and dugouts. Many found lack of water a serious problem. After 1897, when bumper crops were harvested, conditions improved in many places.

By the close of the Territorial period in 1907 there were, according to Marvin Kroeker, 37 Mennonite congregations in Oklahoma, sixteen of which belonged to the General Conference Mennonite Church, twelve to the Mennonite Brethren, three to the Mennonite Church (MC), two to the Old Order Amish, one to the Amish Mennonites, one to the Krimmer Mennonite Brethren, and one to the Church of God in Christ, Mennonites.

Congregations. In 1911, Oklahoma had 33 Mennonite congregations with a membership of 1,944 in the following congregations:

MENNONITE CHURCHES IN OKLAHOMA IN 1911

Name of Church	County	Location	Members
American Indian Mission (GCM)	Blaine	4 m. NW of Canton	74
Bergthal (GCM)	Washita	11 m. NW of Bessie	51
Bethania (GCM)	Woodward	24 m. S of Cold Water	31
Bethel (MB)	Custer	5 m. SW of Weatherford	65
Bethel (GCM)	Caddo	8 m. W of Hinton	23
Caddo (GCM)	Caddo	8 m. W of Hinton	20
Cheyenne Mission (GCM)	Custer	6½ m. E of Hammon	12
Deer Creek (GCM)	Grant	Deer Creek	42
Ebenezer (GCM)	Kiowa	4 m. NE of Gotebo	86
Friedensau (GCM)	Noble	6 m. SE of Perry	23
Friedensthal (GCM)	Kiowa	6 m. SW of Gotebo	74
Geary (GCM)	Blaine	Geary	60
German Springs (OOA)	Alfalfa	Manchester	36
German Springs (MC)	Alfalfa	6 m. SE of Waldron	40
Guymon (OOA)	Texas	7 m. SE of Guymon	13
Gotebo (MB)	Kiowa	Gotebo	65
Herold (GCM)	Washita	5 m. SE of Bessie	125
Medford (GCM)	Grant	2 m. E of Medford	80
Milan Valley (MC)	Alfalfa	3 m. SE of Jet	33
Newkirk (MC)	Kay	5 m. SW of Newkirk	15
Neuhoffnungsthal (GCM)	Woods	½ m. N of Meno	175
Pleasant View (OOA)	Blaine	9 m. SW of Hydro	65
Salem (GCM)	Washita	5 m. NE of Cordell	20
Saron (MB)	Texas	11 m. SE of Hooker	65
Saron (GCM)	Woods	1 m. SW of Orienta	35
School House (OOA)	Grant	Medford	13
Sichar (GCM)	Washita	6 m. NE of Cordell	30
Springfield (GCM)	Caddo	17 m. S of Hydro	54
Thomas (OOA)	Custer	2 m. from Thomas	100
Washita (MB)	Washita	14 m. SW of Weatherford	350
Weatherford (MB)	Washita	Weatherford	
Zemamovo (GCM)	Noble	5 m. SE of Canton	52
Zion (GCM)	Blaine	1 m. S of Lucien	17

(Taken from H. P. Krehbiel, *Mennonite Churches in North America*, published in 1911.)

The following is a list of congregations derived from the official conference reports of the various Mennonite groups of Oklahoma after World War II. The total number of recorded congregations is 40 and the total membership 4,985. The U.M.C. congregations are not listed in these tables.

Mennonite Churches in Oklahoma After World War II

1. General Conference Mennonite in 1956, 17 congregations with 1,902 members: Herold (Bessie) 231, Greenfield (Carnegie) 88, First, of Clinton 49, Bergthal (Corn) 99, Deer Creek 124, Bethel (Enid) 25, Grace (Enid) 119, First of Geary (Geary) 64, Zoar (Goltry) 150, Ebenezer (Gotebo) 52, Bethel (Hydro) 57, Eden (Inola) 147, Medford (Medford) 98, New Hopedale (Meno) 308, Saron (Orienta) 128, West New Hopedale (Ringwood) 67, Friedensfeld (Turpin) 105; *2. Mennonite Brethren in 1954, 13 congregations with 2,260 members:* Balko 131, Bessie 172, Collinsville 72, Corn 626, Enid City 189, Enid Country 203, Fairview 411, Hooker 116, Inola 15, Okeene 89, Weatherford (Indiahoma) 25, Lawton View (Mission) 47, Indiahoma 184; *3. Church of God in Christ, Mennonite, in 1955, three congregations with 406 members:* Plainview (Chickasha) 125, Fairview (Fairview) 235, Pleasantview (Goltry) 46; *4. Mennonite Church (MC) in 1956, three congregations with 257 members:* Zion (Pryor) 108, Pleasant View (Hydro) 130, Oak Grove (Adair) 21; *5. Old Order Amish in 1956, four congregations with 160 members:* South District (Weatherford) 42, North District (Thomas) 66, Choteau District (Choteau) 52, and Mazie District (Mazie, no figure given).

Since World War I. The time preceding and following World War I was marked by definite economic progress for the Mennonites of Oklahoma. The problems and difficulties of pioneer conditions were overcome. During the war some Mennonites suffered because of the general anti-German feeling. Some towns and businesses posted signs, "Use American language only."

In their spiritual and educational efforts the Mennonites of Oklahoma were aided by their mother congregations of Kansas and other states. The Western Conference (GCM) helped to found the Oklahoma Convention (*q.v.*) which takes care of the specific needs and problems of the Oklahoma congregations, although the latter are members of the Western District Conference. The Mennonite Brethren congregations belong to the Southern District M.B. Conference. The M.C. congregations belong to the South Central Conference.

The Mennonite Brethren of Oklahoma established the Corn Bible Academy (*q.v.*) in 1902. The General Conference Mennonites established the Gotebo Preparatory School (*q.v.*) in 1910, and the Oklahoma Bible Academy (*q.v.*) in 1911, which is still functioning. An evangelistic mission-minded fervor is found in most of the congregations. The Mennonites of Oklahoma have supported the mission work among the Indians of the state. (See **Arapahoe** Mennonite Mission, **Cheyenne** Indians, **Indiahoma**.)

The Mennonite population of Oklahoma is still predominantly rural, although the number of those who seek employment in the city and establish businesses is constantly increasing. Some of the towns in and around which Mennonites are located are: Meno, Corn, Enid, Weatherford, Deer Creek, Orienta, Geary, Gotebo, Kremlin, Medford, and Fairview. Only a few, like Meno and Corn, are predominantly Mennonite. During the depression after World War I many Mennonites joined other inhabitants of Oklahoma in their search for better living conditions in California. Numerous Mennonite families established new homes in Los Angeles, Bakersfield, Shafter, Fresno, Reedley, etc.

Since the Mennonite baptized church membership is some 5,000, it can be assumed that the total Mennonite population including children is at present over 10,000 (1957). In the religious and cultural life the Mennonites of Oklahoma in general follow the pattern of the older Mennonite settlements in surrounding states in gradual adjustment to the environment. In most cases English is the primary spoken language, although Low German dialects are still used in some homes. In their worship services English is used almost exclusively, with the exception of the Amish. Although a distinctive ethnic culture in some of the groups can still be traced, many of these characteristics have been more assimilated to the general culture than is the case in the settlements of other states from which they came. Mennonites coming originally from Poland, Molotschna in Russia, Prussia, South Germany, Pennsylvania, and other states have found a new home in a territory which became a state only fifty years ago.   C.K.

Marvin E. Kroeker, "The Mennonites of Oklahoma to 1907" (unpublished M.A. thesis, University of Oklahoma, 1954); Christian Krehbiel, "Beginnings of Missions in Oklahoma," *Menn. Life* X (July 1955); Marvin E. Kroeker, "The Mennonites in the Oklahoma Runs," *Menn. Life* X (July 1955); P. C. Grunau, "North Enid Mennonite Brethren Church," *Menn. Life* IX (October 1954); Herbert M. Dalke, "Seventy-Five Years of Missions in Oklahoma," *Menn. Life* X (July 1955); Diedrich L. Dalke, "Oklahoma Mennonite Pioneers at Enid," *Menn. Life* XI (October 1956).

Oklahoma Bible Academy (GCM). In 1911 a group of the New Hopedale Mennonite (GCM) Church, located at Meno, Okla., contributed money to build the Meno Preparatory School. The school was of elementary rank, with much Bible and German in its course of study, and served primarily the local community. As the need for more advanced training became apparent, it was decided to establish a school to serve all the churches of Oklahoma. In the spring of 1917 at the Oklahoma Convention a plan was formulated for a two-year Bible and high school. A year later the Meno Preparatory School became the Oklahoma Bible Academy, using the original buildings, but with a more advanced course. In 1924-25 with the help of Adam Ratzlaff a new dormitory was built and later a larger school was built, with two dormitories. The school is a full four-year high school accredited by the state of Oklahoma. It also offers four units of Bible. Enrollment in 1951-52 was 58. (*ML* III, 296.)† H.U.S.

Oklahoma Mennonite Convention (GCM) (*Oklahoma Konvention der Mennoniten-Gemeinden*) was organized Sept. 12, 1899, at Shelly, Okla., initiated by representatives of the Western District Conference, patterned after the early Kansas Conference (*q.v.*). The first chairman and secretary were Christian Krehbiel and M. M. Horsch. Krehbiel in his opening address stated that the main purpose of this local conference was to emphasize the devotional and inspirational aspect, make arrangements for pulpit exchange, promote evangelistic services, and to make provision for worship services at places where only a few families were located. H. D. Penner discussed the question of how the educational facilities among the Mennonites of Oklahoma could be improved, suggesting the founding of a teachers' conference and a teachers' institute. The possibility of the establishment of a preparatory school was discussed. The following communities were represented: Washita and Weatherford 49 representatives, Geary 8, Mennoville 7, Omega 2, Cantonment 1, Medford 1, Cleo 1, Lahoma 1, Deer Creek 1, Holt 1, Kansas 17, and Berne, Ind., 1. Of the total of 260-70 who attended the meetings, 90 were registered.

The meetings of the convention were held annually at various places, usually in October or November, lasting from two to three days. At the 1901 session it was decided to change the name from "Oklahoma Lokalkonferenz und Sonntagschul-Konvention" to "Jährliche Konvention der Mennoniten-Gemeinden in Oklahoma." The minutes often speak of "Oklahoma Mennoniten-Konvention" or "Sunday School Convention." Questions raised at these meetings concerned the Sunday-school materials to be used, and whether the sisters of the Sunday school were entitled to vote. It was decided that since they were teaching they should have the privilege to vote when teachers were elected (1903). The contact with the Western District Conference was lively. Representatives from it continued to be present and to appear on the program. The meetings usually started on Sunday with a mission festival and a children's program in the evening. On Monday and Tuesday lectures, discussions, and business matters followed. Deaconess work, the establishment of a Mennonite hospital in Oklahoma, home missions, missions among the Indians, and many other questions were presented. The ministers of Kansas congregations were encouraged to ask their members who had left for Oklahoma to join the Mennonite congregations of their communities. The conference of 1907 wrote to the governor of Oklahoma promising support in the enforcement of the prohibition clause. In 1917 it was resolved, "That a committee of three be created to take in hand the matter of starting an academy." This school was started during the same year in connection with the existing preparatory school of Meno established by J. B. Epp. This newly created school later became known as the Oklahoma Bible Academy (*q.v.*). Some of the outstanding leaders of the early Oklahoma Convention were P. R. Voth, John Lichti, H. Riesen, J. K. Moyer, Chr. Hirschler, Albert Claassen, J. J. Ratzlaff, and J. G. Baergen.

During World War I the Convention dealt with numerous questions pertaining to conscientious objection to war and the anti-German feeling of the day. During this time special sessions took place. For a while the meetings of the convention took place in spring. At present the meeting begins on the Friday of the last week of September. Matters pertaining to the Sunday school are discussed and the reports of the Go Ye Mission are given. On Saturday the reports on the Oklahoma Bible Academy, business sessions, and the Women's Missionary Society program follow. On Sunday afternoon a song festival is given and in the evening the young people's program. The convention has two major committees: the Program Committee and the Church Workers' Committee. The latter sponsors the Church Workers' Conference in spring and young people's retreat and camp at Hydro. C.K.

"Protokoll-Buch der Lokal-Konferenz der Mennoniten-Gemeinden in Oklahoma" (1899-1923), BeCL.

Oklahoma Old Order Amish Mennonites numbered approximately 160 in 1957. They were located in two areas, tne older western settlement in Custer County (*q.v.*), and the newer northeastern settlement in Mayes County (*q.v.*), with 108 and 52 baptized members respectively. Weatherford and Thomas are the addresses of the two congregations in Custer County, while the Amish of the northeastern Oklahoma have the addresses of Choteau and Mazie. The community is south of Pryor. There were two other O.O.A. settlements, now extinct, in the state, one in the southern part and another in the northeastern part of Oklahoma. M.G.

John A. Hostetler, *Annotated Bibliography on the Amish* (Scottdale, 1951).

Ol, Adriaen, an Anabaptist martyr: see **Adriaen Olieu(x).**

Olathe Mennonite Church (MC), now extinct, located in Olathe, the county seat of Johnson County, Kan., about 20 miles southwest of Kansas City, had its beginning in 1884, when the first Mennonite settlers arrived from Lancaster County, Pa. The original nucleus of the settlement was Samuel Ernst and three of his married children. In 1872 Ernst had founded and published the *Weaponless Watchman* in Lancaster, Pa. In 1884 he brought it to Olathe, where it was published until 1888. Additional settlers came from Pennsylvania, Nebraska, and Indiana. Among them were such Mennonite names as Zimmerman, Hershey, Gehman, Wanner, Plank, and Moyer. Originally the group worshiped in the Bethel schoolhouse located about one mile northwest of Olathe. About 1900 they purchased a Presbyterian church in Olathe. Jacob H. Hershey was ordained to the ministry about 1895, but moved to Roaring Springs, Pa., about 1904. The congregation never thrived and shortly after Jacob Hershey left it became extinct. G.G.Y.

Old Colony Mennonite Church is a name given to designate the ecclesiastical organization of the Old Colony Mennonites of Manitoba, Saskatchewan, and

Mexico. The Old Colony Mennonites themselves do not use this name in English and others have started using it only recently. In the memorandum written by the Old Colony Mennonites of Manitoba to the government in February 1919 they spoke of themselves as the "Reinland - Mennoniten - Kirche oder Alte Kirche." President Obregon addressed them on Feb. 25, 1921, as "Reinlaender Mennonitische Altkolonie." "Reinland" refers to the municipality in which the Old Colony Mennonites resided, and has become a part of their name. Even in Mexico the official church seal of the largest group contains it; viz., "Altkolonier Reinlaender Mennoniten Gemeinde." This would indicate that the Old Colony Mennonites went originally under the name "Reinland Mennonite Church," but have later incorporated the term "Old Colony." Old Colony Mennonite churches were located in Hague and Swift Current, Sask., in addition to Manitoba. In Mexico they are subdivided in the following independent churches: Manitoba Old Colony Mennonite Church, Swift Current Old Colony Mennonite Church, and Santa Clara Old Colony Mennonite Church (Loeppke group), Cuauhtemoc, and Patos Old Colony Mennonite Church of Durango (see also **Old Colony Mennonites; Manitoba; Mexico**).   C.K.

Walter Schmiedehaus, *Ein feste Burg ist unser Gott* (Cuauhtemoc, 1948) 61, 81.

Old Colony Mennonites, a socio - religious group originating in Manitoba, deriving its name from "Old Colony" which was the name given to the Chortitza Mennonite settlement as the first (1789) Mennonite settlement in Russia to distinguish it from the "New Colony," viz., the Molotschna settlement, established later (1803). In the pioneer days of Russia the Chortitza or Old Colony Mennonites were poorer, less educated, and more conservative than the Mennonites who came to Russia later. This religious and cultural conservatism furnished the roots for the spirit and characteristics of the Old Colony Mennonites of Manitoba, Saskatchewan, and Mexico. In the total pattern of Mennonite history they can be compared in some respects with the Kleine Gemeinde of the Molotschna, the Hutterites, or the Amish, although more conservative and culturally retarded than any of these. Their utmost concern centers around the preservation of their way of life. From their point of view the total cultural pattern including language, clothing, education, furniture, self-government, mutual aid, village pattern, and all forms of customs are integral parts of their church concept. They have preserved the most extreme form of separation from the world and the practice of church discipline by means of the ban and avoidance. Contact with the outside world is kept at a minimum. As to the church concept and the idea of nonconformity to the world, there is a genuine Anabaptist concern preserved in the Old Colony Mennonite attitude, although largely in a petrified form. Not only is the contact with the outside world reduced to bare necessities, but also the challenge which comes through contact with the other religious groups and the outside culture has been neutralized. Contact with the Ger-

man culture from which the Old Colony Mennonites stem has been completely lost, and contacts with the new environment are not permitted. Thus in the attempt to retain the Mennonite heritage the group deprives itself of the challenges and influences which come through contact with other groups. Even the best concept of the Christian church cannot be realized in a vacuum. New stimulations and a challenge of thoughts and practices by opposing forces and a revitalization through contact with like-minded groups is as important as a sound basic concept. Here lies the strength and the weakness of the Old Colony Mennonites and other conservative groups.

Russia. In comparison with the Mennonite immigrants from Danzig and Prussia to Russia who formed the later Molotschna settlement, the Old Colony settlers of Russia were in general of a less educated class. Those coming later had made greater adjustments to the environment of their home communities, i.e., the German culture. All Mennonites of this area were of Dutch background and used the Dutch language from the 16th to the 18th centuries. The Danzig church record of the early days is written in the Dutch language; the change from Dutch to German occurred throughout the book in 1783-84. At that time the Mennonites of Prussia and Danzig had adjusted to their German environment to the extent of replacing Dutch with High German in school and church, and Low German in their daily life.

The movement to Russia can be considered a protest against adjustment to the environment. When the cycle of adjustment to the German environment was nearly complete the migration to Russia set in, the first Mennonites to go having made the least adjustment, and those coming later being more progressive and more prosperous. This conservative attitude of the Chortitza settlers also prevailed in its daughter colonies, Bergthal and Fürstenland. When the new environment through school and other contacts began to challenge the Mennonite constituency the most conservative element reacted by withdrawing. There had already been severe criticism of the progress made in the realm of education in the days of Cornies. Now around 1870 the Russian government was introducing the Russian language into the schools, raising the requirement in the curriculum, and making the educational system of the Mennonites subject to the Department of Education of Russia. The self-government of the Mennonites in Russia was also being challenged. Complete isolation was becoming extremely difficult. In addition to this some form of service to the government was unavoidable. Thus the news about the possibility of finding a place in the New World where there would be complete freedom along these lines found both willing and attentive ears among the Mennonites of the Chortitza and daughter settlements.

It is interesting to note that the group which became most conservative, the Old Colony Mennonite Church, did not furnish any migration leaders. The elder of the Chortitza settlement, Gerhard Dyck, and his cominister, Heinrich Epp, went to St. Petersburg and attended the Mennonite meetings dealing with the question of compulsory service and the possibility of emigrating to America. Gerhard Dyck was still of the "old school" but does not seem to have considered emigration to America. His co-minister and successor as elder, Heinrich Epp, helped to usher in an era of progress in the Old Colony in Russia. He had received a good training and had taught at the Zentralschule at Chortitza for 19 years when he became elder. He did not favor the emigration. If there were any ministers of the Chortitza settlement who joined the immigrants to Manitoba they were not very influential. The leadership came from the elder of the Fürstenland settlement which had been established about ten years prior to the migration. He was Elder Johann Wiebe who was related to Elder Gerhard Dyck of Chortitza and also to Elder Gerhard Wiebe of Bergthal. However, even before Johann Wiebe left Fürstenland with a group in 1875, some of the Chortitza Mennonites had left in 1874, joining the Bergthal Mennonites of the East Reserve (q.v.) in Manitoba.

Manitoba. Evidently the Bergthal delegation had chosen the East Reserve during their inspection tour in 1873, leaving the West Reserve for the Chortitza and Fürstenland Mennonites, of whom the first arrived at the West Reserve in 1875. Thus the West Reserve became the settlement of the Chortitza and Fürstenland Mennonites, where they founded the Reinland Mennonite Church, which later became known as the Old Colony Mennonite Church. Originally the term was used to distinguish them from the Bergthal Mennonites of the East Reserve. Evidently there has never been any reason to distinguish between the Old Colony Mennonites coming from Chortitza, and the Fürstenland Mennonites, both settling on the West Reserve. The Fürstenland settlement had been in existence only about ten years in Russia and had developed no peculiar characteristics. It was a minority and was therefore included in the name Old Colony Mennonites, the name Fürstenland being dropped in Manitoba.

It has been overlooked by some historians that the majority of the Mennonites who settled on the West Reserve were of the Chortitza or Old Colony Mennonite background and that the Fürstenland group was a small minority. E. K. Francis *(In Search of Utopia,* p. 88) was of the opinion that all Old Colony Mennonites came from Fürstenland and therefore calls them Fürstenländer. D. H. Epp (*Chortitza Mennoniten*) gives information regarding the background of the immigrants, stating that the total number of immigrants who left for Manitoba during 1874-80 from the Chortitza settlement including Fürstenland was 580 families or 3,240 persons. Fürstenland was included because it belonged administratively to Chortitza. This could not possibly have been the number of people coming from Fürstenland, which had been established only about 10 years before, consisting of five villages with 154 family farms. When Johann Wiebe, elder of Fürstenland, wrote to the immigration agent of Hamburg on March 12, 1875, he stated that 169 families consisting of 1,009 persons were ready to leave Fürstenland alone. He must have included almost the whole population of the settlement. The statistics given by Jacob Y. Shantz correspond to the figures given by D. H. Epp. From this we conclude that by far the largest contingent of the total group of 3,240 persons came from Chortitza (Old Colony) proper, and that possibly a third of the total came from Fürstenland.

None of the sources available indicate that there was any basic difference in religious and cultural views between the Old Colony-Fürstenland group settling on the West Reserve and the Bergthal group settling on the East Reserve. The latter had been isolated for some time while the Chortitza Mennonites had been exposed to progressive leadership. If either one was more conservative than the other it would have been the Bergthal group. Differences that developed must have come through conditions in the Manitoba settlements. The roots probably lie in the following explanation. When a religious group adhering to a conservative cultural pattern breaks away from a mother settlement and proceeds to establish a new entity it is likely to make some adjustments in its economic, social, and cultural life to its new environment. For example, the Old Order Amish of Eastern Pennsylvania are somewhat more conservative than those of Ohio and Indiana, who originally came from Western Pennsylvania.

The first differences became evident when a large number of Bergthal Mennonites moved from the East to the West Reserve where they began to adjust themselves to the Canadian system of farming, government, school practices and other forms of culture. The Old Colony Mennonites on the other hand considered the village pattern of community life, self-government, and the parochial school system, which the infiltrating Bergthal Mennonites were willing to sacrifice, an integral part of their way of life and a test of church membership. (For details see **Manitoba.**)

The School Question. Before the Mennonites had come to Manitoba they had made certain that they would have the "privileges" which they had enjoyed in Russia. They obtained from the Canadian government "the fullest privileges of exercising their religious principles" and they had the same privilege extended to "the education of their children in school." The greatest change in matters pertaining to schools came during World War I. The School Attendance Act passed in 1916 did not prohibit private schools provided they conformed to the standards set up by the school administration. However, if a school was found to be inadequate it was condemned. Once a private school was condemned the Minister of Education had the right to appoint school trustees who would establish a public school with compulsory attendance. Naturally, the Old Colony Mennonites were unwilling to have their children thus driven into public schools, and the government was determined to achieve just that. Repeated delegations were sent to the provincial and dominion governments without avail. Numerous petitions were written to the proper authorities. Some of these throw valuable light on the situation and express the Old Colony idea of education very well. They called the attention of the government to the fact that they had had their own schools in Russia and that when this privilege was threatened the Dominion government had graciously granted them the same privileges in a letter dated July 23, 1873, understanding full well the great significance which the Old Colony Mennonites attached to the school question. This correspondence further reveals the Old Colony ideas about their own curriculum and equipment and also that they maintained 22 schools, which were in session 7 months in the year and were attended by all children from the ages of 7 to 13 for girls and 14 for boys. The ministers inspected the schools and enforced regular attendance, with the result that there were no illiterates among them. This petition of Jan. 18, 1917, was signed by Elder Johann J. Friesen and Oberschulze Franz F. Froese. The government was now determined to establish district schools for all, and teachers who hoisted the flag each morning and lowered it again in the evening without a single child attending the school, were hired for the Mennonites. When the Old Colony Mennonites continued to send their children to their own government-condemned schools, the government made public school attendance compulsory. An epidemic of fining and jailing Mennonite preachers started. The government was determined to force the Mennonites to compromise and the more liberal of them gradually did so. Not, however, the Old Colony and Sommerfeld Mennonites. The broken promise, and persecution and suffering for a conviction, were like oil on a fire.

On July 15, 1919, the Old Colony Mennonites decided to send Klaas Heide and Cornelius Rempel of Manitoba, Johann Wall and Johann P. Wall of Hague, Sask., and Julius Wiebe and David Rempel of Swift Current, Sask., to investigate South America for settlement possibilities. On Aug. 23, 1919, they left New York, arriving in Rio de Janeiro on September 9. After losing one of their companions, Johann Wall, and interviewing the authorities of Brazil, Uruguay, and Argentina, they returned without the anticipated results. They were received very cordially everywhere and were made to feel that they were welcome, but when it came to putting in black and white the guarantees or privileges, they found that these countries were not what they were looking for. They wanted a complete exemption from military service and the assurance that they would have no problems pertaining to the schools. Next on the list of consideration were the states of Alabama and Mississippi in the United States. A number of delegations were sent to Mississippi during April and May of 1920. An agent by the name of Peters came to see the Mennonites in Canada, making the offer very appealing to them. In pressing the question pertaining to privileges they got in touch with Attorney-General Palmer of Washington, D.C. The files of the National Archives of Washington contain numerous documents pertaining to this case. The American Legion of the South got very much excited about the prospect of getting nonresistant Mennonites in their states.

At a meeting on June 1, 1920, although the Mennonites had not received the desired "privileges," it was decided to send a delegation of five to make the down payment of $2.00 per acre totaling $250,-000. When the delegates arrived at the United States border they were sent back. David Harder, one of their chroniclers, reports, "We could not find out why the border was closed for us; we were compelled to accept it as guidance from God who wanted to spare us unforeseen hardships. Very likely the offer of freedom was the hoax of a land speculator." In addition to this the American Legion exerted pressure to stop the delegation at the border. But this did not stop the Old Colony Mennonites in their search for a new land. The State of Minnesota and the Province of Quebec were considered with similar outcome.

Mexico. On Jan. 24, 1921, a delegation including Julius Loewen, Klaas Heide, and Cornelius Rempel of Manitoba, and Johann Loeppke and Benjamin Goertzen of Saskatchewan, left for Mexico. At El Paso they met with J. F. Wiebe who brought them a welcome from the President and the Minister of Agriculture. Wiebe, a son of the founder of the Krimmer Mennonite Brethren Church, Jacob A. Wiebe, formerly mayor of Herbert, Sask., and an elder of the K.M.B. Church of that place, became a significant intermediary for the Old Colony Mennonites and the railroad and land agents in Mexico. On February 16 they met President Obregon, his brother-in-law Arturo J. Braniff, and the Minister of Agriculture in Mexico City. They presented their request for privileges and related in great detail their practices and way of life, which evidently found full approval with the highest government officials, so that Johann Loeppke thanked the President with tears in his eyes. They returned with the *Privilegium* approved and signed by the president, addressed to the Old Colony Reinland Mennonite Church, stating: (1) You will not be under obligation to do military service; (2) you will under no circumstances be compelled to swear an oath; (3) you will be given complete freedom to practice your religious principles and to live according to the rules of your church without being molested or in any way restricted; (4) you will have full permission to establish your own schools with your own teachers without any interference of the government; (5) regarding property, our laws are liberal and you are free to follow your own rules along these lines and the government will not interfere if the group will manage its property in its own way.

This statement was taken to Canada as the key that opened the gate to Mexico and became the most cherished document since the days when the Mennonites had received similar invitations and promises from Russia and Canada. Upon their return to Canada this *Privilegium* was hailed as an answer to prayer. Meetings were called immediately to make the necessary preparation to sell the property, to purchase the land in Mexico, and for the trip. After repeated trips to Mexico the delegation returned on Sept. 10, 1921, with reports that they had purchased 230,000 acres of land for the Manitoba Old Colony Mennonites for $8.25 an acre, making a down payment of $2.25 per acre. The land was located in the San Antonio Valley in the province of Chihuahua and was purchased through the agent Charles Newman of El Paso, and J. F.

Wiebe of Herbert, Sask. It was here that the Manitoba Old Colony Mennonites later settled. The Hague group bought 35,000 acres of land near the village of Patos in the province of Durango.

Now the integrity of the group and the spirit of their brotherhood was tested. It was the intention that the group would transfer from Manitoba and Saskatchewan to Mexico as a whole. Those who did not have the means would be helped through the brotherhood. The Waisenamt, a type of savings bank, and other agencies of mutual aid were to take care of this complicated task. The land was to be sold in blocks and not individually by the farmer. It was hard to find buyers of large tracts of land except speculators who tried to take advantage of the situation. At Swift Current 100,000 acres were sold for 44 dollars per acre. The sale, however, became so involved, that it had to be taken to court and resulted in a loss of 10,000 acres to the Old Colony Mennonites. In Manitoba McLeod, Black and Company was willing to serve as agent promising to sell the land by Aug. 21, 1921; but no land was sold by that date, and gradually the land owners began to sell the land individually. Other property, with the exception of that which was to be taken to Mexico, was being sold at auctions. Because of the many sales, prices declined rapidly.

By Feb. 11, 1922, the Oberschulze Franz Froese had a list of immigrants to fill four trains. On March 1 the first train left Plum Coulee, Man., followed by three from Haskett, Man., on March 2, 7, and 11. Two more trains left at this time from Swift Current, Sask. J. F. Wiebe made the arrangements for transportation. All trains arrived safely at San Antonio or Cuauhtemoc, where they were unloaded. Of the 4,526 Old Colony Mennonites in Manitoba in 1922, 3,340 went to Mexico by 1926. This would indicate that about three fourths of the group participated in the migration. Only a little more than 1,000 of the 3,250 (or about one fourth) Swift Current (Sask.) Old Colony Mennonites (who settled right next to the Manitoba Mennonites in Cuauhtemoc) were willing to emigrate. The situation in Hague, Sask., was similar. Only 946 of 3,932 went to Mexico, establishing the Patos settlement in the province of Durango in 1925. Records show that this settlement had a population of only 770 the next year, indicating that some must have returned or transferred to the Cuauhtemoc settlement. (These figures are based on the official Old Colony church record made available through Johann P. Wall of Patos, Durango.)

The question should be raised why only approximately half of the 12,000 Old Colony Mennonites of Canada went to Mexico at that time, and also why the participation among the Mennonites in Saskatchewan was so much smaller. The latter question is answered in part by the fact that resistance to adjustment to environment is usually weaker in daughter settlements. It is also possible that the opportunities to sell their farms were not as good as in Manitoba. In general, failure to sell the land as a unit was a breakdown of an otherwise well-functioning organization and mutual aid system.

The resulting individual responsibility had a disintegrating effect on the morale and the united front of the Old Colony Mennonites. The departure of the strong conservative leaders to Mexico accentuated a slackening in discipline and practice among those who remained behind in Canada. Lack of unity among the leaders was also a disturbing element. Elder Loeppke, originally one of the staunch promoters of the migration, took up temporary residence in Mexico after World War II, and returned to Canada from time to time. Another reason why so many stayed in Canada was the approaching depression, which made it impossible to sell property at the expected price. Without strong conservative leadership the members gradually became accustomed to the prohibited innovations such as cars and other conveniences, and the willingness to pay the price and go to Mexico decreased. Thus there are really two Old Colony Mennonite churches since the departure of the most conservative element to Mexico. Those in Mexico today hardly recognize their Canadian brethren because of the adjustments the latter have made and their unwillingness to pay the price and make the sacrifice of joining them in Mexico. Unlike the Chortitz and Sommerfeld Mennonites the remaining Old Colony Mennonites in Canada made only a few attempts to migrate to a foreign country after World War II. Elder Johann Loeppke led a small group to Mexico, settling with the Kleine Gemeinde at the Los Jagueves Ranch north of Cuauhtemoc. The Sommerfeld minister, Jacob Günther, of Hague, Sask., attempted to reach Costa Rica with a few families in 1951. After an adventurous trip by truck to Mexico and New Orleans they returned, not having been admitted to Costa Rica. In 1934 some families including a number who had been in Mexico moved up the Peace River Valley in Alberta until they reached Fort Vermilion. Some 40 miles from town they established a settlement which has been joined since 1937 by numerous families from Manitoba and Mexico, so that in 1948 there were 65 families or about 400 persons, living far from civilization.

In 1948 a total of c1700 Sommerfeld and Chortitz Mennonites from southern Manitoba and Saskatchewan founded the two colonies of Sommerfeld and Bergthal in southeastern Paraguay. These colonies, like Menno Colony in the Chaco, are not true Old Colony Mennonites.

In Canada the adjustment of the Old Colony Mennonites of Manitoba and Saskatchewan is noticeable not only to their environment but also toward the other Mennonite groups. According to Benjamin Ewert (*Mennonitisches Jahrbuch* 1951, p. 22) the number of Old Colony Mennonites in Manitoba in 1950 was 1,165, of whom 551 were baptized members. They have 6 ministers and 4 places of worship. This would indicate that they have decreased in number. The total number in Saskatchewan is estimated at 2,000 with a membership of 1,000 with 10 ministers and 6 places of worship. If this figure is correct, there are only over 3,000 Old Colony Mennonites in Canada today, whereas there should be about 20,000 if they had increased like their brethren in Mexico. This makes it evident that many of the Old Colony Mennonites in Canada are no longer counted as such.

In 1936 the Manitoba group of Old Colony Mennonites in Mexico numbered 3,340. By 1949 the group had increased to 7,706. In 1953 the number was 8,768. The Swift Current group adjacent to the Manitoba group in Cuauhtemoc numbered 1,000 at the time of their settlement in Mexico. In 1949 it was 2,232 and in 1953 it was 2,694. The Durango group coming from Hague, Sask., originally 946, had 2,861 in 1949 and 3,281 in 1953. In 1946 the North settlement was established as a daughter colony to make provision for settlement by landless families from the Manitoba and Swift Current settlements. It had a population of 2,652 in 1949, and by 1953, 3,590. In 1949 the total population of all Old Colony Mennonites in Mexico was 15,451, which had increased to 18,333 in 1953, in spite of the fact that numerous families had returned to Canada during the years of drought after 1950. This return was particularly noticeable in the Swift Current settlement, which had a population of 2,232 in 1949 and 2,694 in 1953. This slight increase indicates that many of the families must have returned to Canada. No exact figures are available on this movement to Canada. It is likely that next to the Hutterites the Old Colony Mennonites in Mexico are the fastest growing Mennonite group in the world. The Old Colony Mennonites of Mexico aimed to preserve their cherished heritage and the institutions which are a part of it. They have continued the village system with the Schulze and Oberschulze, the Waisenamt, the school system, and the total way of life to which they were accustomed. Some seek better income by going to town or returning to Canada, which is not approved of by the leadership. There were times when the school system was in danger of becoming subject to the Department of Education in Mexico. The greatest

problem, however, is how to maintain and inspire growth in spiritual and cultural values in complete isolation as Mexico offered it to the Old Colony Mennonites. Under the most primitive and sacrificial conditions the Old Colony Mennonites have reprinted the Bible, the *Gesangbuch,* and other educational means. Recently they collected $672.00 among their impoverished church members to purchase 120 copies of the German *Martyrs' Mirror,* which indicates their effort to help the congregation and its members in spiritual growth. However, their complete isolation from other Mennonite groups probably counteracts the few efforts made to improve the cultural and the religious life. In their cultural, home, and family life they illustrate at least outwardly, what Mennonite life in Russia was like 100 years ago. Worship services, singing, linguistic peculiarities, furniture, and family relationships have been preserved here with few changes.

The Manitoba Mennonites in Cuauhtemoc have their own church, the Manitoba Mennonite Church, and also their own civic organization. The same is true regarding the Swift Current group and the North settlement, the Ojo de lad Yegua Church, except that the latter is under the elder of the Manitoba settlement. The Durango or Patos settlement forms an independent civil as well as spiritual entity. These three congregations of Old Colony Mennonites of Mexico work in close harmony and consider each other in good standing. This is not the case with the Loeppke group settling at Santa Clara, north of the Manitoba and Swift Current settlement, nor with those Old Colony Mennonite congregations that stayed in Manitoba and Saskatchewan.

(See also articles **Manitoba, Mexico, Bergthal** Mennonite Settlement, **Bergthal** Mennonite Church, **Chortitza** Mennonite Settlement. For bibliography see **Manitoba.**)   C.K.

OLD COLONY MENNONITE CHURCH, 1958

Congregation	Location	Members	Souls	Elder
Manitoba	Cuauhtemoc, Chihuahua	3,585	8,678	Isaak Dyck
Swift Current	Cuauhtemoc, Chihuahua	1,089	3,059	————
North Settlement	Cuauhtemoc, Chihuahua	1,397	4,293	————
Patos	Durango	1,277	3,673	Peter P. Wiens
	Total in Mexico	7,348	19,703	
Manitoba	Manitoba	521	1,165	Jacob Froese
Hague	Saskatchewan	————	————	
Swift Current	Saskatchewan	————	————	————

Old Elm Hutterite Bruderhof at Magrath, Alberta, was founded in 1918 by Andreas Gross, who had been chosen as minister in South Dakota in 1911 (now deceased). Other ministers, with date of election and ordination, were Andrew J. Wurtz, 1936 and 1946; Jacob J. Wipf, 1947 and 1950; Isaak A. Wurtz, chosen in 1954. In 1947 this Bruderhof had a population of 140, with 60 baptized members. In 1953 Jacob J. Wipf branched out with 16 families, composed of 82 persons, 38 of whom were baptized members, and founded the Bunch Bruderhof at Shaunavan, Sask., which now has a population of

97, with 48 baptized members. Samuel Decker was chosen as minister here in 1954. The Old Elm Bruderhof in 1957 had a population of 100, with 38 baptized members.   D.D.

Old Flemish (Dutch, *Oude Vlaminghen*), a former branch of the Dutch Mennonites: see **Flemish Mennonites.**

Old Flemish Conference (*Sociëteit van Oude Vlamingen*): see **Groninger Doopsgezinde Sociëteit.**

Old Folks' Singing, an annual New Year's Day singing from the *Harmonia Sacra* (*q.v.*) held at the Weaver Mennonite Church near Harrisonburg, Va., since 1903. This music festival developed as an afterglow of the great singing-school movement begun by Joseph Funk and continued by his son Timothy over a period of 50 years in the mid-19th century. It attracts more than a thousand music lovers of various denominations and stands as a symbol of a common musical heritage. Other churches in Rockingham, Shenandoah, and Page counties are similarly preserving the tradition. With a simple organization of moderator and secretary, the singing proceeds throughout the day with different leaders, each choosing two or more favorite songs. The noon intermission, during which a bountiful lunch is served by the local congregation, is an occasion for the renewal of old friendships and the enjoyment of Christian fellowship.   C.K.L.

Old Jacob, an Anabaptist martyr: see **Jacob, de Oude.**

Old Mother Gochenour, one of the last surviving members of the early Mennonite settlement in Page County, Va., lived above Stony Man in the northern part of the county. Her home was one of the last preaching points for Mennonites in Page County at the close of the 19th century.   H.A.B.

Old Order Amish, a segment of the Amish Mennonites (*q.v.*) distinguished by their nonconformist attitudes and resistance to social change, and characterized by worship in private homes, a strictly rural way of life, a horse-and-buggy culture, the use of a dialect of the German language, and "plain" dress resembling that of European peoples two centuries ago. They have no meetinghouses (with minor exceptions), and oppose not only higher education, but most forms of organized church activity, formal missionary work, evangelistic services, and many modern inventions including the ownership of automobiles and telephones and the use of electricity, and in some communities the use of tractors for farming. These attitudes and practices distinguish them from all Mennonite and other Amish bodies, although the Old Order Mennonites (*q.v.*), the Old Colony Mennonites (*q.v.*), and the Hutterites (*q.v.*) to varying degrees share these attitudes and practices.

"Old Order" Amish is strictly an American term which came into usage as some Amish Mennonite congregations resisted "new" methods of church work as well as "new" forms of social organization and technology. One cannot properly speak of "Old Order" before 1850, and its usage came gradually after about 1870, or following the Amish Ministers' Conferences 1862-78, called *Diener Versammlungen* (*q.v.*), which finally crystallized the differences between the more progressive Amish and the Old Order groups. Since the Old Order Amish worship in private homes they are sometimes called "House Amish," to distinguish them from the "Church Amish," who worship in meetinghouses. About one third of the Amish Mennonites existing in 1850 continued in the Old Order, chiefly those in Pennsylvania, Holmes County, Ohio, Elkhart and La-

grange counties in Indiana, and Johnson County, Iowa. These were either (1) the descendants of the colonial Amish who arrived in Lancaster and Berks counties, Pa., 1738-56, from Switzerland and the Palatinate, or (2) part of the descendants of those who came from Waldeck and Hesse-Cassel to Western Pennsylvania 1830-50. The other two thirds, who followed the more progressive "new order," were either (1) almost all of the Amish immigrants of 1820-60 from Alsace, Bavaria, and Montbéliard who came to Waterloo County, Ont., Stark and Fulton counties, Ohio, central Illinois, Washington County, Iowa, and their descendants, or (2) a part of the settlements in Lancaster County, Mifflin County, and Somerset County, Pa., and Holmes County, Ohio, Elkhart and Lagrange counties, Ind., and Johnson County, Iowa, who separated from the Old Order in 1850-1900. These progressive groups formed Amish Mennonite conferences which ultimately merged with Mennonite (MC) conferences in 1916-25. A later separation from the Old Order (1927-50) resulted in what is called the Beachy Amish, who are not yet fully organized into a conference. All these separated groups manifested varying degrees of deviation from the Old Order at the time of separation, although one common mark was the introduction of meetinghouses for worship and the shift away from the *Ausbund* to more modern hymnbooks. They have also developed varying degrees and speed of change since the time of separation. In spite of these successive separations and the loss of many individuals to the more progressive Amish and Mennonite groups, the Old Order Amish have continued to grow, because of their high birth rate and high retention of children in the group. In 1956 they had approximately 17,000 baptized members, almost uniformly above the age of 18, with a total population of some 50,000.

There are currently about fifty geographic Old Order Amish settlements in North America. Each settlement is divided into autonomous "church districts" (congregations) having 15-30 families or an average of about 75 baptized members per district. When a district becomes too large for the management of worship in private homes it is geographically divided. Each new district as soon as possible institutes its own bishop, and each ordains by lot two to four preachers of its own and a deacon.

In 1956 there were a total of 229 Old Order Amish church districts with 17,054 baptized members, distributed in the following 19 states and one province of Canada, in the counties indicated: *Ohio* 69, with 6,378 members: Holmes, Tuscarawas, and Wayne together 44, Geauga 13, Stark 4, Madison 3, Trumbull 2, Defiance 1, Ashland 1, Hardin 1; *Pennsylvania* 52, with 3,979 members: Lancaster with Berks and Chester 32, Mifflin 6, Lawrence 4, Mercer 2, Lebanon 3, one each in Crawford, Somerset, Juniata, and Snyder; *Indiana* 48, with 3,068 members: Elkhart and Lagrange 24, Marshall and Kosciusko 10, Daviess and Martin 5, Adams 3, Allen 2, Howard and Miami 2, Jay 1, Newton 1; *Iowa* 11, with 794 members: Johnson and Washington 6, Buchanan 5; *Illinois* 9, with 672 members: Moultrie and Douglas 9; *Kansas* 6, with 343 members: Reno 5, Anderson 1; *Ontario* 5, with 260(?) members: Perth and

Waterloo 3, Elgin 1, Grey 1; *Michigan* 5, with 226 members: St. Joseph 1, Hillsdale 3, Oscoda 1; *Delaware* 4, with 250 members: Kent 4; *Missouri* 4, with 131 members: Pike 2, Pettis 1, Daviess 1; *Oklahoma* 4, with 160 members: Custer 2, Mayes 2; *New York* 3, with 113 members: Chautauqua 2, Waterloo 1; *Maryland* 3, with 171 members: St. Marys 2, Garrett 1; *Tennessee* 2, with 88 members: Lawrence; *Virginia* 2, with 160 members: one each in Augusta and Fauquier; *Wisconsin* 2(?): one each in Taylor and Clark; *Arkansas* 1, with 12 members: Searcy; *Florida* 1 (seasonal): Sarasota; *North Dakota* 1, with 4 members: Rolette; *Oregon* 1, with 28 members: Yamhill. The Old Order Amish migrate readily and there are therefore a considerable number of extinct communities, and new communities constantly forming.

Technological inventions which radically changed American groups and institutions did not affect the Amish to a great extent until the present century. Because of their isolation and somewhat self-sustaining social, economic, and religious communities they were able to resist change or greatly retard it. Among the culture traits which the Old Order Amish have resisted in the past, and with which some communities have compromised only after a long struggle and others not at all even to the present day, are the following: buttons on coats and vests, wearing a mustache, men's suspenders in various forms, hats for women, "store" clothes, talon fasteners, "bosom" shirts, detachable collars, modern styles of underwear, patterned dress goods, fine shoes, low shoes, ladies' high-heeled shoes, parted hair, parted hair except in the center, meetinghouses, four-part singing, hymnbooks with printed musical notes, laymen's use of Bibles at preaching service, Sunday schools, revival meetings, high-school education, central heating, carpets, window curtains, storm windows and screens, writing desks, upholstered furniture, brightly painted farm machinery, painted wagons, top buggies, "falling" buggy tops, buggy springs, rubber-tired buggies, buggy steps, fancy buggies, whipsockets, dashboards, sausage grinders, lawn mowers, bicycles, windmills, sewing machines, steam threshers, tractors with tires, tractors for field work, tractors at all, elaborately decorated harness, musical instruments, telephones, electricity, automobiles, and many others. Various intrepretations by local leadership on these material cultural items have resulted in numerous divisions among the Amish.

There is evidence that the Old Order Amish not only have retained many of the older traits in their entirety, but have even modified some of them in the direction of greater conservatism. The prescribed length of the haircut for men, for example, is longer today in some localities than it was fifty years ago. This phenomenon may be a kind of reactionary protest against change, which plays some part in cultural survival.

The most conservative of all contemporary Old Order groups are the two districts of "Old School" or "Nebraska" Amish found in Mifflin County, Pa. (see **Gosper County,** Neb.), who do not permit suspenders, colored shirts (they wear white only), traction engines of any kind, projecting roofs on their buildings, screens on windows or doors, curtains, lawn mowers; hair must be shoulder length for men; and women wear black kerchiefs and flat straw hats instead of white prayer caps and bonnets. Buggy tops must be white as distinguished from the yellow tops of the "Byler" group and the black tops of the "Renno" group. Other regional very conservative O.O.A. settlements are the one in Lawrence County, Pa., and five districts of the "Swartzendruber" Amish in Holmes County, Ohio.

Other traits that the Old Order Amish have preserved are a strictly uniform order of worship service, the use of the genuflection at the conclusion of the benediction, silent prayer, and the use of prayerbooks by the ministers in public worship, silent prayer in the homes at the beginning and end of each meal, in some instances tombstones carved by their own members and burial of the dead without embalming, bundling during courtship (in a few local groups), and the "grandfather house," which means provision for retirement of the parents into a small house or wing on the farm which they owned and operated.

Among the 19th-century Amish ordained men known to have been most staunch in holding to the "old way" and adamantly opposed to change were David Beiler (*q.v.,* 1786-1871) of Lancaster County, Pa.; Abram Pitsche (Peachey) (1800-84) of Mifflin County, Pa.; Abner Yoder (1814-83) of Somerset County, Pa., and after 1866 of Johnson County, Iowa; Moses B. Miller (1819-1902) of Somerset County, Pa.; Hannes (John) Yoder of Wayne County, Ohio, and others.

The Old Order Amish subscribe to the *Dordrecht Confession* of 1632 and in formal doctrine differ little from the other Mennonite groups of Swiss descent. They however practice the strict interpretation of avoidance or shunning (*Meidung*) of excommunicated members. At communion time in the spring and autumn they also practice footwashing. Women wear the prayer cap at all times, and small girls begin to wear the cap as soon as they can walk. The youth are admitted to the church at the age of about 17-20, with baptism, usually once a year in the spring after a period of formal instruction by the ministers. Worship services are held fortnightly in the homes of members; on alternate Sundays the families stay at home or visit relatives. Worship starts at about eight-thirty in the morning and dismisses at about one o'clock, followed by a light lunch served in the home. The time varies slightly between localities. The needed store of backless benches is moved from one home to the next.

In theology the Amish have retained the basic doctrines of their forefathers, but have certain characteristic emphases. One of these is the denial of assurance of salvation; they commonly hold that one can only hope to be saved, that it is pride to claim certainty of salvation. There is also little teaching or preaching of conversion, and no pietistic type of piety. There is a strong emphasis on living a righteous life, being and doing good, and obeying the rules of the church.

All the Old Order Amish speak the "Pennsylvania Dutch" dialect in their in-group conversation, but are also conversant in the English language. Most of them read Biblical High German, since German serves as the basis of their Bible reading and worship services. Their hymnbook is the German *Ausbund* (*q.v.*) of the 16th century, which is composed in part of verses written by martyrs and expressing triumphant prayers, sufferings, and wails of sorrow, sung soberly in unison to German folk tunes handed down from memory for hundreds of years but now modified into strange-sounding "slow" tunes. A smaller hymnal (*Unparteiische Liedersammlung*) with faster tunes is used in many places for the Sunday evening young people's "singings."

The Amish ministers follow a traditional outline of Scripture passages and hymn selections from the *Ausbund* arranged for thirty Sundays (meetings only every other Sunday) and special days and events such as Christmas or weddings, *Ein Register von Liedern und Schriften, die in den Amischen Gemeinden gebraucht werden,* first printed edition Elkhart, 1913, but actually much older.

The Old Order Amish, with other Mennonite bodies, have maintained a reputation as excellent farmers, particularly so in Pennsylvania and in the larger settlements. However, this cannot be said for some of the smaller scattered groups. They maintain family-sized farms and do not engage in large-scale farming operations or invest in business enterprises outside their farming operations, except for a few industries related to farming such as mills, blacksmiths, wool carding, etc. Each father wants to own his farm and attempts to make it possible for each of his sons to acquire a farm. The better farms are therefore passed on to succeeding generations by inheritance. The Amish pay high prices to secure additional farms in their settlements and often supplant Mennonite neighbors.

Social scientists, e.g., Walter Kollmorgen, Charles P. Loomis, and Maurice Mook, have in recent years taken considerable note of the Amish as an interesting sociological phenomenon. Well over thirty graduate theses in university libraries treat some phase of Amish life. The most outstanding community research on the O.O.A. to date is probably that made by Walter Kollmorgen for the United States Department of Agriculture, Bureau of Agricultural Economics, published in September 1942, dealing with the Lancaster County Amish. A number of writers of textbooks in sociology and anthropology have used the Kollmorgen report as the basis of their discussion, among whom are C. P. Loomis, John Gillin, Meyer F. Nimkoff, and Earnest W. Burgess.

The general findings developing out of past social research may briefly be summarized as follows: The Amish community maintains certain features of stability through isolation and in-group loyalty. Their stability is accredited to their strong positive interests, religion and farming. Though the group has successfully maintained a distinguished subculture of its own, one of the basic problems of this culture is adaptation to changing situations. There is a gradual slow infiltration of Amish culture by outside patterns, bringing about disintegration of the old values, with the prospect that if acculturation continues the Amish society will eventually disappear. This process is, however, exceedingly slow; more common is the process of breaking away.

The question is frequently asked why the Amish in Europe have completely lost their identity as Amish, while they at the same time survived in America as a group with a distinct and separate culture. (All the Amish in Europe have been assimilated into the Mennonite, Protestant, and Catholic religions.) The reason is not hard to see. The Amish Mennonites in Europe never lived in compact settlements. The scarcity of purchasable land prevented them from forming primary community groupings, since families who fled from one place to another rented or purchased property wherever they were given asylum. Each Amish family became a social unit unto itself, and geographic distance made intercourse between Amish families difficult. As family units (as against community in the New World) the Amish were in an unfavorable position to withstand the pressure toward conformity to the general culture and to European governments in their programs of national unification. However, the European Amish did earlier have a strong sense of separation from the world and its culture in general.

The Amish deviation from Swiss Mennonitism in Europe was largely an ideological difference; in material culture the differences were slight. It was not until their development in America that sharp differences in cultural practices appeared between Mennonites and Amish. The Amish have survived in the New World chiefly because they found freedom —freedom to purchase land, to develop their conservative religion, and to form primary communities where families lived in close proximity to each other. The dominant form of social organization in America is therefore community rather than family.

That the community in America has been an important factor in the maintenance of Amish tradition is well illustrated in the development of a distinct O.O.A. costume. In Europe where family instead of community organization was dominant the Amish wore much the same general style of clothes as their rural non-Amish neighbors. They were seldom conscious of a distinctive costume, except for hooks and eyes. In general appearance and dress the Amish were somewhat similar to thousands of other emigrants from their homeland at the time of their emigration, although there is evidence from the reports of travelers who visited Amish families in Alsace that the Amish were in general culturally backward and looked different in dress to some extent. In America they found themselves for the first time conscious of a really different dress from their frontier neighbors, the Scotch-Irish, Huguenots, Quakers, and the English. This consciousness of difference from others in dress gave them new ground on which to recognize their own kind from others. As protection against change in the strange environment of the New World they traditionalized the dress styles they brought with them, while the world about them accepted the changing styles.

The practice of wearing a beard was common in Europe until about the 18th century, and the Amish who questioned innovations kept the beard as a symbol of something sacred after it disappeared from the general culture. The same was true of hooks and eyes; buttons were first used by the ruling classes as ornamentation, and so it was quite natural that the Amish should retain the old and shun the new. The Amish dress coat, the *Mutze*, broadfall trousers, and black wide-brimmed hats, are adaptations from the ordinary dress of the Palatines a century and longer ago. By comparing old drawings of regional costume in Europe the similarity in dress is established beyond doubt.

The dress of the Amish woman is almost identical with examples in Palatine museums. The white *Häubchen* (prayer cap) of the Amish, the *Halsduch, Leppel,* and the "scoop" hat, were the ordinary dress of the common people in Alsace, the Palatinate, and other parts of Europe. The Amish bonnet of today is an exception; since the Amish migrations to America preceded the bonnet era they adopted this headpiece apparently from a New World source. Both men and women refuse to wear the newer type of overcoat. Amish women still wear only shawls, or in the case of some of the younger women, short coats. Older men and ministers wear the cape overcoat.

It has been pointed out that the Amish attitudes of hostility toward change and their reverence for past traditions is a function of the primary community group. Another principle of Amish survival which seems to be a function of the community has been the perpetuation of the original protest between the Swiss Mennonites and leaders of the Amish division in 1693-97. One of the original protests of the Amish was and still is whether expelled members should be banned in domestic relations or only from the communion table. There is scarcely a community of O.O.A. in America where there are no Amish Mennonites or former O.O.A. members near by, and so the "Meidung" controversy has been a perpetual one in local communities. The many divisions and variations of practice even among the O.O.A. themselves are the result of various interpretations of Meidung. In small Amish communities, particularly in the midwestern states, where associations with non-Amish neighbors are numerous, strict Meidung has been discontinued in favor of a more moderate practice: if the excommunicated member joins another Christian (usually Mennonite) denomination the Meidung is dropped.

Even though their practices differ on some points, the O.O.A. nevertheless maintain certain generalized attitudes of tolerance toward the Mennonites. The Amishman is more sympathetic and socially nearer to the Mennonite faith than to the larger Protestant or Catholic bodies. This explains why Old Order Amish parents frequently permit their nonconforming sons and daughters to become members of the Mennonite Church. By leaving the Amish church entirely, the nonconformist not only obtains freedom from traditional practices, but the O.O.A. group in turn is protected from any further "harmful" association with him. This has probably been an important factor in the survival of the very conservative groups of Amish.

Even though a large proportion (probably one third) of the offspring of Old Order Amish parents do not join the church of their parents, the Old Order Amish are still listed as one of the fastest growing religious bodies in the United States. This is, of course, due to their high birth rate and high retention of children in the group. The Amish do not keep written records of their members, and there is no official enumeration of their own giving membership statistics. The *Mennonite Yearbook* published annually at Scottdale, Pa., lists Amish ministers and congregations with membership. However, since the Yearbook bases its census upon voluntary reports from the local informants the figures are not always reliable and can only be taken as estimates. Memberships in the yearbooks for 1935, 1945, 1955, and 1957 were given as 7,746, 13,407, 15,695, and 17,045. Since membership is restricted to adults, no one knows exactly what the Amish population is, including children and unbaptized young people. Research done in Pennsylvania communities in collaboration with Maurice A. Mook, Professor of Anthropology of the Pennsylvania State University, suggests that actual population is three times the membership.

Amish families are considerably larger than those of the general population in rural areas, as evidenced by the few studies that have been made. A study of Mifflin County, Pa., Amish revealed that the average number of births for O.O.A. families was 7.0, while in a near-by non-Amish rural area the figure was 5.5. Mook reports that in the Atlantic community in Lawrence County, Pa., the average number of births was 7.4, and Howard Good found that in Elkhart County, Ind., the figure was 8.7 births per completed family; there was no noticeable decline in the number of births per family when three generations were compared.

The only major conflict of the Amish with the state has been their refusal to comply fully with the compulsory school laws. O.O.A. parents send their children to elementary schools but object to having their youth enter high school. In recent years parents have gone to jail in support of their stand and a large number of local parochial schools have been built in areas where school consolidation has been put into effect. Amish insistence upon the one-room country school is based upon their desire to maintain the integrity of their way of life, to keep their youth from secular influences such as movies and radio, and to keep them from influences beyond the control of their family and community. They contend that farming and housekeeping do not require higher education and that too much "book learning" is not good for their youth.

The Old Order Amish co-operated with the Conservative Amish Mennonite Conference in publishing *Herold der Wahrheit* in 1912-55, when the latter transferred its interest to the Unaffiliated Amish Mennonite group (Beachy Amish). The present editors are Raymond Wagler for the O.O.A. and Ervin Hershberger for the Beachy group. Some individuals among the O.O.A. have shown considerable interest in missionary work, and following several Amish missions conferences a monthly periodical entitled *Witnessing* was begun in 1953 with Harvey Graber as editor. Bookstores are operated by O.O.A. members as follows: L. A. Miller, Arthur, Ill.; J. A. Raber, Baltic, Ohio; and Benjamin Esh, Ronks, Pa., all of whom do mail-order business and initiate reprints. Because of the widespread use and regular demand for five German books, the O.O.A. of Lancaster County, Pa., have purchased the plates for these books and engage a printer and bookbinder as needed. The five are *Ausbund* (*q.v.*), *Ernsthafte Christenpflicht* (*q.v.*), *Lustgärtlein* (*q.v.*), *Unpartheyisches Gesangbuch* (*q.v.*), and the Holman *Bibel*.

The Old Order Amish are regular contributors to the foreign relief program of the Mennonite Central Committee. Members on this committee have been Eli J. Bontreger 1942-54 and Abe Yoder 1954- .

In the matter of nonresistance the Amish have been very stable. Their record on refusal of military service in any form has been almost 100 per cent. In World War II they accepted Civilian Public Service and even operated one camp of their own. Since 1950 there has been some tendency in a few localities by the ministers to discourage acceptance of the I-W service, partly because of their experience in World War II when some undesirable influences toward progressivism were felt.

The Old Order Amish have long practiced mutual aid, both by lending without interest to young farmers starting out, and by organized fire and storm insurance societies. The first of the latter was apparently the Amish Mennonite Aid Society of Iowa, founded in 1885. The Amish Aid Society of Eastern Pennsylvania started in the early 1890's, and the Amish Aid Plan of Kansas, Oklahoma, and Oregon in 1890. The largest aid societies are those of Ohio and Indiana-Michigan.

(For further information about the Old Order Amish and their practices see the pertinent information in such general articles as describe church organization, ordinances, etc. For the history of the origin of the Amish in 1693-97, see **Amish Division**, and for the later history **Amish Mennonites.**)

J.A.H.

J. A. Hostetler, *Annotated Bibliography on the Amish* (Scottdale, 1951); Calvin G. Bachman, *The Old Order Amish of Lancaster County (Proceedings of the Pennsylvania German Society* XLIV, Norristown, Pa., 1942); Walter Kollmorgen, *The Old Order Amish of Lancaster County, Pennsylvania* (U.S.D.A., 1942); J. C. Getz, "Economic Organization and Practices of the Old Order Amish of Lancaster County, Pennsylvania," *MQR* XX (1946) 53-60, 98-127; John Umble, "Research on the Amish and Source Materials for the Study of the Amish," *MQR* XXV (1951) 128-32; idem, "Old Order Amish of Lancaster County, Pennsylvania," *MQR* XVII (1943) 207-36; idem, "Amish Ordination Charges," *MQR* XIII (1939) 233-50; H. S. Bender, "Some Early Amish Mennonite Disciplines," *MQR* VIII (1934) 90-98; Grant Stoltzfus, "History of the First Amish Mennonite Communities in America," *MQR* XXVIII (1954) 235-62; Maurice A. Mook, "Extinct Amish Mennonite Communities in Pennsylvania," *MQR* XXX (1956) 267-76; D. Paul Miller, "Amish Acculturation" (unpublished M.A. thesis, U. of Nebraska, 1950); J. B. Mast, *The Letters of the Amish Division* (Oregon City, 1950); idem, *Facts Concerning the Beachy A.M. Division of 1927* (Meyersdale, 1950); *ML* I, 56.

Old Order Mennonites, a name applied to certain conservative groups which separated from the Mennonite Church (MC) in the United States and Canada 1872-1901, maintaining the "Old Order" of customs of worship and church life. When the Great Awakening, as H. S. Bender has termed it, came to the Mennonite Church (MC) in the last

third of the 19th century, four "Old Order" divisions occurred in the following areas: (1) Indiana and Ohio, led by Jacob Wisler, 1872; (2) Ontario, led by Abraham Martin, 1889; (3) Lancaster County, Pa., led by Jonas H. Martin, 1893; and (4) Rockingham County, Va., led by Gabriel D. Heatwole, 1900. These groups recognized each other as being one brotherhood, and became known as the Old Order Mennonites, although they had no formal general organization bearing this name. Sometimes the name "Wisler" is applied to the entire group. Locally often the names of the leading bishops are given to the several groups such as "Wenger Mennonites," "Weaver Mennonites," "Martinites," etc., and in Ontario the groups are often referred to under the name of the township in which they reside, e.g., "Woolwichers" (for Woolwich Twp., Waterloo Co.) and "Markham people" (for Markham Twp., York Co.). Subsequent subdivisions occurred in the first three bodies as led originally by Wisler (*q.v.*), Abraham Martin, and Jonas H. Martin. These four groups originated through a reluctance to accept cultural change, and the determination not to adopt the newer agencies for Christian education and evangelism such as the Sunday school, series of evangelistic meetings, and similar new activities and institutions.

Jacob Wisler (1808-89), ordained preacher in Columbiana County, Ohio, in 1833, removed to Elkhart County in 1848, and the year after the death of the aged Martin Hoover (*c*1761-1850) he was ordained bishop by Abraham Rohrer of Medina County, Ohio, the bishop who had ordained Hoover in 1845 just before he migrated to Elkhart County. Wisler, of a conservative turn of mind, was opposed to any change in the life of the church. Joseph Rohrer (1801-84), a preacher of Stark County, Ohio, came to Elkhart County in 1850, and served for some time in the ministry with Wisler. But Wisler did not like the exuberance manifested by Rohrer as he preached, and accused him of having too much of a "Methodist" spirit. Rohrer finally left the church and united with the Evangelical Church, whose house of worship stood one-half mile north of the Yellow Creek Mennonite meetinghouse, 8 miles west of Goshen. In 1864 Daniel Brenneman (*q.v.*), also a preacher, moved from Ohio to Elkhart County, a man similar in spirit to Joseph Rohrer, and was soon, like Rohrer, more popular than the bishop. Brenneman was happy to preach in English and he did not hesitate to sing a strong bass in the Yellow Creek services, although he knew that Wisler favored the old unison singing. A deacon of the Holdeman congregation, Joseph Holdeman, was also critical of Wisler as well as of a number of other leaders through the years. There was considerable dissatisfaction in the church by 1867, the year when John F. Funk (*q.v.*) located in Elkhart County. In October 1867 a committee of 16 leaders from Ontario, Ohio, Pennsylvania, Illinois, and Virginia attempted to adjust the difficulties. The first signer of the Committee of Sixteen was Joseph Hagey of Ontario. The next year, 1868, Tillman Moyer of Ontario made another effort to iron out the difficulties, and he signed his statement "In the presence of Joseph Hagey." In

1869 Tillman Moyer was back again, accompanied by two Ontario and two Ohio Mennonite leaders, and another effort was made to establish permanent peace. In 1870 Bishop John M. Brenneman of Ohio, the strongest leader in the state, came to Elkhart County with the express approval of Bishop Rohrer, who had ordained Wisler and who had served on the Committee of Sixteen in 1867, and Brenneman succeeded in once more effecting peace. But Wisler's dissatisfaction with the Indiana Conference's approval of Sunday schools in 1870 led to fresh trouble in 1871, and in October 1871 a committee of six bishops headed by John M. Brenneman suspended Wisler's bishop function, with the approval of the Yellow Creek congregation. Wisler rejected the decision of the Committee of Six, and on Jan. 6, 1872, the Elkhart County ministers announced to the Yellow Creek congregation that Wisler and his followers, including preachers John Weaver and Christian Bare, were no longer members of the church. It was probably John F. Funk who made the announcement. Thereupon Wisler began to hold separate services and to seek support elsewhere. This support he found in eastern Ohio (Wayne, Medina, and Columbiana-Mahoning counties), where the church divided and the conservative group followed Wisler. In 1907 the Wisler Mennonites of Indiana divided into the more progressive Ramer or Wisler Mennonites and the more conservative Martin or Old Order Mennonites. By 1920 the Ramer and Martin groups had respectively about 150 and 60 members, in 1957 150 and 102. The Ohio congregations in the Wisler group totaled 345 members in 1957, all of the more progressive group. The Indiana and Ohio progressive Old Order congregations constituted a conference which has met annually in June since 1907.

In 1889 a similar schism occurred in Ontario, led by Bishop Abraham Martin of Woolwich Twp., Waterloo County. The other bishops of his group were Christian Gayman of South Cayuga and Christian Reesor of Markham. The issues were the same as in Indiana: Sunday schools, evangelistic meetings, and the like. In 1917 a more conservative faction split off in the Waterloo County area, the "David Martin group," having in 1957 a membership of 116 and listed in the *Mennonite Yearbook* as "not under Conference." In the 1889 meeting to organize the Old Order Mennonites of Woolwich Township, Bishop Christian Shaum of Elkhart County, Ind., Wisler's younger colleague, was present. In the late 1920's a more progressive group broke away from the Woolwichers to found what is now known as the Markham-Waterloo Conference, and which had a membership of 748 in 1957. The original Woolwich Conference had a membership of 1,061 in 1957. (For an account of the O.O.M. in Ontario, see Burkholder, *History*.) Tension had existed between Christian Gayman and the Mennonite Conference of Ontario a number of years before the division of 1889.

Michigan also suffered some schisms. In 1886 the Mennonite congregation of Brutus, Mich., which had its roots in Ontario, divided into the Wisler and non-Wisler group. The Wisler group was for many years much stronger than the remnant which remained with the Indiana-Michigan Mennonite Conference (MC). A few scattered Wisler members lived at Brutus until the 1950's but scarcely any services were held after 1930. There was also a small group of O.O.M. in Tuscola County, Mich., under the leadership of a preacher Daniel Lehman, who died soon after 1920. They settled in Tuscola County c1880, coming mostly from Ontario. Lehman was one of the last members there.

The third area in which a group of O.O.M. arose was in Lancaster County, Pa. George Weaver, a bishop who had served on the Committee of Sixteen in Indiana in 1867, was of a conservative turn of mind, and did not favor Sunday schools. He sympathized with Wisler. When Weaver in his old age wished to ordain a bishop as his successor (in 1881) he rejected Benjamin Horning (1827-1907), an able preacher in his Weaverland-Groffdale District; although Horning received sufficient votes to pass through the lot, Weaver discarded them, saying that he lived too far from the center of the district. Horning continued his ministry, but his preacher-friend Emanuel Newswanger (c1833-1905) stopped preaching in protest against the injustice done Horning. A preacher (ord. 1875) named Jonas H. Martin (1839-1925) was ordained bishop to assist Bishop Weaver. He was of the same convictions as George Weaver and somewhat out of harmony with the Lancaster Conference, which in 1871 had approved Sunday schools, and which in 1872 had endorsed the action of the six bishops in the case of Jacob Wisler. The old custom of the Mennonites in Lancaster County and elsewhere had been to have a table in place of a pulpit, around which the song leaders and preachers sat, and behind which the preacher stood (on a level with his people) to deliver his discourse. When the new Lichty meetinghouse was built in 1889 near New Holland a small pulpit was put into it. A few weeks before the first services someone removed the pulpit from the church by night, arranged the seating in the older arrangement, and installed a neatly constructed table. Bishop Jonas Martin was blamed for secretly approving of the act. Tensions continued to build up because of Martin's conservatism, and he was accused of a lack of integrity. After many efforts to settle the difficulties he announced at a Lancaster Conference meeting in October 1893 that he was withdrawing because (*a*) he and his followers did not favor the bishops and preachers performing marriage ceremonies for nonmembers; (*b*) they were not in favor of Sunday schools; and (*c*) they opposed any Lancaster Conference congregation obtaining a charter from the state. The other bishops of the Conference reciprocated by revoking his ordination. He then proceeded to set up what is now known as the Weaverland Conference. In 1926, the year following Martin's death, Preacher Joseph O. Wenger led a more conservative schism from the Weaverland Conference, and in 1927 Wenger was ordained bishop of his group, which is now known as the Groffdale Conference or Wenger Mennonites. The original Weaverland Conference had a membership of 1,731 in 1957, and the Groffdale Conference had 1,450. There are also other splinter groups of the

O.O.M. in the Weaverland area. (See **Lancaster County**.)

The fourth group of Old Order Mennonites, near Harrisonburg, Va., has always been weak numerically. The founder in Virginia was Gabriel D. Heatwole (1834-1922), a preacher ordained at the Weaver church in 1870 who seceded from the Virginia Conference (MC) in 1901. After his death the leading minister of this group was John Dan Wenger, who served for many years as bishop. In 1922 Bishop Wenger was assisted in the ministry by preachers Lewis P. Good and Emanuel Heatwole. At that time services were being held in the Pleasant View meetinghouse at Dayton, Va., where there were 75 members, at the Pike School in Rockingham County where there were 12 members, and at Mt. Pleasant where there were but three members. In recent years a division occurred, one group being led by Russell Cline. In 1957 there were only two meeting places, Pleasant View and Oak Grove, both near Dayton, with a combined membership of 325, in two factions, one led by Bishop Wenger and one by Bishop Cline. The Virginia group corresponds to the most conservative of the major O.O.M. groups in Indiana, Ontario, and Pennsylvania.

The total for all areas and groups of Old Order Mennonites in 1957 was 5,800 members in 44 congregations. A general cultural and religious conservatism characterizes the entire group. The most conservative groups use only horse-drawn vehicles. The more progressive bodies permit the use of automobiles; traditionally, however, they paint the chrome bumpers black. In most areas the more conservative groups attempt to maintain the use of German for at least parts of the service, but this is becoming increasingly difficult. All groups are still opposed to evangelistic meetings and Sunday schools. By rearing large families the Old Order Mennonites are growing; they have about doubled their membership in the last quarter century.

J.C.W.

L. J. Burkholder, *A Brief History of the Mennonites in Ontario* (Markham, 1935) 197-216; M. G. Weaver, *Mennonites of Lancaster Conference* (Scottdale, 1931) 130, 139, 148, 385-95.

Old Order Mennonites of Virginia. The "Middle District Trouble," involving questions of leadership and methods in church work, resulted in a schism in the Virginia Mennonite (MC) church in 1900. About that time 69 members out of *c*500 total, including the three preachers Simeon, Emanuel, and Gabriel Heatwole, all living near the Bank church, refused to identify themselves with the church and were "published off," i.e., were declared out of fellowship or excommunicated. In 1902 Bishop Jonas Martin of the Old Order group in Lancaster County, Pa., was called in by this group. The Wisler Discipline was read and accepted. A new congregation was organized, and in 1902 the Pleasant View meetinghouse was built 2 miles northwest of Dayton in Rockingham County. The division may be thought of as primarily occurring in the Bank (*q.v.*) church.

On Nov. 15, 1902, Simeon Heatwole was ordained

bishop, and at the same time John Dan Wenger was named preacher. Bishop Heatwole, due to the infirmities of old age, was replaced as bishop by John Dan Wenger in 1912. Wenger has been the most important leader since that time. Another meetinghouse, the Oak Grove church 1½ miles south of Dayton, was built in 1921.

In recent years Bishop John Dan Wenger called into question the preaching and leadership of one of his ministers, Russell Cline. Those who sympathized with Cline sought and acquired recognition for him on the part of the Old Order Church in Pennsylvania and elsewhere, and Cline was ordained bishop for the new group. Warren Showalter and Justus Showalter were ordained to serve as ministers. The membership of this group in 1957 was 200.

John Dan Wenger, the aged O.O.M. bishop in Virginia, believes that he is the rightful leader of the O.O.M. of Virginia. He has ordained his son Paul Wenger as bishop, and Oscar Martin serves as minister. The membership of this group in 1957 was 125. In recent years about 25 of the O.O.M. of Virginia have joined with the "Horning People" (Groffdale Conference) in Pennsylvania. They have purchased an old Baptist church several miles southeast of Mt. Crawford, Va., where they are served occasionally by ministers from Pennsylvania.

H.A.B.

Old People's Home: see **Homes for the Aged** and **Mennonite Old People's Home.**

Old Road (or *White Horse*) Mennonite Church (MC), located near an early family cemetery one mile east of White Horse, Lancaster Co., Pa., is a part of the Hershey circuit of the Lancaster Conference. Until 1841 the congregation met for worship in private homes and in the Pequea Presbyterian church. In 1841 a stone meetinghouse was built along the Old Philadelphia Pike. In 1892 a frame building farther from the road and larger replaced it. This meetinghouse was remodeled in 1947. Martin R. Hershey and Sanford E. Hershey are the ministers, and Clair Eby bishop. The membership in 1957 was 104.   I.D.L.

Old Swiss Mennonites: see **Swiss Mennonites** in the Netherlands.

Old Testament. From its very beginning the Christian church has been faced with a dilemma in its use of the Old Testament. As long as the apostles were alive their authority was accepted on an equal status with the writings of the O.T., but when the church began to wrestle with the formation of a canon of New Testament Scriptures, the problem of authority and place of the O.T. became acute. Jesus, in His teachings, particularly in the Sermon on the Mount, had made His position clear. Paul, following Jesus, used the O.T. freely, but also went beyond it to show that Christ's fulfillment of the O.T. was complete.

The most drastic solution to the problem of the O.T. was advocated by Marcion in the second century, who not only rejected the O.T. entirely, but also expurgated those sections of the New Testament which had a strong Jewish background. All that was left in his N.T. was a drastically revised Luke-Acts, and an "edited" Pauline corpus. Needless to say, the church rejected Marcion as a heretic. Marcion, however, made a contribution by calling attention to the lack of a clearly defined position with respect to the O.T. The Epistle of Barnabas and the Clementine literature were extremely allegorical in dealing with the O.T. and this Marcion rightly rejected. It remained therefore for Irenaeus to develop a "Biblical theology" which took account of the fact that God worked both in the O.T. and the N.T. The theology of Irenaeus represents the first conscious attempt to define the relationship between the O.T. and the N.T. on a historical and not allegorical basis, although the recently discovered Homily on the Passions by Melito of Sardis shows that individual preachers had used certain motifs to bridge the gap between two Testaments, rather than succumbing to abstruse allegory.

Adolf Harnack states that the retention of the O.T. in the church's canon was justified in the early church, but a mere historical accident in the time of the Reformation. Any student of the Reformation will hardly agree with this statement, since in many ways the battles of the first two centuries were again taken up in the 16th. Certainly this is true with respect to the O.T. The Reformers were faced with the problem of the O.T. repeatedly, and part of the reason was that the Anabaptists were critical of the degree of authority given to the O.T. by the Reformers. Unfortunately the issue was obscured by Thomas Müntzer, who breathed deeply from the apocalyptic and vindictive sections of the O.T., thus misreading its true intent, and by the Münsterites who patterned their kingdom at Münster upon the O.T., instituting polygamy, royalty, etc. These events had little to do with the essential development of Anabaptism, but served to obscure the true Anabaptists. At Münster the daily Scripture reading was taken from the O.T., generally from the Prophets. This O.T. Biblicism was criticized by Corvinus, who tried to define the relationship between the O.T. and the N.T. in his attack against Münster.

The Anabaptist estimate of the O.T. was a result of their discussions with the Reformers. It is significant that at each major disputation (e.g., Frankenthal, q.v.) the problem of O.T. authority was discussed at length, especially with reference to its relation to the N.T. As far as the records indicate, the Reformers made no original contribution in these discussions and their solutions have not been accepted by Protestantism. It is quite clear that their arguments about O.T. authority are colored by their desire to retain infant baptism and the state church, as well as to weaken the Anabaptist position on the oath (q.v.), etc. Roland Bainton has shown that with regard to the problem of the immoral deeds of the patriarchs the exegetes of the Reformation developed a number of interesting techniques to justify them, but the end result of this kind of exegesis, seen most clearly in Luther's defense of Philip's bigamy, is that the O.T. can be used as an attenuating ethical standard. On this point the Anabaptists had a much more consistent and clearly defined position.

The enemies of the early Swiss Anabaptists charged them with rejecting the O.T. Bullinger wrote: "The Anabaptists believe that [in regard to salvation] one should not prove anything from the O.T.; the transactions of the O.T. are finished and do not concern us" (Ursprung, 73). Zwingli wrote in his Elenchus of 1527: "In this country they deny the entire O.T., which I have seen with my own eyes. For they wrote to our magistrate that the O.T. has been done away with." Schwenckfeld accused the Anabaptists of living only in the N.T. and disregarding the O.T. Gast, in his Exordio of 1544 (p. 33), attacked the Anabaptist position on the O.T. Wigand, in his De Anabaptismo of 1582, put these words into their mouth: "The O.T. cannot in all respects be held equal to the N.T., but only where it agrees with the New." Since then others have repeated the charge, calling the Anabaptists Marcionites, at least in tendency. An investigation of the sources does not, however, support this charge.

There is first of all the work done by Hans Denk and the marginal Anabaptist Ludwig Haetzer in translating the prophets from the Hebrew into German at the very outset of the Anabaptist movement. Hans Leupold (q.v.), of Augsburg, at his hearing in 1527 asserted that at their meetings the Anabaptists considered God's Word, principally the Gospels and the Prophets. Leonhard Schiemer urges his flock to gather together often and to read mainly from the N.T. and the Psalms. The hidden things of the O.T. will be plain to them in the N.T. It should be noted that Schiemer does not tell his people that they should ignore the O.T., but only urges them to read the O.T. (called shadow) through the eyes of the N.T. (called light). He feels that the Psalms contain everything in the O.T. but that the books of the Kings and the Pentateuch could also be read with profit. However, all things are contained in the N.T., for the apostles are the summary (Auszug) of all the prophets.

The influence of Schiemer continued in the Marpeck brotherhood, which was the only group among the Anabaptists to work extensively on the relation of the O.T. and the N.T. In several aspects of its position the Marpeck group differed from other Anabaptists. This is particularly true of certain exaggerations made by Marpeck in order to establish his point. Already in his confession of 1532, Marpeck referred repeatedly to the difference between the Old Covenant, a covenant of servitude, and the New Covenant, a covenant of sonship. This same distinction appears at some length in the Anabaptist tract of unknown authorship or origin, Von zweierlei gehorsam, and shows that the Anabaptists were interested in a responsible type of Christianity which was not compelled by legalism, but rather based on a vital relationship of sonship. This was viewed as the basic distinction between the two Testaments. In his two booklets of 1531 Marpeck uses the O.T. extensively, explaining that he was compelled to do so because the false prophets whom he was opposing used it wrongly. One of the false prophets was Bünderlin, who repeatedly rejected historical exegesis, explicitly condemning the Antiochian school of exegesis. The alternative which he suggested is an elaborate allegory influenced by neoplatonic values. The same is true of Schwenkfeld, but to a lesser degree. In contrast, Marpeck restricted his use of allegory to examples of allegory in the Bible itself, e.g., Hagar and Sarah, and the Song of Solomon. The historical material was always treated as historical by him, and his greatest objection to both Schwenckfeld's and the Reformers' treatment of the O.T. is that the historical lines of distinction are not observed. He begins with the book of Hebrews and insists that the shadows have now been driven away and the essence has come. The essence, however, is not defined in Platonic terms, but always as a historical person, Jesus Christ. The difference between the two Testaments lies in the Incarnation. The preexistent Christ was present in the O.T., but not in such a way as to give man the benefits which the N.T. saints experienced. To place the O.T. saints on the same level as those of the New, seemed to Marpeck a blasphemy on the work of Christ as found in the N.T. This theme is most fully elaborated in the *Testamenterleutterung* (q.v.).

Beyond and behind the theological issue stood the ethical issue. In the *Clare verantwurtung* Marpeck makes it clear that while the O.T. tolerated revenge, the New definitely forbids it, and that the law of love controls the behavior of the Christian. This same principle was carried into the discussion of the oath when the Reformers insisted on the oath because it was tolerated in the O.T. Over against this the Anabaptists had the clear word of Christ which insisted that the Christian should not swear. The Anabaptist attitude toward the O.T. can be described as desiring above all to give Christ the honor due Him, and not stressing the O.T. revelation except where it is in accord with the New. Darkness is not used to interpret light, but rather light is used to interpret darkness.

Studies of both Marpeck and Menno Simons indicate that they used the O.T. extensively; it is out of the question to consider them Marcionite even in tendency. Their use of the O.T. was, however, such as to draw inspiration from the acts of God in the history of His people, and not to draw an ethic from a time when God's fullest revelation had not yet appeared. The extensive use of the O.T. Scriptures is seen especially in the *Ausbund,* the *Codex Geiser,* Riedemann's *Rechenschaft,* and in the devotional literature, particularly that which had a strong martyrological strain. At a time when they themselves were asked to lay down their lives, the Anabaptists drew inspiration and comfort from the sufferings of the people of God in the past, and were sustained by the conviction that the same God who had worked through His people in the past would also fulfill it in them, no matter how dark the days in which they lived at the time.

It is significant that it was an Anabaptist who in 1531 complained that the Strasbourg preachers were not preaching the Law (O.T.) before preaching the Gospel, and that in the 16th century the Anabaptists rejected the virtual identification of the two covenants seen in Zwingli, Bucer, and Bullinger. In doing so they were ahead of their time in seeing elements of continuity and discontinuity in the two covenants. Perhaps they were inclined to see too clearly the elements of discontinuity, but they did so because they saw what a virtual identification of the two covenants leads to in the area of ethics, and what happens to groups who seek to base a social order on the O.T. Lydia Müller's assertion that the Anabaptists lived strongly in the O.T. must be correctly understood. It was for them literature of edification (*Erbauung*), but the standards of the Christian life were to be drawn from the N.T. Related to this was the conviction that the power to live the Christian life had come only with the New Covenant. Jacques d'Auchy (q.v.), a Dutch martyr of 1559, is a good example, in saying that "we are no longer under the law, but under the gospel" (*Mart. Mir.* E 904) and declaring that the O.T. is to be valued only as it is understood by Christ and the apostles. Conrad Grebel had already declared in his letter to Müntzer in 1524, "We are no longer under the Old Covenant." Hans Denk said in his *Von der wahren Liebe*: "It stands thus with the teaching and work of Moses, David, and the Fathers: wherever love, i.e., Jesus, has surpassed them with something better, one must for the sake of the better consider them bad."

In later years descendants of the Anabaptists have not always taken a wholesome view of the O.T. Legalism, expressed in terms of restrictions on women's dress (not wearing men's clothes) and the beard (q.v.), has been drawn from the O.T. apparently not aware that such arguments run directly counter to the essential Anabaptist position. The difficulty some recent Mennonite theologians have had in reconciling the O.T. ethic with a nonresistant ethic has led to a disparagement of the O.T., while some Mennonite educators even advocate not telling children the story of Goliath because of what it may do to them. These approaches fail to see the essential nature of these narratives, and do little to assist Mennonites in forming a positive opinion of the O.T. in the future. There is no doubt that the O.T. confronts the Christian church with some gnawing problems, but they are not overcome by relegating the O.T. to an irrelevant position. Rather, the church, from Irenaeus through the Reformation even to our time, has seen that the best approach is a historical one in which God is progressively working through His people, preparing them for the fullness of revelation. The O.T. stands as a brilliant testimony to God's working in history to fulfill His purpose among men who yield themselves to His plan. His ways of working have changed, but He still seeks to gather a people around His name. The N.T. insists that everything in the O.T. must be judged in the light of Christ. It is a testimony to the Anabaptist devotion to Christ that they saw this point clearly and insisted on it with courage and steadfastness.

W.Kl.

Hayo Gerdes, *Luthers Streit mit den Schwärmern um das rechte Verständnis des Gesetzes Mose,* 1955; Adolf Harnack, *Marcion, Das Evangelium vom fremden Gott* (Leipzig, 1921) 248 f.; W. Klassen, "Pilgram Marpeck's Hermeneutics with Special Reference to His Understanding of the Old Testament" (unpublished doctoral dissertation at Princeton Theological Seminary, 1959); Roland Bainton, "The Immoralities of the Patriarchs According to the Exegesis of the Late Middle Ages and of the Reformation," *Harvard Theological Journal* XXIII (1930) 39-49; *Corpus Schwenckfeld*. VIII, 221:10 ff.; X, 925; Lydia Müller, *Glaubenszeugnisse* I, 45 (Schiemer); *idem, Der Kommunismus der mährischen Wiedertäufer* (Liepzig, 1927) 25; Heinrich Bullinger, *Von dem einigen vnnd ewigen Testament oder Pundt Gottes* (s.l. 1534); *idem, Der Widertoeufferen Ursprung;* J. Gastius, *De anabaptismi exordio* (Basel, 1544); H. Zwingli, *In catabaptistarum strophas elenchus* (Zürich, 1527); J. Wigand, *De anabaptismo* (Leipzig, 1582); *ML* I, 40.

Oldambt, a region in the Dutch province of Groningen, east of Noordbroek, touching the German border. In the 17th century the southern part was called Wold-Oldambt, the northern part, consisting of polders reclaimed on the Dollard, then was called Klei-Oldambt. In this territory are found the Mennonite congregations of Noordbroek, Winschoten (a union of the former congregations of Beerta, Midwolda, and De Meeden), Pekela, and Veendam. In the 17th century these congregations are sometimes mentioned under the names of Wold-Ampt and Klei-Ampt (also Klein-Ampt). It is not clear which of the now existing congregations formed the Wold-Ampt congregation and which the Klei-Ampt, though it is probable that Beerta and Midwolda were identical with the Klei-Ampt congregation.   vDZ.

Tegenwoordige staat der Vereenigde Nederlanden XXI, Part I (Amsterdam, 1793) 207-36; *Naamlijst, passim;* Blaupot t. C., *Groningen* I and II; *DB* 1879, 5, 86.

Oldeberkoop, a village in the Dutch province of Friesland, formerly the seat of a Mennonite congregation, belonging to the Groningen Old Flemish branch. There is little information about this congregation. It had no meetinghouse, services being held in a private home; the membership must have been very small and it died out about 1700. (*DB* 1879, 3, 91.)   vDZ.

Oldeboorn, a village in the Dutch province of Friesland, where there have been Anabaptists since very early times. Eelke and Fije of Boorn (Oldeboorn) suffered a martyr's death in Leeuwarden, the Frisian capital, in 1549. Eelke had gathered the "God-fearing people and read the New Testament to them." In 1556 five persons were baptized by Leenaert Bouwens in Oldeboorn and soon afterward an additional 21. In 1573 Reytse Aysesz, who lived in the adjacent village of Beetsterzwaag, was seized in Oldeboorn where he had spent the night with fellow believers in his father's house; he was executed by drowning at Leeuwarden on April 23, 1574. The letters that he wrote in prison reveal that his parents, his brothers and sisters, and his wife were also members of the congregation, and that there were numerous "friends," so that we may assume that there was at that time already a congregation of considerable size in Oldeboorn.

Concerning the Oldeboorn congregation in the 17th century not much is known. In 1695 it joined the Frisian Conference, founded in that year. In 1700 there were 118 members who were not supported by the church. In 1738 there was a division (it is not quite clear whether the cause of the divi-

sion was disharmony). For another 150 years two congregations, the "Oude Huis" and the "Nieuwe Huis," existed side by side. In 1838 the former had 142 members, the latter 46; in 1868 the corresponding figures were 251 and 179. The Oude Huis congregation acquired a new church in 1856. The relationship between the two congregations had gradually become quite friendly. In 1882 when the Nieuwe Huis found itself without a minister the two congregations decided to merge; this took place on Jan. 1, 1887. K. Schuiling, the minister in the Oude Huis at that time, became the minister of the united congregation which at that time had about 400 members. The church building (the original Nieuwe Huis) was sold and is now a Reformed church. The membership which in 1900 was 483, is at present (1957) only 182. In 1936 the congregation built a new parsonage to replace the one of 1861.

Both the Oude and the Nieuwe Huis congregations were served by lay ministers chosen from the members of the church until shortly after 1800. S. E. Wieling, called in 1805, was the first educated pastor of the Nieuwe Huis congregation; in the Oude Huis all the untrained preachers retired in 1810 and Jan ter Borg, who had been educated at the Amsterdam Mennonite Seminary, became its preacher. After the merger of 1887 K. Schuiling served until 1889. He was followed by P. Botke 1890-1920, Jacob Hulshoff 1920-30, A. P. van de Water 1935-39, Miss C. Soutendijk 1939-42, E. Daalder 1942-47, H. C. Valeton 1948-50, J. P. Jacobszoon 1951-56, and A. Veldstra 1957- . The church records go back to 1755. The congregation has a Sunday school for children and a ladies' circle.   vDZ.

Inv. Arch. Amst. II, Nos. 2177-83; Blaupot t. C., *Friesland,* passim; Gorter's *Doopsgezinde Lectuur* 1858, 7; *DB* 1887, 147; *Mart. Mir.* D 84 and 677, E 484 and 994; *ML* III, 298.

Oldehove, a hamlet in the Dutch province of Groningen, was shortly after 1530 a center of Anabaptist activity. Later on there were a number of Mennonites here, who with Mennonites of some neighboring hamlets formed the congregation of Humsterland (*q.v.*), also called the Oldehove (*DB* 1861, 152) congregation. According to tradition there was a small meetinghouse at Oldehove. Now the Mennonites living here belong to the Noordhorn (*q.v.*) congregation, a special Mennonite circle of Oldehove-Saaxum-Ezinge having been founded in 1947.   vDZ.

Oldeklooster (or Bloemkamp), a monastery near Bolsward in the Dutch province of Friesland, was seized on March 30, 1535, by about 300 Anabaptists of Friesland, both men and women, led by Jan van Geelen (*q.v.*), an emissary of the Anabaptists of Münster. They thereby won a strong position and from here tried to conquer the entire province—an absurd idea! The imperial stadholder Georg Schenk van Tautenburg was put in charge of capturing the old monastery from the Anabaptists. He supposed that he would be able to do so by a mere turning of the hand, but found himself compelled to conduct a regular siege. On April 1 he decided to bombard the monastery with heavy artillery and tried to storm it. Four times he had to lead his soldiers into the fire. On the third assault they succeeded in taking several positions. Some of the fortifications and the church remained in Anabaptist possession. On April 7 the monastery was finally stormed after a severe battle. Eight or nine hundred Anabaptists are said to have lost their lives, but this number is a gross exaggeraton; there were 300 at the most. Of these who did not lose their lives in the storming, 37 were at once beheaded and 132, both men and women, taken to Leeuwarden, of whom 55 were executed there after a short trial. Jan van Geelen escaped. Among the victims of Oldeklooster was Peter Simons (q.v.), who is erroneously said to have been a brother of Menno Simons. NEFF, vDZ.

Ludwig Keller, *Geschichte der Wiedertäufer und ihres Reiches zu Münster* (Münster, 1880) 2 ff.; Kühler, *Geschiedenis* I, 166-68; K. Vos, *Menno Simons* (Leiden, 1914) particularly 228 f., with a list of the persons executed at Leeuwarden; Mellink, *Wederdopers*, 247-49; *ML* III, 298.

Oldemarkt, a village in the Dutch province Overijssel. Leenaert Bouwens (q.v.) baptized seven persons here in 1563-65. Later there was here a small congregation of the Danzig Old Flemish (q.v.), as there was likewise in Blokzijl, Zuidveen, and Giethoorn, all of which maintained relations with the Flemish congregation at Danzig, Prussia. Roelof Agge Joncker (q.v.) was preacher of the Oldemarkt congregation 1699-1712; his father and grandfather had served in the same office. The Oldemarkt congregation had died out by 1744. (*Inv. Arch. Amst.* II, No. 2184; *DB* 1878, 12; *ML* III, 298.) vDZ.

Oldenburg, a province of Germany (until 1918 a grand duchy), area 2,479 sq. miles, population over 500,000, once consisted of the gravure of Oldenburg and the city of Jever. Anabaptism found its way into this region at an early date from the adjacent province of East Friesland (q.v.). Direct information about Anabaptism here is missing until the middle of the 16th century, but government regulations and statements of Protestant preachers clearly show their presence. In the city of Jever a debate with six Anabaptists was held on Feb. 13 and 14, 1576; they were Hermann Brunsfeld, a scholar, Johannes Gerdes of Hohenkirchen, Nikolaus Hermanni of Altenburg, Henricus Henrici of Wüppels, Jankenius of Sillenstede, and Sara, a pregnant woman (see Schauenburg, 36-43, where the interesting discussion is printed). These Anabaptists were expelled from the country; their case was lost.

In the old gravure of Oldenburg the Anabaptists were apparently mostly of the Münsterite type, such as Bernhard Krechting, a brother of Heinrich Krechting, the chancellor of Jan van Leyden (q.v.). Also David Joris (q.v.) stayed here a short time in 1538. They were expelled. The quiet Anabaptists, who had a large following in the city and the country, finally disappeared. NEFF.

L. Schauenburg, *Die Täuferbewegung in der Grafschaft Oldenburg-Delmenhorst und der Herrschaft Jever zur Zeit der Reformation* (Oldenburg, 1888); *ML* III, 298.

Oldersum, a village in East Friesland, Germany, situated on the Ems, south of Emden, was during the Reformation the seat of Wiard von Oldersum. In 1494 Ulrich von Dornum (q.v.) married Essa, Wiard's daughter. Thus Ulrich obtained half of the castle of Oldersum and some property. He became not only a staunch promoter of the Reformation but also a protector and sponsor of the Anabaptists and spiritualists. The co-owner of the Oldersum castle, Hero, shared his views. Ulrich sponsored a disputation at Oldersum between the Catholic Dr. Laurenz and Jürgen Aportanus, a Protestant minister of Emden, and had the report published in Wittenberg in 1523. In 1530 he wrote to the reformers of Strasbourg regarding the Reformation.

Edzard and Enno, the counts of East Friesland, were strongly influenced by Ulrich. In the controversy as to whether East Friesland was to become Reformed or Lutheran, he followed an independent course and made Oldersum a refuge for the persecuted. When Melchior Hofmann (q.v.) arrived in East Friesland in May 1529, i.e., prior to his association with the Anabaptists, he was in touch with Ulrich von Dornum at Oldersum. During the following year Hofmann dedicated two of his writings in Strasbourg to Ulrich. During the same year Carlstadt (q.v.) found refuge with Ulrich at Oldersum and dedicated one of his writings to him. Because of these contacts Carlstadt was enabled to spend some time and do some work in East Friesland. He was still writing to Ulrich von Dornum from Basel on Dec. 10, 1530, sharing with him his views and problems. In May 1530 when Hofmann reached Emden to start the Anabaptist movement, his former contacts with Oldersum were of help to him, although there seems to be no indication that Ulrich supported him in a special way.

Peter Janss reported that he was baptized by Menno Simons at Oldersum in 1536, which would indicate that Menno Simons found shelter in Oldersum soon after his withdrawal from the Catholic Church in Witmarsum early in 1536. According to tradition Ulrich von Dornum granted Menno shelter for a longer period. Whether that was in the castle (the last part of which was torn down in 1954) or in one of the villages is not known. However, it is likely that Menno Simons had shelter here even after Ulrich's death in 1536. Christoffer van Ewsum (q.v.), who married Ulrich's oldest daughter and lived in the province of Groningen, was also referred to as a "Mennonist," but this is an overstatement. However, Ulrich's daughter Essa married an Anabaptist.

According to Kochs Anabaptists continued to find refuge at Oldersum under Hero after Ulrich's death. Even Sebastian Franck had followers at Oldersum. Johan van Bekesteyn of Oldersum visited Franck in Basel in 1541/42. On this occasion Franck wrote a letter to the Christians of Oldersum who "live like sheep among wolves," admonishing them to seek Christ within themselves and not in creeds and churches. This writing was likely addressed to the Reformed members of the church who had difficulty in maintaining their identity under the influence of Lutherans. Leenaert Bouwens performed baptisms in Oldersum in 1580. Hendrick Derks (d. 1652) was an elder of this congregation, which belonged to the Groningen Old Flemish branch. By 1700 it had either died out or merged with a neighboring congregation. **C.K.**

E. Kochs, "Die Anfänge der ostfriesischen Reformation," *Jahrbuch d. Gesellschaft f. bild. Kunst* ... XX (Emden, 1920); Gerhard Ohling, "Aus den Anfängen der Reformation. Ein Brief des Sebastian Franck ... an die Oldersumer Gemeinde," *Ostfriesland*, 1954, 111-15; *Groningsche Volksalmanak*, 1919, 139 f.; Gerhard Ohling, *Junker Ulrich von Dornum* (Aurich, 1955); Cornelius Krahn, *Menno Simons (1496-1561)* (Karlsruhe, 1936) 36; *ML III*.

Oldesloe, a town of 15,000 (1954) in Schleswig-Holstein, Germany, situated between Hamburg and Lübeck. Oldesloe played a role in the history of Mennonites in that province. In 1554 an Anabaptist printer and his apprentices coming from Lübeck were stopped here by authorities who aimed to suppress their activities. They found with them ten tons of Bibles which were investigated by Balthasar Schröder and Claus Wensin of Segeberg. On Nov. 28, 1554, they reported to Christian III of Denmark that the Anabaptist owner had printed a Bible based on Luther's and a Dutch translation, with a concordance from the Zürich Bible. The Anabaptist insisted that only the death of Christ could save and not baptism. From here he proceeded with his printing press to Fresenburg (*q.v.*), where Bartholomäus von Ahlefeldt (*q.v.*) was a protector of the Anabaptists. Whether this Anabaptist was Menno (*q.v.*) Simons himself, who wrote and printed his books at Fresenburg, has not been established.

Evidently there was never a large number of Mennonites in Oldesloe. The members residing here possibly attended the worship services at Fresenburg. Menno Simons himself ordained Michael Steffens and Dirk Eggerat, who resided in Oldesloe, as ministers. Paul Roosen, the father of Gerrit Roosen, learned the trade of tanning from Dirk Eggerat at Oldesloe. Willem Govers and Karsten von Sintern were other members living there before 1600. With the dispersion of the Fresenburg Mennonite settlers in connection with the Thirty Years' War the Mennonites of Oldesloe must also have moved away. Fr. Bangert, in *Die Geschichte der Stadt und des Kirchspiels Oldesloe* (Oldesloe, 1925), does not mention the Anabaptists. **C.K.**

Robert Dollinger, *Geschichte der Mennoniten in Schleswig-Holstein, Hamburg und Lübeck* (Neumünster, 1930) 4, 29; Cornelius Krahn, *Menno Simons (1496-1561)* (Karlsruhe, 1936) 82 ff.

Oley Mennonite Church (MC), located in Oley Valley, Berks County, Pa., a member of the Ohio and Eastern Mennonite Conference, is the outgrowth of both an agricultural extension and an evangelical outreach from the Conestoga Mennonite Church near Morgantown, Pa. The first family moved into the valley in 1938, and by 1942 there were thirteen families. Sunday-school services were begun in May 1942. On Jan. 3, 1943, Omar Kurtz was ordained as the first pastor. On July 18, 1946, John L. Glick was ordained assistant pastor. For 8 years the services were held in a rented union chapel; but in September 1950 a new church was dedicated. A number from the community have been received into the church, and from here have gone at least six missionaries. The membership in 1957 was 115, with Ira A. Kurtz of the Conestoga congregation serving as bishop. **O.A.Ku.**

Olgafeld, a Mennonite village name transplanted from the Russian Mennonite settlement at Fürstenland, Ukraine, to Hague, Sask., and Cuauhtemoc, Mexico. **C.K.**

Olgafeld, a village in the Fürstenland Mennonite settlement, province of Taurida, South Russia, founded on the lands of a prince; its inhabitants were members of the Fürstenland Mennonite Church, a subsidiary of the Chortitza Mennonites; in 1905 it numbered 242 members with 139 children. (*ML III*, 299.)

Olgino, name of several Mennonite villages in Russia. In the province of Ekaterinoslav (now Dnyepropetrovsk), volost of Novosofiyevka (formerly called Nikolaithal), Schöndorf was founded, later called Olgino, in 1865; in 1910 it had a population of 96. In the province of Semipalatinsk, Siberia, one of the sixteen villages in the Pavlodar settlement was named Olgino. The settlement was made early in the 20th century between Slavgorod and Pavlodar.

In Stavropol province, North Caucasus, a Mennonite settlement was founded in 1895 as a daughter colony of Tempelhof-Orbelianovka, which was a daughter colony of Gnadenfeld, Molotschna, and was named Olgino. There were originally two villages: Olgino with 30 families from the Tempelhof, and Romanovka with 50 families from Orbelianovka. In 1905 and 1910 daughter colonies of these villages were founded and named Loshkarevo and Miropol. The population of the two mother villages was 500 at the time of the founding, with 12,150 acres of land; in 1926 the two villages numbered 600 persons with 10,368 acres of land. The principal occupation of the settlement was agriculture. By introducing the system of fallow, which served as a model for the surrounding native farmers, the yield of land was raised and good crops harvested. Of special interest were fruit growing and viniculture, in which the Mennonites were pioneers. A well-developed social sense is indicated in the organization of institutions such as "Fram" and a credit association. Religiously these settlers were Templers (*q.v.*). (*ML III*, 299.) **T.B., Hege.**

Olijftacxken (*Olive Branch*), a Dutch Mennonite confession of faith (*q.v.*) composed in 1627. The contents are described as follows: "Scriptural instruction, upon what people the Spirit of God rests, also how they are obligated and bound to peace and unity, given in reply to the question: Which are the fundamental, sure, distinctive signs, whereby the children of God and the disciples of Jesus Christ (the Church of God) can and must be identified according to the testimony of the Word of the Lord."

This query is briefly answered: Above all they recognize that Jesus Christ alone is the only cause of the justification of man, of sonship, and the foundation of eternal salvation; the means, however, through which man becomes partaker of the merits of Christ is faith, is derived from God's Word, and is vitalized in man through the Holy Spirit (Rom. 10:17; II Cor. 4:13; Rom. 8:16). And thus man is born of God as he has God as his Father, and Christ as his Brother. These children of God possess all the good and kind gifts of the New Testament, as forgiveness of sin, peace with God, and eternal life. From this follows that the unalterable sign of the children of God and of the disciples of Jesus Christ is the true and only saving faith, which is effective in love (Gal. 5:6; Acts 8:36; 15:11; Matt. 16:18). This faith, which is a firm and sure confidence of the heart, not doubting the things that are promised of God in Christ, is stated in detail on pages 21 to 33. It discusses baptism, its benefit and purpose, communion, the servants of the church, their choice and ordination, footwashing, marriage, secular office, the oath, separation and shunning, the resurrection of the dead and that in their own bodies in which they lived, and finally the last judgment and eternal ruin.

This confession of faith of the Dutch Mennonites was formulated by the four Amsterdam preachers of the Flemish (Lamist) congregation, Tobias Govaertsz (van den Wijngaert), Pieter Jansz (Moyer), Abraham Dircksz (Bierens), and Dirck Dircksz. Inspired by the Waterlander Elder Hans de Ries (*q.v.*), who had given much thought and effort to reuniting the discordant and divided body of the Mennonite church in Holland, they sent a letter to the Dutch congregations in 1626, in which they asked three questions: (*a*) What are the basic marks of a Christian church? (*b*) Are these distinctives only found in Flemish congregations? (*c*) Is making peace forbidden by the Scriptures? When the congregations failed to give adequate answers the four Amsterdam preachers answered the three questions themselves and drew up a confession which was sent with a presentation of peace and a *Brief tot Vreed-Bereydinge* (Letter for Preparing Peace), dated Sept. 16, 1627, to the congregations in the provinces of Groningen, East and West Friesland, Overijssel, Utrecht, Holland, Zeeland, and Flanders. This confession was printed in 1629 and separately reprinted at least four times (Haarlem 1631, 1636, Amsterdam 1647, 1661), and also published in *Algemeene Belijdenissen* (Amsterdam, 1665) and *Handelinge der Vereenigde Vlaemse en Duytse Doopsgesinde Gemeynten* (Vlissingen, 1666). The complete Dutch title is *Christelijcke Geloofs Belijdenisse des Olijf-Tacxken: of Schriftuerlijcke aenwijsingh over wat lieden den Vrede Godts staet, oock hoe deselve tot Vrede en Eenigheyt verplicht ende verbonden zijn.*

The *Olijftacxken* was a messenger of peace. On the basis of this confession of the Flemish and a confession compiled by the Frisians and High Germans (Confession of Jan Cents 1630) an attempt was made to bring about a union between the two factions. A conference was held to that end in Amsterdam, Oct. 2-5, 1630, and after thorough preparation the Flemish and the Frisian High German congregations were united. On April 26, 1639, a meeting was held in the Singel Church of Amster-

dam, which was attended by more than 3,000 persons. NEFF, vDZ.

Kühler, *Geschiedenis* II, 184-200; Schijn-Maatschoen, *Geschiedenis* II, 171 f., where an account is given of the use of this confession in the Hamburg-Altona congregation; *Inv. Arch. Amst.* I, No. 572; II, No. 1242; *ML* III, 301 f.

Olijftak, a Mennonite home for the aged at Heemstede near Haarlem, Dutch province of North Holland, opened on Sept. 15, 1956. (*DJ* 1957, 26-29.)
vDZ.

Olijftak, the name of a new Mennonite church at Amsterdam-Slotermeer, Netherlands, dedicated on Oct. 28, 1956. (*DJ* 1957, 30-33.) vDZ.

Olive Mennonite Church (MC), formerly called the Shaum congregation, a member of the Indiana-Michigan Conference, is located in Olive Twp., Elkhart Co., Ind., 5 miles north of Wakarusa, 1 mile south of Jamestown, and 8 miles southwest of Elkhart. Before 1861-62, the date of the erection of their first Mennonite meetinghouse in this area, the congregation worshiped in a log building along Baugo Creek about one-half mile north of the present meetinghouse. The first preachers were in the Elkhart County Circuit, the center of which was Yellow Creek. Daniel Moyer (1812-64), originally of Bucks County, Pa., moved from Ashland County, Ohio, to a farm west of Jamestown in 1848. He was killed in a train wreck near Hillsdale, Mich., on a preaching trip to Canada on Dec. 21, 1864. Daniel Brenneman served in the Yellow Creek Circuit for ten years, until his expulsion in 1874. In 1871 Henry Shaum (1826-92) was ordained preacher at Olive, and Henry Christophel deacon. In 1888 a new brick meetinghouse was built, which was rebuilt in 1948. In 1896 Jacob Shank (d. 1905), a son of Michael Shank, a preacher living at Lakeville, St. Joseph Co., Ind., and the father of Clarence Shank (ord. 1917), a retired preacher of the congregation, was ordained preacher at Olive. In 1908 the congregation imported D. A. Yoder, a young preacher, from the near-by Holdeman congregation to serve as pastor. In 1910 he was ordained bishop. In 1951 J. C. Wenger, in the North Goshen congregation, was called as pastor and ordained bishop here in place of D. A. Yoder, who was retired at that point, and Elno Steiner, the present pastor, was ordained to the ministry. The membership in 1957 was 260. In 1933 the Olive Mennonite Church established a mission outpost at Crumstown (*q.v.*), which later became independent, and in 1950 at Hudson Lake near New Carlisle, Ind. The deed for the land on which the church stands was granted by Jacob and Mary Shaum to "The Old Menonite Church" in 1872, ten or more years after the erection of the meetinghouse. Olive is said to have had the first Mennonite Sunday school in Indiana, the organizer being John F. Funk (*q.v.*). J.C.W.

Oliver United Mennonite Church (GCM), located near the town of Oliver, B.C., a member of the Conference of the United Mennonite Churches in B.C., began in 1933, when the settlers, Johann Harms, Jakob Harms, and Abraham Spenst, came from the prairie provinces of Canada. The first preacher, Jakob Thiessen, came in 1938. The congregation was organized on June 19, 1938. The first meetinghouse was dedicated in November 1939; it was enlarged in 1942 to seat 100. The members are immigrants from Russia in 1874 and 1923. In 1954 the congregation had 43 members, with G. A. Neufeld as pastor.   C.G.T.

Olivier Willemsz (Willemssens), an Anabaptist martyr, was burned at the stake at Antwerp, Belgium, on Jan. 24, 1574. He was a native of Nijmegen, Dutch province of Gelderland. He had been a Catholic priest at Leeuwen near Nijmegen. When he left the Catholic Church he moved to Antwerp, opened a bookshop in the Steenhouwersvest, and joined the Mennonites. After some time both Willemsz and his wife were arrested. Willemsz was sentenced to death because of his "heretical faith," but his wife escaped from prison and died at the age of 85.   vDZ.

Mart. Mir. D 692, E 1007; Antw. Arch.-Blad XIII, 192, 200; XIV, 96 f., No. 1081.

Olmütz (Czech, *Olomouc*), until 1636 the capital of Moravia, during the Reformation a bishop's see, as well as the most important fortress of the land. From this town Ferdinand issued his mandate of April 21, 1527, to the government of Tirol, Austria, to guard against the spread of the Anabaptists, to search them out secretly, and to bring them to punishment. Of the Hutterian chronicles that have been preserved, the Codex Managetta, the Breslau Codex, and the Codex Dreller, as well as the Schad Chronicle mention executions in Olmütz and Znaim in 1528. One of these was probably in Olmütz if the total figure of four given in the martyr list of the Hutterite chronicle is correct, for in 1538, according to the Olmütz city chronicle, three additional Anabaptist executions took place there; on April 17, 1538, three Brethren were burned at the stake, "one was a tinsmith, the other a maltster, the third a renegade monk." The records of this trial have unfortunately been lost. A special role was played in the movement in Nikolsburg by the suffragan Martin Göschl (*q.v.*) of Olmütz.

The sessions of the Landtag, meeting alternately in Olmütz and Brno, repeatedly dealt with the Anabaptist problem. Thus the Three Kings Landtag in Olmütz ordered the estates not to tolerate any Anabaptists on their lands, a resolution that was frequently renewed, as in the Reminiscere Landtag in 1546, but never carried out. In the 1570's, when the Moravian nobles levied more and more burdens on the Brethren in return for freedom of worship, Olmütz was often the scene of these decisions.

The taxation of the Anabaptists had begun at the Brno Landtag of 1570 with a property tax, to which a poll tax was soon added. This tax was increased by the Olmütz Landtag in 1576, so that for the next ten years an annual tax of five Groschen was levied on all the Anabaptists, male and female. The Brethren found themselves in a difficult position in regard to taxes; they were of course willing to help meet the needs of the country, but did not want to put their means at the disposal of the em-

peror for military purposes, since this was contrary to their religious principles. They therefore refused to pay any taxes that were destined for military needs, and in their place paid the equivalent in goods. The Olmütz Winter Landtag, 1582, imposed a special tax of two Groschen on every male over twenty years of age to defray necessary national expenses. In addition, the Brethren were forbidden to buy grain in the villages except on the market days. The Three Kings Landtag of 1584 assessed all Anabaptists above eighteen years of age with four Groschen per person, payable in two installments; but at the Olmütz July Landtag the tax was reduced by the magistrate Hynek von Waldstein. The *Geschicht-Buch* writes about it: "Therefore we thanked God not a little and took it for a dispensation and intervention of God. For the brotherhood bore much burden of their conscience and worry for a time. Which we often made known to our lords and actually told them that we could not let such a thing happen any more, but would abandon all our farms and would dare to endure a great tribulation for that reason, before we would any longer accept these taxes and let them be taken from us, as they have hitherto themselves taken and reduced the debt, because we would not pay it."

The Olmütz Landtag of 1592 again considered the prohibition of buying and selling grain through the Brethren as well as the serving and sale of wine in their houses. The former should be permitted only on market days; if they disobeyed, the grain was to be confiscated. In respect to the latter, the lords should see to it that the Brethren paid the fee determined for the sale of wine. The January Landtag of 1594 in Olmütz decided that "since the Anabaptists of this land enjoy enough and contribute little in comparison with the national demands," they were to be assessed eight guilders in addition to the twenty already imposed upon each house in which they had a kitchen. But it was left to the lords to collect this fine from their Anabaptist tenants or pay it themselves. Concerning the May Landtag at Olmütz in 1599 the *Geschicht-Buch* reports that since they were unable to pay this tax for conscience' sake, the lords took from them in this year oxen, grain, wine, fat hogs, cows, and sheep.

Further Landtags at Brno and Znaim increased the taxes still further. The July Landtag of 1614 assessed each Bruderhof 100 guilders, together with additional extra taxes. Again the equivalent in goods was taken, since the Brethren, who "a few years ago gave cheerfully, now refused to pay." At the June Landtag of 1618 at Olmütz the tax was raised to 150 guilders per Bruderhof in order to raise money for armies. The Anabaptists did not pay this tax "destined for a wicked war and bloodshed," and therefore "in many places cattle, grain, wine, and other wares were taken, but cheaper than we would have sold them," so that the sorely pressed Brethren, already impoverished by the quartering of soldiers, were burdened anew.

At the Olmütz Landtag of 1625 Cardinal Dietrichstein wished to have the few Anabaptists expelled who were still retained in the service of the nobles on the border of Lower Austria and Hungary. But he did not have his way this time; he therefore requested an imperial mandate to accomplish that end.

The final trace of the Anabaptists is found in the baptismal records of the parish of St. Mauritz in Olmütz, which state that several Anabaptists, probably returning from Hungary, were baptized according to Roman Catholic ritual. P.DE.

Beck, *Geschichts-Bücher;* Paul Dedic, "Die Gesch. d. Protestantismus in Olmütz," in *Jahrbuch für die Gesch. der Protestanten im ehemaligen Oesterreich* LII-LVII (1931-36); Franticek Hruby, "Die Wiedertäufer in Mähren," in *Archiv für Ref.-Gesch.* XXX (Leipzig, 1933-34); Wolkan, *Geschicht-Buch;* Zieglschmid, *Chronik; ML* III, 300 f.

Olyverynken 's Keysers, an Anabaptist martyr, was burned at the stake with Martinken Meere and Janneken Dhanins on Aug. 19, 1573, at Gent, Belgium. Olyverynken was a daughter of Joos van Deinze and a sister of Marie 's Keysers (*q.v.*), who died in prison at Gent on May 13, 1573. During the execution of Olyverynken and her comartyrs, who were gagged to prevent their speaking to the bystanders, an insurrection arose, when the soldiers tried to drive the crowd, which was in sympathy with the victims, from the Vrijdagsmarkt. (Verheyden, *Gent,* 64, No. 230.) vDZ.

Ombu, El: see El Ombu.

Ommelanden, the region around the city of Groningen (*q.v.*), now together with this city forming the Dutch province of Groningen, where Anabaptism found entry as early as 1530. Menno Simons stayed here from the end of 1536 or early 1537 until 1540. Later on there were a number of Mennonite congregations in this area, nearly all belonging to the (Groningen) Old Flemish. (See also **Groningen, Province of.**) vDZ.

DB 1906, 28 f.; Kühler, *Geschiedenis,* 143 ff., 167, *et passim;* K. Vos, *Menno Simons* (Leiden, 1914) 64 f.; *ML* III, 302.

Ommelands(ch) is a Dutch dialect spoken in the Ommelanden (*q.v.*), the area around Groningen. It is very similar to Low German, spoken in Northwestern Germany. vDZ.

Omsk, a city in the Omsk Region, Siberia, located at the confluence of the Irtysh and Ob rivers, a significant railroad center on the Trans-Siberian Railroad, was founded in 1716 and was formerly the capital of Western Siberia and of Akmolinsk province. With the expansion of Siberian trade it became the meeting place of European businessmen and Asiatics seeking an outlet for their products.

Omsk became the gateway of the Mennonites into Siberia. Contrary to their tradition in European Russia, the first Mennonites in Siberia settled in the city of Omsk. Peter J. Wiens, the first Mennonite known to have settled in Siberia, started a business there in 1897, maintaining a general store and a store for farm machinery in Mokraya. In addition he farmed some land. Later he also established a branch of his farm implement store in the city of Slavgorod (*q.v.*). His business in Omsk grew rapidly and he built a large two-story building on the Vtoroy Vsvos in Mokraya. All of his property was confiscated during the Revolution of 1917.

In 1902 Johann P. Isaak and his brother bought some land south of Omsk in Kulomzino on the Irtysh River. Later, when Novo-Omsk, the railroad station of Omsk, located a few miles south, was established here, he sold some of his farm land very favorably. A. A. Lepp sold his mill at Barvenkovo (*q.v.*) in the Ukraine and came to Kulomzino, where he purchased land from Johann P. Isaak on which he built a five-story steam-driven flour mill. Later he sold the mill and built a factory. One of the Mennonites who found their way to Omsk was a banker, Jakob Hildebrand, the son-in-law of P. J. Wiens. Dr. Johann Isaak was an oculist there (1914-20). Some Mennonites found employment in Russian and foreign business enterprises. Jakob Epp of Ivanovka worked in Omsk after the Revolution of 1917 and represented the Mennonites there. In 1911 the Mennonites established a Zentralschule in Kulomzino (see **Omsk Mennonite Zentralschule**).

Omsk was also of significance for the Mennonite settlers in Siberia as the center for agents trying to serve land-hungry Europeans. In this respect Omsk was the gateway for the Mennonites looking for cheap land in Siberia. Some of the land agents tried to take advantage of the inexperienced land seekers (Hildebrand, 28).

During and after World War II Omsk very likely became the residence of Mennonites in exile and dispersion. Numerous letters have come from the city in recent years indicating this. Aganetha Klassen wrote from Omsk that she and her family, formerly of Nieder-Chortitza, were living in the city (*Bote,* April 15, 1955, p. 7). Peter Bärg, formerly of the province of Ufa, also reported that he and his family were living in the city of Omsk (*Menn. Rundschau,* Feb. 24, 1954, p. 5, 8). C.K.

J. J. Hildebrand, *Sibirien* (Winnipeg, 1952); Gerhard Fast, *In den Steppen Sibiriens* (Rosthern, 1957).

Omsk Mennonite Brethren Church: see **Tchunayevka** Mennonite Brethren Church.

Omsk Mennonite Church was established in the Omsk Mennonite settlement (*q.v.*) in Western Siberia in 1906. The church was first known as the "Sibirische Mennonitische Kirchengemeinde" and later as the Alexandrovka Mennonite Church, since the church building was located in the village of Alexandrovka. Originally the Mennonites and Mennonite Brethren settling along the Trans-Siberian railroad west of Omsk forming the Omsk settlement, and who came from the Ukraine and Samara, worshiped together in private homes. When the Mennonite Brethren organized the Tchunayevka M.B. Church (*q.v.*) steps were taken to organize a Mennonite church. B. Fast and Jakob Gerbrandt (*q.v.*) took the initial steps at a meeting held in Margenau in 1906 under the leadership of Jakob Peters, where B. Fast was chosen as the leading minister. Twenty-one baptismal candidates were given instruction and were baptized by Gerbrandt in 1907. On September 22 at a meeting attended by the elders H. Unruh and H. Peters of the Molotschna settlement, a constitution was adopted, and a decision taken to erect a church. On September 24 Jakob Voth was ordained minister. Under the leadership of B. Fast, who visited the scattered members of the large settlement, the congregation grew. P. Bergen, W. Funk, P. Isaak, Käthler, and P. P. Fröse were added as ministers.

On Nov. 27, 1911, the congregation decided to elect its own elder. Peter P. Bergen was elected and ordained by Elder Boschmann. In Kiryanov, the center of the "Apostolische Brüdergemeinde" (q.v.), an Adrian was elected minister. Enns and Wiebe were added to the ministry to serve in the area of the city of Omsk. By 1913 a total of 97 persons had been added to the Omsk Mennonite Church by baptism. On Oct. 6, 1913, the first meetinghouse in Alexandrovka was dedicated.

Unser Blatt regularly carried reports of the work of the Omsk congregations from 1926-27. During this time B. Bergen was the elder. Ministers named are A. Isaak, P. P. Fröse, Harder, B. Fast, and Johann Teichgräf. The congregation was very active in Bible conferences, song festivals, and mission work. It supported the Ob Mission (q.v.). In 1927 the congregation had a membership of over 400. The church observed a harvest festival on Oct. 2, 1927. In addition to the Alexandrovka church there were numerous other smaller congregations about which little information is available. In the smaller communities the Mennonites and the Mennonite Brethren continued to worship together.

P. P. Fröse of Ekaterinovka, reporting on his visit to the scattered members of the church during the winter of 1925, relates that he preached in Neu-Datchino north of Omsk, from where he proceeded to Kiryanovka, Trussovka, Deveterikovka, Khaldeyevka, and Ivanokva, all of which belonged to the followers of Hermann Peters, the "Apostolische Brüdergemeinde" (q.v.), at that time under the leadership of Heinrich J. Warkentin. He found a good reception and had an opportunity to preach in the churches. He particularly visited the Chortitza village in which members of various groups resided but which had no minister.

During the 1930's the organized religious activities had to be discontinued and most of the religious workers were exiled. After Stalin's death in 1953 a revival of interest in religious and church work was noticeable. Helena P. Petkau near Luzino, Omsk Region, wrote that Mennonites have started to meet and worship together because of hunger for the Word of God, although they had no minister (*Menn. Rundschau,* August 1955, p. 14). (See also Omsk Mennonite Settlement.) C.K.

"Ueber Gründung, Stand und Arbeit der sibirischen mennonitischen Kirchengemeinden 1906-1913," *Menn. Jahrbuch,* No. 10, 1913, p. 125 ff.; Gerhard Fast, *In den Steppen Sibiriens* (Rosthern, 1957) 142 ff.; *Unser Blatt* I, 29, 129, 174; II 373; III, 11, 73.

Omsk Mennonite Settlement, formerly in the Akmolinsk Region, now partly in the Omsk Region and Kazakh SSR, Western Siberia, is located between the cities of Petropavlovsk (q.v.) and Omsk (q.v.), extending some 100 miles east to the railroad station of Tatarsk. This was the first Mennonite settlement in Siberia, expanding gradually some 300 miles on both sides of the Trans-Siberian Railroad between Petropavlovsk and Tatarsk, centering primarily around Omsk. Omsk and Petropavlovsk became the gateways for the establishments of this settlement as well as for the establishments of other Mennonite settlements in Siberia, such as Slavgorod (q.v.) and Pavlodar (q.v.). The first Mennonites to settle in this area and in Siberia in general came to the city of Omsk (q.v.), where Peter J. Wiens started a business in 1897.

(1) *Kulomzino.* Kulomzino was the station on the left side of the Irtysh River near the city of Omsk. Johann P. Isaak had bought some land here in 1902 which was later incorporated into the city of Omsk (q.v.).

(2) *Tchunayevka.* In 1899 the families of Johann Matthies, Franz Balzer, Julius Dick, and Peter Dick, of the province of Taurida, and H. Ewert and Gerhard Ewert, of Samara, bought 4,680 acres of land south of the Trans-Siberian Railroad a few miles west of the city of Omsk, and established the village of Tchunayevka. These were the first Mennonite families to settle on land in Siberia. One end of the village was called Orloff because the owner, Heinrich Warkentin, preferred this name. Gerhard Ewert and Peter Engbrecht established a steam-driven flour mill in this area.

(3) *Tchukreyevka* was a Mennonite village located north of the Trans-Siberian Railroad, about three miles west of the city of Omsk. Among the early settlers were Franz, Peter, David Thiessen, and the sons of Johann P. Isaak. In addition to grains the settlers raised vegetables, for which they found a profitable market in the city.

(4) *Maryanovka* was a railroad station west of Omsk. North of the railroad station and five miles east was the village of Sharapov, which had been bought in 1904 by Jakob and Heinrich Dück, Crimean Mennonites. Other families living there were Jakob Goossen, Abram Wiens, and Jakob Schierling. The village had a school. Worship services for the Mennonite Church were conducted by Johann Teichrieb and for the Mennonite Brethren by Jakob Fast. Teichrieb later emigrated to Paraguay. This village achieved considerable prosperity. During the Revolution of 1917 a number of Mennonites were killed. Four miles east of Sharapov near the station of Alonsk was the Renpenning estate, owned by the manufacturer Jacob Renpenning, formerly of Fabrikerwiese, Molotschna. Further east near the station of Luzino was a Mennonite village which bore the same name.

(5) *Moskalenko* is located west of Maryanovka, east of Isil'-Kul, and south of the Trans-Siberian Railroad. This was a business center in which some Mennonites had located. A steam flour mill was owned by a number of Mennonites. A Mennonite village named Ekaterinovka was located in the vicinity of Moskalenko. This was a scattered village with a school. The ministers of the Mennonite Church were Peter P. Bergen, elder, and Peter P. Fröse, who perished in exile. A number of Mennonite estate owners lived in this area, including Johann Rahn and Jakob Konrad.

(6) *Margenau* is located twelve miles east of Isil'-Kul and one mile south of the station of Gorkoye. According to a Russian map of 1946, the station is now called Margenau and not Gorkoye. North of the railroad was the village of Hamberg (Puchkovo). Both villages were located on rented land.

Margenau was the center for a number of smaller hamlets and estates. One mile away was the estate of Ivanovka owned by Heinrich Epp and his children. Three miles south of Margenau was the village of Nikolaifeld, where the ministers Johann Käthler and Peter Isaak were located. Five miles from Margenau was the village of Alexanderkrone with a school taught for a while by H. H. Friesen. In the vicinity was the large estate of Alexeyevka owned by a Reimer. The station Kuyanbar was located six miles east of Margenau (Gorkoye). South of it was the village of Korneyevka named after Cornelius Siemens. The minister of the community was Jakob Heide. South of this village was the large estate of Johann Heinrichs. East of this estate was another, named Grigoryevka after the owner Gerhard Dück. Another place occupied by Mennonites was Bogunovo.

(7) *Isil'-Kul*, a larger railroad center half way between Omsk and Petropavlovsk, attracted a number of Mennonites who established businesses there. Numerous estates and villages were also established in the vicinity. Among them was the estate owned by Peter Funk, who had a large orchard. His married children also lived in the vicinity. Six miles north of Isil'-Kul were the following villages: Friedensruh, Tiegerweide, Rosenort, Feodorovka, Petrovka. The settlers came mostly from Zagradovka. Bückert, the Mennonite Brethren minister, lived in Rosenort.

(8) *Bulayevo*, a railroad station 25 miles east of Isil'-Kul, north of which a number of Mennonite families settled.

(9) *Tokushi* is a railroad station between Bulayevo and Petropavlovsk. Four miles north of Tokushi was the Mennonite village of Friesenov (*q.v*), founded by Peter, Johann, Nikolai Friesen and others in 1901. This place was sometimes called Friesenhof or Perfilyevka after the former owners. Four miles from Friesenov was the Mennonite village of Mikhaylovka. Some of the settlers here were Johann Dück, Wilhelm and Gerhard Janzen, and Peter Harder, ministers. They worshiped in school buildings. East of Tokushi, next to the railroad town of Asanovsky, was located the Mennonite village of Osanovo.

These are the major Mennonite settlements, villages, and estates established by the Mennonites along the Trans-Siberian Railroad between the cities of Petropavlovsk and Omsk. The city of Petropavlovsk also had some Mennonites, among them Johann Friesen, who was the proprietor of a steam flour mill.

North and east of the city of Omsk some additional Mennonite villages and estates were located, as follows:

(10) Apostolic Brethren (Hermann Peters group); Apostolische Brüdergemeinde (*q.v.*), a group founded by Hermann Peters (*q.v.*) in the Molotschna settlement as an independent branch of the Mennonite Brethren, who lived for a while in Crimea, and then moved to Siberia in 1900-1, where they established the village of Trussovka (*q.v.*), 25 miles north of Omsk and Ivanovka. Another group settled northeast of Omsk on the Om River, six and one-half miles from Valerino, and established Kir-

yanovka, Khaldeyevka, and Devyeterikovka. Numerous additional smaller and larger estates and industries were established. The settlers here were industrious and successful farmers, some of them engaging in dairying and the production of barley, oil, milling. Another village of Mennonites and Mennonite Brethren in this area was called Chortitza.

(11) *Maslyanovka* and *Smolyanovka* were located about eight miles north of the station of Novolyubino on the Omsk-Tyumen Railroad east of the Ob River. This land was not purchased like all other land of the Omsk Mennonite settlement, but was obtained through a government grant similar to the Slavgorod settlement land. Masylanovka was a regular Mennonite village with a school and with its own worship services. The minister was Peter Wiebe. Smolyanovka was located six miles distant. The farmers lived on their own land and had their own school. The ministers were Martin Hübert and Nikolai Siemens.

(12) *Other Settlements.* There were some Mennonites at Kremlov, 20 miles from Omsk. Near Barodin not far from Kremlov were some Mennonite estates owned by Philipp Wiebe, Jakob Rehann, David and Peter Unrau, Dietrich Kröker, and others. North of Omsk near Devyeterikovka (Deyatirikovo) there were some Mennonites who had come originally from Grimea. Neu-Dachnoye, south of the Trans-Siberian railroad station of Karatkansk, was the easternmost Mennonite village of the Omsk settlement.

The total population of the Omsk Mennonite settlement was 3,512 in 1926. The amount of land owned and farmed by the Omsk Mennonites is hard to determine. It is variously estimated at 81,000 to 1,080,000 acres. This settlement prospered economically and overcame its pioneering difficulties much more rapidly than did the Slavgorod settlement. This was partly due to the fact that the settlers came with money, and above all that they settled along the railroad lines and did not encounter the severe pioneer difficulties of the Slavgorod settlers. They were as a rule close to the markets, some of them engaging in industry, milling, and business. The cultural level of the settlement was also higher than that of Slavgorod. Although they had difficulties in maintaining schools for smaller groups since they were much more scattered, they usually had qualified teachers and adequate teaching facilities. By 1911 a school board and a Zentralschule had been created in Kulomzino, the railroad station of Novo-Omsk. Among the teachers were Gerhard Gäde, Benjamin Schellenberg, and Jacob Hübert. After World War I a Mennonite secondary school was established in Margenau. Some of the teachers were Abram Schierling, Wilhelm Wilmsen, Jacob Epp, Aron Rempel, Suse Löwen, Agatha Friesen, Hans Braun, and Hans Legiehn. The school building burned down around 1923 but was rebuilt. The school was soon taken over by the Soviets but continued to function.

In 1921 there was a teachers' conference of all German teachers of West Siberia, in which the Slavgorod Mennonite teachers also participated. Some German professors of the University of Omsk were among the speakers. During and immediately after the Revolution the Mennonites of the Omsk settlement suffered severely, particularly those who had attained a certain status of prosperity as estate owners, businessmen, or industrialists. Many were put to death or exiled. In the 1920's some gradually found their way to Canada or later in the 1930's to South America. During the NEP period the economic life of the Omsk Mennonites was revived. They took active part in the program of the All-russischer Mennonitischer Landwirtschaftlicher Verein (AMLV). A. J. Unger reported (*Der Praktische Landwirt,* June-July 1926, p. 11) that their co-operative had established a cheese factory which was functioning satisfactorily, that they had purchased some mills and were going into the milling industry, and that their seed selection program and other business operations were successful. In the same issue J. Epp reported that their co-operative had purchased 25 Fordson tractors and that they had made tremendous progress since 1921 when they had reached the lowest ebb; conditions had improved so much that the "American fever" was gradually disappearing, although some had left for Canada. P. F. Fröse, of Moscow, who visited the settlement during the winter of 1925-26, reported good progress. The AMLV had 500 members in Omsk. Soon collectivization, exile, and the suppression of organized religious activities were similar to those of the other Mennonite settlements. (See also **Omsk** Mennonite Church, and **Tchunayevka M.B. Church**.)

Before, during, and after World War II many of the Mennonites who had been evacuated and exiled from the Ukraine were brought to the Omsk Region, some of whom are now located in the city of Omsk (*q.v.*). Mrs. M. Friesen, formerly of Nieder-Chortitza, reported that she and others were living in Zontsovka, Isil'-Kul, Omsk Region (*Bote,* Aug. 17, 1955, p. 7). Helena P. Petkau wrote that they are living near Luzino in Petrovka, Omsk Region, with other Mennonites; they meet to sing and worship, but have no minister (*Menn. Rundschau,* Aug. 8, 1955, p. 14).   C.K.

Gerhard Fast, *In den Steppen Sibiriens* (Rosthern, 1957); J. J. Hildebrand, *Sibirien* (Winnipeg, 1952); *Unser Blatt* I (1926) 129, 155, 174, 247, 308; II (1927) 333, 373; III (1927) 11, 15, 42, 73.

Omsk Mennonite Zentralschulen. The Mennonites of the Omsk settlement in Siberia early recognized the need for a secondary school. A school board created for this purpose established a Zentralschule in Kulomzino, later called Novo-Omsk, which became the railroad center of the city of Omsk (*q.v.*), in 1911. The first teachers were Gerhard J. Gäde, B. J. Schellenberg, and Jacob Hübert. The school was closed in 1915, during World War I. Whether it was reopened after the Revolution is not clear.

After World War I a Zentralschule was opened in Margenau. Margenau is located on the Trans-Siberian Railroad between Omsk and Isil'-Kul. The following teachers taught there: Abram Schierling, Wilhelm Wilmsen, Maria Wilmsen, Jakob Epp, Aron Rempel, Suse Löwen, Agatha Friesen, Hans Braun, and Hans Legiehn. The Soviet government later took over the school and adjusted it to its educational system.   **C.K.**

Gerhard Fast, *In den Steppen Sibiriens* (Rosthern, 1957) 143; A. A. Töws, *Mennonitische Märtyrer I* (N. Clearbrook, 1949) 332 ff.

Onckel, Aleydt van, a noble lady of Amsterdam, the widow of Vrederick van Onckel, had joined the Anabaptists. In 1536, or even before, she was drowned at Amsterdam because of "Lutheranism" (i.e., heresy) and Anabaptism. Her considerable property was confiscated. (Grosheide, *Bijdrage,* 100 f.)   VDZ.

Oncken, Johann Gerhard (1800-84), the founder of the European Continental Baptist movement, had been influenced considerably by an American Baptist professor of theology, Barnabas Sears, who was attending a German theological school, and so developed the conviction of baptism by immersion as the correct form which should constitute a prerequisite for church membership. He and a group of sympathizers were baptized in the Elbe at Hamburg. He began his service with Pastor Rautenburg at Hamburg, where the first German Sunday school was started in 1825. These influences led Oncken to become the founder of the European Continental Baptist movement in 1834.

During his activities in Hamburg Oncken became acquainted with Jacob Gysbert van der Smissen, a deacon in the Mennonite Church, who freely supported various Christian movements even beyond his own denominational boundaries. Oncken also visited some of the Mennonite churches in Poland (*q.v.*) in 1833, preaching among them six weeks and greatly enjoying their spirituality and their well-attended church services.

When the new movement of the Mennonite Brethren Church began in the Chortitza settlement of Russia, their leader, Abraham Unger, had already become acquainted with Oncken and solicited his visit and influence upon the new movement. Oncken accepted the invitation, and spent ten days visiting some of the newly established, but yet unorganized groups in 1869, and assisted in the ordination of Elder Abraham Unger as elder, and Aron Lepp as minister, and Cornelius Unger and Benjamin Nickel as deacons. Oncken continued his influence upon this group of the Mennonite Brethren Church by correspondence. His influence upon the moral standards of this group, however, was not quite as effective, for Oncken is known to have used tobacco, which several of his admirers in the newly established Mennonite Brethren Church continued to do. Aron Lepp opposed this to the extent that the church excommunicated all those who persisted in the use of tobacco, thus losing ten to twelve influential members.   J.J.T.

J. Lehmann, *Geschichte der deutschen Baptisten* (3rd ed., 1922-23); J. H. Rushbrook, *Some Chapters of European Baptist History* (London, 1929); Ed. Scheve, *Dem Herrn hintennach sehen* (1908); Rudolf Donat, *Wie das Werk begann. Entstehung der deutschen Baptistengemeinden* (Kassel, 1958); *ML* III, 302 ff.

O'Neal (Ark.) Mennonite Brethren Mission Chapel, a frame building 28 x 42 feet, was erected by the Southern District M.B. Conference and dedicated on Feb. 24, 1957. The workers in charge are Mr. and Mrs. George H. Klassen. G.H.K.

Onecho Mennonite Church (GCM), originally known as the First Mennonite Church of Colfax, located at Colfax, Whitman Co., Wash., was organized in July 1893 by J. B. Baer with 24 members of Swiss origin. Paul Aeschliman, the first elder, served for 44 years. He was followed by W. Harley King in 1936 and by P. D. Unruh in 1946. The first church erected in 1895 was replaced by the present building in 1926. The congregation is a member of the Pacific District Conference. In 1954 it had a membership of 134. P.D.U.

Ones, Foppe: see Foppe Ones.

Onnes, a Mennonite family of Groningen, Netherlands, to which belonged Michiel Onnes Mz, b. March 14, 1879, at Groningen, d. June 2, 1950, at Veendam. He was a Mennonite pastor, serving at Hippolytushoef and 't Stroe on the island of Wieringen in 1905-9, Warga 1909-11, Westzaan 1911-29, and at Zutphen from 1929 until he retired in 1946. During his Westzaan period he also took care of the newly founded congregation of Bussum (*q.v.*), and after his retirement served as temporary pastor at Veendam. In *Doopsgezinde Bijdragen* 1907 he published an important historical paper on Jan ter Borg. (*DJ* 1951, 15 f.) vDZ.

Ontario, a province of Canada (pop. 5,405,000). In 1791 the British colony of Quebec, which had been won from the French in 1759, was divided, and the vast area of wild bush country lying west of the Ottawa River became "Upper Canada." The following year some counties were laid out in each of the four districts. Settlement along the lakes and at the points of entry had already begun, and continued over the next fifty years until all available land in the southern part of the province had been occupied. The physical features and natural resources of the province appealed to immigrants. But the rolling land, heavily timbered and well watered by many streams and small rivers suitable for mill sites and as waterways for the settler's small boat or raft, lay for the most part unseen by the white man.

"In 1783 large numbers of United Empire Loyalists flocked to Canada from the United States. The earliest ones went to Nova Scotia. The principal centres around which these immigrants located, however, were in Upper Canada, at Kingston, York (Toronto), and along the Niagara River. It has been estimated that nearly 50,000 came to Canada between 1783-86. The Loyalists who applied for land grants in Canada at this time were required to prove that they had been attached to the British cause and had suffered, as a consequence, the loss of property, and other abuses. The claim was accepted when supported by a single witness. The grants were made very generously. Governor Simcoe (Nov. 6, 1794) made even more generous offers to attract a class of desirable settlers. The immigrant should receive 200 acres of land and some other assistance. He must profess the Christian religion and he must have a good reputation in the country

from which he came. In the first years of his regime Simcoe had advised the British Consul in Philadelphia that Quakers and like societies should be admitted from Pennsylvania, and would be accorded exemption from bearing arms as had been allowed hitherto by the British government. These inducements from Simcoe and the desire to be under the English king (as will be shown later) caused numerous Mennonite families from Pennsylvania to migrate to the fertile wilderness lands in the Home District and along the Grand River. Possibly the difficulty of securing cheap land in the thickly populated settlements in the older Mennonite communities of Eastern Pennsylvania also played a part in the movement" (Burkholder, 14).

The first Mennonites to settle permanently in what is now the province of Ontario came from Bucks Co., Pa., and in 1786 took up land on the "Twenty Mile Creek," so called because of its distance from the Niagara River. This colony was settled among the present towns of Jordan, Vineland, and Campden, and about 1800 may have numbered about one hundred. It was without a minister until 1801 when, upon the advice of the ministers at Deep Run, Pa., to whom they had appealed for help, Valentine Kratz was chosen minister and John Fretz, deacon. The first meetinghouse was built on the farm of Jacob Moyer in 1810.

At about the same time Mennonites from Lancaster and York counties were settling farther south on the north shores of Lake Erie in what is now Welland County. This colony, also known as the "Black Creek" and Bertie settlement, seems to have been more numerous than that on the "Twenty." There were at least three regular places of worship used by the Mennonites here in these early days: in Bertie Township near Sherkston, near Stevensville known as the Black Creek Church, and on the Niagara River near Chippewa, known as the Miller Church (Riverside). There were also Quaker families in this region. In 1837 there were twenty-five Mennonite and two Tunker families in Willoughby Township, Welland County. However, through the years the picture has reversed and the Brethren in Christ have flourishing congregations here while the Mennonites have died out. Lack of capable church leadership in this community seems to have been the reason for its decline.

The largest settlement of Mennonites in the province was made in what is now Waterloo County, in the west central part of southern Ontario. Quoting Burkholder, "The first settlers, Joseph Schoerg and Samuel Betzner, left their homes in Franklin County, Pa., in the fall of 1799 and travelled as far as the Twenty where they wintered. In the next spring, 1800, they, with their families, followed the Indian trail as far as Brantford, and then went north, along the Grand River and settled on its banks in what is now Waterloo County. The location of their farms is now marked by the Waterloo Pioneers' Memorial Tower erected in 1926, four miles south of Kitchener. These two families were the first white families to settle in what is now Waterloo County. During the early spring of the same year, 1800 (according to Ezra Eby), Samuel Betzner, Sr., and John and Christian Reichert came

Ontario

Scale of Miles

0 5 10   20   30   40   50   60

See map of Waterloo County for details.

LAKE HURON

LAKE ONTARIO

LAKE ST. CLAIR

LAKE ERIE

Chesley Lake Camp (MC)

132 air miles to Markstay Mission (MC)

115 air miles to Monetville (MC)

65 air miles to Minden (MC)

85 air miles to Fort Stewart (MC)

Cedar Grove (MC)

Wideman (MC)

Almira (OOM)
MARKHAM
Altona (OOM)
Reesor (OOM)

Wallenstein (OOM)
Moorefield (MC)
Glen Allen (MC)
Riverdale (AM)

Peel, 4th Concession (OOM)
Goshen (OOM)
Berea (MC)
Hagerman (MC)
Warden Park (MC)

West District (OOA)
Mornington (Nafzigers) (OOA)
Blake (AM)
Zurich (MC)
East District (OOA)
Poole (AM)
WATERLOO CO.
KITCHENER

Ontario Hebrew Mission (MC)
Morningside (MC)
Danforth (MC)
Toronto United (GCM)

TORONTO

LAKE ONTARIO

St. Catharines United (GCM)

Virgil (MB)

Tavistock (AM)
East Zorra (AM)
Cassel (AM)

Home for the Aged (AM)
Ailsa Craig Boys Farm
Nairn (AM)

Hamilton Mission (GCM)
United Menn. Home for the Aged
HAMILTON
St. Catharines (MB)

Niagara United (GCM)

Vineland First Mennonite (MC)
Vineland (MB)
Bethesda Mental Hospital
Vineland United (GCM)

Grace (GCM)
NIAGARA FALLS

Good Will Rescue Mission (AM)
Forest City Menn. Mission (AM)
LONDON

South Cayuga (MC)
Rainham (MC)
Rainham (OOM)

Dunnville United (GCM)

BUFFALO

Bothwell (MC)

Erie View United (GCM)
Port Rowan (MB)

DETROIT

Harrow United (GCM)
Leamington (MB)
Leamington United (GCM)

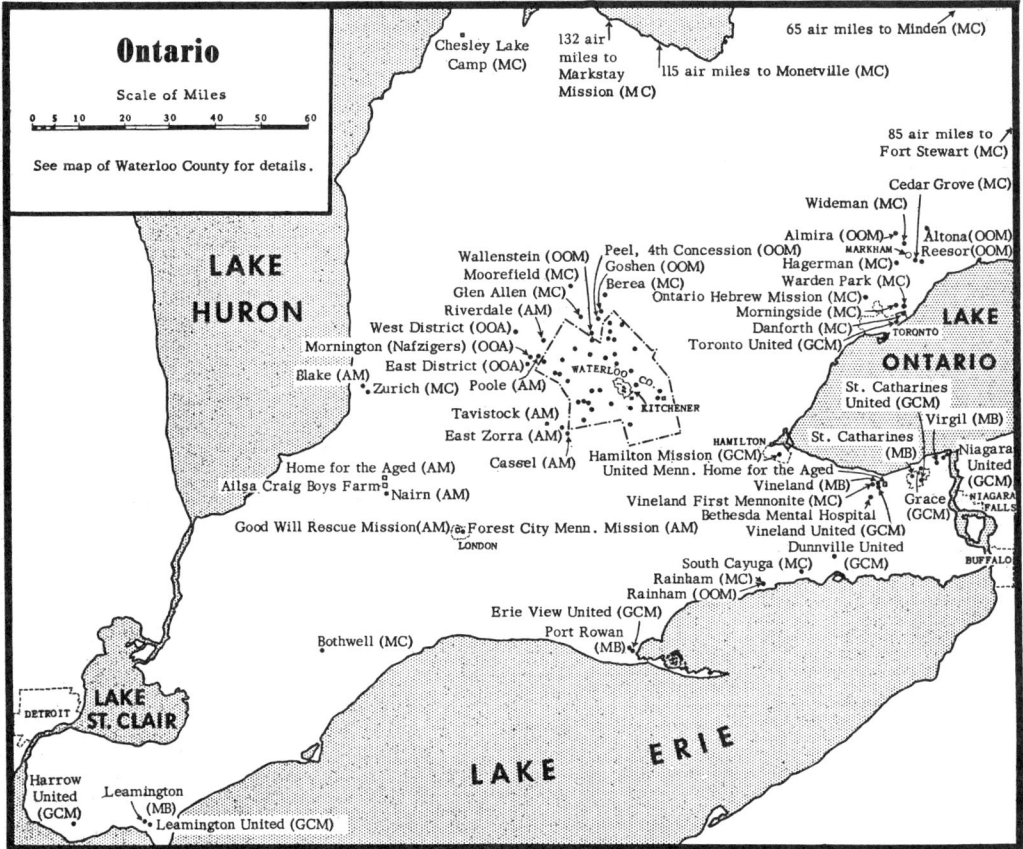

with their families from Lancaster County. David Gingerich of Lancaster County visited the new settlement in 1800 on a tour of investigation and in 1801 came with his family and effects. The same year seven Montgomery County families arrived—three Bechtels, a Kinsey, a Rosenberger, and a Biehn. With them were also several unmarried persons, one of whom was George Clemens. In 1802 a number of other families came from Montgomery, Cumberland, and other Pennsylvania counties. Later in the same year came another company among whom was Joseph Bechtel, who as an ordained man became the first Mennonite minister in the colony, and his family, and John and Samuel Bricker. The general location of these first families was on the east bank of the Grand River near what is now Preston. They organized the first congregation of Mennonites in this part of Ontario, the Hagey (now Preston) church. A little school was started in 1802 near Blair with a Rittenhouse as teacher. The settlement now consisted of at least 25 families with a number of children and young adults.

"These settlers had purchased their lands from Richard Beasley. These farms were part of Block No. 2 of the Six Nations Indians lands. Mr. Beasley was only joint owner, and payment for this land to the Indians, through trustees, was secured by power of mortgage. The titles issued by Beasley were defective because of existing mortgage. Early

in 1803 this defect in the deeds was discovered and the movement to Waterloo immediately stopped. When Mr. Beasley found that his deception was known and that he could not continue to sell the land to the Mennonites, he agreed to sell 60,000 acres of land, practically the whole of the present Waterloo Township, for 10,000 pounds. The matter was taken up by certain Mennonites in Lancaster County and a company was formed and the necessary money was raised. This 60,000 acres was called the German Company Tract. It was divided among the shareholders, by lot, into 134 parcels of 448 acres each. The Company was formed at a meeting held in a home of 'Hannes' Eby, at Hammer Creek, near Lititz in Lancaster County. At this meeting it was urged that the harassed brethren in Canada be given assistance, not for the purpose of material gain, but as a brotherly act. This spirit of helpfulness, without prospect of personal gain, has ever been an outstanding trait in the life of the Mennonites. The Pennsylvania shareholders now became the possessors of lands in Canada. The first installment of $20,000 was carried from Lancaster in solid silver cash in the spring of 1804 and paid over to the proper persons on May 23, 1804. The balance was paid about a year later and clear title was given to the lands of the German Company.

"During the period of uncertainty relative to the land titles, the immigration to Waterloo was halted.

Scarcely any families came during 1803 and 1804. It was during these two years that the Markham settlement north of Toronto began. The Beasley difficulty seems to have been the cause. This difficulty removed, the settlers came again in increasing numbers to Waterloo. Those in Pennsylvania, who had so recently come into possession of fertile lands in the Grand River basin, were desirous of locating upon their holdings. The Lancaster families now predominated among the immigrants. During the years 1805, 1806, and 1807, the Mennonite population more than doubled by immigration. Benjamin Eby, who became the leading figure in the young church in Canada, came from Lancaster in 1807. With him came a large number of Lancaster settlers. This stream of settlers continued with vigor until interrupted by the War of 1812-15" (Burkholder, 34-36).

The Markham settlement was located in York County, north of present Toronto. Henry Wideman, a minister from Montgomery County, Pa., settled near Markham in 1803. In the early years a meetinghouse was erected on his farm and a burying ground begun. Caspar Schoerg (Shirk), brother to the Joseph Schoerg who settled on the Grand River in 1800, came to Markham in 1804 from Franklin County, Pa. Reesors, Hubers, and Stouffers came from Lancaster County the same year. A few years later the Groffs and Barkeys followed. The townships of Vaughan, Pickering, Scarborough, and Whitchurch received some settlers, but the main group was in Markham Township.

"The church in this colony never was large. There were as many as eight regular places of worship, but a few have not been used for some time. Mennonite Brethren in Christ and Wisler divisions decimated the numbers in this county. Neither of the three sections of the church in this area has enjoyed a very marked prosperity following these schisms. Large numbers of the younger generation have gone into other churches. At the present time the three bodies are holding the young people of their families fairly well" (Burkholder, 41).

Other scattered Ontario settlements include Zurich in western Ontario near the shore of Lake Huron, which was established in the 1830's and has continued until the present with both Amish and Mennonite churches. Most of these families came from Waterloo County. In Haldimand County on the shore of Lake Erie, was the Rainham (q.v.) settlement founded by David Hoover of York County, Pa., in 1792. Other Pennsylvania families arrived here, but the group never became large. In 1835-40 numerous families from Welland and Lincoln counties moved into the township of South Cayuga (q.v.) in Haldimand County, while others left for Ohio and Indiana.

Through the years that followed early pioneering, the small, struggling communities grew. The inherent qualities of thrift and industry enabled these Swiss-Germans to prosper and become well-established. Their quiet and simple way of life, coupled with a sense of stewardship of the land they cultivated, very often saved them from mistakes and errors made by their less cautious neighbors, for their own fathers and grandfathers had only lately hewn homes from the wilderness of Pennsylvania.

During the first half century of Mennonitism in Upper Canada (Ontario), agriculture was the predominant occupation. Some operated grist, flour, and saw mills in conjunction with their farms, and a few went into manufacturing enterprises, but they left their mark mainly in the province's agricultural picture. The large bank barn with its deep stone walls, and the neat, well-kept orchard with its variety of fruit trees are only two examples.

However, while good farming and business practices built up the brotherhood in a material way, spiritual zeal and aggressiveness seems to have been often lacking. It is true there were many leaders, Benjamin Eby (q.v.), Jacob Groff, Jacob Moyer, and others, some whose names are not remembered, who were no doubt truly concerned for the well-being and purity of the church. The Methodist and Evangelical churches were very active and they were quick to see that young people with good Mennonite background were desirable members. So over the years there was a gradual, but telling, loss to the Mennonite church. There were also several schisms that divided and weakened the church body. In 1849 Daniel Hoch of Jordan, a minister, separated from the Conference and had sympathizers in each district. In 1855 the Ohio-Canada West Conference was organized at the Carlisle School, Waterloo County. Hoch identified himself with John H. Oberholtzer of Pennsylvania. Hoch's plea for a new life and clean conduct was commended by spiritual people generally, but his method and personality were not acceptable. He worked with the General Conference of Mennonites until 1869, after this with the M.B.C. group; in forming the G.C.M. branch in Canada, he made little progress and his membership dwindled. In 1875 another division took place. Four ministers, three deacons, and several hundred members withdrew and at a conference at Bloomingdale, Ont., formed the United Mennonites. Later, after union with the Pennsylvania (1879) and Ohio (1883) groups, the name "Mennonite Brethren in Christ" was adopted. Some who had harbored dissatisfaction with the parent church from the time of the Hoch schism united actively with the new group. They have been very active in evangelistic work and have grown numerically. In 1949 the name was changed to United Missionary Church. In Ontario (1955) they have 47 congregations and a membership of over 2,400.

Burkholder comments (197), "In the year 1874, when Solomon Eby and John Baer, ministers, and Wm. Hembling and Joseph Schneider, deacons, and many others began what later was known as the Mennonite Brethren in Christ movement, the most aggressive element in the Church was removed. This group desired protracted meetings, prayer meetings and other activities for which the church as a whole was not yet ready, although prayer meetings had been sanctioned by conference in 1847. This schism taught the Church that more active interest must be taken in the gathering of the young into the fold. Some of the methods of the M.B.C. group, in a modified form, would have been acceptable to a large section of the Church, but there were others of a more conservative type who opposed any measure or method to which they had not been accustomed. This conservative group was strongest in Woolwich Township in Waterloo County, but had sympathizers in all the other districts also."

The situation came to a head in 1889 when three bishops and ten ministers and deacons withdrew. They are the "Old Order" Mennonites, sometimes called "Woolwichers" because of their location, sometimes called "Wisler" because of their similarity to the Wisler (q.v.) Mennonites in Indiana, although there never was an organic union or common conference. In 1955 they had 18 congregations and a membership of about 1,800. In 1955 a similar group split off in the Markham and South Cayuga districts.

In 1924 a division took place in the First Mennonite church, Kitchener. About 125 members and their minister, U. K. Weber, withdrew and built their own building on Stirling Avenue, objecting to some of the stricter regulations of the old group. In 1950 they were affiliated with the Eastern District of the General Conference Mennonite Church and had a membership of 475.

Around the turn of the century, a few families from Ontario began to migrate to Western Canada, settling in Southwestern Alberta. Elias W. Bricker left Waterloo County with his family in 1891. Others followed and the colonists became quite numerous. The Ontario Mennonite (MC) Conference appointed S. F. Coffman to spend the year 1901 among the Alberta brethren assisting them in congregational organization. When the congregations had increased sufficiently in number in 1903, a conference was organized known as the Alberta-Saskatchewan Conference, having a present membership of 778.

In Ontario there were also several other immigrant groups besides the Pennsylvania Mennonites, the European Amish, Amish Mennonites, and the Russian Mennonites. Christian Nafziger from Bavaria was the first Amishman to arrive. In 1822, after landing in New Orleans and making his way up through the States, he came to Waterloo and selected a tract of land which comprises the present township of Wilmot. He went to the Governor of Upper Canada who consented to sell 150 acres to each Amish family for a small price and give an additional 50 acres free in return for cutting the trees in the road allowance. Nafziger returned to Germany, coming back to Ontario in 1824, which was the actual beginning of the Amish settlements. Within a few years Amish families from Europe began locating in Wilmot Township. They came from both Bavaria aand Alsace Lorraine. The colony grew and spread west into Perth County and south into Oxford County. Some who originally settled in Ontario later moved to the U.S.A., especially Iowa. However, there are at the present time twelve strong congregations with a total membership of around 2,400. The official name is Amish Mennonite Conference.

In 1886 a division took place in this group. It was decided to build a meetinghouse for worship purposes. Some were not in agreement with this, desiring to continue worship in the homes. They withdrew and are called the "Old Order" Amish Mennonites. They have five congregation and a total membership of about 650.

Russian Mennonites. Another group of Mennonites who are a part of Ontario's history are those who came from Russia in the migrations of 1873 and 1923. During the years from 1874-80, 1,246 families arrived at Toronto en route to Manitoba. Burkholder reports (174), "The immigrants arrived in the summer months, but too late in the season to commence their farming operations in the new country. Because of this, the newcomers were usually distributed among the Ontario Mennonite homes. Large numbers were quartered in Waterloo, 'The Twenty,' and in Markham. In this way opportunity was afforded the newcomers to become partly acquainted with Canadian conditions. It also enabled them to add a little to their capital with which they were about to set up their homes in the western prairie. Contacts were made during this temporary residence in Ontario that were both pleasant and helpful on both sides and lasted for many years." However, these people all went on to Manitoba, none remaining in Ontario. Jacob Y. Shantz (q.v.) of Kitchener rendered great aid to the settlement in Manitoba. Ontario Mennonites raised a large loan for them and furnished the guarantee for a Canadian government loan ($400,000).

After the Bolshevist Revolution of 1917 many more Mennonites were desirous of emigrating. The first group who came to Canada in 1922 went directly to the West. The next year a larger group came and about 800 remained in Ontario, for only a short time; others made their homes here, settling in the Niagara peninsula and in Essex County in the extreme southwestern corner of the province. Some also settled in Waterloo County and others established a colony in Northern Ontario and named it "Reesor" in appreciation of the help rendered them by Thomas Reesor, Markham, who, with S. F. Coffman of Vineland, met these immigrants in Quebec and assisted them greatly. After the second World War (1948-52) many refugees who fled Russia with the retreating German armies were assisted by their relatives and friends in Ontario, and found new homes in the fair province. Most of them have become integrated into existing Russian Mennonite communities. The same is true of the smaller number who came from Paraguay 1950-57. The Ontario Russian Mennonites are in two groups: the Mennonite Brethren, with a total membership of 1,687 in six congregations, and the United Mennonite Church (Canadian District of General Conference) with ten congregations and 2,841 members (1957).

There are also several smaller groups of Mennonites in the province. The Reformed Mennonites have members at several points in Ontario. Their total membership is about 150 in four regular places of meeting. The Hutterian Brethren, whose history parallels that of the Mennonites, also have one "new" colony in the province located near Bright, with a membership of 50, composed largely of Hungarians.

Differences and divisions have lessened the effectiveness of the Mennonite testimony. However, each group has made progress and at the present time there seems to be a greater unity of purpose and more willingness to co-operate with one another than in the past. The main body (Mennonite Conference, MC) has increased numerically, at the present time number 3,840, distributed among 34 congregations. The total membership of all branches of Mennonites in Ontario was 13,333.

The following institutions were operated by the Mennonites in Ontario in 1957: *Schools*—Ontario Mennonite Bible School and Institute at Kitchener (MC, founded in 1907), Rockway Mennonite School (MC, founded in 1945), Eden High School of Virgil (MB, founded in 1945), Mennonite Brethren Bible School at Kitchener (founded in 1943 at Virgil, moved to Kitchener in 1955), United Mennonite Educational Institute at Leamington (GCM, founded in 1946), Emmanuel Bible College at Kitchener (UMC-MBC, founded in 1940); *Homes for the Aged*—Fairview Mennonite Home at Preston (MC, 1943), United Mennonite Home for the Aged at Vineland (GCM, 1955); three rest homes for the aged operated by the Ontario Amish Mennonites: The Maples Rest Home at Tavistock (1952), Craigholm at Ailsa Craig (1953), Milverton Nursing Home at Milverton (1954); Ailsa Craig Boys Farm (1955) operated by the MCC; *Mental Hospitals*—Bethesda Mental Hospital at Vineland (MB, 1937).

Early Ontario Mennonite history has received literary treatment of good quality in two novels by Miss B. Mabel Dunham, the long-time librarian of the Kitchener Public Library: *The Trail of the Conestoga* (Toronto, 1924) and *Toward Sodom* (Toronto, 1927). (See **Literature**, *ME* III, 372.)

P.H.Bu.

L. J. Burkholder, *A Brief History of the Mennonites in Ontario* (Toronto, 1935); A. Eby, *Die Ansiedlung und Begründung der Mennoniten Gemeinschaft in Ontario* (Milford Square, 1872); *Jahrbuch der Ver. Menn.-Gemeinden in Ontario*, 1954 ff.; *Vereinigte Mennoniten Gemeinden in Ontario*, 1956; B. Mabel Dunham, "Beginnings in Ontario," *Menn. Life* V (October 1950); Andrew R. Shelly, "Mennonites of Ontario Today," *Menn. Life* V (October 1950).

Ontario Amish Mennonite Conference is composed of the congregations of the A.M. settlement in Waterloo County, Ont., established in 1824 by immigrants from Alsace-Lorraine and Bavaria, and one small daughter settlement at Zurich, Ont. In 1957 the Conference had 12 congregations with 2,440 members, 7 bishops, 17 ministers, 6 deacons. Although occasional meetings of the ministers of the settlement had been held in the 19th century, these meetings were discontinued about the turn of the century. Attempts at revival in 1918 and 1923 finally resulted in 1925 in a full organization of an annual conference with a constitution adopted June 16, 1925. Not all the congregations in the settlement joined the Conference, the Old Order Amish congregation and the Nafziger and Lichti groups remaining outside. The *Rules and Discipline* of the Conference was adopted in 1926. A small schism was suffered in 1956 when a conservative group withdrew at Milverton under Bishop Valentine Nafziger.

The Conference-sponsored activities include: (1) the Winter Bible School under the administration of a Bible School Board appointed by the Conference (first session 1932); (2) the Mission Board (*q.v.*) organized in 1946, which operates three rest homes and three city missions. A Sunday-school conference has been held annually since 1922. The Amish Mennonite Storm and Fire Aid Union has long been operated (since *c*1865) for the benefit of conference members in co-operation with the other Amish groups in the district.

The Conference has not yet become a member of the Mennonite General Conference (MC), although it is eligible. However, it supports generously all the general activities of the Mennonite Church (MC) including the general boards and institutions, and it elects a member on the General Council of the Mennonite General Conference. The Conference does not elect delegates to the General Conference, although a number of its ministers usually attend its sessions. Proposals have at times been made for a merger with the Ontario Mennonite (MC) Conference, but while good relations obtain between the two, there is at present no serious trend in this direction. O.G.

L. J. Burkholder, *A Brief History of the Mennonites in Ontario* (n.p., 1935); C. Gascho and J. R. Bender, *Bericht der Verhandlungen einer Diener Versammlung der Amischen Mennoniten Gemeinde* (1923).

Ontario Amish Mennonite Mission Board, the home mission agency of the Ontario A.M. Conference (*q.v.*), was organized in 1946. It operates three city missions: the Good Will Rescue Mission in the city of London, Ont., called King Street (1951), the Wellesley Gospel Mission (1953) in Wellesley, Ont., and the Stratford Mission (1952) in Stratford, Ont. It also operates three homes for the aged: Maples Rest Home at Tavistock (1952), Craigholm at Ailsa Craig (1953), Milverton Nursing Home at Milverton (1954). It publishes a joint organ with the Ontario Mennonite Mission Board, the *Ontario Mennonite Evangel* (*q.v.*). H.S.B.

Ontario Conference of Mennonite Brethren Churches. In 1924 a small group of immigrants, members of the Mennonite Brethren and Evangelical Mennonite groups from Molotschna, South Russia, arrived in Waterloo, Ont. They settled in six communities, Kitchener, Hespeler, New Hamburg-Essex County, Port Rowan, and Vineland. On May 24, 1925, these two closely connected faiths amalgamated under the name "Molotschna Mennonite Brethren Church." J. P. Friesen, J. W. Reimer, and J. P. Wiens were instrumental in bringing about this union. Only baptism by immersion was practiced, but other forms of baptism were accepted for transfer members, provided the candidate in question had experienced regeneration.

At first all major transactions of the five affiliated congregations were carried out in Kitchener, even to the extent of having a large annual business session at that church. This arrangement continued until Jan. 31, 1932, when five of these churches united to form a conference, which was registered on July 8, 1932, with the Provincial Government in Toronto as "The Ontario Conference of Mennonite

Brethren Churches." These churches, now autonomous, were as follows: Kitchener 144, Leamington (formerly Essex County) 50, New Hamburg 37, Hespeler 29, and Vineland 27, making a total membership of 287.

The conference showed steady growth and Port Rowan with 33 members was admitted in 1933, Niagara with 48 in 1937, and St. Catharines with 65 members in 1943. In 1952, because of the diminishing size of Hespeler and New Hamburg congregations, and their proximity to Kitchener, they were dissolved, and the members were accepted into the Kitchener church.

The need of belonging to a greater organization was recognized, and on Oct. 25, 1939, the Conference was accepted as a member of the General Conference of Mennonite Brethren Churches of North America as the Ontario District Conference. On June 29, 1946, a change of status took place when the Conference joined the Northern District Conference to form the Canadian Conference of Mennonite Brethren Churches.

The Conference has enjoyed the moderatorship of H. H. Janzen 1932-46, I. H. Tiessen 1946-54, and I. T. Ewert. In August 1955 the Conference noted the following memberships: Kitchener 393, Leamington 181, Port Rowan 123, St. Catharines 399, Vineland 264, and Virgil (formerly Niagara) 483, making a total of 1,843 members. These churches are all located in Southern Ontario not more than 235 miles apart. Since the aims of the Ontario Conference are chiefly directed toward missions, permanent mission stations have been established at Coldwater and Stoney Creek, and a daily vacation Bible school program is actively supported. Services in all six churches are conducted primarily in German, and mission Sunday schools are operated from each center for the benefit of English-speaking children in the surrounding districts.

The Conference sponsors numerous annual conventions, although it convenes semiannually for regular business.

In 1944-47 the Conference owned and operated the Bethesda Home for the Mentally Ill. The institution grew beyond the scope of a small conference; therefore in 1947 the Canadian Conference assumed the responsibility for the project. In 1947 the Conference undertook to administer and finance the Eden Bible and High School at Niagara-on-the-Lake. This school was divided in 1955 and the Bible school moved to Kitchener, while the high school continued at Niagara as Eden Christian College.

J.A.Ku.

Ontario Hebrew Mission (MC) is an organized work under the Ontario Mennonite Conference, established in 1954, directed by J. Ross Goodall, with headquarters in Downsview, Ont., near Toronto. It operates Camp Sholom, a Jewish Mission Camp for family groups, located at Kearney, Ont.

H.S.B.

Ontario Mennonite Bible School and Institute (MC), located in Kitchener, Ont., is an outgrowth of the Bible conference movement. The first extended Bible study class was conducted in 1907 for one week

by S. F. Coffman and L. J. Burkholder, with an attendance of 50-60. The Ontario Conference in 1909 appointed the Bible Study Board to have charge of these classes. The Bible Study Class (later called Bible School) has met annually with the exception of one year, with sessions at first of one or two weeks and later of four weeks or more. In 1918 a course of study was arranged covering the entire Bible, and training in Sunday-school and Christian work extending over a period of six years, and requiring an annual session of six weeks. Attendance and interest in the work were increased by this more regular form of study. In 1929 the course was rearranged to increase the class periods to twelve weeks and shorten the cycle of study to three years. Every year since that time a number of students have finished this course. In 1929 an annex was built to the Kitchener Mennonite Church for the Bible school. Previously the classes had been conducted in the church or in rented quarters in the city. The school is still conducted in the further remodeled First Mennonite Church of Kitchener.

Before 1951 an advanced course was offered to Bible school graduates and others which led the Bible School Board to recommend to Conference the launching of the Ontario Mennonite Bible Institute. It was the conviction of church leaders that there was a need for a Bible course shorter than the regular college Bible course, but more thorough than the Bible school could offer in three months, to meet the need of mature young people who could not attend college. The first session of the Institute was held in 1951-52 for five months, two months before Christmas and three months following.

The teachers who have served or are serving are S. F. Coffman, L. J. Burkholder, Oscar Burkholder, C. F. Derstine, J. B. Martin, Merle Shantz, J. F. Garber, R. S. Koch, Mrs. Arlin Snyder, Osiah Horst, H. S. Bauman, Paul Martin, Arnold Cressman, and Newton Gingrich. Principals in succession were S. F. Coffman for 40 years (1907-47), Oscar Burkholder for 7 years (1948-55), Roy S. Koch 1955-57, and J. B. Martin 1957- . The Ontario Bible School and Institute is well known in Western Ontario and the border states. Its activities, such as tract distribution, singing, and church programs, have been well received for years. The highest enrollment was 226 (1939). The 1957 enrollment of the Ontario Mennonite Bible School (OMBS) was 68; that of the Ontario Mennonite Bible Institute (OMBI) 38, making a total of 106.

O.B.

Ontario Mennonite Brethren in Christ (since 1948 called United Missionary Church). One of the most important sections of the M.B.C.-U.M.C. has been the Ontario Conference, which was in effect in the beginning a separate movement though closely related to the Indiana movement led by Daniel Brenneman. Its real founder was Solomon Eby (1834-1931), a Mennonite (MC) minister ordained at Port Elgin in 1858, who had an unusual spiritual awakening in 1869 which he called his conversion. He immediately began prayer meetings and the promotion of "conversion" among his members with great success. Since his bold advocacy of the new piety and insistence upon the type of conversion experience which he held essential was unacceptable to the Ontario Mennonite Conference, of which he was a member, he was excommunicated (May 1874), followed by the Waterloo County ministers John Bear, Samuel Schlichter, Daniel Wismer, and Moses Erb (the last two soon returned to their former loyalty) and Waterloo deacons William Hembling and Joseph S. Schneider. In the Markham district ministers Abraham Raymer and John Steckley, who had been introducing a similar prayer meeting and revivalistic emphasis and were probably by the 1860's completely outside the Mennonite Church (MC), joined forces with Eby. Daniel Hoch (1806-78) at Vineland, who had been working in the same direction since c1843 and was in difficulty with the old church and who was affiliated with the Oberholtzer group (GCM) 1851-69, together with three small congregations in Ontario (Markham, Vineland, Waterloo), seems to have been drawn into the new Eby movement together with his following.

On May 15, 1874, Eby called a conference to meet in the Kitchener church (MC), which may be considered the actual origin of M.B.C. church in Canada. Daniel Brenneman, who had visited Eby in 1873, was expelled from the Indiana Mennonite Conference in 1874 also, followed by a substantial group of members; they were called New Mennonites. In 1875 the Eby and Brenneman groups formally united at a meeting held in the Snyder Mennonite meetinghouse near Bloomingdale, Ont. (the only congregation that went over completely with meetinghouse to the Eby group, except Port Elgin), on March 23, 1875, calling themselves United Mennonites. The organization formed in May 1874 had been called "Reformed Mennonites." It had two districts, Ontario and Indiana. The Ontario District had its first meeting at Port Elgin on Sept. 18, 1874.

The Dordrecht Confession of Faith was specifically adopted as the doctrinal platform of the group although it did not of course include the specific doctrinal emphases which caused the division. The new body was immediately organized into two conferences—Canada and the United States, with Eby as Presiding Elder for Canada and Brenneman for the United States. In 1879 a merger of the United Mennonites with the Evangelical Mennonites (q.v., Gehman group) of Pennsylvania resulted in the Evangelical United Mennonite Church, which in 1883 became the Mennonite Brethren in Christ when the small Swank faction of the Brethren in Christ (River Brethren) in Ohio joined the E.U.M.

Throughout the years of growth and merger described above the Ontario Conference remained the largest. In 1880 the conference had nine congregations and 19 ministers, with a total of 37 preaching places. By 1955, however, Ontario with 2,471 members in 35 congregations was the second in size in the denomination, having been passed by the Indiana Conference with 2,694.

The proportion of members who left the old conference in Ontario to join the "New" Mennonites is not clear, but possibly at least a third. It was a serious blow to the Mennonite Church (MC) in Ontario. L. J. Burkholder, the historian of the

conference (MC), says, "At least four able ministers and three deacons were lost to us. A much larger number of promising young men who became active ministers of the new branch might well have been used had they remained. A great many devoted families were carried away," among whom was the noted Jacob Y. Shantz (q.v.).

The Ontario M.B.C. Conference showed great spiritual vitality and evangelistic zeal. Much work was carried on in the older Mennonite settlements, and during the 1880's congregations were established at the following places: Berlin (Kitchener), Blair, Bethel, Bright, Breslau, Bloomingdale, Conestoga, Wallace or Maryboro, Port Elgin, Jordan (Twenty), Sherkston, Markham, Scott, Stayner, and Puslinch, largely at the expense of the old church. Among the chief leaders were Solomon Eby, Noah Detwiler, John Bear, Menno Bowman, Amos Eby, Joseph Raymer, John McNally, H. S. Hallman, Henry Goudie, Samuel Goudie, C. N. Good, Ward Shantz, P. G. Lehman, and Michael Houck. In 1908 a group of over 100 left to join the Pentecostal movement, among them the leading ministers Solomon Eby and Amos Eby.

Berlin (Kitchener) has always been the center of the conference; its Bethany congregation is the largest (1957, 320 members). In 1885 the denominational printing plant was moved from Goshen, Ind., to Berlin, and with it the church paper, the Gospel Banner, where it remained until 1909. In 1940 Emanuel Bible College was established in Kitchener as the Bible Institute of the Ontario district.   H.S.B.

J. A. Huffman, History of the Mennonite Brethren in Christ Church (New Carlisle, Ohio, 1920); L. J. Burkholder,, A Brief History of the Mennonites in Ontario (n.p., 1935); Conference Journal, Proceedings of the Ontario Conference of the United Missionary Church (MBC); E. R. Storms, History of the United Missionary Church (Elkhart, 1957).

Ontario Mennonite Conference (MC), formerly known as the Canada Conference, was organized about 1820 soon after the settlements of Mennonites began in the three main areas of Ontario (York, Waterloo, Niagara). It included the congregations in western New York and in eastern Michigan as these were organized. The records of 1831 show that the gatherings were held annually in October. "Die grosse Zusammenkunft" followed a three-year cycle in the areas mentioned. From about 1840 the conference was held on the last Friday of May. In 1889 this became the occasion of dispute and contributed to a division into two conferences, the Old Order (Wisler) Conference and the Ontario Mennonite (MC) Conference.

In the earlier years the conference session was a gathering of bishops, ministers, and deacons. It was the practice to hold communion at the place of conference on the Sunday following, with provision for public gatherings on contiguous days. These conferences were concerned with encouraging order in the churches, temperate living, restraint from forms of worldliness, and godliness in conduct and witness. Council meetings known as semiannual conferences were arranged in each of the three districts. In 1847 the conference authorized the holding of prayer meetings with the caution that the spirit of love and good-will be evident. During the present century two days have been devoted annually to the church conference. Bishop district meetings for counsel on matters of local interest and autumn ministers' inspirational sessions have in the last decade taken the place of semiannual conferences. By 1954 the conference session had become a three-day period. Questions to be considered in open session are arranged in a private session preceding. The year's work of the executive committee is reported for ratification. Since 1949 lay delegates have been included in the conference membership. A conference charter was adopted in 1909. In 1951 the conference was incorporated and now can hold the properties in connection with its institutions. The Finance Committee consists of the treasurers of the various organizations. The deacons of the conference compose the Welfare Board. They meet twice a year and aim to equalize the burdens of the congregations for all major needs, a fund is perpetuated by annual congregational offerings. Child Welfare work is a part of this organization. The Braeside Home Association consists of representatives from all organized churches of the conference and is responsible for the care of the aged. The Association operates through an executive committee of three and a management committee of seven, who meet monthly. Crowded conditions by 1955 led to the erection of an enlarged new building. The outreach of the Conference is made the responsibility of the Mennonite Mission Board of Ontario, organized in 1929. Her teaching program has advanced through the Sunday schools and their conference, established in 1890; through the Ontario Mennonite Bible School since 1907, and through young people's Bible meetings and summer Bible schools of later date.

A major schism affecting the unity of the Conference was experienced as early as 1847, when Bishop Jacob Gross of the Twenty (Vineland) and a number of adherents withdrew to join the Evangelical Association. It was at this time also that Daniel Hoch of the same congregation separated with some following to help form the Ohio-Canada West Conference of Mennonites. This movement caused loss in some twelve congregations of the Conference. Another movement in 1872-74 led to the organization of the Mennonite Brethren in Christ group. The division of 1889 gave rise to the branch known as the Old Order (Wisler) Mennonites of Ontario. In 1924 differences within the First Mennonite Church of Kitchener led to the organization of the Stirling Avenue Mennonite Church, which later joined the General Conference Mennonites.

The bishops who served before the division of 1889 were, in the Waterloo area, Benjamin Eby (ord. 1812), Henry Shantz (1842), Joseph Hagey (1851), Abraham Martin (1867), Amos Cressman (1875), Elias Weber (1879), and Daniel Wismer (1887); in the Markham area, Abraham Grove (1808), Jacob Grove (1837), and Christian Reesor (1867); in the Niagara area, Jacob Moyer (1805), Jacob Gross (1834), Jacob Krehbiel (1839), Dilman Moyer (1850), John Lapp (1862), and Christian Gayman (1875). The present conference body consists also of 47 ministers, 30 deacons, and 42 lay delegates.

The membership of the 42 churches in 1957 totaled 3,928. J.C.F.

Ontario Mennonite Evangel, a 6 x 9 in. 12-page monthly, the joint organ of the Ontario Mennonite and Ontario Amish Mennonite mission boards, published at Kitchener, Ont., beginning November 1956, editor Merle Shantz. The paper was preceded by *Church and Mission News* (*q.v.*), the organ of the above Ontario Mennonite Mission Board 1940-56, and before that by the *Mission News Bulletin* 1936-39. Merle Shantz was editor from January 1945, preceded by Oscar Burkholder who served from the beginning. H.S.B.

Ontdekte veinzing *der hedendaeghsche Gheestdrijvers en Socinianen,* I and II (n.p., n.d., Amsterdam, 1655), are two pamphlets written against Galenus Abrahamsz (*q.v.*) during the "Lammerenkrijgh" (*q.v.*) among the Dutch Mennonites. The author(s) hide their identity under Latin pseudonyms; one of them was probably Salomon van Alderwerelt. (H. W. Meihuizen, *Galenus Abrahamsz,* Haarlem, 1954, pp. 54, 201 f.) vDZ.

Ooltgensplaat, a village in the Dutch province of South Holland on the island Overflakkee, where there was once a Mennonite congregation in conjunction with near-by Bommel. The Mennonites of Ooltgensplaat had some difficulty in 1622 in performing their marriages, which had hitherto been done according to their old customs. By 1676 the congregation had died out (see **Bommel**). (*Inv. Arch. Amst.* II, 2, No. 298 f.; *DB* 1899, 183; 1908, 114; *ML* III, 305.) vDZ.

Oom Jacob Dirksz: see Dirksz, Jacob.

Oortman, a Mennonite family, formerly living at Utrecht (*q.v.*), Netherlands, where they were found from the 17th century, while other members of this family are found at Leiden, Amsterdam, and other places. Many members of this family served as deacons (eleven at Utrecht during the period 1699-1909). Andries Oortman, who obtained his medical degree at the University of Utrecht in 1735 and soon after became city physician of Utrecht, was a deacon of the Utrecht Mennonite congregation, as was his son Andries Oortman, Jr., also a physician. Andries Oortman, Jr., was one of the four members of the Utrecht congregation, who in 1765 gave a pipe organ for the Utrecht church; this was the first organ in any Mennonite church. He also promoted and led the building of a new church in Utrecht, which was dedicated in 1773. Jan Oortman, d. 1887, bequeathed 100,000 Dutch guilders to the A.D.S. (General Mennonite Conference). Johannes Oortman of Utrecht was a minister of the Waterlander congregation at Alkmaar 1734-37. Thereafter he served at Gouda 1737-39 and at Rotterdam from 1739 until his early death in 1741. vDZ.

H. B. Berghuys, *Geschiedenis der Doopsgez. Gemeente te Utrecht* (n.p., n.d.-1926); *Inv. Arch. Amst.* II, No. 1794; *Verslag* (report) of the A.D.S., 1888, 5; 1891, 23.

Oortwijn, a Dutch Mennonite family name; members of this family, many of them having served as deacons, are found in a number of North Holland congregations, e.g., Oostand West-Graftdijk, De Rijp, and Zaandam. vDZ.

Oostburg, a town (pop. 2,313) in the Dutch province of Zeeland (formerly Flanders), between Aardenburg and Groede, where Anabaptist refugees from Flanders were active in 1624 and 1635, giving alms and establishing several new places of meeting. (*DB* 1883, 101-3; 1889, 102; *ML* III, 305.) E.C.

Oosten, Jan, an Anabaptist martyr: see **Hans Marijnsz.**

Oostende (Ostende), a seacoast town in West Flanders, Belgium, was a Mennonite center; there may have been a congregation here in the 16th century; there is, however, no information about it. Claes Leks (*q.v.*) and Lucas de Groot (*q.v.*), both natives of Oostende, were executed there as martyrs in 1548 and 1568. (*ML* III, 14.) vDZ.

Oosterbaan, a Dutch Mennonite family, originally living at Harlingen, Dutch province of Friesland. According to tradition its ancestors, Claes Aryaens and his wife, both Mennonites, residents of Flanders, fled from Brugge, Belgium, to Harlingen because of persecution about 1575. In Harlingen their son Arjen Clasen (d. 1623), a deacon of the Flemish congregation, lived as a merchant. He was married first to Geertie Everts (d. 1614), then to Antie IJsbrands (d. 1655). His descendants too were usually merchants, many of them also serving the church as deacons. The family name of Oosterbaan does not appear before the end of the 17th century. By marriage they were related to other well-known Harlingen Mennonite families such as Roorda, Dreyer, Hanekuyk, Styl, and Stinstra. A member of this family was Heere Oosterbaan (*q.v.*), a Mennonite minister and professor in the Amsterdam Theological Seminary, as well as the following Mennonite pastors: Jacob Everts Oosterbaan, who served 1819-24 at Woudsend, 1824-29 at Den Ilp, and 1829-39 at Workum, in which year he retired. Jacob Oosterbaan, d. 1872, serving at Pieterzij 1860-66 and Midwolda 1866-72. Johannes Arnoldus Oosterbaan (b. 1837 at Harlingen, d. 1901 at Makkum) was pastor of Mensingeweer 1863-66, Giethoorn-Zuid 1866-76, Staveren-Molkwerum 1876-78, and Makkum 1878-1901. His son Pieter Oosterbaan (b. 1873 at Giethoorn, d. 1941 at Hilversum, married to J. Leverland) served at Sint Anna-Parochie 1898-1901, Uithuizen 1901-7, and Huizen-Hilversum 1907-38, in which year he retired. Johannes Arnoldus Oosterbaan, son of the former (b. 1910 at Hilversum, LL.D. 1934, and Th.D. 1953, married to R. C. Lugt), has been a pastor at Broek op Langendijk 1938-40, Barsingerhorn 1940-51, and Haarlem 1951-54. In 1954 he was appointed professor at the Amsterdam Mennonite Seminary and in the same year also at the University of Amsterdam as professor of philosophy of religion and ethics. vDZ.

Oosterbaan, Heere, a Dutch Mennonite theologian, b. Jan. 3, 1736, at Harlingen, d. there Sept. 18, 1807, the son of the merchant Evert Oosterbaan and Grietje Simons Stinstra. As a consequence of scarlet fever he was deaf from his eighth year; but this did not prevent him from becoming a distinguished

preacher. Taught at first by his uncles Johannes and Gooitgen Stinstra (respectively preacher and physician), he attended the Latin school and the Athenaeum at Franeker, obtaining his Ph.D. degree in 1757; then he studied under Professor Tjerk Nieuwenhuis (*q.v.*) at the Amsterdam Mennonite Seminary. In January 1760 he became the preacher of the Mennonite church in Makkum (*q.v.*). In 1761 he was appointed to succeed Nieuwenhuis as professor in the seminary. After the death of Klaas de Vries (1766) he also gave instruction in the natural sciences at the seminary. In 1786 he resigned his professorship and followed his uncle Johannes Stinstra as preacher at the Harlingen congregation, serving until his death in 1807. He was repeatedly one of the delegates of the Friesche Sociëteit (Mennonite Conference of Friesland) and chairman in 1788. His influence in Harlingen and his fatherly attitude in a quarrel in the congregation concerning the management of the "twelve men" is described by Pieter Cool (*DB* 1880, 11-38). He was the author of the missive sent by the Friesche Sociëteit to the Mennonites of Russia at the request of Trapp, the plenipotentiary of Catherine II (printed in Blaupot t. C., *Friesland*). In 1795 he was elected by the popular representation of Friesland to the committee on drafting a constitution. When the *Dictionaire antique Encyclopédique* (Paris, 1769) published an erroneous article on the Mennonites, he managed to have a better one produced. He wrote the *Epistola de Mennonitis* in the *Bibl. Hagana* IV, 133-50 (Amsterdam, 1769); and also *Leerreden ter aanprijzinge van het Instituut tot onderwijzing van dooven en stommen* (Harlingen, 1792): *Ontwerp van eenige schikkingen raakende den openbaren godsdienst* (1792). His lectures (Latin) held at the Seminary, titled *Systema theologicum* (five volumes), are found in the Amsterdam Mennonite Archives. Pastor Freerk Hoekstra, his student and from 1792 his colleague in Harlingen, preached his funeral sermon, *Lijkrede op H. Oosterbaan* (Amsterdam, 1807). In 1760 Oosterbaan was married to Aagjen D. Hanekuyk of Harlingen. K.V.

Blaupot t. C., *Friesland*, 228, 230, 236 f.; idem, *Holland* II, 102; Chr. Sepp, *Johannes Stinstra en zijn tijd* II (Amsterdam, 1866) 289-92; *Naamlijst* 1808, 78 f.; *Inv. Arch. Amst.* I, No. 680; *DJ* 1850, 113-21; *DB* 1880, 1-41 passim; *N.N.B.Wb.* II, 1211; *ML* III, 305.

Oosterend, a village name: see **Burg** and **Texel;** also **Vlieland.**

Oosterhout, a village in the Dutch province of North Brabant. The Mennonites living here joined with those of Geertruidenberg and Breda (*q.v.*) in the 17th century to form the congregation of Brabant. Jan Jansz van de Langerijt and Augustijn Gerritsz Hulstmans as delegates of this congregation in 1664 signed the "Oprecht Verbondt van Eenigheydt" (*q.v.*), which brought about the union of the conservative Mennonites in the Netherlands, later called the Zonsche Sociëteit (Zonist Conference). Of the Mennonites of Oosterhout there is no further information. The congregation of Brabant apparently had died out before 1700. vDZ.

Oostermeer in Friesland: see **Witveen.**

Oosters and Oosters gekleurd ("Eastern" dialect and language with an "eastern" coloring) are two forms of language found in the works of Menno Simons (*q.v.*) and other Anabaptist leaders who migrated from the Netherlands eastward into the German provinces. Menno Simons wrote his *Foundation Book* (*q.v.*) immediately after his withdrawal from the Catholic church when he was living in the province of Groningen and possibly also East Friesland. His native language at home in Witmarsum had been Frisian and the literary Dutch. The language of the earliest writings in his new environment is referred to as "Ooosters gekleurd" (having an "eastern" coloring). This implies that the language east of the Netherlands was considered by the Dutch as having been colored by eastern influences. Later on, after 1550, when Menno Simons settled in Fresenburg (*q.v.*), Schleswig-Holstein, his adjustment to the German environment was even more complete and the writings which were published at this time by his own press are referred to as in "Oosters." Toward the end of his life and after his death, pure Dutch editions of his writings were prepared and published in 1562 and later. They were particularly designed for distribution in the Netherlands.

C.K.

G. E. Frerichs, "Menno's tal," *DB* (1905) 72-111; K. Vos, *Menno Simons* (Leiden, 1914) 272, 296.

Oosterwij(c)k (Oosterwyk), **Matthijs**, d. Dec. 8, 1729, at Leiden, Holland, was a preacher of the Leiden Waterlander Mennonite congregation (serving before 1682), and an elder from 1694. After this congregation had merged with the Flemish congregation he served the united congregation until his death. He was an untrained minister. In 1682 the Waterlander church board of Leiden decided that Oosterwijck should learn some Latin, which was thought necessary for his education, the costs of which were to be paid by the congregation. Matthijs Oosterwijk also preached and baptized at The Hague (*q.v.*), e.g., in 1711. He represented the Leiden congregation (e.g., in 1710) in the Dutch Mennonite Committee of Foreign Needs. His son François Oosterwijk served the Leiden congregation as a deacon a number of times. vDZ.

L. G. le Poole, *Bijdragen tot de kennis van ... de Doopsgezinden te Leiden* (Leiden, 1905) *passim; DB* 1895, 55; 1908, 100; 1918, 53 f.; *ML* III, 306.

Oosterwij(c)k, van, a former Dutch Mennonite family found in a number of towns in Holland. Most of its members were merchants; some were bankers. Willem van Oosterwijk was a deacon in the Mennonite congregation at Utrecht in 1651-56 and 1661-63. In Amsterdam members of the van Oosterwijk family were found in both the Lamist and Zonist congregations, a number of them serving as deacons. A lateral branch of this family was the well-to-do van Oosterwijk Bruyn family, which is descended from Jan Bruyn and Georgina Josina van Oosterhout, who lived at Amsterdam in the 18th century; Willem van Oosterwijk Hulshoff (see **Hulshoff**) also belonged to this family. vDZ.

Oosterwolde, a village in the southeastern part of the Dutch province of Friesland, where a Mennonite circle was organized on May 24, 1949, which now (1957) has a membership of 20. This group belongs to the congregation of Gorredijk (*q.v.*), whose pastor holds monthly services at Oosterwolde. vDZ.

Oost-Graftdijk: see Graftdijk.

Oosthuizen, a village in the Dutch province of North Holland, formerly the seat of a Mennonite congregation. After the Beemster polder had been reclaimed (1608-12), most members of the Oosthuizen congregation, being farmers, gradually settled on this polder; thus a new meetinghouse was built in Midden-Beemster in 1785. Thereupon in 1787 the old meetinghouse at Oosthuizen was sold. The congregation was then known as Beemster and Oosthuizen. Now it is called Beemster (*q.v.*). vDZ.

Oostzaan, near Zaandam (*q.v.*), in the Dutch province of North Holland, was for a few years the seat of a Mennonite circle organized in 1946, which belonged to the Zaandam congregation. From the earliest times Anabaptist-Mennonites lived at Oostzaan; Anabaptist activity here is mentioned as early as 1534. (*Inv. Arch. Amst.* I, No. 125.) vDZ.

Oost-Zaandam, a name formerly given to the congregation of Zaandam-Oostzijde (*q.v.*), i.e., the part of Zaandam situated on the east side of the Zaan River in the province of North Holland. vDZ.

Ootsa Lake, a village in central British Columbia. In 1940 Old Colony Mennonites from Mexico and from other parts of Canada moved to this vicinity. The settlement is extremely isolated. In 1949 John W. Martens was the bishop in charge. J.A.Har.

Oostzee-Collecte (Baltic Sea Collection) was a collection of money raised in the Dutch Mennonite congregations for the relief of a number of West Prussian Mennonite congregations, particularly Rosenort (*q.v.*), Markushof (*q.v.*), Thiensdorf (*q.v.*), and Elbing-Ellerwald (*q.v.*), severely struck by floods on March 17-25, 1888. vDZ.

Opal Union Mennonite Church, now extinct, located in Fauquier County, about 15 miles south of Warrenton, Va. Henry L. Rhodes of Augusta County moved to Fauquier in the late 1880's and asked the Virginia Conference (MC) to send ministers to serve his family and evangelize the community. Other Mennonite and Amish families located here. Land was purchased for the Opal Union Church in September 1892. In 1900 E. J. Berkey, a son-in-law of Henry L. Rhodes, was ordained to serve this church. H.A.B.

Opalinski, Kasimir Johann (d. 1693), Bishop of Culm, Poland (West Prussia from 1772 to 1918), the scion of an old Polish family which was named for the town of Opalencia near Posen. His father was Voivode of Kalisch. He entered a monastery at an early age. His first opportunity to demonstrate his zeal was in driving all the heretics from the estates of the Cistercian monastery at Blesen, of which he was abbot. In 1681 he was appointed Bishop of Culm. To the Mennonites of the Culm (*q.v.*) Marsh, who were needed to drain the land, he issued a document of protection on June 27, 1689, promising the toleration of their religion. H.Wi.

Diecezja Chelminska (Pelplin, 1928); Niesiecki, *Herbarz Polski* VII, 113 (Leipzig, 1841); Orgelbrand, *Encyklopedya Powszechna* II, 99 (Warsaw, 1901); *ML* III, 306.

Open Bible Mennonite Brethren Church, Wichita, Kan., began in connection with the weekly child evangelism Bible classes for children conducted in some of the public schools and homes of Wichita in 1946 under the sponsorship of the Board of Home Missions of the M.B. Southern District Conference and the Wichita M.B. Church. The Supreme Court ruling of 1948 changed the work more to home and release-time classes. In 1957 the Conference discontinued this work as its project. The work was then continued under the support of several M.B. churches of the area. The Open Bible M.B. Church is an outgrowth of the child evangelism classes in the Orienta section of Wichita. In 1957 the membership was 26, with Paul Kliewer as pastor. O.Ha.

Opening, a colloquial expression used in many Mennonite (MC) and Amish congregations in America for the introductory part of a regular Sunday morning worship service, usually called in German "Einleitung" but sometimes "Eröffnung." It included the reading of a portion of Scripture with comments, sometimes brief, sometimes longer, followed by the call to prayer, a prayer which was formerly always kneeling and silent and still is among the Lancaster Conference Mennonites and certain other eastern congregations and the Old Order Amish. The choice of the minister to "make the opening" is made by the assembled ministry in the ministers' anteroom of the meetinghouse, who then after prayer proceed in a body to the bench behind the pulpit. The Amish ministers gather in an upper room to make this decision.   H.S.B.

Ophoorn (Ophoren), Hans (Johan, Jan), a Mennonite elder: see Jan van Ophoorn.

Oppelsbohm, a town in the Winnenden district of Württemberg, Germany. The magistrate at Backnang in 1562 presented to Christoph, Duke of Württemberg, a written report of the oral information he had received from the pastor of Oppelsbohm concerning the Anabaptist Lienhardt: Lienhardt had never come to church nor to communion, had stated that all church ordinances are of the devil, had been four or five years with the Anabaptists in Moravia, and had been in prison as a deceiver several times. His wife was a member of the church and had the children baptized. According to the "Anabaptist Calender" of 1570 the ducal chancellory had admonished Margarethe, the wife of the Anabaptist Feierabend of Oppelsbohm, who had left the country. Adam Epplin of the Oppelsbohm parish was to be locked up and admonished. His daughter had promised obedience before the pastor. Franz Feierabend, though banished from the country, let himself be seen in Oppelsbohm without fear, was therefore to be seized. Feierabend's wife would go to church but not to communion, felt unworthy because she could not keep the Ten Commandments, was to pay three shillings for every sermon she had missed, denied the presence of the body and blood of Christ in the communion emblems. In 1574 Hans Hieber charged his wife Maria with Anabaptism.

The pertinent dean had "refuted her." She would come to church and communion, and would then be watched. In 1575 Franz Feierabend's wife attended church because of the fine, but not to communion, was unteachable. In 1576 her exiled husband slipped into the village again, was seen by the pastor. In 1577 Leonhard Payer and Görg Feurlin had not communed for four years. The latter gave as his reason the hostility of one of the villagers. He was the chosen representative of the community, but was unable to forgive. Margarethe Feierabend had rudely declared to the dean that she would come to communion only under compulsion, "walked out of the room defiantly, said she wanted to be left alone." She also rejected infant baptism. The shoemaker Caspar Mack had not been to communion for three years and declared to the parson that on Sunday he had to deliver shoes and went to church elsewhere. In 1582 Hans Feierabend, Sylvester Siglin, Görg Feurlin, who had not taken communion for six years, offered as excuses their unworthiness, quarrels, and anger, promised to reform, were thereupon watched, and did better in 1583. In 1584 Bartle (Bartholomäus) Weiss had again communed after a lapse of thirty years and had recanted. Marginal note of the church inspector, "Deo Gratias!" In 1586 Margaretha, the wife of the Anabaptist Görg Kurtz, according to her own confession, rarely went to church, and had for ten years not gone to communion; the reason was her husband's exile. For she could not pardon those who had helped to drive away her husband. Besides, she knew of much frivolous living which was not punished, but her pious husband was nowhere tolerated; he was being treated unjustly. To the dean who had spoken to her the fourth time about baptism and communion she refused to answer. The inspector recommended diligent attendance at church and communion, or she would be sent after her husband! In 1587 she took communion.

In 1609 Philip Pfeil, who had gone to the Anabaptists for a year but had returned, could not be found. The dean ordered that he was to be sent to the office if he was seen. In 1611 Konrad Faut, the Swiss Anabaptist, kept all other commands and prohibitions, but neither went to the sermons nor to communion, led no one astray, but persisted in his opinion in spite of all instruction. The 70-year-old man was to be threatened with prison and if he died unrepentant he would be buried without a sermon or church bells. In 1614 Maria, Jakob Faut's wife, was under suspicion of being an Anabaptist, seldom went to church, had not taken communion for three years, had presumably been confused by her father, an Anabaptist. After admonition by the parson she declared that she would avoid sermon and communion. Thereupon she was summoned to the consistory in Stuttgart as a stiff-necked Anabaptist. She was ordered into a women's prison and was there asked pastoral questions. "She answered that she was not misled by any one, but had been instructed by her father. What she believed she believed too. Where her brethren met she did not know and would not betray any one. Judas' betrayal of Christ did him no good." She had five small children, had not been rebaptized, had also had her children baptized. She acknowledged that she was a great sinner. He who does the right is saved. Of a justifying faith she would know nothing. Obedience is due the government. Upon payment of the costs she was released and put in chains at home. Konrad Faut, still "obstinate" in 1615, offered a public recantation in 1617 and went to church and to communion. Maria was still obstinate in 1618, was to be brought to church by the beadle, and if she died impenitent, should be buried without song or bells. *TA Württemberg; ML* III, 306.)   E.T.

Oprecht Verbondt van Eenigheydt (1664): see **Verbondt van Eenigheydt.**

Opwekkende Liederen: see **Liederen en Gezangen.**

Oraibi (Ariz.) Mennonite Mission (GCM) was established among the Hopi Indians in northern Arizona in 1893. H. R. Voth was the first missionary. Others serving in the formative period of the mission were J. B. Epp and J. B. Frey. Later the work was expanded to include the two villages of Hotevilla (*q.v.*), 7 miles west of Oraibi, and Moen Copi (Tuba City), 45 miles west of Hotevilla. By 1929 the membership of the Hopi missions had reached 32 and by 1935 the number was 42. In 1957 12 missionaries were serving in the three stations, 8 of whom were at Oraibi.   M.G.

Orange (*Oranje*), the royal house ruling in the Netherlands. The following members of the house of Orange had previously been stadholders of Holland and Zeeland in the Netherlands: William I 1572-84, Maurice 1584-1625, Frederick Henry 1625-47, William II 1647-50, and William III 1672-1702, while a side branch of the house of Orange ruled in Friesland. William IV 1747-51 and William V 1766-95 were stadholders of all the Netherlands provinces. All of them, but particularly William I (*q.v.*), Maurice (*q.v.*), and William III (*q.v.*), were favorable to the Mennonites.   vDZ.

Oranjeappel, De (The Orange), is the name of a Dutch orphanage, founded in Amsterdam in 1675. The founders were Collegiants (*q.v.*), most of them being at the same time members of the Mennonite Lamist congregation at Amsterdam. The first governors of the orphanage, Anthony Rooleeuw (*q.v.*), Willem Bruin, Adriaan Pieters Dekker, Gerrit Jacobsz Derramout, and Pieter Rijndertsz, were all Mennonites, except Derramout. Until 1920 the orphanage was located on the Keizersgracht in Amsterdam; in this year a building was acquired at the De Lairessestraat. In 1930 the orphanage was moved to Hilversum.

Until the end of the 18th century the orphanage was purely Collegiant, but in 1811 an agreement was made between the governors of the Oranjeappel and the deacons of the Amsterdam Mennonite congregation. Henceforth, the foundation of the Oranjeappel remaining independent, two of the four governors were to be nominated by the Amsterdam Mennonite church board, and all governors were to be members of the Amsterdam Mennonite congregation. After this agreement was made the Mennonite orphanage

of Amsterdam was closed and its 17 orphans were taken into the Oranjeappel.   vDZ.

A. Loosjes, *Het weeshuis der Collegianten, "De Oranjeappel" 1675-1925* (n.p., n.d., -1925).

Oranjewoud, a village in the Dutch province of Friesland, where a Mennonite circle was organized on Jan. 23, 1951. The group, with about 50 members, belongs to the Bovenknijpe (*q.v.*) congregation. Services are regularly held in a rented hall, and catechetical instruction is given by the pastor of Bovenknijpe. There is also a ladies' circle. vDZ.

Orchard Park K.M.B. Church, located in Hutchinson, Kan., was begun in 1954. In 1957 it had 31 members, with Edwin F. Walter as pastor. H.S.B.

Order of Service: see **Worship.**

Ordinances. A term used in nonliturgical churches to designate what is referred to in liturgical churches as "sacraments." There is considerable difference in meaning between these two terms. A sacrament is defined by Thomas Aquinas as a "sign of a sacred thing in so far as it sanctifies man." Augustine referred to it as "the visible form of an invisible grace." "The sign" and the "visible form" became more and more significant and a prerequisite for the appropriation of the "invisible grace." The 16th-century Reformers broke with the medieval concept, although the term "sacrament" was retained in the liturgical Protestant churches; only two sacraments, baptism and the Lord's Supper, were retained. In the Anglican and Lutheran churches a reinterpreted Catholic tradition was retained, while the Reformed, Presbyterians, Anabaptists, and other churches altered the meaning completely, giving usually only a symbolic meaning.

None of the other nonliturgical churches of the Reformation broke as radically with the tradition as did the Anabaptists and Spiritualists. The latter were forerunners in a way of the Quakers, who spiritualized the ordinances completely. But the Biblical Anabaptists retained baptism and the Lord's Supper, and in Holland footwashing, as ordinances of the Lord. The term "ordinance" emphasizes the aspect of institution by Christ and the symbolic meaning. For this reason the use of the term "sacraments" by Mennonites is misleading. Nevertheless, it is being used at times particularly by ministers who have received training in non-Mennonite institutions of liturgical leanings, and was also used at times by the early Anabaptists (see **Sacraments**).

Bernt Rothmann in his *Restitution* stated that the Antichrist had through "his witchcraft" made an idol of baptism. Menno Simons agreed with this statement (Krahn, 131 ff.). Constantly he fought the concept of magical implications and power in baptism and emphasized that only an "inward baptism" can save. After the spiritual baptism of regeneration has taken place, water baptism as a sign of obedience follows. If salvation lay in the outward form, God would have made water, not the blood of Christ, necessary for forgiveness of sin. God has not elevated the elements of water, bread, and wine above other elements but uses them merely as symbols of His forgiving grace.

We use them to demonstrate our obedience and faith. Menno Simons warns, however, against the spiritualization of the ordinances to the point where they become obsolete as was the case among the Spiritualists, e.g., Sebastian Franck and to some extent Hans Denk. Since baptism and the Lord's Supper are symbolic and not absolute conveyors of God's grace, little significance is attached to their precise form. For the early Anabaptists the questions whether baptism should be administered by pouring, sprinkling, or immersion and whether in the Lord's Supper wine or unfermented juice should be used could never have led to controversy.

Dirk Philips spoke of the ordinances as witnesses of the love of God and the deeds of Jesus Christ. However, both he and Menno Simons were very cautious in avoiding the words "signs of grace" for the Lord's Supper and baptism, because they feared that outward forms would again take the place of the atoning death of Christ. The power of the ordinances is not in the sign or symbol but in what these two stand for (Hoekstra, 277).

In addition to the two generally accepted ordinances, most Dutch Anabaptists (not Swiss) and Mennonites, and the Amish as well as the Mennonite Church (MC) and related groups, have practiced and retained footwashing (q.v.) as another ordinance, performed either before or after the Lord's Supper. Menno did not emphasize the ordinance character of footwashing as strongly as that of baptism and the Lord's Supper; it was for him a symbol of unselfish love, hospitality toward the brethren, and humility.

Within the Mennonite churches of later centuries the forms of the ordinances gained in significance and at times obscured their deeper meaning. Controversies about the form of baptism arose because the outward sign had become more important than God's gift and its inward experience. (See also **Baptism.**)

In the Mennonite Church (MC) in the 20th century, largely through the influence of the writings of Daniel Kauffman (q.v.), the idea of seven ordinances arose and has become quite common, though not fixed in any confession of faith or conference disciplines. The seven are listed as baptism, communion, footwashing, prayer veiling for women, anointing with oil, the kiss of charity, and marriage. But J. C. Wenger's *Introduction to Theology* (1954), a widely accepted and influential book, returns to the concept of only two full ordinances, baptism and communion. (See **Communion, Baptism, Footwashing, Prayer Veiling, Kiss, Anointing,** and **Sacraments.**)   C.K.

S. Hoekstra, Bz, *Beginselen en leer der oude Doopsgezinden* (Amsterdam, 1863) 276; Cornelius Krahn, *Menno Simons (1494-1561)* (Karlsruhe, 1936) 129; N. van der Zijpp, *Geschiedenis der Doopsgezinden in Nederland* (Arnhem, 1952) 115; S. F. Rues, *Aufrichtige Nachrichten von dem gegenwärtigen Zustande der Mennoniten* (Jena, 1743) 50; Daniel Kauffman, ed., *Doctrines of the Bible* (Scottdale, 1928); idem, *Mennonite Cyclopedic Dictionary* (Scottdale, 1937).

Ordinances, Hutterite: see **Gemeindeordnungen.**

Ordination of ministers is an act of the church in which the minister-elect (or bishop or deacon) receives confirmation to his office by a ceremony of laying on of the hands of a bishop (elder) and the intercession of the congregation, which gives him the right to lead the congregation in worship and life as pastor, to perform the duties of his office, whatever they may be, to preach the Word of God, to perform marriages, to ordain, to administer baptism and communion, to administer discipline, to administer the alms fund, etc.

Originally and until well into the 19th or even 20th century the Anabaptist-Mennonite tradition everywhere called for an ordination for each level in the ministry, bishop-elder, preacher, or deacon. Hence it was possible for one man to be ordained three times. In Holland formal ordination to all ministerial offices including that of deacon was usual in the 16th and early 17th centuries, and among the Groningen (q.v.) Old Flemish, until c1760, and in a few small conservative groups until the end of the 18th century. But as early as about 1610 the Waterlanders (q.v.) had abolished the laying on of hands for deacons, and by 1665 also for preachers and deacons. But that time the Lamists (q.v.) had also abolished the ordination of deacons. In the 19th century all formal ordination in Holland was discontinued. Since then pastors have been instituted by another minister, usually an older one or a friend. It is customary to ask only whether the new minister will promise to serve the church faithfully. The promise is followed by a prayer. Since c1940 a kind of formal ordination of pastors with laying on of hands has occasionally been reintroduced. In some Mennonite groups in America deacons are no longer ordained. Recently the Ohio and Eastern Mennonite Conference has decided to have only one ordination with charges to the several offices as they are assumed and as may be necessary.

Normally women are eligible for ordination only among the Dutch Mennonites. However, some Mennonite groups in effect give ordination to women missionaries, and the consecration of deaconesses is akin to ordination.

Ordination normally confers a lifetime status. In the older practice, and still in the more conservative group, ministers removed from office for causes such as heresy, or gross sin, or insubordination, or even for lesser causes, were not considered to have lost their ordination, but to have been "silenced," i.e., no longer allowed to preach, and could be restored to office without reordination. Normally also ministers have been accepted on transfer from other Mennonite bodies or from non-Mennonite denominations without reordination. However, when the Kleine Gemeinde elder in Manitoba, Peter Toews, transferred to the Church of God in Christ, Mennonite, in 1882 he and the three ministers who went with him were required to be reordained (also rebaptized). (See **Ministry,** and **Ministry, Call to the.**)   H.S.B.

Ordnungsbriefe (Church Disciplines). The strict Biblicism of the Mennonites logically led to a strict exercise of discipline. In private and family life the fathers sought to regulate matters in such a way as to maintain, to the highest degree possible, the "pure church." For the purpose of formulating their church regulations the elders and preachers of the congregations in Alsace-Lorraine and South Germany met in conference a number of times. (See **Strasbourg Conferences** and **Essingen**,) A record was kept of these meetings and the resolutions passed were announced to the brotherhood as *Ordnungsbriefe,* understood as the norm to be followed as conscientiously as possible. They dealt mostly with matters of congregational life, ministerial service, and church discipline, but reached into the private life of the members. These *Ordnungsbriefe* were never published but were handed down by the elders in writing. Copies of most of them have been preserved in GCL.

The list of known *Ordnungsbriefe* follows:

(1) *Abrede und Verordnung der Diener und Aeltesten in der Versammlung zu Strassburg, im Jahr Anno 1568 and 1607* (with appendix and supplement of Obersülzen and Offstein in 1688). (See **Strasbourg Conferences.**)

(2) *Ordnungsbrief* of April 28, 1752, at Steinselz. (See **Alsace.**)

(3) *Ordnungsbrief* of May 1, 1759, at Essingen near Landau in the Palatinate. This is a supplement to the Steinselz *Ordnungsbrief.* By way of introduction it says, "Today May 1, 1759, we the undersigned have been together at Essingen in order to see how we agree in faith and other opinions, because in the conference at Steinselz on April 19, 1752, we agreed on certain points and have found them offensive to the brotherhood."

(4) *Ordnungsbrief* of Nov. 21, 1779, at Essingen. (See **Alsace.**) This *Ordnungsbrief* (and the previous one of 1759) is printed in full in *Gesch.-Bl.* III (1938) 52-55. The document has the title, *Abrede der Diener und Aeltesten aus vielen Orten und Ländern in der Versammlung zu Essingen bei Landau, den 21. Wintermonat 1779 Jahres.* The sixteen articles of this discipline borrow much from the Strasbourg discipline of 1568. It is in part a repetition of these articles, though in a different order. An addition is the reference to the confession of faith contained in the *Martyrs' Mirror,* and also Article six, which says, "The preachers and elders shall faithfully perform the service laid upon them by the Lord and His church, not in pride or haughtiness, but in lowliness and humility, according to the content of the holy Gospel and shall introduce nothing new or unusual, that they may not be moved aside from the simplicity in Christ."

Also the prescriptions concerning costume and coiffure, from Article 13 on, are not found in the Strasbourg discipline. Responsible preachers and elders were especially admonished in the final article, "to be more careful in preaching and admonition, in baptism and communion in Christian order according to the content of the Gospel." Thirty-nine preachers from 19 congregations signed the document. The Swiss congregations were not represented in these Essingen conferences, but held rather closely to these decisions, including the regulations on dress, etc., until the end of the 19th century. The Ibersheim (Rheinhessen) Conference (*q.v.*) of 1803 had much the same character for the Mennonites of the Palatinate as did the Essingen Conference of 1779 for the Amish.

The European conferences to establish similar regulations (*Ordnungen*) were essentially continued by the Amish in the United States, and the resolutions passed were treated as the *Ordnungsbriefe* had been though not so called. The Amish conferences of 1809 (held in Lancaster County, Pa.), 1837 (Somerset County, Pa.), and 1865 (Holmes County, Ohio), minutes of all of which have been preserved (in GCL), are illustrations. The resolutions are almost identical in form and concern with the earlier *Ordnungsbriefe,* though oriented to the problems of the 19th century in America. To some extent the Mennonite (MC) conferences of the 18th and 19th centuries were essentially the same; their concerns were more in the line of church discipline than theology or church activity. The 20th century broadened the concerns of the conferences when new life and progress came in.

All the *Ordnungsbriefe* and later conference resolutions were conceived basically as guides for the elders to follow in their administration of the congregations and maintenance of the faith and practice handed down from the past. Though not formally binding they had great weight and contributed much to stability, uniformity, unity, and somewhat to rigidity in the congregations.

The Offenthal (*q.v.*) Amish Conference of 1867, by its decision to relax or even discard the older *Ordnung,* was a symbol of the disintegration of the Amish congregations in Hesse and the adjoining territory.   S.G.

Paul Schowalter, "Die Essinger Konferenzen 1759 und 1779," *Gesch.-Bl.* III (1938) 49-55; H. S. Bender, "Discipline Adopted by the Strasburg Conference of 1568," *MQR* I (January 1927) 57-66; idem, "An Amish Church Discipline of 1779," *MQR* XI (1937) 163-68; idem, "Some Early American Amish Mennonite Disciplines," *MQR* VIII (1934) 90-98; *ML* III, 308.

Ordnungsgemein (*Ortnungsgmee* in Pennsylvania German), the Old Order Amish term for the "counsel meeting" (*q.v.*) held preliminary to holding the communion service, when all matters of discipline needing attention were dealt with and the congregation brought into accord with the "Ordnung" or regulations of the church. H.S.B.

Oregon, a state in the United States since 1859, area 96,350 sq. miles, pop. 1,521,341 (1950). West of the Cascade Range, where all the Mennonites are located, the climate is mild and moist. Except for the mission churches (MC) in Portland, Grants Pass, Roseburg, and Blaine, all the Mennonite congregations are located in a strip 40 x 60 miles extending north and south, largely in the Willamette Valley, with Salem, the capital of the state, at the center. Nine tenths of the 3,804 baptized Mennonites in the state live within 30 miles of Salem. Half of them are farmers raising grain, vegetables, and fruit. A few are engaged in lumbering in the foothills of the Cascades, while many are engaged in business and industry.

The first and largest group in Oregon is the Mennonite Church (MC) with 17 congregations and 1,860 members. The first congregation of this group, now extinct, was Eugene, established in

1887. The other old congregations are Zion (1893) with 286 members, near Hubbard; Fairview (1894) with 401, near Albany; Hopewell (1899) with 56, near Hubbard; Albany City (1909) with 227; Bethel (1912) with 54, near Canby; and Sheridan (1923) with 302, near Sheridan. Since 1938 10 smaller congregations have been established, partly as missions, and the Portland Mission, established 1922, has become a substantial congregation with 94 members. Following are the ten congregations: Sweet Home (1938) with 120 members; Porter (1939), near Estacada, with 20; Blaine (1940) with 29; East Fairview (1948), near Lebanon, with 29; Western (1948), in Salem, with 78; Tangent (1950) with 55; Grants Pass (1954) with 27; Winston (1955), at Roseburg, with 18; Lebanon (1957) with 32; and Logsden (1957) at Nashville. The Firdale congregation near Airlie existed 1914-24. The church also has 8 additional missions in the state including a rescue mission and a Jewish Mission in Portland. The M.C. group has established three institutions: Western Mennonite School (1945) nead Salem, Mennonite Home for the Aged (1946) at Albany, and Lebanon Community Hospital, operated since 1948 (but not owned) by the Mennonite Board of Missions and Charities.

The second Mennonite group to come into Oregon were the General Conference Mennonites, who established the Emmanuel Church near Pratum in 1890, now with 239 members; Grace Church at Dallas, which now has 343 members, was in 1932 essentially composed of members who withdrew from the M.C. in the area. Grace Church at Albany, established in 1931, now has 70 members. The remaining three smaller congregations are Calvary at Barlow (1944), with 121 members; Community Chapel at Sweet Home, with 62; and Alberta Community in Portland, with 74. The G.C.M. total in Oregon was 909 in 1957.

The Old Order Amish settlement established in 1895 at McMinnville has remained small; in 1957 it had only 28 members. The other two Amish congregations in the state are classified as Beachy Amish: Harrisburg (1911), with 96 members, a Sleeping Preacher (q.v.) group congregation, and Pleasant Valley at Yoncalla, with 23 members.

The Mennonite Brethren established a congregation at Dallas in 1906, which in 1957 had 319 members. A daughter congregation, the Kingwood Bible Church, was established in Salem in 1940, which had 188 members in 1957. The large Evangelical Mennonite Brethren congregation in Dallas, with 368 members, had its first pastor in 1912, although E.M.B. members had moved into the area by 1890. The Church of God in Christ, Mennonite, very recently (1956?) established a small congregation at Scio, called Evergreen, with 13 members in 1957. The Cloverdale congregation near Creswell, established in 1945, died out in 1957.

The Salem Deaconess Home and Hospital (q.v.) was established in 1917 under the auspices of the G.C.M., E.M.B., and M.B. congregations in the area, but in 1949 it was transformed into a community hospital called Salem Memorial Hospital.

Salem Academy (q.v.) grew out of a Bible school established in 1945, as an inter-Mennonite school representing G.C.M., E.M.B., and M.B. congregations following intergroup Bible study classes conducted from 1930 on. H.S.B.

Orenburg *Mennonite Settlement.* The province of Orenburg, now Chkalov region, its capital having the same name, is located on the Ural River in Eastern European Soviet Russia. The region has an area of 47,787 square miles and a population of 1,677,013 (after World War II). The city of Orenburg (Chkalov), established in 1735, is located on the railroad from Samara (Kuibyshev) to Tashkent; its population was 172,925 after World War II. The population of the province consists of Russians, Bashkirs, Tatars, and many minority groups including Germans. The capital of Orenburg is a significant trading center between Asiatic and European Russia.

Beginning of the Settlement. In 1892-93 the Mennonites of the Chortitza (q.v.) Mennonite settlement in the Ukraine sent a commission to the Deyev, landowning Russians, in the province of Orenburg, who had offered some land for sale. Since the commission made the visit during the winter they did not even see the land, which was located some 35-45 miles from the railroad station and about 50 miles from the city of Orenburg. The price per acre was 9 rubles. The land purchased amounted to 67,500 acres, to which 2,700 acres were added later. The purchase was made by the Chortitza Mennonite volost (administration) and the land was distributed among the landless Mennonites of the Chortitza Mennonite settlement. Each farmer was to have not less than 110 acres and was to be exempt from payment on the land and taxes for two years. One of the Chortitza villages gave each of its families 200 rubles additional aid. The first settlers were already organized into five villages before leaving. They left on four trains from the station of Alexandrovsk (q.v.; now Zaporozhe).

The Orenburg settlement is located on the Tchuran, Uran, and Gusicha rivers. At least 25 villages were established. Karl Fast reports that there were 28 before World War II. In 1894-97 Chortitza, Petrovka, Kantserovka, Kamenka, Deyevka, Nikolayevka, Romanovka, and Feodorovka were established. Starting in 1900 the following additional villages were established: Pretoria, Suvorovka, Dolinovka, Rodnichnoye, Dobrovka, and Kitchkas. All these founded by settlers were from the Chortitza settlement.

Starting in 1895 the Molotschna Mennonite settlement established the following villages adjacent to the Chortitza Mennonite villages: Kubanka, Klubnikovo, Stepanovka, Aliessovo, Karaguy, Kameshevoye, Chernozernoye, Zelenoye. Additional villages were Zabangul, Lyubimovka, and Pogornoye.

The Orenburg settlement never received an "official" name. Sometimes it was known as the Deyevka Mennonite settlement and sometimes the Orenburg Mennonite settlement. After 1917 the settlement was known as Uran Volost.

The first years of the settlement were very difficult. Many of the settlers returned to their mother

Orenburg Mennonite Settlement, Russia

According to P. J. Dyck, _Orenburg am Ural_

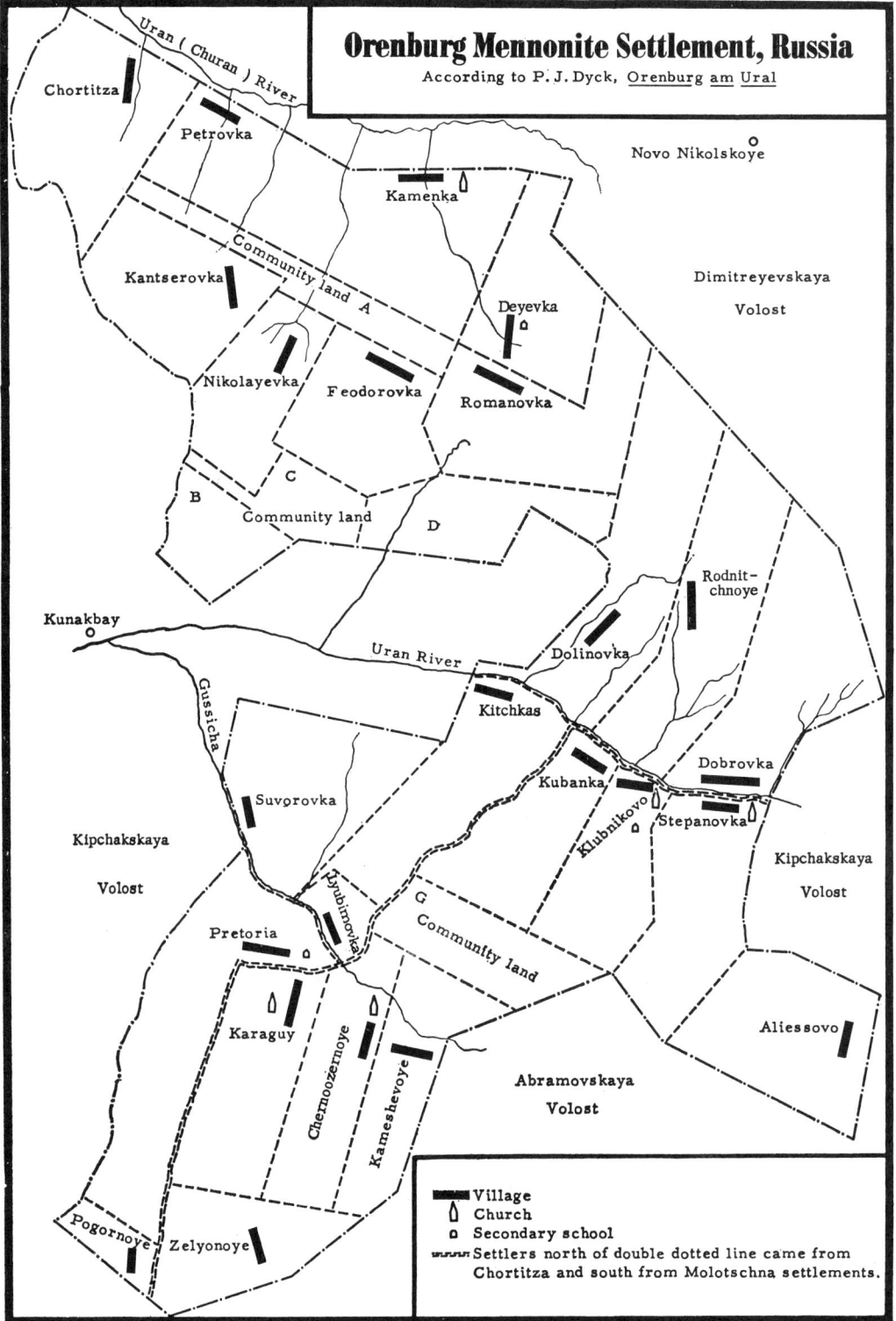

Chortitza

Uran (Churan) River

Petrovka

Kamenka

Novo Nikolskoye

Kantserovka

Community land A

Dimitreyevskaya

Volost

Deyevka

Nikolayevka

Feodorovka

Romanovka

B

C

Community land

D

Rodnit-
chnoye

Kunakbay

Uran River

Dolinovka

Gussicha

Kitchkas

Suvorovka

Kubanka

Dobrovka

Klubnikovo

Stepanovka

Kipchakskaya

Volost

Lyubimovka

G

Community land

Kipchakskaya

Volost

Pretoria

Karaguy

Chernoozernoye

Kameshevoye

Aliessovo

Abramovskaya

Volost

Pogornoye

Zelyonoye

■ Village
⌂ Church
▯ Secondary school
〜〜 Settlers north of double dotted line came from
   Chortitza and south from Molotschna settlements.

settlements. Their reports did not raise the reputation of the new settlement. Poverty, long winters,
poor soil, remote markets, theft by the surrounding
nomadic population, and other factors made the
beginning extremely difficult. Crop failures were
frequent, but the mother settlement was unable or
unwilling to make the necessary loans to give the
settlement a good start. The cycle of crop failures
was as follows: 1901, 1906, 1911, 1916, 1921. The
worst of all was 1906, when the mother and sister
settlements helped by collecting food, clothing, and
money for the settlers. Feed for the livestock had to
be bought in the vicinity.

In 1907-8 many of the Orenburg Mennonite settlers joined the Mennonites from the Ukraine in establishing the Slavgorod (*q.v.*) and Pavlodar (*q.v.*)
settlements in Siberia. Some of the land of those
who left the Orenburg settlement was distributed
among those who remained.

Gradually the economic life of the settlement became more normal. A number of minor industries
were established. About five mills powered by wind
and water were operated to grind the necessary
flour. One of the better-known water-powered mills
was operated by Jacob A. Eckert. The necessary
food oil was produced in the mill operated by Johann J. Löwen. In the carpenter and smith shops
the necessary furniture and tools were made and
repaired. Implement and machinery stores were
operated by Jacob Bergen of Klubnikovo and others. Other business enterprises were set up in the
villages of Pretoria, Klubnikovo, Dobrovka, and
Deyevka. After the Revolution co-operative stores
were introduced.

Administration, Education, Health. The administration of the settlement was the traditional one.
Each village had a Schulze (*q.v.*), and the Chortitza and Molotschna settlements each had an Oberschulze (*q.v.*) or Vorsteher. The Chortitza administration was responsible to the Bashkir volost (*q.v.*)
in Akhmerovo, and the Molotschna villages to the
Russian Abramov volost. At first the position of the
Oberschulze was somewhat unique. He was not
only a servant to the villages, but also to the mother
settlement in the Ukraine, whose interests he had to
represent since the settlement was sponsored by the
Chortitza and Molotschna settlements. Later the
Orenburg settlement became more independent.
Among the officeholders of the Chortitza villages at
Orenburg were Dietrich Lepp, Joseph Friesen, David Froese, Anton Günther, and Isaak Penner. In
1913 under Isaak Penner the Chortitza villages received title of land ownership and thus became independent of the Chortitza settlement. The officeholders of the Molotschna villages were Bernhard
Matthies 1895-99, Abram Fast 1899-1907, and Johann Spenst 1907-17.

After the Revolution the 25 Mennonite villages
were organized into an independent volost with its
seat in the village of Kitchkas. H. H. Löwen became the secretary and Jacob W. Pries the Oberschulze. The volost was subdivided into smaller
districts.

During and after the Russian Revolution of 1917
the settlement underwent the same changes as other communities. In the immediate vicinity of the

settlement the Bashkir and Kirghiz republics were
created, the boundary between the two cutting
across the Mennonite settlement. Both republics
claimed the Mennonite settlement within their
boundaries. The controversy between them was settled when the Bashkirs occupied the Mennonite settlement and took it over. The Mennonites were
constantly open to exploitation under this arrangement until they were transferred to the Kirghiz
Republic. Later developments have been the same
as in the rest of Russia.

Other public activities of the settlement were the
customary fire insurance, with separate divisions for
the Chortitza and Molotschna villages, as well as
the Waisenamt (*q.v.*; i.e., orphanage office). Medical care was primitive in the early days. The usual
midwives and bonesetters (*Knochenarzt*) took care
of the basic needs. Among the midwives were Mrs.
Jacob Giesbrecht and Mrs. Cornelius Kehler. Johann Braun, who settled in Orenburg in 1902, had
some training and experience in the care for the
sick and became known as "Dr. Braun." He did
much to relieve suffering in the settlements. For
a while he was assisted by Dr. Michel from St.
Petersburg. After Braun's death in 1911 a Pole by
the name of Yunovitch practiced medicine until the
outbreak of World War I (1914). In 1922 Dr.
Rudolph A. Klassen, under the sponsorship of
American Mennonite Relief, served the community
until he emigrated to Canada. He was succeeded by
Dr. Lassmann. In 1925 the Soviet government
opened a hospital in the Mennonite village of Rodnichnoye with Dr. Shostakov in charge.

The settlers established an elementary school in
each village. Some of the teachers, e.g., Isaak G.
Krahn, David H. Löwen, and Johann B. Mathies,
had received a normal teacher's training. The annual salary of a teacher in the early days was 350-
650 rubles. Some of the young boys went to the
mother settlements for secondary school training.
In 1919 twelve of the elementry schools had two
rooms.

In 1907 a Zentralschule (*q.v.*) was established at
Pretoria, a secondary school which helped to raise
the educational and cultural level of the settlement.
One of the outstanding leaders of the school board
was P. P. Dyck. Among the teachers of this school
were R. A. Riesen, Franz, F. Lehn, Dietrich J.
Gossen, P. P. Sawatzky, Fr. F. Froese, P. P. Dyck,
D. H. Loewen, D. H. Koslowsky, and F. F. Klassen. In 1918 and 1920 respectively the settlement
established additional secondary schools in Deyevka
and Klubnikovo. By 1925-26 all the schools were
taken over by the Soviet government and administered according to the Marxian philosophy, which
is vividly described by Karl Fast.

In 1923 a Bible school was established in Orenburg by an organization of 61 members. Isaak J.
Töws was the chairman, Peter Paethkau secretary,
and Gerhard Braun treasurer. Jakob Rogalsky was
the first teacher and the instruction was given in the
home of G. Derksen in Karaguy. During the
second year the school had 47 pupils and Jakob
Rempel and Peter Koehn were added as teachers.
The instruction was given in the home of David
Rempel of Kantserovka. During the third year

(1925-26) 67 pupils attended the school and the instruction was given in the Mennonite Brethren church of Kamenka. The pupils came from various other settlements besides Orenburg. The government closed the school in 1927.

World War I and After. During World War I many of the men were drafted for forestry service (*q.v.*) and hospital work. In many instances the women had to do the work in the home as well as on the farm. In 1915 some six thousand German nationals were interned in the Mennonite and surrounding villages. The novel *Das sibirische Tor* by Hans Harder deals at length with this incident. After the war most of them returned to Germany. Only a few Mennonite girls married German nationals and went along to Germany.

During and after the Revolution the Orenburg Mennonites suffered severely, although not as much as some of the Mennonites of the Ukraine. Requisitions of property, grain, horses, etc., were common. In 1921 the settlement experienced a crop failure and starvation set in. In some of the surrounding villages a large percentage of the population perished. The Mennonites organized a relief committee to collect food for distribution among the starving. An attempt was made to take clothing to Siberia in return for food, but it failed. Some help came in 1921 when the American Mennonite Relief reached Orenburg. D. R. Höppner reached Orenburg in March 1922 and supervised the distribution of relief until August 1924. Some fifteen carloads of food supplies were distributed, not only among Mennonites. In addition to this much was done to improve health conditions among the settlers. American clothing was distributed in 1923-24. American Mennonite Relief also established a tractor service to boost agriculture. Thus the crisis of 1921-22 was gradually overcome.

A great problem for the settlement during the Revolution and the years of civil war was the attacks made by the surrounding nomadic population. Some of the young Mennonites organized a Selbstschutz (*q.v.*) to defend their lives and property, although this action was officially condemned by the churches.

In the early days of the Soviets the Mennonites of Orenburg were permitted to do alternative service, supported by the settlement. In 1920-22 they worked on a large near-by estate. Later exemption from military service became impossible.

After the Revolution, during the NEP period, the Orenburg Mennonite settlement revived its economic and religious life (as is recorded in the pages of *Unser Blatt* and *Der Praktische Landwirt*). The results of the crop failures of 1921-22 and the following years were gradually overcome. In 1925 a co-operative was founded to raise the quality of the seed and livestock of the settlement. The co-operatives, which proved to be a success, established tractor stations, dairying, etc. From January 1 to September 1, 36 tons of cheese were produced. Great progress was made in agriculture as well as in the cultural and religious activities of the communities. The total population of the Orenburg Mennonite settlement was 5,767 on Feb. 1, 1926. In 1913 the congregations were centered in Deyevka (since

1899) with 1,103 members and 1,615 minor children, in Klubnikovka with 594 souls, and in Karaguy with 286 souls. The last two belonged to the Mennonite Brethren.

During the NEP period the elders of the Mennonite Church and the Mennonite Brethren Church, Heinrich Rempel and Kornelius Vehr, died and were succeeded by Isaak Krahn and David Janz. The relationship between the two churches improved. One writer states, "As never before the children of God are striving toward unity." Bible studies and song festivals were jointly conducted. Plans were under way to construct one large church for use by both groups. Soon the great change came and religious activities were suppressed and survived only in the hearts of individual believers. Rigid collectivization set in.

Some 300 persons migrated to Canada in 1926 under the leadership of Peter P. Dyck. On Sept. 9, 1926, the group left Orenburg in nine freight cars, arrived at Moscow on Sept. 15, and at Riga on Sept. 18, and proceeded to Canada.

When the NEP period came to a close in 1928-29 and the new collectivization program was inaugurated many regretted that they had not left Russia. Among the thousands of refugees reaching Moscow in the fall of 1929 there were many from Orenburg. Most of them, however, were returned; some reached Paraguay and Brazil. Many of those remaining in Russia were exiled. Walter Quiring lists nineteen leading settlers, teachers, and ministers who were exiled at this time.

When the German army invaded Russia, the Orenburg settlement, unlike most of the other Mennonite settlements of European Russia, was not evacuated. This, however, did not mean that the settlement did not suffer. The exploitation of the settlers during the dark years of the Revolution continued. Again in 1951 the region of the Orenburg settlement experienced a drought. All religious services were forbidden. In 1951 a letter says, "Religious funeral services cannot be conducted but we are permitted to sing. Nothing is offered to the children" (by way of spiritual life) (*Menn. Rundschau,* July 30, 1952, p. 5, 16).

Conditions changed considerably in 1955. Reports reached relatives in America about conversions, religious revivals, and worship services. Not only did the surviving ministers start to preach, but also many of the converted but unordained young men began to conduct meetings and preach. Worship services and Bible study were conducted in the homes and barns of the various villages. It even became permissible to teach some German in the elementary schools. Baptismal services are held. One report states that 98 persons from eight villages were baptized at one time in the village of Petrovka. Numerous ministers were ordained. The writers are enthusiastic about the privilege of worshiping again.

A letter published in *Der Bote* (Jan. 4, 1956, p. 7) reports that a group met regularly for worship services and that the congregation was growing. Abram Dyck is the leading minister. Another letter published in the *Rundschau* (Feb. 1, 1956, p. 6) reports that a group met regularly for worship in the home of Heinrich Unruh at Kubanka and that David Günter was the minister. Thus far seemingly none of the former meetinghouses have been reopened for worship services. In Romanovka the former schoolhouse became a clubhouse and the church was converted into a schoolhouse.

The economic life has changed and improved considerably since World War II. All farming is done on a collective basis. One of the letters of 1955 reports that women do not need to work outdoors during the winter. An old couple by the name of Peter Braun is supported by the collective. A letter published in *Der Bote* (Oct. 12, 1956, p. 8) states that three men have married Russian women, that they have enough food and clothing, and that they had just received electric lights and radios. The correspondence shows that the young men are drafted into the Russian army. There are no indications that this is not taken for granted.　　C.K.

Peter P. Dyck, *Orenburg am Ural* (Yarrow, 1951); Hans Harder, *Das sibirische Tor* (Stuttgart, 1938); Karl Fast, *Gebt der Wahrheit die Ehre* (North Kildonan, 1950); J. Rempel, *Der Sowjet Hölle entronnen* (Kassel, 1935); P. C. Hiebert and Orie O. Miller, *Feeding the Hungry* (Scottdale, 1929) 353 ff.; Adolf Ehrt, *Das Mennonitentum in Russland* (Berlin, 1932); *Der Bote* (Rosthern), Feb. 10, April 7, May 12, 1954; Aug. 17. Sept. 21, Oct. 12, 1955; Jan. 4, Jan. 11, Jan. 18, Feb. 22, April 25, May 2, 1956; Jan. 23, 1957; *Menn. Rundschau* (Winnipeg), June 9, 1948; Jan. 18, 1950; April 18, 1951; Feb. 6, July 30, Aug. 6, 1952; April 14, May 12, Aug. 4, Sept. 15, Sept. 29, Oct. 15, 1954; April 15, April 27, May 18, June 22, July 27, Aug. 10, Aug. 17, Aug. 24, Oct. 12, Nov. 23, Dec. 7, 1955; Feb. 1, March 7, April 11, April 18, May 30, July 18, Aug. 8, Oct. 24, 1956; Jan. 9, Jan. 30, 1957; *Unser Blatt* I (1925) 44; II (1926) 23; III (1927) 91 and 146; *Der Praktische Landwirt* (Moscow, 1926) No. 1, p. 10 ff.; No. 10-11, p. 14; *ML* III, 308.

Oreville (Pa.) Mennonite Home: see **Mennonite Home**, Lancaster, Pa.

Organs: see **Musical Instruments.**

Orienta Mennonite Church: see **Fairview** (Okla.) Church of God.

Original Sin. In the New Testament the term "original sin" does not appear, although the basic idea of the doctrine is found in Paul's epistles, Rom. 5 and I Cor. 15. But it should be noted that Paul nowhere overemphasized this idea; he asserts that men, if reborn in Christ, "will die to sin." It was not until the days of Augustine (d. 430) that the idea became a central issue of Christian anthropology and soteriology. Augustine taught that man became completely corrupt by the fall of Adam; that is he can do no good whatever (denying any freedom of the will), hence has to rely wholly upon God's forgiving grace, which the believer received undeservedly through the atoning death of Christ. Augustine defended this thesis against Pelagius (a British monk), who denied the sinfulness of man and thus asserted that man can do good of his own volition.

The Reformation, both Lutheran and Calvinistic, renewed definitely the Augustinian position of total corruption (or depravity) and of man's inability to do any good, mainly in opposition to both the Catholic doctrine of "Semi-Pelagianism" and the teachings of the humanists, above all Erasmus, who taught that man has a completely free will to decide for or against the good.

The Anabaptists were for the most part outside of all these controversies. With few exceptions they read neither Augustine nor Luther nor Erasmus; therefore the issue of original sin was for them of significance only as they found themselves in religious debates or polemics where they had to defend their position against their Catholic and Protestant opponents. In the rather extensive doctrinal literature of the Anabaptists of the 16th century there are scarcely more than a dozen pages dealing with the issue of original sin; in fact, most doctrinal tracts of the Anabaptist brethren completely by-pass this idea or doctrine. John C. Wenger in his *Doctrines of the Mennonites* (1952) presents only one quotation from Menno Simons in his chapter on "Sin"; and Christian Neff in his article **Erbsünde** in the *Mennonitisches Lexikon* says that the Anabaptists avoided the term "original sin" because it is not found in the Scriptures. Hans Denk declined outright to speak about original sin (with its implication of depravity of man) since he strongly felt that an urge for the good is present in every man. The man who could write the tract *Concerning True Love* naturally had little use for a lamentation concerning man's inability to love. In fact, even Pilgram Marpeck, one of the few Anabaptists who developed specific ideas in this area, also stressed what he calls the *Gegenerb* (counterinheritance), meaning the promise to mankind of the coming reconciliation of man through Christ and the message of brotherly love.

It is therefore fitting to ask how Protestantism and Anabaptism, both deriving their doctrines from the Bible, could develop their teachings in such divergent directions. The clue to this puzzle may be found in two arguments: (*a*) The Anabaptists believed in the freedom of the will, though to be sure not of the Pelagian type but rather in the sense that with the help of divine grace man may overcome evil tendencies in his character and obey the divine commandments. Without this freedom of the will discipleship, the heart of Anabaptism, loses its meaning. (*b*) The Anabaptists believed in and strongly emphasized spiritual rebirth (John 3:3), the transformation of "natural" man into "spiritual" man who now can see his new way, and likewise feels his power (received through a spiritual experience) to resist evil, sin, disobedience to God, pride, and selfishness, which formerly might have dominated his character. Of course, such newly gained strength is never a complete guarantee against possible backsliding (see below, Felbinger's Confession), and life remains a continuous struggle between the two natures of man.

On both points the Reformers took a different direction, remembering Paul's cry of desperation: "For I know that in me dwelleth no good thing" (Rom. 7:18, and similar words), but overlooking his assurance that the believer has actually died to sin. Thus the controversy developed between the Augustinian position on the one hand and the evangelical on the other: the awareness of one's basic corruption versus the divine call to discipleship, something which the Reformers considered well-nigh impossible and indeed held to be a sort of pharisaical self-righteousness and pride.

To understand the Anabaptists' position one must consider their scattered utterances concerning man and his predicament. "One must discriminate between *having* sin and *committing* sin," said Claus Felbinger (*q.v.*) in 1560. Of course, as careful Bible readers the Anabaptists knew very well Paul's thesis that all mankind has inherited from its first parents some corruption, some evil tendencies, and an inclination toward disobedience to God, in short "sin." But this inheritance must under no condition be taken as an inescapable fate which cannot be mended. Hubmaier's booklet *Concerning Free Will* (1527) refers expressly to a passage by the prophet Ezekiel (18:4, and 20) that "the soul that sins shall die" (i.e., the soul may either sin or not die), and he quotes Ezekiel's dictum that "the son shall not bear the iniquities of the father nor shall the father bear the iniquities of the son." This reference to Ezekiel is particularly significant for Anabaptist thought because it removes the fatalistic character of "inherited" sin which became so oppressive in Protestant orthodoxy and so hopeless as to life's possibilities. Later Peter Riedemann (*q.v.*) used the same argument in his great *Rechenschaft* (*q.v.*) of 1540. The *Handbüchlein wider den Prozess* (see **Bedenken**) of 1558, which elaborates on this issue, repeats Riedemann's quotation from Ezekiel.

It is quite probable that the idea of original sin came into Anabaptist thought not so much through the Apostle Paul's writings (where the idea is by no means dominating), but rather through the apocryphal book known as "The Fourth Book of Ezra," which was a favorite of the Anabaptists. In chapters 3 and 7 of this volume, often quoted in Anabaptist and Mennonite tracts, the idea of original sin is elaborated upon and lamented. "O thou Adam, what hast thou done! For though it was thou that sinned, thou art not fallen alone but we all that come of thee" (IV Ezra 7:48). But inasmuch as the Anabaptist brotherhoods were gatherings of "reborn" souls who in accepting baptism upon faith had pledged themselves to walk the narrow path and to fight sin, and to help each other in this fight both by discipline and order, this recognition of man's fall did not at all lead to despair and an exclusive "sola fide" theology, as with the Reformers. "We should fear God," wrote Jakob Hutter (*q.v.*) in 1535, "and be careful concerning our inherent sin and inborn weakness, so that we do not allow that sin any longer to dominate in our mortal body, and also that we will no longer be obedient to sin and the devil and may not use our limbs any longer for sinning." This was the meaning of the pledge given at the time of the believer's baptism.

In dealing with the problem of original sin—mainly on the occasion of debates with authorities or when rejecting accusations—the Anabaptists appropriately distinguished between two separate problems: (*a*) the function of original sin in infants who do not yet know the distinction between good and evil, and (*b*) the role and working of original sin in the life of adults before and after conversion.

(*a*) The first problem deals of course also with infant baptism as considered necessary by the Catholic Church to save these infants from hell. On this point all Anabaptists were unanimous. Although sin, handed down through the generations through the Adamic nature, inescapably leads to temporal or physical death ("The wages of sin is death"—an oft-quoted verse in Anabaptist tracts) of both children and adults, it does not mean condemnation to eternal death or hell, since Christ has died for all mankind (no predestination!) and thus reconciled God and man. Thus He died also for the innocent children. In this regard they were sure of God's bountiful grace made efficacious through Christ's supreme sacrifice. Whether we read Riedemann or Marpeck or Menno Simons or the Hessian Confession of 1578, there is no difference on this point: infant baptism as a saving sacrament has no justification in evangelical faith. Indeed to claim that unbaptized children should be eternally lost was in their eyes a climax of blasphemy and an expression of lack of faith.

(*b*) Quite different is the understanding of the brethren concerning sin in adult life. They did not deny its presence or power in the body, the inclination or tendency toward evil (*Neigung* or *Neiglichkeit*), in a still stronger term also "temptation." It is helpful to remember that the Anabaptists shared the radical dualism of the writers of the New Testament, that is, the contraposition of the world of the devil and darkness and the world (or kingdom) of God and of light. Similarly they accepted the Pauline dualism of flesh and spirit, nature and supernature. "Through conversion," Pilgram Marpeck asserts, "man came from nature into supernature (*aus der Natur in die Uebernatur*) and became a spiritual being." Without such dualism the experience of true conversion and rebirth would completely lose its existential meaning. As soon as man enters the new "covenant of a good conscience with God" (I Peter 3:21), that is through baptism, he is determined to resist this inclination to sin, and will bring his flesh under the discipline (*Zuchtrute*) of the spirit. Only thus can he try to be obedient to God's commandments and be assured that it is possible "to be as pure as the newborn babes" (Ulrich Stadler, 1536, quoting I Peter 2:2).

This was the opinion of practically all Anabaptists and it appears that teachings of this kind must have developed in many places at a rather early date. Sebastian Franck's (*q.v.*) famous *Chronica, Zeitbuch und Geschichtsbibel* of 1531 contains exactly these ideas as the gist of the Anabaptist position concerning original sin. In the section "Chronica der Römischen Ketzer" (Fol. 447) he says:

"Concerning original sin nearly all Anabaptists teach as follows: just as the righteousness (*Gerechtigkeit*) of Christ is of no avail to anyone unless he makes it a part of his own being through faith, so also Adam's sin (i.e., original sin) does not impair anybody except the one who makes it a part of his own being through faith, and likewise brings forth fruit of this sin. For, as foreign righteousness does not save anybody, so will foreign sin not condemn anybody either. [See below, the reference to Ezek. 18.]

"On the other hand, if Adam's sin condemns all men at once merely by its (inherent) nature, it necessarily follows that Christ's righteousness would save all men at once. But if Christ's righteousness saves only those believers who by faith have become transformed into Christ Himself, that is, who no longer live themselves but Christ lives in them, then it follows clearly that Adam's sin likewise condemns only nonbelievers who became Adam not by the mere fact of having been born but by their particular faith or rather unfaith, and by the fact that they bring forth fruit of this kind of faith; in other words, that they are rooted and planted in Him and He in them. That is how they speak of that matter."

On Fol. 446, he says, "Nearly all Anabaptists consider children to be of pure and innocent blood, and they consider original sin not a sin which of itself condemns both the children and the adults. They also claim that it does not make anyone unclean except the one who accepts this sin, makes it his own, brings forth fruits of it and is unwilling to part from it. For they claim foreign sin does not condemn anybody, and in this they refer to the 18th chapter of Ezekiel."

We shall now discuss in greater detail this concept of original sin as held by the southern Anabaptists, examining first several Hutterite doctrinal writings (1536-58) since they furnish relatively the richest yield, and shall then undertake a similar study in the writings of Pilgram Marpeck, the man whom Horst Quiring rightly claimed to have been one of the very few Anabaptist leaders to develop a real doctrine of original sin.

The earliest Hutterite documents on this point are Ulrich Stadler's two epistles of 1536 to the brethren in Crasniktau in Poland. In them he states categorically, "What does not derive from faith is sin." His first letter has clearly two parts: a gloomy one dealing with God's wrath and punishment, and a hopeful one showing that there is a way out. "The spirit in us that does not consent to sin has pleasure in the Law and agrees that it is good." And then he continues that the new man will certainly receive the strengthening help of Jesus Christ so that the spirit will rule in him and *compel* the flesh to become obedient to this spirit.

It is interesting to find exactly the same phrase in Peter Riedemann's *Rechenschaft*. Repentance brings about a real turning point, after which man begins to "bring his flesh into subjection." But of course this is by no means the entire story. As mentioned above, Riedemann affirms that no one may attain what is good unless he is born again. If Christ had not come into the world, there would be no more hope for life. But now, since He became the reconciliation for the whole world (Col. 1:20; I John 2:2), He has brought it about that original sin, "before it stirreth within man, leading to further sin, now causeth physical death only and not eternal, that the word might be fulfilled:

the children shall not bear the iniquities of the fathers but he who sinneth shall himself die. Ezek. 18."

Further, he who is genuinely sorry for his sin must henceforth guard himself against it and flee from it as from a serpent. Ecclesiasticus 21. Do not misinterpret, however, this Hutterite position as gloomy and puritanically stern. Right after this chapter concerning original sin, Riedemann deals joyously with the New Covenant and assures the reader with words taken from the Epistle to the Galatians: "This then is the covenant of childlike freedom of which we also are the children, if and when we submit and surrender ourselves to its working."

In 1558 a Hutterite brother, probably Peter Walpot, drew up a reply to Melanchthon's (and other Lutheran theologians) pamphlet of 1557, called *Prozess wie es soll gehalten werden,* titled *Handbüchlein wider den Prozess.* In its seventh book or chapter, answer is given to Melanchthon's claim that the Anabaptists teach that children have no original sin. In this tract three different connotations of the idea of original sin are presented, which is perhaps the most succinct exposition of the Anabaptist "theology of sin." (1) Adam fell and drew with him all posterity (IV Ezra 7:48), including infants. The result is temporal death for all, infants and adults. But Christ is the reconciliation of the whole world, hence children will gain God's eternal grace, to be sure without any merit on their part. (2) Other original sin is the sinful inclination of man in general which is found in all. However, if this inclination is not yielded to (*nicht ins Werk gebracht wird*), then it does not condemn or lead to eternal death. "There is . . . now no condemnation to them which are in Christ Jesus" (Rom. 8:1). (3) "Inheritance" has no power over the one who believes in Christ (apparently he is thinking here of temptations and *Anfechtungen*). "Whosoever is born of God doth not commit sin" (I John 3:9). The *Handbüchlein* repeats once more the reference to Ezekiel, obviously borrowing from the *Rechenschaft.*

In a more practical vein Claus Felbinger repeats the same ideas in his trial before Bavarian authorities at Landshut in 1560. As the child grows, his inclinations to sin will likewise become stronger. "Therefore one must teach them the fear of the Lord and keep them with the rod until they reach understanding." The adult finally, if he desires to enter into the bond of God and to spend his life in godliness, and if this desire is well proved, will be baptized upon confession of faith. But even the devout are never exempt from original sin, that is, the rising urge in the flesh, evil occurrences, and sinful thoughts. It will trouble and sadden them. Although we have died to sin (Rom. 6), original sin still remains with us; as long as man is in the flesh he must fight against it ceaselessly.

Pilgram Marpeck does not add much to the above "theology" except that his presentation is slightly more intellectual. According to Jan Kiwiet, Marpeck followed strongly the line of Hans Denk (a sort of mysticism of love), mainly in his anthropology. He taught that even after Adam's fall

7

God remained a gracious God and did not withdraw His breath from man. In other words, the "image of God" (also called "breath of God") remains with man and distinguishes him from the rest of creation. Man, created in God's image and capable of loving, therefore has the freedom of conscience to deliberately accept or reject God's commandments, that is, the freedom to either obey or disobey. Not the flesh, not procreation, not any natural process as such is sinful; rather sin must be understood as being rooted in "knowledge": *Die Sünde steht im Wissen.*

Man is born with a tendency toward evil (as we now know), which tendency can be observed even in a young child, but such a tendency may not yet be called "sin," as it has not become a conscious act of the will. Only conscious acts have the quality of obedience or disobedience, faith or sin, and it is only when we are sinning consciously and deliberately that this inborn tendency may be understood as "original sin." It is at the same time that man is called to repentance and conversion. Baptism upon faith is dying to sin, for it means that we have freely decided for Christ.

Original sin draws its inevitable consequences: a troublesome and sorrowful life, and eventually natural death. And it is universal. Marpeck emphasizes the power and inevitability of sin in man as he comes to the time of knowledge. Marpeck therefore rejects Schwenckfeld's charge that he is a Pelagian, and indeed as Bergsten says, his emphasis on the power and universality of sin "saves him from any Pelagian optimism in his concept of man." Marpeck however also holds the idea of the real image of God in man even after the Fall (which was also an idea in Hubmaier's writings). Whatever heritage we have received from Adam does not deprive us of our own final responsibility before God. "The old heart is of no avail, therefore God must give us a new heart." Marpeck like all the other Anabaptists refers expressly to Ezekiel 18 as his main locus against an overworked doctrine of original sin. In the *Vermanung* of 1542 we read: "Inasmuch as Ezekiel says that neither the child shall bear the iniquities of the father nor the father the iniquities of the child, who then will charge the unknowing children with sin?"

Horst Quiring, who analyzed Marpeck's anthropology for the first time, concluded from the fact that Marpeck speaks so seldom of man's sinfulness that there is a certain "optimism" in him with regard to his evaluation of man (somewhat like Hans Denk); in other words, Marpeck believes in man's basic capacity to overcome sin and to return to God as God's child. What characterizes Marpeck in particular is his refusal to identify sin and flesh (as many Hutterites seem to have believed), and to center the concept of sin in the "knowledge of good and evil." Even though fallen, man has never lost sight of God, and the way back, though it may be a hard one, is yet a glorious possibility.   R.F.

The Dutch Mennonites of the present time do not hold the doctrine of original sin. This is not a consequence of predominant Liberalism (*q.v.*), but of Mennonite aversion to this doctrine from the earliest period of Anabaptism. In the numerous accounts written by or about the Dutch 16th-century martyrs, original sin is rarely mentioned. When the doctrine came up for discussion during the trials, as in the cross-examination of Jacques d'Auchy (*q.v.*) and Adriaen Cornelis (*q.v.*), the martyrs rejected the Roman Catholic view. This Mennonite position may have been due in part to the fact that they were usually not scholarly theologians and did not understand fine theological distinctions, but it was still more due to their fundamental aversion to this doctrine. Their denial of the effects of original sin was one of the principal themes during the great disputations held with Calvinists (Frankenthal 1571, Emden 1578, Leeuwarden 1596). Calvinist theologians writing against the Mennonites in the 16th-18th centuries regularly charged them with the heresy of not accepting the doctrine of original sin.

Mennonite authors in general do not give this doctrine much attention. Even Menno Simons and Dirk Philips, the basic "theologians" of 16th-century Mennonitism, only incidentally deal with original sin. Menno uses the term in his *Foundation Book* and says, "We confess and believe that we are all born of unclean seed, that we through the first Adam became wholly depraved and children of death...." The Catholic Church, he continues, claims that we obtain remission of original sin by baptism; but we do not accept this view, since we believe that we receive forgiveness and remission by the death of the Son of God, the second Adam. "By him we have obtained grace, favor, and the forgiveness of our sins" (*Writings,* 130). In his *Een Weemoedige ende Christelycke Ontschuldinge* (*Reply to False Accusations*) (*Writings,* 563), Menno argues similarly: We are all conceived and born in sin and have a sinful nature, and "this is not ineptly called original sin"; but we have been reconciled by Christ and thus "for Christ's sake [the original sin] is not counted as sin unto us."

Dirk Philips (*q.v.*) is somewhat more minute in his expositions on this theme, but basically takes the same view as Menno. He admits the fact—at least theoretically—of total corruption (according to Psalm 51:7; Rom. 5:12, 18 f.). In *Van der Doope* he writes, "Man has become wretched, poor, and bare by Adam and has thus been born from him...," but the Lamb of God has "removed and covered the sin of Adam and of the whole world. For this reason now the sin of Adam and Eve will not condemn nor damn anybody, because Jesus Christ by His death and blood has removed it." At present children are "still" conceived and born in sin, but this "original sin, as it is called, is not imputed to them to damnation for Christ's sake. Children are somewhat like Adam and Eve before the fall, namely, they are simple and good and know neither good nor bad."

The Dutch Mennonite confessions scarcely deal with original sin. Jan Cents' Confession (1630), without mentioning the term original sin, simply states that mankind has fallen in Adam and has been reconciled by the mercy of God (Article 3). The Dordrecht Confession (1632), likewise avoiding the term, writes similarly (Articles 2 and 3).

Only the Cornelis Ris Confession (1766) is somewhat more circumstantial on this topic. Although Ris was somewhat influenced by Calvinism, he nevertheless rejected the consequences of the doctrine of original sin as taught by the Calvinists.

About 1700, when some Dutch Mennonites were leaning toward Calvinism, even adopting the Calvinist views on original sin, e.g., Lambert Bidloo (*q.v.*) and Douwe Feddriks (*q.v.*), influential Mennonite leaders both among the Zonists (*q.v.*) and the Lamists (*q.v.*), such as Herman Schijn (*q.v.*), Galenus (*q.v.*) Abrahamsz, and Jan Klaasz (*q.v.*), plainly rejected the doctrine of original sin. In *Verdediging der Christenen* (1699) Galenus formulates his concept thus: We believe that man, created good and right by God, has by his own trespass and fault fallen from this good estate, but that all has been abundantly restored by the Lord Christ...; that consequently innocent children are not born with damnable and deadly guilt; and nobody will be punished by the righteous God except for his own trespasses and his own sins (*Korte Grondstellingen*, No. XXV). In the 19th century a few Mennonites, influenced by the Reveil (*q.v.*), like Jan de Liefde (*q.v.*), showed some leaning toward the strict Calvinist views on original sin.

In summary it may be said that Dutch Mennonitism has rejected the doctrine of original sin for these three reasons. (*a*) because the term is unscriptural, (*b*) because Christ has removed the consequences of original sin, (*c*) because they could not admit that "the new life" (conversion) was hindered by an unfree will corrupted by original sin.

vDZ.

Torsten Bergsten, "Pilgram Marbeck und seine Auseinandersetzung mit Caspar Schwenckfeld," (Uppsala, 1958, reprint from *Kyrkohistorisk Arsskrift*, 1957 and 1958, 135 pp.), section "Die Erbsünde," 74-82; Heinold Fast, "Pilgram Marpeck und das oberdeutsche Täufertum," *Archiv für Ref.-Gesch.* XLVII (1956) 212-42; Hans Fischer, *Jakob Huter, Leben, Frömmigkeit, Briefe* (Newton, 1956) VI, 47; R. Friedmann, "Claus Felbinger's Confession of 1560," *MQR* XXIX (1955) 158; *idem*, "Peter Riedemann on Original Sin and the Way of Redemption," *MQR* XXVI (1952) 210-15; Jan Kiwiet, "The Theology of Hans Denck," *MQR* XXXII (1958) 3-27; Lydia Müller, *Glaubenszeugnisse oberdeutscher Taufgesinnter* (Leipzig, 1938) 228-34; Horst Quiring, "The Anthropology of Pilgram Marbeck," *MQR* IX (1935) 155-64; Peter Rideman, *Account of Our Religion, Doctrine and Faith* (n.p., 1950) 57; Theodor Sippel, "The Confession of the Swiss Brethren in Hesse, 1578," *MQR* XXIII (1949) 33; John C. Wenger, *The Doctrines of the Mennonite Church* (Scottdale, 1952) 10 f.; George H. Williams, ed., *Spiritual and Anabaptist Writers* (Philadelphia, 1957) 127; W. Wiswedel and Robert Friedmann, "The Anabaptists Answer Melanchthon," *MQR* XXIX (1955) 159; C. Krahn, *Menno Simons* (Karlsruhe, 1936) 23, 60, 130; Menno Simons, *Opera Omnia*, 18, 507 f.; *Writings*, 130, 563; *BRN* X, 74 f.; *ML* I, 603-5.

Orland Mennonite Brethren Church, located in the Capay District of Glen County, near Orland, Cal., a member of the Pacific District, was begun in 1922 when a number of families moved to this area from the Dallas, Ore., community, and later that year other families came from Canada. Services were held in a home and later in a schoolhouse. The same year the congregation was organized and a church building was started, which was completed in 1924 and is still in use after some remodeling.

The membership in 1957 was 111, with M. R. Schimnowski as pastor. M.R.S.

Orloff: see also **Ohrloff.**

Orloff, the name of settlements made by Mennonites in Europe and America. In Russia the spelling has been in some cases changed to Orlow, Orlovo, and Ohrloff besides Orloff.

In West Prussia Mennonite immigrants from Holland founded the village of Orloff in 1550 in what was then Polish territory; until the collapse in 1945 it was still inhabited by Mennonites who belonged to the Ladekopp (*q.v.*) congregation. Mennonites from this village were among the first emigrants to Russia, who in 1789 founded the Chortitza settlement in Ekaterinoslav province, Ukraine. In later settlements the Mennonites frequently transferred the name of the home village to the new one, as they did in the settlement of Deutsch-Wymysle founded in 1762 in Poland, which in 1905 numbered 105 members and 51 children.

One of the oldest villages with this name in Russia is Orloff (Ohrloff) in the southwest of the Molotschna settlement (*q.v.*) in the province of Taurida. It was founded in 1807 by 21 Mennonite families from West Prussia and developed into one of the most important Mennonite communities in South Russia. The number of families had grown to 127 by 1910 in spite of emigration to daughter colonies, and the population to 548. The Orloff congregation, to which the neighboring villages of Tiege, Rosenort, and Blumenort belonged, had a membership in 1905 of 980, with 508 children. Johann Cornies (*q.v.*) was instrumental in having one of the first Zentralschulen built here in 1848, which was later replaced by a splendid new building (picture, *ML* III, 156). In 1908 a girls' school was opened here, and in 1910 a hospital (picture, *ML* III, 157). From Sept. 27-29, 1894, representatives from all the Mennonite congregations in Russia met in conference here, in which it was urged that a theological division be added to the Zentralschule (Ediger, 55). A village in the Rückenau settlement of the Mennonite Brethren in the province of Taurida in 1860 was also named Orloff.

After the introduction of universal military duty in Prussia in 1848, one hundred Mennonite families in West Prussia received from the Russian government the permission to immigrate and to settle on the middle Volga in the province of Samara. Here they founded the Am Trakt settlement in 1855, which grew to 10 villages, and the Alt-Samara settlement (Alexandertal) in 1859 with 8 villages, one village in each settlement receiving the name Orloff. In the province of Kherson Mennonites from the Molotschna settlement founded the Zagradovka settlement in 1871, with 16 villages, one of them bearing the name of Orloff. Here a Zentralschule was built. In 1911 the village had a population of 297.

In the province of Ekaterinoslav, volost Golitsinovka, Bachmut (*q.v.*) district, the Memrik (*q.v.*) settlement came into being in 1885, with 10 villages on the Woltchya, a tributary of the Samara, which flows into the Dniepr. The settlers were Mennonites from the Molotschna, who built the village Orlovo (originally called Bahndorf, *q.v.*) with (1910) 189 inhabitants. Besides agriculture they were engaged in cattle raising, especially the German red cow.

Since 1907 Mennonite settlements have also been made in Siberia. The largest settlement in the province of Omsk is Slavgorod, formerly Barnaul (*q.v.*), with 58 villages, one of which is called Orloff (map, *ML* I, 126). And in the Tchunayevka (*q.v.*) settlement near the city of Omsk a village was given the name Orloff.

In South America the name Orloff in the Fernheim colony was given a village in Paraguay, which was settled in 1930 by Mennonite refugees from the Russian Amur region; in 1935 the village had 20 families.   HEGE.

Dirks, *Statistik* (Gnadenfeld, 1906); Heinrich Ediger, *Beschlüsse der von den geistlichen und anderen Vertretern der Mennonitengemeinden Russlands abgehaltenen Konferenzen* (Berdyansk, 1914); D. H. Epp, *Die Memriker Ansiedlung* (Berdyansk, 1910); *Christlicher Familien - Kalender* (Halbstadt, 1914); *Neuer Haus- und Landwirtschafts - Kalender* (Odessa, 1913); *Mennonitisches Jahrbuch,* No. 10 (Berdyansk, 1914); Jakob Quiring, *Die Mundart von Chortitza in Süd-Russland* (Munich, 1928); *ML* III. 309 f.

Orloff (Ohrloff), a common Mennonite village name which originated in Prussia and was transplanted to the Molotschna and Zagradovka settlements, Ukraine; Alexandertal and Trakt settlements, Samara; Barnaul and Omsk, Siberia; and Fernheim, Chaco, Paraguay. It is likely that the Russian Mennonite village names Orlovka and Orlovo (Memrik) are related to the German Orloff.   C.K.

Orloff, a Mennonite village of the Slavgorod Mennonite settlement (*q.v.*) in Siberia, established in 1908, became the administrative and cultural center of the settlement. In addition to the volost building, a post office and a hospital were erected. The latter was transferred to Halbstadt in 1928-29 where a district hospital was erected. For a while Orloff was the center of the Slavgorod Mennonite Church (*q.v.*). Orloff had a brick factory. A monument was erected in Orloff in 1912, to its benefactor Peter A. Stolypin (*q.v.*). (Gerhard Fast, *In den Steppen Sibiriens,* Rosthern, 1957, pp. 29 ff.) C.K.

Orloff Evangelical Mennonite Church, Zagradovka Mennonite settlement (*q.v.*), Ukraine, Russia, was established on Feb. 27, 1907, when Franz Martens (*q.v.*), elder of the Nikolaifeld Mennonite Church (*q.v.*), withdrew from the congregation with 11 ministers and 2 deacons. Twenty-eight families, consisting of 63 members, established the Altonau, later Orloff, Evangelical Mennonite Church under his leadership. The church emphasized baptism by immersion and the Lord's Supper administered to believers only. The congregation met for seven years in a former store building in Orloff, building a meetinghouse in 1914. In 1932 the congregation had 214 members and a total population of 466. It disintegrated like the others under the pressure of communism, and many members were exiled or went to America. (G. Lohrenz, *Sagradowka,* North Kildonan, 1947, pp. 74, 80.)   C.K.

Orloff Mennonite Brethren Church, in Fernheim Colony, Paraguayan Chaco, in 1957 had a membership of 122 with M. August as leading minister.
                                              H.S.B.

Orloff (Ohrloff) Mennonite Church, oldest congregation in the Molotschna settlement, Ukraine, then known as the Orloff-Petershagen congregation, was founded in 1804, the first year of the Molotschna settlement, with Jacob Enns as elder, followed by Jacob Fast, then Bernhard Fast as elders. Because of the progressive attitude of Elder Bernhard Fast and some other ministers, the greater conservative part of the congregation in 1824 abandoned Orloff and founded the Lichtenau congregation. What was left of the former was now known as the Orloff-Halbstadt congregation and after 1877 as the Orloff - Halbstadt - Neukirch congregation, until 1895, when Halbstadt also became independent. Thereafter it was called the Orloff-Neukirch congregation, with two places of worship, one at Orloff, the other at Neukirch, a village about 10 miles from Orloff.

After the departure of the large Lichtenau group in 1824 the Orloff congregation was for a long time spiritually and culturally the most advanced congregation of the Molotschna as well as the most tolerant. It favored higher education, and the first Zentralschule, known as the *Vereinsschule,* was established at Orloff. Johann Cornies (*q.v.*), the noted Mennonite administrator and cultural leader, was all his life a member of this congregation. During the 1860's, when the Mennonite Brethren Church came into being, Orloff with its elder Johann Harder was the first congregation to recognize it and to enter into friendly relations with it. Three elders of the Orloff church, Bernhard Fast 1821-60, Johann Harder 1860-76, and Abram Goerz 1876-1913, were all outstanding and strong personalities.

The greater part of the population of the following villages belonged to the Orloff church: Orloff, Tiege, Blumenort, Rosenort, Neukirch, Friedensruh, Tiegerweide, and some members from other villages. It was therefore a rural congregation consisting of farmers, numbering about 1200-1500, including children. The language of worship was German; for singing, the *Gesangbuch zum Gebrauch in den Mennonitengemeinden Russlands* was used. As in almost all Mennonite churches in Russia no instrument was used to accompany the singing, but choir singing was introduced at a comparatively early date. Church discipline was applied for moral misconduct.

The Orloff church was built in 1809, the first in the Molotschna settlement, with the money donated by Czar Alexander I. It was later considerably enlarged. The Neukirch church was erected in 1877.

The last elder, Jacob Wiens of Tiegerweide, emigrated to Canada in 1924. In 1926 P. D. Nickel was elected and ordained elder jointly of the Lichtenau and Orloff congregations. He served until 1930, when increasing religious persecution compelled him to leave Orloff. But worship continued until 1932, when the church was closed by the authorities. Even after that meetings were held for some time in private homes, until the last minister, W. H. Janzen, was arrested and banished. The building was then used as a Communist children's home.   H.G.

Orloff (Schönsee) Mennonite Church, located in the Slavgorod Mennonite settlement (*q.v.*) in Siberia, was organized in 1908. This was one of the five congregations of the Slavgorod settlement and the mother church of the others. The congregation served the following seven villages: Schönsee, Lichtfelde, Orloff, Schönwiese, Schönau, Rosenhof, and Friedensfeld. The first leading minister was Peter J. Wiebe, followed by Kornelius D. Harder, who was ordained elder. When Harder (*q.v.*) left for Canada in 1927 he was succeeded by Gerhard Warkentin. Other ministers were Gerhard A. Wiebe, Abram Töws, Cornelius Dück, Johann Fast, Heinrich Wiebe, Bernhard Derksen, Wilhelm Raabe, and Peter G. Wiebe. In 1922 the congregation purchased a house and remodeled it into a church. To what extent the religious life and activities of the congregation, which had to cease in 1932, were revived after 1953 has not become apparent. (See also **Slavgorod** Mennonite Church; Gerhard Fast, *In den Steppen Sibiriens,* Rosthern, 1957, ·p. 69.) C.K.

Orlofferfelde (Ohrlofferfelde), one of the oldest Mennonite congregations in West Prussia, Germany, at first Polish, from 1772 Prussian. It was situated in the Great Marienburg Werder, in the former "Oekonomie" of Tiegenhof. It originated in 1562, when the Loysen banking firm (*q.v.*) had Mennonites settle on the marshy land in the region of Tiegenhof, which the firm had received from the Polish crown in return for a loan, to drain and cultivate it. They settled about 12 miles north of Marienburg in 20 villages and organized a congregation, holding their services in the homes and barns of the members. Not until two centuries later did they receive the consent of the authorities to build a church in Orlofferfelde, in which Cornelius Grunau, an elder from Ohrloff, conducted the first service Dec. 5, 1751. The congregation belonged to the Frisian branch (*q.v.*) and was very active. The number of communicant members rose to more than 500. In the last part of the 18th century their elders Heinrich Donner (*q.v.*) and Johann Donner (*q.v.*) were among the leading personalities of the West Prussian Mennonite brotherhood. In the 18th century the Dutch *Naamlijst* calls this congregation Waterlander. The following ministers are mentioned in the *Naamlijst*: Aldert Aldertsz, Klaes Bestevader, Hendrik Quiring, David Mekelborger, elder *c*1740-71, David Horn 1753-75, Gerdt Albrecht 1754-*c*60, David Bestevader 1753-*c*75, Jan Bestevader 1760-87, Cornelius Grunou 1760-*c*95, Hendrik (Heinrich) Donner 1766, elder 1772, Jacob Penner 1766-73, Hans Horn 1775-after 1802, Jan (Johann) Quiring 1775-after 1802, Peter Dan 1794-?, Cornelis Fröse 1794-?, Jacob Bergthold 1799-1826. Repeatedly the congregation had contacts with the Dutch Mennonites. In 1709 and again in 1788, when its members were severely struck by floods, it received financial support from the Dutch Mennonite Committee of Foreign Needs (*Inv. Arch. Amst.* I, Nos. 1570, 1657, 1739-45; II, Nos. 2646, 2650; II, 2, Nos. 801, 856 f.). In 1852 the baptized membership numbered 315, in 1882, 256.

Besides the Frisian congregaton there was also a Flemish congregation with its seat at Ladekopp (*q.v.*), whose members lived in some of the same villages as the Frisians. When the Prussian law on the corporation rights of the Mennonites of June 1874 was published, which stipulated that the area of the congregation must be geographically defined, David Fröse, the elder of the Frisian group, attempted to co-operate with the Flemish in defining mutually favorable boundaries; after initial failure, these efforts resulted in the union of the two branches in 1882, which Fröse, however, did not live to see. The Orlofferfelde congregation yielded its independence in some respects; the treasury and the economic care of the members were united. But the pastoral care and religious services and preaching remained unaltered in the two branches.

Fröse's successor as elder of the Orlofferfelde congregation was Jakob Penner, a preacher of Platenhof, ordained Feb. 12, 1882, who made it his duty to give the young people of the congregation more thorough baptismal instruction, better suited to the needs of the time. To this end he wished to supplement the Donner catechism, which was also used by the Flemish congregation, in order, as he wrote, "to impress upon the hearts of the children the necessary explanations and admonitions in answering the questions of the catechism presented to them." The conference in Tiegenhagen decided in 1886 to publish a unified catechism for the "United West Prussian Mennonite congregations," and Penner was one of the leading authors of this booklet. But the union did not come to pass. In 1906 the Ladekopp-Orlofferfelde group published a second edition of Heinrich Donner's *Unterricht von der heiligen Wassertaufe* of 1792 under the same title, with the additional phrase, "sowie über das Verhalten der Täuflinge vor, bei und nach der Taufe."

The baptized membership of the Ladekopp-Orlofferfelde-Pordenau congregation (its official name at that time) numbered 756 in 1882, 707 in 1888; there were 1,141 souls in 1927, 1,021 (739 baptized members and 282 children) in 1940. The congregation possessed three meetinghouses, one in Ladekopp (built in 1768), one in Orlofferfelde (1751), and one in Pordenau (1800), and two old people's homes. In this congregation the Orlofferfelde branch had a degree of independence, with its own elder (Bruno Ensz of Tiege, preacher 1933, elder 1935) and preachers.

For the last ministers and the extinction of the congregation, see **Ladekopp.** (*ML* IV, 519.) HEGE.

Orlovo (German, *Bahndorf*), a Mennonite village in the Ukraine, Russia, in the Memrik settlement, post office Zhelannaya, Michailov village council (formerly volost Golitsinovka, Bachmut district, province Ekaterinoslav). In 1885 the village was founded by Mennonites from the Molotschna, province Taurida (see **Bachmut**). The inhabitants were farmers, and formed an artel named Astra with the villages Nikolayevka (Ebental), Marinovka (Nordheim), and Neu-Kalinovo. Orlovo had 2,268 acres of land. Besides agriculture the village also raised cattle. It had a school with thirty-two pupils and a pedagogically trained teacher. Most of the people belonged to the Mennonite Church, the rest to the Mennonite Brethren. The language spoken was Low German. In the school German and Ukrainian were taught (formerly German and Russian). The soil is black, and is well suited to farming. (*ML* III, 310.)　　J.C.

Orono (Maine) Civilian Public Service Unit No. 125, attached to the University of Maine, had a unit strength of ten men engaged in dairy service. Some of the men worked in the university dairy barns, while others worked on experimental farms. The unit was opened in December 1943 and was closed in May 1946.　　M.G.

　Melvin Gingerich, *Service for Peace* (Akron, Pa., 1949) 210.

Orphanage as an Anabaptist prison in Bern: see **Waisenhaus.**

Orphanage Society of the Eastern District Conference (GCM) was organized Nov. 9, 1905, by the conference Ladies Aid societies for the purpose of creating a fund for the care of orphans and the assistance of mothers. Active members consist of members of Mennonite churches who enroll in the society and support the work by freewill offerings. The original purpose, to create a fund to establish an orphans' home, was later changed to provide for orphans' and widows' support to keep families together in their own homes. Little progress was made until the fifth convention held in 1909 at Souderton, when a constitution was adopted and the first officers were elected.

　By the time of the 29th convention, held in Quakertown, Pa., on Nov. 11, 1933, a total of $5,000 had been accumulated. It was decided to create a permanent endowment fund with this money, using the interest for the welfare work of the society. The Orphanage Society has given much aid to needy orphans and widows within the membership of the Eastern District Conference. Contributions have been given to local orphanages. Orphans, nurses, and orphanages abroad have been supported as mission projects. Gifts have relieved war and famine sufferers in Europe and Asia, such as over 1,000 pairs of new shoes for war sufferers.　　G.G.S.

Orphanages (Children's Homes, Child Welfare Work, German *Waisenanstalt*). Because of the strong family and group solidarity among Mennonites, few orphanages have been established to care for Mennonite children except in Holland (see below); where established in modern times they have been service institutions to care for children from orphaned or broken homes outside the brotherhood.

In Europe, except until very recently in France, orphanages were established only in Holland and in Russia. In Russia Abram Harder established an orphans' home at Grossweide, Molotschna, in 1906, including a school, and in 1910 was caring for 27 children. About 1900 Franz Klassen established a school for poor children (*Armenschule*) at Berezovka near Davlekanovo, Ufa province, which Friesen says was "essentially the same" as the Grossweide institution. When Klassen left for America, Jacob J. Martens took over the school. Both institutions were located on farms with residence homes, operated schools, and were supported by donations.

In France the MCC established two children's homes: Mont des Oiseaux (*q.v.*) or Weiler near Wissembourg, Alsace, established in 1945, transferred to the French in 1951, and Valdoie (*q.v.*), near Belfort, established in 1950, transferred to the French in 1955. The Valdoie home had been operated in 1945-50 at Nancy by the MCC. The Association Fraternelle Mennonite (*q.v.*) was organized in 1950 by French Mennonites to operate the children's homes and other charitable institutions, and now owns and operates both Valdoie and Weiler. The MCC has operated a children's home at Bad Dürkheim in the Palatinate, Germany, since Oct. 15, 1949. This home and the two in France are not true orphans' homes since they normally take children only for shorter terms, and from broken or impoverished homes. All three receive substantial grants per child per day from the state, without which they could not operate.

In America the first Mennonite orphanage was established by the Leisy Orphan Aid Society (*q.v.*; GCM) in 1884 on the "Orphan Farm" 1½ miles south of Halstead, Kan., although the work was primarily to place orphans from home mission areas into Christian families. The Mennonite Orphan and Children's Aid Society (*q.v.*), organized in 1893 primarily to raise funds, was merged with the Leisy foundation in 1905 which still exists. The Orphanage Society of the Eastern District Conference (*q.v.*; GCM), organized in 1905, was established as a fund-raising agency, and has never operated an orphanage or placement service. In 1919 the Home Mission Board (GCM) began an orphan placement service which continued for a few years only.

In 1890 the Industrial School and Hygiene Home for Friendless Children (*q.v.*) was chartered in Kansas under a board of directors predominantly K.M.B. and located near the K.M.B Gnadenau Church near Hillsboro. In 1910-15 it gradually changed into a home for the aged and in 1915 was called Salem Home (*q.v.*). In 1898 the Defenseless Mennonites (now Evangelical Mennonites) established the Salem Orphanage, now called Salem (*q.v.*) Children's Home, on a farm 2½ miles southeast of Flanagan, Ill., given for that purpose.

The Mennonite Church (MC) has established three orphanages: the Mennonite Orphans' Home (*q.v.*) at West Liberty, Ohio (1896-1947), operated by the Mennonite Board of Missions and Charities, since 1957 turned into a school for retarded children called Adriel School; Mennonite Children's Home (*q.v.*) at Millersville, Pa., established in 1911 and operated by a local Lancaster Mennonite board; and the Mennonite Children's Home (*q.v.*) at Kansas City, Kan., established in 1917 and operated by the Mennonite Board of Missions and Charities. The only other children's home in North America is the Grace Children's Home (*q.v.*) at Henderson, Neb., established in 1936 and operated by an interdenominational Mennonite board, strongly E.M.B.

Orphans' homes have been established on numerous Mennonite mission fields. The Mennonite Church (MC) has done this in India, where the mission had its beginning in a sense with work done for famine orphans. The M.C. program which began in 1899 resulted in two orphanages, the Boys' Orphanage in Dhamtari and the Girls' Orphanage in Balodgahan, with a maximum total of nearly 500 orphans. The G.C.M. Mission in India, also located in the Central Provinces, began in a similar way two years later and also developed two orphanages, a Boys' Orphanage in Janjgir and a Girls' Orphanage in Birra. The M.B. Mission, begun about the same time but located further south in Madras Presidency, did not develop orphanage work in India. The M.B. board has had an orphanage in Brazil since 1947, located 8 miles from Curitiba, and took over and operated for 10 years, until 1949, the orphanage for Lengua Indian infants, which was started by the Paraguay Mennonites to rescue infants from the infanticide then commonly practiced by the Indians. The Mennonite Brethren in Christ in 1899 established an orphanage in Hadjin, Turkey, to care for Armenian children orphaned by the terrible massacre of 1896, taking a maximum of 305 orphans by 1905, with a home for boys and a home for girls. In 1910 the Boys' Orphanage was transferred to Everek about 25 miles from Caesarea in Cappadocia. The work was closed in 1914 and briefly reopened in 1919-20. The Mennonite (MC) mission in Argentina established an orphanage at Pehuajo in 1926, which was moved to Trenque Lauquen in 1927 and finally was settled in 1936 in Bragado with a new building. The Mennonite (MC) Belgium Mission has operated the Home of Hope at Ohain near Brussels since 1952 as a children's home.

The MCC has operated a home for delinquent boys at Ailsa Craig, near Stratford, Ont., since 1952, called Ailsa Craig Boys Farm. The Mennonite Board of Missions and Charities has since 1949 operated Youth Village, a summer camp near White Pigeon, Mich., for children from city and mission churches. (Friesen, *Brüderschaft*, 663.) H.S.B.

Netherlands. Formerly a large number of Dutch congregations had their own orphanages—not only the largest ones, like the Flemish congregations of Haarlem and Amsterdam, but also smaller ones like Harlingen and De Rijp, and even Ouddorp. Concerning the history of most of these orphanages, except in a few cases, there is not much information and in a number of cases no information at all.

Most of the orphanages were founded in the 17th century: Haarlem (Flemish congregation) 1634, Harlingen 1663, De Rijp 1676, Amsterdam Lamist congregation 1677, Leiden Waterlander congregation before 1681, Zaandam Nieuwe Huys 1712, Groningen 1847. Often in small congregations the orphans were lodged in the old people's home of the congregation. In the first quarter of the 19th century most of the orphanages were closed (Harlingen 1767 or shortly after, Ouddorp earlier), but others sheltered orphans until recent times: Zaandam until about 1900, and De Rijp until 1912. The Amsterdam orphanage was closed in 1800; after this the orphans of the congregation were cared for in the Oranjeappel (*q.v.*) orphanage, among the trustees of which from this date there were always representatives of the Amsterdam Mennonite Church. The reason for closing the orphanages was twofold: through better hygienic conditions and the elimina-

tion of epidemics the number of orphans steadily decreased; and gradually the idea prevailed that orphans could be better cared for in private homes than in sheltered orphanages.

At present there is only one Mennonite orphanage in the Netherlands, in which orphans are actually reared. It is the large orphanage building of the Haarlem Mennonite Church. The present building was opened on June 14, 1874. In 1860 the Vereeniging van Doopsgezinde Gemeenten, commonly called "Haarlemsche Vereeniging," also concerned itself with the Mennonite orphans. Later, when the Haarlemsche Vereeniging was dissolved, a part of its work was taken over by the newly organized Association on Behalf of Mennonite Orphans. Mennonite orphans of several congregations are now placed in homes, in the Haarlem Mennonite orphanage, or sometimes in De Oranjeappel.

The only Mennonite children's home in the Netherlands is operated by the Stichting (*q.v.*) voor bizonderen Noden, and was located at Oud-Wulven (*q.v.*) in 1947-58 and at present at Schoorl. vDZ.

The history of several Mennonite orphanages at Haarlem is described in *De Weeshuizen der Doopsgezinden te Haarlem 1634-1934* (Haarlem, 1934); for those of De Rijp and Zaandam see DB 1918, 20-29, and (S. Lootsma), *Het Nieuwe Huys, Friesch-Doopsgezinde Gemeente West-Zaandam*, 33-43, 139-60.

Orphans' Home (MC), later known as the Mennonite Children's Home, established in 1896 on a private basis by David Garber and S. K. Plank on their farm near Weilersville (not far from Orrville), Ohio, was moved in early 1900 to West Liberty, Ohio, with a formal opening on May 14, 1901. In 1899 it was placed under the Mennonite Board of Charitable Homes established in that year to own and operate this home and the Old People's Home at Rittman, Ohio. This board was merged into the Mennonite Board of Missions and Charities in 1906. It was continued as a standard orphanage for many years, in the 1940's was modified to emphasize orphan placement, was temporarily closed, to be reopened in 1957 as the Adriel School for retarded children. Abram Metzler (1854-1918) was the first and long-time superintendent of the West Liberty orphans' home. H.S.B.

L. L. Swartzentruber, *The Child, A History of the Mennonite Orphans' Home, West Liberty, Ohio* (Scottdale, 1931).

Orrville, a city (pop. 5,153) in Wayne County, Ohio, is the seat of a Mennonite (MC) congregation with 265 members, founded in 1909, and the partial shopping center for an additional Mennonite membership of 1,772 including six M.C. congregations—Kidron, Martins, Pleasant View, Crown Hill, Oak Grove, and Salem—and one G.C.M., viz., Salem, all within a six-mile radius. H.S.B.

Orrville Mennonite Church (MC), in Orrville, Ohio, was established in 1909 as a mission cooperatively by members of the Oak Grove (*q.v.*) Amish Mennonite Church and the Martin (*q.v.*) Mennonite Church. In 1909 the group took over the former Reformed Church building, which had been bought in 1907 by interested Mennonites. In 1911 the mission was taken over by the Mennonite

Board of Missions and Charities who operated it until 1921 when it was turned over to the Ohio Mennonite Mission Board. On April 2, 1922, the congregation was organized as the Orrville Mennonite Mission Church with 100 charter members. On Nov. 22, 1936, it was organized as the Orrville Mennonite Church, and became for the first time an independent congregation, a member of the Ohio and Eastern A.M. Conference, no longer under a mission board. Up to this time it had been treated as a child of the two Ohio conferences who furnished joint bishop oversight. A new brick meetinghouse was erected in 1949. I. W. Royer served as pastor from June 1, 1912, to 1952, when Harold Bauman, who had been associate pastor since 1947, assumed full charge, followed by Lester Graybill in 1958. The membership in 1957 was 265.

H.S.B.

J. S. Umble, *Ohio Mennonite Sunday Schools* (Goshen, 1931).

Ortenburg, a village in Upper Carinthia (*q.v.*), Austria, in which a small Anabaptist congregation was founded in the 16th century. Its preacher was Michael Matschidl (*q.v.*), who was seized there with his wife and Hans Gurtzham (*q.v.*) in 1546, examined by the parson of Villach, and put into prison in Vienna. In a poem of twenty stanzas, published by Beck (131-36), Matschidl describes his seizure in Ortenburg and the execution of his fellow captives Hans Staudach (*q.v.*), Leonhard Schneider (*q.v.*) of Kaufbeuren, Blasius Beckh (*q.v.*), and Anthoni Keim (see **Glait, Oswald**) of Gunzenhausen. Beck (121-23) gives two moving letters written by Matschidl on Nov. 21 and Dec. 5, 1546, from his prison to the brotherhood in Moravia. The congregation in Ortenburg was dissolved after the death of its preacher.   HEGE.

J. Beck, "Ein Beitrag zur Geschichte der Wiedertäufer in Kärnten," in *Archiv für vaterländische Geschichte und Topographie* XI (Klagenfurt, 1867); *ML* III. 311.

Ortlep, Christoph, an Anabaptist martyr, was executed for his faith at Reinhardsbrunn, a monastery in Thuringia, Germany, on Jan. 18, 1530, together with Andreas Kolb (*q.v.*) and four women—Katharina König, Katharina Kolb, Elsa Kunz, and Barbara Unger. Ortlep was arrested in 1529 and subjected to a cross-examination on his faith; after indoctrination by Lutheran theologians he recanted and was released. But he again joined the Anabaptists and was arrested and cross-examined with other Anabaptist prisoners. He declared that he would stand by his faith in all points, in the conviction that the Anabaptist doctrine was the most fundamental truth, from which he would not again depart, even if he must lose his life for it. He did not regret having suffered the penalty imposed on him as shame for the sake of Christ; but he did regret that he had once denied the truth he knew and recanted. A few days later he was sentenced to death and executed at once with the other steadfast prisoners.

The execution aroused general attention, since the condemned were the first blood witnesses in matters of faith under Lutheran government, and there were no civil charges brought against them. The Gotha superintendent Friedrich Myconius, who conducted the hearing and therefore knew the earnest mind of the victims, was shocked by the death sentence and expressed his qualms in a letter to Melanchthon; Melanchthon (*q.v.*) replied in February, trying to quiet his doubts, thereby reversing the attitude of the Wittenberg theologians on the death penalty in matters of faith.   HEGE.

N. Paulus, *Protestantismus und Toleranz im 16. Jahrhundert* (Freiburg i.Br., 1911) 31 ff.; P. Wappler, *Die Stellung Kursachsens und des Landgrafen Philipp von Hessen zur Täuferbewegung* (Münster, 1910) 137; *ML* III, 311.

Ortmann, Friedrich C. (1868-1949), born in Adelhof, Russian Poland, Sept. 20, 1868, immigrated with his parents to near Freeman, S.D., in 1874. On July 24, 1892, he was married to Helena Schmidt, with whom he had one son, and in a second marriage on Mar. 14, 1895, to Maria Schmidt, with whom he had eleven children. He was a lifelong member of the Bethel Mennonite (GCM) Church where he was very active as a layman. He also took a great part in community life. In 1944 he opened his home for other old folks. His daughters are still managing the Home for Aged.   A.F.OR.

Orvel, an Anabaptist martyr. Van Braght's *Martyrs' Mirror* (D 286, E 654; *ML* III, 311) contains an account of three martyrs, Orvel, Jan, and Pleunis, who were drowned in the Rhine at Cologne, Germany, in 1561. This account is inexact and incomplete. Orvel and Jan were very likely the same person, with the name Johann von Orvel. He was a cobbler. On Nov. 29, 1561, after severe torture, he was drowned in the Rhine at Cologne with the tailor Plonius from Emmerich.   vDZ.

Ernst Crous, "Auf Mennos Spuren am Niederrhein," *Der Mennonit* IX (1956) No. 1, p. 11.

Orville, Pieter d', and his son *Jacob Philippe d'Orville,* Dutch merchants and bankers (non-Mennonite) at Frankfurt, Germany, who in 1689 and 1710-14 often intermediated between the Dutch Mennonite Committee for Foreign Needs at Amsterdam and the Mennonite refugees from Switzerland who lived in the Palatinate. (*Inv. Arch. Amst.* I, Nos. 1226, 1272, 1281, 1421, 1425.)   vDZ.

Os, Antony van der, b. 1722 at Zierikzee, d. April 12, 1807, at Zwolle, was a clergyman in the Reformed churches of 's Gravenland in 1746, and Zwolle in 1748, where he soon came into difficulties because he questioned the Reformed doctrine of predestination and in general wanted to accept only the Holy Scriptures and not also the doctrines of the Dordrecht Synod. When he refused to refute Remonstrant views he was suspended on Dec. 21, 1750. Unrest overtook the whole congregation in Zwolle, so that the government had to intervene. The passion with which van der Os carried on this matter caused much offense. In 1755 he was deposed from his office. In 1758 he received a call to the Mennonite congregation of Beverwijk in North Holland, was baptized by Cornelis Loosjes, the minister of the Zaandam Oostzijde congregation, and became its minister. He served Beverwijk until 1764 and then Zaandam-Oost. He was the cause of much disturbance in the Mennonite brotherhood. More than thirty polemics appeared, mostly anonymous, for and against van der Os. Among the opponents were the ministers G. ten Cate Thz of West Zaandam, Jan Beets of Hoorn, and Michiel de Bleyker of Twisk. The stricter Mennonites, especially Cornelis Ris, the elder at Hoorn, feared the influence of van der Os, who had in his confession said that he wished to adhere only to the "Twelve Articles" (the Apostles' Creed) and concerned himself little about the Mennonite confessions. Not until 1767 was he accepted as a member of the Rijper Sociëteit (the Waterlander conference in North Holland). In 1795 he resigned his services among the Mennonites and returned to Zwolle, where he lived until an advanced old age and usually attended the Reformed Church.   vDZ.

Naamlijst 1808, 83-85; *Blaupot t. C., Holland* II, 58-60; *DB* 1872, 69 f.; 1897, 167; 1909, 100; *ML* III, 311 f.; *Inv. Arch. Amst.* I, Nos. 684, 937; *Catalogus Amst.,* 140-46.

Osage County Mennonite Church (MC), now extinct, near Linn, Mo., was started when the Philips family, members of the Pea Ridge congregation in Marion Co., Mo., moved into Osage County, where they were followed by the occasional pastoral visits of J. M. Kreider of Palmyra, Mo. Evangelistic effort in the community brought a few additions. Ezra Bowman, ordained in the Wilson Bend congregation near Carver, Mo., served at Linn until his health failed. Leroy Gingerich of Versailles, Mo., filled appointments for the last few years, and J. R. Shank was given bishop oversight after the death of J. M. Kreider, when only two families were left. These moved to Illinois and the work at Linn came to a close in 1947.   J.R.S.

Osborne County, Kan., the location of a Mennonite church (MC), organized before 1880 under Bishop Abraham Newschwanger (Hartzler and Kauffman, *Mennonite Church History*). In 1893 R. J. Heatwole reported 14 members, many of them Canadians. Through crop failures and dissension the church died out, probably in the early 20th century. M.G.

Osceola County (Iowa) Stauffer Mennonite Church, now extinct, was founded by Stauffer Mennonites from Waterloo Co., Ont., and from Lancaster and Snyder counties, Pa., who wished to establish a congregation far removed in distance from other Mennonites. The first of these families arrived in Osceola County in 1887. Among the early settlers were Jesse S. Bauman, bishop of the congregation, Josiah Martin, minister, and Elias Bowman, deacon, with their families. Other family names in the congregation were Brubacher, Weaver, Stauffer, Auker, Gingrich, and Gehman. These settlers made an attempt to follow a uniform style of architecture in the construction of all of their buildings. This distinctive style marked the location of the former Mennonite community years after the settlement had disappeared. Attempts to enforce uniformity in many areas of life brought about disagreements and the eventual extinction of the congregation. The church was dissolved in 1911, and during the next four years some families moved to Ontario and Michigan, but most located in Lancaster and Lebanon counties, Pa.   M.G.

Melvin Gingerich, *The Mennonites in Iowa* (Iowa City, 1939) 337-41.

Oscoda County, Mich., in the north-central part of the state, is the location of three groups of Mennonites: the large Fairview (*q.v.*) Mennonite Church (MC), the small Comins (*q.v.*) Mennonite Church (GCM), and the very small Old Order Amish group. The Amish began to settle in Oscoda County soon after 1900 and rapidly built up to two congregations, both served by the same ministers. But soon a decline set in, and the group has now dwindled (1957) to 10 or 12 members. Three bishops have served: David Slabaugh, Jacob Gascho, originally of Canada; and Levi S. Troyer. Troyer's death in 1954 was a serious blow to the Amish congregation; Ezra Kauffman, unordained, has been appointed to preach for the group. The Amish now often worship with the Fairview Mennonite Church (MC).   J.C.W.

Oscoda County (Mich.) Old Order Amish settlement dates back to 1900, when four families, Sam Weaver, Jerry Troyer, John Weaver, and Christ D. Miller, moved into the neighborhood of Mio in Oscoda County from Geauga County, Ohio. A congregation was formed in 1901 with the following as ministers: Emanuel Schlabach, David Nissley, Jacob Gascho, Yost Yoder, and David D. Schlabach (ordained as bishop in 1903). The following have served in the ministry since the beginning: Jacob Gascho (ord. 1908) and Levi S. Troyer (1939), bishops; Daniel Miller, Sam Weaver, and Ben Schlabach, preachers. About 60 families both from eastern and western states moved to Oscoda County. In recent years the Amish have been moving away. The membership in 1956 was 20.   L.S.T.

Osiander, Andreas (Hosemann) (1498-1552), a Lutheran preacher in Nürnberg (*q.v.*), Germany, where he became very influential and participated in all the major church affairs. He violently attacked the Anabaptists from their first appearance, so that they were unable to gain a foothold there. One of the first victims of his hostility was Hans Denk (*q.v.*), who was the rector of the school of St. Sebaldus and had joined a group who were dissatisfied with the small improvement in religious and civil life brought about by the Reformation. At Osiander's instigation a course of action was adopted that ended in Denk's expulsion on January 21, 1525, and the later prohibition of the sale of the translation of the Prophets made by Denk aand Haetzer (*q.v.*), even though there was as yet no other German version and the translation was free of anything objectionable.

In the official opinion concerning the punishment of the Anabaptists which jurists and theologians presented to the council in July 1528 Osiander advocated the death penalty for Anabaptist preachers, because they were deceivers. To his opinion he added false and garbled statements on the doctrine of the Anabaptists, asserting that they denied the Trinity and therewith the Deity of Christ; in their teaching nothing is found about Christ, except that "we should do and suffer like Him, as if He were merely an example." They would recognize only works, which "Christ has, however, made unnecessary." It is therefore justifiable before God and man "to punish such error with the sword. . . . In addition, imperial law forbids such Anabaptism upon penalty of beheading; therefore it is clear that it is justifiable before God and man." Baptized persons might be given milder punishment as the deceived, such as prison sentences, branding, or exile. Some of the other theologians also favored branding, but not the death penalty.

Nevertheless, Osiander had had some misgivings as to the effect of such a course upon his own co-religionists, and therefore advocated that "in this time" it was not useful and good "to apply the severest penalty. In the first place, because I know that if their doctrine and their error really came to the light of day, they are so unchristian that I do not doubt that they would fall of themselves. In the second place, because we have among the Catholics errors just as serious as those of the Anabaptists, . . . it would be a bad state of affairs to punish one party with the sword and not resist the other; for it is well known and evil spoken of, what the Papists still do in corners, and that they are not punished for it. In the third place, because it is evident that the Anabaptists die steadfast; that gives their teaching great respect."

Osiander's position on the death penalty for Anabaptists was no doubt further affected by the attitude of Catholic princes, who frequently made no distinction between Anabaptists and other Protestants, killing both alike. When the decision was made by the Swabian League (q.v.) on Feb. 16, 1528, to have the Anabaptists hunted and captured by cavalrymen furnished by Ulm, Kempten, Heilbronn, and Bamberg, Volckmar, the delegate from Nürnberg, protested that "the Protestants would be thrown together with the Anabaptists, and pointed out Würzburg as an example. The door would thereby be opened to all manner of cruelty toward Protestants living in Catholic countries. Also there were many simple misled souls among the Anabaptists, who could be won over by indoctrination." (See Wenzeslaus Linck.)

In a further opinion of May 30, 1531, on the punishment of two imprisoned Anabaptists Osiander expressed the opinion that it would be dangerous to punish them by worldly means, since the intention of these people was good. They should be taught with the Word of God. But if they persisted in their obstinacy, and consequently in their faith, they should be expelled from the country. In case they were preachers the authorities in charge should take a different course.

After the reproaches made against the Nürnberg council following the execution in 1527 of the Anabaptist Wolfgang Vogel (q.v.), the pastor of Eltersdorf, the councillors did not inflict the death penalty on any Anabaptists for refusing to join the Lutheran Church, merely sentencing them to prison and to indoctrination by the clergy. Thus Osiander and his colleagues held many unsuccessful religious discussions with Peter Riedemann (q.v.), who was held in prison in Nürnberg. After a prison term of four years Riedemann was expelled in 1536.

Not many years later Osiander's views on capital punishment for matters of faith underwent a radical change. One of the influences bringing this change about was probably his association with the astronomer Copernicus (d. 1543), whose discovery that the earth revolves around the sun was just as objectionable to church circles as was Anabaptist teaching. Osiander became a sponsor of Copernicus' famous work, De revolutionibus orbium coelestium, which was completed in 1530, but was not published until later. This change is seen in Osiander's booklet, Unterricht und Vermahnung, wie man wider den Türken beten und streiten soll (1542), which expresses views held by the Anabaptists. It is possible that the conversations he held with imprisoned Anabaptists were a factor in bringing this change about. "When God permits the Turks to rule and rage over the Christians, He does nothing other than to deprive by violence the false Christians of the holy Christian name which they still unreasonably keep and bear, who by a wild, rough, and heathenish life have long since despised Christ and through false doctrine lost and rejected Him, just as the badges are torn from a nobleman who has disgraced himself," says Osiander in the booklet. Then he enumerates the sins of Christendom: despising, falsifying, and persecuting the holy Word of God, abuse of the sacraments, false human doctrine, immorality, and unrepentant persistence therein, which are not adequately punished by secular or spiritual authorities. Therefore the Turk must be regarded as "the sharp disciplinary rod of God; one must earnestly repent, and pray God for enlightenment, that all the bishops and preachers preach His holy Word unadulterated, abolish all superstitious practices, spread the Word of God with gentleness and not with the sword and bloodshed, halt offenses by using the ban, give a good example by spotless living, and that all might humbly bow before His divine holy kingdom."

After the Augsburg Interim Osiander moved to Königsberg, Prussia, in January 1549, and became professor of theology at the university founded there five years earlier. Here the debate on his doctrine of justification absorbed his attention to the end of his life (1552). HEGE.

Beck, Geschichts-Bücher, 40; Wilhelm Heberle, "Johann Denk und die Ausbreitung seiner Lehre," in Theologische Studien und Kritiken XXVIII (1855) 835; Chr. Hege, Die Täufer in der Kurpfalz (Frankfurt, 1908) 25 ff. E. Hirsch, Die Theologie des Andreas Osiander und ihre geschichtlichen Voraussetzungen (Göttingen, 1919); Keller, Reformation, 411-17; W. Möller, Andreas Osiander, Leben und ausgewählte Schriften (Elberfeld, 1870) 116, 204, 245 f.; TA Bayern II, 260; G. von Selle, Geschichte der Albertus-Universität zu Königsberg in Preussen (Königsberg, 1944); Wiswedel, Bilder II, 26-28; ML III, 312 f.

Osiander, Lucas, Sr. (1534-1604), a Lutheran divine, the son of Andreas Osiander (q.v.), court chaplain in 1567, was councillor to Louis (q.v.), Duke of Württemberg, 1568-93. Osiander took part in the introduction of the Swabian Concordia Formula drawn up by his brother-in-law Jakob Andreae (q.v.) in 1574 (see Formula of Concord), and in disputes with imprisoned Anabaptists in Württemberg. Thus he cross-examined Paul Glock (*q.v.*), the Hutterite missionary from Moravia, who had been in the Hohenwittlingen prison for 15 years, in the presence of the court chaplain M. Johann Stecher, the pastor of Urach, the *Landhofmeister* and four councillors of the chancellory, and tried to persuade him that the Anabaptist doctrines on infant baptism, communion, and the oath, and their views on Christian government were "not godly"; but he could not refute the Biblically grounded Anabaptist preacher.

Several years later Osiander published a book in defense of infant baptism, titled *Ein Predig Von dem Widertauff. Sampt angehenckter Historien, Welcher gestalt sich die Widertauffer Anno 1534 zu Münster gehalten. Wie selbige geschichten H. Dorpius . . . beschrieben* (Tübingen, 1582; in GCL). In an opinion on Jan. 28, 1584, he opposed all others at the session by sponsoring gentler treatment of Anabaptists on the ground that there were various wings among them, some erring only in matters of faith, and otherwise obedient to authority (Bossert, 579-81). In his *Bauernpostille* of 1597 he warns against "bothering rural churches with subtle disputations."

His son Lucas Osiander, Jr. (1571-1638), was professor of theology and from 1620 chancellor of the University of Tübingen. He also published a book against the Anabaptists titled *Enchiridion controversiarum quae Augustanae Confessionis Theologis cum Anabaptistis intercedunt* (Tübingen, 1605; second edition 1614, in GCL). HEGE.

TA Württemberg, 350-58; Chr. G. Jöcher, *Allgemeines Gelehrten-Lexikon* III, 1751; J. von Walter, *Die Geschichte des Christentums* III (Gütersloh, 1935) 439; *Mart. Mir.* D 714, E 1024; *ML* III, 313.

Osnabrück, a town in Westphalia, Germany. Six Anabaptist emissaries, one of whom was Dionysius Vinne (*q.v.*), traveled from Münster (*q.v.*) to Osnabrück in October 1534 in order to convert this town. They were all arrested before they could begin their work; four of them were executed at Iburg, one died in prison, while Heinrich Graess (*q.v.*), who forsook the Anabaptist principles, was released. Nothing is known of Anabaptism in Osnabrück. (Mellink, *Wederdopers*, 48 f.) vDZ.

Oswald von Jamnitz: see Glait, Oswald.

Ossweil, a town in the Markgröningen district of Württemberg, Germany. In 1559 the Anabaptist Simon Kraushaar of Neckargroningen confessed in cross-examination at Kirchheim-Teck that his baptized daughter Walburga was serving at Ossweil in the home of his brother's son Joseph Kraushaar. In 1570 the *Wiedertäuferkalender* appeared and named some recanting Anabaptists of Ossweil, including Godelburga, an old, ill, unteachable Anabaptist woman; in 1571 the *Urfehde* of Jakob Gantz of Ossweil, who promised diligent attendance at church; likewise Alexander Widmann, called Weber. In 1573 Ossweil is "still the same old nest. The known Anabaptists cannot be found, slip out and in secretly" in spite of all surveillance. In 1574 the pastor of Zuffenhausen announced, "In Ossweil several Anabaptists are staying," and the prelate of Maulbronn reported: "Last summer nearly all sectarian persons moved away." In 1575 he wrote that Maria Weber attend-

ed no church, much less communion, was unteachable. In 1576 the prelate named several others who disregarded communion; the dean had summoned them to the Rathaus and had received several promises to recant. Similarly in 1577 two women were still "stiff-necked"; in 1578 they were summoned to Stuttgart. In 1583 Maria Weber was attending no church; in 1586 after a term in prison she promised to reform. In 1608 she was again arrested, in 1609 likewise, in 1610 was given up as unteachable, in 1612 she finally recanted. (*TA Württemberg; ML* III, 314.) E.T.

Ostens, Jacob, b. 1625 probably at Utrecht, d. Oct. 23, 1678, at Rotterdam, whose ancestors had moved from Flanders to the Netherlands because of persecution, was a physician, who in 1653 was appointed preacher of the Flemish Mennonite congregation at Rotterdam, Holland. Since he was a man of liberal ideas (he is said to have been an anti-Trinitarian, a Spinozist, and a supporter of Collegiant doctrines) trouble soon arose with some of his copreachers. In 1655 he and three other preachers of the Flemish congregation, Jan Ariaens van Raemburgh, Gerrit Jans Veerom, and Huygh Jans Corenhart, left this church and joined the Waterlander Mennonite congregation in Rotterdam. Here Ostens served as a preacher from 1655 until his death. In the Waterlander congregation too he caused some trouble because some members did not agree with his ideas and accused him of Socinianism (*q.v.*). Ostens published *Liefde-son, omstralende de Hoedanigheyt der tegenwoordige genaamde Christenheyt* (Utrecht, 1651). vDZ.

Inv. Arch. Amst. II, 2, Nos. 369-413; K. Vos, *Geschiedenis der Doopsgezinde Gemeente te Rotterdam* (1907, reprint) 17 f., 23, 42 f.; K. O. Meinsma, *Spinoza en zijn Kring* (The Hague, 1896) 228, 341-43.

Osterfeld, one of ten villages in the province of Samara in the Mennonite settlement Am Trakt, which was settled in 1854-73 by Mennonites from West Prussia, Germany (see **Malyschna**). Osterfeld was founded in 1872; its inhabitants were members of the Köppental-Orloff congregation, which had 1,535 members and 760 children in 1905. (*ML* III, 314.) HEGE.

Osterwick, a common Mennonite village name. One of the first of the villages settled by the Mennonites of West Prussia in Russia was Osterwick in the Chortitza (*q.v.*) settlement. It became the seat of one of the largest congregations, with a membership (1905) of 1,571 besides 839 children. In 1812 a village in the same settlement was named Neu-Osterwick. From Russia the name came to the East and West Reserves of Manitoba, to Hague, Sask., and from Canada to Cuauhtemoc, Mex. In Paraguay (*q.v.*) Canadian Mennonites from Manitoba and Saskatchewan founded the village of Osterwick in the west of the Menno (*q.v.*) Colony. In 1932 the first church in the colony was built here, with a seating capacity of 500. In Osterwick there were in 1934 twenty-seven families with a total of 163 persons. (*ML* III, 327.) HEGE.

Osthofen, a market village in Rhenish Hesse, Germany, three miles north of Worms, where there were Mennonites soon after the end of the Thirty Years' War. The register of Mennonite families for 1664 in the archives at Karlsruhe names Peter Schuhmacher, Walruf König (?), Wilhelm Kegi, Thiel Rings, the last as having no property, but employed on the estates. In 1680: Johann Engers, Johann Weber, Johann Rings, Peter Rings, Peter Schuhmacher, Peter Grob (?). The two Rings families are day laborers, Johann Engers a weaver, the other two perhaps hereditary tenants on near-by farms. In 1738: Daniel Schneider, Daniel Engers, Christian Weiss, David Jutzi, Johann Geber, and Johann and Abraham Nold (?). In 1743: David Jutzi, three sons and three daughters; Michael Weiss, one daughter; Ulrich Hackmann, one daughter; Jakob Weiss, Daniel Engers, one son. In 1752: David Jutzi—Katharina 9, Peter 4, Maria 9½ years old. On the Mühlheimerhof Ulrich Hackmann— Barbara 10, Anna Maria 6, and Elisabeth one year old; Jakob Weiss—Jakob 9, Christian 7, Barbara 4 years old. In 1759: David Jutzi widow, 3 children, has her son-in-law as a servant with her. Michael Weiss of Mühlheim — Katharina, Peter, Christian, Elisabeth, Michael; Jakob Weiss of Mühlheim—Jakob, Christian, Barbara, Elisabeth, Maria; Ulrich Hackmann, three children as above; Jakob Engers, linen-weaver, single. In 1768: Jakob Weiss, Georg Schneider, Johann Seutz, Jakob Engers, David Jutzi widow. In 1773: six families, seven sons, four daughters.

The Osthofen families had some difficulties. About 1670 they were summoned before Alzey officials, where they were told that all who had entered the country since 1664 must leave within two weeks and pay a fine of 50 Talers in addition. Thereupon they sent an ardent petition to the elector (undated) not to compel them to leave in winter, since they had cultivated and sowed considerable land. The petition was apparently granted.

The Mennonites of Osthofen have from the first belonged to the Ibersheim congregation. In 1939 three families were living there, two named Weiss and one Stauffer. (ML III, 321.)   NEFF.

Ostorodt, Christoph (d. 1611), a Socinian (anti-Trinitarian) minister of the "Polish Minor Church" (see Polish Brethren) who had several significant contacts with Anabaptists in an attempt to have them unite with his church. He was the son of a Lutheran pastor at Goslar, Germany, and was educated at Königsberg, East Prussia, where he seems to have come into contact with Unitarians. He was converted to Socinianism and in 1585 joined the Polish Minor Church (the only existing church body of that persuasion). He learned the Polish language and soon after became minister of the important church of Smigiel in Greater Poland, near Poznan. In 1598 he accompanied the Polish nobleman Andreas Voydovsky on a missionary journey to Holland, which (according to Wilbur) marked the first introduction of Socinianism into that country, destined to become later the very refuge of that type of Christianity. A few years later he became a minister at Buskov near Danzig. In 1604 he published his *Unterrichtung von den vornehmsten Hauptpunkten der christlichen Religion*, a major dog-matic work of his church, preceding the better-known Racovian Catechism (1605) by one year, and almost on the same level of importance. Wilbur claims that this *Unterrichtung* became a standard manual of Socinian doctrines, and accordingly was also widely attacked by German Protestants. In 1611 Ostorodt died in Buskov.

His activities with regard to influencing if not proselyting Anabaptists may be described according to the three main branches of Anabaptism:

(a) *Swiss Brethren*. In 1590 Voydovsky had made contacts with the Swiss Brethren in Strasbourg in the hope of gaining some footholds there. Returning to Poland, he carried with him a letter of the Strasbourg Swiss Brethren which contained a number of questions as to the Polish beliefs. In 1591 Ostorodt answered this inquiry with a lengthy epistle (16 pages in print), preserved in the State Archives in Bern, Switzerland, and published in full by Theodor Wotschke in 1915. It is a most remarkable source, revealing the spirit of Socinianism as well as the gulf which separated it from the Anabaptists. The tone is irenic and exceedingly warm. "We know all too well," Ostorodt writes, "that prompting factions is just as much a work of the flesh as other sins (Gal. 5:20). For that reason we suffer others and would not shun them if they want only to be obedient to the Lord Jesus Christ [something which Anabaptists always wanted to do] and are ready to recognize us as brethren." The doctrine of the Incarnation, however, was and remained the stumbling block for such a recognition by Anabaptists. "Christ is the son of God in no other sense," Ostorodt confessed, "than that all men are children of God in the spirit." The Strasbourg Brethren studied this document carefully and answered it in 1592 by a lengthy tract entitled "Concerning the Incarnation and Deity of Jesus Christ" (extant in a Dutch print of 1666; see John Horsch in *MQR* 1931, 26, note 136). It states very decidedly that "believing is not a decision of human reason but the acceptance of that which is incomprehensible to reason."

(b) *Dutch Mennonites*. A few years later, in 1598, Ostorodt went to Holland to spread his faith to this country and to try to get a permanent foothold in Western Europe. Naturally, he sought to establish contacts also with the Mennonites of this country, all the more since Mennonites and Socinians had almost identical viewpoints concerning adult baptism and nonresistance. In Amsterdam he debated with the Frisian elder Pieter Jans Twisck (q.v.); he probably also had contact with the Flemish elder Jacques Outerman of Haarlem. In particular he hoped for some success with the most liberal wing of these Mennonites, namely, the Waterlanders (q.v.). Wilbur in his *History of Unitarianism* devotes a lengthy section to this visit of Ostorodt with Hans de Ries (q.v.) of Alkmaar, the spiritual leader of the Waterlanders, and so do also J. S. S. Ballot, the biographer of de Ries (*DB* 1864, 38), and other Mennonite historians. This visit, as could have been assumed, yielded very little in results, in spite of de Ries's spiritualistic, nondogmatic tendencies and certain similar viewpoints on practical matters. In fact, de Ries refused to consider any closer dealings with the Socinians, the main argument being that "the Polish Brethren grossly reduce the glory of Christ" (de Ries, *Ontdeckinghe der dwalingen*, 1627). Soon after the visit of Ostorodt, de Ries wrote a complete refutation of the Socinian position, entitled *Klaer Bewijs van de Eewigheydt ende Godtheydt Jesu Christi*. With this exchange of views the contact of Socinians and Dutch Mennonites came to an end for the time being. Later, more successful contacts and influences, however, do not belong to the scope of this article (see **Galenus Abrahamsz de Haan;** also **Anti-Trinitarianism** and **Socinianism in the Netherlands**).

(*c*) *Hutterites.* It is known that the Polish Socinians showed a strong tendency toward communal living, hence their interest in the experiment of the Moravian Hutterites (*q.v.*) in this regard. Three or four times in the 16th and early 17th centuries visitors from Poland came to study these Anabaptist farm Bruderhofs, but in spite of much friendliness on both sides no real meeting of minds was possible: the genius of Anabaptism and Socinianism was too different as to allow such a rapprochement.

In his letter of 1591 to the Strasbourg Brethren, Ostorodt mentions also that two Polish Brethren went to Moravia in 1590 and there talked "with your brethren" (!) in Auspitz and Pausram. They presented to them a Socinian Confession of Faith but "never received any reply to it." The Hutterite chronicle does not mention this visit at all. It was apparently the report brought back to Ostorodt by these two visitors which prompted him to refute the Hutterite position more elaborately than any Polish brother had done before. Chr. Sand's well-known *Bibliotheca Antitrinitariorum sive Catalogus* (1684, p. 91) shows that Ostorodt had written a pamphlet entitled *Contra Hutterianos seu Moraviensis Communistas Libellus* (no date), to which entry Sand adds: "manuscriptum post obitum ipsius a Joanne Franco possidebatur." The content of this polemical tract is not known. Perhaps it was against this book (or another of Ostorodt's fifteen books and tracts) that the outstanding Hutterite headbishop Andreas Ehrenpreis (*q.v.*) wrote a rejoinder, *Kurze Widerlegung des grossen Streites von Christo Jesu, dem Sohne Gottes, wie er von Christoph Ostorodt in einem im Druck ausgangenen Büchel samt seinem Anhang als Polnische Brüder oder Arianer schimpflich und nachteilig verkleinert ward* (Sobotiste, 1654). Unfortunately, also this reply is known only by its title. An old manuscript copy of it is supposed to exist with the Hutterian Brethren in Canada, but at present its location is unknown. How did Ehrenpreis ever come into the possession of Ostorodt's booklet? It may be reasonably assumed that Ehrenpreis received it from Dr. Daniel Zwikker (*q.v.*), a Socinian physician of Danzig, who had temporarily joined the Hutterite brotherhood in Slovakia. That happened in 1654, the year when Ehrenpreis replied to Ostorodt's dogmatic theses, forty-three years after Ostorodt's death.

(*d*) *Frisian Mennonite congregation at Danzig.* The Polish Brethren also made contacts with the Frisian Mennonites of Danzig in order to try to form a union between the Mennonite church and theirs. An undated letter of about 1609 (*Inv. Arch.*

Amst. II, No. 2926) written by Jan Gerrits, elder of the Danzig Frisian Mennonites, to Hans de Ries, says that the Brethren requested a conversation between Ostorodt and the Mennonite leaders, which was refused by the Mennonites, but the Brethren were urgently insistent on a conversation. Two members were inclined to leave the church and join the Brethren, many of whom were regularly attending the Mennonite meetings. In this letter Ostorodt is said to have denied that Jesus had instituted the ordinance of baptism, rejected the doctrine of satisfaction, and demanded that every preacher know Latin, Greek, and Hebrew.   R.F.

W. J. Kühler, *Het Socinianisme in Nederland* (Leiden, 1912) 53-57, 106-11; E. M. Wilbur, *A History of Unitarianism, Socinianism and its Antecedents* (Cambridge, 1945); Theodor Wotschke, "Ein dogmatisches Sendschreiben des Unitariers Ostorodt," in *Archiv für Reformationsgeschichte* XII (1915) 137-54; Robert Friedmann, "The Encounter of Anabaptists and Mennonites with Anti-Trinitarianism," *MQR* XXII (1948) 139-62.

Ostra, a Moravian village on an island in the March River south of Hrädisch and Bilowitz (Velké Bilovice), in which the Hutterian Brethren had a Bruderhof. Its inmates fled to Hungary at the end of December 1620 because of the brutality of the Bouquoy troops. In desperation one woman threw her child into the river, and the Brethren with difficulty prevented her suicide. In the general withdrawal Ostra and Neudorf had to be abandoned.   P.DE.

Beck, *Geschichts-Bücher,* 43; Wolkan, *Geschicht-Buch;* Zieglschmid, *Chronik;* G. Wolny, *Kirchliche Topographie von Mähren* (Brno, 1855-66); *ML* III, 35.

Ostrovo Kampe, near the hamlet of Ehrental, situated on the east side of the Vistula in Poland, was settled by Mennonites, who were members of the Przechovka (*q.v.*) Old Flemish Mennonite congregation and had their own Mennonite school in the Ostrovo Kampe. Repeatedly struck by floods, most of them left this area about 1765, settling in the Netzebruch (*q.v.*), while the remainder in 1821 moved to Russia and settled at Alexanderwohl (*q.v.*).   vDZ.

J. A. Duerksen, "Przechowka and Alexanderwohl," *Menn. Life* X (April 1955) 76, 78.

Ostrovo-Chortitza, one of the oldest villages of the Mennonites in Russia, was founded in 1789 in the Chortitza (*q.v.*) settlement, province of Ekaterinoslav. The inhabitants belonged to the Kronsweide congregation, which had (in 1905) 1,955 members and 1,055 children. It was also known as Insel-Chortitza. (*ML* III, 326.)

Oswald, a youth of about eighteen, of Augensperg on the Kocher River in Württemberg, Germany, who was seized with a number of Hutterian Brethren near Passau on their way back from Moravia and imprisoned in the Passau (*q.v.*) castle. On Aug. 30, 1535, he was cross-examined. He confessed that he had been baptized by Adam Schlegel at Dillingen in the Oberland. At the same time Hans Fuchs, a boy of sixteen of Bruchsal, baptized in Augsburg by Philip Plener, was examined. The hearts of both the boys had grown strong by the grace of God, so that no skill in argument, nor the thought of perishing wretchedly in the dark, dank holes in the earth of the castle prison was able to deflect them from their conviction. (*ML* III, 326.)   W.W.

Otelia (Pa.) Mennonite Mission (MC) Church began as a mission Sunday school in May 1938. Elmer Yoder and Harry Yoder investigated the possibilities. The Allensville congregation undertook the responsibility and sent workers to the Otelia community. After 18 months of Sunday-school work, A. Roy Payne was appointed as pastor and served until September 1949, when LeRoy A. Zook was ordained and appointed pastor. After fourteen years of work in an abandoned school a new church was erected in 1952. The congregation is now under the Ohio and Eastern Conference. In 1956 the membership was 58, with A. Roy Payne and LeRoy A. Zook as ministers. In July 1957 the Otelia congregation withdrew from the Ohio and Eastern Conference and joined the Allegheny Conference. Also on July 21, 1957, the resignation of LeRoy A. Zook became effective and Joe Esh, of Blountstown, Fla., was installed as pastor.   L.A.Z.

Ottenheim, Matthias von, an Anabaptist martyr: see **Matthias Servaes.**

Otter, Jakob (*c*1485-1547), first a Carthusian monk, later a Protestant churchman of the 16th century, a native of Alsace; educated at the universities of Heidelberg and Freiburg, he became a Lutheran pastor in the Austrian village of Kenzingen in 1522. Expelled in 1524, he fled to Strasbourg, and with the patronage of Hans Landschad, Luther's friend, became pastor in Neckarsteinach. Expelled from there in 1529, he served as pastor in Aarau (Switzerland) and Esslingen (*q.v.*) on the recommendation of Blaurer (*q.v.*) in 1532. Otter also had a letter of recommendation from Bucer (*q.v.*). He was inclined to self-importance, probably to compensate for shortness of stature, and lacked the art of leadership. He injured himself and the Esslingen Church by a lack of respect for Blaurer. For years the Anabaptists of Esslingen could point their fingers at the bitter quarrels between Otter and his colleague Fuchs.

The acclaim given Otter in many biographies of Reformation characters is not deserved. The most recent *Kirchengeschichte von Stadt und Bezirk Esslingen* by Otto Schuster (Stuttgart, 1946) is in this respect pleasantly objective, but contains several errors in the section on Otter. The brief, apt formulation given by Schuster (p. 163) says that in Esslingen it was Blaurer's achievement to lay the groundwork, that of Otter to build the superstructure of the Protestant Church. The regulations formulated by Otter and his colleagues on the order of the services (1533) and church organization (1534), the school regulations (1534) and disciplinary regulations (1536), are now a part of church history and not to be discussed here. But in addition to Schuster's presentation the older one by Th. Keim (*Reformationsblätter der Stadt Esslingen*, 1860) can still be used. Otter's printed works can be found in part in the city library of Esslingen. Schuster's book (1946) shows no knowledge of the articles "Blaurer" by Christian Hege, and "Esslingen" by Christian Neff (*ML* I, 226 and 609). The guild of Reforma-

tion historiography will not permanently be able to close its mind to the fact that the Anabaptist congregation "furnished the best preliminary work for the introduction of the Reformation" (Neff, 609), and that the Anabaptists, won to the church by Blaurer's preaching and pastoral work in 1531-32 and the church discipline he introduced, were again repelled from the church by the return to laxity of discipline and the baneful quarrels between Otter and Fuchs carried on even in the pulpit; the church was therefore to blame for the loss of these Anabaptists. On the other hand it must be admitted that Otter, the self-important polemicist, kindly received Schwenckfeld and Franck, the two spiritualists from the outside who were spiritually akin to the Anabaptists, although he was certainly influenced against them by Bucer, as Brecht was in Ulm. Schwenckfeld went in and out of Otter's parsonage and was permitted to explain to Otter his objections to Luther's doctrine of communion. Blaurer, of course, supported this intercourse by writing warning letters. Otter died in the horror of the Interim in 1547, which destroyed so many churchmen. Still worth reading is his prayer booklet (1537), found in the Landesbibliothek at Stuttgart.   E.T.

Otterberg, a town (pop. 3,000) in the Palatinate, Germany, a former Cistercian monastery, founded by Huguenot Walloons in the 16th century (textiles), since the beginning of the 18th century the residence of several Mennonite families: Lichti (in the "City Mill"), Beutler (in the "Beutler Mill," named for the family), and Reubal (on the near-by Messerschwanderhof). Later came the Engel, Hofli, and Eymann families. In 1957 three Eymann families were living there who belonged to the Sembach (*q.v.*) congregation. Peter Galle, who came to Otterberg through marriage, was the assistant pastor of the Sembach congregation 1800-27, and died of a cerebral hemorrhage during a service. The Otterberg Mennonites own an old cemetery. (*ML* III, 326.)   G.H.

Otterken, Het, a Dutch Mennonite hymnbook: see **Liedtboecxken genaamt het Otterken.**

Ottius (Otto, Otte, Ott), **Johann Heinrich** (*c*1617-82), a Swiss Reformed church historian, was educated at the universities of Lausanne, Geneva, Groningen, Leiden, and Amsterdam, traveled through France and England, and then became preacher in Dietikon near Zürich. He occupied himself with the study of the great Catholic church history by Baronius, and wrote on the question whether and when Peter was in Rome. In 1672 he published the *Annales Anabaptistici* (*q.v.*) *hoc est, Historia Universalis de Anabaptistarum origine, progressu, factionibus & schismatis, paradoxis, tumultibus, colloquiis, pacificationibus, locis & sedibus, scriptis hinc illinc emissis, edictis & judiciis, ac quicquid praeterea ad rem facere videtur. His praemissa prolegomena 1. Ad lectorem. 2. de variis Anabaptistarum fectis tractatio duplex. 3. collatio cum veteribus haereticis. 4. de Donatistis. 5. quomodo tractandi ejusmodi homines; una cum Indice copioso* (Basel, 1672), a chronicle of the Anabaptists year by year from 1521

(Müntzer and Storch!) to 1671. Although Ottius was not very favorable to the Anabaptists and his *Annales* are not entirely unprejudiced, this account of Anabaptist history contains many interesting facts. He spent the years 1634-41 in the Netherlands, industriously collecting the material that he later worked into his chronicle. He must have had an extraordinary acquaintance with the old Anabaptist writings. Later he became a professor at the University of Zürich. He must be distinguished from a number of contemporaries of the same name with variant spellings.   E.C.

Jöchers Gelehrten-Lexikon III (Leipzig, 1751) Col. 1141 and continuation in Vol. V (Delmenhorst, 1816); Cornelius Bergmann, *Die Täuferbewegung im Kanton Zürich bis 1660* (Leipzig, 1916) 146-59; Ernst Correll, *Das Schweizerische Täufermennonitentum* (Tübingen, 1925) 67 f.; Müller, *Berner Täufer,* 166 f.; *ML* III, 327.

Ottmar, Sylvanus, a book printer in Augsburg, Bavaria, Germany, who published contemporaneously with Peter Schöffer in Worms the first German translation of the Old Testament Prophets by Hans Denk (*q.v.*) and Ludwig Haetzer (*q.v.*) in several editions. It appeared first on April 13, 1527, at Schöffer's, and on June 22 was followed by a folio issue of 158 pages; he published a second edition on Dec. 24, and by March 1528 the fifth edition by Ottmar was off the press (Meyer, 211). In Nürnberg Andreas Osiander (*q.v.*) persuaded the council to prohibit its sale (Heberle, 835). Ottmar had already printed several editions of Haetzer's German translation of Malachi with the exegesis by Oecolampadius in Latin on July 17, 1526, the first edition in octavo and quarto, in 1527 in folio (Heberle, 832).
                                                         HEGE.

Wilhelm Heberle, "Johann Denk und die Ausbreitung seiner Lehre," in *Theologische Studien und Kritiken* XXVIII (1855); Chr. Meyer, "Zur Gesch. der Wiedertäufer in Oberschwaben," in *Ztscht des Historischen Vereins für Schwaben und Neuburg,* 1874; *ML* III, 327.

Otto Henry (Ottheinrich) (1502-59), Elector of the Palatinate 1556-59. He had introduced the Lutheran Reformation into his hereditary lands of Neuburg and Sulzbach by 1542. After the defeat of the Schmalkaldian League he had to leave the country; not until the treaty of Passau was signed in 1552 did he again acquire possession of it. By principle he was tolerant. Soon after assuming the government he turned his attention to the Anabaptists, issued a *Kirchenordnung* on April 4, 1556, ordered a church inspection, and held a disputation with the Anabaptists in Pfeddersheim (*q.v.*) near Worms in August 1557. But on Jan. 25, 1558, he felt obliged to issue a mandate against them, obligating the superintendents to watch the parishes carefully. "If they should find among the clergy or the parishioners of their district offensive and injurious errors of the Zwinglians, Schwenckfelders, Osiandrists, Anabaptists, or other evil sects opposed to the Augsburg Confession, they shall deal with them in accord with the Brenz (*q.v.*) *Bedenken.*"

Two years later, on May 9, 1558, Otto Henry released a second mandate, which was to be obeyed in all points on penalty of severe punishment. It is directed against the Anabaptists in Neuburg. He, the prince, had seen "what rubbish the harmful error of Anabaptism bears not alone in the Christian community and church, but also in external police and government. Therefore, in order to counter it in good time, he had a constitution drawn up, which has been decided upon."

And then the alleged errors of the Anabaptists are enumerated: "(1) Since the suffering and death of Jesus there is no original sin, and that all children thereafter are born without original sin. (2) Infant baptism is wrong and useless. (3) They deny the third Person of the Trinity. (4) They hold that the knowledge of God is given to man without the study of the Bible and church attendance. (5) The sacraments are considered by them only as a mark and confession before men and as an outward sign of their brotherhood. (6) Some hold falsely that man is justified before God by holy works and through suffering and fulfilling the law and special illumination. (7) They assert that the reborn cannot fall into the wrath of God. (8) Some teach that temporal rule and temporal judges and the office of prince are sin and condemned and do not rule over Christian people, and judges or princes cannot be at the same time rulers and Christians. (9) They say that all Christians are obliged to give their money and goods to the Christian brotherhood. (10) Item, to accuse others before a temporal court is sin. (11) Item, to render an oath to the ruler or in court is sin. (12) Item, if a married man and woman separate on account of Anabaptism, this is right, together with other unchristian, coarse lies or errors, whereby they and Satan himself who impels them can be recognized."

Since all indoctrination had hitherto remained without result the elector ordered that all his subjects "who are spotted with the damned Anabaptist sect and other abominable errors, desist therefrom and return to the true evangelical Christian Church. Everyone shall also have his children baptized according to Christian order, in six or eight days at the longest after birth. Those who do not do so and regard infant baptism as useless, they shall be punished according to law without delay. Anabaptist elders or leaders shall be sheltered by none, nor given any work. Nor is it permitted to them to hold meetings or preach. He who trespasses against this mandate shall be brought into arrest by the official of the part of the country where the immigrant arrived, and immediately be announced to the government at Neuburg and be punished in accord with the imperial laws.

"But especially shall the officials of the Neuburg district be on a diligent lookout, whether Anabaptists by day or night assemble in the fields or woods and exercise supposed sacraments, as it has happened at other places that they have met secretly and in corners. They shall by deeds oppose such prohibited meetings and bring these insurrectionists and mobsters to prison, and report them to the government, to await the proper penalty.

"Whoever is then contaminated with the disease of Anabaptism and does not allow himself to be turned to the truth after being taught and warned, is to be held as a foul member of the body and shall not be tolerated in the church of God, but shall at least be expelled from the country. And if anyone shows himself so obstinate and ungodly, he might be punished by loss of life."

The church as well as temporal authorities were to see that this mandate was carried out. It was to be proclaimed about once every church year. In consequence of such severe mandates Anabaptism never reached any importance in the principality of Neuburg, though finally the Anabaptists were tolerated by Otto Heinrich.   W.W., E.C.

K. Schottenloher, *Pfalzgraf Ottheinrich und das Buch* (Münster, 1927) in *Reformationsgeschichtliche Studien und Texte*, H. 50-51; discussion in *Zts. für Kirchengesch.* XLVII (1928) 127 f.; Chr. Hege, *Die Täufer in der Kurpfalz* (Frankfurt, 1908) 84-99; *ML* III, 327-28.

Oud Gebruyk van de Vryheit *van spreeken in de Gemeenten der Doopsgesinden* was a book published at Amsterdam in 1665; a second undated edition was published at Harlingen after 1665. This book is a Dutch translation of a Swiss Mennonite booklet, *Verantwortung etlicher so man Töuffer nennt uff die Fragen warum sie nit zur Kilchen gangind*, published by Chr. Froschauer at Zürich in 1561. The Dutch editors, whose names are not found in the preface, were apparently Lamist (*q.v.*) Mennonites and Collegiants (*q.v.*), who favored the practice of speaking freely in the Mennonite meetings. In the preface they emphasize the view that the conservative leaders Bastiaan van Weenighem (*q.v.*) and Jean Boenes (*q.v.*), who had drawn up the *Verbondt van Eenigheyt* (*q.v.*), in which much stress is laid upon well-ordained ministers, who with exclusion of all other brethren are allowed to speak in the Mennonite services, are not in agrement with the old Mennonite practices, as used by the Swiss Mennonites. Besides the translation of the *Verantwortung* the book contains a preface, some extracts of the *Martyrs' Mirror*, a letter of D. V. Coornhert (*q.v.*), and four hymns.   vDZ.

Oud Martelaarsboek (Old Martyrs' Book), common name given by van Braght (*q.v.*) and others either to the first Dutch martyr book, *Het Offer des Heeren* (*q.v.*), or to *Historie der Martelaren ofte waerachtighe Getuygen Jesu Christi* . . . (Haarlem, 1615). The martyr book *Martelaers-Spiegel der werelose Christenen* . . . (Haarlem, 1631) was commonly referred to as the *Groot Martelaarsboek* (Large Martyrs' Book).   vDZ.

Oudaen, Joachim (b. Oct. 7, 1628, at Rijnsburg, d. April 26, 1692, at Rotterdam), a Dutch poet spiritually akin to D. R. Camphuysen (*q.v.*), was the son of Frans Oudaen, a Rotterdam baker who settled in Rijnsburg in 1622 to avoid persecution for his Remonstrant sympathies, joined the Collegiants (*q.v.*) there and became the friend of the van der Kodde family of Warmond, to which the originators of the Collegiant movement belonged, and into which he married. His son Joachim was educated at the University of Leiden and moved to Rotterdam, where a "Collegiant college" had been formed both among the Remonstrants (about 1630) and the Mennonites. He was closely connected with this group, which included François van Hoogstraten, poet and book dealer. His first biographer states that although he was a Remonstrant he was also a deacon in the Waterlander Mennonite congregation of Rotterdam.

That he was a Waterlander deacon is a fact, but that he was a Remonstrant is questionable, though he often attended the Remonstrant church. Some of his descendants were baptized in the Mennonite church. In honor of Menno Simons he wrote a short poem to be used with the etching of Menno; for the Mennonite painter Michiel van Mierevelt (*q.v.*) he composed an epitaph. He met the poets Johannes Antonides van der Goes and Heiman Dullaert in the same circle of God-fearing intellectuals in Rotterdam. As a young enthusiast he was a chiliast and later probably inclined toward Socinianism. He was sharply anti-Catholic.

As a religious poet his chief work was rhyming the Psalms, publishing the first part in 1680, the second a year later (*Uitbreiding der Psalmen*). The Waterlander congregation in Amsterdam adopted many of his rhymed Psalms into the new hymnal in 1684, the Flemish congregation in 1889. In addition he wrote many other religious songs, which were sung by the Rotterdam Waterlander congregation.

In his secular verse Oudaen sought to imitate the great Vondel (*q.v.*, see also **Literature**), though with humble reverence and a mediocre poetic gift. Camphuysen (*q.v.*), whom he adored second only to Vondel, was much more nearly an equal and a more comfortable model. His work also includes dramas and historical poems. A personal trait in his lyric poetry is his lively feeling for nature, and in harmony with it, a conspicuous interest in effects of landscape painting (Jan Porcellis, Adam Willaerts, Hendrik Sorgh, Mierevelt). Oudaen's complete works (*Poezy*) were published in three volumes at Amsterdam in 1712 with a biography by David van Hoogstraten.   H.F.W.J.

G. J. Boekenoogen, "De portretten van Menno Simons," *DB* 1916; Cramer, "Bijdragen tot de geschiedenis van ons kerklied," *DB* 1900, 1902; Arnold Houbraken, *Groote Schouburgh der Nederlandsche Konstschilders* (1718-19); C. B. Hylkema, *Reformateurs* (Haarlem, 1900-2); Gerrit Kalff, *Geschiedenis der Nederlandsche Letterkunde* (Groningen, 1906-12 Dl. IV); W. J. Kühler, *Het Socinianisme in Nederland* (Leiden, 1912); Jakob Prinsen J. L.zn., *Handboek tot de Nederl. letterkundige geschiedenis* (The Hague, 1916); J. C. van Slee, *De Rijnsburger Collegianten* (Haarlem, 1895); *ML* III, 329; J. Melles, *Joachim Oudaen* (Utrecht, 1958).

Oud-Beyerland: see **Beyerland.**

Ouddorp, a village on the island of Goeree in the Dutch province of South Holland. The former congregation in this village was at first often called Goeree (or Goedereede), later usually Ouddorp. The origin and early history of the congregation are still unknown. At first the members met in an attic. In 1624 there were some difficulties with the government on account of two marriages concluded in the congregation. The Mennonites yielded. In 1747 the authorities wanted to compel the Mennonites to trade in arms; the result is not clear. Repeatedly the congregation suffered loss through floods, especially in 1717 and 1953. The congregation, which at first belonged to the Flemish branch and in the 18th century joined the Zonist (*q.v.*) Conference (*Sociëteit*), was always quite small. (The baptized membership in 1645, 44; 1727, 54; 1744, 47; 1807, 25; 1900, 9; 1955, 31.) In the 17th and early 18th centuries this congregation maintained active relationships with the neighboring congregations of Brouwershaven, Renesse, Zierikzee, Middelharnis, Goes, Spijkenisse, and Den Briel, all of which were dissolved in the 18th century with the exception of Goes. Most of the members at that time were quite well-to-do. In 1671 they contributed 473 guilders to the Fund for Foreign Needs; in the course of the 18th century they collected a total of 590 guilders for the brethren expelled from Switzerland and Poland. In the 19th century several families emigrated to North America. It seemed for a moment that the entire congregation would leave; by that time it had become quite poor. The members are almost exclusively farmers. Well-known names found in Ouddorp since the 17th century are Bosland and Mastenbroek. The meetinghouse was probably built before 1771. Few of the ministers of the congregation received training at the Amsterdam Mennonite Seminary. The last ministers were G. Pol 1853-62, T. Schiere 1863-74, H. Koekebakker 1874-78, W. J. Leendertz 1878-81, K. W. Rössing 1882-d.1921, F. B. Kooymans 1924-25, W. Schopenhauer 1926-28, R. Foppema 1930-36, and Jacob Thiessen 1939-46. Since 1946 the pulpit has been vacant.

After a severe flood on Feb. 1, 1953, had devastated a part of the island of Goeree, a Mennonite Voluntary Service unit composed of American and Dutch young men worked at Ouddorp.   vDZ.

Inv. Arch. Amst. I, No. 1065; II, 2, No. 300; *DB* 1876, 72; 1907, 152-69; *DJ* 1954, 38 f.; *ML* II, 131; III, 329.

Oude Friezen (Vriezen), formerly a branch of the Dutch Mennonites: see **Frisian Mennonites.**

Oude Liederen (Old Hymns) is a collection of twelve hymns composed by Joachim Oudaen, Jan Bredenburg Jr., and Reinier Rooleeuw, which was introduced with a new rhymed version of the Psalms in 1684 in the Lam and Toren Mennonite congregation at Amsterdam and used there until 1797. There were a number of reprints: the following unchanged editions are known: Amsterdam 1685 (with notes), Haarlem 1713, Haarlem 1713 (with notes), Amsterdam 1721, Amsterdam 1727, Haarlem 1734, Haarlem 1756, Haarlem 1756 (increased by seven hymns; this edition is entitled *Opwekkende Gezangen*), Rotterdam 1775 (entitled *Liederen en Gezangen*), Amsterdam 1793 (two different editions). A greatly revised edition was published at Amsterdam in 1791. (Copies of most of these editions are found in AML.)   vDZ.

Oude Maeyken, 't (Maeyken Sprincen), an Anabaptist martyr, drowned on Oct. 11, 1559, at the Steen castle at Antwerp, Belgium. She was an aged widow, a native of Maastricht in the Dutch province of Limburg. Her clothing and furniture were confiscated and publicly sold. She was a simple, pious woman, remaining loyal even in temptation and trial, and died steadfast. Maeyken is commemorated in two hymns, (*a*) "Aenhoort Godt, hemelsche Vader" and (*b*) "Babels Raets Mandamenten," both found in the *Lietboecxken* (Nos. 16 and 19). vDZ.

Offer, 566, 581; *Mart. Mir.* D 249, E 623, 639; *Antw. Arch.-Blad* IX, 3, 9, 16; XIV, 26 f., No. 299; Wolkan, *Lieder,* 63, 71 f.; *ML* III, 711.

8

Oude Niedorp: see **Niedorp.**

Oude Pekela: see **Pekela.**

Oude Vlamingen (Old Flemish), a former branch of the Dutch Mennonites: see **Flemish Mennonites.**

Oude Vriezen (Friezen) (Old Frisians), a former branch of the Dutch Mennonites: see **Frisian Mennonites.**

Oude Zijpe: see **Zijpe.**

Oude Zwitsers, a group of Swiss immigrants in the Netherlands: see **Swiss Mennonites in the Netherlands.**

Oudebildtzijl, a village in the Dutch province of Friesland, about ten miles northwest of Leeuwarden. In 1505 a large piece of land was reclaimed from the sea by dykes and was known as the Bildtland, which was drained into the ocean by means of a sluice (*zijl*), near which the village Oudebildtzijl later arose. Many of the peasants who settled in this Bildt-polder are thought to have organized very soon into a Mennonite congregation, the center of which was probably in Sint Anna-Parochie (*q.v.,* at that time usually called Annakerk). The Mennonites living in and near Oudebildtzijl belonged to this congregation. A list set up on the occasion of the organization of the Mennonite Conference of Friesland (*Friesche Doopsgezinde Sociëteit*) in 1695 does not name Oudebildtzijl, which indicates that the members were still part of the Annakerk congregation; this is also the case in 1735, but at that date this congregation is called St-Annakerk and Bildtzijl. Blaupot ten Cate (*Friesland,* 192) writes that in 1695 the St-Annakerk and Oudebildtzijl congregations had already merged and had a total of 118 members, but it is more likely that they had not yet been separated. The congregation had two meetinghouses, one in St-Anna-Parochie and one in Oudebildtzijl. The Oudebildtzijl meetinghouse dated from 1636 or even before. Church records have been preserved since 1642. By 1806 the St-Annakerk congregation had completely disintegrated and the church had been dismantled. In the same year Oudebildtzijl built a new church and became an independent congregation, then numbering 9 baptized members (34 in 1838). In 1812 the congregation called Roelof Schuiling (*q.v.*) to the ministry; he served until 1817, then moving to Hindeloopen. In 1818 Schuiling was called in a second time, the congregation of Oudebildtzijl now having united with the neighboring congregation of Hallum. Schuiling, who lived at Oudebildtzijl, served until 1857. When he left, each congregation decided to call a pastor, and on Sept. 12, 1858, Lamorael Noteboom, who had been the minister in Ternaard, became the first pastor of Oudebildtzijl itself. The church building was enlarged in 1860 and again in 1908, and a parsonage was bought, which was renovated in 1891. An organ was installed in 1896. The Oudebildtzijl church is the only Mennonite church in the Netherlands which has a bell in its tower, which serves as the village clock. When the bell was rung on the occasion of the birth of Princess Juliana on April 30, 1909, it cracked; for its repair a contribution was made by Queen Wilhelmina. The new bell was taken by the Germans in 1944. The congregation, which still consists largely of farmers, now (1957) numbers 140 baptized members (88 in 1861, 98 in 1900).

Pastor Noteboom served here until 1883. He was followed by G. E. Frerichs 1884-90, J. Kooiman 1891-93, A. Hermansz ten Cate 1893-99, B. H. Rudolphi 1900-6, R. Kuipers 1906-14, M. A. Hylkema 1915-22, J. Yntema 1922-26, L. D. G. Knipscheer 1926-31, Miss J. M. Eelman 1932-42, H. Bremer 1942-46, D. Attema, a retired minister of Zaandam, 1946-49, B. K. Homan 1950-54, and M. J. Heynes 1955- . The congregation has a Sunday school for children, a youth group, and a ladies' circle. vDZ.

Blaupot t. C., *Friesland, passim,* see Index; *Naamlijst* 1829, 44 f.; *DB* 1861, 139; 1907, 210; 1909, 191; 1910, 131 f.; *ML* III, 329 f.

Oudeghodt, Pieter, an Anabaptist martyr: see **Pieter den Ouden.**

Oudejan Cornelisz, an Anabaptist martyr: see **Jan Cornelisz.**

Oudekleerkoper, Joris, an Anabaptist martyr: see **Joris.**

Oudenaarden (Oudenaerde, Audenarde), a town in the Belgian province of East Flanders (pop. 6,520 in 1951), was a center of Anabaptist activity during the 16th century. Though there is no information concerning congregational life in this town, at least one martyr was executed here, viz., Adriaen den Burry, on July 10, 1565. About the same period there was live Calvinist activity at Oudenaarden; in 1554-73 thirteen Calvinists died here as martyrs. vDZ.

Bibliographie des Martyrologes II (The Hague, 1890) 798; *DB* 1876, 106.

Oudenaerde (Oudenaarden), (**van**), a Dutch Mennonite family, probably emigrants from the Belgian town of Oudenaarden (*q.v.*), was from the 17th century found at Rotterdam, Netherlands. Willem van Oudenaerde, d. Oct. 27, 1726, at Rotterdam at a very advanced age, a grocer and a linen merchant, married to Wilhelmina van Eyse, was in 1682 appointed preacher of the Rotterdam Flemish congregation and in 1691 elder; in 1694 he moved to Middelburg, and thereupon to Dordrecht, but in 1696 he was back in Rotterdam as a preacher in the Waterlander congregation. After the Flemish and the Waterlander congregations merged in 1700 Willem van Oudenaerde was preacher of the united congregation 1701-5. Some of his descendants served in Rotterdam as deacons. Marinus Oudenaarden published a pamphlet, *Korte Aanmerkingen* (Rotterdam, 1718), against Jan Suderman and Aelbert van Meurs, who had protested against the appointment of David van Heyst (*q.v.*) as preacher. The van Oudenaerde family has died out. vDZ.

Ouderling (Elder; French, *Ancien*), a function found in the Dutch Reformed Church and occasionally also among the Dutch Mennonites in the 17th-19th centuries. This function was not the same as that of an elder among the Mennonites of America, i.e., a minister who has been ordained to bap-

tize, to administer communion, and to perform marriages; such a minister was formerly called "oudste" or "leeraar tot ten vollen dienst," by the Dutch Mennonites. The "ouderling" is a lay member of the church board, whose function among the Reformed is to supervise the local congregation; among the Mennonites the function usually was restricted to the control of the congregational finances. Ouderlingen were found in only a few Dutch Mennonite congregations, particularly at Leiden, where this name and function existed in the Waterlander congregation in the last decades of the 17th century and in the Waterlander and Flemish congregation (united 1701) until 1763. Besides the control of finances, they with the preachers paid annual visits to the members of the church. In the Workum congregation ouderlingen are mentioned in 1692, but in 1710 the name of ouderling was abolished here. In Bovenknijpe the name and function of ouderling was found until 1877. vDZ.

DB 1878, 131; *DJ* 1903, 89; L. G. le Poole, *Bijdragen tot de kennis van . . . de Doopsgezinden te Leiden* (Leiden, 1905) 76, 123-25 *et passim.*

Oudeschoot, a village in the Dutch province of Friesland, where Leenaert Bouwens (*q.v.*) in 1563-65 baptized 14 persons. Since there was no congregation in Oudeschoot, the converts may have joined the Mildam (*q.v.*) congregation. vDZ.

Oudesluis in the Dutch province of North Holland, the seat of a Mennonite congregation, in later times usually called Noord Zijpe. (See **Zijpe.**) vDZ.

Oudste, Dutch name for elder: see **Elder.**

Oud-Wulven, a Mennonite home for children at Houten in the Dutch province of Utrecht. It was founded on Sept. 16, 1947, on the initiative of the Mennonite Foundation for Special Needs (see **Stichting voor Bizondere Noden**) to educate uncared-for children (ages 4-12 or even older). The first directors were Mr. and Mrs. R. de Zeeuw (1947-55). In 1957 about 20 children found shelter in Oud-Wulven. In 1958 the home was moved to Schoorl. vDZ.

Our Bi-Monthly Letter was a four-page M.B.C. missionary periodical published 1913-38 by the United Orphanage and Mission Society, now combined with the United Missionary Society. The first editor was T. Ford Barker and the last Dorinda Bowman. The periodical's interest was that of the Armenians living in Syria, Turkey, and Lebanon. J.A.H.

Out, a Dutch Mennonite family name still found in a number of congregations in North Holland. Jan Pietersz Out was a preacher of the Flemish congregation of Barsingerhorn-Nieuwe Zijpe 1732-*c*52. vDZ.

Outerman, Gilles (Gielis, Jelis), an Anabaptist martyr: see **Jelis Outerman.**

Outerman, Jacques, b. *c*1547, probably in Flanders, Belgium, died at an advanced age before 1639 at Haarlem, Holland. As an elder he played an important role among the Mennonites of the Netherlands. He was also called Jacob Keest, Jacob (**van**)

Reinegom (also Reninge, or Reyninghen). In 1586—he was then a deacon at Franeker in Friesland—he opposed Thomas Bijntgens (Bintgens, q.v.), the elder of the Flemish congregation in Franeker. The consequence was a division of the congregation into two factions known as the Thomas Bijntgensvolk or Huiskopers (Housebuyers) and the Jacob Keestvolk or Contra-Huiskopers. This schism was not induced solely by the purchase of a house, but had its roots in the practice of the ban, the Huiskopers being the stricter, the Jacob Keestvolk the more lenient group. The division was not confined to the Franeker congregation. Soon there were found everywhere Old Flemish (followers of Bijntgens) and Young (or Gentle) Flemish, usually called simply Flemish, the party of Outerman being the more numerous.

Later Outerman was elder of the large Haarlem Flemish congregation "in den Block." About 1616 he was deposed and banned by Jan Luies, the elder of strict Groningen Mennonites; but his congregation remained loyal to him.

Outerman took an active part in compiling the new martyr book, in which the Waterlanders and Frisians also co-operated, which was to replace the smaller *Offer des Heeren* (q.v.). The *Groote Offerboek* appeared in 1615 with a foreword by Hans de Ries (see **Historie der Martelaren**). Outerman for some reason, now unknown, had already finished his contribution to the book.

Outerman must have had a wide influence; the Reformed preachers wrote in warning that the populace looked up to him as to a bishop, shepherd, and master and regarded him as an apostle. Outerman was an unusually prolific writer, writing until a very advanced age. His works are mostly of a polemic character, dealing with the schisms among the Dutch Mennonites. The most important are *Nootwendige Verantwoordinghe . . . tot wederleghhen van de Euangelische mijdinge* (anonymous, n.p., 1595), *Onder verbeteringhe. Verclaringhe met bewijs wt den droevighen handel van Vriesen ende Vlaminghen . . .* (n.p., 1609), and *Copye eens Briefs, soo Jaques Outerman eertijds geschreven heeft*. *. . tot onderrichtinge ven de droevighe Sake, so eertijdts tusschen die men nu Vriesen ende Vlamingen noemt, ghevallen is* (Haarlem, 1634).

In 1608-9 Outerman was attacked by Johannes Zeeuw and Idzardus Nicolai, Reformed preachers, and in 1626 by a Reformed preacher of Haarlem, Johannes Acronius, accusing him of Socinianism, which was heretical on the doctrine of the Trinity, and which the Reformed Church was alertly guarding against at that time. Outerman had to account for his position before the States of Holland. He defended himself and wrote a confession of faith which was signed by nineteen Flemish preachers and presented to the court of Holland on Oct. 8, 1626. This confession deals with the "Eenigen Godt, Vader, Soon en Heyligen Geest" and the incarnation of the Son of God. It was examined and declared Biblical. Outerman had no further difficulties, and the building of the meetinghouse, which the government had halted, could now proceed. But it is a question whether Outerman in his dogmatic rationalism and in his observations on the

Trinity did not deviate too far from the simple words of the Bible and thereby to some extent approach Socinianism.

Outerman's confession was apparently highly regarded by some of the Mennonites. It was included in the book that contains the general confessions (*De algemeene Belijdenissen . . . ,* Amsterdam, 1665). And in 1735, at the meeting called for the founding of a seminary, the more conservative Zonists (q.v.) asked (though in vain) whether Outerman's confession should not be taken as the basis for the seminary.

Little is known about the last years of Outerman's life. In 1637 he was still living, for in this year he published *Een claer Bewijs uyt Godts Woordt, dat Godt . . . alle menschen door Christum . . . voorsien ende verkoren heeft tot den eeuwigen Leven.* Jelis Outerman (q.v.), who died as a martyr in 1561 at Brugge, Belgium, may have been a relative of Jacques Outerman.   vDZ.

Inv. Arch. Amst. I, Nos. 492, 580, 582, 586, 636; II, 2, No. 66; *Bibliographie* II, 503; Kühler, *Geschiedenis* II; *idem, Het Socinianisme in Nederland* (Leiden, 1912) 90-105; *DB* 1870, 59, 63; 1876, 39; 1893, 80; 1899, 103; 1904, 117, 120; 1906, 145, 147; *BRN* VII, 70 f.; *ML* III, 330.

Outgert Jacob Barbierszoon, an Anabaptist martyr, beheaded on Jan. 7, 1539, at Delft, Dutch province of South Holland, together with ten others, who were apparently all David-Jorists (q.v.). Outgert is said to have been a lantern maker from the province of Groningen. (*Inv. Arch. Amst.* I, No. 749; *DB* 1899, 159-60; 1917, 160-67.)   vDZ.

Outrijve, van (originally d'Hauteryve, also Houterijve, Houtryve, Outryve, Autryve), a Mennonite family from French Flanders. In the early 17th century they left Belgium and moved to Aardenburg in Dutch Zealand Flanders and other towns of the province of Zeeland, like Vlissingen, Middelburg, and Goes. Joos(t) van Outrijve (d. year 1682 at Vlissingen) was a preacher of the Mennonite congregation in this town. A collection of his sermons, entitled *De sterre Jacobs of een ligt der Ziende, bestaande in XVIII Predicatien* (Vlissingen, 1688), was published after his death. This book also contains several treatises and some letters by van Outrijve. The letters were separately reprinted at Groningen in 1720. His grandson Joost Pieters van Outryve (d. 1704 at Vlissingen) willed a large part of his property to the Vlissingen Mennonite congregation. (*Inv. Arch. Amst.* II, 2, No. 564.)   vDZ.

Ouwejan(s), Jacob, b. Oct. 29, 1706, at Zaandam, d. Oct. 2, 1781, at Rotterdam, was the scion of a Mennonite family living for more than two centuries at Zaandam, Dutch province of North Holland, where they were mostly engaged in shipbuilding. Some of them were deacons in the United Mennonite congregation in the "Nieuwe Huys" of West Zaandam. Jacob Ouwejan(s), at first engaged in shipbuilding, was made a preacher of this congregation on Nov. 25, 1725, when he was 19 years old. He had received no special training for this position. In 1741 he was called by the Flemish congregation of Danzig, Prussia, to mediate in the dissension that had arisen in this congregation, particularly with Elder Hendrik van Dühren (q.v.). On Sept. 3, 1741, a few days before leaving Holland, he was ordained elder in the Zonist church in Amsterdam by Petrus Smidt; "after a long, difficult, and dangerous journey" he was affectionately received in Danzig. He preached his first sermon in the Flemish congregation in the city on Nov. 5, 1741, and soon succeeded in restoring peace. After only six weeks he received a call from the Rotterdam congregation, and although he was invited to stay in Danzig, he returned to Holland. On June 10, 1742, he preached his first sermon for the United Waterlander and Flemish congregation in Rotterdam, and stayed here nearly thirty years. The new, very handsome church (destroyed in 1940) was dedicated by him on May 28, 1775, with a sermon, *Sions Tempelvreugd* (Rotterdam, 1775). He was extraordinarily strong in body and mind. At that time there was occasional dissension in the congregation. Ouwejans favored the minority group of conservative Flemish, thereby offending the majority. Later he was involved in some difficulty with his more liberal colleague Menalda. He resigned on Sept. 16, 1781, and died after a few weeks. In 1761 he published a collection of sermons, *Hemel en Aarde Verheugd*. His son Jan Ouwejans and his grandson Jan Ouwejan van den Berg served the Rotterdam congregation as deacons in 1782-1810 and 1816-33.   vDZ.

S. Lootsma, *Het Nieuwe Huys* (Zaandam, 1937) 31, 47, 57, 186, 193; *Inv. Arch. Amst.* I, No. 1680; II, Nos. 2673, 2675; II, 2, No. 812; *Naamlijst* 1787, 56-62; K. Vos, *Geschiedenis der Doopsgez. Gemeente te Rotterdam* (1907, reprint) 29, 32, 44; *DB* 1864, 106-8; 1912, 108; *ML* III, 331.

Overbeek, a Dutch Mennonite family, which (according to Blaupot ten Cate, *Groningen* I, 32) originally lived in Münsterland, Germany, from where its members in the 17th century moved to Twente, the southeastern district of the Dutch province of Overijssel, where they are still found. Other descendants have spread throughout the Netherlands. In Twente most of them lived in Hengelo. A few Overbeeks have been ministers. Hendrik Overbeek, a weaver, was a lay preacher of the Groningen Old Flemish congregation at Hengelo from 1727 until he retired in 1743. He died about 1762. Klaas Tigler Overbeek (d. 1847) of Dokkum was a minister of the Franeker Mennonite congregation 1811-46, while his son Pieter Overbeek served the congregation of Terhorne 1841-67. Cornelis Loosjes Overbeek, b. 1793 at Haarlem, d. 1841 at Zutphen, a son of Lucas Overbeek and Engeltje Loosjes, served at Zutphen 1819-38. He then went into business. He left some property to the A.D.S.   vDZ.

Overd'hage, Petrus (Pieter de Zuttere, Suttere), usually called Hyperphragmus, was a Reformed theologian. This remarkable man, who was born before 1530 at Gent, Belgium, joined the local Reformed church and probably was their preacher. He left Gent about 1566 and then lived for some time in Emden, Germany, and later in Rotterdam, Holland. Here he was not admitted to the Reformed pulpit because the strict Calvinists accused him of heterodoxy. In 1581 he was back in Gent, and in 1593 he became a Reformed pastor at Hoogmade, Dutch province of North Brabant, but was dismissed the next year. Of his life not much is known.

Whether he was a relative of the Mennonite de Zuttere (de Sitter) family could not be ascertained. He published a number of theological and devotional books. He was a spiritualist, as is shown from his confession in Latin of 1594 (a confession of 1595, written by Overd'hage in the Dutch language, agrees much more with the Calvinist doctrines); he was thought by some to have been an adherent of D. V. Coornhert (*q.v.*), and by others a follower of Schwenckfeld (*q.v.*).

Overd'hage is of special interest as the editor of Henric Rol's (*q.v.*) book *De Slotel van dat secreet des Nachtmaels onses Heren J.C.* (The Key of the Secret of the Lord's Supper). The assumption of some theologians that the author of *De Slotel* was not the Anabaptist Rol, but Overd'hage himself, is an error, as S. Cramer has proved in *BRN* V, 6-14. Overd'hage was very sympathetic to the Mennonites and is said to have preached sometimes in their meetings.   vDZ.

Bibliotheca Belgica i.v. de Zuttere; DB 1884, 56 f., 58, 60; Chr. Sepp, *Drie Evangeliedienaren uit den Tijd der Hervorming* (Leiden, 1879) 81-122; a study by H. Q. Janssen on Hyperphragmus has been published in *Studiën en Bijdragen, verzameld door W. Moll en J. G. de Hoop Scheffer* IV (Amsterdam, 1880) 321 ff.; J. H. Wessel, *De leerstellige strijd tusschen Nederl. Gereformeerden en Doopsgezinden in de zestiende eeuw* (Assen, 1946) 122; L. Knappert, *Het ontstaan en de vestiging van het Protestantisme in de Nederlanden* (Utrecht, 1924) 190-92.

Overholt, John D. (1797-1878), a great-grandson of Martin Oberholtzer of Frankfurt a.M., Germany, who emigrated to America and settled near Deep Run, Bucks Co., Pa. He was ordained as minister in 1830 for the church in Westmoreland County, Pa. In 1833 he was ordained bishop. In his work as bishop he made annual trips as far west as Columbiana County, Ohio. In 1857 Henry Yother (1810-1900) was ordained bishop to assist John D. Overholt.   W.D.S.

Edward Yoder, "The Mennonites of Westmoreland County, Pa.," *MQR* XV (1941) 151-86.

Overijssel, a province in the Netherlands, area 1,295 sq. miles, pop. 554,000, including 2,700 Mennonites. These are found in the three towns of Deventer, Zwolle, and Kampen, in the northern tip of the province, where the congregations of Blokzijl, Giethoorn, Steenwijk, and Zwartsluis are located, while a smaller congregation in Oldemarkt died out in the middle of the 18th century; also in Twente (*q.v.*) in the southeast of the province, opposite the German border, where the congregations of Almelo, Borne, Hengelo, and Enschedé, formerly also Goor, are located. In the three cities we come upon Anabaptists soon after 1530, and congregations were formed soon after. The congregation in Deventer, concerning which we are well informed, had a very hard time, whereas those at Kampen and Zwolle apparently developed peacefully.

The congregations in the northern point date from the end of the 16th century. In Twente, which remained under Spanish rule until 1626, the Mennonites could hardly expand before that year. Nevertheless there are indications that the congregations of Almelo and Enschedé date back to about 1580. The Mennonite groups were augmented especially by the immigration of weavers and merchants from Westphalia, Germany. (The supposed immigration of a large number of Mennonite weavers from Flanders, Belgium, is very questionable.) They have been of great importance economically. Twente, now a great industrial center, in the manufacture principally of textiles, became what it is largely because of the Mennonites. In Overijssel there was no federation of congregations, as in Friesland; the congregations were too independent for such a step.

Until the beginning of the 19th century the congregations in Overijssel belonged to several Mennonite branches. It is conspicuous that they for the most part were members of the more conservative groups. The more liberal Waterlanders had congregations only in Blokzijl and Zwolle, which were very small. Many congregations belonged to the Groninger Old Flemish, whereas the congregations in Oldemarkt, one in Blokzijl, Zuidveen (later merged with Steenwijk), and one in Giethoorn belonged to the very strictest wing of the Danzig Old Flemish (q.v.).

On the whole, the records of the Mennonites in Overijssel are so scarce that it is impossible to create an exact picture. The magistrates in this province were often very ungracious to the Mennonites. In 1633 they forbade them to have their marriages performed in their own meetinghouses; they were to be performed by the civil authorities after being proclaimed three times in the Reformed churches (these regulations were repeated in 1636, 1649, 1653, 1659, and 1698). In 1625 Mennonite church meetings were forbidden in Overijssel, but in 1631 their meetings were tolerated on the condition that they would not be held publicly. From about 1690 the magistrates became more lenient.

The congregations of Blokzijl, Giethoorn, Steenwijk, Zwartsluis, Kampen, Zwolle, Deventer, are now united in the Zwolsche Ring. The Almelo, Borne, Hengelo, and Enschedé congregations form the Ring Twente.

The eleven congregations in this province had a total baptized membership of 1,202 in 1834 (previous figures not available for most congregations), 1,519 in 1860, 2,031 in 1900, 2,499 in 1929, 2,487 in 1955.   vDZ.

Inv. Arch. Amst. I, Nos. 113, 282, 374; DB 1878, 4 ff.; 1879, 7, 92 f.; 1910, 10; N. van der Zijpp, De Doopsgezinde in Overijssel (repr. 1932); ML III, 289.

Overlanders, a 16th-century term used in Holland for Mennonites of Germany (DB 1864, 26; 1875, 28) and particularly those in South Germany (DB 1905, 77, those in Strasbourg; Inv. Arch. Amst. II, 2, No. 865b, those in Strasbourg and South Germany). Hans de Ries (q.v.), the leader of the Waterlander Mennonites in Holland about 1616, wrote a letter (undated) to the "Overlandsche Broeders," seeking to make peace with them (Inv. Arch. Amst. I, No. 556). But soon, especially after a large number of Mennonites from Germany had moved to the Netherlands, the name of "Overlanders" disappeared, both the Mennonites in Germany and those who had moved to Holland generally being called "Hoogduitsche Doopsgezinden" (High German Mennonites). Alenson (BRN VII, 190) says

that the Overlanders did not accept the view on the Incarnation (q.v.) taught by Menno Simons and the strict Dutch leaders; and it was said (BRN VII, 460, 465) that the Overlanders were mild in the practice of banning. De Hoop Scheffer's idea (DB 1877, 68) that the "Overlandsch" dialect was spoken in North Germany is not correct. (See also **High German Mennonites.**)   vDZ.

Overmeer, a hamlet in the Dutch province of North Holland, formerly the seat of a Mennonite congregation, which had a small membership and at least from 1680 was united with the neighboring congregation at Weesp (q.v.), though in this union Overmeer seems to have had a degree of independence. By 1718 the Overmeer congregation had died out. (Inv. Arch. Amst. II, 2, Nos. 301-3; DB 1872, 67.)   vDZ.

Oversticht, an old name of the Dutch province of Overijssel (q.v.). (See **Stichtsche Handel.**) vDZ.

Overwij(c)k, Harmen R. van: see Reynskes, Harmen.

Owen County, Ind., the seat of the extinct Bower Mennonite Church (MC), the members of which lived in both Owen and Clay (q.v.) counties. The meetinghouse was located in Marion Township, Owen County. One of the early settlers there was Bishop Daniel Funk (1781-1859). Later bishops in the church were Jacob Bower (1803-67), after whom the church was named, Michael Mishler (d. 1871), and Daniel Royer (active in the last quarter of the 19th century). The last two ministers were Jacob Hoffer (1827-1906), ordained in 1872, and Daniel Kinports (1830-1912), ordained about 1885. One of the more active leaders was Deacon George Funk (1812-96), ordained in 1872. The last deacon was Jacob Kilmer (1819-1909). Bishop John M. Brenneman (q.v.) of Elida, Ohio, visited the group and tried to help them, as did also John S. Coffman in 1883. But the group was very conservative and seems to have never started a Sunday school. The first meetinghouse of 1861 was destroyed by a tornado in 1883, and the new meetinghouse built in the same year was sold by the Indiana-Michigan Conference in 1928. Today only the cemetery is left, and it is in poor condition. The father of D. A. Yoder, Peter B. Yoder (1855-1948), was born in Owen County. Some of the Mennonites left the area because of the intermittent fever (ague) which plagued the residents.   J.C.W.

Oyer, Noah (1891-1931), an able educator in the Mennonite Church (MC), was born April 11, 1891, at Metamora, Ill., the son of John P. and Mary Smith Oyer. He secured his high-school and college training at Hesston (A.B., 1919), his seminary training at Princeton (Th.B., 1922), and almost completed an M.A. at Franklin and Marshall College (1922), was ordained preacher Sept. 30, 1923. He served as head of the Bible department at Hesston 1922-24, dean 1923-24, and pastor of the Hesston College congregation. In 1924 he was called as head of the Bible department and dean of Goshen College, serving as the academic leader and pastor of the College church in a crucial period of reconstruction. He played a vital role in the general leadership of the Mennonite Church (MC), as a member of the Mennonite Board of Education for nine years, and as chairman of the General Sunday School Committee for seven years, this committee being a General Conference standing committee. He was married Aug. 9, 1916, to Siddie King. Two of his children, John Oyer and Mary Oyer, are professors at Goshen College. H.S.B.

In Memoriam Dean Noah Oyer 1891-1931 (Goshen, 1931).

Ozark County, Mo., the location of a small Mennonite settlement in the 1890's, is on the Arkansas border. On Nov. 12, 1891, A. B. Kolb wrote to C. Z. Yoder, giving him instructions for a western trip, "Write to Noah D. Troyer, Oak Mound, Ozark Co., Mo. . . . There are only a few families here and no minister, and complain that they have been slighted. There is also a C. K. Miller at Bakersville, Ozark Co., Mo., but I do not know where he lives from Bro. Troyer." M.G.

Ozark Mennonite Brethren Mission: see **Martin Box Chapel.**

P

Pacific Bible Institute of Fresno came into being in response to a long-felt need on the part of the Mennonite Brethren Church on the Pacific Coast to have a Bible School where the young people might avail themselves of a sound Biblical training in an institution organically related to their own conference. On Sept. 18, 1944, the Pacific Bible Institute of Fresno was formally opened with an enrollment of 27 students in Fresno, Cal., in a large residence at 1095 N. Van Ness. Six faculty members, four full-time and two part-time, had been engaged by the Board of Directors. The enrollment increased to 35 students during the second semester of the school year. Toward the close of the first year another building, a former YMCA building, was purchased at 2149 Tuolumne, a three-story structure. In 1954 the Mennonite Brethren Conference of North America initiated a program of unification in its various educational endeavors and the Institute became a General Conference school. A 20-acre site near Fresno has been purchased for a new campus and to be developed over a period of years.

The aims of the school are as follows: (1) To give young people a thorough knowledge of the Bible; (2) To train them in the highest type of Christian living in whatever walk of life they may find themselves; (3) To prepare them for Christian service, at home or abroad; (4) To fortify them against the various unscriptural philosophies of life; (5) To send forth sanctified Christlike personalities, yielded and obedient to the Master.

In keeping with its purpose the Institute has made the study of the Bible the very center of its curriculum. For some time the Institute offered four- and five-year programs granting the Bible College Bachelor of Arts and Bachelor of Theology degrees. In keeping, however, with the program of unification and co-ordination a three-year course is now offered, leading to a diploma in Bible and a two-year course granting the Associate in Arts degree in liberal arts or sacred music.

The Bachelor of Theology has been transferred to the Mennonite Brethren Biblical Seminary, which was established on the same campus in 1956, and there expanded to a Bachelor of Divinity course. The following have served as presidents: S. W. Goossen 1944-46, G. W. Peters 1947-52, R. M. Baerg (acting) 1953-55, and B. J. Braun 1955- . G.W.P.

Pacific Coast Conference (MC) was organized Nov. 1, 1906, to include the three Mennonite churches of Oregon and Idaho which had previously belonged to the Kansas-Nebraska Conference, with a total of 135 members, viz., Nampa (Idaho), Albany (Ore.), and Hopewell (Hubbard) (Ore.). Later, besides additional congregations in Idaho and Oregon, newly established congregations in California, Arizona, and New Mexico were added. The Amish Mennonite congregations in Oregon which had belonged to the Western A.M. Conference joined the Pacific Coast Conference in 1921. Before the merger in 1920 the Pacific Coast Conference had six congrega-

tions with 362 members; the merger added three congregations with 449 members. In 1948 the congregations in Southern California, Arizona, and New Mexico withdrew to form the South Pacific Conference. In 1957 the Pacific Coast Conference had a total membership of 2,174 in 21 organized and 12 mission congregations distributed as follows: Oregon 17 organized and 8 mission congregations with 1,680 members; Idaho three organized and two mission congregations with 293 members; California one organized and one mission with 21 members. Creston, Mont., which had been a member of the Western A.M. Conference until 1916, then joined the Pacific Coast Conference, transferred to the Alberta-Saskatchewan Conference in 1923.

The conference has a district mission board established in 1906 (organ, *The Missionary Evangel*, established in 1944), a Christian workers' conference, a high school (Western Mennonite School) founded in 1945 at Salem, and a Home for the Aged founded in 1946 at Albany. Within the bounds of the conference are also three private elementary schools and the Lebanon Community Hospital, operated but not owned by the Mennonite Board of Missions and Charities. H.S.B.

Pacific District Conference (GCM) was organized in Pratum, Ore., on May 25, 1896. The first meeting was planned and arranged by J. B. Baer, then Field Secretary of the General Conference. P. Steiner and J. Amstutz of Bluffton, Ohio, S. F. Sprunger of Berne, Ind., J. J. Balzer of Mountain Lake, Minn., and C. Kaufman of South Dakota greatly helped to make that first session a success. Three small churches, Irving and Pratum, Ore., and Colfax, Wash., and a Sunday school of Dallas, Ore., were represented at the first meeting; the Amish church of Eugene, Ore., also participated. S. F. Sprunger was elected as chairman of that historic meeting and J. J. Balzer served as secretary. At that session "a Program-Business Committee, consisting of three members, was elected to which all the work was assigned until the appointing of the first Resolutions Committee in 1904 and the election of a permanent Evangelization Committee in 1908. The President and Secretary were elected at the beginning of each session until the close of the third session. From this time on they were elected in advance for the ensuing year."

The second session was held at Eugene, Ore., in 1897. J. B. Baer was elected as president and David Goertz as secretary. At that session it was decided that congregational representation at Conference be granted on the basis of one vote for every ten members. This arrangement is still in effect.

In 1908 the Conference accepted a constitution (German language) which the Business Committee had been instructed to prepare. In 1937 it was revised and translated into English.

According to Article Three, "The purpose of this organization is to promote fellowship among the churches, to co-operate in the spreading and establishing of the Kingdom of God in our own district, and to give united support to the work done by the various boards of the General Conference of the Mennonite Church of North America."

Article Four states their principle as follows: " 'For other foundation can no man lay than that is laid which is Jesus Christ.' The Pacific Conference is not a law-making but an advisory body, and therefore does not consider itself authorized to dictate rules of government to the congregations. It is a union for joint work, and among other things seeks to find ways and means to assist the scattered settlements, by advice and actual help, in the edification and advancement of their congregations, and therefore makes only such regulations as are necessary to carry on this united work. In regard to matters of faith it requires of these congregations who would unite with it that they adhere to the doctrines generally accepted by the Mennonites. By these Mennonite doctrines we understand, baptism on confession of faith, the abstaining from oaths, a Biblical nonresistance, the practice of a Scriptural church discipline, and the inadvisability of membership in secret oath-bound societies, since we consider their principles as contrary to the teachings of Christ and the apostles."

In addition to the regular conference officers, the following standing committees are elected by the delegates: the Evangelization Committee, Education Committee, Peace Committee, and Business Committee.

The Conference has always been interested in missionary work. In 1908 they encouraged the General Conference to open a mission in Los Angeles. In 1928 they started a work in Portland, Ore., in 1949 a new project at Sweet Home, Ore., and in 1954 they helped organize a work at Fresno, Cal., and Filer, Idaho. The congregations have also cooperated in lending assistance to some of the smaller struggling churches of the District.

The Pacific District is the smallest (in membership) of the six districts of the General Conference in the United States, but extends over the largest territory. It includes the area between Canada and Mexico, and the Rocky Mountains and the Pacific Ocean. The great distances between church groups have been a serious handicap in holding frequent fraternal gatherings of the various auxiliary organizations. It has therefore been necessary for them to carry on various phases of the conference activity on a sectional basis. The young people's gatherings are of this nature. Each state conducts its own youth retreats. The California young people conduct an annual Sunday-school and Christian Endeavor convention. They elect their own officers and sponsor their own missionary project.

The Pacific District Conference, which was organized by three small congregations, has now grown into an organization of 23 churches with a total membership of nearly 3,500. Six of these are located in Oregon, six in Washington, eight in California, and three in Idaho.   H.D.B.

D. D. King, "The Pacific District Conference," Mennonite Year Book 1925, 40; P. R. Aeschlimann, "The Pacific District Conference," Mennonite Year Book 1930, 23; idem, "History of the Pacific District Conference," Mennonite Year Book 1932, 32; H. D. Burkholder, "The Story of Our Conference and Churches (N. Newton, 1951).

Pacific District Conference (MB), created in 1913, includes 22 congregations with a total membership in 1957 of 5,070 distributed as follows: Washington one congregation with 187 members; Oregon two, 507; and California nineteen, 4,376. Most of the congregations are located in the San Joaquin Valley of California, with the center in Reedley. A graduate Biblical Seminary was established in Fresno in 1955 alongside a previously (1944) established Junior College and Bible Institute. The first congregations in the conference were established in 1905 at Reedley. In 1942 an Old People's Home was established at Reedley. The Pacific District M.B. Youth Fellowship was set up in 1948. The present conference organization includes among others the Executive Committee, the Home Missions Committee, and the Sunday School Committee.   H.S.B.

J. H. Lohrenz, The Mennonite Brethren Church (Hillsboro, 1950) 159-76.

Pacifism is a term derived from the Latin meaning peacemakers, the word being used in Matthew 5:9. New Testament or Christian pacifism is therefore identical in its meaning with New Testament nonresistance (q.v.), also taught in the Sermon on the Mount and throughout the New Testament. As generally employed, however, the term pacifism is used to cover many varieties of peacemaking, which may or may not be Christian in their orientation. Some modern pacifists oppose all wars and some do not. Some who do oppose all wars find their authority in the will of God and in the word of Scripture, while others find it largely in human reason.

While recognizing these differences and realizing the impossibility of a generalization which covers accurately all cases, the following would seem to be the chief criticisms of modern pacifism generally, seen from the viewpoint of New Testament nonresistance as found in the Anabaptist tradition:

(1) Pacifism too frequently sees peace as an end in itself, whereas the New Testament sees it as "the fruit of the Christian Gospel; peace is the fruit of regenerated individual lives. . . . While it includes social and political reconstruction, these collectivist improvements also root in the radical change necessary in the human heart." Thus, the primary task of the peacemaker is to bring individuals into direct contact with Jesus Christ the Prince of Peace.

(2) Pacifism is frequently too optimistic concerning the possible achievement of world peace. It does not reckon sufficiently with the reality of sin, and too lightly assumes the transformation of the unregenerate social order into the kingdom of God.

(3) Pacifism frequently fails to understand the basic nature of the state as an organization for the maintenance of order by coercive means in a sinful social order. It too lightly essays to administer this state by Christian principles, whereas the police power of the state is in fact the wrath of God at work among men, causing their evil doings to be kept in check by forcible means which are likewise evil. It is freely recognized that some states approach the Christian standard more nearly than do

others, and that some statesmen are men of integrity and Christian character more than others. In the best of states within the unregenerate social order, however, the basic nature remains the same, hence a frequent pacifist assumption that the state may use the Sermon on the Mount as its basic constitution is an illusion.

(4) As a consequence of this misunderstanding pacifism frequently compromises with the coercive methods of the state. In so doing it waters down the high ethic of the New Testament. Its love is not sufficiently far-reaching. Nonresistance, love, and the cross give way to nonviolent coercion or nonviolence (*q.v.*), which in its essence is a form of warfare.   G.F.H.

Don. E. Smucker, "A Mennonite Critique of the Pacifist Movement," *MQR* XX (January 1946) 81-88; Guy F. Hershberger, *War, Peace, and Nonresistance* (Scottdale, 1953); *idem, The Way of the Cross in Human Relations* (Scottdale, 1958); J. R. Mumaw, *Nonresistance and Pacifism.*

Page County (Iowa) Mennonite Church (MC), now extinct, was founded by three families from Allen County, Ohio, in 1864. Among them was John S. Good, who was ordained minister of the new church before these families left Ohio for their new home in the West. During the first two decades of the history of the community, Mennonite families by the names of Good, Horning, Hoffman, Ferguson, Snively, Shellenberger, Lapp, Gehman, and Eberly settled in the community, scattering through four townships in the southeast quarter of the county. By 1878 the church membership had declined to 20. When Andrew Good moved to Missouri in 1890, the Page County church was left without a preacher. That date marked the end of the congregation, although the few families remaining were visited by evangelists every few years during the nineties. The lack of aggressive leadership and the unwillingness of the congregation to organize a Sunday school have been given as reasons for the death of the church.   M.G.

M. Gingerich, *The Mennonites in Iowa* (Iowa City, 1939) 149-55.

Page County (Iowa) United Missionary churches had their origins in a Brethren in Christ congregation which joined the Mennonite Brethren in Christ Church in 1885 or later. The first of the two congregations is the Shambaugh United Missionary Church. When it was incorporated in 1894 it had 25 members. The New Market United Missionary Church was established in 1893 and incorporated the following year with nine members.   M.G.

M. Gingerich, *The Mennonites in Iowa* (Iowa City, 1939) 344-49.

Page County, Va., is situated in the valley drained by the South Fork of the Shenandoah River. This river flows north between the Massanutten Mountain and the Blue Ridge (Shenandoah Forest). It was near Luray, the county seat, that the first and largest settlement of Mennonites was made in Virginia in the second quarter of the 18th century. This area had had a checkered political history before it became Page County. It was at first in Spotsylvania County which originally included all the land in Virginia west of the Blue Ridge. In 1734-38 it was a part of Orange County, 1738-45 of Augusta County, 1745-72 of Frederick County, and 1772-1831 of Shenandoah County. Then in 1831 that part of Shenandoah County lying between the Massanutten Mountain and the Blue Ridge was taken to form Page County.

The Mennonites came to Page County from Bucks, Berks, and Lancaster counties, Pa., as early as 1727, settling along the South Fork of the Shenandoah River and its tributaries. The settlement prospered during its first 25 years. Perhaps one meetinghouse, the old Hamburg church, a union church (still standing), was built at this time. If so, it was the first church which the Mennonites helped to build in Virginia. A *Harmonia Sacra* Singing is held in this old church annually.

This early settlement was not without its hardships. In 1758 an Indian raid, associated with the French and Indian War, practically wiped out the settlement for a short time. The people fled to Pennsylvania, where an appeal was made to the Dutch Mennonites for help in a letter which is found in the Amsterdam Mennonite Archives. This letter, dated Sept. 7, 1758, and signed by Michael Kauffman, Jacob Boner, Samuel Böhm, and Daniel Stauffer, says, "We were thirty-nine Mennonite families living together in Virginia. One family was murdered and the rest of us and many other families were obliged to flee for our lives, leaving all and going empty-handed." The letter goes on to say that in addition to "our brother and companion in the faith Johannes Schneyder, who is contemplating a journey to the friends and brethren in Holland, . . . our minister and elder, Martin Funck," would go along to Holland to assist in presenting the request for help. Funck was "still a single man, and by occupation a miller. He, too, was compelled to flee and leave all behind." Apparently Martin Funck was the bishop of the Page County congregation, which numbered 39 families or about 100 members in 1758.

In 1764 eight Indians led by a white man killed Preacher John Rhodes (Roads) and members of his family. This is known in Virginia history as the "Rhodes Massacre." The house and barn on the old Rhodes homestead were burned.

Decline began when a number of Mennonites joined the Baptist Church prior to and after the American Revolution. A number of Page County Mennonites moved elsewhere. Local leadership in the church was not maintained. The dwindling membership was served by Rockingham County preachers until 1885, when there were not enough members left in Page County to justify the 30 or more miles of travel to serve them.   H.A.B.

"Experience of Mennonite Settlers in Virginia," *Mennonite Yearbook & Almanac* 1911, p. 18; H. A. Brunk, *Early Mennonite Settlements in Virginia* (Harrisonburg, 1959).

Pagitt, Ephraim, author of *Heresiography or A description of the Hereticks and Sectaries of these latter times* (London, ? 2d ed. London, 1645). The author, who was a minister in the Church of England, probably at London, enumerates a large number of "heresies" with a refutation of their "errors."

Among these heresies the Anabaptists and also the Brownists (*q.v.*) occupy a large place. The "Menonists" (Mennonites) are finished off in one sentence. Though the booklet has some value for the enumeration of the many sects found in England in the early 17th century, the information about the Anabaptists given here is of no great value, the author's sources being biased historians such as Bullinger and Niellius.   vDZ.

Pain, an Anabaptist martyr of Swabia, South Germany, was executed with Wolfgang Esslinger (*q.v.*), Martin Zehentmaier (*q.v.*), and four other Anabaptists at Schwäbisch-Gmünd after a year's imprisonment in 1529 (the *Martyrs' Mirror* erroneously gives 1531 as the date). Three songs were written to commemorate their death.   NEFF.

Mart. Mir. D 32, E 439; *Lieder der Hutterischen Brüder* (Scottdale, 1914) 51-55; Wolkan, *Lieder*, 21; *ML* III, 333.

Pakantan, formerly a mission station of the Dutch Mennonite Mission Society on the island of Sumatra, Indonesia (formerly Dutch East Indies), south of Sipıroh, was founded on Jan. 10, 1871, by Heinrich Dirks (*q.v.*). On Aug. 3, 1871, he received the first three converts into the congregation by baptism. When he left to return to Russia in 1881 there were 100 members. The station was taken over by Tilmann Irle (*q.v.*) of the Rhineland Mission, and by Gerhard Nikkel (*q.v.*) in 1888. Nikkel returned to Europe in 1900, and was replaced by Johann Thiessen 1901-9. For a short time David Dirks, the son of the founder, worked here. In 1911 Peter Nachtigal (*q.v.*) took charge of this post and served faithfully until his premature death (1928). Since that time the congregation was without a missionary, cared for by native workers, until it joined the native Christian Batak church. With the support of the Dutch Mennonite Mission Society, a hospital and a school were built at Pakantan.   NEFF.

Menn. Bl., 1879, 30 ff.; several issues of the reports of the Dutch Mennonite Mission Society; *DB* 1891, 40 f.; *De Zondagsbode* XVII (1903-4) No. 13; *Uit Verleden en heden van de Doopsgezinde Zending*, 1914, 20-23, 52, 54; *ML* III, 332.

Palamau, a political district in the province of Bihar, India, on the west side of Hazaribagh District (*q.v.*). Its southern section comprises the western part of the Bihar Mennonite (MC) Mission (*q.v.*) field. In 1956 there were three mission stations in this field, Latehar (*q.v.*), Chandwa, and Bathet. The Palamau field was acquired from the British Churches of Christ Mission. Evangelistic, medical, and educational work are done. There are a number of small village congregations and schools administered by the missionaries and Indian workers. The following missionaries have served in this field with their families: John E. Beachy, Henry D. Becker, S. J. Hostetler, Paul Kniss, S. Allen Shirk, and M. C. Vogt. The Indian evangelists and teachers in 1956 were Kishore Bakhla, Herem Bhengara, D. M. Lakras, Masihdas Minz, Phulchand Minz, Premlata Royan, Daniel Tirki, Joel Tirki, Rabi Tirki, and A. M. Toponos.   S.J.Ho.

Palaeologus, Jakob, an anti-Trinitarian (Unitarian), a native of the island of Chios, came to Transylvania and Poland in 1575, where he became an influential Socinian. Socinus, however, repudiated his teaching that military service and holding worldly office are compatible with the profession of Christianity, and of the non-adoration of Jesus. Palaeologus was burned at the stake as a heretic in Rome in 1585. Worthy of note is his book against infant baptism: *De baptismo liberorum.*   NEFF.

F. S. Bock, *Historia Antitrinitariorum* I (Königsberg, 1784) 583-87; *RGG* IV, Col. 869; *ML* III, 332.

Palatinate, a government district of the German state of Rhineland-Palatinate (since 1945), having Neustadt a.d.W. as its government seat. From 1815 to 1918 it belonged to the kingdom of Bavaria, and still earlier (until 1801) known as the Kurpfalz, which extended across the Rhine and had (until 1720) Heidelberg as its capital and later (until 1778) Mannheim. Enclosed by the Palatinate were the bishoprics of Worms and Speyer. In the realm of the Kurpfalz lay the duchies (e.g., Pfalz-Zweibrücken), several principalities (e.g., Simmern, Veldenz, and Lautern) and graviates (e.g., Leiningen, Falkenstein, Wartenberg, and parts of Sponheim). For a long time the Upper Palatinate (since 1918 in Bavaria) was politically connected with the Palatinate on the Rhine.

Since early times the Palatinate has been splintered politically as well as religiously. In accord with the principle of *cuius regio, eius religio,* most of the population changed its faith five times in the 16th century. Catholic doctrine, supported by Elector Louis V (d. 1544), was followed by the Lutheran under Frederick II (d. 1556) and Otto Henry (d. 1559), the Reformed under Frederick III (d. 1576), again the Lutheran under Louis VI (d. 1583), and finally the Reformed under John Kasimir (d. 1592). These ecclesiastical changes were one of the factors which made it possible for Anabaptism to enter the Palatinate early and to develop—in spite of much resistance—to considerable strength.

Deep inroads were made into the post-Reformation history of the Palatinate by the Thirty Years' War (1618-48) and the French Revolution (1789-1815). Accordingly the 400-year history of the Anabaptists-Mennonites falls into three clearly defined eras: (1) from the origin of Anabaptism c1525 to its almost complete extinction in the Thirty Years' War (100 years); (2) from the immigration of Swiss Mennonites from the middle of the 17th century until the reorganization of the Palatinate c1800 (150 years); (3) from the beginning of the freedom of the 19th century to the present (150 years).

I. The origin of Anabaptism in the Palatinate presumably precedes the formation of the first congregation in Switzerland. Johannes Risser, pastor of the Sembach congregation in 1832-68, says that "already by 1522, and especially after the Peasant Wars (1525)" there were Anabaptists in the Palatinate, although he fails to give any proof for 1522 date. In 1526 Jakob Kautz (*q.v.*), a native of the Palatinate (Grossbackenheim) and a Lutheran preacher at Worms, became an Anabaptist. In 1527 Hans Denk (*q.v.*) and Ludwig Haetzer (*q.v.*) were living in Worms and here published their German

Palatinate
GERMANY

Deutschhof—Mennonite congregations
Kriegsheim*—extinct Mennonite congregations
• small cities
● cities over 15,000
Scale of Miles
0 1 2 3 4 5   10   15

translation of the Prophets, which soon went through thirteen editions. Worms was probably also the scene of the first adult baptisms. "People from the Palatinate who were rebaptized at Worms are persecuted, imprisoned, and the same is happening in other provinces" (Nikolaus Thomae, priest of Bergzabern).

The leading Protestant clergymen of the Palatinate were not completely unsympathetic with the early Anabaptists. When Hans Denk, for example, on his flight from Nürnberg, Augsburg, and Strasbourg came to the Palatinate in early 1527 he was kindly received and heard by Nikolaus Thomae in Bergzabern. He wrote, "In a fraternal manner Denk dealt with us." They parted as friends, although in many respects their ideas differed. "When I accompanied Denk he earnestly admonished me to live a blameless life in accord with the Gospel, for which I am very grateful to him." In a letter to K. Hubert, Bucer's famulus, dated Jan. 28, 1529, he says of five Anabaptists who were employed in

building the prince's castle in Bergzabern that he associated with them "on an entirely friendly basis," for they were "God-fearing and honest people."

Soon after this Hans Denk was in Landau where Johannes Bader (q.v.) was promoting the Reformation. Bader was just on the point of writing his Brüderliche Warnung, a polemic against the Anabaptists who had a considerable following around Landau even before Denk's appearance there. Nevertheless Bader held a debate with Denk on Jan. 20, 1527, on the question of infant baptism. It is worth noting how far Bader, in spite of the sharpness of his opposition, agreed with Anabaptist views, granting, for instance, that the baptism of infants does them no good "unless the parents at the right and proper time remind them of the baptism they have received." Nevertheless Bader did not hesitate to call for their forcible suppression by the state. In early 1528 a mandate was issued in Landau forbidding Anabaptists to stay there or the inhabitants to give them lodging, both on penalty of corporal punishment. But the question of infant baptism occupied Bader to his old age, although he leaned toward Schwenckfeld rather than the Anabaptists in this matter.

Suddenly the sharpest persecution set in against the Anabaptists. On March 5, 1528, the unstable Elector Louis V, 1508-44, upon the insistence of Emperor Charles V, issued a mandate against the Anabaptists referring to the imperial mandate of Jan. 4, 1528, which demanded capital punishment for Anabaptists. Soon many of the prisons were full to overflowing. In Alzey (q.v.) many lay "in arrest," as the elector wrote in 1528, "for a long time." A letter written by J. Cochlaeus (q.v.) to Erasmus (q.v.) on Jan. 8, 1528, contains the information that eighteen Anabaptists were imprisoned for a considerable time at Alzey and had been before the court several times. In Germany their number had reputedly risen to 18,000.

The Anabaptist trial at Alzey created wide excitement. There was general uncertainty concerning the correct judgment of the Anabaptists, from the elector, who sought the advice of jurists and theologians, to the local officials, who kept asking for instructions. The Palatine Chancellor Florenz von Venningen in 1527 wrote an extensive document which argued that since the prisoners had accepted rebaptism they were to be punished by death. The document was sent for consideration to the juristic faculties at Cologne, Mainz, Trier, Freiburg, Ingolstadt, Tübingen, Erfurt, Leipzig, Wittenberg, and Heidelberg. Erfurt and Wittenberg declined to take a position, but the others expressed their agreement.

The Anabaptist prisoners of Alzey were warmly defended by Johann Odenbach (q.v.), the Protestant pastor of Obermoschel. His "Sendbrief und Ratschlag" to the judges tells them that they have treated many criminals better in prison than these poor people who have committed no crime but have merely in error had themselves baptized. "See with what great patience, love, and devotion these people have died, how honorably they have resisted the world! . . . They are holy martyrs of God."

In spite of intercession the Anabaptists at Alzey were executed, the men by beheading and the women by drowning. The exact number of the victims cannot be definitely ascertained. Julius Lober's martyr list mentions fourteen in Alzey, three in Heidelberg, and five in Bruchsal. The Hutterite chronicles give 350 as the total number of martyrs in the Palatinate, based on reports of refugees who escaped to Moravia and related that the Anabaptists were "taken to their execution like sheep to slaughter." One of the last martyrs was Philipp von Langenlonsheim, executed at Kreuznach in 1529.

After 1529 there were probably no Anabaptist executions in the Palatinate. Michel Leubel, the details of whose trial were recently made public and who was drowned in the Rhein at Speyer in 1533, may have been an exception. The Protestant electors, beginning with Frederick II, who became a Lutheran soon after assuming the government in 1544, tried to win the Anabaptists back to the state church by kind methods. Under Frederick II, who was engaged in conflict with Catholicism, Anabaptism seems to have been firmly implanted in the

Palatinate. Hutterite missioners in the second half of the century induced many Anabaptists to go to Moravia, where the brotherhood was enjoying its Golden Age. In the congregations at Worms and Kreuznach serious differences arose concerning doctrine and discipline. The courts were constantly troubled by the property left by the fugitives; in spite of emigration there were continued reports of the spread of the movement.

The church inspection ordered by Otto Henry under the Superintendent of Strasbourg, Johann Marbach (q.v.), confirmed these reports. It was discovered that Anabaptism was strongest where there was a lack of intelligent preachers of the Gospel. Thereupon the pastors were urged to learn what the erroneous articles of the sects were and to counter them in the pulpit, not with noise and derogatory words but with gentleness and honesty; this would be better than prematurely to threaten these people with severe punishment, for they were otherwise honorable, decent, and obedient. However, they should not be allowed to hold official positions, and their dead should be denied a funeral sermon and ringing of the bells.

Upon the request of the Anabaptists a disputation was held at Pfeddersheim in 1557, in which over forty Anabaptists, including nineteen *Vorsteher,* took part. The questions debated concerned infant baptism, government office, the oath, the reason for their leaving the state church, communion, and the ban. The church declared the Anabaptists defeated; but the Anabaptists persisted in their convictions. Soon after this some important Lutheran and Catholic theologians held a disputation at Worms and came to an agreement, not concerning the treatment of Zwinglians and Sacramentists, but on the "condemnation of the Anabaptists." Thereupon Otto Henry issued a severe mandate against the Anabaptists, threatening them with expulsion and punishment according to imperial decree; it was, however, not strictly enforced. Instead, the peaceful Anabaptists were tacitly allowed to stay in the country.

Under the Calvinist Frederick III Anabaptism became still more firmly entrenched in the Palatinate. Frederick was attacked by both the Catholics and the Lutherans; he was blamed for the presence of the Anabaptists in his country. But he continued his practice of trying to convert them by conversations with clergymen. Leonard Dax (q.v.), a Hutterite missioner, described a conversation of this kind in his pamphlet, *Ein pfälzisches Colloquium mit einem Wiedertäufer im Jahre 1567.* Hutterites caught in the Palatinate were generally released. The generosity of the rulers was truly amazing for that time. Duke John Kasimir wrote to Frederick III on Jan. 1, 1566, that since the beginning pious Christians have often been persecuted as sectarians although they were the best Christians and taught and defended the truth.

This was the frame of mind that led Frederick III to institute the Frankenthal disputation in 1571. Foreign, refugee, and native Anabaptists were invited to participate and guaranteed safe conduct for two weeks before and after the debate. To the elector's annoyance, only fifteen Anabaptists announced their coming, including several Swiss Brethren and two Hutterites, but no Dutch Mennonites, whom the elector had particularly meant to attract. The Anabaptist spokesman was Diebold Winter of Wissembourg, Alsace. The representative of the Palatinate Anabaptists was Rauff Bisch of Odernheim. For the established church Peter Dathenus (*q.v.*), the court chaplain at Heidelberg, was the spokesman, with six other theologians, some of whom came from the Netherlands. The debate lasted nineteen days, from May 28 to June 19, with two sessions daily beginning at 6 AM and 2 PM. The elector appeared in person for the opening, and kept himself informed of the course of the debate. He inspected the final record, which was then published as a book of 710 pages, in two editions and in a Dutch translation. The debate dealt with the following subjects: the Scriptures, God, Christ, original sin, churches, justification, the resurrection of the body, marriage, community of goods, government, the oath, baptism, and communion. Inexperienced in dogmatic speculation and disputation, Rauff Bisch made the comment, characteristic of the Anabaptists, "It almost seems to us that you are asking us about matters that are too high for us; for we know nothing else to say about them than what the text simply says." Agreement was reached on very few points. The superintendents were to continue to try to convert the Anabaptists, though these attempts were rarely successful.

The lot of the Palatine Mennonites became harder under the son of Frederick III, the Lutheran Elector Louis VI, 1576-83, who also took sharp measures against the Calvinists. He began to expel the Anabaptists from the country, confiscate their goods to be kept under curators. If an Anabaptist let himself be persuaded to accept the state church, he received his property back after an examination by the superintendent. The superintendents and the pastors were reminded by an "electoral instruction" of Aug. 1, 1579, "to refute Anabaptist errors clearly from the pulpit frequently and to explain thoroughly the practice and benefits of the sacraments." Obstinate Anabaptists were to be imprisoned in the tower on bread and water, but were to be instructed both within the prison and outside several times, "that they may be moved to real conversion." In cases of continued persistence they were to be expelled from the country; this also happened to the Calvinists, one of whom was called "almost an Anabaptist."

Upon the early death of Louis VI his brother John Casimir succeeded to the government, 1583-91, who continued his Reformed father's church polity. His brother's Anabaptist mandate was once more proclaimed, but not strictly enforced. It was opposed by the government officials rather than the clergy. The burgrave of Alzey reminded the government that the state cannot be governed exclusively on confessional lines, but that political and economic principles must also be considered. The government once more urged the church council to conduct another disputation, but was refused on the ground that the others had been fruitless. Thereupon the church council issued a general order to all the inspectors who had to deal with Anabaptists. The pastors were doubtful of results, for the Anabaptists

would, as one of them said, "see nothing in the members of the church but what will hurt them in their hearts and will cause horror and disgust, namely, an unrestrained Epicurean life with cursing, swearing, overeating, drinking, dancing, quarreling, fighting, scolding, fornication, immorality, and the like." In fact the Anabaptists kept replying, "One could read God's Word also outside the churches, since the people who go to church are very wicked." Many a pastor had to work hard with these Anabaptists. One complained that he had "become hoarse and almost sick."

The youthful Elector Frederick IV, 1592-1610, like his uncle wanted peace in church affairs. When complaints were heard about new inroads by Anabaptism, he ordered in 1596 to devote greater care to their conversion. The church councillors, on the other hand, demanded severer proceedings by the government. One week later, June 29, 1596, appeared the order of the councillors, that the Anabaptists were to be strictly watched, "although the pastors of all the villages shall on their part neglect nothing of their constant and zealous instruction and admonition."

By the turn of the century, in spite of oppression and emigration to Moravia, Anabaptism had increased noticeably; for in the Catholic and Lutheran vicinity of Frankfort, e.g., the bishopric of Speyer and the graviate of Leiningen, it was much more seriously persecuted. At the close of 1600 the Reformed councillors reported that the Anabaptists in Dirmstein, Weisenheim a.S., Heppenheim a.d.W., were becoming more established and that at night great numbers of them gathered near Erpolzheim. "When they are ordered to go to church they say they have a large church which has a big roof." In Kriegsheim 66 were reported in 1601. In 1608 it was reported—though later denied—that even the schoolmaster and his son had attended their meeting.

When Frederick V (the "Winter King," d. 1632) became Palatine elector in 1610 and the Thirty Years' War broke out in 1618, there were still some Anabaptists in the Palatinate. Surprisingly, they were living at the same places that after the war became Mennonite centers; e.g., Kriegsheim near Monsheim, Obersülzen near Grünstadt, Dirmstadt near Frankenthal, Rohrbach and Mehlingen near Kaiserslautern, and the Zweibrücken area. There were family names which are still among the Mennonites of the Palatinate; e.g., Herstein, Hüthwohl, and Becker. In the last Anabaptist documents before the Thirty Years' War the church councillors raised serious complaint about the increase in the number of Anabaptists in the district of Alzey. It can certainly be assumed that a number of Mennonite families maintained themselves in the Palatinate throughout the war, and then joined the immigrant Mennonites.

II. During the Thirty Years' War the Palatinate was almost completely depopulated and devastated. The number of Reformed clergymen had been reduced to one tenth of its former number by murder, flight, and emigration. Elector Charles Louis, 1648-80, called back the surviving ones. The repopulation of his lands was a serious concern to him. He was generous not only to the Lutherans and Catholics, but also to the Mennonites. He admitted a number of Moravian Hutterite families to Mannheim (*q.v.*) in 1655, who established a small Bruderhof here, which Duchess Elizabeth Charlotte of Orleans, the elector's daughter, recalled in her letters written in 1718. Soon after the war a Mennonite congregation assembled in Mannheim, to whom the elector assigned space for a meetinghouse. He was especially interested in experienced settlers who could rebuild the country. Thus he also admitted the Mennonites expelled from other countries.

One of the first groups to settle in the Palatinate after the Thirty Years' War came from Transylvania. After severe oppression several of these families emigrated and in 1655 settled in Kriegsheim, Osthofen, Harxheim, Heppenheim a.d.W., and Wolfsheim near Worms. Among them were such family names as Schuhmacher, Kolb, Rohr, and Bonn. Some had become Quakers by 1665; e.g., the Schuhmacher family in Kriegsheim.

The state church was, however, less tolerant than the elector. Already in 1654 voices are heard complaining "about the offensive confusion with the Anabaptists, who despise proper church services and the holy sacraments, let their children run about unbaptized, hold their services boldly in the forests, and even solemnize marriages." From this time on, the church senate continued to warn the government that "it is a necessity to stem the obstinate, fanatical stubbornness of such people and bring them under the discipline of the Reformed Church, marriage, baptism, etc."

In spite of all obstacles the Mennonites made efforts to preserve official toleration and recognition from the elector. In the Palatinate to the right of the Rhine, where also some Anabaptist remnants had been preserved since the 16th century, two Mennonites, Hans Mayer and Hans Körber, decided in 1653 to present a petition to the elector in the name of the congregation, in which they called themselves "Mennists," to obtain permission to meet for worship like their brethren on the left side of the Rhine. But it took a decade, besides the intervention of influential Quakers and even the intermediation of the King of England before Charles Louis was willing to grant them a limited religious freedom. Finally on Aug. 4, 1664, after much effort, they obtained the important general concession which permitted them to meet in groups of more than twenty; but they were forbidden to admit non-Mennonites to the meetings. In return they had to pay an annual fee of six guilders per person as "Mennist Recognition Money," a considerable tax, which was later doubled. Nevertheless this concession was considered a great privilege, meetings having been completely prohibited in 1661. A limit of 200 families was set for the total Mennonite population.

The Mennonites in the Palatinate were increased in number in 1671-72 when persecution in Switzerland reached its climax. The refugees were received as brethren by the Palatine Mennonites and were given generous support from the Dutch Mennonites, who had already intervened in Switzerland for their toleration. On Nov. 2, 1671, Jakob Everling, the preacher of the Obersülzen congregation, reported that 200 persons had come to the Palatinate, some of whom were cripples, old people of 70-90 years, and families of eight to ten children. They arrived destitute with their bundles on their backs and their children in their arms. In January 1672, 215 persons had arrived west of the Rhine and 428 east of the Rhine. The influx of single families and groups continued into the 18th century. Especially in 1709-11 many Mennonite families came from Alsace and Switzerland. Thus the numerous small congregations still existing in the Palatinate were established.

By the end of the 17th century new difficulties overwhelmed the new settlers; economically by the French invasion under Louis XIV, ecclesiastically by the Catholic reaction under the electors of the Zweibrücken-Neuburg line which replaced the Protestant Simmern line. In 1674 and 1689 large areas and numerous towns of the Palatinate were devastated, causing serious losses to many Mennonites. Elector Philip William, 1685-90, who had renewed the Mennonite concession in 1686, died as a fugitive in Vienna. His strictly Catholic son and successor, John William, 1690-1716, was very slow to renew the concession; it was finally granted in 1698 after many petitions, and demanded high protection fees. The early years of his reign saw the expulsion of the Mennonites from Rheydt in 1694, which caused consternation in the entire Protestant world, and also the emigration of a group of Mennonites from Ibersheim to Friedrichstadt in Schleswig-Holstein in 1693.

The first emigration of Palatine Mennonites to North America also occurred at the close of the 17th century. In 1685 a Quaker who had previously been a Mennonite, Peter Schumacher of Kriegsheim near Worms, emigrated to Germantown, Pa. In the spring of 1707 the Kolb brothers—Martin, Johannes, Jakob, and Heinrich—emigrated. Martin Kolb (*q.v.*), who settled at Skippack, was one of the first Mennonite preachers in America. He was probably the instigator of further Mennonite emigration, which increased rapidly under Elector Charles Philip, 1716-42, for he doubled their protection fees, limited their right to purchase land, seeking thus to prevent the number of Mennonite families in the Palatinate to rise above 200. In the spring of 1717 some 300 Palatine Mennonites were in Rotterdam to embark for Pennsylvania where religious liberty was unrestricted; they received financial support from the Dutch Mennonites. With this group a stream of German immigration set in which continued almost without interruption until the second half of the 19th century. By 1732, 3,000 Palatine Mennonites had arrived in America. By 1773 the immigration lists showed over 30,000 Palatine names, mostly non-Mennonite. The Mennonites in America of Palatine origin numbered *c*150,000 souls in 1935, of whom 35,000 were living in Lancaster County alone.

A change in favor of the Mennonites took place during the long rule, 1742-99, of the enlightened Charles Theodore of the house of Pfalz-Sulzbach. Although he was Catholic, he granted extensive liberties to the Lutherans, Reformed, Mennonites, and Jews. The concession to the Mennonites was renewed on Nov. 27, 1743, and the protection fee reduced to six guilders. In return the Mennonites advanced the sum of 10,000 guilders toward the election and coronation expenses. Nevertheless the government at first still worked toward the reduction of "this daily increasing condemned sect." Later, however, it realized "that no better, more industrious, and competent subjects are to be found, who, with the exception of their religion, their faith, and their error, should serve the members of other faiths as an example in morals as well as in working day and night."

Since that time, about the middle of the 18th century, the Mennonites of the Palatinate achieved a leading position in agriculture. "The most perfect farmers in Germany are the Palatine Mennonites," wrote the State Economist Christian W. Dohm in the *Deutsches Museum* in 1778. The official of Hilsbach said about them on Jan. 21, 1794, "They are exemplary, industrious, and intelligent farmers. It would be desirable that every farmer would appropriate their good knowledge of agriculture and stock raising." Jung-Stilling (*q.v.*), the pious physician and economist, described the family life of David Möllinger (*q.v.*) of Monsheim as "the highest ideal of agricultural happiness," calling him the "archfarmer of our Palatine country and perhaps of the Holy Roman Empire," and his friend and brother.

About this time the Mennonites of the Palatinate were also given more and more recognition by the Protestant Church, to which Pietism contributed not a little. Gottfried Arnold (*q.v.*) had already in 1699, in his *Unparteiische Kirchen- und Ketzerhistorie,* defended the Mennonites. Gerhard Tersteegen (*q.v.*), like Jung-Stilling, caried on personal correspondence with the Palatine Mennonites, and called Adam Krehbill, the pastor at Weierhof, "a man according to God's heart." Peter Weber (*q.v.*) of Hardenberg was a zealous devotee of Pietism.

Now nearly all governmental restrictions on the Mennonites of the Palatinate were removed. On April 20, 1769, Jakob Hirschler, elder of the Gerolsheim congregation, wrote to Hans van Steen in Danzig, "Although our ruler is Roman Catholic, nevertheless nearly everywhere Catholics, Lutherans, Reformed, Mennonites, and Jews are living side by side. We are permitted to meet openly for worship wherever we wish, also observe baptism and communion and solemnize marriages. Also we bury our dead openly, and funeral addresses are held, often with many hearers, as in other religions."

At this time the first Mennonite meetinghouses were built in the Palatinate—Weierhof 1773, Sembach 1777, Eppstein and Friedelsheim 1779. The rulers willingly gave their consent, although they stipulated that the church must have the external appearance of a farm building. The names and membership of the congregations are given by Jakob Hirschler for 1769 as follows: "Erpolzheim and Friedelsheim 140, Spitalhof 45, Ruchheim 26, Alsheim and Ibersheimerhof 120. Oberflörsheim and Spiesheim 100, Kriegsheim 52, Wartenberg and Sembach 250, Weierhof 90, Rheingrafenstein 32, Rödern and Schafbusch 45, Böchingen 68, Zweibrücken 94, Gerolsheim, Obersülzen, and Heppenheim 112, Hö-

ningen 54, Eppstein-Friesenheim-Mannheim" (no figures given, but "some 20 households" given for Mannheim). In addition there were numerous scattered Amish families living in the Palatinate around Zweibrücken and Ixheim.

All the congregations were served by lay elders and preachers from their own midst. In 1770 these were: "Abraham Oellenberger in Gönnheim; Daniel Stauffer in Guntersblum; Christian Weber in Oberflörsheim; Johannes Krehbiel in Wartenberg; Jakob Gally in Erbesbüdesheim; Daniel Hirschler, Geisberg; Johannes Schnebele for Zweibrücken; Jakob Hirschler, Gerolsheim; Martin Möllinger, Mannheim." Toward the end of the century a lack of qualified voluntary preachers was painfully felt here and there. The men who had been chosen refused the office. "This error, which may be called disobedience, is unfortunately making serious inroads into the Palatinate," wrote Elder Lorenz Friedenreich of Neuwied on Feb. 27, 1775. Therewith a new development began for the Palatine Mennonites.

Shortly before and after the turn of the century two groups of Palatine Mennonites emigrated. In 1784 twenty-eight Mennonite families followed the invitation of Emperor Joseph II to settle in Galicia (*q.v.*), where they made three settlements near Lemberg-Einsiedel, Falkenstein, and Rosenberg. In 1802 eight families settled in Donaumoos (*q.v.*) in Bavaria. Other Palatine and Alsatian Mennonites followed, until there were twenty-five families, twelve of whom were living in Maxweiler (*q.v.*), which they had founded, and thirteen in the surrounding villages. About the middle of the 19th century most of them emigrated to America.

III. From 1792 until 1813 the Palatinate to the left of the Rhine was under French rule. In 1801 the Kurpfalz was dissolved in the Treaty of Lunéville. After Napoleon's defeat, 1814 f., a large part of the Palatinate on the left of the Rhine fell to Bavaria, a smaller part, Rhenish Hesse, to Hesse-Darmstadt. The part right of the Rhine fell for the most part to Baden (*q.v.*), and a smaller part to Hesse-Darmstadt. With the French occupation in 1803 all the limitations on Mennonite freedom, legal, economic, and ecclesiastical, were removed. Equality of citizenship was gratefully accepted by the Mennonites. But at the same time the leaders feared that this equality of citizenship would lead to complete conformity to their surroundings and the loss of the old doctrines. This concern is clearly seen in the Ibersheim (*q.v.*) Decisions of 1803 and 1805, in which the Mennonites of the Palatinate and of all South Germany expressly endorsed the old Mennonite principles, such as adult baptism, separation from worldly living, and nonresistance. Because soon afterward nonresistance was nonetheless lost, Wilhelm Mannhardt called these Decisions, with some justification, "the evening glow in the sky of orthodox Mennonitism in the Rhineland."

Actually about the turn of the century Palatine Mennonitism underwent a radical change in development which was to give it its characteristic stamp within German Mennonitism. The first element was the sacrifice of the lay ministry, which was maintained only in a few small congregations in the south: Branchweilerhof near Neustadt and Deutsch-hof-Geisberg near Bergzabern, which then joined the Verband (*q.v.*). The small congregation of Altleiningen (*q.v.*) in the heart of the Palatinate almost lost its existence on this account, even though in 1811, under its preacher Christian Goebels (d. 1821), it built its own church. J. Schiller (1812-86) published in *Pfälzer Memorabile* an interesting account of a visit to this church; he had come in order to hear a sermon by a Mennonite lay preacher, but unprepared as he was he was compelled to preach, and thereby changed his whole concept of preaching. The last important lay preachers in the Palatinate were Valentin Dahlem (*q.v.*), the initiator of the Ibersheim Decisions and editor of a formulary, Johannes Goebels of Hertlingshausen near Altleiningen, and Heinrich Koller of Kühbörncheshof.

As the need for preachers in the Palatine congregations increased they began to call theologically trained and professional ministers from their own ranks or from the outside. In 1819 Leonhard Weydmann (*q.v.*) came from Crefeld to Monsheim to gather and re-establish the congregation. He was followed in Monsheim by Johannes Molenaar (*q.v.*), also from Crefeld, 1836-68. In Sembach Johannes Risser (*q.v.*) of Friedelsheim, 1832-68, led the congregation to a new flowering. On the Weierhof Hermann Reeder (*q.v.*) of Neuwied was called, who had attended a Baptist seminary in England. Friedelsheim found two pastors in its own membership—the teacher Jakob Ellenberger (*q.v.*) 1827-79, followed by his nephew with the same name. Ibersheim called preachers from West Prussia—Bernhard Thiessen, 1843-56; then Heinrich Neufeld, 1856-69. Under the ministry of these men new catechisms appeared in 1841, 1854, and 1861; a new hymnal in 1854, 1876; a minister's manual in 1852. Michael Loewenberg (*q.v.*), minister at the Weierhof 1849-74, founded a school there in 1867, which later became the Realanstalt (*q.v.*) am Donnersberg; it was planned as a ministerial training school, but became a secondary school.

The engagement of professional ministers or pastors, most of whom were educated in Protestant seminaries or universities, denoted a deviation from Mennonite tradition, but proved itself as useful for the preservation of Palatine-Hessian Mennonitism. Externally this led to an era of church building. Meetinghouses, still in use, were built at Monsheim in 1820, Ibersheim 1836, Weierhof 1837, and Friedelsheim 1838. In 1853 the small church in Sembach built in 1777 was torn down and replaced by a larger church. The Kühbörncheshof congregation, which belonged to Sembach until 1832, built a meetinghouse in that year. In 1842, 1843, and 1847 churches were built in Deutschhof, Ernstweiler, and Ixheim, the last named being an Amish congregation which did not unite with the others until 1937 and then met with them at Zweibrücken; both churches were abandoned. In the second half of the century churches were built at Obersülzen in 1866, Neudorferhof 1885, and Kohlhof 1888; in 1903 the church at Ludwigshafen was built, but must now (1958) be razed for the rebuilding of the city.

Since 1824 the Conference of the Palatine and

Hessian Mennonite Churches has been meeting more or less regularly in annual sessions, which have greatly strengthened the cohesion of the group. The Conference established a relief fund which was later (1886) called the Mennonitische Hilfskasse. Since 1885 most of the congregations have also belonged to the Vereinigung (*q.v.*). The congregations fall into six groups, each of which is served by one pastor. The groups, with 1958 membership, are composed as follows: (1) Kaiserslautern 72, Kühbörncheshof 163, Zweibrücken 200; (2) Sembach 250, Enkenbach 270, Neudorferhof 196; (3) Weierhof 445, Uffhofen 48, Eisenberg; (4) Monsheim 255, Obersülzen 94, Biedesheim; (5) Ibersheim 165, Eppstein 110, Ludwigshafen 90; (6) Friedelsheim 151, Kohlhof 64, Atleiningen 30.

Leading ministers since just before the turn of the century were "Christian Neff, at Weierhof, 1887-1946; Thomas Löwenberg, Ibersheim, 1883-1917; Abraham Hirschler, Kaiserslautern, 1880-1930; Johannes Hirschler, Monsheim, 1899-1926; Matthias Pohl, Sembach, 1901-29; Johannes Foth, Friedelsheim, 1904-57." In the Palatinate and Hesse there are some 3,200 Mennonites. This figure includes some 1,000 refugees from West Prussia who came to the Palatinate after 1948 and were kindly received by the brethren. A congregation of this kind has arisen at Enkenbach near Kaiserslautern since 1951 with some 270 members including the residents in the Mennonite Home for the Aged, Friedenshort. In 1957 this congregation received a meetinghouse, which, like the entire settlement, was built with substantial aid from German and American brethren. In Kaiserslautern the MCC built the "Mennonite House" in 1956, in which the resident congregation holds its meetings. In Bad Dürkheim the MCC has for years supported a children's home. In Ludwigshafen the Relief Work of the Vereinigung has its center. The active work of these organizations has contributed greatly to the strengthening and revival of Palatine-Hessian Mennonitism as well as German Mennonitism as a whole since World War II.   G.H.

Chr. Hege, *Die Täufer in der Kurpfalz* (Frankfurt, 1908); Manfred Krebs, "Beiträge zur Geschichte der Wiedertäufer am Oberrhein," in *Ztschl für die Geschichte des Oberrheins* LXXXIII (1931) 567-76; Müller, *Berner Täufer; TA Baden-Pfalz;* a large number of documents and letters concerning the Mennonites of the Palatinate are found in the Amsterdam Mennonite Archives and listed in *Inv. Arch. Amst.*, of which only the most important are mentioned here: I, Nos. 1009, 1059, 1130, 1196-99, 1248 f., 1319, 1405-7, 1409, 1414, 1420-26, 1428 f., 1438, 1458, 1470-73, 1476-83, 1495, 1498-1504, 1510 f., 1515, 1517, 1519, 1531 f., 1539, 1750 f., 1866 f., 1881, 2256, 2260, 2267, 2274; Gerhard Hein, "Unsere Gemeinden in der Pfalz vor 200 Jahren und heute," *Der Mennonit* IX (1956) 138-40, 154 f., 170 f.; idem, "The Development of the Mennonite Hof of the Seventeenth Century Palatinate into the Mennonite Churches of Pfalz Rheinland Today," *MQR* (1955) 188-96; *ML* II, 588-600 (*Kurpfalz*), 356-577 (*Pfalz-Zweibrücken*), 357-59 (*Pfälzische Kirchenordnungen*), 492-94 (*Rheinland-Pfalz*); Ernst Crous, "Mennoniten im Regierungsbezirk Trier 1827-1870," *Gem.-Kal.*, 1940, 62-73; idem, "Wie die Mennoniten in die deutsche Volksgemeinschaft hineinwuchsen," *Gesch.-Bl.*, 1939, 13-24 (repr. Karlsruhe, 1939); *Gem.-Kal.* annually contains data on the congregations in addition to numerous articles on congregations and Palatinate subjects which are not here registered; *Namensverzeichniss; Naamlijst; Gem.-Kal.* 1953, 36-44; *ML* III, 490 f.

Paling (Palingh, Palinck, Paeldinck), a family name found among the Dutch Mennonites. Cornelis Michielsz Paling was about 1610 a member of the "bevredigde broederschap" (*q.v.*) at Haarlem. Lambrecht Paeldinck, a preacher or deacon at Schiedam, in 1632 signed the Dordrecht Confession in the name of the Schiedam Flemish congregation. Andries Palinck was a Waterlander preacher, probably at Haarlem. Another Andries Paling(h), who may also have been a Waterlander preacher at Haarlem, published *Verhaal van't gene verhandelt ende besloten is in de by-eenkomst tot Leyden* (Haarlem, 1661), a defense against the accusation of the conservative Flemish leaders that the Waterlanders were not orthodox. He also attacked Galenus Abrahamsz (*q.v.*) in *Aenmerckingen en Aenspraeck op Doct. Galenus Geschrift* (Amsterdam, 1665).

It could not be decided whether the Dutch painters Izaak Paling (d. after 1719 at Leiden) and Willem Jan Paling (1777-1848) were Mennonites and members of this family. (*Inv. Arch. Amst.* I, Nos. 513 f., 525; II, No. 1196; *N.N.B.Wb.* V, 422.) vdZ.

Pallant, Werner von, bailiff of Wassenberg, in the duchy of Jülich, Germany, about 1530, friendly toward the Anabaptists. He declared expressly that he could not act contrary to his conscience in dealing with them. He denied the right of temporal government in religious matters. His castle was a haven for exiled preachers from far and wide (see **Wassenberg "Preachers"**). He was also interested in the development of Anabaptism in Münster (*q.v.*) before this degenerated into extravagant fanaticism, and Johann Klopreis (*q.v.*) wrote a letter to him from Münster, which was delivered by Jacob van Ossenbrug (*q.v.*) in February 1534. Pallant refused to carry out a new instruction for church inspection by Johann III, Duke of Jülich, in the district of Wassenberg. In 1534 he was deposed from office. Even after this he remained the protector of the victims of religious persecution. NEFF.

Rembert, *Wiedertäufer,* 146-50; W. Bax, *Het Protestantisme in het bisdom Luik* I (The Hague, 1937) 57-59 and *passim; ML* II, 332.

Palm Grove Conservative Mennonite Church, located at Sarasota, Fla., a member of the Conservative Mennonite Conference, was organized May 3, 1953, with 19 charter members. They worshiped in the Pinecraft Mennonite Church until Nov. 29, 1953, at which time they met in the Pinecraft school. A church building seating 400 was dedicated Feb. 14, 1954. During the winter tourists from as far as California and western Canada worship with the congregation, raising the attendance to 250. Menno M. Coblentz was bishop and Joseph F. Baer pastor until 1956, when Bishop Andrew Jantzi succeeded them. In 1957 there were 33 members. J.F.B.

Palmer, Christian David Friedrich (1811-75), a Protestant theologian, professor of theology at the University of Tübingen. Through his religious work he had a constructive influence on Mennonite circles. Deserving mention is his book, *Die Gemeinschaften und Sekten Württembergs* (Tübingen, 1877). (*RGG* IV, Col. 878; *ML* III, 332.) NEFF.

Palmken Palmen, an Anabaptist martyr of Born, in the Millen area of the duchy of Jülich, Germany, was burned at the stake in an open field between Sittard and Limbricht, in the present Dutch province of Limburg (then Jülich). He suffered martyrdom with song. In 1535 a Palm who was an Anabaptist was found in Maastricht; shortly before 1550 a Palmen in the district of Born, who may be identical with the martyr Palmken Palmen, was baptized by Elder Theunis van Hastenrath (*q.v.*), who also baptized Petergen Palmen and his wife. In the 17th century a Mennonite Palmen family was found in Amsterdam. NEFF, vdZ.

Mart. Mir. D 98, E 496; W. Bax, *Het Protestantisme in het bisdom Luik* I (The Hague, 1937) 119, 307, 406, 410; *ML* III, 333.

Palmyra Mennonite (MC) Church (now extinct), located two miles east of Palmyra, Marion Co., Mo., a member of the South Central Conference, had its beginning in 1884, when Jacob Rohrer and family moved here, followed by the Isaac Rohrer, E. L. Buckwalter, and J. M. Hershey families. J. M. Kreider was ordained minister for the work in 1898, and moved here with his family, accompanied by the J. H. Hershey family, all of Lancaster Co., Pa. The meetinghouse was built in 1907. The membership in 1955 was 15, with Harry R. Buckwalter and Harold Kreider as ministers. In that year the congregation dissolved. H.R.Bu.

Palo Alto Mennonite Church (MC), Union Street, Pottsville, Pa., is a mission church in the Lancaster Conference. Established in 1948, it had 14 members in 1957. M.G.

Palo Hincado Mennonite Church (MC), located in Barranquitas, Puerto Rico, had a membership of 57 in 1957, with Don Heiser as pastor. M.G.

Pals, van de(r), and collateral branch van Gilse van der Pals, a Dutch Mennonite family found in Rotterdam, Holland, from the early 17th century. Most of them were well-to-do merchants and brokers, and some were deacons of the church. After Gerrit van der Pals in 1786 left the Mennonite Church to join the Reformed, a number of relatives followed him. The Mennonite branch of the family died out in the 19th century. The name seems to indicate that this family stemmed from the Palatinate, Germany, but this could not be ascertained. (*Nederl. Patriciaat* V, 1914, 312-16.) vdZ.

Palsters (i.e., *Pfälzer,* Mennonites from the Palatinate), a name given to Mennonite refugees who moved from the Palatinate (*q.v.*), Germany, to the Netherlands about 1653 settling in or near Groningen (*q.v.*). There is no exact information either concerning this immigration itself nor about the number of immigrants, or about the later adventures of these "Palsters." They may have merged with the 1711 group of Swiss Mennonite immigrants who settled in the province of Groningen in 1711-14. (See also **Swiss Mennonites** in the Netherlands; Müller, *Berner Täufer,* 195; *Inv. Arch. Amst.* I, No. 1193.) vdZ.

Päminger (Bamminger, etc.), **Leonhard** (1495-1567), a German Lutheran poet and hymn writer. His sons Sophonias (d. 1603) and Sigismund (d. 1571) published some of his papers, including the rhymed *Dialogus oder Gespräch eines Christen mit einem Wiedertäufer* (formerly in the Göttingen University Library: Th. Pol. 188b). The *Dialogus* discusses the "three principal errors of the Anabaptist"; viz., their rejection of infant baptism, their attitude toward government (with reference to Matt. 5:39), and their recognition of polygamy (on the basis of the Old Testament); the sons in their foreword made it clear that this "fanaticism" was still flourishing at many places. (*ABD* XXV, 114; *ML* III, 333.) E.C.

Pancratz, a Mennonite family formerly found among the Mennonites of West Prussia, Germany, particularly in the Flemish churches of Schönsee (*q.v.*) and Przechovka (*q.v.*). Here Peter Pancratz was a preacher 1762-d. *c*88, and Andreas Pancratz 1785-after 1802. Later some members of this family moved to Russia. Pancratz may have been a Slavic name, and its bearers of Slavic ancestry. (Reimer, *Familiennamen,* 115; Dutch *Naamlijst.*) vdZ.

Pandora, a village (pop. 717) located in Putnam County in northwestern Ohio. It was first called Columbia, later Pendleton, until changed to Pandora. Approximately 750 Mennonites live in Pandora and on its rural route. Most belong to the General Conference Mennonite Church, although some belong to the Missionary Church Association and several families to the Reformed Mennonite Church.

The Mennonite community extends from 2 miles north of Pandora to about 4 miles south of the village, and from 1 mile west to 4 miles east of the village. About half of the members live in the village. The first Mennonites here were Swiss Mennonites from Florimont (*q.v.*), France, who settled three miles south of Pandora in 1833.

The Grace Mennonite Church (GCM) and the Missionary Church (MCA) are located in the village. The St. John Mennonite Church (GCM) is located 1 mile southeast of Pandora, the Reformed Mennonite Church 3 miles southeast of Pandora in Allen County, but on the Pandora rural postal route.

This area is generally conceded to have some of the best soil in northwestern Ohio and is well known for its crops including cattle, tomatoes, potatoes, and sugar beets. D.L.G.

Pankratz, Johann H. (1867-1952), a Mennonite Brethren evangelist and missionary, was born at Ivanenky, South Russia, on Jan. 14, 1867, the oldest son of Johann J. and Helena Unruh Pankratz. In the summer of 1874 he came to America with his parents and three sisters, settling on a farm in the Lehigh and Goessel, Kan., areas. In 1899 the family removed to Buhler, Kan.

As a young man of 23 years he was converted and on March 15, 1891, he was baptized and received into the Goessel Mennonite Brethren Church. Johann completed his elementary training in a small country school south of Lehigh and attended the Teachers' Normal School in Emporia, Kan., during the school year 1891-92. In 1892-97 he attended the

Baptist Academy and Theological Seminary in Rochester, N.Y., graduating from both schools.

On Sept. 7, 1899, Pankratz married Maria Harms of Hillsboro; they had five children. Pankratz found his first field of ministry in the First Baptist Church in Allentown, Pa. (1897-98). In October 1899 he was appointed evangelist in the Mennonite Brethren Conference. On Oct. 24, 1901, Pankratz and his wife were commissioned to go to India as missionaries for the Mennonite Brethren Conference. Leaving Hillsboro on June 10, 1902, they arrived in India on Oct. 20, having visited numerous churches in Europe en route to India. In the next 39 years (1902-41) the Pankratzes gave to India some 26 years of service: 1902-10, 1913-19, 1921-26, and 1937-41. Pankratz was an undaunted pioneer, a great Gospel preacher, a church builder. He established three mission stations—Mulkapett, Hughestown, and Shamshabad, and a missionary rest home at Ootacamund. He organized the first Telugu Mennonite Brethren Church and ordained the first three Telugu ministers.

While at home on furloughs Pankratz served as evangelist and taught two terms (1911-12 and 1929-30) in Tabor College; in 1930-36 he served the American Baptist Church in Beatrice, Neb. His guiding, inspiring, and upholding Scripture passage was: "As for me, I will behold thy face in righteousness: I shall be satisfied, when I awake, with thy likeness" (Psalm 17:15).

After the death of Mrs. Pankratz on Jan. 25, 1941, Pankratz returned to America, making his home with his daughter Linda, a schoolteacher, first in Los Angeles and later in San Diego, Cal., and died on July 19, 1952. G.W.P.

Panman (Panneman), a Dutch Mennonite family, originally living near Sappemeer, later in Pekela, both in the province of Groningen. Many of the Panman family were deacons of the Mennonite congregations at Veendam, Pekela, and Stadskanaal, and Jan Panneman was from about 1740 until shortly before 1780 a preacher of the Danzig Old Flemish Mennonites at Sappemeer and later of Pekela. vDZ.

Pannabecker (Pannebacker, Pennebacker, Panabaker, Pennypacker, and Pfannebaker), a Mennonite family name going back to the Dutch "pannenbakker" or tile baker. Samuel W. Pennypacker, former governor of Pennsylvania and historian, traces the name back to 1568 at Gorcum, Holland, where Jan Pannebakker and his wife were executed as Anabaptist martyrs, the former at the stake and the latter by drowning. Members of the family fled to Germany whence, *c*1695, Hendrick Pannebecker of Flamborn near Worms in the Palatinate emigrated to Germantown, Pa. There he married Eve Umstadt who had arrived in 1685, and became the progenitor of most of the Pannabeckers in America. A brother Frederick is said to have located in Kentucky about the same time but was not so well known. Hendrick Pannebecker located on the Skippack in Montgomery County, Pa., working as a surveyor for William Penn, where he is said to have surveyed the van Bebber tract. His grandsons

Matthias and Henry Pannebecker were Mennonite preachers, the former being bishop at Phoenixville, Pa. Matthias was zealous in the pulpit and in practical life and took his nonresistant belief so seriously he is reported to have taken the bolts and bars off his house doors and never locked drawers or cupboards. Cornelius Pannebecker, blacksmith and preacher, a great-grandson of Hendrick, migrated in 1810 from Montgomery County to Waterloo County, Ont., and became the ancestor of the numerous Pannebacker families in Ontario. In 1957 S. F. Pannebecker was president of Mennonite Biblical Seminary in Chicago and his brother R. P. Pannabecker was an elder of the United Missionary Church in northern Indiana.   S.F.P.

S. W. Pennypacker, *Annals of Phoenixville and its Vicinity* (Philadelphia, 1872); D. N. Panabaker. "Panabaker Family History," in Waterloo Historical Society, *Twenty-Fifth Annual Report . . . 1937* (Kitchener, 1939); Edith Foster, "In Pursuit of Freedom," in *Christian Living*, January-June 1958; S. W. Pennypacker, *Hendrick Pannebecker* (Philadelphia, 1894).

Pappenheim, Marschalk von, a noble family of the 16th century and later, manorial lords of Kalden in South Germany, prominently connected with Pilgram Marpeck (*q.v.*) and distantly also with Caspar von Schwenckfeld (*q.v.*). Several members of this very distinguished family were patrons of Marpeck, mainly during his Augsburg period (after 1540), and three ladies were even members of the Marpeck Anabaptist brotherhood.

Joachim, Marschalk von Pappenheim (d. 1536), who played a significant role in the political life of his day in favoring the new Protestant movement, seems to have been the first of this family to come into contact with Marpeck.

His sister Magdalena, a nun of the Benedictine order in the convent at Urspring in Swabia, is perhaps the most important of the Pappenheims as far as the Anabaptists were concerned. She was drawn to Schwenckfeld and apparently had expressed her desire to meet him. Something changed her mind, however, for no meeting took place. Instead Schwenckfeld received a document bearing her name, but in all likelihood drafted by Pilgram Marpeck. In a letter dated Aug. 21, 1542, he expressed his regret that she was no longer interested in discoursing with him. He explained that he was not preaching a "proud Christ," and pointed out some of Pilgram's errors to her. Schwenckfeld suspected that she had never read any of his books, but was relying for her opinion of him on Marpeck. To correct this he was sending her a copy of a tract written by Ickelsamer (*q.v.*) against Marpeck's alleged view that Christ could have sinned. Also he indicated to Magdalena why he wrote the *Judicium* against the *Vermanung*. This letter (*CS* VIII, 217-22) should not be regarded as an accurate description of Marpeck's views since Schwenckfeld's aim was to draw Magdalena from Marpeck's influence.

In the letter to Pilgram Marpeck written Sept. 25, 1542, Schwenckfeld defended his action by saying that Marpeck had been depreciating him to Magdalena and others and had thus arrested Magdalena's spiritual growth. His letter was merely an attempt to show Magdalena how much more correct his view of Christ was than Marpeck's. Apparently Magdalena continued this role as a go-between for Marpeck and Schwenckfeld, for on May 27, 1543, Schwenckfeld wrote to Helene von Freyberg (*q.v.*) requesting her to give his reply either to Magdalena von Pappenheim or to Pilgram, since he did not know where to look for Pilgram.

On Sept. 25, 1542, Schwenckfeld wrote a second letter to Magdalena. Her reply to Schwenckfeld's first letter, admonishing Schwenckfeld to read the New Testament more diligently and defending Marpeck, prompted Schwenckfeld to reply with a list of twelve errors of which Pilgram was guilty. Apparently this was the last exchange of letters between Magdalena and Schwenckfeld, although Magdalena replied indirectly to Schwenckfeld in a letter to Helena Streicher (preserved in the Zentralbibliothek at Zürich). It thus becomes apparent that Magdalena was strategic in the literary battle between Marpeck and Schwenckfeld, in which some rather crucial issues were debated. In this struggle Magdalena Streicher remained on Schwenckfeld's side, while the Pappenheims and Helene von Freyberg stayed with the Marpeck brotherhood.

In 1545 Marpeck wrote a letter to Magdalena in Augsburg, "Concerning those who die in sin." This letter was recently discovered in a codex of the Marpeck brotherhood called *Kunstbuch,* copied in 1561. Again on Dec. 9, 1547, he wrote to her on the theme, "Von dreierlei menschen so sich im gericht finden," also concerning the rural nobility (*Kunstbuch,* No. 38). These two letters together with the earlier correspondence prove Marpeck's high regard for this "sister in Christ."

After her death (1571?) Magdalena's copy of the *Verantwortung* came into the possession of her niece Walpurga, Marschalkin von Pappenheim, daughter of Joachim, who had likewise joined the Anabaptists. Schwenckfeld's reaction to her becoming an Anabaptist is found in a variant reading of a manuscript containing a letter to Sibilla Eisler, dated after April 15, 1550. Discussing the way in which many Anabaptists had been tricked into giving up their property, then been disillusioned by the Hutterian Brethren, he said that he had heard that Walpurga von Calde (a Marschalkin) had secretly stolen away from her sister's wedding and gone to Switzerland, and would not return unless safety be guaranteed her. Apparently she had left much wealth, and this along with the confidence with which she replied to her friends surprised Schwenckfeld. He called her "Pilgram's sister" (*CS* XII, 41). The beautiful Zürich codex of the *Verantwortung* bears the note: "Walpurga Marschälkin, 1571" (Loserth). Walpurga is also known as the writer of an Anabaptist hymn, "Du glaubigs hertz, so benedey" (Wolkan, *Lieder,* 124). Beyond this not much is known about her activities.

A third member of this family was Sophie, who had married a Baron von Bubenhofen (South Germany). Of her we know only through a letter in the *Kunstbuch* (No. 36) by Hans Bichel (*q.v.*) of Waiblingen, Württemberg, written to her on Jan. 7, 1555, dealing with her spiritual improvement. Since this letter was carefully preserved, it may be assumed that Sophie was also an active member of the

Marpeck brotherhood somewhere in Bavaria or Swabia.

The story of the Pappenheims is remarkable because not many noble families are known to have shown positive interest in the Anabaptist way of life to the point of sacrifice. (But see **Freyberg, Helene von.**) HEGE, R.F., W.KL.

Loserth, *Verantwortung* (Vienna, 1929); Heinold Fast, "Pilgram Marpeck und das oberdeutsche Täufertum. Ein neuer Handschriftenfund," *Archiv für Ref.-Gesch.*, 1956, 212-42 (concerning the *Kunstbuch); Corpus Schwenckfeldianorum* VII, 35; VIII, 216-22, 280 f.; XII, 41; Wolkan, *Lieder; ML* III, 333; *ADB* (under "Pappenheim").

Paracelsus Theophrastus Bombastus von Hohenheim (1493-1541). As a roving physician ("a doctor should be a wayfarer"), a man of the people, twined about with legend even during his lifetime, characterized by a strong vital personality and an awareness of himself and of his calling, Paracelsus practiced his profession all over Central Europe, not without violent collisions with medical learning, patients, and authorities.

As a writer on medicine, botany, and natural philosophy Paracelsus was amazingly prolific in spite of his roving. His numerous Biblical-theological works, of which 123 are known, have not yet been adequately examined. The *Complete Works* of Paracelsus, edited by Karl Sudhoff and Wilhelm Matthiessen, has published (1922-23) the medical, scientific, and philosophical writings as the first division in 14 volumes in Munich. Of the second division, the theological and religious-philosophical works, only the first volume has been published (Munich, 1923). Of the Bible commentaries, the one on Matthew and the one on the Psalms (1530) should be mentioned here, and of the dogmatic writings, the one on communion addressed to Pope Clemens VII (1530). In this book Paracelsus denies the claim of the Catholics, Lutherans, Zwinglians, and Anabaptists that they are the possessors of the Holy Spirit, as Sebastian Franck (*q.v.*) had done in his song about the four dissentious churches. The two men met at least twice—in 1529 at Nürnberg, in 1531 at Strasbourg. That Paracelsus cured Sebastian Franck of a mental breakdown is mere legend. Franck himself described the doctor as a second Lucianus (i.e., a mocker) and as much more of a mystic than the rationalistic doctor. Nor do the casual meetings with Kaspar Schwenckfeld (*q.v.*) denote a spiritual relatedness. The peaceable, pious Silesian nobleman and the quarrelsome man of the people had little in common. The Schwenckfeld biography by Mrs. Schultz demonstrates the spiritual independence of Schwenckfeld in his relations with Paracelsus. Only ignorance can equate these two opposite spirits with each other or with the Anabaptists.

The fact that Paracelsus had nothing in common with the Anabaptists—except the criticism of the sacrament of communion—in spite of occasional contacts, is seen in the fanatical, unrealistic hope of the doctor for the ultimate restoration of the church by the pope: "In the pope there will be a blessed spirit and thus a blessed spirit in the sheep." No Anabaptist and no convinced Spiritualist thought in such terms in the 16th century. Paracelsus remained a Catholic in life and death.

His retirement to religious literary work probably was due to the Peasants' War. After 1532 he frequently signed himself with a title of doctor of the Holy Scriptures to which he had no right. Much will remain a mystery until more of his theological works appear. The most reliable biography is Georg Sticker's.

The fourth centennial of the death of Paracelsus in 1941 produced a considerable body of literature, which must, however, be used with a critical mind. In addition there are some older works of a biographical and interpretative content. E.T.

Ludwig Englert, *Paracelsus, Mensch und Arzt* (Bücher deutscher Kultur, Berlin, 1941); R. J. Hartmann, *Theophrast von Hohenheim* (Stuttgart, 1904); Fr. Jäger, *Theophrastus Paracelsus 1493-1541* (Salzburg, 1941); Wilhelm Matthiessen, "Theophrast von Hohenheim," in *Arch. f. Ref.-Gesch.* XIV and XV (1917-18); W.-E. Peuckert, *Theophrastus Paracelsus* (Stuttgart, 1941), idem, *Paracelsus, Die Geheimnisse, ein Lesebuch aus seinen Schriften* (Leipzig, 1941); E. H. Reklam, *Die Gestalt des Paracelsus in der Dichtung, Studien zu Kolbenheyers Trilogie* (Leipzig, 1938); G. Sticker, *Paracelsus, ein Lebensbild* (Halle, 1941); *ML* III, 334.

Paradise, a town (pop. 600) ten miles east-southeast of Lancaster, Pa., the center of an old and large Mennonite (MC) community. This was the home of Tanawa, King of the Pequea Indians, and Madame Ferree, a French Huguenot. So beautiful was the sight of this town (a town that cannot be improved) that in 1804 they called it Paradise, and made it a post office on the Lancaster-Philadelphia coach route. David Witmer's hostelry, the schoolhouse, and the later Mennonite church were important points in the early town. Not only were the Mennonites of the vicinity prosperous farmers, but they certainly aided in putting this clean small town on the map. There is a Mennonite meetinghouse in the town. I.D.L.

Paradise Mennonite Church (MC), a member of the Lancaster Conference, located in Paradise, Lancaster Co., Pa., built its first meetinghouse in 1806 on land contributed by David Witmer, the innkeeper. By popular subscription $828 was collected for the building. Forty years later it was replaced by a larger brick church. In 1885 the third church, 45 x 65 ft., also of brick, was built and in 1909 considerably enlarged. The first Sunday school was held in 1887. This was the center of the missionary movement among Lancaster Conference Mennonites, giving J. A. Ressler, A. Hershey Leaman, Mary Denlinger, John H. Mellinger, and John M. Kreider early to the cause. The sewing circle movement started here in 1895 and Mary Mellinger in 1911 became its first conference-wide chairman. The cutting room of the Associated Sewing Circles is near by. A beautiful cemetery is on the hill overlooking Paradise. The church membership in 1958 was 302, with Clair B. Eby as bishop, and Amos W. Weaver and Willis E. King as ministers. I.D.L.

Paradise Mennonite Church (MC), located near Reid, Md., four miles north of Hagerstown. Services were first conducted in a schoolhouse near by in 1892-97, when a brick church was erected on the southeast corner of the Christian Eshleman farm, who also granted the land. In 1925 the building was enlarged and again in 1947. The ministers of the Miller Mennonite Church (*q.v.*), of which it is a branch, have pastoral oversight. Irvin S. Shank was the minister in charge in 1956. It has no separate membership. J.D.R.

Paraditz (Czech, *Boretice*) near Scheikowitz (Czech, *Cajkovice*) in the Göding (*q.v.*) (Hodonin) district, became the seat of a Hutterite Bruderhof, after a house was bought in 1545 by the deacon Thomas Seckler and the interpreter Thomas Schmid. The decision of the Brno Landtag of 1545 was not put into effect in Paraditz until 1547, when the Hutterites emigrated to Hungary. When they were again admitted to Moravia they returned to Paraditz, where in 1570 the preacher Hans Schlachindpfann or Klampferer, "a highly gifted man," died. In 1569 a quarrel developed between the Brethren and the barons, when the latter refused to pay for the work in the vineyards. The Hutterites thereupon stopped working and the baron took away their house and expelled them from his lands. They turned to Koblitz (*q.v.*), a half hour away, where a new Bruderhof was just being set up. But in 1599, ten years later, the new baron Wenzel Hrubcicky von Cechtin of Budkau returned the house to the brotherhood, and the Brethren settled there again. In the middle of July 1605 Paraditz and a number of neighboring villages were burned down by Hungarian troops. It is not definitely known whether the Bruderhof was set up again. It is not named among those that had to be abandoned in 1622. (Beck, *Geschichts-Bücher;* Wolkan, *Geschicht-Buch;* Zieglschmid, *Chronik; ML* III, 334.) P.DE.

Paraguay, a landlocked country, lies in the central part of South America between Argentina, Brazil, and Bolivia. With an area of 157,047 square miles, slightly larger than California, it is one of the smaller South American countries. In point of population, estimated somewhere around one and a half million, it is the smallest.

The Tropic of Capricorn runs through Paraguay at the line where almost equal parts lie on either side. Most of Paraguay proper, however, i.e., the part east of the Paraguay River, lies south of the line. Most of the Paraguayan Chaco, that part of the country west of the Paraguay River, lies in the Torrid Zone. The climate is, therefore, tropical and subtropical. Much of the year is mild, but there is a range from cool to very hot. In the summer months of December, January, and February the temperature frequently rises above 100° Fahrenheit. It can also be hot in other months of the year, even in midwinter. Occasionally there are frosts even on the torrid side of Capricorn. In the drier winter months some parts of the country are at times subject to hot north winds and dust storms. The Paraguay River divides the country into unequal and quite different parts, the eastern section being more rolling and having more rainfall than the western. From the Paraguay River, where the elevation is low, to the Brazilian border on the east, the elevation rises to some highlands which average 1,500

feet or more above sea level. Unlike most of South America, Paraguay has no real mountains. Since transportation facilities within the country are very inadequate, the Paraguay and Parana Rivers are doubly important as channels of commerce.

The natural resources of Paraguay make it well fitted for agriculture. There is some industry and there probably will be more in the future, but the basic ingredients of a great industrial development—coal, or oil, and iron—are lacking. The agricultural products are cotton, tobacco, manioc, corn, sugar cane, rice, peanuts, yerba mate, citrus fruits, melons, sweet potatoes, beans and garden vegetables, pineapples, bananas, and other fruits. Lumbering is also important. In addition to the quebracho tree, which furnishes tannin, there are some types of trees and grasses from which oils can be profitably extracted, including oil of petitgrain, tung, castor, and coconut oils. Cattle raising is an important indusry, providing meat, meat extract, which is largely exported, and hides.

The people are largely a mixture of Spanish and Indian with the Indian (Guarani) predominating. The number of pure Indians and of pure Europeans is not large. There are some Spaniards, a few Italians, Germans, Englishmen, Slavs, and others, besides the Mennonites, who are of Dutch and German ethnic origin.

The Spanish impact on Paraguay goes back to 1537 with the founding of the first settlement, Asuncion. During most of the colonial period Asuncion, the capital of Paraguay, served as the center from which the La Plata section of South America was administered. Since obtaining its independence from Spain in the second decade of the 19th century, Paraguay has had a checkered history. Three dictators dominated the political scene down to 1870, and since that time uprisings and revolutions of one kind or another have frequently plagued the country. Disastrous foreign wars have also contributed to the country's backwardness. One of these was the Chaco War in the 1930's, in which the Mennonites, by settling on territory in dispute between Paraguay and Bolivia, played an unintentional part.

Spain contributed her religious and cultural pattern to Paraguay. The great majority of the people are Roman Catholic, although the attachment on the part of many is no more than nominal. Religious and moral standards are quite low. The number of Protestants in Paraguay is not large, the Mennonites constituting the largest Protestant body. The educational level is also quite low, although the authorities are making heroic efforts to raise it.

It was into this environment that the Mennonites began to come in the 1920's. Some of the most conservative groups of the Mennonites from Western Canada, who had come from Russia in the 1870's, were the first to become interested in Paraguay. They prospered fairly well in Canada until World War I, when the Canadian government began to more fully nationalize its various ethnic elements. This effort included the passing of a law eliminating private elementary schools, and, in the public schools, compelling the use of English and forbidding the teaching of religion. These conservative groups of German-speaking Mennonites considered this a serious curtailment of privileges promised them when they came to Canada, and they began to look for new countries to which they might emigrate. The Old Colony Mennonites in 1919-20 investigated several countries in South America, but then decided to move to Mexico. Another conservative group composed of Sommerfelder, Chortitzer, and a few Bergthaler Mennonites then became interested in Paraguay. Oral promises of special privileges already made to the Old Colony group were now renewed and passed as a law in 1921. This famous and generous *privilegium* provides, among other things, that Mennonites and their descendants shall have the right to practice their religion and to worship with complete and unrestricted liberty, to make simple affirmations in courts of justice, and to be exempt from obligatory military service, combatant and noncombatant, in time of peace and war. They were also given the right to maintain and administer their own schools and to teach their religion and their German language without restriction.

Because of the depression of 1921 and the difficulty of selling their land at satisfactory prices the group which became Menno Colony did not get started on their way to Paraguay until near the end of 1926. With those who came in 1927, a total of 1,778 souls arrived at the river port of Puerto Casado. Since their land, lying slightly more than 100 miles west, bought from the specially formed *Corporación Paraguaya,* was not ready for settlement, these people were bitterly disappointed in their forced prolonged stay in and near Puerto Casado. In addition, tragedy struck in the form of typhoid and other diseases, taking a toll of over 200 lives. Over 300 disillusioned migrants returned to Canada. But the main body was finally able to settle on its own land in 1928 and the discontent was largely dissipated. Very few persons left this colony after actual settlement on the land. They settled in villages (fourteen in 1928), as had been the practice of their forefathers in Russia. This group, known as Menno Colony, was the first Mennonite settlement in South America and the most stable.

The names of a few non-Mennonites who helped in this venture should be mentioned. General Samuel McRoberts (*q.v.*), a New York banker, was contacted by the Mennonites and his interest and help enlisted in the cause. He, together with another banker as a partner, Edward B. Robinette, helped the Mennonites dispose of their holdings in Canada and helped them, through *Corporación Paraguaya* (*q.v.*), buy and settle on their lands in Paraguay. McRoberts hired a Norwegian, Fred Engen, to help him explore and select an area in which the Mennonites might be interested. It was Engen (*q.v.*) who suggested the Chaco area.

The next group of Mennonites who came to Paraguay were refugees from Russia. During the 1920's, as a result of the Communist revolution in Russia, some 21,000 Mennonites came to the United States and Canada, largely the latter. Other thousands, thinking the Communist storm would blow over, and lulled by the partial retreat from Communism under the New Economic Policy (NEP) following

1921, were less inclined to leave at that time. In 1929, after new and more persistent efforts to put Communism with its antireligious aspects into effect, the Mennonites realized too late that the emigration doors were pretty tightly closed. Nevertheless, out of the 20,000-30,000 said to have started for Moscow with the hope of escape, slightly less than 6,000 (including some non-Mennonites) were finally, on Nov. 25, 1929, permitted to leave for Germany, which gave them temporary asylum.

Penniless, these refugees needed help and received it from European and North American Mennonites and also from non-Mennonite Germans. Where these people should be settled permanently was a problem. Germany seemed at that time unable to keep them and doors to the United States and Canada, where they preferred to go, were now closed for the great majority. The Mennonite Central Committee came to their aid and after studying the matter as thoroughly as was possible in the short time at its disposal recommended Paraguay. Brazil was also open and a minority decided to migrate to that country. But Paraguay was one of the very few countries which promised them the freedom they desired and which at the same time was willing to receive the aged, ill, and crippled along with the others. Harold S. Bender was sent as the MCC representative to Germany in January 1930, to help arrange and organize the movement to Paraguay. In Paraguay the MCC arranged for the purchase of land from *Corporación Paraguaya* next to Menno Colony. In 1930-32 a total of slightly more than 2,000 persons from Russia migrated to the Paraguayan Chaco and established Fernheim Colony (*q.v.*). This number included 50 Mennonites who came from Poland and 367 who came from Russia by way of Harbin, China. In the Fernheim migration three Mennonite branches were represented—Mennonites (now GCM), Mennonite Brethren, and a small number of *Allianz Gemeinde* (*q.v.*, corresponding to the Evangelical Mennonite Brethren).

Other than the small temporary settlement at Horqueta near Concepción, the third Mennonite settlement to be established in Paraguay was Friesland. This colony was founded by Fernheim settlers who were dissatisfied with the isolated Chaco and many of whom were also opposed to the colony co-operative. After investigating several places in eastern Paraguay the group decided to settle about 40 miles east of the Paraguay River port of Rosario, or slightly over 100 miles northeast of Asunción. The exodus from Fernheim occurred during the winter months of 1937, and by September 748 persons had settled and established Friesland Colony. The pattern of the new settlement was similar to that of Fernheim—settlement in villages; it also had the same religious organizations (GCM and MB) except that very few families of the *Allianz Gemeinde* had migrated. In time even a business co-operative, which had been so disliked in Fernheim, was formed, but membership was made voluntary. The exodus from Fernheim weakened that colony and caused some bitterness. The MCC discouraged the movement and gave no assistance to the new settlement until some years later. Economically, progress in the Friesland settlement has been disappointing.

In both Fernheim and Friesland considerable dissatisfaction with Paraguay manifested itself during the 1930's and early 1940's and not a little pro-German and pro-Nazi sympathy developed, especially in Friesland, but also in Fernheim; none, however, in Menno. For a while there was more talk of returning to Europe than of further Mennonite migrations to Paraguay, and some actually returned to Germany during the war. After the war, however, this feeling disappeared, and there were actually new Mennonite migrations to Paraguay.

In 1929, when the few thousand Mennonites were able to leave Russia, a larger number was forced to remain behind. During the course of the invasion and occupation of South Russia by the German army in 1941-43, additional thousands of Mennonites fled from Russia to Western Europe. Though many were forced to return to Russia, about 4,500 persons immigrated to Paraguay in 1947-48, besides the 162 persons who came with the group but remained in Buenos Aires. This new immigration to Paraguay was again due to the fact that the doors to other satisfactory countries were closed at this time. The International Refugee Relief Organization (IRO, q.v.) gave the MCC generous assistance in moving these refugees to Paraguay, and the colonies of Fernheim, Menno, and Friesland helped the MCC to get the new immigrants settled on the land. A few of these people settled in Asunción or in the colonies already established, but the majority organized two new colonies. The new Chaco colony of Neuland, located a few miles south of Fernheim, had a population of 2,389 in 1948, and the new colony of Volendam, a few miles north of Rosario on the Paraguay River, had 1,172 inhabitants in that year. The movement to these colonies was somewhat retarded by the Paraguayan revolution of 1947, some groups having been forced to wait several months in Buenos Aires or Asunción.

The most recent Mennonite settlements in Paraguay were founded in 1948 by fellow believers of Menno Colony—Sommerfelder and Chortitzer Mennonites from southern Manitoba, and a smaller contingent from Saskatchewan. Migration conscious ever since the founding of Menno Colony and fearing the impact of continued secularization on their way of life, they finally decided to emigrate. Not satisfied with the Chaco, where their brethren had located, they founded two colonies, Sommerfeld and Bergthal, in southeastern Paraguay between Villarica and the Brazilian border. About 1700 persons emigrated, but because of disillusionment with the primitive and difficult situation they found some 600 returned to Canada in 1948-50.

The Hutterian Brethren (q.v.), distantly related to the Mennonites, in 1941 also formed a settlement in eastern Paraguay near the Mennonite settlement of Friesland. Of a heterogeneous European background, the group numbered 350 in 1941 and grew to 604 by 1950. This Bruderhof is called Primavera (q.v.).

As to the future of the Mennonites in Paraguay, no one, of course, can speak with certainty. Some groups are better satisfied and more stable than others. Menno Colony, as noted, is the most stable. Fernheim perhaps comes next, although a few are still leaving. In the newer colonies of Neuland and Volendam there is considerable dissatisfaction and quite a few have left—and are still leaving—mostly for Canada, where many have relatives. The economic and cultural backwardness of Paraguay together with its political instability has contributed to this unrest. Climate, insects, transportation difficulties, and lack of adequate markets have also made the struggle hard. On the other hand, many appreciate greatly the freedom they have and are willing to continue in hope that most of the discouraging conditions will improve. In this they are probably correct. For progress has been made, and more is likely to be made in the future.   W.H.S.

The Mennonites in the Mennonite colonies of Paraguay are distributed as follows:

	1940	1950	1956
Menno	2020	3169	4265
Fernheim	1512	2339	2524
Neuland	1512	2497	2162
Friesland	822	986	969
Volendam	----	1810	1317
Bergthal	----	574	639*
Sommerfeld	----	626	644*
Asunción	?	?	170†
Total	4354	12001	c13040

* As of 1953.
† Variable figure because of shifting population.

J. Winfield Fretz, *Pilgrims in Paraguay* (Scottdale, 1953); Willard and Verna Smith, *Paraguayan Interlude* (Scottdale, 1950).

Paraguay Mennonite Brethren Mission, "Light to the Indians," in the Paraguayan Chaco was started by missionary-minded members of the Mennonite churches of Fernheim, Paraguay. As early as 1932, soon after the European group of Mennonites settled in the Chaco, the evangelization of the resident aborigines was conceived. The Chaco-Bolivian War delayed a formal beginning until Sept. 17, 1935, when interested friends of missions of the three conferences represented in Fernheim, aided by the KfK (Committee on Church Relations), formed the Fernheim Mission Association and organized a mission under the name "Licht den Indianern." The newly organized mission employed missionary Gerhard B. Giesbrecht, who with subsidies from various church groups in North America and intermittent help hired from the Mennonite settlements kept the mission work going.

In 1937 Bernard P. Epp came from North America to assist Giesbrecht with the study and construction of the Lengua Indian language and the evangelization of the tribe. Other workers labored for shorter intervals. In order to induce the Indians to settle at one place, the mission set out to operate a farm on which employment and living room was offered them. An experiment of eight years proved that these roaming, unevangelized Indians cannot be induced to reside at one place. It was only after the conversion and baptism of the first Indians in 1946 that these new Christians asked for permission to settle in the mission colony in order to withdraw themselves and their families from the pagan and shifting life of their tribesmen and to build a Christian community.

As early as 1943 definite requests were made by
the missionaries as well as by the Fernheim Mission
Association that the M.B. Conference of North
America assume the responsibility. The formal acceptance of the mission by the M.B. Conference took
place in November 1945.

The staff has been increased to include Mr. and
Mrs. Jacob H. Franz from M.B. churches in North
America, Mr. and Mrs. Gerhard B. Giesbrecht, Mr.
and Mrs. Jacob Klassen, Mr. and Mrs. Dietrich
Lepp, Mr. and Mrs. Gerhard Hein, Mr. and Mrs.
David Hein, Mr. and Mrs. Walter Rennert, Mr. and
Mrs. Henry Kroeker, Mary Giesbrecht, Mr. and Mrs.
Albert Enns from the M.B. churches in Paraguay,
and Mr. and Mrs. Kornelius K. Isaak from the Men-
nonite church in Paraguay. Isaak was killed by a
Morro Indian in 1958.

The mission operates stations in Asunción in eastern Paraguay and the Chulupie stations in Filadelfia
and Neuland, as well as the Lengua stations at La-
guna Ipuna and Yalve Sanga in the Chaco. It operates two elementary schools, one for Lenguas and
one for Chulupies. Short term Bible instruction is
given to adults. Dispensary work is carried on by
the nurses. Several Gospels and some doctrinal material and songs have been translated into the Lengua and Chulupie languages. The total number of
baptized believers in 1958 is somewhat over 200.
(See **Licht den Indianern,** which this article supplements.)   A.E.J.
A. E. Janzen, *Glimpses of South America* (Hillsboro,
1943); Mrs. H. T. Esau, *The First Sixty Years of Mennonite Brethren Missions* (Hillsboro, 1954).

Parana, a state of Brazil, area about 77,000 sq. miles,
population (1950) 2,149,509. Its capital is Curitiba,
with a population of 141,349. Parana became the
home in 1935 ff. of some of the Mennonites who
had originally (1930) settled in Santa Catharina,
also a state in Brazil (*q.v.*), some on the Krauel
(*q.v.*), some on the Stoltz plateau (*q.v.*). The settlement at Auhagen on the Stoltz plateau did not
prosper economically; therefore most of the settlers,
75 families with 368 persons, left in 1935-36 and
settled (a few in Blumenau and Sao Paulo) mostly
near Curitiba, the capital of Parana. Later when the
Krauel settlement dissolved most of the group went
to Parana near Curitiba, while others went to Bagé
in the state of Rio Grand do Sul, founding a largely
Mennonite Brethren settlement there in 1949-50.

The first settlement in Parana was made in 1935
by 38 families at the village of Bouqueirao, some 6
miles from Curitiba. In 1936 a second settlement of
28 families was made in the same area, and in 1937
a third with 74 families called Xaxim. In 1948 a
fourth settlement, Guarituba, was founded 12 miles
from Curitiba. In the city of Curitiba itself, in the
suburb Villa Guaira, a Mennonite area developed,
which in 1953 had 75 families. In 1953 the total
Mennonite population in and around Curitiba was
292 families, with 1300 persons. The last Mennonite
settlement in Parana was made in 1951 about 50
miles northwest of Curitiba, and is called New Witmarsum. In 1953 it had 53 families with 319 persons. Thus the total in Parana was 245 families with
1,619 persons. In the Bouqueirao area the settlers
are largely dairy farmers supplying Curitiba with

most of its milk. The New Witmarsum settlers are
largely dairy and cattle farmers.   H.S.B.
Wilhelm Bärg, "Die Mennoniten bei Curitiba in Brasilien," in *Der Bote,* 1948, No. 1283, p. 2 f.; Walter
Quiring, "Auhagen in Brasilien, eine gescheiterte mennonitische Bergsiedlung," in *Der Bote,* 1948, Nos. 1279-
86; *idem, Im Schweisse Deines Angesichts* (Steinbach,
1953); J. W. Fretz, *Pilgrims in Paraguay* (Scottdale,
1953); *ML III,* 335.

Parkesburg Mennonite Church (MC), located in
Parkesburg, a borough of 2,800 in Chester Co., Pa.,
was opened in the Owens Building in 1938, by the
members of the Millwood (*q.v.*) congregation. Noah
L. Hershey was ordained pastor Nov. 13, 1946, and
Amos W. Yoder deacon on June 28, 1950. In 1947-48
a substantial brick building 56 x 36 ft. was built on
Second Avenue. In 1957 the membership was 57.
                                                     I.D.L.

Park View Mennonite Church (MC), located near
Harrisonburg, Rockingham Co., Va., a member of
the Virginia Conference, was organized in January
1954 with 57 charter members, after many years of
group worship on the college campus. Mennonites
in this vicinity had held membership in both the
Northern and Middle districts of the Virginia Conference. The congregation operates with a church
council which has representation from its membership, Eastern Mennonite College administration, as
well as the College and congregational pastors.
Sunday worship services are held jointly with the
students who are living on the campus. The midweek worship service is designed as a distinctly congregational feature. The membership in 1957 was
82; the ministers were John L. Stauffer, bishop, Ira
E. Miller, and Paul H. Martin.   I.E.M.

Parma, Margaret of: see **Margaret of Parma.**

Parnell (Iowa) Mennonite Church (MC) was established in 1948 as a mission under the West Union
Mennonite Church. It became an independent congregation in 1958 with approximately 55 members.
An abandoned church was purchased and moved
into town for the use of the congregation. Paul
E. M. Yoder and John Miller Yoder were its ministers.   M.G.

Partridge (Kansas) Amish community. Partridge
(pop. 221) is located slightly northwest of the center
of Reno Co. (*q.v.*), Kan., on State Highway 61, approximately 10 miles southwest of Hutchinson, the
county seat. The town of Partridge was begun in
1884. A year earlier, 1883, a group of Amish families moved from Shelbyville, Ill., to Reno County
(*q.v.*) and settled in the Partridge and Yoder neigh-
borhoods. The Partridge Old Order Amish settlement in 1955 consisted of three districts with 192
members: North Center District, 58 members, and
South Center District, 70 members, both under
John D. Yoder as bishop (ord. 1944), and East Center District, 64 members, with John N. Mast (ord.
1955) as bishop. The Plainview (*q.v.*) Conservative
Mennonite Church was organized in August 1948 in
the Partridge-Hutchinson community, most of whose
members came from the Partridge Old Order Amish. The Conservative Church (*q.v.*) in 1957 had
97 members.   D.P.M.

Paschen (Paaschen, Paessen), a Dutch Mennonite family, which originally lived at Burgsteinfurt (*q.v.*) in Westphalia, Germany. Here its members were already Mennonites, most of them merchants; Hendrik Gerritsz Paschen, a merchant, was a preacher of the Burgsteinfurt Mennonite congregation in the early 17th century. About 1623 Berent Paschen (b. 1601) moved to Enschedé in the Dutch district of Twenthe, and other members of the family followed. Some of them also settled at Ootmarsum and Hengelo, but the main center of the family was at Enschedé. The branch remaining in Burgsteinfurt died out about 1700. The Paschen family played an important part in the development both of the Mennonite congregation and the town of Enschedé, its members usually being textile merchants. Isaac Paschen (d. *c*1710), a son of Hendrik Gerritsz Paschen of Burgsteinfurt, was a preacher of the congregation. Abraham and Gerrit Paschen, both textile manufacturers, moved to Winterswijk about 1762, where many of their descendants served as deacons of the Mennonite congregation until recent times. By marriage the Paschens became related to a number of noted Mennonite families, such as Stenvers, van Lochem, Blijdenstein, Stroink, Roelvink (all in Enschedé), ten Cate (Enschedé and Almelo), Coster and Hofkes (Almelo), Willink and Walyen (Winterswijk), and Rierink (Zutphen).

Blaupot ten Cate (*Groningen* I, 31) tells an anecdote concerning Hendrik Gerritsz Paschen, a merchant and Mennonite preacher at Burgsteinfurt; being surprised by robbers (*c*1650), he preached them a sermon on Luke 3:14, which made them so ashamed that they left. vpZ.

Uit het Verleden der Doopsgezinden in Twenthe (Borne, n.d.) 57, 61, 97, 104, 134; A. Benthem Gz, *Geschiedenis van Enschedé* (2d ed. 1920) 722; F. C. Fleischer, *De Doopsgezinde gemeente te Winterswijk* (1909) *passim*; the genealogy of the Blijdenstein family (*passim*) in *Ned. Patriciaat* XXXIII (1947) 7-34; P. Beets, *Stamboek der Willingen* (Deventer, 1767) *passim*.

Paschen, Den, a small farm near Zenderen in the district of Twente, Dutch province of Overijssel, was the center and meeting place of the Mennonites in this district, later forming the congregations of Hengelo and Borne. The relation of den Paschen with the Mennonite Paschen (*q.v.*) family is not clear; probably some Paschens lived here. Elder Hendrik Berends (Hulshoff, *q.v.*; 1664-1745) lived at den Paschen. vpZ.

Pasensner von Jesenwang, Martin, ducal inquisitor in Bavaria, Germany, in 1527. Along the Lech regular hunts had been made (for example by the bailiff of Esting according to a report of Dec. 2, 1527), before Martin Pasensner von Jesenwang received the commission, in the spirit of the simultaneous decision of the Swabian League, to hunt down the Anabaptists throughout the country by means of spies and put them into prison; and all officials were instructed to support him. In Bavaria as elsewhere the Anabaptists brought in received no trial, but "the sentence was read at once and the execution followed," for "the secular law is in this case louder." Hege.

J. E. Jörg, *Deutschland in der Revolutions-Periode 1522-1526* (Freiburg, 1851) 721; V. A. Winter, *Gesch. der bayrischen Wiedertäufer im 16. Jahrhundert* (Munich, 1809) 29 f., and 177; *ML* II, 697; III, 335.

Pashnya Mennonite Brethren Church was established in the Slavgorod Mennonite settlement (*q.v.*) of Siberia, and served five villages—Ananyevka, Grigoryevka, Markovka, Ekaterinovka, and Zhelanovka. A meetinghouse was located in Ananyevka. The first leading minister, Gerhard Isaak, was succeeded by Johann Friesen. Other ministers were Heinrich Isaak, Wilhelm Fast, Peter Gäde, Jakob Peters, Jakob Gäde, and Jakob Penner. There were smaller meetinghouses in some of the villages. The present state of the church is unknown. C.K.

Gerhard Fast, *In den Steppen Sibiriens* (Rosthern, 1957) 78.

Pashnya Mennonite Church was located in the Slavgorod Mennonite settlement (*q.v.*) in Siberia and served the inhabitants of Grigoryevka, Markovka, Ananyevka, Ekaterinovka, and Zhelanovka. The first leading minister of the congregation was Jakob Quiring, assisted by Johann Neufeld, David Janzen, Johann Sawatzky, and Johann Boldt. The congregation worshiped in school buildings. (See also Slavgorod Mennonite Church.) C.K.

Gerhard Fast, *In den Steppen Sibiriens* (Rosthern, 1957) 72.

Pasma, a Dutch Mennonite family, living in the province of Friesland, and originally residing at Akkrum, where they were farmers; the family name of Pasma is not found before 1810, but the family is much older and found as early as 1600. It is not clear whether the first generations were Mennonite, but Hendrik Franses, b. *c*1745, was a Mennonite. In 1770 he was married to Wybrich Atzes, widow of Atze Joostes. They were farmers at Snikzwaag near Joure in Friesland, and the curious fact is mentioned that the owner of their farm, Baron Hobbe of Aylva, donated to them the farm on which they lived. Their grandson Hendrik Franses Pasma (1813-91), married to Fokje Jans Fokma, both Mennonites, was a farmer at Irnsum and Haskerdijken. He was an outstanding pioneer in agriculture. Though he had in his youth received little education, he later educated himself by much reading and studying. In 1868 he published an important brochure on the cattle plague and addressed numerous meetings of farmers. In 1879 he was one of the founders of the Fries Rundvee-Stamboek (Frisian Herdbook Association); and on the instigation of the city of Kampen he founded a model agricultural farm near Kampen. He was also active in finding methods for improving the manufacture of butter and made a plan for better drainage of Friesland by building pumping-engines and canals, which project was taken over by the government of Friesland. Hendrik Franses Pasma was an alderman of Haskerland and a member of the States of Friesland, and also a deacon of the Mennonite congregation of Heerenveen. His great-grandson is Frans Hendriks Pasma (b. 1886 at Joure), Mennonite pastor of Mensingeweer 1913-16, Dantumawoude 1916-21, and Grouw 1921-51, who was the moderator of the ADS (*q.v.*) 1940-46, active in behalf of a better pension for retired ministers and ministers' widows, author of

Onze Vermaning (Bergum, 1917), *De Doopsgezinden te Grouw* (Grouw, 1930), *De Friese Doopsgezinde gemeenten in de laatste halve eeuw* (n.p., n.d., 1947), and *Doopsgezind Handboek* (1954). Since about 1850 a number of descendants have joined the Reformed Church.   vDZ.

H. de Haan, *Frans Hendriks Pasma, zijn Voorouders en Nageslacht* (Leeuwarden, n.d.-1956); G. A. Wumkes, *Stads- en Dorpskroniek van Friesland* II, 1800-1900 (Leeuwarden, 1934) *passim,* see Index.

Paso Robles First Mennonite Church, Cal., was organized in 1903 by twenty-five charter members. Originally this group was a part of the San Marcos Mennonite Church (*q.v.*) which dissolved on Nov. 26, 1903, and reorganized as the Willow Creek Mennonite Church (*q.v.*) and the First Mennonite Church of Paso Robles. The group dismantled an old building 15 miles west of Paso Robles and moved it to Paso Robles where the church was erected. Some of the members lived at Estrella, where worship services were conducted on alternate Sundays for a while. The preaching was originally in German, then in German and English, and at present it is in English only.

Jacob Hege served the congregation until 1906, when he moved to Idaho. John K. Lichti succeeded him and was ordained as elder by Michael Horsch. Hege returned to Paso Robles and served as elder 1915-19, succeeded by his son Christian C. Hege 1919-44. Since that time the church has been served by Arlo Kaufman, Ben Rahn, M. S. Galle, and Alfred J. Schwartz, the current (1958) pastor; the membership is 69.   C.K.

H. D. Burkholder, *The Story of Our Conferences and Churches* (1951).

Paso Robles (Cal.) Second Mennonite Church (GCM), since 1954 called Willow Creek Mennonite Church (*q.v.*), before 1943 called San Marcos Mennonite Church (*q.v.*).

Passamentwerker, Geert, an Anabaptist martyr: see **Geert Passamentwerker.**

Passamentwerker, Arent, an Anabaptist martyr: see **Arent Aerssens.**

Passau, a city on the Danube in Lower Bavaria, Germany, once a fortress, where, according to some reports, a small Anabaptist congregation formed at the beginning of the Reformation period. In 1527 Hans Hut (*q.v.*) baptized Hermann Kheil, a citizen of Passau (*Vergicht Passau*, Feb. 4, 1529; Nicoladoni, 28). Wolfgang Brandhuber (*q.v.*), Lienhard Stieglitz (*q.v.*), and other Anabaptist leaders stemmed from Passau. The appendix to Nicoladoni's book contains the records of several Anabaptist trials in Passau. In 1537 about sixty Anabaptists on their way from Moravia to South Germany, were seized in Passau and held in the castle prison for five years. Many died including the song writers Hans Betz (Petz) (*q.v.*) and Bernhard (Michael) Schneider (*q.v.*). The prisoners wrote fifty-one hymns, which are contained in the *Ausbund* (*q.v.*). (See also **Philippites.**)   NEFF.

Beck, *Geschichts-Bücher*, p. X and 132; H. W. Erbkam, *Geschichte der protestantischen Sekten im Zeitalter der Reformation* (Hamburg and Gotha, 1848); Wolkan,

Geschicht-Buch, 74; A. Nicoladoni, *Johannes Bünderlin von Linz und die oberösterreichischen Täufergemeinden* (Berlin, 1893); V. A. Winter, *Gesch. der bayerischen Wiedertäufer im 16. Jahrhundert* (Munich, 1809); *ML* III, 336.

Passau, Jörg von: see **Nespitzer, Georg.**

Passchier Weyns, an Anabaptist martyr, burned at the stake at Gent, Belgium, on Dec. 29, 1568, with Daniel de Paeu and Daniel van Vooren. Particulars are lacking. Van Braght's *Martyrs' Mirror* gives only the year of their execution, not the exact date, nor the method. The names of these martyrs are also found in a song, "Alsmen schreef duyst vijfhondert jaer ende twee en tsestich mede," found in the 1578 and following editions of the *Lietboecxken*. (*Offer*, 652; *Mart. Mir.* D 370, E 726; Verheyden, *Gent*, 50, No. 165.)   vDZ.

Pastor, Adam: see **Adam Pastor.**

Pastoral Messenger, the official organ of the Lancaster Mennonite Conference (MC), is a quarterly, published by the Bishop Board, J. Paul Graybill, editor. The first issue appeared on April 1, 1941. It is now regularly an eight-page paper, printed at Scottdale, Pa.; 6400 copies are printed and sent out gratis to every congregation in the conference.   I.D.L.

Pastorius, Francis Daniel (1651-1719), a native of Sommershausen near Frankfurt, Germany, was one of the signatories of the first protest against slavery in America, which was presented on April 18, 1688. He was educated in several German universities and earned a doctorate in law. In Frankfurt he met Philipp Spener and William Penn. From this contact may have come the idea of emigrating to America. On April 2, 1683, he sailed, arriving in Philadelphia on August 20. His Mennonite and Quaker friends who followed on the *Concord* he greeted with a poem upon their arrival on Oct. 6, 1683. Under his vigorous leadership a plan was at once made for the city of Germantown (*q.v.*). In 1688 he married. His home became the center of a Christian cultured circle. In 1691 he was chosen mayor of Germantown. When the school was built in 1701 he became the first teacher; a log house erected in 1708 served as a school and a church. Pastorius, a Pietist, joined neither the Quakers nor the Mennonites. He wrote many books and much verse that have not been published, in Greek, French, Dutch, English, and Italian. He died at the close of 1719.   NEFF.

Menn. Bl., 1884, 60; 1889, 39; M. D. Learned, *The Life of Francis Daniel Pastorius of Germantown* (Philadelphia, 1908); Whittier's *Pennsylvania Pilgrim* (Boston, 1872); *Comeniushefte*, 1893, 30; 1910, 225; Fr. Nieper, *Die ersten deutschen Auswanderer von Krefeld nach Pennsylvanien* (Neukirchen, 1940) 82 ff.; C. H. Wedel, *Abriss der Geschichte der Mennoniten* (Newton, 1900-4) 131 f.; *ML* III, 336.

Pastwa, a Mennonite village name transplanted from Prussia to the Molotschna settlement, Ukraine, and the East Reserve, Manitoba. (See **Villages.**) C.K.

Pastwa, West Prussia, Germany, a part of the congregation located at Jerczewo, a subsidiary of Heubuden (*q.v.*). In 1854 Jerczewo built a church in

Pastwa and in 1899 united with the Frisian congregation of Tragheimerweide. Pastwa later changed its name to Gutsch and then to Zandersfelde. (*ML* III, 336.) E.C.

Pastwa, a Mennonite congregation in the Gnadenfeld volost in the Molotschna, Russia (*q.v.*), founded in 1820. E.C.

Pati, a city (pop. 22,440) in northwest Java, Indonesia, a former mission of the Dutch Mennonite Mission Association, transferred to the Mennonites by the Reformed Church in 1898. At first Missionary Johann Fast (*q.v.*) had little result here, but after 1930, when a missionary hospital was built, the number of converts from Mohammedanism increased and a congregation was founded, independent since 1940, with a meetinghouse. In 1949 this congregation numbered 102 baptized members and 95 children; the minister is Sardjoe Djojodihardjo (since 1949). Besides this Javanese congregation there is in the town of Pati also a Chinese Mennonite congregation (membership 176 in 1953). E.C., vDZ.

Uit Verleden en Heden der Doopsgezinde Zending, 1937; *ML* III, 336.

Pati (Java) **Mennonite Biblical Seminary.** Before World War II the graduates of the mission-sponsored teacher-training school in Margoredjo received an extra year of Bible training, but only very few of these teacher-lay ministers are still in active church service. A few Mennonite young people had also been sent to and graduated from a Biblical seminary operated by the Reformed Mission Society. One student graduated from the Interchurch Theological Seminary in Jakarta. The Mennonites, however, never had their own preacher training program. Therefore the postwar number of trained ministers in the Mennonite Church was very small. Many congregations and mission stations did not even have an untrained minister. This situation was especially dangerous in the light of the postwar situation. In the newly achieved national independence the Mohammedans became very active. On the other hand, hitherto unknown missionary possibilities were opened. All this clearly called for a large number of trained ministers, and thus, for a program of preacher training.

In February 1950 the Javanese Mennonite church established the Biblical Seminary in Pati. The expenses of this project were shared equally by the MCC, the European Mennonite Mission Board, and the Javanese church. Very simple temporary buildings for classrooms and a dormitory were rented. Twelve young people with the equivalent of junior high school training were admitted as students. Afterwards this number was doubled by the arrival of a group of Batak (Sumatra) students who could not find a place in their own (Lutheran) church seminary. An all-Javanese board supervised the training program, which was headed by two Javanese instructors (S. Djojodihardjo and S. Harso) and two Dutch missionaries (R. S. Kuitse and J. P. Matthijssen). A number of secular courses were taught by several part-time teachers (Javanese and American). The five-year curriculum was in general the same as that of other Indonesian seminaries,

none of which (except the Theological Seminary in Jakarta) leads to any academic degree, but which train young Indonesian Christians to become full-fledged, full-time ministers and missionaries. The Pati curriculum consisted of Old Testament Introduction, Theology and Exegesis of Old Testament; the same of the New Testament; Systematic Theology; Ethics; Church History; History of Dogma; Islam; Ecclesiology; Pastoral Theology; Catechetics; Homiletics; Liturgics; Missiology; New Testament Greek; Mennonite History and Principles; Philosophy, Psychology, and several secular courses, and supervised practical work. After completion of the five-year course during which time no new students were admitted except for a few in a special two-year program, final examinations were held in the spring and summer of 1955.

The financial position of the Javanese church makes it impossible to absorb additional large numbers of ministers in the near future. Thus the number of new students had to be limited. This fact, added to the financial impossibility of maintaining an adequate faculty, motivated the decision to merge the Pati seminary with two others facing the same difficulties (West Java Chinese, East Javanese). This merger took effect as of Aug. 1, 1955. This new interdenominational school, which is located in Malang, East Java, is attended by several Mennonite students and has an excellent joint staff. R. S. Kuitse, who is the Mennonite member of this staff, also teaches several specifically Mennonite courses to those interested. The rest of the former Pati staff is now occupied in a new training school for lay church workers, located in Pati. J.M.

Patijn, a well-known Dutch family of French descent. Andries Jansz Patijn, a Mennonite (b. *c*1559), moved from Rombeke in Flanders, Belgium, to Haarlem, Holland, where he died in 1623. He was a brandy seller and a member of the Haarlem Flemish Mennonite congregation, as was also his son Daniel Patijn (1612-38). Daniel was a skipper, maintaining a regular ship service between Haarlem and Alkmaar; he died at an early age; his wife, a non-Mennonite, had the children educated in the Reformed Church and so the entire Patijn family has become Reformed. It is possible that Lieven Pattin of Maldeghem, Belgium, who is said to have lived there in 1630 as a well-to-do Mennonite, belonged to this family. (*Ned. Patriciaat* IX, 1918, 280 ff.; *DB* 1876, 106, 108.) vDZ.

Pätkau, Jacob H. (1895-*c*1947), a prominent Mennonite elder in the Memrik settlement, South Russia, was born in Nikolaipol, Borrissovo settlement, on April 1, 1895, the son of the miller and preacher Heinrich Pätkau. After graduation from the Chortitza Normal School (*Lehrerseminar*) in 1914 he began teaching in the village school at Schönhorst, Chortitza settlement, but was drafted into alternative service (medical corps) in 1915-17, and resumed teaching in Karpovka, Memrik, in 1917-22, making a brilliant record as an educational leader for the entire settlement. He was ordained preacher in early 1921 by the Kalinovo congregation, and within six months as elder, serving as overseer over the church in 10 villages and beyond. At the request of his church he remained at his post when he could have emigrated to Canada. He was elected a member of the *KfK* (*q.v.*) in January 1925. In the autumn of 1929 he went to Moscow to help those fleeing from Russia, but was arrested and returned to his home. He then fled with his family to the Caucasus, where he continued to serve the church. But he was in constant danger and fled from place to place. He was finally caught in 1937-38, arrested, and sent to Siberia. He was still living in 1945 but dead by 1947. His widow was still living in 1949, working in a children's home.

Taken from A. A. Töws, *Mennonitische Märtyrer* (Clearbrook, 1949) 154-56.   H.S.B.

Patos, an Old Colony Mennonite settlement consisting of 3,000 persons in 1950, is established in the state of Durango, Mexico, about 75 miles north and west of the capital. Patos is the Mexican town that serves as the post office, trading center, and railroad station for the more than sixteen villages that comprise the Mennonite settlement. Mennonites do not live in the town, but in agricultural villages within driving distance of this town. It is of historical interest that originally all of the Old Colony Mennonites now in Mexico had planned to settle in the state of Durango. Land bought there by the large settlement now in the state of Chihuahua was later exchanged for land in Chihuahua before the settlers actually arrived. The Durango colony is about 500 miles south of the larger settlements of Chihuahua.

J.W.F.

Patriots and Mennonites *in the Netherlands.* When William I of Orange in 1568 started the battle against Spain for the freedom of the Netherlands, the Dutch Mennonites supported him loyally with all means except active military service (see **Bogaert**). Not only William I, but also other stadholders of the House of Orange, e.g., Maurice and William III, protected the Mennonites and upheld their privileges of freedom from military service and the oath, granted to them by William I. On their part the Mennonites were warmly attached to the House of Orange. But after the middle of the 18th century and particularly from 1787 on, this changed, and the Mennonites lost much of their sympathy for the Oranges, turning to the views of the Patriots, who were the opponents of the Orangistic group in the Netherlands. Against the conservative views and practices of the Orangists they were progressive and liberal, tending to democracy and demanding a voice in matters of politics. There were a number of causes to make the Mennonites side with the Patriots: the period of the stadholdership of William V of Orange (1766-95), a spineless governor, who was largely influenced by his wife and especially by the group of Orangistic magistrates who often abused the privileges of their office and ranks; the incompetency of the government to restore trade and prosperity, which had been severely weakened by the wars; and the fact that only members of the Reformed Church were allowed to hold government offices. Besides this, the reading of English and French philosophers offered many critical persons new ideas concerning statesmanship and political economy. The War of Independence in America (1776-83), and particularly the Declaration of Independence with its definition of the rights of men, made an enormous impression on the Dutch Patriots. Many of them suffered severely at the hands of the Orangistic party; some were imprisoned, while others were banished from the country. Especially after 1787, when after a short period of hegemony of the Patriots, the reaction of the Orangistic-Reformed party forced many Patriots to go into exile, either voluntary or by the measures of the government. After the outbreak of the French Revolution (1789) and particularly from the moment (1795) when the French armies brought to the Netherlands the realization of the motto of the French Revolution, "Freedom, Equality, Brotherhood," the Patriots became the leading party in the Netherlands. But they soon had the disillusioning experience that the French occupation was no less harsh than the tyranny of the Orangists had been, and many Patriot leaders, disappointed with the new situation, soon withdrew from the local and general offices.

In the Patriot movement there were a large number of Mennonites and many, including Mennonite preachers, were among the leaders. The Mennonites were now for the first time in the Netherlands permitted to hold a public office. It was a consequence of this situation that many then gave up the principle of nonresistance and took up arms. Franciscus Adrianus van der Kemp (*q.v.*), for example, a Mennonite pastor at Leiden, became an officer of a voluntary corps and in nearly every congregation many members joined the free corps. It should, however, be emphatically stated that not all Mennonites then renounced the old principle of nonresistance, as there were also some strict opponents of Patriotism among the Dutch Mennonites, as for example, Pastor Jacob Ouwejans (*q.v.*) of Rotterdam and the banker Archibald Hope in Amsterdam. Particularly in the district of Twenthe, in the Zaan region, and in Friesland, the Mennonites enthusiastically co-operated with the Patriots. Pieter Bel and Pieter Houttuyn, both deacons of the Mennonite congregation in Hoorn, fled to Brussels in 1788 to escape the revenge of the Orange party. Pieter Vreede of Leiden took an active part in the revolution (January 1795); in Friesland it was Pier Zeper of Leeuwarden, later treasurer of the Mennonite conference in Friesland, who upon orders from the *Comité Revolutionair* traveled about in Friesland (February 1795) to dismiss the magistrates who had been in sympathy with the Orangists. Among the first Mennonites to take office were Jan Bernard Blijdenstein in Enschedé and the Mennonite minister of Boven-Knijpe, A. S. Cuperus, while pastor J. H. Floh (*q.v.*) of Enschedé in 1796 became a delegate in the National Assembly and in 1798 its secretary. Many Mennonites were chosen members of the provisional governments, both local and provincial. Rutger Jansz Schimmelpenninck (*q.v.*), who in 1796 became the Grand Pensionary and president of the National Assembly of the Netherlands, stemmed from a well-known Mennonite family. Among the Patriot leaders were the following Mennonite pastors: Petrus Loosjes (*q.v.*) of Haarlem, who with his brother Cornelis Loosjes was editor of *Vaderlandsche Let-*

teroefeningen, a periodical which, founded in 1816, did much to spread the Patriot views; Nicolaas Klopper (*q.v.*) of Harlingen, Andries Scheltes Cuperus (*q.v.*) of Bovenknijpe, Sybren Hofstra of Workum, Jelle Sipkes van Teern (*q.v.*) of IJlst, Abrahams Staal of Leeuwarden, who was forced to give up his ministry, Gerardus ten Cate of Almelo, and Arend Hendrik van Gelder of Zaandam. vDZ.

N. van der Zijpp, *Geschiedenis der Doopsgezinden in Nederland* (Arnhem, 1952) 189, 252; J. Hartog, *De Patriotten en Oranje* (Amsterdam, 1882); J. C. van Slee, *De Rijnsburger Collegianten* (Haarlem, 1895) *passim; Inv. Arch. Amst.* II, 2, No. 178; *DB* 1881, 52 f.; 1909, 70-91; 1912, 107-12; *DJ* 1931, 112-15; 1951, 63 f.

Paturatte, La, in the Bernese Jura, Switzerland. Here in the fields is found a Mennonite school, founded in 1900 by Elder Samuel Gerber of the Sonnenberg (*q.v.*) congregation. In 1955 the schoolroom was remodeled. It is a private school, run without state aid; the number of children was 16 in 1956; teacher is Samuel Gerber. vDZ.

Mennonitisches Jahrbuch (Newton, 1952) 5-11; *Der Mennonit* IX (1956) No. 7, 105.

Paul I, Emperor of Russia 1796-1801, the son of Peter III and Catherine II, was crowned on Nov. 17, 1796, at the age of 42, and murdered on March 2, 1801, by a conspiracy of Count Pahlen. He gave the Mennonites the well-known letter of protection of Sept. 6, 1800. (Friesen, *Brüderschaft,* 90; *ML* III, 337.) NEFF.

Paulding County (Ohio) Mennonite settlement, now extinct, was located in the vicinity of the present village of Junction, eight miles northeast of Paulding. Frederick Geiger of the Putnam Co., Ohio, Swiss Mennonite settlement was attracted to the vicinity in 1862 because of the large amount of uncut timber. He operated a sawmill here and purchased tracts of timber, cleared them and resold the land at a profit. Members of the Hilty, Augsburger, Bandy, and Kemler families from the Putnam County settlement moved there in the next few years. Bishop John Thut of the Riley Creek Mennonite Church (later called Zion Mennonite Church), located about three miles west of Bluffton, Ohio, made several visits to this new settlement, holding services in the homes of various members. Likely other ministers from near-by Mennonite churches also paid occasional visits. Since no Mennonite minister settled here, Frederick Geiger and most of the other settlers returned to the Putnam County settlement in the 1870's. The Kemlers and Bandys remained but were lost to the Mennonite Church. D.L.G.

J. Umble, "Early Mennonite Sunday Schools of Northwestern Ohio: II. Zion (Bluffton) congregation," *MQR* V, No. 3 (July 1931) 182-84; D. L. Gratz, *Bernese Anabaptists* (Scottdale, 1953) 159-60.

Paul(l)ewitz (Pawlovitz; Czech, *Pavlovice*), situated in a valley surrounded by vineyards, a little off the highway, half way between Auspitz and Kostel. The Hutterian Brethren opened a Bruderhof here on the lands of the Baron of Lipa, a house having been purchased in the spring of 1545 by Jakob Seckler, in which "the tall Matthes" served as the first householder. During the persecution of 1547 it was

probably abandoned with the rest; it was not likely reopened, for it is nowhere mentioned again. P.DE.

Beck, *Geschichts-Bücher;* Wolkan, *Geschicht-Buch;* Zieglschmid, *Chronik;* Gr. Wolny, *Kirchliche Topographie von Mähren,* Part II: *Brünner Erzdiözese* II (Brno, 1858) 114 f.; *ML* III, 338.

Pauls (Pauels, Pauwels, Paulsen), a family name common among Mennonites of Prusso-Russian background which was found in the Danzig and Prussian Mennonite churches as early as 1621; e.g., Thiensdorf, Orloff, Danzig, Elbing, Königsberg, Montau-Gruppe, Kazun, and Heubuden. The origin of the name is Paul-sen (son). Heinrich Pauls was a minister of the Mennonite Church in Galicia. Jacob M. Pauls is coelder of the Bergthal Mennonite Church of Manitoba and Wilhelm Pauls is the founder of the Didsbury Bible School, Alberta, and a minister. (Reimer, *Familiennamen.*) C.K.

Paulsheim, a Mennonite congregation in the volost of Gnadenfeld in the Molotschna (*q.v.*), South Russia, established in 1852. (*ML* III, 338.) E.C.

Paulus van Drunen (Druynen), a goldsmith and an Anabaptist elder and martyr, was burned at the stake for the sake of his faith with three other Anabaptists, Michiel Stevens of Oosterhout, Jan Block of Gent, and Adriaen of The Hague, at Vught near 's Hertogenbosch in the Dutch province of North Brabant on Sept. 9, 1538. They had been muzzled before the execution. Two days later four other members of the congregation at 's Hertogenbosch or Vught, of which Paulus van Drunen was the bishop, were put to death; viz., Neelken (the wife of Paulus van Drunen), Jan van Capel, Lysken (the wife of Jan Block), and Geertken Erasmusdochter, of Maastricht. The source of van Braght's report in the *Martyrs' Mirror* was "an old writing" from Friesland. The *Martyrs' Mirror* speaks of 10-17 persons who died as martyrs at Vught at that time. The history has been clarified by Karel Vos in *Doopsgezinde Bijdragen,* 1917. (*Mart. Mir.* D 41, E 447; *DB* 1917, 114, No. 39, and 186 ff., 189; *ML* III, 337.) vDZ.

Paulus Harrouts, an Anabaptist martyr of Somerdijk, i.e., Sommelsdijk (*q.v.*), burned at the stake at Zierikzee, Dutch province of Zeeland, on Dec. 7, 1540, because he did not believe the Catholic doctrine of transubstantiation. (*DB* 1908, 106; *ML* II, 257.) NEFF.

Paulus (Pouwel) **van Meenen** (Paulus van Tielt), a Mennonite elder who was active in Flanders, Belgium, from about 1565. About his private life little is known. He was born at Meenen (Menin) of a prominent family; in 1605 he was still living, then being an elder at Haarlem, Holland. His name is mentioned by some martyrs who had been baptized by him. He was apparently very active in preaching and baptizing. Hans Alenson (*BRN* VII, 215) reported that after the Frisian-Flemish schism of 1566 Paulus van Meenen sided with the Flemish branch, but took a strict position concerning banning. A letter written in prison by Jacob de Rore (*q.v.*) to Paulus van Meenen (found in van Braght's *Mart. Mir.* D 465-68, E 809-12) reveals that Paulus had asked the opinion of his co-elder de Rore as to banning and shunning. De Rore answered by admonishing Paulus van Meenen not to force the issue of the practice of avoidance.   vᴅZ.

K. Vos, "De Doopsgezinden te Antwerpen in de zestiende eeuw," in *Bulletin . . . d'Histoire de Belgique* LXXXIV (Brussels, 1920) 358 f., 377; Verheyden, "Mennonitism in Flanders," ms.

Paulus, Nikolaus (1853-1930), a German Catholic theologian and historian, was chaplain in Molsheim 1878-83, curate in Munich in 1885, wrote among other things the book *Protestantismus und Toleranz im 16. Jahrhundert* (Freiburg, 1911), with strong polemics showing the complete intolerance of the reformers, Lutheran as well as Zwinglian or Calvinist. The objections of Protestant secular and church historians could not invalidate the facts presented by Paulus; especially as Ernst Troeltsch's *Soziallehren der christlichen Kirchen und Gruppen* (Tübingen, 1912) created a generally favorable attitude toward the sects and free churches. Also the *Bilder und Führergestalten aus dem Täufertum* by Wilhelm Wiswedel (2 vv., Kassel, 1930) adopted much from Paulus. (*ML* III, 337.) E.T.

Paulus van Tielt: see **Paulus van Meenen.**

Paur (Baur), **Thomas,** a member of the Anabaptist congregation in Augsburg (*q.v.*), Bavaria, Germany, about 1527, in whose home in the Antoni house on the Honoltzburg their religious services were held. At his home Jörg Nespitzer (*q.v.*), Eucharius Binder (*q.v.*), Leonhard Schiemer (*q.v.*), and Hans Hut (*q.v.*) went in and out, and at times lived there. With the exception of Hut, they were all related by marriage.   HEGE.

Fr. Roth, *Augsburgs Reformationsgeschichte* I (2d ed., Munich, 1901) 232; *ML* III, 337.

Pausram, a market village about four miles from Auspitz, Moravia, in which Philip Blay, a tile maker from Vaihingen, united with the Hutterian Brethren in August 1538, who settled in a house and small vineyard belonging to him. During the persecution of 1547 the Bruderhof had to be abandoned, but when the persecution subsided it was rebuilt on a larger scale. Here the deacon Michael Kern died in 1561, and the preacher Christian Zwickh, called Dietl, a native of Tirol, on Sept. 18, 1580; "he knew Latin well." The property had by this time grown considerably, the Brethren owning nine gardens in one division and four in another, then nine *Gewand* fields with meadows and forests, besides their house, and in addition a polishing and grinding equipment, a fulling machine, a tannery, and a grain mill, for which they paid their baron, Friedrich von Zierotin, an annual rent of fifty-two florins and thirty-two Moravian crowns. Friedrich von Zierotin also owned the land of the colonies in Selowitz (*q.v.*), Pohrlitz (*q.v.*), Nusslau (*q.v.*), Nikolschitz (*q.v.*), and Pribitz (*q.v.*), which housed about 3,000 Huterian Brethren. In Pausram they also had a spa, which was widely known among the Moravian nobility. In this Bruderhof Karl von Zierotin (*q.v.*) dined on Nov. 4, 1588, with his uncle Friedrich, who was a patient at the spa, and whom the Brethren called "our Fritz" because of his benev

olence toward them. In Pausram occurred the death of the deacons Noah Weiss, March 30, 1606; Hans Summer, Sept. 23, 1611; and exactly two years later Philipp Ferber. In December 1620 the Brethren who fled from the destroyed Bruderhofs of Pribitz, Pohrlitz, Maskowitz (*q.v.*), and Niemtschitz (*q.v.*) sought refuge here. In May 1621 the imperial armies came to Pausram; the soldiers took "from the craftsmen and here and there in the house by force what they liked." The captain confiscated the wine; the seven barrels were "drunk up in half a day and all kinds of arbitrariness took place thereby." In Pausram a meeting of all the preachers, householders, buyers, and distributors was held on Feb. 21, 1622, in which the previous Vorsteher Rudolf Hirzel (*q.v.*) was expelled with Burckhart Braitenstainer (*q.v.*) and also Christoph Hirzel in spite of the threats of Cardinal Dietrichstein (*q.v.*)—for betraying the hiding place of the buried money, and Valentin Winter (*q.v.*) was appointed as elder. A few months later Pausram was abandoned.   P.Dᴇ.

Beck, *Geschichts-Bücher;* Fr. Hruby, "Die Wiedertäufer in Mähren," in *Archiv für Kunde österreichischer Geschichtsquellen* III (1850) 72 f.; *ML* III, 337 f.

Pauw (Paauw, Pau, Pou, Pouw), a Dutch Mennonite family, originally living at De Rijp, province of North Holland, where Cornelis Jacobs Pauw (d. 1730) was a deacon of the Waterlander Mennonite congregation. He was probably a member of the Reformed Church, and joined the Mennonites in 1705 with his second wife. A number of his descendants, some of whom settled at Purmerend, were deacons at De Rijp and Purmerend. Ysbrand Arisz Pau(w) (d. July 24, 1793), a son of Aris Jacob Pauw and Neeltje Mars, of De Rijp, was a lay preacher of the Barsingerhorn-Wieringerward congregation in 1783-93.   vᴅZ.

N. H. Slinger, *Het Doopsgezind geslacht Pauw* (Alkmaar, 1938); *Naamlijst* 1794, 63.

Pauwel, an elder of the Frisian Mennonite congregation of Danzig, West Prussia, is mentioned in two letters by Elder Jan Gerrits (*q.v.*), written to the Dutch Waterlander Elder Hans de Ries (*q.v.*) in 1612. By the time of the second of these letters, undated, Pauwel had apparently died. The letter says he is said to have been an excellent leader under whose influence the congregation became prosperous, peaceable, able, and tolerant. The first letter, dated Aug. 25, mentions the death of Elder Simon Martensz and a severe illness of Elder Paulus Bussemaker. If the Pauwel of the second letter is identical with Paulus Bussemaker (*q.v.*), which seems to be the case, the article **Bussemaker** (*ME* I, 485) must include the fact that Bussemaker, having been excommunicated by the Flemish, joined the Frisian congregation at Danzig, and served among them as an elder until his death in 1612. (*Inv. Arch. Amst.* II, Nos. 2925 f.)   vᴅZ.

Pauwels, Pieter, an elder of the Dutch Reformed church at Norwich, England, who wrote a book against the Mennonites. This book, enlarged and corrected, was edited by Herman Moded (*q.v.*) under the title *Grondich bericht, Van de ereste beghinselen der Wederdoopsche Seckten . . .* (Middelburg, 1603). (*N.N.B.Wb.* III, 872.)   vᴅZ.

Pauwels de Roovere, of Leuven (Louvain) in Belgium, a Catholic priest at Heverlee, Flanders, was arrested and imprisoned at Brussels, Belgium, in 1543; in August of this year he was degraded because of heresy and sentenced to life imprisonment in the castle of Vilvoorde. Further information about his fate is lacking. Though the case is not clear and it is not known what the nature of de Roovere's heresy was, it is very probable that it was Anabaptism. (Verheyden, *Courtrai-Bruxelles,* 62 f., No. 11.) vdZ.

Pauwels Vermaete, an Anabaptist martyr, was born about 1498 at Sluis, Dutch province of Zeeland. He was a widower and a basketmaker at Gistel, Flanders, Belgium, and a preacher of the Mennonite congregation of Brugge (*q.v.*). He had been baptized in 1537 or 1538 by Jan van Tricht (*q.v.*) or Jan Matthijsz van Middelburg (*q.v.*). He was seized with a number of members when a meeting of the congregation held near Brugge was surprised by the officials and he was imprisoned for some time. It is said that when he was arrested he had a New Testament, a book containing the Psalms of David, and a martyrbook(?), which were taken away from him. During the examination by the inquisitors he remained steadfast. Together with Martin van de Walle, Jehan de la Beecke, and Hansken van den Brouck he suffered martyrdom at Brugge on Oct. 15, 1558. His daughter Calleken Vermaete, 18 years old, recanted. (Verheyden, *Brugge,* 45, No. 27; *idem, Mennonitism in Flanders, Ms.*) vdZ.

Pavlodar, a town located on the right bank of the Irtysh River of the Pavlodar Region, formerly Semipalatinsk Region, now in Kazakh SSR, Soviet Central Asia, 180 miles northwest of Semipalatinsk, had a population of 20,000 during World War II. The town is located in an agricultural region and on a railroad half way between Akmolinsk and Barnaul.

Near Pavlodar a Mennonite settlement (*q.v.*) originated in 1906. The city was the primary center of the settlement from the beginning. Later the city of Slavgorod (*q.v.*) also gained some significance for some of the Mennonite villages closer to this city. Originally primarily Tatars and Russian businessmen lived in Pavlodar. Because of the good transportation facilities on the Irtysh River, the city developed into a business center. Among the Mennonites who established businesses in the city were Driedger and Voth, who dealt in general merchandise and agricultural machinery. Heinz Görzen had a large steam-driven flour mill, while Schartner and Schmidt maintained a "hotel." Franz F. Fröse was the director of the high school (Gymnasium) of the city of Pavlodar in 1923. It can be assumed that more Mennonites have settled in Pavlodar since World War II. C.K.

Pavlodar Mennonite Brethren Church was organized in the Pavlodar Mennonite settlement (*q.v.*), located in the Semipalatinsk Region, now Kazakh SSR, Soviet Central Asia. Very little information about the organization, development, and religious life of the group is available. The *Adressbüchlein* (1913) by D. H. Epp does not list the congregations. According to Gerhard Fast, the Pavlodar M.B. group

was originally without a minister but met in the home of Johann Janzen. Later Jakob Kröker became the elder, assisted by Johann Voth. A simple adobe meetinghouse was built in the village of Rovnopolye, Taldy-Kuduk. Some difficulties are reported about the two ministers, who were both excommunicated. They were succeeded by Johann Dekker and Jakob Kirsch.

In the Musde-Kul district the Mennonites and the Mennonite Brethren worshiped together in the home of Abraham Unruh. After a revival a baptismal service was held in the M.B. Church, at which 28 were baptized and Unruh was ordained minister, and later elder. Later Jakob Wiens joined this group as minister. In the 1920's Aron Reimer was ordained elder of the Pavlodar M.B. Church. Later Franz Friesen and Daniel Heide were also ordained elders. Both emigrated to Canada in 1925. After this Heinrich M. Janzen was ordained elder; he emigrated to Canada in 1929.

Unser Blatt (October 1926, p. 24) gives a report about a song festival held in the Pavlodar settlement. Five M.B. choirs participated, two coming from Slavgorod, and one from a neighboring Russian church. It can be assumed that this active religious life, typical of the Mennonite congregations in 1924-27, was soon thwarted by the Soviet attack on all organized religious activities. Whether it has ceased or continued on a reduced basis to be revived since 1953 is not known. C.K.

A. H. Unruh, *Die Geschichte der Mennoniten-Brüdergemeinde* (Winnipeg, 1954) 204 (not reliable), 368; Gerhard Fast, *In den Steppen Sibiriens* (Rosthern, 1957) 144 ff.

Pavlodar Mennonite Church originated in the Pavlodar Mennonite settlement (*q.v.*) of the Semipalatinsk Region, now Kazakh SSR, Soviet Central Asia. Very little information is available on the organization, development, membership, and religious life of this church and settlement. In 1925 the total population of the settlement was 2,736. D. H. Epp's *Adressbüchlein* of 1913 names Jakob G. Wiens as the elder of this church in 1913; Wiens kept the church records of all of the main churches of the area. The following affiliated churches or districts and ministers are listed: (1) Rayevka with Abram A. Unruh, (2) Nadarovka with Abraham D. Pötkau, (3) Rovnopol with Jakob F. Kröker, (4) Borissovka with Johann J. Epp.

In addition to this church with its branches, Epp lists two more Pavlodar Mennonite churches: Sabarovka with Johann J. Wiens as minister, and Steinfeld at an earlier date with Johann F. Kröker as minister. Kröker was graduated from the Bethel College Academy at Newton, Kan., in 1899, attended the St. Chrischona Bible School near Basel, Switzerland, and went to India as a missionary (GCM) in 1900. Because of ill health he returned to Russia in 1909, where he served as Reiseprediger (*q.v.*) including the Pavlodar Mennonite Church. Gerhard Fast (p. 151) lists the following ministers: Peter Wiens, Sabarovka; Harder, Sofiyevka; Johann F. Kröker, Rebrovka.

Unser Blatt reports that a baptismal service was held in the church of Halbstadt in the Tas-Kuduk district by the elder, Johann F. Kröker, in 1926.

Choirs of two churches participated, after which the Lord's Supper was observed. During the second holiday a song festival took place in a shed of Jakob Janzen, the leading minister of the Olgino Mennonite Church, in which seven choirs—three of the Olgino Mennonite Church, two of the Konstantinovka Mennonite Church, one of the Borissovka Mennonite Brethren Church, and one of the Rovnopol Mennonite Brethren Church—participated. A similar report was given by Susi Kröker for 1927 (*Unser Blatt*, III, 92). The ministers assisting Kröker on these occasions were Jakob Jansen, Schartner, Bergen, J. Wiens, and Decker. Places of worship are listed on these occasions at Halbstadt, Gnadental, and Olgino.

Judging by general developments, this was no doubt one of the last organized religious activities in the community. The fate of the ministers is not known. Little information is available as to the resumption of worship services and religious activities.

C.K.

Gerhard Fast, *In den Steppen Sibiriens* (Rosthern, 1957); *Unser Blatt*, I (1925) 314; II, 24; III, 11, 92; *Der praktische Landwirt*, 1925-27.

Pavlodar Mennonite Settlement is located in the Pavlodar Region, formerly Semipalatinsk Region, Kazakh SSR in Soviet Central Asia (*q.v.*), formerly Siberia. This settlement was established in 1906 by Mennonites coming from the various European settlements. The first settler to come to this area was David Cornies, who bought the equivalent of three quarters of a section of land on the Irtysh River near the city of Pavlodar. He and his family left Melitopol, Ukraine, on April 13, 1906, and traveled by train to Omsk, Siberia. Here they embarked on a ship and arrived at the city of Pavlodar on May 9. The distance between Omsk and Pavlodar is approximately 342 miles. The first settlement, Rebrovka, was established on the west side of the Irtysh River on purchased land opposite Pavlodar, which is located on the east side. During the 1920's the village Rebrovka was transplanted to the east side of the Irtysh in the vicinity of the Mennonite villages of Tursun-Bay and Mosde-Kul. The rest of the land was located on the right side of the Irtysh and was obtained through the government free of charge similar to that of the Slavgorod settlement. The land was sandy. When the settlers came they found no trees. They raised wheat, oats, barley, linseed, and watermelons in abundance.

Pavlodar had some advantage over the Slavgorod settlement in that some of the settlers were located only some 15 miles from the city and thus had an easy access to market. During World War I, when the Pavlodar-Kulunda-Slavgorod-Tatarsk railroad was built, contact was established with the Trans-Siberian Railroad, which increased the market and traveling facilities of the settlers considerably. Most of the settlers were poor and the pioneering difficulties were great. The winter was severe and the summer hot and dusty. The Mennonites planted trees around their homes. When P. F. Froese visited the settlement during the summer of 1924 he stated that a Mennonite settlement could be recognized from a great distance. He describes four types of villages in the area. The native Kirghiz population

lives during the summer in a special summer aul, and during the winter in a dugout. The Russian village consists of whitewashed adobe houses without any trees or shrubs. The Mennonite houses were also built of adobe or unburned brick patterned after their European architectural styles, but they were surrounded by trees. Most of the surrounding population was Kirghiz.

In addition to Rebrovka there were four groups (*uchastki*) of villages: (1) *Tas-Kuduk* was located 15 miles east of the Irtysh near Pavlodar and consisted of Gnadental, Steinfeld, and Halbstadt. (2) *Taldy-Kuduk* was located 20 miles east of the Irtysh and consisted of Konstantinovka and Rovnopolye. (3) *Tursun-Bay,* located 50 miles east of the Irtysh, consisted of Nadarovka, Reinfeld (Tchistopolye), and Olgino. (4) *Mosde-Kul,* located 60 miles east of Pavlodar, consisted of Sabarovka, Sofieyevka, Dominskoye, and Rayevka.

The Mosde-Kul group of villages or settlement was the closest to the city of Slavgorod (*q.v.*), which these settlers used for marketing their products after the railroad had been completed by 1918.

The nomadic Kirghiz were accustomed to driving their herds of horses from one place to another. In the early days there were some misunderstandings, but soon they became acquainted and got along well. The Kirghiz would come to the Mennonites begging for bread, which they had never known before, since their diet was primarily confined to meat and milk. Some flour mills were established in the villages. Schools were conducted in every village, and worship services were held in private homes or in schools. The Mennonite Church and the Mennonite Brethren often worshiped together.

In 1925 the population of the Pavlodar settlement was 2,736. A report of the administration of the co-operative, named the Cornies-Verband (*Der praktische Landwirt* June-July, 1926, p. 8 ff.), gives an insight as to what happened to the settlement during the Revolution and after. It was doubtless very much the same picture as that described in connection with the Slavgorod Mennonite settlement (*q.v.*). Even in 1926 only eight of 12 village schools were operating because of lack of teachers, in spite of the fact that the settlement had a Zentralschule in Sabarovka started in 1918, which was supported by private individuals until 1924, at which time the Cornies-Verband took it over (see **Pavlodar Zentralschule**).

The Cornies-Verband was represented in all villages, and its 450 members constituted 90 per cent of the families. A report states that many had only one horse and some did not even have one cow. The primary objective of the co-operative was to obtain loans through the government to improve the seed and the cattle and do business for the community. Four dairies, one in each of the settlements, were in operation in 1925. The reporter reveals in his concluding remark that the Cornies-Verband was being influenced by the Marxian terminology when he stated, "We would like to urge all readers loyally and without weariness to continue the work of the co-operative so that we can achieve the goal desired by our forerunner, N. J. Lenin." Later all village schools of the Pavlodar settlement were functioning, and the level of the cultural and religious life rose once again.

Some Mennonites from European Russia probably joined the Pavlodar settlement during World War II and after. A letter written by Johann and M. Dück states that the "Memrik Mennonites who were evacuated were sent mostly to Pavlodar and the Altay regions" (*Bote,* April 4, 1956, p. 7). To what extent these evacuees were placed in the Mennonite villages of Pavlodar is not clear. About present conditions in the Pavlodar Mennonite settlement a letter by Agnetha Boldt reveals that many of those who were exiled during the Stalin regime have died, but those who have survived and are living there now are doing well ("es geht ihnen gut") (*Menn. Rundschau,* May 2, 1956, p. 5). C.K.

Gerhard Fast, *In den Steppen Sibiriens* (Rosthern, 1957); A. H. Unruh, *Die Geschichte der Mennoniten-Brüdergemeinde 1860-1954* (Winnipeg, 1954) 367; *Unser Blatt,* 1926-28, *passim; Der praktische Landwirt,* 1925-27; Helmut Anger, *Die Deutschen in Sibirien* . . . (Berlin, 1930); P. F. Froese, "Durch die Mennoniten-Dörfer in Sibirien" (A. A. Friesen collection, BeCL).

Pavlodar Zentralschule, located in the Pavlodar Mennonite settlement (*q.v.*), Sabarovka, Musde-Kul, was organized by F. F. Fröse of Slavgorod in 1918, privately sponsored and then taken over in 1924 by the Cornies-Verband. A farm of 324 acres was maintained to support this school. Plans were made to add an agricultural department to this secondary school. No information is available as to what happened to the school. C.K.

Gerhard Fast, *In den Steppen Sibiriens* (Rosthern, 1957) 152; *Der praktische Landwirt* (June-July 1926, p. 9).

Pax (Latin for "peace"), the term used to designate the foreign service for I-W men (conscientious objectors drafted into service by the United States Office of Selective Service) administered by the MCC. Established in 1951, Pax men have served in Germany since 1951 in building programs at Niederbieber near Neuwied, Espelkamp, Backnang near Stuttgart, Lübeck, Enkenbach near Kaiserslautern, Bechterdissen near Bielefeld, Wedel near Hamburg; in Vienna, Austria (1955-); in Crefeld; and in Algeria (1955-). The Algerian project has been administered by the Mennonite (MC) Relief and Service Committee of Elkhart, Ind. Pax construction has provided housing for 370 Mennonite refugee families in Germany, meetinghouses for the Mennonite congregations at Niederbieber, Backnang, Enkenbach, Wedel, and Bechterdissen; aid in rebuilding the bombed Protestant Karlsschule in Vienna, aid in constructing a community and youth center for the Crefeld Mennonite Church; and in Algeria some 30 homes for Arab refugees. Other major Pax projects include agricultural improvement in Panayitsa and Tsakones, two villages in northern Greece (1952-); flood cleanup work near Vlissingen, Holland (1953); service to Hungarian refugees in Austria (1956-57); Korean relief (1954-); road building in Peru (1954-) and the Paraguayan Chaco (1956-); various types of service in Jordan, Nepal, Viet-Nam, Liberia, and scattered individuals. A total of over 200 Pax men have served a period of two years (Europe) or three years

10

(Asia) overseas in all the projects. In 1958 the number in service was 110. A few men from Canada have been used in Pax, even though Canada has no draft. Pax has been financed in two ways: (1) by contributions of $75 per month by the Pax man or his denominational service office, or (2) by wages paid by certain employing agencies, such as the LeTourneau Foundation in Peru.

A similar service program for European conscientious objectors, called Eirene (Greek for "peace"), was established in 1957 by conjoint action of the MCC and the Brethren Service Committee. Its first project is one for agricultural improvement in Morocco. H.S.B.

Paxton Mennonite Brethren Church, located on the western prairies of Nebraska about 15 miles southwest of Paxton, was organized in 1919 by John J. Kliewer of Henderson, with H. C. Flaming as leader and a membership of 50. It at first met in a rural schoolhouse. This church has contributed much for missions. A church was built and a parsonage provided. Ministers who have served are H. C. Flaming, John K. Siemens, Geo. H. Jantzen, B. C. Willems, Henry Hooge, and Lavern Loewens. In 1958 the membership was 68, with Edwin A. Schmidt as pastor. H.E.W.

Pays de Gex, the customs-free zone in France just outside the western border of the Swiss city and canton of Geneva. A Mennonite congregation by this name was started in 1909 when Abraham Geiser, elder in the Chaux d'Abel (*q.v.*) Swiss Mennonite congregation, settled here near St. Genis, soon followed by several related families. Upon Geiser's death in 1926 his brother, Elder David Geiser in Chaux d' Abel, had the oversight of the congregation, with David Geiser-Glaus, a son of Abraham, as preacher 1929-40, and Abraham Sommer from 1931. The services were held in German for years in an upper room in a farmhouse of the Zbinden family. Later a Protestant chapel was secured in St. Genis, where the French language replaced the German.

Recently a part of the Pays de Gex congregation began to hold evangelistic services on an interdenominational basis in the city of Geneva in a building called Entr'aide. In 1954 this group ordained Abraham Sommer as elder, in 1956 Jean Sommer and Charles Zbinden as preachers, and Werner and Jean Geiser as missionary preachers. Soon Zbinden and Werner Geiser were made elders. The rest of the congregation continued in the traditional Mennonite way at St. Genis, where in 1957 Albert and Louis Zbinden and Willi Müller were ordained as preachers. No formal schism occurred, but in effect there are two congregations. In 1958 the membership was 64. S.G.

Pea Ridge (Mo.) Mennonite Church (MC), a member of the South Central Conference, located 12 miles west of Palmyra in Marion County, started as an outpost of the Palmyra congregation in 1903, was organized in 1905, when the meetinghouse was built. It burned down and was rebuilt in 1933. J. R. Shank was called to be the first pastor, assisted by Ira Buckwalter, ordained 1907. When Shank was called to Carver in 1908, J. W. Hess came to serve until 1919. In 1955 when Palmyra was dissolved, seven members joined Pea Ridge. In 1957 a new meetinghouse was erected. David A. Hathaway was the pastor, with 33 members.   M.L.K.

Peabody, Kan., originally known as Conesburg, is a town (pop. 1,400) located in the south central part of Marion County. It was incorporated March 15, 1878. Approximately 500 Mennonites live within shopping distance. The various branches are the Church of God in Christ Mennonites, Mennonite Brethren, General Conference Mennonites, Mennonite Church (MC). The C.G.C. group lives largely south of Peabody, the M.B. northwest, the G.C.M. south, and the M.C. north of Peabody.   G.G.Y.

Peace Committee (GCM). The Peace Committee of the General Conference Mennonite Church had its origin in the wake of World War I. At the 20th triennial session of the General Conference held in Meno, Okla., Sept. 2-7, 1914, a committee for the drafting of special provisions was appointed and directed to draft a message to the President of the United States to reaffirm its faith in the principles of peace and to give expression to its opposition to war. A resolution was introduced dealing with the question of conference action in case of actual war, but the importance of such a question was not perceived by the delegates, hence nothing further was done.

At the 21st session of the conference in 1917 a Committee of Seven, later known as the "Committee on Exemption," was appointed. The members of this committee were J. W. Kliewer, Chr., J. F. Lehman, Treas., S. K. Mosiman, Sec., M. H. Kratz, P. H. Richert, H. P. Krehbiel, and Peter Janzen. The work of this committee was limited because of travel difficulties, but individual members of the committee worked with the problems of conscientious objectors in camps and prisons. A Peace Committee of two, H. P. Krehbiel and A. J. Neuenschwander, was appointed at the 1926 conference session, which was active in conferences of pacifist churches and prepared quarterly Sunday-school lessons on peace. The committee was enlarged to three members at the 25th session in 1929, including A. J. Neuenschwander, H. P. Krehbiel, and A. S. Rosenberger, representing the west, middle, and east sections of the country. Since traveling distances made it difficult to carry on the work as a committee, much of the work was planned during the conference, and carried out by individual members working separately and through correspondence. Sunday-school lessons on peace continued and articles appeared in the church papers presenting the work of the Peace Committee. A step forward was taken at the 1933 session of conference when the committee was enlarged to include one member from each District Conference. This committee prepared a resolution embodying the statement of duties and functions of the Peace Committee. The purpose: "The Peace Committee shall in accord with directions of the Conference concern itself with the promotion of the cause of peace as taught and commanded by Jesus, our Lord, and His apostles, and as prophetically foretold in the Old Testament Scriptures."

The years 1926-35 were directed toward war pre-

vention and study conferences with various Christian groups. 1935-41 was marked by an adjustment to the likelihood of war and the consequent need for strengthening individual peace convictions as conscientious objectors. With these areas the committee concerned itself. During this period a literature series was printed: *Christian Peace: According to the New Testament Teaching Outside the Gospels* (1928), by Ernest J. Bohn; *Christian Peace: Four Hundred Years of Mennonite Principles and Practices of the Past Four Centuries* (1938), by C. Henry Smith; *War, Peace, Amity,* by H. P. Krehbiel; *A Brief Catechism on Difficult Questions,* by P. H. Richert; and the conference statement, *A Statement of the Position of the General Conference of the Mennonite Church of North America on Peace, War, Military Service and Patriotism,* adopted at Souderton, Pa., 1941. 1941-50 was a period of inter-Mennonite co-operation through the medium of the Mennonite Central Committee, especially in the Civilian Public Service program of World War II and the Voluntary Service program following the war. This period is also marked by the sense of need for a more aggressive teaching program on peace. A study guide, *The Power of Love,* and Young People's Union Program helps, besides articles in tract form and in the church papers, were published to promote peace education.

The Peace Committee, together with several other service committees, was merged into a larger board, the Board of Christian Service, at the 1950 General Conference, Freeman, S.D.   A.N.

Peace Problems Committee, an important standing committee of the Mennonite General Conference (MC) since 1919, with a membership varying from five at the beginning to six 1925-39, and ten to sixteen since 1939, successor to the Military Problems Committee of 1907-19. It had a United States and a Canadian Section 1925-55. Chairmen have been Aaron Loucks 1919-25, E. L. Frey 1925-35, H. S. Bender 1935- . Orie O. Miller was a long-time secretary 1925-53. Among the long-term Canadian members have been S. F. Coffman 1925-49 and J. B. Martin 1929- . The committee adopted a three point program in 1925: (1) peace and nonresistance education in the church; (2) representation to government in matters affecting military training and service and recognition for conscientious objectors, and (3) the peace witness to other Christians. It has co-operated vigorously with the MCC Peace Section to which it has belonged from the beginning in 1942. It has been an active and influential committee since 1925, and among other things has published or edited a considerable number of pamphlets and books on peace and nonresistance. It has sponsored several important study conferences. H.S.B.

Peace River, Alberta, Old Colony Mennonite settlement, located in a very fertile farming area, was started in 1932 near Carajou by several families from the Saskatoon, Sask., area who moved in 1934 near Fort Vermilion, a small trading post on the banks of the Peace River, some 350 miles north of Edmonton. It expanded rapidly after 1937 and by 1948 had a population of nearly 400, of whom about one third were dissatisfied settlers from the Old

Colony settlement in Mexico. The settlers live on scattered farms, not in villages nor in a compact block. The settlers are grouped in three districts—Rosenfeld, Blumenort, and Rhineland, each with a meetinghouse and preacher. The colony has continued to grow in size and in economic prosperity. The Church of God in Christ, Mennonite, maintains a mission station about 60 miles east of Fort Vermilion. H.S.B.

John A. Hostetler, "Pioneering in the Land of the Midnight Sun," *Menn. Life* III (April 1948) 5-8.

Peace Section of the Mennonite Central Committee was established in January 1942, as successor to the Mennonite Central Peace Committee organized in 1939. It is composed of delegated representatives of the peace committees of the constituent conferences, or in lieu of such, the regular conference MCC members, plus the MCC Executive Secretary ex officio, and two members at large. It functions through an executive committee of five and a full-time executive secretary with office at the MCC headquarters in Akron, Pa. J. Harold Sherk was a long-time executive secretary 1950-58. H. S. Bender has served as chairman continuously from 1942 (1939). The Peace Section has two representatives on the International Mennonite Peace Committee.

The Peace Section has served as an agency for counseling on problems related to conscription and the draft, a representation to government, a center for study, research, and writing regarding the peace position, and a central agency for peace education.

During the years of World War II the Peace Section endeavored to implement the convictions of Mennonites in regard to wartime measures such as Civilian Defense, Red Cross work, and the purchasing of war bonds. For the latter measure the Civilian Bond plan was arranged as a substitute. A counseling service on problems related to the draft was organized. To strengthen the constituency on the Biblical position regarding peace and nonresistance *Must Christians Fight* and *Compromise with War* were published.

The continuation of wartime measures, such as conscription, in the postwar period increased the concerns and activities of the Peace Section. The counseling service for drafted men continued, contacts with government were renewed, the National Service Board for Religious Objectors (NSBRO) continued to function. Besides pamphlet literature two new publications appeared: *The Christian and Conscription* and *Before You Decide*. An increasing concern of the Peace Section related to a testimony to Mennonites abroad. To implement this concern commissioners were sent both to Europe and to the Mennonite colonies in Brazil and Paraguay. Beginning with 1947 a full- or part-time representative has been maintained in Europe. Beginning in 1948 for several years the Peace Section sponsored annual summer peace teams and peace institutes in Europe. *Must Christians Fight* was twice translated into German.

The Peace Section has also maintained a special commissioner in Japan since September 1955: Melvin Gingerich to 1957, and Paul Peachey 1957- .

The Peace Section has been influential in unifying and strengthening the nonresistant position and peace testimony of the Mennonites of North America, and promoting a more vigorous testimony abroad both inside and outside the Mennonite brotherhood. H.S.B.

Peachey Amish Mennonite Church, Belleville, Pa., had two congregations in 1957 with 100 members in the Upper District and 126 in the Lower District. Jesse D. Spicher was bishop of these two Beachy Amish congregations. M.G.

Peake Mennonite Church (MC), located 2 miles northwest of Hinton, Va., a rural mission church of the Middle District of the Virginia Conference, began in 1915, when a Sunday school was organized in a schoolhouse in this highland area. A congregation was established in 1923. Kent Shank and Joseph A. Brunk, active Sunday-school workers, asked permission of the Middle District Council to build the meetinghouse. This was granted if the necessary funds could be raised. H. B. Keener followed by Snively Martin served as pastors of this church for many years; James Shank served here 1947-57. Dewitt Heatwole was the pastor in 1958 with a membership of 47. H.A.B.

Peckh, Hans, an Anabaptist imprisoned in the castle at Passau, Lower Bavaria, Germany. At his cross-examination he confessed that he was baptized by Blasy Khumauf (Blasius Kuhn, *q.v.*) and lived in Greding near Aichstetten; that he had been imprisoned once before, at Eggenburg in Lower Austria; there he was branded by burning through the cheeks and released. He is not to be confused with the Hans Peckh named on page 74 of Wolkan's edition of the *Geschicht-Buch*. But he was no doubt in the group mentioned on page 105 of this chronicle, which was migrating to Moravia in 1533 under Brother Bastl Glaser. "When they arrived in Austria in a village called Hohenwart they were seized. To them Jacob Hutter wrote a beautiful consolatory epistle, which is still extant. They were then taken from Eggenburg, after they had been branded through the cheeks and released." Certainly Hans Peckh was among them.

Hans Peckh was immovable. The authorities were unable to "convert" him in Passau. The court record reports, "he remained firm." (See also **Beck, Hans.**) W.W.

Beck, *Geschichts-Bücher*, 116; Wolkan, *Geschicht-Buch*, 105; Zieglschmid, *Chronik*, 142; *ML* I, 148; III, 339.

Peckstal(l): see **Pöggstall.**

Pedro de Soza, an Anabaptist martyr: see **Peter of Spain.**

Peecke Vulckezoon (name apparently mutilated), an Anabaptist martyr, burned at the stake on July 19, 1550, at Leeuwarden, capital of the Dutch province of Friesland, because "he had been rebaptized and held a bad opinion of the holy sacraments." Further particulars are lacking. vDZ.

J. Reitsma, *Honderd jaren uit de Geschiedenis der Hervorming . . . in Friesland* (Leeuwarden, 1876) 63.

Peeter (Peter) **Mouwe** (Monde), an Anabaptist martyr, a native of Tours in Touraine, France, was beheaded on March 12, 1535, at Antwerp, Belgium. Further information is lacking. (*Antw. Arch.-Blad* VII, 318, 366; XIV, 12 f., No. 137.)   vDZ.

Peeter Symonsz: see Peter Simons.

Pehuajó, Argentina. After making investigating trips practically all over the Republic of Argentina, J. W. Shank and T. K. Hershey, Mennonite (MC) missionaries, began missionary activities in Pehuajó, a city about 250 miles southwest of Buenos Aires. On Feb. 23, 1919, the first Sunday school was conducted with 18 present. On March 6 a hall was rented, and on April 27, the first evangelistic meetings began. Seven new members were instructed and on October 10 baptized. In January 1920 a lot was purchased on which there were two tin shops and a dwelling house. These were remodeled and are still used for the home of the workers and the clinic. In 1923 a church with basement was built. In 1930 a five-room dwelling was built to accommodate additional workers. Practically all of the institutional work was opened in Pehuajó. The orphanage began to function in May 1926 with 12 beds. It was later transferred to Trenque Lauquen and still later to Bragado. The Gospel Printery, purchased in February 1927, began to operate in one of the original tin shops; it has been moved to Trenque Lauquen. The Bible school, organized in 1928, had its beginning in Pehuajó with the local pastor in charge. It was officially organized in 1928. Some of the present national workers were among the first graduates. The Bible institute is now located in Bragado. In 1919 the first kindergarten was begun and Bible reading organized in the homes. Five of the first seven baptized became the first kindergarten teachers and Bible readers.

The missionary activities in Pehuajó are preaching services, young people's meetings, literary society, and visitation work. Most of the people who attend these services represent the working class. Some business and professional men are the product of the Pehuajó congregation. The financial contributions of the church membership show a gradual increase from 11.45 pesos in 1919 to 2,992.55 in 1947.

On Jan. 1, 1948, the records show that 199 have been baptized. Of this number 22 died, 76 moved away (many of whom are members elsewhere), 35 withdrew, and 5 were excommunicated. In 1957 the membership was 58.

The missionaries who have had pastoral oversight are D. Parke Lantz, Nelson Litwiller, L. S. Weber, J. W. Shank, Amos Swartzentruber, T. H. Brenneman, T. K. Hershey, and William Hallman.
          T.K.H.

Peisker, Christoph, a furrier of Quedlinburg, a very successful Anabaptist missionary in Thuringia and Hesse, Germany. Nothing else is known about his life. (See **Christoph** of Meissen; *ML* III, 339.)
          NEFF.

Peisker (Peissger, Peissker, also Döring), **Hans,** an Anabaptist martyr, a miller of Kleinreutersdorf near Orlamünde, Thuringia, Germany, baptized by Melchior Rink (*q.v.*). In his home an Anabaptist meeting was surprised by the police on Nov. 20, 1535. Sixteen persons attending, including Hans Peisker and his daughter Margarethe, were led away prisoners. He bade his wife, who was awaiting the birth of a child, a moving farewell. With four other brethren he was imprisoned in Jena and subjected to a cross-examination under Melanchthon (*q.v.*) and Cruciger (*q.v.*) on Dec. 1. He remained steadfast and was executed with Heinz Kraut (*q.v.*) and Jobst Möller (*q.v.*) on Jan. 26, 1536, at Jena. (Wappler, *Thüringen,* 137-41, *passim; ML* III, 339.)
          NEFF.

Peitz, Hans, an Anabaptist martyr, who died in prison at Passau, Lower Bavaria, Germany, in 1537, is undoubtedly identical with Hans Betz (*q.v.*). (*Mart. Mir.* D 41, E 447.)   NEFF.

Pekela (named for the river Pekel-A). Oude Pekela and Nieuwe Pekela are two adjoining villages in the Dutch province of Groningen, which were founded in the first half of the 17th century, after the peat-moors around the Pekel-A had been dug away and a fertile soil appeared, suited for agriculture. Among the founders of Pekela there were apparently some Mennonites, because as early as about 1660 there was a Danzig Old Flemish (*q.v.*) Mennonite congregation at Pekela. This congregation, always small in membership, was until about 1750 served by preachers chosen from the congregation. Hendrik Wolters was its preacher until about 1750; in 1747 he and his wife Jantje Coops Boon made arrangements that a room in their farm home would in the future be at the disposal of the congregation as it had been until then. From about 1750 until shortly before 1780, when the pulpit was vacant, it was served by Jan Panneman, preacher or elder of the Danzig Old Flemish congregation at neighboring Sappemeer (*q.v.*). Panneman may have moved to Pekela, for his descendants, called Panman, are still found there. Soon after 1780 the Pekela congregation declined or even died out. At least by 1815 there was no longer a congregation (*Naamlijst* 1815, 107), though a number of Mennonites were living both in Oude and Nieuwe Pekela. A new congregation was founded at Pekela in 1851, and a church built, which was dedicated on Sept. 19, 1852. The congregation has always been served by the pastor of Veendam (*q.v.*). In 1900 the baptized membership numbered 40, and 52 in 1958. There is a ladies' circle and a Sunday school for children.
          vDZ.

Inv. Arch. Amst. II, 2185 f.; Blaupot t. C., *Groningen* I, 212 f.; *Zangen bij . . . de eerste godsdienstoefening in de nieuwe Doopsgezinde kerk te Pekela* (Wildervank, 1852); *ML* III, 339.

Pekelharing, a Dutch Mennonite family. Dirk Jelisz Pekelharing (1729-64), living at Zaandam, North Holland, married to Maartje Cornelis Kalf, who made sails for ships and windmills and also compasses, may have been a Mennonite; it is certain that his wife and his descendants belonged to the Mennonite church. His son Cornelis Pekelharing (1760-1800), a sailmaker at Zaandam, belonged to the Oostzijde Mennonite congregation and is said to have been the only adherent of the Orangist party in his congregation, all other members being Patriots (*q.v.*). Cornelis' son Dirk Pekelharing (1783-1857) and his grandson Cornelis Pekelharing (1811-73) were both physicians, Dirk practicing at 's-Graveland and his son Cornelis practicing at Zaandam. Another son of Dirk, Klaas Rutger Pekelharing (1825-85), was a Mennonite minister, serving at Middelburg and Vlissingen 1849-84. He wrote an important paper, "Bijdragen voor de Geschiedenis der Hervorming in Zeeland," which was published in *Archief* VI (1866) of the "Zeeuwsch Genootschap," and also the *Levens-Bericht* of S. de Wind (Middelburg, n.d.). Dirk Pekelharing (1839-1908), a son of Cornelis, was a pastor of the Mennonite Surhuisterveen congregation 1864-1908. Other sons of Cornelis were Baltus Hendrik Pekelharing (1841-?), professor at the technical University at Delft, and Adrianus Cornelis Pekelharing (1848-?), professor in the medical school of the University of Utrecht. Many members of the Pekelharing family served the Zaandam-Oostzijde congregation as deacons, as for example Willem Jan Pekelharing (1851-1933), a merchant who was also for many years a treasurer of the *Zaansche Fonds* (*q.v.*) for the pensioning of retired and disabled ministers. vDZ.

Pekema, a Mennonite family found in the Dutch province of Friesland. Jelle Sippesz Pekema (1863-1942) served as Mennonite pastor at Irnsum-Poppingawier 1890-91, de Rijp 1891-94, and Hilversum 1894-1904, in which year he retired. Engelbertus Pekema, b. April 22, 1877, at Bolsward, d. Sept. 9, 1950, at Enschedé, was a Mennonite pastor, serving at Mensingeweer 1904-7, Monnikendam 1907-9, IJmuiden 1909-12, and Enschedé 1912-42. He wrote a historical paper on the congregation of Enschedé, which is found in *Uit het Verleden der Doopsgezinden in Twenthe* (Borne, n.d.). (*DJ* 1951, 18 f.) vDZ.

Pellertitz (Bellerditz, Czech, *Polehradice*), a market village in Moravia five hours southeast of Brno and north of Niemtschitz. Here on the estates belonging to the Záwis of Wickow the Hutterites expelled from Klein Niemtschitz (*q.v.*) established a small Bruderhof in 1559. But already in 1563 they were driven out by the owner. They returned later, however. In the Polehradice Bruderhof occurred the death of the deacon Abraham Laub on April 8, 1612. The householder Georg Riedel (*q.v.*) caused the Bruderhof great distress by his absorption in alchemy to the neglect of his duties; he was expelled on July 16, 1612, but after making confession he was admitted to the Kostel (Gostal) Bruderhof. The Polehradice Bruderhof suffered severely in the period of the rebellion, being plundered eleven times beginning on Aug. 19, 1619, and "robbed of many horses and much goods." The sisters of the Bruderhof had been hidden in a camp in the woods, but the rude soldiery found them there and raped six of them. The year 1621 brought new misfortune; on February 8 the Bruderhof was plundered by Saxon horsemen, who took away twenty barrels of "rare wine," and on February 19 it was burned down, and was left desolate. P.DE.

Beck, *Geschichts-Bücher;* Wolkan, *Geschicht-Buch;* Zieglschmid, *Chronik;* Gr. Wolny, *Kirchliche Topographie von Mähren,* Part II: *Brünner Erzdiözese* IV (Brno, 1861) 66; *ML* III, 339 f.

Pelsy, Valentin (1870-1925), a Mennonite leader and elder of Alsace-Lorraine, was born in 1870 at Rhodes, near Saarburg, Lorraine. In consequence of a leg fracture in his youth which required many operations he was excused from military service. In 1888 his parents moved to Gosselmingen; there Valentin was responsible for the mill as well as the farm. He was led to study at the Bible school at Chrischona near Basel, Switzerland, by his friend Pierre Sommer (*q.v.*), who had earlier attended that school. Later he and his brother Paul farmed the Mückenhof near Saarburg, which was burned down at the beginning of World War I. The brothers rebuilt it as well as they could and continued their farming. In 1920 Valentin married Marie Wagler of Schneckenbusch and settled on the farm of his grandparents at Gosselmingen.

Valentin Pelsy exerted a deep influence in his home congregation Saarburg (*q.v.*), where he was ordained as preacher and elder in 1898. He also served in the neighboring congregations, such as Morhange (Mörchingen). He had no little part in the spiritual revival in the Mennonite congregations in Alsace and Lorraine. In 1925 he was chosen as president of the newly organized conference of these congregations. With tact and self-sacrifice he served as an organizer and as a pastor. Unfortunately his service was of short duration, for he died on Nov. 23, 1925. S.G.

Almanach Mennonite du Cinquantenaire 1901-1951 (Montbéliard, 1951); *Gem.-Kal.* 1927, 137; *ML* I, 560; II, 340.

Peltner, Hans, an Anabaptist martyr: see **Plattner, Hans.**

Penner, a Mennonite family name occurring in East and West Prussia, Russia, and in North America. The family is found in the Marienburger Werder as early as 1592. In 1776 there were 118 Penner families in West Prussia. In 1936 the members were distributed as follows in Germany: Danzig 56, Elbing-Ellerwald 19, Elbing-Stadt-City 5, Fürstenwerder 21, Heubuden 62, Ladekopp-Orlofferfelde 58, Montau-Gruppe 1, Rosenort 49, Schönsee 8, Thiensdorf-Preussisch Rosengart 88, Tiegenhagen 54, Tragheimerweide 27, Total West Prussia 448; Berlin 13, Gronau 7, Hamburg 1, Total 469. At Hamburg, Germany, Henrich Pender (Heinrich Penner) was in 1669-78 a partner with Carl de Vlieger, also a Mennonite, in the ownership of whaling boats operating near Greenland. Among the outstanding bearers of the Penner name in West Prussia were the following: Elder David Penner (d. 1732), who left Lithuania (*q.v.*) with 120 Mennonite families in January 1724 because of persecution and settled with them at Thiensdorf-Markushof in the Kleinwerder (West Prussia) (*Inv. Arch. Amst.* I, Nos. 1571-79; II, 2, Nos. 708, 736, 751). Abraham Penner of Tiegenhagen was an elder of the Old Flemish congregation of the Grosswerder 1749-67, and Jacob Penner (d. 1794) was a preacher of the Orlofferfelde congregation 1766-73. Gerhard Penner of Irrgang, the nephew of Gerhard Penner, Sr. (*q.v.*), was a preacher at Heubuden in 1861-67. Heinrich Penner (d. 1890), the son of Gerhard Penner, Sr., was the elder of the "emigration congregation," and ministered to those who were compelled to postpone their emigration to Russia. Wilhelm Penner was an elder of the Danzig City congregation and chairman of the church board (picture in Mannhardt, 1904 and 1919, p. 198). Johann Penner of Prangenau (*q.v.*, 1871-1943) was ordained as preacher of the Ladekopp congregation in 1903, and elder 1919, and served as chairman of the Committee of Elders of the Conference of East and West Prussia. Jakob Penner and Johann Penner (*q.v.*) were elders in the Thiensdorf-Preussisch Rosengart congregation.

In Russia the following should be mentioned: Bernhard Penner, b. 1756 at Elbing, d. 1791 at Chortitza, ordained preacher in 1790 and elder 1791 at Chortitza; Wilhelm Penner and Peter Penner were teachers in the Chortitza Zentralschule (*q.v.*; pictures in Friesen, facing p. 618). Another Wilhelm Penner, born in Elbing, a brother of Johannes K. Penner (below), was a preacher at Ak-Metchet and later elder at Aulie-Ata.

In America some of the Mennonite bearers of this name were as follows: Andreas Penner, a younger brother of Gerhard Penner, Sr., was from 1854 preacher of the Heubuden congregation and later in Beatrice, Neb., Gerhard Penner, Sr. and Jr., were preachers in the Beatrice congregation. Two sons of the latter were Cornelius Penner, b. May 17, 1868, at Koczelitzke (Warnau), since 1903 a minister in Beatrice, and Henry Gerhard Penner, b. July 24, 1872, at Marienburg, a physician in Beatrice. Peter A. Penner, b. April 2, 1871, at Bilisirkow, Ukraine, d. 1949, was a missionary in Champa, India. Peter William Penner, b. Feb. 12, 1876, at Prangenau in the Molotschna, was a missionary in Janjgir, India. Jakob B. Penner, b. Feb. 10, 1877, in South Russia, was a minister of the Mennonite Brethren congregation in Kronsgart, Man., as were also Heinrich Daniel Penner and Johannes K. Penner. H. D. Penner was an important G.C.M. minister and writer.   E.C., vpZ.

Franz Crous, "Mennonitenfamilien in Zahlen," *Menn. Gesch.-Bl.* V (1940) 26-45; Friesen, *Brüderschaft*; H. G. Mannhardt, *Die Danziger Mennonitengemeinde* (Danzig, 1919); Dutch *Naamlijst*; W. C. Andreas, "Highlights and Sidelights of the Mennonites in Beatrice," *Menn. Life* I (July 1946); Wanda Oesau, *Hamburgs Grönlandsfahrt* (Glückstadt-Hamburg, 1955) 132 f.; *ML* III, 340 f. See also *Who's Who Among the Mennonites*, 1943, and articles below.

Penner, Abram (d. 1933), was the first elder of the Mennonite church organized in 1894 at Deyevka (*q.v.*) in the Orenburg settlement on the Ural, Russia. He was characterized by a great love for the brotherhood, a firm will, and an unusual gift for organization. Unfortunately, soon after his election serious conflicts arose on the question whether the planned Zentralschule was to be located at Deyevka or Pretoria. In the heat of this strife Penner had to retire from office upon the wish of the congregation. But since he felt himself called by God to the office of elder, he continued to conduct meetings in private homes with a small group of his followers. But before long even these were discontinued. He

died about 1933 without having found his way back into his former congregation.   W.Q.

Penner, Bernhard (Behrent) (d. 1791), the first elder of the Mennonite congregations in the Chortitza settlement in South Russia. With a group of the immigrants to Russia from West Prussia he reached Dubrovka in the Russian province of Mohilev, and since there was no minister in the group he was chosen as minister here and confirmed in this office by the home congregations in West Prussia by letter. In 1790 he was chosen as elder, this office being again confirmed by the home congregations.

The conduct of his office was by no means easy. The severe difficulties of pioneering were heightened by strife in the church life. The poverty was so dire that he had to appear in borrowed boots to conduct communion and baptismal services. In addition to all this, his health was poor. He therefore asked to have a co-elder chosen in 1791; the man chosen, however, declined the office. Penner then wrote an epistle (*Hirtenbrief*) requesting that the congregation choose an elder immediately after his death. He died July 27, 1791, after serving only one year as elder.   B.J.S.

Penner Church, Fairview, Okla.: see **Fairview Church** of God.

Penner, Heinrich D. (1862-1933), a Mennonite (GCM) minister and teacher, was born at Schardau, Molotschna, South Russia, on March 9, 1862. In 1874 he came to America with his mother and stepfather, settling near Hillsboro, Kan. In 1880 he was baptized by Jacob Buller, elder of the Alexanderwohl Mennonite Church. On April 29, 1884, he married Katherina Dalke. He obtained a good education through private study and taught at the Rosenort (Lighthouse) school 1885-89, at the elementary school at Lehigh 1889-93, and at Bethel College 1893-97.

On July 27, ——, Penner was ordained to the ministry by Elder J. S. Hirschler for the Hillsboro Mennonite (GCM) Church. In 1897 he organized the Hillsboro Preparatory School (*q.v.*) and taught there until 1913. In 1913-18 he taught church history and German at Bethel College, and 1913-30 he served as a teacher and spiritual adviser at the Bethel Deaconess Hospital and Home. He then served as copastor of the Mennonite church at Beatrice 1921-26, and at the Geary (Okla.) Mennonite church 1926-33. Penner served on many committees concerned with schools, congregations, and the conference. He wrote the following booklets: *Kurze Andachten fuer die Schwestern und ihre Pflegebefohlenen im Bethel Diakonissenhospital, Newton, Kansas* (n.p.), pp. 118; *Kurzer Leitfaden für den Religionsunterricht in der Kinderlehre* (n.p.), pp. 32; *Leibes- und Seelenpflege bei Kranken* (Newton, 1916); *Our Christian Catechism, Confession and Covenant* (n.p.), pp. 7; *A Short Course of Study in the Rudiments of the Christian Religion for High School Students, Deaconess Probationers, Students in Nurse Training Schools and Lay Workers* (Beatrice, n.d.), pp. 42; *The Twofold Nature of the*

Kingdom (Geary, 1932), pp. 16. He died on Oct. 26, 1933.   C.K.

"Aeltester Heinrich Daniel Penner," *Bundesbote Kalender* (1935) 26; P. J. Wedel, *The Story of Bethel College;* H. D. Penner Collection (BeCL).

Penner, Jakob, an elder of the Mennonite congregation at Orlofferfelde in West Prussia, Germany, b. Jan. 1, 1831, d. Jan. 30, 1909, was ordained elder in 1882. The revision of the Catechism by the Mennonites of West Prussia was chiefly his responsibility; he also shared in the production of a new hymnal. A most significant contribution was the union he brought about between the Frisian and Flemish branches.   NEFF.

Menn. Bl., 1909, 25; Mannhardt, *Jahrbuch,* 1883, 109; *ML* III, 342.

Penner, Johann (1817-89), an elder of the Thiensdorf Mennonite Church in West Prussia, Germany, was born at Thörichthof Sept. 9, 1817, was ordained preacher in 1847 and elder in 1864. He was one of the five elders who traveled to Berlin in February 1869 as deputies of the West Prussian congregations and were given an audience with William I of Prussia to present their position on the military law passed in November 1867. In 1861 Johann Penner had made a previous trip to Berlin on the matter of nonresistance. When the Mennonites were released from military service by an order of cabinet on March 3, 1868, most of the West Prussian Mennonites were satisfied. Some emigrated to America, among them three of the five deputies. Johann Penner remained in Germany and exerted a beneficent influence far beyond the confines of his congregation. He died at Markushof on Feb. 2, 1889. NEFF.

"Heimatbilder aus Westpreussen, nach Oelgemäldern von Marie Birckholtz-Bestvater," *Menn. Jahrbuch* 1951; *Menn. Bl.,* 1889, 42-44; *ML* III, 342.

Penner, Johannes K. (1850-1926), usually called "Lehrer Penner," was born at Elbing, West Prussia, Germany, on Nov. 27, 1850. He attended the school at Elbing and the private school at Bröskerfeld (*q.v.*), where Johannes Claassen (*q.v.*) was his teacher. In 1867 he was baptized by Johann Töws and became a teacher at Bröskerfeld. In 1860 he attended the normal school at Marienburg and in 1870 emigrated with his mother and brother to the Trakt settlement, Saratov, Russia, where he became a teacher. On Oct. 4, 1874, he married Helen Jantzen. In 1875 he was elected minister. In 1880 Penner joined the group which moved to Central Asia (*q.v.*) to escape military service and meet the Lord. Disillusioned, he joined the group who went to America, and arrived in Beatrice, Neb., on Sept. 19, 1884, where he taught in a private school and served as minister. His 50th anniversary in teaching was commemorated on June 16, 1917. He died on Oct. 8, 1926.   C.K.

"Etwas aus dem Leben Pred. J. K. Penner," *Bundesbote-Kalender,* 1926, 28; W. C. Andreas, "Highlights and Sidelights of the Mennonites in Beatrice," *Men. Life* I (July 1946) 22.

Penner, Peter A. (1871-1949), a noted missionary (GCM) to India, was born at Belo Sirko, South Russia, on April 2, 1871, the son of Abraham Penner

and Maria Buhler. His father, who had come from the Bergthal Mennonite settlement, settled in Belo Sirko, and later in Berdyansk, his wife's home. In 1875 the family arrived in Mountain Lake, Minn., where P. A. Penner attended the elementary and preparatory schools. He spent two years at the Minnesota State Normal School at Mankato and two years, 1895-97, at Bethel Academy, Newton, Kan. After this he taught elementary school and attended the Missionary Training Institute, Brooklyn, N.Y. (1899). He was a member of the Bethel Mennonite Church, Mountain Lake, where he married Elizabeth Dickmann (1876-1906) on June 17, 1900. Two children were born to this marriage, Miriam Hilda and Linda Viola. On Oct. 24, 1909, he married Martha Richert, of Goessel, Kan.

In 1900 the P. A. Penners went to India as the first American G.C.M. missionaries, starting a mission at Champa, Central Provinces (now Madhya Pradesh), and establishing the Bethesda Leper Home (*q.v.*). In 1941 Penner returned to Newton. In 1926 he was presented the silver Kaiser-i-Hind medal for distinguished service by the Viceroy of India, to which was added at the time of his retirement a silver bar for the forty years of service. Penner's contribution as a missionary was unique in that he was one of the pioneers with a long and very successful term of service. His reports appeared regularly in the *Christlicher Bundesbote.* Among his writings were *He Was—He Is—He Will Be* (Newton, 1944), and *Kurzer Bericht über die Arbeit unter Aussätzigen* (Champa, 1915). He died at Newton on Oct. 3, 1949.   M.P.S.

Ed. G. Kaufman, *The Development of the Missionary and Philanthropic Interest Among the Mennonites of North America* (Berne, 1931); *Twenty-Five Years with God in India* (Berne, 1929).

Penner, Peter William (1876-1953), a Mennonite (GCM) missionary to India, was born in Prangenau, Molotschna, South Russia, Feb. 12, 1876. When he was two years old, his father, Jakob Penner, migrated to America and settled in the Brudertal community, Hillsboro, Kan. Here he attended the school and was baptized on June 3, 1895, by Wm. J. Ewert, elder of the Brudertal Mennonite Church. In 1902 he married Mathilde Ensz. He attended Bethel College 1896-98, after which he taught school. After taking a teachers' training course at the Mennonite Educational Institute, Gretna, Man., he taught there 1900-4. Then he and his wife attended German (now Baldwin) Wallace College at Berea, Ohio, where he was graduated from the Seminary in 1908. During those years he served the Grace Mennonite (GCM) Church at Pandora and the Sterling Mennonite (GCM) Church at Sterling, Ohio, as minister.

On Sept. 20, 1908, the Penners were ordained missionaries and left for India. On furlough during World War I, he did mission work in Los Angeles and served the Immanuel Mennonite Church 1918-21, after which he returned to India. Besides his heavy evangelistic activities and work in the building program on the mission field, he was the secretary-treasurer of the mission for 25 years. In 1949 he retired after 40 years of service. He died at his home in Hillsboro, Feb. 2, 1953.   C.K.

Pennsville and Stonerville Mennonite (MC) churches, now extinct, were located near Scottdale, in western Pennsylvania. The early Mennonite settlers of this area located on both sides of Jacob's Creek in Westmoreland and Fayette counties about 1790, with Abraham Stauffer as the first minister. The first meetinghouse, a log house, was erected before 1800 near Pennsville, 2½ miles south of Scottdale, and a little later another at Stonerville, 2½ miles north of Scottdale. Both places erected new brick buildings, Stonerville in 1841 and Pennsville in 1852. Both belonged to a single congregation and had services on alternate dates. The congregation flourished, with over 200 members at one time, until about 1840, when a general decline began. Some moved away and others affiliated with other church bodies, finally reducing the membership to about 20. In 1893 a new church was built in Scottdale, which created new interest and became the center of worship. Stonerville was abandoned in 1898 and Pennsville in 1903. The burying grounds are the lone reminders of a once flourishing rural Mennonite settlement surrounding Scottdale.   A.KA.

Edward Yoder, *The Mennonites of Westmoreland County, Pa.* (Scottdale, 1942).

Pennsylvania, one of the original thirteen American colonies along the Atlantic coast, was founded by the English Quaker, William Penn, to whom the land had been granted by King Charles II in 1681. It was named Pennsylvania by the king himself, against the wishes of Penn, who as a Quaker was opposed to any name that might be interpreted as an attempt to glorify himself. The grant was of the proprietary type—that is, Penn as proprietor was granted complete ownership of the land, to dispose of it as he wished, with almost unlimited political power to govern the settlers with such political institutions as he thought best. It was Penn's purpose to establish here on the virgin soil of America a refuge for the English Quakers, who were being severely oppressed in their own country, and also other religious groups in Europe who were still being denied the usual civil and religious rights enjoyed by the established state churches. With this purpose in mind he granted the settlers a liberal frame of government and complete religious liberty.

Immigration. The first settlers were a group of English Quakers who founded the city of Philadelphia in 1681. In the meantime the English Quakers had established several Quaker congregations in Holland and among the Mennonites along the German Rhine (e.g., Crefeld, Kriegsheim in the Palatinate). To these, as well as to all the religious groups that were oppressed by their various governments along the Rhine, Penn issued a cordial invitation, offering them complete toleration—civil and religious—in his new colony. The first to respond to this call was a group of thirteen families from the region of Crefeld, former Mennonites, but by this time victims of Quaker missionary zeal. All of them but one family were now Quakers. The heads of these families were Dirck op den Graeff, Hermann op den Graeff, Abraham op den Graeff, Lenart Arets, Thones Konders, Reinert Tisen, Willem Strepers, Jan Lensen, Peter Keurlis, Jan Siemens,

Johannes Bleikers, Abraham Tunis, and Jan Luykens. This group arrived at Philadelphia on Oct. 6, 1683; and, proceeding some six miles north of the newly established Philadelphia, founded a new settlement which they called Germantown on land which they had purchased from Francis Daniel Pastorius, who had preceded them to America by a few months as agent for the Frankfort Land Company.

One of these colonist families remained a Mennonite; others soon followed from the Lower Rhine region, and later from Hamburg-Altona in Germany, so that a Mennonite congregation was formed by 1690 (or 1702). This was not only the first Mennonite church to be established in America, but the first German settlement of any sort in North America. Germantown is to the Germans of America what Jamestown is to the English. In 1702, a lot was set aside for a Mennonite meetinghouse which was built in 1708 on the site of the present little stone building erected in 1770.

In 1702 Matthias van Bebber started a new Mennonite settlement along Skippack Creek, some 15 miles to the northwest in what is now Montgomery County, which has since grown to numerous congregations in what came to be known as the Franconia (*q.v.*) district, extending 30 miles north and an equal distance west, covering most of the Montgomery County and Bucks County area and spilling over into the counties of Chester, Berks, Lehigh, and Northampton. In 1707 a few Mennonites came from the Palatinate to Germantown.

Beginning with 1710 there was a continuous migration of Mennonites from Switzerland and the German Palatinate, which continued more or less regularly throughout the 18th century up to the time of the French and Indian War (1756-63). Part of these filled up the Franconia settlement. The rest made their way some 60 miles west of Philadelphia, along the Pequea and Conestoga valleys, in what is now Lancaster County, which is today almost solidly Mennonite in most of its rural area. The very first settlers here in 1710 came directly from Switzerland, the rest mostly from the Palatinate. There was little immigration from Europe to Pennsylvania during the wars from 1756 to 1815; after that, Mennonites as well as others who sought greater freedom in America chose the cheaper lands farther west beyond the Allegheny Mountains, so that Mennonite immigration to Pennsylvania was to all intents ended by 1756. The total Mennonite immigration may have reached 3,000 persons. The Lancaster County settlement spilled over into York, Cumberland, Dauphin, and Lebanon counties.

Beginning with 1736 the Amish also followed the Mennonites to the "Paradise of Pennsylvania," but located their first settlement somewhat northeast of the land occupied by the Mennonites in Lancaster, farther out on the frontier, along the Blue Ridge Mountains in what is now northern Berks County. During the Indian Wars which followed in 1754 they were driven south, and the first settlement was abandoned for safer areas in Lancaster and Chester counties on the eastern Lancaster fringe from Morgantown to Atglen. The Amish immigration did not total more than 400 persons.

Mennonite Churches in Pennsylvania

Scale of Miles
0 5 10 20 30 40 50 60

- Old Order Amish Church Districts

(hatched) - Areas Occupied by Old Order Amish

For churches not numbered see:
I - Map of Somerset County
II - Map of Mifflin County
III - Map of Lancaster County
IV - Map of Bucks - Montgomery County

MENNONITE CHURCHES (MC)
1. Sunnyside
2. Meadville
3. Britton Run
4. Beaverdam
5. Masontown
6. Scottdale
7. Kingview
7a. North Scottdale
8. Rockton
9. Pleasant View
10. Altoona
11. Mill Run
12. Martinsburg
13. Barrville
14. Rockville
15. Maple Grove
16. Allensville
17. Mattawana
18. Otelia
19. Shady Pine
20. Rowe
21. Strasburg
22. Pleasant View
23. Chambersburg
24. Marion
25. Pond Bank
26. Rock Hill
27. Williamson
28. Salem Ridge
29. Cedar Grove
30. Buffalo
30a. Beaver Run
31. Crossroads
32. Lauver
33. Locust Grove
34. Susquehana
35. Lost Creek
36. Delaware
37. Diller
38. Meckville
39. Palo Alto
40. Bernville
41. Oley
42. Allentown
43. Steel City
44. Easton
45. Salem
46. Bristol
47. Maple Grove
48. Zion
49. Bethel
50. Birch Grove
51. Media Chapel
52. Sandy Hill

GENERAL CONFERENCE MENNONITE CHURCHES
56. Allentown First
57. Saucon
58. Smith Corner
59. Fairfield
60. Napier
61. Richfield
62. Roaring Spring
63. Springs Second

OLD ORDER AMISH MENNONITE DISTRICTS
64. Crawford County (Atlantic)
65. Mercer County North
66. Mercer County South
67. New Wilmington West
68. New Wilmington North
69. New Wilmington South
70. Enon Valley
71. Selinsgrove
72. Lebanon West District
73. Lebanon East District
74. Juniata County

BEACHY AMISH MENNONITE CHURCHES
53. Maple Grove
54. Peachey, Upper District
55. Peachey, Lower District
55a. Selinsgrove

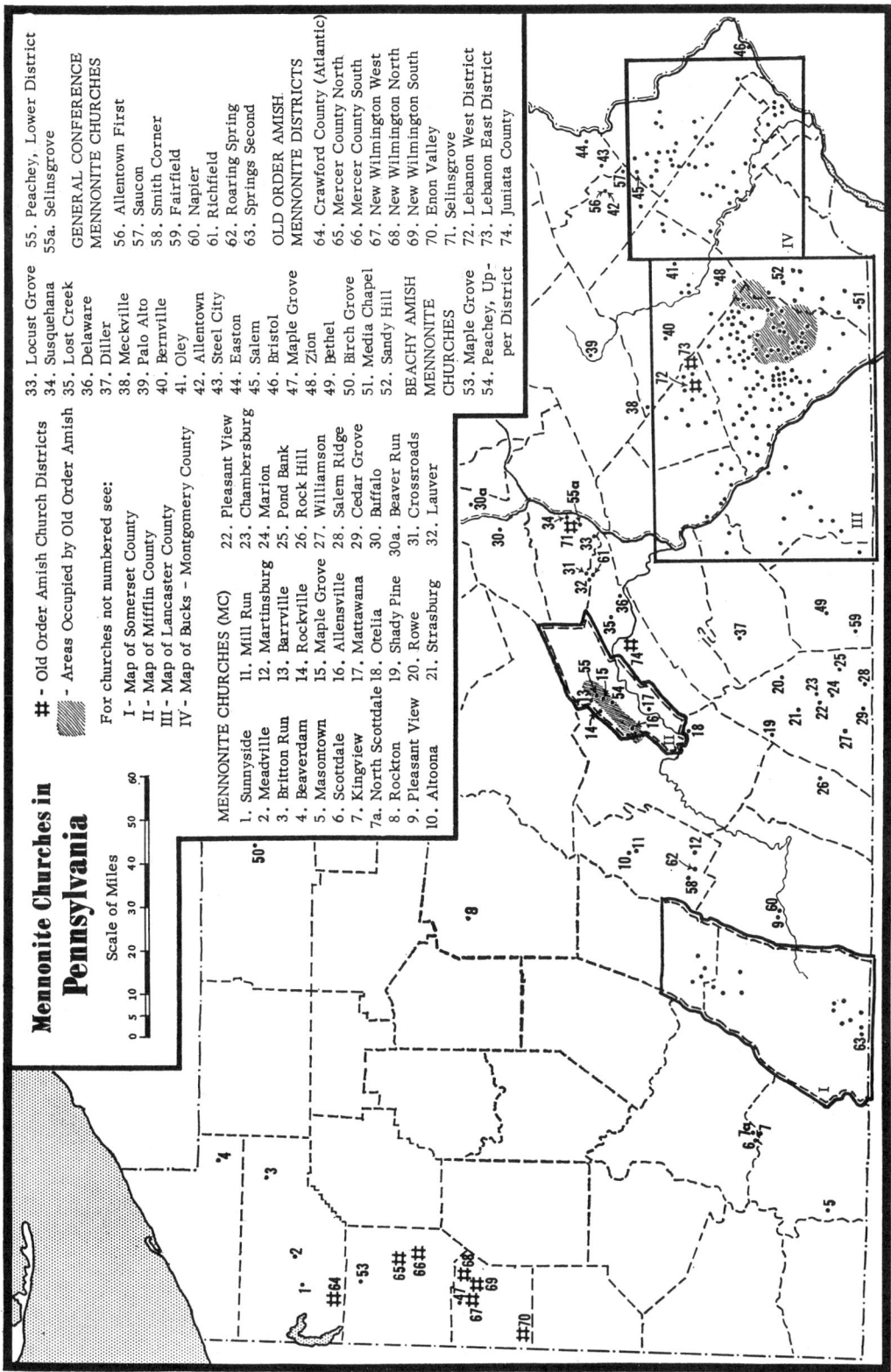

Numerous religious nonresistant German groups and mystics, Dunkards, Schwenckfelders, Moravians, and other smaller German sects soon found their way to the land of freedom from the oppression of the Old World. The smaller nonresistant groups, including Mennonites and Amish, however, formed only a small part of the German migration to Pennsylvania during this period. There was a large influx from South Germany of members of the Protestant state churches—Reformed and Lutheran. These were followed before the middle of the 18th century by the Scotch-Irish, who, finding that the best lands of southeastern Pennsylvania had been taken over by the Germans and the English Quakers, were forced to seek homes farther out on the frontier, along the foothills of the Alleghenies. So by the time of the Revolutionary War (1776), Pennsylvania was settled by the English Quakers, Germans of all religious groups, and the Scotch-Irish (mostly Presbyterians), all enjoying perfect religious liberty, living side by side in peace and contentment. The Mennonites, although they were the first German settlers in the province, formed only a small part of the entire German population by the close of the century. It is estimated that by 1776 there were about 100,000 Germans in Pennsylvania, constituting perhaps about one third of the entire population. Of this number the Mennonites and Amish were not more than 10 per cent.

Most of the Mennonites who immigrated during this time were poor, many of them without sufficient money to pay for their passage. Their Dutch brethren organized the Commission for Foreign Needs, which greatly aided the emigration movement. Some, too, were able to bargain with ship captains for free passage across, in return for which the captain might sell their services (for a number of years) at auction upon their arrival at Philadelphia. These were called "redemptioners." A number of Mennonites came under this head, though the number among them was not as great as among other groups.

The poor economic conditions prevailing throughout the 18th century in the Palatinate, from which came nearly all of the Mennonites and most of the other Germans, together with the arbitrary rule of many of the Palatine counts through the 18th century, were, no doubt, the main cause of the mass migration from this region at this time. But the Mennonites had added reasons for leaving what to them was a land of oppression. Not being one of the three tolerated religious groups guaranteed religious liberty by the Treaty of Westphalia in 1648, they were subjected to all sorts of humiliating civil disabilities and religious intolerance throughout the century. They had to pay an extra tax in the form of protection money; their expansion was limited to 200 families; their young men could not become members of the craft guilds and were thus unable to learn a trade; they were not allowed to live in cities except with special permission; they had only limited rights in the ownership of land; they were not allowed to marry except with the consent of the ruling authorities; nor were they permitted to be buried in the public cemeteries.

All the early Pennsylvania settlements were made in the southeastern corner of the province, within 100 miles of Philadelphia. As they expanded by natural increase and by the addition of new immigrants, and as the land became more valuable and scarce, the second and third generation descendants of the first colonists, as well as the newcomers, were compelled to find new homes farther out on the unoccupied frontiers. Mennonites were always among the pioneer settlers in new territory. As early as 1727 a group of Mennonites were found with the first German immigrants to the Shenandoah Valley in Virginia, although no permanent Mennonite settlement was made in Virginia until about 1780. In that state before the end of the century a number of flourishing congregations were located in the general region of Harrisonburg in what is now Rockingham County. Before 1800, too, the Pennsylvania Mennonites had established new homes along the Juniata in the center of the province, in south-central Franklin County, and in the southwestern corner near the headwaters of the Ohio River in Somerset County and Westmoreland County. In 1786 a number of Mennonites from Franklin County and later (1794) from Bucks and Lancaster found their way to Ontario, first near Niagara, then near what became Berlin, but now Kitchener, where they founded a major colony which has since grown into a large number of flourishing congregations, as well as smaller settlements in Lincoln County (Vineland) and in York County north of Toronto (Markham).

The Amish, too, expanded their settlement before the close of the century into the beautiful Kishacoquillas Valley in what is now Mifflin County, and into Somerset County. During the 19th century both the Mennonites and the Amish formed new congregations in a beeline westward in several states—Ohio, Indiana, Illinois, Iowa, Missouri, Kansas, and Nebraska.

State Relations. As long as the Quakers, who shared with the Mennonites their peace principles and their objection to the oath, retained control of the political machinery, the Pennsylvania government had a considerate regard for the religious scruples of the Mennonites on these questions. In 1717 a special act was passed by the Pennsylvania Assembly relieving Mennonites from any judicial oath; and in 1742 a similar act was passed in behalf of the Amish. In 1754 the Quakers lost control of the Assembly to the non-Quaker element of the population, and the peaceful policy inaugurated by Penn came to an end. During the French and Indian War (Seven Years' War) which followed there were many Indian depredations and massacres along the whole Pennsylvania frontier. Among those who lost their lives was an Amish family by the name of Hostetler. The influence of the Quakers, however, together with that of the other German nonresistant religious groups, was sufficiently strong to guarantee consideration on the part of the government for their special religious scruples throughout the 18th century. During the Revolutionary War Mennonites and others who shared their scruples against the bearing of arms were exempt from military duty upon the payment of a special small fee. When Pennsylvania, together with the other colonies, declared herself an independent state and free from England, demanding a new oath of allegiance from her citizens, some of the small Mennonite communities on the outer fringe of the larger settlements found some difficulty with the local authorities in maintaining their traditional principles regarding both war and the oath. Mennonites opposed the new oath on the grounds of opposition both to any oath at all and also to this new one in particular because it committed them to the support of revolution against constituted government, which was against their religious principles. In the small isolated congregation at Saucon in Lehigh County the whole male Mennonite population was at one time committed to jail for refusal to take the required oath. This was an exceptional case of persecution, however; in the larger, compact settlements, where the Mennonites were better known and understood by their local governments, no such drastic measures were resorted to, although all through the Revolutionary War the Mennonites, to whom respect for civil authority was a fundamental religious principle, were regarded by the superpatriots of the time as unpatriotic and classed with the Loyalists. In 1790 the new state of Pennsylvania passed a law exempting the Mennonites from active militia duty upon the payment of a small fine.

While the Mennonites were unanimous in their refusal to bear arms, there was some difference in certain quarters on the question of paying the special war taxes required by the government. In 1778, Bishop Christian Funk (*q.v.*), son of the pioneer Bishop Henry Funk (*q.v.*), living in Indianfield Township in the Franconia region, insisted on the payment of the special tax, contrary to the general opinion of his fellow Mennonites of this region. As a result of this difference Funk was deposed by the fellowship and with some 52 followers organized an independent congregation which later came to be known as Funkite by those who disagreed with him. These Funkites retained their separate existence until 1850, when they became extinct.

Division. With the exception of the Funk controversy over war taxes, there were no serious controversies among the Mennonites during their first century in Pennsylvania. But during the 19th century there were a number of controversies, usually over minor questions of religious practice, that led to final separation and the organization of separate branches of the church. The first of these was a conservative division led by John Herr, which occurred in Lancaster County in 1812 and resulted in a group called the Reformed Mennonites (*q.v.*). In 1957 there were only 309 members of this group in Pennsylvania in 10 congregations, 221 of whom lived in Lancaster County.

The second division, also a radically conservative one, occurred in Lancaster County in 1845, led by Jacob Stauffer, hence called Stauffer Mennonites. In 1957 the group had less than 300 members in 6 subdivisions.

The third division (GCM) occurred in the Franconia Conference in 1847, led by John H. Oberholtzer (*q.v.*), a young minister who, together with his bishop, John Hunsicker, and a total of 16 of the 70 ministers of the district, because they insisted

upon certain more liberal church practices than those in usage by the church at large at the time, were expelled from the Franconia Conference. The changes advocated by the Oberholtzer group included greater freedom in the choice of the cut of the clerical coat then required for the ministry; a more definite and prescribed form of procedure in conducting the sessions of the ministerial council meetings; and in general, a more liberal attitude toward all social and religious affiliation with the non-Mennonite world.

After its expulsion this group immediately formed a conference of its own, which later assumed the name "Eastern Pennsylvania Mennonite Conference." Under the leadership of Oberholtzer the new conference adopted a progressive program of church extension, establishing Sunday schools, initiating a church paper, advocating an educational institution, and in the main advocating a more liberal association with other churches, both Mennonite and others, in their religious efforts. Oberholtzer was also greatly interested in the union into some sort of common ecclesiastical organization of all the scattered Mennonite churches throughout the country, and consistently advocated this cause in the church paper which he established in 1852, the *Religiöser Botschafter* (*q.v.*). Some years later the congregations in this conference co-operated heartily in the movement that culminated in the formation in 1860 of the General Conference of the Mennonite Church of North America. Today these congregations form the Eastern District of the General Conference. In 1957 its membership in Pennsylvania was 4,041 in 27 congregations.

The fourth division, the Mennonite Brethren in Christ, occurred in 1858, ten years after the Oberholtzer defection, as a division within a division. When William Gehman, a minister in the Upper Milford congregation of the newly organized Eastern Pennsylvania Conference, together with a number of sympathizers, insisted on introducing regular midweek prayer meetings and other evangelistic practices not yet common among even the progressive Oberholtzer following, he was expelled from the conference. This group, too, soon formed a new organization under the name of Evangelical Mennonites (*q.v.*). For a time they were few in number, but in the course of time, by joining with several other like-minded groups from Indiana, Ohio, and Pennsylvania, they formed, in 1883, a new branch of the church under the name of Mennonite Brethren in Christ. In 1947 this branch dropped the name Mennonite, and assumed the name United Missionary Church (*q.v.*), but the Pennsylvania section, which forms a separate Pennsylvania conference, has retained the old name for the present. In 1957 it had 4,507 members in Pennsylvania in 35 congregations.

The fifth division was that of the Old Order Mennonites in Lancaster County in 1893, a part of a larger movement which included scattered groups of conservative Mennonites who, during the latter part of the 19th century, objected to what they considered some of the progressive religious practices then coming into general use among the Mennonite churches at large—Sunday schools, evangelistic meetings, mission meetings, more modern dress, in some cases the use of the English language in the pulpit, and other new religious observances more in keeping with the spirit of the times. In Lancaster they were first called "Martinites" after their leader Jonas H. Martin; in Indiana and Ohio they were called "Wislers" after their leader Jacob Wisler, who broke off in 1871-72; in Ontario the group broke off in 1889, in Virginia in 1900. In 1957 the Lancaster group, with several subdivisions, totaled 3,272 in 18 congregations.

Having lost these various divisions, the Mennonite Church (MC) constituted the main body in Pennsylvania. For convenience it is usually spoken of as the "Old" Mennonites, but the term "Old" is not official and is not recognized by the group. They have not been influenced much by these various defections. They are still largely conservative, especially in matters of dress and affiliation with other religious bodies, though quite progressive in mission work, Sunday schools, relief work, and other forms of progressive religious effort. As a whole they are more conservative in their religious practices than their brethren of the same branch in the states farther west. Their total membership in the state in 1957 was 26,580 distributed over the various district conferences as follows: Franconia, 5,311; Lancaster, 14,663; Allegheny, 2,721; Ohio and Eastern, 1,878; Franklin County, Pa., and Washington County, Md., 682; Conservative Conference, 438; independent congregations, 373; unaccounted for, 514.

Amish. The Amish in Pennsylvania divided *c*1880 into two distinct groups, those who remained unchanged in their forms of worship and church life and practices and hence are called Old Order Amish, and those who followed a more progressive pattern and ultimately joined a Mennonite conference. The second group first joined the Eastern A.M. Conference in 1893, which merged with the Ohio Conference into the Ohio and Eastern Conference in 1925. Later several of these congregations transferred to the Allegheny Conference. Some Old Order Amish joined the Conservative Amish Conference (*q.v.*), formed in 1910, and additional O.O.A. groups (*q.v.*) withdrew to join the Beachy Amish movement which began in 1926. In 1957 the Beachy Amish had 692 members in Pennsylvania in 5 congregations. The Conservative Conference meanwhile had allied itself with the Mennonite Church (MC). The Old Order Amish in Pennsylvania in 1957 numbered 4,168 members in 52 congregations called "districts."

In 1957 Pennsylvania had the largest total number of Mennonites, 39,382, of any state in the Union, twice as large as Ohio, the next in size. This number was distributed by branches as follows:

Mennonite Church (MC)	26,580
Old Order Amish	4,168
General Conference Mennonite Church	4,061
Old Order Mennonite	3,272
Beachy Amish	692
Reformed Mennonite	309
Stauffer Mennonite	300

The Mennonite Brethren in Christ, who do not reckon themselves with the other Mennonite bodies,

had 4,507 members in Pennsylvania in 1957. Thus the total in Pennsylvania carrying the name Mennonite was 43,889.

Institutions established in Pennsylvania by Mennonites include: Mennonite (MC) Publishing House at Scottdale (1908), four high schools (all MC)— Lancaster Mennonite School (1942), Johnstown Mennonite School (1944), Belleville Mennonite School (1945), Christopher Dock School (1954) at Lansdale, and 58 elementary schools operated by either the Amish or the Mennonites (MC) or in a few cases co-operatively by the two groups. Welfare institutions include the following: Mennonite Children's Home (1911) at Millersville, Mennonite Home (1905) at Lancaster, Welsh Mountain Samaritan Home (1898) near New Holland, Bethany Mennonite Home (1954) in Philadelphia, Eastern Mennonite Home (1916) at Souderton, Rockhill Mennonite Home (1955) at Sellersville, Eastern Mennonite Convalescent Home (1942) at Hatfield, and Philhaven Hospital for Mental and Nervous Diseases (1954) near Lebanon. All of these are under the Mennonite Church (MC). The General Conference Mennonites operate the Mennonite Home for the Aged (1896) at Frederick. The Mennonite Central Committee has had its headquarters at Akron, a village ten miles north of Lancaster, since 1937.

The Pennsylvania Mennonites, who were once exclusively rural and have made major contributions to American agriculture through the introduction from their Palatinate homeland of pioneer improvements such as crop rotation, nitrogenous legumes, etc., are now largely urbanized, possibly to 85 per cent. Many have entered into small businesses, a few have become manufacturers on a medium large scale, and an increasing number are entering the professions of teaching and medicine, only a very few into law, and none into politics. Many have become factory workers. The Amish and the Old Order Mennonites have remained exclusively rural.

The literary production of the Pennsylvania Mennonites has been slight, although in the 18th and early 19th centuries the German presses of Christopher Saur (*q.v.*) in Germantown, the Ephrata Cloister, and John Baer in Lancaster, published a considerable amount of German Mennonite literature including hymnals, catechisms, confessions, prayerbooks, and the *Martyrs' Mirror*. The sole Mennonite press before the establishment of the **Mennonite** Publishing House at Scottdale in 1908 was the Mennonitischer Druckverein (*q.v.*) at Milford Square (1856 ff.).

Characteristic Mennonite Names. The most common Mennonite names in Pennsylvania, all of the Swiss-Palatinate background except a very few who descend from the original Germantown settlers from the Lower Rhine, include the following (in modern spelling): Alderfer, Allebach, Bowman, Bleam, Beam, Brenneman, Brubaker, Baer, Bachman, Burkholder, Burkhart, Boyer, Bookwalter, Beyer, Bomberger, Bergey, Betzner, Breckbill, Bechtel, Beidler, Cassel, Clemmer, Clemens, Cressman, Eby, Erisman, Ebersole, Eschleman, Funk, Frey, Fretz, Frick, Freed, Frantz, Gehman, Gingrich, Groff, Good, Geil, Graybill, Glick, Huffman, Hunsicker, Holdeman, High, Hiestand, Hershey, Herr, Hess, Huber, Hagey, Horst, Hunsberger, Hallman, Hoover, Kolb, Kagey, Kratz, Kendig, Kreider, Keyser, Kaufman, Latschaw, Leatherman, Longenecker, Landes, Moyer, Miller, Musser, Musselman, Meylin, Martin, Mellinger, Metzler, Newcomer, Neff, Nissly, Nice, Oberholtzer, Pennypacker, Root, Rupp, Risser, Reist, Rittenhouse, Rosenberger, Swartley, Schantz, Souder, Stemen, Snavely, Shellenberger, Shenk, Stauffer, Snyder, Shoemaker, Shelly, Tyson, Weaver, Witmer, Wismer, Wenger, Wambold, Yoder, Zigler, and Zimmerman. The most common Pennsylvania Amish names include the following: Blough, Beiler, Borntreger, Coblentz, Detweiler, Kenagy, Fisher, Hooley, Hershberger, Hartzler, Hostetler, Kaufman, King, Lantz, Lapp, Miller, Mast, Plank, Peachey, Schrag, Stoltzfus, Smucker, Troyer, Umble, Yoder, and Zook. **C.H.S.**

C. Henry Smith, *Mennonites of America* (Goshen, 1909); *idem, Mennonite Immigration to Pennsylvania in the Eighteenth Century* (Norristown, 1929); *idem, The Story of the Mennonites* (Berne, 1941); J. C. Wenger, *History of the Mennonites of the Franconia Conference* (Telford, 1937); M. G. Weaver, *Mennonites of Lancaster Conference* (Scottdale, 1931); S. W. Pennypacker, *Historical and Biographical Sketches* (Philadelphia, 1883) H. P. Krehbiel, *History of the General Conference of the Mennonite Church of North America* (Canton, 1898); H. S. Bender, "Founding of the Mennonite Church in America at Germantown, 1683-1708," *MQR* VII (1933) 227-50.

Pennsylvania Aid Committee, properly called "Mennonite Executive Aid Committee of Pennsylvania for the Mennonite Congregations in West Prussia, Poland, and South Russia," was formally organized on April 14, 1874, as the over-all relief committee of the Mennonites of Eastern Pennsylvania to raise funds to aid in the resettlement of Mennonites from South Russia in the prairie states of Kansas, Nebraska, Minnesota, and South Dakota. It represented largely the Mennonite Church (MC) in the Lancaster and Franconia conferences, and it was the action of the Lancaster Conference on March 27, 1874, in appointing an aid committee which resulted in the larger committee. Its initial officers were Amos Herr, president, John Shenk, secretary, Gabriel Baer and H. R. Godshall, treasurers. The first four were all of Lancaster County, while Godshall was of Souderton in the Franconia district. The committee co-operated with the Mennonite Board of Guardians (*q.v.*) and the other aid committees, such as the one in Ontario, but continued independently to aid the transatlantic movement (using the Red Star Line of Philadelphia) and to furnish loans to needy immigrant families as well as direct donations for the neediest cases. The servicing of the loans continued for several decades. The further history and organization of the Committee are not known. Caspar Hett of Philadelphia was the business agent of the Committee. **H.S.B.**

C. Henry Smith, *The Coming of the Russian Mennonites* (Berne, 1927); Kempes Schnell, "John F. Funk, 1835-1930, and the Mennonite Migration of 1873-75," *MQR* XXIV (1950) 199-229.

Pennsylvania Dutch (Pennsylvania German) is a dialect spoken widely in southeastern Pennsylvania and in other places to which Pennsylvania Germans have migrated. Fredric Klees estimated that probably more than 300,000 Pennsylvania Germans "are more at home in Dutch than in English" and that there are probably more than 400,000 others who habitually speak English but can make "themselves understood in Dutch if necessity arises." Dr. J. William Frey, author of *Pennsylvania Dutch Grammar* (1950), stated that there were 500,000 in each of these two groups. The principal area in which the dialect or language is spoken is southeastern Pennsylvania, where at least fourteen counties are distinctively Pennsylvania German. Lying directly west of these are eighteen counties having important Pennsylvania German population. Chief areas are the counties of Montgomery, Bucks, Berks, Lancaster, York, Dauphin, Lebanon, Lehigh, Northampton; and the cities of Reading, Allentown, and Bethlehem. During the 18th and much of the 19th centuries nearly all of the Amish and Mennonites east of the Mississippi River and in Ontario, with the exception of those immigrating directly from Holland or Switzerland, spoke Pennsylvania Dutch, and in the 20th century all Old Order Amish Mennonite communities were still using the dialect as their household language, although they used in their religious services a combination of High German and Pennsylvania Dutch. Those wishing to study the dialect have found Amish communities ideal places for their surveys. For instance, Alfred L. Shoemaker did a doctoral dissertation in 1940 at the University of Illinois on "Studies on the Pennsylvania German Dialect of the Amish Community in Arthur, Illinois," while Ruth Bender did a master's thesis at the University of Iowa in 1929 on "A Study of the Pennsylvania-German as Spoken in Johnson County, Iowa." Certain Mennonite communities which have derived much of their membership from the Amish background have also maintained the dialect as a household language. Chief among these areas are the Johnstown and Springs district in Somerset County, Pa., the Holmes County, Ohio, community, and Lagrange County, Ind.

When the pressure of American anti-German feeling during World War I forced the discontinuance of the use of German in public programs, nearly all Mennonite churches in Pennsylvania Dutch-speaking areas which had not done so previously began to use English in their services. The Old Order Amish, however, have continued the public use of German, while the Conservative Amish Mennonites have only recently generally adopted English. The continued use of German by the Amish can be explained by their reluctance to accept any changes in religious practices and partly by the fact that since their music and devotional literature are in German they are fearful of losing their religious heritage by dropping the German. The religious use of German has been an important factor in the retention of Pennsylvania Dutch as the Amish household language. An additional factor in assuring the preservation of the dialect in eastern Pennsylvania has been its widespread use by their Lutheran and Reformed neighbors who originally came to that state from the German Palatinate. English, Scotch-Irish, Welsh, French, and even Negro neighbors learned the dialect from them so that many of these speak it fluently.

The renewed American interest in regional culture and the attempt to popularize Pennsylvania Dutch culture will no doubt prolong the life of this dialect in non-Amish circles and will thus indirectly strengthen its position in Amish life. A growing body of literature on Pennsylvania Dutch culture as well as material written in this dialect has given the Pennsylvanians a pride in their heritage. As long ago as 1941 Otto Springer of the University of Pennsylvania Department of Germanic Languages produced a 16-page mimeographed bibliography listing 223 books and articles for the study of the Pennsylvania German language and its sources. In spite of this interest in the dialect, prophets have predicted that the dialect is doomed to disappear as a living language in America, although it is doubtful that this will happen as long as the Amish preserve their "Old Order."

When thousands of Germans came to Pennsylvania in the 18th and 19th centuries they brought their dialects with them, the chief one of which was the Palatine (*pfälzisch*) German dialect, since the majority of these immigrants came from the Upper Rhine Valley. The Palatine dialect is the basic element in the Pennsylvania Dutch. Although immigrants from other German areas such as Hesse, Baden, and Württemberg, as well as from Switzerland, added words to the Pennsylvania Dutch vocabulary, it is still primarily Palatine German. Even today Pennsylvania Germans visiting in the Upper Rhine Valley have little difficulty in conversing with the natives of that region. While it is true that the Pennsylvanians have adopted some English words into their dialect, these do not comprise more than 5 per cent of the Pennsylvania Dutch working vocabulary. There are slight variations in the dialect between Berks and Lancaster counties in Pennsylvania, and also between Pennsylvania and the western states; but these groups have no difficulty in understanding each other. Klees characterized the dialect thus: "It is not a language possessing dignity or grandeur; it is not a speech fit for tragedy. But it is one in which humor and homely sentiment can be well expressed." One of the most noted pieces of Pennsylvania Dutch literature is a collection of poems by a Reformed minister, Henry Harbaugh, called *Harbaugh's Harfe* (Philadelphia, *c*1870). Chief of several newspaper columns has been *'S Pennsylvaanisch Deitsch Eck* in the *Allentown* (Pa.) *Morning Call*. A number of regular radio programs as well as stage plays in the dialect have entertained large audiences of Pennsylvania Dutch in eastern Pennsylvania.   M.G.

Fredric Klees, *The Pennsylvania Dutch* (New York, 1951) 277-85; Albert F. Buffington and Preston A. Barba, *A Pennsylvania German Grammar* (Allentown, 1954); J. William Frey, *Pennsylvania Dutch Grammar* (Lancaster, 1950); Marcus Lambert, *A Dictionary of the Non-English Words in the Pennsylvania-German Dialect* (Lancaster, 1924); *A Pennsylvania-Dutch Dictionary* (Quakertown, n.d.); A. R. Horne, *Pennsylvania German Manual* (Allentown, 1896); E. F. Robacker, *Pennsylvania German Literature* (Philadelphia, 1943); *Pennsylvania Folklife*, a quarterly now published at Bethel, Pa., beginning in 1949 as the *Pennsylvania Dutchman* published at Lancaster.

Pennsylvania - German Culture. The ethnic group known as the Pennsylvania "Dutch" (from *Deutsch*) has left an indelible impress upon the American way of life. They are a group of people (of Swiss, Alsatian, and Palatine origin) who earlier shared and still share to a certain extent a common High-German Palatine dialect, and who settled mostly in Pennsylvania in the 18th century and later. Religiously there are three general types of Pennsylvania Dutch: (1) "Church People," so called because the adherents belonged to established state churches (Lutheran and Reformed) when they came to this country; (2) the Moravians; and (3) the "plain people" (also called Sects).

Among the "plain people" (so named because of their plainness in dress) are the various groups of Mennonites, Amish, Dunkards or Church of the Brethren, Zion's Children, Brethren in Christ, and earlier the Schwenckfelder group. The Amish are currently photographed and popularized so much that there is a common mistaken notion that all Pennsylvania Dutchmen are "plain." The plain people probably number not more than 10-15 per cent of the total dialect-speaking population; there are about a half million in North America who can speak or understand the Pennsylvania-Dutch dialect.

The Pennsylvania Germans preserved many of the finer features of the group culture which they brought with them from the Old World. Here will be discussed their contributions to the broader scope of American life, with occasional reference to elements of their ethnocentric culture, which of itself is a fascinating field for the sociologist.

Agriculture: Few persons will disagree that these people always have been among the best farmers in America. Accustomed to the intensive cultivation of their fields, they did not adopt the plantation system of the southern states or devote vast acreage to grazing. The farmstead became a fairly self-sufficient economic unit.

Nature is a stern disciplinarian and those who seek her rewards must learn the disciplines of life. The Mennonites, Amish, and other members of the plain people have integrated these disciplines with their spiritual and economic life. Usually the Lutheran and Reformed people also held close to basic principles and practices in agriculture.

The Pennsylvania Germans are credited with the introduction of the willow tree, many varieties of fruit, especially apples, the prevention of soil erosion, the balanced rotation of crops, the building of "bank" barns, the Conestoga wagon, prairie schooner of pioneer days, several types of fences, and numerous other elements found in modern agriculture.

Kitchen Culture: The excellence of Pennsylvania-German cooking is acknowledged by most people. Housewives in Pennsylvania are little concerned with calories and vitamins but ever alert to the virtues of cleanliness, taste, and the complete banishment of hunger from the domains over which they rule. *The Mennonite Community Cookbook,* by Mary Emma Showalter, provides a full fare for those who wish to be initiated. They contributed to our national pantry such delicacies as cottage cheese, scrapple, various types of sausages, pretzels, cole slaw and, of course, sauerkraut.

Crafts: Every ethnic group has its own peculiar Volkskunde; that of the Pennsylvania Germans is of especial interest because of its expertness and the vestiges of Renaissance lore which survived the centuries in a new world. Early craftsmen included cabinetmakers, whose workmanship is attested to this day by antique collectors, weavers, potters, stone masons, wheelwrights, wainwrights, carpenters, smiths, millers, coopers, and processors of farm products.

The young lady of the household filled the dower chest (perhaps one made by a relative and decorated by a friend) with linens made of flax which she spun and embroidered. Her mother quilted bed coverings, braided straw for the making of hats, cut and sewed cloth to furnish garments for her family. Some of these handicrafts are still employed on farmsteads in Mennonite-Amish communities.

The Finer Arts, Fraktur: A style of broken or fractured writing, usually illuminated in brilliant colors, was one of the arts practiced in monasteries by the trained copyists of medieval times. The skills involved and the knowledge of vegetable dyes used, were brought to America by the early Germans. They illuminated their birth certificates, baptismal certificates, *Haus-Segen* (house blessings), and other documents of record. Itinerant artists wrote life data on the flyleaves of Bibles and seamstresses designed and appliqued them to cloth.

This art flourished until 1830 when commercial printing presses began to supply printed forms. Later Currier and Ives attempted to reproduce these forms in color. The invention of four-color printing in the early 1930's has made it possible to reproduce these designs in fairly satisfactory color and theme. Since then the general public has become accustomed to all sorts of advertising materials showing hearts, doves, tulips, stars, and fraktur lettering in glittering hues. The arts of fraktur and illumination are the only forms of folk art transplanted from Europe to American soil.

It should be pointed out here that not all of the church groups participated in the application of designs to the barns, dower chests, chairs, bookmarks, quilts, tombstones, pottery, etc. The practices were not common among Mennonite and Amish sects, who always preferred "plain" living.

After 1830, when the printer, the loom, and the planing mill supplanted the fraktur artist, the seamstress, and the cabinetmaker, respectively, the farmers transferred some of these designs to their barns. To break the monotony of color in an 80-foot expanse of red or white painted boards the owner had attractive designs such as stars, teardrops, sun wheels, etc., painted on barn sides. The credulous, perhaps gullible, persons who know little or nothing of Pennsylvania-German culture have accepted the rather sensational version that these barnscapes are "hex" signs, designed to drive away evil spirits, or witches who might otherwise molest the cattle in the barns.

Music: If the musical capital of the United States had been designated prior to 1830 it would have been located either in Bethlehem or Ephrata, Pa. Remembering that the Puritans of New England were prohibited by the tenets of their faith from participating in any kind of music other than humming and that the plantation of the south knew only the spinet and the fiddle, it becomes quite clear that music could develop only in the middle colonies.

The monks at the Ephrata Cloisters wrote more than 600 hymns. Conrad Beissel, the superintendent of the Cloisters, wrote the first book on harmony written in the New World. As early as 1742 the Moravians in Bethlehem rendered "In Dulce Jubilo." The Brothers and Sisters in Unity (Moravians) composed hundreds of chorales for their religious festivals. To this day the Bach Festival Chorus at Bethlehem continues as one of the finest choral groups in America.

It was the Pennsylvania Germans who built the first church organs, introduced the trombone, the flute, and various types of horns. They formed the first orchestra, rendered the first symphony, and established singing schools in nearly all communities in which they were settled.

Literature: The literature created by people who use a foreign language does not exist for those who do not understand it. The great mass of German literature created before the triumph of English, c1910, is therefore frequently not recognized as a contribution to American life.

Since 1910 all Pennsylvania Germans are completely literate in English and most of them do their thinking in English. The full impact of their contributions is only now beginning to be felt. Among recent writers whose ancestry dates back to early German immigrants are Pearl Buck, Lowell Thomas, Bayard Taylor, William Dean Howells, Joyce Kilmer, Alan Segar, Conrad Richter, Hervey Allen, Neal Swanson, Elsie Singmaster, Joseph Hergesheimer, James Whitcomb Riley, Grace Noll Crowell.

A sizable volume of literature in English has been produced by Pennsylvania German scholars writing for learned societies devoted to the preservation of their history and lore. The result is that the Pennsylvania Germans are probably the most thoroughly recorded group in all America. No group knows its own history better. Not only have professional groups such as the German Society of Pennsylvania (est. 1765), the Pennsylvania German Society (est. 1895), the Pennsylvania German Folklore Society (est. 1935), and the Pennsylvania Dutch Folklore Center (est. 1948) produced much of the literature, but many church bodies, notably the Mennonites, Moravians, and Schwenckfelders, have published great masses of literature relating to their own individual history and statement of faith.

Education: In spite of the assertions made by some writers condemning the Pennsylvania Germans for hostility to secular education the facts prove the opposite to be true. These writers have mistaken the cautious and conservative approach for opposition and benightedness. There are more colleges located in the southeastern segment of Pennsylvania than there are in any similar area in the country; the Language Atlas prepared by Brown University in 1943-44 lists Lancaster, Pa., as the spot where the best English is being used; nearly all the leaders of public education at the state and federal levels are descendants of Pennsylvania - German stock; and the literacy census of 1940 places southeastern Pennsylvania as lowest in the extent of illiteracy in the entire nation. (See **Pennsylvania Dutch.**)   A.D.G.

Emil Meynen, *Bibliographie des Deutschtums der kolonialzeitlichen Einwanderung in Nordamerika, 1683-1933* (Leipzig, 1937); Frederick Klees, *The Pennsylvania Dutch* (New York, 1950).

Pennsylvania Mennonite Church (MC), a member of the South Central Conference, located in Harvey Co., Kan., midway between Hesston and Newton, began in 1872, when Mennonite settlers, most of them from Eastern Pennsylvania, located here. The congregation was organized in 1885. The first meetinghouse, about 30 x 40 ft., was built in 1887. Services were conducted alternately by the Mennonites and Amish Mennonites until they merged in 1892. The Amish Mennonites came to Harvey County from Mifflin County, Pa., between 1885 and 1889. A new frame building 40 x 60 ft. with a seating capacity of 200 was dedicated in 1903, and enlarged in 1947.

Among the historic events in the congregation was the reception into the congregation of 61 members by Bishop T. M. Erb on March 4, 1906—45 by baptism, 16 by confession or letter—following evangelistic meetings by J. E. Hartzler. In 1913 there was a schism in the congregation caused by the Holiness movement, when 50 members withdrew, including two of the three ministers, David B. Zook and J. M. R. Weaver. Weaver returned to the Pennsylvania Church in 1922. R. J. Heatwole, who moved into the Pennsylvania community in 1882, was recognized as an influential layman. He promoted Sunday schools and secured evangelists for the early settlers. T. M. Erb served as minister and bishop 31 years, and his son Paul Erb as minister for 22 years. In 1958 Earl Buckwalter was pastor and bishop of the congregation of 102 members.

G.G.Y.

Emma Risser, *History of the Pennsylvania Mennonite Church in Kansas* (Hesston, 1958).

Pennypacker, Samuel W. (1843-1916), governor of Pennsylvania 1903-7, was a great-great-great-grandson of the Mennonite immigrant Hendrick Pannebecker (b. 1674), who was in Germantown, Pa., by 1699 and settled in the Skippack Mennonite settlement of Montgomery County, Pa., in 1702. Hendrick's grandson was the Mennonite bishop Matthias Pannebecker (1742-1808), and the latter's grandson was Dr. Isaac P. Pennypacker, a physician and teacher of medicine. The doctor's son, Samuel Whitaker, was born at Phoenixville, Pa., on April 9, 1843. He studied law and was admitted to the bar in 1866, became Judge in Common Pleas No. 2 in Philadelphia in 1889, Presiding Judge in this court in 1896, and served as Republican governor of Pennsylvania 1903-7. He was also a historian and bibliophile (collected 10,000 items), and wrote voluminously on the history of eastern Pennsylvania and on his Mennonite forebears and their faith. Worthy of note are his essays on David Rittenhouse, Christopher Dock, and the *Martyrs' Mirror*, in *Historical and Biographical Sketches* (Philadelphia, 1883), also his book, *The Settlement of Germantown* (Philadelphia, 1899).

His brother Isaac R. Pennypacker edited his *Autobiography of a Pennsylvanian* (Philadelphia, 1918). He died Sept. 2, 1916. Whatever merit Daniel K. Cassell's *History of the Mennonites* (1888) possessed was based largely on the materials he used from Pennypacker's research. Pennypacker's grandfather Matthias, son of the bishop, paid for the reprinting of the Dordrecht Confession of Faith at West Chester, Pa., in 1814. Most of the Mennonite section of the Pennypacker book collection was purchased at auction by the Schwenckfelder Library at Pennsburg, Pa., in 1924, where it still remains. J.C.W.

Pension Funds of the Dutch Mennonites. When the trained and salaried ministry became more or less usual in Dutch Mennonite congregations, the matter of supplying pensions for aged and disabled ministers and ministers' widows became a real problem; and so a number of pension funds were established. The oldest fund is the Widows' Fund in North Holland, which dates from 1794 (see **Fonds ter ondersteuning**). Soon after this, funds were founded in Friesland for the pensioning of retired ministers and widows. The Groningen conference founded a widows' fund in 1835; the *Zwolsche Fonds* (*q.v.*) was organized in 1810. The *Algemeen Emeritaat en Invaliditeitsfonds* (*q.v.*), usually called *Zaansche Fonds,* was founded in 1848. In 1917 the Groningen conference established a fund for disabled and retired ministers. The *Pensioenverhogingsfonds* was created in 1929 to supplement inadequate pensions of retired ministers and widows. The functions of all these funds, except those founded by the Groningen conference, are now administered by a new pension fund founded in 1945 by the A.D.S., called the *Algemeen Pensioenfonds.* (F. H. Pasma, *Doopsgezind Handboek,* 1954.)   vDZ.

Pension and Ministers' Aid Committee (or *Committee on Pensions*) of the General Conference Mennonite Church. For a long period of time the leadership of the General Conference Mennonite Church was aware of the need for a plan to pension its ministers and missionaries at retirement age. In the fall of 1945 the Executive Committee appointed a committee called the Pension and Ministers' Aid Committee. The original members of this committee were August Epp, chairman, Clinton Kaufman, secretary, Mrs. J. E. Entz, Mary Bergen, H. Albert Claassen, and Robert Stauffer. The duties of this committee were defined as twofold: (1) To provide aid for needy ministers and widows of ministers and (2) to work out a plan of pensioning for ministers and missionaries commencing at age 65. Provision was made for direct appeal to the committee for help. A well-defined plan for pensioning ministers and missionaries was adopted at the General Conference sessions in August 1947 at Berne, Ind. When the constitution of the General Conference was revised this committee received the name of "Committee on Pensions" operating under the Board of Trustees and Finance (since 1956 called the Board of Business Administration).

In general, those who are eligible to enter the retirement plan are full-time ordained ministers, missionaries, both home and foreign, and full-time employees of the district conferences and the General Conference. As a guide to the employing organizations the committee has recommended that an amount equal to 10 per cent of the employees' salary be paid into the Pension Plan. For a number of years the committee advised that one fourth of the payment into the plan ought to be borne by the participant in the plan and three fourths of the cost be paid by the employing organization, such as the church, the Board of Missions, etc. Of recent years the committee changed its recommendation to the employing organizations in that they have been urging the organizations to pay the entire cost of the Pension Plan, thereby making it possible for the minister to enroll in Social Security and pay the cost himself. Benefits for retirement start at the age of 65, and if the participant dies before that time, a lump sum is paid to the surviving family by virtue of the plan having the factor of life insurance. Since Social Security is available to ministers and missionaries in addition to the Pension Plan of the Conference, it now becomes possible for ministers and missionaries to look forward to an income at retirement which can be considered approaching the point of adequacy. The Pension Plan has not been accepted as fully and promptly as it should have been. To date 46 ministers and 78 missionaries are enrolled in the plan (1957). AU.E.

Retirement Life Income Plan as Adopted by the General Conference (Newton, 1948); *Reports and Official Minutes of the General Conference Mennonite Church 1947, 1950, 1953, 1956.*

Pension Plan: see Pension and Ministers' Aid Committee.

Penthelin, Sebold, a member of the Anabaptist congregation in Augsburg, Bavaria, Germany, in whose house their religious services were held. He was baptized by Jakob Gross. He was seized in September 1527, but declared that he would adhere to his faith and refused to render the oath, and was thereupon expelled from the city with five other Anabaptists, including Anna, the wife of Salminger (*q.v.*). HEGE.

Fr. Roth, *Augsburgs Reformationsgeschichte* I (Munich, 1901) 235; *ML* III, 347.

Pentler, Sigmund: see Peutler, Si(e)gmund.

Penzenauer, Hans, an Anabaptist martyr, a goldsmith of Steyr, Austria. Together with the knifesmith Matthäus Pürchinger, the scissors grinder Hans Schützenecker (*q.v.*), the brushmaker Leonhard Alexberger (*q.v.*), Sigmund Peutler, the woolcarder Hans Muhr (*q.v.*), the blacksmith Paul Hertlmayr, the bowmaker Michael Gruber, and the cobbler Hans Heher (*q.v.*), he was imprisoned in the summer of 1527 by the magistrate of Steyr as an Anabaptist. The cross-examination revealed that they had been confirmed in their belief by the sermons of Hans Hut (*q.v.*). Ferdinand I, to whom the magistrate had reported the affair, ordered on Sept. 10, 1527, that the prisoners be dealt with in accord with the law and pardoned only if they recanted.

In November Wolfgang Künigl (*q.v.*), the prosecutor, arrived in Steyr, and the trial was begun. Künigl advised against too severe a penalty for those willing to recant. But Ferdinand wanted the penalty of Horb (*q.v.*) applied against the penitent; the council in its report of Nov. 15, 1527, objected to this penalty as being too severe, pointing out that six of the prisoners showed signs of penitence. The suggestion of the council was disregarded. On November 20 the king appointed a representative from each of the other six cities in his domain to sit in on the sentencing of the obstinate. The course of the trial has been described in detail in the annals of Steyr written by Preuenhueber. The accused were charged with disregarding the Roman sacrament, heresy, gathering mobs, preaching in corners, and performing baptism.

The examinations, in which the Anabaptists defended their position well with references from the Bible, lasted three days. The prisoners declared themselves willing to stop holding meetings. Künigl replied that this would not be sufficient, and that they must also desist from their Anabaptist views. This they refused to do. In deciding upon the sentence, the minority advocated two months of indoctrination by competent clergymen; the majority, however, out of "human pity," decided upon death by the sword and the burning of the corpses in place of death by fire as the law required.

Ferdinand's decision of March 21, 1528, reproached them for permitting a difference of opinion to arise in judging "so gruesome, damnable, and unheard-of a sect," and ordered death by the sword and the burning of the bodies. On February 28, the condemned men were again tried on the rack, but even torture could not deflect them from their faith. On March 30 the six named at the beginning were executed; in May Heher and five other Anabaptists were beheaded, Schützenecker's wife was drowned, and a number of Anabaptists expelled from Steyr. P.DE.

Alexander Nicoladoni, *Johannes Bünderlin von Linz und die oberösterreichischen Täufergemeinden* (Berlin, 1893); Valentin Preuenhueber, *Annales Styrenses* (Nürnberg, 1740); *ML* III, 347 f.

Peoria, Ill., a city (pop. 111,856; with suburbs 250,512) named after one of the Illini Indian tribes, is located in Peoria County on the western shore of Peoria Lake, an expansion of the Illinois River. It is situated a little north of the center of the state in the heart of an extensive and diversified agricultural area. Part of the city is located on high bluffs along the lake, making beautiful homesites.

The first Mennonites in the area were Amish who settled east of the Illinois River, in Tazewell and Woodford counties, beginning about 1830, coming from Alsace, via Pennsylvania and New Orleans. About 1833 some Mennonites from the East settled in the same areas. The first Mennonite congregation in the city, known as the Mennonite Gospel Mission, was begun on July 19, 1914, by the Central Conference of Mennonites. The second was begun by the Mennonites (MC) on the South Side, on Feb. 16, 1919, and continues as the Ann Street Mennonite Church. Very few Mennonites have settled in the city itself. The present members of these two congregations are largely from non-Mennonite backgrounds. Approximately 200 persons with Mennonite affiliation in all branches now live in the city, with approximately 3,000 persons living within a radius of 25 miles east of the river and city. In 1935 a mission was begun in East Peoria, known as Highway Village, sponsored by the Mennonite Church (MC). The Mennonites in the Peoria area come largely from the M.C., G.C.M., and the Evangelical Mennonites.   J.J.H.

Peoria Gospel Mission (GCM), 1001 N. Adams, Peoria, Ill., under the Central District Mennonite Conference, had 111 members in 1958, with Samuel Ummel as pastor.   M.G.

Peoria Mennonite Church (MC), now known as the "Ann Street Mennonite Church," is located in the southwestern part of the city at 2101-5 West Ann Street, Peoria, Ill. It was started as a mission in a former saloon at the corner of Garden Street and Western Ave., on Feb. 16, 1919, by the Illinois District Mission Board. John Roth served as the first superintendent. In 1921 the work was placed in charge of the Mennonite Board of Missions and Charities, which still sponsors the congregation. On Oct. 29, 1922, the congregation was organized. In 1926 the mission building was sold and the following year the present parsonage and church were erected, greatly enlarged in 1954-58. The membership in 1958 was 86, with J. J. Hostetler as pastor.

In 1938 the congregation opened a branch Sunday school in Bellevue, just west of the city. This work was organized into an indigenous and later unaffiliated congregation, known as the Bellevue Bible Church.   J.J.H.

Perceval van den Berge, an Anabaptist martyr, was burned at the stake at Rijssel (Lille), France, on March 16, 1563, with five other brethren. He was a native of Zwevigem in Belgium, lived in Doornik, and was seized while visiting the preacher Jan de Swart (q.v.) at Halewijn (Halluin) on March 7, 1563. (*Mart. Mir.* D 299 f.; E 664 f.; *ML* III, 349.)
                    vDZ.

Perceux, (Les), is listed in the *Christlicher Gemeinde-Kalender* 1931-41 as a Mennonite congregation in the Bernese Jura, Switzerland, with Eugen Burkhalter as preacher, whose address in 1941 was Perceux-Undervelier. No further information was available.

Pergen (Bergen; Czech, *Perná*), a parish village near Nikolsburg (q.v.), Moravia. Here in 1527 the first colloquy was held between Hubmaier (q.v.) and Hans Hut (q.v.), which was no more successful in leading to an understanding than was the second, which was held soon afterward in the castle of Nikolsburg. When Jakob Wiedemann (q.v.), "one-eyed Jacob," and Philipp Jäger (Philipp Weber, q.v.) grew more and more violently opposed to Hans Spittelmaier (q.v.), who sided with Hubmaier, chiefly on the question of the payment of war taxes and the use of the sword, another debate between the two parties took place in the parsonage of

Pergen. The division resulted in the expulsion of the "Stäbler" (as opposed to the sword) from Nikolsburg by Leonhard of Liechtenstein in 1528; two hundred adults and their children left Nikolsburg and Pergen with Wiedemann and Jäger and went to Austerlitz (q.v.). In Pergen the Bruderhof that joined the Hutterian Brethren was able to continue. Here occurred the death of the preacher Matthias Legeder (q.v.) of Tirol in 1552.

When Adam von Dietrichstein (q.v.) came into the possession of Pergen and summoned the Jesuits, the Hutterites in Pergen were subjected to oppression, in the first place because the Brethren refused to remove their hats before these zealous priests. The preacher of Pergen, who had said that the Jesuits did not conduct themselves like the spiritual persons they pretended to be, was placed in stocks and irons for a day and a half and his mouth stopped with a gag "which was painted with a sticky substance. They beat many Brethren because they did not remove their hats before them." The householder was put into the tower of the Nikolsburg castle in midwinter; with fines and imprisonment they tried to compel the Brethren to attend Mass, but the Brethren steadfastly refused to obey. Siegmund von Dietrichstein, who inherited the lands from his father, expelled the Brethren from Pergen and Voitelsbrunn, in both of which villages they had lived more than thirty years. He gave them eighteen weeks to take away their goods, some of which they sold on the spot, not without considerable loss; they had to leave behind their buildings and the grain in the fields. On May 7, 1591, they moved out, some going to Wastiz (q.v.), the others to Sobotiste.   P.DE.

Beck, *Geschichts-Bücher*; J. Loserth, *Dr. Balthasar Hubmaier* (Brno, 1893) 132 f.; Wolkan, *Geschicht-Buch*; Zieglschmid, *Chronik*; ML III, 350.

Perger, Ulrich, a weaver, an Anabaptist martyr, was beheaded in Wels in Upper Austria (q.v.) on June 5, 1528, with the baker Hans Neumair (q.v.), the furrier Lienhard Haslinger (q.v.), the mason Hans Steinbeck (q.v.), the furrier Jörg Zacherle (q.v.) of Krems, the baker's assistant Jörg Kneutzinger (q.v.), and two cobblers, both named Sebastian; their corpses were burned. The wives of the two furriers, Barbara Haslinger and Barbara Zacherle, were drowned on the following Monday; the execution of Hans Steinbeck's wife was postponed until after the birth of her child. Six Anabaptists who recanted were released.   P.DE.

A. Nicoladoni, *Johannes Bünderlin von Linz und die oberösterreichischen Täufergemeinden* (Berlin, 1893); ML III, 350.

Periwig Dispute in the Danzig Mennonite Church (q.v.), which arose when Elder Hinrich van Dühren (q.v.) refused to admit to church membership a Dutch Mennonite who wore a wig, and excluded him from communion. Then when a considerable number of Danzig Mennonites followed the example of the Dutch and wore wigs, the quarrel assumed more violent forms and brought confusion into the brotherhood. In vain the government was called upon to settle the matter in 1739. Mutual bitterness increased. Finally Jacob Ouwejans (q.v.), a preacher from Holland, succeeded in reconciling the two parties. On Oct. 2, 1740, the entire congregation again observed communion. NEFF.

Inv. Arch. Amst. II, Nos. 2634-75; Horst Quiring, "Der Danziger Perückenstreit," *Gem.-Kal.* XLV (1936) 98-102; *ML* III, 351.

Perkasie Mennonite Church (GCM): see **Bethel** (Perkasie) Mennonite Church, Bucks Co., Pa.

Perkasie Mennonite Church (MC), located at Fourth and Chestnut Streets, Perkasie, Bucks Co., Pa., is a member of the Franconia Conference. The first services were held on Aug. 8, 1909. The meeting house, a brick structure 36 x 50 ft., was used nearly 40 years for conducting a community Sunday school and special services, under the general direction of the Blooming Glen Mennonite Church, and the immediate supervision of three trustees, the first of whom were William M. Moyer, A. M. Hunsicker, and Jacob M. Myers. The interior of the building was considerably redecorated in 1945. In 1948 the regularly attending Mennonite families were organized into an independent congregation of the Franconia Conference, with 45 charter members. The first pastor, Richard C. Detweiler, and deacon, Norman B. Benner, were ordained in 1948 and 1949, and are still serving (1958). The membership in 1958 was 80. In 1949 the congregation purchased a plot of ground near Perkasie for a church and community cemetery. It is frequently noted that the first young people's Bible meeting in the Franconia Conference was held at this church in 1914 and served as the forerunner of Mennonite Sunday evening meetings in the district. It is also considered to be the first mission Sunday school sponsored by Franconia Conference Mennonites. In 1956 a vacated factory building adjacent to the church was purchased, renovated, and annexed to the church to serve as an educational and activity facility. R.C.D.

Perkiomenville Mennonite Church (MC), located at Perkiomenville, Pa., was started as a mission station in 1935, by Clayton Godshall, and was organized as a congregation in 1947, with a membership of 47. Abram Metz was ordained minister in 1944, and Isaiah Alderfer as deacon in 1947. The congregation worships in a remodeled dwelling house. In 1950 a mission outpost was started by workers from the Perkiomenville congregation in an unused Mennonite meetinghouse, known as Bertolet's. It is located about four miles west of Perkiomenville. The membership at Perkiomenville in 1956 was 59, with Abram G. Metz as minister. In the spring of 1954 another mission was begun, also in an unused building, called Hersteins, which in 1956 had 23 members. A few of the members of Perkiomenville are workers there. In July 1957 a building program was started to provide more auditorium space and room for more Sunday-school classes. Dedication services were held on Jan. 19, 1958. A.G.M.

Perle-Bäumli is the name of a hymn by the Swiss Brethren, which contains 100 stanzas and begins with the words: "Was wollen wir singen und heben an zu Ehren dem himmlischen Bräutigam." Motto: The kingdom of heaven is like unto a merchant man, seeking goodly pearls; who, when he had found one pearl of great price, went and sold all that he had, and bought it (Matt. 13). The song was printed in 1767. The full title is as follows: *Ein schön neues geistliches Lied das Perle Bäumli genandt: Gerichtet nach dem Titel des hohen Lieds Salomons, und gegründet auf den Felsen, der Evangelischen Wahrheit und wahrer christlicher Confession, durch A.S. Zu singen wie dasz güldene A.B.C.* (Wolkan, *Lieder,* 156 f.; *ML* III, 350.) NEFF.

Perryton Mennonite Church (MC), located at 319 South Birch Street, in Perryton, Ochiltree Co., Tex., a member of the South Central District Conference, was organized on Nov. 7, 1943. In 1957 there were 50 baptized members. The pastor was Wallace Jantz. R.L.S.

Pershing Street Mennonite Church (MC), located at "C" and Pershing, Hutchinson, Kan., a member of the South Central Conference, is an outgrowth of missionary efforts started in 1931 by the Yoder and West Liberty Mennonite congregations. It was organized as a church on Aug. 7, 1937, with 41 charter members, under the name Hutchinson Mission Mennonite Church. In 1933 a basement was built in which services were held. In 1942 the present frame structure was built. Lay leaders who were prominent in congregational growth are Alf B. Miller, Paul Roupp, and Daniel J. and Susie Headings. The minister who helped in its beginning was Joe F. Brunk. Harry A. Diener and J. G. Hartzler served as bishops. Sanford E. King has been pastor since 1943. The membership in 1958 was 85. Only a few of these are converts of the mission; the majority are of Mennonite background who have made their homes in and around the city. S.E.K.

Persijn, an old Dutch family that can be traced back to 1080. Hippolytus Persijn became known as an enemy of the Mennonites. On Feb. 7, 1544, he wrote a report to the Privy Council against the followers of Menno (preserved in the state archives at Brussels). In a trial presided over by Hippolytus Persijn in 1554 Frans de Cuiper (*q.v.*) recanted his Mennonite convictions. On Jan. 10, 1553, Hippolytus Persijn issued a proclamation against the Mennonites, which gives expression to his fear that the followers of Menno were more numerous than commonly supposed. In 1565 he again urged the severe persecution of the Mennonites. He died on Dec. 3, 1568, at Utrecht.

Hippolytus Persijn was a zealous Roman Catholic, as were other members of this family during the 16th century. Duke Alba (*q.v.*), during his stay in Amsterdam, was the guest of the patrician merchant Jan Persijn; but his brother Pieter Persijn, who favored the Mennonites and was probably a member of the church, was seized on Nov. 27, 1567, on the order of the infamous Blood Council with 37 brethren and put to death without trial in Amsterdam in April 1568, and his property confiscated. It is not known when the family joined the Mennonites. The marriage of Jan Poppesz Persijn with Tettje Bouwens, a granddaughter of the indefatigable Elder Leenaert Bouwens (*q.v.*), on Dec. 11, 1728, shows a close connection. Poppe Jansz Persijn, the son of Jan

Poppesz and Teltje Bouwens, owned a roofing-tile factory at Harlingen, Friesland. Their son Jan Persijn (*q.v.*) was a Mennonite pastor. Others were deacons, as for example his son Jan Hendrik Persijn (1824-1910), an architect, who was a cofounder of the Arnhem congregation and its deacon-treasurer for more than 25 years. Through other marriages the Persijns are related to many well-known Mennonite families. (*ML* III, 350.) J.H.P.

Persijn, Jan, a Dutch Mennonite preacher, b. Aug. 19, 1787, at Harlingen, studied at the Mennonite Seminary in Amsterdam 1807-12. He accepted the pulpit at Hindeloopen in 1813, and was then called to the Mennonite congregation in De Rijp (*q.v.*) in North Holland in 1816. He preached here nearly forty years, retiring in 1855. He preached the dedicatory sermon in 1864, when the church was remodeled, using as his text Psalm 84:2-5. Persijn was untiring in his efforts for the congregation and did a fruitful work. He died as the result of an accident at Arnhem on May 1, 1861, and was buried in De Rijp. Some of his sermons and other historical works were published; e.g., *Een Viertal geschriften betr. de Doopsgez. Gemeente in de Rijp* (Hoorn, 1857). He was married to M. A. M. Sepp. (*ML* III, 350 f.) J.H.P.

Persoons, a former Mennonite family of Nijmegen, Dutch province of Gelderland. Lambert Persoon(s) obtained citizenship at Nijmegen on Sept. 9, 1657, but seems to have lived there for a considerable number of years before that. He was a deacon of the Nijmegen Mennonite congregation before 1656, as his brother Gerrit Persoons also seems to have been. Other members of this family are also mentioned as members of the congregation. His codeacon Jan Godschalks reported that Lambert Persoons died on April 18, 1657, but this cannot be true because he obtained citizenship in September of this year. He may have died in 1658. He and his relatives had moved in from the duchy of Jülich, Germany, probably either from Goch or from Gladbach. The above Gerrit Persoons left the Mennonite church in 1647 and joined the Reformed; in his booklet *Vervolgh van de Vertooninge des Staets en des handels der Mennoniten* (Utrecht, 1663), he tried to convince his former brethren that, although morals were much higher among the Mennonites than among the Reformed, the Mennonite church could not be the true church of Christ because it was divided into various branches. Copies of an earlier book by Gerrit Persoons on the same topic are apparently no longer extant. vpZ.

DB 1874, 13 ff.; 1895, 121; P. C. G. Guyot, *Bijdrage tot de Geschiedenis der Doopsgezinden te Nijmegen* (Nijmegen, 1845) 75.

Perth County, Ont., is significant in Mennonite history because of the westerly part of the Amish settlements in Easthope Township, because of the westerly section of the Old Order Amish of Mornington Township, and because of the Mennonite preaching appointment at a Lehman home in Ellice Township in 1850-65. The Mennonite Church (MC) in Wallace Township was situated also in the upper area of this county. (See also **Lehman, East Zorra, Old Order Amish, Wallace.**) J.C.F.

Peru Mennonite Church (MC), Milam, W. Va., is a mission church established in 1920. Lloyd O. Hartzler was the pastor of its 24 members in 1958. M.G.

Perwanger, Augustin and **Christoph,** two barons of Günzlhofen (*q.v.*) and Vogach in Upper Bavaria, Germany, were beheaded in Munich on Jan. 7, 1528, because they had been baptized as adults. NEFF.

Siegmund Riezler, *Geschichte Bayerns* III (Gotha, 1889) 811; IV (Gotha, 1899) 193 (in *Geschichte der Europäischen Staaten,* edited by Heeren *et al.*); *ML* III, 351.

Peryne (Petronella) **de Corte,** an Anabaptist martyr, burned at the stake at Antwerp, Belgium, on June 6, 1573. Peryne, who was arrested when a Mennonite meeting at Antwerp was surprised by the police, confessed that she had often attended such meetings. She had not yet been (re)baptized. (*Antw. Arch.-Blad* XIII, 118, 121-24, 179; XIV, 90 f., No. 1029.) vpZ.

Pesch, van, a Dutch Mennonite family, since about 1620 living at Utrecht, where many members served as deacons from 1668 until 1875. Originally they were tanners and fur traders, later furriers and bankers. Jacob van Pesch, a deacon, edited Joannes Houbakker's (*q.v.*) sermons (two volumes, published at Amsterdam in 1730 and 1732). There were also some members of the van Pesch family later at Rotterdam, Haarlem, and Amsterdam. Abraham van Pesch, b. 1806 at Amsterdam, d. at Zutphen on Sept. 10, 1850, studied at the Amsterdam Mennonite Seminary in 1826-32 and was a minister in the congregations at Gorredijk-Lippenhuizen 1832-34, and Rotterdam 1834-41; he retired for a year because of illness, and then served at Uithuizen 1842-44 and Zutphen 1845-49. He published *Het Doopsgezinde Kerkgenootschap gekenmerkt door het streven naar Vrijheid* (Rotterdam, 1836). He also copied a large number of the old books and documents of the Rotterdam Mennonite archives; these copies are now in the Amsterdam Mennonite Library. vpZ.

H. B. Berghuys, *Geschiedenis der Doopsgezinde Gemeente te Utrecht* (n.d., 1925); M. Schagen, *Naamlijst der Doopsgezinde Schrijveren* (Amsterdam, 1745) 78; *DB* 1881, 58, 61.

Pestel, Peter, an Anabaptist martyr, a shoemaker, a native of Plauen, Saxony, Germany. In the autumn of 1525 he left his native town and arrived at Linz (*q.v.*), Austria, at the end of 1529 or in early 1530, where he was won for Anabaptism by Franz Intzinger (*q.v.*) and baptized with another convert. He married an Anabaptist woman, but she left him when he migrated to Moravia. When persecution became severe in Moravia he returned to his home town. In Hof he was held a prisoner for seven weeks. He was asked to swear that he would not return to the town; he refused, on the ground that swearing is forbidden the Christian. He was nevertheless released. He stayed here only two weeks, in the home of his brother-in-law Balthasar Pintser and continued his way to Schneeberg, where he was employed by Martin Tubler, a shoemaker. Hardly two weeks later, on April 23, 1536, he was arrested and taken to the castle in Zwickau, and on the next day subjected to a cross-examination in the presence of the clergy (Wappler, p. 76). He confessed himself definitely as committed to Anabaptist teaching, and could not be deflected from his faith even by torture; "He would give his life for it." He said he had neither preached nor baptized, but where it was suitable he testified to his faith and reproved "his fellow men of sin"; he vigorously denied that he or his companions had stirred up revolt, conspiracy, or sedition. Then he was given Melanchthon's booklet, *Verlegung etlicher unchristlicher Artikel Welche die Widderteuffer fürgeben* (Wittenberg, about 1536), which had appeared at the same time as the electoral mandate. After reading it he gave the jailer the reply that there was not a true word in the booklet, that he had no fear of the mandate issued against the Anabaptists, for he had committed himself entirely to his heavenly Father. He would stand by this position. This state of affairs was reported to John Frederick (*q.v.*), Elector of Saxony, who turned the records over to the court in Wittenberg with the request that they pass the sentence. On the next day the sentence was read: Peter Pestel should be executed with the sword because of his heretical views on communion, that in the emblems the body and blood of Christ were not given out, on the person of Christ, that He had not received His flesh from Mary, and on government, that a Christian may not pass sentence as a ruler. The reasons given for the death sentence struck the elector as rather dubious; he could not agree that a man should be put to death merely on account of erroneous religious opinions. But his chancellor Bruck also favored the death penalty, arguing that Peter Pestel should be punished as an obstinate heretic and a violator of the imperial laws. The elector, however, drew up the denth sentence himself and sent it to Zwickau, to the effect that Peter Pestel should be executed with the sword, in accord with the edict of Speyer of 1529. In vain the brother of the condemned man, Valentin Pestel of Plauen, and a cousin Anthonius Pestel, who was the elector's secretary, appealed for modification. The sentence was carried out on June 16, 1536, in Zwickau.   NEFF.

Paul Wappler, *Inquisition und Ketzerprozesse in Zwickau zur Reformationszeit* (Leipzig, 1908) 70-84; *ML* III, 351.

Peter: see also **Pieter.**

Peter, the servant of Peter Planer (*q.v.*), an Anabaptist martyr, was executed with his master at Sterzing in the Adige Valley, Austria, in 1532. (*Mart. Mir.* D 33, E 440.)   NEFF.

Peter van den Broecke, an Anabaptist martyr, was burned at the stake on Aug. 18, 1550, at Antwerp, Belgium. Van Braght's account (*Mart. Mir.* D 128, E 524) that Jan and Pleun died with him is not correct. Jan Lievensz van Gent was executed on August 14, and Pleun, who is called "een Lakenbereider" without the mention of another name, on August 22. Their death is commemorated in the song *Een Liedeken van III Vrienden,* No. 4 in the *Lietboecxken;* it begins with the words, "Ick sal met

vreuchden singen een Liet." Van Braght (*Mart. Mir.* D 99, E 497) mentions the "three friends" but names only Jan Lievensz. Peter van den Broecke, a baker, was born at Komen (Commines) in Flanders; he later lived in Gent.   VDZ.

Offer, 521, the song pp. 521-26; *Antw. Arch.-Blad* VIII, 390, 393; XIV, 18 f., No. 192.

Peter Bruynen (Peter de Bruyne), a native of Weert, Dutch province of Limburg, an Anabaptist martyr, who was put to death at Antwerp, Belgium, on Oct. 22 (van Braght erroneously Oct. 2), 1551. Four others executed with him were Jan van den Wouwer (van Braght calls him Jan de Oude Kleerkooper), Pleunis van den Hoevele (van Braght, Pleun), Martin du Petitz (not mentioned in van Braght), and Jacob Peeters (van Braght: another brother). Peter Bruynen was unmarried. In prison he wrote two letters of farewell, which are little more than a succession of Scripture verses. Peter was baptized in Weert by Anthonis van Asselroye (Theunis van Hastenrath).

The *Groot Offerboek* (Haarlem, 1615) relates the trial of Peter, Jan, and Pleun, which is not found in *Offer des Heeren* or van Braght; all three of the defendants admitted that they had taken part in the breaking of images on the dike at Austruweel, and destroying a cross on the way to Hoboken near Antwerp. This is the only instance of iconoclastic Anabaptism in Holland known to me.

Peter and the four others are the subject of a song which begins with the words, "Tot lof des Vaders, soons, heyligen geest," found in *Offer des Heeren* and taken over in the *Ausbund* (No. 10); it is possible that the song, "Ick sal met vreuchden singhen een Liet" (*Een liedeken van III Vrienden*), found in the *Lietboecxken,* mentions Peter, Pleun, and Jan. Both hymns are found in Wolkan, *Lieder.*   VDZ.

Offer, 177-86; *Historie der Martelaren ofte waerachtige getuygen Jesu Christi* (*Groot Offerboek*) (Haarlem, 1615) 141-47; *Mart. Mir.* D 128-30, E 498; concerning the matter of image-breaking, *Offer,* 177 note 1, and 182 note 2; *DB* 1899, 154 f.; *Antw. Arch.-Blad* VIII, 405, 415; XIV, 20 f., No. 209; Wolkan, *Lieder,* 61, 66, 127; *ML* I, 287.

Peter van Cleve, an Anabaptist martyr: see **Pieter Aelbrechts.**

Peter van Coelen (Pieter van Keulen, van Ceulen, or Peter of Cologne) was by 1568 an elder of the Flemish Mennonites. He is known especially for the public disputations he held with the Reformed clergy. Already in 1578 at the disputation at Emden, Germany, when the elders were worsted by the Reformed preachers, he had saved the honor of the Mennonites. In 1587 he held a disputation with Henricus Antonides at Franeker.

Better known is the public disputation held at Leeuwarden in 1596. When Ruardus Acronius (*q.v.*), the Reformed preacher at Cornjum near Leeuwarden, molested the Mennonites, the States of Friesland ordered a public disputation to be held at the Reformed Galileër Church, in which Acronius and Peter participated and which lasted from August 16 to November 17. In 156 sessions they discussed 11 points set up by the Reformed side (including the Incarnation, the Scriptures, grace, overestimation of human ability, the church). The record (though one-sided) shows that Peter defended his opinions forcefully and with great ability and wide knowledge of the Bible. The only result was an increase in mutual bitterness. The wish of the Reformed synods in the following years to have the Mennonite churches closed is also one of its fruits.

Meanwhile Peter had gone over to the Frisian Mennonites. The Flemish had expelled him because he opposed the strict ban (1589). After the discussion with Acronius he was in Sneek, where he courageously met the violent preacher Bogerman (q.v.) in 1600. A severe edict against the Mennonites resulted. But on the whole the government did not carry it out very rigorously—to the great annoyance of the Calvinists. The date of Peter's death is not known. He died at an advanced age; that he was still active in 1603 is shown by a petition of the Harlingen Reformed Synod to the States of Friesland of that date.   vDZ.

BRN VII, 65, 550; DB 1873, 84-88; 1910, 20 f.; 1917, 132; Kühler, Geschiedenis I, 431, 445, 447 f.; Menn. Bl., 1851, 28-31; Protocol, dat is de gantsche handelinge des ghesprecks, gehouden tot Leeuwarden (Leeuwarden, 1597); Blaupot t. C., Friesland, 132-37; ML II, 524.

Peter Cornelius van Zurick-Zee: see **Plockhoy, Pieter Cornelisz.**

Peter Coster: see **Pieter Claesz.**

Peter (Pieter) Dirks (Dirczn) Snijder, an Anabaptist martyr, a tailor, beheaded at The Hague, Holland, on Nov. 6, 1539. He had been (re)baptized by Pieter de Houtzager (q.v.) and in 1533 was living at Amsterdam. In March 1534 he joined the Anabaptists who sailed from there en route to Münster (q.v.), but was arrested at Bergklooster (q.v.). He was released upon renouncing his faith, but later, "relapsing into his former error," i.e., being again a member of the Anabaptist congregation, he was arrested a second time and put to death. (Inv. Arch. Amst. I, Nos. 219, 745; DB 1917, 103; Grosheide, Bijdrage, 105.)   vDZ.

Peter Frericx, a tailor of Bolsward, Friesland, an Anabaptist martyr, was beheaded because of Anabaptism on March 17, 1537, with two other Anabaptists at Leeuwarden, the capital of the Dutch province of Friesland. His widow Janneken was drowned at Leeuwarden on Dec. 19, 1537. (DB 1917, 90; Mellink, Wederdopers, 242.)   vDZ.

Peter Gael (Pieter Galen), an Anabaptist who after having participated in the revolt and the attack on Amsterdam city hall on May 10-11, 1535, was put to death there in a very cruel way on May 14, 1535. He was typical of revolutionary Anabaptism. His confession contains important information concerning the extent and methods of revolutionary Anabaptism in the Netherlands. He revealed that this group wore a white ribbon on an arm and that they would kill all those not wearing such a ribbon. He also stated that Jacob van Campen, the Anabaptist bishop of Amsterdam, did not agree with their practices and intentions. Peter Gael had been (re)baptized by Claes van Limmen, who is said to have been at Münster during Peter's trial. (Grosheide,

Verhooren, 59-64; Mellink, Wederdopers, passim, see Index.)   vDZ.

Peter van Gheyen (Geyn), an Anabaptist elder in Cologne, Germany, who baptized the martyr Hans van Collen (q.v.) (Coelen) there in 1534. Nothing else is known about him. (Grosheide, Verhooren, 132.)   vDZ.

Peter von Gmunden: see **Riedemann, Peter.**

Peter the Great, Czar of Russia 1682-1725, spent some time in the Netherlands in 1697-98 and returned for a visit in 1717. He had learned to know Dutch business people in Russia and through these contacts he came to the Netherlands. During his stay in Holland he spent about a week in Zaandam to learn shipbuilding. After this he went to Amsterdam to study the same trade on the docks of the East India Company. Naturally his interest went far beyond the shipbuilding industry.

During his stay in the Netherlands Peter must also have established contacts with the Mennonites. Boris Rapchinsky reports that Peter invited among others the Mennonites Jan and Nicolaas van der Heyden, the inventors of fire engines, to come to Russia; they declined (Rapchinsky, 126). Nicolaas Bidloo (q.v.), a Mennonite physician of Amsterdam, accepted such an invitation and became Peter's personal physician and the founder and professor of the first medical school in Moscow.

During his second visit at Zaandam in 1717 Peter is supposed to have been the guest of Claas No(o)men, a Mennonite preacher. When Peter expressed his interest in attending a Mennonite worship service, Nomen took him to church and presented to him "the essence of all admonitions" in the words, "think well, speak well, do well" (Denkt wel, spreekt wel, doet wel). Impressed by this pointed admonition Peter is said to have turned to his Russian priest with the admonition to do likewise. There is, however, a vast number of stories in circulation about Peter the Great's stay and experience in the Netherlands; therefore it may be hard to ascertain whether this incident actually took place. Zaandam has made a monument of the little house in which Peter spent about a week. Of his much longer stay in Amsterdam there seem to be few traces of this nature.   C.K.

Boris Rapchinsky, Peter de Groote in Holland in 1697-98 (Amsterdam, 1925); Menn. Bl., February 1908, 11; June 1911, 44-45; ML III, 124, 352.

Peter auf den Heuren, an Anabaptist martyr, executed at Rheydt (q.v.), Germany, in 1584. (Der Mennonit IX, 1956, p. 123.)

Peter Janssen, an Anabaptist martyr: see **Pieter Jansz.**

Peter Kueper, from Sneek, Dutch province of Friesland, joined the Anabaptists and moved to Münster (q.v.), where he seems to have played a rather important part in the "kingdom" of Jan van Leyden (q.v.). In October 1534 he was one of the "apostles" Jan van Leyden sent out to various Westphalian towns to propagate the views of the "kingdom."

Peter Kueper together with Dionysius Vinne (*q.v.*) and four others went to Osnabrück, where they were apprehended and put to death. (Mellink, *Wederdopers*, 48, 245.) vDZ.

Peter von der Lippe, an Anabaptist living in Westphalia, Germany, was an adherent of David Joris (*q.v.*), and even after 1546 traveled about propagating the ideas of his leader; he also visited David Joris, who was then living at Basel. (Mellink, *Wederdopers*, 101.) vDZ.

Peter Metselaer, an Anabaptist martyr: see **Peter Witses.**

Peter van Norg (Noerich, also Orck; official name, *Gerdt Eike(l)man*) was a leading revolutionary agitator in the Netherlands and adjoining parts of Germany, being a follower of Jan van Batenburg (*q.v.*). Originally he lived at Deventer, Holland. By trade he was a glazier. He can hardly be listed among the Anabaptists, for after 1536 he was nothing but an ordinary bandit. He was burned at the stake on April 30, 1544, at Münster, Westphalia. (*DB* 1917, 141; 1919, 18, 22; Mellink, *Wederdopers, passim,* see Index.) vDZ.

Peter (Pieter) van Olmen, an Anabaptist martyr, burned at the stake on July 27, 1552, at Gent, Belgium. The Dutch martyrbooks, including van Braght's *Martyrs' Mirror,* give no information on the manner of Peter van Olmen's execution or the exact date. There is not much information about this martyr; he seems to have lived earlier in Wervik, Flanders, and hence was also called Peter van Wervick. In prison he wrote a letter to his brethren with admonitions to steadfastness, in which he describes his defense of the faith before the examining theologians. This letter is found in all the Dutch martyrbooks. He was commemorated in a song, "Groot zijn de Heeren crachten" (Great is the power of the Lord), found in the *Offer des Heeren.* The *Lietboecxken* has the "Liet van vrage ende antwoort" (Song of Question and Answer), which is there ascribed to Peter van Wervick. This hymn, which begins with the words, "Een eeuwige vruecht, die niet en vergaet" (An eternal joy, which does not pass away), is included in the Dutch hymnal *Veelderhande Liedekens* of 1556 and following editions (reprinted in Wackernagel, *Lieder*), while a large number of old Dutch Mennonite hymnals contain only the first part of this hymn, which is of much higher literary quality than the last stanzas, probably composed by another poet. HEGE, vDZ.

Offer, 187-94, 594-600; *Mart. Mir.* D 147-49, E 536-38; Verheyden, *Gent,* 18, No. 34; Wolkan, *Lieder,* 64, 66, 78, 84; Wackernagel, *Lieder,* 195, No. 99; *ML* III, 300.

Peter Scheymaker, a Dutch Anabaptist from Baambrugge, province of Utrecht, was in November 1533 one of the twelve "apostles" sent forth by Jan Matthijsz (*q.v.*) of Haarlem. He is identical with Pieter Boekebinder, who is said to have preached "everywhere in Brabant and Münster." There is no further information on him. (*DB* 1917, 98, 103.) vDZ.

Peter Schoenmaker, of Dremmen, a Dutch Anabaptist, who had moved to Münster (*q.v.*), Westphalia, in 1533. In the next year Peter was among the emissaries sent out by Jan van Leyden (*q.v.*) to propagate the ideas of revolutionary Anabaptism. In December 1534 he went to Wesel, Germany, then to the duchy of Jülich and the bishopric of Liége, where all trace of him is lost. (Mellink, *Wederdopers,* 28 f., 52, 370.) vDZ.

Peter Simons (Peeter Symonsz) of Tirns, Dutch province of Friesland, was a follower of Melchior Hofmann and an Anabaptist preacher, against whom the Frisian government issued a decree in 1534. In the spring of 1534 he joined the revolutionary Anabaptists and went to Münster (*q.v.*) in Westphalia, Germany, where he was married to Aeffgen Lystyncx (*q.v.*) and occupied a high rank, becoming major-domo of "queen" Divara, the wife of Jan van Leyden. In early 1535 he returned to the Netherlands. Vos thought he returned as a companion of Jan van Geelen (*q.v.*) to distribute the booklet *Van der Wraecke* and to rouse the Dutch Anabaptists. In March 1535 (according to Vos) he was in the Anabaptist group who stormed the Oldeklooster (Old Cloister) near Bolsward in Friesland, and was killed in the battle when the stadholder of Friesland reconquered it. Mellink is of the opinion that Peter Simons made a journey from Münster to the Netherlands in 1534 and again left Münster in March 1535, but that it is not certain that Peter was killed in the Oldeklooster battle, since all trace of him was lost when he left Münster.

Vos thought this Peter Simons was a brother of Menno Simons, but Kühler is of the opinion that the information of Gellius Faber that "a brother of Menno Simons was killed in the Oldeklooster battle" without further information is unacceptable. Besides this, it is not sure, as Mellink states, and to my opinion even unlikely, that the fanatical Peter Simons was the brother of Menno Simons, for this Peter Simons is said to have been a native of Tirns, whereas a brother of Menno would have been a native of Witmarsum. vDZ.

K. Vos, *Menno Simons* (Leiden, 1914) 2 note 1, and *passim; DB* 1917, 116, Nos. 62; W. J. Kühler in *De Zondagsbode* of Feb. 26, 1928; *idem, Geschiedenis* I, 149, 159; Mellink, *Wederdopers, passim,* see Index.

Peter of Spain (Pedro de Soza, Dutch; *Peter van Spagnien,* official name), an Anabaptist martyr, who was won to the Anabaptist faith by a brother from Amsterdam, Jakob Jansz Ruytenbergh, a merchant whom he had met in Spain. He was baptized in Antwerp, Belgium, and received into the congregation. When he was about to return to Spain to his wife and children he was arrested, and after a valiant confession of his faith was drowned in a tub at Antwerp on Feb. 1, 1560, with two brothers, Gomer de Clercq and Jacob Schot. With many other Anabaptist victims executed at Antwerp, he is commemorated in the song, "Aenhoort Godt, hemelsche Vader," found in the *Lietboecxken.* NEFF, vDZ.

Offer, 567; *Mart. Mir.* D 270, E 640; *Antw. Arch.-Blad* IX, 6, 11; XIV, 28 f., No. 310; Wolkan, *Lieder,* 63, 72; *ML* III, 352.

Peter Vrancken (Vrencken), an Anabaptist martyr, a brother-in-law of the martyr Metken (*q.v.*). In her trial Metken related that Peter had been beheaded at Born, duchy of Jülich, Germany, but did not give the date of his execution. Though the exact date is therefore not known, it must have happened before 1547, when Metken was put to death. vDZ.

W. Bax, *Het Protestantisme in het bisdom Luik* I (The Hague, 1937) 326, 398.

Peter van Wervick, an Anabaptist martyr: see **Peter van Olmen.**

Peter Witses (Wytses, Wietjes, Wiettiezoon), also called Peter (de) Metselaer, an Anabaptist martyr, a mason by trade, was put to death on April 13, 1533, at Leeuwarden, Dutch province of Friesland. During his trial he frankly admitted that he had received baptism on his faith in 1551. In his cross-examination he gave appropriate Biblically grounded answers. To his friends he wrote that they should properly teach simple young souls in the difference in the communion and provide for their own families. "Pray and watch, the times are perilous; and do not forget us in your prayers, and visit us sometimes, it is very edifying." His short letter to his wife is touching: "Abide in God, and mingle not with the wicked; for if the righteous draw back, my soul shall have no pleasure in him, says the Lord. The time of my departure seems to be nigh, may it take place with God. When the hour of parting comes, fear not, but guard your lips. My dear wife, abide in the grace of God given you." He is commemorated in the hymn, "Kermen is ter werlt en geclach, Druck coemt van alle zijden" (There is much moaning and lamenting in the world; persecution comes from all sides), which is found in the *Lietboecxken.* (*Offer,* 437-42; *Mart. Mir.* D 159, E 548 f.; *ML* III, 118.)   Neff.

Peters (Pieters), a Mennonite family in West Prussia, Germany, found there from about 1580 and probably of Dutch-Frisian descent. Many members of this family served as deacons and preachers in various West Prussian Mennonite congregations, especially those of Danzig, Montau, Ladekopp. The Dutch *Naamlijst* names Hendrik Pieters (Peeters) as the elder of the Frisian (Waterlander) congregation in the Elbing Werder 1726-*c*55, and Isaack Peters as preacher in Tiegenhagen 1746-93.

The Peters family furnished a number of prominent leaders in the Molotschna settlement in South Russia. Among these were Abraham Peters (*q.v.*), an M.B. leader who founded the M.B. settlement in the Kuban in 1863; Abraham Peters (*q.v.*) of Fürstenau, who led a group to Turkestan in 1880; Hermann Peters (*q.v.*), the founder of the Peters group called "Brotbrecher"; Bernhard Peters (*q.v.*, 1855-1921), elder at Schönsee; and Isaak Peters (*q.v.*).

In North America in 1957 there were 26 Mennonite ministers bearing the name Peters, distributed as follows: G.C.M.—12: in Kansas 2, Montana 1, Mississippi 1, Manitoba 4, British Columbia 2, Ontario 1, Saskatchewan 1; M.B.—8: Manitoba 6, British Columbia 1, California 1; Old Colony in

Mexico—3; C.G.C.—2: Michigan and Florida. Among these should be mentioned Frank C. Peters (MB), formerly president of Tabor College and now a teacher in the M.B. Bible College in Winnipeg, G. W. Peters, former dean of the M.B. Biblical Seminary in Fresno, Cal., and G. H. Peters, former principal of the Mennonite Collegiate Institute at Gretna, Man.   vDZ.

Peters: see also **Pietersz.**

Peters, Abraham, of Ladekopp (*q.v.*) in the Molotschna (*q.v.*) Mennonite settlement in South Russia, a member of the Petershagen (*q.v.*) congregation, joined the Mennonite Brethren at the founding of that branch, and was chosen deacon. In 1863 he migrated with other Mennonite Brethren to the Kuban (*q.v.*). Here he took an active part in the life of the congregation, serving as Alt-Diakon in the church council in directing the spiritual affairs of the congregation. In 1877-78 the congregation built a new large church and secondary school (Fortbildungsschule) in one building. The school was founded by a board headed by Abraham Peters, who was vigorously interested in the work, and was maintained for several years, until it was united with the settlement school at Wohldemfürst (Velikoknyazhesk) in 1881. (Friesen, *Brüderschaft,* 422; *ML* III, 353.)   A.B.

Peters, Abraham, a minister of the Ohrloff-Neukirch Mennonite Church, Molotschna, Russia, and the leader of a settlement in Aulie-Ata (*q.v.*). Peters was a teacher and was chosen to the ministry in 1873. Under the impact of a revival which swept the Mennonite settlements, the writings of Jung-Stilling, and the introduction of compulsory military service, he—like Claasz Epp (*q.v.*), who led the settlement in Ak-Mechet (*q.v.*)—became the leader of several dozen Molotschna Mennonite families who went to Central Asia in 1880 to seek a refuge from the Tribulation, which they thought was at hand. Peters hoped to secure his ordination as elder at Trakt but failed. Upon arrival at Tashkent his group and Epp's negotiated regarding settlement, the Molotschna group choosing Aulie-Ata. The existence of the two settlements in Central Asia was probably due to rivalry between the two leaders. Ultimately the spirit of Peters predominated. Peters became elder of the Romanovka Mennonite Church (*q.v.*) in 1884, and was succeeded by Johann Regier (*q.v.*). In 1910 Aulie-Ata had a population of *c*1,000, which included also a small M.B. group.   C.K.

Friese, *Brüderschaft,* 409, 480 ff.; Franz Bartsch, *Unser Auszug nach Mittelasien* (North Kildonan, 1948) pp. 40 ff.; *ML* III, 353.

Peters, Bernhard (1816-1912), an elder of the Margenau-Schönsee (*q.v.*) Mennonite congregation in the Molotschna settlement, South Russia, was born at Vierzehnhuben, West Prussia. He married Agatha Wiens in 1846, and had a family of 8 sons and 4 daughters. Peters became minister of the Margenau-Schönsee congregation in 1850 and elder in 1861. He was a member of the "Molotschnaer Kirchenkonvent" and as such was sent twice during the 1870's to St. Petersburg in matters relating to military service for Mennonites. In contrast to most preachers of his day, Peters prepared his sermons himself instead of reading them from a book. He died at the age of 96 at Liebenau, Molotschna. His son Abram Peters, a minister of the Mennonite Brethren Church, now (1951) 92 years old, is living in Winnipeg, Man.

H.G.

D. H. Epp, "Unser Schmerzensblatt, 1912," *Menn. Jahrbuch* 1911-12 (Berdyansk) 139.

Peters, Heinrich (1855-1921), an elder of the Schönsee congregation in the Molotschna settlement of South Russia, was born in 1855 at Gnadenheim, Molotschna, the sixth of the twelve children of Bernhard Peters, elder of the Margenau-Schönsee congregation and his wife Agatha Wiens. In 1879 Peters married Maria Sawatzky; their family consisted of ten children. In 1885 Heinrich Peters was elected minister; in 1903, when the Schönsee congregation became independent, he was ordained its first elder. A great earnestness and devotion to his task characterized his personality and his work. He died in February 1921 during the typhoid epidemic. H.G.

Peters, Hermann (1841-1928), founder and elder of the Apostolische Brüdergemeinde (*q.v.*), was born in Gnadenheim, Molotschna, Russia. He joined the Mennonite Brethren *c*1860 and was apparently among those who expressed their newly found joy of salvation through shouts and the use of musical instruments and in some legalistic forms of piety. When the Mennonite Brethren disapproved of this wing, Peters went his own way. For some time his followers were known as Herman Peters-Brüder. Originally they insisted that since Christ "took the bread and broke it," Christians should always do the same; for this reason they were nicknamed "Brotbrecher."

After this new group, consisting of some 20 families, was organized in 1865-66 in the Molotschna, Peters moved with them to the Crimea, where other Mennonites joined them. In 1900-1 he took the group to Siberia, settling northeast of Omsk near Kiryanovka and Trussovka. Here the group became prosperous and lost some of its narrow views. Common names among them were Peters, Becker, Penner, Unruh, Martens, Voth, and Wedel. Peters died Feb. 10, 1928, and was succeeded as elder by H. J. Warkentin. A small group of Hermann Peters' followers came to America in 1874 and still exists as the Fairview (Okla.) Church of God (*q.v.*).

Other tenets emphasized by Hermann Peters were the refusal to accept any form of government service, extreme separation from the world and all other Mennonite groups, rejection of all innovations, refusal to observe holidays, prohibition of photographs, and maintenance of simplicity. In general, their original attitude was very much like that of the first Kleine Gemeinde (*q.v.*) or the Old Order Amish.

C.K.

Friesen, *Brüderschaft*, 236, 293, 378, 381, 393; J. J. Hildebrand, *Aus der Vorgeschichte der Einwanderung* . . . (Winnipeg, 1949) 78; idem, *Sibirien* . . . (Winnipeg, 1942) 53, 96.

Peters, Isaak (1826-1911), a Mennonite teacher at Fürstenau, Molotschna, and preacher (ordained 1866) and elder (1867) in the Pordenau (*q.v.*) congregation, was born Dec. 1, 1826, at Pordenau, the fifth child of Jacob Peters and Sarah Toews. He was married on Dec. 11, 1849, to Anna Steingardt. P. M. Friesen, who was his pupil, describes him as a "stern and ironclad 'old Mennonite' in all questions of teaching and doctrine relating to society and the state, but also a man who realizes the value of a book, especially of historical and theological works, and is an authority on Mennonite history whose equal we have not yet met." As the elder of the Pordenau congregation "he preached penitence and exercised church discipline in the strictest Mennonite sense." He knew "what a new spiritual life through repentance and the new birth is, and recognized all the evangelical means to that end: live preaching, indoctrination of youth, study of the Bible, and congregational prayer meetings." His strict and rigorous requirements led to a division in the congregation; with his followers he had to withdraw and shortly before his emigration he was expelled from the congregation. He had become a teacher in Fürstenau in 1850.

Isaak Peters was a vigorous opponent of baptism by immersion. The Bible, he asserted, speaks of three kinds of baptism: water baptism, spirit baptism, and blood baptism. Water and spirit baptism belong together. He who has received water baptism without spirit baptism has not yet any part in the blood baptism of Jesus, which alone can save, according to I John 1:7. John the Baptist also said: "I baptize you with water," not in water. Likewise Peters rejected the doctrine of the millennium. He held fast to the doctrine of nonresistance and thus became a leader in the emigration of the 1870's. Because of his open advocacy of emigration he was expelled from the country by the government.

In January 1874 he moved to America, settling near Henderson, Neb. There he and a small group of the Pordenau congregation joined the Bethesda Mennonite Church, which chose him as elder. Since he was unable to carry out the way of life he thought necessary, which included stricter requirements for a separated life as evidence of regeneration, he withdrew from Bethesda with a minority of the congregation in 1880. This was the origin of the Ebenezer Mennonite Church in Henderson, organized in 1882, which, together with the Brudertaler Church of Mountain Lake, Minn., in 1889 formed a new branch of the Mennonites, known at first as the Conference of the United Mennonite Brethren of North America, then as the Defenseless Mennonite Brethren in Christ of North America, and since 1937 as the Evangelical Mennonite Brethren. Isaak Peters was a leader in this move and in the E.M.B. church until he was compelled by ill health to withdraw from active work. He was elder at Ebenezer until 1892.

Peters was a competent writer, and wrote for a number of Mennonite periodicals. He was well versed in the writings of Menno Simons and other older Mennonite writers. Among his literary products are the translation of Georg Hansen's *Ein Fundamentbuch der christlichen Lehre* from the original Dutch into German (335 pp.) (Elkhart, 1893). He wrote *Eine Beleuchtung der Schriften Mennos*, a pamphlet of 40 pages; *Die Christliche Wassertaufe*, of 16 pages, and *Die Auferstehung*, 9 pages, all printed at Elkhart.   H.F.E.

Friesen, *Brüderschaft* II, 73 *et passim*; *A Historical Sketch of the Churches of the Evangelical Mennonite Brethren* (Rosthern, 1939); Jacob Epp, "Aeltester Isaak Peters," *Bundesbote-Kalender*, 1912, p. 26; *ML* III, 353 f.

Peters, Peter: see **Pietersz, Pieter** (de Oude).

Peters, Rhode, listed in van Braght's *Martyrs' Mirror* as one of seven Swiss Brethren teachers (preachers) and elders imprisoned in the penitentiary at Bern, Switzerland, in 1659. Samuel Geiser, however, lists eleven, but does not name Rhode Peters. Is he perhaps identical with "Peter Friedle (Frider) von Biglen" found in the Geiser list, and also in Ernst Müller's list of those banished in 1660? The matter awaits clarification (see **Himmelberg, Anthoni**).

                                                         vDZ.

Mart. Mir. D 826, E 1124; Samuel Geiser, *Die Taufgesinnten-Gemeinden* (Karlsruhe, 1931) 395, 399; Müller, *Berner Täufer*, 179 f., 191.

Petersberg, a castle and village in Tirol, Austria, in the Inn Valley between Imst and Stams, is frequently mentioned in the beginnings of the Anabaptist movement. On Dec. 23, 1527, the government issued to the judge Hans Erlbacher the commission to search for the refugee Anabaptist "seducers" who had fled from southern Tirol to this locality. On April 2, 1528, he was ordered to look for several Anabaptists "who are said to have secretly gone to the jurisdiction of St. Petersberg." The clerk of Innsbruck, Erasmus Oberhauser, was ordered on April 4 to seize Peter Beck and his one-eyed sister who had fled from Hall, and Lorenz Aufleger, who were secretly preaching to the people in Hertenberg, Stams, and Petersberg. On April 7 instructions were issued to Erlbacher to inquire about the persons baptized by Jörg Fasser (*q.v.*) and deal with them according to the articles of Kitzbühel (*q.v.*), burn down the houses in which communion and meetings of this misleading sect were held unless other houses would be endangered by the fire, and in that case to confiscate them, impress upon the ferryman on the Inn to transfer no suspicious persons. In June the government commanded the baroness of Frundsberg to remove from his post the above clerk because he was a renegade and married Lutheran priest who tolerated the Anabaptists; in July the orders were given to remove him within two months. But he was still there in 1529, and on March 19 even received government orders to cross-examine a woman named Venklehnerin, who was being held in Hertenberg, and especially to find out where and by whom she had been baptized. Meanwhile the clerk had himself arrested several Anabaptists, and was ordered by the Innsbruck authorities on May 19, 1529, to question them closely. In autumn a new clerk is found in Petersberg, Ulrich Runger, who received a directive on September 7 to release the penitent and pregnant Anabaptist Susanna Kobel, to promise her fugitive relatives freedom if they would present themselves penitently at the prison.

Several Anabaptists from the Oetztal were imprisoned in Petersberg, and cross-examined by the clerk on Oct. 26 and 27, 1529. The government ordered him on November 9 to question several—like Porst and Kneussl—on several points, on the rack if necessary. An order dated November 19 reveals that seven men were on trial, who seemed inclined to recant. A fugitive Anabaptist, who however returned penitently, Hans Gabel, was to be pardoned in accord with the order of November 24 if he would betray where the others who had escaped with him had gone.

On December 7 and 13 instructions were issued by Innsbruck to pardon Jörg Köberl and Andre Kolb on certain conditions after a recent thorough investigation in which they expressed penitence, which should be tested by a priest. In April 1530 there were still some Anabaptists in prison in Petersberg, whom the government ordered the clerk on April 26 to examine on the rack. On May 3 the command came to bring to the criminal court Mayerl-Fröner (see **Mayrl, Hans**) as a "leader and baptizer of this sect," and others who had abused their pardon.

On June 4 the further order was issued by Innsbruck that in case Fröner repented before his execution he should be given the sacrament and his body buried in consecrated earth. This indicates that the two executions reported in the chronicles for 1529 in Petersberg probably took place in 1530. In May 1531 there were again some Anabaptists on trial, likewise in 1537 and 1544. In 1545 several persons went to Moravia from Petersberg.   P.DE.

Kopialbuch Causa Domini in the Innsbruck National archives, II, fol. 106, 204, 213, 214, 239, 248, 250, 355, 410, 533, 536, 537, 548, 553; III, fol. 89, 91, 92, 105, 211; Beck, *Geschichts-Bücher*; Wolkan, *Geschicht-Buch*; Zieglschmid, *Chronik*; J. Loserth, *Anabaptismus*; *ML* III, 354 f.

Peterschivka: see **Petersdorf.**

Peterschmidt (Peterschmitt), a Mennonite family name of frequent occurrence in Alsace (*q.v.*), but also found in the Palatinate and Baden. It is found in the congregations of Colmar (*q.v.*), Wolfganzen, and Neuf-Brisach, as well as in Pulversheim (*q.v.*), and recently in Le Hang (*q.v.*). As early as 1822 a letter sent to the Birkenhof (*q.v.*) congregation by Colmar (*q.v.*) was signed by Sebastian Peterschmitt. J. Peterschmitt, of Rheinfelderhof near Fessenheim, was one of the two representatives (the other being Pelsy, *q.v.*, of Alsace) in the Conference of South German Mennonites (*q.v.*) in 1912. When communications with the South German Conference declined after World War I and those with France expanded, Elder Benjamin Peterschmitt of Colmar became a member of the conjoint conference. Jean Peterschmitt is the elder of the Neuf-Brisach congregation, Eugene Peterschmitt a minister, and Emil Peterschmitt deacon. Willi Peterschmitt, of Munzenheim, serves as traveling evangelist for the French Mennonite Conference. (*ML* III, 355.)   E.C.

Petersdorf, a village in the Nikolaipol (*q.v.*) district of the province of Ekaterinoslav (*q.v.*), founded about 1833, was the seat of a Mennonite Brethren congregation, which was a subsidiary of the Einlage (*q.v.*) congregation. Petersdorf was later called Petershivka or Nadeshdovka. About 35 years later the Mennonite settlement of Yazykovo (*q.v.*) was established in the same district. (Friesen, *Brüderschaft*, 701, 721; *ML* III, 353.)   E.C.

Petershagen, a part of the Tiegenhagen (*q.v.*) congregation in West Prussia, Germany. There the Mennonites of the Gross-Werder were in 1768 required to build a Catholic chapel on the Moskenberg and maintain it for all time in return for the permission granted by the Bishop of Culm (who in the name of the king of Poland exercised ecclesiastical sovereignty) for the erection of their own chapels in Tiegenhagen, Ladekopp, Fürstenwerder, and Heubuden. The newly built Catholic chapel was burned down by lightning in 1788 and was not rebuilt. The obligation was met with a gift of money. (See **Fürstenwerder**; *ML* III, 355.) M.Kl.

Petershagen, a Mennonite village name transplanted from Prussia to the Molotschna settlement, Ukraine (see **Villages**).   C.K.

Petershagen. Besides the village of Petershagen in West Prussia (*ML* III, 355) and Petershagen on the Molotschna (*loc. cit.*), there was also a Mennonite congregation in Petershagen on the Weser in the principality of Minden, Germany. This congregation is found in the Dutch *Naamlijst* 1766-1810. The congregation is said to have been founded by emigrant Swiss Mennonites. Petrus Staal (Peter Stähli?) was its preacher; the year of his ordination is not stated. Particulars are not known.   vDZ.

Petiscus: see Pitiscus.

Petjanga'an and **Ngeling,** a Mennonite congregation on the Indonesian island of Java, formerly a mission station of the Dutch Mennonite Mission association. It contains the villages of Petjanga'an, Ngeling, and Pendo. In 1953 it numbered 84 baptized members and 100 children. The preachers are (1955) I. S. Siswojo since 1941 and Surant Themotheus since 1949.   vDZ.

Petoskey (Mich.) Mennonite Church (MC) is a mission congregation established in 1950 under the Indiana-Michigan Mennonite Mission Board. In 1957 it had 53 members, with Ivan K. Weaver as bishop.   I.K.W.

Petri, Cunerus, from Brouwershaven, Dutch province of Zeeland, was a Catholic priest of Saint Peter's Church at Louvain, Belgium, and in 1570-78 a bishop at Leeuwarden, Friesland. He died in 1580 at Cologne, Germany. He published *Den Schilt teghen die Wederdoopers . . . bysonder die Mennonisten* (Leuven, 1568). This very prejudiced writing contains no important information, but on the contrary many great errors. For example, Menno Simons is said to have been a schoolteacher. As bishop in Leeuwarden he persistently persecuted the Mennonites; Reytse Aysesz (*q.v.*), executed in 1574, was a victim of his fanaticism.   vDZ.

J. Reitsma, *Honderd jaren uit de Geschiedenis der Hervorming . . . in Friesland* (Leeuwarden, 1876) 152-70, 178.

Petronella, an Anabaptist martyr, the wife of a baker of Holdenstedt, a village near Sangershausen in Thuringia, Germany, who was seized with Hans Höhne (*q.v.*) at Halberstadt in September 1535 and drowned in the Bode at Groningen in October 1535. (Wappler, 133 ff.; *ML* III, 356.)   NEFF.

Petrovka, a Mennonite settlement in Russia, a part of the group of villages called Naumenko in the province of Kharkov, Ukraine, had joined the Mennonite Brethren of Einlage (Kitchkas), the home of their founders, as a subsidiary. In Petrovka and Barvenkovo the settlement had churches. Inadequate connections with the mother church, sharp conflicts with the higher and lower authorities as well as with the Mennonite Church group, combined with economic decline had at times an unfavorable effect on the religious and the intellectual life of this settlement. (See **Kharkov**; Friesen, *Brüderschaft* I, 450 f.; *ML* III, 356.)   M.Kl.

Petter Memorial Mennonite Church (GCM), formerly called the Lame Deer Mennonite Mission Church, is located in the Lame Deer Valley, Rosebud Co., Mont., on the Tongue River Indian Reservation, the home of the Northern Cheyenne Indians. The church was built in 1908 by P. A. Kliewer, who carried on the work from Busby until 1910. Other workers were Mr. and Mrs. Alfred Wiebe 1911-15, Mr. and Mrs. H. T. Neufeld 1915-16, Mr. and Mrs. Rodolphe Petter (*q.v.*) 1916-47, and Mr. and Mrs. Alfred Habegger (d. 1956), who assisted from Busby from 1946, then moved to Lame Deer in 1949. Mrs. Petter continued to help in the work after her retirement. Petter died on Jan. 6, 1947, having served 25 years among the Southern Cheyennes and 30 years among the Northern Cheyennes. Native pastors of this church have been Frank Littlewolf and Milton Whiteman (d. 1958). Over 235 have been baptized since the beginning of the work, with a membership of about 75 in 1947. Both the Cheyenne and English languages are used in the work here. Mr. and Mrs. Donavin Diller have been missionaries at Lame Deer since March 1957. A.H.

Petter, Rodolphe Charles (1865-1947), a missionary (GCM) to the Cheyenne Indians in Oklahoma and Montana, was born Feb. 19, 1865, at Vevey on Lake Geneva, Switzerland, the son of Louis Petter. He attended the local and other schools and the Basel Missionsschule (1883-89). While in military training he became acquainted with a Mennonite, Samuel Gerber, visited the Jura Mountain Mennonites, and heard about the mission interest of the Mennonites in America. J. A. Sprunger (*q.v.*), of Berne, Ind., who was on a tour of the Swiss Mennonite churches, suggested that he consider work among the American Indians. On May 14, 1890, he married Marie Gerber. On August 7 they landed in New York to become missionaries to the Cheyenne Indians under the mission board of the General Conference Mennonite Church. They spent the year 1890-91 at Oberlin College, Ohio, and in 1891 began their work at Cantonment, Okla. After his first wife's death he married Bertha Elise Kinsinger of Trenton, Ohio, Nov. 28, 1911, who was also a missionary to the Cheyennes. In 1916 the Petters took over the Cheyenne mission field at Lame Deer, Mont., where they were active until his death on Jan. 6, 1947.

Petter was one of the most outstanding missionaries and linguists working among American Indians. He created a dictionary of the Cheyenne Indian language (see bibliography), reduced the Cheyenne language to writing, produced a grammar, and translated Bunyan's *Pilgrim's Progress*, portions of the Old Testament, and the entire New Testament. He became a nationally known ethnologist, and his numerous works are found in all leading libraries in this field. His reports about his mission work were published primarily in *Christlicher Bundesbote* and *The Mennonite*. The Rodolphe Petter Collection is on display in the Bethel College Historical Library.

C.K.

Books by Petter: English-Cheyenne Dictionary, published by the author and printed on the Gammeter Multigraph (1915) pp. 1126; *Cheyenne Grammar* (Newton, 1952) pp. 70; *Einiges aus meinen Missionserfahrungen in den vergangenen Jahren* (n.d.) pp. 72; *Reminiscences of the Past Years in Mission Service Among the Cheyenne* (n.d.) pp. 79; *Hosz Maheo Heeszistoz (Portions of the Old and the New Testaments)*, translated and arranged by Rodolphe Petter (Cantonment, 1913) pp. 145; *Maheo Henitae-Histanovestoz Zeoxtoese-Hesetovaomohettoz' Vovoe-Histanova na Maheonoxtoenoe-Manhastova* (Literal and Paraphrastic Translations from the Old Testament Together with Their New Testament Connections) (Lame Deer, 1926) pp. 282; *Zemona Hoemao Maheon-Hoestomohestova . . . (The New Testament in Cheyenne)*, translated by Rodolphe Petter (American Bible Society, New York, 1934) pp. 666; *Nivova-Pavhosto (The Four Gospels)*, translated by Rodolphe Petter (Lame Deer, 1928) pp. 273; *Zesenemeoxtoz (Cheyenne Hymns)* (Lame Deer, 1942), at least seven editions, pp. 40; *Assetosemeheo Heamoxovistavatoz* ("The Pilgrim's Progress" and Some Bible Portions), Printed for the Interest of the Mennonite Mission Among the Cheyenne Indians (Cantonment, 1904) pp. 264; *Zistxuisto* or *Cheyenne Reading Book* (Quakertown, Pa., 1895) pp. 36.

Books and Articles About Petter: Who's Who Among the Mennonites (1943) 191; Mrs. Rodolphe Petter, "Kurze Lebensgeschichte Dr. Rodolphe Charles Petter," *Christlicher Bundesbote*, April 1, 1947, 10; Rodolphe Charles Petter, "How I Became a Missionary," *Mennonite Life* X (January 1955) 4-13; D. J. Unruh, "Rodolphe Petter, Absent from the Body, Present with the Lord," *The Mennonite*, January 1947, 5; "Nachruf des Dr. Rodolphe Petter, Apostel der Cheyennen Indianer" in *Bundesbote Kalender*, 1947, 1-32.

Pettisville Church of God in Christ Mennonite Church, located north of Pettisville, Fulton Co., Ohio, was organized in 1863. The present building with a seating capacity of 150 was erected in 1909; until then the services had been conducted in the homes. M. Seiler, born in Switzerland, was the first minister, followed by Christian Gearig and Peter Eicher, both of whom were ordained in 1872. The ministry is unsalaried. In 1957 the church had a membership of 24, with C. L. Gearig as minister.

C.L.G.

Petz, Hans, an Anabaptist preacher and poet: see **Betz, Hans.**

Petz, Margarethe, an Anabaptist martyr, who was burned at the stake with four other Anabaptists at Bamberg, Germany, on Jan. 30, 1528.   NEFF.

P. Wappler, *Die Stellung Kursachsens und des Landgrafen Philipp von Hessen zur Täuferbewegung* (Münster, 1910); *ML* III, 356.

Peutler, Siegmund, one of six Anabaptist martyrs who were put to death in Steyr, Austria, on March 30, 1528 (see **Penzenauer** and **Austria**).

Peyzel, Conrad, founder of the Ephrata (*q.v.*) cloister: see **Beissel, Johann Konrad.**

Pfalz-Zweibrücken, a duchy in Germany covering scarcely twenty square miles, which lay for the most part in the south and west (not in one block) of the district that later became the Palatinate left of the Rhine; its principal towns were Bergzabern, Zweibrücken, Meisenheim, and Kusel. It also included lesser districts in the Rhine Province, a part of which were, however, made independent in the 16th century, and known as Veldenz. Duke Louis II, who was quite young in the early days of the Reformation, was influenced by his tutors Johann Bader (*q.v.*) and Johann Huttich in favor of the new doctrine. But he was never able to take a positive position or pass decisive measures, even though he was inwardly, in spite of many doubts, favorably inclined toward the Reformation and was supported in this respect by his wife, Elisabeth of Hesse. At the time of his premature death (1532) his son Wolfgang was only six years old. Under his reign, administered by Ruprecht, the brother of the deceased duke, together with the widow, the Reformation was put through. The twelve articles drawn up in 1533 by Johann Schwebel by order of Ruprecht, regulating ecclesiastical affairs in accord with the principles of the Reformation, gradually acquired the status of a church constitution in the entire country. In the education of the young Count Palatine Schwebel exerted a similar influence by having his countryman Caspar Glaser, who had left the services of Baden, appointed tutor of the prince. That the teachings of this man, who was with all his love of peace an outspoken defender of Protestantism, did not fall on infertile soil was to be shown by future events. At first Wolfgang, having assumed the regency in 1543, was hesitant; in spite of all the enticements of his father-in-law Philip of Hesse, he avoided a formal union with the Schmalkaldic League and managed the period of the Interim with a diplomatic finesse unusual in so young a ruler. But after the Treaty of Passau a church inspection of the entire country in 1553 laid the groundwork for a thorough Reformation, which was concluded by the great church constitution of 1557 by the chancellor Ulrich Sitzinger and the superintendent Cunemann Flinsbach. This constitution, revised by Melanchthon and Brenz, essentially based on the patterns established by the constitutions of Neuenburg, Württemberg, and Mecklenburg, was thoroughly Lutheran. A second inspection in 1558 and the establishment in the following year of the Hornbach school, which was put in the charge of Immanuel Tremellius, a former tutor of princes, completed the work of the Reformation.

The origins of the Anabaptist movement in Zweibrücken are still in the dark. It is, to be sure, known that Hans Denk (*q.v.*) was briefly in Bergzabern in 1527 and that he aroused some attention by his disputations, but it is doubtful that there was any connection between this visit and the later spread of the Anabaptist movement in the province. Statements made on the occasion of the first church inspection in 1553 indicate that the movement came in from the outside, particularly from the region of Worms and Kreuznach. Diebold Winter, Claus Sümmerer, and Hans Grecker, who later represented the Anabaptist cause in the disputation of Frankenthal, are named as the prime promoters of the movement in the region of Zweibrücken. In the Bergzabern district the villages of Barbelroth and Frankweiler are named, in the Lichtenberg district besides Achtelsbach and Baumholder, especially Flurskappel, where it is said Kaspar Schmidt was on the point of drawing half the congregation to the Anabaptist side. This wide distribution of the Anabaptists induced the Count Palatine to issue an extensive mandate, which was proclaimed on April 23, 1556 (*Mandat wider die widertaufer und ihre anhenger, auch derselben verfürischen opinionen, etc. Im Fürstentumb Zwaybruck offentlich angeschlagen. Anno 1556*). The mandate, which sets as the minimum penalty for the Anabaptists expulsion from the country, but reserves to the prince the right to impose penalties of life and property in accordance with the imperial decrees, was then incorporated into the church constitution adopted in the following year. In addition the constitution also contained a "warning and command against the error of the Anabaptists," which formed a sort of theoretical counterpart to the constitution and was intended to furnish the clergy with the needed tools to prevent the further spread of Anabaptism by instruction of the "common man." The errors of the Anabaptists are classified in two categories, viz., those that pertain to external physical desires, and those concerning spiritual matters. In the first class they enumerate rejection of temporal government, courts, and punishments; refusal to render the oath; the sinfulness of possessions and demand for community of goods; the right of divorce in the case of deviation in religious practice. As spiritual errors they designate denial of original sin; rejection of infant baptism; justification by works; disregard for the church offices and the sacraments; holiness of the regenerated. The application of Bible references in attacking these rather arbitrarily stated tenets of faith was generally left to the clergy; only in the defense of infant baptism are detailed references given. This constitution was to be put into practice at the next church inspection, planned for 1558. The instructions issued to the inspectors pointed out that the spread of Anabaptism was most serious in the Neukastel district, and especially the village of Frankweiler "more than any others of our towns and villages is in ill repute on this account." The Strasbourg divine, Johann Marbach (*q.v.*), who had charge of the inspection, did not neglect to explain to the clergy the Anabaptist arguments and their refutation. Nevertheless the movement did not decline. In 1561 the pastor of Frankweiler expressed his fears concerning the effect of the adjacent Löwenstein, where a second Moravia was about to be instituted. In 1562 a reprint of the Anabaptist mandate had to be provided, and the clergy were instructed to read the text

once a month from the pulpit. After the middle of the 1560's a definite decrease in the Anabaptist movement is discernible. We hear of emigrations to Moravia, which was at that time in its "golden age," and attracted many; there are also many expulsions from the country. (In 1581 the mason Hans Raidel, a native of Zweibrücken, is named.) The effect of the emissaries from Moravia was rather to promote emigration to Moravia than to consolidate the brotherhood in the district. Toward the end of the century there were only isolated persons in a few regions that attracted the attention of the inspectors.

According to an old document the "congregation of the duchy of Zweibrücken" was founded in 1713. In 1732 there were here 27 Mennonite families and in 1769 the membership numbered 94. The Dutch *Naamlijst* of 1765 lists two congregations in this duchy — Schurburg(?) with preacher Johannes Schönig (Schöny), elder from 1738 (probably 1749), and Zweibrücken with Christian Lohman (Lehmann), elder since 1740. The *Naamlijst* of 1766 lists only one congregation, Zweibrücken - Schurburg, with Johannes Schönig as elder. The *Naamlijst* of the following years mentions a congregation of Freudenberg, Hornbach, and Kirchheimerhof (previously called Zweibrücken) with the elders Johannes Schönig, Joseph Schnebely from 1767 (should be 1762) and the preachers Joh. Lehmann from 1745, Rudolf Schmidt from 1755, and Peter Boer (Böhm, *ME* I, 245, is an error) from 1755; Christian Wels became a preacher in 1774 and an elder in 1781; the *Naamlijst* of 1793 still names Joseph Schnebele as elder and Georg Finger and Ulrich Lehmann as preachers, both from 1783.

Not until the 18th century did the Anabaptist movement find entry into the duchy through the influx of Alsatian Amish Mennonites. Besides Zweibrücken and Ernstweiler, Mennonites were found as renters on the Deutschhof (*q.v.*) in the Barbelroth district, the Neudorferhof (*q.v.*) in the Meisenheim district, and the Kohlhof (Limbach parish close to the former Prussian border). The Ernstweiler (*q.v.*) and the Amish Ixheim (*q.v.*) congregations in this area merged in 1937 to form the Zweibrücken (*q.v.*) congregation.   M.K., vDZ.

Gem.-Kal., 1939, 71; Th. Gümbel, *Die Geschichte der protestantischen Kirche der Pfalz* (Kaiserslautern, 1885); *TA Baden-Pfalz*; Julius Ney, *Pfalzgraf Wolfgang, Herzog von Zweibrücken und Neuburg* (Leipzig, 1912); *Inv. Arch. Amst.* I, Nos. 1433, 1438, 1471 f.; *Gesch.-Bl.*, 1955, 23, 24; *ML* III, 356 f.

Pfastatt Mennonite Church, which has its meetinghouse at Rue de L' Etang 3 in the village of Pfastatt on the northwest side of Mulhouse, was organized in 1912 as a result of a division in the Pulversheim (*q.v.*) congregation, when a minority started to meet in the home of a Mennonite family in Pfastatt. When the Pulversheim meetinghouse was burned during World War I, most of the Pulversheim members began to attend at the Pfastatt location. The necessity of building a meetinghouse resulted in a second division over the question of location, and although the majority built in Pfastatt (1922-23) a minority rebuilt in Pulversheim. World War II damages to the Pfastatt church were severe but were soon repaired. Pfastatt in 1957 was the largest Mennonite congregation in Alsace, with 265 souls including unbaptized children and second in France only to Montbéliard. The elder is Joseph Widmer, of Modenheim, assisted by the ministers Henri Goldschmidt of Bourtzwiller, Hermann Nussbaumer of Wittenheim, Jaques Nussbaumer of Reiningen, and Max Schowalter of Pfastatt. The members live in Bourtzwiller, Isenheim, Modenheim, Willenheim, Upper Asach, and Guebwiller. Heinrich Schneider of Isenheim signed the Dordrecht Confession in 1660. The Conference of Mennonites of Alsace-Lorraine holds its annual meeting at Pfastatt on Ascension Day. E.C.

Almanach Mennonite du Cinquantenaire 1901-1951 (Montbéliard, 1951); *Christ Seul* (December 1951); *ML* III, 359.

Pfeddersheim, a village (pop. 3,500) near Worms, Germany, where an Anabaptist disputation took place with Lutheran theologians on Aug. 25, 1557, on order of Elector Otto Henry of the Palatinate. Some 40 Anabaptists took part, among them 19 bishops (*Vorsteher*). Five topics were discussed: Infant Baptism, State, Oath, Grounds for Leaving the State Church, and Ban. Very little source material is available regarding the disputation, none giving the statements of the Anabaptists. The Stuttgart Staatsarchiv (Rel. S.B. 16) contains a document reporting the statements made against the Anabaptists by their opponents, entitled *Contra Anabaptistarum opinionem, Widerlegung der artikel der Wiedertäufer,* signed at the end, "Written at Worms anno 1557." This is printed verbatim in *TA Württemberg* (pp. 148-61) edited by Gustav Bossert, who states that the document is the report of a disputation, probably the religious disputation at Pfeddersheim in August 1557, and perhaps written by Jacob Andreae, who participated in it. The only other known participant was Dr. Johannes Marbach, who was called from Strasbourg to assist. Diebold Winter, the chief Anabaptist speaker at the Frankenthal (*q.v.*) debate of 1571, stated at that disputation on the opening day that he had been at the Pfeddersheim disputation; he protested that things were printed about the Anabaptist views supposedly stated at Pfeddersheim "which we never thought, much less spoke. Also we protest that thereupon a very sharp mandate was issued. If we were such people as represented in the *Prozess*(?) we would not be fit to stand before your eyes. We want to record this for our defense. This is our complaint and protest, that we were dealt with unjustly at Pfeddersheim. . . . We would like to see such persons as were present at that disputation. If someone is here who can testify to this, and the *Prozess*(?) permits, we would accept correction" (*Protocoll,* 1573, pp. 9 f.).

It is most probable that a booklet written by Melanchthon and others which appeared in 1558(?) titled *Prozess wie es soll gehalten werden mit den Wiedertäufern* deals with the views of the Anabaptists as given at Pfeddersheim. (This would explain the strange term "Prozess" in Diebold Winter's statement.) It is identical with a manuscript in the Stuttgart Staatsarchiv, "Bedenken der Wiedertäufer

halber," which is dated "written at Worms anno 1557" and written Nov. 5, 1557. This document is strangely the outcome of a meeting of Lutheran theologians held at Worms Sept. 11-Oct. 7, 1557, to attempt a reconciliation between the Protestant and Catholic estates by way of a public conference. The experiment failed, but the theologians came to an agreement to recommend to the government of the Palatinate a sharper treatment of the Anabaptists. The *Bedenken* contains their recommendations. Why the Worms theologians should have turned from their failure to solve the Catholic problem to dealing with the Anabaptist problem is perhaps best explained by the results of the immediately preceding Pfeddersheim disputation. Jacob Andreae was a participant in both meetings and no doubt others were also. Diebold Winter's reference to a printed unjust report on the Anabaptist statements at Pfeddersheim could of course refer to a printed *Protocoll,* but none such has ever been discovered. (Recently a trace of a manuscript copy of a set of minutes seems to have been found, but not yet verified, possibly in the princely library at Gotha.) If the *Bedenken-Prozess* is basically an attack on the Anabaptist position as expressed at Pfeddersheim, then the manuscript "Handbüchlein wider den Prozess der zu Worms am Rhein wider die Brüder so man die Hutterischen nennt ausgangen ist im 1557 Jahr" (modern copy in GCL) may well be at least in part a defense of the Pfeddersheim Anabaptist testimony, and may support the idea that Hutterites took part in the Pfeddersheim disputation as they did later in the Frankenthal disputation of 1571.

It is strange that no minutes or record of the important Pfeddersheim disputation have been preserved, a fact which Krebs states in his edition of the *Täuferakten* for *Baden und Pfalz* (1951), p. 153. He prints a report on the disputation (152 f.) contained in a communication from Johann Marbach and Jakob Herman to the Strasbourg City Council dated Aug. 31, 1557, to be found in the Strasbourg Archives. He also prints (footnote, p. 153) a brief report given by Alting in his *Historia ecclesiae Palatinae* (reprinted in L. Chr. Mieg, *Monumenta pietatis* I, Frankfurt, 1702, p. 160). In any case the Lutheran participants declared at the end of the disputation that they had overthrown the errors of their opponents, and summoned them to give up their errors and return "to the fellowship of the true Christian church." But their appeal had no success; the purpose of the Elector in calling the disputation, namely, to bring the Anabaptists back to the fold, was not attained.

Whether there was a congregation of Anabaptists at any time in Pfeddersheim is not clear. Krebs, *Baden und Pfalz,* twice reports Anabaptists at Pfeddersheim. On Aug. 6, 1563, a certain Martinus is named as an Anabaptist. On Oct. 19, 1566, Elector Frederick ordered the Count of Alzey to proceed against the Pfeddersheim Anabaptists, having heard that ten inhabitants of the place had been won to the new faith. On Sept. 14, 1608, a meeting of several hundred Anabaptists is reported as having taken place between Pfeddersheim and Kriegsheim, but these may have been Kriegsheim people since there are numerous reports of Anabaptists at that place.   H.S.B.

Chr. Hege, *Die Täufer in der Kurpfalz* (Frankfurt, 1908); *TA Baden-Pfalz*, 152-54, 157, 163, 242; *ML* II, 593.

Pfeffel, Gottlieb Konrad (1736-1809), an Alsatian writer of fables. In his fable about the wild boar and the birds he has a Mennonite play the part of a frank and courageous friend of the truth: " 'Sir,' said his renter Hans, an intelligent Mennonite, who was just riding past the forest on his way from the market, 'appearances deceive you; from the stirred up earth many a worm creeps forth; with a cry of joy the gay flock of birds pounces upon it, and this fellow thinks that their melody is coined because of his merit' " (free English rendering of German verse). (*ML* III, 359.)   NEFF.

Pfefferlin, Hans, a victim of the Anabaptist persecutions of the Swabian League (*q.v.*), was captured on April 24, 1528, with Eitelhans Langenmantel (*q.v.*) at Leitheim and although he recanted his Anabaptist belief was put to death at Weissenhorn on May 11, 1528. He stemmed from Göggingen near Augsburg, Germany, and had been baptized in his home by Leonhard of Linz (*q.v.*).   HEGE.

Friedrich Roth, "Zur Lebensgeschichte Eitelhans Langenmantel . . ." in *Zts. des historischen Vereins für Schwaben und Neuburg* XXVII (1900) 9, 14, 15, 17, 27-29; *ML* III, 359.

Pfersfelder, Elisabeth, sister of Georg Pfersfelder (*q.v.*), married and living in the region of Bamberg, Germany, owning lands there (according to *Corp. Schwenkf.* VII, 99), "a prominent widow of Wibersbach in the diocese of Bamberg." In the home of her brother, who was friendly to the Anabaptists, she became acquainted with the fanatical Anabaptist Claus Frey (*q.v.*), who had fled from Rottenburg in 1525 leaving his wife and children behind. She then fell to the wiles of this supposed prophet and became his wife without being aware of the fact that he was already married. Her brother was evidently also ignorant of the character of his protégé; otherwise he would certainly have restrained his sister. She followed Frey to Strasbourg as his wife. Here he was, however, rejected by the Anabaptist congregation, for his dual marriage was known there. He was arrested by the Strasbourg council and tried. His designation of himself as "the head of the church" and "fulfiller of the Scriptures" is evidence of an elaborate system evolved by a disordered imagination. The council sentenced Frey to death for bigamy in 1534 and had him executed by drowning. Seriously disturbed in spirit by this trial, even though she was not proved a partner to the deed, Elisabeth requested that the council take her life also, but she was left unmolested and at liberty, evidently remaining in Strasbourg. She came under the pastoral care of Crautwald (*q.v.*), a Schwenckfelder, who wrote a letter to her dated Nov. 14, 1540. Its content is known. Elisabeth had asked Crautwald for the correct interpretation of the passages in Galatians 5:5 and Hebrews 3:14. She also corresponded with Schwenckfeld on the Incarnation of Christ. Schwenckfeld's reply, probably in the summer of 1540, is found in *Corp. Schwenkf.* (VII, 102 ff.). Like her brother, Elisabeth Pfersfelder found the way from the Anabaptists to the Schwenckfelders.   E.T.

Corpus Schwenckfeldianorum IV (Leipzig, 1914) 772 ff.; VII (Leipzig, 1926) 99 ff.; also the older literature there; *ML* III, 359 f.

Pfersfelder, Georg (actually Georg Gross), a baron living and owning property at Weilersburg in the district of Bamberg, Germany, in the service of the city of Nürnberg, was in close contact with Caspar Schwenckfeld (*q.v.*) from 1530 on. The latter complained in a letter of May 1533, that he had received no reply to his letters (*Corp. Schwenckf.*, IV, 772 ff.). This letter clearly indicates Pfersfelder's former connections with the Anabaptists, and warns him in regard to them. Schornbaum's *Quellen* offer conclusive evidence of Pfersfelder's violent and dramatic interference in an Anabaptist trial in Brandenburg-Ansbach in 1531. Anton Schad, the margrave's Protestant pastor in Uttenreuth near Erlangen, in April 1531 had read from his pulpit a mandate of his sovereign against the "fanatics," and had one of his auditors, Anton Schmied, arrested by Hans von Seckendorf, the bailiff of Baiersdorf, for publicly contradicting him. Thereupon Pfersfelder without ceremony arrested the parson and threatened him. After his release Schad accused Pfersfelder to the Ansbach authorities, calling upon them for protection (Schornbaum, 235 f.). As a voluntary counsel for the Anabaptists Pfersfelder wrote a defiant letter to the bailiff, an excerpt from which is found in Schornbaum (231 ff.), and also in Wiswedel (II, 45 ff.). The letter shows Pfersfelder to have been a well-trained opponent of Luther and friend of the Anabaptists, as well as a religiously alert layman who knew how to handle words. A few coarse expressions can be pardoned in that crude century, and especially by Luther's example. Upon the complaint of the chancellor of the margraviate the council of Nürnberg imposed city arrest upon him pending the outcome of the dispute. Meanwhile the Uttenreuth "dreamers" were tried in Baiersdorf and questioned on the rack concerning their contacts with Pfersfelder. Recalling the Peasants' War the authorities suspected social revolutionary intentions. Indeed, as recently as 1527 the Nürnberg parson Vogel of Eltersdorf had after a brief trial been beheaded as an Anabaptist and as an alleged revolutionary (see **Wolfgang Vogel**; also *Bilder* I, 152 ff.). It was not possible to prove such charges against Pfersfelder. Nor were the authorities of the margrave more successful in fastening a charge of disturbance of the peace upon him for his arrest of the Uttenreuth parson. Pfersfelder was, of course, not successful in saving Hans Schmied, whom he had so warmly defended. After weeks of torture on the rack the latter was beheaded on July 10, 1531, on a charge of "setting up a forbidden, illegal, and fundamentally seditious sect and rabble, on account of seductive visionary dreams and ghosts and on account of the dissolving of his marriage." That in the case of Schmied and the other visionaries it was merely a matter of pathological hallucination, medical science was not yet ready to understand. In the Bavarian national archives of Nürnberg (*Religionsakten* XXXIX, 428-39) there is a letter written by Pfersfelder in June 1531, to the "dreamers" imprisoned in Baiersdorf. Its content has not yet been published (*Corp. Schwenckf.* VII, 100). But Pfersfelder's letter of self-vindication written to the margrave on June 23, 1531, is published (in abstract) in Schornbaum (281). In June of that year Andreas Osiander (*q.v.*), the leading theologian of Nürnberg, was commissioned together with Wenzeslaus Linck and several of the Nürnberg councillors, to talk with Pfersfelder concerning his "Anabaptist errors." Pfersfelder did not appear, but presented a statement of his beliefs, a copy of which was taken from an Anabaptist seized in Uffenheim in 1532. A letter written by Pfersfelder to Osiander on June 8, 1531, now in the national archives at Nürnberg in the volume mentioned above (p. 428), has not yet been published, but is mentioned by Schornbaum (p. 332, lines 25 f. and note 5). A colloquy between Osiander and Pfersfelder in 1532 was also fruitless. After the bloody suppression of the Anabaptists in Franconia Pfersfelder transferred to the Schwenckfelders, as did also his sister Elisabeth (*q.v.*). E.T.

    Corpus Schwenckfeldianorum IV (Leipzig, 1914); VI (Leipzig, 1926); *TA Bayern* I; Wiswedel, *Bilder* I and II; J. Jörg, *Deutschland in der Revolutionsperiode von 1522 bis 1526* (Freiburg i.B., 1885); *ML* III, 360.

Pfistermeyer (Meyer), **Hans,** an outstanding Anabaptist leader, of Aarau, capital of the Swiss canton of Aargau (*q.v.*), who was probably won to the Anabaptist movement by Jacob Gross (*q.v.*) of Waldshut in 1525. Little is known of him. On Jan. 26, 1526, the council of Aarau discussed his case. He apparently appeared as a preacher soon after his baptism, whereupon he was apparently banished from the canton. In that year he also preached in Basel. A messenger of the council conveyed to him the order to leave the city. He then went in person to the Protestant mayor, Adelperg Meyer, and received from him a friendly repetition and explanation of the law. But soon Pfistermeyer was in the city again. It was made clear to him that he and his like-minded friends might stay in the city if they would promise not to hold any meetings. To this condition they did not consent and were again expelled. Now they went to the neighboring Therwyl and preached there. They were brought before the council, which demanded from them an oath that they would forever avoid the city and an area with a radius of ten miles around it. They refused to render the oath and were ordered to leave the city, and never to return. Nevertheless Pfistermeyer was in Basel again a year later. "He had heard that good Christian people lived here, and so God led him back and then he worked here." Again he was expelled with a very sharp threat, and apparently did not return. In the following year he was one of the eight Anabaptists who wished to participate in the great disputation held at Bern in 1528, but who were arrested and who were cross-examined after the conclusion of the colloquy, and then expelled from the city and canton. Whither they went is not known. In 1530 he appeared as an Anabaptist preacher. Bern heard that

he frequently preached to crowds of several hundred, though only seven were baptized. Bern then demanded that he be extradited. In March 1531 Pfistermeyer was seized at Mellingen and taken to Bern. On April 19, 1531, the preachers of Bern, Berthold Haller (*q.v.*), Caspar Megander (see **Grossman**), Franz Kolb (*q.v.*), Sebastian Hofmeister (*q.v.*), and Jakob Otherus, engaged in a debate with him, in the course of which he was led to recant. The colloquy has been printed under the title, *Ein christenlich gespräch gehallten zu Bernn zwüschen den Predicanten und Hansen Physter Meyer von Arouw den Widertauff, Eyd, Oberkeyt und andere Widertoufferische Artikel betreffende* (1531) (at GCL). By "the Holy Scripture" it was to be proved that Pfistermeyer was in error with regard to "the faith and the Christian life," and an effort was made "with all friendliness" to lead him from "his ungodly plan" in order that at least "his soul might be won." To attain this goal the preachers dealt with him "with all industry, with gentleness and with patience, out of love." Pfistermeyer was first called upon to account for his statement that the clergy were not preaching God's words but Bern's word. One of the questions dealt with was the Anabaptist view that the New Testament is more important than the Old Testament, a view which Pfistermeyer skillfully defended since Christ "had brought a higher and more perfect teaching." Since everything was to be directed toward faith and life, the swearing of oaths was also discussed by the clergy as being "in accord with faith and love." Pfistermeyer to be sure wanted to stay by a simple yes, but allows himself to be moved far enough on this point that "the swearing of oaths is not different from testifying to the truth" and he would therefore be permitted "to testify to his yes with God."

With regard to taking interest Pfistermeyer asserted that it is not suitable for a Christian to take interest; but the clergy countered with the statement that although the Scriptures do indeed forbid usury taking interest is reconcilable with love. But Pfistermeyer would recognize as real love the kind that according to Matthew 5 shows itself in unselfishness, and he could not "get any farther with the Scriptures."

Concerning the government Pfistermeyer said that no Christian should become involved in such an office. The theologians on the other hand tried to prove by the Old Testament "that a Christian may stay in office." A "Christian government" also had the duty of punishing the wicked. The sword, which Pfistermeyer believed should not be used, saying, "A Christian shall not pronounce a death sentence," was commanded a Christian government as a weapon of love. "Indeed love is precisely the hilt whereby the government shall grasp the sword." They do this "with great sympathy, not arbitrarily or criminally, not out of vengeance or bloodthirstiness, but alone on account of the office of punishing and eradicating the evil for the benefit of the pious." But Pfistermeyer spoke for mercy and pardon, saying that according to the Sermon on the Mount one should not resist evil. It was his opinion that the clergy found so little attention because they "did not follow after Christ," whose teaching was in harmony with His deed, which made a bigger impression on the people than the mere empty word without corresponding deeds.

A lively discussion arose concerning the article of baptism, since Pfistermeyer rejected infant baptism. The circumcision of the Old Testament gave the clergy their foundation for their defense of infant baptism, and baptism denoted being added to the people of God. Pfistermeyer skillfully contended that Christ had commanded to teach and after that to baptize, of which the children were of course incapable. He said that one who was not planted into the kingdom of God by the heavenly Father as a plant, or in other words, added to the people of God, he would be rooted out. Thereupon the clergy said that Christ had promised to the children "the kingdom of heaven." Just as children enjoy civil community without understanding it, so they should also be permitted to participate in the "community of the saints," in baptism. Pfistermeyer, however, found it highly dubious that anybody could be made a Christian through water baptism, without living a godly life.

After a lengthy disputation Pfistermeyer requested time to consider until the next day; this was granted. With the argument that infant baptism is a continuation of the circumcision of the Old Testament and that the latter is based on a definite command of God, Pfistermeyer was finally defeated so that he declared that he knew no further Scripture to oppose it. But since he now "through the grace of God" had been further instructed in the truth, he confessed that he had erred. He would ask God for pardon that He might lead him still further in recognition of the truth.

Now Pfistermeyer considered it to be his task to convert his former companions and brethren to his new view. He failed in this with Heini Seiler, his fellow prisoner, who remained true to his faith until death by martyrdom. This conversation has also been printed (Heiz, 20). After the experiment with Pfistermeyer had succeeded so well, the council of Bern apparently set great hopes on a religious disputation of this kind. Therefore a "friendly teaching from God's Word" was tried again and in 1532 the Anabaptist disputation of Zofingen was instituted, which was to be held like the one with Pfistermeyer according to the rules of "faith and love." That Pfistermeyer was present in Zofingen is not seen in the printed records. In 1533-34 he succeeded in bringing about Friedli Scherger's(?) recantation. In March 1538 he was by letter ordered to appear at the great disputation of Bern (q.v.), since he as a recanting Anabaptist could offer the lords good services. At this point all trace of him is lost. NEFF, S.G.

J. Heiz, Die Täufer im Aargau (Aarau, 1902); S. Geiser, Die Taufgesinnten-Gemeinden (Karlsruhe, 1931); Müller, Berner Täufer; ML III, 360-62.

Pforzheim, city and district in Baden, Germany. Because of its location on the sometimes indefinite borders of the margraviate of Baden, the Palatinate, the bishopric of Speyer, and the duchy of Württemberg, the region of Pforzheim was a favorable

location for the Anabaptists, since they were easily able to escape the hostile measures of one state by moving into another. In the early days of the movement the Anabaptists must have been rather numerous in the city, for the pastor of the city church based his petition for the introduction of a German baptismal ritual in 1532 upon the Anabaptist opposition. ("The Anabaptists may well declare our baptism invalid, since nobody understands it.") For the following period there is no information about the presence of Anabaptists in Pforzheim besides the two executions at Pforzheim mentioned in the Hutterite chronicles and the statement that Georg Rapp, who had emigrated to Moravia in the 1540's, returned to his native town fifteen years later. The apparent decline in numbers may be due to the fact that in 1535 the city became the residence of the lower margraviate and was consequently too closely supervised by the central authorities to permit the growth of separatist groups. So much the more obstinately they maintained themselves in several communities of the Pforzheim district, as in Bilfingen, Dürrn, Ersingen, Eutingen, Hohenwart, Kieselbronn, Königsbach, Niesern, Nussbaum, and Oeschelbronn. In Bauschlott, according to the Hutterite chronicles, an Anabaptist by the name of Georg Baumann was executed about 1529. From most of these towns, especially from Oeschelbronn, there are records of the emigration of Anabaptists to Moravia in the 1570's. As late as 1592, the pastor of Oeschelbronn complained about the great number of Anabaptists who assembled in the forests and fields at night for their secret preaching services. As in the rest of the regions of the Upper Rhine, the congregations, reduced by emigration, exile, and death, disappeared in the storms of the Thirty Years' War. Not until the 18th century is there record of the presence of Mennonite immigrants, who settled on the large estates as renters. In 1755 Pforzheim reported to the authorities of the margraviate that there had been no Anabaptists in the area except on the leased estates of Katharinental (Katharinentalerhof, Göbrichen community) and Karlshausen (Karlshäuserhof, community of Dürrn). The Mennonite lessees Jakob Kurz at Katharinental and Claus Brennemann at Karlshausen in 1763 received permission to live there the remainder of their lives when the authorities of the margraviate took over the management of its estates. Today the Mennonites living in Pforzheim belong to the congregation of Wössingen, located in the district of Karlsruhe. M.K.

Records of the archive of Baden at Karlsruhe; Beck, Geschichts-Bücher; Wolkan, Geschicht-Buch; Zieglschmid, Chronik; TA Baden-Pfalz; ML III, 362.

Pfoutz Valley in Perry County, Pa., extends from the Juniata River at Millerstown to Thompsontown with a ridge in the center to the Susquehanna at Liverpool, between Turkey and Forge Hills. The northwestern valley near Juniata County, in Little Pfoutz Valley, was the home of the Aukers, Lauvers, Brubakers, and Kauffmans in the 19th century. Caspar Auker was the first Mennonite. His son Henry Auker (Sept. 23, 1790-Sept. 24, 1866) and grandsons Deacon Jonas Auker (Nov. 12, 1824-June

18, 1895) and Bishop William Auker (Aug. 18, 1829-July 16, 1908) lived in the valley. For a number of years the Wardville Schoolhouse was used and later Lock Schoolhouse. The Auker Cemetery east of Thompsontown is a mile west of the Wardville Schoolhouse. By 1903 all Mennonites in the area were coming to Delaware for communion. It was always a part of the Juniata-Snyder Bishop District.

I.D.L.

Pfrimmerhof, an estate near the village of Sippersfeld in the Palatinate, which was leased to Mennonites from the beginning of the 18th century, and which has been farmed by their descendants since the beginning of the 19th century as their property. The earlier village Primmen or Prümen, belonging to the monastery of Rosenthal and to the baron of Stauf, was completely destroyed in the Thirty Years' War, and the ruins were inhabited for decades solely by charcoal burners. In 1702 the entire farm (300 Morgen) of desolate land was given by the Nassau-Weilburg authorities to Casimir Lander, his son Hans Jakob, and his son-in-law Hans Jakob Schwarz in hereditary lease. They built three homes, as well as barns, stables, and other buildings, but stayed only a few years. On Sept. 14, 1709, Jost Krehbiel took over the estate; it thus became the home site of the widely ramified Krehbiel family (*q.v.*). Some members of the family emigrated to America, including Jakob Krehbiel, the author of the "Chronik des Pfrimmerhofs," who settled in New York in 1831. Through marriage the names of Stauffer and Bletscher were at times represented on the Pfrimmerhof. Today there are on the Pfrimmerhof in addition to a non-Mennonite family, two Krehbiel families and a Fellmann family, who are members of the Sembach (*q.v.*) congregation.

G.H.

J. Eller, "Die Geschichte des Pfrimmerhofs," in *Pfälzische Zeitbilder,* supplement of the *Pfälzische Presse* (Kaiserslautern, Dec. 12, 1927); *Gem.-Kal.* 1900, 58 ff.; 1905, 143; J. Krehbiel, "Die Chronik des Pfrimmerhofs" (1826, a manuscript in the possession of the Krehbiel family, Pfrimmerhof); *ML* III, 362.

Pfudler, Felix, a cobbler, was a leader of the Anabaptist congregation of Esslingen, Germany, in 1527-28.

Philadelphia (City of Brotherly Love), population over two million, third largest city in United States, has played a very significant role in American Mennonite history. The city was founded by William Penn (*q.v.*) and the Quakers in 1681 and chartered in 1701. The Quakers have played a prominent role in the life of the state and the city. The first permanent Mennonite settlement to be established in America was Germantown (*q.v.*) located 6 miles north of the city at that time, but now incorporated in the city. Ever since the first arrival in 1683 Philadelphia served as a gateway port for most of the Mennonites of Swiss-German background, though very few of them settled in the city. The Germantown Mennonite Church (GCM, *q.v.*) is still in existence with 32 members.

Mennonites moving into the city later (1865) established the First Mennonite Church (GCM) at Diamond and Reese streets (see **Philadelphia First**

Mennonite Church) and the Second Mennonite Church (GCM, *q.v.*, 1899) at Franklin and Indiana. The Norris Square (*q.v.*) Mennonite Church, organized in 1922 (Sunday school organized in 1899), belongs to the Lancaster Conference. The Mennonite Brethren in Christ have the Salem Church at Broad and McFerran and some missions in West Philadelphia and Roxboro.

Philadelphia is a cultural center of the nation and contains in its many libraries and museums, such as the Historical Society of Pennsylvania, the Germantown Historical Society, the Free Library of Philadelphia, the Friends Historical Society, the Carl Schurz Memorial Foundation, significant material pertaining to Mennonite culture and history.

The capital town of the Fernheim Mennonite Colony in the Paraguayan Chaco, Filadelfia, was named after the Pennsylvania city, partly because the owners of the land sold to the Mennonites had their chief residence there, and partly because the idea of emphasizing brotherly love appealed to the refugee settlers.

C.K.

Clarence Fretz, "A Sight-Seeing Tour of Philadelphia." *Menn. Life* II (July 1947) 24-26.

Philadelphia First Mennonite Church (GCM), a member of the Eastern District Conference, located at Fifth and Diamond Streets, Philadelphia, Pa., was organized in October 1865 as the First Philadelphia congregation, with Bishop Moses Gottshall of Schwenksville as the overseer of the work. On Jan. 12, 1867, the chapel was purchased and regular morning and evening services were conducted by visiting ministers. On April 5, 1868, Samuel G. Clemmer became the full-time minister. In 1872 the congregation became a member of the Eastern District Conference. Originally the services were in German but gradually English was introduced. Since 1914 all services have been in English. The language question caused difficulties in 1874 and about one half of the members withdrew and joined the Moravian Church, some of whom later returned. A new brick church building was dedicated in January 1882, which is the present place of worship (Reese and Diamond streets). In 1881 the congregation was incorporated. One of the outstanding ministers of the congregation was N. B. Grubb (*q.v.*), who served the congregation in 1882-1920; under his service the congregation increased to a membership of 470 and introduced more effective methods of outreach. The organization of the Second Mennonite Church in 1899 took some of its members.

A Sunday school was organized in 1868 and a Young People's Society of Christian Endeavour (*q.v.*) in 1886, the first to be organized in a Mennonite church. The congregation had a choir and Ladies' Aid Society from its earliest days. The ministers who have served the church are Samuel G. Clemmer 1868-70, Andrew B. Shelly 1870-72, Levi O. Schimmel 1872-73, Albert E. Funk 1874-82, N. B. Grubb 1882-1920, A. J. Neuenschwander 1921-29, Mary E. Bakewell 1929-30, Carl J. Landes 1930-36, John J. Plenert 1936-47, Wesley C. Ewert 1947-50, H. S. Weiss 1951-52, and Curtis Bedsworth 1952- The membership in 1957 was 173.   J.H.F., C.K.

Fiftieth Anniversary of the First Mennonite Church of Philadelphia (Philadelphia, 1915); *Charter and By-Laws of the First Mennonite Church* (Philadelphia, 1911); *Seventy-Fifth Anniversary of the First Mennonite Church of Philadelphia* (Philadelphia, 1940); "Young People's Association of the First Mennonite Church, Philadelphia, Minutes" 1886-92 (BeCL); J. C. Wenger, *History of the Mennonites of the Franconia Conference* (Telford, 1937); D. K. Cassel, *History of the Mennonites* (Philadelphia, 1888); "History of the First Philadelphia Congregation," *1898 Mennonite Yearbook and Almanac* (Quakertown, 1898).

Philadelphia (Calvary) Mennonite Brethren in Christ Church had 78 members in 1957, with LeRoy S. Heller serving as pastor.   M.G.

Philadelphia (Emmanuel) Mennonite Brethren in Christ Church, 6214 Grays Ave., Philadelphia 42, Pa., had a membership of 60 in 1957. It was organized as a congregation in 1927 and was previously known as the West Philadelphia Mennonite Brethren in Christ Church. John Dunn was the minister in 1957.   N.H.W.

Philadelphia, Paraguay: see **Filadelfia.**

Philhaven Hospital grew out of the experiences of many Mennonite conscientious objectors during World War II who served as attendants in mental hospitals. The Lancaster Conference (MC) appointed a board of 12 trustees in 1948 to establish such a hospital. In 1949 Graybill and Mary Landis donated a farm of 167 acres near Lebanon, Pa., for this purpose; Abram Horst of New Holland was appointed contractor. On May 7, 1952, the building was dedicated. It is on a hilltop overlooking the beautiful Lebanon Valley.

The purpose of this hospital was "to provide institutional facilities for the mentally unfortunate of Lancaster Conference and others . . . regardless of race or nationality." It is a 37-bed active treatment mental hospital. Treatments include psychotherapy, electro-shock, occupational and recreational therapy, and the use of tranquilizing drugs. Since its dedication there have been a total of 1,634 admissions (to Feb. 1, 1958), not including the many outpatients treated. Dr. S. Philip Loucks was the psychiatrist and was succeeded Aug. 1, 1955, by Dr. Henry A. Weitz; on Feb. 25, 1957, a second psychiatrist, Dr. Marjorie Morrison, was added to the staff. Elvin G. Lefever was administrator until November 1953; he was succeeded by J. Horace Martin, the present administrator.

The work grew so rapidly that it became necessary to build (in addition to the original plant): (1) a dormitory 100 x 30 ft. for staff members—the staff having increased from 8 to 33; (2) an annex to the hospital, 31 x 38 ft., to care for acutely disturbed patients. The hospital has served as an outlet for Christian service on a voluntary basis, and as alternative service for CO's.   H.C.S.

Philip I (1504-67), called the Magnanimous, Landgrave of Hesse, Germany, 1509-67, was until 1518 under the regency of his mother Anna of Mecklenburg, introduced the Reformation into Hesse in 1526, founded the University of Marburg in 1527, was one of the most zealous promoters of the Reformation in Germany. Before his death he divided his lands among his four sons, William, George, Louis, and Philip.

In his attitude toward the Anabaptists he showed extraordinary generosity and kindness. He saw in the Anabaptist movement a disorder in religious life, which had its roots in error and weakness in the faith rather than in moral error like sedition and revolt, and which must therefore be treated with lenience and consideration. Characteristic of his attitude are his words: "I see more improvement of conduct among those whom we call fanatics than among those who are Lutheran" (a letter to his sister, Duchess Elizabeth of Saxony, Feb. 18, 1530). "On every hand there is no perfect faith in us, so that we must say: Lord, I believe; help Thou mine unbelief" (Heidenhain, 78). "Alas, how cold love is among us who call ourselves Christian and those who create such offense must give an account before God and bear a grievous judgment" (*Corpus Reformatorum* IX, 762). Above all, he said, one must try to lead them back to the church by persuasion and indoctrination. Expulsion from the country was the severest penalty he would permit; it too must be preceded by teaching. Bishop Franz of Münster asked his advice concerning the punishment of the Anabaptists (letter of Jan. 20, 1534; Cornelius, p. 218), as did also Karl, Margrave of Baden (letter of Oct. 12, 1566). Philip replied, informing him of the decrees that had been issued against the Anabaptists: "not to follow them too strictly, but always deal according to the circumstances and persons, so that the poor people might be converted and brought to the truth" (Hochhut, 554; Franz, No. 150).

At first Philip felt compelled to take steps against Melchior Rinck (*q.v.*). In 1528 Philip had a personal talk with him in the hunting castle Friedewald near Hersfeld (Wappler, II, 53). Then Philip made repeated attempts, but vain, to have him converted by the pastor Balthasar Raidt and the theologians at the University of Marburg. Now Rinck was sentenced to church penance, but remained in the country. Therefore John, Elector of Saxony, sent Philip the printed and manuscript writings of Rinck in order to induce him to take a more rigorous attitude. Soon afterward Rinck was seized on Hessian soil; but the efforts of the elector and his councillors to have a severe punishment inflicted were unavailing. Philip repudiated all interference in this affair. Finally he made up his mind to banish Rinck from Hesse and Saxony, and to extract from him a vow never to return to either of the two principalities. This was done in May 1531 (Franz, No. 5, 13a, 14a).

On the part of Saxony and especially of the Lutheran divines no effort was spared to make Philip, whom they suspected of an open inclination toward Anabaptism, change his opinion and to make clear to him the danger in his present position. Justus Menius (*q.v.*) dedicated to him his libelous booklet, *Der Wiedertäufer Lehre und Geheimnis aus heiliger Schrift widerlegt. Mit einer schönen Vorrede von Dr. Martin Luther* (Wittenberg, 1530). But Philip was not influenced by the polemic. In the matter of the punishment of the Anabaptists living in Eisenach and in the Hausbreitenbach district, which were under the joint jurisdiction of the two rulers, a serious difference of opinion arose. John of Saxony demanded the death penalty; Philip refused to give his consent. At the Schmalkaldic Bundestag at Nordhausen early in December 1531 the matter came up for discussion. The delegates of Saxony demanded the death sentence on the basis of the imperial decree (1529); the Hessian delegates countered that their prince had scruples against putting them to death. If they could not be deflected from their belief by indoctrination, they should be punished by having their hearth fire extinguished. They would then emigrate of their own accord. At most their homes should be barricaded (see the regulation of Philip on the subject of the Anabaptists at the end of 1531 in Wappler, I, 154, Franz, No. 15). The Nordhausen Bundestag (Franz, No. 18) also discussed the case of Melchior Rinck, who had been rearrested on Nov. 11, 1531. Again in vain. Again several of Rinck's writings were sent to Philip, as well as a personal letter from John dated Dec. 21, 1531, which expressed the hope that the old revolutionary be punished with the sword, a course justifiable before God and with a good conscience. John called attention to the fact that the Hessian authorities had agreed to the death penalty in sanctioning the edict of Speyer on April 23, 1529. But Philip was unable to inflict the death sentence on the obstinate Anabaptist. On Jan. 3, 1532, he informed John that he had sentenced the Anabaptist leader to life imprisonment and had taken him to Bürbach in the district of Katzenellenbogen, Wiesbaden area. He added that that he would not be able to reconcile his conscience to executing anyone with the sword in a matter of faith, where there was no other ground for taking his life. Otherwise no Catholics or Jews could be tolerated, for they blaspheme Christ to the highest degree, and would have to be put to death in a like manner (Franz, No. 17, 18b).

Philip likewise refused to consent to the severe penalty for the Anabaptists arrested in Hausbreitenbach. Finally they were divided between Saxony and Hesse; some of the former were executed, the latter were released. In no indefinite terms he also rejected the idea of executing Fritz Erbe (q.v.), who was imprisoned in Eisenach. To Elector John Frederick, who had demanded the death sentence for Erbe on the basis of the opinion of the Leipzig court, he declared in a letter of May 22, 1533, that he had never yet had a man put to death solely on a matter of belief; he had merely banished such or commanded them to sell their goods and move out. Only the obstinate who refused to go had he arrested. Therefore in the case of Fritz Erbe he also favored exile. If Erbe should refuse to leave the country he should be kept in prison until he changed his mind. He could not persuade himself "to punish anyone with the sword because of an error of faith, which is a gift of God, and was adopted at the time, not from malice, but from ignorance." He maintained this position in spite of repeated efforts by the elector, who based his opinion on the imperial law of 1529 and the official opinion of the theologians. Fritz Erbe remained in prison until his death in 1548 (Franz, No. 25).

In July 1533, when 18 Anabaptists were again seized in Hausbreitenbach and the Elector of Saxony again demanded their execution, Philip refused with the words, "Our Lord will give grace that they may be converted." This hope of Philip's was fulfilled in several instances in September of that year when some Anabaptists imprisoned in Mühlhausen recanted. After the revolt of 1525 the protectorate over the city of Mühlhausen was held in turn for a period of one year each by the Elector of Saxony, Duke George of Saxony, and Philip of Hesse. On June 15, 1533, the rule fell to Philip. He had a difficult position to maintain against the other two rulers. But he did not yield, and sent the pastor Raidt to Mühlhausen to convert the Anabaptists imprisoned there; Raidt was surprisingly successful in persuading all to recant, whereupon they were re-released (Wappler, II, 101). The Anabaptists at Sorga near Hersfeld were expelled in September 1533. They emigrated to Moravia (Wappler, II, 102; Franz, No. 28).

Philip's position was made more difficult by the events at Münster (q.v.). From the beginning he gave his attention to developments there. He corresponded with Bishop Franz von Waldeck and the regent and the city council (Cornelius, II); in a letter of March 6, 1535, he requested that the Anabaptists be watched (Becker, 83; Franz, No. 37). He sent his divines Theodor Fabricius and Johann Lening to Münster to convert the Anabaptists and to settle the dispute. After the fall of the city and the capture and condemnation of the leaders of this unfortunate movement, upon his express wish an attempt was made to convert the leaders by the Protestant clergymen Antonius Corvinus (q.v.) and Johann Kymeus (q.v.). With some malicious satisfaction the Elector of Saxony made use of the opportunity to influence Philip to take stronger measures against the Anabaptists. Already on April 25, 1534, he had called attention to the revolt in Münster as an example of the dangers of lenience. Philip did not reply. He was obviously embarrassed. Expulsions from the country did no good. The Anabaptists kept returning. There were instances where they promised three times not to return, but still kept appearing. "In order not to undertake something so very burdensome as concerning the life and body against the Anabaptists," he requested the opinion (May 24, 1536) of the magistrates of the cities of Strasbourg, Ulm, the dukes Ulrich of Württemberg and Ernst of Brunswick-Lüneburg, as well as of the theological faculties of the universities of Marburg and Wittenberg (Franz, No. 47).

Four days later he issued to all the districts of his realm a new mandate against the Anabaptists (Hochhut, 554-57; Franz, No. 47d). It is again unusually lenient for the times. It stipulates that the Anabaptists be summoned and diligently instructed by the clergy. If they persisted in their error they should be commanded to sell all their possessions within two weeks and leave the country with wife and children. If they promised this in a credible manner, they should be given all aid and support in the sale of their goods, "for we desire neither their lives nor their goods." But the houses of the disobedient should be barricaded, and no smoke or fire be allowed in them. Their property should be given them; they should only not live in the realm. All who granted them any aid were threatened with the same punishment as the Anabaptists. But those who were converted and returned to the church should be kindly received and only admonished to avoid "harm and disadvantage" in the future.

Concerning the opinions that were sent to Philip see **Hesse.** To discuss them Philip summoned the most prominent of his councillors, the knights, and his theologians, in addition to several representatives from the cities of his land to Kassel on Aug. 7, 1536 (Becker, 84; Franz, No. 47 P.Q.). This point of time was extremely unfavorable for the Anabaptists. Shortly before, a band of robbers and arsonists posing as Anabaptists was seized and some of its members executed. So it came about that the Hessian chancellor Feige also expressed himself in favor of greater severity toward the Anabaptists. He wanted to have the death penalty inflicted at least on the foreign Anabaptists who returned the third time after as many expulsions; for it was necessary to be on one's guard against them. The sharpest opinions were expressed by the Lutheran preachers Tilmann Schnabel and Justus Winter, who demanded a strict enforcement of the imperial edicts, whereas their colleague Johann Lening, who had been Philip's emissary to Münster, gave this judgment: "One should pray God to correct the errors in his own life and to admonish the Anabaptists kindly and in a friendly spirit. Even if all that they carry on their shield were bad, it is necessary to use caution and not make use of the sword until all other means have been tried."

A new regulation against the Anabaptists was worked out, which was with Philip's consent adopted verbatim in the Hessian church inspection regulations of 1537 (see **Hesse**; Franz, No. 47 R.S.). It sharply insists on the abolition of vices, because the Anabaptists were offended by them. In general it contains a sharpening of the previous regulation: "Foreign preachers of Anabaptists shall be beaten with rods, have a sign burned into their cheeks, and be threatened with death if they ever returned." Natives were ordered to sell all their goods. But if they did not do this within the time set, their houses should be closed up, the hearth fire extinguished, and their goods sold. The proceeds should be kept until they demanded it, and they were to be ordered on penalty of death to leave the country forever. If foreigners should nevertheless return, criminal proceedings should be inaugurated against them and the law take its course according to the imperial mandates. Natives should, on the other hand, in this case be beaten with rods and a sign burned on their faces; if they returned again after this, they should be racked and executed. The same methods should be used against those who were ordered to leave the country but refused to do so. "But no Anabaptist shall be put to death, even after the sentence has been passed, without previously notifying us."

But if someone had not previously baptized, preached, or held meetings, and had perhaps been misled through lack of misunderstanding, but refused to receive instruction, he should, in case he was a foreigner, be expelled from the country for all time, for the first offense. If he should, however, return, he should be beaten with rods and have a sign burned on his cheek; on the third offense he should be put to death. But if he in the face of death recanted, he should be taken back for further consultation and not killed. These severe measures were never put into effect; Philip never confirmed a death sentence. In 1540 he was able to write that in his realm the death sentence had never been inflicted on an Anabaptist. The Anabaptists were given gentle treatment. This was also true of those imprisoned in Wolkersdorf, Georg Schnabel (*q.v.*) and others. On them was found a letter from Peter Tasch with the address: "To the elect and called in the Lord, Jörgen S., my dear brother together with his companions among the wild beasts in tribulation and misery." This letter Philip sent to the Elector of Saxony and the Duke of Jülich, Tasch's sovereign, and recommended to them that they keep a watchful eye on the Anabaptists. Since this letter also mentioned the Anabaptist movement in England, Philip drew up a letter with the Elector of Saxony to Henry VIII, and sent it through the council of Hamburg, notifying him of the presence of the Anabaptists in England (Franz, No. 62).

Philip took pains to induce the Anabaptists imprisoned in Wolkersdorf to recant. He sent them a letter in his own hand (Hochhut, 612; Franz, No. 76), expressing his disapproval of the lenience of their imprisonment; he would therefore have reason to deal otherwise with them, but did not wish to do so, but once more wanted to deal with them graciously and kindly, and was therefore sending them a God-fearing man who wanted to discuss with them in a friendly way their error; they should listen to him, give him good information; they would have to be obstinate indeed and remain stubbornly by their adopted opinion (if they refused to listen to him); "he shall show you the right way, so that you may come to the true knowledge of divine truth, which we would most heartily like to see and would rather hear than to proceed against you with rigor, as is our right, since you refuse to desist from your unchristian sect." To this end he called Martin Bucer (*q.v.*), the reformer of Strasbourg, to Hesse (Philip's letter to the magistrate of Strasbourg, Aug. 9, 1538). This led to complete success. Peter Tasch and his followers declared themselves willing to submit to the church. They presented their modified principles in a document called *Bekenntnis oder Antwort einiger Fragestücke oder Artikeln der gefangenen Täufer und anderer im Land zu Hessen vom 11. Dezember 1538* (Hochhut, 612-22; Franz, No. 85); the statement was accepted by the Lutheran clergy, who then declared that they were "willing to pardon those Anabaptists and accept them in the church." Eagerly Philip accepted the proposal of Bucer to have these converts win their brethren. He did not hesitate to deal with them in person, and to his great joy most of the Anabaptists of his realm returned to the established church.

In 1544 there were once more negotiations between Saxony and Hesse concerning Anabaptists in the Hausbreitenbach district. Again John Frederick wrote to Philip (July 28, 1544; Franz, No. 121), demanding that the imperial edict be enforced against the obstinate Anabaptists, who had had ten years to consider. If Philip hesitated to do this, he should at least not hold it against John Frederick if he (John Frederick) punished them in accord with the imperial edict, which had been confirmed at the last Reichstag at Speyer. Again Philip withheld his reply; his conscience prevented his consenting to the request. To the extreme annoyance of Justus Menius, the superintendent, the Anabaptists in Hausbreitenbach remained unpunished. Philip also protected the Anabaptists in Mühlhausen, whereas George of Saxony had them cruelly put to death and the Elector of Saxony demanded the death penalty for them. In a writing to John Frederick on Aug. 19, 1545, Philip cited his general reasons and also the passages of Scripture, Matt. 13:24-30; Luke 9:52-56; and Romans 14:1-5 and 12 ff., and said, "These quotations block our path to such an extent that we cannot find it in our conscience to proceed with such rigor against a person who errs somewhat in the faith; for the person might accept instruction over night and desist from his error. Now if such a one should straightway be put to death by one of us, we are truly concerned that we may not be innocent of his blood. For if one were to execute all those who are not of our faith, how would the Papists, likewise the Jews, fare, who in this matter err as deeply or even deeper than the Anabaptists? Therefore it pleased us once more, wherever these people are, that they be arrested and indoctrinated by skilled persons with the Word of God; and those who would not return to the church and desist from their error after being instructed should be expelled from the country; if they returned or if they were so completely obstinate that they might infect others they should be kept in prison; the expenses would not be so great" (Franz, No. 128).

This letter is indeed evidence of a generous mind and noble religious tolerance, in which Philip far surpassed his contemporaries and also the reformers Luther (q.v.) and Melanchthon (q.v.); he represented a new era, they were still in the clutches of the Middle Ages. He maintained this position even during his imprisonment by Charles V after the unfortunate outcome of the Schmalkaldian War. In his opinion to John Frederick the Middle of Saxony, on March 7, 1559, he says, "It is so, many Anabaptists have an unchristian evil sect, as was shown at Münster and elsewhere; but they are not alike. Some are simple, pious folk; they should be dealt with in moderation. Anabaptists who deal with the sword may rightly also be punished with the sword. But those who err in faith should be dealt with leniently, and shall be instructed in accord with the principle of love to one's neighbor, and no effort shall be spared, also they shall be heard, and if they will not accept the truth and scatter error like a harmful seed among Christians, they shall be expelled and their preaching abolished. But to punish them with death, as happens in some countries, when they have done nothing more than err in faith and have not acted seditiously, cannot be reconciled with the Gospel. Other Christian teachers like Augustine and Chrysostom also violently opposed it."

This attitude Philip also impressed upon his sons in his will: "To kill people for the reason that they believed an error we have never done, and wish to admonish our sons not to do so, for we consider that it is contrary to God, as is clearly shown in the Gospel" (Franz, No. 148).

Philip's sons and descendants held to this attitude. His spirit of gentleness and reconciliation lived on among them. "And it was due to this lenience toward the Anabaptists to a great extent, that new life and wholesome recollection of nearly forgotten truths of salvation were brought to the church" (Wappler, I, 117). NEFF.

E. Becker, "Zur Geschichte der Wiedertäufer in Oberhessen," in Archiv für hessische Geschichte und Altertumskunde, n.s. X (Darmstadt, 1914); G. Egelhaaf, Landgraf Philipp der Grossmütige (Halle, 1904); Festschrift zum Gedächtnis Philipps des Grossmütigen (Kassel, 1904); A. Heidenhain, Die Unionspolitik Landgraf Philipps von Hessen 1557-62 (Halle, 1890); K. W. H. Hochhuth, "Landgraf Philipp und die Wiedertäufer," in Ztschr für die historische Theologie XXVIII (1858) 538-644; XXIX (1859) 167-234; Philipp der Grossmütige (Festschrift des Hist. Vereins für das Grossherzogtum Hessen, 1904); Urkundliche Quellen zur hessischen Ref.-Gesch. I, 1182 f. (article by Walther Köhler); Paul Wappler, Die Stellung Kursachsens und des Landgrafen Philipp von Hessen zur Täuferbewegung (Münster, 1910); idem, Thüringen; C. A. Cornelius, Die Geschichtsquellen des Bistums Münster (Münster, 1853) 218; TA Hessen (Franz); ML III, 363 ff.

Philip, Margrave of Baden: see **Baden.**

Philip Mutsemeker belonged to a group of Anabaptists at Maastricht (q.v.), Dutch province of Limburg about 1534. In early September 1534 he was baptized by Henric Rol (q.v.). Arrested with many others in January 1535, he was tried and recanted his faith. Thereupon he was beheaded at Maastricht on Feb. 6, 1535. Mutsemeker's trial is very interesting. He was a young man; Steven Mutsemeker, his father, formerly belonging to the Sacramentists (q.v.), also joined the Anabaptists. Philip, who formerly had been a drunkard and a fighter, had turned to a better life after his conversion. He was apparently a poor man, who repeatedly received relief from the Anabaptists; Jan van Genck (q.v.), the deacon, had even had the roof of his house thatched. It was his opinion that infant baptism was not in accord with the Scriptures and that it was not necessary to hold to the institutions of the Catholic Church, such as fasting. Like many of this Maastricht Anabaptist group Philip had a strong tendency to revolutionary practices. vDZ.

W. Bax, Het Protestantisme in het bisdom Luik en vooral te Maastricht I (The Hague, 1937) 91, 98, 119.

Philipp Weber: see **Plener, Philipp.**

Philippites, an Anabaptist group named after Philipp Plener (q.v.), existing as an independent group from c1527 to the middle of the 1540's. Its origins go back to Plener's activities around Bruchsal (q.v.)

in southwest Germany. In 1527 Plener came to Moravia and in 1529 established his own Bruderhof at Auspitz (apparently on a communal pattern), made up in the main of brethren from Plener's home area, Württemberg and Baden. In 1531 Blasy Kuhn (*q.v.*) arrived with the remnants of the old Bruchsal congregation, Kuhn becoming Plener's assistant. There were now three groups in Moravia living communally: the Gabrielites (*q.v.*), mostly Silesians, in Rossitz (*q.v.*), the Philippites, and the Tiroleans (under Schützinger, *q.v.*), both living in Auspitz (*q.v.*). A smaller Bruderhof of the Philippites existed also at Pulgram (*q.v.*), Moravia, which united with the Hutterites in 1538. The Auspitz Philippite group attracted many newcomers and *c*1535 numbered some 400 members. The names of some of these members are recorded in the Hutterite Chronicle and some in the Passau documents, to be discussed below. There were Adam Schlegel (*q.v.*) and Hans Both (*q.v.*), both of whom had shifted from the Hutterites to the Philippites; Hans Haffner (*q.v.*), the author of a remarkable tract; Hans Gentner (*q.v.*), who turned Hutterite in 1538 and thereafter became quite prominent in this group, and two well-known hymn writers, Hans Betz (*q.v.*) of Eger and Michael Schneider (*q.v.*) of Bruchsal.

When persecutions set in in Moravia in 1535 and the brethren were unable to find any place of abode, Plener decided that the entire brotherhood (with the possible exception of the Pulgram people) should return to Germany. Actually the records show that there now existed three different groups 1535-*c*45. (*a*) One group arrived safely in the former home area: the triangle Heilbronn-Worms-Strasbourg, with Bruchsal (in the Kraichgau) roughly in the center. Of this group some facts are revealed in epistles by Peter Riedemann (*q.v.*). Hans Gentner visited them several times 1540-43. Apparently due to a lack of vigorous leadership the group faded out, most likely fusing with the "Swiss Brethren" of that area. This is all the more probable since endeavors toward the unification of all the different Anabaptist groups in the Strasbourg-Worms area were afoot time and again (compare Marpeck's activities in the 1550's).

(*b*) Another group in Upper Austria (see **Austria**) is indicated in certain Riedemann epistles and other Hutterite sources. In Steyr (*q.v.*), Linz (*q.v.*), and Gmunden small brotherhoods existed 1534-41 called "Philippites"; they were presumably the result of Philippite mission work there before 1535. Later Riedemann felt a concern for their spiritual welfare and wrote them many epistles. One name becomes conspicuous in this group; viz., Wolf Brandhuber (*Chronik,* 176), doubtless the son of the leader of the old Linz congregation, Wolfgang Brandhuber (*q.v.*), martyred in 1529. Some of these Upper Austrian Philippites later joined the Hutterites in Moravia, but the majority "turned worldly" and thus disappeared as a distinct group. The Hutterites had not been able to provide them with any leadership outside Moravia. Practically all of these Upper Austrians were urban.

(*c*) The best-known group is the Passau group, 1535-40. Back in Moravia in 1535, Plener in a last

act as bishop had ordained Michael Schneider of Bruchsal as the leader (*Vorsteher*) of a group of about 60 persons (mostly from Bruchsal) who planned to reach their former homes via the Danube route. Catholic authorities, having been alerted, caught the entire group in August and September 1535 around Passau and imprisoned them in the dungeons of the Passau castle (belonging to the bishop of that city). Some were tortured, but no death penalty was imposed. Some of these brethren died in the following years; some recanted and were set free; of the rest nothing is known. Wolkan in his *Lieder* gives the best account of this group, using the "Passauer Religions Akten" of Munich. This source gives the names of some 50 Anabaptists, their origin, and in part their story. The 52 hymns of the oldest part of the *Ausbund* (numbers 81-129) were composed by these Philippite Brethren in Passau. Since some of them later joined the "Swiss Brethren," it is easily understandable that they brought these hymns along from prison and allowed them to be printed (first ed. in 1564) as "hymns of the Swiss Brethren." Of Michael Schneider (the leader) 11 hymns are thus preserved, of Hans Betz 17 (only 11 bearing his signature). One hymn by Betz is also found in the *Lieder der Hutterischen Brüder,* 75-77.

The most remarkable spiritual document coming from the Philippites is the tract *Concerning a True Soldier of Christ* (*q.v.*), written *c*1533-35 by Hans Haffner, of Riblingen near Schwäbisch-Hall. It is a study of what constitutes the proper mental equipment of a disciple: besides love, faith, and hope Haffner emphasizes in particular "Gelassenheit" (*q.v.*) or inner surrender to God. Comparing this tract with the *Ausbund* hymns, one easily discovers a great unity of the genius of both, discipleship, resignation, and love being the main ideas stressed, likewise the inevitability of the cross. Once the principle of community of goods was abandoned (in 1535), it was not too difficult for these brethren to merge organically with the Swiss Brethren of southwest Germany.   R.F.

Robert Friedmann, "The Philippite Brethren: Chapter in Anabaptist History," *MQR* XXXII (1958) 270-97; *idem,* "Concerning a True Soldier of Christ," *MQR* V (1931) 87-99; Zieglschmid, *Chronik; Lieder der Hutterischen Brüder* (Scottdale, 1914); Wolkan, *Lieder; ML* III, 367 f.

Philippus de Keurs, an Anabaptist martyr, a cabinetmaker, died in 1537 at Cassel in Flanders after a valiant confession of his faith. Particulars are lacking. (*Mart. Mir.* D 41, E 447; *ML* II, 486.)
                                          NEFF.

Philips, Dirk: see Dirk Philips.

Philips van Hulle, an Anabaptist martyr, unmarried, a brewer, was burned at the stake with two others on April 13, 1557, at the Vrijdagsmarkt of Gent, Belgium. Further particulars are lacking. (Verheyden, *Gent,* 24, No. 52.)   vDZ.

Philips, J. C., a Dutch artist who made the engravings for the thirty pictures of Dutch Mennonite ministers, including Menno Simons, published at Amsterdam in 1743 by Kornelis de Wit under the title

Verzaameling van Afbeeldingen van Doopsgezinde Leeraaren.   vDZ.

Philips, Lucas, a Dutch Mennonite elder: see **Filips, Lucas.**

Philips, Obbe: see **Obbe Philips.**

Philips Wyntgen van Westbrouck, who was one of the first Anabaptists at Amsterdam, Netherlands, was sentenced to death at The Hague on March 10, 1533, and executed there or at Amsterdam that very day or the next day. His property was confiscated; after the execution, probably by beheading, his head was put on a stake as a deterrent exhibit. Particulars about Westbrouck were not available. (Grosheide, *Bijdrage,* 50, 302.)   vDZ.

Phister, Werner, an Anabaptist martyr, an aged preacher of the brotherhood, who was seized at Wädenswil near Zürich, Switzerland, in 1640 and with his wife and his son's wife put into the Othenbach prison at Zürich. Whereas his wife was released, he and his daughter-in-law were kept in arrest until they died of want and misery. The family name of Phister was later found among the Emmental (*q.v.*) Mennonites. Here Peter Pfister was chosen as preacher in 1809 and (by lot) elder in 1825. NEFF, vDZ.

Mart. Mir. D 819, E 1118; Samuel Geiser, *Die Taufgesinnten Gemeinden* (Karlsruhe, n.d.) 386 f., 467; *ML* III, 371.

Phlein, Christian, a Mennonite elder in the Palatinate, Germany, wrote a letter to David Rutgers at Amsterdam in 1698, which gives information on the material and spiritual conditions of the Palatine congregations. He stated that some of them were planning to emigrate to America, and that the members of the congregations "all stand in peace one with another." There is apparently no further information about this elder. The letter does not indicate which congregation he was serving. (*Inv. Arch. Amst.* I, No. 1428.)   vDZ.

Phoenixville. About 1750 the Mennonites who had settled in the vicinity of Phoenixville in Chester County, Pa., joined in building a union church on the Charlestown road, two miles from Phoenixville. In 1772 the Mennonites built a school and meetinghouse on Main Street in the town, which was later known successively as Buckwalter's and Morgan's Schoolhouse. In 1794 they erected a stone church on the southwest corner of Main and Church streets. Among the ministers who served there were Bishop Matthias Pennypacker and preachers John Buckwalter, Daniel Showalter, George Hellerman, Jacob Haldeman, John Showalter, and Israel Beidler. Beidler went with John Oberholtzer (*q.v.*) in the schism of 1847, and the congregation died out in the next decade. About 1873 Henry A. Hunsicker, the minister of an independent Mennonite congregation and the first principal of the Freeland Seminary (*q.v.*), built a new meetinghouse on the site of the 1794 building in an attempt to establish a new congregation here. He allowed the Lutherans of the city to worship in this building on alternate Sundays. In a few years the Lutherans purchased the meetinghouse, and in 1905 added a Sunday-school annex. They also filled in the cemetery with sufficient soil to bury all but one or two tombstones of the Mennonite cemetery which surrounded the meetinghouse and which contained about one hundred Mennonite graves. According to some authorities there was a meetinghouse on Schuylkill Street before 1750.   J.C.W.

J. C. Wenger, *History of the Mennonites of the Franconia Conference* (Telford, Pa., 1937) 213-15, photograph of the 1794 church following p. 336.

Physicians, Hutterite: see **Medicine, Hutterite.**

Piccards, a mutilation of the name Beghards (*q.v.*), an epithet of opprobrium applied to both the Moravian Brethren (*q.v.*) and the Bohemian Hussites. In government decrees this designation was also used; it thus became so general that the Brethren used it themselves in the title of their writings, often in the following form: "The Brethren who are called Piccards from envy and hate."

The Moravian Piccards of the 15th and 16th centuries were much more radical than those of Bohemia. In Western Europe, particularly in France, the Waldenses (*q.v.*) of the 15th century are often called Piccards.

The theory that the name Piccards is derived from Picardie, a province in Northern France, where the Waldenses were rather numerous, is wrong.

Whether Nicolaus Storch (*q.v.*) and Thomas Müntzer (*q.v.*) were influenced by the Moravian Piccards, as has been suggested, is an open question. (*ML* III, 374.)   NEFF, vDZ.

Pichner, Hans (*Mart. Mir.* D 162, E 550), Hutterite martyr: see **Pürchner, Hans.**

Pickelin, Maeyken, an Anabaptist martyr, a simple, God-fearing woman, who was imprisoned in 1590 (place not given) and died as a result of her sufferings. (*Mart. Mir.* D 777, E 1080; *ML* III, 371.)   NEFF.

Pickert, Veit, from Etzleben, Thuringia, Germany, an Anabaptist martyr, was executed at Sachsenburg, Saxony, in 1527. (Wappler, *Thüringen,* 45, note 6, *ML* III, 371.)

Pierijntgen, an Anabaptist martyr; she is the subject of two accounts in van Braght's *Martyrs' Mirror,* both inaccurate and incomplete. In one instance she is called Pierijntgen van Male, and in the other Pierijntgen Maelbouts. The research by Verheyden has revealed additional facts. Pierijntgen (Pyrinken) van Male was born at Thielt, Flanders, and lived at Malebosch. She was the widow of Jacob de Backere. She and Marijtgen (Martyncken) suffered martyrdom by beheading at Gent, Belgium, on Dec. 12, 1564. The two women are commemorated in the hymn "Alsmen schreef duyst vijfhondert jaer ende twee en tsestich mede," found in the 1578 and the following editions of the *Lietboecxken.* (*Offer,* 652; *Mart. Mir.* D 301, 306; E 666, 670; Verheyden, *Gent,* 30, No. 102; *ML* III, 3.)   vDZ.

Pierken van Cleve, an Anabaptist martyr: see **Pieter Aelbrechts.**

Pierre Messchars, an Anabaptist martyr, a member of the congregation of Brugge, Belgium, who was arrested with a number of other members in March 1568. He was burned at the stake on March 6 or shortly after. Further particulars are lacking. He may have been a member of the Mennonite Messchaert (q.v.) family, which is found later in the Netherlands. (Verheyden, *Brugge,* 52, No. 47.)

vDZ.

Pierre Wandesoye, an Anabaptist martyr, burned at the stake at Antwerp, Belgium, on May 26, 1573, with three others. Pierre was sentenced to death because he had attended Anabaptist meetings. He had apparently not yet been baptized. (*Antw. Arch.-Blad* XIII, 116 f., 178; XIV, 90 f., No. 1027.)

vDZ.

Piers, Wibbe, a Mennonite preacher at Oldelamer in the Dutch province of Friesland, published *Seven Verscheyden Brieven aen den Eersaemen Leser,* printed at Franeker, 1630. The first six letters are by Wibbe Piers, the seventh by Pieter Jansz Twisck (q.v.) in 1629.

vDZ.

Pierson (erroneously Piseron), **Pierken,** a Mennonite from Antwerp, Belgium, who had fled to the Netherlands to escape persecution and settled at Harlingen, Friesland, where he played a part in the Flemish-Frisian strife in 1566. He sided with the Flemish, but in 1574 he is said to have been chosen preacher by the Frisians (stated in a letter by Hans Busschaert, q.v.); he then had some trouble because he refused to "avoid" his former Flemish friends. By trade he was a maker of buttons. (Génard, *Antw. Arch.-Bl.* XII, 25; *DB* 1893, 11 f., 21.)

vDZ.

Pieryntgen (Pierijntje, Périnne, Printgen) **(van) Loosvelt (Losveldt)** (or Peeryntgen Neckers), an Anabaptist martyr, who at the age of 43 was taken prisoner at Meenen (Menin) in Flanders, Belgium, in 1572, while she was visiting a sick woman, and was burned at the stake on Jan. 6, 1573. At no price could she be moved to betray her brethren. She was interrogated on ten points of doctrine, which she answered aptly with Biblical references. When she was led to death she said to the people, "Go and buy testaments and read in them why I am condemned to death and must die." (*Mart. Mir.* D 641, E 962; *BRN* VII, 174 f.; *ML* II, 690.) Neff.

Pieryntgen Ketels, an Anabaptist martyr, who was executed with her mother Leentgen and also Maryntgen and Pieryntgen of Male in 1564, in the abbey of St. Peter in Gent, Belgium. The exact date and method of execution are not known. The names of these martyrs are found in the hymn "Alsmen schreef duyst vijfhondert jaer, ende twee en tsestich mede," which is found in the *Lietboecxken* of 1578 and following editions. (*Offer,* 651; *Mart. Mir.* D 301, E 666; Verheyden, *Gent,* 30, No. 100; *ML* II, 484.) NEFF, vDZ.

Pieter: see also **Peter.**

Pieter Aelbrechts (Pierken van Cleve) of Cleve, Germany, an Anabaptist martyr, was burned at the stake on March 30, 1568, on the Veerle square at Gent, Belgium, together with Jan van Parijs, Hendrik Maelschap (van Braght writes Maelschalk), and Laurens Pieters. When they arrived at the site of execution the Spanish provost compelled the executioner who was to strangle them as the sentence decreed, to burn them. The waiting victims had meanwhile begun a song, "Ik roep U o hemelsche Vader aen" (I call upon Thee, O heavenly Father). So the Spaniards beat them violently and mutilated them terribly, and then burned them alive. They were *aenkomende vrienden* (q.v.), i.e., not yet admitted into the brotherhood by baptism. Pieter and his comartyrs are commemorated in the hymn "Een liedeken van XLI Vrienden," found in the edition of 1578 of the *Lietboecxken.* (*Offer,* 652; *Mart. Mir.* D 367, E 723; Verheyden, *Gent,* 43, No. 137; *ML* I, 364.)

vDZ.

Pieter Andriesz: see **Hesseling, P. A.**

Pieter de Backer(e), an Anabaptist martyr, who is listed in van Braght's *Martyrs' Mirror* as having been arrested at Gent, Belgium, with four other Anabaptists, and executed at the market place of Antwerp in 1557. The official records, collected and published by P. Génard in *Antwerpsch Archieven-Blad,* give the information that Pieter Pluvier, commonly called Pieter de Backere (baker) of Wervik in Flanders was burned at the stake at Antwerp on Jan. 30, 1557. His name is also found in the hymn "Aenhoort Godt, hemelsche Vader" (Hear, O God, heavenly Father), No. 16 of the *Lietboecxken.*

vDZ.

Offer, 564; *Mart. Mir.* D 184, E 568; *Antw. Arch.-Blad* VIII, 433, 437; XIV, 22 f., No. 239; Wolkan, *Lieder,* 63, 72; *ML* I, 102.

Pieter Boekebinder: see **Peter Scheymaker.**

Pieter Claesz (Peter Coster), an Anabaptist martyr, who had been a sexton of the Catholic church at Zaandam, moved to Amsterdam, joined the Anabaptists there, being baptized by Pieter de Houtzager (q.v.), and was ordained as a preacher by Bartholomeus, i.e., Bartel Boeckbinder (q.v.). During his trial he declared that he had baptized only one person. In March 1534 he was among the Anabaptists who sailed from Amsterdam to Bergklooster (q.v.) in order to go on to Münster (q.v.). He was released, and returned to Amsterdam; but shortly after he was betrayed by a woman and seized; because he had been baptized and was preaching he was condemned to death and beheaded on May 25, 1535.

vDZ.

Mart. Mir. D 36, E 50; Grosheide, *Verhooren,* 121 f.; *DB* 1917, 111, No. 24; Mellink, *Wederdopers,* 163 f.; *ML* II, 603.

Pieter Claesz Jansz, an Anabaptist martyr of Wormer, Dutch province of North Holland. Neither the date nor the place of execution is known. According to the *Bibliographie,* he was put to death at Enkhuizen, North Holland. (*Mart. Mir.* D 61, E 464; *Bibliographie* II, 671, No. 136; *ML* III, 352.)

vDZ.

Pieter de Cleercq, an Anabaptist martyr, a miller by trade, burned at the stake on March 4, 1557, on the Vrijdagsmarkt of Gent, Belgium. He had been arrested by treachery. Particulars are lacking. (Verheyden, *Gent*, 23, No. 29.)   vDZ.

Pieter Coerten (Coerte, Courte), a cloth shearer, born at Meenen, Flanders, living at Antwerp and later at Gent, an Anabaptist martyr, was burned at the stake with three others on July 5, 1559, on the Vrijdagsmarkt at Gent, Belgium; on August 7 of that year seven more suffered martyrdom. All were members of the Gent congregation and had been seized on Friday after Pentecost, as Hans de Vette (*q.v.*) relates in his letter, who also gives the names of these eleven martyrs. They all remained steadfast. Their names are commemorated in the hymn "Ick moet een liet beginnen" (I must begin a song), found in the *Lietboecxken*. (*Offer*, 348, 556 ff.; *Mart. Mir.* D 246, E 620; Verheyden, *Gent*, 25, No. 58.)   vDZ.

Pieter Coster, an Anabaptist martyr: see **Pieter Claesz.**

Pieter van Eynoven (Eynhoven), a native of Antwerp, Belgium, a silk weaver 28 years old, had been baptized "according to Christ's teaching" by a certain Leenaert (viz., Lenaerdt Boeckbinder) at Antwerp. He later lived in Rotterdam, Holland, where he was seized and twice horribly tortured, but he remained true to his faith, and was condemned to die by fire with two companions on March 28, 1558, at Rotterdam. While the execution was being carried out a popular uprising broke out, to which he owed his forcible release. (*Mart. Mir.* D 191, E 675; *DB* 1905, 172; *ML* I, 623.)   NEFF, vDZ.

Pieter Florisz of Oosthoven, Flanders (Belgium), an Anabaptist martyr, a native of Nipkerke (Nieppe) in Flanders, renounced his faith, repented of his recantation and earnestly witnessed to his faith, and suffered death at the stake in 1564 at Armentières, France. (*Mart. Mir.* D 301, E 666; *ML* I, 654.)
NEFF.

Pieter Foppes, of Leeuwarden, Friesland, a Dutch Anabaptist martyr, sentenced to death by the Court of Holland on Feb. 15, 1541. The execution took place by beheading, probably at The Hague, Holland. Particulars are lacking. (*Inv. Arch. Amst.* I, Nos. 46, 237, 745.)   vDZ.

Pieter Gerritsz (Wageman), a Dutch Anabaptist martyr, a native of Enkhuizen, province of North Holland, was baptized before Christmas of 1534 by Lenaerdt Boeckbinder (*q.v.*) of Antwerp. He was seized at Zierikzee, Dutch province of Zeeland, together with Adriaen Jorisse of Brouwershaven, who was also baptized by Leenaert, Jan Jansz (baptized in 1535 by Damas Jacobs at Middelburg), and Janneke Melchior Simons of Den Briel (baptized in 1534 by Cornelis Pietersz wt den Briel). They did not believe in the miracle of the Mass. After severe torture they were beheaded early in the morning of Sept. 4, 1536, the corpses burned, and the heads set on poles. Van Braght (*Mart. Mir.* D 38, E 445) names them Pieter Gerritsz, Pieter Jorisz, Pieter Leydekker, and Janneken Mels. (*Inv. Arch. Amst.* I, Nos. 744 f.; *ML* II, 84.)   K.V.

Pieter de Guliker (Peter of Jülich; official name Pieter Aertsz), a Dutch Anabaptist, was arrested with a number of members of the congregation at Nieuwvaart (now the village de Klundert), not far from Breda, Dutch province of North Brabant, on Aug. 5, 1571, while they were attending a worship service in the house in which Pieter de Guliker, a tailor, lived in the front, and Jan Pieters, a weaver, lived in the rear. The meeting was betrayed to the mayor Anthonis van der Broek, while he was in Gerrit Vorster's tavern. After a confinement of two days at this place the prisoners were taken to Breda, where they were brutally tortured. Pieter de Guliker recanted and was beheaded, whereas the others remained steadfast and died at the stake.

W. Meindersma published a study of these martyrs (*DB* 1912), which reveals the following facts about them: Preaching services were held at two places; viz., at Pieter's home and at the home of the widow Elsken Deckers. The records of the trial indicate that there were about 50 persons at the meeting, rather than 100, as stated by van Braght in the *Martyrs' Mirror*. The police raid occurred while Theunis was preaching. Several of the imprisoned women managed to escape. Two were seized on August 24—Hilleken Jacobs, Jacob Cornelis' maid, 25 years old, and Anneken, the wife of Pieter Pieters of Klundert, 58 years old. The execution probably took place in October. The judges were two members of the City Council of Brussels, Desiderius van Sestich and Nikolaus de Zoete. The Meindersma account also includes a letter not found in the *Martyrs' Mirror*, which Pieter wrote to his wife. (*Mart. Mir.* D 603-5, E 929-31; *DB* 1912, 30-48; *ML* II, 198.)   K.V.

Pieter van den Hende, an Anabaptist martyr, a native of Stekene, Flanders, who was living at Gent, Belgium, was burned at the stake with Willem van Ackere (de Camp) on July 11, 1551, at Merelbeke near Gent. Both had been seized at Merelbeke. Pieter was a cabinetmaker. His property was confiscated. Both Pieter and Willem had been baptized by Gillis van Aken (*q.v.*). (Verheyden, *Gent*, 15, No. 28.)   vDZ.

Pieter Hillebrantsz, an Anabaptist martyr, was beheaded on Jan. 10, 1539, at Delft, Dutch province of South Holland, "because he had been rebaptized." Pieter, a "snydere van calckeren," which probably means that he was a tailor of Calcar (on the Rhine, Germany), was apparently a follower of David Joris (*q.v.*). (*Inv. Arch. Amst.* I, No. 749.)
vDZ.

Pieter de Houtzager (Peter Houdtsager), an adherent of the fanatical Jan Matthijs (*q.v.*) van Haarlem, came to Friesland in December 1533. In the Frisian village of Arum he baptized a woman named Hillegond, who suffered a martyr's death by drowning at Kampen in February 1534. In December 1533 he stayed at Leeuwarden, capital of Friesland, where he baptized Dirk Philips (*q.v.*) and tried to win the Sacramentists (*q.v.*) in this town for his Anabaptist ideas and conviction. In a poster the government named Pieter de Houtzager with Melchior Hofmann, Jakob van Campen, Obbe

Philips, and other "misleaders of the populace." He escaped persecution by flight to Amsterdam. He was one of the fanatical leaders who in March 1534 was taking many people by boat to Münster (*q.v.*); but they were halted at Bergklooster (*q.v.*) near Genemuiden. On March 26, 1534, he was beheaded with Bartel (Bartholomeus) Boeckbinder (*q.v.*) (or van Halle) and five others at Haarlem. J.Y.

Inv. Arch. Amst. I, Nos. 24, 27, 745; *BRN* VII, 31, 45, 106, 130; Kühler, *Geschiedenis* I, 76, 105 f., 159; *DB* 1875, 61; 1884, 7-9; 1917, 98, 106 f., 151; Mellink, *Wederdopers, passim*, see Index.

Pieter ten Hove, an Anabaptist martyr: see **Hove, Peter ten.**

Pieter Jansz, of Westzaan, Dutch province of North Holland, an Anabaptist martyr, sentenced to death on May 16, 1534, by the Court of Holland and beheaded the same day or the next, probably at Amsterdam. Pieter was one of the Anabaptists who were arrested at Bergklooster (*q.v.*), having sailed from Amsterdam en route to Münster (*q.v.*) in March 1534. He was then apparently released, but soon after apprehended again. vDZ.

Inv. Arch. Amst. I, Nos. 744 f.; *DB* 1917, 122, No. 151; Mellink, *Wederdopers*, 159.

Pieter Jans(z), an Anabaptist martyr, a native of Blankenham, Dutch province of Overijssel, confessed that he had been baptized about 1536 at Oldersum in East Friesland, Germany, by Menno Simons, and was beheaded at Kampen, Dutch province of Overijssel, on June 14, 1540. Further particulars are lacking. vDZ.

DB 1875, 65 f.; 1906, 4; K. Vos, *Menno Simons* (Leiden, 1914) 243; *ML* II, 392.

Pieter Jansz (Peter Janssen), an Anabaptist martyr who had been baptized by Gillis van Aken (*q.v.*), was burned at the stake on March 20, 1549, at Amsterdam with seven other martyrs. He was a native of "Lininckhuysen" (Lüdinghausen in the bishopric of Münster, Westphalia?), a shoemaker by trade. His wife Trijnken van Dorsten (*q.v.*) was executed on Jan. 15, 1550. Pieter and his comartyrs are commemorated in the hymn "Tis nu schier al/vervult ons broeders getal" (The number of our brethren is now nearly complete), found in the Dutch hymnal *Veelderhande Liedekens* of 1556 and following editions. vDZ.

Mart. Mir. D 82, E 483; Grosheide, *Bijdrage*, 159; F. C. Wieder, *De Schriftuurlijke Liedekens* (The Hague, 1900) 193, No. 473; *ML* II, 390.

Pieter Jansz-Twisckvolk, a branch of the Dutch Mennonites: see **Twiscken.**

Pieter Jeltjes, a Dutch elder and merchant living at Kollum, province of Friesland, and a member of the Old Frisian (*q.v.*) branch of the Mennonites. In 1599 he became involved in a disagreement with Elder Jan Jacobsz (*q.v.*), who was very strict, considering it sin to sell to non-Mennonites, and who at a conference of Old Frisian delegates meeting at Dokkum on Dec. 16, 1599, banned the more liberal Pieter Jeltjes and his adherents. Concerning Pieter's life and work nothing further is known. vDZ.

Lambert Pietersz, *Nootwendighe Verclaringhe van't Verscheel . . . tusschen Jan Jacobsz van Harlinghen . . . ende tusschen Pieter Jelties van Collum* (1624, n.p.); *DB* 1889, 6; 1892, 71; 1912, 66, 68-71.

Pieter-Jeltjesvolk were the adherents of Pieter Jeltjes (*q.v.*), who, after this leader had been excommunicated in 1599, organized congregations at Kollum (*q.v.*) and a few other places in the Dutch province of Friesland. These congregations gradually died out or merged with congregations of other Mennonite branches. The Balk (*q.v.*) congregation, which belonged to this group, later usually called Old Frisians or even Old Flemish, existed until 1853-54, when most of the members emigrated to the United States. vDZ.

Pieter de Jonckheere, an Anabaptist martyr, brother of the martyrs Vijnken, Goudeken, and Janneken de Jonckheere, was burned at the stake on March 12, 1562, at Gent, Belgium. He was born at Merendree, Flanders. Further particulars are lacking, except that he was in prison before Dec. 5, 1561, and that he remained steadfast. (Verheyden, *Gent,* 27, No. 80; *idem,* "Mennonites in Flanders," Ms.) vDZ.

Pieter Jorisz, an Anabaptist martyr: see **Adriaen Jorisse.**

Pieter van Keulen: see **Peter van Coelen.**

Pieter van Leiden, a Dutch Anabaptist preacher, was arrested and imprisoned at The Hague, Holland, in December 1535. Further particulars are lacking. (*DB* 1917, 114, No. 44.) vDZ.

Pieter Leydecker, an Anabaptist martyr, was inhumanly tortured and beheaded with two brethren and a sister at Zierikzee, Dutch province of Zeeland, on Sept. 4, 1536. This is mentioned by van Braght (*Mart. Mir.* D 38, E 445), but the name given here is not quite correct. This martyr's name was probably Jan Jansz(e) (*q.v.*), also called Hansken Schalydecker; he was a native of Tongeren in Belgium. NEFF, vDZ.

Pieter (Pierre) van Maldeghem, an Anabaptist martyr, a native of Nevele, Flanders, was burned at the stake with three others on the Vrijdagsmarkt at Gent, Belgium, on July 16, 1562. Van Braght's *Martyrs' Mirror* only gives the year of execution, not the exact date. These martyrs are commemorated in the hymn "Alsmen schreef duyst vijfhondert jaer ende twee en tsestich mede," found in the 1578 and following editions of the *Lietboecxken.* vDZ.

Offer, 650; *Mart. Mir.* D 289, E 656; Verheyden, *Gent,* 28, No. 87; *ML* III, 3.

Pieter (Pierre) van Male, an Anabaptist martyr, was burned at the stake on July 16, 1562 (van Braght's *Martyrs' Mirror* gives only the year, not the exact date), with three others on the Vrijdagsmarkt of Gent, Belgium. Pieter van Male, who may have been related to the Mennonite van Male family of Flanders, later found at Haarlem, Holland, was 39 years of age and a native of Gent. He had been arrested before Jan. 7, 1562, but, as the Inquisitor Titelman (*q.v.*) complained, the trial had been postponed because the head bailiff of Gent and the bailiff of Den Oudburg disagreed concerning their competence in this case. Pieter's wife Lynken de Meyere (*q.v.*) had already suffered martyrdom on March 24, 1562. Pieter and his co-martyrs are commemorated in the hymn "Alsmen schreef duyst vijfhondert jaer ende twee en tsestich mede," found in the 1578 and following editions of the *Lietboecxken*.   vDZ.

Offer, 650; *Mart. Mir.* D 289, E 656; Verheyden, *Gent*, 28, No. 85; *ML* III, 3.

Pieter Matthijsz, an Anabaptist martyr, who was burned at the stake on Aug. 21, 1552, at Leiden, Dutch province of South Holland. Particulars are lacking. He was probably a brother of the martyrs Willem Matthijsz and Jannetgen Matthijsdochter, executed at Leiden on the same day. (*Offer*, 578, note 1.)   vDZ.

Pieter met den creupelen voet (Peter with the lame foot), an Anabaptist martyr, a cloth dresser, was burned at the stake on Aug. 27, 1555, at Antwerp, Belgium. Neither the *Offer des Heeren* nor van Braght's *Martyrs' Mirror* gives the exact date or the method of execution. His official name was Pieter van Beringen. He was put to death with Hans Borduerwercker, Jan Droochscheerder, and Frans Sweertveger. Their names are found in hymn No. 16 of the *Lietboecxken*: "Aenhoort Godt, hemelsche Vader" (Hear, O God, heavenly Father).   vDZ.

Offer, 564; *Mart. Mir.* D 161, E 550; *Antw. Arch.-Blad* VIII, 426, 429; XIV, 20 f., No. 230; Wolkan, *Lieder*, 63, 72; *ML* III, 352.

Pieter van der Meulen (Peter van der Muelen), an Anabaptist martyr, burned at the stake on Jan. 15, 1564, at Gent, Belgium. The exact date was unknown (not found in *Offer des Heeren* or in van Braght's *Martyrs' Mirror*) until Verheyden published it from the records. Pieter, 27 years old and (re)baptized in 1563, was not a native of Gent; hence his property could not be confiscated. Verheyden mentions a few other van der Meulens, probably relatives of Pieter, who were punished for "heresy." Pieter's name is found in the hymn "Alsmen schreef duyst vijfhondert jaer ende twee en tsestich mede," found in the 1578 and following editions of the *Lietboecxken*.   vDZ.

Offer, 652; *Mart. Mir.* D 301, E 666; Verheyden, *Gent*, 31, No. 104; *ML* III, 173, 352.

Pieter de Meulenaer (Peter the Miller), an Anabaptist martyr, burned at the stake (van Braght's *Martyrs' Mirror* says erroneously beheaded) at Antwerp, Belgium, on May 22, 1557. His official name was Pieter van Beke; he was a miller and a weaver, a native of Petegem, near Deinze, Flanders. His name is found in the hymn "Aenhoort Godt, hemelsche vader" (Hear, O God, heavenly Father), No. 16 of the *Lietboecxken*.   vDZ.

Offer, 564; *Mart. Mir.* D 185, E 569; *Antw. Arch.-Blad* VIII, 434, 438; XIV, 22 f., No. 245; Wolkan, *Lieder*, 63, 71; *ML* III, 180.

Pieter Meynghers: see **Pieter** (de) **Schoenmaker.**

Pieter Neert, an Anabaptist martyr, burned at the stake on Jan. 19, 1554, on the Vrijdagsmarkt at Gent, Belgium. By trade he was a weaver or cloth shearer. Further particulars are lacking. (Verheyden, *Gent*, 19, No. 39.)   vDZ.

Pieter den Ouden (Old Peter), also called Pieter (den) Oudeg(h)od(t), an Anabaptist martyr who was burned at the stake at Kortrijk (Courtrai) in Flanders on April 30, 1569, after being cruelly tortured three times (van Braght's *Martyrs' Mirror* gives only the year). He was executed with five other Anabaptists, and died with the words, "O Lord, stand by Thy servant and strengthen him in this last extremity, and do not hold this evil deed to their account, but convert them; for they know not what they do." He was a native of Kortrijk, living as a cabinetmaker at Meenen (Menin), where he was arrested. His property was confiscated. He had been (re)baptized in 1568.   NEFF, vDZ.

Mart. Mir. D 408, E 759; Verheyden, *Courtrai-Bruxelles*, 38, No. 23; *ML* III, 351.

Pieter Pieters (called Beckjen or Beck), a Dutch Anabaptist martyr, a skipper of Asperen, living at Amsterdam, was sentenced to death after cruel torture, because he had attended the "damned and forbidden meetings of the Mennonites," had furthermore permitted secret meetings of the Mennonites on his ship; although he had not yet been (re)baptized, he was probably a "principal leader"; his two oldest children had been baptized as Catholics, but the youngest was still unbaptized. He confessed that he had not attended the Catholic church for four or five years, and that he had confessed to a priest only once, about twenty years previously; he had never gone to Mass. Notwithstanding torture and much admonition by Catholic priests and by the sheriffs of Amsterdam, he refused to return to the "old faith"; remaining steadfast he was burned at the stake on Feb. 26, 1569, at Amsterdam. His property was confiscated. On the way to the site of execution Willem Jans, also an Anabaptist, called out to him, "Fight bravely, dear brother," whereupon he himself was burned at the stake two weeks later.   NEFF, vDZ.

Mart. Mir. D 385, E 738 f.; Grosheide, *Bijdrage*, 179 f.; *ML* I, 150; III, 372.

Pieter Pieters (Peter Petersz) of Leiden (called Borrekiek, Borrekierck, or Barekiek), an Anabaptist martyr, was beheaded at Amsterdam, Holland, on July 10, 1535 (not May 15 as van Braght states). He was a weaver, who had been (re)baptized in 1534 by Cornelis wt den Briel (*q.v.*). In the spring of 1535 he fled from Leiden to Amsterdam. In his confession he clearly showed that he did not agree with the revolutionary ideas of most of the Leiden Anabaptists. He had not been in the Catholic church for two or three years and emphatically rejected the Catholic doctrine of the Mass. (*Mart. Mir.* D 619, E 765; Grosheide, *Verhooren*, 150-52; *ML* III, 372.)   vDZ.

Pieter Pietersz, of Wormer, Dutch province of North Holland, burned at the stake on May 11,

1534, probably at The Hague (not, as Mellink states, at Amsterdam). Pieter had preached and baptized. He had been in the group who sailed from Amsterdam in March 1534 en route to Münster (*q.v.*), but was arrested at Bergklooster (*q.v.*). (*Inv. Arch. Amst.* I, No. 745; *DB* 1917, 115, No. 56; Mellink, *Wederdopers*, 159, 353.)   vDZ.

Pieter Pietersz (Coman Piet), of Leiden, Holland, apparently a "koopman," i.e., merchant, an Anabaptist martyr, beheaded on May 29, 1536, at The Hague. He had been (re)baptized at Leiden in November 1534. He is charged with the crimes of being rebaptized, having preached in Anabaptist meetings, and having regularly received messages from Jan van Leyden (*q.v.*), then in Münster (*q.v.*). (*Inv. Arch. Amst.* I, Nos. 143, 745; Mellink, *Wederdopers*, 193 f.)   vDZ.

Pieter Pluvier (Plovier), an Anabaptist martyr: see Pieter de Backere.

Pieter Potvliet, an Anabaptist martyr, a native of Thielt in Flanders, a weaver, was beheaded with his brother Jelis Potvliet and Jelis Strings at Wervik, Flanders, Belgium, in 1562 (exact date unknown). They had been sentenced to be burned at the stake, but because the heavy rains had made the wood too wet to burn they were beheaded. (*Mart. Mir.* D 289, E 656; *ML* III, 386.)   vDZ.

Pieter Schoenmaker, an Anabaptist martyr, burned at the stake at Rijssel (Lille) in France on March 16, 1563. Pieter, a native of Eecen, Flanders, whose official name was Pieter Meynghers, son of Josse van Ghelderc, was a shoemaker by trade. On March 7, 1563, a number of Mennonites of Halewijn (Halluin) were arrested including the preacher Jan de Swarte (*q.v.*) and his family, and also Pieter Schoenmaker and his wife Jacomijntgen. They were all conducted to Rijssel, and tried, sentenced, and executed there. Pieter and all the others remained steadfast except Jacomijntgen, who recanted. (*Mart. Mir.* D 299, E 665; *ML* III, 352.)   vDZ.

Pieter Stayaerts (Styaert, Stayert) and his cousin Jan Styaertsz (*q.v.*), two seekers after God, Anabaptist martyrs, who lived with their parents in Mereedor (Meerendree), a village of Flanders, Belgium. Through searching the Scriptures they arrived at the belief that baptism is necessary for the regenerated, and traveled to Germany to look for others of their faith. Being baptized there, but not finding satisfaction, probably because they were averse to the revolutionary views of many Anabaptists, they returned to their home, were seized there, were held prisoner in a vile pit, and then beheaded in 1538 at Vinderhout, a village near Gent, Belgium. This account by van Braght (*Mart. Mir.* D 44, E 449) is correct, as has been shown by the official documents (Verheyden, *Gent,* 4, Nos. 9-10). Van Braght, however, lists another martyr by the same name, Pieter Stayert, who with some others was executed at Gent in 1569 (*Mart. Mir.* D 407, E 759). This Pieter Stayert is commemorated in the hymn "Alsmen schreef duyst vijfhondert jaer

ende twee en tsestich mede," found in the *Lietboecxken*. (*Offer,* 653.) Verheyden (*Gent,* 56) did not find this latter martyr in the records of Gent.
                    NEFF, vDZ.

Pieter Thymans (Peter Thijmanszoon), an Anabaptist martyr of Zutphen, burned at the stake in Amsterdam, Holland, on Aug. 6, 1552. By trade he was a cooper and later a bookbinder; he was baptized by Gillis van Aken (*q.v.*). Pieter was in a group of twenty Anabaptists who were arrested at Amsterdam in May 1552. Only two of them were citizens of Amsterdam; all the others had come to Amsterdam from elsewhere. Pieter had come only eight days before he was arrested. Five were burned at the same time as Pieter, five more on Jan. 6, 1553, and the other nine, who had not been rebaptized and who recanted, were only fined and banished. (*Mart. Mir.* D 142, E 535; Grosheide, *Bijdrage,* 160-62.)   NEFF, vDZ.

Pieter Trijnes of Wormer, Dutch province of North Holland, an Anabaptist martyr, was put to death with Dirk Pieters Krood (*q.v.*), Claes Roders, and Pieter Claes Jans. The date of the execution is unknown. It probably took place at Enkhuizen, Dutch province of North Holland. (*Mart. Mir.* D 61, E 464; *Bibliographie* II, 781, No. 791.)   NEFF.

Pieter Verlonge(n), an Anabaptist martyr, was burned at the stake with Gerrit Vermandele and Willem de Clercq at Antwerp, Belgium, on March 30, 1569. A number of particulars, including the exact date of the execution, not given in van Braght's *Martyrs' Mirror,* have been published by Génard in the *Antwerpsch Archieven-Blad:* Pieter was a native of Kortrijk (Courtrai) in Flanders; he lived at Borgerhout near Antwerp; by trade he was a weaver. About one and a half years before his arrest he was married; his wife also belonged to the church; the marriage had been performed in the presence of the congregation by a certain Herman (probably Elder Herman Timmerman, *q.v.*) in a house at Borgerhout. Pieter rejected infant baptism because this practice is not found in the Scriptures. He was twice tortured very cruelly, but remained steadfast.   vDZ.

Mart. Mir. D 415, E 766; *Antw. Arch.-Blad* XII, 346, 369, 399, 440; XIV, 64 f., No. 715.

Pieter Vettewarier, an Anabaptist martyr, burned at the stake on the market place at Antwerp, Belgium, on Dec. 16, 1558. His name is commemorated in the hymn "Aenhoort Godt, hemelsche Vader" (Hear, O God, heavenly Father), No. 16 of the *Lietboecxken.* Some particulars about this martyr have been published by Génard in the *Antwerpsch Archieven-Blad:* his official name was Pieter Henricx; he had a grocery store with the name "In de Vettewary," hence his name. Génard also lists Pieter van Hese, "vettewarier int Lelyken," who had been arrested on June 11, 1535, and sentenced on Dec. 24, 1535, to a pilgrimage to Nicosie, because he had associated with the Anabaptists and other "Lutherans," i.e., heretics. This man may have been identical with Pieter Vettewarier.   vDZ.

Offer, 566; *Mart. Mir.* D 202, E 583; *Antw. Arch.-Blad* VIII, 454, 465; XIV, 14 f., No. 142; 24 f., No. 270; *ML* III, 352.

Pieter Willemsz was a follower and friend of the Dutch elder Jan Jacobsz (*q.v.*). He lived at Hoorn; Jan Jacobsz, after his banishment from Friesland on April 13, 1600, found shelter in his home. He accompanied Jan Jacobsz on his tours of baptism and after the death of Jacobsz he published his songs under the title *Eenighe Gheestelijcke Liede-kens, gemackt aen verscheyden persoonen door Jan Jacobs zoon van Harlinghen* (Amsterdam, 1612). He also published a songbook entitled *Eenighe Nieuwe Gheestelijcke Liedekens gemaeckt door ver-scheyden persoonen* . . . (Amsterdam, 1612), containing 36 songs, most of which were composed by Pieter Willemsz himself. (Obviously the year 1612 on the title page is an error, because at the end of the book the note is found: "Gedruct bij Nicolaes Biestkens in de Lelye onder de Doornen, Anno 1613" and the last song is dated Dec. 21, 1612.) Pieter Willemsz, who later probably became an elder of the Jan-Jacobsz group, also visited "our friends in Prussia." It is, however, not known which Prussian congregations belonged to the Jan-Jacobsz group. Years of birth (*c*1560) and death and other particulars about Pieter Willemsz were not available.   vDZ.

J. Loosjes, "Jan Jacobsz en de Jan-Jacobsgezinden," in *Nederl. Archief voor Kerkgeschiedenis* XI (The Hague, 1914) issue III, 196 f., 201, 204-6, 239.

Pieters: see also **Pietersz.**

Pieters, a Mennonite family found since the early 17th century at Aardenburg (*q.v.*) in Dutch Zealand Flanders. The members of this family were usually in business, and in the course of three centuries many of them have served the congregation of Aardenburg as deacons.   vDZ.

Pieters, Cornelis: see **Cornelis wt den Briel.**

Pieters, Derk (d. 1566 or 1567), a Dutch Mennonite who lived at the Melkema farm near Huizinge, province of Groningen, was the ancestor of the well-known and large Mennonite Huizinga (*q.v.*) family. He was married to Katrine Tomas.   vDZ.

J. Huizinga, *Stamboek . . . van Derk Pieters en Katrine Tomas* (Groningen, 1883); *Groningsche volks-almanak* 1921, 98, 102, 105.

Pieters, Dirk. About 1600 there were in Holland two Mennonite preachers bearing this name. One Dirk Pieters lived at Hoorn, originally a member of the Frisian branch and an elder of the congregation, later apparently joining the Waterlanders. In 1610 he opposed the union of some English Brownists (see **Smyth**) with the Waterlanders at Amsterdam. He died in 1612.

The other Dirk Pieters, also called Derk Pieters van Nierop, was in 1580 a preacher of the Frisian Mennonite congregation at Nieuwe Niedorp. He is said to have been of a peaceful disposition, trying to eliminate the schisms which had arisen among the Dutch Mennonites. He too joined the Waterlanders and became a preacher at Amsterdam, where he died about 1604. (*Inv. Arch. Amst.* I,

Nos. 480, 531; II, Nos. 834, 1361; *DB* 1876, 37.)   vDZ.

Pieters, Ebbe, a Dutch elder: see **Ebbe Pieters.**

Pieters, Menno, author of *Reys-boecxken, ofte gemeen onderwys in de Christelycke ofte Apostolische Leere* (Gouda, 1616). No information is available concerning him.   vDZ.

M. Schagen, *Naamlijst der Doopsgezinde Schrijveren* (Amsterdam, 1745) 80.

Pieters, Ocke (d. in 1685 at Hamburg, Germany), was ordained as a preacher of the Hamburg-Altona Mennonite congregation in 1671; in 1676 he was ordained as an elder by the elders Jan Sibes Pottebacker of Harlingen and Remmert Jacobs. Pieters preached the first sermon in the new meetinghouse at Altona on March 14, 1675. In 1678 Ocke Pieters, Gerrit Roosen, and Hans Hermans met with Galenus Abrahamsz (*q.v.*), then visiting Hamburg, to investigate his orthodoxy.   vDZ.

C. B. Roosen, *Geschichte der Mennoniten-Gemeinde Hamburg und Altona* I (Hamburg, 1886) 48, 51, 57, 61.

Pieters, Tamme (*c*1650-90), a son of Pieter Michiels of Westeremden, Dutch province of Groningen, was in 1683-90 a preacher of the Groningen Old Flemish Mennonite congregation of Huizinge (*q.v.*). He was a member of the well-known Huizinga (*q.v.*) family. About his marriage to Geertruid Derks in 1678 there is the following information: "Married at Huizinge in the house of Gerit Bennen and performed by Oom Willem Janssen." His son Derk Tammes (1679-1728) was a preacher of the same congregation.   vDZ.

J. Huizinga, *Stamboek . . . van Derk Pieters en Katrina Tomas* (Groningen, 1883) 2; *DB* 1879, 4.

Pietersbierum, a village in the Dutch province of Friesland, where Jacob Teunis, elder of the Jan-jacobsgezinden branch of the Mennonites, baptized a number of persons in 1603-18. Of a congregation at Pietersbierum, however, there is no information. (Blaupot t. C., *Friesland,* 164.)

Pietersz: see also **Peters.**

Pietersz, Jacob: see **Meulen, Jacob Pietersz van der.**

Pietersz, Jacob (also called Jacob Pietersz van de Kooch, Cooch, Coogh) (1599-1671), of Koog aan de Zaan, Dutch province of North Holland, was a preacher of the Flemish Mennonite congregation of Koog and Zaandam-West. He served here from before 1645 until his death. Jacob Pietersz was a peaceable man, as is shown from a letter dated Jan. 30, 1661, in which he urged moderation and peace. On June 9, 1664, he tried to intervene in the quarrels which had arisen in the Flemish congregation at Amsterdam (see **Lammerenkrijgh**), but in vain. He then published *Vrede-basuyn tot verminderingh van de verschillen, voorgevallen onder de Doops-gesinde tot Amsterdam* (Amsterdam, 1664), in which he criticized the quarrels and showed his sympathy with Galenus Abrahamsz (*q.v.*) and the Lamists (*q.v.*). This book was opposed by P(ieter) A(postool) in his *Antwoort op de soo genaemde*

Vredebasuyn (Amsterdam, 1665). Jacob Pietersz had previously published *Veilighe Wech* (Amsterdam, 1631), in which he warned against the practice of strict banning. He also published *Korte Onderwysinge voor de jonge Aenkomelingen . . .* , a catechism (first edition lost; 2nd edition Wormerveer, 1650; 3rd edition, called 2nd on title page, Amsterdam, 1674); *Inleydinge om te koomen tot een recht gebruyck van de tijdelicke Goederen* (Wormerveer, 1649) and *Handelingh of Onderrichtinge om te koomen tot de ware Ruste des Gemoeds . . .* (Amsterdam, 1652), a devotional booklet followed by an appendix which discusses the way in which Mennonite ministers are to be appointed and their authority. He is probably identical with the Jacob Pietersz who was a member of the Frisian Mennonite congregation at Zaandam, but who joined the Flemish congregation with some followers about 1632. vDZ.

Inv. Arch. Amst. I, No. 2032; Biogr. Wb., V, 169; H. W. Meihuizen, Galenus Abrahamsz (Haarlem, 1954) 97; S. Lootsma, Het Nieuwe Huys (Zaandam, 1937) 94.

Pietersz, Jelmer, a deacon or a preacher of the Flemish Mennonite congregation of Harlingen, Dutch province of Friesland, who ardently promoted the reunification of the Dutch brotherhood, divided by schisms. In 1610 his congregation united with the Frisian congregation at Harlingen, which step was greatly censured by most Flemish Mennonites, especially those in the province of Groningen. In 1608 Jelmer Pietersz, in the name of the Harlingen Flemish congregation, had written *Deemoedige Remonstrantie* to plead for the union of Flemish and Frisian Mennonites. (*Inv. Arch. Amst.* I, Nos. 523, 539, 557.) vDZ.

Pietersz, Lambert, author of *Nootwendighe Verclaringhe van 't Verscheel ende Questie, geresen tusschen Jan Jacobsz van Harlinghen met zijne Medehulpers en tusschen P. Jelties van Collum met syne Medestanders* (n.p., 1621). This booklet gives some information about the schism among the Old Frisian Mennonites (see also **Jan Jacobsz,** and **Pieter Jeltjes**). The author was an opponent of Jan Jacobsz and a follower of Pieter Jeltjes. He was a "bishop" of the Old Frisian Mennonite congregation at Bolsward, Dutch province of Friesland, a malt maker by trade, and no doubt the author of some other books, one of which was an attack on the Catholic doctrine of the Apostolic Succession, entitled *Proeve op die Pauselijcke Afkomste ende succesie* (2 vol., Hoorn, 1633). vDZ.

Pietersz, Pieter (German, *Peter Peters*), called "de Oude" (Senior), was born at Alkmaar on Jan. 28, 1574, d. Oct. 14, 1651, at Oost-Zaandam, was a Dutch Mennonite preacher, serving in the Waterlander congregation of De Rijp about 1600-25, and then until his death in the Waterlander or "Komenjannen" congregation at Zaandam. He was a friend of the Waterlander leader and elder Hans de Ries (*q.v.*), and sided with him in the dispute with Nittert Obbes (*q.v.*) and Jan Theunis (*q.v.*). Pietersz is said to have been a gentle, peace-loving, pious man, averse to doctrinal strife: for more than fifty years he worked with unusual effectiveness in the

office of preaching. He was a carpenter or rather a maker of windmills and had no special theological training. On May 25, 1627, after he had preached his sermon at Marken-binnen (*q.v.*), he was compelled to dispute with the Reformed minister Abdias Widmarius (*q.v.*), who accused him of Socinianism (*q.v.*). During his ministry at De Rijp, Pieters had some disagreement with his co-preacher Jan Willems (*q.v.*), caused by views on dogma as well as by personal differences.

Pietersz wrote a number of devotional books, tracts, and sermons. His best-known book is *Wegh na Vreden-stadt: waer in ghewesen wordt hoemen die Vrede mach bekomen* (Way to the City of Peace, in Which is Shown How to Obtain Peace), followed by a prayer and some hymns. This book, written about 1625, went through eight Dutch editions, most of which were undated (nearly all editions now lost). It is a remarkable book, depicting in dialogue form the itinerary to the "heavenly Jerusalem," where is found "the unity of spirit under the palms of peace." "No doubt *Wegh na Vreden-stadt* is a book of fine Christian spirit and moralism. Yet its spirit is far different from all that is known in earlier Mennonite literature, and the book certainly deserves the honor of being one of the very first pietistic writings in Dutch Mennonitism" (Friedmann). Both in method and spirit John Bunyan's *Pilgrim's Progress* (1678) may have been inspired by *Wegh na Vreden-stadt*.

Besides this book Pietersz published *Twee Eenvoudighe stichtelijcke Predicatien . . .* (Amsterdam and De Rijp, 1624); *Toetz-steen om te proeven elck mensche de wegh sijns levens* (De Rijp, 1629); *Spiegel der Gierigheydt* (Hoorn, 1638; 9th ed., 1698); *Hemelsche Bruyloft* (De Rijp, 1641; Amsterdam, 1642 and 1662); *Spieghel der Bermherticheyt* (De Rijp, 1645), followed by *Proeve des Waren Christelycken Geloofs* and *Een Christelijcke Sendtbrief aen alle Doopsgezinden; Predicaties over de Liefde* (De Rijp, 1642), a sermon on the Foolish Virgins and some other sermons. A sermon on the Song of Solomon 2:1-6, "Stichtelycke Predicatie van de Bloem te Saron," is found in *Kort-Verhael van het leven en de Daden van Hans de Ries* (De Rijp, 1644). Finally Pieter Pietersz' *Opera* (Complete Works) were published in Harlingen, 1651 (reprinted Amsterdam, 1666, n.d., but between 1675 and 1686, 1698, 1715, and 1740).

Pietersz' works not only were eagerly read both by Mennonites and non-Mennonites in the Netherlands, but they also have been very popular among the Mennonites of the Palatinate, Prussia, South Russia, and also in America, where they were imported by the Russian Mennonites, especially the Kleine Gemeinde (*q.v.*) in 1874. For this purpose they were translated into German in the early 18th century and maybe even before, but all these old editions are apparently lost. The following editions in German are known: *Weg nach Friedenstadt* (1790); *Spiegel der Gierigkeit* (1827); *Spiegel der Barmherzigkeit* (1865); *Ein Christlicher Sendbrief* (1865); *Ausgewählte Schriften von Peter Peters . . . für die Liebhaber der Wahrheit aufs Neue aufgelegt* (Stuttgart, 1865; reprinted Elkhart, 1901);

the American edition also contains a translation from the Dutch of the *Toetz-steen* under the title *Prüfstein der Menschheit, um für jedermann zu prüfen den Weg seines Lebens, ob er recht gehe nach der Stadt des Friedens, oder hingehe nach Unfrieden und Jammer.* Pietersz' tract, *Himmlische Hochzeit,* translated by the translator of *Prüfstein,* appeared in America in 1906.   NEFF, vDZ.

Schijn-Maatschoen, *Geschiedenis* II (Amsterdam, 1744) 588-96, with a picture of Pieter Pietersz; M. Schagen, *Naamlijst der Doopsgezinde Schrijveren* (Amsterdam, 1745) 80 f.; *DB* 1863, 122; 1864, 15; 1896, 18-26; 1900, 90; 1907, 49 f.; 1917, 30-32; Kühler, *Geschiedenis* II, 171-74, 176, 202; *Amstelodamum* Yearbook XXV (1928) 96, 97, 98, 119, No. 51; *Gem.-Kal.* 1930; *MQR* XIV (1941) 188; R. Friedmann, *Mennonite Piety Through the Centuries* (Goshen, 1949) 106-11; *ML* III, 354.

Pietersz, Pieter, d. Aug. 27, 1680, at Koog aan de Zaan, Dutch province of North Holland, was a preacher of the Koog-Zaandijk Waterlander congregation. He was an ardent Collegiant (*q.v.*) and an advocate of free speaking in Mennonite worship services. J. D. Middelhoven delivered his funeral sermon, *Lykrede, ofte Aenmerking des Doods . . .* (Amsterdam, 1680).   vDZ.

J. C. van Slee, *De Rijnsburger Collegianten* (Haarlem, 1895) 201.

Pieters(z), Syvaert (Sywert), a preacher of the Old Frisian Mennonites at Hoorn, Holland, in temperament and thought like P. J. Twisck (*q.v.*), wrote in collaboration with Twisck the foreword to the Hoorn book of martyrs (1617), which caused great offense by its violent attack upon the Waterlanders (*q.v.*). This foreword contains a confession of faith compiled from the works of Menno Simons. The confession, entitled *Bekentenisse des Gheloofs nae Godes Woort: also de selvighe van vele jaren herwaert ende noch tegenwoordich, by diemen Mennisten noemt: Ghelooft, Gheleert ende Beleeft wordt, . . .* was reprinted twice as a separate edition at Hoorn in 1620 and without date but before 1626.

Pieters is also the author of *Corte aenwijsinghe, voorgestelt in eenighe Vraghen vande voornaemste mishandelinghen der Vlaminghen ende Vriesen, in den twist van den Jare 1566, ende volgens teghen malcanderen bedreven, . . .* (Hoorn, 1634). This book deals with the Frisian-Flemish quarrel and schism. The book, taking the view of the Frisians in a very prejudiced manner, gives some valuable information concerning the schism. Neff's assertion (*ML* III, 372) that Pieters wrote the introduction to the documents of unification between four congregations in Friesland, is a mistake. This unification came into being about 1560, before Pieters was born.   vDZ.

BRN VII, 156, 162 note; IX, 539, 543; *DB* 1864, 56; 1870, 69, 72; 1889, 76 f.; 1893, 1, 4; 1912, 63 f.; Kühler, *Geschiedenis* II, 110; *ML* III, 372.

Pietersz, Wybe: see **Zeeman, Wybe Pietersz.**

Pieterzijl, a hamlet in the Dutch province of Groningen close to the border of Friesland, the seat of a Mennonite congregation until 1892. Of the history of this congregation, always small in membership, not much is known. It may have been founded about the middle of the 16th century. A meeting-house was built in 1664; this made the district governor take action. On the basis of the law of 1651 forbidding the building of Mennonite meeting-houses where they had not existed before, he ordered this meetinghouse to be closed or even pulled down. The Mennonites appealed to the provincial government; the district governor was supported by the Calvinist clergy. It is not clear how the matter ended. In the 17th century the congregation belonged to the Flemish branch; until about 1750 it was generally called the congregation of De Waarden and Pieterzijl. Among the members the de Waard (*q.v.*) family were numerous; many of them were deacons and Jacob Symons and his son Jan Jacobs de Waard, both farmers, were preachers in 1726-*c*60 and 1753-*c*90 respectively. In 1815 a meetinghouse was built in Pieterzijl; it is not known where the congregation met before 1815. In 1827 its baptized membership numbered 21, in 1849 65, in 1860 82. Until 1790 it was served by untrained and unsalaried preachers. Gerben Cornelis van Grouw (d. 1825), serving here in 1792-1814, was its first salaried preacher, and Jan Frederik Boersema, serving 1814-26, its first minister trained at the Amsterdam Mennonite Seminary. In 1891 a new parsonage and in 1892 a new meetinghouse were built, both at Grijpskerk. After that time the congregation was called Grijpskerk and Pieterzijl, now only Grijpskerk. For its history since 1892 see **Grijpskerk.**   vDZ.

S. K. de Waard, *Aanteekeningen uit de Doopsgezinde Geschiedenis van 't Westerkwartier* (Groningen, 1901); G. A. Wumkes, *De Gereformeerde kerk in de Ommelanden . . .* (Groningen, 1904) 39; *DJ* 1850, 60; *DB* 1893, 35.

Pietism is a form of piety originating after the Reformation and during the period of Orthodoxy within the Reformed and Lutheran churches of continental Europe, chiefly in Germany, parallels to which are to be found in Methodism, revivalism, and Fundamentalism in England and America. No other single religious movement has had such an impact on the Mennonites in all countries with the exception of the Netherlands as Pietism. This observation has led some to believe that there is a close historical kinship between Anabaptism and Pietism (Max Goebel, Albrecht Ritschl).

Background and Basic Principles. Pietism as a movement came into being at the end of the 17th century in the midst of Reformed and Lutheran Orthodoxy in which adherence to the doctrinal and confessional heritage was strongly emphasized. In opposition or as a supplement Pietism emphasized a "heartfelt" religion accompanied by a self-analysis based on a personal emotionally experienced conversion resulting in the application of this experience in daily life in doing good works and in certain forms of nonconformity, abstaining from such entertainments as the dance, card playing, the theater, worldly literature, and at times alcoholic beverages. Pietism also emphasized the second coming of Christ. Its adherents met frequently for private devotional exercises.

Major representatives of Pietism in the Reformed Church were Gisbert Voetius (Utrecht) and Gerhard Tersteegen (Mühlheim). The father of Pietism within the Lutheran Church was Philipp Jakob Spener (1635-1705), who was active as a minister in Frankfurt, Dresden, and Berlin and started the movement through his *Pia desideria* (*Pious Wishes*) in 1675, in which he emphasized more diligent use of the Bible, the spiritual priesthood of laymen, a reform of preaching and the study of theology. Through group Bible studies, prayer meetings, and special meetings for children he introduced institutions which later were accepted by Protestant churches generally. August Hermann Francke (1663-1727) emphasized home mission work and the spread of the Bible. Nikolaus Ludwig, Count von Zinzendorf (1700-60), gave Pietism a more emotional emphasis. He became the great leader of the Moravian Church and promoted foreign missions by sending missionaries out to the West Indies, Greenland, and America. He had received the remnant of the Moravian Brethren on his estate in Silesia, where they founded the village of Herrnhut. His successor was August Gottlieb Spangenberg (1704-92). Particular brands of Pietism originated in Württemberg, promoted by men like Johann Albrecht Bengel, who introduced special private Bible studies known as "Stunden" (see **Stundism**).

Various waves of Pietism have influenced European Christendom. In France, Switzerland, and the Netherlands, "Reveil" (*q.v.*) became another form which influenced the Mennonites particularly in Holland. Later the Baptist (*q.v.*) movement spread from England to Germany and other countries influencing the Mennonites of Russia, Prussia, and Poland. The Gemeinschaftsbewegung (*q.v.*) of the 19th century was another form of much the same movement, which influenced the Mennonites of the Palatinate. Pietism also affected Anglican Christianity through the Moravians. John Wesley was influenced by Moravian missionaries in his work in England. The Moravians established outposts in Holland, England, and Pennsylvania. The various awakenings and revivals of North America were closely related to continental Pietism. The assertion that the Great Awakening during the first half of the 18th century, primarily promoted by Jonathan Edwards and George Whitefield, had its beginnings among the Mennonites has not been clearly established. The revival movements of the 19th century centering around Charles G. Finney, Dwight L. Moody, J. Wilbur Chapman, Billy Sunday, and Billy Graham have very much the same emphasis as Pietism, although each has peculiarities and methods of its own, and although the mass type of evangelism was seldom practiced in Europe.

Netherlands and North Germany. Along the Lower Rhine in Northwest Germany, the Mennonites had early contacts with leading pietists. The devotional writings of Pieter Pietersz (*q.v.*), Jan Philipsz Schabalje (*q.v.*), and others also reveal pietistic tendencies prior to the actual introduction of Pietism. Johannes Deknatel (*q.v.*) of Amsterdam was strongly influenced by the Moravians. John Wesley was a guest in his home. Deknatel influenced the South German Mennonites toward Pietism (see **Weber, Peter**). Before Deknatel the Collegiant movement (*q.v.*) had definite pietistic traits

13

and influenced the Dutch Mennonites very strongly. Galenus (*q.v.*) Abrahamsz, the leader of the Lamists (*q.v.*), was its main representative. The Reveil (*q.v.*) movement of the Netherlands, led by Willem Bilderdijk (1756-1831), influenced the Mennonites. Among the Mennonite leaders in it were Willem de Clercq (*q.v.*), Jan ter Borg (*q.v.*), and Jan de Liefde (*q.v.*), who promoted a "return to the Bible." The Gemeentedagbeweging (*q.v.*) after World War I had also some pietistic leanings.

The Mennonites of Crefeld (*q.v.*) were under the influence of Pietism. Gerhard Tersteegen (*q.v.*) had friends among the Mennonites and preached in their church. The Crefeld Mennonites were also influenced by the Quakers and the Dunkards. Ernst Christoph Hochmann (*q.v.*) von Hohenau associated with them. The Mennonites of Hamburg-Altona were strongly influenced by Pietism. The van der Smissen family, originally very successful in business, directed its interest to a large extent to the cause of Pietism. The strongest representative was Jacob Gysbert van der Smissen (*q.v.*), who was in touch with the pietistic leaders of his day and supported their cause. Jacob Denner (*q.v.*) followed pietistic leanings to the degree that he broke away from the Mennonite church and established a Dompelaar church.

Germany. The Mennonites of Prussia were early in contact with representatives of Moravian Pietism. It was particularly the case with the Mennonites along the Vistula River and the congregation of Brenkenhoffswalde (*q.v.*) near Driesen. Joh. N. Lederer-Lentz and J. H. G. Jahr were ministers of the Moravian Church who visited the Mennonites of Brenkenhoffswalde and the Vistula River between Graudenz and Marienburg in the early 19th century prior to their migration to Russia and helped them when the revival broke out. Mrs. von Krüdener also visited these churches emphasizing sanctification of life. Moravian literature was read by the Mennonites of West Prussia and Poland. The writings of Johann Arndt, Krummacher, and Hofacker were much used by most of the Mennonites.

Among the Mennonites in South Germany the Pietism of Württemberg was influential. The movement of J. M. Hahn (*q.v.*) influenced three small groups to break away and form the Hahnische (*q.v.*) Mennoniten. A similar pietistic influence was found among the Mennonites of Switzerland and Alsace-Lorraine. As soon as the Mennonites of these areas began to attend schools in preparation for the ministry or simply to strengthen their religious convictions they attended pietistic institutions. The Missionary Institute of Basel founded by Christian G. Blumhardt (1840), the Bible school at Beuggen in southern Baden, the Bible school at Muristalden near Bern, the Evangelical Ministerial Training School of Basel founded in 1876, and the St. Chrischona school near Basel founded in 1835 were attended by Mennonites of Germany, Russia, Switzerland, and France. In Switzerland the Mennonites have been closely associated with the Free Evangelical churches, which were of pietistic background.

Russia. The Mennonites of Russia, particularly

those who had been in touch with the Moravians in Prussia, underwent pietistic influences during the first half of the 19th century. Additional influences came through Württemberg Pietism and its chief promoter Eduard Wüst (*q.v.*), who was the minister of a neighboring Evangelical separatist church near the Molotschna settlement. Some of the Mennonite leaders, such as August Lenzmann (*q.v.*) and Cornelius Jansen (*q.v.*), became his close friends and introduced him to the Mennonite churches and settlements. Nicholai Schmidt (*q.v.*), who traveled in South Germany, became acquainted with the teachings of Christoph Hoffman (*q.v.*), a separatist of Württemberg. The forces at work among the Mennonites of Russia through these influences aimed to raise the educational, cultural, and spiritual levels and to free the Mennonite brotherhood from a "dead orthodoxy" in favor of a pietistic experience of salvation, which led to the founding of a number of new groups within the Mennonite brotherhood and the revitalization of the total brotherhood. In addition to the influence of Pietism of Moravian and Württemberg background, the German Baptist influences must be mentioned. The Mennonite Brethren (*q.v.*), with their emphasis on abstinence and the emotional side of Christian experience, were most influenced by Pietism. However, the Mennonites of Russia in general were strongly influenced by this movement. The young men who obtained a training for the ministry and teaching profession attended not only the schools of Switzerland already named, but also the Johanneum of Barmen, established in 1886, the Missionsanstalt of Neukirchen near Mörs, Lower Rhine, established in 1882, and the Bible School of Berlin, established in 1905 and later transferred to Wiedenest. These schools, although differing widely in educational standards, were all originally inspired by Pietism and had also a definite influence on the Mennonites of Russia and consequently on those in America. The mission society Licht im Osten, organized in Wernigerode am Harz in 1918 under the leadership of Jakob Kroeker (*q.v.*), was intended to serve evangelical Christendom in Russia. The Blankenburg Alliance Conference of Germany, at which Jakob Kroeker was a frequent speaker, was quite regularly attended by Mennonites from Russia and Germany. The Plymouth Brethren, founded in 1824 in England by J. N. Darby, influenced the Mennonites through traveling evangelists and Bible teachers, such as Baedeker, and in current times Erich Sauer.

America. From the earliest Mennonite settlements at Germantown to the present time, characteristics and influences of Pietism can easily be traced among the immigrants coming from Europe. Pietism of European background prevailed for a long period, not only in groups like the Mennonite Brethren and Evangelical Mennonite Brethren, but also in the older churches. The American revival movements also influenced the Mennonites. John Oberholtzer (*q.v.*), in organizing a conference of like-minded congregations and ministers and introducing Sunday schools, publications, and mission activities, revealed pietistic influence at work among the Mennonites of his day. Carl Justus van der Smis-

sen (*q.v.*), called from Germany to teach at Wadsworth, successfully promoted pietistic views in this country. Most of the Mennonites who came from West Prussia, Poland, and Russia and settled in the prairie states and provinces had been touched by European pietistic trends, except those who settled in Manitoba as the Bergthal and Old Colony groups. A freer and more spontaneous informal church service with greater emphasis on a personally experienced salvation, the use of musical instruments, Gospel songs, the introduction of Sunday schools, prayer meetings, Bible studies, the emphasis on conversion and serious holy living are all characteristics of Pietism which leavened the old Mennonite heritage. Some of these influences have revitalized church practices and traditions which at times were fossilized, and given new meaning and significance to Mennonite traditions. Even such a conservative group as the Amish is being somewhat influenced by this form of piety, although usually those coming under this influence break away from the Old Order Amish.

As soon as the Mennonites of America adopted the English language and the American way of life they were also challenged by American revivalism (*q.v.*) and more recently Fundamentalism (*q.v.*). Some of the forms of Christian outreach and the expression of Christian life found in some Mennonite groups today are the result of American revivalism and Fundamentalism rather than European Pietism. One of the major differences between the old form of Pietism and contemporary Fundamentalism is that the former was born in opposition or as a supplement to orthodoxy, while the latter is combating Modernism and Liberalism in American theology. In some of their promotional and sensational methods revivalism and Fundamentalism are typical American accents, the extremes of which are not readily accepted by Mennonite churches.

Evaluation. Has Pietism had a positive influence on the Mennonites since it penetrated the congregations? How do the basic beliefs of Anabaptism differ from those of Pietism? What would have happened to the Mennonites if they had completely rejected Pietism? In general, it is apparent that pietistic influences have been beneficial in Mennonite history, in many areas revitalizing the rather dead and traditional Mennonite orthodoxy. The emphasis on a personally experienced salvation, on the Christian outreach at home and abroad, and the use of newer forms of spreading the Gospel is particularly due to the revitalization which came through Pietism. That some of the standards and basic Anabaptist ideals and emphases, which had already been obscured by the dead weight of tradition, were altered is true. The Anabaptist emphasis on the church of believers within which each member is challenged to discipleship differs from what is commonly found in an emotionally experienced conversion of the pietistic fundamentalist practice. Particularly dispensationalism brought into the Mennonite fold by millennialism in the 20th century is foreign to Anabaptism. Also it weakens the witness pertaining to peace and nonresistance. Pietism and Fundamentalism have some decided weaknesses and can serve only as a supplement. The core of any

Christian church is found in the Gospel and the confessions of faith. The latter are usually minimized since Pietism considers the personally experienced conversion as the cornerstone of Christendom. The classic Christian tradition considers this aspect an overemphasis of the subjective element of Christianity and a minimizing of the objective act of God in Christ Jesus expressed in the creeds of Christendom. It is likely that a continuous exposure to a theological liberalism could have influenced the Mennonite churches negatively and weakened their witness.

The exact relation of Anabaptism and Pietism has not yet been fully studied, both as to possible influence of Anabaptism on the origins of Pietism, and their theological relationship. Ritschl's (q.v.) theory that Anabaptism was a direct forerunner of Pietism has not found support among careful scholars. Robert Friedmann, who has delivered the only thorough theological comparison of the two movements (Mennonite Piety), concludes that they are substantially different, and that when Pietism came into the Mennonite fold it at the very least blunted the essential thrust of Anabaptism as discipleship in conflict with the world, and at the most, substantially changed and redirected Anabaptist-Mennonite theology and piety from a sturdy movement to conquer the world by bringing men under the lordship of Christ into a subjective emotionalized search for inner peace and godliness which lost its readiness to defy the world for the sake of its understanding of the Gospel and the Christian ethic. Pietistic Mennonitism, he claims, was much more ready to accommodate itself to the prevailing culture and abandon such characteristic Anabaptist teachings as nonresistance and nonconformity.

C.K.

General: "Pietismus," RGG IV; H. Bornkamm, Mystik, Spiritualismus, und die Anfänge des Pietismus (Giessen, 1926); A. Ritschl, Geschichte des Pietismus, 3 vv. (Bonn, 1880-86); W. Hadorn, Geschichte des Pietismus in den Schweizerischen Reformierten Kirchen (Constance, 1901); Werner Mahrholz, Der deutsche Pietismus (Berlin, 1921); George Eisenach, Pietism and the Russian Germans in the United States (Berne, 1948); W. Goeters, Die Vorbereitung des Pietismus in der Reformierten Kirche der Niederlande (Leipzig, 1909); Max Goebel, Geschichte des christlichen Lebens in der rheinisch-westfälischen evangelischen Kirche, 3 vv. (Koblenz, 1849-60); Paul Fleisch, Die moderne Gemeinschaftsbewegung (Leipzig, 1912?); W. W. Sweet, Revivalism in America. Its Origin, Growth and Decline (New York, 1945).
Mennonite: Dirk Cattepoel, "Das religiöse Leben in der Krefelder Mennonitengemeinde des 17. und 18. Jahrhunderts," Beiträge zur Geschichte rheinischer Mennoniten (1939) 5-28; Ernst Crous, "Mennonitentum und Pietismus," Theologische Zeitschrift (Basel, July/August 1952) 279-96; idem, "Vom Pietismus bei den altpreussischen Mennoniten im Rahmen ihrer Gesamtgeschichte 1772-1945," Gesch.-Bl. XI (1954) 7-29; Robert Friedmann, Mennonite Piety Through the Centuries (Goshen, 1949); Emil Händiges, "Der Pietismus," Der Bote XXVI (1949) No. 50; 51; XXVII (1950) No. 1-7, 9-12; 14; 15; 19; 21; 22; 24; 26-28; Friedrich Nieper, Die ersten deutschen Auswanderer von Krefeld nach Pennsylvanien (Neukirchen, 1940); Chr. Neff, "Peter Weber, ein mennonitischer Pietist aus dem 18. Jahrhundert," Gem.-Kal. 1930, 61-102; J. J. Wolleb, Gespräch zwischen einem Pietisten und einem Wiedertäufer, in welchem einige Vorurteile und Lehrpunkten der Wiedertäufer untersuchet und worinnen wahre Pietisten von ihnen zu unterscheiden sind (Basel, 1722, copies in GCL and AML); W. Leendertz, "Johannes Deknatel, een pietist onder de Doopsgezinden." Geloof en Vrijheid (1887); Nachrichten aus der Brüdergemeinde (1830) 243, 308; 1839, pp. 78, 118; Alexander Glitsch, Geschichte der Brüdergemeinde Sarepta (1865) 276; Friesen, Brüderschaft, 83, 118; Ernst Crous, "Anabaptism, Pietism and Rationalism," in Recovery of the Anabaptist Vision (Scottdale, 1957); ML III, 372-74.

Pigeon (Mich.) Mennonite Church (MC) was organized in 1894 by Bishop Daniel Wismer of Berlin, Ont. Samuel S. Bowman was sent by the Ontario Conference in 1897 as the first minister of the congregation. The first meetinghouse was built in 1897 in Berne, one mile north of Pigeon. Berne was then the largest settlement. In 1897 Peter Ropp was ordained minister. Other ministers who were ordained and served here were Alfred Weidman 1917-24, S. J. Miller 1926-43, and Sherman Maust 1934-44. In 1916 the Berne congregation was transferred from the Ontario Conference to the Indiana-Michigan Conference and Menno Esch, of Fairview, Mich., was appointed bishop. The present meetinghouse was built in 1934 on a new site in Pigeon. In 1957 the membership was 101, with Donald King as minister and bishop. D.E.K.

Pigeon River Conservative Mennonite Church, located near Pigeon, Huron Co., Mich., several miles south of Saginaw Bay, a member of the Conservative Mennonite Conference, had its beginning in 1900 when several C.A.M. families from Croghan, N.Y., moved into this community. M. S. Zehr, one of this group, was ordained to the ministry. With several families who came from Ontario in 1902 they organized a Sunday school in that year under the leadership of Jacob M. Bender, bishop of the Ontario group. Solomon J. Swartzendruber, bishop, had charge of the work in 1904, when a meetinghouse was built. This church was enlarged in 1909 and replaced by a new one in 1957. The membership in 1957 was 275, including three mission outposts conducted by the congregation. Former ministers were S. J. Swartzendruber, M. S. Zehr, Jacob Yoder, Dan Shetler, Edwin Albrecht, Raymond Byler, and Emanuel Swartzendruber, bishop. The ministers in 1957 were Willard R. Mayer, bishop, and Earl J. Maust, minister. E.J.M.

Pigeon River Mennonite Mutual Auto Aid, a mutual insurance company covering automobile accidents (not liability and property damage), was organized Jan. 1, 1950, at Pigeon, Mich., to serve Conservative Mennonites of the local area. It had 75 members in 1953. H.S.B.

Pigot(t), Thomas, an English refugee living at Amsterdam, Holland, who was a Brownist (q.v.) of John Smyth's (q.v.) party, which had separated from the main Brownist body. Smyth and his party, including Pigott, had been influenced by the Mennonites and accepted the doctrine of believers' baptism. After Smyth's death in 1612, Pigott became the preacher of this group, which in 1615 joined the Mennonite Waterlander congregation at Amsterdam. Because of the difference of language, the English group continued to meet separately in their former meetinghouse called Jan Munter's bakehouse. Pigott, who had been ordained as an elder by the

Waterlander elder Pieter Andriesz Hesseling in 1620, served until his death in 1639. Then the English group discontinued its separate meetings. After Smyth's death Pigott published Smyth's *Retraction of Errors and Confirmation of the Truth,* adding a preface in commemoration of Smyth and a confession drawn up by Smyth. The Amsterdam Mennonite library contains a written copy of John Smyth's Confession and Life (of 1612) by Pigott. Four other members of the Pigott family also joined the Mennonites in 1615.   vDZ.

Kühler, *Geschiedenis* II, 95 f.; J. G. de Hoop Scheffer and W. E. Griffis, *History of the Free Churchmen* (Ithaca, n.d.-1922) 148, 163-68; *Inv. Arch. Amst.* II, No. 1351.

Pijper, Frederik, a Dutch Reformed theologian, b. 1859 at Hoogwoud, d. 1926 at Leiden. He was professor of church history at the University of Leiden, and coeditor with Samuel Cramer (*q.v.*) of the *Bibliotheca Reformatoria Neerlandica,* in which he edited a number of rare 16th-century Reformed books. After Cramer's death he edited volume X, containing the writings of Dirk (*q.v.*) Philips, with notes and an introduction. In the *Nederl. Archief voor Kerkgeschiedenis* (II, 1903, 299) he published an article, "Een nieuw entdekt Doopsgezind Martelaarsboek," in which he expressed himself quite critically about it. Besides a number of other books and papers on church history, he published *Martelaarsboeken* (The Hague, 1924), in which he dealt with the martyr books by Jean Crespin (*q.v.*), Adriaan van Haemstede (*q.v.*), the *Offer des Heeren,* and later Mennonite martyr books, and the book by Ludwig Rabus (*q.v.*). (Kühler, *Geschiedenis* I, 259; *ML* III, 374.) NEFF.

Pike County (Mo.) Old Order Amish settlement, near Bowling Green, Mo., began in December 1947, when Jacob M. Beachey and his sons moved here from Jay County, Ind. A church was organized on Feb. 29, 1948, with Jacob J. Miller as minister of the group, and Christ M. Bontrager of Buchanan County, Iowa, as bishop. The congregation is now (1958) divided into two districts, the South District having 55 members, with Jacob J. Miller as bishop and Joseph E. Miller and P. M. Borntrager as preachers, and the North District, 68 members, with Peter Girod as bishop and Jacob J. Schwartz, John M. Schwartz, and Jacob W. Eicher as preachers.   J.J.Mi.

Pike Mennonite (MC) Church, located two miles west of Elida, Ohio, originated as a daughter of the Salem (*q.v.*) congregation in 1874, when the first meetinghouse was built, although services had been held soon after Sunday school was started in the Pike area in 1860. The second meetinghouse, built in 1888, which burned in 1930, was replaced in 1934. J. B. Smith (1870-1951) was senior minister at Pike from 1922 to his death. In 1957 Paul Smith and Harold Good were the ministers, with 238 members. The Pike congregation was supporting two mission congregations in Kentucky—Wildcat (1949) and Newfound Mission (1951). The Central Mennonite Church (*q.v.*) was established in Elida

in 1925 by a group of members expelled from the Salem and Pike congregations.   H.S.B.

Pike Mennonite Church. In a disagreement over the treatment of an orphan girl in 1845 the two ministers at Groffdale, Lancaster Co., Pa., Jacob Stauffer and Jacob Weber, led a small schism, with Jacob Brubaker of Juniata County as their bishop. They were granted a small meetinghouse near Hinkletown and built one in Snyder County on Port Trevorton Route 2. They are today called the Weaver Mennonites. There were in 1955 60 members, with Weaver Zimmerman as bishop and Martin S. Weaver and Peter L. Weaver as ministers. The Stauffer Mennonites, 218 in all, are in two congregations, with Jacob S. Stauffer as bishop and Joseph O. Brubaker as minister at the Pike church, worshiping in the same house as the Weaver group, and at Loveville, Md., Harry Stauffer and John M. Brubaker, ministers. There are a few other small schismatic groups in Snyder County.   I.D.L.

Pike Mennonite Church (MC), Harrisonburg, Va., located 5 miles south of the city on Route 11, was established in 1825, with Frederick Rhodes and Abram Nisewonger as ministers. It was then known as "Moyers Church." In 1957 it had 162 members, with Aldine Brenneman and John E. Kurtz as ministers.   H.A.B.

Pilgrim Fathers, the name of a group of English Congregationalists (*q.v.*) who came to America on the *Mayflower,* arriving in Massachusetts on Dec. 11, 1620, the first settlers in this area. These English Separatists had lived for some time at Leiden in the Netherlands. In their strict church life they were somewhat akin to the Anabaptists. They were influenced in the origin of their group (about 1595) by Dutch Mennonites, but soon adopted more Calvinistic views on baptism and predestination.   NEFF.

H. G. Wood, *Venturers for the Kingdom* (London, n.d.-1919); D. Plooy, *De "Pilgrim Fathers"* (Utrecht, 1919); *HRE* X, 684 f.; *ML* III, 375.

Pilgrim Mennonite Church, Amelia, Va., established in 1956, had 53 members in 1957. Harvey J. Mast and Levi D. Kramer were the ministers.   M.G.

Pilgrims Amish Mennonite Church, Allendale, S.C., is an independent Sleeping Preacher (*q.v.*) church, attempting to establish a more conservative church than the Oregon group from whom they separated. The bishop of their 13 members in 1957 was LeRoy S. Stoltzfus.   M.G.

Pilgrims, Veit (Fitus tho Pilgrams), an Anabaptist martyr, a native of South Germany, who was apprehended in 1532 and imprisoned at Gladbach, then belonging to Jülich, Germany. By the aid of friends he was able to escape from prison. But he continued his activity and was again arrested. After being cruelly tortured he was burned at the stake at Gladbach (*q.v.*) in 1537, because he loyally confessed his faith. (*Mart. Mir.* D 33, E 440; Rembert, *Wiedertäufer,* 15, 437; *ML* III, 375.) NEFF.

Pil(l)owitz (Bil(l)owitz; today, Velké Bilovice), a village located 20 miles west of Göding (*q.v.*) in Moravia, in which the Hutterian Brethren acquired a house with all its equipment in 1545. Here occurred the death of deacon Gregor Pehem. Johann von Zierotin (*q.v.*), the proprietor of Pillowitz, gave the Brethren a meadow in 1571 for a vineyard. One day in 1595 "in broad daylight" a fire was set in the roof of the Hutterite school, destroying not only the Bruderhof, but also a large part of the village. In April and June of 1600 the cavalry of Count Thurn caused a vast amount of damage. The Brethren fared even worse at the hands of the troops of the revolting Hungarians who had crossed into Moravian territory and on May 7, 1605, burned Pillowitz to the ground, after murdering four Brethren. For years the site remained desolate. In 1614, at the wish of the new Baron Ladislav Velen von Zierotin, the Brethren erected a new Bruderhof, which was burned down by Dampierre's soldiers in 1619. The Hutterites rebuilt once more, but in 1622 had to leave Pillowitz for good. (Zieglschmid, *Chronik; ML* III, 375.)   P.DE.

Pilraust, Erhard: see **Polrus, Erhard.**

Pincher Creek Hutterite Bruderhof, of the Dariusleut (*q.v.*), located at Pincher Station, Alberta, was founded in 1927 by members of the Raley brotherhood. Their preacher Jakob Hofer was chosen in 1924 by the Raley Bruderhof, and with several families from this Bruderhof founded Pincher Creek. Paul Gross was chosen preacher here. In 1950 this Bruderhof had 85 souls, including 30 baptized members.   D.D.

Pincher Creek Mennonite Brethren Church was affiliated with the Coaldale, Alberta, M.B. Church until 1948, when it was organized as a separate congregation and built its church building. In 1957 the presiding minister was D. Duerksen, with 23 members.   A.A.T.

Pinder, Wolfgang, an Anabaptist martyr found in van Braght's *Martyrs' Mirror* (D 539, E 874): see **Binder, Wolf.**

Pine Crest Church of God in Christ Mennonite Church, Louisville, Ga., is located 5 miles northwest of the town. It had 97 members in 1958, with Reno L. Hibner as pastor.   M.G.

Pine Grove Mennonite Church (GCM), located at Bowmansville, Montgomery Co., Pa., had its beginning in 1848, when certain members were excommunicated from the M.C. congregations for bringing suit in protest against the state's taking over the schools. In 1852 they organized a congregation, and in 1854 dedicated a new meetinghouse. A tablet originally facing the highway, bearing the legend, "Pine Grove Fersamling House 1854," is now in the church. Ministers who have served are William Shelly 1856-58, Solomon Ott 1859-1913, Raymond Stubbs 1929-48, Leroy Albright 1950-53, and John Wesley Muffley 1953-55. In 1957 the membership was 42, with Howard T. Landes as pastor.   J.W.M.

Pine Hill Hutterite Bruderhof (colony) near Penhold, Alberta, belonging to the Dariusleut (*q.v.*) branch. In 1950 the population was 86 with Peter Hofer as head preacher.   VDZ.

Pinecraft Mennonite Church (union), Sarasota, Fla., is controlled by trustees representing A.M., C.M., and M.C. groups. The church is open for services to each of these groups, and consequently the Pinecraft Mennonite Church (*q.v.*) of the Lancaster Conference worships here. The union services began with a Sunday school in 1941. The present building was occupied in 1946 and accommodates an average winter attendance of over 700.   M.G.

John Umble, "The Mennonites in Florida," *Menn. Life* XII (1957) 108-15.

Pinecraft Mennonite Church (MC), Sarasota, Fla., a member of the Lancaster Mennonite Conference, was organized from among those attending the Union Mennonite Church in the Pinecraft area. It had a membership of 30 in 1957, with Joseph M. Nissley and Otho B. Shenk serving as preachers.   J.M.N.

Pinegrove Mennonite Church (MC), located south of Stryker, Ohio, on Route 6, was established in 1951. In 1957 it had 106 members, with D. Wyse Graber as pastor.   M.G.

Pinesburg Mennonite Mission (MC), located midway between Williamsport, Md., and Clear Spring, Md., is the outgrowth of a Sunday school begun in a schoolhouse. In 1925 it was organized as a congregation under the Washington Co., Md., and Franklin Co., Pa., Mission Board, by persons living in the community. In 1957, the membership was 35, with Oliver H. Martin as minister. The present frame building was built in 1939.   J.D.R.

Pingjum, a village in the Dutch province of Friesland, about three miles west of Witmarsum (*q.v.*) where Menno Simons was born. Menno is supposed to have spent his youth at Pingjum and after his studies he officiated here as a Catholic priest in 1524-31. The Catholic church in which he served has been replaced by a new one (now Reformed), but its old tower is still standing. It is not known when Mennonitism arose here. Wabbe Lysbethsdochter of Pingjum had as early as March 1535 been among the Anabaptists who assaulted the Oldeklooster (*q.v.*) near Bolsward. Leenaert Bouwens (*q.v.*) baptized 14 persons here in 1563-65, and 12 in 1568-82. At least since that time there has been a Mennonite congregation at Pingjum. Concerning this congregation there is only scarce information. In 1695 it numbered 32 baptized members. During the 18th century the (lay) preachers of Pingjum also served in the neighboring congregation of Arum (*q.v.*). In 1827 the Pingjum congregation united with that of Witmarsum, from then being served by the ministers of Witmarsum. The old and characteristic meetinghouse of Pingjum was restored in 1950.   VDZ.

Menn. Life V (January 1950) 44-46; *DB* 1864, 125 f.; *DJ* 1951, 21-26; K. Vos, *Menno Simons* (Leiden, 1914) 30, 229; *ML* III, 375.

Pinto Mennonite Church (MC), located in Pinto, Allegany Co., Md., a member of the Allegheny Conference (formerly Southwestern Pennsylvania), was organized in 1927 with a membership of 46. D. H. Bender was the first Mennonite minister to preach in that community, about 1915. Milton B. Miller, of Springs, Pa., served as minister. Chester M. Helmick was ordained as minister in 1929, and the following year Robert P. Dayton was ordained to the ministry. The church building, a cement block structure which seats 250, was built in 1927. In the present (1957) membership of 100 there are representatives of ten denominations who have been received into fellowship. The ministers in 1956 were A. Lehman Longenecker and Chester M. Helmick.   C.M.H.

Pioneer Evangelical Mennonite Church, located in Pioneer, Williams Co., Ohio, was organized in 1912, built its first church in 1916, and was served by E. M. Slagle its first pastor. It had 55 members in 1958, with Gaylord E. Gerig as minister. G.E.G.

Pioneer Mission (Mennonite Pioneer Mission), which in 1957 was made the official mission board of the Canadian District Conference of the General Conference Mennonite Church, was a mission agency of the Bergthaler Mennonite Church (largely of Manitoba) 1945-57. It was started to take over the missionary effort which Ronald Groening had begun in 1942 among the Tarahumau Indians of Mexico, assisted by Mr. and Mrs. Heinrich Gerbrandt in 1945-48, but which had to be discontinued in 1948. In 1948 work was begun among the Indians on Matheson Island in Lake Winnipeg, to which two additional Indian stations have recently been added (Paungassi and Cross Lake). The Pioneer Mission also raises funds for the support of missionaries from the Canadian Conference constituency serving under the Congo Inland Mission (*q.v.*; two in 1957) and those serving under the G.C.M. Mission Board in India (one), Japan (two), and Formosa (one). In 1957 there were three missionary couples working among the Indians in Northern Manitoba. The official organ, *Mennonite Pioneer Mission,* has appeared twice per year as a 12-page 6 x 9-inch journal at Altona, Man., since 1945. The headquarters of the organization have been at Altona.   H.S.B.

Pioneers Memorial Hospital, Rocky Ford, Col., though owned by the community, has been administered since 1954 by the Mennonite Board of Missions and Charities (MC). It has a capacity of 31 beds and 9 bassinets.   J.H.F.

Pirenne, Henri (1862-1935), was professor of history in the University of Gent, Belgium, in 1896-1930. Among his numerous books and papers on the history of Belgium is the outstanding *Histoire de Belgique* (7 vols., 1899-1932, also translated into German and Dutch). The third volume deals with the rise of Anabaptism in Belgium. He describes Anabaptism largely as a socio-economic movement, the Anabaptists in his view having been the poor, the proletariat. Pirenne's views deeply influenced

the Dutch Mennonite historian Karel Vos (*q.v.*).
                                                    vDZ.

Pirkheimer, Willibald (1470-1530), a Humanist, one of the outstanding leaders in the active intellectual and religious life of Nürnberg, Germany. At the beginning of the Reformation he sided with Luther, but in 1524 returned to the Catholic Church. When Hans Denk (*q.v.*) was made rector of the school of St. Sebaldus upon recommendation of Oecolampadius (*q.v.*), he must certainly have come in contact with Pirkheimer. There is no information on the matter. In Denk's dispute with Andreas Osiander (*q.v.*) Pirkheimer took the latter's side. He wrote an unfavorable opinion concerning Denk to Basel. Oecolampadius wrote two letters to Pirkheimer, Feb. 26, and April 25, 1525, to defend his recommendation of Denk to the rectorate of the school of St. Sebaldus.   NEFF.

Ernst Staehelin, *Briefe und Akten zum Leben Oekolampads* (Leipzig, 1927) 359, 364 f.; *ML* III, 375.

Pistor, Georg, an Anabaptist of the Palatinate and Zweibrücken, Germany, who stemmed from Alsace (Hagenau). Under Capito (*q.v.*) and Bucer (*q.v.*) he was a Protestant preacher in Strasbourg, and was sent by Bucer to Zweibrücken at the request of Johann Schwebel, the reformer of Zweibrücken; Pistor was given the pastoral charge of the neighboring village of Ernstweiler. His Anabaptist views soon brought him into conflict with Schwebel. "Stripping baptism and the breaking of bread of all sacramental significance and denying their necessity as means of salvation, the demand for the moral integrity of the one administering them as a necessary condition for the validity of the rite; the assertion of the incompatibility of true Christianity with holding a government position or with the possession of worldly goods; in addition the disregard and defamation of a salaried ministry"—these were the Anabaptist views that Pistor held and that Schwebel attacked. The Strasbourg reformers were called in a futile attempt to arbitrate the matter. Ruprecht, the Count Palatine, also entered the breach. In 1538 Georg Pistor was expelled from the country. All trace of him is lost.   NEFF.

Fritz Jung, *Johannes Schwebel, der Reformator von Zweibrücken* (Kaiserslautern, 1910) 107 ff.; *ML* III, 375 f.

Pistorius, Johannes (Jan de Bakker or Jan Jansz van Woerden), b. 1499, was the first victim of the Inquisition in the Netherlands. He was a Roman Catholic priest who rejected the doctrine of the Mass and other Catholic doctrines. From July 11 to Sept. 7, 1525, Pistorius was interrogated by the inquisitor Ruardus Tapper (*q.v.*). He was arrested in May 1525 and imprisoned at The Hague. One of his prison mates was Guilhelmus (Willem) Gnapheus (*q.v.*), to whom he dictated the questions of the inquisitors and his own answers and who then wrote a circumstantial account of the cross-examinations of Pistorius. In the sentence he is called a Lutheran, but this means merely that he was a Sacramentist (*q.v.*). He was burned at the stake at The Hague on Sept. 15, 1525.   vDZ.

J. G. de Hoop Scheffer, *Geschiedenis der Kerkhervorming in Nederland . . . tot 1531* (Amsterdam, 1873) 360-89 and *passim*.

Pius IV (b. 1499), a pope 1560-65, successor of Paul IV, is said to have been a lenient ruler, but less merciful to "heretics." In 1564 he complained to Marco Soranza, the emissary of the republic of Venice, concerning the lax attitude toward heretics; in consequence the two imprisoned "Anabaptists" Sega (*q.v.*) and Rizzetto (*q.v.*) were sentenced to die by drowning on Feb. 8, 1565. The sentence stated that this mode of execution rather than the usual one of burning was passed "for definite reasons on the strength of a special authorization granted this tribunal by the Holy See." The drowning was performed at night to keep it quiet. NEFF.

K. Benrath, "Geschichte der Reformation in Venedig," in *Schriften des Vereins für Ref.-Geschichte* V (Halle, 1886) No. 18; pp. 99, 101; *idem*, "Wiedertäufer im Venezianischen," in *Theol. Studien und Kritiken*, 1885, 9-67; *ML* III, 376.

Plaats, van der, a Dutch Mennonite family, from the 17th century found at Harlingen, Friesland, where in the early 18th century Folkert van der Plaats Jzn was a deacon of the Mennonite congregation and owner of a publishing house, which printed a number of books by Johannes Stinstra (*q.v.*). His son Folkert van der Plaats Jr. continued this publishing house until his death in 1806. The business was then run by Melle van der Plaats, a son of Folkert Jr. Some members of this family were noted physicians and lawyers in Friesland.

A descendant of this family was Jan Daniel van der Plaats, b. 1837 at Leeuwarden, d. 1890, who after finishing his studies at the Amsterdam Theological Seminary served as pastor at Hindeloopen-Molkwerum 1851-56 and Woudsend 1856-83. He published the sermons delivered in 1858-59 to commemorate the last service in the old meetinghouse and the first service in the new one at Woudsend: *Twee tempel-psalmen* (Sneek, 1859). VDZ.

G. A. Wumkes, *Stads- en Dorpskroniek van Friesland*, 2 vv. (Leeuwarden, 1930 and 1934) *passim*; Blaupot t. C., *Friesland*; *De Zondagsbode*.

Placcaten, official edicts issued by the Dutch government against the Anabaptists and Mennonites: see **Mandates.**

Placement Committee. With the transition from the lay ministry in the General Conference Mennonite Church to the trained and professional ministry, a need arose for the mediation between churches and prospective candidates for pulpits which had become vacant. In the 1929 session of Conference a temporary committee of five members was created, known as the Placement Committee. For some time this committee was continued by special resolution from session to session.

To begin with, this committee was charged with the sole responsibility of finding available qualified ministers and recommending them to congregations looking for a minister. The committee sought to meet the needs of the particular congregation with the qualifications of the man recommended. By 1945 the functions and responsibilities of the committee had been enlarged and widened so that it recognized the following areas: (*a*) The placement of ministers; (*b*) Recruiting young ministers; (*c*) The training of ministers; (*d*) Keeping in touch with ministerial students; (*e*) Ministerial internships; (*f*) Responsibility to Mennonite students in non-Mennonite schools; (*g*) Guidance of young ministers; and (*h*) Obtaining facts and information regarding candidates and congregations.

With the adoption of the new constitution in 1950 the Placement Committee was replaced by the Committee on the Ministry, with greatly enlarged functions. Some of the additional responsibilities with which this new committee is charged are the ordination of ministers and the preparation of an all-conference ordination questionnaire, an ethical code for ministers and congregations, ministers' salaries, ministerial certification, scholarships for ministers, the orientation of new ministers, standards for the ministry, and keeping in touch with ministerial students. The Committee on the Ministry is also responsible for setting up and promoting retreats for ministers and other Christian workers. It is responsible to the Board of Missions, and the members of the Committee are appointed by this board. P.K.R.

Plae, Jean le (Jan de Pla), was a preacher of the French-speaking Mennonite Waterlander congregation of Leiden, Holland. He was chosen to the office before 1630, and was still serving in 1647, when as a delegate from his congregation he attended a Waterlander conference held at Amsterdam. He also intermediated in the schism of 1627 in the Amsterdam Waterlander congregation between Nittert Obbes (*q.v.*) and his co-preachers. VDZ.

L. G. le Poole, *Bijdragen tot de kennis van . . . de Doopsgezinden te Leiden* (Leiden, 1905) 41, 62 f., 83, 215; *Inv. Arch. Amst.* II, 2, Nos. 341-43.

"Plain" Coat. In Colonial America the man's coat was a frock coat without lapel, and buttoned to the throat. It had a long, split tail for convenience in horseback riding. In the early 19th century the collar rose higher and higher on the back and finally turned over to form the modern roll collar and lapel. At the same time the tail shortened to form the modern sack coat. The ministers in general, and some of the laity, in the more conservative Mennonite groups objected to these changes, and clung to the old-fashioned frock coat with its long tail and no lapel. In the strictest groups such as the Old Order Amish the old collarless coat, known as the "plain" coat, is still worn by ministry and laity alike, and is fastened with hooks and eyes rather than buttons. In the eastern sector of the Mennonite Church (MC) (Franconia, Lancaster, Washington-Franklin, and Virginia conferences) the ministers generally still wear the split tail frock coat (somewhat shortened) with the "plain" collar, while some of the laity wear a collarless sack coat, and others wear the conventional sack coat with roll collar and lapel. In the remainder of the church (MC) the standard practice of the ministers is to wear the sack coat with the "plain" collar, but most laymen wear the conventional coat with lapel. (See also **Dress.**) Mennonite deviations in dress from the conventions of the surrounding culture are regarded by many as symbols of nonconformity to the world.

The Amish congregations descending from the Alsatian Amish immigrants of 1815-60 did not bring the "plain" coat with them from Europe and did not adopt it generally until well into the first quarter of the 20th century and then only for the ministers, not for laymen. In the course of the first quarter of the century most of the Mennonite and Amish conferences (MC) adopted regulations requiring the "plain" coat for the ministers and recommending it for the laity, hence the "plain" coat is often called the "regulation" coat. The high tide of the movement was about 1920-30. In the Lancaster Conference in recent times all male church workers, including Sunday-school teachers, are required to wear the "plain" coat as a condition for service. Further west the trend seems to be toward less wearing and less requirement of the "plain" coat, even for ministers. In some sections the "plain" vest is also worn with the plain coat. Because in most sections of the church west of the Allegheny Mountains very few laymen wear it, the plain coat has in effect become a preacher's coat or clerical coat, and has indeed a very similar appearance to the clerical coat worn by some Roman Catholic and Episcopalian clergymen. Its origin, however, has no connection with the clerical coat.

The Church of the Brethren, which formerly had the custom of wearing the "plain" coat similar to the Mennonite custom herein described, has now largely dropped it. Among the Quakers it has completely disappeared. The Brethren in Christ still retain it.   J.C.W.

Plains (for a time Plain) Mennonite Church (MC), located in Hatfield Township, west of Lansdale, Pa., is a congregation in the Franconia Mennonite Conference. The name is derived from the plain on which Lansdale is built. The first log school and meetinghouse was built between 1760 and 1769 on land contributed by Henry Frey. It remained in use until 1813, when a stone meetinghouse was built. A third stone building was erected in 1867, and the present stone (white stucco) building in 1922. Before the Revolutionary War the circuit system was in use. Bishop Isaac Kolb (1711-76) is thought to have considered this his home church after 1764. He was ordained bishop in 1761. The first minister definitely known to have been ordained for this church was John Krupp (1799-1842), ordained in 1816. Others who served this church were Joseph Cassel (1799-1868); Jacob Kulp (1798-1875), ordained minister 1838 and bishop in 1843; Jacob C. Loux (1822-95), ordained minister 1867; Henry Godshall (1834-1908), ordained 1874, relieved in 1905; Jonas Mininger (1852-1937), ordained minister 1895, bishop in 1905; Jacob C. Clemens (1874-1965), ordained 1906; John E. Lapp (1905-   ), ordained minister 1933, bishop 1937; Wayne Kratz (1913-   ), ordained 1949. Burials were made in the cemetery as early as about 1764. A Sunday school was organized in 1888. The last three of the above ministers were still serving in 1956, with a membership of 254.   J.E.L.

J. C. Wenger, *History of the Mennonites of the Franconia Conference* (Telford, 1937) 163-66.

Plainview Church of God in Christ Mennonite Church is located 6 miles west of Chickasha, Grady Co., Okla. The first members, among whom was J. B. P. Schmidt, came here from Pauls Valley in 1902. The church building, erected in 1920 and enlarged in 1952, has a seating capacity of 250. The first pastor was Sam A. Nichols. Ministers ordained here include Andrew Nightingale, P. W. Decker, Edward Unruh, and Eben Nightingale. In 1958 Abe D. Koehn was pastor and the membership was 147.   E.U.

Plainview (Kan.) Conservative Mennonite Church. In 1948 five Amish families, feeling the need for more spiritual activities in the church, such as young people's Bible meetings, prayer meetings, more mission work, etc., decided to ask the Conservative Mennonite Conference for help to organize a Conservative church here. On Aug. 1, 1948, the church was organized with 24 members. Nevin Bender of Greenwood, Del., and Emanuel Swartzendruber of Pigeon, Mich., were in charge of the work. Noah Miller was pastor for two years. A new church building was dedicated on Dec. 18, 1949, located 4 miles south and 4 miles west of Hutchinson. In 1958 the baptized membership was 105, with Valentine Headings as bishop and Jonas P. Yoder as minister.   C.Y.M.

Plainview Mennonite Church (MC), near Aurora, Ohio, a member of the Ohio and Eastern Conference, was founded by Amish Mennonites from Nebraska. Several Stutzman families arrived in 1906 but their first minister was Eli B. Stoltzfus of West Liberty, Ohio, who had been ordained for Long Green, Md., in 1908, but moved to Portage County in 1909, and was ordained bishop in 1916. The congregation enjoyed economic and religious growth. Membership increased from 35 in 1908 to 100 in 1912. In that year the congregation built the present meetinghouse. Members of the congregation helped to found the Britton Run Amish Mennonite Church (*q.v.*) in Crawford Co., Pa., and still assist actively in the Burton Mennonite Church (*q.v.*) in Geauga County and in the Gladstone Mennonite Mission in Cleveland. The membership of Plainview in 1957 was 136. Development of the congregation is being hindered by inflationary land values and the encroachment of wealthy buyers of land for rural estates. The resident bishop in 1957 was Elmer Stoltzfus and the minister Eugene Yoder.   J.S.U.

Vern L. Miller, "The History of the Plainview Mennonite Church . . ." (1950, unpublished paper in GCL).

Plainview Mennonite Church (GCM), now extinct, at Dalhart, Tex., was listed in the *Minutes and Reports of the Western District Conference* for 1932 with a membership of 46. The congregation had no minister at that time. J. W. Bergen served the church 1933-35; then the church was dissolved. It was a home mission church of the Western District Conference.   C.K.

Plaitner, Virgil: see **Plattner, Vigilg.**

Planer, Andre, an Anabaptist, a scythe smith in Welsberg, South Tirol, Austria. In his house the first followers of Jakob Hutter (*q.v.*) met. One meeting was raided on May 26, 1529, but Hutter managed to escape. (*ML* III, 377.) P.DE.

Planer (Plaver), **Peter,** an Anabaptist martyr, was imprisoned with Lamprecht Gruber (*q.v.*), Hans Beck (*q.v.*), Lorenz Schuester (*q.v.*), Hans Taler (*q.v.*), and Planer's servant Peter in Sterzing in South Tirol, Austria (now Italy), in 1532. In spite of the use of the rack they were true to their faith and were therefore put to death by beheading. The letters they wrote in prison have been preserved. P.DE.

Beck, *Geschichts-Bücher; Mart. Mir.* D 33, E 440; Wolkan, *Geschicht-Buch,* 74; Loserth, *Anabaptismus;* Zieglschmid, *Chronik,* 102; *ML* I, 145; III, 377.

Planerkolonie, located north of the Sea of Azov between Mariupol and Berdyansk, Ukraine, was a German settlement established in 1822. The name was derived from a "plan" which was worked out by the government for the settlement. The settlers of the original 17 villages came from the Marienburg, Danzig, and Elbing area of Prussia where the Mennonites also came from. Although these settlers spoke Plattdeutsch and established homes and villages similar to those of the Mennonites and some had "Mennonite" names they were not Mennonites. The village names were primarily given in memory of those from which they had come. The settlers had spent some years in the Molotschna settlement and were later joined by others coming from South Germany. The original Planer settlement was located just north of the five Mennonite villages of Bergthal. When the Bergthal Mennonites left for America in 1874 their villages became a part of the Planer settlement.

The original Planer settlement consisted of 27 villages and the five Bergthal Mennonite villages, of which Grünau, Ludwigstal, and Bergthal were the district seats. The Planer mother settlement spread into the surrounding territory of Mariupol, establishing 19 additional villages. The settlement also spread into the East, establishing a daughter settlement in the Don Basin. The 20 villages had names like Liebental, Grüntal, and Gnadenfeld. Another daughter settlement was established north of Berdyansk with the following villages: Neuhoffnung, Rosenfeld, Neuhoffnungstal, and Neu-Stuttgart.

In this area the evangelist and minister Eduard Wüst began his evangelistic work, which caused a great revival among the German population in South Russia, spreading into the neighboring Molotschna settlement. Cornelius Jansen of Berdyansk was a friend of Wüst. From here the revival movement also spread eastward into the mother settlement of Mariupol and the daughter settlement in the Don area. For a time there was a Mariupol Mennonite Brethren Church (*q.v.*). Wüst's activities caused breaks in the Protestant churches and the founding of Pietistic and separatist movements. Some joined the Baptist Church. C.K.

J. A. Malinowsky, *Die Planerkolonien am Asovschen Meere* (Stuttgart, 1928); G. J. Eisenach, *Pietism and the Russian Germans in the United States* (Berne, 1948).

Plank, a Mennonite family name found principally in Pennsylvania, Ohio, and Indiana, but also repre-

sented in Illinois, Iowa, Missouri, and Kansas, as well as other western states. In 1958 there were five Planks in the ministry of the Amish and Mennonite churches. Among the prominent representatives of the family was David Plank (1833-1912) (*q.v.*), an Amish Mennonite bishop of Logan County, Ohio, and a descendant of Melchior Plank. Samuel Plank (1809-79), David's father, who moved to Logan County from Mifflin County, Pa., in 1845, served as an Amish Mennonite deacon for thirty years. Solomon K. Plank (1837-1912) served as deacon for forty-two years, mostly in Wayne County, Ohio. D. J. Plank was ordained bishop by the Douglas County, Ill., O.O.A. in 1892. Peter Plank, who served as bishop in the Conestoga, Pa., A.M. Church 1808-31, was a great-grandson of a French Huguenot doctor who settled in Berks County, Pa. Perhaps through the influence of his wife, he became a Mennonite. He was the successor of the first bishop of the Conestoga A.M. Church. Following him as bishop was John Blank (1831-35) (C. Z. Mast), who may possibly be an ancestor of the A.M. Blanks in eastern Pennsylvania, although other Blank families were among the early immigrants to Pennsylvania. C. Henry Smith listed Hans Blank and Christian Blank for 1751, and Jacob Blank, Nickolas Blank, and Frederick Plank for 1752.

There is confusion concerning the relationship of the Blanks and Planks. John Horsch listed Blank as a Mennonite Palatinate name of Swiss origin. Christian Blank was an active participant on the Amish side of the Ammann-Reist controversy in Switzerland in 1693. The name Blank was found among South German Mennonites as late as 1940. In America evidently some members of the family changed the name to Plank.

Most of the Mennonite Planks of the central states, however, are descendants of Melchior Plank, or more specifically Johann Melchior Blankenberg, who arrived in America from Holland and was sold as an indentured servant for a five-year term to Jason Cloud on Nov. 27, 1767. In Berks County, Pa., on Jan. 16, 1769, Jason Cloud assigned his servant to Howard Hughes for the remainder of his term and on June 22, 1772, Hughes dismissed Blankenberg upon his payment of five pounds, as shown by the photostatic copy of the indenture in the Goshen Archives of the Mennonite Church. According to family tradition Blankenberg was a Swiss Mennonite in Holland, who with his wife visited friends sailing for America on a ship docked in a Dutch port. While they were on board ship it left the harbor.

To the Melchior Planks were born six children, the oldest of whom was Jacob (1768-1851). To Jacob and his wife Mary Yoder Plank were born 12 children, 3 in eastern Pennsylvania and 9 in Mifflin County, Pa. In 1821 Jacob moved to Wayne County, Ohio. The Planks of Wayne County, Ohio, and Lagrange County, Ind., are descendants of Jacob. M.G.

Plank, David (1833-1912), bishop of the South Union (*q.v.*) and Walnut Grove (*q.v.*) Amish Mennonite congregations in Logan County (*q.v.*), Ohio, from 1895 to 1912, was born in Mifflin County (*q.v.*), Pa., the son of Samuel (later, deacon) and Juliana Hertzler Plank. With his parents he moved to Union Township, Logan Co., Ohio, in 1845. In 1856 he was married to Mary Hertzler. After his ordination in 1859 he sided with the more progressive neighboring Champaign County bishop, John Warye, in his controversy with the Logan County leaders. Always alert for new ideas and plans for Christian work, he attended a Brethren Sunday school near his home and in 1863 with the consent of his bishop and the unanimous vote of the congregation he organized in Logan County the first Amish Sunday school in America, held in an Amish meetinghouse. The next year he organized a similar school in the Hooley Amish meetinghouse in Champaign County (later known as the Oak Grove Church, *q.v.*). He served as both superintendent and teacher for a number of years. Following the complete break between the two districts in the late 1860's he and his father had charge of the seceding Logan County group, which alternated services with the Champaign congregation and in 1875 erected the Walnut Grove Amish Mennonite Church (*q.v.*) in Union Township near Plank's home. Plank was successful in his small farming operations and had special talent in drawing, carpentry, and cabinet-making. After the bishop at South Union moved to Kansas, the congregation at that place was left without a bishop. Following the organization of the Ohio Amish Mennonite Conference (*q.v.*) in 1893 earnest efforts to reconcile differences between South Union and Walnut Grove resulted in a decision to place the Walnut Grove and South Union ministers in the lot for bishop and to ordain for both congregations whoever was chosen. David Plank was chosen and ordained in 1895 and served until his death in 1912, when A. I. Yoder (*q.v.*), as son of the South Union minister, was installed as Plank's successor. Plank did much to heal the breach between the two factions.   J.S.U.

John Umble, "Early Sunday Schools at West Liberty, Ohio," *MQR* IV (1930) 6-50, *passim*.

Plantenga, Broer Pieter, b. Dec. 15, 1865, at Zutphen, d. May 28, 1929, at Haarlem, a Dutch Mennonite pastor serving at Meppel 1893-98, Wormerveer 1898-99, Arnhem 1899-1901, and Haarlem 1901-27. In 1927 he resigned because of his health. Among his many offices in the Dutch brotherhood should be mentioned his membership (secretary) on the committee for the Mennonites in the Diaspora (see **Verstrooiing**) and on the board of curators of the Mennonite seminary. He also served for a number of years as a trustee of the Dutch (liberal) Protestant Union. (*DJ* 1930, 21-26.) vpZ.

Plantinus. There have been three Dutch Mennonite ministers by this name: Petrus Plantinus, serving as preacher at Schiedam 1732-d.41, Jan Plantinus (b. c1783 at Dokkum, d. ?), minister of Drachten and Ureterp 1809-50, and his son Doede Plantinus (b. 1815 at Drachten, d. 1890 at Holwerd), minister of Rottevalle-Witveen 1839-45, Uithuizen 1845-47, Warga 1847-49, and Holwerd-Blija 1849-85. Jan and Doede Plantinus received their theological training at the Amsterdam Mennonite Seminary. Doede

Plantinus was the author of a catechetical book, *De Leer des Heils* (1st ed. n.d.; 2d ed. 1882), and *Blijf in hetgene gij geleer leerd hebt* (Drachten, 1864), a sermon to commemorate his 25 years in the ministry. (*De Zondagsbode* III, 1889-90, No. 29.) vpZ.

Plarre, Ernst Martin (1684-1717), an official in the military secretariat in Berlin, Germany. In 1701 he wrote his first book, *E. M. P. Epideigma sive specimen historiae anabaptisticae*. It is based on the *Histoire des Anabaptistes* (Paris, 1695), and upon its predecessor, *Historia Tumultuum Anabaptisticorum* (Basel, 1548) by Lambertus Hortensius. Hence Münster (*q.v.*) and the Netherlands (*q.v.*) occupy the foreground of his observations, followed by David Joris (*q.v.*). Other areas in which the Anabaptists appeared are given less consideration; of these England (*q.v.*) is most extensively treated.
          E.C.

Christian Gottlieb Jöcher, *Allgemeines Gelehrten-Lexicon* III, and the continuation by Henrich Wilhelm Rotermund, *op. cit.*, IV; *ML* III, 377.

Plato Mennonite Church (MC), Lagrange, Ind., established in 1949, had a membership of 90 in 1957. Willis C. Troyer was the minister.   M.G.

Plattdeutsch (Plautdietsch), a Low German language spoken by Mennonites who originally came largely from the Netherlands and settled in Danzig and along the Vistula River whence they spread into Russia and North and South America. All Mennonites are primarily of two ethnic and linguistic backgrounds, the Swiss-German (see **Pennsylvania German**) and the Dutch-German or Low German.

Dutch Background. When the Mennonites from the Netherlands settled along the Vistula, they adhered to their Dutch language until the second half of the 18th century. Individuals of different backgrounds joining the Mennonites simply learned this foreign language. The native language of the country was a form of Low German or Plattdeutsch with pecular local characteristics, spoken in some form in all of North Germany. It is linguistically related to Dutch and English. That the similarities between Low German, Dutch, and English are in some respects greater than those between Low German and High German, the official language of German-speaking countries, can be seen in the word for water: Dutch *water,* Low German *woata,* and High German *Wasser.* Until the 17th century it was a literary language. Whereas Dutch has remained a literary language, most of the Low German dialects are now colloquial languages, although there is a large body of Low German literature, and the dialect has been used by some of the great writers. A current classification divides the Low German language and dialects by the following geographical areas: Westphalia, Hanover, Oldenburg, Bremen, Hamburg, Lübeck, Holstein, Mecklenburg, Pomerania, Braunschweig, Brandenburg, West Prussia, and East Prussia. Most of these areas or countries have many local dialect forms.

From Dutch to Low and High German. Although the Mennonites of this area lived at times under Polish sovereignty, they were little influenced by the

Polish language. In their daily life they accepted the Low German spoken in their territory. The question has been raised why the Mennonites in America coming from Russia and Poland speak different forms of Low German. Some scholars have pointed out that this is related to their religious background such as the Flemish or Frisian church affiliations (Quiring). Others consider it due to the different localities in Danzig and West Prussia from which they moved to Russia (Mitzka). The Mennonites accepted the Low German of their environment gradually, at times retaining some Dutch peculiarities. Mitzka has pointed out that some of the notebooks of Mennonite farmers of the 17th and 18th centuries contain a mixture of Dutch and German. This was the time when they were becoming more and more exposed to the German culture and language. C. Wiens, in his study of the Dutch linguistic influence on the vocabulary of this area, has shown that the shift from Dutch to Low German in daily life was completed before Dutch was replaced by High German in worship services, correspondence, etc. In rural areas this change in worship services was completed earlier than in cities like Danzig. Some ministers, e.g., Buhler in the Grosswerder, began to preach in German in 1757, although the congregation did not like it. In 1762 the first German sermon was preached in the Mennonite church of Danzig, for which the minister received special permission, but no appreciation was expressed. The last elder to insist on Dutch preaching in Danzig was Hans von Steen (*q.v.*), who died in 1781. The Danzig church record was henceforth kept in German (in BeCL). The first German Mennonite hymnal replacing the Dutch was printed in 1761. In 1788, when the first Mennonites migrated to Russia, some were still using Dutch. Dutch Bibles and other books were taken along to Russia, some of which even reached the prairie states and provinces of the United States and Canada during the migration of 1874. However, the first migrants to Russia, coming from the poorer classes of the Danzig and Elbing area and settling at Chortitza (*q.v.*), primarily spoke Low German. Dutch was no longer in use and High German was still a foreign tongue. It is particularly this form of Low German which has been perpetuated among the more conservative Mennonites of Manitoba and Mexico, and which has been investigated by such scholars as Quiring and Lehn.

Those Mennonites who stayed in Danzig and West Prussia longer followed the prevalent trend, accepting High German more fully for worship services and literary intercourse. Better education, particularly among the more well-to-do, hastened this development. In 1803, when the Molotschna settlement was established in the Ukraine, the new settlers, being a little more prosperous, had made a greater shift from Dutch to Low German as well as to High German. Also the Low German spoken by them had been considerably altered by High German influences. The difference between the Chortitza and Molotschna Low German is still discernible in the settlements of North and South America. There was, however, a general tendency in Russia toward accepting this "more cultured" form of Low

German in the areas where Mennonites from both settlements were mixed, such as in secondary schools, forestry service camps, daughter settlements, and especially in the North and South American settlements, where a mixing of various backgrounds has taken place on an unprecedented scale. Among those Mennonites who left Danzig and Prussia in 1850-80, going to Samara (Russia), Nebraska, and Kansas, the shift from Low to High German had almost been completed before the emigration. In the family the parents spoke mostly High German, but knew Low German well enough to converse with servants and those who preferred it. Their High German, to be sure, revealed peculiarities as a remnant of their Low German background. This phenomenon was true of many of the Mennonites of Prussia up to the time of their dispersion in 1945. At that time Low German was still spoken by the non-Mennonite population, especially by the laboring and poorer classes, in the Prussian communities from which Mennonites had gone to Russia and America, and in which Mennonites still resided. Mitzka, who made a study of the Low German spoken by the Mennonites of Russia and the areas from which they originally came in West Prussia, states that a geographic shift of the Low German had taken place in their home country.

Low German in America. In the great Mennonite migration from Russia to North America in 1874 the Chortitza or Old Colony Mennonites went to Manitoba and later some to Mexico and South America. They have preserved the original Low German in its purest form, although it also shows Russian and English influences. They have only a very limited mastery of High German and English, and in Mexico and South America of Spanish. The Molotschna Mennonites went primarily to the United States, settling in Kansas, Nebraska, the Dakotas, and Minnesota, although some settled in Manitoba. Mennonites from Poland settled in Kansas and Dakota. The Low German of the Polish group differs more from that of the Molotschna and Chortitza than these do between themselves. The Molotschna Mennonites did not all speak the same form of Low German, nor had they lived together long enough to achieve complete uniformity. The later Molotschna settlements, such as Waldheim and Alexanderwohl, had very definite linguistic characteristics which have been retained and are even today noticeable in Kansas.

Russian and English Influences. Gerhard Wiens's study of the influences of the Russian language on Low German makes some startling observations: "This study of mine may indeed shock some of my people," because their Low German "was not nearly so pure as we were proud to claim." He presents examples of how new words were introduced from the new environment and assimilated, how Russian neologisms entered and Low German words were given a Russian form. Quiring also made a study of Polish and Russian influences on Low German, while C. Wiens has done similar work on Dutch influences on Low German. J. John Friesen and J. W. Goerzen have pointed out the relationships between Plattdeutsch and English. No one has fully investigated the influence of the English language on Low

German in Canada and the United States, or the Spanish and Portuguese upon the Low German in Mexico and South America, although such influences are noticeable.

Among the Mennonite groups of Russian background in the United States, Low German is still spoken or understood in solid Mennonite communities such as Goessel, Buhler, Inman, and Hillsboro in Kansas, Henderson in Nebraska, and Mountain Lake in Minnesota. However, by far not all the young people are able to converse in Low German. It can be expected that Low German will gradually disappear within a few generations among the Mennonites in the United States, but will likely remain in use for some time to come in Canada and particularly in Mexico and South America where the bearers of this language are living in much greater isolation. A Plattdeutsch religious radio program has been broadcast over CFAM in Altona, Man., by the Mennonite Radio Mission since 1957, and another at Swift Current, Sask. During World War II, when the use of the High German was not permitted, the Mennonites of Brazil used Low German in worship services. The Old Colony Mennonite ministers frequently change from High to Low German since many of the young people understand very little High German. Many of the Indians living in the vicinity of the Chaco Mennonites in Paraguay speak some Low German. Thus far the studies dealing with the Low German as spoken by the Mennonites have been devoted primarily to synchronic, diachronic, and phonetic investigations (Quiring, Goerzen, Lehn). Only few attempts (Mitzka) have been made to trace the origin, spread, and differences among the various Low German dialect forms spoken by Mennonites, their relation to each other, as well as the structural development of each.

There is a noticeable culturally restrictive effect of the continued use of the dialect, particularly in groups where the isolation from the main stream of German or English culture is marked. Most of those who speak Low German as their major language read practically no literature, since there is very little modern Low German literature available especially of a religious character. (See Language Problem.)

The Low German and Pennsylvania German languages have been used by the conservative Mennonites and Amish as barriers against "worldly" influences. Like other forms of nonconformity, such as dress restrictions, they have been at times a positive and at times a negative factor in the development of a wholesome Mennonite church and community life. (See also Pennsylvania German and Language Problem.)

Low German Mennonite Literature. Among the Mennonites of Russia, J. H. Janzen was the first to write Low German plays. They were primarily designed to be given in schools and deal particularly with questions pertaining to education. He continued his writing in Canada and was succeeded by Arnold Dyck, who wrote *Dee Fria,* a comedy, *"Wellkaom op'e Forstei!"* and a number of other Low German plays and numerous narratives and short stories, such as *Koop enn Bua op Reise; Koop enn Bua faore nao Toronto; Die Millionäa von Kosefeld;* and *Onse Lied.* These plays are still being given in Mennonite communities of North and South America where Low German is spoken. This is generally the case in Canada, Mexico, Brazil, and Paraguay.   C.K.

Jacob Quiring, *Die Mundart von Chortitza in Süd-Russland* (München, 1928); H. Grimme, *Plattdeutsche Mundarten* (Leipzig, 1910); C. Wiens, "Niederländischer Einfluss im Wortschatz der Weichselwerder," *Ztscht des Westpreussischen Geschichtsvereins,* 1916; Walter Isaak Lehn, "Rosental Low German, Synchronic and Diachronic Phonology" (unpublished Ph.D. dissertation, Cornell University, 1957); J. W. Goerzen, "Low German in Canada, a story of 'Ploutdietsch' as Spoken by Mennonite Immigrants from Russia" (unpublished University of Toronto Ph.D. dissertion 1952); Walter Mitzka, "Dialektgeographie der Danziger Nehrung," *Ztscht für deutsche Mundarten* XVII (1922) 117-35; idem, *Deutsche Mundarten* (Heidelberg, 1943); idem, "Die deutsche Sprache in Westpreussen," *Staat und Volkstum* (Berlin, 1926) 487-95; idem, *Grundzüge Nordostdeutscher Sprachgeschichte* (Halle-Salle, 1937); idem, *Handbuch zum deutschen Sprachatlas* (Marburg, 1952); idem, "Die Mennoniten in Russland und ihre Beziehungen zu Westpreussen," *Staat und Volkstum* (Berlin, 1926) 471-87; idem, "Niederpreussisch," *Ztscht für deutsche Mundarten* XVI (1921) 151-54; idem, *Sprachausgleich in den deutschen Mundarten bei Danzig* (Königsberger deutsche Forschungen II, Königsberg, 1928); idem, "Die Sprache der deutschen Mennoniten," *Heimatblätter des deutschen Heimatbundes* VIII (Danzig, 1930; also as a reprint 1931); V. Schirmunski, *Die deutschen Kolonien in der Ukraine* (Moscow, 1928); Unruh, *Hintergründe;* E. Wagner, "Ueber die Mundart der Thorner Stadtniederung" (unpublished University of Königsberg doctoral dissertation, 1912); W. Ziesemer, *Die ostpreussischen Mundarten* (Breslau, 1924); Gerhard Wiens, "Russian in Low German," *Menn. Life* XIII (April 1958) 75; J. John Friesen, "Romance of Low German," *Menn. Life* II (April 1947) 22; J. W. Goerzen, "Plautdietsch and English," *Menn. Life* II (April 1947) 22.

Plattner (Basseyrer, Passeier, Peltner), **Hans,** an Anabaptist martyr, a tailor, was beheaded in 1574 at Rotenholz in Tirol in the Inn Valley. "He was . . . conducted forth to the place of execution, where he admonished the people to desist from sin and repent. Then he kneeled down, turning his face to the East, . . . lifted his hands to heaven and poured out an earnest prayer to God his heavenly Father, thanking and praising Him for all the grace and benefits shown him, and that He had made him worthy to suffer for His name. He also prayed for all people who were worthy, that God would put repentance and amendment into their hearts. Finally he commended his spirit into the hands of God, for whose name he was willing to offer up again his life and body (which he had received from Him), and to testify to His truth even to his last drop of blood, as he had promised Him on baptism, and would thus expect to be received of Him into His gracious arms. . . . When he had finished praying, he rose and went boldly toward the executioner, so that neither his face nor his color changed, but he knelt down again so intrepidly, that the executioner was consternated by his valiant praying and undaunted mind, and became afraid to execute him."

Plattner is the author of two hymns: "Ach hilf mich leid und sehnlich klag all Tag" (three stanzas) and "Hilf, Herr, in dieser Not, sieh an die schwere Pein" (13 stanzas). He is also the subject of the hymn: "Hört zu, was wir euch singen thon, ir Gottes hausgenossen" (43 stanzas), an acrostic on the name "Hans Blatner aus Passeir, ein Schneider."

NEFF.

Mart. Mir. D 676, E 993; *Lieder der Hutterischen Brüder* (Scottdale, 1914) 703-7; Wolkan, *Lieder*, 234; Zieglschmid, *Chronik*, 474; Wolkan, *Geschicht-Buch*, 366; Beck, *Geschichts-Bücher*, 266; *ML* III, 377.

Plattner (Plaitner), **Vigilg** (Vigil), an Anabaptist martyr, previously a people's priest in Rattenberg in Tirol, Austria, joined the Anabaptist movement. The severe persecution breaking out in North Tirol made him withdraw to another place. He was probably on his way to Moravia, when he was seized at Schärding. He defied all attempts to convert him, "would not deviate to the right or to the left." Condemned to death, he was beheaded in 1529 at Schärding (at that time in Bavaria). He is the author of a hymn, in which he gives "testimony to God in the truth": "Wach auf, mein Seel, wann es ist an der Zeit" (with 17 stanzas). P.DE.

Zieglschmid, *Chronik*, 64; Beck, *Geschichts-Bücher*, 33; *Mart. Mir.* D 23, E 432; Wolkan, *Geschicht-Buch*, 46; *Lieder der Hutterischen Brüder* (Scottdale, 1914) 45; Wolkan, *Lieder*, 15; *ML* III, 377.

Platzer, Jacob, of Prad in the Vintschgau, Tirol, Austria, an Anabaptist martyr, a locksmith, was seized together with three other Anabaptists, Sier, Mareez, and Rauchenpüchler, on May 6, 1585, by Jost Tausch, called Aichele (*q.v.*), who was hunting down the Anabaptists (see **Lienz**). At his cross-examination he refused to name those who had lodged him. The four men had been sent by the Hutterian Brethren in Moravia to Tirol to visit the Anabaptists there and to win new converts for Moravia. On July 5 Platzer recanted, as the others also did before and after him. He explained that it was not the doctrine, but only the life and conduct of the Anabaptists that attracted him. He enjoyed his freedom for a long time; on June 19, 1591, he was again arrested in the village of Sillian in eastern Tirol, having apparently again adopted Anabaptism. During the eight weeks of his imprisonment he could not be persuaded to recant. He accepted his death sentence "with good cheer"; "he was not at all sorry to have to die for his faith." His steadfast martyrdom is the theme of the hymn, "Ir liebhaber der Warheit guet, lasts euch erzellen mit freiem muet" (with 30 stanzas). P.DE.

Beck, *Geschichts-Bücher*, 308-10; Wolkan, *Geschicht-Buch*, 434; Zieglschmid, *Chronik*, 562; J. N. von Kripp, *Ein Beitrag zur Geschichte der Wiedertäufer in Tirol* (*Das achte Programm des II. Staatsgymnasiums zu Innsbruck*, 1857) 3-60; *Lieder der Hutterischen Brüder* (Scottdale, 1914) 790; J. Loserth, *Der Anabaptismus in Tirol* I and II (Vienna, 1892-93); Wolkan, *Lieder*, 236; *Mart. Mir.* D 779, E 1082; *ML* III, 377 f.

Platzer, Melchior, a Hutterian Brethren martyr, an apothecary, was arrested in Zürich, Switzerland, with Ludwig Dörcker and David Falch in 1574, subjected to a cross-examination, and then released (Bergmann, 46; *Geschicht-Buch*, 367 f.). In 1583 he was seized in the village of Rankweil in Tirol, Austria, and taken to Feldkirchen, where he was put into the tower of the castle. He was again cross-examined. A priest was summoned from Bregenz to convert him, and hoped to gain honor and fame by this colloquy. But when he was soon defeated he said, "Did the devil bring me here and deceive me with this Anabaptist?" It was hoped that Lutheran clergymen would have better suc-

cess. But they too failed. Thereupon Platzer was accused of being a misleader of the people. In 1581-82 he had been very active in the Bregenz Forest (*q.v.*) area, converting many persons and persuading them to emigrate to Moravia (*q.v.*). The government required that he render an oath in order to be released; he could then go where he had come from. But he refused. He was then returned to Rankweil and there beheaded and burned on Nov. 6, 1583. At the site of execution he admonished the people, who showed great sympathy for him; he urged them to repentance and warned them of the false prophets who were misleading them. He is the author of the hymn, "Hörent jhr Kinder Gottes rein, was wir euch wellen singen." NEFF.

Cornelius Bergmann, *Die Täuferbewegung im Kanton Zürich* (Leipzig, 1916); *Mart. Mir.* D 751, E 1058; Wolkan, *Geschicht-Buch*, 367 f., 413-15, 435; Zieglschmid, *Chronik*, 477, 533 ff.; Beck, *Geschichts-Bücher*, 283; *Lieder der Hutterischen Brüder* (Scottdale, 1914) 756; Wolkan, *Lieder*, 235; *ML* III, 378.

Plauschwarren, a village in East Prussia, formerly German, now Russian, where Mennonites from West Prussia settled in the 18th century. They founded the Lithuanian congregation about 1758 (usually called Memel-Niederung, *q.v.*, after 1918) near Tilsit (*q.v.*), membership 233 in 1774, and 239 in 1788, and built a church at Plauschwarren in 1767. In 1831 this meetinghouse was abandoned and a new meetinghouse was built at Adlig-Pokraken, then the center of the congregation. The old meetinghouse of Plauschwarren was remodeled in 1884 and used again until 1897, when it was sold. vDZ.

Herbert Wiebe, *Das Siedlungswerk der westpreussischen Mennoniten* (Marburg a.d. Lahn, 1952) 44 f.

Pleasant Grove Mennonite Church (MC), Brewton, Ala., a mission congregation established in 1949 under the Lancaster Conference, had a membership of 10 in 1957. M.G.

Pleasant Grove Mennonite Church (MC), Salix, Pa., had 27 members in 1958. Norman Teague was its licensed minister. It was started in 1900 in an abandoned Lutheran church near Elton by L. A. Blough, organized as a congregation the same year, erected a new meetinghouse in 1910 remodeled in 1940. M.G.

Pleasant Grove Conservative Mennonite Church, located 5 miles southeast of Goshen, Ind., was built in 1948 as a branch of the Townline and Griner churches. The first services were held here Aug. 15, 1948. Services were held in all three of the churches every Sunday, the ministers alternating between the three churches. In 1956 the congregations organized separately. The membership of the Pleasant Grove congregation at that time was 260, with Clarence A. Yoder (ordained in 1948, as bishop 1950), Menno S. Schrock (transferred from O.O.A.), and Edwin J. Knepp (ordained in 1954).

In 1954 the Bethel Church was built 4 miles northeast of Nappanee, and a congregation was organized as a branch of the Pleasant Grove congregation with Homer Miller as bishop; in 1957 it had 85 members, while Pleasant Grove had 240. S.T.E.

Pleasant Grove Mennonite Church (MC), located in Pendleton County, W. Va., is a member of the Northern District of the Virginia Conference. Services were first held at this place in an old tannery and in near-by schoolhouses beginning about 1885, under the leadership of bishops John Geil and Abraham Shank. In 1903 a frame church was built, which still serves the congregation. Until this time the ministry was supplied from Rockingham County, Va. The membership in 1956 was 54, and the pastor Lloyd O. Hartzler, who was ordained in 1945. T.S.

Pleasant Grove Mennonite Church (MC), now abandoned, was erected in 1900 about 3 miles southwest of Martinsburg, Blair Co., Pa., as a branch of the Martinsburg (*q.v.*) congregation, having their worship together on alternate Sundays. Pleasant Grove was abandoned in 1945, and since that date all services are held in the Martinsburg church, only a beautifully kept cemetery near by remaining. A.KA.

Pleasant Hill Amish Mennonite (MC) Church, now extinct, located near O'Neill, Neb., was listed in the Mennonite *Family Almanac* in 1892 for the first time under the name "Slocum," which was used interchangeably with "Holt" until 1922 when it was listed as the Pleasant Hill congregation, with 23 members. It was last listed in 1944, with one member. In 1905 it had had 40 members with Christian Ernst as minister. It reached its highest membership, 51, around 1916. M.G.

Pleasant Hill Mennonite Church (MC), earlier known as the Pleasant Hill Rural Mission, a member of the Illinois Conference, and located about 4 miles northwest of Morton, and 5 miles southeast of Peoria, Ill., was organized as a congregation on March 8, 1924. In 1958 it had a membership of 91, with Wayne King as pastor. R.D.R.

Harry F. Weber, *Centennial History of the Mennonites of Illinois* (Goshen, 1931) 314 f.

Pleasant Hill Mennonite (MC) Church, now extinct, located in Fairfield County, Ohio, a member of the Ohio and Eastern Conference, was founded in the early 1800's by settlers from Rockingham County, Va. The first settler (1799), Martin Landis, Sr., built a log meetinghouse at an early date. Henry Stemen (*q.v.*), who came in 1803, was ordained minister and later bishop and served the congregation until 1841, when he moved to Allen County, Ohio. In the early years the congregation built a meetinghouse on the farm of Henry Brenneman, father of John M. and George (bishops), Daniel (preacher), and Henry (deacon) Brenneman. Nearly the entire membership moved away from the "Fairfield County hills" to land better suited for farming. The church building was moved across the road just north of the Pleasant Hill cemetery. Later it was sold and the proceeds used to fence the now badly neglected cemetery. J.S.U.

John Umble, "Extinct Ohio Mennonite Churches," *MQR* VI (1932) 5-29.

Pleasant Hill Mennonite Church (MC), located in Milton Twp., Wayne Co., Ohio, is a member of the Ohio and Eastern Mennonite Conference. The original meetinghouse was built in 1880 as one of the two meeting places of the Oak Grove congregation, remodeled in 1910 and again in 1950. (For the history of this congregation before 1947 and the names of its ministers, see **Oak Grove** Mennonite Church.) The present congregation was organized in 1947 as a schism from the Oak Grove congregation when the latter withdrew from the conference. The ministers since 1947 were Wm. G. Detweiler 1947-52, Gerald C. Studer 1947- . The membership in 1957 was 180. In 1959 it built a new meetinghouse at the edge of the town of Smithville. G.C.S.

Pleasant Retreat, a mission station of the Lancaster (MC) Conference, was opened in West Cocalico Twp., Lancaster Co., Pa., 3 miles east of Cocalico in 1928. For 15 months Sunday school was held in the afternoon every two weeks, followed by preaching, but in 1931 the work was combined with Cocalico. I.D.L.

Pleasant Ridge Mennonite Church (MC), erected in 1882 in Vermilion Twp., Ashland Co., Ohio, replaced an earlier Mennonite church built (probably c1840) on land donated as a public burying ground by John Beutler, a Palatine immigrant. Soon after 1830, the ordained men here were Peter Beutler and John Risser (*q.v.*), immigrants from the Bavarian Palatinate, John Nusbaum, Isaac Kilmer, and either John or Christian Kauffman, probably a deacon. Bishop Jacob Nold of Columbiana County, Ohio, ordained Isaac Kilmer as bishop. Internal dissension, incompetent leadership, financial reverses, and defection to the River Brethren (Brethren in Christ) contributed to the early dissolution of the congregation. Before 1860 the Beutlers moved to Mahaska County, Iowa; the Kilmers, first to Crawford County, Ohio, and then to Elkhart County, Ind.; John Nusbaum and many others also to Elkhart County. The few remaining members joined with the small number of survivors of the Salemskirche (*q.v.*, GCM) and their Lutheran and Reformed neighbors to found the prosperous Stone Lutheran Church five miles south of Ashland. J.S.U.

John Umble, "Extinct Ohio Mennonite Churches," *MQR* XIX (1945) 227-37; Melvin Gingerich, *Mennonites in Iowa* (Iowa City, 1939) 138-45.

Pleasant Valley Amish Mennonite Church, Yoncalla, Ore., a Sleeping Preacher (*q.v.*) church, which broke away from the Harrisburg (Ore.) congregation. Roy J. Headings was bishop of its 23 members in 1957. Before 1953 it was called Roseburg (*q.v.*). M.G.

Pleasant Valley Church of God in Christ Mennonite Church, Ordway, Col., is located 1¼ miles northeast of Crowley. In 1958 it had 34 members with deacon D. J. H. Schmidt in charge. M.G.

Pleasant Valley Mennonite Church (MC), now extinct: see **DeKalb County, Ind.**

Pleasant Valley Mennonite Church (MC), sometimes known as Sandtown, located 8 miles south of Iowa City, Iowa, and 2½ miles southeast of Hills, was organized as a congregation July 23, 1956. In 1948 the East Union and Lower Deer Creek congregations began a rural mission in the area, using an abandoned Methodist church, which is still used as a meetinghouse. The membership in 1958 was 20. Herman J. Smucker was pastor of the church.

H.J.Sm.

Pleasant Valley Mennonite Church (GCM), located at Kismet, Kan., was organized by Mennonite families coming from eastern Kansas at the beginning of the century. The first report of the congregation, under the name Schöntal Mennonite Church, appeared in the Western District Conference minutes of 1915. In 1930 P. B. Kopper was listed as leader, and the membership was 48. In 1957 the minister was Harold H. Jantzen, and the membership 38.

C.K.

Pleasant Valley Mennonite Church (MC), located in Harper Co., Kan., a member of the South Central Conference, was organized in 1888 with 15 charter members. The first meetinghouse, a frame structure, was built in 1897. The present meetinghouse was built in 1915. The first minister was Jacob Holderman. R. M. Weaver became pastor in 1907 and served the congregation for 39 years. Other ministers who have served the congregation are Andrew Good, Ephraim Shellenberger, Simon Hetrick, George Hinkle, Ben Horst, Noah Ebersole, J. P. Berkey, H. J. King, John Thut, Stephen A. Yoder, Wilbert Nafziger, and Waldo Miller (present pastor). B. F. Hamilton, S. C. Miller, T. M. Erb, David D. Miller, Milo Kauffman, and Gideon G. Yoder served the congregation as bishops. The membership, most of which is rural, was 188 in 1957.

G.G.Y.

Pleasant View Amish Mennonite Church, now extinct, Holden, Mo.: see **Johnson County, Mo.**

Pleasant View Amish Mennonite Church, located near Berlin, Holmes Co., Ohio, a member of the Conservative Mennonite Conference, was organized in May 1912 with about 20 members under the leadership of Bishop John B. Zook. Ministers who have served the church are P. V. Yoder and Dan Miller. Ministers who have been ordained by this church are John Swartzendruber, Joe Schlabach, Abe J. Schlabach, M. J. Swartzendruber, and Harry Stutzman. In 1933 there was a split in the church and the congregation began again with 21 members. In 1945 the congregation organized another worship service in Wayne Co., Ohio, north of Tragy Station on U.S. 30. In 1955 the combined membership of the two groups was 250, with Bishop Harry Stutzman and ministers Moses M. Miller, David L. Stutzman, and Andrew Stutzman in charge. HA.S.

Pleasant View Beachy Amish Mennonite Church, Hartville, Ohio, was organized in June 1947. It had 132 members in 1957, with Samuel J. Otto as bishop (ord. 1948).

M.G.

Pleasant View Church of God in Christ Mennonite Church is located on the northeast edge of Goltry, Alfalfa Co., Okla. The first members settled here in 1900. The congregation was organized in 1905, using a district school for a place of worship until 1935, when the present church was built. In the early years the church was served by ministers from Kansas. A Sunday school was organized in 1923, and a sewing circle in 1940. The majority of the members are farmers and industrial workers. In 1958 Reuben J. Koehn and Leroy Wedel were the ministers, with a membership of 45.

R.J.K.

Pleasant View Mennonite Church (MC), located 4 miles north and ¾ mile west of Goshen, Ind., was established in 1936 as a mission Sunday school by the Prairie Street Mennonite Church. In 1958 it had a membership of 153, with John S. Steiner serving as bishop.

J.S.S.

Pleasant View Mennonite Church (GCM), located near Aurora, Neb., was organized in 1886 under Christian Rediger and again in 1892 as the "German Mennonite Church," one of the twelve charter member congregations of the Central Conference of Mennonites. Ministers who have served the congregation were Andrew Oesch, Jacob Donner, George Donner, Eugene Augspurger, Edwin Gossen, and Herbert Roszhart. The membership in 1957 was 161, with Leo D. Thomas as pastor. The original church built in 1886-87 was remodeled in 1949.

H.Ro.

Pleasant View Mennonite (MC) Church, North Lawrence, Ohio, dates back to 1837, when a group of 36 from Farmersville, Lancaster Co., Pa., settled in the vicinity, arriving there after fifteen days of travel by Conestoga wagons and buggies. Family names included Horst, Eschliman, Dague, Doll, Shisler, Oberlin, Hartel, Keffer, and Buchwalter. The land was homesteaded in 1811 and some of the old deeds, still preserved, bear the signature of President James Madison. The first church building was erected in 1856. Ministers who have served the church in order of succession are Henry Martin, Jr., and Benjamin Horst (ordained 1857), Michael Horst (1877), I. J. Buchwalter (1893), Alva Wengard (1935), Elmer E. Yoder (1952), and David E. Hostetler (1953). In 1956 the membership was 91, with Elmer E. Yoder as minister. D.E.H.

Pleasant View Mennonite Church (MC), located 9 miles southwest of Hydro, Okla., a member of the South Central Conference, began in 1896-97, when the B. B. Miller family came from Kansas and the W. C. Lantz family from Indiana. The congregation was organized by Bishop Joseph Schlegel of Milford, Neb., in 1898. In 1900 another Joseph Schlegel, who lived in Lyon County, Kan., became its bishop. In 1906 he settled on the quarter of land where the church is located, and served until 1914. In 1902 a meetinghouse was built, 8½ miles southeast of Thomas, across the road from the cemetery, which is now used by the Old Order Amish. In 1915 the old church was replaced by a larger one and the present structure was built in 1924-25. In 1906, in order to locate it more centrally, the meetinghouse was moved 2½ miles east and 2 miles south. About one fourth of the members, past and present, came from non-Mennonite homes.

The ministers in charge of the congregation of 130 members in 1956 were John Slagell, pastor, and Alva Swartzendruber, bishop.   J.S.

Pleasant View Mennonite Church (MC), located 2½ miles west of Chambersburg, Franklin Co., Pa., is a member of the Washington Co., Md., and Franklin Co., Pa., Conference. The church was built in the summer of 1909 by members of the Marion and Chambersburg congregation and was dedicated on Aug. 15, 1909. Ministers serving this congregation have been George W. Ernst 1909-52, Walter H. Lehman 1929- , and John B. Sollenberger 1949- . The membership was about 35 in 1909, and 104 in 1958.   W.H.L.

Pleasant View Mennonite Church (MC), Schellsburg, Pa., a member of the Allegheny Conference, had a membership of 29 in 1957. Aldus Wingard was bishop and Charles R. Shetler minister. It was started by settlers from the Johnstown region in 1872, but no meetinghouse was erected until 1910. The congregation was organized fully in 1914.   H.S.B.

Pleasant View Old Order (Wisler) Mennonite Church, located in Mahoning County, Ohio, is a congregation of about 80 members. In 1872 preacher Samuel Good (1810-83) and deacons David Weaver (1819-90) and Christian Lehman (1832-1912) with about 16 families withdrew from the Columbiana-Mahoning congregation with Bishop Jacob Wisler. Local issues which precipitated the division were the use of the English language in preaching, elevation of the pulpit and ceiling in the new Oberholtzer meetinghouse, and funeral customs. This group used the three meetinghouses of the Columbiana-Mahoning congregation in 1872-98. The Columbiana-Mahoning (MC) congregation held three services a month, alternating between the Oberholtzer church at Columbiana, the Nold church at Leetonia, and the Metzler church at North Lima. The Wisler group used one of the two churches which were vacant. In 1897 a meetinghouse, still used, was erected west of the present Midway church. The congregation was organized with 40 charter members in 1898. Ministers who have served are Samuel Good (1810-83), Jacob Tyson (1850-1914), who moved from Wood County, Ohio, Jacob L. Weaver (1846-1921), Harvey Horst, and Abraham Brubaker. In 1957 the ministers were Daniel C. Witmer, Israel Snyder, and David Weaver, with a membership of 85.   W.D.S.

Pleasantview Home for the Aged, at Kalona, Iowa, a 46-room home built and operated by the Mennonite Benevolent Association consisting of 33 members representing the Mennonite, Conservative Mennonite, and Beachy Amish congregations of the community. It was built in 1957-58 at an approximate cost of $250,000, and was opened for service on April 14, 1958.   E.G.S.

Pleasantview Mennonite (MC) Church, near Brethren, Manistee Co., Mich., had its origin in 1903, when William Lantz, the first Mennonite to locate in the area, settled here. Other settlers followed, mostly from the Howard-Miami Amish Mennonite

(now MC) congregation near Kokomo, Ind. E. A. Mast, bishop of the Howard-Miami congregation, organized the Manistee Amish Mennonites into the Pleasantview congregation on Sept. 9, 1904. Included among the first members was Joseph S. Horner (1864-1945), a preacher. The new congregation in Manistee County worshiped in a log cabin until 1906, when a church building was erected in Brown Township. Four years later, in December 1910, Horner moved back to his home congregation, Howard-Miami. At about that point the membership was 48. But soon a decline set in as families moved away. Finally only one family remained. In 1917 the church building was sold to the Church of the Brethren, only to revert later to Mennonite ownership. Two years later, in May 1919, C. C. Culp was placed in the Pleasantview congregation by the district mission board to serve as pastor and mission worker. He served there until his death in 1953. Lester Wyse also served as a minister in the congregation for a number of years until his removal to Ohio. In 1957 the minister was Warren Shaum, with a baptized membership of 30. The congregation is not independently organized but is under the sponsorship of the mission board. J.C.W.

Plempsche Doopsgezinden, or **Plempsche gemeente** (congregation), nickname of the Old Frisian Mennonite congregation at Hoorn (*q.v.*), Holland, "de Plemp" being the name of a house in which this congregation held its meetings. Because of the fanaticism of the elder Pieter Jans Twisck, Jr., this group, then numbering 30 members, had separated from the Frisian congregation in 1690. Its members merged with the main body in 1723. (*Inv. Arch. Amst.* II, 2, Nos. 111-13; *DB* 1867, 78-90.)   vDZ.

Plener, Philipp (also called *Blauärmel,* blue sleeves being the sign of the dyers' craft, or *Weber,* i.e., weaver for his profession), the leader of an early Anabaptist group in 1527-35. His birthplace is not known; in some records he is called Philipp of Strasbourg, in others "of Bruchsal," indicating, however, the places of early activity rather than his birthplace. Gustav Bossert Jr. assumes that he comes from Zaisersweiher near Bruchsal, Baden, Germany, and that his real name was Loyer, Layer, or Löwe (*TA*, 52). W. Wiswedel follows this conjecture; but it is hard to see how Plener and Loyer could coincide. In any case, he was won for Anabaptism by 1526 or early 1527, most likely in Strasbourg. He then concentrated his work in and around Bruchsal in the Kraichgau, where he won and baptized Blasius [or Blasy] Kuhn (*q.v.*), who later became his most loyal and effective co-worker, Hans Gentner (*q.v.*), who later was an important link with the Hutterites, and a great number of others. In 1530/1 the Bruchsal congregation was said to have numbered about 500, Julius Lober (*q.v.*) being their minister for a time. Plener moved on. For two months in 1527 he lived in Augsburg in the home of the widow of Hans Leupold (*q.v.*), the martyred Anabaptist leader; he worked in and around Augsburg with Jörg Schachner of Munich. Persecution drove him on to Moravia, where he at first worked hand in hand with Gabriel Ascherham (q.v.) at Rossitz (1527). As the group grew by newly arriving Anabaptists from the Palatinate, Hesse, Swabia, and Baden, all seeking a safe refuge in Moravia, Plener moved on to Auspitz on grounds belonging to the Abbess of Maria Saal (Brno). In 1529 the principle of community of goods was established, most likely at first for economic reasons rather than Christian principles. From now on the brethren lived in Bruderhof communities. In 1531 Blasy Kuhn brought the remnants of the Bruchsal congregation also to Moravia, swelling the Auspitz group to (allegedly) a total of 2,000 souls.

There were now three Anabaptist groups in Moravia practicing community of goods: the Gabrielites (mostly Silesians) in Rossitz, led by Gabriel Ascherham and his assistant Peter Hueter, who in 1537 joined the Hutterite group; the Philippites (mostly Southwest Germans from Swabia, Baden, and the Palatinate) in Auspitz with Philipp Plener as leader and Blasy Kuhn as his assistant; and third the Tyroleans, also in Auspitz, under the leadership of Sigmund Schützinger (q.v.), and later Jakob Hutter. In 1531 these three groups loosely fused, with Ascherham as their bishop. To be sure there were other Anabaptist groups in Moravia, living on private property; they were collectively called the "Swiss Brethren." When, in 1533, Jakob Hutter came to Moravia, rivalries soon developed. It appears that no principles of Christian living were involved; it was rather a question of leadership, perhaps one could better say of "charismatic leadership." No doubt Hutter was spiritually superior to all the others involved, a true leader in the prophetic sense of the word. Since, however, neither Schützinger, Ascherham, nor Plener was willing to step back, sad and unpleasant conflicts arose. Schützinger was eliminated from the Tyrolean group, which thus became "Hutterite" in the later sense of the term. Ascherham became the exclusive leader of the Gabrielites at Rossitz; after his death in Silesia most of them united with the Hutterites. Plener now became the leader of the Philippite Brethren in Auspitz—supposedly a total of 400—at least for the short yet significant years 1533-35.

Then in 1535 intermittent persecutions began also in Moravia. Ascherham and his group emigrated to Silesia. The Hutterites tried to stay on, in spite of great privations and misery (Jakob Hutter returned to Tirol and was martyred there in 1536; Hans Amon became the new bishop). Concerning the Philippites the only information extant is what the Hutterite chronicles report, understandably in not too sympathetic terms. The Abbess had driven them away from Auspitz, and they camped somewhere in the open, deeply discouraged. Plener and his assistant Blasy Kuhn went on horseback hither and thither to find other places to settle. As they were unable to find anything, they told the crowd (Wolkan, *Geschicht-Buch*, 109) that everyone should look out for himself as best as he could.

With these few remarks both Plener and Kuhn disappear from the records; that is, the Hutterites had no further information about them. Certain Philippite brethren stayed on and later joined the
14

Hutterites (1538/9); the majority, however, returned to Germany; for their history, see **Philippites**. Since the later trial records of this group contain no complaints concerning Plener's behavior, it is apparent that he did not really abandon his flock, even though no document reveals his later fate. Since there were Philippite Brethren in many parts of Western Germany until the mid 1540's, it may be rightly conjectured that Plener returned to Württemberg (or Baden) with a group, but that he died or was martyred soon afterward. In 1539 Peter Riedemann (q.v.) had talks with these brethren in Heilbronn, but nothing was recorded about Plener.

Concerning his teachings and spiritual leadership the chief source is Hege's report on the early days of Bruchsal. To be sure, some main ideas of the brotherhood are known, but it cannot be said with certainty whether they were ideas of Plener himself or of some of his co-workers at Auspitz. In any case, the principle of community of goods was observed by the Philippites both in Moravia and in Upper Austria, but was abandoned by the West German groups. Thus it was not too hard for the two first-named groups to join the Hutterites several years later, while the others, the Southwest German groups, being leaderless, joined the Swiss Brethren in their respective areas in the 1540's.

R.F.

TA Württemberg, 52; Beck, *Geschichtsbücher*; Wolkan, *Geschicht-Buch*; Zieglschmid, *Chronik*; Chr. Hege, *Täufer in der Kurpfalz* (Frankfurt, 1908) 60 ff.; Wiswedel, *Bilder* III, 146-49; *ML* III, 378.

Pleshanovo (Neu-Samara), a Mennonite settlement in the Luxemburg district of the province of Samara, South Russia, was founded by the Molotschna settlement in 1890. The settlement covered an area of 96,376 acres and included 14 villages and 9 separate farms, with a Mennonite population of 3,670. In 1917 the settlements organized a volost, whereas up to that time they had belonged to Bashkir and Russian volosts. The settlement suffered less during the Revolution than some of the other Mennonite settlements. During the civil war the front passed over the settlement several times, but aside from the much requisitioning and occasional plundering did relatively little damage. In 1919-20 the Pleshanovo and Orenburg (q.v.) settlements were incorporated into the newly established Bashkir republic. The Bashkirs, an Asiatic Mohammedan race on a culturally inferior plane, had difficulty in adapting themselves to the role of ruler of the relatively wealthy Mennonites.

The Tok-Churan province, to which the two Mennonite settlements belonged, moved its seat from the Bashkir villages into the Pleshanovo settlement, beginning for the Mennonites a period of requisitioning and oppression; for since the Bashkirs owned practically nothing, they had to depend on the Mennonite farms for everything. Even the obligation of the settlers to transport the innumerable petty officials of the clumsy government organization meant a heavy burden, so much the more serious because the crop failures of 1920-21 made it difficult to feed the horses adequately. The employees of the province and the army had to be supported by the settlements. At the end of 1921 a Mennonite delegation in Moscow managed to have the Mennonite settlements separated from the Bashkirs and attached to the Russian regional government.

Pleshanovo had three steam-driven mills, two of which were ruined during the Revolution (1917); there were no funds available for repairing them. A large Mennonite water mill on the Tok filled the needs of the settlement for a time.

In 1905 a post office was built in Pleshanovo, and in 1907 a Mennonite hospital was founded by G. G. Voth; it passed into the hands of the district, and was enlarged in 1912. The school (a three-class Zentralschule) was built at Lugovsk in 1908.

Mennonite villages in the Pleshanovo settlement were: Krassikov with 221 souls on 45 farms with 4,860 acres of land; Podolysk with 263 persons on 47 farms with 5,000 acres and a steam mill; Lugovsk with 64 families, 305 persons, on 31 farms with 3,248 acres; Pleshanovo with 49 families, 258 persons, on 22 farms with 4,700 acres, with a post office, a Mennonite church, a Mennonite co-operative, and a hospital; Donskaya with 58 families, 298 persons, on 45 farms with 4,860 acres; Bogomazov with 65 families, 284 persons, on 34 farms with 3,672 acres; Annenskoye with 93 persons on 15 farms with 2,025 acres; Ishalka with 38 families, 212 persons, on 22 farms, 2,700 acres; Klinok with 246 persons on 44 farms, 4,700 acres; Yugovka with 175 persons on 35 farms with 3,780 acres; Kaltan with 251 persons on 45 farms with 4,860 acres; Kuterlya with 195 persons on 40 farms with 4,320 acres.

According to Ehrt the settlement had a population of 3,071 in 1926. After the Revolution many were exiled but the settlement was not completely disrupted during World War II as was the case with most of the European Mennonite settlements, and as erroneously stated in the article **Neu-Samara**. Numerous communications published in the Mennonite papers indicate that the settlement has continued some activity, although on a different level. Regular reporters have been Jacob and Anna Wiens. They state that many of the homes have been changed considerably. The traditional barns and sheds have been removed and the dwelling places have been altered to accommodate more families. Between the villages of Bogomazov and Dolinsk an electric power station has been erected for the industrial centers and the surrounding villages. A large carpenter shop, sawmill, blacksmith shop, flour mill, secondary school, hospital, clubhouse, garage, and barns and sheds for cattle, horses, and poultry as well as grain bins have been established. All the five sons of the Wienses served in the Russian army during the war and three of them did not return. Another report states that the churches of Lugovsk and Donskoye are being used as schools. The Donskoye collective farm planted an orchard of 32,123 acres.

Regarding the religious life recent letters have also given encouraging information. Wilhelm Sawatsky, a minister of Lugovsk, celebrated his golden wedding anniversary, for which occasion many people came. In both the afternoon and the evening three ministers preached. Another minister

named in the letter is Peter Engebrecht. Even in 1949 religious funeral services were conducted. All the old ministers are gone, but young ones have taken their place, and revival meetings and baptismal services are common occurrences. Greater religious freedom prevails in the settlement since the death of Stalin. (See **Neu-Samara**, which this article corrects and supplements.)   J.Q., C.K.

Der Bote, June 27, 1956, 7; July 25, 1956, 7; March 19, 1958, 4; *Menn. Rundschau*, Aug. 10, 1955, 2; June 6, 1956, 11; June 13, 1956, 2; Adolf Ehrt, *Das Mennonitentum in Russland* (Berlin, 1932) 152; *ML* III, 378 f.

Pleshanovo (Neu-Samara) **Mennonite Church**, Samara, Russia, was established in 1891, the early days of the Pleshanovo settlement (*q.v.*). In 1905 the baptized membership numbered 1,034, and the total number of souls was 2,689. The elder at that time was Daniel Boschmann, assisted by Johann Isaak, Peter Stobbe, Heinrich Peters, David Warkentin, Heinrich Unruh, and Johann Braun. The church was located in the village of Pleshanovo.

The settlers, in distinction from the "Old Samara" settlement, came from the Molotschna settlement and not directly from Prussia. Contact with other settlements was lively. The Revolution disrupted the economic and religious life, but gradually an adjustment took place and religious activities were resumed. *Unser Blatt* reported regularly in 1925-28 on song festivals and other activities of the church. In 1926 there was a song festival and a course for choir directors in Lugovsk in which nine choirs and 200 singers participated. In 1927 ministers from the settlements conducted a Bible study conference in the villages of Pleshanovo. The Mennonite settlement did not disintegrate during World War II as stated in the article **Neu-Samara**, but is still in existence although great changes have taken place. Few of the old ministers have remained but young ones have taken their place. Revival meetings and baptismal services have been common occurrences since the death of Stalin. Ministers named in letters include Wilhelm Sawatsky of Lugovsk and Peter Engebrecht.   C.K.

H. Dirks, *Statistik*, 1905, 32, 64; Friesen, *Brüderschaft*, 717; *Unser Blatt* I, 176; II, 112, 275; III, 168.

Pletscher (Plätscher), a Mennonite family of Swiss descent, living since the last decades of the 17th century in the Palatinate, Germany. Jakob Plätscher was a preacher at Immelhausen (*q.v.*) in Baden from 1761, and Heinrich Plätscher a preacher at Eppstein (*q.v.*) near Frankenthal from 1764, both serving until after 1802. This Heinrich Plätscher was married to Katharina Brenneman; they lived at Friedelsheim. Their son Johannes with his family emigrated from Friedelsheim to the United States in 1833. Other relatives moved from Friedelsheim to America in 1841-55. The martyrs Jacob and Melchior Platzer (*q.v.*) may have belonged to this family. A Pletscher family migrated from Schleitheim (*q.v.*) to the Palatinate *c*1650.   vDZ.

Dutch *Naamlijst*; *MQR* XXX (1956) 142, No. 28; 146 f., No. 38; 147, Nos. 39-41; 151, No. 50.

Plett, Gerhard (1860-1933), elder of several congregations in the Molotschna, Taurida, Russia, was born at Hierschau, Molotschna, in 1860. In 1882 he was married to Elizabeth Klassen, and in 1892 to Katharina Willms. The family consisted of three sons and six daughters. He supplemented his elementary education by evening instruction from the local teacher and later by extensive reading and private study, and then served for several years as a teacher, first in a village of the Crimea, then at Sparrau in the Molotschna. Then he took over a farm at Hierschau. In 1899 Plett became the minister of the Margenau congregation, in 1908 its elder, in 1909 elder of the newly formed Landskrone congregation, and in 1910 elder of the Alexanderwohl congregation. Before becoming minister Plett served for several years as district (*Volost*) judge at the Gnadenfeld office and later for many years as a member of the Molotschna Church Council (*Kirchenkonvent*) and the Molotschna School Board (*Schulrat*). Gerhard Plett was arrested in 1919 and spent some time in prison; in 1931 he was driven from his home and, broken in health, led the life of a fugitive until his death in April 1933. Devotion to duty and sound judgment were outstanding features of his character.   H.G.

Pleun(is): see **Plonius.**

Pleun (Pleunis), official name, Ampleunis van den Hoevele (Huevele), an Anabaptist martyr, burned at the stake at Antwerp, Belgium, on Oct. 22, 1551 (not Oct. 2, as is stated in van Braght's *Martyrs' Mirror*). Peter Bruynen, Jan de Oude Kleerkoper, Martin du Petitz, and Jacob Peeters suffered martyrdom with him. Pleun was a linen weaver, born at Kortrijk (Courtrai) in Flanders. These martyrs have been commemorated in the hymn "Tot lof des vaders, soons, heyligen geest" (To the praise of the Father, Son, and Holy Ghost), found in *Offer des Heeren* and also in the *Ausbund* (No. 10); and the hymn "Ic sal met vruechden singen een Liet" (With joy I will sing a song), found in *Lietboecxken* (No. 5), was written in memory of Pleun, Peter, and Jan.   vDZ.

Offer, 177, note 1, 184 ff., 521 ff.; *Mart. Mir.* D 128, E 524; *Antw. Arch.-Blad* VIII, 405, 415; XIV, 20 f., No. 210; *Bibliographie* II, 756, No. 631; *DB* 1899, 83, 154; Wolkan, *Lieder,* 61, 66, 127; *ML* III, 379.

Pleuntgen van der Goes (Apollonia Lonts Jansdochter), an Anabaptist martyr from Goes, Dutch province of Zeeland, was drowned in a tub on March 19, 1559, in the Antwerp prison called the "Steen," together with Naentgen, a leather merchant, and the midwife Fransken, because they persisted in their faith. They are celebrated in the hymn "Aenhoort Godt, hemelsche Vader" (Hear, O God, heavenly Father), found in the *Lietboexken*. Further particulars about Pleuntgen are lacking. K.V., vDZ.

Offer, 566; *Mart. Mir.* D 244, E 618; *Antw. Arch.-Blad* VIII, 460, 472; XIV, 26 f., No. 283; Wolkan, *Lieder,* 63, 72; *ML* II, 133.

Plockhoy (Ploquoy, Pluckoy, Plokhoy, Pluquooij), a Mennonite family found in the Netherlands, probably emigrants from Flanders, Belgium. Pieter Cornelis Plockoy (*q.v.*) belonged to a branch of this family formerly living at Zierikee (*q.v.*). During the 17th and early 18th centuries a number of Plockhoys were living in Amsterdam as members of the Lamist (*q.v.*) Mennonite congregation.   vDZ.

Plockhoy, Pieter Cornelisz (1620?-1700?). *The Netherlands.* Living in the "Golden Age" of Dutch political independence and cultural achievement, Plockhoy came to Amsterdam from the city of Zierikzee in Zeeland, as did also Galenus Abrahamsz de Haan, the noted physician and minister of the Amsterdam Mennonite Church. These two men were both influenced by the Collegiant movement and were associated in bringing into the Amsterdam Church Collegiant ideas, which caused much dissension and eventually divided the church into the Lamists and Zonists. Plockhoy was also associated with a radical Collegiant group of poets in Amsterdam known as the Reformateurs. In the light of his Collegiant connections he has little significance in the history of thoroughgoing Mennonitism except as a by-product of the transitory period of the Amsterdam congregation in 1650-64.

England. In Puritan England Plockhoy has more significance as a religious and social reformer during the late months of the Cromwell government. He published various editions of the following two tracts dated 1659:

1. *The Way to the Peace and Settlement of these Nations fully discovered* . . . published the letters that he had submitted to the Cromwell government in his attempt to reform in the area of the state church by supplanting it with all-embracing interdenominational assemblies based on principles of freedom, discussion, and toleration, all of which were typical Collegiant ideas. His attempt at reform on such a big scale had little chance for success.

2. *A Way Propounded to Make the Poor in these and other Nations Happy* . . . comprised an alternative scheme with more practicality as a solution to the immediate socio-economic needs of the day. It was a plan for co-operative settlements with communitarian production and consumption. Although colonies were actually begun in London, Southampton, and Ireland, and others were projected for locations in the Isles and even on the Continent, the Restoration of Charles II in 1660 put an end to these and other reform movements of the English revolutionary period. There is some evidence that in England Plockhoy had connections with other radical reformers of this period: Levellers Giles Calvert and William Walwyn; utopian, Samuel Hartlib; and possibly the poet-statesman, John Milton.

Colonial America. Plockhoy's determination to establish communitarian settlements culminated in the planting of a colony of Dutch emigrants along the Delaware in New Netherland in 1663, following a long series of negotiations with the Amsterdam burgomasters begun in 1661. In addition to the two English tracts mentioned above, there are also extant a third and fourth published in the Netherlands in 1662 and coming out of the negotiations in Amsterdam:

3. *Kort Verhael van Nieuw Nederlant* . . . (Brief Account of New Netherlands) published the seven anonymous letters which Plockhoy and his com-

pany submitted to the burgomasters in petition for a colonization contract.

4. *Kort en Klaer Ontwerp* (Brief and Concise Plan) bears Plockhoy's signature and was the actual colonization prospectus which he published to enlist emigrants for his settlement. According to a separate document, a group of twenty-five "Mennists" had already been enlisted and promised financial support by the Amsterdam government. The identity of these Mennonites has never been established, and the colony was not itself a Mennonite colony in the usual sense.

A settlement of 41 persons was made in America in 1663 at Horekill on the Delaware, but was destroyed after a brief year of existence in the Anglo-Dutch war of 1664. Plockhoy's active career apparently came to an abrupt end, due in part no doubt to the fact that he became blind. Although he and his wife continued to reside in the neighborhood of Lewes, Del., under English rule for thirty years, they finally sought and found refuge in the new Mennonite settlement at Germantown, Pa., where they lived as public charges for their last six or more years (1694-1700).   L.HA.

H. P. Quack, *De Socialisten* (1899) I, 186-207; Leland Harder and Marvin Harder, *Plockhoy from Zurik-zee* (Newton, 1952); Leland Harder, "Pioneer of Christian Civilization in America," *Menn. Life* IV (January 1949); *idem,* "Plockhoy and His Settlement at Zwaanendael, 1663," *MQR* XXIII (1949) 186-99; Irvin B. Horst, "Pieter Cornelisz Plockhoy, An Apostle of the Collegiants," *MQR* XXIII (1949) 161-85; *DB* 1884, 76; Friedrich Nieper, *Die ersten deutschen Auswanderer von Krefeld nach Pennsylvanien* (Neukirchen, 1940) 104; *ML* III, 379.

Ploeg, van der, a Dutch Mennonite family. The first generations of this family, as far as known, were in the early 17th century living at Bolsward and Franeker in the province of Friesland; many members of the Franeker branch were potters. They gradually spread over the Netherlands. This family has produced a number of Mennonite ministers: Feike Hiddes van der Ploeg (b. 1736 at Franeker, d. 1790 at Dokkum) studied at Franeker University and the Amsterdam Mennonite Seminary and was a preacher at Hindeloopen 1767-72 and at Dokkum 1772-87. In 1787 he retired and left Dokkum; the probable reason for his retiring was his Patriotic (*q.v.*) sympathies. In 1788 he was back in Dokkum to give all his time and energy to a publishing house which he had founded in 1778. He was the author of a book of poems for children, which was once very popular. He also published a *Naamlijst* (List of Names) of the Mennonite congregations in Friesland with their ministers (*N.N.B.Wb.* VI, 1158; *Inv. Arch. Amst.* I, No. 1693). Both of his sons were Mennonite preachers: Hidde Wibius van der Ploeg (b. in 1769 at Hindeloopen, d. at Goch, Germany, in 1853), serving at Cleve 1789-93 and Crefeld 1793-1818; then he resigned, but in the next year he accepted a call from Goch, where he served 1819-50, also serving at Emmerich 1821-49 and at Cleve 1822-49. He published a sermon on Eph. 5:15-16 which he had preached at Crefeld, and a collection of sermons, *Christelijke Leerredenen* (Haarlem, 1813). The other son of Feike Hiddes was Johannes Aeschinus van der Ploeg (b. 1778 at Dokkum, d. 1859 at Grouw), who was a minister

at Grouw in 1802-52. Two sons of the latter were also Mennonite ministers: Feico van der Ploeg (b. 1805 at Grouw, d. 1883 at Burgsteinfurt, Germany), who served at Ouddorp 1829-42 and Enschedé 1842-71, and Hidde Wibius van der Ploeg (b. 1815 at Grouw, d. there 1903), who was a pastor of Middelie 1839-92. Feico's son Jan van der Ploeg (b. 1834 at Ouddorp, d. 1917 at Wildervank) also went into the ministry (serving at Baard 1858-63, Monnikendam 1863-83, and Veendam 1883-98), as did also his cousin Sybrand Feico van der Ploeg (b. 1854 at Middelie, d. 1942 at Apeldoorn), a son of Hidde Wibius; he served at Burg on the island of Texel 1880-84, Drachten-Ureterp 1884-87, Noordhorn 1887-89, Pieterzijl (Grijpskerk) 1889-91, and Leer in East Friesland 1891-1920. He was married to Emma van der Goot, a daughter of the well-known Amsterdam Mennonite pastor Pieter van der Goot. Two other Mennonite pastors were members of this family: Folkert van der Ploeg (b. 1865 at Grouw, d. 1947 at Apeldoorn) married to Albertje Wuite, of Tjalleberd, minister of Tjalleberd 1893-96, Wolvega 1894-96, Veendam 1896-1906, and Groningen 1906-31, and his cousin Tjalke van der Ploeg (b. 1876 at Grouw, d. 1938 at Amsterdam), who served as pastor at Mensingeweer 1901-3, Heerenveen 1903-8, Zaandam-Oostzijde 1908-25, and Apeldoorn 1925-38. With the exception of Feike Hiddes van der Ploeg, who had no special training for the ministry, and Hidde Wibius, who was appointed as a ministerial candidate (*proponent*) by the Conference of Friesland (F.D.S.) in 1839, all of these ministers received their training at the Amsterdam Mennonite Seminary. In addition, many members of this family served as deacons in various Dutch Mennonite congregations. (*Ned. Patriciaat* XVII, 1927, 282-93.)   vDZ.

Plonius (Pluen, Pleunis), an Anabaptist martyr, was drowned in the Rhine on Nov. 29, 1561, at Cologne, Germany, with Johann von Orval (*q.v.*). The account in van Braght's *Martyrs' Mirror* is brief and incorrect. He only mentions the year of execution and not the date; he reports that two other martyrs, Orvel and Jan, were executed with him. This must be a mistake; Orvel and Jan were the same person, viz., Johann von Orvall (*q.v.*). Plonius was a tailor, a native of Emmerich, Germany.   vDZ.

Mart. Mir. D. 286, E. 654; *Der Mennonit* IX (1956) No. 1, p. 11.

Plovier (Plouvier, Plovyer, Pleviers), a Mennonite family found in the 16th-17th centuries at Haarlem, Holland. They were weavers or tailors, natives of Meenen (Menin) in Flanders, who fled to Haarlem because of persecution. By marriage they were related to other Mennonite families such as van Heuvel, van Robaix, Verschoten, and Alderwerelt. Very likely the martyr Lenaert (*q.v.*) Plovier, executed in 1560 at Antwerp, Belgium, was a member of this family. (Church records of Haarlem: *Inv. Arch. Amst.* II, No. 1855.)   vDZ.

Pluen, an Anabaptist martyr: see **Pleun** (van Hoevele).

Pluevo: see **Nepluyevka.**

Plum Coulee, a village (pop. 500) located 9 miles west of Rosenfeld, Man., on a creek named Plum Coulee, because delicious wild plums grew on both sides of the creek. It began in 1888 when the Canadian Pacific Railroad completed the Pembina branch. It was incorporated as a village municipality in 1901 and officially opened as such Jan. 1, 1902, with A. A. Harder as its first mayor. In 1897 Plum Coulee had seven grain elevators; a large surrounding area shipped all its grain to this spot. The town had four churches in 1958: Sommerfelder, built in 1917, the Bergthaler, the largest in membership, built in 1926, the Rudnerweide church and the Church of God in Christ Mennonite Church, built only recently. John J. Hooge served the Bergthaler congregation for many years. The village is noted for its tree-lined streets where formerly there was only open, bald prairie. H.H.H.

Plum Coulee Mennonite Church, a congregation of the Rudnerweide (*q.v.*) Mennonite Church, located in Plum Coulee, Man., was organized about 1945 as a schism from the Sommerfelder (*q.v.*) Mennonite Church. The ministers take the pulpit in rotation according to a schedule. They are unsalaried. The membership in 1957 was about 120. H.H.H.

Plum Creek Mennonite Church (MC), 2 miles east and 2½ north of Beemer, Cuming Co., Neb., a member of the Iowa-Nebraska Conference, was organized in 1895 with 14 charter members, with Jacob D. Birky the first resident minister, ordained here in 1895. The first meetinghouse was built in 1907 on the present site, and has been twice enlarged. The membership in 1956 was 142, with Samuel Oswald as bishop and P. O. Oswald minister. S.O.

Plumstead Mennonite Church: see **Groveland.**

Pluvier, Leendert, an Anabaptist martyr: see **Lenaert Plovier.**

Pluys, Jan (name probably garbled), was a preacher of the Mennonite congregation of Monjou (Monschau, *q.v.*) in the Eiffel, Germany, who because of persecution in 1711 moved to the Dutch province of South Holland, where he was engaged in farming. Further particulars are lacking. (*Inv. Arch. Amst.* I, No. 1305.) vDZ.

Plymouth Church of God in Christ Mennonite Church, now extinct, located near Plymouth, Neb., was organized in 1885 with David Hiebert and Peter Yost as ministers. Its membership grew to about 30. Upon the death of David Hiebert, Peter Yost and John Yost served as lay ministers. After the death of Peter Yost in 1906 the congregation began to dissolve by members moving to other congregations, mostly to Kansas, until by 1919 it was extinct. A.L.Y.

Pochtitz (Bochtitz; Czech, *Bohutice*), a village and estate in the parish of Wolframitz near Kromau (*q.v.*) in Moravia (*q.v.*). Because of a strong influx of Anabaptists, the Hutterian Brethren, after es-

tablishing a Bruderhof at Gopschitz (see **Gobschitz**), bought a house "on the heath" in Pochtitz in 1545-46 of Gallus Kusy von Mukodel and settled in the domain of the Kusy von Mukodel family; soon afterward they acquired a mill in Klein-Selowitz. During the time of persecution they had to abandon this Bruderhof but re-established it in 1560.

Whereas they had been favored by Stefan Kusy, their position deteriorated under his son Hans to such an extent that an open break occurred. On April 13, 1597, Kusy's men entered the house and severely damaged it, compelling the Brethren to leave on the following day, with their "aged, widows, and orphans and little children," losing all their possessions. The chronicles estimate the loss, including unpaid wages due for more than a year, at 5200 florins. The baron soon discovered his loss in their departure, and "upon his repeated desire and persistence" they returned in 1598.

In 1602 Gopschitz was abandoned "with the good will of the baron," but the Pochtitz Bruderhof remained. In 1605 it suffered at the hands of the Altheim regiment, in 1610-11 through the mismanagement of Georg Riedel, who purchased the grain too late (see **Pellertitz**). On Aug. 1, 1619, it was "hard plundered" by Dampierre's troops; on Dec. 19, 1620, Spaniards, Neapolitans, French, and Polish soldiers behaved so barbarously that the Brethren decided to flee.

After some time the refugees returned to Pochtitz, where on Aug. 26, 1621, the preacher Konrad Blösi died. On Jan. 5, 1622, the imperial troops, composed of all kinds of rabble, burned down the dwelling house; the remaining buildings were plundered and burned ten days later by cavalry from Lower Austria. The Brethren, driven out by these acts of violence, did not return; the settlement was abandoned. P.DE.

Beck, *Geschichts-Bücher;* Wolkan, *Geschicht-Buch;* Zieglschmid, *Chronik;* G. Wolny, *Kirchliche Topographie von Mähren* II: *Brünner Erzdiözese* (Brno, 1858) 311 ff.; *ML* III, 380.

Podolsk Mennonite Settlement in Samara: see **Pletchanovo.**

Podusilna, a former Mennonite congregation in Galicia (*q.v.*), located 15 miles southeast of Przemysl. It was one of the later settlements which developed out of the original settlement in 1789. In 1872 several families settled here, followed by others in the following spring. Among the most common names were Bachmann, Brubacher, Ewy, Hubin, Müller, and Rupp. Jakob Müller was the first elder, ordained on July 8, 1877, d. Jan. 25, 1878. He was followed in office by Peter Bachmann, chosen to the ministry in 1878 and as elder in 1897, d. in 1901. In 1881 many of the families emigrated to America. In 1909, as a result of a general reorganization of the Galician Mennonites, the "Christliche mennonitische Gemeinde Kiernica-Lemberg" (*q.v.*) was organized, which incorporated all the earlier organized groups. During World War II the Mennonites left Galicia, most of them to settle temporarily in the Warthegau (*q.v.*). In

1945 they fled to West Germany. Finally most of them emigrated to Uruguay, although a few got to Canada.   NEFF, E.C.

P. Bachmann, *Mennoniten in Kleinpolen* (Lemberg, 1934) 280 ff.; *Menn. Bl.*, 1878, 16, 23; *ML* III, 380 f.

Poeldijk, a village in the Westland district south of The Hague, Dutch province of South Holland, was in February 1536 the center of a revolutionary movement. Perhaps as many as 40 Anabaptists, both men and women, gathered in the home of the wealthy Jutte Ewouts (*q.v.*). The leader of this group was Adriaen Adriaensz (*q.v.*), a fanatic who claimed to be called by God to punish the world. On March 8-9, 1536, the Jutte Ewouts' house was surrounded by the police and finally taken. A number of the Anabaptists were killed, including Adriaen Adriaensz. (He did not escape, as is assumed in the article in *ME* I, 14.) A few succeeded in escaping; the others, including Jutte, were arrested, and in the next few days thirteen of them were put to death at The Hague, and some of the others were banished from Holland.   vDZ.

Inv. Arch. Amst. I, Nos. 166-72, 176, 178 f.; E. van Bergen, "De Wederdopers in het Westland," in *Bijdra-*

Pöggstall (Peckstall), a village northwest of Melk (*q.v.*) in Lower Austria, became the center of an Anabaptist congregation, which was gathered by Georg Fasser (*q.v.*), who had just been released from prison in Mödling (*q.v.*). He was captured and suffered a martyr's death in 1537 or 1538. The records do not agree on the date or the method of execution. (Beck, *Geschichts-Bücher;* Wolkan, *Geschicht-Buch;* Zieglschmid, *Chronik;* ML III, 381.)   P.DE.

Pohl, Matthias (1869-1934), a Mennonite preacher, born in Emmendingen, Baden, Germany, on March 26, 1869, was a typesetter and proofreader in Langnau in the Emmental, Switzerland, where he also served the Mennonite congregation as preacher. In 1896 he was called as a co-worker on the *Zionspilger* (*q.v.*) and wrote several articles for this periodical. He also had some poetic gift and published some of his verse in a small volume, *Blumen am Wege.* In 1898 he became editor of the *Zionspilger* and kept this position until he returned to Germany in 1900. In that year he was elected preacher in Sembach (*q.v.*) in the Palatinate. His work here was blessed until he retired in 1929. He spent his last years at the Thomashof. As an author he was unusually active, contributing devotional, narrative, and historical articles to the *Gemeindeblatt* and the *Christlicher Gemeindekalender,* thereby creating for himself a lasting monument of grateful appreciation. Matthias Pohl died at the Thomashof (*q.v.*) on May 13, 1934. (*Gem.-Kal.* 1935, 54-63; *ML* III, 381.)   NEFF, S.G.

Pohrlitz (Boherlitz; Czech, *Pohorlice*), a market village on the Iglava in Moravia (*q.v.*), belonging to the Zierotin domains of Selowitz (*q.v.*) in 1581, when the Hutterian Brethren began to settle there. The next year they bought a small house with the land belonging to it of Josef Kowar, the resident of Pohrlitz, and expanded it to a proper Bruderhof. The buildings were located on the Waitzen highway, and were later known as the "old post office." In 1593 the Bruderhof comprised a considerable amount of land, for which they paid a fee to the barons. Although Johann von Zierotin (*q.v.*) favored the Anabaptists, he was nevertheless displeased by the intention of the widow of a Lutheran preacher to join the Brethren. The Bruderhof was greatly damaged by the Teuffenbach cavalry in 1608. On Dec. 16, 1619, the deacon Dietrich Pfingshorn died here. In summer of 1620 Bouquoy's troops plundered the Pohrlitz Bruderhof, murdered two of the Brethren, wounded three others fatally, and took away all the horses. Under the impact of this violence the Brethren fled, but soon returned. But on Dec. 29 the Bruderhof was again attacked, plundered, and partly burned. It was scarcely restored, when it had to be finally abandoned in 1622.   P.DE.

Beck, *Geschichts-Bücher;* Wolkan, *Geschicht-Buch;* Zieglschmid, *Chronik;* Gregor Wolny, *Kirchliche Topographie von Mähren* II; *Brünner Erzdiözese* II (Brno, 1858) 229; *ML* III, 381.

Pokraken, Adlig, was the center of the Mennonite Memel-Niederung (*q.v.*) congregation in East Prussia after 1831, when a meetinghouse was erected here. Until 1831 the meetinghouse had been at Plauschwarren (*q.v.*).   vDZ.

Pol, a Dutch Mennonite family, which is said to have come from Münsterland, Westphalia, Germany. (1) Jan Jansz Pol, b. about 1665, a weaver, spent his winters in Zaandam, Holland, and is supposed to have joined the Mennonites there. About 1700 he settled at Borne in the district of Twenthe, Dutch province of Overijssel, from where this family later spread over the Netherlands. By marriage they have become related to many prominent Mennonite families of Twenthe, such as Hulshoff, ten Cate, Doorencate, Nijenhuis, Paschen, Stroink, Stenvers. In Borne the Pol family, which in the first generations was engaged in weaving and textile business, were Groningen Old Flemish Mennonites. (2) Jan Jansz Pol (1740-1806), a textile merchant and grandson of (1) Jan Jansz Pol, was in 1766-1806 a lay preacher of the Borne congregation. From 1779 he was a "commissaris" (trustee, and at the same time elder) of the Groningen Old Flemish Mennonite conference. (3) Adam Pol (b. 1782 at Borne, d. 1872 at Workum), son of (2) Jan Jansz Pol, after receiving his training from Pastor Pieter Beets (*q.v.*) of Zaandam, served as Mennonite preacher at Hippolytushoef (Wieringen) 1810-19 and at Hindeloopen 1819-50. The following ministers from this family received their training at the Amsterdam Mennonite Seminary: (4) Jacob Pol (b. 1787 at Hengelo, d. 1848 at Weesperkarspel), a son of Jan Hendriksz Pol of Hengelo, served at Hoorn 1814-43. His brother (5) Jan Pol (b. 1804 at Hengelo, d. there 1849) was the pastor at Leeuwarden in 1827-49; a half brother of (4) Jacob and (5) Jan was (6) Gerhard Pol (b. 1815 at Hengelo, d. 1895 at Apeldoorn), who was a minister at Baard 1840-53, Ouddorp 1853-62, and Kromwal (Ytens)

1862-83. Finally (7) Johannes Pol (b. 1815 at Hippolytushoef, d. 1888 at Norden), a son of (3) Adam Pol, served at Warga 1839-47 and at Norden, East Friesland, Germany, 1847-84. His picture was published by Jan ten Doornkaat Koolman in his history of the Norden Church (1904).

Some of them published sermons and other writings: (4) Jacob Pol published a *Leerrede* (sermon) at Hoorn in 1839, commemorating his 25 years of serving and also his farewell sermon at Hoorn (Hoorn, 1848). (6) Gerhard Pol published his farewell sermon preached at Baard, *Afscheidsrede* (Harlingen, 1854), and (7) Johannes Pol *Iets uit mijn Katechisatiewerk* (Norden, 1886). Many members of the Pol family have served as deacons at Borne as did some members of the Hulshoff Pol lateral branch. vDZ.

Ned. Patriciaat XXVIII, 1942, 227-44; Naamlijst 1829, 33, 43 f., 58; DJ 1840, 40; DB 1891, 54; 1897, 5 f., 8; ML III, 381.

Poland, located between Germany and Russia, has undergone many changes in its history as a "buffer state" and played a significant role in the history of the Mennonites who moved eastward from the Netherlands and South Germany. West and East Prussia were added to Poland in 1466 under the Jagellon dynasty (1386-1572) in a conflict with the Teutonic Knights. After 1530, therefore, when the Mennonites started to come from the Low Countries to settle along the Vistula River, they settled in Polish territory. Both privileges (*q.v.*) permitting them to settle under certain conditions and edicts prohibiting their settlement as "heretics" were issued in early times, primarily by Polish rulers. They were mostly valid only during the lifetime of a ruler. The Mennonites were tolerated only because some estate owners or officials derived benefits from them as expert farmers and drainers of the swampy areas along the Vistula River. In many instances they were unfairly exploited by government officials. After Willibald von Haxberg, the representative of the king of Poland, had unjustly exploited them, King John Casimir (1648-68) issued two "privilegia," July 16 and Nov. 28, 1650, which were renewals of a privilegium of 1642 and applied to the Mennonites of the Marienburg and Graudenz lowlands. The Mennonites and other Dutch immigrants became known as experts in various trades, particularly in draining swamps. Numerous favorable privileges and restricting edicts were issued in the following years. A special manner of settling, i.e., the pattern by which the "Hollanders" settled and rented their land, became known throughout Poland.

Starting in Danzig around 1535 Mennonite settlers moved into the unoccupied areas along the Vistula River establishing "Holländer" villages in the triangle between Danzig and Elbing and Marienburg. Some of the areas were the Danzig Werder (*q.v.*, i.e., marsh), Scharpau (*q.v.*), Tiegenhof (*q.v.*), Marienburg Werder (*q.v.*), Heubuden (*q.v.*), Herrenhagen (*q.v.*), and Einlage (*q.v.*).

As the land in this triangle became occupied the descendants and newcomers proceeded south along the Vistula River, establishing themselves in Schwetz

(*q.v.*), Graudenz (*q.v.*), and Culm (*q.v.*). From here they proceeded into the interior of Poland. During the late 18th century they established the Mennonite settlements of Deutsch-Kazun (*q.v.*) and Deutsch-Wymysle (*q.v.*) near Warsaw and farther southeast Michalin (*q.v.*) near Makhnovka, Karolswalde (*q.v.*) near Ostrog in Volhynia (*q.v.*) which meanwhile had become Russian Poland.

During the 18th century Swiss Mennonites and Amish from South Germany and Alsace-Lorraine settled near Lemberg (*q.v.*) in Galicia (*q.v.*), which was ceded by Poland to Austria in 1772. In Volhynia such villages as Kutuzovka (*q.v.*) and Neumanovka (*q.v.*) were established. Most of these Swiss-Volhynian and Swiss-Galician Mennonites emigrated to the United States around 1874 (see also **Volhynia**).

Since the fate of Poland is so varied most of the Mennonite settlements shared in the same vicissitudes. The history is related in greater detail in the articles dealing with the individual provinces, settlements, and villages.

During the Reformation period Poland experienced its greatest expansion when its territories extended from the Baltic Sea to the Black Sea, including West and East Prussia, Galicia, Volhynia, and other parts of the Ukraine and Lithuania. Lithuania was lost in 1635 and parts of the Ukraine in 1667. During the first partition of Poland (1772) West Prussia, not including Danzig and Thorn, became a part of **Prussia, and East Galicia of Austria.** During the partitions of 1793 and 1795 other parts of Poland—Danzig, Thorn, Plock, and Warsaw—were added to **Prussia, and** Volhynia to **Russia.** The Volhynian and some other Mennonite settlements were in Russian Poland when the great migration of Mennonites to America took place in 1874.

After World War I Poland again became independent, and Danzig (*q.v.*) became a free city. Many of the Mennonite settlements were located in Polish territory or the Polish Corridor. At the beginning of World War II Germany and Russia divided Poland once more, and the Mennonite population in Russian-occupied Poland was transferred to the German part. Since 1945 all of the areas in which Mennonites lived in Danzig, Prussia (except the Königsberg-Memel area, now Russian), and Poland belong to Poland and are under Polish rule. The Mennonite population either fled from this territory during World War II or the German collapse in 1943-45 or they were evacuated or have fled since that time. No organized Mennonite community or church exists today (1957) along the Vistula River or any other part of Poland. Two women are known to be still living in Danzig and Elbing who survived because of intermarriage with Poles.

American Mennonites did relief work in Poland in 1940-41 and 1947-49. M. C. Lehman was in charge of the Mennonite Central Committee work in 1940-41, when needy Poles and the Deutsch-Kazun Mennonites were helped. In 1947 relief work was resumed by the Mennonite Relief Committee (*q.v.*) and the MCC. In the Danzig area and in Nasielsk north of Warsaw some 245 tons of food and 31 tons of clothing were distributed in 1947-48. In 1947 the MCC established a demonstration farm near Pelplin south of Danzig. At its peak this unit had 23 men. The MCC was also instrumental in helping some remaining Prussian, Polish, and Russian Mennonites to leave for Western Germany.

The relation of the Mennonites to the Poles and Poland, the attitude of the Polish rulers toward the Mennonites, and their contribution to the country have not been thoroughly investigated. Much of the source material is not accessible at this time or has been destroyed. Some of the church records have been rescued and are located in the Bethel College Historical Library, the Mennonite Research Center at Weierhof (Germany), and in private hands. In some instances the Mennonite communities were fertile soil for the Baptist movement, which entered Poland in the mid-19th century. Some Mennonites joined the Baptists and helped the spread of this movement, which ultimately reached not only the German Protestant churches, but also the Polish Catholic churches. Today the Polish Baptists are primarily Polish nationals, since the German population has fled or been evacuated from Poland.

There is some evidence that intermarriages have taken place between the Mennonites and Poles since the early days of their settlement. In some instances, since it was forbidden to proselyte among non-Mennonites, Polish nationals went to Holland to become members of the Mennonite Church, and after their return married a Mennonite and transferred their membership to the local church. Some of the names which are still common among Mennonites which are likely of Polish origin are Dellesky, Ratzlaff, Rogalsky, Sawatzky, Schepanski, Tetzlaff, Tilitsky, and Utesch. Quiring (107) lists fifty words in the Low German language which are of Polish background. These are adaptations made by Mennonites while living in a Polish environment. (See also **West Prussia, Danzig,** and other cities.)

C.K.

General: Richard Winkel, *Die Weichsel* (Leipzig, 1939); Viktor Kauder, *Das Deutschtum in Polen* (Leipzig, 1940); Kurt Lück, *Der Mythos vom Deutschen in der polnischen Volksüberlieferung und Literatur* (Leipzig, 1938); Walter Kuhn, *Deutsche Blätter in Polen* (Posen, 1928); Hans Schadewaldt, *Polish Acts of Atrocity* (New York, 1940); Kurt Kauenhowen, "Das Schrifttum zur Sippenkunde und Geschichte der taufgesinnten niederländischen Einwanderer (Mennoniten) in Alt-Preussen und ihrer Abzweigungen," *Mitteilungen der Niederländischen Ahnengemeinschaft* I (Hamburg, 1939); Postma, "Literatuurlijst over Nederlandsche Mennoniten in Pruisen, Polen en Rusland" (manuscript, 1942).

Mennonite: C. Henry Smith, *Story of the Mennonites* (Newton, 1957); Abraham Hulshof, *Tentoonstelling van Kaarten, Boeken Plaatwerken Nederland-Danzig 15 April-15-Mei 1942* (Utrecht); Wilhelm Mannhardt, *Die Wehrfreiheit der Altpreussischen Mennonisten* (Danzig, 1863); Unruh, *Hintergründe;* H. G. Mannhardt, *Die Danziger Mennonitengemeinde* (Danzig, 1919); Horst Penner, *Ansiedlung mennonitischer Niederländer im Weichselmündungsgebiet von der Mitte des 16. Jahrhunderts bis zum Beginn der preussischen Zeit* (Weierhof, 1940); *idem,* "West Prussian Mennonites Through Four Centuries," *MQR* XXI (October 1949) 232-45; William T. Schreiber, *The Fate of the Prussian Mennonites* (Göttingen, 1955); Walter Kuhn, "Deutsche Täufersiedlungen im westukrainischen Raume," *Zeitschrift für Ostforschung* IV (1955) 481-505; Peter Bachmann, *Mennoniten in Kleinpolen* (Lemberg, 1934); Zdzislaw Ludkiewicz, *Osady Holenderskie na nizinie Sartawicko-Nowskiej* (Torun, 1934); *Namenverzeichniss der Aeltesten, Lehrer und Diakonen oder Vorsteher der Taufgesinnten Mennonitischen Gemeinden in Ost- und West-Preussen, Litthauen, Polen*

und den neu angesiedelten Kolonien in Russland (Elbing, 1835, 1843, and Danzig, 1857, 1881); Jacob Quiring, *Die Mundart von Chortitza in Süd-Russland* (München, 1928); Edward Kupsch, *Geschichte der Baptisten in Polen 1852-1932* (Zdunska-Wola, 1932); Walter Kuhn, "Swiss Galician Mennonites," *Menn. Life* VIII (January 1953); Herbert Wiebe, *Das Siedlungswerk niederländischer Mennoniten im Weichseltal* (Marburg, 1952); Felicia Szper, *Nederlandsche Nederzettlingen in West-Pruisen gedurende den poolschen tijd* (Enkhuizen, 1913); Mannhardt, *Jahrbuch,* 1883; *Gnadenberg Mennonite Church; from Michalin to Gnadenberg, 1811-1950* (North Newton, 1950); W. Kerber, *Mennoniten in der Weichselniederung* (Bromberg, 1936); Christian Neff, "Die Mennoniten in Deutschland, Danzig und Polen in Vergangenheit und Gegenwart," *Allgemeiner Kongress der Mennoniten* (1936) 40-47; Martin Schrag, "The Swiss-Volhynian Mennonite Background," *Menn. Life* VII (October 1954); John D. Unruh, *In the Name of Christ* (Scottdale, 1952); *ML* III, 381 f.

Polau: see **Pollau.**

Polehraditz: see **Pellertitz.**

Polderman de Zeeuw: see **Cornelis Polderman.**

Poliander (Gramann, Graumann), **Johann** (1487-1541), a Lutheran clergyman, was a pastor at Königsberg, the reformer of East Prussia (*q.v.*), Germany, attacked Schwenckfeld (*q.v.*) and the Anabaptists at the colloquium at Rastenburg (*q.v.*) in 1531 and again in 1535 (*HRE,* 525). His hymn, "Nun lob, mein Seel, den Herren," was included in the hymnal of the Mennonites of the Palatinate and Hesse. (*ML* III, 382.)   Neff.

Polish Brethren: see **Socinianism.**

Polk County (Iowa) Amish Mennonite settlement, now extinct, was founded near the Story County line by five families from Johnson County, Iowa, in 1868-69. John Mishler, an Amish deacon who moved to Johnson County from Ohio in 1859, was dissatisfied with the progressivism and the leadership of the Iowa Amish church, and when he ceased to co-operate with the Iowa church leaders his church office was taken from him in 1864, and he became one of the leaders of the dissatisfied group which moved to Polk County in 1868-69. Because, contrary to expectations, only five families moved to Polk County and no church was established, two families left the community, one joined the Methodists, and two attended the services of the Church of the Brethren.   M.G.

Melvin Gingerich, *The Mennonites in Iowa* (Iowa City, 1939) 124-26.

Polk County (Iowa) Mennonite Church (GCM), now extinct, was organized in 1858 in the home of John B. Neuenschwander of Polk City. In August of that year Christian Sutter ordained Joseph Schroeder as minister and John B. Neuenschwander as deacon. Two years later Schroeder was a delegate to the first General Conference of the Mennonite Church of North America, held in Lee Co., Iowa, in 1860, and was appointed a member of the committee that prepared plans for the union of the Mennonites of America. Schroeder had been trained for the Catholic priesthood, later rejoined the Catholic Church, and died in that faith in 1893.

The Polk County Mennonite community was

founded by the Neuenschwanders and Nussbaums, who moved there from Putnam Co., Ohio, in 1849. Other families in the congregation were the Singers, Gehmans, Snyders, Gefflers, Berrys, Beutlers, and the Leichtys. In 1863 John Singer was ordained minister for the congregation and Peter Neuenschwander bishop. When, a few years after this date, Singer and John B. Neuenschwander moved to Missouri, the church was left without leadership and passed out of existence. In 1933 the only family name of the above list still represented in the community was Leichty.   M.G.

Melvin Gingerich, *The Mennonites in Iowa* (Iowa City, 1939)) 146-49.

Poll Tax: see **Taxation.**

Pol(l)au, a village in the domains of Lord Leonhard von Liechtenstein situated on the slope of the Polau Mountains between Nikolsburg (*q.v.*) and Auspitz (*q.v.*) in Moravia (*q.v.*), in which some Swiss Brethren had settled. Their preachers Hans Klopfer (*q.v.*) with four other brethren left the group on account of differences on several points of doctrine. Later on the congregaton joined the Hutterian Brethren. The Bruderhof had several vineyards and a fishpond in lease from the barons of Nikolsburg. When the domain passed into the hands of the fanatically Catholic Dietrichsteins (*q.v.*), the Jesuit Cardaneus, who had been called in by the barons to force the Brethren to become Catholic, together with Christoph Erhard, the Nikolsburg dean and priest, caused the Brethren to be expelled from Polau in 1590.   P.DE.

Loserth, *Communismus;* Wolkan, *Geschicht-Buch;* Beck, *Geschichts-Bücher;* Zieglschmid, *Chronik; ML* III, 382.

Polonie Jansdochter Lonts, an Anabaptist martyr: see **Pleuntgen van der Goes.**

Polrus (Pulrus, Pilraust), **Erhard,** an Anabaptist martyr, baptized by George of Staffelstein in Esperstedt, near Frankenhausen in Thuringia, in 1529, was arrested in early January, but released when he recanted. But he almost immediately returned to the Anabaptists, was seized in the middle of 1530 with six fellow believers, and since he again recanted was released with the penalty of having his cheeks burned through. Soon, however, he was persuaded by the Anabaptist leader Alexander to return to the brotherhood. He was arrested the third time and executed with two companions in mid-November 1532 at Allstedt. (Wappler, *Thüringen,* 92-97; *ML* III, 382.)   NEFF.

Poltzinger (Boltzinger), **Hänsel,** an Anabaptist martyr, a tailor, was captured with Marcus Eder (*q.v.*) on April 24, 1605, at Mernbach in Bavaria, now Upper Austria, and taken to Ried (*q.v.*), where the two men lay in prison for 15 weeks, tormented by judges and priests, besides two Jesuits from Oetting (*q.v.*), and were twice tortured on the rack. On Aug. 26, 1605, they were beheaded and then burned. Their death is the theme of a hymn (with 20 stanzas), which begins with the words, "Hört, hört und merkt, ir Gotteskindt, die ir liebhaber Gottes sind."   NEFF.

Beck, *Geschichts-Bücher,* 789-90; *Mart. Mir.* D 803, E 1103; Wolkan, *Geschicht-Buch,* 481; Zieglschmid, *Chronik,* 626 f.; *Lieder der Hutterischen Brüder* (Scottdale, 1914) 812; Wolkan, *Lieder,* 236; *ML* III, 382 f.

Polzinger, Leonhard, an Anabaptist martyr, a maker of clocks: see **Boltzinger, Leonhard.**

Pond Bank Mennonite Church (MC), located 10 miles southeast of Chambersburg, Franklin Co., Pa., a member of the Washington Co., Md., and Franklin Co., Pa., Conference, began as a rural mission April 3, 1910, and was organized as a congregation in July 1942, when Andrew Lehman was ordained deacon. William W. Hege, a minister from Marion, was largely responsible for the beginning of the work. In 1921 Hege was succeeded by Harvey E. Shank, who was ordained bishop in 1946. The latter's son Luke J. Shank was ordained to the ministry Dec. 29, 1946. They were still serving in 1957; the membership was 57.   H.E.S.

Pondman, Dutch Mennonite family. G. Pondman P. Az. was with an interruption of one year from 1886 until his death in May 1917 a deacon of his home church at Zaandam-West. A. B. F. A. Pondman, professor of medicine at the Groningen University, has since 1951 been a curator of the Amsterdam Mennonite Seminary.   vDZ.

Pontanus, Isaac (*c*1625-1710), a Remonstrant (*q.v.*) minister at Friedrichstadt, Brielle, and Amsterdam, and after 1666 professor in the Remonstrant seminary, was the author of *Tractaet van de sichtbare Kerke Christi op aerden* (Amsterdam, 1660), in which he opposes the spiritualistic views of Galenus Abrahamsz (*q.v.*). The treatise is followed by an *Aensprake* (address) *tot de Vereenigde Duitsche, Friesche en Waterlandsche Gemeenten* and by *Van de Vrijheidt van spreeken in de Gemeente der Geloovigen tegen Laurentius Klinkhamer* (*q.v.*).   vDZ.

Poole (Ont.) Amish Mennonite Church, established in 1874, had a membership of 270 in 1957. It is a member of the Ontario A.M. Conference.   M.G.

Poole, Le, a Dutch Mennonite family. Anthony le Poole (d. 1658) of Hondschoote in West Flanders, Belgium, moved to Leiden, Holland, where he obtained citizenship in 1627. He may have emigrated because of his faith and settled at Leiden about 1625. His descendants have been loyal members of the Mennonite Church and many of them have served as deacons at Leiden. They were usually prosperous textile manufacturers. Anthony's son Jacob le Poole (b. 1624 at Hondschoote, d. 1693 at Leiden), a jute manufacturer, bequeathed a sum of money to the Waterlander Mennonite congregation, of which he was a member. His son Jacob le Poole (Leiden, 1651-1704), a textile manufacturer and a deacon of the Waterlander congregation, took part in the Collegiant (*q.v.*) meetings. The son of this Jacob le Poole, also named Jacob le Poole (1693-1750), a dealer in grain and a deacon of the church, was appointed as administrator by the last remaining members of the congregation of The Hague (*q.v.*), when this congregation was about to die out (*DB* 1896, 60). Lodewijk Gerardus le Poole

(b. 1848 at Leiden, d. there 1908), secretary of the church board at Leiden, studied the archives of this congregation and wrote its history: *Bijdragen tot de kennis van het kerkelijk leven onder de Doopsgezinden, ontleend aan het archief der Doopsgezinde gemeente te Leiden* (Leiden, 1905). This outstanding work also contains many particulars about the le Poole family. (*Ned. Patriciaat* X, 1920, 354-59; *ibid.*, XLI, 1955, 291-305.)   vdZ.

Poor, Care of. Organized care of the poor was unknown in the pre-Christian era; it is a product of Christianity. The Old Testament frequently emphasizes the duty of aiding and supporting the poor according to ability, but only in the New Testament do we find congregational care of the poor. This was the object of the ordination of the seven deacons in Acts 6. In the second century the provision was fully organized. The necessary funds were raised by voluntary donations, partly gifts in kind given at the communion service; there was no compulsion. II Cor. 9:5. Only those really in need and worthy of help received support. Special provisions were made for widows and orphans. In the original Christian church none suffered want. This orderly provision for the poor came to an end when, after Constantine, the church accumulated greater and greater wealth. Ineffectual mass provision for the poor followed.

In the Reformation the Anabaptists were pioneers in the care of the poor. They made it one of their first obligations from the very beginning, at a time when the established churches let other duties have priority over the care of the poor, even though the Anabaptists had no church or monastery property to draw on as the large churches had. They appointed deacons to manage funds voluntarily given for that purpose. The first of these deacons were probably those chosen by the nonresistant group who left Nikolsburg (*q.v.*) in the spring of 1528; they were Jakob Mändel and Franz Itzinger.

The opponents of the Anabaptists disliked and frequently attacked this arrangement, charging the Anabaptists with rating good works above faith. Even in the more recent literature the purpose of this provision for the needy is completely misunderstood; Hermann Hering of Halle, for instance, says about the Mennonites, "More than in true baptism, their interest lay in other ideals, which, playing in apocalyptic and eschatological colors, had as their end happiness in this life." In Augsburg the Protestant clergy argued that the Anabaptist practice of caring for the poor was dangerous to the state. Friedrich Roth (p. 399) has shown the invalidity of this charge: "There was among them [Augsburg Anabaptists] no thought of proposals that would tend toward community of goods . . . yet the common purse from which the funds were taken to provide for the poor—not only those of their own brotherhood—was in the eyes of the council an absolutely illegitimate arrangement, because it interfered with civic care of the poor and still more because it attracted foreign Anabaptists and other sectarians."

The principle that no one should suffer want in a Christian brotherhood has always been considered a sacred duty in the Anabaptist-Mennonite churches. Wherever there was need, brotherly love gave aid. It was the particular task of the deacons (*q.v.*) to take an interest in the poor and to supervise their relief. The larger congregations in Holland and Germany built homes to take care of their poor. (See **Homes for the Aged in Europe.**)

The Chortitza Mennonite Church, the largest and oldest in South Russia, maintained the institution of caring for the poor to the end. Deacons managed the funds given by voluntary donation, and gave an annual report, usually between Christmas and New Year, on their work and their use of the money. Chortitza had no building dedicated to this care, since it was thought better to provide for the poor in private homes, for which suitable remuneration was given. Though the other congregations did not have so thorough an organization for this purpose, there was some provision everywhere. The congregations of the Molotschna settlement built a large home for their needy aged. The provisions for orphans in orphanages were similar and based on a long tradition dating to the early days in Holland. These institutions and practices were transplanted from Russia to the prairie states and provinces of North America and to Mexico and South America, where they are perpetuated in similar or modified forms. (See also **Alms, Homes for the Aged, Mutual Aid, Orphanages.**)   HEGE, NEFF, D.H.E.

Hermann Hering, "Die Liebestätigkeit der deutschen Reformation," in *Theologische Studien und Kritiken*, 1885; Beck, *Geschichts-Bücher*, 75; J. Loserth, "Die Wiedertäufer in Steiermark," in *Mitteilungen des historischen Vereins für Steiermark* (1894) 127; Friedrich Roth, *Augsburgs Reformationsgeschichte* II (Munich, 1904) 399; *Menn. Bl.*, 1896, 87; *ML* I, 84.

Poperinge, a town in West Flanders, Belgium, where Anabaptists were active as early as 1538. Later there was a Mennonite congregation here, concerning which there is little information. This congregation is said to have been wiped out in 1561 by Inquisitor Titelman (*q.v.*), but in 1568 Mennonites at Poperinge still held meetings in the home of Augustijn Gloribus, who in this year escaped arrest by flight. A few Mennonites of Poperinge died as martyrs in other Belgian towns. In the 16th century Mennonites moved from Poperinge to Holland, particularly to Haarlem, bringing their craft of linen bleaching with them.   vdZ.

Poperinghe, Willem van, an Anabaptist martyr: see **Willem de Clercq.**

Popitz, a parish village southwest of Auspitz (*q.v.*) in Moravia (*q.v.*), in which the Hutterites had a Bruderhof on the lands of the barons of Lomnice in 1537. In the great persecution of 1570 the Brethren had to flee and concealed themselves in holes and caves, the *lochy* (*q.v.*). The Polau Mountains, especially Mt. Maydenberg (Mayberg) near Popitz, offered possibilities for hiding. The Hutterite chronicle records that especially around the Mayberg they had in many places pits and holes concealed in clumps of bushes, in which they with their children lived for a time, also "in the clefts of the rocks in the valley and in the high rocks of the Mayberg, the same at other places in the country, wherever they could." At Popitz the authorities were about to smoke them out of the caves, but were prevented. In their former Bruderhof the householder Gabriel Aichhorn died in 1551. But they did not really begin to live there again until 1573. In 1599 the deacon Thomas Pruckner died in the Popitz Bruderhof. The Thurn cavalry did much damage in 1600. Popitz is not named among the Bruderhofs abandoned in 1622. P.DE.

Beck, *Geschichts-Bücher;* Wolkan, *Geschicht-Buch;* Zieglschmid, *Chronik,* 242; *ML* III, 383.

Popkes, Tiete (1695-1770), in 1721 became a lay preacher and in 1732 an elder of the Groningen Old Flemish congregation in Humsterland (*q.v.*) in the Dutch province of Groningen. He was a farmer, living near Oldehove. By order of the Groningen Old Flemish Mennonite conference he drew up a confession of faith, *Een beknopt ontwerp of schets van de Geloofsbelydenisse der Mennonyten onder de benaminge van oude Vlaamingen,* published at Groningen in 1749. His son Jacob Tietes (1734-1821), a farmer at Ter Horne near 't Zandt in the province of Groningen, who was a preacher of the Leermens (*q.v.*) Mennonite congregation after 1763, took the family name of Huizinga (*q.v.*). The grandson of Tiete Popkes, also called Tiete Popkes (1772-18?), took the family name of Gaaikema (*q.v.*). VDZ.

J. Huizinga, *Stamboek van Derk Pieters en Katrina Tomas* (Groningen, 1883) 6, 7; *idem, Stamboek van Fiepke Foppes en Diver Olferts* (Groningen, 1887) 5, 6; *DB* 1879, 4; 1890, 104, note 106.

Poplar Grove Mennonite Mission (MC) was begun in May 1908 by the Missions Committee of the Weaverland (MC) congregation to serve eighteen members of the congregation with twenty-seven children, who were living on rented farms in Chester County, Pa. The services were held in a schoolhouse on the farm of A. S. Wenger. By 1911 it was a prosperous and self-supporting work, but in 1912 the work was abandoned and by 1914 all the families had moved nearer to Lancaster County churches, to be replaced by Old Order Amish families. I.D.L.

Poplar Point Hutterite Bruderhof in Manitoba, founded in 1938. Their preacher Joseph Waldner, chosen Oct. 15, 1905, by the Bon Homme Bruderhof in South Dakota, confirmed March 17, 1907, by the Huron Bruderhof in South Dakota, left the Huron settlement with 11 families, bought land and built the necessary buildings at Poplar Point, Man. In 1939 Friedrich Waldner was chosen preacher. When Elder Joseph Kleinsasser died in 1947, Joseph Waldner was chosen in his place.

In 1950, 75 persons from the Poplar Point Bruderhof, including 21 baptized members, established the Springfield Bruderhof at Vivian, Man., with Joseph Waldner (d. 1951), the elder of the entire body of Schmiedeleut (*q.v.*), as preacher. Samuel S. Waldner was chosen as assistant pastor in 1950 at Poplar Point for the Springfield Bruderhof. Friedrich Waldner, the present pastor at Poplar Point, confirmed in the ministry at the Huron Bruderhof in 1946, stayed at Poplar Point with 80 persons, 26 of whom were baptized members. The present (1958) membership at Poplar Point is 42, in a population of 151. John Waldner was chosen as assistant pastor in 1957. D.D., F.W.

Popodin (Pobudin), a village in the neighborhood of Holitsch (*q.v.*) in Slovakia (*q.v.*), not far from Göding (*q.v.*) in Moravia, where some Hutterian Brethren settled during the period of persecution in Moravia, which began in 1547, in the domain of Peter Bakich de Lák (*q.v.*), who was at first their protector, but later proved to be one of their most violent opponents. In Popodin the deacon Michel Kramer died in 1551, who "made the song of the great Hungarian tribulation, how the brotherhood fared at that time," and in 1553 occurred the death of Simon Waindl, who had been ordained only the year before at Kutí (Gätte in the chronicles). (Beck, *Geschichts-Bücher;* Wolkan, *Geschicht-Buch;* Zieglschmid, *Chronik; ML* III, 383.) P.DE.

Poppingawier, a village in the Dutch province of Friesland (*q.v.*), where there has been a Mennonite congregation since earliest times. It was usually united with the Irnsum (*q.v.*) congregation. Only in 1871-79 did it have its own preacher (J. J. Honig 1871-75, G. Vrijer 1875-79). Nothing is known of its early history. Until 1848, when a church was built, the congregation met in a private home. The baptized membership in 1899 was 95, and in 1958 it was 41. (*DB* 1870, 140 note, 152; 1872, 191; 1887, 147; *ML* III, 383.) VDZ.

Pordenau, a Mennonite village name transplanted from Prussia to the Molotschna settlement, Ukraine, Russia. (See **Villages.**) C.K.

Pordenau Mennonite Church was located in the village of Pordenau, Molotschna settlement (*q.v.*), South Russia. The village was established in 1820, and in 1869 consisted of 48 farms with 4,676 acres. The settlers were primarily "Flemish" and belonged originally to the "Grosse Gemeinde" (*q.v.*) of the Molotschna. When Elder Jakob Warkentin was deprived of his office in 1842, Pordenau became one of the three congregations emerging from the Grosse Gemeinde or Ohrloff-Petershagen-Halbstadt Mennonite Church (*q.v.*). In 1887 Pordenau had 984 baptized members and 1,033 children.

The first elder was Heinrich Töws (*q.v.*) of Pordenau, succeeded by Isaak Peters (*q.v.*) who migrated to America in 1874. After this the congregation was subject to Elder Diedrich Barg of the Margenau Mennonite Church for a number of years. The following elders were Gerhard Regehr (*q.v.*) and Peter Epp (*q.v.*). Other ministers who served this church were Isbrand Friesen, Franz Töws, Peter Dyck, Johann Görzen, Johann Neufeld, Isaak Braun, Johann Töws, Peter Ewert, Jakob Dyck, Jakob Gerbrandt, and Gerhard Dürksen.

The first church building was erected in 1828 which was replaced in 1860 by a larger building. In 1905 the congregation had a total population of 1,771 and membership of 806. Little is known about the later development of the congregation. (Friesen, *Brüderschaft,* 706; Dirks, *Statistik,* 1905, 20, 63; *ML* III, 383.) C.K.

Porrentruy (German, *Pruntrut*), a government district in the northwestern part of the Swiss canton of Bern on the Alsatian border, with a capital by the same name, close to the French border.

Mennonite families have been living in this area for decades. They first attended the meetings of the neighboring congregations of Grand Lucelle (*q.v.*) and Florimont (*q.v.*), and also maintained connections with the Seigne (*q.v.*) congregation in France, whose members were of Swiss descent. Since they were too far away from the other congregations Isaak Gerber (*q.v.*), who had leased the mountain farm called Vacherie-Mouillard, began to hold meetings in his home, at first occasionally, and after 1895 every month. This was the beginning of the Porrentruy congregation. The first meetings were conducted alternately by Heinrich Schmutz of La Lave of the Seigne congregation and Samuel Gerber (*q.v.*) of Paturatte (*q.v.*), Bernese Jura.

At the outbreak of World War I Heinrich Schmutz had to flee from France because he was a German citizen. Deprived of all his possessions, and leaving his wife behind in an internment camp in southern France, he escaped with his two children to Switzerland and found a temporary home with the David Gerber (son of the above) family in Mavaloz near Porrentruy.

The Porrentruy congregation soon increased, making it necessary to provide a larger room for their meetings. In 1918 a suitable hall was rented for this purpose in the western part of the city on the farm of the old tile factory. The first meeting at this place was held on May 12, 1918, and from that time on twice a month. For twenty years this simple room served the congregation as a place of meeting.

As the congregation grew inwardly and outwardly, the young people organized a chorus, and the small room was no longer suitable. After lengthy consultation a members' meeting decided on Jan. 6, 1938, to build a new chapel on the farm of Elder Schmutz in Courgenay (*q.v.*), where this family was now living. This has become one of the most beautiful of the Mennonite churches in Switzerland. It was dedicated on Jan. 22, 1939.

A factor in the development of the Porrentruy congregation was the annual Bible course, which was usually conducted by Mennonites from the outside.

For a time the congregation was affiliated with the Alsatian Mennonite Conference but for a considerable period it has been affiliated with the Swiss Mennonite Conference.

For many years Elder Heinrich Schmutz was the only preacher of the Porrentruy congregation. His first co-minister was Samuel Geiser, who was living in this area at that time and served for two years, until he moved away to the Kleintal congregation. In 1932 two men were ordained to the ministry—Christian Schmutz, a son of the elder, and Jakob Lehmann. In 1941 Daniel Nussbaumer, formerly of Basel (*q.v.*), and two "trial" preachers, Abel Baumgartner and Gaston Gerber, preached for a while. In 1955 the elder was Christian Schmutz of Courgenay, the preachers Albert Nussbaumer, Gaston Gerber, and Abel Baumgartner. The baptized membership in 1958 was 140. (*Gem.-Kal.* 1951; *ML* III, 402 f.)   S.G.

Port Rowan Mennonite Brethren Church, located near Port Rowan, Norfolk Co., Ont., a member of the Canadian Conference, was organized on Nov. 20, 1932, under the leadership of Jakob Penner. The first meetinghouse was an old frame church which was at first rented, then bought and remodeled. Ministers who have served the congregation are P. Reimer, Abraham Pauls, Peter Lodde, and J. A. Penner. The pastor in 1958 was P. Reimer; the membership was 131.   H.H.J.

Port Elgin Mennonite (MC) Church: see **Bruce County**, Ont.

Portage County, Ohio, south of Cleveland, was formed from Trumbull County in 1807. It is so named from the old Indian portage path seven miles long between the Cuyahoga and Tuscarawas rivers. It is the home of the flourishing Plain View Mennonite Church (*q.v.*) located between Kent and Aurora.   J.S.U.

Porter Mission (MC) in the foothills near Estacada, Ore., was established in 1939 as an outgrowth of a rural visitation project of the Bethel Mennonite Church of Canby, Ore. In 1956, 20 members organized as a congregation of the Pacific Coast Conference. Ernest J. Bontrager was the minister in charge. Services were held weekly in a small church built in 1943.   O.G.M.

Portielje (originally *Portille*), a Dutch family, which is thought to have fled from French Flanders because of persecution, moving to Amsterdam. The first generations of this family seem to have been Mennonites, but in the 17th century they became Reformed. The descendants of Pieter Portielje (1781-1847), who was married to Clara van Aken (a Mennonite), however, became Mennonites, and some of the family have been very active members of the church. David Abraham Portielje (Amsterdam, 1814-52), married first to Catharina van Eeghen and after her death to Alida Johanna Fock, studied law and then became a director of the Dutch Association of Life Insurance Companies (*Hollandsche Sociëteit van Levensverzekeringen*), founded in 1807 at Amsterdam by Anthonie Hartsen, also a Mennonite. His son Jan Pieter Portielje (1843-1909), married to Cécile Dorothée Fock, studied law, and became a director in the same company. Besides this he was a trustee of the Collegiant-Mennonite orphanage Oranjeappel (*q.v.*), treasurer of many Mennonite corporations, and a trustee of the A.D.S. 1893-1909. His son David Abraham Portielje (1872-1927), married to Anna Helena Voûte, also studied law and was like his father and grandfather a director of the life insurance company at Amsterdam. He was also a trustee of the Oranjeappel orphanage, manager of the "Christina Stichting" (*q.v.*), a trustee of the North Holland Widows' Fund, and member of the church board at Amsterdam. As a member of the executive committee of the A.D.S. he was active in the matter of pensioning retired and invalid pastors. He was also a curator of the Mennonite Theological Seminary. P. B. Westerdijk commemorated him in a warmhearted *In Memoriam,* found in the *Doopsgezind Jaarboekje* of 1928. vDZ.

Ned. Patriciaat VI, 1915, 314-16; DB 1910, 202-10; DJ 1928, 21-30; De Zondagsbode XXII (1908-9) No. 53; XL (1926-27) No. 42.

Portier, Hermanus, a Mennonite of Harlingen in Friesland, Netherlands, who on March 14, 1739, wrote a "Remonstrantie" (petition) to the States of Friesland in behalf of Wytze Jeens Brouwer (*q.v.*) and Pieke Tjommes (*q.v.*), two Mennonite preachers of Heerenveen who had been suspended from their ministry in 1738 on the charge of teaching Socinian (*q.v.*) views, and whose suspension was extended on March 13, 1739. In this petition Portier wrote that the States were committing practices of intolerable inquisition, and this word "inquisition" so offended the authorities of Friesland that the petition was fruitless. Portier also published *Omstandig en Waaragtig Bericht* (Harlingen, 1742), in which he particularly attacked Daniel Gerdes (*q.v.*), of Groningen, who supported and defended the States of Friesland in their intolerant attitude toward the Mennonites. (Blaupot t. C., *Friesland,* 209; *Catalogus Amst.,* 139.) vDZ.

Portland, Ore., chief city (pop. 375,690) and largest in the state, and county seat of Multnomah County, situated just above the confluence of the Willamette and Columbia rivers, the "vacation capital" of the Pacific Northwest, in the midst of a magnificent landscape.

There are over 300 churches in Portland; but of Mennonite churches there are only the Mennonite (MC) Mission Church, the Rock of Ages Rescue Mission (MC), and the Alberta Community Church (GCM) in this vast area. There are only some 125 Mennonites living in Portland's vicinity; within 100 miles to the south of Portland there are approximately 1500 Mennonites, most of whom are farmers. Directly north of Portland across the Columbia River which is the Oregon-Washington line, there is a small U.M.C. group. The Mennonites came to Oregon in 1890, and to Portland in 1922. G.M.H.

Portland Mennonite Church (GCM): see **Alberta Community Church.**

Portland Mennonite Church (formerly called Mennonite Gospel Mission and later Mennonite Mission Church), located at 2235 Northwest Savier Street, Portland, Oreg., was opened by the Pacific Coast District (MC) Conference on Nov. 12, 1922, and organized as a church July 27, 1924, with 23 members. In 1955 it became an independent congregation. During its first 25 years the following served as superintendents: Allan Good, Henry Yoder, Paul Roth, Glen Whitaker, Marcus Lind, Paul Yoder, and Claud M. Hostetler. In 1947 there were 58 members; in 1958 there were 93. The erection of the church building in 1927 was a church-wide project. A city-wide evangelistic campaign in 1939 conducted by C. F. Derstine of Kitchener, Ont., helped to present the church and her doctrine to the public. M.MI.

Portner (Portzner), **Jakob,** an Anabaptist evangelist in Upper Austria, had been chaplain of the baron of Regensdorf in the castle at Steyr until Hans Hut (*q.v.*) arrived in town (June 15, 1527). He introduced Hut into the homes of the respected citizens and saw to it that Hut could preach soon after his arrival. Soon afterward Portner was chosen by lot with three other Anabaptists, Jerome Herrmann (*q.v.*), Leonhard Schiemer (*q.v.*), and a former people's priest from Nürnberg, to go out as Anabaptist evangelists. The ceremony of the lot was conducted by Hans Hut. The government ordered the council of Steyr on September 20 to pursue Portner with placards. In Augsburg (*q.v.*) he was imprisoned. When Charles V (*q.v.*) came to Augsburg in 1530 he demanded that Portner be turned over to imperial authorities. His accusers asserted that he had misled the entire community. The prisoner was transferred after the Emperor had assured the council that this transfer would not diminish their jurisdiction (Roth, 255). Nothing more is known with certainty concerning Portner's fate, but it may be assumed that an Anabaptist leader like Portner who fell into Charles's hands would be executed. HEGE.

J. Jäkel, "Zur Geschichte der Wiedertäufer in Oberösterreich," in *47. Bericht des Museums Franciscus-Carolinus* (Linz, 1889) 30, 31, 39; Fr. Roth, *Augsburgs Reformations-Geschichte* I (Munich, 1901) 255; *ML* III, 384.

Pos, Heyndrick Jacobs, a Dutch Mennonite of the 17th century who probably lived in Edam or Middelie, is the author of the booklet *Geestelycken Comeet* (Edam, 1665); he also composed the 131 hymns of the *Middelieer Lied-boeck* (*q.v.*). vDZ.

Posen (Polish, *Poznan*), a province in the valley of the Warta (Warthegau), formerly belonging to Prussia (*q.v.*), now to Poland. In 1939-45 Mennonites from Galicia (*q.v.*) and Russia (*q.v.*) found temporary asylum here, being settled on lands provided by the German government. (*ML* III, 385.) E.C.

Posjager, C. A., was a Dutch Mennonite preacher of the Waterlander branch, serving at Noordeind van Graft. In collaboration with E. A. van Dooregeest (*q.v.*), the Mennonite preacher of neighboring De Rijp, he published a book for the use of Mennonite sailors, who were numerous in the congregations of De Rijp and Graft, and who often had to leave their home towns for long periods when they sailed for herring fishing or for whaling as far as Greenland. This book is entitled *Ryper Zeepostil* (Amsterdam, 1699). It contains twenty-two sermons, a number of prayers, and a short history of Holland, especially of the home towns of the sailors, Schermer, Graft, and De Rijp. Concerning Posjager there is no further information. He is supposed to have been the son of Albert Cornelisz Posjager, who was probably also a Mennonite preacher at Noordeind van Graft, and who was once in 1655 for some unknown reason fined by the magistrate when he was preaching in De Rijp. Posjager died about 1730. (Schijn-Maatschoen, *Geschiedenis* II, 572 f.; *DJ* 1837, 96; *DB* 1917, 35-38.) vDZ.

Post: see **Steinbach Post.**

Post Oak (Indiahoma), a mission station of the
Mennonite Brethren Church of North America serving the Comanche Indians of Oklahoma, situated on
a 160-acre farm one mile east and 4 miles north of
the village of Indiahoma, near Lawton, Okla., was
opened in 1894 when Henry Kohfeld and his wife
were appointed for this work, assisted by a conference committee which included E. C. Deyo, a Baptist missionary to the same Indians, and Dr. Mor-
row, supervisor of all Baptist Indian Missions in the
United States. The opening of the work was made
difficult by the indifference of Chief Quanah Parker. Finally, however, yielding to the pleas of the
missionary and some of his own people and one of
his wives, Parker led the missionary to the place
where he believed the mission should be founded.
He cut a sign to indicate this location in a post oak
tree; hence the mission was named Post Oak. The
religious indifference of the Indians was gradually
overcome. The first converts were baptized in
1907; approximately 400 adults have been baptized
at the station. At present some 150 members constitute the Post Oak Comanche Mennonite Brethren Church.

The congregation has yielded some fine assistant
workers such as George Koweno, Deacon Urheyah,
Shelby Tenequer, and Ruben Tabbytosavita, all four
of whom have died. Those specially active today
are the deacons Felix Koweno, James Chebahtah,
and Pete Coffey, and the lay members Herman
Asenap and Max Pahcheka. The last named deserves special credit for having opened a promising
work at the Fort Sill Indian School for children near
Lawton, conducting Sunday school and worship
services there.

The work in the main has been of an evangelistic
type, but in 1948 a school for Indian children was
opened at Post Oak under the supervision of D. J.
Gerbrandt with Ruth Wiens as teacher. In 1949 the
school was transferred to a new building in Indiahoma. There are some 60 to 70 Indian children and
four teachers in the first eight grades.

Missionary families who have served at Post Oak
are as follows: Henry Kohfeld 1894-1907, A. J.
Becker 1901-40, J. S. Dick 1941-42, C. E. Fast 1942-
44, J. J. Wiebe 1944-45, D. J. Gerbrandt 1945 (now
at Indiahoma), H. J. Neufeld 1949, who is now
(1954) in charge of the Post Oak Mission. Among
the helpers who have served on special occasions we
mention only Mrs. Anna Hiebert Gomez, who has
been with the mission since 1911 in various capacities, and is still doing a very commendable work,
especially among the women.   J.H.L., G.W.P.

G. W. Peters, *The Growth of Foreign Missions in the
Mennonite Brethren Church* (Hillsboro, 1947).

Post und Volksblatt was a weekly German newspaper edited by H. P. Krehbiel and C. E. Krehbiel
and published by the Western Book and Publishing
Co. (*q.v.*) at Newton, Kan., 1904-9. It was formed
by combining the *Hillsboro Post* and the *Kansas
Volksblatt.* The 1904 volume of *Post und Volksblatt*
was volume 18. In 1910 the name was changed to
Der Herold (*q.v.*) but the volume numbers were
kept in consecutive order. The *Kansas Volksblatt*
had at one time been edited by D. Goerz and W. J.
Krehbiel and sold by them to the Newton *Kansan*
in 1899. D. R. Krehbiel served as editor until the
Kansan sold the *Kansas Volksblatt* to the western
Book and Publishing Co. (*q.v.*).   J.F.S.

Newton Kansan, Fiftieth Anniversary Edition, 1922;
Post und Volksblatt (BeCL).

Postel, Wilhelm (Elias Pandocheus, pseudonym), a
mystic and friend of the Anabaptists of the 16th
century, used the pseudonym for reasons of personal
security, wrote books advocating religious tolerance,
e.g., *Panthenosia* (1547), was a friend of Jean Ban-
tin of Basel, Switzerland, the physician of David
Joris (*q.v.*), of Joris (*q.v.*) himself, and of Blesdijk
(*q.v.*), the son-in-law of Joris. He testified at the
trial of David Joris in 1559, but said nothing personally detrimental to Joris. He ascribed great religious illumination to Joris, which had, however,
been misused through the sumptuous living of the
sectarian leader, who had grown wealthy from gifts
of love.   E.T.

Roland H. Bainton, in *Nederlandsch Archief voor
Kerkgeschiedenis* XXIV, II (1931) 17 f.; idem, "David
Joris," in *Archiv für Ref.-Gesch.,* supplementary volume
VI (1937); *ML* III, 385.

Posthuma, Folkert Evert, b. May 20, 1874, at Leeuwarden, a Dutch Mennonite, who studied agriculture at the National Agricultural College at Wageningen and the University of Halle, Germany, and
then was engaged in agricultural and dairy industries and director of the farmers' national co-operative bank. In 1914 he was made Dutch minister of
Agriculture and Trade and organized the distribution of food in the Netherlands during World War
I. By his executive ability he managed to keep the
Dutch population adequately fed. He remained a
state cabinet minister until 1918. During this period
he lived at The Hague, and was a trustee of the
Hague Mennonite congregation. During World
War II Posthuma sympathized with the National-
Socialist principles and co-operated with the German occupation authorities. Consequently he lost
the sympathy of both the Mennonite brotherhood
and the Dutch nation. In 1942 he was shot by
Dutch partisans.   vDZ.

Postlawitz (Poslawitz; Czech, *Bohuslavice*), a village near Gaya in Moravia, belonging to the domains of Bucovice. In 1545 the Hutterian Brethren
acquired a house here with a mill, in the spring of
the following year another house, and on May 7,
1547, the third house. Although this seems to have
been one of the larger Bruderhofs, it was apparently abandoned later. Nothing more is heard of it,
nor is it mentioned in the list of the Bruderhofs
vacated in 1622. (Beck, *Geschichts-Bücher;* Wolkan,
Geschicht-Buch; Zieglschmid, *Chronik,* 249; *ML* III,
386.)   P.DE.

Potbaker, Jan Sibes: see **Sibes, Jan.**

Potemkin, Prince Gregor (1739-91), appointed governor general of New Russia by Catherine the Great,
whose favorite he was, with instructions to open
and settle the newly acquired territory in the South.

Potemkin accomplished this task by resettling Russian peasants and settling foreign pioneers, by founding cities (see **Kherson** and **Ekaterinoslav**), developing roads, and planting forests and vineyards. The war with Turkey, which broke out in 1787, came inopportunely for him, but the acquisition of Crimea (*q.v.*) in 1783 was one of his achievements. Upon the suggestion of Count Peter Rumiantsev (d. 1796), a Russian general, Catherine sent George von Trappe as her plenipotentiary to invite foreign settlers, with an especial commission to the Danzig Mennonites, whose pioneering capabilities had come to the attention of the Russians in the Seven Years' War. As governor general of Little Russia Count Rumiantsev was much interested in agriculture, and in 1770 he had permitted the Hutterian Brethren, who had been designated as Mennonites by the immigration laws, to settle on his Vishenka estate in the province of Chernigov. After Rumiantsev's death the Hutterian Brethren established a Bruderhof at Radichev (*q.v.*). In other respects also the Hutterian Brethren were the forerunners of the Mennonites in settling in Russia. Potemkin, whose colonizing achievements have been described by Theresia Adamczyk, in 1786 received in Dubrovna on the Dnieper Jakob Höppner (*q.v.*) and Johann Bartsch (*q.v.*), the delegates sent by the Danzig Mennonites to examine the land offered by Catherine. In the spring of the following year the delegates were received at Kremenchug by Catherine in the presence of her dignitaries, and also, on the return journey, by Paul, the heir apparent to the throne. They had selected the region of Berislav, not far from Kherson, for settlement, but "on account of warlike events" (Heese) were compelled by Potemkin to settle in the Chortitza area in the district of Ekaterinoslav, the capital of which Potemkin was planning to make the center of the Black Sea region.   B.H.U.

Theresia Adamczyk, *Fürst G. A. Potemkin, Untersuchung zu seiner Lebensgeschichte* (dissertation, Berlin and Emsdetten, 1936) 28-49; Alexander Klaus, *Unsere Kolonien* (translated into German from Russian by Jakob Töws, Odessa, 1887); Margarete Woltner, *Die Gemeindeberichten von 1848 der deutschen Siedlungen am Schwarzen Meer: Sammlung Georg Leibbrandt* IV (Leipzig, 1941) p. 3, note 1, and p. 4, note 5; *ML* III, 385.

Pott, Nicolaas (d. May 7, 1872), was a Dutch Mennonite minister, about whose training little is known; he studied at the Amsterdam Mennonite Seminary 1812-*c*13, and was appointed ministerial candidate in 1816 by the trustees of the Mennonite conference in Friesland. He served as Mennonite pastor at Warns 1821-24 and at Hippolytushoef on the island of Wieringen 1824-68. He married a Catholic wife, which seems to have been well accepted by the congregation. At Hippolytushoef, even after her marriage, she kept a vegetable shop, in which she also sold liquors. She gave up the sale of liquors when the church board censured this business.   vDZ.

DB 1891, 54 f., 56; 1900, 55; 1901, 87 f.; *De Zondagsbode* LII (1938-39) No. 17.

Pottere (Potbacker), **Bastiaen de**, an Anabaptist martyr: see **Bastiaen.**

Pottinga, a Mennonite family at Harlingen, Dutch province of Friesland. A descendant of this family was Jetze Pottinga Hz. (b. 1846 at Harlingen, d. 1927 at Apeldoorn), who after completing his studies at the Amsterdam Theological Seminary in 1866-71 served the following Mennonite congregations: Noordhorn 1871-74, Hindeloopen 1874-78, IJlst 1878-80, Irnsum-Poppingawier 1880-86, Joure 1886-90, Hoorn 1890-93 and 1893-1912; in 1912 he retired. His son Dirk Pottinga Jz. (b. 1876 at Hindeloopen, d. June 1925 at Arnhem) studied at the University and the Mennonite Seminary of Amsterdam and served the congregations of Baard 1903-6, Veendam-Wildervank 1906-8, Purmurend 1908-12, and Arnhem 1912-25.   vDZ.

Pottstown First Mennonite Church (GCM), now extinct, was located at Oak and Evans Streets, Pottstown, Pa. The first public service was held Jan. 27, 1894, in a rented hall. In the fall of 1894 a brick building 27 x 49 ft. was erected and dedicated April 21, 1895. The congregation was organized on Dec. 30, 1895, with William S. Gottshall as the pastor. Congregational difficulties arose and the church was discontinued about 1904.   W.S.S.

J. C. Wenger, *History of the Mennonites of the Franconia Conference* (Telford, 1937) 374.

Pottstown Mennonite Church (MC), located in Pottstown, Montgomery Co., Pa., a member of the Franconia Conference, began as a mission station under the Franconia Conference Mission Board on Nov. 23, 1930, with Elmer G. Kolb as superintendent, who was ordained as pastor June 7, 1938. A new church building with a seating capacity of 180 was dedicated May 4, 1952. On March 6, 1954, the congregation was organized with a membership of 60, mostly rural. Norman H. Bechtel (ordained 1953) also serves as minister.   E.G.Ko.

Potvliedt (Potvliet), a Mennonite family at Amsterdam, members of the Flemish and later of the Zon (*q.v.*) congregation. This family, now extinct, originally came from Flanders. Probably the martyrs Jelis (*q.v.*) and Pieter (*q.v.*) Potvliet belonged to the same family.   vDZ.

Potzbach, a somewhat remote village in the northern Palatinate, Germany, between Otterberg (*q.v.*) and Winnweiler, where since the beginning of the 18th century several Mennonite families had been located who were members of the Sembach (*q.v.*) Mennonite congregation. Deacon "Weissebutzbach," who is named by Ernst Müller (*Berner Täufer*, 212), was Hans Weiss of Potzbach, who was one of the first leaders and deacons of the Sembach congregation. Until 1784 there was a Mennonite cemetery in Potzbach. The group here has greatly declined, partly through emigration and partly through mixed marriages and transfers of memberships to other churches. Some families, such as Beutler and Fuchs, have died out. In 1951 the names Bally, Blickensdörfer, and Krehbiel were still represented.   G.H.

Ernst Crous, "Mennoniten im Regierungsbezirk Trier 1827-1870," in *Gem.-Kal.*, 1940, 62-73; *ML* III, 386.

Poughkeepsie, N.Y., is the location of the Hudson River State Hospital, an institution with more than 5,000 mental patients. Civilian Public Service Unit No. 144 was located here from April 1945 to April 1946. Nearly all of the men in this Mennonite unit were in relief training and pursued courses of study designed to prepare them for relief service in war-devastated countries. The thirty members of the 1945 women's summer service unit also took courses in relief training.   M.G.

Melvin Gingerich, *Service for Peace* (Akron, Pa., 1949) 242-46.

Poutschy (Eduardsdorf), a village in Volhynia (*q.v.*) situated some fourteen miles west of Dubno, was the leading center of the Swiss-Volhynian Mennonite group in 1815-61. It was settled by Swiss Amish Mennonites from the Polish villages of Urszulin and Michelsdorf (*q.v.*), who had come from Montbéliard, France, in 1791. Dissatisfaction with farming conditions at Urszulin-Michelsdorf and a liberal offer by Prince Edward Lubanirsky were the basis of the move to Poutschy. Families found their way to near-by villages, such as Zahoris (*q.v.*), Futtor, and Hecker.

The Poutschy settlement was reinforced by some members of a small group of Swiss Amish Mennonites who had settled near Dubno (*q.v.*) in 1801-2. In the course of time the two groups, those at Poutschy and those located nearer Dubno in the villages of Wignanska and Futtor, merged. The group near Dubno had its historical roots in the movement of Mennonites from South Germany to Galicia.

The land at Poutschy was leased from the Prince for periods of 24 years. New names added to the church roster here were Waldner, Wedel, Archlus, Strauss, and Prieheim. The traditional earlier family names were Albrecht, Flickinger, Gering, Krehbiel, Miller, Schrag, Stucky, Sutter, Voran, and Zerger. In its earlier years the congregation adhered to the Amish Discipline of 1779, but there is some evidence that by 1860 the distinctive practices were waning. Officials of the church were Joseph Schrag, Johann Albrecht, Johann Müller, Johann Schrag, Johann Gering, and Jacob Stucky. Almost the entire Eduardsdorf group moved to Kutuzovka and Neumannovka (*q.v.*) in 1861. The families who remained related themselves to the congregation found in the villages of Zahoris and Futtor.   M.H.S.

Martin H. Schrag, "European History of the Swiss-Volhynian Mennonite Ancestors of Mennonites now living in Communities in Kansas and South Dakota" (unpublished master's dissertation, Eastern Baptist Theological Seminary, 1956).

Powder Spring Mennonite Church (MC), now extinct, located 12 miles west of Mt. Jackson, Shenandoah Co., Va., was probably the first rural outpost under the Virginia Conference. The meetinghouse was originally built in 1858 for school and church services by three denominations, the Lutherans having one-half interest, and the Brethren and Mennonites each one-fourth interest. Here the Mennonites held services once a month and sometimes twice a month until the Woodland Tabernacle

was built in 1944. A more permanent church was built in 1954. James Gross was ordained pastor in 1957. The work here was never flourishing, since it was in the midst of a strong German Lutheran community.   T.S.

Powellsville, Md., near which was located Camp Pocomoke, a former Civilian Conservation Corps camp, which the Friends operated as a Civilian Public Service camp in 1942-44. In the latter year the Mennonites took charge of this soil conservation project and continued the work of building a 14-mile drainage canal. By the autumn of 1946, the labor expended had already lowered the water table of the surrounding farms sufficiently to improve 34,000 acres of farm land and to make arable 37,000 additional acres that were formerly unproductive. Camp No. 52 was closed in March 1947.   M.G.

Melvin Gingerich, *Service for Peace* (Akron, Pa., 1949) 123-24.

Powwowing, a superstitious custom, no doubt descending from medieval European folk superstitions, which professes to heal sicknesses by the pronouncement of a mysterious formula handed down from one practitioner to another, still practiced to some extent among the Pennsylvania Dutch of Pennsylvania and other regions. Some Mennonites and Amish have indulged in the practice. According to the theory the ability to powwow (i.e., to cure by powwowing) is handed down from a male to a female and then in turn from a female to a male practitioner. Powwowing is not "faith healing" nor healing by prayer. Similar practices involve the ability to cast off "the evil eye" which may have been "cast" upon beast or man by a person able to do so.   H.S.B.

Practical Christianity rather than theology was the actual primary concern of the Anabaptists and Mennonites. A brief comparison of the first Anabaptist confession of faith, the seven articles of the Schleitheim Confession of 1527, and the general Protestant confession, viz., the Apostles' Creed, makes this very clear. As early as 1526 Hans Denk (*q.v.*) expressed this interest in his familiar words, "No one can truly know Christ without following Him in life." Hänsel Gremser (*q.v.*), who was on trial in 1533, said that the Anabaptists, in case they were asked, recognized each other by the phrase, "I do Christian works." In his *Reply to False Accusations* Menno himself defends the Anabaptists and their charitable deeds: "No one among them is allowed to beg. They take to heart the need of the saints. They entertain those in distress. They take the stranger into their houses. They comfort the afflicted; assist the needy; clothe the naked; feed the hungry; do not turn their face from the poor; do not despise their own flesh." And about 150 years later, in 1693, George Thormann (*q.v.*), the Reformed pastor of Lützelflüh in the Emmental, used very similar words concerning the Bernese Mennonites in his book, *Probierstein* (*q.v.*). Only on such a basis could the church ban and church discipline in general become of such importance to the Anabaptists. With their aversion to all luxury, their ethics lean toward sanctification and good works, and criticize the one-sidedness of Luther's doctrine of justification. Their home missions, and homes for the poor, the aged, and the orphans are expressions of this inclination. Indeed, relief and nonresistance have always appeared as two sides of the same principle. The Mennonite relief organizations, such as Christenpflicht (*q.v.*), Mennonitische Flüchtlingsfürsorge (*q.v.*; relief organization of the Vereinigung, *q.v.*), the Dutch Committee for Foreign Needs (*q.v.*), and Stichting voor Bizondere Noden (*q.v.*), the Mennonite Central Committee (*q.v.*), as well as the numerous orphanages, old people's homes, and hospitals in several countries where Mennonites are living, are evidence of this fact, as well as the history of all the various groups which at times gave and at other times received help, from Switzerland to Lithuania, in the Ukraine, and in mission fields, especially in Java (*q.v.*) and India (*q.v.*).   E.C.

Ernest Crous, "Hilfswerke der Mennoniten in früherer Zeit," *Unser Blatt* III (1949) No. 42; also *Gem.-Kal.*, 1952, 68-72; Menno Simons, *Complete Writings*, 558; *ML* III, 387 f.

Prader, Carius, an Anabaptist martyr, who was put to death in the territory of Salzburg, Austria, in 1529. He was locked into a house with several other Anabaptists, which was then set afire. Van Braght gives no further particulars. Zieglschmid's (*Chronik*, 66) suggestion that he is identical with Eucharius Binder (*q.v.*) is very plausible. (*Mart. Mir.* D 24, E 433.)   vDZ.

Prague (Czech, *Praha*) (pop. 932,000), capital of Bohemia and since 1919 of Czechoslovakia, the center of the Hussite movement of the 15th century. In 1521-22 Thomas Müntzer (*q.v.*) visited the city and on Nov. 1 and 25, 1521, announced his peculiar religious views in his "Manifesto of Prague." Volkmar Fischer (*q.v.*), an Anabaptist of Hesse, was imprisoned at Prague in 1532. Julius Lober's (*q.v.*) list of martyrs (1531) names four martyrs beheaded in Prague, and the list of the *Geschicht-Buch* names eleven by 1542. The archives of the Ministry of the Interior contain some source materials on Anabaptist history. No Anabaptist congregation was ever established here.   E.C.

Beck, *Geschichts-Bücher*, 312; Wolkan, *Geschicht-Buch*, 182; F. Hruby, "Die Wiedertäufer in Mähren," in *Archiv f. Ref.-Gesch.* XXX (1933) 1-36, 170-211; XXXI (1934) 61-102; XXXII (1935) 1-40; *TA Reichsstädte* (*Bayern* II); *ML* III, 387.

Prairie Rose Evangelical Mennonite Church (Kleine Gemeinde) is located near Lorette, Man., in a different municipality (county) from the other three church districts, about half-way between Steinbach and Winnipeg. This district was settled in 1918-19, by rural people of the other districts, with H. R. Reimer as minister. Two others, Bernhard D. Reimer and Franz D. Reimer, both sons of H. R. Reimer, were later elected as ministers. Bernhard D. Reimer left this district and moved to the Steinbach district. In later years Abram P. Unger and Vernon Reimer were elected as ministers, and Franz D. Reimer was ordained as bishop. A modern meetinghouse has been erected. The baptized membership in 1957 was 285 (besides 275 not baptized). A German young people's meeting is held every four weeks,

alternating with an English young people's meeting also held every four weeks.   D.P.R.

Prairie Street Mennonite Church (MC), located at 1316 Prairie St., Elkhart, Ind., a member of the Indiana-Michigan Conference, was organized by John F. Funk (*q.v.*), a minister who had moved into the city in 1867 and set up a publishing company there. Preaching services had been held in the city every two weeks in the homes of the members since Dec. 4, 1870. The meetinghouse was built at the present site in 1871 and the first service held in it on Nov. 26, 1871. Elkhart at that time had a population of some 3,000.) The meetinghouse, a frame building, which was enlarged in 1895 and 1901, burned to the ground in 1935 and was replaced by a brick building seating 550. Its membership in 1957 was 288. Two daughter congregations have developed in Elkhart out of mission outposts: Belmont in 1929 and Roselawn in 1949, with (1957) memberships of 100 and 44 respectively, making a total membership in Elkhart of 492. The chief ministers in the congregation have been J. F. Funk 1871-1935, J. S. Coffman 1879-99, J. S. Lehman 1892-1904, G. L. Bender (deacon) 1907-21, J. E. Hartzler 1910-14, W. B. Weaver 1914-23, J. S. Hartzler 1923-33, J. E. Gingrich 1933-53, J. B. Shenk 1953-57, and Howard Zehr 1958- . The congregation was organized in 1871.

The Prairie Street congregation has been one of the most progressive and active M.C. congregations, partly because of the presence of the Mennonite Publishing Company (*q.v.*) and the early progressive leadership of Funk, who was also bishop of the congregation from 1891 until his removal from that office in 1900. Here the Mennonite Aid Plan (*q.v.*) was organized in 1882, the Mennonite Evangelizing Committee (*q.v.*) in 1882, which developed into the Mennonite Board of Missions and Charities (*q.v.*), which has always had its headquarters here, and the Elkhart Institute (*q.v.*) in 1894, which developed into Goshen College in 1903. The first Young People's Meeting (MC) was started here in 1897, and the Mennonite Book and Tract Society (*q.v.*) was organized in 1894. In the Prairie Street church the first M.C. foreign missionaries were consecrated in 1899, viz., W. B. Page and his wife and J. A. Ressler. Prairie Street was also one of the first M.C. congregations to engage a seminary-trained minister and adopt the one-pastor system, when it engaged J. E. Hartzler in 1910.   H.S.B.

Minutes of the Indiana-Michigan Mennonite Conference 1864-1929 (Scottdale, 1929) contains a brief historical sketch of the congregation.

Prairie View Hospital, a mental hospital located near Newton, Kan., established by Mennonite Mental Health Services, Inc. (*q.v.*), a section of the Mennonite Central Committee, and operated by a local board representing ten Mennonite groups in the central area of the United States, is a treatment center for acute mental illnesses and longer term rehabilitation with limited service for care of the chronically ill. There is room for 41 inpatients. Possible expansion to 100 beds is envisioned. Outpatient services reach a large number of former inpatients and others not requiring hospitalization. The hospital,

15

a one-story brick construction on a 50-acre tract east of Newton, was opened on March 15, 1954. The cost of the plant and equipment was approximately $280,000, nearly all of which was given by the MCC constituency in the central area of the United States. The total staff averages about 40 including professional and nonprofessional personnel. The hospital, with other Mennonite mental hospitals, grew out of a concern for better treatment of the mentally ill which developed during World War II when Mennonite conscientious objectors served in state hospitals. It furnishes an outlet for Christian service for young people on a voluntary service or remunerative basis. This includes many young men giving alternative service to military training. Plans are in progress to include a training program for graduate nurses wishing to specialize in psychiatric nursing.
M.Eb.

Praktische Landwirt, Der, a periodical published monthly by the Mennonites of South Russia. It was proposed on Oct. 11, 1922, by a Mennonite conference in the Alt Samara settlement, but it was not established until three years later. The conference chose a committee to found an association for the purpose of promoting the re-establishment of Mennonite agriculture and related industries in close cooperation with existing German agricultural organizations and the authorities, and of serving the neighboring populace. They cited the precedent of the Alexandertal seed co-operative as an example of what a Mennonite organization was able to achieve even without state funds (*Praktischer Landwirt,* 1926, No. 12, p. 2). The efforts to form a closer association led to the founding of the All-Russian Mennonite Agricultural Association (*q.v.*) with its seat at Moscow. As the organ of the organization *Der Praktische Landwirt* was called into being with P. F. Froese as editor, a valuable specialized journal, which gave the German farmers practical suggestions for successful management, and also published statistics on the Mennonite settlements in Russia. The first number appeared on May 15, 1925. The office of censorship put difficulties in the way of publication, so that the journal had to cease with its December number in 1926. A complete file is found in GCL, except for the first two numbers. Hege.
Bericht über die Mennonitische Welthilfskonferenz, 1930, in Danzig (Karlsruhe) 54; ML III, 387 f.

Pralitz (Prahlitz, Präles), a market village situated on the right bank of the Iglava, Moravia, southeast of the neighboring Kanitz, usually called Präles in the Hutterian chronicles; they used this form to identify the near-by Bruderhof of Klein-Niemtschitz ("ob Präles"; see **Klein-Nembschitz**), in order to distinguish it from other Moravian towns having the same name.
P.De.

Prangenau, a village in the Marienburg Werder (*q.v.*), West Prussia (now Poland), four miles northwest of Neuteich. Located in the area of the Ladekopp (*q.v.*) community, it was rather late in receiving Mennonite settlers. Some of these settlers lived on the three farmsteads (*Höfe*) "built into the field." One of these farms belonged to Johann Penner (see **Penner** family), the elder of the Lade-

kopp congregation until his death in 1943. Since he was also chairman of the Committee of Elders of the Conference of the Mennonite Churches of East and West Prussia (*q.v.*), this village became one of the better-known villages. (*ML* III, 388.) H.Q.

Prangenau, a village in the Molotschna Mennonite settlement in South Russia, was established in 1824 on the right bank of the Yushanlee River, about 50 miles from Berdyansk. The first elder, Gerhard Wall, proposed that the village be named for Prangenau of West Prussia. Originally the village had 23 families, about half of whom had come from the Chortitza Mennonite settlement of South Russia, and the others from the Marienburg and Tilsit areas of Prussia. B.H.U.
Margarete Wolter, "Die Gemeindeberichte von 1848 der deutschen Siedlungen am Schwarzen Meer," in *Sammlung Georg Liebbrandt* IV (Leipzig, 1941) 151 f.; ML III, 388.

Prater, a former Mennonite family on the Dutch island of Ameland; its members usually were sailors and skippers. Pieter Jacobs Prater was a preacher of the Janjacobsgezinden (*q.v.*) congregation of Ameland 1793-d.1831. (*DB* 1889, 179.) vDZ.

Prayer (Dutch Mennonites). The martyrbooks such as the *Offer des Heeren* and T. J. van Braght's *Martyrs' Mirror* emphasize that it was prayer that strengthened the Anabaptists in prison, gave them the power to endure trials and torture; and that with prayer on their lips they faced execution. If the executioner permitted them to do so, they knelt on the scaffold or near the stake and prayed. The old martyr literature gives striking testimony to their fervent prayers. Though there is little information, it may be assumed that in their early secret meetings the Anabaptists and Mennonites not only read and explained the Scriptures, but also prayed. Of an Anabaptist meeting at Maastricht in 1534 and of one in Amsterdam about the same time it is expressly said that "they knelt down to send up their prayers to the Almighty God."

Later on, after conditions had improved and religious life had become settled, prayer became a regular element of the worship service. They then used to pray twice in a service. Prayer was then always silent (*stil gebed*): the preacher admonished his hearers to pray and thereupon all knelt down and silently offered their individual prayers. The conservative groups, like some Old Flemish and the Janjacobsgezinden, maintained this practice of silent prayer until the end of the 18th century; on the island of Ameland it continued until 1809, in Balk until 1853, in Giethoorn until 1865, in Aalsmeer until 1866. The Waterlanders (*q.v.*), under the influence of their elder Hans de Ries (*q.v.*), had by 1590 abolished the practice of silent prayer, introducing the audible prayer (then called *stemmelijk gebed*) by the minister, as was the practice in other Protestant churches. The Flemish and Frisian Mennonites adopted audible prayer shortly after 1640. With the abolition of silent prayer, the practice of kneeling for prayer was also dropped. For some time, in a few country churches in Friesland until recently, the men in the congregation sometimes arose for prayer, as is often done in Reformed churches. In some congregations the change to audible prayer led to discord, as for example in Grouw (*q.v.*), where the magistrate had to settle the quarrel.

After about 1665 both the Lamists (*q.v.*) and the Zonists (*q.v.*) adopted the practice of prayer at worship services similar to the present Mennonite practice; i.e., the service is opened with a *votum* and closed with a benediction. Besides these two prayers, which are short, there are two longer prayers, one before the sermon and one after. This practice undoubtedly was taken over from the Reformed Church liturgy.

It is probable that after audible prayer had been adopted, the Lord's Prayer was rarely used, the minister composing his own "free prayer." At present the Lord's Prayer is very often used, perhaps nearly always used, either before or after the sermon.

Family worship has never been very popular among the Dutch Mennonites, though it has been held occasionally. Formerly it was customary to offer prayer, usually silent, before and after meals; in many Mennonite families this is still the practice.

There are no special Dutch Mennonite prayerbooks. In the early days sometimes a few prayers were added to hymnals, to confessions, to collections of sermons, or to devotional books.　　　　vdZ.

J. de Backer, *Kort onderwijs van de christelyke gebeden* (Amsterdam, 1707); F. S. Knipscheer, "Geschiedenis van het stil en stemmelijk gebed bij de Doopsgezinden," *DB* 1897, 77-120 and 1898, 55-77; S. F. Rues, *Tegenwoordige Staet der Doopsgezinden* (Amsterdam, 1745) 42 f.; *Inv. Arch. Amst.* I, Nos. 611, 712 f.; *DB* 1863, 147 f.; 1864, 2; 1877, 81; 1890, 6; 1891, 46; 1892, 57; F. H. Pasma, *De Doopsgezinden te Grouw* (Grouw, 1930) 9 f.; Blaupot t. C., *Groningen* II, 143; Kühler, *Geschiedenis* III, 26 f.; N. van der Zijpp, *Geschiedenis der Doopsgezinden in Nederland* (Arnhem, 1952) 110 f.

Prayer Books, Mennonite. Collections of prayers by Mennonite authors for use by Mennonite preachers in public worship or in private devotions were first published in Holland. Hans de Ries (*q.v.*, 1553-1638), the noted Waterlander preacher of Alkmaar, was probably the author of the first prayer collection, a group of 11 prayers attached as an appendix to the Waterlander confession of faith prepared by him and Lubbert Gerrits and published at Amsterdam in 1610 and 1618 as *Corte Belijdenisse des Geloofs* (numerous reprints). This collection of "eenige aandachtige Gebeden" was added to the hymnal edited by de Ries called *Gesangh Boeck,* published in 1643, also (with 3 additional prayers) to a book by Jan Gerrits, *Vijf stichtelijke Predicatien,* published in 1650. It also appeared in *Korte Belijdenisse des geloofs,* published at Amsterdam in 1700. The second collection was by a Flemish preacher, François de Knuyt (*q.v.*), who added a small prayer collection to his *Corte Bekentenisse onses Geloofs,* first printed at Amsterdam in 1618 (many reprints). The third Dutch prayer collection, containing 18 prayers, was by Leenaert Clock (*q.v.*), published in Dutch in 1625, entitled *Forma eenigher Christelijker Ghebeden,* the first distinct prayer book. This was translated into German and as *Formulier etlicher Gebäthe* appeared as an appendix to the first German Mennonite confession of faith,

the Prussian confession of 1660 (Elbing?) with only 13 of the 18 prayers, and T. T. van Sittert's first German edition of the Dordrecht Confession of 1632, published at Amsterdam in 1664, which had the full 18 prayers of Clock's *Forma.* Through these two books, both of which were often reprinted, Clock's collection became the standard "prayerbook" model for all German Mennonites and their descendants. However, neither Dutch nor German Mennonites have used any of these prayer books since the middle of the 19th century.

The Clock collection, enlarged by 2-20 prayers, was made a part of the Swiss Brethren devotional book, *Güldene Aepffel in Silbern Schalen* (Basel? 1702, 1742, and Ephrata, Pa., 1745), where the title became simply *Etliche christliche Gebett* without the *Formulier* heading. A second Swiss Brethren devotional book of c1715, *Send-Brieff von einem Liebhaber Gottes wort,* took over 12 of the Clock prayers from the *Güldene Aepffel* and added 3 new prayers taken from Johann Arndt's *Paradiesgärtlein* of 1612, and gave the whole a new title, *Gebeten auf allerhand Anliegen und Nothen gerichtet.* It also added an 8-page *Schönes Gebett* made up of parts of two Clock prayers and the prayer of *Hans Reist* (which had been published in booklet form about 1700).

But the outstanding German Mennonite prayer book was *Die ernsthafte Christenpflicht* (*q.v.*), *darinnen schöne, geistreiche Gebätter, darmit sich fromme Christenherzen zu allen Zeiten und in allen Nothen trösten.* The first edition was at Kaiserslautern in 1739, followed by at least 10 other editions in Europe to 1852, and at least 24 editions in America between 1745 and 1940. It finally became the prayer book of the Amish. Early editions contained 36 prayers, later increased to 50 and finally 53. It is used by the Amish as the exclusive source of prayers for the minister to use in public worship, as well as being a private devotional book. Its prayers come from varied sources, the *Formulier* (later editions contain all its prayers), Caspar Schwenckfeld's *Deutsches Passional* of 1539 represented by five prayers, Johann Arndt's *Paradiesgärtlein,* with 3 (from the *Send-Brieff*), and others.

The last Swiss prayer book was *Kleines Handbüchlein, darinnen Morgen- und Abendgebetter,* of which six European editions are known from 1786 in the Palatinate to 1867 at Biel, Switzerland, with two American imprints of 1835 and 1872. It contained 12 prayers, 8 from the *Formulier.*

The Elbing *Katechismus* of 1778, later called the "Waldeck Catechism," with many reprints, contained a collection of 14 prayers for children. The 1727 edition of the *Christliches Gemüthsgespräch* by Gerhard Roosen has an appendix of 28 prayers which was not included in later editions.

It is worth noting that none of the Dutch or German prayer collections have ever been translated into English. English-speaking American Mennonites have never produced nor used prayer books in public worship, and seldom, until recent times, in private or family worship.

Non-Mennonite prayer books used by Mennonites include Johann Habermann's *Gebetbuch,* first published in 1567, which was used by Mennonites chiefly in the smaller form, *Der kleine Habermann,* Johann Arndt's *Paradiesgärtlein,* first published in 1612, Johannes Zollikofer's *Neueröfneter himmlischer Weichrauchsschatz* of 1691, and Johann Friedrich Starck's *Tägliches Handbuch* of 1727. But the most popular prayer book of this character among Mennonites was doubtless the *Geistliches Lustgärtlein,* which appeared at least as early as 1787, and in later editions was called *Neu vermehrtes geistliches Lustgärtlein frommer Seelen.* Several times the *Ernsthafte Christenpflicht* appeared in combination with part of the *Lustgärtlein,* the last time at Scottdale in 1915 for the express use of the Amish.   H.S.B.

Robert Friedmann, "Mennonite Prayer Books, Their Story and Their Meaning," Chap. VI of *Mennonite Piety Through the Centuries* (Goshen, 1949) 176-202, on which the above article is based; F. S. Knipscheer, "Geschiedenis van het stil en het stimmelijk gebed bij de Nederlandsche Doopsgezinden," DB 1897, 77-120; 1898, 55-77.

Prayer Guide, officially the *Daily Prayer Guide for Missions, Relief, and Home Activities of the Mennonite Church,* is issued by the Women's Missionary and Service Auxiliary of the Mennonite Board of Missions and Charities (*q.v.*), Elkhart, Ind. The *Booklet of Prayer for Missions of the Mennonite Church* was first issued by the Mennonite Women's Missionary Society for 1925. In 1936 "Handbook of Information" was added to the title. By 1940 the title had become *Booklet of Prayer and Handbook of Information for Missions and Institutions of the Mennonite Church.* Six years later it became the *Daily Prayer Calendar for Home and Foreign Work of the Mennonite Church.* Its present title and format (1958-59) were established in 1951. It is a 5¼ x 7½ in. 136-page booklet. A Bible reading, meditation, and prayer suggestions, followed by birthdays of missionaries and their children, are given for each day. The last 17 pages list officers of the women's missionary organizations and church boards, all missionaries serving under the Mennonite Church (MC), and a missionary book list. In 1958-59 Mrs. Fred Gingerich was editor. Since the daily Bible readings follow the International S.S. Lessons, the *Guide* is used widely in Mennonite family worship.
        M.G.

Prayer, Kneeling Posture, in public services seems to have been a custom of the Basel Anabaptists of the Reformation period. Paul Burckhart says, "As soon as they entered the house where their services were held, they fell upon their knees, and after inexpressible, soundless sighs they arose, wiped the perspiration from their faces, and urged each other to expound the Holy Scriptures." Ernst Müller says of the Bernese Anabaptists, "At their services they sang from the *Ausbund,* the chorister (*Vorsänger*) reading two stanzas aloud before they were sung. For prayer they knelt together, continuing the custom until the beginning of the century." Ludwig Keller says, "The congregation always knelt for prayer. This was also the custom in the previous century in many Mennonite churches." He cites Anna Brons, but her description concerns the Swiss Mennonites in Holland. In West Prussia the kneeling posture was observed until the dissolution in 1945. From Switzerland and South Germany the custom of

kneeling in prayer was brought to Pennsylvania and became the universal practice among Mennonites and Amish of all groups of this background in America. Only in the past 10-15 years has the custom been changing in the Mennonite Church (MC) in some sections. The Mennonites in Russia all practiced the kneeling posture, as did their descendants of all groups who came to America. However, only the most conservative groups of this background (Old Colony, for example) have maintained the practice; the others have discontinued it for some considerable time.   NEFF, H.S.B.

Prayer Meetings, gatherings of Christians for prayer and mutual admonition and edification, are held in many Mennonite congregations in North America weekly, usually on a midweek evening, either in the meetinghouse or in a member's home. The term cottage meeting or cottage prayer meeting is sometimes used in the latter case. Leadership of the meeting may be in the hands of a layman or in the hands of the pastor. In the latter case the pastor may conduct a Bible study or give a devotional address. A common practice is for a number of those present to offer testimonies or admonitions, possibly based upon a portion of Scripture assigned in advance as the basis of the evening session.

The prayer meeting was borrowed from other Protestant groups, especially of the Pietistic type, and its introduction into American Mennonite circles earlier frequently caused trouble and even schism. The Evangelical Mennonites (*q.v.*) of the Gehman group arose as a schism in the Oberholtzer (GCM) group in Eastern Pennsylvania in 1858 when 24 members of the Upper Milford congregation were expelled because they refused to accept the conference decision forbidding such meetings. The attempt to introduce prayer meetings into the Mennonite Church (MC) in the period of 1870-90 caused serious trouble in Indiana and elsewhere and contributed to the schisms of the Old Order (Wisler) Mennonites and the Mennonite Brethren in Christ (Daniel Brenneman group) in Elkhart County in 1871 and 1875, as well as of the Solomon Eby group in Waterloo County, Ont., about the same time.

The counterpart of prayer meetings in Europe, called Gebetsstunde or Bibelstunde, were and still are important aspects of Pietism and the Gemeinschaft (*q.v.*) movement. Through the influence of such movements they have been introduced into some Mennonite areas in France, Switzerland, and South Germany, although they are seldom regular features of the church life, because of the scattered rural membership. Such meetings were more readily held in the village type of settlement in Russia, where they were a prominent feature of the Mennonite Brethren movement. Mennonite educational institutions in North America commonly have student or faculty prayer meetings on a regular weekly (or even daily in some cases) basis.   H.S.B.

Prayer Veiling, also known as the devotional covering or worship veil, is worn in worship and prayer services by the women members of certain American Mennonite bodies, and formerly by most Mennonites of Europe as well. Indeed the principle that women should worship with veiled heads can be called a historic Christian practice. Catholic women are still generally not permitted to enter the church with uncovered head, as is largely also true of the Anglicans. In the 18th century the Reformed churches of Switzerland required women to wear a *Tuechli*, or head covering, when they attended church services. The ancient church father Tertullian (c160-c230) reports that it was customary in most of the churches founded by the apostles for the women to worship veiled, including the virgins. The Episcopalian *Church Encyclopedia* (1883) reports that in England as well as in some American parishes it was customary for women and girls who were confirmed to wear "a light veil." One of the last remnants of the worship veil in general Christendom is the wedding veil.

The Biblical basis for the worship veil is I Cor. 11:2-16. In the section in I Cor. 11 dealing with the practice of the Lord's Supper in the church and the exercise of the gifts of the Spirit in the assembly, the apostle treats of the worship veil. He begins by commending the Christians of Corinth for obediently following his instructions (the Greek term does not mean ancient traditions, nor does it assign the status of a sacrament or ordinance to the veil). He then expounds the order of creation as to the headship of man; he likens this relationship of equal persons, the one of whom is to serve as "head," to the relationship which obtains between God and Christ (Paul does not make a four-level hierarchy: God, Christ, man, woman; he simply makes an illuminating comparison to clarify the meaning of man's headship). The symbol of man's administrative headship is his bared head as he worships. The symbol of woman's role in the order of creation is her veiled head. The apostle is evidently correcting the socially revolutionary practice of some Corinthian women who cast aside their veils in the mistaken notion that the equality of men and women in grace had destroyed the order of creation as to their relationship on earth. He says severely that if a woman wishes to abandon her true role as given her by the Creator when He made her nature, she might as well also abandon her true role as a Christian woman and shave and shear off her hair as the women of the street did in Corinth in that day. The woman ought therefore to wear a sign-veiling that she accepts man's leadership in the church. It should also be noted that Paul does not limit this veil to the married, for it is with man as male and with woman as female that he is concerned. The relationship has to do with the very nature of each sex, and is not confined to the home. Finally Paul appeals to the universal Christian practice in the churches; all of them, he declares, support him.

Although social propriety still generally calls for a covered head in worship in the Western culture of the mid-20th century, American denominations generally make no point of requiring this, either by custom or regulation. The more conservative Mennonite groups, however, have clung to the traditional veil. This veil still resembles that portrayed by Rembrandt in his painting of 1641, "The Mennonite Minister Cornelis Claesz Anslo," which painting shows the preacher strengthening a veiled woman through the ministry of the Word. It is also similar to that shown in the painting of a Lancaster Mennonite Woman by Jacob Eichholtz about 1815 (*ME*, I). S. F. Rues reports (*Aufrichtige Nachrichten*, 1743, 50) observing a baptism among the Mennonites in Holland where the bishop pushed the cap (*Haube*) back from the woman's forehead before pouring the water. In Elbing c1869, according to an eyewitness report in *Mitteilungen des Sippenverbandes* (February 1937, p. 67), "every married woman had to wear a cap (*Haube*) on entering the church. Every unmarried woman, regardless of age, had to wear a hat."

In modern times the prayer veiling in the Mennonite (MC) and related groups has become a small light cap made of a fine organdy or similar material, usually white in color, but sometimes black. The form of the veil in the past 150 years in America has always been that of a cap, not a true veil, formerly almost always tied with strings. The strings are now seldom used except in the most conservative sections, and the cap is usually pinned lightly to the hair. In the Russian Mennonite groups the veil took the form of a kerchief or head-shawl, customarily black. In the Church of God in Christ and Evangelical Mennonites (Kleine Gemeinde) the kerchief is still black and has become quite small. In the Ohio (MC) churches of Swiss extraction as well as in certain A.M. churches of Alsatian extraction (e.g., Central Illinois and Croghan, N.Y.) the cap was black (still worn by a few).

John A. Hostetler has shown that the Pennsylvania Mennonite veiling or cap was probably imported from Europe and is very similar to the cap worn by Palatinate women universally in the 18th century. The last Mennonite women of Europe to wear the prayer veiling (a black lace kerchief called a *Fischelein* from the French *fichue*) were those of the Badischer Verband in South Germany. The practice gradually disappeared there in the first quarter of the 20th century.

Historically the veil was also once worn (uniformly) by the women of certain Protestant denominations: the Society of Friends (note Whistler's painting, "My Mother"), the Church of the Brethren, the Brethren in Christ, and other denominations. The Mennonites of Russia had the veil for married women only. The North American Mennonite bodies which observe the wearing of the veil are the Mennonite Church (MC), the Old Order Amish, the Old Order Mennonites, the Conservative Mennonites, the Holdeman Mennonites (CGC), the Evangelical Mennonites of Canada (KG), the Hutterian Brethren, the Old Colony Mennonites, and related groups. In the Mennonite Church (MC) the leaders of the congregations east of Ohio have since about 1900 taught the constant wearing of the veil throughout the day and this practice is now fairly uniform in the Eastern United States. Elsewhere it has been worn usually only in public worship, or in some places also at the table. J.C.W.

Clayton Beyler, "Meaning and Relevance of the Devotional Covering, A Study in the Interpretation of

I Corinthians 11:2-16" (unpublished Th.M. thesis, Southern Baptist Theological Seminary, 1954); Harold S. Bender, "An Exegesis of I Corinthians 11:1-16" (Ms in GCL); *The Catholic Encyclopedia* XV, "Veil, Religious"; Arthur M. Climenhaga, "The Doctrine of the Veiling" (unpublished M.A. thesis, Taylor University, 1938); Mahlon M. Hess, "The Devotional Head-Covering" (unpublished Th.B. thesis, Eastern Mennonite School, 1941); Daniel Kauffman, "Christian Ordinances," *Doctrines of the Bible* (Scottdale, 1928) 378-439; D. D. Miller, "The Devotional Covering," *Bible Doctrine* (Scottdale, 1914) 416-27; Paul M. Miller, *The Prayer Veiling* (Scottdale, 1956); Albert C. Wieand, "The Prayer Veil" (Ms in GCL); J. C. Wenger, *Separated unto God* (Scottdale, 1955) 207-12; Richard Detweiler, *The Christian Woman's Head-Veiling: A Study of I Cor. 11:2-16* (n.p., n.d.-1958).

Preacher (German, *Prediger;* Dutch, *Predikant;* French, *Predicateur*), a widely used title among Mennonites in all countries, especially in former days. In those groups which have adopted the practice of a single minister-pastor the title pastor or minister has been introduced. "Preacher" has generally been displaced by pastor or minister in America, in Germany by *Pfarrer* (South Germany) or *Pastor* (North Germany), and in the Netherlands by *Dominine*. In all these cases the function of the office is more than simply preaching, and includes pastoral care and full responsibility for leadership. Preacher is then reserved for those ordained or licensed men who have no exclusive pastoral charge but serve with other ministers (bishops, elders, or preachers) in a given congregation. Among the Mennonites of Russia the titles *Pfarrer, Pastor,* or *Diener* were never used; only *Prediger* and *Aeltester* (elder) were used. Among the Hutterites the title *Diener am Wort* (*q.v.*), and among the Amish *Diener zum Buch* were used instead of *Prediger* or preacher. In the Netherlands in former times the title *Leeraar* (teacher) was used, and in North Germany the corresponding term, *Lehrer,* also *Vermaner* (Dutch) and *Vermahner* (German), meaning "admonisher." The term preacher or its equivalent is still the standard term in the Badischer Verband (*q.v.*) in South Germany, in France, Switzerland, South America, and the more conservative groups and areas in North America, as also in the German-speaking bodies in Canada. *Predikant* is still used some in Holland.   H.S.B.

Predigerfonds, a fund established in Germany for the improvement of Mennonite ministers' salaries, pensions for retired ministers, support of ministers' widows, etc. Such funds were once established in the North German city congregations. A general fund for salaries was established in 1897 by the German Mennonite Conference known as the Vereinigung (*q.v.*), also a fund for widows' support. In 1921 a third fund for ministers' pensions was created. Each of these funds is independently established and is operated apart from the general treasury of the Vereinigung, on the basis of using only the income from invested capital. In 1918 the total capital of the three funds was as follows: Salary Fund DM 75,785.65, Widows' Fund DM 39,-733.55, Pension Fund DM 15,500.00. Unfortunately the capital funds were almost wiped out in the inflation of 1923, and again in 1948. The current status is very weak. (*ML* III, 390 f.)   H.S.B.

Prele (Präle), **Paul** (in Beck erroneously called Pretten), of Esslingen, Palatinate, Germany, was seized in Neuffen on April 15, 1573, together with Matthias Binder (*q.v.*) or Schneider, a preacher, on a journey through Württemberg. Prele had come to Württemberg previously as an apostle of the Hutterian Brethren in Moravia. This is inferred from a letter Paul Glock (*q.v.*) wrote to Peter Walpot (*q.v.*) on Sept. 29, 1570, which says that Prele brought Glock a veil as a greeting from Moravia. He was acquainted with the country; Glock referred to him when he wrote of imprisoned Anabaptists. Thus Glock reported that Lienhard Sommer of Necklinsberg, one of the Swiss Brethren with whom he shared a prison on Hohenwittlingen, and with whom he had many an argument on the differences between Hutterian Brethren and the Swiss Brethren, must be acquainted with Prele. After their arrest Prele and Binder were held for several days in Neuffen. On April 24 they were cross-examined by a committee consisting of Johann Rucker, dean of Kirchheim, three clergymen, the magistrate Isaak Jäger, and a nobleman, probably Klaus von Greifeneck. The two were supposed to collect a debt in Frickenhausen, but the mayor arrested them and turned them over to the magistrate Isaak Jäger. Binder's cross-examination was lengthy, Prele's quite brief. In a letter written by Binder to Walpot dated May 16, they reported that they were well and that they were together in prison. At that time the magistrate said: "I have never heard of a Hutterite in this country who recanted his faith." On May 15 they were both questioned again. Prele was informed that by order of the prince he was to swear to leave the country permanently. He refused to render this oath, and was released without it. His petition to permit Binder to leave with him was rejected. Binder was held in Maulbronn and later in Hohenwittlingen. Presumably Prele took Binder's letter with him to Moravia. Nothing more is known of Prele. (*TA Württemberg;* Wolkan, *Geschicht-Buch,* 381 f.; Zieglschmid, *Chronik,* 491 ff.; *ML* III, 392.)
                                                  G.Bos.

Premont, Tex., a town (pop. 2,500) located in the southern part of Jim Wells County in southern Texas. There are 59 Mennonites living within shopping distance of Premont, who represent the M.C. and M.B. groups, each of which has a church. There have been Mennonites in this area for 30 years. The surrounding area is largely agricultural and ranch country, with some oil and gas. The Mennonite Brethren maintain a mission for Latin Americans.
                                                  H.F.R.

Premont Mennonite Brethren Church, located in Jim Wells County, southern Texas, had its beginning in settlement of a number of M.B. families in 1927. On Nov. 3, 1929, this group organized as a local church and at a subsequent meeting elected Elder H. H. Flaming as leader and pastor. Meetings were at first held in homes and in other buildings. In 1935 the congregation purchased some land and built its own church. Elder H. H. Flaming was followed by J. P. Kliewer 1941-47, John W. Duerksen 1947-52, Lewis H. Boese 1953-56 and 1958—, Ruben Wedel 1956-58. In 1958 the membership was 53. The church now has a parsonage and Sunday-school annex.   J.W.D.

Prenner (not Renner, as in *ML* I, 142), Jakob (Jörg), an Anabaptist martyr, a day laborer of Schmiechen, Upper Bavaria, Germany, who baptized about eighteen persons, was beheaded at Munich (*q.v.*) in 1528.   W.W.

S. Riezler, *Geschichte Bayerns* IV (Gotha, 1899) (*Geschichte der europäischen Staaten* LVIII) 194; J. E. Jörg, *Deutschland in der Revolutions-Periode von 1522 bis 1526* (Freiburg, 1851) 745; *ML* III, 392.

Prenzlau, a town 60 miles north of Berlin, Germany, was the location of one of the three camps (the other two Mölln in Lauenburg, and Hammerstein) provided by the German government for the temporary quartering of Mennonite refugees from Russia from November 1929 to the late summer of 1930, while they were waiting to move on to Brazil and Paraguay.   H.S.B.

Preparatory Schools (*Vorbereitungsschulen*) were schools among the Russian Mennonites of the prairie states and provinces, which came to their bloom at the turn of the last century. In the complex system and development of education among the Mennonites of this area the following criteria can be used to establish whether a certain school falls under this category or not: (1) the age of pupils was usually fourteen or above; (2) the curriculum included Biblical and high-school subjects; (3) the more advanced preparatory schools prepared students for teaching or college entrance. Originally the preparatory school was modeled after the Russian Mennonite Zentralschule (*q.v.*) and later more after the American high school. In this process of adjustment a number of the schools, not having enough students to develop according to the original plan, had to be satisfied to convey an elementary knowledge of the German language and Bible. These became known as Bible schools (*q.v.*).

The terms "Zentralschule" and "Fortbildungsschule" were used when the Emmatal School (*q.v.*) was established (1878). Already before this Peter Balzer had been teaching secondary courses in his school. Those preparatory schools able to pursue their goal to prepare students for teaching and college entrance later became known as academies (Bethel, Tabor, Freeman, etc.) of which some have been discontinued or have become colleges. Some are still functioning in this category, e.g., Meno and Corn, Okla., the Mennonite Collegiate Institute at Gretna, Man., and Rosthern Junior College in Saskatchewan. Recently established academies are Central Kansas Bible Academy (*q.v.*) and the Berean Academy (*q.v.*).

Two of the most prominent preparatory schools were the Hillsboro Preparatory School (*q.v.*), with H. D. Penner (*q.v.*) as founder, and the Mountain Lake Preparatory School (*q.v.*). The following is a partial list of the schools which fall under the category of preparatory schools (not included are those which have become colleges): Beatrice Bible Academy, Berean Academy, Central Kansas Bible Acad-emy, Corn Bible Academy, Emmatal Fortbildungsschule, Goessel Preparatory School, Gotebo Preparatory School, Henderson Bethesda Preparatory School, Hillsboro Preparatory School, Hoffnungsau Preparatory School, Meade Bible Academy, Mennonite Collegiate Institute, Moundridge Preparatory School, Mountain Lake Preparatory School, Oklahoma Bible Academy, Rosthern Junior College, Zoar Bible Academy.

The catalogs of the various preparatory schools which have been preserved are quite uniform in content. The one prepared by H. D. Penner for the Hillsboro Vorbereitungsschule probably served as a model for most of them. It states that the objective of the school is to prepare Mennonite youth for a higher school, for a special vocation, or for an intelligent concept of duties of life in general, and that boys and girls of at least fourteen years of age were accepted. The school year consisted of two semesters beginning September 28 and closing March 26. The tuition per semester was $7.50 and board and room $2.00 per week. The nine rules of the school emphasized standards of conduct generally observed in schools even in our day. Among the subjects offered in the first catalog were Bible history, world history, language, singing, and geography. During the second year two new subjects, church history and composition, are included in the curriculum. These schools usually had a two-year course. (See **Secondary Education.**) C.K.

Preparatory Service, the name given to the regular Sunday morning service preceding the communion service, or to a special service held on Saturday afternoon or evening preceding communion Sunday (as in the Franconia Mennonite MC Conference district in Eastern Pennsylvania) at which the intent of the sermon and the entire worship is to contribute to an inner preparation of the congregation for a better celebration of the communion. The custom is no longer as common as it once was among the Mennonites of North America or other countries. It is to be distinguished from the Counsel Meeting (*q.v.*), whose function, though also in a sense preparatory to the communion, was rather to deal with matters of church discipline. H.S.B.

Pressburg: see Bratislava.

Preston, a town (pop. 8,819) in Waterloo County, Ont., is situated 8 miles south of Kitchener and 60 miles west of Toronto. Led by George Clemens about 1800, the first Mennonite settlers here (from Pennsylvania) were soon followed by others. The settlement grew and prospered with the construction of a grist mill and sawmill. Known first as Cambridge, later Preston, it became a village in 1833. An important industrial center today, it has over 35 diversified industries. The Mennonites first met in homes for worship until 1842, when a church building was erected north of the town, called Hagey's. Twice destroyed by fire, it is now located within the town limits. Early leaders were Joseph Bechtel, first minister; Benjamin Eby, bishop and organizer; Martin Baer, David Sherk, and John Baer ministers. A 26-capacity home for the aged (Braeside) was dedicated in 1943. It was replaced by a new and larger building at the north edge of the town in 1956 called Fairview Mennonite Home.   H.E.Sn.

Preston (Ont.) Mennonite Church (MC), a member of the Ontario Conference, was from 1842 to 1953 known as the Hagey church because of the Hagey families in the congregation and because it was located at Hagey's crossing about one mile northwest of Preston. The meetinghouse, erected in 1842, was destroyed by fire in 1950; its successor was likewise destroyed by fire in 1953. The present brick meetinghouse at 791 Concession Road was dedicated May 16, 1954. In 1957 the membership was 119, with Howard Good as minister.

The Preston area was the place of earliest Mennonite settlement in Waterloo County, which began in 1799. The first ordained man in the area was Jacob Bechtel, a deacon who arrived in 1800. The first minister was Joseph Bechtel, who arrived in 1802 and was ordained preacher in 1804. Other ministers, with dates of arrival and ordination, were Martin Baer 1801 and 1808; Abr. L. Clemens, deacon, 1809 and 1815; John Baer, a son of Martin, ordained in 1838, but withdrew to join the "New Mennonites" (MBC) in 1874; Jacob Hagey, deacon, 1822 and 1832; Joseph Hagey 1822 and 1844, bishop 1857-76; David Sherk (1801-82), the most important early preacher of the congregation, ordained 1838; and Ben B. Shantz, 1908. Howard Good, the present pastor, was ordained in 1948.

Although the Preston area settlement was the oldest in Waterloo County, the history of the Hagey congregation before 1842 is obscure. The congregation must have met in the homes of the members for some time, since the first meetinghouse in the county, at Kitchener, was erected in 1813. There is some evidence that a meetinghouse was erected near Preston about the same time. The Wanner (q.v.) congregation (first meetinghouse 1829) has always been closely related to Hagey, and apparently for a long time the ministers served both the Hagey and Wanner congregations. For a time the Weber (Strasburg) (q.v.) church was included in the circuit. This area has for the past 70 years been progressive in outlook and activities.   H.S.B.

Pretle, Hans, an Anabaptist martyr, named in van Braght's *Martyrs' Mirror:* see **Brötli, Johannes.**

Pretoria, a Mennonite village name of the Orenburg and Terek settlements, Russia, given to the newly established villages because of sympathy for the Boers of South Africa during their independence struggle (see **Villages**).   C.K.

Pretoria Zentralschule. This four-class school, located in the village of Pretoria in the Orenburg Mennonite settlement of the Orenburg province, Russia, owed its existence to the energy and sacrificial spirit of Peter P. Dyck, a minister now living at Rosemary, Alberta. In 1907 Dyck organized an association to raise the educational standards of the Orenburg Mennonites, and in the same year began a school by teaching about 25 students in a private home in Pretoria. The attendance soon rose to

about 100. During World War I instruction was halted on government orders. It was resumed in 1918-19, with as many academically trained teachers as possible. Beginning in 1921, the school passed gradually into Soviet hands, leaving no authority to the Mennonite settlement. But in 1907-21 the school was of great benefit to the settlement, for many of the preachers, most of the teachers, and many other local officials attended it and then worked successfully for the settlement and the congregations.   W.Q.

Pretten, Paul: see **Prele, Paul.**

Pretty Prairie Amish Mennonite Church, now extinct, located about 10 miles north northeast of Lagrange, Ind., the meetinghouse of which, built in 1872, is still standing on the farm of Simon Bontrager. Early settlers were Christian K. Mast (born in Lancaster County, Pa., in 1822) 1864, Christian J. Plank of Adams County, Ind., 1859, Christian Nafziger (served as a preacher), Christian Stuckey, Christian Plank, Joseph Borntrager, and Jacob Hooley. Other ministers who served at Pretty Prairie were Christian Warye, who moved to Johnson County, Iowa, in 1884, Jonas C. Yoder, who moved to Logan County, Ohio, and Jonathan B. Hartzler (1850-1950), ordained preacher May 18, 1879, but who did his lifework in the Crown Hill (MC) congregation in Ohio. At the communion service in 1869 bishops J. D. Troyer of Marshall County, Ind., and Isaac Smucker of Lagrange County (Hawpatch congregation at Topeka) were in charge. Daniel Brenneman visited the congregation as early as 1866. The congregation had died out by 1915. The membership never exceeded 40.

                                            J.C.W.

Pretty Prairie First Mennonite Church (GCM), located 3 miles east of Pretty Prairie, Kan., a member of the Western District Conference, was organized Oct. 10, 1884, with 88 members of Swiss German descent, from Volhynia (q.v.), under the leadership of J. J. Flickinger, the first pastor. The first services were held in the homes of John B. Graber and Andrew Schwartz.

In 1886 the first meetinghouse was moved on the church ground. This church was sold in 1891. The second church, built in 1891, was destroyed by a tornado in 1897. A third structure, built in the same year on the same foundation, burned down in May 1905. The fourth church, built in 1905, was replaced in 1927 by a larger building, which seats 900. The parsonage was acquired in 1919. This church has a Sunday school, Christian Endeavor, and a sewing society.

Ministers who have served this congregation are: J. J. Flickinger 1884-1919, with John G. Graber assisting 1887-1917, J. B. Epp 1919-21, N. W. Bahnmann 1922-25, J. W. Lohrenz 1925-32, S. M. Musselman 1932-37, P. P. Tschetter 1937-48, and Howard G. Nyce 1948-58. The membership in 1957 was 622.   H.G.N.

Arthur J. Graber, "The Swiss Mennonites—Pretty Prairie," *Menn. Life* V (April 1950).

Pretscher, Friedrich, an Anabaptist martyr, a cleric at Nordheim in Franconia, South Germany. Pretscher had previously been a monk but, perhaps out of sympathy for his brother Martin Luther, he left the monastery. On a suspicion that Pretscher was an Anabaptist, the Bishop of Würzburg had him arrested on Feb. 17, 1528, and taken to Würzburg. George, Margrave of Brandenburg, having heard of his arrest through the magistrate of Kottenheim, interceded for him and a lengthy correspondence ensued, in which the bishop asserted that according to the testimony of two executed Anabaptists as well as his own confession Pretscher was guilty of performing adult baptisms. Thereupon the margrave withdrew his petition for clemency. Pretscher was put to death on April 15, 1528.   W.W.

H. Clauss, "Kleine Beiträge zur Geschichte der Wiedertäufer in Franken," in *Ztscht für bayrische kirchengesch.* XVI (Erlangen, 1941) 174; K. Schornbaum, "Zur Einführung der Reformation in die Herrschaft Schwarzenberg," in *Jahresbericht des Hist. Vereins für Mittelfranken,* No. 58 (Ansbach, 1911) 136 f.; *TA Brandenburg; ML* III, 394.

Preubler, Andreas, an Anabaptist leader around Steyr in Upper Austria (*q.v.*). Little is known of his life and work except that he was a shoemaker, and the author of a booklet of "seventeen pages" on baptism, which has, however, not yet come to light. Its contents are known through a refutation by the Lutheran scholar Gall Steininger (in 1566 appointed as preacher in Peuerbach, Upper Austria, and in 1584 the author of a book on original sin, attacking the Flaccians), who indulged in violent accusations against the Anabaptists, using vulgar expressions, hardly to be duplicated in any other writing against them.

According to Preubler's booklet the Anabaptists taught as follows: the nations should first have the Gospel preached to them, and then, if they accept the Word, they should be baptized; since little children cannot be taught, they should not be baptized. The apostles first gave instruction in the mysteries of faith and did not baptize until that was done. The baptism of children should be postponed until they are grown and able to understand the doctrine. Those who let baptism precede indoctrination are not messengers of Christ, but of Antichrist. All who are to be baptized must first through the Holy Spirit acknowledge the forgiveness of their sins through the preaching of mercy in the New Testament, otherwise baptism has no value. Infant baptism was invented by men and was instituted and preserved by the spirit of Antichrist. Only through faith in the name of Christ is one saved, and not through infant baptism, nor indeed through adult baptism nor through other good works. Christ has given to all, while we were yet dead in sin, life with Him; by faith in Him one is born anew. If justification comes through Christ's righteousness, it cannot come through baptism. God accepts little children by grace, even without baptism or other service of the church, in case of early death. But the baptizers of infants wish to make children acceptable to God through baptism, which is a work of the law, thereby denying God's grace. By trying to make little children acceptable to God by baptism faith

is extinguished and the Word, the office, and the work of Christ are weakened and blasphemed. The Jewish infants who died before they were circumcised on the eighth day were certainly not damned. Likewise our children are not damned without baptism. He who attaches his salvation to external ceremonies honors the creature more than the Creator; this is what baptizers of infants do, for they attach salvation to baptism. They thereby deny the finished work of Christ, who has won and sealed our salvation with His blood. The Holy Spirit alone is the assurance of our salvation, and not infant baptism. Christ says (John 15): Ye are clean through the Word; hence one is not made clean through baptism. Christ urges inner purification (Matt. 23); but infant baptism is only an external cleansing, a work performed by man. True inward cleansing and washing away of sins is done through the Spirit of our God (I Cor. 6; Heb. 8, 9, and 10).

Steininger expressed his opinion that such terrible blasphemies against Christ and His sacraments had never before been heard; such a devilish rascal should have his tongue pulled out of his throat; the Jews would not have tolerated such a blasphemer, but would have stoned him, especially since God has commanded it. (Source: Collection of Joseph Beck's papers in the Moravian Archives at Brno; *ML* III, 394 f.)   W.W.

Preussisch Holland (Polish, *Paslek*), originally called simply Holland, a town (1946 pop. 3,278) in East Prussia southeast of Elbing (since 1945 in Olsztyn, formerly Allenstein, a province of Poland), in which there were a few Mennonites until the collapse in 1945, members of the Heubuden and Thiensdorf-Preussisch Rosengart congregations. The articles of the founding of the town, dated Sept. 29, 1297, mention that it was named for settlers from Holland. In 1527 a new immigration from the Netherlands set in, at first east of the city toward Bardeyn, consisting of Sacramentists (*q.v.*). Others, including Anabaptists, under the leadership of Hermann Sachs, on Feb. 1, 1539, received permission to settle the village of Schönberg (and also Judendorf) north of the town in the district of Preussisch Holland (document printed in Schumacher, 176-78). Their names and the occupations of some are given by Schumacher (184). Their deviation from the religion of the duchy, however, soon became apparent; hence they were expelled by the great church inspection of 1542-43; only a few adjusted themselves to the dominant church in order to be permitted to remain in the country. (See **East Prussia.**)   E.C.

Mennonitisches Adressbuch (Karlsruhe, 1936); Bruno Schumacher, *Niederländische Ansiedlungen im Herzogtum Preussen zur Zeit Herzog Albrechts 1525-68* (Leipzig, 1903); Felicia Szper, *Nederlandsche nederzettingen in West-Pruisen gedurende den poolschen tijd* (Enkhuizen, 1913); B. H. Unruh, "Kolonisatorische Berührungen zwischen den Mennoniten und den Siedlern anderer Konfessionen im Weichselgebiet und der Neumark," *Deutsches Archiv für Landes- und Volksforschung* IV (1940) 256-60; Hans Egon Wolfram, *Die Niederlande und der deutsche Osten* (Berlin, 1943); *ML* III, 397.

Preussisch Rosengart, a village (1944 pop. 367) in the Marienburg district of West Prussia, in which 55 Mennonites, members of the Thiensdorf-Preussisch Rosengart congregation, were living in 1945. In 1776 and again in 1888 there were 23 Mennonite families here; in 1936 there were only 17. In 1888, when the Nogat River dam broke, the church at Markushof (q.v.) was severely damaged. Without awaiting an appeal for help to come from West Prussia, Pastor van der Smissen of Hamburg issued an appeal for aid to the victims of the flood. A committee composed of pastors van der Smissen of Hamburg, Mannhardt of Danzig, and Harder of Elbing, requested permission of the Dutch Mennonites to set aside 18,000 Marks of the Dutch relief fund for the erection of a church for the congregations of Thiensdorf and Markushof, which had been divided into two congregations for about a century. Thus they were reunited. The church was built (1891) in Preussisch Rosengart, rather than in Markushof, which was too close to Thiensdorf. This church was one of the few Mennonite churches to have a bell. With the assistance of a Wiehler family, Eva von Tiele-Winckler (q.v.) built two homes for the homeless here in 1916-18.   G.R., E.C.

Mennonitisches Adressbuch (Karlsruhe, 1936); Eva von Tiele-Winckler, *Nichts unmöglich!* (Dresden, 1929) 206-13, 311; *ML* III, 397.

Pribitz (Priebitz), a Hutterite Bruderhof located several miles south of Selowitz (q.v.) in Moravia on an elevation on the left bank of the Iglava; when the Brethren settled here in 1565 it belonged to the Selowitz domain, which had been acquired by their great benefactor Friedrich von Zierotin (q.v.), who later became lord of Moravia. The Brethren built the entire Bruderhof; it soon developed into one of the best in the land. On Feb. 17, 1572, this Bruderhof confirmed Wendel Holba (or Müller) and Rupp Gellner (q.v.) as preachers, and on April 19, 1573, three additional preachers, and again on April 27, 1575, three preachers. On May 23, 1575, five more were confirmed by the elder by the laying on of hands. Here the deacon Valtin Preindl died in 1576, and the well-known Peter Walpot (q.v.) on Jan. 30, 1578, one of the three elders, "highly endowed with the Spirit of God and an ornament of the entire brotherhood." Here also occurred the death of the preacher Josef Doppelhammer (or Schuster) on Dec. 24, 1580, "who from his youth had been with and was raised in the brotherhood." In 1582 the deacon Christian Häring (q.v.) died, who had served the brotherhood for forty years and was one of the Brethren who had been condemned to the galleys, but who escaped in Trieste; also on Dec. 30, 1586 (in some manuscripts Feb. 2, 1587), occurred the death of the preacher Georg Planer or Uhrmacher.

A thriving industry in Pribitz was that of clock making; its fame was spread throughout the land. The town of Mödritz obtained a tower clock from the Bruderhof in 1572 for the price of thirty florins. But also the medical arts were given special attention here as they were also in Nikolsburg (q.v.). Especially the noblemen preferred to employ the Pribitz physicians (barber-surgeons). The baron of Vostitz (Wastitz) and Pürschitz (q.v.), Franz, Count Thurn Valsassina, for instance, summoned Tengler, a physician of the Bruderhof, to care for his son, who was wounded in the war against the

Turks in 1583; the treatment was successful in restoring him.

According to a tax list of the Selowitz domain the Bruderhof in the 1590's owned a smithy with a garden, a meadow, some vineyards, a hop garden, a river fishery, and a cemetery, for which an annual tax of 16 florins had to be paid. On Jan. 8, 1594, occurred the death of Jakob of Hinnen (or Kiss), and on Sept. 2, 1599, David Hasel (see **Michael Hasel**), both preachers; on Jan. 10, 1606, Johann Rath, "an outstanding preacher of the Gospel." Here Michel Grossman was confirmed as an elder on Feb. 5, 1606, and two brethren were chosen to the office of preacher. On Feb. 12, 1609, the deacon Mathes Pühler died here.

In 1609 the parish of Freiberg in Moravia purchased of the Pribitz Brethren a clock for the church tower for 250 florins. For Franz, Cardinal of Dietrichstein (q.v.), they made a clock in 1613 for the sum of 170 talers, and an equally costly one for the Archduke Maximilian, who requested their baron, Johann Dionys von Zierotin, to place the order for him.

In Pribitz occurred the death of the two deacons, Michel Ritter on Feb. 27, 1615, and Merthin Hederich on May 1, 1616; also the death of the preacher Hänsel Stam on Dec. 1, 1616. In autumn 1619 the fateful invasion of Moravia by Dampierre's troops took place; twelve Bruderhofs fell as victims to them. The Pribitz Brethren sought to escape the danger by removing the sick and aged as well as the children to Austerlitz (q.v.). On their return on September 14 the aged, the ill, and the children, being brought home from Austerlitz and Lettonitz on twelve wagons, fell into the hands of Dampierre's men, who at once shot down three Brethren accompanying the caravan, scattered the women and children into "the water, moor, and reeds," raping four of the women. The troops took all the wagons with their provisions and forty horses. The scattered victims did not venture to come out of hiding for three or four days, and "there was in this crowd such great misery, fear, and terror and distress, also a lamentable crying and weeping of the young and old that it would have moved a stone to pity."

But the Pribitz Bruderhof was to be visited by even greater disaster. On July 28, 1620, on a Tuesday morning at three o'clock, "while all the people were lying in bed without worry," the Bruderhof was attacked by imperial horsemen and musketeers, mostly Poles, who in less than three hours murdered 52 of the Brethren, including a young mother with her child, "tortured some for money" by burning them with glowing irons, cutting wounds into the calves of the legs and setting fire to powder placed into the cuts, pouring hot fat over their naked bodies, pinching off fingers, and other satanic measures. In addition about sixty persons were seriously wounded, "shot, stabbed, and beaten," some of whom died of their wounds; a total of 71 persons lost their lives. Most of the women, "married and single, also some girls of ten or twelve years," were abused before the eyes of their families. The wounded Vorsteher Hans Jakob Wolf, a large number of women, and several men, a total of 70 persons, "together with an inexpressibly severe robbery, also all the horses, cattle and oxen, all the cows, and much food, were taken away." The "Pribitzer Lied" describes this in detail. In December, when the neighborhood was plundered and pillaged, the brotherhood of Pribitz fled to Pausram (*q.v.*). On Jan. 5, 1621, the Pribitz Bruderhof was robbed and burned down by imperial troops. By order of Cardinal Dietrichstein one of the five caches of money betrayed by Vorsteher Hirzel (*q.v.*) was dug up by Count Breuner on July 23; after a long search a second was found on July 30. Adam von Waldstein, who acquired the Selowitz lands in 1616, complained to the Cardinal about the removal of this money; the latter referred him to the imperial court from whom the Cardinal claimed to have received a letter sanctioning the course. In October 1622 Pribitz had to be evacuated and all that they had rebuilt left behind. P.DE.

Beck, *Geschichts-Bücher;* Wolkan, *Geschicht-Buch;* Franticec Hruby, "*Die Wiedertäufer in Mähren*," in *Archiv für Ref.-Gesch.* XXX-XXXII (1935); Th. Unger, "Ueber eine Wiedertäufer-Liederhandschrift des 17. Jahrhunderts," in *Jahrbuch der Gesellschaft für die Gesch. des Protestantismus in Oesterreich* XV (1894) 24 f.; Gregor Wolny, *Kirchliche Topographie von Mähren* II: *Brünner Erzdiözese* I (Brno, 1856) 294; II (Brno, 1858) 235 f.; the "*Priebitzer Lied*" is found in Beck, *Geschichts-Bücher,* 379, 380, 382, 383, 385, 387; *ML* III, 397 f.

Prijntgen Maelbouts, an Anabaptist martyr: see **Pierijntgen van Male.**

Primavera, a Hutterite colony in East (Alto) Paraguay (*q.v.*), located about 80 miles northeast of Asuncion. This colony was founded in 1941 when the inhabitants of the Cotswold Bruderhof in Wiltshire, England, because of the outbreak of World War II, were forced to leave England. The movement to Paraguay was made with the assistance of the Mennonite Central Committee and the American Friends Service Committee, and the settlement was made adjacent to the Mennonite Colony of Friesland to the east. The colony consists of three separate village communities—Isla Margarita, established in 1941, Loma Jhoby, 1942, and Ibate, 1946. The total population was 350 in 1941, 650 in 1951, and 650 in 1958. Of the 650 persons in 1951, 350 were children under fifteen. Eighteen different nationalities (about 50 per cent are English, about 20 per cent are German) and 90 family names are found among the Primavera Hutterites. The chief source of income is agriculture; some industry has developed, particularly the extraction and bottling of orange juice, tangerines, and grapefruit. By their education programs and their hospital (Sanatorio Primavera) the community has proved to be very helpful to the native Paraguayans. The official corporate name in Paraguay is Sociedad Fraternal Hutteriana (*q.v.*). It maintains a home and business office in Asuncion (40 persons 1958). vDZ.

J. W. Fretz, *Pilgrims in Paraguay* (Scottdale, n.d.-1953) 53-59; *ML* III, 398.

Princess Anne County (Va.) Amish Mennonites. Old Order Amish families moved to this county first in 1907 from Somerset and Lancaster counties, Pa.

Early arrivals were the families of Ben Smucker, Daniel Hershberger, Elias A. Yoder, Noah E. Yoder, Milton E. Yoder, and Peter D. Kinsinger. The first resident bishop was Daniel D. Yoder. William S. Yoder, Simon D. Schrock, and Jonas H. Hershberger were later bishops. A meetinghouse was erected in 1913 midway between Norfolk and Virginia Beach; it was enlarged in 1927 and in 1948.

In 1941 a division occurred, which resulted in a migration of many Old Order Amish members to Stuarts Draft, Va. Those remaining conceded the use of automobiles, and are now known as the Kempsville Amish Mennonite Church (*q.v.*), which belongs to the Beachy Amish group. The congregation has had a Sunday school since 1922, and has supported an elementary church school since 1946. The community is located in a favorable market area, with dairying and vegetable farming in the vicinity. The membership in 1957 was 136. J.A.H.

Prins, a common Dutch family name both Mennonite and non-Mennonite. A widely ramified Mennonite family by this name is found in the province of North Holland, originating from de Rijp, where Arent Claesz Prins, b. *c*1635, was a shipbuilder and shipowner, as were his descendants until *c*1750. They gave up shipbuilding after de Rijp was no longer an important shipping and whaling center. Members of this family thereupon moved to Purmerend and Wormerveer. In Wormerveer Simon Jansz Prins (1738-1814) was a merchant in grains and the founder of a starch factory, which business was also run by his son Cornelis **Simonsz Prins (1771-1843, who was 1811-d.43 at the same time a burgomaster of Wormerveer)** and his grandson Simon Cornelisz Prins (1796-1871) who added a linseed oil factory, gradually also becoming engaged in limited liability companies, running similar businesses.

In de Rijp some members of this family have been trustees of the Mennonite orphanage; in Wormerveer some of them were deacons. As far as known none of them served as a minister of the church. vDZ.

Ned. Patriciaat XII (1921-22) 120-30; information by J. Aten, Wormerveer.

Prins, A. Winkler: see **Winkler Prins, A.**

Prischib, a village and volost of a Protestant and Roman Catholic German settlement west of the Molotschna River and the Molotschna Mennonite settlement in the Ukraine, Russia, province of Taurida, was established in 1804 and consisted of 125,000 acres and 27 villages. The village of Prischib, 33 miles north of Melitopol, was the administrative center of the settlement just across the Molotschna River from the Mennonite administrative center of Halbstadt (*q.v.*). In 1913 the population was 810, in 1919, 1,185. Numerous business enterprises and a Zentralschule, established in 1873, a girls' school, an institution for the deaf, and a bookstore were located in the village. Gottlieb Schaad published the *Molotschnaer Volks-Kalender* at Prischib from 1881 on. There was a lively exchange of cultural and economic values between the Molotschna Mennonites and their Prischib neighbors.   C.K.

Emil Blank, "Die Prischiber Volost," *Neuer Haus- und Landwirtschafts-Kalender* (Odessa, 1913) 107 ff.

Privileges (*Privilegium*), i.e., grant of privilege or special license, known sometimes as letters of protection, were documents which granted a release from military service and the oath, usually issued by a ruler; they occurred in Mennonite history principally in the 17th century, but also as late as the 20th century. Following is a list of all known Privileges:

(*a*) *Netherlands* (*q.v.*): Jan. 26, 1577, Prince William of Orange; printed in van Braght's *Martyrs' Mirror* (D 747, E 1054); printed in *DJ* 1930, 120-23.

(*b*) *Palatinate* (*q.v.*): Aug. 4, 1664, Elector Charles Louis (*q.v.*); printed in *ML* II, 461 f.

(*c*) *Wied* (*q.v.*): Dec. 16, 1680, Count Frederick I for Neuwied (*q.v.*); printed in *Beiträge zur Geschichte rheinischer Mennoniten* (Weierhof, 1939) 152 f.

(*d*) *East Friesland:* May 26, 1626, Count Rudolf Christian (*q.v.*); printed in J. P. Müller, *Die Mennoniten in Ostfriesland vom 16. bis zum 18. Jahrhundert* I (Emden, 1887) 41.

(*e*) *Holstein* (*q.v.*)-*Gottorp*: Feb. 13, 1623, Duke Frederick III (*q.v.*) for Friedrichstadt (*q.v.*); printed in *Corpus Statutorum Slevicensium* III 1 (Schleswig, 1799) 587.

(*f*) *Denmark* (*q.v.*): June 6, 1641, King Christian IV for Altona (*q.v.*); printed in Johann Adrian Bolten, *Historische Kirchennachrichten von der Stadt Altona* (Altona, 1790/91) 283 f., and Berend Carl Roosen, *Geschichte der Mennoniten-Gemeinde zu Hamburg und Altona* I (Hamburg, 1886) 37 f.

(*g*) *Prussia* (*q.v.*): Jan. 30, 1721, King Frederick William I (*q.v.*) for Crefeld (*q.v.*); printed in *Beiträge zur Geschichte rheinischer Mennoniten* (Weierhof, 1939) 56 f. March 27, 1780, King Frederick II (*q.v.*) for West Prussia (*q.v.*) and East Prussia (*q.v.*), also printed in Reiswitz and Wadzeck, *Beiträge zur Kenntnis der Mennonitengemeinden* (Berlin, 1821) 212 ff., and in Max Beheim-Schwarzbach, *Hohenzollernsche Colonisationen* (Leipzig, 1874) 420.

(*h*) *Poland* (*q.v.*): Dec. 22, 1642, King Ladislaw IV (*q.v.*); printed in Wilhelm Mannhardt, *Die Wehrfreiheit der Altpreussischen Mennoniten* (Marienburg, 1863) LX-LXI (1, Lat.) and 80 ff. (German)—Aug. 22, 1694, King John III (*q.v.*); printed in Wilhelm Mannhardt, *Die Wehrfreiheit der Altpreussischen Mennoniten* (Marienburg, 1863) LXV-LXVI (4, Lat.) and 87 ff. (German)—Oct. 12 (or 18), 1732, King August II (*q.v.*); printed in Wilhelm Mannhardt, *Die Wehrfreiheit der Altpreussischen Mennoniten* (Marienburg, 1863) LXVII-LXVIII (5, Lat.) and 90 f. (German), also printed in Hermann Nottarp, *Die Mennoniten in den Marienburger Werdern (Schriften der Königsberger Gelehrten Gesellschaft, geisteswissenschaftliche Klasse* VI, 2, Halle, 1929) 89 f.—Sept. 19, 1750, King August III (*q.v.*); printed in Wilhelm Mannhardt, *Die Wehrfreiheit der Altpreussischen Mennoniten* (Marienburg, 1863) 93 ff. (German).

(*i*) *Russia* (*q.v.*): Sept. 6, 1800, Czar Paul I (*q.v.*); printed in David Heinrich Epp, *Die Chor-*titzer *Mennoniten* (Odessa, 1889), also in Anna Brons, *Ursprung, Entwickelung und Schicksale der . . . Mennoniten* (Amsterdam, 1912) 278 ff.

(*j*) *Mexico* (*q.v.*): Aug. 26, 1921, Declaration of President Alvaro Obregon; printed in J. Winfield Fretz, *Mennonite Colonization in Mexico* (Akron, 1945) 11 (English) and also in *ML* III, 120 (German).

(*k*) *Paraguay* (*q.v.*): July 26, 1921, Law No. 514; printed in *Las Colonias Menonitas en el Chaco Paraguayo* (Asuncion, 1934) 5 ff. (Spanish and German), also in Walter Quiring, *Russlanddeutsche suchen eine Heimat (Schriftenreihe des Deutschen Ausland-Instituts* 7, Karlsruhe, 1938) 51 ff., in *Der Mennonit*, March 1950, 32 (German), in Sanford C. Yoder, *For Conscience Sake* (Scottdale, 1945) 275 ff., and in Willard H. Smith and Verna Graber Smith, *Paraguayan Interlude* (Scottdale, 1950) 174 ff. (English).   E.C.

E. Crous, "Die Mennoniten in Deutschland seit dem Dreissigjährigen Kriege," in *Der Mennonit* III (1950) 7; *ML* III, 398 f.

Proba Fidei: see **Valerius de Scholmeester.**

Probier-Stein. *Oder Schrifftmässige und auss dem wahren innerlichen Christenthumb Hargenommene Gewissenhaffte Prüfung dess Täufferthums In der Forcht des Herrn Herrn zu Allegemeiner Erbauung Abgefasset* (Bern, 1696) is a small octavo volume of 610 numbered pages, besides 82 pages of introductory material including a short history of Anabaptism, written by a Reformed minister, Georg Thormann (1655-1708), at that time serving as pastor at Lützelflüh in the Swiss canton of Bern. It was prepared at the request of both the civil and ecclesiastical authorities of Bern and printed by the government printery. The author states his purpose to be to give the common people a book which will strengthen them against the "strongly growing" Anabaptism, and indicates that he intends to do this in a good way, different from the usual polemics. He even states that he will not use the term "Widertäuffer," because "it is so hated by them," but will use "Täufer" instead.

Thormann actually presents a very fair picture of the Bernese Anabaptists, making no effort to show them in a bad light. He says repeatedly that his readers are well informed concerning the doctrine of these people and their commendable life and conduct. He writes, "Among our country people the opinion prevails in general that whoever sees an Anabaptist sees a saint, a person who is dead to the world, having experienced true conversion, and that there are no more earnest and consecrated people than they." And again, "If among all Christian communions there is one which seems to be upright and give assurance of personal salvation to the soul, it is certainly that of the Anabaptists. And this is true to such an extent that their religion appears to very many of our country people as by far the surest way of salvation." And again, "Their regard for them is such that many look upon them as saints, as the salt of the earth and the very kernel of Christendom. Their opinion concerning them is so favorable that many believe a good Christian and an Anabaptist to be one and the same thing." The latter part of the book contains earnest challenges to follow the good example of the Anabaptists. Thormann's book gives abundant light on the question why the Bernese in spite of tremendous effort found it impossible to exterminate them. It was because the general population in the area where the Anabaptists lived sympathized with them and gave them assistance and help in every possible way.

The book is divided into four parts described by the author as follows: (1) "an account of the apparent reasons why the country people have such a great regard for the Anabaptists"; (2) "a discussion of the points of difference: infant baptism, preacher's office, ban, oath, war, etc., and which shows that it is quite unnecessary to be an Anabaptist to be saved"; (3) "proof that it is rather highly dangerous to one's salvation to be an Anabaptist"; (4) "conclusion, directions showing how a true Christian among us should live and serve the Lord to all pleasing, and should fulfill all righteousness in spirit and in truth."

This is one of the most remarkable books ever written by an enemy of the Anabaptist-Mennonites, and is very valuable for a knowledge of these people in the Emmenthal in the canton of Bern in the late 17th century. The above description is taken in part from John Horsch's account of the book in his *Mennonites in Europe* (Scottdale, 1942), pp. 398-40. The Goshen College Library copy of the *Probier-Stein* was once the possession of Adolf Fluri (*q.v.*) of Bern.　　　　　　　　　　　　　　　　　H.S.B.

Proefdienaar. This former Dutch Mennonite term was used in two different senses: (*a*) When a member of a congregation was chosen as preacher or deacon he was frequently "beproeft" (examined) by the elder(s) who were present concerning his views on the basic principles and doctrines of the church, and asked whether he was willing to accept the call. If the examination was satisfactory, he was called a "proefdienaar" and after a longer or shorter interval he preached his installation sermon. This practice existed, for example, on the island of Ameland (*q.v.*) until the middle of the 19th century. (*DB* 1889, 28-30.) (*b*) In a somewhat different sense the word is found in the congregation of Leiden and other Dutch congregations, where a chosen candidate had to "in de proeve staan," i.e., he was obliged to deliver two or three or even more sermons to show his capacities in speaking and expounding the Scriptures, and was during this period called a "proefdienaar."　　vDZ.

Proentgen (Peronne, Pronken, Pierrine, Pierrette, Pierotte Pertrijs), an Anabaptist martyr, the daughter of Willem van Meteren, wife of Karel van de Velde (*q.v.*), and sister of Claesken, who was the wife of Françoys de Swarte. She was arrested at Hondschoote in Flanders, with Claesken and her husband and three other Anabaptists. The others were burned at the stake; but she and her sister were secretly drowned there in a tub on Oct. 3, 1562. "One of the women, when she saw that they intended to put her to death secretly, complained of it, since she would have preferred to testify publicly

to the truth with her death, whereupon her sister said: 'It is all the same, for God sees it; He will reward us and avenge our wrongs.'" (*Mart. Mir.* D 298, E 663; *ML* III, 399.)　　　　　　　　　E.C.

Proentgen, an Anabaptist martyr, wife of Karel Tancreet, was put to death with eleven other Anabaptists at Gent, Belgium, in 1559. This meager account found in van Braght's *Martyrs' Mirror* can be amplified by information published by Verheyden from the records. Peronne Witgans (her official name) was a native of Belle (Bailleul) in Flanders. Her execution took place on July 5, 1559, at seven o'clock in the morning. She was burned at the stake with five other martyrs, while on July 4 four others, arrested several days earlier, had been burned at the stake, among whom was Karel Tancreet, Proentgen's husband. These martyrs are commemorated in a hymn, "Ick moet ein Liet beginnen" (I must begin a song), found in the *Lietboecxken.* (*Offer,* 348, 556; *Mart. Mir.* D 246, E 620; Verheyden, *Gent,* 25, No. 66; *ML* III, 400.)　　　　　　　vDZ.

Proeve, Een Christelijke, *ende overlegginge ofte rekeninge, waerin dat allen B. en S. vermaendt worden tot een scherp ende neerstich ondersoec haers selfs, ende der gantscher menichte,* is a Dutch Mennonite book, published in 1570, reprinted in 1610 (n.p.) and at Haarlem in 1626. It was published after the Dutch Mennonites had been divided by the Frisian-Flemish schism, in which the Zierikzee (*q.v.*) congregation had remained neutral, and were therefore called *Stilstaanders* (*q.v.*). They were banned both by Frisians and Flemish. In *Een Christelijke Proeve* they give the motivation of their neutrality, criticizing the dissentious groups and urging peace and reconciliation.　　　　　　　　　　vDZ.

H. W. Meihuizen, *Galenus Abrahamsz* (Haarlem, 1954) 8-12.

Prook, a Dutch Mennonite family found at Aalsmeer, province of North Holland, since at least the 17th century. Some members of this family have been preachers of the "Oude Vermaning" (Frisians) on the Uiterweg, viz., Cornelis (Pieters) Prook serving 1746-c80, Gerrit Jansen Prook 1786-c1825, Pieter Gerrits Prook, preacher 1810, elder 1850-d.55, and Willem Cornelis Prook 1855-d.60.　　vDZ.

W. Tsj. Vleer, *De aloude Aalsmeerse familiën* (De Kaag, n.d.-1953); *Naamlijst;* Gorter's *Doopsgezinde Lectuur* (1856), appendix 30 f.

Prophets, Worms Translation of, by Hans Denk (*q.v.*) and Ludwig Haetzer (*q.v.*): see **Worms Translation.**

Proponent, Dutch designation for a ministerial candidate. Formerly and particularly in the last decades of the 18th and early 19th centuries a young man who had been trained by a Mennonite minister was in many cases examined by a local church board, and if the outcome was satisfactory he was appointed "proponent." The students of the Amsterdam Mennonite Seminary (*q.v.*), founded in 1735, were until 1810 examined and appointed as proponents by the church board of the Amsterdam congregation and after 1811 by the trustees of the

A.D.S. (Dutch General Mennonite Conference) or by a committee appointed by the A.D.S. for the examinations, as is done today. Occasionally, but not since 1849, the Mennonite Conference of Friesland also appointed proponents.   vDZ.

Propst, Jörg: see **Rothenfelder, Jörg.**

Protection Fee: see **Taxation.**

Protection Mennonite Church (MC), six miles south of Protection, Comanche Co., Kan., a member of the South Central Conference, was organized March 7, 1907. Services were first held in a schoolhouse two miles south of Protection. Early ministers included Bishop George R. Brunk, and ministers N. E. Ebersole, Ben Horst, and C. W. Miller. When George R. Brunk moved away, S. C. Miller assumed bishop oversight. On Nov. 1, 1908, the first church was dedicated. In 1917 the church was enlarged. The membership increased from 37 in 1907 to 86 in 1956. D. D. Miller served as minister (1917) and as bishop 1927-41. Charles Schweitzer served 1935-53. From 1956 Sanford C. Oyer was the minister in charge.   C.Sc.

Protestantenbond Hymnal: see **Nederlandse Protestantenbond.**

Protocol dat is, *de gantsche handelinge des ghesprecx ghehouden tot Leeuwarden* . . . : see **Leeuwarden Disputation.**

Protocol. Dath is, *alle handelinge des gesprecks tho Emden in Oistfrieszlandt mit den Wedderdöperen* . . . : *see* **Emden Disputation.**

Protocoll of the religious disputation of Leeuwarden, 1595: see **Leeuwarden.**

Protocoll, *Das ist Alle handlung des gesprechs zu Franckenthal inn der Churfürstlichen Pfaltz, mit denen so man Widertäuffer nennet:* see **Frankenthal Disputation.**

Protokoll, *dat is alle handelingen des Gesprecks tot Emden:* see **Emden.**

Protzka (Czech, *Broczko,* today *Brodsko*), a Slovak village in Hungary, now in the Nitra (German, *Neutra*) province of Czechoslovakia. During the severe persecution of 1547 the Hutterian Brethren who had to flee from their Bruderhofs in Moravia turned to Hungary, where they were given domicile in Berencs (Präntsch) by Count Franz Nizry von Bedek and in Holitsch and Schossberg by Peter Bakich de Làk (*q.v.*). Here, with considerable difficulty in clearing the land, they built houses. One of the Bruderhofs set up at that time was Protzka. Here in 1554 the deacon Jörg Ladendorfer died, and on Dec. 1, 1556, in his fiftieth year, Peter Riedemann (*q.v.*), the revered leader, whose confession of faith, the noted *Rechenschaft* (*q.v.*), was printed probably by 1545 and who was also the author of a long series of letters, which are among the principal sources for the study of Anabaptist doctrine, as well

as nearly fifty songs. He had been a preacher for twenty-seven years.

On March 4, 1597, Hans Zuckenhammer (*q.v.*) was publicly excommunicated in Protzka. After serving as a preacher for seventeen years, he proved himself unworthy by his unjust decisions and other wrong deeds, and finally rebelled against his removal from this office in Lewär. Before his death he "made his peace" with the brotherhood, and was restored to fellowship; he died in Protzka on April 29, 1598.

On May 4, 1605, rebel Hungarians attacked the Bruderhof here. Most of the Brethren succeeded in escaping before the soldiers plundered and burned the house. Three men and several women who had remained were mistreated. Not until 1616 did the Brethren rebuild, having first concluded a new contract with the current owner, Michael Czobor, who wanted them to resettle there. Work was begun on June 4. But by Feb. 6, 1621, the Bruderhof was attacked by Polish auxiliaries of the imperial army and pillaged anew. On the afternoon of April 28, 1623, a fire broke out in the smithy, which destroyed half the house with the goods in it, as well as some of the cattle. In the late fall the Bruderhof was involved in the conflict between Gabriel Bethlen and the emperor. When Janos Czobor plundered Lewär, others following his example fell upon Protzka on October 28, plundering, driving away the cattle, and finally burning down the whole house including the newly rebuilt part. But in spite of these bitter experiences the Brethren again rebuilt their house, completing it in a few months.

In 1625 the Brethren were struck by new misfortune. Without any justification the baron demanded of the Brethren a tribute of 200 talers, several knives, and a piece of cloth. The Brethren pointed out that their house in Protzka had been burned twice in three years, and that they had been charged an extremely high price by the baron for protection during the Turkish invasion, and were therefore unable to pay the required sum. Because of this refusal the householder and the purchaser, "two aged Brethren," were arrested. The brotherhood sent a delegation consisting of a preacher and two lay Brethren to the baron, who was not at home, but "several miles behind Kascha(u)," to ask for the release of the prisoners. After his return from the Landtag at Oedenburg, Czobor summoned the elders of Protzka and Sobotiste (*q.v.*) "to settle the debt once for all." Czobor owed the Brethren 313 florins, which he wished to cancel against a debt of 80 florins the Brethren owed him, and also demanded the payment of 2,000 talers in return for the protection he had given them during the Turkish disturbance, in order to pay for the fields the Turks had devastated, though Czobor had fully compensated himself for the lodging he had given the Brethren by confiscating all their hogs. When they rejected this demand he threatened to have the Bruderhof plundered by his Hussars, and could only with difficulty be deflected from this plan. After lengthy negotiations he finally agreed on a sum of 100 florins and a quantity of grain and promised to observe the terms of the contract signed with the Brethren by his father.

Scarcely was this danger past, when a band of fifty imperial cavalrymen of Wallenstein's army plundered Protzka on Sept. 21, 1626, and took nearly all the cattle. On Feb. 20, 1627, the Bruderhof was attacked by wandering Croats, and more cattle taken away. When more and more imperial troops continued to threaten the Moravian-Hungarian border, the Brethren were compelled to seek safety in the castle. In 1628 their oppressor Czobor died, and his widow demanded a payment of 40 florins. The refusal of the Brethren to make this payment was countered by her taking their four best oxen.

On March 5, 1632, a band of newly recruited Croats and Hungarians fell upon the Protzka Bruderhof at night, and robbed it of much woolen and linen cloth. The new baron, Emmerich von Czobor, had his Hussars pursue the robbers and recover the booty, but the Brethren did not get half of it back. An imperial army under Puchheim's command crossed into Hungary in 1644 and plundered Protzka, even finding the caches where the Brethren had hidden some goods, and took everything away. On July 27, 1645, Protzka was plundered again; all the buildings but the tannery and the mill went up in smoke, and the tanner was murdered.

In 1662 the householder and deacon Hans Schütz died in Protzka. After an abnormally cold spring the crops failed and famine set in, "so the brotherhood came into dire poverty, for at Lewär, Protzka, and Johanni they had only empty straw to harvest." The attack by the Turks in 1663 finally brought the Bruderhof to an end. On Sept. 4, 1663, the house in Protzka was robbed; even the persons who had fled to the woods were carried away by the Turks. After making an attack in Moravia the arsonists returned, finished plundering Protzka, drove away the cattle, about 100 oxen and cows and 1,350 sheep, and burned down what was still standing. In the neighboring St. Johannes the Brethren were able to maintain themselves, but Protzka was apparently abandoned for good.   P.De.

Beck, *Geschichts-Bücher;* Wolkan, *Geschicht-Buch;* Zieglschmid, *Chronik; ML* III, 400 f.

Providence Conservative Mennonite Church, located 1½ miles southwest of Kempsville, Va., on Providence Road, was started in 1952 as a Sunday school conducted by a small group from the Kempsville Amish (Beachy Amish) Church. In the same year the church was organized by the Executive Committee of the Conservative Mennonite Conference. The meetinghouse was built in 1953. Simon Coblentz, a minister from the Maple Grove C.A.M. Church, Hartville, Ohio, was called to take charge of the congregation of 16 members, and was ordained as bishop on October 11 of the same year. A few other families also moved in from Ohio. The membership in 1957 was 65, with Noah Miller as minister.   S.J.C.

Providence Mennonite Church (MC), a small congregation located in Upper Providence Twp., Montgomery Co., Pa., is a member of the Franconia Mennonite Conference. It originated about 1815 (although some claim 1740) and has been a part of the Skippack circuit, which includes the Skippack, Worcester, and Providence congregations. By 1890 the congregation had grown to 65 members; in 1936 the membership had dropped to 40, and by 1957 reached 65 again. The minister in that year was Jesse M. Mack. Providence had the oldest meetinghouse in the Franconia Conference, probably built in 1815. It was razed in 1958 and replaced by a new one.   J.C.W.

J. C. Wenger, *History of the Mennonites of the Franconia Conference* (Telford, 1937) 110-11.

Providence Mennonite Church (MC), located south of Versailles, Mo., in the hill country, was formerly called the Wilson Bend congregation. In 1930 the Wilson Bend meetinghouse had to be disposed of because of a dam built in the Osage River. In 1947 the present church was built, about five miles from the former location. Meanwhile the work was carried on in schools and abandoned churches. When the land was flooded, many members had to move away. The congregation was last listed in the *Yearbook and Directory* in 1956; the minister was J. R. Shank. There were only seven members in 1954. Before the move across the creek to Wilson Bend the congregation was called Carver.   J.R.S.

Providence Mennonite Church (MC), Denbigh, Va., located on Route 60 near Oyster Point, is a member of the Ohio and Eastern Mennonite Conference. The congregation was organized in 1900 and its church dedicated the following year. D. Z. Yoder was the first minister. It had 31 members in 1957. Wilbur H. Smoker was minister.   M.G.

Fifty Years. Building on the Warwick (Denbigh, 1947) 32-35.

Provo, Utah, the location of the Utah State Hospital, had a Civilian Public Service unit, under Mennonite administration, from January 1943 to April 1946. The twenty-five men in Unit No. 79 served in various positions in this institution of 1,150 mental patients.   M.G.

Melvin Gingerich, *Service for Peace* (Akron, Pa., 1949) 227-28.

Prozess wie es soll gehalten werden . . . (1557): see **Bedenken;** also **Handbüchlein wider den Prozess.**

Pruckh, Leonhard von, a participant in the Martyrs' Synod (*q.v.*) held at Augsburg (*q.v.*), Germany, on Aug. 20, 1527. He was sent with Leonhard Spörle (*q.v.*) as an Anabaptist missionary to Bavaria. His identity is not clear, and his fate unknown. (*ML* III, 402.)   E.C.

Pruckmaier: see **Bruckmaier.**

Prugner, Nicolaus, formerly a Reformed preacher at Mühlhausen, was the coauthor with Balthasar Fridberger (Hubmaier, *q.v.*) of *Acht unnd dreyssig schlussrede so betreffende ein gantz christlich leben war es an gelegen ist* (n.p., 1524). A copy of this rare booklet is found in the Amsterdam Mennonite library. About Prugner no further information was available.   vDZ.

Pruntrut: see **Porrentruy.**

Pruschanek (Pru(t)schän) is a Moravian village situated between Kostel and Göding (q.v.), which belonged to the domain of the Závis of Vitchkov in 1566, when the Hutterian Brethren settled there. It suffered great hardship during the wars of the 17th century. It was plundered and burned by Bocskay's troops on July 12, 1605; four of the inmates were murdered, thirty-five kidnaped—men as well as women. The householder Cornelius Harb was held responsible for their seizure and was expelled from the brotherhood; he was later restored to fellowship. In spite of the high price demanded by the Turks and Hungarians for their captured Hutterites, the women priced at 100 or even 200 ducats depending on their appearance and age, the elders decided to redeem them. They were apparently not successful in this undertaking, for in 1607 complaints from the sisters held in Ofen were still reaching Prushanek, and Sigel (Sigmund) Pühler was in this year tardily called to account for his negligence in providing for the safety of the sisters. Salomon Böger (q.v.), a miller, whose wife and son were among the victims taken into slavery in Turkey, made a courageous journey into Turkey to try to redeem them as well as the others.

In 1609 the Brethren began to clear away the rubble and to rebuild the Bruderhof; but after another decade, on Sept. 23, 1619, it was again burned down, this time by Dampierre's troops. Scarcely had the Brethren completed rebuilding it, when Polish auxiliaries and peasants pillaged it on Jan. 12, 1621, murdering the householder, Hans Walmann. It was not reopened. In 1624 the Jesuits of Olomouc purchased the Tscheikowitz estate and built the chapel of St. Catherine in Pruschanek.   P.DE.

Robert Friedmann, "Adventures of an Anabaptist in Turkey, 1607-1610," *MQR* XVII (April 1953) 73-86; Beck, *Geschichts-Bücher;* Wolkan, *Geschicht-Buch;* Zieglschmid, *Chronik,* 421 f.; G. Wolny, *Kirchliche Topographie von Mähren* II: *Brünner Erzdiözese* II (Brno, 1858) 197; *ML* III, 403.

Prussia was an earlier designation for the territory that later became the provinces of East and West Prussia (previously Polish Prussia), and in 1701 the Kingdom of the Hohenzollerns, which, having originated from the Electorate of Brandenburg, became after World War I a Free State, and after World War II was dissolved. In 1914 Prussia consisted of the "old provinces" (acquired before 1866) of East Prussia, West Prussia, Pomerania, Posen, Brandenburg, Saxony, Westphalia, and the Rhine Province, and of the "new provinces" (acquired in 1866) of Schleswig-Holstein, Hanover, and Hessen-Nassau. In 1850 the principalities of Hohenzollern were added. In 1854 the principality of Neuenburg and Valengin (today the Swiss canton of Neuchâtel) was given up. The rulers were Frederick I until 1713, Frederick William I until 1740, Frederick II (the Great) until 1786, Frederick William II until 1797, Frederick William III until 1840, Frederick William IV until 1861, William I until 1888, Frederick III 1888, and William II until 1918.

In Pomerania, Posen, and Silesia there were no great numbers of Mennonites. Within the other parts of the state the various groups of Mennonites long developed in regional independence of each other, also in relation to the state. Frederick William I (q.v.) took a very different attitude toward the Mennonites in East Prussia than to the Mennonites in Crefeld. Frederick II (q.v.) granted specific privileges to the settlements in the Netzebruch (q.v.) in 1765 and to the Mennonites in the East in 1780. In 1830 Frederick William III, after careful preparation, issued a law particularly designed for the Mennonites in the West. But the Order of Cabinet of 1827 concerning the oath was valid for the entire state; likewise the elimination of exemption from military service of 1867, the permission granted the old Mennonite families to do noncombatant military service, and in 1874 the law concerning the rights of the Mennonite churches to incorporate.

E.C.

The 1925 German census gives the following statistics (total population) for the Mennonites in Prussia:

District Königsberg	251	
" Gumbinnen	491	
" Allenstein	40	
" West Prussia	3120	
Total Province of East Prussia		3902
Berlin, city		599
District Potsdam	144	
" Frankfurt/Oder	74	
Total Province of Brandenburg		218
District Stettin	40	
" Köslin	50	
" Stralsund	9	
Total Province of Pomerania		99
Province of Grenzmark Posen-West Prussia		24
District Breslau	128	
" Liegnitz	11	
Total Province of Lower Silesia		139
Province of Upper Silesia		10
District Magdeburg	105	
" Merseburg	62	
" Erfurt	9	
Total Province of Saxony		176
Total Province of Schleswig-Holstein		227
District Hanover	75	
" Hildesheim	29	
" Lüneburg	49	
" Stade	24	
" Osnabrück	34	
" Aurich	231	
Total Province of Hanover		422
District Münster	131	
" Minden	16	
" Arnsberg	159	
Total Province of Westphalia		306
District Kassel	46	
" Wiesbaden	89	
Total Province of Hessen-Nassau		135
District Koblenz	66	
" Düsseldorf	1121	
" Cologne	76	
" Trier	33	
" Aachen	5	
Total Rhine Province		1301
Hohenzollern		21
Grand Total		7599

CITIES—MENNONITE POPULATION

Berlin	599	Frankfurt/Main	35
Königsberg	78	Wiesbaden	47
Stettin	15	Essen	43
Breslau	74	Düsseldorf	59
Magdeburg	38	Duisburg	21
Halle/Saale	14	Barmen	8
Erfurt	6	Elberfeld	19
Kiel	29	Crefeld	791
Altona	87	Mühlheim/Ruhr	8
Hanover	66	Hamborn	11
Münster	7	München-Gladbach	2
Dortmund	31	Oberhausen	32
Bochum	15	Cologne	58
Gelsenkirchen	12	Aachen	2
Kassel	20		
		Total	2227

(See also pertinent articles in this ENCYCLOPEDIA.)

Prussian Lithuania: see Lithuania.

Prutschän: see Pruschanek.

Pruyckmair, Georg: see Bruckmaier, Georg.

Pruys Liedtboeck (Prussian Songbook) is a Mennonite hymnal in the Dutch language, which was used by the Mennonites of Prussia, Germany. Its author was J. J. (Jan Jansz?) of Danzig. It was printed at Amsterdam in 1604 and contains 205 pages with 44 hymns without notes. Most of the hymns are composed by the editor, who signs with the motto "Ledigh-gangh leert veel quaets." The *Doopsgezind Jaarboekje* (1837, 64) mentions a *Pruys Liedtboeck* by H. v. D. (i.e., Hans van Dantzich). This is the same as the above hymnal, Jan Jansz being identical with Hans van Dantzich (or Dantzig). Of a *Tweede Pruys Liedtboeksken* by S. H., published at Alkmaar in 1607 (mentioned in *DJ* 1837, 65), nothing is known. vDZ.

Pruyt, Hendrik, an Anabaptist martyr: see Hendrik Spruit.

Przechovka (German, *Wintersdorf*), West Prussia, was formerly the seat of an Old Flemish congregation, the mother congregation of the Brenkenhoffswalde congregation (*q.v.*) in the Netzebruch (*q.v.*) and of Alexanderwohl (*q.v.*) and Gnadenfeld (*q.v.*), the leading congregations in the Molotschna Mennonite settlement. It was situated inland from the villages of Deutsch-Konopath and Divorczieka (German, *Wilhelmsmark*) and along the Vistula River with the villages of Glugovka, Kossovo, and Christkovo (German, *Christfelde*), southwest cf Schwetz with Ostrov (German, *Ehrenthal*) up the Vistula in the Klein-Schwetz marsh, south of the Frisian communities of Montau-Gruppe (*q.v.*) and Schönsee (*q.v.*). Przechovka and Divorczieska were royal villages, Deutsch-Konopath, Kossovo, and Christkovo noble villages, Glugovka part royal and part noble. The settlements are thought to have originated about 1540; in 1661 they were a part of the Groningen Old Flemish Sociëteit, which held most tenaciously to the old traditions. In the 18th century there were settlements of Old Flemish to the northwest in the noble village of Jeziorka (Ger-

man, *Kleinsee*), straight north in Tuchel, and northeast across the Vistula in Schönsee, Posterwolde, Horst, Ausmass, Jamerau, and Dorposch.

The estate of Przechovka was originally sold to five Mennonites from the Netherlands by the heirs of a Polish nobleman; these settlers attracted other Anabaptists, so that the village community finally embraced 15 home sites. The first contract of lease was granted to the village in 1642 for 50 years. In 1653 there was an association of Dutch inhabitants for the support of the schoolteacher, the burial of members of other faiths; in 1668 a "Manist Johannes" touched his breast as affirmation instead of an oath. The privilege granted by John II Kasimir (*q.v.*) was confirmed a number of times; on Feb. 9, 1672, it was confirmed expressly for Przechovka, Kossovo, and Christkovo.

Early in the 18th century the elders Alle Derks (*q.v.*; 16?-1733) of Groningen (*q.v.*) and Hendrik Berents Hulshof (*q.v.*; 1664-1745) of Zenderen, near Borne, in the province of Overijssel (*q.v.*), visited their brethren here, Derks in 1723 and about a decade earlier Hulshoff in 1719 and 1733. In 1732 they had a collection taken in the Dutch congregations for the needy fellow members in Prussia and Poland. Both listed the families they visited. The baptized membership was as follows:

	Derks	Hulshoff
Przechovka	39	57
Deutsch-Konopath	32	52
Posterwolde	10	14
Schönsee	9	13
Horst	3	21
Jamerau	1	—
	94	157

In general, children were not counted, especially by Derks. At Deutsch-Konopath there were Lutherans living among the Mennonites. The most common Mennonite names were Ratzlaff, Unrau, Becker, Voht, Nachtigal, and Wedel. Hulshoff, whose diary of 1719 is extant, stayed at Przechovka July 5-17, and on the other side of the Vistula in Posterwolde and Schönsee July 18-29. On Sunday, July 9, Wednesday, July 19, and Tuesday, July 25, he preached on Ephesians 6:11-13, Hebrews 1, and on the fruits of the Spirit in general. On Thursday, July 13, two preachers, Abraham Unrau in Przechovka and Jakob Isaaks in Posterwolde, were chosen, and on the following Sunday confirmed. On a Sunday they observed footwashing. One or two days before the official actions Hulshoff spent "with the books." The Polish brethren had requested the Dutch to send them Biestkens Bibles (*q.v.*), old hymnals, martyr books, and Menno Simons' and Dirk Philips' works. The joy caused by their visit is mentioned several times. Rye was at that time the outstanding crop. In 1738 and 1765 collections were again taken among the Dutch Mennonites for those in this region.

The first recorded elder was Berent Ratzlaff (b. 1660?). The Dutch *Naamlijst* (1759-1805) gives the following names of elders and preachers: Benjamin Wedel, elder before 1719-c47; another Benjamin Wedel (grandson of the former?), preacher? elder

1747-85; Jacob Wedel, preacher 1779, elder 1785-91; Abraham **Richert, preacher** 1785, elder 1791-99; Benjamin Wedel, preacher 1791, elder 1799-?; and the following preachers: Jacob Isaac, d. before 1755; Hans Voet (Voht, Foth) 1719-after 1755; Abraham Unrau c1723-c60; Peter Ratzlaff, before 1743-c80; **Jacob Wedel 1747-65; Laurens Sparling 1718-?; Ernst Schmidt (Smit)** c1760-75; Jacob Schmidt (Smit) c1765-74; Hans Ratzlaff c1765-?; Heinrich Unrau 1779-?; Andreas **Pankratz 1785-?; Heinrich Ratzlaff** 1791-?; Hans Unrau 1799-?

Under the leadership of Peter Wedel and Heinrich Buller most of the Mennonites left in the Schwetz area emigrated to the Molotschna Mennonite settlement in Russia in 1819-20 and 1823-24, and founded the Alexanderwohl congregation. Concerning the end of the congregation Stobbe reports: "The meetinghouse was in the present school yard. . . . In 1832, when the town of Przechovka built its own school and wanted to rebuild the Mennonite meetinghouse for that purpose, the few remaining Mennonites opposed the move and sold it to be dismantled. What happened to the meetinghouse cannot be ascertained, since the records of the town were destroyed by a fire in 1857. The last elder was a Richart and lived in Deutsch-Konopath. The congregation that at the end of the 18th century had about 300 members was extinct by about 1830. The few remaining old Flemish united with the Frisians in 1849." E.C.

Friesen, *Brüderschaft*, 90; H. Ch. Hulshoff, "Bezoekreis van Hendrik Berents Hulsholt aan de Doopsgezinde gemeenten der Oude Vlamingen in Pruisen en Polen in 1719," in *Bijdragen en Mededeelingen van het Historisch Genootschap* 1936, 32-82; Hans Maercker, "Eine polnische Starostei und ein preussischer Landratskreis. Geschichte des Schwetzer Kreises 1466-1873," in Wegner, *Geschichte des Schwetzer Kreises* II, in *Zeitschrift des Westpreussischen Geschichtsvereins*, 17-19 (Danzig, 1886, 1887, 1888) Wilhelm Mannhardt, *Die Wehrfreiheit der Altpreussischen Mennoniten* (Marienburg, 1863); (August Gottlieb) M(eissner), *Leben Franz Balthasar Schönberg von Brenkenhof* (Leipzig, 1782); Józef Paczkowski, *Opis królewszczyzn w wosewodztwach Cheminskim, Pomorskim i Malborskim w roku 1664* (Societas Literaria Toruniensis, *Fontes* 32) (Torun, 1938) 237 and 246; Horst Penner, "Die Westpreussischen Mennoniten im Wandel der Zeiten," in *Gesch.-Bl.* VII (1950) 17-31; Georg Leopold, Freiherr von Reiswitz, and Friedrich Wadzeck, *Beiträge zur Kenntniss der Mennoniten-Gemeinden in Europa und America* (Berlin, 1821); Leonhard Stobbe, *Montau-Gruppe* (Montau and Gruppe, 1918); Felicia Szper, *Nederlandsche nederzettingen in West-Pruisen gedurende den poolschen tijd* (Enkhuizen, 1913); B. H. Unruh, "Die Mennoniten in der Neumark," in *Gem.-Kal.* 1941, 58-76; Herbert Wiebe, *Das Siedlungswerk niederländischer Mennoniten im Weichseltal zwischen Fordon und Weissenberg bis zum Ausgang des 18. Jahrhunderts* (Marburg, 1952); *Menn. Bl.*, 1918, 93; 1919, 5, 10, 36, 37, 55, 80; *Inv. Arch. Amst.* I, 1702; II, 2, Nos. 738, 740; J. A. Duerksen, "Przechowka and Alexanderwohl," *Menn. Life* X (April 1955) 76-82; *ML* III, 404-7.

Psalmen Dauids, De C.L., *ende eenige Schriftuurlijcke Lof-sangen . . . Met de Belijdenisse des geloofs ende eenige al-gemeine Gebeden,* printed at Emden, was published by Karel de Fleger (De Vlieger) at Hamburg, Germany, in 1652. This collection, all in the Dutch language, contains a complete psalter after the rhymed version of Dathenus (*q.v.*) with notes, 92 hymns also with notes, the Apostolic Creed, the Jan Cents (*q.v.*) Confession of 1632, and a number of prayers. The preface is undated and unsigned. vdZ.

F. C. Wieder, *De Schriftuurlijke Liedekens* (The Hague, 1900) 175, No. CXXXIV.

Psalmen Davids, De, *nieuwlyx op rym-maat gestelt,* a Dutch psalter containing the 150 psalms rhymed by Joachim Oudaen, Dirk R. Camphuyzen, Joost van den Vondel, Antonides van der Goes, Anslo, van Hoogstraten, Galenus Abrahamsz, and others. This version was made by order of the church board of the Amsterdam Lamist (*q.v.*) congregation. The preface is dated April 10, 1684. There are copies of the editions of 1684, 1685 (with notes), 1721, and 1727; of other known editions there are no copies. This version was introduced in the Amsterdam Lamist congregation to replace the rhymed version by Dathenus (*q.v.*). It was used until 1793. (*DB* 1865, 69 f.; Kühler, *Geschiedenis* III, 34-36) vdZ.

Psalmen Davids, De, *in't Nederduyts berijmd,* a Dutch psalter, edited by the church board of the Peuzelaarsteeg Mennonite congregation at Haarlem. The first edition is of 1713; the following editions, 1734 and 1756, are with notes. This psalter contains the whole collection of 150 Old Testament psalms. In this edition a number of old psalms were taken from the Amsterdam psalter of 1684, but most of them were revised (by Vondel, Pieter Cornelisz Hooft, Reinier Rooleeuw, Jacob Westerbaen, and others). This psalter was also introduced in the Mennonite congregation of De Rijp and a few other congregations. In Haarlem it was used until about 1804. (*DB* 1865, 70 f.; 1910, 88 f.; Kühler, *Geschiedenis* III, 36 f.) vdZ.

Psalmen Laus Deo, a Dutch rhymed version of the Psalms: see **Laus Deo, Salus Populo.**

Psalms as Hymns: I. *Switzerland and Germany.* The earliest known edition of a Protestant translation of the Psalms as a hymnal appeared in Paris in 1541 and contained 30 Psalms, which Calvin (*q.v.*) republished at Geneva in 1542. It was the work of Clement Marot (c1419-1544). In 1543 appeared a third edition increased by 20 new Psalms and with a foreword by Calvin. The rest of the psalms were translated by Theodor Beza (*q.v.*) in 1550-52. In 1552 appeared the first complete Psalter with a poetic foreword by Beza. Melodies for most of these Psalms were composed by Loys Bourgeoucs; the four-part version of the music was composed by Claude Goudimel (the martyr of the massacre of St. Bartholomew's night in 1572 at Lyon). This *Psalter* became the hymnbook of many Reformed churches.

This precious treasury of songs soon became the common possession of German church music. The French Psalms by Marot and Beza were translated into German by Ambrosius Lobwasser (1515-85), and published in 1573 in Leipzig as *Die Psalmen Davids nach französischer Melodey in deutsche Reymen gebracht durch Dr. Ambrosius Lobwasser.* It was inevitable that the verse suffered some deterioration in the process of translation. Nevertheless the work was used in Reformed circles, especially in Switzerland. In the 17th century the Bern government commissioned Johann Ulrich Sulzberger, the music director of Bern, to revise the music and re-publish the *Psalter*. This revision with Lobwasser's text, of which several editions were printed, soon became the common possession of the Swiss Reformed Church.

In the course of the 18th century the inadequacy of this translation of the Psalms became more and more apparent. Johann Jakob Spreng (1699-1768), a professor at the University of Basel, therefore undertook the task of producing a rhythmically improved edition of the Psalms. A little later, Johannes Stapfer (1719-1801), a professor of theology at the University of Bern, revised the Lobwasser Psalms on the basis of Spreng's edition. The new revision of the Psalms for Germany was made by Mathias Jorissen (1739-1833). The work of these men made a real contribution in poetic improvement. Their texts follow the Scripture closely. Musically these Psalms are also valuable. The leading voice (cantus firmus) lies in the tenor. In the 19th century when many of these Psalms were included in the newer hymnals the leading voice was changed to the soprano part.

Among the Swiss Mennonites the Lobwasser Psalms were used until the late 19th century, rarely also the Stapfer version. In order that these strictly conservative Anabaptists would not feel that this was a state church hymnal, the title page with the imprint of the Bernese government was simply torn out of their copies. With the appearance of modern hymnals, especially of those of English melodies, the old books of Psalms had to yield. In Switzerland many of these old well-bound books can still be found. In more recent times an effort has been made to revive at least a few of the beautiful old Psalms. The Lobwasser *Psalms* were also taken to Lancaster County, Pa., by Swiss Mennonite immigrants in the early 18th century. (See **Hymnology.**)

In Anabaptist circles (see **Hymnology**) Sigmund Salminger (*q.v.*) of Munich was the first to make a translation; in 1537 he issued *Der gantze Psalter, das ist alle Psalmen Davids an der Zahl 150 in gesangweiss gestellt* (Keller, 426). Jakob Dachser (*q.v.*), also an Anabaptist preacher, made a rhymed version of several Psalms and in 1538 published *Den gantz psalter Davids nach ordnung und anzahl aller Psalmen*. The Hutterite Chronicles relate concerning Wolf Sailer (*q.v.*), that he rhymed the entire Psalter, "as we have and sing it in the brotherhood" (*Geschicht-Buch,* 257). Unfortunately little is known about these songs. This translation is said to be in the Archiepiscopal library in Gran as Manuscript III, 190. S.G.

Wolkan, *Geschicht-Buch;* Zieglschmid, *Chronik;* L. Keller, *Die Reformation u. die älteren Reformparteien* (Leipzig, 1885); *ML* III, 407 f.

II. *Netherlands.* In the early 16th century and even before, some of the Psalms had been translated into Dutch; they were usually called *Souterliedekens*. A complete rhymed version of all the Psalms, published in 1540 at Antwerp, went through at least ten editions, and other rhymed versions of the whole psalter or parts of it were published in the same period. These *Souterliedekens* may have been sung by the early Anabaptist-Mennonites in the Netherlands. But until the end of the 16th century the Dutch Mennonites preferred to sing the hymns composed by the martyrs and the songs dealing with their faith and sufferings (see **Hymnology**). The Waterlanders (*q.v.*) were the first among the Dutch Mennonites to use Psalms; by 1581 the singing of Psalms was usual in the Waterlander congregations. This was largely due to the influence of Hans de Ries (*q.v.*). In his hymnal of 1582 he included a number of Psalms, and the 1618 edition of his hymnal contained all the Psalms. In the early 17th century it was an exception, not only among the Waterlanders, but also among the Flemish Mennonites, to sing any hymn but a Psalm. Harmen Hendriksz van Warendorp (*q.v.*), who had given a meetinghouse to the Amsterdam Mennonite congregation (see **Lamist Church**) in 1632, stipulated in his will that a fine was to be paid whenever a hymn other than a Psalm was sung. The Psalms used by both the Waterlanders and the Flemish were in the Dathenus (*q.v.*) version. Since the artistic quality of this version was not very satisfactory, efforts were soon made to get a better version. It is not clear why the excellent rhymed version of D. R. Camphuysen (*q.v.*) was not used by the Mennonites. In 1684 the Amsterdam Lamist congregation introduced a new version, rhymed by Joachim Oudaen, Joost van den Vondel, Antonides van der Goes, Anslo, van Hoogstraten, Camphuysen, Galenus Abrahamsz, and others. In 1713 the Peuzelaarsteeg congregation of Haarlem introduced a new version, different from the 1684 Amsterdam version; this psalter was also used by a number of other congregations. A version, rhymed in 1759 by the rhetorical society "Laus Deo, Salus Populo," was introduced in 1762 in the Amsterdam Zonist congregation, and soon after in the Amsterdam Lamist congregation and other churches. In 1900 this version was still used by three Mennonite congregations. The new version introduced in the Dutch Reformed Church in 1773 was also used by the Mennonites; in 1900 at least 81 congregations were using it. In 1900 (reprinted in 1906) an anthology of Psalms in a somewhat revised version was published in the *Leidsche Bundel* (*q.v.*). The present *Doopsgezinde Bundel* (*q.v.*) (Mennonite hymnal) of 1944 contains 46 Psalms. (*DB* 1865, 69-83; Kühler, *Geschiedenis* III, 33-37.) vDZ.

Publication, Board of, a former organization of the General Conference Mennonite Church, consisted of 6 members and was elected directly by the Conference. It was in charge of publishing the church papers—*The Mennonite, Der Bote,* the *Junior Messenger,* and *Der Kinderbote;* the Sunday-school quarterlies—*Sonntagschul-Lektionen,* the *Mennonite Adult Quarterly, Mennonite Junior Quarterly,* the *Mennonite Junior Quarterly Teacher's Handbook,* the *Mennonite Young People's Quarterly,* as well as the *Mennonite Hymnary,* and many other special publications in the field of theology, Mennonite history, doctrine, etc. In 1950 at the General Conference held in Freeman, S.D., this board was merged with the Board of Education to form the Board of Education and Publication (*q.v.*). H.J.A.

Publication Committee of the Mennonite Brethren Conference was called into being at the 1884 General Conference sessions when a committee of three was elected to (1) work toward a written history of the brotherhood; (2) arrange to have the conference reports printed; and (3) establish a periodical for the denomination. Largely through the efforts of this committee, the *Zionsbote,* Conference Yearbooks, Sunday-school material, and other literature as well as the Mennonite Brethren Publishing House were brought into being. From its inception until 1936, the committee consisted of three to five members. In 1936-51 it consisted of five members, and since that time seven members. Since the establishment of the conference publishing house in 1904 the major effort of the committee has been the operation of this enterprise on a sound financial basis. Since 1954 this committee has been known as the Board of Publications.   O.H.

Publication Society *of the United Missionary Church.* The work of publication was begun when the church, since 1947 called the United Missionary Church, was known as the Evangelical Mennonite Church. The first publication was the *Gospel Banner,* an 8-page semimonthly, which was begun in July 1876. In the early years this periodical was published in Goshen, Ind., and was printed part in English and part in German. It still continues as the church organ, has 16 pages, and is published weekly. For twenty years, 1900-20, the publication work of the church was carried on in Kitchener, Ont. Besides the church organ, the Publication Society published the disciplines, songbooks, and some other church literature.

In 1910 the Bethel Series of Sunday School Literature using the International Uniform Series was launched for the church by an independent publishing company, the Bethel Publishing Company, headed by J. A. Huffman, an ordained minister in the church. Headquarters of this publishing house were first at New Castle, Ohio, and then Dayton, Ohio. In 1920 the publication work of the church under the Publication Society was merged with that of the Bethel Publishing Company and was located in Elkhart, Ind., in 1928. Since the change made in 1920, the recognized publishing house of the church has continued to be known as the Bethel Publishing Company, under the management of the Publication Board of the church and with an Agent employed by that board.   J.A.Hu.

Publications of the Dutch Mennonites. In addition to privately published books and hymnals (see **Hymnology**), some editions of the confessions (*q.v.*), and accounts of peacemaking among the divided branches and of other meetings, such as *Handelinghe (q.v.) der Doopsgezinde, ghenaemt de Ver-eenigde Vlaemsche en Duytsche Gemeynte,* the first—semiofficial—publication was the *Naamlijst* (*q.v.*), appearing first in 1731, at first at long intervals, then annually 1759-76 and 1778-94, and finally biennially 1796-1810, the last editions being 1810, 1815, and 1829. It contained an enumeration of the Dutch Mennonite ministers; most issues of the *Naamlijst* also listed the congregations in Germany and elsewhere. From 1788 they also contained some items of church news (*Kerknieuws*).

The *Naamlijst* was succeeded by the *Jaarboekje voor de Doopsgezinde gemeenten in de Nederlanden,* commonly called "Muller's Jaarboekje" (*q.v.*), published in 1837, 1840, and 1850. This contained a list of the congregations, news about the congregations, and also a number of historical papers. It was succeeded by Gorter's *Doopsgezinde lectuur* (1854, 1856, 1858) and *Doopsgezinde Bijdragen* (*q.v.*), which was published annually from 1861 to 1919 (except 1866, 1871, and 1913-15). In 1887 the first number of the *Zondagsbode* (*q.v.*), a weekly, was published, which appeared until June 21, 1942. Since 1942 it has been the official periodical of the A.D.S. In 1945 the A.D.S. published *De Noodbrug* (June 1945, and monthly from August 1945 to September 1946), and from October 1946 the *Algemeen Doopsgezind Weekblad* (*q.v.*).

From about 1911 to about 1943 most congregations or groups of neighboring congregations published their own periodicals, usually monthly. After 1947 some congregations again undertook this kind of publication.

Other regular publications are *Verslag wegens de Staat der Algemeene Doopsgezinde Sociëteit* since 1811, the annual report of the Dutch Mennonite Mission Association since 1849, *Brieven* (*q.v.*) of the Vereniging voor Doopsgezind Broederschapswerk (*q.v.*) 1918-56, *De Hoeksteen,* a monthly periodical of the youth organization, since 1935, the *Doopsgezind Jaarboekje* (*q.v.*) since 1901, an annual calendar 1937-57, *Stemmen uit de Doopsgezinde Broederschap* since 1952, and *Koers,* a monthly edited by the youth organization. Most of these publications did not appear during World War II, because they were forbidden by the German occupying forces or could not appear because of lack of paper.   vDZ.

"Doopsgezinde periodieken in Nederland," in *Stemmen uit de doopsgez. broederschap* I, No. 1 (January 1952).

Publishers, Mennonite: *Holland*—Though there have never been any special Mennonite publishing houses in the Netherlands, and books written by Mennonites have from the very beginning been published by non-Mennonites, as for example as early as 1577 by Gillis Rooman (*q.v.*), who probably was not a Mennonite, yet there have been a large number of Mennonite printers and publishers, who have also published Mennonite books. Among those to be mentioned, the first is Nicolaes Biestkens (*q.v.*), who at first operated a printing shop at Emden, and from *c*1580 one at Amsterdam; his business was taken over by his son A. Biestkens. Reiner Wylicks at Utrecht published Mennonite books in 1593. About the same time Passchier Wesbus(ch) (*q.v.*) was a Mennonite publisher at Haarlem as were his son Hans Passchiers van Wesbusch and his grandsons Passchier and Isaac van Wesbusch. They published numerous Mennonite books. Other Mennonite publishers of the 17th century were J. A. Calom (*q.v.*) at Amsterdam, Zacharias Jansen (Harteveldt) and his son Pieter Sacharijasen at Hoorn, Jan Theunisz (*q.v.*) at Amsterdam, Claes Jacobs at de Rijp, Pieter Arendsz at Amsterdam, Geleyn Jansz (*q.v.*) and his son Jan Geleynsz at

Vlissingen, and Pieter van der Meersch at Leiden. In the 18th century we find Isaac Tirion (*q.v.*) at Amsterdam, Denys van der Schuere, Jan Bosch, and Isaac van der Vinne at Haarlem, Folkert van der Plaats at Harlingen, and Hendrik Rintjes (*q.v.*) at Leeuwarden. In the 19th century there were several members of the Plantinus family at Drachten, Johannes Müller at Amsterdam, and in the 19th and 20th centuries the publishing houses of François Bohn and Tjeenk Willink (*q.v.*) at Haarlem, the J. H. de Bussy publishing house at Amsterdam, H. Born and L. Hansma (*q.v.*) at Assen, J. Over and son at Borne, D. Rooda (firm A. H. Schut Azn) at Groningen, and A. H. Veenbaas (G. Taconis Lim) at Wolvega. The ADS (*q.v.*) has recently issued several pamphlets under its name, thus being in a sense the only official church publishing agency, except possibly a committee of the ADS called De Commissie tot de Doopsgezinden in de Verstrooiing, which published a series of pamphlets, 61 in number, from 1897 to 1940, under the general title *Geschriftjes ten behoeve van de Doopsgezinden in de Verstrooiing.*   vDZ.

Germany, Switzerland, and France—Mennonites in these countries have never had an official conference publishing agency, and very few Mennonites here have ever gone into the printing or publishing business. No Anabaptist presses were known except the one which operated for a time in Lübeck and later in near-by Wüstenfelde which published a number of Menno Simons' writings *c*1550-61, and Simprecht Sorg, called Froschouer, who followed Hubmaier to Nikolsburg in 1526, where he published some of the latter's writings. In modern times the South German Mennonite Conference (1885) published a few pamphlets and the hymnbook of the conference. Heinrich Schneider, a Mennonite minister and printer in Karlsruhe, Germany, has published a number of Mennonite books since 1930 and printed others. Recently some evidence has been uncovered to suggest that Pilgram Marpeck had a printing press.

United States and Canada—The first Mennonite publishing agency in the United States was established at Mountain Valley (Singers Glen), near Harrisonburg, Va., in 1847 by Joseph Funk (*q.v.*, MC) and continued as Joseph Funk & Sons until 1862, when Funk died. His sons, who were not Mennonites, continued the business. John H. Oberholtzer (*q.v.*, GCM) published alone at Milford Square, Pa., 1848-56 (press from 1852), followed by the Mennonite Printing Union (Mennonitischer Druckverein) 1856-66, a semiofficial private company, which was taken over by J. G. Stauffer 1867-1908(?), a Mennonite who did some Mennonite printing for about 20 years. John F. Funk (*q.v.*, MC) started publishing in Chicago in 1864, moved to Elkhart, Ind., in 1867, and established there in 1875 the Mennonite Publishing Co. (*q.v.*), which continued as a vigorous and influential private company with a substantial Mennonite publications list until 1908, when most of the business was sold, although Funk operated the MPC until 1925 for the full length of its 50-year charter. David Goerz and others operated the Western Publishing Co.

(*q.v.*, GCM) at Halstead, Kan., 1875-81. The Mennonite Book and Tract Society (*q.v.*, MC) operated under several addresses 1889-1908.

The era of official conference publishing agencies began with the Evangelical United Mennonite Publication Society (MBC) in 1875-85 (Goshen, Ind.), followed by the Mennonite Brethren in Christ Publication Society 1885-1908, and the Bethel Publishing Co. (1910, as a private concern, from 1920 as an MBC conference agency, from 1928 at Elkhart, Ind.). The next conference publisher was the Christliche Central-Buchhandling der Allgemeinen Conferenz (*q.v.*, GCM) at Berne, Ind., and Halstead, Kan., 1882-93, followed by the Mennonite Book Concern (1893- ? *q.v.*), which in turn was followed by the Mennonite Publication Office (*q.v.*) at Newton, Kan., 1939- . A private publishing agency was established at Newton in 1900 by members of the G.C.M. Church, called Western Book and Publishing Co. (*q.v.*). It has continued to the present, operating since 1920 under the name Herald Publishing Co. D. W. Friesen & Sons have operated at Altona, Man., as publishers largely for the Manitoba Mennonites since 1933.

The official publishing agency of the Mennonite Church (MC) since 1908 has been the Mennonite Publishing House (*q.v.*) at Scottdale, Pa., owned and operated by the Mennonite Publication Board (*q.v.*). It was preceded 1905-8 by the Gospel Witness Co. at Scottdale. The Board bought out this latter company and the periodicals of the MPC at Elkhart. The MPH has become a relatively large agency, and has been for years the major Mennonite publishing agency in the western hemisphere, the only one with a substantial list of Mennonite books and pamphlets. The Amish Publication Society, started in 1912, represents most Old Order Amish interests in a church paper, the *Herold der Wahrheit,* though a purely private organization. Several individuals of the O.O.A. group, such as L. A. Miller at Arthur, Ill., and J. A. Raber at Baltic, Ohio, have for many years served as publishers for sections of the group.

The official Mennonite Brethren Publishing House was established as a conference agency in 1915 at Hillsboro, Kan., displacing several previous private M.B. publishers. A Canadian M.B. minister established the Rundschau Publishing House in 1923 at Winnipeg, Man., to serve the Canadian M.B. churches. This agency became the Christian Press, Ltd. in 1940, owned in part by the Canadian M.B. Conference and in part by private persons. The K.M.B. Publishing House was established at Chicago in 1915 as a conference agency of the K.M.B. Church. The Central Conference Publication Board served the Central Illinois Conference 1910-58.

A number of private publishing agencies have been established, most of which have had only a limited publishing scope, and some of which continued only a short time. Chief of these is the Echo Verlag founded at Winnipeg in 1944, which has published a notable historical series on the former Mennonite settlements in Russia. Others to be noted are the Warte Verlag (A. B. Dyck) at Steinbach, Man., the Prairie Press (Jacob Regehr) at North Kildonan, Man., the Salem Publishing House

(J. H. Klassen) at Inman, Kan., Peniel Publishing House (J. W. Tschetter) at Chicago, Ill., Bethel College Press at North Newton, Kan., which became the Mennonite Press (*q.v.*), jointly owned by the college and the General Conference. Sometimes the term Press means only a printing shop; sometimes it is equal to "publisher." H.S.B.

Pudespitz (Putschowitz, Butschowitz; Czech, *Bucovic*), a market village east of Austerlitz, Moravia, in which the Hutterites set up a Bruderhof in 1537. Ulrich Stadler (*q.v.*) of Brixen, Austria, who had led the Brethren (*q.v.*) from Austerlitz to Poland during the persecution in Austerlitz, had returned to Moravia and united with the Hutterites, bringing with him about 100 persons, and served as Vorsteher in Butschowitz. He is known for the letters he wrote advocating an extension of the authority of the preachers. He died here in 1540. Five years later an additional five hundred Gabrielites (*q.v.*) united with the Hutterian Brethren here. The persecution of 1547 apparently brought this Bruderhof to an end. (See **Bucovic**, which the present article supplements.) P.DE.

Wolkan, *Geschicht-Buch;* Zieglschmid, *Chronik;* Gregor Wolny, *Kirchliche Topographie von Mähren* II: *Brünner Erzdiözese* IV (Brno, 1861) 2; *ML* III, 408.

Pueblo (Col.) Mennonite Brethren Church existed for a number of years as a small city congregation under the leadership of John H. Boese. It was last listed in the M.B. Yearbook in 1914. H.S.B.

Pueblo (Col.) Mennonite Church (MC) had its inception in 1941 when Mennonites working in the city began to hold regular fellowship and Bible class meetings. The use of a building and lot was secured in July 1942. The congregation was organized in 1947, with 19 charter members. Marcus Bishop served as pastor until 1956. He was followed by Cletus S. Miller. The membership in 1956 was 30. The meetinghouse serves as the church home for the Mennonite student nurses who affiliate with Pueblo hospitals. For 18 months (1952-54) 36 conscientious objectors performed their I-W service here. M.McC.

Puerto Casado, Paraguay, situated on the west bank of the Paraguay River, 190 miles north of Asuncion, was founded in 1889 by the Carlos Casado Company of Buenos Aires, Argentina, with 50 Paraguayan families. Serving largely as the center of the large tannery and cattle ranch owned by the Casado Company, it gained significance as a Chaco river port with the coming of the Mennonites, and was, until the establishment of the air service, almost exclusively the port used by the three Chaco Mennonite colonies for all travel, exports, and imports. Narrow-gauge railroads run into the interior to facilitate the shipment of logs to the tannery. One of these railroads is used up to Kilometer 145 (Station Fred Engen) by the Mennonite colonists. It operates one train weekly and has special small cars (*autovia*) for passenger hire. Many of the 130 Mennonites who died in the typhoid epidemic in 1927-28 are buried in the town cemetery. Puerto Casado today has approximately 6,000 inhabitants, most of

whom are in the employ of the Carlos Casado Company factories. It has one Catholic church. The town is approximately 240 feet above sea level. During the Chaco War of 1932-35 the port became invaluable to the Paraguayan army as a railhead and supply center. C.J.D.

Walter Quiring, *Russlanddeutsche suchen eine Heimat* (Karlsruhe, 1938); Philip Raine, *Paraguay* (New Brunswick, 1956).

Puerto Rico, an island about 100 miles long and 35 miles wide, is the smallest of the four Greater Antilles (Cuba, Jamaica, and Hispaniola). San Juan, the capital of Puerto Rico, is 1600 miles southeast of New York City, and 1000 miles southeast of Miami. The island's 3,435 square miles of land surface support a population of 2,276,000 (1957) or a density of 663 persons per square mile, with a 10 person per square mile increase each year. The island was discovered by Columbus in 1493, and remained a Spanish colony for 400 years. It was ceded to the United States in 1898 following the Spanish American War, and in 1952 became an American commonwealth with almost complete self-government. Puerto Rico has a subtropical climate; its chief agricultural products are sugar cane, tobacco, and coffee. Puerto Rican culture is more Spanish than American, though Spanish customs have been modified considerably by American influence. During a ten-year period Puerto Rico intensified its industrial economy. More than 400 American industries have entered Puerto Rico, changing the economy from an agricultural to an industrial one. The average family income increased from $660 in 1940 to $2,400 in 1956.

Mennonite interest began in 1943, when the Mennonite Central Committee responded to an invitation of the Brethren Service Committee to establish a CPS medical and social service program in the La Plata Valley. The Brethren CPS unit was begun at Castaner in August 1942, after the door was closed to CPS men in foreign countries. The MCC service program included medical, recreational and educational, and agricultural service. In January 1950 the MCC service program was transferred to the Mennonite Relief Committee, an agency of the Mennonite (MC) Board of Missions and Charities, which had begun evangelistic work at Pulguillas in December 1945. In 1947 a Mennonite (MC) church was also organized at La Plata.

The present Mennonite program in Puerto Rico includes a service and evangelistic program administered by the Mennonite Board of Missions and Charities. The service and evangelistic programs were merged into one administration on April 1, 1958. MRSC continues to supply personnel to assist with the service aspects of the church program in Puerto Rico. Included in the program are a 32-bed modern hospital in Aibonito and a number of medical clinics in rural communities, a community agricultural program and a community center program in La Plata. There are eleven congregations and outstations and an elementary and junior high school. There is also a language school and the Spanish radio (see **Radio Broadcasting**) program. The total church membership was

339 in 1957 with an active Sunday school and summer Bible school. The Bethany Mennonite School (Escuela Menonita Betania), with grades one to nine, at Pulguillas had an enrollment of 165 in 1957. Approximately 65 American Mennonite workers are engaged in the service and evangelistic program in Puerto Rico. A number of other Mennonite workers are also serving in Puerto Rico with the Ulrich Foundation, a Mennonite service agency with headquarters in Roanoke, Ill. J.G.H.

Justus G. Holsinger, *Serving Rural Puerto Rico* (Scottdale, 1952); *The Power of the Gospel in a Changing World,* Mission Board Report, 1954; *ML* III, 408-10.

Puerto Rico Mennonite Church (MC), the result of mission work by the Mennonite Board of Missions and Charities, is the outgrowth of the work of the Civilian Public Service unit at La Plata near the center of the island, which was sponsored by the MCC during World War II. The first Mennonite meetinghouse on the island was built at La Plata by the MCC and was dedicated on March 18, 1945. The congregation was organized in 1947. A second center was opened and a congregation organized at Pulguillas, 12 miles from La Plata, in 1947. In 1948 the Mennonite Board of Missions and Charities purchased from the Puerto Rico Reconstruction Administration the entire La Plata Unit, consisting of the hospital, community center, store, dwelling houses, and other buildings, and operated the work conjointly with the MCC, for the benefit of the community, until 1953. In 1957 the hospital at La Plata was discontinued and is now operated as a clinic. In the same year a new 32-bed hospital of fire- and hurricane-proof construction was opened at Aibonito, where a new nurses' home is in process of erection. In addition to the hospital there are now (1958) four medical clinics and one dental clinic, staffed by three doctors and one dentist. There are now on the field a language school, a Bible school, an elementary and junior high school, and a broadcasting station, *Luz y Verdad,* which reaches 21 stations scattered throughout the Latin countries of the world. There are 8 organized congregations, 3 mission stations with a membership of 339 in charge of 7 ordained and 3 licensed ministers. In 1955 the churches of Puerto Rico were organized into a conference which was admitted to membership of the Mennonite General Conference in that same year. In addition there is also maintained under private management a farm project, store, and related interests for the benefit of the people of the community.   S.C.Y.

Puerto Rico Reconstruction Administration (PRRA) was established under the (U.S.) Congressional Emergency Relief Appropriation Act of 1935. During a five-year period, PRRA purchased more than 40,000 acres of coffee, tobacco, and sugar absentee-owned land and redistributed it as small farms among poor rural people. PRRA constructed more than 12,000 new homes, thirty-eight modern concrete second-unit schools, and sixty-four rural medical dispensaries. Extensive agricultural, recreational, and social service programs were organized in the larger resettlement projects. In 1942, when money was no longer available to finance the extensive social service and medical programs, PRRA made available government community center property at three different locations to the Brethren Service Committee, the Mennonite Central Committee (La Plata, *q.v.*), and the Friends Service Committee, for CPS medical and social service programs. PRRA also became the government-sponsoring agency of the CPS program in Puerto Rico and worked in close co-operation with the Brumbaugh Reconstruction Unit, the central agency of the three church service organizations.   J.G.H.

Justus Holsinger, *Serving Rural Puerto Rico* (Scottdale, 1952) 5-18.

Pulaski Mennonite Church (GCM), located 3 miles southwest of Pulaski, Davis Co., Iowa, a member of the Middle District Conference, was organized in 1861. Christ Kropf and Christ Sharp from Indiana were the first preachers for the group, which was made up of Mennonite settlers from Canada, Ohio, Illinois, and Indiana. Meetings were held in homes and schools until the first church was erected in 1866. The second was dedicated in 1885, with extensive remodeling in 1914. Among those who have served were two pastors, Philip Roulet from Ohio and W. W. Miller from Indiana, whose two terms totaled more than 60 years. The pastor in 1958 was Kenneth Shelly, from Pennsylvania, with a membership of 154, mostly rural.   V.E.S.

Pulaski Street Mennonite Church (MC), 223 S. Pulaski, Baltimore, Md., established in 1952, is a mission congregation under the Lancaster Conference. It had 26 members in 1957, with Lloy A. Kniss as pastor.   M.G.

Pulgram (Pulgern), a village about 10 miles east of Nikolsburg in Moravia, situated on the Thaya River, belonged to the Nikolsburg domain of Liechtenstein (*q.v.*). In the period of persecution of 1535 Hans Tuchmacher or Amon (*q.v.*) gathered the Anabaptist brotherhood "between Nikolsburg and Pulgern in the Föhrenwald," and secretly administered the "glorious and beautiful memorial of the Lord's Supper with great peace."

When persecution subsided, a group of Philippites (*q.v.*) settled in Pulgram; in the fall of 1538 they joined the Hutterite brotherhood, whereby the latter came into the possession of a stately Bruderhof which included "the bake house, also the great house in which the school was located, the smithy, and the new house below the smithy." Other buildings were soon erected.

But in the next year danger threatened under the pressure of royal decrees. Amon wrote that the Brethren were about to be expelled from Pulgram, "and the sick and the children put out without pity." In 1545, on a shallow pretext but with the consent of the authorities, a quantity of cattle, leather, and wine were taken from them; in 1547 the great persecution brought with it greater damages.

In 1551 the preacher Peter Hag died here, who was one of the Brethren taken to the galleys from the Falkenstein castle, but managed to return home and memorialized his fate in a song.

In this year also, with the silent consent of the

government, the settlement was robbed of much goods by a butcher Kunther and his associates, and the Brethren driven into the forest for a time. Later they prospered and were even able to lease a dairy farm from the Nikolsburg lords. In 1591 Siegmund von Dietrichstein (q.v.) expelled them and also the Swiss Brethren from Bergen and Voitelsbrunn. Some of them settled in Wastitz (q.v.), and others in Sobotiste (q.v.). In 1619 Dampierre's troops quartered in Pulgram and severely damaged the Bruderhof at Neumühl (q.v.).   P.De.

Beck, *Geschichts-Bücher;* Loserth, *Communismus,* 190; Wolkan, *Geschicht-Buch;* Zieglschmid, *Chronik;* Gregor Wolny, *Kirchliche Topographie von Mähren* II: *Brünner Erzdiözese* II (Brno, 1858) 93; *ML* III, 410 f.

Pulrus: see Polrus.

Pulversheim, a village (pop. 1,040) in the Upper Alsace lowland, Guebwiller area, located at the intersection of the Guebwiller-Mulhouse and Sennheim (Cernay)-Ensisheim highways, the seat of a Mennonite congregation. It is situated between the congregations of Colmar (81 members in 1951) and Neufbrisach (108 in 1951) in the north, and Pfastatt (263 in 1951) in the south, and further, Altkirch (95 in 1951) and Birkenhof (77 in 1951). Of the 23 families in the congregation, four have the name Tschantz and three Peterschmitt; one has Amstutz, one Widmer, names which are found particularly in Birkenhof and Pfastatt.

In the Reformation time there was a substantial Anabaptist movement in this region. According to Sebastian Franck, 600 (probably exaggerated) Anabaptists were executed in Ensisheim, which is only about 6 miles from Pulversheim. In spite of the severest measures it is probable that Anabaptism was never completely uprooted in this region, but the modern Mennonite community here had its origin in the immigration of Swiss Mennonites who were welcomed by the princes in this area after the close of the Thirty Years' War in 1698, to help repopulate and restore the partially devastated lands. The first documentary evidence of a Mennonite congregation in this area is from the end of the 18th century, when a "Mühlhausen" congregation is mentioned. This congregation became the largest in Alsace but suffered from a constant stream of emigration. At first families in search of land moved to Austria and Germany, and about the turn of the century particularly to Galicia and Bavaria (Augsburg to Regensburg). After the Napoleonic Wars the tide turned toward America (Waterloo County, Ont., 1824, Lewis County, N.Y., 1833, Central Illinois 1829 ff., etc.), a major purpose being to escape military service.

Before 1856 the congregation met in homes in rotation. In that year a former inn in Pulversheim was purchased and a room in it renovated as a meeting room, a Mennonite family occupying the rest of the building. The purchase was made in the names of two members, Joseph Eicher of Pulversheim and Jacob Zimmermann of Mühlhausen, and the congregation now received the name Pulversheim. In 1888 it had 150 baptized members. At the turn of the century a number of families moved in from Switzerland. By 1911 it had 185 baptized

members and 78 children. By an unfortunate division in 1912 a portion of the membership withdrew to establish a congregation in Pfastatt (q.v.), a few miles distant at the edge of Mulhouse. In 1951 the membership was 101 with 11 children, in 1958 72 including children.

The church, destroyed in 1914, rebuilt in 1923, was again severely damaged in 1939-45. On the map *Reichskarte 642* it is called "Wiedertäuferkirche." During World War I services were held in St. Georgenhof. Later the congregation was united for a time with Pfastatt, and then for a time it was served by the Alsatian Conference. Later Emil Kempf, of Colmar, was the pastor. Albert Peterschmitt, of Ungersheim near Ensisheim, has succeeded Jean Peterschmitt, of Strohstadt-Biesheim, as elder. Worship services are held on the second and fourth Sundays of the month; on the second Sunday a Bible study is conducted in connection with the worship service. A Bible course is held in the winter, and the harvest festival of thanks in October. Communion is observed four times a year. (See articles **Alsace, Altkirch, Birkenhof, Colmar, Pfastatt.**)   E.C.

Gem.-Kal., 1903 ff.; *Almanach Mennonite du Cinquantenaire 1901-1905* (Montbéliard, 1951); *Christ Seul,* Christmas issue, 1951; "Die Mennonitengemeinde Pulversheim im Elsass," *Gem.-Kal.* 1958, 61-63; *ML* II, 411.

Punishment of the Anabaptists. A general discussion of this theme will be found in the article **Juridical Procedures.** The article **Mandates** gives further information and contains a fairly exhaustive list of decrees against the Anabaptists including prescription of punishments. The articles on **Luther** and **Melanchthon** discuss the changing attitudes of these leading Reformers toward punishment of the Anabaptists. The articles on the individual rulers of the various states which took legal action against the Anabaptists give detailed information on the legal measures taken. See also the article **Persecution** in the Supplement, and the article "Bestrafung der Täufer" in *ML* I, pp. 201-9. The following article treats the punishment of Anabaptists in one area, the Low Countries.   H.S.B.

Punishment of the Anabaptists in the Low Countries. Concerning the Netherlands and Belgium, which in the 16th century constituted the "Netherlands" of the empire of Charles V, the following is to be said.

The question of the punishment of the Anabaptists and the Mennonites in the Netherlands and Belgium is an extremely complicated problem, not only because the laws of the various provinces were very dissimilar, but also because at the time of the rise of Anabaptism in the Netherlands (1530) Charles had not yet gained possession of all the provinces. The present Belgium and the southern provinces of the present Netherlands, Holland and Zeeland, were hereditary lands belonging to Charles. Here persecution was most severe. In 1524 Charles conquered Friesland, in 1528 Utrecht and Overijssel (and Drenthe); in 1536 Groningen passed into his possession and finally Gelderland in 1543. In these newly conquered territories persecution was usually not severe; although the number of Anabaptists in Groningen and Friesland was very large from the beginning, the number of victims of persecution is not nearly so great here as e.g., in Holland and Flanders. In the province of Friesland there was not a single martyr.

Charles V, who like his son Philip II, was firmly determined to eradicate heresy in his lands, had a number of proclamations (*placcaten*) issued, some of them intended for the entire empire, and some only for the Netherlands, in which a "falling away" from the Roman Catholic Church was made punishable by death, as was also the possession or printing of heretical books. The proclamation of June 1535 was issued specifically against the Anabaptists.

In order to combat Anabaptism Charles created a new form of the inquisition for the Netherlands. Whereas previously the bishops were responsible to keep heresy out of their territory, Charles appointed imperial inquisitors who were authorized to appoint regional inquisitors. By this act Charles made the conflict with heresy a matter of state, although the fact that the inquisitors appointed by the emperor were all members of the clergy, who also usually (but not always) received the pope's approval, gave the matter an ecclesiastical stamp. The first imperial inquisitor was Frans van der Hulst, 1522-24. The Anabaptist martyrs had to deal with the following inquisitors: Barend Gruwel of Grouwel, appointed in 1546; Pieter Titelman, who worked in Flanders; Lindanus, appointed in 1563. In addition to the inquisitors appointed by the emperor there were also inquisitors serving by papal appointment, while the bishops and their assistants also remained active. Thereby and also because the inquisitors did not receive exactly determined commissions and were not assigned to well-defined territory, the question of the inquisition became extremely involved. Some insight is given by an instruction for the inquisitors defined by the emperor and issued on Feb. 28, 1546.

Actually there were two crimes for which the heretics were persecuted, viz., real heresy, and disobedience to the imperial mandates. There was also some mention of disrespect for divine and human or temporal majesty (*lese majeste*). This double aspect carried with it some ambiguity and haziness, in the trial as well as in the sentence. The sentence usually stated that the heretic was condemned to death because he "disregarded the doctrine [or: the sacraments] of the Holy Church, and contrary to the faith and ordinances of the same church, the written laws and proclamations of the Imperial Majesty, our gracious lord."

The course of the trials was usually as follows: whenever the inquisitors, the clergy, or anyone else noticed a heretic, he had the heretic arrested; the prisons, usually foul, dark, unwholesome dungeons in the towers of castles, were used only to confine the heretics. (Imprisonment as punishment for a crime dates back only to the 17th century.) After a longer or shorter time the prisoner was cross-examined by the court. These were secular courts, to which usually clergymen were added, and on which also the inquisitors sometimes sat.

The Anabaptists were tried either by the city courts or by the provincial courts.

The cities had their own courts, known as the *schepenbank;* in addition there was in most provinces a *Hof,* i.e., a supreme provincial court (thus Anabaptists were tried, e.g., by the *Hof* of Holland or the *Hof* of Friesland). There was in principle no difference between the trial before a city court or a provincial court. Frequently the city governments did not wish to transfer the heretics to the provincial court for trial. They based this refusal on the ancient privilege that no citizen was to be sentenced outside the limits of the city (*ius de non evocando*). A second point of controversy between the city and the Hof, true particularly in the province of Holland, was the question of the confiscation of the property of the defendant. Usually the possessions of Anabaptist martyrs were declared forfeit to the use of the emperor, while sometimes the accuser received some of this property as a reward. (The proclamation of 1535 stipulated that anyone who reported an Anabaptist should receive one third of his goods.)

However, while the Hof, which represented the affairs of the emperor, demanded the entire inheritance, the city authorities, on the basis of the privilege noted above, simply claimed a part of the possessions of the condemned man. These privileges were abolished in 1549. There were other points of controversy between the city governments and the Hof; whereas the emperor strove for centralization in authority as well as in courts, and to this end wanted to give the Hof greater authority, the cities opposed this policy. Finally the city of Amsterdam, especially in the beginning, refused to send Anabaptists to the Hof in The Hague, because it wanted to protect them.

We have in van Braght's *Martyrs' Mirror* sufficient accounts of trials to be able to conclude that these took a fixed course. The inquisitors apparently made use of a prepared list of questions. One fixed point in the cross-examinations of martyrs (concerning the questions of the sacraments of the Roman Catholic Church) is the question where the defendant was baptized, by whom, and who was present. If these questions were inadequately answered, which was usually the case, the "sharp examination" took place, i.e., the victim was racked by the executioner in the torture chamber (*pijnkelder*) in the presence of the judges. Very often the Anabaptist martyrs, in spite of the most brutal torture, refused to betray their fellow believers. Then the "sharp examination" was sometime later repeated. If the unfortunate one then named some names, then his confessions were read to him later, with the assertion that the suspect had made these confessions "without torture or force."

Whether the trial had come to this desired result or whether the martyr remained silent, an effort was made to convert him. This end was served not only by the cross-examinations, but more especially by visits made to the prisoner in his dungeon by priests and monks, who even after the death sentence had been pronounced accompanied the condemned man to the site of execution.

Finally the sentence was pronounced; in the early period, until 1536, burning at the stake was not as frequently pronounced as was beheading for men and drowning for women. Later the penalties became more severe. On Oct. 4, 1540, Charles V announced as an eternal edict that those who would recant (*peniteeren*) and return to the Catholic Church would, in the case of men, be executed by beheading, and in the case of women, by burying alive ("executed with the sword and the women with the pit"). If, however, the victim persisted in his error, both men and women were to die at the stake ("be executed with fire"). This then became the general practice, although there were many exceptions; in Amsterdam the names are known of many persons who repented and were not put to death but exiled. In a few instances an Anabaptist was also put to death in the Netherlands without the process of the law. But this was contrary to law and order; the government wanted a regular hearing, especially since by this method it was possible to obtain names and other facts concerning the leaders of the Anabaptist movement. This practice was very deliberately followed in order to be able to arrest the leaders, so that the rest, like sheep without a shepherd, would be conveniently scattered. But in this respect the authorities were mistaken. Although most of the elders and preachers were executed, the movement continued. The prophetic words of one of the martyrs, "But know, where they kill one, a hundred shall arise," were fulfilled.

The first Anabaptist martyr in the Netherlands was Sicke Freerks Snyder, executed for his faith at Leeuwarden on March 20, 1531, and the last martyr who fell in the northern Netherlands was Reytse Aysesz, also executed at Leeuwarden, on April 19, 1574. In the southern Netherlands, now Belgium, Anneken van den Hove (Uyttenhove), executed on July 19, 1597, at Brussels, closed the long list of martyrs. vDZ.

Offer; Mart. Mir.; I. M. J. Hoog, De martelaren der Hervorming in Nederland tot 1566 (Schiedam, 1885).

Puppius Robertus was a Reformed minister at Middelie and after 1617 at Edam, who attacked the Mennonites, especially the Waterlander preacher Anthony Jacobsz (*q.v.*), in three books: *Bewijs van den Kinder-doop, dat de selve uyt Gode is, ende niet uyt den Menschen* (Amsterdam, 1614); *Bewijs van den Weder-doop, dat de selve uyt den Menschen is, ende niet uyt Gode; teghen den Mennisten* (Amsterdam, 1614), and *Bescherminghe des Kinder-doops, teghen Anthoni Jacobsz* (Amsterdam, 1617 and 1629). Puppius was opposed by Cornelis Jacobsz in his *Proces op en tegen het Protest gedaen van R. Puppium aengaende den Kinder-doop* (Amsterdam, 1618). vDZ.

Schijn-Maatschoen, Geschiedenis III, 278-83; M. Schagen, Naamlijst der Doopsgezinde Schrijveren (Amsterdam, 1745) 52.

Pur, Bartlime, also called Bartlime Pfister (i.e., baker), belonged to the Zürich group around Grebel und Manz. The letter of Sept. 5, 1524, sent by this group to Thomas Müntzer was also signed by Pur.

About him there is no further trace in Anabaptist history. His wife was a member of the first Zürich congregation, baptized by Hans Oggenfuss (*q.v.*). (*TA Zurich*, 19, 65, 385.) vDZ.

Pürcher, Andreas (Andries Pirchner), an Anabaptist martyr, a tile-maker, born in Stertzing, Tirol, Austria (now Italy), resident in Scharlach in the Engadin, was captured on May 26 (June 5), 1584, at Latsch on the Adige, a village in the Vintschgau not far from Schlanders; he was taken to Goldrain and brutally tortured. He was commanded to report where and with whom he had lodged. This he refused to do, since he would not be a Judas to those who had been kind to him. As concerned his faith, he would remain by the vows he had taken at his baptism, and not become a liar to God, even if he should have to suffer death in consequence. Neither the arguments of the priests nor the request of sympathizers influenced him. Thus he willingly suffered martyrdom on Oct. 19, 1584, at Schantzen near Schlanders. He is the author of the song of 36 stanzas which begins, "Singen wollen wir unserem Gott, der die Frommen in ihrer Not." NEFF.

Beck, Geschichts-Bücher, 289 f.; Mart. Mir. D 752, E 1058; Wolkan, Geschicht-Buch, 416 f.; Zieglschmid, Chronik, 536; Lieder der Hutterischen Brüder (Scottdale, 1914); Wolkan, Lieder, 235; ML III, 413.

Pürchinger, Matthäus, a knifesmith, one of the six Anabaptist martyrs executed at Steyr, Austria (*q.v.*), on March 30, 1528. (See **Penzenauer;** *ML* III, 413.) E.C.

Pürchner (Pichner), **Hans,** an Anabaptist martyr of Saalen, a village near Bruneck, Austria (now Italy), was captured in 1555 at Kortsch in the Adige (*q.v.*) on a missionary tour with Gelg Federspiel and taken to Schlanders. Federspiel escaped. Pürchner was brutally tortured to make him betray where and with whom he had lodged; but he betrayed none of them. After the trial he was unable to stand or to raise his hands to his mouth to eat. For six months longer he was held in a dark dungeon with chains on his hands and feet. Many learned men, priests, monks, noblemen, and others "beset him hard for two days and an entire night," to bring about his conversion; but he remained "steadfast in the Lord." Since he was unable to kneel he was leaned in a sitting position against a pillar and thus beheaded. One of the priests who debated with him was Leonhard Dax (*q.v.*), who later became an Anabaptist.

Two songs were written to commemorate his death: "Fröhlich wollen wir singen jetzund in Gottes Nam," by Sigmund Hosauer (*q.v.*), and "Mit Freuden wollen wir singen, wie wir's beschlossen han," by Claus Felbinger (*q.v.*). Zieglschmid suggests that both of these hymns may be revisions of a hymn written by Pürchner. NEFF.

Beck, Geschichts-Bücher, 240; Wolkan, Geschicht-Buch, 262; Zieglschmid, Chronik, 346 f.; Ethelbert Stauffer, "Märtyrertheologie und Täuferbewegung," Ztscht für Kirchengeschichte, 1933, 591; Lieder der Hutterischen Brüder (Scottdale, 1914) 436-46; Wolkan, Lieder, 209 f., 229; Mart. Mir. D 162, E 550; ML III, 413.

Purmerend, a town (pop. 6,737, with 164 Mennonites) in the Dutch province of North Holland. In 1534 it was noted that the Anabaptists were numerous here; many of them belonged more or less to the revolutionary wing of Anabaptism; 30 Anabaptists of Purmerend who had joined the trek to Münster in March 1534 were seized en route. On Sept. 22, 1540, Lambrecht Jacobs Grootboot of Purmerend, a follower of Jan van Batenburg (*q.v.*), was executed. But there were also peaceful Anabaptists and Mennonites. At the end of the 16th century there were three Mennonite congregations in Purmerend, a Waterlander, a Frisian, and a Flemish. Of their history not much is known. Delegates of the Purmerend Waterlander congregation attended a general Waterlander conference at Amsterdam in 1581. In 1695 the Waterlander and Frisian congregations merged and in the next year built a new church on the Pottenmarkt. A Flemish congregation had merged with the Frisians before 1695. In 1727, 1733, and 1734 it contributed liberally for the needs of the oppressed Prussian Mennonites. The Purmerend congregation, which in the 18th century belonged to the Waterlander Conference as well as the Zonist Conference, was at that time in a state of serious decline. During 1731-94 it had no preacher, in 1795 only 33 members. In the 19th century it began to increase: 67 in 1836, and 246 in 1899. Then it declined again, having 220 members in 1926, and 164 in 1958. The present meetinghouse with organ was built in 1864. In 1944 the congregation joined the Beemster (*q.v.*) congregation for preaching service and religious instruction. Since 1794 the following ministers have served here: Klaas Honig Jzn 1794-1832, P. Cool, the first minister serving here who had been educated at the Amsterdam Seminary, 1833-36, L. G. Bavink 1836-73, L. F. Goteling Vinnis 1873-90, J. Westerman Holstijn 1891-1908, D. Pottinga 1908-12, F. ten Cate 1912-16, M. J. Kosters Gzn 1917-23, F. J. de Holl 1926-29, W. Banga 1930-44, Miss Aafke Leistra 1944-56, and A. Zwartendijk 1957- . There is a ladies' circle, a youth group, a church choir, and a Sunday school for children. vDZ.

Inv. Arch. Amst. I, Nos. 37, 56, 60, 80, 98, 232, 474, 745, 1180; II, Nos. 2187-93; II, 2, Nos. 304-31; *DJ* 1837, 16; Blaupot t. C., *Holland* I, 24, 28, 252, 354; II, 68, 201 f., 204, 232; *DB* 1864, 176; 1865, 167; 1872, 57; 1877, 79; 1910, 71; 1917, 111; *Naamlijst* 1796, 58 f.; *ML* III, 413.

Pürschitz, an estate near Selowitz (*q.v.*) in Moravia, which Burian Zabka of Limberg in 1563 sold to Albrecht von Boskowitz and Cernáhora. The latter maintained friendly relations with the Anabaptists, had them build for him an ornamental carriage and lay the water pipes in his house in Brno in 1569, and also had them help in building his Wostitz (Wastitz) castle. Their Vorsteher he addressed in a letter as "Brother Bastl, good friend." In 1571 he turned the estate over to his brother John Schembera von Boskowitz, who sold it together with Wostitz and Urspitz to Franz, Count of Thurn. The fate of the Brethren in the Wostitz Bruderhof under him and under his son John Jacob, who married the Countess Magdalene Serenyi, is recorded at length in the chronicle. P.De.

Wolkan, *Geschicht-Buch;* Zieglschmid, *Chronik;* Franticec Hruby, "Die Wiedertäufer in Mähren," in *Arch. für Ref.-Gesch.* XXX-XXXII; Gregor Wolny, *Die Markgrafschaft Mähren II* 2 (Brno, 1837); *ML* III, 413.

Puslawitz: see Postlawitz.

Puslinch, a "preaching appointment" (MC) in Wellington County, Ont. The Mennonite Conference of Ontario shared in holding services in the Union Church (Puslinch) at the crossroads of the Cober settlement, east of Hespeler, about 1878. This work failed, but was revived about 1892. The Brethren in Christ (Tunkers) and the Mennonites, both having families in this community, alternated services in this church. The adjoining cemetery carries considerable history. Neighboring churches supplied ministerial help. By 1899 meetings were discontinued. Most of the Mennonite families moved to organized congregations in Waterloo County. No Mennonite congregation was ever organized at Puslinch. J.C.F.

Pustertal (Puster Valley), one of the most important routes of traffic in Tirol (formerly Austria, now Italy), falls into two halves. One half, traversed from east to west by the Rienza River, has a number of villages extending from the Toblach plateau to the Mühlbach cove, which are frequently named in Anabaptist history, such as Welsberg, St. Lorenzen, Bruneck, Ehrenburg, Vintl, and Mühlbach. The other half, traversed by the Drave River from Toblach via Lienz (*q.v.*), has Innichen, Sillian, Abfaltern, etc., though these enter the Anabaptist scene later than those in the half lying nearer the center of the movement.

The Anabaptist movement entered the Pustertal in a southeasterly direction from Stertzing (*q.v.*) and in a northeasterly direction from Brixen (*q.v.*). The first traces of the movement are found in the region of Welsberg, Bruneck, Toblach, and Michelsburg in April and May 1529. From the Michelsburg parish thirteen Anabaptists were taken to the court in Brixen in April of this year, four of whom were executed on June 4, one of them being Gregor Weber (*q.v.*), a preacher and the friend of Jakob Hutter (*q.v.*).

Though the Pustertal has fewer blood witnesses than the Adige (*q.v.*) Valley and the Inntal (*q.v.*), Michelsburg shows the considerable figure of twenty-four, Sillian two, Taufers (*q.v.*) one, Rodeneck four, and Schöneck four. But this list is incomplete, as the court records show. As early as 1529 Anabaptists were brought to trial from Lienz and St. Lorenzen, among them Agnes, Jakob Hutter's sister; Hutter had not yet come to public attention. Benedict, a former people's priest of Bruneck, was also seized. In the Schöneck jurisdiction Anabaptists were arrested, taken to Brixen, and sentenced.

St. Lorenzen (*q.v.*), near Bruneck (*q.v.*), was Hutter's home town; he, however, apparently first became acquainted with the Anabaptists in Klagenfurt. As their apostle he now made his first appearance in the Pustertal. He was the leader of the small group at Welsberg. Persecution began here in May 1529. Soon the Tirolese Anabaptists—a large group from the Pustertal—were emigrating to Moravia (*q.v.*). In Schöneck and Rodeneck the prisons were filled with Anabaptists in 1532. Also in Lienz the presence of Anabaptist leaders was suspected in 1533; in Sillian some were arrested and reported to Vintl.

The trial of Anton von Wolkenstein as well as his family falls into this period and this region. He belonged to one of the first families of the Tirolean nobility and was closely associated with the Anabaptists, and for a long time resisted the attempts of the Catholic clergy to convert him.

In the period just preceding and during Hutter's imprisonment the Anabaptist movement was extremely active throughout the Pustertal; later, though it still continued, it was no longer so successful. However, Anabaptists were arrested in Lüsen, Michelsburg, and Schöneck.

The attitude of the populace toward the Anabaptists is shown by a letter written by the church councillors of Brixen to the authorities in Innsbruck on June 17, 1527, which states that in this persecution the people could not be trusted. And it was still possible for members of the nobility to join the Anabaptists, as did Agnes von Waltenhofen, the widow of the clerk of Michelsburg, and her daughter. Since it was feared that others might follow their example, orders were issued in 1539 not only to apprehend her, but also to recruit men to "exterminate Anabaptist persons in the realm of Michelsburg, Schöneck, and Lüsen."

The vigorous steps taken by the authorities set a limit to the spread of the movement in the Pustertal as elsewhere. In the next few years fewer Anabaptists were brought to trial. The villages of Ehrenberg, Schöneck, Michelsburg, Uttenheim, and Heunfels still had Anabaptists, and as late as 1548 the Innsbruck authorities demanded of the governor (*Stadthalter*) and the councillors of Brixen that they restore order in the Pustertal. Some Anabaptists were found in the villages in 1551 and 1554 and 1561. In 1569 it was reported that Anabaptism was becoming increasingly troublesome in the Pustertal. In 1580 the priest of Taufers reported to Brixen that several leaders of the Anabaptist sect were stirring up the people, and two years later large crowds were reported to be on their way to Moravia, a movement which lasted into the 1590's. In 1590 Georg Wenger was seized in St. Lorenzen and put to death on Aug. 5, 1591, after a lengthy trial. On June 19, 1591, Jakob Platzer (*q.v.*) was arrested in Sillian and beheaded on August 7 of the same year. Not until the situation of the Hutterites in Moravia deteriorated did the migrations thither diminish; they ceased altogether when disaster struck the Moravian brotherhood in 1622. In the Pustertal there were still some Anabaptists in the early years of the 17th century—in Mühlbach, in the Rodeneck parish, in Bennfels, Sillian, Vintl, and Lüsen. After this the records contain no further evidence of the presence of Anabaptists in the Pustertal. (Loserth, *Anabaptismus;* ML III, 413 f.)

LOSERTH.

Putnam County, Ohio, lies in the "Black Swamp" area of northwestern Ohio and was formed from Old Indian Territory in 1820. The land is level and wet but very fertile when drained. Between 1834 and 1850 a large Swiss Mennonite settlement sprang up in southeastern Putnam and northeastern Allen counties (*q.v.*). The struggling Blanchard Mennonite Church (*q.v.*) (MC) was founded in the west-central part of the county in 1836. J.S.U.

Putschowitz: see Pudespitz.

Q

Quadendorf, a village 3 miles southeast of Danzig, in which Mennonites appeared for the first time in 1571. In 1845 the Neunhuben Mennonite congregation built a church here as a subsidiary of the Fürstenwerder congregation, which remained in use until 1945. (*ML* III, 415.)　　　　　　H.P.

Quakers: see **Society of Friends.**

Quakertown, Pa., a town (pop. 6,000) located in the southeastern part of the state in Bucks County. There are about 1500 Mennonites living within the shopping area, belonging to three branches: M.C., G.C.M., and M.B.C. The earliest known settlement of Mennonites in this area dates back to 1717, when Pastor Valentine (Felty) Clemmer arrived here from the Palatinate in Germany. Quakertown derives its name from early Quaker settlers. It was incorporated as a borough in 1855.

There are ten Mennonite churches in town and vicinity. The M.C. group has established a school near the town. Mennonites of the area also have an interest in such near-by institutions as the Eastern Mennonite Home at Souderton, the Mennonite Home for the Aged at Frederick, the Grandview Hospital at Sellersville as well as the Quakertown Community Hospital.　　　　　　A.S.R.

Quellen zur Geschichte der Täufer (before 1940, *Wiedertäufer*), a series of possibly fifteen volumes of Anabaptist archival sources, published by the German Society for Reformation History (*Verein für Reformationsgeschichte;* hereafter indicated as VRG) in its series *Quellen und Forschungen zur Reformationsgeschichte* beginning in 1930. The series was planned and its preparation directed by the Kommission zur Erforschung des Täufertums (Commission for Anabaptist Research) appointed by the VRG in 1920. To date the following volumes have appeared: I. *Herzogtum Württemberg* (1930) 1199 pp., edited by Gustav Bossert Sr., completed by his son, Gustav Bossert Jr.; II. *Markgraftum Brandenburg (Bayern, I. Abteilung)* (1934) 375 pp., Karl Schornbaum, editor; III. *Glaubenszeugnisse oberdeutscher Taufgesinnter* I (1938) 270 pp., Lydia Müller, editor; IV. *Baden und Pfalz* (1951) 574 pp., Manfred Krebs, editor; V. *Bayern, II. Abteilung* (1951) 314 pp., Karl Schornbaum, editor; VI. *Strasbourg I* (1958) 500 pp., edited by Karl Adam, J. Rott, and Manfred Krebs. Volumes in preparation include: *Strasbourg II* (Adam, Rott), *Alsace* (Adam, Rott), *Glaubenszeugnisse II* (Müller, Robert Friedmann), *Epistel der Hutterischen Brüder* (Friedmann), *Württemberg II, Niederrhein* (G. Goeters). A volume on *Silesia* was assigned to Theodor Wotschke (Breslau) before the war, but nothing has been delivered. Unassigned as yet are three more volumes on Bavaria including such important places as Augsburg and Nürnberg. The section on Switzerland, originally assigned to Leonhard von Muralt, was withdrawn from the German series, and is now being published as a Swiss series of 4-6 volumes,

Quellen zur Geschichte der Täufer in der Schweiz, of which *I. Zürich* (1952) 428 pp., edited by L. von Muralt and Walter Schmid, has appeared. Additional volumes planned include *Berner Gespräch* of 1538, *Canton Bern, Basel,* and *Ostschweiz.* The volume on Hesse, *Wiedertäuferakten 1527-1626,* 574 pp., edited by Walther Köhler, Walter Sohm, Theodor Sippell, and Günther Franz (1951), appeared in Volume IV of *Urkundliche Quellen zur hessischen Reformationsgeschichte,* which was Volume XI of *Veröffentlichungen der Historischen Kommission für Hessen und Waldeck.* For a report on other Anabaptist source publications see **Historiography.**

The VRG, a German learned society founded in 1883, undertook in the period following World War I the publication of all the documents in the German language area of Europe bearing on the history of the Anabaptist movement from its beginning in 1525 down to the Thirty Years' War (1618). This great undertaking was made possible by the grant of a generous subsidy from the Prussian state. Attempts to secure financial support in America failed. Unfortunately the inflation of the German currency in 1922-23 reduced the amount of the subsidy so much that the project was handicapped from the beginning. In spite of this, the editors for the various projected volumes were chosen and the majority of assignments completed before World War II, although only three volumes were actually published. Only one of these, Vol. I, *Herzogtum Württemberg,* prepared by Gustav Bossert, a stately volume published in 1930, appeared in full size according to plan with documents *in extenso* and full indices, although even this volume was not exhaustive. Volumes II and III, published in 1934 and 1938, appeared largely in extract form, and with meager indexing. Four additional *Täuferakten* volumes had been largely completed in manuscript before World War II, but not published since even the reduced subsidy from the Prussian state was finally canceled, and the resources of the VRG were too slender to continue without outside help, which was not forthcoming in adequate amount although the Mennonite Historical Society (*Mennonitischer Geschichtsverein, q.v.;* founded by Christian Hege; hereafter designated as MGV) made a small annual cash grant of 200 Marks for this purpose from 1937 to 1942. The publisher of the first three volumes, M. Hensius—Paul Eger Nachfolger in Leipzig, who was the publisher for all the publications of the VRG, being now in the Russian Zone and operating only on a restricted basis, surrendered his publication rights in 1947.

When it became fully clear after the close of World War II that the VRG would be unable to continue and complete the original *Täuferakten* undertaking, the MGV, encouraged by the prospect of American Mennonite financial aid and stimulated by the initiative and urgings of Eberhard Teufel of Stuttgart, decided at its annual meeting in May 1948 to undertake the project with the consent and co-operation of the VRG. The procedure set up by the MGV for the revived *Täuferakten* project was the creation of a Täuferakten-Kommission (TAK) to be composed of three representatives of the MGV and two of the VRG. The two societies function as joint publishers of the remainder of the series beginning with Volume IV. The VRG will make available all its completed manuscripts, and the MGV will endeavor to furnish the necessary finances through its American Mennonite connections. This is being done by direct subsidy contributions by the Historical Commissions of the two largest Mennonite bodies in North America, the Mennonite Church (MC) and the General Conference Mennonite Church, and by subsidy purchases of 200 copies per edition by the Mennonite Publishing House, Scottdale, Pa. All net profits from sales are pledged to further publications in the series.

The TAK was formally organized at a meeting in Heidelberg on July 5, 1948, as follows: chairman Ernst Crous (MGV), vice-chairman Heinrich Bornkamm (VRG), secretary Eberhard Teufel (MGV), treasurer H. S. Bender (MGV). Later Cornelius Krahn and Manfred Krebs were added. Upon the death of Eberhard Teufel in 1957, Heinold Fast was elected secretary.

The publication of the Anabaptist documents of the 16th century as envisaged in the above plans is an enterprise of the greatest importance not only to Anabaptist historiography but to church history as a whole. After centuries of neglect and even abuse, the Anabaptist movement is coming into its own in the modern understanding of the history of the Christian Church particularly in the Reformation period. The comprehensive and exhaustive account of the movement which is so urgently needed and which is essential for a final evaluation of Anabaptism awaits the publication of these documents and other source materials.   H.S.B.

H. S. Bender, "The Täufer-Akten Publication Series of the Society for Reformation History," *MQR* XXIII (1949) 48-52; Walter Eisenbeis, "Anabaptist Sources and Research," *Menn. Life* XII (1957) 69 ff.; Roland H. Bainton, "Anabaptist Source Materials," *Menn. Life* VIII (1953) 69 ff.; *ML* III, 417 f.

Quelles, Les (sometimes written Yquel) Mennonite Church was a continuation of the Salm congregation (*q.v.*), which was renamed after the death of Elder Nicolas Augsburger (1890) to correspond with the new meeting place in the hamlet of Les Quelles, a short distance south of the hamlet of Salm. The congregation grew weaker, but revived somewhat with the visits of ministers of the Colmar congregation, especially Henri Volkmar, the first Reiseprediger (*q.v.*), of the Alsatian Conference. In 1924, one of the families living in near-by Bénaville offered its home as the meeting place, hence the congregation was renamed Bénaville (*q.v.*). Actually Salm-Les Quelles-Bénaville was a continuing congregation, and Blanc-Rupt was a schismatic daughter of Salm.   H.S.B.

Quese, a former Mennonite family of merchants in Friedrichstadt (*q.v.*), Germany. Gerrit Jansz Quese was preacher of the Friedrichstadt church 1698-c1745, and his brother (?) Jacob Jansz Quese c1730-c40.   vDZ.

Questincx (Questincksz), **Tobias,** a Dutch Anabaptist martyr: see **Tobias Quintincxsz.**

Quincy (Mo.) Amish Mennonite Church: see **Hickory County.**

Quins, a Mennonite family of Hamburg-Altona, Germany. Its ancestor was Hans Quins (b. 1557 in Flanders, d. of the plague 1597 at Hamburg), whose wife's name was Rinske, and who was a cutler and a sword-maker. About 1580 he moved from Flanders, probably from Diest or its surroundings, to Hamburg. His daughter Jannecke (Hannchen, d. 1663 at Altona) was married to Paul Roosen (b. 1582 at Oldesloe, d. 1649 at Altona).   vDZ.

B. C. Roosen, *Gesch. der Mennoniten-Gemeinde zu Hamburg und Altona* I (Hamburg, 1886) 12, 22.

Quirijn Jansz (better called Jan Quirijnsz as in the *Martyrs' Mirror* and the *Mennonitisches Lexikon*), an Anabaptist martyr, a boatman, born at Utrecht but a citizen of Amsterdam, was baptized by the Mennonites about 1562. He rejected the attempts of the Catholic priests and the city council to convert him and was therefore sentenced to death. After two questionings on the rack (March 4 and 5) he was burned at the stake at Amsterdam on March 12, 1569. The *Martyrs' Mirror* contains a letter written by him. (*Mart. Mir.* D 490, E 832; Grosheide, *Bijdrage,* 181; *ML* III, 418.)   E.C., vDZ.

Quirijn (Quirinus) **Pietersz,** b. at Kruiningen, Dutch province of Zeeland, an Anabaptist martyr who lived at Groningen and died at the stake at Amsterdam, April 16, 1545, because he was (re)baptized. It was Menno Simons who had baptized him in 1539 in Groningen. He steadfastly confessed his faith.   NEFF, vDZ.

Inv. Arch. Amst. I, 323 f.; *Mart. Mir.* D 73, E 474; *DB* 1864, 141; 1906, 14 f.; K. Vos, *Menno Simons* (Leiden, 1914) 67, 247; *ML* III, 372.

Quirin Vermeulen: see **Meulen, Quirijn van der.**

Quiring (Quiering), a Mennonite family name, occurring first as a Christian name in Quirin van der Meulen (d. c1600), the second elder of the Danzig congregation, who latinized his Frisian name Kryn. The final *g* is the Frisian patronymic; Quiring means "son of Quirin." The name was most frequently found in the Ladekopp, Orlofferfelde, and Tragheimerweide congregations. Many preachers and deacons in the West Prussian congregations since 1650 had this name. Johann Quiring (*q.v.*) was a minister in Russia.

From Russia the name Quiring spread to North and South America. Today it is found in Canada, the United States, and South America. Outstanding representatives were Johann Quiring (*q.v.;* 1851-1912), elder of the Trakt Mennonite Church, Samara, Russia; his son Jacob Quiring, evangelist and Old Testament scholar, who taught at Bluffton College and Witmarsum Theological Seminary; Walter Quiring, educator and journalist, since May 1955 editor of *Der Bote,* Rosthern, Sask.; Horst Quiring, minister, Mennonite historian, formerly pastor in Berlin, and now manager of the Evangelische Missionsverlag of Stuttgart, Germany. (See also **Meulen, Quirijn van der.**)   H.Q.

Quiring, Johann (1851-1912), a Mennonite teacher and elder in Russia, was born at Fessendorf near Marienburg, West Prussia, Germany, on Sept. 12, 1851. In 1855 his parents settled at Köppental (Trakt settlement), Samara, Russia. He obtained his teacher's certificate in 1870, upon completion of the course at the Marienkirchenschule, Saratov. He taught at Köppental 1870-89, and after the school was reorganized into a secondary school (*Ministerialschule*) he was instructor in Bible there 1898-1911. He served on the school board 1884-1911.

On Oct. 25, 1881, Johann Quiring was elected minister and in 1884 elder to succeed David Hamm (*q.v.*). Quiring was a very gifted and successful teacher and preacher and became known far beyond his own settlement. He was active in the work of the Bundeskonferenz (General Conference of Russian Mennonites), of which he attended many sessions and served as chairman for three years. He also administered baptism and the Lord's Supper in the neighboring provinces of Ufa and Orenburg and made a trip to St. Petersburg in behalf of all the Mennonites. Jacob Quiring (*q.v.*), evangelist, educator, and scholar, who went to America, was his son. Johann Quiring died at Köppental on April 9, 1912.

C.K.

D. H. Epp, "Unser Schmerzensblatt, 1912," *Menn. Jahrbuch 1911-12* (Berdyansk) 137-39; J. J. Dyck, *Am Trakt* (North Kildonan, 1948) 48 ff.

Quitt, the title of a novel written in 1891 by Theodor Fontane (1819-98), one of the leading German novelists of the later 19th century; the novel is of importance to the Mennonites in that the second half of it has its setting in a Mennonite (GCM) home and community in Oklahoma.

Lehnert Menz, a young West Prussian, shoots a game warden and leaves him for dead. Later he hears the warden call, but is morally unable to go to the rescue. When the authorities are about to apprehend him he flees to America and finally comes to the farm of Obadja Hornbostel, a Mennonite elder. Lehnert confesses his crime to Hornbostel and becomes a member of his congregation. Lehnert meets his death from a fall while out looking for the son of the family, who has supposedly come to some harm. While awaiting death he has the conviction that he has atoned for his crime and is now "quits."

Fontane's charming and sympathetic portrait of Hornbostel is carefully drawn, based probably, as Zieglschmid has shown, on reports given by his friend Paul Lindau, who visited the American Mennonite settlements in 1883. The story, however, has some rather un-Mennonite pietistic and Calvinistic characteristics which invalidate certain aspects of Fontane's interpretation of the Mennonite faith. (See the excellent discussions by Ernst Correll, "Theodor Fontane," *ML* I, 661, and Paul Schowalter, "Literatur," *ML* II, 665.)

E.H.B.

Elizabeth H. Bender, "The Mennonites in German Literature," especially the chapter "Theodor Fontane's Novel *Quitt*, 1891" (M.A. thesis, Minnesota, 1944); Ernst Correll, "Theodor Fontane's *Quitt*," *MQR* XVI (1942) 221 f. (reprint from *ML* I, 661); Otto Schowalter, "Die Mennoniten in der allgemeinen deutschen Literatur: Bibliographie," *Beitrage zur Geschichte der Mennoniten* (Weierhof, 1938); A. J. F. Zieglschmid, "Truth and Fiction and Mennonites in the Second Part of Theodor Fontane's Novel *Quitt*: the Indian Territory," *MQR* XVI (1942) 223-46.

Quynende Kercke *der Waterlandse Doops-gesinde tot Wormer-veer* (Amsterdam, 1677) is an 18-page anonymous pamphlet which deals with a conflict in the Mennonite Waterlander congregation of Wormerveer (*q.v.*), Dutch province of North Holland, during 1669-76. This booklet is clear evidence of the growing conservatism among the Dutch Waterlander group about the second half of the 17th century. The authors of the booklet were probably Pieter Adriaensz (Hardloop) and Sijmen Pietersz Schilp.

vDZ.

R

Raabe, Friedrich, was elected minister of the Karassan Mennonite Church (*q.v.*), Crimea, Russia, in 1874 and elder in 1883. In 1884 he became the elder of the Busau Mennonite Church (*q.v.*), and served until 1890, when he was relieved of his responsibilities as elder. **C.K.**

Friesen, *Brüderschaft*, 709; H. H. Friedrichsen, "Die Geschichte der Busauer Menn.-Gemeinde," *Unser Blatt* II, No. 8 (May 1927) 236-38.

Rab, a Mennonite family found from the 17th century on the Dutch island of Texel (*q.v.*), many of whose members have served as deacons. Some Rabs were skippers of Greenland whalers, the last of whom was Willem Rab in the early 19th century. **vDZ.**

Rabbit Lake is a village about 100 miles northwest of Saskatoon, Sask., with the Hoffnungsfeld General Conference Mennonite Church of 100 members (1957) a few miles outside the town. In 1926 the first settlers, who came to Canada from Russia in 1923 ff., settled here. In 1927, after clearing the land, the first crop was totally frozen. But the newcomers did not give up. Soon two more stations to the east, Mullingar (*q.v.*) with an M.B. church which has been razed and Mayfair with the Hebron G.C.M. church of 26 members (1957), were settled, and two stations to the west, Bornemouth with a G.C.M. church which has been razed and Glenbush with an M.B. church of 144 members (1957). The churches in Mullingar and Bornemouth were razed when the boom of the Rabbit Lake country collapsed in the 1930's. At present there are in the area roughly 250 each of the M.B. and the G.C.M. groups. **J.G.R.**

Rabe (Rabus), **Ludwig** (1514-92), was born at Memmingen, Germany, went to Strasbourg (*q.v.*) about 1540 to assist Matthäus Zell (*q.v.*), a reformer and Lutheran pastor, and became his successor in 1548. In 1556 he was appointed church superintendent at Ulm. As a church leader he opposed the doctrines of the Anabaptists and the Schwenckfelders (*q.v.*).

Rabe is to be specially mentioned for his martyr book. In 1552 he published at Strasbourg *Tomus I de S. Dei confessoribus, veterisque ecclesiae martyribus.* A German edition of this first volume appeared at Strasbourg in 1554, entitled *Historien der Heyligen Auszerwöllten Gottes Zeugen, Bekennern und Märtyrern.* The first volume was followed by seven more. There are a number of reprints, of which the best known is the folio edition in two volumes (Strasbourg, 1571-72) titled *Historien der Märtyrer.* All the editions are illustrated by woodcuts and deal with 209 persons. Rabe's book is somewhat different in character from other martyr books such as the *Offer des Heeren* and van Braght's *Martyrs' Mirror.* Rabe listed not only persons who had suffered and died for their faith, but also men like Luther who had been defenders of the faith. (The discussion on Luther occupies 488 pages of volume IV.)

Rabe's martyr book includes three Dutch Anabaptist martyrs, Wendelmoet (Weynken) Claes (*q.v.*) and the two noble ladies of Beckum (*q.v.*) (all in volume III, 1557). The account on Wendelmoet follows an old pamphlet under the title *Ein wunderliche Geschycht . . . von . . . Wendelmoet Clausen dochter.* For the article on Maria and Ursula van Beckum Rabe used other sources than those used by the *Offer des Heeren.* He adapted two songs, both found in the *Bibliographie des Martyrologes Protestants Néerlandais* (Vol. II, 553-59). The first song begins, "Allhie will ich übersummen, was ich in kurtz hab vernummen, von zweyen Junckfrauen sagen," and the second, "Nun lasst uns fröhlich heben an und Gott zu Lobe singen, von zweyen Junckfrauwen wolgethon." It is possible that the account on Wendelmoet Claesdochter in the *Offer des Heeren,* which does not occur here until the fourth edition (1570), was borrowed from Rabe's book. **vDZ.**

Offer, 422 f., note 1, 509, note 1; *Bibliographie* II, 533-82; F. Pijper, *Martelaarsboeken* (The Hague, 1924) 120-33.

Rabensburg, a castle and village in Lower Austria near the confluence of the Thaya into the March. In May 1605 three Hutterian Brethren were murdered here. Rabensburg was the home of Gabriel Krettle who wrote about Pilgram Marpeck's *Verantwortung.* (See Codex III, 19 at Olomouc.) Krettle is thought to have united with the Hutterian Brethren (according to H. Maier in 1592). **E.C.**

Beck, *Geschichts-Bücher,* 341; Wolkan, *Geschicht-Buch,* 485; Zieglschmid, *Chronik,* 632; *ML* III, 419.

Rabenska (Rabentzkj; Czech, *Rovenszko*), a village between Sobotiste and Senitz in the province of Nitra (Neutra), Czechoslovakia, the site of a Hutterite Bruderhof in Hungary which was settled in 1547, and burned down by Bethlen Gabor's (*q.v.*) troops on Nov. 21, 1623.

Beck, *Geschichts-Bücher,* 420, 443; Wolkan, *Geschicht-Buch,* 241, 572, 595; Zieglschmid, *Chronik,* 319, 759, 791, 817; *ML* III, 419.

Raber (Räber, Reber), a Mennonite family name, found in Switzerland. In 1567 Peter Räber, of Buchholterberg near Diesbach, canton of Bern, was arrested; after severe torture he recanted and promised to swear an oath of allegiance. About 1670 the Räbers lived in the Emmental (*q.v.*). In 1711, when a number of Bernese Anabaptists were compelled to leave the country and to settle in the Netherlands, Samuel Räber then was arrested and finally released to be conducted to the ship. He seems to have left the ship at Mannheim (*q.v.*) with others of this group and joined the Mennonites who had settled here some years earlier.

In 1837 Jacob Raber with his wife and six children emigrated to America from Germany. The 1955 history of this Amish family lists 1571 descendants, many of whom live near Baltic, Ohio; others are widely scattered in Indiana, Michigan, Illinois, and

Iowa. In this group of descendants over 280 bear the name Raber and 99 are or have been ministers, mostly in the Old Order Amish Church. In 1957 three Rebers and eleven Rabers were in the Mennonite (MC) and Amish ministry. J. A. Raber of Baltic, Ohio, has been publishing *(Der) Neue Amerikanische Calendar (q.v.)*.

Christian Raber, very likely an older brother of the above Jacob, also emigrated to America in 1837 and with his family settled north of Cincinnati, Ohio, where he served as an Amish preacher. Later he moved to Lee County, Iowa, where he continued his ministry. Some of Christian's descendants moved to Hickory County *(q.v.)*, Mo., from where they have scattered to many Mennonite communities. Among Christian's descendants was Daniel B. Raber, a widely known Mennonite minister, who worked among the mountain people of Southern Missouri. Daniel's son Frank was for twenty years the pastor of the Detroit (Mich.) Mennonite Gospel Mission *(q.v.)*.

John Reber, born in Alsace in 1820, came to America as a young man to escape military service. He was ordained to the Amish ministry in Elkhart County, Ind., but in perhaps 1853 moved to Johnson County, Iowa. His descendants are found principally in Iowa, Kansas, Michigan, and Illinois, among whom have been the following ordained Mennonite ministers: David Reber, Joseph Reber, George Reber, and Don D. Reber.   vDZ., M.G.

Samuel Geiser, *Die Taufgesinnten-Gemeinden* (Karlsruhe, 1931) 194 f.; Delbert Gratz, *Bernese Anabaptists* (Scottdale, 1953) 48, 61 f.; Daniel J. Raber, *Raber Family History 1837-1937* (n.p., n.d.); David M. Raber, Mrs. Roman E. Yoder, and Joe D. Yoder, *Descendants of Jacob Raber 1794-1955* (Nappanee, 1955).

Raber, J. A., an Old Order Amish book dealer, born Sept. 8, 1885, who has maintained a bookstore at his farm, 2 miles south of Charm, Holmes Co., Ohio, since 1915. He has supplied Amish readers with numerous German publications and published the following reprints: *Die vollständigen Werke Menno Simon's* (1926), Nagler's *Handwörterbuch der heiligen Schrift* (1934), the *Märtyrer-Spiegel* (1950), and numerous smaller works. An annual publication by Raber since 1930 has been *Der Neue Amerikanische Kalender,* which contains a register of Amish ministers.   **J.A.H.**

Räbl, Wilhelm, was a leader of the Hutterites at Austerlitz *(q.v.)*, who in 1531 disagreed with Jacob Widemann *(q.v.)*. Räbl was supported by Jörg Zaunring *(q.v.)*. (Wolkan, *Lieder,* 25.) vDZ.

Rabus, Ludovicus: see Rabe, Ludwig.

Race Relations. By the mid-20th century the rights of subject peoples, especially those of color, had become a burning social and political issue throughout the world. With other Christians, Mennonites found it necessary to speak out on this question, especially on the Christian attitude toward persons of a color other than one's own.

It could be pointed out that Mennonites have never owned slaves, that slavery was forbidden in the Plockhoy *(q.v.)* colony of 1663, and that in 1688 the Germantown Mennonites had a share in the first public protest against slavery on record in America.

In 1955 the Committee on Economic and Social Relations *(q.v.)* and the Mennonite Community Association *(q.v.)*, both of the Mennonite Church (MC), sponsored a conference on Christian race relations; a significant pronouncement, "The Way of Christian Love in Race Relations," was drafted here and was later that year adopted by the Mennonite General Conference (MC) as its official position. The statement proclaims the unity of man in the order of creation and in the order of grace, and the unity of the one fellowship in Christ. It holds that the Scriptural teaching and New Testament practice are opposed to distinctions based on race or color and that racial discrimination is a recent phenomenon and a sin, in that it does wrong to the victim, scars the soul of the offender, contributes to social tension and hatred, is a major cause for war, invalidates the central meaning of redemption, discredits the Christian church and the Gospel before the world, and weakens its missionary program. The statement includes a confession of the failure of the church to witness against this sin as it ought and a commitment to a renewed emphasis on the way of Christian love in race relations.

Obviously the members of the younger Mennonite churches in Africa and Asia are persons of color. In the United States, however, both the Mennonite Church (MC) and the General Conference Mennonite Church had a Negro membership with at least one Negro minister in each group in 1958. These groups as well as others were conducting church extension work, voluntary service units, and other forms of evangelistic and social service work among Negroes, Latin American, Indian, and other non-Caucasian groups. (See **Negro Missions**.)

In 1956, 1957, and again in 1958 the Peace Section of the MCC sent a group of visitors to the South to study race conditions there and to encourage Christians who were engaged in a witness against racial discrimination. In 1957 a group of students from Goshen College gave a week of service to Koinonia Farms in Georgia. While prejudice and discrimination were not completely overcome in all Mennonite groups, there was positive teaching against these evils. All Mennonite schools and colleges, even in the South, were open to persons of color without discrimination, although this was not true of all homes for the aged. Attempts were being made to maintain Mennonite congregations and institutions on an integrated basis, and there was a limited amount of intermarriage among American Mennonites of Caucasian background with Latin Americans, Puerto Ricans, Filipinos, and Negroes.   G.F.H.

Christian Race Relations: Proceedings of the Conference on Christian Community Relations (Scottdale, 1955); C. N. Kraus, *Integration: Who's Prejudiced* (Scottdale, 1958).

Rack (Räck), Jörg (Georg) (Georg Mair), a Hutterite martyr, a deacon from Pfons, a village under the jurisdiction of Steinach, Tirol, Austria, was seized with Hans Mändl *(q.v.)* and Eustachius Kotter *(q.v.)* on Nov. 15, 1560, in the neighborhood of Rosenheim. On Jan. 26 and 27, 1561, he was cross-examined both without and with the use of the rack. He remained steadfast. The confession of faith made by the three martyrs has been preserved in the library of the University of Vienna. On June 10 they were sentenced to death and were executed at Innsbruck on the same day. Kotter was beheaded first, then Räck, who died happily with the words, "Here I forsake wife and child, house and property, life and body for the sake of divine truth." He is the author of two songs: "Ich ruf zu dir, o Vater mein" (nine stanzas), and "Mein Gott, ich tu dich bitten von ganzem Herzen mein" (ten stanzas). Loserth's statement (*ME* III, 454) that Rack wrote three songs is apparently inaccurate. Jörg Rack, Hans Mändl, and Eustachius Kotter are the subjects of a hymn by Andreas Ehrenpreis (*q.v.*). NEFF.

Beck, *Geschichts-Bücher*, 210, 222-25; Zieglschmid, *Chronik*, 398, 403-6; Wolkan, *Geschicht-Buch*, 302, 308-10; *Die Lieder der Hutterischen Brüder* (Scottdale, 1914) 634-36; Wolkan, *Lieder*, 280, 282; *Mart. Mir.* D 276, E 645, where he is called Juriaen Raek; *ML* III, 424.

Rackschitz (Rakschitz), a Bruderhof of the Hutterian Brethren near Kromau (*q.v.*) in Moravia (*q.v.*), was founded in 1545 by the purchase of a house. At this time the village belonged to the baron of Lipa-Kromau. Johann von Lipa, who came from a line noted for its tolerance, accepted the Brethren on his estate.   HEGE.

Beck, *Geschichts-Bücher*, 164; Wolkan, *Geschicht-Buch*, 195, 240; Zieglschmid, *Chronik*, 250, 316; *ML* III, 424.

Racovian Catechism: see **Rakow** and **Socinianism.**

Rade vorm Walde, a town (1944 pop. 13,861) in the Düsseldorf area of the Rhine Province of Prussia, Germany. A "Catalog of the Anabaptists in Rade vorm Walde in 1638" lists fourteen Mennonite families, mostly embroiderers, who were expelled from the town. They had come from the area of Jülich (*q.v.*) and Berg (*q.v.*). After the expulsion Andreas Linnich went to Friedrichstadt (*q.v.*); the von Voss and Wienenberg families settled on the Lower Rhine (*q.v.*). One of the refugees, destined to become the most important, was the embroidery worker "Entgen, widow ahn der Leyen," the mother of Adolf van der Leyen (*q.v.*); he moved from Rade vorm Walde to Crefeld (*q.v.*) in 1656. From a tailor, Isaak Becker, who was presumably a Mennonite, and who was living in Rade vorm Walde in the middle of the 18th century, Jung-Stilling (*q.v.*) found religious encouragement and inspiration.
E.C.

Wilhelm Niepoth, "Der 'Catalogus der Widdertauffer zu Rade vorm Walde Anno 1638,'" *Zeitschrift des Bergischen Geschichtsvereins* LXXIII (1952) 74-84; idem "Zur Frühgeschichte der Familie van der Leyden," *Die Heimath (Krefeld)* XXI (1950) 156-58; *ML* III, 424.

Radecke (Radecius), **Matthäus** (1540-1612), was born at Danzig, educated at Königsberg, served as city clerk of Danzig 1566-92. He was christened a Catholic, and later became successively Lutheran, Reformed, Mennonite (baptism by aspersion), and Socinian (*q.v.*; baptism by immersion). In 1592 he was deposed from his office because of his Socinian beliefs and left the city with his wife and eight children. After a brief stay at Schmiegel, near

Posen, he went to Buskow in 1593 and then to Rakov (*q.v.*; Poland) in 1608. Here he died on March 29, 1612. (He is erroneously called Martin Radecke in *ME* I, 76.)   E.C.

F. S. Bock, *Historia Antitrinitariorum* I, Part 2 (Leipzig, 1716) 700-9; Matthäus Radecke, *Ursachen, warumb sich Matthäus Radecke, welcher der Stadt Dantzigk, 26 Jahre lang, für einen Secretarium gedienet, von dar gemachet, undt sich mit den seinen ahn andere Ort begeben hab* (Rakow, 1593); *RGG* V, Col. 660; *ML* III, 424.

Radegundis (Saint Radegundis), a hamlet southwest of Augsburg, Bavaria, Germany, where in the spring of 1528 the Anabaptists assembled in the open (see **Augsburg**).   E.C.

Fr. Roth, *Augsburgs Reformationsgeschichte 1517-1530* (Munich, 1901) 246; *ML* III, 425.

Rademacher (Radermecher), **Reinken,** an Anabaptist martyr, who baptized Theunis van Hastenrath (*q.v.*), is probably identical with Remken Remakers (*q.v.*), who was put to death at Sittard in 1550. (*DB* 1890, 58; 1909, 120, 124; *Mart. Mir.* D 98, E 497; *ML* III, 424.)   NEFF.

Radical Reformation, a collective term for all those groups of religious innovators of the 16th century on the European continent who were neither Lutherans, nor Zwinglians, nor Calvinists. Occasionally all these groups are broadly conceived as the "Fourth Reformation." No doubt the Protestant revolt against Rome opened the floodgates for all forms of separatism which continued what is often called "medieval sectarianism." In German official church history it has become customary to call all those who opposed the Lutheran Reformation *Schwärmer* (Enthusiasts, *q.v.*) or *Ketzer* (hence *Ketzerhistorie, q.v.*), a derogatory term which did grave injustice to all dissidents. In the 20th century the conceptions have changed somewhat under the impact of the new science of sociology of religion. Now these groups are often simply distinguished as "sects" in contrast to "church" (*Kirche*), i.e., state church. Ernst Troeltsch was a leader in this reclassification. In America the church historians, having no use for these typically continental concepts (since in America all churches are "denominations"), had to find another type of classification. In 1941, Roland H. Bainton of Yale proposed the generic term "Left Wing of the Reformation," using the political connotation of "left" and "right" for a characterization of the different groups. "Left" then meant opposition to the state-church idea (the established church), and championship of the free or nonconformist church idea. (But Bainton also thought in part of a "left" wing in theology, namely, anti-Trinitarianism.) Bainton also at times used the term "Anabaptists" for all these groups, since most (though by no means all) advocated adult baptism. By this broadening of the term Anabaptism a Menno Simons and a Michael Servetus, for instance, were lumped together in a strange fellowship. In spite of its vagueness, the term "Left Wing of the Reformation" was rather widely accepted, chiefly for lack of a better term, and to a certain extent proved its usefulness in American church historical studies. Franklin Littell and recently Leonard Verduin showed also an inclination to use the term "Restitutionism" for the greater part of these groups. Littell pointed out (50) that the idea of restitution (q.v.) binds together Anabaptists and Spiritualists, Schwenckfelders and Polish Brethren, etc., even though it must be admitted that not all Spiritualists had the vision of the restoration of the primitive church.

That a common term for all these "dissident" groups is hard to find must be granted, even though the need for it is obvious. Certain men who were for a time Anabaptists adopted anti-Trinitarian views (Adam Pastor, apparently also Ludwig Haetzer), while certain anti-Trinitarians accepted adult baptism though otherwise far from any of the well-known evangelical Anabaptists. Müntzer was just as disinterested in the question of baptism as was Sebastian Franck or Bünderlin. Particularly difficult is the delineation of "Spiritualism" (Rufus Jones's "Spiritual Reformers") because of the extreme individualism of its defenders. In the Netherlands a section of evangelical Anabaptism was always "spiritualistically minded," while the Swiss Brethren opposed this trend radically. "Unitarians": H. Richard Niebuhr has suggested a strange and unusual subclassification of "Unitarianism of the Father"—Socinians; "Unitarianism of the Son"—Schwenckfeld, Swedenborg; "Unitarianism of the Holy Spirit"—Spiritualists.

In view of the motley nature of the "Fourth Reformation," the proposal by George H. Williams of Harvard Divinity School (1957) of a new and rather adequate descriptive term together with a more refined subclassification of the historical phenomena is welcome as a real aid in the understanding of the spiritual life of the 16th century. Williams distinguishes between "magisterial Reformation" (also called territorial Protestantism), where the princes were the real heads of the church with magisterial prerogatives and an excessive ecclesiasticism (establishment), and its opponents, called "Radical Reformation." Common to all the radical reformers is their opposition to "the suffocating growth of ecclesiastical tradition," to the above-named prerogatives, and above all to the compromises and adjustments of the new territorial churches to the "world" in its broadest sense. No one of these radical reformers had any place for state powers within the church. All of them wanted to cut back to the Biblical roots of faith and order.

Among these radical reformers Williams then distinguishes three clearly separated groups: (a) the Anabaptists, (b) the Spiritualists, and (c) the Evangelical Rationalists. (See the similar classification by Johannes Kühn, q.v.) The first two groups are mainly Germanic (German, Dutch, Swiss), while the Evangelical Rationalists belonged pre-eminently to the Romance cultural area—Italy, Spain, and to a lesser degree France (Juan de Valdés, Servetus, Ochino, Castellio, Biandrata, Socinus, etc.).

While the Protestant reformers advocated the medieval idea of a *corpus Christianum,* a Christian society composed of saints and sinners, this concept was absolutely unacceptable to the radical reformers. They visualized a selected society of true believers, that is a *Corpus Christi,* as their final ideal. As to how such a Corpus Christi should look, ideas naturally differed. Some would look back to the apostolic model, the primitive church and the church under the Cross (1st—3rd centuries); they would then represent the "restitutionists" proper (by and large the Anabaptist group). Others of the radical reformation took their lead from the Book of Revelation and looked into the future for the kingdom or new world to come. Some would simply wait for this event, others would fight (like Müntzer). Williams claims that this look into the future is nearer to the spiritualistic type than to the Anabaptist one, although this is not always true.

Williams sees three distinct groups in each of his three main sections, namely:

Anabaptism: (1) evangelical (Swiss Brethren, Mennonites, Hutterites, etc.); (2) revolutionary (the Münsterites above all; Troeltsch called them "Taborites," Littell suggests the term "Maccabeans"); (3) contemplative (mainly Hans Denk, to whom the inner word or inner Christ is more important than any external form).

Spiritualism: (1) evangelical (Schwenckfeld and Gabriel Ascherham); (2) revolutionary (Thomas Müntzer, also the Zwickau "prophets" and perhaps Karlstadt); (3) rational (Sebastian Franck, Paracelsus, and many more).

Evangelical Rationalism: here Williams does not offer any subdivision except that he finds some staying in their old church, "evangelical Catholics" (Erasmus, LeFevre, Valdes), while others broke away (Servetus and Ochino), being either lonely wanderers over the earth, or founders of conventicles or churches like Faustus Socinus (Polish Brethren, Transylvanian Unitarians).

The Anabaptists are the representatives of the idea of restitution in its broadest sense; the question is only what they aim to restore. The evangelical Anabaptists look back to the apostolic church; that is, to them the New Testament is the only norm, while the Old Testament has but figurative or allegorical value. They look to a church *(Gemeinde)* of discipline and order, with ban, shunning, and inner-worldly asceticism. The revolutionary Anabaptists (Münsterites) in contradistinction accept the Old Testament as their norm, desiring to erect the New Jerusalem in the here and now; hence the sword, which was abhorred by the evangelical brethren, is here glorified (as it is also by Müntzer). The contemplative Anabaptists finally (if there are such) are more indifferent to the externals of discipline, and thus draw nearer to the Spiritualists. Only the evangelical Anabaptists, emphasizing discipleship, know also the idea of a suffering church, called "theology of martyrdom" by Ethelbert Stauffer.

Spiritualists hold the inspiration by the Holy Spirit above the word of the Scriptures (inspirationism). The revolutionary group among them are strongly influenced by the books of Daniel and Revelation; they are visionary and apocalyptically minded. The evangelical Spiritualists, among whom Williams also counts Schwenckfeld (this classification is open to debate), base their teachings primarily upon the Johannine writings, in which the "spirit" or light is emphasized. The rational Spiritualists, finally—individualists through and through

—are the nearest to what Rufus Jones called "spiritual reformers," a sort of bridge between rationalism proper and Christian mysticism.

Here might then be found also the bridge to the Evangelical Rationalists, who in spite of their strong reliance upon reason (see **Reason and Obedience**) nevertheless resist a complete surrender to a humanistic rationalism (which eventually leads to rational philosophy). They do accept the Holy Scriptures, but are inclined to interpret them by the light of natural reason. Hence their inclination either to anti-Trinitarianism or to a moral Pietism, as it is so well known from the later 17th and 18th centuries (Dutch Collegiants, Galenus Abrahamsz).

It is clear that no classification can do absolute justice to the many-sidedness of the actual historical phenomena, but the suggestions by Williams are useful and may help to clarify terms and stereotypes. (See **Anabaptist** and **Kühn, Johannes.**) R.F.

George H. Williams, *Spiritual and Anabaptist Writers, Documents Illustrative of the Radical Reformation* (Library of Christian Classics, Vol. XXV) (Philadelphia, 1957); R. H. Bainton, "The Left Wing of the Reformation," *Journal of Religion* XXI (1941) 127 ff.; John T. McNeill, "Left Wing Religious Movements," in *A Short History of Christianity*, ed. by Archibald G. Baker (Chicago, 1940); H. Richard Niebuhr, "The Doctrine of the Trinity and the Unity of the Church," *Theology Today* III (1946) 371 ff.; Robert Friedmann, "Concept of the Anabaptist," *Church History* IX (1940) 341-65; *idem*, "Recent Interpretation of Anabaptism," *Church History* XXIV (1955) 132-51; Johannes Kühn, *Toleranz und Offenbarung* (Leipzig, 1923); Franklin H. Littell, *The Anabaptist View of the Church* (American Society of Church History, 1952; second ed. Boston, 1958); George H. Williams, "Studies in the Radical Reformation: A Bibliographical Survey," *Church History*, March and June 1958.

Radichev on the Desna, a village in the Russian province of Chernigov, a Hutterite Bruderhof. Count Peter Rumiantsev (*q.v.*) brought the Hutterian Brethren to Vishenka (*q.v.*) in the province of Chernigov, Ukraine; but his son restricted the liberties promised them. Therefore they were given some crown land at Radichev in 1801, and established a new Bruderhof there. Soon, however, a decline set in. Health conditions were poor; of the fifty families only two persons passed the age of fifty, and the natural increase for half of a generation was only 58. More serious was the division within the settlement, one group under elder Johann Waldner wishing to retain the ancient practice of community of goods, and the other group under Jakob Walter wanting to give it up. The government authorities summoned from St. Petersburg were unable to establish peace. The Walter group left the Bruderhof, but many of them returned within a year. The old Bruderhof buildings burned to the ground. The groups then remained together but abandoned community in 1819, for the second time in Hutterite history. In 1820 Johann Waldner died. The settlement made some recovery in the ensuing years. New villages were established in the Molotschna at Hutterthal (*q.v.*), Johannesruh, Neuhutterthal, and again a Bruderhof Hutterdorf. In 1874 Hutterdorf emigrated to South Dakota; in 1877 Hutterthal and Johannesruh followed, and the rest in 1879. E.C.

Alexander Klaus, *Unsere Kolonien* (translated from the Russian by Jakob Tōws) (Odessa, 1887) 46-92; C.

Henry Smith, *The Story of the Mennonites* (Newton, 1950) 380-83; Zieglschmid, *Klein-Geschichtsbuch; ML* III, 425.

Radio Broadcasting, Mennonite. 1. *The Mennonite Church (MC).* Commercial radio broadcasting began in the United States in 1920. By the early 1930's numerous evangelical Christian groups were producing religious broadcasts. The first Mennonite radio broadcast program, so far as is known, was begun in November 1936 by William Detweiler (d. 1957), a Mennonite minister of Smithville, Ohio, and was called "Calvary Hour." It began as a weekly half-hour broadcast with one station at Canton, Ohio; in 1939 a station in Pennsylvania was added; finally 20 stations were included. It is still broadcasting. The broadcast is managed by a family type incorporated board, with the two minister sons of the late William Detweiler continuing in their father's stead as the radio preachers. The second broadcast was established in 1940 at Kitchener, Ont., by a layman, who offered a musical program by a "Nightingale Chorus" for shut-ins, but which discontinued after about six months. By 1951 a total of 32 broadcasts had been started in local congregations, about one third by laymen; some 15 had been discontinued. Only one broadcast was sponsored by a conference, namely, the Ontario Mennonite Conference project begun in 1945. A Spanish language broadcast was begun at La Junta, Col., in 1945 by the local Mexican Mennonite Church; it is still on the air. In August 1947 Lester Hershey started a Spanish broadcast from Puerto Rico, where he was engaged in mission work; it is still on the air, affiliated with the Mennonite Hour. The 32 broadcasts started were sent over a total of 76 stations distributed as follows: Ohio 13, Pennsylvania 10, Ontario 8, Illinois 7, Maryland 5, Puerto Rico 4, Indiana 3, Kansas 3, Iowa 3, Virginia 3, Oregon 2, New York 2, Michigan 2, and one each in Florida, Colorado, Missouri, Louisiana, Washington, Nebraska, California, Ecuador, Costa Rica, Panama, and Haiti. Discontinuance of programs, which often were short-lived, was due chiefly to lack of financial support and difficulty in securing talent.

The year 1951 marked a significant change in radio broadcasting work in the Mennonite Church. By action of the General Council of the Mennonite General Conference in that year, the Mennonite Board of Missions and Charities was urged to establish a national Mennonite broadcast under its supervision. By 1953 the board had established a national and international broadcast operated through the Mennonite Crusaders, Inc. (*q.v.*), a local group established at Harrisonburg, Va., in June 1951 to operate the Mennonite Hour (*q.v.*), which had been established in March 1951 on the campus of Eastern Mennonite College, using a college musical group. The Mennonite Crusaders was supplanted by Mennonite Broadcasts, Inc. (*q.v.*) in 1956. B. Charles Hostetter has served as radio pastor since January 1952. The Mennonite Hour was broadcasting over 70 stations in early 1957, of which 56 were in the United States, and 2 in Canada, plus broadcasts in Ceylon, Costa Rica, Ecuador, Jamaica, Liberia, Panama, the Philippines, Puerto Rico, and Viet-Nam. The weekly listening audience was estimated at 5 million, with broadcasts in English, Spanish, and Japanese. Since then an Italian language broadcast in Italy and a Navajo Indian language broadcast in Arizona have been added, and plans are being made for German, French, and Russian broadcasts in Europe. The European headquarters is at Basel. Since 1958 Menn. Broadcasts sponsors the Heart-to-Heart program, a weekly women's broadcast by Ruth Stoltzfus, which she began in 1950. Mennonite Broadcasts is normally self-sustaining, being supported by the contributions of the listeners.

Partly because of the establishment and the development of the Mennonite Hour, most of the local broadcasts have been discontinued or have been replaced by local sponsorship of the Mennonite Hour. Except for the Calvary Hour, the Spanish broadcast at La Junta, and the Sunday School Hour at Sarasota, Fla., started respectively in 1936 and 1945 and 1946, no other Mennonite broadcast started before 1950 was still in existence in 1958. Seven other local broadcasts however were still operating, started respectively in 1950, 1951 (2), 1953 (2), and 1957 (2). The day of local broadcasts is pretty well past in the church.

2. *Other Mennonite Bodies.* The radio broadcasting work has not found extensive use in other Mennonite bodies in North America. In 1952 Andrew Shelly reported only five broadcasts in the General Conference Mennonite Church in the United States, two of which were Bethel College and Freeman College, and one was the Mountain Lake (Minn.) Mennonite Home. Shelly reported only two broadcasts by Mennonite Brethren Churches—Buhler, Kan., and Delft, Minn. Grace Bible Institute at Omaha, Neb., also had a broadcast. Ed. J. Peters, an M.B. layman, owned and operated a private station at Wasco, Cal., broadcasting only good musical and religious programs. The M.B. churches at Kitchener and Virgil, Ont., also had broadcasts. Tabor College now broadcasts "The Chapel Hour" over at least 10 stations.

Bethel College has presented weekly "Chapel Meditations" over KFH, Wichita, every Sunday since 1951, consisting of meditations presented by Erland Waltner and at present by D. C. Wedel, and choir music by the Mennonite Singers under the direction of W. H. Hohmann. The General Conference Mennonite Church has been conducting a radio ministry twice daily since 1953 over KJRG, Newton, Kan. The First Mennonite Church of Newton has been broadcasting its Sunday worship services over KJRG for a number of years. Other churches, as for example the First Mennonite Church of Beatrice, Neb., are also broadcasting their worship services.

J. G. Rempel's report of 1952 on Mennonite radio broadcasts in Western Canada reported somewhat more broadcasting in that area by both G.C.M. and M.B. groups. He listed nine programs in the Western provinces—Manitoba two, Saskatchewan 5, Alberta one, British Columbia one; by conferences G.C.M. four, M.B. four, and E.M.B. one. Several Mennonite programs in this area were integrated into nondenominational broadcasts or were sponsored by the Canadian Sunday School Mission.

Numerous individual Mennonites were appearing on nondenominational broadcasts. The first Western Canadian Mennonite program was the M.B. broadcast from Saskatoon in 1940, the second the G.C.M. program in the same city in 1948.

A radically new development in Canada, and the only one of its kind anywhere, was the establishment of a Mennonite-owned and operated radio station, CFAM at Altona, Man., by the Southern Man. Broadcasting Co. (*q.v.*) (A. J. Thiessen, pres. D. K. Friesen, sec.-treas.). It went on the air on March 13, 1957. It is intended to serve "the economic, cultural, and religious needs of Southern Manitoba." It furnishes a good outlet for a considerable amount of religious broadcasting by Mennonites of several branches in the area. The Mennonite Radio Mission, the radio arm of the Manitoba Mennonite Conference (GCM), sponsors several broadcasts in three languages, English, German, and Low German. Several of the Mennonite programs in other provinces broadcast in two languages and some in Low German also. A group in Steinbach has also applied for a broadcast license.

In 1957 the Mennonite Brethren started a Russian language broadcast over a station in Winnipeg, designed to reach Russia. The M.B. broadcast is under the name "The Gospel Light Hour" in German, English, and Russian. Reports by letter from Russia indicate that both Russian and German religious broadcasts are being received by Mennonites in Russia.

The Janz Brothers, a small M.B. group, originally attached to the Prairie Bible Institute at Three Hills, Alberta, have been broadcasting in German with headquarters in Basel and in Canada. They operate on an independent basis. Theodore Epp, a former G.C.M. minister in Nebraska, has been broadcasting on a large scale through the Back to the Bible Hour, Inc., with headquarters at Omaha. This is also independent and nondenominational. Eastern Mennonite College (1957, 10 watt power) and Goshen College (1958, 250 watt power) operate local FM stations broadcasting over a radius of about 15 miles, 2-3 hours daily, partly as an opportunity for student experience.

The purpose of the Mennonite religious broadcasts has been uniformly primarily evangelistic, but also edificatory and devotional, and intended to reach the general public as well as Mennonites. Without doubt much has been accomplished, especially by the stronger programs, but probably little direct increase in membership of the Mennonite church can be attributed to the broadcasts.

The first reaction of the more conservative Mennonites to the use of the radio and radio broadcasting was rather negative. A number of more conservative conferences in the Mennonite Church (MC) in the East at one time had regulations forbidding the use of the radio in the home. This attitude has now changed, although one conference still maintains an official ban. H.S.B.

Andrew R. Shelly, "Mennonites on the Air," *Menn. Life* VII (1952) 65-71; J. G. Rempel, "Mennonites on the Air in Western Canada," *ibid.*, 125-27; Earl Meyers, "Mennonite Radio Broadcasting 1936-1951," unpublished manuscript in GCL (1951); Eugene Sauder, "A Radio Broadcasting Program for the Mennonite Church," ms in GCL (1952); "The History of the Radio Ministry of the General Conference Mennonite Church," ms in BeCL; Frank H. Epp, "Radio as It Should Be," *Menn. Life* XIV (January 1959).

Raduga ("Rainbow"), a Mennonite publishing company established at Halbstadt, Molotschna settlement, Russia, after H. J. Braun (*q.v.*) had purchased of P. Neufeld the print shop in Halbstadt. At first (1904-9) the imprint was "Druck und Verlag von H. J. Braun." In 1909 the Raduga Publishing Company was organized. Among the directors and shareholders were H. J. Braun, A. J. Kroeker (*q.v.*), and J. S. Prochanov, the leader of the Evangelical Christians. The company purchased the bookstore of Jakob Löttkemann of Halbstadt and had an interest in the bookstore of David P. Isaak of Schönwiese. Later a subsidiary was established in St. Petersburg.

Among the most important publications were the semiweekly *Friedensstimme* (*q.v.*), a devotional calendar, *Abreisskalender,* in German and in Russian (highest circulation 45,000), *Liederperlen,* a monthly periodical containing songs (first published in 1889), P. M. Friesen, *Die Alt-Evangelische Mennonitische Brüderschaft in Russland (1789-1910) im Rahmen der mennonitischen Gesamtgeschichte* (1911) (*q.v.*), B. H. Unruh, *Leitfaden für den Religionsunterricht,* (1913), and *Choralbuch zum Gebrauch für Kirche, Schule und Haus* . . . of the General Conference of Russia (1914).

A. J. Kroeker was the manager of Raduga and the editor of the *Friedensstimme* and the *Christlicher Familienkalender* (*q.v.*). Jacob Kroeker (*q.v.*) also had an active part in the publishing enterprise particularly as writer and editor. In 1910 he went to Germany. In addition to the books and periodicals mentioned, Raduga published, printed, and distributed many tracts and much devotional literature in the Russian and German languages which made a substantial contribution to the spread of the evangelical movement in Russia. After the Revolution H. J. Braun went to Germany and A. J. Kroeker to the United States.　　　　　　　　B.H.U., C.K.

"Abraham J. Kroeker—Writer and Publisher," *Menn. Life* VII (October 1952) 165; Friesen, *Brüderschaft,* p. 669 ff.; A. Kroeker Jr., "Abraham J. Kroeker" (manuscript); *ML* III, 425.

Raegh-besem, *seer bequaem om sommige Mennonitische Schuren te reynigen van de onnutte spinnewebben, sotte grollen en ijdelheden eeniger Geest-drijveren* (Dustmop to Clean Some Mennonite Barns of Noxious Cobwebs, Dull Notions and Vain Ideas of some Rattle-brained [i.e., spiritualistic] Fanatics) (Amsterdam, 1625) is a book written by Nittert Obbesz (*q.v.*). It was published without the knowledge of Obbesz by Jan Theunisz (*q.v.*), one of his followers, under the pseudonym of Nicodemus Letterknecht van Wt-gheest, appearing during a conflict in the Mennonite Waterlander congregation of Amsterdam, Holland, in which Obbesz was a preacher, when Obbesz accused his co-preachers Reynier Wybrands (Wybma), Cornelis Claesz (Anslo), and Pieter Andriesz (Hesseling) of neglecting the Scriptures (*verminderingh vant beschreven Woordt Godts*) in favor of the inward working of the Holy Spirit. Not only the preachers

of the Amsterdam congregation but particularly Hans de Ries (*q.v.*), the leader of the Waterlander group, was attacked in the book because of his spiritualism. About this conflict and its issue see Nittert Obbes(z).　　　　　　　　　　vDZ.

W. J. van Douwen, *Socinianen en Doopsgezinden* (Leiden, 1898) 146-63; W. J. Kühler, *Het Socinianisme in Nederland* (Leiden, 1912) 115-30.

Raek, Juriaen, an Anabaptist martyr: see **Räck, Jörg.**

Raemburg, Jan Ariens van, of Rotterdam, Holland, was appointed preacher of the Flemish Mennonite congregation in his home town about 1650, but by 1655 van Raemburg and three of his co-preachers and many members left this congregation to join the Waterlanders. The reason for this act was that the Flemish congregation was at this time growing more and more conservative; e.g., it did not tolerate the free-speaking meetings of the Collegiants (*q.v.*). In the Rotterdam Waterlander congregation van Raemburg was an elder 1655-March 1677; he died at Schiedam in 1678 at 55 years. He was a well-to-do merchant, who is said to have been a good Christian, humble, pious, and always a good example by his efforts to maintain peace.　　vDZ.

DB 1909, 158, 160; K. Vos, *Geschiedenis der Doopsgezinde Gemeente te Rotterdam* (reprint Rotterdam, 1907) 17, 42, 43.

Raermakers, the wife of Severin, and also her son and daughter were executed in March 1536 at Limburg, Belgium, because of their Anabaptist convictions.　　　　　　　　　　　　　　vDZ.

L. E. Halkin and F. Lemaire, "Un procès d'Anabaptistes a Limbourg en 1536," in *Bulletin de la Comm. Royale d'Histoire* CXXI (1956, repr.).

Ra(e)rop: see **Ransdorp.**

Rahusen, a Mennonite family, which, according to a family tradition based on a record in an old family Bible at Leer, but as yet unproved, came from Switzerland. The first Rahusen on record is (1) Gabriel Otto Rahusen at Hamburg, Germany, who in 1695 married Anna Roosen, of Altona. His grandson was (2) Reinhard Rahusen (*q.v.,* 1735-93), a Mennonite preacher. Another grandson, (3) Herman Rahusen, b. 1738 at Hamburg, moved to Leer in East Friesland, where he died in 1799. He was a grocer and tobacconer, married to Margaretha Vissering of Leer, and after her death, her sister Elske Vissering. He had a large posterity, mostly living at Leer, later also at Emden, Norden, and Amsterdam. Most of the family in Emden and Norden left the Mennonite Church to join the Lutherans. (4) Herman Rahusen, a son of (3) Herman, b. 1766 at Leer, moved to Amsterdam, where he died in 1839, as did his half brother (5) David Jacobus Rahusen, b. 1786 at Leer, d. 1830. In Amsterdam they founded a trading company, which was continued by their descendants, who, however, gradually turned to banking. By marriage the Amsterdam branch became related to prominent Mennonite families like de Clerq, Huidekoper, van Eeghen, and van Lennep. The Amsterdam Rahusens have been loyal Mennonites, and from 1796 to 1947 eleven of them served as deacons, some serving three or four periods. (6) Herman Jan Rahusen (1817-75), married to Jacoba van Eeghen, a merchant at Amsterdam; (7) David Rahusen (1823-83), married to Elisabeth J. van Lennep, a banker; (8) Pieter Rahusen (1827-92), married to H. J. Hooglandt, a vintner; and (9) Eduard Nicolaas Rahusen (b. 1830-19?), unmarried, a lawyer, were sons of (5) David Jacobus Rahusen. (9) Eduard Nicolaas Rahusen was a delegate of the Dutch government to the Peace Conference at The Hague in 1901; in 1898, when the government introduced a law on compulsory military service which was to abolish the system of substitutes, which had made it possible for Mennonites (and others) to avoid military service, Rahusen, then a member of the First Chamber, as a Mennonite declared that he had no objections to compulsory service and that the Dutch Mennonites had abandoned the old doctrine of nonresistance; this view was opposed by Enno ten Cate Fennema (q.v.), a Mennonite who was also a member of the First Chamber. (10) David Rahusen (1858-1932), of Amsterdam, married to Jkvr. A. L. Hooft, a son of (8) Pieter Rahusen, was a managing director of the Dutch State Bank; he was also a deacon of the Amsterdam congregation and a trustee of the A.D.S. (Dutch General Mennonite Conference) from 1899 to 1929, serving as its chairman 1902-3 and its treasurer 1915-29. His son (11) Gerrit Hendrik Rahusen, b. 1905 at Amsterdam, also engaged in banking, was a deacon of the Amsterdam Mennonite congregation 1935-42 and treasurer of the A.D.S. 1941- . Another branch of the Rahusens has been prominent in the Mennonite congregation in Gronau (q.v.), Germany, where Reinhard Rahusen (d. 1952) was an elder. vDZ.

Ned. Patriciaat V (1914) 326-30; G. ten Cate, Geslachtslijst der familie Vissering (1903); DB 1898, 128-30; Zondagsbode XLIV (1931-32) No. 25.

Rahusen, Reinhard, b. Aug. 23, 1735, at Hamburg, Germany, d. March 8, 1793, the son of Hermann Rahusen and Sara Janssen. He was educated at the University of Leiden. He married twice. His first wife was Catharina van Calcar, of Groningen, and his second wife Catharina van Hoorn, of Leer. His son died in 1770; only one daughter survived him. He served as pastor of the Mennonite congregations of Enkhuizen 1760-63, Leer 1763-85, and Hamburg 1785-93, with unusual success, both as preacher and as pastor. He introduced German preaching in the Hamburg Mennonite Church. Rahusen was a prolific writer in both Dutch and German, publishing a large number of writings, especially sermons and smaller catechetical and devotional works. Some of the titles follow:

Die lieblichstärkenden Erquickungen der guten Streiter Jesu Christi (Hamburg, 1754); *Erweckliche und erbauliche Anwendungen einiger Sprüche heiliger Schrift* (Hamburg, 1757); *De zalige Werkzaamheid van Jesus met de Ziel* (Leiden, 1757); *De uitmuntende Heilbelofte aan de geestelyke Overwinnaars toegezegt, een gezang uit het hoogduitsche vertaald* (Enkhuyzen, 1761); *Messias herders last het volk des Heeren te weiden . . . en Davids onwankelbaar . . . volyverig aankleeven aan zynen*

Verbonds God, of Afscheids Reden te Enchuisen en Intreerede te Leer (Groningen, 1765); *Het Gode betamentlyke Stilzwygen in harddrukkende Beproevingsweegen* (Groningen, 1766); *Het gelukkige lot der geestelyke Overwinnaars door den Dood* (Groningen, 1766); *Verhandeling over het borgtogtelyke gelove onzes Zaligmakers* (Groningen, 1768); *Afgeperste Verdediginge van de Eere en Leere der Mennoniten te Leer in Oostfriesland* (Groningen, 1768); *Catechetischer Entwurf der christlichen Lehre* (Hamburg, 1778); *Catechetischer Unterricht über alle hohen Feste* (Hamburg, 1778); *Tweetal van Leerredenen* (Groningen, 1782); *Sammlung einiger Predigten und Reden bey feyerlichen Gelegenheiten, nebst Beygefügten Ceremoniel* (Bremen, 1784); *Broes der nachdenkende Christ,* translated from the Dutch (Bremen, 1784); *De geloofsvolle en blyde Roem eenes in den Heere stervenden Leeraars,* a funeral sermon for Pastor Arisz of Norden (Aurich, 1785); *Kurze Abhandlung über das wahre Christenthum* (Minden, 1786), also in Swedish (Gothenburg, 1787); *Katechetische Verhandeling der 3 eerste Versen van het Kerkgezang: O Zion, loof den Heer der Heeren* (Altona, 1786); *Empfindungen des Herzens bey dem tödtlichen Hintritt des Hrn. S. Deknatel's* (Altona, 1787); *Tiental van Leereden en over de wyze en dwaaze Maagden* (Altona, 1787); *Etwas von dem Leben der seeligen Frau Wittwe E. van Eden* (Altona, 1788); *Gedachtenisreden over wylen den Heer B. Roosen* (Altona, 1788); *Zweite Sammlung einiger Predigten bey feyerlichen Gelegenheiten, nebst einer kurzen Beschreibung des Ursprungs und der jetzigen Beschaffenheit der Mennoniten* (Bremen, 1788); *Kurze Erläuterung des wichtigen Passions-Liedes: Brich durch, mein angefochtnes Herz* (Altona, 1789); *Handboeck over den H. Doop en het H. Avondmaal . . . ten Dienst der aankomende Jeugd . . .* (Altona, 1790); *De beste en vertigste Troostgronden waardoor wy ons den anderzins hoogstmarte lyk en dood onzer naebestaende Bloedsverwanten verzagten en verligten kunnen* (Altona, 1790); *Denkmal der Hochschätzung und Freundschaft der im Herrn entschlafenen Frau Witwe Alida van der Smissen, geb. Veen, errichtet* (Altona, 1790); *Väterliche Empfindungen bey dem frühzeitigen Tode seines einzigsten Sohnes, H. G. Rahusen* (Altona, 1790); *Freundschaftliches Trostschreiben an Hrn. J. G. van der Smissen bey dem schmerzlichen Tode seiner Ehegattin, Helena van der Smissen* (1790); *Etwas über den Zustand Europens* (Altona, 1793); *Nachrichten vom gegenwärtigen Zustande der Mennoniten* (in Christian Wilhelm Franz Walch, Neueste Religionsgeschichte XIX, Lemgo, 1782, 303-18); Essays in *Aussätze aus dem Briefwechsel der Deutschen Gesellschaft thätiger Beförderer reiner Lehre und wahrer Gottseligkeit* I-III (Basel, 1783-85).

NEFF.

Menn. Bl., 1854, 36 f.; Johann A. Bolten, Historische Kirchen-Nachrichten von der Stadt Altona und deren verschiedenen Religions-Partheyen I (Altona, 1790) 305-8; Blaupot t. C., Groningen, Overijssel en Oost-Friesland 228; Berend Kordes, Lexikon der jetzt lebenden Schleswig-Holsteinischen und Eutinischen Schriftsteller (Schleswig, 1797) 490; J. G. Meusel, Lexikon der vom Jahr 1750 bis 1800 verstorbenen teutschen Schriftsteller II (Leipzig, 1811) 13-15; B. C. Roosen, Geschichte der

Mennoniten-Gemeinde zu Hamburg und Altona II
(Hamburg, 1887) 71-77; J. A. Starck, *Geschichte der
Taufe und Taufgesinnten* (Leipzig, 1789) 391; *ML* III,
425 f.

Raid (Raide, Raidt, Reide, Rhaide), **Balthasar,** of
Fulda, pastor of Hersfeld (*q.v.*), Germany, 1525-
65, "the first really Protestant preacher of the city
church" (Freudenstein, 35). He was frequently
called to debate with the Anabaptists of Hesse; by
1544 he claimed to have dealt with three hundred
of them, among whom he had many a success. In
1533 he wrote against Georg Witzel (*q.v.*): *Wid-
der das lester vnd lügen büchlin Agricole Phagj,
genant Georg Witzel antwort* (Wittenberg). In
1539 followed *Concordia vnnd vergleichung der
Papisten, Widderteuffer, Rotten, Witzelianer vn
Lutheraner jnn vnnd mit der heiligen catholischen
Christlichen kirchen, an die zween Ept zu Fulda
vnd Herssfelt* (Erfurt), both with a foreword by
Luther. Both are in the Library of the University
of Göttingen.   E.C.

TA Hessen, Nos. 5, 5a, 17, 24, 27, 28, 54, 115, 121,
124; Erich Freudenstein, *Bilder aus der Kirchengeschichte Hersfelds* (Hersfeld, 1938); Wappler, *Thüringen,* 53, 74, 102, 180, 294-302, 329, Nos. 30, 40b; *ML*
III, 426.

Raiffer, Hans, a Hutterite martyr, missioner, and
hymn writer, d. 1558 at Aachen: see **Schmidt, Hans.**

Rainham Mennonite Church (MC), once known as
"Stoney Creek" and also as "Lake Shore," a member of the Ontario Conference and located in Rainham Twp., Haldimand Co., Ont., was founded by
Jacob Hoover (d. 1810), of York County, Pa., who
settled here in 1790 with his family of five sons and
three daughters. Among the early names were
Strickler, Shank (a preacher here in 1816), Swartz,
Byers, and Miller. Trouble apparently arose early
in its history because of the westward movement
in Ontario, for the Wayland List of Ministers and
Deacons of the Mennonite Church in Canada (1853)
names those of Cayuga Township but omits the
neighboring Rainham group entirely. The Mennonite ministers of the Rainham congregation were
probably out of fellowship with the Conference
(MC) at that time. The center of the schism was
at the Twenty (Vineland), the home of the leader,
Daniel Hoch, only 50 miles from Rainham. The
profusion of cemeteries is also indicative of division.
There are two small burial grounds south of Selkirk;
there are also plots in Walpole to the west, Fisher-
ville to the north, Sweet's Corners to the east, and
the principal one at Hoover's Point on the lake.
There was also a settlement of Mennonites from the
Strickler (*q.v.*) church of Clarence, N.Y., who came
to Selkirk after the middle of the 19th century. In
1956 the membership of the Rainham congregation
was 39, with A. Lewis Fretz as minister and bishop,
who also serves the South Cayuga congregation.
(See also **Strickler** Mennonite Church and **Miller**
Mennonite Church.)

When the first meetinghouse was built is not
known, possibly in 1836, when the first deed was
granted for church purposes, although the oldest
marker in the cemetery is for a death occurring in
1812. The present meetinghouse, located 2½ miles
east of Selkirk and one mile north of the Lake Erie

shore, was erected about 1870. The only other Mennonite congregation near by is South Cayuga, with
a meetinghouse 9 miles east. The two congregations
have been served by one pastor since 1887. J.C.F.

Rainham Old Order Mennonite Church, located in
Haldimand County, Ont., was formed in 1889 as a
schism from the Rainham Mennonite (*q.v.*) Church
(MC) under the influence of Christian Gayman,
bishop of the adjoining South Cayuga Old Order
Mennonite Church, who left the Ontario Mennonite
Conference in 1889. The Rainham Mennonite minister, Leonhard Hoover (1842-90), identified himself with the Old Order group in 1889, as did the
deacon Andrew Sherk (1827-1908). For lack of
aggressive work many of the young people drifted
into other churches or made no profession. The
small congregation was long served by John Sherk,
preacher at South Cayuga, and later by ministers
of Waterloo and York counties. The membership
in 1957 was only three, without a minister.
                                                 J.C.F.

Rainy River Mennonite Church (MC), International
Falls, Minn., had 26 members in 1957. Lester Mann
was its minister. The North Central Conference
district mission board established it as a mission in
1950.   M.G.

Rakov (Rackau), a town in Poland, near Cracow,
was in the early 17th century the center of Socinianism (*q.v.*), a unitarian movement. Here the annual
synod of the Socinians was held 1603-37. In Rakov
they had their seminary, where Lutherans, Reformed, Mennonites, and even some Catholics attended the lectures of their learned professors. In
Rakov too was the printing and publishing house
of these "Polish Brethren," which printed many
theological books, including their catechism, drawn
up by Fausto Sozzini (Faustus Socinus). The first
edition in the Polish language appeared in 1605,
followed by a German edition in 1608 and a Latin
edition in 1609 (the Latin edition was reprinted at
Amsterdam, Holland, in 1665, 1680, and 1684). A
Dutch edition was published at Amsterdam in 1659.

After some students of the seminary had wantonly damaged a Catholic crucifix, the Polish diet on
May 1, 1638, resolved to put an end to "this blasphemous anti-Trinitarian heresy." The printing shop
at Rakov was closed, the school was destroyed, and
the church was confiscated and given to the Catholics. This was the end of Socinian activity in Rakov
and soon in all of Poland; it continued for some
time in the Netherlands.   vDZ.

W. J. Kühler, *Het Socinianisme in Nederland* (Leiden, 1912) 9, 135 f., 139 f.; E. M. Wilbur, *A History of
Unitarianism: Socinianism and Its Antecedents* (Cambridge, 1946).

Rakowitz (Räkowitz, Rakvic), a Bruderhof of the
Hutterian Brethren, today a village with 1600 Slavic
inhabitants, north of Eisgrub in Moravia, where the
Anabaptists purchased several houses and settled in
1540. Johann von Lipa sold and also leased some
lands to them. The chronicles relate that a brother
was killed here on July 16, 1605.   HEGE.

Beck, *Geschichts-Bücher,* 149, 344 f.; Wolkan, *Geschicht-Buch,* 157, 175, 240, 487; Zieglschmid, *Chronik,*
223, 316, 636; *ML* III, 427.

Rameaux, Jean (Jan) **des,** was a preacher of the Flemish Mennonite congregation of "den Blok" at Haarlem, Holland, about 1650. With his colleague Koenraad van Vollenhoven (*q.v.*) he took the side of the more progressive Galenus Abrahamsz (*q.v.*) of Amsterdam, against Isaac Snep (*q.v.*) and other conservative leaders of the Haarlem Flemish congregation. This led to serious discord in 1665 and to a schism in this congregation in 1671. (*DB* 1863, 137 f.) vpZ.

Ramer Mennonite Church, a local designation for the progressive wing of the Wisler Mennonite Church in Elkhart (and St. Joseph) County, Indiana. The origin of the group was as follows: Over a period of time a degree of tension and loss of mutual confidence arose in the Wisler Mennonite Conference of Ohio and Indiana. The respective leaders were Henry Hursh (1839-1916), bishop of the County Line and Chestnut Ridge congregation in Wayne County, Ohio (progressive), and John W. Martin (1852-1940), bishop of the Yellow Creek and Blosser and County Line congregation, in Elkhart County (conservative). The tension came to head, ostensibly over the use of the telephone, at the spring conference of 1907 which met in the County Line meetinghouse, St. Joseph County, Ind. John Weaver, a preacher who had played a major role in the division of 1872 (Wisler-Funk), tried earnestly to prevent a schism in the Wisler Conference in 1907, but in vain. Bishop Martin withdrew from the conference, taking along all of his fellow ministers (Christian Z. Weaver, Henry Schrock, and Martin Ramer, besides the deacons Elias Z. Martin and Isaac Martin) into his new Old Order Mennonite Conference. The majority of the lay members of Elkhart County, however, refused to follow the ministers; they stood rather with the aged preacher John Weaver, a feeble old man who died on Sept. 2, 1907. About six months after the division Martin Ramer (1858-1928), a preacher who had been ordained about 1886, reconsidered his stand and transferred to the progressive side in Indiana. Meanwhile the progressives had chosen Levi Ressler (brother of J. A. Ressler, *q.v.*) as deacon, and his son Christian L. Ressler as preacher. In 1911 Ramer was chosen bishop of the progressive group. In 1919 his son William Ramer was ordained as preacher, and in 1929 as bishop. Because the ministerial leadership has been in the hands of the two Ramers, father and son, since 1907, the group has come to be known locally as the Ramer Mennonites. They themselves prefer the name Wisler Mennonites, while the Martin group call themselves the Old Order Mennonites. The chief differences relate to the adoption of new cultural items such as the automobile. Neither group has a Sunday school. The Ramer services are held largely in English, while the Martin services are largely in German. Both groups use the two jointly owned meetinghouses, Yellow Creek Frame and Blosser's, alternating Sundays. The Ramer group numbers 200 members, the other group 102. J.C.W.

Ramond (Raemund, Raymond, Rémon, Raemond), **Florimond** (c1540-1601), a lawyer of Bordeaux, France, concerning whom it was said, "He judged without conscience, wrote books without knowledge, and built without money." His principal work was *Histoire de naissance, progres, et décadence de l'hérésie de ce siècle,* which was published after his death (Paris, 1605) and was translated into Latin, German, and Dutch, appearing in many editions. It refutes Protestantism with temporary effectiveness, and concerning the Mennonites it says (following Stanislaus Hosius, *q.v.*): At the same time the Mennonites arose, under the banner of Menno Simons, a crippled Frisian who had been a Lutheran preacher in Wismar. These miserable people deny that Christ, the Son of God, was born from the body of Mary and took His body from hers; they think instead that He brought it from heaven, and like Luther they say that He is to judge the angels and the princes of this world. It is Ramond who stated that Obbe Philipsz (*q.v.*) returned to the Catholic Church after his apostasy, a misconception accepted by some Mennonite historians, e.g., Kornelius van Huyzen (*q.v.*) and Herman Schijn (*q.v.*). E.C., vpZ.

Karel Vos, *Menno Simons* (Leiden, 1914) 320; Hans Joachim Schoeps, *Von himmlischen Fleisch Christi* (Tübingen, 1951) 47; *BRN* VII, 95; *DB* 1884, 17 note 1; *ML* III, 467.

Ramos Mejía, Argentina, located about 19 miles from the center of the Argentine capital, belongs to the Greater Buenos Aires, that is, the part of this great metropolis that lies outside the federal district. Pastor Albano Luayza with his family moved to this city in 1942 to open a Mennonite (MC) mission. The work was actually started on May 3, 1942. The first believers were baptized in August and the first communion service with 13 participating was celebrated in September of the same year. In December 1954 there was a membership of 52 in a well-organized church with Sunday school, young people's and women's organizations. The Mennonite Board of Missions contributed land on which the congregation built a church, dedicated in 1955. In December 1954 Pastor Agustin F. Darino became the leader of the congregation, Luayza having reached the age of retirement. N.L.

Rampersdorf, a Hutterite Bruderhof in Moravia (*q.v.*), located between Kostel (Gostal) and Lundenburg. As early as 1545 the Brethren here and at Pulgram and Schäckowitz were plundered by Anderle von Villach, who wanted to take back into his own possession the estate which his brother Stoffel von Villach had granted the Hutterian Brethren when he united with them. In 1576 Johann von Zierotin confiscated four horses; "he needed them down in Hungary for use in war or things in which we do not help; therefore he took them by force; he, to be sure, repaid a part, but spoiled enough." In the Hungarian war a brother was killed and three persons taken away on June 28, 1605. At the beginning of the Thirty Years' War, Sept. 19-20, 1619, Rampersdorf was plundered and burned, and on Oct. 8, 1621, the miller's wife was drowned. E.C.

Beck, *Geschichts-Bücher,* 163, 268, 356, 374, 402; Wolkan, *Geschicht-Buch,* 204, 369, 371, 486, 496, 539, 561; Zieglschmid, *Chronik,* 263, 478, 481, 634, 649, 711, 742; *ML* III, 427.

Ramseier (Ramseyer, Ramsayer), a Mennonite family name originating from Eggiwil, Signau, and Trub in the Emmental (*q.v.*), canton of Bern, Switzerland. The name was given to persons who came from a village named Ramsey (*Ram,* raven; *ei,* flat meadow near a stream).

The first mention of an Anabaptist member of the family occurred in a list of 1710, where Hans Ramseier was one of 57 persons listed for deportation to America. However, he escaped en route. During the early 18th century the Ramseyers with other Anabaptist families from the Emmental fled to the Jura (*q.v.*). Some who had a brief time before become followers of Jakob Ammann (*q.v.*) settled in the Prussian owned province of Neuchâtel (*q.v.*). Peter Ramseier (*q.v.*; b. 1706) lived on the Münsterberg in the Jura. He was chosen as minister in 1730 and elder in 1732. He took a prominent part in bringing accord among the Palatinate brethren in 1760-84, making at least four trips to them for this purpose.

From the Jura, members of the family moved to western France. From Neuchâtel and France most of the Ramseier families migrated to America during the 19th century settling especially in Stark and Wayne counties, Ohio, central Illinois, Ontario, and the "thumb" of Michigan. The ancestor of most of the families living in Ohio was John Ramseier (1776-1853). His son Peter settled in Stark County, Ohio.

Prominent members of the family include Joseph E. Ramseyer (*q.v.;* 1869-1944), a founder of the Missionary Church Association, Lloyd L. Ramseyer (1899-   ), president of Bluffton College, 1938- , and Edna Ramseyer, a professor at Bluffton College.   D.L.G.

Ramseyer, C. Auguste, a Swiss Baptist, author of the *Histoire des Baptistes* (Neuchâtel, 1897), which P. M. Friesen used repeatedly in his *Geschichte der Alt-Evangelischen Mennoniten-Brüderschaft in Russland* (Halbstadt, 1911), (*ML* III, 427.) NEFF.

Ramseyer, Joseph Eicher (1869-1944), one of the chief founders and for forty-four consecutive years president and spiritual father of the Missionary Church Association (*q.v.*), was born Feb. 7, 1869, near New Hamburg, Waterloo Co., Ont., the son of Michael and Mary Ramseyer, members of the Amish Mennonite Church. His father died when the boy was only four years old, and he was reared in his grandfather's home near New Hamburg. The family moved to Zurich, Hay Co., Ont., and from there in 1890 to Elkton, Mich., in the Huron Peninsula. While living at Zurich Joseph had a conversion experience in 1885, influenced in part by reading the biography of George Müller of Bristol. Soon after his arrival in the Elkton community he felt the call to preach and began preaching in his home community, though he was not yet ordained. He was ordained in March 1892 by Bishop Joseph Rediger of Gridley, Ill., and Joseph Egly of Berne, Ind., both leaders in the Defenseless Mennonite Church. He served as pastor of the Elkton church (meetinghouse erected in 1894) until his evangelistic work became too heavy. He had been baptized (by pouring) several years before as a member of the Defense-

less Mennonite Church by Bishop Henry Egly (*q.v.*), founder of that church.

Ramseyer began his very effective evangelistic work in January 1893 in the Defenseless Mennonite Church at Archbold, Ohio. On Aug. 11, 1896, he had himself baptized by immersion while attending a Christian and Missionary Alliance conference at Cleveland, Ohio. On Dec. 8, 1896, he was expelled from his church by action of its General Conference, meeting near Berne, Ind. The grounds of the excommunication were his teaching of such doctrines as the second work of grace (baptism by the Holy Spirit subsequent to the new birth), premillennialism, and baptism by immersion. The struggle in the Defenseless church over these matters had lasted for 5 years (1891-96).

In August 1898 the Missionary Church Association was organized at Berne. Elements from the Defenseless Church and the Christian and Missionary Alliance united to form the new denomination (see **Missionary Church Association** for the full account of the origin and subsequent history of this group). Ramseyer was the leading spirit in the group throughout the remainder of his life, almost 50 years. It is clear that Alliance influence was a strong factor in Ramseyer's life and theology as well as in the M.C.A.

Ramseyer became the first superintendent of the Bethany Bible Training School founded on Nov. 1, 1895, at Bluffton, Ohio, which continued until 1901, serving in that office 1895-97. However, the school of the Missionary Church Association was to be the Fort Wayne Bible Institute (now called the Fort Wayne Bible College) founded in January 1904, largely due to the efforts of Ramseyer, who served as president from 1923 until his death.

Ramseyer was married Oct. 27, 1896, to Katherine Zeller of Bluffton, Ohio, who died in 1899. His second wife was Mary Garth of Union City, Tenn., whom he married May 1, 1902. He had no children. He died in Fort Wayne on Jan. 25, 1944, and was buried in Lindenwood Cemetery there.

Ramseyer was a man of unusual ability as a preacher and evangelist and of undoubted spiritual power, universally beloved and respected. At his death his denomination had grown to 6,500 members, and his school to an enrollment of 300 students. "He was an honorary vice-president of the Christian and Missionary Alliance for many years and carried on a wide and influential ministry in other denominations" (Lugibihl and Gerig, 53).
                                              H.S.B.

M. G. Ramseyer, *Joseph E. Ramseyer—Yet Speaking* (Fort Wayne, 1945); W. H. Lugibihl and J. F. Gerig, *The Missionary Church Association, Historical Account of its Origin and Development* (Berne, 1950).

Ramseyer (Ramseier), **Peter** (b. 1706), of the Münsterberg in the Bernese Jura (*q.v.*), Switzerland, was ordained as a minister in 1730 and as an elder in 1732. Ramseyer was one of the most important leaders of the Mennonites of the Jura of that time. One of the responsible services of these Jura preachers was the care of the orphaned Emmental Mennonites following the last severe persecutions and emigrations. Traveling was in those days no easy matter. The official records found in the state archives at Bern report that meetings in the neighborhood of Thun were held by brethren from the Jura in 1767. On the other hand, young couples of the Emmental traveled to the Jura to be married by Ramseyer.

In the spring of 1762 Peter Ramseyer went to the Palatinate (*q.v.*), Germany, with two other preachers and brought back a certificate signed by 25 elders and preachers, showing that these three men "paternally and sincerely comforted the congregations in the Palatinate and pointed them to true constancy in the faith." In 1766 the Jura ministers were again called to the Palatinate to try to settle a serious difference that had arisen among the preachers there in consequence of the pietistic preaching of Peter Weber (*q.v.*). The matter was to be discussed at a conference of the Palatine brethren and the Swiss visiting ministers. In September Abraham Zeisset (*q.v.*) wrote the letter of invitation with the following address: "An den bescheidenen Petter Ramseyer zu Minster im bischofsgebit brunatrut [Pruntrut, *q.v.*] 12 stund ober Basel." (To the humble Peter Ramseyer at Münster in the bishopric of Pruntrut—*q.v.*—12 hours above Basel.)

Believing that the matter had come to a peaceful settlement, the Swiss preachers returned to their homes. But only a few months later the dissension had become so general that the Easter communion service of 1767 was omitted throughout the Palatine congregations, the laymen demanding of their preachers that they first make peace among themselves. A further attempt at unification was made by the Jura brethren in 1770, though with the same negative result. More letters were sent from Illfingen near Biel dated May 24, 1779. In 1782 the aged Peter Ramseyer made a final journey to the Palatinate, accompanied by Hans Lehmann (*q.v.*), Bendicht Wahli, Hans Steiner, and David Baumgartner; they met at the Himmelhäuserhof, and this time succeeded in restoring peace. On July 13, 1784, he and the other ministers wrote a letter at Biderichgraben to Johannes Weber on the matter of the Amish division, and on April 24, 1787, he received a letter from a number of brethren in the Palatinate. Nothing more is known about Peter Ramseyer. S.G.

"Geschichtliche Beiträge aus den Mennonitengemeinden," *Gem.-Kal.*, 1928, 118-33; 1929, 139-44; 1930, 91-102; Samuel Geiser, *Die Taufgesinnten-Gemeinden* (Karlsruhe, 1931) 452, 456 f.; *ML* III, 427 f.

Randall, Gilles (*c*1600-50), an English clergyman concerning whose life little is known. He was the son of Edward Randall of Chipping Wycombe, Bucks, and earned his bachelor's degree at Oxford in 1626. In 1643 he was charged with having preached Anabaptism, Familism, and Antinomianism. In the fall of 1644 he was deposed from his office as a clergyman "on account of his Anabaptism." He apparently held confused ideas. HEGE.

Rufus M. Jones, *Spiritual Reformers of the Sixteenth and Seventeenth Centuries* (London, 1914) 253-63; *RGG* IV, Col. 1698; *ML* III, 428.

Randt, Erich Otto (1887-1948), a historian and archivist at Berlin, Germany, was born at Neu-Paleschken, East Prussia, on May 17, 1887, the son of the preacher (*Lehrer*) Richard Randt. He received his elementary instruction at Mausdorf in the Elbing district, and later attended the Gymnasium at Marienburg for eight years and studied geography and history at the universities of Breslau and Königsberg. In 1912 he published his dissertation, *Die Mennoniten in Ostpreussen und Litauen bis zum Jahre 1772*, a thorough piece of research, which gives detailed information on the origin of the Mennonites of East Prussia and their life and achievements in the early period. He became an archivist and died at Berlin on May 6, 1948. (*ML* III, 428.) HEGE, E.C.

Randville Bible Church (E.M.B.), located near Iron Mountain, Mich., in 1957 had 20 members with Max Eisenbraun as pastor. It is a mission church subsidized by the conference, started *c*1944, and for a time had a second place of meeting at Chinning. The church building, formerly a store, has been remodeled. H.S.B.

Ransdorp (often Ra(e)rop), a village near Amsterdam, Holland, formerly the seat of a Flemish Mennonite congregation. About its history very little is known. The martyr Thijs Joriaensz van Rarop, executed at Muiden in 1569, was from here. In 1563-65 Leenaert Bouwens (*q.v.*) is said to have baptized 82 persons at Ransdorp, but this is not correct, since 49 of these 82 were not baptized at Ransdorp, but at Weesp (*q.v.*). From this time until the late 17th century a Flemish church existed at Ransdorp, which throughout the 17th century was without a preacher. At the Flemish conference held at Haarlem in 1649 it was represented by Sievert Arentsz and Hendrik Dirksz. About 1665 it sided with the conservative Zonists (*q.v.*), but it soon dissolved or perhaps merged with the Zonist congregation in Amsterdam. (*Inv. Arch. Amst.* I, No. 412; *DB* 1892, 108.) vDZ.

Ransom Mennonite (MC) settlement, now extinct, in Ness County, Kan., was founded by Shellenberger, Ummel, Schrock, Miller, Troyer, and Stutzman families; the date of the founding is not known. E. M. Shellenberger, a Mennonite minister from Freeport, Ill., lived in the community for a few years, but the congregation was never organized. Services at first were held in a store building and later in a schoolhouse in Ransom. In 1918 fourteen members of the Ransom community were received into the West Liberty (*q.v.*) Mennonite Church. Monthly preaching appointments were held at Ransom until 1925. Preacher S. C. Miller moved to Ness County in 1886, and a year later was ordained bishop, but in the following year moved back to McPherson County. M.G.

Ransom First Mennonite Church (GCM), located in the small town of Ransom, Ness Co., Kan., a member of the Western District Conference was organized in 1886 by the Abraham Ummel, Julius Jaehde, and Jacob Aeby families. They held their regular meetings in a small sod school located three fourths of a mile east of Ransom until 1900, when the church was built in Ransom, replaced in 1956 by a brick church. When Jacob Aeby returned to Missouri, Abraham Ummel (d. 1921) became the elder. Not only Mennonites, but also Lutherans joined the church. The congregation had 115 members in 1957; the pastor was R. L. Siemens.

M.J.

Ranst, Jan van, b. 1634 at Rotterdam, Holland, d. there March 1684, a flax-dealer, married to Neeltgen Conincs, was from 1661 until his death a preacher of the Rotterdam Waterlander congregation. Through his activity, his honesty, and his forethought, he was of importance not only for his Rotterdam home church, but also for the Dutch brotherhood in general. He was the first to draw up a "resolutions book" of the Rotterdam Waterlander congregation, writing down all that seemed to him worth remembering. His notes are an important source of information concerning this Rotterdam congregation. He was very broad-minded, participating in the Collegiant (*q.v.*) movement; and after the failure of an attempt by his church to merge with the Flemish Mennonite congregation in Rotterdam he considered a union with the Remonstrants (*q.v.*) at Rotterdam, which proposal was, however, declined by the Remonstrants.

When the needs of the Swiss Mennonites who had been expelled from Switzerland and emigrated to the Palatinate became known in Holland in 1671, the Rotterdam Waterlander congregation, on the initiative of van Ranst, made a proposal to help them by bringing them all to the Netherlands and settling them there at the expense of the Dutch Mennonites; but this plan was not carried out because the Swiss Brethren wished to stay among their coreligionists in the Palatinate, even hoping to have an opportunity to return to Switzerland, which indeed some of them clandestinely did.

Van Ranst also initiated the founding of the Waterlander or South Holland Conference in 1675. Although this conference was short-lived it was of the highest importance for the future practice of training ministers, for van Ranst in 1675 and again in the following yearly meetings proposed the founding of a seminary. He called attention to the fact of the decay of most of the (Waterlander) congregations, which van Ranst thought was largely caused by the lack of preachers (many pulpits were vacant) and the incompetence of many untrained preachers. The seminary was not realized at this time, mostly because of the unwillingness of the Haarlem congregation; nevertheless one result was that the Amsterdam Lamist congregation in 1680 directed its preacher Galenus Abrahamsz (*q.v.*) to train young men for the ministry.

Besides all this, van Ranst in 1681 traveled to Friesland and Groningen, combining business and church matters, and visited a number of congregations in this area, stimulating them to unite into a conference. This had no direct result, but led to the founding in 1695 of the Mennonite Conference of Friesland.

Cornelis van Ranst and Reyer van Ranst, apparently both sons of Jan van Ranst, were deacons of the Rotterdam congregation, Cornelis from 1689 and Reyer from 1705.   vDZ.

K. Vos, *Geschiedenis van de Doopsgezinde Gemeente te Rotterdam* (reprint 1907) 25, 43; *Inv. Arch. Amst.* I, No. 1060; II, No. 2208; II, 2, No. 378; *DB* 1872, 61, 64, 66; 1918, 49; J. C. van Slee, *De Rijnsburger Collegianten* (Haarlem, 1896) 109, 114.

Raphaël (Raphel) **van de(n) Velde,** an Anabaptist martyr, who after being tortured several times was burned at the stake on the Veerle Square at Gent, Belgium, on July 14, 1576, together with Jeronimus Scheepens. The Dutch martyr books, including van Braght's *Martyrs' Mirror,* contain six letters written in prison by this martyr. All of these letters, four of which were written to his wife, one to his son Raphelken, and one to the Gent congregation, bear witness of his strong faith. The letters are undated except the first (to his wife), which bears the date of May 24, 25, 1576.

In the first letter to his wife he wrote of the terrible tortures he suffered, but gave thanks to God, who strengthened him. With striking words he proclaimed his tender love to his wife and his child. He thanked his wife in very moving words for all the good she had conferred upon him, comforting her with the coming bliss in the Lord, admonishing her to faith and fidelity. To his son he wrote a "Testament" (*q.v.*): "See, my dear son Raphelken, . . . the Lord has so ordered it, that I must be taken from you . . . . My dear son, walk in the way of the Lord, . . . depart from evil, . . . love not the world, neither the things that are therein; . . . my dear son, though you lose me, be not impudent to your mother, but obey her the more . . . . I commend you and your mother to the Lord. . . . Written by me, your father. Adieu, my dear son, whom I love more than any silver or gold or precious stones; but God must be the dearest. . . ."

Verheyden has published some particulars about this martyr from the official records: Raphael van de Velde was a master mason, a citizen of Gent, living on "Abeelestraete." He was apparently a rather young man, since his only son was still a small child. His wife was also a member of the congregation.

Other members of the van de Velde (*q.v.*) family also suffered martyrdom. Karel van de Velde (*q.v.*) was executed at Gent (not at Hondschote as stated in *ME* III, 151) in 1562, Janneken van de Velde (*q.v.*) died as a martyr at Antwerp in 1573, Sebastiaen van de Velde, who was arrested at Gent in 1563 and condemned to the galleys, may also have been a relative.

Since the 17th century there has been a Mennonite van de Velde family at Amsterdam. This family is said to stem from the van de Velde family at Gent. *(Mart. Mir.* D 715, E 1026; Verheyden, *Gent,* 65 f., No. 236.)   vDZ.

Rapp, Georg, the name of two Anabaptists of Pforzheim (*q.v.*), Germany, who were arrested in Vaihingen, examined by Johannes Brenz (*q.v.*) in Stuttgart in 1577, but released, since they were merely passing through the country. One of them had spent five years in Moravia (*q.v.*) in the 1540's. (*ML* III, 428.)   E.C.

Rappenau *(Bad),* a village (1945 pop. 2,688) in northern Baden, Germany, 10 miles southeast of

Sinsheim. In 1766-1862 the neighboring Martinshof (*q.v.*) was the seat of a Mennonite congregation. In 1862 the center was transferred to Rappenau. In 1887 the congregation had 50 members besides 33 children. In 1914 and 1924 there were 48 members. The *Adressbuch* of 1936 lists 19 baptized members: a Hotel family living in Rappenau, Fellmann and Schmutz in Fürfeld, Fellmann and Glück in Wimpfen. Jakob Glück of Wimpfen had been elder since 1919, and Oskar Fellmann, also of Wimpfen, preacher since 1935. The congregation was listed for the last time in the *Gemeinde-Kalender* of 1940; its members joined the Heilbronn (*q.v.*) congregation.   E.C.

Menn. Adressbuch (Karlsruhe, 1936) 160; *Gem.-Kal.*, 1914, 141; 1924, 135; 1935, 133; 1939, 127; Mannhardt, *Jahrbuch* (Danzig, 1888) 32; *ML* III, 429.

Rappites, or **Harmonists**, an American Christian communistic society founded in 1804 by Johann George Rapp (1757-1847), a peasant linen weaver of Württemberg, Germany, who separated from the Lutheran Church of that region and gradually built up, under persecution, a following of some 300 families. He emphasized a simple Biblicism, including particular emphasis on the imminent Second Coming of Christ, and criticized vigorously the social order of the time which he held to be in strong contrast to the New Testament way of life.

In 1803 Rapp emigrated to America to find a home for his group where they might be free of persecution. He bought 5,000 acres of land in the Conoquenessing Valley north of Pittsburgh, Pa., and in 1804 settled there with 600 of his followers who had emigrated from Germany. In a colony called Harmony, located within the limits of the town of Ambridge, they soon adopted communism as their economic order. In 1807 they decided to adopt celibacy. They also rejected infant baptism.

In 1814 the group sold Harmony and relocated on a large tract south of Evansville, Ind., on the Wabash River, founding the New Harmony Colony. This they sold in 1824 to Robert Owen. The group then relocated a second time near the first Harmony location, naming their new colony Economy. Economy was highly successful. Rapp died in 1847. After this the colony declined but did not dissolve until 1892, at the death of the leader Jacob Heinrici, who had emigrated from Grosskarlbach in the Palatinate and had become a leader in 1868.

It is of considerable interest to note that in 1884-85 the Rappists negotiated an agreement with the Hutterites in South Dakota whereby the entire group was to leave South Dakota and take over a large tract of land owned by the Economy colony, located near Tidioute, Pa. At that time there were about 380 souls in the Hutterite group. The Hutterites accepted the offer but were unable to carry it through because of difficulty in selling their Dakota land. The Tripp Bruderhof, however, sold its land and arrived at Tidioute on May 1, 1884, with 19 families, 3 families having moved in 1883. The land, located 4 miles south of the city of Tidioute in Warren County, was too difficult to farm. Hence in two years the entire group returned to South Dakota, arriving there on July 2, 1886.

The Rappists had been very generous in lending money to the Hutterites in South Dakota at different times, and there were long-continued warm and friendly relations between the two groups. The first loan was granted for the building of a mill, requested on May 31, 1875, by the Bon Homme Colony. The first visit of a Rappist to Bon Homme was in September 1875, when Jonathan Lenz came. A considerable correspondence between the two groups has been preserved, and was to be published by Professor Karl J. Arndt (according to Zieglschmid).   H.S.B.

J. A. Bole, *The Harmony Society: A Chapter in German-American Culture* (Philadelphia, 1904, reprint from *German-American Annals* XXI); Karl J. Arndt, "The Harmonists and the Hutterians," *American German Review* X (1944) 24-27; Zieglschmid, *Klein-Geschichtsbuch*, 461; Mark Holloway, *Heavens on Earth, Utopian Communities in America 1680-1888* (New York, 1951).

Rasquert, a village in the Dutch province of Groningen, formerly the seat of a Mennonite congregation belonging to the Groningen Old Flemish branch. This congregation probably existed as early as 1550. The following ministers are named: Jacob Derks (d. 1620) from *c*1560, Luy (Luirt) Cornelisz *c*1685, Jacob Lippes (d. 1735), Waalke Eises from 1729, Tjaard Michiels (d. before 1754), Tonjes Klassen (Teunis Clasen) 1736-d.65, Tamme Pieters (Huizinga) 1741-70, Luitje Olferts Wiersema 1757-91, and Hendrik Bakker 1792-95. Tjaard Michiels and Teunis Clasen were at the same time elders of the Groningen Old Flemish Conference. All of these preachers except the last were chosen from the congregation of Rasquert; they were farmers, and had no training for the ministry. After 1795 the pulpit remained vacant.

The Rasquert congregation was small: in 1710 there were about 100 baptized members, 97 in 1733, 59 in 1754, 22 in 1809. It built a plain meetinghouse in 1708, which is reported to have been in a state of ruin in 1815. The members, most of whom were farmers, lived around the village of Rasquert or near-by Baflo; hence the congregation is sometimes called Baflo. In 1686 and again in 1717, when the ocean dikes burst and the country was flooded, the congregation suffered great damage and lost some of its members. In 1816 the Rasquert congregation merged with Den Hoorn and Obergum-Winsum, together forming the new congregation of Mensingeweer (*q.v.*).

Karel Vos surmised that after Menno Simons left the Catholic Church in January 1536, he lived for a time at Rasquert, enjoying the hospitality of Christoffer van Ewsum, a rural nobleman, who possessed a country house at Rasquert.   vDZ.

Blaupot t. C., *Groningen* I, 127, 131, 140, 142, 202; II, 54, 224, 225; *DJ* 1840 (table facing 52); *DB* 1879, 5; *Naamlijst* 1829, 65; *Groningsche Volksalmanak* 1918, 149-64; 1919, 139-46.

Ratheim, Gisbert von (Gys van Rothem) (*c*1500-36 or after), one of the "Wassenberg preachers," was identical with Gisbert von Breberen, but not with Gillis von Aachen (*q.v.*). The difference in their Christian names (Gisbert and Gillis, which is the equivalent of Aegidius) makes it impossible to consider them a single person. His confessions give some facts about his life, his doctrinal views, and the occasion of his journey to Münster. (Two of his confessions are found in Redlich; Cornelius published a third one, which conflicts with some of the statements of the first two.)

Gisbert was born about 1500 in or near Breberen, the son of Gys in Broich and Lyssken van den Dyck. He was a chaplain in Hoengen in the Millen district in Jülich. The records of the church inspection of 1533 show that he was still drawing some income from this position, though he was no longer there. It says of him, "Herr Gys, he also became Luther's." In February 1531 he married Gertrud Valkenbergh, a nun who had fled from the convent of Nieuwenhof in Maastricht on account of pregnancy. His marriage was performed in Wassenberg (*q.v.*) in the home of Johann Klopreis (*q.v.*) either by Klopreis, or by Heinrich von Tongern (see **Slachtscaep**) in Klopreis's presence. His wife was the sister of the Mayor Valkenbergh of Nieuwstad near Sittard, who later vainly attempted to assist Jan Revens, a sexton of Hoengen imprisoned in Maastricht, to freedom.

Under the influence of the Wassenberg preachers, of whom Dionysius Vinne (*q.v.*) and Heinrich von Tongern had been preaching in Hoengen, especially however under the influence of Klopreis, Gisbert resigned his priestly office in the year of his marriage and became the chaplain of the Stadholder Heinrich von Olmissen, called Mülstroe, at Haus Hall near Ratheim, a protector of these preachers. Here he continued to preach Protestant doctrine, served the Lord's Supper in both forms, performed marriage ceremonies, and had large audiences. In 1531 Slachtscaep preached in his home. Between them a dispute arose concerning communion, in the course of which the usually gentle Gisbert showed him the door. The ducal regulation expelling heretical preachers compelled Gisbert to leave Ratheim. For a few days he was able to stay with Junker Hermann auf der Erft (Arft). He could stay nowhere for any length of time—neither with the aged Baron von der Heyden at Tüschenbroich, nor with Junker Wilhelm von Kinsweiler at Müdersheim, nor with his wife's brother at Maastricht, nor with the Baronesses von Elssen, near Schynnen in the Valkenberg area, in Hoengen and Havert, nor in Cologne. He fled from place to place until through the mediation of the elder and younger lords of Mülstroe the magistrate (*Vogt*) of Heinsberg permitted him to stay in the country if he would promise to be quiet.

At the end of 1533 Gisbert lodged in his home the Münsterite agitators Jacob von Ossenbrug (*q.v.*) and Peter Schonemacher of Dremmen. They described to him the splendors of the "New Jerusalem" so convincingly that "he should not have looked at this matter." Under the leadership of Jacob and Gisbert 40 men and women, chiefly from the region of Hückelhoven and Dremmen, met at Eschenbroich east of Heinsberg, and went to Neuss via Odenkirchen (*q.v.*). There they boarded a boat but were stopped at Düsseldorf on Feb. 28, 1534, and imprisoned. Gisbert was examined on March 4. His statements concerning his doctrinal views were extremely cautious and indefinite. Concerning infant baptism he believed it to be sufficient for salvation! Concerning the office of the Mass, he thought that it was a true symbol of the body and blood of Christ if it was observed as the Lord had instituted it. When he was asked whether it was not in essence the body and blood of Christ he remarked that on this point he was still too weak but wanted to be instructed in it. He and his wife had not been rebaptized and were not going to be rebaptized. After this examination he was apparently released. Shortly after he was living in Maastricht (*q.v.*), Dutch province of Limburg, where he conversed with the Anabaptist Ruth Ketelbueter (*q.v.*) and attended a baptismal service conducted in a home by Jan Smeitgen (*q.v.*).

Gisbert von Ratheim as well as the other Wassenberg preachers had left the old church but, judging from his confessions, they were all, with the exception of Campanus, unclear, indefinite, and wavering in their convictions. Gisbert had no precise doctrine and is not to be reckoned with the Anabaptists. For two years he remained in the custody of the Duke of Jülich. In 1536 he was handed over to Electoral Cologne with the priest Herman Tack of Cleve and imprisoned at Kaiserswerth. At this point all trace of him is lost.   W.N.

Rembert, *Wiedertäufer*, 339 ff.; C. A. Cornelius, *Die Geschichtsquellen des Bistums Münster* II (Münster, 1853) 223; O. R. Redlich, *Jülich-Bergische Kirchenpolitik* II (Bonn, 1911) 506, 854-58; Peter Bockmühl, "Die Anfänge der reformatorischen Bewegung in der Stadt Neuss," *Monatshefte für Rheinische Kirchengeschichte*, 1914, 203 ff.; Willem Bax, *Het Protestantisme in het bisdom Luik en vooral te Maastricht 1505-1557* (The Hague, 1937) 52-57; *ML* III, 429 f.

Rattenberg, Tirol, Austria, a small fortified town situated on the Inn River about 25 miles east of Innsbruck, with some copper mines near by. Ruins of the fortress are still present; also the picturesque town remains almost unchanged since the 16th century. In the 1520's Anabaptism was very vigorous here as everywhere else along the Inn (see **Inn Valley**), perhaps because of the miners (*Bergknappen*), the most alert section of the population. The Hutterite *Chronik* reports (up to 1542) a total of 71 martyrs from this town alone. Only Kitzbühel (*q.v.*) with 68 martyrs and Schwaz, another mining town of the Inn Valley, with 20, had such large numbers. Kirchmaier, in his contemporary *Chronicle of the Bishopric of Brixen* (Tirol), reports that a thousand "heretics" were executed in Tirol prior to 1530, and that fagots were burning continually all along the Inn Valley.

Unfortunately little is known about the inner history of the Rattenberg congregation which had so many martyrs; no doubt it was a strong and vigorous group. Only two facts are certain: (1) The Anabaptist "bishop" Leonhard Schiemer (*q.v.*) was caught in this town on Nov. 25, 1527, and beheaded on Jan. 14, 1528; and (2) Pilgram Marpeck (*q.v.*) was born and educated here, became a mining magistrate (*Bergrichter*) and in 1525 a member of the inner council of the city. Very likely about 1527 he came into contact with Anabaptism, either in Augsburg or in Kitzbühel (see **Freyberg, Helene von**), and was baptized. Since he refused to hunt

Anabaptists among the miners, as was demanded by the government, he was removed from his position (Jan. 22, 1528), and soon afterward went to Strasbourg and other places. That he was strongly influenced by the Anabaptist tradition of the Inn Valley (or of Rattenberg) is beyond doubt. The *Kunstbuch* (*q.v.*), a work of the Marpeck group, contains writings by Schiemer and Hans Schlaffer (executed at Schwaz in February 1528), among them even items otherwise unknown, which suggest Marpeck's dependence on this tradition.

Fortunately the Hutterite epistle books (see **Epistles, Hutterite**) allow us at least a few glimpses into the situation of these exciting years of the 1520's at Rattenberg (in the sources usually called Rottenburg or Rothenburg am Inn). Lydia Müller's *Glaubenszeugnisse*, Volume I, contains four epistles by Leonhard Schiemer to the Rattenberg congregation written in prison in 1527 (a fifth epistle or brief sermon for the Rattenberg brethren is found in the *Kunstbuch*). In one case he signs his name, "Leonhard Schiemer, humble servant of you all and unworthy bishop, elected by God and His church" (Müller, 77). This suggests that he was the *Vorsteher* or bishop of the Rattenberg congregation at least for a short while, all the more since he also commends his wife Bärbl to the care of the congregation. But in his "Confession" (Müller, 80-1) he claims that he was made a *Lehrmeister* (i.e., minister, preacher) at Steyr, Upper Austria, and was sent out as a missioner by that group, went to many places and was seized at Rattenberg on the very first night of his stay. Be that as it may, he felt himself a true shepherd for his flock; all his letters are full both of concern for the brotherhood and of teachings and guidance in the true faith. Thus it is probably correct to call the Rattenberg congregation the real congregation of Leonhard Schiemer.

Not long after the death of Schiemer (1528), Wolfgang Brandhuber (*q.v.*), the Vorsteher or bishop of the congregation of Linz, Upper Austria, sent a long and unusually profound and moving pastoral letter to the now orphaned Rattenberg church, a true document of the spirit of early Anabaptism. Its exact date is not known, but no doubt Brandhuber had been deeply concerned about life and discipline of the Rattenberg congregation, in spite of considerable geographic distance between Linz and Rattenberg. It is most characteristic of the spirit of brotherhood, that one cares for those brethren who have lost their leader, wherever they may be. Brandhuber admonishes his brethren (whom he, most likely, had never seen) telling them of the great law of love which requires also a certain sharing of worldly goods with the brethren, telling them of the need for inner discipline and of the inevitable conflict with the "world." One year later, 1529, he himself had to seal his faith with his life, being burned at Linz, thus leaving fatherless not only his own congregation but also the one in distant Tirol.

The Chronicle of the Hutterites reports for the year 1529 a *Gemeindeordnung*, "Regulation or Discipline of the Church: How a Christian Should Live" (*Geschicht-Buch*, 60). Since at that time Hutterites did not yet exist as a group, the chronicler

Caspar Braitmichel may have found this document later among his many sources (perhaps a small notebook or loose paper as such material still exists today among the Hutterites in Canada), and arbitrarily inserted it at the year 1529. Several codices of the Hutterites in North America contain the same *Ordnung* immediately following Schiemer's epistles, so that the likelihood is great that this church discipline had been drawn up also by Schiemer for the Rattenberg brotherhood, for which he felt so obviously responsible and concerned. That it is unsigned is nothing unusual among Anabaptist sources, and no argument against our conjecture. Its brevity (two pages in print) rather indicates the incipient condition of the group which needed just a few guiding principles, such as brotherly sharing (not full community of goods) and the idea of the suffering church which must expect martyrdom and accept it with a willing heart, etc.

The Rattenberg brotherhood, beginning so strong, was deprived too soon of leadership. Though the miners all along the Inn Valley continued to resist persecution, the Rattenberg group finally could not maintain an orderly life as a church *(Gemeinde)*, and either collapsed or moved to Moravia (*q.v.*).

Rattenberg is mentioned again in the Chronicle in 1541, when the Hutterite brother Christoph Gschäll, on a mission trip, spent a whole winter there. But then the records cease, as they do of nearly every other place in Tirol.   R.F.

Wolkan, *Geschicht-Buch;* Lydia Müller, *Glaubenszeugnisse* I; Loserth, *Anabaptismus;* R. Friedmann, "The Oldest Church Discipline of the Anabaptists," *MQR* XXIX (1955) 162-66; Kirchmaier, *Denkwürdigkeiten des Stiftes Brixen (Fontes Rerum Austriacarum* I, 1854). See also the Bibliography for the article "Marpeck." The Canadian sources have not yet been made available in print.

Ratzlaff (Raatslaf, Retzlaff), a family name found among the Mennonites of West Prussian and Danzig background in Russia and North and South America. The name appeared particularly among the Flemish Mennonites of Kleinsee (Jeziorka; *q.v.*), Przechovka-Konopath, and Kazun, and is supposed to have been derived from the Slavic name Ratislav. The Przechovka-Konopath congregation had the following ministers: Berent Ratzlaff (*c*1660), Peter Ratzlaff (1689-1775), Hans Ratzlaff (1727-88), Heinrich Ratzlaff (1742-1805), and Jacob Ratzlaff (1765-?). At Kleinsee-Jeziorka Peter Ratzlaff (b. 1742) became elder and Berent Ratzlaff, minister both in 1785. When the Przechovka Mennonite Church moved to Russia it was known as the Alexanderwohl Church (*q.v.*). The Ratzlaffs spread in Russia, many of them later coming to America, particularly to Kansas. Abraham Ratzlaff (d. 1939) was a minister at Buhler, and Abraham K. Ratzlaff is a physician in Goessel, Kan. Mary Ratzlaff has charge of the Salem Home for the Aged at Hillsboro, Kan.
vDZ., C.K.

Reimer, *Familiennamen*, 116; J. A. Duerksen, "Przechovka and Alexanderwohl," *Menn. Life* X (April 1955) 76; *Naamlijst 1766-1802;* Unruh, *Hintergründe*, 369, 371.

Ratzlaff, Benjamin (1791-1874), an elder of the Rudnerweide Mennonite Church (*q.v.*), Molotschna, South Russia, was born April 1, 1791, in Jeziorka,

West Prussia (*q.v.*), a son of Peter Ratzlaff, and moved to Franztal, West Prussia. He was ordained minister in 1819, and emigrated to the Molotschna in 1820, where he was chosen elder of the Rudnerweide Mennonite Church in 1835. He was active at the time of the revival and signed many documents and letters pertaining to the origin of the Mennonite Brethren. In 1874 he joined a group migrating to America. He died at Buhler(?), Kan., three weeks after his arrival.   C.K.

B. H. Unruh, *Hintergründe*, 369; Friesen, *Brüderschaft*, 139, 167, 192, 197, 208, 499; Franz Isaac, *Die Molotschnaer Mennoniten* (Halbstadt, 1908); *ML* III, 430.

Ratzlaff, Berent, was born about 1660 and was the first known elder of the Przechovka (*q.v.*) Old Flemish Mennonite Church near Schwetz in Poland. He was the grandson of the first Ratzlaff in this church. His grandfather was a soldier in the Swedish war. After hearing about the Mennonite peace teachings, he thrust his sword into a post and joined the Mennonite Church. Berent Ratzlaff lived in the village of Przechovka.   J.A.D.

Rauffer, Wolf(gang), a martyr of the Hutterian Brethren, a tailor, hence also called Wolf Schneider, was taken prisoner with Hans Zuckenhammer (*q.v.*) in 1579 at Tittmoning in Upper Bavaria but released; he returned safely to the brotherhood in Moravia (*q.v.*). In two songs Hans Zuckenhammer described the arrest and imprisonment. Wolf Rauffer was seized again on the Wednesday following Easter in 1585 with Hans Aichner (*q.v.*) and Georg Bruckmaier (*q.v.*) in the vicinity of Ried (at that time belonging to Bavaria, now Upper Austria), taken to Burghausen on the Salzach, and executed on Aug. 14, 1585. He is the author of the beautiful song, "Weil ich so arm und elend bin."   NEFF.

Beck, *Geschichts-Bücher*, 274, 293; *Mart. Mir.* D 754, E 1060 f.; Wolkan, *Lieder*, 237 f.; Wolkan, *Geschicht-Buch*, 418-21; Zieglschmid, *Chronik*, 541-44; *ML* III, 430.

Rauschenbusch, August (1816-99), German and American theologian, was born Feb. 13, 1816, at Altena, Westphalia, Germany, the son of Dr. August Ernst Rauschenbusch, descendant of five generations of Lutheran pastors. He served as German professor at the Rochester Baptist Theological Seminary, Rochester, N.Y., 1858-70. August Rauschenbusch began his service as a Lutheran pastor in 1840, and resigned in 1845 to go to America to serve the large number of German immigrants there, working under the American Tract Society 1846-53. In 1850 he joined the Baptist Church, of which he remained a member until his death. In 1851, on a 5-week trip to Ontario, he met the Mennonites. His biographer refers to this visit as follows: "The contact with the numerous Mennonites of that region served a preparatory purpose. The moral seriousness and the church life of the Mennonites had had a significant influence, but they lacked spiritual power; they had no mission work and did not insist on conversion, so that none of those reached by the Awakening joined them. Only their preacher Daniel Hoch preached repentance at that time and he therefore met much opposition" (p. 168).

Rauschenbusch early became interested in the history of baptism and also of Anabaptism. In 1868/69 he visited numerous university libraries doing research on Anabaptist history, preparatory to writing a comprehensive work, visiting also Professor C. A. Cornelius (*q.v.*) in Munich, whose work on Münster he admired. He adopted the correct theory of the origin of Anabaptism in the Reformation period in contrast to the widely prevalent Baptist construction of Anabaptism as a part of a chain of apostolic succession. He never produced his intended history of Anabaptism but did write a number of articles in encyclopedias and journals, among them articles on the history of the Baptists, Mennonites, and Tunkers for Schem's *Deutsch-Amerikanisches Konversations-Lexikon* (N.Y., 1873). J. G. de Hoop Scheffer published in the *Doopsgezinde Bijdragen* for 1873, pp. 23-29, an article on the Mennonites in North America, based upon the above article by "my good friend A. Rauschenbusch," which the latter had sent him. The German Mennonite *Gemeindeblatt* (*q.v.*) published in its issue of November 1884 (pp. 84 f.) a reprint of Rauschenbusch's article from the same Lexikon entitled "Geschichte der Mennoniten in den Niederlanden, Westpreussen, Russland und der Schweiz." The *Mennonitische Blätter* (*q.v.*) of Aug. 1, 1888 (pp. 89 f.), published an original article by Rauschenbusch, "Verfolgung der Täufer in Salzburg im Oktober und November 1557." His major historical work was *Die Entstehung der Kindertaufe im dritten Jahrhundert nach Christi und die Wiedereinführung der biblischen Taufe im 17. Jahrhundert nach Christi* (Hamburg, 1897, sec. enlarged edition 1898).   H.S.B.

Leben und Wirken von August Rauschenbusch, angefangen von ihm selbst, vollendet und herausgegeben von seinem Sohne Walter Rauschenbusch (Cassel, 1901); *ML* III, 430-32.

Rauschenbusch, Walter (1861-1918), an American Baptist theologian of great influence in the development of the "social gospel," Professor of Church History at the Rochester Baptist Theological Seminary, Rochester, N.Y., was born Oct. 4, 1861, at Rochester, the son of August Rauschenbusch of the seminary faculty. Following his graduation from Rochester Seminary he served in 1886-97 as a pastor in a slum section of New York with a strongly pietistic spirit. He was gradually driven into a deep social concern by his experience in New York, and modified his theology in a liberal direction to include a strong social dimension in redemption. He served as Professor of New Testament Interpretation in the German department at the Rochester Seminary 1897-1902, thereafter until his death, as Professor of Church History in the English department. He now became the leading figure in what was known as the "social gospel" movement in America. His *Christianity and the Social Crisis* (1907) made him a national figure, and his later books increased his influence: *Christianizing the Social Order* (1912), *The Social Principles of Jesus* (1916), *A Theology for the Social Gospel* (1917). Rauschenbusch was definitely interested in Anabaptism and made it a vital part of his lectures in church history. In 1905 he published in *The Ameri-

can Journal of Theology IX (1905), 91-106, a translation of Conrad Grebel's letter of 1524 to Thomas Müntzer with an introduction and commentary, "The Zurich Anabaptists and Thomas Müntzer." Don. E. Smucker holds, in his 1957 doctoral dissertation on Rauschenbusch of the University of Chicago, that Anabaptism, communicated in part by his father August, in part the result of his own study, had an appreciable influence on the development of Walter Rauschenbusch's theology.   E.C., H.S.B.

Dictionary of American Biography XV (1935) 392 f.; C. H. Hopkins, *The Rise of the Social Gospel in American Protestantism 1865-1915* (New Haven, 1940); Don. E. Smucker, "Walter Rauschenbusch" (unpublished dissertation, University of Chicago, 1957); *ML* III, 432.

Ravens (Raven, Rave), a Mennonite family name, found during the 17th and 18th centuries in the Lower Rhine area, Germany, and particularly at Rees (*q.v.*). In the 18th century a Ravens family lived at Gladbach. The martyr Wendel Ravens (*q.v.*) may have been a member of this family. Since about 1620 a Raven(s) family, which had moved in from the Rhineland, has been found in Amsterdam.
          vDZ.

Ravens, Wendel (Windel Rauens), an Anabaptist martyr, executed at Cleve (*q.v.*), Germany, with Willem de Kistenmaker (*q.v.*) in 1551. (*Mart. Mir.* D 131, E 525; *ML* III, 430).   NEFF.

Rawley Springs Mennonite Church (MC), a rural mission located 12 miles west of Harrisonburg, Va., near Hinton, was established in 1932 under the Virginia Mennonite Conference. In 1957 its minister was Ralph Heatwole and its membership 79. M.G.

Rawlinsville Mennonite Church (MC), a member of the Lancaster Conference, began in 1929 under the ministry of the Byerland-New Danville District when it leased the old Muddy Run Presbyterian meetinghouse which had been a Presbyterian center 1742-1916. In 1948 a new brick church was built by the District and the Mission Board. In 1958 David N. Thomas was bishop, and John Miller minister, assisted by Amos M. Hess; the membership numbered 61. A few Puerto Rican families (four of whom are members) are included in this community, served by the County Migrant Pastor.
          I.D.L.

Reading, Pa., county seat (pop. 114,000) of Berks County in the heart of the Pennsylvania-German culture area of Pennsylvania, is the seat of the second largest congregation of the Mennonite Brethren in Christ (373 members in 1957, 87 in 1911) and one congregation (started in 1922) and two mission stations of the Lancaster Mennonite (MC) Conference with a total of 82 members. The Lancaster Conference also operates the Mennonite Girls' Home in the city, founded in 1935. The city lies outside the basic Mennonite settlements in Eastern Pennsylvania, the nearest congregation of the old established settlements lying some 15 miles to the south and southeast. It is a very strong center of the Pennsylvania-German culture area.   H.S.B.

18

Reading (Pa.) Mennonite (MC) Mission was opened as a result of the study of the Book of Acts in the Gehman District of Lancaster Conference. The first service was held on Jan. 8, 1922. Jacob Gehman became the first superintendent in January 1923. The center was moved to 558 North 11th Street and in 1926 to the former Lutheran church at 12th and Windsor Streets. In 1958 Arthur Good and Paul Angstadt were the ministers, with a membership of 40. The first regional Bible school was held here in 1955. The Girls' Home (see **Mennonite Girls' Home**) has been an aid to the Mission over the years.   I.D.L.

Reading Girls' Home: see **Mennonite Girls' Home** (Reading).

Realanstalt am Donnersberg, a Mennonite school at the Weierhof (*q.v.*), Palatinate, Germany. Michael Löwenberg (*q.v.*), the pastor of the Weierhof congregation, established a small school called the "Lehr- und Erziehungsanstalt," which opened at the Weierhof on Dec. 2, 1867. Responsibility for the school was borne by the School Association composed of Mennonite friends living at Weierhof and vicinity. Classes met in Löwenberg's home; the students were lodged in the "Weavers' Cabin." It was the purpose of this school to give the boys two years of training, particularly religious training, beyond the public school, similar to that offered in the Zeller institutions at Beuggen, Switzerland, and in the schools of the Moravian Brethren. The plan was to add a Bible school to train Mennonite ministers. The attendance was good.

A school building was erected slightly north of Weierhof and opened Sept. 22, 1869, with financial support from the Mennonites of the community, and also especially from Crefeld (*q.v.*). In 1873 the enrollment consisted of 25 resident students and 25 day students. There were probably three teachers. The plan for a ministerial school was dropped for lack of patronage. A crisis arose when the state insisted on the fulfillment of its requirements in the school and the founder died in 1874. Following this there were many changes in the office of principal.

In 1884 Ernst Göbel, a former student at Weierhof, consented to become principal of the school, which then had 9 resident students and 15 day students. He had been a teacher at the Rauhes Haus (*q.v.*) at Hamburg. The objective he set for himself was to give the boys a thorough secondary education as well as family style religious and moral training. In the autumn of that year the school was made a six-year Realschule with a dormitory. Under the direction of Ernst Göbel and his brother Gustav Göbel, who came to the school in 1892 and served on the teaching staff and as business manager, and the co-operation of David Krehbiel (*q.v.*) besides younger teachers, the school made rapid progress, becoming, in spite of tremendous difficulties, one of the outstanding secondary schools in the Palatinate. In the course of time the plant was also developed to provide for normal extracurricular activities. In 1935-36 the enrollment was 246, of which 20 were Mennonites. The local Mennonite pastor for almost 50 years, Christian Neff, regularly taught the Bible and religion classes, but the school otherwise did not have a particularly Mennonite character, even though the Board of Directors was Mennonite.

In 1936 the school was taken over by the Nazi Party, and after World War II (1945) by the French occupation forces. In 1957 the American military, which had used the school for several years for a specialized training school, promised to return it to the Mennonite owners. Meanwhile despairing of regaining the school property the Board had purchased in 1952 a building in Kirchheimbolanden, two miles from the Weierhof, to serve as a boarding and rooming dormitory (Schülerheim) for Mennonite and other boys attending the Kirchheimbolanden high school, using the rent received from the military authorities for the Weierhof school property to help maintain the new student home. In 1957 a total of 90 boys were occupying the student home, of whom however only 20 were Mennonites. There are in addition 30 Mennonite day students, making a total of 50 Mennonite boys in the school. No other such concentration of Mennonites in any school is found in German- or French-speaking Europe. The assistant principal, Dr. Horst Penner, is a Mennonite, several other Mennonite teachers from the old Weierhof faculty are on the Kirchheimbolanden school staff, and a Mennonite couple are serving as house parents for the student home. The Weierhof Mennonite pastor has been teaching Bible for the Mennonite students since 1953.

The Weierhof Board since about 1930 has no longer been exclusively Mennonite, even though the majority of the members still are. It is clear that the Mennonites are not able to finance a school alone, nor do they have a sufficient faculty. It also seems uncertain whether there will ever be enough Mennonite students to make the Weierhof school, should it be reopened, a predominantly Mennonite school. This would be highly regrettable, since the Weierhof school could fill a major role in German Mennonitism as a center for Mennonite education and activity. The Weierhof school board hoped to reopen the school in 1959.   C.G., H.HA.

Gustav Göbel, "Ernst Göbel," *Gem.-Kal.*, 1936, 47 ff.; Emil Händiges, "Zum fünfzigjährigen Jubiläum der Real- und Erziehungsanstalt auf dem Weierhof am Donnersberg," *Menn. Bl.*, 1920, 91-97, with five photographs; Paul Schowalter, "Die Schule auf dem Weierhof," *Gem.-Kal.*, 1958, 47-60; Helmut Haury, "Die Weierhöfer Schule," *Menn. Jahrbuch* 1955, 17 ff.; *ML* III, 432 f.

Reason and Obedience (to divine commands), one of the basic problems in the life of an earnest Christian, and in particular an issue in Anabaptist polemics. The Scriptural text from which the discussion proceeds is II Corinthians 10:5, "We destroy arguments and every proud obstacle to the knowledge of God, and take every thought captive to obey Christ" (with Luther: ". . . und nehmen gefangen alle Vernunft unter den Gehorsam Christi"; note that *Vernunft* is a far stronger term than "thought"). It is a perennial problem concerning the use of reason and its limitation by the unconditional obedience in faith to the Word of God, with-

out further speculation. Rationalists have called this attitude a "blind faith," while Anabaptists would consider their opponents simply lacking that concrete faith which leads to evidencing or witnessing.

With the exception of its earliest period, Anabaptism had only a few scholars among its members. Only Grebel, Hubmaier, Denck, and a few more had humanistic training; only Hubmaier was a "doctor" of theology. This stood in sharp contrast to the state churches of the time in which university training was considered a necessary prerequisite for the ministry. A Hutterite tract of the 16th century entitled "Why Are There no University Graduates (*Hochgelehrte*) in our Midst?" answers that intellectual sophistication kills simplicity and with it faith, as Anabaptism understood the latter. Pilgram Marpeck, himself a learned engineer, praised Christ as "the unlettered son of a carpenter out of whom your [Schwenckfeld's] philosophy has fabricated such a high Christ" (*Verantwortung, 55*). All this seems to indicate that Anabaptism had chosen the type of faith which embraces the revealed truth with a simple heart no longer in need of theological speculation. But this acceptance of God's Word in obedience and discipleship in no way means dullness of the mind; it rather means the significant distinction between reason and "understanding" (the latter term used in the King James version at many places: Luke 2:47; Eph. 3:4; Col. 1:9 and 2:2; II Tim. 2:7; Rev. 13:18, etc.), that is, between logical (Greek) rationality and Biblical spirituality.

In the age of Reformation this tension between reason and obedience appears particularly impressive in the debates (*Gespräche*) between Anabaptists and anti-Trinitarians (Socinians, Polish Brethren, etc.). Naturally, the controversy with this group was much more relevant for Anabaptists than a controversy with Humanism (*q.v.*) since the latter had hardly any appeal to Anabaptists. Anti-Trinitarianism (*q.v.*) represented at that time the rationalistic wing of the "Radical Reformation" (*q.v.*) which for reasons of intellectual integrity could not accept the doctrine of Trinity and with it the doctrine of the divine sonship of Christ. We know of numerous contacts which these anti-Trinitarians had with some Anabaptist groups and of the different approaches of the two groups toward a closer union (see **Ostorodt**). Since they accepted adult baptism and the simple life of discipleship, and since they even experimented with communal life, they felt rather close (morally) to both Hutterites and Mennonites, and could not understand the cool reception they received by both groups. In this connection a correspondence is revealing which in 1571 the Hutterite bishop Peter Walpot (*q.v.*) carried on with an elder of the Polish church in Cracow by the name of Simon Ronemberg, an apothecary. (This correspondence is inserted into the great Hutterite *Chronicle* at the year 1571.) "You give the impression," writes Walpot, "that you have already surrendered yourself to the obedience of God and have taken your reason captive unto His obedience. To this I say . . . you have indeed given obedience, but only to act according to your own free will, desire and pleasure, . . . which obedience is not that which Paul and the apostles sought to establish among the heathen" (*MQR*, 1945, 35). The letter goes on in this rather sharp vein and it may be assumed that the Polish brother wondered about this apparent lack of Christian love. But without such strictness, or full surrender as Walpot calls it (see **Gelassenheit**), Anabaptism would not have been able to carry on a life of discipleship in a world utterly unsympathetic to this idea. In a later letter Walpot writes to the Poles: "Those of you who were sent to us desired to teach us, which we could not accept at all; it would have meant letting ourselves be judged by those who have not completely renounced the world and the heathen way of life" (*ibid.*, 39, 40) (see also Friedmann, "Encounter").

That was in 1571. In 1833 a simple minister of the Kleine Gemeinde (*q.v.*) in Russia, Heinrich Balzer (*q.v.*), wrote a treatise for his church (which had recently separated from the main body of Mennonites in Russia for reasons of conservatism), which treatise sounds almost like a paraphrase of Walpot's letters. Balzer gave his tract the strange sounding title *Verstand und Vernunft* (Understanding and Reason—Simple Opinions Regarding the Difference Between Understanding and Reason According to the Teachings of the Gospel). Essentially it is a tract on the tension between reason and obedience, between intellectuality and spirituality, characteristic of both Anabaptists and conservative Mennonites. (For an English translation see bibliography.) The term *Verstand* the author seeks to explain as "Verstand des Herzens" (understanding of the heart), somewhat like Blaise Pascal's *raison du coeur* in the 17th century, which alone leads to a grasp of the genius of the Gospel message. Balzer approvingly quotes Paul's daring statement that "knowledge (i.e., Greek rationality) puffeth up" (I Cor. 8:1), and refers to II Cor. 10:5, just as it was used previously by Walpot and other Anabaptists.

The emphasis here as elsewhere is on simplicity (which alone enables absolute obedience and *Nachfolge*); but again this simplicity of the mind should not be understood as a renunciation of the gift of thinking. In 1560, when Claus Felbinger (*q.v.*) stood before inquiring authorities he told them that he intends to stay in the "simplicity of Christ," whereupon the interrogating officer answered, "I do not think that you are so simple. I think there would not be one in a hundred who could give an account of himself (his faith) as you do" (*MQR*, 1955, 141). But in spite of the clear distinction between the two forms of thought, whereby obedience is compatible with "understanding" but not with reason, the tension continues to exist and to face the Christian of the 20th century with the same dilemma which existed four centuries ago.   R.F.

R. Friedmann, "The Encounter of Anabaptists and Mennonites with Anti-Trinitarianism," *MQR* XXII (1948) 139-62; idem, "Reason and Obedience, an Old Anabaptist Letter . . . and Its Meaning," *ibid.*, XIX (1945) 27-40; idem, "Faith and Reason, the Principles of Mennonitism Reconsidered in a Treatise of 1833," *ibid.*, XXII (1948) 75-93; idem, *Mennonite Piety Through the Centuries* (Goshen, 1949), Chapter XI, "Concept of the Spirit Among Anabaptists," 81 ff., also 43; Robert Kreider, "Anabaptism and Humanism, an Inquiry . . ." *MQR* XXII (1952) 123-41.

Reber (Räber), **Samuel**, a Mennonite living at Trub in the Emmental (*q.v.*), Swiss canton of Bern (*q.v.*), "having endured much persecution, oppression, and chains," was put on board a boat on March 18, 1710, with 44 men and 12 women and taken down the Rhine to be deported to America. He escaped and returned to Switzerland contrary to his promise, and was sentenced to life imprisonment. The Dutch ambassador at Bern, Runckel (*q.v.*), intervened and had him released. Reber was then, at the age of 75, against his will, put on a boat with Hans Bürky (*q.v.*) and taken down the Rhine to be settled in the Netherlands. But he left the boat at Mannheim with other passengers, mostly followers of Hans Reist. Then all trace of Reber is lost. (Müller, *Berner Täufer*, 277, 296, 302, 304, 307; *ML* III, 433.)   E.C.

Rebstock, Jakob (d. 1654). a Hutterite barber-surgeon, was chosen to the ministry on March 13, 1649, and confirmed at Sobotiste (*q.v.*) in 1651. Among his effects was found a manuscript, *Kurtzes denkbuechl, darinen zum tail Begriffen, was sich von dem 1525 Jar biss auff gegenwirtig Zeit in unsserer gemain zugetragen . . .*, now Codex F ("Codex Rebstock") of the Moravian national archives at Brno.   NEFF.

Beck, *Geschichts-Bücher*, XXV, 477, 483; Wolkan, *Geschicht-Buch*, 634, 642; Robert Friedmann, "Die Briefe der österreichischen Täufer," in *Archiv für Reformations-Geschichte* XXVI (1929) 44; *Inv. Arch. Amst.* I, Nos. 1317, 1339; *ML* III, 433.

Rechenschafft unserer Religion, Leer und Glaubens *Von den Brüdern so man die Hutterischen nennt ausgangen* was written by Peter Riedemann (*q.v.*) in 1540-41. Among the not too numerous doctrinal tracts of the 16th-century Anabaptists, Riedemann's *Rechenschaft* (*Account of our Religion, Doctrine and Faith*, the title according to I Peter 3:15, "Be ready to give an answer to every man that asks you a reason of the hope that is in you") is one of the most important and significant documents, a basic source for the knowledge of Anabaptist doctrine and theology, a true spiritual foundation for the Hutterite branch of Anabaptists, but beyond that, characteristic of this great movement at large, save for the one specific doctrine concerning community of goods. It is a book of much inner beauty and spirituality which did much to enable the Hutterites to survive through the centuries more or less loyal to their beginnings. Together with the great *Article Book* of 1547 (and 1577) (*q.v.*) and the *Handbüchlein wider den Prozess . . .* (*q.v.*) of 1558, it represents the official position of the Hutterites in matters both of doctrine and practice. That the *Rechenschaft* was better known to the outside world than the other two statements was mainly due to the fact that it is one of the few Hutterite books ever to have been published in print (1565).

The history and theology of this unique work has not yet been given a thorough study, although there have been some recent attempts in this direction. Thus it was not known until the present that Riedemann (who began this *Rechenschaft* during his imprisonment in Hesse, 1540-41, at the castle of Wolkersdorf) got the idea for this work when he wished to inform Landgrave Philip of Hesse about the true Anabaptist doctrine. "Since he has never interrogated us personally . . . since perhaps others slander us, he should at least know why he is keeping us imprisoned" (Epistle 21, of 1540-41, sent to Hans Amon and Leonhard Lanzenstiel).

The original manuscript is very likely lost; yet two old manuscript codices are still extant: one in the primatial library in Esztergom (*q.v.*), signature IV, 1, dated 1614, having 364 leaves in 16°, very carefully written, apparently intended as a pocket "companion"; and a second in private possession in Freeman, S.D. (of which no description is available). In 1545 the book came out in print; its last page says: "This year the Confession was reprinted by Philips Vollanndt." Nothing is known about this printer, and it may be assumed that he was an itinerant printer who chanced to pass by the Hutterite settlements in Moravia, offering his services to everyone, and there (perhaps at Neumühle, the seat of Bishop Peter Walpot; see **Neumühle**) accomplished this work. It was the Golden Age of the brotherhood, and the Brethren probably felt that each of the many Bruderhofs in Moravia and Slovakia should have a copy of this basic work. Nevertheless, the edition must have been small since only a very few copies have come down to our time (list at end of this article). The expression "reprinted" has puzzled scholars regarding the possibility of an earlier print, but it can hardly mean this since no such print has ever been discovered. Apparently it means: first written by hand but now also printed. In modern times the book has been republished three times (1870, 1902, 1938) and also translated into English (1950), thus making the text easily available to anyone interested (list of editions at end of article).

Although the *Rechenschaft* is the work of but one man, it must be assumed that the brotherhood after careful study promptly approved of it as an official church document. When the Brethren in their dire predicament in 1545 sent a collective letter to the Lords of Moravia (Beck, 169-73), they enclosed a copy (apparently in manuscript) of this *Rechenschaft* to inform the authorities about their stand both as to doctrine and practice. The work has kept its place of pre-eminence throughout Hutterite history because of its excellence and clarity.

The *Rechenschaft* is divided into two unequal parts (in the English edition of 1950 of 127 and 86 pages respectively), the first part being the more important while the second is made up of seven lengthy meditations on various topics, not considered as part of the official "Account." The first part is made up of ninety articles, most of them brief. The initial group of twenty-nine articles represents an interpretation of the Apostles' Creed, followed by the articles "What faith is," "Why God created man," "What sin is," "Concerning original sin," "Concerning remorse,—repentance," "Concerning the baptism of children," and the refutation of the arguments for infant baptism. Then follow articles about the Lord's Supper, community of goods (less than 4 pages), separation from the world, etc. The first part is concluded by a set of articles concerning practical matters: government, warfare, taxation, manufacture of swords (forbidden), litigation and swearing (both forbidden), traders, innkeepers, standing drinks (all forbidden), education of the young, ban and readmission, and finally an article concerning the whole life: conduct, dress, adornment, etc.

It is impossible to give here an adequate presentation of the ideas of this comprehensive document; reference to literature at the end of this article will be of some help as well as several other articles in this ENCYCLOPEDIA. That the theological emphasis is thoroughly different from that of Luther, Zwingli, and Calvin, is worth mentioning. The great issue of original sin (in many Anabaptist documents completely missing) is here dealt with on not more than three pages. Justification "by faith alone" is not mentioned at all, and the classical loci used by Luther for his basic doctrines are conspicuously absent. In short, Riedemann was not familiar with the Lutheran theological tradition. His sources are rather various texts from the Scriptures. Thus, for instance, baptism is called, after Titus 3:5, "the bath of rebirth"; and as for "the harm wrought by original sin" Riedemann refers back to the Old Testament locus in Ezekiel 18:20, where it is said that children shall not bear the iniquities of their fathers. "The mother of sin," however, Riedemann emphatically declares (English text, 56), "is disobedience" to the commandments of God, alluding to Romans 5:16-19. There is but one reference to Luther (English text, 35), followed by a passionate denial that the Brethren taught "work righteousness." "To this we say 'no,' for we know that all our work, in so far as it is our work, is naught but sin, but in so far as it is of Christ and *done by Christ in us,* so far it is truth, just and good" (English text, 36). There is nowhere an explicit theology of atonement but there is the emphasis that redemption follows repentance and inner rebirth: "fleeing from sin as from a serpent"(English text, 59). Thus "man is grafted into Christ." "We, redeemed from death through Him, might [thus] be the children of His covenant" (English text, 63) (Acts 3:17-26); indeed a "covenant of childlike freedom" (English text, 68) (Gal. 4:4). The emphasis is thus laid not so much upon justification from sin but upon sanctification of life, which is the very proof of inner rebirth and obedience, i.e., discipleship.

The church, however, of these reborn children of the "new covenant" (67) is basically a spiritual thing. "It is a lantern of righteousness" (39) in which "the light of grace is borne and held before the whole world." "Whosoever endures and suffers the work of the Spirit of Christ is a member of this church." It is the Spirit and not man who leads men to this church (39-41). This church, then, in the concrete here and now, is defined as "the fellowship of the Lord's Table" *(Abendmahlsgemeinde),* the assembly of the reborn ones. Such a fellowship, to be sure, is not established by the Lord's Supper, but the latter is rather an expression of this fellowship previously entered into. It is a church, as far as humanly possible, "without spot and wrinkle," and in order to achieve this end separation from the world and inner discipline are needed. This leads to all the ensuing statements concerning conduct of life and the practice of the ban ("exclusion," 131 f.).

For the world "which is without" (I Cor. 5:12) no further concern is expressed, for this world will eventually be judged by God Himself.

It is obvious that a document of such inner richness could not be drawn up without some forerunners who prepared the spiritual framework in which Riedemann developed the ideas which are specifically Hutterite in character. In 1894 Johann Loserth presented the thesis that the theological framework of this *Rechenschaft* was taken in its entirety from the work of Balthasar Hubmaier (*q.v.*) and that therefore the *Rechenschaft* is not so much an original work as an adaptation of ideas developed by Hubmaier in 1525-27 and assiduously studied later by the Hutterites in Moravia. Loserth's claim was challenged by Franz Heimann in a doctoral dissertation (Vienna, 1927), in which he concludes that Riedemann borrowed from Hubmaier only in those parts which deal with the doctrines of baptism and the Lord's Supper, doctrines which are common to all Anabaptists. The assimilation of these ideas from Hubmaier does not detract from the originality and genuine spiritual eminence of Riedemann's comprehensive work. Hubmaier's most outstanding contribution to the Anabaptist vision is his very convincing discussion and refutation of the several arguments in favor of infant baptism. This discussion Riedemann takes over point by point into his *Rechenschaft* (English text, 70-77), according to Heimann.

Otherwise, Heimann emphasizes, in all practical and ethical items Riedemann is by and large independent of Hubmaier, rendering Loserth's theory invalid. It must not be forgotten, for instance, that Hubmaier approved the "sword," i.e., the right of the government to use force in the execution of its laws, while the Hutterites, like all evangelical Anabaptists, stood passionately for nonresistance and non-co-operation with any government.

Finally, Riedemann was not solely dependent upon Hubmaier in the shaping of his Anabaptist doctrines. He must certainly also have known the ideas of his earliest teachers such as Hans Hut, Hans Schlaffer, and Leonhard Schiemer. But no such research has as yet been undertaken. It is also possible that Riedemann was influenced in part by Ulrich Stadler (*q.v.*), the most important doctrinal thinker of the 1530's in Moravia, but again this question has never been studied. Since Riedemann's Biblical spiritualism was shaped in the second half of the 1520's, one might think of Hans Denk as a strong influence; but this was again the general Anabaptist vision of that time. The value and genuine contribution of the author himself should not be diminished by pointing to some forerunners. Since the work was written in prison in Hesse, it is very likely that Riedemann had no reading material on hand, and his formulations must be considered as his original personal viewpoints and conceptions arising out of his own spiritual pilgrimage.

Of the original *Rechenschaft* edition in 1565 only a few copies are known to exist: one at the British Museum in London (sign. 3908 a8), one in the University of Chicago Library, one in the National Museum of Brno, Moravia, one at a Bruderhof in the United States (formerly at Rockport, S.D., but now of unknown location), one used in 1870 by Calvary but supposedly acquired by the Prussian State Library, one reported by Beck to be in the University of Breslau Library, and one at the National Library of Vienna, Austria.

The following are known—modern reprints: (1) *Mittheilungen aus dem Antiquariat S. Calvary* (Berlin, 1870) 254-417, reprinted from a 1565 copy; (2) A reprint from the Chicago copy as *Rechenschaft unseres Glaubens, . . . , neu herausgegeben von den Brüdern in Amerika* (Berne, 1902). This edition was probably edited by John Horsch, who lived in Berne at that time, and who had been in close contact with Elias Walter, the leading Hutterite elder of that period. (3) A reprint from the copy in the British Museum in 1938 by the Society of Brothers (Plough Publishing House in England); (4) an English translation, *Account of our Religion, Doctrine and Faith, . . . ,* published by Hodder and Stoughton (London) in conjunction with the Plough Publishing House in 1950, 283 pages. The English translation is by Kathleen E. Hasenberg. In this edition the nearly 1,800 Bible references are all collected in a special appendix of nearly 38 pages (229-66). (See **Riedemann**.)   R.F.

Besides all major treatments of the Hutterites such as those by Loserth, Wolkan, Horsch, etc., see Franz Heimann, "The Hutterite Doctrine of the Church and the Common Life: A Study of Peter Riedemann's Confession of Faith of 1540," in *MQR* XXVI (1952) 22-47 and 142-60 (doctoral dissertation, University of Vienna, 1927, translated by Robert Friedmann); Robert Friedmann, "Peter Riedemann on Original Sin and the Way of Redemption," *MQR* XXVI (1952) 210-15; W. Wiswedel, "Peter Riedemann, ein Gefangener Jesu Christi," in his *Bilder* I, 169-94; Lydia Müller, *ML* III, 500-5.

Rechlinger, Ulrich: see **Rehlinger, Ulrich.**

Rechperger, Henslin, an Anabaptist martyr, was put to death with several other Anabaptists at Ipfhofen in Middle Franconia, Germany, in January 1528. (Wappler, *Thüringen,* 36 and 283; *ML* III, 433.)
                                                                    NEFF.

Reck-Malleczewen, Friedrich (1884-1945), a German literary figure, was born at Malleczewen, Lyck district of East Prussia, on the Russian border, descended from an old landed family, studied medicine, but also lived in the world of music, literature, and history. After an extended tour of America in 1912 he settled in Stuttgart and later in Munich and in the Chiemgau of Upper Bavaria. In 1925 he made a journey to Africa. "In 1933 he joined the Catholic Church, which seemed to him the last bulwark against increasing brutalization and impersonalization." In despair he wrote *Bockelson, Geschichte eines Massenwahns* (Berlin, 1937, and Wiesentheid, 1946), a belletristic historical study based on the Münster revolt of 1534 f. (see **Jan van Leyden**). It is hardly surprising that in his view of the Münsterite (*q.v.*) "kingdom" as the preview of the Nazi regime he saw in Anabaptism only fanatical chaos and spiritual disease which resulted in maniacal behavior. The treatment is based on some older works, viz., the source work, *Geschichtsquellen des Bistums Münster,* the collection of documents by Niesert and Neudecker, Löffler's collection of documents, contemporary presentations such as Hamelmann, Bolandus, and Dorpius, and six contemporary reports. More recent works used by Reck-Malleczewen were those of Fässer (1852), Ranke's history of Germany, and unpublished letters in the archives at Cassel. Recent material, which must have been available in Munich in 1937, is untouched. Reck believed that all revolution has the same source, in alienation from native culture and real religion, and that as the Münsterite revolution resulted in catastrophe, so the Nazi revolution would follow the same course. Hitler he viewed as a parallel to Bockelson. Reck was taken to the Dachau concentration camp on Dec. 31, 1944, and died there without trial or sentence on Feb. 17, 1945.   E.C.

Mary E. Bender, "The Anabaptist Theme in Modern German Literature, unpublished Master's thesis, Indiana University, 1958; *ML* III, 438.

Reconstruction Work in France. During World War I, as early as November 1914, English Quakers had begun reconstruction work in war-devastated areas of France. In April 1917, the month in which the United States entered the war, the American Friends Service Committee was organized at Philadelphia, Pa. In June a commission of investigation was sent to France following which an AFSC reconstruction unit was set up under the general direction of the civilian service of the American Red Cross.

In July 1917 a unit of 100 men, including one Mennonite, was gathered at Haverford, Pa., to be trained for the French service. It was the hope of the AFSC that this service would be recognized by the War Department as noncombatant service. On Sept. 4, 1917, 54 of the Haverford unit men, including the Mennonite, started for France, with the understanding that any men subject to the draft could be called back. In March 1918 the War Department declined to recognize the project for purposes of assignment, but Congress enacted the "furlough law" providing that men in the army might be furloughed for other essential work. The War Department now applied this law to the CO's and by the close of the war 1,300 CO's in the army had been recommended for furlough, of whom 200 (including a number of Mennonites) were assigned to the AFSC.

In January 1918 the Mennonite Relief Commission for War Sufferers (MC) took official action to support the AFSC project in France and began processing Mennonite applicants for this service. By the close of the war (Nov. 11, 1918) less than a dozen Mennonites had arrived in France, but after the armistice the men were processed more rapidly, and eventually 54 Mennonites joined the AFSC reconstruction unit, a number of them following release from prison at Fort Leavenworth. Those who had gone to France as furloughed soldiers were given their discharges at discharge camps in France and then continued with the AFSC as civilians.

The French reconstruction work was located in the region between Verdun and Paris, which for four years was ravaged by the constant moving back and forth of the opposing armies. The earlier work was concentrated in the Marne region west

of the Argonne Forest. In 1919, when the Mennonites began to arrive, the AFSC center shifted to Clermont-en-Argonne at the edge of the Meuse-Argonne battle front west of Verdun. Here the AFSC medical work centered in a Catholic hospital in the city which had been taken over by the army and was largely ruined by shell fire. The AFSC rebuilt the hospital and operated an inpatient and outpatient service.

In 1919-20 the AFSC headquarters were located at Grange-le-Compte, an estate near Clermont-en-Argonne. From Grange-le-Compte and its subsidiary warehouse refugees and war sufferers were supplied with food, clothing, and various forms of first aid. An important part of the work was the construction of temporary prefabricated housing for the homeless; in many cases whole villages had been wiped out. Before the Mennonites arrived the Quakers had built 543 such homes and repaired others in the Marne-Somme area. In 1919 the AFSC was assigned 40 villages in the Verdun area and later the assignment was enlarged. In the village of Neuvilly, where a number of Mennonites were stationed, 70 houses were built. In comparison with other areas the AFSC construction work advanced the return of the refugees to their villages by at least a year.

The AFSC agricultural department introduced machinery to restore ruined land to cultivation, and distributed young fruit trees, rabbits, chickens, goats, sheep, bees, and hatching eggs to enable farmers to begin their work. When the French program ended on April 1, 1920, most of the Mennonites had been with the service a year and a very few two years. Several gave additional service with the AFSC in other parts of Europe. (See **Relief.**)

In the summer of 1919 S. E. Allgyer and Vernon Smucker visited the French project as representatives of the MRCWS. They visited the various work units, held religious services with the Mennonite men on a number of successive Sundays, and on June 20-22 attended a conference of Mennonite reconstruction workers at Clermont-en-Argonne. Smucker then sailed for home on July 6, while Allgyer spent two weeks with the French and Alsatian Mennonites. He then went to Paris with A. J. Miller, J. C. Meyer, and J. Roy Allgyer, where from July 30 to August 2 they interviewed a number of government officials and relief administrators including Herbert Hoover of the Allied Food Commission regarding further opportunities for relief work in Europe. Allgyer sailed for home on August 9 and following his report the MRCWS appointed A. J. Miller and J. Roy Allgyer to investigate further relief needs in Europe, and these two men named A. E. Hiebert as the third member of the committee.

A significant outcome of the Mennonite work in France was the visits of reconstruction workers and of S. E. Allgyer with the French and Alsatian Mennonites. Pierre Sommer (*q.v.*) at the conference at Clermont-en-Argonne in June 1919 appealed for help from America in rebuilding the scattered Mennonite congregations in France. The conference then asked the Mennonite Board of Missions and Charities (MC at Elkhart) to "consider the advisability of rendering to these churches such **personal** help as could be given in this their time of great need." In addition, S. E. Allgyer was also asked to present this matter to the Mission Board personally. It was not until 1927, however, that the Board took action in this matter.

The French reconstruction work represents a significant event in recent Mennonite history. The young men who served in the project regarded the manner in which the church supported the new relief program as "the crucial test of her sincerity" with respect to nonresistance and they believed that "the future of the church is closely related to the present problem of reconstruction." In evaluating the Mennonite contribution to the AFSC program Rufus M. Jones said: "The young men stood the test of the [military] camps with insight and with much bravery. They had the backing of their church and they were conscious that they were its standard bearers. They became closely united in fellowship with our men in the camps and they shared with them the desire to make a positive contribution to service abroad. . . . They were excellent workers and they brought a fine spirit of devotion and co-operation to the mission." The American Mennonites contributed a total of $291,000 for the support of the French reconstruction work.

Out of the experience of the Mennonite (MC) workers in France came the stimulus for the initiation of the Young People's conference (q.v.), a forward-looking movement in the Mennonite Church (MC). G.F.H.

Rufus M. Jones, *A Service of Love in Wartime: American Friends Relief Work in Europe, 1916-1919* (New York, 1920); *Report of General Conference of Mennonites in France in Reconstruction Work (June 20-22, 1919)* (n.p., n.d.).

Recreation: see Amusements and Holidays.

Red Moon Mennonite Mission Church (GCM): see **Hammon Cheyenne** Mennonite Church.

Red River Valley Mennonite Church (MC), located in Casselton, Cass Co., N.D., is a member of the North Central Conference. In the spring of 1928 the families of I. S. Mast and Daniel L. Martin, now a minister in Sheldon, Wis., moved into this community. The following spring several families moved in from Nebraska, and on June 19, 1929, the congregation was organized with 15 charter members. I. S. Mast was chosen as pastor. In 1942 Mast left the district; the congregation was without a resident pastor until July 27, 1947, when Abraham J. Stoll was ordained, who was still serving in 1956, with a membership of 47. A.J.S.

Red River Valley Mutual Insurance Company of Altona, Man., was founded in 1941 as a private commercial mutual insurance agency, which took over some of the members of the former Mennonite Church fire insurance association in the West Reserve, which had been founded in 1900 as a breakaway from the East Reserve association (see **Canada and States** Mennonite Insurance Association), but which had had its own "insurance elder" under the East Reserve plan since the original settlement in the West Reserve in 1875. The remaining members continued in the Manitoba Mennonite Mutual Insurance Company (q.v.) with headquarters at Steinbach, Man., which was incorporated in 1940, one year earlier. The Red River Company, which does not restrict its patrons to Mennonites as does the Manitoba Mutual, but serves the general public (although the majority of its policyholders are still Mennonites), had 5,800 policyholders in 1955, with about $37,000,000 property coverage. Approximately one third of its 5,520 members were members of the Evangelical Mennonite Church (Kleine Gemeinde, q.v.). D.P.R.

Red Run Mennonite Church (MC), near Denver, Pa., formerly called Martin's, a member of the Lancaster Conference, in 1957 had a membership of 50, but actually was considered a sub-congregation of Bowmansville (q.v.) and served by the ministry of that congregation. A Sunday school was conducted here 1912-27 in the Martin's Schoolhouse between Fivepointville and Terre Hill by the Weaverland (q.v.) congregation, and thereafter preaching once a month until in June 1946, when the Sunday school was reopened. More recently preaching services have been held every two weeks. I.D.L.

Red Run Mennonite Church (MC), Grantsville, Md., established in 1947, is a mission in the Allegheny Mennonite Conference. In 1957 it had a membership of 15, with Vernon Yoder as pastor.

Red Top Mennonite Church (MC), located 30 miles north of Glendive, Mont., and 5 miles east of Bloomfield, a member of the North Central Conference, was organized in March 1917 with 18 charter members. Services were held in a little red top schoolhouse. With increased membership came the need of a church building and a pastor. The new church was dedicated on April 12, 1936. The 1957 membership was 68, with Elmer Borntrager as minister. L.B.

Red Well Mennonite Mission (MC), now extinct, located on the western fringe of Welsh Mountain, Lancaster Co., Pa., was opened in 1896 with John R. Buckwalter and John H. Hershey as superintendents. When they moved to Missouri, John Musselman and Amos H. Hershey became the next superintendents. In 1899 a large frame meetinghouse was built for the growing congregation. The first Sunday-school Meeting held in Lancaster County met here on Nov. 22, 1904. This was the first evangelistic field for John W. Weaver in 1909. The highest membership was 65. By 1929 the members had moved away, and the work was consolidated with the Welsh Mountain (q.v.) Samaritan Home, the building itself being razed to enlarge the Home. Recently a cottage meeting has been conducted in the neighborhood. I.D.L.

Redemptioners, a term used to denote immigrants to the United States who "redeemed" their fare by working for it upon arrival. Usually, upon landing in Philadelphia, Pa., they were auctioned off. An adult usually had to work four or five years to pay off the debt, and a child until he reached the age of 21. Many Mennonites came to America as redemptioners. E.C.

C. Henry Smith, *The Story of the Mennonites* (Newton, 1950) 543 f.; *ML* III, 438.

Rediger, Joseph (1826-1904), a minister of the Defenseless Mennonite Church, was born in Lembach, Baden, Germany, the son of Jakob and Veronica Rediger. Jakob came to America in 1834, living in a log hut near Peoria, Ill. Joseph visited him there and returned to Germany to help the rest of the family emigrate. With his mother, two brothers, three sisters, and a number of others he arrived in America and settled near Peoria. Joseph married Veronica Oyer (d. 1872) in 1850. Five sons and eight daughters were born to them. Their youngest son, Benjamin, served long as chairman of the Board of Directors of Salem Children's Home. In 1876 Joseph married Anna Oyer (d. 1897).

Joseph Rediger was received into the Mennonite Church (MC) at age of sixteen and chosen minister in 1863. After a period of service as minister he joined with Bishop Henry Egly and his newly formed Defenseless Mennonite Church in efforts to spread the Gospel. He started the Waldo (now Gridley) church and traveled extensively with Egly in Kansas, Nebraska, and Missouri, also visiting churches in Ohio and Indiana. Rediger was one of the pioneers in the Defenseless Mennonite Church to promote foreign missions. In his later years he lived at Meadows, where he died on March 8, 1904. He was buried in the Waldo cemetery. E.E.R.

Reed City Church of God in Christ Mennonite Church, now extinct, located near Reed City, Osceola Co., Mich., was organized in the late 1870's. At first the small group of about 30 members was ministered to by John Holdeman, Mark Seiler, and Frank Seidner from Ohio. Later Jacob Litwiller, Dan Buerge, and Peter Yost became their local leaders, and held regular Sunday morning worship services. In 1883 some members moved to other congregations. The church was revived under the leadership of ministers Peter Litwiller and F. C. Fricke, but they too and others relocated with other congregations. Meetings ceased in 1914. P.G.H.

Reeder, Hermann (dates of birth and death not known), a Mennonite minister in the Palatinate in the 19th century, concerning whose life few particulars have been discovered. He probably stemmed from non-Mennonite parents, but he is reported to have been reared by Mennonites and to have been baptized by a preacher Dahlem (letter by David Kaege of Offstein to Johannes Galle of Monzernheim, Jan. 1, 1836). He was educated in a Baptist seminary in England, and was then ordained as an elder by Dahlem. This Dahlem is apparently not Valentin Dahlem (*q.v.*) of Rosenköppel, since there is no mention of this ordination in Dahlem's letters although he casually mentions Reeder.

For a time Reeder served in the small congregation of Neuwied (*q.v.*). Having had his attention directed to the Palatinate by the Baptist preacher Angas (*q.v.*), he visited the Mennonite congregations there, and preached sermons to deepen the spiritual life and cultivate the newly awakened missionary spirit. There is definite information on a visit by Reeder to the Weierhof (*q.v.*) in August 1832, when he was given money collected for the Baptist mission. A letter written by Reeder on Sept. 22, 1832, to Jakob Krehbiel (*q.v.*) indicated he was already considering moving to the Weierhof, However, housing difficulties frustrated this plan.

In 1835 the Weierhof congregation decided to extend a formal call to Reeder, and thus acquired its first professional and trained minister, though not without opposition from the conservative element led by Johannes Galle (*q.v.*) of Monzernheim. Reeder lived for a time in Kirchheimbolanden, four miles distant.

In a short time Reeder succeeded in reviving the congregation, so that both the inner and outer growth were soon evident. In two years (1837) the new, larger church was built, modeled externally after a Baptist meetinghouse in Tottenham, England, which Reeder had doubtless seen. Much of the cost of the building was raised by Reeder himself on a tour via Elberfeld to England.

In 1836 Reeder also took charge of the Uffhofen (*q.v.*) congregation near Alzey, which had almost disintegrated. His first sermon there, delivered on March 6, 1836, was printed and distributed in the interest of the Weierhof church. Reeder built a parsonage at Weierhof out of his own funds, including a barn, which he used in farming as a secondary source of income. He is thought to have been the first to use a team of horses at Weierhof. He also set up a sort of boarding home for young Englishmen in his home and engaged a tutor for them. By means of these supplementary sources of income Reeder was probably finally able to support himself without the rather small salary at first offered him by the congregation, returning the money for the education of Michael Löwenberg (*q.v.*), who was to be his successor.

Reeder left Weierhof in 1848 or 1849, apparently on account of the disturbances of the German revolution of that year. It is not known whether or not he accepted another pastorate. At any rate he was still living at Bad Kreuznach in 1853 with his wife, Therese Keetman. He apparently had no children. In 1852 he sold his property in Weierhof to Johannes Kaegy, and in 1853 he gave the Weierhof congregation a gift of 400 guilders. Most of this money came from the sale of his book, *Predigten an Festtagen und bei besonderen Veranlassungen, gehalten von Herm. Reeder, Prediger der Taufgesinnten-Gemeine Weyerhof,* which was printed, perhaps gratis, by Karl Tauchnitz (*q.v.*) at Leipzig in 1842. (*ML* III, 439 f.) P.S.

Reedley, Cal., a city (pop. 5,683) situated in Fresno County, approximately midway between Los Angeles and San Francisco, in the center of the rich San Joaquin Valley. The combined Mennonite membership within the Reedley shopping area is approximately 2,000. The community has Mennonite Brethren, General Conference Mennonites, Evangelical Mennonite Brethren, and a few Krimmer Mennonite Brethren who attend church near Dinuba. The Mennonites have settled all around Reedley, with a lesser concentration across the river to the west. Of the G.C.M. families, 134 live in the country and 219 in the city. Of the M.B. families one third operate farms and business, while two thirds are wage earners or retired.

The M.B. congregation was organized with 11 charter members on June 12, 1905. The present church, dedicated on May 4, 1952, seats 2,200. The membership in 1957 was 1,436. The G.C.M. church was organized on June 10, 1906, with 25 charter members. The membership in 1957 was 593; this represents a slight decline due to the recent organization of the G.C.M. church in Fresno. The E.M.B. church, with 36 members, was dedicated May 26, 1952.

Important Mennonite institutions in Reedley include the Mennonite Brethren Home for the Aged with 52 guests and the Immanuel Bible Academy with an enrollment of 220. Kings View Homes, the West Coast Mennonite Central Committee psychiatric hospital, is located near Reedley.

Reedley is a rich fruit-growing center. Its soil and water conditions grow citrus fruits, plums, peaches, grapes, tomatoes, celery, and nuts, to name only a few products. Up to 4,400 carloads of fruits and vegetables have been shipped in a year from its group of packing houses. Reedley is called the "world's fruit basket." It serves a trading area of approximately 20,000.   A.J.

Arnold C. Ewy, "Grape and Raisin Industry," *Menn. Life* V (October 1950) 4.

Reedley Bible School: see Immanuel Academy.

Reedley (Cal.) Evangelical Mennonite Brethren Church, called Grace Church, was started in 1950 as a conference-subsidized congregation. In 1957 it had 30 members, with C. A. Wall as pastor. Its church building was dedicated in 1952.   H.S.B.

Reedley First Mennonite Church (GCM), a member of the Pacific District Conference, had its beginning in 1903, when Daniel T. Eymann and a few other families came to Reedley through the Santa Fe Immigration Department to look over its possibilities. In June 1906 the Mennonites who had settled in Reedley organized a congregation. In 1908 the first meetinghouse was erected, which was enlarged in 1914 and remodeled in 1944. The membership of 593 consists largely of immigrants from South Germany and from Russia and their descendants. A majority at the present time live in the country and are fruit farmers, although many live in Reedley. Ministers who have served the congregation since its beginning are H. J. Krehbiel, J. M. Regier, J. H. Langenwalter, P. K. Regier, and Aaron J. Epp, the present pastor (1957).   P.K.R.

The First Mennonite Church (1906-1956), Reedley, California. Fiftieth Anniversary Program and a Brief History of the Church.

Reedley Mennonite Brethren Church, located in Reedley, Fresno Co., Cal., in the fertile San Joaquin Valley, a member of the Pacific District, was organized June 12, 1905, under the leadership of D. T. Enns, whose family had come with others from the Middle West to settle in the area. The church of

less than 20 charter members has grown to a membership of 1,436 in 1957, the largest Mennonite congregation in the Western Hemisphere of any branch. In 1907 a building with a seating capacity of approximately 150 was constructed, enlarged in 1910 to seat 300 and in 1919 to 1,200. In 1952 a fireproof structure with 2,000 seats was built. The membership, which is 30 per cent urban and 70 per cent rural, migrated from Kansas, Oklahoma, Nebraska, and Minnesota, approximately 100 coming from Russia. The church is well organized in all phases of church work. It practices footwashing. Pastors who have served the congregation are D. T. Enns, Abr. Buhler, Johann Berg, D. C. Eitzen, G. B. Huebert, J. B. Toews; Dan Friesen was serving as pastor in 1957, with H. R. Wiens as assistant pastor. J.J.T.

Reekalf, Goossen Jansz, a burgomaster of Amsterdam in 1535, was kindly disposed to the Anabaptists in this town, though he was not an Anabaptist himself. In May 1535 he took stern measures to stop the assault of the small group of revolutionary Anabaptists on the city hall in Amsterdam. (Kühler, *Geschiedenis* I, 177, 179.)   vDZ.

Reense (Rhenense, Rhijnse) Veen: see Veenendaal.

Rees, a town (1944 pop. 4,792) on the Lower Rhine, in the duchy of Cleve (*q.v.*), Germany, in which there was formerly a Mennonite congregation. Little is known concerning this church and its history, since the church records were not preserved. Mention is made of a Mennonite congregation in Rees as early as 1570 in a letter by Hans Busschaert. On May 1, 1591, Louijsz Boudewijns, very likely a Flemish immigrant, signed the Concept of Cologne (*q.v.*) for the Rees congregation. Until 1680 it was an independent congregation with preachers, deacons, and elders. On Aug. 6, 1680, Jakob Welsing of Rees married Helene van Voorst, the daughter of the minister of the Emmerich congregation. Later the congregation gave up a measure of its independence, for although Jakob Welsing is named as the preacher of Rees, its baptisms and most of its marriages were solemnized at Emmerich (*q.v.*). The congregation later became independent again for a time. The *Naamlijst* of 1731 names the following as preachers of Rees: Harmen Leendertz from 1707, Pieter Koenders 1727, Isaac Welsin(g)k 1727; the *Naamlijst* of 1743 states that these three preachers had died, Hendrik Welsing being the only preacher of the Rees congregation at that time. He served until 1761-62 and was the last preacher of Rees. The Emmerich records for this period contain no entries concerning Rees. On Feb. 11, 1738, Rees purchased a house and land on Deelstrasse, sold the house, and built a church on the site of the barn (archives of the town of Rees). At that time it was one of the small Mennonite congregations. In 1721 its share of the recruiting fee levied on the six Mennonite congregations of Cleve-Mark was fixed at 10 per cent of the total. In 1752 certain Rees members were again mentioned in the Emmerich church records. The membership continued to decline, and died out in the first half of the 19th century. The church on Deelstrasse stood until the end of 1944.

The Mennonite families in Rees in the 18th century were Rave(ns), Welsing, Korsten, Leenders (Leendertz, q.v.), Braakman, van Zutphen. Some were buried in the Protestant cemetery, and the rest in the Catholic cemetery. W.N., vDZ.

W. Mannhardt, *Die Wehrfreiheit der Altpreussischen Mennoniten* (Marienburg, 1863); the letter by Hans Busschaert was published by Karel Vos in *Bulletin de la Commission Royale d'Histoire de Belgique* LXXXIV (Brussels, 1920) 384 f.; *Naamlijst* 1731, 1743, 1755, 1757, 1759; *Mennonitisches Adressbuch* (Karlsruhe, 1936) 45, 74; *Inv. Arch. Amst.* II, Nos. 2571, 2850; *ML* III, 440.

Reesch: see **Resch.**

Reesema, a Mennonite family in the Netherlands: see **Sieuwertsz van Reesema.**

Reesor: see also **Risser.**

Reesor, Christian (1833-1915), an Old Order Mennonite leader, was born in Markham Twp., York Co., Ont., on April 16, 1833, the son of John Eby Reesor, a Mennonite preacher, and Maria Burkholder. His home was on the site of the present Reesor (Wisler) Mennonite Church. His brothers Simeon and Noah were older; Benjamin and Susanna (Diller) were younger. He farmed directly south of Cedar Grove in Scarboro. His first marriage, in 1856, was to Esther (1838-68), daughter of John Hoover. His second marriage, in 1885, was to Rebecca Miller (1837-1917), of Pennsylvania. He was ordained minister in 1863 and bishop in 1867. In the schism of 1889 in Ontario he allied himself with bishops Abraham Martin of Waterloo and Christian Gayman of Cayuga. This was the beginning of Old Order Mennonites in Ontario. Christian Reesor died Dec. 26, 1915. One of his sons was Thomas Reesor (q.v.). J.C.F.

Reesor, Thomas (1867-1954), Mennonite immigration leader, was born March 18, 1867, on the old homestead in York County, Ont., the fourth child of Christian Reesor (q.v.) and Esther Hoover. In 1891 he married Adeline, the daughter of Joseph and Diana Grove. They had five children. Thomas was ordained to the ministry in 1916. He helped to organize the Non-Resistant Relief Organization of Ontario and assisted conscientious objectors in 1917-18. In 1924 he aided Russian immigrants in finding homes, and in 1925, employed by the Canadian Pacific Railway, he acquired land from the government for a settlement of Russian Mennonites in northern Ontario, west of Cochrane. This point, Reesor Station, flourished, growing to a population of 150 by 1935, but then deteriorated as the urban centers and frontiers expanded. Thomas Reesor died March 20, 1954. He was an Old Order Mennonite of the Markham branch. J.C.F.

Reesor Old Order Mennonite Church, located on the border between York and Ontario counties, Ont., formed a single congregation with the Altona group until 1956. In 1911 its membership was 46. A meetinghouse built in 1857 on the farm of the preacher John E. Reesor became the possession of the Wisler group at the time of the division in 1889.

In 1957 Fred Nighswander was the minister and the combined membership with Altona was 105. E.C.

L. J. Burkholder, *A Brief History of the Mennonites in Ontario* (Markham, 1935) 119 f., 197-200, with picture of meetinghouse; *ML* III, 521.

Reesor United Mennonite Church (GCM), now extinct, located at Cochrane, Ont., was organized in May 1927 by Jacob H. Janzen. The settlement was situated along the Trans-Canada Highway, where Mennonite refugees from Russia in 1925 took up homesteads in the woods. It was organized in the traditional Russian Mennonite manner, with Toews as district man, Rempel as Schulze (q.v.), Penner and Lepp as ministers, and Heidebrecht as schoolteacher. The settlement prospered at first, reaching a membership of 75 in 1932, but declined rapidly during the depression. The congregation was dissolved on Jan. 5, 1948, most of the families having moved away. The congregation was named after Thomas Reesor (q.v.), who aided in establishing it. J.C.T.

Reformed Amish Christian Church (*Christliche*), an independent Mennonite congregation located 4 miles northwest of Berne, Ind., listed in H. P. Krehbiel's *Mennonite Churches of North America* as having 69 members in 1911. It had divided from the Old Order Amish group in Adams County sometime earlier. The ministers then were David Schwartz, Jacob J. Schwartz, and Daniel Mazelin. The group was dissolved in 1952. M.G.

Reformed Authors *against Mennonitism in the Netherlands.* When the war of independence (Eighty Years' War) of the Dutch against Spain broke out in 1568, the power of the Catholic Church in the Netherlands collapsed with the overthrow of Spanish domination. This meant at the same time a rapid rise of Calvinism in this country. The Calvinists did not persecute and execute the Mennonites as the Catholics had done, but the Calvinists were also far from tolerant. They persistently tried to influence the government to restrain the Mennonites, for example, by prohibiting their meetings. Moreover, they published many books of warning against Mennonite teachings and of opposition to their views.

Preceded by such authors as John à Lasco (q.v.) and Martin Micron (q.v.), who attacked Menno Simons, it was Guy de Brez (q.v.) who made a first major attack on the Mennonites with his book *La Racine, source et fondement des Anabaptistes* (1565), of which a Dutch translation appeared in 1570 (reprinted 1589, 1608) with the title *De Wortel, den oorspronck ende het fundament der Wederdooperen.* As his sources de Brez mentions Calvin, à Lasco, and Heinrich Bullinger. His arguments against the Mennonites are as follows: they originated in the heresy of Jan van Leyden (q.v.) and Münster; they have false ideas on baptism, the oath, and the magistracy. In the introduction de Brez argues that the Mennonites (de Brez always calls them *Wederdoopers* or *Anabaptists,* i.e., "rebaptizers") are recognizable by three distinguishing marks: (*a*) they have a remarkable knowledge of the Scriptures ("it seems that they have eaten the Bible"), by which they deceive and seduce the simple people; (b) they teach that their faith is proved by their good conduct, but "can a good life outweigh a bad faith?"; (c) they impress the people by their patient endurance of suffering, torture, and death; but this does not prove that their faith is from God, because it is "not the pain and death that make the martyr, but the cause for which he suffers"; only those who suffer and die for the truth are real martyrs, for "they suffer for the sake of Christ, which the Anabaptists do not do, because they are suffering for the doctrine of Antichrist." The magistrates should not tolerate the Anabaptists, even though to all appearance they are peaceful at the present time. Their history at Münster and Amsterdam and their ungodly doctrines reveal their real face. Menno Simons is a hypocrite; if he and his followers had a chance, they would conduct themselves as outrageously as their predecessors had done.

De Brez's arguments and his bitterly hostile tone became dominant for a large number of polemic writings by Reformed authors, of which only the most outstanding or influential publications are listed here: Caspar Heidanus (q.v.), *Cort en claer Bewys van de h. doop* (1581); Jean Taffin (q.v.), *Onderwysinghe teghen de dwalinghen der Wederdoopers* (1590); Marnix van Sint Aldegonde (q.v.), *Ondersoeckinge . . . der Geestdrijverische Leere . . . der Wederdooperen* (1595); Herman Moded (q.v.), *Grondich bericht van de eerste beghinselen der Wederdoopsche Seckten* (1603); Hermann Faukelius (q.v.), *Babel, dat is verwerringhe der wederdooperen onder malkanderen* (1621); Johannes Cloppenburch (q.v.), *Gangraena Theologiae Anabaptisticae, dat is: Cancker vam de leere der Wederdooperen* (1625; Latin editions 1645, 1656); Dooreslaer (q.v.) and Austro-Sylvius (q.v.), *Grondige en klare Vertooninghe van het onderscheydt in de voornaemste hooftstucken der Christelijcke Religie, tusschen De Gereformeerde ende de Weder-dooperen* (1637, repr. 1649; this work was composed on the instigation of the Reformed Synod of North Holland); Petrus Bontemps (q.v.), *Kort Bewijs van de menighvuldighe doolingen der Wederdoopers ofte Mennisten* (1641, repr. 1653, 1661); Fredericus Spanhemius (F. Spannheim, Sr. q.v.), *Variae disputationes anti-anabaptisticae* (1643-48); Johannes Hoornbeek (q.v.), *Summa controversiarum religionis* (1653, repr. 1697); Christiaan Schotanus (q.v.), *Van de Gronden der Mennisterij* (1671; against van Braght's *Martyrs' Mirror*); Fredericus Spanhemius (F. Spannheim, Jr., q.v.), *Controversiarum de Religione Elenchus historico-theologicus* (1687, repr. 1694 and 1757).

These books were countered by Mennonite authors. Menno Simons wrote against à Lasco and Micron. Outstanding polemics by Mennonite authors were as follows: Jacob Pietersz van der Meulen (q.v.), *Declaratio* (1600); Claes Claesz (q.v.), *Bekentenisse van de voornaemste Stucken des Christelijcken Gheloofs* (against Faukelius; 1624, repr. 1650); Anthoni Jacobsz (q.v.) Roscius, *Babel d.i. Verwerringe der Kinderdooperen onder malcanderen* (against Faukelius; 1626); Joost Hendricksz (q.v.), *Wederlegginge van de Argumenten, voor-*

gestelt door P. Bontemps (1643); E. A. van Dooregeest (q.v.), *Brief aan den Heer F. Spanhemius* (1693, repr. 1693, 1700); Galenus Abrahamsz (q.v.), *Verdediging der Christenen, die Doopsgezinde genaamd worden* (against Spannheim, Jr. 1699); Herman Schijn, *Korte Historie der protestante Christenen, die men Mennoniten of Doopsgezinden noemt* (1711), and other works by Schijn.

In the 18th century a few of these Reformed polemic books were reprinted, but no new polemics by Reformed authors against Mennonitism were published. The Reformed Church had grown more tolerant, though there was still a hidden aversion among the Calvinists against the Mennonites, as is shown by the novels by Wolff and Deken (q.v.), and occasionally by some Reformed writings. Even in the 19th century, as late as 1883, Abraham Kuyper, a Calvinist divine, who in 1886 had separated from the main Dutch Reformed Church to found a separate Reformed church, warned his followers in an introduction to a new edition of Adriaen Haemstede's (q.v.) martyr book against using the wrong martyr book, i.e., that of van Braght.

Occasionally the antiquated and historically wrong perception of the descent of the Mennonites from the Münsterities is still found in modern Reformed books, but better information by such Reformed historians as L. Knappert and J. Lindeboom has cleared away false interpretations. Besides this the growing ecumenical movement has opened the way for better mutual understanding. (See also **Historiography IV:** *Netherlands*.) vDZ.

Reformed Mennonite Church, a body founded in 1812 by John Herr (q.v.), of Strasburg, Lancaster Co., Pa., the son of Francis Herr, who had been a member of the Mennonite Church in West Lampeter Twp., Lancaster Co., but had been expelled for reasons no longer clear, probably about 1798. According to the son John Herr and Daniel Musser, chief historian of the later Reformed Mennonite Church and himself a member, Francis gave as his reason for leaving the church the fact that the Mennonites had departed far from the beliefs and practices of their founder Menno Simons and that the church leaders had become too lax in disciplining those members who had become careless in their religious life and social practices. The small group of sympathizers who had been expelled or had withdrawn from fellowship with the old church with Francis, finding no church with which they felt they could affiliate, and desiring to continue as Mennonites, continued to meet in their various homes for informal religious services consisting of praying, singing, and exhortations in which each took part, though Francis Herr was apparently the chief exhorter. Francis also preached the funeral sermons for members of the group. He always spoke in a sitting position, however, since he felt that only a regular ordained minister could properly speak while standing and preferably before a pulpit. These meetings had not gone beyond the informal state at the time of his death in 1810.

After the death of Francis, the son John Herr, 28 years old at the time, and before this not a member of any church but probably one of the informal group above mentioned, now assumed leadership of the group and continued his father's cause. It was not his intention at this time to start a separate church, but on May 30, 1812, at a meeting in his home, he was selected as pastor and bishop of a new church organization, even though not yet baptized. In this dilemma, the group followed the only course possible, and like the first two members of the original Anabaptist church in Zürich, Switzerland, in 1525, who baptized each other, so too Abraham Landis, who as a former member of the Mennonite Church had already been baptized, but now no longer regarded this baptism as valid, baptized John Herr, who in turn rebaptized Landis. The new group called itself Mennonite, the only "true" Mennonite Church. By others, however, in order to distinguish them from the old church they were sometimes spoken of as "New" Mennonites, occasionally merely as "Herrites" and later as Reformed Mennonites, which latter term finally became the official name of this group.

The new Reformed Mennonite movement began almost as a family affair. In addition to a few of Francis Herr's old associates, John's wife, five sisters, and three brothers-in-law, some of whom had never been members of their father's church, formed the first organized church. John Herr, who possessed some ability as a public speaker and writer, with a rather wide knowledge in church history, now began an aggressive campaign in behalf of his father's cause and his own religious views, and soon had organized a number of small congregations in Lancaster and several of the surrounding counties, as well as in several of the neighboring states. But with his death in 1850 expansion of the movement practically ceased. It is probable that it never reached a baptized membership exceeding 2,500 at any time.

John Herr wrote a number of books, in which he freely expressed his own religious views and especially assailed the old church in strong terms, insisting as his father had done before him that it was a "dead" church, and claiming that the Mennonite Church of that day had departed far from the traditions and practices of the original teachings and practices of Menno Simons. "Back to Menno" might well be called a fitting slogan of the new movement. Herr says, "So far as the evening is from the morning, of darkness from light, are [the Mennonites] separated from our first reformer's doctrine, or the community of Christ." Musser in the same strain says, "Those who departed from the distinctive features of Menno's profession are not fairly entitled to the name Mennonite."

Among the "carnal" practices of Mennonites of that day censured by the Herr following were voting at elections and taking part in political campaigns, foolish talking and jesting, attending county fairs, observing race-ridings, excessive drinking, and especially the failure of many members to observe footwashing and avoidance of excommunicated members and the kiss of peace, and laxity on the part of the elders in admitting members and in disciplining unfaithful members.

The following statement of the doctrines, practices, and attitudes of the Reformed Mennonite Church in 1958 has been supplied by two present bishops of the church in Lancaster County, Pa., Jacob L. Kreider and J. Henry Fisher, both of Lancaster City.

"The Reformed Mennonites are a small body of people who adhere to the doctrines and principles of love taught in the New Testament, and practiced by true Christians in all ages since the church was established on the day of Pentecost. They are not a part or branch of any other organization. They believe that Menno Simons, from whom they derive their name, and with whose teachings they are in full agreement, was not a founder of the original Church of Christ. Likewise, John Herr, who in 1812 helped to organize the group now known as Reformed Mennonites, did not establish a new church. It was under his leadership that a number of persons, who could not at that time find an organization which they felt sincerely carried out the teachings of the New Testament, were drawn together to worship, and subsequently organized into church fellowship.

"The Reformed Mennonites believe the church is the effect of the power of the Holy Spirit, that there could be no true Christian organization without it, and that the continuity and succession of the church is dependent on the presence and guidance of God's Holy Spirit. They do not believe outward forms of religion can save anyone, but that the divine power or principle begotten within the soul by the combined influence of the Father, Son, and Holy Spirit will result in repentance, regeneration, and a hope of salvation, bringing about love, unity, and peace among believers. Without love and unity in the church, the Reformed Mennonites feel it would be impossible to keep the commandments and observe the ordinances given by Christ. They practice adult baptism upon faith and the evidences of a consistent life, believing that baptism is an outward symbol of the spiritual baptism within the heart. Their communion, too, is closed, for to them communion signifies not only fellowship between God and the believer, but also with one another.

"They carry out the plain commandment of laboring with an erring one as explained in Matthew 18:15-17, even to the extent of applying the ban when there is evidence that the spiritual life has been lost, so that the church may be kept pure, and with the hope that such a one may become sensible of his situation, and penitently return to the Lord. The Reformed Mennonites believe this labor is a duty devolving not alone upon the ministry, but also upon each individual member of the church. This labor of love, as well as the original washing of regeneration and the daily need of forgiveness by the Lord, is exemplified for them by the ordinance of feetwashing, which is participated in by all the members of the church. The laity, as well as the ministry, also 'greet one another with the kiss of charity.'

"The Reformed Mennonites are entirely nonresistant and do not sue at law. They ask to be excused from military service; for this reason they do not vote or hold any office in government. They believe Christians are called out from the worldly kingdom into Christ's kingdom in nonconformity to the world. They try to live in simplicity, abhor strife, contention, and worldliness. Their manner of dress is plain, and the women wear a head covering at all times as commanded in I Corinthians 11:1-14. This head covering, as well as their clothing, is of generally uniform design throughout the church, both in the United States and Canada, where their congregations are located.

"They feel they cannot consistently and conscientiously participate in the worship of those who do not live in harmony with the doctrines of Christ, for in so doing, they would be bidding them Godspeed, as taught in II John 10, 11. Because of love for the souls of all mankind, they would not want to encourage anyone in a course at variance with Christ's teachings, but by withdrawal from all divided religious services, quietly but earnestly and firmly testify to their belief that the power of God's Spirit will lead regenerated persons in unity and love and away from the saying of 'Lo here is Christ, and Lo there' manifest by the many professions of Christianity. They believe the Scriptures clearly indicate that there can be but one true Church of Christ in any one place because Christian love draws Christ's followers together into one, as was the case on the day of Pentecost. 'There is one body . . .' (Eph. 4:4-6)."

In methods of church work the Reformed Mennonites confine themselves principally to Sunday morning worship services, having no Sunday schools, young people's work, or mission work, although they cordially invite others to attend their services. Their ministers are selected by vote and serve without pay. They have the threefold ministry of bishops, ministers, and deacons. In 1958 there were five bishops in the United States and two in Canada. The church has remained relatively unchanged in doctrine, practice, forms of dress and worship, and organization since John Herr's death in 1850.

Their children, however, so long as they are not members of the church, are permitted and expected perhaps to live the normal life of the young people of the community, and are in no way limited in their political, social, or cultural contacts with the rest of the community. The radical transformation from this free and easy way of life to the rather rigid regulations of membership no doubt accounts partially for the fact that so few of the children of Reformed Mennonite parentage join the church of their fathers.

The Reformed Mennonites, though very strict and very conservative, live up to their convictions unusually well. In their daily life they are an upright people, honest, industrious, conscientious, law-abiding citizens. Their religious exclusiveness does not extend to their business enterprise except that there are no partnerships with nonmembers. In this field they are frequently unusually successful. Among those in their line of descent, though himself never a member, was the late Milton Snavely Hershey (1857-1945), the Pennsylvania chocolate candy king, whose mother was a member. His grandfather, Abram Snavely, was a bishop of the church 1830-67. In the professions open to them, such as medicine and dentistry, they also succeed above the average.

The membership of the Reformed Mennonites has manifested a steady decline apparently throughout the past fifty years at least and probably longer. The Census of 1906 reported in the United States 2,079 members, that of 1936 only 1,044; in 1958 there were only 616. In 1910 there were 34 congregations with 29 meetinghouses and 1,655 members according to the Census, but in 1958 there were only 19 congregations with 616 members. The United States Census of 1890 reports 34 congregations with 1,655 members.

The 1948 distribution of Reformed Mennonite congregations was as follows: United States, 24 meeting places with 733 members; Canada, 6 congregations with 217 members, a total of 950 members. In 1958 there were only 616 members in the United States and 211 in Canada. Following is a list of congregations in 1958, with (where known) year of founding, year of building of first meetinghouse, and membership: Pennsylvania, 10 with 309, in Lancaster County 5 meeting places (all within 20 miles of Lancaster City) with a total of 221 members as follows: Landisville (1869), Lancaster (1864), Longenecker's (1812), New Danville (1830), Shirk's near Brownstown (1889) (including former Denver and Steinmetz); other Pennsylvania locations—Hershey's near Hershey, Dauphin Co. (1833) 9, Worcester near Lansdale, Montgomery Co. (1864, meetinghouse 1890) 15, Falling Spring near Chambersburg, Franklin Co. (1841, 1847) 12, Middlesex near Carlisle, Cumberland Co. (1870) 28 (including former Plainfield, 1882 and former Winding Mill, 1870); Waynesboro, Franklin Co. (1827 beginning at Ringgold, Md., 1876 at Waynesboro) 24; Ohio, 5 with 150 as follows: Lauber Hill near Archbold, Fulton Co. (1852) 70; Bluffton, Allen Co. (1876) 47; Marshallville, Wayne Co. (1820, 1860) 24; Medway, Clark Co. (1872, now sold) 3; Whitehouse, Lucas Co. (1852) 6; Indiana, 1 at Valparaiso (1860) 24; Michigan, 1 at Shelby, Oceana Co. (1868) 52; Illinois, 1 at Sterling (1820, 1868) 52; New York, 1 at Williamsville, Erie Co. (1834) 29. In Canada there were 6 congregations with 211 members, all in Ontario as follows: Humberstone (1825) 44 and Stevensville (1835) 41, both in Welland County, Rainham near Selkirk in Haldimand Co. (1825) 5, Hostetler's near New Hamburg (1844) 52, and Kingwood near Wellesley (1850) 27, both in Waterloo County, and Amulree near Stratford in Perth County (1850) 42. The group operates two homes for the aged, known as Lancaster Church Home (in Lancaster City) and Waynesboro Church Home (in Waynesboro). The only Reformed Mennonite church paper ever published was *Good Tidings,* published at Lancaster, Pa., July 1922 to July 1932. It is a 32-page, 13½ x 9½ inch quarterly, edited by Jacob Kreider. The address of the church is 734 S. West End Ave., Lancaster, Pa.   C.H.S., H.S.B.

John Herr, *The True and Blessed Way* (Harrisburg, 1816); idem, *Erläuterungs Spiegel* (Lancaster, 1827); John Herr, *Complete Works* (520 pp.) (Buffalo, 1890); Daniel Musser, *The Reformed Mennonite Church, Its Rise and Progress with Its Principles and Doctrines* (Lancaster, 1873); John F. Funk, *The Mennonite Church and Her Accusers* (Elkhart, 1878); J. S. Hartzler and Daniel Kauffman, *Mennonite Church History* (Scottdale, 1905); M. G. Weaver, *The Mennonites of Lancaster Conference* (Scottdale, 1931); I. D. Rupp, *An Original History of All the Religious Denominations in the United*

States (Philadelphia, 1844) contains a section (pp. 502-10) "The Reformed Mennonite Society," which had "the sanction of the Rev. John Herr of Strasburg, a Bishop of this Society"; Wilmer J. Eshleman, "History of the Reformed Mennonite Church" in *Papers read before the Lancaster County Historical Society* XLIX (1945) 85-117, containing also a complete list of the 47 bishops and ministers ordained 1812-1940 in the Lancaster County Reformed Mennonite Church.

Reformer und Agriculturist und Allgemeiner Neuigkeits-Berichter, Der,

a weekly (first and for a short time issued as a daily) local newspaper (16 x 22 in., 4 pp.) of general interest, published from July 4, 1867, to at least 1879 in German by John G. Stauffer, a Mennonite printer and publisher living at Milford Square in Bucks County, Pa., reported here only because it was published by a Mennonite (GCM) and had a considerable circulation among Mennonites in Eastern Pennsylvania. It is listed in a brief report in *Zur Heimath* for Oct. 1, 1879, in an anonymous article, "Ein flüchtiger Blick auf die mennonitische Literatur der Gegenwart." It was merged with *Patriot und Reformer* in 1878 or 1879, and continued publication by John G. Stauffer to October 1886, by U. S. Stauffer and A. B. Shelly for one further year, by Daniel Stauffer 1887-1905, and by David M. George to July 14, 1910. *Der Reformer und Pennsylvania Advertiser* was a weekly, published in English and German, edited by John G. Stauffer and A. B. Shelly, and published by the Mennonitischer Druckverein (*q.v.*), which appeared 1867-71(?). *Der Bucks County Patriot*, still another weekly paper, also apparently edited by John G. Stauffer, appeared under this name July 4, 1867-77, then as *Der Bucks County Patriot und Reformer und Agriculturist* 1878-80, as *Der Bucks County Patriot* May 6, 1880-81, and again as *Der Patriot und Reformer* 1881-1910. The above listing of titles and dates may not be wholly accurate, as May E. Olson indicates, who furnished much of the information. For an evaluation of Stauffer's newspapers, see Ralph Wood's article "Journalism among the Pennsylvania Germans" in *The Pennsylvania Germans* (Princeton, 1942), especially pp. 148-50.   H.S.B.

Refugee Camps

(*Flüchtlingslager,* later called Mennonite Homes, *Mennonitenheime*), shelters for the remnants of Mennonite refugees from Russia, located at Mölln, Wandsbeck, and Altona on the Elbe, established in 1929. About 16,000 Mennonites and other Russians of German descent at that time left their homes under terrible pressure of the Soviet government to go to Moscow and from there to Canada and the United States. The refugees who managed to escape at all made their way via Germany. Here they were temporarily lodged in refugee camps at Hammerstein, 4,000 persons; Prenslau, 1,500 persons; and Mölln. They were cared for in the best possible manner under the direction of the German government committee in charge of aid to Germans escaping from Russia and the German relief committee Brüder in Not (*q.v.*). They enjoyed frequent visits by German Mennonite preachers. Special services were rendered by Mayor and Mrs. Wolff in Mölln, Pastor Braun, and B. H. Unruh. In April 1930 the Prenslau camp was dissolved, and at the end of the year the Hammerstein camp also.

The remaining refugees stayed in Mölln. On Feb. 1, 1931, acting on a resolution passed by the Mennonite World Relief Conference, the refugee camp was turned into a Mennonite home. After eighteen months, when the lease on the building at Mölln expired, the home was moved to Wandsbeck; later another building was rented in Altona, which sheltered 50 persons. Nearly all the inmates of the Altona home soon left for America. The few who remained were provided for elsewhere.

On May 1, 1936, the Mennonite Home was closed, terminating an important phase of the work of Brüder in Not. (*Menn. Bl.,* 1930, 7; 1931, 5, 7, 14, 41; 1932, 91; 1934, 27; *ML* III, 106.)   NEFF.

Refugee Relief: see **Relief Work.**

Regeer: see **Regier.**

Regehr family: see **Regier.**

Regehr, Cornelius: see **Regier.**

Regehr, Jakob, elder of the Alexandertal Mennonite Church, Samara, Russia, was born at Heubuden, West Prussia, in 1841 and moved to Mariental, Alexandertal settlement, where he resided the rest of his life. He was elected minister in 1896 and elder in 1897, succeeding Johann Wiebe. In 1918 he was succeeded by his son, Eduard Regehr, who was exiled under the Communist government. (See also **Alexandertal.**)   C.K.

Friesen, *Brüderschaft,* 720; H. Dirks, *Statistik* (1905) 26.

Regehr, Johann, elder of the Romanovka Mennonite Church (*q.v.*), Aulie-Ata, Central Asia, was elected minister in 1878 and elder in 1884, in which office he succeeded A. Peters who had led the group from the Molotschna settlement to Central Asia. Little else is known about his life and work. C.K.

H. Dirks, *Statistik* (1905) 36; Friesen, *Brüderschaft,* 720.

Regel, Anna: see **Regel, Georg.**

Regel, Georg (Jörg) (d. 1547), the scion of an old patrician family of Donauwörth, Bavaria, Germany, became a citizen of Augsburg by his first marriage. In 1510 he married as his second wife Anna Manlich(in). In 1517-25 he lived on his estate Lichtenberg on the Lech. Here he read the Gospels to the peasants and took communion in both forms. The dukes of Bavaria, from whom he had acquired the estate, then had him and his wife arrested and imposed a heavy fine upon them; then they returned to Augsburg. Georg carried on an active correspondence with Zwingli (*q.v.*) in 1527-28.

Ludwig Haetzer (*q.v.*) had been a guest in the Regel home in 1524. Georg Regel assisted Hans Denk (*q.v.*) in 1525-26 in finding a position as a teacher of Latin and Greek at Augsburg. Hans Hut (*q.v.*) probably baptized Georg and Anna and their two maids Apollonia and Dorothea in the spring of 1526. Anna, however, recanted in October, and Georg in the following February. But then they were "driven back into the old track," so that they were compelled to flee from Augsburg at the time of the arrests at Easter in 1528. They fled to Constance in May 1528. By the time Ludwig Haetzer arrived there, between Nov. 20 and Nov. 28, the Regels had no doubt already left Constance.

In the autumn of 1528 Ludwig Haetzer was tried in court in Constance. The charge was that "he had a wife here, whose name was Apollonia, and in addition he also married the wife of Jörg Regel of Augsburg, and took the liberty of persuading her and others that she might take him, since Jörg Regel . . . was not a brother in Anabaptism. This Haetzer has also written much about the Trinity and other articles of the Christian faith, but contrary to the Holy Scriptures; hence these unworthy books were done away with." The report says that when the sentence of death was read to Haetzer he said he was satisfied with it, and commended his father and his wife Apollonia to the mayor and the magistrate. Haetzer was executed on Feb. 4, 1529, and in the same year the Regels were readmitted to Augsburg upon recanting and doing penance. The Hutterite chronicles do not mention any guilt; Christian Neff speaks only of "unproved accusations," and Fritz Blanke doubts the correctness of the charge. Others, however, have given sharper verdicts. Goeters says, "It was not only justice that was satisfied in this suit. The accusers were intent on eliminating the man whom they wanted removed as a teacher of heresy. Haetzer's moral lapse —to be sure, at an opportune moment—furnished the formal reason, but the ends pursued extended further. The lawsuit of Constance . . . is one of a series of major actions in the attempt to subdue South German Anabaptism." The charge, for example, was issued from Augsburg; Haetzer was merely transiently in Constance when he was arrested.

Later the Regels definitely turned their interests to spiritualism (q.v.). Georg aided his fellow countryman Sebastian Franck (q.v.) especially by means of a loan, and Anna attached herself to Kaspar Schwenckfeld (q.v.). In 1532-33 Georg was an intermediary in settling the friction between Leo Jud and Heinrich Bullinger (q.v.). Finally, in 1538, Georg was again admitted to patrician society. He died childless in 1547; his will, made in 1542, bequeathed his wealth for the establishment of a charitable foundation. HEGE, E.T., E.C.

Fritz Blanke, "Beobachtungen zum ältesten Täuferbekenntnis," Archiv für Reformationsgesch. XXXVII (1940) 245, note 1; Corpus Schwenckfeldianorum VIII (1927) 432 ff.; J. F. Gerhard Goeters, Ludwig Haetzer (Gütersloh, 1957); Alfred Hegler, Beiträge zur Geschichte der Mystik in der Reformationszeit, in Archiv f. Reformationsgesch., supplement vol. I (Berlin, 1906) 102, 120, 121, 169, 186; W. Hans Herwarth von Bittenfeld, "Zur Geschlechtskunde der Regel von Altisheim," Ztscht des Historischen Vereins fur Schwaben und Neuburg XVIII (1891) 93-100; TA Bayern I, 454-67; Wilhelm Renn, Cronica newer geschichten, ed. Friedrich Roth (Die Chroniken der Deutschen Städte XXV) 1896, 57 ff.; Friedrich Roth, Augsburgs Reformationsgeschichte I (1517-1530) (Munich, 1901); Eberhard Teufel, "Täufertum und Quäkertum im Lichte der neueren Forschung," Theologische Rundschau, n.s. XIV (1942) 148-50; ML III, 444 f.

Regensburg, the capital (1952 pop. 80,000) of the Oberpfalz, Bavaria, Germany, formerly an imperial city, was in the earliest time of the Reformation the seat of an Anabaptist congregation. It may have been founded in the fall of 1527 (by Ludwig Haetzer, q.v.), when several persons were baptized. In that year several Anabaptist leaders stopped here en route to other places—Oswald Glait (q.v.), Hans Schlaffer (q.v.), Wolfgang Brandhuber (q.v.), and probably also Hans Hut (q.v.). Hut is named in a warning about the Anabaptists sent to Regensburg by the Nürnberg city council on March 18, 1527. At the end of the year the congregation was discovered by the authorities. Some of its members, mostly Austrian Anabaptists, including Leonhard Freisleben (see **Eleutherobios**), were imprisoned and crossexamined on Nov. 15, then expelled from the city. A worse fate befell the Augsburg schoolteacher Augustin Würzlburger (q.v.). He was captured on May 21, 1528, and executed on Oct. 10 of that year; he is the only Anabaptist who died as a martyr in Regensburg.

Until 1534 there is no further mention of Anabaptists in the city. It was then reported that hundreds of Anabaptists were on their way to Linz (q.v.) or to Moravia (q.v.) by way of the Danube. Daily large numbers passed through the cities on the Danube. The cathedral preacher Laurentius Hochwarth boasted it was due to his preaching that Regensburg was saved from the fate of Münster (q.v.). In a letter of June 30, 1534, Luther warned the city council about the Anabaptists. Scarcely a year later (June 11, 1535) the council issued a severe mandate against them, and in 1537 took active steps. Several were banned from the city, but upon recantation readmitted. Nothing is heard of enforcing the imperial mandates. This may have led to an increase in the number of Anabaptists in the city. In 1539 the council estimated their number at several hundred. Twenty persons were summoned before the court; most of them were expelled, but those who recanted remained in the city. This lenience evoked an ungracious letter from King Ferdinand demanding severe punishment for the Anabaptists. It was not heeded. Captured leaders were expelled from the city.

Slowly the movement receded. In the 16th century it is heard of only occasionally, and in the 17th not at all.

Since the beginning of the 19th century there has been a Mennonite congregation with Regensburg as its meeting place. It was formed by families from Alsace and Lorraine who leased the larger farms in the vicinity of Regensburg; most of the members are still farmers. The first preacher was Jakob Ackermann (1785-1841), who had a large farm in lease at Köfering near Regensburg. The congregation was reduced in size by emigration to America, and even more by the transfer of members to the Lutheran Church. It has at present (1957) a membership of 128 baptized members; the families are scattered over 33 villages. Meetings were held in rotation in the homes of the members until 1893, when they rented the use of the Bruderhaus church in Regensburg. Services are held twice a month.

The Regensburg congregation formerly belonged to the Amish (q.v.) branch, but most of the distinguishing characteristics have been dropped, although footwashing (q.v.) was practiced until 1908.

On July 8, 1908, some changes were made in the organization. The congregation decided to cooperate with those at Munich (*q.v.*) and Eichstock (*q.v.*) in engaging a minister; they chose Emanuel Landes (b. 1879 at Kradolf, Switzerland, now retired), who served at Munich and Eichstock 1905-54 and in Regensburg 1908-54. On the above date (1908) they joined the Vereinigung (*q.v.*), and replaced the Waldeck Catechism (*q.v.*) and the Dordrecht Confession (*q.v.*) with the *Christliches Lehrbüchlein*, published by the Committee of Elders (see **Aeltestenrat**) of the Gemeindeverband (*q.v.*). Since Jan. 1, 1908, the congregation has kept a church record. Since 1955 lay ministers have again been serving the congregation. In 1957 they were Albert Schantz, Ludwig Krehbill, Ernst Horsch, and Heinrich Funck.　　　　　　　　　　E.L., E.C.

Gerhard Hein, "Quellen zur Geschichte der Täufer in Bayern," *Gesch.-Bl.*, 1953, 54-56; Hermann Nestler, *Die Wiedertäuferbewegung in Regensburg* (Regensburg, 1926); *TA Bayern* I, 1-86; Leonhard Theobald, *Die Reformationsgeschichte der Reichsstadt Regensburg* (Munich, 1936) 176-87, 231-37; Eberhard Teufel, "Täufertum und Quäkertum im Lichte der neueren Forschung," *Theol. Rundschau*, 1942, 151-53; Wiswedel, *Bilder* II, 87-97; *Gem.-Kal.* 1957, 45 f.; *ML* III, 443 f.

Regensburger Ordnung *(Constitutio)*, a set of regulations passed at Regensburg, Bavaria, Germany, on July 7, 1524, at a conference of twelve South German Catholic bishops or their representatives, with Cardinal legate Campeggi as chairman, in the presence of Archduke Ferdinand (see **Ferdinand I**) as well as the dukes of Bavaria. The rulers of the South German states countered the stormy progress of the Reformation in Middle and South Germany by a staunch adherence to Catholicism. It was especially the Wittelsbach family in Bavaria (*q.v.*) who organized a union of the South German princes in 1523 to present a united front against the ecclesiastical innovations. Cardinal Campeggi was successful in eliminating the greatest obstacle, viz., the jealousy between the Hapsburgs and the Wittelsbachs. He gathered the South German estates about him at Regensburg in June 1524, and there in July the principles were laid down for the procedure in blocking the progress of the Reformation. The estates obligated themselves to carry out the Edict of Worms of 1521 and to oppose all changes in matters of faith and worship in their provinces, suppress the writings of the innovators, etc. The object of the *Constitutio* was, first of all, to bring about a reformation in the life of the clergy; for, as Campeggi said, the disorderly conduct of the clergy played no small part in the rise of heresies. It was decided to institute commissions composed of clergymen and laymen to investigate the life of the parishes and to remove abuses. It was of great significance for the Catholic Church in South Germany.

In Austria (*q.v.*), especially in Lower Austria, the spread of the Anabaptists in 1528 was the immediate occasion for the passing of regulations similar to the *Regensburger Ordnung* there. On Jan. 16, 1528, King Ferdinand issued to all bishops, prelates, etc., who had authority in spiritual matters a mandate (*q.v.*) to this effect, which was to be read from the pulpits at specified times. A commission was organized to visit all parishes in Upper Austria; it reported to the king on June 27, 1528.

　　　　　　　　　　　　　　LOSERTH, HEGE.

Josef Jäkel, "Zur Geschichte der Wiedertäufer in Oberösterreich und speziell in Freistadt," in *47. Bericht des Museums Franciscus-Carolinus* (Linz, 1889) 25, 26, 71 f.; Walter Friedensburg, "Der Regensburger Convent von 1524," *Historische Aufsätze dem Andenken an Georg Waitz gewidmet* (Hannover, 1886) 502-39; *ML* III, 444 f.

Regewart (Regenwort), Hermann, a Catholic priest of Warendorf (*q.v.*) in Westphalia, Germany, who was converted by the Anabaptist elder Hendrik van Maeren (*q.v.*) and joined the Anabaptists in early 1534. On Feb. 17 of this year Regewart and some 30 other Anabaptists, all converted by van Maeren, accompanied him to Münster (*q.v.*). Here Regewart became a follower of Jan van Leyden (*q.v.*), who sent him with seven others to Coesfeld, Westphalia, as an emissary of his policy. Upon arrival at Coesfeld they were all arrested; Regewart was executed there in January 1535. (Mellink, *Wederdopers*, 24, 27, 48.)　　　　　　　　　　vDZ.

Regier (Regehr, Regeer), a widespread Mennonite family found in West Prussia, Germany (105 Regiers and 85 Mennonite Regehrs in the Vistula Delta in 1936), Russia, and North America. The spelling was often interchangeable in earlier times, Regehr being probably the older form. There were two lines in West Prussia, one going back to Peter Regier (b. 1669) and one to Cornelius Regier (b. 1743). The Regiers were found in large numbers in the Heubuden congregation, and furnished a large number of ministers and elders here and elsewhere. Cornelius Regier (1743-94), elder at Heubuden from 1771, was an outstanding leader; he died May 30, 1794, in the Chortitza Mennonite settlement, Ukraine, whither he had been called to assist in solving the serious church problems which had arisen. Other Regiers who served the church were Peter Regier (*q.v.*), a brother of Cornelius; Abraham Regier (*q.v.*; 1774-1851), a son of Cornelius, Heubuden elder 1804-51; Peter Regier (*q.v.;* 1776-1814), a brother of Abraham, elder 1809-14; Peter Regier (*q.v.;* 1798-1856), a son of Abraham, elder of the Gross-Werder congregation 1833-56. Three of the four sons of the above Peter Regier (d. 1856) were active in the ministry of the Gross-Werder congregation—Peter Regier (1825-97), elder at Fürstenwerder, Abraham Regier (1831-1909), elder at Tiegenhagen 1885-1909, Cornelius Regier (1835-1916), preacher at Tiegenhagen.

A Peter Regier (1851-1925) of Rückenau, elder of the Rosenort congregation from 1888, emigrated to the Rosthern, Sask., community, in 1893, where he founded and became the first elder of the Rosenort congregation there, dying at Tiefengrund in 1925. (David Toews became his assistant elder in 1913.) His son Johannes Regier became assistant elder to David Toews at Rosenort in 1929, then moved to British Columbia, where he has served as elder of the Bethel congregation at Aldergrove since 1947. Bernhard Regier (1810-92), a preacher in the Heubuden congregation from 1838, left his homeland in 1880 because of his strong convictions for nonresistance and settled in Newton, Kan., where he joined in founding the First Mennonite Church (GCM) and served as preacher until his death. A son of his, Bernhard Regier (1855-1940), served as minister of the First Mennonite Church of Newton 1903-40, and a nephew of his, Jacob W. Regier, served as pastor of the Zion Mennonite Church at Elbing 1919-39. Ernst Regehr was chosen elder of the Rosenort congregation in West Prussia in 1934, emigrated to Uruguay in 1948, and has been elder of the El Ombu congregation there since then, and moderator of the Uruguay Mennonite Conference. In the United States and Canada there are six Regehrs and two Regiers serving as ministers in the M.B. Church, and nine Regehrs and two Regehrs as ministers in the G.C.M. Church. J. M. Regier (1885-) served pastorates in Reedley, Cal., and Hillsboro, Kan., while P. K. Regier (1891-) has been executive secretary of the G.C.M. Church since 1952. A. J. Regier (1884-1947) was president of Freeman Junior College 1916-27, and professor at Bethel College 1927-46; D. A. Regier (1887-1956) was long a minister in the E.M.B. Church at Mountain Lake, Minn., and a leader in the E.M.B. Conference; C. C. Regier (1884-1950) was a professor of history, serving at Bethel College and then at a series of other colleges. (*ML* III, **441-43; 445-50.**)   O.R., H.S.B.

Regier, Abraham (1774-1851), the son of elder Cornelius Regier (*q.v.*), was born Feb. 2, 1774. In 1794, upon his father's death, he took over the farm in Heubuden (Gurken). He was chosen as preacher in 1800, and as elder in 1804 for the Heubuden congregation. The first decade of his eldership was a very trying period for the West Prussian congregations.

Abraham Regier maintained conscientious church discipline. He was in close connection with the Gross-Werder congregation. In 1809 Abraham Regier ordained Jacob Kröker as elder of the Elbing-Ellerwald congregation and his brother Peter Regier (*q.v.*) as elder of the Gross-Werder congregation. When his brother died, he conducted a vote for a replacement in the three "quarters" of the Gross-Werder congregation (Ladekopp, *q.v.*; Tiegenhagen, *q.v.*; and Rosenort, *q.v.*). The vote resulted in a tie; the lot, used to break the tie, fell on Abraham Wiebe (who later married a daughter of elder Peter Regier, d. 1814). In 1833 an election for elder occurred to replace Abraham Wiebe. This was conducted at Rosenort, and also resulted in a tie. The lot fell on his son Peter Regier (*q.v.*), who, however, refused to assume the office of elder for the large district. Abraham Regier died on Aug. 8, 1851, at Heubuden. The congregation erected a tombstone.

Other ministers who served with Abraham Regier were Johann Regier of Heubuden (1777-1830), Gerhard Regier of Tralau 1831-d. 59, Cornelius Regier (*q.v.*) of Tralau, and Bernhard Regier (*q.v.*) of Sandhof. The relationship of these Regiers has not been established. In the branch of Cornelius and Abraham Regier was the Abraham Regier of Klein-Lichtenau (1877-1909), a preacher in the Heubuden congregation. (*ML* III, 446 f.)   O.R.

Regier, Bernhard (1810-92), a Mennonite minister of West Prussia and Kansas, was born at Sandhof near Marienburg in West Prussia, Germany, in 1810. He learned to read at home, and by the age of ten had read the entire Bible three times (the Bible and the hymnal were usually the only books in the homes). He received his education in a private Mennonite school in Rodlofferhuben, where the gifted Wilhelm Lange (*q.v.*) was teaching. The school was later transferred to Bröskerfelde (*q.v.*). In 1839 he was chosen to the ministry in his home congregation, and served without salary until the age of seventy.

He took an active part in the Danzig Missionary Association (founded 1829). The monthly meetings were held in Mennonite homes; the annual missionary conference, in which Lutherans and Reformed also took part, met in a roomy granary of a member of the Association. He was also interested in the temperance movement.

Bernhard Regier gathered in Germany the material for the Regier family history. When the German Mennonites lost their nonresistant privileges he emigrated to Newton, Kan., in 1880, and took part in the establishment of the first Mennonite (GCM) church in Newton, as well as of Bethel College. He died at the age of 82 after a ministry of 54 years. (*ML* III, 449.)   C.H.R.

Regier, Cornelius (1743-94), a Mennonite elder, born in Rosenort (*q.v.*), West Prussia, Germany, later living in Altmünsterberg and Heubuden (Gurken), became a teacher in 1765, succeeded his father-in-law Gerhard van Bergen (1704-71) as elder of the Heubuden (*q.v.*) congregation. Concerning his inner life there is information in his correspondence with Isaak van Dühren (*q.v.*), the minister of the Danzig Frisian Mennonite congregation.

According to the church record, Cornelius Regier was loved by the Heubuden congregation; throughout his life his influence was conciliatory. By preaching in various churches he sought to bridge over the differences between the Frisian (*q.v.*) and the Flemish (*q.v.*) Mennonites. He maintained close contact with the Danzig (*q.v.*) congregation. The Danzig church archives show that his advice was frequently asked in church matters. His close connection with the Danzig Flemish congregation is also indicated by the fact that in 1780 he ordained Peter Epp (*q.v.*) as elder and in 1790 Jacob de Veer. His sermons as a guest preacher were no doubt widely announced and must certainly have strengthened the bonds between the elders of the various congregations.

Cornelius Regier was an elder in an age filled with disturbance for West Prussia. During his eldership the Werder (*q.v.*) was transferred from Poland (*q.v.*) to Prussia (*q.v.*) (1772). (See **Regier, Peter.**) For their exemption from the bearing of arms (see **Nonresistance**) the Mennonites had to pay 5,000 talers annually from June 1, 1773, for the military training school at Culm (*q.v.*). A conference (1775) presented a petition to the King in Berlin for the confirmation of the privileges (*q.v.*) acquired from the rulers of Poland and for the remission of fees to the local Catholic and Protestant congregations. In 1788 the "Wöllner" religious edict was passed which made a distinction between the principal creeds and the remaining religious groups, the Mennonites being counted with the latter, which, though tolerated, were subject to restrictions. Further restrictions were caused by the edict of July 30, 1789, which decreed that the Mennonite landowners must pay certain fees to the Catholic and Protestant clergy, and limited their acquisition of land. Under such conditions Mennonite emigration to Russia set in (q.v.). For the families of the Gross-Werder and the congregation of Danzig and Elbing-Ellerwald (see **Elbing**), 152 families with 919 persons, Cornelius Regier preached the farewell sermon in the Rosenort Mennonite Church.

The young Russian congregations had serious difficulty in regulating their church life, and urgently wanted an elder from West Prussia to come to help them. Cornelius Regier was chosen for the task. (Peter Epp, who was first chosen, died during his preparations for the journey.) On March 14, 1794, he and Cornelius Warkentin, a minister of Rosenort, began the perilous journey to Russia, and on April 29 arrived at Chortitza (q.v.). Cornelius Regier at once began his work of unification. After three weeks, during which he preached eight times, he succeeded in restoring peace. Then a fatal illness, probably typhus, struck Regier. Before he died he ordained Warkentin as elder, and asked him to preach a simple funeral sermon for him on Rom. 14:7, 8. His funeral was attended by Baron von Brackel, the director of the Chortitza settlement. A monument was erected 100 years later. (*ML* III, 445 f.)　　　　　　　　　　　　　　　　**O.R.**

Regier, Heinrich H. (1855-1934), a Mennonite (GCM) elder, was born Sept. 12, 1855, at Alexanderkrone in the Molotschna Mennonite settlement, South Russia. During the migration of the Mennonites from Russia to America he settled in Mountain Lake, Minn. He attended the Baptist Theological Seminary at Rochester, N.Y. In 1888 he became the first minister of the Bethel Mennonite Church (q.v.), and elder on Nov. 18, 1890. He married Maria Görtzen March 30, 1884. On Jan. 1, 1927, he resigned from his office and died Jan. 4, 1934. He baptized 157 candidates, ordained 12 elders, and served on the aid committee of the General Conference for many years.　　　　**C.K.**

"Ältester Heinrich H. Regier," *Bundesbote-Kalender,* 1935, p. 29; J. John Friesen, "Early Mountain Lake Churches," *Menn. Life* XI (July 1956) 133-37.

Regier, John S. (1879-1918), an evangelist and Bible lecturer of the Mennonite Brethren Church, was born in the village of Klippenfeld in the Molotschna Mennonite settlement in South Russia on March 6, 1879, the oldest of the four children of John J. and Maria Schellenberg Regier. In the summer of 1879 the family emigrated to America, first settling in Boone County, Neb., and a few years later in York County, Neb., where the father became the first elder of the Henderson M.B. Church and where the children grew up. Regier married Anna Wall on June 7, 1900. To them seven children were born.

They established their home first at Henderson. Later they lived at Reedley, Cal., Hillsboro, Kan., and again returned to Henderson. After his conversion Regier was received into the M.B. Church by baptism about 1896. At an early age he entered the Christian ministry and in 1901-18 he was very active as a traveling evangelist and Bible lecturer among the M.B. churches. He was especially qualified for Biblical exposition. Tabor College frequently called him to lecture at its annual Bible conferences. He died on Aug. 22, 1918, and was buried in the local M.B. cemetery.　　　　　　**J.H.L.**

Regier, Peter, of Tralau (Feld), West Prussia, Germany, a brother of Cornelius Regier (q.v.), was at the same time as he a minister (from c1764) in the Heubuden Mennonite Church. His home was the scene of a meeting of the ministers of all the Mennonite congregations in West Prussia (Flemish and Frisian) held concerning participation in the ceremony of obeisance for Frederick the Great (q.v.) on Sept. 27, 1722, in Marienburg, when a petition for the free exercise of religion and release from military service was presented to the King. From this year the two branches met together in an annual conference, usually held at Heubuden. In 1775 the Conference of East and West Prussian Mennonite Churches (q.v.) delegated elder Heinrich Donner (q.v.), of Orlofferfelde, and Peter Regier to present to the King at Berlin a petition for the confirmation of the privileges and the remission of fees. Like his brother, Peter Regier's work was conciliatory in an attempt to heal the breach between the Frisians (q.v.) and the Flemish (q.v.). In 1774 he was censured by many in his Flemish congregation for preaching a guest sermon in a Frisian congregation. (*ML* III, 446.)　　　　　　**O.R.**

Regier, Peter (1776-1814), an elder of the Grosswerder Mennonite Church, West Prussia, Germany, was born at Altmünsterberg, West Prussia, on March 10, 1776, the second and youngest son of elder Cornelius Regier (q.v.). He married a daughter of Gerhard Wiebe (q.v.) of Ellerwald and settled at Sparrau in the area of the Elbing-Ellerwald (q.v.) congregation. In 1798 his congregation chose him as minister, but he declined the office, because he was planning to move to the Grosswerder. In 1799 he moved to Siebenhuben and was chosen as minister by the Ladekopp congregation. In 1809 he was consecrated as elder by his brother Abraham Regier in the Orlofferfelde (q.v.) church. The time of his service there was a difficult period. In 1811 he and Johann Donner (q.v.), of Orlofferfelde, and Cornelius Wiens, the treasurer, journeyed to Marienwerder (q.v.) to present to Frederick William III (q.v.) a gift of 10,000 talers for use for the state. At a conference meeting in Marienburg (q.v.) in 1813 Donner and Regier were delegated to go to Königsberg (q.v.) to request exemption from military service for the Mennonites. An account of his mission is found in Donner's autobiography. On their return they had to wade to their knees through icy water caused by a flood. Regier became ill in consequence. His trouble was heightened by the lack of understanding and appreciation for their work; he and Donner were violently opposed by their members. On Feb. 26, 1814, at the age of 37 years, he died, and was buried at Orloff (*q.v.*), near his home.

Peter Regier served as elder only six years. He was the last elder serving the entire Grosswerder group of congregations—Rosenort, Ladekopp, Fürstenwerder, and Tiegenhagen. In 1809 he agreed to the appointment of an elder for Fürstenwerder (*q.v.*). *ML* III, 447.) O.R.

Regier, Peter (1798-1856), an elder of the Grosswerder Mennonite congregation, was born Jan. 31, 1798, at Heubuden, West Prussia, Germany, the son of Abraham Regier, elder at Heubuden. He was chosen as preacher in 1825, and as elder in 1833 (by lot; he had received 104 votes and Jakob Wiebe of Ladekopp 102) by the Grosswerder congregation. He, however, declined to carry the office alone, on the ground that each of the component congregations was entitled to an elder of its own, and that his father and Isaac Schulz, co-elders of the large district, had found the work too difficult. The Ladekopp congregation then chose Jacob Wiebe as elder, whereas the Rosenort congregation continued to be served by the elder of Tiegenhagen until 1857.

Peter Regier was active in the congregations. He conducted elections for elder at Fürstenwerder (1841), Ellerwald (1846), Heubuden (1852, to replace his father, who died in 1851), and Ladekopp (1853). In 1853 he officiated at an election for minister in Ladekopp, where his brother-in-law Peter Regier, of Mierau, was chosen. He died at Tiegenhagen on March 9, 1856.

All four of Peter Regier's sons served in the ministry in the Grosswerder congregations. (1) Peter Regier (1823-96/97), elder of Fürstenwerder; (2) Abraham Regier (1831-1909), preacher 1856, elder 1855 at Tiegenhagen; (3) Cornelius Regier (1835-1916), preacher 1867 at Tiegenhagen; (4) Gerhard Regier (1837-1902), deacon 1879 at Tiegenhagen (he declined the office of preacher to which he was chosen in 1881). (*ML* III, 448.) O.R.

Regier, Peter (1851-1925), a Mennonite elder of Prussia and Canada, was born in Prussia Jan. 14, 1851. He received his elementary and secondary education in Prussia. He married Anna Enss on Dec. 16, 1873, after which he lived in Rückenau, Marienburg. On Sept. 7, 1879, he was elected minister of the Rosenort Mennonite Church, and on July 1, 1888, was ordained elder by his father Peter Regier, elder of the Fürstenwerder Church. Because the Mennonites of Prussia were gradually yielding their principle of nonresistance he emigrated to Canada in 1893. After a stop at Gretna he settled at Tiefengrund, Sask., in 1894, where he organized a new Rosenort Mennonite Church. Other Mennonites from Prussia followed him. Other congregations were organized which became subsidiaries of Rosenort. He died at Tiefengrund on April 11, 1925. C.K.

J. G. Rempel, *Fünfzig Jahre Konferenzbestrebungen 1902-1952* I (Steinbach, n.d.) 26; *ML* III, 448 f.

Regina (Sask.) Mennonite Brethren Church was organized in February 1941 under the leadership of Abram Klaassen. Despite financial difficulties the little group with brave efforts was able to build its own church. In 1957 there were 18 members. The Regina M.B. Church is affiliated with the Herbert M.B. Church. J.I.R.

Register of the Names *of the (Professors and) Ministers of the Mennonites in the Netherlands (and Adjacent Countries):* see **Naamlijst** and **Namensverzeichnis.**

Regius, Urban: see **Rhegius, Urban.**

Rehlinger (Rechlinger, Rhelinger), **Ulrich** (d. 1547), an important mayor of Augsburg (*q.v.*), Bavaria, Germany, 1523-35, a zealous promoter of the Reformation, belonged to the local Schwenckfelder (*q.v.*) circle with his wife Ursula, née Gossenbrot, and his son Jacob. The noted Johann Rehlinger who was often consulted by the Regensburg (*q.v.*) council was his brother. E.T.

ABD XXVII, 597 ff., "Rehlinger"; Friedrich Roth, *Augsburgs Reformationsgeschichte 1517-1530* (Munich, 1901); *TA Bayern* II, No. 23, 26; Selina Gerhard Schultz, *Caspar Schwenckfeld of Ossig (1489-1561)* (Norristown, Pa., 1946); idem, *Corpus Schwenckfeldianorum;* Leonhard Theobald, *Die Reformationsgeschichte der Reichsstadt Regensburg* (Munich, 1936); *ML* III, 450.

Rehoboth Mennonite Church (MC), St. Anne, Ill., was established in 1953. It had a membership of 20 in 1958, with Mark Lehman as pastor.

Reichenberg, a village in the Danzig (*q.v.*) Werder, was a "Holländerdorf" (see **Villages**). As early as 1547 the locator (colonization agent) Philip Edzema distributed the territory to the immigrants, who apparently came from the Dutch province of Friesland, with the charge to cultivate the land and to construct windmills and sluices. They probably were Mennonites. Their descendants in the early 17th century moved east to the great Marienburger Werder, among whom was Peter Giesebrecht in 1607, a builder of sluices. vDZ.

Horst Penner, *Ansiedlung Menn. Niederländer im Weichselmündungsgebiet* (Schriftenreihe III, Weierhof, 1940) 12, 23, 31.

Reichenberger, Hans, was active as an Anabaptist missionary in South Bohemia about 1527-28. (*ME* I, 382.)

Reichsweiler (French, *Ricqueviller*), near Rappersweiler, a few miles from Colmar, was one of the first villages in Alsace to admit Swiss Mennonites fleeing from oppression in the canton of Bern. With the help of Beatus Fischer, a patrician of Bern, they settled here as early as 1671. vDZ.

Delbert L. Gratz, *Bernese Anabaptists* (Scottdale, 1953) 38.

Reidenbach Mennonite Church (OOM) (also called the "Thirty-Fivers") is a small group who in 1946 left the Groffdale Conference of Old Order Mennonites in Lancaster County, Pa., to form a separate congregation. During World War II, the Groffdale Conference had some boys in Civilian Public Service and some in jail. By 1946 a group of their constituency, led by Mrs. Rufus Martin, demanded that the CPS boys be excommunicated. When Bishop Joseph Wenger refused to take this action, the Mrs. Martin group refused to attend services. This led to their excommunication. Mrs. Martin and her son-in-law David Hoover moved to organize a separate group. By lot in the summer of 1947 Henry Martin was ordained by one of them to the ministry, and later to the office of bishop. Another minister and a deacon were also ordained. In 1948 they built a meetinghouse near Reidenbach's store in the Weaverland Valley, where they now worship with possibly forty members. The official name of their church is Reidenbach Mennonite Church. They have no Sunday school or missions, but are attempting to hold to the practices of the forefathers, using nothing containing rubber and no conveniences, not even poultry brooders. They are farmers. I.D.L.

Reiff Mennonite Church (MC), formerly known as Witmer's Church, is located near Maugansville, Washington Co., Md. In 1833 a group of families from Lancaster County, Pa., settled on homesteads in this community. Families represented were Reiff, Horst, Weber, Eshleman, and Martin. They worshiped in the near-by home of David Reiff until 1840, when a church was built on the present site and named for the man who granted the deed. In 1867 it was enlarged, and in 1891 it was replaced by a new brick building. The present building, the largest in the district, was erected in 1928. The first bishop, Peter Eshleman, was ordained in 1838. Ministers who have served the congregation were John Summers, Michael Horst (later bishop), Abr. Ebersole, Jacob Risser, George Keener, C. R. Strite, Martin E. Risser, D. R. Lesher, Moses K. Horst (present bishop), Stanley H. Martin, and Reuben E. Martin. The membership in 1957 was 389. J.D.R.

Reimann, Heini, an Anabaptist martyr, of Grüningen (*q.v.*) in the Swiss canton of Zürich. He was one of the most loyal of Conrad Grebel's adherents and a zealous preacher of Anabaptist doctrine in 1525 f. With Jakob Falk (*q.v.*) he baptized several persons and was therefore imprisoned. Both Falk and Reimann had been imprisoned previously, and in April 1525 they were again arrested at Appenzell (*q.v.*), but were apparently soon released. On a Sunday in May 1526 they were attending a meeting in the Herrliberg forest between Bubikon and Wetzikon, which was disbanded by the magistrate Berger; 15 participants were arrested, including Reimann and Falk, and imprisoned in Grüningen. They boldly confessed to Berger that they had been baptized and had also baptized others, although they knew that such baptism was forbidden on a penalty of death, and declared that they intended to continue the practice.

Now the Grüningen Landtag was faced with a serious decision as to whether Reimann and Falk should be sentenced to death "according to law." The Landtag refused to pass this sentence, thereby clashing with the Zürich council, which insisted on death on the basis of the mandate of March 7, 1526. Zürich decided that if these Anabaptists were not immediately drowned they would appeal to the court of Bern. Bern's verdict, favoring Zürich, was pronounced in 1528. The prisoners were then lodged singly in various Zürich prisons for two weeks on bread, water, and "Mus." Reimann and Falk, as the "rabble rousers," were again examined. Upon their persistence in their faith they were sentenced to death by drowning. On Sept. 5, 1528, in the early afternoon, they were drowned in the Limmat. This was the second Anabaptist execution in Zürich, the first victim having been Felix Manz (*q.v.*). S.G.

Emil Egli, *Die Züricher Wiedertäufer zur Reformationszeit* (Zürich, 1878) 58, 82 f.; Paul Peachey, *Die soziale Herkunft der Schweizer Täufer in der Reformationszeit* (Karlsruhe, 1954) 121; *TA Zürich*, 54, 211, 214 f., 217 f., 220, 225, 257, 264, 266, 268, 273 f., 305; Samuel Geiser, *Die Taufgesinnten-Gemeinden* (Karlsruhe, 1931) 146 f.; *ML* III, 453.

Reimann, Valerian Maximilian, a student of theology who delivered a Latin address on Menno Simons with the title, *Mennonis Simonis qualis fuerit vita vitaeque actio exponatur* (Life and Works of Menno Simons). The address was made on May 30, 1893, at Jena, probably at the instigation of Friedrich Nippold (*q.v.*), who was a professor of theology at the University of Jena 1884-1907. It was published (Jena, 1893) as a university paper, but was not meant for distribution, hence is rather scarce. It is found in the Mennonite Library of Amsterdam, in the National Library of Paris, and in the Library of the University of Göttingen. (*ML* III, 453 f.) E.C.

Reimer, a Mennonite family name. It is probable, but not certain, that the name originated in the Netherlands and that it was brought to West Prussia by religious refugees. At any rate members of the Reimer family took part in the reclaiming of the land north of Tiegenhof (*q.v.*) in the great Marienburg Werder.

In 1626 a Michel Reimer is named in Glabitsch north of the Vistula at Elbing. Two decades later he became a councilor of this village, an area that had just emerged from the fresh-water lake about 1600. In the neighboring Poppau, Isebrandt Reimer took part in the draining of this land which is below sea level. Also in the Scharpau, which was still an ideal fishing area in the time of the Teutonic Knights, the Reimers were active settlers; a Franz Reimer on the "Polish Hube" passed his land on to a Wiens about 1640, and a Wilm Reimer was living on the Schröderskampe near Altebabke about 1650. Johann Reimer was one of the founders of the village called Reinland (*q.v.*), whose lands did not become arable until 1725.

In the course of the centuries the Reimers in the Werder (*q.v.*) moved to the south. In 1936 there were 14 in the Fürstenwerder congregation (*q.v.*), 5 in Tiegenhagen (*q.v.*), 28 in Ladekopp (*q.v.*), 18 in Rosenort (*q.v.*), 76 in Heubuden (*q.v.*), 15 in the Danzig congregation (*q.v.*), 1 in Elbing-Ellerwald (*q.v.*), 2 in Thiensdorf-Preussisch Rosengart (*q.v.*), 5 in Tragheimerweide (*q.v.*), and 1 in the Ludwigshafen congregation in the Palatinate; this makes a total of 165. There were also Reimers among the West Prussian Mennonites who emigrated to Russia. Gustav Reimer (*q.v.*; 1884-1955), a deacon in the Heubuden congregation, was long prominent in the West Prussian Conference; he moved to Uruguay in 1950.

The Reimer family furnished an unusual number of leaders among the Mennonites of Russia. Klaas Reimer (*q.v.*; 1770-1837) was the founder of the Kleine Gemeinde (*q.v.*) in 1812, and the Reimers have ever since furnished a large number of ministers and family heads in this group, both in Russia and in Canada, among them currently elder David P. Reimer and preacher P. J. B. Reimer. Jakob Reimer (*q.v.*; 1817-91) was one of the founders of the Mennonite Brethren in the Molotschna (*q.v.*) Mennonite settlement in 1860. Jacob W. Reimer (*q.v.*; 1860-1948) was an outstanding preacher and Bible teacher in the M.B. group in Russia and after 1924 in Canada. Jakob A. Reimer (1844-1917) was an outstanding layman in the General Conference Mennonite Church, sharing in the founding of the Zagradovka (*q.v.*) settlement in the Ukraine, and serving as the leader (1908) and Oberschulze (*q.v.*) of the Slavgorod (*q.v.*) settlement in Siberia. There are Reimer families in certain areas of the Russian Mennonite settlements (GCM and MB) in the United States and Canada, but few have been found among the ministers.   H.P., E.C.

Franz Crous, "Mennonitenfamilien in Zahlen," *Gesch.-Bl.*, 1940, 26-45; Horst Penner, *Ansiedlung mennonitischer Niederländer im Weichselmündungsgebiet* . . . (Weierhof, 1940); Reimer, *Familiennamen; ML* III, 454.

Reimer, Gustav (1884-1955), a Mennonite leader of West Prussia and Uruguay, was born Oct. 17, 1884, at Heubuden (*q.v.*), West Prussia, Germany. In 1919 he was chosen as deacon by his home congregation. He was commissioned by the Mennonites of West Prussia to bring suit against the Protestant churches for requiring Mennonite landowners to pay them taxes. This task Gustav Reimer carried through successfully all the way to the imperial court in Leipzig. He saved many a church record from destruction and established a card index of the West Prussian Mennonites and their forebears.

After the flight from the East in 1945 he began to look after the religious and material needs of the Mennonites in Jeetzel, Hannover, where he was temporarily quartered, and promoted emigration to Uruguay (*q.v.*). In World War II he lost three of his five sons; in 1948 his wife, Frieda Reimer, also died. He therefore left without hesitation, settling in Montevideo, where he had a fruit farm and where he again served his brethren as deacon. He died there on July 19, 1955.   H.P., E.C.

Gustav E. Reimer, "Rescued Documents Relating to the History and Genealogy of the Mennonites of Former West Prussia," *MQR* XXIII (1949) 99-104; "Zum 70. Geburtstag von Diakon Gustav Reimer . . . ," *Der Mennonit* VII (1954) 141 f.; obituary, *Der Mennonit* VIII (1955) 127; *ML* III, 454 f.

Reimer, David: see **Felsenthal**.

Reimer, Jacob Wilhelm (1860-1948), a noted Mennonite Brethren preacher and Bible expositor in Russia and Canada, was born in Alexanderkrone, Molotschna Mennonite settlement, South Russia, on March 9, 1860, the son of Wilhelm and Helena (Klassen) Reimer. He entered the Orloff Zentralschule at the age of 13. At 17 he began to teach in Mennonite schools, which he continued for six years. He was converted at the age of 23 through

the preaching of F. W. Baedeker of England, who was at that time visiting South Russia. He resigned from the teaching profession, joined the M.B. Church through baptism, and began to preach. Meanwhile he gained a most remarkable knowledge of the Bible through intensive study. Reimer was married twice. In 1887 he married Gertrud Neustädtler (d. 1920) and settled in Rückenau. They had six sons and four daughters. His second wife, whom he married in 1923, was Margaret (Peters) Rempel.

The M.B. Conference in Russia appointed Reimer as itinerating minister (*Reiseprediger*) and ordained him to the ministry in 1900. He had a most effective period of ministry for 35 years and conducted meetings in all the M.B. congregations in Russia as well as among many other circles, his tours extending to Turkestan and to the Siberian Mennonite settlements. Seventeen times he visited the Kuban settlement in the Caucasus; twice he visited Germany, serving as Bible lecturer at the Blankenburg (*q.v.*) conferences. He found open doors for preaching among influential circles in St. Petersburg. For some time he accompanied the evangelist Baedeker as his interpreter. In 1899 he visited America and held meetings in many M.B. churches. In 1913 Reimer was largely instrumental in establishing the Mennonite Zentralschule in his native Alexanderkrone, and served on its board of directors (*Schulrat*) until the Revolution.

In July 1924, J. W. Reimer and his second wife emigrated to Canada, making their home in Ontario for four years; then after a stay of ten months in Winnipeg they settled in Steinbach, Man.

In Canada Reimer, though advanced in years, traveled much and preached in many M.B. churches. His ministry also extended into other circles. He wrote valuable articles for Mennonite papers. His book *Der wundervolle Ratschluss Gottes mit der Menschheit* has been widely read. He continued to preach up to his 87th year. He was largely responsible for the widespread introduction of premillennialism in the M.B. Church.

In October 1942 Reimer moved to Sardis, B.C., where he died on March 6, 1948, and was buried in the local cemetery.   J.H.L.

Reimer, Jakob (1817-91), one of the founders of the Mennonite Brethren Church in Russia, was born in the village of Kronsgarten in the Molotschna Mennonite settlement in the Ukraine, the son of David Reimer and Maria Neufeld, grew up on his father's farm Felsenthal (*q.v.*), was a close friend of his teacher Heinrich Franz I (*q.v.*), whom he followed to Gnadenfeld (*q.v.*) for a year. There he was admitted to the church by baptism. He would have preferred baptism by immersion, having been convinced in 1837, by reading the life of Ann Judson, that it was the proper form. Later he married in Gnadenfeld and became an outstanding member of the village and of the congregation. Inspired by the revival preaching of Eduard Wüst (*q.v.*), he joined the revival movement in the late 1840's and promoted it on his travels in the Mennonite churches with Johannes Claassen (*q.v.*) and Wilhelm Bartel (*q.v.*). Gradually his group left the large church and founded the Mennonite Brethren (*q.v.*). On May 21, 1861, he was baptized by immersion by Heinrich Hübert (*q.v.*). He was one of the signatories of the petition to the government for permission to settle in the Kuban, which was granted on March 4, 1864. After he had worked in Friedrichsfeld and Blumenau, he spent some time in Kuban and returned to the Ukraine and founded Wiesenfeld where he died in 1891. Jakob Reimer made important contributions to the development of the Mennonite Brethren Church. He opposed the emotional excesses of the early period with determination, and was excommunicated for this reason by his opponents in the group in 1864 through Benjamin Becker. In the next year he was, however, restored and the differences reconciled. From then on he worked quietly in a smaller circle. (Friesen, *Brüderschaft*, 81 ff.; *ML* III, 455.)   NEFF.

Reimer, Jakob A. (1844-1917), was born in the Molotschna Mennonite settlement in Russia. He took part in the establishment of the Zagradovka Mennonite settlement in 1872, settling in Neu-Schönsee. He served as Oberschulze (*q.v.*) of the settlement for 16 (perhaps 18) years. Energetic and progressive, a man of vision, with a special gift for dealing with superior government officials, he was known as a "Mennonite Moses." Although he had the confidence of the people at times, he was somewhat harsh in his methods of promoting the cause of the settlement and in 1896 resigned from his office.

In 1908, when the Slavgorod Mennonite settlement in Siberia (*q.v.*) was established, Reimer immediately became the leader of this movement and the Oberschulze of the settlement. In fact, the establishment of the settlement is very closely connected with the person of Reimer. On one occasion when important visitors from St. Petersburg visited Slavgorod and all the officials of the surrounding community were gathered there for the event, Reimer was singled out by the St. Petersburg representative with the words, "You are no stranger in St. Petersburg because we have heard much about you and your settlement in the Kulundin Steppes," before the officials were greeted. Reimer had not only friends and followers, but also opponents. In 1914 he accompanied 200 young military draftees to the city of Tomsk, and there convinced the government of their status as conscientious objectors. Meanwhile some of his opponents had denounced him at the government office in Slavgorod and when he returned he was deprived of his office of Oberschulze. He retired to the home of his son, where he died in 1917. One of his particular friends was Cornelius D. Harder (*q.v.*), the elder of the church.

                                                            C.K.

Gerhard Fast, *In den Steppen Sibiriens* (Rosthern, 1957) 87; *Der Bote*, Aug. 13, 1952; G. Lohrenz, *Sagradowka* (North Kildonan, 1947) 45 f.

Reimer, Klaas (1770-1837), the founder of the Kleine Gemeinde (*q.v.*) (now Evangelical Mennonites), was born in Petershagen near Danzig, Germany. He married the daughter of Elder Peter Epp and moved to the village of Neunhuben. On Sept. 1, 1801, he was elected minister of the Flemish Danzig Mennonite Church of which his father-in-law was elder. Reimer's autobiography relates that he studied the Bible and *Martyrs' Mirror* diligently. Encouraged by his dying father-in-law he decided that there was no future for the Mennonites in the Danzig area. He left with some thirty members of the church for Russia in 1804. During a stop at the Old Colony he became acquainted with a likeminded minister, Cornelius Janzen. From here Klaas Reimer and his group proceeded to the Molotschna settlement where he established a home in Petershagen near Halbstadt. Reimer soon found himself in disagreement with the leader of the church, Jakob Enns, and the religious conditions of the church. He was opposed to the contributions made to the Russian government during the Napoleonic War, to the punishment of miscreants in the Mennonite community, and to some "worldly" practices among the Mennonites. In 1812 he and a small group of the Flemish congregations began to hold separate meetings in private homes. Cornelius Janzen had meanwhile joined this group. Klaas Reimer was elected elder in 1814 in the presence of Elder Heinrich Janzen of the Schönwiese Mennonite Church of the Old Colony who, however, refused to ordain him as elder. Thus Klaas Reimer assumed the responsibilities of an elder without official ordination. Cornelius Janzen, his co-minister, preached an installation sermon and a group of some eighteen to twenty members considered itself organized and soon became known as the Kleine Gemeinde in distinction from the "Grosse Gemeinde" (the main body of Mennonites). Reimer and his followers were for some time not recognized as a separate body of Mennonites. Reimer died on Dec. 25, 1837.

Reimer's writings and concerns reveal that he was genuinely concerned in promoting and reforming the Mennonites in accord with the traditions of the church and the writings of Menno Simons, Dirk Philips, and Peter Peters. These books were cherished by him and his followers. On the other hand, Reimer had a very poor formal education and had some narrow views on the basic concepts of Christianity and Mennonitism. In the history of the Kleine Gemeinde the latter long overshadowed the good intentions and zeal of the founder and the leader of the group.   C.K.

Valuable sources on Reimer's life are the diaries of Klaas Reimer, Abraham Friesen, the ministers' list of the Kleine Gemeinde, the Danzig Church record, etc., all found in the original, transcript, or microfilm in BeCL and GCL; some originals are in possession of Elder David P. Reimer of Giroux, Man.; C. Krahn, "From Russia to Meade," *Menn. Life* VI (July 1951) 18; Friesen, *Brüderschaft*, 75 ff.; "Zum 100jährigen Gedenktag des Vorältesten Klaas Reimer, Gründer der Kleingemeinde," *Christlicher Familienfreund* (Winnipeg), December 1937, 2 f.; *ML* III, 455.

Rein (Reyn) **Edes**, the brother-in-law of Menno Simons (*q.v.*). His wife was Griet, a sister of Menno's wife. In his letter of Sept. 1, 1558, to the brotherhood in Waterhorne Menno addressed to Rein his moving words of grief over the division in the brotherhood. Karel Vos and Cornelius Krahn, however, assume that this letter was written to Hoyte Renix (*q.v.*).   NEFF.

K. Vos, *Menno Simons* (Leiden, 1914) 139; Cornelius Krahn, *Menno Simons* (Karlsruhe, 1936) 92; the letter is found in Menno Simons, *Opera* (1681) 392, and *Writings*, 1055; *BRN* VII, 236; *ML* III, 455.

Reincke, a Mennonite family name, found at Danzig, West Prussia, Germany, since 1641. A Wilhelm Reincke of Danzig was married to Anna Suderman about 1680. In Königsberg (*q.v.*), East Prussia, a Wilhelm Reincke is mentioned; he was a brewer who had moved in from Danzig. He is very likely identical with Wilhelm Reynke, who was named in the *Naamlijst* as a preacher of the Königsberg Mennonite congregation 1751-58. Giesbrecht Reincke, a "Dutch weaver," and Johann Reincke, "in trade with silk, wool, and camel's hair yarns," who are named in 1777 and 1789 as Mennonites, may have been sons of Wilhelm. Johann was a well-to-do citizen. There were formerly some members of this family in the Hamburg-Altona Mennonite congregation.   vDZ.

Reimer, *Familiennamen*, 116; *Gesch.-Bl.*, 1956, p. 28, Nos. 80-82; *Naamlijst* 1755.

Reinders, a Mennonite family name, found since the early 18th century at Sappemeer, Dutch province of Groningen, where Reinder Luitjes (d. 1758) and his son Luitje Reinders (d. *c*1800) (his descendants assumed the family name Reinders) were farmers. Jacob Luitjes, a member of this family, was a (lay) preacher of the Sappemeer congregation from 1780 to *c*1807. Recently two members of the Reinders family served as Mennonite ministers after studying at the University and Mennonite Seminary at Amsterdam. Uko Jan Reinders (1868-1917) served at Ternaard 1897-99 and Dantumawoude 1899-1916, and was very active in the cause of state pensions for the poor. He published a historical paper on Jan ter Borg in *Doopsgezinde Bijdragen*, 1897. His brother Luurdo Reinders (1870-1948) served as Mennonite pastor at Berlikum 1897-1937.   vDZ.

Reindertsz (Reynersz, Renicx), **Tjaert:** see **Renicx, Tjaert.**

Reinegom (Reynegom, Reninge), **Jaques van:** see **Outerman, Jacques.**

Reinfeld (Rheinfeld), a Mennonite village name which originated in Russia and was found in the Mennonite settlements of the Don region, Ukraine; Pavlodar and Amur, Siberia; East and West Reserves, Man.; Hague and Swift Current, Sask.; and Cuauhtemoc and Durango, Mexico. (See **Villages.**)   C.K.

Reinfeld Mennonite Brethren Church, located near the village of Reinfeld, Sask., a member of the Northern District (Herbert Division), was organized in 1927 under the initiative of C. C. Penner, with a membership of 18. The meetinghouse was built 20 miles southeast of Swift Current in 1928. The first leader was Jacob Derksen, succeeded by C. C. Penner and Heinrich F. Klassen; the latter was still serving as leader and pastor in 1957, with a membership of 20. The name had been changed to McMahon.   J.I.R.

Reinfeld Mennonite Church, located in the Slavgorod Mennonite settlement (*q.v.*) in Siberia, was composed of the residents of the eight villages of Reinfeld, Protassov, Alexeyfeld, Tiege, Gnadenfeld, Schöntal, Nikolaipol, and Berezovka. The congregation was founded in 1908; its first leader was Franz Buller, who was one of the delegates to inspect the land for settlement. He was succeeded by Heinrich Sawatzky. Other ministers were Johann Bergmann, Gerhard Warkentin, Peter Zacharias, Peter Löwen, and Heinrich Sawatzky, Jr. After World War I the congregation remodeled a home in the village of Protassov into a church. Whether this congregation was revived after the death of Stalin in 1953 is not yet known. (See also **Slavgorod** Mennonite Church.)   C.K.

Gerhard Fast, *In den Steppen Sibiriens* (Rosthern, 1957) 70.

Reinhardsbrunn, a village (pop. 800) in the government district of Hausbreitenbach, Thuringia, Germany, which now belongs to Friedrichroda, but in the 16th century belonged to the duchy of Gotha. Reinhardsbrunn is of importance in Mennonite history in the fact that here and in the castle nine Anabaptists were imprisoned in January 1530 and cross-examined by Friedrich Myconius (*q.v.*), the superintendent of Gotha. Six of them remained steadfast—three recanted—and were put to death on Jan. 18, 1530. Their joyful martyrdom attracted much attention in the electorate of Saxony (*q.v.*). No seditious charges could be proved against them; they were executed for their faith. They were Andreas and Katharina Kolb (*q.v.*), Christoph Ortlep (*q.v.*), Katharina König (*q.v.*), Elsa Kuntz (*q.v.*), and Barbara Unger. In August 1533 another Anabaptist was held here and examined by Friedrich Myconius, but was released upon recanting. NEFF.

Wappler, *Thüringen*, 12, where an excerpt is given from the book by Justus Menius (*q.v.*), *Der widderteuffer lere vnd geheimnis, aus heiliger Schrift widerlegt*, and 135, where the trial is described and the Anabaptist defendants named; *ML* III, 455 f.

Reinier Wybrands(z): see **Wybema, R. W.**

Reinken Ramakers (Rademacher): see **Remken Ramakers.**

Reinland (*Rheinland*), a common village name which originated in West Prussia and was found among the Old Colony Mennonites of the West Reserve, Man., from where it was transplanted to Swift Current and Hague, Sask.; Cuauhtemoc and Durango, Mexico; and Menno in the Chaco, and Villarrica, Paraguay. (See **Villages.**)   C.K.

Reinland, a village in West Prussia, Germany, was one of the later village areas to be cultivated, being covered by a forest until 1725. The first settlers had predominantly Dutch names. The settlers were given permission to build walls and dams, dig trenches, and build windmills and sluices for drainage. They were released from work on the main dam. They were permitted to sell their land only to relatives. In 1936 there were still seven Mennonite families there, who were members of the Tiegenhagen (*q.v.*) congregation.   E.C.

W. Crichton, *Zur Gesch. der Mennoniten* (Königsberg, 1786) 28; E. J. Dormann, *Gesch. des Kreises Marienburg* (Danzig, 1862) 73; Horst Penner, *Ansiedlung mennonitischer Niederländer im Weichselmündungsgebiet* . . . (Weierhof, 1940) 56; *ML* III, 456.

Reinland Mennonite Church or "Altkolonier Reinlaender Mennoniten Gemeinde," the name of the Old Colony Mennonite Church (*q.v.*) at Cuauhtemoc, Chihuahua, Mexico, which was transplanted from Manitoba, where it was also known as the "Reinland-Mennoniten-Kirche." The church was transplanted under the leadership of Elder Johann J. Friesen, who was succeeded by the present Elder Isaac Dyck (1958). The membership of the church including children was 3,340 in 1936, 7,706 in 1949, and 8,768 in 1953. The church has a number of places of worship in the various villages. (See also **Old Colony** Mennonites and **Old Colony** Mennonite Church.)   C.K.

Reintal, a Mennonite village name which originated on the West Reserve of Manitoba, from where it was transplanted to Cuauhtemoc in Mexico, Menno in the Chaco, and Villarrica, Paraguay. See **Villages.**)   C.K.

Reiseprediger (English, itinerant preacher), an office established in the second half of the 19th century by the Mennonites of South Germany, Switzerland, France, and Russia, and still maintained in the southeast German Verband (*q.v.*) and in France. Its purpose has been essentially to furnish pastoral ministry to individual families, often widely scattered, and to supplement the work of the local preachers with a special preaching ministry for various special occasions. Although the Reiseprediger has usually been appointed by a conference, with a salary guaranteed by the conference treasury, part of the support has often been provided by direct contributions from the families served and by offerings at the special meetings. At times the Reiseprediger has been conceived of as an evangelist and Bible teacher available for service both within and outside the conference appointing him. Elder Christian Schmutz of Rappenau (*q.v.*), a leader in the Verband, advocated this concept as early as 1866 (*Menn. Bl.,* 1866, p. 11) and urged the establishment of a training school for such Reiseprediger and evangelists.

The Verband was the first Mennonite conference to inaugurate the Reiseprediger system, partly because it had the largest number of scattered families and partly because it wanted to supplement the work of its exclusively rural and untrained ministry. Since 1871 the Verband has had continuously one or two Reiseprediger. The list is as follows: Christian Herrmann 1871-74(?), Michael Landes (*q.v.*) 1873-75, Jakob Hege of Reihen (*q.v.*) 1876-1911, Johannes Hirschler (1853-1931) 1883-86, G. van der Smissen (1859-1923) 1886-1923, Michael Fellmann ?-1936, Daniel Pohl (d. *c*1943) 1935(?)-40, Ulrich Hege (b. 1892) 1945- , Adolf Schnebele 1956- . Christian Schnebele, first appointed by the South German Conference, served the Verband 1922-58. The South German Conference had the following Reiseprediger: Emil Händiges (1871-) 1912-18, Christian Schnebele 1918-20, Abraham Warkentin (1885-

1947) 1918-20, and Christian Guth (1879-1952) 1923-52. All but Herrmann Händiges, Ulrich Hege, Warkentin, and Adolf Schnebele were products of St. Chrischona and carried the Chrischona emphasis in doctrine and piety with them. In Switzerland the Mennonites never had their own Reiseprediger, but Reiseprediger from Germany (e.g., Jakob Hege) and from non-Mennonite circles have served them. The Alsatian Conference appointed Henri Volkmar in 1913; he was succeeded in 1921 by Fritz Goldschmidt, who served until World War II. About 1950 Willi Peterschmitt was appointed. The French-speaking Mennonites have had Pierre Sommer and later André Goll, and for a time Pierre Widmer.

The North German and West Prussian Mennonites never adopted the Reiseprediger practice, although it was vigorously advocated by outstanding leaders. The Vereinigung (*q.v.*) included a provision for Reisepredigt service in its 1934 constitution but without practical result. One Reiseprediger served in the West Prussian area 1901-29, viz., Nikolai Wiebe of Lichtenau (Molotschna settlement in Russia), who had served as a missionary in Sumatra 1889-1901.

In Russia the first "Reiselehrer" of the Mennonite Brethren Church (*q.v.*) was Benjamin Bekker (*q.v.*), ordained in 1861. The character of the Reiseprediger and their work in the M.B. Church was described about 1872 in a number of their diaries. Their reports were sewed together in a single volume and were sent from congregation to congregation on a specified route. Some of the evangelists were Jakob Dirksen, Jakob Jantz, Jakob Reimer (1817-1891, *q.v.*), Christian Schmidt (1833-1905, *q.v.*), Abraham Unger (1820-80, *q.v.*), and Abraham Wall.

"Systematic Reisepredigt in the Mennonite congregations as far as we know arose first in the private Reiseprediger committee, which was formed for the purpose of sending Bernhard Harder (1832-84, *q.v.*) to Halbstadt (*q.v.*) about 1880 and was organized through the initiative of Heinrich Lettkemann of Halbstadt and then carried on for a long time by Heinrich Janz. Then the matter of the Reisepredigt was taken up by the General Conference (*Bundeskonferenz*). The appointed Reiseprediger were Bernhard Harder, Jakob Quiring (educated at the Weierhof, *q.v.,* and the Evangelical Seminary at Basel), who later went to America, Gerhard Harder, Elder Jakob Gerbrandt, and missionary Johann Kröker. . . . In addition elders and preachers frequently traveled as delegates of the church conference of this or that group and of the General Conference (*q.v.*). Much information concerning the Reisepredigt in the Mennonite Church is found in the *Mennonitisches Jahrbuch* (*q.v.*) published at Berdyansk in 1909."

In America the Reiseprediger concept found formal expression only among the General Conference Mennonites and the Mennonite Brethren. Daniel Hoch (d. 1863) was the first to be appointed by the General Conference in 1861, the Conference at its organization in 1860 having expressly stated as one of its objectives the provision of a Reisepredigt ministry. He was followed by Christian Krehbiel. In 1868 the Conference appointed three Reiiseprediger, L. O. Schimmel for the East, Ephraim Huns-berger for the Central area, and Christian Krehbiel for the new West. The Kansas Conference (first session 1877), later called the Western District, made provision for preaching visits and later appointed Reiseprediger. In 1880 a Reisepredigt Committee was created. Christian Krehbiel was appointed Reiseprediger 1881-83, followed by David Goerz 1883-84. In 1884 the Reisepredigt was made a full-time assignment, with J. B. Baer appointed, followed in 1890 by N. F. Toews. Wilhelm Ewert served 1885-86. In Canada Benjamin Ewert served as Reiseprediger 1921-38. The above list is by no means complete.

The Canadian Mennonite Brethren have never had an official Reiseprediger, although individual ministers have been called by provincial conferences for special service of this sort, visiting the congregations in the district area. In the United States the Committee on Evangelism of the U. S. Area Conference (beginning in 1957) appoints a Reiseprediger. In 1958 he was Waldo Wiebe.

In the Mennonite Church (MC), although there were never any official Reiseprediger, numerous ministers of their own volition traveled widely in the 19th century visiting scattered families and small congregations. The Evangelizing Fund and Evangelizing Committee established in 1882 as forerunners of the later Mission Board were essentially provision for a sort of modest Reiseprediger service. (Condensed from the article "Reisepredigt" by Ernst Crous, *ML* III, 456-60). H.S.B.

Friesen, *Brüderschaft*, 385, 397, 430 ff., 762 f.; II, 45, 137; Mannhardt, *Jahrbuch*, 1888, 96; *ML* III, 456-60.

Reisswitz: see Reiswitz.

Reist (Reyst), **Hans** (also called Hans Hüsli) (dates of birth and death not known), of Obertal, an elder in the Mennonite congregation in the Emmental (*q.v.*), Switzerland. Not much is known about his life and work, though he was without doubt an important preacher and elder. In the official documents of Trachselwald of 1670-71 Hans Reist is named as having left the country with his wife, who like him adhered to Anabaptist teaching; his leaving was probably not voluntary, however, for about that time about 700 persons were expelled from the canton of Bern (*q.v.*). The farm home of Hans Reist in Rothenbaum, near Affoltern in the Emmental, was confiscated and sold. In the "Täufergeltstage," in the state archives of Bern, his estate is listed. The stock of grain, two cows, a calf, a pig, hay and straw, seven beds with furnishings, a loom, and furniture were sold at public auction. After paying the debts and other expenses, a sum of 854 pounds remained, which was added to the Anabaptist fund (*q.v.*).

But Reist, like many other Emmental Anabaptists, returned from his exile. In 1686 the court record reads, "Hans Reist of Sumiswald, brother-in-law of Tobias Heininger, has been summoned to court, because he called for Heininger's wife at Waltrigen to take her to an Anabaptist meeting. He did not appear." In the prebendary manual of Dürrenroth, under date of Feb. 6, 1701, there is a notation that

"Hans Reischt" promised the magistrate, who had summoned him to answer for his Anabaptism (*Teufferey*), to attend church services and accept the sacraments. But by May 1704 the charge was made that Hans Reist's wife, "Baby Ryser," did not come to communion services, but instead went with her husband to an Anabaptist meeting on Saturday night and did not return until the next morning.

The Bernese Mennonites had a severe struggle to undergo in the storms of persecution of the 17th century; but a still worse struggle was brought upon the leaders by internal dissension. This was especially the case with Hans Reist, when Jakob Ammann (*q.v.*) demanded a strict enforcement of avoidance in marriage and in eating (see **Avoidance**), thus causing a deep schism in the brotherhood. When he was asked his position on this point by Ammann, who was making a round of the congregations as Nikolaus Moser (*q.v.*), the elder of Friedersmatt, and Peter Giger, of Reutenen, near Zäziwil, and others had done, Reist, at that time a preacher in Utzingen, near Worb, rejected such a strict interpretation of the ban. Avoidance at the table is wrong, said Reist, for it is not what goes into a man's mouth that defiles him. Peter Giger advocated calling all the Swiss elders together to examine the matter in the light of the Bible and then to act in accord with its teaching. Then a number of preachers and elders met at the home of Nikolaus Moser to discuss the question, when word came that Reist and his followers would not come. Peter Giger was grieved, as he wrote, when Ammann began to criticize the brethren. Giger begged them not to create a schism, "for if ye bite and devour one another, take heed that ye be not consumed one of another" (Gal. 5:15). But Ammann began to call Reist and six of his co-elders rabble rousers who should be expelled from the brotherhood as liars and shunned. The brethren begged him to exercise patience; open transgressors who persist in their sin should be excluded with the counsel of the entire brotherhood, but not brethren on account of difference of opinion. Ammann, however, cut off fraternal relations with the opposing group and pronounced the ban (*q.v.*) on them. There were several violent arguments. Hans Reist now became the leader of those who opposed Ammann.

Soon afterward Ammann wrote a warning letter demanding that the brethren yield to his "Biblical views" within a short period. Such ultimatum-like demands resulted in a complete break, which defied all attempts at reconciliation, between the Amish (*q.v.*) and the Reist or Emmental group. Other points of difference, such as footwashing (*q.v.*), and strict regulation of clothing, were added to the points in dispute and became prominent issues.

The division extended into Alsace (*q.v.*) and the Palatinate (*q.v.*). Ammann visited the Alsatian congregations, everywhere banning those who did not yield to his views. In March 1694 the preachers of the Palatinate (*q.v.*) reached an agreement with the Swiss, confirming their adherence to the milder application of the ban. This paper was signed by Hans Reist and nine other preachers and elders of the Swiss congregations, including Peter Giger, and seven of the Palatinate.

Again the brethren met in Markirch (q.v.) on Nov. 8, 1697, to take a position against the harsh attitude of the Amish. Elder Hans Rudolf Nägele wrote a letter at Altkirch to Hans Reist severely criticizing Ammann's view that without his interpretation of the ban there was no salvation. It was his view that when the knowledge of the Word of God increased and the light of truth shone more brightly it would be clear whether salvation is to be sought in the ban or in the merit of Jesus, and that Ammann's position made the suffering of Jesus of no avail; the Amish were like wolves who did not spare Christ's flock (Acts 20), and who avoided neither lies nor deception to secure a greater following.

The dissension was bitter; the brethren found it difficult to be just to one another. Both sides called the other heretics. The Markirch congregation wrote another letter to the Emmental brethren on Dec. 23, 1697, stating that Ammann had called them false teachers, excommunicated liars, indeed, servants of the devil. In a letter of Oct. 16, 1699, Jakob Gut advised that the subject be dropped and all condemnation cease, for each would have to answer for his own deeds before the Judgment Seat of Christ. Ammann later rued his harsh action, and in a letter of Feb. 7, 1700, confessed his wrong to the Reist group, requesting their forgiveness. But it was too late; the schism could not be healed. Among the emigrants to Holland in 1711 the two groups were sharply distinguished. The "Reistschen" in general were less willing to join the emigration than the Amish, and many of the Hans Reist group obstinately refused to leave the country. Their elder then was Peter Hahbegger; Peter Spaar (?), Hans Gärber, Ulrich Säger, Peter Oberley, and Christian Jacob were the preachers of this group, who are said to have lived particularly in the "Unterland." Daniel Grimm and Benedict Brechbühl (Brechbill, q.v.), both of whom had been banished before but had secretly returned, were also very influential in persuading the Reist followers not to leave with the Amish.

Though nothing more is known about Reist's work, his spirit is evident in a prayer, which has been preserved in printed form, asking that God might come to the aid of the scattered believers who lived in tribulation, care, anxiety, and distress, and save them from the hands of those who did not know God. "Turn from us all unreasonable undertakings and attacks of men, who persecute, despise, insult, hate, and defame us, and . . . draw us all together in Thy great love and let no dissension or scattering come among us any more, but rather see, O Lord of Harvest, how great the harvest is, but how few Thy faithful workers are; so rouse up among us faithful workers, shepherds and teachers, preachers and elders, who may proclaim and reveal Thy Word."

Hans Reist is also the author of the song, "Es ist ein wunderschöne Gaab," 46 stanzas, which was long in use in the Swiss congregations. It has the heading, "A Scriptural Story of Abraham and His Son."   S.G.

Inv. Arch. Amst. I, No. 1334; see also Nos. 1255a, 1255c, 1331, 1337, 1339, 1341; Milton Gascho, "The Amish Division of 1693-1697 in Switzerland and Alsace," *MQR* XI (1937) 235-66; Samuel Geiser, *Die Taufgesinnten-Gemeinden* (Karlsruhe, 1931) 417 f.; Delbert Gratz, *Bernese Anabaptists* (Scottdale, 1953); John B. Mast, *The Letters of the Amish Division* (Oregon City, 1950); Müller, *Berner Täufer*, 314-19; Wolkan, *Lieder*, 156; *ML* III, 460-62.

Reist Mennonite (MC) Church, now extinct, met every fourth Sunday about 1850-70 near or in the home of deacon Peter Reist, who lived 6 miles east of Breslau, Waterloo Co., Ont. There is no indication of organization. According to arrangement by the Ontario Conference, ministers were likely supplied. Jacob Miller, a Mennonite minister of south of Niagara Falls, owned property in this community, and one member of his family lived there. Peter Reist was ordained deacon for the Wanner Church several miles to the south in 1873.   J.C.F.

Reist Mennonite Meetinghouse, built on original Reist lands of Sun Hill, southeast of Manheim, Pa., was used both for church and school purposes by the Mennonites living between Erisman and Erb, and in the circuit. The site was abandoned in 1860, when the congregation built the Kauffman church on the Lancaster-Manheim Pike.   I.D.L.

Reistschen (Reystsche Anabaptisten, Hans-Reist-volk), the followers of Hans Reist (q.v.).

Reiswitz (Reisswitz), **George Leopold, Baron of** (1764-1828), royal councilor and knight of the order of St. John, a friend of the Mennonites, was born of an old family of Silesian nobility at Moschen, Upper Silesia, Germany, on Feb. 7, 1764. He and Friedrich Wadzeck (q.v.) published the book *Beiträge zur Kenntnis der Mennoniten-Gemeinden in Europa und America, statistischen, historischen und religiösen Inhalts* (Berlin, 1821). The foreword presents the purpose of the book to be to protect the Mennonites from persecution by an objective illumination of their history, their principles, their life, and their attitudes. It contains 392 pages, and contains information on the Mennonite congregations in Prussia, privileges (q.v.), confessions (q.v.) of faith, also a collection of laws and regulations passed against them, as well as on Menno Simons (q.v.) and the Münsterite (q.v.) and Müntzer (q.v.) "abominations," with proof that the Mennonites had nothing in common with them, and also opinions concerning the Mennonites in France (q.v.), and concerning the "Sauds in East India, a religious sect that conspicuously resembles the Mennonites and Quakers," a very inexact and incorrect list of the sources on the history of the Mennonites, the account of a legal battle (see **Riesen, David van**), the census of the Mennonite congregations in Prussia, and information on the Mennonite settlements in South Russia and Caucasia. The statements and assertions are in many cases out of date, and thus detract from the value of the book.

The second part of the book appeared eight years later under the title, *Beiträge zur Kenntniss der taufgesinnten Gemeinden oder der Mennoniten, statistischen, historischen und religiösen, auch juristischen Inhalts.* It was published by Reiswitz, Wadzeck having died in the interim, at Breslau in 1829. Its contents are as follows: (1) "Notes of a scholar of the Mennonite faith concerning information on the Mennonite congregations, which has been furnished by several recent authors." (2) "Presentation of the organization of the West Prussian Mennonite congregations, with respect to their payment of dues to the church, parish, and schools to other religious parties and other organizations." (3) "Concerning the Mennonites" (an attempt at a historical presentation by means of excerpts from various writings). (4) "Concerning the creed of the various denominations similar to the Mennonites and yet essentially different from them" (Waldenses, Quakers, and Methodists). (5) "Concerning the attitude of the Mennonites toward government and their participation in public offices." (6) "Additional information on the life of Menno Simons." (7) "Directory of all the Mennonite congregations in Europe." (8) "Information on the origin of the Mennonite congregations in East Prussia (*q.v.*) and Lithuania (*q.v.*), according to Crichton and some manuscript data," and "Privileges (*q.v.*) of the Mennonites of West Prussia (*q.v.*) and Lithuania." (9) "Concerning the emigration of the Mennonites to Russia and the principles of government established for that purpose (a historical presentation)." (10) "Concerning the right of the Mennonites to possess property." (11) "Concerning the refusal of the Mennonites to render military service." (12) "Historical presentation of the various legal stipulations concerning the military obligations of the Prussian Mennonites." Then follows an appendix containing supplementary facts on refusal to do military service, statistics of the congregations of the Bavarian Rhine district, a law on the oath (*q.v.*), the number of Mennonites in America, the English language periodicals of the Anabaptists, a list of villages in Lithuania where Mennonites had settled, names of Mennonites who owned land in Lithuania, a list of the elders and preachers of the Mennonites in South, East, and West Prussia, Lithuania, Poland, and the recently settled colonies in Russia. This book of 375 pages has at the end a directory of Mennonite families in the "Marienwerder and Danzig Cammer-Departement," besides two pictures of the Mennonite church in Danzig and a map of the lands of the Mennonites and other German settlers in the province of Ekaterinoslav, Russia (*q.v.*). The numerous misprints and inexact statements as well as the omissions are very annoying. Nevertheless both books are of value for the history of the Mennonites. (*ML* III, 462 f.)

NEFF.

Baron von Reiswitz and Friedrich Wadzeck published in 1824 a *Glaubensbekenntnis der Mennoniten und Nachricht von ihren Colonien, nebst Lebensbeschreibung Menno Simons.* Concerning the origin of Anabaptism in Switzerland and its spread to South Germany, Holland, and to West Prussia the authors apparently lacked information, for by way of introduction they say, "The origin of this Christian religious party is very obscure." Their discussion in general does not go beyond Menno's leaving the Catholic Church, the confession of faith by Cornelis Ris, and the history of the Mennonites in Prussia, with the exception of the emigration to Rus-

sia. A detailed account of a legal contest on the question of the nonresistance of the Mennonites of West Prussia is presented. On the whole the authors try to do justice to the Mennonites and approach the Anabaptist movement with a respectable understanding.

S.G.

Reitzes, Uilke: see Dijkstra, Uilke Reitses.

Rekker, a Dutch family name, borne by four Mennonite ministers. Meindert Huyberts Rekker was a lay preacher of Sneek 1723-*c*57. Jan Pieters Rekker was a lay preacher of the congregations of Veenwoudsterwal *c*1740-49, Groningen (united Flemish and Waterlander congregation) 1749-51, and Winsum-Obergum 1751-*c*75. Gerlof (Gerlaicus) Rekker, of Dokkum, studied at the University of Franeker and the Mennonite Seminary at Amsterdam and served the congregations of Den Hoorn on the island of Texel 1754-56, Bolsward 1756-59(?), and Vlissingen 1759-d.1809. His son Bartholomeus Rekker (1768-1844) was a merchant and writer. Sicco Rekker (1767-1835), also of Dokkum, and apparently a relative of Gerlof's, studied at the Amsterdam Mennonite Seminary and was a minister at Middelburg 1790-1832. His son Pieter Rekker served there as a deacon for many years.

VDZ.

Naamlijst: F. Nagtglas, *Levensberichten van Zeeuwen* II (Middelburg, 1893) 502-4; *DB* 1884, 50; 1885, 92, 95.

Relics of the Martyrs, i.e., objects or portions of objects left by the martyrs, portions of their bodies, or articles connected with their death. In the Catholic Church there is a certain superstitious veneration of these objects on the assumption that they possessed miraculous powers of grace and benefit. There is no such veneration among the Mennonites. It is merely a matter of the loyal appreciation of several objects pertaining to their martyrs. So far as we know, there are three such objects: a fragment of a tablecloth owned by Thomas von Imbroich (*q.v.*), the pear of Maeyken Boosers (*q.v.*), and the tongue screw used on Hans Bret (*q.v.*). The first two are kept in the archives of the Mennonite Church of Amsterdam, and were shown to visitors at the Mennonite World Conference held June 29-July 3, 1936. The tongue screw is in the possession of the de Hoop Scheffer family. A thorough investigation of the authenticity and history of these relics was made by Samuel Cramer. (*DB* 1898, 107 ff.; *ML* III, 53.)

NEFF.

Relief, Colonization, and Public Service, Incorporated, of the church of God in Christ, Mennonite. In the early 1930's, during and before the great drouth in western Kansas and eastern Colorado, Sam Dirks and A. L. Yost took a special interest in resettlement of needy families. In 1933 the General Conference chose five men of the Western District to form a Colonization Board, with one additional member from each of the other two districts. The board operates under the General Conference and serves in both home and foreign relief and rehabilitation work. The board has been instrumental in forming settlements at Fredonia, Kan.; Bonner's Ferry, Idaho; Burns, Kan.; La Junta, Chih., Mexico; Huron, S.D.; Atmore, Ala.; and Stapleton, Ga.

P.G.H.

Relief (Ken.) Mennonite Church (MC), established in 1943, is a mission station of the Virginia Mennonite Home Mission Board. In 1957 it had 7 members.

Relief News Letter began as the *Relief Trainees' News Letter,* issued monthly February-October 1944; the title was then changed to *Relief News Letter,* and continued monthly until September 1946, with 32 issues. It was a mimeographed paper, 8½ x 11 in., with 8-10 pages plus a 4-page supplement, published by the MCC headquarters at Akron, Pa. The supplement featured book reviews and articles on foreign relief activities. The *Relief News Letter* had the following editors: John E. Bender, Irvin B. Horst, Ruth L. Hilty, J. Richard Blosser, Delbert L. Gratz, David A. Shank, and Ralph K. Bargen. The purpose of the *Relief News Letter* was to present news concerning the MCC foreign relief program to MCC Civilian Public Service men and other young people in training for relief service.   J.N.B.

Relief Work. The Anabaptist emphasis on discipleship and brotherhood required the material possessions of the Christian to be brought under the lordship of Christ. The extremes of luxury and poverty were to be avoided. Material aid and generous sharing and co-operation in economic matters were to be freely practiced; and after the manner of the Good Samaritan the needy were to be helped. Hans Leopold, a Swiss Brethren martyr of 1528, said of his brethren: "If they know of anyone who is in need, whether or not he is a member of their church, they believe it their duty, out of love to God, to render help and aid." Menno Simons, in an enumeration of qualities of the saints, says: "They show mercy and love. . . . They entertain those in distress. They take the stranger into their houses. They comfort the afflicted; clothe the naked; feed the hungry." Both the Dordrecht and the Ris confessions of faith in their statements on nonresistance emphasize the duty of the Christian to feed, clothe, and help his needy fellow men.

Anabaptist-Mennonite history is filled with illustrations of this brotherhood and "Good Samaritan" faith in action. In 1553 occurred the well-known incident in which the followers of Menno Simons at Wismar in North Germany gave asylum to a group of English Calvinist refugees who had been driven from home by the Catholic queen and then were refused admission to his country by the Lutheran king of Denmark. The Hutterite chronicles of the 17th century record the presence in their communities of numerous strangers receiving bread and alms during a time of famine.

During the 17th and 18th centuries the Dutch Mennonites gave much material assistance to their persecuted and needy brethren in Switzerland, the Palatinate, Danzig, Poland, and Moravia. In 1666 the Amsterdam city authorities, in a formal protest made to the Swiss government at the request of the Dutch Mennonites against the persecution of the Mennonites, included the following sentence: "The Mennonites are a people which at no opportunity have failed to extend noteworthy charity toward the people of the Reformed faith. Only recently, when

our brethren, the Waldenses, were so cruelly driven from their homes [by the duke of Savoy], they have in this city, simply upon our recommendation, contributed the sum of about 7,000 pounds in Holland money, for the support of the aforesaid Waldenses." Following the revocation of the Edict of Nantes in 1685 the Dutch Mennonites contributed similar assistance to the French Huguenots.

In 1710 the Dutch Mennonites organized the Foundation for Foreign Relief (Fonds voor Buitenlandsche Nooden, *q.v.*), which carried on an active relief program for half a century and which was not finally liquidated until 1803. In 1711 this organization assisted 400 refugees from Switzerland to settle in the Netherlands. Other settlers followed in 1713 and subsequently. During the 1720's and 30's large sums were contributed by the Dutch organization for the assistance of Mennonites migrating from the Palatinate to Pennsylvania. It is estimated that in 1709 the Dutch Mennonites contributed more than 270,000 guilders for foreign relief work, for the aid of both those who were going to America and those who settled in Holland. When the Mennonite World Relief Conference was held in Danzig in 1930 G. Fast in an address enumerated a long list of cases, first in which the West Prussian Mennonites had been assisted by the Dutch, and then in which the Prussian Mennonites gave aid to their brethren in West Germany and in Russia.

The new settlements of Mennonites in America continued the tradition of helping the needy. As early as 1756 the Franconia Mennonites in Eastern Pennsylvania organized a small relief program for the help of the Moravian communities of Northampton County who had suffered loss of life and property because of Indian raids. In 1775, when the war spirit of the revolutionary era was running high, the Mennonites joined the Dunkers in a petition to the Pennsylvania Assembly declaring it according to their principles "to feed the hungry and give the thirsty drink; we have dedicated ourselves to serve all men in everything that can be helpful to the preservation of men's lives, but we find no freedom in giving, or doing, or assisting in anything by which men's lives are destroyed or hurt." During the war the Mennonites used the facilities of the Brethren Cloister at Ephrata for hospital purposes. A Mennonite minister, John Baer, and his wife died, evidently of a contagious disease, while ministering to sick soldiers at this place. One writer says: "we may be sure from what we know of their character and customs, that many a weary straggler, invalid soldier, or destitute refugee received aid and comfort from the rich farms and hearths of the Pennsylvania pacifists." Even British fugitives received such aid. In 1783 some British soldiers who had been imprisoned in Lancaster escaped and called at Mennonite homes northeast of the city, where they received help. Local officials regarded this as an act of treason and insisted that the Mennonites be punished. Only through an appeal to George Washington himself were these Mennonites saved from a prison sentence. But they had to pay a fine.

The immigration of 18,000 European Mennonites, chiefly from Russia, in the decade following 1873, was the occasion for a large-scale relief and aid program on the part of the Mennonites of Canada and the United States. Three committees were organized for carrying on this work. The first was the Mennonite Board of Guardians (*q.v.*) organized in 1873 with Christian Krehbiel and David Goerz of Summerfield, Ill., as president and secretary, and John F. Funk of Elkhart, Ind., as treasurer. The second committee known as the Mennonite Executive Aid Committee was organized in Eastern Pennsylvania under the leadership of Preacher Amos Herr of the Lancaster Conference. The third committee was formed by the Ontario Mennonites and was known as the Canadian Aid Committee, with Jacob Y. Shantz of Berlin (now Kitchener) as president. These three committees co-operated very closely and did a remarkable piece of work. They distributed literature throughout the Mennonite communities of south Russia, giving detailed instructions as to procedures for taking advantage of the provisions being made by the American committees. They had representatives in Hamburg and New York who met the immigrants and helped them with the details of their travel and transportation arrangements. They helped them make contact with the proper railway companies and arranged for very cheap immigrant fares, and gave assistance in the location and purchase of lands on which to settle. It is estimated that the assistance in money and services given by the Mennonites in the United States to the Russian immigrants amounted to more than $100,000. The Ontario Mennonites secured a loan of $88,000 from the Canadian government to assist the immigrants who came to Canada. In addition, private loans and gifts brought the aid given by the Canadian Mennonites also considerably above $100,000.

The next important relief project of the American Mennonites was in response to the India famine of 1896-97. In 1897 the *Home and Foreign Relief Commission* (*q.v.*) was organized at Elkhart, Ind., under M.C. auspices and for a decade contributed grain for famine relief aid funds for the support of orphans. The HFRC came to an end in 1906. The *Emergency Relief Commission* (*q.v.*) of the General Conference Mennonite Church, organized in 1899, carried on a similar work in India. This board continued in existence until it was merged with the Board of Christian Service in 1950. It served as a relief agency to aid members in needy North American congregations after the work in India was completed. An important outcome of these projects was the founding of two India Mennonite missions (*q.v.*), the M.C. in 1899 and the G.C.M. in 1900. The M.B.C. Church in 1898 started orphanage work at Hadjin, Turkey, for Armenian survivors of the Turkish massacres.

The *Mennonite* (MC) *Relief Commission for War Sufferers* (*q.v.*), organized in 1917 at Elkhart, was the official agency through which the Mennonite Church (MC) supported the Friends reconstruction work in France and other European Relief projects as well as the Near East relief following World War I. (For a treatment of the French work see **Reconstruction Work** in France.)

In 1919 the MRCWS appointed a committee of three reconstruction workers then serving in France,

A. J. Miller, J. Roy Allgyer, and A. E. Hiebert, to investigate opportunities for relief work in other parts of Europe. Leaving Paris on Oct. 9, 1919, they spent three and one-half days in Berlin, traveled through Leipzig, Dresden, and Prague, and spent five and one-half days in Vienna; then continued through Budapest and Bucharest and spent six days in Odessa and Kherson, South Russia. They visited hospitals, welfare centers, and charitable institutions, and reported great shortages of food, clothing, and fuel, accompanied by suffering, want, and disorganization wherever they went; the opportunities for a Mennonite relief work were great, working either independently or in co-operation with the *American Friends Service Committee*. In the meantime, however, the MRCWS had committed itself to the Near East work, its first workers having sailed in January 1919. Hence no extensive work was undertaken in any of the countries visited by the above team except Russia.

In 1920, however, John J. Fisher was stationed in Vienna, where he engaged in child feeding work under the Quaker organization. Russell Lantz transferred from the French Reconstruction Unit to Poland, where he worked under the Quaker relief organization. Four workers transferred from France to Germany; Atlee Hostetler, Homer Hostetler, and Ora R. Liechty assisted in chief feeding work under the AFSC, and Solomon E. Yoder visited families of German prisoners of war who had worked for the AFSC reconstruction unit in France, and remunerated them for their service. Russell Lantz worked for a time in Poland under the AFSC. The AFSC administered the entire German section of the European Children's Fund program which began in February 1920. At one time this organization was feeding 1,000,000 German children daily. The AFSC asked S. E. Allgyer to organize support for this program among all branches of American Mennonites. This offer was not accepted, however, because of commitments by the MRCWS in the Near East and Russia.

The American Mennonites did, however, give considerable support to the South German Mennonite relief organization, *Christenpflicht* (*q.v.*), founded in 1920 under the leadership of Michael Horsch (*q.v.*). In 1922 Horsch visited the American Mennonites in behalf of this work and in 1930 he reported that during this period the total receipts of Christenpflicht had been about $62,000, of which $44,000 had been contributed by the MRCWS, $8,500 by the Emergency Relief Commission (GCM), $6,500 by other American Mennonite sources, and the remainder by the European Mennonites. Closely associated with Christenpflicht was the *Mennonitische Flüchtlingsfürsorge* (*q.v.*), later called *Deutsche Mennoniten-Hilfe* (*q.v.*), also organized in 1920, with headquarters at first at Heilbronn, for the assistance of Mennonite refugees from Russia. This organization operated a refugee camp at Lechfeld (*q.v.*).

Near East Relief (*NER*). Another needy relief field was the Near East. For many years the Armenians and other Christians had been persecuted by the Turks. Perhaps a million had been killed or died as a result of mistreatment. Perhaps another three quarter million lived as refugees and orphans in various parts of the old Turkish Empire. In addition to the obvious need of the sufferers, this field of service appealed to the American Mennonites because its location was in Bible lands which it was believed would provide opportunities for a new mission field.

As early as November 1915 the American Committee for Armenian and Syrian Relief, later known as the Near East Relief, was organized. The NER was able to do a small amount of work during the war. As soon as the war was over, however, it was ready to operate on a large scale, using missions and mission schools throughout the region as the base of operations. A plan was launched to raise $30,000,000 during the winter of 1918-19. The cause was promoted through American Sunday schools, who were asked to raise $2,000,000. The General Sunday School Committee of the Mennonite Church (MC) co-operated in this plan.

On Jan. 4, 1919, the MRCWS accepted an invitation from the NER to co-operate in its work by contributing personnel and funds. Five days later payment of $20,000 as the first financial contribution to the NER was authorized. On Jan. 25, 1919, the *Pensacola* sailed for Beirut carrying 42 relief workers and 5,000 tons of relief supplies. Among the relief workers were nine Mennonites, seven young men going out as workers under the direction of Aaron Loucks and William A. Derstine, the latter two men having the responsibility to locate and organize a field of work and to determine its relation to the Near East Relief. It was hoped that a semiautonomous work could be organized under the general administration of the NER, conversations with the NER headquarters in New York apparently having suggested this possibility. It was also hoped that the Mennonite relief program in the Near East would lead directly to the establishment of mission work. After further study, however, the idea of a semiautonomous Mennonite unit was abandoned. Loucks and Derstine then sailed for home, while the seven young men remained in Beirut in the service of the Syrian area of the NER under the direction of James H. Nicol.

The reasons for abandoning the original plan for a Mennonite relief unit were (1) the inexperience of the Mennonite Church; (2) confusion within the administration of the NER, particularly lack of understanding between its New York office and its Constantinople director; (3) the poor prospects for a mission in the area since the field was covered by other long-established missions; (4) the need for the services of the Mennonite workers within the NER organization at Beirut.

Of the seven men in the first contingent Orie O. Miller became administrative assistant to Nicol and assistant director of the Syrian area extending from Port Said to Mardin, in which at least 7,000 orphans were located; David Zimmerman was construction engineer; Ezra Deter was engaged in transport in the Beirut district; William Stoltzfus and Silas Hertzler had charge of orphanage work in Sidon; B. F. Stoltzfus was assistant director of an orphanage in Jerusalem; and C. L. Graber was director of a refugee camp and industrial work in Aleppo. Dur-

ing 1919 nine more Mennonites entered the NER service and in the next two years 13 more men and two women did so, making a total of 31 Mennonite NER workers. The work of these men and women was similar to that of the original seven. One of the men, Menno Shellenberger of Kansas, who sailed with the last group in July 1921, died on the field. The total financial contribution of the Amercian Mennonites to NER was $339,000, of which $326,000 was contributed through the *Mennonite Relief Commission for War Sufferers* (MC) and the Eastern Mennonite Board of Missions and Charities. While the original hopes for the establishment of a semiautonomous or even an independent Mennonite relief project in the Near East were not realized, the workers on the field and the American Mennonites as a whole gained much valuable experience through their co-operation with NER, as well as earlier with the AFSC in the French reconstruction work.

Russian Relief. As early as 1919 M. B. Fast, W. P. Neufeld, and B. B. Reimer, Mennonites of Reedley, Cal., collected funds, clothing, and relief supplies amounting to more than $40,000 for the suffering Mennonite communities in Siberia, which were at that time not under Soviet rule. Fast accompanied the shipment in person and was joined later by Neufeld. Following their return the Emergency Relief Committee of the Mennonites of North America was organized Jan. 4, 1920, at Hillsboro, Kan., with P. C. Hiebert as chairman and M. B. Fast as general secretary; but it soon found the door to Siberia closed by military developments.

In June 1920, however, the Studienkommission (*q.v.*), composed of four Mennonite delegates from Russia, came to America to solicit help for their people who were suffering from famine, many of whom desired to emigrate. In response to this need and appeal the MCC was organized in July 1920 for the operation of a joint Mennonite relief program. The Emergency Relief Committee of the Mennonites of North America now joined its forces with the new movements as did the MRCWS, the Emergency Relief Committee of the General Conference Mennonite Church, the Eastern Mennonite Board of Missions and Charities, the Krimmer Mennonite Brethren, and the Mennonite Brethren Church. P. C. Hiebert was elected as chairman (serving until 1952) and Levi Mumaw as executive secretary (serving until his death in 1937), after which Orie O. Miller was chosen to fill his place (serving until 1958).

The Constantinople Unit. In August 1920, a church-wide program was launched for the gathering of new and used clothing, and in September twenty-five tons of clothing were shipped and three men sailed from New York to open the work in Russia, these being Orie O. Miller, Arthur W. Slagel, and Clayton Kratz. They reached Constantinople on September 27 and found numerous refugees from Russia, including some Mennonites, in the city. Slagel then remained in Constantinople with the shipment of goods and acquainted himself with the work of the NER, while Miller and Kratz went to Sebastopol, arriving on Oct. 6, 1920, from whence they pushed up into the Mennonite territory to survey the needs and complete plans for carrying on the work. After spending a few days there Miller returned to Constantinople to bring in the supplies in company with Slagel, while Kratz remained in Russia.

Although the Soviet government was now about three years old, the opposition forces had not been completely subdued, and at the time when Miller and Kratz came into Russia the White army of General Wrangel was in control of much of the area of the Mennonite settlements. Before Miller returned from Constantinople, however, Wrangel's forces were defeated and Clayton Kratz was caught behind the Bolshevik lines. He was later taken into custody by Bolshevik authorities and has never been heard from since. It is assumed that he died at their hands. Another result of Wrangel's defeat was the flight of about 130,000 refugees, including 200 Mennonites, from Russia to Constantinople. When they arrived many of them were unable to leave their ships for almost a month. The condition of these people was so appalling that the MCC found its first task to be that of helping to care for them. An orphanage was opened for the care of the children, and a department was opened for the distribution of the clothing which had been sent over. A home was opened for women and girls, and also a Mennonite home to care for the Mennonites on the refugee ship. Besides these four projects the MCC had charge of four smaller camps outside the city where they distributed soap, fuel, clothing, medicine, and other necessaries. This work in Constantinople was finally closed in July 1922. The total amount expended for the work of the Constantinople unit was over $200,000. Of this amount more than $14,000 was used to assist a group of sixty-four Russian Mennonite refugees to come from Constantinople to America. In addition to Arthur W. Slagel, the workers comprising the Constantinople unit were B. F. Stoltzfus, J. E. Brunk, Vesta Zook, and Vinora Weaver.

Relief Work in Russia. Early in 1921 Alvin J. Miller, who had been with the reconstruction service in France, was appointed by the MCC as director of relief work in Russia, which was now almost completely under Soviet control. He came to Constantinople on Jan. 29, 1921, and then early in April, in company with Arthur W. Slagel, he sailed for the port of Novorossisk on the Black Sea, but they were refused entry into Russia. Miller now turned to Western Europe to make contact with Soviet diplomatic missions there, particularly in London. The Soviet government was very suspicious of all outside influences; therefore Miller's task was a very difficult one. But after making many contacts with the Red Cross, with Herbert Hoover's American Relief Administration, with the Quaker organization, and other agencies, Miller finally found his way to Moscow and gained an audience with the head of the Russian Central Commission for Combatting Famine, who signed an agreement on Oct. 1, 1921, stating the terms whereby the MCC would be permitted to carry on relief work in South Russia. Although the American Relief Administration had received permission in August 1921 to open work

in Russia, authorization to do so in the Ukraine was not granted until January 1922, three months after the MCC agreement was signed.

The MCC operated in that part of Russia where the Mennonites lived, but relief was given to the entire population regardless of race or creed. Extensive work was carried on in some villages where no Mennonites lived at all. The method of work was to establish feeding kitchens in villages and distribute food to the needy. By May 1922 the Mennonites were feeding 25,000 persons daily, and by August the figure had reached 40,000. The feeding kitchens continued in operation through the summer of 1924. In addition to this service the MCC distributed food packets sent by Americans directly to their relatives and friends in Russia. Fifty or more Fordson tractor plow outfits were also shipped to the Mennonite villages by the MCC, these to take the place of the horses lost to the villages during the time of the war. The American Mennonites spent a total of about $1,200,000 for the relief work in Russia, and this was supplemented by several hundred thousand dollars contributed by the Mennonites of Holland, who also sent two Dutch representatives to the field in Russia. The total amount contributed by the American Mennonites and distributed through its own organizations for the relief of war sufferers in Europe and the Near East during World War I and immediately afterwards is estimated at about $2,500,000. In addition to O. O. Miller, A. J. Miller, and Clayton Kratz, the Mennonite relief workers in Russia included G. G. Hiebert, P. C. Hiebert, D. R. Hoeppner, Barbara Hofer, D. M. Hofer, C. E. Krehbiel, Daniel Schroeder, A. W. Slagel, P. H. Unruh, and H. C. Yoder. In August and September 1921, Jacob Koekebakker, pastor of Middelburg, as a representative of the Dutch Mennonite Committee for Foreign Needs, negotiated with the authorities at Moscow, where he worked with Orie O. Miller. Pastor F. C. Fleischer (*q.v.*) had charge of the food and clothing shipments of the Dutch Mennonites in the Ukraine from early 1922 until the summer of 1923. R. J. C. Willink was the director of the Dutch relief action in Russia. For particulars see **Fonds voor Buitenlandsche Nooden.**

Emigration from Russia to Canada. Besides its relief program in Russia, MCC had an important part in the migration, although at first several other Mennonite organizations were effected to carry on this task. One of these was the Mennonite Board of Colonization (*q.v.*) organized in 1920 at Newton; the other, the more important one of the two, was the Canadian Mennonite Board of Colonization (*q.v.*) with headquarters at Rosthern, Sask., organized in 1922 under the leadership of David Toews. The Canadian Pacific Railway and Steamship Company welcomed the prospect of new immigrants to settle the lands in western Canada, especially since it had confidence in the Mennonites because of the splendid record of the immigrants of the 1870's in repaying the loan which they had received from the government.

In the summer of 1923, therefore, the railway company readily entered into an agreement with the

Canadian Mennonite Board of Colonization to transport 3,000 Mennonites from Russia to Canada at the rate of $140 per person on a credit basis. To this was to be added the railway fare from the port of entry to their final destination. The credit was extended without collateral, the Board of Colonization, with no assets, alone being liable for payment; individual members of the board assumed no financial responsibility. When the first 3,000 immigrants had arrived the contract was renewed. Renewal was repeated from time to time until by 1927 about 20,000 Russian Mennonites had arrived in Canada. The railway and steamship company extended a total credit of $2,000,000. In spite of the long depression years about two thirds of this amount had been repaid as early as 1940, and by 1945 the entire debt had been liquidated. In 1925-26 about 600 immigrants were brought from Russia to Mexico with the aid of the Mennonite Board of Colonization of Newton. Later, however, most of these removed to the United States or Canada. The few who remain live in a little settlement of their own at Cuauhtemoc, near the larger colony of Mennonites from Canada.

During the years following the Russian revolution, while some of the Mennonites were finding their way from Russia to America, many others were trying to restore the life of their old communities, hoping that the Soviet government would develop a policy of tolerance making it possible for Mennonite life to continue in a normal way. During the period of the New Economic Policy, 1921-28, it seemed as if this hope might eventually be realized; but after Stalin introduced his Five Year Plan in 1928 for the complete communization of Russia this hope was brought to an end. Those Mennonites who had the courage to maintain their individuality and their religious life soon found their property confiscated and sold, and themselves deported to northern Russia, where they suffered untold hardships and perished in large numbers. By 1929 the situation was so desperate that thousands of them determined to leave the country at any cost.

In the late spring of 1929 a few families from Siberia went to Moscow to secure passports for emigration. Finally, in August permission was granted them to leave. As soon as the news reached the Mennonite settlements there was a literal march on Moscow to secure passports. In a short time 15,000 would-be emigrants, chiefly Mennonites, were in the city, and it was estimated that 40,000 more were on the way. "It was a mass movement, unplanned, unorganized, hysterical almost." The government refused to grant passports, however, and made desperate efforts to stop the movement. Police were sent to the colonies to prevent Mennonites from boarding the trains and leaders were imprisoned. Thousands of the would-be emigrants encamped about Moscow were arrested and shipped, in unheated, sealed stock cars, to South Russia or Siberia in the cold of November and December.

Of this large number who sought to emigrate 6,000, two thirds of whom were Mennonites, however, received passports. But then they discovered that the Canadian government would not admit those without funds, unless they had friends who

could guarantee that they would not become public charges. For a time it appeared that they would not be able to leave, but fortunately the German government admitted them to Germany temporarily, giving them time to decide on their final destination. The German Reichstag appropriated 6,000,000 Marks, as a loan for the aid of the refugees; various philanthropic organizations, including the German Red Cross, operating in an over-all organization known as "Brüder in Not," helped to care for them, and the Mennonites of Germany and Holland also organized an effectual relief work among them. Benjamin H. Unruh, one of the four Studienkommission delegates from Russia, who had remained in Germany as the agent for the Russian Mennonites and had done great work in the 1922-27 emigration, now served as the liaison with the Mennonites of Western Europe and America in caring for the 1929-30 movement.

Unruh now appealed to the MCC for help. Since emigration to the United States was impossible, and since the door to Canada was also practically closed because of the economic depression, the MCC turned to Paraguay as the best place to which the refugees in Germany might look for a home, and made plans to colonize as many as possible there. Harold S. Bender was then sent to Germany in early 1930 as special commissioner of the MCC, charged with the task of supervising the migration, arranging transportation, and purchasing basic equipment. At the same time C. G. Hiebert was sent to Paraguay. Eventually almost 1,000 of those who had close relatives and friends in Canada found their way there. Another 1,200 settled in Brazil under the auspices of the German government. These were joined later by a group of Russian Mennonite refugees from Harbin, China, making the total immigration to Brazil about 1,300. The remaining 1,700 were brought to Paraguay and settled on land near the Manitoba settlement formed in 1926-27, called the Menno Colony. The new Russian colony was called Fernheim. To these were added about 300 refugees from Harbin, besides a few immigrants from Poland. By 1938 the total Mennonite population in Paraguay was 4,757.

In addition to the 29,000 or more refugees who found their way from Russia to permanent homes in Canada, Brazil, and Paraguay in 1922-32 there were also numerous individuals or small groups who escaped from Russia. One man who was sentenced to forced labor succeeded in having his family brought to him and then together they escaped across Turkestan and the Himalayas to the Mennonite mission at Champa, India. In 1931 three young women fled through eastern Siberia, across the Amur River into China, and then across the Pacific to America. Some fled across the Caucasus into Persia. Others escaped from the lumber camps of northern Russia by British lumber steamer to England or Germany. Many who tried to do so perished in the attempt. Many who remained in Russia also perished at the hands of the Soviets.

Continuing Assistance in Paraguay. Since the colonization of the Mennonite refugees in Paraguay in 1930 the MCC has followed the policy of keeping in close touch with the settlers, providing the assistance necessary in the struggles and hardships of pioneer life. The original expenditure of the MCC in settling the refugees in Paraguay was nearly $200,000. At the time of immigration the settlers had contracted to purchase their land from the Corporación Paraguaya. As time went on, however, it became advisable for the MCC to purchase the Corporación Paraguaya and all its holdings. This purchase of an area more than twenty by twenty-five miles in extent, comprising 330,000 acres, was made in 1937 for some $57,500, with funds loaned to the MCC by the Mennonites of North America. The Paraguayan settlers now purchased their individual holdings from the MCC at one dollar (paper) per hectare, instead of the original eight dollars (gold) which they had contracted for with the Corporación Paraguaya. In 1943 a cancellation of approximately one half of the loan debt was actually carried through.

The program of aid to the new settlers in Paraguay has been continuous and vigorous from the beginning. It was being carried on in reduced form in 1958. Money was sent down for direct relief, but more important was such aid as the sending of a succession of doctors and a dentist for short-term service in the colony and the training of practical nurses and even "practical" dentists. Shipments of new and used clothing, new and used farm implements and tools, a large bulldozer with a trained operator, support of a mental hospital, support of an experimental farm, support of hospitals, and the support for the preparation of schoolteachers of Fernheim Colony in Switzerland were among the forms of aid. In 1957 a group of Pax men was sent down to aid in the construction of the Trans-Chaco roadway. In 1958, through the good offices of the MCC a U.S. government loan of $1,000,000 was made available for colony development through the Paraguayan government.

Spanish Relief. In June 1937 the Mennonite Board of Missions authorized a program of relief to be administered by the Mennonite Relief Committee (see **Mennonite Relief and Service Committee**) in Spain, which was then engaged in civil war. Funds and clothing were gathered and D. Parke Lantz and Levi C. Hartzler were sent to the field in November 1937, followed later by Clarence Fretz, Lester T. Hershey, Wilbert Nafziger, and Ernest Bennett. When the program closed in the spring of 1940 cash contributions and gifts in kind amounting to about $57,000 had been contributed for this work by the American Mennonites. The Dutch Mennonite Peace Group had also contributed about $1,500 to the work. The MRC work in Spain was closely co-ordinated with that of the AFSC. In addition to the Mennonite contributions the MRC in Spain distributed a large amount of food supplied by the International Commission for the Assistance of Child Refugees in Spain. The MRC work was on the Loyalist side.

World War II. With the coming of World War II the Mennonite relief ministry was expanded beyond anything which had been conceived in World War I. As a result of the earlier experience the MCC had now developed into an agency co-ordinating the relief work of Mennonites everywhere. It

was an efficient and effective agency which had found its place in a world of relief agencies, both public and private, and was equipped to send funds and workers as needed anywhere in the world, operating independently or in co-operation with other agencies as the occasion might require.

Within three months after the opening of World War II the first MCC representative was in Europe to begin negotiations for a relief program in Poland. A modest work was carried on there from March 1940 until the entrance of the United States into the war. In the spring of 1940 work was opened in southern France for the care of Spanish refugees. Following the German occupation of northern France the work was extended to child feeding in Lyons and other cities and to the care of refugees from German-occupied territory. This phase of the work came to an end in 1942 after the Germans took over the southern French territory.

Early in 1940 the MCC began work in England among refugees from Austria, Poland, and Turkey. The work was later extended to include assistance to old people and children who had been bombed out of their homes in the cities, as well as a ministry to German prisoners of war and other services. The London center was now the European headquarters of the MCC. In addition to carrying on the work in that country plans were being made to open an enlarged work on the continent as soon as the opportunity presented itself. As the war drew to a close the headquarters were moved to Amsterdam and later in 1945 to Basel. (In 1952 it was again moved, this time to Frankfurt.)

As rapidly as possible, now, new relief projects were opened in practically all countries of western Europe. By the end of 1945 the MCC reported 14 workers in France, nine in Holland, three in Belgium, and two at the general headquarters. The work consisted of building reconstruction, emergency relief in the form of food and clothing, and the care of refugees.

In 1946 the MCC work was extended to Germany, Denmark, and Austria. By 1947 the relief program in Germany was in full swing. During that year alone 43 MCC workers distributed 4,538 tons of food, clothing, and other supplies in Germany. The over-all work of the MCC was co-ordinated with CRALOG (the Council for Relief Agencies Licensed for Operation in Germany), and Evangelisches Hilfswerk, the Protestant relief organization. Assistance to Mennonite refugees from Russia and East Germany was co-ordinated with German Mennonite relief agencies: Christenpflicht, the south German agency, and the Hilfswerk der Vereinigung Deutscher Mennonitengemeinden, the organization operating in the Palatinate and North Germany. The MCC had food distribution centers in many cities. In June 1947 alone MCC supplied food to 80,000 people in Germany. Work was extended into Poland (part MRSC), Hungary, Italy, and Belgium (MRSC).

A major portion of MCC work was devoted to Mennonite refugees from the east, who came in large numbers to Denmark, Germany, and even into Holland. In February 1947 the *Volendam* carried 2,304 of these refugees from Bremerhaven to

20

Buenos Aires on their way to Paraguay. Of these passengers 329 were gathered from Dutch homes, 1,071 from a refugee camp near Munich, and the remainder came from Berlin. In 1947 the MCC opened two refugee camps in Germany, one at Gronau and the other at Backnang. These camps served as processing centers from which as many as possible were moved to Canada and South America, and a few to the United States, in many cases with assistance from the International Refugee Organization (*q.v.*). From 1946 to 1951 the MCC assisted a total of 13,980 European refugees in finding new homes in the Western Hemisphere. Of those who remained in Germany permanently, many have been settled in new housing projects with MCC help through its Pax (*q.v.*) services, in which the labor of young American Mennonites, engaged in alternative service under conscription, served as the down payment for the house which was then financed by the German government. Such housing projects are located at Wedel near Hamburg, Bielefeld, Backnang, and Enkenbach.

Pax units are also located in other countries, as in Greece where the work is devoted to agricultural improvement, in Algeria (MRSC) as a housing project, and in South America where it is road building. Additional forms of aid in Germany and elsewhere in Europe have been maintenance of children's and old people's homes and community centers.

In addition to Europe the MCC and Mennonite relief agencies associated with it had operations following the beginning of World War II in Jordan, Egypt, and Ethiopia in the Middle East. The work in Egypt in 1944-45 concentrated on aid to Greek and Yugoslav refugees; that in Ethiopia on hospital and medical service; and that in Jordan on help to the Arab refugees from Israel. In the Far East following 1942 work was opened in India, China, the Philippine Islands, Java, Sumatra, Japan, Korea, Formosa, Viet-Nam, and Nepal. One of the most significant projects of the MCC was that in Puerto Rico (*q.v.*) which began as a CPS unit in 1943, but which employed other personnel engaging in medical and hospital work, and in agricultural and community services.

From 1941 through 1950 the MCC and its affiliated organizations expended more than $12,000,000 in cash and kind for relief purposes. To this must be added perhaps several millions more for the resettlement of refugees. Bringing this help in the name of Christ represented a direct personal ministry of perhaps 700 or more men and women, besides occasional short-term commissioners. After 1948 the relief program had passed its crest. Even so, the annual meeting of the MCC in March 1950 reported a total of 156 workers still on the field, distributed as follows: South America 21, Ethiopia 15 (MRSC), Palestine 5, Far East 26, Europe 59. The latter group had 59 workers in Germany, 8 in France, 4 in Belgium, 4 in Italy, 4 in Austria, 5 in Holland, and 7 in Switzerland, the latter constituting the personnel of the headquarters office in Basel.

Relief in some form somewhere seems to be a continuing need. The annual meeting of the MCC in January 1958 reported a total of 211 Mennonite workers on the field in 1957, distributed as follows:

relief workers 115, Pax men 96. Of the total 61 were in Germany, with 30 additional in Europe (Austria, France, Holland, Switzerland), 24 were in Paraguay with 11 additional in South America (Brazil, Uruguay, Peru), 14 were in Korea, and 42 additional in the Far East (Viet-Nam, Indonesia, Formosa, Japan, India, Nepal); 16 were in Jordan and 9 were in Algeria (MRSC).

From such a long list of persons who served in Mennonite relief since 1940 it is impossible to mention by name all who rendered even outstanding service. Among the names which have become almost household words, however, are those of C. F. Klassen, the father of the refugees, who died in the service in Germany in 1954, and Peter and Elfrieda Dyck, who led the refugees on the *Volendam* to South America in 1947. In 1957 Peter Dyck was serving as general director of the MCC in Europe. The only MCC relief worker who died in the line of duty in Europe was Marie Fast, who lost her life in 1945 in the Mediterranean Sea while assisting in the repatriation of Yugoslav refugees returning from Egypt; however, two Pax boys died in Greece while swimming and one in Africa, and two girls serving under the MCC died in Korea while recreationing.

The world-wide Mennonite relief work which has developed beginning with World War I and especially since the formation of the MCC in 1920 represents both a cause and an effect of a reawakened and an increasingly ecumenical Mennonitism. In 1915 the European and American Mennonites did not know each other and even many of the Mennonite groups in America had little in common. Even in 1925 only two Americans were present at the first Mennonite World Conference in Basel, Switzerland. The events which followed in the wake of World War II, however, changed this picture completely. By the time of the 1957 World Conference at Karlsruhe, Germany, the existence of a world Mennonitism, in which Mennonites from all parts of the world including the younger churches, as those of India and Indonesia, share in common faith and life and work, had become a fact which was recognized by all.

The two-century-old tradition of active relief work in the Dutch Mennonite brotherhood is carried on today by the *Stichting* (*q.v.*) *voor Bijzondere Noden in de Doopsgezinde Broederschap en Daarbuiten,* organized in 1948 as the successor to the prewar *Algemeene Commissie voor Buitenlandsche Nooden.* It has been active in sending relief to Austria and Germany, and particularly since 1955 in Berlin. It took the lead in organizing the International Mennonite Relief Committee in 1955, with the specific purpose of strengthening the relief work for East Zone Mennonites through the Berlin Mennonite Church.

In Germany the *Hilfswerk der Vereinigung der Deutschen Mennonitengemeinden,* established in 1948 to help care for the Mennonite refugees from the East (West and East Prussia), has continued to serve especially in aiding the relief work carried on by the Berlin Mennonite Church for the East Zone Mennonites. Mennonitische Heime was organized in 1948 to establish homes for aged refugees, which are subsidized by the German government through per capita per diem payments for inmates. The MCC has also helped by contribution of relief food. Three such homes have been established: Enkenbach, Leutesdorf, and Pinneberg. Additional German Mennonite organizations have been established to work in the field of resettlement of refugees: *Mennonitische Siedlungshilfe* (1953) and *Genossenschaftliches Flüchtlingswerk* (1954). G.F.H.

John D. Unruh, *In the Name of Christ: A History of the Mennonite Central Committee* (Scottdale, 1952); P. C. Hiebert and Orie O. Miller, *Feeding the Hungry* (Scottdale, 1929); S. C. Yoder, *For Conscience Sake: A Study of Mennonite Migrations Resulting from the World War* (Goshen, 1940); Irvin B. Horst, *A Ministry of Goodwill: A Short Account of Mennonite Relief, 1939-1940* (Akron, 1950); M. C. Lehman, *Mennonite History and Principles of Mennonite Relief Work, an Introduction, Students Edition with Syllabus and Annotated Bibliography* (Akron, 1945); W. J. Kühler, "Dutch Mennonite Relief Work in the 17th and 18th Centuries," *MQR* XVII (1943) 87-94; Christian Neff, ed., *Mennonitische Welt-Hilfs-Konferenz vom 31. August bis 3. September 1930 in Danzig* (Karlsruhe, 1931); see also the reports and addresses on relief and refugee work in the printed reports of the other Mennonite World Conferences (1936 at Amsterdam, 1948 at Goshen and Newton, 1952 at Basel, 1957 at Karlsruhe); C. Krahn, J. W. Fretz, and R. Kreider, "Altruism in Mennonite Life," in P. A. Sorokin, *Forms and Techniques of Altruistic and Spiritual Growth, a Symposium* (Boston, 1954) 309-28.

Religious Liberty (freedom of conscience, toleration). Toleration of a variety of religions or religious groups and opinions within the boundaries of a single state has often been a major problem, under both Christian and non-Christian governments. The Roman Empire was not completely intolerant when Christianity was established. On the contrary, it symbolized its tolerance by the erection of the Pantheon at Rome, in which all the gods were to be represented. When it became clear that Christianity was not a part of Judaism and would not give the Roman Emperor divine honor and worship, it was declared an illegal religion (*religio illicita*), in the time of the Emperor Trajan (*c*96). After the failure of the policy of persecution became clear, edicts of toleration were issued in 311 and 313 making Christianity a permitted, i.e., tolerated religion. The pendulum then swung to the opposite extreme so that in 380 an edict was issued by the Emperor Theodosius making Christianity the state religion and the only tolerated religion. From that time on in the Empire, the only Christianity recognized was that of the ecumenical creeds (Nicea, Chalcedon, etc.). Not only were the heathen religions not tolerated but no form of deviant (i.e., heretical) Christianity was permitted. Heresy, as defined by the state church (Roman or Greek), became a crime against the state and punishable by death. There was no religious liberty, except for the one recognized religion. The Constantinian compromise of the essence of the church by union with the state meant the end of toleration. This was the state of affairs down to the Reformation.

But the Reformation brought no freedom of conscience or religious liberty to Europe. On the contrary, the Reformers, in spite of early declaration seemingly supporting freedom of conscience, finally turned out to be as intolerant as the Roman Church. (See **Luther.**) They were intolerant not only toward the Roman Church, but also toward other forms of Protestantism, and in particular bitterly intolerant of Anabaptism. When the principle of territorial churches, coextensive with the civil state, was established, in both Lutheran and Reformed areas, with only one religion tolerated, the rulers were often perplexed as to what to do with deviants from the established faith, particularly the Anabaptists, who were so persistent and earnest in witnessing to their faith and establishing their voluntary congregations. Seeking counsel from the religious leaders, such as Luther and Melanchthon, they received lengthy documents, numbers of which have been printed, commonly counseling complete intolerance and usually calling for severe persecution including death. While without doubt the motives of both rulers and Reformers were mixed, including fear for the established political and social order if toleration should be granted, yet the basic fact is that religious liberty was denied. The bitter persecution of the Anabaptists everywhere, almost from the beginning, ordered on the basis of such sweeping decrees as that of the Diet of Speyer in 1529, is irrefutable evidence of the intolerance of both Catholic and Protestant civil and religious authorities.

The victory for religious liberty was not won in Western Europe until the 17th and even 18th centuries (in certain Eastern European, and even Western European Catholic countries, not until the late 19th or even 20th century, and in some parts is not yet secure, notably Spain and Soviet Russia), and then it was to a large extent due not to the will of the dominant Christian churches, whether Catholic or Protestant, but to the will of rulers exhausted by religious wars and determined to find a basis for peace in the European community which would transcend the warring religious parties; or it was due to the growing rationalism, secularism, and materialism of the ever more powerful emerging middle class, which often placed religion low in the scale of cultural values.

A. *Anabaptist-Mennonite Experience of Religious Liberty.* The record of the suffering of the Anabaptists and Mennonites under this policy of intolerance is reported in the various articles in this ENCYCLOPEDIA covering countries, regions, and political units in general, and in the biographical articles on a number of emperors, kings, etc., and need not be repeated here. (See for instance **Germany, Netherlands,** etc.) Suffice it to say that often the rulers and landholders were tolerant toward the Mennonites of the 17th century and later, because of their economic value, and frequently had great difficulties with the intolerant clergy of their domains. The fact also that citizenship was not a universal right, but a privilege to be granted or withheld by the rulers or granted conditionally, had a direct bearing on toleration. In some areas in Germany, especially Mennonites were not granted full and unconditional citizenship until the second half of the 19th century.

By contrast the New World was a land of religious liberty and therefore a most attractive place of settlement for the harried Mennonites of Europe (outside the Netherlands, which as early as 1572 granted partial toleration to the Mennonites). While certain of the American Colonies had established churches (Massachusetts, e.g., down to 1844, Virginia, etc.) and in the early days were rather intolerant, complete tolerance soon became the general rule and full religious liberty was written into the federal constitution (1787) and into the several state constitutions. William Penn's colony of Pennsylvania (established 1681) from the beginning offered complete religious liberty (except for Catholics); in fact Penn planned it as a haven of refuge for persecuted Quakers and other persecuted religious minorities. The Mennonites who settled in Pennsylvania from 1683 on enjoyed complete religious freedom and have suffered no persecution anywhere in the New World, except by mob action, or by punishment for violation of certain regulations or aspects of the legislation requiring military or civil service. Difficulties arising out of conscription do not invalidate, however, the basic principle of religious liberty and freedom of conscience which has been a fundamental and deeply cherished principle of the American nation from its beginning. The same holds generally true for Canada.

There has been occasional persecution of Protestant minorities in Latin-American countries where Catholicism is the established or dominant religion. Mennonite missions or colonies established in these countries have generally enjoyed full liberty of worship and propagation of their faith. A recent outbreak of intolerance and persecution in Colombia has caused some tribulation for the Mennonite Brethren and General Conference Mennonite Missions there.

The most serious case of denial of religious liberty for Mennonites in modern times has been Soviet Russia. It is true that Czarist Russia forbade proselyting of Greek Orthodox people, and in this sense certainly did not allow full freedom of propagation of faith (although allowing it among the non-Greek Orthodox people), but full freedom of worship was guaranteed to the Mennonites and other settlers immigrating into Russia in 1788 and later, and this right was consistently maintained. The constitution of Soviet Russia guarantees full freedom of worship, but denies freedom of propagation of religion. In actuality freedom of worship was severely restricted in 1929-41 through the closing of churches, imprisonment, deportation, and even execution of clergy, severe limitation of religious activities such as instruction of children under 18, and all types of religious organizations except direct congregational structure. At times religious persecution was carried on under the guise of breaking resistance to collectivization of agriculture; and it is clear that the leadership of the Soviet state sought to break up any type of solidarity of religious, ethnic, or economic groups, which might conceivably be or become a source of continuing resistance to the communist regime or ideology in any form. Religion, particularly for Mennonites, was one of the strongest bonds for the maintenance of a spirit of nonacceptance of the Marxist ideology. Mennonites in Russia were never guilty of any disobedience to the Soviet authorities or forcible resistance to government measures, but they did endeavor to maintain their church and community life as long as possible, and to nurture their children in the faith of their fathers. The clash with the Soviet state was inevitable and resulted in untold suffering, including the death of thousands in Russia, in forced labor camps, and in exile. Mennonite church life was completely broken up. Religious services were no longer held; probably no organized worship was conducted from 1935 to 1943. Since 1943, at first in a very slight and tentative way, and since 1953 more openly and extensively, Mennonite worship has been reviving, with regular preaching, choir singing, prayer meetings, etc. A severe handicap has been the death of ordained ministers, since very few survived the ordeal of 1935-43. A further difficulty is the fact that liberty of worship is permitted by law only to registered congregations, and it has been impossible for the Mennonite congregations to secure legal recognition and registry since they have again emerged from the period of persecution.

Mennonite suffering in Russia has been further compounded by the fact of their German culture, language, and sympathies. It is difficult at times to determine whether their tribulations were due to their Germanic character, their economic skill, their sturdy non-Marxianism, or their religious steadfastness. Perhaps the very combination of several undesirable (from the Soviet point of view) qualities made their lot more difficult. Certain it is that the Evangelical Christians and Baptists in Russia, though also subject to a certain amount of persecution in the dark days, have since 1943 enjoyed much more liberty than the Mennonites. A major reason may well be their Slavic character.

B. Advocacy of Religious Liberty. The Anabaptists were the only Reformation group consistently advocating religious liberty, separation of church and state, freedom of the individual conscience, and toleration of divergence in religious matters, although individuals like Sebastian Franck and Sebastian Castellio were outstanding exceptions, particularly the latter. The Anabaptists did not produce any extensive literary defense of their position, as did Castellio, but from the very beginning of the movement they gave constant witness to their strong convictions on this great principle. It was not only their Biblicism with its desire to follow both the commandments and example of Christ which motivated them, but their fundamental conception of Christianity as a matter of voluntary commitment and free choice, their insistence on love to all as a universal Christian obligation with its corollary of nonviolence and nonresistance, their understanding of suffering as the way of victory or a theology of martyrdom, and their belief that faith is a gift from God and hence impossible to create by compulsion of man.

The place of Anabaptism in the history of religious liberty has been recognized by a few scholars such as Ernst Troeltsch, Johannes Kühn, and Rufus M. Jones, but it has as yet not been brought out in sufficient clarity and strength to become a part of the commonly accepted understanding of the development of toleration, although certainly all who are at all seriously conversant with Anabaptist history are aware of the general Anabaptist position. It must be admitted that the break-through to religious liberty and toleration in Western Europe was due primarily to other forces, but the Anabaptists were the prophets before their time, the pioneers who had to raise their voices in a wilderness, who had to go counter to the entire spirit of their age, the 16th century. Professor Walther Köhler of Heidelberg declared that "they dare to claim a place in history as the pioneers (*Bahnbrecher*) of the modern world view with its freedom of conscience and freedom of faith." Ernst Troeltsch says, "All this [i.e., toleration, liberty, the rise of the modern free man, etc., in England] is not actually the work of Protestantism, but rather the work of a revived Anabaptism and Spiritualism (merged with a radicalized Calvinism), which thus received a belated compensation for the boundless suffering which this religion of toleration and personal convincement of conscience endured at the hands of all the confessions in the 16th century. Here the stepchildren of the Reformation finally enjoyed their great historical hour." Bradford Smith in his biography, *Bradford & Plymouth* (1951), does not hesitate to identify the Pilgrim libertarian tradition which ultimately won out over Puritan authoritarianism in New England as essentially Dutch and Anabaptist in character.

C. *Anabaptist Testimonies on Religious Liberty.* Out of the fullness of material cited in H. S. Bender's "The Anabaptist and Religious Liberty in the Sixteenth Century" (*MQR* XXIX, 1955, 83-100) the following typical statements are here cited. Conrad Grebel in the letter to Thomas Müntzer (1524) wrote: "The Gospel and its adherents are not to be protected by the sword, nor are they thus to protect themselves." Felix Manz, in Zürich court records of 1525 and 1526, admitted teaching that those of other faiths are to be left undisturbed in their practice. Balthasar Hubmaier in his four-page pamphlet *Concerning Heretics and Their Burning* (January 1524), which is called the first Protestant declaration for religious freedom, said, "So it follows that the slayers of heretics are the worst heretics of all, in that they, contrary to Christ's teaching and practice, condemn heretics to the fire." Hans Denk (1527) said, "Everyone should know that in matters of faith everyone should proceed as free, voluntary, and uncompelled." Kilian Aurbacher of Moravia wrote in a letter to Bucer in Strasbourg (1534): "It is never right to compel one in matters of faith, whatever he may believe, be he Jew or Turk. . . . And thus we conduct ourselves according to the example of Christ and the apostles and proclaim the Gospel according to the grace that He has entrusted to us; we compel no one. . . . That this then also is an open truth, that Christ's people are a free, unforced, and uncompelled people, who receive Christ with desire and a willing heart, of this the Scriptures testify." An appeal of the Zürich Anabaptists to the Zürich Council of 1589 asserts that "the state authorities have no place in the church of God, no right to control and persecute the conscience, and that this principle is one which they, the Swiss Brethren, have recently proved out of Scripture." Heinrich Bullinger, in his *opus magnum* against the Swiss Brethren, *Der Widertöufferen Ursprung* (1560), sets forth clearly and emphatically the Anabaptist belief in freedom of conscience, tries to refute it point by point, and

defends the Zürich policy of intolerance and persecution. Among other things he charges that they asserted, "One cannot and should not use force to compel anyone to accept the faith, for faith is a free gift of God." Menno Simons said, "Say, good reader, where have you, in all the days of your life, read in the apostolic Scriptures that Christ or the apostles have called upon the power of the magistracy against those who would not hear their doctrine or obey their words" (726)? "Faith is a gift of God. . . . It cannot be thrust upon a man by external force or by the sword" (605). The Hutterite Chronicle (in section written before 1542) says: "Faith is not to be compelled but is a gift from God." These testimonies are typical and could be multiplied from many sources. H.S.B.

H. S. Bender, "The Anabaptists and Religious Liberty in the Sixteenth Century," *MQR* XXIX (1955) 83-100, also the same in *Archiv für Reformationsgeschichte* 44 (1953) 32-50; R. H. Bainton, "The Struggle for Religious Liberty," *Church History* X (1941); idem, *The Travail of Religious Liberty* (Philadelphia, 1951); idem, *The Development and Consistency of Luther's Attitude to Religious Liberty* (Cambridge, 1929); idem, *David Joris, Wiedertäufer und Kämpfer für Toleranz* (Leipzig, 1937); M. S. Bates, *Religious Liberty; an Inquiry* (New York, 1945); J. H. Cockburn, *Religious Freedom in Eastern Europe* (Richmond, 1953); Balthasar Hubmaier, *Von Ketzern und ihren Verbrennern* (1524); Hans Denk's (q.v.) *Widerruf*; Sebast. Franck, *Paradoxa* (ed. Ziegler, Jena, 1909); Caspar Schwenckfeld, *Ein Bedenken von der Freiheit des Glaubens christlicher Lehre, Urteils, und Gewissens* (1547); H. Bullinger, *Der Widertöufferen Ursprung, Fürgang, Secten, Wäsen, fürnemen und gemeine irer leer Artickel* (Zürich, 1560); Bluntschli, *Geschichte der Rechte der religiösen Bekenntnisfreiheit* (1867); K. Völker, *Toleranz und Intoleranz im Zeitalter der Reformation* (Leipzig, 1912); W. Koehler, *Reformation und Ketzerprozess* (Tübingen, 1901); P. Wappler, *Inquisition und Ketzerprozesse zu Zwickau* (Leipzig, 1908); idem, *Die Stellung Kursachsens und des Landgrafen Philipp von Hessen zur Täuferbewegung* (Münster, 1910); N. Paulus, *Protestantismus und Toleranz im 16. Jahrhundert* (Freiburg, 1911); Ernst Troeltsch, *Protestantism and Progress* (New York, 1912); J. Kühn, *Toleranz und Offenbarung* (Leipzig, 1923); Rufus M. Jones, *Studies in Mystical Religion* (London, 1909) 369; *ML* I, "Duldung," 484 f.; II, "Gewissensfreiheit," 108-10, "Glaubensfreiheit," 120 f., "Glaubenszwang," 121 f.; Menno Simons, *Writings*; Filip von Sesen, *Des Weltlichen Standes Handlungen/ und Urteile wider den Gewissenszwang* . . . (Amsterdam, 1665); Sape van der Woude, "Gestaltung der Toleranz," in *Castelliana* (Leiden, 1951); J. Kühn, "Das Geschichtsprobem der Toleranz," in *Autour de Michel Servet et de Sebastian Castellion* (Haarlem, 1953); see also *ML* articles "Gewissensfreiheit," "Glaubenszwang," etc.

Rem van Hoorn: see **Rem Pieters.**

Rem Pieters (Rem de Pelser), a Dutch Anabaptist, who was very active by preaching in Amsterdam in 1534. He was arrested and charged with preaching and possessing forbidden books, among which is mentioned the "Deutsche Messe" by Oecolampadius (*q.v.*). The sentence was remarkably mild: Rem was banished from Amsterdam for six years. Rem undoubtedly belonged to the revolutionary wing of Anabaptism. He was later at Monnikendam, from where he was banished in December 1535. About his further life nothing is known.

Rem van Hoorn, a follower of David Joris (*q.v.*), who was active at Alkmaar, North Holland, is probably identical with Rem Pieters. vDZ.

Inv. Arch. Amst. I, Nos. 142 f., 285; Grosheide, *Verhooren*, 161-65; *DB* 1909, 17, 30; *ibid.* 1917, 114, No. 43; Mellink, *Wederdopers, passim.*

Rembrandt Harmensz van Rijn (Ryn) (1607-69), probably the greatest painter of the Western world, was born July 15, 1607, at Leiden, and died Oct. 4, 1669, at Amsterdam. In an age when the tradition of Christian painting had been practically abandoned in the Netherlands under the influence of the Dutch Reformed spirit, Rembrandt devoted about one third of his life's work to the depiction of Biblical scenes. Contrary to the trend of contemporary art, in which the "genre" picture, still life, and seascapes predominated, he founded a new style of interpretation of the Bible. To be sure, the young painter frequently drew his themes from the Bible because of the wealth of dramatic material found there, especially in the Old Testament. But after the death of his wife Saskia in 1642 an increasing religious sincerity becomes evident in Rembrandt's work. Especially his etchings and drawings (there are about 600 of these showing Biblical scenes) show Rembrandt's reactions to the message of the Gospel.[1]

Officially Rembrandt was a member of the Reformed Church, and as yet there has been no evidence that he severed this connection[2] in spite of serious conflicts with the church council, such as the exclusion of Hendrickje Stoffels from communion in 1653, who lived with him after his wife's death. Nevertheless there is some indication that Rembrandt was in close contact with Mennonite circles and from them received essential religious motivations.[3]

Against the assumption that Rembrandt did not enter Anabaptist circles until Saskia's death recent research in archives has shown that at least outwardly Rembrandt was in contact with Mennonite families in his first years at Amsterdam.[4] Of greater importance is the contemporary tradition which originated with the Italian Baldinucci, a writer on art, and which says that about 1642 Rembrandt belonged to the "religion of the Menists." This statement, as Michel has shown, goes back to Bernhard Keihl, one of Rembrandt's students.[5] Hitherto this tradition was doubted because it was believed that Keihl came to Rembrandt's studio in 1648, when any close contact between Rembrandt and the Mennonites was improbable (financial collapse, illegal living with Hendrickje).[6] But a re-examination of Baldinucci's statements about Keihl's life shows that Keihl came to Rembrandt's studio as early as 1641-42.[7] In that year Rembrandt painted and etched portraits of the Waterlander Mennonite preacher C. C. Anslo. In January 1641 Samuel Hoogstraaten entered Rembrandt's studio, and he was demonstrably a Mennonite. All these data relate to the same period, and become important because it was at this very time, following Saskia's death, that Rembrandt's growing religious perceptivity is evident.

But beyond these historical facts, there are in Rembrandt's Biblical portrayals numerous traits that presuppose Mennonite rather than Reformed influences. With respect to the Old Testament the following can be asserted: Rembrandt sees the Old Testament accounts not from the point of view of prophecy and fulfillment; each Old Testament account contains for him its own religious lesson within in itself. He does not hesitate—as in the Abraham scenes—even to depict God. He especially loved the

Apocrypha, particularly the little book of Tobit. All of this was in contrast to the point of view of the Reformed Church. With respect to the New Testament, he strongly stresses the figure of Christ as the teacher and healer, whereas the artists preceding him had depicted preferably the stories of Jesus' birth and death (the dogmas of the Incarnation and atonement). Christ does not wear the stereotype halo, but is rather understood as the one who must "in all things be like His brethren." At the same time, however, by means of a symbol of radiation, Rembrandt puts emphasis on the particular moment in which Jesus of Nazareth discloses Himself as the Christ of God to a human being who meets Him.[8] This stress on a very personal encounter with Christ in the act of receiving an insight of faith is suggestive of Mennonite influence. His frank portrayal of Mary is suggestive of the love of the Mennonites for Mary as the mother of the Lord, which was not burdened by confessional polemics. In the story of the death of Christ it is not the physical suffering and the related doctrine of reconciliation (satisfaction) that Rembrandt stresses, but rather the spiritually tempted Christ. Rembrandt's concept of the sacraments is also illuminating. The Lord's Supper, as has often been noticed, is unimportant in Rembrandt's work. Instead it is the Emmaus scene that dominates: the exalted Lord breaks bread for His church (communion as a ceremony of the "breaking of bread"). Also the interest in the picture of John the Baptist, in the baptism of the Ethiopian (adult baptism), in the blessing of the children (Hundred Gulden Print), as well as the act of washing the disciples' feet, point to an Anabaptist understanding of the sacraments. In the 1650's his presentations frequently take on the character of an immediate proclamation, which corresponds with the lay witness of the Mennonites.

The question whether Rembrandt was a member of a Mennonite church is not answered with all of this. His name is not found in any Mennonite membership list (these are, however, not intact). To become a member of a Mennonite congregation included the necessity of being baptized as an adult. It is unlikely that Rembrandt took this step. "Hundreds and more hundreds at that time reckoned themselves among the Mennonites without having taken this last step," and lived so to speak in the "courts of the real congregation." Certain facts indicate that in the last years of his life, i.e., after 1656, Rembrandt associated with a Mennonite circle with Collegiant (q.v.) inclinations and took part in their Bible discussions, which were conducted by laymen. One of the evidences for this is the portrait of Catherina Hoogsaet, the wife of a preacher with Collegiant interests, and his relationship with Collegiant-minded Anabaptist circles derived from this fact.[9]

In spite of all that is still unanswered with regard to the question, "Rembrandt a Mennonite?" this may be said in summary: In the early 1640's he experienced a deep contact with the piety of the Mennonites. His own Christian personality is stamped by this fact. His presentations of Biblical scenes may from this time on be evaluated as witnesses and self-statements of the Christian Rembrandt.[10] Venturi's *Lives* says that the Spirit of Rembrandt's art was Mennonite.   H.M.R.

(1) This as yet theologically unexploited treasure of interpretation of the Bible is best accessible in W. R. Valentiner, *Rembrandt. Handzeichnungen* I (1925), II (1934) in the series *Klassiker der Kunst*. In process of publication since 1954 is O. Benesch, *Rembrandt's Drawings* (6 vv., London).

(2) All the official documents (also the entries in the church records) are printed in Hofstede de Groot, *Die Urkunden über Rembrandt (Quellenstudien zur holländischen Kunstgeschichte* III, 1906). Also for the supposed membership of Rembrandt's son Titus in a Mennonite congregation, which was assumed by W. Molenaar and Christian Neff on the basis of a lecture delivered in 1907 by Alfred Seltzer, a professor at the University of Heidelberg (see *Menn. Bl.*, 1908, 18, and on the opposite side Samuel Cramer, *ibid.*, 29; also *Menn. Bl.*, 1933, 92), there is no evidence, according to N. van der Zijpp, who at my request examined the archives of the Mennonite Church of Amsterdam.

(3) In the discussion on the question of whether Rembrandt was a Mennonite, which was going on before the war but became somnolent during the war, Samuel Cramer took the negative view in his article, "Rembrandt menist?" (*De Zondagsbode*, 1906, No. 27), and C. N. Wybrands the affirmative, "Rembrandt doopsgezind?" (*ibid.*, 1906, Nos. 35-41), besides the articles mentioned above. The first thorough investigation was made by Karel Vos, "Rembrandts Geloof" (*De Gids*, 1909, 49 ff.). Carl Neumann follows the Vos arguments in the chapter "Rembrandt und das religiöse Leben in Holland" of his monograph on Rembrandt. A careful summary of the discussions on the question "Rembrandt doopsgezind?" is given by N. van der Zijpp in the *Doopsgezind Weekblad*, 1948, No. 43. Recent affirmative answers to the question have been made by J. Rosenberg in his Rembrandt monograph, Vol. I, pp. 107 ff., discussed by Cornelius Krahn in *Menn. Life* VIII (1953), No. 1; H. E. van Gelder, *Rembrandt en de heilige Schrift* (Amsterdam, 1948) 59; *idem*, in *Oud Holland*, 1943, 35-37; Kühler, *Geschiedenis* I, 58, speaks of the "Doopsgezinde Rembrandt," without giving the source. See also K. T. Gorter, "Een Doopsgezind Kunstenaar?" in *DJ* 1953. H. R. Rotermund, the author of the present article, a Lutheran, has treated the views summarized here in an article, "Rembrandt und die religiösen Laienbewegungen seiner Zeit," in *Nederlandsch kunsthistorisch Jaarboek*, 1952, pp. 104-92. Hendrik van Loon's book, *R. van Ryn*, makes the flat assertion, without explanation, that Rembrandt was a Mennonite. (See also *Art*.) W. A. Visser 't Hooft in *Rembrandts weg tot het Evangelie* (Amsterdam, 1956; this essay had previously been published in French and English, and there is also a Spanish translation) takes the view that Rembrandt was not a Mennonite and that his piety was not typically Mennonite.

(4) See W. F. H. Oldewelt, "Rembrandts relatie met de familie Bruyningh," in *Amsterdamsche archiefvondsten* (1942) 158 ff.; also the articles by H. F. Wijnman noted in (9).

(5) F. Baldinucci, "Cominciamento e progresso dell' arte . . ." (Florence, 1686) 78; printed in Hofstede de Groot, document 360, par. 4 (see note 2 above). E. Michel, "Francesco Baldinucci et les biographes de Rembrandt," in *Oud Holland*, 1890, pp. 167-72.

(6) Also held by W. A. Visser 't Hooft, *Rembrandt et la Bible* (1947) 23 ff. See also P. R. Musculus, "Remarques sur Rembrandt, le Calvinisme et les Mennonites," in *Bulletin de la societé calviniste de France,* May 1932.

(7) As early as the article "Bernhard Keihl," in Thieme-Becker, Künstler-Lexikon XX (1927) 66-68. J. Six in *Jaarboek der Koninkl. Akad. van Wetensch.*, 1925/26, 233.

(8) Hans-Martin Rotermund, "The Motif of Radiance in Rembrandt's Biblical Drawings," *Warburg Journal* XV (1952) 101-21.

(9) H. F. Wijnman, "Een drietal portretten door Rembrandt," in *Jaarboek Amstelodamum 1934*, 90 ff. See also H. F. Wijnman, "Nieuwe gegevens omtrent den schilder Lambert Jacobsz," *Oud Holland* XLVII, 145-57, and LI, 241-55.

(10) Critical of this view, W. A. Visser 't Hooft, *Rembrandts Weg zum Evangelium* (Zürich, 1955), and *Rembrandts weg tot het Evangelie* (Amsterdam, 1956). (See also the Rembrandt issue of *Mennonite Life*, October 1956.)

Rembrandtsz, Dirk (1640-83), of Nierop (i.e., Niedorp in the Dutch province of North Holland), was a Mennonite cobbler who was an able astronomer. He is the author of the *Nieroper Graadboek* (a travel book for seamen), which went through fourteen editions. The book proved useful to mariners, and was republished in 1725 and 1730 in revised editions, edited by Jan Albertsz van Dam, the Mennonite preacher at Hoorn. He also published some books on astronomy and mathematics. He corresponded with internationally noted mathematicians, e.g., Christiaen Huygens and Nicolaes Witsen.   vDZ.

N.N.B.Wb. V, 373; Winkler-Prins *Encyclopedie* XIV (Amsterdam, 1952) 509; Marten Schagen, *Naamlijst der Doopsgezinde Schrijveren* (Amsterdam, 1745) 70 f.; *ML* III, 253.

Remcken: see Remken Ramakers.

Remke, Govert, a Mennonite of Crefeld, who in co-operation with Wilm van der Leyen procured the release from prison for his brethren of Rheydt. On April 11, 1683, he purchased a tract of 1,000 acres in Pennsylvania, signing a contract with William Penn. He never took possession of the land, however, for he did not emigrate to America. He sold it on Jan. 14, 1686, to Dirk Sipman.   NEFF.

Friedrich Nieper, *Die ersten deutschen Auswanderer nach Pennsylvanien* (Neukirchen, 1940) 32 and 89; William I. Hull, *William Penn and the Dutch Quaker Migration to Pennsylvania* (Swarthmore, 1935) 243, 253 f.; *ML* III, 466.

Remken Ramakers, an Anabaptist martyr, who was executed at Sittard in the duchy of Jülich, Germany (now Dutch province of Limburg), in 1550. He is probably identical with Reinken Rademaecker, who baptized Theunis van Hastenrath (*q.v.*).   NEFF.

DB 1890, 58; 1909, 120; *Bibliographie*, No. 655; *Mart. Mir.* D 98, E 497; *ML* III, 425, 427.

Remkes, Johann (1714-70), the last lay preacher of the Crefeld (*q.v.*) Mennonite congregation, was born March 16, 1714, and was ordained to the ministry on Oct. 17, 1754, by Winand Wynands (b. 1702, preacher 1727-77). On June 13, 1769, Remkes as preacher and Heinrich van der Leyen (*q.v.*) as deacon, both aged men, wrote an illuminating letter to the Lam en Toren congregation of Amsterdam asking for ministerial help. The letter gives much interesting information on the Crefeld congregation (see a long excerpt, *ML* III, 647). Remkes died Jan. 3, 1770. The first educated minister was then called in 1770; it was not de Vries, but Wopko Molenaar (*q.v.*) and Zino van Abbema.   E.C.

Beiträge zur Geschichte rheinischer Mennoniten (Weierhof, 1939) 47, 81 f., 86 f., *et passim; ML* III, 467 f.

Remonstrantie en deductie *over de Leere, en conventiculen der Mennisten der Stede Deventer* (Deventer, 1670) (Inquiry and Conclusion Concerning the Doctrines and Meetings of the Mennonites in the City of Deventer) is a pamphlet by an anonymous (Reformed) author addressed to the magistrate of

Deventer (*q.v.*), Dutch province of Overijssel, for the purpose of having the Mennonite meetings in this town prohibited. Shortly before, another pamphlet had appeared: *Redenen waerom de . . . Magistraet den Mennisten tot Deventer niet magh toelaten Conventiculen te houden* (Deventer, 1670) (Reasons Why the Magistrates of Deventer Should not Allow the Mennonites to Hold Meetings). These reasons are repeated in *Remonstrantie en deductie;* they are partly theological and partly political, viz., that the Mennonites were Socinians (*q.v.*), rejected the magistracy, and were of Münsterite (*q.v.*) origin.

Abraham Willemsz Cremer (*q.v.*), the Mennonite minister of Deventer, opposed both the *Redenen* and the *Remonstrantie en deductie* in the pamphlets *Nootwendighe ontschuldinge* (Necessary Apology) (Deventer, 1670) and *Antwoorde* (Answer) (Deventer, 1671).

The magistrates of Deventer officially decided to close the two Mennonite churches in this town, but actually they made no serious attempts to stop the Mennonite meetings, and the Mennonites continued to meet without hindrance. (*DB* 1919, 48-61.)

vdZ.

Remonstrants, a Protestant denomination in the Netherlands, founded in 1619. Soon after Calvinism had become predominant in the Netherlands, divergent views on a number of doctrines became apparent among the theologians within the Reformed Church. Particularly the doctrine of predestination as taught by Calvin became a point of controversy. Shortly after 1600 this dogmatic quarrel became very violent. Franciscus Gomarus, a professor at the University of Leiden, defended the doctrine of predestination to its utmost consequences, whereas Jacobus Arminius (*q.v.*), of the same university, championed a rather moderate view. In 1610 the followers of Arminius, who had died in 1609, addressed a petition to the Dutch government, which formulated "five articles of remonstrance." Hence the moderate Calvinists were called Remonstrants. At first they were also called Arminians (after Jacobus Arminius), but this name soon disappeared in the Netherlands. Outside the Netherlands Remonstrantism is generally known as Arminianism (*q.v.*).

The national Dutch Reformed synod held at Dordrecht in 1618-19 had to discuss and come to a decision in this matter. But the synod, composed of opponents of Arminius' views and presided over by the strict Calvinist Johannes Bogerman (*q.v.*), hardly permitted the Remonstrants to defend their opinions, dismissed the Remonstrants, and condemned their teachings. Two hundred Reformed preachers who embraced the Arminian views were deposed. Only a few of them were willing to submit to the resolutions of the synod. Most of the others went into exile, particularly to Antwerp, and as early as 1619 they organized the "Remonstrant Reformed Brotherhood," which has remained the official name. Soon some of the exiled pastors clandestinely returned to Holland and organized Remonstrant congregations. Notwithstanding the opposition and obstruction of the Reformed Church, they indeed succeeded in building up a number of congregations, particularly in the province of South Holland. Outstanding leaders in this first period were Simon Episcopius (Bisschop) (1583-1643), theological professor at the Leiden University in 1612-19, later professor in the Remonstrant seminary, who was the great leader, and Johannes Uytenboogaert (1557-1644),

In the course of time the Remonstrants were tolerated; in 1630 they were allowed to build a (hidden) church in Amsterdam, in 1632 in Rotterdam. In 1634 they founded a seminary at Amsterdam for the training of preachers (this seminary was moved to Leiden in 1872).

The Remonstrant Church has remained limited to the Netherlands; there is only one foreign congregation, i.e., Friedrichstadt in Holstein, Germany. About 1750 they had 34 congregations in the Netherlands with a total membership of about 3,000. In 1956 these figures were 34 congregations and nine circles (*Kringen*), with 21,000 members.

The Remonstrants, whose teachings have been influential far beyond the Dutch borders (see **Arminianism**), always have been moderate in their views as to basic Christian theology. In the 19th century the whole Remonstrant brotherhood adopted theological liberalism (modernism). Among its leaders in this period there were outstanding liberal theologians, such as H. C. Rogge, C. P. Tiele, and J. A. Beyerman. Their appeal for liberal Christianity caused a considerable increase in their membership about 1860, since many members of the Reformed Church, dissatisfied with the conservative orthodoxy in their church, joined the Remonstrants.

There have been rather close ties between the Mennonites and the Remonstrants. During the first years of their existence Remonstrant congregations often used the confession of faith of the Waterlander elder Hans de Ries. At the rise of Remonstrantism the Mennonites generally sympathized with these fellow Christians who were likewise oppressed by the Reformed state church and the government. Both the Mennonites and the Remonstrants objected to Calvinist dogmatism. S. F. Rues (*q.v.*), who visited the Netherlands in 1741, was of the opinion that there was not much difference between the Remonstrants and the Lamist (more liberal) Mennonites; hence he called the Lamists "Remonstrantsche Doopsgezinden" (Remonstrant Mennonites). Mennonites and Remonstrants met each other regularly in the meetings of the Collegiants (*q.v.*). Some of both groups believed that their churches were rather similar in views and doctrines; for this reason attempts were made to merge: in 1658 and in 1669-70 a merger of the Waterlander Mennonite congregation at Rotterdam and the Remonstrant church was planned, but for some reason the union was not achieved. Only in a much later period at Dokkum (*q.v.*) in Friesland did the Remonstrant and Mennonite congregations merge, in 1796; the names Remonstrant and Mennonite were dropped and the new congregation henceforth was called the "United Christian Church."

Church letters were given when Mennonites wished to join the Remonstrant congregation, and many Mennonites who lived in places where there was no Mennonite church became (often temporarily) members of the Remonstrant church. The reverse happened less frequently, obviously because the Mennonite congregations were more "closed" than those of the Remonstrants, although many Remonstrants worshiped with the Mennonites and (in Lamist congregations) participated in their communion services.

During 1706-35 a number of Mennonites were educated for the ministry in the Remonstrant theological seminary, but then the differences immediately became clear. The Remonstrants maintained infant baptism, rejected by the Mennonites. Besides this, the Mennonites objected to Remonstrant theology and usually opposed any kind of theological system.

During 1731-1806 the Remonstrants and the Mennonites together published the *Naamlijst* (*q.v.*), a booklet, containing a list of congregations with their pastors, appearing at first irregularly, later annually.

During World War II there was a movement among some of the Remonstrant and Mennonite pastors toward a general union of the two churches, but especially the Mennonites questioned the desirability of such a step, and the discussion was not continued.

In recent times there has been among some Remonstrant leaders an orientation toward the Dutch Reformed Church, and a few wish to guide their flock back to the old church from which they were expelled some three and a half centuries ago. vDZ.

De Remonstranten, een Gedenkboek (Memorial Book) (Leiden, n.d.-1919); Lucie J. N. K. van Aken, *De Remonstrantsche Broederschap in verleden en heden* (Arnhem, 1947); Blaupot t. C., *Friesland*, 364-66; Chr. Sepp, *Johannes Stinstra en zijn tijd* I (Amsterdam, 1865) 200; Karel Vos, *Geschiedenis van de Doopsgezinde gemeente te Rotterdam* (repr. Rotterdam, 1907) 23 f.; *DJ* 1850, 90-92, 109, 111; *DB* 1875, 87; 1880, 64 f.; 1901, 33; 1918, 70-74; *Inv. Arch. Amst.* II, Nos. 2884-91; S. F. Rues, *Tegenwoordige Staet der Doopsgezinden* (Amsterdam, 1745) 82; *ML* III, 467.

Rempel, a widely ramified family name among the Mennonites in West Prussia and America. It is derived from Raganbald or Raganbold (meaning a brave council); it is not of Dutch origin, as is the case with most of the Mennonite names of West Prussia and Russia, since Raganbald and -bold had already become Rempaud and Remboud at an early time in the Dutch language; but in South and Middle Germany it had become Rempel. Its geographic distribution area in the late Middle Ages was Franconia, the Lower Rhine, Thuringia, and Silesia. From which of these areas the first Mennonite bearer of this name came is still to be investigated.

In West Prussia (*q.v.*) the Rempel family appeared first exclusively in the Flemish congregations of Elbing, Danzig City (since 1673), Tiegenhagen (since 1723), Ladekopp, Rosenort, and Heubuden. It cannot now be determined whether it appeared any earlier in the congregations named besides Danzig and Tiegenhagen. Representatives of this name were serving the congregations to a lesser degree than later was the case in Russia and America. Only once was there a preacher with this name (in Rosenort 1813-38) and in more recent times a *Vorsteher* in Königsberg. All other bearers of this name were probably exclusively farmers. In 1936 there were living in Germany 36 bearers of this name; 11 in

Heubuden-Marienburg, 4 in Königsberg, 5 in Rosenort, 5 in Thiensdorf-Preussisch Rosengart, 7 in Tiegenhagen, and 2 in Berlin.

In Russia (*q.v.*) the Rempel family was far more strongly represented in the service of the church. The series begins in 1832 with Aron Rempel. The next preachers of this name were chosen in 1864 and 1878, and from this time on the name becomes much more frequent in the last two generations and it closes with the outstanding Elder Jakob Rempel (*q.v.*). Some of the ministers of this name in the Mennonite churches were: 3 elders—Hermann A. Rempel (*q.v.*), Hermann D. Rempel (*q.v.*), and Jakob A. Rempel; 21 preachers of whom 11 died a natural death, 2 in the 1920's escaped to Canada, while of the 7 remaining in Russia 6 went the way of martyrdom and the 7th probably as well: (1) Abram Rempel of Hochfeld-Yazekovo (*q.v.*); (2) Gerhard D. Rempel of Kantserovka No. 2, Orenburg (*q.v.*); (3) Gustav A. Rempel of Gnadenfeld (*q.v.*); (4) Gustav G. Rempel of Gnadenfeld; (5) Jakob D. Rempel of Kantserovka No. 3, Orenburg; (6) Johann D. Rempel of Klubnikovo, Orenburg; (7) Johann J. Rempel, last in Einlage (*q.v.*); 2 deacons, the first (chosen 1842) died a natural death, the second, Abram D. Rempel of Kantserovka No. 3, Orenburg, trod the way of martyrdom already in 1929 and as late as 1947 was still living in exile; 6 preachers, of whom one died a natural death, and another escaped to Canada, 4 on the other hand demonstrably entered the way of martyrdom: (1) Abram Rempel of Central, Voronezh area; (2) David D. Rempel of Kantserovka No. 3, Orenburg; (3) Johann D. Rempel of Davlekanovo, Ufa (*q.v.*); (4) Peter Rempel of Central, Voronezh area.

In America (North and South) a number of Rempel families should be mentioned: 3 elders, 20 preachers, 2 deacons, 2 teachers, and 3 professors. In summary there were (1) in the ministry: 7 elders, 42 preachers, and 5 deacons or Vorsteher; (2) in the professions: 3 professors, 1 engineer, 8 teachers, and 1 artist; (3) in agriculture: 1 estate owner, 2 mill owners, 1 factory owner, 3 merchants; besides founders and cofounders of the Kronsfeld Mennonite settlement (*q.v.*). Among these are J. G. Rempel, elder of the Rosenort (GCM) congregation at Rosthern, Sask., and H. S. Rempel, elder of the E.M.B. congregation at Steinbach, Man. The Rempels are almost unknown, however, in the United States, and are found mostly among the newer immigrants of 1922-25 to Canada. Among these is C. J. Rempel, of Kitchener, Ont., for some years MCC director for Canada. (Reimer, *Familiennamen*; *ML* III, 467-74.) A.R.

Rempel, Cornelius, of Manitoba, was one of the delegates of the Old Colony Mennonites (*q.v.*) sent to South America in 1919 to find a place of settlement. After investigating some other possibilities, including the United States, the delegation went to Mexico where a purchase of land was made resulting in the migration of most of the Old Colony Mennonites to that country. Cornelius Rempel was one of the leaders of the settlement. C.K.

Walter Schmiedehaus, *Eine feste Burg ist unser Gott* (Cuauhtemoc, 1948) p. 72.

Rempel, David, of Swift Current, Sask., was one of the six delegates of the Old Colony Mennonites of Canada sent to South America in 1919 to investigate settlement possibilities. Rempel's diary is an important index of the things they were looking for, their impressions, and their reactions. Again, when a delegation was sent to Mexico in 1921 he kept a diary reporting of the findings and developments.

C.K.

Walter Schmiedehaus, *Eine feste Burg ist unser Gott* (Cuauhtemoc, 1948) 72 ff.

Rempel, G. J., Press. G. J. Rempel, of Blumenort, Cuauhtemoc, Chih., Mexico, an outstanding leader (*Vorsteher*) of the Cuauhtemoc Old Colony Mennonite settlement, has done much for the economic and cultural development of the conservative Mennonites. Among other things he established a small hand press to produce the most needed supplies for the schools and community life. On this press the whole Bible according to the translation of Martin Luther was printed in 1941 and the Russian Mennonite *Gesangbuch* in 1940 and 1943. The setting of the type and the printing were done primarily by the son of J. A. Enns, Rempel's brother-in-law. The book by Walter Schmiedehaus, *Eine feste Burg ist unser Gott,* was printed in Rempel's shop in 1948. Many other items have been printed in this little shop.

C.K.

Rempel, Heinrich, elder of the Deyevka Mennonite Church (*q.v.*), Orenburg settlement, Russia, was elected minister in 1899 and elder in 1911. He served the congregation until his early death in 1924. He was succeeded by Isaak G. Krahn. C.K.

Peter P. Dyck, *Orenburg am Ural* (Clearbrook, 1951) 61 ff.; Friesen, *Brüderschaft,* 902.

Rempel, Hermann Abraham, the first elder of the Mennonite congregations at Karassan in the Crimea (*q.v.*), then the founder and elder of the Evangelical Mennonite Brethren at that place. Educated in his parental home of Gnadenfeld (*q.v.*) and later in the Zentralschule in Halbstadt (*q.v.*), he obtained a position as teacher in the Mennonite elementary school at Karassan. At the same time he was a member of the Mennonite school council in the Crimea, but he gave up his calling as a teacher and became a farmer. In 1903 he was chosen preacher and after the retirement of Elder Abraham Friesen he was chosen as elder of the Karassan congregation. His election as elder must have taken place after 1910, since in Friesen's book Abraham Friesen is named as the last elder here in 1910.

Following a Bible conference in 1920 a doubt stirred in Hermann Rempel "whether he had really been born again." One day he turned to Abraham H. Unruh with the words, "I was indeed at least born again when I went to baptism, but my conversion was not normal." Unruh reported later about this: "Later he asked me to go with him to the field. There we knelt down and Brother Rempel on his knees before the Lord judged his entire life down into the smallest detail. Deeply moved he rose from his knees and from that hour there was in him a deep calm assurance, and a sure course in pastoral care." From now on he worked together

with the other preachers toward a "revival of his brotherhood." He was oppressed to see that "many members of the congregation lived indifferent lives," and he retired from his office as elder after Unruh had prevented him, when he was still the official elder, from accusing so-called believing members of his congregation of unfaithfulness and publicly challenging them to leave the congregation. He justified his withdrawal from office by saying that he was no longer in a position to distribute the communion emblems to "unconverted persons." After this he left the church "with a large group of like-minded persons" and with them in 1921 founded the "Evangelische Mennoniten-Brüderschaft" in the Crimea, serving as their elder. They built a meetinghouse in the Lustigtal. In the course of time this brotherhood developed into a rather large congregation, "in close working fellowship with the Mennonite Brethren (*q.v.*) and in Bible conferences also with the Karassan Mennonite church."

In the fall of 1929 Rempel came with his family to the gates of Moscow to emigrate; like many others he was forcibly sent back and went to Memrik (*q.v.*). Therewith began for him and his family a difficult road of suffering. In order to maintain his family he had to work in stone quarries and coal mines at Yuzovka (today Stalino in the Donets basin). He, however, did not give up even here in Memrik the ministry to the Mennonite brotherhood. During a vacation he even visited once again his orphaned congregations in the Crimea in order to serve them. Later he was banished to Siberia, to which place his wife voluntarily followed him. Also three of his sons were sent into exile. Of the daughters some probably remained in Memrik. In exile father, mother, and two of the sons, it is definitely known, found a martyr's death and one day also the third son became silent; it is to be assumed that he also became a martyr. A.R.

Friesen, *Brüderschaft,* 709; Aron A. Töws, *Mennonitische Märtyrer* (Winnipeg, 1949) 90 ff.; ML III, 469.

Rempel, Hermann D. (d. 1924), elder of the Mennonite congregation of Deyevka in the Orenburg Mennonite settlement (*q.v.*) in Russia. He was by vocation a farmer and was chosen as minister in 1899. In that year the congregation of Deyevka, which had been founded in 1894 as a subsidiary of Old Chortitza, organized as an independent congregation. Its first elder was Abram Penner. He retired in May 1910, and his successor, Hermann D. Rempel, was chosen in 1911. During Rempel's eldership there was an important revival movement as the consequence of the house visits made by the preacher and missionary Johann J. Peters of Susannovo in nearly all the families. After a service of 12 years as a preacher and 13 additional years as elder Rempel died in 1924. A.R.

Peter P. Dyck, *Orenburg am Ural, Die Geschichte einer mennonitischen Ansiedlung in Russland* (Clearbrook, 1951) 62, with portrait; ML III, 469.

Rempel, Jakob A. (1883-   ), one of the most prominent leaders of the Mennonite Church in Russia, elder of the Neu-Chortitza and Nikolaital Mennonite congregations, was born on April 8, 1883, the first of 13 children of Aron A. and Justina Peters

Rempel, at Heuboden in the Borozenko settlement, Ukraine. He served as village schoolteacher 1901-5. He studied theology, philology, and philosophy at the Predigerschule and the University in Basel, Switzerland, 1906-12. In 1913 he became a teacher in the Zentralschule in Chortitza and was ordained preacher there. He was transferred by the governmental school authorities in 1915 to Stalino (formerly Yuzovka) as teacher of German and French, and in 1916 to the Nikopol gymnasium where he was also acting principal. In 1918 he became private lecturer at the newly founded University of Ekaterinoslav, where he was recommended as professor, though this was not carried through until 1920 when he was called as professor to the University of Moscow. While he was considering whether he would accept another call as elder of the Neu-Chortitza congregation, the Moscow University rector declared him deposed from the professorship because he was considering a religious office. He was ordained elder May 2, 1920, and soon thereafter accepted the call to serve also as elder of the Nikolaital congregation. He located in the village of Grünfeld. His bishopric now covered a territory some 40 x 60 miles in area including 22 villages, in which he averaged 40 communion services per year, in addition to a heavy load of pastoral duties and teaching in Bible conferences, and the ordination of many new preachers due to the death or emigration of a large number of preachers. Rempel also served the brotherhood at large. In 1921-25 he rendered special service in Zagradovka by request of the church there. In 1922 he was chosen chairman of the KfK (q.v.) at the General Conference in Chortitza, a position with heavy responsibilities for negotiations in Moscow which he held until 1925, when he refused reelection on the ground that it would be wiser to change leadership. However he continued in a leading position in the KfK and was counted on to head the ministers' training school which he was asked to organize. He was sent as a delegate to the first Mennonite World Conference in Basel in August 1925, but was denied a Swiss visa; so he made a three months' tour of the Mennonite congregations in Germany. He was appointed special commissioner of the KfK in 1928 to continue negotiations with the government. He continued to serve widely in Bible conferences, in 1929 for instance for two weeks in the Orenburg settlement.

On Sept. 8, 1929, Rempel was expelled from Grünfeld, and on Oct. 13, 1929, his property was confiscated and his family expelled. On Nov. 16, 1929, he was arrested in Moscow as he was seeking emigration papers. He was held seven months in Moscow in arrest, was placed under heavy pressure to renounce his faith, and offered a professorship in the University if he would do so. Upon his obdurate refusal he was sentenced to 10 years of hard labor in the Solovki camp on the White Sea. He escaped from Solovki on Jan. 24, 1932, but was arrested again on March 13, 1936, at Khiva and was brought to trial and sentenced at Piatigorsk in the North Caucasus. He was imprisoned first at Vladimir near Moscow and then at Orel. His last letter to reach the West was dated June 12, 1941. It

was long assumed that he had died or been executed but recently there are indications that he may have survived and may be still alive. His family, which reached Canada (one son remaining in Germany), has 116 letters from Rempel written during the years 1930-41 in addition to much other material. (Condensed by H.S.B. from the article on Jacob A. Rempel by Alexander Rempel, his son, in ML III, 470-74.) A.R.

Peter A. Rempel, *Aeltesten J. A. Rempel's Lebens- und Leidensgeschichte* (Gretna, 1946); A. A. Töws, *Mennonitische Märtyrer* I (Abbotsford, 1949); II (North Clearbrook, 1954); *Unser Blatt* (1926-29) *passim*.

Rempel, Johann D. (b. 1874), a Mennonite Brethren minister of Russia, was born on Nov. 2, 1874, at Hoffnungsort, Chortitza, South Russia, a son of David Rempel and Anna Thiessen. On Jan. 6, 1898, he was married to Katharina Krahn, and in 1906 moved to Rodichnoye in the newly established Orenburg (q.v.) settlement. In 1910 he was chosen to the ministry of the Mennonite Brethren Church of Klubnikovo. By attending Bible courses and by private study he acquired an extensive and deep knowledge of the Scriptures. On March 2, 1929, his wife died.

In connection with the "peasant flight" to Moscow in 1929 Rempel was arrested and banished with his son Johann to Archangel, and from there to the forests of Pechora in the northern Urals. Here he spent 3½ years. His good performance of the assigned work and also his general personality earned for him the respect of his fellow prisoners as well as of the GPU officials, a respect which gave him certain privileges easing the imprisonment. In 1933 he was released and returned home. Since he was not permitted to serve in his office of preacher and knew that further imprisonment awaited him, he went to the Ukraine, settling as a day laborer in the village of Einlage near Zaporozhe. Here he secretly served small Mennonite circles. Soon he was again arrested, but acquitted after an imprisonment of seven months. During this time his second wife died. His third wife, the widow Maria Klassen, took him into her home, but he could not rest long. During the night of July 20, 1938, he was arrested. His further career is unknown. HA.R.

Rempel, Peter Paul (1865-1938), a Mennonite Brethren evangelist, teacher, and elder, was born Aug. 12, 1865, in Russia, the oldest son of Peter P. and Gertrude Rempel. At the age of 28 he was converted and joined the M.B. Church through baptism. For his theological training he attended the St. Chrischona Bible School at Basel, Switzerland. On July 31, 1897, he married Theresia Esau. A son and two daughters were born to them. He began to do evangelistic work in the M.B. Church in Russia and was ordained to the ministry in 1900.

In 1900 Rempel emigrated to America, establishing his home in Kansas, where he continued his studies, especially in English. For eight years he was chiefly engaged as traveling evangelist in the M.B. Church Conference and was much in demand for such service. With the beginning of Tabor College 1908 he served on its faculty five years, teaching chiefly theological subjects. The Hillsboro (Kan.) M.B. Church elected him to the pastorate in 1909 and ordained him elder the following year. This position he held until 1914, when he moved to California. There he held pastorates in several M.B. churches: at Los Angeles 9 years, at Shafter 4 years. He died at his home in Shafter on April 7, 1938, and was buried in the local M.B. cemetery. J.H.L.

Rempel-Wall und Reinländer Waisenamt is the name of one of the two companies which were organized by the Old Colony Mennonites in Manitoba in 1921 to purchase and distribute the land of the Manitoba Mennonite settlement (*q.v.*) at Cuauhtemoc, Chihuahua, Mexico.   C.K.

Renata is a small town on a stump peninsula in the Arrow Sea, about 20 miles northwest of Castlegar, B.C. It is reached by ship. This settlement sprang up in the primeval forest about 50 years ago and was settled by 5 Mennonite (GCM) families from the Rosenort (*q.v.*) Church near Rosthern, Sask. Climatic and agriculture conditions are favorable and there are about 50 homes in this settlement now. The main occupation of the settlers is fruit raising. But many Mennonites have left Renata in the last years, and there are now only about 10 Mennonite families left. The first ministers to visit Renata were D. J. Unruh, Herbert, Sask., in the early 1920's, and C. F. Sawatzky from Laird, Sask. Abraham Hamm, an immigrant preacher, arrived in 1923. In 1938-53 P. P. Dyck from Rosemary, Alberta, preached here the six months of each year while he was living in Renata.   J.G.R.

Renesse, a town on the island of Schouwen, Dutch province of South Holland, was the seat of a (Flemish) Mennonite congregation in the early 17th century. The congregation, which bought a house in 1644, where "public Mennonite meetings" were held, and of which Jan Aelwyns was a preacher in 1646, occasionally received financial support from the Rotterdam congregation. It had only a very small membership and died out before 1660. (*DB* 1883, 110; 1907, 153, 168.)   vDZ.

Rengers, a Mennonite family found in the Dutch province of Groningen. The first known member of this family was a man with the Christian name of Renger, who lived in Leens or Ulrum about 1600. Some of his descendants took Rengers (a patronymic meaning the son of Renger) as their family name (found since about 1760); others assumed the name Arkema, Doornbos, and Huizinga (*q.v.*), all of which are still familiar names in this province. A number of them have been Mennonite preachers, e.g., Jacob Melles (Rengers), serving at Leens 1649-83.

There was also a noble Rengers family in the province of Groningen, which was not related to the Mennonite family of this name. A member of this family was Johan Rengers ten Post, a contemporary of Menno Simons, who wrote a chronicle,

Kronyk, in which he described the Anabaptist troubles at 't Zandt (*q.v.*).   vDZ.

J. Huizinga, *Stamboek van Derk Pieters en Katrina Tomas* (Groningen, 1883) *passim; DB* 1905, 97.

Renicx van Kimsward: see **Hoyte Riencx.**

Renken, Melchior: see **Rink, Melchior.**

Renner: see **Prenner.**

Reno County (Kan.) Old Order Amish settlement was organized as a congregation in 1883, when the families of Christian H. Miller, Christian C. Miller, Tobias Schrock, and Peter Schrock came from Shelby County, Ill. The first ministers were Christian E. Bontrager, bishop, and John D. Nissley and Noah T. Schrock, ministers. The two districts, North Haven and East Haven, formed in 1899 and 1923 respectively, had a combined membership of 109 in 1957. A third district, West Haven, was discontinued in 1943. The Yoder Mennonite Church (MC), founded in 1917, was organized largely by former members from the Amish congregations.
     L.S.K.

Paul D. Miller, "Amish Acculturation" (M.A. thesis, University of Nebraska, 1950).

Repaix, a village in Lorraine (*q.v.*), near Blamont, the seat of a Mennonite congregation that in 1871-1918 lay on both sides of the German-French boundary. In 1888 it had 85 baptized members and 65 children. The elders were Fougond on the (at that time) German side, and Mosimann on the French side. Baptism was performed after instruction upon desire at the age of thirteen or fourteen. Footwashing was celebrated with the Lord's Supper. In 1908 there were 73 baptized members living in ten villages. The elders were Christian Lehmann on the German side and Pierre Sommer Jr. on the French side. In 1928 the congregation was reported to be dying out; the elder was Jean Lidviller. In 1938 the congregation merged with Lunéville (*q.v.*). In 1907 Repaix-Avricour was the scene of a meeting of the French congregations, which resulted in the organization of a conference.   E.C.

Almanach Mennonite du Cinquantenaire 1901-1951 (Montbéliard, 1951) 43; *Gem.-Kal.,* 1902, *passim;* Mannhardt, *Jahrbuch* 1888, 43; *ML* III, 475.

Reporter for Conscience' Sake is a monthly paper published since July 1942 by National Service Board for Religious Objectors, 401 Third St. N.W., Washington 5, D.C. The *Reporter* contains news about conscientious objection to war, including laws and regulations, CO court cases, the alternate service program, CO's in jail and in the armed forces, and other general information about conscientious objectors and their problems. It is a four-page paper, 8½ x 11 in., with an average circulation of 5,000 copies monthly.   E.ME.

Request met bygevoegde Deductie *voor het Regt van de Vryheid van Geloove, Godsdienst, en Conscientie op den naam van de Doopsgezinde Gemeenten in Friesland ingeleverd aan de E.M. Heeren*

Staaten der gemelde Provincie (Request with Attached Conclusion in Behalf of the Right of Freedom of Faith, Worship, and Conscience, in the name of the Mennonite congregations in Friesland handed in to Their Highnesses, The States of the forementioned Province) was published in 1740 (n.p.). The *Request* numbers four pages in large octavo, the *Deductie* 24. The reason for this request and deduction was as follows: In 1738 the States of the Dutch province of Friesland had suspended Wytze Joens (Brouwer, *q.v.*) and Pieke Tjommes (*q.v.*), both Mennonite preachers at Heerenveen, on the charge of teaching Socinianism (*q.v.*). The Mennonite Conference of Friesland (Friesche Doopsgezinde Sociëteit, *q.v.*) held special meetings (on Oct. 9 and 23, 1739, and Jan. 8, 1740) to discuss the matter. They feared that as in 1722 (see **Thomas Jan**) the Frisian States, stirred up by the Reformed synods under the pretext that Socinianism was being taught in Mennonite churches, would require the Mennonite preachers to sign a confession drawn up by the Reformed ministers, and forbid the Mennonite meetings. They therefore resolved to present a petition to the States of Friesland. This petition, followed by an explanation, was drawn up by Joannes Stinstra (*q.v.*), Mennonite pastor at Harlingen and at this time moderator of the Frisian Conference.

After the *Request* and *Deductie* had been published, an anonymous Reformed author, calling himself "Liefhebber der Waarheit" (Friend of the Truth), attacked the Mennonites. Others who opposed the Mennonites were Daniel Gerdes (*q.v.*) and Gerardus Kulenkamp (*q.v.*). Both the *Request* and the *Deductie* were reprinted in *Het Regt der Vryheid van Geloove . . .* (three editions, all at Harlingen, 1740).

The States of Friesland adopted no special measures against the Mennonites in general at this time, and Pieke Tjommes and Wytze Jeens were in 1743 again permitted to preach in their congregation; Stinstra, however, was suspended by the States in 1742 and not readmitted to the pulpit until 1757.

vDZ.

Resch, Ambrosius, a Hutterite brother, died December 1592 at Schäkowitz (*q.v.*) in Moravia. He gained a certain significance as the author of a chronicle of the Hutterites, which because of its completeness and style was often copied and also used as model for similar books. Joseph Beck (*q.v.*) used it extensively for the text of his *Geschichts-Bücher* (1883), calling it "Codex A." Its title runs as follows: *Ein kļaines gründliches Denkbüechel, darin wirt begriffen und angezaigt, was sich seit dem 1524 Jar mit den recht christ glaubigen und fromen menschen hat zutragen, und wie sich die gamain gots wiederumb hat angefangen und vermört ist worden* (small octavo, 146 leaves). The chronicle begins with 1524 and was continued by other writers up to 1640. At present it is in the city archives of Bratislava (*q.v.*). Resch also copied the Bible concordance of 1530 by Leonhard Brunner (**see Concordances**), but enlarged its contents by including references to the Apocrypha. The original manuscript is lost, but a copy made in 1642 is still extant in the library of the canons of the Bratislava cathedral. It is remarkable for its unusual size, a handwritten book of 1040 leaves folio size.   R.F.

Beck, *Geschichts-Bücher,* pp. 3-4 prints the "Vorrede an den Leser" by Resch; *op. cit.,* 318; Ernst Crous, "Wandernde und versteckte Täuferhandschriften," *Gesch.-Bl.,* 1938, 61 f.; Robert Friedmann, "Eine dogmatische Hauptschrift . . . ," *Archiv für Ref.-Gesch.,* 1931, 225 f.; Frantisek Kraus, *Nove prispevky k dejinam habanov na Slovenska* (New Research and Documents about the Habaners of Slovakia) (Bratislava, 1937); this work is based largely on the Resch chronicle, excerpts of which are presented in Slovakian translation; *ML* III, 475.

Resinex: see Resinx.

Resius, Johannes *(et Lubbertus Gerardi), Praecipuorum christianae fidei articulorum brevis confessio* (Amsterdam, 1723), is the Latin translation of the Mennonite confession of 1610 by Hans de Ries (*q.v.*) (and Lubbert Gerritsz).   vDZ.

Ressler, Jacob Andrews (1867-1936), pioneer Mennonite (MC) missionary and editor, the son of Martin B. and Magdalena Andrews Ressler, was born near Ronks, Pa., July 28, 1867; died Oct. 3, 1936; interment in Scottdale cemetery. He received his education in the public schools and in Millersville Normal School, Millersville, Pa., from which he graduated in 1891. He was a teacher in the public schools of Lancaster and Westmoreland counties, Pa., for a number of years. In 1891 he married Elizabeth Bachman of Lancaster County, Pa. She died Aug. 3, 1898, leaving one child, Emma (Mrs. George Townsend), of Masontown, Pa. On June 18, 1903, he was married to Lina Zook of Sterling, Ohio, a former worker in the Mennonite Mission in Chicago, Ill. Two children of this marriage, Ruth and Rhoda Ressler, have served as missionaries in Japan.

Ressler was converted and united with the Mennonite Church (MC) at Strasburg, Pa., at the age of seventeen. In 1895 he moved to Scottdale, Pa., and in July of the same year he was ordained to the ministry at the Alverton Mennonite Church, three miles from Scottdale. In 1898 at a missionary meeting at Elkhart, Ind., he was unanimously chosen by the bishops and the congregation present to head a small group of missionaries to open up work in India. Before sailing he was ordained as bishop at Springs, Pa., on Jan. 5, 1899. He and Dr. and Mrs. W. B. Page sailed from New York on Feb. 22, 1899, and landed at Bombay, India, March 24. This was the beginning of the Mennonite Mission (MC) at Dhamtari, India. He returned to America for a brief furlough in 1903. During this year he married his second wife, Lina Zook, who returned with him to the field in December 1903. In 1908, owing to his wife's failing health, the family returned to America.

After his return from India Ressler lived near Sterling, Ohio, until 1911, when he was called to Scottdale to serve as editor of Sunday-school literature. This proved to be his longest field of service. For 25 years he edited the *Advanced Sunday School*

Lesson Quarterly, and for the greater part of this time also the *Words of Cheer* and *Beams of Light.* He was for many years Associate Editor of the *Gospel Herald.* He was the author of a number of books and pamphlets, three of which were *Stories from India* (1916), *Junior India* (1927), and *Elementary Studies in Prophecy* (1917).

"J. A.," as he was popularly known, also served the church as evangelist and Bible instructor and was active in General Conference, serving as moderator in 1922-23, and in the conference and mission board of the Southwestern Pennsylvania (now Allegheny) District. (*ML* III, 476.)   J.L.H.

Restitution, a term said to derive from a concept of early canonical law, *restitutio in integrum,* meaning the restoration (of some institution) to its original state. Further back the term points to the still better known New Testament use in Acts 3:21, where it denotes "the restoration of all things" (*apocatastasis panton,* in the Vulgate *restitutio omnium*) on the Day of the Lord. The 16th-century Anabaptists understood the term *restitutio* primarily in the sense of a restoration of the church to its former position, from which it had fallen under the Emperor Constantine the Great (A.D. 313) when state and church had become allied and later fully unified, thus belying the original meaning of the idea of the church. The idea of restoration or restitution then assumed a twofold meaning. (1) It meant an immediate concrete attempt at actual restoring the primitive church, something which the state churches would consider either heresy (*Ketzerei*) or sectarianism (*Abspaltung*), and consequently would persecute as a threat to peace. On the other hand, those who advocated such restitution would consider their new beginnings the true church, which must needs be separated from the "world" and be nonconformist to it, while the depraved "world" had to be left to its unhappy destiny. Some modern authors speak in this connection of these people as "restitutionists" and also of a "restitutionist movement." (2) Restitution could also mean a sort of dream or romantic hope that the true church will one day, most likely soon, be restored again by divine fiat, implying that secular history will then come to its final end. Such a view represents a stronger apocalyptic interpretation of history, going back in the main to the vision (and periodization of history) of the Abbot Joachim of Fiore (*c*1200), and continued in the age of Reformation by a number of eschatologically oriented persons such as Melchior Hofmann (*q.v.*), David Joris (*q.v.*), and Michael Servetus.

The study of the entire attitude toward "restitution" and its meaning owes a substantial debt to some American church historians (Bainton, Littell, Wray, etc., see II below), although the facts as such have long been known also among European historians of the period. Attention has been drawn to the fact that a considerable number of 16th-century books and tracts bear the term *restitutio* on their title page or use it otherwise as a leading concept in the text itself. Karl Rembert was perhaps the first to discover this idea in Anabaptism (1899); it was discussed in a more general fashion by K. Borinski (1919) and J. Huizinga (1930) without connecting the ideas too closely with Anabaptism. It has also been recognized that the idea of restitution is always intertwined with the idea of the fall of the true church (see e.g., G. J. Heering, *De Zondeval van het Christendom,* 1928) and is a part of a general outlook which A. Lovejoy aptly termed "Christian primitivism" (1935).

The Main Works Witnessing to This Trend and the Subsequent Polemics Connected with These Books. The first work here to be considered is that by Johannes Campanus (*q.v.*), *Göttlicher und heylliger Schrifft vor vilen jaren verdunckelt und durch unheylsame leer und leerer . . . verfinstert-restitutio und besserung . . .* (1532) (Restoration and Reformation of Divine and Holy Scriptures, Darkened and Obscured by Unwholesome Teachings and Teachers Many Years ago, . . .). This work is actually a shortened edition of his (now lost) work *Contra totum post apostolos mundum* (for contents see **Campanus**). It was soon widely read and became influential for the "Wassenberger preachers" (*q.v.*), Henrik Rol, and others who in turn influenced Bernhard Rothmann (*q.v.*), one of the promoters of the New Jerusalem to be erected in the city of Münster (*q.v.*).

Rothmann treats the idea of restitution in two works: first in his *Bekenntnis van den beyden Sacramenten* (1533) and then in his more elaborate work, *Eyne Restitution edder Eine wedderstellinge rechter vnnde gesunder Christliker leer, gelouens vnde leuens vth Gades genaden durch de gemeinte Christi tho Munster an den dach gegeuenn* (1534) (A Restitution or Restoration of Sound Doctrine, Faith and Life Brought to Light out of God's Grace by the Church of Christ at Münster). This is an extensive defense of the principles and institutions of the Anabaptist "kingdom" in Münster. It teaches that just as the Jews restored their temple after their return from Babylonian exile, so also the true "Israelites" today must now restore the kingdom and eliminate the heathen and unbelievers. Rothmann took his ideas so seriously that he did not hesitate to send a copy of his book to the Margrave Philip of Hesse (*q.v.*), known as an open-minded and tolerant Christian ruler. Philip took a critical look at this strange book, and with the help of two court theologians, Corvinus (*q.v.*) and Lenning, he came to the conclusion that it contains teachings which "began well but ended rather badly." In 1536 Rothmann's book was also critically answered by the Lutheran polemicist Urban Rhegius (*q.v.*) in a pamphlet, *De restitutione regni Israelitici, contra omnes omnium seculorum chiliastes.* Also Dirk Philips (*q.v.*) felt urged to answer the book, opposing Rothmann's idea of establishing the "kingdom" by way of the sword. Since the kingdom is a spiritual one, says Philips, it cannot be restored in any other way than by that which the Dutch brethren have chosen. This is the leading idea of Philips' *Van de geestelijcke restitution, dat is hoe dat al wat van de beginne gheschiet is, in Christo Jesu geeste-*

lijck vervult, weder gehaelt ende weder gebracht (Spiritual Restitution, that is: Christ Jesus has Spiritually Fulfilled, Restored and Made Restitution for All Things that Were Done from the Beginning). This pamphlet shows that the Dutch Anabaptists were by and large rather cool to the idea of "restitution." To them discipleship and obedience to the divine commands were more central than restitutionism, even though some elements of it also appear in their thinking.

Other men of the 16th century who dealt with this idea follow: Hendrik Niclaes (*q.v.*), a native of Münster, who established the "House of Love" somewhere around the middle of the century, speaks of the restitution of "original complete justice" (*erste vollkommene Gerechtigkeit*). Wilhelm Postell, the former Catholic mystic and enthusiast, likewise uses this idea prominently in his rather abstruse *Panthenosia* (1547). David Joris (*q.v.*), who calls the fourth part of his famous *'T Wonderboek* (1542 and 1551): *Dat vierde deel, daer die restitutio oder wederbrenginghe Christi . . . gheopenbaerdt werdt* (Fourth Part in Which the Restitution or Restoration of Christ is Revealed). Joris and Niclaes knew each other quite well and carried on a brief literary dispute. The last name to be noted is a man of a very different type of vision—the anti-Trinitarian Michael Servetus (*q.v.*), Calvin's famous victim at Geneva. In 1553 he published his *Restitutio Christianisme,* in which he (Völker in *RGG*) "dissolves rationalistically the doctrine of the church . . . in order to reveal Christ as the mediator of a spiritualized transcendental kind of life, to which adult baptism was to open the way." This pneumatic Christianity then was to represent the true and genuine "restitution" of the original (invisible) church.   NEFF, E.C., R.F.

* * *

II. The Meaning and Significance of This Idea for the Radical Wing of the Reformation. Following the lead of Roland H. Bainton (1936), Franklin H. Littell and Frank J. Wray have developed the thesis that the idea of restitution of the true church, whether sectarian realization or eschatological dream, was the real tie which bound together Anabaptists and Spiritualists, Schwenckfelders and Polish Brethren (anti-Trinitarians). (Leonard Verduin in a yet unpublished study calls them all "restitutionists," where Bainton would have applied the term "Anabaptists" generically. See **Radical Reformation** and **Anabaptist**, Sixteenth Century Usage.) Characteristic of all was their antagonism to secular culture, which they judged corrupt and decadent, and also their expectation of the imminent triumph of the true church here on earth (Littell). "History in the eyes of sixteenth-century Anabaptists" (Wray) appears then as a tripartite affair: fall, redemption, restitution, whereby between redemption and restitution two more periods have to be inserted: a temporary fall in the days of Constantine, and a temporary restitution by true believers which continues until the Day of the Lord. (Rothmann, however, taught a number of successive falls

and restitutions.) These true believers, among themselves called brethren and by their opponents called heretics or sectarians, are then a sort of trustee of this true church until the day when all the world will be redeemed and the true restitution (Acts 3:21) will come to pass. This was the idea of David Joris as much as of Sebastian Franck or, in due distance, of Michael Servetus. Whether or not it was also the idea of the evangelical Anabaptists is still an open question. To all of these men the great church history of Eusebius (*q.v.*) was a very welcome tool, undergirding their vision by an old and accepted authority, while the more radical spiritualists and millennialists liked to refer to Joachim of Fiore and his work.

Franklin H. Littell, who devotes an entire chapter in his *Anabaptist View of the Church* to this idea of restitution, and another to the idea of the fall, defines Anabaptism proper as that section of the "Left Wing of the Reformation" which gathered and disciplined a true church upon an apostolic pattern (50). He expressly says that the Anabaptists were pledged "to re-live in studied fashion" the life of the New Testament community in all of its phases. The term "biblicism" is therefore not specific enough, and this type of life should rather be called "Christian primitivism," that is, a restitution grounded in the New Testament. This restitution follows a very definite pattern to which belong believers' baptism, spiritual government (ban, shunning, shepherds, deacons, etc.), the practice of community of goods in some form, nonresistance and nonswearing of oaths, the great commission (missioners being called apostles or *Sendboten*), the Lord's Supper as a testimonial sign of true fellowship in the Lord, etc. These people also became the earliest champions of the "free church" idea and of freedom of conscience in matters of faith (toleration, Christian voluntarism). Simplicity and purity of life were understood as undisputed external forms of such a church (in which life and worship become one). Also pacifism in the sense of nonresistance and absolute non-sword-bearing belong to the picture as a whole.

Frank J. Wray elaborates still further on this idea in his dissertation "The Anabaptist View of History," calling restitution the "fundamental concept among Anabaptists," using the term in the broader sense developed by Bainton, which, however, is not generally accepted by Mennonite scholars. After discussing the close ties between restitutionism and eschatological vision (Hofmann, Rothmann, etc.), Wray concludes, "Although the radical fringe connected the restitution with the Day of the Lord more closely than did the main stream of Anabaptists, setting a definite date, Anabaptists in general believed that the restitution was a prelude to greater things to come." And again, "The term was used more frequently by those on the fringe of Anabaptism than by the representatives of the main stream of the movement." These are significant restrictions to the general thesis discussed above, but we will presently see that even under this new aspect the thesis is still open to debate, stimulating though it is in the endeavor of an understanding of the essence of Anabaptism.

In his essay "Recent Interpretations of Anabaptism" (1955) Robert Friedmann tried to analyze this thesis of Bainton, Littell, and Wray as far as the evangelical Anabaptists were concerned. Does restitution mean that the Anabaptists actually and consciously planned such a (historic) restoration as two millenniums earlier the Israelites had planned the rebuilding of their temple (Rothmann)? Does it mean a historic consciousness, an emulation of earlier patterns? If attitudes are considered (as they are in this context), it should be said that what actually concerned the brethren was not such an historic re-establishment of something previously lost but rather obedience to the divine will without reservation (see **Reason and Obedience**). Obedience is another term for discipleship, something extremely non-historical, and certainly it does not mean a "return" at all. Furthermore, many Anabaptists of the first generation were most emphatic with regard to the idea that what they were really striving after was nothing but a *continuation* of the true apostolic church. "We are not wrong," wrote Pilgram Marpeck in 1545 (*Verantwortung*, 405), "in wishing to consider our church in Christ equal to the first apostolic church." Ludwig Keller wrote in this connection of the invisible continuity of "old-evangelical brotherhoods" (*q.v.*). In other words, the opinion prevailed that the true church was never lost but existed as a timeless and perennial community of believers both before and after Constantine. From an interpretation of Anabaptism as discipleship (see **Anabaptist,** Modern interpretation), it follows that restitution has too strong a historical connotation to fit a description of the Anabaptist genius. The books enumerated above seem to indicate that the term was significant only to some fringe figures of the Age of Reformation, who dreamed of restitution or attempted its realization in Münsterite fashion. The larger body of evangelical Anabaptists (Swiss, Dutch, Austrian), however, did not have too much use for it, all the quotations in recent literature notwithstanding.

To clarify the situation still further, it might be useful to quote an unpublished remark by Bainton in a letter to this writer (1953): "The ideal of restitution or restoration was common in the Age of Reformation, and all parties desired to restore something. The difference was only as to what, and as to how far back one would go. Luther wished to restore the church of the early Middle Ages, since for him the great corruption [of the church] was the rise of the temporal power of the papacy in the eighth century. The Anabaptists went back further than any of the other groups, and turned exclusively to the New Testament. Even within the New Testament they tended to neglect Paul and to push back to Jesus. That is why the ideal of restoration tends to coincide with the ideal of the imitation of Christ."

R.F.

K. Rembert, *Wiedertäufer*, 241 ff.; K. Borinski, "Die Weltwiedergeburtsidee in der neueren Zeit," *Sitzungsberichte der Bayr. Akad. d. Wiss. phil.-hist. Kl.* (1919);

J. Huizinga, *Wege der Kulturgeschichte* (Munich, 1930) 124-27; K. W. Bouterwek, *Zur Literatur und Geschichte der Wiedertäufer* (Bonn, 1864); L. Keller, *Geschichte der Wiedertäufer und ihres Reiches zu Münster* (Münster, 1880) 149-51; E. Braune, *Die Stellung der hessischen Geistlichen zu den kirchenpolitischen Fragen der Reformationszeit* (Marburg, 1932) Chapter I: "Hessische Geistlichkeit im Kampfe gegen die Wiedertäufer von Münster"; G. Franz, *Urkundliche Quellen zur hessischen Reformationsgeschichte* II (Marburg, 1954) 214-24; Roland H. Bainton, "Changing Ideas and Ideals in the Sixteenth Century," *The Journal of Modern History* VIII (1936) 428 ff.; Franklin H. Littell, *The Anabaptist View of the Church* (Am. Society of Church History, 1952), Chapters 3 and 4; Frank J. Wray, "The Anabaptist Doctrine of Restitution of the Church," *MQR* XXVIII (1954) 186-96 (this essay is a chapter of the unpublished Yale doctoral dissertation, 1953, "History in the Eyes of the Sixteenth Century Anabaptists"); R. Friedmann, "Recent Interpretations of Anabaptism," *Church History* XXIV (1955) 132-51, particularly 137; Leonard Verduin's book on the "Restitutionist Movement" has not yet been published; *BRN* V, 504, 559-64; *ML* III, 476 f.

Reublin (Röuble, Röblin, Reeblin, Reble, Räbel, Reubel, or Reiblin), **Wilhelm** (1480/84-after 1559), an early Anabaptist, is one of the most interesting figures of the century of the Reformation. Among the Anabaptists of his time he is one of the most frequently named; his fate as well as his career are among the most remarkable.

He was born between 1480 and 1484 in Rottenburg on the Neckar, died after 1559, probably in Znaim (*q.v.*) in Moravia (*q.v.*). He had already received a clerical consecration while a student at the University of Freiburg. On Aug. 21, 1509, he went to Tübingen. His parish of Griessen (between Schaffhausen and Waldshut) he committed to the care of others, and in 1510 he gave it up. For the following years his trace is lost. In the spring of 1521 he appeared with the title of *Magister* and on June 24 he entered St. Alban's Church in Basel as people's priest. His powerful advocacy of the new faith won him a large following, particularly among the trade guilds. According to the Basel chronicles he explained "the holy Scriptures so well that the like had never been heard before." His audience numbered up to 4,000. He preached against the ceremonies of the old church and its hierarchy, the vigils, annual Masses and Masses for the dead, the regulations of fasting, and offered to give an account on all these points from the Bible. When he began to preach against the Mass the bishop raised a complaint with the council. The populace sided with the bold preacher, since he proclaimed the pure Scripture, and the council had to let him go. But on June 13 he declared the Gospel to be the true sacred object, and the monstrance to contain only dead bones; he was then expelled from the city, in spite of the intervention of his friends, on June 27, 1522. He at once received an appointment as people's priest at Lauffenburg on the Rhine, but could not remain under Austrian dominion. In the autumn of 1522 Reublin appeared in Zürich (*q.v.*) without a position, and at once joined the Reformation circles and became one of its most radical proponents. "God-fearing people gave him the necessary support at first." He preached repeatedly in the Fraumünster and was made assistant preacher in Wytikon (*q.v.*) and Zollikon (*q.v.*), subsidiaries of the prebendary foundation (*Chorherrnstift*) of Zürich. In Wytikon the peasants chose him as pastor in 1523, to the great displeasure of the prebendaries. In Zürich he also advocated a radical course, deliberately broke the fasts, incited the peasants to rebel against the tithe, and criticized the government and the monastic system. In his sermons he even used obscene expressions in speaking of the secret sins of the nuns. On April 18, 1523, he married Adelheid Leemann; he was the first priest to take this step in Switzerland.

Reublin was the first in the canton of Zürich, in early 1524, to preach against the baptism of infants; by Easter a number of parents in his congregation did not present their children for baptism. He said, "If I had a child I would not have it baptized before it came to maturity and could choose its own godparents." He was arrested and imprisoned for a time.

The opponents of infant baptism during this time gathered around men like Felix Manz (*q.v.*) and Conrad Grebel (*q.v.*). In the debate between them and Zwingli and his party on Jan. 17, 1525, Reublin was a participant. Zwingli considered him simple of mind and foolishly bold, garrulous, and unwise. After the debate the Anabaptists were expelled from the canton, including Reublin.

Reublin, accompanied by his friend Brötli (*q.v.*), went first to Hallau (*q.v.*), and stayed a while in the region of Schaffhausen (*q.v.*). While here it is assumed that he also visited his former parish of Griessen. But nothing is definitely known about such a visit. Specifically, there is no evidence that Reublin, Grebel, and Manz paid a visit to Thomas Müntzer (*q.v.*), who is thought to have stayed at Griessen three months previously. From Hallau Reublin went to the Austrian city of Waldshut (*q.v.*). There he won Balthasar Hubmaier (*q.v.*) and with him the city for the Anabaptist cause, carrying through a baptism of 300 persons on Easter Day. In March 1526 he was in Strasbourg (*q.v.*), where he was probably received by the tailor Jörg Ziegler (*q.v.*). He debated on baptism with Capito (*q.v.*) in Capito's home. Capito wrote to Zwingli that Reublin appeared to be a pious and honorable man, but not a diamond in dependability. He evaded a colloquium, but started a rumor that the preachers had yielded to him and accepted Anabaptist doctrine but did not dare to take the position in the open for fear of the secular authorities. He was challenged three times to a discussion on infant baptism, but rejected it, saying that it was unnecessary, and left the city.

Reublin now turned toward his home town Rottenburg. Here and in Horb (*q.v.*) he was active in the Anabaptist cause. He called Michael Sattler (*q.v.*) to take charge of the work in the region of Horb. When Sattler and his followers, including Reublin's wife, were seized by the Austrian government and taken to Binsdorf, Reublin fled to Reutlingen (*q.v.*), where a married sister was living. Here he wrote a brief account of the death of his friend Michael Sattler and his companions, and of

the tribulations of the Anabaptists in Swabia. His wife remained in prison a long time; the mayor of Zürich, at the request of her relatives, sent a petition in her behalf. She was probably released upon recantation and an oath, for Reublin reported to Zollikon that all the women with the exception of Sattler's wife had recanted. But the Zürich copyist of the letter written by Reublin to the Swiss Brethren (after July 17, 1527) added the sentence, "William's wife with her eighteen-months-old son is lying in prison with others at Horb in a tower, and has been lying thus since the second week after Easter" (Easter fell on April 21).

From Reutlingen Reublin went to Ulm (*q.v.*), probably by way of Esslingen (*q.v.*), where there was a large Anabaptist congregation. In Ulm he met Hans Denk (*q.v.*). He soon returned to Esslingen, and there, as his enemies reported, "he conducted a regimen like the infallible pope." But there were also other influences at work in Esslingen. The Anabaptists of Esslingen, embittered by the execution of Anabaptists at Rottenburg (*q.v.*), wanted to take up arms against those who believed differently, in the name of the true government in heaven. Reublin was sharply opposed to Leonhard Lutz (*q.v.*), who had fled to Reutlingen, and who with his group had been persuaded by the Lutheran clergy that the Anabaptist position on baptism was too harsh and severe. Reublin bitterly reproached him and his party. But Reutlingen was not open to Anabaptist doctrine. In 1528 Reublin was expelled from Esslingen with the lash, and Stephan Böhmerle —and in the next year four other Anabaptists—was put to death by beheading. The leaders of the Swabian League had demanded that Esslingen take a more active attitude against Anabaptism. Reublin was considered by them "a very wicked and seditious person"; on Feb. 20, 1528, the "shepherd, or Brother Wilhelm," as he was called, had disappeared from the city.

Reublin next went to Strasbourg. There he worked with Jakob Kautz (*q.v.*), who had recently been expelled from Worms, and Hans Bünderlin (*q.v.*) of Linz. Reublin was also acquainted with Pilgram Marpeck (*q.v.*), of Tirol, and Jakob Widemann (*q.v.*), of Memmingen. Reublin soon became known as an Anabaptist leader; his followers, for the most part refugees from other cities, held their meetings on Saturday, and also on other days; they had a proper congregational organization, with deacons who gathered contributions from the members and others in the vicinity. Since Reublin and Kautz everywhere attacked the clergy of Strasbourg, the council intervened. On Oct. 22, 1528, an Anabaptist meeting was interrupted by police and Reublin and Kautz arrested. Reublin tried to flee, but failed and was imprisoned in the tower of the "Ratsbote" Thomas. On Jan. 5, 1529, they were summoned to give an account of themselves. Ten days later they presented a statement of their faith: water baptism is the enrollment of the believers in the visible church of God. "If he desires it, he shall not be refused, if he has heard the word of penitence and consented to it in his heart. A confessed faith . . .

21

must precede and not follow baptism. Thus it is clear that infant baptism is contrary to the command of Christ." "Again, we know from experience that your preachers are comparable to poor carpenters, who have, to be sure, torn down the church of the pope, but have not yet built a church of Christian order; thus their call is not of God, not divine, but earthly." Thereupon the clergy were again sent to the two for further discussion. Reublin and Kautz demanded a public trial. Bucer (q.v.) and his colleagues favored their request, but the council insisted that the debate be fought out in writing. The result was inconclusive. The prisoners were released and expelled from the city and bishopric on threat of drowning if they reappeared. During his imprisonment Reublin had become crippled; he returned to his home to recuperate. He and his wife and children then went on to Moravia (q.v.). A group of his former flock had already gone there. In vain he had tried to settle in Constance (q.v.).

In early 1530 Reublin arrived in Austerlitz (q.v.), Moravia. The elements that had assembled here were too heterogeneous to function without friction. Satan, say the chronicles, attacked the people at their most vulnerable spot, namely, their elders, upon whom their whole life depended. During the summer they had held their meetings in the open; but during the winter, when it was too cold to meet outside, they found no place large enough to hold them. Therefore they were divided into three groups and a preacher assigned to each group. This step proved costly. The teaching differed from one group to another. One taught that Christ was a citizen in Capernaum; therefore they too might perform civic duties and the oath. Others, as Jakob Widemann, were not competent as preachers. They preached that the sisters should marry, else the brethren must be given heathen wives. Girls were bothered by peculiar questions. Some of the preachers showed signs of pride, eating and dressing better than their brethren. The Tirolese complained that the preaching here was not as edifying as it had been at home, and appealed to Jörg Zaunring (q.v.), their compatriot, concerning "judgment" and "discipline of children." At this point Reublin intervened. He was not received with the cordiality he wished, but rather with distrust. He was not permitted to preach, "because they had had no experience with him." Was Widemann acquainted with Reublin's restlessness, and did he have a premonition of his lack of integrity? Perhaps he feared Reublin's sharp judgment, which had accused the Strasbourg clergy of being able only to tear down, but not to build up. Here Reublin was no more optimistic than there.

In Auspitz Reublin became the leader of an opposition party and began to speak about the abuses in the brotherhood. For a time he filled the place of the preacher Kilian; this fact he took as a justification to step in here. Concerning the reasons for this dispute with the elders he wrote to Pilgram Marpeck on Jan. 26, 1531 (letter in Cornelius, II, 253 ff.). The original letter was taken from Julius Lober (q.v.), on April 8, 1531, by Albrecht Gailing, magistrate in Hoheneck near Ansbach (Bergdolt, 109). This letter says that one evening after the common meal near the close of 1530 he began to read aloud, and, since the people gathered around him, to explain the Scripture; likewise on the next evening. On the third evening the elders drove the people out of the room. Then they went to the schoolroom and listened to Reublin there. Jakob Widemann thereupon called the people together, spoke of the wonderful works he and his fellow preachers had performed at Nikolsburg (q.v.) and Austerlitz, and gave orders that only the preachers he specified be allowed to preach; the others were to listen. But Reublin's friends asked him to continue. Thus a break was inevitable.

On New Year's Day of 1531 Widemann summoned all the elders and announced that Reublin taught at inconvenient times and contrary to their order, that the people were running after him, and that he was a false prophet. Reublin's friends refused to have the reading of the Word denied them in their house. When Widemann asked all those who considered his preaching right to come to his side, Zaunring and others remained on Reublin's side and demanded that Reublin's answer be heard. Reublin refused, "for they had already been sitting in the cold all day. They would have liked to turn the people from us, but the people understood the matter." On January 3 the elders demanded that Reublin and his immediate group give an account of themselves for calling the elders false preachers and prophets. Reublin replied that they would do so only before the assembled brotherhood. On the next day Reublin then presented his charges to the assembly as follows: the leaders of the brotherhood did not constitute a Christian church in one God, one faith, and one baptism; for they not only showed no fruits, but also prevented others from doing so. In the second place they grieved the Christian brotherhood which has its strength and being in the Holy Spirit, and thus wasted the fountain of divine grace in depriving preachers and hearers of the strength of the spirit of grace. Thirdly, they permitted the wealthy to have their own houses with rich food and clothing; the wives of some of the wealthy had never been seen at the common table. In the fourth place they held baptism alone to be the work of justification, whereas it should be faith. In the fifth place, though they taught that every person awakened by the Holy Spirit was a true apostle, nevertheless they did not allow him to preach. Other complaints dealt with the poor training of the children. Many a person had contributed fifty guilders to the brotherhood, and then had to see his own child go hungry. From such false prophets one must part. Thereupon Reublin was put out of the brotherhood as "one who incites and makes unhappy."

Reublin gathered his followers; on Jan. 8, 1531, they "shook the dust off their feet" and withdrew, about 300 persons, not including children. With great difficulty they reached Auspitz (q.v.). One of Reublin's friends by the name of Kaspar had gone to Auspitz some time earlier. "Let every one consider how burdensome such a journey with so many children was in winter in such poverty." Johanna von Boskowitz, a noblewoman and abbess of Mariasaal near Brno, gave them residence and in the village of Steurowitz (*q.v.*) in a parsonage, "in which we now have about fifty brethren." In particular the sick and the children were lodged here. The beginnings were difficult enough in Auspitz and Steurowitz. "The people were not trained in agriculture and in the work in the vineyards." Attacks by robbers also caused some trouble. But still more serious was the fact that the Brethren were unable to achieve unity even here. There were justified complaints against Kaspar and especially against Reublin, who had rudely rejected a preacher of Swabia who wished to join them with a small group of his own. Reublin had organized a brotherhood on strictly communistic lines. But while the members suffered want though performing difficult work, forty guilders were found on Reublin during a severe illness. And so he, the leader of the Anabaptists, and the preacher of community, lost his good name, and was banned as a "lying, unfaithful, treacherous Ananias." He himself confessed that this judgment had come upon him with reason. But in spite of his repentance he was apparently not taken back into the brotherhood. Reublin's name then disappeared from the chronicles of the Hutterian Brethren.

But in July 1531 Reublin appeared in the vicinity of Rottenburg. He was presumably making an attempt to collect the remnants of his former congregation here in his home area. Near Esslingen he found about 300 persons. But they had scarcely met, when they were dispersed by the Swabian League.

The next information comes in 1535, when Reublin wrote a letter to Heinrich Bullinger (*q.v.*), the leader of the Reformed Church in Zürich. Reublin had returned from Moravia with a demand against his brother-in-law Felix Leeman, and asked Bullinger (probably successfully) for support. The letter shows that Reublin had withdrawn from Anabaptism. His residence was in Znaim in Moravia. Ten years later (1545/46) he made two journeys from Znaim to Zürich, serving as a letter carrier between Soerin, a clergyman at Ulm, and Bullinger. On his second return trip to Moravia in June 1546 he was the leader of the Zürich citizens Hans Hug and Meinrat Oggenfuss, who with letters of recommendation from the Zürich city council went to Moravia for some unknown reason (but not as Anabaptists) and returned in August.

In August 1554, at the age of seventy, Reublin appeared in Basel in poor health and asked a shelter for himself and his wife for the short time of life remaining to them, and a small sum for their support; he offered to supply the sick and the aged in particular with distilled goods. But he was sent to a spa with a considerable gift of money (Burckhardt).

On Feb. 8, 1559, King Ferdinand wrote to the authorities at Innsbruck that Wilhelm Reble of Znaim had repeatedly requested the release of his inheritance in Rottenburg, which was being withheld. He was inclined to be gracious to Reble, and would like to see him come into his possessions if only in consideration of his advanced age—Reublin was at that time between seventy-five and eighty years old. It is not known whether Reublin lived to see the restoration of his property. Did he manage to conceal his past, so that Ferdinand was not aware that he was the "renegade Lutheran priest" whom he had once in great anger commanded to be seized? Had Reublin in his last days returned to the bosom of the Catholic Church? Could the love of money have taken him so far? It is not known, just as his character in general is a puzzle. At times he appears in a very dubious light, and at other times his tragic fate and often deeply moving words reach across the centuries. But his attachment to the Anabaptists was without question permanently broken in the 1530's.

(Based on material left by Johann Loserth and Gustav Bossert, written by Gustav Bossert, Jr., supplemented by Eberhard Teufel and Heinold Fast.)
G. Bos.

Beck, *Geschichts-Bücher*, 86, note 1; Wolkan, *Geschicht-Buch*, 66-68, 70; Zieglschmid, *Chronik*, 48, 92 f.; Johannes Bergdolt, *Die freie Reichsstadt Windsheim im Zeitalter der Reformation (1520-1580)* (Leipzig, 1921) 109; Gustav Bossert, "Die Täuferbewegung in der Herrschaft Hohenberg," *Blätter für württembergische Kirchengeschichte* IV (1889) Nos. 10-12; V. (1890) Nos. 1 and 2; Paul Burkhardt, *Die Basler Täufer* (Basel, 1898); C. A. Cornelius, *Geschichte des Münsterischen Aufruhrs* II (Leipzig, 1860) 16, 252 ff.; *Corpus Schwenckfeldianorum* VIII, 675 ff Heinold Fast, "Neus zum Leben Wilhelm Reublins," *Theologische Zeitschrift* XI (Basel, 1955) 420-25; Camill Gerbert, *Geschichte der Strassburger Sectenbewegung zur Zeit der Reformation 1524-1534* (Strasbourg, 1889); Abraham Hulshof, *Geschiedenis van de Doopsgezinden te Straatsburg* (Amsterdam, 1905); J. Loserth, *Doctor Balthasar Hubmaier und die Anfänge der Wiedertaufe in Mähren* (Brno, 1893); idem, *Communismus*; idem, "Die Stadt Waldshut und die vorderösterreichische Regierung 1523-1528," *Archiv für österreichische Geschichte* LXXXVII; *TA Zürich*, Nos. 10-11, 36, 41, 42, 45, 55, 157, 249, 250, 253, 296, 303, 340-42, 391, 393; Paul Peachey, *Die soziale Herkunft der Schweizer Täufer* (Karlsruhe, 1954); J. C. Wenger, "A Letter from Wilhelm Reublin to Pilgrim Marpeck, 1531," *MQR* XXIII (1949) 67-75; *ML* III, 477-81.

Reusner (Reyssner), **Adam** (1496-1575), of Bavaria, Germany, a Schwenckfelder (*q.v.*) writer of hymns, one of which is No. 51 in the *Ausbund* (*q.v.*). (*ML* III, 481; *Der Mennonit* IX [1956] No. 7, p. 100a.)

Reusse, Hans, an Anabaptist martyr, husband of the martyr Ottilie Franke (*q.v.*) probably a native of Frankenhausen in Thüringen, Germany, where he suffered a martyr's death in 1534.   NEFF.

Eduard Jacobs, "Die Wiedertäufer am Harz," in *Zeitschrift des Harz-Vereins für Geschichte und Altertumskunde*, 1899, 423-536, 631-33; Wappler, *Thüringen*, 109, 159; *ML* III, 481.

Reusse (Ruse), **Peter,** a successful Anabaptist leader in Thuringia, Germany, by trade a feed-cutter, stemmed from Esperstedt near Frankenhausen, moved with his wife and children to Sandersleben in Anhalt, baptized many in the villages in the neighborhood also in Mühlhausen (*q.v.*), including Appolonia Kaiser (*q.v.*), and probably introduced the fraternal kiss and footwashing. His name occurs in the records of 1530-37.   NEFF.

Eduard Jacobs, "Die Wiedertäufer am Harz," in *Zeitschrift des Harz-Vereins für Geschichte und Alter-

tumskunde, 1899, 423-536, 631-33; Wappler, *Thüringen*, 106 f., 110, 118, 124, 126, 128, 157, 160, 224; Nos. 38, 45, 48, 52, 54; *ML* III, 481.

Reusser: see **Risser.**

Reutlingen, a town (1951 pop. 45,000) of Württemberg, Germany, on the Echaz, 20 miles south of Stuttgart, until 1802 a free imperial city. The preacher Matthäus Alber (1495-1570) thoughtfully introduced the Reformation here. Neither the dispute on communion, the Peasants' War, nor the Anabaptist movement gained much ground here. Wilhelm Reublin (*q.v.*) could accomplish nothing here in 1527. In the spring of 1527 some Anabaptists fled from Rottenburg to Reutlingen, where some of them found refuge with Friedrich Frick, master of the shoemakers' guild, and some in the "tile hut." On Feb. 28, 1528, the council prohibited the admittance of refugee Anabaptists. With friendliness and patient explanation Alber and his fellow preachers converted the Esslingen refugee Anabaptists back to the Lutheran faith, among them Leonhard Lutz, the master of the guild of vine dressers, so that they were permitted to return to Esslingen (*q.v.*).

In the first decades of the 20th century several Mennonite families settled in and around Reutlingen. At first they were members of the Stuttgart congregation. In 1948, when the division of Germany into military zones (1945) hindered travel, a congregation was organized here. Increased by refugees who settled in the neighborhood, the congregation numbered 73 baptized members in 1957, with Fritz Hege and Daniel Schneider as elders.

(Based on articles by Horst Quiring and Gustav Bossert.)   E.C.

ADB I, 178; *Blätter für württembergische Kirchengeschichte* XXX (Stuttgart, 1926) 198 ff.; Gustav Bossert, "Der Reutlinger Sieg vom Jahre 1524" in *Für die Feste und Freunde des Gustav-Adolf-Vereins* (Barmen, 1894) 178; F. G. Gayler, *Historische Denkwürdigkeiten der ehemaligen freien Reichsstadt Reutlingen . . . bis 1577* (Reutlingen, 1840); Julius Hartmann, *Matthäus Alber, der Reformator der Reichsstadt Reutlingen* (Tübingen, 1863); Karl Theodor Keim, *Reformationsblätter der Reichsstadt Esslingen* (Esslingen, 1860); Fredrich Keppler, *Die Marienkirche in Reutlingen . . .* (Reutlingen, 1947); Karl Pfaff, *Geschichte der Stadt Esslingen* (Esslingen, 1840); Albrecht Ströle, *Matthäus Alber, der Reformator Reutlingens* (Reutlingen, 1895); Julius Volk, "Das Verhör des Reutlinger Reformators Dr. Matthäus Alber," *Blätter für württembergische Kirchengeschichte*, 1926, 198 ff.; *ML* III, 481 f.

Reve, Hans van der (Hans von Reve), listed in van Braght's *Martyrs' Mirror* as an Anabaptist martyr who was burned at the stake at Klausen (*q.v.*) in Tirol, Austria, in 1529 with Georg Blaurock (*q.v.*), is presumably identical with Hans Langegger (*q.v.*). The execution took place on Sept. 6, 1529. (*Mart. Mir.* D 22, E 432; *ML* I, 233; II, 506, 617.)   vDZ.

Réveil, name given to an early 19th-century revival movement in Holland: see **Revival: Netherlands.**

Review, The, an illustrated periodical edited and published by H. P. Krehbiel starting in April 1899, as an 8-page monthly, 9 x 11 inches, at Canton, Ohio. It was transferred to Newton starting with the December 1900 issue, where it was published by the Western Book and Publishing Company (*q.v.*),

which was managed by H. P. Krehbiel. With the issue of August 1903 the paper was enlarged to 11 x 14 inches. Starting with the December 1904 issue Krehbiel merged the *Review* with the *Post-und Volksblatt* (*q.v.*), which was in its 18th year of publication. In 1922 Krehbiel started the *Mennonite Weekly Review* (*q.v.*). (Complete set of *The Review* in BeCL.)   C.K.

Revival (German, *Erweckung;* French, *Réveil*), a term commonly used to refer to renewal and intensification of spiritual life in an existing religious congregation, denomination, region, or country, without implying a doctrinal or organizational change or a basic reform. Revivalism has come to mean a technique by which emphasis is placed upon frequent religious renewal through specific methods adopted to produce a mass religious response on a smaller or larger scale, largely through special meetings with considerable appeal to religious emotions and definite personal commitment.

"Revival" as a descriptive term is not applied to movements of renewal or religious stir in Roman or Greek Catholicism, although certainly such renewals have taken place at various times and places in Christian history. Even for Protestantism the term is usually limited to revival movements since the 18th century, beginning in Germany with Pietism (1670-1750) including Zinzendorf and the Moravians (1722 ff.), in England with the Wesleyan movement (1738 ff.), and in the American Colonies with the Great Awakening of Jonathan Edwards and others (1734-44). The following sections will report on the revival movements in (1) North America, (2) Netherlands—*Réveil,* (3) French Switzerland and France, (4) Germany, and (5) Russia, as they influenced Mennonites in those areas or developed among Mennonites themselves.

North America. Nowhere else in the world has revivalism had so wide a spread and so powerful an influence as in the United States, beginning early in the 18th century and continuing into the 20th. As W. W. Sweet explains in his excellent survey *Revivalism in America, Its Origin, Growth and Decline* (New York, 1944), this was due primarily to the specific religious situation in Colonial America produced by the great migrations of generally lower-class European peoples to the New World, the freedom and individualism of American life especially on the frontier, and the extreme weakness of organized religion. As late as 1760 not more than 8-10 per cent of Americans were members of any church, and in the middle colonies of New York, Pennsylvania, New Jersey, Delaware, and Maryland, probably not more than 5-6 per cent. Not only manners but morals were crude, culture was low, educated leaders were scarce, and formal religion had little power. Under these circumstances only a powerful emotionalized, personal religion had much chance to convert America. The conversion was a slow process but it was gradually accomplished, largely as the result of revivalistic methods. Those denominations which operated on this level were the greatest beneficiaries of its results, hence the Methodists and Baptists and related groups have become the largest and most influential religious bodies in America.

The first great revival, called the Great Awakening, began in the 1720's with Theodore Frelinghuysen in New Jersey, a pietistic Reformed immigrant preacher, followed by the Presbyterian Tennents in the same area. With the great Jonathan Edwards at Northampton, Mass., it broke out in full power (especially 1734-36) in New England, where 60,000 and more new members were swept into the Congregational and other churches, and the old members greatly revived. George Whitefield, the Calvinistic Methodist from England, made seven journeys to America in 1738-70, becoming the great over-all unifying revival preacher, building up all denominations open to the movement. Thus German Pietism, English Methodism, and New England Calvinism all played a role in this tremendously significant Colonial revival movement. The Moravians in their own way (arrived in Pennsylvania 1738) made their contribution, particularly among the Germans. "Colonial revivalism brought religion to the common man" (Sweet).

It is not clear how much the Colonial Mennonites in Eastern Pennsylvania were involved in or affected by the Great Awakening and its side effects. The claim that they influenced Frelinghuysen or shared in his movement, made by some reputable historians, is unsubstantiated. But that the Mennonites were influenced by Pietism, both before they left the Palatinate (1707 ff.) and in America, especially by pietistic literature, is beyond question. It is highly doubtful, however, that they adopted the revivalistic preaching techniques or doctrinal and emotional emphases. They resisted the Moravian influences. The German Tunkers (Dunkards or later Church of the Brethren), who arrived in Eastern Pennsylvania in 1719-22, being themselves Pietists, joined vigorously in the revivalistic movement and profited greatly by it, winning many Mennonites to their membership.

Thereafter the Mennonites resisted and rejected the revivalistic influences and example until late in the 19th century. The second Great Awakening (1793-1810), the Charles G. Finney revival of 1824-27, the revival of 1853, and others of the first half of the 19th century had little influence upon the Mennonites except to tear large numbers of sheep from the folds of traditional staid Mennonitism. The newer revivalistic German denominations such as the United Brethren, founded in 1800 in Eastern Pennsylvania by the former Reformed preacher Otterbein and the former Mennonite bishop Martin Boehm (q.v.) of Lancaster County (who was followed by other Mennonites such as Newcomer), and the Evangelical Church, also founded in 1800 in Eastern Pennsylvania by Jacob Albright, gathered in many dissatisfied Mennonites in Pennsylvania, Maryland, and Virginia, and later in Ohio, Ontario, and Indiana. The Church of God (Winebrennerian), founded in Harrisburg, Pa., in 1836, had a similar attraction for Mennonites. Martin Boehm (q.v.; 1725-1812) is the most striking case of the revivalistic impact on Pennsylvania Mennonites. Ordained preacher in 1753 and bishop in 1759, he came

in contact with Whitefield in Virginia in 1761 and thus was drawn into the Great Awakening. In 1767 he participated in the famous meeting in Isaac Long's barn in the Conestoga Valley in Lancaster County, where he met Otterbein. His ever more extensive revivalistic ministry outside the Mennonite Church and his general revivalistic practices and beliefs led to his excommunication in 1777. In his later years Boehm greatly influenced the spread of Methodism in the Lancaster area, and his funeral sermon was preached by his friend, Bishop Francis Asbury, the first Methodist bishop in America. The whole course of American Mennonite history in America might have been vastly different if Boehm had succeeded in "revivalizing" it in his day. The Brethren in Christ (River Brethren), who arose in Lancaster County about 1770, were a fruit of the revivalistic impact on Mennonites.

Whereas the early revivalism largely took Mennonites out of the church of their fathers (or led to their expulsion), the revivalism of D. L. Moody and others in the 1870's and following more often had the indirect effect of setting revival influences going in the church itself. An outstanding case of this in the M.C. group is J. F. Funk (q.v.; 1835-1930), who came directly under Moody's influence in Chicago in the 1860's and was his associate in mission Sunday-school work there. Funk attributed a very strong influence from Moody directly upon himself, which motivated him in turn in his important progressive work in the Mennonite Church. The first M.C. revival meeting (q.v.) was held by Funk and Daniel Brenneman (q.v.) in 1872. J. S. Coffman (q.v.) was the great carrier of revivalism into the church 1879-99. By 1900 the church was won over to this method, although it was conservative in its use and did not promote the emotionalistic emphasis and the Calvinism or Wesleyanism which often characterized it in general.

Daniel Brenneman (q.v.) in Indiana and Solomon Eby (q.v.) in Ontario did adopt this emotionalistic method and emphasis and formed the Mennonite Brethren in Christ Church (q.v.) in 1875, which has been deeply stamped by this point of view.

In the Amish Mennonite Church, Henry Egly (q.v.; 1824-90) came under the influence of revivalism and founded the small Defenseless (now Evangelical) Mennonite group in Adams County (Berne), Ind., and elsewhere in 1866. Out of this group later came the Missionary Church Association (q.v.; 1898 at Berne, Ind.).

The General Conference Mennonites, whose major elements were the Oberholtzer group (1847) in Eastern Pennsylvania, Swiss Mennonites in Ohio and Indiana coming in 1818 ff. and 1838 ff., and Russian Mennonites in the western states and provinces since 1874, have undoubtedly also been influenced by Pietism and revivalism, although Gehman and his Evangelical Mennonites (formed from the Oberholtzer group in 1858) represent a revivalistic influence which was excised from the G.C.M. Daniel Hoch (q.v.; 1806-78) of Ontario (ordained bishop by Oberholtzer in 1851) left the group with his followers in 1869 to join the later Mennonite Brethren in Christ.

The Mennonite Brethren (*q.v.;* formed in 1860 in Russia; in the United States since 1874) represent the revivalistic movement in a wholesome way and are joined in this by the Krimmer Mennonite Brethren (*q.v.;* formed in Russia in 1869; in the United States since 1874) and the Evangelical Mennonite Brethren (*q.v.;* formed from the G.C.M. in 1889).

In general the revivalistic influence has been wholesome in those groups which have remained Mennonite in basic and historic character. The groups which have left the Mennonite brotherhood have adopted a more emotionalized type of piety, together with general Wesleyan emphasis on "holiness" and the second work of grace or also entire sanctification (*q.v.*) or perfectionism. The "Camp Meeting" was adopted by the Mennonite Brethren in Christ from the earlier Methodistic revivalism.

In the Mennonite Church (MC), as well as in the Mennonite Brethren Church and related groups, the general adoption of the revivalistic pattern for securing new members led to the use of this method for bringing the children of the church into church membership in place of the older method of catechetical instruction and baptism at a traditional age of 14-18 years. The revivalistic emphasis upon personal conversion and decision is in principle, so long as it is not pressed upon children at too early an age or induced by emotionalized pressures, in accord with the Anabaptist understanding of faith as personal, voluntary acceptance of Christ as Saviour and Lord. Apart from undesirable excesses revivalism may therefore be understood as a renewal in a sense of the central Anabaptist emphases. (See also **Evangelism, Revival Meetings,** and **Pietism.**)

H.S.B.

W. W. Sweet, *Revivalism in America, Its Origin, Growth and Decline* (New York, 1944); F. G. Beardsley, *A History of American Revivals* (New York, 1904); H. S. Bender, *Mennonite Sunday School Centennial* (Scottdale, 1940); W. W. Sweet, *The Story of Religion in America* (New York, 1950); K. S. Latourette, *A History of the Expansion of Christianity* III, IV (New York, 1939, 1941); C. Henry Smith, *The Story of the Mennonites* (Newton, 1957).

* * *

Europe. The term *Réveil* is applied to a revival movement in the renewal of Pietism (*q.v.*) in the train of the Romantic movement in the early 19th century in western Europe, especially Holland. It is treated in the following series of articles.

1. *West Switzerland and France.* As early as 1805 several inspired members of a small congregation of Bohemian Brethren in Geneva, viz., Ami Bost (1790-1874), Henri Louis Empaytaz (1790-1853), and others, met with some late adherents of Pietism. Soon external influences were added. In 1813 Mrs. von Krüdener (1764-1824), converted in 1807, appeared, in connection with Jung-Stilling (*q.v.*), in 1816 Robert Haldane (1764-1846), who was giving an exegesis of the epistle to the Romans in Geneva and with whom other Scots were working. The Anabaptist concept of "a church after the pattern of the apostolic church, which recognizes only converted persons and rejects infant baptism, was accepted by many awakened Christians" (Hadorn,

431). In 1841, after theological professors and pastors had rejected a reformation, and a transfer to the Catholic Church had been briefly considered, the first free church arose, known as the New Church (*nouvelle église*). Others then began to preach in the established church the forgotten doctrines of Calvin, such as original sin, predestination, etc. When Cesar Malan (1787-1864) was refused a pulpit he opened in his garden the Chapel of the Testimony (*chapelle du temoignage*), which in 1823 became the second free church. This was the origin of the Free Evangelical Churches. Louis Gaussen (1790-1863) was one of the founders of the Evangelical Association, for the defense of the evangelical faith within the established church. He was soon deposed from his pulpit; he then accepted a teaching position in the theological faculty of the Evangelical Association, which was founded in 1832, and in his *Theopneustia* (1840 and 1842) he taught the doctrine of the verbal inspiration of the Old and New Testaments.

The movement spread into France (Free Church in 1832, Evangelical Association in 1833, the Monod brothers as leaders), and also to the cantons of Vaud and Lausanne in Switzerland, where Alexander Vinet (1797-1847) was the leading personality and where a Free Church and a free theological faculty came into existence, and into Neuchâtel, where a revival had begun in 1817, though the Free Church and the free faculty were not instituted until Frederic Godet initiated them.

In Bern a Free Church was begun in 1829 and an Evangelical Association in 1831.

The Evangelical Association of the canton of Bern (*q.v.*), as well as the Free Protestant churches, have had many contacts with the Mennonites in the canton of Bern. The Mennonite *Der Zionspilger* (*q.v.*) was called *Der freie Zeuge* in 1918-21. Since 1868 and particularly since 1912 the Swiss Mennonites have been connected with revival movements.

North Switzerland and Adjacent South Baden. The revival movement here was an outgrowth of the German Association for Christianity (*Deutsche Christentumsgesellschaft*) with its seat in Basel, Switzerland, which was founded by Johann August Urlsperger (1728-1806) in 1780 for the promotion of pure doctrine and true godliness (*Gottseligkeit*). Friedrich Steinkopf (1773-1859), who was the secretary of this association 1795-1800, brought in English inspiration. William Carey (1761-1834) had founded the Baptist Missionary Association in 1792; the Religious Tract Society was founded in 1799; and the British and Foreign Bible Society in 1804. Gottlieb Blumhart (1779-1838), the revivalistic pastor of St. Peter's Church in Basel and long-time secretary of the Association for Christianity, was under the same influence. At times in 1816 f., Mrs. von Krüdener with her stormy enthusiasm stayed in and around Basel. Christian Friedrich Spittler (1782-1867), like Steinkopf and Blumhardt a native of Württemberg, but a layman, also a secretary of the Association for Christianity in 1801 f., "a personality who believed and achieved the incredible" (Hadorn, 493), formed the focal point with his organization. In 1804 the Basel Bible Society came into being. In 1815 in the castle Beuggen am Rhein, which the Grand Duke of Baden put at their disposal under the leadership of Christian Heinrich Zeller (1779-1860), a seminary was organized for the training of teachers for the schools of the poor and a rescue home for neglected children of the poor. In 1840 Spittler's favorite work, St. Chrischona, near Basel, was founded as an institution for the training of workers for home mission work, in 1865-83 and 1890-1909 under the leadership of Heinrich and Dora Rappard (1837-1909 and 1842-1923). The school at Beuggen educated many a Mennonite, among them Jakob Ellenberger (*q.v.;* 1800-79) and Michael Löwenberg (*q.v.;* 1821-74), the founder of the school at Weierhof (*q.v.*). "Between Zeller and the Mennonites there was a fraternal relationship and mutual confidence. He never entered into theological arguments with them, but he told the Mennonites, 'If you cannot decide to have your children baptized, you should at least bring them to Jesus in a ceremonial service, and ask Him to bless them' (Thiersch, 676)." The Pilgermission school at St. Chrischona educated the Mennonite elders Fritz Goldschmitt, Samuel Nussbaumer, Samuel Gerber, Hans Rüfenacht, and Theo Loosli of Switzerland, and Pierre Sommer of Montbéliard, France, and in Germany the ministers Johannes Hirschler of Monsheim (*q.v.*), Matthias Pohl (*q.v.;* 1860-1934) of Sembach (*q.v.*), Michael Landes (*q.v.*), Jakob Hege (*q.v.*), Gysbert van der Smissen (1859-1923), Emanuel Landes, the son of the above Michael Landes, and Christian Schnebele, the superintendent of Thomashof (*q.v.*).   E.C.

2. *Germany.* In Württemberg leading spirits in the movement at this time were Ludwig Hofacker (1798-1828, converted 1816), whose sermons were much read by German Mennonites (even in South Russia, where they contributed to the rise of the Mennonite Brethren), the poet Albert Knapp (1798-1864), and J. C. Blumhardt (1805-80). Noteworthy is the establishment of the millennialistic community of Korntal near Stuttgart (1819), also the emigration of separatistic groups of revivalistic type to South Russia about 1843, among whom was Eduard Wüst (*q.v.;* 1817-59), who was a major influence in the rise of the Mennonite Brethren.

In Berlin the movement found leaders in several professors at the universities of Berlin (August Neander, 1789-1850, E. W. Hengstenberg, 1802-69) and Halle (August Tholuck, 1799-1877). In Hamburg the Mennonite deacon J. G. van der Smissen (1746-1829), influenced by the bookseller Friedrich Perthes, became much involved, serving as secretary of the Hamburg Bible Society (founded 1814). He was also connected with Johann Gossner (1773-1858). In the Lower Rhine-Westphalia region Barmen became a center, where a mission school was started in 1828, which was later attended by a number of Mennonites (Heinrich Dirks, 1842-1915, the first Russian Mennonite missionary. Thomas Löwenberg, 1849-1928, preacher at Weierhof and Ibersheim, and Ernst Regehr, elder at Rosenort in West Prussia and later at El Ombu, Uruguay). Early leaders of the movement in this general area were the Krummachers (Friedrich Adolf, 1767-1845, and

Friedrich Wilhelm, 1796-1868). Isaak Molenaar (*q.v.;* 1776-1834), preacher at Leiden, Holland, 1813-18 and from 1818 on at Crefeld, was influenced by the movement.

The imported Anglo-Saxon Methodist (1831), Baptist (1834), Plymouth Brethren (1848), and Evangelical Association (1850) groups prospered in Germany largely as a result of the revival movement, as did also the Free Evangelical Church, which entered Germany from Geneva via Lyons in 1854. The Baptist Seminary in Hamburg-Horn was attended by a number of Mennonites from Russia (Jacob Kroeker studied here 1894-98, J. G. Wiens 1899-1903, and Abraham Warkentin 1912-15). (See also **Pietism**.)   E.C.

* * *

3. *Netherlands.* About 1820, influenced by revivalist movements in Geneva and the canton of Vaud in Switzerland, and by Scotch and English revivalism, a religious revival arose in the Netherlands, which is usually known as the "Réveil."

The Réveil was opened by the Dutch poet and historian Willem Bilderdijk (1756-1831), who continuously and fervently attacked the halfheartedness and lack of Biblical fundamentalism of the Reformed Church of Holland. Bilderdijk became the spiritual leader of a number of close followers, among whom were the converted Jews, Isaac da Costa (1798-1860), who in 1823 published *Bezwaren tegen den geest der eeuw* (Complaints Against the Spirit of this Age), attacking political and religious liberalism quite in the style of Bilderdijk, and Abraham Capadose (1795-1874), both of Amsterdam. The Réveil, which at first had its center at Amsterdam, also had a group of followers at The Hague from about 1832. Its aim was to fight rationalism and liberalism, with a plea "back to the Bible"; hence their leaders conducted numerous Bible courses (particularly da Costa) and founded Sunday schools for children. Great stress was laid upon the experience of knowing Jesus Christ as the Saviour and Redeemer. In the large cities missions were started, rousing the people to personal conversion. The Réveil had a typically pietistic background, which, though distrusted by da Costa and others, was never denounced, and predominated in the activities of Jan de Liefde (*q.v.*) and others.

The Réveil movement gathered its followers particularly from the upper classes. From about 1830 it took a keen interest in charity, at this time greatly neglected by the churches, and much was done for the relief of social needs. The "Christian Friends," as they often called themselves, made contact with kindred spirits abroad and often followed their examples. Thus in 1844 a deaconess hospital was opened in Holland on the pattern of the Theodor Fliedner's deaconess house at Kaiserswerth, Germany. The Réveil also prepared the way for the founding of special Christian schools.

In 1834 a number of members left the Dutch Reformed Church, to restore the church on the basis of Calvinism as formulated in the resolutions of the national Dutch Reformed synod held at Dordrecht in 1619. This caused a difference of opinion in the Réveil group, some of whom joined the separatists, who founded a new Reformed church, while others held to the (old) Reformed church, as did da Costa, who said that their position should not be juridical but medical ("Together we have become sick, together we should recover"), hence no separation. After 1850 the Réveil lost much of its strength and influence, but its adherents continued their activities and meetings until after 1865.

Although the Réveil as a movement was favored particularly by the Reformed, a number of Mennonites were actively engaged in it. The most prominent of these was Willem de Clercq (1795-1844; q.v.), of Amsterdam, who was for many years a close friend of da Costa. Others were Willem Messchaert (1790-1844; q.v.), of Rotterdam, Jan ter Borg (1782-1847; q.v.), a Mennonite minister at Amsterdam, and in later times Jan de Liefde (1814-69; q.v.) and Pieter van der Goot (1817-77; q.v.), who was also a Mennonite minister at Amsterdam.

The Mennonites who became interested in the Réveil were all more or less dissatisfied with the spiritual atmosphere of the Dutch Mennonite brotherhood. As was also the case in the Reformed Church, spiritual life in the church was at this time at a low level, the sermons being rationalistic or moralistic lectures rather than evangelical messages. Most of the Mennonite friends of the Réveil left the Mennonite Church—Messchaert in 1829; de Clercq, who from 1825 took a great interest in the development of the Reformed Church and had his children baptized, officially terminated his membership in the Mennonite Church in 1831; ter Borg resigned his office in 1829, but did not leave the church; de Liefde left the Mennonite pulpit and his congregation in 1845; van der Goot tried to realize some of the Réveil principles in the Mennonite congregation of Amsterdam.   vDZ.

Ernst Crous, "Mennonitentum und Pietismus," *Theologische Zeitschrift* VIII (1952) 279-96; *idem*, "Vom Pietismus bei den altpreussischen Mennoniten . . . 1772-1945," *Gesch.-Bl.*, 1954, 7-29; W. Hadorn, *Geschichte des Pietismus in den Schweizerischen Reformierten Kirchen* (Constance, 1901); Ludwig Tiesmeyer, *Die Erweckungsbewegung in Deutschland während des XIX. Jahrhunderts* I-IV (Kassel, 1901-12); M. E. Kluit, *Het Réveil in Nederland* (Amsterdam, 1936); *ML* III, 482-84; W. Goeters, *Die Vorbereitung des Pietismus in der Reformierten Kirche . . .* (Leipzig, 1911).

Revival Meetings (German, *Erweckungsversammlungen*), a name given in North America to a series of meetings, usually one or two weeks in length, although they may continue as long as six to eight weeks, held in Mennonite and other Protestant churches for the purpose of stimulating spiritual life and activity among professing Christians. The name is often confused with "evangelistic meetings" (see **Evangelism**), whose ostensible purpose is to win unbelievers to faith in Christ. Often the two purposes are combined and accordingly the names are used interchangeably. Usually an outside preacher is brought into a congregation who is expected to preach on the great central themes of the Gospel and to urge more complete consecration, or renewal of careless members, in addition to appealing for unbelievers to accept Christ as Saviour. Sometimes a song leader or a musical team accompanies the preacher.

Revival meetings first entered the Mennonite churches in North America through outside influences, and usually against opposition. It is not clear whether Daniel Hoch (q.v.) of Vineland, Ont. (1806-78), who was ordained in the Mennonite Church (MC), then for a time (1850-60) joined the Oberholtzer (GCM) group and finally the Mennonite Brethren in Christ, introduced revival meetings, and if so in which group, certainly not in his original congregation. The same is the case with William Gehman (q.v.), founder of the Evangelical Mennonites (q.v.) in Pennsylvania, who was expelled by the Oberholtzer group in 1857. The first revival meetings in the M.C. group were held in 1872 by Daniel Brenneman (q.v.) of Goshen, Ind., assisted by John F. Funk (q.v.) at Masontown, Pa. In 1875 he was expelled by his church in Indiana, apparently for too vigorous promotion of new methods of church work including revivalism, and led the formation of a new Mennonite body, with Soloman Eby (q.v.) of Ontario, which ultimately became the Mennonite Brethren in Christ Church (q.v.) and which used the revivalistic method extensively and effectively.

John S. Coffman (q.v.; 1848-99) was the pioneer in the use of the revivalistic method in the Mennonite Church (MC), beginning in 1879 when he moved to Elkhart, Ind. By 1900 the method was widely accepted in the church, and by 1920 it had become practically a universal custom for each congregation and each church college to have at least one series of revival meetings annually.

The Mennonite Brethren, who brought the revivalistic spirit with them from Russia, have followed a similar practice. Groups influenced by either of these two groups or drawing their inspiration directly from American Protestant revivalism have followed a similar pattern. These include the Conservative Mennonites, the Evangelical Mennonites, the E.M.B. and K.M.B. groups, and lately the Church of God in Christ Mennonites and the Evangelical Mennonites (Kleine Gemeinde). In the G.C.M. group some congregations have also followed this pattern (e.g., Berne, Ind.).

The revivalistic procedures borrowed from the outside were usually altered and adapted somewhat to suit the Mennonite genius and spirit.

In recent years two organized revival efforts have appeared in the Mennonite Church (MC), which have conducted inter-Mennonite revival meetings in numerous larger Mennonite communities as well as in the M.C. congregations. These are Brunk Revivals, Inc. (q.v.), founded in 1951 by George R. Brunk, Jr., and Christian Laymen's Tent Evangelism, Inc., founded in 1952 by Howard Hammer, later led by Myron Augsburger. Both organizations aim to evangelize unbelievers as well as to revive church members, but the major effort usually turns out to be the latter.   H.S.B.

Rexton Mennonite Church (MC), Rexton, Mich., was established in 1947 under the Indiana-Michigan Mennonite Mission Board. The membership was 34 in 1957, with Joe Swartz as pastor.   M.G.

Reyer Dirks, an Anabaptist martyr, a skipper by trade. Having been a member of the Anabaptist group for three years he was executed at Amsterdam on Aug. 16, 1550, after "terrible torture." NEFF.

Mart. Mir. D 104, E 502; *Inv. Arch. Amst.* I, No. 364; Grosheide, *Bijdrage,* 158 f.; *ML* I, 451.

Reyer Egberts, an Anabaptist martyr, died at the stake with five brethren at Amsterdam on Aug. 6, 1552, having been brutally tortured on June 28. During his trial and torture he admitted that he had left the Roman Catholic Church; he had not gone to the confessional for 15 or 16 years and had not taken the holy sacrament for 5 or 6 years. Reyer Egberts had not yet been baptized on the confession of his faith, because Gielis (Gillis van Aken, *q.v.*) had refused to baptize him, saying that he had not adequately examined and studied the Scriptures. Reyer was a citizen of Amsterdam and a weaver by trade. (*Mart. Mir.* D 142 f., E 536; Grosheide, *Bijdrage,* 160 f., 309; *ML* I, 507.)   VDZ.

Reyer Willemsz (Reynier Franchynmaker, i.e., maker of parchment), of Leiden, Holland, was arrested in 1542 at Leiden, when a number of Anabaptist books by David Joris (*q.v.*) were found in his house. After trial and torture, in which he admitted that he had printed and distributed "heretical books," the trial was delayed because of a jurisdictional conflict between the city magistrates of Leiden and the Court of Holland at The Hague. On Oct. 19, 1545, Maria of Hungary, regent for the King of Spain at Brussels, authorized the Court of Holland to bring the trial to a close. There is no further information about this case. Probably Reyer was executed; but it is also possible that he died in prison. It is not clear whether Reyer Willemsz was an Anabaptist.   VDZ.

Inv. Arch. Amst. I, Nos. 257, 261, 330 f.; *DB* 1864, 145; Mellink, *Wederdopers,* 205, 417 f.; *N.N.B.Wb.* V, 1030 f.

Reyers, Johannes (Jan), d. 1680, a practicing physician, was from 1661 until his death a preacher of the Waterlander Mennonite congregation at Amsterdam, Holland. His congregation merged with the Amsterdam Lamist (*q.v.*) congregation in 1668. Reyers wrote *Kort vertoog van de Nootsakelyke voorwaarde der Saligheid* (Amsterdam, 1672) and *Paulus en Jacobus eens gevoelende in de Leer der Regtvaardigheid* (Amsterdam, 1677). Reyers' collection of books became the basis of the present Amsterdam Mennonite Library. The Amsterdam Mennonite Archives have his autobiography. VDZ.

Inv. Arch. Amst. I, Nos. 771, 805; Marten Schagen, *Naamlijst der Doopsgezinde schrijveren* (Amsterdam, 1745) 83; *ML* III, 486.

Reyn Christelijck Vermaeck was the title of a Mennonite hymnbook published at Haarlem in 1672, of which there is apparently no copy extant.   VDZ.

Martin Schagen, *Naamlijst der Doopsgezinde schrijveren* (Amsterdam, 1745) 88; *DJ* 1837, 65.

Reyniere van der Vere, of Veere, Dutch province of Zeeland, is said to have been an Anabaptist preacher, active in the province of Zeeland in 1534. Particulars are lacking. (Mellink, *Wederdopers,* 318.)   VDZ.

Reynskes (Reintjes, Rynskes), **Harmen** (Harmen R. van Overwij(c)k) (d. 1737 at Amsterdam), a Dutch Mennonite preacher at Warns, Friesland, then from 1689 at the neighboring village of Molkwerum, where he became involved in a quarrel with his colleagues Homme Heeres and Ruurd Durks, the preacher at Warns, because of his leaning toward the Reformed doctrine of predestination, was finally removed from office by vote of the congregation on Feb. 2, 1695, and retired to Hindelopen. In November 1696 he was called to the Amsterdam Zonist (*q.v.*) congregation after publishing his defense, titled *Een verklaringe over het ongenoegen der soo genoemde Doopsgesinde Christenen in Molqueern. Over haren Leeraer Harmen Reynskes* (Workum, 1695, reprinted Amsterdam, 1696). In Amsterdam he served 1696-1716 and 1717-29, and then retired. In 1716 he was suspended from his office because of a quarrel with his colleague David van Heyst (*q.v.*), who resigned that year. In 1717 Reynskes was allowed to take up his office again. He was rather conservative and somewhat disputatious, in discord with many people within and without the congregation. One of these opponents was Kornelius van Huyzen (*q.v.*), who in 1715 attacked van Overwijk in *De grondslag van de Leere der Doopsgezinde Christenen, verdeedigd . . . tegen H.R.V.O.* Reynskes published a number of books: the funeral sermon he delivered for his colleague Samuel Apostool (*q.v.*), *De Heerlyckheit van een gestorven Gunstgenoot des Heeren* (Amsterdam, 1699), *Ondersoek over de Natuur van het Leeraar Ampt* (Amsterdam, 1712), *Eenige Vraagen en antwoorden over het verschillend gevoelen in de Doopsgesinde Gemeente de Zon* (Amsterdam, 1717), *Over den H. Evangelist Mattheus,* followed by *Over de Instellinge en bedieninge van den H: Waterdoop* (Amsterdam, 1722), *Gods Alwetende en Voorsienige Bestieringe aangetoont* (Amsterdam, 1727), *De Hoogste Trap, in de Godsdienstige Deugd, namentlyk de Liefde* (Amsterdam, 1730), *Ondersoek over de volstrektheyt van het Goddelyke Zyn en Werkinge* (Amsterdam, 1726, reprint 1731).

NEFF, VDZ.

Inv. Arch. Amst. I, No. 927; *DB* 1895, 111 ff.; 1898, 78, 80, 88, 99 f.; 1901, 103 note; Marten Schagen, *Naamlijst der Doopsgezinde schrijveren* (Amsterdam, 1745) 73 f.; *ML* III, 331.

Reynx (Renicx), **Huyte** (Hoyte), a Dutch Mennonite elder: see **Hoyte Riencx** (Renicx).

Reytse Aysesz (Reitse Aitses), an Anabaptist martyr, was drowned in Leeuwarden, Dutch province of Friesland, on April 23, 1574. On Sept. 18, 1573, he left Beetsterzwaag, where he lived, to visit his parents in Oldeboorn (*q.v.*), and was there arrested by the magistrate Andries Grijpen (Gryf), having been betrayed by a friend. He was imprisoned in Leeuwarden, the capital of Friesland. The *Martyrs' Mirror* contains an exact account of his trial and his confession before his inquisitors. Again and again in painful detail they cross-questioned him about the most important articles of faith, especially baptism and communion. Reytse Aysesz confessed that he had never been in the Catholic church for confessions of sins and the holy sacrament, and that he agreed with Menno Simons' doctrine of the Incarnation; i.e., that Jesus had not taken His flesh from Mary. But he repeatedly embarrassed his opponents with his ready replies, amazing them by his knowledge and understanding of the Bible. No threats or tortures shook his steadfastness; nor did the most insidious questions of his opponents confuse him. Reytse's letter to his mother shows a victorious readiness to suffer death: "Finally I . . . said very joyfully, 'Do what you will and you can answer for before God, for I do not want to forsake my faith, for either life or death.' " To the bishop he replied to the charge that he based his faith on the doctrine of Menno, who was a seducer and vagabond: "I rely not upon Menno or human doctrine, but only upon the Word of God; in this I desire by the help of the Lord to live and to die." Finally they questioned him anew on all the articles, and again he confessed his faith. Thereupon his sentence was read: because he was a heretic, unwilling to be instructed in the regulations of the holy church, he was committed into the hands of the judges (executioners). The assertion of the bishop that "he would rather fast two weeks with bread and water than pass sentence upon me" betrays qualms of conscience, as does also the act of the bishop's commissioner when he washed his hands "like Pilate, and thought he would be clean of my blood and that I must now await the verdict."

Reytse urged his fellow believers to be steadfast and consoled his parents with the glory awaiting him; he was deeply concerned that his two sisters and his young brother accept the faith. He also comforted his wife, from whom he was separated at the age of twenty-five after a marriage of two years, and urged her to be steadfast. He tried to convert his fellow prisoners by proclaiming God's Word to them. While he was being taken to the torture tower he sang the hymn "Ick roepe u, o hemelsche Vader, aen, wilt myn geloove stercken" (I call on Thee, O heavenly Father; wilt Thou strengthen my faith). This was a familiar Mennonite hymn, and was later included in the Dutch Mennonite hymnals *Groot Hoorns Liedtboeck (q.v.)* and *Kleyn Hoorns Liet-boeck (q.v.).*

The *Bibliographie des Martyrologes Protestants Néerlandais* mentions a booklet written in prison by Reytse Aysesz, *Sommige Belijdingen, schriftlijcke Sent-brieven ende christelicke Vermaningen.* This assertion is, however, not very probable, for the booklet closes with an account of the execution and two hymns composed to commemorate the death of Reytse: "Wilt aenhoren een liedeken recht, men salt u gaen verbreden" (Listen to a song; you will be informed), and of Douwe Eeuwouts. The fact is that the letters and the account of the execution were gathered soon after his death and were published as a booklet about 1577, probably by Gillis Roman at Haarlem. Only one copy of this very valuable booklet is extant; it is found in the library of the Dutch Association for Literature at Leiden, Holland; the Amsterdam Mennonite archives have a handwritten copy of it. Most of this material has been included in all the Dutch martyr books from

1615 on, including the *Martyrs' Mirror,* which contains six letters written by Reytse Aysesz—two to his father in Oldeboorn, who was a member of the church, one to his mother, also a Mennonite, two to his wife, and a general letter about his trial. This letter to his friends contains the interesting information that the Mennonites sang hymns (*liedekens*), and not the Psalms as the Reformed did. The *Martyrs' Mirror* also gives an account of his sufferings and death. In a letter not found in the *Martyrs' Mirror* Reytse Aysesz thanks a brother in F. (probably Franeker, *q.v.*) for sending a book to him in prison, and a brother in L. (Leeuwarden) for a gift of brandy, cake, sweet wine, and wheat bread. (*Mart. Mir.* D 677-91, E 994-1004; *Bibliographie* I, 19-29, 646 f.; *DB* 1865, 68; *ML* I, 100 f.) E.H., vDZ.

Rheensche (Rhenensche) Veen: see Veenendaal.

Rhegius, Urban (1489-1541), a Lutheran theologian, reformer of Augsburg (*q.v.*), Germany. He attended the University of Freiburg and like Balthasar Hubmaier (*q.v.*) went to Ingolstadt with Johann Eck. In 1517 he was crowned imperial orator and poet laureate by Emperor Maximilian, settled in Constance, became the good friend of Johannes Faber (*q.v.*), and upon his recommendation was transferred to Augsburg in 1520. Here he soon became active in the cause of the Reformation and had to leave the city in 1521-24. Upon his return he was a zealous and active Lutheran. The Anabaptists he persecuted without mercy. He bears the principal blame for the expulsion of Hans Denk (*q.v.*). In 1530 he was compelled by order of Charles V to leave the city. He went to Celle and there promoted the Lutheran cause until his death. He also attacked the Anabaptists with his pen. In 1527 he wrote the pamphlet *Wider den newen Taufforden* against Jakob Dachser's *Ein Göttlich unnd grundtlich Offenbarung von wahrhafftigen wiederteuffern.* Other writings along this line were: *Zwen wunderseltzam sendbrieff zweyer Widertäuffer an ire Rotten gen Augspurg gesandt, Verantwurtung aller irrthum diser obgenanten brieff durch Urbanum Rhegium* (1528); *Ein sendbrieff Hans Huthen etwa ains furnemen Vorsteers im wiedertauff ordenn* (1528); *Widderlegung der Münsterischen newen Valentinianer und Donatisten Bekentnus an die Christen zu Osnabrugk in Westfalen, Mit einer Vorrede Doctor Martin Luthers* (Wittenberg, 1535); *De restitutione Israelitici, contra omnes omnium seculorum chiliastes* (1536); *Ein bedencken der Lüneburgischen, Ob einer Oberkeyt gezymme die widerteüffer oder andere ketzer zum rechten glauben zu dringen . . .* (1538); *Wie man die falschen Propheten erkennen, ja greiffen mag, Ein predig zy Mynden jnn Westphalen gethan* (Brunswick, 1539). NEFF.

Menn. Bl., 1886, 89; S. Calvary & Co., *Verzeichniss seltener und werthvoller Werke* (Berlin, 1870) 56 f.; Samuel Geiser, *Die Taufgesinnten-Gemeinden* (Karlsruhe, 1931) 220; Ludwig Keller, *Ein Apostel der Wiedertäufer (Hans Denk)* (Leipzig, 1882) 102, 122 ff.; G. Uhlhorn, *Urbanus Rhegius, Leben und ausgewählte Schriften* (Elberfeld, 1862); *ML* III, 486 f.

Rheinbund (Rhine Union), a federation of several German states established in July 1806 by Napoleon,

the area left (west) of the Rhine having already been incorporated into France. The participant states, including Bavaria (*q.v.*), Württemberg (*q.v.*), Baden (*q.v.*), Hesse (*q.v.*), and Nassau (*q.v.*), were required to furnish troops. Universal military service was enforced, alleviated by the permission to hire a substitute actually meant for the upper classes. From this point on, the Mennonite principle of non-resistance was gradually but steadily lost. (*ML* III, 487.)
E.C.

Rheinfelderhof, a large farm in the Upper Alsace, about 12 miles southeast of Colmar, which was the seat of a Mennonite congregation from the 18th century until 1924, when a meetinghouse was built at Neuf-Brisach (*q.v.*), which then became the center of the congregation. A number of the members are still living at the Rheinfelderhof.
vDZ.

Rheingau, an area in the government district of Wiesbaden, formerly Nassau (*q.v.*), Germany. As early as 1537 there was an Anabaptist congregation at Lorch (*q.v.*), led by a bishop, Peter Nyerup, of Calcar. Toward the end of the 18th century Amish families settled here around Eltville, the principal town of the area, but left after 1880. The Dutch *Naamlijst* (1765 ff.) names as preachers: Bäntz Güngerich in the Nassau-Siegen congregation; Valentin Dahlem (*q.v.*) and David Steiner in the Nassau-Usingen congregation (Mosbach near Wiesbaden); Peter Schantz, Hans Naftziger, and Peter Unsicher in the Nassau-Weilburg congregation. About 1830 a family of eight was living at the Eberbach monastery and another of the same size at Neuhof. In 1894 Spielmann (*Annalen,* 143) listed the following families: at Massenheim a Müller family of six; at Eschborn three families, 22 persons, named Dahlem, Hiestand, and Christoph; at Schafhof a Krehbiel (Staufer) family of five; at Wiesbaden three families, 16 persons, named Dahlem, Hüttwohl, and Steiner; at Rosenköppel the Dahlem family of eight; at Schierstein a Gossmann family of seven; at Mosbach three families, 18 persons, named Borkholder, Kopper, and Kaltwasser. The statistics of Hesse-Nassau show for the Rheingau 22 Mennonites (Amish) in 1871, 29 in 1880, 6 in 1890, 5 in 1910, and one in 1925.
E.C.

Ernst Correll, *Das schweizerische Täufermennonitentum* (Tübingen, 1925) 131 f.; C. Spielmann, "Die Mennoniten und ihre Bedeutung für die Kultur in Nassau," *Annalen des Vereins f. Nassauische Altertumskunde und Geschichtsforschung* XXVI (1894) 137-44 and (somewhat shortened) *Menn. Bl.*, 1895, 19-21, 27-29, 36 f.; *Naamlijst,* issues of 1765-1802; F. W. E. Roth, "Zur Geschichte der Wiedertäufer am Mittelrhein, insbesondere im Rheingau," *Menn. Bl.*, 1893, 89-91; *ML* III, 487.

Rheingrafenstein, a village near Kreuznach in the former Prussian Rhine Province, now Rhineland-Palatinate, Germany, is named in the Dutch *Naamlijst* of 1766 as the seat of the Mennonite congregation of Rheingrafenstein, Erbesbüdesheim, and Weierhof. Services were held weekly alternately at the Rheingrafenstein castle and Dimrotherhof. Ulrich Ellenberger was the elder of this congregation in 1743-67. In 1768 the congregation divided into its three component parts, each with its own deacons and preachers, but served by one elder,

Jakob Galle of Uffhofen, who was ordained in 1767. In 1769 the baptized membership numbered 32. The preacher of the Rheingrafenstein congregation was Christian Moser (d. 1790), who was ordained as preacher in 1766 and as elder in 1782. Jakob Schowalter was a preacher of the Rheingrafenstein congregation from 1774 and elder from 1805 until after 1820. In November 1816 the seat of the Rheingrafenstein congregation was transferred to Neudorferhof (*q.v.*). The membership of the Neudorferhof congregation in 1956 was 138 including the children. The pastor was Gerhard Hein, of Sembach (*q.v.*), who was also serving the Altleiningen (*q.v.*), congregation.
E.C.

Naamlijst, issues of 1766-1802; *Gesch.-Bl.,* 1955, 24; *Der Mennonit* IX (1956) No. 9, p. 138; *ML* III, 487 f.

Rheinische Missionsgesellschaft, a missionary association founded at Mettmann, Germany, on Sept. 28, 1828, by the union of three smaller societies of the Lower Rhine area—Elberfeld, Barmen, and Cologne. It maintained a mission school at Barmen and mission stations in South and Southwest Africa and among the Chinese in New Guinea. In addition its missionaries, doctors, teachers, and deaconesses served the Batak (*q.v.*) and Nias churches in Sumatra, Nias, and Mentawei. For the Mennonites this missionary association was particularly significant in that a number of Mennonite preachers and missionaries received their training in Barmen; e.g., Thomas Löwenberg and Abraham Hirschler, and the missionaries Heinrich Dirks (*q.v.*), Gerhard Nikkel, and Nikolai Wiebe. On Sumatra, where the Association developed an extensive work among the Batak, it was closely associated with the former Dutch Mennonite mission. When Heinrich Dirks left the field in 1881 Tilmann Irle (*q.v.*) of the Association looked after the work at Pakantan (*q.v.*) until 1887, and at the death of Peter Nachtigal (*q.v.*) in 1928 the management of Pakantan was taken over until 1940 by native workers under the direction of the Association and since then under the direction of the Batak church. A considerable number of Mennonites from Russia attended the mission school at Barmen. NEFF, G.M.

Alfred Bonn, *Ein Jahrhundert Rheinische Missionsgesellschaft* (Barmen, 1928); Eduard Kriele, *Geschichte der Rheinischen Missionsgesellschaft* I (Barmen, 1928); *Menn. Bl.*, 1889, 101; *ML* III, 488.

Rheinpfalz: see Palatinate.

Rhenish Hesse: see Rhineland.

Rheydt, a city (pop. 45,124) in the Rhine Province of Prussia, Germany (since 1929 part of Gladbach-Rheydt), formerly under the dominion of the duchy of Jülich (*q.v.*); here, depending on the greater or smaller dependence of the governor upon the duke, the Anabaptists for longer or shorter periods found refuge from oppression in the adjoining Jülich and Cologne territories. The sources on the Mennonites in Rheydt are rather meager until the expulsion of the Anabaptists; for this occurrence there is full information. It would be most peculiar if the populace of the district had been untouched by the preaching of the Anabaptists and if there had been no Anabaptists in Rheydt in the 16th century, when numerous Anabaptists were living in the region all around. Not until the end of the 16th century does the veil lift somewhat.

Otto von Bylandt (*q.v.*), the Baron of Rheydt, confidential adviser and chancellor of Duke William the Rich of Jülich, was eager to make Rheydt an imperial city, and thus became involved in a legal battle with the duke. He also oppressed his subjects with additional taxes and services. This course led to lawsuits in the imperial court, in the course of which the Mennonites of Rheydt are mentioned. In 1584 Peter auf der Heuren is called an Anabaptist. The defense statement by Bylandt's lawyer in 1594-95 states that "among the plaintiffs [the subjects] there are some who are suspect of Anabaptism, who have resisted their proper and inherited government" (since the Anabaptists did not wish to be subject to any temporal authority). Otto von Bylandt's son, Arnold Adrian, who remained Catholic, summoned five witnesses to report on Sept. 26, 1594, about the Anabaptists in the area. These witnesses named more than 25 persons who had for a year or two been "running to the corner preachers" and avoiding the parish church in Rheydt. In Altgen Cüper's house the people of the Gladbach area and other neighboring places were meeting in broad daylight. Their singing could be heard daily, especially in the evening. One witness testified that he had often seen these persons passing through the courtyard at night toward Hockstein, to the Gladbach windmill, to "Hanssen Newissen" sons, who were acknowledged Anabaptists (Hans Neues, of Gladbach-Lürrip, was the ancestor of the Mennonite te Neues family in Crefeld), or to Wettschewell (Wolter of Wetschewell signed the Concept of Cologne on May 1, 1591, for the Odenkirchen—*q.v.*—congregation). The persons named were, however, suspected only of Anabaptism. Thus it happened that at the *Hochgeding* of Jan. 29, 1595, the village neighbors pointed out only one, namely, "Thomas Velbereiter as unbaptized." These were all statements in a lawsuit in which the opponents were trying to blame one another. In 1599, when the Anabaptists in Gladbach were once more subject to severe oppression, several fled into the domain of Rheydt. The baron was suspected of having received them in his domain and giving them shelter in the castle. The bailiff of Jülich with his police fell upon Rheydt to take back what the Gladbach Mennonites had brought with them. The report names particularly Clasz Wolters (see **Claes Wolters Kops**), the "chief preacher and leader of the Gladbach congregation," who was in Sittard (i.e., Sittard Street in München-Gladbach). He is the same "Clasz Wolters, the preacher," who according to the register of Mennonites in Gladbach in 1622, lived outside the parish of Gladbach. He was apparently the son of "Herr Wolter," who was pastor of Odenkirchen (*q.v.*) in 1540, and later preached in Hüls, Kempen (*q.v.*), and Crefeld (*q.v.*), the forest ranger (*Waldläufer*) "with the long white beard."

With the beginning of the Reformed church records in Rheydt it is noted that Mennonites were **transferring** their membership to the Reformed Church, but the minutes of the consistory also show transfers to the Mennonites. This proves that in the first half of the 17th century there were Mennonites in Rheydt, some of whom belonged to native families, others of whom had married into Rheydt, or had immigrated. The deacons (*Armenpfleger*) mentioned in the court records of Rheydt in 1646-48 were members of the Rheydt and Gladbach Mennonite congregations. The Mennonites of Rheydt were at that time probably united in a single congregation with those of Gladbach. Theunes Comes, who signed the Concept of Cologne in 1591 as the delegate of the Mennonites of Gladbach and who was named in 1611 as a preacher of the Mennonite congregation in Gladbach, also owned property in Rheydt.

The decree of the Duke of Jülich of 1652, on the basis of which the Mennonites were expelled from Gladbach, was ineffectual in Rheydt. A list of "Mennonites staying in the domain of Rheydt" in 1664 named only four persons who owned a home. On Nov. 6, 1669, the Duke wrote to the Baron of Rheydt "on account of the abomination of Anabaptism," which had "again slipped secretly into the district of Rheydt," complaining that the Baron did not seriously take steps against "the damned sect," even when the Count Palatine renewed his demand in 1658. Indeed (said the letter), he admitted the Mennonite refugees from the vicinity and gave shelter to some in the castle grounds. The Mennonites from Dahlen (the present München-Gladbach-Rheindahlen) had in 1652 escaped to the imperial domain of Wickrath (*q.v.*). In the 1670's they were compelled to leave this place of refuge and settled in Rheydt and in Dohr, in Zoppenbroich, a domain of the Elector of Cologne. Now the Mennonites in Rheydt were so numerous that they could organize a congregation of their own. In the church records of the Mennonites of the Lower Rhine (especially Goch) there are certificates signed by the preachers of the congregations from which they came. Thus on March 11, 1690, Maryken Arents, daughter of Arent Claessen (van Aken) from Rheydt, brought a certificate to Goch which was signed by Jans Peter Camp and Derck Kouters (or Koeters), "preachers of our Mennonite congregation in Reid." Thus it is known that Rheydt had a firmly established Mennonite congregation in 1690, with a significant membership, some of whose members stemmed from Rheydt, others from their former home towns, frequently persons expelled from other places finally coming to rest in Rheydt. Here they acquired a home, paid a protection fee to the baron, and were quietly and industriously engaged as weavers and merchants.

This way of making their living became their doom. Their Reformed neighbors felt the competition and were angered by the fact that they had to perform so much the more guard duty at the castle and turnpikes, whereas the Mennonites were excused from this service upon payment of a fee. Then on May 16, 1694, about fifty houses of the town of Rheydt, including the monastery building, were destroyed by fire. The Mennonites were accused of arson. In Düsseldorf lived the splendor-loving Elector Palatine John William, whose conscience had been alerted by his confessor Splinter to consider the extirpation of the Mennonites as a work pleasing to God. His councillors made it clear to him that in this matter "100,000 Oberland guilders with interest would be won by His Highness." The time was well chosen. In 1692 a quarrel had broken out between the branches of the Bylandt family concerning the succession in Rheydt. A factitious letter from the Rheydt community arrived, making charges against the Mennonites, and the elector took vigorous action. He struck a final blow, which he hoped would finally clear his land of the "damned sect." A sad picture of religious and social intolerance unrolled in a rapid flow.

In the night of July 16, 1694, the officials of the elector suddenly arrived in Rheydt with 200 peasant marksmen, led by Baron Hermann von Bongart of Paffendorf an der Erft, Palatine privy councillor and bailiff at Kaster. The Mennonites were driven together in the village, struck and kicked until blood flowed. The next evening they were taken in chains to Jüchen together with the women and children of the seven families living in the castle, whose men had fled to Crefeld. In Jüchen they were cross-examined and threatened with death if they refused to become Catholic. But their lives would be saved if they would make a contribution of 12,000 talers to the elector. They finally agreed upon 8,000 talers. But since they were unable to find security for the money in such a short time, the prisoners were chained on Aug. 1, 1694, and taken to Paffendorf on the Erft and there given unworthy lodging and tortured in many ways.

In Rheydt their possessions were sold—houses, land, cattle, furniture, and looms. Their property was estimated by their account books and confiscated. The duke received his share in bolts of linen, etc. Meanwhile William (III, q.v.) of Orange, Stadholder of the Netherlands and King of England, who as Duke of Mörs was also sovereign of Crefeld, came to the aid of the prisoners (see **Mörs**). But before his aid became effective, the prisoners managed to collect in Crefeld the 8,000 Talers required "for expenses." The money was delivered by Govert Remkes (q.v.) and Wilhelm von der Leyen (q.v.), both citizens of Crefeld. In their presence the seventeen prisoners were interrogated for the last time, to make certain that they were subjects of the Duke of Jülich and that the conduct of the duke was therefore legal. They were given a receipt and released on Aug. 29, 1694. Most of them went to Crefeld and with the aid of William of Orange received back the property that had been sold (decree of Aug. 17, 1697). (The fate of these Mennonites is given in detail in the article **Instrumentum publicum.**) A number of Mennonites from Rheydt went to the Netherlands, where they were aided by the Dutch Mennonite Committee for Foreign Needs and the Conference (Sociëteit) of Friesland in settling in the province of Groningen. In the 1720's some Mennonites living in Crefeld sold the last of their possessions in Rheydt.

Since 1694 no Mennonites have lived in Rheydt. For one hundred years the town sank into economic

insignificance, while Crefeld moved toward its great prosperity brought about by the Mennonites. W.N.

Instrumentum publicum wegen desjenigen, was bey denen Churfl. Pfaltzischen Herrn Commissarien gegen die Protestante Mennoniste zu Rheydt in Anno 1694 in facta vorgenohmen vnd sich zügetragen (Crefeld, 1696), reprinted in *Gem.-Kal.*, 1933, 126-31; Dutch translation by Godschalk Godschalks (Crefeld, 1771), English translation by N. B. Grubb (Philadelphia, 1909); Friedrich Nieper, *Die ersten deutschen Auswanderer von Krefeld nach Pennsylvanien* (Neukirchen, 1940); Wilhelm Niepoth, *Zur Geschichte der Mennoniten in Rheydt* (n.d.); Rembert, *Wiedertäufer* (Berlin, 1899); Ludwig Schmitz, *Geschichte der Herrschaft Rheydt* (Rheydt, 1897); Ernst Weydmann, "Ueber die Vertreibung der Mennoniten aus Rheydt und deren Einwanderung in Crefeld im Jahre 1694," in *Menn. Bl.*, 1891, 21, 22, 25, 26; *Inv. Arch. Amst.* I, Nos. 1427, 1749; Blaupot t. C., *Friesland*, 197 f.; *ML* III, 494-96.

Rhineland (German, Rheinland), since 1815 divided among the Prussian Rhine Province, Rhenish Hesse (Rheinhessen), the Bavarian Rhenish Palatinate (Rheinpfalz), and since 1945 divided into North Rhine-Westphalia and Rhineland-Palatinate. For Rhineland-Palatinate see **Palatinate.**

1. *Rhine Province,* since 1824 embracing the Rhenish possessions of Prussia; the former principalities of Cologne and Trier, the former duchies of Cleve (q.v.) and Jülich (q.v., but without the Born district, which in 1814 was ceded to the Netherlands), Berg, the gravures of Mörs with Crefeld (q.v.) and Wied with Neuwied (q.v.), and imperial cities including Aachen (q.v.) and Wetzlar (see **Lower Rhine**). The total Mennonite population in 1812-27 of about 1,200 in this area were enumerated as follows: in the government district of Cleve (later a part of Düsseldorf) a total of 141 Mennonites in 1812, the city of Cleve having 51, Goch 39, Issum 8, Kalkar 9, Xanten 2, Wesel 4, Emmerich (1815) 23, and Rees (1815) 5. The government district of Düsseldorf (original area) had in 1819 a total of 720, distributed in Crefeld with 696, the rest scattered. In the government district of Cologne there were in 1817 two Mennonites. In the district of Coblence there were in 1827 a total of 278 Mennonites, the Neuwied area having 218, Altenkirchen area 12, Braunfels area 27, and Kreuznach area 21. The government district of Aachen had in 1827 four Mennonite families, one living in the Heinsberg area, two in the Aachen (Burtscheid) area, and one in the Düren area. The government district of Trier had in 1827 a total of 15 Mennonite families, one living in each of the areas of Wittlich, Trier, Saarbourg, Merzig, and Ottweiler, three in Saarlouis, and seven in Saarbrücken.

In 1925 the Düsseldorf government district had a total of 1,221 Mennonites living as follows: Crefeld 791, München-Gladbach 2, Hamborn 11, Oberhausen 32, Duisburg 21, Mülheim (Ruhr) 8, Essen 43, Düsseldorf 59, Elberfeld 19, Barmen 8, in other villages 227. The government district of Cologne had 76 Mennonites, 58 of whom were living in the city of Cologne. Coblence had 66, Aachen 5, and Trier 33.

Reiswitz lists for 1829 the congregations of Cleve, Emmerich, Rees, Crefeld, and Neuwied; Goch and settlers in the district of Trier who had been transferred from the Palatinate.

In addition to the liberal city congregations, which

Wageningen · Rhine → Arnhem 4 miles Doetinchem Winterswijk Gronau ↑ 22 miles Münster 10 miles →

Waal Rhine Rhine WESTPHALIA Coesfeld ·

NIJMEGEN Emmerich † Anholt Bocholt Borken · Dülmen ·

CLEVE † Rees †

Ravenstein GERMANY Lippe Haltern

Grave Gennep Goch · Xanten · Wesel † Dorsten · RECKLINGHAUSEN

NETHER- Rhine HERNE

Well · Dinslaken · GELSENKIRCHEN

Venray · Rheinberg · OBERHAUSEN BOCHUM

Helmond · Geldern · Kamp · DUISBURG † ESSEN

Eindhoven 6 miles → Aldekerk · Moers · Ruhr

LANDS Wachtendonk · RHEINHAUSEN MÜLHEIM

Niers VENLO · Kempen · WUPPERTAL

Kaldenkirchen · CREFELD DÜSSELDORF

Steyl · Süchteln · REMSCHEID

Weert · Born · Dülken · Viersen · Neuss

Brüggen · MÜNCHEN-GLADBACH †

Bree · ROERMOND · RHEIDT · Liedberg

Stevensweert Vlodrop · Wildenrath · Wickrath Odenkirchen GERMANY

Monfort · Burgelen · Holtum Opladen ·

Maaseyck Roosteren · Wassenberg · Erkelenz · Venrath · Grevenbroich · Leverkusen ·

Vissersweert Dieteren · Ratheim · Küchhoven ·

Susteren · Heinsberg · Hückelhoven · Hüchelhoven ·

Holtum · Waldenrath · Dremmen · Lövenich ·

Millen · Havert · Brachelen · Bedburg ·

Born · Gangelt · Linnich · COLOGNE †

Sittard · Geilenkirchen · Beeck ·

Berg · Jülich ·

Heerlen Kerpen · Brühl · Siegburg ·

Valkenburg · Herzogenrath · Erft

MAASTRICHT † Würselen · Weiden · Eschweiler · Düren · Lechenich ·

Vaals Volkenrath · Hastenrath · Kornelimünster BONN Oberpleis ·

AACHEN † Stolberg · Zülpich · Bad Godesberg · Königswinter ·

Vossenack · Euskirchen · Homref ·

LIEGE Eupen · Lammersdorf · Schmidt · Rheinbach · Remagen Linz

Limburg · Simmerath · Steckenborn · Ruhrberg · Münstereifel · Ahrweiler ·

Verviers · Imgenbroich · Wolfseiffen · Gemünd Sinzig

Monschau · Dedenborn · Herhahn ·

Dreiborn · Olef · Schleiden ·

Ettelscheid · Neuwied 8 miles →

SCALE OF MILES
I   5   10   15   20

KEY TO MAP OF

LOWER RHINE

were of the Dutch Mennonite type, and all of which except Crefeld and Neuwied gradually died out, there were Amish settlements; viz., the rural congregation of Neuwied, which extended over Andernach as far as Münstermaifeld, and which in 1857 (besides the city congregation of 35 members) had 200 baptized members. It also disappeared. Whereas the city congregation of Neuwied adopted the Cornelis Ris (q.v.) Confession of Faith, the Amish held to the Dordrecht (q.v.) Confession. As late as 1818 the Landrat of Braunfeld expressed serious distrust of the quiet and sober, industrious and competent Amish farmers, because they let their beards grow, wore no buttons, took part neither in (state) church services nor religious instruction, and married only in their own group.

The Prussian government at once sought to reach an understanding with the Mennonites living in its Rhenish possessions. On June 7, 1815, Chancellor Hardenberg, in the midst of the Congress of Vienna, wrote a letter to the *Oberpräsident* in reply to his report that there were many Mennonites living there. His letter inquired what attitude the Mennonites had taken under French rule and how they were planning to help in the defense of the country. In 1818 the small Amish congregation near Dierdorf (Neuwied area) wrote a letter to the chancellor and received a prompt reassuring reply. The Crefeld congregation was in constant communication with the king and the *Oberpräsident*. Individuals also, e.g., Hermes and Winkelmann of the Crefeld congregation, personally fought the issues of nonresistance and the oath through to the highest instance. Meanwhile the Berlin government was also working on the problem. On July 8, 1817, the Minister of the Interior, and on Feb. 8, 1819, the Council of State, presented to Frederick William III (q.v.) a report based on Menno Simons, the confessions of Dordrecht (q.v.) and of Cornelis Ris q.v.), the writings of Schijn (q.v.), Zeidler (1698), Rues (q.v., 1643), Crichton (q.v., 1786), Starck (q.v., 1789), and others. Shortly before the question of the oath was settled in 1827 by an order of cabinet, the king requested that all Mennonite heads of families be questioned on their position on nonresistance. The question was not settled for them until May 16, 1830. Most of the Mennonites had accepted military duty, but all those who remained nonresistant, including the Quakers, were to be excused from service, but must pay a 3 per cent income tax; they should be admitted to local offices but not to state offices; they were not permitted to acquire land, and the settlement or reception of new members was prohibited. By 1848 Hermann von Bekkerath (q.v.) was in a position to say in the Frankfurt Parliament that the Mennonites in the Rhineland with few exceptions had accepted military service, and that they did not regard the rejection of this service as a necessary part of their doctrine.   E.C.

Ernst Crous, "Wie die Mennoniten in die deutsche Volksgemeinschaft hineinwuchsen," in Gesch.-Bl., 1939, 13-24 (reprint, Karlsruhe, 1939); idem, "Mennoniten im alten Reich und Staat," in Die Heimat (Crefeld), 1939, 137-44; idem, "Mennoniten im Regierungsbezirk Trier 1827-1870," in Gem.-Kal., 1941, 62-73; J. Mannhardt, Namens-Verzeichniss . . . (Danzig, 1857); Georg L. von Reiswitz, Beiträge zur Kenntniss der . . . Mennoniten II (Breslau, 1829); ML III,

2. *Rhenish Hesse* (German, *Rheinhessen*), since 1815 the possession of the Grand Duke of Hesse, situated on the left bank of the Rhine, viz., the northern edge of Rhineland-Palatinate (q.v.) (Alzey district). For the distribution of the Mennonites in the areas of Mainz, Alzey, Bingen, Oppenheim, and Worms in 1871-1925, see Hesse. The Mennonite membership in congregations follows:

	1857	1887	1914	1934	1954	Church built
Uffhofen	45	72	62	53	62	1829
Ibersheim	300	233	160	156	185	1836
Monsheim	180	280	260	230	286	1820
	525	585	482	439	533	

The Uffhofen (q.v.) congregation is under the care of the pastor of Weierhof (q.v.); Ibersheim (q.v.), Eppstein (q.v.), and Ludwigshafen-Friesenheim (q.v.) are united, as are Monsheim (q.v.) and Obersülzen (q.v.), disregarding the new political divisions. The change from a lay ministry to a professional ministry began in the Hessian congregations. In 1817-22 a merger was formed between the Lutherans and the Reformed, which the Mennonites were also urged to join. This they refused to do; and believing that they would be in a better position to assert their independence if they had professional ministers, the Kriegsheim (q.v.) congregation, which in 1820 transferred its center to Monsheim, in 1818 called Leonhard Weydmann (q.v., 1793-1868) as the first minister of this kind, who had been educated at the universities of Basel, Amsterdam, and Berlin. The second trained minister was called in 1832 to Sembach in the Rhenish Palatinate, viz., Johannes Risser (q.v., 1810-68), educated at the universities of Heidelberg, Erlangen, and Bonn. The third was the older Jakob Ellenberger (q.v., 1800-79), called to Friedelsheim; he had studied in the Zeller Institute at Beuggen, east of Basel. In 1835 Weierhof in the Rhenish Palatinate followed with a trained minister, and in 1843 Ibersheim in Rhenish Hesse.

Outstanding Mennonite farmers of Rhenish Hesse were Christian and August Dettweiler (q.v.); Peter Dettweiler (q.v.) was a leading physician in combating tuberculosis; Jakob Finger (q.v.) as Minister of State governed the entire province in 1884-98. (For bibliography see **Palatinate**.)   E.C.

3. *North Rhine-Westphalia*, a state in West Germany, formed in 1947 of the government districts of Aachen, Düsseldorf, and Cologne of the Prussian Rhine Province, of Westphalia, and of Lippe. Its capital is Düsseldorf and its population (1952) 13,147,100 (56 per cent Catholic, 39 per cent Protestant). The state is divided into the government districts Aachen, Düsseldorf, and Cologne; Arnsberg, Detmold, and Münster; in 1949 small border areas were ceded to the Netherlands and Belgium.

The old Mennonite congregations of Crefeld (q.v.) and Gronau (q.v.) were located here, and also the new refugee congregations of Bergisches Land (q.v.) and Espelkamp (q.v.). Of the congregations belonging to the Westphalian group, Bielefeld, Detmold, Münster, and Recklinghausen belong to North Rhine-Westphalia, while Hameln,

Rinteln, and Osnabrück are reckoned with Lower Saxony.

	1940	new members	influx
Crefeld	c800	1,605	805
Bergisches Land		275	275
Total	c800	1,880	1,080
Gronau	c70	110	40
Espelkamp		135	135
Westphalia (part of)		400	400
Total	70	645	575
Grand Total	c870	2,525	1,655

These figures show that in 1955 the membership in this area included about 900 members in the original families and an increase of 1600 refugee members, mostly from West Prussia. The Neuwied congregation (*q.v.*), formerly closely connected with the Crefeld congregation in the Rhine Province, now belongs to the Palatinate.

The churches at Crefeld and Gronau, which had been destroyed in World War II, were rebuilt in 1950. The refugee congregation of Espelkamp acquired its meetinghouse in 1953 in a remodeled munitions storehouse. With the help of the Mennonite Central Committee (*q.v.*) and later the Pax (*q.v.*) boys the refugees were given supplementary food and clothing (of the nine areas in West Germany under the care of the MCC in the period of want following 1945, three lay in North Rhine-Westphalia, viz., Crefeld, Gronau, and Brakel) and later also assistance in building settlements. After World War II the MCC built a refugee camp with a hospital in Gronau, which published a periodical *Unser Blatt* (*q.v.*) from Oct. 8, 1947, to June 15, 1950. Settlements were built at Espelkamp (north of Bielefeld) in 1951 and at Bechterdissen (south of Bielefeld) in 1955. In general, the refugee congregations have rarely been able to retain the West Prussian organization of elder, preacher, and deacon; in most cases a pastor now serves under a church board of several members. The general organization of North German Mennonite congregations formed in 1951 and known as the "Gemeindenausschuss" was joined at once by the congregations in Bergisches Land and "Westphalia," i.e., Crefeld and Gronau. In 1948 the second Mennonite student conference (*Studententagung*) met in Crefeld. In Gronau the Vereinigung (*q.v.*) and the German Mennonite Historical Association (see **Mennonitischer Geschichtsverein**) met in 1948; the Historical Association decided to establish the Research Center (*Forschungsstelle*) at Göttingen, the home of the director Ernst Crous. In 1954 the Vereinigung met at Crefeld. Youth organizations were formed at Cologne and Espelkamp. In May 1955 a ministers' retreat (*Predigerrüstzeit*) was held at Espelkamp. The Crefeld Mennonite minister took a leading part in a petition for offerings on Dec. 11, 1946, on behalf of relief. This appeal was to be presented to the Christians of all creeds throughout the world, and a sacrificial offering for the needy of Crefeld was to be made in all the churches of the city. In Heerewegen (*q.v.*), near Utrecht, representatives of the Dutch and Northwest German congregations

met on May 7, 1954, to try to renew old bonds of co-operation and find new ways of working together.

Gustav Kraemer (1863-1948) served as pastor of the Crefeld congregation for many years; he was followed by Dirk Cattepoel 1937-51, and Daniel Reuter 1951- . Hendrick van Delden (1872-1950), an elder of the Gronau congregation, and Reinhard Rahusen (1883-1951), a minister of the same congregation, were of great importance for the entire Mennonite brotherhood. The large textile firm M. van Delden & Co. celebrated its centennial in 1954.

E.C.

Gem.-Kal., 1941 and 1951; printed matter on the appeal for relief funds (*Bitt- und Opfergang*) in the Göttingen Research Center; *ML* III, 491 f.

4. *Rhineland-Palatinate,* a state of West Germany, which was formed on Aug. 30, 1946, by order of the French military government, of the government districts of Coblence and Trier of the Prussian Rhine Province, of parts of Nassau, of Rhenish Hesse, of the Bavarian Rhenish Palatinate (hence essentially the core of Kurtrier, Kurmainz, and Kurpfalz). Its capital is Mayence, and its population (1952) 2,993,700 (59 per cent Catholic, 39 per cent Protestant); it is divided into the government districts of Coblence, Trier, Montabaur, Rhenish Hesse, and Palatinate.

Statistics for the old Mennonite congregations in this area follow.

Congregation	1940	1955	Increase	Decrease
Branchweilerhof	46	65	19	
Deutschhof	198	122		76
Friedelsheim	140	180	40	
Kohlhof	45	70	25	
Ibersheim	162	185	23	
Eppstein	121	120		1
Ludwigshafen	127	90		37
Kaiserslautern	60	91	31	
Kühbörncheshof	122	209	87	
Zweibrücken	304	245		59
Saar		70	70	
Monsheim	200	310	110	
Obersülzen	100	121	21	
Sembach	350	400	50	
Neudorferhof	110	138	28	
Altleingen	44	40		4
Weierhof	370	560	190	
Uffhofen	44	58	14	
Neuwied	25	500	475	
	2,568	3,574	1,006 net	

There are in this area about 2,600 members of local old Mennonite families and 1,000 recent additions, mostly refugees from West Prussia. The increase occurred principally in the congregations of Neuwied (formerly closely associated with Crefeld in the Rhine Province), Weierhof, and Monsheim. The loss in the Deutschhof congregation is due to the fact that the Alsatian part, Geisberg, became independent; the loss in the Zweibrücken congregation is due to the fact that the members living in the Saar area had to form an independent organization.

Almost half of the German Mennonites are now living in the two Rhenish states, as a regional survey clearly shows:

Area	1940	1955	Increase
Rhineland-Palatinate	2,568	3,574	1,006
North Rhine-Westphalia	870	2,525	1,655
Lower Saxony	434	1,793	1,359
Baden and Württemberg	922	1,177	255
Berlin	406	1,122	716
Hamburg	338	935	597
Schleswig-Holstein	25	855	830
Bavaria	651	736	85
Bremen		500	500
Frankfurt and South Hesse		170	170
	6,214	13,387	7,173

The churches in Deutschhof and Ludwigshafen, which were destroyed in World War II, were restored in 1949-50. In the area of Rhineland-Palatinate two homes for the aged were built, especially for the refugees from West Prussia, viz., Leutesdorf, near Neuwied, and Enkenbach, near Sembach, in 1949-50. In 1955 the refugee settlements in Niederbieber (q.v.), Torney, near Neuwied (q.v.), built a church besides the one in Neuwied, which belonged to the small original congregation. Since the school at Weierhof (see **Realanstalt am Donnersberg**) was not released by the occupation authorities, an organization was formed which opened a dormitory (*Schülerheim*) in Kirchheimbolanden for Mennonite (and other) students attending the secondary school in that town. Refugees were not admitted into the French zone until 1948. In that year they began to come into the Palatinate and were assisted by American relief. The settlement in Neuwied (Niederbieber/Torney) was begun in 1949, the one in Enkenbach in 1943. An organization to help refugees get settled (*Genossenschaftliches Flüchtlingswerk*), founded at Weierhof (q.v.) in 1949 by Otto Zerger and Johannes Driedger, included local Mennonites and refugees who wished to settle, for the purpose of support in assuming rented farms. Thus, on the Offweilerhof near Zweibrücken three farms, called "Werderhof," were established, and by 1954 thirty Mennonite refugee families had been helped to find homes and a chance to earn a living. The association called Mennonite Settlement Aid (*Mennonitische Siedlungshilfe*) serves a wider clientele; it originated in Ludwigshafen (q.v.) on July 24, 1953, under the direction of Fritz Stauffer. The HVDM (the relief organization of the Vereinigung, q.v.), the corporation Mennonite Homes for the Aged (*Mennonitische Altersheime*), and the voluntary service organization MFD (*Mennonitischer Freiwilligendienst, q.v.*) maintain a common office with Mennonite Settlement Aid in Ludwigshafen, headed by Richard Hertzler. The chairman of the German Mennonite Missions Committee is Abraham Braun, former pastor of the Ibersheim congregation.

Various conferences and committees have resumed their activities. The Conference of the Palatine and Hessian Mennonite Churches (q.v.) meets annually either in Neustadt a.d.W. or Ludwigshafen. Since 1953 the congregational ministers and leaders of the Palatinate and Hesse have been meeting annually for a study conference. In 1950 the fourth edition of the hymnal (see **Hymnology**) was published.

There have been conferences for youth, and at Monsheim (q.v.) one for the aged. The *Gemeindekalender* has been edited by Paul Schowalter, pastor of Weierhof, and the *Mennonit* by Gerhard Hein, pastor of Sembach. Several ministers have retired: Johannes Foth in 1953, at the age of 75; Emil Händiges in 1951, at the age of 70; he was succeeded by Alexander Prieur in 1954; Hugo Scheffler who emigrated to Canada in 1951 was replaced by Theo Hotel. Abraham Braun has been succeeded by Daniel Habegger, who served as his assistant 1952-57. In Neuwied Otto Wiebe, formerly a preacher of Heubuden (q.v.), became the elder.   E.C.

Rhineland Agricultural Society was organized in February 1931 to serve the citizens of the Rural Municipality of Rhineland (q.v.) and adjoining areas of southern Manitoba. Its headquarters are in Altona, where its annual fall fair is held. Although it is not a church organization, most of the society's officers and members have been Mennonites. From 1931 through April 1937 it published *Rhineland Agricultural Society's Quarterly* and since then has continued the publication of its *Annual Fall Fair Prize List*. The society assists the farmers in the control of crop and livestock diseases and in obtaining seeds of new and better varieties of crops, promotes interest in agriculture and works for the improvement of rural life, sponsors agricultural and homemaking schools, short courses, correspondence courses, and lectures on agricultural problems, and holds agricultural fairs. Its financial support comes from the Manitoba Department of Agriculture and the Rural Municipality of Rhineland, as well as from private organizations and individuals and the members of the society. Since the early 1940's a full-time agriculturalist has been serving the society, who in addition to giving direct aid to the farmers supervises boys' and girls' clubs, in which thousands of young people have been enrolled. The annual fairs avoid the kind of amusements often associated with these events, although they do feature sports, music, and instructive educational lectures, as well as contests in livestock, poultry, grains, grasses, fruits and vegetables, and in junior educational exhibits.   M.G.

Rhineland, Rural Municipality of, equivalent to a county in the United States, was established in 1884 as a local government unit by the Manitoba government. First called Douglas, it was renamed Rhineland in 1891 at the request of its citizens. It covers an area of 18 townships, a block roughly 18 x 18 miles, 360 sq. miles, or 230,400 acres, extending north from the United States border just west of the Red River. It includes the towns of Altona, Gretna, Plum Coulee, Horndean, and Rosenfeld, and 15 villages, including Sommerfeld and Halbstadt. Altona is the civic and business capital of the area. Its area is almost identical with the original West Reserve grant. In 1949 it had a population of 8,000, in 1959 some 6,500, then being the most densely populated rural district in Manitoba. It is a prosperous rural area with almost 100 per cent of its land under cultivation. It has probably the largest concentration of Mennonite population in compact block in North America, with very little admixture of population of non-Mennonite stock. The reeves, secretary-treasurers, and members of the Municipal Council have almost always been exclusively Mennonite. H. T. Hamm of Altona served as secretary-treasurer 1913-43. The largest body of Mennonites in the area is the Bergthal Mennonite Church. The former Sommerfeld and Old Colony group were largely replaced by newer immigrants from Russia in 1922-26. The Rudnerweide group had its origin here and has most of its members in the municipality. (See also **Manitoba, Old Colony Mennonites.**)   H.S.B.

H. H. Hamm, *Sixty Years of Progress, 1884-1944, Diamond Jubilee, The Rural Municipality of Rhineland* (n.p., n.d., Altona, 1944); E. K. Francis, *In Search of Utopia* (Altona, 1955).

Rhineland-Stanley Teachers' Association includes the teachers of the rural municipalities of Rhineland and Stanley in southern Manitoba, most of whom are Mennonites. This association was organized by H. H. Ewert of Gretna, Man., in the 1890's to further the cause of education among the Mennonites of this province. The members of the association hold a two-day convention each fall. Before World War I the second day of the convention was always conducted in German, but now both days are in English. The locale of the convention alternates between the main towns of the two municipalities. The 1949 convention was held in Winkler; 145 teachers attended. By 1958 the RSTA area was organized into two divisions with 220 teachers, though still meeting in one convention. N. G. Neufeld has been convention secretary for the past ten years.

                   P.Br.

Rhodes: see also **Roth.**

Rhodes, John (d. 1764), a Mennonite minister, born near Zürich, Switzerland, emigrated to America in 1728, settled in Shenandoah County, Va., in 1730, and later moved to Page County, Va. In August 1766 eight Indians led by a white man massacred eight members of this family. Two daughters escaped and one son was held captive two years by the Indians in their camps west of the Ohio River.

                   W.D.S.

Rhodius, Marianne (1814-1902), a Mennonite philanthropist, was born Oct. 12, 1814, at Crefeld, Germany. After the death of her husband Christian Rhodius in 1873 she lived quietly in retirement, finding her happiness in making others happy. The records of the "Rhodius petitions" which she quietly granted, have been preserved in the archives of the Crefeld city poor-law administration. Of these petitions there were in poor years about 2,400; in 1892-93, 2,191 were granted; after 1884 Mrs. Rhodius contributed 25,000 Marks annually for this purpose alone. In addition she was the first contributor in all undertakings for the common welfare (e.g., 100,000 Marks for the erection of the Kaiser Wilhelm Museum). Almost unnoticed were her contributions to all institutions and associations as well as for the support of talented students in the universities or art schools, regardless of creed. When she came into the inheritance of the property of her uncle Cornelius de Greiff (*q.v.*) she contributed the business house of the firm of her grandfather, Cornelius and Johann Floh, for the initial care of the

poor; four years later 25,000 Talers to enlarge the city hospital; and in 1867, 50,000 Talers for the support of fifty needy families (see **de Greiff**). Later she gave 40,000 Marks for the building of a market hall, and in her will, under the name of "Cornelius de Greiff'schen Unterstützungsfonds," she bequeathed to the city for benevolent purposes 1,800,-000 Marks, to the Linn community 100,000 Marks, and for institutions and communities at other places, including the Mennonite congregations at Weierhof, Neuwied, and Monsheim, 54,000 Marks. Her residence, which the city acquired in 1905 from the heirs, houses the Crefeld city library. A portrait of this benefactress has been placed in the library. (*Menn. Bl.*, 1902, 195; *Die Heimat*, 1939; *ML* III, 496 f.)   K.R.

Rhönbruderhof (Bruderhof Neuhof, Fulda district, Germany), the name given in 1934 to the settlement of Hutterian Brethren, originally called simply "Bruderhof," which was founded in the foothills of the Rhön Mountains of Germany in 1926 by the Sannerz brotherhood, and which existed until 1937. The contract of its founding, dated Dec. 5, 1926, which was the expression of "the fundamental common expression of the direction of the will and the work for all time," says: "The publications of the Eberhard Arnold-Verlag and the work of lecturing connected with it shall be continued in the spirit of the hitherto published books, writings, and periodicals; likewise the daughter congregation in the spirit of the Sannerz letters and the *Wegwarte*. Above all the open door and the community of life and goods of the early Christian church are to be kept open and carried on. . . . The contracting parties on the occasion of the hereby established founding of the Bruderhof express their unanimous will that this agreement shall remain unconditionally and without a break directive also for all successors of both parties." The name Bruderhof was adopted from the older Hutterite terminology.

To the original small peasant farm Hansahof two additional adjacent farms were added, thus giving the Rhönbruderhof about 250 Prussian Morgen of fields, meadows, pastures, and woods. By 1934 a small communal settlement had been erected by new buildings and remodeling of old ones, which offered simple subsistence to about 140 persons. From this colony Eberhard Arnold set out to visit the Hutterite settlements in the United States and Canada in 1930-31. Through the union established at that time with the Americans the inner and outer structure was continued under the deep impact of the four-hundred-year-old history of the genuinely fraternal communal living of the Hutterites. The elder (*Wortführer*) was supported by one or two assistant preachers (*Diener am Wort*). Together they bore the responsibility for all the internal and practical affairs, assisted by the householder in business matters, the work supervisor (*Weinzedel*) for the systematic distribution of labor, the treasurer (*Kästner*) for provisions, and the housemother for feminine concerns. Several additional brethren (*Zeugnisbrüder*) were called on for support in making important spiritual decisions; each field of work was supervised by a responsible member of the brotherhood. But the final authority in all inner and outer matters lay, as in all Hutterite communities, in the Spirit-led, united brotherhood as the bearer of the reality of the church.

The divisions of work included agriculture with the gardens, the community school with the children's home, the publishing house with its printing and distribution of books, the office, the various workshops for trades and building; in addition there were, besides the care of the smaller children, also the various household activities. The infants were cared for in the nursery and "creeping-room." At the age of two or three years they were placed in the kindergarten until they were of school age. Young people were educated according to their gifts and abilities. In the children's home orphans and children from difficult social circumstances were supported and educated with the children of the commune in the spirit of true brotherhood. Among the older children there were frequent conversions which led to an inner union with the brotherhood. In the publishing house and the printery which was instituted in 1931 the work begun in Sannerz was continued, especial attention being given to research, collection and publication of the old Hutterite writings. In 1932 the printing of the *Klein Geschichtbuch* by Johannes Waldner was begun, and in that year as well as in the next an epistle was issued to the Hutterian Brethren of North America. With the Nazi rise to power in 1933, the death of Eberhard Arnold in 1935, and other difficulties, the work on the old manuscripts was seriously hindered, and the printing of the *Klein Geschichtbuch* could not be completed. The preaching of the Word among the brethren and the numerous guests and assistants on the Bruderhof was, besides the education of the children and public witness in spoken and written word, the most important work of the missionary community on the Rhönbruderhof, so that the brotherhood grew from a membership of 40 in 1927 to 130 in 1934 through the influx of persons from Germany and other countries, who had convictions favoring the communal life.

In spite of the difficulties evoked by the Nazi government, the Bruderhof attempted to continue its work in the same spirit as before. But by November 1933, the Gestapo instituted a search of the buildings, closed the school and the children's home, and forbade the care of strangers on the Bruderhof. Since the distribution of literature in Germany was also restricted, a daughter colony was founded early in 1934 in the principality of Liechtenstein. The school, children's home, and publication were transferred to the Almbruderhof (*q.v.*) there. In consequence of the emigration of a part of the Bruderhof and the departure of a number more when military training became obligatory in Germany in 1935, the Rhönbruderhof was seriously weakened. By such measures as heavy taxation, foreclosure of mortgages, and other economic regulations the state tried to compel the Bruderhof to close; but with the assistance of the Almbruderhof and the Cotswold Bruderhof, the Rhönbruderhof was able to maintain itself until it was forcibly closed by the Gestapo. Eberhard Arnold died on Nov. 22, 1935, in the midst of this severe struggle. His *Innenland,* revised in 1932, was published soon after his death, as well as the booklet, *Eberhard Arnold, Sein Leben für die*

Bruderhöfe. At the end of 1936 the Cotswold Bruderhof in England took over the printery and the extensive library. In April 1937 two American Hutterite elders, David Hofer of James Valley, Man., and Michael Waldner of Bon Homme, S.D., visited the Bruderhof and were witnesses of its dissolution on April 14, 1937, the arrest of the three directing members of the corporation, the confiscation of endowments, and the expulsion of the members with their children from the grounds. Through negotiations the expelled group succeeded in obtaining permission to emigrate to Liechtenstein and Holland. David Hofer gives an account of these events in *Der Pflug* (Vol. I, no. 3) and *The Plough* (Vol. I, no. 3) in the form of pages from his diary, titled "Die Auflösung des Rhönbruderhofes in Deutschland." A few of the exiles were admitted to the Almbruderhof; most of them for two months enjoyed the hospitality of the Dutch Mennonites in Bilthoven and Elspeet, until they could proceed to England and enter the Cotswold Bruderhof. After three months the three imprisoned brethren were released and permitted to join their families in England. The Rhönbruderhof was sold at auction by the authorities.

In Liechtenstein and in England the brotherhood was able to live according to its faith, until it was compelled by reasons of war to emigrate to Paraguay. Three Bruderhofs were established in Primavera, Paraguay, whereas in England the communal life was revived in 1942 in the Wheathill Bruderhof (*q.v.*). In all four of these settlements the work was carried on in the spirit of the contract of founding as a work of re-establishment of the primitive Christian and primitive Anabaptist church. Later a Bruderhof was established at Woodcrest (*q.v.*), Refton, N.Y.   E.C.H.A.

Menn. Bl., 1937, 86 f.; *Gbl.* 1937, 62; Michael Horsch, *Die Auflösung des eingetragenen Vereins Neuwerk Bruderhof, Post Neuhof, Kreis Fulda* (Hellmannsberg, 1937); *Zondagsbode* (1936-37) Nos. 32, 38; *ML* III, 497.

Rhynsburg: see **Rijnsburg.**

Ribeauville, a town (pop. 3,866) 9 miles north of Colmar in Upper Alsace, the seat of an early Anabaptist congregation and also of an 18th-century Mennonite congregation, long since extinct. Two Anabaptists arrested in Basel in 1534 stated under torture that Anabaptist meetings were being held at Ribeauville and also near Colmar, and that a service attended by 300 persons had met in a forest between Colmar and Ingersheim. In all this region, they said, their doctrine was making progress; Hunawihr, near Ribeauville, was almost completely won over, and the brethren were numerous at Riquewihr and Kaysersberg. There continued to be Anabaptists in the region of Colmar until in the 17th century. Immigration from Switzerland after the Thirty Years' War established a considerable Mennonite settlement northeast of Colmar, with meeting places in various villages in this area, which also changed as the places of settlement of the members changed. Whether one of these places of meeting was Ribeauville in this and the later period down into the 19th century is not definitely known.   H.S.B.

Pierre Sommer, "Historique des Assemblées, 41. Vieilles Assemblées de la Haute Alsace," *Christ Seul* (July 1932) 7-9.

Rich (Riche, Richen, Reich, Ricken, Rijkens) is a widely spread Mennonite family name. The Rich(en) family stems from Frutigen in the Bernese Oberland of Switzerland; it is also found in Hochstetten, west of Langnau in the Emmental (q.v.). Persecution in the canton of Bern (q.v.), lasting into the 18th century, compelled many Mennonites to emigrate. The "Amnesty Proclamation" issued by the Bernese government on Feb. 11, 1711, permitting them to leave freely with all their possessions, had as a consequence a mass emigration, in which the Richen family was included.

Among the refugees settling in the Netherlands was Daniel Richen (Ricken) (c1681-c1755), an Amish Mennonite preacher, who had previously been banished to Neuchâtel (q.v.) and then at the age of thirty served as supervisor on the emigrant boat sailing for the Netherlands in 1711, settled first in Deventer (q.v.) and later became an elder and organizer in the congregations of the Nieuwe Zwitsers (see Swiss Mennonites in the Netherlands), in Groningen (q.v.) and Sappemeer (q.v.). Peter Ricken (d. 1772), probably a brother of Daniel, was a preacher here in 1740-72. They were all farmers and lived near Groningen, where some descendants are still living (Rijkens). David Ricken (d. 1779), a son of Daniel Ricken, was a preacher of the Old Flemish congregation in Norden, East Friesland, 1777-79.

A second place of refuge for the Swiss Mennonites was Montbéliard (q.v.), now in the French department of Doubs. There were Richens here since 1715. A Hans Richen, a well-to-do farmer with eight children, was for many years an elder in the congregation of Swiss origin, a leading personality. The congregation met every second week in his home; in 1730 he began to keep a church record. In April 1787 he assisted in the ordination of an elder in the Schänzli (q.v.) congregation of Basel (q.v.), and in June of that year he recommended two brethren of the Chaux de Fonds (q.v.) congregation in the Bernese Jura to the office of elder (see his note in the Bernese dialect, ML III, 498). He also traveled to the Netherlands as one of the elders from Alsace called to the New Swiss (q.v.) congregations in 1766 to arbitrate a dispute among them. A century later Pre. Isaac Rich (d. 1878), who grew up in the Seigne (q.v.) congregation and attended the Mennonite (GCM) school at Wadsworth (q.v.), Ohio, established a school in Etupes, near Montbéliard, which was soon moved to Exincourt and continued there until 1876. Other members of the Rich family served as preachers or deacons in the Montbéliard congregation until the 20th century. Peter Rich was the elder of the Birkenhof (q.v.) congregation in Upper Alsace 1788-c1820.

In Mennonite circles in Switzerland—Bernese Jura and Basel—and in France—Montbéliard, Altkirch, and Florimont—the name continues. It is also found in Ohio, Iowa, Kansas, and other states. Willis E. Rich and Ronald L. Rich are on the faculty of Bethel College. Olive G. Rich is on the faculty of Goshen College. Eldon S. Rich is a practicing physician in Newton, Kan.   S.G., NEFF, E.C.

Almanach Mennonite du Cinquantenaire 1901-1951 (Montbéliard, 1951) 12; Blaupot t. C., Groningen, 186,

207; Inv. Arch. Amst. I, Nos. 1317, 1319, 1325 f., 1329, 1348, 1351, 1360, 1366, 1889, 1908, 1911, 1920; Huizinga, Stamboek . . . van Samuel Peter en Barbara Fry (Groningen, 1890) 38, 39, 61, 62, 67, 69, 114, 115, 117; DB 1872, 109, 112 ff.; 1873, 113-18, 136, 138; 1885, 20 f.; 1895, 91-98; H. Dassel, Menno's Volk in Groningen (Groningen, n.d.-1950) 42; Gem.-Kal. 1906, 160; 1936, 138; Charles Mathiot, Récherches historiques sur les Anabaptistes de l'ancienne principauté de Montbéliard, d'Alsace et des regions voisines (Belfort, 1922); Menn. Bl., 1872, 17; 1870, 37, 38; Müller, Berner Taüfer, 309, 321, 323, 325; Delbert L. Gratz, Bernese Anabaptists (Scottdale, 1953) 49, 65, 92, 135, 199; ML III, 498 f.

Richardson, Samuel (1689-1761), owner of a publishing house at London, England, and a novelist, some of whose novels (Pamela, 1740; Clarissa Harlowe, 1747-48; and Charles Grandison, 1753) have been translated into Dutch. Johannes Stinstra (q.v.) translated Clarissa Harlowe in eight volumes (Harlingen, 1752-55); for Volumes 3, 5, and 7 Stinstra wrote prefaces of 60, 32, and 28 pages, in which he explained and defended Richardson's moralism. In 1752-56 Richardson and Stinstra exchanged a number of letters, which were published in The Correspondence of Samuel Richardson (London, 1804). Richardson's novels were very popular in the Netherlands, influencing such authors as Wolff and Deken (q.v.), and were read with special interest by the Mennonites.   vDZ.

Chr. Sepp, Johannes Stinstra en zijn tijd I (Amsterdam, 1865) 7 f.; II (Amsterdam, 1866) 243-52.

Riche: see Rich.

Riche (Ricquere, de Rijker), Guiljame, an Anabaptist martyr: see Willem de Rijken.

Richert (Richertz, Richaert, Richers, Riggert, Riggers), a family name which originated among the Mennonites of Prussia and spread to Russia and America. The earliest appearance of the name in Mennonite records is found in 1632. It was found in Danzig, Schönsee, and Przechovka. The Alexanderwohl church record has had many bearers of this name during more than 300 years. The first bearer of the name, Knels Richert, a shoemaker, joined the Mennonites in 1632. He was an ancestor of the Alexanderwohl Richerts. From Goessel, Kan., the name has spread over numerous states.

Among the prominent members of the family have been Heinrich Richert (q.v.), an outstanding leader of the Goessel Mennonite community, and his son Peter H. Richert (1871-1949), former pastor of the Tabor Mennonite Church of Goessel and a G.C.M. leader. A second son, David H. Richert (1875-   ), was for many years professor of mathematics and astronomy at Bethel College. Peter Richert (1850-1937) served as pastor of the Reedley M.B. Church. Herbert C. Richert (1900-   ) is professor of music at Tabor College. John Henry Richert (1883-   ) is a minister in the M.B. church at Dinuba, Cal., and Irvin Richert is pastor of the G.C.M. church at Buhler, Kan.   C.K.

Reimer, Familiennamen, 116; C. H. Wedel, "Heinrich Richert," Bundesbote-Kalender (Berne, Ind., 1897) p. 28: Alexanderwohl Church Record.

Richert, Heinrich (1831-95), an outstanding Mennonite (GCM) teacher, minister, and leader, born May 23, 1831, the oldest son of David Richert, at

Deutsch-Kunopath, West Prussia, where he became a member of the Przechovka Mennonite Church. Before he was a year old his parents moved to Russia and settled in the village Alexanderwohl of the Molotschna settlement. He attended the school at Lichtfelde and passed the teacher's examination in 1851, after which he taught in Nikolaidorf. In 1849 he was baptized by Elder Peter Wedel and in 1856 he married Anna Schmidt. In 1859 he was elected minister. Soon his influence in the congregation became noticeable. He favored active participation in mission work and some changes in traditions. The first Mennonite missionary, Heinrich Dirks (*q.v.*), came from this church. In 1860 Richert accepted the call to teach in the neighboring school of Gnadenheim where he had from seventy to eighty pupils. In 1869 his wife died, leaving him with eight children. His second wife was Helena Unruh.

In August 1874 Richert joined a group of Alexanderwohl Mennonites who emigrated to Kansas and established the Alexanderwohl or Goessel Mennonite community. Here he continued his work as minister and was particularly active in promoting the educational and missionary efforts of the General Conference Mennonite Church. After attending the General Conference sessions in South Dakota in 1890 he suffered a cerebral hemorrhage which paralyzed him. On Oct. 16, 1895, he died.　　C.K.

C. H. Wedel, "Heinrich Richert," *Bundesbote-Kalender* (Berne, 1897) 28; H. P. Krehbiel, *The History of the General Conference of the Mennonites of North America* I (Newton, 1898) p. 442; Friesen, *Brüderschaft,* 495 and 1195; Cornelius Krahn (ed.), *From the Steppes to the Prairies* (Newton, 1949) p. 22 ff.

Richert, Peter H. (1871-1949), a teacher and leader in the General Conference Mennonite Church, was born Aug. 11, 1871, at Gnadenheim, province of Taurida, South Russia, the son of Heinrich and Helena Unruh Richert. In 1874 he came to America with his parents, with whom he experienced the hardships of pioneer life. He grew up near Goessel, Kan., attended Halstead Seminary, and completed the Bible course at Bethel College in 1897. On Aug. 16, 1900, he married Eva Schmidt and to them were born five children.

Richert taught five years in the district schools and fifteen years at the Bethel College Academy. In 1896 he was elected evangelist in his home church of Alexanderwohl and several years later elected minister of this church. In 1908 he was elected as pastor of the newly organized Tabor Mennonite Church, and on Oct. 2, 1910, ordained as its elder; he served here until 1946, when he suffered a stroke which partially paralyzed him.

Peter Richert's dream of serving as a foreign missionary never materialized, but was partly fulfilled in the tremendous amount of work which he did as secretary of the Foreign Mission Board in 1910-46. Reports sent in by the foreign missionaries were published in the *Mission Quarterly,* which he edited 1924-31. In 1913 he served as vice-president for the All-Mennonite Convention. 1914-18 found him president of the Kansas Ministers' Conference, and 1920-29 president of the Bethel College board of directors. For seven years he was president of the Western District Conference.

Richert's preaching was mainly expository; very frequently he preached about the cause he loved most, viz., missions. He was also deeply interested in the promotion of peace. In 1940 he wrote a catechism entitled *Some Difficult Passages Concerning the Use of the Sword.* He died on Oct. 24, 1949.　　R.E.F.

Richfield Mennonite Church (GCM), located in Richfield, Juniata Co., Pa., a member of the Eastern District Conference, began in 1883, when about 125 members, the larger part of the Cross Roads (*q.v.*) congregation, with three ministers, Solomon and Thomas Graybill and William Bergey, and deacon Abel Shirk, withdrew from the Lancaster County (MC) Conference to form an independent congregation. A meetinghouse was built in 1886 and enlarged in 1914 and 1950. A Sunday school was organized in 1914. In 1928 the congregation joined the Eastern District Conference. The membership in 1958 was 270, with Walter J. Dick as pastor. Biweekly worship services were held until 1948, when weekly Sunday morning and evening services were begun.　　W.J.D.

Richmond, the capital (pop. 230,000) of Virginia, is located in the eastern part of the state. The National Heights Mennonite Church (MC), organized in 1951, had a membership of 27 in 1957, with Truman H. Brunk as bishop in charge. The university and seminary in the city attract an increasing number of Mennonite students.　　E.W.C.

Rich(s)t (Rixt, Ryxt), an Anabaptist martyr, also called Richt Heynes because she was the wife of Heyne Renicxzoon Schuytemaker (maker of boats), living at IJlst, Dutch province of Friesland, was arrested there on Oct. 12, 1556, and taken to Leeuwarden, the capital of Friesland. Her husband, also a Mennonite, escaped. After she had given birth to a son in prison, Richt was tried and severely tortured and, "desiring not to part from Christ," was finally sentenced to death. On March 14, 1557, she was executed by being put in a sack and drowned. During the trial she admitted that she had been rebaptized, and had regularly taken part in the meetings of the "sectarists," i.e., the Mennonites, at IJlst. Both van Braght's *Martyrs' Mirror,* and the *Bibliographie des Martyrologes Protestants Néerlandais* state that Richt was put to death about 1547, but this has been proved an error.　　vDZ.

Mart. Mir. D 80, E 481; *Bibliographie* II, 703, No. 307; J. Reitsma, *Honderd jaar uit de Geschiedenis der Hervorming . . . in Friesland* (Leeuwarden, 1876) 63; *DB* 1899, 109; *ML* II, 312.

Richter (Henkel), **Adrian,** an Anabaptist martyr from Emseloh, a village near Sangerhausen (*q.v.*) in Thuringia, Germany, the servant of a slater, Georg Knoblauch (*q.v.*), stayed with his family in the Lutter forest near Lauterberg (Osterode district), was drowned in the Bode in the city of Gröningen on the Bode on Sept. 20, 1535, with Hans Höhne (*q.v.*) and Petronella (*q.v.*), after a steadfast confession of his faith.　　NEFF.

Eduard Jacobs, "Die Wiedertäufer am Harz," in *Zeitschrift des Harz-Vereins für Geschichte und Altertumskunde,* 1899, 525-28; Wappler, *Thüringen,* 107, 134, *passim; ML* III, 500.

Ricken (Richen): see **Rich.**

Ridderus, Franciscus (François) (*c*1618-83), was a Dutch Reformed minister, who served at Schermerhorn, Brielle, and Rotterdam. He is known for his religious poems and devotional books; his *Bloedspiegel der Religie,* which deals with Christian martyrs (no Mennonites), went through several editions. Besides these he published *Doop, Avondmaal en Discipline van de tijden Christi af vervolgens tot den jaare 1672* (Amsterdam, 1672). Though he defended infant baptism and rejected Mennonite doctrines, Ridderus is one of the few Reformed authors who did not repeat the calumny that the Mennonites are descended from the Münsterites (*q.v.*). In *Doop* (p. 698) he gave Menno Simons and the Mennonites this favorable testimonial: "When Menno Simons came to rebaptism, the Münsterite revolt broke out, but Menno showed clearly that he detested this wicked rebellion and he vigorously attacked it. The Doopsgezinden (Mennonites) in Holland too have always been quiet, honest, and peaceful people. During and after the Münster rebellion there were violent revolts by those who called themselves Wederdopers (Anabaptists), but these men came from abroad, and one should take care not to blacken all the Mennonites."   NEFF, vDZ.

B. Glasius, *Biographisch Woordenboek van Nederlandsche Godgeleerden* III ('s Hertogenbosch, 1856) 172-74; Schijn-Maatschoen, *Geschiedenis* I, Preface, p. LXXXIX f.; K. Vos, *Menno Simons* (Leiden, 1914) 316; *Bibliographie* II, 586 ff.; *ML* III, 500.

Rideman, Peter: see **Riedemann, Peter.**

Ridge Valley (GCM) Meeting, Bucks County, Pa. A deed of Dec. 12, 1792, conveyed a parcel of land in West Rockhill Twp., Bucks Co., Pa., to "the Lutheran and Reformed Calvinist societies." A log school on the tract was used as a house of worship at least until 1833 when it was renovated. It is not known when the Mennonites began to share in the use of this union house of worship, possibly before 1833, but in 1854 the Lutherans, the Reformed, and the Mennonites united to build a meetinghouse for their common use. The building committee consisted of one representative from each group, the Mennonite being Jacob Roth. It appears that the Mennonites who united in this project were of the Oberholtzer group (GCM). The Mennonite services seem to have soon died out, but were resumed about 1881, only to be discontinued permanently in 1886.   J.C.W.

J. C. Wenger, *History of the Mennonites of the Franconia Conference* (Telford, 1937) 244, 245.

Ridgeway Mennonite Church (MC), Harrisonburg, Va., established in 1949, is a mission station under the Virginia Mennonite Home Mission Board. In 1957 Daniel M. Smucker, Jr., was pastor of its 12 members.   M.G.

Rieckher: see **Rieger.**

Ried, a town (pop. 12,000) in Upper Austria, until 1779 and again in 1810-16 belonging to Bavaria (*q.v.*). Anabaptism came to Ried in the early days of the movement. Wolfgang Brandhuber (*q.v.*), of Passau, had won a group here for the Anabaptist

cause in 1528. In the 1530's the Philippites (*q.v.*) settled here after their withdrawal from Moravia; Riedemann (*q.v.*) visited them in Ried. But in the early 1540's they disappeared from the town. Hutterite missioners were martyrs here: Hans Blüetl (*q.v.*) 1545, Hans Aichner (*q.v.*) 1585, Georg Bruckmaier (*q.v.*) 1585, Wolf Rauffer (*q.v.*) 1585, Marcus Eder (*q.v.*) 1605, Hänsel Poltzinger (*q.v.*) 1605.   E.C.

Konrad Meindl, *Geschichte der Stadt Ried in Oberösterreich* (Munich, 1899); Beck, *Geschichts-Bücher;* Zieglschmid, *Chronik; ML* III, 500.

Riedel (Ruedl), **Georg,** a Hutterite elder, chosen preacher on Jan. 19, 1579, at Pribitz (*q.v.*) and chosen elder on March 14, 1599, at Niemtschitz (*q.v.*) and Pochtitz (*q.v.*). In 1610, he was deposed from his office on account of the "disgraceful and seducing art of alchemy" and laxity in performing his duty. He was then admitted as householder at Pellertitz (*q.v.*), but because of his offensive attitude he was expelled on July 16, 1612. He died at Pribitz on April 1, 1616.   NEFF, E.C.

Wolkan, *Geschicht-Buch,* 446, 459, 519-23; Zieglschmid, *Chronik,* 580, 596, 679 ff.; *ML* III, 500.

Riedemaier: see **Riedmair.**

Riedemann (Rideman, Rydeman, Ryedeman), **Peter** (1506-56), Hutterite bishop, missionary, and outstanding doctrinal writer, by some called the second founder of the Hutterite brotherhood. Because of his height he was also called "the tall Peter," and because of his first imprisonment in Gmunden (*q.v.*), Upper Austria, was also known as "Peter of Gmunden."

Riedemann was born in 1506 in Hirschberg, Silesia, Germany, where he learned the shoemaker's trade. In 1529 he is encountered for the first time, imprisoned in Gmunden for his Anabaptist faith. Apparently he had joined the Anabaptist Brethren in Upper Austria (*q.v.*) sometime before, where Hans Hut (*q.v.*) and later Wolfgang Brandhuber (*q.v.*) had been active as missioners, mainly around the cities of Linz, Steyr, and Gmunden 1527-29. Riedemann had been ordained as "Diener des Wortes" in 1529. During his three years' imprisonment (1529-32) Riedemann wrote his first great doctrinal work, *Rechenschaft unseres Glaubens geschrieben zu Gmunden im Land ob der Enns im Gefencknus,* a work of deeply spiritual qualities, which placed Riedemann doctrinally very near to his contemporary brethren Hans Schlaffer (*q.v.*) and Leonhard Schiemer. (A complete publication of this work is planned for the second volume of *Glaubenszeugnisse,* to be published in the *Täuferakten* Series in 1960.) Even though Riedemann at the time of writing this work had not yet joined the Hutterites, they have faithfully preserved this "Account of Our Faith" in numerous manuscript books. Besides its main part, this work contains also two separate pieces of great beauty not strictly belonging to the confession proper: (1) *Wie man das Haus Gottes bauen soll und was Haus Gottes sei,* and (2) *Von den sieben Pfeilern an diesem Hause* (Proverbs 9:1).

In 1532 Riedemann escaped from prison. He worked first with the Brethren in Linz (*q.v.*), but soon thereafter joined the Hutterite brotherhood in Moravia (*q.v.*) then still in its formative years. In 1533 he was sent out for the first time as a missioner (*Sendbote*) into Franconia, to spread the Anabaptist message. On his way he revisited the remnants of the older Anabaptist groups in Upper Austria, inviting them to join the Moravian group. In 1533-37 he was again jailed for the sake of his faith in Nürnberg (*q.v.*), but little is recorded of him in this period. In July 1537 he was released from prison upon his promise not to preach in Nürnberg, and he now returned home to Moravia, again via Upper Austria. Here he met the remnants of the Philippite Brethren (*q.v.*) and took them into his care as if he were their bishop. Four epistles from his hand (1537-39) written to these Philippite Brethren in Linz, Steyr, and Gmunden, and two more (1537-38 and 1540) to other Philippites in Germany (Württemberg, Palatinate, etc.) are still extant. These epistles give a strong impression of pastoral care for this almost leaderless group, some of whom later joined the Hutterites in Moravia.

About 1532, prior to the above journey, Riedemann married an Anabaptist sister Katharina, called familiarly "Treindl." Among his many letters there are six very lovely ones sent to his "marital sister." In 1539 the Brethren sent him again on a mission trip to Hesse (*q.v.*) mainly to straighten out an unpleasant affair with Hans Both (*q.v.*), a friend of Melchior Rinck (*q.v.*) and a former Philippite. At Holzhausen Riedemann composed an important epistle. Returning in the same year 1539, he arrived at the brotherhood a few days after the unfortunate government raid at Steinabrunn (*q.v.*), Lower Austria. Several letters of comfort written to the imprisoned in Falkenstein (*q.v.*) are extant, which again show Riedemann as a true pastor, loving and full of concern. Two months later he was again on his way to Hesse through Austria, Tirol (*q.v.*), Württemberg (*q.v.*), and Swabia (Lauingen, *q.v.*), visiting all the groups he could reach. In Hesse he seems to have been very successful, since large numbers (up to 90-100) were now making their way to Moravia. Some of these newly won members were imprisoned in Württemberg en route; Riedemann comforted them too in the genuine fashion of a shepherd.

Not long thereafter, most likely toward the end of February 1540, Riedemann himself fell into the hands of the authorities of Hesse and was chained in a dark and severe prison in Marburg (*q.v.*). It should be noted that Philip (*q.v.*) of Hesse did not permit Anabaptists to be put to death. The numerous letters written by Riedemann during this imprisonment (1540 to early 1542) show that his condition was soon eased. He was permitted to help the jailer by making shoes, and then he and another brother were removed to the near-by castle of Wolkersdorf, where the administrator (*Vogt*) was sympathetic to Anabaptist ideas and somewhat ashamed of all the imprisonment. Riedemann now had full freedom of movement, but he felt obligated to remain at the castle. His activities were manifold. He received visitors from Hesse and from Moravia (his old friend Hans Gentner (*q.v.*), a former Philippite from Austria, but now a Hutterite, was sent to consult him concerning a difficult case at home), and he continued to dispatch newly won brethren and sisters to Moravia. In 1541 his correspondence became more sparse; it may be assumed that at that time he was working on his great doctrinal work, the *Rechenschaft* (*q.v.*). One of the letters (No. 21) indicates that his main motive for writing this confession was to inform Philip of Hesse about the true beliefs and viewpoints of the Anabaptists. (This fact was not known heretofore.) Since he had full leisure, the book became rather lengthy and carefully worked out. More trouble in the Moravian brotherhood and the death of the Vorsteher Hans Amon (*q.v.*) in February 1542 prompted the Brethren to ask him to come home if he could manage it without hurting his conscience.

Late in February 1542 Riedemann was back in Moravia, where after Hans Amon's death Leonhard Lanzenstiel (*q.v.*) was chosen Vorsteher of the brotherhood. Riedemann was now made co-bishop, and this co-operation worked out very well. Lanzenstiel was more of a practical man, while Riedemann was the great spiritual teacher and leader. From now until his death in 1556 Riedemann remained with the brotherhood, leading it forcefully through years of severe persecution and trial. In 1545 the brotherhood presented to the lords of Moravia a petition (found in Beck, 169-73, incomplete) which can safely be assigned to Riedemann's hand. A copy of the *Rechenschaft* of 1540 was enclosed with this appeal.

The years 1547-51 brought the severest persecution which the brotherhood had to endure before their total expulsion from Moravia in 1622. The Brethren were homeless as hounded game, moving hither and thither, and digging underground tunnels (in Czech called *lochy, q.v.*) as temporary abodes. Many fell away, but the strong core remained loyal. In fact the group was augmented by newcomers from Silesia (former Gabrielites, *q.v.*). One of Riedemann's letters of this period was addressed to these Silesian brethren and spoke frankly about their suffering. One can almost feel the strong spiritual forces that bound the brotherhood together in those days, Riedemann, Lanzenstiel, and Walpot (*q.v.*) being responsible leaders. The *Rechenschaft* may well have added to the strength of their conviction, as the church now had available a statement which was well argued and documented by not less than 1,800 Bible references. One last letter by Riedemann (of 1549-50) was addressed to those brethren who were now scouting for new and safer homes east of the Carpathian Mountains in (then Hungarian) Slovakia.

In December 1556 Riedemann died on the Bruderhof of Protzko (*q.v.*), Slovakia, at the age of fifty, having been a minister of the Divine Word for 27 years, and having suffered in prison for 9 years. The Hutterite Chronicle contains a lengthy obituary, in which all his achievements are listed with the comment, "For he was rich in all divine secrets and the gift of the spiritual language issued forth from him like a spring which gushes over. All souls who heard him gained peace. . . . On his deathbed he comforted his brethren with the words of Ezra 8:3 and 9" (presumably IV Ezra). Shortly before his passing he composed the hymn "Quitt, ledig, los hat uns gemacht Christus vom Tod, des Teufels Macht" (*Lieder der Hutterischen Brüder,* 516).

Riedemann's written work is quite considerable and has not yet been fully studied. It may be classified in three divisions: doctrinal writings, epistles, and hymns. (*a*) *The doctrinal writings* comprise two large works, (1) the *Gmundener Rechenschaft* (1529-32), one of the very strong expressions of early Anabaptism, biblicistic and yet thoroughly spiritual (well called "Biblical spiritualism," as over against the general spiritualism of the Sebastian Franck type); and (2) the great *Rechenschaft unseres Glaubens,* written in 1540-41, one of the few books ever to have been printed by the Hutterian Brethren, published in 1565. (See **Rechenschaft unserer Religion.**) To this day it has remained the basic doctrinal statement of the Hutterites.

(*b*) *The Epistles.* Next to nothing was known about Riedemann's epistles until recently. Wolkan refers to them as "a major source of our knowledge of the Hutterite doctrinal position," but only four epistles were incorporated in the *Chronicle* and were thus known to him. As far as could be ascertained, only one manuscript codex (at a Bruderhof in Montana) and several recent copies of it contain a nearly complete collection of these most valuable documents, 34 in number (six of which are addressed to "Treindl"). To them must be added the epistle to the lords of Moravia (*Landesherren*) of 1545, mentioned above. The present biographical sketch has been partly drawn from the contents of these epistles. They express a deep and concrete Christian faith, a genuine brotherly love, and a pastoral concern for the fellow brethren and sisters, whom he calls his "dear little children." No prison or persecution could stop him in these acts. The epistles will be published in full in a *Täuferakten* (*q.v.*) publication in the near future.

(*c*) *Hymns.* The *Lieder der Hutterischen Brüder* (Scottdale, 1914) contain (pp. 450-537) forty-five hymns by Riedemann. One additional hymn, "O Herr, wie reichlich tröstest du," composed in 1529, was discovered by Riedemann which the editor of the *Lieder,* after the publication was out, and another, the "Glaubensbekenntnis" (*Ausbund,* No. 2): "Wir glauben all an einen Gott," is likewise ascribed to Riedemann, even though the Brethren think it was composed by Siegmund Wiedemann (*Rechenschaft,* new edition, Berne, 1902, last page). Hymn 37 in the *Ausbund,* "Komm Gott Vater vom Himmel," is likewise by Riedemann (*Lieder,* 483), composed while imprisoned in Gmunden in 1529, which praises the martyr death of Hans Langenmantel. It is possible that still more hymns were written by this outstanding man. Rudolf Wolkan, who carefully studied these hymns (*Lieder,* 185-206), considers Riedemann the greatest Hutterite hymn writer. The hymns are found in numerous Hutterite codices in both Europe and America.

One may safely say that the fact that the brotherhood weathered the critical years of 1545-51 and kept its spiritual testimony so high that they could continue unspotted until far into later centuries was due not least to the work of this man, a true bishop of his flock. His writings are preserved in numerous codices and are still being copied today by the Hutterian Brethren in America.   R.F.

Beck, *Geschichtsbücher,* 88, 169-73, 195; Zieglschmid, *Chronik,* 194, 356 f.; Loserth, *Communismus;* Schimmelpfennig, "Huterische Wiedertäufer in Mähren und Peter Riedemann, ihr Vorsteher," in *Jahresbericht der Schlesischen Gesellschaft für vaterländische Kultur* (1885) 295-315; Anonymous, "Peter Riedemann aus Hirschberg, ein schlesischer Wiedertäufer," in *Literaturblatt zu den schlesischen Provinzialblättern,* September 1793 (according to S. Calvary, 1870); Wolkan, *Lieder,* 185-205, 483; Wilhelm Wiswedel, "Peter Riedemann, ein Gefangener Jesu Christi," in *Bilder* I, 169-94, including extensive excerpts from the *Rechenschaft* (180-93); F. Mencik, "Ueber ein Wiedertäufergesangbuch," in *Sitz.-Ber. der kgl. Böhmischen Ges. der Wissenschaften* (1896) No. XI, mentions a hymn by Riedemann which is not found in the *Lieder der Hutterischen Brüder* (according to Wiswedel, 193); for the several editions of the *Rechenschaft,* see that article; the recent editions published by the Society of Brothers in England (1938, 1950) contain a brief appreciation of Riedemann; *ML* III, 500-5.

Riedmair (Riedemaier, Riedmaier), **Bärthl** (Bartholomäus), also called Schlesinger. He was at first a preacher (*Diener*) of the Gabrielites (*q.v.*), but was removed from his office by Ascherham (*q.v.*). On Jan. 16, 1545, he with some followers united with the Hutterian Brethren at Schäkowitz (*q.v.*), became a preacher here, and died at Tracht (*q.v.*) in Moravia on April 10, 1571. (Zieglschmid, *Chronik,* 250-57, 459; *ML* III, 505.)   E.C.

Riedselz, a village south of Wissembourg in Lower Alsace. By 1735 Dettweiler (*q.v.*) families were leasing the Riedselz castle. In 1818 Johann Dettweiler moved to the Hammerhof near Eichstock (*q.v.*), Bavaria.   E.C.

Richard Ringenberg, *Familienbuch der Mennonitengemeinde Eichstock* (Munich, 1942); *ML* III, 505.

Riegel (erroneously Ringel in the Hutterite chronicles), **Bärtl** (Bartholomäus), of Gündelbach, Maulbronn district, Württemberg, Germany, chosen preacher at Sobotiste (*q.v.*) in 1553. In 1557 he and Burkhart Bämerle (*q.v.*) were arrested and tortured. He was active in his office until his death in December 1572 at Neumühl (*q.v.*) in Moravia. He also wrote two hymns: "O Mensch, kehr dich von Sünden" (27 stanzas) and "O reicher Gott, lass uns von Herzen singen" (44 stanzas).   G.Bos.

Beck, *Geschichts-Bücher,* 198, 260; Wolkan, *Geschicht-Buch,* 259, 323, 361; Zieglschmid, *Chronik,* 343, 422, 470; *Die Lieder der Hutterischen Brüder* (Scottdale, 1914) 305, 308, 312; *ML* III, 505.

Rieger (Rieckher, Rücker), **Johannes,** a Hutterite (see **Hutterian Brethren**) preacher 1648 or 1649-62, then Vorsteher until 1687. He took part in the negotiations with Elector Charles Louis (*q.v.*) of the Palatinate in 1654 regarding the establishment of a Bruderhof in Mannheim (*q.v.*), with the archbishop of Gran (*q.v.*) in 1674-76, and with the Hungarian Stadholder Georg Szelepcsenye; his co-worker and successor was Johannes Milder (*q.v.*). On April 20, 1665, in the name of the brotherhood in Lower Hungary, he wrote a letter to the Dutch Mennonite congregations requesting financial aid. His letter of thanks for the gift received, sent from Sobotiste, is now in the archives of the Amsterdam

Mennonite Church. Another Johannes Rieger was a deacon in 1616-20. E.C.

Inv. Arch. Amst. II, 419, No. 2851; Beck, *Geschichts-Bücher,* 381, 476, 503, 527-29, 531, 552; Zieglschmid, *Chronik,* 678, 760, 846, 859, 871, 897; idem, *Klein-Geschichtsbuch,* 180, 183, 196, 221; *ML* III, 505 f.

Riehl, Wilhelm Heinrich (1823-97), a German historian and important writer of historical fiction, was born at Biebrich, a suburb of Wiesbaden, Germany. He was educated at the universities of Marburg, Tübingen, Giessen, and Bonn. From 1845 to 1853 he served on the editorial staff of several newspapers. In 1854 he was appointed as professor at the University of Munich. He wrote innumerable articles (745 by 1853) and over fifty Novellen, which were published in seven volumes. His most important work was *Die Naturgeschichte des Volkes als Grundlage einer deutschen Social-Politik,* which appeared in four volumes—*Land und Leute* (1853), *Die bürgerliche Gesellschaft* (1851), *Die Familie* (1855), and *Wanderbuch* (1869). In 1857 his *Die Pfälzer, ein rheinisches Volksbild* appeared. He was an outstanding folklorist.

Riehl had many Mennonites contacts. In the Rheingau, where he grew up, there were Mennonites and Amish. Riehl's father was the manager of the castle of the Nassau regents, and thus had contact with the outstanding Mennonite farmer and elder Valentin Dahlem (*q.v.*), who had leased the Koppenstein land at Wiesbaden. It is possible that this was the Mennonite farm depicted in Riehl's first work. His maternal grandfather, who lived in Marnheim, near the Weierhof (*q.v.*), is said (Schmidt) to have been related to Mennonites there (as yet unproved). On his lecture tours Riehl frequently stopped at Crefeld in the 1870's and 1880's and also visited Johannes Molenaar (*q.v.*), the Mennonite minister at Monsheim.

It is possible that Riehl's attention was called to Anabaptist history by Carl Adolf Cornelius (*q.v.*), who was about the same age as he and lived in the same general area. Both were professors at Munich in related fields at much the same time. In the 1872 issue of *Raumers Historisches Taschenbuch,* which Riehl edited 1871-80, Cornelius published an article, "Die Eroberung der Stadt Münster im Jahre 1535."

In 1846 Riehl published a novel, *Richard Zürbach,* in the literary supplement of a Frankfurt newspaper; this novel he reworked in 1848, and called it *Die Geschichte vom Eisele und Beisele.* The mother of the hero was the daughter of a Mennonite, or rather Amish, family which disowned her for marrying a Protestant minister. Riehl describes the mother and her father as healthy, frugal, and sensible, but intellectually dormant, with rather expressionless faces.

In 1852 Riehl published in the *Allgemeine Zeitung* an essay concerning the permission granted by Russia for West Prussian Mennonites to settle in the province of Samara, giving them the doubtful tribute of having contributed more to agriculture than to church history. In his 1857 book *Die Pfälzer* Riehl describes the Mennonites in the Palatinate, distinguishing between the Mennonites and the Amish, and praising the learning of some of the

Mennonite ministers. In 1869 Riehl's *Wanderbuch* speaks of the contribution made to Crefeld's (*q.v.*) prosperity by the Mennonites and other Separatists, and describes the monument erected in Crefeld to Cornelius de Greiff (1781-1863), one of Crefeld's great philanthropists.

In 1875 Riehl published in the volume *Am Feierabend* the Novelle *Mein Recht* (*q.v.*), which deals sympathetically with the Mennonite position of nonvengeance. The hero, Henneke Gülzow, has set his heart on obtaining justice for his brother who met his death in a scuffle. When at the end it is apparent that he has been in error in seeking vengeance, even though his motive was the preservation of order in the world, he loses his mind and dies. The psychological conflict is excellently portrayed. The book deserves wider reading than it enjoys at present.

Through all these works Riehl's attempt to be fair to the Mennonites is obvious. An occasional error in historical fact or in interpretation may be pardoned. (See **Literature.**) E.C., E.H.B.

Elizabeth H. Bender, "The Anabaptist Novelettes of Adolf Stern and Wilhelm Heinrich Riehl," *MQR* XVIII (1944) 179-85; Viktor von Geramb, *Wilhelm Heinrich Riehl, Leben und Wirken (1823-1897)* (Salzburg, 1954-56); Albert Krehbiel, "Wilhelm Heinrich Riehl, Zu seinem 100sten Geburtstag," *Gem.-Kal.,* 1923, 65-68; B. J. C. Schmidt, "W. H. Riehl, seine geistige Entwicklung bis zur Uebernahme seiner Professur in München" (doctoral dissertation, Strasbourg, 1913); a long, thorough article by Ernst Crous in *ML* III, 506-9.

Rieme Douwedochter, of Jelsum, Dutch province of Friesland, was arrested on April 7, 1535, during the recapture of the Oldeklooster (*q.v.*) near Bolsward, which had been taken by revolutionary Anabaptists. She was brought to Leeuwarden, capital of Friesland, and drowned there with a number of other victims on April 14, 1535. (K. Vos, *Menno Simons,* Leiden, 1914, 229.) vdZ.

Riemer (Rinner), Hans, a tailor of Altenbergen, Gotha district of Thuringia (*q.v.*), Germany, was arrested as an Anabaptist in Reinhardsbrunn (*q.v.*) in 1530, but recanted and was released. Nevertheless in 1532 he allowed himself to be baptized by Jakob Schmiedeknecht in a barn. In 1533 he was arrested and on July 7 cross-examined by Friedrich Myconius (*q.v.*) at Gotha (*q.v.*). Concerning baptism and communion his answers followed the Anabaptist concepts. But in his attack on the Lutherans he accused Luther of having dethroned the pope and seated himself on the throne. When he was thereupon, upon command of Electoral Prince John Frederick (*q.v.*) of Saxony, sentenced to death as an Anabaptist and Sacramentist (*q.v.*) in accord with the mandate of Speyer of 1529, he recanted again. (Wappler, *Thüringen,* 89, 223, Nos. 44 a-d; *ML* III, 509.) E.C.

Riemmich, Hans: see Rümmich, Hans.

Rienks, a Mennonite family in the Dutch province of Friesland, where there are still many Mennonite members of this family. Originally (mentioned as early as 1618) they lived in or near Hallum (*q.v.*) and soon after also at Holwerd, Oudebildtzijl, St. Anna-Parochie, and other villages in Friesland. At first they were all farmers, and many have served the church as deacons.

An outstanding member of this family was Sieds Johannes Rienks (1770-1847), who lived near Ferwerd in Friesland until c1820 and later at Berlikum. He was a farmer and also a maker of telescopes, and built a famous telescope for the astronomical observatory at Leiden about 1830. In 1825 he constructed lightning rods, then a novelty. In 1828 he moved with his family to Leiden, and there manufactured instruments.

An Yde Rienks, of Hyum near Hallum, was a (lay) preacher in the United Flemish-Waterlander congregation at Sneek (q.v.) in 1726-45. In 1746, after confessing his agreement with the Old Flemish confession, he was ordained as preacher of the small Groningen Old Flemish congregation at Sneek, serving until Sept. 11, 1763. He died at Sneek on Oct. 7, 1763. Yde Rienks probably did not belong to the same family as Sieds Johannes Rienks.   vDZ.

G. Terpstra, *Famyljeboek fan de Rienksen* (Leeuwarden, 1955); G. A. Wumkes, *Stads- en Dorpskroniek van Friesland* II (Leeuwarden, 1934) 79, 94, 138, 602; *DJ* 1932, 74 ff.; *DB* 1890, 103-6.

Ries, Hans de (also de Rys, de Reis, de Rycke, le Riche, which may have been his official name), b. Dec. 13, 1553, at Antwerp, Belgium, d. Sept. 14, 1638, at Alkmaar, Holland, was an important leader of the Dutch Mennonites. Originally, when he found himself at variance with Roman Catholic doctrine, he united with the Reformed church of his native city; but he did not feel at ease among them either, because they carried arms when they went to their religious meetings, and possibly also because of their strictly dogmatic spirit. He was drawn to the Anabaptists, but hesitated to join the congregation at Antwerp, which was rather conservative. Then he became acquainted with the somewhat more liberal spirit of the Waterlander (q.v.) branch in Holland and journeyed to De Rijp (q.v.) in North Holland, where he was baptized upon confession of his faith by Simon Michiels (q.v.) in 1575 or 1576. Soon he returned to Antwerp, and on Jan. 4, 1577, he stood beside the stake at which his friend Hans Bret (q.v.) suffered martyrdom for his faith. He married the mother of his friend, and probably soon afterward left the insecurity of Antwerp. His employer—de Ries was a bookkeeper and is therefore also known as Hans Cassier—rode after them on horseback, and the noble-minded Catholic gave them a purse of money: "Take this and use it in your need." In September 1577 de Ries was in Alkmaar, where he with other Waterlander preachers drew up a confession of faith of 25 articles, the first known Dutch Mennonite confession (printed in *Doopsgezinde Bijdragen* 1904, 145-56). Later he did much traveling. He is thought to have spent some time in Aachen (a.v.), Germany, and in April 1578 he was in Middelburg, the capital of the province of Zeeland, where he was imprisoned, but released after a month on condition that he leave the area of the city within 24 hours. Then he went to Emden (q.v.), where he had his headquarters until about 1600. In 1600 or a little earlier he was back in Alkmaar as leader of the Water-

lander congregation, a position he held until his death.

The influence of Hans de Ries was profound on the Mennonites of the Netherlands, especially the Waterlander branch. He was a friend of Dirk Volkertsz Coornhert (q.v.), whom Kühler calls the "Sebastian Franck of Holland," and like Coornhert he thought little of the external (visible) church. He was a Spiritualist (q.v.), i.e., he believed that the believer must be completely open to the Spirit of God. Church constitutions, regulations, offices, sacraments, ban, and the church itself are of minor importance. Apparently, under the influence of Coornhert, de Ries even laid aside his preaching office in 1578, but it was only for a short time, for soon he was actively on duty again. Later on he also grew more conservative, although throughout his life he did not rate the organization and authority of the church and its elders as highly as most of the Frisians and Flemish did at that time. In the Waterlander congregations the ban was little applied, avoidance not at all, and marriage with non-members was not considered serious.

In many areas de Ries was an outstanding leader. With great joy he watched the merger take place between the High Germans and the Frisians in 1591 on the basis of the Concept of Cologne (q.v.). Throughout his life he worked for the unification of all Mennonites; he wanted to "heal the breach." Unfortunately he saw very little visible result. But the beginning seemed promising. After the union between the High Germans and the Frisians effort was made to bring the Waterlanders into this merger, and de Ries strove untiringly for this goal. Gradually many of the Waterlander congregations joined the union, and in 1601 the Bevredigde Broederschap (q.v.), i.e., the brotherhood that had made peace, was accomplished, and more and more Waterlander congregations joined. But about 1610 it became clear that this union was after all somewhat artificial, because the views of the Frisians and the High Germans, especially regarding the ban and outside marriage, were not those of the Waterlanders; therefore a large part of the Frisians and High Germans withdrew as Afgedeelden from the Bevredigde Broederschap in 1613. This must have been a bitter experience for de Ries.

The loss was balanced by a gain; in 1615 in Amsterdam a group of English Brownists (q.v.) united with the Mennonites (see **Smyth, John**). For this union de Ries, in co-operation with Lubbert Gerritsz (q.v.), a Frisian elder who had joined the Waterlanders via the Bevredigde Broederschap and was at the time a leader of the Amsterdam Waterlander congregation, drew up a confession of faith of 38 articles, which was later, with two additional articles, printed and is known as the Confession of Hans de Ries.

Of great importance is de Ries's work in martyr literature. The old first martyr book, *Het Offer des Heeren,* had contained reports on only a few of the martyrs. When the need of a new edition became apparent, de Ries decided to issue an entirely new and more complete edition. For years he had been collecting reports and records on the martyrs and had stimulated others to do the same, e.g., Jacques Outerman (*q.v.*) among the Flemish. On the basis of this preliminary work he published in 1615 his *Historie der Martelaren ofte waerachtighe Getuygen Jesu Christi*, with an important introduction in which he urged love and peace and asked that the Mennonites bury their dissensions. Unfortunately this admonition was little heeded. The new martyr book, however, was very welcome; after it had been reprinted with slight alterations in 1617, 1626, and 1631, T. J. van Braght used it as the basis for his *Martyrs' Mirror* in 1660 and 1685.

De Ries also gave the church a hymnal, published first in 1582 with the title *Lietboeck* (*q.v.*), and in six later editions under different names, e.g., *Lie(d)tboeck, Het Boeck der Ghesangen*, and *Gesangboeck*. In 1624 the book appeared in a completely revised edition. In this edition the rhymed version of the Psalms by Dathenus (*q.v.*) was added. De Ries's high evaluation of the Old Testament Psalms was probably due to his temporary sympathy with the Reformed Church; it was in turn due to his influence that the Psalms gradually replaced the *Liedekens* in the assemblies of the Dutch Mennonites. His authority is also seen in the Waterlander custom of partaking of communion while seated around a table (*Avondmaal bij aanzitting*), whereas in other branches the emblems were taken by the ministers to the members, who remained seated (*Avondmaal bij Rondgang*).

De Ries was one of the first Mennonites to replace silent prayer with audible prayer by the minister (*stemmelijk gebed*). He apparently also introduced the practice of admitting members of the Reformed Church without (re)baptism; for this he was severely criticized by the conservative branches like the Frisians and the Flemish. About the end of the 17th century this became the practice of the Lamists (*q.v.*), and is now the general practice among the Dutch Mennonites. Thus Hans de Ries was in many regards an innovator who steered the brotherhood into new paths.

The library and the archives of the Mennonite church in Amsterdam contain a number of documents in de Ries's own handwriting, as well as many letters written by and to him. In addition to his *Lietboeck* and the confession, published in 1610, 1614, 1618, 1624, 1634, 1640, 1643, 1654, 1658, 1681, 1686, 1700, 1716, 1740, 1741, all in Dutch, a French edition (n.p., 1684), a Latin (Amsterdam, 1723), and a German (Amsterdam, 1741), the following books by de Ries are still extant (other tracts may have been lost): *Cort ende claer bewijs, dat de twaelf Jongheren, daer d'Euangelist Lucas van meldet, Act. 19, vers 1. twee mael met water ghedoopt zijn* (Amsterdam, 1597), and *Ontdeckinghe der dwalingen, misduydinghen der H. Schrift ende verscheyden mis-slagen, begrepen in seecker Boek, ghenaemt Raech-besem* (Hoorn, 1627), directed against Nittert Obbesz (*q.v.*). After de Ries's death two tracts were published with *Kort Verhael van het Leven en de Daden van Hans de Ries*; these tracts were *Een seer stichtelijck Tractaet, by maniere van een Vaderlijcke onderwijsinghe . . . ghestelt 1581*, and *'t Fonteyntien, zijnde: een corte onderrichtinge*. This volume also contains a letter of 1630

by de Ries: *Eenen brief gheschreven aen M.T.* His *Klaer Bewys van de Eeuwigheydt ende Godheydt Jesu Christi* appeared at Haarlem in 1672 and was reprinted at Leeuwarden and at Haarlem in 1688. Marten Schagen mentions the following additional writings by de Ries: *Seyndt-brief waer in begrepen is een corte Bekentenisse bevesticht met de H. Schrift, van eenige stucken betreffende de Mensheyt Christi*, followed by *Bewijs uyt der H. Schrift, dat Maria is van den Sade ofte Geslachte Davids* (Amsterdam, 1604).

De Ries was a man of great authority. At times his action seems headstrong and imperious, for which reason some of his opponents called him "Pope Hans." He was a very beloved preacher, and is said to have moved his hearers to tears, especially in his prayers. He was frequently called by other congregations to settle disputes or to arbitrate in matters of discord. In 1608 he was in Haarlem to intermediate between Leenaert Clock (*q.v.*) and Claes Wolter Kops (*q.v.*); in 1618 he presided at a conference of elders and preachers at Workum, which met to examine charges made against elder Rippert Eenkes (*q.v.*); in 1626 he was asked to settle the quarrel between Nittert Obbesz and the leaders of the Waterlander congregation at Amsterdam.

Hans de Ries carried on an extensive correspondence with many congregations and preachers. The Danzig congregation asked him for advice in countering the persistence of the Socinians and even bade him come over for a disputation with their leaders. He was engaged in controversy with many opponents both within and without the Mennonite fold. The great number of these polemics, of which only a few were printed, complete the picture of a man who served the kingdom of God faithfully and without regard for consequences. At the age of 84 he allowed himself to be persuaded to undertake a journey by boat to Zaandam to preach a sermon. Once more he served his church at Alkmaar (in early August 1638). Three weeks later he became bedfast; he died on Sept. 14, 1638. Three days later he was buried in the Reformed Church (Groote Kerk) at Alkmaar. The Haarlem preacher Denys van der Schuere delivered his funeral sermon. He married three times. His first wife, the mother of Hans Bret, apparently died soon after they fled from Antwerp; concerning his second wife nothing is known, not even her name; his third wife was Guertje Jansdochter, whom he married in Alkmaar, and who died on July 3, 1638, a few months before his death. His portrait was painted by Michiel Mierevelt.   vDZ.

Kort Verhael van het Leven en de Daden van Hans de Ries (De Rijp, 1644, reprinted 1655); J. S. S. Ballot, "Hans de Ries, zijn leven en werken," *DB* 1863, 104-24; 1864, 1-74; Schijn-Maatschoen, *Geschiedenis* II, 156, 157; III, 482-94; Marten Schagen, *Naamlijst der Doopsgezinde schrijveren* (Amsterdam, 1745) 83-85; *N.N.B.Wb.* II, 1209-11; Kühler, *Geschiedenis* I and II, *passim*; III, 18 f., 27, 34, 44 f.; J. H. Wessel, *De leerstellige strijd tusschen Nederlandsche Gereformeerden en Doopsgezinden in de zestiende eeuw* (Assen, 1946) 22 f., 114; *Inv. Arch. Amst.* I, II, and IIa, numerous letters; the most important are I, Nos. 424 f., 430, 468 f., 483, 488, 495 ff., 501 ff., 528, 533, 543, 555, 642-58; II, Nos. 1193 f., 1198, 1207 ff., 1345, 1355, 1367, 1375, 1692, 2624 f., 2926 ff., 2934; II, 2, Nos. 334, 338, 364, 655 ff., 864; *DJ* 1837,

94 ff.; 1840, 145 f., 150 note; *DB* 1877, 79, 84 f., 87 f., 92; 1891, 8; 1897, 103, 109 f., 113 f., 164 f.; 1900, 76, 84 f.; 1903, 59-74; 1904, 141 f.; 1907, 70; 1908, 33, 40; 1909, 43-48; 1910, 25; *ML* III, 509-11.

Riesen, van (von), a Mennonite family found in a number of West Prussian churches (Danzig, Ladekopp, Tiegenhagen, Heubuden, Elbing) from the early 17th century. David von Riesen (*q.v.*) was a Mennonite preacher. (See also **Peter von Riesen**.) Cornelius von Riesen (b. 1754) who in 1789 moved from Damfeld in the area of Marienburg, Prussia, to Neuendorf, Russia, was from 1794 a preacher of the Frisian Mennonite Old Colony (Chortitza) congregation.

Cornelius Jansen (*q.v.*) married Helena von Riesen, the daughter of Peter von Riesen (*q.v.*), who printed Menno's writings. David Goerz (*q.v.*) also married a Helene Riesen. Some of the Riesens who joined the Kleine Gemeinde changed their name to Friesen. Many of them settled in Jansen (*q.v.*), Neb., and Manitoba. Some of the Riesens established the Brudertal Mennonite Church (*q.v.*) near Hillsboro, Kans., and others settled in Beatrice, Neb. Ronald von Riesen, a G.C.M. minister, served as president of Freeman College 1951-58.   vdZ.

Reimer, *Familiennamen*, 116; G. E. Reimer and G. R. Gaeddert, *Exiled by the Czar* (Newton, 1956) 4 ff., 191.

Riesen, David von, a member of the Mennonite congregation of Elbing-Ellerwald (*q.v.*), West Prussia, Germany, was expelled from membership for serving in the army in the War of Liberation in 1815, and sought to be reinstated into this congregation or into the Danzig (*q.v.*) congregation by way of the courts, but after lengthy negotiations his suit was rejected by the royal court in Berlin on Jan. 24, 1818. Riesen's fate was the basis of Wildenbruch's drama *Der Mennonit* (*q.v.*).   NEFF.

Johann Donner, Autobiographical sketch, *Gem.-Kal.*, 1932, 101-3; G. L. von Reiswitz and F. Wadzeck, *Beiträge zur Kenntniss der Mennoniten-Gemeinden in Europa und America* (Berlin, 1821) 233-315; *ML* III, 511.

Riesen, Peter von, a Mennonite of Schidlitz, near Danzig, (then) Germany, who had close connections with the Kleine Gemeinde (*q.v.*) in Russia. He was the father-in-law of Cornelius Jansen (*q.v.*). His name is associated with a revision of the German translation of Menno Simons' (*q.v.*) *Foundation Book* (*q.v.*) and its printing in 1834 in an edition of several thousand copies. His associates in this undertaking were his brother Abraham von Riesen and perhaps another brother Klaas von Riesen, Abraham and Klaas being ministers in Russia. The brothers Abraham and Klaas appear later with the name Friesen (=von Riesen?). Gustav E. Reimer, however, is of the opinion that Klaas was Klaas Reimer (*q.v.*), the founder of the Kleine Gemeinde and the brother-in-law of Peter von Riesen.

J. W. Mannhardt (*q.v.*) gives the following account of the "strange" story of this publication: Right after publication the book fell into the hands of a non-Mennonite who was offended by several arguments used by Menno in defending himself against Lutheran and Reformed theologians. Fearing further offense, the church board compelled the publishers to hide the entire edition in a church in the swamps of the lowlands. Twenty years later,

when the von Riesen heirs demanded it as their property, a committee went to Königsberg to ask timidly whether the release of such books was permissible. The leader of the opposition was apparently Peter Regier (*q.v.*), the elder of the Tiegenhagen congregation 1833-56, whose father, Abraham Regier (*q.v.*), elder of Heubuden 1804-51, stopped the sale in Russia. But also David Epp, a leader in the revival movement, in his correspondence attacked the publication and offered to send several hundred tracts to convert the Kleine Gemeinde. On the other side Abraham Friesen protested that the foundation of the first nonresistant Christians was thereby rejected (see the *Martyrs' Mirror*). Wilhelm Mannhardt was right in assuming that the fear of the loss of their privileges played a role here. But a declaration of the 29 ministers on Aug. 10, 1835, bases the withdrawal of the books on love for members of other faiths. Later the elders permitted the exportation of some copies to Russia, whence they have found their way to America. Copies are in GCL and BeCL.   E.C.

Robert Friedmann, *Mennonite Piety Through the Centuries* (Goshen, 1949) 140; Friesen, *Brüderschaft*, 75 f., 11-13; *Menn. Bl.*, 1869, 38 (Wilhelm Mannhardt); 1903, 85 f.; *Gesch.-Bl.*, 1954, 14 f. (Ernst Crous); P. Töws, *Eine seltsame Begebenheit, Angehend der durch Peter von Riessen von Schidlitz, bei Danzig in Preussen in Druck gegebenen Menno Simons Schriften* (Gretna, 1911); G. E. Reimer and G. R. Gaeddert, *Exiled by the Czar* (Newton, 1956) 4 ff.; *ML* III, 511 f.

Rietmaker (Rietmacher), **Abraham,** was a preacher of the Mennonite congregation of Aachen (*q.v.*), Germany, in the early 17th century. The Amsterdam Mennonite Archives contain five letters written by Rietmaker to the Waterlander leader Hans de Ries (*q.v.*), in which he informed de Ries on the situation of the congregations in the Rheinland, the progress of the unions between the High German Mennonites, the (Young) Frisians and the Waterlanders, the troubles in this united group at Haarlem, where Leenaerdt Clock (*q.v.*) and Claes Wolters Kops (*q.v.*) were in discord, and the relation between the Mennonites and the Socinians (*q.v.*) in Danzig. The first of these letters is dated Dec. 29, 1613, the last Oct. 7, 1614.

Rietmaker was a defender of a plain Christianity; about 1620 he censured Claes Wolters Kops, who was then living at Gladbach (*q.v.*), for his wealth and his luxurious estate.

Particulars about the life of Rietmaker are not available. It is not very likely that he is identical with Abraham Dirks (Bierens, *q.v.*), an elder of the Flemish congregation at Amsterdam from 1617, who is also called Abraham Rietmaker, and who was also a *rietmaker* (maker of baskets or of cane chairs).   vDZ.

Inv. Arch. Amst. I, Nos. 543, 555; *Ztscht des Aachener Geschichtsvereins* VI (1884).

Rieu, Adriaen du, an Anabaptist martyr: see **Adriaen Olieu(x).**

Rieuwertsz (Rieuwers), **Jan** (1617-c85), was a publisher at Amsterdam, and from 1675 the official printer of this city. He published a large number of books by Mennonite authors, including Schabaelje, Galenus Abrahamsz, Reynier Wijbrandsz,

Tieleman Jansz van Braght (several editions of *Schole der Deught*), Abraham Verduin, and many Galenist (*q.v.*) pamphlets during the "Lammeren-krijgh" (*q.v.*). Rieuwertsz also printed books by D. R. Camphuyzen and the philosopher Descartes.

Rieuwertsz was a member of the Flemish (Lamist) Mennonite congregation of Amsterdam and a warm adherent of Galenus Abrahamsz (*q.v.*), whom he supported in the conflict with the conservatives. Rieuwertsz' well-known bookshop, "Het Martelaarsboek," was located on Dirk-van-Hasselt-steeg and later on Beursstraat. This shop was the meeting place of the Collegiants and other "enlightened spirits." In 1646 the Collegiant meetings in this bookshop were prohibited by the magistrates of Amsterdam.

Rieuwertsz played an influential part in the Amsterdam Mennonite life of the 17th century, as well as in Protestant liberalism in general. His friendship with the Jewish philosopher Spinoza was severely censured by the more conservative Mennonites.

Barend Rieuwersz was a deacon of the (Groningen) Old Flemish Mennonite congregation at Amsterdam about 1625. No relationship has been ascertained between this Barend Rieuwersz and Jan Rieuwertsz.   vDZ.

Inv. Arch. Amst. II, Nos. 1237-40; *N.N.B.Wb.* II, 1211; K. O. Meinsma, *Spinoza en zijn kring* (The Hague, 1896) 105, 362, 452, *et passim.*

Rijcen (Rijken, de Rijcke, Rycaen), **Christiaen,** an Anabaptist martyr; see **Christiaen de Rijcke.**

Rijkmans (formerly Ryckmans), a Dutch Mennonite family at Zuidveen (*q.v.*), province of Overijssel, where Matthys Ryckmans was a member of the Mennonite congregation as early as 1600. The Rijkmans family in the 18th century was less conservative than most members of the Zuidveen congregation; this caused some friction. In 1768 Berend Thijssen Rijkmans was banned from the congregation because he opposed the decision of the elder and the deacons to rebaptize his wife, who had come from the Borne (*q.v.*) Mennonite congregation. Rijkman Roelofs (*q.v.*) belonged to this family. The Rijkmans family has played an important part in the Zuidveen congregation, which since 1848 has been called Steenwijk (*q.v.*), and in which many of its members served as deacons. (*DB* 1878, 6 f., 16, 26, 28; Steenwijk church records.)   vDZ.

Rijnsburg, a village a few miles west of Leiden, Dutch province of South Holland, was the center of the Collegiant (*q.v.*) movement; its adherents were therefore also called "Rijnsburger Collegianten" or Rijnsburgers. They met here twice a year, at Pentecost and in August. The meeting place, called Groote Huis, was a country estate. Here they held their communion services and performed baptism by immersion. The first of these "great meetings," attended by Collegiants from everywhere, was held about 1640 and the last one in 1787; thereafter only occasional baptismal services were held at Rijnsburg, the last one in 1801. The Groote Huis and other properties were sold in 1828.

Besides members of other churches, many Mennonites joined the group at Rijnsburg. Some of the many Mennonites baptized here were Willem van Maurik of Amsterdam in 1730, Hendrik Koeke-bakker of Wormerveer in 1737, Daniel Hovens of Haarlem in 1735, Aagje Deken (*q.v.*) of Amsterdam in 1760, Maria Bavink of Amsterdam in 1762, Pieter Vijgh of Rotterdam in 1775, and Pieter Zeper of Leeuwarden in 1781. Mennonites, both ministers and laymen, often addressed the Rijnsburg meetings and conducted the communion and baptismal services. Among these there are familiar names, such as Koenraad van Diepenbroek (*q.v.*) of Haarlem, Agge Roskam Kool (*q.v.*) of Beverwijk, Pieter Klaasz de Jong (*q.v.*) of Krommenie, Joost Daams and Daniel Hovens (*q.v.*) of Haarlem.

The conservative Mennonites, e.g., the Zonists (*q.v.*) and many Waterlanders (*q.v.*), were opposed to the progressive Collegiant ideas and in many congregations the members who attended the Rijnsburg meetings were excluded from the communion service in their home churches. In 1673 a number of Waterlander congregations in North Holland decided not to admit to the pulpit any ministers who were leaders and speakers at Rijnsburg.

It was at Rijnsburg that Richard Blount (*q.v.*), one of the founders of the Baptist Church in England, was baptized by immersion.   vDZ.

J. C. van Slee, *De Rijnsburger Collegianten* (Haarlem, 1895) 187, 288-312, 412-16, 437-42, and *passim*; S. F. Rues, "Opregt Berigt van den tegenwoordigen Staet der Collegianten of Rynsburgers," in *Tegenwoordige Staet der Doopsgezinden* (Amsterdam, 1745) 275-330; P. K. de Jong, *Aanteekeningen van de Personen, die gesproke hebbe . . . op de Reynsburgse Vergadering: sedert het Jaar 1727* (manuscript in AML): *Inv. Arch. Amst.* I, Nos. 892, 896; II, Nos. 2947 f., 2952, 2954.

Rijnsburgers: see Collegiants.

Rijnse Veen ('t Rijnse Veer): see **Veenendaal.**

Rijntgen Boens, an Anabaptist martyr: see **Truyken Boens.**

Rijp, De, a village in the Dutch province of North Holland (1947 pop. 1490, with 86 Mennonites). In the 16th century, before reclamation of the lakes, it was situated on an island, and so offered good protection to the persecuted Mennonites. There were Anabaptists here at a very early date; Arent Jacobs (*q.v.*) of this town was drowned with his wife and son at Monnikendam (*q.v.*) about 1539 because they had been rebaptized. A congregation soon formed, and by the end of the 16th century the village was practically all Mennonite.

The De Rijp congregation belonged to the Waterlander (*q.v.*) branch, although in the 17th century a more conservative tendency was noticeable here than was usual among the Waterlanders; for this reason it joined the Zonist Sociëteit (*q.v.*) in 1664. In the 16th century it was the most outstanding Waterlander congregation in the Netherlands. In 1576 Hans de Ries (*q.v.*) was baptized here. De Rijp was one of the first congregations to join (1601) the union of the High German and Young Frisian Mennonites (see **Bevredigde Broederschap**). The congregation had excellent preachers, such as Jacob Jansz Scheedemaker (*q.v.*) from 1557, the principal author of the Waterlander confession of faith of 1577; Pieter Pieters de Oude (*q.v.*) 1600-25; Jan Willemsz (*q.v.*) 1610-d.60, who was also a physician, and Engel Arentsz van Dooregeest (*q.v.*) 1666-d.1706. In the 17th and early 18th centuries some of the Mennonites of De Rijp took active part in the Collegiant movement (*q.v.*), often attending the meetings at the Collegiant center at Rijnsburg, which was severely censured by the rather conservative leaders of the congregation.

The relations with the Reformed Church and the magistrates of De Rijp were better than in most Dutch towns. As early as 1574 a Mennonite preacher is reported to have preached in the Reformed Church; in the 17th century Mennonites occupied magisterial offices and were often very influential. In the 18th century this prosperous congregation suffered a rapid decline, principally for economic reasons. The herring and whale fishing industries and their subsidiary industries such as shipbuilding, in which many Mennonites were engaged, grew less and less important. A large number of the De Rijp Mennonites moved to Amsterdam. The membership, which was still 472 in 1670, decreased from that time on. There were 403 members in 1704, 167 about 1800, some 200 in 1809, 160 in 1847, 184 in 1900, and 68 in 1958.

The first meetinghouse burned down in 1654; the replacement was considerably renovated in 1853. The present church was dedicated on Dec. 13, 1953. The congregation once possessed an orphans' home, mentioned first in 1676. The institution was completely rebuilt in 1866; but since 1912 there have been no orphans. In the 17th and 18th centuries the congregation had great wealth; most of the property has been lost since then.

One of the outstanding lay members of this congregation was Jan Adriaensz Leeghwater (*q.v.*) (1575-1650), the noted mill builder and "engineer," to whom North Holland owes the initiative for the reclamation of the many lakes, and partly also the execution of this task.

A complete list of preachers and deacons from 1557 to the present has been preserved. The first minister of De Rijp who was trained at the Mennonite Seminary at Amsterdam was Anthony de Vries, 1770-71; he was followed by two lay preachers, Johannes van Grouw 1771-79 and Pieter Hartman 1780-1815. Since that time all the ministers have been educated at the Amsterdam Seminary: Pieter Hollenberg 1805-15, Jan Persijn 1816-60, Jan de Verwer 1855-71, S. Kutsch Loyenga 1872-73, W. J. van Douwen 1874-87, W. I. Leendertz 1888-90, J. S. Pekema 1891-94, P. Sijbolts 1894-1901, J. P. Smidts 1902-8, G. Fopma 1908-13, J. Scherpenhuysen 1914-23, P. Keuning 1925-52, and L. Koopmans 1954-57. The pulpit is now vacant.

Since July 1949 the pastor of the De Rijp congregation also serves the Graftdijk (*q.v.*) and Noordeind van Graft (*q.v.*) congregation. Church activities include a ladies' circle and a Sunday school for children (in co-operation with the Reformed Church). De Rijp has been the seat of the Rijper Sociëteit (*q.v.*) since the middle of the 17th century. A well-known Dutch hymnal was the *Rijper Liedt Boecxken* (*q.v.*).   vDZ.

Den Rijper Zeepostil (Amsterdam, 1699) 269-372; J. Persijn, *Een viertal geschriften betr. de Doopsgezinde*

Gemeente in de Rijp (Norden, 1857); G. Fopma, "Uit de Geschiedenis der Doopsgezinde Gemeente in de Rijp," *DB* 1917, 9-65; 1918, 1-42; *Inv. Arch. Amst.* I, Nos. 708, 892, 896; II, No. 2927; II, 2, 462-64; *DB* 1863, 110; 1872, 57; 1876, 36 f.; 1877, 79; 1900, 89, 109; 1909, 169-72; *DJ* 1955, 21-27; Blaupot t. C., *Groningen* I, 270; *idem*, *Holland* I and II, *passim*; *Nieuwe Rotterdamse Courant*, April 28, 1956; *ML* III, 512 f.

Rijp, van de, a Dutch Mennonite family, in the 17th and 18th centuries found at Amsterdam and Haarlem. In Amsterdam they were members of the Waterlander (Toren) congregation and after the merger of this congregation with the Lamist church (1668), of the United Lam and Toren congregation. At Haarlem Johannes van de Rijp was a trustee of the Mennonite orphanage on the Klein Heiligland from 1673, as was his wife Judith ten Cate from 1699. In Amsterdam Arend van de Rijp (d. 1729) was for many years a trustee of the Collegiant Oranjeappel (*q.v.*) orphanage.

Gerrit van de Rijp (d. March 1735) bequeathed his property to his nephews Jan and Job van de Rijp Centen (the sons of his sister Maria van de Rijp and Gozewijn Centen) on condition that they contribute 20,000 guilders of this property to the founding of an old ladies' home. In 1736 his heirs bought some small houses on the Rozengracht, which were remodeled for this purpose and were called the Rijpenhofje. On Dec. 14, 1747, Jan and Job van de Rijp Centen transferred the title to this home to the deacons of the Lam and Toren Mennonite congregation, who still govern the Rijpenhofje. The home was completely rebuilt in 1913. (*Inv. Arch. Amst.* II, Nos. 521-32, 3188, 3190.)   vDZ.

Rijpenhofje, an old ladies' home at Amsterdam: see **Rijp, van de.**

Rijper Achterhofken, Het, an appendix to the Dutch hymnbook *Rijper Liedt Boecxken* (*q.v.*).   vDZ.

Rijper (Ryper) Liedt Boecxken (also called *Rijper Gesangboek*), a formerly much-used Dutch Mennonite hymnal, the first editions of which were printed at De Rijp (*q.v.*), whence it took its name. It contains 450 hymns without notes, divided into three parts: (*a*) *Schriftuurlijcke liedekens,* (*b*) *Geestelijcke liedekens* (Spiritual Hymns), and (*c*) an appendix, called *Achterhofken* (Back Garden). Copies of six editions are still extant and are found in the Amsterdam Mennonite Library (except the first, which is found only in the Goshen College Library): Wormerveer 1647, Alkmaar 1664 (also in GCL), Saerdam (Zaandam) 1669, 1682, and 1693, and Amsterdam 1716. (This last edition also contained *Geestelyck Kruydt-Hofken.*) But there were without doubt other editions. The preface of this hymnal is dated Aug. 25, 1624; hence there must have been an edition of 1624 or 1625 at De Rijp. Marten Schagen and Blaupot ten Cate mention also editions at De Rijp 1647 and Krommenie 1647. The poet H. A. Hoejewilt (*q.v.*) of De Rijp was the author of many of the hymns. The *Rijper Liedt Boecxken* was particularly used in Waterlander congregations.   vDZ.

DJ 1837, 65; Gorter's *Doopsgezinde Lectuur* III (1858) 195 ff.; Marten Schagen, *Naamlijst der Doopsgezinde schrijveren* (Amsterdam, 1745) 88; Blaupot t. C., *Hol-*

land III, 212; a reproduction of the title page of the 1664 edition is found in *ME* II.

Rijper Sociëteit is the name of a conference of Waterlander (*q.v.*) Mennonite congregations in the Dutch province of North Holland (*q.v.*), established about 1640. The fixed place of meeting has always been De Rijp; hence its name. In 1841 the Frisian Sociëteit of North Holland united with the Rijper. It differs from the usual pattern in that its annual conferences are attended by the deacons rather than the ministers, for the reason that its purpose is the financial support of needy congregations. From 1693 to 1798 this conference also called a meeting at which the ministers were present, its purpose being to provide for vacant pulpits. vpZ.

Blaupot t. C., *Holland* II, 53-70; *Inv. Arch. Amst.* I, Nos. 882-84; "De Vereenigde Waterlandsche en Friesche Doopsgezinde Sociëteit in Noordholland," *DJ* 1942, 35-43; 1943, 38-48; *ML* III, 513.

Rijper Zeepostil, Den, is the title of a Dutch book published at Amsterdam in 1699; it was composed by the Mennonite ministers E. A. van Dooregeest (*q.v.*) and C. A. Posjager (*q.v.*), and was designed to be taken along by the Dutch seamen and whalers, who were numerous at De Rijp (*q.v.*) and who often had to leave their home town for months. It contains 22 sermons, 16 prayers, and a history of Holland, especially of North Holland and De Rijp. The *Zeepostil* was used during the services held on the boats on Sunday mornings and on special occasions. vpZ.

Rijsdijk (Rysdyk), **Jacobus,** b. *c*1690 in Norden, East Friesland, Germany, a Dutch Mennonite preacher, serving in Almelo 1716-23, Zwolle 1723-28, Groningen 1728-42, and again Almelo 1742-44, where he died in November 1744. He was an educated preacher of the United Waterlander and Flemish congregation, a defender of the Zonist (*q.v.*) principles, opposing rationalism and Socinianism (*q.v.*), with a leaning toward the Reformed Church, which his son is said to have joined. He distinguished between "true Mennonites" like himself, and "the so-called Doopsgezinden (*q.v.*), who hid behind the name Mennonite," and fought the latter, including his colleague Jan Commes in Zwolle and his uncle and colleague Eppo Botterman (*q.v.*), over his activity in the Collegiant (*q.v.*) movement in Groningen, where the congregation vainly tried to mediate in 1730-31, and finally also Johannes Stinstra (*q.v.*), a preacher in Harlingen.

Jacobus Rijsdijk wrote both polemical and doctrinal works. Of his polemic writings the following should be mentioned: *Verdediging van de Regtzinnigheid der Ware Mennoniten* (Groningen, 1729); *Ongeveinsd en Zedig Antwoordt over de beschuldiging hem aengedaen door Jan Commes* (Groningen, 1730), which was a reply to the attack on Rijsdijk by Commes titled *Den Veynzaart ontmaskert* (Zwolle, 1729); and *Zedige Aanmerkingen* (Groningen, 1735) against Botterman. The following doctrinal works should be mentioned: *Eerste Beginzelen van de Lere des Geloofs* (Groningen, 1733; 2d ed. 1740; 5th ed. Amsterdam, 1784); *Korte Schets van de Lere der Waarheid* (Groningen, 1733, 1747, 1756, 1764); *De Waarheid van Jesus Messiasschap* (2 vv., Gronin-

gen, 1735, reprinted 1745, 1749); *Eerste Waarheidsmelk* (Groningen, 1742); *Godtgeleerde Aanmerkingen* (2 vv., Groningen, 1742-44). Besides these he published his farewell sermon at Zwolle and first sermon at Groningen: *Afscheidts en Intre-predikaatzien, zo van de Gemeente te Zwolle als in die van Groningen* (Groningen, 1729).

As late as Dec. 23, 1789, a plan for contracts for future ministers drawn up at Emden (*q.v.*), Germany, stipulated that they should build the church and instruct the youth "in accord with the confession of faith of the Zonist Sociëteit as published and taught by Hans de Ries (*q.v.*), Pieter Arends, Herman Schijn (*q.v.*), and Jacobus Rijsdijk. The books written by Schijn and Rijsdijk were regularly used in the brotherhood; their spirit should prevail in any other books to be introduced." E.C., vpZ.

N.N.B.Wb. X, 863; Blaupot t. C., *Groningen* I, 137, 167; *DB* 1895, 121; W. J. Kühler, *Het Socinianisme in Nederland* (Leiden, 1912) 263 f.; Schijn-Maatschoen, *Geschiedenis* II, 672; Marten Schagen, *Naamlijst der Doopsgezinde schrijveren* (Amsterdam, 1745) 87 f.; Christiaan Sepp, *Johannes Stinstra en zijn tijd* I and II (Amsterdam, 1865-66), particularly I 104-7; II 97-99; H. Dassel, *Menno's Volk in Groningen* (Groningen, n.d.) 36-38; N. van der Zijpp, *Geschiedenis der Doopsgezinden in Nederland* (Arnhem, 1952) 165, 167, 179; J. C. van Slee, *De Rijnsburger Collegianten* (Haarlem, 1895) 231-35; *DB* 1868, 65; 1878, 48; 1895, 121; *Catalogus Amst.*, 135, 136, 167, 219, 248, 261; Catalog of the library of the Mennonite Church of Hamburg-Altona (Altona, 1890) 40, 43, 45, 52; *ML* III, 513.

Rijssel: see **Lille.**

Rijswijk, Govert Jan van, b. 1764 at The Hague, d. 1838 at Amsterdam, was an outstanding Dutch Mennonite preacher. He did not have a specifically theological training. He was at first the manager of a type foundry (1784-1800), and during this time he frequently addressed the meetings of the Rijnsburg Collegiants (*q.v.*). In 1797 he took part in an essay contest on "Indifference and Carelessness in Attendance at Religious Meetings," and won an honorable distinction. He therefore decided to devote his life to the ministry. In 1800 he became the preacher of the Hengelo congregation and served until 1806, followed by service at Monnikendam 1806-8, Joure 1808-17, and Den Hoorn on Texel 1817-24. In 1824 he had to resign because of approaching blindness; he soon lost his vision completely. He spent his last years in Leiden.

Van Rijswijk published a number of theological and devotional books: *Proeve van Onderzoek over de oogmerken van het Lijden en Sterven van Jezus Christus* (Amsterdam, 1792); *Schets der christelijke Leere . . .* (Amsterdam, 1809, 2d ed. 1816, 3d ed. 1842); *Lijkrede op Jezus* (Amsterdam, 1813); *Het Hoofdzakelijke der Christelijke Leere . . .* (Amsterdam, 1814, 2d ed. 1825); *Leerredenen en Kerkelijke Redevoeringen* (2 vv., Amsterdam, 1816 and 1825); *Vragen betrekkelijk de kennis en het goed verstand der heilige Schriften . . .* (Amsterdam, 1826).

Van Rijswijk owned a good collection of Mennonite works, including some rare ones. He gave them to the Library of the Amsterdam Mennonite Church. vpZ.

B. Glasius, *Godgeleerd Nederland* III ('s Hertogenbosch, 1856) 248 f.; *Catalogus Amst.*, 223, 312, 313, 325; *DJ* 1837, 113 f.; *DB* 1861, 35; 1869, 95; 1875, 27; 1896,

166 f.; *Inv. Arch. Amst.* II 620 f.; *Naamlijst* 1829, 32, 34, 50; *ML* III, 514.

Riley Creek Mennonite Church: see **Zion**.

Rinck, Melchior: see **Rink, Melchior**.

Ring, a Dutch word meaning a regional association of ten or twelve neighboring Mennonite congregations for the purpose of assisting one another, especially in the case of pulpit vacancy. The objective of the general organization was to avoid the extinction of congregations, which was a common occurrence in the 18th century. The first Ring, viz., Ring Akkrum, was founded in 1837 upon the initiative of Steven Blaupot ten Cate (*q.v.*), who was the minister in Akkrum 1830-39. Soon two more Rings were founded for Friesland, viz., Ring Bolsward (*q.v.*) in 1840 and Ring Dantumawoude (*q.v.*) in 1850. In 1844 Ring North Holland (*q.v.*) followed their example; in 1862 Ring South Holland and Zeeland was established. Other similar regional associations were Ring Zwolle (*q.v.*) for the northwest, and Ring Twente (*q.v.*) for the southeast of the province of Overijssel. The province of Groningen has no Ring; the functions of the Ring in this province are performed by the Groningen Conference (Sociëteit van Doopsgezinde Gemeenten in Groningen). After World War II Ring Utrecht and 't Gooi (*q.v.*) and Ring Arnhem (*q.v.*) were reorganized. There are at present ten Rings in the Netherlands.   vDZ.

Verslag (Report) *wegens de staat der Algemene Doopsgezinde Sociëteit over de periode 1946-1947* (Kollum, 1947) 57 f.; *DJ* 1956, 135 f.; *ML* III, 514.

Ring, Melchior: see **Rink, Melchior**.

Ringel, Bärtl, of Gundelbach: see **Riegel, Bartl**.

Ring(h) (Ryngh), **Yeme** (Jeme, Ieme, Ime) **Jacobsz de,** a Dutch Mennonite preacher, b. Nov. 17, 1574, at Harlingen, Dutch province of Friesland, d. there April 10, 1627, served the Waterlander congregation in his home town until his death. As an elder he was very active, especially in the province of Friesland, visiting the congregations regularly, baptizing and administering communion; in 1613-18 he intervened in Workum (*q.v.*), where complaints had arisen against elder Rippert Eenkes. At first he took a rather strict position in church discipline, disagreeing with Hans de Ries (*q.v.*), the leader of the Waterlanders in North Holland; but in the course of time his views became more lenient. On Sept. 7, 1626, with five colleagues, he signed the thirteen articles of faith intended to mediate the dispute between the preachers Reinier Wybrandsz (*q.v.*), Pieter Andriesz Hesseling (*q.v.*), Cornelis Claesz Anslo (*q.v.*) on the one side, and Nittert Obbesz (*q.v.*) on the other. When he died a sentimental poem appeared: "Lament of the Oppressed Spirits Concerning the Death of the Virtuous, Blessed, and Eloquent Yeme Jacobsz de Ring," which is a living testimony to his esteem in the brotherhood. Three writings of de Ring's have been preserved; they are *Predicatie over Proverb: 30 vers 24-28*, in *Kort Verhael van het Leven van Hans de Ries* (De Rijp, 1644); an excellent funeral sermon, *Lijkpredicatie,*

on II Sam. 3:38 in memory of Anthoni Jacobsz (*q.v.*) Roscius (Hoorn, 1624); and *Tractaet teghen het Straffen der Buyten-Getrouden zonder Onderscheyt* (Jan. 1, 1627). This "Tract" attacks a High German (*q.v.*) preacher, probably Leenaert Clock (*q.v.*), who took a stricter position in applying the ban to persons guilty of marriage with outsiders. Formerly the "Tract," which was signed with the pseudonym Ben Israëls, was ascribed to Anthoni Jacobsz Roscius; but Schijn-Maatschoen, *Geschiedenis* III, 154 f., proves that the author was de Ringh. Yeme de Ringh had his portrait painted by Lambert Jacobsz (*q.v.*).

A Jacob de Ring(h) was a preacher of the Young Frisian Mennonites at Harlingen in 1590. He was probably Jeme de Ring's father. Auke de Ring, of Zaandam (*Inv. Arch. Amst.* II, Nos. 1779-84), was a Mennonite preacher at Gouda, Dutch province of South Holland in 1728-33, and died there on Feb. 6, 1733.   NEFF, vDZ.

Inv. Arch. Amst. I, No. 527; II, Nos. 1358 f., 1890; II, 2, Nos. 661, 666, 669; *DB* 1864, 15, 63, 68; 1903, 58 f., 62, 64, 71 f., 81-83; Marten Schagen, *Naamlijst der Doopsgezinde schrijveren* (Amsterdam, 1745) 85; Kühler, *Geschiedenis* II, *passim*; Schijn-Maatschoen, *Geschiedenis* III, 119, 147-67; *BRN* VII, 236; *ML* III, 514.

Ringmacher, Lorenz, of Augsburg, Germany, author of the hymn, "O Jesu, der du sehlig machst Die bossfertige hertzen," No. 74 in the *Ausbund* (*q.v.*). (Wolkan, *Lieder,* 142; *ML* III, 514.)   NEFF.

Ringmacher, Peter, leader of the Anabaptist congregation of Augsburg (*q.v.*), chosen to the office with Hans Schleifer (*q.v.*) on April 4, 1528. They were sent to Regensburg (*q.v.*) to comfort the brethren there. (*ML* I, 95; III, 514.)   NEFF.

Rink (Rinck, Ring, Ringk, Grink), **Melchior** (1494-after 1545), an Anabaptist martyr of Hesse, Germany, the outstanding leader of the Anabaptists in Hesse. He was educated at the universities of Leipzig and Erfurt, some of his professors being humanists. His nickname "the Greek" is probably an allusion to a good mastery of Greek. He was said to have participated in the fanatical disturbances of the Zwickau (*q.v.*) prophets in Wittenberg as early as 1520 or 1521 (Ottius, 7); but this is probably an erroneous assumption. The first certain information about him after this time says that he was a schoolmaster (chaplain) in Hersfeld (*q.v.*; not in the village, but in the city and the *Stift*) in 1523. Here he became the good friend of the pastor Heinrich Fuchs, and worked enthusiastically with him to promote Luther's ideas. The Stift authorities, however, induced the abbot to dismiss him; when this happened in December 1523 some disturbances occurred. The landgrave then had Rink and Fuchs arrested, but they were released; they were then permanently expelled from Hersfeld and Hesse.

The two friends now turned to Thuringia (*q.v.*) where Rink secured a pastorate in Oberhausen near Eisenach and later in Eckardtshausen. He married Anna, the daughter of Hans Eckard. He soon fell under the influence of Müntzer and (according to a report by Eberhard von der Tann) took an active part in the Peasants' War, especially in the battle at Frankenhausen. Fuchs lost his life, but Melchior

Rink tried to continue Müntzer's (*q.v.*) work by means of strong polemics against Luther's doctrine of justification, the proper fruits of which he thought he missed everywhere. Henceforth he was homeless and led the life of a wanderer. In the spring of 1527 he is thought to have met Hans Denk (*q.v.*), Ludwig Haetzer (*q.v.*), and Jakob Kautz (*q.v.*) in Worms and with them signed the seven articles for the disputation with the Lutheran clergy. In 1528 he stayed most of the time around Hersfeld on the Thuringian border, preaching Anabaptist doctrine. There is no sign of seditious intentions on his part. His principal concern was the refutation of infant baptism and the gathering of quiet Christians, tried and tested in life and in suffering, who would enter upon the discipleship of Jesus. He attacked infant baptism because "original sin does not condemn before the person reaches the years of reason and wills to sin." He asserted that a man must first be taught of God before he is baptized, for faith comes by hearing; but without faith baptism is nothing; the child is not a Christian and must first be taught the Word like adults. From this faith issues, and afterwards baptism; for with the heart one believes and by confession one secures salvation. He rejected the bodily presence of Christ in the Lord's Supper, but did not venture into speculation or dispute on this point.

Rink found a considerable following, and therefore ventured to ask permission to preach openly in Hersfeld. His request reached Philip of Hesse (*q.v.*), who summoned him to a personal conversation in his hunting lodge Friedewald and gave him a choice between recanting and presenting his teachings to the theologians of the faculty of the University of Marburg. Rink chose the latter, and thus a disputation was held at Marburg (*q.v.*) on Feb. 17 and 18, 1528, the rector of the university acting as chairman. The debate was led principally by Balthasar Raid (*q.v.*), a Hersfeld clergyman. Raid sent an exact report of the course of the debate to Philip (given verbatim in *Thüringen*, 294-302). Melchior Rink was required to present his doctrines in five points in written form. The first three concerned the creation of man and his fall and need of redemption. On these there was no difference of opinion. The difference of opinion arose when the question of baptism was opened. Since no agreement could be reached on this subject, the last point, concerning communion, was not touched at all.

As a penalty for his obstinacy Rink was sentenced to imprisonment upon the insistence of John the Steadfast (*q.v.*), Elector of Saxony, and paid this penalty in Haina on the Wohra. But records of this punishment vary. Hochhuth says he was sentenced to public church confession, and Wappler says that he was expelled from the country. But undeterred by all the persecution Rink at once resumed his quiet gathering of converts. The elector, however, had him sharply watched by his bailiff on the Wartburg, Eberhard von der Tann. But he was not apprehended on Saxon soil; if he had been, his life would certainly have been forfeit. When he was seized in Hesse, Saxony tried by all the means at its disposal to influence Philip to institute a formal heresy trial with the obvious intention of having him executed.

Philip did not yield, but punished Rink with a light sentence of imprisonment, and after half a year released him upon the sole condition that he would never again set foot upon the soil of Hesse or Saxony.

During his arrest Rink wrote a letter to the Wartburg bailiff concerning the attempt by his father-in-law Hans Eckard to have Rink's marriage with his daughter annulled; Rink had not seen his wife since the days of the peasant uprising. Rink's reply reveals poignantly his homelessness: "After I have been for so long persecuted by both the Papists and the Lutherans, that is, by the entire abomination of antichrist, not only as a heretic and fanatic, but also as a seditionist, contrary to all reason (as God is my witness and as the facts have abundantly shown my adversaries), from village to village, from town to town, and from country to country, there now comes to light the deceit and unfaithfulness of my supposed wife and her parents, and heaps upon me such grim and untruthful charges that even my judges, if they only would, could well without my answering to them recognize my innocence and clear me of the charges they make." He accused her of unfaithfulness in that "she took me not for love and a free heart, but out of a desire for quiet days and on the compulsion of her parents."

Rink had not long to enjoy his liberty. On Nov. 11, 1531, he was again seized, in Vacha on the Werra, with eleven companions, while he was preaching on Mark 16:16, one of his favorite texts. Again Saxony interfered and in a personal letter the elector insisted that Philip impose the supreme penalty on Rink on the basis of the edict of Speyer of 1529 and the official opinion of 1531 by the theologians of Wittenberg. But in vain. Rink was condemned instead to perpetual imprisonment, having rejected the plea of his friend Georg Witzel, who had just paid a visit to his native town of Vacha, to recant his views on baptism and to stop performing it. He was taken to Bärbach in the district of Katzenelnbogen, and was still there in 1551. In 1540 his chains were eased upon Bucer's (*q.v.*) intervention after Peter Tesch joined the established church. He probably died in prison, since Peter Tesch had tried in vain to convert him.

All of Rink's writings but three have been lost. One of these is an epistle written conjointly with Antonius Jacobsz, which was actually a broadside (*Flugschrift*) on infant baptism. It was published by *Cramer* (*BRN* V, 642-44). Another writing was the letter to Eberhard von der Tann, written in prison at Haina, published by both Wappler (*Kursachsen*, 149-52) and Franz (*TA Hesse*, No. 14a, pp. 33-37). Both are effective evidence of his earnest Christian attitude.

In 1958 a hitherto unknown writing by Rink, *Widerlegung einer Schrift, so Johannes Bader . . . Pfarrher zu Landau, neulich than hat, den Kindertauff als christlich zu erhalten* (manuscript), was discovered in the Frankfurt University Library (see *Gesch.-Bl.*, 1958, 48 f.).

Rink baptized Hans Peisker (*q.v.*) on Jan. 26, 1536. Others whom he is known to have baptized were Gilg Scherer (also called vom Berge), of Motzfeld, the leader of the congregation at Sorga, near

Hersfeld. Among his most loyal followers were Hans Both (*q.v.*) and Margaretha, "the old cook" (Garköchin).   P.S.

BRN V; *TA Hesse;* C. A. Cornelius, *Geschichte des Münsterischen Aufruhrs* II (Leipzig, 1860); *Corpus Reformatorum, Opera Melanchthon's* II; *Grouwelen der voornaemster Hooft-Ketteren* . . . (Leiden, 1623); *HRE* XVII, 17, Carl Mirbt with an exact bibliography; K. W. H. Hochhuth, "Mitteilungen aus der protestantischen Sektengeschichte in der hessischen Kirche: Landgraf Philipp und die Wiedertäufer," in *Ztscht für historische Theologie,* 1858, 541-53; Eduard Jacobs, "Die Wiedertäufer am Harz," in *Ztscht des Harz-Vereins für Gesch. und Altertumskunde,* 1899, 427, 428, 434-36, 440 f., 466 f., 480, 501, 522, 526, 528, 531; W. I. Leendertz, *Melchior Hofman* (Haarlem, 1885) 341-48, Supplement 1, "Overzicht van het Leven van Melchior Rinck"; F. O. zur Linden, *Melchior Hofmann, ein Prophet der Wiedertäufer* (Haarlem and Leipzig, 1885) 74 and 171; W. Maurer, "Gestalten aus der hessischen Täufergeschichte I: Melchior Rinck," in *Pastoralblatt für Kurhessen-Waldeck* (1953) No. 1, pp. 10-12; J. H. Ottius, *Annales Anabaptistici* (Basel, 1672); *RGG* IX, Col. 2039 (article by Walther Köhler); Paul Wappler, *Die Stellung Kursachsens und des Landgrafen Philipp von Hessen zur Täuferbewegung* (Jena, 1913); idem, *Thüringen;* Wiswedel, *Bilder,* 108 ff.; Wilhelm Dersch, "Das Vorspiel der Reformation in Hersfeld," in *Ztscht des Vereins für hessische Geschichte,* 1909, 91 ff.; *ML* III, 515 f.

Rinkes, a Mennonite family, formerly living at Joure (*q.v.*), Dutch province of Friesland. From the early 18th century the members of this family were usually ships' chandlers and grocers. In the early 19th century they adopted Rinkes as their family name. Inne Wouters (Rinkes) was a lay preacher in the Oude Huis congregation of Joure 1780-d. 1814, and some members of this family were deacons of the church, e.g., Jan Innes Rinkes (1849-1935), who was its treasurer and moderator from 1892 to 1931.

Another member of this family was Simke Heeres Rinkes (1829-65), professor of Latin and Greek at Arnhem and state school inspector, who was active in the promotion of better education for Dutch teachers.   vDZ.

Rinner, Hans: see **Riemer, Hans.**

Rinske Obbedochter was taken prisoner when the soldiers of the governor of Friesland recaptured the Oldeklooster (*q.v.*) near Bolsward on April 7, 1535, which had been taken by a group of revolutionary Anabaptists a few days before. She was conducted to Leeuwarden, capital of Friesland, and on April 14, 1535, sentenced to be executed by drowning. (K. Vos, *Menno Simons,* Leiden, 1914, 229.)   vDZ.

Rintjes (Rintsius), **Hendrik** (1630-98), a preacher of the Waterlander congregation in Leeuwarden, Dutch province of Friesland, and a book printer there. He had contacts with important scholars of his time and from 1656 on published a number of collections of verse. His own verse, of which he published several editions, mediocre in quality, includes *Gedachten op den Jongsten dag, in versen vertoont* (1681, reprinted 1685), *De Morgenstond in haer somersche Vermaeklijkheden vertoont* (Leeuwarden, 1684), and *Ziele-Zucht aan God* (Leeuwarden, 1698). Rintjes apparently also wrote a number of hymns found in the Mennonite hymnal *Geestelijke Goudschale* (*q.v.*).   E.C., vDZ.

B. Glasius, *Godgeleerd Nederland* III ('s Hertogenbosch, 1856) 179 f.; Marten Schagen, *Naamlijst der Doopsgezinde schrijveren* (Amsterdam, 1745) 85; Blaupot t. C., *Friesland,* 235, 385; A. M. Ledeboer, *Alfabetische Lijst der Boekdrukkers, Boekverkoopers en Uitgevers in Noord-Nederland* (Utrecht, 1876) 142; *Chronologisch Register* (Utrecht, 1877) 20; *ML* III, 516 f.

Rio Linda Mennonite Church (MC), Roebla, Cal., was established in 1953 and had 21 members in 1957. It is a member of the Pacific Coast Conference.

Rippert Eenkes, a Dutch Mennonite elder: see **Eenkes, Rippert.**

Ris, a widely ramified Dutch Mennonite family, many of whose members, usually conservatives, served the church as preachers and deacons. It seems to have had its origin in Hoorn (*q.v.*), province of North Holland; branches of this family were found as early as 1650 at Westzaan and Krommenie in this province.

The most outstanding member of this family was Cornelis Ris (*q.v.;* 1717-90), preacher at Hoorn 1747-90 and composer of the Ris confession of faith (1766); his son Jan Ris (b. 1756 at Hoorn, d. 1784 at Hamburg) was a preacher of the Hamburg-Altona congregation in 1777-84, whose baptismal sermon preached at Altona on March 28, 1784, entitled *De Christelyke waterdoop,* was published at Hamburg in 1784. Cornelis Willemsz Ris was also a lay preacher at Hoorn 1766-85. Deacons at Hoorn were Gerrit Pieters Ris in 1646-69 and Pieter Ris (1742-1808), a brother of the preacher Cornelis Ris and married to Cornelia van Vollenhoven, from 1783 until his death. Pieter Ris, like his brother, ardently defended the old Mennonite principles, in the Waterlander (Rijper) and also in the Frisian conference. A number of his writings entitled *Christelijke brieven en overdenkingen,* were published after his death (Hoorn, 1812).

In Hoorn the Ris family was engaged in business and trade; they were among the most active owners of whaling boats and were well-to-do. This family has died out here.

At Wormerveer in 1675 Pieter Jans Ris, a member of the Waterlander congregation, together with some other members insisted that the confession of Hans de Ries (*q.v.*) should be maintained in the congregation, and that no preacher should be admitted to the pulpit who did not agree with the confession.

At Westzaan, Jan Willems Ris was an untrained preacher of the Frisian congregation in the early 18th century. His writings, *Israels Blijdschap, Dank-Predikatie over den vrede van Utrecht* (Haarlem, n.d.); *Redenvoering, geschickt om in een Sterfhuys voorgedraagen te worden* (Haarlem, n.d., 1744); and *Verzaameling van Boet- en Bedestoffen, of Bedestonds redenvoeringen, uitgesproken in de jaaren 1702 tot 1712* (Haarlem, 1747), were edited by Agge Wynalda, the Mennonite minister of Haarlem.

One of the descendants of Jan Willems Ris was Klaas Ris, b. *c*1795 at Westzaan, d. 1852 at Joure, who was trained for the ministry at the Amsterdam Lamist seminary and served the congregations of Makkum 1820-23 and Joure 1823-52. He published

Naamlijst van allen, die . . . hunne studiën aan de Kweekschool begonnen en voleindigd hebben (Leeuwarden, n.d.-1841).

A. A. Ris was the sexton of the Haarlem Mennonite Church in 1900-29. Klaas Ris Taconis, b. 1844 at Nieuwe Niedorp, d. 1876 at Graft, a son of Pastor Inne Taconis and Aagtje Ris, after studying at the Amsterdam Mennonite Seminary, served at Noordeind van Graft in 1872-76. He retired because of poor health (*DB* 1876, 129). His farewell sermon, *Laatste Toespraak,* was published at Joure in 1876. He died soon after.   vDZ.

Inv. Arch. Amst. I, Nos. 870, 900; II, 2, Nos. 125, 139, 168, 171 f., 199, 210; *DJ* 1935, 34 ff.; 1940, 57-63; M. Schagen, *Naamlijst der Doopsgezinde schrijveren* (Amsterdam, 1745) 83.

Ris, Cornelis, b. 1717 at Hoorn, Dutch province of North Holland, d. there April 18, 1790, a Zonist (*q.v.*) Mennonite preacher, stemmed from the influential Ris (*q.v.*) family of Hoorn. On March 12, 1746, Cornelis was installed as one of the ministers of the Hoorn Frisian congregation. In the 17th century Hoorn had an unusual number of Mennonite branches; in 1747 the Frisians (*q.v.*) and the Waterlanders (*q.v.*), then the only remaining congregations, merged. Ris served at Hoorn until his death. His colleague Jacob Spis delivered his funeral sermon.

An address to the Hoorn congregation said, "There was namely besides the Waterlander congregation, which had adopted the Confession of Hans de Ries, also a Frisian congregation, which gave considerable approval to another (confession), signed at Dordrecht on Sept. 27, 1632, by a number of ministers: when these two congregations united in 1747, the third article of the agreement stipulated the following: The confessions of faith now adhered to by the two congregations will not be changed now; nor will the ministers and members be required to give a more specific declaration than that given when they were installed in office or admitted into the congregation; but when the two congregations are united, an attempt will be made to unify the two confessions wherein they may differ: And if an admission of members is planned, as has hitherto been customary, to proceed with such moderation that too much will not be demanded of such as are weak of understanding and tender spirits are spared" (Foreword of the German edition of the Confession of Cornelis Ris, Hamburg, 1776).

Thus it became a special concern to Cornelis Ris to gather into a single confession and merge the confessions of faith (*q.v.*) that seemed definitive in the *Algemeene Belydenissen* (1665) of the Zonists (*q.v.*); viz., the Concept of Cologne (*q.v.*), 1591; Outerman's (*q.v.*) Confession, 1626; *Olijftacxken* (*q.v.*), 1627; Confession of Jan Cents (*q.v.*), 1630; Dordrecht Confession (*q.v.*), 1632. Besides consideration for the two congregations at Hoorn, he was moved by the desire to check the rapid decline of the congregations of his time by steering them toward the old foundation of the recognized confessions (whereas van der Zijpp has shown that the congregations that were more faithful to the confessions were declining even more rapidly than the more liberal ones). In 1759 the church council of the Hoorn congregation decided to present Ris' proposal to the Zonist Sociëteit. This body approached the problem with hesitation. Nevertheless Cornelis Ris was able to present a concrete sketch in 1762 and to publish it in 1766. His caution in this matter is shown by the title of the fourth article; at first it read, "How this one God is further to be distinguished in the Holy Scriptures"; the later version says more plainly, "Of the Holy Trinity." Not until 1773 did the Sociëteit formally approve the confession. But in spite of this approval it found no enthusiastic reception by the Zonists, the Lamists (*q.v.*), or the Old Flemish (*q.v.*). Concerning the previous history and the difficulties in having this confession approved Ris wrote *Kort Berigt van't voorgevallene over de Geloofsleere* (Hoorn, 1776).

The Confession of Cornelis Ris was given the significant title *De Geloofsleere der waare Mennoniten of Doopsgezinden.* Nevertheless Cornelis Ris, like the orthodox wing of the Dutch Mennonites in general at that time, also sought contact with Calvinism, the established faith; his confession, which expressly attaches itself to the Mennonite tradition, has a certain Calvinistic inclination (the doctrine of election in article IX was later moderated or left open by insertions). His 36 articles deal with all the major points of theology.

This confession, like the Dordrecht Confession, had only temporary significance in the Netherlands (*q.v.*), but attained a true and wide significance outside its home. For the Confession of Cornelis Ris its relations to the Hamburg-Altona (*q.v.*) congregation and to America were important.

Besides the Hoorn congregation, the only other congregations to support it were Westzaan in North Holland and Almelo (*q.v.*) in Overijssel, where Pieter Beets (*q.v.*), a nephew and collaborator of Cornelis Ris, was the pastor. He took a position in favor of the confession in a "Brief Report."

The bridge to the Hamburg-Altona congregation was built by members of the Beets (*q.v.*) family, some of whom lived there and others in Hoorn. Jan Beets (*q.v.*; 1708-88), of Hoorn, a follower of Count Zinzendorf (*q.v.*) and a successful revival preacher, was a faithful adherent of Cornelis Ris. His cousin Gerrit Beets (*q.v.*; 1707-76), elder of the Hamburg-Altona congregation, fought all his life, like Ris, "that the ancient pillars should not be removed." Pieter Beets (1727-76), a nephew of Jan Beets and of Cornelis Ris, who had also been "awakened" in the early 1750's, was called from Almelo to Hamburg-Altona, recommended by his uncle Cornelis Ris, and began his service there in 1771. He was succeeded not long after by Jan Ris (1756-84), a son of Cornelis Ris, whom Pieter Beets had instructed in Hamburg-Altona, and who became a ministerial candidate in 1775, a minister in Hamburg-Altona in 1777, and an elder in 1779.

In Hamburg the Confession of Cornelis Ris was translated into German and published in 1776. The Foreword explains that it was intended for Mennonites of Dutch extraction who were now using German in their services, and for the congregations in Southwest Germany and Alsace and their "colonies" in America; it expresses the hope that the Protestants would graciously accept this work. The translator reproduced some 12 pages of the original author's 52-page introduction and added some pages of his own, making a German introduction of about half the length of the Dutch. For 1791 B. C. Roosen reported in his history of the Hamburg-Altona congregation (II, p. 55), "when the preachers of our congregation in 1791 suggested in the church council that competent preachers be sought from the outside, they added the wish that only orthodox ones adhering to the confessions of Hans de Ries and Lubbert Gerrits, Gerrit Roosen, or Cornelis Ris be invited for a visit." The same history records that on May 29, 1803, it was unanimously decided to adopt the Confession by Cornelis Ris, and that for many years each newly chosen preacher and deacon signed a copy of this confession.

In the early 19th century, when Prussia organized its Rhine Province (see **Rhineland**) and sought information about its Mennonites, the Dordrecht Confession was presented as that of the stricter branch (Amish), and the Cornelis Ris confession as that of the more lenient branch.

The Confession of Cornelis Ris acquired new effectiveness in the 19th and 20th centuries through the work of Carl Justus van der Smissen (*q.v.;* 1811-90), who was the minister in the Friedrichstadt (*q.v.*) Mennonite congregation 1837-68, and was then called to America to serve as a teacher in the school at Wadsworth (*q.v.*), Ohio. He revised the German translation of this confession "in order that it may not be lost to our congregations." His revision, without the Scriptural proof texts, was published as a manuscript in 1850.

In America Carl Heinrich Anton van der Smissen (*q.v.;* 1851-1950), a son of the above, a Mennonite pastor in Summerfield, Ill., published the Cornelis Ris Confession in 1895 as an appendix to a short history of the Mennonites. This edition contained some new proof texts added by his father and Berend Roosen (*q.v.*). This confession seemed more liberal, in America as well as in Europe, than the Dordrecht Confession, and was published by the General Conference Mennonite Church in English in 1902 and 1904, and 1904 (with title of 1895 edition) and 1906 in German, as its recognized confession.

In 1778 and 1779, Cornelis Ris also published thirty sermons by his nephew after his early death. Furthermore, his glance extended beyond the ecclesiastical matters. He had since 1777 promoted the establishment of a "Patriotic Association for Shipping and Trade," and in the service of this association (which became a victim of the years of the French Revolution) he composed in 1871 his *Algemeen Christelijk-Catechisatieboekje voor de kinderen van verschillende gezindten op de educatieschool der Vaderlandsche Maatschappij te Hoorn.* E.C.

Biogr. Wb. XVI, 356; *N.N.B.Wb.* X. 817 f.; *Inv. Arch. Amst.* I, Nos. 933, 935 f., 938 f.; *DJ* 1837, 46; 1840, 116; 1940, 58; *DB* 1898, 14 f.; *Naamlijst* 1791, 62; Bender, *Two Centuries,* 103, 108, 109; Blaupot t. C., *Holland* II, 36, 87, 180; Ernst Crous, "Wie die Mennoniten in die deutsche Volksgemeinschaft hineinwuchsen," *Gesch.-Bl.* 1939, 13-24 (reprint Karlsruhe, 1939); R. Dollinger, *Geschichte der Mennoniten in Schleswig-Holstein, Hamburg und Lübeck* (Neumünster, 1930) 58-61, 182; Robert Friedmann, *Mennonite Piety Through the Centuries* (Goshen, 1949) 135 f., 253; B. C. Roosen, *Geschichte der Mennoniten-Gemeinde zu Hamburg und Altona* II (Hamburg, 1887) 50-55, 65, 68, 83; C. Henry Smith, *The Story of the Mennonites* (Newton, 1950) 680-82, 747, 772; N. van der Zijpp, *Geschiedenis der Doopsgezinden in Nederland* (Arnhem, 1952) 165, 167-69, 179; idem, *De Belijdenisgeschriften der Nederlandse Doopsgezinden* (Haarlem, 1954) 21 f.; *Catalogus Amst.,* 173, 220, 243, 247, 253, 265; *ML* III, 517-19.

Ris, Hans de: see **Ries, Hans de.**

Risser (Reeser, Reesor, Reusser, Rieser, Rüssor), an old Mennonite family stemming from Signau in the Emmental (*q.v.*) of Switzerland. In 1597 Daniel Reusser "is a disobedient Anabaptist" and a Rüsserin of Brienz returns to the church. Among the Swiss Mennonites who emigrated to the Netherlands in 1711 were Stephan Rüsser, of Hilterfingen, a member of the Reformed Church, with his second wife and Michael Rüsser (1684/5-c1759), a son of his first marriage. Michael, who was arrested for his faith in 1710, was at the time of his emigration a preacher. In the Netherlands, farming near Groningen (*q.v.*), he became a preacher and soon after an elder of the Nieuwe Zwitsers. (See **Swiss Mennonites in the Netherlands.**) In 1680 the Anabaptist Hans Rüsser of Hartlisberg zu Thun was for years reported out of the country; his property had been seized by the church and "should he return he shall be punished with rods and sent away again as a hard wicked Anabaptist" (Bern Archives). In 1672 Babe Ruesser, over 80 years old, Hans Reuscher and his wife and son Daniel, and Hans Reysscher and his wife were among the refugees in the Palatinate. In 1702 a Kaspar Risser successfully eluded the "Täuferjäger."

In 1715 and again in 1749 Hans Rüsser or Johannes Risser is found in the Palatinate as a hereditary leaseholder in Friedelsheim (*q.v.*). In 1773 Abraham Risser or Rüsser is found in Erpolzheim (*q.v.;* see **Leiningen**). A Johannes Risser was a preacher (from 1832) and elder (1833) at Sembach (*q.v.*) and another Johannes Risser (*q.v.*) was preacher in Friedelsheim; the former was in the middle of the 19th century one of the leaders in the Palatine-Hessian congregations, and the latter emigrated to America in 1832. In 1870-71 H. Risser was a teacher in the school at the Weierhof (*q.v.*) and preached occasionally in Altleiningen (*q.v.*). The Mennonite *Adressbuch* of 1936 lists 27 Risser families in Germany.

Members of the Risser family are reported to have emigrated to America as early as 1712. At any rate, in 1737 a Peter Risser (d. 1804 at the age of 91) emigrated from Switzerland and settled in Lancaster County, Pa. He enjoyed telling that he had emigrated in order to avoid being chosen by lot to the ministry; but immediately upon his arrival the lot fell upon him; thus it became clear to him that it is impossible to flee from the presence of God. He became an outstanding preacher and served a longer term in the ministry than any other Lancaster preacher before or after him. Eight children were born to him in America. His son Christian in 1774 married Fanny Reif(f) and settled near Markham, Ont. His son Jacob married Mary Snyder and remained in the home community. They were the ancestors of all the Mennonite Rissers, Reesors, and Reesers of Lancaster, Dauphin, and Lebanon counties, Pa., and Markham, Ont. Some of the original land is still in the family name. Among the descendants in the ministry were Jacob Risser, his son Martin E. Risser (d. 1905), and his grandson John D. Risser (d. 1952) in Washington County, Md., and Christian Risser (d. 1826) and John Risser (d. 1870) of the Risser congregation, Bishop Christian Risser (d. 1910) and John Risser (d. 1873) of the Hammer Creek congregation, Peter Risser (d. 1864) of Chestnut Hill, Bishop Noah W. Risser (1877-) of the Stauffer congregation, and Abram Risser of the Hernley congregation, all in Lancaster County, Pa., and Jacob and Martin Risser (d. 1926) of Lebanon County, Pa. In 1911 Christian B. Risser (or Reeser) (d. 1923 at the age of 103) was an Amish preacher in Roanoke, Ill. James Reusser is a minister (GCM) in the Salem Church near Dalton, Ohio. The family is also found in Kansas and Oklahoma.   I.D.L., E.C.

L. J. Burkholder, *Reesor Family Reunion, The Reesor Family in Canada* (n.p., 1950); H. P. Krehbiel, *Mennonite Churches of North America* (Berne, 1911); Müller, *Berner Täufer*, 201, 310, 341; *MQR* XXX (1956) 148-53; M. G. Weaver, *Mennonites of Lancaster County* (Scottdale, 1931); J. C. Wenger, *History of the Mennonites of the Franconia Conference* (Telford, 1937); Daniel Kauffman, *Mennonite Cyclopedic Dictionary* (Scottdale, 1937); Ethel Arlene Cosco, *Christian Reeser, the Story of a Centenarian* (n.p., 1952); Franz Crous, *ML* III, 519 f.

Risser, Johannes (1810-68), a minister of the Mennonite congregation at Sembach, Germany, was born in Friedelsheim (q.v.), Nov. 21, 1810. He was educated at the universities of Heidelberg, Erlangen, and Bonn. On Sept. 16, 1832, he entered the ministry at Sembach. He vigorously cultivated the spiritual life and intellectual interests of his congregation. (The church record books contain his notes on the history of the Mennonite churches in Palatinate.) His influence extended far beyond his congregation. He was an active co-worker on the *Mennonitische Blätter* (q.v.). He was closely associated with his co-preachers Jakob Ellenberger (q.v.) and Johannes Molenaar (q.v.). He had a prominent part in the compilation of the *Formularbuch* (q.v.), which is still in use, and of the new hymnal (see **Hymnology**) of 1854. Also the questions of the creating of a ministerial fund (*Predigerfonds, q.v.*) and of the traveling ministry (see **Reisepredigt**) occupied him. His attempts to bring about a union with the Amish Mennonites of the Palatinate were only temporarily successful, but are a testimonial to his warm love for the brotherhood, his broad view, and his generous mind. He died at Sembach on May 23, 1868.   NEFF.

Chr. Hege, *Die Täufer in der Kurpfalz* (Frankfurt, 1908) 6; "Johannes Risser, Prediger in Sembach," autobiographical sketch in *Gem.-Kal.*, 1914, 47-72; *ML* III, 520 f.

Risser, Johannes (John), a minister in the Mennonite congregation at Friedelsheim (q.v.), Palatinate, Germany, 1825-32, where among other things he conducted missionary meetings. He was born at Friedelsheim, Nov. 27, 1788. In 1813 he married Katharina Weber, who was related to the Mellinger family. In 1832 he emigrated to America. They as well as their relatives who had previously emigrated to Mellingers (q.v.) in Pennsylvania sent reports on travel and on America to their old home. Excerpts of these have been published in the *Mennonite Quarterly Review*. The German originals were probably published early in the 20th century in a newspaper of Worms. German excerpts were printed in the *Wappenkunde* of the Palatinate shortly before the appearance of the English version. Johannes Risser purchased some land and settled in Mifflin Twp., Richland Co., Ohio, not far from Mansfield in 1833. In 1845 he published a booklet on baptism, *Glaube und Lehre von der Taufe der Mennoniten in Deutschland. Verfasst von Johannes Risser, Mitglied dieser Kirche, und hieher nach Amerika eingewandert, welchem dort zwar der Beruf als Prediger geworden, aber ohne in eine andere Schule als eine gewöhnliche Volksschule gekommen zu seyn, folglich kein Gelehrter ist, und daher die Leser wegen der vorkommenden Unvollkommenheiten um freundliche Nachsicht bittet.* It appeared in the shop of Heinrich Eby (q.v.) at Berlin (now Kitchener), Ont. It is an expansive treatment, in two parts, dealing respectively with the historical and the practical aspects.   NEFF, E.C.

Bender, *Two Centuries*, 21; *idem*, "The Correspondence of Martin Mellinger . . . ," *MQR* V (1931); Fritz Braun, "Auswanderer aus der Mennonitengemeinde Friedelsheim im 19. Jahrhundert," in *Pfälzische Familien- und Wappenkunde*, 1955; Don Yoder, "The Risser Letters (1832-1833)," *MQR* XXX (1956) 44-64; *ML* III, 521.

Risser (Rissers) Mennonite Church (MC), located 4 miles east of Elizabethtown, Pa., a member of the Lancaster Conference, originated in 1737. The first meetinghouse was built in 1760 in a grove on Peter Risser's (q.v.) land. This was enlarged in 1865, and in 1887 replaced by the present frame church 50 x 70 ft. It is beautifully located, with a schoolhouse adjoining and a well-kept cemetery. In 1957 the membership was 138; Noah W. Risser and Clarence E. Lutz were the bishops, Walter W. Oberholtzer and J. Harold Forwood the ministers. It formerly shared its ministers with the Stauffer congregation at Bachmanville.   I.D.L.

Rissler, Daniel and **Moses**, preacher and deacon respectively of the New Holland O.O.M. Church, Lancaster Co., Pa., were brothers who led a schism of the Weaver Mennonites, a branch of the Pike Mennonites (q.v.), and then disagreed among themselves. The combined group consisted chiefly of the members of these two families and never numbered more than seven.   I.D.L.

Rissler Old Order Mennonites. Samuel Bowman (1822-1902), bishop at the Pike church of the Stauffer Mennonite (q.v.) group, New Holland, Pa., led a faction, following the Civil War, which was more conservative than the main Stauffer group. He appointed Philip Rissler minister of the conservative group, which met in private homes. As a bishop Bowman again joined the main Stauffer group in 1916, only to be expelled with 11 members in 1919. Later Deacon Moses Rissler expelled his brother, Minister Aaron Rissler, from the Rissler group.

Aaron Rissler after that was the leader of a small group of followers until his death in March 1950.

I.D.L.

Ritschl, Albrecht (1822-89), one of the outstanding German liberal theologians of the 19th century, professor of theology 1852-64 at the University of Bonn and 1864-89 at Göttingen, wrote twice at length concerning Anabaptism, both times in connection with his investigation of the origin and history of Pietism. Under the influence of Max Goebel's *Geschichte des christlichen Lebens in der rheinisch-westfälischen evangelischen Kirche* (Coblence, 1849, 1852, 1860) he held Pietism to be in a sense a revival of Anabaptism; hence he attempted to show the relationship of the two by analyzing their basic ideas and showing the similarity. In tracing the origin of Pietism to Anabaptism he felt it necessary to trace the origin of Anabaptism, which he did by tracing its roots back to medieval Catholicism, particularly the Franciscan tertiaries or spirituals.

Ritschl first set up his theory of the origin of Anabaptism in an article in *Zeitschrift für Kirchengeschichte* II (1878) 1-55, entitled "Prolegomena zu einer Geschichte der Pietismus." Here he asserted a direct connection with Franciscan tertiary congregations. When Ritschl published his *Geschichte des Pietismus in der reformierten Kirche* (Bonn, 1880) he modified his theory (p. 70) to say that since he had found no documentary proof of direct connection he claimed only a general derivation of Anabaptist ideas from Franciscan tertiary ideas.

More important than the matter of the specific origin of Anabaptism is Ritschl's attempted characterization of Anabaptism as in effect a revival and continuance of medieval Franciscan tertiary ideology in contrast to the Lutheran and Zwinglian Reformation, which succeeded in overcoming medieval Catholicism altogether and operated with a radically different concept of church reform. According to Ritschl, Lutheranism (and Zwinglianism) was the exact opposite of Anabaptism on this point. (Calvinism, he thought, had certain Anabaptist-Franciscan elements.) Here Ritschl departed from his mentor Goebel's favorable evaluation of both Pietism and Anabaptism. Contrary to Goebel's view that "Anabaptism was the more thorough, decisive, and complete Reformation, a child of Luther's and Zwingli's Reformation, which was surrendered by Luther in 1522 and by Zwingli in 1524," Ritschl insists that Luther had an entirely different concept of the reform of the church, and never intended what the Anabaptists wanted. He sought to reform doctrine and worship and the clergy, working only indirectly for a reform of life and raising of moral standards, while the Anabaptists like the Franciscans sought basically a reform of life based upon a restoration of a New Testament apostolic moral and social order and institutions on a legalistic monastic-ascetic basis, which meant withdrawal from ordinary occupational and state life, "a flight from the world." Luther by contrast emphasized justification by faith, freedom from legalism, and participation in occupational and state life—no withdrawal. The Anabaptists wanted to establish a pure church by discipline, while Luther wanted to improve the general morals and behavior of the people through the general

moral education of the people by the state. So, says Ritschl, one cannot rate Anabaptism as a better Reformation unless one prefers (1) social withdrawal and rejection of the state, (2) communism of goods and regulation of costume, (3) prohibition of cheerfulness and merriment, (4) imagined sinlessness which leads to antinomianism.

Ritschl admits that both Luther and the Anabaptists claimed to base their principles on Scripture, hence the decision between the two in Reformation times could not be made by using Scripture, but only by force, which meant the physical suppression of Anabaptism.

For Ritschl Anabaptism was basically a revival of the monastic-ascetic legalistic ideal of holiness as the Christian way of life which was taught and practiced by the Franciscan tertiaries for 300 years before the Reformation. Both movements treat the New Testament as a code of law. He insists that Anabaptist teaching and regulations can be shown to reproduce precisely the Rule of the Tertiaries (in part). The tertiaries had prohibition of worldly amusements, regulation of costume, restrictions on the oath and the bearing of arms. The Anabaptists, it is true, made the latter two points absolute, but Melchior Hofmann fell back precisely to the tertiary position of restriction on the oath and arms, rather than absolute prohibition.

Ritschl adduces two secondary aspects of Anabaptism, mysticism and chiliasm, and claims that these were also drawn from Franciscan backgrounds. He goes so far as to claim that "all Anabaptists taught the return of Christ and the establishment of His earthly millennial kingdom."

Having surrendered his theory of the direct derivation of Anabaptism from tertiary congregations, Ritschl is at some pains to show the route by which Anabaptists got tertiary ideas. He concedes that the Anabaptists had been direct adherents of Luther (*q.v.*) and Zwingli (*q.v.*) in the early years of the Reformation, but says this does not at all mean that they got their ideas from Luther and then carried them on to more complete and logical expressions. He propounds the following theory. All Anabaptists, even their educated leaders, came from the lower artisan classes of the cities. Since it was precisely in these classes that the Franciscans had preached and worked with success, these classes thought of reform in the medieval Franciscan sense of moral reform—of an application of monkish-ascetic holiness to the common people. They held their ideal under the title of "preaching the Gospel" and believed it was based upon the New Testament Scriptures. When Luther came he professed to (1) preach the Gospel, (2) base his work solely on Scripture, and (3) reform the church. Hence the city masses thought he was going to carry out their previously held ideals of reform and rushed to follow him. When they discovered that he was not at all going to do this, they forsook him and his Reformation. At this point the Anabaptist movement came along and the disappointed masses followed them.

What better sources does Ritschl have to support this thesis than he had for his earlier thesis of direct connection, for which he confesses he had no documentary sources? He offers no proof for his claim that all Anabaptists came from the artisan classes of the cities nor even for the claim that these classes were shot through with tertiary ideas. His chief cited source for Anabaptist principles is Heinrich Bullinger's (*q.v.*) *Der Wiedertäufer Ursprung* (Zürich, 1560), which he unquestioningly accepts. He has one footnote reference to Cornelius' (*q.v.*) *Geschichte des Münsterischen Aufruhrs* II (1859), and Erbkam's *Geschichte der Protestantischen Sekten im Zeitalter der Reformation* (Hamburg, 1847), both of which he lightly puts aside.

Goebel's book, of course, he was familiar with. Ludwig Keller's basic works on Anabaptism had not yet appeared (Ritschl's preface is signed Jan. 20, 1880). Ritschl gives no evidence of any thorough study of Anabaptism. His method is, in fact, basically that of comparative theology. He draws conclusions about genetic relationships from similarities in ideologies. This method has some value, but at most it can only classify ideas without proving any genetic relationships. Ritschl cites no Anabaptist literary sources or archival records. He names in passing a few Anabaptist leaders, Conrad Grebel (probably based on Cornelius), Hans Denk (*q.v.*), and Hans Hut (*q.v.*), and seemingly includes Carlstadt (*q.v.*) and Müntzer (*q.v.*) in the Anabaptist group. Where he got his erroneous assertion that Hans Hut's group "as the true Israel undertook to root out all Canaanites by force" is unknown. Nor does he prove his impossible claim that all Anabaptists were chiliasts. He does admit that most Anabaptists were peaceful and nonresistant (he had to in line with his thesis of Franciscan ideological origin) but cites Hut and the Münsterites as examples of the use of violence. His claim of antinomianism among the Anabaptists (where it is not merely a logical deduction) must have come from Bullinger.

One cannot escape the impression that Ritschl basically operates with two central ideas which are imposed upon his material *a priori* rather than derived from the evidence: (1) Luther's Reformation is preferable as a movement which transcended medieval Catholic monastic-ascetic, papal, and hierarchical Christianity of works by its proclamation of the Gospel of justification by faith, freedom from legalism, rejection of following the New Testament example in ethics and social institutions, and promotion of a Christianity which works toward the gradual improvement of moral and the social order through education. (2) All other types of reformation are basically the opposite of this in all points, in essence a continuation of the medieval Catholic idea of moral reform bearing an essentially legalistic monastic-ascetic character. This latter strain came to the fore in the mendicant orders, especially the Franciscans, and there particularly in the tertiaries or Spirituals. Since the Anabaptists, as conceived by Ritschl, bear this same character, they must have arisen out of this background.

The specific construction of Anabaptist origin and character advocated by Ritschl has had no substantial support by other historians. The idea that Anabaptism was monastic in essence, a monkish movement, was of course often charged in the Reformation period, by Luther and Melanchthon for instance, as well as by Bullinger and by superficial

observers since that time. This is a strange misunderstanding of the central Anabaptist motivation to be "earnest" Christians in full discipleship and to establish a church of this character kept pure by discipline. On the other hand, from the very beginning there have, of course, been individuals and even groups who went to extremes and became legalistic, both Anabaptists and Mennonites. That this has ever had any direct or even indirect relation to any historic aspect of Roman Catholic monasticism is most unlikely, and certainly has never been proved from acceptable documentary sources.

Heinrich van der Smissen, Mennonite pastor in Hamburg-Altona, Germany, reviewed Ritschl's book in 1882 in the *Mennonitische Blätter* XXIX, pp. 19-22, 28 f., 37 f., 45 f., 58 f., analyzing at length and refuting Ritschl's hypothesis. Karl Barth describes Ritschl's position as follows in his *Die protestantische Theologie im 19ten Jahrhundert* (Zollikon-Zürich, 1947) p. 598: "Christianity is world view and morality (*Weltanschauung und Sittlichkeit*), but in no sense an immediate relationship with God. Catholicism and Anabaptism of any sort are accordingly thereby eliminated (*erledigt*) in one stroke, since they claim to know of a Christianity and indeed a more perfect Christianity in the moral sphere than the conscious and actuated sonship of God."   H.S.B.

Otto Ritschl, *Albrecht Ritschls Leben* 2v. (Tübingen, 1892, 1896); *ML* III, 460.

Rittenhouse (Rittinghuysen, Rittinghausen, Ruddinghuysen, Rittershausen), a Lower Rhine Mennonite family name dating back at least to 1591. There is no trace of the Rittenhouse family among the European Mennonites after William Rittenhouse came to Pennsylvania in 1688. Willem (William) Rittinghausen (1644-1708) was born in the Rhineland near Mühlheim, Germany, and was living in Amsterdam before he emigrated to America in 1688. He became the first Mennonite minister in America and builder of the first paper mill at Philadelphia in 1690. The American Mennonite Rittenhouses all descend from him.

Most of the American Rittenhouses have remained in the place where they first settled (near Philadelphia in Montgomery, Bucks, and Berks counties), but some of them went to Canada with the Bucks County migration of 1799-1800. A few families moved to Wayne County, Ohio, and one can still find a few Rittenhouses scattered in Indiana and Michigan, and even a few in Alberta. A considerable number of the descendants of the original family have joined other faiths. Some notable members of the family besides the pioneer William Rittenhouse have been Matthias Rittenhouse (1770-1832), a minister in the Skippack (Pa.) Mennonite (MC) congregation of the Franconia Conference, and Nicholas (Claes) Rittenhouse (1666-1734), son of William, one of the subscribers to the Dordrecht Confession of Faith (*q.v.*) at the 1725 conference. There is one Mennonite minister today bearing the name Rittenhouse, Jacob Z. Rittenhouse, pastor of the Lansdale (MC) congregation in the Franconia Conference. The most famous person bearing the family name was David Rittenhouse (1732-96), the Philadelphia astronomer and scientist and the first director of the United States mint, who was a son of Matthias of the third generation in America. He was not a member of the Mennonite Church.

J.R.C.

D. K. Cassel, *A Genea-Biographical History of the Rittenhouse Family* (Philadelphia, 1893-97, 6 vv.); Samuel W. Pennypacker, *Historical and Biographical Sketches* (Philadelphia, 1883) 59-88; Edward Ford, *David Rittenhouse. Astronomer-Patriot 1732-1796* (Philadelphia, 1946).

Rittenhouse, William (1644-1708). To this man goes the distinction of being the first Mennonite preacher in North America. He was born at Broich in Westphalia, Germany. In 1678 he became a citizen of Amsterdam, signing as Willem Ruddinghysen of Muelheim, papermaker. Ten years later (1688) he was in Germantown, Pa., and in 1690 joined in building the first paper mill in the American colonies, located on a branch of the Wissahickon Creek in what is now Fairmount Park, Philadelphia. This paper mill was in the Rittenhouse family for over a century. It was probably in 1690 that Rittenhouse was chosen as the first preacher of the Germantown (*q.v.*) Mennonite congregation, a group of Lower Rhine (chiefly Crefeld) immigrants, which had been without a leader from its beginning in 1683-85. For many years no baptismal or communion services were held because Rittenhouse was not a bishop and did not therefore feel free to proceed in such bishop work. The Germantown Mennonites wrote to the ministers at Altona, Germany, in 1702 asking that a bishop come to America and ordain a bishop for them, so that baptism and communion could be performed. The Altona ministers replied that the trip to America was too great to undertake, and advised the Germantown ministers to proceed with the administration of the ordinances. Rittenhouse was not convinced. In 1706 he wrote to the Amsterdam Mennonites and got the same advice. He eventually felt sufficiently persuaded of the soundness of this advice to proceed, but became ill and died on Feb. 18, 1708, before he was able to perform the services. It was probably D. K. Cassel who started the fiction that Rittenhouse was bishop. The man who actually carried out the instruction of the Altona preachers was Jacob Gottschalk (*q.v.; c*1666-1763), who had been ordained as assistant preacher to Rittenhouse in 1702.

One other bit of information is known about Rittenhouse. He made an effort to have the Dordrecht Confession of Faith (*q.v.*) translated into English, but the price asked was so high that the project was abandoned. Jacob Gottschalk then took up the matter with the Amsterdam Mennonites, who successfully accomplished the task in 1712 (reprinted in Philadelphia, 1727).

William Rittenhouse had some distinguished descendants. His son Nicholas Rittenhouse (1666-1734) served as a Mennonite preacher at Germantown. Nicholas had a son Henry, who located in what is now Montgomery County and who granted the land for the Worcester meetinghouse to the "Mennonist Society" in 1739. J. C. Clemens, minister in the Plains Mennonite Church and long-time secretary of the Franconia Conference, is a direct descendant. Henry Rittenhouse had a brother Mathias who became the father of the famous mathematician, scientist, and astronomer, David Rittenhouse (1732-96), thus a great-grandson of William the preacher. David built orreries for Princeton University and for the University of Pennsylvania. He also built an observatory and a transit telescope. In 1776 he was a member of the Pennsylvania Assembly. He served as treasurer of Pennsylvania 1777-89, and as the first director of the United States mint 1792-95. He was president of the American Philosophical Society 1791-96, succeeding Benjamin Franklin.

J.C.W.

G. Allen, "Rittenhouse Paper Mill and Its Founder," *MQR* XVI (1942) 108-28; H. S. Bender, "William Rittenhouse, 1644-1708: First Mennonite Minister in America," *MQR* VIII (1934) 58-61; C. I. Kephart, "William Rittenhouse, First Mennonite Bishop in America," *MQR* XVIII (1944) 49-55; H. S. Bender, "Was William Rittenhouse the First Mennonite Bishop in America?" *MQR* XVIII (1944) 42-47; *idem*, ". . . A Reply to Dr. Kephart," *MQR* XVIII (1944) 55-58; S. W. Pennypacker, *Historical and Biographical Sketches* (Phila., 1883) 59-88; Edward Ford, *David Rittenhouse, Astronomer-Patriot 1732-1796* (Phila., 1946).

Ritter, Georg, a well-to-do grocer of Bern, Switzerland, who played an important part in the emigration of Swiss Mennonites. He and a certain Louis Michelle, who traveled in the Pequea region of Pennsylvania in 1704-5, organized a land company whose holdings were to be settled by Swiss Mennonites. This project did not materialize, although in 1710 Swiss Mennonites did establish the Lancaster Mennonite settlement. In 1712 Ritter, in co-operation with the Bernese magistrates, undertook to conduct to the English colony of Carolina in America a transport of some 56 Mennonite prisoners at Bern, and a few poor Bernese residents. He was promised 45 Thalers for each Mennonite whom he safely delivered across the ocean, to be taken from their confiscated property, and for the poor a lump sum of 500 Thalers. But the plan miscarried because the prisoners were released by the Dutch officials when their ship arrived at Nijmegen. In the next year, through the intervention of the Dutch government (see **Runckel**), a number of Swiss Mennonites were permitted to leave the country to settle in the Netherlands; then Ritter was the leader of the transport of five boats which sailed from Basel on July 16, 1711, arriving at Amsterdam on August 3. For his care and pains Ritter received a gift of 200 Rix-thalers.

vDZ.

Inv. Arch. Amst. I, Nos. 1321, 1326, 1339, 1349, 1763; Müller, *Berner Täufer,* 258-302, 319 f.; *ML* III, 524.

Rittinghausen: see Rittenhouse.

Rittman, a town (pop. 3,810) in Wayne County, Ohio, near which are located the Crown Hill (*q.v.*) Mennonite Church, with 139 members in 1956, and a Mennonite Home for the Aged, which was established in 1901 as a foundation by D. C. Amstutz. The building burned down in 1919, but was rebuilt in 1939. In 1911 there was also a "Swiss" congregation with 50 members, and a Christian Apostolic Church with 40 members.

E.C.

"A Home for Old People at Rittman, Ohio," *Menn. Community* V (July 1951) No. 7, pp. 7-9; *ML* III, 524.

Rivageois, the inhabitants of Jemeppe and other villages of the Meuse River, south of Liége, Belgium, who in 1531 rebelled against the government of the Catholic bishop of Liége. This revolt is often said to have been a result of the rise of Anabaptism in this area, but there is no indication of Anabaptist origin. The rebellion of the Rivageois was merely an economic protest.   vDZ.

J. Meyhoffer, *Le Martyrologe Protestant* (n.p.-Brussels, 1907) 149; W. Bax, *Het Protestantisme . . . in het Bisdom Luik* I (The Hague, 1937) 10 f.

River Brethren, a popular name long used for the denomination known since 1862 officially as the Brethren in Christ (*q.v.*). The name is supposedly due to the fact that the group had its beginnings (*c*1770) in an area of western Lancaster County, Pa., near the Susquehanna River.   H.S.B.

River Corner Mennonite Church (MC), located 2 miles south of Conestoga Center in southern Lancaster County, Pa. Benedict Eshleman deeded one acre of land for a cemetery and meetinghouse upon which a meetinghouse was built about 1774. It was named Miller's after Martin Miller, who obtained the first deed in 1794. A stone building in 1828 replaced this, and another beautiful stone church of colonial design was built in 1882, which was enlarged in 1947. The congregation is a part of the Byerland-New Danville circuit. The membership in 1958 was 73 with David N. Thomas as bishop and Mylin Shenk minister. A large, old well-kept cemetery adjoins the church.   I.D.L.

Riverdale Amish Mennonite Church, located at Millbank, Perth Co., Ont., began as a mission in a former Presbyterian church, purchased in 1946 by the Mission Board of the Ontario Amish Mennonite Conference. A number of Mennonite families from surrounding congregations began to worship in the church. Menno Zehr and Valentine Nafziger were superintendents of the mission. Preaching services were supplied by neighboring congregations. In January 1948 Menno Zehr was ordained minister, and in June 1948 a congregation was organized with about 60 charter members, which bought the meetinghouse from the mission board. In early 1956 the bishop, Valentine Nafziger, withdrew with 23 members to form a strictly conservative church called Bethel. In 1958 the Riverdale congregation had 120 members, with Menno Zehr as minister.
                                                O.G., V.N.

Riverside Conservative Mennonite Church, Au Gres, Arenac Co., Mich., until 1945 called the Augress River Church, had a membership of 93 in 1957, with Levi Swartz and Elmer Jantzi as ministers. The church was first listed in the 1919 *Mennonite Year-Book and Directory*, with 17 members.   M.G.

Riverside Evangelical United Brethren Church, located 3 miles north of Fulks Run, Va., is used once a month by the Mennonites (MC) as a rural mission in behalf of the seven members who live in the community. The Mennonite appointment is in the care of L. P. Showalter, Broadway, Va.   T.S.

Riverside Hutterite Bruderhof of the Dariusleut (*q.v.*) group, located at Glenwood, Alberta, was founded in 1939 by Preacher Lorenz Tschetter (d. 1957), who was chosen preacher in the Stand-Off (*q.v.*) colony in 1933 and confirmed there in 1938. He was succeeded as leader of the Bruderhof by his brother Peter A. Tschetter who was chosen to the ministry here in 1944 and confirmed in 1948. In 1958 the number of souls in the Bruderhof was 104, the number of baptized members 47. Plans are under way for 50 persons of the Riverside Bruderhof to establish a new Bruderhof at Estuary, Sask., in the summer of 1958.   D.D., P.A.T.

Riverside Hutterite Bruderhof, known as the Riverside Hutterian Mutual Corporation, located one and one-half miles south of Arden, Man., was founded in 1933 by a group from the Iberville Bruderhof, led by the preacher Paul Gross, who died in 1943. He was succeeded by John R. Hofer, who left with a group of families to found the Bloomfield Bruderhof at Westbourne, Man. The present minister is John J. Hofer, chosen in 1949 and confirmed in 1957. The population in 1958 was 82, with 26 baptized members.   D.D., J.J.H.

Riverside Mennonite Church (MC), Welland Co., Ont.: see **Black Creek.**

Riverside Mennonite (MC) Mission Church, near Harman, Randolph Co., W. Va., under the Virginia Conference. The work was begun near 1900, and services were held in Dry Fork, Bonner Mountain, and Pennington schoolhouses previous to the building of the Riverside church in 1932. The 1957 membership was 70, with Menno J. Brunk as minister.
                                                O.M.K.

Riverstix Church of God in Christ Mennonite Church, now extinct, located at Riverstix, Medina Co., Ohio, was organized in 1871 with 6 members; services were held in homes. Later the membership increased to 18 and services were held in schools, one of which was later purchased for a church building. Henry Leatherman, who was ordained in 1879, and Sam Leatherman, were their first ministers. Later C. G. Buerge served as pastor for many years. The congregation dissolved by members moving away. It ceased to exist about 1943.   P.G.H.

Riverview Conservative Mennonite Church, located at White Pigeon, Mich., on Highway 103 near the Indiana-Michigan line, had a membership of 184 in 1957; Orie Kauffman was the bishop and Noah Zehr and Jonas D. Miller the ministers. The church was first listed in the 1953 *Mennonite Yearbook.* In 1952 it was formed of former members of the Townline and Griner Conservative Mennonite congregations.   M.G.

Rixtel, van, a Dutch Mennonite family name, probably of Flemish origin, found at Rotterdam, Haarlem, Amsterdam, and a few other towns in the 16th-18th centuries. Pieter van Rixtel, a Mennonite, lived in Elbing (*q.v.*), West Prussia, Germany, until 1709. Another Pieter van Rixtel (1644-73), of Haarlem, was a poet of mediocre gifts. He often stayed at the inn of Jan Zoet (*q.v.*) near Amsterdam, called "Parnassus aan het Y," a poets' center, where van Rixtel met with Karel Verloove (*q.v.*) and other Collegiant-Mennonite makers of verse.   vdZ.

N.N.B.Wb. II, 1216; *Inv. Arch. Amst.* I, No. 1569; G. Kalff, *Geschiedenis der Nederlandsche Letterkunde* IV (Groningen, 1910) 462 f., 467, 475; K. O. Meinsma, *Spinoza en zijn Kring* (The Hague, 1896) 135, 141, 145.

Rizzetto, Antonio (d. 1565), a Hutterite martyr, was baptized around 1551 in his house in Vicenza, Italy, by the anti-Trinitarian Anabaptist minister Marcantonio of Asolo, an associate of Pietro Manelfi (*q.v.*). Late in 1551, following the exposure of the north Italian evangelical movement by Manelfi, the Inquisition began to arrest members of the sect, forcing Rizzetto to flee. He sought refuge in Thessalonica, accompanied by Bartolomeo of Padua and the latter's wife and daughter. Upon Bartolomeo's death Rizzetto married the widow. After living some time in Thessalonica, Rizzetto returned alone to Italy, perhaps prompted by a letter from Francesco della Sega (*q.v.*). In 1561 he visited the Hutterites in Moravia in the company of Bartolomeo of Ferrara, Lucrezia of Vicenza, and one of his daughters by an earlier marriage. He was accepted as a member of a community there, so must have renounced his anti-Trinitarian beliefs, if he in fact ever held them. He went to Moravia, says Rizzetto, "because I had learned that there were there good people who lived saintly lives; and seeing their lives and actions, I was pleased, and thus I determined to remain there and I stayed and I left my daughter there." He now made arrangements to have his wife, Caterina, and his stepdaughter, Paola, join him. To effect this he went to Venice in 1562 with della Sega and paid a merchant twenty-five ducats to bring his family from Thessalonica. (Paola died in Thessalonica; Caterina was attempting to return to Italy in 1563.) Rizzetto himself was about to go back to Moravia with several other persons when a financial dispute led a member of the party to betray them to the authorities at Capodistria, and Rizzetto, della Sega, Nicola Buccella, and Rizzetto's young son were arrested (Aug. 27, 1562). Interrogations followed, at Capodistria and then at Venice, and in the course of these Rizzetto supplied not only the information given above but also some descriptions of the doctrines and ceremonies of the Hutterites. All efforts of the Inquisitors to bring him to recant failed, despite arguments, prolonged confinement, and the pleas of his son. On Feb. 8, 1565, together with della Sega, he was sentenced, as an impenitent Anabaptist heretic, to be drowned. When the executioner told him della Sega was considering an abjuration, Rizzetto, much disturbed, replied, "Unhappy soul! But if he has lost his soul, I do not want to lose mine: What I have said, I have said." Exhorted further, he answered simply, "Do your deed." Thus he died not knowing for sure whether della Sega had recanted.

The execution was a tragic and moving scene. As the boats carrying the party moved under cover of darkness toward the sea, a priest urged Rizzetto to kiss the Crucifix, but he refused and warned those with him to come to Christ that they might escape eternal damnation. When the boats stopped, a plank was extended between them, and the executioner passed around Rizzetto's waist a chain attached to a heavy stone. Turning his face to the heavens Rizzetto cried, "Father, forgive them, for they know not what they do." Then, saying, "O God, into Thy hands I remit my spirit," he rolled off the plank into the sea.   DeWind.

Beck, *Geschichts-Bücher*, 243; V. Bellondi, *I battisti, pagine della Inquisizione veneta* (Rome, 1881); K. Benrath, "Wiedertäufer im Venetianischen um die Mitte des 16. Jahrhunderts," *Theologische Studien und Kritiken* LVIII (1885) 9-67; E. Comba, *I nostri protestanti* (Firenze, 1897) II, 589-602; H. A. DeWind, "Anabaptists in Thessalonica?" *MQR* XXIX (1955) 70-75; idem, "Italian Hutterite Martyrs," *MQR* XXVIII (1954) 163-85; *ML* III, 524 f.

Roanoke Mennonite Church (MC), located 2 miles west and 2 miles south of Roanoke, Woodford County, Ill., is a member of the Illinois Conference. Settlers from Ohio, Alsace-Lorraine, and Germany settled in the vicinity in 1829, including David Schertz, the first minister. In 1875 the first frame church was erected and dedicated. This was replaced by a brick church in 1920 with a seating capacity of 185, which was enlarged in 1957 to accommodate 325. The majority of the members are farmers, active and retired. The outstanding early bishop was John Smith (1843-1906), ordained preacher 1887, bishop about 1890. Ezra Yordy, of Eureka, was ordained bishop on Sept. 25, 1925, and served until 1957. The membership in 1958 was 316. John L. Harnish, ordained minister on Dec. 24, 1922, served until 1952. Wesley Jantz became pastor in 1957.   J.D.H.

Roaring Run Mennonite Church (MC) belonging to the Virginia Conference, located 3 miles north of Onego, W. Va., was established in 1870. In the early 1920's it had a membership of 27 but in 1957 it had only 10.   M.G.

Roaring Spring Mennonite Church (GCM), located in Roaring Spring, Blair Co., Pa., had a membership of 24 in 1957; its minister was Kenneth H. Ross. Its first meetinghouse was built in 1898. Among its early ministers was Abram Snyder, who was listed with the congregation in the Southwestern Pennsylvania Conference (MC) as late as the 1908 *Mennonite Year-Book.* The next issue of the Year-Book (1913) no longer carried the church as a member of this conference district, but it was not until the conference of 1920 that it was listed with the General Conference Mennonite congregations in the Eastern District Conference.   M.G.

Robbertsz, Robbert (Le Canu), b. 1563 at Amersfoort, d. after 1627 at Hoorn, Holland, was a teacher of navigation and the instructor of noted Dutch explorers, e.g., Jacob van Heemskerck at Amsterdam from about 1586, and at Hoorn from 1610. At the close of his life he was living at Hoorn, earning his living by selling brandy.

Robbertsz was at first a member of the Frisian Mennonite congregation of Amsterdam. In 1589, when a schism arose in this congregation, dividing it into conservative Old Frisians and moderate Young Frisians, Robbertsz took the side of Lubbert

Gerritsz (*q.v.*), the leader of the Young (or Mild) Frisians; but soon after, probably by 1590, Robbertsz was banned even from this moderate group for his advanced ideas. Robbertsz defended himself in *Verantwoordinghe oft ontschulddinghe* (1592). With a few others he then founded the Robbert Robbertsz congregation, which had some adherents also in other Dutch towns (called Robbert-Robbertsvolk). To this group also belonged Tymen Claesz Honich (*q.v.*), who dedicated his hymnal *Schriftuerlijck Lied-Boecxken* (n.p., n.d.) to Robbertsz. It could not be ascertained how long this congregation existed, but it is fairly certain that it dissolved in a few years. Robbertsz himself seems to have left the Mennonites. In later years he called himself a "Neutralist," saying, "The church of Christ is a majestic cathedral with many doors, all leading to the center," with this metaphor expressing his idea that one church is as good as another. He is said to have had his children baptized in different Protestant churches.

Robbertsz wrote a number of pamphlets, some of which pertain to the Mennonites: in 1591-92 against Lubbert Gerritsz, in 1596 against Jacob Jansz Kist (i.e., Jacob Schedemaker, *q.v.*). In 1627 he published a booklet, *Disputatie tusschen twie Huyslieden*, which defended Jan Theunisz (*q.v.*) and attacked the preachers of the Amsterdam Waterlander congregation. He also attacked Reformed leaders such as Herman Moded (*q.v.*). A reprint of some of his pamphlets and poems was published at Makkum in 1646.   vdZ.

N.N.B.Wb. I, 561-65; C. P. Burger, *De Amsterdamsche boekdrukkers en uitgevers* III; *Amstelodamum* Yearbook XXV (Amsterdam, 1928) 98, note 2, 104 f., 120, No. 54; Blaupot t. C., *Holland* I, 259; II, 210; K. O. Meinsma, *Spinoza en zijn Kring* (The Hague, 1896) 14-24; *Catalogus Amst.*, 193, 197, 212; *DB* 1897, 103, note; *ML* III, 525.

Robson, Isaac (1801-85), an English Quaker (*q.v.*), was delegated with Thomas Harvey (1812-84) to visit the Mennonites living in South Russia in 1867. They first made contact with the Mennonites of South Germany living in the area of Neuburg (*q.v.*), Bavaria; the Oesch family and a Jakob Hege are named in their report. In Berdyansk they established long-lasting connections with Cornelius Jansen (*q.v.*), who was then the Prussian consul. Guided by him, they went on to the Molotschna (*q.v.*), visiting Gnadenfeld, Halbstadt, Felsenthal, Neukirch, Orloff, Rudnerweide, Steinbach, and Tiegenhagen, namely, those congregations that in comparison with Petershagen and Pordenau (*q.v.*) were considered more progressive. At the beginning of 1868 Robson sent an open letter to the South Russian Mennonites, more specifically to Jansen, urging them to spread the Gospel in their vicinity. The publication of this letter was stopped by Russian censorship. The connections with Cornelius Jansen, however, remained. The original with Cornelius Jansen's German translation is preserved in the Cornelius Jansen Collection in BeCL. The English Quakers gave the Mennonites emigrating to America generous financial support. On Feb. 8, 1879, they sent a letter to the immigrant Mennonites in America, which was printed in that year at Elkhart, Ind. (Copy GCL.)   E.C.

Bender, *Two Centuries*, 45; Owen Gingerich, "The Relations Between the Russian Mennonites and the Friends During the 19th Century," *MQR* XXV (1951) 285-94; G. E. Reimer and G. R. Gaeddert, *Exiled by the Czar, Cornelius Jansen and the Great Mennonite Migration 1874* (Newton, 1956) 33-37, 102-6; *ML* III, 33-37.

Rock Lake Hutterite Bruderhof, of the Schmiedeleut (*q.v.*) branch, located one mile west of Grossisle, Man., was founded in 1947 by Michael Gross, preacher of the Iberville (*q.v.*) Bruderhof, and nine families with 70 persons including 25 baptized members. By 1958 the population of Rock Lake was 124, with 36 baptized members.   D.D.

Rock Mennonite Church (MC), located in Berks Co., ½ mile northwest of Elverson, Pa., was begun in 1920, when the few remaining members of the Rock Baptist Church asked the Conestoga A.M. congregation to start Sunday school in this meetinghouse, built in 1845. In 1936 a congregation was organized by Bishop J. S. Mast, which is affiliated with the Ohio and Eastern Mennonite Conference. The meetinghouse was enlarged in 1937 and 1956. A number of former members are serving the church in other communities. The membership in 1957 was 66, with Ira A. Kurtz as bishop, and Christian J. Kurtz and Harry Hertzler as ministers.   C.J.K.

Rock of Ages Church of God in Christ Mennonite Church is located at Maysville, Ohio. The 1957 membership was 22; the minister in charge was Paul Swartley. Most of its members were formerly Amish.   M.G.

Rockhill Mennonite Church (MC), near Telford, Montgomery and Bucks counties, Pa., a member of the Franconia Conference, formerly called Bechtel's, then Gehman's (the name Rockhill only since about 1910), was organized between 1744 and 1764. The first meetinghouse was erected between 1737 and 1773. In 1838 the second meetinghouse was erected, and in 1925 the third. Early preachers were Isaac Kolb 1744-76, Samuel Bechtel 1764-1802, Abraham Gehman 1770-92, and Samuel Gehman 1799-1845. The first deacon was Michael Derstine (d. 1777). A small faction left in 1848 to join the new Oberholtzer (GCM) group. In 1957 the congregation had 221 members, with Arthur D. Ruth as bishop, and Edwin A. Souder, Clinton D. Landis, and Alfred A. Detweiler as preachers.   H.S.B.

Rockingham County, Virginia (pop. 45,889, area 869 sq. mi.), is beautifully located in the Shenandoah Valley on the far western side of the state, between the Blue Ridge Mountains on the east and the Appalachian Mountains on the west, bounded by Augusta County on the south, and Shenandoah and Page counties on the north. The chief towns are Harrisonburg, the county seat (seat of Eastern Mennonite College and Madison State Teachers College), Timberville, Broadway, Edom, Mt. Clinton, Keezletown, Elkton, Dayton, Mt. Crawford, and Bridgewater (seat of Bridgewater College of the Church of the Brethren). It was formed in 1777 out of Augusta County. The area had an early settlement of the German element from Eastern Pennsylvania and still has many people of German descent. Mennonites,

MENNONITE CHURCHES IN **ROCKINGHAM COUNTY, VIRGINIA**

● Home Base Congregation
▲ Mission Point Developed Into Established Congregation
▲ Mission Church
★ Sunday School and Preaching Held in Schoolhouse
✸ Old Order (Wisler) Mennonite
○ Towns

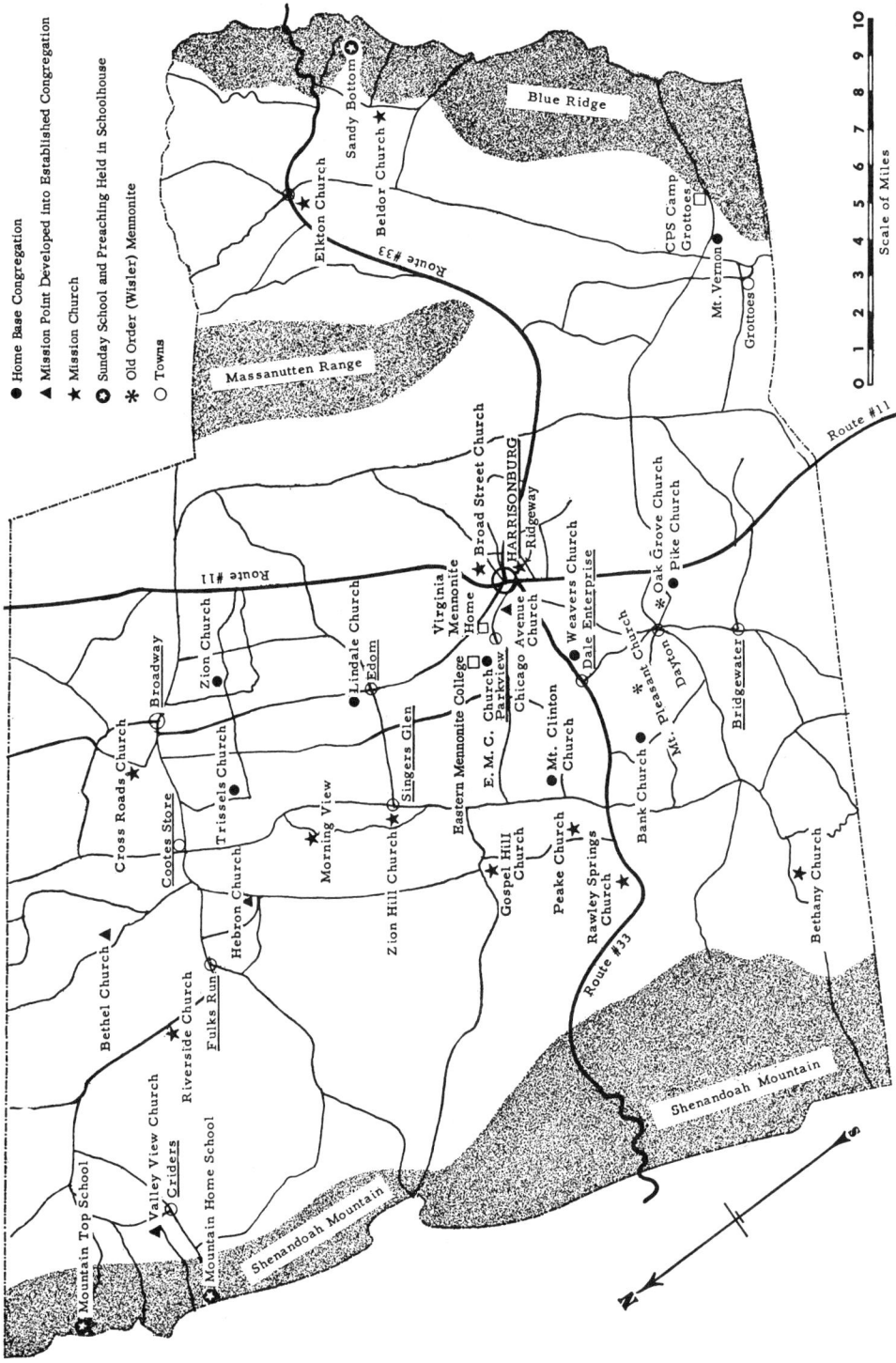

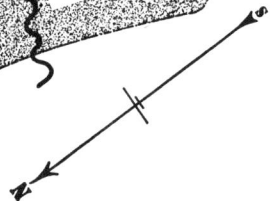

Scale of Miles
0 1 2 3 4 5 6 7 8 9 10

Blue Ridge

Massanutten Range

Sandy Bottom

Beldor Church

Elkton Church

Route #33

CPS Camp
Grottoes

Mt. Vernon

Grottoes

Route #11

Broad Street Church

HARRISONBURG

Ridgeway

Virginia
Mennonite
Home

E. M. C. Church
Parkview

Eastern Mennonite College

Chicago Avenue
Church

Weavers Church

Dale Enterprise

Oak Grove Church

Pike Church

Mt. Pleasant Church

Dayton

Bridgewater

Mt. Clinton
Church

Bank Church

Bethany Church

Broadway

Zion Church

Lindale Church

Edom

Singers Glen

Cross Roads Church

Cootes Store

Trissels Church

Morning View

Zion Hill Church

Gospel Hill
Church

Peake Church

Rawley Springs
Church

Route #33

Hebron Church

Route #11

Bethel Church

Riverside Church

Fulks Run

Valley View Church

Criders

Mountain Home School

Mountain Top School

Shenandoah Mountain

Shenandoah Mountain

N
S

and the Church of the Brethren coming a little later, have always formed a substantial part of the population.

Rockingham County is the location of the oldest permanent settlement and largest part of the Mennonites in Virginia. Eighty per cent of the membership in the base congregations in the Shenandoah Valley are in this county, and 20 per cent in Augusta County. Fifty-two per cent of the total conference membership lives in Rockingham County. The first Mennonite settlers were probably Daniel Stover and John Shenk who came in 1773, and Henry Funk from Montgomery County, Pa., who came in 1780. The Mennonites came largely from the Pennsylvania counties of Montgomery, Lancaster, and York. The oldest present congregations date from 1820-30, Trissels near Broadway (1822), and Pike (1825) and Weaver (1827), both near Harrisonburg, but there is reason to believe that there was an organized congregation at least as early as 1790 in this area. In 1957 there were 15 congregations in the county with a membership of 1,832, and 12 rural mission churches with 613 members and two city missions, one for Negroes and one for whites, with a combined total of 25 members, a total of 2,470. The above churches are responsible for 27 meeting places outside the county. All these are organized into two bishop districts, established about 1840, called the Middle and Northern districts. This is the heart of the Virginia Mennonite Conference. Here are located Eastern Mennonite College (since 1917) and the Virginia Mennonite Home for old people (since 1954). Singers Glen on the west side of the county was the location of the Joseph Funk Mennonite press c1847-62. An Old Order Mennonite schism formed in 1900 has two congregations in the county with 300 members. The Church of the Brethren has 20 congregations in the county with about 5,000 members. H.S.B.

Noah D. Showalter, *Atlas of Rockingham County, Virginia* (Harrisonburg, 1939; J. W. Wayland, *A History of Rockingham County, Virginia* (Dayton, Va., 1912); idem, *Virginia Valley Records: Genealogical and Historical Materials of Rockingham County, Virginia, and Related Regions* (Strasburg, Va., 1930); Harry M. Strickler, *Old Tenth Legion Marriages, Marriages in Rockingham County, Virginia, from 1778 to 1816* (Dayton, Va., 1928); J. Lewis Peyton, *History of Augusta County, Virginia* (Bridgewater, 1953); Samuel Kercheval, *A History of the Valley of Virginia*, 4th ed. (Strasburg, Va., 1925, first ed. 1833); H. A. Brunk, *History of the Mennonites of Virginia* (in preparation).

Rockport Hutterite Bruderhof, of the Schmiedeleut (*q.v.*) branch, 6 miles southwest of Alexandria, S.D. The site was settled first in 1891 by a Lehrerleut (*q.v.*) group from the Old Elm Spring (*q.v.*) Bruderhof with the preachers Jakob Wipf and Johann Kleinsasser. This group branched out in 1931 and founded the Hutterville (*q.v.*) Bruderhof near Magrath. In 1934 they sold Rockport and moved to Alberta, founding the O.K. Bruderhof near Raymond. The present occupants came from the Bon Homme (*q.v.*) Bruderhof with twelve families and Preacher Joseph Waldner. Daniel S. Wipf was chosen as minister here in 1934; later John J. Waldner was chosen, who is now in the Riverside Colony, Huron, S.D. In 1945 they branched out to found Rosedale (*q.v.*) in South Dakota, and in 1949 Huron, S.D. David Wipf was chosen as assistant

minister in 1954. The membership of Rockport was 32 in 1958, and the total population 123.
D.D., D.S.W.

Rockton Mennonite Church (MC), located in the northeastern part of Clearfield County, Pa., a member of the Allegheny Conference, had its beginning in 1839, when John Brubaker, the first minister and bishop in the new settlement, located here. Other names of early settlers were Lininger, LaBorde, Hummel, Brilhart, and Hollopeter. The first meetinghouse was built in 1860 and the Sunday school was established in 1864. Revival meetings in 1897 by A. D. Wenger strengthened the church by 23 new accessions. The membership in 1957 was 25, with Paul L. King as minister in charge. G.M.S.

Rockview Mennonite Church (MC), 235 Rockview Ave., Youngstown, Ohio, sponsored by the Ohio and Eastern Mennonite Mission Board, was established in 1947. It had 40 members in 1957, with Fred E. Augsburger as pastor. It is a Negro congregation. M.G.

Rockville Mennonite (MC) Mission, located at Honeybrook, Pa., was established in 1951. In 1957 Millard Shoup was the pastor, with a membership of 62. It belongs to the Ohio and Eastern Conference.
M.G.

Rockway Gospel Chapel (MC), East Minot, N.D., is a mission station locally sponsored. It was established in 1951 and had 12 members in 1957, with John H. Stoll as pastor. M.G.

Rockway Mennonite (MC) **School**, 142 Doon Road, Kitchener, Ont., is a secondary school offering the work of grades 9 to 12 inclusive, operated by a board appointed by the Ontario Conference. Finances are supplied from tuition and by gifts of churches and friends. The school opened in September 1945 in a dwelling on a fourteen-acre farm which had been purchased for the purpose, on the outskirts of Kitchener. The house is still the only dormitory available, housing about 15 per cent of the students. The school accommodations have been increased in three major steps. In the summer of 1946 a barn on the property was converted into a school with four rooms and dining facilities. In 1948 four classrooms were added to the remodeled barn, and in 1954 the first permanent building was erected, consisting of four classrooms and administration quarters. The enrollment has steadily increased to its present level of 167 for 1957-58. Harold D. Groh served as principal until 1956. There are now eight teachers on the staff, including the principal, Ross T. Bender, 1956- . The courses offered are those outlined by the Ontario Department of Education, which accredits the school and issues the diplomas to the graduates. In addition students are required to take a unit of Bible, and this is supplemented by a daily devotional period. H.D.G.

Rockwell Mennonite Church (MC), now extinct, located in Sheffield, Bureau Co., Ill., was organized in 1945 under the District Mission Board of the Illinois Conference. The first services, in 1943, were held in homes; later they were held in the Danish Lutheran Church in Sheffield. The 1948 member-

ship of 17 consisted largely of Mennonites who had moved there from other communities. Ministers who served the congregation were John S. Detwiler 1945-47 and John I. Byler 1948-?. It was last listed in the Yearbook of 1950, when it had 22 members.
E.I.C.

Rocky Mountain Mennonite Camp Association, Divide, Col., was organized in 1951. Since 1952 it has been conducting a summer camp in "the shadow of Pikes Peak," at an elevation of 9,660 feet. During the 1956 season it served more than 1,600 persons. The president is Harold Dyck, of Hesston, Kan., and the executive secretary Jess Kauffman, of Colorado Springs, Col.
M.G.

Rocky Ridge Mennonite Church (MC), located 2 miles southeast of Quakertown, Pa., began as a mission in 1931, with Linford D. Hackman as superintendent. It became a congregation of the Franconia Conference in 1949. The meetinghouse was built in 1948, services having previously been held in a private home. The membership in 1957 was 87; Ernest K. Moyer and Abram K. Landis were the ministers in charge.
E.K.M.

Roden, a town (1947 pop. 6,596, with 48 Mennonites) in the Dutch province of Drente. Mennonites living here in 1937 formed a Fellowship (*Kring*), which was at first served by the pastor of the Den Horn (*q.v.*) congregation. In 1950 the circle joined the Groningen congregation and was under the care of the pastor of this congregation, from 1951 under Miss C. E. Offerhaus. In 1954 the circle organized as an independent congregation and built a church, which was dedicated on March 6, 1955. The Roden congregation in 1958 numbered 42 baptized members. It has a ladies' circle and a Sunday school for children. Miss Offerhaus served until 1957; since 1958 C. de Groot has been pastor, serving also the recently established Haren congregation. (*DJ* 1956, 33-36.)
vDZ.

Rodenbach, a village near Grünstadt in the Palatinate, Germany, formerly belonging to the graviate Leiningen (*q.v.*), in the 17th and 18th centuries, perhaps also earlier, the residence of several Mennonite families. In 1685 the Mennonite lists of Karlsruhe name 10 or 11 persons. Toward the end of the 18th century only two Mennonite families were left (Jansson and Christophel). The cemetery, which was laid out by the Mennonites, was used by Mennonites of the vicinity, members of the Altleiningen congregation (*q.v.*), until the middle of the 19th century. The Mennonite *Adressbuch* of 1936 lists for Rodenbach only one Mennonite. Mennonites have occasionally also lived in two other villages named Rodenbach, both in the Palatinate—Rodenbach near Kaiserslautern and Rodenbach **near** Germersheim. (*ML* III, 526.)
G.H.

Rödern, a Mennonite congregation in Alsace: see **Niederrödern.**

Roderwolde, located near Roden (*q.v.*) in the Dutch province of Drente, is named in 1639 as the seat of a small Mennonite congregation which had its own preacher. Concerning the history of this congregation nothing is known, either before or after 1639. (*ML* I, 478b.)
vDZ.

Rodlofferhuben, a hamlet between Heubuden (*q.v.*) and Kalthof, near Marienburg (*q.v.*), West Prussia, Germany. Here the Mennonite congregations of Danzig (*q.v.*) and Heubuden established a Christian school in 1826 under the leadership of the teacher Friedrich Wilhelm Lange (*q.v.*) of Brenkenhoffswalde (*q.v.*). The Lutheran clergy of Marienburg charged Lange with Pietism and had the school closed in 1836. It was then moved to Bröskerfelde (*q.v.*), near Neuteich.
E.C.
Ernst Crous, "Vom Pietismus bei den altpreussischen Mennoniten . . . ," *Gesch.-Bl.*, 1954, 7-29; Ludwig Tiesmeyer, *Die Erweckungsbewegung in Deutschland* . . . (Kassel, 1910); *ML* III, 527.

Roelan(d)t Staey(a)ert was an Anabaptist martyr executed at Gent, Belgium, in 1569. Particulars about this martyr are lacking. Verheyden did not find his name in the official records. His name is commemorated in a hymn in the *Offer des Heeren* (edition of 1578), beginning "Alsmen schreef duyst vyfhondert jaer, ende twee en tsestich mede." Roelant is listed as No. 30 in this hymn. (*Offer*, 652; *Mart. Mir.* 407, E 759; Verheyden, *Gent*, 56.)
vDZ.

Roelantsz, Jan, a Dutch Mennonite, living at Haarlem about 1600, who was a partisan of Jacob Pietersz van der Meulen (*q.v.*) of the Flemish and who in 1605 negotiated with Hans de Ries and the Waterlanders to bring about a merger of the Haarlem Flemish congregation with the Waterlanders, which, however, failed. Roelantsz probably was a deacon of the Haarlem Flemish congregation. (*Inv. Arch. Amst.* I, Nos. 507, 510-14.)
vDZ.

Roelof Martens: see Adam Pastor.

Roelofs (Rulfs), **Berend,** was called from Sluys (Oudesluis) in De Zijp, Dutch province of North Holland (*q.v.*), to the Hamburg-Altona (*q.v.*) Mennonite congregation in 1650 to serve as pastor. But on Nov. 30, 1659, he resigned his pastorate. He "spoke against baptism, communion, and the office of preaching with contempt, so that great sorrow arose in the congregation and offense outside" (Roosen). With his entire family he united with the Quakers (see **Society of Friends**), who were propagandizing in Hamburg. When this group was expelled from Hamburg, on June 24, 1660, Roelofs and his family went to Alkmaar (*q.v.*), his native town. Here or in Oudesluis an ancestor of Roelofs' had at the turn of the century, influenced by a debate between the Reformed and the Mennonites, left the Reformed Church to unite with the Mennonites, giving up his position as sexton in the Reformed Church, because he considered the Mennonite views more Scriptural, and had become a Mennonite preacher.
E.C.
Blaupot t. C., *Holland* I, 194; *DB* 1909, 43; B. C. Roosen, *Geschichte der Mennoniten-Gemeinde zu Hamburg und Altona* I (Hamburg, 1886) 44 f.; Schijn-Maatschoen, *Geschiedenis* II, 649, 650; N. van der Zijpp, *Geschiedenis der Doopsgezinden in Nederland* (Arnhem, 1952) 138; *ML* III, 527.

Roelofs, Oeds, b. 1765 at Murmurwoude, d. Nov. 8, 1848, at Terhorne, both villages in the Dutch province of Friesland, served the Terhorne Mennonite congregation as pastor from 1791 until he retired in 1836. Roelofs had no special training for the ministry, nor did he receive a salary (perhaps, however, a small remuneration), but supported himself as a baker. Oeds Roelofs assumed the family name of Dantuma in 1810; a number of his descendants are still found in Friesland, many serving the church as deacons. Three uncles of Oeds Roelofs served as lay preachers of the Dantumawoude (*q.v.*) congregation about 1800. (*Naamlijst* 1792, 61; *DJ* 1837, 28.)

vdZ.

Roelofs, Rijkman, a member of the Rijkmans (*q.v.*) family, b. *c*1750, was baptized at Zuidveen, Dutch province of Overijssel, by a preacher of the (New) Flemish Mennonite congregation of Giethoorn (*q.v.*) Zuid; but this baptism was not recognized in the Old (Danzig) Flemish congregation of Zuidveen. Disagreements of this sort led to dissension and division in the congregation, and thus also to strife about the meetinghouse and possessions of the congregation. Whereas the conservative congregation, which was much the smaller of the two, died out early in the 19th century, the larger one persisted, and built a new church at near-by Steenwijk (*q.v.*) in 1848. In this congregation Rijkman was a leader. In 1774 he was one of two deacons chosen by the congregation. In 1796, when a new preacher had been chosen, Roelofs was asked to confirm him as elder. On this occasion Roelofs presented the preacher, Reinder Pieters Veen, with three questions: (1) whether he considered his choice by the congregation good and in accord with requirements; (2) whether in his preaching he was willing to remain on the foundation of the Old and New Testaments and Anabaptist principles; and (3) whether he was ready to serve the congregation with the signs of the covenant, i.e., baptism and communion. The preacher answered the questions affirmatively and promised, with the help of the Lord, to fulfill these requirements.

In 1802, when an assistant preacher was considered necessary, Roelofs again circulated a document inquiring whether the appointment of a new preacher was considered necessary and how much the members would be willing to contribute to his support. The questions were answered affirmatively and a relatively high sum was collected. When the next pulpit vacancy occurred Roelofs appealed to Professor Hesselink (*q.v.*), of the Amsterdam Mennonite Seminary, since they did not want an untrained preacher. In other instances as well, Roelofs took serious interest in the welfare of the congregation, finally as secretary of the church council. In 1806 he and his sister gave the congregation an organ, and in 1816 he enlarged the church building at his own expense.

E.C.

A. J. Bijl, "De Scheuring in 1774 onder de Doopsgezinden te Zuidveen," *DB* 1878, 1-37; Blaupot t. C., *Groningen* I, 102, 104, 218, 239; II, 68; *ML* III, 527.

Roermond, an old city (1951 pop. 22,500) and fortification at the confluence of the Roer with the Maas, in the 16th century a part of the duchy of Gelre (*q.v.*), today belonging to the Dutch province of Limburg (*q.v.*), has been a Roman Catholic bishop's see since 1569. It is not known when Anabaptism arose in and around Roermond, but by 1540 Gillis van Aachen (*q.v.*) was preaching here. About 1545 Menno Simons had come by boat to Roermond from Vischersweert. Persecution of the Anabaptists set in only gradually. The court of Gelderland (*q.v.*) then moved to Venlo to cope better with the situation, and upon receiving a report from a commissar sent to Roermond moved into that city. Already at the end of July 1551 (not 1550) Tijs van Lind (*q.v., more correctly Thys van Lin, but also Thijs Hille or Thijs op den Bergh*) was burned here at the stake. Two other Anabaptists recanted. Heresy and persecution continued in this area. Many Anabaptists of Roermond are reported to have settled in the Wassenberg (*q.v.*) district. A report from Roermond dated 1565 mentions the wife and children of Tys van Lind, and also a weaver Lenart Boymers as having Anabaptist leanings. In that year the Anabaptists held meetings in or near the city attended at times by 100 persons. At these meetings Teuwalt (Theobald of Worms? Theodor was an elder of Worms; see **Farwendel**) and Henrich of Cologne, both about fifty years old, are reported to have preached. Hence it is probable that there was at this time a congregation in Roermond; but since nothing more is known about it, it likely died out soon after these events.

E.C., vdZ.

W. Bax, *Het Protestantisme in het bisdom Luik* I (The Hague, 1937) 333-36, 341-48, 352-55; Rembert, *Wiedertäufer*, 341 f., 436, 515; *De Zondagsbode* XXII (1908-9) No. 21; *ML* III, 528.

Roes(s)elare (Roulers), a town in the Belgian province of West Flanders, in which, according to information given by the Inquisitor Titelman (*q.v.*), there were Mennonites in 1561. Concerning the history of the Mennonites in this town not much is known. There was a congregation here in 1545, for in that year its deacons signed a letter written by Adriaen van Kortrijk (*q.v.*) to the Mennonite congregation at Antwerp. In 1556 Elder Jacob de Rore (*q.v.*) preached in Roesselare. After 1561 there is no evidence of the presence of Mennonites in Roesselare. It is possible that the congregation was wiped out in that year by Titelman. (Verheyden, "Mennisme in Vlaanderen," manuscript.)

vdZ.

Roeters, a Dutch Mennonite family, probably from Emmerich, Germany (a Pauwels Roeters was a cloth merchant there about 1650), found at Amsterdam since the early 17th century. One branch of the Roeters family belonged to the Old Frisian Mennonite and later the Zon (*q.v.*) congregation. Another branch was Lamist (*q.v.*); one of these was Abraham Roeders (Roeters), a deacon of the Lamist congregation in 1667, who also took part in the meetings of the Collegiants (*q.v.*) and was a warm supporter of Pastor Galenus Abrahamsz (*q.v.*). A number of other members of the Roeters family served as deacons of the Amsterdam Lamist church.

A lateral branch of this family is the Roeters van Lennep family, whose progenitor was Jacob Roeters van Lennep (1740-1808), the son of David van Lennep and Perina Roeters. He was a deacon of the Amsterdam congregation, as was also his grandson Herman Christiaan Roeters van Lennep (1820-79).

(*Ned. Patriciaat* XLIV, 191 ff.; Amsterdam Church Records.) vDZ.

Rogel, Hans, author of the beloved hymn, "Ach Gott verleih mir dein genad, Dass ich die grosse wunderthat," which is No. 53 in the *Ausbund* (*q.v.*).

Wolkan, *Lieder,* 125; Max Radlkofer, "Die künstlerischen und schriftstellerischen Leistungen des Hans Rogel, Schulmeisters und Formschneiders in Augsburg," in *Ztscht des hist. Vereins für Schwaben und Neuburg* XXIV (Augsburg, 1897) 1-23; Joh. P. Classen, "Taufgesinnte Liederdichter," *Der Mennonit* IX (1956) 100; *ML* III, 528.

Rogge, a Dutch Mennonite family, found at Zaandam, Dutch province of North Holland. During the 17th and 18th centuries the Rogge family was outstanding in the area along the Zaan River in shipbuilding. Others were whalers or in other industries (lumber dealers and paper manufacturers). Jan Lijns Rogge (d. Feb. 9, 1759) was a merchant and shipowner at Zaandam and from 1721 until his death also a preacher of the Frisian Mennonite congregation of West Zaandam. He was well educated, though not specifically trained for the ministry. He knew many languages. In co-operation with the preachers Adriaan Loosjes (*q.v.*) of the Zaandam Nieuwe Huys congregation and Marten Schagen (*q.v.*) of Utrecht he translated the works of Josephus from Latin into Dutch.

Some members of the Rogge family served the West Zaandam Frisian congregation as deacons. Adriaan Rogge (1736-1826), also a deacon of this church, was one of the leaders in the meetings held regularly in the church on Sunday evening during the winter, in which the Bible was explained both by the preachers and the lay members of the congregation, and in which every brother of the church was entitled to a free expression of his thought.

Grietje Rogge, who died unmarried in 1828, willed her considerable fortune to the Frisian Mennonite congregation of West Zaandam. A branch of this Rogge family was found at Amsterdam as early as 1690. vDZ.

S. Lootsma, *Het Nieuwe Huys* (Zaandam, 1937) 47, 63, 70, 75, 113, 190, 192, 196; *Naamlijst* 1810, 72; *DJ* 1837, 99.

Roggenacher, Anthoni, a furrier of Schwyz, Switzerland, and his wife Dorothea were among the members of the first Anabaptist congregation at Zürich (*q.v.*) in 1525-26. Roggenacher, who was baptized by Blaurock (*q.v.*) on Feb. 26, 1525, had given 100 crowns to the church, "that there might be no want." Interrogated concerning this gift he declared before the government officials that it was not his view that the believers should hold their property in common (*das guot zuosammen schütten*). In March 1526 he was in prison at Zürich with Felix Manz (*q.v.*) and others, but they escaped. Probably he was soon rearrested and recanted. (*TA Zürich, passim.*) vDZ.

Roggeveen, a Dutch Mennonite family, found from the 17th century in some country churches of the province of North Holland, now spread all over the Netherlands. Members of this family have served as deacons in many congregations. C. M. Roggeveen,

of Blaricum, has been secretary of the Dutch Mennonite Missions Association since 1952. vDZ.

Rogne, Antoine, an Anabaptist martyr of Douai, France: see **Anthonie (de) Rocke.**

Rohatetz (Rohatec), a Hutterite Bruderhof (*q.v.*), near Göding, Moravia. (Zieglschmid, *Chronik,* 323, 324, 325, 633; *idem, Klein-Geschichtsbuch,* 66; *ML* III, 528.)

Rohrbach, a southern suburb of Heidelberg, Baden, Germany, where there were Anabaptists from the Reformation to the Thirty Years' War, and again since that war. About 1564 Georg Hailmann preached Anabaptist doctrine in the fields and elsewhere to numerous followers. About 1596 the Protestant pastor at Rohrbach wrote that the Anabaptists were increasing very rapidly, whereupon the *Landschreiber* at Heidelberg received orders to investigate the matter, and, if possible, to arrest the leader. In 1605 "only one poor woman" is named as being suspect of Anabaptism; the rest had "partly died off, partly been converted, and had partly gone to Moravia."

It is worthy of note that after the Thirty Years' War it was at Rohrbach that the Anabaptist-Mennonites again found a gathering point. Throughout the 18th century the government lists of Mennonites mention Mennonites at Rohrbach. Some of the family names were Fellmann, Bühler, Stauffer, and Lehman, which are still found among the Mennonites of Baden and the Palatinate. There are today no Mennonites in Rohrbach. G.H.

TA Baden und Pfalz, No. 163 (1564), 216 (1596), 220 (1605); *ML* III, 528.

Rohrbach, a small village in the Palatinate, Germany, situated near Kaiserslautern, between Sembach (*q.v.*) and Wartenberg (*q.v.*). Anabaptists were tolerated here even before the Thirty Years' War under Kolb von Wartenberg. An official report of July 25, 1605, says, "The deceased Konrad Kolb did not keep his agreement not to admit other Anabaptists after the death of the three living there then. In Rohrbach on the Kolb estate there is still an old Anabaptist, Hans Gramm, a miller with five sons, who have their meeting at Frankenstein; outwardly their attitude is friendly and neighborly, but they mislead the members of the parish who are employed in their service."

At Rohrbach there is still a Mennonite family, whose forefathers, however, came from Switzerland after the Thirty Years' War. G.H.

TA: Baden und Pfalz, No. 220 (in the Index of Places erroneously called "BA Bergzabern" instead of "BA Kaiserslautern").

Rohrer, a Mennonite (MC) family name, meaning "inhabitant of the swamp land," originating in the Swiss Emmental. Gertrud Rohrer and Margreth Rorer, both farmers' wives, are named as early as 1529 as Mennonites. Anna Rohrer, of Habstetten, arrested in 1567 but released after recanting, was apprehended again in 1571; she was tried on Nov. 27, 1571, at Bern and gave interesting information concerning the congregational life of the Swiss Mennonites. Notwithstanding severe torture she refused to give the Bernese officials any information on other members of the church.

Among the Swiss Mennonites emigrating to the Netherlands in 1711 there was Barbara Rohrer (b. 1671), of Bollingen, the wife of the Reformed Veits Sagimann. She died on the journey at Amsterdam. In the 1690's some Rohrers emigrated to Alsace (q.v.) and from there c1732 to America.

The first Rohrer members to sail the Atlantic were Johannes and Johann Gottfried, who came Sept. 11, 1732. Johannes married Elizabeth Snavely in 1735, settling in East Lampeter Twp., Lancaster Co., Pa. He had seven sons and a daughter, hence the name soon spread. A grandson Henry Rohrer (1784-1840) went to the Shenandoah Valley, Va.; a second grandson, Isaac Rohrer (1787-1840), located near Canton, Ohio, and another, Abraham Rohrer, an ordained preacher (1788-1878), moved to Medina County, Ohio, where he became bishop. Among the ordained men in Lancaster Conference were Ephraim Rohrer (1811-91) of Manor, John Rohrer (1827-1908) of East Petersburg, and Israel D. Rohrer. Michael Rohrer (1816-93), a bishop at Canton, Ohio, 1865-93, and Samuel D. Rohrer (1879-1955), a preacher of Wadsworth, Ohio, are among the ordained Rohrers. Hinke mentions thirteen Rohrer immigrants, but Johannes is the only one known to the Mennonite church. I.D.L., vDZ.

Strassburger and Hinke, *The Pennsylvania German Pioneers* I, 212, 214, 215; Weiss and Getz, *A History of Johann Rohrer* (1939).

Rohrerstown Mennonite Church (MC), located 3 miles northwest of Lancaster, Pa., a member of the Lancaster Conference, started at Abbeyville about 1750 with Bishop Benjamin Hershey (q.v.), three Hans Brubachers, Peter Swarr, and others on the land immediately west of Hickory Town, now Lancaster. In 1791 they moved on Brubaker land, north of Rohrerstown, where a beautiful cemetery still marks the spot. After 63 years a new meetinghouse was placed on the same site. In 1895 a brick church was built on the third site south of the square in Rohrerstown, 50 x 75 ft. This building was completely renovated in 1955-56. These churches have been the scene of the spring sessions of the Lancaster Mennonite Conference from time immemorial until 1953, when it was first held at East Petersburg. This was the home of two bishops named Benjamin Hershey, Bishops Jacob and John Brubaker, Preacher John K. Brubaker, and John Shenk. It is a part of the Rohrerstown-Millersville circuit and in recent years most of the ministers were from the Millersville area. The membership in 1957 was 173, with Christian K. Lehman as bishop, Jacob G. Hess, J. Herbert Fisher, and Paul H. Gochnauer as ministers. I.D.L.

Rohrhof, an estate in the district of Schwetzingen, Baden, Germany, about 8 miles east of Mannheim, was formerly the seat of a Mennonite congregation, usually called Rohrhof-Bruchhausen. A list of 1731 reports that the congregation consisted of 16 families and had Jost Eschbacher of Eppelheim (?) and Jakob Fälman of Bruchhausen as preachers, and Christian Neukomm of Rohrhof as deacon. Jakob Fellmann and his son(?) Jakob Fellmann, the latter
24

from 1765, were its elders in the 18th century. In 1822 the congregation numbered 57 members, 22 of whom lived at Rohrhof. After the emigration of most of the Rohrbach Mennonites to America in the 1830's, meetings were held only at Bruchhausen and by 1840 the congregation of Rohrhof had disappeared. (See also **Bruchhausen.**) (*ML* III, 529.)
G.H.

Röhrich, Timotheus Wilhelm, author of the following works: *Geschichte der Reformation in Elsass, und besonders in Strassburg*, 3 vv. (1830-32); "Die Gottesfreunde und die Winkeler am Oberrhein," in *Zeitschrift für historische Theologie* I (1840); *Evangelisten der Reformationszeit* (reprint from *Ztscht für Historische Theologie*, 1845); *Mitteilungen aus der Geschichte der evangelischen Kirche des Elsasses*, 3 vv. (1855); *Zur Geschichte der Strassburgischen Wiedertäufer in den Jahren 1527 bis 1543* (reprint from *Ztscht für Historische Theologie*, 1860, 3-121). He is not to be confused with G. G. Roehrich, the author of *Essai sur la vie, les écrits et la vie de l'Anabaptist J. Denk* (1853), who may have been his nephew. (*ML* III, 529.) E.C.

Rol, Heinrich: see Henric(k) Rol.

Rolette County (N.D.) Old Order Amish Settlement, now extinct. In the spring of 1894 four Amish families and an unmarried man left their homes in Lagrange County, Ind., and moved to Rolette County, N.D.—John D. Bontrager, Rudolph A. Yoder, Joni Hershberger, Moses H. Hochstetler, and John A. Yoder. Four of these soon left the community. In 1895-1900 a number of Amish came to North Dakota, among them Eli J. Bontreger, who had been ordained in Indiana, until by 1900 there were some fifty families located there. Ministers ordained there were Eli D. Weirich 1895, Moses S. Miller 1907, Eli N. Hochstetler 1900, Reuben L. Bontrager 1901, Daniel J. Miller 1902, Moses M. Yoder and Rudolph A. Yoder 1903, Jacob Graber 1907. In June 1901 Eli J. Bontreger was ordained bishop, but moved to Wisconsin in 1910. By that time a number of families including some of the ministers had moved away. Other ordinations were as follows: Abraham Gingerich 1910, Jacob Graber (d. 1921), bishop 1913; Abraham Gingerich (d. 1930), bishop 1922; John C. Gingerich was ordained 1930; Mahlon Yoder 1932, bishop 1935; and Amos Graber 1937. About 1930 Dan Coblentz, a deacon, moved in from Montana. The other ministers all moved away. Until 1938 the former bishop Eli J. Bontreger returned occasionally to help in the church. After 1938 conditions arose that caused more and more families to leave; in 1948 preaching services were discontinued. E.J.B.

Rolfe (Iowa) Amish Mennonite settlement, now extinct, was established in Pocahontas County in 1897-98, when families from Illinois and Minnesota located near the town of Rolfe. Among the family names were Good, Zimmerman, Miller, Horsch, and Shantz. Sunday school was held regularly in a schoolhouse on Joseph Good's farm, 3½ miles northwest of Gilmore City, but there was never an organized church, although ministers from Henry County, Iowa, preached there occasionally. The first family left the community in 1902 and the last one perhaps thirty years later. **M.G.**

Melvin Gingerich, *Mennonites in Iowa* (Iowa City, 1939) 336-37.

Roll, Hen(d)ric(k) (Heinrich): see **Henric(k) Rol.**

Rol(l)wagen, Jan Claes (Jan Claes Codt, or Coodt): see **Kotte, Johann Clausen.**

Romanovka, a Mennonite village name found in the Russian settlements of Ignatyevo and Olgino, Ukraine; Orenburg and Auli Ata, Central Asia (see **Villages**). **C.K.**

Romanovka, a village near Olgino (*q.v.*), province of Stavropol in the foothills of the Caucasian Mountains, Russia, was established in 1895 by fifty families of the Temple Church (*q.v.*) who had previously resided at Orbelianovka (*q.v.*) near Tempelhof. The Romanovka Temple followers were of Württemberg separatistic background and not Mennonites like those of Olgino. **C.K.**

Friesen, *Brüderschaft,* 679; H. Sawatzky, *Templer mennonitischer Herkunft* (Manitoba, 1955) 32.

Romanovka Mennonite Church, located near Aulie-Ata, Central Asia, was organized in 1884 under the leadership of Abraham Peters (*q.v.*) by a group who had left the Molotschna settlement in the Ukraine to meet Christ at His second coming in Central Asia. Most of the settlers of Aulie-Ata (*q.v.*), which was founded in 1812, had come from the Molotschna. Peters was succeeded as leader by Johann Regehr (*q.v.*). In 1905 Regehr was assisted by the following ministers: Hermann Epp, Franz Abrams, Gerhard Kopper, Hermann Wall, Kornelius Wall, and Jakob Hamm. At that time the total membership of the church was 406, of whom 196 were baptized. Before World War I some of the members came to America, settling in the Newton, Kan., and Beatrice, Neb., areas. According to a report published in *Unser Blatt* (1925) the congregation was also known as the Köppental Mennonite Church, and had a membership of 197 in 1925. By that time the congregation had introduced baptism by immersion. In addition to this congregation there was at Aulie-Ata the Gnadental Mennonite Brethren Church and the Nikolaipol Free Church. **C.K.**

H. Dirks, *Statistik,* 36, 64; Friesen, *Brüderschaft,* 720; F. Bartsch, *Unser Auszug nach Mittel-Asien* (North Kildonan, 1948; reprint of first edition of 1907); *idem,* "Meine Reise nach Turkestan," *Unser Blatt* I (October-November 1925) 9-10, 26-27; J. Janzen, "Mennonite Colony in Turkestan," *MQR* IV (October 1930) 182-289.

Rombout Smit, an Anabaptist martyr: see **Rommeken.**

Römer, Hans, an Anabaptist of Hesse (*q.v.*), Germany, a native of Eisenach in Thuringia, a furrier by trade, at first a follower of Thomas Müntzer (*q.v.*), was expelled from his native town for participating in the Peasants' War; leaving his wife behind, he began a life of wandering. With his fellow Anabaptists, Christoph Peisker (*q.v.*), Volkmar Fischer (*q.v.*), and Christoph von Meissen (*q.v.*), he was an unusually successful propagandist for the Anabaptist cause. After Müntzer's death he attached himself

entirely to the peaceful Anabaptists. In August 1534 he was taken prisoner in Göttingen. By recanting he escaped a martyr's death, and was probably punished with a prison term. (Wappler, *Thüringen,* 40 ff.; *ML* III, 531.)

Rommeken, an Anabaptist martyr, who was burned at the stake at Antwerp, Belgium, in 1555. His name is found in hymn No. 16, "Aenhoort God, hemelsche Vader" (Hear, O God, heavenly Father), of the *Lietboecxken.* Van Braght's short account in the *Martyrs' Mirror,* which states that he died valiantly, follows the information given in the *Offer.* The exact date of the execution and a number of details about this martyr have been published by P. Génard in the *Antwerpsch Archieven-blad.* His official name was Rombout Smit, and he was a native of Antwerp, by trade an engraver on glass. He was a master craftsman and from 1543 a member of the painters' guild of St. Luke. He was burned on the market place of Antwerp on Dec. 10, 1555. **vDZ.**

Offer, 564, No. 7; *Mart. Mir.* D 162, E 550; *Antw. Arch.-Blad* VIII, 428, 429; XIV, 20 f., No. 232.

Ronse (Renaix in Flanders), **Dean of,** a Roman Catholic inquisitor who persecuted the Anabaptists: see **Titelman.**

Ro(o)leeuw, a Mennonite family of Amsterdam, Netherlands. Anthony Rooleeuw is found there in 1625 as a deacon of the (Groningen) Old Flemish congregation. But most of the members of the Rooleeuw family were somewhat liberal, and belonged to the Waterlander Toren (*q.v.*) congregation, and after the merger of this congregation with the Lamist church, in 1668, to the United Lam and Toren congregation.

Isaac Jacobsz, b. about 1600 at Amsterdam, was a son of Jacob Theunisz (*q.v.*) and a brother of Anthoni Jacobsz (*q.v.*) Roscius and Lambert Jacobsz (*q.v.*). He married Itien Reiniersdochter and adopted the family name of Rooleeuw (after the house in which his father lived, which had the sign of a red lion—*Roode Leeuw*). He had a silk business and was a member of the Waterlander congregation.

Isaac's youngest brother was Jacobus Rooleeuw (*c*1605-70), who was a lay preacher of the Waterlanders. The years of his service are uncertain; he is said to have been called to the ministry in 1628, but he was definitely appointed in 1638, in which year he, however, requested some delay. In 1647 and in 1652 he was at any rate actually serving. By trade he was a dyer and cloth merchant. He married Catharina Hooghsaet (*q.v.*), usually called Trijn Jacobs, whose portrait was painted by Rembrandt (*q.v.*) in 1657. Like his father Jacob Theunisz he was a friend of the poet Joost van den Vondel (*q.v.*). He seems to have been a man of somewhat advanced ideas.

Some members of the Rooleeuw family served as deacons in the Waterlander congregation and also later in the Lamist church. Among these was Anthony Rooleeuw (d. 1700), a son of Isaac Jacobsz and married to Cornelia Block; he was a leading textile merchant; in 1672 he was delegated with three other deacons of the Amsterdam congregation to visit the Swiss refugees in the Palatinate, Germany, to investigate their living conditions. Both he and his wife participated in the Collegiant (*q.v.*) movement and attended the Collegiant meetings, which were for some time held in his home on the Keizersgracht.

To this family also belonged Abraham Rooleeuw, also a son of Isaac Jacobsz, b. *c*1636 at Amsterdam, d. there in 1693, married to Elisabeth van Alderwerelt, of an old Mennonite family. Abraham Rooleeuw, a wealthy man who conducted a textile business, was a member of the Mennonite church, but his sympathies were largely with the Collegiants, whose meetings were for some time held at his house. In 1675 he was one of the founders of the Oranjeappel (*q.v.*) Collegiant orphanage, to which he contributed a large sum of money.

Reinier Rooleeuw (Amsterdam, 1627-84), also a son of the above Isaac Jacobsz, unmarried, was a physician at Amsterdam. He was an interested participant in the Collegiant meetings and also promoted the founding of the Oranjeappel orphanage. He is particularly to be mentioned here for a number of his writings, including *De Schat der Ziele ofte Begeerden* (Amsterdam, 1678; 3d ed. 1684), which was illustrated with the oldest known engravings of Jan Luyken (*q.v.*), and a songbook entitled *Schriftuurlyke Gezangen, gerijmt en op nieuwe Zangwijzen gesteld* (four editions, 1681, 1686, 1702, 1725, all at Amsterdam). A number of hymns of this songbook were included in the Mennonite hymnal *Liederen en Gezangen* (Haarlem, 1713). For the *Stichtelyke Rijmen* by D. R. Camphuisen (*q.v.*) Reinier Rooleeuw composed new melodies (editions Rotterdam 1688, Amsterdam 1690, Rotterdam 1702, 1713, 1737, and 1759; besides these a few editions without place or date of publication). He also translated the New Testament from Greek into Dutch (published after his death, Amsterdam, 1684). Kühler believed that Reinier Rooleeuw was influenced by the Racovian Catechism (*q.v.*) of the Socinians (*q.v.*).   vDZ.

Inv. Arch. Amst. I, Nos. 1196, 1412 f.; II, Nos. 1237-40, 1757; *DB* 1865, 71; *N.N.B.Wb.* VII, 1064 f.; J. C. van Slee, *De Rijnsburger Collegianten* (Haarlem, 1895) *passim*; W. J. Kühler, *Het Socinianisme in Nederland* (Leiden, 1912) 190-92; H. F. Wijnman, "Een drietal portretten van Rembrandt," *Amstelodamum* Yearbook XXVIII (Amsterdam, 1931) 81-86.

Ro(o)man, Gillis (d. *c*1610), a printer of Haarlem, Holland, who printed a number of Mennonite books, particularly letters and confessions of the martyrs. Probably as early as 1577 he printed (and published?) *Sommige Belydingen . . .* by Reytse Aysesz (*q.v.*). In 1579-88 he printed *Martelaersbrieven*, a collection of letters written by martyrs, which included letters by Hendrick Alewijnsz (*q.v.*), Jacob de Keersmaecker (de Rore, *q.v.*), Joost Verkindert (*q.v.*), Thijs Joriaensz (*q.v.*), and Jan Woutersz van Cuyck (*q.v.*). In 1588 he published *Tgetuygenisse ende de naeghelaeten Schriften van Christiaen Rijcen* (Christiaen de Rijcke, *q.v.*). Some of this material was printed in the Dutch martyr books, including van Braght's *Martyrs' Mirror*. Gillis Rooman was probably also the printer of the "Schottland Bible" (*q.v.*) for Krijn Vermeulen (*q.v.*) at Danzig in 1598.

It is not known whether or not Gillis Rooman was a Mennonite. His son and successor Adriaen Rooman obviously was not, for in 1617 he printed the second edition of the Dutch translation of Heinrich Bullinger's (*q.v.*) book, supplemented by Gerardus Nicolai (*q.v.*), *Teghens de Wederdoopers*, which violently attacks the Mennonites.   vDZ.

Bibliographie I and II; *Catalogus Amst.*, 99-101; *DB* 1918, 108; *BRN* VII, 164, note, 288 f.

Roos, a common Dutch family name. There have been a number of Mennonite families with this name, some apparently unrelated; nearly all have died out.

A branch of the Roos family was found at Middelie and Edam in the province of North Holland. Dirk Cornelisz Roos (d. 1729) was a preacher in the Frisian congregation at Edam in 1724-29, and Pieter Cornelisz Roos in the Waterlander congregation of Wormer-Jisp in the early 18th century.

Other branches were found at Amsterdam, Haarlem, Groningen, Harlingen, Workum, and Sneek. The Haarlem branch had probably come from Flanders, Belgium, in the early 17th century (see **Roose**). A part of the Amsterdam family seems to have been related to this Haarlem branch. Another part of the Amsterdam family, as well as those in Groningen, Harlingen, Sneek, and Workum, seems to have had a common progenitor, Harke Roos, who lived in Workum, Friesland, about 1600. His descendants living in the last four cities were usually in business, such as lumber. Most of the Workum Roos family in the 17th and 18th centuries were shipowners. Some of them, e.g., Jelle Sipkes Roos (d. 1789), a deacon of the Workum Mennonite congregation, were very wealthy. Epke Sipkes Roos, b. 1702 at Workum, d. 1794 at Sneek, probably a brother of Jelle, founded a fund for the training of young men of the congregations of Sneek, Workum, and Grouw for the ministry at the Amsterdam Mennonite Seminary. Other members of the Roos family at Sneek were among the last members of the conservative Old Flemish congregation.

At Amsterdam some of the Roos families were members of the Lamist congregation and Collegiants (*q.v.*) at the same time. Others belonged to the conservative Old Frisian "Arke Noë" congregation; their descendants joined the Lamists (*q.v.*) about 1730.

Some branches of the Roos family, especially that of Haarlem, may have been related to the Mennonite Roosen (*q.v.*) family. Members of this family occasionally spelled their names Ro(o)se or Ro(o)sen; but hasty conclusions must be avoided, for the spelling of Dutch family names was very slovenly, often as late as the 19th century.

A Mennonite de Roos family is still living at Staveren, Friesland.   vDZ.

Gorter's *Doopsgezinde Lectuur*, 1858, 327-30; *DB* 1887, 128; 1898, 85; 1903, 109 f.; 1905, 41; *Inv. Arch. Amst.* II, Nos. 1152, 2500-2; *Verslag* (Report) of the A.D.S., 1813, 5, 14, 20; 1817, 9 f.; 1818, 10; 1823, 13; 1824, 9; G. van Mesdag, *Het Geslacht Mesdag* (n.p., 1943-46) 106, 140, 142; J. C. van Slee, *De Rijnsburger Collegianten* (Haarlem, 1895) 187, 439; church records of the Amsterdam congregation.

Roose (Rose, Ro(o)sen, Rooze), a Mennonite name found in Flanders, Belgium, and after their emigration because of persecution, in Holland. Gilles (*q.v.*) Rooze, of Bellegem near Kortrijk, died as a Mennonite martyr at Brugge, Belgium, in 1568. In 1583

Vincent Rooze, a Mennonite citizen of Gent, Belgium, when this town was under a (temporary) Calvinist government, was banished forever, because he had refused to swear an oath of allegiance, professing that his faith forbade him to swear an oath. From the early 17th century the Roose family, sometimes spelling their name Roos, no doubt having emigrated from Flanders, were found among the members of the Mennonite Flemish congregations of Leiden and Haarlem, and soon after also of Amsterdam. Jan Rose (Roose) was a preacher of the Leiden Flemish church from shortly after 1600 until at least 1640. He was extremely conservative, and with some adherents, called Jan Rosensvolk (*q.v.*), split off from the main Flemish church. In 1669 a Samuel Roose is mentioned as a member of the Mennonite congregation of Rotterdam. Among the Mennonites at Königsberg, Prussia, were Johann Roos(e) and his son Cornelius Roose (b. 1753), both brandy distillers, mentioned in the reports of the city in 1751 and 1809 respectively. Whether some of these Rooses were related or not with the Hamburg Roosen (*q.v.*) family could not be ascertained.　　　　　vDZ.

Inv. Arch. Amst. II, 2, Nos. 436, 443a.; *DB* 1863, 56; Kühler, *Geschiedenis* II, 195, 197; *Gesch.-Bl.*, 1956, 28, Nos. 85-86; Verheyden, "Mennisme in Vlaanderen," Ms.; *ME* III, 81.

Roosen, a prominent German Mennonite family attached since 1532 to the Anabaptist movement. Its progenitor Coord Roosen (1495-*c*1533) joined the Anabaptists in his home town of Korschenbroich in the duchy of Jülich-Cleve, Germany, and fled to Holstein with his four children when persecution set in. He settled in the village of Steinrade near Lübeck and supported his family by farming and manufacturing gunpowder. His fifth son, Gerlinck (Geerlinck, Geerling), born in 1532 in Korschenbroich soon after the flight to Holstein, followed the family to Holstein in 1554 when his mother died. By that time his father was also dead. In 1566 Geerlinck leased the farm Holskamp near Lübeck, united with the Lübeck or Fresenburg Mennonite congregation, and in 1565 married Elisabeth von Sintern. He without doubt met Menno Simons, who was living at Fresenburg. He died in 1611. Geerlinck's oldest son and then his oldest grandson leased the farm Holskamp after him. His fourth son, Paul (1582-1649), married to Janneken Quins, settled in Altona in 1611 as a tanner and leather dealer became quite well-to-do, and acquired considerable property, which the Count of Schauenburg placed at the disposal of Mennonites, Reformed, and other victims of persecution, and which was called the "Freiheit." The congregation was at that time known as Flemish, since it was largely composed of Mennonite immigrants from Flanders. Later the congregation called itself the United Congregation of Flemish, Frisians, and High Germans, toward the end of the 17th century "Mennonisten," and one hundred years later "Mennoniten." Paul Roosen became a deacon in this congregation. He placed a building at its disposal for use as a meetinghouse, which the congregation later bought. On this site the congregation built a church in 1674, and after the razing of Altona by the Swedes in 1714, another church, which was used until within the 20th cen-

tury. Of Paul Roosen's sons, Gerrit Roosen (*q.v.*), the oldest, became the most important member of the Roosen family. His brother Herman (1627-96), married in 1657 to Maria Stockmann who was an important merchant in Hamburg, was also a deacon, and for a short time a preacher as well. Herman's daughter Anna (1670-1714) married Gabriel Otto Rahusen, a well-known Mennonite merchant of Hamburg, in 1695.

In the following century two of Gerrit's grandsons, Berend and Salomon Roosen, were deacons in the Altona congregation. Berend Roosen (1705-88), married to Elisabeth Kramer, became the greatest merchant of the family and one of the greatest of Hamburg. He lived at 3 Vorgesetztenstrasse, in a house built by Sonnin, the architect of the Michaeliskirche in Hamburg. He owned about twenty ships. A major part of his business was Greenland shipping and whaling, which was engaged in by most Mennonite merchants of the late 17th century and all of the 18th. He owned a wharf on the Reiherstieg, a canal which connected Hamburg with the Elbe. Salomon Roosen (1717-95), married to Sara Koopman, was likewise a wealthy merchant of Hamburg. The business of the brothers was carried on for several generations by their heirs, many of whom served the congregation as deacons. Roosen Bridge was named for Berend.

In the next generation, which included the trying period of the French occupation, two Roosens were deacons in the Altona congregation: Hermann Roosen (1778-1853) and Berend Roosen (1757-1820), both merchants. The latter was married to Elisabeth de Vosz. In the next generation, which experienced the great Hamburg fire, five Roosens were deacons: Berend Roosen (1778-1853), Hermann Roosen (1786-1864), B. Paulus Roosen (1792-1875), Salomon Roosen (1793-1863), and Berend Roosen (1795-1860). In the second half of the 19th century there were again several deacons of the Roosen family: Johannes Roosen (1823-1907), the architect B. Otto Roosen (1832-1912), and the shipper Berend Roosen (1835-87). Of special importance to the congregation was Berend Carl Roosen (*q.v.*), a preacher. The 20th century also lists two Roosens as deacons of the Mennonite congregation of Hamburg: the merchant brothers Paul Roosen (1867-1907) and Hermann Roosen (b. 1861).

Government positions were not accepted by the Mennonites of the 17th and 18th centuries. Article 28 of the *Glaubenslehre der wahren Mennoniten* (Hamburg, 1776) by Cornelis Ris (*q.v.*) is an express warning on this point. But in the progressive 19th century men of the Roosen family accepted honorary positions in the government, served as members of the popular "Bürgerschaft," and in 1890 the merchant Rudolf Roosen (1830-1907) was chosen senator of the Free City of Hamburg. In 1700 a Paul Roosen and his wife Anna, Mennonites of Hamburg, leaving Altona on March 5, 1700, emigrated to Germantown, Pa., but soon after returned to Hamburg. No member of the Roosen family born since 1901 is now a Mennonite.　　　　　G.A.R.

B. C. Roosen, *Geschichte der Mennoniten-Gemeinde zu Hamburg und Altona* (Hamburg, I in 1886, II in 1887); *idem, Geschichte unseres Hauses* (Hamburg,

1905); Wanda Oesau, *Hamburgs Grönlandsfahrt* (Glück-stadt-Hamburg, 1955) 133-50; *MQR* VII (1933) 236; *ML* III, 531-33.

Roosen, Berend Carl (1820-1904), a Mennonite minister of Hamburg, Germany. After the completion of his theological studies he was chosen as pastor of his home church, the Hamburg-Altona congregation, on Oct. 12, 1845, serving for nearly sixty years until his death. Roosen is said to have been a man of short stature with a kind face and vivid eyes. He was a man of sincere, moderate, somewhat liberal convictions. The long period of his service was one of great calm. Materially the church prospered and its spiritual life also flourished under Roosen's intelligent leadership. Roosen maintained friendly connections with the Lutheran pastors of Hamburg and Altona and enjoyed their high regard. He was active in many areas of church life, including home missions. In his honor the meetinghouse of the home mission society organized by Wichern, which was located in the section of Hamburg known as Winterhude, was named the Roosenhaus. He also was much interested in the foreign Mennonite missions, vigorously supporting the Dutch Mennonite Missions Association (*q.v.*) at Amsterdam, of which he was a trustee. He died at Hamburg on Dec. 20, 1904.

Roosen published a biography of Menno Simons: *Menno Symons den evangelischen Gemeinden geschildert* (Leipzig, 1848); his biography of his ancestor Gerrit Roosen (*q.v.*) appeared in 1854 at Hamburg: *Gerhard Roosen weiland Prediger der evangelischen Mennoniten-Gemeinde zu Hamburg und Altona, geb. 1612, gest. 1711, geschildert.* His *Geschichte der Mennoniten-Gemeinde zu Hamburg und Altona* I and II (Hamburg, 1886, 1887) is the product of serious historical study. In 1893 he wrote a history of his family, which was published by his daughter after his death: *Geschichte unseres Hauses* (Hamburg, 1905). A sermon of his, *Neujahrspredigt gehalten am 1. Jan. 1886,* was published in the *Mennonitische Blätter* of 1884, No. 4.   vDZ.

Inv. Arch. Amst. I, No. 1003, 2; *DB* 1875, 106 f., 111 f.; 1887, 19, 1905, 202; Robert Dollinger, *Geschichte der Mennoniten in Schleswig-Holstein, Hamburg und Lübeck* (Neumünster, 1930).

Roosen, Gerrit (Gerhard; he signed one of his writings as Geeritt Roosen), b. at Altona, near Hamburg, Germany, on March 8, 1612, d. there Nov. 20, 1711, a wealthy businessman; one of the industries in which he was dominant was whaling in the waters of Greenland. He lived on Blömken Street in Hamburg. In 1640 he married Maria (Mayken) Amoury, the daughter of the Mennonite deacon and merchant Hans Amoury. His grandmother had had personal contact with Menno Simons. Through his life of nearly a century Gerrit Roosen spent much of his time, devotion, and money for the Mennonite congregation of Hamburg-Altona. He was chosen as deacon in 1649 and as preacher in 1660. For 50 years he served as preacher and from 1664 as elder, delivering over 700 sermons, and defending his flock in all internal controversies and against all attacks by the Lutheran clergy. At the age of 96 he still administered communion. He began a church record of Hamburg-Altona in 1650 and continued it until he was 88 years old. Besides caring for his own con-

gregation, he gave much attention to the brotherhood in general, traveling through Holstein and the Netherlands and in 1676 visiting the churches in Prussia and Poland with Preacher Jan Sibes Potbacker of Harlingen. During their stay of 42 days they visited the congregations of Orloff, Nieschewski, Montau, Kassou(?), Lunau, Markushof, and Danzig. In all these congregations they administered communion and in some of them they baptized. Roosen was interested in the difficulties of the oppressed Mennonites in Switzerland and the fate of the refugees in the Palatinate. He seems to have promoted the idea of colonizing the Swiss Mennonites in Prussia.

Roosen was a man of deep piety and moderate views. He preached in the Dutch language, but gave his catechetical instruction in German. He published a catechism, *Christliches Gemüths-Gespräch von dem geistlichen und seligmachenden Glauben* (1st edition 1702; it went through at least 22 editions, from 1857 also in English; see **Christliches Gemütsgespräch**). It was much used in the congregations of Germany as late as the 19th century. He also published a defense of Mennonitism, which had erroneously been accused of Münsterite tenets. This book bears the title *Unschuld und Gegen-Bericht der Evangelischen Tauff-gesinnten Christen, so Mennonisten genandt werden* (Ratzeburg, 1702). Parts of this book were published in the Dutch language in Schijn-Maatschoen, *Geschiedenis* III. This same volume also contained a confession of faith in twelve articles drawn up by Roosen from the Dutch *Algemeene Belydenissen* (*q.v.*). Besides this Roosen published *Predigt . . . gehalten am Sonntage nach Ostern in der Tauffgesinneten Gemeine (zu Altona)* (Ratzeburg, 1702).

Roosen retired in 1708. On his 98th birthday he presented a manuscript to his relatives and the ministers of the Hamburg-Altona Mennonite congregation, a kind of spiritual testament, in which he rendered an account of his church leadership. Unable to write because of poor vision he dictated it to a friend. This writing was also reproduced by Schijn-Maatschoen, *Geschiedenis* III.

Roosen made several liberal endowments to the congregation, but he did not forget his home town, partly financing, for example, the tower of St. Michael's church (Lutheran) at Hamburg.

G.A.R., vDZ.

B. C. Roosen, *Gerhard Roosen* (Hamburg, 1884); idem, *Geschichte der Menn.-Gemeinde zu Hamburg und Altona* I (Hamburg, 1886) 30, 33 f., 41, 44, 46, 55, 57, 61, 64, 73 f.; Schijn-Maatschoen, *Geschiedenis* III, 320-431 (with portrait); *Inv. Arch. Amst.* I, Nos. 1357, 1422; *DJ* 1840, 64; *DB* 1881, 36 ff.; 1882, 41 f., Robert Dollinger, *Geschichte der Mennoniten in Schleswig-Holstein, Hamburg und Lübeck* (Neumünster, 1930); R. Friedmann, *Mennonite Piety Through the Centuries* (Goshen, 1949) 142-51, discusses Gerrit Roosen's writings, their background and significance; *ML* III, 533 f.

Ro(o)sevelt, Hendrik van, was a Mennonite elder in Flanders, Belgium. Concerning his life and work little is known. In 1566, probably shortly after Easter, on the invitation of the Mennonite emigrants from Flanders to the Dutch province of Friesland, he went to Friesland and stayed in Harlingen or Franeker until August 1566. The Flemish had invited him to help in settling their discord with the Mennonites of Friesland, who had received them kindly but soon objected to some differences in the manner of dress and living. Van Roosevelt tried to mediate, but he showed partiality to the Flemish. The discord culminated in a schism and the Frisian Mennonites were banned by Dirk Philips; then Hendrik van Roosevelt likewise banned the Frisians. In 1568 van Roosevelt stayed in Emden, East Friesland, and in the fall of 1569 he was sent with Jan van Ophoorn (*q.v.*), an elder of Emden, and a certain Laurens, an elder at Franeker, to Cleve to arbitrate a dispute in that congregation. At that point van Roosevelt disappears from history. He probably returned to Flanders, where under his influence the congregations, particularly those of Antwerp and Gent, sided with the Flemish party against the Frisians. This Hendrik van Ro(o)sevelt may be the Hendrik (van) Rosenfelt, of Antwerp, who came to Montau (*q.v.*), West Prussia, in 1586, and was the progenitor of the Mennonite Rosenfeld (*q.v.*) family.   vDZ.

DB 1893, 21, 26 f., 31, 33, 51 f., 68, 76; Kühler, *Geschiedenis* I, 411; *Inv. Arch. Amst.* I, No. 466; *BRN* X, 555 note, 603 note.

Ropp, a Mennonite family name: see **Rupp.**

Rosanna of the Amish (319 pp.), a semifictionized biography, written and published in 1940 by Joseph W. Yoder, of Huntingdon, Pa., himself a lifelong member of the Mennonite Church (MC), relates the life story of his mother, an Irish Catholic orphan, who was reared in an Old Order Amish home, married a young Amishman, Crist Yoder, and remained a loyal member of the Amish church until her death. The book gives an unusually clear and accurate picture of the brighter side of Amish life and culture. It is frankly autobiographical and contains the name of only one fictitious character, Simon Riehl, who is introduced to describe an Amish excommunication and the consequent "Meidung." Commendable Amish traits, German, perhaps, as well as Amish, receive proper emphasis: honesty, frugality, humility, hard work, joy in the completion of a task well done, friendliness, and neighborliness, all suffused with a deep religious piety. The volume catches with remarkable success the happy, joyous community spirit where interest in the simple, homely virtues and in one another's welfare enables the group to face life with an upward look and a clear conscience. It also records faithfully the religious and cultural practices of the Old Order Amish in Mifflin County, Pa. In spite of evident literary shortcomings the volume deserves the popularity that has made numerous reprintings necessary. The pen sketches by George Daubenspeck add interest and value to the volume. (Reviewed in *MQR* XV, April 1941, 143-47.)
                                                J.S.U.

Rosario, Mexico, a former settlement of refugee Mennonites from Russia after World War I, located some miles west of the large Old Colony Mennonite settlement in the state of Chihuahua about 240 miles south of El Paso, Tex. The settlement was made in 1924 on a ranch which, with help of the Mennonite Board of Colonization in the United States, was rented with an option to buy. The original group consisted of 36 families but a number of families joined later. The Rosario settlement effort resulted in failure. Some of the families moved to Irapuato (*q.v.*) and others who were able to get Mexican citizenship after two years of residence in Mexico emigrated to Canada. Within two years the last of the Mennonite families had left Rosario.   J.W.F.

Röschingen in Württemberg, Germany, is named in the *Naamlijst* of 1775 as a Mennonite congregation with David Musselmann as preacher from 1772. In later issues (1784 ff.) Röschingen is included in a united Willenbach, Prutzenhof(?), Dürrhof, and Röschingen congregation, of which Abraham Zeisset (*q.v.*), of the Rauhof, was the elder and David (from 1772), Michael (1781), and Christian Musselmann (1783) the preachers.   vDZ.

Roscius, Anthony, a Dutch minister: see **Jacobsz, Anthoni.**

Rose, Jan: see **Roose.**

Roseburg (Oregon) Civilian Public Service Unit No. 151 was authorized by Selective Service in December 1945, the last camp approved by this agency. Under Mennonite Central Committee administration, a unit of twenty-four men arrived in Roseburg in January 1946. The men worked in the Roseburg United States Veterans' Hospital, serving the mental patients in this institution, until the close of the unit in December 1946.   M.G.

Melvin Gingerich, *Service for Peace* (Akron, Pa., 1949) 274.

Roseburg Conservative Amish Mennonite Church (independent), Sutherlin, Oreg., was first listed in the 1950 *Mennonite Yearbook,* with 32 members. In 1953 its name was changed to Pleasant Valley (*q.v.*), with 17 members; it is one of the "Sleeping Preacher" congregations.   M.G.

Rosedale Church of God in Christ Mennonite Church, located at Crooked Creek, Peace River District, Alberta, was organized in 1939. Church services began in 1930 with the coming of Gerhard de Veer from Swalwell, Alberta. The first church building of 1931 was followed by another in 1938, built of logs, with room for 150 persons. One minister and two deacons have been ordained in the history of the church. The meetings include weekly Sunday morning services, biweekly Sunday evening services, a monthly Christian Endeavor, and midweek Bible study. The church in 1957 had a membership of 127; the ministers in charge were Peter I. Thiessen and Alvie Esau.   J.T.E.

Rosedale Hutterite Bruderhof of the Schmiedeleut group, located near Mitchell, S.D., was founded by several families from the Milltown Bruderhof, including Joseph Hofer, a minister. In 1904 Paul Gross was chosen as preacher. In 1918 this Bruderhof was sold, and the Brethren moved to Canada and established the Rosedale Bruderhof near Elie, Man. In 1945 Joseph Waldner Sr., with ten families from the Rockport (S.D.) Bruderhof, bought the original Rosedale farm and re-established the Bruderhof. Joseph A. Waldner, chosen to the ministry in 1950 and ordained in 1957, was the minister in 1958. In 1947 there were 30 baptized members and a total population of 87; in 1958 there were 47 members. D.D., J.A.Wₐ.

Rosedale Mennonite Brethren Church, located 10 miles west of Bakersfield, Cal., a member of the Pacific District, was organized in November 1911. The church was the host church of the first conference session of the Pacific District in the late fall of 1911. The first pastor of this church was John Boese from Colorado. Ministers who have served this church were John Boese, John Berg, Henry Kohfeld, K. G. Neufeld, J. D. Hofer, H. D. Wiebe, Walter L. Penner, and P. N. Hiebert, who was still serving in 1957, with a membership of 173. The first missionary couple, Mr. and Mrs. Ivan Elrich, of this church were sent to the foreign field in 1955. P.N.H.

Roseland (La.) Mennonite (MC) Church, now extinct, located 70 miles north of New Orleans, was reported in the *Herald of Truth* of Oct. 1, 1894. Sunday school and church services were held every Sunday. Their first communion service was observed in October 1894. Jonas T. Nice, the minister, was last listed under Louisiana in the 1899 *Family Almanac.* M.G.

Roseland Mennonite Church (MC), located near Roseland, Neb., a member of the Iowa-Nebraska Conference, was organized on March 20, 1880, with 26 members, with Albrecht Schiffler as bishop and Samuel W. Lapp as deacon. A meetinghouse was built about two years later, replaced in 1898 by a new one, at which time the membership numbered 160. Daniel Lapp was ordained bishop. Ministers who have served the congregation are John L. Reasoner, Jonas Nice, Andrew Good, John M. Nunemaker, Abraham Stauffer, Samuel G. Lapp, Noah Ebersole, J. Kore Zook, Edward Diener, and Alton Miller. Missionaries from this church sent to India were Mahlon C. Lapp, Jacob Burkhard, George Lapp, Esther Ebersole Lapp, and Velma Lapp Hostetler. In 1957 the bishop was Peter R. Kennel, and the membership was 17. S.S.B.

Roselawn Mennonite Church (MC), Elkhart, Ind., was established in 1949. It is an unorganized mission congregation under the Prairie Street (*q.v.*) Mennonite Church. In 1957 it had 52 members, with Verle Hoffman as its pastor. M.G.

Rosemary (Alberta) Mennonite Brethren Church, now extinct, was organized in 1945. The group had previously been affiliated with the M.B. Church at Gem, Alta. The last leader and minister of the Rosemary church was F. Friesen and the membership was 16; in 1950 it ceased to exist. A.A.T.

Rosenberger, a Mennonite family found largely in southeastern Pennsylvania, especially in the Franconia Conference (MC), and also in the Brethren in Christ Church in Bucks and Montgomery counties, Pa. According to tradition the family came from Zweibrücken, Germany. The first immigrant by this name was Henry Rosenberger Sr. Henry Jr., Benjamin, Daniel, and John Rosenberger are thought to

have been his sons; his daughters were Mary and Sarah. John Rosenberger (1724-1818) was a Mennonite trustee in the Lexington congregation of the Franconia Conference. Henrich Rosenberger (1725-1809) was a deacon in the Franconia congregation (MC). John Rosenberger (1790-1883), a son or grandson of the above John, was a Mennonite farmer in Hatfield Twp., Montgomery Co., Pa. One of his sons was John H. Rosenberger (1832-1910), preacher in the Lexington congregation; another son was Henry H. Rosenberger (ordained bishop at the Silverdale, Pa., Brethren in Christ Church in 1886); and a third son was Samuel H. Rosenberger (1836-1918), who helped build the Silverdale Brethren in Christ house of worship in 1883, where he was ordained a deacon in 1886, and a preacher in 1891. Samuel H. Rosenberger had a son Edwin C. Rosenberger (b. 1886), who is also serving as a Brethren in Christ minister in Silverdale and Souderton. Henry B. Rosenberger (1844-1921) was an unusually influential man in the Blooming Glen Mennonite congregation and community; he was ordained preacher in 1885, and bishop in 1895. One of the leaders of the Eastern District Conference (GCM) is Arthur S. Rosenberger, minister in Quakertown, Pa., and sometime president of Bluffton College. The family is also represented in Canada, Virginia, and other areas to which migrations took place from eastern Pennsylvania. J.C.W.

Francis C. Rosenberger, *Some Notes on the Rosenberger Family* (Richmond, 1950); Edward Matthews, *The Rosenberger Family of Montgomery County* (Harleysville, 1892); A. J. Fretz, *Descendants of Henry Rosenberger* . . . (Milton, N.J., 1906).

Rosenfeld (*Chistopol*), a Mennonite village name which was found in the following settlements: Barnaúi, Siberia; East and West reserves, Man.; Swift Current and Hague, Sask.; Jansen, Neb.; Cuauhtemoc, Mexico; and the Bergthal settlement of Villarrica, Paraguay. (See **Villages**.) C.K.

Rosenfeld (Rosefeldt, Rosfeld, Ro(o)sevelt, Roosenfelt), a family name found among Mennonites of Prussia, Russia, and South America. The name occurs in the Montau-Gruppe congregation as early as 1586 with the coming of Hendrik (van) Roosevelt (*q.v.*) to Montau from Antwerp, Belgium. The name was also found in Lithuania and Kazun. A contemporary of this family is the M.B. Elder G. Rosenfeld of Brazil. (Reimer, *Familiennamen; ML* III, 540.) C.K.

Rosengart, a Mennonite village name which was transplanted from the Chortitza settlement in the Ukraine to Neu-Rosengart, Ukraine; the East and West reserves of Manitoba; and Cuauhtemoc, Mexico. (See **Villages**.) C.K.

Rosengart, West Prussia: see **Preussisch Rosengart**.

Rosenhof, a Mennonite village name found in the following settlements: Brazol, Ukraine; Barnaul, Siberia; West Reserve, Man.; Swift Current, Sask.; Jansen, Neb.; Cuauhtemoc, Mexico; and Menno (Chaco), Paraguay. (See **Villages**.) C.K.

Rosenhof (Rosenort) Evangelical Mennonite Church (Kleine Gemeinde), located near Morris, Man., between the two school districts, formerly villages, Rosenhof and Rosenort, west of the Red River, was founded in 1874 by K. G. immigrants from Russia. Church services were held in the village schools from 1874 until about 1920, when the meetinghouse was erected between the school districts. Jacob B. Kroeker served as bishop 1923-54, followed by P. L. Friesen. The ministers serving in 1957 were Jacob B. Kroeker, Franz B. Kroeker, Cornelius P. Dueck, P. J. B. Reimer, and Frank P. Kroeker; the baptized membership was 501, most of whom were rural people.   D.P.R.

Rosenort, a Mennonite village name transplanted from Prussia to the Molotschna settlement, Ukraine. From here it was transplanted by the Kleine Gemeinde to the West Reserve, Man., and Jansen, Neb. It was also found in Swift Current, Sask.; Cuauhtemoc and Durango, Mexico; Fernheim (Chaco) and Volendam, Paraguay. (See *ML* III, 543 ff.)   C.K.

Rosenort Church of God in Christ Mennonite Church, located 10 miles northwest of Morris, Man., and near the village of Rosenort, was started in 1882 with a membership of 36 as a part of the group that withdrew from the Kleine Gemeinde (*q.v.*). John Enns was the first residing minister, serving 1882-d. 1917. Other ministers who served were Abr. Klaassen, David Hiebert, and G. K. Goossen (1906-d. 37). Services were held in homes and schoolhouses until the first church was built in 1919. The present church, seating capacity 300, was built in 1949. The present ministers are G. F. Goossen and J. D. Penner, both ordained in 1924, and J. P. Isaac and W. P. Goossen, ordained in 1943. Most members are farmers and are predominantly of Molotschna descent and speak Plattdeutsch in their homes. Church services are now mostly conducted in English. Midweek Bible study and singing meetings are held. Musical instruments are not used. Footwashing is practiced at communion services. The membership in 1958 was 188.   J.D.P.

Rosenort Evangelical Mennonite Church: see **Rosenhof.**

Rosenort Home for the Aged, at Rosthern, Sask., was established in 1944, when Isaac P. Friesen gave his house in Rosthern for this purpose. The Rosenort congregation (GCM) owned another house in Rosthern for the same purpose, in which the boys of the Rosthern Bible Academy lived for a few winters while the Academy girls lived in the Friesen house. In 1945 the house was dedicated as a home for the aged, and was gradually filled with aged persons, who could help themselves. The others were taken into the Invalid Home on the Youth Farm. In 1953 an addition was built to the Rosenort Home, making accommodations for 16 persons.   J.G.R.

Rosenort Mennonite Church, a congregation in West Prussia, Germany, originally a part of the Gross-Werder congregation, originated south and east of the town of Tiegenhof (*q.v.*) through the immigration of Dutch Mennonites, to whom the banking firm of Hans Simon and Steffen Loysen (*q.v.*) in 1562 granted land near Danzig to be made arable. At first the congregation, belonging to the Flemish wing, was served in communion and baptism by the elders of the Danzig (*q.v.*) church. After 1639 they chose elders of their own. The first elder was Hans Siemens (d. 1644), chosen on Sept. 22, 1639.

Until the middle of the 18th century the Dutch language was used in the religious services. Their meetings had to be held in their homes, granaries, barns, and sheds. On anniversaries and festive occasions there were sometimes 1,000 persons at a meeting, as in July 1741, when 51 persons were baptized. Not until 1754 did the congregation receive permission to build a church in Rosenort. The first communion service in the new church, held on March 2, 1755, was observed by 1,566 members. By 1787 the congregation had grown to a membership of 1,836. They were almost exclusively farmers, but in 1774 they together owned only 129 Hufen and twelve Morgen of land, or a little more than two Morgen per person.

In order to improve their condition they sent two members to Berlin in 1787, Cornelius Warkentin and Elder Donner, to negotiate with the government concerning their old charter and also to get permission to acquire more land. During their ten weeks in Berlin they found little understanding. Therefore, many families of the West Prussian Mennonites accepted the invitation of Catherine the Great (*q.v.*) to settle in Russia. The first train of emigrants, 152 families with 919 persons, including 41 families of the Rosenort congregation, gathered on July 28, 1788, for a great farewell service in the Rosenort church. The Mennonite emigration to Russia continued for 50 years and took all the overflow of the West Prussian congregations to the still uncultivated steppes of South Russia (*q.v.*). How difficult it was for the Mennonites to take up the wanderer's staff is made clear in a petition presented by the Rosenort congregation in 1791, which asks: "Do the king's most loyal subjects not need to fear to leave the land into which we did not push ourselves, but into which our forefathers were invited more than two hundred years ago, the land which our forefathers for the most part made arable?" (Regehr, 6). The name Rosenort was repeated in their new lands, as in the Molotschna (*q.v.*), Saskatchewan (*q.v.*), Manitoba (*q.v.*), in Mexico (*q.v.*), and in Paraguay (*q.v.*).

On Jan. 19, 1812, the church in Rosenort burned down, but was rebuilt and put into service on Nov. 20, 1814. It seated 600. In the fire the church records kept from Nov. 1, 1772, to 1809, were destroyed. Later the record of 1840-55 was lost in a flood. All that remained were the notes of 1810-40 and the record begun in 1857. After 1754 the cemetery around the Rosenort church belonged to Rosenort and after 1883 another was acquired in Zeyersvorderkampen, both of which had a funeral hall. Several times the Rosenort congregation suffered severe damage by floods, e.g., in 1681, 1848, and 1888.

The baptized membership stood at 622 in 1852, 636 in 1882, and 606 in 1887 (plus 335 children); number of souls was 725 in 1928, and about 800 in 1941. The last elders of the congregation were Peter Regier, of Rückenau, preacher 1879, elder 1887, Eduard Dyck, of Tiegenhof, preacher, 1894, elder 1908, and Ernst Regehr, of Rosenort, preacher 1930, elder 1934, who migrated to Uruguay in 1948.

In the last years before the collapse of 1945 the congregation was served by an elder and five preachers, and in 1942 had a membership of 514 besides 291 children, living in 32 villages. The congregation was a member of the Conference of the East and West Prussian Mennonite congregations and also of the Vereinigung (q.v.).

On Jan. 24, 1945, the area between the Vistula and the Nogat was evacuated before the oncoming masses of Russians. Four hundred years of history of the settlement and over three hundred years of congregational history found its close on these days. Of the 800 souls in the Rosenberg congregation in 1939 not even 150 announced their arrival in the western zones of Germany and in Denmark in 1947. Many fell in the struggles lasting many years, many froze to death on the flight over snow-covered roads or in the floods of the Baltic Sea, many died of starvation or were killed at home, many lost their lives on the road to Siberia or in hopeless imprisonment.

HEGE, E.RE.

J. Ellenberger, *Bilder aus dem Pilgerleben* III (Eichstätt, 1883); H. G. Mannhardt, "Die Mennoniten unter den preussischen Königen" in *Gem.-Kal.*, 1902; H. G. Mannhardt, *Jahrbuch* 1883, 17, 19; *idem*, 1888, 10; E. Regehr, *Geschichts- und Predigertabelle der Mennoniten-Gemeinde Rosenort* (2d ed., Elbing, 1939); *ML* III, 544-47.

Rosenort Mennonite Church (GCM), located in the Rosthern district of Saskatchewan, 50 miles north of Saskatoon, began in 1891, when five families came to the prairies at Rosthern. On July 2, 1894, Elder Peter Regier (q.v.), who had come from the Rosenort church in West Prussia the year before, helped the Rosenort Mennonite Church to organize. In 1896 the first Rosenort church was dedicated in Eigenheim, six miles west of Rosthern. It was rebuilt in 1902. The next year the church in Rosthern was built. In 1910 three churches were built: in Aberdeen (on the right side of the South Saskatchewan River), about 25 miles south of Rosthern, and in Laird and Tiefengrund, 13 miles and 18 miles west and northwest of Rosthern. In 1911 Hague, about 14 miles south of Rosthern, built a church. All of these belonged to the Rosenort congregation. In 1913 David Toews (q.v.) was elected as elder. In 1929 Johannes Regier, son of Elder Peter Regier, was elected as elder to help David Toews, who was commonly called bishop, especially by the government and the daily papers. Eigenheim became self-sustaining in 1929. Besides Hague, churches were acquired at Hochfeld and Neuanlage. The church in Hague was rebuilt in 1929. In 1945 a church was built at Hochfeld and in 1946 the old Hague church was moved to Neuanlage. The Osler church, about 10 miles south of Hague (built in 1928), joined the Rosenort church in 1931. In 1932 Saskatoon organized a congregation which joined Rosenort until 1938. Capasin, about 100 miles northwest of Rosthern, built a church in 1933. The Garthland and Horse Lake (about 25 miles north of Rosthern) congregations, which have their own meetinghouses, also belong to Rosenort. In September 1946 Johann G. Rempel was ordained as elder.

In 1954 the Rosenort congregation divided into two parts because of its unwieldy size. The congregations are now known as the Rosenort Mennonite Church (Tiefengrund, Garthland, Capasin, Hague, Hochfeld, Neuanlage, and Aberdeen) with Arthur Regier of Tiefengrund as their elder, and the United Mennonite Church of Saskatchewan (Rosthern, Osler, Laird, and Horse Lake) with Jacob C. Schmidt of Rosthern as elder. They were both ordained at Rosthern by Elder Johann G. Rempel on Aug. 8, 1954. The United Mennonite Church has about 700 members, and the Rosenort Mennonite Church has about 650 members. Assistant ministers of the Rosenort Mennonite Church are Henry T. Klassen (Hague), John Janzen (Neuanlage), Frank Koop (Aberdeen), A. E. Regier (Tiefengrund), J. J. Pauls (Garthland), George Heppner (Capasin), and of the United Church they are Art Friesen (Laird), Willie Janzen (Horse Lake), and J. H. Pauls (Osler).

J.G.R.

J. G. Rempel, *Die Rosenorter Gemeinde in Saskatchewan in Wort und Bild* (Rosthern, 1950).

Rosental Evangelische Mennoniten-Gemeinde, commonly known as *Allianz-Gemeinde* (q.v.), was organized in Rosental near Chortitza, Ukraine, in the 1920's under the leadership of A. G. Klassen (b. March 12, 1883, d. in exile) and patterned after the Evangelische Mennoniten-Gemeinden (q.v.) elsewhere. This group was characterized by a more tolerant attitude than the Mennonite Brethren toward other Mennonites and a strong evangelistic emphasis. The movement spread into other villages such as Schöneberg, Osterwick, Einlage, and Neuenburg. The Council of Elders (*Aeltestenrat*) consisted of A. G. Klassen, A. Froese, and B. B. Dyck, who were assisted by the following ministers: J. K. Janzen, P. G. Klassen, Dietrich Klassen, and G. P. Schröder. The group was very active also among the Russian population. A. G. Klassen, B. B. Dyck, and others perished in exile, while other ministers and members of the group found their way to Canada and South America.

C.K.

A. A. Töws, *Mennonitische Märtyrer* (Abbotsford, 1949) 148-50, 233-35.

Rosenthal (*Kantserovka*), a Mennonite village of the Chortitza settlement in the Ukraine, transplanted to the Amur settlement, Siberia; the East and West reserves of Manitoba; Jansen, Neb.; Cuauhtemoc and Durango, Mexico; and Fernheim, Paraguay. (See **Villages**; *ML* III, 548.)

C.K.

Rosevelt, Hendrik van: see **Ro(o)sevelt.**

Roseville (Ont.) Mennonite Church (MC): see **Detweiler** Mennonite Church.

Rosiane 't Kemels, an Anabaptist martyr, was executed at Aalst in Belgium, in August 1539. She was born at Gent, Belgium, and was the wife of the martyr Lieven van de Walle (q.v.), who was executed on June 5, 1536, at Gent. After her husband's arrest Rosiane fled to Aalst, where there was also a Mennonite congregation. She was arrested here in February 1536 and imprisoned for some 170 days. Rosiane was put to death by being buried alive.

vDZ.

A. L. E. Verheyden, "La Réforme à Alost pendant le XVIe Siecle," in *Revue Belge de Philologie et d'Histoire* XXIX (Brussels, 1951) 1155 f., 1161.

Rosner(in), Katharina, an Anabaptist martyr, who was executed by burning at the stake with four others at Bamberg, Germany, on Jan. 30, 1528. They confessed that they had been meeting at Mühlhausen (q.v.).

Paul Wappler, *Die Stellung Kursachsens und des Landgrafen Philipp von Hessen zur Täuferbewegung* (Münster, 1910) 45 and 238; ML III, 549.

Rossach, a Mennonite congregation 1820-1914, located near Schönthal, in the Jagst Valley, Württemberg, Germany, named after the residence of its elder Johannes Horsch who served 1820-56. In 1857 it had 31 baptized members, 35 in 1881, 27 in 1887, 26 persons including unbaptized children in 1914. In 1915 the Möckmühl (q.v.) congregation took its place. The congregation was a member of the Badischer Verband (q.v.). (ML III, 549.)
E.T., E.C.

Rossitz, a small market town and manorial estate ten miles west of Brno (q.v.), Moravia. In the 16th century it belonged successively to the noble lords of Pernstein (1522-49), of Lipa (1549-60), and of Zierotin (q.v.) (1560-1628). In 1527 Anabaptists under the leadership of Gabriel Ascherham (q.v.), of Silesia, began to settle there, and in 1529 started a communal Bruderhof in Rossitz where they flourished until they were expelled in 1535. Then they returned to Silesia. In 1527-29 Philip Plener (q.v.), of Baden, and his group, known as the Philippites, also lived in Rossitz together with the Gabrielites, but they separated later and set up their own Bruderhof in Auspitz (q.v.), 12 miles east of Brno. The third group, the Tyroleans, since 1533 called Hutterites (q.v.), settled in Auspitz and Austerlitz (q.v.) but not at once in Rossitz. In 1533 a serious conflict arose between the Hutterites and the two other groups. Ascherham thereupon called a conference of all three groups to Rossitz, which however ended negatively in a complete break of fellowship between these groups, at least for the time being. After the exodus of the Gabrielites and the cessation of persecution about 1536-37, the Hutterites began to settle in Rossitz under the tolerant lords. This Rossitz Bruderhof then existed uninterruptedly until 1622, when Anabaptists were expelled completely from all of Moravia.

According to Beck, Bohemian Brethren (q.v.) or Piccards had also settled in Rossitz, but nothing is known about contacts between Hutterites and Bohemian Brethren. This may be due to two reasons—the language barriers (German and Czech) and the differing genius of the two groups. (Beck, *Geschichts-Bücher*, 69; Zieglschmid, *Chronik;* ML III, 549.)
R.F.

Rossmere Mennonite Mission (MC), in the northeastern sector of Lancaster, Pa., was opened by David B. Groff in 1935. He with Jere Fenninger, under the East Chestnut Street Mennonite Church, conducted the work in rented quarters until their brick meetinghouse, 30 x 50 ft., on Janet Avenue was dedicated on Jan. 1, 1940. Earl W. Mosemann was ordained as pastor on Dec. 21, 1941, and was followed by Daniel E. Miller, ordained Nov. 3, 1946, who was still serving in 1957, with a membership of 42.
I.D.L.

Rossville and Buck Creek (Ind.) Mennonite settlement, now extinct, was located in two distinct districts, one near Rossville and the other near Buck Creek. Their farms were located in the counties of Tippecanoe, Carroll, and Clinton. They were attracted to this area by cheap land and good springs.

The first Mennonites in this area were the brothers John and Christian Zimmerman, who came from Missouri in 1870. Both were ministers. They organized the first congregation of Mennonites, which soon became affiliated with the "Egly-Amish." Other families moving there in the 1870's and 1880's and likely of Amish background were the Schonbecks, Gerbers, Ehresmans, Schrocks, Hirsheys, Gingerichs, and Wises. The Swiss Mennonite settlement in Putnam County, Ohio, contributed a large number of families, including the following names: Amstutz, Mellinger, Basinger, Bucher, Lutz, and Lehmann. Some of these soon left the Mennonite Church and joined the German Reformed Church or Dunkard Church near by. Until 1890 the Mennonite church services were held in the homes. At that time a meetinghouse was erected near Buck Creek on the Chris Schonbeck farm. The membership varied from 30 to 35 in 1906-28. Besides the Zimmerman brothers, other ministers were Christian Gerber, Levi Mellinger, Sam Ehresman, and John Rediger. In 1944 the last church services were held in Buck Creek. In 1941 a Defenseless Mennonite Church was started in Lafayette, some 15 miles away. Most of the families from Buck Creek and Rossville have moved away. Some of the remaining ones worship at Lafayette.
D.L.G.

Delbert L. Gratz, *Bernese Anabaptists* (Scottdale, 1953) 166-67.

Rosthern, Sask., is a town (pop. 2,000) half way between Saskatoon and Prince Albert. It was started in 1902 by Gerhard Ens; the first settlers were Mennonites. Now it has many nationalities and ten churches, of which the Mennonite church is the largest. Most of the stores are owned by Mennonites, especially Friesens. Rosthern was also the seat of the Canadian Mennonite Board of Colonization 1922-47, the time when David Toews (d. 1946) of Rosthern served as chairman, through which over 20,000 Mennonites were brought into Canada, mostly from Russia, and the seat of *Der Bote*, which has been printed and published here from the beginning.
J.G.R.

Rosthern Bible School dates back to 1932, when it was established as a supplement to the Rosthern Junior College (q.v.), then called the German-English Academy. For the first three years Jacob J. Nickel of Aberdeen taught this school, which had a term of about 5 months (November-March). In later years a month was added. In 1935-49 John G. Rempel served as principal of the Bible School. The number of students rose from about a dozen to over 50. In 1939 the Bible School moved into a separate house. H. T. Klassen is now the principal of the Rosthern Bible School. In 1956 it had 25 students.
J.G.R.

Rosthern Junior College dates back to 1905. For many years this school was called the German-

English Academy. Its purpose was to keep Mennonitism alive; study of the Bible and of German were to help in achieving this aim. The first meeting was held by Elder Peter Regier, but soon Elder David Toews was the leader in this affair. The opening of the school took place on Nov. 14, 1905. There were 24 students that year. Herman Fast ("with a beard") was the first teacher, then David Toews took the leadership of the school, teaching until 1917, when he resigned to give his time to the alternative service program. Cornelius D. Penner taught in this school and served as principal in 1921-23 and 1925-31. Another teacher was Kornelius G. Toews, in whose time 1938-51 the enrollment of the school went over 150. David Toews (d. 1946) was chairman of the school board until 1944. A new school building was erected in 1910. Lack of money hindered the school for many years. In the summer of 1945 a dormitory with three stories and a basement was built for the girls and shortly afterwards one for the boys. The enrollment in 1957 was well over 100; it had eight teachers, nearly all of them with a B.A. standing. The principal was Elmer Richert. About 70 per cent of the students, boys and girls, live and board at the school. The four grades of high school are taught.   J.G.R.

Rosthern United Mennonite Church: see **United** Mennonite Church of Saskatchewan.

Rostock, a city (pop. 114,869) in Mecklenburg-Schwerin, Germany. The Anabaptist movement found entry to this place very early. Evidently the soil had been prepared by the Bohemian Brethren, who had members living in the city and its vicinity for many years. The pastor of the church of St. Mary and Dr. Johann Oldendorp, the syndicus of the city, were friendly toward the Anabaptists. The mandates of the Hanseatic League were for a while not published. All violent measures were avoided. However, in 1535, Rostock was represented at a conference of Protestant theologians at Hamburg, which stated that God was punishing the world with the Anabaptists and asked the government to make Anabaptism punishable by law.

The idea that Bernhard Rothmann (*q.v.*) was living in Rostock (derived from a letter written by the council of Löeck to that of Rostock on June 6, 1537) is probably an error. It is more likely that Obbe Philips (*q.v.*) lived here for a time. This was reported to Johann Gartzen, pastor of the church of St. Peter in Hamburg, by Joachim Kükenbiter, a pastor in Schwerin in 1538, with the information that Philips was trying to lure his brethren in other towns of Mecklenburg to Rostock. Obbe Philips presumably wrote his important confession (*Bekentenisse, q.v.*) in Rostock. From this place twenty important tracts were sent to the Mennonites in Holland.

On July 28, 1548, the council of Rostock issued a new decree against the Anabaptists. All persons who had come to the city from the Netherlands within the previous four years were required to present to the authorities within eight days a testimonial from their former residence showing that they were not poisoned by the wicked error of Anabaptism and had lived an honest life there. Those

who were unable to do this were requested to leave the city and its environs within eight days. From that time nothing more is heard of Anabaptists in Rostock. They may have remained quietly in the city for a long time; a large part of them migrated to Prussia and Lithuania or joined the Lutherans. In 1912 fifteen Mennonites were counted in the city.   Neff.

Menn. Bl., 1912, p. 87; C. M. Wichmann, *Mecklenburgs altniedersächsische Literatur* II, 1600-25 (Schwerin, 1885); R. Dollinger, *Geschicte der Mennoniten in Schleswig-Holstein,* . . . (Neumünster, 1930) 193; *ML* III, 550.

Rotgans, a Dutch Mennonite family found on the island of Terschelling (*q.v.*) from the 17th century, and from *c*1720 also on the island of Ameland (*q.v.*). They were usually skippers. One of them was Gerrit Siebesz Rotgans, of Terschelling, who in 1733 transported a number of Mennonite expellees from Lithuania (*q.v.*), with their furniture from Danzig to Holland. Theunis Cornelisz Rotgans, also a skipper, was a resident of Königsberg in East Prussia *c*1800. Both at West-Terschelling and Nes on Ameland some members of this family served as deacons. A noted member of this family is Jacob Wybrands Rogtans (Terschelling, 1859-Baarn, 1948), who studied medicine, practiced in Groningen, thereupon becoming professor of surgery at the Amsterdam University. Some Rotganses moved from Terschelling to Amsterdam *c*1745, where they were members of the Lamist (*q.v.*) church.   vDZ.

Inv. Arch. Amst. II, 2, No. 782; church records of Terschelling and Amsterdam; *Gesch.* 1956, 28, No. 87.

Roth, a Mennonite family name of Swiss origin, found in France and North America. Jakob Rott, a farmer of Bülach, canton of Zürich, and Nesy Rott, of Bipp, canton of Bern, are named among the early Swiss Anabaptists in 1533 and 1538. As early as 1527 Hans Roth preached at Kitzbühel, Austria, and baptized a number of persons at Münichau. Othmar Rot(h), of St. Gall, is the author of hymn No. 53 in the *Ausbund* (*q.v.*), composed in 1532. In the 17th century Mennonite Roths were living at Diesbach in the area of Thun, and a Mennonite Rot family in the lower Aargau. Hans Roth was among the Mennonite emigrants to the Palatinate in 1670, and other Roths emigrated from Switzerland to the Alsace at the end of the 17th century. Among the Swiss Mennonites settling in the neighborhood of Groningen, Netherlands, in 1711, were Ulrich Roth, of Diesbach, with his wife and three children, and another Ulrich Roth, a miller of the Emmental, aged 55, with his wife Elsbeth Steyner and four children. In the 18th century a Martin Roth is mentioned, who was a preacher of the congregation at Alwinc (*q.v.*) in Transylvania, and who under the threats of the Jesuit priest Delphini (*q.v.*) left the church.

In 1750 the Montbéliard Mennonite church record lists Hans Roth, formerly of Aux Gouttes, later at Exincourt, likely the progenitor of Nicolaus Roth, who married Veronica Zimmerman in Europe and died in 1834, leaving seven children. His widow came to the United States in 1837, probably from Baden, Germany. Several of his children immigrated to America, settling near Hamilton, Ohio, before his widow came to Hamilton in 1837 with the remaining children, several years later moving to Morton, Ill. One daughter, Barbara Roth, who married Joseph Zehr in Europe, settled near Tavistock, Ont. Descendants of Nicholas Roth are found most frequently in central Illinois, since six other children settled in localities of Morton, Groveland, Fairbury, El Paso, and Gibson City, although descendants are scattered throughout the United States. There were in 1955 approximately 2,364 descendants of Nicolaus Roth with approximately 300 bearing the Roth name. Outstanding personalities bearing the family name are Daniel Roth, youngest child of Nicolaus, who served as the minister of the Pleasant Grove (Amish) Mennonite Church at Tremont, Ill., and his grandson Roy Daniel Roth, former pastor of the Pleasant Hill Church at East Peoria, Ill., now president of Hesston College. *A Genealogical Study of the Nicolaus and Veronica (Zimmerman) Roth Family (1834-1954),* written by Ruth C. Roth and Roy D. Roth, published under auspices of Daniel Roth Family Reunion in 1955, is the first work written regarding the Nicolaus Roth family.

Obituaries in the *Herald of Truth* and other Mennonite periodicals reveal that Roths have lived in sixteen states and provinces, with Iowa, Ohio, Nebraska, Ontario, Oregon, Pennsylvania, and Illinois leading in this order. These are mostly descendants of many 19th-century immigrants from Europe, who were not necessarily closely related to each other. Paul M. Roth, Mennonite minister of Masontown, Pa., is a grandson of one of these immigrants, Benjamin Roth from Alsace, who settled at Bellefontaine, Ohio. His brother Daniel's descendants live principally in Oregon. Their half brother Joseph settled in Wayne County, Ohio, in 1868, but his descendants live principally in Henry County, Iowa. In 1947 there were 19 Roth Mennonite ministers in North America and Europe, of whom 13 were serving in the Mennonite Church (MC). R.C.R., vDZ.

Ruth C. Roth and Roy D. Roth, *A Genealogical Study of the Nicolaus and Veronica (Zimmerman) Roth Family (1834-1954)* (Elkhart, 1955); Harvey Reeser and Norma Hamilton Reeser, *The Genealogy of Christian and Catherine (Rich) Roth* (n.p., 1953?).

Roth, Friedrich (1845-1932), a teacher in the Gymnasium of Augsburg, Germany, the city of his birth, author of the four-volume *Augsburgs Reformationsgeschichte* (Munich, 1889) and the four-volume *Augsburgs Reformationsgeschichte* (Munich, 1901-11); "Zur Geschichte der Wiedertäufer in Oberschwaben"; I, "Die Anfange des Wiedertäufertums in Augsburg" (Christian Meyer); II, "Zur Lebensgeschichte Eitelhans Langenmantels von Augsburg"; and III, "Der Höhepunkt der wiedertäuferischen Bewegung in Augsburg und ihr Niedergang in Jahre 1528," in *Zeitschrift des Historischen Vereins für Schwaben und Neuburg* XXVII (1900) 1-45, and XXVIII (1901) 1-154; "Der Meistersinger Georg Breuning und die religiöse Bewegung der Waldenser und Täufer," in *Monatshefte der Comeniusgesellschaft,* 1904, 74-93; *Leonhard Kaiser, ein evangelischer Märtyrer* (Halle, 1900); *Willibald Pirkheimer . . . Der Einfluss des Humanismus und der Reformation auf die Erziehung und Schule* (Halle, 1898). The "Höhepunkt" article of 1901 is extraordinarily valuable, with an exhaustive exploitation

of the archival documents relating to the Augsburg Anabaptists. (*ML* III.) NEFF.

Roth, Leonhard, a Hutterite song writer, who was seized with 150 brethren at Steinabrunn (*q.v.*), Austria, on Dec. 6, 1539, and taken to the Falkenstein castle (*q.v.*), where they were held for six weeks and subjected to repeated rigorous examination. Thereupon Roth was sent to the galleys at Trieste with ninety of the Brethren; with several others he escaped and returned to Moravia. In the following year (1541) he died at Schackowitz (*q.v.*). In the Falkenstein prison and in Trieste he wrote three letters to the brotherhood. He also wrote the following three songs: "Ach Gott im höchsten Reiche, Du starker Schirm und Schild" (15 stanzas), "O Gott Vater in Ewigkeit, Dir sei ewig Lob, Ehr bereit" (29 stanzas), "Herr Gott Vater vom Himmel, wir bitten dich gemein" (25 stanzas), called the Steinabrunn hymn. Several stanzas of the first hymn are found in the new German Lutheran hymnal, hymn No. 203. NEFF.

Beck, *Geschichts-Bücher,* 144-47; Wolkan, *Geschicht-Buch,* 156, 178; Zieglschmid, *Chronik,* 227; *Lieder der Hutterischen Brüder* (Scottdale, 1914) 89 ff.; Wolkan, *Lieder,* 173; *ML* III, 551.

Rothe(i)m, Gys van: see **Ratheim, Gisbert van.**

Rothen, David, a schoolteacher and hymn writer of the Palatinate, Germany, stemmed from Switzerland and was received by baptism in the Mennonite congregation at Friedelsheim (*q.v.*) on May 21, 1830, and then served as a teacher on the Branchweilerhof (*q.v.*). In 1832 he emigrated to America. Eight of his hymns were adopted into the hymnal of the Mennonites of South Germany. (*ML* III, 551.) NEFF.

Rothenburg ob der Tauber, a town (pop. 11,200) in Bavaria, Germany, in which there were a few Anabaptists in the early 16th century. As an imperial city since 1172 it had some rural territory attached to it. Karlstadt's (*q.v.*) presence here from December 1524 to the end of May 1525 had some influence. Anabaptist preachers and teachers had penetrated Rothenburg territory in 1527/28 from near-by Windsheim, among them Georg Nespitzer (*q.v.*), a weaver of Passau, George Utz, a dyer of Munich, and Marx Maier from Alt-Erlangen. In 1529 several Anabaptists were arrested in Rothenburg—Hans Bassauer, a blacksmith, Hans Hartmann, a tailor, and Christine, the wife of the dyer Veit Merkur. Both men recanted and were expelled. In 1529 Markus Schmidt, the leader of a small Anabaptist congregation in Schmerzbach, a rural village below Rothenburg, was forced to recant but was not expelled. In 1536 the Anabaptist Endres Kentlein (Keller), a citizen of Rothenburg, was arrested and submitted an extensive confession of faith (16 printed pages), but finally swore the required oath promising to leave and not return (*Urfehde*). In 1564 the Anabaptist Hans Kress, a brewer, was expelled from the city. Schattemann concludes that the Anabaptist movement never played a major role in Rothenburg, and that there were only scattered individuals of the group. E.C.

Paul Schattemann, *Die Einführung der Reformation in der ehemaligen Reichsstadt Rothenburg o.d.T. (1520-1580)* (Munich, 1928) 50-71, 72 ff., 83, 141; *TA Bayern* II, 163-238, where the confession by Markus Keller is printed, pp. 193-209; *ML* III, 552.

Rothenfelder, Jörg Propst (also called **Jörg Maler**), the compiler and copyist of the recently (1955) discovered *Kunstbuch*, a codex containing 42 epistles written by members of the Marpeck brotherhood, and a hitherto little-known Anabaptist leader. He became an Anabaptist in 1532 when he was baptized by Sebold Feichter in the home of George Nessler in Augsburg. Feichter's recantation on March 29, 1533, may have had a negative effect on Maler's stability. At any rate the Augsburg *Straffbuch* shows that on Sept. 18, 1533, Maler also recanted and took an oath (*Urfehde*), after which he was expelled from the town. It is in this period that a "recantation" by Maler belongs which is now in the Augsburg Archives (III Fasc. No. 24. Ms. Copy from Box Catalogue in Schwenckfelder Library, Pennsburg). In this statement Maler said that he would reply to the five articles submitted to him. (1) Concerning the place of the external Word Maler cites Romans 10 and says that it refers to both the inner and the outer word; Peter's sermon at Pentecost, Philip's sermon to the Eunuch, and other passages of Scripture show that the inner and the outer word cannot be separated. (2) Concerning infant baptism, he said that under the influence of the Anabaptists he had hitherto considered it to be a human ordinance, and had allowed himself to be baptized. Since the important matter is the content of baptism, not the time, he would not quibble about it. Salvation does not depend on the external element in any case, but rather on the death of Christ. By this he did not wish to invalidate what Christ had commanded, for good deeds to friends and foes would endure. (3) Concerning the Lord's Supper, the important thing is faith. To the extent that a man believes he will partake of Christ. (4) Concerning government, Maler did not deny that a ruler could be a Christian, for after all, as one can be a father who rules his family, so also a ruler can be a Christian, as Paul wrote in I Tim. 6. (5) When asked if a Christian can swear an oath, Maler replied, "Yes, wherever it relates to the honor of God and love for the neighbor." The Christian has no law, even though he is subject to the law of God. Over perjurers stands the law of wrath. He did not understand either Christ or James as prohibiting the oath, but rather swearing by creatures as the scribes had done. He says that according to the understanding of many Anabaptists Paul must have erred (II Cor. 2) when he called God to witness over his soul. Maler closes with a prayer that God might be merciful to the many Anabaptists who were still imprisoned in the chains of conscience.

The striking similarities between this recantation and Hans Denk's appear to indicate literary dependence. Fortunately, Maler himself explained this recantation in 1550 when the Augsburg Council questioned him about it. He told them that when he had just come to faith (1532) and was in prison, Musculus (*q.v.*) and other preachers were unable to move him. Then Bonifacius (Wolfhart), the pastor

of St. Anne's Church, tricked him into signing the four or five articles by stating that they meant little since the council was divided between papists and Lutherans. Maler admitted that he had not given sufficient thought to the matter and that he had been hypocritical in not denying and opposing the letter which was read to him; therefore he had soon been found again among the Anabaptists (1535) and again asked to desist. This time he refused because his conscience would not allow him to comply. He learned then that the council did not agree with Bonifacius' presentation of the matter to him in prison. Other than that, Maler insisted he had never openly recanted.

Maler was apprehended at a large Anabaptist meeting at Augsburg on April 4, 1535, in a ravine (*Grube*) in Rosenau. His court records of April 5 and 7 indicate that since his earlier stay in the city he had been in Switzerland and Moravia, and was suspected of bringing a letter from there to the brotherhood at Augsburg. On April 15 he was driven out of town with a whip.

For six years following this (1535-41), Maler lived in St. Gall, and then for nearly eight years (1541-48) in Appenzell. While here he was in correspondence with Pilgram Marpeck, whom he had learned to know through his excellent work at St. Gall in getting water to a fulling mill. While in Appenzell he received a letter from Pilgram Marpeck attempting to iron out some difficulties among the Appenzell Brethren (*Kunstbuch*, #8, dated 1543). Maler was apparently an elder here, for he baptized two persons. He learned the trade of weaving. He left Appenzell on account of some disagreement. The Brethren there, for example, rejected the oath entirely; he thought that where it served the needs of the Brethren and contributed toward the preservation of righteousness or truth it was permissible. The Brethren rejected all bearing and use of the sword; Maler rejected only its misuse. The Brethren would not concede that one could take an unbelieving wife or one with whom one did not agree, but Maler thought this wrong in view of Paul's advice. The Brethren did not want any of their number who was a weaver to weave anything colored or bold; Maler could see no wrong in it. The Brethren felt that one should not punish or strike his wife, no matter how angry he became; Maler believed punishment of one's wife to be justified in certain cases just as a father punishes his child. Finally, the Brethren refused to report their marriages to the government, whereas Maler felt that since the government was instituted by God and had authority over adultery, it should also be informed about marriages. That Maler was nonresistant is clear from his refusal to answer the call to arms to protect Appenzell, which resulted in an order to leave the city. He arrived in Augsburg about Feb. 7, 1548, and joined Marpeck (*q.v.*).

When Maler was taken into custody on April 23, 1550, he was stronger in faith than he had been on his previous arrest (1533) and refused to recant. He was then imprisoned, and since a visit by the preachers in October 1551 failed to bring results, he was ordered to remain in prison until April 22, 1552. The visit of the clergy is no doubt the one described by Maler in the *Kunstbuch* (fol. 164), when he was sentenced to remain in prison until he recanted. But on May 5 they had spared him torture because he had a very sore leg, which had recently deteriorated, and because he was weak in constitution.

When he was summoned on April 22, 1552, the judges, out of pity for his condition, wanted to release him. On April 25 they promised to do so if he would refrain from propaganda or holding meetings, either within or without the city limits. Although such a proposition must have been a severe temptation to the sick man, he replied that he understood the proposition well, and had given it careful consideration, but because of his conscience he could not accept it, since he did not know what God desired to do with him. Otherwise, as far as temporal matters were concerned, he was happy to obey the government, even as his life has hitherto been blameless, only he must be unrestricted as far as God's Word and his faith were concerned. The council decreed that he must leave town and re-enter it only upon pain of corporal punishment. On July 4, 1553, Sigmund Bosch addressed a letter of comfort to Maler admonishing him to be patient in all tribulation (*Kunstbuch*, #26).

That Maler was considered a leader in the brotherhood (*Kunstbuch*, fol. 164, 168 f.) is indicated by references to him in the correspondence between Marpeck and the Moravian Anabaptists. Marpeck reported that he was sending Maler to them, and they replied that they were happy to have him come. Since this was written soon after Maler was released from prison, it can be assumed that he resumed his church work at once.

Besides the *Kunstbuch* Maler left two confessions of faith, probably written because of differences with his colleagues, and an important epistle to Ulrich Agemann. The first confession, *Rechenschaft des Glaubens* (Fol. 228-35b in the *Kunstbuch*), was written at Appenzell in 1547. It is a typical Anabaptist confession of faith in that it consists almost entirely of a series of Scriptural quotations dealing with such matters as the necessity of suffering and cross bearing, discipleship, and the purity of the church. The margin contains many citations from the Old and New Testaments as well as the Apocrypha. There is no indication of the context within which this confession was drafted, but throughout it breathes the spirit of Anabaptism.

The second confession of faith, the *Bekenntnis des Glaubens,* dated 1554, is also brief (Fol. 331b-35b) and is patterned on the Apostles' Creed. The margins again are filled with references to Scripture passages; it is the concordance type of confession very common among Anabaptists. The union of his confession with the Apostles' Creed indicates also the interest of many Anabaptists in the Christian creeds. At this point they were definitely not heretics but part of the universal church. In all points this confession of Maler's is in harmony with Anabaptist theology.

The third writing by Maler in the *Kunstbuch* is his epistle to Ulrich Agemann, who was friendly toward the Anabaptists but never joined them. This epistle, dated at St. Gall on Oct. 15, 1562 (Fol. 144-57), urges Agemann to make an open confession of faith, accept baptism, and become a member of the covenant community, Christ's suffering body. He begins by pointing out that the kingdom of Christ is not one of force, but one which each member has joined of his own free will. Maler's second point, stressing the importance of a clear distinction between the church and those without, leads him to discuss the nature of Christian baptism, in which he again stresses the nature of the covenant. Baptism is not for the unknowing, as practiced among those opposing Christ (the term "Widerchristen" used here was obviously a reply to the term "Wiedertäufer" and had been used by Eleutherobion—*q.v.*— in 1528), but only for those who have faith. The order (*Ordnung*) of Christ must be observed, and the three witnesses (spirit, water, and blood) must be kept together. Nor should one have only the inner baptism (as certain perverted spirits teach); rather, the inner faith demands an outer witness, else faith is dead. Outside the order of the Holy Spirit and of Christ there is no grace, good pleasure, or forgiveness of sin. Maler further details the order of Christ, using the same general approach found in all South German Anabaptism—Denk, Marpeck, Hut, etc. The order is derived from Mark 16 and Matt. 28 and insists that teaching must precede baptism.

Inserted after this epistle (Fol. 157) in the *Kunstbuch* is a discussion of the oath in reply to a question put to the author. This was likely also written by Maler, and represents a variation from the typical Anabaptist position, at least as it was expressed at Schleitheim (*q.v.*). The position expressed is, however, in harmony with the position of Hut (*q.v.* in *ML* but not *ME*), Denk, and Marpeck in the *Kunstbuch*. Whereas Schleitheim insisted that the asseverations of Paul were merely instances of calling God to witness, and hence not oaths, Musculus (*q.v.*) in his booklet on the oath in 1533 had argued that Paul and Christ both used the oath; hence the restrictions on the oath enjoined in the Sermon on the Mount and in James are not to be taken in an absolute sense. This argument, starting from a Biblicistic presupposition, must have had an appeal to Anabaptists like Maler. At any rate the statement in the *Kunstbuch* reflects the position of Musculus.

The relationship of Maler to the larger Anabaptist movement is not too clear. Along with his copying of the *Kunstbuch,* there are also some critical comments against Marpeck and his group, as well as positions which directly oppose the Marpeck brotherhood's position. This is true of his interpretation of II Cor. 2, "The letter kills," which Scharnschlager (*q.v.*) and Marpeck both insisted refers only to the Old Testament. In the *Kunstbuch* (Fol. 152b) Maler takes the opposite position, although he does not develop it in polemical opposition to anyone. This may indicate that after Marpeck's death and Scharnschlager's removal from Augsburg, Maler developed in a direction not completely in harmony with their position.

George Maler is not to be identified with Gregory Maler (*q.v.*) of Chur; their names preclude such identification, although some reasons for their identification can be adduced.

The date of Maler's death is not known. Since the *Kunstbuch* (assembled in 1561) contains a letter written by Maler in 1562, it is probable that he died soon after that somewhere in Switzerland, possibly in St. Gall. W.KL.

Friedrich Roth, *Augsburg Reformationsgeschichte* II, 411, 420, 422; IV, 614 ff., 640 f.; Oskar Vasella, "Von den Anfängen der bündnerischen Täuferbewegung," *Zeitschrift für Schweizerische Geschichte* XIX (1939) 180 f.; Heinold Fast, "Pilgram Marbeck und das oberdeutsche Täufertum," *Archiv für Reformationsgeschichte* 47 (1956) 212-42; Jan J. Kitwiet, *Pilgram Marbeck; ein Führer in der Täuferbewegung* (Kassel, 1957); Walter Fellmann, ed. *Hans Denck, Schriften* II, 110; Christian Meyer, "Die Anfänge des Widertäuferthums in Augsburg," *Zeitschrift des Historischen Vereins für Schwaben und Neuburg* I (1874) 228.

Rothenfels (Königseck-Rothenfels), since 1805 belonging to Bavaria, Germany, previously a gravure in Allgäu (capital, Immenstadt). In the spring of 1528 horsemen and several hundred foot soldiers were organized to find Anabaptists. A number of the Anabaptists were caught, but most fled. They were probably refugees from Switzerland (Bern, Zürich, and St. Gall). The magistrate and officials of the strictly Catholic lords of Montfort had the prisoners tried by the executioner of Kempten, who had long been willingly handling such cases. He was to proceed in accord with the decision of the Swabian League (*q.v.*) of February 1528, which stipulated that persons suspected of Anabaptism were to be removed from their proper jurisdiction and put to death without trial. The executioner could not make up his mind to do this. After a consultation lasting four hours his superiors rejected the decision of the League; they wanted to execute only those who refused to recant. The Rothenfels authorities turned to Memmingen to find an executioner, but very likely in vain. Probably it was impossible to eradicate the Anabaptists. The communities were all Protestant when, in 1546, a Smalkaldian army camped in Allgäu. The preachers were then admonished to convert the Anabaptists. If the Anabaptists were obstinate they were to be banished from the country and their possessions given to their children. In the adjacent Rettenberg territory (in the south of the bishopric of Augsburg, now Sonthofen district) Anabaptists were arrested in 1566 and 1568, who maintained contact with Moravia (*q.v.*). In 1595 a church inspection revealed that "Anabaptists have again taken root . . . and had protection and lodging from our people." Books were confiscated, and their owners banished and threatened with loss of property and life. The neighboring prince-abbot of Kempten (*q.v.*) had seven Anabaptists executed at that time. In 1630 some Anabaptists were found in near-by Alpsee; this is the last evidence of Anabaptists here. R.Do.

City archives of Memmingen; *Allgäuer Geschichtsfreund*, 1921, No. 1; Franz Ludwig Baumann, *Geschichte des Allgäus* III (Kempten, 1890); *ML* III, 552.

Rothmann (Rotmann, Rottman), **Bernhard** (Bernd) (c1495-c1535), a theologian and an Anabaptist of Münster, Westphalia, Germany, was born at Stadtlohn in the bishopric of Münster. He served as a teacher in Warendorf, pastor of the church of St. Moritz at Münster after 1529, went to Wittenberg where he became a friend of Melanchthon, traveled over South Germany, especially Speyer (*q.v.*) and Strasbourg (*q.v.*). He returned to Münster and was appointed pastor of the Church of St. Lambert, and introduced the Reformation into the city in 1532. He joined the "Wassenberg" (*q.v.*) preachers in 1533 and finally allied himself with Jan Matthijs van Haarlem (*q.v.*) and Jan Bockelson van Leyden (*q.v.*), who had come from Holland in early 1534, in whose service he wrote a number of important pamphlets. Nothing definite is known about his death, but it is very likely that he lost his life in the siege of the city in June 1535. His most important works are as follows (all in Low German):

(1) *Bekentnisse van beyden Sacramenten, Doepe unde Nachtmaele der predicanten tho Münster* (Münster, November 1533). A copy is to be found in the Amsterdam Mennonite Library; reprint, H. Detmer and R. Krumbholtz, *Zwei Schriften des Münsterschen Wiedertäufers Bernhard Rothmann* (Dortmund, 1904) 1-85. It is a declaration by Bernhard Rothmann, Hendrik Rol (*q.v.*), Johann Klopreis (*q.v.*), Dionysius Vinne (*q.v.*), Hermann Staprade (*q.v.*), and Gottfried Stralen (*q.v.*); it was printed in Rothmann's own print shop on Nov. 8, 1533, and showed Rothmann (according to Detmer) as an Anabaptist of the peaceful wing.

(2) *Eyne Restitution edder Eine wedderstellinge rechter unde* (in another edition vnnde) *gesunder Christliker leer gelouens unde leuens vth gades genaden durch de gameynte Christi tho Munster an den dach gegeuenn* (Münster, 1534). It is to be found at The Hague; reprint: Bernhard Rotmann, *Restitution rechter und gesunder christlicher Lehre*, published by Andreas Knaake in *Flugschriften aus der Reformationszeit* VII, in *Neudrucke deutscher Litteraturwerke des XVI. und XVII Jhs. 77/78* (Halle, 1888).

The *Restitution* (*q.v.*), Rothmann's most important work, is imbedded in a presentation of his view of history; viz., the fall of man in the old covenant from Adam on, and the restoration by Christ, was followed by a second fall in the new covenant from the second century on by scholars and by princes, and a second restitution from Luther (*q.v.*) to Melchior Hofmann (*q.v.*), Matthijs, and Bockelson; but now not only some parts, but all must be restored, not by and for the learned, but precisely for the common man. The *Beschlussreden*, however, deal with the resisting and avenging hand of Christ and several miraculous acts of God; i.e., the events in Münster since the beginning of 1534. Many a chapter has a genuine Anabaptist tone. Again and again stress is laid on doing the will of God, whatever it might cost. But then again there are chapters from which Melchior Hofmann speaks: in Chapter 4 is the doctrine of the Incarnation, claiming that Christ did not assume sinful flesh from Mary; Chapter 11 teaches that a voluntary sin committed after conversion cannot be forgiven; Chapter 17 teaches the imminent coming of Christ. Besides these there are the outspokenly Münsterite ideas. In Chapter 3 we read that the Old Testament is by no means antiquated. Chapter 12 teaches community of goods. "We have not only made all our possessions common by placing them into the hands of the deacons, but are also ready to promote one another with service of all kinds. All that has served selfishness and possession, buying and selling, working for money, income and interest, misusing our neighbors by fattening ourselves by their labor, etc., has been completely done away." Chapter 15 proclaims that a man has the liberty of having more than one wife; this teaching is based in part on the Old Testament example and the creation, in part on the idea that a man should be allowed to express himself with a good conscience. Chapter 18 teaches that the true and Christian government has received authority from God to act as a servant of God, protector of the innocent and just, avenger of evil, and then shows from their own history where Christians are permitted to use the sword against an ungodly government. These ideas do not originate with Rothmann; but he believes, after conscientious examination, that he can adopt the most radical of them and prove them theologically, indeed, that he must do so, on the basis of his pronounced power over the masses. Philip of Hesse (*q.v.*) rejected this book and Rothmann's former friend Melanchthon wrote *Etliche Propositiones wider die lehr der Widerteuffer*, precisely against this *Restitution*.

(3) *Eyn gantz troestlick bericht van der Wrake vnde straffe des Babilonischen Gruwels, an alle ware Israeliten vnd Bundtgenoten Christi, hir vnde dar vorstroyet, durch de gemeinte Christi tho Munster, Anno M. CCCC. xxx iiij yn Decembre*. This book was printed in Münster, but is preserved in a manuscript copy found in the Staatsarchiv of Düsseldorf. Reprinted in K. W. Bouterwek (*q.v.*), *Zur Literatur und Geschichte der Wiedertäufer, besonders in den Rheinlanden* (Bonn, 1864) 66-80. This pamphlet heightens the language concerning the time and place of vengeance found in the *Restitution*, since distress has been increasing: "Therefore, dear Brethren, arm yourselves for the battle, not only with the humble weapons of the apostles for suffering, but also with the glorious armor of David for vengeance (the day of the return of Christ is the day of vengeance!) in order with divine strength and help to eradicate all ungodliness."

(4) *Van verborgenheit der schrifft des Rykes Christi, vnde van dem daghe des Heren durch de gemeinte Christi tho Münster (Münster, Februar 1535)*. This pamphlet is extant in two printings (*Catalogus Amst.*, 62); reprint in *Bernhard Rothmanns Schriften*, ed. K. W. H. Hochhuth (Gotha, 1857). As the true key for the understanding of the Scriptures this work—Rothmann's last—he claims "the live understanding of the Spirit, which is won by the actual accomplishment of the divine will," as was the case in Münster. In sharp polemics against Catholics and Protestants it proclaims, certain of victory, the assurance that now "a new heaven and a new earth" are coming, "in which righteousness dwells" (Detmer, 127-99).

(5) *Van erdescher vnnde tytliker gewalt* (May 1535). A manuscript copy of this writing is found in the Staatsarchiv at Münster. It is printed in Heinrich Detmer and Robert Krumbholtz, *Zwei Schriften des Münsterschen Wiedertäufers Bernhard Rothmann* (Dortmund, 1904) 86-129. This unfinished fragment takes up ideas of the *Restitution* (Chapter 18): Temporal force became necessary only through

the sin of man and must be abrogated in the dawn of the new kingdom (Detmer, 127-99).

In these works of Rothmann the Protestant zur Linden (*q.v.*) found a gaping abyss between the current presentations of the Münster revolt and the spirit prevailing in the Münsterite writings. Also the Protestant Detmer (*q.v.*) pointed out not only the graphic Low German language of Rothmann (127-99), but, in spite of all his disagreement with the ideas, also speaks appreciatively of the earnestness with which the deepest religious problems are treated. Detmer says that in this misled misleader the religious side of the entire movement is incorporated (129-201). The Catholic Hast (*q.v.*) even calls Rothmann one of the most outstanding men of his time.

NEFF, E.C.

ADB XXIX, 364-70, article by Ludwig Keller, reprinted in *Menn. Bl.*, 1890, 9 f., 13-15, 21 f.; *Catalogus Amst.*, 50-58, 62 f.; C. A. Cornelius, *Geschichte des Münsterischen Aufruhrs* I (Leipzig, 1855) 121 ff., 281, 284; Heinrich Detmer, *Bilder aus den religiösen und sozialen Unruhen in Münster während des 16. Jahrhunderts* II (Münster, 1904); Johann Hast, *Geschichte der Wiedertäufer, von ihrem Entstehen zu Zwickau in Sachsen bis auf ihren Sturz zu Münster in Westfalen* (Münster, 1836); *HRE* XIII, articles by Walther Köhler on "Münster" and "Wiedertäufer"; Kühler, *Geschiedenis* I, 74 f., 80 f., 84 f., 119, 126, 129, 141, 151, 171; *Archiv für Ref.-Gesch.* XLVII (1956) 243-51; R. Stupperich, *Das Münsterische Täufertum* (Münster, n.d.-1957); F. O. zur Linden, *Melchior Hofmann, ein Prophet der Wiedertäufer* (Haarlem and Leipzig, 1885) 349-74; *RGG* IV, article by Walther Köhler; Rembert, *Wiedertäufer*; Christiaan Sepp, *Geschiedkundige Nasporingen* I Leiden, 1872) 55-157; Mellink, *Wederdopers*.

* * *

Modern historians dealing with the person and life of Rothmann are unanimous in their praise of the genius of this man, a trained theologian and one who early assumed a position of leadership in the evangelical church at Münster. Rothmann's travels, which were meant to keep him faithful to the Reformed cause, served rather to broaden his outlook. He was thrilled with what his friend Capito (*q.v.*) showed him in Strasbourg (*q.v.*) in 1531, where he also met Schwenckfeld (*q.v.*; although Schwenckfeld never admitted this acquaintance; he said he had seen Rothmann once). Likely he did not meet Bucer (*q.v.*) personally since Bucer was out of the city when Rothmann visited there. Rothmann called Strasbourg the crown and palm of all Christian cities and churches. Of his time spent traveling from April to July 1531 he spent from the middle of May until July there. When he returned to preach in Münster at the beginning of July 1531, he was thoroughly evangelical in his preaching.

The unsettled state of the bishop's tenure in Münster (there were three in rapid succession) made it possible for Rothmann to rise to a position of honor and power. Related to this was the control which the guilds exercised over the council. He was supported by an atmosphere of reform and so began to agitate for his religious views. On Jan. 23, 1532, he published his confession of faith (found in Kerssenbroch, 176-89). This confession contains thirty articles which include the main points under discussion by the Reformers. It is thoroughly Lutheran and divergent from Wittenberg only in the points dealing with the sacraments, where it shows clear influence from Capito and Zwingli (*q.v.*), for the sacraments are considered memorial signs. There are no indications of Anabaptist leanings, and the separation between the spiritual and the physical realms reminds one of Luther. On August 10, after a number of struggles, the evangelical preachers took over the churches in Münster, and six days later Rothmann along with the preachers published a notice of the abuses of the Catholic Church containing sixteen articles. Here Zwingli's influence is very clear. Article six speaks directly against Luther and for Zwingli.

This divergence from Lutheran views caused both Melanchthon (q.v.; an acquaintance of Rothmann's) and Luther to warn Rothmann, who was suspect also because he practiced the Lord's Supper outside the church, using ordinary bread sprinkled with wine. At the end of 1532 Luther warned Rothmann regarding Zwingli, and felt it necessary to call the attention of the Münster council to the danger of the Anabaptist movement.

As far as Rothmann was concerned this warning was not needed, for on Sept. 6, 1532, he wrote to the humanist Hermann von dem Busche sharply criticising the Anabaptists. This situation, however, soon changed after Philip (q.v.) of Hesse intervened on Feb. 14, 1533, to confirm the six evangelical preachers in Münster, and after the election of the council had resulted in a victory for the evangelical party and the guilds in March 1533. Then a reformation was undertaken in an evangelical sense. For this reason church and disciplinary orders were to be created. Rothmann was entrusted with the working out of a church order. Even the strictly Lutheran John von der Wieck did not oppose him in spite of his suspicion that Rothmann was an Anabaptist. This church order has been lost, but the broad outlines indicate sufficiently that Strasbourg's arrangements and Zwingli's teachings serve as the prototype. Philip's demand that the articles on baptism and the Lord's Supper be changed (April 17, 1533) indicates how little this church order was based upon Lutheran presuppositions.

Through the strong influence of the Wassenberg preachers (q.v.), who entered Münster in the course of 1532, Rothmann began to change his views. The domineering personality of Hendrick Rol, whom he may have learned to know in Strasbourg in 1531, exerted a strong pressure on Rothmann's subsequent development. In any case Rothmann was on the road to a complete rejection of Lutheranism and on May 6, 1533, he made his position against infant baptism very clear. An open division thus came about between the conservative Lutheran party in the council under the leadership of the syndicus von der Wieck, which saw its hope in the Smalcald League, and the party under the leadership of Rothmann supported by the guilds and influenced by the Wassenberg preachers. The result of this was that Rothmann wrote to his friend Bucer and shared his reservations on infant baptism. The reply which Rothmann received was not favorable to his views as he had expected but indicated that infant baptism must be retained to keep the unity of the church. This led Rothmann even further in the rejection of infant baptism, an attitude which resulted in a very important public disputation in Münster on August

7 and 8, 1533. For the Lutheran party and for the Catholic party this disputation was intended to end the influence of Rothmann and the preachers. For this reason the brilliant and well-trained humanist, von dem Busche, was invited to speak for the city council to present its point of view on the sacraments. The preachers, especially Rothmann and Rol, were accused of calling infant baptism an abomination and denying that anyone who had been baptized as an infant could be a Christian. The preachers, with Rothmann as spokesman, thoroughly defeated the opposition in the course of the disputation. Even though at this time Rothmann did not defend rebaptism, or put adult baptism in the place of infant baptism, his arguments against infant baptism were so effective that the council decided to call off the disputation after two days, ostensibly because the aged von dem Busche was tired. A modern historian who described this disputation believes that never at any time did the opponents of infant baptism have such a clear-cut victory in a disputation. To the embarrassment of the council they had to reinstate Rothmann in his ministerial office upon pressure from the guilds, which they did on October 3. Apparently a continual seesawing between the council and the preachers took place in which the preachers were banished and then reinstated, although Rothmann himself was allowed to stay in Münster even though he could not preach.

Another important influence in Rothmann's life now came to fuller expression. Since the summer of 1533, adherents of the sect of the Melchiorites had been coming to Münster (see Münster Anabaptists). Though many things separated them from Rothmann's coterie, their common opposition to Lutheranism drew them together. Rothmann's desire to increase his following naturally made him anxious to have the support of this group. It was through his act that Jan Matthijsz (q.v.), who since November 1533 had been turning many of the Melchiorites into a radical direction, and the revolutionary element which later became so strong in Münster got a foothold. Rothmann's writings show clearly how this change came about. The writing called Bekentnisse, which was written in collaboration with five other preachers and completed on Oct. 22, 1533, and published in Rothmann's own print shop on November 8, bears no evidence of this apocalyptic revolutionary mood. Indeed, as Wray has shown, this confession was translated by the Marpeck brotherhood in an effort to rally the splintered Anabaptist movement of the 1530's together into a united group. Published in 1542 under the title Vermanung (q.v.), it was revised considerably to coincide with the theology of the Marpeck group. Greater stress was laid upon the difference between the Old and the New Testaments; Rothmann's treatment of the circumcision-baptism analogy was dropped and a clearer one presented in its stead; the Marpeck brotherhood went out of its way to insert nonresistant passages, and added numerous admonitions to continue faithful unto the end. A detailed comparison of these two documents shows clearly how the theology of the Marpeck brotherhood formed. Obviously they knew the tragic end which had befallen Rothmann, but they also saw the intrinsic value in the confes-

25

sion of the Münster preachers. Its concise and clear rebuttal of all the arguments against infant baptism could not be allowed to go unnoticed and unused.

Even in this writing the tension between Rothmann's Lutheran background and the influences received from Strasbourg is not completely reconciled. Bucer, writing to Rothmann in December 1533, replied against Rothmann's reservations on infant baptism. Not only did Bucer refute Rothmann, but all of the Strasbourg preachers together wrote a polemical book in March 1534, in which they dealt point by point not only with the published minutes of the disputation held in Münster on August 7 and 8, 1533, but also with the published *Bekentnisse*. This rebuttal by the Strasbourg preachers—Capito, Hedio, and Bucer—sent first in the form of a letter to Münster, was thought so valuable that it was published and sent especially to Augsburg. The title is: *Bericht auss der heyligen geschrift von der recht gottseligen anstellung vnd hausshaltung Christlicher gemeyn/ Eynsatzung der diener des worts/ Haltung vnd brauch der heyligen Sacramenten. Vom heyligen Tauff/ vnnd das die kinder zu teüffen/ mit satter schrifftlicher widerleggung was biss her hie wider vffbracht. Von dem H. Sacrament des leybs/ vnnd bluts vnsers Herren Jesu/ vnnd Christlicher eynigkeit in disem handel zehalten. Durch die Prediger des heyligen Evangeli/ zu Strassburg/ der Stat/ vn kirchen zu Münster in Westfal/ erstlich geschriben.* The writing is important because the *Bekentnisse* incorporates the best of Anabaptist thought. The latter book reveals clear dependence upon a book by Christoff Freisleben (*Vom wahrhaften Tauff Joannis*) (see **Eleutherobios**), and in other respects is a concise rebuttal of the arguments for infant baptism. Also the Strasbourg preachers gave considerable thought to the problem of infant baptism, and as they are fond of pointing out in the *Bericht,* they had read all the literature which the Anabaptists had produced in the previous eight years.

Rothmann's authority in Münster continued to ebb and flow. In November 1533 a new church order was introduced, and because Rothmann opposed it he was directed to leave the city on December 11. Yet he remained, and Philip of Hesse and Wieck planned by means of another disputation to drive him from Münster. This became impossible and on Jan. 23, 1534, an edict by Franz von Waldeck, bishop of Münster, called for the imprisonment of all Anabaptists, especially Rothmann.

Through the influence of Jan Matthijsz (*q.v.*) and Jan van Leyden (*q.v.*) affairs in Münster soon took an abrupt turn. Rothmann's precise role from this point is not clear, but since he had always been impressionable, he very likely came under the influence of these men, who used his gifts of expression and leadership to their own ends. Finally on Jan. 5, 1534, Rothmann along with the Wassenberg preachers was rebaptized; in his home many others were secretly baptized. In the ensuing perversion of power that took place in Münster (see **Münsterites**) Rothmann assumed an ambiguous role. He opposed many of the changes at first, and yet bowed to the pressure of the more revolutionary leaders. Kerssenbroch reports that he took nine wives when polyg-

amy was instituted. His real importance for Münster was his gift of public speaking and of writing. It is a tribute to his writings that Kerssenbroch, the 16th-century chronicler of the Münster revolution, did not give the contents of the writings in German because he did not want to contribute to the spreading of his ideas.

The lasting influence of Rothmann has come through the confession which he wrote with the Wassenberg preachers. This confession lived on in translation and revision (*Vermanung*) in the Marpeck brotherhood, and is still somewhat an Anabaptist classic. Just how much he had to do with its actual writing is not clear. Nevertheless it remains one of the tragedies of early Anabaptism that this gifted man, in spite of all his expressions of humility, yielded to the desire for honor, and finally could not resist the influences which came to bear upon his life. And yet Detmer, his modern biographer, may be correct when he implies that Rothmann inevitably had to take the way that he did because the Reformed party would not give him a serious hearing in the 1533 disputation and ignored his victory.

The last days of Rothmann are not known. It may be that he escaped when the city of Münster was attacked, but it is more likely that he chose a courageous death in battle rather than the miserable life of a fugitive driven from place to place.   W.KL.

Heinrich Detmer, "Das Religionsgespräch zu Münster am 7. und 8. August 1533, Ein Beitrag zur Geschichte B. Rothmanns . . ." in *Monatshefte der Comenius-Gesellschaft* IX (1900) 273-300; idem, *Hermanni A. Kerssenbroch Anabaptistici Furoris . . .* (Münster, 1900); idem and Robert Krumbholtz, *Zwei Schriften des Münsterschen Wiedertäufers Bernhard Rothmann* (Dortmund, 1904); Frank J. Wray, "The 'Vermanung' of 1542 and Rothmann's 'Bekentnisse,' " in *Archiv für Ref.-Gesch.,* 1956, 243-51; P. Bahlmann, *Die Wiedertäufer zu Münster* (Münster, 1894) 10, No. 7; *Corpus Schwenckfeldianorum* V, 28, 323, 402; T. Schiess, *Briefwechsel der Brüder Ambrosius und Thomas Blaurer I* (Freiburg, 1908) 450; Friedrich Brune, *Der Kampf um eine evangelische Kirche im Münsterland* (Witten-Ruhr, 1953) 11, 16, 18 ff., 34, 36, 43; Robert Stupperich, *Die Schriften Bernhard Rothmanns* (Münster, 1970); C. Krahn, *Dutch Anabaptism* (The Hague, 1968) 145-164; *ML* III, 552-54.

Rotholz (Rotenholz, Rothholz), a village in the Inn Valley, near Jenbach, Tirol, Austria, one of the villages in which Anabaptists were found in the early period. In November 1527 it was ascertained that "foreign persons" were in the village, "who take the liberty of stirring up our subjects on Anabaptism and other seductive articles." A search was ordered and carried out. Two Anabaptists lost their lives at the stake at that time. In 1574 the Hutterite Hans Plattner (*q.v.*) was put to death in Rotholz; the Hutterite chronicles relate that an epileptic woman recovered her health by drinking the blood of this martyr.   E.C.

Beck, *Geschichts-Bücher,* 366 f.; Wolkan, *Geschicht-Buch;* Zieglschmid, *Chronik,* 234, 474-76; idem, *Klein-Geschichtsbuch,* 101; Loserth, *Anabaptismus,* 26, 90 f.; *ML* III, 554.

Rothrock Mennonite Church (MC), now extinct, was located near Richmond, Northampton Co., Pa. The meetinghouse, probably built before 1794, was sold by the Franconia Mennonite Conference in

1909: the congregation presumably died out in the first quarter of the 19th century. M.G.

John C. Wenger, *History of the Mennonites of the Franconia Conference* (Telford, 1937) 236-37.

Rotmann, Bernhard: see **Rothmann, Bernhard.**

Rottenbauer, a village (1944 pop. 736) in the Würzburg area of Bavaria (*q.v.*), Germany, became the seat of a Mennonite congregation about 1810, founded by Mennonites from Baden. The center of the congregation was later moved to Giebelstadt and Würzburg. By 1936 there were no Mennonites living in Rottenbauer. In 1839 the congregations of Rottenbauer and Bildhausen (*q.v.*) published a hymnal of their own with 575 hymns, *Christliches Gesangbuch zunächst für Mennoniten. Herausgegeben von der Mennoniten-Brüder Gemeinschaft in Unterfranken* (Würzburg, 1839).

In 1857 the congregation had 110 baptized members; Heinrich Landes of Albertshausen was the elder (preacher 1824, elder 1839), and the preachers were Jakob Horsch (from 1835), Michael Bachmann (1835), Samuel Mosemann (1845), and Heinrich Burkholder (1852). (*ML* III, 554.) E.C.

Rottenburg, a town (pop. 9,500) on the Neckar, between Horb (*q.v.*) and Tübingen (*q.v.*), Württemberg, Germany, until 1806 the seat of the Austrian rule of Hohenberg (*q.v.*), now the seat of a Catholic bishop and of a Catholic seminary.

In the spring of 1526 Wilhelm Reublin (*q.v.*), a native of this town, appeared here with his wife, and stayed in the home of Jörg Schuhmacher. In both Rottenburg and Horb he won and baptized a large number of followers. He called his friend Michael Sattler (*q.v.*) to Horb. In February 1527, when the authorities became aware of the Anabaptists, Reublin fled to Reutlingen (*q.v.*), while Sattler with his wife and his fellows was arrested and taken to Binsdorf (see **Horb**). On May 17 a court session was held in Rottenburg, and on May 21 the inhuman execution of Sattler was carried out. On the next day his wife was drowned in the Neckar. Of his companions some were put to death and some exiled. In 1528 eleven persons were sentenced, some to death and some to exile. In 1529 Anabaptists who had lain in prison 157 days were driven from the town with rods after the executioner had burned an image of the devil on their foreheads.

Thus Anabaptism was exterminated from Rottenburg. For some time longer Lutheranism tried to maintain itself, but finally the Austrian authorities were successful in keeping it a Catholic town.

On Aug. 16, 1957, the Sixth Mennonite World Conference dedicated a memorial plaque to Michael Sattler in the Lutheran parish church in Rottenburg, at which time a special memorial service was held. G.Bos., E.C.

Beschreibung des Oberamts Rottenburg I (Stuttgart, 1899) 379-412; Gustav Bossert, articles in *Blätter für württembergische Kirchengeschichte* I (1866) 25 f.; II (1887) 1-89; III (1888) 4-65; n.s., VIII (1904) 148 ff.; XVI (1912) 148 ff.; *idem*, "Das Blutgericht von Rottenburg," in *Christliche Welt* (Leipzig, 1891) 22 ff.; reprint (Barmen, 1928); *ML* III, 554 f.

Rotterdam, a city (1958 pop. 720,000, with some 1,750 Mennonites) of the Dutch province of South Holland. The fact that two Anabaptist martyrs, Anneken (*q.v.*) Jans and Christina (*q.v.*) Michiels Barents, were drowned here on Jan. 24, 1539, does not prove the existence of a congregation here at that early date, for both women were merely passing through the city when arrested.

Nevertheless there was some Anabaptist activity here in 1534, led by Jan (*q.v.*) Jansz Schot, and an Anabaptist congregation was doubtless established at Rotterdam soon after 1540, which conducted itself quietly. Since the government here was more tolerant than, for example, in Amsterdam or Antwerp, or perhaps because there were fewer Anabaptists living here than at some other places, there were relatively few martyrs at Rotterdam—a total of about 24 in 1534-68, besides a number who were expelled from the city. One of the anonymous martyrs of 1544 was a girl of fourteen, who left a song. In 1558, at the scene of an Anabaptist execution, when the executioner was clumsily strangling Jan Hendricks (*q.v.*) preliminary to burning him, the crowd released the other four prisoners. Concerning the death of Hendrik (*q.v.*) Arentsz in 1568, van Braght's *Martyrs' Mirror* gives a full account. Little is known of the congregation in the early period. In 1556 it met in a home in Houttuyn. Leenaerdt Bouwens (*q.v.*) visited it repeatedly, baptizing 15 persons here in 1554-56, 7 (or 15) in 1557-61, and at least 100 in 1563-75. Soon thereafter there was an influx of persecuted Anabaptists fleeing from Flanders, Belgium.

In the last three decades of the 16th century the Rotterdam congregation, like most of the Dutch congregations, was divided by doctrinal dissension. About 1590 there were at least five congregations here: Flemish, Old Flemish, Waterlander, Frisian, and High German. By 1620 the Waterlanders, Frisians, and High Germans had united; but there was still a splinter of the High German group, perhaps identical with the Claes Woutersz group, and in addition a congregation of Flemish and one of Old Flemish, both in existence since 1590. It is hardly possible to form an actual picture of the various mergers and divisions in the 17th century before 1671. In that year there were three congregations: (*a*) Old Flemish, (*b*) Flemish, also called Flemish and High German, with which the conservative Frisians had united, and (*c*) Waterlander, to which the progressive (Young) Frisians and Mild Flemish belonged.

The (*a*) Old Flemish were extremely conservative; they co-operated with the group known as the Danzig Old Flemish, an association of Mennonite congregations, which included seven small congregations in the Netherlands and some conservative congregations in West Prussia. This Rotterdam congregation was always small, usually 20-30 members, and met in a home called Het Arkje, behind the Lombardstraat. By 1740 its pulpit was vacant and by 1770 the congregation was extinct.

The (*b*) Flemish congregation met in a meetinghouse behind Leeuwenstraat from 1609. The meetinghouse was enlarged in 1645. In 1650 the membership was some 200. This group had important elders in the 17th century. One of these was Bastiaan van Weenighem (*q.v.*) 1659-86, who often visited other Mennonite congregations, e.g., Hamburg-Altona in 1661. He was followed by Herman Schijn (*q.v.*), who moved to Amsterdam in 1690. In 1656 a call was given to the influential Dordrecht elder Tieleman Jansz van Braght (*q.v.*), but he declined. This Rotterdam congregation was a sort of mother church to a number of small Flemish congregations in the vicinity, giving repeated financial aid and free ministerial service to those at Brielle (*q.v.*), Delft, Geervliet, Gouda, Middelharnis, Oosterhout, Schoonhoven, Spijkenisse, Zevenhoven, and Zuidland, all of which nonetheless died out around the turn of the century. In 1632 the deacons Balten Centen Schoenmaker and Michiel Michielsz signed the Dordrecht Confession for the Flemish congregation.

In 1652 and the following years the Rotterdam Flemish congregation was threatened by a serious division because a number of its members were Collegiants (*q.v.*); in 1655 order was restored when five preachers were expelled with their following. The congregation was now very conservative (no contact with Collegiants, close communion, strict church discipline). In 1664 it joined the Zonists (*q.v.*). Gradually the conservatism relaxed; in 1675 religious instruction for children was introduced, which had previously been given by the parents. In 1682 the Biestkens Bible (*q.v.*) was replaced by the state translation (*Statenvertaling*). A union with the Waterlanders was in prospect.

The (*c*) Waterlander congregation, which was represented in 1579 at a Waterlander conference at Emden (*q.v.*) and at Amsterdam in 1581. It was far less important than the Flemish in numbers, wealth, and influence, held its meetings at the Quakernaat (probably from 1592, at any rate from before 1620). It was less conservative in the use of the ban (*q.v.*), mixed marriages (*q.v.*), and the admission of members of other creeds (other Mennonite branches, Remonstrants—*q.v.*—and Reformed) to communion. Dissatisfied Flemish transferred their membership to the Waterlanders; in 1592-1620 an entire Frisian congregation made the transfer. The influx of the Flemish contributed to the involvement of the Waterlanders in the Collegiant dispute; the congregation was divided into two parties in 1655-72, one in favor of and one opposed to the Collegiants.

In 1647 and again in 1655 an attempt was made to unite the Waterlanders with the Flemish; but the offers were rejected by the Flemish. Twice there was talk of merger with the Remonstrants; in 1658 the Remonstrants seem to have taken the initiative, and in 1669-70 the Waterlanders led; both attempts failed. Since 1664 the congregation had belonged to the Lamists (*q.v.*). In the conference meetings of the Lamist or South Holland Sociëteit Jan van Ranst, a Rotterdam preacher, began in 1676 to urge the establishment of a theological seminary. The Waterlander congregation had begun religious instruction (1672) three years earlier than its sister church. A member was appointed to visit the sick, and in 1687 the first salaried preacher, Hendrik Toren, a baker, was engaged. In October 1696 negotiations were inaugurated leading to a merger

with the Flemish congregation. This merger became reality in 1700. The old partisan names that had caused so much damage, were buried; the congregation was now called the United Mennonite Church. Abraham van Loon, of Gouda, preached the sermon of unification on June 6, 1700.

Both meetinghouses were used until 1776, when the Waterlander "preaching house" at the Quakernaat was sold. The congregation had built a stately church with room for all on the site of the Flemish meetinghouse on Leeuwenstraat. This building was made possible by the legacy of the brothers Pieter and Jan Bisschop (*q.v.*), wealthy yarn merchants, the latter of whom died in 1771 at the age of 91. The dedicatory sermon for the church, a fine specimen of baroque architecture and furnished with an organ, was preached by the pastor, Jacob Ouwejans (*q.v.*).

In spite of the unification and the agreement to forget the ancient quarrels, tensions remained throughout the 18th century between a group of Flemish origin and a group of the more liberal Waterlanders. Especially after Ouwejans' death, who had served from 1742 to 1781 and given it a conservative stamp, the old strife threatened to flare up again, but was permanently settled in 1786 with the choice of the pacific Wytse Sytses Hoekstra (*q.v.*) as pastor.

In 1700 at the time of the merger there were 400 members—143 men and 257 women. In the 18th century certain names recurred: Dekker, van Gilse, Jansen, de Koker, Lommen van Lil, Messch(a)ert, van der Pals, van Rijkevorsel, van Rijnbach, van Sleiden, Staal, Verloove, van Vollenhoven, Wynands. In the 19th century the following names were added: Altmann, Cupedo, Dutilh, Gerpot, Hulshoff, de Monchy, Rueb, and Sieuwertsz van Reesema. Most of these old families have died out or moved away; only Altmann, de Monchy, Rueb, Staal, and Verloove remain. The membership, which was 400 in 1700, had dropped to 250 by 1771, and 102 by 1808. Since then there has been a rapid increase: 195 in 1847, 234 in 1861, 498 in 1900, 1,031 in 1918, 1,252 in 1940, but dropped to 835 in 1945 (effects of war), 990 in 1958.

Jacob Ouwejans served as pastor 1742-d.81, Jan Menalda 1771-d.1800, Keimpe Dam 1773-d.1810, Wytze Sytses Hoekstra 1786-d.1801, Nicolaas Messchaert (*q.v.*) 1802-33 (he died of cholera), Abraham Jacobus van Pesch 1834-41, Pieter van der Goot (*q.v.*) 1842-51, Sytse Hoekstra Bz (*q.v.*), who later taught in the Seminary at Amsterdam, 1852-57, J. P. Müller 1857-62, Jacobus Craandijk 1862-84, Johannes Dyserinck (*q.v.*) 1884-1901. Under Craandijk and particularly Dyserinck Modernism found its way into the congregation, without, however, causing any difficulties or dissension. Since 1902 the preachers have been A. Binnerts Szn 1902-7, F. Dijkema 1907-16, S. H. N. Gorter 1916-46, Miss D. Groeneveld 1924-28, Miss S. Goossen 1928-34, Mrs. H. C. Voorhoeve-ten Bruggencate 1936-48, N. van der Zijpp 1946- , and D. E. W. Siccama 1950- .

The Mennonites of Rotterdam have always been on good terms with the city government. Only occasionally, during the 17th century, some obstacles were placed on their path. Permission to enlarge the meetinghouses was always willingly granted. In 1629 the Waterlander preacher Edward Nabels was excused from assuming the office of sheriff, which he rejected for reasons of nonresistance, upon payment of a "gift" of 25 guilders for the Reformed poor (*Inv. Arch. Amst.* I, No. 447). A good testimonial is given the Rotterdam Mennonites in a letter written on Feb. 19, 1660, by the magistrate of Rotterdam to the city of Bern, Switzerland, in behalf of the suppressed Bernese Anabaptists (*Inv. Arch. Amst.* I, No. 1746). Once or twice the burgomasters made serious difficulties: in 1693 the deacons and preachers of the Waterlander congregation were summoned to court on a charge of Socinianism (*q.v.*). In 1718 Pastor David van Heyst (*q.v.*) was called before the burgomasters of Rotterdam on a charge of unorthodoxy. On both these occasions an oral confession of faith was sufficient. The matter was cleared by a visit of a committee of the church council to the burgomasters. In 1795, when military conscription became law, it took some effort to establish the release of the Mennonites from armed duty; the beautiful new church was used for political meetings and even for military drill. At that time, as everywhere in the Netherlands after 1796, the Mennonites took part in the city government. The Mennonites have had an active part in the economic rise of Rotterdam; especially the van Vollenhoven and de Monchy families are engaged in trade and shipping.

On two occasions the Rotterdam congregation, which had previously been very active in supporting oppressed Mennonites elsewhere, as in 1660 and 1710 those in Switzerland, in 1690 those in the Palatinate, and after 1730 those in Prussia, was of particular importance for Mennonitism in other countries. In the first half of the 18th century, especially in 1709-34, many Mennonite emigrants from Switzerland and the Palatinate went to America by way of Rotterdam. They were generally cared for by the church board, and sometimes even clothed, and considerable sums were used by the congregation to transport them to London, the port of exit for Pennsylvania. Some were helped to sail directly from Rotterdam to America. In 1709 the preacher Hendrik Toren (*q.v.*) and the deacon Jan van Gent are said to have promoted the transportation to England of the Palatine Mennonites who had come to Rotterdam; over 1,000 of them, however, were persuaded by Toren and van Gent to return to the Palatinate. In 1735, 180 Mennonite emigrants were shipped to Pennsylvania by Archibald and Isaac Hope, members of the Rotterdam Mennonite congregation, and again 3,000 in 1753 and 4,000 in 1765, all from the Palatinate. The second time when Mennonites, expelled from their homes, traveled to the New World via Rotterdam began in 1924, when the Dutch Mennonite Emigrant Bureau was established for the benefit of the Russian Mennonite refugees. Led by S. H. N. Gorter, J. Th. de Monchy, C. S. Altmann, and J. N. de Jong, the Bureau did an extensive work. Over 1,000 of these Mennonites left Europe for Canada and Brazil via Rotterdam in 1924-31. On Jan. 27, 1947, the *Volendam* sailed from Rotterdam with 442 Russian Mennonites, and after stopping at Bre-

merhaven to pick up 1,863 more refugees, went on to Paraguay.

World War II brought unspeakable distress to Rotterdam—occupation, bombs, destruction, hunger, and death. The Mennonite congregation was also hard hit. In consequence of losses through bombing, hunger, compulsory resettlement of elderly persons in the country and of younger persons into foreign lands, the membership dropped from 1,252 to 835. A great misfortune struck the congregation in the early days of the war, in May 1940, when with the heart of the city their beautiful church was burned down. Little was saved. A valuable collection of portraits was lost, as well as the six costly silver communion cups acquired in 1780, the silver baptismal plate, and two antique pewter wine jars from the 17th century; some of the archives, however, were saved, for they had temporarily been stored elsewhere. During the war and occupation, congregational life was carried on as well as possible. Services were held at various places with many changes. Plans were made before the war was over for the rebuilding of the church, but it took some years after its close before the plans of the young architect Gerrit Kuiper, a member of the congregation, could become reality. On Oct. 27, 1950, the moderator H. G. J. de Monchy started the machine that drove the first concrete pillar into the ground. On Dec. 21, 1951, the new church, with its spacious side buildings, could be used. Both pastors preached on the occasion. The building was made possible only by the sacrificial giving of the entire congregation and the generous support of the entire Dutch Mennonite brotherhood. The fine pipe organ, acquired in 1957, was largely a munificent gift by one of the members.

The congregation is led by a church council, which consists of the ministers and twelve members who are chosen for five-year terms. Until 1921 the church board was self-perpetuating; the trustees are now elected by the congregation. The church council is assisted by the *Oude dienst,* i.e., a committee of retired deacons. Since 1952 there has also been a committee of twelve lay members, which cares for the financial and social needs of the congregation, the fund for this work being provided by the church council. The church has a choir, four women's groups, a youth circle (ages 18-35), a section of Menniste Bouwers (ages 12-18), a West Hill Sunday school (ages 4-12), and a study group of the Peace Group.   vDZ.

Inv. Arch. Amst. I, Nos. 143, 207, 216, 384-89, 393 f., 447, 613, 778, 781, 784, 801, 804, 806 f., 815, 835, 885, 907, 1060, 1064, 1066, 1133, 1188, 1248, 1543, 1746, 1788, 2248, 2251 f., 2256, 2258 f., 2264 f., 2268, 2274-79; *idem* II, Nos. 2123-41, 2194-2213, 2242, 2477, 2479, 2955, 3304, 3313, *idem* II, 2, Nos. 332-461; *DB* 1861, 171 f.; 1862, 110 f.; 1864, 102-23; 1869, 120-24; 1872, 57; 1877, 86; 1892, 103, 117-27; 1896, 55; 1897, 78-82, 97 ff.; 1900, 94; 1905, 169-75; 1906, 141-45; 1908, 89-104; 1917, 122, No. 159, 152; 1918, 49; *Mart. Mir.* D 70 f., 143-45, 191-96, 383; E 472 f., 453 f., 574-78, 736; Blaupot t. C., *Holland* I and II, *passim;* K. Vos, *Geschiedenis der Doopsgezinde gemeente te Rotterdam* (Rotterdam, 1907); W. Bezemer, "Geloofsvervolgingen te Rotterdam 1534-39," in *Archief Nederl. Kerkgeschiedenis* VI (1897) 52 ff.; Mellink, *Wederdopers,* 222-26; J. Verheul Dzn, *De Doopsgezinde Gemeente en haar Kerkgebouw te Rotterdam* (Rotterdam, 1907); H. C. Hazewinkel, *Geschiedenis van Rotterdam* (Amsterdam, 1940) I, 159-63; II, 214 f.; *DJ* 1953, 34-37; S. H. N. Gorter, "Destruction and Reconstruction of Mennonite Churches in Holland," *Menn. Life* I (January 1946) 31; *ML* III, 554-58.

Rotterdamsch Lied-boeck, a Dutch Mennonite hymnal, mentioned in van Braght's *Martyrs' Mirror* (D 665, E 983). No copy of this hymnal is extant.

vDZ.

Rottevalle, a village in the Dutch province of Friesland, the seat of a Mennonite congregation, which was originally centered in the neighboring hamlet of Witveen. Here Mennonites settled about 1620-40 to cultivate the moors and to dig peat. In the second half of the 18th century the congregation, known at that time as Witveen-Rottevalle, had a meetinghouse in each of the two villages. Gradually the congregation center shifted to Rottevalle. Soon after 1830 the Witveen meetinghouse was dismantled because it was dilapidated and also because very few members were living there; the church in Rottevalle was remodeled and enlarged in 1838. An organ was installed in 1931. The membership was 108 in 1751, 72 in 1847, 101 in 1900, and 142 in 1958. In 1734 Witveen joined the Conference (Sociëteit) of Friesland, followed in 1778 by Rottevalle. The last lay preacher in this congregation was Volkert Klazes Klosma ("Volkert Oom"), who served from 1799 to 1830. After his retirement the pulpit was vacant for nearly ten years. Since 1839 the ministers of the Rottevalle congregation have all been educated at the Amsterdam Mennonite Seminary. H. A. van Cleef served 1839-51, A. Loosjes 1852-53, P. Bruyn 1854-55, A. Käyser 1856-58, J. van Delden 1859-61, B. Cuperus 1861-63, H. C. Hofkes 1863-68, H. ter Meulen 1869-73, S. Wartena Jr. 1873-80, L. Hesta 1882-84, A. K. Kuiper 1889-95, P. J. Glasz 1896-98, E. Engelkes 1899-1902, J. Hulshoff 1903-9, A. Stiel 1910-25, Miss S. E. Doyer 1926-43, Miss M. J. van Hamel 1946-54, A. Zwartendijk of Surhuisterveen, in charge 1954-57, and again Miss S. E. Doyer 1957-. Church activities include Sunday school for children, Menniste Bouwers (ages 12-15), youth group, and ladies' circle.

vDZ.

Blaupot t. C., *Friesland,* 189, 248, and 306; *DJ* 1840, 22; *DB* 1872, 33-42; 1900, 109, 122 note 1; *Inv. Arch. Amst.* II, Nos. 2214-18; *ML* III, 558.

Rottmann, Bernhard: see **Rothmann, Bernhard.**

Rottmannshart, a hamlet (pop. 33) near Manching, south of Ingolstadt (*q.v.*), Bavaria, Germany, was the seat of a Mennonite congregation from 1891 to 1905. It was founded by Mennonites from Baden (*q.v.*), and later transferred its seat to Ingolstadt. In 1956 an elder, Eduard Landes, and a preacher, Richard Landes, of the Ingolstadt congregation were living in Rottmannshart. (*Gem.-Kal.,* 1957, 90; *ML* III, 558.)

E.C.

Rowe Mennonite (MC) Church, located 4 miles west of Shippensburg, in Franklin County, Pa., was organized in 1840. In 1957 it had 108 members, with Amos E. Martin as bishop and Paul C. Martin as minister. It is a member of the Washington Co., Md. and Franklin Co., Pa. Conference.

H.S.B.

Royen (Roey), **Abraham van,** an Anabaptist martyr: see **Abraham (van Royen).**

Royer Mennonite Church (MC), a member of the Lancaster Conference. Jacob Royer (1771-1850) and his wife, Catherine Hammer, lived on a farm near Richland, Pa. He was a son of Daniel Royer and a great-grandson of the pioneer Sebastian Royer. Jacob Royer donated the ground on which the Tulpehocken Church of the Brethren was built in 1840. This was erected by the "Old Brothers Society of the Conestoga Family," an outpost of the Bareville Church of the Brethren in Lancaster County, the first meetinghouse of that denomination in Lebanon County. It was a stone building, 35 x 40 ft., in which a school for the community was held. An annex of 25 ft. was added. This Jackson Township school and church had two sets of trustees. The adjoining cemetery was "for anyone who had clean and honest deaths, and the house should be open for any preacher for these funerals." This church was used by the Brethren for a century. Then it was leased for some years to the Old Order Mennonites. In January 1947 the building was leased by the Millbach Mennonite group, and soon it was used exclusively by these workers. Noah N. Burkholder became their minister, and Earl B. Horst was ordained as assistant minister in 1953. The membership, through colonization, was 95 in 1957. Amos Horst and Mahlon Zimmerman are the bishops. The Royer congregation has an outpost at Texter, opened on May 10, 1953, with Willard Eberly, Peter M. Risser, and Levi Burkholder as superintendents; Texter had 34 members in 1957. The ministers are those of the Royer Mennonite Church. A new meetinghouse was built in 1957-58.

I.D.L.

Royersford (Pa.) Mennonite Brethren in Christ Church was organized in 1889, when a chapel was built, replaced in 1898 by the present church. In 1957 the membership was 72, with Earl M. Hosler as pastor.

P.E.B.

Rozenhofje is a home for the aged at Rozengracht 149, Amsterdam, Holland. It was founded in 1743 by the Amsterdam Collegiants (*q.v.*). Since 1770, when Collegiantism in Amsterdam died out, it has been administered by a committee usually consisting of Mennonites. It contains 30 apartments for aged women. The facade was rebuilt in 1890, but the interior court is still in the old picturesque style. vDZ.

Ruchat, Abraham (1678-1750), a Swiss Reformed theologian, served as pastor in a number of congregations, and as professor of literature and theology of the Academy of Lausanne, a versatile writer. In 1721-27 he wrote his *Histoire de la Réformation de la Suisse,* and published it in six volumes at Geneva in 1727 f. It earned for him the title of Father of Protestant Historiography (RGG) in Switzerland. For 1536 the presentation is complete, but becomes more sketchy with each succeeding year: from 672 pages for 1536 to 96 pages for 1537 and 80 for 1538-57. A second edition appeared at Nyon in 1835-38 in seven volumes, "with appendices and a sketch of the life and works of Ruchat by L. Vulliemin." This edition was welcome, for the original covered only the years 1516-36 and was so persecuted by the church board and city council of Bern that the second part, covering the years 1536-66, could not be published in full as planned. The catalog of Calvary says, "The present (second) edition embraces the complete work, the first section . . . in four volumes and the previously unprinted section according to the original manuscript in three volumes. Court records, letters, and documents, which were not accessible to the author or which he was perhaps not permitted to publish, are added. Ruchat's work is the first critical book on the Swiss Reformation. A considerable part is occupied by the history of the Anabaptists in Switzerland; the presentation of the history of Anabaptism in Romance Switzerland, in Geneva, Wallis, and Tessin, which is attempted here for the first time, deserves consideration."

NEFF, E.C.

S. Calvary & Co., *Verzeichnis seltener und werthvoller Werke aus dem antiquarischen Lager* (Supplement to *Mittheilungen aus dem Antiquartiate von S. Calvary & Co.*) I (Berlin, 1870) 32 f.; *HRE* XVII, 184-86 (H. Vuilleuwier); *RGG* IV, Col. 2,129 (Otto Erich Strasser); *ML* III, 559.

Ruchheim, a village (pop. 1,451) in the district of Ludwigshafen, Germany, was settled by Mennonites of the Eppstein (*q.v.*) congregation in 1732. The deacon for Ruchheim was Ludwig Gross. In 1766 it was united with Erpolzheim (*q.v.*), Friedelsheim (*q.v.*), and Spitalhof (*q.v.*); in 1787 united with Assenheim (*q.v.*); in 1805 independent with Melchior Eberly and Johannes Wiesler as preachers, both ordained in 1775, and after 1790 as elders. In 1888 the Ruchheim congregation, together with Flomersheim, Hessheim, and Oggersheim, again belonged to the Eppstein congregation. (*ML* III, 559.)   E.C.

Rückenau, the name of two villages in West Prussia (*q.v.*), Germany, one in the Elbing area, with inhabitants, 157 and the other in the Gross-Werder area, with 290. In the latter there were in 1936 15 Mennonite families, of whom 11 were farmers, a total of 62 souls, who belonged to the Rosenort (*q.v.*) Mennonite Church in West Prussia. Their names were Braun, Friesen, Haese, Hein, Janzen, Klaassen, Neufeld, Penner, Regehr, Schröder, and Wiebe.   E.C.

Mennonitisches Adressbuch (Karlsruhe, 1936) 167; *ML* III, 560.

Rückenau, a village in the Molotschna Mennonite settlement, Russia, founded in 1811, consisting of 4,978 acres (14 full farms and 12 half farms). In 1895 a home for the aged was established by Peter Martin Friesen in Rückenau which he turned over to the local Mennonite Brethren Church. The home took care of fifteen persons.   C.K.

H. Görz, *Die Molotschnaer Ansiedlung* (Steinbach, 1951) 17, 115; Friesen, *Brüderschaft*, 661.

Rückenau Mennonite Brethren Church in the village of Rückenau, located in the heart of the Molotschna settlement of South Russia, became the nerve center in the development of the M.B. movement. M.B. interest had concentrated sufficiently in this area in 1874 to buy a tavern and convert it into a meetinghouse. Church activities outgrew this building by 1883 when a new structure, 84 x 42 ft., was erected providing a seating capacity of 600. The highest estimated membership was 3,000, including several affiliated congregations. The early M.B. leaders also exerted considerable influence in this congregation.

After Elder H. Hübert left for the Kuban in 1873, Abr. Schellenberg was elected elder, and when he moved to America in 1879, Johann Fast succeeded him. Jacob Dirksen, David Schellenberg, David Dürksen, Jacob Reimer, and Jacob Thiessen were other leading personalities. The annual M.B. Conference was held in this church and from it determining influences radiated into other M.B. congregations. The congregation remained strong until the Revolution in the early 1920's. Many, including a number of the leaders, emigrated when religious liberty was suppressed. During World War II, with the retreat of the German army, many of these settlements were wiped out, all the Mennonites leaving. Nothing further is known of the congregation, which at one time was the heart of the Mennonite Brethren movement.   J.J.T.

Ruddinghuysen: see **Rittenhouse.**

Rüdiger, Ottilia, an Anabaptist martyr, who was drowned with Hans Hentrock (*q.v.*) in the Unstrut between Mühlhausen (*q.v.*) and Ammern in Thuringia, Germany, on Jan. 17, 1538. (Wappler, *Thüringen,* 164; *ML* III, 560.)   NEFF.

Rudnerweide, a village in the Stuhm (*q.v.*) Lowlands near the Vistula in West Prussia, Germany. Mennonites expelled from the Tilsit (*q.v.*) marshes, East Prussia, settled here in 1724, draining and reclaiming the swampy area. The family names of these settlers were Arendt, Block, Ediger, Flamming, G(o)ertz, Jantzen, Nickel, Penner, Quiring, Schroeder, Unrau, and Wichert. In the Dutch *Naamlijst* the congregation is called "Stuumsche Needering op Swijngrube." It was later called Tragheimerweide (*q.v.*) or Zwanzigerweide (*q.v.*). It belonged to the Frisian (*q.v.*) branch, also being called Waterlander.   vDZ.

Herbert Wiebe, *Das Siedlungswerk niederl. Mennoniten im Weichseltal* . . . (Marburg, 1952) 40, 85.

Rudnerweide, a Mennonite village name of Prussian background, transplanted to the Molotschna settlement, Ukraine; the West Reserve of Manitoba; Cuauhtemoc, Mexico; and Menno (Chaco), Paraguay. (See **Villages.**) (*ML* III, 560.)   C.K.

Rudnerweide Mennonite Church, a Mennonite branch found chiefly in Manitoba. A schism occurred in the Sommerfeld (*q.v.*) Mennonite congregation in southern Manitoba (*q.v.*) in 1937, the more progressive members advocating a more active, spiritual church life, and the more conservative section strongly opposed to this movement. As a result a new more active congregation was organized, composed of former members of the Sommerfeld church, with four of the twelve Sommerfeld ministers, Isaac A. Hoeppner, George Froese, P. S. Zacharias, and William H. Falk, as ministers. Of these, William H. Falk, of Schoental, was chosen as elder or bishop. This congregation has from the beginning been interested in home and foreign missions, as well as education and Bible schools. The Rudnerweide Mennonites stress true conversion, a clean manner of life, and good fellowship in the church. They adhere to the same tenets of faith and use the same catechism as the original group, but hold evangelistic gatherings and Bible and prayer meetings, as well as taking part in Sunday-school work, young people's endeavor, and choir practice. Their elected ministers are free to deliver their sermons directly from a Bible text, instead of merely reading sermons handed down from the past as is the case in the mother Sommerfeld church. Fourteen foreign missionaries have been sent out by this congregation and are now supported by it.

This congregation has as yet not joined any of the existing conferences. It has in Manitoba about 600 families with 3,200 souls and 1,200 members, served by 20 ministers in 14 meetinghouses. The total baptized membership in 1958 was 1,700, with 500 scattered throughout Western Canada, not attached to any local meeting. It owns ten meetinghouses and holds Sunday services also at a number of smaller stations. Twenty ministers serve in circuit at all the stations of the congregation in Manitoba. In 1954 Jacob H. Friesen was elected as elder. The main meeting places, all in Manitoba, are located as follows:

Meeting	Post Office
Bergfeld	Plum Coulee
Eigenhof	Gretna
Glencross	Morden
Lowe Farm	Lowe Farm
Neubergthal	Altona
Altona	Altona
Plum Coulee	Plum Coulee
Reinland	Winkler
Winkler	Winkler
Rosenfeld	Rosenfeld
Winnipeg	Winnipeg

There are also two meetinghouses northwest of Portage La Prairie, and a branch in Saskatchewan near Hague, founded about 1940, which now has 300 members with 3 meetinghouses.

H.H.H., G.H.P.

Rudolph Christian, Count of East Friesland 1625-28, son of Enno III (*q.v.*), issued a letter of protection (*Schutzbrief*) to the Mennonites on May 25, 1626, which became the pattern for all succeeding letters of protection (see **Privileges**), and which secured to the Mennonites a legal status; the matters of the oath and military service were reserved for a later time. The letter of protection is printed *in extenso* in *ML* III, 562 f.   NEFF.

J. P. Müller, *Die Mennoniten in Ostfriesland vom 16. bis zum 18. Jahrhundert* (Emden and Borkum, 1887) 41; *ML* III, 562 f.

Rudri, a former station of the Mennonite (MC) Mission in Madhya Pradesh, India, situated 4 miles south of Dhamtari. The site of 50 acres was bought by the Mission in 1902. It had been felt by the missionaries then in charge of the orphanages that the boys and girls should live in separate stations; the girls' orphanage was therefore built at Rudri in 1904. In 1912, however, when the Canal Department of the government decided to construct a large irrigation system with Rudri as its headquarters, it requisitioned all the buildings of the station. The mission then moved the orphanage to Balodgahan. The Mission was reluctant to give up Rudri because of its strategic position near a large river and also among

villages where evangelistic work could be carried on. The Rudri Christian families moved to Maradeo, owned by an Indian convert, in which settlement is now a small but very active Christian community. A small grove by the riverside one mile from Rudri became the permanent camping place for the annual conferences and meetings for the deepening of spiritual life.   G.J.L.

Rueb, a Dutch family of German descent, whose ancestor was Johann Peter Rueb (d. 1707), of Trarbach on the Moselle. His grandson Johannes Stephanus Rueb (d. 1788), a Lutheran, moved to Dordrecht, Holland, where he was a wine merchant. A son of Johannes Stephanus was Christoffel Rueb (1775-1865), a sugar broker at Rotterdam. He married Petronella van Heukelom (1782-1852), a Mennonite of Leiden. Then most of his descendants became Mennonites, including his son Adolph Stephanus Rueb (1805-54), a physician at Utrecht, and the following members, all living at Rotterdam: Pieter Rueb (1810-48), Jan Rueb (1807-71), Pieter Rueb (1812-94), Willem Rueb (1855-1944), Adolph Stephanus Rueb (1880-1948), Pieter Rueb (1888-1958), and Willem Rueb (b. 1917), all of whom served the Rotterdam Mennonite congregation as deacons. At Rotterdam the Rueb family has a vinegar distillery.   vDZ.

Ned. Patriciaat II (1911) 413-19; XV (1925) 435-45; Kobus and de Rivecourt, *Biographisch Woordenboek* II, 731.

Rueg(g)er, Hans, an Anabaptist martyr, a cabinetmaker of Hallau (*q.v.*) in the Swiss canton of Schaffhausen, was sentenced to die by the sword on Nov. 13, 1527, (*a*) because he had permitted himself to be rebaptized and had sheltered Anabaptists; (*b*) because he had defended the peasant revolt and the insurrection of the vinedressers and fishermen; and (*c*) because he had bought a small house without having the funds to pay for it in the hope that in the course of the progress of the Gospel such payments as well as interest and tithes would be abolished and all things become common property.

"This is the first death sentence in Schaffhausen pronounced on an Anabaptist and no doubt carried out. We see that in this instance Anabaptism and treason were linked in the charge; to be sure, not a single revolutionary deed could be proved against this poor man, but only some improper words and thoughts, which may have been extorted from him on the rack" (Bächtold, 102).   E.C.

Carl August Bächtold, "Die Schaffhauser Wiedertäufer in der Reformationszeit," *Beiträge zur vaterländischen Geschichte* . . . VII (Schaffhausen, 1900) 71-118, especially 101 f.; Karl Schib, *Quellen zur neueren Geschichte Schaffhausens* (Thayngen and Schaffhausen, 1948) 27-31; Paul Peachey, *Die soziale Herkunft der Schweizer Täufer* (Karlsruhe, 1954) 42, 65, 114, No. 112; *ML* III, 563.

Rüegsau, Ulrich of, an Anabaptist martyr, a peasant of Rüegsau, Emmental, Switzerland, one of nine martyrs put to death in the canton of Bern (*q.v.*) in 1537. His actual name is not known.

Mart. Mir. E 1192; Samuel Geiser, *Die Taufgesinnten-Gemeinden* (Karlsruhe, 1931) 182; Theodor de Quervain, *Kirchliche und soziale Zustände in Bern unmittelbar nach der Einführung der Reformation (1528-1536)* (Bern,

1906) 149; Paul Peachey, *Die soziale Herkunft der Schweizer Täufer in der Reformationszeit* (Karlsruhe, 1954) 141; *ML* III, 563.

Rüegsegger, Steffen (Rüegsecker, Stäffen), an Anabaptist martyr, a peasant, one of the nine martyrs put to death in the canton of Bern (*q.v.*) in 1538. He was executed at Lake Thun on Nov. 8, 1538.

Mart. Mir. E 1192; Samuel Geiser, *Die Taufgesinnten-Gemeinden* (Karlsruhe, 1931) 182; Theodor de Quervain, *Kirchliche und soziale Zustände in Bern unmittelbar nach der Einführung der Reformation (1528-1536)* (Bern, 1906) 150; Paul Peachey, *Die soziale Herkunft der Schweizer Täufer in der Reformationszeit* (Karlsruhe, 1954) 136; *ML* III, 563.

Rues, M. Simeon Friedrich, a German Lutheran clergyman, made a journey through the Netherlands and wrote the book, *Aufrichige Nachrichten von dem gegenwärtigen Zustande der Mennoniten oder Taufgesinnten wie auch der Collegianten oder Reinsburger, beyderseits ansehnlicher kirchlicher Gesellschaften in den vereinigten Niederlanden* (Jena, 1743). This important work falls into five divisions: Concerning the Old Flemish or the Frisians, Flemish, Waterlanders, and United; Concerning the dissensions of some Mennonites with the Reformed clergy; Concerning the Collegiants or Rijnsburgers; Concerning the government of Friesland, and the Reformed and other clergy in the United Netherlands. The book was translated into Dutch by Marten Schagen (*q.v.*) and published with corrections and illustrations in Amsterdam in 1745 under the title *Tegenwordige Staet der Doopsgezinden of Mennoniten in de Vereenigde Nederlanden* [en] *een Berigt van de Rynsburgers of Collegianten.* (*DJ* 1840, 125; *ML* III, 563 f.)   E.C.

Ruff, Barbly, was seized on account of her faith in the district of Knonau in Switzerland in 1643. Because she was pregnant she was chained in her brother-in-law's house. After the birth of her child she escaped, but died soon after in consequence of this mistreatment. She was probably a member of the Mennonite Rupp (Ropp) family. (*Mart. Mir.* D 822, E 1121; *ML* III, 564.)

Ruggensberger, Sebastian, a monk and prior of a Roman Catholic monastery, joined the Anabaptist movement at St. Gall, Switzerland, in 1525, and was active in preaching until 1528, when he left the Anabaptists.   vDZ.

Paul Peachey, *Die soziale Herkunft der Schweizer Täufer* (Karlsruhe, 1954) 25 f., 75, 109, No. 14.

Rügsau, Hans von: see Schweitzer, Hans.

Ruisdael (Ruysdael), **van,** a Dutch family of painters. Isaac de Goyer, or Ruisdael, born 1599 at Naarden, d. 1677 at Haarlem, and his brother Salomon van Ruisdael, born shortly after 1600 at Naarden, d. 1670 at Haarlem, were both Mennonites, but after they moved to Haarlem, Isaac joined the Reformed Church about 1630. Salomon seems always to have been a Mennonite, though it is not known whether he was a loyal member. He purchased his release from civil guard duty. Isaac's son was Jacob van Ruisdael, b. *c*1628 at Haarlem, d. 1682 at Amsterdam. He was the most outstanding of the Ruisdael family, and his paintings, mostly landscapes, are

world-famed. Thieme-Becker asserts that he joined the Reformed Church in 1657, but the records of the Amsterdam Lamist Mennonite Church have an entry showing that both Jacob van Rusidael and his wife, whose name is not mentioned, were received into the Amsterdam congregation in 1666 upon the presentation of a certification from the Flemish Mennonite Church at Haarlem, signed by the preacher Koenraad van Diepenbroek and the deacons Adriaen van den . . . (illegible) and Mattheus Gryspeert. Jacob van Ruisdael (1629/30-82), the son of Salomon van Ruisdael, was also a Mennonite. He seems to have lived extravagantly, for the Flemish congregation of Haarlem in 1681 offered to pay his board in the city poorhouse.   vDZ.

Thieme-Becker, *Allgemeines Lexikon der bildenden Künstler* XXIX (Leipzig, 1935) 188-94; H. F. Wijnman, "Het Leven Ruysdael's," in *Oud Holland* XLIX (1932) 49-60, 173-81, 258-75; *ML* III, 564.

Rümmich (Riemmich), **Hans,** one of the Anabaptists (see **Philippites**) who were arrested in Passau (*q.v.*), Bavaria, on their flight from Moravia in 1533. At his cross-examination on August 30 he confessed that his home was two miles from Schwäbisch-Hall (in Marbach); that in Bruchsal (*q.v.*) 500 persons had assembled; that he had been baptized by Blasy (see **Blasius Kuhn**) in Austerlitz (*q.v.*) about eighteen months previously. He could not be persuaded to recant. His wife Judith confessed that she had been baptized at Heilbronn (*q.v.*) three years before by Wolf of Gritznis (Griesbach?), who was executed at Pretouw (Bretten, *q.v.*) on the Rhine. She too remained steadfast. (Wolkan, *Geschicht-Buch,* 30 f.; *ML* III, 564.)   W.W.

Rumiantsev, Peter Alexandrovitch (1725-96), was a Russian general and later field marshal who received the honorable name Zadunaysky because he crossed the Danube River in the Russo-Turkish War (1770-74). During this campaign on the border between Moldau (Moldavia) and Poland he met the Hutterian Brethren who had to leave Walachia and were interested in settling in Russia, and invited them to settle on his estates in the Ukraine near Kiev, granting them very favorable privileges.

Under the protection of an officer the Hutterites proceeded through Poland to Vishenka (*q.v.*), on the Desna River, where they arrived on Aug. 1, 1770. Rumiantsev continued to be their protector and defender until his death in 1796. At this time three Brethren were sent to express their sympathy to the family and to negotiate with the heirs regarding their lease. Because of difficulties with the heirs they left Vishenka in 1802 to settle on crown lands at Radichev (*q.v.*), where they enjoyed for a while the privileges of the Mennonites of Russia. Later they settled near the Molotschna Mennonite settlement.   C.K.

Zieglschmid, *Klein-Geschichtsbuch;* Arthur Kleinschmidt, *Drei Jahrhunderte russischer Geschichte (1598-1898)* (Berlin, 1898); *ML* III, 566 f.

Rump, Ludwig, of Elbing (*q.v.*), West Prussia, Germany, served in the 18th century as an intermediary between the Dutch Mennonite Committee for Foreign Needs and the Mennonites of East Prussia (then Lithuania) and West Prussia, who repeatedly requested financial support from Holland. The Mennonite Archives at Amsterdam contain some letters by Rump and a statement of account for 1723-43, in which he reports on the gifts of the Dutch Committee which he presented to the Lithuanian and Polish (West Prussian) Mennonites. One of these letters states that he acted as early as 1711. Rump was particularly active in 1726, when a group of 120 Mennonite families, compelled to leave East Prussia, moved to Markushof in West Prussia. Concerning Rump's private life nothing is known. In one of the letters he is called secretary, and a letter written by his widow, dated April 23, 1743, notes that he had died, probably shortly before.   vDZ.

Inv. Arch. Amst. I, Nos. 1231, 1571-75, 1681, 1689; II, 2, Nos. 698, 731, 743, 792.

Run(c)kel, Johann Ludwig, a friend of the Swiss Mennonites, Dutch ambassador to Switzerland, had his seat first at Schaffhausen and later at Bern as secretary of the embassy. In 1710-11 he took an active interest in the Mennonites, who were subjected to oppression and persecution by the government. The Amsterdam Mennonite archives contain more than 70 letters, documents, and statements of account sent by Runckel to the Dutch Mennonite Committee for Foreign Needs (see **Fonds voor Buitenlandsche Nooden**). In the first of these letters (Jan. 22, 1710) he alerted the Dutch Mennonites to the plight of the Swiss Mennonites, and from then his detailed letters gave the Committee at Amsterdam an exact idea of the situation, including the names of the prisoners. Runckel acted in the name of the Dutch Mennonites; his authority was based on his function as ambassador of the Dutch States General, whose secretary, François Fagel (*q.v.*), supported him both morally and financially. Runckel negotiated with the Bernese officials and spoke with the Swiss Mennonites, many of whom were unwilling to leave the country, and distributed to them the money sent by the Dutch Mennonites and the confessions of faith (more than 120 were sent from Holland). With great difficulty he obtained permission for the Mennonites to leave Bern and a guarantee that they could sell their property and take along the money, and undertook the difficult and time-consuming task of administering the whole business. He had previously mediated in the (bootless) plan to colonize the Swiss Brethren in Prussia. It was Runckel's suggestion in his letter of Nov. 8, 1710, to settle all the Swiss Mennonites in the Netherlands, which was adopted by the Dutch Committee and favored by the Dutch States General, and after much negotiation with the Bernese government and the unwilling Mennonites, who being divided by the Ammann-Reist (*q.v.*) schism refused to move together, Runckel finally saw his great effort crowned by the emigration of a large number of Mennonites to the Palatinate and the Netherlands. Runckel's last letter to the Dutch Committee concerning this matter is dated July 11, 1717. (See also **Bern** and **Swiss Mennonites in the Netherlands**.)   vDZ.

A. van Gulik, "Uit de geschiedenis van de overkomst der vervoldge Zwitzers in 1710 en 1711," *DB* 1919, 136, 145 ff.; C. Henry Smith, *The Mennonite Immigration into Pennsylvania in the Eighteenth Century* (Norristown, 1929) 70-74; Müller, *Berner Täufer,* 221; Runckel's

most important letters are *Inv. Arch. Amst.* I, Nos. 1219 f., 1255b, 1271, 1285, 1287, 1290 f., 1293, 1301, 1310, 1312, 1316-19, 1321, 1330 f., 1334, 1337-45, 1353, 1373; *ML* III, 566.

Rundbriefe (Circle Letters). A fellowship among young German Mennonites was created following World War I through the youth work of the South German Mennonite Conference, which was carried on through a circle letter and occasional fellowship meetings. It reached its height 1938-39, at which time the list of participants totaled 183, distributed as follows: South Germany 74, West and East Prussia and Danzig 17, Berlin 8, Hamburg 14, Germany scattered 19, Holland 19, Poland 9, Switzerland 7, France 1, Paraguay 13, Mexico 2. The movement was subdivided into sub-circles which reached a total of 26, each with 8-10 in intimate fellowship. The publication of the movement was *Mitteilungen für die mennonitischen Jugend-Rundbrief-Freunde.* The movement was concerned with spiritual renewal on a Biblical basis for individuals and the church. (Condensed from Walter Fellmann's article in *ML* III, 566.)

Rundschau: see Mennonitische Rundschau.

Rundschau-Kalender, Der, an annual almanac, published 1927-35, at Winnipeg, Man., by the Rundschau Publishing House. In 1935 the almanac section was replaced with a simple calendar for the year. Earlier issues included Bible readings. Beginning in 1929 the Sundays of the church year were named. Serious articles on Mennonite themes by recognized Mennonite Brethren authors mark most of the earlier issues. With the 1933 issue these were replaced by articles of general information. The lists of ministers published in 1927 and 1928 were almost identical with those in the *Mennonite Yearbook and Directory* (*q.v.*) for 1926 and 1927. No ministerial lists appeared in 1929 and 1930. Beginning with 1931 ministerial lists and statistical information were restricted to Mennonites of various branches in Western Canada and Mennonites of Russian background in Ontario. With the exception of the first and last issues, each issue had 64 pages. There was a minimum of advertising.   N.P.S.

Rupelmonde (Rijpermonde), a town in Belgium, the scene of the execution of the martyrs Hendrik (*q.v.*) Verstralen and Maeyken (*q.v.*) Deynoots in 1571. In a letter Verstralen expressed his expectation that the congregation of which he was a member would take care of his wife and children. (*Offer,* 638; see also 628 note.) This may refer to a congregation of Rupelmonde, but nothing further is known of it.   vDZ.

Rupp (Ropp, Ruff), a Mennonite family of Swiss origin. At the disputation at Bern in 1538 (see **Bern,** section 4) Uli Rupp of Stauffen (probably near Lenzburg in Aargau) and Kläwi Rupp of Signau (see **Emmental**) are named. In 1540 Hans Rupp, a peasant, is listed among the Anabaptists. Rulandt Rupp, of Lucerne, an Anabaptist, emigrated in 1571. In the early 18th century a Rüby (Rubi) of Frutigen, and a Rupp of Sigriswil moved to Clémont and Montbéliard in 1709, and Hans Rupp, of Gunten near Sigriswil, emigrated to Nijmegen in the Netherlands, and later settled at Deventer. Among the Swiss emigrants to Holland in 1711 were Hans Ruff and Christen Ruff, of Sigriswil, with their families.

In Alsace, Jakob Rupp was living at Markirch (q.v.), and a Christian Rupp of Kühnheim (north of Neuf-Brisach) intervened for the expellees from Switzerland; he may be identical with the Christian Rupp who also settled in Deventer. In 1779 Hans Rub signed the Ordnungsbriefe (q.v.) for the Colmar (q.v.) congregation. In 1805 Jakob Rupp was an elder at Colmar. In 1950 the name occurred only in the form Ropp(e). Dr. Martha Ropp, of Mulhouse, was a missionary in Indonesia (Java) c1950- .

In the duchy of Berg a Rupp family occurred in the 17th century. Thiell (Thilmann) Rupp, a son of Heinrich Rupp, was named in 1624; in 1638 he was at Oberdollenhof and Obercassel (Löwenberg, q.v., area); in 1650 he settled at Heddesdorf (or Gönnersdorf) near Neuwied (q.v.), joined the young congregation there, and died in 1666. The Privilege (q.v.) granted by the Count of Wied in 1680 names Heinrich Rupp and his sons Thielmann Rupp and Peter Rupp among the founders of the congregation. Heinrich Rupp (1637-after 1700) was the leader of the Neuwied congregation; from 1698 to 1768, when the church was built, a large room in his house served the congregation as a place of meeting. Peter and Thielmann (b. 1649/56) were, however, his brothers and not his sons. Tillmann was the leader of the congregation for 26 years, and his son Leonhard (b. 1683, baptized at Crefeld in 1703) for 18 years; Leonhard's niece Anna (b. 1711) married Lorenz Friedenreich in 1745. In 1837 an endowment by the Rupp family aided the congregation in its period of decline.

In the Palatinate Philipp Raup (or Rupp), of Nussloch near Heidelberg, was tried on May 1, 1529, with other followers of Philipp Plener (q.v.), but remained constant. Some members of the Swiss Rupp family were found later in the Palatinate: in 1717 Peter Rupp in Ludwigshafen (q.v.), 1732 Heinrich Rupp, deacon of the Oberflörsheim (q.v.) congregation, living in Gundersheim near Worms; 1742 Johann Rupp in Heppenheim (q.v.) near Alzey. In 1786 Jakob Rupp, of Heppenheim, exchanged correspondence with Abraham and Rudolph Landes in the Deep Run congregation. In 1936 there was only one Mennonite in the Palatinate with this name.

Some Rupps participated in the Mennonite settlement in Bavaria (q.v.). Jakob Rupp, of Odenheim, near Bruchsal, was one of the founders of the Maxweiler (q.v.) congregation (1882); Johann Rupp was a former member of the Eichstock (q.v.) congregation.

Among the Palatine Mennonites who emigrated to Galicia (q.v.) in 1784 f. there were also Rupps; Heinrich Rupp (1760-1800), of Harxheim, and Johann Rupp (1745-87), of Alzey, settled in Einsiedel (q.v.) and Rosenberg (q.v.) respectively. Johann's death and burial gave rise to the "cemetery scandal," in which the peasants were compelled by the military to grant him burial in the Greek Catholic cemetery. Peter Bachmann sketched the family trees of both lines of the Rupps. Johann Rupp (1849-96) was the first to become a soldier under the law of Dec. 5,

1868; although he was assigned to the hospital corps, his fellow members bade him farewell as if he were doomed to death. The Rupps did not share in the emigration to Russia in 1796, but the poorest of them were among the emigrants to America in 1880 ff. The Heinrich Rupp branch of the family was active in the life of the church. Daniel Rupp (1817-1905) was a preacher (1849) and elder (1855) in Horozana wielka (q.v.); in 1909 Heinrich Rupp (b. 1856) was leader of the new congregation at Kiernica-Lemberg (q.v.); Dr. Johann Rupp (b. 1883, portrait ML III) was a founder of the "Mennonite Geselligkeitsverein." Another Heinrich Rupp (1855-1929) was curator of the congregation 1918-21; Jakob Rupp (b. 1877) was a district judge. His cousin Theodor Rupp was a teacher at the Gymnasium and a collaborator on the Mennonitisches Lexikon.

After the departure to the Warthe area in 1939 and west, Richard Rupp (b. 1913), a son of the curator Rupp, took a prominent part in the establishment of the refugee settlement of Backnang (q.v.) in Württemberg.

Rupp and Smith report that Peter Rupp came to America on the "Harle of London" in 1736; Johannes and Peter Rupp on the "Phoenix" in 1749; Johannes and Christian Rupp (Rub!) of Montbéliard on the "Brotherhood" in 1750, and Johann Jonas Rupp of Reihen, near Sinsheim, with the "Phoenix" in 1751. Johann Jonas Rupp settled first in Lebanon County, Pa., and in 1772 moved to Cumberland County opposite Harrisburg. Most of the Mennonite Rupps are still found here. In the Slate Hill (q.v.) congregation three served — Henry Rupp (1752-1810), George Rupp (1798-1888), and Henry Rupp (1828-98), the first two as preachers, and the third as a deacon.

The fourth of the fourteen children of George Rupp, who was a son of Johann Jonas Rupp (1729-1801), was Israel Daniel Rupp (q.v., 1803-78), "the father of the local history of the southeastern counties of Pennsylvania"; he was baptized into the Reformed faith by John Weinbrenner (1797-1860, ord. 1820, founder of the Church of God).

In the 19th century a second immigration of Rupps to America occurred. The Rupps of Maxweiler (q.v.), Bavaria, settled in Lee County, Iowa (q.v.), joining the Zion congregation near Donnellson, in 1866 moved northward into Washington County and in 1874 to Kansas (q.v.), where in 1911 an H. Rupp was an assistant pastor in the Einsiedel congregation near Hanston, and Jacob Rupp, at the age of 84, told the long story of the long journey from Maxweiler to Kansas.

A Rupp-Ropp family of Amish origin settled in Fulton County (q.v.), Ohio (q.v.), and in Illinois and other states of the Midwest. Two important bishops of this family were Andrew and Christian Ropp. Later most members of the family joined the Defenseless Mennonites (now Evangelical Mennonite Church) or the General Conference Mennonites. Among these was Benjamin Rupp, a preacher and leader, first superintendent of the Salem Children's Home (q.v.) and then of the hospital at Bloomington, Ill.   E.C.

Genealogy of the Neuwied and Crefeld Rupp family, which died out in 1839 with Elisabeth Rupp, the wife of Christian Passarin of Crefeld, written by Richard Wolfferts (copy in the Neff library at Weierhof); *Almanach Mennonite du Cinquantenaire 1901-1951* (Montbéliard, 1951); Peter Bachmann, *Mennoniten in Kleinpolen* (Lemberg, 1934); Dirk Cattepoel, "Die Neuwieder Mennonitengemeinde," *Beiträge zur Geschichte rhein. Menn.* (Weierhof, 1939) 144-53; Ernst Correll, "Die Mennoniten im Donaumoos," *Gem.-Kal.*, 1922, 80-91; Christian Hege, *Die Täufer der Kurpfalz* (Frankfurt, 1908); Daniel Kauffman, *Mennonite Cyclopedic Dictionary* (Scottdale, 1937) 319; *TA Baden-Pfalz*, No. 140; H. P. Krehbiel, *History of the General Conference of the Mennonite Church* (Canton and Newton, 1898 and 1938) 15, 23, 35; Miller, *Berner Täufer*, 80, 211, 255, 270, 278, 291, 292, 321, 341, 369, 372; Charles Mathiot, *Recherches historiques sur les Anabaptistes de l'ancienne Principauté de Montbéliard . . .* (Belfort, 1922); Paul Peachey, *Die soziale Herkunft der Schweizer Täufer in der Ref.-Zeit* (Karlsruhe, 1954); Richard Ringenberg, *Familienbuch der Mennonitengemeinde Eichstock* (Munich, 1942); Walther Risler, "Täufer im bergischen Amt Löwenberg," *Gesch.-Bl.*, 1956, 39 f.; Jakob Rupp, *Entstehung und Auflösung der Gemeinde zu Maxweiler . . . und erste Pionier Jahre in Amerika* (Moundridge, 1924); I. D. Rupp, *A Brief Biographic Memorial of Joh. Jonas Rupp, and Complete Genealogical Family Register of his Lineal Descendants, from 1756 to 1875* (Philadelphia, 1875); Richard Rupp, "Neue Heimat in Württemberg, die Mennonitensiedlung in Backnang-Sachsenweiler," *Gem.-Kal.*, 1956, 43-53; D. L. Gratz, *Bernese Anabaptists* (Scottdale, 1953); *ML III, 567-69.*

Rupp, Benjamin (1862-1928), a minister of the Evangelical Mennonite Church, was born Aug. 19, 1862, near Archbold, Fulton Co., Ohio, the son of Jacob Rupp of Switzerland, and Catharine Freienberg of Alsace. Benjamin Rupp was married to Lydia Steiner of Bluffton, Ohio, on Jan. 28, 1886. Three sons and three daughters graced this union: Dennis, Edna, Eldon, Ruth, Libby, and Harvey.

Rupp specialized in dairy farming. He was a member of the Defenseless Mennonite Church, now Evangelical Mennonite Church. He loved music and became chorister in his church and later minister. Soon after his ordination he was called to take charge of a newly founded Orphans' Home at Flanagan, Ill., now known as Salem Children's Home, serving as superintendent 1900-17. He then became superintendent of the Mennonite hospital at Bloomington, Ill., serving 1919-27. In 1926 he was appointed president of the Board of Directors of the Salem Orphanage and served there until his death. In addition he was also engaged in evangelistic work, and served as chairman of the conference for a number of terms. His life was one of continual sacrifice, for he served in most of the above capacities without stipulated pay. He died May 12, 1928, at Flanagan, and was buried in the Waldo cemetery near the church and orphanage he served. E.E.R.

Rupp, Israel Daniel (1803-78), "father of local history in the southeastern counties of Pennsylvania," was born in Cumberland County, Pa., the son of George Rupp, and grandson of Johann Jonas Rupp (a Mennonite) of Reihen near Sinsheim, Baden, Germany, who emigrated to Pennsylvania in 1751. I. D. Rupp was baptized in the Reformed faith. Rupp was a self-taught scholar who learned to read eight or nine languages, was for some 20 years a schoolteacher, but devoted his great energies to a variety of literary, editorial, and research pursuits, the producer of a large number of volumes on Pennsylvania history, translations of eleven works, some large, from German or Dutch into English, and English into German. He published six volumes of his-

tory on a total of 23 counties of Pennsylvania, the first being his *History of Lancaster County* (1844). His *He Pasa Ekklesia, An Original History of the Religious Denominations . . . United States* (1844), contains the first sketches of Mennonite and Amish history published in America, a short article by Christian Herr on the Mennonites and one by Shem Zook on the Amish. *A Collection of Thirty Thousand Names of German . . . Immigrants in Pennsylvania . . . 1727 to 1776* (1856, new ed. 1876) is valuable for Pennsylvania Mennonite immigrant names. His German translation of the Foxe Martyr Book, *Geschichte der Märtyrer* (Cincinnati, 1830, new ed. 1832), was published in another edition as *Allgemeine Geschichte des Christlichen Marterthums* in 1840 in Philadelphia, which contained an added lengthy section on Mennonite history (185 pp.) entitled (first part) *Geschichte und Lehre der Taufgesinnten* (35 pp.) and (second part) *Verfolgungen der Mennoniten* (150 pp.), the latter taken largely from van Braght's *Martyrs' Mirror.* The *Wandering Soul,* edition of Philadelphia 1833, the first in English, was translated by Rupp, as was the edition at Lancaster 1835 of Menno Simons' *Foundation and Plain Instruction* published by John Herr, the Lampeter (Lancaster County) 1837 edition of the *Martyrs' Mirror,* published by David Miller, and the Lancaster edition 1849, of the Waldeck *Catechism* published by the Oberholtzer (GCM) Mennonite group. All of these were the first English editions. Rupp deserves the credit of having introduced these basic Mennonite writings to English-speaking readers. The Funk edition of the *Complete Works* of Menno Simons (Elkhart, 1871) made use of the Rupp translation of the *Foundation and Plain Instruction* of 1837 (reprint 1863), with some modifications. Rupp was in general reliable in his writings and rescued a vast amount of information which would otherwise no doubt have been lost.

E.C., H.S.B.

Dictionary of American Biography XVI (1935) 225 f., based largely on Oswald Seidensticker, "Memoir of Israel Daniel Rupp, the Historian," *Pennsylvania Magazine of History and Biography* XIV (1890, not 1891 as cited in *ADB*) 403-13.

Rupschitz (Hrubschitz, Hrubcic), a Hutterite Bruderhof situated on the Iglava near Eibenschitz (*q.v.*), Moravia (*q.v*), purchased by Hans von Feuerbach and Hans Mändl on Oct. 5, 1545. In 1552 Schluchter Hans and a group of other Brethren rebelled against the preachers and elders of the Brotherhood, and he was expelled. E.C.

Beck, *Geschichts-Bücher*, 165, 197; Wolkan, *Geschicht-Buch*, 205, 240, 258; Zieglschmid, *Chronik*, 263 f., 316, 341 f.; *idem, Klein-Geschichtsbuch*, 61 f.; *ML III, 569 f.*

Rur River (Dutch, *Roer*), with a course of 130 miles from Botranche near Malmedy (now in Belgium) to its confluence with the Meuse River at Roermond, played a significant role in Anabaptist history. On its banks lie (from south to north) Montjoie (*q.v.*), Einrichr, Nideggen, Düren, Jülich (*q.v.*), Linnich (*q.v.*), Wassenberg (*q.v.*), and Roermond (*q.v.*), all of significance in 16th-century Anabaptist history. (*ML III, 570.*) E.C.

Rural Missions, evangelism focused on church extension in rural areas: see **Home Missions.**

Russia, now officially the Union of Soviet Socialist Republics (USSR), is the largest country in the world, with an area of 8,358,567 square miles and a population of 203,000,000 (1950). Russia is populated basically by Slavic peoples, although a large number of minority groups are found in the country, some of them belonging to the Mongolian race which invaded Russia from time to time in its early history. Other nationalities have immigrated into Russia, during its early history coming from Scandinavia, and more recently, when rulers were interested in occupying the vast uninhabited areas along the Volga River and in the Ukraine, from Western Europe.

I. *Russian Immigration Policy.* Already under the rule of Elizabeth "Nine Articles" were drawn up on Sept. 26, 1752, to promote immigration into Russia. On Dec. 4, 1762, Catherine II issued a manifesto inviting foreign settlers from Western European countries to settle in the vast uninhabited areas of Russia, which was followed by the better known second Manifesto of July 22, 1763, patterned after the Potsdam Edict of 1685. Prospective settlers were extended the following rights and privileges: (1) free board and transportation from the Russian boundary to the place of settlement; (2) the right to settle in any part of the country and to pursue any occupation; (3) a loan for the building of houses, etc.; (4) perpetual exemption from military and civil service; (5) exemption from payment of taxes for a period of years; (6) free exercise of religious practices, and to those who founded agricultural settlements, the right to build and control their own schools and churches; (7) the right to do mission work among non-Christians; (8) the right of local self-government for agricultural communities; (9) the right of every family to import its possessions free of duty; (10) to those who established factories with their own capital, the right to buy serfs and peasants.

In order to inaugurate and supervise a large-scale immigration and colonization program, the Bureau of Guardianship of the Foreign Colonists was established. It supervised the work of recruiting colonists (by agents), making land available to them, the actual settling, etc. This Bureau had the status of a separate ministry which was responsible to the empress. Gregory Orlov was its first chairman.

The Manifesto of 1763 was publicized in foreign countries through embassies and agents. In some countries which did not favor emigration the publicity failed. The only countries in which the Russian representatives met no obstacles in making known the colonization policy of their government were the small states of South and West Germany. In some of these there was widespread discontent and a desire for emigration, but even here the number of those who responded to the call was small. In 1764, when the government employed professional agents, the picture changed. Copies of the Manifesto and numerous broadsides were distributed, which created an emigration fever in some of the German states. German settlements were established in the province of St. Petersburg in 1765-66. However, the largest originated along the lower Volga River, where over 100 villages were founded in 1764-67. None of these were Mennonite.

II. *Ukraine.* The major goal of foreign settlers during the remainder of the 18th century and the beginning of the 19th century was New Russia, later known as the Ukraine (*q.v.*). This territory, located in South Russia and inhabited only by nomadic peoples and Cossacks, finally came under complete possession of Russia with the annexation of the Crimea in 1783. Beginning in 1774 this territory was administered by the Viceroy Potemkin (*q.v.*), who was interested in colonizing this largely uninhabited area. Much of the land was granted to court officials, army officers, and government officials. A large number of peasants from central Russia were settled on the Dniepr River. Potemkin's agents tried to induce citizens of Danzig, Albania, Greece, Sweden, and other countries to settle in the Ukraine. Some Greek, Armenian, and Swedish settlers established settlements in 1778-81. In Danzig Potemkin's agent Georg von Trappe began his campaign on June 19, 1786. Some non-Mennonite families established the Old Danzig settlement in the province of Kherson.

About this time the Russian Count Rumiantsev-Zadunaisky (*q.v.*), who had frequently been through the Mennonite settlements in the vicinity of Danzig, called the attention of the Russian government to them as prospective settlers. Georg von Trappe also called Potemkin's attention to the Mennonites whom he had met. In August 1786 an invitation was extended to the Mennonites, and von Trappe became the chief agent for their immigration into Russia.

At first the Mennonites received this invitation with great reserve in order not to antagonize the Danzig city council, which was opposed to the emigration. Jakob Höppner (*q.v.*) and Johann Bartsch (*q.v.*) were sent to Russia to inspect the land and make necessary arrangements for the immigration. After inspecting the proffered land and interviewing Potemkin and Catherine II (May 13, 1787) and other authorities, they returned to report their findings to their constituency. Meanwhile von Trappe had been active in promoting the emigration in Danzig. In a printed broadside dated Dec. 29, 1787 (*Menn. Life,* April 1951, 37), he praised the conditions of the settlement highly and invited those interested to meet on Jan. 19, 1788, at the Russian Embassy in Danzig. During that year 228 families left for Russia, followed by additional groups, a total of 462 families (B. H. Unruh, 231) who established the first Mennonite settlement, Chortitza (*q.v.*), in the province of Ekaterinoslav (*q.v.*) in the Ukraine. The Chortitza settlement is also known as the Old Colony since it was the first settlement. Between 1798 and 1802 the stream of immigrants subsided, until new difficulties in the home country caused a new wave of immigration to Russia.

On Feb. 20, 1804, Alexander I issued another Manifesto. During 1803-6 some 365 Mennonite families went to Russia, some of which stopped at the Chortitza settlement. Beginning in 1804, they settled in the province of Taurida (*q.v.*) on the Molotschnaya, a river from which the name of the Molotschna settlement (*q.v.*) was derived, some 100 miles southeast of the Chortitza settlement. From time to time additional groups followed until gradually 60 villages were established. In 1835 the migration to the Molotschna came to a close with an estimated total of 1,200 families or 6,000 persons.

MENNONITE
SETTLEMENTS

in European
Russia

Based on <u>Die Mennoniten-Gemeinden</u>
in <u>Russland</u> (Heilbronn, 1921).

50   0   50   100   150   200   250

Scale is in Kilometers

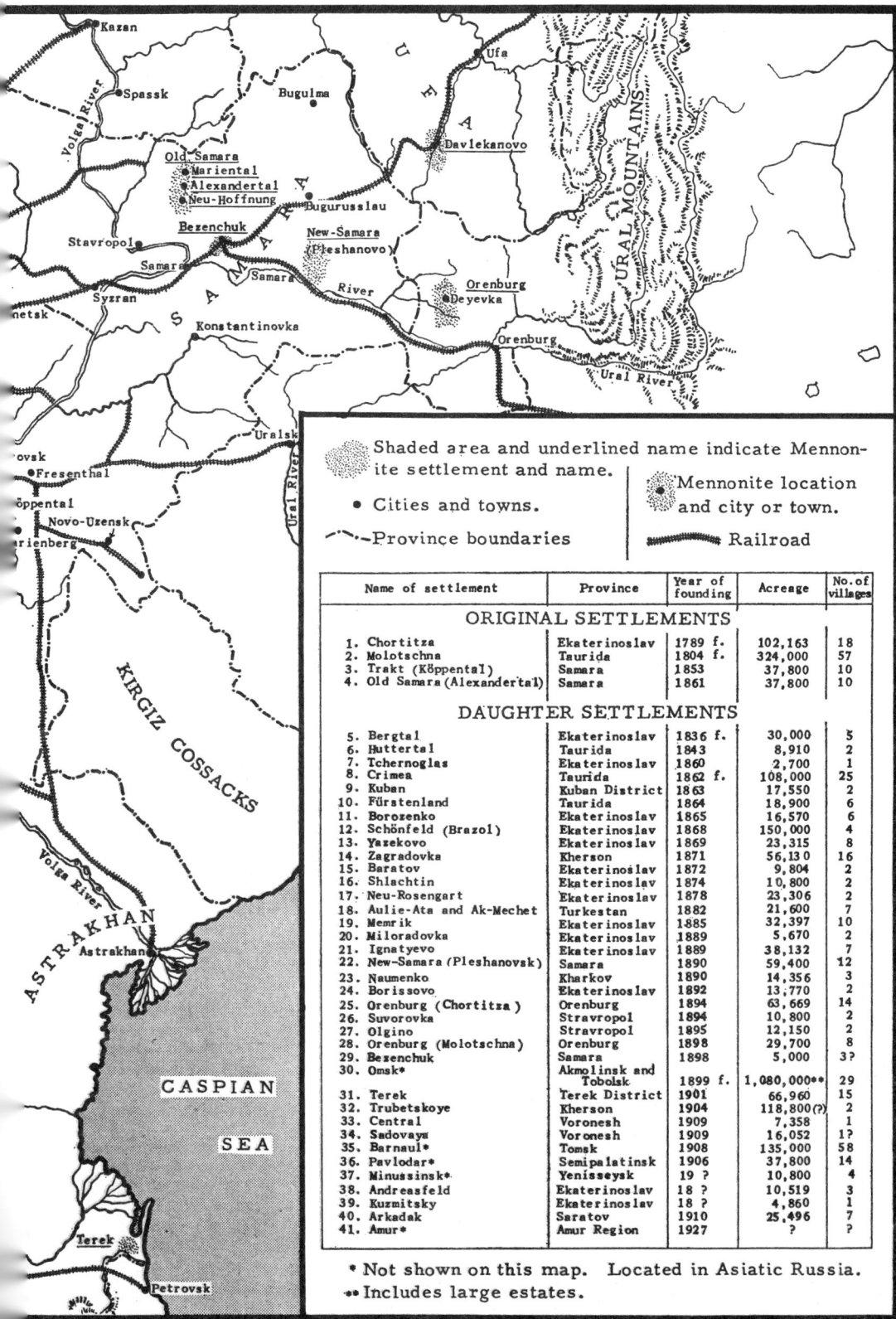

Shaded area and underlined name indicate Mennonite settlement and name.

• Cities and towns.

‧Mennonite location and city or town.

⁀‧Province boundaries

🔗🔗🔗 Railroad

Name of settlement	Province	Year of founding	Acreage	No. of villages
ORIGINAL SETTLEMENTS				
1. Chortitza	Ekaterinoslav	1789 f.	102,163	18
2. Molotschna	Taurida	1804 f.	324,000	57
3. Trakt (Köppental)	Samara	1853	37,800	10
4. Old Samara (Alexandertal)	Samara	1861	37,800	10
DAUGHTER SETTLEMENTS				
5. Bergtal	Ekaterinoslav	1836 f.	30,000	5
6. Huttertal	Taurida	1843	8,910	2
7. Tchernoglas	Ekaterinoslav	1860	2,700	1
8. Crimea	Taurida	1862 f.	108,000	25
9. Kuban	Kuban District	1863	17,550	2
10. Fürstenland	Taurida	1864	18,900	6
11. Borozenko	Ekaterinoslav	1865	16,570	6
12. Schönfeld (Brazol)	Ekaterinoslav	1868	150,000	4
13. Yazekovo	Ekaterinoslav	1869	23,315	8
14. Zagradovka	Kherson	1871	56,130	16
15. Baratov	Ekaterinoslav	1872	9,804	2
16. Shlachtin	Ekaterinoslav	1874	10,800	2
17. Neu-Rosengart	Ekaterinoslav	1878	23,306	2
18. Aulie-Ata and Ak-Mechet	Turkestan	1882	21,600	7
19. Memrik	Ekaterinoslav	1885	32,397	10
20. Miloradovka	Ekaterinoslav	1889	5,670	2
21. Ignatyevo	Ekaterinoslav	1889	38,132	7
22. New-Samara (Pleshanovsk)	Samara	1890	59,400	12
23. Naumenko	Kharkov	1890	14,356	3
24. Borissovo	Ekaterinoslav	1892	13,770	2
25. Orenburg (Chortitza)	Orenburg	1894	63,669	14
26. Suvorovka	Stravropol	1894	10,800	2
27. Olgino	Stravropol	1895	12,150	2
28. Orenburg (Molotschna)	Orenburg	1898	29,700	8
29. Bezenchuk	Samara	1898	5,000	3?
30. Omsk*	Akmolinsk and Tobolsk	1899 f.	1,080,000**	29
31. Terek	Terek District	1901	66,960	15
32. Trubetskoye	Kherson	1904	118,800(?)	2
33. Central	Voronesh	1909	7,358	1
34. Sadovaya	Voronesh	1909	16,052	1?
35. Barnaul*	Tomsk	1908	135,000	58
36. Pavlodar*	Semipalatinsk	1906	37,800	14
37. Minussinsk*	Yenisseysk	19 ?	10,800	4
38. Andreasfeld	Ekaterinoslav	18 ?	10,519	3
39. Kuzmitsky	Ekaterinoslav	18 ?	4,860	1
40. Arkadak	Saratov	1910	25,496	7
41. Amur*	Amur Region	1927	?	?

* Not shown on this map.   Located in Asiatic Russia.

** Includes large estates.

Chortitza and Molotschna constitute the two original Mennonite settlements of the Ukraine; from them most of the daughter settlements in Russia originated.

Although by this time the Russian government was no longer interested in settling foreigners in Russia, two more settlements, with some 500 families, were established in the province of Samara (q.v.), viz., the Trakt (q.v.) settlement (begun in 1855) and the Alexandertal (q.v.) settlement (begun in 1859). The total immigration of Mennonites from Danzig and Prussia to Russia during the years 1788-1870 was about 2,300 families, of whom approximately 462 families went to Chortitza, 1,200 to the Molotschna, and 500 to Samara; 80 families supposedly remained in Vilna on their way to the Ukraine. B. H. Unruh (230) estimates that the total number of immigrants was 10,000. These families came from the following communities and churches: Danzig, Marienburg, Elbing, Tiegenhof, Heubuden, Orloff, Ladekopp, Fürstenwerder, Rosenort, and Tiegenhagen. By no means all the immigrants were experienced farmers. Particularly the first group settling in Chortitza was largely composed of poorer laborers, primarily because it was harder for the well-to-do class to obtain permission to leave the country. The Molotschna and Samara settlements, having numerous prosperous and experienced farmers and better land, made more rapid progress economically and culturally than did Chortitza.

III. *Reasons for Migration*. The Mennonites of Danzig (q.v.) and Prussia (q.v.) had always been a minority in their homeland, tolerated at times because of the economic advantages which the rulers derived from them and at other times oppressed because of their peculiar religious views, their unwillingness to serve in the army, and their rapid spread in the rural areas. In the early days they had been welcomed as good farmers who drained and cultivated the uninhabited swamps of the Vistula River. As Mennonites, however, they were not considered full-fledged citizens. At any time when their service was not needed they were oppressed. The occupations open to them were restricted from time to time (see Danzig Edict of Nov. 10, 1749, *Menn. Life,* April 1951, 36). In 1789 a new "Mennonite Edict" prohibited the Mennonites from purchasing new land, basically because the Mennonites with their large families were buying large quantities of land and thus weakening the rural manpower available for military service. In 1748 the Mennonites in 21 villages of the Werder possessed 392 Hufen (a Hufe is about 40 acres) of the 2,418 of this territory; by 1788 they owned 683 Hufen, thus in 40 years nearly doubling their holdings. In 1772 they purchased a total of 400 farms in Prussia. In 1783-87 the number of families increased from 2,240 to 2,894, which was an increase of 654 families or 3,083 persons in four years (H. Quiring, *Menn. Life,* April 1951, 37).

Thus the reasons for the great interest of the Mennonites of the Vistula River in emigration become apparent. Their rapid increase in numbers, combined with the restrictions in the purchase of land and the occupations open to them, in addition to the uncertainties regarding the preservation of their religious heritage, e.g., the practice of nonresistance,

induced them to consider invitations to other countries.

The Mennonites, however, as noted above, were not the first to receive the invitation to settle in Russia. Catherine II and her agents had tried to attract citizens of many other countries before their attention was called to the Mennonites. And the Mennonites never constituted more than a minority in the total number of immigrants coming to Russia from Germany and other countries. The total population of people of German descent in Russia during World War I was estimated somewhere around 2,000,000, of whom only some 100 to 120 thousand (5 per cent) were Mennonites. Special "privileges" accorded Mennonites when they went to Russia have probably been overstated. There was, to be sure, some variation in the conditions under which settlements in general were established, but they were probably not due to the fact of differing religious faith (Mennonite or non-Mennonite). Even exemption from military service, which had already been offered as an inducement in the Manifesto of 1763, was granted also to non-Mennonite settlers. The ultimate differences in treatment between the Mennonites and others were possibly due rather to the fact that the Mennonites, because of their deeply rooted religious convictions, more persistently claimed exemption from military service when this "privilege" was threatened. However, 1874-80 when one third of all Mennonites from Russia moved to the United States and Canada, many thousands of non-Mennonite Russo-Germans including Catholics, Lutherans, Reformed, and Pietists also moved to North and South America partly because of the loss of their "privileges."

IV. *Privileges and Administration*. The rights, privileges, and administration of the foreign settlers were not stable and uniform throughout all times nor for all settlements. In general the settlers were under the laws and jurisdiction specifically made for "foreign colonists," who were originally responsible to the Bureau of Guardianship of Foreign Colonists, which had its quarters in St. Petersburg. In 1818 a Fürsorge-Komitee (q.v.; Guardian's Committee) was established by the Russian government, with its seat first at Kherson, later at Ekaterinoslav, and finally at Odessa, which was originally subject to the Minister of Interior. In 1871 the Fürsorge-Komitee was abolished and the foreign settlers including the Mennonites became subject to the local authorities of their respective districts. The German system of self-administration under a Schulze (q.v.) in the village and an Oberschulze (q.v.) of the settlement was practiced by the Mennonites from the beginning until the Revolution of 1917 removed all semblance of privilege and independence from the Mennonites of Russia.

The basic condition under which all colonists were admitted to Russia was Catherine's Manifesto of July 22, 1763 (for a complete text, see D. H. Epp, *Chortitzer Mennoniten,* 1889, 3). In general this remained the policy for all settlements, although the conditions were not always so generous. In recent times, particularly in America, the charge has been made that the Mennonites of Russia promised not to do any evangelistic or missionary work in Russia.

The fact is, however, that none of the Mennonite "privileges" contained such a restriction. Hence this charge must have reference to the original Manifesto of 1763, which states (VI, 1) that the foreign colonists settling in Russia were to have the right to exercise their religion freely in accord with their church rules and practices without any molestation, but that "everyone is warned that none of the Christian believers residing in Russia should under any pretext be persuaded or misled to accept or join the faith and the church" of the foreign colonists. This restriction is followed by a statement that "all the nationalities of the Mohammedan faith living within Russia can be persuaded to accept the Christian religion without any restriction." This makes it clear that the restriction was meant to protect the Russian Orthodox Church against proselyting, but that the foreign settlers had ample opportunity to do mission work among non-Christian citizens of Russia. This Manifesto was dated 1763, and the first agreement made between the Mennonite settlers and the Russian government was dated March 3, 1788, which was 25 years later. Neither this first agreement of 1788 nor any of the following contains a clause restricting mission work in Russia. It is likely that very few Mennonites who settled in Russia ever heard of the restricting clause of the Manifesto of 1763.

The twenty articles (German text in D. H. Epp, 25 ff.) which Höppner and Bartsch presented to Potemkin and which were later confirmed by the government in St. Petersburg including Catherine II contain the terms under which the Mennonites would come to Russia; the first deals with religious freedom, the second with the settlement conditions, the third and fourth with tax exemptions, the fifth and sixth with the development of industry and a loan by the government, the seventh and eighth with the guarantee of freedom of religion and exemption from military service for "eternal ages." The remaining articles, the ninth to the twentieth, deal with the details of travel to Russia and the settlement there. On the margins the government representatives approved or qualified the requests. Articles seven and eight, pertaining to the guarantee of religious freedom and exemption from military service "for all times," are thus annotated, "This shall be done in accordance with their practice" and "they shall be exempted from military service." In 1800 the Mennonites of Russia received a *Privilegium* under Czar Paul I confirming the rights they had received before (printed by D. H. Epp, 97). Special rights were given to the Mennonites who settled later in the province of Samara.

V. *Early Developments (1789-1850)*. The Chortitza settlement, being the first, established in an entirely new environment, under the most primitive conditions differing greatly from those of the Vistula Delta, and by settlers who were poor and inexperienced in agriculture, underwent the greatest hardships, affecting the economic, cultural, and religious life. The leaders Bartsch (*q.v.*) and Höppner (*q.v.*) were not trusted, and there were no ordained religious leaders. Only under the greatest privations were the early difficulties of pioneering overcome. The promises of the government were either not fulfilled at all or not according to schedule. Theft by officials was common. The Molotschna settlers, many of whom had stopped at the Chortitza settlement, gained much information and experience and settled under more favorable conditions. Many of them were more prosperous to begin with and of a better cultural and spiritual background. This second settlement soon made greater cultural, economic, and religious advances.

A great promoter was Johann Cornies (*q.v.*; 1789-1848). Through his personal work and as the chairman of the Agricultural Association (*q.v.*) he did much to improve the economic and educational life of both settlements, particularly of the Molotschna. Gradually the Mennonites shifted the emphasis from the raising of cattle, sheep, and horses to that of grains, particularly winter wheat. Primitive agricultural machinery was replaced by advanced implements produced in Mennonite factories. Chortitza (*q.v.*), Alexandrovsk (*q.v.*), Halbstadt (*q.v.*), and Orloff (*q.v.*) were leading towns in industrial enterprises and in cultural development. By the time of the death of Johann Cornies the foundation for this development had been laid. But in the matter of providing settlement opportunities for the landless (*q.v.*) population of both settlements only a beginning had been made by a spear-heading group. The conservative landowning class of farmers did not yet realize their responsibility toward the less fortunate majority of the population of both settlements. Only gradually was the traditional system of mutual aid broadened, which enabled the Mennonites of Russia to establish many daughter settlements not only in the Ukraine, but also in other provinces of European Russia and Siberia, through co-operative purchase of land and loans to new settlers.

In educational and religious practices the pioneers in Russia were extremely conservative, preserving the practices of the old homeland. Ministers read their sermons monotonously. Very little progress was made in challenging the congregations and individuals in their ethical and religious practices and in awakening their social, missionary, and evangelistic responsibilities. The schools were primitive and restricted to the teaching and reading of the Bible and Bible stories, the catechism, the primer, and elementary arithmetic. Teachers were poorly prepared and the school buildings and equipment inadequate.

VI. *Daughter Settlements*. The number of landless (*q.v.*) Mennonites increased from generation to generation, particularly since the government did not permit the subdivision of a farm, which consisted as a rule of 176 acres (65 dessiatines). The large surplus land tracts in connection with the settlements were generally rented by the well-to-do farmers. The landless usually obtained a small parcel of land at one end of the village and worked as farm hands, industrial workers, etc. They were known as *Anwohner* (*q.v.*). A typical situation was that in the Molotschna settlement in 1865, when there were 1,384 landed farmers and 2,356 landless workers in the villages. Only the landowners, comprising less than one third of the population, had civic and economic rights; the other two thirds had none. A committee known as the *Landlosen-Kommission* (*q.v.*) was formed in 1863 to represent the cause of the landless and appeal to the Fürsorge-Komitee for remedial action. Finally the surplus land of the Molotschna settlement was distributed among the landless. In addition to this, a fund was established for the purchase of land for oncoming generations. By painful experience the Mennonites of the Molotschna and Chortitza learned to help and to provide for the new generations of landless by establishing daughter colonies.

J. Ewert's study of the increase of the population and the land owned by Mennonites from 1789 to 1910 reveals that approximately 8,500 (the estimate is now 10,000) immigrants established the Chortitza, Molotschna, Alexandertal, and Trakt settlements, which had a population of 34,500 by 1859, while the occupied land area remained the same, viz., 501,400 acres. After the great emigration of the Mennonites to America in 1874-80, the population again rapidly increased. In 1910 Ewert estimated the population of Mennonites in Russia as 100,000, owning a total acreage of 1,798,948, or an average of 18 acres per person (*Der Praktische Landwirt,* December 1926, No. 12, pp. 12 ff.). (Some estimates are higher. See *ME* I, 25.) Adolf Ehrt estimates that in 1860 the Mennonites averaged 14 acres per person, and in 1914 16 acres. However, this land increase took place primarily in the daughter settlements. The acreage of the mother settlements remained more or less unchanged (Ehrt, 84). In 1860 the mother colonies owned seven times as much land as the daughter colonies, and in 1914 they owned equal amounts (Ehrt, 83).

The increase in property owned by the Mennonites of Russia can be estimated from the taxation for the maintenance of the forestry service or alternative service program. The records reveal that in 1908 the reported property value was 194,000,000 rubles, while by 1914 this had increased to 276,000,000 rubles (Ehrt, 70). No doubt this is an underestimate, since probably not all persons had been reached by the census. Land holdings by Mennonites increased proportionally beyond the growth of the population. The large increase of land ownership was partly due to the purchase of scattered large estates outside the main settlements. Before World War I there were 384 large Mennonite estate owners, who owned 810,000 acres, making an average of 283 acres; the average evaluation of such an estate in 1914 was 200,000 rubles. The large estate owners, though numbering only 1.9 per cent of the Mennonite population, contributed one third of the total, or 80,000 rubles, annually for the maintenance of the forestry service on the basis of an assessment on owned land. The largest Mennonite estate consisted of 50,000 acres (Ehrt, 87).

During the second half of the 19th century the establishment of daughter settlements was restricted primarily to European Russia, first in the territories immediately surrounding the two settlements, then in the Crimea, then in the foothills of the Caucasian Mountains, and later (after 1890 except for Turkestan 1882, 1884) in the eastern provinces of Central European Russia, such as Orenburg, and in Asiatic Russia. Following is a list of the settlements with name, province, the year of founding, number of villages, acreage, and population. Separate articles on each of the settlements are to be found in the ENCYCLOPEDIA. The Russian names, usually Germanized, appear here in an Anglicized form, while the German ones have been retained. (See also article **Villages.**)

A. Mother Settlements

Name	Province	Founded	Villages	Acreage	Population
1. Chortitza	Ekaterinoslav	1789 ff.	19	1789: 89,100 1917: 405,000	1819: 2,888 1941: 13,965
2. Molotschna	Taurida	1804 ff.	60	1835: 324,000	1835: 6,000 1926: 17,347
3. Trakt	Samara	1853 ff.	10	1897: 44,134	1897: 1,176
4. Alexandertal	Samara	1859 ff.	8	1870: 26,500 1917: 53,500	1913: 1,144

B. Daughter Settlements

Name	Province	Mother Settlement	Founded	Villages	Acreage	Population
1. Bergthal	Ekaterinoslav	Chortitza	1836–52	5	30,000	1874: 3,000
2. Jewish Settlement (Judenplan)	Kherson	Chortitza	1847	6	5-6 families per village	
3. Chernoglaz	Ekaterinoslav	Chortitza	1860	1	2,700	130
4. Crimea	Taurida	Molotschna	1862 ff.	c25 & estates	1929: 108,000	1926: 4,817
5. Kuban	Kuban	Chortitza and Molotschna	1862	2	17,550	1904: 2,000
6. Fürstenland	Taurida	Chortitza	1864–70	7	19,000	1874: 1,100
7. Borozenko	Ekaterinoslav	Chortitza	1865–66	6	18,000	1910: 600
8. Friedensfeld (Miropol)	Ekaterinoslav	Molotschna	1867	1	5,400	
9. Brazol (Schönfeld)	Ekaterinoslav	Molotschna	1868	4 & estates	1868: 14,000 1910: 187,000	1917: 2,000

Name	Province	Mother Settlement	Founded	Villages	Acreage	Population
10. Neu-Schönwiese (Dmitrovka)	Ekaterinoslav	Schönwiese-Chortitza	1868	1	3,788	
11. Tempelhof	Stavropol	Molotschna	1868	2		
12. Yazykovo (Nikolaifeld)	Ekaterinoslav	Chortitza	1869	6	23,315	1930: 2,200
13. Nepluyevka	Ekaterinoslav	Chortitza	1870	2	10,800	1910: 550
14. Andreasfeld	Ekaterinoslav	Chortitza	1870	3	10,620	
15. Baratov	Ekaterinoslav	Chortitza	1872	2 (4)	1872: 9,800	1905: 2,569
16. Zagradovka	Kherson	Molotschna	1871	16	57,445	1922: 5,429
17. Shlachtin	Ekaterinoslav	Chortitza	1874	2	10,800	1910: 1,000
18. Neu-Rosengart	Ekaterinoslav	Chortitza	1878	2	1,800	1910: 250
19. Wiesenfeld	Ekaterinoslav	Chortitza	1880	1	23,306	
20. Aulie-Ata	Turkestan Central Asia	Molotschna	1882	6	21,600	1910: 1,000
21. Ak-Mechet	Khiva Central Asia	Trakt	1884	1	13	25 families
22. Memrik	Ekaterinoslav	Molotschna	1885	10	32,400	1,367
23. Alexandropol	Ekaterinoslav	Molotschna	1888	1	?	15 families
24. Samoylovka	Kharkov	Molotschna	1888	2	?	1905: 239
25. Milorodovka	Ekaterinoslav	Chortitza	1889	2	5,670	1910: 200
26. Ignatyevo	Ekaterinoslav	Chortitza	1889–90	7	38,132	1910: 1,400
27. Naumenko	Kharkov	Chortitza Molotschna	1890	4 (3)	14,350	1905: 700
28. Neu-Samara (Pleshanovsk)	Samara	Molotschna	1890	14	1922: 91,000	1922: 3,670
29. Borissovo	Ekaterinoslav	Chortitza	1892	2	13,770	1910: 400
30. Davlekanovo	Ufa	Molotschna Samara	1894	19 & estates	1926: 30,000	1926: 1,831
31. Orenburg (Deyevka)	Orenburg	Chortitza	1894	14	63,660	1910: 1,400
32. Suvorovka	Stavropol (Caucasus)	Zagradovka	1894	2	10,800	80 families
33. Orenburg (Molotschna)	Orenburg	Molotschna	1898	8	29,700	1910: 1,000
34. Olgino	Stavropol (Caucasus)	Mixed	1895	2 (4)	12,150	80 families
35. Bezenchuk	Samara	Alexandertal	1898	3?	5,400	75
36. Omsk	Akmolinsk & Tobolsk	Mixed	1899	29 & estates	108,000	
37. Don (Millerovo)	Don Region	Molotschna	1900–3	*	10,800	
38. Terek	Terek (Caucasus)	Molotschna	1901	15	66,960	1905: 1,655
39. Rovnopol (Ebenfeld)	Samara	Molotschna	1903	1	8,250	
40. Trubetskoye	Kherson	Molotschna	1904	2	118,800 (?)	400
41. Pavlodar	Semipalatinsk	Mixed	1906	14	37,800	
42. Sadovaya	Voronezh	Chortitza	1909	1?	16,052	
43. Slavgorod (Barnaul)	Tomsk	Mixed	1908	58	135,000	1925: 1,373
44. Zentral	Voronezh	Chortitza	1909	1	7,358	
45. Arkadak	Saratov	Chortitza	1910	7	25,500	1925: 1,500
46. Bugulma	Samara	Alexandertal	1910	1	2,700	
47. Kistyendey	Saratov	?	1910?	1		
48. Minusinsk	Yeniseysk	Ignatyevo	1913	2 (4)	10,800?	1918: 32 families
49. Amur	Eastern Siberia	Mixed	1927	20		1927: 1,300
50. Kuzmitsky (Alexandrovka)	Ekaterinoslav	Chortitza	?	1	1910: 4,860	1910: 200
51. Eugenfeld	Ekaterinoslav	Chortitza	?	1		
52. Alexeyfeld	Kherson	Molotschna	?	1		

* Millerovo, Masayevka, Nikolaipol

Sources: Friesen, *Brüderschaft;* H. Dirks, *Statistik; Die Mennoniten-Gemeinden in Russland;* J. Quiring, *Die Mundart von Chortitza.*

C. Settlements in Russian Poland, including the Hutterian Brethren

Name	Province	Mother Settlement	Founded	Villages
I. Prussian Settlements				
1. Deutsch-Wymysle	Warsaw	Przechovka	1762	1
2. Deutsch-Kazun	Warsaw	Culm-Graudenz	1776	1
3. Wola-Orsczynska	Plock, Warsaw			
4. Karolswalde	Ostrog, Volhynia	Culm-Graudenz	1780–85	6
5. Michalin	Kiev	Graudenz	1880	
II. Swiss Volhynian Settlements				
1. Vignanka-Futtor	Dubno, Volhynia	Galicia	1801	2
2. Michelsdorf-Urszulin	Lublin, Poland	France	?	2
3. Eduardsdorf-Zahoriz	Dubno, Volhynia	Michelsdorf	1815	2
4. Horodyszcze	Novograd-Volynsk, Volhynia	Michelsdorf	1837	2
5. Kotozufka-Neumanufka	Novograd-Volynsk, Volhynia	Eduardsdorf	1861	2
III. Hutterian Settlements				
1. Vishenka	Tchernigov	Transylvania	1770	1
2. Radichev	Tchernigov	Vishenka	1802	1
3. Hutterthal	Taurida	Radichev	1843	1
4. Johannesruh	Taurida	Hutterthal	1853	1
5. Hutterdorf	Taurida	Hutterthal	1857	1
6. Neu-Hutterthal	Taurida		1857	1

Explanation Regarding Russian Poland and Hutterian Brethren. Mennonites living in the Vistula Delta area gradually moved up the river into Poland, and Swiss Mennonites from Alsace-Lorraine and South Germany settled in Poland. Some of these settlements shared the political fate of Poland (*q.v.*) and passed under Russian rule in the Partitions of Poland (1772-95) when Russian Poland was established (1815) and when it became a Russian province (1836-1914).

The Prussian Mennonites established Deutsch-Wymysle (*q.v.*), Deutsch-Kazun (*q.v.*), and Wola-Orsczynska (*q.v.*) at Plock, all near Warsaw; Karolswalde (*q.v.*) near Ostrog in Volhynia (six villages); and Michalin (*q.v.*) in the province of Kiev.

The Swiss Mennonites established the settlements of Vignanka-Futtor (*q.v.*) at Dubno in Volhynia, Michelsdorf-Urszulin (*q.v.*) near Lublin in Poland, Eduardsdorf-Zahoriz at Dubno in Volhynia, Horodyszcze (three villages) at Novograd-Volynsk in Volhynia, and Kotozufka-Neumanufka at Novograd-Volynsk in Volhynia (two villages). All of the Swiss and most of the Prussian Mennonites of Volhynia and Russian Poland went to the United States in the 1870's when the universal conscription law was introduced in Russia. Contact between the Mennonites of Russian Poland and those of Russia proper was infrequent. Some from Russian Poland later settled in the Molotschna, through whom a contact was established (see also **Waldheim** and **Poland**).

The first settlers of the Anabaptist-Mennonite family to enter Russia were the Hutterites (*q.v.*), who established themselves on the estate Vishenka (*q.v.*) of Count Rumiantsev (*q.v.*), on the Desna River in the Ukraine, in 1770. The basis of this settlement was originally a private arrangement between the landowner and the Hutterites. Later the Hutterites shared in the Mennonite privileges and were treated similarly. Soon the Bruderhof was moved to the crown land of Raditchev, whence the Hutterites transferred to the Molotschna settlement near Meli-

topol, establishing the villages of Huttertal, Johannesruh, Hutterdorf, and Neu-Huttertal. All the Hutterites emigrated to the United States in 1874-77.

VII. *Period of Growth and Achievement* (1850-1917). The reason for the rapid spread of the Mennonite settlements in Russia was their increase in population. Ehrt comes to the conclusion that of the 120,000 Mennonites in Russia after World War I, 75,000 were found in the Ukraine and 45,000 in the other parts of Russia including Siberia. His analysis was based on the statistics of the AMLV (*q.v.*). In 1926 there were 19,267 Mennonites living in Siberia, 1,545 in Turkestan, 4,017 in the Crimea, 3,246 at the foothills of the Caucasian Mountains, 7,596 in the province of Samara, 5,655 in the Volga region, and 2,175 scattered, or a total of 44,304 in the RSFSR (USSR outside of the Ukraine). His statistics, based on the official report of the KfK of 1926, give a total of 46,830 for the Ukraine, which makes the total of 91,134 in all USSR for the year 1926, in spite of the emigration of over 20,000 Mennonites to America 1922-26 (Ehrt, 152 ff.).

What is the Mennonite population of Russia today? No definite answer can be given to this question. However, here is an estimate. In 1920 the Mennonites of Russia had a population of about 120,000. Annually there was an increase of around 3,000. By 1929 Ehrt (159) estimates that there had been an increase of 20,700. However, a total of some 23,000 left for America (1923-29), leaving a population of 117,800 in 1929. On this basis we could continue with the estimate that the population normally increased by 3,000 annually. During the years of exile and disrupted family life the increase declined and there may actually have been times when the loss, due to concentration camps, etc., was greater than the increase. In spite of the great loss during the exile and evacuation and the reduced increase because of the separation of the families and the emigration of some 12,000 to Canada and South America in connection with World War II, the total population of Mennonite descent, although many may have given up their identity in belief and culture, may possibly be estimated at about 100,000.

Hand in hand with the expansion of the population and the establishment of new settlements went the total economic development of the Mennonites of Russia. The improvement of agricultural machinery enabled the Mennonites to produce hard winter wheat on a large scale. A prosperous milling industry and the establishment of many businesses enabled them to market their products. The Mennonites were by no means restricted to rural occupations. Towns like Chortitza, Alexandrovsk, Halbstadt, Berdyansk, Ekaterinoslav, and Millerovo had become centers of Mennonite industry. Of all the businesses and industries owned and operated by Mennonites before World War I, 30 per cent were located in Chortitza. Of the total production of agricultural machinery produced in the Ukraine, 10 per cent was produced in Mennonite factories, while of the total output in Russia, 6.2 per cent was produced in Mennonite factories. By 1914 the commercialized or capitalistic enterprises of the Mennonites of Russia in agriculture, industry, and business had grown considerably, consisting of one third of the total Mennonite capital investment. This means that two thirds still followed the traditional agricultural pattern with some additional small home industries, while one third had gone over to large-scale capitalistic enterprises. Only 2.8 per cent of the population were the bearers of this commercialized and capitalistic tendency, owning three fourths of the total Mennonite capital (Ehrt, 91-96). (See **Agriculture Among the Mennonites of Russia, Business,** and **Industry.**)

The general cultural achievement of the Mennonites ran parallel with their economic progress. Schools, hospitals, and other institutions designed for public service were established. Centers of cultural progress were found in Gnadenfeld, Orloff, and Halbstadt, all in the Molotschna; and in Chortitza. Progressive leadership in education and spiritual life broke the lethargy of the early days and ushered in a well-developed educational system which had been inaugurated by Johann Cornies before 1847. Among the pioneer educators were Tobias Voth, Heinrich Heese, Heinrich Franz I, and Fr. W. Lange. The first secondary schools (see **Zentralschule**) were established in Orloff, Gnadenfeld, and Chortitza. Various organizations promoted the educational institutions and standards among the Mennonites, particularly in the early days the Fürsorge-Komitee, the Agricultural Association, and the Molotschnaer Mennonitischer Schulrat (*q.v.*).

Problems in connection with education arose when the Russianization policy of the government gradually subjected the Mennonite educational system to the Department of Education of Russia. This speeded up and reinforced the desire of many in the 1870's to emigrate to North America. All of the school subjects, with the exception of Bible and German literature, came gradually to be taught in the Russian language. In 1920 the Mennonites of Russia had about 450 elementary schools with about 16,000 pupils, and 27 secondary schools (Zentralschulen) with about 2,000 pupils and a teaching staff of 100. With the Revolution of 1917 and the introduction of the antireligious Marxian philosophy in education,

the Mennonite educational system was gradually wiped out. Many of the teachers emigrated to America, were exiled, or chose another vocation. Some adjusted themselves to the Soviet philosophy. The well-developed educational system produced by the Mennonites of Russia, which has never been equaled anywhere else among Mennonites, disintegrated (see **Education** Among the Mennonites in Russia).

Religious life among the Mennonites of Russia was on a comparatively low plane at the outset. Leadership was lacking and had to be selected from an untrained constituency which at times also lacked spiritual qualities. Gradually, with the help of the mother church of Prussia, the church life was organized and made some progress. One of the earliest schisms took place when Klaas Reimer (*q.v.*) of the Molotschna, an ultraconservative leader, separated and organized the Kleine Gemeinde (*q.v.*) in 1814.

Progressive leadership and a more vital religious life came through some of the groups who immigrated to Russia later and established villages and congregations such as Gnadenfeld in the Molotschna. They introduced the practice of abstinence, mission festivals, and other pietistic and evangelistic views. Some of these Mennonites who came from Prussia had been in contact with the Moravian Brethren of Germany. Another source of influence came from Eduard Wüst (*q.v.*), who was a Württemberg Pietist and the minister of an Evangelische Brüdergemeinde at Neuhoffnung near Berdyansk. He promoted evangelism, mission festivals, prayer meetings, etc. Some of the Mennonite leaders, e.g., Cornelius Jansen, Bernhard Harder, and August Lenzmann, were his personal friends. Soon his sermons were attended by Mennonites, and he was also at times invited to preach in the Mennonite villages. A strong emphasis on a personal acceptance of salvation and conversion was typical of his preaching. A group of eighteen heads of families in the village of Gnadenfeld who had been influenced by Wüst asked their elder August Lenzmann to administer the Lord's Supper to them as a special group. When he denied the request, this group of eighteen not only observed the Lord's Supper independently, but also drew up a document (Jan. 6, 1860) stating why they desired to start a new church. This act was the official founding of the Mennonite Brethren Church (*q.v.*). Through the Baptists this group was further influenced in certain religious practices, e.g., the introduction of baptism by immersion (*q.v.*). The struggle between this group and the leaders of the old church continued for a while during which time both sides made mistakes and expressed more zeal than brotherly love. The new group was extreme in denouncing the church from which they had seceded, and some of the Mennonite leaders took an unbrotherly attitude toward the new group. Among those who did much to improve the relationship were Johann Harder (*q.v.*), Bernhard Harder (*q.v.*), and Leonhard Sudermann (*q.v.*). These were the men who favored a more spontaneous expression of the joy of salvation and newer methods of promoting the Gospel, similar to the founders of the General Conference Mennonite Church which had originated slightly earlier in North America and was led by men like John Oberholtzer, Christian Schowalter, Daniel Hoch, and Daniel Hege.

The growth of the Mennonite Brethren group in Russia was notable. In 1888, 95.7 per cent of all Mennonites of Russia belonged to the Mennonite Church, while 4.3 per cent belonged to the Mennonite Brethren Church and other groups (Ehrt, 61). In 1925-26 74.9 per cent belonged to the Mennonite Church while 22.5 per cent belonged to the Mennonite Brethren and 2.6 per cent to other groups. The growth of the Mennonite Brethren is particularly noticeable in the daughter settlements. In 1925-26 81.2 per cent of the total Mennonite population of the Ukraine, in which the mother settlements were located, belonged to the Mennonite Church, 15.5 to the Mennonite Brethren, and 3.3 to other groups. In the RSFSR, that is, the rest of Russia outside of the Ukraine, consisting primarily of daughter settlements, the percentage differed considerably. To the Mennonite Church belonged 60.5 per cent, to the Mennonite Brethren 38.2 per cent, and to other groups 1.3 per cent. This makes it clear that the strongest increase in Mennonite Brethren, which was due primarily to winning members from the Mennonite Church, was found in the daughter settlements. It could also indicate that the Mennonite Brethren of the mother settlements were more active in the establishment of daughter settlements (Ehrt, 85).

Bible study, prayer meetings, song festivals, evangelistic meetings, publication efforts, conference organizations were among the results of this general spiritual revival, which gradually affected all the Mennonites of Russia. The Allgemeine Bundeskonferenz der Mennonitengemeinden in Russland (*q.v.*), founded in 1883, was also attended from 1906 and officially from 1910 by the Mennonite Brethren, who had their own conference from 1872. Beginning in 1910 a Kommission für Kirchenangelegenheiten (*q.v.*), usually called KfK, functioned as the executive committee of the Bundeskonferenz.

Other new groups which originated in Russia were the Krimmer Mennonite Brethren (*q.v.*) in 1869, the Mennonite section of the Temple Church (*q.v.*) or Friends of Jerusalem in 1863, the followers of Hermann Peters (*q.v.*) in 1866, and the Evangelische Mennoniten-Gemeinden (*q.v.*) in 1905. Another result of the general pietistic influence was the migration of Mennonites from the Molotschna and the Trakt under the leadership of Abraham Peters (*q.v.*) and Claas Epp (*q.v.*) to Central Asia (*q.v.*) in 1880 to avoid all military or alternative service and to meet the Lord at a designated place of refuge in the East.

Two of the most disturbing factors during the second half of the 19th century were the introduction of a universal military conscription law and the inauguration of a general program of Russianization of foreign settlers in Russia. They caused one third of all Mennonites of Russia to leave for the United States and Canada in 1874-80. Only the compromise of the Russian government in granting the Mennonites the privilege of fulfilling their state obligations in forestry service (*q.v.*) prevented a more or less general exodus. Some 18,000 Mennonites went to North America, where the largest Mennonite settlements were established in Kansas (*q.v.*) and Manitoba (*q.v.*). The Manitoba settlers were primarily from Chortitza (*q.v.*), Fürstenland (*q.v.*), and Berg-

thal (*q.v.*), some of which became known as the Old Colony Mennonites (*q.v.*), most of whom later went to Mexico because of their ultraconservative attitudes. The Mennonites settling in the United States were primarily those coming from the Molotschna settlement, Prussia, Russian Poland, and Galicia, including the Hutterites, most of whom went to Canada after 1918. The Mennonites remaining in Russia fulfilled their duty toward the government in forestry service and also in World War I in part in hospital service. Even under the Soviet government they were for a while exempted from military service; this privilege was rescinded *c*1935.

At the beginning of the 20th century the need for educated ministers had grown to the extent that the advisability of establishing a theological seminary was repeatedly discussed. The same was true regarding the publication efforts. The anti-German feeling of the Russian government was not conducive to the promotion of these plans. Young men received their education more and more in Germany and Switzerland at Bible schools, theological seminaries, and universities. Some studied at Russian universities. Semiofficial periodicals such as the *Botschafter* (*q.v.*) and the *Friedensstimme* (*q.v.*) and almanacs served the constituency after 1903-5 with interruptions.

VIII. *Under Communism (1917-57)*. The overthrow of the Czarist government, the Civil War, and the ultimate establishment of the Communist regime starting in October 1917 caused most radical changes for the Mennonites of Russia. The first period was characterized by the Civil War, confiscation and nationalization of property, starvation, and general confusion, which ended with the full working establishment of the Communist government.

The Mennonite way of life was undermined in its basis by laws like the following issued April 8, 1929: "Religious organizations are forbidden to (a) organize mutual aid and co-operatives; (b) give material support to church members; (c) organize special meetings for children, youth, women, and prayer, and other meetings as well as general Bible literature, sewing societies, work groups and religious instruction groups, circles, and arrange for excursions and entertainment for children, for libraries and reading materials, and to organize hospitals and medical aid."

At the General Conference meeting of the Mennonites of Russia which took place in Moscow in January 1925, the following eight points were stated as the minimum requirement for the Mennonites to survive: (1) undisturbed religious meetings and discussions in church and private homes for adults and children; (2) undisturbed religious societies, choirs, instruction in religion and doctrines especially for children and youth; (3) undisturbed founding of Mennonite orphanages with Christian education; (4) undisturbed erection of new church buildings and the exemption of church and ministers from special taxes; (5) undisturbed acquisition of Bibles and aids and other Christian literature including periodicals for the congregations; (6) undisturbed Bible courses conducted for the preparation and the deepening of the knowledge of ministers; (7) recognition of the schools as a neutral territory where neither religious nor antireligious propaganda takes place and where exclusively knowledge is taught by teachers who have freedom in their private life; (8) exemption from military service and basic military preparation, the granting of a useful alternative service, and exemption from the oath for Mennonites who make a simple promise. A conference resolution made the following assertion: "These eight points of the KfK in the memorandum to the Central Executive Committee of the USSR regarding the fundamental questions of Mennonite church life the meeting considers the minimum prerequisite for the continued existence of the Mennonites as a religious fellowship." This request was declined, but the conference appealed again to the government on Jan. 16, 1925, the petition closing with these words, "Give us our children, give us freedom to train and educate them in accord with the commands of our conscience" (Ehrt, p. 141 f.). These were some of the last organized efforts of the Mennonites of Russia to obtain rights to continue their religious life in accord with their basic beliefs.

At this time (1922-27) some 23,000 Mennonites left Russia since they saw no hope for a better future. Exemption from military service was still possible for a time, possibly until 1930-35. Each individual had to apply for exemption and each case was separately examined by a court. The questions which the court decided were whether the religious group to which the applicant belonged actually were conscientious objectors, and whether the applicant actually believed and lived in accord with this tradition. If he was exempted, he could do alternative service. The Soviet law made ample provision for exemption from military service, which other groups besides Mennonites, such as the Dukhobors, followers of Tolstoy, and Baptists made use of. However, soon the practice was found to be in conflict with the original democratic theory. Ehrt reports that of 131 young Mennonites who applied for exemption in 1925, only 64 were freed, 20 accepted full military service, and 47 were imprisoned. Of 22 young men imprisoned in the Caucasus area, four died of typhoid fever and 14 were shot. In 1926 there were 70 Mennonite young men imprisoned in Kiev who were to be sent to forced labor camps because of their objecting to military service (Ehrt, 143 ff). The alternative service camps resembled slave labor camps in severity of treatment and difficulty of physical survival. In the beginning of the 1930's it became almost impossible to be exempted from military service. Gradually young men were forced to serve in the regular army. No organized spiritual fellowship was possible since the leaders and the ministers had been exiled. Whether and to what an extent some of the young men refused in these years to serve in the army is not yet known. When Hitler invaded the Ukraine, a systematic effort was made to remove from the Red army all people of German background including the Mennonites, although some remained in the army in spite of this effort.

Stalin's harsh program of collectivization and exile caused some 13,000, not all Mennonites, to flee to Moscow in 1929, of whom only some 5,000 were permitted to leave, settling mostly in Brazil (*q.v.*) and Paraguay (*q.v.*), although perhaps 1,000 got to Canada. The ruthless destruction of the Mennonite religious and cultural life was a part of the total program of dictatorship, through which many families were disrupted by exile and death, particularly among the leaders such as ministers and teachers.

With the outbreak of hostilities between Russia and Germany in 1941, an attempt was made to send eastward the remaining German-speaking males west of the Volga, including Mennonites. When the German army invaded the Ukraine, an attempt was made to move all the Mennonites (Germans) of the Ukraine to the east of the Dnieper River. This attempt was only partially successful. Most of the Chortitza Mennonites remained in German-occupied territory. During this time the cultural and religious life was restored to some extent but only for a short time (1941-43), and some of the churches were again being closed. When the German front collapsed in Russia and the retreat began, the remaining Mennonite population of the Ukraine was evacuated by the retreating German army by trains or wagon caravans starting in the fall of 1943 with the goal of settling them in the Warthegau (*q.v.*), former western Poland, along the Vistula River, near the general area where they had come from 150 years before. With the collapse of Hitler's empire, these Mennonites fled westward; one third ultimately reached Canada and South America; the majority, however, were returned to Russia and only a very few remained in Germany. It is estimated that some 35,000 Mennonites were taken along to Germany by the German army in 1943, of whom nearly two thirds were forcibly repatriated by the Red army, while one third or some 12,000 went to Canada and Paraguay, where they established the Volendam (*q.v.*) and Neuland (*q.v.*) settlements. Meanwhile many have left South America and joined their relatives in Canada. Many of the Russian Mennonite men were drafted into the German army in 1941-45. Practically all the Russian Mennonites in the Warthegau, together with other Russian Germans, were naturalized en masse by the German authorities in 1943.

Since the death of Stalin (1953), conditions in Russia have somewhat changed. During the last years the picture is becoming clearer as to what happened to those Mennonites who remained in Russia and those who were sent back to Russia from Germany. The original assumption that the Chortitza and Molotschna settlements as well as the daughter settlements of the Ukraine were severely damaged and that no Mennonites remained there has been proved correct. But there are some indications that a few families have returned since Stalin's death, since there is greater freedom for the civilians to move about. In some of the settlements east of the Volga like Orenburg, Pleshanovo, and particularly in Siberia, large numbers have been allowed to remain in their original homes. To some extent they have retained some phases of their cultural and religious life, which is illustrated by the fact that conversions and baptismal and worship services have taken place quite regularly during the last several years. A large concentration of the exiled, evacuated, and uprooted Mennonites is noticeable in the Asiatic Russian regions and territories immediately east of the Ural Mountains in Soviet Central Asia (*q.v.*), especially Kazakh S.S.R. etc., and Siberia (*q.v.*). The old Mennonite settlements of Slavgorod (*q.v.*), Omsk (*q.v.*), and Pavlodar (*q.v.*) have been relatively undisturbed as geographic units. Karaganda has become the center of a large congregation. The settlements in Old and New Samara and the Caucasus were also completely destroyed.

It can be estimated that Russia again had a total of 100,000 Mennonites at the time when Hitler invaded the Ukraine (1941) in spite of the fact that some 25,000 had migrated to America. Of these 100,000 probably one fifth was exiled under Stalin, and one fourth was evacuated eastward when the German army invaded Russia in 1941. This would mean that 45,000 of the 100,000 Mennonites were either in forced labor camps or evacuated to uninhabited places by the time of the outbreak of World War II in Russia. There were still some 35,000 Mennonites left in the Ukraine who were taken along by the German army in 1943. Of these some 23,000 were repatriated and sent to uninhabited places, primarily to Asiatic Russia. This would indicate that of the *c*100,000 Mennonites living in Russia today, only some 30,000 live in their former home communities; the majority are scattered all over the Ural region and farther east. Many of them spent ten to twenty years in labor or concentration camps.

Typical as to the number of people exiled is the Chortitza Mennonite settlement (*q.v.*). In 1929-41, 1,456 Mennonites of the total population of 13,965 were exiled. The worst years were 1929-30 and 1937-38. In 1929, 153 were exiled; in 1930, 244; in 1937, 361; and in 1938, 465. Of the 1,456, 1,148 were men, 43 were women, and 44 were young people. It is not known where 973 of them were sent. Six were sent to the Far East, 18 to Siberia, 332 to the Ural Mountains, 4 to Kazakhstan, 66 to the northern parts of European Russia, 6 to Central Russia, and 57 to Southern Russia (Stumpp).

These camps were scattered all over European and Asiatic Russia. Dallin and Nicolaevsky listed 125 camps or clusters of camps while B. Yakovlev listed 165, some of which were clusters of camps. Both sources state that their lists are incomplete. There was hardly a part of Russia which did not have camps. Dallin and Nicolaevsky subdivided the camps according to geographic location and listed 58 camps in European Russia, many of which were located in the northern region. In Asiatic Russia they listed 67 camps located in western, northern, and eastern Siberia, and Central Asia. Since the days when Stalin developed these labor camps, some changes have taken place. Many of the camps have been closed. Recently those who have served their terms in camps or had been forcibly settled at places have obtained greater liberties to move about. On the other hand, it is clear that Khrushchev places great emphasis on settling uninhabited places in Asiatic Russia. Of particular interest to him is the Kazakh S.S.R. in Soviet Central Asia (*q.v.*), where a great increase in population is being reported. Many people settled here "voluntarily." It has become apparent that many of the Mennonites are now located in the Kazakh S.S.R. and other parts of Soviet Central Asia. No doubt many were sent there when they were repatriated, others were exiled into that region, still others may have been attracted to this area because of the concentration of Mennonites here. It can be assumed that of the Mennonites in the U.S.S.R. today, some 80 per cent are located east of the Ural Mountains and some 20 per cent in European Russia, of whom only a small number are found in the old Mennonite settlements such as Orenburg and Pleshanovo. The number of Mennonites living in their original settlements can be estimated as follows: Orenburg settlement (*q.v.*), 5,000 (Europe); Pleshanovo settlement (*q.v.*), 2,500 (Europe); Slavgorod settlement (*q.v.*), 14,000 (Siberia); Omsk settlement (*q.v.*), 4,000 (Siberia); Pavlodar settlement (*q.v.*), 2,500 (Siberia), and Amur settlement (*q.v.*), 2,000 (Siberia). This makes an estimated total of 30,000. Of these, only some 7,500 live in European Russia.

To what extent a concentration of Mennonites in these old and new settlements in Asiatic Russia and a revival of religious and cultural traditions through an organized program will be possible depends very much on the development of civil and religious freedom in Soviet Russia, including the rights for minority groups. Being of Germanic background and of a group with deep religious motivations, resisting the antireligious Marxian philosophy of life, the Mennonites as some other minority groups of Russia were distrusted and uprooted before and during World War II. Now that they have lost their religio-cultural foundation and stronghold in the Ukraine, a perpetuation of their cultural values, which were based on their settlements and educational system, may be extremely difficult. Even if greater freedom is granted to them, an adjustment to their Russian environment including intermarriage and the rapid loss of the German language is unavoidable unless a radical change takes place. Of course, a strong Christian faith and church life can be built without the German language and culture. The very changeover to the Russian language may be the door to a much wider and more effective Mennonite witness in Russia.

Looking over the 150 years that Mennonites lived in Russia, it can be said that they had unparalleled opportunities for establishing and maintaining communities on the basis of their understanding of Biblical truth and their heritage. They carried out the mission for which they were called; namely, to transform barren steppes into a garden spot and granary of Russia and to show the surrounding Slavic and nomadic population an exemplary Christian life in family and community and model methods of tilling the soil. Men like Johann Cornies and the settlements as a whole had a great influence on the surrounding population. But this influence was not restricted to the economic and social life. The Evangelical movement of Russia was influenced strongly by the Mennonites for nearly a century. This contact is continuing even in our day. The Mennonites of Russia had an opportunity for a self-realization and witness which they discharged with great success. (See "Russian Baptists and Mennonites," *Menn. Life*, July 1956, 99). **C.K.**

This is a selected bibliography. For a complete list of books and periodicals, see the bibliographies of the dissertations by A. Ehrt and D. J. Rempel. For additional information see also the various articles dealing with settlement and institutions of Russia.

A. *General:* Clarence A. Manning, *The Story of the Ukraine* (New York, 1947); Eugene M. Kulischer, "Europe on the Move," *War and Population Changes in 1917-47* (New York, 1948); Theodor Mundt, *Kampf um das Schwarze Meer* (Braunschweig, 1855); George Hume, *Thirty-Five Years in Russia* (London, 1914); Lothar

König, *Die Deutschtumsinsel an der Wolga* (Dülmen, 1938); *Der Wanderweg der Russlanddeutschen* (Stuttgart, 1939); Otto Auhagen, *Die Schicksalswende des russland-deutschen Bauerntums in den Jahren 1927-1930* (Leipzig, 1942); Alexander Petzholdt, *Reise im westlichen und südlichen europäischen Russland im Jahre 1855* (Leipzig, 1864); *Ukraine mit Krim*, Part 3: *Dongebiet und Kaukasus;* Part 4: *Die deutschen Siedlungen in der Sowjetunion*, Sammlung Georg Leibbrandt (Berlin, 1941); Karl Lindemann, *Von den deutschen Kolonisten in Russland. Ergebnisse einer Studienreise 1919-21* (Stuttgart, 1924); G. Pisarevskij, *Iz istorrii innostranoj kolonizacii v Rossii v XVIII v. Moskva 1909* (Iz V T., Zapisok Mosk. Archeologiceskogo Instituta); G. Bonwetsch, *Geschichte der deutschen Kolonien an der Wolga* (Stuttgart, 1919); K. Stumpp, *Die deutschen Kolonien im Schwarzmeergebiet, dem früheren Neu- (Süd-) Russland. Ein siedlungs- und wirtschaftsgeographischer Versuch* (Stuttgart, 1922); David J. Dallin and B. L. Nicolaevsky, *Forced Labor in Soviet Russia* (New Haven, 1947); B. Yakovlev, *Concentration Camps in the USSR* (Russian) (Münich, 1955).

B. *Periodicals: Der Botschafter* (Ekaterinoslav, 1905-14); *Friedensstimme* (Halbstadt, 1903-14); *Unser Blatt* (Grossweide, 1925-28); *Der praktische Landwirt* (Moscow, 1925-28); *Der Bote* (Rosthern, Sask., 1924-); *Mennonitische Rundschau* (1877- , Winnipeg, 1924-); *Mennonite Life* (North Newton, 1946-); *Mennonitisches Jahrbuch*, ed. Heinrich Dirks (Gross-Tokmak, 1901-14); *Mennonitisches Jahrbuch*, ed. Cornelius Krahn (Newton, Kan., 1948-); *Christlicher Familien-Kalender*, ed. A. Kröker (Halbstadt, 1897-1919);

C. *Books and Articles Specifically on Mennonites:* A. Ehrt, *Das Mennonitentum in Russland* . . . (Berlin, 1932); D. G. Rempel, "The Mennonite Colonies in New Russia. . ." (unpublished doctoral dissertation, Stanford University, 1933); Martin H. Schrag, "European History of the Swiss-Volhynian Mennonite Ancestors of Mennonites now Living in Communities in Kansas and South Dakota" (unpublished M.A. thesis, Eastern Baptist Theological Seminary, May 1956); Horst Quiring, "Die Auswanderung der Mennoniten aus Preussen 1788-1870," *Menn. Life* VI (April 1951); P. Hildebrandt, *Erste Auswanderung der Mennoniten aus dem Danziger Gebiet nach Südrussland* (Halbstadt, 1888); A. Klaus, *Unsere Kolonien* (Odessa, 1887); Gerhard Fast, "The Mennonites under Stalin and Hitler," *Menn. Life* II (April 1947) 18 ff.; S. D. Bondar, *Sekta Mennonitov v Rossii* (Petrograd, 1916); D. H. Epp, *Die Chortitzer Mennoniten. Versuch einer Darstellung des Entwicklungsganges derselben* (Rosental, 1889); Friesen, *Brüderschaft;* Abr. Kröker, *Pfarrer Eduard Wüst, der grosse Erweckungsprediger in den deutschen Kolonien Südrusslands* (Leipzig, 1903); H. G. Mannhardt, *Die Danziger Mennonitengemeinde. Ihre Entstehung und ihre Geschichte von 1569 bis 1919* (Danzig, 1919); W. Mannhardt, *Die Wehrfreiheit der Altpreussischen Mennoniten* (Marienburg, 1863); *Die Mennoniten-Gemeinden in Russland während der Kriegs- und Revolutionsjahre 1914-1920* (Heilbronn, 1921); J. Quiring, *Die Mundart von Chortitza in Süd-Russland* (Munich, 1928); C. Henry Smith, *The Story of the Mennonites* (Newton, 1957); Franz Isaac, *Die Molotschnaer Mennoniten* (Halbstadt, 1908); A. A. Töws, *Mennonitische Märtyrer* I and II (North Clearbrook, 1949, 1954); H. Görz, *Die Molotschnaer Ansiedlung. Entstehung, Entwicklung und Untergang* (Steinbach, 1950); P. C. Hiebert and Orie O. Miller, *Feeding the Hungry, Russia Famine 1919-1925* (Scottdale, 1929); C. Henry Smith, *The Coming of the Russian Mennonites* (Berne, 1927); Gustav E. Reimer and G. R. Gaeddert, *Exiled by the Czar* (Newton, 1956); Benjamin H. Unruh, *Die niederländisch-niederdeutschen Hintergründe der mennonitischen Ostwanderungen im 16., 18. und 19. Jahrhundert* (Karlsruhe, 1955); Heinrich H. Schröder, *Russlanddeutsche Friesen* (Döllstadt, 1936); Leonhard Froese, *Das pädagogische Kultursystem der mennonitischen Siedlungsgruppe in Russland* (Göttingen, 1949); Waldemar Gutsche, *Westliche Quellen des russischen Stundismus* (Kassel, 1956); George J. Eisenbach, *Pietism and the Russian Germans in the United States* (Berne, 1948); *Jahresbericht des Bevollmächtigten der Mennonitengemeinden in Russland in Sachen der Unterhaltung der Forstkommandos im Jahre 1908;* A. H. Unruh, *Die Geschichte der Mennoniten-Brüdergemeinde* (Winnipeg, 1954); J. H. Lohrenz, *The Mennonite Brethren Church* (Hillsboro, 1950); Gerhard Lohrenz, *Sagra-*dowka (Rosthern, 1947); Cornelius P. Toews, *Die Tereker Ansiedlung* (Rosthern, 1945); J. J. Dyck, *Am Trakt* (North Kildonan, 1948); J. Hildebrand, *Sibirien* (Winnipeg, 1952); *Die Kubaner Ansiedlung* (Steinbach, 1953); H. Goerz, *Memrik* (Rosthern, 1952); David H. Epp, *Johann Cornies* (Berdyansk, 1909 and Rosthern, 1956); idem, *Heinrich Heese* and Nikolai Regehr, *Johann Philipp Wiebe* (Steinbach, 1952); *ML* III, 573-81.

Russian Missions of the Mennonite Brethren Church had their beginning soon after the establishment of the M.B. Church. Early preachers to the Russians were Johann Wieler 1883-89, Jacob F. Froese, Adolf Penner 1906-? and Hermann Fast (*q.v.*) 1892-? Fast was for some time active in St. Petersburg and in Rumania, and after 1901 among the Russians in Canada. The M.B. Church of Russia established a special fund in 1905 which supported eight Russian evangelists. Some of the Brethren were given prison sentences for disregarding the law against proselyting among the Greek Orthodox; among these were Froese and A. H. Unruh. After the revolution of 1917 work was taken up more freely by tent evangelism (Jacob J. Dyck, 1919), in which a number of Mennonite Brethren were engaged. With few exceptions they were later murdered by the Machno (*q.v.*) bandits.

After the establishment of the M.B. Church in America following the immigration of 1870 ff., M.B. preachers repeatedly conducted Gospel meetings in the Russian settlements in North Dakota and Saskatchewan, Hermann Fast and John F. Harms (*q.v.*) serving as evangelists and pastors to the converts. In 1905 the conference published a small Christian periodical, *Golos* (i.e., Voice), with Fast as editor. Congregations were organized at Kief and Dogden, N.D., and at Arlee and Blaine Lake, Sask., which were to some extent affiliated with the M.B. Conference, but which also held their own conferences. Luke Kravchenko has been one of their outstanding ministers. The Board of Foreign Missions of the M.B. Church has for a number of years supported workers among the Russians of Canada. In 1949 the Canadian Conference was supporting Peter Schroeder at Grand Forks, B.C., who worked among the Dukhobors, D. B. Wiens at Arlee, Sask., and A. Huebert, an itinerant preacher. (See **Evangelism**.)

H.H.J.

A. H. Unruh, *Geschichte der Mennoniten-Brüdergemeinde 1860-1954* (Hillsboro, 1954); John H. Lohrenz, *The Mennonite Brethren Church* (Hillsboro, 1950).

Rusterhel (Ruster[holz]), **Jakob,** an Anabaptist martyr, a cabinetmaker by trade, of Horgerberg in the Swiss district of Grüningen, was arrested in Zürich (*q.v.*) and imprisoned in the Oethenbach prison, where he was so unmercifully treated that in a weakened condition he promised to attend the (Reformed) church services. But he repented and was rearrested, and sick as he was he was taken to prison in chains and died there. S.G.

Cornelius Bergmann, *Die Täuferbewegung im Kanton Zürich bis 1660* (Leipzig, 1916) 128 f., 172; Samuel Geiser, *Die Taufgesinnten-Gemeinden* (Karlsruhe, 1931) 386; *Mart. Mir.* D 815, E 1114; *ML* III, 579.

Rutgers, a common Dutch family name, formed as a patronymic from the Christian name Rutger, of which there are many branches in the Netherlands, both **Mennonite** and non-**Mennonite**.

Since the 16th century there have been two Mennonite Rutgers families in Amsterdam, not related to each other. (1) A Rutgers family which belonged to the Flemish Lamist branch. The genealogy of this family is rather well known and has partly been published in *Nederlandsch Adelsboek*. The ancestor of this family as far as is known, was Nicolaes Rutgeers, surnamed Pels (probably because he was a fur dealer). He was a citizen of Antwerp, Belgium, and died there in 1561. His son David Rudtgheerts (b. c1520 at Antwerp, d. 1587 at Cologne, Germany), married Agneta de Bie, of Antwerp, was a silk merchant. He apparently was a Mennonite and left Antwerp on account of persecution. From father to son the name David was passed on; they were all Mennonites. David Rutgers I (Antwerp, 1555-Amsterdam, 1623), married Josyntje Lambers, a Mennonite of Rees, in 1585, was a textile merchant, at first at Cologne, where he was a member of the Mennonite church and apparently a deacon; he signed the Concept of Cologne (*q.v.*) for the Cologne congregation. In 1595 he was expelled from Cologne because of his Mennonite faith. He thereupon moved to Haarlem and later to Amsterdam. David Rutgers II (Haarlem, 1601-Amsterdam, 1668) was a cloth merchant at Amsterdam, also engaged in banking. He married Suzanna de Flines, of Amsterdam. From 1654 he was a deacon of the Amsterdam Lamist congregation; during the disputes between the ministers Galenus Abrahamsz (*q.v.*) and Samuel Apostool (*q.v.*) (see **Lammerenkrijgh**) he sided with Galenus and published a pamphlet in which he urged reconciliation: *Vredes-presentatie* (Amsterdam, 1664). David Rutgers III (Amsterdam, 1629-1706), married Margaretha Blok, of Amsterdam, ran a mill weaving velvet and flowered silk materials. He was a rather wealthy man; in 1697 he was knighted by Emperor Leopold I and received for himself, his oldest son, and further descendants the title *jonkheer*, the family name becoming Rutgers van Rozenburg (after his country estate Rozenburg near Amsterdam). David Rutgers III was a deacon of the Lamist congregation of Amsterdam in 1684-89, 1694-99, and 1704-6. He lived in a stately home on the Singel at Amsterdam and later in the splendid country home called Groenenvecht, near Breukelen. David Rutgers IV van Rozenburg (Amsterdam, 1658-1731) was a wealthy merchant and banker, living at the Heerengracht at Amsterdam. He was married to Cornelia van Hoeck and served as deacon in 1689-94, 1700-5, and 1712-17. David Rutgers V van Rozenburg (Amsterdam, 1682-1757), married Maria de Neufville, was a silk merchant at Amsterdam and also a loyal member of the church, as were also Leonard Rutgers I van Rozenburg (Amsterdam, 1723-91, a son of David Rutgers V) and Leonard Rutgers II van Rozenburg (Amsterdam, 1760-1831, a son of Leonard Rutgers I), both merchants and bankers. Other members of the family serving as deacons of the Lamist congregation were Abraham Rutgers 1678-83 and Adriaan Rutgers 1707-12 and 1717-? and Dirk Rutgers (1667-1781) 1708-?

A number of members of this Rutgers family rendered valuable service to the oppressed Mennonites in the Palatinate (*q.v.*) and Prussia. David Rutgers II was for some time treasurer of the Mennonite Committee of Foreign Needs and in 1687 and 1694

collected funds for the Swiss Mennonites who had emigrated to the Palatinate (*Inv. Arch. Amst.* I, Nos. 1145, 1197, 1200, 1203, 1204-6, 1252 f., 1425, 1428, 2245). Isaac Rutgers, a son of David Rutgers II, who lived at Danzig, West Prussia, as an agent of the banking firm of his father and later of his brother, in 1680 represented the Dutch Committee of Foreign Needs on behalf of the Prussian Mennonites. He received a considerable sum of money from Holland, which he distributed among the Mennonites at Montau (*q.v.*) and other congregations, who had suffered severely from floods and crop failure (*Inv. Arch. Amst.* I, Nos. 1566-68). His grandson Isaac Rutgers, also living at Danzig for business in 1767, served as an intermediary of the Amsterdam committee in supporting the Mennonites of the Klein-Werder (*q.v.*), especially at Thiensdorf (*q.v.*), who had been struck by several calamities and in the spring of 1767 by a terrible flood. In 1776 he sent support to the people of Kleinsee (Jeziorka, *q.v.*), who, on account of war and pillage, were unable to pay their rent. In 1779 he was still active in relieving the needs of the Kleinsee congregation (*Inv. Arch. Amst.* I, Nos. 1707-19, 1728 f.). Nothing is known concerning his private life. Until about 1790 all of this family was Mennonite; but after 1800 nearly all of them joined the Reformed Church.

(2) A Rutgers family which belonged to the Waterlander (Toren) congregation at Amsterdam until 1668 and after the merger of this congregation with the Lamists in 1668, to the United Lam and Toren congregation at Amsterdam. Concerning this family only scant information is available. The ancestor of this branch was Rutger Willemsz (d. 1630 at Amsterdam), who was a cabinetmaker; he had moved from Kampen to Amsterdam, where he was received into the Waterlander congregation without baptism about 1612 and served as a deacon from 1620. In 1623 he sided with Nittert Obbesz (*q.v.*) in the conflict between Obbesz and the preachers. Among his descendants who bear the family name of Rutgers there were a number of craftsmen who were loyal members of the church until the family died out in the last decades of the 18th century.

Concerning Swaen Rutgers at Emden, see **Rutgers, Swaen.**

vDZ.

Nederlandsch Adelsboek 1916, 421-30; *ibid.*, 1950, 388-90; *Inv. Arch. Amst.*, besides the items mentioned above also II, Nos. 1257, 3175; *Amstelodamum*, Yearbook (Amsterdam, 1928) 85, 100; Kühler, *Geschiedenis* II, 165, 168, 174.

Rutgers, Swaen: see Swaen Rutgers.

Ruth (Rutt), a Swiss family represented in the Lancaster and Franconia conferences (MC) of eastern Pennsylvania. In Lancaster the name is spelled Rutt, and in Franconia, Ruth. Henry Ruth settled in Montgomery County, Pa., c1720. Some outstanding persons of this family in the history of the Franconia Conference Mennonites were David Ruth (d. 1820), bishop of the Plains and Lexington congregations; Benjamin Ruth (1849-1904), deacon of the Towamencin congregation; Joseph G. Ruth (1857-1928), bishop of the Line Lexington congregation; and the latter's nephew, Arthur D. Ruth (1892-   ), senior bishop of the Franconia congregation in the mid 20th century. In the Lancaster Conference Martin

Rutt (1840-1905) served as bishop in the Risser district; he was a strong figure in the conference. Abraham Rutt (1838-98) was a deacon in the Strickler congregation, and Edwin Rutt, his son, succeeded him as deacon. Albert B. Rutt, a Lancaster Mennonite, served for a time as a missionary in Chicago early in the 20th century, but later went into business. J. L. Rutt served for a number of years as a missionary (MC) in Argentina. In the Wisler division of 1872 in Indiana and Ohio the Rutts of Ashland County, Ohio, followed Jacob Wisler. The references to Swiss Mennonite church leaders of 1645 bearing the name Ruth as an apparent Christian name are not entirely clear. (*Mart. Mir.* D 823, E 1122.) J.C.W.

According to the "Haus und Hand-buch für die Familie David Ruth zu Eichstock, 1852" (in BeCL), Gerhard Ruth and his family migrated from the Rhein area to Upper Bavaria in 1819, where he purchased the Eichstock estate near Dachau. About 1852 his son David Ruth (*q.v.*), emigrated from Eichstock to Franklin Center, Iowa, and there he served as a preacher. From here family members moved to Halstead, Kan., and have also spread to other states. The children of David Ruth were John W., Susanna A., who married Christian Krehbiel, David C., Henry G., Jacob E., and Gerhard B. Ruth. The "Haus und Hand-buch" contains historical and genealogical data about the family in Bavaria, Iowa, and Kansas. The original German narrative has been translated into English. C.K.

Ruth Ketelbueter: see Ketelbueter.

Rutt, Martin N. (1841-1905), a bishop and leader in the Lancaster Mennonite (MC) Conference, was born Feb. 8, 1841, on a large Donegal farm in Lancaster County, Pa., the son of Jacob S. Rutt and Elizabeth Nissley. He married Fannie Ebersole (1841-1904). At the age of thirty he was called to the ministry at the Bossler Mennonite Church and on March 11, 1880, he was ordained bishop for the Strickler-Stauffer-Bossler Bishop District. He had a share in writing the first discipline in the 1890's, when Jacob N. Brubacher, Isaac Eby, and he were the leaders of the Bishop Board. He was an early promoter of Sunday schools, serving as superintendent at the home congregation from 1883 until his death. In the Martinite division his counsel was well considered. He traveled far over the conference district in the horse-and-buggy days, whenever duty called. His greatest achievement came in the fall conference season at the Mellinger church in 1905, when he pleaded at midnight for permission to have revival meetings, after the Conference had twice rejected his request, and he won. He did not live to see the wisdom of this move, for he died on Nov. 7, 1905, before the Elizabethtown meetings were held in February 1906. He was buried in the Bossler cemetery. I.D.L.

Rutschmann, Rudolf, a member of an old peasant family at Zollikon (*q.v.*), near Zürich, Switzerland, was one of the earliest Anabaptists. He was baptized during the first week of the existence of the brotherhood, between January 22 and January 29, 1525. Soon after this event fourteen of the leaders of the Anabaptist movement were placed under arrest in

the Augustinian monastery for investigation; Rudolf Rutschmann was the first of these to be questioned. He openly confessed that he had been (re)baptized. Since he was now a "servant and subject of God" he would continue to do "what the Spirit of God instructed, taught, and commanded" him to do. He would therefore not allow himself to be deflected by any secular authority. In other respects he would be obedient to "the gracious lords of Zürich" in so far as "it was not contrary to the Word of God." All of the accused agreed with this confession. The sentence of the council, Feb. 8, 1525, released them upon promise to desist and a total fine of 1,000 guilders, with the admonition that they had acted "unreasonably against God and against man with offense." Rutschmann, however, refused to pay the fine.

In a cross-examination at the end of June 1525 it was related that Rudolf Rutschmann had read aloud one or two chapters of the Bible at a Bible study meeting in a peasant house at Nenikon. On the way home he was asked by several women to come into their homes and read to them. After initial hesitation he did so, reading a chapter on the love of God. He had kept his promise of February and had baptized no one, and had only read from the Bible in private homes, as the councillors had permitted him to do. He was released, but compelled to swear an oath that he would leave off baptizing and preaching. He was summoned to the court again and tried in August 1525, where he confessed that he had attended a Bible reading, but that nothing had been said there about baptism. At this point all trace of him is lost. S.G.

Fritz Blanke, *Brüder in Christo. Die Geschichte der ältesten Täufergemeinde (Zollikon 1525)* (Zürich, 1955); *TA Zürich; ML* III, 579 f.

Ruysch Jansz (Ruysch Jan Beths) was a burgomaster of Amsterdam, who was in sympathy with the Anabaptists in 1531-35, like some other magistrates of Amsterdam, such as Jan Hubrechts, Pieter Colijn, and Heyman Jacobsz. He protected them against persecution and was accused of permitting a large number of them to set sail from Amsterdam en route to Münster (*q.v.*). Ruysch was, however, not an Anabaptist. vDZ.

Inv. Arch. Amst. I, No. 20; Kühler, *Geschiedenis* I, 68; Mellink, *Wederdopers,* 33, 103, 105 f., 141, 176.

Ruysdael; see Ruisdael.

Ruytenburg, Jacob Jansz: see Peter of Spain.

Ruyter, Jan (Hans) de, an Anabaptist martyr: see **Hans Ruyter.**

Rypert Claesz, an Anabaptist martyr of Driesum in Friesland, Netherlands, was beheaded with two others at Leeuwarden, capital of Friesland, on March 17, 1537. He confessed "that he belonged to the sect of the Anabaptists, but had not yet been (re)baptized"; this, however, was not due to lack of desire on his part, but to want of an elder to administer the rite. He wished to receive baptism on his faith as soon as possible. vDZ.

Inv. Arch. Amst. I, No. 746; J. Reitsma, *Honderd jaren uit de Geschiedenis van de Hervorming . . . in Friesland* (Leeuwarden, 1876) 23; *DB* 1917, 90.

S

Saar Amish Mennonite Church, sometimes known as the Moselle congregation, now extinct, whose members lived in the Rhine Province of Germany and in Luxembourg. The congregation was founded by Mennonites emigrating from Lorraine about the beginning of the 19th century. The first elder was a Planck of Helleringen. The services, at which the *Ausbund* (*q.v.*) was used into the 20th century, were conducted every four weeks in German in a deaconess home. For the instruction of their youth the 1880 catechism (see **Catechisms**) printed in Zweibrücken was used. Footwashing was observed in connection with communion services, and church discipline applied. The congregation of one hundred members, mostly farmers and millers, lived scattered in seventeen villages. The congregation had a fund for the support of the poor. Nikolaus Nafziger was long an elder of the congregation. In 1936 when it had 32 members and Otto Schertz as preacher, the congregation merged with Ixheim (*q.v.*) which in 1937 in turn merged with the Ernstweiler (*q.v.*) congregation to form the Zweibrücken (*q.v.*) congregation, which since 1952 has been in effect combined with the Kaiserslautern (*q.v.*) congregation. The Saar congregation was listed under various names in the *Christlicher Gemeinde-Kalender* in the past 50 years. Often the word Luxembourg was combined with it, and the present Luxembourg (*q.v.*) congregation was once a part of Saar. Saargebiet was the most common name and the one used at the last, although as late as 1927 it was called "Luxembourg und Saargebiet." During the French occupation of the Saar territory (1945-57) the Mennonites living in the territory were organized as a separate Saarland congregation (1949), which in 1957 had 62 baptized members. H.S.B.

Saarburg: see **Sarrebourg.**

Saargemünd: see **Sarreguemines.**

Saarland Mennonite Church: see **Saar.**

Sabatisch: see **Sobotiste.**

Sabbatarian Anabaptists. The question of the relevance of the Old Testament (*q.v.*) was solved in one aspect by a small group of Anabaptists by saying that the Ten Commandments were still valid; hence they observed the Sabbath. The most prominent leader of this group was Oswald Glait (*q.v.*), who along with Andreas Fischer and Hans Bünderlin (*q.v.*) was active in Silesia about 1528. When Glait published his *Entschuldigung* at Nikolsburg in 1527 he was not yet a Sabbatarian (as point 7 of the booklet shows) and there is no clue to indicate why he became one. He left Nikolsburg after Hubmaier's martyrdom in May 1528, and while in Silesia working with Andreas Fischer met both Valentine Crautwald and Caspar Schwenckfeld. Shortly after this encounter, Glait wrote a booklet in which he defended Sabbatarian views, to which booklet Crautwald replied. Neither of these books is extant. Glait then asked Andreas Fischer to reply to Crautwald.

Fischer was of the Anabaptist congregation at Linz, but had been a missionary and overseer at Passau, Obernberg, and Wels. At Nikolsburg he adopted the Sabbatarian beliefs of Glait. Fischer's reply to Crautwald is not extant, but Crautwald's second treatise is preserved and bears the title: *Bericht und anzeigen wie gar one Kunst und guotten verstandt, Andreas Fischer. vom Sabbath geschrieben . . .* (manuscript copy of printed book is in Schwenckfelder Library at Pennsburg, Pa.).

The Sabbatarian movement upset Leonhard von Liechtenstein; so he wrote a letter to Capito (*q.v.*) enclosing a copy of Glait's book on the Sabbath and requesting a critique of it. Capito, burdened with work, turned the task over to Schwenckfeld, who wrote a reply (*Vom Christlichen Sabbath und Unterschied des A.T. und N.T.,* 1532), which has been preserved and published in the *Corpus Schwenckfeldianorum* (IV, 444-518).

That the Sabbatarian movement did not die out at once is evident from Luther's concern with it in his *Brief wider die Sabbather* (Erlangen Ausgabe XXI, 416). That it continued for some time is evident from the mention of the Sabbatarians in George Eder's (*q.v.*) *Evangelische Inquisition* (1573), in Christoph Erhard's (*q.v.*) history of the Münsterite Anabaptists (1588), as well as in Stredovsky's (about 1600) and Varotto's (1567) list of Anabaptist sects. In a letter to the Swiss Brethren (wrongly dated 1531?) Pilgram Marpeck (*q.v.*) discusses the Ten Commandments and goes into some detail in his discussion of the third commandment. He rejects any legalistic application of this commandment, and concludes by saying, "That is in short against those who wish to reinstitute the physical Sabbath. Jesus Christ is Lord over all ceremonial laws of the Old and New Testament" (*Kunstbuch,* fol. 46b, 38b). W.Kl.

Henry A. DeWind, "A Sixteenth Century Description of Religious Sects in Austerlitz, Moravia," *MQR* XXIX (1955) 44-53; Letter of Schwenckfeld to Leonhard von Liechtenstein, Jan. 1, 1532, *Corpus Schwenckfeld.* IV (Leipzig, 1914) 444-518; Wilhelm Wiswedel, "Oswald Glait von Jamnitz," *Zeitschrift für Kirchengeschichte* LVI (1937) 550-64.

Sach, Franciscus von der: see **Sega, Francesco della.**

Sachs (Sax, Sass), **Konrad,** a cooper in Stuttgart, Germany, was the delegate of the city of Stuttgart to the Württemberg assembly of the peasants on the Wunnenstein and at Bietigheim in the Peasants' War of 1525. After the Peasants' War he became an Anabaptist and was presumably a leader of the South German Anabaptists by 1530, when he baptized Barbara Löffler, the wife of a shoemaker in Stuttgart. He found shelter with Konrad Thumb of Neuburg, Württemberg, in his village of Stettin in the Remstal, where Schwenckfelders and Jews were also admitted and where the Schwenckfelder Burkhard Schilling was the pastor. He worked at his trade in Stuttgart and is called the leader (*Vorsteher*) of the Swiss Brethren in 1539 and 1545, and won a large following in the vicinity of Stuttgart and Esslingen. Nothing is known of the close of his life. G. Bos.

TA Württemberg, 1048; *Württembergisches Jahrbuch für Statistik und Landeskunde 1923-24,* 100.

Sackmann(in), Anna (Aendle), of Rueten, an Anabaptist martyr, was put to death at Tauffers (*q.v.*) in the Adige (*q.v.*) Valley, Austria. (Beck, *Geschichts-Bücher,* 278; *ML IV.*)

Sacrament. The word "sacrament" came into usage in the church's vocabulary because the church of the West translated the word "mystery" used by the Greek Mystery Religions for their initiatory rites with the word *sacramentum* and applied it to baptism and the Lord's Supper. As is the case with many other terms in Western Christendom, the man mainly responsible for its adoption into Christianity is Tertullian (*q.v.*). The term had a legal and military connotation and involved the idea of commitment or responsibility, often being used for an oath.

The term embedded itself in the Christian Church so securely that even during the Reformation period it was never questioned, although there was considerable discussion as to the significance of the practices it referred to. While Luther declared that the church is present wherever the Gospel is truly preached and the sacraments correctly administered, and Calvin as where the Gospel is truly heard and the sacraments correctly administered, Anabaptists took over this same term (Rothmann, Marpeck, and Menno Simons) but defined it to fit their own view of the sacraments.

The Confession of Schleitheim (*q.v.*) discusses both baptism and the Lord's Supper but does not accord them the constitutive role which they had in the larger Reformation. Conrad Grebel (*q.v.*) called them simply "ceremonies," and for the most part Anabaptism was heavily indebted to the symbolic interpretation of Zwingli as far as the Lord's Supper is concerned. Baptism was for them a deeply moving experience, the first baptism having been preceded by a genuine time of penitence and real searching (see Blanke, below). Full appreciation has never been given to the vital place which both sacraments played in early Anabaptism; certainly no slavish literalism prompted such a radical break with **tradition.**

The term "ceremonies" is used also by Hans Denk, along with a certain depreciation of their place in the religious experience of both the individual and the church, which is continued and hardened in men like Jacob Kautz (*q.v.*) and Hans Bünderlin (*q.v.*), both of whom insisted (the essence of religion being spiritual) that there was no need for the external ceremonies in the life of the mature church. Bünderlin insisted that the ceremonies in the apostolic church were a concession to its Jewish members and that these rites were no longer needed. His book *Erklärung durch vergleichung* (1530) is meant to show the folly of continuing to use the ceremonies. The same stress is seen also in his other books.

Since the Anabaptist brotherhood at Strasbourg read Bünderlin's books in their meetings, and Pilgram Marpeck attempted to organize the brotherhood there in 1530, it was necessary to take a position on the place of the sacraments. The result was the publication of the *Clare verantwurtung* (*q.v.*) of 1531, which dealt with all of Bünderlin's major arguments not only in his books but also in conversations. It may be that this is the booklet Schwenckfeld says was written against him (in a letter to Johann Bader, *q.v.,* dated Sept. 24, 1531) since it certainly does deal with some of the arguments Schwenckfeld advanced against the Anabaptists. At any rate the *Clare verantwurtung* represents the clearest argument in Anabaptism for the practice of the ceremonies such as baptism and the Lord's Supper, as well as footwashing, etc.

Marpeck uses the word "ceremonies" rather than "sacraments" in his confession and also in some of his later writings (*Kunstbuch,* fol. 44b and 46b). However, in his most important works, both the *Vermanung* (*q.v.*) and the *Verantwortung* (*q.v.*), he uses the term "sacrament" and accepts Rothmann's long section which explains the term and justifies its use by Christians as long as it is correctly interpreted. Here the explanation is the same as that offered by Oswald Glait (*q.v.*) in 1527, i.e., that *sacramentum* means a vow or an oath, and so the element of commitment (*verpflichtung*) must be taken seriously. This is indicative of the ingenuity with which a term was taken, and redefined, the traditional wrappings having been removed to open the way for what the Anabaptists considered a Biblical interpretation of these practices in the life of the church.

One of the alternatives open to the Anabaptists was to accept the sacraments as "mere symbols," as was done by Bucer and Zwingli. The spiritualistic tendency which both Zwingli's and Bucer's attacks against Anabaptism took made them wary of taking this approach. If the sacraments are "mere symbols," Bucer's argument that a mere symbol should not divide the Christian brotherhood has some force. Over against this Marpeck insisted in his Confession (1532) that the sacraments, specifically baptism, should not be called a sign or symbol but rather a "witness." In all of his writings he stressed this aspect of the sacraments again and again, and the term "cotestimony" (*Mitzeugnis*) became central in his thought. At one point in his revised translation of the *Bekentnisse* (see **Vermanung**) he translates "teken" (sign) as "Mitzeugnis." This is evidence of the fundamental importance which Marpeck attributed to the sacraments of the church. Inner experience demands an external witness; if none is forthcoming, the inner experience is belied. For this reason he was so sharp in his criticism of Schwenckfeld, whose approach to the sacraments could lead only to their complete cessation. Marpeck insisted that until Christ returns we have need of these external rites which serve us in that they witness to the world and to the church that we accept the order of Christ. Along with this is a sense of realism in the performance of the sacraments, baptism becoming a part of Christ's body, the Lord's Supper a testimony to the unity of Christ's body which we share. Needless to say he rejects all sacramentarian views in that he does not see the metaphysical presence of Christ in the bread, but rather sees Christ present in the gathered church and in His preached word. Hence the "real presence" is taken seriously by Marpeck; but not in a mechanical way, but rather in the experience of the participating believer. Where the element of cotestimony is lacking, there sacraments are merely external acts without any meaning whatever. While Marpeck says that perhaps it would be better not to use the term "sacrament" since it does not occur in Scripture, he says further that the same is true of the term "sign"; hence the usage of the term is not the decisive matter. His close co-worker who probably collaborated in all of his writings, Leopold Scharnschlager (q.v.), stressed the idea that baptism is a covenant, and in this he was following the main stream of Anabaptism.

In Dutch Mennonitism the position does not differ greatly from the Swiss-South German views. Menno Simons uses the word sacrament in his writings, sometimes also the term "sacramentelycke teeckenen" (Sacramental symbols) and repeatedly warns against Roman Catholic views on baptism and communion (Mass), which he considered idolatrous. Occasionally he uses the word "ordinantie" (ordinance). See Index to Opera Omnia (1681) and to Complete Writings (1956). Dirk Philips is somewhat more precise in his terminology and usually avoids the word sacrament, instead by preference speaking of "de Goddelijcke Ordeninghe(n) van der Doope ende des Nachtmaels" (the divine ordinance(s) of baptism and communion). The Dutch confessions of faith scarcely deal with this theme, obviously because it was not necessary to discuss the question, in which all Mennonites of the several branches agreed. The Olijftack Confession (1626) speaks of "uytwendighe sienlijcke teeckenen" (external visible signs), which are ordinances of Jesus Christ. The Jan Cents Confession (1630), Article XI, has "baptism, the Lord's Supper, and other Christian ordinances." The Dordrecht Confession (1632) calls them "uytwendighe ceremonies" (outward ceremonies). The Flemish preacher Claes Claesz (q.v.) uses the term "ceremoniale geboden" (ceremonial commands).

The sacraments, particularly the Mass, were a frequent topic in the discussions of the Roman Catholic clergy with the Anabaptist-Mennonite martyrs during their trials. The martyrs all reject the Roman Catholic doctrines, often in bold and rude expressions: "I have never read in the Scriptures of a Holy Sacrament, but of the Lord's Supper" (Elisabeth); the sacrament is "a God of bread" (Jeronimus Segersz); "the sacrament is an idol, only a bit of flour" (Jooskindt), and Jacques d' Auchy, upon being asked his opinion of the sacrament (Mass), frankly replied, "Do you mean the breakers of the bread?" Except Joriaen Simansz no martyr found in the Offer des Heeren uses the word sacrament. For the martyrs baptism and communion are "ordinances of Christ," signs, ceremonies; the Lord's Supper is "a memorial sign," a symbol.

The early Waterlander Mennonites with their spiritualistic tendencies avoided the word sacrament; baptism and communion are "mere symbols." Hans de Ries in his confession (1610) calls them ordinances (insettingen), together with footwashing

as "the service of love." Galenus Abrahamsz (Korte Grondstellingen, 1699, No. LI) speaks of "ceremonial or solemn commands." In later Dutch Mennonitism there is practically no discussion about the character of the "sacraments."

There never has been any question of overestimating them. Occasionally baptism and the Lord's Supper were undervalued. This was a result of mystical or spiritualistic individualism, already found in Obbe Philips, in this point a follower of Sebastian Franck, who was opposed by Dirk Philips, and like Menno Simons attacked all those who depreciated the ceremony of baptism, saying, "What is the use to us of a handful of water?" This dislike of the "sacraments" in 19th-century Dutch Mennonitism sometimes led to making baptism optional or even to abolishing baptism and the Lord's Supper altogether. This radicalism is now past. In varying degrees later Mennonitism has attempted to prevent a degeneration into any idea that sacraments are inherently efficacious. The use of the term "sacrament" is however more or less incidental to this attempt as is seen by its use interchangeably with "ordinance" in a recent Mennonite book on theology (see Wenger).

As in the other aspects of worship, a major problem in the use of the sacraments (ordinances) has been to maintain a balance between undervaluation and overvaluation. Mennonites have been more inclined to the latter. Too little attention has been given to a good theology of the sacraments which will prevent a lapse into mere traditionalism.

W.KL., vDZ.

Harold Bender and E. H. Correll, "Conrad Grebel's Petition of Protest and Defense to the Zürich Council in 1523," Goshen College Record Review Supplement XXVII (January 1926) 23, 25; Complete Writings, 143 note 740, passim; John C. Wenger, Introduction to Theology (Scottdale, 1954) 231-42; Fritz Blanke, Brüder in Christo (Zürich, 1956); Walter Fellmann, Hans Denck, Schriften (Gütersloh, 1956) 54, 104, 108, 109; A. Nicoladoni, Johannes Bünderlin (Berlin, 1893); Johannes Bünderlin, Erklärung durch vergleichung der biblischen geschrifft, das der Wassertauff sampt anderen eüsserlichen gebräuchen. . . . On Gottes befelch und zeugniss der Geschrifft von etlichen dieser zeit wider eefert wird (n.p., 1530); Torsten Bergsten, "Pilgram Marbeck und seine Auseinandersetzung mit Caspar Schwenckfeld," Kyrkohistorisk Arsskrift 1957-58; Corpus Schwenckfeldianorum IV, 259 passim; John C. Wenger, "Pilgram Marpeck's Confession of Faith . . ." MQR XII (1938) 187; Gedenkschrift zum 400jährigen Jubiläum . . . (Ludwigshafen, 1925) 185-282, especially 190 f. and 254 (Vermanung); Verantwortung, 90-95 (in Quellen und Forschungen) published by Johann Loserth (Vienna and Leipzig, 1929); Wilhelm Wiswedel, "Oswald Glait von Jamnitz," Zeitschrift für Kirchengeschichte LVI (1937) 561; Jan J. Kiwiet, Pilgram Marbeck (Kassel, 1957) 134-41; Karl Barth, The Teaching of the Church Regarding Baptism (London, 1948); F. W. Dillistone, Christianity and Symbolism (Philadelphia, 1955); Donald Baillie, The Theology of the Sacraments . . . (New York, 1957); Markus Barth, Die Taufe ein Sakrament? (Zollikon-Zürich, 1951); The Believers' Church (Newton, 1955); Offer II, 121, 129, 191, 233, 252, 278, 285, 327, 423.

Sacramentists (Dutch, Sacramentisten, Sacramentariërs), the designation in the Netherlands of those who from about 1520 did not believe in the efficacy of the sacraments of the Roman Catholic Church and particularly denied that the host in the Mass was the real body and blood of Jesus Christ. Besides their doubt or unbelief concerning the doctrine of transubstantiation, they criticized certain Catholic practices, calling indulgences, pilgrimages, etc., mere idolatry, and at the same time were severely critical of the low moral standards and conduct of the clergy.

One of the first to censure Catholic abuses was a certain Wouter, a Dominican monk at Utrecht, who is said to have "preached the evangelical truth" as early as 1516. Jelle Smit (Gellius Faber, *q.v.*), in later times an opponent of Menno Simons, then a Catholic priest at Jelsum in Friesland, is said to have preached evangelical doctrine from 1516; but this is incorrect, for Smit was not yet a priest in 1516 (as Vos has pointed out). Nicolaes Peters, a Franciscan monk, published in 1520 an anti-Catholic booklet, "Hier beghinnen de Sermonen . . . ." Cornelius Grapheus, city clerk of Antwerp, influenced by Erasmus, was arrested in 1522 and tried at Brussels, because he had attacked the Catholic Church. Like many of these first Sacramentists he recanted his heresies. Grapheus even died at an advanced age after a successful life as a loyal son of the Catholic Church. Others were less inclined to bend. Cornelis Hoen (*q.v.*) of The Hague was the first in the Netherlands to formulate an evangelical doctrine of the Lord's Supper (*c*1521). He presented his formulation first to Luther, who rejected it, thereupon to Zwingli, who agreed with it; in this way Hoen's interpretation, that bread and wine in the Communion were merely a commemoration of the suffering and death of Christ, became the doctrine of the Zwinglians and also of the first Anabaptist church in Zürich, Switzerland. Hoen died in prison at The Hague in 1523. Other influential Sacramentists were Hinne Rode (*q.v.*), Johannes Sartorius (*q.v.*), and Willem Gnapheus (*q.v.*).

These Sacramentists, or Evangelicals (*Evangelischen*) as they have sometimes been called, were influenced by Erasmus and other Biblical humanists such as Wessel Gansfort (*q.v.*). Luther's attitude against the Catholic Church, and his writings circulating in the Netherlands and eagerly read by the Sacramentists, also greatly stimulated them. Most of them, severely critical of the Catholic Church, remained members of the church. Only at Delft and perhaps a few other places was something like a separate evangelical church formed. Emperor Charles V, always a keen enemy of heresy, soon took measures to extirpate Sacramentism. In 1522 Frans van der Hulst was appointed imperial inquisitor-general of the Netherlands, but because of the opposition of the city magistrates, who maintained the rights of the cities to adjudicate the cases in their own territories, van der Hulst was not as successful as the emperor wished, especially because many magistrates in the Netherlands sympathized more or less with the Sacramentists. Nevertheless some of them were put to death; in September 1525 Jan Jansz de Bakker, usually called Pistorius, formerly a priest at Woerden, was burned at the stake at The Hague for his evangelical principles and doctrines. Others escaped the inquisitors by fleeing from the country. A large number of Dutch "evangelicals" are said to have settled in Prussia, Germany, before 1530.

The Sacramentist movement, especially during its rise about 1520-25, found its adherents among the well-educated classes, and priests and schoolteachers often promoted its ideas. But soon its views also found an echo among the masses of the Dutch people, particularly in the larger towns. For example, a considerable group of Sacramentists, all craftsmen, were found in Maastricht in the province of Limburg.

The Anabaptist movement rising in the Netherlands in the autumn of 1530 largely attracted the Sacramentists, and most of them joined the newly founded Anabaptist congregations. This was also the case in Maastricht (*q.v.*), where nearly all the Sacramentists became active Anabaptist leaders. The line between Anabaptism and Sacramentism was not always clear, and until 1534-35 Anabaptists were often called Sacramentists and also the contrary. The Sacramentist martyr Wendelmoet (Weynken) Claes(dochter) (*q.v.*), of Monnikendam, executed at The Hague on Nov. 20, 1527, was listed among the Anabaptist martyrs and commemorated in the *Offer des Heeren* and the following Mennonite martyr books, including van Braght's *Martyrs' Mirror*. This is not surprising. Sacramentists and Anabaptists had much in common; they both rejected Roman Catholic doctrines and practices, though the Anabaptists were more radical than the Sacramentists, and in their plea for Biblical-Evangelical Christendom they spoke the same language. Yet the Sacramentists did not practice baptism upon confession of faith and, with few exceptions, did not found special congregations.

Whereas most Sacramentists from the beginning joined the Anabaptists, others, averse to the radical principles of Anabaptism, later formed a group of Reformed, among whom should be mentioned Anastasius Veluanus (*q.v.*). vDZ.

J. G. de Hoop Scheffer, *Geschiedenis der Kerkhervorming in Nederland van haar ontstaan tot 1531* (Amsterdam, 1873) *passim*; L. Knappert, *Het Ontstaan en de Vestiging van het Protestantisme in de Nederlanden* (Utrecht, 1924) 79 f., 111-61; W. Bax, *Het Protestantisme in het bisdom Luik en vooral te Maastricht* I (The Hague, 1937) 179-93; Kühler, *Geschiedenis* I, *passim*; Mellink, *Wederdopers*, 331-45; *Inv. Arch. Amst.* I, Nos. 1, 113, 117; K. Vos, *Menno Simons* (Leiden, 1914) 19.

Sadovaya, a Mennonite settlement of one village, Anna, in the district of Bobrov, province of Voronezh, Russia, established in 1909 on 16,062 acres by some 40 families with 200 persons. (Friesen, *Brüderschaft*, 678; see Ssadovoye.) C.K.

Säemann, (Der), was a 4-page 6x9 monthly Mennonite publication started in April 1897 under the name Säemann, by the Salem Publishing Concern, Hillsboro, Kan., as a "Biblical, unsectarian leaflet." Jacob F. Wiebe (KMB Church) was the publisher. By 1913 the place of publication was Lehigh, Kan., and the size of the paper had been enlarged to 9x12 inches. Some of the printing was done in the Christliches Verlagshaus, Erfurt, Germany. What is more confusing, there are also some issues entitled *Der kleine Säemann,* of which Jacob J. Wiebe, Jr., was the editor and publisher, who was also connected with the publishing of *Der Säemann.* He died in Hillsboro in 1958. BeCL has the second volume, January to December 1899, of *Der kleine Säemann* and an incomplete set of *Der Säemann* spread over 16 volumes, 1897-1912. J. J. Wiebe was the publisher in 1912. C.K.

Saerken van Duerhoven, an Anabaptist martyr, burned at the stake with Barbelken Goethals outside the city gate at Gent in Flanders, Belgium, on Nov. 22, 1570. Particulars are lacking. (*Mart. Mir.* D 534, E 870; Verheyden, *Gent,* 57, No. 197; *ML* I, 484.) vDZ.

Saga, Francesca della: see **Sega.**

Sager, Bernhard, of Bremgarten, was an early Swiss Anabaptist leader who was present at the first Bernese disputation on May 21, 1527. About the same time he was active in the surroundings of Basel. vDZ.

D. L. Gratz, *Bernese Anabaptists* (Scottdale, 1954) 15; S. Geiser, *Die Taufgesinnten-Gemeinden* (Karlsruhe, 1931) 160.

Sagradowka: see **Zagradovka.**

Sahorez (Sahores), a Mennonite village in Volhynia: see **Zahoriz.**

Sailer, Appolonia: see **Seiler, Appolonia.**

Sailer, Leonhard: see **Lanzenstiel, Leonhard.**

Sailer, Wolf(gang), a cabinetmaker by trade, had interesting connections with Pilgram Marpeck (*q.v.*) and Caspar Schwenckfeld (*q.v.*). Apparently he was the latter's comrade (*Stallbruder*) in 1529-32 in Strasbourg (*q.v.*), and Schwenckfeld became reluctant to accept Anabaptism partly because of Sailer's affinity with it. Sailer was more eager to seek out the Anabaptists in those years than to converse with Schwenckfeld.

Sailer left Strasbourg probably about the same time as Marpeck, January 1532, and most likely went to Moravia (*q.v.*). From here he wrote a letter to Schwenckfeld on June 4, 1540, reporting that Marpeck had visited him at Austerlitz and that when Marpeck last saw Schwenckfeld the latter had indicated surprise that Sailer had apparently forgotten him. In this letter Sailer referred to Marpeck as his "special friend and brother in the Lord," but did not call Schwenckfeld a brother, an omission which irritated Schwenckfeld, but is evidence that Sailer was now an Anabaptist brother. Apparently he also was somewhat critical of Schwenckfeld's work, for the reply he received was quite defensive of his methods.

Schwenckfeld's reply was written on Aug. 10, 1540, and shows that Schwenckfeld was not happy with the picture as Marpeck had described it to Sailer. He was disturbed that the relations between him and Sailer had deteriorated, and said that Sailer was incorrect in assuming that he (Schwenckfeld) wrote only for the preachers and those outside of the church, for he did not presume to be wise or highly educated as Sailer charged. Apparently Sailer interpreted Schwenckfeld's condemnation at Schmalcald in a way displeasing to Schwenckfeld, for Schwenckfeld remarked that he could also interpret Sailer's "cross" in that way, but that he would not do so. Sailer was chosen to the ministry at Auspitz, Moravia, in 1547. He may then have been a Hutterite.

Nothing further is known of Sailer. His name does not occur in the Marpeck correspondence, and it seems that he belonged to the Pilgramites in Moravia and later to the Hutterites, but the relationship of these two groups to each other is not clear. He is an important link in the relationship between Marpeck and Schwenckfeld. Two years later the tensions between Marpeck's brotherhood and Schwenckfeld came to a climax through the publication of the *Vermanung* and letters which Marpeck and Schwenckfeld exchanged. Sailer died at Saitz, Moravia, in 1550. W.Kl.

* * *

Sailer was one of the most prolific of the Hutterite hymn writers. The translation of the Psalms which he made for congregational use is still extant. But since it lacks poetic rhythm it has never been adopted. He gives a melody for each psalm. Of the thirty-fourth and fifty-first Psalms he notes, "own melody." Wolkan (*Lieder,* 180-85) gives the beginning of fourteen of his songs and points out his lack of talent with several illustrations. This is also borne out in the fifty songs which are given in the *Lieder der Hutterischen Brüder* (Scottdale, 1914), 133, 161, 178-297. He was widely imitated, though most of the imitations are improvements over his songs. In the Hutterite brotherhood he was highly regarded. NEFF.

Beck, *Geschichts-Bücher,* 165-67; *Corpus Schwenckfeldianorum* (ed. E. E. S. Johnson) VII (Leipzig, 1926) 161-67; Torsten Bergsten, "Pilgram Marbeck und seine Auseinandersetzung mit Caspar Schwenckfeld," *Kyrkohistorisk Arsskrift* 1957-58 (Uppsala, Sweden) p. 4 f.; Wolkan, *Lieder,* 180-5; *ML* IV.

Saimer, Peter, an Anabaptist martyr, beheaded on July 8, 1588, at Freiburg in Bavaria, Germany. After his arrest at Freiburg he was taken to Berkhausen (?), but was soon brought back to Freiburg. Here he was tried. Both the officials and his friends tried to save him but Peter said, "I have one head; if I had two, or even more, I would rather suffer them all to be cut off than to renounce my faith." Thus he died valiantly. Van Braght says that his head, cut off, turned around facing the executioner, which made a deep impression on the crowd gathered around the execution place. He is the author of the first eight of the eighteen stanzas of the song, "Fröhlich will ich singen." vDZ.

Beck, *Geschichts-Bücher,* 301; *Mart. Mir.* D 764, E 1069; Wolkan, *Geschicht-Buch,* 427 f.; Zieglschmid, *Chronik,* 551 f.; *Die Lieder der Hutterischen Brüder* (Scottdale, 1914) 488 ff.; *ML* IV.

St. Agatha Mennonite Church (MC) is located one-half mile west of the village of St. Agatha in Wilmot Twp., Waterloo Co., Ont. The meetinghouse, seating capacity 350, was built in 1885. Services were originally held alternately in this church and the Steinman church (*q.v.*) at Baden. Since services are now held regularly at each place the two have actually become two separate congregations except for the fact that the same ministers serve both churches.

The original building at St. Agatha was also of frame structure but was completely rebuilt in 1953 with a basement. (For membership, see **Steinman Mennonite Church.**)   O.G.

St. Catharines Mennonite Brethren Church, located at St. Catharines, Lincoln Co., Ont., a member of the Canadian Conference and General Conference of the M.B. Church, was organized Nov. 6, 1943, under the leadership of Gerhard J. Epp. The congregation met in a rented hall in the city until 1949, when a church was built. Gerhard J. Epp was the minister and H. Janzen the leader of this congregation. In 1958 the membership was 498, with Henry P. Penner as leader and minister, and A. H. Redekop as assistant leader and minister; other assistant ministers were D. Duerksen, Abraham Block, and Peter Dick.   H.H.J.

St. Catharines United Mennonite Church (GCM), located on Garnet Street on the east side of St. Catharines, Ont., was organized in 1946 by 16-18 families who had moved to the city or settled on neighboring fruit farms, led by W. Schellenberg from the Essex County United Mennonite Church in Leamington, Ont., who served as its first pastor until 1950, when he retired from active duty. The St. Catharines United Mennonite Church belongs to the Conference of the United Mennonite Churches of Ontario and to the Conference of the Mennonite Churches of Canada. The first church was built in 1946, replaced in 1948 by a larger church seating about 450. Its membership in 1957 was about 430, with P. J. Heinrichs as pastor.   F.J.A.

St. Elizabeth Mennonite Church (MC), now extinct, located 25 miles south of Winnipeg, Man., began in 1915 when the Seth Miller family and others moved here in 1915-18. These settlers organized a Sunday school on March 1, 1919, with A. A. Zook and Seth Miller as superintendents. The largest membership was 15. They were affiliated with the Dakota-Montana Conference (now North Central), and ministers from the district filled monthly appointments. At different times Allan Good and J. M. Kreider held special meetings. The work was discontinued because of the depression, prejudice against German-speaking people, and lack of a resident minister.   F.E.K.

St. Gall (St. Gallen), the capital (pop. 67,865) of the canton of St. Gall, Switzerland, the next canton east of Zürich, was the seat of a brief but substantial early Anabaptist movement in 1525-27. The Reformation in St. Gall was secondary to that of Zürich, as was the Anabaptist movement. Joachim von Watt, called Vadian, who returned in 1519 from the University of Vienna, where he had been an outstanding humanist teacher (also a physician) but not a priest or theologian, became its leader. He served as burgomaster of the city 1526-32. Although he was a brother-in-law of Conrad Grebel, and although Grebel tried to persuade him to at least tolerate if not join the Anabaptist movement, he followed Zwingli completely in his opposition to it. Since in St. Gall the Reformation was borne by the people rather than by the clergy, Anabaptism had a greater opportunity to rise in the midst of the people. Johannes Kessler's "Bible study" group, a week-

27

ly (Sunday) popular meeting in which Kessler (b. 1502), who had returned in December 1523 from a period of study in Württemberg and in early 1524 had begun (with knowledge and approval of the church authorities) to teach evangelical doctrine through Bible exposition (I John, Romans, etc.), furnished the starting point for Anabaptism proper. (Note the similar situation in Zürich, where Castelberger's "Bible study" of 1522, followed by the Grebel and Manz "Bible study" of 1523-24, was the starting point for the Anabaptist movement there. In St. Gall, however, Kessler did not become an Anabaptist as did the leaders in Zürich, nor was the Zürich Bible study ever approved by the authorities. Zwingli overshadowed all.) Lorenz Hochrütiner, a native of St. Gall, who had lived for a time in Zürich and in 1522-23 was a member of the Grebel group but had returned to St. Gall in November 1523, was the channel for the first introduction of pre-Anabaptist ideas. In the summer of 1524 he challenged infant baptism in Kessler's meeting, supported by a letter from Grebel which condemned Kessler's teaching on baptism. But it was Wolfgang Uolimann (*q.v.*), of an old upper-class St. Gall family, a former monk of St. Lucius in Chur, who took charge after the city council forbade the Kessler meetings on Sept. 15, 1524, and in November began public preaching in the open, and later in the weavers' guild house. In February 1525 he was baptized by Grebel in the Rhine near Schaffhausen. Grebel himself appeared in St. Gall in April (two weeks' stay) and on Palm Sunday baptized several hundred in the Sitter River at the edge of the city. Upon his leaving, Anthoni Roggenacher (*q.v.*) and Hippolyt Eberli (see **Bolt, Eberli**), who probably had accompanied him from Zürich, joined with Uolimann in the leadership of the newly established Anabaptist congregation. The movement spread rapidly, also into the surrounding countryside. There is evidence that it had sympathizers in the city council. The leaders were invited to a discussion in the burgomaster's residence. The movement reached a remarkable height.

But soon measures of suppression were taken. The foreign leaders were expelled from the city. Eberli was executed in Schwyz about this time, the first Anabaptist martyr. Uolimann was called before the council, where a lengthy discussion on baptism, "communion, and other matters" took place. Uolimann was first requested, then commanded to cease for a time conducting baptism and communion. The council promised a thorough consideration of the issues. A disputation, with written statements from both sides, was ordered. Vadian submitted a paper, and the St. Gall Anabaptists called on Grebel, who sent a lengthy document. Unfortunately both papers have been lost. Zwingli's chief anti-Anabaptist book, *Vom Tauf, Wiedertauf und Kindertauf,* dedicated to St. Gall, appeared just in time to be used; it was ordered read to the people in the St. Lorenz church by the St. Lorenz schoolmaster Zili. In the course of the reading, two Anabaptists, Uolimann and Giger, interrupted, and opened a discussion which finally led to the leaving of the church by the Anabaptist element. Tension mounted in the city and surroundings. It seemed likely that a majority of the peasants in the countryside, who had already been stirred by a peasants' agitation, would swing over to the Anabaptists. Actually the village of Toblatt was won over by Hans Kern (Krüse) of Klingnau. On June 5 Vadian read his anti-Anabaptist paper in the presence of the council and representatives of the Anabaptists. The next day the Anabaptists read to the same gathering their reply to Vadian (no longer extant). A disputation followed, which resulted in a negative decree by the council. All irregular Anabaptist meetings were now forbidden, although special privilege was granted them to hold meetings in the St. Lorenz church on open Sundays. The mandate, dated June 7, 1525, called for fines for those who had themselves baptized, and exile for those who attended the irregular Anabaptist meetings. A special militia of 200 men was sworn in to handle a possible revolt. It was forbidden to receive foreign visitors who might teach and baptize. Hans Denk apparently appeared in St. Gall about this time, as Kessler reports (*Sabbata*, p. 229), but nothing further is known of his work here.

The measures of repression broke the back of the Anabaptist movement in St. Gall as they did in Zürich. By the end of 1526 little was left of a once powerful movement. Manz appeared here for a brief time in 1526. Uolimann, banished from the city, worked elsewhere after 1526. There must still have been a few Anabaptists in St. Gall for some decades as well as in the adjoining canton of Appenzell.

Some Anabaptists from other regions appeared in the city in 1529, coming from Zürich, the district of Allgäu in South Germany, and from the Adige Valley in Tirol. Niklaus Guldi, formerly an active Anabaptist preacher, was "converted in Strasbourg in 1530, returned to St. Gall where he was rehabilitated," and became a major source for Kessler's reports on the Anabaptists in his *Sabbata*. In 1532 there was a mild revival of Anabaptism, led by Hans Marquart, a former priest of Wissenborn. The Anabaptists made a formal request for toleration as a free church, but were refused. Vadian held a disputation with them in 1532. Jörg Maler, the copyist of the important recently discovered collection of Anabaptist documents called the *Kunstbuch*, lived here 1535-41. Pilgram Marpeck addressed several letters to him. In 1553 a disputation was held in the castle of Lütisburg near St. Gall with some imprisoned Anabaptists who rejected infant baptism along with the teaching that baptism cleanses from original sin. As late as 1639 the St. Gall official records refer to an Anabaptist schoolmaster by the name of Joseph Hochrütiner. Marpeck was employed by the city as a water engineer in the late 1530's.

After the forcible suppression of Anabaptism in St. Gall excesses appeared. As reported by Kessler they included infantile expressions demonstrating "becoming as little children" and other extreme literalistic applications of Biblical passages, which are reported at length by Egli, who recognized them as a fanatical excrescence (*Ausartung*) of the Anabaptist movement. The notorious Thomas Schugger, who is reported to have beheaded his brother, has been shown by John Horsch to have been a marginal figure rather than an Anabaptist. H.S.B.

Emil Egli, *Die St. Gallen Täufer* (Zürich, 1887), on which the above article is largely based; *Johannes Kesslers Sabbata*, ed. Ernst Götzinger; *ML* IV.

St. Jacobs is a village (pop. 725) 9 miles north of Kitchener, Waterloo Co., Ont. Approximately 250 Mennonites live in the village with another 1,000 or so near by. The M.C. group has a church of 400 members in the village. Three Wisler Mennonite (OOM) churches are within two miles of the village. Mennonites own a blacksmith shop, a general store, a produce market, two woodworking shops, two garages, an implement agency, a paint shop, and a weaver shop. Practically all the inhabitants speak the Pennsylvania-German language. R.S.K.

St. Jacobs (Ont.) Mennonite Church (MC), a member of the Ontario Conference, built its first log meetinghouse 2 miles west of St. Jacobs in 1844-45, to serve also as a school; it was called the Conestoga Church. The congregation was divided by the Wisler split that affected a large part of Ontario in 1889. The Wisler (Old Order Mennonite) group used the meetinghouse until the fall of 1892. The present congregation started using the building on Jan. 1, 1893. In 1915 a new church was built in St. Jacobs, its present location, and the congregation adopted the name St. Jacobs Mennonite Church. The meetinghouse was enlarged twice, in 1936 and in 1949. Roy S. Koch (ordained as minister in 1936 and as bishop in 1950) served the congregation until 1957. He was succeeded by Raymond Kramer. The membership in 1958 was 415. R.S.K.

St. John Mennonite Church (GCM), one mile east and a quarter south of Pandora, Ohio, on State Highway 12, is a member of the Middle District Conference. Originally there was only one Swiss Mennonite church in the community; but as the membership increased and the community grew, more churches were built. In 1888 the St. John Mennonite Church building was erected four miles north of the Ebenezer Mennonite Church.

Before 1893 the organization of the church was rather informal and the only officers were the pastors and deacons. No regular congregational meetings were held, nor their proceedings recorded. On Jan. 2, 1893, the congregation adopted a constitution and in October joined the General Conference. In 1956 the pastor was John P. Suderman, who took charge on June 13, 1954. The membership in 1957 was 206. J.P.S.

St. Mary's County (Md.) Old Order Amish Settlement. Amish families began to settle in this county around Mechanicsville in January 1940. The first arrivals were Stephen and Benjamin Stoltzfus and John L. Fisher from Lancaster County and Israel Swarey from Mifflin County, Pa. John L. Fisher was the first minister. In 1953 the district divided into two districts, known as the Southwest District or District A, and the Northwest District or District B. Both are served by John B. Fisher as bishop. The total baptized membership in 1956 was 86. J.B.F.

Ste-Marie-aux-Mines: see Markirch.

St-Mihiel, an extinct Mennonite congregation in France formed about the middle of the 19th century by families of the Meuse (*q.v.*) congregation who lived around the city of St-Mihiel. It died out in 1870 with the death of André Greebill, its only known elder, since no one was found to assume the responsibilities of the ministry. Most of the families joined the Reformed Church; others moved away or became Catholic. Among the family names were Moser, Muller, Hodler, Esch, Géni, and Lebé.

H.S.B.

Pierre Sommer, "Assemblée de Saint-Mihiel," *Christ Seul,* November 1932, 7 f.

St-Saphorin, François Pesme de, a nobleman of the canton of Vaud, Switzerland, b. 1668, of a prominent family of Geneva, who as the Swiss ambassador to Holland played a prominent part in the negotiations concerning the deportation of Bernese Mennonites to America in 1710.   NEFF.

C. H. Smith, *The Mennonite Immigration to Pennsylvania* (Norristown, 1929) 62-74; *Inv. Arch. Amst.* I, No. 1331; *DB* 1909, 139-49; Müller, *Berner Täufer,* 265-99; *ML* III.

St-Victor, the seat of a Mennonite congregation in Lorraine 1922-40: see **Diesen.**

Salem Academy, located two miles west of Salem, Ore., an interdenominational evangelical school, had its beginning in small Bible classes held in the Dallas Mennonite churches in 1930-38 with N. N. Hiebert, H. H. Dick, and Herman D. Wiebe as instructors. In 1938 a district school building was secured and what was then known as Beacon Bible School was organized by a Bible School Society composed of interested members of the Grace Mennonite, Evangelical Mennonite, and Mennonite Brethren churches of Dallas.

In 1944 an evening Bible Institute of an interdenominational nature was begun in the Mennonite Brethren Church in West Salem. In 1945 the efforts of Dallas and Salem together with interests of others of the area were united and the Salem Academy came into being. Classes were begun in the West Salem Mennonite Brethren Church with an enrollment of 75, John W. Ediger as principal, and A. A. Loewen as the first chairman of the Board of Trustees.

In 1946 the present site was purchased and in 1947 the present large concrete block building was erected on an imposing twenty-four-acre hill site campus. Enrollment has risen to and maintained itself at 200-250 during the ensuing years. A teaching staff of some 15 offers fully accredited instruction in grades 7-12, with competent Bible instruction included. Beside the administration building housing offices, 8 large classrooms, laboratory, shop, cafeteria, and chapel stands an unimposing music building and a fully standardized gymnasium-auditorium in the background.   G.H.J.

Salem Children's Home, Flanagan, Ill., an organization of the Evangelical Mennonite Church (*q.v.*) of North America, had its beginning in 1896, when Mr. and Mrs. Daniel King gave their 100-acre farm, located one-half mile east and two miles south of Flanagan, for an orphans' home. The first building was erected in 1898, and additions have been made as the work has grown. At present provision is made for 80 to 90 children, besides rooms for the staff members. Farm lands include 300 acres in the surrounding community given by legacies of Henry Broad, Flanagan, Ill., and Joseph Wagler, Groveland, Ill. The Home is directed by a board chosen from the delegates of the Evangelical Mennonite Church, who in turn appoint staff members from volunteers to help unfortunate children. The Home has influenced the lives of some 1,050 children through the services of over 100 workers. In 1956 the superintendent was E. Dean Short, followed in 1957 by Vernon W. Zimmerman.   E.D.S.

Salem Church of God in Christ Mennonite Church, located 8 miles north and 3 miles west of Copeland, Haskell Co., Kan., began in 1917, when the first members settled here, going to Montezuma for worship services until 1922. Jacob N. Yost was the first resident minister. In 1925 a new church was built, which was remodeled in 1947 to seat 300. Four ministers and two deacons have been ordained in the history of the church. Sunday school was started in 1922, and a sewing circle in the later 1920's. In 1957 the church had a membership of 175; the ministers were Vernon Nightengale, Orlan Wedel, and John Nightengale.   E.S.

Salem Deaconess Home and Hospital, located at Salem, Ore., was founded in 1917 under the auspices of the local General Conference, Mennonite Brethren, and Evangelical Mennonite Brethren churches, with Franz B. Wedel as superintendent. The main unit of the hospital had 60 beds. Franz B. Wedel was also the editor of the *Salems Stern* (*q.v.*). After he died in 1930 his son Frank F. Wedel became the superintendent. Under him the south unit was added to the main building. In 1948 the hospital administration was reorganized by creating a board of twelve members consisting primarily of local business people, and the name was changed to Salem Memorial Hospital. By this time the hospital had lost its Mennonite denominational character. At present Irwin F. Wedel, the son of Frank F. Wedel, is superintendent. A west unit is being added to the building. The hospital now has 155 beds and two clinics. (*Salems Stern,* 1919-30.)   C.K.

Salem Evangelical Mennonite Church, near Gridley, Ill., formerly known as the Defenseless Mennonite Church, had its origin in a schism in the **Waldo** Amish Mennonite (MC) congregation during the Civil War, after 1863, due to the new insights of the minister into Christian experience with emphasis upon conversion, and the influence of Henry Egly of Indiana, the founder of the Evangelical (Defenseless) Mennonites. The first meetinghouse was erected in 1875, and the second, which has been remodeled twice, in 1893. Joseph Rediger, who was ordained to the ministry in the Amish Mennonite church in 1863, was the first minister. Other ministers who have served the church are John Rediger, Christian King, C. R. Egle, Christian Rediger, Eli J. Oyer, Benjamin E. Rediger, Benjamin Rupp, H. E. Bertsche, I. R. Calhoun, Edward Enns, and C. L. Zimmerman. Several ministers and missionaries have come from this congregation. The membership in 1957 was 196. The congregation is now called the Gridley Mennonite Church.   E.E.Z.

H. F. Weber, *Centennial History of the Mennonites of Illinois* (Goshen, 1931) 342-56.

Salem (Ore.) Evangelical Mennonite Brethren Church was organized in July 1933 as a result of a division in the Dallas (Ore.) E.M.B. Church. The membership was at one time 70. The congregation disbanded in December 1941, but was reconstituted in 1957, with Frank Wiens as pastor.   O.H.W.

Salem Home for the Aged began on March 17, 1889, when a frame building was dedicated as a "Home for the Friendless." A group of Krimmer Mennonite Brethren ministers and laymen of the Gnadenau congregation, with Tobias Martin and Amanda Dohner and other public-minded citizens, agreed to operate an orphans' home 2½ miles southeast of Hillsboro, Kan. On Oct. 23, 1893, it was decided that a larger building was needed and a four-story stone structure, 40 x 50 feet, was completed and dedicated on Oct. 18, 1896, as the "Industrial School and Hygiene Home for the Friendless" (*q.v.*). The institution owned 105 acres of land. On May 10, 1915, the institution was rechartered as the "Salem Home and Hospital," and rearranged to serve the aged and ill. On April 29, 1944, the building was struck by lightning and completely destroyed by fire and the inmates were moved to the Salem Hospital Annex at Hillsboro. In 1956 a new modern hospital was built at a different site and the entire former Salem Hospital and Annex was converted into a larger home for the aged, known as the "Salem Home for the Aged." The remodeled building was dedicated Nov. 3, 1957. Mrs. Ed. Penner and Mrs. Frank V. Wiebe are the superintendents of the institution. At the time of dedication the home had 43 inmates. More facilities are to be added. The Salem Home for the Aged is operated by a corporation (Home for the Aged, Inc.) representing seventeen churches of the Hillsboro area, including G.C.M., M.B., K.M.B., and non-Mennonite congregations.   D.V.W.

Salem Hospital, at Hillsboro, Kan., was built and sponsored by the Krimmer Mennonite Brethren Conference. It was opened in 1918 with a capacity of 18 patient beds. The administration of the hospital for many years was vested in a board of six members and a supervisory nurse; later three additional members were added to the board, one each from the Chamber of Commerce, the First Mennonite Church (GCM), and the Mennonite Brethren of Hillsboro. During the 1920's the hospital conducted a course in nurses' training, which was later dropped. A resident staff of two and three doctors served the hospital.

In 1951 the Krimmer Mennonite Brethren Conference sold the hospital to the Hillsboro community. A new Salem Hospital corporation was formed by the elected delegates representing 14 evangelical churches of the community and the city chamber of commerce. The hospital was operated by an administrator under a nine-member board. A $260,000 32-bed modern hospital was built in 1955. A new

nurses' home was built near the new hospital by the Hillsboro Chamber of Commerce at a cost of $20,000 and then donated to Salem Hospital, Inc. The original hospital together with an annex which was built some years ago have been converted into the Salem Home for the Aged (*q.v.*), which is operated under a board separate from the hospital board.
                    S.L.L.

Salem Krimmer Mennonite Brethren Church, now extinct, located near Jansen (*q.v.*), Neb., was organized Jan. 1, 1881, at which time two ministers, Peter Thiessen and Peter Fast, were elected from the group under the direction of Elder Jacob A. Wiebe. By this time 34 persons had been converted and baptized as a result of a revival. Homes and a schoolhouse served as meeting places until 1885, when a frame meetinghouse was built. It was replaced in 1905 by a brick building, which was moved to Hillsboro, Kan., in 1947, as an addition to the Old People's Home. In 1912 there was a membership of 68. The congregation was dissolved in 1930.   C.F.P.

Salem Krimmer Mennonite Brethren Church, located in the rural municipality (township) of Laird, Waldheim, Sask. Its original eight members immigrated from Bon Homme and Turner counties, S.D., in April 1899, and possibly organized the following month when services, including Sunday school, were conducted in farm homes. In 1905, after a great revival, the first meetinghouse was built, which was destroyed by fire in 1934, but was immediately replaced by the present frame structure with a seating capacity of 350. The membership in 1956 was 125. Heinrich A. Goossen served as elder and leader from 1899 to 1936, followed by Edwin T. Schmidt. The minister in 1956 was Ed H. Epp.   E.T.S.

Salem Krimmer Mennonite Brethren Church, located 10 miles southwest of Bridgewater, Hutchinson Co., S.D., was organized on Nov. 25, 1886, with a membership of 16. In 1900 a frame church was built as the first meetinghouse. Under this a full basement was built in 1917, and in 1944 the building was remodeled and enlarged. The leaders who have served the congregation are Henry A. Goosen 1889-99, Dietrich Goosen 1899-1910, Jacob J. Hofer 1910-19, and David M. Tschetter 1919- . In 1956 the membership was 237, with J. J. Kleinsasser serving as leader.   D.W.T.

Salem Mennonite Brethren Church, sometimes known as the Colby Mennonite Brethren Church, now extinct, located 4 miles southwest of Mingo, Thomas Co., Kan., was organized in 1922, with P. E. Dahl as leader. From 1920 on, when Mennonite Brethren and General Conference Mennonite families moved into the area, members of both conferences met for worship under the leadership of D. J. Heinze. When additional families of both groups arrived each organized separately. Because of disunity and the depression members moved to Colorado and California. The congregation was dissolved in 1934. The highest membership was approximately 40. The church building has been preserved by a former member for possible future use.   I.G.N.

Salem (Ore.) Mennonite Brethren Church, since 1953 called Kingwood Bible Church (*q.v.*), was previously also called the West Salem Church.

H.S.B.

Salem Mennonite Brethren in Christ Church, Broad and McFerran St., Philadelphia, Pa., was organized in 1900 through the work of the Gospel Herald Society of the Pennsylvania Conference. In 1956 the congregation had 225 members, mostly urban, with J. E. Golla serving as pastor. W.H.F.

Salem Mennonite Brethren in Christ Church, Allentown, Lehigh Co., Pa., was organized in 1901. In 1957 the congregation had 102 members, mostly urban, with R. H. Gehman serving as pastor.

H.W.H.

Salem Mennonite Church (MC), located near Tofield, Alberta, dates back to 1910, when several families, including Bishop N. E. Roth, moved into the area from Nebraska. The congregation was organized under the Western Amish Mennonite Conference; with the arrival of more settlers, including most of the Mayton (Alberta) Mennonite congregation, it affiliated with the Alberta-Saskatchewan Mennonite Conference. The meetinghouse was built in 1911, enlarged in 1915 and 1926, and replaced by a new one, 52 x 80 ft., in 1954. Former ministers include N. E. Roth, bishop 1911-39, and J. K. Lehman. This congregation, with 253 members in 1957, is the largest in the Alberta-Saskatchewan Conference district. The congregation is active in the support of missions. An extension church is located at Round Hill, about 6 miles southwest, where Sunday school and church services are held each Sunday. In 1957 John B. Stauffer was the bishop, and Milo D. Stutzman, Paul L. Voegtlin, and Harold Boettger the ministers of the Salem congregation. M.D.S.

Salem Mennonite Church (GCM), Aberdeen, Idaho: see **Aberdeen** First Mennonite Church.

Salem Mennonite Church (MC), located one-half mile south and 5 miles west of New Paris, Elkhart Co., Ind., a member of the Indiana-Michigan Conference, was organized by R. J. Smid (1814-93) in 1889. About one half of the charter members were Mennonite immigrants from Balk (*q.v.*), Friesland, Netherlands, who had arrived in 1853 and had held Dutch services in homes and schoolhouses, and also attended German services in the Christophel Mennonite church, an alternate meeting place for the Yellow Creek (*q.v.*) Mennonite Church. The meetinghouse was built in 1889 and enlarged in 1919. Ministers of the congregation have been R. J. Smid (Schmidt), J. H. Bare (ordained 1906), Ray F. Yoder, the present bishop (ordained 1918), and Francis E. Freed (ordained 1939) and Harold D. Myers, the present ministers (1958). The membership is 166. R.F.Y.

Marie Yoder, "The Balk Dutch Settlement near Goshen, Indiana, 1853-1889," *MQR* XXX (1956) 32-43.

Salem Mennonite Church (GCM), now extinct, located about 5 miles southwest of the present town of Wellman, Washington Co., Iowa, was probably organized in 1865. The Rupps, Desters, Schmitts, and possibly others from Lee County, Iowa, established the settlement. William Galle served for a time as elder and as the teacher in the parochial school. The largest number observing communion service was 31, in October 1876. About this time the members began moving to Kansas. The last business meeting of the church of which there is a record was held in November 1880. M.G.

Melvin Gingerich, *The Mennonites in Iowa* (Iowa City, 1939) 86-92.

Salem Mennonite Church (GCM), located in Munich, N.D., was organized in 1901 by Henry Quiring of Mountain Lake, Minn.; Martin Fast and Isaac Friesen were elected as ministers. Other ministers who have served are Hellmuth F. Ortmann and George Hoffman. The meetinghouse was built in 1906, and remodeled and enlarged in 1946. The membership in 1957 was 152, with John J. Hofer as pastor. H.F.O.

Salem Mennonite Church (GCM), now extinct, member of the Northern District Conference, in Butterfield, Watonwan Co., Minn., was organized in 1896 under the sponsorship of the Bethel Church of Mountain Lake, a neighboring town. A church building was erected that same year. In 1915 the Menno Simons congregation in Butterfield, of Swiss origin, merged with the Salem Church. In a few years friction developed between the two groups which caused the Swiss members to leave Salem in 1921 and build a new church in 1922, known today as the Mennonite Church of Butterfield. The "Gemeinde-Chronik" of Salem has no membership list, but an aged former member reports that it never had more than 50 members. The separation of the two groups left the Salem congregation in a weakened position. On Oct. 2, 1926, the congregation decided to sell the church and dispose of all church property. The last entry in the official record is made July 16, 1934, when the Salem Church organization was formally dissolved. A few of its former members had died, some moved away, and others joined neighboring congregations. J.J.F.

Salem Mennonite Church (MC), four miles southeast of Shickley, Neb., was organized in 1891 by P. P. Hershberger and Chris Beller. Services were held in a township hall until 1904, when a meetinghouse was erected. In 1957 the membership was approximately 265 with Peter R. Kennel serving as bishop and Fred C. Reeb as minister. P.R.K.

Salem Mennonite Church (GCM), now extinct, located 6 miles southwest of Wisner, Neb., a member of the Northern District Conference, was organized in 1889 by August Leisy, Henry Leisy, Rudolph Leisy, Jacob Risser, and Chris Risser. The meetinghouse was built in 1889. In 1954 there was no minister in charge and the church was only semi-active, with 12 members. It was not listed in the 1956 Yearbook. A.J.L.

Salem Mennonite Church (GCM), located 4 miles southwest of Dalton, Ohio, and 2½ miles northeast of Kidron, Ohio, was organized May 20, 1886, with

18 charter members, of the Sommer, Kirchhofer, Lehman, Zuercher, Moser, Steffen, Amstutz, and Geiger families, as a schism from the Sonnenberg (*q.v.*) Swiss congregation. The first meetinghouse was dedicated on Nov. 28, 1886. A. A. Sommer was chosen as the first regular pastor. The present building is a result of additions and four remodeling programs. The congregation in 1957 had 204 baptized members, with James R. Reusser as minister.

I.L.B.

Salem Mennonite (MC) Church, a member of the Ohio and Eastern Mennonite Conference, located 2½ miles northeast of Elida, Allen Co., Ohio, was organized in 1841 with 48 charter members. The first families came in part from near Harrisonburg, Va., and in part from Fairfield County, Ohio, near Columbus. The first meetinghouse, according to tradition, was erected in 1843, but the lot was purchased in 1847.

It was first called Sherrick's (Sherk's) church because of the numerous families by that name, but after the Civil War it was renamed Salem, because peace had been secured, *Shalom* being the Hebrew word for peace. In 1857 a frame building was erected, replaced by a larger building (40 x 60 ft.) in 1883. In 1860-94 a part of the congregation which had moved westward began worshiping near Gomer, and in 1874 erected a meetinghouse and formed the Pike (*q.v.*) congregation. The two congregations worked closely together and for many years held services alternately in the two meetinghouses. In 1925 a group expelled from the Salem-Pike congregation organized the Central (*q.v.*) Church in Elida.

The first minister and bishop at Salem was George Stemen, who had been ordained bishop shortly before in Fairfield County (*q.v., 1846-95*). An outstanding leader was Bishop John M. Brenneman who had been ordained bishop in Franklin County before (1849) moving to Allen County in 1855. J. M. Shenk (1848-1935) was a long-time leader, ordained minister in 1874 and bishop in 1884. In 1957 Richard E. Martin was a pastor at Salem, with 92 members.

H.S.B.

Salem Mennonite Church (MC), located 2 miles southeast of Smithville, half way between Orrville and Wooster in Wayne County, Ohio, a member of the Ohio and Eastern Conference, was founded in 1891 as a daughter congregation of the Martins church (*q.v.*), the meetinghouse being built in that year. Actually the origin of the congregation was largely due to David Hostetler and Solomon Plank, preacher and deacon respectively in the Oak Grove Amish Mennonite Church (*q.v.*), who, being dissatisfied with some of the conservative practices of the congregation, transferred to the Martins congregation in 1890, and became the first ministers of the Salem congregation. A few Oak Grove members followed them to Salem, but the total initial group was not large. In 1905 the membership was 55. In 1957 the membership was 45, with Daniel Hilty and Paul Showalter as ministers.

H.S.B.

Salem Mennonite Church (GCM), located 5 miles northeast of Cordell, Washita County, Okla., with

H. D. Schmidt as minister and a membership of 20, was listed by H. P. Krehbiel, *Mennonite Churches of North America* (1911). The *Minutes and Reports of the Western District Conference,* starting 1913, list a Salem Mennonite Church at Weatherford, Okla., which is likely the same congregation. The last time the church is mentioned in the *Minutes* was in 1918, at which time it was represented by R. Riesen.

C.K.

Salem Mennonite Church (MC), located in the village of Shelly, Pa., a member of the Franconia Conference, was organized in August 1950 by Elmer M. Mack, chairman of the Franconia mission board. The church auditorium is in a four-story brick building, formerly a factory, which also contains the pastor's residence. The membership in 1958 was 87, with Lester K. Moyer as pastor.

M.D.R.

Salem Mennonite Church (GCM), located at Freeman, S.D., had its beginning during the summer of 1907, when the Swiss Mennonite settlement east of Freeman decided to divide as a congregation. The northern half of the settlement remained with the original Salem-Zion congregation, and the southern half withdrew and became the Salem Mennonite Church. Land was purchased 2½ miles south of the Salem-Zion church and a meetinghouse was built, dedicated on May 24, 1908. On Jan. 2, 1909, a constitution was adopted. In 1913 a cemetery was begun. In the fall and winter of 1916-17 the church building was greatly enlarged to its present size. In 1920 a large parsonage was erected south of the church. Ministers who have served the Salem church are Christian Mueller 1908-10 and 1919-20, Christian Hege 1911-19, E. J. Neuenschwander 1920-24, W. S. Gottschall 1924-30, P. R. Schroeder 1930-40, Willard Claassen 1941-52, and J. Herbert Fretz 1953- . The membership of the Salem congregation in 1957 was 542. The common names are Preheim, Waltner, Kaufman, Graber, Gering, Miller, Ries, and Schrag. Recent missionaries from the congregation are Mrs. Orlando Waltner in India, and Mrs. Verney Unruh and Mrs. Raymond Reimer in Japan.

J.H.F.

Salem Mennonite Church (MC) is a rural mission church at Needmore, Hardy Co., W. Va., under the Virginia Conference. Either before or soon after the Civil War (1861-65) ministers from Broadway, Va., traveled 45 miles to Bean Settlement, 6 miles north of this church, and preached at a schoolhouse, giving pastoral care to a few members living there. Later they also preached at the Mine Spring schoolhouse near by.

In 1927 a church was built here, which was enlarged in 1948 by adding two Sunday-school rooms. This congregation is the result of one of the first efforts of rural evangelism of the Northern District of the Virginia Conference. The membership in 1957 was 113; the pastor was Samuel A. Shank.

T.S.

Salem Publishing House, Inman, Kan., was owned and operated 1934-58 by the J. H. Klassen family, members of the Krimmer Mennonite Brethren. It printed several Mennonite church papers, such as the *Wahrheitsfreund, Christian Witness, Zion's Tid-*

ings, and *Gospel Tidings,* and also the *Sower* for the Northern Bible Society of Duluth, Minn. They also did binding and rebinding of worn Bibles. The firm had its beginning in a low one-room building, but later acquired a brick and tile building, 35 x 100 ft., with a stock room and a small retail bookstore. In 1958 this firm changed its name to The Klassen Bookbindery and sold its printing equipment and bookstore. It still rebinds worn Bibles as a hobby.

J.H.K.

Salem Ridge Mennonite Church (MC), Route 3, Greencastle, Pa., was established in 1946 and had 60 members in 1957, with Charles E. Shank as minister. Its location is 3 miles south of Greencastle and one-half mile east of Route 11.

M.G.

Salems Stern, an 8-page 8½ x 11½ monthly publication of the Salem Deaconess Home and Hospital of Salem, Ore., edited by F. B. Wedel, first issue March 1919, last issue February 1930. The primary purpose of the paper was to promote the interests of the Salem Deaconess Home and Hospital (*q.v.*) of which F. B. Wedel was the manager. The German language was used primarily, although there was an occasional report in English.

C.K.

Salemskirche (Salem Mennonite Church), a brick building erected in 1847 six miles south of Ashland, Ohio, by John Risser (*q.v.*), a Mennonite preacher, and his fellow immigrants from the Bavarian Palatinate, following Risser's unsuccessful attempt to work harmoniously with the local American Mennonites at Pleasant Ridge (*q.v.*). It replaced another log church-school building erected near by in 1835, three years after Risser and his family arrived. Risser lost interest in preaching soon after the church was built and permitted the German Reformed and Lutheran groups, served by their own pastors, to hold services in the building. The Mennonite congregation worshiped with them. After the middle of the century an attempt to hold English services was thwarted by the discovery that the deed to the property prohibited holding any but German services in the building. Assistance from the Mennonite school at Wadsworth revived interest, but conditions were not conducive to healthy congregational growth. Risser's coreligionists from the Palatinate, some destined to rise high in later Mennonite circles, stopped briefly in Ashland County and then continued west to Summerfield, Ill., or Donnellson, Iowa. The last pastors of the congregation were Carl H. Anton van der Smissen (*q.v.*), later of Newton, Kan., 1874-79, and his illustrious father, Carl Justus van der Smissen (*q.v.*), who had come from Hamburg-Altona in Germany to teach the German theological courses at the Wadsworth Mennonite school. But even before the latter's death in 1890 some of the younger members preferred English services. Most of the remaining members at Salem, a few from the old Mennonite congregation at Pleasant Ridge, and practically all of their German Reformed and Lutheran neighbors united to build the "Stone" Lutheran church a half mile north of the Salem church. The Salem church has been removed to enlarge the cemetery. The Stone Lutheran congregation is a flourishing organization. J.S.U.

John Umble, "Extinct Ohio Mennonite Churches," *MQR* XX (1946) 5-52.

Salem-Zion Mennonite Church (GCM), located 5 miles east of Freeman, S.D., a member of the Northern District Conference, was formed out of two congregations which had their origin in Russia, coming from two separate Russian villages in Volhynia (*q.v.*) in 1874, the Salem group from Horodyszcze and the Zion group from Waldheim. After worshiping for a number of years in homes, they built separate meetinghouses and continued to worship separately until 1902, when the Zion church was destroyed by a cyclone. Then the two congregations merged, forming the Salem-Zion church. The first ministers immigrated with their congregations in 1874. With the Salem group came Peter Kaufman as elder and Christian Graber as minister. In 1878 the Salem church elected Christian Kaufman as elder and Christian Mueller as minister. In 1907 a group organized the present Salem Mennonite Church (*q.v.*) with Christian Mueller as minister. When the Zion church was destroyed, Joseph Kaufman of that church served in the Salem-Zion church. In 1957 the congregation had a membership of 426, with Olin A. Krehbiel as pastor, who succeeded Russel L. Mast. A new meetinghouse was dedicated in 1958. R.L.M.

Salford Mennonite (MC) Church was one of the early Mennonite settlements in what is now Montgomery County, Pa. The first house of worship was built sometime prior to the first purchase of land by the congregation in 1728. The grantors of the land were Henrich and Modlena Ruth, and the grantees were Henry Funk (*q.v.*), Dielman Kolb (*q.v.*), Christian Meyer, and Abraham Reiff. These men were or later became ordained Mennonite church officials, Funk a bishop, Kolb a preacher, and Meyer and Reiff deacons. Services were conducted exclusively in German for almost two centuries. The first English-speaking preacher was ordained in 1915. Salford is remembered as the location of one of the schools taught by the noted Mennonite schoolmaster, Christopher Dock (*q.v.*), whose other school was at Skippack. About 1770 the original Salford meetinghouse was replaced by a larger one. D. K. Cassel (*q.v.*) taught school in this meetinghouse in 1839. It was replaced by another in 1850, which was enlarged in 1897, but was torn down in 1924, when the present house of worship, the fourth, was built, 56 x 88 feet in size. Perhaps the most noted minister in the past century was Henry S. Bower (1836-1909), ordained in 1865. In 1958 the ministers were Rein A. Alderfer and Henry L. Ruth. The membership was above 250 in 1884; in 1958 it was 420.

J.C.W.

J. C. Wenger, *History of the Mennonites of the Franconia Conference,* 131-37.

Salisbury (in the documents *Sarum*), the seat of one of the five Anabaptist (Baptist) congregations of England, who on Nov. 12, 1626, wrote a letter to Hans de Ries (*q.v.*) and Reinier Wybrands (*q.v.*) and their (Waterlander) Mennonite congregations in Holland, in which they declared that they had read with full agreement the confession of faith by Hans de Ries and Lubbert Gerritsz, and made a proposal to form a union with the Dutch Waterlanders. The union, however, did not come about. (See also **Coventry** and **England;** *Inv. Arch. Amst.* I, Nos. 1372-75.)　　　　　　　　　　vDZ.

Salland, a Mennonite home for the aged at Colmschate near Deventer in the Netherlands, founded in 1955, dedicated February 1955. The pastor of the Deventer (*q.v.*) congregation is in charge of this home. (*DJ* 1956, 37-40.)　　　　　　　　vDZ.

Salm, a Dutch Mennonite family of Amsterdam, Netherlands, members of the Old Frisian (Arke Noachs) congregation from the 17th century, and later also in the United Mennonite Church. Many of them were deacons, but none was a preacher. The ancestor of the family, as far as is known, was Claes Sybrandtsz Salm (1609-64), of Amsterdam, who was a builder of barges and later was a salmon merchant, from which the name was derived. The Amsterdam Salm family became very wealthy in the 18th and 19th centuries (most of them were sugar, tobacco, etc., brokers). Abraham Salm Gz (d. 1915 at Amsterdam), for some time a deacon of the Amsterdam congregation, was an architect. Members of the Salm family were formerly also found at Zaandam.　　　　　　　　　　vDZ.

(J. J. A. Wijs), *Stamboom van de familie Salm* (n.p., n.d.-1936); Blaupot t. C., *Holland* I, 241; Supplement of the *Nederlandsche Leeuw,* 1950, 118 f.; church records of Amsterdam.

Salm (Salmer), a former small Mennonite congregation in the Bruche Valley of Upper Alsace (*q.v.*), about 50 miles southwest of Strasbourg in the Vosges Mountains, now extinct. It is not clear when the congregation was established, certainly it existed at the time of the expulsion of the Mennonites from Markirch in 1712, possibly already in the 17th century. A second group, closely related to Salm, located at Blanc-Rupt (*q.v.*), which separated from Salm after the middle of the 19th century as a result of a schism. The Dutch *Naamlijst* of 1769 mentions that it was formed by Swiss emigrants with Christian Ringe(n)berg as elder. The *Naamlijst* of 1775 states that Jakob Kupferschmidt (d. 1813) served as its elder from 1766, Hans Rube also being an elder and Peter Gerber a preacher. The names of the same ministers are found in following *Naamlijsts,* but not in those of 1793 and after; then Christian Ringenberg is again named as its elder. Other known elders with dates were Michel Saltzmann (1759), Hans Guengerich, Jogi Mosimann, Christian Gerber (d.1824), Andrée Shirch (1822), Nicolas Augsburger (d.1890), Pierre Sommer (d.1878), Hans Beller (d.1892), Joseph Beller (1874, d.1910), Henri Neuhauser (ord. 1882). In 1837 it numbered 60 souls, children included. In 1881 it still existed, then numbering 50 souls, with three elders, one preacher, and one deacon. When the congregation disappeared is not certain.

After the death of Elder Augsburger the congregation relocated its worship somewhat south of Salm at a place called Les Quelles (*q.v.*). The congrega-

tion known as Bénaville (*q.v.*) was formed in 1924 from former members of the Salm congregation. The book by Alfred Michiels, *Les Anabaptistes des Vosges* (Paris, 1860), describes the Salm Mennonites, including a visit in the home of Elder Augsburger.　　　　　　　　　　vDZ., H.S.B.

Naamlijst; ML I, 561; Mannhardt, *Jahrbuch* 1888, 37; Pierre Sommer, "Assemblée de Salm (Les Quelles-Bénaville)," *Christ Seul,* 1932, 5 f.

Salminger, Sigmund, a former monastic priest (a Franciscan) of Munich, Bavaria, Germany, was one of the founders of the Augsburg Anabaptist congregation (*q.v.*). He and his wife Anna (*q.v.*), who was a faithful companion to him, were baptized in March 1527 by Hans Hut on the occasion of his second visit to Augsburg, which lasted nine or ten days, and was chosen by lot as Vorsteher of the Augsburg congregation at its first organization. He was, however, seized soon after Sept. 15, 1527. Among those he baptized was the "Mangmeisterin" Plöck(in), who was expelled from the city with her infant of eight weeks. In addition he baptized several peasants who did not live in Augsburg, as well as Sebastian Vischgatter, a citizen, Elisabeth, the wife of Gall Vischer, and Katharina, wife of Hans Kunig, the stone mason, who had recanted on Oct. 3, 1527, but was rearrested in May 1528.

After spending more than three years in prison Salminger recanted on Dec. 17, 1530, and was released. His written recantation and also a letter he wrote to the council requesting permission for his wife's return to the city (already previously published by Greiff) were published by Schletterer (180, 182). Penniless and a physical wreck Salminger left the prison. Since he was unable to pay his board he was ordered in March 1531 to leave the city; but it was impossible for him to comply on account of the inclement weather and the state of his health. He was granted a brief respite, but at its expiration was just as wretched as before. He therefore wrote a petition to the council, asking permission to stay and offering his services.

Wackernagel published four of Salminger's hymns (pp. 807-11). Salminger had poetic and musical gifts which poured themselves out in religious songs. In the oldest hymnal of Augsburg some of the finest hymns are those from Salminger's pen.　　　HEGE.

Greiff, *Beiträge zur Geschichte der deutschen Schulen* (Augsburg, 1858) 146; H. M. Schletterer, in *Monatshefte für Musikgeschichte* XXI (1889) 177-86; Wackernagel, *Kirchenlied* III, 807-11; Friedrich Roth, "Zur Geschichte der Wiedertäufer in Oberschwaben," *Zt. des hist. Vereins für Schwaben und Neuburg* I (1874) 212; XXVIII (1901) 4, 114 f.; *ADB* XXX (1890) 270-72; Karl Schottenloher, *Philipp Ulhart* (Munich, 1921) 81-83; *ML* IV.

Salmuth, Johann (b. 1552), court chaplain at Dresden, Germany, an opponent of the Anabaptists, the son of Heinrich Salmuth who was Superintendent of Leipzig and professor of theology at the local university. He published a Calvinist edition of the Bible in 1591, in which he attacked Luther and mingled attacks on the Anabaptists into his accusations. Like a red thread the struggle against the Anabaptists goes through his entire Bible. The line of demarcation between Calvinism and Anabaptism is drawn exceedingly sharply. The editors rejected the Anabaptist position on the oath (Deut. 6:13). In opposition to the Anabaptists they recognized the legitimacy of just wars (Deut. 20:1). They opposed the Anabaptist separation of church and state, stating that it is the duty of the government to take the work of the Reformation in hand and that participation in the work of the government is a service to one's neighbor which promotes the glory of God (Gen. 41:40; Num. 36:1). They specifically attacked community of goods as introduced by the Anabaptists (Num. 32:5), arguing that riches do not necessarily lead to unbelief (Gen. 13:2). Also in opposition to the ascetic earnestness of the Anabaptists, they frequently advocate a certain joy in the world; to be happy is not wrong as the Anabaptists fanatically believe, only one must not forget God and one's neighbor in being happy (I Chron. 13:40). And in the reference to Thomas Müntzer (Judg. 7:18) and the Peasants' War (Num. 16:3) a warning was given against the abuse of Christian liberty: revolt is not at all permissible and even against a tyrant the people have no right to rebel (I Sam. 8:5). Here the comment is expressly added: "To refute the seditious conduct of the Anabaptists on the annihilation of temporal regents." HEGE.

Hans Lebue, "Die sächsische calvinistische Bibelausgabe vom Jahre 1591," in *Archiv für Ref.-Gesch.* XXVII (1930) 56; *ML IV.*

Saltillo Church of God in Christ Mennonite Church, located about 55 miles south of Saltillo, Coahuila, in Nuevo Leon, Mex., was founded in 1945 by several Koehn families from Cuauhtemoc, Mex., who had previously migrated from Oklahoma, including the minister, Henry B. Koehn. However, after enduring a few years of drought they left and Saltillo became a mission outpost. In 1958 there were 24 members. Originally services, both English and Spanish, were held in the home of the minister. At present services are conducted only in Spanish.

P.G.H.

Salto Mennonite Church (MC), located in Salto (pop. 8,000), Argentina, the seat of Ugarte County, in the province of Buenos Aires, on a branch line of the Central Buenos Aires Railroad. A mission was opened by William G. Lauver under the Mennonite Board of Missions and Charities in August 1941, and a congregation was organized in September 1942. In 1957 there were 15 members, with Ross Goldfus as pastor. E.V.S.

Salunga Mennonite Church (MC), now extinct, located 9 miles northwest of Lancaster, Pa., was a member of the Lancaster Conference; through the instrumentality of Deacon Jacob M. Greider a brick meetinghouse, 50 x 65 ft., was built in 1893. It was a part of the Landisville-Chestnut Hill circuit. In 1954 the building was turned over to the Eastern Board of Missions and Charities for its headquarters, and the congregational activities completely merged with those of the Landisville congregation. I.D.L.

Salzburg. The struggle against the Anabaptists could be carried on with much greater vigor in Salzburg than in the Austrian hereditary lands, since here the temporal and spiritual authority were combined in the archbishop. In Salzburg there were resident Anabaptists as early as 1526. Of Jörg Zeller it is related that he had brought the symbol "which is called rebaptism" to his home in Franconia from Salzburg, and several of the Anabaptists seized early in 1528 in the Bavarian district of Auerbach came from Salzburg; among these were Antoni, who had commissioned Hans Stieglitz to baptize, and Gilg, a former priest, then a leader of the Anabaptists, who had received his commission from Dorfbrunner (*q.v.*).

The extensive spread of Anabaptism in the bishopric of Salzburg is seen in the numerous mandates as well as the complaints of Archbishop Matthäus, who wrote on July 4, 1527, that he had to work day and night with his councillors to stamp out Anabaptists in his bishopric. One of the mandates warns the populace on penalty of death not to become involved in "such unchristian acts of rebaptism." The judges were ordered to pursue the matter with vigor, and prevent meetings "in which such seducing deeds are perpetrated," organize posses, and especially to proceed against foreigners who were found in these meetings, in accord with the mandate which was to be nailed to the door of the city hall and read in all public places (Oct. 25, 1527).

In two days another mandate appeared warning against involvement with Anabaptism either in word or deed; books were to be burned; giving an Anabaptist food or shelter was punishable by having the house of the perpetrator destroyed. All Anabaptists from the outside were to leave within eight days. The next decree (Nov. 14, 1527) was issued to the pastors of Hallein, Tittmoning, Laufen, and Radstadt, notifying them that two Anabaptists had been punished and several had recanted; it was known that there were still several in the country, and to prevent the spread of their evil doctrines instructions were sent showing the common man how to deal with them, what questions were to be asked of them, and how the recantation formula was to be worded. Suspects were to be questioned concerning any possible communistic ideas, views on government, the deity of Christ, and the Lord's Supper, the number of persons any one might have baptized, the sending out of missioners, their views on the Last Judgment, whether it is possible to be saved without rebaptism, etc.

The consequences of the severe persecution in Moravia and Austria on the one hand and Tirol on the other would naturally be evident in Salzburg. Indications of this are seen in the *Neue Zeitung* of 1528, whose author claims to have been an eyewitness: "Here (in Salzburg?) the guest Brethren have gathered, preached, and established their rebaptism. Thirty-two persons were surprised and arrested. They would not desist from their errors nor name their brethren and sisters." "Ten of them including their preacher were punished." Those who would not recant were burned at the stake in the Fronhof. Five who confessed their error were beheaded and then burned. A woman and a girl of sixteen, daughter of the goldsmith Georg Stein (see **Steiner, Georg**), the friend and companion of Hans Hut, who could have saved their lives by recanting, were sentenced to death. The executioner took the

girl in his arm, carried her to the horse trough, and
held her under the water until she died. She
laughed at the sight of the water. Cases of this kind
were in the mind of the lawyer Hepstein, when he
protested to the city council of Augsburg on Jan. 25,
1529, that nothing could be achieved by slaughter-
ing the Anabaptists: "In Austria the young girls
come running and request to be put to death." On
November 1 four were put to death, among them
Wolf Paumann, the judge of Tittmoning; although
he recanted and offered to give all his goods he was
beheaded. In the same manner three brethren ended their lives in Mühldorf. On November 5 ten
women and several men were driven out of the city,
although they had recanted. Eleven women and
sixteen men together with their preacher were
seized at a meeting in a solitary place about a half
hour from Salzburg and taken to Halle. Refusing to
recant, they were locked into the house where they
had met and were burned with it. This was also
the fate of two other houses in which the Anabaptists had been meeting. "There are therefore about
forty-one persons still languishing in prison," says
the *Neue Zeitung*.

The Hutterite chronicles also write of such executions. "The elect saints," writes Leonhard Schiemer (*q.v.*) on Dec. 3, 1527, "who at this time are
praising God in Salzburg and at other places with
their martyrdom, must have bathed in tubs of oil,
else they would not have remained constant in
faith." "Pray to God," he writes in a second epistle,
"for our brother Schreiner from Brixlegg, who lies
in prison with his wife in Lofer."

But there were still some Anabaptists known to be
in Salzburg. The watch on foreigners was sharpened. A new directive issued on Jan. 4, 1528, prohibited discussion of Lutheran (Protestant) doctrine
with travelers. The archbishop noted that the Anabaptists were moving to Tirol to gain a foothold. At
the same time he informed the administrator of
Passau, who had also seized many Anabaptists at
this time, of the situation in Salzburg. The penalties of the preceding year were increased. Whereas
the previous mandate ordered death by burning for
all Anabaptists, those who recanted were to be beheaded before being burned; those who were only
misled and had not themselves baptized, but had
given food and shelter to the Anabaptists, should be
drowned. Now those who gave shelter were to have
their houses destroyed, pay a fine, be imprisoned,
have their clothing removed, and the foreigners to
be placed in the stocks and beaten with rods. All the
penalties were defined, even for carelessness in this
matter. Thereby Salzburg set the pattern for its
neighbors; it was even followed in Nürnberg (*q.v.*).
Only rarely did an Anabaptist meet a kind fate in
Salzburg, such as that of Asmus Gschöll, who after
he had finished his prison term appealed to Innsbruck that he should not again be tried for his Anabaptism. Of course, as persecution in Tirol increased, many Anabaptists returned to Salzburg,
causing grave concern to the rulers. On June 4,
1533, Ferdinand I wrote to the archbishop that he
had definite information that the Anabaptists were
creeping into Rattenberg, Kufstein, Kitzbühel, and
into the valleys of the bishopric of Salzburg, and

that it was very urgently necessary to send three
spies thither at once. The archbishop hastened to
comply. Among the Anabaptists there was in general greater activity at this time. Early in 1534 "a
goodly number of persons of Berchtesgaden came to
Anabaptism," of whom more than twenty persons
of property fled. The bailiff of Mosham, Wolf Kent-
scherner, was instructed on February 16 to arrest
these Anabaptists and to look for those who had
fled to Lungau. He arrested the mine superintendent Jörg Weisshempt and his wife as Anabaptists.
Both begged for mercy; it was granted in return for
recantation and security. The bailiff was informed
that some, under the pretext of being related to the
miners, were able to penetrate far into the mountains, lodge with remote peasants, and fill the people with their teaching. On May 6, 1534, Kent-
scherner received orders to be doubly vigilant, with
reference to events at Münster. A similar uprising
was feared at Salzburg, and all measures were adopted to fortify the country as if for war. The archbishop kept himself informed about the progress of
events at Münster. All arrested Anabaptists were
questioned to establish any possible connections.
The statements of the prisoners show very clearly
that no such connection existed, for the Anabaptists
of the South had little connection with those of the
North. Konrad Siebenburger, seized with other
Anabaptists, recanted on May 14 at St. Johann. In
November an officer of Burghausen reported that
he had drowned Margarethe Moser and her daughter Walpurg without trial because they had been
rebaptized. In the following year many Anabaptists
on their way from Moravia to and through Bavaria
were captured in Passau. Among them was a leader,
a tailor. Many recanted and were released; others
were still in prison. In 1541 and 1542 several Anabaptists were put to death by fire or water. The Hutterian chronicles relate a bit of valor on the part of
Leonhard Bernkopf at the stake. "This side is now
roast enough; turn me to roast the other side now."
. . . "Therefore he will on the other side have a harp
in his hands." From Golding the Anabaptists in the
spring of 1531 migrated into Lungau territory by
way of the Radstatt valleys, and from there to
Moravia. In Lungau and in Golding there were still
some Anabaptists; their presence annoyed the archbishop. The bailiff of Mosham reported that no
Anabaptist passed through the defiles there, though
they may have crossed the mountains at some other
place. The regulations of 1529 against the Anabaptists were renewed in 1544 and proclaimed in all
Salzburg. Nevertheless there were still some present. In 1547 two of them were arrested in Lungau.

The great provincial synod of 1549 issued strict
regulations against the Anabaptists in general and
against their publications in particular. In consequence of the watchfulness of the clergy it became
impossible for the Anabaptists to maintain themselves except in the mountains, and they were now
in close contact with those expelled from Moravia.
A church inspection instituted in 1555 by Archbishop Michael Koenberg revealed some scattered
Anabaptists in Golling and Gastein, and a mandate
issued in September 1558 gave strict orders that children must be brought to baptism. Concerning the

next year the chronicles report that Wolf Maier and a Hueber were put to death with the sword at Tittmoning in the Salzburg district.

On April 20, 1567, the archbishop ordered the provost of the Zillertal to evaluate the confiscated property of a citizen who had become an Anabaptist; there were very likely some Anabaptists among the "sectarians" whom the archbishop ordered the authorities of Rattenberg, Kitzbühel, and Kufstein to find and bring to judgment.

Of especial interest is the story of the clockmaker Veit Grünberger from the Pinzgau, a Vorsteher of the Anabaptists, who visited Tirol nearly every year after 1564 and held his "revier" in the vicinity of Imst. In 1570 he was seized in a forest in the Pinzgau. His replies in the cross-examination indicate that people of this kind found sympathy not only among the lower classes, but also among the educated. Not until the third year of his arrest was he brought to trial. In the seventh year of his imprisonment, after suffering much misery and tribulation he managed to escape through a window. The castle guards said it was impossible to escape by that route; Veit said, "With God all things are possible." On Aug. 1, 1576, he reached his brethren in Moravia.

In July 1573 the archbishop again issued a mandate against the Anabaptists, "because this shameless sect will not clear out of the country." Six years later Hans Zuckenhammer, a smith, and Wolf Raufer, a tailor, who had been sent to Württemberg by the brotherhood in Moravia, were seized in Tippmening and taken to Hohensalzburg; they were released in 1580. Two hymns deal with Zuckenhammer's imprisonment.

In the following years the authorities had little trouble with the Anabaptists. Their chronicles are inexact when in the table of martyrs they put the archbishopric of Salzburg in the ninth place: at Salzburg 38, Berchtesgaden 18, Martel-Lofer 2, Ruckeltal 3.

On the other hand, the Hutterian chronicles of 1584 again tell of a Salzburg Anabaptist, Leonhard Sumerauer, who was arrested at Tittmoning, having boarded a boat en route to Moravia. He managed to escape at Burghausen, but was recaptured, tortured, and beheaded at Burghausen on July 5, 1585. In his case, too, the attitude of the populace was apparent. When he was told to deny only the doctrines of baptism and communion, Sumerauer replied, "Leave me in peace. I want to die upon my faith." Thereupon the executioner said, "I do not like to put you to death; but if I do not do it, another will." His death was commemorated by the Brethren in a hymn.

Great zeal in persecuting the Anabaptists was shown by Archbishop Wolf Dietrich von Raitenau. In a decree of July 1, 1593, he ordered that Anabaptists should be killed by fire and sword, and the property of fugitives be confiscated. The last Anabaptists were no doubt, with few exceptions, wiped out by the Counter Reformation, which had already been carried out in the neighboring Inner Austrian provinces in 1598.   LOSERTH.

Beck, *Geschichts-Bücher;* Zieglschmid, *Chronik;* Wolkan, *Geschicht-Buch;* Johann Loserth, "Geschichte der Wiedertäufer in Salzburg," in *Mitteilungen der Gesellschaft für Landeskunde* LII; *ML* IV.

Salzman, Thomas, a sheath maker in Strasbourg, Alsace, was put to death by beheading in 1527 on a charge of denying the deity of Christ. In his trial he approved of "the plans of the Anabaptists," but it is not known that he belonged to an Anabaptist group.   HEGE.

T. W. Röhrich, "Zur Gesch. der strassburgischen Wiedertäufer," in *Ztscht für historische Theologie,* 1860, 14, 30; *ML* IV.

Sam, Konrad (1483-1535), reformer of Ulm (*q.v.*), Germany, pastor at Brackenheim near Heilbronn, came to Ulm in 1524, and died there in 1535. According to Calvary (p. 33) he "leaned strongly toward Anabaptist teachings, namely, those of Johann Hut," in his book *Ain schöner wolgeteütschter gründlicher bericht, für den gemeinen menschen, ob der leyb Jesu Christi im himel zu der Rechten Gottes zu eren, und im Geist zu suchen oder auff erden im brot wesentlich zu verhoffen sey* (Ulm, 1526). This assertion has not yet been investigated.   NEFF.

ADB XXX, 304-5; G. Bossert, "Zur Biographie von Konrad Sam," *W. Vjh.* 1889, 28; H. Hermelink, *Geschichte der Evangelischen Kirche in Württemberg von der Reformation bis zur Gegenwart* (Tübingen, 1949); K. Th. Keim, *Die Reformation in der Reichsstadt Ulm* (1851); J. Rauscher, *Württembergische Ref.-Gesch.* (Stuttgart, 1934); R. Schmid, *Ref.-Gesch. Württembergs* (Heilbronn, 1904); S. Calvary, *Verzeichnis seltener und wertvoller Bücher* (Berlin, 1868); *ML* IV.

Samara (now Kuibyshev), a province of Russia located on the Volga River, also the name of the capital of the province. To the north it borders on the province of Kazan, in the west on Simbirsk, in the south on Astrachan, and in the east on Ufa, Orenburg, and the Ural Mountains. It consists of 20,000 square miles and had a population of three million at the turn of the century.

In 1853 Mennonites direct from Prussia established the Trakt (*q.v.*) settlement consisting of 10 villages and an acreage of 37,800 in the southern part of the province near the Volga River. In 1859 a second settlement of Prussian Mennonites was started in the province known as Alexandertal (*q.v.*) or Alt-Samara consisting of 8 villages and an acreage of 26,500, which later was nearly doubled.

In 1890 the daughter settlement of Pleshanovsk (*q.v.*) or Neu-Samara, consisting of 12 villages and an acreage of 59,400, was established east of Alexandertal. In 1897 a small group of Alexandertal Mennonites established a settlement near Bezentchuk (*q.v.*) in the vicinity of the city of Samara. Originally the settlement consisted of some 75 persons with an acreage of 5,400.

Before World War II these four settlements in the province of Samara consisted of a total of approximately 35 villages, and a population of 6,750 with an acreage of 176,580. Samara and Saratoff were the provinces on the Volga River in which large non-Mennonite German settlements were established, which under the Soviets were organized for a while as the German Volga Republic. According to available information, most of these German settlements, including those of the Mennonites, disintegrated before and during World War II. Most of the population was sent beyond the Ural Mountains.   C.K.

Die Mennoniten-Gemeinden in Russland (Heilbronn, 1921); Jacob Quiring, *Die Mundart von Chortitza in Süd-Russland* (Munich, 1928).

Sambsfeuer, Wilhelm, an Anabaptist martyr, was executed at Michelsburg (*q.v.*) in Tirol, Austria, on June 17, 1529.   HEGE.

Samen Een is the name of a conference center, particularly for camping and youth activities, on a lake near Giethoorn (*q.v.*), Netherlands. Samen Een has been in operation since July 1932.   vDZ.

Samer, Peter: see **Saymer.**

Samland, an area near Königsberg (*q.v.*) in former East Prussia. Mennonites from West Prussia settled here in 1714 and organized a congregation, which soon numbered about 250 members. For the history of this congregation see **Lithuania, Bagdannen,** and **Tilsit.** (*Inv. Arch. Amst.* I, No. 701.)   vDZ.

Sammlung Georg Leibbrandt is a series of publications dealing with the former German population in Russia, prepared under the direction of Ernst Meynen. Georg Leibbrandt, after whom the series is named, had written numerous books on the German population in Russia and was prominent in this field during the days of Hitler and the occupation of Russia during World War II. The full series appeared in several subsections.

Of special significance for Mennonite research are the volumes III, IV, and VI of the section *Quellen und Materialien zur Erforschung des Deutschtums in Osteuropa.* They are: Hans Rempel, *Deutsche Bauernleistung am Schwarzen Meer, Bevölkerung und Wirtschaft 1825* (108 pp., Leipzig, 1941); Margarete Woltner, *Die Gemeindeberichte von 1848 der deutschen Siedlungen am Schwarzen Meer* (230 pp., Leipzig, 1942); and Otto Auhagen, *Die Schicksalswende des russland-deutschen Bauerntums in den Jahren 1927-1930* (197 pp., Leipzig, 1942). Of great significance are also the two publications by K. Stumpp which appeared in the *Sammlung Georg Leibbrandt* (Publikationsstelle Ost, Berlin, 1943) under the titles *Bericht über das Gebiet Chortitza* and *Bericht über das Gebeit Kronau-Orloff.* (Orloff is the Zagradovka Mennonite settlement.) These two books consist primarily of tables on the Mennonite economic and cultural life of these settlements, report at length about the economic and human losses sustained by these settlements from the Revolution to the evacuation in 1943. It is not known whether similar reports exist for other settlements.

Another section of the *Sammlung Georg Leibbrandt,* entitled *Die deutschen Siedlungen in der Sowjetunion,* consisted of five volumes (Berlin, 1941), which have the special inscription *Sonderausgabe. Nur für den Dienstgebrauch.* These booklets deal with regions having a German population and contain large maps of the areas enclosed in pockets in the back. They list names of places and provinces, German population statistics, and the geographical location. Of special interest for Mennonites are volume III, *Ukraine mit Krim,* and volume IV, *Dongebiet und Kaukasus.*

Unfortunately very few copies of some of these publications survived World War II. In some instances only one or two copies are extant (Hans Rempel's book). Although these publications appeared during the height of Hitler's campaign and propaganda, they contain very valuable and factual information about the Mennonites of Russia and have been used extensively in the ENCYCLOPEDIA articles.   C.K.

San Joaquin Valley, a 250-mile-long valley in central California, separated from the Pacific Ocean by the Coast Ranges, and extending some 70 miles wide eastward to the Sierra Nevada. It extends from the Tehachapi Mountains in the south to Stockton in the north. The river gets its water largely from the Sierra Nevada. The development of the valley began during the Gold Rush of the last century. One hundred years ago it was a barren, worthless desert. Today, through irrigation, it is one of the most productive, diversified, and richest farming areas in the nation.

A total of some 5,100 baptized members of five Mennonite conferences live in the valley, grouped into three major geographical areas: Bakersfield-Shafter in the southern end of the valley with 1,025 members (4 MB congregations with 969 members, 2 in Shafter, one in Bakersfield, and one in Rosedale, and one GCM in Shafter with 56); the central area 70-100 miles to the north (from Dinuba to Fresno and Madera) with 3,323 members (7 MB congregations with 2,440, including 4 in Fresno with 585, Reedley with 1,436, Dinuba with 381, and Madera with 38, 2 GCM with 645, including Reedley with 593 and Fresno with 52, and one KMB at Dinuba with 238); the northern area 60 miles north of Fresno with 627 members (2 CGC with 433, including Winton with 143 and Livingston with 290, one MC at Winton with 75, one GCM at Winton with 68, and one MB at Winton with 51). There are also two small MB churches above Stockton at Lodi (114) and Victor (25). Thus there are in the valley by conferences: MB 3,599, GCM 769, CGC 433, KMB 238, MC 75, a total of 5,114.

In the Shafter-Wasco area near Bakersfield the potato and cotton industries are predominant. Mennonites have settled here since the beginning of the 20th century, and have established prosperous communities with churches at Shafter (*q.v.*), Rosedale, and Bakersfield (*q.v.*).

North of this area in the Reedley-Fresno area the Mennonites established themselves around the turn of the century. The first Mennonites came to Reedley in 1903. In 1905 the M.B. church was organized and by 1906 the G.C.M. church. Some of the early settlers came from Kansas and Minnesota. At that time the land consisted mainly of grain fields as far as it was cultivated. New methods of cultivation and the problem of marketing their products caused many difficulties. Irrigation was also a major problem. Gradually the grape and raisin industry was accepted also by Mennonites. They raise wine grapes, raisin grapes, table grapes, and sweet grapes, the table and raisin varieties being the most extensively grown. For raisins the Thompson and Muscat varieties are

San Joaquin Valley, California

Churches ● ⊘ Churches in towns   ○ Towns and cities
⬡ Largest cities   ▫ Institutions

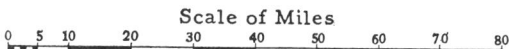

Scale of Miles
0 5 10   20   30   40   50   60   70   80

Name of Church

GENERAL CONFERENCE MENNONITE (GCM)

1. Mennonite Community (Fresno)
2. First Mennonite (Paso Robles)
3. Willow Creek (Paso Robles)
4. First Mennonite (Reedley)
5. First Mennonite (Shafter)

MENNONITE BRETHREN (MB)

6. Bakersfield
7. Dinuba
8. Fresno, Bethany
9. Fresno, Butler Ave.
10. Lodi
11. Madera
12. Reedley
13. Rosedale (Bakersfield)
14. San Jose
15. Shafter
16. South Shafter

17. Winton
18. Sunset Gardens (Fresno)
19. West Park (Fresno)

MENNONITE (MC)

20. Sharon (Winton)

KRIMMER MENNONITE BRETHREN (KMB)

21. Zion (Dinuba)

EVANGELICAL MENNONITE BRETHREN (EMB)

22. Grace (Reedley)

CHURCH OF GOD IN CHRIST MENNONITE (CGCM)

23. Winton
24. Livingston

INSTITUTIONS

25. Pacific Bible Institute (Fresno)
26. Kings View Hospital (Reedley)
27. Immanuel Bible Academy (Reedley)
28. Mennonite Brethren Home for the Aged (Reedley)
29. Mennonite Brethren Biblical Seminary (Fresno)
30. Mennonite Central Com. Clothing Center (Reedley)
31. Mennonite Central Com. Personnel Center (Reedley)

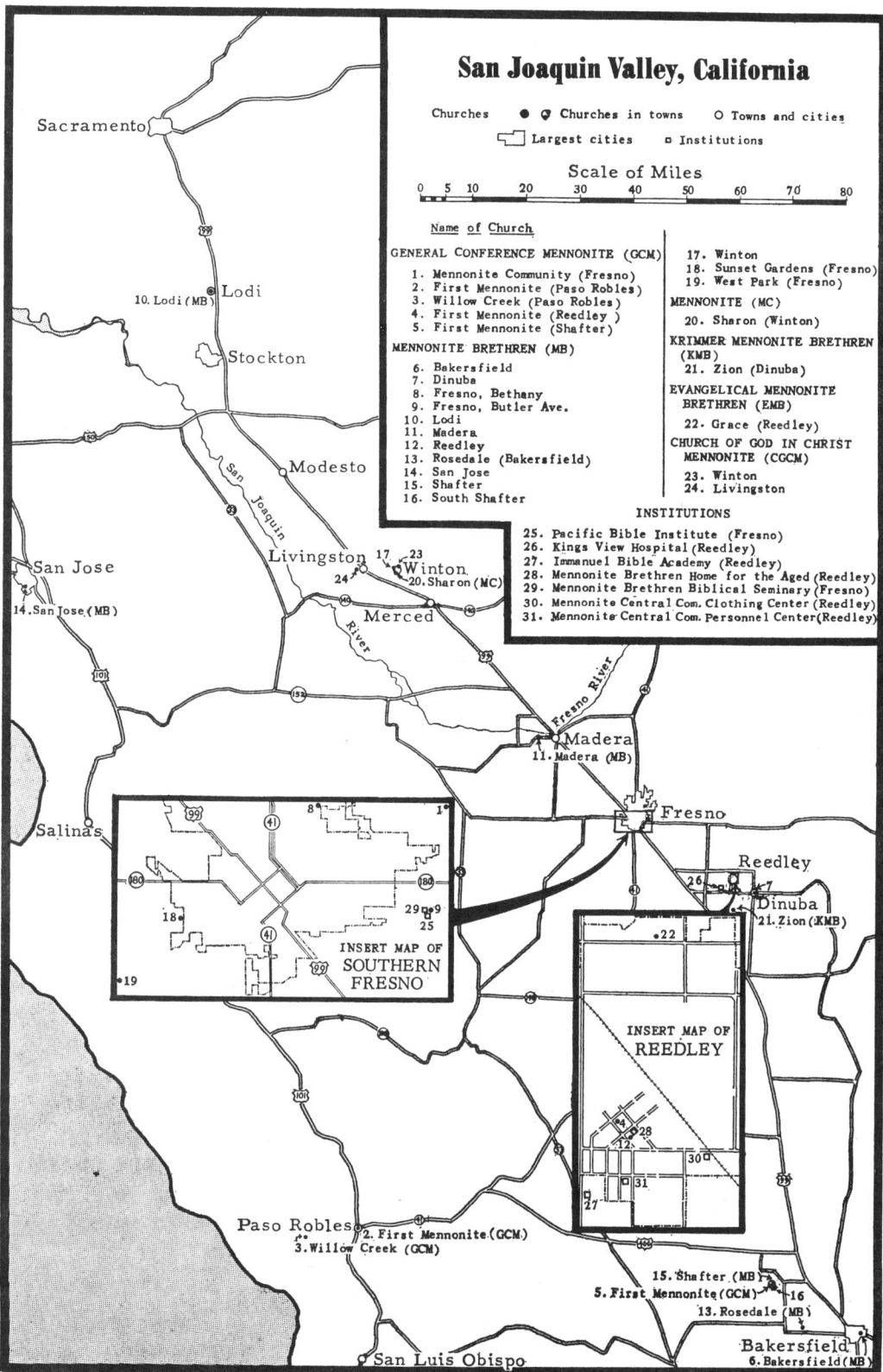

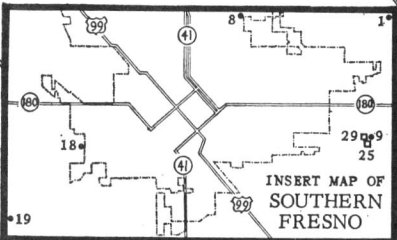

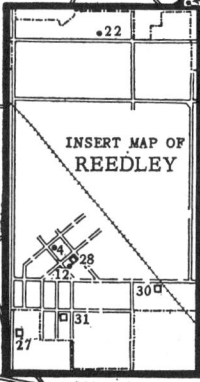

Sacramento
10. Lodi (MB) Lodi
Stockton
Modesto
San Jose
14. San Jose (MB)
Livingston 17 23 Winton
24 20. Sharon (MC)
Merced
San Joaquin River
Fresno River
Madera
11. Madera (MB)
Fresno
Reedley
26 4 7
Dinuba
21. Zion (KMB)
Salinas

INSERT MAP OF SOUTHERN FRESNO
8 1
18
29 9
25
19

INSERT MAP OF REEDLEY
22
4
12 28
30
31
27

Paso Robles 2. First Mennonite (GCM)
3. Willow Creek (GCM)
15. Shafter (MB)
5. First Mennonite (GCM) 16
13. Rosedale (MB)
Bakersfield
6. Bakersfield (MB)
San Luis Obispo

the most suitable. In 1950 the purchase price of a good bearing vineyard varied from $300 to $1,000 per acre including buildings and frequently some equipment. Ninety per cent of commercially grown grapes in the United States are grown in California, primarily in the San Joaquin Valley.

Eighty-six per cent of the Mennonites of California live in the valley, including almost a third of the M.B. membership in the United States.   C.K.

Arnold C. Ewy, "The Grape and Raisin Industry," *Menn. Life* V (October 1950) 4-9; Vernon Neufeld, "The Shafter-Wasco Community," *Menn. Life* VII (October 1952) 158-64; Arlene Sitler, "M.C.C.–San Joaquin Valley Project," *Menn. Life* VI (July 1951) 407; Walter Goldschmidt, *As You Sow* (New York, 1947).

San Jose Mennonite Brethren Church, located at 1195 Clark St., in San Jose, Cal., 45 miles from San Francisco, was organized on Oct. 20, 1940, with 20 charter members. Five pastors have served the congregation: D. J. Gerbrandt, J. J. Gerbrandt, A. Nickel, J. K. Warkentin, and William Neufeld, the present (1957) pastor. The congregation has used five places of worship. It began in a small Legion Hall until a small building on Montgomery Street could be purchased. Later a larger building was secured on Delmas Street. After this building was sold and until the present church was built (1951), the congregation met in Germania Hall. The membership in 1957 was 365.   W.NE.

San Juan Colony, near the city of Irapuato, Mexico, a short-lived (1924-25) colonization effort by a group of Mennonite refugees from Russia, sponsored by H. P. Krehbiel and other Mennonites of Kansas, as a well-intended but nevertheless a rival colony to the Rosario Colony (*q.v.*). See also **Irapuato** and **Mennonite Colonization Board.**   H.S.B.

San Luis Potosi, one of the 28 states of Mexico. A small settlement of six Old Order Mennonite and Old Order Amish families was made in 1944 in a tropical area of this state about 130 miles inland from the gulf coast town of Tampico, led by Aaron Martin, of Lancaster County, Pa. The move to Mexico was made partially in protest to the governmental restrictions brought on by World War II; Martin and his followers were protesting against the militarization of America. For a short time (1943) these families lived with the Old Colony Mennonites in Chihuahua. In 1944 they settled in this isolated section of San Luis Potosi. The settlement effort was brief. After a few years Martin died and the rest of the families scattered, most of them returning to the United States.   J.W.F.

San Marcos Mennonite Church (GCM), located at Chimney Rock near Paso Robles, Cal., was the first Pacific District Conference church to be organized in California. In 1896-97 six Mennonite families from Beatrice, Neb., settled 10 miles northwest of Paso Robles, including the minister, A. J. Wiebe. During these years another Mennonite settlement was established in the Estrella district, east of Paso Robles, among whom was Jacob Hege, a preacher. In 1897 these two groups, though rather far apart, organized a congregation. Hege was elected elder and Wiebe his assistant. In 1898 the congregation built its first church at Chimney Rock, northwest

of Paso Robles. Since the two settlements were so widely separated, and transportation was difficult, it became necessary to establish two meeting places, one group continuing to meet at the new church with Wiebe, while the other group met in an adobe church near Estrella with Hege. Monthly union meetings were conducted in order to maintain the spirit of fellowship between them.

In the fall of 1901 John K. Lichti was called to assist Hege at Estrella. In May 1903 a joint council was called at Paso Robles to discuss various problems within the congregation. The discussion became so acute that the congregation was ordered dissolved. The group at Estrella immediately organized as the First Mennonite Church of Paso Robles (*q.v.*). The western group organized in 1904, with 39 members, taking the name San Marcos Mennonite Church. F. F. Jantzen was the first elder, with A. J. Wiebe continuing as minister. The San Marcos meetinghouse was moved to Willow Creek in 1911, but the congregation continued to be called San Marcos. In 1943 the name was changed to Second Mennonite Church of Paso Robles, and in 1954 to Willow Creek (*q.v.*). In 1958 the membership was 122, with J. M. Galle as interim pastor.   H.D.B.

H. D. Burkholder, *The Story of Our Conference and Church* (1951) 37-43.

Sanctification (German, *Heiligung*). This theological term, seldom used in older Mennonite writing, refers historically to the process by which the Christian who has come to faith in Christ and been justified and regenerated or born again is made holy. The meaning of the term will therefore depend upon the meaning put into the word "holy." In common Christian usage "holy" means morally pure and righteous as God is pure and righteous. Sanctification is therefore generally used to mean the deliverance of the personal life of the Christian from the impurity and power of sin. Actually the original meaning of the New Testament (also Old Testament) word for "make holy" is to dedicate or consecrate to God and His use, and it is used thus of Christ sanctifying Himself (John 10:36 and John 17:19), but it is also so used of disciples and even of things. The derivative meaning of make clean or purify is, however, also clearly used (I Cor. 1:2; I Thess. 5:25; Rom. 15:16; Eph. 5:36, etc.). The two meanings should not be separated, and they are often apparently both intended in the one expression.

The fact of the two meanings has contributed to theological confusion, in addition to confusion caused by varying understandings of the nature of redemption and the agent of sanctification, whether the Holy Spirit, God, Christ, or the Christian himself. As a consequence some view sanctification as an immediate act of God or the Spirit following justification, thus in effect confusing it with the latter. Most hold it to be a process in which the grace of God, working through the Holy Spirit, in cooperation with the endeavors of the individual to lay hold upon truth and grace, to resist temptation, to exercise piety and devotion, and to perform conscious obedience (though with the real possibility of sudden or large progress as well as reversals and decline), combine for growth in grace, in holy living, and in conformity to the image of Christ. The direct appeals of Paul (Rom. 12; Rom. 6; Gal. 5) as well as Christ Himself (Sermon on the Mount) clearly justify this assumption.

Some consider sanctification to be an instantaneous act of the Holy Spirit subsequent to conversion and distinct from justification and the individual's own efforts at holy living. This view, commonly called "second work of grace," or "second blessing," derives from Wesleyan teaching, and has been accepted by a few Mennonites (e.g., United Missionary Church, *q.v.*) under Wesleyan influence. Experientially it has a certain measure of support in the experience many Christians have of a conscious renewal or reconsecration, either after an inadequate experience due to too early conversion or to lack of proper teaching and understanding of the realities and possibilities of God's gracious working through the Holy Spirit and the necessity for full surrender, consecration, and living up to the privileges of the believer in Christ. To elevate this to a dogma of a necessary second experience for all in the form of an act of God in the plan of salvation is quite another matter.

Further differences arise out of the understanding of the degree of sanctification. The Wesleyan doctrine of perfectionism or near perfectionism was meant by Wesley primarily as an assertion of perfectibility, i.e., the possibility of real victory over sin and the attainment of a growing and ultimate high degree of holiness. To turn this into the doctrine of instantaneous entire sanctification or total eradication of sin, as some do, is something quite different and is contrary to the description by Paul, for instance, of the continuing conflict in the Christian's experience between the spirit and the flesh (Gal. 5) and the need for "mortifying" the flesh (Rom. 6) and "putting off the old man," and "putting on the new man" (Col. 3), or even the reference to "carnal" Christians (I Cor.). This doctrine has found very little, if any, entry into Mennonite circles.

The general Wesleyan ideas on sanctification, and the modifications or even perversions of these by later followers and groups, have produced, especially in the United States, what is often called the Holiness Movement with a number of new sects and subdivisions arising particularly in the second half of the 19th century. The schisms in the Methodist Church itself in the 19th century did not usually produce extremist sanctification emphases, but a rather wholesome type, while of course including the "second blessing" and perfectionist or eradication doctrines. These were the Methodist Protestant (1830), Wesleyan Methodist (1843), and Free Methodist (1860) churches, of which the latter two are still continuing as small denominations. There are many other "holiness" churches, some of which include the adjective "Methodist" in their titles. The Mennonite Brethren in Christ (*q.v.*) are a group with a moderate holiness emphasis. The Brethren in Christ (*q.v.*) on the whole can be classed here, although the specific holiness doctrines are not uniformly held among them today. Many of the moderate "holiness" denominations are members of the National Holiness Association.

The more extreme groups (now often moderated) are usually associated with the National Holiness Movement, which arose about 1867, out of which certain denominations emerged. One such is the Church of the Nazarene, which was formed out of a series of mergers with name changes, assuming its final form in 1919; it forms the "right wing" of the Holiness Movement. The Pilgrim Holiness Church (1897) is very similar to the Nazarene Church. The Christian and Missionary Alliance (1887), founded by A. B. Simpson, a Presbyterian perfectionist, as an alliance of congregations, is in effect a denomination. It developed a strong doctrine of faith healing, rejecting ordinary medical practice. The Church of God (Anderson) is also a moderate holiness denomination. But there are several "Churches of God" who are among the more extreme groups, which fall into the Pentecostal or radical wing of the Holiness Movement. The Pentecostal movement has in the 20th century had an extraordinary growth in the United States, and abroad by missionary activity. It has added to the usual "holiness" emphasis the charismatic teaching about the revival of certain pentecostal gifts, usually only two, the gift of tongues and the gift of healing. One of the most rapidly growing of these groups is the Assemblies of God.

Mennonites on the whole have been relatively untouched by either the radical holiness or pentecostal influences, although individuals have occasionally fallen victim, e.g., in France and in the United States and Canada. Prompt disciplinary action has usually excised the threat, or the individuals have withdrawn. About 1913 the entrance of moderate "holiness" teaching caused a schism in the Pennsylvania Mennonite (MC) congregation near Hesston, Kan., resulting in the formation of an independent group, locally called the David Zook Church.

Because of the above connotations, most Mennonites have been disinclined to use the term. Actually the insistence on real sanctification of life and true holy living is a major basic Anabaptist concept. The concept of discipleship includes holiness as its ethical aspect. But the twin idea of dedication to Christ and His cause is also an integral part of discipleship. The Anabaptist insistence on "newness of life," on bringing faith into "evidence," on the full lordship of Christ and obedience to His commands, on the development of Christian character and separation from the world of sin, all this is "holiness" in its best sense. The fruit of this emphasis was a rather uniformly high quality of moral life and holy behavior among the Anabaptists, which was testified to even by their enemies again and again. The Anabaptists were even accused of "hypocrisy," of putting on a pious life to attract members. (It is true that their sincere holy living was a powerful attraction.) The eagerness to be strict in holy living did lead at times to a certain amount of moralism and legalism, of which their enemies, the Reformers, were all too ready to accuse them. In response to the Reformers' charge of a "Scheinheiligkeit," the Anabaptists brought the charge against the Reformers of a "Scheinglauben," quite in the spirit of the Book of James.

The Mennonite demand for true holiness and discipleship has persisted throughout the history of the brotherhood, but has often been threatened or perverted by the twin dangers of moralism and legalism. The group has been charged with perfectionism and claiming to be a perfect church, especially during Anabaptist times, because of its insistence upon striving to attain the ideal of a church "without spot or wrinkle" (Eph. 5:27). But this charge is easily refuted by the simple observation that insistence upon discipline, including the ban, presupposes the possibility of failure in life and apostasy in faith. The endeavor to attain the spotless state has at times led to another very serious consequence, namely, censoriousness and divisiveness, and has produced not a few schisms, not only in the 16th century but also later. It has been noted that practically all Mennonite schisms have arisen out of differences as to the degree of "holiness" or discipline to be required of members. These perversions, however, in no way invalidate the major principle that Christ requires of His disciples absolute holiness and perfection (Be ye perfect, even as your Father in heaven is perfect) properly understood, that the Father's will is to be done on earth as in heaven. Paul calls repeatedly for perfect, i.e., mature members (*teleioi*). To surrender this ideal with the concept that in a sinful world it is impossible to attain such an ideal, and that therefore the Christian is at liberty to compromise and that the church should not discipline for sin, but that all Christians should live in trustful hope for the attainment of the ideal outside of history, placing the major emphasis "in the here and now" on forgiveness, is in the Anabaptist-Mennonite understanding not only unscriptural but indeed a betrayal of the lordship of Christ. H.S.B.

H. S. Bender, "The Anabaptist Vision," *MQR* XVII (1944) 67-88; G. F. Hershberger, editor, *The Recovery of the Anabaptist Vision* (Scottdale, 1957); "Special Anabaptist Theology Number," *MQR* XXXII (1950); Cornelius Krahn, *Menno Simons* (Karlsruhe, 1936); Elmer T. Clark, *The Small Sects in America* (New York, 1949); *ML* II, 277-79.

Sander Hendriksz, an Anabaptist martyr, executed (probably by beheading) in the Steen castle at Antwerp, Belgium, on Nov. 19, 1558. He is named as No. 34 in the hymn "Aenhoort, Godt, hemelsche Vader," No. 16 in the *Lietboecxken* (*q.v.*). The brief information on this martyr found in van Braght's *Martyrs' Mirror* is borrowed from this hymn. Génard has published more particulars about Sander, including the exact date of execution. He was known as Alexander de Bode (i.e., Messenger), and was probably a "weetdoener" of the Antwerp congregation, who visited the members to announce the time and place of the next meeting. Sander was a cabinetmaker by trade. (See **Alexander de Bode,** which this article supplements.) vD Z.

Offer, 566; *Mart. Mir.* D 202, E 639; *Antw. Arch-Bl.* VIII, 452, 465; XIV, 24 f., No. 269; *ML* II, 282.

Sander Woutersz, an Anabaptist martyr, burned at the stake on Sept. 3, 1572, at Amsterdam, Netherlands. He was a native of Bommel, i.e., Zaltbommel in the Dutch province of Gelderland, and a tailor by trade. Evert Hendriks (*q.v.*) of Warendorp was executed with him. They were the last two Anabaptists to die in Amsterdam. Van Braght in the *Martyrs' Mirror,* though publishing the sentence in full, does not give much information about these martyrs. Grosheide has published some particulars from the records: Sander moved to Amsterdam in 1534 or 1535; he also lived in a village near Dordrecht, but the last years before his arrest he was living again at Amsterdam. About 1560 he was baptized by Joost Verbeek (*q.v.*). In his house sometimes meetings were held in which he or one of the brethren read a chapter from the Bible, followed by a "vermaning" (sermon). He was tortured on the rack, but did not reveal particulars concerning the congregation. His property was confiscated. (*Mart. Mir.* D 620 f., E 944; Grosheide, *Bijdrage,* 184 f.) vD Z.

Sanders van Gremberghe (Grimberge), the son of Gillis, an Anabaptist martyr, a native of Gent in Flanders, Belgium, was executed there on March 2, 1560, at the age of thirty-one by burning at the stake on the Vrijdagsmarkt, together with Joos de Vinck, Joos de Vlaminc, Michiel van Houcke, and Joos van de Velde. Further particulars are not available. (Verheyden, *Gent,* 26, No. 72.) vD Z.

Sandhill Community Church, located about 6 miles northeast of Clarence, N.Y., was used by the western New York Mennonite (MC) congregation that took rise in 1920 when several families of Mennonites were attracted by low-priced farms in the vicinity of Lockport, Akron, and Clarence. The Rural Mission Board of Ontario gave aid for organization and ministerial help. In 1923 a congregation was organized in a brick church east of Akron. Soon the place of worship moved to the Sandhill church. For a few years from 1923 Irvin E. Burkhart ministered to the congregation. Others who preached here were Chris L. Ressler, D. D. Kauffman, and Jacob W. Birky. In 1928 this congregation joined the Mennonite Conference of Ontario. The membership grew to almost 200. In the late 1930's a new meetinghouse was built nearer Clarence (see **Clarence** Mennonite Church), and Sandhill fell into disuse for the Mennonites. J.C.F.

Sandhill Hutterite Bruderhof, near Beiseker, Alberta, belonging to the Dariusleut (*q.v.*) branch, was founded in 1936 by a group from the Springvale (*q.v.*) Colony, with the preacher Jacob K. Wurz. The Sandhill Bruderhof has in turn founded the Ferrybank Colony at Ponaka, Alberta, and is in process of establishing a Bruderhof at Leask, Sask. Ministers ordained by Sandhill are Frank A. Wollman and John M. Wurz. In 1958 the baptized membership was 46, and the total number of souls 160. J.M.W.

Sandy Bottom Mennonite Church (MC), Swift Run, Va., established in 1946, is a mission congregation. Aldine Brenneman was the pastor of its 18 members in 1957. M.G.

Sandy Hill Mennonite Church (MC), located at Sadsburyville, Pa., was established in 1947. In 1957 it had 80 members with R. Clair Umble as pastor, in the Ohio and Eastern Conference. M.G.

Sangerhausen, a town of Thuringia, Germany, in the vicinity of which the Anabaptist movement won a large following during the Reformation. The movement was brutally suppressed. In or about 1535 twelve Anabaptists were put to death for their faith. But it took several years to stamp it out completely. (Wappler, *Thüringen; ML* IV.)

Sanitarium, Bethesda, at Hillsboro, Kans., was opened in 1920 by J. V. Wiebe in a two-story building adjacent to the Salem Hospital (*q.v.*) for the purpose of caring for the sick, poor, and aged. Later the building was taken over by the Salem Home for the Aged of Hillsboro. (*A Guide to Hillsboro,* 1940, 54.)   C.K.

Sankra (Zion) Mennonite Church (MC), located in Madhya Pradesh, 18 miles west of Dhamtari, a member of the India Mennonite Conference, began as a mission in 1908, under M. C. Lapp, P. A. Friesen, and G. J. Lapp, and was at first called the Zion Evangelistic Station. The first Christians came from other mission stations. Worship services were conducted on the veranda of the bungalow. In 1912 the Malguzar of Sankra offered a small plot of land in the hamlet for a church building, and in 1913 a small meetinghouse was built. The Christian community grew rapidly during the famine of 1920-21 when many people came to this and other mission stations for relief and responded to the appeals of the Gospel. A new and larger church was built in 1925 at the mission station, a mile from the village. Under Dr. Friesen a larger medical dispensary with an operating room and several wards was built in 1926. The missionaries also conducted roadside medical clinics. Soon after the Christian community was established at Sankra an elementary school for the children of the community was opened. The government school was some distance away. The children received more kindly consideration in the church schools. In 1946 the name appeared in the Yearbook (Scottdale) as Zion. In 1957 the membership was 102, with O. P. Lal and S. Paul Miller as ministers.   G.J.L.

Sankt Johann (Johanniskirchen): see **Johann, Sankt.**

Sankt Johann (Sant Johannes), a Hutterite Bruderhof in Hungary. Its inmates fled into the forest on Nov. 4, 1623, when it was attacked by Turks and Tatars. Twenty-six persons were abducted (women and children); only two returned, and one of these had to leave her child behind. In September 1663 the house was plundered by Turkish troops; two brethren who had remained were murdered and two boys carried away. In the following years the Bruderhof declined rapidly, so that by 1757 only six families remained. On March 12, 1761, the decree of the chancellor (see **Sobotiste**) was announced which compelled them and all the other Bruderhofs in Hungary to adopt the Catholic faith. The leader, Johannes Mayer, was arrested and transferred to the Jesuits in Stuhlweissenburg. Meanwhile the Brethren refused to attend the services of the Jesuit priests (see **Hildesheim** and **Halle**). Mayer finally declared himself willing to take the required step and was released on October 2. At the end of October he arrived at St. Johann, a sick and broken man. Jacob

Schulz, the lay member who resisted the violent conversion most vigorously, was also delivered to the Jesuits in Tyrnau. The brotherhood at St. Johann had no property in common at this time. Most of the members were not to be persuaded by kind words or by violence to become Catholic, declaring that the mandates were contrary to their principles. But finally those who did not flee yielded to force. By March 11, 1763, seventy-nine persons, fifty of whom were married, declared their transfer to the Catholic faith. (Beck, *Geschichts-Bücher;* Zieglschmid, *Klein-Geschichtsbuch; ML* IV.)   HEGE.

Santa Catarina, a coastal state in Brazil (area 36,435 sq. mi., pop. 1,578,159), lying between Parana on the north and Rio Grande do Sul on the south, in 1930 became the home of two colonies settled by Mennonite refugees from Russia, Krauel (*q.v.*), called Witmarsum, and Auhagen (*q.v.*) on the Stoltz Plateau. Both colonies were sponsored by the German government and settled on land purchased from the Hanseatische Kolonisations-Gesellschaft. The Auhagen Colony was abandoned in 1934, the settlers moving to Curitiba. The Krauel Colony was dissolved in 1952, and most of the families have moved away, some earlier to Curitiba, others at the very end to Bage in Rio Grande do Sul. Heinrich Martens, the original leader of the colony, early settled in Blumenau, the capital of the state, where he remains as one of the few Mennonites left in Santa Catarina.   H.S.B.

Santa Clara Sommerfeld Mennonite settlement at Chihuahua, Mexico, located north of the Manitoba Mennonite settlement, was established in 1926(?) by some 600 Sommerfeld Mennonites from Manitoba. For a while, *c*1950, the Mennonite Central Committee operated a hospital there. The General Conference Mennonite Mission Board was operating an elementary school at this place in 1957. C.K.

Santa Fe Railroad Company (or Atchison, Topeka and Santa Fe Railway Company) was founded by Cyrus Holliday and incorporated in 1859. The Santa Fe deserves considerable credit for a large number of Mennonites settling on its land north and south of Newton, Kan., in 1873 and later. The railroad had reached Newton by 1871 and had received a land grant of three million acres from the federal government. Interested in settling this land, the railroad employed successful agents and produced literature to attract settlers. One of the earliest leaflets carried the title "If You Want a Farm or Home You Should Buy of the Atchison, Topeka and Santa Fe Railway for the Following Reasons." Many of these promotional pamphlets were translated into foreign languages and distributed not only among people arriving in America, but also among prospective immigrants in Europe. One was entitled *Die Mennoniten Niederlassung auf den Ländereien der Atchison, Topeka und Santa Fe Eisenbahn-Gesellschaft in Harvey & Marion Co., Kansas,* which was published by the "Committee zur Ordnung der Ansiedlerangelegenheiten der Mennoniten . . ." and written by David Goerz. The committee consisted of Christian Krehbiel, Jakob Leisy, David Lehmann, Bernhard Warkentin, and Abraham Naufer, of Sum-

28

merfield, Ill. The pamphlet *Die Deutschen Ansiedlungen in Süd West Kansas auf den Ländereien der Atchison, Topeka & Santa Fe Eisenbahngesellschaft*, published in Topeka in 1878, was possibly also written by David Goerz (*q.v.*) and appealed particularly to the German and Mennonite settlers. It contains numerous illustrations of Mennonite farms.

The earliest Mennonite settlers in the Santa Fe territory were the Amish near Hutchinson. Eli M. Yoder purchased 300 acres of land which resulted in this settlement. The agents Case and Billings of Marion Center sold 5,000 acres to M. W. Keim and his friends of Johnstown, Pa., in 1869-70. With the coming of the Mennonites from Russia, Mennonites from Summerfield, Ill., also became interested in settling in Kansas. Christian Krehbiel (*q.v.*) became a promoter of this venture. A. E. Touzalin, George Heriot, and C. B. Schmidt were the early Santa Fe agents through whom the contacts were made. Peter and Jacob Funk established themselves in Marion County in 1873. Bernhard Warkentin was an early promoter of the settlement of the Santa Fe land and established himself with the Summerfield Mennonites at Halstead, Kan. When Touzalin resigned as land commissioner for the Santa Fe, he was replaced by A. S. Johnson under whom C. B. Schmidt (*q.v.*) of Lawrence, Kan., worked among the German-speaking settlers. When the Alexanderwohl group arrived in 1874, Schmidt met them in New York.

C. B. Schmidt received a commission from the Santa Fe to visit Russia to encourage immigrants to come to Kansas, in order to settle on the Santa Fe land. He left New York on Feb. 1, 1875, with many letters of introduction from Mennonites in Kansas to their relatives and neighbors. He also stopped in West Prussia. Schmidt had been in contact with some of the twelve delegates who came to investigate the land of the Great Plains. Of the 1,275 Mennonite families who came to America in 1874, six hundred families came to Kansas. The Santa Fe had considerable competition from other railroads, particularly the Kansas Pacific and the Burlington. The large groups of immigrants were met in New York and other places and the agents tried to persuade them to settle on the lands of their respective companies. In spite of C. B. Schmidt's trip to Russia in 1875, the preceding year, 1874, remained the peak year for the Mennonite migration to settle on Santa Fe land in Kansas, when nearly 3,000 Mennonites came to Kansas. The Santa Fe deserves a considerable amount of credit for this large-scale successful settlement. (See also **Kansas** and **Newton**.)   C.K.

C. J. Dyck, "Kansas Promotional Activities with particular emphasis on Mennonites" (M.A. thesis, University of Wichita) 1955; C. Henry Smith, *The Coming of the Russian Mennonites* (Berne, 1927); L. L. Waters, *Steel Trails to Santa Fe* (Lawrence, 1950); Helen B. Shipley, "The Migration of the Mennonites from Russia, 1873-1883, and Their Settlement in Kansas" (M.A. thesis, University of Minnesota) 1954; C. B. Schmidt, "Reminiscences of Foreign Immigration Work for Kansas," Kansas State Historical Society, *Transactions*, IX: 485-97 (1906); G. D. Bradley, *The Story of the Santa Fe* (Boston, 1920); James Marshall, *Santa Fe, the Railroad That Built an Empire* (N.Y., 1945).

Santa Rosa (Argentina) Mennonite Church, located at Santa Rosa, F.C.O. Pampa, Argentine Republic. Santa Rosa (pop. 20,000) is the capital of La Pampa. It is located about 360 miles west of Buenos Aires. Work was started here in 1921 by D. Parke Lantz and his wife, who moved here simply to hold the town. Later in the same year meetings were begun by Albano Luayza who had come with his wife from the Alliance Church. The following year the congregation was organized; the Luayza family lived here until 1939, during which time 75 persons were baptized. Santa Rosa is a center of Catholicism and the work was started under much opposition. The pastor has always been an Argentine. The membership in 1957 was 36, with Pedro Lanik as pastor.   L.S.W.

Santen, van: see **Zanten, van**.

Santfirderrijp (Santvoorderrijp), a hamlet in the Dutch province of Friesland, where Elder Leenaert Bouwens (*q.v.*) baptized 17 persons in 1554-56 and another 16 in 1563-65. From this time a Mennonite congregation existed here, of which however there is only scarce information. T. H. Siemelink has surmised that during the period of persecution Santfirderrijp, surrounded by lakes and pools, was the meeting place of the Workum (*q.v.*) Mennonite congregation, and that the martyr Claesken (*q.v.*), executed in 1554, who is said to have been baptized "near Workum in the fields," received her baptism here about 1549. But this could not be proved. In any case, besides the Workum congregation there was an independent congregation at Santfirderrijp in the 17th century. In 1695 this congregation, then numbering 24 baptized members, joined the Sociëteit (conference) of Mennonite churches in Friesland. In 1726 it contributed ten guilders to the Dutch Committee of Foreign Needs for the relief of the Mennonites in the Palatinate. During the early 18th century Douwe Djurres was its preacher, serving until about 1750 (his son Djurre Douwes was a preacher of the congregation at Koudum, Friesland, 1741-78). Soon after, at least before 1765, the congregation of Santfirderrijp died out; the few remaining members joined the Workum congregation. Probably Elder Hoyte Riencx (*q.v.*), who was also called Hoyte Renix Santvoort, came from here.   vDZ.

Blaupot t. C., *Friesland*, 89, 188, 306; *Naamlijst* of 1731-57; *DB* 1895, 17, 20; 1899, 33-35; 1902, 39.

Santvoort, Huyte Renicksz: see **Hoyte Riencx**.

Sao Paulo, the largest city of Brazil with an approximate population in 1958 of 3,000,000. In 1958 there were about 150 Mennonites, mostly young women, living in this city. Mennonite women have been in great demand as domestics and as governesses for the well-to-do Brazilian families since the early thirties, soon after the first permanent Mennonite settlements were made in Brazil. There are very few young men or Mennonite families in Sao Paulo. In 1947 the MCC sent Mr. and Mrs. John E. Kaufman to Brazil to establish a home for Mennonite girls where they could meet regularly for fellowship, wor-

ship, and counseling. Later directors of the home
have been Mr. and Mrs. J. J. Jantzen, Mr. and Mrs.
Frank Wiens, Mr. and Mrs. David Quapp, Emma
Schlichting, and Mr. and Mrs. Abram J. Dick, the
present directors who have served since 1952.

J.W.F.

Sappemeer, an industrial town in the Dutch province of Groningen (pop. 7,224 in 1947, with 180
Mennonites), which together with the adjacent town
of Hoogezand (pop. 13,194 in 1947, with 225 Mennonites) is the seat of a Mennonite congregation,
in the 19th century mostly called Hoogezand-
Sappemeer, and now officially Sappemeer, the town
where the meetinghouse is found.

In 1618 a large lake east of Hoogezand, called
Sap-meer or Sappemeer, was reclaimed, and in 1621
the first houses of what later was the town of Sappemeer were built on its grounds. In 1628 the adjacent
wild peat moors had been opened up and the
reclaimed land immediately settled. Among the
settlers there were a number of Mennonites, some
of them coming in from the province of Friesland.
As early as Aug. 10, 1629, the Reformed Synod of
Groningen made mention of Mennonite activities
here, and by 1631 there existed at Sappemeer a
Flemish and a Frisian Mennonite congregation.
Complaints about Mennonite activity were then
made to the magistrates of the city of Groningen,
which at this time was the owner of the reclaimed
grounds.

Soon the Mennonites must have been rather numerous at Sappemeer. There were at least nine
different Mennonite congregations: (1) Frisians,
(2) Flemish, (3) Ukowallists (a branch of the Old
Flemish, followers of Uko Walles, *q.v.*), (4) Danzig Old Flemish, (5) Waterlanders, (6) Groningen
Old Flemish, (7) from about 1680 also Paltsers
(Mennonites from the Palatinate, Germany), and
from the early 18th century (8) Oude Zwitsers (Old
Swiss Brethren), and (9) Nieuwe Zwitsers (New
Swiss). Of some of these congregations there is
little information. (1) Of the Frisians nearly nothing is known but the fact of their existence in the
earliest period. This group probably claimed Heero
Jans and his son Berend (Bene) Heeres (from
which the Benes family descended, still found at
Hoogezand-Sappemeer), who in 1631 with a number of other Mennonites moved in from de Wijn-
gaarden near Heerenveen, Friesland, and who
settled at the Oude Friese Compagnie, later called
Kalkwijk (*q.v.*) at the south part of the reclaimed
area. This Frisian congregation apparently soon
merged either with the Flemish or the Waterlander
congregation. (2) Concerning the Flemish congregation there is no more information; it also existed
from the very beginning. It had a meetinghouse
in the Kleine Meer (the former little lake, also
reclaimed) in the southeast section of Sappemeer;
this meetinghouse was renovated or rebuilt in 1691.
About 1730 this congregation merged with the
Waterlanders.

(3) Ukowallists (Uke-Wallesvolk) are mentioned
at Sappemeer first in 1640. This group of the
Mennonites especially had much trouble with the
magistrates. In the conference of the Reformed

Classis at Groningen, May 30, 1636, it was reported
that the Mennonites at Sappemeer were building "a
church to hold their meetings in it"; the magistrates
of Groningen were requested to prevent this, and
in 1640, apparently before the meetinghouse was
complete, Johan de Mepsche, estate steward of the
city of Groningen, bought this house by order of
the magistrates. Consequently it could not be used
as a meetinghouse. This house was located on the
main road in the west part of Sappemeer. Probably
this occurrence pertained to a planned meetinghouse
of the Ukowallists. In 1647, when the new lands of
the Borger Compagnie were distributed, a condition
was made that the landowners were not allowed to
sell their land to the "people of the Uke Walles sect."
In 1642 the Ukowallists are said to have held their
meetings on a farm belonging to Macke Gerkes van
Dam (the family name of van Dam is still found
at Sappemeer) on the Jouwerswijk. This was a
canal, dug in 1630, along which farms were established, partly occupied by Mennonites moving in
from Joure in Friesland, from which it took its
name. It could not be ascertained whether the
Ukowallists were identical with the group which
later was called Groningen Old Flemish, or were
a separate independent group. If the latter, they
soon, at least before 1670, merged with the Groningen Old Flemish.

(4) The Danzig Old Flemish Mennonites are
mentioned in the 18th century, but they obviously
had a small congregation at Sappemeer from about
1650 or even before. They held their meetings in
the homes of members, most living at the Kleine
Meer. Hindrick Coops Boon, a well-to-do proprietor
of land reclamations, peat merchant, and shipowner,
the ancestor of the Boon family still living at Sappemeer, was about 1700 an elder of this church, which
in 1699 acquired a meetinghouse on the Jouwerswijk. Jan Panneman and Jan van Dalen were
preachers of this group about 1740-70. Jan Panneman at the same time served the Danzig Old
Flemish congregation at Pekela (*q.v.*), to which
town he seems to have moved about 1665. In 1777
the Danzig Old Flemish congregation of Sappemeer
died out after most members in course of time had
joined the Groningen Old Flemish church.

(5) The Waterlander congregation at Sappemeer
also dates from an early period. In 1647 this congregation was represented at a large Waterlander
conference at Amsterdam by Egbert Harmsz and
Doede Harmsz, apparently its preachers. During
the first decades they held their meetings in private
homes; later they had a meetinghouse in the Kleine
Meer. In 1695 this Waterlander congregation, then
numbering about 30 baptized members, joined the
Sociëteit (conference) of Mennonite congregations
in Friesland, and remained a member until 1769.
About 1730 the Waterlander congregation merged
with the Flemish congregation (2). Henceforth it
is called either Flemish and Waterlander or Waterlander and Flemish or simply the Flemish congregation. This congregation contributed liberally to
the needs of the Mennonites in Prussia and Poland in 1734. It was a member of the Flemish-
Waterlander Humsterland (*q.v.*) conference *c*1756-
65. Outstanding families in this congregation have

been Mulder (*q.v.*), Mandema, and Benes. Hendrik Jacobsz was a preacher here in 17? -*c*1733, Harm Jacobsz 1730-72, Watse Joukes (Mandema) (d. 1763) 1710-60, and Roelof Sebes 1764-72. In 1772 the Waterlander-Flemish congregation merged with the Groningen Old Flemish Mennonites.

(6) The Groningen Old Flemish had the largest congregation at Sappemeer. No figures as to the membership are available for the 17th century; in 1710 they numbered 140 baptized members, about 120 in 1750, and 116 in 1767. At first they too held their meetings in the homes of members, nearly all farmers living on the Kalkwijk, the Jouwerswijk, and the Borger Compagnie. At least in 1734, but probably some decades before, they had a rather large but very plain meetinghouse in the eastern section of the town (Borger Compagnie). This meetinghouse was used until 1847. The Groningen Old Flemish congregation was a member of the Old Flemish conference (sociëteit). Next to the congregation in Groningen (city) it was by far the largest Old Flemish congregation in the Netherlands. Like all Old Flemish congregations it was served by untrained preachers chosen from the members. Of the preachers of the 17th century only a few names have come down; they are Jacob Alberts and Harke Pieters, mentioned in 1681, Asink Abels in 1683. The first Dutch *Naamlijst* (1731) lists for 1731 Engelbert Jochems, Maarten Obbes, Maarten Garbrands, and Evert Hendriks. Maarten Garbrands (d. 1762) served 1704-*c*60. Not only did Maarten Obbes (1676-1736) serve for a long period, but also his sons Obbe Meertens (1703-82), serving 1733-79, when he retired, and Hinrick Meertens, serving 1736-80, as well as his grandson Meerten Obbes (Ubbens), serving 1774-d.86, were able and active preachers of the church. Others were Sjoert Clases, serving 1736-*c*50, Alle Feyes mentioned in 1734, Jan Harms in 1748. Koert Izaaks Verveld (1719-1804) served from 1756 until his death, Harm Jacobsz, formerly preacher of the Waterlanders, from the union in 1772 until 1780, Sybolt Aans 1782-85(?), Jacob Luitjes (Reinders) 1780-1807, Pieter van Kalker (Calcar) 1786-*c*1813, Hayke Harms (Mulder) 1786-d.1833, Rigt Eppes 1786-*c*1812. Pieter Hendriks (*q.v.*), the author of *Schriftuurlijke Catechismus* (1744), was very probably also a preacher of this congregation. In the course of time a number of members of other Mennonite branches joined the Old Flemish congregation; in 1772 the Waterlander-Flemish congregation (5) merged with the Old Flemish, in 1777 the few remaining Danziger Old Flemish (4) joined them, and about 1802 also the remnant of the Swiss congregation (8-9). From then we can trace the united church of Sappemeer (10).

(7) According to tradition, which, however, is not proved by documents, a number of Mennonites from the Palatinate, Germany, emigrated to Sappemeer in 1680-90, settling as farmers in the easternmost parts of the reclaimed area. If this tradition is true, they may have joined the Swiss Brethren, who settled here in 1711 ff.

(8) In 1711 a number of Mennonites came to the Netherlands from the Swiss canton of Bern. (See **Swiss Mennonites** in the Netherlands.) A number of them settled in the Dutch province of Groningen, partly in and near the city of Groningen, partly near Sappemeer. They were soon (1726?) divided into two separate groups—the Oude Zwitsers (Old Swiss) being more conservative in life, dress, and doctrines, and using the German language in their church services until the end of the 18th century, and the Nieuwe Zwitsers (New Swiss) being more progressive and soon using the Dutch language in their meetings. The Old Swiss living at Groningen and at Sappemeer formed one congregation, meeting alternately at Groningen and at Sappemeer; the New Swiss of Groningen and Sappemeer also founded a single church, meeting alternately at Groningen and Sappemeer. Swiss Mennonite families settling at Sappemeer in 1711-14 were Ancken (Anken), Baur (later called Boer, also de Boer), Fruttiger, Furrer, Gerber (Gerwer), Gut(h), (Goet, later de Goede), Kneubühl (later Kneubel), Gautschy (later Kousie), Krähenbühl (Krejenbul, later Kreiboer and Kraaiboer), Krätzer (Kratzer, Kraster), Krebs (Kreps), Lang (Lange), Lienders (Leenders), Lörts (Leurts), Lötscher (Latscha, Leutscher), Maihuser (Meihuizen), Mayer (Meyer), Moerer (Murer, Muur), Rich or Richen (Ricken, Righen, Rijkens), Roth (Root), Rüsser (Risser) or Reuscher (Ruysser, Ruischer), Sarbach, Schabels, Stauffer, Steiner, Stähly (Stehle, Stelli), Stucky (Stukje), Stutsman, Thöne(n) (Teune), Teutscher, Witwers and Sorg (Zorge). A number of these families after a few years moved elsewhere in the Netherlands or back to the Palatinate, while others came in from Kampen, Deventer, and Groningen. Most of them were provided with farmlands and houses through the agency of the Dutch Committee of Foreign Needs at Amsterdam and the Groningen Old Flemish conference. Especially Alle Derks (*q.v.*), an elder of Groningen, deserved well of these Swiss immigrants, many of whom took along considerable amounts of money for the rest, which enabled them to run their businesses without the usual difficulties of settling in a foreign country. In 1811 descendants of the following Swiss immigrant families were still found at Hoogezand-Sappemeer: Anken, Boer, Gerber, Kneubel, Kousie, Kraaiboer, Kraster, Kreps, Leenders, Leutscher, Meihuizen, Meyer, Rijkens, Schabels, Stukje, and Teune. At the present time the church records of the Sappemeer Mennonite congregation still contain the names of members of the Boer, Meihuizen, and Rijkens families.

The Oude Zwitsers held their meetings in a home in the Kleine Meer. There is no information about the number of their members, and the list of their ministers is somewhat unclear. The first *Naamlijst* in which they are mentioned is that of 1755. Ministers then were Abraham Loover (Lauffer), living at Groningen, from 1726, an elder, and Claus Gerber (from 1739) and Peter Riegen (Ricken) preachers. Other ministers were Jacob Stehle (Stähly) and David Righen (Ricken) from 1767. Claus (Nicolaas) Gerber served 1739-61, Peter Righen 1740-d.72, Jacob Stehle 1736-57. Abraham Loofer served until his death in 1774; Preacher David Righen then became elder, serving until his death in 1796. David Righen lived at Sappemeer; until the end he preached in German. A copy of *Die ernsthafte Christenpflicht, darinnen schöne geistreiche Gebätter damitt sich fromme Christen-Herzen zu allen Zeiten und in allen Nöthen trösten können,* which copy was owned and used by Ricken, is now the property of G. N. Schutter at Sappemeer. In the Old Swiss congregation, after the preacher had finished his sermon, other brethren spoke briefly to express their agreement with the sermon or to add a few words from the Bible. They knelt for (silent) prayer and practiced footwashing in connection with their communion services. They seem not to have used a confession of faith; their hymnal was the German *Ausbund.* After the death of David Righen the Old Swiss seem to have merged with the New Swiss.

(9) The Nieuwe Zwitsers (New Swiss) also had a room on a farm at the Kleine Meer, probably the same as the one used by the Old Swiss, where they met every two weeks. Figures concerning the membership of this group are also not available. This group may have been somewhat smaller than the Old Swiss group, and in the course of the 18th century some of them, through marriage, joined the Danzig and particularly the Groningen Old Flemish congregations. They too practiced silent prayer and footwashing, but soon used the Dutch language in their services. They were not as strict in their dress regulations as the Old Swiss were, tolerating buttons instead of hooks and eyes, and shoes instead of boots. They used a Dutch confession of faith, drawn up by Jan van Koomen (*q.v.*), *Belijdenisse des Geloofs onder de doopsgezinde Christenen* (1744), and also Dutch hymnbooks. Some of the Old Flemish Mennonites who had moved from Deventer (*q.v.*) to Hoogezand-Sappemeer in 1720 soon after joined the New Swiss congregation. Ministers of the New Swiss were Hans Ancken, serving from 1712, Michiel Ruysser, serving 1711-59, elder, Peter Leenders, 1711-57, elder, Jan van Ko(o)men, d. 1743, Anthony Kratzer 1740-79, elder from 1760, Christiaan Ancken 1754-70, Jan Leenders 1754-59(?), Rudolf Leutscher 1755-61, Jan van Kalker (Calcar) 1755-75(?), Balster Franszen 1762-82, Hendrik Cornelis 1770-1808, elder from 1794, Isaak van Kalker (Calcar) 1772-96, Roelof Jans 1781-d.90, Alle Cornelis 1791-1800, Ties Hansen Top 1791-97. Most of these New Swiss preachers lived at Groningen. Van Komen and both the van Kalkers were not of Swiss decent. Obviously after 1800 meetings were only at Groningen, the Swiss brethren living at Sappemeer all having joined the main Mennonite congregation. In 1802 the deacons of the "former Swiss congregation" sold a house and a tract of land on the Kalkwijk, which had been the property of this church. The remaining Swiss congregation in Groningen merged with the main Mennonite church in this town in 1824. Not all descendants of the Swiss Mennonites remained Mennonites. Some of them may have joined the Reformed as early as the last decades of the 18th century, but more left particularly when the Mennonite Sappemeer congregation called a salaried preacher (see below), and again in 1847 when the old meetinghouse was abandoned for the new one, more in the center of the town. All of the Kneubel

and Kreps families left the church in 1847, joining the Separate Reformed Church, and many members of other families, e.g., Kraster, Rijkens, and Stukje, also left.

Among the outstanding Mennonite families of Sappemeer there is also the van Calcar (van Kalker) family. This family originally lived at Deventer, Dutch province of Overijssel. In 1720 Hendrik van Calcar and his wife moved from Deventer to Sappemeer and joined the New Swiss Mennonites. Hendrik's son Izaak van Calcar was married here to Maria Brunner, widow of Peter Lienders. Izaak van Calcar bequeathed his farm to Pieter Leenders (the son of Peter Lienders and Maria Brunner) on the condition that he assume the family name of van Calcar. Thus Pieter Leenders became Pieter van Calcar (married in 1783 to Dievertje Verveld, a daughter of the preacher Koert Izaaks Verveld); they have numerous descendants.

Other settlers at Sappemeer were Georg Grüber and his family, refugees from East Prussia, who emigrated to the Netherlands and after living a few years on the island of Walcheren (*q.v.*), settled at Sappemeer in 1744.

(10) Since the Flemish-Waterlander and Groningen Old Flemish had merged congregations in 1772 and the Swiss Mennonites had joined them about 1800, there has been only one Mennonite church at Sappemeer. Until 1847 this congregation used the Groningen Old Flemish meetinghouse, which was remodeled and provided with an organ in 1808. A new church was built in the center of Sappemeer, dedicated on Feb. 21, 1847. A parsonage had been built here in 1838.

The membership of this united congregation was about 270 in 1790, 300 in 1834, 438 in 1861, 464 in 1900, 345 in 1926, 265 in 1958.

The last untrained and unsalaried minister at Sappemeer was Heyke Harmens Mulder (Hayke Harmze) serving 1786-d.1833. In 1790, because of lack of able men in their own group, the congregation decided to call a preacher from outside who was to be salaried. This was Foeke Wigles Gorter, a self-made man, not specially trained for the ministry, then preacher at Knijpe (*q.v.*). Gorter served at Sappemeer until 1836. During his ministry a second minister was called; this was Pieter Feenstra, who had been trained at the Amsterdam Mennonite Seminary. He served at Sappemeer 1824-27 and again 1837-71. He was followed by S. G. Binnerts, serving 1872-1913, S. H. N. Gorter 1914-16, F. ten Cate 1916-35, B. Dufour 1935-40, R. de Zeeuw 1941-47, and G. M. Kosters from 1947. Since 1946 the pastor of Sappemeer has also been in charge of the Noordbroek (*q.v.*) congregation.

Church activities now are a Sunday school for children, a Youth Group (ages 12-15), Youth Circle (ages 18-35), Brethren Circle, and Ladies' Circle.

The Mennonites have always occupied an important place in the economic and cultural life of Hoogezand-Sappemeer. Until the end of the 18th century they were mostly farmers, a few being engaged in business, e.g., the Mulder family, who owned a tannery. The wealthy Boon, Boer, and Reinders families were large landowners, often engaged in land reclamation elsewhere. The Meihuizen and van Calcar families, who were farmers at Kalkwijk in the 18th century, later spread over the other peat colonies (Pekela, Veendam, Wildervank) of the province of Groningen, but many of them from the early 19th century had other trades and became millers, grocers, distillers, tanners, grain merchants, wood dealers, etc. The later generations have spread all over the Netherlands and both the Meihuizen and van Calcar families are now dying out at Sappemeer. In the 18th and 19th centuries some Mennonite families also were shipowners (Boon, Romkes, van Calcar, van der Goot, and Meihuizen). The Romkes and van der Goot families particularly have been wood dealers. The Calkema family, now extinct, owned an important lime burning business in the Oude Vriese Compagnie which was called Kalkwijk after this business.

The Mennonites also owned a number of sawmills. Some of the businesses at Sappemeer under Mennonite direction and in part Mennonite owned are: the van Calcar distilleries (until 1896), Benes' flour mills, Smit's shipbuilding yard at Westerbroek, shipbuilding yard of Coops Brothers, engineering works of Douwe E. Gorter, dairies, a potato-flour mill, the Dijkhuis printing shop, Brand Brothers Lumber Yard and sawmills. Many Mennonites have been outstanding in the cultural and political life of Hoogezand-Sappemeer. The Hoogezand-Sappemeer section of the Maatschappij tot Nut van't Algemeen (q.v.) and the public library have largely been stimulated and led by Mennonites. A number of burgomasters of Hoogezand have been Mennonites.

G.N.S., vdZ.

Tegenwoordige Staat der Vereenigde Nederlanden (Amsterdam, 1793) XXI, 203 ff.; *Inv. Arch. Amst.* I, Nos. 1893, 1896; II, Nos. 1839 f., 2219; Blaupot t. C., *Groningen* I, *passim*, see Index; II, 144; *idem, Friesland,* 187 f., 200; *Naamlijst* 1829, 62 f.; *DJ* 1850, 55 f.; *DB* 1861, 153; 1879, 5 f.; 1919, 74-76, 97-109; J. Huizinga, *Stamboek . . . van Samuel Peter (Meihuizen) en Barbara Fry* (Groningen, 1890); *Stamboek van het geslacht Meihuizen 1400-1945, opnieuw samengesteld en angevuld door J. Meihuizen* (n.p., n.d.—1946) 41-67; M. G. de Boer, "Vom Thunersee zum Sappemeer," repr. from *Berner Zeitschrift für Geschichte und Heimatkunde,* 1947; "Van de oevers van de Thunerzee naar Sappemeer," in *Tijdschrift voor Geschiedenis* LXVIII (1955) No. 2, 146-68; Blaupot t. C., *Voorlezing over de opkomst van de Veenkolonien Hoogezand en Sappemeer* (Sappemeer, 1854); *Gedenkboek Hoogezand-Sappemeer 1628-1928,* particularly pp. 72-75; J. Lindeboom, "Sectewezen in Stad en Lande," in *Groningsche Volksalmanak 1945,* 53-79; H. W. Meihuizen, *Foeke Wigles Gorter* (n.p., n.d.).

Sarasota, Fla., a city (pop. 40,000) in Sarasota County on the west coast, 50 miles south of Tampa. The population doubles in winter. About 300 Mennonites are living permanently in the area, winter visitors increasing this number to 1,000-1,500. Both permanent settlers and winter tourists are scattered throughout the city and surrounding vicinity, the largest concentration being in Pinecraft just outside the city limits to the southeast. The first settlers came in 1927, then there was a very gradual increase until 1945, since when there has been a sharp increase annually.

There are five organized Mennonite (MC) churches in the Sarasota area as follows: Bay Shore (Ohio Conference), membership 187, within the city; Tuttle Avenue (Virginia Conference), membership 93, within the city; Newton Community Chapel (colored mission, Virginia Conference), membership 12), within the city; Pinecraft (Lancaster Conference), membership 30, in Pinecraft; and Palm Grove (Conservative Mennonite Conference), membership 40, in Pinecraft. Some Old Order Amish also hold services in homes in Pinecraft in winter but have not organized a congregation. Practically all branches of Mennonites and Amish are represented in the thousands of Mennonites who spend some time here each winter. The number of young married and retired couples who are establishing their homes here is on the increase. There is no important industry in the city, many Mennonites depending upon the building industry for a livelihood.   T.H.B.

Saratov Mennonite Brethren Church was established in the early days of the Slavgorod Mennonite settlement (q.v.), Siberia, and served the following four villages: Saratov (89), Khoroshye (89), Nikolayevka (75), and Silberfeld (86). The first leading minister was Bernhard Wiens, who was succeeded by Daniel Heide. Other ministers were P. P. Löwen, Jakob Dück, David Löwen, and David Nachtigall. In 1914 a church building was erected in Saratov. Additional smaller places of worship were located in other villages.   C.K.

Gerhard Fast, *In den Steppen Sibiriens* (Rosthern, 1957) 78.

Sarcerius, Erasmus (1511-89), a German Lutheran clergyman. Of his numerous writings, mention should be made of his book, *Wider die Secten Rotten und falsche Lerer* (Eisleben, 1560), in which he includes the Anabaptists.

Sardis First Mennonite Church (GCM), a member of the Canadian Conference, located at Sardis, B.C., a town 65 miles east of Vancouver. The first Mennonite church to be organized here began in 1929, when the first settlers came to Sardis. The first meetinghouse was built in 1940, enlarged in 1941, and replaced in 1947 by a new church seating 1,200. The members are farmers, most of them in berry farming. Services are conducted every Sunday in German; there is a Sunday school for the children, a chorus, a young people's organization, and three women's missionary societies. Footwashing is not observed. The first elders were Nicolai Bahnmann and Johann Klassen. The ministers assisting them were David Hausknecht and Abram Warkentin. After a period of difficulty in the congregation Elder Wilhelm Martens of Alberta was called as elder of the congregation in 1946. Isaak Harms and Gerhard Peters were called to the ministry. In 1957 the membership was 262, with Bruno Enss as pastor.   C.G.T.

Sardis Mennonite Brethren Church: see **Greendale** M.B. Church.

Sargent Avenue Mennonite Church (GCM), Winnipeg, Man., a member of the Canadian Conference, first called "Winnipeg Mennoniten Stadtmission," in 1950 renamed Winnipeg Mennonite Mission Church, and in 1955 renamed Sargent Avenue Mennonite

Church, was organized in 1949 with 11 members, and in 1958 had 265 members. Two thirds of the members immigrated as refugees from Russia after World War II. The meetinghouse was purchased in 1951. In 1958 the congregation was served by three ministers, Gerhard Lohrenz, Johann Adrian, and George Epp. J.RE.

Saron Mennonite Church (GCM), located one mile south of Orienta, Okla., a member of the Western District Conference, was organized in 1897 with 11 charter members, under the leadership of Christian Ramseier, assisted by John Bartel. The first meetinghouse was dedicated in 1906 and was replaced in 1940 by a brick structure built on the original site. The membership in 1957 was 124, with A. C. Siebert as pastor. W.J.F.

Sarrebourg (German, **Saarburg**), a Mennonite congregation in Lorraine, France. Though it is not possible to trace the origin of many of the Mennonite families who now comprise the Sarrebourg congregation, it is known that there have been Mennonites living here since the beginning of the 19th century. They were not known (nor are they for the most part today) as Mennonites, but as "Anabaptistes" in the French-speaking villages and "Täufer" in the German-speaking ones.

Thus the books of Erkmann-Chatrian describe the Anabaptist Pelsy, who lived in a remote mountain region of the Vosges Mountains, and their community; a résumé of his account follows: Most of the families still hold firmly to their manner of worship, and since they live great distances apart they have to cover many miles on foot to attend the meetings. Some of the older persons still recall starting out at three in the morning and returning after dark. Until about 30-40 years ago most of the members were engaged in agriculture or some trade in the village. The farms were often quite remote from the towns. They were thus removed from the temptations that accompany city life, and God could grant these simple rural people many a spiritual blessing in heavenly goods in their rough and laborious existence; most of these blessings have since been lost or have passed into formalism or traditionalism. But our faithful God, in view of the forefathers, will not permit their descendants to be easily submerged in the darkness and the enticements of this world. For many years meetings were held in the homes on various farms, as for example in Schacheneck, Imling, and Sarrebourg; later a meetinghouse was built in Sarrebourg, which was a rather central point for most of the families. For many years Valentin Pelsy (q.v.) served as elder, a faithful, devoted witness of the Lord. He avoided no effort, and his affectionate nature helped in reminding the members of their duty and responsibility. But in spite of all these admonitions the spirit of the world has found its way into the congregation, so that in many cases the simple and childlike faith of the fathers has been lost and the enemy of souls has reaped a rich harvest, many a heart turning to the world for its joy and contentment. But the Lord has been watching and has

given them a period of repentance and revival, when Emile Kremer was chosen elder after the death of Valentin Pelsy. A happy time of revival began, and many committed themselves to the Lord and placed their lives at His disposal. Thus many of the members of the congregation are not of Mennonite descent.

The present Sarrebourg congregation meets twice a month in a chapel in Sarrebourg. In 1957 the membership, including children, was 142. The elders were Emile Kremer and René Pelsy, and the minister Ernst Stalter. R.P.

Pierre Sommer, "Assemblée de Sarrebourg," *Christ Seul*, January 1932, 5-8; *ML* IV.

Sarreguemines (German, *Saargemünd*) Mennonite church, located in northeastern France, was organized in 1927 by Reiseprediger (q.v.) Henri Volkmar under the direction of the Alsatian Mennonite Conference after attempts by Reiseprediger Christian Guth, of Germany, beginning in 1920, had failed. The twenty or more families forming the group were a remnant of the former Bitscherland (q.v.) congregation (dissolved c1902) who had thereafter transferred to the Ixheim (q.v.) congregation just across the German border. (Up to 1918 Alsace-Lorraine was a part of Germany and there was no national border.) Since 1918 Sarreguemines has been politically French, although the Mennonites have continued the German language like those living in Alsace. Sarreguemines, a city of c12,000 population, lies on the French-German border. In 1957 the congregation had 35 members and was served by Elder Willi Hege. H.S.B.

P. Sommer, "Assemblée de Sarreguemines," *Christ Seul*, September 1931, 4 f.; *ML* IV.

Sartorius, Johannes (Jan Snyder), b. c1500 at Amsterdam, d. 1570 at Delft, Dutch province of South Holland, was a Dutch Sacramentist (q.v.) who by his Biblical preaching and teaching promoted the development of the evangelical faith in the Netherlands. Sartorius was influenced by the Dominican monk Wouter (q.v.). As early as 1525, severely critical of the doctrines and practices of the Roman Catholic Church, Sartorius preached salvation by faith, and published a treatise (Latin) on the Lord's Supper in which he rejected the Catholic doctrine of transubstantiation. In the same year he was imprisoned at The Hague on a charge of heresy, and upon recanting was set free. But he continued his evangelical preaching. A few months later he was a schoolteacher at Amsterdam, protected by its liberal magistrates. He is said to have taught at the Groote School at Amsterdam that "all the people are seduced by monks and priests." He taught in Amsterdam until 1535. For some time he was head of a Latin school at Noordwijk near Leiden, influencing and stimulating the evangelical-minded of Leiden and Haarlem. He also stayed at Zutphen, and c1545 at Basel in Switzerland. In 1558 he became the leader of a group of evangelicals at Delft, Holland, the only town, as far as is known, where the Sacramentists had a sort of congregation. Unlike most Sacramentists, Sartorius did not join the Ana-

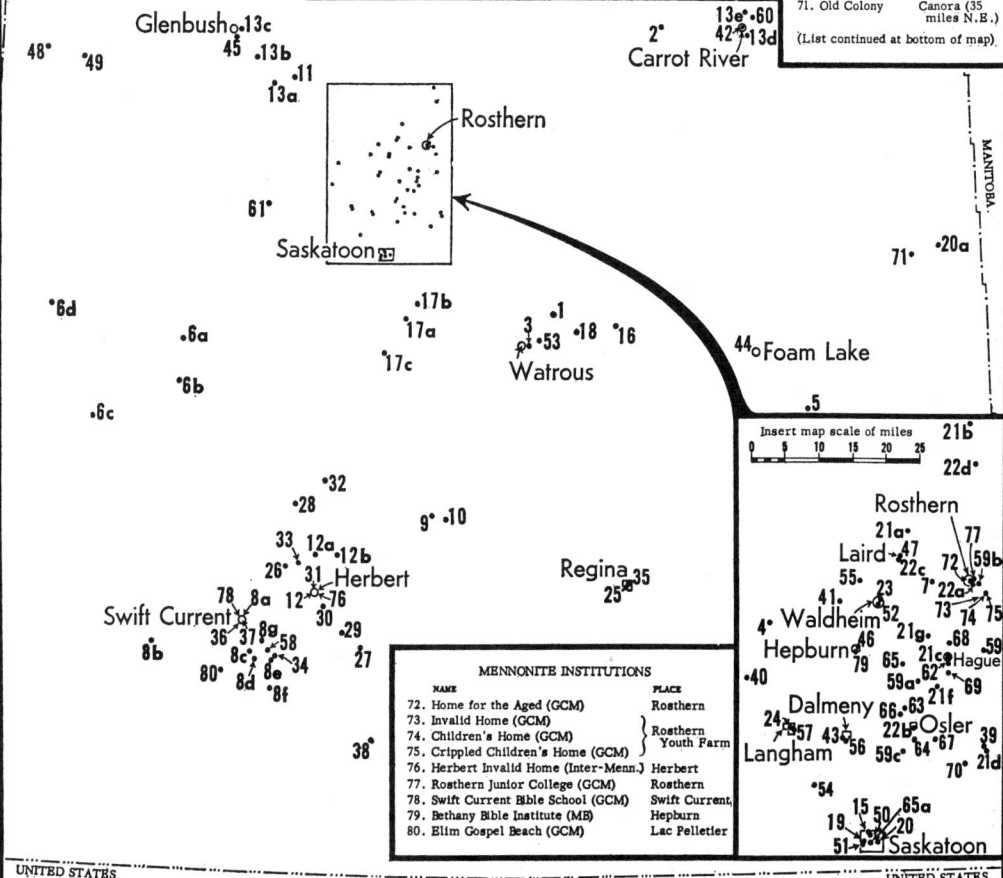

Saskatchewan

Scale of Miles

0   10   20   30   40   50   60   70   80   90   100   110   120   130   140   150

MENNONITE (MC)

NAME OF CHURCH	PLACE
1. Sharon	Guernsey

GENERAL CONFERENCE MENNONITE (GCM)

2. Bethany	Lost River
3. Bethany	Watrous
4. Bethel	Great Deer
5. Ebenezer	Fitzmaurice
6. Ebenfeld	
6a. Herschel	Herschel
6b. Fiske	Fiske
6c. Glidden	Glidden
6b. Superb	Superb
7. Eigenheim	Rosthern
8. Emmaus	
8a. Swift Current	Swift Current
8b. Gull Lake	Gull Lake
8c. Wymark	Wymark
8d. Schoenfeld	Schoenfeld
8e. McMahon	McMahon
8f. Pella	Neville
8g. Rhineland	Wymark
9. Eyebrow	Central Butte
10. Eyebrow First Mennonite	Eyebrow
11. Hebron	Mayfair
12. Herbert	Herbert
12a. Gouldtown	Gouldtown
12b. Glen Kerr	Morse
13. Hoffnungsfeld	
13a. Mayfair	Mayfair
13b. Rabbit Lake	Rabbit Lake
13c. Glenbush	Glenbush
13d. Carrot River	Carrot River
13e. Petaigan	Petaigan
14. Immanuel	Barnes Crossing
14a. Immanuel	Daisy Meadow
14b. Immanuel	Compass
14c. Immanuel	Pierceland
14d. Immanuel	Meadow Lake
14e. Immanuel	Dorintosh
15. Mayfair	Saskatoon
16. Jansen-Watson	Lampard
17. Nordheim	
17a. Nordheim	Dundurn
17b. Nordheim	Dundurn
17c. Nordheim	Hanley
18. North Star	Drake

19. Pleasant Hill	Saskatoon
20. Saskatoon First	Saskatoon
20a. Swan Plain	Swan Plain
21. Rosenort	
21a. Tiefengrund	Laird
21b. Garthland	Garthland
21c. Hague	Hague
21d. Aberdeen	Aberdeen
21e. Capasin	Capasin
21f. Neuenlage	Hague
21g. Hochfield	Hague
22. United	
22a. Rosthern	Rosthern
22b. Osler	Osler
22c. Laird	Laird
22d. Horse Lake	Horse Lake
23. Zoar-Waldheim	Waldheim
24. Zoar-Langham	Langham
25. Victoria Avenue	Regina

MENNONITE BRETHREN

26. Bethania	Main Centre
27. Elim	Kelstern
28. Beechy (Friedensheim)	Beechy
29. Gnadenau	Flowing Well
30. Greenfarm	Greenfarm
31. Herbert	Herbert
32. Lucky Lake	Lucky Lake
33. Main Centre	Main Centre
34. McMahon	McMahon
35. Regina	Regina
36. Swift Current	Swift Current
37. Swift Current	Swift Current (south side)
38. Woodrow	Woodrow
39. Aberdeen	Aberdeen
40. Borden	Borden
41. Bruderfeld	Hepburn
42. Carrot River	Carrot River
43. Dalmeny	Dalmeny
44. Foam Lake	Foam Lake
45. Glenbush	Glenbush

46. Hepburn	Hepburn
47. Laird	Laird
48. Lashburn	Lashburn
49. Maidstone	Maidstone
50. Saskatoon	Saskatoon
51. Saskatoon West	Saskatoon
52. Waldheim	Waldheim
53. Watrous (Philadelphia)	Watrous

KRIMMER MENNONITE BRETHREN

54. Emmanuel	Langham
55. Salem	Waldheim

EVANGELICAL MENNONITE BRETHREN

56. Dalmeny	Dalmeny
57. Langham	Langham

SOMMERFELDER MENNONITE

58. Swift Current Area (20 villages south of Swift Current, with approximate population of 3000).
59. Rosthern Area (15 villages south of Rosthern, with a population of approximately 2000).

59a. Bergthaler	Gruenthal
59b. Bergthaler	Rosthern
59c. Bergthaler	Warmen
60. Carrot River	Carrot River
61. Sonningdale	Sonningdale

RUDNERWEIDE MENNONITE

62. Chortitz	Hague
63. Neuhorst	Hague
64. Rudnerweide	Osler
65. Rudnerweide	Hague
65a. Rudnerweide	Saskatoon

OLD COLONY MENNONITE

66. Old Colony	Neuhorst
67. Old Colony	Kronsthal
68. Old Colony	Hague
69. Old Colony	Hague
70. Old Colony	Aberdeen
71. Old Colony	Canora (35 miles N.E.)

(List continued at bottom of map)

ALBERTA

MANITOBA

Carrot River

Glenbush

48°

49

Rosthern

61°

Saskatoon

6d

6a

6b

6c

Watrous

Foam Lake

71°

20a

Insert map scale of miles

0   5   10   15   20   25

21b

22d

Rosthern

Laird

Waldheim

Hepburn

Dalmeny

Osler

Langham

Hague

Saskatoon

Regina

Herbert

Swift Current

MENNONITE INSTITUTIONS

NAME		PLACE
72. Home for the Aged (GCM)		Rosthern
73. Invalid Home (GCM)		Rosthern Youth Farm
74. Children's Home (GCM)		
75. Crippled Children's Home (GCM)		
76. Herbert Invalid Home (Inter-Menn.)		Herbert
77. Rosthern Junior College (GCM)		Rosthern
78. Swift Current Bible School (GCM)		Swift Current
79. Bethany Bible Institute (MB)		Hepburn
80. Elim Gospel Beach (GCM)		Lac Pelletier

UNITED STATES   UNITED STATES

baptists; nevertheless by his Biblical teaching he undoubtedly stimulated the Anabaptist movement.

vdZ.

J. G. de Hoop Scheffer, *Geschiedenis der Kerkhervorming in Nederland van haar ontstaan tot 1531* (Amsterdam, 1873); L. Knappert, *Het Ontstaan en de Vestiging van het Protestantisme in de Nederlanden* (Utrecht, 1924).

Sarum: see **Salisbury.**

Saskatchewan, a province of Canada, is the central one of the three prairie provinces in Western Canada. On the east is Manitoba and on the west is Alberta. The name Saskatchewan is an Indian name meaning rapidly flowing river. In fact, two rivers of this name flow through Saskatchewan—the North Saskatchewan River and the South Saskatchewan River, which originate far apart in the West in the Rocky Mountains and meet just east of the city of Prince Albert, then continue as one to Lake Winnipeg.

Regina is the capital of the province. One of the first members of the parliament was Gerhard Ens (*q.v.*), of Rosthern, a Mennonite, who later joined another church. In Regina there are also a Mennonite Brethren church and a General Conference Mennonite church.

The second city is Saskatoon, where a university and a teachers college are located which usually have a good number of Mennonite students. Saskatoon has four Mennonite churches—two M.B. churches and two G.C.M. churches. Prince Albert and North Battleford also have G.C.M. churches.

The first Mennonite settlers came from Russia to Manitoba in the 1870's, but because of their large families they were soon looking for new land. The first five families from Manitoba arrived in Rosthern, 50 miles north of Saskatoon, in 1891-92. Soon the adjoining districts of Eigenheim, Laird, and Waldheim were settled. Some came directly from Russia to this district. Some Mennonites from Prussia settled in the Tiefengrund district, which is only a few miles north of Laird. In the main, these districts formed the Rosenort Mennonite Church, which now has about 1,500 members. In the beginning of this century, the Old Colony Mennonites, mostly from Manitoba, took land near Hague and Osler and settled in many villages. Some went across the South Saskatchewan River, where the town of Aberdeen is located. They were joined by other Mennonites and generally live on separate farms. A somewhat milder branch of the Old Colony Church is called the Bergthaler Church. In the early 1920's a large part of the two groups emigrated to Mexico and Paraguay, because they were dissatisfied with the requirement of the public school system in Canada that the English language be used in instruction. In the southern part of Saskatchewan, near Swift Current, a number of villages were settled by Old Colony Mennonites. Other Mennonites came from Minnesota, Nebraska, and the Dakotas and settled near Langham, Dalmeny, and up to Mennon and Hepburn. Many of these were Mennonite Brethren, whose church interests are centered mainly in Hepburn and Dal-

meny. South of Langham a group of Krimmer Brethren settled, where the names of Waldner and Stahl predominate. Across the North Saskatchewan River from Waldheim and Langham Mennonites also settled, and here the small town of Borden is located. A greater party from Kansas and Oklahoma settled near Drake about 100 miles southeast of Saskatoon. Not far away from these, near Guernsey, there is an M.C. group.

The southern part of Saskatchewan also received Mennonite settlers. Besides the Old Colony Mennonite settlement near Swift Current other settlers located at Herbert, between Regina and Swift Current, and in surrounding districts. In Herbert (*q.v.*) and in Swift Current (*q.v.*) there are both M.B. and G.C.M. congregations.

Later smaller and larger colonies of these first settlers were established in the northern parts of Saskatchewan, near Meadow Lake, Carrot River, Lost River, and other places. When the immigrants in the 1920's came from Russia, larger settlements were established near Herschel, Fiske, Kindersley, and Superb (Ebenfeld congregation) in the western part of the province; also at Rabbit Lake and Glenbush (Hoffnungsfeld) the congregation in the northern part of this province, which is more or less settled; and also in the Hanley and Dundurn districts south of Saskatoon. Somewhat northwest of Regina is the Eyebrow Mennonite Church.

In 1957 there were about 20,000 (pop.) Mennonites in Saskatchewan, who in the main belong to seven branches.

The yearbook (1954) of the Conference of the Mennonites in Canada gives the following statistics of its congregations in the province:

Name of Church	Location	Membership
(1) Bethany	Lost River	162
(2) Bethany	Watrous	91
(3) Bethel	Great Deer	30
(4) Capeland	Main Centre	24
(5) Ebenezer	Fitzmaurice	28
(6) Ebenfeld	Herschel	261
(7) Eigenheim	Rosthern	199
(8) Emmaus	Swift Current	210
(9) Eyebrow	Tugaske	64
(10) Hebron	Mayfair	25
(11) Herbert	Herbert	127
(12) Hoffnungsfeld	Carrot River	114
(13) Hoffnungsfeld	Petaigan	31
(14) Hoffnungsfeld	Rabbit Lake	103
(15) Immanuel	Meadow Lake	76
(16) Leroy group	Jansen	15
(17) Nordheim	Dundurn	271
(18) Rosenort	Rosthern	1,375
(19) First Mennonite	Saskatoon	291
(20) Saskatoon	Mayfair	66
(21) Plain group	Swan Plain	15
(22) Trossacks group	Trossack	26
(23) Zoar	Langham	167
(24) Zoar	Waldheim	213
(25) Scattered		25
Total Baptized Membership		4,009
With Children		7,157

The 1954 M.B. yearbook lists the following membership status:

South Saskatchewan:

(1) Bethania	Beaver Flat	40
(3) Eyebrow	Kelstern	52
(2) Elim		16
(4) Friedensheim	Beachy	26
(5) Gnadenau	Flowing Well	40
(6) Greenfarm	Herbert	63
(7) Herbert		170
(8) Loreburn		9
(9) Main Centre		221
(10) Regina		16
(11) Reinfeld	McMahon	30
(12) Swift Current		46
(13) Woodrow	near Herbert	66

North Saskatchewan:

(1) Aberdeen		41
(2) Borden		84
(3) Bruderfeld	near Waldheim	80
(4) Mission Station	Compass	28
(5) Dalmeny		238
(6) Foam Lake		17
(7) Glenbush		161
(8) Hepburn		261
(9) Laird		47
(10) Lashburn		18
(11) Mullingar		8
(12) Maidstone		8
(13) Saskatoon		231
(14) Warman		14
(15) Waldheim		92
(16) Watrous		82
Total Membership		2,205

This would give us the following totals of population: Canadian Conference GCM, over 7,000; Mennonite Brethren, 4,000; Bergthaler (statistics of individual congregations not available), 3,000; Old Colony, 1,000; MC, one near Guernsey 136; the Krimmer Brethren two at Waldheim and Langham, 175, and others. The latest congregation is the Rudnerweide Church near Osler and Hague. The total baptized Mennonite membership in Saskatchewan in 1957 was c9,000.

In 1903 Mennonites (GCM) of Rosthern and surrounding districts gathered in Eigenheim, near Rosthern, to consider the question of establishing a Mennonite high school. In 1905 the German-English Academy was opened in Rosthern and still functions as the Rosthern Junior College. This school was incorporated in 1908 under a special Act under the name German-English Academy. During these 50 years the school had many ups and downs, but in the last years it had well over one hundred students.

In 1932 the Rosthern Bible School was opened in connection with the German-English Academy, now Rosthern Junior College. In 1939 the Bible School moved into a separate building which it occupied until 1957, when it was again united with RSC.

Until recently Rosthern was the Mennonite center in Saskatchewan. In the last decades, however, many Mennonites have been moving into larger cities, and at present Saskatoon (pop. 72,858) has the largest Mennonite population. In 1922 the Canadian Mennonite Board of Colonization was founded with its office in Rosthern and in 1923 the immigrants from Russia started to come in. Up to 1930 over 20,000 Mennonite immigrants came to Canada, mostly from Russia. The Canadian leader of this immigration was David Toews, elder of the Rosenort Mennonite Church in Saskatchewan, who was living in Rosthern. After World War II a new stream of immigrants to Canada set in when J. J. Thiessen of Saskatoon was chairman of the Canadian Mennonite Board of Colonization which has now moved to the city of Saskatoon.

The Mennonite Youth Farm, located on the Experimental Farm near Rosthern, was discontinued as such by the government, because the Agricultural Department of the University of Saskatchewan in Saskatoon, only 50 miles south, was doing a similar work. In the winter of 1943-44 the Experimental Farm with 640 acres was bought by the Youth Organization of Saskatchewan. In 1944 the Invalid Home was opened on the Youth Farm and now (1955) has 80 patients in two separate buildings. In 1945 the Elim Gospel Beach (q.v.) in South Saskatchewan was bought. In 1946 the first Children's Home on the Youth Farm in Rosthern began and in 1953 another home, the Crippled Children's Home, was opened on the same Farm. Combined these homes are able to take 20 children. In 1949 the pasteurization plant on the Youth Farm was built. This Farm has about 30 cows and supplies the town of Rosthern with pasteurized milk. In 1951 the Invalid Home in Herbert, South Saskatchewan, was built by the Youth Farm. It now has about 20 patients.

The Rosenort Mennonite Church of Saskatchewan has now (1954) divided into two churches. It had 11 districts and now has the names of United Mennonite Church (Rosthern, Osler, Laird, and Horse Lake) and the Rosenort Mennonite Church of Saskatchewan (Tiefengrund, Hague, Hochfeld, Neuanlage, Aberdeen, Garthland, and Capasin).

Besides these there are four Bible schools. The G.C.M. have one at Swift Current; the E.M.B. have one at Dalmeny, and the M.B. one at Herbert, founded in 1913, and Bethany Bible Institute at Hepburn. The General Conference maintains a bookstore at Rosthern.   J.G.R.

Leo Driedger, "A Sect in a Modern Society. A Case Study. The Old Colony Mennonites of Saskatchewan" (M.A. thesis, University of Chicago, 1955); idem, "Hague-Osler Settlement," Menn. Life XIII (January 1958) 13 ff.; idem, "The Saskatchewan Old Colony Mennonites," Menn. Life XIII (April 1958); J. G. Rempel, Fünfzig Jahre Konferenzbestrebungen 1902-1952; ML IV.

Saskatchewan Conference of the Mennonite Brethren Church was organized in 1946 as an annual gathering of ministers, including two subdistricts (North and South) with semiannual gatherings. In 1957 it had 26 congregations with a total baptized membership of 2,301 (North 1,467, South 834). As is the case in other Canadian M.B. provincial conferences, the conference devotes its attention to matters of local or provincial nature, including home missions, ministers' conferences, Bible conferences, etc.   H.S.B.

Saskatchewan Mennonite Youth, a 6-page monthly, edited by Isaac Epp, was started in 1944 and published in Rosthern, Sask. The last issue in the Bethel College Historical Library was dated March 1949.
C.K.

Saskatoon, Sask., population 72,858, chief commercial center of central Saskatchewan and site of the provincial university, has five Mennonite churches (3 GCM: First, 348 members; Mayfair, 115; Pleasant Hill, 28; 2 MB: Saskatoon, 302; and City Mission Chapel, 22), and the headquarters office of the Canadian Mennonite Board of Colonization (*q.v.*) since 1947. The Mennonite Brethren began work in the city in 1927, the G.C.M. Church in 1930. The Mennonite population in the city is over 1200, including children. The nearest Mennonite congregations are 20 miles to the northwest at Dalmeny (MB, 262 members; EMB, 212), 30 miles northwest at Langham (EMB, 87; GCM, 178), 30 miles north at Hepburn (MB, 241), and 30 miles south at Dundurn (GCM, 293). Rosthern (*q.v.*) is 60 miles north.
H.S.B.

Saskatoon First Mennonite Church (GCM), located in Saskatoon, Sask., a member of the Canadian District Conference and the Conference of Mennonites in Canada, had its beginning with the coming of the Mennonites from Russia after World War I. Mennonites who settled in Saskatoon were at first served occasionally by visiting ministers and students at the university. In 1930 Jacob John Thiessen was stationed here by the Home Mission Board. In 1932 a congregation was organized as a branch of the Rosenort Mennonite Church of Saskatchewan and Thiessen was ordained as minister. A new church was dedicated on Oct. 18, 1936. In 1937 the congregation was reorganized as an independent church, and in 1938 Thiessen was ordained as its elder. The congregation began the Pleasant Hill and Mayfair mission centers; the latter is now known as the Mayfair Mennonite Church. The membership of the First Mennonite Church in 1957 was 348, with J. J. Thiessen as elder.   J.J.Th.

Saskatoon Mennonite Brethren Church, located in Saskatoon, Sask., began in 1927, when members gathered for worship under the leadership of Peter Funk. As more Mennonite Brethren moved into the city a congregation was organized under the leadership of Gerhard Penner, which met for services in a Baptist church. The first church was built on the corner of Avenue C and 25th Street West in 1935, and H. S. Rempel became the leader of the city mission and also of the congregation. As the work grew the congregation was separated from the mission and a new church was built in 1954 on the corner of Avenue C and 33rd Street. Other pastors who have served the church have been H. H. Epp, Dan Wiebe, Art Martens, and G. L. Braun, the last of whom was serving in 1957, with a membership of 302.   J.H.E.

Sattler, Michael. *Sattler's Pre-Anabaptist Life.* Michael Sattler, an outstanding Anabaptist leader and martyr of South Germany, was born at Staufen in the Breisgau near Freiburg, Germany, about 1490.

The Hutterite chronicle relates that he was a learned man. All of his writings show that this was a fact. He was familiar with the original languages of the Bible; for in his trial he offered to prove his teaching from these languages. But where he was educated is not yet known. His name is not on the matriculation lists of the University of Freiburg; nevertheless it is possible that as a monk in the nearby Benedictine monastery of St. Peter he attended lectures at Freiburg. Nor is it known when he entered the monastery. In the monastery he reached the office of prior, second only to the abbot, as is reported in the *Berner Chronik* (V, 185 ff.) of Valerius Anshelm, whose wife was a native of Staufen. This also agrees with the mocking question why he did not remain a lord in the monastery, put to Sattler by the soldiers just before his death in Rottenburg in 1527, to which Sattler replied, "According to the flesh I would be a lord; but it is better so."

The Reformation caused great excitement in the Breisgau area; Freiburg seethed. In Kenzingen Jakob Otter preached evangelical doctrine, in Neuenburg Otto Brunfels, in Schlatt the venerable dean Peter Spengler. Sattler began to study the Pauline epistles in the monastery, and soon discovered that the way to righteousness before God was not the one required by the old church and the monastic life. The earnest, morally upright monk was horrified by the unspiritual life of the priests and monks. He knew the dangers of celibacy as required by the Catholic Church. He therefore left the monastery and married a Beguine, whom Anshelm called "a talented, clever little woman." But now he could no longer stay at home, since Ferdinand I of Austria, the ruler of the Breisgau, under the influence of Cardinal Campegio, had ordered the extirpation of heresy. He went to Zürich in 1525, and there, probably under the influence of Reublin, he joined the Anabaptists. With Muntprat of Constance and Konrad Winkler of Wassberg, near Ufter, he zealously preached in forests, and among others won Jakob Zander, of Bülach, called Schmid, for the Anabaptist cause. It is improbable that he attended the first Zürich disputation with the Anabaptists, Jan. 17, 1525, or the second, March 20, 1525; but it is certain that he was present at the third on Nov. 6, 1525, for the authorities were now aware of him and expelled him on Nov. 18. He returned to his home town, but could not stay under the bloody regimen of Ensisheim (the seat of the Austrian government of the Breisgau in Alsace). He turned to Strasbourg (*q.v.*), where Capito (*q.v.*) received him in his home.

The Theology of Sattler and Denk Compared. At Strasbourg Sattler met Hans Denk (*q.v.*); but very soon the great difference in their views became apparent. Sattler adhered to the principles of the Zürich Brethren, whereas Denk was more independent. Sattler clung to the letter of the Scripture, whereas Denk rated the inner Word, the revelation of God in the human spirit, above the written Word. Both questioned the Lutheran doctrine of justification and also held works to be important to man's salvation, but they differed on Christ's work of redemption. Sattler agreed with Protestant teaching:

"Who gave himself for us, that he might redeem us from all iniquity, and purify unto himself a peculiar people, zealous of good works" (Titus 2:14). Denk rejected the concept of total depravity, for every man, he said, bears in him a spark of God's Spirit, and is related to God. Christ is our example and shows the way to become one with God. The confession of Christ's death or reconciliation he disregarded. Though he did not expressly deny that Christ's suffering is reckoned to the believer, he put it into the background. On the other hand, he stressed that Christ by fulfilling the law has opened the path which no man could find alone. In other words, Denk's emphasis was on Christ as an example rather than as a sacrifice.

Sattler wanted to build a church of Christ, pure, God-fearing, and genuine, cleansed by the blood of Christ to be holy and blameless before God and men. His brethren were God's obedient children, who had separated from the world. Denk's writings contain practically nothing about the church and the world. Nowhere, except in the debated conclusion of his booklet *Von der wahren Liebe,* does he discuss the relation of the church to the world and its attitude toward government, to military service, or other requirements.

Sattler and Denk also differed on the value of baptism. Sattler believed that through baptism the believer was admitted into the church of the saints. Denk did not place much value on the sacraments, which were for him nothing more than external symbols. Denk's entire concept of church and baptism is derived from the great influence of Mysticism, as represented by Tauler, *Deutsche Theologie,* and the *Imitation of Christ.*

Sattler, like the Reformers, taught that Christ came to save all who believe on Him, but that he who does not believe will be condemned. Denk taught that Christ died for all, and that God has destined all men for salvation. In Denk is seen the bold flight of the spirit which wants to penetrate into the deepest questions of faith. Sattler clung to humble simplicity and withdrew from highflying spirits and theologians (*Schriftgelehrte*).

Sattler's Discussion with Bucer and Capito in Strasbourg. After Denk, Ludwig Haetzer (*q.v.*) was staying in Capito's home; but the serious, quiet, and upright Sattler was repelled by the restless and impure man. His association with Capito and Bucer (*q.v.*) was so much the more sincere. He presented to them a summary of Anabaptist teaching after consultation with the Anabaptists of Strasbourg, which shows a mystical-quietistic piety, but at the same time a deep inwardness and holy earnestness. The points of discussion between them were baptism, communion, power or sword, oath, and the ban. Sattler drew up his articles of faith as follows:

(1) Christ has come to save all who believe in Him.

(2) He who believes and is baptized will be saved, but he who does not believe will be condemned.

(3) Faith in Christ reconciles us with the Father and gives access to Him.

(4) Baptism seals all the believers into the body of Christ, who is now their Head.

(5) Christ is the head of His body, that is, of the believing church.

(6) As the Head, so shall the body be.

(7) The predestined and called believers shall be conformed to the image of Christ.

(8) Christ despises the world; His children shall do the same. He has no kingdom in this world; the world is against His kingdom.

(9) The believers have been chosen out of the world; therefore the world hates them.

(10) The devil is the prince of all the world; through him all the children of darkness reign.

(11) Christ is the prince of all spirits; through Him live all that walk in the light.

(12) The devil seeks to destroy, Christ to save.

(13) The flesh is at enmity with the spirit, the spirit with the flesh.

(14) The spiritual are Christ's; the carnal belong to death and the wrath of God.

(15) Christians are quite at rest and confident in their Father in heaven, without any external worldly armor.

(16) Christ's citizenship is in heaven, not on the earth.

(17) Christians are the family of God and citizens of the saints, not of the world.

(18) But they are the true Christians who do the teachings of Christ with works.

(19) Flesh and blood, display, worldly honor, and also the world cannot comprehend the teachings of Christ. In short, Christ and Belial have nothing in common.

Capito and Bucer discussed these points with Sattler in "brotherly discipline and peace," but did not reach an agreement. Sattler realized the untenability of his situation. On the one hand, he must have feared that the learned theologians would influence him to change his mind, which would for him denote a denial and blasphemy of God. On the other hand, he feared that if he persisted in his views he would fall into the hands of the authorities.

The Schleitheim Conference. It is probably right to assume that in the last months of 1526 (not in 1527) Sattler went into the Hohenberg territory in Württemberg in response to an invitation by Reublin. There he wrote a letter of farewell to Capito and Bucer, defending his departure. Reublin and Sattler divided the Hohenberg region between them, Reublin taking the work south of Rottenburg (*q.v.*), and Sattler in the north, with his headquarters in Horb (*q.v.*). Sattler was very successful and won a large following for the Anabaptist movement in and around Horb. His influence is indicated by the fact that he presided at the conference at Schleitheim (*q.v.*) on Feb. 24, 1527, which adopted a confession of faith drawn up in seven points and sent to the brotherhood in the form of an epistle (see **Brüderlich Vereinigung**). Though these articles did not attain the status of a full confession of faith, they offered a firm foundation for the High German and Swiss Anabaptists, and at the same time rejected the libertinism of a man like Haetzer. The goal set by Sattler for the Brethren was the creation of a holy church, which was forbidden all association with persons of other faiths, all participation in the religious services of Catholic or Protestants, all association in civilian life including trade, all acceptance of public office, all use of weapons and legal compulsion, and all swearing. At the same time Sattler created a proper organization. Each congregation was to choose and dismiss its "shepherd." The "shepherd" had the leadership of the congregation in his hand in the broadest sense, especially the conducting of worship services, communion, reading, admonishing, teaching, reproving, banning, and audible prayer. Very carefully Sattler provided for the preservation of the office of preaching during persecution, so that the congregations should never lack a firm hand, even though their preacher should be banished or killed. The seven articles of the Schleitheim Confession testify to Sattler's holy zeal and his unfeigned warmth and devotion.

Sattler's Arrest and Trial. When Sattler returned from Schleitheim, the Anabaptists had already been discovered at Rottenburg, without Sattler's having any premonition of it. Then at the end of February he with his wife and Reublin's wife, Matthias Hiller, and Veit Veringer of Rottenburg, and a number of men and women of Horb were arrested. The government had made a valuable catch. For on Sattler were found not only the seven articles, but also some important written notations on the plans and activities of the Swiss Brethren. The authorities did not trust the feeling in Horb, and the prison was not strong enough or large enough for the great number of prisoners; they feared a revolt. Therefore the prisoners were led by Count Joachim von Zollern and the foremost officials, with fourteen horses, to the more secluded town of Binsdorf. Here Sattler wrote a letter of consolation to the congregation at Horb. He admonished them to be steadfast and bade them farewell. For he was constantly threatened, now with the rope, now with fire, and now with the sword. But these did not terrify him; with his wife and brethren he had committed himself entirely to the will of the Lord, but he knew that martyrdom awaited him.

The Innsbruck (Austria) authorities, under whose jurisdiction this territory fell, had decided to hold court in Rottenburg, and on March 18 the towns of Ueberlingen, Radolfszell, Stockach, and Villingen received orders to send two judges each to Rottenburg. The University of Tübingen was also required to send two doctors of the imperial law, since it was feared that laymen might pass an unsuitable verdict, and also because they wanted to be protected against public opinion, which might have accused the government of dealing too lightly with so serious a matter as a religious trial in committing it solely to the laity. The trial was set for April 12; but all sorts of hindrances interfered. Horb refused to deliver the prisoners to the court. The government was acquainted with the mood of Horb and had therefore taken the four Anabaptist leaders to Binsdorf.

The strictly Catholic University of Tübingen also flatly refused to send two lawyers, for they knew that the outcome would be a death sentence, which would disqualify them for the priesthood; some had already taken the first steps toward entering the priesthood, and others were planning to do so soon,

and they could not be consecrated if they took part in a criminal court. The university also raised the objection that it had a burden of work accruing from the courts in its own principality, whereas Rottenburg belonged to another rule. And finally they noted that the Rottenburg parish belonged to the University of Freiburg, which should therefore be interested in an ecclesiastical trial in Rottenburg. Did the government feel that the real motive behind the university's refusal was horror of the capital punishment its representatives were to approve?

With amazement the authorities noted the large number of appeals for mercy for the prisoners, an indication of the mood of the people. For Count Joachim, a man of indolent calm, and his officials the entire case, which was creating so much work, was most inconvenient. How easily they could have been relieved of the work of holding court by simply calling in the imperial provost Aichele (*q.v.*) to hang the Anabaptists quietly on the nearest tree, as the Swabian League did! The Count actually made this proposal to the government. The government replied contemptuously that the honor of the house of Austria did not permit execution without trial and sentence. Even Ferdinand, who in his hasty manner declared "the third baptism," i.e., drowning, the best antidote to Anabaptism, and who had expressed the wish that Sattler be drowned without delay by Aichele, but felt that for the others there was no need to hurry, was persuaded to postpone the court session to May 17. Ehingen was added to the towns mentioned above which were to send representatives to Rottenburg. Freiburg also sent two men, though they were not members of the university. The Innsbruck authorities appealed to Stuttgart to use its influence on the University of Tübingen to send two jurists; they were not to be doctors of spiritual law, but of temporal law, who were laymen. Once more the university protested that it had no jurists but those who were now priests or about to take orders, and claimed papal and imperial law. Indeed, on May 6 the university sent two of its members to Stuttgart to present their refusal to send delegates. Stuttgart rejected the appeal, for it wanted to please Innsbruck. A clever evasion was agreed upon, probably suggested by Stuttgart. Two doctors actually went to Rottenburg; they were better paid than was usual for the first court session; they were, however, not doctors of law, but of the arts. They were Georg Farner of Kirchheim and Balthasar Stumpp of Waiblingen.

Now Innsbruck also considered it necessary to call two men from Ensisheim because of their wealth of experience in religious trials. But there was no other government with so bad a reputation as Ensisheim. Their lack of earnestness and strength was matched by an ambitious attitude, full of sycophancy toward their superiors and bloodthirstiness toward their inferiors. The men sent by Ensisheim had no lack of experience in or of inclination for "Blutgericht." They were the city secretary Eberhard Hofmann and Jodokus Gundersheim, the city secretary of Neuenburg.

Michael Sattler and his wife, Veit Veringer, and Matthias Hiller, who had thus far spent eleven weeks and three days in jail, were taken to Rottenburg by the mayor of Binsdorf, Peter Putz with twenty-four horsemen. Since Count Joachim feared a revolt in the town fifty-six additional foot soldiers were drawn from the villages of the lower district and sent to Rottenburg.

On Wednesday, May 15, 1527, the judges called to the trial were already assembled, so that the court could open. According to the Villingen chronicle the court consisted of twenty-four judges. The chairman was the "Landeshauptmann" Count Joachim of Zollern. The attorney for the defense was the mayor of Rottenburg, Jakob Halbmayer, whom Sattler made responsible for the outcome of the trial; but he appeared only at the beginning and the end of the trial. During the trial, feeling inadequate to the position, he had Hofmann speak for him. The assumption is probably correct that this eloquent legal expert was the conspicuous character in the affair and that he was responsible for the cruel sentence, which aroused great excitement.

There are four accounts of the course of the trial; the simplest and most credible has the title, *Ayn newes wunderbarliches geschicht von Michael Sattler zu Rottenburg am Neckar sampt andern 9 mannen seiner lere und glauben halben verbrannt und 10 wyaber ertrenkt, 1527* (copy in the Wolfenbüttel library, photostatic copy in GCL). This account is based on the narration of Klaus von Graveneck, a Swabian who had presumably been forced to come to Rottenburg with arms to protect the court. He was a Protestant. In the Peasants' War he had in person gathered a company of peasants and was therefore arrested, and not released until May 5, 1526. His sisters Kunigunde and Margarete had been nuns in the Königsfelden convent, but had married Zürich clergymen. The account was probably written by a brother-in-law of Klaus von Graveneck and printed in Zürich. The second account appeared as an appendix to the *Brüderlich Vereinigung* and was headed, *Folgen die Artikel und Handhabung, so Michael Sattler zu Rottenburg am Neckar mit seinem Blut bezeuget hat* (Walther Köhler, *Flugschriften* II, no. 3). This appeared in a Dutch translation with some of Sattler's writings as early as 1560 (reprint 1565). The third account is *Eines Wiedertäuffers Nachricht an die Brüder und Schwestern des Schweizerlandes von Hinrichtung einiger ihrer Secte zu Rothenburg am Neckar und der dabei vorgefallenen Wunderzeichen,* printed in *Füsslin* (II, 374-88), written by Reublin and sent to the Brethren in Zollikon, Grüningen, Basel, and Appenzell. A fourth account is found in the chronicles of the Hutterian Brethren, published by Josef Beck (pp. 26 ff.). A fifth account, written by Johannes Schlegel of Ravensburg, first prebendary at Zürichberg, then assistant in Dübendorf, then three years in Bernese territory, about 1525 assistant in Höngg, 1528 pastor in Otelfingen, 1530 in Elgg, d. 1552, has not yet been found. Christian Friedrich Sattler gives brief but independent data certainly based upon material in the state archives.

The trial opened on Friday, May 17, and continued on Saturday. On the bench of the accused sat Michael Sattler, his wife, Matthias Hiller, Veit Veringer of Rottenburg, and seven other men and eight other women. According to the Villingen chronicle there were fourteen defendants. First they were given their choice of attorney. Sattler, speaking for the group, declined the offer, since it was not a legal matter. The way of law was forbidden them by God's Word; he was willing to be shown the contrary from the Word of God. Sattler spoke in a courteous, modest, but definite manner. Very wisely he called the judges the servants of God, thereby on the one hand recognizing their authority, though of course only to the extent that it did not concern religious matters, and on the other hand he appealed to their conscience by calling attention to their responsibility. Sattler briefly questioned the competence of the court. But no attention was paid to this objection, for they had been appointed by the Austrian government, and were therefore competent.

The Charges Against Sattler. Count Joachim now had the charge read. It comprised nine articles, seven of which pertained to all the defendants, and two to Sattler alone. The charge is not unskillfully written, but it reveals that there was no understanding for the Anabaptist case, and that the authors did not even have the pertinent facts about the Anabaptists. An analysis of its contents follows.

The first article accused the Anabaptists of trespassing against the imperial mandates. Anabaptism was therefore to this court not only a religious crime, but also a civil crime. It meant not only the overthrow of the Roman Church, but of the entire Christian Church, an unchristian attack against the faith, which placed the Anabaptists on the same level as the Turks; and in addition it was a secret revolt. The mandates had been posted in all the churches and town halls. This being the case, the court was of course competent. The emperor was the protector of the church—this was the premise and conclusion of medieval history—and the church was none but the Roman Catholic Church. This church, its doctrine, its organization, and its law were alone valid on Austrian soil. What had been going on for ten years to prove the untenability of this medieval view did not exist for Austria; and where it showed itself it was to be extinguished like a dangerous fire.

The first article concerned the law of the church acknowledged by the empire; the others were concerned with the splendors of this church in its means of grace and miracles, first of all with its sacraments. The second article accounts the Anabaptist denial of the Roman doctrine of transubstantiation, indeed of the presence of Christ in the emblems, as a crime; the third, their rejection of infant baptism; the fourth, their rejection of the extreme unction. The seventh article, which is incorrectly placed, belongs here. It reproaches the Anabaptists with an unheard-of practice in the communion; they broke bread and wine together into a dish and took them together. It is not known where this charge originated. The Schleitheim Confession presupposes the Biblical manner of breaking bread. It must be assumed that a false rumor played a part here, connected with the term "breaking" the bread, which was foreign to the judges. From the Roman Catholic point of view breaking the bread was in itself unthinkable, since the bread was the body of Christ. The fifth article accused the Anabaptists of despising the "Mother of God" and the saints. The sixth dealt with their refusal to swear an oath to the government. These were the charges made against all the Anabaptists.

The last two articles applied to Sattler alone. The eighth charged him with the crime of abandoning the monastic order and marrying; his appointment as an Anabaptist preacher was evaded. In the ninth article a statement of Sattler's, perhaps taken from one of his writings, was cleverly put at the conclusion, which made him an especially dangerous man in the eyes of any Austrian. He was accused of having taught that if the Turks came into the country, no resistance should be offered; indeed, if war could be morally justified, he would rather fight against the Christians than against the Turks. This charge could not fail to make the deepest impression on the court. The Turks for years had been considered the worst foe of the empire and the Christian faith. Vast sums of money had been sacrificed by the faithful and paid as a Turkish war tax to make war on this archfoe of Christendom. The Turks had caused Ferdinand inexpressible distress; at great pains he had aroused the German estates and raised an army to fight the Turks. And now the Turk was to be considered less dangerous than he and the representatives of the old faith. To be sure, Sattler was not charged, as other Anabaptists had been, with having made an alliance with the Turks, but the charge that was made was sufficient to make him an archtraitor to the empire.

A glance over the nine articles shows that the center of gravity rests in the first article, and that besides it only the sixth and ninth were important. Accusations concerning the erroneous views on the sacraments and disregard for the saints were actually the concern of the ecclesiastical court at Constance and not of the secular court at Rottenburg. How was the secular court to consider a man a criminal on the basis of a question of the communion or baptism or for marrying, when no other crime could be proved against him? Was Sattler not right in claiming that the court was not competent?

But the accusation was based on the law of the empire. The faith of the Catholic Church was the only legitimate one in the empire. This had been confirmed by all the imperial mandates since the Diet of Worms in 1521; and these mandates were alone valid in Rottenburg. The view of the law was still that of the Middle Ages. Opposed to it stood a new world in the person of Sattler and the Anabaptists. They sponsored the principle of faith and freedom of conscience and adherence to the Word of God, but this concerned only a minority and was not the law of the empire. To the representatives of the medieval world it must have appeared as arbitrariness, or even sedition. But the course of the trial was even for that time a horrifying one. Responsibility for this state of affairs must be placed on the indolence and bungling of the presiding judge and the venom of the secretary of Ensisheim.

Sattler's Defense. Sattler now consulted the other defendants as to the manner of the defense. Then he began, unafraid, skillfully, but modestly, to discuss each article in its turn. At first he tried to refute the charge that the Anabaptists were disobedient to the imperial mandates; for these required that the Lutheran doctrine and error should not be followed, but alone the Gospel and the Word of Christ. This the Anabaptists had done. But the mandates threatened not only Lutheran doctrine, but all deviation from the Gospel as Rome understood it; to the Catholics, the Anabaptists were merely a Lutheran sect.

On the second article Sattler admitted at once that the Anabaptists rejected the teaching of the presence of the body and blood of Christ in the communion and attempted to prove his point as Luther and Zwingli had done: Christ had gone to heaven and was seated at God's right hand. If He is in heaven, He is not in the bread and cannot be eaten. Also on the third article Sattler admitted the charge. He did not try to conceal that the Anabaptists repudiated infant baptism. The command to baptize has faith precede baptism. Baptism is merely the symbol of the covenant with Christ. On the extreme unction Sattler made a distinction between oil as a creation of God, which is good, and the pope's oil. The pope had never created anything good. The oil mentioned by Mark and James was not the pope's oil. Here Sattler had a good point, but he assumed too much on the part of the judges.

The charge that the Anabaptists despised Mary and the saints Sattler could deny with a good conscience; but he had to admit that they believed that Mary was not yet elevated, but, like all men, awaiting the judgment; they did not accept her as a mediator and intercessor. But in the eyes of the court, such an attitude was contempt. As saints Sattler would acknowledge only those who live and believe. Dead believers he called the "blessed ones."

The charge that they refused to render an oath Sattler justified wth Matt. 5:34 and 37. Sattler hardly found it necessary to refute the charge that the Anabaptists ate bread mingled with wine as the Lord's Supper; at least none of the accounts of the trial recorded it.

After Sattler had answered the charges against the Anabaptists in general he turned to the accusations made specifically against him. He justified his departure from the monastery with the knowledge derived from the study of the Pauline epistles, that the monastic position was an unchristian, deceptive, and dangerous one; and from his own experience of the life and conduct of the monks and priests, their show, deception, usury, and their great fornication in seducing this man's wife, that one's daughter, and the third man's maid. Paul had prophesied this in I Tim. 4:3.

Concerning the last point Sattler admitted that he had taught that if the Turk should come, no armed resistance should be made, for it is written, Thou shalt not kill. We should not resist any of our persecutors with the sword, but with prayer cling to God, that He may resist and defend. Sattler even admitted having said that if war were right, he would rather march against supposed Christians who persecute, capture, and kill the God-fearing. The Turk knows nothing about the Christian faith; he is a Turk according to the flesh. But you want to be considered Christians, boast of being Christ's, and still persecute His pious witnesses. You are Turks according to the spirit. To this strong admonition to the conscience of the court, Sattler added in conclusion that it was their calling to punish the wicked and protect the good. He could bear witness that the Anabaptists had done nothing contrary to God and the Gospel. Likewise the closest examination would substantiate that he and his brethren had never opposed the government by any act or word, neither in revolt or sedition nor in any other way. He demanded that experts be called and the Bible used in the original languages; a debate should be arranged. The Anabaptists were ready to be taught from the Bible. If they were proved to be in error, they would gladly bear the punishment. "But if we are not shown to be in error, I hope to God that you will accept teaching and be converted." The idea that the judges might be taught and converted by Sattler seemed so peculiar to them that they put their heads together and burst out laughing. The secretary of Ensisheim snapped at Sattler, "Yes, you rascal of a monk, should we dispute with you? Yes, the hangman shall and will dispute with you." The chairman found not a word to say in defense of the accused. Sattler did not allow himself to be disturbed and replied, "What God wills, will happen." His calm earnestness irritated the city secretary, so that he cried, "Indeed, it would be good if you had never been born, you archheretic; you have seduced pious people. If they would only acknowledge their error and commit themselves to mercy!" Sattler replied, "Mercy is with God." One of the other defendants said, "It is wrong to deviate from the truth." Now the wrath of the secretary reached its limit. He cried, "Yes, you desperate rascal, you archheretic, I say, if there were no hangman here, I would hang you myself and be doing God a good service thereby." Reublin reports that he had partly unsheathed his sword and said, "If you do not desist, I will execute you myself with this sword." Reublin probably confused a later scene with this one.

The Sentence and the Execution. The secretary may have felt that his poisonous attitude was making an unfavorable impression on the court, and began to speak in Latin with Sattler; this Klaus could not record, for he did not understand it. He remembered only Sattler's last word, "Judica." Now the city secretary became aware that he was playing a role that was not his. He therefore turned to Count Joachim with the words, "He will not cease this chatter today anyway. Therefore you may proceed with the sentence; I call for the decision of the court." Now Joachim asked Sattler whether he wished to ask for the verdict. Sattler replied, "You servants of God, I am not sent to judge the Word of God; we are sent to testify; but we are not for that reason removed from being judged, and we are ready to suffer and to await what God is planning to do with us. We will continue in our faith in Christ as long as we have breath until we are shown from the Scripture to be wrong."

Again the city secretary replied instead of the chairman, repeating the threat, "The hangman will instruct you and will debate with you, you archheretic!" Sattler replied, "I will appeal to the Scriptures." At this point the discussion was broken off. The judges withdrew to consult on the verdict. Their discussion evidently did not proceed as smoothly as the city secretary had imagined, for it lasted one and one-half hours.

The Anabaptists were then committed to the soldiers. Sattler saw himself subjected to scenes similar to those his Lord and Master had experienced. One cried to him, "When I see you get away, I will believe in you." Another seized his sword from the table, drew it, and said, "See, with this we will dispute with you." Klaus von Graveneck was horrified by all these words of contempt which were not at all fitting to the gravity of the situation; he felt that in such a situation one would have pitied the worst murderer, and here he saw innocent people tormented with no defense. Sattler's silence toward all personal insults annoyed the soldiers. One of the prisoners said, "Pearls should not be cast before the swine." Once more Sattler began to speak when someone asked him why he had not remained a lord in a monastery. It seemed incomprehensible to the man that anyone would for the sake of his faith sacrifice the haughty rank of a priest and the comfortable life of a prior in a monastery. Then Sattler answered, "According to the flesh I would have been a lord, but it is better so," and then showed from the Scriptures that his exchange was a fortunate one.

The period of painful waiting came to an end. The judges reappeared; the verdict was read. It read, "...Michael Sattler...shall be committed to the executioner. The latter shall take him to the square and there first cut out his tongue, then forge him fast to a wagon and there with glowing iron tongs twice tear pieces from his body, then on the way to the site of the execution five times more as above and then burn his body to powder as an archheretic."

Klaus von Graveneck adds, "All this I saw myself. May God grant us also to testify of Him so bravely and patiently." Reublin says that the trial lasted two days, that the verdict was read on Saturday, May 18, and that when the sentence was read, Sattler's wife comforted him with great joy in the sight of the entire crowd.

Before the prisoners were led away, Sattler had another conversation in a private chamber with the mayor of Rottenburg, whom Sattler had made responsible for the final verdict, although it is to be assumed that the city secretary of Ensisheim bore most of the guilt for the sentence. Sattler said to the mayor, "You know that you with your fellow judges have sentenced me contrary to law; therefore take care and repent. If you do not, you will with them be condemned to eternal fire in God's judgment."

Three more days were granted Sattler. Reublin is probably correct when he says, "What fear, conflict, and struggle flesh and spirit must have undergone, cannot be imagined." Sattler had agreed with his group to give a sign as evidence of his constancy and cheer. There is a difference of opinion concerning the day of Sattler's death. The Anabaptist chronicles and the *Ausbund* give May 21 as the day of his martyrdom. Klaus von Graveneck gives May 20. Reublin says, "Sattler lay in prison from Saturday to Monday and was executed on that day." It is most likely that the Anabaptist chroniclers became confused in their counting by the termination of the imprisonment "until the third day," and thought Sattler was executed on Monday, May 20. This is also the opinion of Hulshof (p. 65) and Baum, *Capito und Butzer* (p. 373).

First Sattler was taken to the market place and a piece cut from his tongue, but not enough to prevent speech. Then pieces were torn from his body twice with glowing tongs. Then he was forged to a cart, and between the city gate and the place of execution the tongs were applied five times again. The number of times the tongs were used is variously given. The sentence ordered two and five applications, Reublin speaks of six, Capito in his letter to the Council of Horb of two and five. The place of execution is a quarter hour's walk from the town close to the highway to Tübingen. The tortures of the unfortunate victim under the tongs, a monstrous heightening of the execution, must have been unspeakable, but nothing could shake Sattler. On the market place and the site of the execution he prayed for his persecutors and Klaus von Graveneck. When he was bound to the ladder with ropes to be pushed into the fire, he admonished the people to be converted, to repent and fear God, and to intercede for his judges. Then he turned to the judges. He especially remembered the mayor and the admonition given him in private. The mayor replied defiantly and angrily that Sattler should concern himself now only with God. Then Sattler prayed, "Almighty, eternal God, Thou art the way and the truth; because I have not been shown to be in error, I will with Thy help on this day testify to the truth and seal it with my blood."

Reublin says that a sack of powder had been tied around Sattler's neck to hasten his death. He was now thrown into the fire on the ladder; then his voice could be heard bright and clear with prayer and praise. Soon the ropes on his hands were burned through. He could now raise the two forefingers of his hands, thereby giving the promised signal to his group, and prayed, "Father, I commend my spirit into Thy hands."

Reublin could not avoid adorning Sattler's death with miracles. He reports that Sattler's right hand and his heart did not burn. The executioner cut the heart to pieces, the blood spurting high toward heaven. In the night after Sattler's death the sun and moon were seen for three hours above the site of execution with golden letters in them. The glow had been so bright that everyone thought it was midday. The authorities forbade anyone's speaking of it under oath, in order to suppress the matter. The death of Sattler, steadfast to the end as a martyr to his faith, does not need adornment from Reublin's imagination.

Three other Anabaptists were executed, among them Matthias Hiller. The furrier's apprentice of St. Gall, the wife of Stoffel Schuhmacher, and Salome Katler(in) of Rottenburg had recanted publicly. These like all other recanting Anabaptists were lighted out of Rottenburg with burning torches, and expelled forever from Austrian territory. Veit Veringer, who had first recanted and then returned to the Anabaptists, lay in prison at Schömberg for over thirteen weeks and was then executed. Valerius Anshelm relates that the countess of Hechingen, i.e., the wife of Joachim von Zollern, tried to persuade Sattler's wife to desist from her faith and stay at her court. But she declared that she would be true to her Lord and to her Christian husband, and was drowned in the Neckar on the eighth day after her husband's death. She would have preferred to die in the fire with him. According to some reports she was drowned on Wednesday, May 22.

The Reaction of the Public. Sattler's character lies clearly before us. He was not a highly educated divine nor an intellectual; but his entire life was noble and pure, true and unadulterated. The impression made by his death sentence in Rottenburg was profound. Klaus von Graveneck's horror is clearly felt in his report. It is as if the hand of Heinrich Hug, the chronicler of Villingen, trembled when he concluded his narrative about the Anabaptists in Rottenburg with the words, "It was a miserable affair, they died for their conviction" (*Publikation des Literarischen Vereins* 164, p. 459). Especially great was the impression on Strasbourg, where Sattler was personally known. Word had scarcely been received there that four others had been executed in addition to Sattler, and that still others lay in prison, when Capito seized his pen and on May 31 wrote to the council of Horb, "This Michael is known to us here in Strasbourg and he was somewhat in error, which we showed him through the Scriptures; but since he saw a lack in our preachers and other preachers of the true doctrine, especially in the outward life of the congregation, he perhaps paid less attention to our admonition. But at the same time he showed such great zeal for the honor of God and the church of Christ, which he would have pure and blameless and without reproach to those who are outside. We never censured this but praised it highly, but his method and the articles of his faith we always kindly rejected, and that after mature reflection before God. Now we did not agree with him herein. He wanted to make pious Christians through a fixed creed and outward compulsion, which we considered the beginning of a new monkery. But we desired to correct the life of the believers through consideration of God's good deeds, which He has shown us in body and soul, that it might be a fruit of love and gratitude, for this is the way and the order of salvation" (Baum, 373). Bucer speaks with equal respect in his *Getreue Warnung* (July 1527): "We do not doubt that Michael Sattler, who was burned at Rottenburg, was a dear friend of God, although he was a leader of the Anabaptists, but much more skilled and honorable than some."

Reublin's booklet seriously embarrassed the Austrian government, which would have liked to issue a counter report, but feared that nothing fruitful would result, and rightly so. But one consequence of the enormous excitement caused by Sattler's execution can be observed. In Württemberg the authorities now had the Anabaptists indoctrinated by clergymen, at this time by the Tübingen professor Käuffelin, to persuade them to recant.

The Anabaptists ascribed to Sattler the hymn, "Als Christus mit seiner wahren Lehr," which is in the *Ausbund* of 1583. Keller (*ADB* XXX, 412) considers Sattler the author of the leaflet, *Wie die Gschrift verstendiglich soll unterschieden und erklärt werden* (n.p., n.d.). Michael Sattler was as deserving of a monument at the site of his execution as John Huss in Constance.

On Aug. 16, 1957, the Sixth Mennonite World Conference dedicated a memorial plaque to Michael Sattler in the Lutheran parish church in Rottenburg, at which time a special memorial service was held. G.Bos., H.S.B.

Beck, *Geschichts-Bücher;* J. C. Füsslin, *Beiträge zur Kirchen- und Reformationsgeschichte des Schweizerlandes* II (Zürich, 1742) 374; III (Zürich, 1747) 249; Emil Egli, *Aktensammlung zur Geschichte der Züricher Reformation* (Zürich, 1879), No. 1366; J. Ottius, *Annales Anabaptistici* (Basel, 1672); Veesenmeyer, "Von Michael Sattler," in *Kirchenhistorisches Archiv* (1826) p. 476; C. A. Cornelius, *Geschichte des Münsterischen Aufruhrs* (Leipzig, 1855-60); J. Baum, *Capito und Butzer* (Elberfeld, 1860); *ADB* XXX, 411; Gustav Bossert, "Michael Sattler," in *Blätter für württb. Kirchengeschichte* (1891) 67-69, 73, 75, 81-83, 89, 90; (1892) 1-4, 9-10; Camill Gerbert, *Geschichte der Strassburger Sektenbewegung* (Strasbourg, 1889); G. Bossert (Introduction only), *Beschreibung des Oberamtes Rottenburg* I (1899) 409 ff.; idem, *Das Blutgericht von Rottenburg* (Barmen, 1892); idem, *HRE* XVII, 492-94; XXIV, 451; A. Baur, *Zwinglis Theologie* (Halle, 1885 and 1889) 186; *Zwinglis Werke* III (Leipzig, 1914) 357 ff. *BRN* V; Walther Koehler, "Brüderlich Vereinigung etzlicher Kinder Gottes, sieben Artikel betreffend, Item ein Sendbrief Michael Sattlers an eine Gemeine Gottes samt seinem Martyrium" (1527), in *Flugschriften aus den ersten Jahren der Reformation* II, No. 3 (Leipzig, 1908) 277-338; Wolkan, *Lieder;* Abraham Hulshof, *Geschiedenis van de Doopsgezinden te Straatsburg van 1527 tot 1557* (Amsterdam, 1905) 24 ff.; Valerius Anshelm, *Bernische Chronik* V (Bern, 1896) 185 f.; Friedrich Spitta, "Michael Sattler als Dichter," in *Ztschr für Kirchengesch.* XXXV (1914) 393-402; Christian F. Sattler, *Geschichte des Herzogtums Würtenberg unter der Regierung der Herzogen* II (1771) 171 ff.; *TA Zürich;* G. Bossert Jr., "Michael Sattler's Trial and Martydom in 1527," *MQR* XXV (1951) 201-18; *ML* IV.

Saucon Mennonite Church (GCM), a member of the Eastern District Conference, is located on the Old Bethlehem Pike between Coopersburg and Center Valley, Pa., in Upper Saucon Twp., Lehigh Co. The first meetinghouse, a log building, was erected in 1735-38. It had one room for the church and one room for the church school, separated by a swinging partition. In 1749 the following trustees were appointed to build another meetinghouse: George Bachman, Philip Geissinger, John Rieser, Samuel Newcomer, and Samuel Bechtel. The deed, dated 1751, is well preserved. More than a dozen Indians worshiped regularly in the services. In 1782 a schoolhouse was built on the grounds near the highway. It was abandoned when the Penn Schoolhouse, a public school, was built by the township. In 1847 (1841?) a beautiful stone meetinghouse replaced the old building.

In the Oberholtzer division of 1847 in the Franconia Conference most of the Saucon members followed Oberholtzer, so that the congregation became a charter member of the Eastern District Conference (GCM). The small group which stayed with the old conference continued to use the meetinghouse for some years. The last resident Franconia Conference (MC) minister who preached to the small M.C. flock at Saucon was Samuel Moyer (1806-77); he himself first went with the majority into the new conference, but returned to the Franconia Conference about 1861. The last M.C. member died in 1899. In 1957 the pastor of the Saucon church was M. Lawrence Smith, and the membership was 64. S.F.S., J.C.W.

J. C. Wenger, *History of the Mennonites of the Franconia Conference* (Telford, 1937) 224 f.

Sauder (Sauter, Souder), a Swiss Mennonite family name no longer found in Europe but strongly represented in the Mennonite Church (MC) in the Franconia and Lancaster Conference districts in Eastern Pennsylvania and to some extent in Ontario, as well as in the Amish Mennonite area in Fulton County, Ohio. In 1746 two Souder brothers settled in Montgomery County. Of their descendants the following have served in the ministry of the Franconia Conference: Mahlon D. Souder (1859-1924) and Edwin A. Souder (1882-1957) at Rockhill, and Menno B. Souder (1892-) at Franconia. John D. Souder, a brother of Mahlon D., was prominent as a historian and artist in illuminated manuscripts. The town of Souderton, founded in 1860 and named Souderton in 1876, was named for the many Souders in the community.

In Lancaster County some of the Sauders who have served in the ministry are John M. Sauder in the Weaverland congregation as preacher from 1895 and as bishop from 1926, his son Eli G. Sauder, minister at Groffdale since 1920, Noah N. Sauder, minister at New Holland since 1923, J. Paul Sauder (b. 1902) at Tampa, Fla., and two other congregations. Roy Sauder is bishop at the Tedrow congregation near Archbold, Ohio. Levi S. Sauder was long superintendent of the Millersville (Pa.) Children's Home. Elvin R. Souder, of Souderton, Pa., is an active church and conference worker (GCM) and attorney. H.S.B.

Saur (written both Saur and Sauer by the family itself, Sower being the later anglicized form), **Christopher** (1693-1758), a noted Dunkard (Church of the Brethren) printer and publisher of Germantown, Pa., was born in Laasphe, Wittgenstein, Germany, emigrated to Germantown in 1724, and was baptized a member of the Dunkard church in 1728. After a residence near Ephrata in Lancaster County as a farmer, he returned to Germantown and in 1738 began his notable career as the first German printer and publisher in America. His annual almanac, *Der Hoch-Deutsch Americanische Calender* (1739-77), and his newspaper, *Der Hoch-Deutsch Pennsylvanische Geschicht-Schreiber* (1739-77), had wide circulation among the Germans of Pennsylvania and Maryland and had great influence among the German sects, including the Mennonites. In these and other publications he spoke out against war and slavery. His son's (Christopher Saur, Jr.) *Ein Geistliches Magazien* (1764-73), the first religious journal in America, published hymns and other writings of the Mennonite schoolteacher Christopher Dock (*q.v.*), the good friend of both the father and the son. It was the father who persuaded Dock to write his famous *Schulordnung* in 1750, which was published by the son in 1770. The Saur Press published the first European language Bibles in America (German in 1743, 1763, and 1776); copies of the first edition are still found in some Mennonite (MC) pulpits in the Franconia Conference.

The Saur Press, carried on by the son until its confiscation by the Revolutionary authorities in 1778, printed the following Mennonite books: *Ausbund* (1742, 1751, 1767); Henry Funck, *Ein Spiegel der Taufe* (1744); and J. P. Schabalie, *Die Wandlende Seel* (1768, 1771). The other colonial Mennonite printer, the Ephrata Cloister Press, handled seven imprints during the same time: *Güldene Aepffel* (1745); *Das Andenken einiger heiligen Märtyrer* (1745); *Die ernsthafte Christenpflicht* (1745, 1770); *Der blutige Schau-Platz oder Märtyrer-Spiegel* (1748-49); and *Christliches Gemüths-Gespräch* (1769, 1770). H.S.B.

G. H. Genzmer, "Christopher Sower" and "Christopher Sower, Jr.," in *Dictionary of American Biography* XVII (1935); Oswald Seidensticker, "Die beiden Christoph Saur in Germantown," *Bilder aus der Deutsch-Pennsylvanischen Geschichte* (N.Y., 1885); idem, *The First Century of German Printing in America 1728-1830* (Philadelphia, 1893); John S. Flory, *Literary Activity of the German Baptist Brethren in the Eighteenth Century* (Elgin, 1908); W. R. Steckel, "Pietists in Colonial Pennsylvania; Christopher Saur, Printer, 1738-1758" (Ph.D. dissertation at Stanford University c1949); E. Gordon Alderfer, "Pioneer Culture of the Plain People," *Menn. Life* V (October 1950) 32; Edward W. Hocker, *The Sower Printing House of Colonial Times* (Pennsylvania German Society, Norristown, 1948).

Savary (Savery, Savry), a Dutch Mennonite family of artists (painters, copper engravers, sketchers), originally from Kortrijk (Courtrai) in Flanders, Belgium, from where Jacques (Jacob) Savry moved to Amsterdam, where he died in 1602. One of his pictures, "Jephtha's daughter," is found in the Rijksmuseum at Amsterdam. His son Salomon Sav(a)ry (Amsterdam 1594-1665), married to Maria Levynsdr Panten, was a copper plate engraver as was his son Jacob (Amsterdam 1617-66). It could not be ascertained whether Roelant Savery (Kortrijk c1578-Utrecht 1639), who obviously was a brother of Jacques and the most prominent of all Savrys, was a Mennonite.

Another Savary family, probably related to the former, was found at Haarlem, Holland; here Marten Savry, married to Margaretha Snep, was from 1687 a trustee of the Flemish-Waterlander orphanage. vDZ.

N.N.B.Wb. V, 660; Thieme-Becker, *Allg. Künstler Lexikon* XXIX (Leipzig, 1935).

Sawatzky (Sawatzki, Sawadsky, Sabatzke), a family name which originated among the Mennonites of Prussia and was found in the church records of Tiegenhagen, Ladekopp, Rosenort, Fürstenwerder, and Elbing. The name is of Slavic origin. No information is available as to when it first appeared among the Mennonites. Han Sawatzky (*Naamlijst* 1743) was a preacher in the Elbing district of the Marienwerder (Frisian) Mennonite congregation.

From Prussia the name spread to Russia and to North and South America.

Franz Sawatzky, a pioneer minister (GCM) at Herbert, Sask., and his son Jacob F. Sawatzky, Newton, Kan., and his grandson, Victor Sawatzky, minister at Pawnee Rock, Kan., are representatives of the Sawatzky family which came to Canada in 1874. J. G. Rempel lists as G.C.M. ministers in Canada also A. Sawatzky, F. Sawatzky, J. J. Sawatzky, and G. W. Sawatzky. Some descendants of Abr. A. Sawatzky of Schönfeld, Russia, are now located in Ontario. Peter C. Sawatzky is Principal of United Mennonite Educational Institute, Wheatley, Ont.; Jacob Sawatzky, of Hague, Sask., is chairman of the Board of Rosthern Junior College, Rosthern, Sask.; Peter G. Sawatzky is a minister of the Mayfair Mennonite (GCM) Church in Saskatoon. C.K.

Reimer, *Familiennamen;* J. G. Rempel, *Fünfzig Jahre Konferenzbestrebungen* (Steinbach, 1952).

Sawyer County (Wis.) Old Order Amish Mennonite Settlement, now extinct. In 1908-13 about 15 Amish families moved to Exeland, Wis., among them Bishop Eli J. Bontrager and family of Mylo, N.D., formerly of Indiana. In September 1913 Rudolph Hochstetler was ordained to the ministry. In 1916 Bontrager returned to Indiana for church and personal reasons. A minister, Ira Nissley, was ordained in 1919 and with two ministers the church prospered, as a number of other families moved in. After another bishop who lived close by took over the bishop care of the church, however, the unity of the church suffered and the families started to leave. The settlement was dissolved. E.J.B.

Sawyer Mennonite Brethren Church, located 7 miles west of Sawyer, N.D., a member of the M.B. Central District Conference, was organized by Christian Reimche in 1909 with nine members. Reimche, the first pastor, served the church for many years with the assistance of other ministers. The first church building was erected in 1909. This was replaced by a new building in 1924, which was again enlarged and remodeled to 20 x 58 ft. in 1947. Ministers who have served the congregation include D. J. Gerbrandt, J. F. Thiessen, and Gustav Faul. In 1957 the membership was 84; the pastor was John D. Block. A.A.D., J.F.T.

Saxony existed as an electorate in Germany 1356-1806, then became a kingdom and in 1918 a free state. It was the cradle of the Lutheran Reformation in the 16th century, promoted and protected by the electors of the Ernestine line of the Wettin-Saxon princely house, who lived in Wittenberg at the time. Among them were Frederick the Wise (1486-1525), his brother John (*q.v.*) the Steadfast (1525-32), and his son John Frederick (*q.v.*) the Magnanimous (1532-47), who was compelled after the battle at Mühlberg (1547) to give the electoral honors and lands to Duke Moritz of the Albertine line resident at Leipzig, which turned Catholic in 1697 and ruled until 1918.

As freely as Lutheranism was permitted to develop, so violently was Anabaptism attacked and suppressed by both the spiritual and temporal leaders. It was feared that there lurked within this religious lay movement the revolutionary and fanatical spirit of a Thomas Müntzer (*q.v.*) and the "Zwickau prophets" (*q.v.*).

Early in February 1527, in the district of Königsberg (*q.v.*), a Saxon enclave in Würzburg territory, where the movement gained an early foothold through the efforts of Hans Hut (*q.v.*), Volk Kolerlin, and other Anabaptist apostles, the first Anabaptists were seized. On Feb. 26, 1527, the elector issued the public order, "that no one, be he citizen, peasant, or anyone else, except the regular clergyman, preacher, and chaplain, to whom pastoral care is entrusted and who is qualified at each place is permitted to preach, baptize, or exercise other similar offices in his house or other places owned by him." Soon afterward he had the Königsberg (*q.v.*) citizens, Beutelhans (*q.v.*), Wolf Schominger (Schreiner), and ten other men besides a woman put to death as Anabaptists.

On Jan. 7, 1528, a new mandate was issued against the Anabaptists and the dissemination of their doctrine by spoken or written word, after the church inspectors had on June 16, 1527, been ordered to summon to court all those suspected of false doctrine, question them, and if necessary hear the testimony against them. Those who persisted in their error must sell their possessions and leave the country; those who acted contrary to the mandate should be arrested.

In 1528 Luther wrote his booklet, *Von der Wiedertaufe an zwei Pfarrherren,* in which he gave the assurance that there had not yet been an Anabaptist in Saxony. He adds, "I do not yet know exactly what is the cause and foundation of their faith."

The Saxon reformers approved of the elector's violent measures, so that on April 23, 1529, at Speyer he could without qualms of conscience give his consent to the well-known Anabaptist mandate (see **Punishment** of the Anabaptists) and henceforth strove to act in accord with it.

In 1529 ten Anabaptists were imprisoned at Reinhardsbrunn, and the six who remained steadfast were put to death on Jan. 18, 1530, causing great excitement among the people. The reformers now found it advisable to formulate a vindication of the right to punish heretics. To this end Justus Menius, the superintendent of Eisenach, wrote *Der Widdertauffer lere und geheimnis aus heiliger Schrift widderlegt,* with a preface by Luther and a dedication to Philip of Hesse (who, they were convinced, was too lenient), dated May 4, 1530; and Melanchthon drew up a formal opinion addressed to the elector of Saxony at the end of November 1531.

In a long-drawn-out dispute with Philip concerning the penalizing of several Anabaptists in the Hausbreitenbach district, which was under the joint jurisdiction of Saxony and Hesse, the elector insisted on their execution. In the end the prisoners were divided between Saxony and Hesse. Of those allotted to the elector at least three were put to death: Berlet Schmidt, Hans Eisfart, and his wife. Later he also insisted upon the execution of the Anabaptist leaders, Melchior Rinck (*q.v.*) and Fritz

Erbe (*q.v.*), who were held by Philip. They died in prison.

In Schweinitz near Wittenberg death in prison terminated the many cross-examinations and long martyrdom of Hans Sturm of Steyer, though he had neither preached nor baptized in Saxony. His countryman Peter Pestel of Linz, also a victim of the intolerance of the Wittenberg theologians and jurists, was beheaded on Friday after Corpus Christi at Zwickau in 1536.

After the fall of Münster in 1535 the elector's severe attitude was, of course, sharpened. On Nov. 21, 1535, Hans Peissker of Kleineutersdorf near Orlamünde was arrested in his own house with his sixteen-year-old daughter Margarethe and fourteen others; he was taken to the Leuchtenburg, and after a minute cross-examination, attended by Melanchthon, put to death with Heinz Kraut (*q.v.*) and Jobst Möller in Jena at the end of January 1536. Of the four prisoners who were transferred to Neustadt a. d. Orla because of lack of prison space in the Leuchtenburg, Heinrich Möller sealed his faith with his death.

On April 10, 1536, a new mandate was issued in Saxony against the "Anabaptists, Sacramentists, and fanatics," which was composed by Melanchthon, and also a polemic from the same pen, *Verlegung etlicher unchristlicher Artikel, welche die Wiederteuffer furgeben,* which every pastor in Saxony had to read and explain to his congregation on each third Sunday.

In January 1538 the elector had two men executed who were caught conversing with Fritz Erbe in the tower of the city wall of Eisenach, and who persisted in their faith in spite of all efforts to convert them. They were Hans Köhler (*q.v.*) of Eyerode and Hans Scheffer of Hastungsfelde. Other admirers of Erbe recanted on the rack.

In the territory of Mühlhausen, an imperial city, where after the Peasants' War in 1525 the Duke of Saxony had the protective magistracy every third year alternating with the elector of Saxony and the langrave of Hesse, Georg Köhler and Klaus Ernfart were among those who suffered death. A large number of Anabaptists were drowned in the Unstrut between Mühlhausen and Ammern and buried on the bank; among these were Jakob Storger and Klaus Scharf besides eight women on Nov. 8, 1537, and Hans Hentrock of Amra and Ottilia Goldschmidt, a Mühlhausen girl, on Jan. 17, 1538.

In spite of the frightful severity of the measures taken to suppress Anabaptism in and around Saxony, representatives of the movement now and then ventured to appear, especially in the Hausbreitenbach district, where on Jan. 7 and 8, 1544, a group of sixteen persons was tried at Berka (*q.v.*). Six of them escaped death by the intervention of Philip of Hesse; the rest were executed.

In 1543 John Frederick had Peter Rube (*q.v.*) beheaded. After the catastrophe of Mühlberg (1547) he apparently adopted a more lenient attitude; in 1551 he wrote to his son John Frederick the Middle, "To threaten heretics with the fear of fire and not to instruct them from the Scriptures we cannot consider Christian or right."

Under the Albertine electors, however, Anabaptism continued to be a capital offense and was completely eradicated. Early in 1584, under Elector August, who succeeded his brother Moritz, the Anabaptist Hans Dohn ended his life at the stake.

G.H.

P. Wappler, *Die Stellung Kursachsens und des Landgrafen Philipp von Hessen* (Münster, 1910); idem, *Thüringen*; idem, *Inquisition und Ketzerprozesse in Zwickau zur Ref.-Zeit* (Leipzig, 1908); the original of Luther's letter is found in Wolfenbüttel: see Keller, *Reformation*, 370; N. Paulus, article on Wappler in *Theol. Jahresbericht* XXX (1911), showing that heresy was a capital crime; *ML* IV.

Saymer, Peter: see **Saimer, Peter.**

Scabalie: see **Schabaelje.**

Scarboro Mennonite Mission (GCM) of Calgary, Alberta, was opened by the Alberta Conference in July 1944 and taken over by the General Conference in 1945. The building, formerly a United Church, was purchased in 1945. In 1957 there were 188 members, with J. J. Sawatzky as pastor. J.J.SA.

Schabaelje (Scabalie, Scabalje, Schabaellie), a Dutch Mennonite family found at Amsterdam, Netherlands, in the 17th and 18th centuries as members of the Waterlander (Toren) congregation and after the merger (1668) of this congregation with the Lamist (*q.v.*) church, of the united Lam en Toren congregation. Jan Philipsz Schabaelje (*q.v.*), the renowned author of *Lusthof des Gemoets* and many other books, belonged to this family. Dirk (Philipsz) Scabalie (Jan's brother), b. at Zoutelande, Dutch province of Zeeland, about 1590, d. at Amsterdam after 1641, a member of the Waterlander congregation at Amsterdam, was a miller (also called Dirk Philipsz Molenaar), who had made much money by an invention for making white flour from buckwheat. This Dirk Scabalie was during his lifetime noted as a dramatic poet; his play *Spel des Gheschils tot Athenen*, a paraphrase of Acts 17, was played in the city theater of Amsterdam in 1617. He also published *Aerdige comedie van Eigenbaet* and *Spel van des Heeren Wyngaert* (Amsterdam, 1614), a tract on Romans 9 (Amsterdam, 1616) and *Spel des Oproers tot Efesen* (Amsterdam, 1641). With his brother Jan Philipsz Schabaelje he published a hymnal called *Walchers Liedboeck* (Vlissingen, 1611). His father Philips Scabalie seems to have been a rather liberal Mennonite, who for some time shared the radical views of Robbert Robbertsz (*q.v.*).

Carel Scabalje was a deacon of the Waterlanders 1659-61, and of the Lam en Toren congregation 1683-88. Pieter Schabaelje was a public notary at Amsterdam 1695-c1735.

The Schabaelje family at Amsterdam died out in the early 18th century. VDZ.

Mennonite church records of Amsterdam; M. Schagen, *Naamlijst der Doopsgezinde schrijveren* (Amsterdam, 1745) 88 f.; *N.N.B.Wb.* V, 660; *Amstelodamum* yearbook XXV (Amsterdam, 1928) 103, 120, No. 120.

Schabaelje (Scabalie, Scabalje), **Jan Philipsz** (Philipsen), b. at Amsterdam about 1585, d. there in April 1656, and buried at Alkmaar, was a member of the Mennonite Waterlander (Toren) congregation at Amsterdam. At first he, together with his brother Pieter, owned a grain mill and was rather wealthy; later he lost his money. In 1620 he was chosen deacon of his home congregation, and soon decided to devote himself to study; he then moved to Alkmaar, where he in 1636 or 37 was called to the ministry of the Waterlander congregation as a colleague of Hans de Ries (*q.v.*). After a few years, however, he was dismissed on a charge of offensive conduct with his housekeeper, whom he later married. The exact years of his service at Alkmaar are not known. After his dismissal he returned to Amsterdam, where he opened a bookshop in the Langestraat. This business did not prosper, and gradually Schabaelje's circumstances became rather poor; then he was appointed visitor of the sick in the Amsterdam Waterlander congregation with a small salary.

Schabaelje published a large number of writings, partly because he was forced to earn his living in this way, partly also because he felt an inner call to do so. With his brother Dirk Philipsz Scabaelje he published a hymnal entitled *Walchers Liedboeck* (Vlissingen, 1611). His other publications are *Harmonia ofte Eendrachtighe Vertellinghe der Vier Evangelisten* (Amsterdam, 1624); *Sommarium ofte corten inhoudt des Bijbels*, followed by a *Historielied van het leeven onzes Heeren Jesu Christi* and two other hymns (Amsterdam, 1629, repr. Haarlem, 1654); *Tractaet teghen de Successie der Pausen van Romen* (Amsterdam, 1633); *Dialogus van den Corinthischen twist . . . op deesen onsen tijd gepast* (de Rijp, 1640); *Aenmerkingen, of Gulden Annotatien* (Hoorn, 1641; with a somewhat revised title reprinted De Rijp, 1641, and Amsterdam, n.d.); *Den grooten Figuer-Bibel*, a Biblical history with 477 copper engravings (Alkmaar, 1646); *Historische Beschrijving van het Leeven Jesu Christi*, 1069 pages with illustrations (De Rijp, 1647; 3d ed. Leeuwarden, 1707, 4th ed. Amsterdam, 1716; 64 pictures found in the third edition of this book are taken from the N. Visscher's *Prentenbijbel*); *Bibelsche Figueren anders ghenaemt Spiegel des Evangeliums* (Amsterdam, 1648); *Emblemata Sacra* (1653); his *Metamorphosis ofte Transformatie onses tijdts waar in Poetischer Wijze beweezen word de groote, en wonderbaarelijke veranderinge der Menschen uit hunne waare scheppinge: gesteld by maniere van Zaamensprekinge tusschen eenen welbelezen Historicus en eenen Pelgrim* (Alkmaar, 1657) appeared after his death. Of his book *Corte Maniere om de Siecken in haer wtersten te troosten* the first edition has been lost. A second revised and enlarged edition was published at Amsterdam in 1682. He also wrote a booklet on *De eeuwige Godtheyt Christi*; of this book no separate edition seems to be extant; it is only found in a volume, published at Leeuwarden in 1688, containing (*a*) Hans de Ries' *Van de eeuwigheyd ende Godtheyd Jesu Christi*, (*b*) Schabaelje's *De eeuwige Godtheyt Christi*, and (*c*) Menno Simons' *Van den eenigen eeuwigen ende waren Godt, Vader, Soon ende H. Geest*. Besides these and a number of his hymns found in Mennonite hymnals such as *Gheestelijck Kruydt-Hofken* (*q.v.*) and Stapel's (*q.v.*) *Lusthof der Zielen*, two of his publications have been of outstanding significance for the Mennonites, viz., *Lusthof des Gemoeds* and *Vereenigingh van de principale Artijckelen des Geloofs.*

In 1635 Schabaelje published at Alkmaar a devotional book, *Lusthof des Gemoets inhoudende verscheyden geestelijcke Oeffeningen met noch twee Collatien der wandelende Ziele met Adam en Noach* (The Mind's Garden of Pleasure, Containing Various Spiritual Exercises with Two Dialogues of the Wandering Soul with Adam and Noah). This book has gone through more than 50 Dutch editions and has been the most widely read Mennonite book, also very popular among non-Mennonites. The second and following editions were augmented by a dialogue with Simon Cleophas, the title henceforth reading: *Lusthof des Gemoeds . . . met nog drie Collatien der Wandelende Ziele met Adam, Noah en Simon Cleophas.* In the second and following editions also a number of small additions were added. Most editions have a few rather primitive pictures and an illustrated title page; a 1724 edition has some copper engravings by Jan Luyken (*q.v.*). The last Dutch edition is dated 1768.

The last part of this book was separately published in a German translation, entitled *Die Wandlende Seele, das ist: Gespraech der Wandlenden Seelen mit Adam, Noah und Cleophas, verfasset die Geschichten von der Erschaffung der Welt an biss zu und nach der Zerstoerung Jerusalems.* This translation was made by B.B.B., who was very probably Bernhard (?) Benedict Brechbühl (Brechbill, *q.v.;* 1665-1720), who was among the Swiss refugees who came to Holland in 1710 and later emigrated to America. The German translation was edited in Europe at least 13 times, chiefly at Basel and Frankfurt-Leipzig.

It was very popular among the Mennonites in America, where 18 German editions of *Die Wand(e)lende Seel(e)* are known (first ed. Germantown by Chr. Saur, 1768) and 9 English editions of *The Wandering Soul.* As in Europe the American editions of this book, both German and English, were widely read by non-Mennonites. (See **Wandering Soul.**)

In 1640 (at Amsterdam) Schabaelje published: *Vereenigingh van de principale Artijckelen des Geloofs eeniger Doops-ghesinde Ghemeynten, diemen noemt Waterlanderen, Vlaminghen, en Duytschen, getrocken uyt hare uyt-gegevene Confession, waer uyt men sien kan het klein en nietigh verschil der selver Confessien, Tot dienst van alle vreed'-lievende, door I.P.S.* (Combination of the Principal Articles of Faith of Some Mennonite Congregations, called Waterlanders, Flemish, and Germans, Extracted from Their Published Confessions, from Which One Can See the Slight Difference Between These Confessions, in the Service of All Peaceful [Christians]). A second edition of this book appeared at Amsterdam 1674, 3d ed., Rotterdam 1739. In this book, written for the promotion of greater unity among the Dutch Mennonites, Schabaelje compares the Waterlander Confession by Hans de Ries and Lubbert Gerritsz, of 1610, and the Jan Cents High German-Frisian Confession of 1630, showing that the differences in the main doctrines are insignificant. Schabaelje's book was much appreciated by Schijn (*q.v.*) and other leading Dutch Mennonites.   vDZ.

Schijn-Maatschoen, *Geschiedenis* II, 581-88; *N.N.B.Wb.* II, 1268-70; *DB* 1864, 44; 1891, 2, 8; Marten Schagen, *Naamlijst der doopsgezinde schrijveren* (Amsterdam, 1745) 89 f.; the Amsterdam Mennonite library has a copy of this *Naamlijst* in which Schagen himself made handwritten annotations of a large number of editions of *Lusthof des Gemoeds,* now lost; Harold S. Bender, *Two Centuries,* 4 and *passim;* C. Henry Smith, *The Mennonite Immigration to Pennsylvania* (Norristown, 1929) 346-48; Robert Friedmann, *Mennonite Piety Through the Centuries* (Goshen, 1949) 111-15; I. B. Horst, "The Wandering Soul, a Remarkable Book of Devotion," *MHB* XVIII, 4, pp. 1, 2, 4, 8.

Schachner, Georg, a leader (*Vorsteher*) of the Anabaptist congregation in Augsburg (*q.v.*), Germany, a native of Munich, who served the Augsburg congregation after the execution of Hans Leupold (*q.v.*) until its final disbanding.   NEFF.

Schad, Georg (Jörg), an Anabaptist of Zollikon, Swiss canton of Zürich, was required to give an account of his faith before the court. He confessed that he had once lived in vice and sin, but through the grace of God had come to the knowledge of salvation and therefore desired baptism and faith, "the sign of brotherly love," whereupon Felix Manz (*q.v.*) baptized him with water. Later, when he was again summoned to answer for his faith, he confessed openly that he had himself baptized more than forty persons in the region of Zollikon, Höngg, and Küssnacht. Nothing more is known of Schad. Among the Mennonites of France, Schad is a family name of frequent occurrence, corrupted in English to Short.   S.G.

J. C. Füsslin, *Beiträge zur Schweizer Kirchen- und Reformations-Geschichte* (Zürich, 1741; repr. Bern, 1912); Fritz Blanke, *Brüder in Christo* (Zürich, 1955); *ML* IV.

Schaefer, Katharina, an Anabaptist martyr of Widdershausen, Thuringia, Germany, a village not far from Hersfeld on the Werra, was drowned in the Unstrut between Mühlhausen and Ammern on Nov. 8, 1537. (Wappler, *Thüringen,* 159 ff.; *ML* IV.)

Schaeff (Schaef), **Catharina** (d. 1692 at The Hague, Netherlands), was one of the last members of the Mennonite congregation of The Hague, which died out soon after, but was re-established in 1881. Catharina Schaeff, who never married, was undoubtedly well-to-do, for she made a number of legacies, including one to the congregation of The Hague and one to Bastiaen van Weenighem (*q.v.*), who was her cousin. She had a remarkable collection of books; among them were some old Dutch Bibles, a copy of the oldest Dutch martyr book, *Offer des Heeren,* and other martyr books, the *Foundation Book* by Menno Simons, Dirk Philips' *Christelyk Handboecxken,* a number of old Mennonite hymnals, Sebastiaen Franck's "Wereltboeck" (obviously his *Chronica . . . , q.v.*), the poetical works of Vondel and Camphuysen, writings of Galenus Abrahamsz and Bastiaen van Weenighem, and a collection of devotional books. It is not known what became of these books after her death. (*DB* 1896, 55-58; *De Zondagsbode* VI, 1892-93, No. 17.)   vDZ.

Schaerwyde, a Mennonite home for the aged near Zeist, Dutch province of Utrecht, has been in operation since Oct. 13, 1951. (*DJ* 1953, 41-44.) vpZ.

Schafbusch, a large farm (*Gutshof*) 2 miles east of Wissembourg in Alsace, just south of the German border, was formerly the center of the Deutschhof-Geisberg (*q.v.*) Mennonite congregation. Mennonite families expelled from Switzerland about 1700 settled here as renters and joined with other Mennonites of the vicinity to form the Geisberg-Niederrödern (*q.v.*) congregation. The *Naamlijst* of 1776 calls it the Schafsbusch-Röderen-Geisberg congregation. The family names of Schowalter, Borkholder, Müller, Schmitt, Hirschler, and Krämer occur in the 18th century. Services were held in a room reserved for the purpose, called the "Kirchenstube." Later, when the meetings were held in rotation on the various farms the communion services were still held at Schafbusch. In 1860, when the estate passed into non-Mennonite hands, Geisberg (*q.v.*) became the meeting center. Consequently the name Schafbusch has been dropped from the name of the congregation.

The church records, begun in 1855, and depending for their information on oral and written tradition, list the ministers and dates of ordination as follows: Johann Krehbiel of Niederrödern 1716, Johannes Borkholder of Schafbusch 1739, J. Weldy of Bühl 1775, Elias Dettweiler of Haftelhof 1780, Christian Hirschler of Schafbusch 1786, Johannes Müller of Schafbusch 1790, Heinrich Schmitt of Haftelhof 1790, Johannes Lehmann of Geisberg 1807, Christian Hirschler of Geisberg 1810, Jacob Hauser of Haftelhof 1813, Heinrich Hirschler of Niederrödern 1827, Johannes Lehmann of Niederrödern 1832, and Jacob Schowalter of Deutschhof 1839. This list, compiled so late, is, of course, not complete. Other sources fill in some of the omissions. Ernst Müller names Daniel Hirschler 1762, Hans Greiebüiel (Krehbiel), Jakob Lähmen (Lehmann), Hans Schowalter, and Johannes Miller (Müller). The Dutch *Naamlijst* names the first three, with the note that Daniel Hirschler held the office of elder from 1736 on.

Schafbusch is now the home of Philipp Hege (ordained elder in 1943), a descendant of Peter Hege of the Branchweilerhof (*q.v.*) who purchased it in 1912. The buildings of Schafbusch and Geisberg were severely damaged during World War II, but have been rebuilt. P.So.

Menn. Bl., 1855, 41; *Gesch.-Bl.,* 1938, 89; Pierre Sommer, "Assemblée de Deutschhof-Geisberg," *Christ Seul,* December 1931, 5-9; Müller, *Berner Täufer,* 212; *ML* III.

Schaffhausen, city and canton in the north of Switzerland almost entirely surrounded by Baden, Germany. Dr. Sebastian Hofmeister (*q.v.*) is found very early in Schaffhausen working for the Reformation. He was a close friend of Zwingli's and was one of the presidents of the religious disputation held in Zürich in October 1523. Hofmeister must have been a very ready debater. The favorable outcome of this disputation encouraged Hofmeister to take further steps in introducing the Reformation into his home town. At the third Anabaptist disputation held in Zürich (Nov. 6-8, 1525) he was

one of the four presidents; and in the Anabaptist disputation held at Zofingen (*q.v.*), July 1-9, 1532, he was one of the leading preachers who debated with the Anabaptists.

In September 1524 Balthasar Hubmaier (*q.v.*) of Waldshut (*q.v.*), who later became an Anabaptist leader, came to Schaffhausen. His influence here was not very great, however, for he left the city after a few weeks and returned to Waldshut on October 19.

Anabaptist refugees who had been expelled from the canton of Zürich came to Schaffhausen in 1525 hoping to win Hofmeister for their cause. Johannes Brötli (*q.v.*), who baptized many in Hallau in the canton of Schaffhausen, as well as Wilhelm Reublin (*q.v.*), came to Schaffhausen. Obviously their work here was not without success. Brötli even wrote that Dr. Sebastian agreed with them in the matter of baptism. The rumor was spread that Schaffhausen would arrange a disputation on the question of baptism. In Zürich there was much concern about it since there were some doubts whether the matter of baptism would be solved in agreement with their ideas in Schaffhausen. But the council of Schaffhausen assured the people of Zürich in reply to a question that had been raised by Zürich: "We are also of the mind to baptize our young children and not to desist from this practice at this time."

Also Conrad Grebel (*q.v.*) had come to Hofmeister in February 1525 in the hope of influencing his opinion in the matter of baptism. But although Hofmeister at the beginning doubted the genuineness of infant baptism, he finally accepted it, certainly under some influence of Zwingli. As already mentioned, Hubmaier was also in Schaffhausen though without any great results. After he had been baptized by Reublin in April 1525, he worked with full conviction for baptism upon confession of faith and in this matter of baptism he also corresponded with Hofmeister. In his book published in 1526, *Der uralten und gar neuen Lehrer Urteil, dass man die Kinder nicht taufen solle,* Hubmaier reports that Hofmeister had written to him how they (the Anabaptists) publicly rejected infant baptism before the council; if Zwingli confirmed it he would not be walking according to the truth of the Gospel (*ML* II, 335). In this matter, Hubmaier writes, he has Hofmeister's own handwriting. This is proof for the assertion that Sebastian Hofmeister not only doubted the Scripturalness of infant baptism but even repudiated it.

On Feb. 8, 1525, the Zürich council wrote to the authorities of Schaffhausen that there had been "error and dispute about infant baptism," wherefore a public religious debate had been arranged in which it was recognized, "that infant baptism is not anything wrong." Thereupon a mandate was issued ordering young children to be baptized. At the same time it was stated that the theologians of Zürich had recognized the Anabaptist teaching as false and that Zwingli would very soon publish a writing clarifying the matter of baptism, *Vom Touf, Wiedertouf und Kindertouf.* This was the occasion for a definite reversal in Hofmeister's doctrinal opinions. The entire course of the development shows a strong dependence of the city of Schaffhausen on

Zürich in religious matters. On Feb. 11, 1525, the Schaffhausen council issued a mandate "that young children shall be baptized."

Whereas in the city an impasse was reached, in the country, at least in Hallau, under the work of Brötli Anabaptism made some progress. Most of the inhabitants were baptized. Brötli mentions in a letter that he and his companion Wilhelm Reublin had come to Hallau and then had gone "toward Schaffhausen and found our dear brother Conrad Grebel there." When the authorities of Zürich heard of Brötli's successful work, they at once wrote to Schaffhausen to warn them against this deceptive dangerous mission. The letter dated April 4, 1525, is new evidence of the concern felt in Zürich in behalf of Schaffhausen; it had a decisive influence there. In consequence, the council of Schaffhausen ordered Brötli's expulsion from Hallau; the Hallau people, however, refused to comply.

While Conrad Grebel was in Schaffhausen, Wolfgang Uolimann (q.v.) of St. Gall also came, to receive instruction and baptism from him. Uolimann had met Grebel in Schaffhausen and become a convert; he did not want to have the customary basin of water poured over him, "but was pushed down naked into the Rhine by Grebel" (Kessler).

After the Peasant Revolt (1525), when the matter of the Reformation was somewhat dubious in Schaffhausen, Hofmeister himself had to leave; he was accused of having preached from the pulpit that the Sacrament of the Mass, the baptism of young children, and also the confessional were the work of the devil. "Hofmeister," writes Bächtold, "did not promptly learn to distinguish between Reformation and Revolution or between intellectual religious rebirth and political and social regeneration."

An event of great importance for all of Anabaptism was the Synod of Anabaptist leaders held in the territory of the canton of Schaffhausen on Feb. 24, 1527, at Schleitheim (q.v.). The Chronicler Rüegger speaks of it in his Chronicle: "At the time of the Reformation the enemy did not neglect always to build a chapel in these places beside the churches of Christ with the weeds of the seditious, quarrelsome, and obstinate Anabaptists," and that they had worked out their confession of faith there and published it with the title *Christenlichen Gloubens-Bekantnus der Kinderen Gottes zu Schleitheim am Randen* (i.e., the "Brüderliche Vereinigung").

In August 1527 the worried authorities of Zürich issued a warning that Hans Denk (q.v.), the well-known Anabaptist leader, was thinking of traveling to Schaffhausen, Constance, and Augsburg and that they should be careful that he does not sow tares.

In the meantime, since the Anabaptist movement was increasing more and more and Zürich and the other Protestant cities were applying sharp measures of violence against the Anabaptists, the council of Schaffhausen also let itself be persuaded to apply severe means to dam up Anabaptism. In the *Abschid* (Resolution) *des Gehaltenen Tags zu Zürich der nachfolgenden Orten, Zürich, Bern, Basel, Schaffhausen, und St. Gall.* On Sept. 8, 1526, the penalty for Anabaptism was decided upon. With satisfaction Zürich learned that the delegates "of our dear confederates of Basel and Schaffhausen ... did not have less displeasure in such Anabaptism and the following of the same." The initiative for opening common consultation among the evangelical cities in their struggle against Anabaptism was taken by Zürich. Schaffhausen was also invited to the common Concordat against the Anabaptists of Aug. 12-14, 1527, at Zürich (*ML* II, 542). From this time on fines of money, imprisonment, and expulsion were the order of the day.

This conference of the evangelical cities resulted in a mandate published by the council on Sept. 13, 1527: "We the mayor and the council of the city of Schaffhausen proclaim to our citizens and to our people everywhere in our canton: since it is known that at present all kinds of tramps, rascals, Anabaptist preachers and the like who have been expelled elsewhere and are not allowed to stay in their fatherland are now keeping themselves in our city and canton ... preach to the common and simple people and thereby mislead and confuse them the more rather than bring them to the true faith ... so that henceforth no one shall lodge such or that kind of vagabonds ... no one shall listen to their preaching, but shall arrest such people and commit them into our hands."

In this period occurred the first death sentence imposed in Schaffhausen, carried out on Nov. 13, 1527, against Hans Rüeger. He was charged with plans for a political revolt in addition to his Anabaptist faith, but there is no evidence for any revolutionary deed. On April 14, 1529, the second death sentence was pronounced against Jakob Schuffel from the Schufelberg. The records of the charge reveal that he had to give his life "on account of Anabaptism which cannot by any means be maintained with the Holy Scriptures and Christendom but is everywhere being rooted out of Christendom and is considered erroneous and heretical." Schuffel had been imprisoned in Zürich for one year and 18 weeks on account of his Anabaptist faith. On account of his "unchristian conduct" he was executed with the sword. It is reported concerning him: "he died firmly in his faith and rejects infant baptism which is not valid and states that his baptism is right and good and firm."

Numerous Anabaptists including some women were imprisoned in 1530 who were to be visited by the clergy in order "to lead them to the right way." Verena Mayer, also called Häckerin, the sexton's wife, who "had seen her error," was dismissed from prison upon payment of a fine of a silver mark; she also had to swear an oath not to return and had to stand in the pulpit of the cathedral and recant before the assembled congregation and ask for pardon. In spite of her public recantation she again went to the Anabaptists and was arrested. Since this imprisonment and the repeated visits of the clergy were fruitless, she was tried in the criminal court on Feb. 25, 1531, and sentenced by expulsion from the country. Because of her loyalty to her faith she was not permitted to come within four miles of the territory of Schaffhausen, otherwise "she should be executed in life and body." In this year "a series of obstinate subjects of my gracious lords" appeared before the council on account of Anabaptism. Most of them came from Hallau and were fined. While the strictly moral Anabaptists were treated thus, a frivolous life was quite noticeable in the masses of the people.

From the year 1532 there is extant a *Memorial der Geistlichen* in which the offensive conduct of the populace is reproved. In conclusion this document says: "From these above-stated articles it follows that the Anabaptists take a reason to separate themselves from us and make secret meetings in the city and canton saying that no improvement is noticed among us and that all vices are increasing; and because they do not have an understanding of the Scriptures they err grievously in some articles for which error we give them reason with our offensive living." This document of the clergy was not without its effect upon the "gracious lords." This is shown by the mandate of July 29 against gambling, cursing, drinking, etc., and finally against Anabaptism. After a lengthy warning against this "Anabaptist sect," persistence in the Anabaptist faith was threatened with punishment "against body, life, and property."

In 1535 Anabaptism seems to have reached its climax in Schaffhausen since the records of the council mention Anabaptists 41 times. The council saw itself compelled to issue a new mandate against the Anabaptists on March 31. They declared that such schismatics should be summoned before the council and warned. If that didn't do any good, they must emigrate. Further it is commanded with sharp threats of punishment: "because the Holy, divine Word is the true food of the soul, therefore in the future all who live in our city and canton . . . old and young shall at least once a week come to the true worship service and submit to the sermon." A letter written by an Anabaptist to the council has a somewhat ironic tone. It says that to be sure the papacy had been eliminated but one could still see no fruits of the true teaching. The strife over communion "had only given offense. . . . The Father enlightened others so they have recognized your mischief, but those you will not endure. But if you had remained in Christ's teaching you would be Christ's disciples, then your light would have shown so that men would have been reformed." Their position to Christ, the letter continues, and to His people is like that of the wolf to the sheep (Sirach, Chapter 13). One of the most important Anabaptist leaders of Schaffhausen was Martin Weniger, also called Lincki (*q.v.*). He was one of the principal speakers on the Anabaptist side in the disputation of Zofingen (*q.v.*) in July 1532. There is extant a document written by him, *Rechenschaft marti Weningers gen. Lingki's, us was ursachen sich die Töufer von unserer Kirchen, Gottesdienst und Predigten absöndern.* Lincki applies to the clergy in this document everything uncomplimentary found in the Bible about the scribes and Pharisees. He saw in the Protestant church the "world" which walks in darkness. In conclusion he points to the persecutions of the Anabaptists and says: "If the Lord were not with us, they would have devoured us alive so that none of us would be left over. Our protection and shield is God. Overcoming by the faith and patience of Christ we overcome our enemies accord-

ing to the example of Christ. All praise and honor only be to God and to his church in Christ Jesus." Lincki had to answer before the criminal court, was kept in prison for some time and then it is stated concerning him: "Because Martin Lincki has desisted from the Anabaptist faith he shall recant upon both pulpits, swear an oath not to fall back; then he may dwell in my lord's city and canton." The records of the Anabaptist disputation in Bern (*q.v.*) on March 11-17, 1538, mention the backslidden Lincki; also a Heinrich Wininger of Schaffhausen is named as a representative of the Anabaptists.

Beginning with 1536 the movement visibly declined. The sharp measures of the government succeeded in subduing the fire. The Anabaptist mandates were from time to time confirmed and renewed. In the 1570's and 1590's a powerful emigration to Moravia took place, and the congregations in the canton of Schaffhausen soon were dissolved. Bächtold gives them the testimonial that he cannot find in the records the least trace of "madness or fanatical childishness." S.G.

C. A. Bächtold, *Die Schaffhauser Wiedertäufer in der Reformationszeit* (in *Beiträge zur vaterländischen Geschichte*, Schaffhausen, 1900); J. C. Füsslin, *Beiträge zur Erläuterung der Kirchen-Reformations-Geschichten* (Zürich, 1741); S. Geiser, *Die Taufgesinnten-Gemeinden* (Karlsruhe, 1931); G. Strasser, *Der schweizerische Anabaptismus zur Zeit der Reformation* (in *Berner Beiträge zur Geschichte der Schweizerischen Reformationskirchen*, Bern, 1884).

Schaffhouse, a former Mennonite congregation in Lower Alsace, France, known only because it sent two delegates to the Essingen Conference in 1759—Benedikt Fischer and Hans Steiner. H.S.B,

Pierre Sommer, "Assemblées diverses de la Basse-Alsace et des pays voisins et qui ont disparu," *Christ Seul,* November 1931, p. 6.

Schäffler, Oswald, an Anabaptist martyr, who was beheaded for his faith at Munich, Germany, in 1527. (Beck, *Geschichts-Bücher,* 24; *ML* IV.)
NEFF.

Schagen, a Mennonite family, formerly of Alkmaar, Dutch province of North Holland, members of the Waterlander and later the united congregation. Pieter Gerrits Schagen was a deacon in 1674; Pieter Schagen was four times a deacon in 1737-54; Pieter Schagen Jr. 1749-51, and Jan Regter Schagen four times in 1777-1814. Members of this family are the preachers Marten Schagen (*q.v.*) and his son Petrus Schagen (*q.v.*). There was also a Reformed branch of this family at Alkmaar. (Church records of Alkmaar.) vDZ.

Schagen, Ma(a)rten (b. Oct. 24, 1700, at Alkmaar, d. Oct. 20, 1770, at Utrecht), was a son of Pieter Martens Schagen and Grietje Jacobs Volder. He was baptized in Alkmaar (Frisian congregation) in 1718 and in the same year he moved to Amsterdam, where he opened a bookstore and a publishing house on the Nieuwedijk in 1723. He printed and published a number of books, the most outstanding of which was a Dutch translation of the works of Josephus by A. Loosjes (*q.v.*) and J. L. Rogge (*q.v.*) in 1732. In the meantime he made a thorough study of languages (German, French, Latin, even Greek and Hebrew), literature, and theology. In 1727 he was called to be a (unsalaried) preacher of the Frisian congregation (Arke Noachs) at Amsterdam, serving here until 1738, at the same time running his business. In October 1737 he took the initiative in holding weekly meetings in a room of the church to explain and discuss the New Testament. In 1738 he was called to serve the Waterlander and Frisian congregations (then united) at Alkmaar (salary 750 Dutch guilders; 1,000 guilders after 1739); he served here only three years, in 1741 accepting a call from the Utrecht congregation, which he served until his death. By his activity, his wise policy, and his strong faith he succeeded in raising the Utrecht congregation, which had fallen into a serious decline, to great prosperity. After his death his colleague Joannes Cuperus (q.v.) delivered a funeral sermon in his memory—M. Schagen . . . plegtig gedagt in eene Lykrede (Utrecht, 1770), in which both his assiduity and his tolerance are highly praised.

This self-made man was highly renowned for his knowledge and his erudition. In 1766 he was one of the founders of the "Maatschappij der Nederlandsche Letterkunde" (Association of Dutch Literature), which still exists. He published a large number of translations of theological books. The following sermons were published by Schagen: De Messias Uitgeroeit (Amsterdam, 1735, reprinted 1736, enlarged edition Haarlem, 1739); "Drie Proeven van Aenmerkingen over den Lastbrief aen de Efezische Kerk" in Vols. II, IV, and VI of Leerzame Verlustiging; Kerkrede over het oude geloof en 't goede geweten (Utrecht, 1742); 't Genadeloon der welaengelegde Twee Talenten, a funeral sermon for his son Petrus Schagen (q.v.) (Haarlem, 1755), Vryheid en zuivere Godsdienst (Haarlem-Amsterdam-Utrecht, 1762), De Muziek in der openbaeren godsdienst gewettigd. Predicatie by de inwijding van het eerste kerkorgel in de Doopsgezinde Kerk te Utrecht (Utrecht, 1771), Het eerst Kapittel van Joëls Profetie verklaert en op 's Lands Toestand gepast, six sermons (Haarlem, 1745). De Heilige Week of Nieuw Avondmaalsboekje (Haarlem, 1753) is a devotional book. Schagen tried to elevate catechetical instruction by writing and publishing some manuals: Korte Schrifuurlyke Stellingen tot onderwys der Doopsgezinde Geloofsleerlingen (Alkmaar, 1738, repr. Haarlem, 1751), Voorbereidende Overdenkingen tot het Ontfangen van den H. Doop (n.p., n.d.), Eenvoudige Handleiding tot de Algemeene Waerheden van het Christendom (Alkmaar, 1741), and Aanhangzel over de Byzondere Leerstukken des Geloofs, welke de Doopsgezinden handhaven (n.p., 1743).

But Schagen's special interest in study was church history. In this field he published a book on the Waldenses, Historie der Christenen, die men gemeenlyk Waldensen noemt tot den Jaere 1200 (Amsterdam-Haarlem, 1732, repr. 1765, 1769), and two apologetical books on the Dutch Mennonites: De Kerk der Nederlandsche Doops-gezinden in derzelver Reformatie vertoont, three sermons (Haarlem, 1743), and De Reformatie der Nederlandsche Doops-gezinden, en deselve met de Kerkhervorming in't gemeen tegen alle Bezwaering verdeedigt

(Haarlem, 1744). A book which is still of great value is the translation by Schagen of S. F. Rues' Aufrichtige Nachrichten von dem gegenwärtigen Zustande der Mennoniten oder Taufgesinnten wie auch der Collegianten oder Reinsburger in den vereinigten Niederlanden (Jena, 1743), which with numerous notes and corrections by Schagen was published under the title Tegenwoordige Staet der Doopsgezinden of Mennoniten in de Vereenigde Nederlanden (en) een Berigt van de Rynsburgers of Collegianten (Amsterdam, 1745). The additions by Schagen give the translation superiority over the original edition. In 1745 Schagen published a bibliography containing the names of Mennonite authors and their books with exact annotations; mentioning all reprints. Of this valuable book, entitled Naamlijst der Doopsgezinde Schryveren en schriften van 1539-1745 (Amsterdam, 1745), the Amsterdam Mennonite Library has a copy, in which Schagen himself annotated new editions and reprints published after 1745.

Schagen possessed a rich library of Mennonite books including many rare editions, which he bequeathed to the congregation of Utrecht; the catalogue of this library numbers 72 pages. In 1834 the books were sold for 250 Dutch guilders to the Amsterdam Mennonite library, where they are at present. The Amsterdam Mennonite archives also contain a handwritten copy of a sermon by Schagen on Matt. 22:31-32 and also a number of historical annotations made by himself, including the manuscript of his translation of Rues' book. vDZ.

N.N.B.Wb. I, 1452-55; Inv. Arch. Amst. I, Nos. 673-76, 719, 733-36, 754-56; II, No. 1411; II, 2, Nos. 56, 68; DJ 1837, 62, 96-100; 1840, 111, 113, 125; 1850, 137; DB 1863, 22 note, 85 f., 91, 126, 129; 1864, 130; 1868, 95 f., 101-5; 1881, 106-10; 1890, 75; 1901, 120 f.; (de Lange) Beknopte Geschiedenis der Doopsgezinde gemeente te Alkmaar (n.p., n.d.-1927) 42-44; H. B. Berghuys, Geschiedenis der Doopsgezinde gemeente te Utrecht (n.p., n.d.-1926) 52-57; J. C. Sepp, Johannes Stinstra en zijn tijd (Amsterdam, 1865-66) I, 75, 139, 215; II, 99 f.

Schagen, Petrus (Pieter), b. about 1725 at Amsterdam, d. Nov. 11, 1753, at Westzaan, was a son of Marten Schagen (q.v.). He studied medicine, obtaining his M.D. degree at Utrecht in 1747; he then studied theology at the Amsterdam Lamist Seminary in 1747-51. From 1751 until his early death he served as preacher in the Frisian congregation of Westzaan-Zuid, practicing medicine at the same time. Petrus Schagen was one of the last of the many Dutch ministers who combined the ministry with a medical practice. He published a few medical studies and a treatise in Latin on earthquakes (1747). His theological-philosophical tract Oratio de Summo Bono was published at Haarlem, 1741. After his death his father edited five of his sermons: De Natuur en Zalige gevolgen van't ware Christelijke Leven (Haarlem, 1755), together with a funeral sermon, which Marten Schagen preached in commemoration of his son at Westzaan on Dec. 16, 1753, entitled 't Genadeloon der welaengelegde Twee Talenten. (N.N.B.Wb. I, 1455; DJ 1837, 105; 1850, 85, note.) vDZ.

Schagerbrug: see **Zijpe, Noord.**

Schäkowitz (Schackowitz, Schakowic), a Bruderhof of the Hutterian Brethren one-half mile south of Auspitz, Moravia, the Hutterite center; it was founded in 1533. The region was at that time the possession of the barons of Lipa-Kromau. In 1535, at the outbreak of persecution in Moravia, the Brethren were driven from the houses they had just recently built; for a long time they were compelled to camp with their children and their sick on the site of the desolate village of Starnitz (identical with Starlitz?, *q.v.*) near Tracht on the Thaya, on Liechtenstein territory.

In 1582 the Brethren bought the Bruderhof at Schäkowitz for the third time. On July 12, 1605, it was burned down by Hungarian troops; two brethren were also killed. In 1609 the school was transferred to Gostel (*q.v.*). In October 1622 the Brethren were driven out of Schäkowitz, with the loss of all their property. They settled in Hungary and Transylvania. (See also **Scheikowitz**, which in the variable spelling of the day was also called Schakowitz.) HEGE.

Beck, *Geschichts-Bücher,* 104, 117, 281, 396, 408; Wolkan, *Geschicht-Buch;* Zieglschmid, *Chronik; ML* IV.

Schalmeye, inhoudende veel geestelycke Liedekens, is a Dutch Mennonite songbook, of which Marijn den Brauwer was the author. It was published at Haarlem in 1614 and contains 112 hymns without notes. The same author, of whom there is no further information, published the hymnal *Het Otterken* (*q.v.*). vDZ.

Schantz: see also **Shantz.**

Schantz, Peter (1853-1924), an outstanding leader in the Central Mennonite Conference, was born at Congerville, Ill., April 14, 1853, the son of Jacob Schantz, an immigrant from Hesse-Darmstadt, Germany, in 1847. He became an orphan at the age of twelve and was reared in the home of Christian Imhoff, a minister. In 1872 he was baptized in the North Danvers church, in 1875 married Anna Kinsinger, the daughter of Michael Kinsinger, locating on the Kinsinger farm in 1877, then living on a farm in the White Oak district in 1892 until 1910, when he moved to Normal, Ill. He died there on July 24, 1924. He was ordained preacher at North Danvers in 1892, and in 1900 as bishop. He was secretary of the Mission Board *c*1907-16, and field secretary of the conference 1916-21. He was a man of vision and a good organizer, and did much in church extension work. Next to Joseph Stuckey he was the most important leader of the conference, and was followed by Emanuel Troyer in that capacity, the three men being the real fathers of the conference. H.S.B.

W. B. Weaver, *History of the Central Conference Mennonite Church* (Danvers, 1926); H. F. Weber, *Centennial History of the Mennonites in Illinois* (Goshen, 1931).

Schanzenfeld, a Mennonite village name found in the West Reserve, Man.; Swift Current, Sask.; and Cuauhtemoc, Mexico. (See **Villages.**) C.K.

Schärding, a town on the Inn River, 8 miles from Passau in Upper Austria (formerly in Bavaria), where there was strong Anabaptist activity by 1527, Wolfgang Brandhuber (*q.v.*) preaching here. Concerning the Schärding congregation there is little information. Virgil Plattner (*q.v.*) was executed here in 1529, Wolf Binder (*q.v.*) in 1571. vDZ.

Scharf, Klaus, an Anabaptist martyr of Mühlhausen (*q.v.*) in Thuringia, Germany, was drowned on Nov. 8, 1537, together with Martha Scharf and others in the Unstrut between Mühlhausen and Ammern. (Wappler, *Thüringen,* 162; *ML* IV.)

Scharfenberg together with Landau and the Sperlingsdorfer Bruch, in the Danzig Werder, West Prussia, were colonized by Dutch farmers as early as 1547. At least the second generation of settlers were Mennonites, the family names of Jantzen, Philippsen, Peters, and Giesebrecht, soon also those of Andres and Froese being predominant. If it may be assumed—as is probable—that the first generation of settlers were Mennonites from the Netherlands, this area was the first settlement of Mennonites in Prussia. vDZ.

Horst Penner, *Ansiedlung Menn. Niederländer im Weichselmündungsgebiet . . .* (Weierhof, 1940) 12 ff.

Scharnschlager, Leupold (Leupold der Seifensieder), d. 1563, an Anabaptist elder who belonged to the Brotherhood of Marpeck (*q.v.*), a native of Tirol, Austria, where he owned an estate at Hopfgarten near Kitzbühel. His wife Anna probably belonged to a prominent family. Her father, Konrad Honigler, stemmed from Hall in Tirol, her mother Margaret Rieper, from Gossenass at the southern foot of the Brenner. A brother of her mother, Dr. Johannes Rieper, was the deacon and cathedral provost in Brixen, and there were other clergymen in her relationship. Her sister Veronica was married to Hans Steger, a judge and later clerk in Kitzbühel. Anna's first husband was Gallus Steger, the brother of this judge, upon whose death she married Scharnschlager. One daughter, Ursula, is mentioned, born about 1510; it is not known whether of the first or second marriage.

About 1530 Scharnschlager united with the Anabaptists and had to leave his home with his wife and daughter. His estate was confiscated in March 1531. They fled directly to Strasbourg (*q.v.*), probably invited by their compatriot Marpeck, who had been expelled from Tirol in 1528. Scharnschlager lived and worked in Strasbourg in 1530-34, but his activity in the Anabaptist cause extended as far as Speyer, where he baptized a certain Kaspar Schuhmacher (*q.v.*) as early as 1530, who, however, recanted. About this matter he wrote a letter to Michael Leubel (*q.v.*), an Anabaptist of Speyer, in 1532. The doctrinal portions of the letter, dealing with original sin and baptism, already contain the ideas found in the books he and Marpeck wrote together in 1542-48. The Anabaptists who were expelled from Speyer, Hans "the Servant" (Knecht) and Margareth "the maid," had free access to his home. At Christmas of 1532 Thomas Adolf, a citizen of Speyer, visited him and desired to be baptized by him or Pilgram Marpeck. Marpeck had, however, been expelled from the city earlier that year, and Scharnschlager had been forbidden to perform baptisms for the time being, and so

Thomas Adolf had to return without having his purpose fulfilled, taking with him the letter to Michael Leubel (the original of which is in the state archives of Speyer, Fasc. 492). A confession made by Thomas Adolf before the court in Speyer on Jan. 8, 1533, reveals that Leopold Scharnschlager is identical with Leupold der Seifensieder (the Soapmaker), whom Melchior Hofmann (*q.v.*) called an opponent in his trial on May 29, 1533 ("who was opposed to him in the principal doctrine"). Whether Scharnschlager actually practiced soapmaking is not known; Thomas Adolf said he had not seen him at his work.

Scharnschlager's daughter Ursula married a clockmaker, Hans Felix, in Strasbourg, whom Scharnschlager names in his letter to Leubel; he sends greetings from "Hans Uhrmacher," who had visited him in the city of Speyer. The young couple must have gone to Moravia soon after; in 1533 the mother wrote to her brother that her daughter had married a clockmaker two years before; "they are at present in Moravia." A letter from the son-in-law dated Austerlitz, Oct. 28 or 29, 1538, indicates that he had been converted to the Anabaptists by Scharnschlager, probably in Strasbourg.

The Strasbourg *Täuferakten* contain Scharnschlager's moving appeal which Scharnschlager made to the city council for freedom of religion when he was expelled in 1534. This document clearly shows that Scharnschlager was well acquainted with the major literature of the early Reformation. He brilliantly points out the inconsistencies between the early position of the Reformers and the course of the Reformation at that time. In many respects the appeal to the council reminds one of Marpeck's dealings with the council only two years before. Where Scharnschlager went from Strasbourg is not known, but no doubt both he and Marpeck lived a transient existence in the Grisons and the Augsburg area. Around 1540 Marpeck was already in Augsburg, and since he and Scharnschlager together published a revised and translated form of the Rothmann *Bekentnisse* in South Germany in 1542, it seems logical to assume that he lived in South Germany during this time. No evidence of a sojourn at Augsburg has been published to date.

Hans Felix in his letter of 1538 twice said that his parents-in-law were living "oben," whence he himself had come to Moravia, but they could not stay there either. It is possible that he meant Strasbourg (Schiess thinks it means Tirol, and ten Doornkaat-Koolman, South Germany in general). In the ensuing years at any rate Scharnschlager was no doubt close to Marpeck, who was living in Augsburg. Here they worked at the *Vermanung,* which was published in 1542. The book names as its authors "the believing comrades of the covenant and of the suffering that is in Christ." Pilgram Marpeck is regarded as the principal composer; Caspar Schwenckfeld, however, speaks at one place of two "scribenten," doubtless referring to Scharnschlager in addition to Pilgram Marpeck. At another place Schwenckfeld says that he had less to do with Leupold than with Pilgram. Scharnschlager is also named as the second of the coauthors of the *Verant-*

wortung, the first part of which was completed in 1544 and the second in 1546. The striking similarity of doctrine concerning baptism and original sin in this book and in Scharnschlager's letter of 1532 indicates that he took a major part in drafting the work. It is in the first place the teaching, also accepted by Luther, that in baptism the inner cannot be separated from the outer, and in the second place the specifically Anabaptist idea that children "before the use of reason have no sin but the inherited weakness, which does not endanger their salvation until it breaks out into actual sin. Therefore baptism was not instituted for them." In the *Verantwortung* this teaching is based on an otherwise unknown point of doctrine held by the Brethren of Moravia, which Scharnschlager may have learned from his son-in-law. It is not definitely known whether Scharnschlager stayed in Moravia for a time.

From 1546 on Scharnschlager and his wife were at Ilanz in Grisons. They were probably compelled to flee from Bavaria, where, according to a note left by his wife, they had to pay a fine of 40 guilders. For nearly two decades they were able to live unmolested in Ilanz. Scharnschlager turned his knowledge to account b teaching the youth of Ilanz, and his wife restored contact with her home in Tirol and tried to regain her former property. On occasion their son-in-law visited them; during his stay Scharnschlager repaired the village clock and "bietzte," as a witness of that time testified. They renewed their connections with Moravia and Upper Germany, and Scharnschlager again placed his energy at the disposal of the brethren. From a letter of reply written by Valentin Werner, one of the younger coauthors of the *Verantwortung,* dated Augsburg, Aug. 26, 1559, it is known that Scharnschlager was at that time the leader of an Anabaptist congregation in Grisons. Werner's letter, which has been preserved attached to the Zürich copy of the manuscript of the *Verantwortung,* acknowledges the "manifold trouble and work" Scharnschlager had in making a copy of the *Verantwortung,* and also mentions another of Scharnschlager's writings, "Vom gericht," for which the brethren in Augsburg sent their "cotestimony" (*mitzeugnus*); "please accept them in the love of Christ, for which love may you continue to serve us in one thing and another, and lead us as a father with the treasure and riches entrusted to you by the Lord where need requires it and love constrains you, though to put too heavy a burden on your old age is not our intention."

The regard of the brethren for Scharnschlager throughout his life and beyond is revealed by a letter written by Wernhard Riepl from Klein-Teschau on Feb. 15, 1571, which has been preserved in the Olomuce manuscript of the *Verantwortung.* In this letter Riepl tells of dissension among the brethren Adam and Uhrmacher and others "on account of the Holy Scripture and the dead letter, through which spirit and life come." To settle the question Riepl called a number of the brethren together and presented to them an explanation of the matter in one of Scharnschlager's writings, known as the *Unterscheid.* It may have been the well-known

Testamenterleutterung . . . zu dienst und fürderung ains Klaren urteils von wegen unterscheid Alts und News Testaments (q.v.).

Recent studies in South German Anabaptism (Kiwiet, Bergsten, Herbert Klassen, William Klassen) indicate that Scharnschlager must be given a place of greater importance in the total movement. The discovery of the *Kunstbuch* has shown that he was regarded as an elder (so he often signs his letters, while Marpeck never uses the term to refer to himself) and that he had an important place in the brotherhood. Of the 42 epistles and tracts in the *Kunstbuch,* six were written by Scharnschlager, while one was written by Marpeck to him (#27, dated 1545, "Concerning the Inheritance of Sin"). Of these six, two deal specifically with questions of church order, one (#19) being a brief church order divided into seven articles dealing with (1) the importance of continuing to meet as a church, (2) the place of leadership in the church, (3) the care of the poor, (4) the support of the ministry, (5) the true community of goods (he rejects the enforced communism of the Hutterites, and advocates a common fund), (6) church discipline, (7) doctrine, baptism, and the Lord's Supper, in which apostolic practice and Christ's order is to be observed. This church order, unfortunately, is without a date, but its polemic against enforced community of goods indicates that it was written after 1535. While there are some similarities to the church order of Leonhard Schiemer (q.v.), they are not so striking as to indicate direct borrowing.

The second writing dealing with church order is entitled "General Admonition and Reminder to the Edification of the Body of Christ" (#20). It is also without date, and no destination is given. The tone of this epistle indicates the fervor with which Scharnschlager worked for the Anabaptist church. It deals first of all with the lukewarmness creeping into many Anabaptist congregations where man and wife have actually joined the church, but take little interest in the affairs of the church. Related to this is his criticism of many of the Brethren who were more concerned about getting rich and leaving a large inheritance for their children than about taking the cross of Christ seriously. Next Scharnschlager deals with the attitude of those who refuse to submit to brotherly admonition, hiding behind the excuse that everyone has faults. He rejects this, saying that all submit to brotherly admonition according to the Scriptures. Finally he deals with the problems of marriage. Many are marrying because of the desire to be rich; others marry "outsiders" and then do not remain true to the Anabaptist cause. Some even justify their marriage because they desire to be strengthened in their faith by their partner, but Scharnschlager insists that marriage must remain on a Pauline basis. This epistle is one of the clearest indications that Anabaptism was moving from its early days to the second generation when the dynamic thrust of the early movement had to be consolidated into living and continuing congregations.

Another short tract by Scharnschlager bears the title "Whether a Christian May Be a Government Official," and it too is without date or destination.

It covers only two leaves, and is clearly written as a reply to questions about Scharnschlager's position. He replies that the important thing is whether one is living according to the will of Christ, and that a distinction be made between the realm of Christ and that of the world. In supporting his argument he appeals to the booklet by Michael Sattler (q.v.), whom he mentions by name, and then quotes the article from the Schleitheim Confession which deals with this subject. This quotation by a prominent South German elder of a Schleitheim article indicates that it is risky to drive a wedge between the Anabaptists who drew up the Schleitheim articles (calling them the Swiss Brethren) and the South Germans. There is no evidence that the Marpeck Brotherhood was critical of Schleitheim at any time, even though there were tensions between the Marpeck Brotherhood and some "Swiss Brethren."

Another epistle, dated May 24, 1544, is an epistle of comfort, directed to Martin Blaichner (q.v.) when he was driven out of Chur by persecution. He acknowledges Martin's letter and then comforts the recipients of the letter in their affliction. Tribulation is the very nature of the Christian faith and is a test of being a true son of God. He supports this with a number of quotations from the Bible and one from the book of Judith. He asks them to read this epistle to the church, especially to the sisters, and to preserve this epistle for him, since he failed to make a copy of it.

Another epistle dealing with the same theme (#30) has no date or destination. It deals with the strong temptation to yield a little here and there and in that way to avoid persecution. This temptation must be rejected, says Scharnschlager, and he admonishes his readers to remain faithful, comparing their persecutions with those which the earlier Anabaptists had to endure. In this letter he mentions the epistle written to Martin Blaichner, hence it must have been written after May 24, 1544.

While the above writings all deal with church order or intend to strengthen the brotherhood for tribulation, Scharnschlager's only extant theological treatise bears the title, "A Report on True Faith and Common Salvation in Christ" (#32). It is the longest of all his writings in the *Kunstbuch,* extending from folio 254a to 263b. This epistle (according to a marginal note) was directed to the Anabaptists in Alsace, but is without date or place of composition. Its contents include also an admonition to remain faithful in assembling and a discussion of the two types of nourishment that Christians need, physical and spiritual bread. The heart of this epistle deals with the nature and importance of faith. It is through faith that we live, says Scharnschlager (quoting Romans), and not through external works, as certain of the Swiss (Anabaptists) insist. This reference to "certain of the Swiss" is the only indication in all the writings of Scharnschlager of a critical attitude to some Swiss Anabaptists. Apparently he did not disagree with them to the same extent as Marpeck. Faith consists basically of two things: (1) faith in the death of Christ Jesus, the Son of God, which results in forgiveness and the appeasement of the wrath of God; (2) faith in the future kingdom of God with its heavenly essence and glory. External works can spring up only from this faith, which is a living active work and which only Christ can give. This faith is not a dead, historic (*historisch*) faith, but rather a living union with Christ, as James saw clearly when he wrote his epistle. It is apparent that Scharnschlager is here in conversation with both Schwenckfeld, who accused the Anabaptists of being tied to a "historisch" faith, and the Lutheran group which had little use for James. After a definition of faith, Scharnschlager defines the result of such a faith. These results are atonement and a clearer perspective on this world, since it gives one an inner eye to see beyond the earthly to the heavenly essence. This separates one from the love for creatures, and results in the true "Gelassenheit of which also the *Theologia Deutsch* and the *Imitation of Christ* write." This reference to the booklet about the *Nachfolge Christi* indicates again that Scharnschlager was well read, and it may be that he supplied the references to the *Theologia Deutsch* in the *Verantwortung* (*q.v.*). In the rest of the epistle he deals with the themes of love, good works, and the strength of this kind of faith. It was to help his readers to withstand the Papists, Lutherans, Zwinglians, and even the false Anabaptists. The epistle closes with an admonition to be obedient to the elders and to support the "Vorsteher" so that the latter would not have any lack or need to spend their time trying to earn a living to the neglect of the cause of the church.

It is apparent from this that Scharnschlager must be considered as an important South German leader. He was much more than merely an assistant to Marpeck; they were no doubt equals in every sense of the word. The epistle which Marpeck wrote to Scharnschlager (*Kunstbuch* #27) indicates clearly the intimate relationship between them, and there is no evidence of friction. In this letter Marpeck mentions a previous letter he had written to Leupold, and discourses at length about the many false servants of Christ abroad. The reason he does so is that the brethren in Moravia have written him about the divisions and deceptions taking place there. May the Lord protect us, he adds.

If an attempt must be made to say what is distinctively Scharnschlager's in the literature of the Marpeck Brotherhood, a comparison must be made on the basis of Scharnschlager's letters in the *Kunstbuch* with the other writings. This would reveal that Scharnschlager's insistence on the union of the inner and outer (a powerful weapon against spiritualism), whether it be in baptism or in his view of the Word of God, no doubt helped Marpeck's Brotherhood to overcome the arguments of Schwenckfeld. Any attempt to analyze differences between Marpeck and Scharnschlager is, however, futile, because in their writings we have what Horst Quiring first called a type of "Gemeindetheologie." In this type of thought individualism is replaced by a corporate search for truth, especially as this truth is revealed in God's Word.

The *Ausbund* (No. 57) preserves a hymn by Scharnschlager. It is a song in praise of love (I Cor. 13) and has seven stanzas (printed in Wackernagel III, No. 519).

Scharnschlager died in Ilanz in 1563. His wife lived a few years longer, but was in poor health and sent a messenger for her daughter, who, after the death of Uhrmacher, had married a weaver named Stoffel Krieger, and requested her to come with her husband to care for her and to receive the inheritance. But she did not see her daughter again, for she died in that year. The daughter also died soon afterwards in Moravia. The inheritance, probably considerable, was given to grandsons of Scharnschlager in March 1566 by the court of Ilanz. We owe many a bit of information about Scharnschlager to the lawsuit caused by the false claims made on the estate by a carpenter.   G.H., W.KL.

J. ten Doornkaat-Koolman, "Leupold Scharnschlager und die verborgene Täufergemeinde in Graubünden," in *Zwingliana* IV (1926) 329-37; G. Hein, "Täufer in Speyer," in *Festschrift für D. Christian Neff* (1938); idem, "Leupold Scharnschlager, ein Mitarbeiter Pilgram Marbecks," *Gesch-Bl.* IV (1939) 6-12; idem, "Leupold Scharnschlager, 1563, Anabaptist Elder and Hymn Writer," *MQR* XVII (1943) 47-52; idem, "Two Letters by Leupold Scharnschlager," *MQR* XVII (1943) 165-68; Loserth, *Anabaptismus;* T. Schiess, "Aus dem Leben eines Ilanzer Schulmeisters," in *Beiträge zur Geschichte St. Gallens in der Ostschweiz* (St. Gall, 1932) 229-45; Wackernagel, *Kirchenlied* III (Leipzig, 1870); T. W. Röhrich, *Ztscht f. d. hist. Theol.* 1860, 71; J. J. Kiwiet, *Pilgram Marbeck* (Kassel, 1957); Torsten Bergsten, "Pilgram Marbeck und seine Auseinandersetzung mit Caspar Schwenckfeld," in *Kyrkohistorisk Arsskrift* (Uppsala) 1957 and 1958; Herbert Klassen, "Some Aspects of Hans Hut's Teachings" (M.A. Diss., Univ. of British Columbia, 1958); William Klassen, "The Hermeneutics of Pilgram Marpeck" (Th.D. Diss., Princeton Theological Seminary, 1959); Heinold Fast, "Pilgram Marbeck und das süddeutsche Täufertum," *Archiv für Reformationsgeschichte*, 1956, 212-42; *TA Baden und Pfalz*, 419-24; *ML IV*.

Schartner, a family name among the Mennonites of Prussia, spread to Russia and America. The first member of the family to join the Mennonites was Friedrich Schartner, who during the 18th century left Königsberg to avoid conscription. A widower, he married Maria Jantz, a Mennonite, at which time he joined the Mennonite church in the village of Karolswalde, Volhynia, Polish Russia. Four of his thirteen children became ministers. His oldest son, Johann Schartner (*q.v.*), went to Russia and served as minister of the Alexanderwohl Mennonite Church (*q.v.*). His son Gerhard Schartner is an educator and minister among the Fernheim Mennonites in Paraguay. In 1874 the family was transplanted to South Dakota during the migration of the Mennonites to America. Friedrich Schartner (1842-1916) was a leader of this group. He and his son Jacob F. Schartner served as ministers of this group. Representatives of this family, small in number, are found primarily in South Dakota and Russia.   C.K.

Eldon E. Smith, *The History and Record of the Schartner Family* (Marion, S.D., 1952).

Schartner, Johann (1827-1912), a Russian Mennonite elder, was born at Karolswalde, Volhynia, Polish Russia, on Aug. 22, 1827, a son of Friedrich Schartner. He was ordained to the ministry at Karolswalde in 1852. Before or at the time of the great migration of the Polish Mennonites to America Schartner went to the Molotschna (*q.v.*) settlement in Russia, where after the exodus of the Alexanderwohl congregation he was elected elder of the newly organized church in 1877. As elder he frequently visited the Mennonites of Poland, particularly those who had been left without a minister. His contribution lay in his knowledge of the Bible, Christian sincerity, and a brotherly and tolerant attitude in matters of congregational life. He was first married to a Becker and later to Elisabeth Schmidt. To the first marriage twelve and to the second eleven children were born. He died at Landskrone, Molotschna, on Aug. 12, 1912.　　　　　　　C.K.

E. E. Smith, *A History and Record of the Schartner Family* (Newton, 1952); G. Harder, "Unser Schmerzensblatt, 1912," *Menn. Jahrbuch* 1911-12, by H. D. Epp (Berdyansk) 140-43.

Scharwoude. Noord- and Zuid-Scharwoude are two small villages a few miles north of Alkmaar in the Dutch province of North Holland. There was some Anabaptist activity here in 1534-35. Reinier Brunt (*q.v.*), an attorney-general of the Court of Holland, adopted harsh measures against the Anabaptists at Scharwoude in the spring of 1535, demolishing the house of the widow of Jan Zyboetszoon, probably because Anabaptist meetings had been held in it. In 1541 a few Anabaptists of Zuid-Scharwoude escaped their persecutors by flight. There was later no congregation at Scharwoude; the Mennonites living here joined the congregation of neighboring Langendijk (*q.v.*). (*Inv. Arch. Amst.* I, No. 240; *DB* 1909, 15.)　　　vDZ.

Sch(a)ufelberg(er), Jakob, an Anabaptist leader in the district of Grüningen, Swiss canton of Zürich, in 1525 together with Jacob Falk (*q.v.*) and Heini Reimann. In January 1527 he was arrested in Appenzell, and in 1528 he was imprisoned in the "Täuferturm" in Zürich. At first he refused to recant, but after a long imprisonment he did so and was released on Sept. 9, 1528. (*TA Zürich.*)　　vDZ.

Schedme, Ulrich (Ully): see **Schneider, Ulrich.**

Sche(e)demaker, Jacob Jansz, a Dutch Mennonite elder: see **Jacob Jansz.**

Scheemder-Hamrik: see **Nieuw-Scheemda.**

Scheerer, Jörg: see **Wennlin.**

Scheffer, Hans, an Anabaptist martyr of Hastungsfeld, a village on the Hörselberg near Eisenach, Germany, who was seized with Hans Köhler (*q.v.*) in November 1537, as they were conversing with Fritz Erbe (*q.v.*), who was a prisoner. They were executed in Eisenach at the end of January. The record of the trial contains their remarkable confession of faith. (Wappler, *Thüringen,* 172-74; *ML* IV.)　　　　　　　NEFF.

Scheffer, J. G. de Hoop: see **Hoop Scheffer, J. G. de.**

Scheffman, Christoph, a hymn writer of the Hutterian Brethren, d. 1570 at Klein-Nemscha in Moravia. Wolkan lists the following hymns from his pen: (1) "Ach Gott, was soll ich singen, mein Harpfen will nicht klingen"; (2) "Herr Gott Vater, lass mir gelingen, dass ich mit gsang mög firner bringen"; (3) "Nun hörent Gottes Wunder viel, davon ich jetzund singen will"; (4) "O reicher Gott in Himmelsthron, wir, deine kindt, bitten dich alle sambt gar schon"; (5) "Trost, Fried und Freud im Gwissen, Sieg Ueberwindung frei." The *Lieder der Hutterischen Brüder* prints four of these songs (179 ff., viz., nos. 3 and 4 above) and in addition (6) "Christlich Lieb und Eigenschaft mehr sich bei euch durch Gottes Kraft"; (7) "Wo soll ich mich hinkehren, ich arms Brüderlein."　　　NEFF.

Beck, *Geschichts-Bücher,* 324; *Lieder der Hutterischen Brüder* (Scottdale, 1914); Wolkan, *Lieder,* 230; *ML* IV.

Scheikowitz (Schäckowitz, Schaikowitz; Czech, *Cajkovice*), a village in Moravia, where the Hutterite Brethren had a Bruderhof (not to be confused with the Schäkowitz, *q.v.*, north of Auspitz), founded in 1545, at that time owned by Závis von Wickow. Scheikowitz was northeast of Kostel. In 1558 the Brethren were expelled by Lord Säbisch, Závis of Wickow; they settled at Paraditz (*q.v.*). On Sept. 20, 1619, the Bruderhof was burned down by soldiers.　　　　　　　HEGE.

Beck, *Geschichts-Bücher,* 164, 209, 374; Wolkan, *Geschicht-Buch;* Zieglschmid, *Chronik; ML* IV.

Schelben, a shoemaker of Schlicht in the Upper Palatinate, Bavaria, Germany, was considered as belonging to the Anabaptists with his wife and children. For seven years, says the court record, this family "partook of communion only in the spirit when they broke bread at home with their children, because Christ's body and blood were in heaven, and with us only in the spirit." They were expelled in 1535. On May 23, 1534, the Count Palatine had ordered this mild penalty "for this sect without loss of life." There were only isolated Anabaptists in the Upper Palatinate.　　W.W.

Fr. Lippert, *Die Reformation in Kirche, Sitte und Schule der Oberpfalz,* 1520-1620, p. 27; *ML* IV.

Schelhamer, Johan, author of the book, *Widerlegung der widertäuferischen hellischen Grundsuppen des letzten Seculi in der vermeinten Postillen Valentin Weigels ausgeschüttet und Warnung in alle Welt* (Hamburg, 1623). Schelhamer was a pastor in Hamburg, a violent opponent of Valentin Weigel (*q.v.*). (*ML* IV.)

Schellenberg (Schellenbarg, Schöllenbarg, Schellingbarg, Schellenberger), a Mennonite family name found in Switzerland, Germany, Russia, and America. It is a German family name that first occurs in Liechtenstein, and appears in the early Middle Ages in the records of Bavaria, Württemberg, and Upper Franconia. Early in the 14th century a branch of the family settled in Switzerland. The American "Schellenbergers" are of Swiss origin and are traceable to Johannes Schellenberger, who arrived in Philadelphia on the *Pennsylvania Merchant* on Sept. 11, 1732. A branch of the family also migrated from Emmenthal, canton of Bern, Switzerland, to join the Anabaptists of the Netherlands, and its descendants later migrated to Prussia and Russia. The Alexanderwohl church record names a Tobias Schellenberger, who was a refugee from Moravia and joined the Przechovka Mennonite Church in Prussia in 1634. His son, who remained with the Mennonites, had no male offspring. The name appeared as early as the 17th century in

Danzig, Tiegenhagen, and Rosenort. Among the Mennonites of this name migrating to Russia were Anton, Aron, Bernhard, Georg, Gerhard, Jakob, Johann, and Paul Schellenberg.

Prominent leaders of the Mennonite Brethren Church were Abraham Schellenberg (*q.v.*), Abraham L. Schellenberg (*q.v.*), and David Schellenberg (*q.v.*). Töws lists Johann J. Schellenberg, who was killed during the Revolution, as an M.B. minister in Russia. J. G. Rempel lists Wilhelm Schellenberg as a minister of Russia and Canada, Peter P. Schellenberg, minister in Coaldale, Alberta, and B. J. Schellenberg as an educator. *Who's Who Among the Mennonites* lists Peter E. Schellenberg, professor of psychology, former president of Tabor College, who since 1957 has been dean of Bethel College, and Theodore R. Schellenberg, Assistant Archivist of the United States National Archives, Washington, D.C. A Schellenberg of Saskatoon, Sask., is the founder of the O. K. Economy grocery chain. Some of his sons have changed their name to Shelly.

C.K., T.R.Sc.

Gustav Reimer, *Familiennamen*, 117; Alexanderwohl Church Record; Danzig Church Record; *Mennonite Life* X (1955) 80; J. G. Rempel, *Fünfzig Jahre Konferenzbestrebungen* (Steinbach, 1952) 274, 384; B. H. Unruh, *Hintergründe*, 427; A. A. Töws, *Mennonitische Märtyrer* I (Clearbrook, 1949) 137; Müller, *Berner Täufer*, 308.

Schellenberg, Abraham (1845-1920), an elder and outstanding leader of the Mennonite Brethren Church, was born in the village of Halbstadt, Molotschna Mennonite settlement, South Russia, on Aug. 29, 1845. His father was a calico dyer. In Abraham's early life his parents lived in Tiegerweide and Tiege. At the age of fifteen he began to work in his father's shop. He married Katharina Lohrenz on Feb. 25, 1868, and they established their home in Tiegerweide. They had seven children. In 1864 Schellenberg was converted and baptized the following summer. He soon became active in his home church at Rückenau, where he was elected minister in 1869 and elder 1875. Until 1879 he was a very influential minister and leader of the Mennonite Brethren Church in Russia, traveling extensively and preaching very effectively in all of its congregations.

In the spring of 1879 Schellenberg emigrated with his family to America and settled on a farm southwest of Moundridge, Kan. In 1884 his first wife died. He married Suzanna Flaming on Feb. 17, 1885. To them twelve children were born.

Elder Schellenberg was very active in the M.B. Church from his arrival in America until his death. He was at once chosen as the pastor of the newly organized Ebenezer M.B. Church east of Buhler and served for thirty years. Under his ministry this congregation developed into one of the strongest of the M.B. Conference. Elder Schellenberg filled a very important role in the M.B. Conference. In the two decades 1880-1900 he was elected moderator eighteen times. He served much as an itinerating minister, being a gifted public speaker and Bible expositor. He was one of the first of the M.B. leaders to urge foreign missions and was chairman of the Foreign Mission Board for many years. His oldest daughter, Dr. Katharina L. Schellenberg, became the first medical missionary of the M.B.

Church. Schellenberg took a leading part in establishing the mission endowment fund for the support of its foreign missions.

Among the other phases of Conference work in which Schellenberg had an important part was that of publication. He urged the establishing of its church organ, the *Zionsbote*, and advocated the establishing of a Conference publishing house. His oldest son, A. L. Schellenberg, carried out this plan and served as its manager for many years. Schellenberg also contributed valuably to the cause of education in the M.B. Church. Largely through his influence the Conference established a German Department School in conjunction with McPherson College, McPherson, Kan., in 1898. He later also encouraged the establishment of Tabor College and faithfully supported this institution.

In 1907 Schellenberg moved with his family to Escondida, Cal., where he organized an M.B. Church and served as its pastor until 1915. He then returned to Kansas, and after living on his farm four years, retired to Buhler, until his death April 11, 1920. He was interred in the Ebenezer M.B. cemetery east of Buhler.   J.H.L.

Schellenberg, Abraham L. (1869-1941), editor and publishing house manager of the Mennonite Brethren Church, was born in the Molotschna Mennonite settlement, South Russia, May 30, 1869, the oldest child of Elder Abraham and Katharina (Lohrenz) Schellenberg. When he was ten years of age, the family moved to America and settled on a farm southwest of Moundridge, Kan. Here Abraham grew up and received his early schooling. Later he attended school at McPherson College and at Rochester, N.Y. He taught in country schools in the vicinity of Buhler, Kan., for twelve years. He was converted in 1897 and joined the Ebenezer M.B. Church east of Buhler. On Feb. 27, 1898, he married Sarah Schroeder. To them ten children were born. In 1907, when the M.B. Publishing House was transferred to McPherson from Medford, Okla., Schellenberg became manager of the M.B. publishing work and editor of the church organ, the *Zionsbote*. He served the Conference as business manager of the Publishing House and editor of the *Zionsbote* 1907-19 and again 1923-29, a total of 19 years. In 1913 he built the M.B. Publishing House at Hillsboro, Kan., to which the publishing work was then transferred. He also edited and published *Der Deutsche Westen* while at McPherson, and the *Hillsboro Vorwaerts* 1913-29.

Schellenberg served the M.B. General Conference as its secretary 1907-15. He was deeply interested in the educational activities of his church and served for some time as chairman of the Board of Directors of Tabor College. While living at Littlefield, Tex., 1919-23, he was engaged in farming. After retiring from the publishing work in 1929 he settled on a farm at Coldwater, Tex., where he also served the M.B. Church as minister. He died at Hooker, Okla., April 11, 1941, and was interred in the M.B. cemetery east of Buhler.†   J.H.L.

Schellenberg, David (1852-1919), a Mennonite Brethren elder in Russia, was born in Neukirch, Molotschna, Sept. 13, 1852, the son of Abram and

Maria Pauls Schellenberg. He supplemented his elementary education with extensive reading. In 1879 he married Lena Enns, a daughter of Daniel and Maria Peters Enns. Four children were born to this union. His wife died in 1903, and in the following year he married Sara Koop (nee Klassen). After years of Sunday-school teaching he was called to the ministry at the age of 24 and ordained on April 15, 1878. When his older brother, Elder Abraham Schellenberg, left Russia on May 15, 1879, to emigrate to America, he took a part of his church with him and David Schellenberg was elected as elder of the remainder on April 14, 1881, and ordained to the office on May 23, 1882.

P. M. Friesen pays the following tribute to David Schellenberg: "The elder was modest and wise and gladly recognized the talents of others. Many blessings accompanied the earlier part of David Schellenberg's eldership. This changed however later, until circumstances developed in 1909 which brought the office of elder in Rückenau to a standstill." The leadership was henceforth given to a church council. The last ten years of his life were spent in quiet but in full fellowship with his church. His funeral was held on March 3, 1919, when the Molotschna settlement was overrun by the Machno bands.

J.J.T.

B. B. Janz, a contemporary of David Schellenberg, in consultation with other contemporaries, wrote a biography in the German, of which the above is an abbreviated translation.

Schellinger, a Mennonite family, now extinct, found at Amsterdam, Holland, in the 17th and 18th centuries; they were usually ironmongers and in the 18th century came to great prosperity. Some members of this family belonged to the Old Frisian (Arke Noach) Mennonites at Amsterdam, among whom was Abraham Pieters Schellinger, who was a preacher of this church 1718-d.66. Members of the family were found in the Jan-Jacobsz, Lamist, Zonist, and (in the 17th century) Waterlander congregations. A few members of this family were warmly interested in the Hernhutter (*q.v.,* Moravian) Brotherhood and some joined them at Zeist, as did Jacob Schellinger (b. 1706) and his brother Cornelis. Both were members of the Amsterdam Lamist church and were won over to the Hernhutters by Johannes Deknatel (*q.v.*), the Lamist minister, who was a warm friend of the Hernhutters. Jacob married Magdalena Beuning, and Cornelis married Sophia Centen; both women were Mennonites. In 1736 Jacob Schellinger provided the money for the purchase of a tract of land near IJsselstein in the Dutch province of Utrecht, where a suitable building was then erected for the Hernhutter colony, which was named 's Heerendyk. In 1745, 's Heerendyk having become too small, Cornelis Schellinger bought a manor with a large area of land at Zeist near Utrecht (for 155,000 guilders). He also contributed generously to the furnishing of the manor at Zeist, to which the Brethren now moved from 's Heerendyk. Cornelis Schellinger and his family lived for a number of years in a wing of this castle; Jacob Schellinger and other families lived here temporarily. Count Zinzendorf (*q.v.*) also lived there for some time; his eldest daughter was mar-

30

ried in the castle chapel, which had also been built largely by Cornelis Schellinger's contributions. About 1749 discord arose between Cornelis Schellinger and Count Zinzendorf. In 1752 the former was involved in the financial difficulties of the Hernhutter group; in 1767 after some disappointment he sold the castle and most of the other property to Count von Dohna, Zinzendorf's son-in-law, and left Zeist, without, however, entirely leaving the Hernhutters.

vDZ.

Amsterdam church records; W. Lütjeharms, *Het Philadelphisch-Oecumenisch Streven der Hernhutters in de Nederlanden in de achttiende eeuw* (Zeist. 1935) *passim.*

Schellingwou (Schellinckwou), **Jan Jansz** (not to be confused with the Anabaptist leader Jan van Schellingwou, *q.v.*), was in the early 17th century a Waterlander preacher (congregation unknown) in the Dutch province of Friesland. In 1610 he and some other Waterlander preachers and elders, e.g., Hans Matthysen (Matthijs, *q.v.*), Dirk Doedes, Ane Anes, and Yeme de Ringh (*q.v.*), opposed the plan of the Waterlander congregation of Amsterdam to merge with the English (Brownist) church of John Smyth (*q.v.*). (*Inv. Arch. Amst.* I, No. 538; II, Nos. 1358, 1362 f., 2933; *DB* 1903, 59.) vDZ.

Schellinkhout, near Hoorn in the Dutch province of North Holland, was formerly the seat of a Mennonite congregation, of whose origin and history very little is known. It belonged to the Frisian branch and died out or merged with Hoorn before 1700. (Blaupot t. C., *Holland* I, 251; II, 45.) vDZ.

Schelte Aedelezoon, an Anabaptist martyr, from Friesland, Netherlands, was burned at the stake at Leeuwarden, the capital of Friesland, on May 13, 1553, because he was rebaptized, opposed the Roman Catholic sacrament of the Mass, saying "that all that is done in the (Catholic) church is idolatry." He refused to recant and died loyally for his faith. (*Inv. Arch. Amst.* I, No. 746.) vDZ.

Scheltema, a Mennonite family, from the 16th century found at Harlingen and from the 18th century at Franeker, both in the Dutch province of Friesland, where they were engaged in business. A descendant of this family in the female line was Jan Jansen Agricola (1658-94), of Franeker, who later also took the family name of Scheltema. He was a merchant and a preacher of the Franeker Mennonite congregation. His son and further descendants joined the Reformed Church. One branch of this family has taken the family name of Scheltema de Heere. Elder Jan Jacobsz (*q.v.*), who according to tradition was a son of Jacob de Heere, may have been a son of a Jacob whose great-grandson took the name of Scheltema. (*Ned. Patriciaat* XXVII, 1941, 208-81.) vDZ.

Schen(c)k: see also **Shank** and **Shenk.**

Schenck van Tautenburg, George (d. Feb. 2, 1540, at Vollenhove, Netherlands), was a German nobleman, who was a stadholder of Emperor Charles V (*q.v.*), governing the province of Friesland in 1524-40. Being a convinced Catholic, he fought Sacramentism and Anabaptism with all his power. He personally led the attack on the cloister of Bloemcamp (Oldeklooster, *q.v.*) near Bolsward in March 1535, which had been taken by revolutionary Anabaptists some days before. During Schenck's government, besides those who had participated in the Oldeklooster uprising, all of whom were put to death, 19 Anabaptists were executed whose names are known; the number of anonymous Anabaptist martyrs in Friesland during his rule is estimated at about 80.

In 1534 Schenck, as a confidential agent of the emperor, negotiated with Franz von Waldeck, Bishop of Münster, Westphalia; the emperor wished to have the territory of the bishopric added to his dominion. Though the negotiations were strictly secret, something of the imperial plans became known and were opposed by the Protestant princes in Germany, particularly Philip of Hesse. Schenck also seems to have dealt with Jan van Geelen (*q.v.*) the ambassador of Jan van Leyden, in order to acquire the city of Münster for the emperor. vDZ.

J. Reitsma, *Honderd jaren uit de Geschiedenis der Hervorming . . . in Friesland* (Leeuwarden, 1876) *passim;* Mellink, *Wederdopers, passim.*

Schenk: see also Shank.

Schenk, a Mennonite family found at Wormerveer, Dutch province of North Holland, since the 16th century, and formerly belonging to the Frisian congregation. In the 18th century some members of this family were adherents of the Collegiant (*q.v.*) movement, particularly Jan Gerrit Schenk (d. June 25, 1760, at Wormerveer), who in 1726-52 repeatedly addressed the Collegiant meetings at their center at Rijnsburg (*q.v.*). He also contributed liberally to the building of the large brick baptismal tub at Rijnsburg in 1736 (for baptism by immersion as practiced by the Collegiants) and bequeathed 40,000 Dutch guilders to the general fund of the Collegiants for the maintenance of the buildings at Rijnsburg. vDZ.

J. C. van Slee, *De Rijnsburger Collegianten* (Haarlem, 1895) 199 f. and *passim;* information by J. Aten at Wormerveer.

Scheppach, Peter, an artist of Augsburg, Bavaria, Germany, a member of the Anabaptist congregation at that place, was compelled to recant and then expelled from the city (see **Augsburg**). NEFF.

"Zur Gesch. der Wiedertäufer in Oberschwaben," in *Ztscht des hist. Vereins für Schwaben und Neuburg* I, 227; *ML* IV.

Scherer, Peter: see Walpot, Peter.

Scherk: see also Shirk.

Schermanch(h)owitz, a Bruderhof of the Hutterian Brethren in Moravia (*q.v.*). In 1620 it was attacked by soldiers and in 1621 plundered. In October 1622 "upon command of Emperor Ferdinand, through the instigation and incitation of the Cardinal of Dietrichstein," they were expelled, leaving all their possessions behind. They settled in Hungary. (Zieglschmid, *Chronik; idem, Klein-Geschichtsbuch; ML* IV.) HEGE.

Schermer, a Mennonite family at Wormerveer, Dutch province of North Holland, members of the Frisian congregation (Wormerveer op't Noord). Cornelis Schermer of Wormerveer was a Mennonite preacher of Den Ilp 1770-80, Hindeloopen (Nieuwe kerk) 1780-90, and Uithoorn-Aalsmeer 1790-1804. His son Klaas Schermer (d. Dec. 31, 1854), trained for the ministry by his father, served as preacher in the Wormerveer op't Noord congregation 1800-49. Lucas Schermer, a merchant at Wormerveer, was a representative to the national Dutch parliament meeting at The Hague in 1796. vDZ.

Schermerhorn, a hamlet in the Dutch province of North Holland, formerly situated beside Lake Schermer, which was reclaimed in 1632-35. A Waterlander congregation existing here sent delegates to the Waterlander conference at Amsterdam March 4-7, 1581. A letter of 1673 mentions the congregation of (Groot) Schermer, which probably means Schermerhorn. There is no further information about this congregation; it very probably died out or merged with a neighboring congregation soon after, at least before 1700. vDZ.

Inv. Arch. Amst. I, No. 892; *DB* 1872, 57; 1877, 80; Blaupot t. C., *Holland* I, 251; II, 45.

Schertz, a Mennonite family name of Swiss origin, found in the Palatinate after 1664. In 1940 twenty-two persons bearing the Schertz name were members of the Ixheim-Saar Mennonite Church in South Germany. A Johann Heinrich Schertz, possibly Amish, arrived in Philadelphia in 1742. Some 19th-century Amish Schertz immigrants settled in Butler County, Ohio, but more of them located in central Illinois, where most of the Mennonite Schertzes are found today. Over 75 per cent of the obituaries of members of the Schertz family in Mennonite periodicals are from Illinois. Among the early Amish immigrants arriving in Illinois were David Schertz and his father, who settled in Tazewell County near Peoria, in 1831, and whose descendants were found largely in the Metamora congregation. Harry Weber (*History of the Mennonites in Illinois*) refers to more than twenty individual members of the Schertz family. Among the Illinois Mennonite (MC) ministers have been Peter D. Schertz (1848-1928), Christian S. Schertz (1851-1937), and Henry R. Schertz (1886-1954), bishop of the Metamora Mennonite Church (*q.v.*). M.G.

Scheure, van der: see Schuere, van der.

Scheuten, Mennonite family of Crefeld, named from the farm "uf der Schutten" in the parish of München-Gladbach. Daem (Adam) Scheuten (1607-18) came to Crefeld in 1654, became a citizen there in 1679; he was a dealer in linen. As lay preachers of the Crefeld congregation mention should be made of his son Adam (1639-68) and his grandson Leonard Ewalds (d. 1743). His grandson Adam Scheuten (1697-1765), married to Aletta von der Leyen (1699-1757), the sister of Friedrich (1701-78) and Heinrich van der Leyen (1708-82, *q.v.*), was a versatile industrialist in Crefeld. With his brothers Johann (1699-1757) and Hermann (1702-49) he was engaged in distilling brandy and vinegar, curing tobacco (a business he probably acquired with his wife's dowry); they also established a linseed oil plant and manufactured starch and barley grits. He also sold silk goods manufactured by his brothers-in-law, and built a warehouse in Essenberg (on the Rhine, opposite Ruhrort) in 1743 for better disposal of his wares. In the list of taxpayers in Crefeld he ranked among the most highly assessed, second only to his brothers-in-law. His grandson Adam Wilhelm Scheuten (1753-1801) endowed by bequest the "Scheutensche Lehranstalt," which later became the Crefeld Realgymnasium. The male line of the family died out in 1914. "Sammlung Scheuten" is a collection of genealogical notes on the history of the old Mennonite families of Crefeld, an important and reliable source, probably begun by Abraham Scheuten (1707-89), who was also a lay preacher, a grandson of Daem.   W.R.

Beiträge zur Gesch. rheinischer Mennoniten (Weierhof, 1939) 123 f.; Die Heimat (Crefeld) IX, 274 ff.; XVII No. 4.

Schiebach: see Skippack.

Schiedam, a city (1956 pop. 77,500, with about 100 Mennonites) in the Dutch province of South Holland, near Rotterdam, in which Anabaptists were found as early as 1534. During the winter of 1534-35 Leenaerdt Boeckbinder (q.v.) and Jan Claesz Cock (q.v.) baptized a number of persons here. In September 1535 twenty-five Anabaptists of Schiedam saved their lives by flight. In 1539 Claes Claesz (Snyder), a deacon of the Schiedam congregation, was arrested at Leiden and on November 16 severely tortured at The Hague; he was beheaded at Leiden on Dec. 20, 1539. Claes Willems, a (non-Mennonite) bailiff of Schiedam, was charged in 1545 with having protected the Anabaptists and other heretics in this town. Elder Leenaert Bouwens (q.v.) baptized 14 persons at Schiedam during his visits in 1563-65.

Soon after, at least by 1580, there were three Mennonite congregations at Schiedam, a Flemish, a Frisian, and a High German or Waterlander. Jan Hendriksz, at this time a preacher or elder of the Frisian church, soon after sided with Lubbert Gerritsz (q.v.) and the progressive Young Frisians. The moderate views in his congregation and also in that of the High Germans led to a merger of these two groups, probably as early as 1591, but in any case before 1620. Negotiations opened about 1625 between the Frisian-High German group, now mostly called Waterlanders, and the Flemish with a view to union miscarried. The Flemish congregation, being rather conservative, rejected the offer of the Waterlanders; particularly the Flemish preacher Cornelis Cornelisz Bom van Cranenburgh, who served 1623-50, opposed the merger. Lambert Lambertsz Paeldinck and Lubbert Wolfertsz (van Vollenhoven) of the Flemish congregation in 1626 signed the Outerman (q.v.) confession. The information by P. J. Twisck (Blaupot t. C., Friesland, 117) that about 1628 the Flemish Mennonites of Schiedam held their meetings in the same house as the High German or "Overlanders" is not clear, unless he means that the united High German and Frisian congregation, then called Waterlanders, were

about this time preparing for this merger, and were using the same meetinghouse for this purpose.

At a conference of conservative Flemish delegates held at Leiden, June 1660, of which T. J. van Braght (q.v.) was the moderator, it was reported that the Flemish congregation had just merged with the Waterlanders (this indeed had happened in 1650) and that the united congregation was inclined to the liberal views of Galenus Abrahamsz (q.v.).

In the meantime some difficulty arose in the newly united church of Schiedam between a progressive and a more conservative faction. About 1655, the progressives, then in the majority, invited Galenus to preach at Schiedam; but in 1671 after an address of the conservative elder Bastiaen van Weenighem (q.v.) of Rotterdam, the congregation promised to follow the views of the conservative Zonists (q.v.). A few years later, however (1675), the Schiedam congregation sided with the Galenists or Lamists (as this group was mostly called then), and in this year it joined the Lamist South Holland Sociëteit (conference). During this tumultuous period Jan Huygen van der Linden (d. 1678), who had already been a Waterlander preacher before the merger of 1650, served the congregations until 1677. He was followed by Jan Ariens van Raemburg, a preacher of the Rotterdam Waterlander congregation, who had moved to Schiedam in March 1677, but who died in the course of the year. Thereupon Melis Ates Spinneker (q.v.), subsidized by the Lamist South Holland conference, was a preacher at Schiedam until his death in December 1681. He was followed by Jan de Jager, serving 1682-c90. After de Jager had been dismissed, Petrus van Loon served at Schiedam until about 1705, followed by Jan Arkenbout 1721-22, Dirk van Beek 1721-25, Simon Buys 1726-28, Jan Visser 1728-31, Petrus Plantinus 1731-41, and Hendrik Seije, the last preacher of Schiedam, 1741-47. In 1747 discord arose and he was dismissed; thereupon the few remaining members joined the neighboring Rotterdam congregation.

To this survey can be added a few facts. In 1642 the Mennonites of Schiedam were granted permission to have their marriages performed in their meetinghouses. Concerning these meetinghouses there is not much information. The united congregation used one that had been built shortly after 1610 on the Schie River in the center of the town. This meetinghouse, probably rebuilt at least once, was sold to the Lutherans in 1756. The membership was always small. Figures of early times were not available; in 1675 the united congregation numbered 30 baptized members, in 1745 only 14. From about 1670 it was financially supported by the Rotterdam church and the Lamist church of Amsterdam. Three members of the noted van Vollenhoven (q.v.) family, which later moved to Rotterdam, Amsterdam, and Haarlem, served the church as deacons; viz., Lubbert Wolfertsz van Vollenhoven, deacon of the Flemish church from 1630, Anthony van Vollenhoven and Koenraad von Vollenhoven, both deacons of the united congregation in 1712-41 and from 1732 respectively. Another Koenraad van Vollenhoven (1611-79), a member of the same family, was a preacher at Schiedam 1636-40, probably of the Frisian-High German congregation. In 1640 he moved to Haarlem.

Jan van der Beest, a Mennonite, was a public notary at Schiedam from 1622, and was exempted by the States of Holland from taking an oath.

In the early 17th century the Collegiants (*q.v.*) had some warm adherents among the Mennonites of Schiedam. One of them, Pieter Vijgh, was baptized in 1729 "in the manner of the Collegiants," i.e., by immersion. Preacher Hendrik Seije also regularly attended the Collegiant meetings.

The Mennonites now living at Schiedam are members of the Rotterdam congregation.   vDZ.

DB 1899, 181, where Jan van der Beest is erroneously called N. Beest; 1909, 156-68; *Inv. Arch. Amst.* I, Nos. 206, 216, 220, 225, 321, 445, 564, 582, 593, 601 f., 781, 907 f., 1180; II, Nos. 1837 f., 2207, 2220-43; II, 2, Nos. 358, 428, 465-86; *DB* 1863, 130; 1872, 67; 1892, 103, 124, 126 f.; 1893, 81, note 1; 1899, 181; 1918, 50, 52; Mellink, *Wederdopers,* 223, 225; *De Zondagsbode,* Sept. 19, 1898.

Schiemer, Leonhard, of Vöcklabruck, Upper Austria (the *Martyrs' Mirror* erroneously calls him Leonhard Schöner of Becklasburg), one of the outstanding Anabaptist leaders and martyrs of the very beginning (died 1528), whose significance for the entire movement has been but recently recognized. He belongs to the line of South German Anabaptists roughly characterized by the names Denk (*q.v.*) and Hut (*q.v.*), to which group also Hans Schlaffer (*q.v.*), Ambrosius Spittelmayr (*q.v.*), and Hans Nadler (*q.v.*) belonged. They all represent a stronger spiritualistic emphasis in their Christian faith. The "outer word" alone does not suffice for a true understanding, Schiemer would say; rather the true light of the Holy Spirit is needed which shines in our heart.

Of his life some details are known from his *Bekanntnus* (Müller, 80-81), which he submitted to his judge in January 1528. He was brought up at Vöcklabruck and Vienna by God-fearing parents, and desired to enter the Catholic priesthood. But when he found little godliness in the life and teaching of the priests he joined the Barefoot Friars (Franciscans), noted for their piety. But again he found nothing but strife and hypocrisy; finally, having tried this life for six years he fled from the monastery at Judenburg, Styria. A kind citizen of that city gave him some clothing and a guilder for his needs. Now he began to wander about: first he went to Nürnberg where he learned the tailor's trade (and probably met some of the leading men of the Radical Reformation). Thence he went to Nikolsburg, Moravia, to hear Hubmaier's teachings —having vigorously opposed them in his former days. From here he turned to Vienna to learn more about true Christianity from Hans Hut. He related that the assembly "in the Kärntnerstrasse" was greatly embarrassed when he entered, suspecting him to be a spy. After two days of talks, however, he accepted believer's baptism from Oswald Glaidt (*q.v.*) in the spring of 1527. From Vienna he went to Steyr, the industrial city in Upper Austria, known as a place of great readiness for radical ideas. Here he stayed for a time earning his living by his trade and baptizing many converts to the new faith. The brotherhood made him a preacher (*Leermeister*) and soon sent him into many lands (Salzburg, Ba-

varia, Tirol) to spread his new message. Although he was well aware that several monasteries in Austria were trying to apprehend him as a renegade monk he obeyed his call without hesitation, and was caught in the city of Rattenberg (*q.v.*) on the Inn, Tirol (in the documents always written Rotenburg), Nov. 25, 1527, scarcely six months after his conversion. In Rattenberg, he claims, he had worked only one day, and yet he signs one of his epistles to the local brotherhood as "your unworthy bishop." We cannot completely reconstruct the story of that Rattenberg Anabaptist congregation but there is little doubt that Schiemer's influence was tremendous, in spite of the fact that he was in prison until his execution by the sword seven weeks later, Jan. 14, 1528. The district judge Bartholomeus Angst was most lenient to his prisoner (Beck, 61 note), allowing brethren to go in and out and to give him paper and ink to write as much as he wanted. Thus these seven weeks are among the most fruitful ones in the long and bitter story of South German and Tirolean Anabaptism. His writings were soon collected in a pamphlet or booklet presumably for the local congregation, but they found wide distribution afterwards in Moravia, Germany, and Switzerland. The Hutterites as well as Pilgram Marpeck and his people were greatly indebted to this outstanding Anabaptist teacher.

At one time Schiemer tried to escape (Müller, 76) but was caught again. Now his imprisonment was made harder. Torture and hunger made him miserable in the flesh, and the dread of death made him shudder. But he gained new strength by the thought, "If I did not place all my confidence in the Lord, I would fall; but the Lord is my comfort and my confidence; he forsakes none who trusts him" (Müller, 76). The government in Innsbruck urged Judge Angst to greater rigor and requested the speeding up of the case. Schiemer was condemned to death by fire in accordance with the mandates of King Ferdinand (*q.v.*), but the sentence was moderated to beheading and burning the corpse afterwards. "After him about 70 others testified to their faith [in Rattenberg]," writes the Hutterite Chronicle, thus demonstrating the amazing spiritual vitality of this "Schiemer congregation."

The writings produced by Schiemer in prison are found in numerous Hutterite codices (best perhaps in the oldest one extant, 1566, now at a Bruderhof in Montana) and, surprisingly, also in the *Kunstbuch* (*q.v.*) of 1561, which originated in the Marpeck group. The numbering and counting of these writings is not easy because the items are sometimes written together and sometimes separated, sometimes considered as "epistles" and sometimes taken as tracts or sermons. Their tremendous appeal and effectiveness in the shaping of the Anabaptist genius and tradition cannot be doubted. Fortunately, the majority of Schiemer's writings have been published by Lydia Müller (*Glaubenszeugnisse*); others will follow in *Glaubenszeugnisse* II and in the forthcoming edition of the *Kunstbuch*. The list is roughly as follows:

(1) *Eine hübsche Erklärung der 12 Artikel des christlichen Glaubens,* contained in an epistle to the church in Rattenberg (Müller, 44-58; *Kunstbuch,*

No. 10). The oldest codex of the Hutterites (1566) has this item too, supplemented by two pages containing a remarkable diagram of four circles: /the Will of God/ Adam/ Creature/ Christ/, plus accompanying text (not yet published).

(2) *Was die Gnad sey. Eine Vorred*, and a tract "concerning threefold grace." The term *Vorred* means with the Hutterites always "sermon" but at this place it might also mean "introduction" (Müller, 58-71; *Kunstbuch*, No. 9). This is a real gem of Anabaptist writing. In the article concerning "the second grace" there is a lengthy insertion called *Auslegung des Vater Unser*, a paraphrasing of the Lord's Prayer (reissued side by side with a similar piece by Hans Langenmantel, *q.v.*, in *Glaubenszeugnisse* II). In the *Kunstbuch* this item runs over without interruption into item

(3) *Vom Fläschl* (Müller, 72-74), concluded by a lengthy epistle to the congregation of Rattenberg, dated Dec. 4, 1527 (Müller, 74-77). The *Kunstbuch* has *Fläschl* and epistle all under No. 9. It might be said that Schiemer was never more profound and close to the spirit of the great medieval mystics than in this item. The ensuing epistle is more personal; the writer suddenly interrupts his "Lehr" (instruction) by being overwhelmed by his predicament and now wants to pour out his troubled mind to his brethren.

(4) *Von der Tauff im Neuen Testament*, also called *Von dreyerlei Tauff* (namely, by the Spirit, by water, and by blood), very much a counter piece to the *Dreyerlei Gnad* (above No. 2; Müller, 77-79). The *Kunstbuch* includes this item in No. 10 (see above, item 1) as a sort of appendix. The Hutterite codices call this item "the third epistle by Leonhard Schiemer," apparently meaning the third item which Schiemer sent from prison. The term "epistle" is not quite correct as this item does not contain personal communications. The *Kunstbuch* presents these four items as Nos. 9 and 10.

(5) *Trostbrief an einen schwachen Bruder*. In many Hutterite codices but not in the *Kunstbuch* or in Müller.

(6) *Ein wahrhaft kurz Evangelium, heut der Welt zu predigen*, found only in the *Kunstbuch*, to be published in *Glaubenszeugnisse* II, a rather short piece, a kind of sermonette.

(7) *Ein Bekanntnus vor dem Richter zu Rotenburg* (most likely January 1528) (Müller, 80-81; not in the *Kunstbuch*), a brief biography with a concluding apologetic paragraph.

These are the known items of Schiemer's work, all produced for his Rattenberg brethren during the seven weeks of his imprisonment. The writer of this article, however, is inclined to ascribe to Schiemer also a number of anonymous items found in Hutterite codices, usually following Schiemer's "epistles" and apparently serving a similar purpose—organizing the Rattenberg church and giving it guidance, direction, and order.

(8) *Ordnung der Gemein, wie ein Christ leben soll*. In the Hutterite Chronicle (Wolkan, 60-61), inserted by the writer of the Chronicle for 1529 without much argument, taken most probably again from the afore-mentioned (hypothetical) booklet of Schiemer's writings. The *MQR* (1955, 162-66) published an English translation of the fuller text (as found in codices). It is a skeleton church discipline, a true model of Anabaptist thought concerning ordering life in the congregation, much shorter than the Schleitheim articles of the same year (1527), only laying the groundwork for all future attempts in the same direction. Most likely Schiemer drew it up tentatively (in 12 points) that the brethren of the incipient congregation might have some guidance after his death.

(9 to 13) Anonymous tracts of similar purpose. One is a catechism; the rest contain more or less moral instructions. The *Lieder der Hutterischen Brüder* (1914, p. 19) assigns all these items expressly to Schiemer.

Besides these writings several hymns are likewise ascribed to Schiemer: (1) Dein heilig statt hond sie zerstört (Müller, 82-83, after Beck 58-59, note); (2) Wir bitten dich, ewiger Gott, neig zu uns deine Ohren (*Ausbund*, No. 31); here the author is named Leonhard Schöner whence the *Martyrs' Mirror* may have taken the name; also in *Lieder der Hutterischen Brüder*, 28-29; (3) Sollstu bei Gott dein wohnung han (*Lieder der Hutterischen Brüder*, 28-29). According to an old codex in Esztergom this hymn is said to have been composed by Schiemer, but according to Wolkan (*Lieder*, 12) it was written by Ludwig Haetzer; (4) Wie köstlich ist der Heil'gen Tod (Wiswedel, 185, who took it from the Beck collection in Brno, file No. 45). No further reference found.

Schiemer's "Theology" and Main Teachings. One might easily agree with Wiswedel's statement (184) that both Schiemer and Schlaffer (*q.v.*) had been strongly influenced by medieval mysticism (while being priest or monk), in the main by Tauler and the *Deutsche Theologie*, just as Hans Denk and some of the early Spiritualists had been. Christ must be born in us, we must suffer with Him, be crucified and be buried with Him, also descend into Hades with Him, in order to be raised with Him (Müller, 53). Schiemer prefers the translation "The Word became flesh and dwelleth *in* us," rather than "among" us, as we likewise believe "in" God not "on" God (German: *an* Gott), etc. (Müller, 61). Justification without sanctification loses its deeper meaning (Müller, 78), countering Paul's thesis by references to Matt. 25. In such an outlook naturally the old problem of "the inner and outer Word" (see **Bible, Inner and Outer Word,** also **Spiritualism**) becomes a most urgent issue although this emphasis on the inwardness of God's Word never leads to a quietistic enjoyment but rather to an active witnessing and following of Christ.

This becomes perhaps most impressive in the beautiful small tract *Vom Fläschl*: "A reply to those who say we drink something from a small flask, of which the devil himself does not know what it contains." Very well, says Schiemer, let it be called a flask. But the drink in it is nothing but a contrite, crushed, and sad heart, pounded by the mortar of the cross. The grapes in it grew in God's vineyard and were pressed under the press of tribulation. From such a flask Christ drank on the cross. And as a flask is narrow at the top but wide at the bottom, thus is also the way of salvation: once a man has overcome all agony and tribulation the flask gets wide and he receives God's comfort and consolation.

Schiemer teaches three kinds of grace: the first is the Word given us by the Father as a divine light (the law). This divine light in man shows him what sin is (*anzeigen was sind sey oder nit*). Although this light is the same in all men, not all accept it and use it in the same way (Müller, 63). The second grace is Christ or divine righteousness (*Gerechtigkeit*). The first light is our taskmaster (*Zuchtmeister*), preparing us for the other light which is Christ (apparently Christ *in us*). But in order to see this second light one needs to go through the "furnace of suffering" (Luther: *Feuer der Trübsal*, Eccl. 2:5, also I Peter 1:7, "gold tested by fire"; the Anabaptists changed the word into *Schmelzofen der Gelassenheit*), "for the uncrucified Christ is like untried metal" (Müller, 67 and 78). In other words, an untested faith is no faith at all. Thus the second grace might also be called "the cross." The third grace, finally, is a grace of joy and rejoicing. It is the promise of the Holy Spirit and His glory. While the life of the "world" begins merrily but ends sadly, the life of a God-fearing man has a sad beginning but eventually the Holy Spirit comes to him anointing him with the oil of unspeakable joy.

As there are three kinds of grace there are also three kinds of baptism, well known from the Scriptures themselves: the first baptism is with the Holy Spirit, the second is with water, and the third with blood. Baptism with water is a confirmation of faith and an inner covenant with God. When one has written a letter he seals it. But no one would seal a letter without knowing what it contains. Whoever baptizes a child acts like a man who seals an empty letter (Müller, 79).

It would be an attractive task to search for the spiritual roots of these teachings. Herbert Klassen in his study of Hans Hut strongly suggests that many a thought of Schiemer, Schlaffer, Ambrosius Spittelmayr, and others goes back to this dynamic and dedicated leader, as far as we are able to reconstruct his doctrines. This is most likely correct. But it is certainly also true that a great many of these ideas are derived from Schiemer's own spiritual experiences condensed as they were into the unbelievably brief span of perhaps nine months. The wide use of his writings throughout the Anabaptist brotherhood, including Pilgram Marpeck, and the unique heroism of the Rattenberg congregation (72 martyrs within a few years) give vivid testimony to the spiritual force of these tracts, suggesting that also the 16th century knew something of the charismatic and pneumatic experiences of the apostolic church.

R.F.

Beck, *Geschichts-Bücher;* Wolkan, *Geschicht-Buch;* Loserth, *Anabaptismus; Lieder der Hutterischen Brüder* (Scottdale, 1914); A. Nicoladoni, *Johannes Bünderlin* (Berlin, 1893); Wiswedel, *Bilder* II (Kassel, 1930), "Leonhard Schiemer, der erste Täuferbischof Oberösterreichs." 174-86; Lydia Müller, *Glaubenszeugnisse oberdeutscher Taufgesinnter* (Leipzig, 1938); L. Müller and R. Friedmann, eds. *Glaubenszeugnisse oberdeutscher Täufer* (Gütersloh, 1960), quoted as *Glaubenszeugnisse* II; Heinold Fast, "Pilgram Marbeck und das oberdeutsche Täufertum, ein neuer Handschriftenfund,"

Archiv für Reformationsgeschichte XLVII (1956) 212-42; "Das Kunstbuch" (typescript copy in GCL); Herbert Klassen, "Hans Hut" (unpublished master's thesis, University of British Columbia, 1958; copy in GCL); R. Friedmann, "The Oldest Church Discipline of the Anabaptists," *MQR* XXVIII (1955) 162-66; *Mart. Mir.* D 13 f., E 424 f. (here called "Schoener"); *ML* IV.

Schiere, a Mennonite family found at Harlingen, Dutch province of Friesland, from the 17th century, members of the Waterlander and later of the united congregation. They were usually merchants and active members of the church, as was Jan Symons Schiere in 1695. In the 19th century one branch was engaged in book printing and publishing at Harlingen. By marriage they were related with other Mennonite families at Harlingen, such as Hingst, Roos, Menalda, van Schouwenburg, and Fontein.

Teunis Schiere (b. 1836 at Boornbergum, Friesland, d. May 19, 1907, at Arnhem), who may have belonged to the Harlingen family, studied theology at the University of Groningen and the Amsterdam Mennonite Seminary, and served as a Mennonite minister at Ouddorp 1861-74 and at Den Ilp 1874-97, when he retired.   vDZ.

Schijn, a Dutch Mennonite family, found at Amsterdam in the 17th and 18th centuries, members of the Zonist church. Herman Schijn (*q.v.*) was a noted elder and voluminous author. His brother(?) Laurens Schijn (d. May 11, 1713) was a deacon of the Rotterdam Flemish congregation from 1686 and from 1700 (merger of the Flemish and Waterlanders) of the united Rotterdam Mennonite church. Jacob Schijn, a son of Dr. Herman, served from 1721 as a deacon of the Amsterdam Zonist congregation. The Schijn family died out in the 18th century.   vDZ.

Schijn (Schyn), Herman (Hermannus, Hermanus, Harmannus), b. Aug. 3, 1662, at Amsterdam, d. there Nov. 25, 1727, studied medicine at the universities of Leiden and Utrecht, obtaining his M.D. degree at Utrecht in 1682, practiced medicine at Rotterdam until 1690 and then until his death at Amsterdam. At the same time he devoted himself to the interests of the Mennonite church. In 1685 he was appointed deacon of the Rotterdam Flemish congregation and in 1686 called to the ministry in the same congregation, serving as preacher until 1688, when he became an elder. In 1690 he moved to Amsterdam and served as an elder of the Zonist (*q.v.*) church from 1690 until his death. Herman Schijn had two sons.

Schijn was the great leader of the conservative Mennonites (Zonists) in the Netherlands. Besides this the Dutch brotherhood is deeply indebted to him for his historiography, Schijn being one of the first Dutch scholarly historians. As a member of the Dutch Mennonite Committee of Foreign Needs (*Commissie voor Buitenlandsche Nooden*) he was active in behalf of the oppressed Mennonites in Switzerland and Prussia. In 1707-8 he carried on a correspondence with the Mennonites in Germantown, Pa. As a conservative leader Schijn was much disturbed when his former church of Rotterdam in 1700, then merging with the Waterlander congregation, resolved to admit to the communion services "all Christians," not only those who were members of other Mennonite churches or other Christian denominations, but even unbaptized persons who considered themselves Christians. Against this liberal formula of *benodiging* (*q.v.*, i.e., invitation) with its Collegiant (*q.v.*) spirit Schijn published *Aenmerkingen op het formulier van benodiging* (Amsterdam, 1703).

Schijn wrote a large number of books; besides the *Aenmerkingen* and his historical works (listed below) they are: *Zalige Na-gedagtenis* (Amsterdam, 1695), a funeral sermon for his co-preacher Michael Fortgens; *Salomons tempelbouw* (Amsterdam, 1697), a sermon preached at Amsterdam; *Kort onderwys des christelyken Geloofs* (Amsterdam, 1697, repr. 1698, 1710, 1723, 1740, all at Amsterdam), a catechetical book, written by order of the Zonist conference; *Zeedige Verantwoording der Mennoniten op zeeker placcaat, door de regeerders der Stadt Bern tegen de z.g. Weederdoopers uitgegeeven* (n.p., n.d.-c1710); *Eerste Beginselen van den christelyken godsdienst* (Amsterdam, 1718, repr. 1723, 1736, 1783, all at Amsterdam), a catechism; in collaboration with H. van Dam, *De Kerkeraadt en Gemeente der Doopsgezinde te Amsterdam . . . verdeedigt* (Amsterdam, 1719); *De mensch in Christus of het geestelyk leeven der geloovigen* (Amsterdam, 1721, repr. Amsterdam 1725, 18 sermons); *Zeedige en rechtmaatige verdeediging tegens den E. David Bramen* (Amsterdam, 1724); *Beletzelen des geestelyken leevens* (Amsterdam, 1727), containing 21 sermons; *Heilige Keurstoffen* (Amsterdam, 1737), a collection of sermons published after his death.

Of special interest is a book by Schijn (published at Amsterdam in 1723, repr. there 1738) entitled *Ontwerp tot vereeniging der doopsgezinde Christenen (Project for the Unification of the Mennonite Christians)*. In this mild and wise book the author deals with the desirability and possibility of a unification of the different branches of Dutch Mennonites, and particularly of a merger between the Lamists (*q.v.*) and the Zonists. Previous attempts made to unite these two largest groups of Mennonites had failed. The Lamists accused the Zonists of putting too much importance on the confessions of faith, while the Zonists complained that the Lamists were guilty of a "considerable indifference" (*aenmerkelyke lossigheid*) concerning the basic principles, and objected to the Collegiant and even the Socinian (*q.v.*) views prevalent among the Lamists. Schijn's deacon, Lambert Bidloo (*q.v.*), severely attacked the Lamists because of their "unlimited tolerance" (*onbepaelde verdraegsaemheyt*). The book by Schijn on this matter is very moderate. His position is as follows: all possible efforts should be made to bring about a unification; for many of the differences between the Lamists and the Zonists are insignificant, such as footwashing, the question of silent or "spoken" prayer, of strict or mild banning and shunning, and a number of minor questions. But on two points Schijn maintains Zonist doctrines: the practice, ignored by the Lamists, that no unbaptized person should be admitted to the Lord's Supper and that the congregation should have a confession. Schijn believed that choosing one of the outstanding confessions would cause no difficulty.

Since J. Ph. Schabaelje (*q.v.*) in his *Vereenigingh van de principale artijckelen des Geloofs* (1640) had shown that on the major points the differences between the confessions of faith were slight, it was not important which of the confessions was to be used in the brotherhood; Schijn himself preferred the confession by Hans de Ries. Schijn's book closes with a cordial encouragement to unity: "So we entreat the Doopsgezinden by the mercies of God and the precious blood of His only begotten Son, that they . . . now make an end of their divisions and follow peace, without which no man shall see the Lord." Schijn's admonition, however, was fruitless. Not until 1801 was the Zonist-Lamist schism healed by the union of the congregations at Amsterdam.

Herman Schijn is especially known for his historical works. In 1711 he published at Amsterdam his *Korte historie der protestante Christenen, die men Mennoniten of Doopsgezinden noemt*. In order to bring their principles before the learned world, which then often had misconceptions concerning their origin and doctrines, Schijn resolved to publish his book in a Latin translation, and thus a somewhat enlarged Latin edition appeared, *Historia Christianorum qui in Belgio Foedere inter Protestantes Mennonitae appellantur . . .* (Amsterdam, 1723). A Dutch translation of this Latin work was made by M. van Maurik, *Geschiedenis der Protestante Christenen in 't Vereenigd Nederland genaamt Mennoniten . . .* (Amsterdam, Utrecht, 1727). A greatly enlarged edition of Schijn's book, revised by himself, but published after his death, was *Historiae Mennonitarum Plenior deductio* (Amsterdam, 1729), of which a Dutch translation by van Maurik appeared at Amsterdam in 1738: *Uitvoeriger Verhandeling of vervolg van de Geschiedenis der Mennoniten . . . .* A new translation of the *Historiae* of 1729 was made by Gerardus Maatschoen. Maatschoen was a colleague of Schijn in the Amsterdam Zonist church. He not only translated Schijn's book, but also thoroughly revised and greatly enlarged it. He added a long preface and a new volume composed by himself. The title of this Maatschoen edition reads as follows: *Geschiedenis dier Christenen, welke in de Vereenigde Nederlanden onder de Protestanten Mennoniten genaamd worden . . .* (three volumes, Amsterdam 1743-45).

The first volume of this new edition by Maatschoen contains eleven chapters: (1) Origin of the name Wederdopers (Anabaptists) and in how far the Mennonites differ from them; (2) On the baptism of Jewish proselytes; (3) Views of the Mennonites concerning baptism; (4) Proofs adduced by the Roman Catholics, Lutherans, and Reformed as to infant baptism; (5) History of the followers of Menno Simons; (6) History of the Anabaptist doctrines in the 16th century in Germany and elsewhere; (7) Confession of faith by Hans de Ries and Lubbert Gerritsz (here found *in pleno*); (8) Clear testimonies of Menno Simons, showing the difference between the Mennonites and the Anabaptists; (9) The fore-mentioned differences explained from the Confessions; (10) The differences shown as to the practices of life, and according to testimonies of some great princes; (11) An explanation why the Mennonites always have been averse to fanaticism

(*Geestdryverye*). Volume II contains four chapters on the origin of the Mennonites (here Schijn points out the similarity of Mennonite principles and those of the Waldenses), the name of the Mennonites (preferring to call them Mennonites and not *Doopsgezinden,* as the Lamists did), their doctrines and their confessions. After these four chapters this volume contains 24 biographies and bibliographies on Dutch Mennonite leaders, including Menno Simons, Dirk Philips, Hans de Ries, Reinier Wybrandsz Wybema, Pieter Jansz Twisck, Tieleman van Braght, Galenus Abrahamsz de Haan, and Jan Philipsz Schabaelje. Volume III, not written by Schijn but by the editor Gerardus Maatschoen, is entitled *Aanhangzel, Dienende tot een Vervolg of Derde Deel van de Geschiedenisse der Mennoniten.* It contains some 19 more biographies of Dutch Mennonite leaders.

This edition of 1743-45 has some fine pictures of baptism, communion service, footwashing, and other ceremonies of the Dutch Mennonites as practiced during this time, and a large number of engraved portraits of the leaders whose lives and books are described. Schijn's portrait is found in Volume I, facing page 1.

Schijn's historical works are not historiography in the modern sense of the word, describing a number of historical facts or events in chronological and logical order, but can be characterized as a kind of apology and dogmatics, elucidated and illustrated by facts from Mennonite history. Schijn's main thesis is that the Mennonites did not take their origin and doctrines from the revolutionary Münsterites (*q.v.*) as generally was stated by Reformed authors and other opponents, but that from the very beginning down to the Middle Ages, they had been a peaceful group of Biblical Christians, in the 16th century gathered and led by Menno Simons. This apologetical intention is the main trend of Schijn's work. At the present time the books of Schijn are valuable especially for a large number of particulars about Mennonite leaders and about books, many of which are now lost, since Schijn related their contents.

Herman Schijn was a highly esteemed leader not only among his own group, but also among his opponents. He was a very beloved preacher in the Amsterdam Zonist church. After his death Maatschoen delivered a commemorative sermon in the Zonist church at Amsterdam on Dec. 28, 1727: *Eeuwigdurende Gedagtenis des Rechtvaardigen . . . Lykrede op H. Schyn* (Amsterdam, 1728). In 1727 Maatschoen and others published *Ter Lijkgedagtenisse van H. Schyn, leeraar der Doopsgezinden in de Zon en Med. Doctor te Amsterdam.†* vDZ.

HRE XVII (Leipzig, 1906) 574 f.; Schijn-Maatschoen, *Geschiedenis* II, 662-67; *Inv. Arch. Amst.* I, Nos. 1074-77, 1254 a and b, 1281, 1602, 2247; II, 2, No. 816; *DJ* 1837, 39 note, 44, 49, 106; 1840, 111, 116, 124; *DB* 1892, 27; 1897, 163; 1898, 5, 8, 78 ff.; 1905, 73; 1908, 65 ff.; Christian Sepp, *Johannes Stinstra en zijn tijd* (Amsterdam, 1865-66) I and II *passim,* see Index, particularly II, 95 f.; J. C. van Slee, *De Rijnsburger Collegianten* (Haarlem, 1895) 183, 271, 400-3; *MQR* VII (1933) 44-46.

Schilthuis, a Mennonite family found at Groningen, Netherlands, since the early 18th century, where they were grain merchants. According to a family tradition Uko Walles (*q.v.*) was one of its ancestors.

One of the most outstanding members of this family was Ulferdus Gerardus Schilthuis (1799-1856), a grain dealer at Groningen. He was a member of the Provincial States of Groningen and from 1837 a justice of the peace at Groningen. He was the promoter of new branches of trade and agriculture in the province of Groningen, and through his initiative a school of agriculture (*Landhuishoudschool*) was founded at Groningen. He married Coenradine Catherina van Delden (1797-1871). At present a branch of this family is also found at Rotterdam; Ulferdus Gerardus Schilthuis, a lawyer at Rotterdam, is a member of the church board of the Rotterdam congregation. vDZ.

Schimmelpennin(c)k, a Dutch Mennonite family, found since the 16th century at Zutphen, Deventer, Almelo, Zwolle, and in later times also in other towns. Johan Schimmelpenninck, the ancestor of this family, who died before 1573 at Zutphen, was a wine merchant. The members of the Zutphen-Deventer branch were usually wine merchants; the Almelo branch was engaged in the textile business. Many of the Schimmelpennincks, particularly at Zwolle and Almelo, were Mennonite deacons. Thomas Schimmelpenninck, of Zwolle, represented the Zwolle congregation at the large Flemish delegates' conference at Haarlem in 1649. Gerrit Schimmelpenninck (b. 1727 at Almelo, d. Oct. 30, 1792, at Goch), after studying at the Mennonite Theological Seminary at Amsterdam, served as a preacher at Goes 1757-74 and Goch, Germany, 1774-92. To this family also belonged Rutger Jan Schimmelpenninck (b. 1761 at Deventer, d. 1825 at Amsterdam), a noted Dutch statesman, at first a lawyer at Amsterdam, in 1795 an influential member of the national Dutch Convention, then an ambassador of the Netherlands at Paris and London, 1805-6 Grand Pensionary of the Batavian (i.e., Dutch) Republic, knighted by Napoleon as a count of the empire and from 1815 a member of the First Chamber of the Netherlands. His father, Gerrit Schimmelpennick, a wine merchant at Deventer, was a Mennonite; Rutger Jan, however, and all the other children of Gerrit Schimmelpenninck became members of the Reformed Church as their mother was. The Mennonite branch of this family has died out in the male line. vDZ.

Ned. Patriciaat I (1910) 410-13; XIII (1923) 322 f.; *Inv. Arch. Amst.* II, Nos. 1743 f., 2777; *DB* 1881, 91 f.; 1888, 55; 1912, 109; *N.N.B.Wb.* IV, 1225.

Schindlberger, Kaspar, is named by Wolkan (p. 247) as the author of a Hutterite hymn, "Christliche Arth mit meinem Mundt." A very similar hymn, "Christliche Art, Eifer und Trieb" (*Lieder,* 697 ff.), was written by Kaspar Braitmichel (*q.v.*). In all probability the former is a variant of the latter. Nothing else is known of Kaspar Schindlberger. (Wolkan, *Lieder,* 247; *ML* IV.)

Schlabach (Slabaugh, Schlabaugh, Slabach, Schlappach), a Mennonite family name of Swiss origin. Peter Schlapbach, of Signau, canton of Bern, was an Anabaptist in 1538. The name is found among the Swiss Mennonite refugees in the Palatinate after 1664. Jakob Schlabach (*q.v.*) was expelled from the canton of Bern in 1660 for being an Anabaptist. Peter Schlabach (*q.v.*), who was an elder in an Amish congregation in Upper Hesse, Germany, served in the Prussian Landtag in the latter part of the 19th century. Johannes Slabach, who arrived in Philadelphia in 1733, may have been Amish and if so was perhaps the first representative of the Amish Schlabachs to come to America. Other Schlabach immigrants arrived in the 19th century. The brothers John and Christian Schlabach arrived in Somerset County, Pa., in 1819. Their parents and family joined them the following year, and about five years later the entire family settled in Holmes County, Ohio, where numerous descendants are found today. A Daniel Schlabach arrived in Fairfield County, Ohio, perhaps in 1834. Nearly all of his numerous descendants live in Holmes and Geauga counties, Ohio. Daniel's brother John settled in Fairfield County, Ohio, around 1838, but after his marriage he moved to Johnson County, Iowa, in 1851, where most of his descendants live. Another John Slabaugh who settled near Johnstown, Pa., has descendants in Howard County, Ind. Obituaries in Mennonite periodicals show that the family is scattered in at least twelve states, with Ohio, Indiana, Illinois, and Iowa leading. In 1937, at least seven bearing the family name were ministers in the Mennonite Church (MC), one in the Conservative Mennonite Church, and ten in Old Order Amish Mennonite churches, particularly in Holmes County, Ohio.

M.G.

Schlabach (Schlebach, Schleppach), **Jakob** (Jegi, Jegly), an Anabaptist of Oberdiessbach in the Swiss canton of Bern, was imprisoned in Bern in 1660 with a number of other Swiss Brethren, and later transported to the Netherlands as an obstinate Anabaptist. (*Mart. Mir.* D 826, E 1125 f.; Müller, *Berner Täufer*, 179; *ML* IV.)   NEFF.

Schlabach, Peter (1834-1906), an elder of the Amish congregation in Upper Hesse, was married to Anna Güngerich of the Albacherhof, leased the estate of the deceased Unzicker in Frielingen, Hersfeld district, and later a grain business in Wetzlar, became bookkeeper of a savings bank, and was elected the conservative representative to the Prussian Landtag. He took his office with an affirmation instead of an oath: "I, Peter Schlabach, promise that with my yea, which is yea, besides the handshake, that I will be true and faithful to His Royal Majesty the King and will conscientiously follow the constitution." He also attended the conference of the Mennonites of South Germany and was loyal to the brotherhood until his death. (*Menn. Bl.*, 1900, 71; *ML* IV.)
          NEFF.

Schlachtin, a Mennonite settlement in the district of Verkhnedneprovsk in the province of Ekaterinoslav, Russia, consisting of two villages, Grünfeld (*q.v.*) and Steinfeld, established in 1874. The acreage of the settlement was 10,800, on which about 200 families with about 1,000 persons settled. The settlement formed an administrative unit with the Baratov Mennonite settlement (*q.v.*) and belonged to the Neu-Chortitza Mennonite Church (*q.v.*). See also Grünfeld.) (Friesen, *Brüderschaft*, 677-701.) C.K.

Schladahl (Sladal), a suburb of Danzig, West Prussia, Germany, located outside the Neugarten Gate, was the seat of the Danzig Frisian Mennonite congregation. The meetinghouse built there in 1638 was destroyed. (*ML* IV, 62.)   vDZ.

Schladming, a mining town (pop. 1500) in the Enns Valley in Styria, Austria, was one of the first communities to become Protestant in the 16th century. In the Peasants' War of 1525 it played a prominent part on the side of the revolting peasants, who defeated Sigmund von Dietrichstein on July 3, 1525, but were in turn defeated by Duke Nicolas von Salm. The town was destroyed and the inhabitants severely punished for its part in the insurrection. The restoration proceeded very slowly, and under the protection of the Protestant Baron of Grünbichel its inhabitants became Protestant; in the Counter Reformation they changed their faith (1600). That there were Anabaptists there in the 1520's is seen in a report made to the authorities, found in the archives in Steyer. (*ML* IV.)
          LOSERTH.

Schlaffer, Hans, an Anabaptist martyr (d. 1528), highly regarded by Anabaptists as a true preacher of the Word of God, and a "highly gifted man" (Chronicle). His "Account" (*Verantwortung*) before the magistrate of Schwatz, Tirol, in 1527 (Müller, 115-21) states that he had entered the Catholic priesthood in 1511, and served in Upper Austria. With the coming of Luther he began to preach the pure Gospel but soon was forbidden to do so. In 1526 he resigned his priesthood, realizing that "it was the estate of a false prophet." For a time (1526-27) he stayed with the Protestant Lord Zelkin at his castle Weinberg near Freistadt (*q.v.*), Upper Austria. It was either then or still earlier that he had come into contact with Anabaptists, most likely with Hans Hut. It is not known when or by whom he was baptized but Grete Mecenseffy shows how heavily the Anabaptist congregation of Freistadt leaned on Schlaffer, who followed more or less the line of Hut. In any case he left the area, beginning a period of wandering, the sequence of places being not quite clear. He visited Nikolsburg in 1527 where he heard the dispute between Hubmaier and Hut, which happened prior to Hut's coming to Upper Austria. He may have been converted to Hut's ideas on that occasion and returned temporarily to Freistadt, establishing an Anabaptist congregation there; but it is also possible that he was in Nikolsburg even before he came to Lord Zelkin. In any case Freistadt soon became an unsafe abode, and he then went to Bavaria. First he went to Augsburg where he met Jacob Wideman (*q.v.*), and again Hans Hut; he may have been present at the "Martyr Synod" (*q.v.*) of Augsburg. Next he went to Nürnberg where he met Hans Denck and Ludwig Haetzer in September 1527 (Fellmann), "two excellent, in God learned men"; finally he went to Regensburg where he met Oswald Glaidt (*q.v.*) and Wolfgang Brandhuber (*q.v.*), two more of the then leading men in the growing Anabaptist movement.

From Regensburg he turned south to the Inn (*q.v.*) Valley of Tirol, to Brixlegg and Rattenberg (*q.v.*), where he had some relatives. But after a brief stay due to sickness he went on toward Hall on the Inn for the winter. On his way he attended a meeting of Anabaptists in the mining city of Schwatz on the Inn, a few miles west of Rattenberg, on Dec. 5, 1527, but was caught by the authorities and imprisoned in the near-by Frundsberg castle, together with the brother Linhard Frick (or, as the *Kunstbuch* calls him, Funck). He was brought before the magistrate and submitted a written *Verantwortung* which was sent to the provincial government in Innsbruck. His defense was very dignified: he had sought nothing evil but only divine truth; nothing was further from his mind than rebellion. Children, he contended, should not be baptized, for "they were the Lord's as long as they were in innocence, and they would not be damned." The Innsbruck government sent instructions to Judge S. Capeller for conducting the case. The statements of the prisoners would be sent to the authorities in Bavaria who also wanted to try these men. Orders were further given to convene the court with twelve jurymen to pass sentence on the two prisoners. At the same time a secret report should be made by the judge on the attitude of the jurymen, as it was known that some of them did not approve of death in such cases. Finally the death sentence was pronounced and Schlaffer and Frick were beheaded at Schwatz on Feb. 4, 1528.

Schlaffer left nine writings, all well preserved in numerous Hutterite codices. His long prayer written in the night before the execution is also found in the *Kunstbuch* of 1561 as No. 12. Of these writings only one rather short piece was composed while Schlaffer was still free, most likely in Freistadt, for the local brotherhood; it is a sort of shortened paraphrase of Hut's *Vom Geheimnus der Tauff* (Mecenseffy). All the other writings were written in prison between Dec. 6, 1527, and Feb. 3, 1528, slightly more than eight weeks. These are the writings:

(1) *Kurzer Bericht eines christlichen Lebens* (also *Kurzer Bericht und Lehr eines rechten christlichen Lebens*); it is made up of the "Hut paraphrase" (Müller, 94-96) and two prayers (*ibid.*, 96-98; Beck, 651). Already in the first document we recognize Schlaffer's greatest potential: his profound gift of praying or communicating with his God.

(2) *Ein einfältiger Unterricht zum Anfang eines gotseliges Lebens,* again introduced by a beautiful lengthy prayer (Müller, 84-94). This tract, written Dec. 19, 1527, likewise reveals strongly Schlaffer's dependence on Hut (Müller, 85, note).

(3) *Kurze und einfältige Vermahnung von der Kindertauff, und wie derselbige nit mag beibracht werden aus Heiliger Schrifft.* It was written Jan. 2, 1528 (Müller, 98-105).

(4) *Brief an einen schwachen Bruder, Antwort auf etliche Fragstück,* also Jan. 2, 1528 (Müller, 105-10).

(5) *Von der Art und Gestalt Christi, was er geistlich und leiblich sey geformieret* (unpublished, found in Canadian Hutterite codices).

(6) *Bekandtnus und Verantwortung* [dem Richter zu Schwatz] *schriftlich überantwortet,* no date (Müller, 110-15).

(7) *Die andere Verantwortung: Antwort auf* [fünf] *Fragstück vor dem Richter* (Müller, 115-21). From this item all the biographical information was gained. This account was apparently first given orally before the judge, and later written down by Schlaffer for his brethren.

(8) *Ein Bericht seiner Verantwortung vor der Obrigkeit getan an seine Geschwistriget im Herren zugeschickt, Pfingstag vor Pauli Bekehrung,* January 1528 (Müller, 121-25). This is another summary of Schlaffer's defense. He informed his brethren (perhaps the congregation of Schwatz) that the authorities in Innsbruck had falsified his written statement (No. 6), completely changing its meaning; for that reason he wanted to inform his brethren about what he had actually written. Thus we have three different documents (Nos. 6 to 8) in which Schlaffer gives account of the major ideas of South German Anabaptism as it had evolved at that time.

(9) *Ein einfältig Gebet,* also called *Gebet, Beicht und öffentlich Bekanntnus, Hans Schlaffers Testament und eigen Bekanntnus gegen Gott,* written Feb. 3, 1528, in the night before his execution. This is found in the *Kunstbuch* No. 12, and in many Hutterite codices (also Beck, 652, as a very inadequate version of this prayer). In the typescript copy in the GCL this prayer covers 18 pages; in a narrowly written Hutterite codex (1566) it covers eight leaves. This prayer is no doubt one of the most profound and moving documents in the entire German devotional literature. Like Augustine in his *Confessions* he talks to God at great length about his life and thoughts, strengthening his mind during the agonizing hours before his death. It is most likely here that Schlaffer's greatest power is to be found and also his greatest contribution to Anabaptist tradition.

Schlaffer composed also two hymns: "Ungnad begehr ich nit von dir," No. 32 in the *Ausbund,* and pp. 22-23 in *Lieder der Hutterischen Brüder;* the hymn was also circulated as a pamphlet in 1527, and reprinted in 1550 and 1551 in Nürnberg; "Herr Gott, mein ewiger Vater" (with the acrostic "Hanns Schlaffer") in *Lieder der Hutterischen Brüder,* 21-22; it was written in the last hours of his life, either before or after the above prayer.

Schlaffer's teachings: As was pointed out above, Schlaffer's main ideas are not his own but were taken from Hans Hut, often to the point of verbatim borrowing. But this was nothing unusual in those days (compare Marpeck and Rothman); what really mattered was the particular emphasis or slant given to the ideas. In all Schlaffer's writings we meet the same spiritualistic or pneumatic atmosphere as in those of Schiemer, Ambrosius Spittelmayr, Hans Nadler, and other men connected with Denk and Hut. "Even if Christ had died a hundred times, it would avail nothing if the spiritual Christ is not preached also" (Wiswedel, 197, quoted from a copy in the Beck collection, file No. 46, in Brno). "Who ever descends into Hades with Christ, that is *in* Christ, will also be led out of Hades by God" (Müller, 96). Pilgram Marpeck some twenty years later liked to indulge in speculation of this kind in exactly the same way (see **Nicodemus, Gospel of**).

Schlaffer is aware that suffering is a keynote of the Christian in the "world," and his writings abound in such thoughts. "All Scriptures speak of nothing but of the suffering of the elect, from Abel to the apostles; that is why the lamb has been killed ever since the beginning of the world" (Müller, 88). "Who ever suffers in the flesh stops sinning" (*ibid.*, 89). And in the Account: "Here I stand as a lamb which does not open its mouth as it is being slaughtered, to which may Christ . . . grant me strength and help" (Müller, 124). "Only he who follows Christ is a Christian." Of particular appeal is a short passage in his first *Bericht und Lehr* where he speaks of the "Tiefe Christi," meaning Christ's lowliness (*Niedrigkeit*) and resignation. "It might also be called Hell, that a man could imagine himself deserted by God and all creatures. This lowliness (*Tiefe*) is the sign of Jonah. Into this lowliness one has to enter if one wants to be saved in Christ" (Müller, 96). This is a thought which was repeated twenty years later nearly verbatim by Pilgram Marpeck in his "Epistle to the Brethren in the Grisons, Appenzell and Alsace," Feb. 1, 1547, dealing with *Von der Tiefe Christi* (*Kunstbuch,* No. 35; see Fast, 235).

Grete Mecenseffy compared this entire tract of Schlaffer (Müller, 94-96) with the Confession of the Freistadt Anabaptists (Nicoladoni, 250-52) and Hut's *Vom Geheimnus der Tauff*, and found a near identity of all three, at least in certain sections. She thinks that the major ideas were borrowed from Thomas Müntzer, Hut's first spiritual awakener, but this remains a debatable question. Rather one could think of the influence of late medieval mysticism as the true root of this line of tradition. In any case it remains a "gospel of the cross" which became particularly real as this cross was being experienced in the agony and dread of death.

In his "Letter to a Weak Brother" Schlaffer tries to answer certain scruples of that brother concerning difficult doctrinal issues; his reaction here might be called again typically Anabaptist. "One should not worry too much," he writes, "concerning certain secrets as if it would hurt you not to grasp their meaning. Rather one should take into captivity all thought and reason in obedience to Christ (II Cor. 10:5)" (Müller, 107). This answer is found time and again in Anabaptist sources (see **Reason and Obedience**). On the delicate issue of the meaning of the Trinity, Schlaffer answers, again typically for pneumatic Anabaptism: "God is neither this nor that" (Müller, 108; here Lydia Müller refers to a stanza of a hymn by Ludwig Haetzer which says exactly the same thing and must have been known to Schlaffer, *ML* II, 231 or Beck, 34). But Schlaffer does not deny the truth of the Trinity; in fact he defends it to the best of his ability.

Schlaffer and Schiemer are usually mentioned together, and rightly so. They both had been Catholic clergymen, had become true apostles of budding Anabaptism, both pursuing mainly the Denk-Hut line. Both died as martyrs within the span of two and a half weeks, not more than five or six miles apart in the Inn Valley. Both left a valuable legacy to their brethren, who kept their memory and also their teachings alive. Schiemer was no doubt more

the "bishop" who cared fatherly for his congregation or church; Schlaffer never had one to care for. His accounts and tracts are rich sources of instruction and of strength, but his most lasting contributions are his numerous prayers. No other Anabaptist ever produced documents of this type as profound and spiritual as Schlaffer. R.F.

Beck, *Geschichts-Bücher*, 63 note; L. Müller, *Glaubenszeugnisse oberdeutscher Taufgesinnter* (Leipzig, 1938); Loserth, *Anabaptismus*, 35 ff.; *Lieder der Hutterischen Brüder* (Scottdale, 1914) 21-23; A. Nicoladoni, *Johannes Bünderlin* (Berlin, 1893); Wiswedel, *Bilder* II, chapter "Hans Schlaffer, ein ernster Beter und eifriger Verteidiger der göttlichen Wahrheit," 191-212; Heinold Fast, "Pilgram Marpeck und das oberdeutsche Täufertum," *Archiv für Ref.-Geschichte* XLVII (1956) 212-42; Grete Mecenseffy, "Die Herkunft des oberösterreichischen Täufertums," *Archiv für Ref.-Geschichte* XLVII (1956) 252-59; W. Fellmann, *Hans Denck, Religiöse Schriften* (Gütersloh, 1956) 18; Herbert C. Klassen, "Ambrosius Spittelmayr," *MQR* XXXII, 251 ff., especially 266 f.; *ML* IV; he does not appear in the *Martyrs' Mirror*.

Schlatten am Randen, a village near Engen in the Hegau, Baden, Germany; not to be confused with Schleitheim (*q.v.*).

Schlebach, Iegh, an Anabaptist martyr: see **Schlabach, Jakob**.

Schlegel (Slagel, Slagle, Slagell), a Mennonite family name of Swiss origin now found chiefly in Illinois, Oregon, and Ontario. A Nicholas Schlegel was one of the early members of the East Zorra (*q.v.*) Amish Mennonite Church in Ontario. Christian Schlegel settled in the Amish community of central Illinois in 1835. He is perhaps the Christian Schlegel (1819-84) who served as an Amish Mennonite bishop in Livingston County. His son Joseph Schlegel (1847-1914) was ordained an Amish Mennonite bishop in 1891, serving the Pleasant View (*q.v.*) congregation at Hydro, Okla. Joseph's son John Slagell is now a minister in this congregation. Joseph Schlegel (*q.v.*, 1837-1913), a native of Alsace, was ordained bishop at Wayland, Iowa, in 1868. In 1879 he moved to Milford, Neb., where he served the rest of his life. Daniel W. Slagel (1864-1947) was a minister in the Waldo Mennonite Church (*q.v.*) and Emmanuel Slagle (1869-1944) served as bishop of the Pioneer and Archbold Evangelical Mennonite churches in Ohio. Arthur Slagel, of the Waldo church, served in relief work in Russia after World War I. Five representatives of the family were in the ministry of the Mennonite Church (MC) in 1957. M.G.

Schlegel (Schlögl), **Adam**, early Anabaptist of unknown origin (Bavarian, Swabian?). In 1528 he joined the Moravian "Stäbler" (*q.v.*, see **Moravia**) under the leadership of Jacob Wideman (*q.v.*) and was soon made Diener des Wortes (minister), at the same time as Franz Intzinger, Jacob Mändl (*q.v.*), and others. In 1531 he allowed certain liberties in the brotherhood (*fleischliche Freiheiten*—whatever that may mean), and thereupon was expelled from the brotherhood, along with Burckhardt von Ofen. He now turned to the Philippite Brethren (*q.v.*) in Auspitz, Moravia, where he was kindly received and confirmed in his function as a minister. Among the Philippites he seems to have gained an important position, for he baptized many persons in Auspitz in 1531-35. Then the Philippites left Moravia and nothing more is heard of him. It is possible that he returned to South Germany as many others did. (Zieglschmid, *Chronik*.)		R.F.

Schlegel, Hans, a Hutterite from Württemberg, Germany, a tailor by trade, was chosen to preach on Jan. 25, 1568, at Nembschitz (see **Niemtschitz,** Moravia) and confirmed in the service three years later. He died at Maskowitz (*q.v.,* in Moravia), Feb. 21, 1587. He is the author of the song, "Nun harret alle eben in diesem Jammertal."		NEFF.

TA Württemberg, 422; Wolkan, *Geschicht-Buch,* 326, 425; *Lieder der Hutterischen Brüder* (Scottdale, 1941) 164; *ML* IV.

Schlegel, Joseph (1837-1913), was born near Mulhouse, Alsace, Nov. 11, 1837, and as a youth migrated to Ontario, and a few years later to Davis County, Iowa. He was ordained to the ministry in the Amish Mennonite Church at Wayland, Iowa, in 1867, and the next year was ordained bishop. In 1879 he moved to Milford, Neb., where he died Dec. 25, 1913. He was the first moderator of the Western District Amish Mennonite Conference (*q.v.*) and served either as moderator or assistant moderator ten times between 1890 and 1904. He attended at least nineteen sessions between 1890 and 1913, preached eight conference sermons, and was appointed to important committees. He was known as a forceful speaker and his ability as a mediator was widely recognized.		M.G.

M. Gingerich, *The Mennonites in Iowa* (Iowa City, 1939); *idem,* "Ten Leaders of the Western District Amish Mennonite Conference," *MHB,* October 1940.

Schleifer, Hans, an Anabaptist of Augsburg, Bavaria, Germany, was chosen with Peter Ringmacher (*q.v.*) on April 1, 1528, as bishop (*Vorsteher*) of the Augsburg congregation and sent to Regensburg to comfort the brethren. (See **Augsburg;** *ML* IV.)

Schleitheim, capital of the district of the same name in the Swiss canton of Schaffhausen, also called Schlatten in the local dialect, not to be confused with Schlatten am Randen (*q.v.*), a vicarage with about 1700 inhabitants. Schleitheim was one of the first communities entered by the Anabaptist movement. In 1522 Sebastian Hofmeister (*q.v.*) preached the Reformation in Schaffhausen, and from here it spread to the neighboring Schleitheim, proclaimed by the chaplain Nikolaus Spöhrlin. Spöhrlin's personal life was, however, not favorable to the promotion of the new teaching. This may be the reason why Anabaptism found such early entry into the town. The source of the first appearance of the movement is no longer altogether clear. Thomas Müntzer (*q.v.*), who was preaching in the village of Griessen in the fall of 1524, was reported by Brenz (*q.v.*) to have also visited Schleitheim. At about the same time (September to October 1524) Balthasar Hubmaier (*q.v.*) was staying in Schaffhausen; but neither of these had anything to do with Anabaptism in 1524. Conrad Grebel (*q.v.*) was engaged in a debate with Hofmeister in Schaffhausen early in 1525 and led members of the most prominent families into the Anabaptist movement.

The entry of the movement into Schleitheim probably came from Schaffhausen. On Feb. 24, 1527, the first Anabaptist synod was held here, led by Michael Sattler (*q.v.*), which drew up the principles of the Swiss Brethren in seven articles known as the *Brüderlich Vereinigung* (*q.v.*), which became a widely accepted confession of faith of the Swiss and South German Anabaptists.

On Sept. 18, 1527, the first known member of the Swiss Brethren at this place was cast into the prison of Schaffhausen, but was later released upon payment of a fine and expulsion from the town, and a confession that he had erred on the question of baptism. In 1535 Martin Lincki of Thengen was compelled to recant in Schleitheim. At first the authorities hoped to be able to convert the Anabaptists back to the Reformed Church, and had the pastor conduct a number of debates with "obstinate Anabaptists." When these proved futile, severer measures were adopted. "Wetzelmayer's daughter" was threatened with drowning. Meetings in private homes were prohibited. In 1544 Heinrich Wininger was fined for lodging Anabaptists. The Anabaptists now met in the woods, in the "Kehle am Randen," by the "Täuferwegli" (Anabaptist path, a footpath still in existence by that name between Schleitheim and Merishausen). In 1560 this place was discovered and the cabin razed. But the congregation still persisted. In 1577 another disputation was arranged, which was also fruitless. It was followed by further repressive measures, such as prohibition of the use of communal property in 1580. Under this pressure several Anabaptists migrated to Moravia, and lost their citizenship. The following names are given: "Hans Bley called Rouchly with his wife and children. Zentz the son of the Stammwirt with his wife and children. Marx Wäber called Gebhart with his youngest son. Bucheler's son with his children. Michael Thigen's boy. The hatter with his wife and children. Jacob Bletscher the servant with his wife and children." Orders were issued that the Swiss Brethren remaining should be reported; this was, however, not done, for the citizenry sympathized with the Swiss Brethren and honored the refugees or martyrs. Even the officials sometimes failed to obey the government orders, and several were punished; the sheriff was imprisoned in the tower.

In 1594 J. J. Rüger, the Schaffhausen clergyman and chronicler, with two councillors, betook himself to Schleitheim once more, "to remind each Anabaptist kindly of his error." Concerning this visit he writes, "At the time of the Reformation or change in religion the enemy did not neglect to build chapels beside the Christian churches, with the tares of the seditious, obstinate, and constant Anabaptists, who have increased since the Reformation to such an extent that the honorable Christian government has not been able to get rid of it, much less to uproot it. These intractable Anabaptists have had their confession of faith publicly printed. . . . Indeed, they are fine 'children of God,' while they are more infamously and obstinately rejecting their God's ordinances and are disobedient to his commands! and because they may not hold their meetings in the village they have used wildernesses and solitary places (chiefly the Küetal) in their neighborhood, but these have been shut off and forbidden by the honorable government." The outcome was the military occupation of the village in 1595, to compel the Swiss Brethren to attend church and to baptize their children by force. In spite of all this, a marked increase of the movement was noted. A new warning was issued, threatening dire punishment. The Anabaptists were forbidden to pasture their cattle with the common herds. Hans Russenberger, who had led others to Anabaptism, was ordered to leave the village within a week. Josef Rössler and his wife had refused to be married in the church (both of them "stiff-necked Anabaptists"); the man was expelled. In 1612 all the Anabaptists but five old men (Christian, Georg and Vinzenz Russenberger, Hans and Melchior Meyer) were expelled. Christian Russenberger was soon after put into prison, since he had baptized Baschian Müller of Löhningen, the husband of Anna Wanner of Schleitheim. Two women who refused to leave the village were punished by the removal of all their furniture and the doors and windows. In 1620 twenty more had to leave. They fled into the neighboring communities, but were returned, lest they find shelter with relatives. Similar treatment was given Georg Gering, Bürckly Wanner, Thomas Pletscher, and others, who were extradited by Maximilian von Pappenheim in 1617, when they had fled to Stühlingen. Nevertheless the congregation blossomed. When Hans Meyer, a weaver, was unable to pay a fine, 65 sheaves of rye and 34 of oats were taken from his barn. Melchior Meyer and his two sons were put in prison, but escaped. When they were caught, each had to pay a fine of 100 florins. A man, whose wife was an Anabaptist, was ordered to leave by morning. Wanner, apparently the leader of the congregation, was put into the "Anabaptist prison." By day he had to thresh, and by night he was in ankle chains. The same lot befell the "stubborn" Georg Pletscher. Finally all the cattle were taken from the Anabaptists. The response was eight additions to the Swiss Brethren. The government again answered with imprisonment and compulsory labor. In the second half of the Thirty Years' War the Mennonites had to pay for a substitute in the protection of the national boundaries, and later they had to board and lodge him.

In spite of all these oppressions the congregation by no means declined. In 1640 an ultimatum was issued for their conversion. It was fruitless. In 1641 the village was again occupied by the military. All the men who were Mennonites were taken to Schaffhausen and placed in irons. Five of them broke out, but were caught and put into a chain gang, the chains being provided with bells. Christian Bächtold was whipped with the lash. Meanwhile the wives and children of these men were suffering the direst want. The children were reared Reformed. After some time the men were released from their chains, and it seemed that quiet had descended upon the village. But the movement was not yet quite extinct. In 1642 an order was issued imposing a fine of 100 florins on anyone who kept an Anabaptist overnight, and twenty for talking to one.

In 1648 the council of Schaffhausen learned that the Anabaptists were again refusing to send their children to school and to church. They were thereupon ordered to sell their goods and move out. When they refused, the magistrate was ordered to sell their property. But no buyers could be found, and so the government assumed the farming. Now many Mennonites were compelled to emigrate to the Palatinate. Others at least wanted to send their children there, so that they could be raised as Mennonites. These children the council threatened with loss of citizenship and banishment. Unfortunately no record of this emigration has been preserved. The congregation was now small, and still persecuted with the same severity. On Feb. 8, 1661, Nikolaus Hess was ordered to leave the town with his wife and parents-in-law; but the order was rescinded when he returned to the church. Upon his death in 1680 his widow, Margaretha Bächtold, with two children emigrated to the Palatinate, where her seven children were living, leaving one son in Schleitheim. She was probably the last Mennonite of Schleitheim. The struggles of the congregation had lasted 150 years. The Mennonite Pletscher and Bechtel families (Palatinate and later North America) almost certainly come from Schleitheim. W.Pl.

C. A. Bächtold, "Die Schaffhauser Wiedertäufer in der Ref.-Zeit," in Beiträge zur vaterländischen Gesch., No. 7 (Schaffhausen, 1900); H. Böhmer, Urkunden der Gesch. der Bauernkriege und der Wiedertäufer (Bonn, 1911); P. B. Burckhardt, Die Basler Täufer (Basel, 1898); Ernst Correll, Das schweizerische Täufermennonitentum (Tübingen, 1925); Walther Köhler, Flugschriften aus ersten Jahren der Reformation (Leipzig, 1905) (1907)?; J. Loserth, Doktor Balthasar Hubmeier und die Anfänge der Wiedertäufer in Mähren (Brünn, 1893); L. v. Muralt, "Glaube und Lehre der schweiz. Wiedertäufer in der Ref.-Zeit," in 101. Neujahrsblatt zum Besten des Waisenhauses in Zürich für 1938 (Zürich); J. J. Rüeger, Chronik der Stadt und Landschaft Schaffhausen (Schaffhausen, 1884); Chr. H. Wanner, Gesch. von Schleitheim (Schleitheim, 1932); Jacob Wipf, Ref.-Gesch. der Stadt und Landschaft Schaffhausen (Schaffhausen, 1929); Histor. biogr. Lexikon der Schweiz (Neuenburg, 1931); Ernst Crous, "Auf Spuren der Täufer am Oberrhein: Schleitheim," Der Mennonit X (1957) 90-93, 122-23; Werner Pletscher, "Wanderwege einer Mennonitenfamilie," Badische Heimat XXXII (1952) 57-61; ML IV.

Schleitheim Confession: see Brüderlich Vereinigung.

Schleswig-Holstein, a state of the Federal Republic of Germany, was Danish during the Reformation and later. The Anabaptists found refuge there early in the 16th century, particularly in the rural areas. Evidently as early as 1528 action was taken against Anabaptists. Anabaptists were found early near Lübeck (q.v.), where among others the Roosen (q.v.) family was located. In eastern Holstein the king issued an edict against the Anabaptists and Sacramentists in 1553. In southern Holstein, Anabaptists were found in Wandsbeck, Pinneberg, and Oldesloe (q.v.).

In the southwest the Anabaptists were important in the economic life, transforming certain aspects of agriculture; i.e., farmers changed from cattle raising to the production of milk and cheese. Some of the places mentioned are Wilster, Brockdorf, and Wewelsfleth. As in East Friesland the first Anabaptists in Schleswig-Holstein were primarily refugees from the Low Countries.

In Steinburg the Mennonites had to report to the government on Aug. 6, 1635, with the result that an edict was issued against them and they were asked to join the Lutheran Church. Another edict followed in 1642. From the early days the Mennonites enjoyed full privileges in Wüstenfelde (q.v.) near Oldesloe, Glückstadt (q.v.), and later in Altona (q.v.). Gradually the Mennonites disappeared from the rural areas, surviving only in such cities as Friedrichstadt, Altona, and Hamburg. A law of July 14, 1863, made it possible for Mennonites to settle and move freely throughout Schleswig-Holstein.

The Wüstenfelde congregation near Oldesloe, where Menno Simons and his followers found refuge, is unique. Menno Simons (q.v.) spent the last years of his life at Wüstenfelde, where he published his books, died, and was buried. The Wüstenfelde settlement was destroyed during the Thirty Years' War and most of the Mennonites moved to Altona. Here the Mennonites became city builders as in the case of Crefeld (q.v.). Outstanding was the van der Smissen (q.v.) family.

Only a few of the early Mennonite churches have survived, among them Friedrichstadt (q.v.) and Hamburg-Altona (q.v.); the latter has grown considerably since World War II because of the influx of Mennonite refugees from the East. Additional Mennonite congregations and groups have been established in Kiel (q.v.), Lübeck (q.v.), and the group known by the name of Schleswig-Holstein (q.v.), with one meetinghouse at Wedel, built in 1958.

Mennonite settlements were established in 1952 at Pinneberg-Rellingen. The MCC helped the refugees of Schleswig-Holstein first with Kiel as a center (1946-47) and later from Hamburg (1948-56). In 1950 the Mennonite refugee population of Schleswig-Holstein was 4,300, and in 1958 the total number affiliated with Mennonite congregations was about 2,000.   C.K.

Robert Dollinger, *Geschichte der Mennoniten in Schleswig-Holstein, Hamburg und Lübeck* (Neumünster, 1930); Heinz Münte, *Das Altonaer Handlungshaus van der Smissen* (Altona, 1932); Cornelius Krahn, *Menno Simons* (Karlsruhe, 1935); ML IV.

Schleswig-Holstein Mennonite Church is one of the newly organized congregations in the province by that name, consisting in 1957 of 380 Mennonite refugees from East Germany. The elder was Arthur Goetzke. In 1958 a meetinghouse was built with the help of Pax boys (q.v.) in Wedel (q.v.). Other places of meeting are Nordhastedt, Itzehoe, Elmshorn, Heiligenhafen, Lensahm, Eutin, Schleswig, Flensburg, Husum, Friedrichstadt.   C.K.

Schlüsselberg, Conrad, a German Lutheran clergyman, church superintendent at Stralsund, author of the book *Catalogus Haereticorum* (1592-99), in which he also attacks the Anabaptists.   NEFF.

Schmaus, Cuntz, an Anabaptist preacher, stemmed from Kupferberg near Würzburg, Germany, was won to the Anabaptists by Hans Hut (q.v.), and probably baptized by him in Vienna in 1527. From Vienna he went to Waldeck, where the two founded an Anabaptist congregation of one hundred brethren in two weeks. After Hut's departure Schmaus was chosen as their preacher. But he soon fell into the hands of Mattheus Lang von Wellenburg, Archbishop of Salzburg, who sent the results of the hearing, which contained valuable information, to the council of Augsburg on Nov. 27, 1527. Nothing further is heard of the fate of Schmaus. Very likely he was one of the thirty-eight persons who were locked into a house in Salzburg (q.v.) and burned with it in 1527.   HEGE.

Beck, *Geschichts-Bücher,* 57; Josef Jäkel, "Zur Geschichte der Wiedertäufer in Oberösterreich und speziell in Freistadt," in *47. Bericht des Museums Franziscus-Carolinus* (Linz, 1889) 57; Christian Meyer, "Die Anfänge des Wiedertäufertums in Augsburg," in *Ztscht . . . für Schwaben und Neuburg* I (Augsburg, 1874); ML IV.

Schmellentin, Joannes Christophorus, a physician at Amsterdam, who translated the confession of Hans de Ries (q.v.) from the Dutch into the German and edited it with a preface: *Ein Kurtz Bekäntnüsz der fürnämsten Hauptstückken des Christlichen Glaubens . . .* (Amsterdam, 1741). He also published a Dutch edition of this confession: *Een korte belydenis der voornaamste Artykelen des Christelyken Geloofs . . . En nu met een Voorreden voorzien en uitgegeeven* (Amsterdam, 1741).   VDZ.

Schmerbach, today a vicarage in the Mergentheim district, near Rothenburg o.T., Germany, occurs twice in Anabaptist court records of the trial of Marx Maier (*TA Bayern* I, 177 and 192).   E.T.

Schmid, Bastl, also called Bastl (Wastl) Anfang, a Hutterite preacher in Moravia, was seized with two companions, Heinrich Schweitzer and Uhl Schuster, on a missionary journey through the canton of Bern, Switzerland, on May 15, 1585. In the first two weeks Bastl was questioned three times by the Reformed clergy. In the fourth week all three were tortured to make them reveal the names of those who had sheltered them. Bastl was threatened with hanging, and even had the noose around his neck. The authorities finally saw that all questioning and torture were futile, and returned them to prison. After 20 weeks in prison, when the council had made preparations for the execution and had given them their "final" meal, popular vote opposed the execution. The council therefore decided to release the prisoners. Heinrich and Uhl were beaten "with rods and burned through the ears with hot irons," and whipped to the border. Then Bastl was released without further penalty, even though he refused to vow never to return to Bern. The three Brethren safely reached the community in Moravia. (See also **Anfang, Wastl,** which this article supplements.)
                                                      S.G.

Beck, *Geschichts-Bücher,* 295; Zieglschmid, *Chronik,* 544 f.; Wolkan, *Geschicht-Buch;* ML IV.

Schmid, Hans (Hänsel), also called *Raiffer,* probably because he was born in the Tirolean village of Raiffach, a Hutterite leader and martyr (d. 1558), successful missioner, composer of hymns, writer of letters and doctrinal tracts, a strong and leading personality, one of the noblest representatives of the second period of Anabaptism. The data of birth and conversion are not known. In 1548 (a period of severe persecution in Moravia) he was made minister and four years later was confirmed in this office. Soon thereafter he began his successful mission work in Germany: in 1555 he was in Hesse (district of Nidda), in 1556 in the Rhenish Palatinate around Kreuznach and Worms, where he won over a group of "Swiss Brethren" to the Hutterite way after long and serious debates, in 1557 he worked along the Lower Rhine and around Aachen, winning the important Swiss Brother Hans Arbeiter (*q.v.*) and other Swiss Brethren, most of whom now moved to Moravia like those from Kreuznach. Next his work led him into the Eifel district of Western Germany and again to Aachen. Here, on Jan. 9, 1558, during a meeting, he was surprised by city authorities and together with five brothers and six sisters (all of the former Hans Arbeiter group) he was imprisoned.

On the events between January 9 and the day of his execution, October 19, there is much detailed information thanks to the 35 extant letters and the 15 hymns written in prison, which material the Chronicle used for its graphic account. Raiffer had cherished some hope of finding leniency at the hands of the City Council, but of the twelve Anabaptists imprisoned five men were finally executed, the sixth recanted and was thereupon released (he returned to Moravia, repented, and was reaccepted by the Brethren), and the six women were flogged and driven out of the city. At one time all twelve were allowed to be together from 4 a.m. to 10 p.m., but then were separated again in different prisons. They sang overly loud as often as they could to comfort each other (see **Singing, Hutterite**), and they wrote letters to each other between their confinements, as well as letters to the Rhineland Brethren and those in Moravia. Schmid was badly racked but remained steadfast, defending his faith courageously and helping others to do likewise. Of his 35 letters from prison 15 were addressed to his "marital sister" (wife) Madlen (Magdalena) in Moravia. Apparently messengers could communicate freely with the prisoners. A wealthy woman in Aachen sent them extra food, but Schmid refused it unless she would change her mind and allegiance. All attempts to persuade him failed as they did with nearly all Anabaptists; accordingly the city authorities finally had to obey the imperial mandates issued by the "new" emperor Ferdinand I (*q.v.*). In October 1558, all five brethren were publicly strangled and then burned.

Of this unusually strong personality we get a vivid picture from his numerous writings, which places him on the level of Peter Riedemann (*q.v.*). *Letters* —The letters are found in many Hutterite codices, which proves their popular appeal. Of the 37 letters the 35 written in Aachen are described above (excerpts of one are to be found in Wolkan's *Geschicht-Buch*, 292, note). Seventeen of these are scheduled to be published in a forthcoming volume of Anabaptist epistles edited by the present writer. One letter (perhaps of 1557), written to Romies Caltenburg and dealing with the Incarnation, is extant in a codex in Bratislava. Schmid discussed this topic several times (*Chronik*, 384 and 387), repeating more or less the Nicene creed. One letter of 1555

(now in Darmstadt) written to the Rentmeister of Nidda (*TA Hesse*, 332-36) contains a defense against slander and a sort of summary of Anabaptist teaching.

Doctrinal Writings—Of Schmid's doctrinal writings the following are known: (*A*) *Eine Rechenschaft vom Abendmahl und seiner rechten Bedeutung*, written in prison in Aachen and sent to his fellow prisoners as well as to the Brethren in Moravia, obviously a repetition of his oral defense before the authorities. This document (to be published in *Glaubenszeugnisse* II, as No. 12) has two parts: (*a*) a defense of the Zwinglian theology of the Lord's Supper (the symbolical interpretation); (*b*) *Vom rechten Gebrauch . . .*, which explains the idea of community (*Gemeinschaft*) both with Christ and with the Brethren (excerpts of this tract in Wiswedel, *Bilder* III, 97-99). (*B*) *Brüderliche Vereinigung zwischen uns und etlichen Schweizer Brüdern* (1556), containing the debate with Lorenz Huef and others at Kreuznach, a statement of the Hutterite position in seven articles (*Chronik*, 361-66) in which the main differences from the Swiss Brethren position are formulated. Andreas Ehrenpreis (*q.v.*) reprinted this piece in his *Sendbrief* of 1652. The article concerning marriage and divorce is very informative, and so is the one concerning ministers and their special honors (see **Ministers, Hutterite,** etc.). (*C*) One year later Schmid discussed 17 articles with Hans Arbeiter, the titles of which are named but their contents not published. Here we find also two theological items: Concerning Original Sin, and Concerning the Incarnation of Christ. One may safely assume that Schmid's views coincided with those of Riedemann.

Hymns—The *Liederbuch der Hutterischen Brüder* (pp. 551-611) contains 15 hymns by Schmid (hymn No. 3 is not by Schmid but about him), and six hymns by his coprisoners, most of them of great beauty and depth. Wolkan (211-28) discusses them at great length, reprinting five of them in full, and claiming that with Schmid and Riedemann Hutterite hymn composition reached its climax. Wiswedel (99, note 5) claims that Schmid composed 24 hymns, but does not report further. One hymn is printed by Wackernagel, *Kirchenlied* III, 812. One hymn, "O herre Gott vom Himmelreich merck auff und sieh die worte . . . ," composed by Schmid and Jörg von Ingenheim, is found in the rare German hymnal *Ein Schon Gesangbüchlein* (*q.v.*). The main theme of all these hymns is love, obedience to God, community, and Gelassenheit (*q.v.*), a key attitude of the Anabaptists. Of particular beauty is hymn No. 4, "Fröhlich so wollen wir singen," a deeply felt praise of Christian love. Many a hymn shows the typical Anabaptist acrostic—a hidden message composed by the first words of each stanza. (For details see *Chronik*, 385 note.)

The names of the brethren who were martyred with Schmid are Heinrich Adam, Hans Weckh, Matthias Schmied, and Tillman Schneider. R.F.

Wolkan, *Geschicht-Buch;* Zieglschmid, *Chronik;* Wolkan, *Lieder,* 211-28; Wiswedel, *Bilder* III, 95-101 and 210-13; L. Müller and R. Friedmann, *Glaubenszeugnisse oberdeutscher Täufer* II (to be published in 1960) No. 12; *TA Hessen,* 332-36; *Liederbuch der Hutterischen Brüder* (Scottdale, 1914) 551-611; Josef Hansen, "Wiedertäufer in Aachen," *Zeitschrift des Aachener Geschichts-vereins* VI (1884) 295-338 (contains extensive excerpts from Schmid's writings); excerpts are also found in K. W. H. Hochhuth, "Mittheilungen aus der protestantischen Secten-Geschichte in der hessischen Kirche," *Zeitschrift für die Historische Theologie* XXX (1860) 267-71; Wackernagel, *Kirchenlied* III, 812; *Mart. Mir.* D 209-13, E 588-90; *Der Mennonit* IX (1955) 10.

Schmid, Konrad (1467-1531), a Swiss Reformed clergyman, born at Küssnacht on Lake Zürich, was appointed as commander (Comtur) of the Johannite monastery in 1519. Soon after, he became a close friend of Ulrich Zwingli (*q.v.*) and zealously promoted the Reformation in Zürich, publicly advocating the Reformation in the second disputation, Oct. 26-28, 1523. The topics of the debate at this large, important meeting were the unscripturalness of the images of saints and the veneration of the saints, and the Catholic Mass. In the course of the debate Konrad Schmid said tactfully that everything must proceed from God's Word, the pure Gospel, which teaches us to acknowledge Christ as the only Mediator, to whom alone honor is due. He was trying to say thereby that iconoclasm was not the essential of the Reformation, but the acceptance of Jesus Christ as Saviour. His well-meant admonitions, however, did not find universal acceptance. Even Zwingli was not altogether satisfied with him, and declared to him, "When . . . the commander remarks that everyone should first be instructed in the divine Word, that pleases me very well; if the priests had preached the Word, the populace would not have followed unfruitful things, and it would never have reached the point where one could learn to know Christ only through paintings. But if one were to postpone the removal of the images until it could create no offense, it would never happen."

On the afternoon of the third day there was a lively discussion on the Mass. Opinion as to its abolition was divided, although Zwingli had recognized the Mass as reprehensible idolatry. During this indecision Conrad Grebel (*q.v.*) urged the immediate abolition of the Mass by vote of the meeting, since it was not a sacrifice, but was sufficiently shown from the Scriptures to be an error, and all abuses should be uncovered and eliminated. Balthasar Hubmaier (*q.v.*) supported Grebel and tried to explain that the Mass was nothing but a distortion of the symbols of the communion: the body and blood of Christ. He demanded that the Mass should be read in the mother tongue. Zwingli agreed with both and added that anything that had forced its way into the church without Christ's institution was an abuse of the divine, and must be countered with God's Word. But he wanted to leave the matter of eliminating the abuses to the government, whereupon Simon Stumpf (*q.v.*) replied that he had no right to submit the decision in spiritual matters into the hands of temporal government.

Then Konrad Schmid made an important speech, summarized as follows: Although God has completed everything in Christ people still practice superstition. It is the duty of the council to issue orders to honor, worship, and call upon God alone, and not to worship images. Christian regents should issue Scriptural decrees "that in their lands and realms none but Christ should be called upon, worshiped, and honored, and recognized as the only comforter and helper in need and Lord of all things." Paul too was protected by temporal authority when the Jews were about to kill him. If the Gospel is again brought to the world cheerfully and clearly, Christ's reign will be established. "You have hitherto assisted many a temporal prince to regain his rule for the sake of money, now for the sake of God assist Christ our Lord to regain His kingdom." "If Christ were permitted to be the only Lord and Master of all things, so that He could reign in us and fulfill His work, we would have brotherly love among us, Christian peace, divine grace and mercy here in time and afterward eternal life."

This address of Konrad Schmid's was a clever defense of an ecclesiastico-political, theocratic view. It made an enormous impression on the hearers, but more important, it brought about the union of the temporal power with the spiritual. This was the formal introduction of the Reformed State Church. From this time on the clergy saw in the church only an institution of the state, which in accord with the ordinance of God (Rom. 13) was authorized to dictate faith and if necessary use the sword against the "unbelieving."

This union, however, became the point of division between the Swiss Brethren and Zwingli. Zwingli and Schmid acquired power that developed into a dictatorship, beside which no other view was permitted. Then a committee was appointed to carry out the work of the Reformation: Zwingli, Wolfgang Joner, Heinrich Brennwald, Heinrich Engelhard, Leo Jud, four councillors, and Konrad Schmid.

In the late fall of 1525 Schmid was one of the four presidents of the third disputation on the question of baptism, the others being Wolfgang Joner of Kappel, Dr. Sebastian Hofmeister of Schaffhausen, and Joachim von Watt (Vadian) of St. Gall. It seems that at that point he abandoned his moderate point of view in matters of faith and became a violent opponent of the Swiss Brethren.

At the great disputation at Bern in the summer of 1528 where the Reformation was decided upon, Konrad Schmid was again one of the four presidents. Having in his home town participated in the bitter struggle against the Swiss Brethren, Schmid may have been so much the more annoyed to meet some of them at the Bern disputation. He published a polemic against them with the title, *Verwerffen der Artickeln und stucken so die Widertöuffer uff dem gesprach zu Bernn, vor ersamen grossen Radt fürgewendt habend. Durch Cunraden Schmid, Commenthur zu Küssnacht am Zürich See.* Its purpose was to induce the leaders to adopt the same policy as had been adopted at Zürich. This pamphlet, filled with epithets from the animal and demon worlds, contains many falsehoods and perversions. Schmid went so far as to assert that the Swiss Brethren were "the worst enemies of the cross of Christ, the like of which has never yet been found in any history." They were the ones who annul Christ and in His place pour forth their devilish baptism." It was his opinion that they could expect nothing but eternal damnation, and "would be cast into the lower world as the Gadarene swine had been cast into the sea, unless they returned to the unity of the Christian church, besides which there is no way to bliss." "What the devil has spun, the Swiss Brethren have reeled"; yet these erring ones had at the disputation of Bern in 1528 been quite kindly dismissed by the honorable council (with prison and threat of death)!

It is sad that so influential and gifted a man as Konrad Schmid allowed himself to be led to such boundless distortions. Hubmaier reports in his letter from Zurich, "The Johannite priest, Commander at Küssnacht," in whom there is in truth nothing but talk and pomp, "was one of those most to blame for the severity of the government measures against the Anabaptists."

Schmid served in both Kappel wars, 1529 and 1531, as an army chaplain. Like his friend Zwingli he died in battle in 1531. After his death Bullinger wrote of him, "This Conrad Schmid was a pious man, helped much in the Reformation, as can be seen in all the records." S.G.

K. R. Hagenbach, *Kirchengeschichte* III; Samuel Geiser, *Die Taufgesinnten-Gemeinden* (Karlsruhe, 1931); J. C. Füsslin, *Beiträge zur Erläuterung der Kirchen- und Reformationsgeschichte des Schweizerlandes* (Zürich, 1741); J. H. Yoder, "The Turning Point in the Zwinglian Reformation," *MQR* XXXII (1958) 153-61; *ML* IV.

Schmidt (Schmid, Smit, Smet, Schmitt, Smith) is a common Mennonite name, particularly among the Mennonites of Prusso-Russian background. The name appears in the early church records of Thiensdorf, Orlofferfelde, Danzig, Elbing, Jeziorka, Przechovka, Konopat, and Kazun. Particularly from the latter groups the name was transplanted to Russia and America. The first records of the name in Prussia date back to 1586. Hilchen (Hiltje) Smet (Smid) was elder of the Montau Mennonite Church in 1588. Hans Schmidt, a Hutterite preacher of Moravia, who was an evangelizing missionary in Württemberg, died in 1602. From the Przechovka-Alexanderwohl church record we learn that the first bearer of the name fled in 1634 with Tobias Schellenberger from Moravia to Hungary and then to Przechovka. He is supposed to have received the name because he was a master smith. Most of his descendants lived in the villages of Przechovka, Konopat, and Jeziorka. Some of them settled later in the Polish-Russian villages of Heinrichsdorf and Michalin.

Several Schmidts from Przechovka joined the group of Mennonite immigrants to the Molotschna settlement, where they established the village and congregation of Alexanderwohl (*q.v.*). In 1874 most of them settled in the community of Goessel, Kan., while those from Heinrichsdorf and Michalin established the congregations and communities of Gnadenberg, Canton, Pawnee Rock, Kan., and Avon, S.D. Later the family spread over most of the states and provinces west of the Mississippi River. The name was also transplanted to Canada and South America. The Alexanderwohl church, with its 991 members, has 135 whose surname is Schmidt (1954). Some of the bearers of the name, particularly of South German background, have changed the name to Smith. The connection be-

tween the Schmidts among the Mennonites of South German and Prussian background has never been fully investigated. It is likely that they are not of the same ancestry.

Among the Mennonite leaders of Russia were Nikolai Schmidt and Johann Schmidt, members of the Board of the Gnadenfeld Bruderschule and cofounders of the Friends of Jerusalem (Templers). P. P. Schmidt (1860-1910) of the Molotschna settlement was a cofounder of the Evangelical Mennonite Church. Hermann Schmitt of South Germany was a missionary under the Dutch Mennonite Mission Board in Indonesia. *Who's Who Among the Mennonites* (North Newton, 1943) lists the following: Albert G. Schmidt, minister; August Schmidt, teacher and minister; Augusta Schmidt, missionary; H. U. Schmidt, minister; H. R. Schmidt, M.D.; J. R. Schmidt, M.D.; R. Schmidt, minister. Others are H. B. Schmidt, minister; John F. Schmidt, professor. John Smith (1843-1906), a prominent bishop in the Mennonite Church (MC) at Roanoke, Ill., was of Alsatian Amish stock. C. Henry Smith (*q.v.*) was his son. Professor Willard Smith of Goshen College is his grandson, as is Tilman R. Smith, president of Hesston College 1959—. J. B. Smith (*q.v.*, 1870-1951), a prominent Mennonite (MC) minister at Elida, Ohio, and sometime president of Eastern Mennonite College, was of an Ontario Mennonite family. His son Paul and nephew Norman are ministers (MC) at Elida and Cloverdale, Ohio. P.U.S., C.K.

Przechovka-Alexanderwohl Church Record; J. A. Schmidt, *Schmidt Family Record* (Vermillion, 1948); Reimer, *Familiennamen*; P. U. Schmidt, *The Unruh Genealogy . . .* (1941).

Schmidt, Berlet, an Anabaptist martyr of the Hausbreitenbach (*q.v.*) district (Germany) who was executed with Hans Eisfart (*q.v.*) and his wife at Eisenach in 1532, at the command of Elector John of Saxony.

Paul Wappler, *Die Stellung Kursachsens und des Landgrafen Philipp von Hessen zur Täuferbewegung* (Münster, 1910) 36; *ML* IV.

Schmidt, C. (Carl) **B.** (Bernhard) (1843-1921?), who because of his activities as land agent for the Santa Fe in promoting the Russian Mennonite immigration to Kansas became known as "the Moses of the Mennonites," was born Sept. 7, 1843, in Dippoldiswalde, Saxony, Germany. In 1863 he became foreign correspondent in a commercial house at Hamburg. In 1864 he went to America, living in St. Louis until he came to Kansas in 1868. He became a grocer in Lawrence, later also becoming an implement salesman. As a correspondent for several German newspapers he established contact with people who wished to migrate to America.

In 1873 Schmidt began his service for the Santa Fe. Through his contacts with Cornelius Jansen (*q.v.*), the Board of Guardians (*q.v.*), and individual leaders, Schmidt influenced thousands of the Mennonites to settle in Kansas, concluding the sale of 100,000 acres of land in October 1874. In 1875 he went to Russia to persuade more Mennonites to come to Kansas. He served the Santa Fe until most of the railroad land was sold. He became personally acquainted with the Mennonite leaders; the files of David Goerz (*q.v.*), Christian Krehbiel (*q.v.*), and others in the BeCL contain extensive correspondence signed by C. B. Schmidt.

After dissolving his association with the Santa Fe Schmidt managed the Equitable Trust Company in Omaha, Neb. In 1880 he set up the London office of the Santa Fe. In 1895 he went to Pueblo, Col., as manager of the Suburban Land and Investment Company and director of the Bessemer irrigation ditch. Later he became commissioner of immigration of the Rock Island Lines, and 1914-16 he was a colonization agent of the Wyoming Development Company, with offices in Chicago. He again carried on an extensive correspondence with Mennonites, particularly H. P. Krehbiel, in an endeavor to sell lands in the area of Wheatland, Wyoming. J.F.S.

"Reminiscences of Foreign Immigration Work for Kansas," *Kansas State Historical Collection* IX (1905-6); Board of Guardians File, H. P. Krehbiel Collection (BeCL).

Schmidt, Christel, a Hutterite hymn writer, was excommunicated in 1564 on account of his views on divorce. Wolkan states that Schmidt is the author of a story about Judith. The *Lieder der Hutterischen Brüder* does not include him. Horsch mentions an "Epistel an Claus Braidl aus seinem Gefängnis 1586." NEFF.

Beck, *Geschichts-Bücher;* Wolkan, *Geschicht-Buch;* John Horsch, *Kurzgefasste Geschichte der Mennoniten-Gemeinden* (Elkhart, 1890); *Lieder der Hutterischen Brüder* (Scottdale, 1914); Wolkan, *Lieder; ML* IV.

Schmidt, Christian (1833-1906), an elder of the Mennonite Brethren in Russia, was born at Constantinograd in 1833. He was a cabinetmaker by trade, and lived in Tokmak in 1864. In the church he opposed the "Ueberfröhlichen," presented to the councillor Brun on Dec. 6, 1865, an important document, the Selbstbekenntnis (Confession of faith), which contains exact information on the Mennonite Brethren. In 1872 he was appointed traveling evangelist with Jakob Jantz, and published an account of the journey in a yearbook the two founded in 1865. In 1868 he moved to the Kuban (*q.v.*). He was ordained as elder in Friedensfeld (*q.v.*) on June 15, 1875. He died there in 1906. (*ML* IV.)

Schmidt, Hans, an Anabaptist martyr: see **Schmid, Hans.**

Schmidt (Schmied), **Hans,** an Anabaptist martyr of Uttenreuth, was beheaded in June 1531 at Baiersdorf, Bavaria, Germany. (*TA Bayern,* 369; Wappler, *Thüringen,* 37.)

Schmidt, Hans, von Rommelshausen (d. 1602), a Hutterite brother from Württemberg whose experiences on a mission in his native country in 1590 are graphically described in a very remarkable epistle. This epistle relates that he had been won for Anabaptism in 1581, and had left Württemberg and gone to Moravia, joining the Hutterites. Here he married. In 1590, he was sent to his home country to spread the Gospel, and after many months of suc-

cessful work was caught by the authorities and now badly treated, being moved from prison to prison, each worse than the one before. In Schorndorf (*q.v.*) he met his father and his brothers who pleaded with him to return to their (official) church, but also gave bond for him to the authorities. The most interesting passage in the epistle is the discussion concerning the "sword": the bailiff (*Vogt*) of one of the castles where he was kept asked him whether, if Turks were to invade the country, he would not want to defend it by the sword. Thereupon Schmidt answered: "The Turk prides himself on being a Turk; but he is a Turk; but the alleged Christians pride themselves on being Christians according to the flesh, but then they persecute the true Christians . . . they are Turks according to the Spirit" (Bossert, 656). These are almost the same words with which Michael Sattler (*q.v.*) answered his judges at his trial in 1527 (when the Turkish danger was imminent). Obviously Schmidt was familiar with the booklet in which Sattler's trial was described.

Schmidt was badly racked and tempted by all kinds of means; but he did not yield. Eventually, upon the intercession of his father he was released and expelled from the country without having pledged never to return. He had been kept in prison from the middle of August to Dec. 4, 1590. After his release he sent the epistle with all these details home to Moravia. In one codex this epistle covers not less than 24 leaves, in Beck's copy (now at Brno) it covers 54 handwritten pages, in print 13½ pages folio, allowing a deep insight into the life, thought, and technique of these missioners—all at the end of the 16th century when many had assumed that Anabaptism was on its way out.

Having returned to Moravia, Schmidt was chosen preacher in 1591, and was confirmed in this office in 1596. He died in 1602 at the Stignitz Bruderhof near Moravian Kromau. R.F.

Zieglschmid, *Chronik; TA Württemberg,* 625-65; Wiswedel, *Bilder* III, 36-39; *ML* IV.

Schmidt, Johann, was ordained minister in 1894 and elder in 1896 in the Deutsch-Wymysle Mennonite Church (*q.v.*) near Warsaw, Poland, when his predecessor Johann Khewer (*q.v.*) joined the local Mennonite Brethren congregation. In 1907 he also joined the Mennonite Brethren leaving the Deutsch-Wymysle congregation without an elder. The observance of baptism and Lord's Supper in the remaining small congregation was supervised by the elder of the Deutsch-Kazun Mennonite Church. Johann Schmidt moved to Deutsch-Kazun in 1930, where he died on Feb. 26, 1936. (Friesen, *Brüderschaft,* 719; see also **Deutsch-Wymysle.**)

C.K.

Schmidt, Johann, cofounder of the Gnadenfeld (*q.v.*) Bruderschule and the Templer (*q.v.*) movement and an elder of the Olgino (*q.v.*) Tempelhof church and settlement. His oldest son, Johann Schmidt (d. 1882), a businessman, died in Berlin in 1950. C.K.

H. Sawatzky, *Templer mennonitischer Herkunft* (Winnipeg, 1955) 49-51; Franz Isaac, *Die Molotschnaer Mennoniten* (Halbstadt, 1908).

Schmidt, Mat(t)hias, a Hutterite martyr, a preacher and missioner, who was arrested with Hans Schmid (Raiffer) (*q.v.*) and ten other Anabaptists at Aachen in 1558 and put to death on Jan. 4, 1559, with Tillmann Schneider (*q.v.*). Two songs by Matthias Schmidt have been preserved: "Merkt auf, ihr Völker, alle gleich in diesen letzten Zeiten," and "Wacht auf, ihr Streiter, Kämpfer, ihr Kinder Gottes rein."   NEFF.

Beck, *Geschichts-Bücher,* 233; Wolkan, *Geschicht-Buch,* 299; Zieglschmid, *Chronik,* 385 f., 389, 393; *Mart. Mir.* D 221, E 588-90; *ML* IV.

Schmidt, Nikolai (1815-74), primarily responsible for the founding of the Templer (*q.v.*) movement among the Mennonites of the Molotschna settlement, Russia, was born July 20, 1815. During his journeys in Germany he became acquainted with the educational institute Kirschenhardthof, Württemberg, under Christoph Paulus. Johannes Lange (*q.v.*) was sent to attend this school and became the first teacher of the Gnadenfeld (*q.v.*) Bruderschule (established in 1857), of which Nikolai and Johann Schmidt (*q.v.*) were board members. This school became the testing ground which led to the founding of the Mennonite Brethren and the Templer movements. Nikolai Schmidt was an outstanding leader of the movement, transplanting the ideas of the Templer movement from South Germany into the Mennonite environment of the Molotschna and in the establishment of the Tempelhof (*q.v.*) settlement at Kuban (*q.v.*). He went to Palestine to investigate settlement possibilities and died on the way to Palestine at Toganrog, on Sept. 14, 1874, while migrating with a group.

His son, Nikolai Schmidt II, born Sept. 29, 1839, as well as grandson, Nikolai Schmidt III, born April 13, 1876, also played a significant role in the movement. The latter was mayor of the Templer colony of Jerusalem after World War I and leader of the group during the trying years of World War II. He died in Australia, Jan. 10, 1953.   C.K.

H. Sawatzky, *Templer mennonitischer Herkunft* (Winnipeg, 1955) 22, 46-49; Franz Isaac, *Die Molotschnaer Mennoniten* (Halbstadt, 1908) 207-66.

Schmidt, Peter, was chairman of the Molotschna Mennonite Agricultural Association and chairman of the Molotschna Mennonite School Council. He owned and lived on the estate Steinbach (*q.v.*), where he had his office. He also established a secondary school on this estate, taught by Peter Neufeld. Peter Schmidt was very influential in the cultural life of the Mennonites of the Molotschna settlement. He was a nephew of Klaas Wiens, the founder of the Steinbach estate. The exact dates of his life are not known, but the peak of his activities was *c*1850-69.

Another Peter Schmidt (1860-1910) of Steinbach (*q.v.*), an elder of the Steinbach congregation, was evidently a son of the above. He was a great benefactor to various Mennonite causes, including the Morija (*q.v.*) Deaconess Home. P. M. Friesen speaks highly of his consecrated Christian living. He died on May 30, 1910, at the age of fifty. (Friesen, *Brüderschaft,* 162, 166 f., 645 ff., 659, 725.)   C.K.

Schmiedeleut, one of the three Hutterite kinship groups (the other two being the Dariusleut, *q.v.*, and the Lehrerleut, *q.v.*), so named because its founder, Preacher Michael Waldner, was a blacksmith (*Schmied*) in Russia. Michael Waldner was the first to re-establish communal living in Bruderhof form, which he did in 1859 in one end of the village of Hutterdorf in the Ukraine (see **Dariusleut**). The Waldner Bruderhof migrated to South Dakota in 1874 and settled the Bon Homme Colony near Yankton. This was the first Hutterite Bruderhof in America and is commonly, though wrongly, thought of as the mother Bruderhof of all Hutterites in America. The second kinship group, the Dariusleut, which was established in 1860 in the same Hutterdorf village in Russia, arrived in South Dakota later in 1874 and did not establish its first Bruderhof (Wolf Creek) until the next year, 1875. The Schmiedeleut Bruderhofs in the United States are now all in South Dakota, and those in Canada are all in Manitoba, and they are the only group having Bruderhofs in these two locations. Their leader or bishop is Peter Hofer, James Valley Colony, Starbuck, Man., who was chosen in 1951. Following is a list of the Schmiedeleut Bruderhofs as they existed in 1957. It should be noted that the Forest River Bruderhof, Fordville, N.D., was dissolved in 1955, because a considerable number of families joined the New Hutterites (Society of Brothers) and moved away.   H.S.B.

CENSUS OF SCHMIEDELEUT BRUDERHOFS

Name of Colony	Address	Founded	pop. 1957	Head Preacher
Schmiedeleut Bruderhofs in South Dakota				
Bon Homme	Tabor	1874	90	Jacob Waldner
Glendale	Frankfort	1949	130	John Waldner
Gracevale	Winfred	1948	104	Sam Wipf
Huron	Huron	1944	135	Jacob Wollmann
Jamesville	Utica	1937	95	Paul Wurz
Maxwell	Scotland	1949	113	Joseph Hofer
Millerdale	Miller	1949	74	John Waldner
New Elm Spring	Ethan	1936	145	Sam Wollmann
Pearl Creek	Iroquois	1949	130	Michael Waldner
Platte	Academy	1949	102	Joseph Waldner
Riverside	Huron	1949	80	John Waldner
Rockport	Alexandria	1934	123	Dan Wipf
Rosedale	Mitchell	1945	114	Joseph Waldner, Sr.

Spink	Frankfort	1945	142	John Wipf
Tschetter	Olivet	1942	144	David Decker, Sr.
Clark	Raymond	1955	75	Fred Waldner
Blumengard	Wecota	1950	73	Jacob Hofer
			1869	

Schmiedeleut Bruderhofs in North Dakota — Forest River, settled 1950, closed 1955

Schmiedeleut Bruderhofs in Manitoba — census for Manitoba as of April 1958

Barickman	Headingly	1920	124	David Hofer
Bloomfield	Westbourne	1954	65	John R. Hofer
Blumengard	Plum Coulee	1922	107	Jacob Waldner
Bon Homme	Elie	1918	155	Joseph Wollman
Crystal Springs	St. Agathe	1954	91	Jacob Kleinsasser
Elm River	Newton Siding	1934	105	Jacob Z. Hofer
Gruenwald	Dencross	1956	92	Joseph P. Hofer
Huron	Benard	1918	123	Joseph Glanzer
Iberville	Headingly	1919	131	Andreas Gross
James Valley	Starbuck	1918	98	Peter Hofer
Lakeside	Headingly	1946	126	George Wipf
Maxwell	Headingly	1918	135	George Waldner
Milltown	Benard	1918	84	Michael Waldner
New Rosedale	Portage la Prairie	1944	191	Jacob Maendel
Oak Bluff	Morris	1954	89	David J. Hofer
Poplar Point	Poplar Point	1938	151	Fred Waldner
Riverdale	Gladstone	1946	140	David Wurz
Riverside	Arden	1934	81	John J. Hofer
Rock Lake	Gross Isle	1947	124	Michael Gross
Rosedale	Elie	1918	206	Jacob K. Hofer
Spring Valley	Brandon	1956	87	Jacob Waldner
Sturgeon Creek	Headingly	1938	104	Samuel Kleinsasser
Springfield	Anola	1950	126	Samuel Waldner
Sunnyside	Newton Siding	1940	125	Joseph Kleinsasser
Waldheim	Elie	1935	106	Michael Waldner
Rose Valley	Graysville	1958	69	David Waldner
Total			3035	
Grand Total			4904	

Schmitt, Hermann, a German Mennonite of the Deutschhof (*q.v.*) congregation, was sent out in November 1926 by the Dutch Mennonite Missions Association as a missionary on Java (*q.v.*), serving at Tajoe (*q.v.*) and Margoredjo (*q.v.*). During World War II the ship on which Schmitt and his brother-in-law Otto Stauffer (*q.v.*), also a missionary, were transported was torpedoed in the Indian Ocean on Jan. 18, 1942, and both perished.   vDZ.

Schmitt Mennonite Church (MC), now extinct, at Edgely in the Mennonite settlement of Vaughan and York townships in York Co., Ont., was located 15 miles north of Toronto and 12 miles west of the Markham settlement. The families came from Pennsylvania about 1800. Peter Musselman was the first minister. Christian Troyer was ordained after Musselman's death in 1830. Daniel Brundage became minister about 1845. The meetinghouse, the oldest Mennonite church in Ontario still standing, was erected in 1824. The membership, about 50, was strongest about 1875. Since then the Mennonite Brethren in Christ Church has been more active. After the division of 1889 there were few members for either party, and the congregation died out. The Brethren in Christ were active in Vaughan Township throughout the 19th century.   J.C.F.

L. J. Burkholder, *A Brief History of the Mennonites in Ontario* (n.p., 1935) 120 f.

Schmucker: see **Smucker.**

Schmutz, a Mennonite family name, originating in Switzerland. In 1717 the name is listed for the first time in Anabaptist Registers of the Palatinate, South Germany, when a Christian Schmutz was living at Helmstadt (now Baden). Some members of the family probably emigrated to America at the end of the 18th century, and to England in the middle of the 19th century. It is now most numerous among the South German Mennonites. In 1755, according to the *Naamlijst,* Abraham and Christian Schmutz were preachers in the congregation called Hasselbach, Martinshof, Helmstedt, and Sennfeld. Christian Schmutz (*q.v.,* 1799-1873), of Rappenau, Baden, called "Christel-Vetter," was an outstanding leader and preacher in the congregations of the Gemeindeverband (*q.v.*).   U.H.

Friedrich Schmutz, *Zweihundertvierzig Jahre Familiengeschichte [1692-1935]. Ein Stammbaum der Familien Schmutz* (Leuterstal, 1936); ML IV.

Schmutz, Christian (1799-1873), an elder of the Mennonites in Baden (*q.v.*), Germany, was born Oct. 19, 1799, at Rappenau, Baden. An invalid from his youth, he visited a spa in Cannstatt in Württemberg at the age of twenty-two, and was deeply impressed by some Christian believers at the place. Upon the death of his father he took over the home farm. In 1858 he gave up farming in order to devote all his time and strength to the service of the brotherhood. At the age of thirty he was chosen preacher, and five years later elder. His work extended far beyond the borders of his brotherhood. In the early volumes of the *Mennonitische Blätter,* 1855 and 1856, he wrote three excellent articles on "Die Mennonitengemeinden im Grossherzogtum Baden," and in 1858 on the Mennonites of Switzerland. In 1860 he sharply opposed the proposed *Menno-Stiftung* (*q.v.*) and any human honoring of Menno, and at the same time opposed a trained ministry. Special mention should be made of his six open letters to all the ministers, in which he expressed his religious views without reservation. When the *Gemeindeblatt der Mennoniten* appeared in 1870, which was founded at his instigation, he was one of the most devoted collaborators. He wrote a series of valuable articles for it. In 1865 he published a catechism under the title *Christliches Lehrbüchlein,* which is used by Mennonites outside Baden and was adopted by the Swiss Mennonites. His manuscript became the basis for the Ministers' Manual of the Gemeindeverband (*q.v.*), *Leitfaden zum Gebrauch bei gottesdienstlichen Handlungen* (1876). He died Nov. 18, 1873. (*Menn. Jugendwarte,* 1920, 12 ff.; ML IV.) NEFF.

Schmutz, Christine, of Rappenau, Baden, Germany, published in 1880 a booklet called *Samenkörner der Wahrheit, ausgestreut für wahrheitliebende Herzen,* which, redolent of the spirit of the Temple Church (*q.v.*), was expressly repudiated by the conference of elders of the Baden Mennonites. (*Gbl.,* 1800, 23; ML IV.)

Schnabel, Georg, a Hessian Anabaptist preacher, previously a treasurer in Allendorf, a town on the Werra near Kassel, Germany, was seized with thirty other Anabaptists at a meeting in an abandoned church at Gemunden, and imprisoned with ten brethren at Wolkersdorf. From there he and three others who were regarded as second offenders were taken to Marburg.

Soon they were returned to the Wolkersdorf prison. Their confinement was rather mild; they were allowed some freedom of movement. Georg Schnabel confessed to the magistrate at Marburg that he had repeatedly left the prison and baptized about thirty persons. When Noviomagus (*q.v.*), a professor at the University of Marburg, and Fabricius (*q.v.*), the pastor of Allendorf, were sent to Wolkersdorf by Philip of Hesse in August 1538 to convert the prisoners, Georg Schnabel was already at home with his family.

But they found a copy of the booklet Schnabel had written, *Verantwortung und Wiederlegung der Artikel, so jetzund im Land zu Hessen über die armen Davider, die man Wiedertäufer nennt, ausgegangen sind.* It was written with the purpose of refuting the charges raised by the church inspection committee against the Anabaptists, and to strengthen his brethren in the faith. With an amazing knowledge of the Bible Schnabel presents Anabaptist teachings and with determination repudiates the charges of communal possession of property and of wives, as well as the rejection of government.

For two years all the untiring efforts of the landgrave to convert the Anabaptists were in vain. Finally Bucer (*q.v.*), the reformer of Strasbourg, who had been summoned by Philip, succeeded in a disputation held on Oct. 30 to Nov. 1, 1538, in persuading the imprisoned Anabaptists to recant. They signed the "Bekenntnis oder Antwort etlicher Fragestücke oder Artikeln der gefangenen Täufer und anderer im Land zu Hessen," which was drawn up by Peter Tasch (*q.v.*), and were received into the church. W.W.

W. Diehl, *Zur Geschichte der Konfirmation* (Giessen, 1897) 4 f.; Paul Wappler, *Die Stellung Kursachsens und des Landgrafen Philipp von Hessen zur Täuferbewegung* (Münster, 1910) 57 ff.; an account of the colloquy of 1538 is found in *Ztsch für die historische Theologie,* 1858, 626-44; ML IV.

Schnebele (Schnebeli, Schnebly, Schnebel, Snavely), a Mennonite family name of Swiss origin, found especially in the Palatinate. In 1533 Bernhart Schnewli, of Affoltern, Swiss canton of Zürich, is named as an Anabaptist. In 1660 Jakob Schnebely, of Baldenheim in Alsace, signed the Dordrecht Confession in Ohnenheim (*q.v.*). In 1706 Hans Jakob Schnebely is named in Mannheim; in 1710 and later he corresponded with Dutch and Alsatian Mennonites in the cause of the Swiss refugees. As a preacher or elder he obviously held a position of trust. Other members of the family were living on the Rohrhof and at Gräfenau.

Jakob Schnebele (1727-76) came to Fischbach (*q.v.*) by way of the Mückenhäuserhof, near Ibersheim. Christian Schnebele (1739-1808), living either at Frankenstein or Diemerstein, was a preacher 1765-? and an elder 1781-1808, first in the Diemerstein congregation, and later in Sembach. Some descendants of Jakob went to Wartenberg, Mehlingen, Rohrbach, etc. Others emigrated to the United States in the 19th century. Among these was Jakob Schnebele, of Ernstweiler, a preacher who in 1852 led a group of Mennonites from Eichstock (*q.v.*) in Bavaria to Iowa. A Joseph Schnebele, of Hornbach, a preacher of the Zweibrücken congregation (*q.v.*) in 1766 gave information for the Dutch *Naamlijst* (*q.v.*) to Peter Weber (*q.v.*).

Another descendant of the Wartenberg-Rohrbach branch is Christian Schnebele (1888-   ), a son of Jakob and Elisabeth Kinsinger Schnebele. He married Emma Pohl, a daughter of Matthias Pohl (*q.v.*) of Sembach. Schnebele was educated for the ministry at St. Chrischona, near Basel, Switzerland, in 1906-9, and then served in home and city missions, especially at Worms; in 1924 he was appointed housefather of the "Bibelheim Thomashof" (*q.v.*) and at the same time served the Badischer Verband (*q.v.*) as traveling evangelist (*Reiseprediger*). Since 1925 he has been the editor of the *Gemeindeblatt der Mennoniten* (*q.v.*). His son Adolf Schnebele (1922-   ), a minister, is a Reiseprediger for the Verband. P.S.

TA Zürich, 330; Müller, *Berner Täufer,* 195, 225, 290; Peter Weber's correspondence, copies in the Neff library at Weierhof; *Mennonitisches Adressbuch* (Karlsruhe, 1936) 22; *Gesch.-Bl.,* 1936, 22; J. Snively, *Genealogical Register of the . . . Descendants of John Jacob Schnebele . . .* (Chambersburg, 1858); ML IV.

Schneevo(o)gt: see **Voorhelm.**

Schneider, Adam, a young Hutterite, who was seized with Anderle Schlosser at Oettingen (q.v.) in April 1578, while they were on their way from Tirol to Moravia; they were severely tortured and subjected to many attempts to convert them. They, however, made a marvelous escape from prison and reached the brotherhood in Moravia. (Wolkan, *Geschicht-Buch,* 389-91; *ML* IV.)

Schneider, Bernhard, an Anabaptist martyr, "a young fellow" from Frisingen near Laubingen, baptized in Neckarweihingen, Württemberg, Germany, was imprisoned with other brethren at Passau (q.v.) and confessed on Sept. 18, 1535, that he had joined the Anabaptists two years before and then moved to Auspitz (q.v.), Moravia, and lived there until now. "They have no permanent place," but move from one place to another, "wherever God leads them, to places where they are permitted to work and stay." With the Münsterites they had nothing to do, nor were they opponents of government, "if it is with God." Only government that is contrary to God he would not obey, but would not rebel against it either, but leave vengeance to God. He is the author of the hymn, "O Herr Gott, mein Not tu ich dir klagen." He also wrote one stanza of the song "Mit freuden wolln wir singen." (See **Philippite Brethren.**) Neff.

TA *Württemberg,* 1180, under "Neckarweihingen"; Wolkan, *Lieder,* 30 f., 38, 39, 255; *ML* IV.

Schneider, Gallus, of Wädiswyl in the Swiss canton of Bern, an Anabaptist martyr, died in the prison of the Oethenbach monastery at Zürich in 1640, having been "kept in irons sixteen weeks and very harshly treated." (*Mart. Mir.* D 819, E 1118; *ML* IV.)

Schneider, Kaspar: see **Braitmichel, Kaspar.**

Schneider, Leonhard, an Anabaptist martyr of Kaufbeuren, Germany, was seized with Hans Staudach (q.v.), Anthoni Keim, and Blasy Beck (see **Beckh, Blasius**) en route to Moravia on Aug. 3, 1546. They were taken to Vienna and beheaded on Nov. 22, 1546. Their death is commemorated in two hymns written by Wolf Sailer (q.v.) and Hans Gurtzham (q.v.). Neff.

Beck, *Geschichts-Bücher,* 165-67; Wolkan, *Geschicht-Buch,* 206 f.; *Lieder der Hutterischen Brüder* (Scottdale, 1914) Nos. 133 and 136; Zieglschmid, *Chronik,* 265-67; *Mart. Mir.* D 74, E 475; *ML* IV.

Schneider, Leopold (Liepolt Snyder), an Anabaptist martyr: see **Leupold, Hans.**

Schneider, Michael, a Philippite Anabaptist and hymn writer, originally of Bruchsal (q.v.), Baden, where he joined the group of Philipp Plener (q.v.) in 1527. With Plener he went to Moravia and lived at the Bruderhof at Auspitz (q.v.). When, in 1535, the entire brotherhood of the Philippites broke up into several groups to return to Southwest Germany, Plener in a last act as bishop ordained Michael Schneider as leader (also called "bishop") of a group of about 60 souls who seem to have had

Bruchsal as their destination. In August and September of 1535 this "Schneider group" was caught at Passau and imprisoned there 1535-40. We know something of these people through the *Passauer Religionsakten* (used by Wolkan) but unfortunately the records concerning Schneider are lost. Schneider's wife was among the prisoners, and all the prisoners deposed that Schneider had been their "bishop" or leader. He was also one of the prisoners, as related in the oldest part of the *Ausbund* (q.v.), which contains the hymns of these Passau Philippites. In the dungeons of the Passau castle 52 hymns were composed, eleven of which had Schneider as author, namely, Nos. (in modern editions) 82, 85, 87, 93, 95, 96, 97, 99, 101, and together with Hans Betz or Petz (a.v.) as coauthor, Nos. 102 and 103. Wackernagel (III and IV) also prints them.

In his *Lieder der Wiedertäufer,* Wolkan analyzed all these hymns in great detail and rated Schneider as "a true poet" and a composer of great depth of feeling and power of expression. In fact he rates Schneider as more profound than Betz. Schneider's main concern is discipleship, which becomes possible only by practicing *Gelassenheit* (q.v.), that is, surrender to God in the hour of testing. Even in his agony Schneider prays for his enemies (No. 85, stanza 3). Hymn No. 87 is one great praise of the power of love. He has a deep grasp of the meaning of martyrdom for the true disciple of Christ. Wolkan points out that Schneider avoids all dogmatic questions, touching only the Lord's Supper.

Nothing is known about Schneider's fate. Since no death penalty was practiced in Passau, he either died in prison with many others (e.g., Betz), or was finally freed. But no details are recorded. The Hutterite Chronicle omits his name. (Wolkan, *Lieder;* Wackernagel, *Kirchenlied; see* **Philippite Brethren.**) R.F.

Schneider, Sicke: see **Sicke Freerks.**

Schneider, Tillmann (Dileman Snijder), a Hutterite martyr, was put to death on Jan. 4, 1559, at Aachen, Germany, together with Matthias Schmidt (q.v.). (*Mart. Mir.* D 209, E 588; Wolkan, *Geschicht-Buch,* 299; Zieglschmid, *Chronik,* 393.)

Schneider, Uhl, a Hutterite missioner imprisoned in Bern, Switzerland, for 20 weeks in 1585, with Bastl Anfang and Heinrich Schweitzer. For his story, see **Anfang, Wastl; Schmid, Bastl;** and **Schweitzer, Heinrich.**

Schneider, Ulrich, an Anabaptist martyr of Lützenpfluhe (Lützelflüh) in the Swiss canton of Bern, who was executed at Bern. Particulars are not known.

Adolf Fluri, *Beiträge zur Geschichte der Bernischen Täufer* (reprint from *Blätter für bernische Geschichte und Altertumskunde,* 1912) p. 14.

Schneider, Ulrich (Uhl), an Anabaptist martyr, was seized on Sept. 23, 1635, in Wädiswyl, in the Swiss canton of Zürich, and died in chains in the Oethenbach (q.v.) prison in Zürich in 1639. His two sons were then imprisoned in the same place but escaped. Meanwhile the authorities sold their home for 7,000 guilders, and put the children out among strangers. (*Mart. Mir.* D 815 f., E 1115; *ML* IV.) Neff.

Schneider, Walser (Walser=Balthasar; *Mart. Mir.* has Wolfert), an Anabaptist martyr, who was executed in 1533 (not 1536 as in *Mart. Mir.*) at Gufidaun (*q.v.*) in the Adige Valley of Tirol, Austria, with Christian Alseider, Valentin (Valtan) Gsäl (*q.v.*), Hans Beck (*q.v.*), Wölfl of Götzenberg, Hans Maurer (*q.v.*), and Peter Kranewetter (*q.v.*), on account of his faith. (Beck, *Geschichts-Bücher,* 108; *Mart. Mir.* D 38, E 444; Zieglschmid, *Chronik,* 104; *ML* IV.)   NEFF.

Schneider, Wolf (Wolfer, Wolphart, Wolfert): see **Rauffer, Wolf.**

Schniftenbergerhof near Alzey (*q.v.*) in Rhenish Hesse, Germany, is listed in the Dutch *Naamlijst* of 1794 (p. 44) as a Mennonite congregation with Christian Eicher as preacher (from 1786) and Jacob Gally as elder (1767). Gally (Galle) was also the elder of the Weierhof (*q.v.*) and Spiesheim (*q.v.*)-Wallertheim congregations. Of the Schniftenbergerhof congregation little is known. Probably meetings were held for some time at this farm, which was the center of a group of Mennonites and a more or less independent congregation, soon after 1794 merging with a neighboring church, either Weierhof or Oberflörsheim (*q.v.*).   VDZ.

Schobbelant Bertels, a Calvinist martyr (erroneously listed by Génard as an Anabaptist) executed at Antwerp, Belgium, on July 9, 1568. The court records at Antwerp state that he was hanged, the *Antwerpsch Chronykje* that he was burned at the stake. (*Antw. Arch.-Bl.* XII, 295, 393, 400; XIV, 56 f., No. 648.)   VDZ.

Schoen, a Mennonite family found in the Zaan district, Dutch province of North Holland, from the 16th century. Willem Jansz Schoen, a baker at Wormerveer, was a preacher of the Wormerveer Frisian Mennonite congregation 1699-c1745. His three sons did not bear the family name of Schoen, but different names—Jan Willemsz Blaauw, Melis Willemsz La(a)keman, and Dirk Willemsz Breeuwer. Jan Willemsz Blaauw and Dirk Willemsz Breeuwer are the ancestors of the Blaauw and Breeuwer families, whose descendants are still found in many Mennonite congregations of North Holland. The Schoen family is also found at Zaandam. Here Simon Schoen was on friendly terms with Czar Peter of Russia, who lived at Zaandam for a time in 1697. There were many Schoens at Zaandam-West; some of them were deacons of the congregation and governesses of the Mennonite orphanage. In Zaandam is the famous dye factory of Pieter Schoen and Son Limited, which developed from a dye mill of the 17th century owned by Pieter Schoen, who was a Mennonite, as were his descendants. In other towns of the Zaan district, like Zaandam-Oost, Westzaan, and Koog, there were also some members of this family. Most of the Schoens were Mennonites, some belonged to the Reformed Church, and a few were Roman Catholics.   VDZ.

Naamlijst, 1731 and 1743; S. Lootsma, *Het Nieuwe Huys* (Zaandam, 1937) 114, 195 f., 200; G. Voet, "Schoen, een typisch Zaans Geslacht," in *De Typhoon* (a Zaan district newspaper) May 5-21, 1953.

Schoener, Leopold: see **Schiemer.**

Schoenfelder Mennonite Church (GCM), located at Pigeon Lake, Man., 25 miles west of Winnipeg, in St. Francois Xavier Municipality, a member of the Canadian Mennonite Conference, was organized on Jan. 25, 1939, by Johann Driedger. The first settlers arrived in 1924-25, purchased a church in 1929, which was enlarged in 1940 and 1953. In 1957 the membership was 151, with David Abrahams as pastor.   D.AB.

Schoental Mennonite Church, at Kismet, Kan.: see **Pleasant Valley** Mennonite Church.

Schoenwiese: see also **Schönwiese.**

Schoenwiese Mennonite Church (GCM) of Manitoba, a member of the Canadian Mennonite Conference, consists of a group of congregations. When the Mennonite refugees from Russia came to Canada in 1923, Elder Johann Peter Klassen of Schönwiese in Russia gathered 22 new Mennonite settlements in Manitoba into one church, which was first called the Starbuck Mennonite Church, but changed to its present name in 1929. The Schoenwiese congregation has expanded into the following churches: Springstein 1939, Schoenfeld 1939, Steinbach 1942 (in part from other congregations), Niverville 1944, Glenlea 1945, and North Kildonan 1956.
The present (1958) Schoenwiese Mennonite Church consists of the following groups: First Mennonite Church of Winnipeg, 1,026 members; Oak Lake Mennonite Church 75, Petersfield Group 17, Steinbach Group 24, and scattered 135; the total membership is 1,277. The elder is Johann Hermann Enns, successor of Johann Peter Klassen.   J.H.EN.

Schoerg: see also **Shirk.**

Scholtens, Harm(en) (May 2, 1703-74), was a minister of the Groningen Old Flemish Mennonite congregation at Groningen, Netherlands. In 1738 he was appointed preacher, in 1755 elder (later called *opziener*). Like other elders of this denomination he paid an annual visit to all congregations in his district. In 1766, accompanied by other elders, he negotiated at Amsterdam concerning a merger of the Groningen Old Flemish group and the Zonists (*q.v.*), but this union did not come into being because most of the Old Flemish congregations opposed it. Scholtens did much in behalf of the oppressed Mennonites in West Prussia, Germany. Though co-operating with the (general) Dutch Committee of Foreign Needs at Amsterdam, the Old Flemish also organized a special relief action of their own, particularly for the (Old Flemish) congregations of Przechovka (*q.v.*) and Brenkenhoffswalde (*q.v.*) in 1766. Scholtens was the soul of this action. He also acted as an intermediary between the Amsterdam Committee of Foreign Needs and the Swiss Mennonites who had settled near Groningen and Sappemeer.   VDZ.

Blaupot t. C., *Groningen* I, 133, 150, 161; H. Dassel Sr, *Menno's Volk in Groningen* (n.p.; n.d.) 35; *Inv. Arch. Amst.* I, Nos. 1111 f., 1702, 1898 f., 1901 f.; II, 2, No. 853; *DJ* 1840, 41-48; *DB* 1879, 4, 69; 1890, 107 f., 110; 1892, 92, 97; 1919, 82, 93.

Schominger, Wolf, also called Wolf Schreiner, a carpenter by trade, an Anabaptist martyr of Königsberg (*q.v.*) in Lower Franconia, Germany, beheaded in March 1527 with several others. His home was the center of the local Anabaptist congregation. In January 1527, when the preachers Eukarius Kellermann (brother-in-law of Schominger) and Kilian Volkaimer, of Grosswalbur, again appeared in the region of Königsberg their meetings came to the attention of the authorities. In February 1527 seven Anabaptists were arrested—the miller of Aurach, Kaspar Spiegel, Beutelhans (*q.v.*), Hans Furster (the brother-in-law of Beutelhans), Wolf Schominger, and two others. For the trial and sentence, see **Beutelhans** and **Königsberg.**   E.H.B.

Paul Wappler, *Die Stellung Kursachsens und des Landgrafen Philip von Hessen zur Täuferbewegung* (Münster, 1910); *idem, Thüringen,* 538; *ML IV.*

Schon Gesangbüchlein, an old hymnal whose full title was *Ein schon ge-/ sangbüchlein Geistlicher lieder / zusamen getragen, Auss dem Alten und / Newen Testament, Durch frome Christen / und liebhaber Gottes, welcher hie für / etliche getruckt seindt gewesen, aber / noch vil darzue gethan, wel / che nie im truck auss- / gangen seindt. /* (Ornament) *// In welchen auch ein recht leben vnd funda- / ment des rechten Christli- / chen glaubens ge- / lehrt wirt. // Colossern.* iii. *// Lehrend vnd ermanendt euch selbst mit / gesangen vnd lobgesangen, vnd geist- / lichen Liederen in der gnad, und / singend dem Herren in ewe- / rem hertzen.* This is apparently the hymnal of the German-speaking Anabaptists of the Lower Rhine area, although none of its editions give any indication of the place of printing. The first edition title page printed at the head of this article must have appeared after March 9, 1563, and before June 30, 1565, since it contains a hymn telling of the martyrdom of Jörg Friesen who was executed on March 9, 1563, at Cologne, but does not contain the hymn telling of the martyrdom of Matthias Servaes, executed on June 30, 1565, at Cologne, which appeared in the second edition. It contains, besides a preface of two pages, 123 hymns on 212 folios, and 3 folios of an index and conclusion. Five of its hymns appeared in the first edition (1564) of the second part of the *Ausbund (q.v.),* called *Etliche schöne Christlich geseng.* The fact that the title of the first edition carries the phrase "[hymns], some of which were printed before, but many more added to, which never have appeared in print," does not require that a previous edition of the entire book had appeared, but rather indicates only that "some were printed before," probably in small leaflets or pamphlets as the custom was. The second edition must have appeared between June 30, 1565, and Jan. 5, 1570, since it contains the Servaes hymn but not the hymn telling of the martyrdom of Arent von Essen, who was executed on Jan. 5, 1570. It contains 133 hymns on 234 folios, but the last four hymns of the first edition were replaced by others, so that actually the second edition has **16 new hymns.** On folio 203a of the section reprinted from the first edition the following note appears before the added hymns: "Several new hymns, which previously were not in and

now are added by pious Christians." The title is almost identical with that of the first edition. The second part of the *Ausbund* (1583 ed.) also contains five of the added hymns of this second edition. The third edition appeared between 1570 and 1583, since it contains the hymn on Arent von Essen, while the *Ausbund* of 1583, which contains a total of 22 hymns from it, clearly depends on it, according to Wackernagel. It contains 141 hymns on 243 folios, including six hymns by L.(eenaerdt) K.(lock). The fact that Klock's first hymnal, called *Vier en twintig schriftverlijcke Liedekens,* was not published until 1589 does not require dating the third edition after that year. The title of this edition is as follows: *Ein schon ge/sangbüchlein, darinn/begriffen werden vielerhandt/schöner Geistlicher Lieder auss/ dem Alten vnd Newen Testament,/ durch fromme Christen zu-samen gezogen. // In welchem auch ein recht le-/ben vnd Fundament dess rechten/ Christlichen Glaubens ge-/lehrt wirdt. // Jetzo von newen widerumb vbersehen,/ ahn vielen orthen gebessert, vnd mit/etlichen newen Liedern/vermehret etc./ Colossern 3./ Lehrendt vnd vermanendt euch selbst mit/gesangen vnd lobgesangen vnd Geist-/lichen Liedern in der gnadt, vnd/singendt dem Herren in ewe//-rem Hertzen.*

This edition was in octavo format; the first and second editions were in identical smaller format.

The hymns contained in *Ein schon gesangbüchlein* are of both Swiss and Dutch origin, so that this hymnal represents a true merging of the two main streams of Anabaptist life and tradition. Rosella Duerksen comments further as follows: "The influence of the German *Volkslied* in Anabaptist hymnody is perhaps nowhere more evident than in the *gesangbüchlein.* Here the imitation of lines and phrases from secular texts reaches its height, and the folk tune is borrowed without restraint. First lines of hymns which are copied outright from secular love songs are such as *Ich stund an einem Morgen,* or *Ich sag ade wir zwey wir müssen scheyden,* or *Von deinetwegen bin ich hie.* The language used is basically High German, coupled with heavy borrowings from the speech of the Low Countries. In subject matter the hymns are similar to those of the *Ausbund,* concerning themselves with stories of martyrdoms as well as with a wide range of doctrinal and devotional topics."

The only known copy of the first edition was located in 1956 in the Stadtbibliothek of Trier, Germany, by J. P. **Classen of Winnipeg.** Microfilm copies are in his possession and in GCL. The second and third editions, copies of which were then in the Prussian State Library in Berlin, were used by Wolkan in his careful descriptive analysis of this hymnal in his *Lieder* (90-118). Wackernagel reprinted the title of the third edition together with an exhaustive bibliographical collation in his *Kirchenlied* (I, 484), using the Berlin copy. Wolkan showed that the preface (found in all three editions with minor typographical variations) was an almost word for word translation of the preface of the Dutch Anabaptist hymnal of 1562 called *Veelderhande Liedekens,* from which also at least 8 hymns were translated. Wolkan asserts (102) that the greater part of all the hymns in *Ein schon gesang-*

büchlein are translations from the Dutch, and that only some 23 are German originals. He is certain that the collection was made somewhere in the region of Cologne near the Dutch border. If so, it was most probably printed in Cologne or near by. It is almost impossible to determine which of the two hymnals, the Swiss *Geseng* or the German *Schon gesangbüchlein,* was printed first. It is quite possible that both were printed in the same year and that neither borrowed from the other. Wolkan speculates that the German book may have gotten its Swiss hymns from a corrupted manuscript, since the text of the same hymns varies so substantially (though in minor points) in the two books that it is scarcely likely that one copied directly from the printed form of the other. Both could have translated their German versions of Dutch hymns directly from the Dutch *Veelderhande Liedeķens.* The German book used many Dutch hymns, the Swiss book only five. These five hymns are, however, found in identical German form in the two books, with only slight editorial revisions in the Swiss book.

H.S.B.

J. P. Classen, "Editions of the *Ausbund,*" *Menn. Life* XII (1957) 47 f.; *idem,* "Ein schon gesangbüchlein Geistlicher lieder" (unprinted ms), which claims to know 5 editions; Rosella Duerksen, "Early German Anabaptist Hymn Books," *Menn. Life* XII (1957) 61-63, 96; *idem,* "Anabaptist Hymnody of the Sixteenth Century" (unpublished doctoral dissertation, Union Theological Seminary, N.Y., 1956).

Schön, Max, a statistician, a son of the teacher R. Schön in Orloff near Tiegenhof (*q.v.*) in West Prussia, Germany, the author of the book *Das Mennonitentum in Westpreussen* (Berlin, 1886), which with pregnant brevity gives a generally correct description of the Mennonites of West Prussia. (*Menn. Bl.,* 1880, 6 and 1; *ML* IV.) NEFF.

Schönau, a Mennonite village name transplanted from Prussia to the Molotschna settlement in the Ukraine and the Alexandertal settlement, Samara, Russia. This name was also found at Barnaul, and Minussinsk, Siberia; East and West reserves, Man.; Cuauhtemoc, Mexico; and Menno and Fernheim (Chaco), Paraguay. (See **Villages.**) C.K.

Schöneberg, a Prussian Mennonite village name transplanted to Chortitza in the Ukraine; the East Reserve, Man.; and Cuauhtemoc, Mexico. (See **Villages.**) C.K.

Schöneck, Kaspar von, an Anabaptist martyr: see **Schuester, Casper.**

Schönfeld Mennonite Church was established in the Schönfeld settlement in the district of Alexandrovsk, province of Ekaterinoslav, Russia, in 1868. Smaller subsidiary churches of the settlement were located at Rosenhof (*q.v.*) and Blumenfeld (*q.v.*). All of these congregations remained subsidiaries of the Lichtenau-Petershagen Mennonite Church (*q.v.*) of the Molotschna settlement. The elder of this church officiated at baptismal services and the Lord's Supper. The elders were Jakob Töws and Bernhard Epp. During the Revolution, Johann Klassen of the Schönwiese Mennonite Church served the congregation as elder.

In 1883 the first church building was erected at Schönfeld. Prior to this the congregation had worshiped in an old home. Rosenhof and Blumenfeld also each had a church building. Some worship services were conducted in private homes. In 1905 the number of souls in the Schönfeld Mennonite Church was 585, of whom 276 were baptized. The other two congregations had a total of 178, of whom 90 were baptized.

The first minister was Peter Neufeld who was elected on Jan. 12, 1873, and died in 1898. Other ministers were Kornelius H. Epp (1845-1916) who was elected by the Rosenhof church, and Jacob Enns who served the Rosenhof church and was an itinerant minister. Enns received training at a Bible school in Berlin. Jakob L. Dyck (Dück) (1852-1922) was elected minister March 1, 1881. When he came to Schönfeld in 1888 he was elected the leading minister of the church, which position he held until the settlement was dissolved. Gerhard Töws (1861-1924) was elected minister in 1892. Johann Driediger (b. 1871), elected minister in 1909, now lives in Canada. Nikolai Thiessen and Johann Hübert, missionaries in Java, were sons of the Schönfeld Mennonite settlement. The Schönfeld church building was destroyed in 1920. C.K.

Gerhard Töws, *Schönfeld. Werde- und Opfergang einer deutschen Siedlung in der Ukraine* (n.p., 1939).

Schönfeld Mennonite Settlement was located in the district of Alexandrovsk, province of Ekaterinoslav, Russia. The nucleus of the settlement was the estate consisting of 14,000 acres which was purchased from D. M. Brazol (*q.v.*), July 20, 1868. This land was located north of the Molotschna settlement and east of the Chortitza settlement and differed from most of the other Mennonite settlements of Russia because it was primarily purchased by individuals and scattered over a large area interspersed by numerous other German settlements and Russians. Only a few of the villages resembled the traditional pattern. Most of the dwelling places were scattered on estates. A second purchase of land was made in 1869 from the nobleman Chonuk. As in the first case the settlers came from the Molotschna. Two families, Cornelius Epp and Peter Epp, coming directly from Prussia purchased the Hutterian Bruderhof Kovalicha. The Hutterites then migrated to America. This total settlement became known as Schönfeld.

In 1885 a number of settlers purchased an estate consisting of 1,458 acres from the owner Samoylenko. The settlement became known as Schönbrunn. As a result of further purchases the Rosenhof settlement consisting of the estates Rosenhof, Tiegenhof, Blumental, Solenaya, Hochfeld, Schönberg, Bergtal, Oleyev, and Krukov, originated between 1855 and 1875. This settlement consisted of representatives from both the Molotschna and Chortitza settlements. Between the years 1875 and 1879 the villages Blumenheim and Kronberg and the estate Eichental were established by settlers coming from the Molotschna. A village, Silberfeld, near the station Pologi, had been previously established.

According to a table presented by Töws, the whole settlement consisted of 202 farms, 132,838 acres, and a population of 1,056. Among the railroad stations used by the settlers were: Gaichur, Mechetnaya, Obshaya, and Gulay Pole. The settlement had fourteen schools and one Zentralschule supported and administered by the Mennonites. Since the farms of the village were so scattered, most of the villages had more than one school. The three churches were located in Schönfeld, Blumenfeld, and Rosenhof (see **Schönfeld** Mennonite Church and **Rosenhof** Mennonite Church). The Mennonites obtained the right for self-administration of this scattered settlement known as the Schönfeld Volost (*q.v.*) (administration).

The Schönfeld settlement consisted primarily of farmers but soon a large network of industries developed. In Rosenhof Kornelius Epp and Abr. A. Sawatzky had brick factories. In Schönfeld there were a number of brick factories. Later flour mills originated in all areas. The Russian population in the surrounding territory made use of them. Schönfeld had a wagon factory and other factories, a foundry, and two sunflower seed presses. At the station Sofiyevka, Heinrich Neufeld had a factory for agricultural machinery. There were numerous business establishments in the villages. The annual fairs were attended by people from far and near.

In the realm of agriculture the Mennonites raised sheep, cattle, hogs, and horses. At the turn of the century hard winter wheat had generally been accepted. In matters of health the community was taken care of originally by the traditional "Knochenarzt," midwives, and chiropractors. Before World War I some trained physicians were available.

During World War I and the Revolution this settlement suffered similarly to the others. The settlement was occupied at one time by the German army, then again by the White army, and finally by the Red army. Before this happened the Mennonite settlement was dissolved. During the chaotic years of 1918-20 the bandits of the surrounding territory robbed the settlement and killed many inhabitants; those remaining fled to the other near-by settlements. After the establishment of the Soviet government some returned to their estates. Many of the homes were destroyed. The Schönfeld church was destroyed in 1920. The former inhabitants shared the fate of the Mennonites of other settlements. Some were exiled and others found their way to Canada and South America.   C.K.

Gerhard Töws, *Schönfeld. Werde- und Opfergang einer deutschen Siedlung in der Ukraine* (n.p., 1939).

Schönfeld Mennonite Volost (administration) came into being with the new Schönfeld Mennonite settlement in the district of Alexandrovsk, province of Ekaterinoslav, Russia. Since this settlement was scattered, it was difficult to persuade the local government to grant the Mennonites the customary privilege of self-government. After much effort, particularly by Peter Harder, the first secretary, the government recognized the Schönfeld Volost in 1873. The following villages belonged to it: Schönfeld, Silberfeld, Blumenheim, Kronberg, Rosenhof, and Blumenfeld. Schönfeld was in the center of the settlement and some of the villages were about twenty miles away. The following served the settlement as Oberschulze (mayor): Abraham Driediger,

Johann Cornies, Johann Dyck, and Heinrich Wiens. Secretaries were Peter Harder and David P. Dyck. In 1902 a new brick building was erected for the Schönfeld Volost.   C.K.

Gerhard Töws, *Schönfeld. Werde- und Opfergang einer deutschen Siedlung in der Ukraine* (n.p., 1939).

Schönfeld Mennonite Zentralschule of the Schönfeld Mennonite settlement (*q.v.*) was established in 1907 with Hermann A. Rempel as teacher. The first year instruction was given in the Schönfeld elementary school. During this year a dwelling place for the teacher which served as a temporary school was built. A second teacher Jacob J. Dueck was employed. In the fall of 1909 an impressive Zentralschule building was completed and Abraham P. Töws was added as third teacher. Hermann Rempel was succeeded by Franz Ediger, and Töws by G. Schroeder. Later teachers were Aron Rempel, Heinrich Neufeld, Peter Sawatzky, Susanna Loewen, Helena Froese, Jakob Thiessen, and Jakob Neufeld. First the school was for boys only but later it became coeducational. Two additional residences for teachers were built.   C.K.

Gerhard Töws, *Schönfeld. Werde- und Opfergang einer deutschen Siedlung in der Ukraine* (n.p., 1939) 49 ff.

Schönhorst, a Prussian Mennonite village name transplanted to the Chortitza settlement of the Ukraine; the East and West reserves of Manitoba; and Neuland, Paraguay. (See **Villages.**)   C.K.

Schönsee (Schoensee), a Prussian Mennonite village name transplanted to the Molotschna and Zagradovka settlement in the Ukraine; Barnaul and Amur, Siberia; East Reserve of Manitoba; and the Sommerfeld settlement, Villarrica, Paraguay. (See **Villages.**)   C.K.

Schönsee, a village in the Molotschna settlement, Taurida, South Russia, situated about 70 miles from the seaport of Berdyansk at the Sea of Azov, was one of the 18 oldest villages of the Molotschna, founded in 1804-6 by Mennonite settlers from Prussia. In 1812, the site having been found unsuitable, the village was transferred to another site some ten miles east. A typical Molotschna village of medium size, it contained 20 farms of about 160 acres each and a number of smaller farms of 40 acres each. At the end of the village were a number of houses whose inhabitants possessed no land but were craftsmen of different kinds (see **Anwohner**). The total land area was 4,200 acres, the population around 500 souls, who before World War I were almost exclusively Mennonites. The village contained a general store, a small factory manufacturing agricultural machinery and employing around 30 workers, a large flour mill, a blacksmith shop, and outside the village on a hill a large windmill of the Dutch type. But this type of mill, of which there were several in the Molotschna, was not used for pumping water as in Holland but for milling feed grain on a large scale. The school contained two classrooms and employed two teachers. At the eastern end of the village stood the new church completed a few years before World War I.

With the Russian revolution hard times began for the villagers, and a general decline followed. During the Civil War in 1919, Schönsee for several months was in the front line between the warring armies and suffered considerable damage. A number of the inhabitants were killed. During the 1930's a great number of people who had been prosperous were branded "kulaks" and banished to Siberia, mostly men. From the village of Schönsee alone this number reached 72.

Toward the end of World War II most of the remaining Mennonite inhabitants succeeded in escaping from Russia with the retreating German armies. But the greater part of these refugees were rounded up by the Russians in Poland and forcibly returned to Russia. As far as is known, they were not taken to their former homes but to Kazakhstan, a desolate province of central Asia. Only a very few inhabitants of Schönsee reached the Western Zone of Germany, from where in due time they emigrated to Canada or South America. The final fate of the village after the departure of the Mennonite population is unknown. H.G.

Schönsee (Polish, *Sosnovka*), a village in Poland, from 1772 until 1919 belonging to West Prussia, Germany, situated ten miles north of Culm (*q.v.*), about two miles from the right bank of the Vistula River, where Mennonites from the Netherlands settled as early as 1553 to reclaim and drain the swampy lands along the Vistula, being the first Mennonite settlement in the Culm region. The first land lease is lost, but a second one, of 1594, between the city of Culm, to which this territory belonged, and the farmers, still exists. In this and following leases only farming was allowed to the settlers; no handicrafts were permitted except weaving, tailoring, and shoemaking for private use. They were allowed to fish in the Vistula. The settlers, who lived at Schönsee and also in the surrounding villages and hamlets such as Jamerau, Dorposch, Lunau, and Schöneich, were explicitly granted the privilege of free exercise of their religion, including teaching in schools. The following Mennonite families are named in the land leases in 1695 after that: Unrau (Unruh), Siefert (Siebert), Hube(?), Block, Voth (Foth), Funk, Jans (Jantz), Buller, Köhn, Sperling, Stephan (Stevens, Steffens), Wilhelm (Willems), Boltz (Bolt), Stob (Stobbe), Tomasche (Thomsen), Meister, Decker, Penner, Brümmer(?), Mentz, Schümann (Schoman), Frantz, Abraham (Abrams), Pödker (Boetscher), Voutsche(?), Siedau(?), and from 1725 also Nickel, Bartel, Schröder, Nachtigal, Weitgraff (Weidegraf), Pancratz, Arndt (Arentsz), Eckert (Eggert), and Plener (Plenert). Besides these there are found in the list drawn up by Elder Hendrik Berents in 1719 the names of Schellenberg, Isaack, and Riggers (Richert). Since a number of these names are not Dutch-Frisian, other settlers must in the meantime have joined the original settlers.

As early as about 1570 there were two Mennonite congregations at Schönsee, one Flemish, whose meetinghouse was called "die kleine Schule" (small school), which sided with the Groningen Old Flemish (*q.v.*), and one Frisian (also called Waterlander),

whose meetinghouse, built in 1618, was called "die grosse Schule" (large school). They are small and very plain buildings (pictures in *Siedlungswerk* taken in 1940-41).

Concerning the early history of the Mennonites of Schönsee there is not much information. Social and religious development seems to have been favorable in the 16th and 17th centuries. Sometimes they were struck by calamities like floods and crop failures, but their tenacity and energy, and aid from their benevolent landlords, the city magistrates of Culm, easily overcame their blows. Both congregations of Schönsee were small in membership; the Frisians, concerning whom there is no further information, formed the larger one; in 1719 the Flemish numbered 48 baptized members. This Old Flemish group then belonged to the same congregation as Przechovka (*q.v.*, Wintersdorf) and Konopath on the left bank of the Vistula in the territory of Schwetz, and Posterwolt on the right bank. Although Schönsee was a part of this congregation, it obviously had its own preachers by this time. In 1760 a separation was made for practical reasons. Schönsee then became independent and its preacher Laurens Sperling was appointed elder. Repeatedly the Flemish Mennonites in this area were visited by elders from the Netherlands; mentioned are Jan Siebes (Seebes), Gerrit Roose, and Stieve Sand(?) in 1676. About 1700 Alle Derks (*q.v.*), the noted elder of the Old Flemish congregation at Groningen, visited the Old Flemish congregations in Prussia, including Schönsee, and in 1719 and again in 1733 Elder Hendrik Berents (Hulshoff, *q.v.*) was in Schönsee to perform baptism and administer communion and also to exercise church discipline. Of his visit Hendrik Barents made a circumstantial report, mentioning the names of the members and their conditions.

In 1727 a few Mennonites of the Frisian (Waterlander) branch, who had been expelled from East Prussia, settled near Schönsee. Among them were Heinrich Nickel and Gabriel Frantz, both preachers. They corresponded with the Dutch Committee for Foreign Needs at Amsterdam and both their letters and copies of the answers to these letters are in the Amsterdam Mennonite archives. This correspondence affords a clear idea of the situation of the Mennonites in this area about 1730. Both congregations were then using the same meetinghouse and the preacher of the Frisians, in the letters always called Waterlanders, was Derk Wichert. About this time the Catholic bishop of Culm insisted on harsh measures against the Mennonites, which could be prevented only by paying heavy taxes; they lived in constant fear of expulsion. The estates were flooded by the Vistula, and there were many years of crop failure and even of famine. The Dutch Mennonites supported their coreligionists in these misfortunes.

In 1765 a number of Old Flemish Mennonites from Przechovka and Schönsee moved to Brenkenhoffswalde (*q.v.*) and Franztal in the Neumark; others emigrated to Deutsch-Kazun (*q.v.*) about 1780 and still others to Volhynia (*q.v.*) in the early 19th century. These emigrations appreciably decreased particularly the number of Flemish Mennonites in this area.

The Dutch *Naamlijst* from 1743 to 1802 also names the ministers in the Schönsee congregations. In the Old Flemish congregation the ministers were Laurens Sperling, elder 1760; Peter Pancratz, preacher 1760; Jacob Wedel, preacher; Peter Jantz, preacher 1773; the *Naamlijst* of 1780 names only Peter Pancratz; in 1786 Pancratz is missing; the preachers are Benjamin Wedel and Tobias Jantzen, both appointed in 1785. The list of ministers of the Frisian congregation is more complete; they were Peter Dirks before 1743-*c*58; Gabriel Frantz, Sievert Tjart, Jan Siebrandt before 1743-*c*50; Peter Nickel before 1743-*c*80; Cornelis Frantz, elder *c*1750-58; Andries Gertz, preacher *c*1750-62; Hendrik Cornelissen 1757-59; Peter Tjart 1757-62; Gertgen Knoop 1759-*c*81; David Bartel *c*1752-65; Cornelis Frantz, preacher 1763, elder 1776-*c*88; Heinrich Siebrandt 1786-? ; Peter Baltzer 1771-*c*96; Jacob Gertz 1775-*c*98; Heinrich Tjart 1788-after 1802; Timotheus Boltz 1788-after 1802; Jacob Frantz, preacher 1791, elder 1794-after 1802.

On Oct. 12, 1849, the small Old Flemish congregation of Schönsee, then numbering 39 souls, merged with the Frisian congregation. The Flemish meetinghouse was abandoned; the old Frisian meetinghouse of 1618, somewhat remodeled, was used until 1945. The united Schönsee congregation numbered 364 baptized members in 1852, 320 in 1880, 273 in 1927, 179 in 1941. Johann Stobbe, preacher 1851, was elder 1875-1906, Johann Bartel, preacher 1898, elder 1906-1945). The congregation had its own home for the aged.

In the spring of 1945 with the coming of the Russian armies the congregation of Schönsee was wiped out.   vdZ.

Herbert Wiebe, *Das Siedlungswerk niederländischer Mennoniten im Weichseltal* (Marburg a.d.Lahn, 1952) 8, 35 f., 37, 56 note 45, 57 note 16, 81 f., 87-91, 95 f.; "Bezoekreis van Hendrik Berents Hulshoff aan de Doopsgezinde gemeenten der Oude Vlamingen in Pruisen en Polen," in *Bijdragen en Mededeelingen van het Historisch Genootschap* LIX (Utrecht, 1938) 32-82, particularly 64, 76 f., 80; *Inv. Arch. Amst.* I, *passim*, particularly Nos. 1097 f., 1581, 1597, 1599 f., 1604 f., 1611-14, 1641 f., 1647; *Naamlijst* issues 1743-1802; Mannhardt, *Jahrbuch* 1882, 17, 19; 1888, 15; *Menn. Bl.*, Dec. 1939, 75 f.; *Gem.-Kal.*, 1941, 115; *Cosch.-Bl.* IV (1939) 34-36; *Menn. Life* X (April 1955) 76, 78; *ML* IV, 88.

Schönsee Mennonite Church, Molotschna, Taurida, South Russia, was until 1842 a part of the large Lichtenau congregation and from then until the beginning of the century a part of the Margenau congregation. In 1903 it became independent under its own elder, Heinrich Peters. The greater part of the inhabitants of the following villages belonged to the Schönsee congregation: Fürstenau, Fabrikerwiese, Schönsee, Liebenau, Wernersdorf, about one quarter of Hamberg and Klippenfeld, and some of the large estates lying at some distance from the Molotschna in a southeasterly direction, altogether about 1500 souls. Almost without exception they were farmers whose forefathers had come from the Danzig district of Prussia at the beginning of the 19th century. Sunday school was introduced only after the revolution, when religious instruction was prohibited at the day schools. The congregation had a choir but there was no instrument to accompany the singing.

The first church building was erected in 1831 behind the orchards of the village of Schönsee, all of wood in the old Prussian church style. Later it was surrounded by mighty trees and, although simple and small, had a beauty of its own. In 1909 a new church was built at the eastern end of the village of much larger size and in a more modern style, one of the largest and most beautiful Mennonite churches in Russia.

Some of the more prominent ministers of the congregation were Elder Heinrich Peters (*q.v.*), who served his congregation with great devotion as minister from 1885 and as elder from 1903 until his death in 1920 during the great typhoid epidemic; Jacob Renpenning (1885-1922), owner of a large agricultural machinery factory in the village of Fabrikerwiese, who was a good speaker and earnest Christian; and Bernhard Wiens 1903-30, who besides being an outstanding minister for 19 years, served the village of Schönsee as a very efficient schoolteacher. But the most important minister the congregation ever had was Alexander Ediger (*q.v.*), who was called to the ministry at an hour (1922) when the storms of the revolution and the civil war swept the country. He was a man of exceptional intellectual and spiritual power, whose influence extended far beyond the boundaries of the Molotschna. In 1931 Elder Ediger was imprisoned at Melitopol and later banished to Murmansk. Johann Görz, a young minister, continued to conduct services for a while in private homes until he also was banished. The church building was first turned into a granary and then into a communist club. A large stage was erected at the front with a curtain picturing the goddess of beauty. Between the windows on the walls life-sized pictures of Lenin, Stalin, and other leaders of the revolution were placed. During the German occupation the building again for a short time was used as a church. (Friesen, *Brüderschaft.*)
                                                          H.G.

Schönsee Mennonite Church (GCM), located at the eastern edge of Tofield, Alberta, a member of the Canadian Conference of Mennonites, was organized on June 15, 1936, by Mennonite immigrants from Russia who began to arrive in 1924. The congregation has seven ordained ministers. David A. Heidebrecht has served the congregation as minister since 1929 and as elder since 1942. A new church was dedicated in 1937. In 1958 the leader was Johann Neufeld, and the assisting ministers were David Boese, Abraham Epp, Peter Regehr, Gerhard Franz, and Abraham Heidebrecht. The membership in 1958 was 189.   D.A.H.

Schöntal, a Mennonite village name found in the Bergthal settlement in the Ukraine, in the Barnaul settlement in Siberia, in the East and West reserves of Manitoba, the Old Colony settlement at Swift Current, Sask., Cuauhtemoc (twice) and Durango, Mexico, and in the Menno and Neuland colonies in the Chaco, Paraguay. (See **Villages.**)   C.K.

Schöntal Mennonite Brethren Church, established in the early days of the Slavgorod Mennonite settlement (*q.v.*), Siberia, served the following 10 villages: Schöntal, Rosenwald, Nikolaipol, Reinfeld,

Alexeyfeld, Protassov, Gnadenfeld, Tiege, Grünfeld, and Berezovka. The first leading minister was Aron Reimer; he was ordained elder in 1920. When he went to Canada in 1925 he was succeeded by Abram Janz and later by Dietrich Görzen. Other ministers were Peter Neufeld, Jacob Wall, Heinrich Franz, David Thielmann, Wilhelm Federau, Cornelius Plett, Andreas Nachtigall, Johann Klassen, Heinrich Dück, Heinrich Funk, and Jakob Bergen. The congregation erected a church building in Schöntal 1910. C.K.

Gerhard Fast, *In den Steppen Sibiriens* (Rosthern, 1957) 76.

Schöntal Mennonite Church: see **Pleasant Valley Mennonite Church.**

Schönwiese: see also **Schoenwiese.**

Schönwiese (Schoenwiese), a common Mennonite village name transplanted from Schönwiese near Chortitza in the Ukraine to Barnaul, Siberia; East and West reserves of Manitoba; Swift Current, Sask.; Cuauhtemoc, Mexico; Menno in the Chaco, and Villarrica in the Sommerfeld settlement, Paraguay. (See **Villages.**) C.K.

Schönwiese, a former Mennonite village, which became a suburb of Alexandrovsk (Zaporozhe) on the Dniepr in 1911. After the destruction of Neukronsweide, Schönwiese was the center of the Kronsweide Mennonite Church, with a church (erected in 1862) and a school. The settlement was founded on the "beautiful meadow" on the Moskwa, a tributary of the Dniepr, in 1797, by seventeen families of stragglers in the great emigration from West Prussia in 1789. They were given such large advances by the Russian government that they were able to build small homes the first winter in Russia. It was a very important center for all the German settlements in Russia. Geographically the place offered many advantages with Alexandrovsk, a railroad center, in the north and the wide navigable Dniepr in the west. The largest milling firms and factories for the manufacture of mowers in all Russia were located in Schönwiese, all with Mennonite owners.

From the first, the milling industry here did a thriving business. In the 1850's and 1860's a dozen German windmills stood in a close circle. Peter Bock became a widely noted builder of mills, and employed as many as fifty workers in his factory; he supplied the entire Ukraine with wind- and treadmills. The settlers of Schönwiese at first engaged in agriculture and sheep raising, but soon found industry more profitable. They sold most of their land, keeping only the Dniepr lowlands. During World War I, when liquidation threatened, they sold even this land, about 3,240 acres, to the town of Alexandrovsk. Schönwiese suffered severely during the war and the Revolution, especially because it was the seat of a number of very prosperous Mennonite firms: Lepp and Wallmann, A. Koop, Hermann Niebuhr, Hildebrandt and Priess, and J. Badowsky (Lutheran). During the Civil War the front passed over Schönwiese twenty-three times, and all industry was halted. Not until the Soviet

government had restored order could work be resumed, but then the plants were nationalized.

Among the older leaders there were some striking personalities. One of these was the minister Andreas Vogt (1854-1914). Since the Lutherans and Roman Catholics of the town had had no pastor for decades, "Uncle" (*Ohm*) Vogt helped all with their spiritual problems. Kornelius Hübert (1835-97) was a teacher, chorister, and faithful counselor in all kinds of spiritual and material, legal and commercial matters. A pupil of Heinrich Franz (*q.v.*), he taught the village school for twenty years. (For later developments, see **Zaporozhe.**) D.H.E.

Schönwiese Mennonite Brethren Church was established in the early days of the Slavgorod Mennonite settlement (*q.v.*), Siberia. The first leading minister was Peter Bergen, who was succeeded in 1923 by Heinrich Janzen, who in turn was succeeded in 1926 by Heinrich H. Klassen. The last leading minister was Heinrich Matthies. Additional ministers were Heinrich Janzen, Abram Friesen, and Nikolai Franz. In 1911 a church building was erected in Schönwiese. Originally this congregation was a part of the Alexandrovka M.B. Church. C.K.

Gerhard Fast, *In den Steppen Sibiriens* (Rosthern, 1957) 75.

Schönwiese Mennonite Church, Alexandrovsk, Ukraine, was a branch of the Kronsweide Mennonite Church (*q.v.*). Some of the ministers who served the church and lived in the village of Schönwiese (*q.v.*) were Peter Krahn, Jakob Janzen, and Peter Janzen. A meetinghouse was erected in Schönwiese in 1862. In distinction from the Chortitza Mennonite Church, which was of Flemish background, this church was Frisian. C.K.

D. H. Epp, *Die Chortitzer Mennoniten* (Odessa, 1889) 105; Friesen, *Brüderschaft,* 702.

School and College Journal was the first official publication of Bethel College, published by the board of directors January 1895-December 1902. It was succeeded by the separate language editions, *Monatsblätter aus Bethel College* and *Bethel College Monthly.* The *School and College Journal* was an 8-page, 8½ x 11½, monthly periodical, published in both German and English, and printed by A. Wiebusch and Son Printing Co., St. Louis, until August 1896, when this work was transferred to Newton. The contents consisted of editorials, news of Bethel College, financial reports, and general cultural and religious articles. David Goerz edited the *Journal.* J.F.S.

Schoolmeester, Valerius de: see **Valerius.**

Schoonhoven, a town in the Dutch province of South Holland (1947 pop. 4,869; 2 Mennonites), was formerly the seat of a Mennonite congregation, which belonged to the moderate Flemish branch. Concerning this congregation, which was always a small one, there is only scant information. Of its origin nothing is known. Albert Jans(s)en was its preacher about 1608. In 1614 Leenaert Clock (*q.v.*) moved from Haarlem to Schoonhoven and lived here for some time, serving the congregation together with Jan Lammersz. In 1641 Esaias Janse van Nottelen, a Flemish preacher at Rotterdam, accepted a call of the Schoonhoven congregation, but already in 1649 it was without a preacher and in the following decades only occasionally preachers from Gouda, Rotterdam, Dordrecht, and Utrecht conducted services at Schoonhoven. The congregation died out some time before 1700.   vDZ.

Inv. Arch. Amst. I, No. 531; Blaupot t. C., *Holland* I, 222, 330; *DB* 1863, 96, 102.

Schoorl, a village in the Dutch province of North Holland, in the neighborhood of which is found a Mennonite Brotherhood Home (*Broederschapshuis*), operated since July 1, 1932. A church was dedicated on July 16, 1951. This home is used during the summer for conferences and special meetings and also as a vacation center. From November 1950 until December 1956 a number of aged "displaced persons" from Eastern Europe were sheltered in the Van-de-Water House, a building not far from the Brotherhood Home. Since February 1958 the Van-de-Water House has also been sheltering a number of children (formerly at Oud-Wulven, *q.v.*), who are being educated here under the care of the Dutch Mennonite Bijzondere Noden foundation. (*DJ* 1950, 49 f.)   vDZ.

Schopfheim, a town (pop. 4,649) in Baden, Germany, about 10 miles northeast of Basel, is the seat of a small Mennonite congregation which is a member of the Gemeindeverband (*q.v.*) and was organized in 1949 by members of the Ueberlingen (*q.v.*) congregation living in or near the town. In 1957 the membership (baptized and children) was 31. Services were held in Steinen i. Wiesental by visiting ministers since there was no resident minister.

H.S.B.

Schorant, Wolfgang: see Uolimann, Wolfgang.

Schornbaum, Karl (1875-1953), a Lutheran scholar of Bavaria, Germany, church historian and research specialist in Anabaptist history, was born in Thundorf, Lower Franconia, studied theology and philosophy at the universities of Erlangen, Greifswald, and Kiel, was vicar in Thalmosing 1897-99, instructor in catechism at Nürnberg 1899-1907, received his doctorate in philosophy at Erlangen in 1907, was pastor at Alfeld 1907-22, received his doctorate in theology at Erlangen in 1910, was dean at Roth near Nürnberg 1922-31, director of the state church archives in Nürnberg 1931-46, and retired in 1946. In 1932 he received the chair of Bavarian church history at Erlangen, and the title of honorary professor in 1945. He was the editor of the *Zeitschrift für bayrische Kirchengeschichte* and chairman of the Association for Bavarian Church History, and also of the Association for the History of Nürnberg. He wrote many books and articles on Franconian church history; e.g., *Markgrafen Casimir und Georg von Brandenburg.* A major contribution to Anabaptist history was his publication of the *Täuferakten* (*q.v.*) for Bavaria, *Quellen zur Geschichte der Wiedertäufer* (*Bayern* I, 1934, *Bayern* II, 1950.) He died in 1953.   E.T.

Schorndorf, a city (pop. 12,268) in Württemberg, Germany, fifteen miles east of Stuttgart, in the fertile Rems Valley.

Joseph Beck records only one Anabaptist martyr for Schorndorf in 1527-31; the court records do not mention him. Nevertheless there are frequent references to Anabaptists in Schorndorf during that time. In 1528 Hans Glut of Schorndorf was tried on the rack, and said he had been baptized in 1527 at Hainebach near Esslingen. A court record of 1533 points out the spread of the Anabaptists in this region.

Under Duke Ulrich there were more Anabaptists in Schorndorf and the vicinity after 1535. Hans Volmar of Geradstetten had been in Moravia and was banished from the town in 1535; the same lot befell Katharina Schneck in 1536, Wendel Rumel of Hebsack in 1533, Michel Weber of Rohrbronn in 1533, Stephan Jetzlin and Endris Sigwart of Steinenberg, and in 1539 Jakob Hüll of Schorndorf. For a while the persecution apparently stopped. In 1545 a woman of Schorndorf fled to Stetten, an Anabaptist haven, likewise a cooper Hans Walch; at the same time Heinrich Walch, presumably a brother of Hans, and mayor of Schorndorf, was banished, because he had "been somewhat careless" (*sich etwas übersehen*).

After the interim the search for Anabaptists began anew under Duke Christoph. In 1545 the duke had been informed of Anabaptist disturbances in the vicinity. The trials of Stoffel Schuhmacher of Beutelsbach in 1555 and Jakob Wachter in 1557 show that there was ground for suspicion. On April 2, 1558, Sixt Weselin, the magistrate (*Vogt*) of Schorndorf, reported that Peter and Endris Stirmmer (Sturmmer?) of Rudersberg with his family, and Ulrich Lemblin's wife had emigrated to Moravia at the instigation of Paul Glock (*q.v.*) and Hans von Schrotsberg, leaving all their property. Three trials of this year—Lienhart Rauch, and Martin and Georg Weller of Manoldsheim—indicate the vigor of the Moravian emissaries. Not all of the converts were pleased with the Moravian life. In 1559 Sixt Weselin reported to the government that Michel Honacker and Hans Braun had fled to Moravia from Mittelschlechtbach with their families in 1558, but had now returned. They were examined in Stuttgart, had to recant before the mayor and the court, and were assigned a special pew in the church.

In 1560 Stephan Haug, called Jetzlin, who had twice joined the Anabaptists, was expelled from the village, and Hans Peter of Weiler from the countryside. In 1561 the Anabaptists were stirring in Necklinsberg. Apollonia Geiger, a widow, was under indoctrination in Stuttgart. In Schnait a property confiscated from Anabaptists was leased out. Stoffel Schuhmacher of Beutelsbach had backslidden and was tried in Stuttgart in 1562; in Leonberg he was examined on the rack and then expelled from the country. In Esslingen, an imperial city, the following Anabaptists of the Schorndorf region were tried before officials of Württemberg: Bastian Weber of Beutelsbach, Lienhard Sommer of Necklinsberg, Stephan Utzlin (Jetzlin), called Haug, of Steinenberg, Peter Lang of Schorndorf, Abraham Halbgewachsen and Hans Kugelin of Schnait, Ulrich Hauwer of Krähwinkel, and Jörg Bichler (Bühler) of Miedelsbach. Bastian was thought to be a *Vorsteher* on account of his determination, and Stephan Haug proved to be one. Peter Land and Halbgewachsen were put under oath not to return to Esslingen. The fate of the others is not known.

In 1563 the citizens of Rudersberg asked for the property of Peter Hasel and his wife, who had emigrated to Moravia in 1555. In 1564 Anna Krauter, young Hans Heutling's wife, of Schorndorf, and Bastian Schuhmacher's wife, of Hebsach, left their homes; in 1565 Claus Frey of Beutelsbach likewise, though he returned in 1569 and asked for a hearing. In 1570 the authorities expelled from the country Leonhart and Hans Sommerer of Necklinsberg, Caspar Dautel of Hosslinswart, Apollonia Trieber of Kleinheppach, Christian Seiferlin and Friedrich Bauer of Endersbach, Aquila Schöberlin of Schorndorf, Jous Gump and Marx Wellhaf of Strumpfelbach, Bastian Weber of Beutelsbach, Anna Weissgarber of Winterbach, Maria Schmid of Heppach, Marx and Barbara Schöberlin of Schorndorf, Andas Dilgen, and the daughter of Beutelsbach. Blasius Greiner of Walkersbach was required to recant in Schorndorf in 1569 before the entire congregation in church; the formula of recantation prescribed for him became the model. In 1573 the district (*Amt*) of Schorndorf was inspected for Anabaptists and special attention was paid them in the future. The Greiner family (*q.v.*) in the remote Walkersbach caused the authorities much trouble, likewise the family of Marx Schöberlin. In 1582 Simon Kress, an apostle from Moravia, was seized in Oberurbach. This community was closely watched until the Thirty Years' War; in 1633 there were still some Anabaptists there, besides "many disorderly people."

The confiscated Anabaptist property in the Schorndorf area was valued at 6,838 guilders and 31½ kreutzer in 1580-1613. Schorndorf was also the home of Johannes Walch (*q.v.*) of Nürtingen, deacon there 1578-82, who was dismissed as a Swiss Anabaptist. (*TA Württemberg; ML* IV.) G. Bos.

Schotanus, Christianus (1603-71), was a Reformed pastor and from 1639 a professor at the University of Franeker, Friesland, Netherlands, where he at first taught Greek and history and later also theology. His most outstanding book was *De Geschiedenissen kerkelyck ende wereltlyck van Friesland oost ende west . . . tot op het jaer 1583* (Franeker, 1658), which, though antiquated in its first part, is still of importance for the history of the 16th century. Schotanus was a bitter antagonist of the Mennonites and attacked them in *Van de Gronden der Mennisterij, ofte Waerschouwinghe over 't Bloed-tooneel der Doopsgesinde van Thieleman Jans van Bracht* (Leeuwarden, 1671). This book, written by order of the Reformed Synod in Friesland, severely criticizes van Braght's *Martyrs' Mirror* (*q.v.*), first edition of 1660. Schotanus' main theses are: the Waldenses have not preserved the Apostolic traditions; the Mennonites have their origin in the Münster (*q.v.*) revolt; the government should be on guard as to the Mennonites; because of ungodly revolutionary principles in the past, they should not be granted toleration. This book by Schotanus is very biased and has no historic value. vDZ.

N.N.B.Wb. V, 700; *Bibliographie des Martyrologes Prot. Néerl.* II (The Hague, 1890) 597-99.

Schot(t)land: see **Danzig.**

Schottland Bible: see **Meulen, Quiryn van der.**

Schotvanger, Jan Dirksz (d. 1737 at Amsterdam, Netherlands), was a preacher of the Old Frisian (Arke Noachs) congregation at Amsterdam in 1707-35. He was one of the lay preachers who led this church for a number of years, others being Cornelis Lely (*q.v.*), Cornelis Schellinger (*q.v.*), and Marten Schagen (*q.v.*). Though there is not much information concerning Schotvanger, it is known that he was pious, capable, and hard-working. Cornelis Lely delivered his funeral sermon. (Blaupot t. C., *Holland* II, 187.) vDZ.

Schouten, common Dutch family name. There was a Mennonite Schouten family in the Waterlander congregation of Amsterdam from c1580, where Lourens Jans Schouten was a deacon from 1612, as were some other members of this family. The Schoutens of Amsterdam were engaged in business and well-to-do. Maerten Schouten was a lay preacher at Knollendam (*q.v.*) 1754-c74. (*Inv. Arch. Amst.* I, No. 520, and church records of Amsterdam.) vDZ.

Schouwenburg, van, a prominent Dutch Mennonite family, originally of Harlingen in Friesland, where they were owners of brickyards and tileworks from the early 18th century or before. Some of its members were deacons at Harlingen and later at Zaandam, where a branch of the Schouwenburgs lived from the 19th century. A side branch is the Menalda van Schouwenburg family. vDZ.

Schowalter: see also **Showalter.**

Schowalter, Christian (1828-1907), was born in Assenheim, Palatinate, Germany, of Swiss ancestry, on Nov. 11, 1828 (1829?). In 1845-46 he attended a Bible school at Beuggen and then for three years the normal school at Schiers, Switzerland, from which he was graduated in 1849. After teaching for one year at Deutschhof, Bavaria, he emigrated to Ohio. After three years of teaching in Ohio he was called to the parochial school of the Zion Mennonite Church at Donnellson, Iowa, and served as teacher here, which position he filled for thirty-six years, 1853-89, with an interruption of two years. Here he married Rosina Heffner (Haffner) on Oct. 25, 1855.

In 1858 a movement arose for greater unity among Mennonite churches. Schowalter, then a teacher, was one of the promoters of this vision. In 1860 he was chosen as secretary of a meeting held at West Point, Iowa, to outline steps for such a unification. He became a member of the committee that drew up the "Plan of Union" which was the beginning of the General Conference Mennonite Church (*q.v.*). He was a member of the committee that prepared the handbook for ministers, and served as the president of the Foreign Mission Board 1896-1902.

When the question of higher education for Mennonite youth came up in Conference circles Schowalter mapped out a course of instruction and principles on which a school could be conducted. His plans met with favor and on Jan. 2, 1868, he was induced to become principal of the Wadsworth School, Ohio, and was the first man ever to head a Mennonite institution of higher learning in America. He held this position nearly two years and at the end of his principalship visited Germany with his family.

In 1861 Schowalter was chosen by lot to succeed the pastor of the Zion Mennonite Church (*q.v.*) and was ordained to the ministry by David Ruth in 1862. He introduced the Sunday school in his church as well as a young people's society. He wrote a German catechism for the General Conference in 1871 which was accepted in 1881. In 1907 he retired from the ministry because of failing health, and died April 13, 1907.   C.K.

"Rev. Christian Schowalter, A Memorial Biography," *Bethel College Bulletin* (April 20, 1938); H. P. Krehbiel, *The History of the General Conference of the Mennonites of North America* I (Canton, 1898) 417-21; Melvin Gingerich, *The Mennonites in Iowa* (Iowa City, 1939) 81-82.

Schowalter Foundation, Inc., a Mennonite philanthropic organization, was founded in 1954. Its chairman in 1957 was O. O. Miller, Akron, Pa., and its president and general manager H. J. Andres, Newton, Kan. Its six trustees represent the G.C.M., M.C., and C.G.C. Mennonite branches, the three groups named in the will of J. A. Schowalter (1879-1953), which bequeathed most of his assets to the Foundation, the income from which is to be used for relief work, training of ministers and missionaries, and for the promotion of peace. The total appraised value of the estate was more than $1,157,000. Schowalter immigrated to America from Germany in 1883 and soon settled in Harvey County, Kan., where he lived the rest of his life. He acquired his fortune through wheat farming, land investments, and oil. He was active in the G.C. Mennonite Church as a layman and contributed liberally to missions, relief, and church institutions. He served two terms in the Kansas state legislature (1934-36 and 1936-38).   M.G.

Schräffl, Georg, an Anabaptist martyr of Rungen in Tirol, Austria, was executed with his servant at Michelsburg (*q.v.*) in the summer of 1531. They had been seized by Christoph Ochs, the judge of Michelsburg, with a number of "simple minded folk," who were released. But Schräffl and his servant were sentenced to death as backsliders. (*ML* IV.)
                                              NEFF.

Schrag (Schrock, Shrock, Schrack, Schragg), a Mennonite family name of Swiss origin found in the Palatinate after 1664. From Germany members of the family migrated to Galicia in 1773, and from there to the Russian province of Volhynia. In 1874 members of the Schrag family left Russia in the migration of the settlement to America and located in Kansas and South Dakota, where they are generally members of the General Conference Mennonite Church. In 1937, three were in the G.C.M. ministry. Martin Schrag of the faculty of Messiah College, Menno Schrag, editor of the *Mennonite Weekly Review,* and John Schrag, on the faculty of Grace Bible Institute, are representatives of the Volhynia branch of the family.

Other members of the Schrag family emigrated directly from Germany and Switzerland to America.

As early as 1766 a Johannes Schrag landed in Philadelphia. Casper Schrock, born in Switzerland *c*1745, came to America as a young man and settled in Somerset County, Pa. His son Peter (1795-1846) was an Amish Mennonite minister in Wayne County, Ohio. Many of his descendants live in Ohio and Indiana. Among the early members of the East Zorra (*q.v.*) Amish Mennonite Church, organized *c*1837 in Ontario, were Daniel Schragg, John Schrag, and Joseph Schrag. Daniel Schrag (1813-91) was born in Bavaria, lived in Pennsylvania, and settled in Ontario, where he became a minister of the East Zorra Church in 1849. Descendants of the Ontario Schrags live in New York and Ontario.

The genealogy of the Tobias Schrock (Schrag) family shows many of his descendants living in Amish communities in Illinois, Iowa, and Kansas. He was born in Holmes County, Ohio, in 1823. Obituaries in Mennonite periodicals show the Mennonite (MC) and Amish branches of the family to be most numerously represented in Indiana, followed by Ohio, Kansas, and Illinois. In these two branches of the church 32 Schrock (Shrock) ministers were serving in 1937. Among the better-known members of the family was Andrew A. Schrock (1863-1949), for many years the bishop of the Metamora Mennonite Church (*q.v.*), at Metamora, Ill., and Tobe Schrock (1897-   ), bishop of the Bowne Mennonite Church (*q.v.*) at Elmdale, Mich. M.G.

Schregel, De, a former Mennonite family of Leiden, Holland, where between 1680 and 1769 seven of its members served as deacons, one of them for six terms.   vDZ.

Le Poole, *Bijdragen tot de kennis van . . . de Doopsgezinden te Leiden* (Leiden, 1905).

Schreiner, Wolf: see **Schominger, Wolf.**

Schrijver, a Dutch Mennonite family of Flemish descent. To this family belongs Gillis (*q.v.*) Schrijver, a Mennonite elder in Flanders, who played a part in the Flemish-Frisian quarrels at Harlingen in 1666-67. In the early 17th century a branch of this family was living in Utrecht; from here the family spread over a number of North Holland towns. Cornelis and Coenraad Schrijver were Mennonite merchants at Amsterdam in the 18th century. Pieter Schrijver (*q.v.*) was a Mennonite minister. A Tobias Schrijver, a Mennonite, managed a lace factory at Kampen from 1760. About 1650 a Mennonite Schrijver (Schryfer) family was living at Goch, Germany. (Blaupot t. C., *Holland* I, 329 note 2; *DB* 1881, 96 f.; *Inv. Arch. Amst.* II, Nos. 2573 f.)   vDZ.

Schrijver, Pieter Arends (b. Nov. 11, 1665, at Hoorn, d. April 11, 1742, at Haarlem), was a preacher of the Waterlander congregation at Hoorn 1691-1706 and of the united Flemish, Frisian, and High German congregation on the Klein Heiligland at Haarlem 1706 (elder 1710) until his death. He was known for his conservative views and his attachment to the old Mennonite confessions. A volume of his sermons, *Evangelische Genade-Leere betoogd in predicatien,* appeared after his death (Amsterdam, 1746). He married Maria Maatschoen, who died in 1727; in the same year two of his sons died, aged 23 and 27. By trade he was a dyer. It is very curious that this conservative man was among the first Mennonites to wear a fashionable wig with powdered curls (see his portrait). vDZ.

Schijn-Maatschoen, *Geschiedenis* III, 484-91, where Schrijver's portrait is found; *DB* 1873, 42, 51; *ML* IV.

Schrobenhausen, a town in Upper Bavaria (*q.v.*), Germany, in which there was a small Anabaptist congregation in the middle of the 16th century, which met in the home of a shoemaker, Hans Lohr. It was violently disbanded in 1559. (See **Bavaria;** *ML* IV.) NEFF.

Schrock: see also **Schrag.**

Schrock, Andrew A. (1863-1949), a Mennonite (MC) bishop, was born in Alsace, France, on Oct. 28, 1863, and came to the Metamora community from Alsace at the age of six. On Jan. 12, 1888, he married Barbara Bachman; eight children were born to this union. On July 8, 1894, he was ordained as a minister and on April 24, 1898, as bishop. He served the Metamora congregation faithfully and was also used widely in other congregations in the Western A.M. Conference. He was moderator of this Conference on six different occasions.

Andrew A. Schrock was a kindly man with an absorbing interest in the welfare of the church and his responsibility for preserving the faith. He was able to adapt himself to the times in such a way that the congregations under his oversight were able to make the necessary transitions without undue friction. Bishop Schrock was singularly humble and sincere, and a faithful and worthy servant of the church during a very difficult period. He died April 7, 1949. T.R.S.

Schröder (Schroeder, Schroeter), a family name originally found among Mennonites in Danzig and West Prussia. The name was recorded as early as 1605 and appeared in the congregations of Tiegenhagen, Fürstenwerder, Orloff, Tragheimerweide, Montau-Gruppe, Schönsee, Danzig, Königsberg, and Elbing. From here the name was transplanted to the Ukraine (see B. H. Unruh and H. H. Schröder). Peter Schroeder, of the Crimea, was a Mennonite representative in the Duma in St. Petersburg. "Franz and Schroeder" was an agricultural machinery factory of Halbstadt, Molotschna, and Heinrich Schroeder, of Halbstadt, was a manufacturer of motors. Johann Schroeder (*q.v.*) was the second elder of the Michalin Mennonite Church (*q.v.*), Poland, and the first elder of the Gnadenberg Mennonite Church (*q.v.*), Kansas. P. R. Schroeder (*q.v.*) was a leading G.C.M. minister. Elizabeth A. Schroeter, of Reedley, Cal., wrote a fictionalized account of the Mennonite migration from the Ukraine to America, entitled *From Here to the Pinnacles* (New York, 1956). The name is found in Canada, the United States, and South America. C.K.

Reimer, *Familiennamen,* 117; *Who's Who Among the Mennonites* (Newton, 1943) 215; Heinrich H. Schröder, *Russlanddeutsche Friesen* (Döllstädt, 1936) p. 96; B. H. Unruh, *Hintergründe,* 427; *ML* IV, 97; *Gem. Kal.,* 1906, 89.

Schroeder: see also **Schröder.**

32

Schroeder, Johann (1815-99), the second elder of the Gnadenberg Mennonite Church of Michalin, Polish Russia, was born in Michalin in May 1815, a son of Johann and Rebecca Isaac Schröder. He was baptized in 1833, and elected minister of the congregation in 1848, and ordained elder Sept. 17, 1852. (The *Christlicher Bundesbote* states that he was elected minister 1843 and elder the following year.) He married Helena Nickel on May 25, 1847, and with the entire Michalin congregation he and his family came to America in 1874, settling east of Newton, Kan., where he continued as elder of the congregation, which was renamed the Gnadenberg (*q.v.*) Mennonite Church (GCM), established in 1875 near Newton. Five children lived to maturity. Elder Schroeder died April 19, 1899. J.F.S.

Christlicher Bundesbote, June 8, 1899; Church Record of Gnadenberg Mennonite Church on deposit at Bethel College Historical Library; *Namensverzeichniss der . . . Mennoniten-Gemeinden* (Danzig, 1857).

Schroeder, Peter R. (1888-1941), was born Aug. 22, 1888, at Mountain Lake, Minn., where he attended the elementary school, German school, and high school. He graduated from Bethel College in 1912 and took some additional work at the University of Chicago, at the School of Theology at Winona Lake, and the University of South Dakota. On Sept. 1, 1910, he married Susie T. Nickel of Mountain Lake. In June 1912 Schroeder became the assistant pastor of the Berne (Ind.) Mennonite Church, although he and his wife had planned to go to India as missionaries. Four daughters were born to them: Celeste, Vernell, Louise, and Esther Ruth. Schroeder was ordained in 1914 by S. F. Sprunger. During his ministry at Berne the church grew in membership from 776 to 1042, as well as growing in other areas. In 1928-30 he served as president of Freeman Junior College, at Freeman, S.D. In 1930 he resigned and became the pastor of the Salem Mennonite Church at Freeman, but continued as Bible teacher of the college until 1936.

In 1933 Schroeder was elected president of the General Conference Mennonite Church. This office he held for two terms, a total of 12 years. In 1936 he attended the third Mennonite World Conference in the Netherlands. In 1940 he became pastor of the Bethel Mennonite Church of Mountain Lake. He died on April 16, 1941, at the age of 52.

P. R. Schroeder had excellent leadership qualities and influenced many young people to go into the ministry and mission work. His emphasis was on a warm Bible-centered concept of the Gospel and Christianity. He was active in evangelistic **work** and Bible lectures in many states and provinces of North America. C.K.

Celeste Schroeder Dehnert, "Peter R. Schroeder—Pastor and Conference Worker," *Menn. Life* IV (July 1949) 38-41.

Schrot, Anna, the wife of Bernhard Schrot (*q.v.*), baptized by Hans Hut of Bibra; she shared her husband's fate. W.W.

Schrot, Bernhard, an Anabaptist who was imprisoned in the Oberhaus, a castle in Passau (*q.v.*), Germany, in 1535. With 14 brethren he was questioned on Sept. 16, 1535, by the judges of Wegscheid, and confessed that he stemmed from Württemberg. Concerning his faith he confessed that he had been baptized five years previously by Andreas von Weiss, who had been executed at Neuenburg on the Danube; concerning the Münsterites he knew nothing; nor were they his brethren, for they shed blood, something that his group did not do; he had no news of them either by word of mouth or writing; it had never occurred to him to join the Turks; he intended to stay by his faith. (*ML IV.*)   W.W.

Schubert, Hans von (1859-1931), Protestant theologian active in Anabaptist research as executive manager of the Verein für Reformationsgeschichte. He was a professor of church history at the universities of Strasbourg, Kiel, and Heidelberg, the author of numerous books, including *Kirchengeschichte Schleswig-Holsteins* I (1907), *Der Kommunismus der Wiedertäufer zu Münster und seine Quellen* (1919), and his biographical work, *Lazarus Spengler und die Reformation zu Nürnberg* I (Leipzig, 1934). (*ML IV.*)   NEFF, E.T.

Schuere (Schure, Scheure), **Denys** (Dionys) **van der** (also Verschuren), a Dutch Mennonite preacher and elder, d. 1673 at Haarlem, who served the Waterlander congregation of Amsterdam 1639-71 and Haarlem 1671-73. During his Amsterdam period he conducted at the same time a printing office and bookshop. Among his editions are Bibles and Schabaelje's *Vereenigingh van de Principale Artijckelen das Geloofs.* His descendants were also printers and booksellers at Amsterdam. Van der Schuere descended from a Mennonite family which had emigrated from Flanders.

In 1640, after Joost Hendriksz (*q.v.*) had attacked the Waterlanders and accused them of holding unbiblical views concerning the satisfactory death of Christ, Denys van der Schuere and Jacob Cornelisz van Dale (*q.v.*), his co-preacher in the Amsterdam Waterlander congregation, published *Korte Vertooninghe van de onware beschuldigingen . . .* (Amsterdam, 1640). After the death of the Waterlander leader Hans de Ries (*q.v.*) in 1638 van der Schuere published *Lijck-Predicatie over 't Afsterven van Hans de Ries* (Amsterdam, 1638). vDZ.

Schijn-Maatschoen, *Geschiedenis* III, 296; *DB* 1863, 124, 138; 1898, 56; *Inv. Arch. Amst.* II, 2, No. 376.

Schuester, Casper, a Hutterite martyr, who suffered death by beheading at Michelsburg in the Puster Valley (*q.v.*) with Martin (*q.v.*) of Vilgraten in 1538. His death is sung in the hymn (*Ausbund,* No. 33, where he is called Kaspar von Schöneck), "Merkt auf und nehmt zu Herzen, wie Gott will suchen heim." The *Martyrs' Mirror* names both martyrs twice: once as Vilgard and Caspar of Schoeneck who died in 1528 (*Mart. Mir.* D 19, E 429), and again as Martin of Vilgraten and Caspar Schumacher who died in 1538 (*Mart. Mir.* D 43 f., E 449). The Hutterite chronicle calls them Casper Schuester and Marthin aus Vilgrädten. Under the name of Kaspar Schumacher the *Lieder der Hutterischen Brüder* (Scottdale, 1914, p. 86) gives a beautiful hymn, "Erzürn dich nicht, o frommer Christ!" (See **Caspar of Schöneck,** *ME* I, 522, which

this article supplements.) (Beck, *Geschichts-Bücher,* 135; Zieglschmid, *Chronik,* 187; *ML* II, 489; *ML* IV.)   NEFF.

Schu(e)ster, Lorenz (Laurence Schumacher), a Hutterite martyr, who was executed at Sterzing, Tirol (now Italy), in 1532, together with Lamprecht Gruber (*q.v.*) and four other brethren. (Beck, *Geschichts-Bücher,* 105 f.; Zieglschmid, *Chronik,* 102 f.; *Mart. Mir.* D 33, E 440.)

Loren(t)z Schu(e)ster was also the name of two other Hutterian Brethren—a deacon at Schäckowitz (*q.v.*), chosen in 1538, and (perhaps the same?) a deacon at Urschitz (*q.v.*), near Dämberschitz, who died in 1561. (Zieglschmid, *Chronik,* 185, 407; *ML* IV.)

Schuhknecht, Christoph, an Anabaptist martyr, the son of Andreas Zimmermann, who had previously been executed as a martyr, was put to death with Valentin Luckner and two other companions at Michelsburg (*q.v.*) in the Puster Valley (*q.v.*) of Tirol, after Oct. 20, 1552 (1553?). They had been caught by Christoph Ochs, the judge of Michelsburg, at a meeting of some twenty Anabaptists in a forest, at which Hans Amon had preached.   NEFF.

Schuhmacher, Caspar: see Schuster, Casper.

Schuhmacher, Fridli, a shoemaker of Zollikon (*q.v.*) near Zürich, Switzerland, who was baptized on Jan. 22, 1525, by Johannes Brötli (*q.v.*) at the village fountain of Hirslanden. His wife was baptized a few days later by Blaurock (*q.v.*). In February 1525 Brötli addressed two letters to Fridli, who was apparently one of the leaders of the first Anabaptist congregation of Zollikon. Arrested soon after, Fridli recanted, but when released he continued his activity. In July 1525, he was again in prison. The last information on him is dated Aug. 9, 1525, when he confessed before the judges that he had been baptized, which was "not against God," and that he would stand by it. (*TA Zürich.*)   vDZ.

Schuiling, a Dutch Mennonite family, whose descendants are still found in the province of Friesland; they have usually been engaged in farming. Roelof Roelofs Schuiling (b. June 1783 at Kalkwijk, d. July 12, 1871, at Oudebildtzijl) was a son of Roelof Schuiling, a (Reformed) koffskipper and later a farmer at Kalkwijk (*q.v.*) near Sappemeer in the province of Groningen. Young Roelof Roelofs was baptized in his infancy in the Reformed Church, but joined the Mennonite Church, the church of his mother Elsbet Schuiling, who was a descendant of the Swiss Mennonite Meihuizen (*q.v.*) family. With independent study and the assistance of a friendly Mennonite pastor (whose name is not given) he became a Mennonite preacher, serving 1812-17 at Oudebildtzijl, 1817-18 at Hindeloopen, and 1818-57 at Oudebildtzijl again, at the same time serving the congregation at Hallum. In 1857 he retired. Though he had little formal education, his good intellect and his untiring devotion made him a man of great influence in Friesland, particularly in the Friesche Doopsgezinde Sociëteit (Mennonite Conference of Friesland), of which he was a trustee for many years. He married Klaaske Thyssen Rienks, of Hallum, of a well-known Frisian Mennonite family.

One of their sons was Klaas Roelofs Schuiling (b. May 9, 1831, at Oudebildtzijl, d. June 11, 1907, at Veenwouden), who after studying at the Amsterdam Mennonite Seminary served as pastor of the Oldeboorn Oude Huis congregation from 1857. In 1887, when on the instigation of Schuiling a merger was effected between the Oude Huis and the Nieuwe Huis congregations, Schuiling became the pastor of the united congregation, serving until 1889, when he moved to Veenwouden, serving here until 1897, in which year he retired. For many years Klaas R. Schuiling was a trustee of the A.D.S. (Dutch General Mennonite Conference) and a curator of its seminary. He was also on the executive board of the conference of Friesland and a trustee of the Dutch Mennonite Mission Association. Many of the Schuiling family have served the church as deacons.   VDZ.

J. Huizinga, *Stamboek . . . van Samuel Peter en Barbara Fry* (Groningen, 1890) *passim; Naamlijst* 1829, 44 f., 58; *DB* 1907, 189-95, with portrait of K. R. Schuiling; *DB* 1910, 131 f.; *DJ* 1908, 57-68; 1928, 119; 1936, 68 ff.

Schulfreund, Der, a 4-page, 8½ x 11, published semimonthly starting August 1917, at Rosthern, Sask., by the Mennonite congregations of Saskatchewan in the interest of the Rosthern Academy, edited by David Toews and N. W. Bahnmann. It is not clear when publication ceased. Bethel College Historical Library has the first volume.   C.K.

Schulrat: see **Mennonite Board (Council) of Education.**

Schultbekentenisse (Confession of Guilt) **van Jan Hendricksz van Schiedam,** published in 1590 (n.p.), is a notable booklet in which Jan Hendricksz, elder of the Frisian (*q.v.*) congregation of Schiedam, Holland, lamented the Frisian-Flemish schism of 1566-67. His confession of guilt, signed by him and ten other preachers and deacons, was an introduction to the merger of the (Young) Frisians and the High German Mennonites on the basis of the Concept of Cologne (*q.v.*) in 1591.   VDZ.

Schulteboat is the Low German name of a meeting of the Mennonite farmers of a village in Russia, Manitoba, Mexico, and Paraguay, under the leadership of the Schulze (*q.v.*). The meeting included originally only the owners of farms but was later opened to other male members of the village. All questions pertaining to the economic, social, and cultural life of the village were acted upon at these meetings. Only religious matters were left in the hands of the ecclesiastical leaders. J. H. Janzen (*q.v.*) wrote a Low German play under the title *Schulteboat* which describes the activities of such a meeting.   C.K.

Schultz, Peter, was born March 2, 1853, in Gnadenheim, South Russia, the seventh child of Heinrich and Helena Fast Schultz. He came to America in 1874, settling at Mountain Lake, Minn. On Jan. 6, 1878, he married Anna Klassen. Thirteen children were born to them, of whom one son and two

daughters died in infancy. Four sons were ministers: G. P. Schultz (deceased), Chicago; H. P. Schultz, Saskatchewan (deceased); D. P. Schultz, South Dakota and Oregon; and Jacob P. Schultz, Saskatchewan (deceased). Schultz was a member of the Brudertal (EMB) Mennonite Church of Mountain Lake until 1903, when he moved to Langham, Sask., where he became a charter member of the Bruderthal Church at that place. He was a minister of the Langham Bruderthal Church from 1903, and elder from 1909 until 1930.

Peter Schultz's contribution to his community and conference was one of personal work, sound Biblical preaching, and loving church leadership. He was one of the ministers associated with the founding of the Evangelical Mennonite Brethren Conference. His occupation was farming; with this he combined the work of the ministry. He died April 13, 1930, at Langham and was buried in the Bruderthal cemetery.   O.H.W.

Schultze, Daniel Severin (1645-1712), a German Lutheran theologian. He had no pastoral charge, but made a name for himself through his polemics against the Catholics and other non-Lutherans. Of especial interest to Mennonites is his pamphlet against Jakob Denner (*q.v.*): *Wohlgemeinte Warnung für die Gemeinschaft des Gottesdienstes der Mennonisten, zur Ehre Gottes, zur Erbauung der Glaubens-genossen, und zur Besserung der Mennonisten dargestellt* (Hamburg, 1706).

At the beginning of his booklet the author speaks of two kinds of Mennonites who meet for worship in Altona (*q.v.*), near Hamburg; in the smaller meeting a dyer by the name of Jakob Denner preached every Sunday and holiday, and some Lutheran citizens of Hamburg faithfully attended his sermons in order to learn from him the way of life. Denner, Schultze reported, had published eighteen of his sermons under the title, *Eenige christelijke uitbreidingen over schriftuuerlijke Texten.* One of these booklets was sent to him with the request that he admonish his coreligionists not to neglect their own beautiful services; this is what he wished to do after carefully examining the book.

The booklet is an expression of the annoyance of the learned Lutheran clergy at the successful preaching of the simple Mennonite dyer, before whom they were fundamentally helpless.   NEFF.

Schulverein, Christlicher: see **Ohrloff Schulverein and Vereinsschule.**

Schulz (Schultz, Schult), a family name found in Danzig (1674), Tiegenhagen, Ladekopp, Königsberg, and Montau-Gruppe, whence the name was transplanted to Mennonite settlements in Russia and America. The name is likely derived from the office of Schulze (mayor). Among the members of the Schultz family representatives prominent in Mennonite (GCM) church work have been: David Schulz, of Altona, elder of the Bergthal church in Manitoba; J. J. Schulz, manager of the Concordia Hospital at Winnipeg, Man.; Peter Schulz, a minister at Steinbach, Man.; Peter Schulz (*q.v.*), E.M.B. elder at Langham, Sask.; and Jacob S. Schultz, a former dean of Bluffton College. In the E.M.B.

Church George P. Schultz (1880-1957) was long a leader in the Church and pastor in Chicago; his brother David P. Schultz was pastor at Marion, S.D. A son of George P., Arnold C. Schultz, is now professor of Old Testament at Northern Baptist Theological Seminary in Chicago; he was formerly at Bluffton College. (Reimer, *Familiennamen*, 117.)

C.K.

Schulze is the German title for a village mayor in a Mennonite settlement in Prussia, Russia, Manitoba, Mexico, and Paraguay. The Schulze calls meetings (see **Schulteboat**) and is the responsible civic leader of a village (*q.v.*) and was in turn responsible to the Oberschulze (*q.v.*) of the Mennonite settlement. (See also **Government** of Mennonites in Russia.)

C.K.

Schumacher (Schuhmacher, Schomacher, Schomecher, Shoemaker), a Mennonite family name. Among the early Swiss Anabaptists there are found the names of Fridli (*q.v.*), Gabriel, Annli, Felix, Caspar (*q.v.*), Hans, and Verena Schumacher. A Mennonite Schumacher family of Swiss descent, originally from Safenwil, Aargau, was in the 17th and 18th centuries found in Alsace, the Palatinate, and later in America. In Hamburg, Germany, there was a Mennonite Schomacher family in the 17th and 18th centuries, some of whose members were deacons; Johann Janssen Schomacher and his brother Paul were well-to-do owners of Greenland whaling vessels 1654-96. Another (not related) Schomecker Mennonite family was living at Niederdollendorf near Bonn in 1650, whose members shortly after moved to Kriegsheim (*q.v.*) in the Palatinate.

Among the first Mennonite-Quaker settlers in Germantown, Pa., was Jacob Schuhmacher, of Kriegsheim, who emigrated in 1683, as a servant of J. D. Pastorius (*q.v.*). He was of Mennonite descent, but had joined the Quakers, like his relatives (?) Peter and Isaac Schumacher, arriving in Philadelphia in 1685, and the children of Georg Schumacher, arriving there in 1686. Some of their descendants later became Mennonites. In America they changed the name to Shoemaker (*q.v.*).   VDZ.

Paul Peachey, *Die soziale Herkunft der Schweizer Täufer in der Ref.-Zeit* (Karlsruhe, 1954) 114, No. 115, 118, No. 212, 119, No. 213, 138, Nos. 653-56; Fritz Blanke, *Brüder in Christo* (Zürich, n.d.-1955) 22 f., 50, 59, 60; D. L. Gratz, *Bernese Anabaptists* (Scottdale, 1953); C. Henry Smith, *The Mennonite Immigration to Pennsylvania* (Norristown, 1929) 94 *et passim*; *Gesch.-Bl.* XIII (1956) 40 f.

Schumacher, Hans, of Wynstägen (erroneously called Wünistern by van Braght), Safenwyl, in the Swiss canton of Aargau, an Anabaptist martyr who was executed in Bern on June 3, 1539. After his execution his family and relatives fled to the canton of Basel. Kaspar Schuhmacher of Safenwyl, who was an Anabaptist preacher in Basel early in the 17th century, no doubt belonged to this family.

E.H.B.

J. Heiz, *Täufer im Aargau* (Aarau, 1902) 158; *Mart. Mir.* E 1139.

Schuster, Claus: see **Braidl, Klaus.**

Schuster, Peter, an ironmonger of Leoben, Styria, Austria, in whose cross-examination records is found the note: "Peter Schuster has become an Anabaptist. To be investigated." On April 21, 1529, Ferdinand (from Speyer) sent to his chamberlain Veit Zollner the property of the two Anabaptists Franz Intzinger (*q.v.*) and Peter Schuster. (See **Leoben**.)

Schütt, Jelle Jansz, mayor, and leader of the Mennonite congregation at Friedrichstadt on the Eider (*q.v.*), Germany, b. in Ameland in Holland, Nov. 11, 1802, d. Jan. 18, 1895, rendered outstanding service to the congregation in fifty years of untiring devotion and work. On Jan. 3, 1886, he celebrated the fiftieth anniversary of his service. In the Hamburg-Altona congregation the name Schütt is also found among the outstanding leaders.   NEFF.

R. Dollinger, *Gesch. der Menn. in Schleswig-Holstein, Hamburg und Lübeck* (Neumünster, 1930) 61 f.; *Menn. Bl.*, 1885, 21; *ML* IV.

Schütz, Johann, an Anabaptist martyr, the author of the song "O Heer, ick magh wel klagen": see **Jan Schut.**

Schützenecker, Hans, an Anabaptist martyr, a scissors grinder by trade, was seized at Steyr (*q.v.*) in Upper Austria in June 1527 with other members of an Anabaptist congregation. They refused to make the required recantation and said that the learned priests were themselves in error, they (the Brethren) would adhere to the doctrine taught them by Hans Hut (*q.v.*) from God's Word, as long as they were not shown something better from the teaching of Christ.

The report of the council of Steyr to the government at Vienna was followed by the order of King Ferdinand of Sept. 10, 1527, that "the imprisoned Anabaptists should be dealt with according to the law and the penalty." Those who recanted should be pardoned; "They must swear an oath that they will desist from the erroneous, seductive, heretical articles and doctrines that they have learned and received from Brother Hans Hut or his aides and related persons, will avoid them and take care not to go to any secret meeting and corner preaching, but will adhere henceforth all their life to the holy Christian church. Furthermore they shall on three successive holidays, when people are going to church, walk around the church in black clothing, bare head, and uncovered face, holding a lighted wax candle in the right hand. Then while the Mass is being sung they shall kneel before the high altar and beseech Almighty God for mercy, for correction of their fall into error and the sin which they have committed, and after the ceremony, with the permission of the priest, return to their homes. The mourning clothing shall be worn for four months. On the holiday or Sunday after the third Sunday each one shall confess to the priest or his assistant and receive the sacrament of the altar. In their homes the penitents shall have no company, avoid all meetings, . . . nor accept any office, bear no weapons nor have them carried after them for an entire year from the first day of the penance. Finally, they shall not change their place of residence for a year if they are living in Steyr or Burgfried, nor sell their home, nor dispose of them in any other way, nor leave Burgfried at all without the knowledge and consent of the government, and they shall also to the best of their ability repay the costs accumulating to His Majesty and to the city of Steyr in their case."

Now began the trial against the Anabaptists who persisted in their faith. Künigl (*q.v.*), who was appointed as prosecutor by the king, made the charge that they have involved themselves in seductive, heretical, Hutian and Zwinglian doctrine and sect, have practiced the same and still believe them, that they have banded themselves together, attended corner preaching in and out of the city, have also received rebaptism, which they call the sign and covenant of the Lord, which was previously never heard of in the Christian church, disparage infant baptism and the sacrament of the altar, still believe it, and will not let themselves be directed back to the right way: he therefore demands their punishment. The accused Anabaptists replied with a written *Verantwortung*. It said in effect: It had never been their intention to act contrary to the mandates of His Imperial Majesty, contrary to brotherly love and Christian order. They were well aware of the divine command: Give to Caesar that which is Caesar's, and also of the verse, Be subject to all human authority for the Lord's sake. In this obedience they would persevere to the end with body and possessions.

It was true that they had met several times in order to instruct one another in brotherly love in the Word of God, but not with the intent of fomenting evil or sedition. Furthermore they offered to abstain from such meetings hereafter. But the doctrine which they teach is not new, but the teaching of Christ (Mark 16; Matt. 28; I Cor. 2, 8, and 10; John 3:4 and 5; Rom. 6; I Cor. 15; Luke 12); they knew of no other baptism than the one which they taught. Concerning the sacrament of the altar there was nothing in Scripture, but the Lord's Supper, as He instituted it, they regarded very highly. But from the words of its institution, as described by the holy evangels and Paul, it could be clearly understood that the body of Christ is not in the form of the bread, nor did they believe that it was. For Christ said: If anyone will say to you, Lo here is Christ, or lo he is there, believe him not (Mark 13). God, who made the world and all that is therein, does not live in temples made with hands, nor is He cared for with human hands as one who has need of anything. He Himself gives life and breath to all!—Künigl replied with violence and demanded the death penalty. But only a part of the jury voted for the death sentence, most of them favoring more lenient measures, another two months' period of indoctrination, and finally expulsion from the country. King Ferdinand heard this report with annoyance. He vigorously demanded their death, and the authorities complied. On Monday, March 30, 1528, the six captured Anabaptists (Hans Schützenecker, Sigmund Peutler, Mathäus Pürchinger, Hans Muhr, Hans Penzenauer, and Leonhard Alexberger) were executed with the sword and their bodies burned. Schützenecker's wife was drowned. In May

Hans Heher (*q.v.*) and later five other Anabaptists seized in the country suffered the same fate as the six named.   NEFF.

A Nicoladoni, *Johannes Bünderlin von Linz und die oberösterreichischen Täufergemeinden in den Jahren 1525-1531* (Berlin, 1893) 74-84; *ML* IV.

Schützinger (Schitzinger), **Simon** (Sigmund), an early Anabaptist, born in Rattenberg (*q.v.*) in Tirol (according to Widmoser), a co-worker of Jakob Hutter (*q.v.*) and his assistant in Tirol in the late 1520's. We know of him only through the Chronicle and one letter by Peter Riedemann (*q.v.*); no writings by Schützinger are known. Twice Hutter and Schützinger made the trip from Tirol to Moravia together to help the beginning communities there to become established on sound Christian principles. At that time there was one Bruderhof in Austerlitz, entrusted to another Tirolean brother, Jörg Zaunring (*q.v.*), populated in the main by Tirolean newcomers; in 1531 it was moved to Auspitz. At that time three groups of Anabaptists lived communally in Moravia: the Gabrielites in Rossitz, and the Philippites and the Tiroleans in two groups in Auspitz. For a while they lived in friendly co-operation and unity. Then, in 1531, after an unpleasant affair involving Zaunring's wife it was decided that not Zaunring but Schützinger should become the shepherd or "bishop" of the group, in fact the leader of all three groups.

Then, in 1533, Jakob Hutter came to Moravia for the third time, this time to stay. Now a lamentable conflict arose which seriously injured brotherly unity and peace. Hutter felt called by God to become the very shepherd of all brethren who lived in community of goods, but Schützinger showed no intentions to yield the office. Philipp Plener (*q.v.*) suggested that both should become coleaders as he and Blasy Kuhn (*q.v.*) were among the Philippites; Gabriel Ascherham (*q.v.*) opposed this solution; Schützinger felt badly about even the suggestion of sharing in the leadership. The congregations were confused and not able to decide (according to the description of Caspar Braitmichel, the writer of the Chronicle, and most likely an eyewitness). Then a situation arose reminiscent of the story of Sapphira in Acts 5, involving the wife of Jörg Fasser (*q.v.*). Hutter now proposed spontaneously to see whether or not such a breach of trust might not also have happened among the elders of the community, and a search was undertaken in Schützinger's house. Here they found money hidden under the roof, and Schützinger readily admitted that he had known of this reservation of private money without mentioning it to the brotherhood. Then on Oct. 5, 1533, the congregation convened and excommunicated Schützinger, their former leader. Eight days later Hutter was made bishop of the entire group; but the conflict with the Gabrielites and Philippites continued and led eventually to a complete break in fellowship. Unfortunately, Braitmichel does not say anything about the later fate of Schützinger, who simply disappears from the pages of the Chronicle. It is likely that he returned to his native Tirol. (Zieglschmid, *Chronik;* Loserth, *Anabaptismus.*)   R.F.

Schuurmans, Hermanus Jz (1867-1942), was a Dutch Mennonite pastor serving at Giethoorn 1894-1910, Den Horn 1910-12, and Sneek 1912-33. He is the author of a volume of novelistic sketches of the Giethoorn people, entitled *Van de Oude Garde* (Amsterdam, 1907) and of a few sermons. vdZ.

Schuurmans, N. D. (d. 1908 at Haarlem), was a missionary of the Dutch Mennonite Missions Association (*q.v.*). Being an orphan, he was trained in the Oranjeappel (*q.v.*) orphanage to be a blacksmith; but he desired to devote his life to Christian missions, and was accepted by the Dutch Mennonite board as a future missionary. After studying in the mission house in Rotterdam, he undertook a journey to visit all the Mennonite congregations in the Netherlands, married C. S. Portugies, and on March 18 (1863) entered the service of the mission. He went to Java to support Pieter Jansz (*q.v.*) in his work. In August 1863 he took up his work in Japara. His especial work was with the schools. On March 27, 1875, he sent a warm letter of thanks to the Sembach "Groschenverein" with a description of his work. He also wrote a letter to America. He thus maintained close contact with his brethren. But in a few years his wife and child became ill and his own health broke down; in 1878 he had to give up his work. On the journey home he suffered a serious shipwreck, in which he lost all his goods. At home he again devoted himself with zeal to the cause of missions. His account, *Overzicht van het Zendingsveld in Nederlandsch Indien*, has historical value. NEFF, vdZ.

DB 1886, 87; 1890, 48-51; 1892, 39, 41, 44 f.; 1893, 111 f.; *Jaarverslagen* (Reports) of the Dutch Missionary Association.

Schuursma, Roelof, b. 1871 at Meppel, a Dutch Mennonite pastor, serving at Den Horn 1897-1902, Baard 1902-3, Westzaan-Noord 1903-10, and Zutphen 1910-29. He wrote a novel on the martyr Elisabeth (*q.v.*) Dirks, entitled *Van Elisabeth, die een Bagijntje was* (Enschedé, 1921). vdZ.

Schuyring, N. Joannes, a Reformed minister at Beetsterzwaag, in the Dutch province of Friesland, published in 1661 *Doolhof der Mennisten, beplant met 84 vruchteloose Boomen, een Cort Begrijp van de voornaemste Dwalinghen der Mennisten, getrocken uyt hare Schriften, ende kortelyck wederleyt uyt Gods H. Woort, tot dienste van de Verdoolde Schapen onder de Mennisten van Opsterlandt ende andere eenvoudighe Christenen meer.* This work, which attacks the Mennonites, tries to refute a number of quotations from the *Protocol* of the Emden disputation, the books of Twisck, Claes Claesz, François de Knuyt, and other Mennonite authors. Schuyring's refutation, approved by the Reformed classis of Zevenwolden and dedicated to the governors of the Frisian district of Opsterland, is picayune and not very convincing. (*DB* 1897, 117.) vdZ.

Schwäbisch-Gmünd: see **Gmünd.**

Schwärmer, a derogatory term for the Anabaptists, used by the Reformers and the official church historians mainly in Lutheran lands, best translated as "enthusiasts" (*q.v.*), with the connotation of "fanatics." The real Schwärmer of the 16th century were the Inspirationists who relied on inner inspirations and visions, such as the Zwickau Prophets, Thomas Müntzer (*q.v.*), and David Joris (*q.v.*). R.F.

Schwar(t)z: see **Swartz.**

Schwarz, Rupprecht, an Anabaptist of Mainz, Germany, was arrested in Strasbourg and examined on May 29, 1539. Nothing else is known about him.

T. W. Röhrich, "Zur Gesch. der Strassburger Wiedertäufer in den Jahren 1527 bis 1543," in *Ztscht f. d. hist. Theologie,* 1860, 115; ML IV.

Schwarzenau Anabaptists. The early followers of Alexander Mack in Germany, later in America called the Church of the Brethren (*q.v.*), first organized at Schwarzenau a.d. Eder, Germany, in 1708, were frequently called "Täufer" or "Anabaptisten" by their critics and opponents. They actually had much in common with the earlier Anabaptists, as Don Dürnbach has shown in his doctoral dissertation, *The European Origins of the Church of the Brethren* (Elgin, 1958). H.S.B.

Schwartzentruber: see **Swartzentruber.**

Schwaz (Schwatz), a town on the Inn near Innsbruck in Tirol, Austria, was like Rattenberg (*q.v.*) and other towns in this area a center of Anabaptist activity 1526-50. In 1526-42 twenty Anabaptists died as martyrs at Schwaz, including Hans Schlaffer, (*q.v.*) and Leonhard Frick (*q.v.*) both arrested in 1527 and executed in 1528, and Ludwig Fest (*q.v.*) in 1533. In 1544 many Anabaptists moved from Schwatz to Moravia (*q.v.*) to join the Hutterite communities. vdZ.

Schwebel, Johannes (1490-1540), the reformer of Zweibrücken, a town in the Palatinate, Germany, served on the Ebernburg from June to October 1522, was then pastor in Landstuhl, the residential town of Franz von Sickingen, and then in Zweibrücken from April 1523 until his death. In 1532 he felt himself compelled to take up strenuous battle with Anabaptist views. He became involved in a dispute with Georg Pistor (*q.v.*), his colleague in Ernstweiler, who was favorably inclined toward the Anabaptists, in consequence of which Pistor had to leave Zweibrücken. But the Anabaptist movement was not wiped out. Several years later a Christian Schuhmacher and a certain Nader were forced to recant their Anabaptist views. Schwebel was also used in other places in the suppression of the Anabaptists. He wrote the book, *Eine freundliche Vermahnung und Unterricht an etlich, die des Wiedertaufs verdächtig sind in Bischweiler* (*q.v.*) (1535?). NEFF.

Fr. Jung, *Johannes Schwebel, der Reformator von Zweibrücken* (Kaiserslautern, 1910); ML IV.

Schweblin, Johannes, a Reformed clergyman of the Reformation period, assistant to Cratander (*q.v.*), who sympathized with the Anabaptists, first in Basel and later in Strasbourg.

Paul Burckhardt, *Die Basler Täufer* (Basel, 1898) 19; T. W. Röhrich, "Zur Gesch. der Strassburger Wiedertäufer 1527-1543," in *Ztscht f. d. hist. Theologie* XXX, 33; ML IV.

Schweiger (*Silentes,* i.e., Silent Anabaptists) were a group of unknown number and origin who apparently observed an absolute rule of silence. Several authors reported on this group, the earliest of whom was Sebastian Franck in his *Chronica* of 1531 (folio 446). It may be that all subsequent writers mentioning the group relied on Franck. At any rate the next reference to them occurs in the correspondence between Caspar Schwenckfeld (*q.v.*) and Sibilla Eisler concerning her maid who was apparently an Anabaptist and who refused to greet people or thank them. Sibilla asked Schwenckfeld's advice on the matter. Schwenckfeld pointed out that the maid's attitude was due to a faulty exegesis of Luke 10:4 ("Greet no one on the way"), but was uncertain of the relationship between the "Schweiger" and the Anabaptists. However, he called them Anabaptists and claimed that they rejected all external oral Christian teaching, and despised the Holy Scriptures and edifying books. He located them as a group in Allgäu, a region south of Ulm toward the Bavarian Alps.

The Silentes are also mentioned in Gabriel Prateolus' *De vitis, sectis et dogmatibus omnium haereticorum* (Cologne, 1569). (See **Nicoladoni.**) The Schweiger are No. 15 in George Eder's list of 1573, and Erhard's list of 1589.

At the time when Franck was in Strasbourg writing his *Chronica* the Anabaptists had the practice of not greeting people on the street who were not a part of their fellowship. Bucer accused Marpeck of not speaking to him on the street, but wanting to discuss matters pertaining to the Christian faith behind closed doors in the council chambers. It may be that as a result of this practice some began to dub the Anabaptists "Schweiger," although it is also possible that a sect called "Schweiger" actually existed. If so, and if Schwenckfeld's description of them is accurate, it is clear that they did not belong to Anabaptism proper, for Anabaptism always placed a high value on preaching and the oral reading of the Word of God.   W.Kl.

A. Nicoladoni, *Johannes Bünderlin* (Berlin, 1893) 120; Henry A. DeWind, "A Sixteenth Century Description of Religious Sects in Austerlitz, Moravia," *MQR* XXIX (1955) 44-53; *Corpus Schwenckfeldianorum,* ed. by E. E. S. Johnson (Leipzig, 1907-   ) XII, 24 ff.; 103 f.

Schweingrube in the district of Stuhm (*q.v.*) in West Prussia, the seat of a Waterlander Mennonite congregation, formerly also called Stühmsche Niederung, later Tragheimerweide (*q.v.*).   vDZ.

Schweitzer, Hans, of Rügsau, an Anabaptist martyr, put to death in Bern, Switzerland, in 1537.

A. Fluri, *Beiträge zur Gesch. d. bernischen Täufer* (Bern, 1912) 14; *Mart. Mir.* E 1129.

Schweitzer, Heinrich, a Hutterite missioner from Moravia, who with Uhl Schuester and Bastl (Wastl) Anfang (*q.v.*), the latter a minister, was arrested near Bern in Switzerland in 1585, and imprisoned in Bern for 20 weeks. After three doctrinal examinations (in the first 14 days) and repeated vain attempts to get the brethren to disclose where they had secured lodging, the council made preparations for the execution and gave them their "final" meal. But popular vote opposed the execution. Heinrich

and Uhl were beaten and had their ears burned through and were whipped to the border. Later Bastl was also released. All three returned safely to the brotherhood in Moravia. See also **Schmid, Bastl.**)   E.H.B.

Schweitzer, Philipp, a Catholic priest of Montbéliard (*q.v.*) in France, but probably a native of Switzerland, joined the Anabaptists and was active in Basel and Lucerne, Switzerland. He is said to have converted and baptized eight Catholic priests. Schweitzer was executed in 1539 at Lucerne.   vDZ.

Paul Peachey, *Die soziale Herkunft der Schweizer Täufer* (Karlsruhe, 1954) 23 note 1, 25 f., 109, No. 17.

Schwenckfeld, Caspar: also **Kaspar;** see *Supplement.*

Schwenckfelder Church, a body in Pennsylvania taking its name from the Silesian nobleman, lay evangelist, and reformer, Caspar Schwenckfeld von Ossig (1489-1561). Within the first two decades of the 16th-century Reformation there were Christians in Europe known as Lutherans, Zwinglians, Anabaptists, and Schwenckfelders, the followers of Caspar Schwenckfeld. Here and there in Silesia whole congregations and their pastors supported the teaching of the last named. Later on this was also true in isolated cities and areas of South Germany. Schwenckfeld never permitted his followers to form a body under his name. Nor would he countenance the establishment of another ecclesiastical division. His followers were spoken of as brethren or brotherhoods; he himself came to speak of them as Confessors of the Glory of Christ. There never was an organization of them in Europe, where thousands adhered to them, from the Prussian shores of the Baltic, in parts of Poland, Silesia and Glatz, through South Germany to Lake Constance and to Strasbourg.

The persecutions they suffered even unto death for two hundred years were extremely bitter. But all this did not prevent peasants and artisans, merchants and professionals, statesmen and nobles, both Catholic and Protestant from following after them. However, by the end of the Thirty Years' War they had apparently disappeared from South Germany. Thereafter we find them only in Lower Silesia and in an area west of the cities of Liegnitz and Goldberg in the villages of Harpersdorf, Langneundorf, Armenruh, Lauterseifen, Hohenau, and Laubgrund. Here they were addressed by letter before 1670 by Philipp Jakob Spener (*q.v.*), and the Quaker Roger Longworth in 1675 visited their physician Martin John Jr. (1624-1707) in Laubgrund, who was the first to notice that wax is a product of the body of the honeybee. They were given to diligent and intensive study of the Scriptures. From the time of Schwenckfeld himself they pursued the study of languages and mathematics; he had from 1523 on, the service and support of the erudite Valentine Crautwald, lector at Saint Thomas in Liegnitz, as his linguist. The Schwenckfelders have throughout their history been noted for their interest in education and learning, with extensive literary activity.

In Silesia the Anabaptists and Schwenckfelders were close c1570, for the latter often had Anabaptist writings.

When it was found that they were not to be won for the established churches either by persecution or by persuasion it was reported to the Austrian authorities that in the Lower Silesian villages there were these unchurched heretical people. The eminent schoolman and 19th-century Schwenckfeld research scholar, A. F. H. Schneider (1806-90) of Berlin, believed that about 1719-20 they had at least 1,250 members. Emperor Charles VI authorized the creation of an especial Jesuit mission to convert them to the Roman Catholic faith. Such a mission, composed of Johan Milan for Harpersdorf and Carolus Regent for Langneundorf, made its appearance in December 1719. Although the Schwenckfelders sent able representatives to the Austrian court in Vienna, who presented seventeen petitions pleading for toleration, by 1724 it was clear that their only hope for preservation was to flee from their homes and country. But where were they to go? Through the kindness of Count Zinzendorf (q.v.) they found temporary asylum on his estates in and around Herrnhut and Berthelsdorf in Saxony. They fled by night, a few families at a time, leaving cattle in the stall and their farms abandoned. About 500 men, women, and children fled in 1725-36. However, only a brief respite was given them. By 1730 there were signs that they must move again. In 1731 one of their young men reached Philadelphia; in 1733, when they were given a year's time to dispose of their property, 14 more came to Philadelphia; on Sept. 22, 1734, the main body, 171 souls, arrived in Philadelphia; in 1736 eight more came, and a final 14 in 1737. The number of those who came to Pennsylvania in that period did not exceed 212. Melchior Dorn, the last survivor of those who remained in Europe, died in Harpersdorf in 1826.

The Mennonites of the Netherlands had come to the assistance of the Schwenckfelders during their sojourn in Saxony. When they set out for Pennsylvania Hinrich van der Smissen, a Mennonite minister in Hamburg, was host to them; he entertained the larger body of 1734 for ten days in Altona and fitted out three sailing vessels in which he had them transported to Amsterdam. Cornelis van Putten, the Mennonite pastor, showed them great kindness, and the Mennonite van Buyssant family in Haarlem munificently entertained them and in addition paid for their passage on the "Saint Andrew," besides an additional fund of 224 Rixthalers for their poor. They sailed from Rotterdam on June 19, 1734.

On Sept. 23, 1734, the day after the arrival of the larger body in Philadelphia, the Schwenckfelder group gave their promise of loyalty to the Crown of England, sealing it with a handclasp. The following day was designated as a day of thanksgiving for their deliverance and safe arrival in Pennsylvania. Each succeeding year they and their descendants have held a service of remembrance on September 24, calling it their "Gedächtnistag."

The Schwenckfelders settled in southeastern Pennsylvania on lands lying today in the counties of Philadelphia, Montgomery, Berks, and Lehigh. Their first minister in Pennsylvania was Georg Weiss (1687-1740), whom they chose before their arrival. Through the first 55 years of their life here their worship services were conducted in their homes; their first meetinghouse was built in 1789. To avoid total disintegration they finally, in 1782, organized themselves into the Society of Schwenckfelders, and under that name they functioned until 1909, when they were incorporated as the Schwenckfelder Church. Since then the five congregations have been individually incorporated. At the end of 1953 their total church membership was 2,540.

The Schwenckfelder Board of Missions was organized in 1895, their Board of Publication in 1898, succeeding the Publishing Committee appointed in 1884; under the combined auspices of the Schwenckfelder Church and the Hartford Theological Seminary it has published the *Corpus Schwenckfeldianorum,* a complete scholarly edition of the writings of Caspar Schwenckfeld. Volumes I to XV were issued in 1907-39. The Board of Charities has a fund resting back upon the 224 Rixthalers of 1734, now exceeding $12,000.

The General Conference is the official body of the Schwenckfelder Church. All its officers are laymen. Under its direction a committee began operations in 1885 which led to the creation of the Schwenckfelder Library, incorporated in 1946, at Pennsburg, Pa. Similarly also the General Conference in 1891 purchased the property of the Perkiomen Seminary, since 1916 known as Perkiomen School, originally founded in 1874-75. This is a college preparatory school for boys, enrolling 200 each year. The polity of the Schwenckfelders is congregational. For them the kingdom of God is a spiritual one revealed in Jesus Christ. The Scriptures are the record of the voice of the Word of God. The Word of God is that which transcends whatever is written or printed whether on parchment or paper. The Christian must be free and unfettered by human creeds and human authority. The spirit must have free course to follow the light of truth as it advances. Government essential to maintain an orderly society has no right to interfere with or influence religious convictions.

The *Schwenckfeldian,* published monthly since 1903, is the official organ, published at Philadelphia. Of literature mention may be made of Howard W. Kriebel, *The Schwenckfelders in Pennsylvania* (Lancaster, 1904); Elmer Schultz Gerhard, *A Vindication of Caspar Schwenckfeld von Ossig: An Elucidation of His Doctrine and the Vicissitudes of His Followers,* translated from the German and edited (Allentown, 1942); *Formula for the Government and Discipline of the Schwenckfelder Church* (1948), *Beliefs and Teachings of the Schwenckfelder Church* (Norristown, 1956). The secretary of the General Conference is Wilber C. Kriebel, of Chester, Pa.　　　　　　　　　　　　　　　W.C.K.

Schwendimann, Peter, of Grosshöchstetten, was an early Swiss Anabaptist leader. He was present at the Bernese Disputation of 1538.　　　　　vDZ.

S. Geiser, *Die Taufgesinnten-Gemeinden* (Karlsruhe, 1931) 179.

Schwer(d)tler (i.e., bearers of swords), a name given to the faction of the Anabaptists at Nikolsburg, Moravia, led by Balthasar Hubmaier (q.v.) and Hans Spittelmayer (q.v.), which defended the use of the sword in a war of defense, though not in self-defense or for the protection of one's own property. They also defended the payment of war taxes. The faction of the Anabaptists led by Jacob Widemann (*q.v.*) and Philipp Jäger (*q.v.*), which stood for complete nonresistance and carried the staff in place of the sword, were called Stäbler. The definite break between the two groups occurred at the debates held on these questions at Nikolsburg (*q.v.*) in 1526, at which Hans Hut (*q.v.*) took the side "against the sword," while Hubmaier defended the sword. The "Schwertler" party died out by 1529, while the Stäbler developed into the Hutterites. The Hutterite *Chronik* (Zieglschmid, 86) states that the Schwertler "now (=1542?) are called Sabbather and have the Münsterite spirit. By this spirit Lord Leonard Liechtensteiner (*q.v.*) . . . expelled Jacob Widemann and Philipp Jäger together with their other brethren." H.S.B.

Schwetzer Niederung (Lowlands near Schwetz), a district (*starostei*) on the Vistula in West Prussia, until 1772 belonging to Poland. Dutch colonists reclaimed this swampy area in the 16th and 17th centuries. In the Schwetzer Niederung were found the villages of Deutsch-Westfalen, Brattwin, Schönau, Kleinsee (Jeziorka, *q.v.*), Neunhuben, Wintersdorf, Christfelde, and Kossovo. Wintersdorf (Przechovka, *q.v.*) was the first Mennonite settlement (c1540). About 1650 there was a considerable number of Mennonites in all these villages, and some villages were completely Mennonite. Until the early 18th century the Mennonites enjoyed many privileges such as the freedom to organize their own schools, and exemption from military taxes and quartering soldiers. By their able land-draining and their skillful farming the Schwetzer Niederung became very prosperous, but repeated floods, exploitation by the rulers and officials, and restrictive economic regulations caused the Mennonites to move away from 1765 to 1850 (to Brenkenhoffswalde and Deutsch-Wymysle); by 1850 most Mennonites had left this area. (*ML* IV, 141-143.) vDZ.

Felicia Szper, *Nederl. Nederzettingen in West-Pruisen gedurende den Poolschen tijd* (Enkhuizen, 1913) 140-46; H. Wiebe, *Das Siedlungswerk niederl. Mennoniten im Weichseltal* . . . (Marburg, 1952) 29-31 and *passim.*

Schwindern (Swinderen), **Hans van** (von), a Dutch immigrant to Schidlitz, a suburb of Danzig, West Prussia, where he was a preacher of the Flemish Mennonite congregation from c1565. Of his life and activity nothing is known but the fact that he sided with the elder Quiryn van der Meulen (*q.v.*). Both van der Meulen and van Schwindern were banned in 1586. For further information see **Meulen, Quiryn van der.** vDZ.

Schwiser, Michael, of Saytarn (?) near Speyer, Germany, was imprisoned in the Upper House at Passau (*q.v.*) with a number of his brethren on Sept. 16, 1535. At his trial on September 16 he confessed that he had been baptized by Hans Schwaigern near Heilbronn, and had been an Anabaptist for 1½ years. Schwiser was among those who remained steadfast. (Wolkan, *Lieder,* 30, where he is called Schuester; *ML* IV.) W.W.

Schyn, Hermannus: see **Schijn, Herman.**

Science Ridge Mennonite Church (MC), located two miles north of Sterling, Whiteside Co., Ill., is a member of the Illinois Conference. The first Mennonites to arrive in this area (1852) were Benjamin Stauffer and wife from Lancaster, Pa. In 1865 a group of 55 came from Franklin County, Pa. The church was organized in 1858. At first the preaching was all in German, and services were held only every two weeks. Sunday school was not attempted until 1882. The greatest spiritual awakening came with the John S. Coffman revivals in 1889, when at one time 45 were added to the church. A. C. Good (ordained preacher in 1906, bishop in 1934) served as pastor 1906-52. In 1957 the membership was 208, with J. Frederick Erb as pastor and bishop. A.C.G.

Scott, Clifford Isaiah, was born in Emporia, Kan., Oct. 19, 1871, the son of Isaiah and Harriet Sinks Scott. He married Olive Shelley on Nov. 10, 1896. He served as pastor of various churches in the Indiana and Ohio Conference, and also in the Nebraska Conference of the United Missionary Church. In 1906-8 he was district superintendent of the Ohio District of the Indiana and Ohio Conference; 1914-33 district superintendent of the Nebraska Conference. He was a delegate to the Quadrennial General Conference five times, and chairman once. He died in 1933. J.A.Hu.

Scott Church of God in Christ Mennonite Church, located 12 miles north and 7 miles west of Scott City, Scott Co., Kan., began in 1943, and was organized in 1945, at which time a house of worship was built. In 1957 it had 93 members, with Ervin Nightengale and Albert Dirks as the ministers in charge. A.Di.

Scott County (Missouri) Old Order Amish. An Amish settlement consisting of about 35 members at the most lived in Scott County about 1924-36. The original settlers, the families of Dan P. Bontrager, Sam S. Miller, Christ M. Bontrager, Joe Schrock, John S. Miller, and Sam Mast, came to Scott County from Butler County about fifty miles west, having moved there from Reno County, Kan. M. E. Bontrager served as bishop and Christ M. Bontrager as minister. D. Roy Nisley was ordained in 1929. The congregation was discontinued in 1934. All of the families moved to Indiana, Michigan, and Buchanan County, Iowa, the last family leaving in 1936. J.M.B.

Scottdale, situated on the southern boundary between Westmoreland and Fayette counties, Pa., was incorporated on Feb. 7, 1874. It was laid out on the farms of Jacob S. and Peter S. Loucks, both grandsons of the Mennonite pioneer settler, Peter Loucks, who moved to this vicinity from Berks County, Pa., in 1800. The population is about 6,500, but with the surrounding community there are about 10,000 inhabitants. It is the home of the Mennonite Publishing House (since 1908) and of its predecessor, the Gospel Witness Company, founded in 1905. The Scottdale Mennonite Church, built in 1893 and rebuilt in 1939, is located in the city. There is another church in Kingview, about a mile east in Fayette County, and a place of worship at North Scottdale in East Huntingdon Township, about a mile to the north. These churches are the successors of two earlier places of worship — at Pennsville, Fayette County, and Stonerville (Alverton), Westmoreland County.   J.L.H.

75 Years of Progress, Scottdale, Pennsylvania, 75th Anniversary Booklet (1949).

Scottdale (Pa.) Mennonite Church (MC) is an outgrowth of the Mennonite settlement in the Jacobs Creek Valley of Fayette and Westmoreland counties, Pa., which began in 1789. A log meetinghouse was erected at Pennsville, in Fayette County, some time before 1800, and another at Stonerville (now Alverton), in Westmoreland County, about 1800. The settlement grew during the first fifty years, reaching a membership of 200 or more in 1840. The next fifty years was a period of decline for various reasons, such as shift of population as people moved west, use of the German language after it was outmoded, failure to use progressive methods of Christian work such as the Sunday school, and lack of adequate resident leadership, until the membership dropped to 16 in 1892. The first step toward revival was the ordination of Aaron Loucks to the ministry on Sept. 18, 1892. A new meetinghouse was built on the corner of Market and Grove streets in Scottdale and dedicated on Dec. 3, 1893. It superseded the use of the other two buildings in about ten years. It was replaced by a larger building on the same site in 1939. By 1905 the congregation numbered 50 members. Through the influx of people drawn into the community by the publishing interests established in Scottdale in 1905 and an active missionary program the congregation grew to a membership of 273 in 1954.

In 1906 a mission Sunday school was opened at East Scottdale and in 1934 a similar effort was begun in North Scottdale. In 1952 a new church, called the Kingview Mennonite Church, was built in East Scottdale. The congregation was organized in January 1955 with 50 charter members, a number transferring from the home congregation; in 1957 the membership was 59. The school building at North Scottdale was purchased in 1954. In 1958 the building was remodeled and a congregation of some 55 organized.   J.L.H.

Edward Yoder, *The Mennonites of Westmoreland County, Pennsylvania* (Scottdale, 1942); J. S. Hartzler and D. Kauffman, *Mennonite Church History* (Scottdale, 1905); J. L. Horst and A. Kaufman, *Seventy-fifth Anniversary Observance of the Southwestern Pennsylvania Mennonite Conference* (n.p., 1951).

Scroll, College, a 6-page bimonthly journal published by the Canadian Mennonite Bible College, Winnipeg, Man., since 1947, edited by students and alumni.   C.K.

Seagoing Cowboys, a term applied to the men in CPS Reserve, a unit in Civilian Public Service (*q.v.*), also known as the UNRRA (*q.v.*) Reserve Unit. These men served as attendants with livestock shipments going to Europe. The first men assigned to this duty sailed on a cattle boat Feb. 12, 1946. Of the 366 CPS men in the program, 167 were listed as

Mennonite and Brethren in Christ. Most of the ships left from Newport News, Va., most of them carried horses instead of cattle, and their destination was generally Greece, Yugoslavia, or Poland. Some of the men made three or more trips each. Ben Bushong of the Brethren Service Commission, who was responsible for selecting attendants for the UNRRA livestock ships, eventually chose many Mennonite young men and farmers who had not been in CPS or who had been demobilized to serve on these boats. The total number of Mennonites accompanying the UNRRA livestock shipments was very likely over 300. These trips gave most of these men their first experience with ocean travel, their first contacts with Europe, and their first opportunities to engage directly in foreign relief service. The total effect of these experiences on the life of the churches remains to be evaluated. (M. Gingerich, *Service for Peace,* Akron, 1949, pp. 187-89.) M.G.

Seamen's Mission (MC) is a home mission project among the Oriental seamen who work out of Newport News, Va., operated by the Virginia Mennonite Board of Missions and Charities. It was founded in 1951, and in 1958 had 14 members, with Lloyd Weaver in charge.   H.S.B.

Seckler, Hans, of Basel: see **Hansmann, Hans.**

Second Mennonite Church (GCM), of Philadelphia, Pa., was established in 1894 when the First Mennonite Church of Philadelphia started a mission on Janney Street. In 1897 a private home at 3007 North Sixth Street was rented for worship services. On April 4, 1899, the present church was dedicated at the corner of Franklin Street and Indiana Avenue and on May 5, 1899, the congregation was officially organized with 36 members and with Silas M. Grubb as pastor. Until 1912 the congregation was supported by the First Mennonite Church. In 1915 the congregation had a membership of 190.

The congregation was served by S. M. Grubb from 1899 until 1938, from 1938-41 by Erland Waltner, from 1942-43 by Edwin M. Crawford, from 1943-49 by Walter J. Dick. In 1958 Curtis Lehman was pastor; the membership was 85.   C.K.

Fiftieth Anniversary of the First Mennonite Church of Philadelphia (Philadelphia, 1915); *50th Anniversary, Second Mennonite Church of Philadelphia, Pa.* (1949).

Second Mennonite Church (GCM), Springs, Pa., was established c1925, when a group of excommunicated members of the Springs Mennonite Church (MC) formed a new fellowship, which c1944 joined the Eastern District Conference (GCM). Edward Miller, a minister of the Springs M.C. congregation but living at Inwood, W. Va., some 100 miles distant, was called as supply preacher c1928, serving once a month, but soon only for two communion services per year. In 1958 the membership was 18. They used the Brethren meetinghouse in Salisbury, some 6 miles north of Springs.   H.S.B.

Secondary Education, the level of education between the elementary school (usually ages 6-14 in North America, and 6-10 or 14 in Europe) and (in North America) the college or (in Europe) the university.

This article treats only the regular secondary school, not specialized schools such as Bible schools (*q.v.*).

No Mennonite secondary schools were ever established in Holland, France, or Switzerland. In Germany one Mennonite secondary boys' school was established at Weierhof (*q.v.*) in the Palatinate (see **Realanstalt am Donnersberg**) in 1867, which developed into an excellent institution under private Mennonite management and with a Mennonite principal and part Mennonite faculty, but with only a small number of Mennonite students. The Weierhof Mennonite pastor customarily taught religion in the school. It was taken over by the Nazi regime in 1941, and then used by the French and American armies 1945-57. The school was finally reconstituted in 1959. The Russian Mennonites, however, developed a strong secondary school program, which had a total of at least 23 schools in the Ukraine at its height in 1910, seventeen for boys, five for girls, and one coeducational, with an enrollment range per school of 70-200 pupils, and three to six teachers, usually with a three-year program, although several schools had four years. These were called Zentralschulen (*q.v.*) since they were thought of as central schools for a district.

The first secondary school in Russia was established in 1822 at Ohrloff in the Molotschna colony by the School Association led by Johann Cornies (*q.v.*). It was planned as a school to prepare teachers, although it taught only content subjects, no educational methods or theory subjects. This school became the pattern for others to follow. Three outstanding Russian secondary school pioneer educators were the first two principals of the Ohrloff school, Tobias Voth (*q.v.*) 1822-29 and Heinrich Heese (*q.v.*) 1829-42, and Heinrich Franz (*q.v.*), principal of the Chortitza secondary school 1846-58. In the first 50 years only two additional schools were established, Halbstadt in the Molotschna (1835) and the Chortitza school in the Old Colony (1842). Growth was slow until the early part of the 20th century. The only new boys' schools until 1905 were Gnadenfeld in the Molotschna (1874) and Neu-Schönsee in the Zagradovka settlement (1895). The first girls' secondary schools were at Halbstadt in the Molotschna (1874) and Chortitza (1895). By 1910 some 200 Russian Mennonite youth were attending Russian schools and colleges, in addition to the 2,000 attending the Mennonite secondary schools. Zentralschulen were also established in the Crimea, and in the Orenburg, Ufa, and Slavgorod daughter settlements from 1908 on and even after the Revolution.

At first the secondary curriculum was determined by the Mennonite administration of each school, although it was commonly patterned after the first two schools, Ohrloff and Chortitza. After the new military service law of 1874 permitted graduates of an approved secondary school to reduce the period of military service from six to three years, the Mennonites planned a new curriculum to qualify their schools for approval, which was granted by the Russian Department of Education in 1876. Besides the common general subjects, this curriculum included for every year Bible study and church history (including Mennonite history and faith) and both German and Russian languages and choral singing. This curriculum called for a six-year program, but later the four-year program was restored, which continued until 1920.

A regular two-year teacher-training course (Normal School) was added to the Halbstadt Zentralschule in 1878. In 1890 a similar program was adopted at the Chortitza Zentralschule. These two schools trained most of the Mennonite elementary teachers until 1917. Plans to create a separate 3-4 year normal school could not be carried out until 1917. It was perfected in 1921 as the "Molotschnaer Mennonitisches Lehrerseminar."

Girls were not refused admission to the Zentralschulen until 1870, although but few actually enrolled. The first effective girls' secondary school was established at Halbstadt in 1874, which finally developed into an 8-year Gymnasium. The first regular coeducational school was established in 1908 at Davlekanovo in the Ufa settlement.

The graduates of the Mennonite Zentralschule were not eligible for admission to the Russian state higher schools. The Halbstadt Kommerzschule (8-year program) established in 1908, patterned after the German Realgymnasium, was equal to the Russian Commercial or Realschule, hence its graduates could now enter the state schools, but not the universities, which required graduation from a classical Gymnasium. No Mennonite secondary school in Russia ever attained this standard. The Kommerzschule also offered training for entrance into business activities. Students coming from the Zentralschule were admitted to the fifth year of the Kommerzschule.

In addition to the "official" secondary schools under the management of colony-appointed boards, a number of private secondary schools were in operation, usually financed and promoted by wealthy estate owners.

All Mennonite education in Russia was under the supervision of the Mennonite ministers until 1843. This was the standard ruling of the Russian government for all foreign immigrant groups in Russia, especially the Germans. This worked satisfactorily for the Lutherans and Catholics, whose ministers were trained and salaried, but not for the Mennonites, whose ministers were untrained and self-supporting. In 1843 the government placed the Mennonite schools under the Agricultural Association (*q.v.*), which also was not logical, since education was only a secondary responsibility for it. After the death of Cornies (1848) the situation deteriorated until boards of education were organized to operate the schools (in the Molotschna and Chortitza colonies in 1869). From 1881 to 1905 the Russianization pressures of the government handicapped the schools, threatening their independence and Mennonite character. In 1905, the year of proclamation of new liberties in Russia (Manifesto of Czar Nicholas), the Mennonite school program took on new life, and several new secondary schools were established. A Mennonite Teachers' Association (*q.v.*) was soon formed which gradually took over many of the functions of the boards of education, which had been forced almost out of action. Due to the drafting of many teachers in 1914-17 (World War I) the schools suffered. The return of the teachers in

1917 repaired the damage, and in spite of many troubles five new Zentralschulen were established in 1917-20. One of these schools was still operating in 1931. But the program of the new Soviet Communist state, which soon led to the nationalization of all schools, created increasing difficulties for the Mennonite schools. Religious instruction was forbidden, although continued for a brief time under the guise of Mennonite history. By 1928 the government had succeeded in setting up and bringing into operation its own program of education. From now on the Mennonite teachers were forced out as rapidly as Russian communist teachers could be supplied. Under Stalin all teachers had to sign an atheist questionnaire. Most Mennonites refused to sign and lost their jobs. This was the final end of Mennonite secondary education, at least in the Ukraine. It is not clear when the secondary schools in the Ural region and in Siberia were closed.

Under the German occupation of the Ukraine in the fall of 1941 the German schools and churches were to be reopened and religious instruction allowed. The Chortitza Zentralschule was reopened and celebrated its 100th anniversary in 1942. The dominant Nazi ideology soon began to interfere with real freedom, but before other Zentralschulen were reopened the Germans evacuated the Ukraine in 1943, taking the German population with them.

United States. The first Mennonite secondary school in the United States was the school at Wadsworth, Ohio, operated by a board of the General Conference Mennonite Church, 1868-78. Although its purpose was the training of ministers, it was actually largely a secondary school to which a program of Biblical and theological courses was added. (Mention should be made of Freeland Seminary founded in 1848 at Collegeville, Pa., by Abraham Hunsicker, at that time a preacher in the GCM Church, which ultimately became Ursinus College. Henry Hunsicker, son of Abraham, was principal 1848-65. Both Abraham and Henry were expelled from the Mennonite Church in 1851, after which they were nonsectarian.)

Meanwhile the new Mennonite immigrants from Russia, with their tradition of education provided by the church, finding no high schools in their new settlements in Kansas, Nebraska, Minnesota, and the Dakotas, established a series of German preparatory schools (*q.v.*), the first of which was founded at Goessel, Kan., in 1879, which finally developed into Halstead Seminary, established in 1883 at Halstead, moved in 1893 to what became the Bethel College campus in North Newton, and continued there as Bethel College Academy. Other schools were established at Mountain Lake, Minn. (1886); Buhler, Kan. (1889); Beatrice, Neb. (1890); Hillsboro, Kan. (1897); Whitewater, Kan. (1900); Henderson, Neb. (1902); and nine others in 1906-38. These schools gradually all died out. (See **Preparatory Schools.**) Bethel College Academy was discontinued in 1927 with a brief revival during World War II (1944-46).

In addition to the Bethel College Academy, a series of Mennonite secondary schools called academies, all of which have developed into colleges, were established 1894-1917 as follows: Elkhart Institute (MC) 1894 (to Goshen in 1903), now Goshen College; Central Mennonite College (GCM) at Bluffton, 1900, now Bluffton College; Hesston Academy (MC) at Hesston, Kan., 1909, now Hesston College; Freeman Academy (GCM), Freeman, S.D., 1903, now Freeman Junior College; Eastern Mennonite School at Harrisonburg, Va., 1917, now Eastern Mennonite College; and Tabor Academy (1908), now Tabor College. At Hesston, Harrisonburg, and Freeman the academies have continued as high-school departments alongside of the colleges. At Goshen, Bluffton, and Tabor they were discontinued.

Two Mennonite secondary schools developed in Western Canada about the same time, which have continued and have not grown into colleges—Mennonite Collegiate Institute at Gretna, Man. (1889), and Rosthern German-English Academy at Rosthern, Sask. (1908).

A new day came for Mennonite secondary education in the United States after 1940, partly as a result of the pressure of World War II. A series of Mennonite high schools were established in the Mennonite Church (MC) as follows: Lancaster (Pa.) Mennonite School 1942, Bethel Springs School (Culp, Ark.) 1944, Johnstown (Pa.) Mennonite School 1944, Iowa Mennonite School (Kalona) 1945, Belleville (Pa.) Mennonite School 1945, Rockway Mennonite School (Kitchener, Ont.) 1945, Western Mennonite School (Salem, Ore.) 1945, Christopher Dock Mennonite School (Lansdale, Pa.) 1954, Bethany Christian High School (Goshen, Ind.) 1954, and one planned to open at Kidron, Ohio, in 1959. These are mostly conference-owned and -operated schools.

Two similar schools have been established by private groups in the General Conference Mennonite Church: Oklahoma Bible Academy (Meno) 1917 and Berean Academy (Elbing, Kan.) 1946. Central Kansas Bible Academy (Hutchinson), est. 1948, is inter-Mennonite (GCM, KMB, MB), as are Meade Bible Academy (Kan.) 1945 (EMB and GCM), Immanuel Academy (Reedley, Cal.) 1944 (MB and KMB), and Lustre Bible Academy (Mont.) 1947 (GCM, EMB, MB). One Mennonite Brethren secondary school has been operating since 1902, the Corn (Okla.) Bible Academy.

In 1956 the total enrollment of the 17 Mennonite secondary schools in the United States (including Hesston and EMC) was c2,300, of which c1,650 were in the 10 MC schools.

In 1958 Canadian Mennonites were operating 11 high schools, 5 MB, 4 GCM, 1 MC, and 1 inter-Mennonite. Two of the GCM schools, Gretna and Rosthern, were of the old type, but all the rest were new type, founded since World War II, and all but Rockway and Steinbach (Man.) by the newer Russian Mennonite immigrants of 1922-27. These include the MB Collegiate Institute in Winnipeg, Man. (1945), Mennonite Educational Institute at Clearbrook (formerly Abbotsford), B.C. (1944, with one GCM congregation participating), Alberta Mennonite High School, Coaldale, Alberta (1946), Sharon Mennonite Educational Institute, Yarrow, B.C., and Eden Christian College, Niagara-on-the-Lake, Ont., and two GCM schools: the United Mennonite Educational Institute at Leamington, Ont. (1944), and Mennonite Educational Institute, Winnipeg (1958).

Steinbach (Man.) Bible Academy was founded in 1946 (closed and then restarted in 1953) as an independent inter-Mennonite private school supported chiefly by EMB, Kleine Gemeinde (now EM), and Immanuel Mennonite members. The total attendance at the eleven schools in Canada in 1958 was c1900. Two earlier high schools in the Fraser Valley, B.C., at Yarrow (1945-49) and Greendale-Sardis (1948-59), were of short duration. The Mennonite Educational Institute operated at Altona, Man., 1908-26, when its building burned down.

All the Mennonite high schools in the United States and Canada today maintain a strong emphasis on their Christian character, and most of them also emphasize their Mennonite character and their particular denominational loyalty. All are supported by private donations and tuition fees. Most of them also maintain high academic standards equal to the public high schools or better, and a number of them are accredited by the states or provinces in which they are located. The six Canadian schools operated by the newer immigrant groups also emphasize German language teaching.

The Mennonite foreign missions in the Far East and Africa generally have established secondary schools in their areas as soon as feasible. Dhamtari (India) Christian Academy (MC), for instance, was established in 1913. In the Latin-American countries, because of the relatively high level of education, this was not done.

The new Mennonite settlements established 1930 and later by refugees from Russia in Paraguay have produced three 4-year secondary schools, the Filadelfia Zentralschule in Colonia Fernheim, Chaco, the Zentralschule in the central village in the Friesland Colony in East Paraguay, and the Neuland Zentralschule in the Chaco. The Filadelfia school has added a two-year teachers' institute.

In Brazil a Zentralschule was established in Witmarsum in the Krauel Colony (c1938), but in World War II all private schools in Brazil were nationalized and the use of the German language in schools was suppressed. In 1954 a Mennonite Zentralschule was established near Curitiba.   H.S.B.

Friesen, *Brüderschaft;* P. J. Braun, "The Educational System of the Mennonite Colonies in South Russia," *MQR* III (1929) 168-82; L. Froese, "Das pädagogische Kultursystem der mennonitischen Siedlungsgruppe in Russland" (doctoral dissertation, Göttingen, 1949); M. S. Harder, "The Origin, Philosophy, and Development of Education Among the Mennonites" (doctoral dissertation, University of Southern California, 1949); Ira E. Miller, "The Development and the Present Status of Mennonite Secondary and Higher Education in the United States of America" (doctoral dissertation, Temple University, 1953); J. E. Hartzler, *Education Among the Mennonites of America* (Danvers, 1925); Silas Hertzler, "Attendance at Mennonite Colleges and Secondary Schools," an annual statistical report in the *MQR* begining with 1929, includes the statistics for secondary schools up to and including the school year 1951-52.

Secret Societies, commonly called lodges, are oath-bound fraternities with more or less secret grips, signs, ritual, and the like, the most significant perhaps being the Freemasons. Persons unite with secret societies for the fellowship they provide, for the sense of security they afford, sometimes for financial benefits, and for the religious ritual they offer. It is often also a matter of prestige to be a member of a lodge. One of the oldest lodges is the Ancient Order of Free and Accepted Masons, a fraternity which probably had its beginnings in the trade guilds of the Middle Ages but which claims to have been originated by King Solomon in ancient Israel. Until the 19th century no Mennonite would have wanted to join a lodge nor would he have been accepted into lodge membership. But in the last hundred years, as Mennonites have become somewhat more culturally assimilated, there has been a tendency in the less strict congregations to tolerate lodge membership on the part of members.

The official position of the various Mennonite groups has remained one of opposition to lodge membership, however. There are five reasons for this opposition. For one thing Mennonites in all lands have always been opposed to the oath, and secret societies are oath-bound. Christ said, "But I say unto you, Swear not at all" (Matt. 5:34). In his excellent exposition of this prohibition of the oath (*q.v.*) Christian Neff shows that Christ intended His words to be taken at their face value, for lesser oaths involving the temple or its altar are wrong precisely for the reason that they ultimately involve a real oath taken in the name of God. Matt. 23:16-22. It would therefore be impossible for a Christian who rejects the oath to unite with an oath-bound organization. But more than that, the oaths sworn by various lodges are particularly offensive by their severe sanctions, so that even some Christian denominations which do not oppose a simple legal oath nevertheless object to the oaths sworn by the Masons; this is true of the Orthodox Presbyterian Church, for example.

A second reason for the Mennonite objection to membership in secret societies is the desire to be free and open witnesses for Christ and His Gospel. Christ Himself said that He had taught nothing in secret. His teaching and program were open to all. He had no secrets. John 18:20. Mennonites, seeking to follow their Lord in this respect, do not believe that it is right for a Christian to have a part in organized secrecy.

The Mennonites as a brotherhood type of church seek to avoid any inconsistent use of titles. They feel that the church should consist of believers who are spiritually on one level. Historically they called each other brother and sister. It is therefore impossible for them to reconcile the teaching of Jesus (Matt. 23:8-10) against employing such common titles as Rabbi, Father, or Teacher, or such near-blasphemous titles as Worshipful Grand Master, as are used in secret societies. The hierarchy of the lodge is for Mennonites irreconcilable with New Testament Christianity.

A fourth objection which is sometimes raised against lodges is their supposedly sub-Christian ethics. A lodge member, for example, may swear not knowingly to have carnal relations with the wife, sister, or daughter of a fellow lodge member. Why not, ask some Christians, simply become a Christian and live a holy Christian life? It is of course recognized that many lodge members would not stoop to immorality of any kind.

The most serious objection to membership in such secret societies as the Masons is their offering salvation to those who keep the rules of the lodge. All members expect to go to the "Grand Lodge Above" fully prepared to meet the "Supreme Architect of the Universe." This position is held whether or no the member believes in Christ. But Christians hold fast to the clear word of Christ that He is the only Door, that no man can come to the Father but by Him. John 10:1-18; 14:6. The apostolic message was that only through Christ could men be saved. Acts 4:12.

The Mennonite position on secret societies is set forth in the various constitutional and disciplinary standards of the several groups. In the Mennonite Church (MC) all district conference disciplines forbid lodge membership. The Rules and Discipline of the Lancaster Conference (MC) of Oct. 7, 1881, for instance, indicate in section 20 that membership in secret societies is "strictly forbidden." Article XIII of the "Christian Fundamentals" adopted by Mennonite General Conference (MC), Aug. 24-26, 1921, declares that secret orders are "antagonistic to the tenor and spirit of the Gospel." In its "Declaration of Commitment in Respect to Christian Separation and Nonconformity to the World," adopted by the General Conference (MC) on Aug. 26, 1955, it is stated: "We also reaffirm our age-long opposition to secret and oath-bound fraternities and lodges, holding that the principle of organized secrecy is wrong in itself, that the swearing of oaths is prohibited the Christian by the plain word of our Lord, that the hierarchical titles of the lodge are unbecoming to humble followers of Christ, that Christians ought not to be unequally yoked with non-Christians, and that in many cases lodges erroneously offer salvation to their members on other grounds than the shed blood of Jesus Christ. Lodge membership is therefore a test of membership in the Mennonite Church."

The current constitution of the General Conference Mennonite Church (1953) declares that the General Conference "believes that membership in oath-bound secret societies . . . is contrary to such apostolic admonitions as: 'Be not unequally yoked with unbelievers (II Cor. 6:14-15).'" The earlier constitution (1896) contained a long article against secret societies, declaring that "no congregation which tolerates among its members those belonging to secret societies shall be admitted into Conference." The G.C.M. General Conference long had a "Lodge Committee," whose assignment was to produce literature and promote teaching against "the lodge." Among the resolutions reported by this committee and adopted by the Conference was the following (1899): "Resolved that the General Conference takes a positive stand against every kind of secret society, and that the conference considers it as necessary in order to maintain this position, that the member churches declare at the Conference, if and with what success they have laboured at cleansing their churches from members of secret societies and the Conference herewith announces that if it is found that some churches still tolerate secret society members to remain unmolested in the church, that such churches shall no longer be considered as members in the Conference." However, in spite of the vigorous position historically taken by the G.C.M.

Church, the autonomy of the local congregation and social pressures have resulted in some lodge membership in certain areas, especially east of the Kansas-Nebraska line.

The Mennonite Brethren Church also has maintained a strong position on secret societies. Its Confession of Faith contains the following declaration: "Concerning the joining of lodges or secret societies we believe and confess that there is no scriptural basis which would permit Christians to join with lodges and secret societies in view of the many unchristian practices of these organizations such as horrible oaths which members must take and because the name of our blessed Lord and Saviour is omitted or rather excluded from them." In former years all baptismal candidates were required to promise that they would not join a secret society. In many churches this practice is still continued.

The constitution of the Evangelical Mennonite Church (Kleine Gemeinde) states (1956) that church members "should not belong to a worldly or secret lodge." Other smaller Mennonite bodies have similar positions. There is no evidence of a position against secret societies by European Mennonites. However, except for the Masonic Lodge, there are few such societies in Europe. Occasionally more liberal Mennonites in Holland and North Germany have joined the Masons.   J.C.W.

J. F. Funk, "Freemasonry Again," *The Herald of Truth*, August 1868, 113-15; J. E. Hartzler, "Secret Societies," *Bible Doctrine* (Scottdale, 1914) 560-74; Daniel Kauffman, "Secret Societies," *Doctrines of the Bible* (Scottdale, 1928) 522-31; H. P. Krehbiel, *Unsere Stellung zu den Geheimen Gesellschaften und Warum* (Berne, 1898); *Voices Opposing the Lodge or Secret Societies Heard at the General Conference of the Mennonites of North America* (Berne, 1901, German ed. same year); *An Article on Secret Societies* (Published by the Lodge Committee of the General Conference of Mennonites of North America, n.d.-1915); H. P. Krehbiel, *History of the General Conference of the Mennonite Church of North America* II (Newton, 1938) 73 f., 271-79. R. B. Kuiper *et al.*, *Christ or the Lodge. A Report on Masonry* (Philadelphia); "The World of Hiram Abif," *Time*, July 25, 1949; J. C. Wenger, *Separated unto God* (Scottdale, 1952) 191-96; Clayton F. Derstine, *The Yawning Pit of Lodgery* (Eureka, Ill., 1921); J. H. Oberholtzer, "Geheime Gesellschaften," *Der Wahre Character von J. H. Oberholtzer* (1860) 50-54; H. R. Voth, *Gibt es Verhältnisse unter uns, die ein Werben von seiten der geheimen Gesellschaften unter unsern Gliedern begünstigen? Und wie begründen wir unsere Stellung diesen Gesellschaften gegenüber?* (Gretna, 1910); David Schroeder and Esko W. Loewen, "Loyalty and Lodges," *Studies in Church Discipline* (Newton, 1958) 173-81.

Sedlmaier, Hans, a peasant of Oberhaim in the Landshut (*q.v.*) area of Bavaria, Germany, was won for the Anabaptist movement by Augustin Würtzlburger (*q.v.*) and was baptized with his wife and two sons, Paul and Wilbold, and his daughter Katerina. Soon afterward, in 1528, he was arrested and taken to Landshut, where he was tried on the rack. Sedlmaier confessed that Würtzlburger had been with him twice in Oberhaim, and had baptized him; he did not consider this a second baptism, since his baptism as an infant was not a true baptism. He had partaken of the sacrament at Easter, but only as the bread of thanksgiving. But he refused to confess that Würtzlburger had been rebaptized "even if they would tear him to pieces." He ended his confession by saying that he would die for his faith. He was presumably beheaded, for not long afterward the Landshut council reported to Augsburg that an Anabaptist had been thus executed.

NEFF.

V. A. Winter, *Gesch. der baierischen Wiedertäufer* (Munich, 1809) 26 ff.; *TA Bayern II*, 21 ff.; *ML IV*.

Seemann, Enoch, Jr. (1694-1744), the son of Enoch Seemann, Sr., (*q.v.*), was also a painter, specializing in still life. Some of his father's pictures have been erroneously ascribed to him; the subjects of the portraits were no longer living at Enoch's time. He became a well-known portraitist in London, where he painted several members of the royal family. A self-portrait hangs in the Dresden Art Gallery; it is reproduced in *Mennonite Life* for July 1949. He died in London in 1744.   F.H.

Alfred Muttray, "Der Danziger Maler Enoch Seemann" in *Mitteilungen des Westpreussischen Geschichtsvereins* XVI (1917) 59-61; Georg Cuny, "Die Maler Deneter und Seemann," *ibid.*, XII (1913) 48-54; Kurt Kauenhoven, "Mennonite Artists Danzig and Koenigsberg," *Menn. Life IV* (July 1949) 17; H. G. Mannhardt, *Die Danziger Mennoniten-Gemeinde* (Danzig, 1919) 78; *ML IV*.

Seemann, Enoch, Sr. (1661-?), the son of Isaac Seemann (*q.v.*), surpassed his father in artistic ability; he learned painting in the studio of his brother Isaac, then made extensive journeys, returned to Elbing in 1680, and was received into the Mennonite congregation there at the age of nineteen. In 1683 he moved to Danzig and on December 5 of that year married Susanna Ordonn. On the basis of his work he was made a "free master," and was permitted (outside the guild) to paint only portraits and could not keep apprentices. He served as "City Painter" (Stadtmaler) 1683-98. At first all went well. But soon the elder of the congregation, Georg Hansen (*q.v.*), forbade him to paint portraits, suggesting that he paint landscapes instead. Seemann replied that the signs on the shops were then also wrong and should be removed. When after a time these signs were not removed, and the guild of landscape painters made trouble for him, he again began to paint portraits, thereby drawing the renewed censure of the elder, who placed him under the ban in 1697. Seemann published *Offenbahrung und Bestraffung des Gergen Hansens Thorheit* (Stolzenberg, 1697), in which the story is given. About 1698 he went to Warsaw and served at the royal court until 1704, then went to London, where he died (date unknown). Seven children were born to him; four were named in publications, but only two are recorded in the church books of the Danzig congregations. (*ME I*, 167, 171; *ML IV*.)   F.H.

Seemann, Isaac, the descendant of a Flemish Mennonite family, a good portrait painter, several of whose works were reproduced in copper etchings. He was a preacher (*Vermahner*) of the Elbing-Ellerwald Mennonite congregation in West Prussia, moved to Danzig in 1683, went to London about 1700, and died there in 1730 at the age of ninety. His son Enoch Seemann, Sr. (*q.v.*), was also an able painter. (*ML IV*.)   F.H.

Sega (Saga, Saag, von der Sach), **Francesco della**, a Hutterite martyr, was born in 1528 or 1532 at Rovigo in the Venetian Republic. He went to Padua

to study civil law in the 1540's and lived there the life of a typical young student. Stricken with illness brought on by excesses and chided by a pious craftsman, he turned to the Scriptures, determined to model his life after Christ's. His conversion was complete: he even abandoned law for the tailor's craft, subjecting himself to the ridicule of family and friends. He evidently went directly over to the evangelical movement then current in northern Italy and was probably baptized by some leader of the movement, which around that time was coming under the influence of anti-Trinitarianism. Unfortunately we do not know when or by whom he was baptized, but since he was later accepted into the Hutterite communion without having to undergo adult baptism, he must have been baptized in Italy.

Della Sega's activities during the early 1550's are obscure. Around 1557 he visited Vienna and then traveled with a Hungarian friend in Hungary and Slovakia. He learned of the Hutterites from a Moravian servant, and, enlisting the latter as a guide, visited several Hutterite communities. Much impressed by them he requested and was granted admission to membership, perhaps first in Slovakia, but later in Moravia. There he married a woman from the Grisons and settled down to his humble craft.

In 1559, receiving the news of his father's death, he traveled to Italy to see about the inheritance, and other trips followed, on which he carried word of the Hutterites to friends. Because of this activity it has been assumed that he was a minister (Beck, 212), but he later told the Inquisition, "I have not baptized anyone because I am neither priest nor minister. I am a simple tailor." Perhaps he was accorded special position as an emissary, without full ordination.

In 1562 on one of these expeditions to Italy in the company of Nicola Buccella of Padua and Antonio Rizzetto of Vicenza (*q.v.*) he was preparing to lead some twenty new recruits from the Cittadella community to Moravia when an unfortunate incident occurred. A man who claimed to have been defrauded by Buccella's brother complained to the authorities at Capodistria. Captain Lando, in charge there, arrested della Sega, Rizzetto, and Buccella (Aug. 27, 1562), but allowed the other members of the party to go on their way. Upon examining their documents the officer realized that he had stumbled upon a case of heresy, and at once communicated with the Inquisition at Venice, sending the prisoners there for further examination. They were imprisoned at San Giovanni in Bragora, where Giulio Gherlandi (*q.v.*), who had fallen into the hands of the authorities the preceding year, was being held. The fellow believers quickly made contact and were able to speak to each other in the weeks that ensued.

Della Sega was questioned Sept. 26, 1562, about his personal history and beliefs. Pressed concerning the latter, he agreed to prepare a statement. His confession, dated Oct. 20, 1562, is the source of much of the above information. The principal points of his faith were these: salvation is by faith, not works; baptism should be reserved for believers;

confession should be to God, not to priests; one should seek to obey God's commandments. There is no sign of the anti-Trinitarianism to which he was almost certainly exposed earlier in Italy. There followed a series of examinations conducted by the famed Spanish Jesuit theologian Salmeron, among others. Throughout these interviews della Sega continued to stress his devotion to the Scriptures.

Early in 1563 della Sega directed a letter to Leonhard Sailer (q.v.) (Lanzenstiel) and Peter Scherer (Walpot, q.v.) as well as to the whole community in Moravia (letter in the Hutterite Codices of 1563). This epistle, about whose means of delivery we are left to speculate, is of exceptional interest, breathing as it does a pure faith and love: "I would not let the occasion pass while I am yet in this tabernacle of desiring for you the grace of the salvation of the omnipotent God. I have loved you all sincerely; but I love you even more now that I have been deprived of your presence, which deprivation is a great tribulation to me. And when the end comes, I will love you with the love that I have through Christ Himself, because you are members of His body, yea, bone of His bone, flesh of His flesh. And you have loved me sincerely; through you I have received of God innumerable benefits for which I have not repaid you, and thus I remain your debtor. But I desire to bear this my humiliation with patience, for love of you; yea, I would, through love of you, bear being rejected and cast out and finally led to the execution." He continues with exhortations directed to the pastors and to the community as a whole, as well as to his fellow Italians who had joined the group. "I say to you, my dear ones, especially love and fear the Lord and see to it that you never forsake the brotherhood and church but keep always before your eyes Christ's parable of the vine. . . . Think what grace you have received from God through being led from the deepest shadows to His marvelous light, and love one another with a pure heart, with all sincerity and fullness of heart, without pretense." The letter ends with greetings to his friends, to his wife, and to his mother-in-law Florentina.

A decree of the Venetian Council of Ten, issued April 7, 1564, providing for the expulsion of heretics (Cantu, III, 139), raised in della Sega the hope that it might apply to him. He wrote the court July 18, 1564, asking release from his imprisonment. His arguments were ignored. In November the Inquisitor Fra Adriano prepared a report on his case in which he listed the chief heresies of della Sega and Rizzetto: their rejection of the Roman Church, of infant baptism, and of confession to priests; and their union with the Hutterites. An interrogation of Dec. 12, 1564, showed della Sega still firm in his faith despite the abjuration one week earlier of his companion Buccella.

It must have been around this time that della Sega addressed a letter to his mother and brothers in Italy. This undelivered letter, characterized by Benrath as "one of the most moving documents to come out of the whole Anabaptist movement," reproaches his brethren for ignoring his efforts to bring them to see the light. "May God pardon you and summon you to repentance. I pray you for the last time to consider why you have come into the world, and calling yourselves Christians, to do what Christ teaches. . . . I exhort you still to desire His grace and to observe His commandments. I pray it of you with all my heart, now that I am about to die. In place of my last testament, since I have no money to leave, that which I have and know for divine grace I manifest to you, and anew with great sorrow of heart and with tears in my eyes, I plead with you to seek God while He is to be found. . . . And do not put off your conversion, because we do not know what tomorrow will bring. Think that if God is merciful, His wrath is great toward the rebellious. . . . Now, if this letter should not please you, I know nought else to say. God will not save you by force. It remains to me, in this case, to ask you only to pass this letter to some other who may have the desire to do good and live a Christian life."

Sentence was passed on della Sega and Rizzetto Feb. 8, 1565. Della Sega wavered momentarily when the executioner came for him. He appeared undecided in the presence of Salmeron, Feb. 20. The Court reproved him for his indecision on Feb. 22, but in the end he remained true to his faith. On the night of Monday, Feb. 26, 1565, in the accustomed manner, he was cast into the depths of the sea. "But the sea will give up its dead at the Judgment Day of God."   DeWind.

Beck, Geschichts-Bücher, 211-12, 241-43; K. Benrath, "Wiedertäufer im Venetianischen um die Mitte des 16. Jahrhunderts," Theologische Studien und Kritiken LVIII (1885) 45 ff.; C. Cantu, Gli eretici d'Italia (Turin, 1865-66) III, 139; E. Comba, I nostri protestanti (Florence, 1897) II, 521-54; H. A. DeWind, "Italian Hutterite Martyrs," MQR XXVIII (1954) 163-85; "Eingabe des Francesco della Sega an die Inquisition (18. Juli 1564)," Gem.-Kal. 1938, 93-95; Mart. Mir. D 298, E 664; R. Wolkan, Geschicht-Buch, 313-18; Zieglschmid, Chronik, 408, 410, 413 ff.

Segenschmid, Bastl: see **Anfang, Wastl** and **Schmid, Bastl.**

Segers(z) (Seghers): see **Zegers, Herman.**

Seid, Katharina, an "obstinate Anabaptist," the wife of Andreas Klaiber (q.v.), was arrested in Strasbourg, Alsace, and tried on Nov. 23, 1534. Her confession of faith gives some insight into early Anabaptism. She said she had been baptized in her home two years previously by a man who had come from over the Rhine; his name she did not know. Years previously Matthias Zell (q.v.) had preached that others, more genuine than they, would come. Therefore she prayed that God would give her true understanding. Then the brethren called Anabaptists had come, who had rightly explained the Scriptures and had first showed her the truth; by the grace of God she hoped to remain steadfast in it. She knew of no preacher of the established church who could give better instruction and doctrine. Baptism by water was not essential to her, but the knowledge of Christ; this she had, and by God's grace she would maintain it. When she was urged to desist from such error and be taught by the Reformed preachers, she replied that she was too simple for them, since she was not educated. But she was sure of her faith. She would let each depend on his own faith, since each was responsible for himself.

There had indeed been learned men among the Anabaptists, but the people had not been able to learn from them. "They departed from us, but we do not depart." She trusted God, who had led her from bondage to salvation, to help her understand His truth.

Then the sentence of expulsion was read to her. She responded that she had spoken nothing but what Christ her Lord had commanded her, and she asked for the sake of the Lord to be allowed to stay; she visited only the sick who had need of her, and if she could serve anyone she would gladly do it. When asked who belonged to her sect she said she knew no Anabaptists and could say nothing about it; she would not betray them. She went nowhere and knew only Melchior Hofmann (*q.v.*), who was in prison here, "of whom my lords say that he is an Anabaptist"; she had been fined a pound four years previously for lodging him and his wife and child; his wife did not want to stay in Strasbourg. Katharina was probably expelled.   NEFF.

T. W. Röhrich, "Zur Geschichte der strassburgischen Wiedertäufer in den Jahren 1527 bis 1543," *Ztscht für die historische Theologie* XXX (1860) 79 f.; *ML* IV.

Seidel (Seidl, Seyel, Seydel), **Hans,** an Anabaptist martyr of Murau, who was seized with Hans Donner (*q.v.*) of Wels at St. Veit in Carinthia, Austria, on the Wednesday before Christmas in 1538. Both were beheaded after a valiant confession of their faith. (Zieglschmid, *Chronik,* 193; *Mart. Mir.* D 44, E 450; *ML* IV.)   NEFF.

Seidenkohen, Cunas, of Constance, an Anabaptist martyr, who was put to death at Bern, Switzerland, on March 28, 1538.

A. Fluri, *Beiträge zur Geschichte der bernischen Täufer* (Bern, 1912) 14; *Mart. Mir.* E 1129; *ML* III.

Seidl, Johann (1804-75), a poet of Vienna, Austria, author of *Die Wiedertäufer,* a poem describing a hunt for Anabaptists; one of them, Richard Willemson, is seen by the bailiffs, but he succeeds in escaping. The executioner, pursuing him over a frozen lake, breaks in. Willemson saves his life, is himself seized, and ends his life at the stake. It is the story of Dirk Willems (*q.v.*), found in van Braght's *Martyr's Mirror.* It was published in 1876. (*Menn. Bl.,* 1891, 6, supplement; *ML* IV.)   NEFF.

Seidensticker, Oswald (d. 1894), an American historian, author of the valuable works, *Die ersten deutschen Einwanderer in Amerika 1683* (Philadelphia, 1883); *Ephrata, eine amerikanische Klostergeschichte* (1883); *Bilder aus der Deutsch-Pennsylvanischen Geschichte* (1885); *William Penn's Travels in Holland and Germany* (1878); *Die beiden Christopher Sauer in Germantown* (1881); *Geschichte der Deutschen Gesellschaft in Pennsylvanien 1676-1876* (Philadelphia, 1876).   H.S.B.

Seifensieder, Leupolt: see Scharnschlager.

Seifensieder, Michael (Michiel Zeepzieder, also Michl Böhem), an Anabaptist martyr. While traveling from Wallern in Bohemia to Tirol in 1536, he was betrayed and arrested at Vienna (*q.v.*), Austria, and burned at the stake on March 31, 1536, with his

brethren Hieronymous Käls (*q.v.*) and Hans Oberecker (*q.v.*). Loserth's assertion (*ML* III, 11) that he was identical with Hans Mändl is incorrect.
                    VDZ.

Mart. Mir. D 39, E 445; Wolkan, *Lieder,* 170; Zieglschmid, *Chronik,* 158-60.

Seigne (Sennergemeinde) Mennonite Church, Alsace, France, now extinct, had its place of worship on a farm called by that name on the left bank of the Doubs River opposite the village of Vaufrey, near the French border east of Montbéliard, in the county of Montjoie. The Mennonite community here must have been started very early by Swiss refugees from the canton of Bern, probably in the latter 17th century. The area was isolated and rugged and furnished a quiet retreat. The first definite data about the group date from 1750, when it had close relations to the congregations at Montbéliard and in the Swiss canton of Neufchatel (Chaux de Fond). At times it is difficult to distinguish Montbéliard and Seigne, especially before the meetinghouse was built at the former place (1833). Thereafter Seigne was completely independent, with its meetings in the homes of the members. In 1888 there were 76 baptized members. Due to emigration to America and removal to the Montbéliard (*q.v.*) and Courgenay (*q.v.*) congregations, Seigne declined. About 1918 the congregation dissolved, and the few remaining members joined or moved to Montbéliard. The Courgenay congregation was built up largely from Seigne. In 1903 Elder Pierre Ramseyer, who had been ordained in 1896 at Seigne, moved to Courgenay. Elders at Seigne from 1830 on were Peter Rich (d. 1849), Hans Rich (d. 1877), Jean Staehli (ord. 1859, d. 1865), Jean Ramseyer (ord. 1866, moved to Alsace 1897, d. 1920), Pierre Ramseyer (ord. 1896, moved to Switzerland 1903).   H.S.B.

Pierre Sommer, "Assemblée de Seigne," *Christ Seul,* February 1930, pp. 8-10.

Seije(n): see Seye.

Seil(e)maker: see Seylemaker.

Seiler, Friedrich (1642-1708), a Reformed pastor in Basel, author of *Wiedertäuffer-Geheimnusse* (Basel, 1680). The book is listed in the Calvary catalog, *Verzeichnis seltener und wertvoller Bücher* (Berlin, 1870, 59), with the title *Anabaptista larvatus, das ist Verstellter Wieder-Täuffer. Entdeckt beydes In einem historischen Entwurff aller uns bekandter Wieder-Täufferen Vrsprungs. Wie auch Einer dogmatischen Widerlegung aller derselben Irrthumen, seltzamer Meynungen, vnd hin vnd wieder erweckter Unruhen* (Basel, 1680) (copy in GCL). The first part, 182 pp. plus 22 pp. of preface and introduction and 25 pp. of contents, indices, etc., contains an "Anabaptist History" in 12 chapters, of which the last five chapters treat of the Swiss Anabaptists, including those of Zürich, Bern, Basel, and Schaffhausen-St. Gall, based largely upon secondary sources, especially Bullinger and Ottius. A complete three-page list of sources used is given. The second part, the "Dogmatic Part," devoted to a description and refutation of the Anabaptist "errors," occupies 510 pp., plus 30 pp. of contents and indices. The

33

topics covered are: God and the Trinity, Creation of Man, Preservation and Government of all Things, Adam's Fall, Original Sin, Free Will, Redemption, Election, Scripture, Saving Faith, Justification, Incarnation, The Church, Ministers, The Ban or Church Discipline, Baptism, Communion, State, Oath, and Future Life. Much more time is spent on the exposition and defense of the author's position as a Reformed theologian than on a statement of the Anabaptist position. And although the author freely used the Franckenthal and Emden debate protocols, he drew the Quakers, Schwenckfelders, Weigelians, and other radicals into the orbit of his discussion alongside the Anabaptists and Mennonites. H.S.B.

Seiler, Heini (Heinrich), an Anabaptist martyr, a hatter of Aarau, Switzerland, who suffered death by drowning at Bern in July 1531 together with Hans Seckler (see **Hansmann**) and Hans Dreier. He was one of the eight Anabaptists who had planned to take part in the great religious colloquy of 1528 in Bern (q.v.) but were arrested, tried after the colloquy, and expelled from the city and canton. Seized the second time, Seiler was examined on May 24, 1529, with the two men mentioned above and held prisoner for two years longer. An account of the trial is found in **Hansmann, Hans.** On April 19, 1531, he had a conversation with Hans Pfistermeyer (q.v.).   Neff.

J. Heiz, *Die Täufer im Aargau* (Aarau, 1902) 11-13; Müller, *Berner Täufer*, 44; *Mart. Mir.* E 1129; *ML* IV.

Seiler, Leonhard: see Lanzenstiel.

Selden (Kan.) Amish Mennonite Church, now extinct, was a member of the Western A.M. Conference (MC). Selden is in northwest Kansas in Sheridan County, but the settlement is sometimes known as the Decatur County congregation because many of its members lived in that county, which adjoins Sheridan. The first settlers came from Illinois before 1887, when the congregation was organized. The meetinghouse was built in 1888-89. A. B. Kolb after a western trip wrote in November 1891 concerning Selden, "There are some 12 or 15 families here. I think they are nearly all Amish." The highest membership, about 100, was reached in 1897. By 1905 it had dropped to 20. Ammon E. Stoltzfus served as minister 1897-1910. The drought was the chief factor in its becoming extinct. It was last listed in the 1918 Year-Book, with 22 members and C. C. Steckley as minister. The cemetery at the site of the former church still exists.   G.G.Y., M.G.

Seli, an Anabaptist martyr, who is reported by van Braght to have been burned at the stake at Amsterdam in 1542. Van Braght calls her the wife of Jacob van Wormer (q.v.). It seems, however, that van Braght is in error; no martyr by this name is found in the official records. Seli is probably identical with Cecilia Jheronimusd (q.v.), wife of Jacob Claesz van Landsmeer, who was burned at the stake at Amsterdam on Nov. 9, 1549, together with her husband.   vdZ.

Mart. Mir. D 61, 85, E 464, 485; *Inv. Arcn. Amst.* I, No. 357; *DB* 1917, 173; Grosheide, *Bijdrage*, 158, 308; *ML* II, 386.

Seligental, a former name of the Adelsheim (q.v.) Mennonite congregation.

Selowitz, a village in Moravia in which the Hutterian Brethren built a Bruderhof, which they abandoned in 1583 to move to near-by Nusslau (q.v.), where the landowners promised them greater liberty in cultivating wine and hops. In Selowitz they occupied what is now house No. 37. (Zieglschmid, *Chronik*.)

Sembach, a village in the Palatinate (q.v.), Germany, not far from Kaiserslautern, since the end of the 17th century the seat of a Mennonite congregation, with a membership in 1957 of some 250 baptized members; most of the families live in the villages and on the farms around Sembach: Wartenberg-Rohrbach, Mehlingen-Neukirchen, Enkenbach, Neuhemsbach, Langmeil, Potzbach, Schmitterhof, Otterberg, Münchhof, Randeckerhof, and Pfrimmerhof (q.v.). The original families of the congregation — Krehbiel, Eymann, Eichelberger, Würtz, Schnebele, Beutler, Latschar, Kinzinger, Höfli — immigrated from the Emmental (q.v.), Switzerland, in 1660-1710.

Religious services were held in private homes in Sembach, Wartenberg, Fischbach, and Diemerstein until 1777, when the church was built. The first preacher was Ulrich Trüssel, of Sumiswald, who was imprisoned in Bern in 1710 and came to the Palatinate in 1711. He was succeeded in 1760 by Johannes Krehbiel, of Wartenberg, who saw the erection of the church, dedicated in 1778 by Jakob Galle, Erbesbüdesheim; substantial financial assistance was given by the Mennonites of Crefeld and the Netherlands. Among the more prominent elders and lay preachers were Heinrich Würtz, Johannes Eymann, and Peter Eymann (q.v.).

In 1832 Johannes Risser (q.v.), of Friedelsheim, became the pastor, and under his ministry the congregation experienced inward and outward strengthening. In 1842 a parsonage was built, in 1853 the church was substantially enlarged, and in 1859 a constitution was adopted. The church records begun by Risser in 1832 and kept until his death in 1864 contain much that is of interest and value for the history of the South German Mennonites, besides the record of baptisms, births, marriages, and deaths in the congregation. The congregation continued to develop along the lines established by Risser under the succeeding preachers, Johannes van der Smissen (q.v.) 1869-79 and Samuel Blickensdörfer 1879-99. Services were held every Sunday, and communion twice a year. Baptism was administered on the first Sunday in September. In 1892 the congregation was incorporated. Among the chairmen (*Vorsteher*) of the congregation Jakob Krehbiel was outstanding and left a series of valuable diaries.

In 1900-29 Matthias Pohl (q.v.) was the preacher in Sembach; he was noted far beyond his congregation as a speaker and writer. He vigorously countered many a symptom of decline in the congregation. In 1904 the congregation joined the Vereinigung der Mennonitengemeinden im Deutschen Reich. The congregation declined in membership through marriage with persons of other creeds. Consciousness of membership in a brotherhood seems to be disappearing in many Mennonite families. In 1887 the baptized membership numbered about 400, in 1940 only about 110.

Hugo Scheffler, a native of West Prussia, served as minister of the Sembach congregation 1929-35. In 1935 Gerhard Hein, of Russia, took charge of this congregation with that at Altleiningen (q.v.) as a subsidiary, serving until October 1958. World War II left Sembach relatively undamaged. In 1948 an influx of about 100 Mennonite refugees from West Prussia strengthened it. In 1948, with the aid of the American Mennonites they rebuilt a dilapidated barn connected with the parsonage into a hall for the youth of the congregation, which was dedicated on Dec. 19, 1948.   G.H.

Gerhard Hein and Matthias Pohl, "Beiträge zur Familiengeschichte der pfälzisch-hessischen Mennonitengemeinden: Geschichtliches aus der Gemeinde Sembach" (Pohl), and "Ein Kirchenbuch gibt Auskunft" (Hein), Gem.-Kal. 1939, 86-121; Inv. Arch. Amst. I, 1472, 1543 f.; II, 2857-59; ML IV.

Seminaries, Mennonite Theological. The first Mennonite theological seminary was the Amsterdam Mennonite Theological Seminary (q.v.) organized in 1735. Before this time the Dutch Mennonite ministers who secured theological training did so either at the Remonstrant Theological Seminary, or by private instruction from Mennonite ministers in service. The idea of establishing a seminary had been proposed as early as 1675, but met sufficient opposition to block it until 1735, when the Amsterdam Lamist and Toren congregation established it on its own authority and with its own support. When the congregation could no longer carry the seminary alone, the General Mennonite Conference (ADS) was organized in 1811, its main purpose being to take over the seminary. The seminary has never had a full faculty, limiting its instruction to dogmatics, ethics, practical theology, and Mennonite history. The remaining subjects were taken by the students at the University of Amsterdam (theological faculty established in 1876) or its predecessor the Athanaeum. The full Mennonite professors (formerly two, at the moment only one) are also professors on the university theological faculty. This seminary is on the graduate level, comparable to other European theological schools.

The Mennonites of Germany and of Russia considered establishing theological schools in the second half of the 19th century, but did not finally reach this goal. Such German or Russian ministers as secured training have attended either the Protestant theological schools at the state universities, or Bible schools of lower academic rank, such as St. Chrischona (Basel), Switzerland, or the Baptist Theological Seminary at Hamburg, Germany.

The first attempt at a school for ministerial training in North America was in the General Conference Mennonite Church, which operated a training school for ministers at Wadsworth, Ohio, 1868-78, called "Christliche Bildungsanstalt der Mennoniten-Gemeinschaft." It was not on the graduate level, and even though it had a department of theology, it was essentially a secondary school with a Bible department and a majority of course offerings in secular fields. The first graduate theological seminary was established at Bluffton College in 1914, when the institution's name was set as Bluffton College and Theological Seminary, operated by a board of trustees representing five Mennonite branches, although not all five were officially represented by their own appointed trustees. Actually the major part of the student body and faculty were from the General Conference Mennonite Church. The Mennonite Seminary was an integral part of Bluffton College until 1921, when it became a separate and independent institution under a separate corporation with trustees representing six Mennonite branches, again not serving as official representatives in most cases, and actually as predominantly a school serving the General Conference Mennonite Church. The organized school was now given the name Witmarsum Theological Seminary (q.v.), and under this name it operated until 1931 as a standard graduate seminary offering the B.D. degree. It also had a department called the Theological College offering a combined four-year college and theology curriculum based upon high school and leading to the Th.B. degree.

The Goshen College Biblical Seminary (q.v.) at Goshen, Ind., a school of the Mennonite (MC) Church (until 1946 called Bible School), began in 1933 to offer a two-year theological course based on two years of college and leading to the Th.B. degree. In 1942 the theological course was enlarged to three years with the same degree; this course was discontinued in 1956. In 1946 the standard three-year graduate seminary course based upon college graduation and leading to the B.D. degree was added. The GCBS is an autonomous division of Goshen College, with its own dean and academic faculty and student body, but integrated into Goshen College with a common president and financial administration. A separate set of buildings was erected for it in 1959 at the south edge of the Goshen College campus.

The next theological seminary was the Mennonite Biblical Seminary (q.v.), which was opened in Chicago in 1945 as a new institution chartered by the General Conference of the General Conference Mennonite Church, but to be considered in a sense as a reorganized Witmarsum Theological Seminary, which transferred its assets in endowment, property, and library to the new school. However, during its stay in Chicago 1945-58, the MBS was not a full seminary; even though it had its own headquarters, library, and residence halls at 4614 Woodlawn Ave., it was affiliated with the Bethany Biblical Seminary of the Church of the Brethren in such a way that the students were enrolled in Bethany Biblical Seminary and secured their degrees from it. The several members of the MBS faculty taught their courses as members of the Bethany faculty. This arrangement paralleled that of the Amsterdam Mennonite Seminary. The MBS also operated a college level department called the Mennonite Bible School, with a very small enrollment. In 1958 the MBS moved to a new campus at Elkhart, Ind., where it began operations as a full seminary with a complete faculty and curriculum, offering its own degrees. This move was made in connection with affiliation with the Goshen College Biblical Seminary under a plan of co-operation called the Associated Mennonite Biblical Seminaries, which is described below.

The Associated Mennonite Biblical Seminaries is the name given to a group of seminaries which have agreed to an affiliation calling for a close co-operation in the academic program while maintaining full independence of government and financing. The plan calls for a Joint Co-ordinating Committee representing the boards of control and a Joint Administrative Committee representing the schools. There is also a Joint Library composed of all collections of the associated schools. A certain number of joint courses will be offered, permitting students to take up to one third of the B.D. curriculum in such courses, in addition to the privilege of cross-registration in all associated schools. However, each school grants its own degrees. Two seminaries have entered the plan to begin with, the Mennonite Biblical Seminary at Elkhart and the Goshen College Biblical Seminary at Goshen. It is hoped that other conferences will join the plan in the course of time so that the Associated Seminaries will become a center for Mennonite ministerial training in North America. The headquarters of the associated institutions is the Elkhart campus of the MBS. The Institute for Mennonite Studies, operated jointly by the Associated Seminaries, and located on the Elkhart campus, is also a part of the program. The total program went into effect in September 1958.

The first graduate theological seminary in the Mennonite Brethren Church was opened at Fresno, Cal., in 1955 as the Mennonite Brethren Biblical Seminary, offering the standard three-year graduate theological program leading to the B.D. degree. The Bible School at Tabor College was at that time discontinued, which had been offering the Th.B. and B.R.E. degrees for a two-year program of Biblical study based upon two years of college. The Mennonite Brethren Bible College (q.v.) at Winnipeg, Man., established in 1944, offers a similar four-year Th.B. and B.R.E. program. The Canadian Mennonite Bible College of the General Conference Mennonite Church, also at Winnipeg, founded in 1947, also offers a similar four-year B.C.E. curriculum.

Eastern Mennonite College (MC) at Harrisonburg, Va., has offered a Th.B. degree through its Bible School since 1938, first as a two-year theology course based on two years of college, increased in 1946 to a three-year course and in 1948 to a combined six-year course, of which two years are in graduate theology.

Grace Bible Institute at Omaha, Neb., founded in 1943 as an inter-Mennonite school, though largely G.C.M. and E.M.B., has from the beginning offered the equivalent of seminary training on a college level, a four-year course with two years of theology, but gives only B.A. and B.R.E. degrees.

In 1950 the Indonesian Mennonite Church established a theological school at Pati, which was of secondary school grade, with teachers from Holland. In 1955 Pati was merged with the theological school of the Reformed Church of East Java in Malang under a combined Reformed and Mennonite board and with teachers from both groups.

In 1955 the Mennonite Biblical Seminary at Montevideo, Uruguay, was established under an inter-Mennonite South American board of trustees, but sponsored and supported by the mission boards of the MC and GCM groups in North America. It is not a graduate theological seminary, but offers a three-year course based upon high school. It is designed to offer theological training in the Spanish and German languages for Mennonites from all over South America, especially Paraguay, Argentina, Uruguay, and Brazil who plan to enter mission work or serve as pastors in Mennonite congregations in these countries.   H.S.B.

Sendbrieff von einem Liebhaber Gottes Worts, the last written genuinely Anabaptist document in existence, a true martyr epistle in the great style of the beginnings, written in 1715 by an unknown Swiss brother in the darkness of prison in Bern, Switzerland. It is contained in a booklet of 40 pages, entitled *Ein Send-Brieff samt einem schönen Gebätt und geistlichen Lied. Worbey noch etliche andere Christliche Gebätt, in vielen Anligen und Nöthen zu gebrauchen. Wie auch etliche geistliche Lieder. Gedruckt im Jahr, Da wahre Busz vonnöthen war,* probably printed by the Mechel (q.v.) publishing house in Basel c1720 (title page reproduced in Friedmann, *Piety,* plate III). In Europe this booklet is extremely rare and not mentioned in literature. H. S. Bender found several copies in Mennonite homes of Swiss background in Pennsylvania and Ohio, now in GCL. It appears in a Sammelband (several writings bound together as one) of 100 pages, the rest consisting of prayers and hymns of typical pietistic character.

The "Sendbrief" is addressed to "the fellow members of the household of faith" and contains a strong and moving call to steadfastness and loyalty in the face of trial and danger of life; it closes with an admonition to the true "fear of God." This term is most characteristic, as it used to be the watchword of 16th-century Anabaptism, together with the word "obedience," replaced in the later pietistic trend by the term "godliness." The book also contains six songs, one by the author, two by Leonardt Klock (Clock, q.v.), one taken from the *Ausbund* (q.v.), and two of unknown origin.

Thus the unknown editor of this book combined under one cover two very different moods, belonging to two different historic times: discipleship on the one hand (strongly defended by the imprisoned brother) and a sweet godliness on the other hand by which the spirit of the entire publication becomes changed. As such the book seems to have been a real success, one of the few genuine Swiss Anabaptist devotional books ever printed. (Compare **Ernsthafte Christenpflicht.**)   R.F.

Robert Friedmann, *Mennonite Piety Through the Centuries* (Goshen, 1949) 165-67; Wolkan, *Lieder,* 155 f.

Seneca County (Ohio) Mennonite (MC) Church (now extinct), founded by Troxel families from Frederick County, Md., and Stark County, Ohio, by Hunsicker families from Montgomery County, Pa., and by other land-hungry immigrants from eastern states and even from Germany c1825-40, who erected a hewn log meetinghouse at an early date on the farm of George Muckley 2½ miles east of Bloom-ville. Shortly before his death in 1842, Muckley deeded the acre on which the church and cemetery stood to "Henry Troxel, Jacob Rothgabe and Isaac Boren (Rohrer) and the Manomenist Congregation of Bloom Township." Early members of the con-gregation bore the names Troxel, Legron, Brandt, Detweiler, Newcomer, Bachman, Rothegabe, All-derffer, Muckley, Bowman (pronounced Bau-man), Kroft (Kraft?), Zutavern, Behm, and Lehman. Bishops (nonresident) were Henry Stemen (*q.v.*) followed by John M. Brenneman, the latter serving until the Wisler (*q.v.*) controversy arose in 1871; ministers, David Martin and Isaac Rohrer. Even before Martin died and Rohrer followed his brother Abraham Rohrer, of Medina County, into the Wis-ler branch, the congregation declined. Denied Sun-day-school privileges the young people united with the German Reformed or the Methodist Church. The last services were held in 1879 about the time that Isaac Rohrer and his wife moved to the Wisler congregation in Mahoning County, Ohio. The church building was sold and razed in 1888. Many of the later burials in the cemetery were exhumed and reinterred in the Woodlawn cemetery west of Bloomville. A few of the remaining members re-turned to the older Wisler congregations in western Wayne, Medina, and Mahoning counties. Unlike other extinct Mennonite congregations in Ohio, Sen-eca County supplied few if any accessions to Men-nonite congregations in Indiana.   J.S.U.

John Umble, "Extinct Ohio Mennonite Churches," *MQR* XVIII (1944) 186-92 and 225-37.

Sennergemeinde: see Seigne.

Sensenig (Sensenich, Senseny, Senseney), a Swiss name found especially among the Mennonites of Lancaster County, Pa. The ancestor of many mem-bers of the family was immigrant Jacob Sensenig, who married Maria Krey. Jacob's children married into the Wenger, Witwer, and Martin families. The Sensenig family is distinguished by an unusual num-ber of physicians. One line had a doctor in every generation for five generations. In the Midwest the best-known member of the family was Aaron Stauf-fer Sensenich (1849-1919), a physician of Wakarusa, Ind., whose son Roscoe L. Sensenich served as presi-dent of the American Medical Association. Arthur S. Sensenich's widowed mother took for her second husband Christian Good, a Brethren in Christ min-ister. The only members of the family to serve as Mennonite ministers in North America were in the Stauffer (*q.v.*) and Wisler (*q.v.*) branches of the church. Daniel S. Sensenig is a missionary (MC) in Ethiopia.   J.C.W.

Barton Sensenig, *The "Sensineys" of America* (Phila-delphia, 1943).

Sent, Jan, a Dutch Mennonite, author or composer of the hymnal usually called *Jan Cents Liedboeck*. There have been at least two editions, 1628 and 1679. The official title reads *Nieu* (*q.v.*) *Sangh Boec*. It is doubtful that Jan Cents was a member of the Senten (Centen, *q.v.*) family of Amsterdam.   vDZ.

Sepp, a Dutch Mennonite family, whose ancestor (1) Christian Sepp was born about 1700 at Goslar, Germany, where his father was the assistant rector of the Latin school. Christian Sepp was a merchant, first at Hamburg, then at Amsterdam. Here he founded a bookshop and printing office, which for nearly one hundred years was leading in the Nether-lands. It is not clear whether this Christian Sepp joined the Mennonite Church. He died in 1775 at Amsterdam. His son was (2) Jan Christiaan Sepp (1739-1811), whose first wife was Sara Focking (1745-73) and who was a renowned map engraver and bookseller in Amsterdam. He was well known for his fine collection of butterflies and insects, and edited a number of famous books on flowers (*Flora Batava*), insects, and birds. In collaboration with Cornelis Nozeman, a Remonstrant minister of Rot-terdam, he published *Nederlandsche Vogelen* in five volumes; after the death of Nozeman and Sepp this work was continued by Martinus Houttuyn. Sepp himself made some of the beautiful pictures in this book. Besides these and other books (*Beschouwin-gen der Wonderen Gods*) he also managed the pub-lication of some Mennonite hymnals. Sepp was a man of great influence in Amsterdam; he was one of the founders of the association "Felix Meritis," which promoted public lectures on scientific themes, many of these lectures having been held by Sepp himself. In 1781 he was chosen as preacher of the Danzig Old Flemish (*Bij de Kruikjes*) congregation of Amsterdam; in 1787, when this congregation merged with the Zonist (*q.v.*) church, he became a Zonist minister until he retired in 1801.

Among his sons were: (3) Christian Sepp (1773-1835), who was superintendent of the police at Am-sterdam, a pious man, who translated and published some works by Jung-Stilling into Dutch; (4) Jan Sepp (1778-1853), like his father the manager of the bookshop and printing office at Amsterdam, and (5) Hendrik Albert Sepp (1807-31), who was a lay minister at Knollendam 1830-31. (6) Cornelis Sepp (1810-68), the son of Jan Sepp (4), continued the printing and publishing business of his father and his grandfather. Another son of Jan Sepp (4) was (7) Christiaan (*q.v.*) (1820-90), a Mennonite minis-ter and church historian. (8) Jan Sepp, a son of Cornelis (6) (b. 1847 at Amsterdam, d. 1905 at Beverwijk), studied at the Amsterdam Mennonite Seminary and served as minister at Witmarsum-Pingjum 1871-73 and Beverwijk 1873-1905. He pub-lished *Gedachten des Bijbels* (1876), *Gedachtenis aan Doopbediening en eersten Avondmaalsgang* (Beverwijk, 1889), and some sermons; his paper, "De nieuwe gezangbundels der Amsterdamsche ge-meente," is found in *Doopsgezinde Bijdragen* of 1872. He and H. Boetje (*q.v.*) composed a new hymnal for the Dutch Mennonite congregations, usually called *Leidsche Bundel* (*q.v.*).

(9) Alidus Anne Sepp (b. 1881 at Beverwijk), a son of Jan Sepp (8), was at first an office clerk; after studying theology at the University and the Men-nonite Seminary of Amsterdam he served as minister in the following Mennonite congregations: Witmar-sum-Pingjum 1914-18, Edam 1918-26, Veenwouden 1926-30, Westzaan 1930-34, and Zaandam-Oost 1934-

44. He published *Achter de Maaiers* (Hillegom, n.d.), a few Biblical plays, and a set of catechetical booklets. In 1932-42 he was secretary of the A.D.S. Because of Nazi sympathies during World War II he took residence in Germany and never returned to Holland.   vDZ.

N.N.B.Wb. III, 1168, V, 719-25; *Inv. Arch. Amst.* II, No. 1417, II, 2, No. 231; *Naamlijst 1815*, 49 f.; *DB* 1898, 21 note 2; 1902, 12 ff.; 1905, 208.

Sepp, Christiaan, b. April 3, 1820, at Amsterdam, d. May 10, 1890, at Wijk aan Zee, a son of Jan Sepp and Christina Bakker, was a Dutch Mennonite minister and an outstanding church historian of the Netherlands. He was married in 1848 to C. E. A. Spin of Amsterdam. Sepp studied theology at the Amsterdam Mennonite Seminary in 1837-43, and served as minister at Westzaan-Zuid 1843-48, Zaandam-Oost 1848-54, and Leiden 1872-79, then retiring and moving to Amsterdam. Sepp was a beloved preacher and a loyal pastor; he was one of the leading Dutch ministers of the 19th century. During his service at Leiden he also took charge of the Mennonites living at The Hague and promoted the founding of the Hague congregation in 1881. He was a trustee of the A.D.S. and a curator of its seminary. He opposed radical liberalism, and was a friend of Pietism, always maintaining Biblical supranaturalism against the theological trend of monism and antisupranaturalism. "His Christianity was mild and Biblical," says Binnerts.

Sepp was also a man of learning. As early as 1837, at the age of 17, he started his many translations of German theological works into Dutch. His study in Latin on the doctrines of St. Paul was awarded a gold medal by the University of Utrecht in 1843. Other books published by Sepp were: *Herinneringen uit het leven van een hulpprediker* (Amsterdam, 1846), *Johan Albrecht Bengel, een waardig discipel van dem Heer* (Amsterdam, 1848), *De leer des Nieuwen Testaments over de Heilige schriften des Ouden Verbonds* (Amsterdam, 1849), *Proeve eener Pragmatische geschiedenis der theologie in Nederland 1787-1858* (Haarlem, 1860, repr. Amsterdam, 1860; Leiden, 1868), *Johannes Stinstra en zijn tijd* (Amsterdam, 2 vv., 1865, 1866), *Geschiedkundige Nasporingen,* 3 vv. (Leiden, resp. 1872, 1873, 1875), *Het Godgeleerd Onderwijs in Nederland in de 16de en 17de eeuw,* 2 vv. (Leiden, 1873-74), *Drie Evangeliedienaren uit den tijd der Hervorming* (Leiden, 1879), *Polemische en irenische theologie* (Leiden, 1881, repr. Leiden, 1882), *Bibliographische Mededeelingen* (1883), *Kerkhistorische Studiën* (Leiden, 1885), *Bibliotheek van Nederlandsche Kerkgeschiedschrijvers* (1886), *Verboden Lectuur* (1889), *Uit het predikantenleven van vroeger tijden* (Leiden, 1890); after his death his *Het staatstoezicht op de godsdienstige literatuur in de Noordelijke Nederlanden* was published by L. Knappert and J. Sepp.

Besides these books Sepp published many articles, particularly in *Godgeleerde Bijdragen,* a periodical of which he was the editor; a devotional book *De Zeven Kruiswoorden, voor vrienden van Jezus verklaard* (Amsterdam, 1856); a few sermons, two funeral sermons, one in memory of Matthijs Siegenbeek (q.v.) (Leiden, 1855), and one to commemorate Daniel Tieboel Siegenbeek (q.v.) (n.p., n.d.-Lei-

den, 1866). For the Association of Dutch Literature, of which Sepp was a member, he wrote obituary biographical notices for K. Sybrandi (1873), Samuel Muller (1876), and others.

Apart from his book on Stinstra, Sepp did not publish much about Mennonite history; he was, however, well informed in it. A few papers on Mennonite history are found in his *Geschiedkundige Nasporingen.* His article "Menno Simons in de eerste jaren zijner Evangeliebediening 1536-39" is found in his book *Uit het Predikantsleven.*

Sepp was a member of a number of learned associations. In 1875 the University of Leiden awarded him an honorary degree in theology. The biographical notice for Sepp published in the records of the "Maatschappij voor Nederlandsche Letterkunde" was written by Samuel Cramer.   vDZ.

J. Sepp, *Ter gedachtenis aan Christiaan Sepp, Theol. Dr en rustend predikant* (1890); S. Cramer, *Levensbericht van Chr. Sepp* (Leiden, 1891); *N.N.B.Wb.* V, 720-24; *DB* 1867, 110-41 (review of Sepp's book on Stinstra); 1889, 64; 1892, 1 ff.; 1896, 64-66; 1905, 89; *DJ* 1905, 21-31 with portrait.

Serarius, Petrus (Pierre Serrurier), a Mennonite of French descent, who according to tradition was born in Flanders in 1636, and to another more probable tradition, at London, England, in 1600, and who died at Amsterdam in 1665. He was a businessman and lived at first in London and then (before 1659) at Cologne, Germany, where he was a member and probably a deacon of the Mennonite congregation; later he lived at Amsterdam. Whether he joined a Mennonite congregation in Amsterdam or not is not certain. In his youth he had belonged to the Reformed Church. During his Amsterdam period he called himself "a preacher of God in His general church." Meinsma called him "a Mennonite Collegiant." In Amsterdam he was an adherent of Galenus Abrahamsz (q.v.), whom he defended against Jan Jansz Swichtenheuvel (q.v.). More and more he came to the opinion that of all churches on earth none could be considered the true church of God; but he considered the Mennonite Church, as founded by men of good will, to be nearest to the true church. The present churches, he says, have the devil as their founder. This idea Serarius may have borrowed from Christian Entfelder (q.v.), whose book *Von den manigfaltigen im glauben zerspaltungen dise jar entstanden* he translated into Dutch. On the ground of his astronomical observations he expected the coming of Christ in the near future, and gathered around him a group of chiliasts including some Mennonites.

Serarius published a large number of books both in Latin and in Dutch, some of them having been reprinted as late as the 18th century. The most important are: *De Vertredinge des Heyligen Stadts* (Amsterdam, 1659), *Naerder Bericht wegens die groote conjunctie* (Amsterdam, 1662), and *Een Blijde Boodschap aen Jerusalem* (Amsterdam, 1665).   vDZ.

B. Glasius, *Godgeleerd Nederland II* ('s Hertogenbosch, 1856) 344-46; Gottfried Arnold, *Kirchen- und Ketzer-Historie* II, 900; H. W. Meihuizen, *Galenus Abrahamsz* (Haarlem, 1954) 45, 63, 80; K. O. Meinsma, *Spinoza en zijn Kring* (The Hague, 1896) 212, 269, 291; C. B. Hylkema, *Reformateurs,* 2 vv. (Haarlem, 1900 and 1902) *passim,* see Index.

Sermons. Preaching has always been the center of Anabaptist-Mennonite public worship, hence the presence of the pulpit in the center of the Mennonite meetinghouse and the total absence of the altar. Very soon after the founding of the Anabaptist movement in 1525 the congregations chose individuals as leaders who were then ordained. The major office, called shepherd (*Hirt*) in the Schleitheim Confession of 1527, was that of preacher; one or more were in every congregation. From among a plurality of preachers one was chosen to be elder (*q.v.;* or bishop, *q.v.*), who was responsible for general oversight, administration of the ordinances and discipline, and provision of ministers. However, elders were also, and still are, chiefly preachers. The Schleitheim Confession defines the office of shepherd as follows: "This office shall be to read, to admonish and teach, to warn, to discipline, to ban in the church, lead out in prayer for the advancement of all the brethren and sisters, to lift up the bread when it is to be broken, and in all things to care for the body of Christ, in order that it may be built up and developed, and the mouth of the slanderer be stopped."

The character of the preaching was indicated by the early titles used for this office: "Minister of the Word" or "of the Book" (*Diener zum Wort, q.v.*) was intended to emphasize the function of the preacher to proclaim the message of the Bible. The Amish later preferred to use "Minister of the Book" (*Diener zum Buch*) for the same concept. The most common term, however, in Holland, North Germany, and Prussia was "teacher" (*leeraar, Lehrer*), or "admonisher" (*vermaner, Vermahner*). Both of these terms emphasize the function of the preacher to bring to the congregation the message of the Bible as something to be accepted and followed. The term "preacher" (*preeker, prediker, predikant, Prediger*) is neutral so far as indicating the character of his message, and was probably borrowed from Protestantism.

The early Anabaptist sermons were without doubt conceived as simple forthright declarations of a hortatory and devotional character, except when used for evangelistic purposes. They were certainly not expected to be rhetorical orations prepared and finished according to the practice of learned men. It was assumed that any member of the church could admonish the congregation out of his general knowledge of the Scriptures, his experience in life, and the help of the Holy Spirit. Sermons were not written and read but given ex tempore. The tradition from the early times took two directions however. On the one hand the tradition of completely ex tempore preaching persisted in some groups of the Swiss-South German type, with the strict understanding that no written text, not even outlines or notes, should be used at preaching time. On the other hand, the tradition of writing and reading sermons developed in the Prussian-Russian line, climaxing finally in the strict requirement that one should not even write his own sermons but only recopy and read the sermons of the past, with ultimately some minor modifications allowed; to preach ex tempore was condemned as pride. This was once the tradition among all the Mennonites in Manitoba and is still the case among all groups of Old Colony Mennonites. It is clear that few if any sermons of the ex tempore type would be preserved. Exceptions are noted for a few 19th-century preachers of this type who did write down sermons which have been preserved (or were they written to be memorized and not read perhaps?). In West Prussia and some descendant groups the concept of preacher hardened into the idea that the preacher's office was only to preach from the pulpit and not to do any pastoral work. A similar idea developed among the Mennonites of Eastern Pennsylvania and elsewhere, with the plural ministry, namely, that the preachers were to do nothing but preach, leaving the pastoral work to the bishop and deacons.

The publication of sermons, as distinct from tracts and treatises, though common among other Protestant groups from the early days of the Reformation, was almost unknown among the Anabaptists. One anonymous sermon by a South German Anabaptist was identified by Ludwig Keller in Eitelhans Langenmantel's *Exposition of the Lord's Prayer* published at Augsburg in 1527. No published sermons by Swiss Brethren or their direct descendants to the present day are known, in Switzerland, France, or Austria, although a few sermons by South German Mennonites of the 19th century have appeared. The writing out of sermons (which precedes their printing) was not done by the lay-preachers of these areas, nor did the Anabaptists and their descendants of the first two hundred years have much interest in printed, theological sermons in any case. It was only later, largely after they had begun to read Lutheran and Reformed books of sermons, particularly under the influence of Pietism in the 18th century, and especially after they had begun to use trained ministers, that Mennonites had a real place for printed sermons. Here they followed pietistic influences. Popular sermon writers were Bogatzky, Hollaz, Hübner, and Funck.

The Dutch were the first among the Mennonites to publish sermons, and the most prolific. Beginning with Pieter Pietersz (1624) and Joost Hendricksz (1647), an almost endless stream of printed sermon collections appeared. The Amsterdam *Catalogus* lists to 1919 almost 400 titles in Dutch, of which almost 200 were printed before 1800. This includes single sermons as well as collections. The first printed sermons by a German preacher were also in Dutch, those of Willem Wynantsz of Hamburg-Altona (1660). The first printed sermon in German was by Peter Verhelle of the same place (1702). The Hamburg Dompelaar Jacob Denner's tremendous sermon collection (1730, 1718 pages) was not only the largest but probably most influential collection of Mennonite sermons ever printed. Most numerous of the sermon authors were the preachers of Hamburg-Altona, Crefeld, and Danzig. Mennonite sermons printed in Russia appeared mostly in yearbooks and periodicals after the close of the 19th century.

Why were sermons printed? To be read from the pulpits by other preachers? Hardly. To be used as models? Probably. To be read in family worship? Certainly this was the case in later times. The two volumes of West Prussian sermons *Predigten aus*

Mennoniten-Gemeinden 1891-99 (1906) and *Predigten vorgetragen in den Mennoniten Gemeinden Westpreussens 1906-09* (1909), were expressly printed for this purpose according to the title page, "Zum Gebrauch für Hausgottesdienst." Perhaps such books were also to be used as private devotional books. The reprints of Wynantsz, Deknatel, and Denner in the 19th century in America no doubt had this as their primary purpose. In 1773 Pennsylvania Mennonites were using "many other books which our old preachers published and left behind for us, as Joost Hendricks, Willem Wynands, Jacob Denner, and many others" (*MQR* III, 1929, 231). The translation of Wynantsz in 1830 was made by the Amishman David Zug, and all three American editions of this book were for the Amish. Festival sermons had historical value, such as funeral, ordination, beginning of service (*Antrittspredigt*), retirement (*Abschiedspredigt*). Baptismal sermons may have been printed as souvenirs for the families involved.

Apart from reprints of European sermon collections (1830, 1835, 1852, 1860, 1871) and the curious sermons of the sleeping-preacher Noah Troyer, printed after his death (1879, 1880), the only original American Mennonite printed sermons before 1900 were: the sermon on "Christianity and War" (1863) by John M. Brenneman (MC) and a collection of New Year's sermons (1885) by the noted S. F. Sprunger (GCM) of Berne, Ind. Sprunger also published a unique international Mennonite sermon collection in 1891, *Festklänge,* with selections from preachers of the United States, Russia, Switzerland, and Germany. The 20th century in North America has produced a representative series of sermon books: J. E. Hartzler (1908), J. A. Huffman (1915), G. P. Schultz (1924), A. H. Unruh (1935), J. H. Janzen (1942, 1945), Wm. G. Detweiler (1943, 1949, 1951, 1952), George R. Brunk (1953), and a collection of Mennonite Brethren sermons. The radio, with its weekly sermon hour, has led to the printing of many Mennonite sermons in recent years.

H. S. Bender and N. D. Springer published in *MQR* XXVII (1953), 143-57, under the title "An Annotated Bibliography of Published Mennonite Sermons," an extensive list of separately printed Mennonite sermons, whether in collections or as single sermons. Full titles are given, with bibliographical data and locations in BeCL, GCL, AML, and Hamburg Mennonite Library. Sermons printed as parts of conference proceedings, church bulletins, periodicals, biographical volumes, etc., are not reported. The list is in three parts, (1) Europe, aside from Holland, (2) North America, (3) Holland, of which only the first two parts have appeared.

The only known published discussion of the history of Mennonite preaching outside of Holland is that by H. G. Mannhardt in *Mennonitische Blätter* XXXVIII (1891), 18 f., 22 f., 28 f., 37 f. (1891), entitled "Geschichte der Predigt in den deutschen Mennoniten-Gemeinden." Roy Umble's doctoral dissertation, *Mennonite Preaching, 1864-1944* (Northwestern University, Evanston, Ill., 1949), is a study of the preaching of eleven leading American Mennonite (MC) ministers of that period. It has not

been published. But see his article, "Characteristics of Mennonite Preaching," *MQR* XXVII (1953) 137-42.   H.S.B.

Sermons, Hutterite. The existence of a large number of written sermons of Hutterite origin, mostly of the 17th century, was completely unknown until the publication of the *Klein-Geschichtsbuch der Hutterischen Brüder* in 1947. Even since the printing of excerpts in the *Klein-Geschichtsbuch,* no publication offers any reference or information concerning this material. When around 1800 Johannes Waldner (*q.v.*), then bishop of the Hutterites in Vishenka, Ukraine, decided to provide his brotherhood with another "Chronicle," summarizing the contents of the old (called "big") Chronicle and continuing it up to his own day, he felt that some of the sermons found at Vishenka should also be included to give posterity an adequate picture of the spiritual life of the brotherhood in its best time, the era of Andreas Ehrenpreis (*q.v.*). Thus shorter and longer excerpts of not less than 26 such sermons are given in the text of the *Klein-Geschichtsbuch* (pp. 204-14, and 218-21), all of them deriving from 1652-59. Most of these texts originated at a Bruderhof at Kesselsdorf (*q.v.*) in Slovakia, where apparently a kind of seminary for preachers existed. Even though Waldner does not mention names, at least six Hutterites are known who composed these sermons: H. F. Küentsche (*q.v.*), who was the major contributor, Caspar Eglauch (*q.v.*), Mathias Binder, Johannes Milder, Tobias Bertsch, and Benjamin Poley. But there were also other sermon writers, above all Ehrenpreis himself.

In 1954 the present writer visited a number of Hutterite colonies in Canada and the Northwest of the United States, and was shown the originals from which these sermon excerpts had been taken. Between 300 and 600 original sermon booklets exist, dating from the early 17th century to 1665 (not one later), modest notebooks written in pencil or poor ink, which have been reverently preserved in the brotherhood through the centuries.

In the 18th century Johannes Waldner and several co-workers decided to revive the time-honored custom of reading sermons during the worship hour, and thus they began collecting the contents of most of these booklets in carefully written sermon books, many of them of considerable size. The oldest of these volumes, still extant, is of 1786; then follows one of 1789 (the Mathias Müller book), and so on up to 1804 and slightly later. All this material, old and new, was brought to America. When a brother is elected preacher it is his first duty to make for himself as complete a copy as possible of the entire sermon material. Each of the hundred odd Bruderhofs today has a collection of 30-60 carefully handwritten and well-bound books of sermons for all occasions. None has ever been printed, and it is the pride of each preacher to keep adding new sermon books to his bookshelves, written in excellent penmanship. All the long winter days are filled with this work. The selection changes slightly depending on whether he belongs to the Dariusleut (*q.v.*), Schmiedeleut (*q.v.*), or Lehrerleut (*q.v.*); some of them have more, some less. All are written and read in High German, even though the Hutterites speak a sort of Tirolean-Bavarian German dialect among themselves. Why are only old sermons read among the Hutterites today? The brethren would answer that these sermons are so perfect that no one could improve upon them. More likely is the assumption that the tradition-minded Hutterites are simply continuing a custom which was widely accepted in all churches during the 17th and 18th centuries.

The oldest exegetical books of the Hutterites, as far as is known, date back to the later part of the 16th century: 1566 and 1579 (both codices in Budapest), 1593 (in Esztergom), 1598 (in Brno), and 1599 (Bratislava). Although these codices were known to European scholars they were never recognized as the prototype of the later (not known) Hutterite sermon books. There are about 15 codices in European libraries, containing such exegeses ("Erklärungen") of different books of the Old and New Testaments (including the Book of Revelation, see **Olivi**), which are rather similar to the "Lehren" (homiletic instructions) as practiced by the brethren at least since 1629 if not earlier. After that time the datable production increased tremendously up to 1665 and then suddenly stopped. Innumerable undated sermons which to all appearance belong to the same period—that of Ehrenpreis—are also extant. A rigid series of pericopes for the entire church year, including holidays, provided the texts for most of these sermons. To these must be added sermons for other church events, such as baptisms, weddings, or funerals, for which also standard texts were and still are being used. The sermon production then worked around this program, interpreting the texts from many angles, but always in a conservative Biblicistic way, rarely indulging in the fashion of budding Pietism (q.v.). Thus the sermons lack emotional elements and are distinctly more hortatory than edificatory. The style and ideas of these sermons would deserve a detailed analysis, but in the absence of this no final appreciation can be offered.

Hutterite sermons are basically of two types: **Lehren** and **Vorreden**. The *Lehr'* is usually an exegetical sermon interpreting a certain chapter of the Scriptures verse by verse, often very long-windedly, and (at least today) rarely read in its totality. In former times, to be sure, sermons lasted two hours or more. This *Lehr'* always occupies the second part of the worship program; the first part is filled (besides prayer and hymns) by a *Vorred*. This is a general expository sermon centered around a special verse. Also the traditional ceremonies of the church, such as baptism, have this dual type of homiletics.

The information as to the number of existing written sermons varies greatly: the late bishop Elias Walter (q.v.) of the Dariusleut counted 196 Lehren and 25 Psalm interpretations (a total of 221) besides 55 general Vorreden and 25 Vorreden for holidays, making a grand total of 301 sermons. The Lehrerleut, however, claim 250 Vorreden and 350 Lehren, while another preacher claimed 180 Vorreden and 230 Lehren (totaling 410). One of the preachers added the information that some of these sermons are said to have been copied from the Jacob Denner (q.v.) sermon collection (German editions since 1730), which most likely explains the difference in the counting of the existing written sermons.

The prevailing church tradition concerning sermons includes the following. Christmas being celebrated for three days requires three Lehren; New Year's Day needs one Lehr, and Epiphany (January 6), another. Palm Sunday, the usual day of the baptismal ceremony with its elaborate, prescribed ritual (see **Taufreden**), requires one Lehr. On Good Friday another Lehr is read, while Easter, celebrated for three days, requires four Lehren (Sunday morning and afternoon; the Easter Sunday morning sermon deals with the Lamb of Exodus 12 as its traditional theme); Easter Monday is the day for the Lord's Supper with a lengthy sermon, usually lasting two hours; Tuesday is celebrated as resurrection day. Ascension Day requires one sermon, while Pentecost, celebrated for three days, has three Lehren. The Day of Annunciation (*Mariae Verkündigung*) is celebrated by the Schmiedeleut only, who use one Lehr for the morning worship; in the afternoon everyday work is resumed. There are also sermons for weddings (Eph. 5), funerals, election of ministers, confirmation of ministers, election of bishops, a total of at least 21 standard sermon assignments.

At this place no complete list of the Bible chapters and verses used can be offered. A scrutiny of the datable sermons shows, however, that of the Old Testament most-used books were Isaiah (predominant), Ecclesiasticus (their favorite Old Testament book), Jeremiah, Psalms, Proverbs, and Tobit. In the New Testament preference is given to the Gospels, Acts, Romans, Corinthians, Ephesians, John, Peter, James, and Hebrews.

The entire worship of the Hutterites, as it developed during the Ehrenpreis era, is strongly ritualized and formalized. When the preacher reads the Scripture text of his sermon, the congregation rises; the reading itself is done in chanting fashion. Since the daily prayer hour comes after a long day of hard work, it should not be surprising that now and then a member of the congregation falls asleep. Actually some of the sermons which Johannes Waldner collected in the *Klein-Geschichtsbuch* contained a complaint about "the sleepy audience" (206), and quote the admonition "that one should not sleep even if the sermon should last for two hours" (207). The reading of the sermon (at least today) sounds often more as a ritual than as a living instruction or exhortation; certain passages are most likely no longer fully understood. Due to the uncompromising Biblicism of all sermons they call their reading "sharp preaching" in contrast to the "soft preaching" in other churches (cf. *Klein-Geschichtsbuch*, 577). The brethren are very fond of this "sharp" preaching, that is, of the outspokenness of the instruction concerning the meaning of the Scriptural text and its application in everyday life, realizing that it is this Biblical radicalism which distinguishes their piety and life from all their surroundings. Hence they like their worship period, with its sermons, prayers, and singing (q.v.), both on workdays (daily at 6 p.m.) and on Sundays. Needless to say that perfect attendance by all is taken for granted.

The minister, wearing a black frock coat almost

down to the knees, enters the meeting room (usually, but not always, the schoolroom) first, then follow slowly the elders and those who have any office, taking their seats next to the preacher, facing the congregation. Next the congregation enters, men right (from the view of the preacher), women left, children in front, again boys separated from girls. At the conclusion of the worship, the exit takes place in the reverse, children first, and the minister last, who then locks the house. In 1957 the average Sunday service lasted 1½ hours, the Lord's Supper service lasted 2½ to 3 hours, and the ordination of a minister sometimes up to 4 hours.

The facts here described in no way exhaust the meaning and character of the Hutterite devotional life. Closer study of this subject would be needed, foremost by analyzing the sermon texts proper and comparing them with earlier and later texts from elsewhere. Therefore the material given above should not be taken as the final word.   R.F.

Servaes, Matthias, an Anabaptist martyr: see **Matthias Servaes.**

Servaes Vuegen (Voegen), a Sacramentist (*q.v.*) of Maastricht, Dutch province of Limburg, who about the fall of 1534 became a member of the Maastricht Anabaptist congregation, having been baptized by Jan Smeitgen (*q.v.*). Arrested with many other members, he renounced his faith and was beheaded at Maastricht on Feb. 6, 1535. His confession before the officials is very remarkable; he says that he was baptized by Jan Smeitgen (*q.v.*) during a meeting of the congregation in a private home; before baptism was administered Smeitgen had preached on Mark 16:16, teaching that faith should precede the ceremony of baptism. He also confessed that they were interested in the events at Münster (*q.v.*) and that those of Münster "had chosen a king."   vDZ.

W. Bax, *Het Protestantisme in het Bisdom Luik* . . . I (The Hague, 1937) *passim,* see Index.

Servant of Peter Planer, an Anabaptist martyr, executed in 1532 at Sterzing, Austria: see **Planer.** (*Mart. Mir.* D 33, E 440.)   vDZ.

Servant of Pieter (Peter) **de Gulicker,** an Anabaptist martyr: see **Claes Denysse.**

Servetus, Michael (1511-53), a native of Spain, was much exercised over the problem of the conversion of the Jews and the Moors. The great obstacle appeared to him to be the requirement of belief in the doctrine of the Trinity. Great was his relief to discover that the technical language of that doctrine is not to be found in the New Testament. At the same time he learned from the Occamist theologians how many logical contradictions the doctrine entails. He concluded that the formulation of the essentials of the doctrine at the council of Nicaea constituted the fall in the history of the Church. His own view affirmed one God, operative through His Word, which is coeternal with Himself and His agent in creation. This Word was united with the man Jesus, born of a virgin, to become the Son of God, who thus had a beginning in time and was not coeternal with God. The term "Christ" was applied to the Word, whether before or after the

incarnation. This doctrinal position was set forth by Servetus in his *De Trinitatis Erroribus* printed at Hagenow near Strasbourg, and thus on Protestant soil, in 1531 (English translation by E. Morse Wilbur, *Harvard Theological Studies* XVI, 1932). The work, issued before the censors were alerted, received a wide dissemination and exerted a marked influence upon the anti-Trinitarians (*q.v.*).

By reason of this book Servetus was safe neither in Protestant nor in Catholic territory. He took refuge under pseudonymity and lived as Michel de Villeneuve in France, where for several years he supported himself as an editor. Everything he did gave offense. An edition of the Bible had notes which said that the prophets of the Old Testament were referring to events of their own times and were not predicting the future. An edition of Ptolemy's geography contained a passage denying that Palestine was a land flowing with milk and honey. Servetus then studied medicine in Paris and became the discoverer of the pulmonary circulation of the blood. For twelve years he practiced as a physician at Vienne near Lyons.

In 1553 he brought out clandestinely his great work, the *Restitutio Christianismi,* which repeated the views of the *De Trinitatis Erroribus* with the addition of two new elements. The first was Anabaptism which he had presumably imbibed during his previous stay at Strasbourg. With vehemence he denied the rightfulness of infant baptism, and recommended the postponement of baptism to the thirtieth year in imitation of Christ. The very title of the book, the *Restitution of Christianity,* is reminiscent of several Anabaptist works and the idea is precisely the Anabaptist ideal of the restoration of primitive Christianity. With the chiliastic Anabaptists he looked for the speedy return of the Lord and assigned to himself some ill-defined messianic role in that Michael Servetus would assist the archangel Michael. But Servetus was not an Anabaptist in his view of the church, which he held to be only a spiritual fellowship, nor in his conduct, since as a Nicodemite he attended mass.

The second new element was the Neoplatonism of the Florentine academy with which he became acquainted through the medical humanists of France. In accord with this tradition he interpreted Christ to be the light of the world in terms of the metaphysics of light. Servetus was not a systematic thinker. His writing is marked by bold speculation and by passionate outbursts of lyrical piety.

Through channels unknown to us the full circumstances of Servetus' identity and of the publication of his book came to be known in Geneva and were brought to the attention of John Calvin with whom Servetus some time previously had carried on an exacerbated correspondence. A certain Guillaume Trie, a Protestant of Geneva, had betrayed Servetus to the Inquisition at Vienne and then, being challenged for evidence, inveigled Calvin into supplying the necessary documentation. Servetus escaped, however, from the prison of the Inquisition and after wandering for three months turned up in Geneva on Aug. 13, 1553.

There he was recognized and was denounced to the Town Council on the capital charge of heresy at the instance of John Calvin. After a trial of two months Servetus was condemned as guilty of the two religious crimes subject to death in the code of Justinian, namely, the repetition of baptism and the denial of the Trinity. He was sentenced to be burned at the stake. Servetus petitioned for death by the sword lest he recant and lose his soul. Calvin seconded his request, but it was denied by the Council. From the flames Servetus called upon "Christ, the Son of the eternal God." Had he been willing to shift the position of the adjective and call upon "Christ, the eternal Son," he might have been saved. The *Restitutio Christianismi* was so effectively suppressed that only three copies survive, though there is an 18th-century reprint.

The execution on Oct. 27, 1553, marked the beginning of the toleration controversy (*q.v.*) on an extensive scale in Protestant churches. The reformers of the established Protestant churches endorsed the action of the Geneva Town Council and of Calvin, for example, Melanchthon and Brenz. (Luther was dead.) But many were deeply troubled. Vergerio was aghast. David Joris entered a plea for the accused during the trial. Catherine Zell, Postell, and Curio voiced disapproval. The most influential protest was that of Castellio (*q.v.*) in his *De Haereticis* (1554, actually printed at Basel). R.H.B.

R. H. Bainton, *Hunted Heretic* (Boston, 1953); S. van der Woude, *Verguisd Geloof* (Delft, 1953) 49-144; B. Becker *et al.*, *Autour de Michel Servet et de Seb. Castellion* (Haarlem, 1953); W. Köhler, *Reformation und Ketzerprozess* (Tübingen, 1901); *ML* IV.

Services Bulletin, an 8-page 8½ x 11 in. monthly periodical published by the Mennonite Central Committee at Akron, Pa., first issue March 1947, last issue April 1956, at which time the circulation was 7,500 copies, distributed free. The following have served as editors: Ernest W. Lehman, Paul Holdeman, Ruth Hess, Emma Schlichting, Marion W. Kliewer, and Margaret Jantzi. The purpose of the *Services Bulletin* was to give in a concise form a review of the various services sponsored by the MCC, namely, foreign relief, refugee resettlement, voluntary service, peace, and mental health. In April 1958 the periodical was reactivated under the name *Report* and published as a quarterly interpreting the MCC program to 2500 church leaders and educators. Each issue of this 6⅞ x 9½ in. booklet is devoted to a section of MCC activity. This periodical is edited by the Information section of the MCC.
J.N.B.

Settlement Mennonite (MC) Church, now extinct, was organized by Mennonite families (MC) in Northampton County, Pa., in 1802, when a meetinghouse was built, evidently as the continuation of the older Siegfried (*q.v.*) congregation, the first meetinghouse of which was built on what is now Twenty-first Street, Northampton, Pa., in 1760 or earlier. The trustees in 1802 were Jacob Baer, Jacob Histand, John Ziegler, and Samuel Landis. As was usual in Pennsylvania prior to the adoption of the Public School Law of 1834 the land was given for both church and school purposes. The Mennonites built on this lot a frame building, 26 x 30 feet in size. But the effort to revive the congregation did

not succeed. For the next hundred years there was a weary struggle for survival. Franconia Conference preachers, General Conference Mennonites, and even independents, all made efforts to keep the congregation alive, but in vain. Finally in 1908 the property was sold and converted into a dwelling. The Cement National Bank of Siegfried, Northampton, Pa., is custodian of a trust fund for the care of the cemetery, which has about 60 marked graves. J.C.W.

J. C. Wenger, *History of the Mennonites of the Franconia Conference* (Telford, 1937) 229-31.

Seu, Johannes (Jan Seeus), a native of the Dutch province of Zeeland, d. 1613 at Middelburg, capital of Zeeland, was a Reformed minister. At first he was a schoolteacher at Frankenthal, Germany. As pastor he first served in Germany, in 1575 being preacher of the Calvinist refugees at Frankfurt on the Main. From 1576 he was a Reformed clergyman at Middelburg, Holland. Seu was a bitter opponent of the Mennonites. It was obviously Seu who caused the imprisonment of Hans de Ries (*q.v.*) at Middelburg in 1578, when de Ries visited this town. When later the Mennonites of Middelburg refused to take an oath and to bear arms Seu tried to press them into the military civil guard, and if they should refuse, to close their shops. By the intervention of Prince William of Orange (*q.v.*) the Mennonites of Middelburg could live in peace, being exempted from the oath and the military service (1577-78, 1580). But Seu continued to attack the Mennonites and tried to persuade the magistrates to forbid the public exercise of their religion. Again Prince William brought relief. Seu also wrote some books against the Mennonites: *Schriftmatige Artykelen tegen de ongeschickte en valsche dwaelingen der wederdoopers* (Middelburg, 1599), *Corte Beschrijvinge van het ampt der overheid ende wederlegginge van een boucxken dat eenen Wederdooper met verswijging zijns naems . . . heeft laten uitgaen . . . tegen het recht gebruijk des crijchs* (Middelburg, 1600). In his *Waeraghtighe grondige bewijsinge . . . van den Kinderdoop* (Leiden, 1601) he defended infant baptism, attacking believers' baptism; it is the duty of the magistrates to eradicate the Mennonites by forbidding their meetings and removing their preachers. In 1608 he published *Antwoordt op een boecxken gemaeckt door eenen wederdooper Cornelis de Cuyper genaemt: eenvuldighe verantwoordinghe . . .* (Middelburg, 1608), which severely attacks the Mennonites, saying that they are worse than the Pope and his idolatry. (*N.N.B.Wb.* I, 1470 f.; *DB* 1908, 21-26, 33, 42; *ML* III.) vDZ.

Seventh Street Mennonite Mission (MC) is located at 347 South Seventh Street in Reading, Pa. The work is an outpost of the Twelfth and Windsor Mission established in Reading in 1938 among the colored. In 1957 the minister was William M. Weaver and the membership 22. I.D.L.

Seventh Street Mennonite (MC) Church (known until 1947 as the Alpine Street Mennonite Church), located on Seventh at Campus Avenue, Upland, Cal., was organized in 1942 with 25 members as a member of the Pacific Coast District Conference (now South Pacific Conference). A new church was dedicated on Aug. 17, 1948. The first minister was William Jennings. In 1957 the membership was 104, with Sherman Maust as pastor.   J.D.L.

Seward County, Neb., is located in the east central part of the state. The Mennonite settlement of the county is in and around Milford, a town of 951 population, in the south central part of the county. The four Mennonite churches (MC) in the county, West Fairview (*q.v.*), East Fairview (*q.v.*), and Milford (*q.v.*), and a new congregation formed in 1958 by members of East Fairview, had a combined membership of *c*650 in 1958. The first settlers were Amish Mennonites from Walnut Creek, Ohio, arriving in the spring of 1873; others came later from the Wayland (Iowa) neighborhood and from Central Illinois. In 1958 the Bellwood (MC) congregation was established with 55 charter members. A new congregation has also been formed with 22 members in Lincoln, Neb., of former members of the Milford, West Fairview, and East Fairview churches, who are now living in Lincoln.   A.M.M.

Sewel, William (Dutch, **Willem Sewel**) (Amsterdam, 1653-1720), an outstanding Quaker historian and author of *Historie van de Opkomste, aanwas en voortgang der Christenen, bekend by den naem van Quakers* . . . (Amsterdam, 1717), of which book there is also an English translation, *The History of the Rise, Increase and Progress of the Christian People Called Quakers* (London, England, 1722), was of Mennonite descent. His grandfather William Sewel, a painter, belonged to the Brownists (*q.v.*), who moved from England to the Netherlands in 1589. This William Sewel's son was Jacob Sewel (who often spelled his name "Zeenwel"), a surgeon at Amsterdam, who married Judith Zinspenning. Both Jacob and his wife were members of the Utrecht Mennonite Church and later of the Amsterdam Flemish congregation until about 1656, when Quakerism arose in the Netherlands; under the Quaker influence especially of William Ames (*q.v.*) both Jacob Zeenwell and his wife left the Mennonite Church. Especially Judith Zinspenning was an ardent Quaker, charging that the spirit of true conversion was lacking in Mennonite sermons and meetings, and that they held too much to the "outward (i.e., visible) church," considering baptism and communion as divine orders, while neglecting enlightenment by the Spirit of God. Thus she wrote in her book *Eenige Schriften en Zendbrieven* (Amsterdam, 1684). Her son William Sewel repeated these charges in his book.   vDZ.

N.N.B.Wb. IX, 1017-21; C. B. Hylkema, *Reformateurs* I and II (Haarlem, 1900-2); H. W. Meihuizen, *Galenus Abrahamsz* (Haarlem, 1954) 58 f., 112; W. I. Hull, *William Penn and the Dutch Quaker Migration to Pennsylvania* (Swarthmore, 1935); idem, *Willem Sewel of Amsterdam 1653-1720* (Swarthmore, 1933).

Sewing Circle, a term widely used in the Mennonite Church (MC) and Conservative Mennonite Church for women's meetings generally held once a month to make clothing and bedding for distribution by missionary and relief workers among needy people in America as well as in foreign lands. See Women's Missionary and Service Auxiliary and Women's Missionary Association.   M.G.

Sewing Circle Committee, General, the name applied to the committee supervising women's sewing circles in the Mennonite Church (MC). In the 1932 *Mennonite Year-Book,* the name appears for the first time, replacing the earlier Women's Missionary Committee. In 1947 the General Sewing Circle Committee became the Women's Sewing Circle Organization and in 1955 the latter became the Women's Missionary and Service Auxiliary (*q.v.*). M.G.

Seye (Seyen, Seijen, Sye, Sije, Sijen), a Dutch Mennonite family, now extinct, formerly largely represented in the Waterlander congregation of Amsterdam, later also found at Haarlem, Leiden, and Rotterdam. Many members of the family served as deacons in Amsterdam as well as in Haarlem and Leiden. There were at least three Mennonite preachers of this family: Jacob Seyen was a preacher of the Waterlanders at Amsterdam 1642-d.70. Hendrik Seye served the Flemish and Frisian Kruisstraat congregation of Haarlem 1715-*c*50. Hendrik Seye Jr, after serving as assistant pastor at Friedrichstadt (*q.v.*) in Holstein, Germany, was the last minister of the Mennonite congregation of Schiedam (*q.v.*), serving there 1741-47. He was at the same time an ardent Collegiant (*q.v.*), often speaking in the Collegiant meetings at Rotterdam and at Rijnsburg (*q.v.*). Whether a Jacob Seyen was a preacher at Alkmaar in the early 18th century is questionable.
          vDZ.

Church records of Amsterdam and Leiden; *DB* 1909, 161-67; *Inv. Arch. Amst.* II, Nos. 1466, 2241-43; II, 2, Nos. 469-71, 474, 477.

Seyel, Hans: see **Seidl, Johannes.**

Seyfried, Johann, a preacher at the Lutheran church of St. George in Augsburg, Germany, was tolerant to the Anabaptists in the city and was one of the few clergymen of the Reformation period to defend them. He is reported to have frequently said from the pulpit, "One finds nowhere in the Scripture that the Anabaptists should be punished to the extent to which they are punished" (*Literaliensammlung des Augsburger Stadtarchivs,* July 4, 1528). When Martin Zehentmaier (*q.v.*) was heard by the council of Augsburg on Nov. 27, 1528, he asserted that he had conversed with Master Hans Seyfried; he did not condemn rebaptism, but said if anyone came to him desiring rebaptism, he would rather baptize him himself.   HEGE.

Fr. Roth, "Zur Gesch. der Wiedertäufer in Oberschwaben," *Ztscht des Hist. Vereins für Schwaben und Neuburg* XXVIII (1901) 86; *ML* IV.

Seylemaker (Seil(e)maker), a Mennonite family, formerly found at Hoorn, Dutch province of North Holland, where Volkert Maertensz Seylemaker, a sailmaker, lived in the 16th century. Brandt called him "a man of knowledge and loyalty among the Mennonites, now called Frisians" and says that it was Seylemaker who told that when he was visiting Menno Simons, who lay on his deathbed, Menno said, "Be not a servant of men, as I have been." Volkert Maertensz was probably well-to-do, for his youngest son Dirk studied medicine at Leiden and in Italy, obtaining his medical degree in 1594 at the famous University of Padua. This Dirk Volkertsz Seylemaker (b. 1572 at Hoorn, d. there 1630) after finishing his medical studies was a physician in his home town; after a fashion of that period he used a Latin name, Theodorus Velius, and Velius became the family name of his descendants. He was married first to Martha des Muliers, a Mennonite refugee from Flanders (d. before 1599), and then to Aef Ewouts. Velius was a man of erudition and also wrote some poetry. He is specially known for a historical chronicle, *Chronijck van de Stadt Hoorn* (first ed. Hoorn, 1604, reprints 1617, 1648, 1740), which gives some information about the Mennonites. His son Pierre Velius, a physician like his father, left the Mennonite Church, as did most of his descendants. Mennonite descendants called Velius were found at Leiden and Amsterdam in the 16th and 17th centuries.

Willem Maertens Seylemaker (1626-81), a grandson of the above Volkert Maertensz, was married to Aechtje Sleutel. He and most descendants took the family name of Sleutel (*q.v.*) instead of Seylemaker. He was a preacher of the Frisian Mennonite congregation at Hoorn from 1649 and elder from 1657. Two of his sons, Jan Willems Sleutel (1654-92) and Gerrit Willem Seylemaker, were preachers of the same congregation, Jan Willems from 1678 after his father died, and Gerrit Willems from 1688. vpZ.

DB 1867, 72, 77 f.; 81, 84; 1875, 30; 1889, 76; 1899, 104; G. Brandt, *Historie der Reformatie* (2d ed. Amsterdam, 1677) 186 f.; *N.N.B.Wb.* I, 1518 f.; *ML* III, 175.

Seyler, Friedrich: see **Seiler, Friedrich.**

Shady Pine Mennonite Church (MC), located at Willow Hill, Pa., member of the Washington-Franklin Mennonite Conference, is a mission congregation under the district mission board. It was established in 1948, and had 25 members in 1957, with Howard Lehman as pastor. M.G.

Shafter (Cal.) **First** Mennonite Church (GCM), a member of the Pacific District, had its beginnings with the migration of Mennonites to the area in 1918-19, stimulated by H. J. Krehbiel of Reedley. Meetings were held in homes, the Santa Fe school, and later in a small church erected on Scaroni Avenue. Herman Janzen was the first leader. When some of the Mennonites moved away, those remaining joined other denominations for a time, but when Krehbiel returned to Shafter in 1935, the congregation reorganized and in 1937 built the present church at the corner of Golden West and Wall Streets. The congregation had 56 members in 1957, with Ramon H. Jantz as pastor. J.Ba.

Shafter (Cal.) Mennonite Brethren Church, a member of the Pacific District Conference, was organized in the fall of 1918, when a number of recent settlers met in the home of Henry Kohfeld. Deacon Frank C. Penner, formerly of Escondido, Cal., also assisted in the organization. For a time the congregation met in private homes and later in the local school. In 1919 a tabernacle was built near the center of town at the corner of Kern and California Streets. The membership in 1958 was 522 with H. H. Dick as the pastor in charge, and D. W. Nikkel assistant pastor. E.Si.

Shamshabad, a Mennonite Brethren mission station in India, located near the large village of Shamshabad, 10 miles southwest of Hyderabad, Madhya Pradesh (formerly Central Provinces), was opened in 1920, and in the following years the Mission built two bungalows for missionaries, a church, two school buildings, hostels for school boys and girls, a hospital, and living quarters for workers and students. Mr. and Mrs. J. H. Pankratz began the work in this area and resided at this station one year. Dr. Katharina L. Schellenberg and Anna Hanneman have lived and worked here many years. In 1957 the missionaries were Mr. and Mrs. P. V. Balzer, Emma Lepp, Helen Harder, and Marie Riediger.

Regular worship services and other church activities have been conducted at the station from its beginning. A middle and primary school has been conducted since 1920. In 1946-48 the mission high school was located here, and the Bethany Bible school 1930-45. In 1927 the hospital was built and it is still in operation. The Shamshabad station field, comprising an area of 1,000 square miles and having a population of 160,000, in 1957 had a growing Christian community with a church membership of 800. J.H.L.

Shank (Shenk, Schenk, Schenck), a Mennonite family name formerly found in Switzerland in the Emmenthal in the 16th and 17th centuries. Some of the family emigrated to Moravia in the 1530's, others to the Palatinate, Germany, in the 1670's, among whom was Michael Schenk, of Mühlibach, Emmenthal, who in 1671, at the age of eighty-one, settled in Osthofen in the Palatinate, leaving his wife and 14 children in Switzerland. He was accompanied by one son with his wife and children, and his brother(?) Christian, aged ninety-five, with two daughters. Since 1800 the name is not found among the Swiss Mennonites.

In Pennsylvania a Michael Shank (Schenck) (d. 1744) and his son Michael Shank (d. 1785) were on the naturalization list of 1729. There was also a Henry Shank (Shenk) on the Strasburg Strettle tract. These lived and died in Lancaster County, Pa., and are the ancestors of all Mennonites with this name. Some outstanding bearers in the Lancaster Conference were bishops Henry Shenk (1794-1865) of Conestoga Township, and Daniel Shank (1832-1906) in Adams County.

The first bishop in Virginia was Henry Shank (1758-1836), ordained in 1810 to have the oversight over all the congregations in the Shenandoah Valley; his son Samuel Shank (1790-1863) was bishop in the Lower District in Virginia, and the latter's son Abraham Shank (1829-1901) was bishop in the same district. Samuel Shank (1821-1901), a minister, a brother of Bishop Abraham Shank, was a leader in the Virginia Conference, serving a number of years as moderator. Three of his sons, Lewis, Joseph, and Perry, and several of his grandsons followed him in the ministry. Lewis Shank (1855-

1942) was bishop of the Lower District in Virginia from 1901 until his death. J. Ward Shank (1904-) has been serving as bishop in the Lower District since 1954. John H. Shenk (1911-) is a minister at Denbigh, Va., and John F. Shank (1911-) a minister at Broadway, Va.

Deacon Jacob A. Shenk (1900-50) established the successful Shenk Hatcheries at Harrisonburg and was active in church work, especially in missions, serving as president of the Virginia Mennonite Mission Board until his untimely death in a plane crash. Aaron M. Shenk was a bishop in the Lancaster Conference at Myerstown, Pa.

In Allen County, Ohio, the successor of Bishop John M. Brenneman (q.v.) was John M. Shenk (1848-1935). J. W. Shank (1881-) was a Mennonite missionary to Argentina 1917-49. His brother J. R. Shank (1877-1958) served as a rural missionary in Missouri from 1905. David Shank, their nephew, is a missionary in Belgium. Stanley C. Shenk (1919-) was a minister and writer at West Liberty, Ohio, and his brother Charles J. Shenk is now a missionary in Japan. Harvey E. Shank (1887-) is a bishop at Chambersburg, Pa., and G. D. Shenk (1878-) a bishop at Sheridan, Ore. Dozens of ministers in the Mennonite Church (MC) have borne the name Shank or Shenk. In 1957 there were 32 such, of whom 19 were Shank and 13 Shenk, in Pennsylvania, Maryland, Virginia, Ohio, Idaho, Indiana, and Oregon.   J.C.W.

J. Clayton Shank, "Panoramic Pageantry of Shank Family Names," *Journal of the Lancaster County Historical Society* XLII (July 1958) 169-74.

Shank, John Robert (1877-1958), a Mennonite (MC) bishop and editor, was born Aug. 19, 1877, at Versailles, Mo., a son of Lewis and Mary Wenger Shank. Ordained a minister in 1905, he served first at Pea Ridge, Mo., until 1908, then at Carver, Mo., and in the surrounding Osage River district. In 1941 he was ordained bishop. Besides his rural missionary work he served widely in Christian educational work as editor and writer for the Sunday-school periodicals of the Mennonite Church, and editor of YPBM topics. He was secretary of the Missouri-Kansas Conference 1907-34, and long-time member of the Mennonite Publication Board. He was married to Clara M. Brubaker; there were no children. He died April 26, 1958.   H.S.B.

Shantipur Leper Homes, situated 4 miles southwest of Dhamtari near the Dhamtari-Balodgahan highway, Madhya Pradesh (formerly Central Provinces), India. During the famine of 1899-1900 the lepers among the thousands who came for food and shelter were placed in separate huts and were fed from separate kitchens. The British government and the municipality of Dhamtari gave grants of money and private individuals subscribed sums for their later maintenance.

In 1901 J. A. Ressler (q.v.), an American Mennonite (MC) missionary, was asked to assume the responsibility for founding an institution for the lepers. He received financial aid from the Mission to Lepers in India and the East, with headquarters in Edinburgh, Scotland. The American Mennonite Mission was to have free access to the lepers for re-

ligious work and for organizing and supervising the living and work of the lepers and also built up a Christian staff of overseers and helpers.

The first leper asylum was located on a plot of ground donated by Dhamtari at the southern edge of Dhamtari, where a group of lepers had previously lived in little bamboo matting huts, subsisting by begging. The first substantial buildings were constructed in 1902-3. Much of the material was donated by the Government Forest Department. Gradually kitchens for cooking, a medical dispensary, a house for the caretaker, and a chapel were built. Ultimately the Government provided a per-capita grant for the maintenance of the lepers to supplement the sum given by the Mission to Lepers. To care for the increasingly large number of lepers applying for admittance it was found necessary to find a larger site. Accordingly in 1920 the Mission to Lepers sanctioned a scheme for a project estimated at $60,000 which would provide for Leper Homes with all the facilities for their care and treatment. By this time the enrollment of inmates was 251 of whom 227 were baptized Christians and 22 were applicants for baptism. In 1922 an area of 115 acres of land was purchased from a village for $2,400. The estimated cost of the entire plant to accommodate about 500 inmates with medical and other facilities would be about $60,000 of which Government and the Mission to Lepers each would provide half.

In 1924 the lepers were transferred from Dhamtari to Shantipur. By 1929 there were cottages to house the 450 lepers and healthy children of lepers, two large hospital wards, a large medical dispensary with laboratory, school buildings for leper and non-leper children, buildings for administration and hospital staff, and the bungalow for the missionary superintendent. The medical staff had at their disposal all the latest remedies for the treatment of the lepers. Shantipur became one of the largest leper homes in the interior of India.

A word of tribute must be given to Dr. C. D. Esch who untiringly gave his time and effort to the building up of Shantipur.   G.J.L.

Shantz (Schantz, Shanz, Tschantz, Johns), a Swiss Mennonite family, with few representatives in Europe today (Albert Schantz is a preacher in the Regensburg, Bavaria, congregation and chairman of the relief committee known as Christenpflicht, q.v.), but early represented in Pennsylvania (Jacob Schantz, immigrant to Montgomery County, Pa., in 1737, Hans Tschantz, third bishop in the Lancaster County, Pa., colonial Mennonite settlement, active c1742; a cemetery plot donated by him still called "Hans Tschantz cemetery"), and since 1800 a prominent family in the Mennonite Church (MC) in Ontario. There the following ordained men bearing the name Shantz have served or are serving: bishops, Henry Shantz (1864-77), Detweiler congregation from 1842; Israel R. Shantz (1863-1910), moved from Waterloo to Carstairs, Alberta, c1903; Moses H. Shantz (1884-1938) at Blenheim, Ont., many years moderator of the Ontario Conference (MC) and for a time president of the Mennonite Publication Board; Benjamin B. Shantz (1880-),

Hagey congregation; Stanley D. Schantz (1914-), Guernsey, Sask.; preachers, Merle Shantz, Wanner congregation, Ont.; Irwin Schantz, Loman, Minn. Jacob Y. Shantz (*q.v.*) was a prominent layman (MC) in Kitchener, Ont., joining the M.B.C. Church *c*1875 when it was started. John Schantz (1774-1855) and his son Joseph (1814-81) were ministers in the Upper Milford (Pa.) congregation which joined the Oberholtzer group (GCM) in 1847, and J. W. Schantz (1878-1916) was a minister (GCM) at Schwenksville (Pa.) and Zion at Souderton (Pa.) 1907-16.

An Amish branch of the family came to America *c*1768. Joseph Schantz (1749-1810), who changed his name to Johns, was in Somerset County, Pa., by 1793, and in 1810 founded the city of Johnstown on his land. Some of his descendants moved to Elkhart County, Ind., where Daniel J. Johns (1850-1942) was an outstanding leader and two of his sons also, Ira S. Johns (1879-1956), preacher at the Clinton Frame congregation near Goshen and long secretary of the Indiana-Michigan Mennonite (MC) Conference, and Otis N. Johns, bishop of the Beech congregation near Louisville, Ohio, and long secretary of the Mennonite Publication Board. Joseph Schantz (1856-1934), a preacher at Ingolstadt, Bavaria, where his father and grandfather had been bishops in the Amish congregation, emigrated to the Midwest, finally locating at Wisner, Neb., in the M.C. congregation. Two brothers, Daniel and Andrew Schantz, also came with Joseph to the Midwest. Descendants of the three men are scattered in Nebraska, Oklahoma, and other midwestern states. Other Amish Schantzes came from Europe to Central Illinois, including Christian Schantz to Tiskilwa *c*1840, Jacob Schantz from Hesse-Darmstadt, Germany, to Congerville, Ill., in 1847. A son of Jacob, Peter (*q.v.*; 1853-1921?) Schantz, was an outstanding leader in the Central Mennonite Conference.

The earliest known mention of a member of the family among the Anabaptists is in 1541 in the canton of Bern, Switzerland. In 1567 a Hans Tschantz of Kiesen, canton of Bern, was imprisoned for his faith. Oppligen and Röthenbach in the same canton were mentioned in connection with the family. In the fore part of the 18th century members of the family moved to the Bernese Jura district, also to Montbéliard and Alsace. In 1824 a Johannes Tschantz and his son Abraham left their Jura home and settled in the Sonnenberg district in Wayne County, Ohio, where many of their descendants still live. **H.S.B.**

Daniel Kauffman, *Mennonite Cyclopedic Dictionary* (Scottdale, 1937).

Shantz, Jacob Yost (1822-1909), of Berlin (now Kitchener), Ont., for many years a promoter of the Mennonite settlements in Manitoba, was born on May 2, 1822, the eighth child of Jacob and Maria Yost Schantz, of Montgomery County, Pa., who had purchased a farm in what is now East Kitchener. The son's interests soon extended beyond his vocation of farming. Fruit growing, maple sugar production, and the operation of a sawmill were added to his activities. Later he entered the building and contracting business. He promoted various industries in his city, the chief being the Dominion Button Works. For 27 years he served on the Berlin school board and in 1882 was unanimously chosen as mayor of Berlin, but he resigned the position after four days in office.

Shantz's chief public contribution, however, lay in the promotion of Mennonite immigration to Manitoba. In 1872 as a representative of the Canadian government Shantz accompanied Bernhard Warkentin (*q.v.*), who represented the prospective Mennonite immigrants from Russia, on a land inspection trip to Manitoba. The Canadian Department of Agriculture published Shantz's report under the title *The Narrative of a Journey to Manitoba,* which became a history-making pamphlet going through various editions with a total circulation of several hundred thousand. During the next 35 years, Shantz made many trips to Manitoba, the twenty-seventh and the last in his 85th year. His work consisted in assisting the Mennonite immigrants who wished to settle in Manitoba with transportation and supplies, as well as helping them settle on the land. By November 1874 it was reported that 1,400 Mennonites had been placed in Manitoba and five years later the number had grown to over 7,000. Shantz not only obtained most favorable travel rates for the immigrants but often used money from his $100,000 personal credit fund in a Berlin bank to assist his friends from Russia by helping pay their transportation costs, equipment, and farm machinery. Shantz was also placed in charge of the $100,000 Canadian government loan to the Russian Mennonites, guaranteed by the Ontario Mennonites. As treasurer of the "Aid Committee of Ontario" Shantz also dispensed the funds loaned to the immigrants by his fellow Mennonites. He lived to see the day when all of these loans were repaid, the final settlement having been made in his 85th year. In 1893 Shantz began promoting Alberta land and here again future developments proved his business judgment and vision. (In his German correspondence he usually spelled his name "Schantz.")

Shantz became a member of the Mennonite Church (MC) at an early age. In 1875, desiring a more progressive church, Shantz became a member of the group later to be known as the Mennonite Brethren in Christ. For eighteen years he served on the Managing Committee of the *Gospel Banner* (*q.v.*) and for at least 8 years on his denomination's Foreign and Heathen Missionary Society. In his last years he showed interest in Christian Science but died a member of the M.B.C. church. He was always deeply interested in the temperance movement and a defender of Biblical nonresistance.

Although Shantz was a quiet and unassuming man, his voice had a deep, organ-like tone that people did not forget. He was married three times, in 1843 to Barbara Biehn, in 1853 to Nancy Brubacher, and in 1871 to Sarah Sherk. Two sons and three daughters were born of the first marriage, and three sons and four daughters to the second. Shantz was buried in the East End Mennonite Cemetery of Kitchener.† **M.G.**

M. Gingerich, "Jacob Y. Shantz, 1822-1909, Promoter of the Mennonite Settlements in Manitoba," *MQR* XXIV

(July 1950) 3, 230-48; *From the Steppes to the Prairies,* C. Krahn editor, "Jacob Y. Shantz," by Melvin Gingerich (Newton, 1949) 92-97; Gustav E. Reimer and G. R. Gaeddert, *Exiled by the Czar* (Newton, 1956).

Shantz Mennonite Church (MC), located in Waterloo County, Ont., north of Baden and about 8 miles west of Waterloo, is a member of the Ontario Conference. It is locally also known as the Upper Street Church. It was founded in the 1830's, the first settlers having been George R. Schmitt and John Schmitt, from Alsace. George Schmitt (d. 1882) was the first minister. The first meetinghouse, a stone structure, was built in 1853 and remodeled in 1900. It was replaced in 1929 by a red brick building. Among the other ministers who served the Shantz congregation were Tobias Bowman (ord. 1875), Orphen H. Wismer (ord. 1898), and Leslie Witmer (ord. 1937), the pastor in 1958.

It is improbable that the Ohio-Canada West (GCM) movement greatly affected the Shantz congregation. However, at the neighboring Geiger church, south of Baden, Ulrich Geiger, a minister, was influenced by this movement and was out of fellowship with the main body for a time. Divisive influences seem to have touched the Shantz congregation. The Wayland List of 1853 indicates that Amos Cressman, a deacon, was not in fellowship, though he lived close to the Shantz church. He is buried in the little Crosshill Mennonite plot several miles north, although the Cressman family plot is in the Shantz cemetery. (See also **Wellesley**). J.C.F.

Sharon Bethel Amish Mennonite Church, unaffiliated, located 5 miles north of Kalona, Iowa, was organized in 1946, under D. O. Burkholder of Nappanee, Ind. The congregation held its services in a Lutheran meetinghouse until 1952, when it dedicated its own meetinghouse. In 1954 Jonathan M. Miller was the bishop. J. C. Helmuth and Mose E. Yoder the ministers, with 52 members. J.M.M.

Sharon Conservative Mennonite Church, located at Ragersville, Ohio, was established in 1951 and had 51 members by 1957. Harry J. Stutzman was its bishop.   M.G.

Sharon Mennonite Brethren Church, located at Hooker, Okla., was organized Jan. 8, 1936, with a membership of 30. Henry S. Voth was the first leader. The following have served as pastors of the church: H. S. Voth, Abraham Cornelsen, H. B. Pauls, B. C. Willems, H. H. Hiebert, and M. R. Schimnowski. Mr. and Mrs. P. V. Balzer have gone out as missionaries to India. The first church building was built in 1905, and the present building in 1925. The 1957 membership was 117. In 1957 the name was changed to Adams M. B. Church.
                                                H.H.Hie.

Sharon Mennonite Church (MC), located on Winton Way Street, Winton, Cal., a member of the South Pacific Conference, was organized March 15, 1931, with 23 members. J. P. Bontrager was appointed pastor and bishop, and L. E. Weaver minister. The meetinghouse was built in 1935 with a seating capacity of 180. The membership in 1957 was 75, with Wilbert R. Nafziger, Luke E. Weaver, and Leonard Garber as ministers.   J.P.Bo.

Sharon Mennonite Church (MC), 3 miles southeast of Plain City, Ohio, a member of the Ohio and Eastern Conference, was organized Jan. 15, 1933, most of the members having come out of the Madison County Old Order Amish (*q.v.*) church. Abram Kaufman (ordained bishop in 1948) has been the pastor from the beginning. Sunday-school work was begun in 1926 in an abandoned church which was used until 1938. In that year a new building was erected, which burned down just before completion. It was at once rebuilt and dedicated in January 1940. In 1957 the membership was 163.   Ab.K.

Sharon Mennonite Church, located in Steelton, Pa., at 401 Main St., a colored congregation (MC), an outpost of the Elizabethtown congregation of the Lancaster Mennonite Conference, opened in 1952.

Sharon Mennonite Church (MC), located near Guernsey, Sask., a member of the Alberta-Saskatchewan Conference, had its origin in the winter of 1903-4, when a committee from Berlin (now Kitchener), Ont., inspected the Saskatchewan Mennonite Reserve. In 1905 the first settlers left from Ontario, followed in 1906 by another group. The first sermon was preached by Eli S. Hallman. Early services were held in the home of Aaron S. Biehn, and later, until 1911, at the Waterloo School. In 1911 a meetinghouse, 30 x 40 ft., was built. The following ministers have served the congregation: Eli S. Hallman, Moses H. Schmitt, Isaiah S. Rosenberger, Burton Weber, Daniel Schlabach, Stanley Schantz, Aaron S. Biehn, Edwin Bowman, and Arnold Shantz. Prominent family names are Bowman, Biehn, Snyder, Shantz, Weber, and Gingerich. The membership in 1957 was 136, with Bishop Stanley D. Shantz as pastor.   E.S.

Sharon Valley Mennonite Church (MC), now extinct, located at Ulen (hence also called the Ulen church), Clay Co., **Minn.**, was organized in 1924 with I. S. Mast as pastor. The highest membership, about 40, was reached in 1925. In the following years the families moved into other communities. By 1938 Mennonite church activities in the area had ceased.   F.F.K.

Shelby Reformed Mennonite Church, located 3 miles east of Shelby, Oceana Co., Mich., is the only congregation of this branch of Mennonites in Michigan. The congregation was organized in 1888 and the meetinghouse, a frame structure with a seating capacity of 160, was built in 1893. The organizers of the church were Ambrose Bearss, John Near, and Peter Roth, Bearss serving as minister and Near as deacon. Other ministers who have served the congregation are Eli Near, Al Near, and Jesse Fogelsonger. In 1952 Omar Near was the minister. In 1958 the membership was 52.   R.N.

Shelby County, Ill., is located in the southern half of the state, approximately 50 miles southeast of Springfield. In 1872 a small Old Order Amish settlement was established in the county by settlers from Elkhart and Lagrange counties, Indiana, and Holmes County, Ohio. Among them were Jacob Miller, a minister, and Christian Borntreger, later ordained minister. Because of a disagreement among the organizers, most of the settlers moved away in 1883, principally to Reno County, Kan.

In 1907 John D. Kauffman (*q.v.*) and his followers established another Amish Mennonite settlement in the county near Shelbyville. Their church, named Mt. Hermon, was built in 1912. The membership had declined to 41 by 1957. Joseph D. Reber was bishop. M.G.

Harry F. Weber, *Centennial History of the Mennonites of Illinois* (Goshen, 1931) 550, 558.

Shelby County, Missouri: see **Mount Pisgah** Mennonite Church.

Shelbyville (Ill.): see **Mount Hermon** Amish Mennonite Church.

Sheldon Mennonite Church (MC), located 4½ miles northwest of the town of Sheldon, Rusk Co., Wis., a member of the North Central Conference, was organized on July 15, 1936, by B. B. King of Elida, Ohio, and built its church in 1937. In 1957 the membership was 73, served by Daniel L. Martin and Norman H. Witmer as ministers. D.L.M.

Shelly, a Mennonite family which, according to tradition, is of English origin, but which under the religious persecution of Queen Mary fled to Holland. About 1725-30 Abraham Shelly, a recent Mennonite immigrant from Switzerland, purchased from William Penn and his brother a tract of land in what is now Milford Township in Bucks County, Pa., about 35 miles north of Philadelphia. The family is now scattered in many of the states and Canada. The greatest concentration of Shellys is still in the Milford Square area of Bucks County.

Andrew B. Shelly (*q.v.*; 1834-1913) was a contemporary of John H. Oberholtzer and a leader and organizer of the General Conference of Mennonites. Anthony S. Shelly (*q.v.*; 1853-1928) taught in the Wadsworth Mennonite school 1877-79, and for ten years served as editor of the *Mennonite* (*q.v.*). Other members of the Shelly family in the ministry were Elwood Shelly and Harvey Shelly. G.C.M. ministers of the present include Ward W. Shelly of Lancaster, Pa.; Paul R. Shelly, Bluffton College; Andrew R. Shelly, Mennonite Biblical Seminary; Maynard Shelly, North Newton, Kan.; Wilmer S. Shelly, Frederick, Pa.; and Kenneth Shelly, Pulaski, Iowa. W.S.S.

Shelly, Andrew B. (1834-1913), was an outstanding leader in the Eastern District Conference and in the General Conference Mennonite Church for 50 years, from about 1865 until his death. His leadership was revered in his pastoral ministry, his district conference activities, and in his many tasks in the General Conference. He was born in Bucks County, Pa., on Sept. 23, 1834, the only son and oldest child of Joseph and Elizabeth Bauer Shelly. His great-great-great-grandfather on both his father's and mother's side was Abraham Shelly, who with his two brothers immigrated to this country from Switzerland about 1720.

Shelly always enjoyed studying, having an inquisitive mind. At the age of seven he went to the parochial school conducted by the West Swamp Church for one year and then went to public school

during the winters until he was nineteen. He worked on his father's farm during these summers. After this he began to teach. He further prepared himself for teaching by going to an academy for nine months. He taught school until 1863, when he devoted all of his time to farming. Another of his activities in this period was teaching "singing school." On Oct. 15, 1858, Shelly married Fannie Weinberger, daughter of Joseph and Mary Shelly Weinberger. They had three sons and two daughters, one son and one daughter preceding their parents in death.

Shelly began his work in a local church as a layman. In 1857 he became superintendent of the Sunday school in the West Swamp Mennonite Church. This has been referred to as the first G.C.M. Sunday school. Later he helped to organize the Sunday School Convention of the Eastern District Conference. The first meeting of this group was held on Oct. 2, 1876. His first contribution to the life of the church in wider circles was in the field of editing and writing. In 1866 he became editor of the *Mennonitischer Friedensbote,* serving until 1881 when this paper was merged with *Zur Heimath* and the *Christlicher Bundesbote.* He served as assistant editor of the new paper until 1884. Seeing the need of an English church paper he urged that one be started. He was on the original board which published the *Mennonite,* the first issue being printed in October 1885.

Shelly was ordained to the Christian ministry on March 25, 1864, to serve as associate minister to John H. Oberholtzer. He was pastor of the First Mennonite Church of Philadelphia 1869-71. On Aug. 22, 1872, he was ordained as bishop of the West Swamp, East Swamp, Flatland, and Saucon congregations. He served as pastor at West Swamp throughout his further life and for part of this time he was also pastor of one or more of these other churches. In addition to his work as pastor, he engaged in an unusually large number of conference activities. He was president of the Eastern District Conference 1871-82 and of the General Conference 1874-96. He was also active on various boards. His major contribution in this area was his service on the G.C.M. mission board 1874-1911, when he resigned because of his age. He was secretary of this board 1889-1911. He was elected to the educational board at the 1913 session of the General Conference. He attended all the sessions of the General Conference from 1866 to 1913. He died while visiting N. B. Grubb in Philadelphia on the morning of Dec. 26, 1913. The funeral and burial took place on New Year's day of 1914 at the West Swamp Mennonite Church. His wife died on Oct. 13, 1913.

Shelly was said to be conservative yet aggressive in his leadership. He promoted causes even though the church as a whole was not ready for them, such as the organization of the General Conference, the educational program of the church, an English paper, etc. He was said to have been conscientious and painstaking in his pastoral work and always anxious to develop lay leadership. P.R.S.

N. B. Grubb, *In Memoriam, Rev. Andrew B. Shelly* (Quakertown, 1914); *Mennonite Year Book and Almanac* (Berne, 1927); H. P. Krehbiel, *The History of the General Conference of the Mennonites of North America*

(Canton, 1898); *idem, The History of the General Conference of the Mennonite Church of North America* II (Newton, 1938).

Shelly, Anthony S., was born on Feb. 28, 1853, in Milford Twp., Bucks Co., Pa., the third of the seven children of Levi and Barbara Shelly Shelly, who were members of the West Swamp Mennonite Church (GCM). He grew up during the leadership of John H. Oberholtzer and Andrew B. Shelly in the West Swamp Church.

Shelly enrolled for one year at the G.C.M. school in Wadsworth, Ohio, in 1870. After teaching in Pennsylvania two years he entered Millersville State Normal School in 1873, graduating in 1875. Again he taught two years in Pennsylvania and then taught English in the school at Wadsworth in 1877-79. Following a period of teaching in 1879-84 in Newtown, Bucks Co., Pa., he taught at the Mennonite Academy at Halstead, Kan., 1884-86. He then returned to Pennsylvania and became a partner in the newspaper business with U. S. Stauffer, his brother-in-law in Quakertown. He was married to Percilla S. Stauffer in 1875. They were parents of five children, three sons and two daughters. He began his ministry in Halstead, Kan. In 1886 he was given an evangelist's license by the Eastern District Conference and assisted Andrew B. Shelly in the West Swamp Church. He became pastor of the Hereford Mennonite Church, Bally, Pa., in 1890 and served there for 25 years. He was pastor of the Upper Milford Mennonite Church, near Zionsville, Pa., for 16 years, and the Menno Simons Mennonite Church, Boyertown, for 9 years, serving these churches concurrently with his pastorate at Bally. He was pastor of the Mennonite Church at Upland, Cal., for three years and the First Mennonite Church of Bluffton, Ohio, for two years. He was superintendent of the Bluffton hospital for one year. His final pastorate was at Germantown, Pa., where he was pastor for six years. He died on Jan. 5, 1928. The memorial services for him were held in the Germantown and West Swamp churches with the burial at West Swamp.

Shelly's conference activities were numerous. He was president of the General Conference Mennonite Church for fifteen years, five times serving a three year term. For ten years, beginning in 1892 he served as the editor of the *Mennonite.* He was a member of both the Home Mission and Foreign Mission boards of the G.C.M. Church. In addition he was active in the Eastern District Conference program, serving on the Board of Managers of the Mennonite Home for the Aged at Frederick, Pa., for a number of years. He translated the Ris Confession into English.　　　**P.R.S.**

Mennonite Year Book and Almanac (Berne, 1929); H. P. Krehbiel, *The History of the General Conference of the Mennonites of North America* (Canton, 1898); *idem, the History of the General Conference of the Mennonite Church of North America* II (Newton, 1938).

Shelly Mennonite Church (MC), now extinct, located one mile west of Richfield in Monroe Twp., Juniata Co., Pa., was built in 1800. Until 1815 it was also used as a school. One of the oldest cemeteries in the Valley is found here. Under George Leiter a schism occurred, both sides using this meetinghouse for 40 years, until Bishop Leiter returned to the Lancaster Conference. This necessitated a larger, brick meetinghouse in 1868. In connection with the Solomon Graybill schism in 1884 a historic bill in equity was initiated in the Juniata County courts to obtain the use of this church for the new group. In 1886 the General Conference Mennonites built a church on the edge of Richfield. The Mennonites (MC) used this church until larger meetinghouses were built at Cross Roads and Lauver, and a decade later regular services were discontinued. It serves as a home for the sewing circles of the Valley now.
　　　I.D.L.

Shelly Mission Station Oklahoma: see **Washita Mission.**

Shelton Mennonite Church (GCM), now extinct, near Rocky Ford, Otero Co., Col., had 15 members in 1911. C. R. Voth was the minister.　　　**M.G.**

Shenk, John M. (1848-1935), a bishop in the Ohio Mennonite (MC) Conference, was born in Hocking County, Ohio, Jan. 19, 1848. His grandfather, Jacob Shank, was born in Lancaster County, Pa., and moved to Rockingham County, Va. There his eldest son Henry, father of John M., was born. Henry Shank left Harrisonburg, and married Susanna, sister of John M. Brenneman (*q.v.*), whom they followed to Allen County, Ohio, about 1855. At the Salem Church (*q.v.*) at the age of nineteen John M. Shenk was baptized and at once took an active part in the Sunday school. At twenty-one he married Frances Good; ten of their eleven children grew to maturity. At Salem he was chosen by lot and ordained to the ministry in 1874 by George Brenneman, his bishop uncle. Ten years later he was ordained bishop by Abraham Shank of Virginia. From 1920 to 1927, when the Ohio Mennonite Conference merged with the Ohio and Eastern A.M. Conference, he was the only Mennonite bishop in the western half of the state. He was much interested in the missionary and charitable activities of the church. He seldom missed a meeting of General Conference or of the state conference and long worked for the union of the Amish Mennonite and Mennonite Conferences.　　　**J.S.U.**

Shepherd, A, from Gorsleu (i.e., Gors op Leeuw in Flanders, Belgium), an Anabaptist martyr, was burned at the stake on March 6, 1544, at Liège in Belgium. Particulars are lacking.　　　**vdZ.**

W. Bax, *Het Protestantisme in het bisdom Luik . . .* I (The Hague, 1937) 162.

Sheridan Mennonite Church (MC), located in the city of Sheridan, Yamhill Co., Ore., about 35 miles from the Pacific Ocean, is a member of the Pacific Coast Conference. The church was organized in December 1923 with 35 charter members, as the outgrowth of a branch Sunday school started near McMinnville, Ore., by the Hopewell congregation of near Hubbard, Ore. The first ministers were Bishop Jacob D. Mishler and Daniel F. Shenk. In 1957 the membership was 302, with Gabriel D. Shank and Raymond Mishler as bishops, and Daniel F. Shenk, LeRoy Cowan, and Oscar Wideman as ministers.
　　　R.M.

Sherk (Sherrick, Scherch, Shirk, Schoerg, Shurk, Sharig), a Mennonite family name which has been traced to Sumiswald in the Emmenthal in the Swiss canton of Bern. As a result of persecutions in Switzerland members of the family moved first to the Palatinate; later some migrated to Pennsylvania. The family name is found today in Karlsruhe, Germany, and in Luxembourg as well as in the United States and Canada. The first of this name in America was Joseph Schoerg, who arrived in Philadelphia in 1727 and settled in Lancaster County, Pa. Others of Joseph Schoerg's family came in at various times up to 1747 and settled in Pennsylvania. Several descendants moved to Upper Canada (now Ontario) about 1799 and later. A grandson, also named Joseph Schoerg, was the first settler in what is now Waterloo County, the largest Mennonite settlement in Ontario. David Sherk (*q.v.*) was a leading minister (MC) in Waterloo County. The name occurs frequently in eastern Pennsylvania and in Ontario, and is found occasionally in Alberta and British Columbia and in Ohio, Indiana, Michigan, Illinois, Iowa, Kansas, and other states. Records show the names of many members of this family who have served as missionaries, ministers, bishops, and in other capacities in Mennonite and other churches. Others were teachers, doctors, lawyers, businessmen, etc.

J.HA.S.

R. B. Strassburger and W. J. Hinke, *Pennsylvania German Pioneers* I (Norristown, 1934); Ezra E. Eby, *History of Waterloo Township* (Kitchener, 1895 f.); Ira D. Landis, *I Must See Switzerland* (Bareville, 1954).

Sherk, David (1801-82), a leading Mennonite (MC) minister, was born in 1801, the fourth son and sixth child of Joseph Schoerg, who came to Waterloo County, Ont., in 1800, from Franklin County, Pa. David was married to Elizabeth Betzner (1811-94) in 1827. They had ten children. Two of his daughters were successively the wives of Jacob Gingerich (1840-1920), preacher of the Hagey and Wanner congregations. About 1837 David Sherk was ordained deacon for the Hagey Mennonite Church and the following year as minister for the three churches, Strasburg, Hagey, and Wanner. In his time he was considered one of the leading ministers of the Ontario Mennonite (MC) Conference. He was the author of *Nonconformity to the World* (72 pp., Elkhart, 1882). He died in 1882.   J.C.F.

Sherkston Mennonite Church (MC), now extinct, located in Bertie Twp., Welland Co., Ont., lay north of Lake Erie some 12 miles west of Buffalo. The deed was given in 1828 to the "Mennonite Society" by Samuel Sherk. No record exists of the nature of the building until a brick church was built in 1853. This was replaced by a cement block church in 1917. Ministers who served are George Zavitz, Christian Herschi, John Zavitz, **Benjamin Hershey,** Peter Sherk, John Hershey, Nelson Michael, Gilbert Bearss, Howard Stevanus, Noah Hunsberger, and Simon B. Martin. For about 20 years before the building of the church in 1917 the congregation was nearly extinct. With declining membership the church was sold to the Brethren in Christ ("Tunkers" in Canada), whose families dot the area (1931). This was a very early settlement of Mennonites in Ontario, Jacob Zavitz (Sevitz) having come from Lancaster County in 1788. A score of families may have been the extent of the Bertie settlement, with as many or more in Willoughby Township further north near Niagara Falls. Their activity in the Mennonite Conference of Ontario was apparently never very great.   J.C.F.

Shetler, Samuel Grant (1871-1942), a prominent Mennonite (MC) evangelist and Bible teacher, was born Jan. 13, 1871. He was baptized Dec. 13, 1892, at the Stahl Mennonite Church, where he was ordained deacon in 1894 and minister in 1897. He was ordained bishop in 1915 at the Hopewell Mennonite Church near Hubbard, Ore., where he was temporarily residing and serving as pastor. He was an energetic promoter of summer Bible schools and in 1920 established the Johnstown Winter Bible School at the Stahl church in addition to promoting and teaching in various winter Bible schools (*q.v.*) in other parts of the church. He was widely used as an evangelist for many years, holding revival meetings in almost every section of the Mennonite Church (MC). In 1919 he served as moderator of the Mennonite General Conference; he also served in various offices in the Southwestern Pennsylvania Conference.   H.S.B.

Shirati Mennonite Church, located about 30 miles north of Musoma, East Africa, along the Kenya-Tanganyika boundary, is in the Luo tribe. It is the oldest congregation of the Mennonite mission in East Africa. Mission work was begun at Shirati on May 26, 1934, by John H. Mosemann and Elam W. Stauffer. The church was begun on Sept. 15, 1935, when at the first baptism and communion services held, fifteen persons were baptized and six others received into fellowship, a total of twenty-one. The membership in 1956 was 511. John Mosemann had first pastoral oversight of the church until his furlough in 1939. The succeeding pastors have been J. Eby Leaman, Clinton Ferster, Noah Mack, Merle Eshleman, Elam W. Stauffer, and James Shank. In 1956 the ministers were J. Lester Eshleman, Robert G. Keener, and Zedekea Marwa Kisare, with Simeon W. Hurst as bishop.   E.W.S.

Shirk's Mennonite Church, now extinct, located in Hanover Twp., Lebanon Co., Pa. The area was settled by the Dohner, Miller, Peiffer, Moyer, Getze, Hain, and other families. On Oct. 26, 1823, Peter and Barbara Sherick deeded to Jacob Sherick 73 perches for the building of an "Unpartheyish Menist Gemeinhouse." After a few decades (1845), the United Brethren claimed most of the membership and the house for many years. Today it is still intact, a large unused unpainted frame house, a bleak reminder of a religious ancestry. A cemetery lies east of the church.   I.D.L.

Shirk's Reformed Mennonite Church, located near Brownstown, Lancaster Co., Pa., is one of the 5 meetinghouses of the Reformed Mennonites in Lancaster County which are counted as one congregation, which had a total of 221 baptized members in 1958. The meetinghouse was built in 1889. H.S.B.

Shirksville Mennonite Church (MC), located 7 miles north of Lebanon, a member of the Lancaster Conference, is the oldest (founded 1740) and most northerly of Mennonite churches in Lebanon County, Pa. Caspar and Barbara Shirk moved from Chestnut Hill to the farm from which the site for the meetinghouse was taken. When the deed was given to Christian Newcomer, Peter Graff, Peter Wolf, and Christian Lentz in 1776, the meetinghouse was already erected and the cemetery ground provided. It served the congregation until the present frame church was built on the same site in 1895. Most of the original families have been lost to the church, but others have moved in, especially during the last decade; the membership in 1957 was 60, with Lester C. Shirk as minister.   I.D.L.

Shisler Mennonite Church (MC), located in Humberstone Twp., Welland Co., Ont., is one of two points where the Mennonite Brethren in Christ worshiped in 1880-1900. The church was located a few miles west of the Sherkston Mennonite (MC) Church in Bertie Township and close to Lake Erie at Shisler's Point. The membership was small. Ministers from the Twenty, 40 miles north, usually supplied. Organized work was discontinued about 1900 and the church was disposed of to the Brethren in Christ (Tunkers). Since the Brethren bought the Sherkston (MC) church in 1931 the Shisler church has fallen into disuse.   J.C.F.

Shoemaker, Joseph S. (1854-1936), an outstanding bishop in the Mennonite Church (MC), was born Feb. 1, 1854, at Philadelphia, Pa., but early located on a farm near Freeport (Dakota), Ill., where he spent his active life. He married Elizabeth Brubaker on Dec. 6, 1877. Among their 9 children were Charles B. Shoemaker of Scottdale, Pa., long an officer of the Mennonite Publishing House, and Stella (Mrs. A. E. Kreider). He was ordained preacher in 1892 and bishop in 1902. He was president of the Mennonite Board of Publication 1908-33, secretary of the Mennonite Board of Missions and Charities 1906-20, many times moderator of the Illinois Mennonite Conference, moderator of the Mennonite General Conference in 1905 and 1909, and a member of the Mennonite Board of Education 1903-20. He was publisher and a coeditor of the *Church and Sunday School Hymnal* (1902), writer of the section on the "Ministry" in the *Christian Worker's Manual* Vol. I (1915), author of *The Ideal Christian Home* (1925), and coauthor of *Among Missions in the Orient and Observations by the Way* (1912). He was a widely used evangelist, a great influence for unity and progress, and for many years one of the most widely known and beloved leaders in his denomination.†   H.S.B.

H. F. Weber, *Centennial History of the Mennonites of Illinois* (Goshen, 1931) 620 f. and *passim*.

Shope Mennonite Church (MC), located a few miles southeast of Harrisburg, Pa., one mile east of the Lancaster Pike at Steelton, was first called the Mumma Mennonite congregation, since they worshiped in Frederick Mumma's home. By 1815 a church-schoolhouse, 20 x 30 ft., of log with comb roof was erected, and later weatherboarded. It was replaced in 1873 by the present brick church. The cemetery was started in 1877 on the elevation. Bishop Nathaniel Shope was the first to be buried there. It is a part of the Strickler-Shope circuit of the Lancaster Conference, with communion at the Strickler church. The total membership in the circuit in 1957 was 87. Harry L. Longenecker was the minister at the Shope church. A separate Sunday school of 50 is maintained. (See **Strickler.**)   I.D.L.

Shore Mennonite Church (MC), a member of the Indiana-Michigan Conference, is located one mile south and one mile east of Shipshewana, Lagrange Co., Ind., on State Road 20 near Shore Lake. In the early 1860's church services were held in a barn or homes of members. A few years later a schoolhouse was used for services. At this time the name Shore was given to the small village, the school, and the lake. The members residing in this community held membership with the Clinton Brick Mennonite Church, and many years after the church was organized the ministers served both congregations. In 1874 a site was donated by William Wiler, and a church 30 x 40 ft. was built on the west side of Shore Lake. The membership then was about 200. In 1893 this building was moved across the road and enlarged; it was replaced by a new church in 1929.

Some of the early ministers who served at the Shore Mennonite Church were John Nusbaum, Henry A. Miller, and J. J. Weaver (who preached in English), P. Y. Lehman, James J. Mishler, John Garber, and P. J. Miller. In 1957 the bishop was Lee J. Miller (ordained 1945), and Josiah J. Miller and Percy J. Miller (ordained 1933) the ministers. The membership was 333.   V.C.

Showalter (Schowalter), a Mennonite family name of Swiss origin found in the Palatinate and across the border in Alsace, chiefly at Deutschhof, Kaplaneihof, Schafbusch, and Geisberg. In 1717 a Bernard Schowalter lived at Lambsheim, Palatinate. About 1720 a Johannes Schowalter was living at Geisberg and a Peter Schowalter at Schafbusch. In 1740 a Christian Schowalter lived at Mechtersheimerhof. About 1750 a Jakob (Christian Schowalter) came to the Haftelhof. In 1787 a Joseph Schowalter of Klein-Bunderbach near Zweibrücken purchased the Kaplaneihof, where there are still four Schowalter families. In 1794 Jakob Schowalter purchased part of the Deutschhof. Pastors Otto Schowalter of Hamburg and Paul Schowalter of Weierhof stem from the latter two communities. In 1936 Schowalter, with 98 persons, was the third most common name in the Mennonite congregations of the Palatinate, exceeded only by Krehbiel and Stauffer. The chief congregations with numerous Schowalters were Deutschhof-Geisberg (24), Monsheim-Obersülzen (20), Neudorferhof (17), and Ludwigshafen (8).

Christian Schowalter (*q.v.;* 1828-1907), a prominent minister and leader in the formation of the General Conference Mennonite Church in the 1860's, pastor at Donnellson, Iowa, 1861-1907, came from Assenheim in the Palatinate to America in 1850. Jacob A. Schowalter (1879-1953), a G.C.M. layman of Halstead and Newton, Kan., born at Friedelsheim in the Palatinate, came to Kansas in 1883, served in the Kansas State Legislature 1934-38, and established upon his death the J. A. Schowalter Foundation, a charitable trust for Mennonite purposes, with assets of some $1,200,000.

In 1750 five Schowalters arrived on the *Brotherhood* at Philadelphia—Jacob Sr., Jacob, John, Christian, and Peter. By 1759 Jacob Sr., John, and Joseph owned land in Whitehall Twp., Northampton Co., Pa., Jacob Sr. being a leader in the newly established Siegfried (*q.v.*) (MC) congregation. The removal of John, Joseph, and Jacob (Jr.?) in 1771 to other places was a severe blow to the congregation, which soon died out. Of Jacob Sr.'s eight sons, Christian Showalter moved to Lancaster County, Peter and Jacob Showalter died in Bucks County, John and Joseph Showalter in Chester County, Pa., while three, Daniel, Valentine, and Ulrich Showalter, moved to Rockingham County, Va. Three Showalters were preachers in Chester County, Pa., Joseph (d. *c*1802) at Charlestown (MC) and John and Daniel (d. 1840) at Phoenixville (MC). In 1824 David was a trustee at Charlestown. Additional immigrants were John (1744) and Christian (1764) Schowalter. The original Showalters have apparently died out in Eastern Pennsylvania.

In 1788 Daniel Showalter, apparently ancestor of most of the Virginia Mennonite Showalters and the few MC families by this name living farther west, settled near Broadway, in Rockingham County, Va. Among his descendants are an unusual number of Mennonite ministers. Serving the Northern District churches in the Shenandoah Valley were his son Daniel (1802-89) Showalter and the latter's grandson, George B. Showalter (1859-1931). Four of George's sons have served in the same area: Bishop Timothy Showalter (1887-1957), G. Paul Showalter (1890-   ), Lewis P. Showalter (1890-   ), and Mark Showalter (1891-   ), and a daughter, Elizabeth Showalter, serves as editor at the Mennonite Publishing House at Scottdale, Pa. Three grandsons of George B. Showalter are also Mennonite ministers: Elmer Showalter at Lebanon, Pa., Omar Showalter at Pipersville, Pa., and Paul Showalter at Wooster, Ohio. A great-grandson of the first Daniel, Earl Showalter (1890-   ), served at La Junta, Col., and elsewhere. A younger descendant, Richard L. Showalter, served at Perryton, Tex. Mary Emma Showalter, a great-granddaughter of the first Daniel and a daughter of Howard D. H. Showalter, is professor at Eastern Mennonite College, and Amos M. Showalter, a great-grandson of Daniel and son of Cyrus who moved from Virginia to Kansas in 1910, is professor at Madison College, both of Harrisonburg, Va. H.S.B.

P. M. Showalter, *Family Record of the Showalters* (Maugansville, Md., 1943); Elizabeth Showalter, *Our Family, Facts of the George B. Showalter Family* (n.p., 1955); Franz Crous, "Mennonitenfamilien in Zahlen," *Gesch.-Bl.* V (1940) 26-45; J. C. Wenger, *History of the Mennonites of the Franconia Conference* (Telford, 1937); Robert Schrag, "The Story of a Mennonite Millionaire, Jacob A. Schowalter 1879-1953," *Menn. Life* XI (1957) 64-69.

Shroud, in Mennonite circles a white gown in which the dead are buried, which was made over a specified pattern. In the 19th century its use was prob-ably universal in the Mennonite Church (MC). The more conservative areas of the Mennonite Church (MC) such as the Franconia Conference still make some use of the shroud, and such groups as the Wisler Mennonites still use it as a general practice. Funeral directors have each shroud made to order.

Mennonite funerals tend to be somewhat differentiated from general Christian practice in various respects. Earlier this meant the use of a coffin rather than a casket, the coffin being tapered gently from the shoulder point toward both ends, while the casket was completely rectangular; the body was clothed in a shroud rather than in conventional dress; there was congregational singing rather than special music; no flowers were brought to the meetinghouse; the body was viewed outside the meetinghouse; and burial occurred before the memorial service was held. By the mid-20th century many of these distinctive practices had been lost except in the more conservative groups, and in the more conservative areas of the Mennonite Church (MC). (See also **Funeral Customs.**) J.C.W.

Siberia, a part of Northern Asia and of the RSFSR of the Soviet Union, lying between the Ural Mountains and the Pacific Ocean, consists of one third of the Asiatic continent, 4,887,223 sq. miles, with a population of 30,000,000 (1956). It comprises seventeen divisions of the RSFSR, some of which are regions, some territories, some republics. The following are the most significant of them from the west to east: Perm, Tyumen, Sverdlovsk, Chelyabinsk, Kurgan, Omsk, Novosibirsk, Altai, Tomsk, Kemerovo, Krasnoyarsk, Irkutsk, Chita, Maritime Territory, Khabarovsk. Old Mennonite settlements are located in the Omsk (see **Omsk** Mennonite settlement) and Altai (see **Slavgorod** Mennonite settlement) regions. The Semipalatinsk region of the Kazakh SSR, now Soviet Central Asia (*q.v.*), was formerly also considered a part of Siberia, in which the Pavlodar Mennonite settlement (*q.v.*) is located.

Today Mennonites can be found in almost all of the regions, territories, and republics of Siberia. Exile and evacuation from the Mennonite settlements of European Russia, particularly the Ukraine (*q.v.*), have scattered them over the older Mennonite settlements in Siberia as well as in most of the other regions and territories.

1. Opening Siberia. During the 14th century a Tatar kingdom called Sibir was located on the Irtysh River in Siberia. The Cossack Yermak subdued the Tatars in 1582, and Tobolsk became the capital of the established government. By 1875 the Russians had occupied all of Siberia including the island of Sakhalin and in the 1890's the Trans-Siberian railroad was built, reaching Vladivostok. Previous to that time, Russian population had been moved into Siberia, some of whom were political and religious exiles. With the coming of the railroad and a systematic plan of the government to populate this vast territory, Russian population, particularly from the Ukraine, was attracted by generous offers from the government. The Mennonites were among the first to follow this invitation and to establish daughter settlements in Siberia. As early as 1860, however, Martin Riediger and Bernhard Warkentin had made

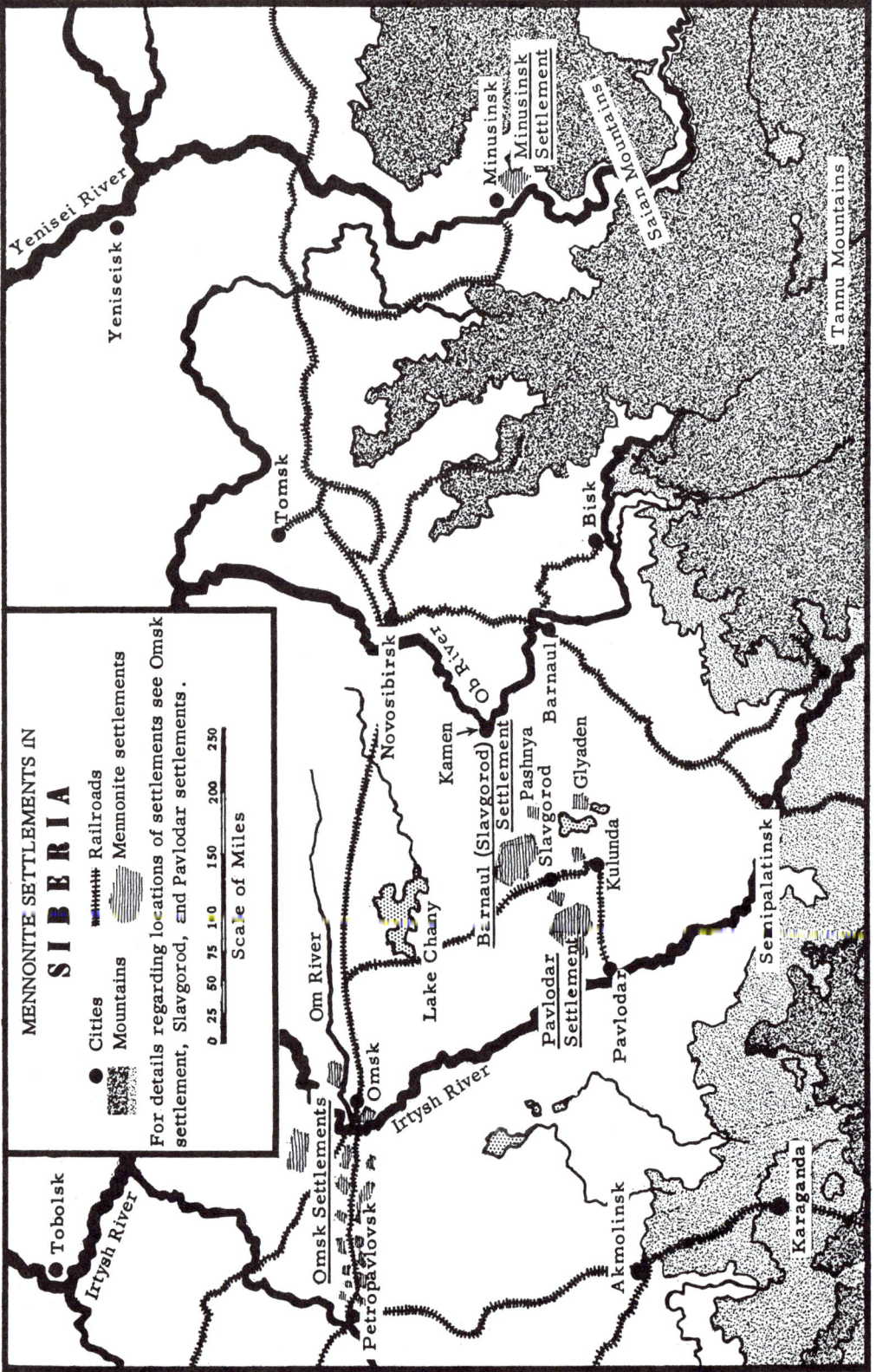

MENNONITE SETTLEMENTS IN
S I B E R I A

- Cities
  Mountains
● Railroads
▨ Mennonite settlements

For details regarding locations of settlements see Omsk
settlement, Slavgorod, and Pavlodar settlements.

0 25 50 75 100 150 200 250

Scale of Miles

Yenisei River

Yeniseisk ●

Tobolsk ●

Irtysh River

Om River

Omsk Settlements

Petropavlovsk

Omsk

Irtysh River

Novosibirsk

Lake Chany

Tomsk ●

Kamen

Ob River

Barnaul (Slavgorod) Settlement

Pashnya

Slavgord

Glyaden

Kulunda

Barnaul

Bisk ●

Minusinsk ●
Minusinsk Settlement

Saian Mountains

Tannu Mountains

Pavlodar Settlement

Pavlodar

Semipalatinsk

Akmolinsk

Karaganda

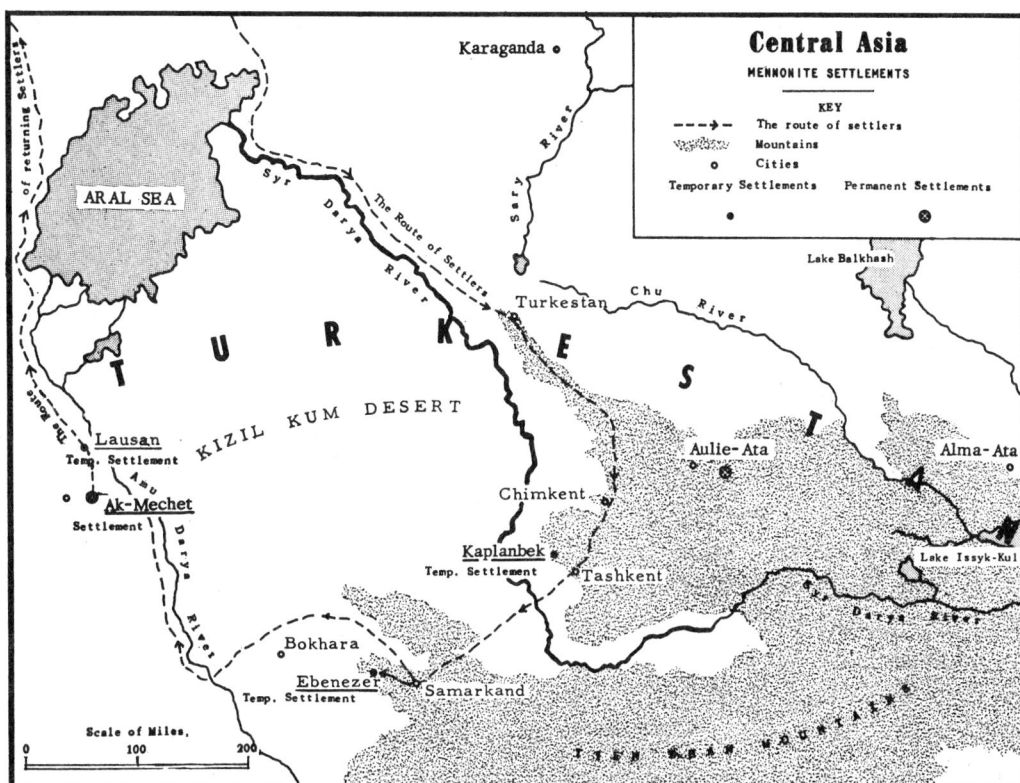

Central Asia
MENNONITE SETTLEMENTS
KEY
— — —➔ — The route of settlers
Mountains
o Cities
Temporary Settlements • Permanent Settlements ⊗

a trip to the Amur region, now Khabarovsk, in order to investigate settlement possibilities. At that time Crimea was opened for settlement, and as a result nothing came of the plans to settle in the Far East.

The first Mennonite to settle in Siberia was Peter J. Wiens from Schönau, Molotschna, who established a business enterprise in agricultural machinery in the city of Omsk (q.v.) in 1897. Others followed from the various settlements and established themselves along the Trans-Siberian railroad between Petropavlovsk (q.v.) and Omsk (q.v.). This settlement became known as the Omsk Mennonite settlement (q.v.).

2. Old Mennonite Settlements. In 1906 official announcements were made by the government about the availability of land in Siberia. A delegation representing the settlements of Zagradovka, Ufa, Samara, and Orenburg was sent to the Kulundian Steppes between the Irtysh and the Ob rivers in the Omsk region to investigate the land. They made a trip to Barnaul (q.v.) and some even continued the journey again to investigate the Amur region. They found the land near Barnaul more suitable. In 1910 the city of Slavgorod (q.v.) was established here and the settlement became known as Slavgorod Mennonite settlement (q.v.). The delegates reserved 58,441 acres of land for 1,443 persons, with the following privileges: (1) reduced fare; (2) exemption from taxes for five years; (3) exemption from governmental services for three years; (4) loan of 160 rubles and a credit of 160 rubles. The land was free of charge.

In 1908 the settlement consisting of 59 villages on some 135,000 acres was finally established. The cities of Kameny and Pavlodar (q.v.) were each about 130 miles from the settlement. The city of Slavgorod (q.v.) was ten miles away and became the Mennonite business center. Barnaul was 250 miles away on the Ob River. Many of the non-Mennonite Germans and also Ukrainians settled on the Kulundian Steppes (see Barnaul Mennonite Settlement and Slavgorod Mennonite Settlement).

The Pavlodar Mennonite settlement (q.v.) was started in 1906 near the Irtysh River, some 15 miles from the city of Pavlodar which was later connected with the Trans-Siberian railroad to the north. The settlement consisted of 12 villages. The city of Pavlodar (q.v.) had a number of Mennonite enterprises. Under the Soviet regime the villages of the Pavlodar settlement became a part of Kazakh SSR in Soviet Central Asia (q.v.).

The Minusinsk Mennonite settlement in the Province of Yenisei (now Krasnoyarsk Territory) was established in 1913, consisting of two villages, Rozovka and Krasnovka. During the Revolution of 1917 this settlement suffered so severely that it was gradually dissolved (see Yenisei).

The latest Mennonite settlement voluntarily established was the one in the Amur (q.v.) region in 1927. From here many Mennonites moved to Harbin (q.v.) in 1929 and later, from where they proceeded to the United States and South America. Of significance is also the Ob Mission (q.v.) established in northern Siberia c1926.

3. Mennonite Exiles and Evacuees in Siberia. Thus

far the story of Mennonite settlements established voluntarily has been related. The most recent chapter deals with the information pertaining to Mennonite movements to Siberia under the Soviet government mostly because of exile, forced labor (*q.v.*), and the evacuation from the Ukraine, a practice introduced by Stalin. At that time thousands of men were exiled to northern parts of European Russia (see **Vologda**) and also Siberia and Soviet Central Asia (*q.v.*).

This forced movement of the Mennonites to Siberia occurred primarily during the years 1931-32 and 1937-38, at the outbreak of World War II (1941), and again later when Mennonites who had been evacuated from the Ukraine by the German army were repatriated by the Soviet army (1945-46). It is estimated that 25,000 Mennonites were returned from Germany to Soviet Russia, many of whom were sent to Siberia.

How many Mennonites have been exiled and evacuated from European Russia and how many of them are located in Siberia? No exact answer is possible to this question. There were some 100,000 Mennonites in Russia when the German army invaded the Ukraine (1941). We proceed with the assumption that approximately one fifth, that is, 20,000, had been exiled by that time. The German invasion of the Ukraine was the reason for an evacuation of all people of German background. Stalin succeeded in evacuating a large percentage of the Mennonite population of the settlements which were close to the front. This involved about one fourth of the total population making it about 25,000. Some 35,000 were taken along by the retreating Germans in 1943 of which the Red army repatriated nearly 25,000 who were sent primarily beyond the Ural Mountains into Asiatic Russia including Siberia. This makes 70,000 uprooted or exiled and evacuated Mennonites out of a total population of 100,000. Of these remaining 30,000 some 6,000 are found in the Orenburg settlement (*q.v.*) and some 4,000 in the Pleshanovo settlement (*q.v.*), which are the two major settlements of European Russia which were not completely disintegrated and uprooted during the war. The remaining 20,000 Mennonites who stayed in their homes and settlements are found in the Slavgorod (*q.v.*), Omsk (*q.v.*), Pavlodar (*q.v.*), and Amur (*q.v.*) settlements of Siberia. According to these figures 30,000 Mennonites are still in their former homes and 70,000 are living in dispersion.

We proceed with the assumption that of these 70,000 Mennonites no longer living in their home communities some 20,000 live in European Russia particularly in the Vologda (*q.v.*) and Arkhangelsk regions from which they were exiled but also in many other parts of Russia particularly since many have obtained permission to move about more freely. Some have even returned to their former homes. Adding to this number the 7,500 who have remained in their communities it can be assumed that there are some 27,500 in European Russia.

Of the remaining 50,000 Mennonites who have lost their homes we can assume that half are in Siberia and half in Soviet Central Asia (*q.v.*). Many of these Mennonites who have come to Siberia under

the Soviet government have found their way to the Mennonite settlements of Slavgorod (*q.v.*), Omsk (*q.v.*), and Pavlodar (*q.v.*). Most of them, however, are located in regions in which until recently no Mennonites were found. A great number are found in the regions of Perm (formerly Molotov), Tyumen (*q.v.*), Sverdlovsk (*q.v.*), Chelyabinsk (*q.v.*), Akmolinsk, Aktyubinsk, Kurgan, Novosibirsk (*q.v.*), Altai, Tomsk (*q.v.*), Karaganda, Alma Ata, Stalinabad, Tashkent, Frunze, and other industrialized areas in the far south of Central Asia.

What do the Mennonites do and how do they live in these areas? Those who were exiled mostly worked in mines in the Ural Mountains, forestries, railroad and other building projects, and agricultural units. Living conditions were extremely difficult and many thousands perished. The complete record is not available and what is available has not been investigated and systematically used. Of the 76 labor camps in Asiatic Russia listed by Dallin and Nicolaevsky 68 were located in Siberia, many in the Ural Mountain area. Even if the inhabitant of a camp survived the 10-20 years of slave labor his record did not permit him to move freely. Since 1955-56 changes have come about. This is clearly recorded in the correspondence coming from Russia, and was reported by Bender and Wiens as a result of their trip to Russia in 1956. Many leave their place of labor and move to other places in order to improve their living conditions and above all in order to unite with their family members and relatives. A considerable number now live in and around Karaganda.

The fate of the evacuees of 1941 and those repatriated by the Red army in 1945-47 was probably not as severe as that of the exiles, nevertheless they too have endured severe hardships during the last ten years. But their conditions also seem to have been improved. According to a recent study made of letters the Mennonites are located in rural areas as well as in large cities. They follow almost any occupation. They are tractorists on collective farms, students in agricultural and medical schools, workers in factories, engineers, etc. The children attend public schools and are often unable to speak German except some Low German. Intermarriages with non-Mennonites are frequent, although not as frequent as one could expect after all the movements and shifts of the population. The general revival of interest in religious life is noticeable in Siberia as at other places.

4. Bibliographical Information. Siberia is "a dark chapter" in Mennonite research. The settlements originated just before World War II and were far removed from the cultural centers of the Mennonites in the Ukraine. Occasional reports or letters are the major sources of information. P. M. Friesen (*Mennonitische Brüderschaft,* 1911) contains little information about the settlements in Siberia. Some information is contained in the annual reports (*Jahresbericht*) of the forestry service in Russia compiled for taxing Mennonite property. The almanacs, such as *Mennonitisches Jahrbuch,* edited by H. Dirks and D. H. Epp (see 1913), *Christlicher Familienkalender,* edited by A. Kröker, and the

Haus- und Landwirtschafts-Kalender (Odessa) contain lists of villages and other statistical information up to 1914.

The two periodicals, *Der Botschafter* and *Die Friedensstimme,* contain announcements about the planned settlements in Siberia, the movements of the Mennonites to Siberia, the beginning and pioneer experiences, and the developments up to the time that the papers ceased publication during World War I. After the Russian Revolution, the Siberian Mennonite settlements were in touch with the Allrussicher Mennonitischer Landwirtschaftlicher Verein and were visited by representatives of this organization and reported regularly. These reports have been preserved in the A. A. Friesen Collection of the Bethel College Historical Library and some were published in *Der Praktische Landwirt* (*q.v.*). The reports about the cultural life and religious activities, such as song festivals, baptismal services, visits by ministers from other Mennonite settlements, appeared regularly in *Unser Blatt* (*q.v.*) from 1926 on, which was discontinued in 1928. From there on, there was silence. Otto Auhagen published some letters from Siberia in *Die Schicksalswende des russlanddeutschen Bauerntums in den Jahren 1927-1930* (Leipzig, 1942).

Of some significance are scattered reports written by non-Mennonites. Jakob Stach, who was serving the Lutheran churches of Slavgorod, Pavlodar, etc., immediately after the Russian Revolution, reported about it in his books, *Meine Feuertaufe* (St. Gallen, 1924) and *Das Deutschtum in Sibirien, . . . bis in die Gegenwart: Geschichte und Selbsterlebtes* (Stuttgart, 1939). The novelist Edwin Erich Dwinger, in his *Zwischen Weiss und Rot* (Jena, 1930) (reportage), relates that the retreating White army stayed overnight in one of the Mennonite villages which he describes vividly. The cultural life of the Mennonites of the Slavgorod Mennonite settlement is described in greater detail in the novel *Beata* (Heilbronn, 1935) by Ernst Behrends. In this book Jürgen, a German soldier, who became a prisoner of war and was sent to Siberia, met Daniel Hooge of Rheinfeld, who took him home to his parents, where he fell in love with Daniel's sister Beata. However, Jürgen returned to Germany and Beata married someone else. Later Jürgen met her, a widow with three children, in the refugee camp in Mölln, Germany. This novel describes in a sympathetic and accurate way the cultural traits of the Mennonites of Slavgorod.

Of descriptive nature is H. Anger, *Die Deutschen in Sibirien. Reise durch die deutschen Dörfer Westsibiriens* (Berlin and Königsberg, 1930), who presents valuable information about the German settlements including the Mennonites. Walter Quiring in "Die russlanddeutschen Flüchtlinge in China" (in *Der Wanderweg der Russlanddeutschen,* Stuttgart, 1939) relates the story of the escape of the Mennonites of the Amur settlement to Harbin, China. The story of the Amur (*q.v.*) settlement has been related in greater detail by A. Loewen and A. Friesen, *Die Flucht über den Amur* (Steinbach, 1946).

The first attempt to present the story of the Mennonites in Siberia in general was made by J. J. Hildebrand in *Sibirien* (Winnipeg, 1952). His book is subdivided into two parts, the first one dealing with Siberia in general and the Mennonite settlements of Omsk (*q.v.*) and Slavgorod (*q.v.*), and the second part specifically with the Mennonite group under the leadership of Hermann Peters known as Apostolische Brüdergemeinde (*q.v.*), which is the most detailed account found anywhere on this subject. This part also contains the author's account of his effort in trying to help young men of Siberia establish the status of conscientious objectors to war during the years following the Revolution.

The most recent book dealing with the Mennonites of Siberia was compiled and edited by Gerhard Fast under the title *In den Steppen Sibiriens* (Rosthern, 1957). Numerous accounts of eyewitnesses and participants in the early settlements in Slavgorod were collected and edited which contain more information on this subject than any other source. The Omsk, Pavlodar, and Amur settlements are sketched only briefly.

Many hundreds of letters have been published in *Der Bote* (Rosthern) and *Mennonitische Rundschau* (Winnipeg). Virginia Claassen, Peter Neufeld, and Vern Q. Preheim, in a Mennonite Seminar of Bethel College under the direction of Cornelius Krahn (1947), checked this correspondence and prepared an alphabetical index including names, locations, economic, cultural, religious, and occupational conditions, etc., of the Mennonites of Russia as portrayed in the correspondence. The findings were presented in "Glimpses of Mennonites in Russia 1948-57." To a large extent, this information which originated in Siberia and Soviet Central Asia was made use of in this and other articles written for this ENCYCLOPEDIA.

The only eyewitness who has visited a part of the Mennonite settlements of Siberia (Slavgorod) since World War II is Klaus Mehnert, who gave illustrated accounts in *Christ und Welt* (Stuttgart, June 21, 1956), *Quick* (Munich, July 7, 1956), and *Bote* (Sept. 5, 12, 19, and 26, 1956).

The account of the relief activities among the Mennonites of Slavgorod was presented by Alvin J. Miller in *Feeding the Hungry* (Scottdale, 1929, p. 312 ff.). M. B. Fast reported about his visit in Siberia in *Geschichtlicher Bericht . . .* (Reedley, 1919). The best studies on forced labor and concentration camps in Siberia and other parts of Russia are those by David J. Dallin and B. I. Nicolaevsky, *Forced Labor in Soviet Russia* (New Haven, 1947), and B. Yakovlev, *Concentration Camps in U.S.S.R.* (Munich, 1955). Siberia in general is treated by Juri Semjonow in *Sibirien, Eroberung und Erschliessung der wirtschaftlichen Schatzkammer des Ostens* (Berlin, 1954), which presents a very valuable bibliography, and by Donald W. Treadgold in *The Great Siberian Migration* (Princeton University Press, 1957).   C.K.

Sibes, Jan, surnamed Pot(te)backer, was an elder of the Mennonite congregation of Harlingen in Friesland, Netherlands, in the 17th century. Concerning this elder there is not much information. He may have been identical with the Jan Sybesz who was a member of the Glückstadt (*q.v.*) Mennonite congregation in 1633. Sibes often preached in the congregation of Hamburg-Altona; in 1676 he there ordained Ocke Pieters as a preacher. In the same year during a trip of 42 days with Elder Gerhard (Gerrit) Roosen (*q.v.*) of Hamburg he visited a number of congregations in West Prussia, preaching and baptizing in Orloff, Nieschevski, Montau, Kassou(?), Lunau, Markushof, and Danzig. Maatschoen (*q.v.*) mentions a poem by Jan Sibes written in Danzig, which describes their trip and was published by Roosen, but is lost.   vdZ.

B. C. Roosen, *Geschichte der Mennoniten-Gemeinde zu Hamburg und Altona* (Hamburg, 1886-87) I, 48, 60, 61; II, 34; Schijn-Maatschoen, *Geschiedenis* III, 348 f.

Sibrandt Sibrandtszoon, a revolutionary Anabaptist, was arrested at the Oldeklooster (*q.v.*) on April 7, 1535, and executed at Leeuwarden one week later. (K. Vos, *Menno Simons,* Leiden, 1914, 229.) vdZ.

Sibrant Smit, of whom there is little information, was in the last decades of the 16th century an elder of the Flemish Mennonites together with Hans de Wever (Hans Busschaert), Jacob Pieters van der Meulen, Pieter van Coelen, and others. It is said that Smit took a less strict and more tolerant attitude as to the practice of banning, and was therefore banned by the other Flemish elders. He is also said to have founded a special branch of Mennonites, of which however nothing further is known. Nor is it known where he served. This information is found in V.P., *Successio Anabaptistica,* printed in 1603 at Cologne, Germany, and reprinted in *Bibliotheca Reformatoria Neerlandica* VII. (*BRN* VII, 69.)
vdZ.

Sichar Mennonite Church (GCM), now extinct, located at Cordell, Okla., was organized on April 14, 1896, with the help of Elder Jacob Toews of Newton, Kan., by a group of Mennonite settlers who withdrew from the Bergthal Mennonite Church (*q.v.*). The first minister was Peter Pankratz. In 1896 Michael Klaassen was ordained minister. The first services were held in a schoolhouse. In 1897 a church located on the Jacob Janzen farm was dedicated. In 1899 the congregation divided, the part called the Herold Mennonite Church (*q.v.*) obtaining possession of the church building. The other group, under the name Sichar Mennonite Church, in 1900 erected a new church building 2½ miles south of the Herold church. Gradually members began to affiliate with the near-by Herold Mennonite Church. During November 1947 the church agreed to dissolve.   C.K.

Western District Conference Minutes, 1900-48; H. P. Krehbiel, *Mennonite Churches of North America* (Canton, 1911); Marvin Kroeker, "Mennonites in the Oklahoma 'Runs,' " *Menn. Life* X (July 1955) 114; Menno H. Kliewer, "History of the Sichar Mennonite Church, Oklahoma" (term paper, Bethel College, 1944).

Sichel und Sense, published by Deutsche Mennonitenhilfe, Heilbronn, Germany, in 1922 in the form of a newspaper of eight pages reporting about starvation in Russia. It is not known whether more than one issue appeared (BeCL).   C.K.

Sichem, van, a Roman Catholic family of Dutch artists, particularly engravers, who for four generations made and published a large number of engrav-

ings both as illustrations for books and as loose pictures. Christoffel van Sichem, called "de Oude" (1546-1624), of Amsterdam, who lived at Basel, Switzerland, for a few years, published at Amsterdam in 1606 a number of loose sheets, most of them drawn and engraved by himself, on which were pictured a number of "Anabaptists" such as Jan van Leyden, David Joris, and Knipperdolling. Beneath each picture was a biographical sketch. In 1608 these pictures, augmented with some new ones, were published in book form, entitled *Historische Beschreibüng unnd abbildünge der fürnembste Haupt-Ketzer so . . . für Schwärmer unnd irrige gaister verbannt . . . seind, durch C.V.S.A., zu Amstelredam Bey Cornelis Niclausz, 1608.* This book contains the following seventeen pictures: Bishop Arius, Lodewyck Hetzer, Johannes Hut, Johan Matthis von Haarlem, Johan Böckelsz von Leyden, Melchior Hoffman, Michael Servetus, Adam Pastor, David Görgen (i.e., David Joris), Hendrick Niclaus, Balthasar Hubmor (i.e., Hubmaier) von Fridberg, Herman Schoenmaker op 't Sant, Bernhard Knipperdollinck, Dietrich Schneyder Adamyt (see **Dirck Jansson**), Melchior Rinck, Thomas Muncer (i.e., Müntzer), and Machomet den Aertsketter. All these pictures have a letterpress in the German language. Another Dutch edition with the same seventeen pictures is titled *Historische beschrijvinge . . .* (Amsterdam, 1608). The Latin version has the title *Iconia et Historica descriptio praecipuorum haeresiarcharum . . .* (Arnhem, 1609). There may have been other editions; as late as 1677 *Het Tooneel der Hooft-Ketteren, bestaande in verscheyde Afbeeltsels van Valsche Propheten, Naackt-Loopers . . . in 't Koper gesneden door C.V. Sichem* appeared at Middelburg. This is an enlarged edition, containing in addition to the former seventeen pictures also pictures of Menno Simons (the familiar picture!), Doctor Faustus, Christoffel Wagenaar (Wagner), and Broer Cornelis van Dordrecht, "prediker tot Brugge" (i.e., Cornelis Adriaensz, *q.v.*).

Greuwel der vornehmsten Haupt-Ketzeren, so wohl Wiedertauffer als auch andern (Leiden, 1608), and its Dutch version, *Grouwelen der voornaemster Hooft-ketteren,* of which the first known edition was published 1623 at Leiden, contain a number of pictures, for which probably the van Sichem engravings were used, but they are all altered and aesthetically less satisfying; moreover the reviser did slovenly work. The person representing Thomas Müntzer, for instance, is the one who in the original van Sichem editions is indicated as Jan Matthys. The Dutch *Grouwelen* has only nine of the seventeen pictures.

The historical verisimilitude of the pictures by van Sichem is probably not too great, though it is possible, even probable, that the author occasionally used old pictures.   vdZ.

N.N.B.Wb. IX, 1023-28; *Catalogus Amst.,* 7 f., 248; *DB* 1890, 65-68; 1916, 37, 52-58.

Sicily Mennonite Mission (MC) was established in 1942 under the Virginia Mennonite Board of Missions and Charities. The work developed out of early contacts with MCC workers and visits by Mennonite ministers and others from America. There have never been any permanently stationed American workers; the work has been self-propagating and by 1957 had 82 members, all living in Palermo, where a congregation has been established with national leadership. Truman Brunk has bishop oversight.   H.S.B.

Sicke Freerks (Frerichs, Frericx; also called Sicke Snyder), an Anabaptist martyr, who was beheaded March 20, 1531, at Leeuwarden, Dutch province of Friesland. Menno Simons writes, "Afterwards it happened, before I had ever heard of the existence of brethren, that a God-fearing, pious man, named Sicke Snyder, was beheaded at Leeuwarden, for being rebaptized. It sounded strange to me to hear a second baptism spoken of. I examined the Scriptures assiduously and meditated on them earnestly, but could find nothing in them concerning infant baptism." Van Braght's account of the execution in the *Martyrs' Mirror* contains several errors; the date is 1531 instead of 1533 as he has it; nor does Reitsma, who has examined the relevant archives, know anything of the torture van Braght mentions.

Early in 1531 Sicke Freerks, an honest and quiet tailor of Leeuwarden, was accused of heresy and given a trial. In the cross-examination it was revealed that he not only confessed Protestant doctrine, but considered faith a prerequisite for baptism. Two weeks before Christmas he had confessed his faith and been baptized at Emden.

Because he persisted in his faith he was condemned to death by the court of Friesland. He was beheaded; his body was tied to the wheel and his head put on a pole. Sicke was the first Anabaptist martyr in the Netherlands. The execution was publicly performed and made a deep impression. A drummer among the soldiers, who was a friend of Sicke's, began a tirade against Catholicism and had to flee. His wife Hadewyck (*q.v.*) later became an Anabaptist and was imprisoned with Elisabeth Dirks (*q.v.*), but managed to escape.

Through his preaching Sicke Freerks founded a small circle of Anabaptists, who were adherents of Melchior Hofmann's (*q.v.*) doctrine, peacefully awaiting the return of Christ, and hoped that in 1534 the New Jerusalem would be established. They called themselves *Bondgenooten* (*q.v.*; i.e., Covenanters). Prominent leaders emerged from this circle, including Obbe Philips (*q.v.*) and Dirk Philips (*q.v.*). About January 1534 Pieter de Houtzager (*q.v.*), the emissary of Jan Matthijsz of Haarlem, led a number of this circle into fanaticism; Obbe and Dirk Philips rejected Houtzager's proposals. The followers of Obbe were called Obbenites. This was the group that Menno Simons joined in January 1536.

Sicke Freerks was obviously a convert of Melchior Hofmann's, as well as Jan Volkertsz Trypmaker (*q.v.*) of Hoorn, who was baptized at Emden, Nov. 15, 1530, and was sent to preach in Amsterdam and North Holland. Sicke was presumably baptized by Trypmaker and sent out to Leeuwarden to spread the new faith there.   K.V.

J. G. de Hoop Scheffer, *Geschiedenis der Kerkhervorming in Nederland* . . . (Amsterdam, 1873) 490, 621 f.; J. G. Reitsma, *Honderd Jaren uit de Geschiedenis der Hervorming in Friesland* (Leeuwarden, 1876) 38-41; *Inv.*

Arch. Amst. I, No. 5; *Mart. Mir.* D 35, E 441; *DB* 1904, 7; 1919, 135; Kühler, *Geschiedenis* I, 65, 162 f.; K. Vos, *Menno Simons* (Leiden, 1914) 24, 182; *ML* I, 695.

Sicke Snyder: see Sicke Freerks.

Sideling Hill Civilian Public Service Camp No. 20, Wells Tannery, Pa., operated by the Mennonite Central Committee, was opened in October 1941 and closed in October 1944. The work project was divided between landscaping and erosion control on the Pennsylvania Turnpike and soil conservation. The camp had a capacity of 120 men.   M.G.

Melvin Gingerich, *Service for Peace* (Akron, 1949) 121.

Siebenacher, Gerhard, a native of Sittard (*q.v.*) in the present Dutch province of Limburg, is the author of the hymn "Genad und Fried vom Herren," found in the old German Mennonite hymnal *Ein Schon (q.v.) Gesängbüchlein.* (Rembert, *Wiedertäufer*, 494; Wolkan, *Lieder*, 100.)   vDZ.

Siebenbürgen: see Transylvania.

Siebrandt, David, first elder of the Michalin (Gnadenberg) Mennonite Church, Galicia, was born at Kommerau on the Vistula River, Oct. 25, 1778, a son of Heinrich Siebrandt. He was baptized in 1799. In 1811 he was married to Catarina Harms, daughter of Heinrich Harms. In the same year he was chosen minister and in 1816 elder. He died July 1, 1851. (Church Record of Gnadenberg Mennonite Church on deposit at BeCL.)   J.F.S.

Siedsma, Jelle Ulbes, b. c1750, d. May 1838 at Sneek, was trained for the ministry by Pastor Pieter Beets (*q.v.*) of Altona, and served 1775-1838 as elder of the Kleinzand (Old Flemish) congregation at Sneek (*q.v.*) in Friesland, from 1814 until his death also as justice of the peace at Sneek. (*DJ* 1840, 25.) vDZ.

Siegenbeek, Matthijs (b. June 23, 1774, at Amsterdam, d. Nov. 26, 1854, at Leiden), a Dutch Mennonite pastor and scholar, studied at the Mennonite Theological Seminary at Amsterdam and became a ministerial candidate in 1795. Accepting a call of the Mennonite congregation of Dokkum (*q.v.*) in Friesland, he served here from March 1796 until July 1797. He then left Dokkum where soon after his departure the Mennonites and Remonstrants (*q.v.*) —very probably not without Siegenbeek's influence —merged as the "United Christian Congregation." Siegenbeek moved to Leiden, where he had accepted a professorship in Dutch elocution at the University. In 1799 he taught also the Dutch language and literature and from 1815 also national Dutch history. He published a number of literary books and papers. His project for better spelling of the Dutch language (spelling-Siegenbeek) was accepted by the government in 1804. Siegenbeek gave much energy to the Association for Dutch Literature (*Maatschappij der Nederlandsche Letterkunde*), of which he was secretary 1803-22, and president 1822-47.

At the same time Siegenbeek gave much of his time and his care to the Mennonite brotherhood. In 1804-29 he served the congregation of Leiden as an assistant pastor, in 1814-45 he was a trustee of the A.D.S. (Dutch General Mennonite Conference), several times its president and also a curator of its seminary 1814-45. Even after his death his love for the seminary was shown by an important bequest for the purpose of rewarding prominent students.

In *Archief voor Kerkgeschiedenis* (VI, 1835, 203-24) Siegenbeek published a paper, "Over hetgeen het kerkgenootschap der doopsgezinden in de laatste vijftig jaren tot verspreiding van redelijke Godskennis, handhaving van het zuiver Christendom en verbetering van de predikwijze heeft toegebracht." In 1808-10 he was active in behalf of a new Mennonite hymnal, forming a committee with P. Beets, J. van Geuns, and J. de Vries, which prepared the edition of *Uitgezochte Liederen* (*q.v.*) in 1810.

Matthijs Siegenbeek married Geertuida Tieboel, of Dokkum. They had two sons, both born at Leiden on Feb. 23, 1806, but one of them soon died. The other, Daniel, bearing the family name of Tieboel Siegenbeek (d. Jan. 11, 1866, at Leiden), studied literature and law at the University of Leiden and became a lawyer in his home town; in 1858-66 he was burgomaster of Leiden. He married Elizabeth van Heukelom, and served as a deacon in the Leiden congregation 1838-65. He sponsored his cousin Daniel van Heukelom (1850-1900), who adopted his family name and was called Daniel Eliza Siegenbeek van Heukelom; he was a medical professor at the University of Leiden and served the Leiden congregation as deacon 1874-76 and from 1886 until his death. Matthijs Siegenbeek was commemorated in a funeral sermon by Christian Sepp (*q.v.*); Samuel Muller published an obituary notice for the Dutch Association for Literature. vDZ.

N.N.B.Wb. V, 735-41; II, 1317; IV, 742; S. Muller in *Levensberichten* (Leiden, 1855) 83-135; L. G. le Poole, *Bijdragen tot de kennis van . . . de Doopsgezinden te Leiden* (Leiden, 1905) *passim; Naamlijst* 1798, 57; 1804, 64; 1829, 34; *DB* 1865, 76; 1900, 111; 1912, 107; *Algemeen Doopsgezind Weekblad* X, No. 10 (May 14, 1955); *Inv. Arch. Amst.* II, No. 2544.

Siegfried Mennonite Church (MC), now extinct, called "Lehay" (Lehigh) in the letter written by the Franconia bishops to Holland in 1773, was located on what is now Twenty-first Street, Northampton, Pa. Common names in the congregation were Showalter, Basler, Funk, Ziegler, Hiestand, Landis, and Siegfried. The log meetinghouse was built about 1760. The land for the cemetery was conveyed to four trustees in 1770: Joseph Showalter, Henry Funk, Peter Fried, and Jacob Baer. In 1802 the congregation built the Settlement meetinghouse (*q.v.*) and the Siegfried church building and cemetery were abandoned. In 1829 Jacob Funk, a survivor of the Siegfried congregation, was legally empowered to sell the remaining unused portion of the cemetery lot. A stone wall was built around the cemetery, which contained almost one hundred graves. In 1885 Tilghman Seiple, a grandson of Henry Funk, raised money by popular subscription to put an iron fence around the cemetery. Later the cemetery was filled in and all but two headstones were covered. It is traditional that the services of the Siegfried congregation were sometimes disturbed by Indians.   J.C.W.

J. C. Wenger, *History of the Mennonites of the Franconia Conference* (Telford, 1937) 226-28.

Siemelink, Tjaard Hendrik (1864-1928), married to G. Gaastra, a Dutch Mennonite pastor, serving at Workum 1890-1908 and at Vlissingen-Goes 1908-27.

He was well versed in Mennonite history and published a painstaking study on the history of the Mennonites at Workum in *Doopsgezinde Bijdragen* 1899, 1903, and 1905. He further published a sermon in commemoration of the second centennial of the Workum meetinghouse (Workum, n.d.-1895) and *Het beginsel der Hervorming en de opkomst der Doopsgezinden* (booklets published by the Committee for the Mennonites in the Diaspora, Nos. 45, 48, and 49; Amsterdam, n.d.). (*De Zondagsbode* XLI, 1927-28, Nos. 22 and 23.)   vDZ.

Siemens (Siemons, Simon, Siemen, Ziemens) is a family name originating among the Mennonites of Prussia and Danzig which was transplanted to Russia and America. One of the earliest records of the name is found in the church record of Danzig (1665). The name was common in Elbing, Königsberg, Tiegenhagen, Rosenort, Fürstenwerder, and Tragheimerweide. The name was presumably derived from Simon. It is a common German name. Among the Russian Mennonites B. H. Unruh lists as ministers Franz Siemens, George Siemens, Peter Siemens; and A. A. Töws names D. J. Siemens. Jan Siemen was one of the first Germantown settlers. J. Siemens had a large flour mill at Nikopol, Ukraine, and another J. Siemens was Oberschulze at Fernheim, Chaco. J. G. Rempel lists as ministers (GCM) J. J. Siemens, a minister in Winkler, Man., Gerhard Siemens, and F. F. Siemens. Rubin L. Siemens is a minister (GCM) at Ransom, Kan. Nikolai Siemens is a leader among the Mennonites of Paraguay, and was long editor of the *Menno-Blatt*. J. J. Siemens was a business leader of Altona, Man.   C.K.

Reimer, *Familiennamen*, 118; H. H. Schröder, *Russlanddeutsche Friesen* (1936) 96; Unruh, *Hintergründe*, 426; A. A. Töws, *Mennonitische Märtyrer* II (North Clearbrook, 1954).

Siemens, Gerhard, an elder of Naumenko Mennonite Brethren Church (*q.v.*), Russia, from 1903 until he went to North America in 1905. Upon his return to Russia in 1907 he continued as elder of the church at least as late as 1910. (Friesen, *Brüderschaft,* 450-51.)   C.K.

Siemens, Nikolai (1895-1958), a leader of the Mennonites in the Fernheim Colony, Paraguay, was born March 15, 1895, in Johannesfeld in the Crimea, South Russia, died Sept. 24, 1958, in Fernheim. In 1910 his family moved to Smolyanovka, Omsk district, Siberia, where he was baptized at 15 in the M.B. Church and early chosen as preacher. In 1923-25 he attended the Bible School at Tchongrav, Crimea, and the following year the Orenburg Bible School, after which he returned to Smolyanovka to become leader of the M.B. congregation there. In 1929 he emigrated to Paraguay and settled in Fernheim in 1930. Here he became editor of the *Menno-Blatt,* which he edited and published for 25 years. He served for varying periods on the KfK (*q.v.*), on the Missions Committee, and as director and teacher of the traveling Bible school, the forerunner of the Fernheim Bible School. He was the guide and teacher of many young ministers, was active in youth work, was a warm advocate in inter-Mennonite co-operation, and a loyal and firm supporter of Fernheim Colony. (*Menno-Blatt,* Oct. 16, 1958.)   H.S.B.

Sieswerdus Klerick (erroneously sometimes Kurick), a schoolteacher in Geldern, Rhineland, Germany, was an Anabaptist leader, of whom there is no further information but that he was present at the conference of Anabaptist leaders at Boekholt (Bocholt, *q.v.*) in Westphalia in August 1536.   vDZ.

Sieuwertsz van Reesema, a Dutch Mennonite family whose ancestor was Willem Sieuwersze, a maker of camlet (a fabric of camel's hair or wool), b. 1643 at Emden, East Friesland, Germany, who moved to Amsterdam, Holland, where he died in 1688. He and his wife Susanna van Gent were members of the Mennonite church as were their descendants for many generations, found at Amsterdam, Haarlem, Leiden, Rotterdam, and other towns of the Netherlands. They first were textile merchants and manufacturers, but later also bakers and lawyers. Some of them served the Mennonite congregation at Rotterdam as deacons. Abraham Sieuwertsz van Reesema (Leiden, 1786-Rotterdam, 1848), a lawyer and deacon of the Rotterdam church, was a close friend of Pastor Nic. Messchaert (*q.v.*), whom he assisted morally and financially in his efforts for the welfare and better education of his fellow citizens. Albert Cornelis Sieuwertsz van Reesema (1853-1911) was a deacon at Rotterdam and in 1873-86 a trustee of the A.D.S. (Dutch General Mennonite Conference). Most of his descendants have now left the church. In 1690 a Sievert Sievertsen van Reschema was found at Danzig, West Prussia, who may have been a member of the same family.   vDZ.

Ned. Patriciaat V, 1914, 335-39; *Schriftenreihe des Menn. Geschichtsvereins* No. 3 (1940) 118.

Sigelsbach: see Thomae.

Sigismund II (1520-72), King of Poland 1548-72, united Lithuania, West Prussia, Volhynia, and the Ukraine with Poland in 1569 and granted general religious freedom in 1572. He did not at first tolerate the Anabaptists, whom he considered a threat to the state. When he heard that Dutch Mennonite refugees were settling in Elbing he issued a mandate in 1556 ordering their expulsion, but later he confirmed the contract of lease concluded by the barons of Loysen with the Mennonites.   NEFF.

W. Mannhardt, *Die Wehrfreiheit der Altpreussischen Mennoniten* (Marienburg, 1863); *ML* IV.

Sigismund III, King of Poland 1587-1632, confirmed the contracts of lease made with the Mennonites and on Oct. 20, 1623, accorded special privileges to the lacemakers of Schottland, most of whom were Mennonites. But he refused to grant them any new rights or liberties. Upon the complaint of the city council of Elbing that the Mennonites broke up marriages without having previously informed the authorities (i.e., they practiced avoidance), married one another, and divided property at their pleasure, he forbade the Mennonites, upon penalty of a fine of 100 guilders, to marry without the foreknowledge of the authorities, and ordered that the Mennonites should be given no special rights. When the Mennonites nevertheless requested release from all civil handicaps, especially from military defense of the city and the court oath, he decreed on April 26, 1615, that they should do their duty like others.

But the ruling was not enforced. On April 26, 1626 (1635, as given by Mannhardt, p. 72, is impossible because he was no longer on the throne at that date), the king sent the following orders to the magistrate of Elbing: Because he had heard that they had accepted Anabaptists and Mennonites and given them liberties, so that they "without swearing to him and the city, carried on trade and crafts, bought houses, snatched food from the citizens, and tolerated them free of all that citizens must assume, and, what was not the least, their testimony at court was counted as valid as an oath, all of which is contrary to the public and special laws and offended his royal regard sorely and threatened to do harm," therefore these "people shall be held to sworn obligations to the king and the city, to take up all civil burdens." Sigismund placed wild hordes of Cossacks and Poles at the disposal of his brother-in-law, Ferdinand II, of Austria, which burned and sacked the Hutterite Bruderhofs at Schädowitz, Wätznobis, and Göding, killing many of the people.   NEFF.

Wilhelm Mannhardt, *Die Wehrfreiheit der Altpreussischen Mennoniten* (Marienburg, 1863); Zieglschmid. *Chronik*, 724; *ML* IV.

Signau, a large village and former government center (*Landvogtei*) in the Emmental, Swiss canton of Bern, where the Anabaptists early found adherents. At the great Anabaptist colloquy at Bern in 1538 (*q.v.*) Hans Krähenbühl represented the Signau congregation. A formal hunt was organized against the Anabaptists in the Emmental in these years, which was very rewarding in Signau, the bailiff of the Emmental receiving six pounds, and another man eight pounds for hunting Anabaptists there. About five persons were put to death in the Signau district in 1537-66, among them the well-known Wälti Gerber (*q.v.*) of Röthenbach (which belonged to Signau), who was beheaded in Bern on July 30, 1566. Strict orders from Bern that the Anabaptists were to be punished were sent to the Signau district in 1564; these regulations were even proclaimed from the pulpits. Bernetta Blindenbach was taken from Signau to Bern the second time in 1566, and imprisoned and tortured because she refused to name her brethren.

In the 17th century also the Anabaptist movement spread in Signau. The ancient mandates were renewed. In February 1649 the Mennonite preacher Joseph Widmer (*q.v.*) was caught in the territory of Signau and taken prisoner to Bern. Among the Mennonite preachers delivered in chains to the new penitentiary and orphanage (*q.v.*) in Bern was Hans Zaugg of Signau. All of this indicates that the Anabaptist movement was comparatively strong in the region of Signau. Johannes Frisching, magistrate at Signau, wrote to Bern in 1663 that his subordinate officers were unwilling to be used in the seizure of Mennonites on account of blood relationship. Among the Mennonites expelled from the canton in the 18th century there were many from the territory of Signau.   S.G.

Samuel Geiser, *Die Taufgesinnten-Gemeinden* (Karlsruhe, 1931); *ML* IV.

Sijbolts, Pieter (1867-1906), studied at the university and the Mennonite seminary at Amsterdam and was pastor at Warga 1892-94, De Rijp 1894-1901, and Middelburg 1901-6. A volume of his sermons, titled *Preeken,* was edited by A. Binnerts Szn (Assen, 1907).   vDZ.

Sijbrant Jansz, an Anabaptist martyr, executed at Hoorn, Holland, on June 7, 1535, with Hendrik Gijsbertsz, of Kampen, Steven Benedictus, Femmetgen Egberts, and Welmoet Jans. Sijbrant and the two other men were beheaded; the two women were drowned. In March of the same year they had been arrested, and though Catholic theologians tried hard to make them recant, they all remained steadfast. The Court of Holland ordered them to be executed without pardon and without delay. Their execution stirred Hoorn deeply; even most city magistrates abhorred the executions.   vDZ.

Mart. Mir. D 36 f., E 443; *Inv. Arch. Amst.* I, No. 131; Mellink, *Wederdopers,* 168 f.; *ML* II, 391.

Sijen (Syen): see **Seye.**

Sijmensma, Ruurd Jacobs (1816-54), preacher of the Mennonite congregation at Balk (*q.v.*) in the Dutch province of Friesland, chosen in 1842, who because of his opposition to the general trend of liberalism developing among the Dutch Mennonites, and particularly because he wished to maintain the principle of non-bearing of arms, decided to emigrate. With Ruurd Johannes Smid (*q.v.*), an elder of this congregation, and 17 of its members and a few non-Mennonites he left Balk on April 9, 1854; via Rotterdam and Liverpool (England) they arrived at Philadelphia, Pa., on May 6. On June 1 a few of their company including Sijmensma arrived at Goshen, Ind., ten miles southwest of which they settled. In August their families, which they had left behind at Dover, Ohio, joined the pioneers. Sijmensma died in 1854, not quite a year after the emigration. Five letters written by Sijmensma and Smid to the Mennonites remaining at Balk, describing their travel and their settling in the United States, are printed in *Doopsgezinde Lectuur.* The first two of these letters were written by Sijmensma. His grandfather Ruurd Symens was an elder of the Balk congregation at the close of the 18th century.   vDZ.

The adventures of these Balk immigrants (the first group of April 1853 was followed by a few others; 19 members of Balk with their families, a total of 52 souls, moved to America) are related in the article by Marie Yoder, "The Balk Dutch Settlement Near Goshen, Indiana, 1853-1889," *MQR* XXX (January 1956); the five letters are found in *Gorter's Doopsgezind Lectuur,* 1854, 261-300; *DB* 1861, 130 f.; 1887, 112; Carl F. Brüsewitz, "The Mennonites of Balk, Friesland," *MQR* XXX (January 1956) 19-31; idem, "De Doopsgezinden van Balk," *Stemmen uit de Doopsgezinde Broederschap* V (1956) No. 4, 81-95.

Sijntgen, an Anabaptist martyr, the aged mother of the martyr Steven de Graet (*q.v.*), was burned at the stake with her son on April 7, 1564, at Gent in Flanders, Belgium. The information given in the *Offer des Heeren* and in van Braght's *Martyrs' Mirror* is rather incomplete, stating neither the exact date nor the manner of execution. Verheyden was able to give some details from the official records: Sijntgen's full name was Jozyne Steghers; she was born at Kortrijk in Flanders, and was the widow of Cornelis Segaert (the name of de Graet is apparently a corruption of Segaert). Both Sijntgen and her son are commemorated in the hymn "Als men schreef duyst vijfhondert jaer ende twee en tsestich mede," found in the *Lietboecxken.* (*Offer,* 651; *Mart. Mir.* D 301, E 666; Verheyden, *Gent,* 30, No. 98.)   vDZ.

Sijntgen (*Kreupel;* i.e., Lame Sijntgen), an Anabaptist martyr, who was beheaded on July 19, 1576, at Gent in Flanders, Belgium, together with Lippijntgen Roetsaert and Barbele Pieters. The account in van Braght's *Martyrs' Mirror* on this martyr incorrectly gives 1573 as the year of execution; van Braght calls her a cripple and relates that she was carried to the scaffold on a chair. Verheyden has added some particulars from the official documents: her official name was Jossyne Bornaige, or Barninge; she was a daughter of François and was born at Kortrijk in Flanders; she was the widow of Maerc de Smet. She had been baptized upon her faith at Wervik, Flanders, by Joachim (i.e., Elder Joachim Vermeeren, *q.v.*) in 1561.   vDZ.

Mart. Mir. D 648, E 968; Verheyden, *Gent,* 67, No. 241; *ML* I, 127.

Sijntgen van Gelder (Cynken in *Offer*), an Anabaptist martyr, burned at the stake on July 21, 1562, at Gent in Flanders, Belgium. Her official name probably was Josynken (Srijnken) Cruels, b. at Kortrijk in Flanders; she was the widow of Adriaen Brave. These details have been published by Verheyden, who also found in the records both the exact date and the manner of her execution, not mentioned in *Offer* and van Braght's *Martyrs' Mirror.* Four other women were put to death with Sijntgen, viz., Vijntgen, Goudeken, Janneken de Joncheere, and Betgen van Maldegem. These women are commemorated in the hymn "Als men schreef duyst vijfhondert jaer ende twee en tsestich mede," found in the *Lietboecxken.*   vDZ.

Offer, 650; *Mart. Mir.* D 289, E 664; Verheyden, *Gent,* 29, No. 89; *ML* II, 47.

Sijntgen van Roesselare, in the official documents called Synken Snellaerts or Syntgen van Roselaer, an Anabaptist martyr, burned at the stake at Antwerp, Belgium, on Nov. 19, 1573 (van Braght's *Martyrs' Mirror* does not state the day of execution). In prison she wrote a letter to S.I.H., a sister of the congregation; this simple pious letter, full of fitting quotations from the Bible, admonishes to steadfastness and loyalty; she thanks God for His mercy and is prepared to die for His name. "Greet with the peace of the Lord, in my name, your people where you live, and all dear friends, known and unknown, especially your brother and sister Passchier, my familiar acquaintances. My fellow prisoners greet your love cordially with the peace of the Lord. Pray the Lord heartily for us; we will most gladly do the same for you according to our weak ability. And let us always persevere steadfastly, that no one may take our crown, but that we may with the wise virgins enter into joyful rest. Amen." This letter, found in the *Martyrs' Mirror,* indicates that Sijntgen was not only a pious Christian but also a well-educated woman. In the letter she calls herself the wife of Jeronymus.   vDZ.

Mart. Mir. D 644, E 965; *Antw. Arch.-Blad* XIII, 133, 181; XIV, 92 f., No. 1042.

Sijntgen Wens, also called Sijntgen (Joosyne) Swynts (Swints), and Syntgen de Wind, an Anabaptist martyr, who was secretly strangled on April 13, 1589, with Joos de Tollenaer and Michiel Buyse within the 's Gravensteen castle at Gent, Belgium, and then hanged. She was 33 years of age and the wife of Pieter Dierkens. She had been (re)baptized at the end of 1588 during a meeting held outside the city of Gent. Before she was baptized she had already taken part in the meetings of the congregation for six or seven years. The account of this martyr by van Braght in the *Martyrs' Mirror* is rather short. He mentions that Sijntgen was arrested on Jan. 10, 1589, at ten o'clock in the evening. Verheyden found the particulars (given in this article) in the official records. (*Mart. Mir.* D 764, E 1069; Verheyden, *Gent,* 69, No. 248.)   vDZ.

Sijntgen Vercoilgen, an Anabaptist martyr, the mother of Jan Vercoilgen, was put to death at Courtrai in Flanders on March 9, 1569. (*Mart. Mir.* D 388, E 740.)

Silberfeld, a Mennonite village name found in the following settlements: Barnaul, Siberia; East and West reserves of Manitoba; twice in Cuauhtemoc, Mexico; and the Bergthal settlement, Villarrica, Paraguay. (See **Villages.**)   C.K.

Silesia (German, *Schlesien;* Czech, *Sleszko;* Polish, *Slask*), a region in east central Europe along both sides of the Oder River. Most of it is divided between Poland and Czechoslovakia. In almost all the principalities and duchies of Silesia there had been Anabaptists from 1525. Half the village of Stolz, near Frankenstein, was Anabaptist at this time. A particularly active Anabaptist in these regions was the furrier Gabriel Ascherham (*q.v.*). In Breslau an Anabaptist butcher, Claus Salb, won some adherents and was expelled. Other Anabaptist preachers, such as Ernst von Glatz, Behmisch David of Schweidnitz, Bärtl Riedmaier, who was the leader of one of the seventeen Hutterite congregations in Schäckowitz (*q.v.*), Veit Uhrmacher or Grünberger, Walter Schlesinger, and Peter Riedemann (*q.v.*, also called the "Silesian"), are named. Also Hans Hut (*q.v.*) and a certain Oswald (Glait?) and a brother Hess caused the government and established church some uneasiness in the region of Breslau (*q.v.*), Glogau, and Glatz, "whereby many people were misled." According to a virulent attack, *Wiedertäuferisches Gesindleins in Mähren und Schlesien seltsame Beschaffenheit,* Ascherham was considered the founder of a number of the Anabaptist congregations in Silesia. On Aug. 1, 1526, King Ferdinand issued a harsh mandate against not only the Anabaptists and Schwenckfelders, but also the Lutherans. Duke Frederick of Liegnitz therefore protested at the court against this mandate, promising to take suitable steps to suppress the Anabaptists in his lands, but refusing to re-establish Catholic ceremonies. From that time on, Anabaptists who would not desist from error were to be placed in stocks and have an ear cut off. Luther advised the Protestant pastor Johann Hess, who complained that the Anabaptists were getting the upper hand, that he should not report them to the authorities, but let them betray themselves; then the senate would expel them.

To evade these strict measures Gabriel led his followers, also known as Gabrielites (*q.v.*), to Moravia. But when persecution began there in 1535, many Anabaptists who had emigrated from Silesia returned, causing a sudden increase in the movement in Schweidnitz, Guhrau, Jauer, and Habelschwerdt. But they had a bitter opponent in the Breslau preacher Ambrosius Moibanus (*q.v.*), who wrote a tract against them, for which Luther wrote a foreword. On July 28, 1529, the returning Anabaptists presented a petition to the princes and estates assembled at the Silesian Landtag requesting safe conduct to the assembly so that they might defend their religious views on the basis of Scripture, assuring the assembly that they gave to the emperor what was the emperor's and to God what was God's. They called themselves "the faithful subjects of the prince's grace and authority and obedient brethren and integrated members of Christ's covenant" (Kaster, 61). But the assembly did not consider this appeal. On March 30, 1530, Ferdinand ordered Frederick II to take sterner measures against the Anabaptists, since he feared a revolt and a treaty between them and the Turks. On Oct. 13, 1533, the city council of Breslau wrote to Frederick that several Anabaptists were living under the Baron of Bernstein, among them a certain Clement, who preached and induced all kinds of people to move away. Frederick replied that Clement had been imprisoned in the Wohlen tower for several weeks and had again been expelled from the district. Clement was beheaded at Glogau in 1535.

In 1538 the churches in Habelschwerdt were not being attended, because the Schwenckfelders were meeting in private homes. Pastor Petrus Eiserer left the town and gave the keys of the church to the city council. But the Anabaptists laid no claim to the church either. "For them the whole city was a temple; in private homes of citizens they held their meetings. The Neisse and the Weistritz were the great baptistries, into which adults were immersed and made members of their covenant." Immersion was apparently practiced here. In Weizenrode, in the principality of Schweidnitz, when a tailor was about to be arrested in 1536, "an entire little congregation was discovered," to which the servants of the mayor and the miller's wife belonged.

Such proceedings of course precluded any congregational organization. It seems that the Anabaptists continued in Silesia as Schwenckfelders, since the latter often had possession of Anabaptist writings. But as late as the 1570's individual Anabaptists were found in the country.   W.W.

Kaster, *Archiv für die Geschichte des Bistums Breslau,* 61; *Korrespondenzblatt des Vereins für Geschichte der evangelischen Kirche Schlesiens* (Breslau, 1887) 38 f.; *Luthers Schriften,* ed. de Wette III, 263; L. Rabus, *Historie der heiligen auserwählten Gottes Zeugen* (1555) 12; *Schriften des Vereins für Reformationsgeschichte* (1891) 68-71; Friedrich Thudichum, *Die Deutsche Reformation II* (Leipzig, 1909) 135-37; Volkmer, *Geschichte der Stadt Habelschwerdt in der Grafschaft Glatz* (1897); ML IV.

Silver Lake Mennonite Brethren Church (sometimes called the Dolton M.B. Church), Hutchinson

Co., S.D., was organized by about 30 members under the leadership of P. H. Unruh in 1889. In 1891 a church was constructed east of Silver Lake and about three miles southwest of Dolton. P. H. Unruh was succeeded by Peter Fast, who served 1909-23, J. J. Adrian 1923-46, G. S. Warkentin 1946-?. In 1920 a new church with a seating capacity of 275 was erected. In 1957 the membership was 140, with John Regehr as pastor.   J.A.W.

Silver Street Mennonite Church (GCM), located in Clinton Twp., Elkhart Co., Ind., a member of the Central District, was organized by former members of the Clinton Frame Amish Mennonite Church (*q.v.*) in Indiana. Due to a number of disagreements regarding church government and ordinances, particularly the prayer covering and the bonnet, in early 1892 the congregation divided into two groups, conservative and progressive, the progressive being the minority group, but including the bishop, Benjamin Schrock. The two groups used the same building for worship services for some months until June 1892, the progressive group using it on Sunday afternoon. The climax came when the progressive group invited Joseph Stucky and Peter Tschantz of Illinois to hold meetings for two weeks in June. On Oct. 23, 1892, the progressive group dedicated a new meetinghouse, the membership being 87, and Benjamin Schrock the pastor, with Jacob Smoker, Daniel Smoker, and Christian Mehl as deacons. The name Silver Street Mennonite Church was adopted. In 1893 J. C. Mehl was asked to provide services in the Topeka area and within the first year a new congregation had begun, members coming from the Silver Street mother church and from the Topeka area. In 1913 a second offspring was born when Alvin K. Ropp, then pastor of the church, organized the Eighth Street Mennonite Church in Goshen. By this time the church had joined the Central Illinois Conference. The Silver Street congregation reached its peak of 250 members in 1924 under the leadership of Allen Yoder. In 1958 it had 130 members.

The Silver Street church has had the following pastors besides Benjamin Schrock 1892: John C. Mehl 1892-1906, M. A. Niswander 1906-11, A. K. Ropp 1911-13, Allen Yoder 1913-35, Harry Yoder 1935-41, Robert Hartzler 1942-45, H. E. Nunemaker 1946-53, William Klassen 1953-54, Daniel Graber 1954- .   D.J.G.

Sim(m)erauer, Hans: see **Zimmerauer, Hans.**

Simoda Mennonite Church (MC), Riverton, W. Va., established in 1954, is a member of the Virginia Mennonite Conference. It had a membership of 13 in 1957, with Melvin G. Myers as pastor.   M.G.

Simon Fyts (Fijts) was a preacher of the Mennonite congregation on the Dutch island of Texel in 1569. The 1626 edition of the Dutch martyr book mentions that the accounts in this book on the martyrs Thijs Joriaensz (*q.v.*), Jan Claesz (*q.v.*) van Weesp, and Jan Smit (*q.v.*), which are reproduced in van Braght's *Martyrs' Mirror* (pages D 481, 641, E 823, 962), were given by Simon Fyts, who had visited Thijs and Jan Claesz in prison and observed their execution, and who was a close friend of Jan Smit.

In 1606 he ordained Jan van der Voort as elder of the Flemish congregation at Utrecht (*q.v.*). Further particulars about Fyts were not available. (*DB* 1873, 141; 1899, 104, 120.)   vDZ.

Simon Janssens, an Anabaptist martyr: see **Hans** (Jan) **Symonsz.**

Simon den Kramer (Simon the Shopkeeper), an Anabaptist martyr, burned at the stake in 1553 (exact date unknown) outside the town of Bergen op Zoom, Dutch province of North Brabant. Van Braght's *Martyrs' Mirror,* which is the only source concerning this martyr, relates that Simon was a market vendor (*kramer*), and while standing near his stall refused to give homage to the Roman Catholic "idol" (probably the Holy Sacrament passing in a procession), whereupon he was arrested. Van Braght also relates that the sheriff (*drossaert*), upon coming home from the execution, fell ill and died soon after, filled with doubt whether Simon's execution was just. (*Mart. Mir.* D 149, E 540.)   vDZ.

Simon Maertsz Vernouwen, a Dutch Anabaptist, an adherent of the revolutionary wing led by Jan van Batenburg (*q.v.*), was sentenced by the Court of Holland on July 31, 1544, to be burned at the stake, and executed that day or the next at The Hague. He had been active at Alkmaar, North Holland, where he lived, but also in the neighborhood of Brugge and Gent in Belgium, in Münster (*q.v.*) in Westphalia, Germany, and in other towns. This man's career shows both that revolutionary Anabaptism still was active at that late date, and also that long journeys were made by its adherents to propagate their ideas.   vDZ.

Inv. Arch. Amst. I, Nos. 281, 744 f.; DB 1909, 22, 28 f.; Mellink, Wederdopers, 174, 410, 414.

Simon Michielsz (Machielsz) was an elder of the Waterlander congregation at De Rijp (*q.v.*), Dutch province of North Holland. In 1575-76 Michielsz baptized Hans de Ries (*q.v.*) here, who soon became an influential elder and leader of the Waterlanders. In 1577, at a conference of Waterlander elders and preachers held at Alkmaar, a resolution was passed that Jacob Jansz (*q.v.*) Scheedemaker and de Ries should draw up a confession of faith, assisted by Simon Michielsz and others. Again in 1581 a Waterlander conference at Amsterdam discussed the question of drawing up a confession; it was then resolved that de Ries should write it with the assistance of Michielsz and Scheedemaker, which confession, after approval by the congregations, would be printed.

Later Michielsz was an elder at Haarlem, where he and Scheedemaker adopted a stricter practice in banning than a part of the congregation favored, which led to some trouble. Simon Michielsz probably died in 1587, for after this year there is no information about his activity. His brother Cornelis Michielsz was also a Waterlander preacher. In 1592 he refused to sign the Concept of Cologne (*q.v.*), because he believed that the strict regulations concerning banning and shunning as found in the Concept were too much "human views" and not Scriptural.   vDZ.

DB 1863, 110; 1864, 20; 1876, 36; 1877, 79, 81, 82, 84; 1897, 93, 110; 1904, 142, 144; Blaupot t. C., *Holland* I, 46, 116 f., 119; Kühler, *Geschiedenis* I, 351, 355, 370; *ML* III, 129.

Simon van Vliermaal, a locksmith, was burned at the stake in 1534 at Curingen (Curanges) near Hasselt, Belgium. He confessed that he was an Anabaptist, and that his coreligionists were planning to bathe the country in fire and blood. This Simon of Vliermaal shows that revolutionary Anabaptism was at this time also found in northeastern Belgium.

vDZ.

L. E. Halkin, *La Réforme en Belgique sous Charles-Quint* (Bruxelles, n.d.-1957) 81.

Simons, Menno: see **Menno Simons.**

Simplicissimus: see **Grimmelshausen.**

Simplicity, a Christian virtue stressed by the Anabaptists and the Mennonites, closely related to sincerity, humility, and forthrightness, and applying to many aspects of life, including the manner of address and communication, forms of worship and type of meetinghouse, character of homes and furniture, costume, etc. It is closely related to the principle of nonconformity (*q.v.*), and hence it is at times difficult to distinguish the motivation for simplicity of expression, whether it is grounded in sincerity and opposition to prideful expression, or in the intent to be different from the world. It is also related to such attitudes as oppose materialism and complexity. At times it has been closely related to ruralism and anti-urbanism, since many Mennonites have been farmers, and also to traditionalism as opposed to change. At times it has been strongly identified with simplicity in dress. It is therefore not always easy to assign to the concept of simplicity particular expressions of behavior. Much of what might be referred to here is treated in the articles **Nonconformity** and **Dress.**

The earliest testimony to the Anabaptist emphasis on simplicity is found in Kessler's *Sabbata,* written in 1525, describing the Swiss (St. Gall?) Brethren: "They shun costly clothing, they shun expensive food and drink, clothe themselves with coarse cloth, cover their heads with broad felt hats. Their entire manner of life is completely humble." Sebastian Franck (*Chronica,* 1531) refers to Anabaptist regulations on simplicity of clothing. Bullinger (1561) wrote: "They reproved sharply covetousness, pride, profanity, the frivolous talking and inordinate life of the world"; and at another place, "They reproved earnestly all vain display, all intemperance in eating and drinking." The Strasbourg Conference of 1568 directed that "tailors and seamstresses shall hold to the plain and simple style and shall make nothing at all for pride's sake" and that "brethren and sisters shall stay by the present form of our regulation concerning apparel and make nothing for pride's sake." The Catholic Franz Agricola, evidently describing the Hutterites, wrote in 1582: "Among the existing heretical sects there is none which in appearance leads a more modest, better, or more pious life than the Anabaptists. As concerns their outward public life they are irreproachable. No lying, deception, swearing, harsh language, no intemperate eat-

ing and drinking, no outward personal display is found or discernible among them, but humility, patience, uprightness, meekness, honesty, temperance, straightforwardness in such measure that one would suppose that they have the Holy Spirit of God."

Menno Simons said: "We acknowledge, teach and seek no other kingdom than that of Christ, which shall endure forever, in which there is no pomp, splendor, gold, silver." At another place he said that Christ's kingdom is not one "in which a display is made of gold, silver, pearls, silk, velvet and costly finery, as is done by the proud, wicked world."

It is clear that all early Anabaptists of Swiss, Dutch, or Hutterite type and background stressed simplicity consistently in all aspects of life. It is also clear that growing wealth and acceptance in society became a weighty influence militating against the maintenance of simplicity in certain aspects, especially in housing and clothing. This is clearly revealed in the following article on simplicity in the Netherlands. A similar development took place in North Germany and in West and East Prussia, as the second article below indicates. However, simplicity in worship was retained in all these areas, and ceremonialism and liturgical forms never made their way into Mennonite worship anywhere, unless one would rate the introduction of musical instruments as a violation of the original simplicity of Anabaptist worship.

Anabaptist-Mennonite simplicity was on the whole retained in Europe in the rural Mennonite communities in Switzerland, France, and South Germany, even though any prescribed forms of plain dress have long since disappeared; and there is still a spirit of simplicity and resistance to modern fashions and ornamentation in many areas.

The traditional simplicity of Mennonite meetinghouse architecture in Europe and America has been due in part to sincere insistence upon a modest, functional, and economical character of the meetinghouse. However, the severe restrictions placed upon the "churchly" appearance of Mennonite meetinghouses by the governmental authorities in Holland and elsewhere, as well as the desire by the once persecuted Mennonites to avoid all occasion for calling attention to themselves, and possibly the carryover from the house meetings into the first meetinghouses, have also contributed to keep Mennonites from following prevailing ecclesiastical styles, such as Gothic or ornate later styles, with towers, belfries, stained glass windows, etc. In Pennsylvania the influence of the plain Quaker meetinghouse may have been a factor.

The first Mennonites who came to America in 1683-1756 settled in Pennsylvania and came under Quaker influence, the dominant cultural and political group at that time, who strongly emphasized simplicity in many aspects of life including plain dress. Their later neighbors, the Dunkards, the Moravians, the Schwenckfelders, and the Amish, all emphasized simplicity and plainness. All these groups manifested or developed plainness in garb, somewhat like the Quakers, hence the intensification of the "plain" spirit in this area was natural, and all these groups gradually became thought of and often labeled as "the plain people" or "the plain sects."

35

The Eastern Pennsylvania, Maryland, and Virginia areas of the Mennonite Church (MC) as well as the Old Order Mennonites who broke away from them, as well as the various groups of Amish and Amish Mennonites, have maintained a strong emphasis on simplicity and plainness, including certain aspects of a prescribed "plain" costume. Simplicity at times may have become perhaps too exclusively identified among them with "plain dress," although the spirit of plainness is carried through in other aspects of life as well. It is interesting to note that an early source described the Mennonite immigrants of 1710 to the Lancaster area in the following terms: "The dress of both female and male was domestic, quite plain, and of coarse material, after an old fashion of their own." J. C. Wenger cites Morgan Edwards, a Baptist historian writing in 1770, as describing the Mennonites as people who dressed very plainly and as claiming that some men had been expelled for wearing buckle shoes and outside coat pockets.

But the first Eastern Pennsylvania Mennonites and Amish and their descendants were not the only American Mennonites to emphasize simplicity and to apply it concretely to costume as well as other things. The same was true of the Alsatian Amish immigrants of the first half of the 19th century, and of the Swiss immigrants of the same period who later joined the General Conference Mennonite Church. Such groups as the Church of God in Christ Mennonites, the Evangelical Mennonites (Kleine Gemeinde), and the various conservative Manitoba groups (Old Colony, Sommerfelder, etc.) still continue to stress simplicity and plainness.

The increasingly higher level of income, the gradual acculturation to the contemporary manner of life in society in general, and the powerful pressure of clever and materialistic advertising, press hard upon the general Mennonite desire to maintain the simple life. Among the American Mennonites of Swiss-South German background, the principle in general is being maintained, although certain outward forms are changing, particularly in costume, but vigorous action in teaching and discipline will be necessary to maintain to the full any valid expression of simplicity in the contemporary situation.   H.S.B.

J. C. Wenger, *Separated unto God, A Plea for Christian Simplicity of Life and Scriptural Nonconformity to the World* (Scottdale, 1951); *idem, Historical and Biblical Position of the Mennonite Church on Attire* (Scottdale, 1944); John Horsch, *Mennonites in Europe* (Scottdale, 1942).

• • •

Netherlands. Simplicity of dress, food, and furniture, if not a doctrine, was nevertheless the style of former Dutch Mennonite life, which was inspired by Matt. 5:19 ff. Though the main groups of the Dutch Mennonites, such as the Waterlanders, (Young) Frisians, and (Young) Flemish, never prescribed what degree of simplicity of life was necessary, various incidental references suggest that simplicity was held to be a desirable Christian virtue. During the 17th century in the prosperous Dutch "Golden age," when particularly Mennonite merchants at Amsterdam, Haarlem, Leiden, and other towns became well-to-do and even wealthy, they be-

gan to wear costly dress, to build stately homes and country seats, and to furnish their homes with costly furniture and treasures of art. Preachers like Jacob Cornelisz van Dalen (Waterlander), Tieleman Jansz van Braght (Flemish), and Galenus Abrahamsz de Haan (Lamist) ardently protested against the growing luxury and for the retention of simplicity, but seemingly without much success. In 1647 a large Waterlander delegates' meeting held at Amsterdam resolved to remind the preachers of the resolutions taken in the conference of 1581, "to impress both by their lives and teachings" the members of the church of the dangers of "the great pomp of clothes, wedding parties, funerals, meals, decoration of the homes," and similar things.

At the same time or somewhat before, both Old Frisians and Groningen Old Flemish occupied themselves with the same matter. In 1639 the (Old) Frisian Conference of North Holland drew up twelve articles in some of which simplicity of dress and furniture was emphatically demanded. These articles, expanded in the following years, were always read at the beginning of the yearly meetings of the conference. They are found in Blaupot ten Cate, *Holland* II, 223-28.

In 1656 the Groningen Old Flemish Conference, meeting at Loppersum, resolved to adopt a number of articles in which the members, on penalty of excommunication, were urged to avoid luxury. These regulations were rather rigorous: forbidden were such things as colored clothing, fashionable shoes, the use of smoothing irons, luxurious bedding, chinaware, silver cups and spoons, colored harness for horses, gaudily painted carriages, long hair for men, paintings or pictures on the walls, fire screens with pictures, Delft tiles on the walls, etc. An incomplete copy of these regulations is found in Blaupot ten Cate, *Friesland,* 307 f. After the last decades of the 18th century they fell into disuse.

In 1698 H. L. Bentheim, a Lutheran opponent of the Mennonites, wrote: "Although there is need of guarding against the errors of these people, one can learn much from them that is good, namely, humility, contentment, sobriety. . . . Above all, they insist on modesty in respect to clothing, although there are some in Amsterdam who are attracting attention by using periwigs and other indications of worldliness. However, in Friesland and in Groningen one will see them in plain dress, although they also as a class are well-informed and well-to-do."

But still in the 19th century, particularly in some conservative rural congregations like Aalsmeer, Balk, Warns, and Ameland, Mennonites held to simplicity. On the island of Ameland, Mennonite homes were generally not painted red, white, green, but a sober brown. Occasionally mention is made of "Menistblauw" (blue), and in my youth I often heard it said that my grandfather refused to wear a gold watch, always using a simple silver one.   vDZ.

N. van der Zijpp, *Geschiedenis der Doopsgezinden in Nederland* (Arnhem, 1952) 152-56.

• • •

Prussia, Russia, and Descendants in America. The practice of simplicity among the Mennonites of

Prussia and Russia was very similar to that of the Swiss and the Dutch. Through their isolated life they developed some specific beliefs and practices as to what constitutes a true, consecrated Christian life and what is "worldly." This was noticeable in their manner of life, their clothing, homes, furniture, worship services, entertainment, etc. Through group action, cultural patterns developed which were acceptable and variations became difficult to promote because of church discipline or group pressure. Mannhardt (p. 111) reports in detail the changes that took place in the Danzig Mennonite Church. The baptismal candidates were not accepted during a certain year because of their "worldly" clothing which included such items as wigs and scarves. However, being exposed to the culture of the surrounding cities, they gradually adjusted to their environment, although they retained certain characteristics of simplicity.

In Russia, because of greater isolation, patterns of simplicity could be preserved more readily. With later agricultural and economic progress the enforced "simplicity" of the pioneer days gradually disappeared. Contact with the German and Russian culture changed the pattern in clothing, furniture, and buildings. There is, however, very little reference to disciplinary action along these lines. Such features as clothing and head covering did not assume the religious significance and were not considered prerequisites for a simple Christian life to the same degree as among the Amish and other conservative Pennsylvania-German Mennonite groups, although some of the same problems are noticeable.

Particularly the migration of the Mennonites of 1874 must be viewed in connection with the process of an adjustment of the Mennonites to the higher standards of living and culture in Russia. Some of the more conservative groups, such as the later Old Colony Mennonites (*q.v.*) who settled in Manitoba (*q.v.*), left Russia not only because of the threat of military service but also because they felt that their simple way of life at home and particularly in the schools was threatened. In Manitoba and Mexico they developed very much along the same lines as the Amish and Hutterites in that they "froze" or "petrified" certain forms of culture in their belief and emphasis on the simple Christian life. The traditional head covering for men and women, clothing, and even the leather boots for the ministers, received religious significance. The objection to electricity and motor-driven vehicles and many other modern cultural and religious practices was due to their concept of simplicity and nonconformity.

To some degree some other conservative Mennonite groups from Russia who settled in the United States and Canada, such as the Kleine Gemeinde and smaller congregations, have emphasized simplicity similarly and objected to the introduction of some common American cultural customs and practices. The cutting of women's hair, attendance at motion pictures and other theatrical amusements, and at places the introduction of the radio have in some congregations caused disciplinary action on the basis that they were undermining the simple Christian life. This has been the case of some of the con-

gregations of the G.C.M., M.B., K.M.B, E.M.B., and other groups of Russian background. As a rule there have not been great controversies or differences of opinion along these lines which led to separation, with the exception of the conservative Manitoba Mennonites where for instance one division in recent times was caused in part by a dispute regarding the wearing of white bridal gowns instead of the traditional black. It is generally emphasized that a stable consecrated Christian life will find an expression in daily living which will be in harmony with the traditional Biblical Mennonite concept of simplicity. C.K.

H. G. Mannhardt, *Die Danziger Mennonitengemeinde* (Danzig, 1919); Cornelius Krahn, "Menno and Discipleship," in *Studies in Church Discipline* (Newton, 1958).

Sinclair Church of God in Christ Mennonite Church, located 3 miles north of Sinclair, Man., was organized in 1953, the church erected in 1955. In 1958 the membership was 40, with H. H. Barkman as minister. H.H.B.

Singel (Singhel, Cingel, Singele) **van,** a former Dutch Mennonite family, found in the 16th-18th centuries at Amsterdam, where Pieter Jans van Singhel was a preacher of the Danzig Old Flemish congregation from 1619. In the 18th century members of this family lived at Utrecht, Alkmaar, and Leiden. Pieter van Cingel (Singele) was a preacher of the Frisian Mennonites at Alkmaar 1703-48. The Mennonite van Cingel family of Scheemda, province of Groningen, most of whom were farmers and often deacons, was apparently not related to the above Amsterdam family. (*Inv. Arch. Amst.* II, Nos. 116 f.; II, 2, No. 5; *DB* 1891, 10.) vDZ.

Singel Mennonite Church, the name popularly given to the meetinghouse of the Amsterdam Mennonite Church, which is located on the Singel Canal, No. 452. In 1608 Harmen Hendriksz van Warendorp (*q.v.*) had this meetinghouse built for the Flemish congregation; it was enlarged in 1639. It received the name *bij't Lam* because it was located near a brewery which had a lamb as its gable sign. (See **Amsterdam.**) vDZ.

Singing, Hutterite, at Worship. Like the delivery of their sermons (*q.v.*) the congregational singing of the Hutterites of today is also strongly formalized, a practice which undoubtedly goes back to certain usages of the 16th and 17th centuries. Some of its characteristic features were mentioned in the article **Lieder der Hutterischen Brüder;** some further observations will be briefly summarized here. A. J. F. Zieglschmid reports in a footnote of the *Klein-Geschichtsbuch* (580, n. 3) that in the singing of hymns during the worship hour the preacher (*Diener des Wortes*) reads and sings one line of the hymn from the *Liederbuch,* whereupon follows the congregation sings this line in unison; then follows the second line in the same fashion, and so forth. Since most of the hymns are extremely long, only a few stanzas are sung. The singing itself is rather devoid of musical beauty; it is not only sung in unison but extremely shrill and loud. The tunes are known by all through oral tradition. The texts are taken from two printed hymnals, the Lieder der Hutterischen Brüder (1914) and Das Kleine Liederbuch (1930). The tunes derived originally from old secular folk tunes (mostly medieval) but they lost most of their melodiousness and freshness by the above described formalization.

There is good reason to ask what has made this overly loud, rather unmusical singing the congregational practice. A good conjecture would be that in the beginning it was introduced intentionally by brethren who were imprisoned and who wanted to be heard both by their fellow brethren in other parts of the jail and by outsiders that they might stop and listen to their testimonies of faith. Jeronimus Käls (q.v.), martyred at Vienna 1536, reports in one of his epistles from prison that at night the brethren in separate cells sang so loudly that they could hear each other and thus give each other mutual comfort; moreover by so doing they tried to allay their own agony (ME III, 340; also Arch. f. Ref. Gesch. 1929, 80).

Similarly Hans Schmid (q.v.) or Raiffer, martyred at Aachen 1558, wrote to the brethren in Moravia that "once God brought all of us together in jail; there I began to pray and sing as loud as I was able to raise my voice. Thereupon people came running to find out what was going on. The warden (Amtmann) came and threatened that unless we lowered our voices he would never again allow such a meeting. But," he concluded, "the brethren did not heed his words and continued in this loud manner so that everyone [outside] could hear how they stood to each other and how they were giving testimony for each other" (letter unpublished, but text also in part in the Chronik, 388 f.). The Scriptural basis for this attitude was Isa. 58:1, in Denk's translation: "So lasst uns schreien dass uns der Hals kracht."

All this indicates that congregational singing is neither folk singing nor artistic singing but a testimony to the praise and glory of the Lord.

As to the tunes used, Oliver S. Beltz (a professor at Mission College, Takoma Park, Md.) made a number of tape recordings of actual Hutterite singing both in Canada and in South Dakota in 1946-47. His material is now deposited in the Folk Song Collection of the Library of Congress. Transcripts in notation may be found likewise in the Music Section of this Library, and also at Concordia Theological Seminary, St. Louis, Mo. Beltz himself plans to publish his findings both from a musicological point of view and by comparison with earlier studies in this area of "folk music turned sacred music." A certain similarity is noticeable with the singing of the Old Order Amish, but thus far no study of any kind has been undertaken in this direction. The late A. J. F. Zieglschmid (q.v.) is said to have had a manuscript ready dealing with the remarkable phenomenon of tune transfers, but it seems to be lost. R.F.

Singing, Old Colony Mennonite. The singing of the Old Colony Mennonites (q.v.) of Chihuahua, Mexi-

co, by far the largest body of this group, is here used as the basis for a brief descriptive account of Old Colony singing in the regular worship services, based upon an extensive and thorough monograph, "The Church Music of the Old Order Amish and Old Colony Mennonites," MQR XXVII (1953), pp. 34-54, by Charles Burkhart, who spent a year in close contact with the Chihuahua group, carefully observing their musical practices. Old Colony singing has remarkable similarities to Old Order Amish singing (q.v.), which are not, however, noted in the following account. For a discussion of hymns and tunes, see **Hymnology** and **Tunes.**

Old Colony church singing is led by a number of song leaders called Vorsänger or choristers (q.v.), who are seated on a platform adjoining the pulpit at the front of the meetinghouse. The office of Vorsänger carries much prestige and is actually very important since, because of the absence of printed notes in the hymnal, the propagation of the tunes and mode of singing from generation to generation depends almost entirely on them. Because of the difficulty of learning the music much practice is necessary and few young men ever become proficient enough to become leaders.

Old Colony music is monodic and is sung by men and women together an octave apart. The natural voice is not used; instead the singing is nasal. Since no dynamics are consciously observed, all sing about mezzo forte in the middle of their range. The resulting tone quality is quite piercing and resonant. Use is made of simple responsive singing between the Vorsänger and the congregation. The former sings all the time, the latter making short pauses at specific points. At the end of each line the congregation stops singing on the first tone of the last syllable group, but the Vorsänger adds a few more tones of his own composition, after which the congregation, having caught a new breath, begins to sing again on the first syllable of the succeeding line. Thus there is no break in the sound, since the leader waits to catch his breath until the congregation has begun the next line. The tempo gives the impression of being very slow, partly because a single syllable is often sung to a fairly long melisma (melodic embellishment), although there are really few long notes. Nearly every syllable is sung to a melisma of anywhere from three to nine tones. Every syllable may be embellished, although the ornamentation is more florid for some than for others. Besides this primary type of ornamentation there is a secondary type composed of quite short tones, frequently inserted by the Vorsänger and naturally difficult for the congregation to follow. In addition to specific ornaments certain melodic formulas constantly recur which contain a number of short ornaments. The mediants sung by the leaders while the congregation catches its breath vary from one leader to another and actually serve as musical cues for the congregation's re-entrance, since the leader makes absolutely no physical gesture in his leading. Since part of the ornamentation is improvised, no two singings of a hymn are ever exactly alike. It is interesting to note that the mediants have something of a counterpart in the cadence formulas of the Psalms for the

Gregorian vesper service. Being strictly monodic, the Old Colony style of singing lends itself to modality, both major and minor modes being used, as well as church modes and *musica ficta*. H.S.B.

Singing, Old Order Amish, in worship. In their regular biweekly worship service most of the Old Order Amish use the *Ausbund* (*q.v.*) exclusively. The hymnbooks are the property of the congregation and are gathered by the oldest hymn leader after each service and carried home in a satchel-like box. For the next service he selects the hymn sung traditionally with the Scripture suitable for that season of the year. (See "Amish Service Manuals" in *MQR* XV, 1941, 26-32.) Before the next meeting he marks with a piece of bluish-gray yarn in each book the first hymn to be sung. Arriving at the home where the service is to be held, he distributes the books along the benches in the rooms where the worshipers will sit. As the time for the service approaches, each one present takes up a book and turns to the marked page. Each congregation has several hymn leaders ("Vorsänger"), who decide among themselves who is to lead each hymn. Since the hymns of the *Ausbund* are sung to well-known medieval or Reformation folk tunes, and the books contain no music notation, hymn leaders must learn them by ear. Very few ever are able to learn all of the twenty-one tunes used by the Amish; many can lead only six or eight with complete confidence. Because leading a hymn is the only congregational activity usually engaged in by a layman, many members chosen for the lot when a minister is to be selected have first served as hymn leaders.

The Amish leader usually sings all but the last word or syllable of the first line alone, the congregation joining in unison at that point. The entire congregation sings the air; the men and women an octave apart; there is no four-part singing. The second hymn in every Amish worship service is the *Loblied* (hymn of praise), page 770 in the *Ausbund*, known in northern Indiana as the *Lobgesang*. Amish tunes have become embellished, down through the years, with so many glides and grace notes and are sung so slowly that the singing of a single stanza requires many minutes. The *Loblied* with its four seven-line stanzas seems to be the only one ever sung in full. If the ministers enter the room from their half-hour pre-service counsel meeting before the congregation finishes the *Loblied*, the singing stops at the end of the next line even though the hymn is not finished. If the ministers have not appeared by the time the *Loblied* ends, one of the hymn leaders announces further singing by saying, for example, "Page 492, stanza 25." Hymns always are announced by the page and the number of the stanza. When the ministers enter, the singing ends at the end of the next line even though the sentence is not complete. There is no further singing until *after* the benediction, which is spoken with both speaker and audience remaining seated. One of the hymn leaders then announces two or more stanzas from an appropriate hymn. After the service on the Sunday nearest Christmas, for instance, he says, "Page 545, stanzas 14 and 15," two stanzas dealing with the Incarnation and taken from a doctrinal hymn of 32 nine-line stanzas. On certain occasions Amish young people sing faster tunes like "Beulah Land," adapted to their Amish hymns. This is true of the celebration following a wedding service and at the Sunday evening "singings." Amish young people are fond of singing and usually have good, though untrained, voices. J.S.U.

Singing Schools. Church music among the Protestant groups was at its lowest ebb in the early 18th century. The Puritans sang only metrical versions of Psalms and possibly used no more than a dozen tunes, the Quakers sang not at all, and the Mennonites used the old hymns and slow monophonic tunes of the *Ausbund*. One of the earliest texts for teaching music was written by Thomas Walter of Roxbury, Mass., entitled *The Grounds and Rules of Music Explained,* and published in 1721. The book used shaped notes and bar lines.

Nathaniel D. Gould in *Church Music in America* explains how singing schools were organized in the New England states in the latter part of the 18th century. When the singing had become insufferable in a given church interested members of the congregation would form a committee to secure subscribers to underwrite a singing school. Then a teacher was selected and a place of meeting. According to Gould, this was frequently located in the village tavern for want of a better place. Instruction consisted of the simple elements of notation and vocal exercises. Gould lists 115 singing schools which he taught between 1799 and 1844.

Lowell Mason (1792-1872) was a musician with a talent to write, to teach, and to arrange singable tunes for church and school. He was founder of Boston Academy of Music and director of the Handel & Haydn Choral Society. He, with George J. Webb, had music festivals and short courses for singing class teachers that were attended by large numbers. In New York City William Bradbury and Joseph Holbrook were also promoters of school music and singing classes. Singing classes were found everywhere in the United States after the early part of the 19th century.

The earliest music enthusiast among the Mennonites was Joseph Funk, born in Berks Co., Pa., in 1777. He with his wife moved to Virginia, where he built a log cabin by the spring where the town of Singers Glen is now located. He introduced music in the schools where he taught, and was recognized as a leader of singing schools. The crowning work of his life was the publication of his collection of *Genuine Church Music* in 1832. With the fourth edition the name was changed to *Harmonia Sacra*. This was the great book of the early Mennonite singing schools. These schools were often community gatherings rather than a church-sponsored effort and were not held in the church, but usually in the school.

In 1875, the Mennonite Publishing Company, Elkhart, Ind., published a new book for singing schools, the *Philharmonia,* compiled by Martin D. Wenger of Virginia, which contains 37 lessons on music theory. All the tunes in this book have four-part harmony. The singing class teachers of the last quarter of the 19th century should be given credit for the style of music used in the M.C. Mennonite churches today. Besides Martin D. Wenger there was also Christian H. Brunk of Virginia who traveled widely among the Mennonites organizing Sunday schools and teaching singing. J. F. King of Orrville, Ohio, was a teacher and publisher of two singing class books, *Silver Star* and *Singer's Joy*. Abraham B. Kolb of Elkhart, Ind., and Aaron C. Kolb of Kitchener, Ont., gave much of their time and talent to the development of good singing in the Mennonite churches. Chauncey King of Wayne Co., Ohio, and Simon Hartzler of Cass Co., Mo., spent many years teaching singing classes among the Amish Mennonite churches of Indiana, Ohio, Illinois, and Missouri. The work of Joseph W. Yoder, Belleville, Pa., will long remain a dominant influence in the singing of the churches in the "Big Valley" and the Mennonite churches of the Franconia, Pa., district.

It was not until late in the 19th century or early 20th century that singing classes were permitted to be held in the churches. During the years from 1906, when John D. Brunk came to Goshen College to inaugurate the Music Department, until his health would not permit, he was a firebrand for better hymns and hymn singing in the M.C. churches. He was an excellent teacher and a well-trained Christian musician. His book, *Educational Vocal Studies*, was written and compiled for singing class use in the church. He opened each session with a devotional period; next a review and practice on points taught in previous lessons. He used a blackboard to present the new theory, then turned to *Educational Vocal Studies* for exercises and songs illustrating the point discussed; finally turned to the *Hymnal* for songs bearing on the new theory just taught. He closed the session with one or two good hymns for interpretation, in order that he might close on a high spiritual plane as well as a high musical experience. Singing classes are still held in some Mennonite congregations, though not as commonly as earlier. In the East they sometimes close with a public program at which heavier music may be sung.   **W.E.Y.**

Singings, Amish, the name usually given to the Sunday evening gatherings of the Old Order Amish young people. (There are some "old folks' singings" for the purpose of transmitting the unwritten chants used in Amish church services.) The young people's singings are of long standing; they were begun to provide an activity of Christian fellowship for the young people.

In earlier times the singing consisted primarily of German hymns; however, not the slow tunes used in the church services. Today the singing is mostly English Gospel songs and hymns. In some communities there is 100 per cent participation in the singing. The evening is begun with Scripture reading and prayer, and usually the group disperses quite promptly after the closing prayer. In some other communities the singing is no longer of importance, since not more than 5 per cent of those present participate.   **H. Gr.**

Singmaster, Elsie (1879-1958), in private life Mrs. Harold Lewars, an American author who wrote outstanding "local color" fiction with Eastern Pennsylvania as a major locale. Since she was of Pennsylvania-German stock, some of her works naturally deal with the "plain people," including the Mennonites. Most of the short stories in her collection *Bred in the Bone* (1925) center around the Reformed Mennonites; a few deal with young Amishmen. These characters and their problems Miss Singmaster treats with sympathy and gentle (never derisive) humor. Her home was at Gettysburg, Pa., where her husband was a professor at Gettysburg College. She was the author of over 300 novels and children's stories, including twelve major novels, most of them dealing with American history, especially of Pennsylvania.   **E.H.B.**

Sinntal Bruderhof, a community of the Society of Brothers founded in 1955 at Bad Brückenau in northern Bavaria. In 1959 the population was some 60, most of them having returned from Paraguay. The Sinntal Bruderhof earns its living by toymaking and some market gardening and is particularly active in reaching out to the younger generation in Germany. It publishes *Der Pflug,* the German edition of *The Plough.*   **E.C.H.A.**

Sinsheim Mennonite Church, in Baden, Germany, the central Mennonite congregation of northern Baden (Elsenzgau and Kraichgau), an area which was formerly a part of the Palatinate, which meets every first, third, and fifth Sunday of the month in the county seat Sinsheim (pop. 5,430), 13 miles southeast of Heidelberg. Most of the members are farmers and come from a radius of 10-20 miles to the services. The congregation was formed in 1912 out of two congregations, one of them probably the oldest congregation in all South Germany, viz., Immelhausen (*q.v.*, 1650-1912), combined in 1841 with Bockschaft and Streichenberg (*q.v.*, 1655-1841), and Ittlingen (*q.v.*, 1841-1912). Later two other congregations were merged with it, Mönchzell, formerly Meckesheim (1896-1914), and Dühren (c1675-1945). None of these congregations had a meetinghouse except Immelhausen (*q.v.*), which was really the direct ancestor of the Sinsheim congregation. The only other congregation remaining in this area is Hasselbach (*q.v.*). From this area a considerable emigration to Pennsylvania took place in the first half of the 18th century. In 1957 the membership was 101, plus 19 children; elders were Heinrich Fellmann, Heinrich Kreiter, and Ulrich Hege. Within the congregation is the oldest continuously occupied Mennonite farm in all South Germany, and possibly in all Europe, the Immelhäuserhof, probably occupied since 1650. The chief places in which members of the congregation live are Bockschaft, Daisbach, Dühren, Hoffenheim, Ittlingen, Immelhäuserhof, Kloster Lobenfeld, Mönchzell, Oberhof, Reihen, Sinsheim, and Weiler.   **H.S.B.**

Sintern (Sinteren), van, a family found in the Mennonite congregation of Hamburg-Altona, Germany, in the 16th-19th centuries. Pieter van Sinteren, whose daughter Elisabeth (1533-1624) was married to Geerlinck Roosen, of Steinrade, Holstein, Germany, in 1565 or 1566, was a Mennonite and had probably moved from Holland or Flanders to Holstein about 1555. Heinrich van Sintern, a grandson of Pieter, was a tailor at Altona about 1600. Another Heinrich van Sintern was baptized at Lübeck in 1710. A Hinrich van (von) Sintern and Isaac van Sintern with his wife Neeltje Claesen and their children emigrated from Altona to Pennsylvania in the spring of 1700, where they joined the Germantown (q.v.) Mennonite congregation.   vDZ.

B. C. Roosen, *Geschichte der Mennoniten Gemeinde zu Hamburg-Altona* I (Hamburg, 1886) 16, 21 f., 35, 58, 63; II (Hamburg, 1887) 85 f.

Siouw Harmen Thysdochter, a revolutionary Anabaptist; she was arrested at the Oldeklooster (q.v.) on April 7, 1535, and drowned at Leeuwarden a week later. (K. Vos, *Menno Simons,* Leiden, 1914, 229.)   vDZ.

Sipke Sitszoon, an Anabaptist martyr executed at Leeuwarden, capital of the Dutch province of Friesland, on April 14, 1535, because he was rebaptized. He was a weaver of Pietersbierum, Friesland. (K. Vos, *Menno Simons,* Leiden, 1914, p. 229.)

Sipkema, a Dutch Mennonite family, formerly living near Joure, Friesland, where some of them were deacons until recent times. Ane Sipkema (b. 1845 at Broek, d. 1926 at Amsterdam), at first engaged in farming, became a student at the Amsterdam Mennonite Seminary in 1868-74 and was a pastor 1888-1912, serving at Mensingeweer 1874-81, Borne 1881-88, and Edam 1888-1912. Johannes Wibrandus Sipkema (b. 1914) studied at the university and the seminary at Amsterdam, thereupon serving the congregations of Terhorne 1938-42, Drachten 1942-47, Eindhoven and Breda 1947-56, and Aalsmeer 1956-   vDZ.

Sipkes, Jelle: see **Teerns, J. S. van.**

Sipman, Dirck, a Quaker of Crefeld, Germany, probably a Mennonite before the Quaker meeting was established in 1679, with Jacob Telner (q.v.) and Jan Streypers, one of the promoters of the Germantown (Pa.) settlement of 1683 ff. He bought 5,000 acres in Pennsylvania from Benjamin Furly, Penn's agent in Rotterdam, in 1682 but never emigrated. He sold his land to other settlers in 1685 and 1698.   H.S.B.

W. I. Hull, *William Penn and the Dutch Quaker Migration to Pennsylvania* (Swarthmore, 1935).

Sippe Claeszoon, of Winsum in Friesland, a revolutionary Anabaptist, arrested at the Oldeklooster (q.v.) on April 7, 1535, and beheaded at Leeuwarden on April 10, 1535. (K. Vos, *Menno Simons,* Leiden, 1914, 228.)   vDZ.

Sittard, a town in the Dutch province of Limburg (pop. c24,000; 94 per cent Roman Catholic), which until 1794 belonged to the duchy of Jülich (q.v.), was, like some of the neighboring villages, e.g., Hoingen, Millen, Gangelt, and Nieuwstad, a center of Anabaptist activity about 1530-34; later also some Anabaptists lived here. Lenart (q.v.) van Ysenbroek and Theunis van Hastenrath (q.v.) baptized in this vicinity about 1550; the latter baptized Herman van Sittart, a surgeon. Remken Ramakers (q.v.) was burned at the stake at Sittard in 1550.

Gerhart Siebenacker (q.v.), the author of some beautiful hymns, was from this town, as apparently were also Gijsbertus Sittart (q.v.), a Mennonite (Flemish) preacher at Leiden until 1679, and the van Sittert (q.v.) family at Amsterdam and Haarlem.   vDZ.

Rembert, *Wiedertäufer,* 450; W. Bax, *Het Protestantisme in het bisdom Luik* I and II (The Hague, 1937, 1941); Wolkan, *Lieder,* 100; DB 1909, 125.

Sittart, Gijsbertus, apparently a physician, was a preacher of the Waterlander congregation at Leiden, Holland, serving there from before 1670 until at least 1679. In 1671 he negotiated with the trustees of the Leiden Flemish congregation concerning a merger of the Waterlanders with the Flemish, but without result. (The two congregations united in 1701.) In 1675 Sittart, called to account by the city magistrates, promised not to teach the doctrines of Socinus (q.v.). Sittart was the author of *Jeugd-Oefening in de Ware Godsdienst Zo als de zelve onderwezen werd in de gemeente Christi (diemen de Waterlandsche Doops-gesinde gemeente noemd) binnen Leiden* (Leiden, 1675; repr. there 1683 and 1704, and at Alkmaar, 1726). His daughter Remberta was married to Johannes Bremer, the Remonstrant pastor at Leiden, whose son Johannes Bremer (q.v.) was a well-known Mennonite pastor at Amsterdam. Hendrik Sittart, probably a descendant of Gijsbertus Sittart, was a deacon of the Leiden congregation from 1690.   vDZ.

L. G. le Poole, *Bijdragen tot de kennis van . . . de Doopsgezinden . . . te Leiden* (Leiden, 1905) *passim.*

Sitter, de (de Sutter, de Zuttere), a Dutch Mennonite family, originally living in Flanders, Belgium. Some of them, who were farmers, moved to Dutch Zeeland Flanders in the early 17th century and joined the Aardenburg (q.v.) congregation. In the 17th and 18th centuries the de Sitters, then usually engaged in business such as textiles, one of them a manufacturer of white lead paint, are found in Rotterdam, where some of them were deacons of the Mennonite church.   vDZ.

F. K. van Lennep, *Verzameling van Oorkonden betrekking hebbende op het geslacht van Eeghen . . .* (Amsterdam, 1918) *passim;* K. Vos, *Geschiedenis der Doopsgezinde gemeente te Rotterdam* (1907, repr. 45, 47 f.).

Sittert, van, a Dutch Mennonite family found at Amsterdam and Haarlem in the 17th and 18th centuries; in the 18th century a branch of this family was living at Zutphen and Winterswijk. Tieleman Tielen van Sittert (q.v.) was a member of this family; his son Sander van Sittert (d. c1690), married first to Anneken van Limburg, then to Clementia van Vollenhoven, was a noted cloth merchant at Amsterdam.   vDZ.

Sittert, Tieleman Tielen van (d. 1664 at Amsterdam), was a Dutch Mennonite elder, originally belonging to the High Germans, a friend of Elder

Leenaert Clock (*q.v.*). In 1630-39 he served as an elder of the united Frisian and High German congregation and, after the merger (1639) of this church with the Flemish, in the united Flemish-Frisian-High German congregation *bij 't Lam* until June 1664. After the Lamist-Zonist schism in June 1664 he served in the Zonist congregation for a few months until his death. Van Sittert, often called Tieleman Tielen without his family name, was conservative, strictly maintaining the old doctrines and ardently defending his view that his church was the only truly Christian church. Among the Flemish-Frisian-High German delegates assembled at Haarlem in 1649 it was especially van Sittert who advised the rejection of the request of the Waterlanders to merge with the Flemish. From about 1650 he showed himself a fierce opponent of Preacher Galenus Abrahamsz (*q.v.*) and Collegiant (*q.v.*) ideas. Meihuizen is of the opinion that the pamphlet *Commonitio ofte Waerschouwinghe aen de Vlaemsche Doops-gesinde Gemeynte binnen Amsterdam* (n.p., 1655) was drawn up (probably Cornelis de Vries was the author) with the help and at any case in the spirit of van Sittert. In this booklet, whose author calls himself a "voorstander" (deacon) and member of the Amsterdam Flemish congregation, Galenus, David Spruyt, and Frank Beuns are severely attacked and charged with Socinianism. Tieleman Tielen was a noted personality among the conservative leaders and often conducted services, particularly baptism and communion services in other congregations, for example, at Utrecht and Hamburg-Altona.

Tieleman Tielen co-operated with Jan Cents (*q.v.*) and others in drawing up the Jan Cents confession of faith of 1630, on the basis of which the merger of the Frisian-High German group with the Flemish came about in 1639. He was the editor (publisher) of *Christliche Glaubens-Bekentnus der Waffenlosen und fürnehmlich in den Niederländern (unter dem nahmen der Mennonisten) Wohlbekanten Christen, wie auch Etliche Christliche Gebähte eben derselben Glaubensbekenner* . . . (Amsterdam, 1664, 1686, and 1691; n.p. 1711; Basel, 1822); an English edition was printed at Amsterdam in 1712 in behalf and upon the request of the Mennonites in Pennsylvania; a large number of reprints were published in America, both in English and German. This *Christliche Glaubens-Bekentnus* is a translation of the Dordrecht Confession (*q.v.*) of 1632. To the translation van Sittert added a number of prayers, seven hymns (written by Leenaert Clock), and an essay on historical theology. This book was popular among the South German, Alsatian, and American Mennonites; in places it is still used.   vDZ.

Schijn-Maatschoen, *Geschiedenis* III, 241; H. W. Meihuizen, *Galenus Abrahamsz* (Haarlem, 1954) *passim*; DB 1863, 80; 1898, 62; Wolkan, *Lieder*, 115-18; Robert Friedmann, *Mennonite Piety Through the Centuries* (Goshen, 1949) 118 f.

Skalitz (Gallitz; Slovak, *Scalica*), a village located between Hosterlitz and Stignitz (Trstenice) in Mährisch-Kromau (Muravsky Krumlov), was the seat of two Hutterite Bruderhofs in the 16th century, the first founded in 1563. They were among the "upper households." In 1592 one of the Bruder-

hofs was abandoned, presumably because of heavy taxation. In 1605 much burning, murdering, and robbing was done in the remaining Bruderhof by the Bocskay troops. (Zieglschmid, *Chronik*.)

                                                        E.H.B.

Skippack, a village in Skippack Twp., Montgomery Co., Pa., with a population of 3,224 (1950), near which are two Mennonite congregations, the Lower Skippack (*q.v.*) independent congregation, and the Upper Skippack congregation, usually called simply Skippack, of the Franconia Conference (MC). Skippack is also the site of the publication of a number of Mennonite books in the 19th century: the Dordrecht Confession of Faith, 1836; Henry Funck's *Spiegel der Taufe*, 1853 (German and English editions); Menno Simons' *Fundament-Buch*, 1851; the Waldeck *Katechismus*, 1848. A Skippack Mennonite preacher named Henry Bertolet started a monthly religious periodical entitled *Der Evangelische Botschafter* in 1836, but was unable to continue it beyond one issue. The name Skippack is spelled Schipbach in the introduction to *Zwey Erbauliche Lieder*, 1764, where Christopher Dock is called "Schulmeister an der Schipbach." This spelling is probably reminiscent of the Swiss name Schüpbach near Signau in the Emmental, canton of Bern. The Skippack is a small creek, a tributary of the Perkiomen.

On May 8, 1742, and on Oct. 19, 1745, the congregations in the Schiebach (Skippack) area wrote letters to the Zonist Mennonite congregation of Amsterdam, asking advice on how to retain the privileges granted to them by the King of England. They said that particularly the freedom from military service was endangered by the threat of war. They also asked for advice concerning translating into German and printing 1,000 copies of T. J. van Braght's *Martyrs' Mirror*, which they wanted especially for their youth.   J.C.W.

Skippack Mennonite Church (MC) in Skippack Twp., Montgomery Co., Pa., is affiliated with the Franconia Conference (*q.v.*). Skippack was settled in 1702 by Johannes Custer, Claus Jansen, Jan Krey, and others. In 1717 the wealthy Matthias van Bebber, Mennonite owner of the 6,000-acre tract on which the Mennonites settled, conveyed 100 acres to 7 Mennonite trustees named Sellen, Jansen, Ziegler, Custer, and three Kolb brothers, Henry, Martin, and Jacob. A meetinghouse was built here c1725, replaced in 1844 by a new one.

Preacher Martin Kolb had settled at Skippack by 1709, and Jacob Godshalk, who functioned as a bishop, arrived three or four years later. Henry Kolb also served as a preacher. Jacob Kolb was probably a deacon, for he was treasurer of the church funds. Claes Jansen and Michael Ziegler were preachers. The congregation has kept an alms book since 1738, which is a valuable source of information because the ordained men audited and signed it annually. Perhaps the ablest minister in the history of the congregation was Bishop Henry Hunsicker (1752-1836), ordained preacher 1781/82 and bishop soon thereafter. His son John Hunsicker (1773-1847) was the senior bishop in the Franconia

Conference in the division of 1847 and with Ober-holtzer withdrew from the conference. John Hun-sicker's younger brother, Abraham Hunsicker (1793-1872), was ordained as preacher at Skippack on New Year's Day of 1847. He followed Oberholtzer in the division. In 1848 he and his son Henry A. Hunsicker established Freeland Seminary (*q.v.*) at Collegeville, Pa. (now Ursinus College). (See also **Hunsicker.**) The history of the portion of the congregation which withdrew from the Franconia Conference in 1847 is given under **Lower Skippack.** The portion which remained with the conference built a new meetinghouse one and one-fourth miles northwest of the old meetinghouse site in 1848. This building was replaced in 1950. The most prominent minister since 1847 was Jacob B. Mensch (1835-1912), preacher from 1867, antiquarian and unofficial secretary of the Franconia Conference from 1880. In 1958 the ministers were Jacob T. Landes and Daniel Reinford; the membership was 102.

J.C.W.

J. C. Wenger, *History of the Mennonites of the Franconia Conference* (Telford, 1937).

Slabaugh: see Schlabach.

Slackwater Mennonite Church (MC), located on Route 1, Millersville, Pa., was established in 1950; by 1957 it had 31 members, with Frank K. Garman as pastor. It is a member of the Lancaster Conference.

M.G.

Slag(h)regen, a former Mennonite family of Amsterdam, Holland, members of the Flemish congregation and after the schism in 1664 of the Zonist (*q.v.*) Mennonite congregation, some of them serving as deacons. The Slagregens were also found in the Haarlem Waterlander congregation, where a few of its members were trustees of the congregational orphanage in the 17th and 18th centuries. Jacob Slagregen, d. 1853, a stone merchant at Amsterdam, was a trustee of the Oranjeappel (*q.v.*) orphanage in 1823-53 and a cofounder of the Dutch Mennonite Mission Association. This family died out in the 19th century.

vDZ.

Slappe Vriezen (Lax Frisians), a former branch of the Dutch Mennonites: see **Frisian Mennonites.**

Slate Hill Mennonite Church (MC), located in the beautiful Cumberland Valley, 7 miles west of Harrisburg, Pa., began when David Martin (1767-1822), oldest son of Bishop Henry Martin of Weaverland, settled here. In 1810 the scattered members built a brick meetinghouse called "Martin" on an elevation on his farm. In 1831 the ministers were his brother David (1807-75) and William Westhafer (1782-1851). The second brick church was built in 1875. This has always been the strongest Mennonite congregation in the Cumberland Valley. It was the home congregation of Bishop Benjamin F. Zimmerman (1851-1930), Samuel Hess (1854-1948), and the present Bishop William M. Strong. The first Sunday school, headed by Jacob Mumma (1809-76), was held in 1872. The first Sunday-school meeting in the Lancaster Conference was held here on Nov. 5, 1896. In 1957 the ministers were Christian W. Zimmerman and Norman L. Zimmerman; the membership was 124.

I.D.L.

Slavgorod, a city in the region of Tomsk in the Kulundian Steppes, Siberia, was established in the vicinity of the Barnaul (later Slavgorod) Mennonite settlement in 1909. The engineers in charge of building this city were Belyayev and Tchernov. Tchernov in particular, as a direct representative of the St. Petersburg government, helped the Mennonites in establishing the Slavgorod settlement (*q.v.*). The city was planned so that lots 140 x 175 ft. could be rented. By 1913 the streets were lighted. Slavgorod soon developed into a business center, particularly for the Mennonites. A number of Mennonite businesses were established here. Cornelius P. Wiens, Peter A. Friesen, and Jakob Dück had grocery and dry goods stores. Peter P. Friesen and Franz P. Friesen operated a flour mill. Mills were also owned by Peter F. Klassen, Jakob C. Friesen, H. Hamm and H. Miller, David Hübert, and Heinrich Hübert. Among the dealers in farm machinery were Bernhard Friesen and Peter J. Wiens. All these businesses were confiscated after the Revolution of 1917. After World War II the town had a population of 16,000. It is located on a branch of the Trans-Siberian railroad, 250 miles west of Barnaul.

In 1927 J. Wall, an M.B. minister, preached and conducted Bible conferences in the large Baptist church, which had been built in the previous year.

Klaus Mehnert, who visited Slavgorod in 1955, reports that the population was about 30,000, of whom approximately one third were of German background. He found a Baptist church, which is also attended by the Mennonites. At the time of his visit German services were not yet permitted. Meanwhile this permission has been granted. The minister told Mehnert that they had 300 registered members, but that the attendance was larger than the capacity of the church. Permission had not yet been granted to enlarge the church. (See also other articles under **Slavgorod.**)

C.K.

Klaus Mehnert, "Deutsche—vom Sturme verweht," *Der Bote,* Sept. 5, 12, 19, 1956; Gerhard Fast, *In den Steppen Sibiriens* (Rosthern, 1957) 27 f.

Slavgorod City Mennonite Brethren Church was founded in Slavgorod in 1914, in the center of the Slavgorod Mennonite settlement (*q.v.*), Siberia. Worship services were originally conducted in private homes. After World War I a church was located on Sadovaya Street and later the old post office on Moscow Street was purchased and remodeled into a church. The first leading minister was Dietrich Friesen, followed by P. P. Friesen. They were assisted by Heinrich Hiebert and Gerhard Wiens. The church served the growing Mennonite population of the city of Slavgorod. Under the Soviets this church was closed. According to latest reports, Mennonites worship in the Baptist church of Slavgorod, which conducts some services in the German language. A report dated Feb. 8, 1927, states that J. Wall (MB) was working among the Russian Baptists, conducting Bible discussions and explaining the plan of salvation.

C.K.

Gerhard Fast, *In den Steppen Sibiriens* (Rosthern, 1957) 79.

Slavgorod (Kulundian) Mennonite Brethren Church was established in the Slavgorod Mennonite settlement (*q.v.*), Siberia, in 1908. A minister, Sawatzky, of Alexandertal, Samara, served the group in 1908. In 1909 the following ministers joined the group, coming from various settlements: Aron Reimer, Jakob Bergen, Abram Ratzlaff, Peter Bergen, and Heinrich Janzen. The Mennonite Brethren were divided into five independent congregations known under the following names: Schönwiese, Schöntal, Alexandrovka, Gnadenheim, and Grishkovka. Quarterly meetings of the leading ministers took care of business and problems of a general nature. Each congregation had a church council and its regular congregational meetings. Periodically all the congregations joined in a meeting by sending one delegate to represent each 25 members.

In 1917 the Slavgorod Mennonite Brethren had 12 congregations, located at Schönwiese, Schöntal, Alexandrovka, Gnadenheim, Grishkovka, Fernheim, Saratov, Pashnya, Svistunovo, Tchayachy, Glyaden, and the town of Slavgorod. The first general elder was Johann Wiens, who organized congregations, ordained ministers and deacons, and led Bible discussions and ministerial courses. In 1910 he went to the Pavlodar settlement. He was succeeded by Aron Reimer, who left for Canada in 1925. Daniel Heide and Franz Friesen succeeded him. When Friesen emigrated to Canada, Heinrich Janzen took his place until 1929, when he also emigrated to Canada. Of special significance were the Sunday schools conducted on Sunday afternoons, the church choirs, and the harvest festivals. The Mennonite Brethren supported the Ob Mission (*q.v.*) among the Ostyaks. The following paragraphs report on the congregations with names beginning with letters preceding "O" which have not been taken care of in the ENCYCLOPEDIA. Congregations under "O" and following can be found under the following separate articles: **Schönwiese** M.B. Church, **Saratov** M.B. Church, **Pashnya** M.B. Church, **Tchayachy** M.B. Church, and **Slavgorod** M.B. Church.

Alexandrovka M.B. Church served the four villages of Alexandrovka, Orloff, Friedensfeld, and Tchernovka. The leading minister was Johann Schmidt, who left for Canada in 1926 and was succeeded by Cornelius Funk. They were assisted by Wilhelm Giesbrecht and Heinrich Teichrieb. Tina Hübert from this congregation served as a missionary among the Ostyaks in the Ob Mission (*q.v.*).

Gnadenheim M.B. Church served the villages of Gnadenheim, Blumenort, Ebenfeld, Kleefeld, Shumanovka, Halbstadt, and Hochstädt. The first leading minister was Isaak Braun, who was succeeded in 1926 by Heinrich M. Janzen, who was ordained elder. Other ministers were Heinrich Konrad, Peter Esau, Jakob Rogalsky, Bernhard Klassen, Franz Friesen, and Herman Klassen.

Grishkovka M.B. Church served nine villages: Grishkovka, Markovka, Karatal, Chortitza, Stepnoye, Golyenkoye, Alexanderkrone, Dolinovka, and Suvorovka. A church was erected in Grishkovka. There were smaller places of worship in other villages. The first leading ministers were Abram Ratzlaff and Jacob Ott, assisted by Gerhard Giesbrecht, Peter Krause, Johann Pätkau, and David Janzen.

Fernheim M.B. Church served three villages: Fernheim, Gnadental, and Sergeyevka. A church was erected in Fernheim during World War I. The

leading minister was Cornelius Klassen, assisted by Johann Wiebe, Nikolai Kliewer, Peter Dück, and David Friesen.

Glyaden M.B. Church served the four villages of Lichtfelde, Ebenfeld, Ivanovka, and Sluchaynoye. The leading minister, Jakob Peters, was assisted by Franz Wiens, Peter Enns, Gerhard Neumann, and Heinrich Unger. A church was erected in Sluchaynoye in 1912.

A smaller congregation was founded in *Svistunovo* serving the villlages of Volinovka and Tchernyevka, with the ministers Jakob Löwen and Wilhelm Löwen.

During the Revolution and after the establishment of the communistic regime, severe hardships were inflicted on the faithful believers and worshipers. Gradually the tax for the ministers and the meetinghouses became unbearable. Many ministers were exiled. By 1932 organized religious activities including worship services were impossible. Since the death of Stalin in 1953 some of the religious activities and work have been resumed. Worship services are conducted at various places and conversions and baptismal services are taking place. (See also **Slavgorod Mennonite Church.**)

C.K.

Gerhard Fast, *In den Steppen Sibiriens* (Rosthern, 1957) 72 f.; A. H. Unruh, *Die Geschichte der Mennoniten-Brüdergemeinde* (Winnipeg, 1954) 208.

Slavgorod Mennonite Church was established in 1908 in the Slavgorod Mennonite settlement (*q.v.*) in Siberia. Originally worship services were held in the village schools. In 1909 a congregational meeting was held in Orloff attended by Elder Jacob Gerbrandt and the ministers Franz Buller, Johann Bergmann, Peter J. Wiebe, Gerhard Wiebe, Dietrich Epp, and Isaak Löwen. In this brotherhood meeting the Slavgorod (Orloff) Mennonite Church was divided into five districts: (1) Orloff with 6 villages, (2) Grünfeld 5, (3) Reinfeld 8, (4) Kleefeld 8, and (5) Markovka 6. All ordained ministers were recognized as such, and Jakob Gerbrandt, who had attended Bethel College, North Newton, Kan., was charged with the responsibility of baptizing, administering the Lord's Supper, and the ordination of ministers and deacons in all the districts. However, each district had its own leading minister. Between Easter and Pentecost the traditional catechetical instruction took place, and at Pentecost the first baptismal service and Lord's Supper were observed in the large shed of Johann Klassen, of Grünfeld. First the church of the settlement was known as Orloff, but later as Schönsee. This article treats this general area church under the name of the settlement, Slavgorod. The church records and the handing out of church certificates were in the hands of P. J. Wiebe.

When Kornelius D. Harder (*q.v.*) came to the Slavgorod Mennonite settlement in 1912, he was ordained elder of the Orloff (Schönsee) Mennonite Church. Another of the outstanding elders was Franz Buller, who was one of the delegates to look for land in the Kulundian Steppes. During the first years the responsibilities of the elder originally assigned to Jakob Gerbrandt were probably shared by some of the leading ministers. Gradually each of the congregations, particularly the larger ones, became independent. Of the churches listed above, those which should have been treated in the preceding volumes of this ENCYCLOPEDIA will be reported in the following paragraphs. The others are found in alphabetical order in this volume. (See Schönsee [Orloff] Mennonite Church, **Reinfeld** Mennonite Church, **Pashnya** Mennonite Church, **Tchayachy** Mennonite Church, and **Svistunovo** Mennonite Church.)

Grünfeld Mennonite Church comprised five villages: Grünfeld, Nikolaidorf, Alexandrovka, Rosenwald, and Tchernovka. The first elder was Jakob Gerbrandt (*q.v.*), who was originally elder at large. He was assisted by the ministers Isaak Löwen, Dietrich Epp, Peter P. Epp, and Martin von Kampen. Later were added Abram Block, Heinrich Unruh, and Heinrich Krahn. Jakob Gerbrandt was soon succeeded by Peter P. Epp as leader of the general congregation. The congregation did not have a church building, but worshiped in schoolhouses.

Kleefeld Mennonite Church served the following eight villages: Kleefeld, Shumanovka, Halbstadt, Alexanderkrone, Gnadenheim, Blumenort, Ebenfeld, and Hochstädt. The first leading minister was Abram Dück, who was succeeded by Cornelius Wiens (d. 1918) as elder. Wiens was succeeded by Jacob Harder, who emigrated to Canada. After him Johann Goossen became the leading minister. In 1918 a spacious, beautiful church was erected in Kleefeld. Other ministers who served the congregation were Jacob Kliewer, Wilhelm Hübert, Jacob Voth, and Dietrich Geddert.

Markovka Mennonite Church served the following eight villages: Markovka, Chortitza, Stepnoye, Golyenkoye, Grishkovka, Karatal, Dolinovka, and Suvorovka. The first leading minister was Jacob Enns; he was succeeded by David Bäcker, who was ordained elder. Other ministers of the congregation were Anton Löwen, Peter Enns, Isaak Wiebe, Franz Derksen, Jacob Spenst, David Heidebrecht, and Peter Konrad. In 1913 the congregation built a church in Markovka. In 1923 Jacob Nickel started a Jehovah's Witnesses group in this congregation.

Khoroshoye (Nikolayevka) Mennonite Church served four villages: Khoroshoye, Nikolayevka, Saratov, and Silberfeld. The first leader was Dietrich Görzen. He was assisted by the following ministers: Jacob Harder, Abram Penner, Johann Derksen, Johann Krüger, Peter Voth, Jacob Enns, Abram Wiebe, and Salomon Derksen. In 1924 the congregation built a church in Khoroshoye.

Gnadental Mennonite Church served three villages: Gnadental, Fernheim, and Sergeyevka. The first leading minister was Isaak J. Fast, who was assisted by Franz Harder, Abram Unruh, Cornelius Penner, and Peter Wiens. The congregation started the building of a church under the Soviet government, which was then prohibited. C.K.

Glyaden Mennonite Church served the following four villages: Lichtfelde, Ebenfeld, Ivanovka, and Sluchaynoye. The elder of this congregation was Jacob Warkentin, assisted by Jacob Boldt, Samuel Boldt, and David Harder, who became a communist. The congregation built a church in Lichtfelde

in 1920. At this place an Adventist group originated under the leadership of Peter Thiessen.

The Slavgorod Mennonite Church was unique in difficulties to be surmounted. The congregations had barely been organized and had barely overcome the first pioneer difficulties when World War I broke out, which ended with the Revolution of 1917 ushering in a civil war and finally the communistic regime. All the congregations, although they had been registered in Tomsk in 1912, had to be registered now under the new Soviet government in Omsk. The hardships and antireligious attitude of the government, together with the accompanying exile of ministers and the taxation of church property, resulted in the cessation by 1932 of all official religious and worship activities. A few church leaders had left for Canada; most had been exiled, and many perished in exile. Since the Slavgorod Mennonite settlement, unlike the settlements of the Ukraine, was not completely disrupted, religious activities have been resumed more readily since the death of Stalin (1953) than among some of the scattered Mennonites in other regions.

It has not become apparent to what extent the Slavgorod Mennonite settlement has benefited by the greater religious liberty which is noticeable throughout the Asiatic communities in which Mennonites live. However, great changes have taken place. A letter written by Margarete Koop, who is living in the Slavgorod settlement, states that she had not been able to attend any worship services for a number of years (published in *Menn. Rundschau,* Dec. 12, 1956). Franz Thiessen, of Blumenort, Slavgorod, writes that there was no preaching of the Gospel in 1931-55. Now many, including Thiessen, are starting to preach. Scarcity of Bibles and hymnals compels them to copy hymnals by hand (*Menn. Rundschau,* Oct. 10, 1956, p. 6). Another letter reports that many people have been converted and that some, of whom it was never expected, have started to preach the Gospel (*Bote,* Jan. 2, 1957, p. 7). The Baptist church of the city of Slavgorod (*q.v.*), which Klaus Mehnert visited in 1955, was attended by many Mennonites when there was no other possibility for Mennonite public services. The church did not yet have permission to enlarge its facilities, but in 1956 it received permission to have German preaching. A letter written by the daughter of Margarete Boldt, in Orloff, Slavgorod, states that Peter Voth is to serve as elder in the neighboring church which has just been opened (*Bote,* Jan. 25, 1956, p. 7 f.). Anna Stobbe of Ivanovka, Glyaden, Slavgorod, writes that many conversions are taking place and that a new Mennonite Brethren church has been organized (*Menn. Rundschau,* Dec. 12, 1956, p. 11). Such information indicates that general revival of religious life and the permission for Mennonites to meet even though they are not registered are also noticeable in the Slavgorod Mennonite settlement. C.K.

Gerhard Fast, *In den Steppen Sibiriens* (Rosthern, 1957); D. H. Epp, *Adressbüchlein* (Berdyansk, 1913); J. J. Hildebrand, *Sibirien* (Winnipeg, 1952); *Unser Blatt,* I, 45, 128, 279; II, 182, 208, 210, 277; III, 11-13, 15-16; Ernst Behrends, *Beata* (Heilbronn, 1935); see also bibliography under "Slavgorod Mennonite Settlement."

Slavgorod Mennonite Orphanage was organized in 1919, when Peter Löwen, of Halbstadt in Slavgorod Mennonite settlement (*q.v.*) of Siberia, placed his newly established home at the disposal of the settlement for the purpose of caring for the orphans of the community. The dedication took place in September 1919. Some 50 orphans had been accepted. Mr. and Mrs. Nikolai Friesen, of Gnadenheim, were the house parents, assisted by a Vollrat, of Germany. Jacob Derksen, of Schöntal, was the teacher. The Mennonite community was responsible for the support of the institution. Help for the workers was received from private sources and through the Mennonites of America. Of the two freight car loads of clothing which came from North America to Slavgorod, the orphanage received a considerable share. Soon the Communist Party caused difficulties. Under pressure of the Soviet government the orphanage dissolved and the children were distributed in families.   C.K.

Gerhard Fast, *In den Steppen Sibiriens* (Rosthern, 1957) 80.

Slavgorod Mennonite Settlement, also known as Barnaul (*q.v.*) Mennonite settlement, is located in the Kulundian Steppes between the Irtysh and the Ob rivers in West Siberia, a part of the USSR in the Altai Territory (formerly Tomsk). The settlement was at first called Barnaul, since this was the only city in the area at the time of the settlement in 1907. In 1911, when the city of Slavgorod was established ten miles from the settlement, the settlement took this name.

(1) *The Settlement.* When the government in 1906 announced the availability of land in the Kulundian Steppes, Mennonites became interested and sent representatives from the settlements of Zagradovka, Ufa, Samara, and Orenburg. In the Orenburg (*q.v.*) settlement Heinrich Neumann and a Hiebert took the initiative and called a meeting for Aug. 20, 1906, at which a committee of eight was elected. On September 20, Heinrich Krüger and Jakob B. Peters were delegated to investigate the Kulundian Steppes. In October the two delegates reported about their findings. At the end of April 1907 Krüger and Peters were sent again to Siberia for final arrangements. Here they met with the following representatives from Zagradovka: Franz Buller, J. D. Wiebe, Abraham Dück, Isaac Friesen, and Jakob B. Peters. The Davlekanovo Mennonites of Ufa also had investigated the settlement possibilities and had been in touch with others. Jakob A. Reimer met Stolypin (*q.v.*), who recommended the Barnaul area for settlement. When Franz Buller was in St. Petersburg in the interest of this matter, he was asked to investigate land along the Amur River. The representative from Samara was Heinrich Lohrenz. Jakob B. Peters of Orenburg, Jakob A. Reimer of Ufa, and Isaac Friesen and Abraham Dück of Zagradovka continued the trip to the Amur (*q.v.*) region to investigate land. Upon their return, Reimer and Peters stopped in Barnaul to make arrangements for settlement in the Kulundian Steppes near Barnaul.

Fifty-nine villages consisting of Mennonites from all the major settlements of European Russia were established in the Slavgorod settlement on some 162,000 acres (60,000 dessiatines). They were given a reduction in railroad fare to the place of settlement, were exempted from taxes for five years and from government services for three years, received a loan of 160 rubles and also a credit loan of 160 rubles, and the land free of charge. The beginnings were especially difficult because of the distance from the railroad. The nearest railroad stations and also the harbor of Pavlodar on the Irtysh River were 150 miles away. The settlers raised wheat, oats, and other grains. The winter set in early and lasted long, leaving a short season for raising the grains and harvesting them. Of the promised 160 rubles only 100 were actually paid out. The lumber for building had to be gotten from the royal forest about 70 miles away. It was hard to obtain even the essential food supplies such as flour until Mennonites established their own mills.

An outstanding leader of the pioneer days was the Oberschulze Jacob A. Reimer (*q.v.*), from Zagradovka. With the establishment of Slavgorod (*q.v.*) as a city and district, this also became a business and industrial center, which improved the conditions of the new settlement. The government representative was located here and supervised the establishment of the settlement. Stolypin (*q.v.*), the premier of Russia, paid a visit to the Mennonites in 1910, which helped the development of the settlement.

The surrounding population consisted to a large extent of descendants of former Czarist exiles known as Chaldony. This population was extremely hospitable and honest, and of great help to the Mennonites in the pioneer days. In addition to these there were also the descendants of religious exiles such as the Baptists. Ukrainians and other Germans had also settled in this territory. The administration of the settlement was located in Orloff (*q.v.*). In 1920 an additional administration district was established in Chortitza.

The original settlement consisted of 36 villages. Later additional border settlements were added consisting of three to five villages each. Thirty miles from Slavgorod, Fernheim, Sergeyevka, and Gnadental were established in 1910 with 38 farms each. In 1912 four more villages were established some 20 miles southeast of Slavgorod, viz., Nikolayevka, Silberfeld, Khoroshoye, and Saratov.

In 1908 the Glyaden (*q.v.*) or Lichtfelde settlement, with four villages, originated some 80 miles from Slavgorod, consisting of Lichtfelde, Ebenfeld, Ivanovka, and Sluchaynoye. Another settlement, which was a part of the Slavgorod area in 1912, became known as Pashnya (*q.v.*) and consisted of the five villages of Grigoryevka, Markovka, Ananyevka, Ekaterinovka, and Zhelanovka. The location was about 70 miles from Slavgorod. Another settlement was Tchayatchy, consisting of the three villages of Nikolayevka, Alexeyevka, and Tatyanovka. Some settlers from here went to the Amur (*q.v.*) area in 1924.

(2) *Agriculture and Industry.* The villages of the settlements were similar to those of the mother settlements in European Russia. Summer wheat was the predominant grain produced. The farms followed the four-field rotation system. Summer was

short and much work had to be done during this
time. Products were very cheap during the first
years because of lack of markets and transportation
facilities. Farm machinery had been brought along
from the old settlements. The first industrial undertakings were the common blacksmith shop and
carpenter shops in which the farm implements were
repaired. J. Walde, Lichtfelde, had a wagon and
fanning mill factory. Windmills and mills driven
by horsepower were established in order to produce
the necessary flour. In 1911 Abram Tjart erected a
steam flour mill for $67,500, which was nationalized
in 1923 by the Soviet government. Jacob Martens
erected another steam flour mill in Alexandrovka.

Some of the villages had grocery stores and other
business enterprises: Franz Dyck in Orloff, Johann
Abrahams in Rosenwald, Jacob Dyck in Slavgorod.
Other businesses, such as farm machinery sales and
mills, were established in Slavgorod. A Danish-
Siberian company had numerous stores in the Mennonite and surrounding settlements. Co-operative
stores, dairies, seed stores, etc., became common,
particularly after the Revolution. The dairy co-
operatives enabled the Mennonites to sell butter at a
favorable price. In 1916 the Slavgorod Mennonite
settlement was connected with the Trans-Siberian
railroad by a branch line leading from Tatarskaya
to Slavgorod, which was extended later to the city
of Pavlodar (*q.v.*). This was a great improvement
for the settlement.

The Slavgorod settlement built a hospital in Orloff village in 1911, in which Gerhard Fast served
for a while as doctor. A number of midwives did
significant work; e.g., Mrs. David Thielmann, Mrs.
Jacob Voth, and Mrs. Franz Derksen. In 1919 the
Slavgorod orphanage (*q.v.*) was opened for 50
orphans in the village of Halbstadt. In addition to
the many elementary schools there was a Zentralschule in Orloff and later for a while in Grishkovka
and Schöntal.

The judges of the volost court were Johann Fast
and Andreas B. Siebert. The first secretary was
Peter Renpenning. In 1916 the second volost was
established in Chortitza so that the settlement was
under two separate administrations. The first Oberschulze of Chortitza was Jacob Nickel, and the first
secretary Peter Töws. In 1922 the two administrations of Orloff and Chortitza were merged with the
neighboring Russian administrations. Thus the Mennonite self-administration came to a close. In 1927
a district government (*rayon*) was established in
Halbstadt, which included all German settlers. Later
this was discontinued.

(3) *From World War I to World War II.* During
World War I the young men of the Slavgorod settlement were drafted to serve in forestry and as
hospital workers on the Caucasian front. In September 1916, 161 of the 200 men aged 42-43 were drafted
and went to the Caucasus to serve in offices and hospitals. Some died of typhoid fever. The majority
of the drafted men did forestry service. After the
Revolution in 1917 most of the young men returned.
Siberia was a battlefield between the White army
led by Kolchak and the Red army, ending with a
victory of the latter. Some Mennonites were drafted
into the White army.

After the Revolution the German settlers organized a Slavgorod section of the Union of German
Citizens of Russia (*Verband deutscher Bürger
Russlands*), of which Peter A. Friesen was the chairman. At this time there were some hopes that Siberia would become an independent country in
which the German element would have its own
state. When the Soviets gained power the Union
was dissolved.

In 1923 a section of the All-Russischer Mennonitischer Landwirtschaftlicher Verein (AMLV) was
organized in Slavgorod with its headquarters in Orloff. As in European Russia the purpose was to promote agriculture and cultural objectives in general.
The report made to the AMLV by H. Friesen, a
representative of the Slavgorod Mennonite settlement, on Feb. 12, 1922, stated that the total Mennonite population in December 1921 was 14,890; the
city of Slavgorod had 254 Mennonites in a total German population of 30,500, consisting of Mennonites,
Lutherans, and Catholics. He pointed out that in
1921 they had been able to send food to the Mennonite settlements of Samara and the Volga district
to help the starving. By 1922 the situation had
changed considerably; because of the heavy requisi-
tion of grain no seed wheat was left for 1923. American Mennonite Relief furnished aid. However, P. F.
Froese's report given in August 1924 on the extended trip he made with other representatives of the
AMLV, including Alvin J. Miller of the American
Mennonite Relief, through the Mennonite settlements of Siberia and particularly Slavgorod, says
that there was actual starvation, lack of clothing and
bedding, machinery, horses, and cattle. His report,
although not hopeless, was extremely gloomy, and
indicated dire need.

Some of this help was furnished when W. P. Neufeld and M. B. Fast of Reedley, Cal., collected clothing and sent it to Siberia via Vladivostok. The
poverty-stricken non-Mennonite population was also
helped by the American Mennonite Relief, through
seed loans, wool, flax, and cotton, for the processing
of which spinning wheels and looms were furnished
(Unruh, 22). Decline and disruption was caused by
the Revolution of 1917 and the ensuing civil war,
crop failures, and the excessive expropriation of food
stocks by the Soviet government.

The American representative, Alvin Miller, and
the president of the Russian Verband, Peter F.
Froese, attended a meeting held in the Slavgorod
settlement in 1924. The seat of the organization was
transferred to Slavgorod. Gradually the Slavgorod
Mennonites overcame the extreme crisis. In 1925
P. B. Epp reported that gradual improvement was
noticeable. Particularly the co-operative organized
in 1923 and the stimulation which came through
the branch office and headquarters of the AMLV in
Moscow did much to improve economic conditions.
The settlement co-operated in the selective seed program and the establishment of co-operative dairy
organizations. By 1925 the AMLV had 960 members in this area. Froese, who attended the local
meeting in 1926, could report more optimistically
about the conditions. Epp reported that a new spirit
had seized the settlers; buildings were in progress
and improvements and repairs were noticeable ev-

erywhere. J. Epp found 26 Fordson tractors acquired by the co-operatives. He still found some signs of "America fever," but only a few had left for Canada. In the 1930's this revival of personal initiative came to a close and a complete and radical collectivization program was inaugurated similar to that found everywhere in the Soviet Union.

According to a report given by H. Friesen, a representative of the Mennonites of the Slavgorod settlement in 1922, this settlement was divided into seven rayons (districts) in 1917. The population was expected to deliver grain to the government regardless of what had been harvested. A general retrogression was noticeable, as is evidenced in the following table: in 1920 the settlement had 3,005 horses, 1,530 cows, 1,702 sheep, and 710 pigs; in 1927 there were only 1,752 horses, 1,205 cows, 1,600 sheep, and 515 pigs. Similar retrogression was reported in farm machinery. For education the barest necessities were not available.

Confiscation, inflation, and various other policies of the newly established Soviet government, including the NEP, followed in rapid succession in Siberia. The NEP period was characterized by an increase in dairy organizations. However, by 1922 many were considering emigration to America. Two delegates were sent to Moscow in 1922 to inquire about the possibilities. Peter B. Epp, while attending a meeting of the Verband in Moscow in 1925, and others went to the GPU in the Lubyanka office to get information about emigration possibilities. Some Slavgorod families left in 1925. The following year a larger number followed. A committee was organized and an English physician came to examine the emigrants. Among those leaving were Elder Kornelius A. Harder and Peter B. Epp. The emigrants, which did not exceed 200, went to Canada and Mexico. (NEP = New Economic Policy).

Meanwhile Stalin introduced his five-year plan and with it sealed the fate of the farmers. Since the conditions became more difficult, a few farmers went to Moscow in 1929 hoping to obtain permission to leave the country. When they succeeded, large numbers followed them. Some received permission to leave, but the vast majority were returned in freight trains. Those who had sold everything had very difficult times. Most of those who emigrated finally got to Paraguay and settled in the Fernheim (q.v.) colony.

In 1930-31 all the villages were organized as collective farms. Many farmers and families were exiled, and great numbers perished. A number of the European Russian Mennonites who were exiled to Siberia under Stalin's rule, or were evacuated eastward in 1941 when the Germans occupied the Ukraine, doubtless found their way to the Slavgorod settlement after completing their term as exiles. Letters received by relatives in America indicate this.

A vivid description of conditions among the Slavgorod Mennonites is given by Klaus Mehnert in the article "Deutsche—vom Sturme verweht" (*Der Bote*, issues of Sept. 5, 12, 19, 1956). He visited the Mennonites through the publication office of the paper *Arbeit* in Barnaul. He judges that in the Kulundian Steppes there are some 200,000 to 250,000 people of German background. He had an extensive visit on the collective farm composed of five Mennonite villages consisting of 289 families with 1,025 persons. The 571 workers are divided into three groups, one taking care of the farming, the second the animals, and the third the buildings, homes, sheds, etc. A considerable amount of virgin land had been added to the collective farm. The farm had 514 cows, 356 pigs, and 512 sheep, and had been distinguished at the Moscow agricultural exhibition. For 1955 the monthly wages of an individual were 257 rubles and 110 kilograms of grains.

Mehnert found that the children were unable to understand High German, but they still spoke "Mennonitisch" (Plattdeutsch). The school was conducted in the Russian language. Recently the area was given permission to use the German language but decided to stay with the Russian. From his German point of view, the writer stated that he had never found a German settlement in all his journeys throughout the world which depressed his heart more than that of Slavgorod. It was not so much the poverty as the general despondency and apathy of the people, who no longer knew whence they had come and whither they were going. (Regarding the latest developments in the realm of religious life, see **Slavgorod** Mennonite Church.)

C.K.

Gerhard Fast, *In den Steppen Sibiriens* (Rosthern, 1957) 27; *Der Praktische Landwirt*, 1925-27; A. A. Friesen Collection, BeCL; J. J. Hildebrand, *Sibirien* (Winnipeg, 1952); Ernst Behrends, *Beata* (Heilbronn, 1935); P. C. Hiebert and O. O. Miller, *Feeding the Hungry. Russia Famine 1919-1925* (Scottdale, 1929) 313 ff., 390; A. Loewen and A. Friesen, *Die Flucht über den Amur* (Steinbach, 1946); H. Anger, *Die Deutschen in Sibirien. Reise durch die deutschen Dörfer Westsibiriens* (Berlin and Königsberg, 1930); Jakob Quiring, *Die Mundart von Chortitza in Süd-Russland* (Munich, 1928) 39-41; *Unser Blatt* I, 45, 128, 279; II, 182, 208, 210, 277; III, 11-13, 15-16; M. B. Fast, *Geschichtlicher Bericht wie die Mennoniten Nordamerikas ihren armen Glaubensgenossen in Russland jetzt und früher geholfen haben* (Reedley, 1919); H. Unruh, "Die Mennonitischen Ansiedlungen in West-Sibirien," *Bundesbote-Kalender*, 1913; John D. Unruh, *In the Name of Christ* (Scottdale, 1952).

Slavgorod Mennonite Volost (administration) came into being with the establishment of the Barnaul (Slavgorod) Mennonite settlement (*q.v.*) in the Kulundian Steppes of Siberia. The seat of the administration (volost) was in Orloff. The first Oberschulze was Jacob A. Reimer (*q.v.*), who was followed by Abram Koop, Abram Wittenberg, Abram Fast, Gerhard Klippenstein, Abram Töws, and Heinrich Friesen. Reimer did much for the establishment of the settlement. The first secretary was Peter Renpenning. The Oberschulze received 300 rubles and the secretary 500 rubles per year. In connection with the volost there was a court which met a number of times monthly to take action on minor offenses. Judges were Johann Fast and Andreas B. Siebert. The volost building at Orloff had a small jail.

In 1916 the Slavgorod settlement was divided and a second administration was created in the Chortitza Volost. Nine villages belonged to this district. No special building was erected. The first Oberschulze was Jacob Nickel, and the secretary was Johann

Löwen, who was succeeded by Peter Töws, H. Philippsen, and Helen Friesen. In 1920 Peter B. Epp became the Oberschulze of the Chortitza Volost, later succeeded by Heinrich Goossen and Isaak Derksen.

In 1923 the two Mennonite volosts of Orloff and Chortitza were merged with the Russian volosts of that region. The Orloff administration was transferred to the Russian volost of Znamenka and the Chortitza administration to the volost of Slavgorod. This brought the Mennonite self-administration to a close. In 1927 the German settlements of the Slavgorod region were merged into one district (*rayon*) with the seat of the administration at Halbstadt. All Mennonite, Lutheran, and Catholic German villages were under this administration, which was dominated by Communists, who received their directives from the Communist Party. In the 1930's this administration was dissolved and the pattern of administration established in 1923 was revived.

After the Revolution of 1917, when efforts were made to establish an independent Siberian government in Tomsk, the Mennonites also sent their representative, Franz F. Froese, to the Siberian Duma. After a defeat of the Communists in 1918, and a revival of the Duma with the help of the Czechoslovaks, Mennonites were again represented by such men as Franz F. Froese, Johann Penner, Peter Boldt, and Heinrich Boldt. Kolchak, the leader of the White army, dissolved the Duma.

The Mennonites also participated in the establishment of the *Verband Deutscher Bürger Russlands* (Union of German Citizens of Russia) in 1917, which aimed to establish an autonomous Siberia with an independent German state. Mennonite representatives in this Union were Peter A. Friesen, Franz F. Froese, H. H. Wiens, and others. This organization aimed to prepare a legal pattern for a better future of the settlement.

Another organization which played a significant role was a Slavgorod section of the *All-Russischer Mennonitischer Landwirtschaftlicher Verein* (*q.v.*), of which Heinrich Friesen, Johann Görz, and Abram Friesen were the first officers. After the permanent establishment of the Soviet government, Mennonite self-administration and organizations in any form disappeared. (See also **Slavgorod Mennonite Settlement.**)   C.K.

Gerhard Fast, *In den Steppen Sibiriens* (Rosthern, 1957) 87.

Slavgorod Mennonite Zentralschule was first established in Slavgorod, Siberia, in 1917 through the Deutscher Verein with Franz F. Fröse, Aron Rempel, and Miss Neumann as teachers. This school operated only one year. In 1918 the Mennonite Church established a Zentralschule in Orloff with Heinrich D. Willms and Anna A. Chechulin as teachers. The Mennonite Brethren established a Zentralschule in Schöntal with Gerhard Fast and Olga G. Pobedimov as teachers. After the first year the schools were merged and transferred to Gnadenheim. Heinrich D. Willms and Eugenia G. Pobedimov served as teachers. In 1921-22 Jacob Wedel taught German and Bible. Wassily S. Modin and his son and daughter were also on the teaching staff. After this the school was closed.

Sponsored by Heinrich Wiens, of Grishkovka, the proprietor of a mill, Anton A. Löwen (*q.v.*) started a Zentralschule in 1918. Löwen's death in 1921 was soon followed by the death of the sponsor, and the school was discontinued. By this time it had become impossible to maintain a religious secondary school in Siberia.   C.K.

Gerhard Fast, *In den Steppen Sibiriens* (Rosthern, 1957) 87.

Slee, Jacobus Cornelis van (1841-1929), a Dutch Reformed pastor, whose last term of service, at Deventer 1891-1913, is of interest for Mennonite history, was the author of *De Rijnsburger Collegianten* (Haarlem, 1895), a treatise which was awarded the Teyler (*q.v.*) Foundation gold medal. Van Slee received an honorary Th.D. degree from the University of Groningen in 1914.   vDZ.

Sleep of the Soul, the doctrine that the human soul passes into a state of sleep or dormancy at death, from which it will not awake until Christ appears for judgment. Many of its adherents understood it to be a state of forgetfulness, a sort of dream life without consciousness. Thus the ancient Greeks had the concept that the departed would drink of the stream of forgetfulness (Lethe), which obliterated all memory of their past life. Similar views are found in Christendom. Paulsen, for instance, says, "The imagery of the soul's sleep expresses the nature of the interim state of the soul; the idea that the soul sleeps is substantiated by those who have been roused from the dead, inasmuch as the awakened ones can give no information about death, as would be the case if they had remained fully conscious." Others, on the other hand, understand the sleep of the soul to be a sleep with consciousness (Schleiermacher in *Morgenstern*, No. 5, p. 98). Of Luther it is said that he "imagined the fathers and likewise the pious dead to be in a state of sleep, which was peaceful for them, because they were preserved and held in the faith in God's Word as in a womb" (Loofs, 779, note 8).

Calvin (*q.v.*), in his *Psychopannychia* (1544), counts the Anabaptists as one of the groups believing in the sleep of the soul, which is, however, obviously an error (see especially Hulshof, 188, note 2). Also Friedrich Spannheim (*q.v.*) asserts that the Mennonites held the belief in the sleep of the soul; the assertion is vigorously refuted by Maatschoen. Karl Müller, the church historian of Tübingen, thought the doctrine was definitely held by the Anabaptists in the Romance countries. The fact is, there is no convincing evidence that such a belief was held by the Anabaptists or Mennonites anywhere.   NEFF.

A. Hulshof, *Geschiedenis van de Doopsgezinde te Straatsburg van 1525 tot 1557* (Amsterdam); Fr. Loofs, *Leitfaden zur Dogmengeschichte* (1906); Schijn-Maatschoen, *Geschiedenis* III; Karl Müller, *Kirchengeschichte* II (Tübingen, 1919) 121, *passim*; John Calvin, *Psychopannychia* (1544, new edition by Walter Zimmerli, Leipzig, 1932, copies of both editions in GCL); *ML* IV.

Sleeping Preacher Churches, a term sometimes applied to those Amish Mennonite churches which had their origins about 1907 in the teachings and influence of John D. Kauffman (*q.v.*), the Amish bishop who preached full sermons while apparently in a trance. In 1957 six congregations with a total membership of 540 had this background, although several of these churches have deviated considerably from the practices of their first congregations. Sermons in those churches most loyal to the original pattern make frequent mention of Kauffman's teachings, referring to his statements as the preaching of the Spirit, so that one hears the statement, "The Spirit taught us . . . ." His biographer, Pius Hostetler, explains that they think of his discourses as "Spirit preaching," i.e., actually the words of the Holy Spirit. What Kauffman taught in his periods of trance is therefore regarded as an authoritative interpretation of the Bible and as completely binding upon his followers. Thus Kauffman's teaching that men below 30 years of age should not be ordained to preach would be regarded as authoritative in those churches adhering most strictly to their early standards.

Originally these congregations had only German services, and no Sunday schools, prayer meetings, evangelistic meetings, nor youth and women's organizations. Their first congregation, Mt. Hermon (q.v.) near Shelbyville, Ill., now has English services and little is said about "Spirit preaching," which is also true of the Linn Township (q.v.) congregation. The third congregation in Illinois, Fairfield (q.v.), which broke away from the Mt. Hermon church in 1933 and was established in Henry County in 1938, is perhaps the most conservative of all, using German in its services and emphasizing Kauffman's "Spirit preaching." It has no fellowship with the Linn Township church but recently has had with the Mt. Hermon congregation. The Harrisburg (q.v.), Ore., congregation no longer considers itself a Sleeping Preacher church, although some of its members are related to those in the Illinois congregations and there is social fellowship between them. With its English services, Sunday school, prayer meetings, sewing circle, young people's meeting, Bible school, and missionary outreach, it is following the pattern of the Conservative Mennonite Conference, although not affiliated with this body. A split in this congregation led to the establishment of a more conservative group, the Pleasant Valley (q.v.) Church at Yoncalla, Ore. This congregation in turn was divided when its most conservative faction moved to Allendale, S.C., establishing the unorganized congregation of Pilgrims (q.v.), which is attempting to establish a "Spirit preaching" church similar to the Fairfield congregation. M.G.

Sleeswijk, a Dutch Mennonite family, formerly found in the province of Friesland. Frederick Samuelsz (c1605-April 22, 1680), from 1668 calling himself Sleeswij(c)k, was a Mennonite preacher at Harlingen; he had a yarn and linen shop, and was also engaged in a shipping ring; he was probably well-to-do. He married Antie Salomons, whose father, Salomon Jansz Buylaert, had in his youth immigrated with his parents from Gent, Flanders. His son Sicke (Sixtus) Sleeswyck (b. 1644 at Harlingen, d. 1705 at Workum), married to Catalina Jans Mesdag(h), of Alkmaar, was a physician at Workum, whose son Gillis (Jillis) (d. 1743) was a baker at Workum, and whose grandson Rienk (d. 1789) was

a merchant at Workum. They were all Mennonites, but some branches of the Sleeswijk family left the Mennonite Church in the 18th century. vDZ.

Jierboekje fan it Genealogysk Wurkforban (Ljouwert, 1955) 64.

Sleupner, Dominicus, a Lutheran preacher at the church of St. Sebald in Nürnberg, a sharp opponent of the Anabaptists. (*TA Bayern* II, 259; *ML* IV.)

Sleutel, a former Mennonite family at Hoorn, Dutch province of North Holland, descended from Elder Jan Willems (*q.v.,* d. 1588), of Hoorn, who had nine children. The oldest of them was Pieter Jansz Lioren (*q.v.*); Jacob Fransz (1608-71), a grandson of Jan Willems, took the family name of Sleutel. He joined the (Old) Frisian congregation at Hoorn, of which Pieter Jansz Twisck (*q.v.*) was the elder. Jacob Sleutel wrote a number of hymns found in Claes Stapel's *Lusthof des Gemoeds.* His sister Aechtjen (Aagtje) was married to Willem Maartens Seylemaker (*q.v.*); their children usually also took the family name of Sleutel. Among them was Jan Willems Sleutel (1654-93), who in 1678 was appointed preacher (later elder) of the Frisian congregation of Hoorn; the elder of the congregation was Pieter Jans Twisck Jr., who was conservative and ambitious like his grandfather. Jan Willems Sleutel, being more progressive and mild in the practice of ban and avoidance, became involved in trouble with Elder Twisck, and in 1687 withdrew, in the next year however serving again. In 1690 a schism arose and Twisck with about thirty members left the main body, forming the "Plempsche" (*q.v.*) congregation. Shortly before his death Jan Willems Sleutel succeeded in merging the Frisian and the Flemish congregations at Hoorn. vDZ.

DB 1867, 51-90; *Inv. Arch. Amst.* II, 2, Nos. 105, 107; *N.N.B.Wb.* I, 1476.

Sleyden (Sleiden), **van (der),** a Dutch Mennonite family, formerly living at Leiden and Rotterdam, where they were members and often deacons of the Flemish congregations. Isaack Leensz van Sleyden was a deacon of the Leiden Flemish church in 1683-87, as was his brother Samuel from 1689. Their brother Laurens at the same time took part in the Collegiant (*q.v.*) movement, as did also most members of the Rotterdam branch of this family, e.g., Anthony van Sleyden, the son of Barend van Sleyden, and Barendina Bredenburg. The Rotterdam van Sleydens were outstanding merchants (wine, textiles). Both the Leiden and Rotterdam branches died out in the 19th century. (Church records of Leiden and Rotterdam.) vDZ.

Slocum (Neb.) Amish Mennonite Church: see **Pleasant Hill.**

Slotel, Die, van dat Secreet des Nachtmaels (The Key to the Mystery of the Communion) is an important treatise in the Dutch language on the doctrine of the communion, both on the Last Supper of Jesus with His disciples and on the communion services as observed in the Christian churches. The author combats the doctrine of transubstantiation as taught by the Roman Catholic Church: the words of Christ, "This is my body," and "This is my blood," do not mean that bread and wine really became His flesh and blood, but that they represented His flesh and blood. Again and again the author emphasizes that "those who go to the communion table to obtain forgiveness of sin" have "a blind doctrine." He also attacks Luther's doctrine of consubstantiation.

Then the author broadly presents his own view: The Christian communion is an analogy to the Jewish Passover. It was not the eating of the Pascal lamb that saved them, nor does the eating of the bread in the communion service redeem Christians. The Jews ate their Passover with thankful hearts that they were freed from the Egyptian slavery; in the same way the Christians eat the bread in gratitude for release from the power of sin and from death and hell. During the first eating of the Passover the Jews in Egypt had not yet actually been liberated, but they praised God for His promise, which would surely be realized. In the same way the disciples of Christ praised God in joyful thankfulness, because they believed in the promise of God, then not yet fulfilled. God's promise was fulfilled at Calvary's cross. Therefore the believers should meet and hold their Lord's Supper in joyful gratitude; "The spirit of the heart must eat and not only the mouth." The author attacks the views of Carlstadt (q.v.) and Campanus (q.v.), who believed that communion services were of little value.

The author also deals with the question of who should be called to the communion services and who is allowed to eat the bread and to drink the wine. In Israel, he says, only those were admitted to the Passover lamb who bore the token of circumcision. Among the Christians only those should approach the communion who are "inwardly circumcised, i.e., who believe in Christ and who are baptized." It is not clear, however, whether the author means here baptized by water or by the Holy Ghost. But one thing is evident: all those, who are still living according to the flesh, are not allowed to draw near to the table of Christ. The communion should be held in the congregation of believers, which is identical with the body of Christ. Those who wish to take part in the communion must be "alive" (i.e., faithful), not "sick" (i.e., doubting the grace of God). They must be "hungry" (i.e., desiring to proclaim the glory of God) and "thirsty" (i.e., longing for salvation).

There is not much uncertainty as to the author of *Die Slotel van dat Secreet des Nachtmaels.* Though the treatise is anonymous, a number of old witnesses, e.g., Klopreis (q.v.) and de Zuttere (q.v.), have ascribed it to Henric Rol (q.v.). Samuel Cramer believes it to have been written between 1531 and Nov. 8, 1533. The first and second editions have been lost; a third edition appeared without date about 1563. This edition, also containing *Eyne rechte Bedijnckung hoe dat Lichaem Christi van onsen lichaem tho onder-scheyden isz,* probably by the same author, was edited by Pieter de Zuttere (Petrus Overd'hage, q.v.). It was republished from this third edition, copies of which are very rare, in *Bibliotheca Reformatoria Neerlandica* V (The Hague, 1909) and provided with introduction and notes by Samuel Cramer. vDZ.
36

BRN V, 1-94; C. A. Cornelius, *Geschichte des Münsterischen Aufruhrs* II (Münster, 1860) 163 ff.; Chr. Sepp, *Kerkhistorische Studien* (1885) 1-90.

Sloten (Slooten), a town in the Dutch province of Friesland (1947 pop. 711; 20 Mennonites), formerly the seat of a Mennonite congregation. This congregation was founded in the 16th century, likely by the activity of Elder Leenaert Bouwens (q.v.), who between 1551 and 1582 repeatedly visited Sloten, baptizing 59 or perhaps 62 persons, a number of whom may, however, have lived in surrounding villages. Of the history of the Sloten congregation there is not much information. In later times it belonged to the more progressive Waterlander branch. In 1695 it numbered about 50 members (there were 47 members who did not receive financial support from the deacons). In the *Naamlijst* of 1731 it is called Sloten and Lemmer, but this is not quite correct; the Lemmer (q.v.) and Sloten congregations did not merge until 1748. In 1731 there were three lay preachers; one of them was Ruurd Douwesz Kooyman, who served 1720-65. After 1781 the pulpit remained vacant. The *Naamlijst* states that the Sloten congregation was united with that of neighboring Legemeer (q.v.); but this union did not save the congregation, for in 1789 the Sloten congregation was dissolved, the few remaining members joining the Balk congregation. vDZ.

Blaupot t. C., *Friesland,* 89, 188, 193, 306; H. J. Busé, *De verdwenen Doopsgezinde gemeenten in Friesland* (reprint from *De Vrije Fries* XXII, 14 f.); *DB* 1895, 12, 20; *Naamlijst* 1808, 88.

Slovakia, formerly the northwestern section of the Kingdom of Hungary (called Upper Hungary), now part of the Czechoslovakian Republic. It is situated between Danube in the south and the Carpathian Mountains in the north, between the March River on the west (Austrian border) and the Gran River on the east; it is rich in mineral ores (gold, silver, etc.) and warm springs. Its capital is Bratislava (German *Pressburg,* Magyar *Pozsony*). It was here that the kings of Hungary (Hapsburgs) were crowned and the Diet met until, after the defeat of the Turks (c1700), the center shifted back to Budapest.

In the 16th-18th centuries this country was occupied mainly by manorial lords called "magnates," most of whom were of the Hungarian Reformed faith (Calvinists), strongly independent of the Hapsburg government in Vienna. They were organized under a Palatine or viceroy who represented the king in Hungary but frequently refused to accept orders from Vienna. The country bordered on that part of Hungary which was occupied by the Turks (1526-1700), and consequently suffered much by the numerous Turkish invasions, although the more remote mountain areas were less molested than the area along the Danube road. The lords were for the most part as tolerant as the Moravian nobles and were glad to receive Anabaptists as their tenants or "neighbors" (the Anabaptists always tried to buy land rather than to rent it; everywhere they were independent and free).

From 1546 on Slovakia was a refuge for Moravian Anabaptists (Hutterites), although the number of Bruderhofs in Slovakia never exceeded 14 or 15, as compared with the 80 to 90 in adjacent Moravia. (*ME* II, 859 f., lists all the known Bruderhofs of Slovakia, and gives a map showing their locations.) In the 18th century, when the Hapsburgs eventually gained the upper hand also in Hungary (the Turks had been driven out by Prince Eugene of Savoy, the imperial generalissimo, by 1700) and the independence of the Hungarian magnates was broken, the Jesuits entered this former Calvinistic sanctuary and the Anabaptists were doomed. Those who accepted Catholicism could remain (see **Habaner**); the rest had to leave as best they could, migrating to the Ukraine (see **Hutterites**).

The story of the Slovakian settlements of the Hutterites is closely related to their story in Moravia (*q.v.*) and is in part understandable only in the total context. Though somewhat more sheltered than Moravia, the new Bruderhofs did not produce any great spiritual leader; thus Slovakia became a place for the preservation of the faith and ways of the fathers rather than aggressive new ideas. All the outstanding Hutterite personalities are intimately connected with Moravia, the only exception being the great Vorsteher Andreas Ehrenpreis (*q.v.*), active in 1630-62. He could be called "the second founder of the brotherhood" inasmuch as the Hutterites of today are to a much greater extent Ehrenpreis's people than Hutter's people.

In 1546 Sobotiste (German, *Freischütz*), in the northern part near the Moravian border, became the first settlement of the Hutterites in Slovakia; some of the old houses still exist at this place, though the unique clock tower dates back only to 1753. The brethren were invited by the lord Franz Niary of Bedek, lord of the Branc castle (in the *Geschicht-Buch* phonetically written as Bränitsch, Brainisch, or Präntsch; Magyar, *Berencs*), but the area belonged actually to not less than thirteen manorial estates, and it was certainly not easy to satisfy all these self-willed lords. Great hardship began in 1548 when King Ferdinand (*q.v.*) prevailed upon the lords, at least temporarily, to expel the Anabaptists. Now they had to find other places, wandering from Slovakia to Austria, thence to Moravia and back again to Slovakia. At times they had to live in underground tunnels (called Lochy, *q.v.*). But by 1554 the Hapsburgs had so many other tasks on hand that they had to leave Slovakia (then a part of Hungary) to itself again. Thus the "Golden Period" set in—1554-1600. In 1588 the lord of Gross-Schützen (Slovakian, *Velke Levary*), Hans Bernhard von Lembach, imperial cupbearer, invited the brethren to start a Bruderhof on his estate, not too far from the Austrian border, and gave them a charter (*Stiftungsbrief*, the text of which Zieglschmid published in 1940) containing all the needed protection.

But peace did not last. In 1605 Turkish and Hungarian satellite armies (under Bocskay) invaded the area, killing and plundering everywhere. The Sobotiste Bruderhof remained uninhabited for eight years; then in 1613 the lords urged a resettlement, giving the brethren a new and stronger charter (*Hausbrief*, excerpts of which are given in Beck, 364 note), which was renewed once again in 1640 (text in *Klein-Geschichtsbuch*, 128 note). The Brethren

were granted full liberty of conscience, the right to withdraw from the land at their pleasure, but with financial compensation, freedom from payment of taxes and tithes, compulsory labor only every third year, etc. The lords were to buy all their wares, yet at reduced prices; otherwise the brethren were free to carry on their trades as they wished. It was also understood that the Brethren would not take refuge in litigation, which meant that friendly arbitration should replace manorial court procedure.

In 1621 an exodus took place, in which some of the Hutterites in Slovakia moved on to Transylvania, invited by the prince of that land, Bethlen Gabor, who at that time lived under the suzerainty of the Turkish sultan. On April 1, 1621, the preacher Franz Walter (see **Walter** family, the oldest living Anabaptist family on record) together with 185 persons moved to Alwinz (*q.v.*), where the settlement soon made remarkable progress, perhaps due to Walter's aggressive leadership (see **Transylvania**). The Thirty Years' War (1618-48), though fought mainly on German and Bohemian land, was strongly felt also in Slovakia. In 1626-27 great sufferings are reported all over the country, caused mainly by marauding soldiers. Since Moravia had expelled all its Anabaptists without exception by 1622 (though Loserth claims that hidden nests of Hutterites were found in Moravia as late as 1650), newcomers to near-by Slovakia swelled the Anabaptist settlements. The Archbishop of Esztergom (Gran) tried to stem this tide by a sharp letter to the royal court in Vienna (1629, text in Beck, 436), complaining among other things about the success which these simple Christians had among the rural population of the area. But since the Catholic clergy had but little power in this part of the Hapsburg land, the Brethren remained by and large unmolested.

Time of Andreas Ehrenpreis (1630-62). Concerning this period there is much material in both the Great and the Small Chronicle of the Hutterites. Surprisingly it is also described in the great contemporary novel *Simplicissimus* by Grimmelshausen (*q.v.*), who draws a glowing picture of these people, their peace, thrift, and inner happiness; in short, he confesses that, were it not for their faith, he would not hesitate to join their community. In 1633, an unpleasant incident happened in Sobotiste, when Brethren used brute force to prevent the taking away of horses by a haughty manorial lord. Much misery followed, but what really matters is a model ordinance by Ehrenpreis in 1633 concerning the nonresistant attitude of a genuine Christian, even if that should involve loss of property (*Klein-Geschichtsbuch*, 168-72, translated by Friedmann in *MQR*, 1951). As far as Hutterites are concerned this was the only known case of "self-defense" ever recorded. Ehrenpreis's strong leadership became noticeable at once. In 1639 when he was elected Vorsteher, he at once set about reviving and amplifying the old regulations of the church, called *Gemeindeordnungen* (*q.v.*). A large handwritten book (codex), most likely written by Ehrenpreis himself, has been preserved (now in Esztergom, *q.v.*) in which all these ordinances are collected and supplemented. The *Klein-Geschichtsbuch* (519-32) also contains at least one of these ordinances (of 1651), all of which greatly strengthened the inner discipline of the now rather static brotherhood.

Not insignificant was also the attention given to the medical needs of the group: there were a number of excellent barber-surgeons and even a physician among the Brethren during this period, one of these men practicing in the mineral bath of Trenchin-Teplice. A medical codex of that time has also been preserved. Another characteristic feature of the Ehrenpreis period was the new custom of writing down the sermons for all the services throughout the year and for special occasions (see **Sermons, Hutterite**). Henceforth sermons were read, and the preacher who dared to extemporize a new sermon was frowned upon. The Bruderhof at Kesselsdorf (*q.v.*) was apparently a particular center of such sermon writing, and the brother Küntsche (*q.v.*) seems to have been the most productive of all these sermon writers. Some Ehrenpreis sermons, written with pencil in small notebooks, are still preserved by the brethren in Canada; in fact the entire collection of 300-500 sermons of the Ehrenpreis era has been copied and recopied up to the present and represents a most influential element in present-day Hutterianism.

It was also under Ehrenpreis that the last attempts were made at mission work in foreign lands. Brethren were sent to Danzig on the Baltic Sea where contacts were made with a Socinian group. One of this group, Dr. Daniel Zwicker (*q.v.*), a physician by profession and a humanist, even came down to Slovakia in the early 1650's to see for himself what the Anabaptist life was like. Eventually he joined the group (though with some mental reservations), only to leave soon again for Danzig, giving up his pledge and other ties.

Since the Brethren were not permitted to start new settlments in Slovakia, they experimented with a new Bruderhof in Germany, setting up a small unit in Mannheim (*q.v.*) in 1654, which however never showed much inner life and was soon abandoned, most likely due to lack of leadership (the charter of the Hof in Beck, 492).

In 1650 Ehrenpreis put together for the last time all the essentials of the ancient Hutterite faith in a booklet (printed in 1652) entitled, *Ein Sendbrief . . . brüderliche Liebe . . . betreffend*. One more positive event of this period deserves mention. When Leopold I became Emperor of the Holy Roman Empire in 1657 and at the same time King of Hungary (though only of a rump of that realm), he showed a certain willingness to protect even his non-Catholic subjects. The fervor of the Counter Reformation (*q.v.*) and of the Thirty Years' War was over, and peace and prosperity were at this time of prime importance for Austria's recovery. Thus, on Jan. 29, 1659, Leopold issued an Imperial Privilege which specifically placed the Hutterites under royal protection, "that all brethren should receive protection (*Schutz und Schirm*) against violence and persecution" (Beck, 496; see **Leopold I**). This Privilege covered the Anabaptists of three Hungarian districts (comitats), Bratislava, Neutra, and Trenchin. It is certainly a unique document in the entire history of the Hutterites, but unfortunately, it was soon forgotten, discounted, or disregarded.

The great time of Anabaptism was now over, and a decline set in soon after the death of Ehrenpreis. Poverty and misery of all sorts prompted the Brethren to send a delegation to the Mennonites in Amsterdam asking for material help (the letter of 1665 to these Mennonites closes the Great Chronicle; Wolkan, 666-71). Apparently this action was successful, for the Mennonite Archives in Amsterdam contain a letter of thanks for the generous help received, dated Nov. 24, 1665 (*Inv. Arch. Amst.* II, 419). This help, however, could not stop the decline (*Verfliessen*) of Hutterite life. The principle of community of goods was in part abandoned in the later years of the 17th century, and the old discipline began to wane. At the same time the power of the Jesuits began to grow, and after 1700 the Anabaptist Brethren faced a challenge to which their spirituality was no longer a match. Already in 1688 Cardinal Kolonitch tried to insist that from now on infants in Velke Levary, his estate, must be baptized, an order obeyed by the more timid members. In 1733 another order or mandate was issued likewise requiring general infant baptism on the threat of severe penalties for the nonconforming parents. The details of the ensuing bitter struggle are recorded by Johannes Waldner in his *Klein-Geschichtsbuch* (197-239); as a whole it is a pathetic story of suffering and agony though of a different nature from the 16th-century martyrdom. Only a small fraction managed to leave Slovakia for the Ukraine; the majority eventually succumbed to the pressure and accepted Catholicism, though with much resistance and inner reservation. It was then that mass confiscations of their codices began (30 today in Bratislava, another 30 in Esztergom, 10 in Budapest, and many more simply destroyed), while here and there books were hidden behind walls or under the floors (see **Habaner**). Even the Edict of Toleration of the enlightened Emperor Joseph II in 1781 was of no help; Brethren from Slovakia went to Vienna for an audience with the Emperor, but he had little understanding for their way of life (though he permitted Mennonite settlers to locate in Galicia at the same time; see **Galicia**). Thus nothing was achieved. As soon as the Brethren turned Catholic, the Jesuits allowed them all the rest of their time-honored ways of life; the Bruderhof institutions remained unchanged, a common treasury was kept (almost up to 1914), and to this day people continue to live in the old Hofs. Also their most treasured craft, ceramics (Habaner fayence), was practiced far into the 19th century, creating some particularly beautiful pieces before and after 1800. When two American Hutterite Brethren revisited the old Slovakian homesteads in 1937, they joyfully recognized the familiar patterns of life as their own. But the genius had faded away and after a few hospitable days they parted, conscious that Hutterite life was no longer at home in Slovakia, Transylvania, or the Ukraine, but was to be found only in the far away prairie areas of Canada and the United States. R.F.

Beck, *Geschichts-Bücher*, 302, 364, 436, 492, 496, 570; Wolkan, *Geschicht-Buch*, 246, 666-71; Zieglschmid, *Chronik; idem, Klein-Geschichtsbuch*, 128, 168-72, 179-239, 519-32; A. J. F. Zieglschmid, "An unpublished Hausbrief of Grimmelshausen's Hungarian Anabaptists," in *Germanic Review* XV (1940) 81-97; Robert Friedmann,

"Anabaptist Pottery: The Story of Habaner Fayences," in *Menn. Life* XIII (July 1958); *idem*, "An Anabaptist Ordinance of 1633 on Nonresistance," *MQR* XXV (1951) 116-27; *idem*, "Hutterite Physicians and Barber-Surgeons," *MQR* XXVII (1953) 128-36; Johann Loserth, "Decline and Revival of the Hutterites," *MQR* IV (1930) 93-112. The diary of the two Hutterites who visited the colonies in 1937 is to be published in translation in the *MQR* in 1959.

Sluys, van der (Versluys, van Sluys), a Dutch Mennonite family, whose ancestors lived in Belgium. Guilliame Versluys (d. *c*1628) was a burgomaster of Waerschoot, Flanders; his widow with three sons and one daughter, all Mennonites, moved to Cadzand in Zealand-Flanders, Netherlands, in 1629. Among them was Guiliame van der Sluys, called de Oude, who later lived at Aardenburg as a wool and cloth merchant, and died there about 1675, whose son Maerten married Maria van Eeghen. Jan Versluys, a farmer at Zomergem (*q.v.*), Belgium, moved to de Biezen near Aardenburg with his family, all Mennonites, about 1620. Another Guilliame van der Sluys, called de Jonge, lived about 1667 at Zierikzee, Dutch province of Zeeland, where he owned a thriving textile business. Martin van der Sluys, the husband of the martyr Grietgen van Sluys (*q.v.*), probably belonged to the same family. Another member of this family was Guillaume van der Sluys, of Rotterdam, a member and deacon of the Flemish Mennonite congregation, who in 1661 with others signed the letter of Dutch Mennonite congregations to the city of Bern, to intervene with the Bernese government in behalf of the oppressed Mennonites, and who signed the Verbondt van Eenigheydt (*q.v.*) in 1664 for the congregation of Rotterdam. In 1663 he was present when Tieleman Jansz van Braght (*q.v.*) disputed with Pastor Aemilius (*q.v.*) at Oud-Beyerland. Most members of this family left the Mennonite Church to join the Reformed in the 18th century.   vDZ.

F. K. van Lennep, *Verzameling van Oorkonden betrekking hebbende op het geslacht van Eeghen* . . . (Amsterdam, 1920) *passim; DB* 1876, 102, 104, 108; 1877, 11 f.; 1879, 33, 38, 46; 1881, 5, 12; 1884, 39; 1889, 95; Müller, *Berner Täufer*, 192.

Smalcius (Schmalz), **Valentinus** (d. 1622), was a preacher of the Polish Brethren (Socinians, *q.v.*) at Rakov, Poland. In 1610 Smalcius and the Socinian elder Moscorovius (*q.v.*) had a conversation at Lublin with three Mennonite leaders of Danzig and the surrounding congregations. Thereupon Smalcius drew up a confession of faith, which was widely spread among the Mennonites of Poland. The Socinians wished to have closer contacts and even a merger with the Mennonites, since they held that there were only slight differences between their doctrines; but the Mennonites opposed this union. Smalcius and other leaders of the Brethren, including Ulrich Pius Herwarth, a preacher of the Brethren at Danzig, insisted that Jan Gerrits van Emden (*q.v.*), a Mennonite preacher at Danzig, and other Mennonite leaders in Poland have a debate with them in order to prepare the merger. Jan Gerrits wrote a number of letters to Hans de Ries (*q.v.*), Leenaert Clock (*q.v.*), Reiner Wybrands (*q.v.*), and other Mennonite leaders in Holland, urgently asking them to come to Danzig to dispute with the Brethren leaders, because they felt unequal to the theologically well-trained polemical Smalcius and other Socinian leaders. The Dutch elders, however, declined, de Ries writing a letter to Jan Gerrits. The union of Mennonites and the Brethren did not come about; in 1628 the Polish Brethren church was dissolved by order of the Polish government. (*Inv. Arch. Amst.* II, Nos. 2928-36.)   vDZ.

Smid (Smit), a Mennonite family at Balk (*q.v.*), Dutch province of Friesland, found there from at least 1672. Many of its members served as deacons, preachers, and elders in the Balk congregation, which more than other Dutch congregations held to the old Mennonite principles and practices—ban, nonresistance, lay ministry, difference of the functions of elder and preacher, plain dress, Biestkens (*q.v.*) Bible. From 1800 to his death in 1844 Meine Ob(b)es was at first a preacher and then an elder of this church. Of great significance and blessing was Johannes Obes (*c*1765-1828), who assumed the family name of Smit (Smid), being a blacksmith. In 1814, at his own expense, he reprinted for the congregation the *Klein Hoorns Liedboek* (*q.v.*), a 17th-century Dutch Mennonite hymnal which was used at Balk until 1848, when the *Uitgezochte Liederen* were adopted to be used together with the *Hoorns Liedboek*. In 1824-25 he reprinted Tieleman van Braght's *Schole der Deugd* and Pieter Boudewijn's *Onderwijzinge des Christelijken Geloofs*. In 1828, after Johannes' death, his eldest son Obe Smid (1802-50) became a preacher of the congregation. He was a good leader with great gifts of heart and head. He diligently studied the writings of Menno Simons, Dirk Philips, and Pieter Jansz Twisck. Besides a diary he wrote a number of doctrinal and devotional tracts, one of which, entitled *Verklaring van 't groote gebod Gods*, was published at Sneek in 1848. A list of the manuscripts he left behind is found in *MQR* XXX (1956) 130 f. Obe Smid, who was unmarried, died in 1850, apparently somewhat disappointed in the spiritual development of the congregation, which had partly left the old paths.

Ruurd Johannes Smid (1814-93), the third son of Preacher Johannes Smid, was appointed preacher in 1847 and elder in 1849. On May 9, 1853, together with Preacher R. J. Sijmensma (*q.v.*), he led the emigration of a large part of the Balk congregation to the United States. For this exodus (19 of the 30 Balk members, with their children 52 souls, emigrated) there were different reasons: not only, though predominantly the desire to maintain the old Mennonite principles and practices, particularly that of nonresistance, but also because economic conditions had become difficult for them. In five letters, three by Smid and two by Sijmensma, they informed the part of the Balk congregation which had not joined the emigration, of their trip and their first experiences in America. (These letters were published in Gorter's *Doopsgezinde Lectuur*, 1854.) The Balk group first moved to Dover, Ohio, from where some pioneers, including Smid, moved to Indiana where they found farm land near Goshen. The group, apparently because of its small size, did not organize a church here, but worshiped with some German-speaking Mennonites (MC) in "the Christophel Meeting House" (Yellow Creek area). Ruurd Smid (he soon Americanized his name as Smith) preached sometimes in this church as he did later in the Salem church. In 1874 "the Christophel Church, including the Holland brethren" was "under charge of R. J. Schmidt" (Smith). During the first years after the immigration, when the Balk people were not yet well acquainted with the English language, Ruurd Smid often preached in the homes of the members. Mrs. Smith's diary relates that Ruurd Johannes Smid became sick on April 20, and died on April 26, 1893. Mrs. Smith, nee Grietje (Margaret) Sijmensma, was a sister of Preacher R. J. Sijmensma (1820-1911).   vDZ.

C. F. Brüsewitz, "The Mennonites of Balk," and Marie Yoder, "The Balk Dutch Settlement near Goshen, Indiana," in *MQR* XXX (January 1956); C. F. Brüsewitz, "De Doopsgezinden van Balk," in *Stemmen uit de Doopsgezinde Broederschap* V (1956) No. 4; *DJ* 1950, 49 f., 195 f.; *DB* 1861, 130; 1887, 112.

Smidt, Petrus (Pieter), b. Nov. 10, 1707, at Amsterdam, d. there Aug. 12, 1781, whose great-grandfather was Gerrit Smidt, a Mennonite preacher of Hamburg-Altona, was an elder of the Amsterdam Zonist (*q.v.*) congregation from 1728 until his death. When the Amsterdam Lamist congregation started a seminary for the training of Mennonite ministers and some Zonists desired a good training for their ministers too, the Amsterdam Zonist congregation decided to open a Zonist seminary, appointing Petrus Smidt as theological professor in 1753. Smidt taught until 1780, when the Zonist seminary was closed; the number of students had always been very small. Smidt did not publish any writings except a sermon in 1728.

Petrus Smidt seems to have been a man of means. Besides a stately home at Amsterdam, first on the Singel, later on the Heerengracht, he owned a country home at Uithoorn. He married Sara de Koker (1702-58). His daughter Maria Smidt was married to Pastor Hendrik van Gelder (*q.v.*), whose descendants, still numerous in the Netherlands, bear the family name of Smidt van Gelder.   vDZ.

Inv. Arch. Amst. II, Nos. 2953, 3146; *DB* 1872, 55; 1890, 110; 1918, 78; J. M. van Gelder, *Stamboek van de familie van Gelder* (Amsterdam, 1899) 178-83.

Smissen, van der, a Mennonite family which has played a significant role in the church and community life. The origin of the family has been traced to Brabant, Belgium, where it was also called Bogaard; during the 15th century it was a patrician family of Brussels. Gysbert I van der Smissen escaped from Belgium around 1576 during the days of the Inquisition and lived in Goch, on the Lower Rhine. When he joined the Mennonites is not known. After 1583 he resided in Haarlem, Holland. His son Jan was a Mennonite minister in Haarlem. Another son, Daniel, settled in Friedrichstadt, Holstein, which became a Mennonite refuge. His son Gysbert II (b. April 8, 1620) settled in Glückstadt in 1644 and founded a bakery and a whaling company. In 1677 he moved to Altona and established a bakery. His oldest son, Daniel (b. 1646), continued his father's enterprise. The ninth child of Gysbert II was Hinrich I (*q.v.*; Jan. 24, 1662-1737), who followed his father to Altona in 1677. He was a suc-

cessful businessman and occupied a significant position in the growing city. He has been given the name "city builder" because he laid the foundation for Altona's prosperity. He was also an active supporter of the Altona Mennonite Church (*q.v.*). His two sons, Hinrich II (b. 1704) and Gysbert III (b. 1717), continued the father's business. During this second generation the business reached its peak. During the third generation Hinrich III (b. 1742) and Jacob Gysbert van der Smissen (*q.v.*) (b. 1746) were the outstanding representatives of the family. Jacob had strong pietistic leanings. Toward the end of his life the firm collapsed.

Münte states that there was a certain degeneration noticeable in the fourth generation partly because of intermarriage in the family. Johann W. Mannhardt (*q.v.*), who married Anna van der Smissen, and some of his descendants are significant representatives of the family. A detailed study of the ups and downs of the van der Smissen family and their enterprises is found in Münte's book *Das Altonaer Handlungshaus van der Smissen 1682-1824* (Altona, 1932). Seldom have Mennonites had such influence in the affairs, growth, and prosperity of a city as was the case in Altona.

Some of the van der Smissens, e.g., Jacob Gysbert, turned from their interest in business to religious work and had strong pietistic leanings. Carl Justus van der Smissen (*q.v.*) was a minister in Glückstadt and one of the first of the Mennonites of Germany to receive a full theological training. He migrated to America in 1868 and was a teacher of Wadsworth Seminary (*q.v.*). His son Carl H. A. van der Smissen (*q.v.*) made an outstanding contribution to the Mennonites of America as an editor and minister. (See **Germany**.)   C.K.

Among the writings on the family may be listed an original genealogy entitled *1743 Stam Boom ende Geslagt Register der Van der Smissen in de Linie van Daniel Van der Smissen Voort Stammende of den Stamhouder Gysbert van der Smissen* (BeCL). In addition to the book by Münte, see W. Oesau, *Hamburgs Grönlandfahrt auf Walfischfang und Robbenschlag vom 17.-19. Jahrhundert* (Hamburg, 1955) and R. Dollinger, *Geschichte der Mennoniten in Schleswig-Holstein, Hamburg und Lübeck* (Neumünster, 1930). BeCL has Jacob Gysbert van der Smissen's original Journal and correspondence, as well as other early material brought to America by the van der Smissen family, all of it in the "Van der Smissen Collection." *ML* VI, 187-192.

Smissen, Carl Heinrich Anton van der (1851-1950), a Mennonite (GCM) minister and editor, was born at Friedrichstadt, Schleswig-Holstein, Germany, on Dec. 4, 1851, the son of the Mennonite preacher Carl Justus van der Smissen (*q.v.*). He attended the local elementary and high schools, the universities of Basel (1870-72), Tübingen (1872-73), and Halle (1873-74), and the Wadsworth (Ohio) and Haysville (Ohio) academies (1875-80). In 1874 he came to America to join his parents. He served churches while a student and taught public school at Coshocton, Ohio (1880-81). He served the Upper Milford and Hereford Mennonite churches of Zionsville and Bally, Pa. (1881-90), and the Summerfield Mennonite Church, Ill. (1890-1911). He was the editor of the *Bundesbote* and the *Bundesbote-Kalender* 1911-29, of the *Kinderbote* 1911-36, of the *Mennonite* 1912-14, and of the German Sunday-school quarterlies

1920-43. In 1911-32 he lived at Berne, Ind. He served as the secretary of the Eastern and Middle district conferences and the General Conference (1896-1902) and was a member of the General Conference Board of Education and Publication (1887-90) and the Board of Foreign Missions (1890-96, 1902-11). He preached in many churches and held many other offices. He and his father were the first American Mennonite teachers and ministers with a full standard theological training.

In 1881 he married Mary E. Knight, who died in 1892. From this marriage were born two children. In 1892 he married Elizabeth B. Ruth. To them were born six children. In 1932 he retired from his active duties and resided in the Home for the Aged at Newton, Kan. On June 30, 1950, he died, having nearly attained the age of one hundred years of an active life. He was the author of *Kurzgefaszte Geschichte und Glaubenslehre der Altevangelischen Taufgesinnten oder Mennoniten* (Summerfield, 1895) and *Der Eid*. (Elkhart, 1894).   C.K.

"C. H. A. van der Smissen," *Mennonite Yearbook and Almanac*, 1927, 34; 1931, 28; "Autobiography of Carl H. A. van der Smissen" (BeCL).

Smissen, Carl Justus van der (1811-90), a Mennonite (GCM) minister and educator, was born at Altona, Germany, on July 14, 1811, the son of Jacob van der Smissen (*q.v.*). He attended school at Friedrichstadt and Ratzeburg. He was baptized in 1826, in which year he went with his parents to Danzig where his father received a call as a minister. There he learned the trade of bookbinding. With the mediation of Johann E. Gossner he spent some time in this line of work in St. Petersburg, Russia. In 1832 he began his study at the Missionshaus of Basel, preparing for the ministry. After three years he spent two years at the University of Erlangen. In 1837 he accepted the call of the Mennonite church of Friedrichstadt, and married Sarah van der Smissen. Among the eight children born to them were Carl H. A. (*q.v.*) and Hillegonda Jacoba (*q.v.*). Under the influence of such pietists as Gossner, van der Smissen caused a revival in the congregation. In 1850 the war compelled the family to go to Hamburg. The following year he returned to his work.

In 1867 the General Conference Mennonite Church extended a call to van der Smissen to become the teacher of theological subjects at the Wadsworth School (*q.v.*) in Ohio. The family moved to Wadsworth in 1868. For ten years he taught at this school. Many leaders and ministers of the General Conference received their training under him, the first American teacher and minister with a formal theological training. After the close of the school, van der Smissen became the minister of the Salem Mennonite Church at Haysville, Ohio, in 1879. He served for many years as secretary of the Board of Missions (1872-90) and edited the mission paper, *Nachrichten aus der Heidenwelt* (1877-81). He remained active in his pastoral work almost to the close of his life, which occurred on May 29, 1890. His sermons have been preserved in the van der Smissen Collection (BeCL).   C.K.

H. P. Krehbiel, *The History of the General Conference . . .* (1898) 436-40; C. H. A. van der Smissen and S. F. Sprunger, "Lebensbeschreibung von Carl Justus

van der Smissen," *Christlicher Bundesbote*, June 12, 1890, p. 4.

Smissen, Dominicus van der (1704-60), an artist, born at Altona, Germany, in 1704, a nephew of Hinrich van der Smissen. He was a pupil of Balthasar Denner (*q.v.*), whose sister Catharina he married in 1730. Little is known about his life. He was active as an artist at Dresden, Braunschweig, Amsterdam, and London, in addition to Hamburg-Altona. He died in 1760. Lichtwark says that a generation ago a number of his works of art were in the possession of families in Hamburg: some landscapes, portraits, and still lifes, which have become very scarce. The Kunsthalle of Hamburg possesses a considerable number of his works, including a Self Portrait (Catalog, No. 432), Portrait of the Senator and Poet B. H. Brockes (34), Portrait of the Poet Hagedorn (41), Portrait of Dr. Vincent Rumpf (165), Portrait of a Hamburg Mayor (167), Portrait of the Wife of the Mayor (166), Portrait of a Captain (433), Still Life (434), and Hinrich I van der Smissen, "The City Builder." Dominicus also painted Meta Moller, Klopstock's first wife. All the above are oil paintings. As a rule van der Smissen closely followed Denner's style, although he portrays forms of the body in greater detail. Additional paintings of his are found in Braunschweig and in private possession. The Bethel College Historical Library has colored slides and black and white reproductions of most of his works.   C.K.

Alfred Lichtwark, *Das Bildnis in Hamburg* I (Hamburg, 1898) 144 ff.; *Kunsthalle zu Hamburg; Katalog der alten Meister* (1921) 155.

Smissen, Hillegonda Cornelia van der (1848-1949), was born at Friedrichstadt, Schleswig-Holstein, Germany, on June 30, 1848, a daughter of Carl Justus van der Smissen (*q.v.*), and came to the United States with her parents in 1868 where they resided at Wadsworth, Ohio. Ten years later her parents moved to Haysville, Ohio, and in 1890 she followed her mother to Summerfield, Ill. In 1908 she became the supervisor of the household of the Bethel Deaconess Hospital at Newton, Kan. On Sept. 16, 1909, she was consecrated as a deaconess, continuing her service to the hospital. She wrote *Unsere Arbeit in den Missionsvereinen* (n.d.), pp. 30; *The History of Our Missionary Societies* (n.d., p. 72) translated by Mrs. J. Quiring; *Bilder aus meinem Leben* (Bethel Deaconess Hospital, Newton, n.d.), pp. 86; *Sketches from My Life* (Bethel Deaconess Hospital, n.d.), pp. 54. During her last years of a long and fruitful life she was a resident of the Home for the Aged where she died on Sept. 29, 1949, being more than 101 years old.   C.K.

"Sister Hillegonda Cornelia van der Smissen," *In the Service of the King*, October-November 1949.

Smissen, Hinrich I van der (1662-1737), known as "City Builder," was born Jan. 21, 1662, at Glückstadt, Holstein, where his father, Gysbert II, had a bakery and a business. In 1677 his father moved to Altona. In 1679 Hinrich I finished his apprenticeship as a baker and in 1684 he took over his father's bakery in Altona. He started a transport business in addition to the bakery and purchased land including the present "Van der Smissen Allee," where he built numerous houses. In a short time he became a prosperous and respected man. He became a member of the committee to rebuild Altona when it was destroyed by the Swedes in 1713, through which he earned the name "City Builder." He was generous in his support of the city as well as the Altona Mennonite Church (*q.v.*). He was one of the most successful businessmen of the van der Smissen family. He was married to Marie de Voss, May 14, 1693. Of his six children the two youngest, Hinrich II and Gysbert III, inherited his business. He died on June 1, 1737.   C.K.

Heinz Münte, *Das Altonaer Handlungshaus van der Smissen 1682-1824* (Altona, 1932) 9 ff.; Paul Th. Hoffmann, *Neues Altona* (Jena, 1929) 224 ff.; Robert Dollinger, *Geschichte der Mennoniten in Schleswig-Holstein, Hamburg und Lübeck* (Neumünster, 1930); *ML* VI.

Smissen, Hinrich van der (1851-1928), a German Mennonite leader, was born at Altona (*q.v.*), Germany, on Dec. 14, 1851, attended the local Gymnasium, studied at the universities of Halle and Göttingen until the outbreak of the Franco-Prussian War in 1870. As a volunteer in the medical corps of Hamburg he took part in the entire campaign. In September 1872 he was chosen to the ministry by the congregation of Ibersheim, Eppstein, and Friesenheim. For ten years he served the congregation faithfully and was a leader in the work of the conference of the Palatinate and Hesse, the board of the school at Weierhof (*q.v.*) as secretary (1875-79) and president (1879-85); in 1875-79 he was coeditor of the *Mennonitische Blätter* with his cousin Johannes van der Smissen (*q.v.*) and in 1879-1923 he was sole editor. In 1880 it was he who brought about the establishment of the General Central Relief Fund, which later became the Mennonite Relief Treasury (*Mennonitische Hilfskasse, q.v.*). In 1882 he became assistant preacher of the Hamburg-Altona congregation (*q.v.*) and in 1885 the pastor of the same congregation. Here again his service and influence were extensive. For many years he was chairman of the *Vereinigung der Mennonitengemeinden im Deutschen Reich*, which he helped to found. He made extended journeys, visiting nearly all the Mennonite congregations in Germany, Switzerland, Holland, Russia, and some in America. He died March 3, 1928. His father was Hinrich T. van der Smissen.†   NEFF.

Christian Neff, "Hinrich van der Smissen," *Gem.-Kal.* 1929, 70-99 with picture; *ML* IV.

Smissen, Jacob II van der (1785-1846), a son of Jacob Gysbert van der Smissen (*q.v.*), was born at Altona, Germany, in 1785. After his training under J. W. Mannhardt, in the Ritterakademie in Uhyst, and in Rotterdam, he was engaged in business and agriculture. He lost most of his property in 1812 and lived at Hanerau. He married Sophie W. F. Weihe in 1805. In 1813 he purchased a bakery in Hanerau, tutored, and was engaged in home mission work. He served as pastor of the following Mennonite churches: Friedrichstadt 1818-26, Danzig (the first salaried minister) 1826-35, Neustadt-Gödens 1836-42. He retired to Ottensen and died at Altona in 1846. He was a gifted speaker and perpetuated the pietistic heritage of his father. Carl Justus van der Smissen (*q.v.*) was his son. (*ML* VI, 189.)   C.K.

Smissen, Jacob Gysbert van der (1746-1829), an outstanding member of the van der Smissen (*q.v.*) family during the 18th century when there was a turn in the family from successful economic enterprise to a pietistic emphasis. He was born on Jan. 1, 1746, the son of Gysbert III van der Smissen. For five years he was an apprentice in Rotterdam, after which he worked in his father's business in Altona, becoming a shareholder in 1781. He was married to Helena Linnich in 1770, who was a niece of his mother. Their children were Gilbert (Gysbert IV), Hinrich II, and Jacob II. Jacob II (*q.v.*) later became the Mennonite minister at Friedrichstadt. His wife died in 1790. In 1796 he married Hillegonda Jacoba Deknatel, the daughter of Johannes Deknatel (*q.v.*) of Amsterdam.

Van der Smissen was deeply influenced by Pietism and the Moravian Brethren. His correspondence with a large circle of friends far beyond the Mennonite fold, which has been preserved, is an unusual source of information on not only the religious development and views of the writer, but also those of his day in general. Many of his letters as well as those written to him were preserved in the original form or copied. Among his friends were the Moravian minister Briant, Jung-Stilling, Lavater, Matthias Claudius, Perthes, Gossner, and other leaders of the pietistic movement. He was a member of the organization "Deutsche Gesellschaft zur Beförderung reiner Lehre und Gottseligkeit," of Basel, and cofounder of the paper *Basler Sammlungen*. He wrote for this paper and promoted it. He was active in promoting other religious organizations. He was particularly interested in promoting Pietism in opposition to the Rationalism of his day, not stressing denominational lines. Purely cultural questions and organizations did not interest him.

In 1810 he suffered a stroke from which he never recovered fully. In 1824 the large van der Smissen business enterprise suffered a collapse, partly because of the post-Napoleonic developments. On March 3, 1829, he died, a relatively poor man, although he had some income from the Deknatel estate. His wife had died in 1817. His children received a very good education. Johann Wilhelm Mannhardt (*q.v.*) was their private tutor. Later some attended the Moravian educational institute at Christiansfeld. As a deacon of the Altona Mennonite Church Jacob Gysbert was active in upholding the Mennonite traditions and rights within the environment in which they lived.   C.K.

Heinz Münte, *Das Altonaer Handlungshaus van der Smissen 1682-1824* (Altona, 1932); Robert Dollinger, *Geschichte der Mennoniten in Schleswig-Holstein, Hamburg und Lübeck* (Neumünster, 1930) 172-82; Jacob Gysbert van der Smissen's Journal and Letters, or "Dies Buch Welches lauter geistliche Sachen enthaelt . . . ," Oct. 23, 1824," in BeCL; Paul Th. Hoffman, *Neues Altona* (Gena, 1929) 226 f.; correspondence with his daughter Helena Elisabeth, Pieter Beets, Cornelis Ris, Georg Gottlieb Bärenbruck, etc. Jacob Gysbert van der Smissen was the grandfather of Carl Justus van der Smissen (*q.v.*) who came to America and through whom a part of the family collection was brought along and consequently became a part of the Bethel College Historical Library. *ML* VI, 189.

Smissen, Johannes van der (1808-79), a German Mennonite leader, was born on July 17, 1808, at Altona in Schleswig-Holstein, Germany, studied mathematics and the natural sciences at the universities of Copenhagen and Berlin, also attending lectures in theology. After completing his course he held positions as private tutor in Altona, the Baltic provinces, and in Danzig; here he was persuaded by Jakob Mannhardt (*q.v.*) to make further preparations for the ministry. In 1856 he accepted the very difficult position of minister of the Kiernica (*q.v.*) congregation in Galicia and there married Elisabet Vlaar, of the Altona congregation, on April 18, 1858. In 1868 he accepted the call to Sembach (*q.v.*) in the Palatinate, to occupy the Mennonite pulpit left vacant by the death of Johannes Risser (*q.v.*). He was an energetic worker for the *Mennonitische Blätter*. In 1875-79 he was its coeditor with his cousin Hinrich van der Smissen (*q.v.*). He also performed an important service as chairman of the board of the school at Weierhof and in reviving the conference sessions of the Palatinate and Hesse. On April 28, 1879, he died, deeply mourned by his congregation. (*Menn. Bl.*, 1879, 33, 42, 44; *ML* IV.)   NEFF.

Smit (Schmidt), Hilchen, was an elder of the Frisian Mennonite congregation at Montau, West Prussia, in the second half of the 16th century. About this leader there is only scarce information. He was probably of Dutch descent (his Christian name Hilchen may have been a corruption of the Frisian name Hylke), but he was not among the first Dutch Mennonites who settled at Montau in 1568. The years of his serving are unknown. In 1588, at Danzig, Hilchen Smit, being authorized by the Frisian congregation of Haarlem, Holland, banned Cryn van der Meulen (*q.v.*, Vermeulen) and Hans von Schwindern (*q.v.*), an elder and preacher of the Danzig Frisian congregation, who were planning a union with the moderate Waterlanders. After 1588 nothing more is known about Smit.   vDZ.

Smith: see also **Schmidt.**

Smit(h), John see Smyth, John

Smith, C. Henry (1875-1948), an outstanding American Mennonite historian, was born June 8, 1875, at Metamora, Ill., one of the eight children of Bishop John (*q.v.*) and Magdalene Schertz Smith, his grandfathers Schertz and Smith having immigrated from Alsace-Lorraine *c*1829. He married Laura Ioder Dec. 26, 1908; there were no children. He was educated at Illinois State Normal University, 1896-98, University of Illinois (B.A., 1903), and the University of Chicago (B.A., 1903, Ph.D., 1907), the first known American Mennonite to secure the Ph.D. degree and continue in the church. His chosen career of teaching included three years of elementary school near home (1893-96), Elkhart Institute 1898-1900, Goshen College 1903-5 (also librarian) and 1908-13 (first dean of the college 1909-13), and Bluffton College 1913-48. His major field was history, in which he did outstanding work at the University of Chicago (Phi Beta Kappa), and which he taught well for almost 50 years. He taught for one year (1922-23) at Bethel College. He also en-

tered the banking business, serving for years as president of the Citizens National Bank of Bluffton and vice-president of the First National Bank of Pandora. With ample private means he could devote himself to research and writing in his special field of interest, Mennonite history. In his church he was a member of the Board of Publication of the General Conference Mennonite Church 1940-48, and in the district conference a member of the Peace Committee.

Smith's interest in Mennonite history continued throughout his life. His doctoral dissertation (1907) was *Mennonites of America,* published by the author in 1909. His outstanding work was *The Story of the Mennonites* (Berne, 1941), an enlargement of his earlier work *The Mennonites: A Brief History of Their Origin and Later Development in both Europe and America* (Berne, 1920). Two other larger monographs came from his pen: *The Coming of the Russian Mennonites: An Episode in the Settling of the Last Frontier 1874-1884* (Berne, 1927), and *The Mennonite Immigration to Pennsylvania in the Eighteenth Century* (Part XXXIII of A Narrative and Critical History of the Pennsylvania German Society, Norristown, Pa., 1929). He shared in the writing of *The Story of Bluffton College* (Bluffton, 1925, edited by E. J. Hirschler and C. Henry Smith). Smaller sketches and booklets include: *Mennonites in History,* an address delivered in Philadelphia (Scottdale, 1907); *Menno Simons, Apostle of the Nonresistant Life* (Berne, 1936); *Christian Peace: Four Hundred Years of Mennonite Peace Principles and Practice* (Newton, 1938); *One Hundred Years Ago,* an address delivered at the first Home-Coming celebration of the old Partridge congregation near Metamora in 1940; *Mennonites in America* (Akron, 1942, number II in the series *Mennonites and Their Heritage,* published by the Mennonite Central Committee for use in CPS camps); and *Metamora* (Bluffton, 1947). His autobiographical book, *The Education of a Mennonite Country Boy,* was written in 1925, but published in 1943 at Bluffton in 15 mimeographed copies. He wrote some 15 articles for the *Mennonitisches Lexikon* and a similar number for the MENNONITE ENCYCLOPEDIA. He was a central figure in the planning of the ENCYCLOPEDIA, serving as coeditor until his death, and in this connection was first president of the Mennonite Research Fellowship. He wrote numerous articles in some 16 Mennonite periodicals and yearbooks. A complete bibliography appears in *MQR* XXIII (1949), "A Bibliography of the Writings of C. Henry Smith," by N. P. Springer.

His work will remain a challenge to complete objectivity, to scrupulous fairness and justice, and to effective and winning presentation of insights gained. Mennonites owe to him a great debt for his pioneer and creative work, particularly in the field of American Mennonite history. He was a valiant fighter, not only for historical truth, but for the best in the Mennonite heritage, particularly the testimony for peace and nonresistance. With malice toward none, and charity toward all, he hoped for and worked toward a better understanding and eventual reunion of the divided Mennonite brotherhood. As a historian, Smith was unquestionably the greatest of the historians produced by the Mennonites of America and the peer of any of the European Mennonite historians. With his five major works, written over a period of thirty-five years, he published more full-length historical works than any other Mennonite historian. His particular gift was that of synthesis of masses of material into well-written, interesting, integrated accounts. He was pre-eminently the general Mennonite historian who took the great sweep of our history in both Europe and America and put it into clear, easily read volumes that will remain standard works for years to come.

C. Henry Smith was a member of the Mennonite Church (MC) until his withdrawal to Bluffton, when he joined the General Conference Mennonite Church. The initial "C" has been erroneously assumed to stand for "Christian." It was simply an initial adopted by Henry himself.† H.S.B.

Willard H. Smith, "C. Henry Smith 1875-1948: A Brief Biography," *MQR* XXIII (1949) 7-15; H. S. Bender, "C. Henry Smith: A Tribute," *ibid.*, 5 f.; C. Henry Smith, "The Education of a Mennonite Country Boy" (mimeographed autobiography); N. E. Byers, "C. Henry Smith as I Knew Him," and Carl M. Lehman, "Smith as a Business Man," *Menn. Life* V (April 1950).

Smith Corner Mennonite Church (GCM), located 3 miles west of East Freedom, Blair Co., Pa., a member of the Eastern District Conference, was started in 1908 by Jacob G. Snyder and Herman Snyder, of Roaring Spring, Pa., formerly ministers in the Mennonite Church (MC), with a nucleus of members from that community. The church was built in that same year. The pastor in 1957 was Walter D. Fry, and the membership was 61. W.T.S.

Smith, Jacob Brubaker (1870-1951), a leading minister and educator in the Mennonite Church (MC), was born at St. Jacobs, Waterloo Co., Ont., the son of George and Mary Schmidt. His education included work at Elkhart Institute and Ohio Northern University at Ada, Ohio, and Temple University. He was ordained preacher in 1897, serving several years as pastor of the Bethel (MC) congregation of Garden City, Mo., then 1901 ff. in the Bethel (MC) congregation of West Liberty, Ohio. In 1922 he moved to Elida, Ohio, where he served as minister in the Salem Church for many years. He died at Elida on Sept. 23, 1951.

Smith's greatest service was in the field of teaching and writing. He served on the faculty of Hesston College 1910-17 and 1927-29, and as the first president of Eastern Mennonite College 1917-22. He was the author of *One Thousand Best Bible Verses* (Chicago, 1924) and *Greek-English Concordance to the New Testament* (Scottdale, 1955). On March 17, 1901, he was married to Lena Burkhardt. Among their seven children were Mrs. Truman Brunk and J. Harold Smith, formerly a professor at Hesston and Goshen colleges. H.S.B.

Smith, John (1843-1906), a Mennonite (MC) leader and bishop, was born near Metamora, Woodford Co., Ill., Nov. 27, 1843. His parents, Christian and Catrina Smith, both born in Alsace, came first to Pennsylvania and then in 1833 came to the pioneer settlement in the Black Partridge Creek area the year the Partridge Amish congregation was organized. In 1865 he married Magdalena Schertz. Ten children were born, seven of whom grew to adulthood. His son Joseph D. Smith was for many years superintendent of the Home for the Aged at Eureka, and another son, C. Henry Smith (*q.v.*), was a pioneer historian of the Mennonites in America.

John Smith was ordained to the ministry in 1887 at the Roanoke Mennonite Church (MC) by Christian Ropp, and a few years later was ordained bishop. He served the Western Conference six times as secretary and three times as moderator.

He was a person of more than ordinary ability and was recognized as a leader in secular as well as in spiritual affairs. He was considered broad-minded but was one of the first to speak from the pulpit against the evils of tobacco and alcohol. He was conservative but willing to accept changes which would promote the welfare of the church. He actively supported the infant mission and educational interests of the church. His last years were given over almost entirely to the work of the church. He was one of the first in his area to use the English language in preaching. He died of a heart attack at his home on July 6, 1906. T.R.S.

Smithville, Ohio, is a town (pop. 800), located in Wayne County, northeast quarter of the state. Probably 1,500 Mennonites live within a ten-mile radius, mostly of the M.C. group, with some Conservative Amish, Old Order Amish, Old Order (Wisler) Mennonites, and General Conference Mennonites included. Chief settlements are north, east, and south, with about thirty Mennonite families living in Smithville. Amish Mennonites were among the first settlers in the area, coming from Pennsylvania about 1817. Three Mennonite (MC) churches in the immediate vicinity (Oak Grove, Smithville, Salem); Rittman Mennonite Home for the Aged is five miles northeast. Smithville is in Green Township, one of the most productive agricultural regions in the nation. V.M.Ge.

Smithville (Ohio) Mennonite Church (MC) is the former Pleasant Hill Mennonite Church (*q.v.*). In 1958 the congregation built a new meetinghouse at the eastern edge of Smithville village, leaving its old meetinghouse unoccupied. H.S.B.

Smoketown: see **Lichty Mennonite Church.**

Smucker (Schmucker, Smoker, Smuker, Smooker). Records show this family living in Switzerland and near Heidelberg, Germany, in the 18th century. Christian Schmucker emigrated from Switzerland to Berks County, Pa., in 1752. He is the ancestor of approximately 8,000 descendants living in Mennonite communities, chiefly in Pennsylvania, Ohio, Indiana, and Illinois. The first Smucker pioneer to push westward from Pennsylvania was Christian Schmucker, grandson of the immigrant ancestor, who settled in Wayne County, Ohio, about 1819. In 1841, Isaac Schmucker, an Amish preacher, moved from Ohio to Elkhart County, Ind., and conducted the first Amish Mennonite service in Indiana. In 1843 he was ordained bishop. His son Jonathan P. Schmucker (*q.v.*) was ordained bishop in 1878. The latter was active in promoting Sunday schools among the Amish Mennonites, and was one of the originators, of the Indiana-Michigan Amish Menn. Conference. Four ministers living today and well known in Mennonite circles are Ralph Smucker (MC), a former missionary in India, George R. Smoker (MC), a missionary to Africa, Don. Smucker (GCM), a former professor in the Mennonite Biblical Seminary, and Jesse N. Smucker (GCM), editor of *The Mennonite* and former president of the General Conference Mennonite Church. S.J.S.

Gladys Johns, "Christian Heroes, Biography of Jonathan P. Schmucker," *Youth's Christian Companion,* June 21, 1936; C. Z. Mast and R. E. Simpson, *Annals of Conestoga Valley* (Elverson, 1942) 201.

Smucker, Jonathan P. (1834-1903), a leader in the Indiana-Michigan Amish Mennonite Conference (now MC), was born in Wayne County, Ohio, May 8, 1834, the son of Bishop Isaac Schmucker (1810-93), the first Amish bishop in Indiana, and the great-grandson of Swiss immigrant Christian Schmucker from Bern and Barbara Stoltzfus of Zweibrücken. Jonathan moved with his parents to Knox County, Ohio, in 1838, where his father was ordained preacher. In November 1841 Isaac Schmucker and family located in Elkhart County, Ind., where two years later he was ordained bishop. Jonathan Smucker's first wife was Salome Pecht (d. 1893). To this union eleven children were born. In 1873 Jonathan Smucker joined the small Amish Mennonite settlement at Grovertown in Starke County, Ind., where he was ordained deacon and later preacher that same year by Bishop Jonas D. Troyer. (Troyer was the leader of the progressive Amish Mennonite schism from the Old Order Amish in Elkhart County in 1854.) In 1875 Smucker moved to west of Nappanee and took charge of the small Amish Mennonite congregation which worshiped on West Market Street in Nappanee. In 1878 he was ordained bishop in this congregation by bishops Joseph Stuckey and Isaac Smucker. In 1895 he married Mary Stutzman Kauffman, and then located east of Goshen, where he died Nov. 23, 1903. He was active in Amish Mennonite circles from Pennsylvania to Oregon, and was a strong promoter of church unity. He was buried in the Union Center Cemetery northeast of Nappanee.   J.C.W.

Gladys Johns, "Christian Heroes, Biography of Jonathan P. Schmucker," *Youth's Christian Companion,* June 21, 1936.

Smyth (Smith), John (c1565-1612), was born in East England. He studied theology at the University of Cambridge in 1586-93, and probably also medicine, and became a minister in the Church of England at Lincoln. In 1602, after nine months of doubt and deliberation, he left the state church. About this time or shortly before he was won to the principles of the Puritan Brownists (*q.v.*), whom he had previously attacked in a polemical tract. After leaving the state church he seems to have traveled and preached for some months. Early in 1603 he was invited by a number of Puritan manufacturers of Gainsborough to be their preacher, and for nearly four years he served as the leader of the Gainsborough Brownist congregation. But the oppression of the Nonconformists was becoming more and

more severe during the reign of King James I; Smyth left England, and with a number of adherents went to Amsterdam in October or November 1607. Here he found a Brownist congregation led by Francis Johnson (*q.v.*) and Henry Ainsworth (*q.v.*). Smyth and his followers, however, did not join this congregation, but founded a second English (Brownist) church, apparently because he did not agree with Johnson's views, who leaned toward Calvinist doctrines, such as predestination. While serving this congregation as minister, Smyth made his living by the practice of medicine. The Smyth congregation, at first rather small in membership, increased, particularly in 1607 when the Brownist congregation of Scrooby, of which John Robinson (*q.v.*), "the father of the Pilgrims," had been the preacher, also moved to Amsterdam. Some of its members, including Thomas Helwys (*q.v.*), joined the Smyth group. In the meantime Smyth had come to a deeper understanding of the nature of the church, and believed that the church should be a church of believers and only those should be admitted to the church who were converted to the faith, infant baptism being unscriptural. He severely attacked the Johnson group, accusing them of idolatry while they maintained the legality of infant baptism and ministers' ordination received in the state church, and reproaching them with accepting money from unbelievers. Smyth's reproofs were not all fair, and caused a sharp paper war with Johnson, Robinson, Clyfton, and others.

Smyth, convinced of the truth of his newly acquired views, and with the approval of his congregation, step by step turned to Anabaptism, and finally, holding that the baptisms he performed were not valid because he himself had not received the right baptism, in the fall of 1608 "in the solemn divine service, before them all (i.e., the members), baptized himself on confession of faith." This baptism was severely censured by the Johnson leaders, and even in his own group some did not agree and left the Smyth congregation. Soon Smyth himself came to the conclusion that his baptism was un-Biblical and repented it. About the same time, Smyth with some 40 followers acquired Jan Munter's (*q.v.*) bakehouse for their meetings. Repenting his self-baptism and trying to bring his congregation to a more Biblical pattern, he sought to contact the Waterlander Mennonite congregation of Amsterdam, of which Jan Munter had informed him. As an introduction he sent a letter to this congregation, where Lubbert Gerritz (*q.v.*) was the elder at this time. In this letter he included a list of members, signed by 14 men and 17 women, all of whom declared that the self-baptism of Smyth was wrong; he added a confession of faith of 20 articles in Latin. (Later Smyth delivered a still more detailed confession in 102 articles.) It was obviously the intention of Smyth to form a union or even a merger between the Waterlander Mennonite congregation and his own. But not all of Smyth's followers agreed; about ten of them, including Helwys, refused to sign the letter to the Mennonites. Though they wished to be on friendly terms with the Waterlanders and sharing the Mennonite views concerning baptism, they did not favor a merger. Helwys, in the name of the dissidents, wrote a letter to the trustees of the Waterlander congregation, asking them not to consent to Smyth's proposal. Helwys also drew up a confession of faith (19 articles) pointing out that the Brownists in many respects agreed with the Mennonites, but differed on the nonswearing of oaths and nonresistance. Helwys severely attacked Smyth, charging him with apostasy and sin against the Holy Ghost, and soon after excommunicated Smyth and his followers.

The letter by Smyth was cordially received by the Amsterdam Waterlanders, though they hesitated to take Smyth's outstretched hand; the warning of Helwys as well as the objections raised by some Waterlander country churches in Friesland deterred them from precipitate action, though both Lubbert Gerritsz and the preachers of Amsterdam as well as Hans de Ries (q.v.), the outstanding Dutch Waterlander leader, urged a union with "the English." Lubbert Gerritsz and de Ries together drew up a confession of faith of 38 articles, an English translation of which was sent to the Smyth group. After a number of debates and negotiations, the union finally came about in 1615. By this time both Lubbert Gerritsz and Smyth had died.

Smyth published a large number of writings; besides two confessions of faith and a volume of sermons, *The Bright Morning Starre* . . . (1603), he is the author of many polemical tracts, including *The Character of the Beast* (1609), in which he explains his motives in his baptism and his proposal to unite with the Mennonites against Helwys. Most of these tracts by Smyth give the impression that in accord with the fashion of his time he was a disagreeable theological polemicist, but this view is one-sided, because this man, successively an Anglician divine, a Puritan, a Brownist, an Anabaptist, a Mennonite, through his whole life passionately sought after the truth of God. At the end of his life he found peace. Overwhelmed by the bitter polemical writings of his opponents, he kept silent. A few years before his death he wrote, "If any man say, why then do you not answer the books written in opposition? my answer is, my desire is to end all controversies among Christians rather than to make and maintain them, especially in matters of the outward church and ceremonies; and it is the grief of my heart that I have so long cumbered myself and spent my time therein. . . . And now from this day forward do I put an end to all controversies . . . and resolve to spend my time in the main matters wherein consisteth salvation."   vDZ.

Inv. Arch. Amst. II, Nos. 1345-55; T(homas) P(igott), *John Smyth's Confession and Life* (1612; a copy of 1875 in AML); R. Barclay, *The Inner Life of the Religious Societies of the Commonwealth* (London, 1876) 52 f., 68, 70; H. Morton Dexter, *The True Story of John Smyth* . . . (Boston, 1881); A. H. Newman, *A History of Anti-pedobaptism* (Philadelphia, 1897) 376-93; W. H. Burgess, *John Smith, the Se-baptist, Thomas Helwys* (London, 1911); W. T. Whitley, *The Works of John Smith,* 2 vv. (Cambridge, 1915); J. G. de Hoop Scheffer and W. E. Griffis, *History of the Free Churchmen* (Ithaca, N.Y., n.d.-1922) 88-115, 145, 147-62, 197-207, 211-18, 231-53.

Sneek, a town in the Dutch province of Friesland (1952 pop. 19,530; 640 Mennonites), the seat of a Mennonite congregation. Little is known of its early history. Elder Leenaert Bouwens (q.v.) baptized 54 or 55 persons at Sneek during several visits in 1551-82. In the early 17th century there were here three congregations: a Flemish, a Groningen Old Flemish, and a Waterlander congregation. Of the Flemish and the Groningen Old Flemish there is no further information; the Flemish united with the Waterlander church likely about 1620, the Groningen Old Flemish died out before 1731. The Waterlander (sometimes also called Flemish and Waterlander) congregation steadily increased in membership and in general could meet undisturbed except in the years 1600-1. Shortly before 1600 the Reformed ministers of Sneek, G. Geldorp and Johannes Bogerman (q.v.), tried to destroy the Mennonite congregation; they several times entered into the meetinghouse during services in order to address and "to convert" the Mennonites; they repeatedly held debates with the noted Mennonite leader Pieter van Ceulen (q.v.), who was living at Sneek. But all their efforts failed. Thereupon they made a petition to the city magistrates, asking them to forbid the Mennonite meetings, and even to expel the Mennonites on the ground that there should be only one church and one confession in the state, namely, the true Reformed church and confession. The magistrates, more intimidated by their audacity than convinced by their arguments—they were afraid of losing a good number of substantial merchants and skillful and industrious artisans—refused to expel the Mennonites as in particular Bogerman had demanded, yet resolved in 1601 to proclaim a mandate forbidding the Mennonites to hold meetings either in their meetinghouse or in private homes, on pain of heavy fines. Barend Jacobsz, however, one of the Mennonites, braving the mandate, organized a meeting in his home, and being fined, refused to pay the fine; thereupon some of his furniture was publicly sold. The mandate was, however, in the course of the year not strictly enforced and the Mennonites could meet again rather freely.

At first the Waterlander congregation held its meetings in a large room of a private quarter near the city wall, but in 1654 a meetinghouse was erected on the Singel, which held 600 persons. This meetinghouse, being rather uncomfortable and moreover in a dilapidated condition, was rebuilt in 1842 (dedicated on April 10) and in 1855 provided with a beautiful entrance hall. It is still used by the congregation. A large hall, called "Mennozaal," used for all kinds of congregational activities, was built in 1927 close to the church. A parsonage next to the church was built in 1900-1.

In 1695 (earlier figures are missing) the membership numbered about 200; 392 in 1796; 310 in 1838; 347 in 1861; 434 in 1900; 452 in 1958.

During the 18th century not all Mennonites living at Sneek belonged to the Waterlander congregation; a small number, more conservative in maintaining the old Mennonite doctrines and church discipline as well as in simplicity of dress, were members of the Groningen Old Flemish congregation at neighboring IJlst (q.v.). In 1746, however, the 17 members of this congregation who lived at Sneek, particularly it seems on the instigation of Wouter Berends, a wealthy brother of advanced age, separated from IJlst and founded an independent Groningen Old Flemish congregation at Sneek. A house on the Kleinzand belonging to Wouter Berends was adapted as a meetinghouse, and Yde Rienks was called as their pastor, serving 1746-d.63. The membership soon increased: 34 in 1754, 43 in 1767. Such outstanding families as ten Cate and Veen belonged to the Kleinzand congregation. Pastor Rienks was followed by Hidser S. Hoekstra, serving 1764-72, and J. U. Siedsma 1775-d.1838, from 1831 assisted by the preachers of Kromwal and IJlst. In the course of time, particularly from about 1790, most members of the ten Cate and Veen families and some others left the Kleinzand church to join the "Groote Huis" or Singel congregation. In 1839 the Groningen Old Flemish group merged with the Singel congregation, after an attempt at such a merger in 1813 had miscarried.

The congregation meeting on the Singel had always been served by ministers chosen from the brethren until the early 18th century. In 1746 Klaas Bruin, called from the outside, was the first salaried preacher, serving until about 1773; he had not been trained at the Amsterdam Mennonite seminary. The first minister from the seminary to serve here was Albertus van Delden 1773-97, followed by Pieter Wepkes Feenstra 1797-1842, Izaak de Stoppelaar Blijdenstein 1842-57, J. A. J. Verstege 1858-88, L. Hesta 1889-90, V. Loosjes 1890-1912, H. Schuurmans 1912-33, W. Mesdag 1934-46, and M. van der Meulen 1946-

Church records have been preserved since 1667. Church activities now include a ladies' circle, men's circle, and a Sunday school for children.   vpZ.

Inv. Arch. Amst. I, Nos. 607-9; II, Nos. 2244 f.; II, 2. No. 487; *DJ* 1840, 25 f., 1850, 47 f.; *DB* 1861, 141 f.; 1873, 88 f.; 1890, 87-123; 1892, 89-98; 1901, 15; G. Brandt, *Historie der Reformatie* II (Amsterdam, 1674) 3, 12-14.

Snep, a former Mennonite family at Haarlem, Holland. Jan Snep in the early 17th century settled at Haarlem, probably coming from Goch (*q.v.*), Germany. In Haarlem he joined the High German-Frisian Mennonite congregation, but during the troubles in this congregation he left it to join the Flemish congregation of "den Blok" (*q.v.*). His son was Isaac Snep, b. at Goch in 1612, d. at Haarlem 1681, married to Grietje Teyler (d. 1681), who was from before 1649 an elder of the Flemish Den Blok congregation. Serving in a period in which the Flemish Mennonites partly became more progressive, Isaac Snep was throughout life a champion of the old Mennonite doctrines and practices. In June 1660 he attended the "Leydse Synode" (*q.v.*), a Flemish conference of conservative leaders who wished to face the growth of liberalism, which under Collegiant (*q.v.*) influences was propagated by such ministers as Galenus Abrahamsz (*q.v.*) of Amsterdam and Willem van Maurik (*q.v.*) at Utrecht. At this meeting in Leiden Snep and three other preachers were appointed to draw up a new confession of faith out of the four outstanding Dutch Mennonite confessions; this new confession, however, never appeared. In 1661 Snep was among the "buitenmannen" (ministers from elsewhere) who took measures to suspend four progressive preachers at Utrecht (*q.v.*). When in 1664 (see **Lammerenkrijgh**) a part of the Flemish congregation *bij't Lam* in Amsterdam led by the preacher Samuel Apostool

left this church, Snep conducted the first service of this group on June 22, 1664, at the Oude Teertuinen. They were then called "Apostoolsen," but the name was soon changed to "Zonists" (*q.v.*). In his own congregation at Haarlem Snep also became involved in complications with a progressive group; he and Preacher Pieter Marcusz, defending the old principles and the authority of the Mennonite confessions, were opposed by two other preachers of the church, viz., Koenraad van Vollenhoven (*q.v.*) and Jan des Rameaux, who were followers of Galenus. After a few years of mutual reproaches and accusations the conflict exploded; in vain the burgomasters of Haarlem tried to reconcile the embittered opponents. Finally in 1670 the conflict ended in a schism; most of the members (1360) sided with Snep, while 508 took the part of van Vollenhoven. A brick wall was built in the meetinghouse, dividing it into two separate meeting places. Isaac Snep seems to have been a popular preacher, and often conducted services in other congregations, some as far away as Hamburg in Germany.

His son Thomas Snep (Haarlem, 1636-92), married in 1655 to Magdelena Bontemps, served the church of his father as a preacher. In 1680 he had some difficulties with his co-preacher Jan Evertsz (*q.v.*), who with the majority of the members separated from the main body and began to hold meetings on the Bakenessergracht, later at the Kruisstraat. Though Jan Evertsz seems to have been a troublemaker, Snep's conduct was not the best either; it seems that Snep, who was well-to-do and had influential business relations, played up Evertsz' financial weakness. Thomas Snep also preached at times at Hamburg.

In the 18th century some members of the Snep family at Haarlem were deacons of the church and trustees of the Mennonite orphanages.   vpZ.

DB 1863, 131-59, *passim;* 1898, 65; 1900, 33; 1916, 170, 176, 190; H. W. Meihuizen, *Galenus Abrahamsz* (Haarlem, 1954) 72, 98; B. C. Roosen, *Geschichte der Mennoniten zu Hamburg und Altona* I (Hamburg, 1866) 42, 60.

Snijder (Snyder), Sicke, an Anabaptist martyr; see **Sicke Freerks.**

Snow Hill Mennonite Church (MC), located 3 miles north of Snow Hill, Md., is a member of the Ohio and Eastern Conference, established in 1953. It had 31 members in 1957 and Omar Stoltzfus was its pastor.   M.G.

Snyder (Snider), a Mennonite family of Swiss origin, found today in Germany solely in Baden-Württemberg in the form Schneider, where Daniel Schneider is elder in the Reutlingen congregation and Fritz Schneider is elder in the Heilbronn congregation, while Heinrich Schneider is preacher in the Karlsruhe-Durlach congregation and a well-known Mennonite printer and publisher with a shop in Karlsruhe. In North America the name was Anglicized to Snyder or Snider, and is found almost exclusively in the Mennonite Church (MC) and largely in Ontario, where a number have served in the ministry. Among them were the bishops Jonas B. Snider (1858-1944) at Waterloo and Oliver D. Snider

(1878-) at Elmira, and the preachers Elias Schneider (1815-90) at Waterloo, Absalom B. Snyder (1861-1936) at Wanners, his grandson John W. Snyder (1925-) at Bloomingdale, Elvin Snyder (1900-), a missionary from Ontario in Argentina and Puerto Rico, his son Mario (1931-) in Chicago, and Howard W. Snider (1923-), formerly of Saskatchewan, now Edmonton, Alberta. In Lancaster County, Heinrich Schneider (1722-62) was the ancestor of numerous Mennonite descendants. In 1758 John Schneider, a Virginia Mennonite, made a trip to Holland to secure aid for needy Mennonites in Virginia. Of the Snyders in Juniata County, Pa., a Christian Snyder (1819-72) moved to Freeport, Ill., where he was ordained minister in 1864, while Jacob Snyder (1793-1865), who was ordained preacher in 1816, moved to Huntingdon County and became a leader in the Morrisons Cove (Blair Co.) district. Four of his five sons were ordained to the ministry, Christian, Abram, Herman, and Jacob Snyder, the latter two also as bishops. Jacob Snyder led his small congregation at Roaring Spring into the G.C.M. Church about 1908. His son William Snyder has been executive secretary of the MCC since 1958. A branch of the Snyder family (MC) has been represented in the Midwest at Alpha, Minn., Plainview, Tex., and Kalona, Iowa.   H.S.B.

Joseph M. Snyder, *Hannes Schneider and His Wife . . . Their Descendants* (Kitchener, 1940?).

Snyder County (Pa.) Amish settlement. Several families of the "Zook Church" in Mifflin County, Pa., moved to Selinsgrove in Snyder County, in 1948, when the majority voted to permit electricity. Among them were Bishop Jacob S. Peachey and two preachers, Jess and Jonathan Peachey. In 1956 the Snyder County group divided. Jonathan Peachey, with assistance from the "Zook Church" (which in 1954 affiliated with the Beachy Amish), led a separate congregation that permitted automobiles. The membership of the O.O.A. group in 1958 was 30, and in the Beachy group 21.   J.A.H.

Snyder Mennonite Church (MC), located one mile west of Bloomingdale, Waterloo Co., Ont., a member of the Ontario Conference, was organized about 1824 when Henry Weber was chosen as the first minister. The first meetinghouse was erected in 1826, when Jacob Snyder (settled here in 1806 and owned 3,000 acres including the site of the present village of Bloomingdale), after whom the church is named, granted the land for the building. So many of the members followed the M.B.C. movement in the 1870's that the congregation was in effect suspended until about 1882. The present brick building, erected in 1878, was used by the M.B.C. group. Menno Bowman, at that time a deacon in the Snyder congregation, left to become a leading minister in the M.B.C. Church. In 1957 the congregation had 61 members, with John W. Snyder as pastor. H.S.B.

Soblahof(f) (Soblahov, Zobelhof), a Bruderhof of the Hutterian Brethren near Trentschin (Trencin) in Hungary (*q.v.*) (now Czechoslovakia). The household was purchased for 150 Talers from Hieronimus Thaus on Dec. 6, 1622, by Hutterites who were expelled from Stiegnitz (*q.v.*). On Oct. 23,

1623, Count Caspar von Illésházi received the refugee Brethren and gave them permission to furnish the Bruderhof according to their requirements and gave them a piece of wasteland in addition to all sorts of rights and privileges. In 1626 the Brethren acquired two more barren fields. In 1630 Caspar released the Brethren from the payment of fees which the Lutheran Church had required. In 1651 his sons, Gabriel and George Illésházi, confirmed the contract and all the liberties which Caspar had granted them, and in 1652 George gave them half the "Session" Holgasovska there (Beck, 484). On Oct. 5, 1652, Turkish troops plundered the Bruderhof and set it afire. Twelve persons were abducted or killed. It was abandoned in 1688.   HEGE.

Beck, *Geschichts-Bücher;* Wolkan, *Geschicht-Buch;* Zieglschmid, *Chronik; ML* IV.

Sobotiste (German, *Freischütz;* in Hutterite sources *Sabatisch*), a town in Slovakia near the Moravian border, the site of a large Hutterite Bruderhof which is still inhabited by descendants of the Hutterites, the only Bruderhof which continued in existence throughout the entire period of Hutterite history in Central Europe (1546-1762). In the 16th century this market village belonged to the manorial nobleman Franz Niary of Bedek, lord of the castle of Branc (in the Chronicle *Bränisch*). Since he needed good tillers of the soil and tenders of the vineyards he invited the Hutterites from near-by Moravia to settle on his estate in 1546. Soon times of great hardship set in (see **Slovakia**), but in 1554-1605 the peace was not disturbed. Then followed a Turkish invasion, and it was not until 1613 that the brethren began anew to build a Bruderhof. From then on until today this Bruderhof has existed nearly unchanged. All the Vorsteher or "bishops" of the Hutterite brotherhood lived here, including particularly Andreas Ehrenpreis (*q.v.*). The lords gave the brethren a charter of privileges (*Hausbrief*) in 1613 and another in 1640 (see *Klein-Geschichtsbuch*, 128 n); the latter is still in the possession of the Hof and was reported in 1937 and 1938. In 1621, Franz Walter started an exodus of some 180 Brethren from here in Transylvania (see **Alwinz**). The best time was the Ehrenpreis period, 1630-62, which might be called the high point of the Sobotiste congregation.

In 1665 a marked decline set in. A delegation was sent to the Mennonites in the Netherlands for material help, but even though this was granted it could not stop the rapid deterioration of the Sobotiste group, both economically and spiritually. Eventually the practice of complete community of goods was given up, although many elements of it still remained. The 18th century saw the coming of the Jesuits (*q.v.*) and with it a real crisis set in. The brotherhood was no longer strong enough to resist the aggressive manipulations of both the Jesuits and the governmental authorities (details in Beck, *Geschichts-Bücher,* and in the *Klein-Geschichtsbuch*). The last Vorsteher was Zacharias Walther, a descendant of the oldest still living Anabaptist family (see **Walter family**). In his days the congregation numbered about 220 souls, and in 1753 they built a clock tower (Beck, 574; a picture of it in Friedmann, *Habaner*) and in 1754 a "Bet-Haus" (i.e., a meetinghouse; picture in Lydia Müller). Beck found records of these years showing that Hutterite, or more correctly now Habaner, midwives were very popular and much in demand with the local population. In 1748 and again in 1752, Walther wrote to the Mennonites in Amsterdam, apparently hoping again to receive both material and moral support in the hard struggle of the time. (All the correspondence both of 1665 and of 1748 and 1752 is found in the archives of the Mennonite Church of Amsterdam.) But in 1761 the Jesuits decided to act: a number of brethren were taken into custody, including Zacharias Walther, who was sent into a monastery in Budapest where eventually he yielded and became Catholic in 1763, Heinrich Kuhn who turned Catholic in 1762, and Tobias Pullman (or Polman) who did the same in 1763 in the city of Neutra (*Klein-Geschichtsbuch*, 238, note; Beck 606, 610, 613, 617).

These conversions, however, were of little value. Privately these Sobotiste people continued in their old Hutterite faith as far as possible (infant baptism was obligatory now), and thus much hypocrisy developed. The brethren knew of course of the new settlements in the Ukraine which had been started by the Transylvanian group, and there was much discussion about whether or not to leave everything behind and try to join these brethren. One of the strongest in character among the men of Sobotiste was a Jacob Walter, of whom the *Klein-Geschichtsbuch* relates an interesting story. In 1782 he left Sobotiste alone, and traveled via Herrnhut (the German center of the Moravian Brethren Church, *q.v.*) to Vishenka (Wischenka), Ukraine, where the new Bruderhof had been started *c*1770. The next year he came back in order to take his wife and child along to these brethren; one daughter had to be left behind as she had married a Catholic. With the help of several other brethren who were sent back from Russia to assist Sobotiste, eleven families managed to escape the surveillance of the clergy, and some 56 souls eventually reached the new Ukraine Bruderhof, 1782-83 (the *Klein-Geschichtsbuch*, 373-74, lists all their names; some of them were also from nearby Velke Levary, *q.v.*). The last visit of these Vishenka brethren in Sobotiste occurred in 1795, but after 1782 no further transfers took place. Those who decided to stay in Sobotiste were resigned in their new religion (Catholicism), glad that the clergy allowed them at least to continue most of their old communal institutions.

In 1937 two American Hutterite brethren visited this place, and from the unpublished diary of David Hofer we learn the following details. The Bruderhof buildings had survived essentially unchanged since 1613, consisting all in all of 39 straw-thatched houses, dominated in the distance by the ruins of the former castle of Branc. Some of the names of the inhabitants were Baumgartner, Pullmann, and Tschetterle (Ceterle, Tschetter), all well-known Hutterite names (see **Hutterite Family Names**). All in all there were about 40 families who still lived in this large-scale Hof or colony. All of them spoke German besides the native Slovakian. In 1937 the mill, the dye house, the inn, the wine cellars, and the woods were still held as communal property by the present-day Habaner. The mill, erected in 1739, was still working. The Chapel was still standing,

but the clock and bells had been removed from the old clock tower during World War I. In the Town Hall the visitors found an old clock of their forefathers. In the cemetery most tombstones had disappeared except one of 1755, for Tobias Seidel. The once famous pottery workshop (producing the famous Habaner fayence; see **Ceramics**) no longer existed, but some people had started digging and had found in the ground potsherds and a few fine specimens of this lost art. (Most of the Habaner fayence that has survived is found in museums in Bratislava, Budapest, and elsewhere.) In the houses and in the Town Hall the visitors found ancient heavy oak tables of Hutterite origin and other household goods, even old books. The charter of 1640 (*Hausbrief*) was likewise shown to the guests from America, who were received with warm hospitality by these Catholic Habaner. But, naturally, they showed little interest in their own history and the tradition of a time long gone by. Nothing of the old things described was for sale, hard as the American brethren tried to buy a few souvenirs.

In 1945 in the wave of anti-German feeling following the war, most of the German-speaking people were expelled from Czechoslovakia, and it must be assumed that this fate also hit most of the Habaner of Sobotiste, unless they declared themselves openly as Slovaks.   R.F.

Beck, *Geschichts-Bücher;* Zieglschmid, *Chronik* and *Klein-Geschichtsbuch;* Robert Friedmann, "Die Habaner in der Slowakei," *Wiener Zeitschrift für Volkskunde,* 1927 (illustrated); Lydia Müller, *Kommunismus* (with good illustrations); R. Friedmann, "Hutterites Revisit Their Old Homesteads: the Diary of David Hofer, 1937," in *MQR* XXXIV (1960); *ML* IV, 212-16.

Social Background of the Anabaptists: *General*— The Anabaptists of the 16th century represented a radical challenge to the current social order and to the corresponding Catholic and Protestant social philosophies. Where the status quo represented a cultural monism with the whole society and culture grouped around a central religious motif, Anabaptism postulated a cultural pluralism which allowed for spontaneous and restrictive association, on the premise that by the very nature of the case complete homogeneity is not possible.

To the guardians of the social order the voluntary and exclusive assemblies appeared as a stab at social order and unity. Both Catholic and Protestant religious and civic leaders therefore felt that the movement had to be suppressed at all costs, even at the cost of contradicting their own religious professions. Their polemical declarations against the Anabaptists are filled with invectives against men who appear as society's worst enemies. These declarations became the basis for the interpretation of these stirring events until modern scholarship succeeded in placing the struggle into a more valid perspective.

A second ideological attempt to interpret 16th-century Anabaptism in its social development came in modern Marxist and Socialist thought. Marxist writers saw Anabaptism as an early stage of modern class warfare and as part of the Peasant Revolt (Engels). More moderate Socialists likewise saw it as the religious garb of class struggle (Kautsky) or as "the culminating effort of medieval Christian

Communism" (Belfort Bax). From a completely different viewpoint Anabaptism became linked to the spirit of the French Revolution (Alexandre Weill), and Christian Socialists became interested in the social passion of this movement (Leonard Ragaz).

In both the 16th-century polemic and the modern social philosophies, interest was directed first of all to the dynamic or motivation of Anabaptism. While the Reformers did not deny the religious concern of the Anabaptists, they saw in their efforts nevertheless a revolt against duly constituted political and religious authority. In Switzerland Anabaptists were thought to have "sucked their poison" from Thomas Müntzer (q.v.). After the Münster (q.v.) uprising (1534-35), it became customary to accuse all the 16th-century dissenting religious parties of clandestine revolutionary intention. In this way the religious aspirations of even the nonrevolutionary dissenters were buried beneath the odium of supposed sedition.

In the hands of the Marxists the alleged revolutionary character of Anabaptism was likewise asserted. But now this became the glory of the movement. Whatever religious coloring it may have had, it was seen as nothing other than the class struggle in the economically determined course of history. The common denominator of the 16th-century Anabaptist bands was simply the proletarian status of their members.

Modern serious scholarship, however, has placed 16th-century Anabaptism into a completely new perspective. On the one hand there were liberal thinkers like Ludwig Keller and Ernst Troeltsch who recognized the genuine religious impulse underlying this movement. On the other hand there were the objective historical inquiries which have made available important historical data which had lain unused in the archives of European cities since the 16th century.

The first result of these inquiries of importance to us here is clear proof of the religious character of 16th-century Anabaptism. While admittedly the movement is quite complex in character, and nonreligious factors are also discernible, an examination of the testimonies of the Anabaptists themselves and of their contemporaries shows that the movement can be understood only by understanding their religious experience.

In the second place, it follows from this that their radical social views must be interpreted in the light of their religious outlook and not vice versa. One of the major issues at the time of the Reformation was the payment of tithes to the church. This the Anabaptists rejected, because they repudiated an institutional church such as medieval Catholicism. But the civil tithe or tax they paid because the Scriptures commanded it, even though they rejected the magistracy in the sense of holding government office. They stoutly maintained that governments were divinely ordained and therefore must be obeyed. There are records of Anabaptists under torture addressing the officials under whom they suffered as ministers of God.

Finally, the social composition of 16th-century Anabaptism was far too diverse to allow interpretation in terms of class conflict. The initial communities in Switzerland contained members from all classes, as did those in South Germany and Moravia. The center of the movement lay in the cities in the enlightened intellectual and "middle class" circles, including both clergy and laity. From the outset there were also peasants and occasional members of the aristocracy, though admittedly the latter were few, probably for the reason that these were hostile to all reform efforts.

As to the earliest Dutch Anabaptism, Karel Vos, and in his footsteps A. F. Mellink, tried to prove that in the period 1530-44 with only a very few exceptions the Anabaptists came from the "lower class" and even from the dregs of the population, expecting from Anabaptism the improvement of their material conditions. W. J. Kühler and N. van der Zijpp have shown, however, that the vast majority of the Anabaptists in Holland and Flanders came from the "middle class," for a large part being craftsmen and artisans, and that the movement was purely or at least fairly predominantly of religious character.

In the wake of severe persecution, however, the descendants of the original Swiss Brethren, who today are to be found in Switzerland, France, Germany, and North America, rapidly lost out in the cities and developed a strong agrarian ethos. In the Netherlands, on the other hand, while strong rural communities developed, the city churches were able to perpetuate themselves and today strong city churches are to be found in centers like Amsterdam, Haarlem, The Hague, Groningen, Leeuwarden, Rotterdam, Leiden, and Utrecht.

Having recognized the religious motivation of 16th-century Anabaptism, however, we must note also the important conditioning role of the complex social forces operative at the time. There was the urban ferment of the city state of medieval Europe now caught up in the emergent mercantilistic nation state of the 16th and 17th centuries. There was the impact of modern political, economic, and religious theory on the peasantry. And there was the new learning carried forward by the men of letters and their busy printing presses. All of these helped to pave the way for the tremendous burst of spiritual energy released in the Protestant Reformation, which was then to be divided so tragically as the new wine was forced back into the old skins of the *corpus christianum*, and the Anabaptists arose to protest.

The motivation of the 16th-century Anabaptist movement was religious, but it did not occur in a social vacuum. Born in a time of intense groping, it brought perspectives to bear on the social struggle which were born of profound religious insights, and which were to play an influential role in modern history.   P.P.

H. S. Bender, "Die Zwickauer Propheten, Thomas Müntzer und die Täufer," *Theologische Zeitschrift* VIII (Basel, 1952); Ernst Correll, *Das schweizerische Täufermennonitentum* (Tübingen, 1925); Paul Dedic, "The Social Background of the Austrian Anabaptists," *MQR* XIII (1939); Cornelius Krahn, "The Dutch Mennonites and Urbanism" (*Proceedings of the tenth Conference on Mennonite Educational and Cultural Problems, 1955*); R. Kreider, "Vocations of Swiss and South German Anabaptists," *Menn. Life* VIII (January 1953); Paul Peachey, *Die soziale Herkunft der Schweizer Täufer* (Karlsruhe,

1954); *idem*, "The Social Background . . . of the Swiss Anabaptists," *MQR* XXVIII (1954); B. H. Unruh, "Das Täufertum und die Bauernrevolution," *Gedenkschrift* (Karlsruhe, 1925); K. Vos, "Revolutionnaire Hervorming," in *De Gids*, 1920; Mellink, *Wederdopers;* W. J. Kühler, "Het Anabaptisme in Nederland," in *De Gids,* 1921; N. van der Zijpp, "Menno en Munster," in *Stemmen uit de Doopsgezinde Broederschap* II (1953) No. 1.

* * *

Anabaptists in the Hapsburg Territory, mainly Austria and Moravia. It used to be a common assumption that Anabaptism was basically a "proletarian" movement, made up in the main of "common people," i.e., laborers and peasants, plus a few artisans, while the upper strata of society everywhere joined the new state churches (Swiss Reformed or German Lutheran) or remained Catholic. This picture is certainly incorrect as far as the earlier period of the movement is concerned, that is, the first and second generations, 1525-70. About 1600 the situation greatly changed, at least for the South German and Swiss area and for Moravia and Slovakia. As the fervor of the beginning waned, the movement became more and more rural, and the economically and intellectually stronger sections of population dropped out. But for the earlier period the picture is by no means uniform: there were priests among the Anabaptists as well as nobility, also a goodly number of citizens of some means; the number of learned men, however, was never large, as the simplicity of the Anabaptist faith did not have much appeal to the "humanists."

As for Austria and the Hapsburg realm (which includes Moravia and Slovakia) our knowledge is based on two brief studies, one by Paul Dedic, which are, however, sufficient to allow certain conclusions:

(1) *Clergy*—Dedic lists the following names: Hubmaier, Schiemer, Schlaffer, Thomas Waldhauser, Canon Martin Göschl, Oswald Glaidt, Jörg Blaurock (though Swiss he was also active in Tirol), and perhaps Wolfgang Brandhuber. All these men belonged to the first few years of the movement up to 1530. To later decades belong the names of Leonhard Lochmaier, Leonhard Dax, and Virgil Plattner.

(2) *Nobility*—The best known is Leonhard Liechtenstein, Lord of Nikolsburg, the patron of Hubmaier and of the "Schwertler." He died in 1534. (His nephew Hans Liechtenstein, though sympathetic to the Anabaptists, was never baptized by them.) Of the strong Tirolean nobility there were Helene von Freyberg (*q.v.*), mistress of the castle of Münichau near Kitzbühel, who joined the Marpeck group; the Barons Anton and Siegmund von Wolkenstein, of South Tirol, who for a while joined the Anabaptists; a Bavarian nobleman, Michael Veldtaler (*q.v.*), who joined the Hutterites in Moravia in 1555 and became one of the most active members, being imprisoned several times and working as a missioner for many years. Dedic names also the wife of the Imperial Captain Katzian and a Tirolean noblewoman Agnes von Waltenhofen. Perhaps also the von Pappenheim (*q.v.*) family should be mentioned, supporters of Marpeck, although only distantly related to the Austrian territory.

(3) *Burghers,* the urban middle class of the 16th century, patricians, scholars, etc. The most outstanding representative of this class was, no doubt, Pilgram Marpeck of Rattenberg, Tirol, a successful mining and water engineer. Ulrich Stadler of Sterzing, Tirol, a mining official, and Onophrius Griesinger, likewise a mining official in Salzburg, belong to the same class; also Marpeck had originally been a mining official. The two brothers Freisleben or Eleutherobios (*q.v.*) of Upper Austria were outstanding examples of humanists among the Anabaptists (they, however, returned later to Catholicism). (Bünderlin, named by Dedic, was not an Anabaptist in the narrower sense.) Antoni Erfordter was a substantial burgher of the city of Klagenfurt, Carinthia, and a highly educated man. Jeronymus Käls, a schoolmaster of Tirol, was martyred in 1536. Later in the 16th century the apothecary Melchior Platzer (*q.v.*) suffered martyrdom in Vorarlberg in 1583. The number of physicians and barber-surgeons among the brethren was by no means small (see **Medicine among the Hutterites**): Georg Zobel (*q.v.*), a physician; Josef Hause, a barber (*c*1600); Balthasar Goller, a physician (d. 1619); and Sebastian Dietrich (*q.v.*), a barber. There is no doubt that a number of well-to-do burghers had joined the brotherhoods here and there, mainly in Tirol (Dedic), but the sources rarely give their names. In Upper Austria Anabaptism centered around urban places like Linz, Steyr, and Wels, also Freistadt (before 1530), which implies that here the movement was predominantly urban.

(4) *Artisans,* both master craftsmen and journeymen. To this class, no doubt, the majority of Austrian (Moravian) Anabaptists belonged; nearly all the leading men came from this background. Since they belonged to the lower middle class, the Anabaptist movement may sociologically be considered an offspring mainly of this stratum, in spite of certain exceptions. Certainly Anabaptism was not "proletarian" in the narrow sense of the word.

A scanning of the list of the better-known men among the Hutterites and related groups shows names like Jacob Hutter, allegedly a hatter, Hans Amon, a weaver of wool, Peter Riedemann, a shoemaker, Peter Walpot, a warper, Leonhard Lanzenstiel, a ropemaker, Veldt Grünberger, a clockmaker, Andreas Ehrenpreis, a miller, Gabriel Ascherham, a furrier, and Philipp Plener, a weaver. One of the noblest crafts among the Hutterites was pottery (see **Ceramics**), and much fame came to the brethren for their beautiful "fayence." But strangely, not one potter's name ever appears in the sources, just as no cutler is mentioned, another Hutterite trade of high repute.—Every new member of the brotherhood had to learn a trade; even the former nobleman Veldtaler had to comply and learned joinery. In fact the elaborate *Gemeindeordnungen* (*q.v.*) are a good indication of their major occupations.

It is characteristic of this class of artisans not to hold too high an appreciation for scholarship. A tract of *c*1590 inquires "Why no scholars (*Hochgelehrte*) are found in our midst." Answer: because too much studying is a hindrance to a simple and straightforward faith. But, says Dedic, even though there were no scholars among the brethren, there were no illiterates either. With a few exceptions all the men were literate, and many were truly masters of the art of letter writing. Thus the educational standards of this group were definitely high.

(5) *Peasants*—In Tirol a great number of free peasants joined the Anabaptists, but again names are rarely given. Dedic thinks that only in Tirol did Anabaptism find response among this less educated class. In Upper Austria the movement took roots primarily in urban centers.

(6) *Laborers*—The only group to be considered here would be the miners (*Bergknappen*). It is known that the miners were a most alert and open-minded element of the 16th-century population. In the Inn Valley (Tirol) copper was mined near Rattenberg (*q.v.*), Schwatz, and Brixlegg, and salt near Hall. All these places quickly became centers of Anabaptism—to be sure, only during the earliest period (up to perhaps 1535-40). Of later decades no information is available.   R.F.

Paul Dedic, "The Social Background of the Austrian Anabaptists," *MQR* XII (1939) 5-20; R. Friedmann, "Epistles of the Hutterites," *MQR* XIX (1946) 153 f.

Sociedad de Hermanos, Spanish official name of the Society of Brothers (*q.v.*) in Latin America. For the group in Paraguay, see **Primavera.**

Sociëteit is the Dutch designation for what in America is called an organized conference. At present there are the following Mennonite Sociëteiten in the Netherlands: (1) Algemeene (*q.v.*) Doopsgezinde Sociëteit (ADS), founded in 1811; (2) Rijper (*q.v.*) Sociëteit in North Holland, formerly called Waterlandsche Sociëteit, founded in the 17th century; (3) Sociëteit van Doopsgezinde gemeenten in Friesland (FDS; see **Friesland, Sociëteit**), founded in 1695; (4) Sociëteit van Doopsgezinde gemeenten in Groningen en Oostfriesland (see **Groninger Doopsgezinde Sociëteit,** 3), founded in 1826; and (5) a conference with the same function as a Sociëteit, viz., the Zwolsche (*q.v.*) Vereeniging.

Formerly there were also: (6) Vriesche (Friesche) Sociëteit in Noordholland (see **Noordholland Sociëteit**), which in 1841 merged with the (2) Rijper Sociëteit; (7) Sociëteit van (Groninger) Oude Vlamingen (see **Groninger Doopsgezinde Sociëteit,** 1), dissolved in 1815; (8) Waterlandsche Sociëteit in Zuidholland, also called Lamistische Sociëteit (see **Zuidholland Sociëteit**), which existed briefly in the last decades of the 17th century; (9) Humsterlandsche Sociëteit (see **Groninger Doopsgezinde Sociëteit,** 2); (10) Zonsche (*q.v.*) or Zonistische Sociëteit, founded in 1674 and active until 1796.   vDZ.

N. van der Zijpp, *Geschiedenis der Doopsgezinden* (Arnhem, 1952) 129-32, 192 f.

Society of Friends, popularly called Quakers (a nickname given in 1650), founded in England by George Fox (1624-91), who began preaching in 1647-48, calling his followers Friends of Truth. His teaching was a vigorous attack on the Christianity of his day, the Church of England and the Presbyterians in particular, calling for a thorough transformation of the ecclesiastical system and the restoration of true Christianity conceived as a simple, completely dedicated following of Christ, under the authority of the Bible and led by the "inner light," a spark of which

is in every man. He called for simplicity and brotherhood in all things, high and holy living, and a worship without any sacraments, ordinances, clergy, or liturgy. He held a vision of the ultimate conquest of England for his faith. Accordingly Quakerism was from the very beginning strongly evangelistic and missionary. William Penn (*q.v.*; 1644-1718), sometimes called "the second founder of Quakerism," was a very effective leader. By the end of the 17th century the Quaker growth was extraordinary; they numbered about 100,000.

Almost from the beginning the Quakers completely repudiated violence and warfare, standing for full nonresistance, and refused the oath. They suffered severe persecution for decades in England and elsewhere, but could not be suppressed. They developed a close-knit effective organization with strong discipline.

So much in the Quaker principles is similar to the principles of the early Anabaptists (not the form of worship or polity) that it seems impossible that there could have been no influence from Anabaptism upon the origin and ideas of the movement. However, the most intense search, by both Quaker and non-Quaker historians, has failed to uncover direct connections. There is a very real possibility, however, that the spirit of Continental Anabaptism, which was transferred to England (*q.v.*) in 1530 and continued to influence English religious life with results in the earlier Congregationalist (*q.v.*) and Baptist (*q.v.*) movements, had an indirect influence upon Fox and the early Quakers.

Although the Quakers of the first two hundred years retained a Biblical and evangelical orthodoxy along with their emphasis on the inner light and ethical matters, the 19th century saw a substantial change, completed in the 20th century, by which a large block, especially in America, adopted liberal theological positions while retaining the Quaker forms of worship and polity, although a majority of the Quakers retained and intensified the evangelical type of theology but surrendered typical Quaker worship and polity to accommodate themselves to American Protestantism. (However, certain groups of Quakers have retained Quaker worship forms along with evangelical theology.) Also, while Christian pacifism has remained fairly strong among English Friends, it has declined relatively among American Friends, even though outstanding individuals are active in Pacifist causes, and even though on both sides of the ocean official statements are uniformly pacifistic. The principle of personal freedom of conscience and the relative abandonment of discipline have opened the door to toleration of relatively any position on pacifism as well as in theology. The social service motive has remained strong, however, and both British and American Quakers have made large contributions in the fields of idealistic social service, social reform, and international good will. Outstanding in this field has been the work and influence of the American Friends Service Committee (*q.v.*), founded in 1917 at Philadelphia, of which Rufus Jones was long chairman and Clarence Pickett was long executive secretary. Most groups of evangelical American Quakers have also carried on extensive foreign mission work.

37

The distribution of Friends throughout the world in 1957 was as follows:

I. *English-speaking Base Congregations*		145,097
United States	119,469	
British Isles	23,574	
Australia and New Zealand	1,358	
Canada	696	
II. *Continental Europe*		969
Germany	547	
Scandinavia	250	
France, Holland, Switzerland	272	
III. *Foreign Mission Fields*		46,721
Kenya	28,222	
Madagascar	7,700	
Latin America	8,260	
Other	2,530	
	Total	192,787

In 1937 the Friends World Committee was created which convenes a World Conference every 15 years. Outstanding work in relief, social service, and peace has been done by the Friends Service Committee of England and the American Friends Service Committee of America. The two together were awarded the Nobel Peace Prize in 1947.

The chief purpose of the rest of this article is to trace relations between Quakers and Mennonites, which fall in general into three periods: (1) Mennonites under Quaker evangelism on the European Continent, 1655-1750; (2) Mennonites and Quakers in Colonial Pennsylvania; and (3) Mennonite and Quaker contacts and co-operation in North America in the time after World War I, especially since 1935.

Mennonites Under Quaker Evangelism on the European Continent, 1655-1750. It is noteworthy that the Quakers in Holland and Germany had missionary success almost only among the Mennonites. This was due in part to the similarities of the principles of the two groups, but also to the fact that attempts to convert members of the state churches in most cases brought severe persecution. The first missionaries came to Holland in 1653—John Stubbs and William Caton, who preached in Middelburg and Vlissingen. William Ames (*q.v.*) reached Amsterdam in the spring of 1656; John Higgins, Steven Crisp, William Bale, Joseph Cal, and others followed. Ames was the most aggressive and most successful of the group. They succeeded in assembling a small congregation in Amsterdam, composed almost solely of former Mennonites. Among them were the parents of the noted Quaker historian William Sewel (*q.v.*), both of whom had belonged to the Lamist congregation. Ames and others also went to Rotterdam and Haarlem. Ames went from Amsterdam to Germany as far as the Palatinate, where in 1657 he gathered a small congregation at Kriegsheim, composed of eight former Mennonite families, which lasted, in spite of severe tribulation, until 1685, when it emigrated to Pennsylvania. (William Penn visited them in 1677.) Upon Ames' return to Amsterdam he was expelled from the city and went to Schiedam, Rotterdam, and Gouda, where he won a small group of former Mennonites. His continued success led to the calling of an anti-Quaker synod of the state church in 1657. Ames was imprisoned for

a time, but this did not stop him. In 1659 a second synod issued an urgent warning to all the clergy to resist the Quaker inroads. Ames wrote back to England typically that he found the Mennonites "near to the kingdom" and "white unto harvest." (See Hull's *Rise of Quakerism* for exhaustive details.)

In 1658 Ames went to Friesland and in 1659 reached Hamburg, where he won the preacher of the Flemish Mennonite congregation, Berend Roelofs, and his four adult children. The Quaker mission aroused deep unrest in the city. Because of the Quakers the Mennonites developed serious internal difficulties as well as getting into external trouble. The state church preachers wrote pamphlets of warning against the foreign agitators, as did the Mennonite preacher Gerhard Roosen. On June 24, 1660, the Hamburg city council issued a mandate requiring all Quakers to leave the city within four days, as a consequence of which Roelofs and his group went to Alkmaar in Holland. However, a small group of Quakers persisted in Hamburg.

Ames apparently next went to Friedrichstadt in Holstein, where in 1660 he won a following among the Mennonites. On June 21, 1677, George Fox came to Friedrichstadt. The congregation here grew substantially through transfers from Bremen, Danzig (de Veer family), and Elbing. With the help of financial support from England, it was able to build a meetinghouse in 1678. The plan of the city government to expel the group was blocked by Fox through a written appeal to Duke Christian Albrecht of Holstein-Gottorp. As a result in part of conflicts with the authorities in 1706 and 1711 the group declined sharply in number through emigration and death. By the middle of the 18th century it ceased to exist.

Ames arrived in Danzig in June 1661, apparently seeking out the Mennonites. Although he was expelled from the city within a month, he succeeded in winning a few followers, not Mennonites this time, who were imprisoned for a time in 1663. Fox secured toleration for them in 1677 through a written appeal to King John III, the Polish ruler of the area.

Ames returned to Holland in 1661, where he spent some time working in the provinces of Gelderland and Overijssel, visiting practically all the Mennonite congregations, then moving on to Friesland. Although he had little direct success, a few Mennonites, Socinians, and others began to hold religious meetings patterned on the Quaker style. As a result in 1662 the Frisian government issued a decree forbidding the entrance into the country of "Quakers, Socinians, and immersionists," and ordering a 5-year imprisonment at hard labor for such as might nevertheless venture to come. In the same year Jan Roelofs and William Caton published a defense against the Alkmaar Mennonite preacher Pieter Joosten de Colder, entitled *Een rechtvaardigke Verdediginghe der Waerheyt onses Godts* (Hoorn, 1662). The number of Quakers in Alkmaar at this time must have been large. In Harlingen unusually severe prison sentences were imposed upon Quakers because of their riotous behavior. They complained bitterly about this, also about the attitude of the Mennonites as well as Reformed in the city (*Menn.*

Bl., 1854, pp. 55 f.). Among the writings of the Quakers against the Dutch Mennonites at this time and later were: William Caton, *De Oorsaeck van de Pest* (Amsterdam, 1665); George Keith, *Het Decksel gescheurt* (Amsterdam, 1670); Stephen Crisp, *Uytroepinge tegen de Vervolginge,* 2 vv. (n.p., 1670-71); *idem, Een Geklanck des Alarms* (Amsterdam, 1671); Judith Zinspenning, *Eenige Schriften en Zend-brieven* (Amsterdam, 1684). The meeting of William Penn and George Fox with Galenus Abrahamsz (*q.v.*) in Amsterdam in 1677 is of much interest (see Sewel's account).

In 1662 Ames succeeded in winning a small following among the Mennonites in Emden which received official toleration in 1686, after much tribulation, but by 1688 there were few Quakers left in the city.

In Crefeld a small Quaker group was organized by former Mennonites, apparently in 1667, as the result of a visit by Stephen Crisp. Crisp visited them again in 1677, when he also visited Wesel and Cleve, where there were interested persons who apparently did not finally become Quakers. The Crefeld Quakers suffered much at various times, and since they never found real toleration, they finally emigrated to Germantown, Pa. Twelve of the original thirteen families who settled Germantown in 1683 were Crefeld Quakers. Stephen Crisp reported on May 6, 1685, that the Crefeld (and Kriegsheim) Quaker meetings had been discontinued, since all members had gone to Pennsylvania.

By the end of the 17th century, the British intensive Quaker mission work on the Continent had come to an end, as had also all Quaker meetings. Many English and American Quakers visited cities across the continent as far as Russia, throughout the 18th and 19th centuries, but these visits seldom resulted in the formation of Quaker congregations. Minden and Pyrmont, Germany, in 1790, were exceptions. But until after World War II there were no significant contacts with Mennonites in Holland or Germany. In Germany Bernhard Brons (*q.v.*) of Emden was an advocate of contacts with the Quakers (*Menn. Bl.,* 1894 and 1897). Pastor Gustav Kraemer of Krefeld occasionally attended the Quaker Yearly Meetings at Bad Pyrmont in the first third of the 20th century.

In Holland a significant influence of British Quakerism on the Mennonites was the result of attendance of some Mennonites at the Quaker school and center at Woodbrooke, near Birmingham, England, which had been founded in 1903 and had become the channel of a renewal among the British Friends. Among those who attended were T. O. Hylkema, J. E. van Brakel, and C. Nijdam, all of whom became influential pastors in Dutch Mennonite churches. The Gemeentedagbeweging (today called Broederschapswerk, *q.v.*), which has meant a great deal for the renewal of the Dutch Mennonite brotherhood, was the direct outcome of Woodbrooke influence. T. O. Hylkema was the originator of the new movement, whose first annual conference (Gemeentedag) was held on Aug. 2, 1917.

Later contacts between British Quakers and Dutch Mennonites were almost exclusively in the area of the peace testimony, largely channeled through the European Continuation Committee of the Historic Peace Churches (1947-), which is described below.

The visits of British and American Friends to the Mennonites in Russia in the 19th century, and the substantial aid of British Friends to the Russian Mennonite settlers in the United States in 1874-75 form an interesting story, of which little was known until the appearance of Owen Gingerich's account in the *MQR* for October 1951, from which the following material is taken. The first visitors were Stephen Grellet and William Allen, British Friends who spent May 13-29, 1819, in both the Chortitza and the Molotschna settlements. A warm letter of appreciation from Elder Jacob Fast of Halbstadt has been preserved. John Yeardley made a visit about the middle of the century, of which little is known.

Very important was the visit of Thomas Harvey and Isaac Robson, official delegates of the London Yearly Meeting for religious service in South Russia, chiefly among the Molokans. After a stop with Mennonites at Neuburg a.D. in Bavaria in August 1867, they reached Berdyansk in the Ukraine on October 9, where they were guests of Cornelius Jansen, who was their guide on a visit to the Mennonite settlements. Correspondence between Jansen and Harvey continued for about ten years, even after Jansen emigrated to the United States in 1873. The interest of Harvey and Robson in the difficulties of the Mennonites with the Russian government which arose in 1870 as well as in the emigration of 1874 ff. ultimately led to the raising of funds from British Friends for the needy Mennonite settlers in the United States. In 1875, for instance, $10,000 was raised and sent to Jansen and others in America. Much informational material was published in the *British Friend* by Harvey in the years 1873-76. In 1872 Harvey and Robson published a small informational pamphlet, *The Mennonites of South Russia,* which included strong advice to the Russian Mennonites against accepting hospital service in the army (*Sanitätsdienst*). In 1879 they wrote another small pamphlet, *An die in den Vereinigten Staaten aus Süd-Russland eingewanderten sogenannten Mennoniten,* containing words of encouragement, which was published by the Mennonite Publishing Company at Elkhart, Ind.

The last item of interest here is the visit of the American Quaker Barnabas Hobbs, later a president of Earlham College, to St. Petersburg in 1878, accompanied by Charles Taylor, an English Friend from Manchester, England. Hobbs carried a message from American Friends to Czar Alexander on behalf of the nonresistant privileges of the Russian Mennonites. He failed to get an audience with the Czar himself, but presented to a high Foreign Office official his memorial on behalf of the Mennonites together with a historical statement on the policy of the United States toward conscientious objectors.

Mennonites and Quakers in Colonial Pennsylvania. The assertion has often been made that the Mennonites came to Pennsylvania on invitation of William Penn, who is supposed to have visited them in Germany. While it is true that literature advertising Pennsylvania was published in Germany and distributed in Germany (Penn pamphlets of 1681 and 1684, Pastorius' book *Umständige geographische*

Beschreibung of 1700, and other material), and it is also true that Penn was eager to secure settlers from Germany as well as to aid persecuted Christians (Mennonites) everywhere by furnishing them opportunity for a secure haven in his Pennsylvania, there is no evidence that Penn either personally or in writing ever specifically invited Mennonites from Germany to come to Pennsylvania, or that he even thought about German Mennonites as a specific separate group. Certainly he never had any personal interest in the Swiss Mennonites. His agent in Amsterdam, Benjamin Furly, a good land agent, of course, had business dealings with Mennonite land buyers. Penn's journey to Germany, July to October 1677, was made as a Quaker missioner before he came into possession of Pennsylvania (he petitioned for the grant of Pennsylvania June 24, 1680, and received the charter for it March 14, 1681). In any case, although on this trip he visited several places in Holland where he came in contact with Mennonites, he did not visit any Mennonite community in Germany. He did visit the Kriegsheim Quakers and the Frankfurt "Saalhof" Pietiests. The contact with the Crefeld Quakers and Mennonites was made through Jacob Telner (*q.v.*), an Amsterdam and Crefeld Quaker (former Mennonite) merchant of considerable wealth, who had business connections in Amsterdam, Rotterdam, and London, and who in March 1682, with two friends, Dirck Sipman of Crefeld and Jan Streypers of Kaldenkirchen, purchased 15,000 acres of land in Pennsylvania with the purpose of founding a colony (deed signed personally by Penn and executed in London). Even in the absence of direct solicitation by Penn, however, the promised religious tolerance in Pennsylvania with freedom from war and the oath, and enticing economic opportunity was sufficient to move the first fifty or more Crefeld-Lower Rhine Mennonite and Quaker families to leave their homeland between 1683 and 1708. And without doubt the Kriegsheim Quaker emigrants from the Palatinate in 1685 sent favorable reports back to their relatives (some Mennonite?) in their homeland. At least the 1707 forerunners of the great Palatine Mennonite emigration of 1711-56 came from territory near Kriegsheim. The Swiss emigrants of 1709-10, who came to the Lancaster County, Pa., area, were handled by an agent, François Michelle, who found the land for them and negotiated for them with Penn for its purchase, and were not personally responsible for the choice of Pennsylvania. Earlier attempts had been made by the government of Bern to settle them in North Carolina.

Wm. I. Hull (*Dutch Quaker Migration to Pennsylvania*) has shown that most of the thirteen original families settling Germantown in October 1683 were a group of closely related Quaker families from Crefeld, former Mennonites, of course, but not Mennonites at that time as had long been supposed. Only one at least continued as a Mennonite. The Mennonite group in Germantown was in the minority for some years and was in danger of being swamped by the Quakers. In 1690 it finally began to hold separate meetings, and gradually organized in the traditional Mennonite way, but did not build a meetinghouse until 1708, nor hold a baptismal or communion service until that year. The famous Protest against Slavery of 1688 has often been attributed, erroneously however, to Mennonites, only one of the four signers was a Mennonite, and the protest was actually delivered to a Friends monthly meeting as a protest against Friends holding slaves. The most Mennonites can claim is that three of the signers had once been Mennonites, and that no English Friend was among the signers.

The relations between Mennonites and Quakers in Pennsylvania in colonial times were friendly, largely because of the common stand against war and oaths, and probably also out of sense of gratitude on the part of the Mennonites for their new homeland. Evidence shows that the Mennonites, along with the other nonresistant German groups, gave the Quakers strong support at the polls, and made it possible for them to continue in control of the provincial assembly long after Quaker votes alone would not have been enough. Other German nonresistant groups, such as the Moravians, Schwenckfelders, and Dunkards, no doubt also contributed to this result.

It is also most likely that the well-known position against war and the oath held by the very influential Quaker groups in several of the colonies was the chief reason for the introduction of specific provisions in many of the colonial and later state constitutions guaranteeing freedom of conscience on these points. In fact, where any specific group is mentioned in such provisions, usually Quakers and Mennonites (and Moravians) are mentioned together. Quakers certainly have made the major contribution to the establishment of the strong tradition in American life which recognizes the religious conscience which is opposed to military service and oath-taking.

It is also probable that the Quaker simplicity of costume, which was a principle brought along from England and which established uniform costume for both men and women, had some influence on Mennonite costume. Mennonites did not bring from Europe the principle or practice of a uniform costume, although they did bring the principle of simplicity with them. The great similarity of Mennonite and Quaker "plain" costumes in Eastern Pennsylvania suggests definite Quaker influence.

Good relations between the Philadelphia Quakers and the Eastern Pennsylvania Mennonites have persisted to the present day, without any direct connections. There is one exception: for many years during the 19th and early 20th centuries Philadelphia Quaker representatives made annual visits to a Mennonite Sunday service in Montgomery County, where they were always invited to preach.

Mennonite and Quaker Relations in North America Since World War I. About 50 young Mennonite CO draftees, who were given furlough for this purpose by the United States Army, volunteered for service in the Friends Reconstruction Unit in France under the American Friends Service Committee, which had been organized for this purpose in 1917. These men were largely from the Mennonite Church (MC) and were largely supported by the Mennonite Relief Commission for War Sufferers (*q.v.*) beginning in 1918, although the workers were appointed directly by the AFSC. There was no direct co-operation between the Mennonites and Friends during World War I in working on CO problems as there was later in World War II.

The Friends initiated the movement which came to be known as the Conference of Pacifist Churches. The first meeting was held in August 1922 at Bluffton, Ohio, where besides the Mennonites, Brethren, and Friends, Schwenckfelders and Moravians were invited. The latter two did not join the movement permanently, but the three other groups continued together in the conferences (1923, 1926, 1927, 1929, 1931). In October 1935, under the leadership of H. P. Krehbiel, a conference met at Newton, Kan., which was called the Conference of Historic Peace Churches. The name HPC was either coined or fixed in connection with this meeting, which resulted in the creation of a Continuation Committee of the HPC to carry on further interrelations in the interest of the historic peace testimony of the three groups, particularly in relation to the prospect of a World War, which actually came to Europe in 1939 (America 1941). This committee is still functioning and has rendered a valuable service, not as an operating committee, but as a contact committee which furnished the stimulus for the administrative agencies to act. It was also the channel for the creation of a similar and identically named Continuation Committee of the HPC in Europe, created in 1947, in which a representative of the British Friends, the Mennonite Central Committee, the Brethren Service Committee, and ultimately also of the International Fellowship of Reconciliation meet occasionally for contact, stimulus, and certain co-operative activities on the European Continent or in England. When World War II came, the Mennonites, Friends, and Brethren organized the National Service Board for Religious Objectors (q.v.) with its office in Washington, D.C., as a common liaison with Selective Service and the United States Congress and other governmental offices. The Friends withdrew active participation in 1946, but have remained in close touch with its work.

Until the MCC was fully ready to operate as a general foreign relief agency on behalf of the Mennonites, it depended upon the aid of the AFSC. For instance, the MCC relief work in France in 1939-41 was carried on through the good offices and administrative channels of the AFSC, as was the relief work in Spain carried on in 1937-41 by the Mennonite Relief Committee (Elkhart). Since then, the AFSC and the MCC have been on friendly terms but each agency has gone its own way.

The AFSC sponsored a series of Institutes of International Relations between the two world wars and beyond, at various centers in the United States. One of these centers was Bethel College, North Newton, Kan., where an institute was held annually in the second half of the 1930's, with co-operation of members of the college faculty in the management. The Institute was moved to Wichita in 1941. The Conference of Historic Peace Churches in Ontario, founded in 1945, has from the beginning included the small body of Canadian Quakers.

The intermingling of a small number of Mennonites and Friends in the ways mentioned above has served as a stimulus to both sides and no doubt served common interests usefully. There has not been, however, any appreciable drawing together of the groups as a whole because of this, either in recent times or earlier. H.S.B.

William Sewel, The History of the Rise, Increase, and Progress of the Christian People Called Quakers (London, 1722); Robert Barclay, The Inner Life of the Religious Societies of the Commonwealth (London, 1678 and many later editions including Dutch and German 1876); W. C. Braithwaite, The Beginnings of Quakerism (London, 1912, 2nd ed., 1955) idem, The Second Period of Quakerism (London, 1919); Rufus M. Jones, The Later Period of Quakerism 2 vv. (London, 1921); Robert Barclay, Apology for the True Christian Divinity (London, 1678); Sidney Lucas, The Quaker Story (New York, 1949); Rufus M. Jones, The Faith and Practice of the Quakers (London, 1927); Margaret E. Hirst, The Quakers in Peace and War, an Account of Their Peace Principles and Practice (London, 1923); Auguste Jorns, The Quakers as Pioneers in Social Work (Eng. tr. N.Y., 1931); Isaac Sharpless, A Quaker Experiment in Government 2 vv. (Philadelphia, 1898); G. F. Hershberger, Nonresistance and the State; the Pennsylvania Quaker Experiment in Politics 1682-1756 (Scottdale, 1926); A. G. Dorland, A History of the Society of Friends in Canada (Toronto, 1927); A. M. Gummére, The Quaker; a Study in Costume (Philadelphia, 1901); Wilhelm Hubben, Die Quäker in der deutschen Vergangenheit (Leipzig, 1929); Friedrich Nieper, Die ersten deutschen Auswanderer von Krefeld nach Pennsylvanien (Neukirchen, 1940); Dirk Cattepoel, "Mennoniten oder Quäker," Gem.-Kal. 1939, 52-58; Karl Rembert, "Zur Geschichte der Auswanderung Krefelder Mennoniten nach Amerika," Beiträge zur Geschichte Rheinischer Mennoniten (Weierhof, 1939) 161-84; Walter Fellmann, "Kriegsheimer Mennoniten und Quäker in ihrer religiösen Verschiedenheit," Beiträge zur Geschichte der Mennoniten (Weierhof, 1938) 19-24; Owen Gingerich, "Relations Between the Russian Mennonites and the Friends During the Nineteenth Century," MQR XXV (1951) 283-95; DJ 1840, 46; DB 1877, 129; C. B. Hylkema, Reformateurs 2 vv., esp. I, 48-72 (Haarlem, 1900, 1902); H. W. Meihuizen, Galenus Abrahamsz (Haarlem, 1954) 58-60; G. E. Reimer and G. R. Gaeddert, Exiled by the Czar (Newton, 1956) 33-37, 79-87, 103-8; Ernst Troeltsch, The Social Teachings of the Christian Churches (New York, 1931, German ed. Tübingen, 1912); in the Swarthmore College Monographs on Quaker History by W. I. Hull, the following: William Sewel of Amsterdam (1934), The Rise of Quakerism in Amsterdam 1655-1665 (1938), Benjamin Furly 1636-1714, and the Rise of Quakerism in Rotterdam (1941), William Penn and the Dutch Quaker Migration to Pennsylvania (1935); H. S. Bender, "The Founding of the Mennonite Church in America at Germantown, 1683-1708," MQR VII (1933) 227-50; H. H. Brinton, ed., Children of Light (New York, 1938) contains a chapter by W. I. Hull, "The Mennonites and the Quakers of Holland"; M. D. Learned, The Life of Francis Daniel Pastorius (Philadelphia, 1908).

Socinianism is the theology and the doctrines projected and drawn up by Laelius (Lelio) Socinus (q.v.) and in particular by his nephew Faustus Socinus (q.v.), and taught in the Socinian or Polish Brethren Church. This theology is best known from the Racovian Catechism (first ed. Polish 1605, then German 1608, Latin 1609, Dutch 1659; revised reprints Latin 1665, Dutch 1666). Socinian doctrine differs from the main Protestant theology, both Lutheran and Calvinist, by (a) its anti-Trinitarianism, (b) its rejection of the deity of Jesus Christ, (c) its rejection of the atonement by the blood of Christ (satisfaction), (d) its strong emphasis on the free will of man, his reasonableness and his natural knowledge of God. The center of Socinianism is its denial of the Trinity. This doctrine is rejected by arguments borrowed from the Scriptures (Ex. 20:3; Matt. 24:36; 27:46; Luke 18:19) and from the reason (ratio). There is but one divine Person, not three. Christ is not a person of the Trinity, but a human being, though His birth was supernatural and His resurrection a historical fact. He performed miracles, because God had given Him the ability to prove His godly mission in this way. Much stress is laid upon Christ as a moral teacher; as such, men should be His disciples and followers. Men are sinners, but have preserved liberty to choose the way of righteousness. The justification of man is principally an act of the grace of God. This is, however, to be understood in this way: Christ died for men, to awaken them from sin and (moral) death. Justification is not the direct result of Christ's atonement, but the indirect consequence of His death. The main doctrine of Protestantism, viz., justification by faith, is formally upheld, but essentially undermined by the concept that faith really means obedience to the commands of Christ. Of course it is admitted that man's human good works never are satisfactory, but God by His endless love and goodness attributes complete justification to those who earnestly strive to be obedient to the commandments of the Lord.

The church is a body of believers who are converted; in it strict discipline is to be exercised according to Matt. 18:15-17. Baptism and Communion are not mysteries with sacramental overtones, but merely acts of confession. Though infant baptism was not quite abolished in the Brethren church of Poland, it was not considered strictly necessary to their salvation and baptism (by immersion) was regularly administered to adults.

The Socinians were opposed to taking oaths for the same reasons as the Mennonites. One of their principles was also nonresistance; the members of the Brethren church did not take military service and also refused to take government offices.

These Socinian views have widely influenced modern thinking; their theological and philosophical principles are the common possession of the philosophies of the 18th century; Unitarianism has also borrowed much from Socinianism. Socinian doctrines are the backbone or at least the background of modern Liberalism (q.v.). Yet there are striking differences between Socinianism and Liberalism (Modernism) in particular as compared with present American Modernism. Both Socinus and the Racovian Catechism as well as later Socinian theologians consciously built their dogma within the framework of the Scriptures; they accepted the Bible as the Word of God, His revelation, and did not yet apply subjective criticism, which is fundamental in modern Liberalism and Unitarianism. Moreover religion was limited to and identical with Christianity.

It cannot be denied that in the theological system of Socinianism there is a strong element of intellectual ambition and speculation, which often strains the very heart of religion. This was felt by Socinians themselves at times. The later revised editions of the Racovian Catechism (from 1665) are much less rationalistic and much more orthodox than the first editions; for example, in the 1609 Latin edition, the question why it was necessary that Christ suffer so much is answered, "Because all whom He might save are subjected to such a death and suffering," but in the 1665 Catechism is found the answer, "Christ by the will of God suffered for our sins, and resigned Himself to the shameful death as an expiatory sacrifice." Also in the writings of later Socinian theologians like Sandius (1644-86), Jeremias Felbinger (1616-c90), Daniel Zwicker (1612- ?), and Andreas Wiszowaty (1608-78) the accent is more that of evangelical piety. All these authors lived in the Netherlands and approached more or less the Remonstrant (q.v.) views.

Yet the strong emphasis in the Socinian writings put upon Christian morals as a fruit of conversion according to Matt. 7:17-23 was wholesome in a period in which the large Christian churches neglected the problem of Christian ethics and usually paid little attention to "good works."

The church of the Brethren in Poland contributed much to education and scholarship; its university at Rakow, Poland, was led by capable and learned professors, and students from every part of Europe attended its lectures in great numbers. There is an important body of literature by Socinian scholars. Among these scholars should be mentioned besides Faustus Socinus: Christoph Ostorodt (q.v., d. 1611), the author of popular theological books, the medical professor Ernst Soner (d. 1612), the systematic theologian and philosopher Johannes Völkel (d. 1618), the polemist Valentinus Smalcius (q.v., Schmalz, d. 1622), Johannes Crell (Crellius) (d. 1631), the author of dogmatic and ethical writings, the Bible exegete Johann Ludwig von Wolzogen (d. 1661), the apologist Jonas Schlichting (d. 1661), the Prussian statesman Samuel Przypkowski (d. 1670), Andreas Wiszowaty (d. 1678), the historian, theologian, and editor of the well-known Bibliotheca Fratrum Polonorum (1656 ff., 8 vv.), and his son Benedictus Wiszowaty, the historian and man of letters Christophorus Sandius (d. 1686), particularly known as the editor of Bibliotheca Anti-trinitariorum (1684).

There were about 300 Polish Brethren congregations. In 1603-37 an annual synod of delegates was held at Rakow. Until 1638 the Brethren church could meet undisturbed, protected by independent and liberal noblemen. In this year, however, through the machinations of the Jesuits, the parliament of Poland resolved to stop Socinian education by closing the Rakow University and even demolishing its buildings. Also their printing shop was closed. From then the suppression of the Brethren church began. A number of its preachers were banished from the country; others voluntarily went into exile. The congregations only secretly and with great danger could meet for worship. This too came to an end in 1658. Then the parliament forbade the Socinian confession on pain of death. Only those who were willing to embrace the Roman Catholic creed were allowed to remain in the country. Thereupon most of them left Poland, emigrating to adjacent countries like Hungary (Transylvania) and Germany (predominantly to Silesia, but also to Prussia), but also England, where they in spite of much interference prepared the way for an important Unitarian movement, at the same time feeding the 18th-century philosophy of Deism, whereas the Netherlands also gave shelter to the expelled Brethren. The elector of the Palatinate, Germany, permitted them in 1663 to settle at Mannheim, but by 1666 they were forced to leave the country. It was particularly in the Netherlands that most of its scholars and theologians settled.   vDZ.

Stanislaus Lubienecki, *Historia Reformationis Polonica* (1685); Friedrich Samuel Bock, *Historia Antitrinitariorum,* 2 vols. (1776-83); O. Fock, *Der Socinianismus* (Kiel, 1847); *HRE* XVIII, 3d ed., 459-80; A. Harnack, *Lehrbuch der Dogmengeschichte* III, 4th ed. (Tübingen, 1910) 784-808; Earl M. Wilbur, *A History of Unitarianism* (2 vv., Cambridge, 1945, 1952).

* * *

Socinianism in the Netherlands: I. *Polish Brethren in the Netherlands.* Soon after Socinianism had risen in Poland two of its representatives, viz., the preacher Christoph Ostorodt (*q.v.*) and Voydovsky, a nobleman, visited the Netherlands in order to look after some Polish students at the University of Leiden, and probably also to make contacts with Dutch theologians. They arrived at Amsterdam in August 1598; soon their books were confiscated and in October of the same year they were banished from the country, though they did not leave until 1599. During their stay at Amsterdam they met the Mennonite elder Pieter Jansz Twisck (*q.v.*), and visited Hans de Ries (*q.v.*), the elder of the Waterlanders at Alkmaar. In the course of time some other missionaries from Poland clandestinely stayed in the Netherlands, but they apparently had little success at that time in spreading their doctrines in this country. There was a rather large increase of Socinians when their seminary at Rakov was closed in 1638 by the Polish government. Some of their scholars settled at Amsterdam, and often had their books printed there. Their ideas (see **Socinianism**) found acceptance with some circles of the Collegiants (*q.v.*), some of whom—Camphuyzen, Joachim Oudaen, Adam Boreel, Daniel de Breen, Joan Hartigveldt, Frans Kuyper, and more or less Johannes Bredenburg—appropriated Socinian ideas; the Socinian practice of baptism by immersion (*q.v.*) became common among the Collegiants. Among the Mennonites too they had some influence (see II). Also a few Remonstrants (*q.v.*) were accessible for Socinian concepts, though later on (from about 1650) Socinian theologians, such as Wiszowaty and Sandius, learned more from the Remonstrants than the Remonstrants did from the Socinians. Samuel Crell (1660-1747), a grandson of the early Socinian professor of Rakov, Johannes Crell, was trained for the ministry at the Remonstrant seminary at Amsterdam, and after having served as a minister of a Socinian congregation near Berlin, Germany, returned to Amsterdam in 1727.

From the very beginning Calvinism vigorously fought Socinianism. Repeatedly Calvinist synods expressed their deep horror of "Socinian errors," and "Socinianism" became for more than a century and a half the epithet of heresy in general, as "Lutheranism" had been a common name for all kinds of deviation from Roman Catholicism in the early 16th century. Calvinist polemicists for more than a hundred years wrote thorough refutations of Socinian doctrines. The Calvinist preachers and synods induced the Dutch government to issue numerous mandates particularly from 1639, forbidding their

teaching and the printing and sale of their books in 1651, 1654, 1659, 1662 (Friesland), 1674, 1685 (Friesland). Yet Socinians could live in the Netherlands rather freely; for example, Andreas Wiszowaty (b. 1608 in Poland, d. 1678 at Amsterdam), a grandson of Faustus Socinus (*q.v.*) and editor of the revised Racovian Catechism (1665), who lived in Amsterdam from 1666 until his death, and Christophorus Sandius (b. 1644 at Königsberg, Prussia, d. 1686 at Amsterdam), who lived at Amsterdam 1668-80, where he had his *Bibliotheca Anti-trinitariorum* printed (1684). Numerous other Socinian books were printed at Amsterdam, though rather secretly. The places of publication named in the books, Irenopolis, Eleutheropolis, Freistadt, Stauropolis, all mean Amsterdam. The most important of these publications was *Bibliotheca Fratrum Polonorum* (8 vv. from 1656), edited by Wiszowaty, containing the theological, ethical, and philosophical writings of Faustus Socinus, Johannes Crell, and other Socinian leaders. Socinian books were secretly sold in the noted Mennonite bookshop of Jacob Aertsz Calom (*q.v.*).

During the 18th century Socinianism in the Netherlands disappeared from the scene, but left a distinct trace in the philosophy of the Enlightenment and in the theology of the non-Calvinist churches and groups, such as Remonstrants, Mennonites, and Collegiants.

II. *Socinianism Among the Mennonites.* Socinianism undoubtedly had some attractions for Dutch Mennonites: its emphasis on practical Christianity and Christian morals was in the spirit of Mennonites, and they liked the Socinian doctrine of the freedom of the will. Moreover their practice of adult baptism, nonresistance, nonswearing of oaths, and their reluctance or even refusal to accept government offices—none of which were found in the surrounding Christian churches—deeply impressed the Mennonites. Though the conservatives like the Zonists and the "fijne Menisten" all rejected Socinianism because they wanted to hold Trinitarianism and the deity and satisfaction of Christ, the more progressive groups, the Waterlanders and particularly the Flemish and later the Lamists (*q.v.*), were in sympathy with some (not all) of the Socinian doctrines. They usually did not adopt the Socinian anti-Trinitarian views; they mostly did not deny the deity of Christ, though they emphasized His commandments as the Polish Brethren did. And as to the doctrine of satisfaction (atonement by the blood of Christ), which dogma was rejected by the Socinians, this doctrine was not expressly denied by the progressive Mennonites, even not by Galenus Abrahamsz, but the idea that "good works" are necessary to obtain the grace of God largely undermined the strictness of the doctrine of the satisfaction of Christ. As a whole, Socinianism was never accepted by the Mennonites, probably partly because they wished to avoid the punishments threatened by the mandates issued by the government against those "who were infected with the errors of Socinus"; but mainly for these two reasons: (*a*) The Mennonites did not want and did not like to have a theological system of any kind; Socinianism was a system, a dogmatic creed, and Mennonite spiritualism conflicted with every kind of dogmatic theology; (*b*) Socinianism, being largely intellectual and rationalistic, generally lacks the real piety and devoutness so much honored by the Mennonites. Granting these facts, Joh. Hoornbeek's statement in *Summa Controversiarum* (1650) can be admitted: *Anabaptista indoctus Socinianus, Socinianus autem doctus Anabaptista* (A Mennonite is an unlearned Socinian; a Socinian, however, is a learned Mennonite). This, of course, concerned only the more progressive liberal Mennonites.

The first Polish Brethren leaders who visited the Netherlands in 1598, Ostorodt (*q.v.*) and Voydovsky, made contact with some Mennonite leaders; e.g., Hans de Ries (*q.v.*), Pieter Jansz Twisck (*q.v.*), and probably also Jaques Outerman (*q.v.*). Twisck at once and completely rejected their teachings; de Ries, though politely and discreetly, rejected them too; only Outerman (according to Kühler's view) was open at least to some aspects of Socinianism. Charged with Socinianism by the Reformed synod in 1625, he was compelled by the magistrates to write a confession of faith, in which he formally repudiated Socinian concepts. Shortly after 1610 Jan Gerrits (*q.v.*) van Emden, the elder of the Waterlander (also called Frisian) congregation of Danzig, Prussia, requested the aid of his Dutch brethren, e.g., Hans de Ries and Leenaerdt Clock (*q.v.*), to help them resist the advances of the Socinians, who wanted to merge their congregations in Danzig and elsewhere with those of the Mennonites (see **Moscorovius** and **Smalcius**). A married couple (according to Jan Gerrits) had already left the Mennonites to join the Socinians at Danzig; it was probably Matthis Radeken, who after joining the Polish Brethren, promoted the union. The Danzig Waterlander church and the neighboring churches, however, were not in favor of this attempt and finally retired from Socinian obtrusiveness. About 1625 a serious dissension arose in the Amsterdam Waterlander congregation, in which Nittert Obbesz (*q.v.*) opposed the other preachers of this church. Hans de Ries clearly pointed out that the teachings of Obbesz, so different from those of the other preachers, had their roots in Socinianism. In 1663 Galenus Abrahamsz (*q.v.*), accused by his Mennonite opponents of teaching Socinian views as early as 1655, was summoned by the Reformed Church Board at Amsterdam to answer to the Court of Holland; but the Court declared him to be a "good Mennonite." Yet Galenus, who at this time had many contacts with the Amsterdam Collegiants (*q.v.*), among whom Socinianism found a rather favorable reception, may in some respects have been influenced by Socinian doctrines. His statement in opposing his co-preacher Samuel Apostool (*q.v.*) that the doctrine of satisfaction as taught by Apostool was dangerous for a sound moral life, in any case smacks of Socinianism. Foecke Floris (*q.v.*) was imprisoned at Leeuwarden in 1687 by order of the government of Friesland, on a charge of having taught the doctrines of Socinus. Jan Klaasz (*q.v.*) van Grouw openly avowed about 1700 that he was a Socinian; others, though usually with more caution, admitted their sympathy with Socinian ideas. The notorious mandate against Socinians, Quakers, and Dompelaars issued in 1662 by the States of Friesland and

repeated in 1678 was sometimes used against the Mennonites. Jan Thomas (*q.v.*), a preacher of Knijpe, Friesland, was suspended in 1719 because of Socinianism, and nineteen years later three other preachers, Wytze Jeens (Brouwer), Pieke Tjommes, and Wybe Pieters (Zeeman), were suspended for the same reason. Johannes Stinstra (*q.v.*), the noted preacher of Harlingen, was also charged with Socinianism, but unjustly, and was suspended from his office by the States of Friesland in 1742; he was not allowed to preach again until 1757. In 1771 the Reformed Church in Friesland was still exhorting its synods "to guard against and oppose the pernicious doctrine of Socinus among the Mennonites." Outside the province of Friesland the magistrates were apparently more tolerant from about 1650. Only in Deventer, province of Overijssel, Abraham Willemsz Cremer and his colleague Jan Lambertsz ten Cate had some difficulty with the magistrates in 1669-70 concerning supposed Socinian teachings. In the province of Zeeland there were also some difficulties. Adriaan van Eeghem (*q.v.*) of Middelburg was summoned before the city magistrates in 1665 and suspended for a time; in the same town Gerardus de Wind (*q.v.*), a preacher of the same congregation, had to answer for his "Socinianism" in 1726-28. Twelve questions drawn up by the Reformed minister Cornelis Gentman (*q.v.*) (see **Geuzenvragen**) were used as a basis for the questioning of the Mennonite preachers.

The conservative Zonists not only repudiated Socinianism, but also attacked the Lamists, censuring their sympathy with Socinianism. Lambert Bidloo (*q.v.*) did so, bitterly, in *Onbepaalde Verdraagzaamheyd de Verwoesting der Doopsgezinden* (1701), and Douwe Feddriks (*q.v.*) in *Mennonitische Ondersoek op de Korte Grondstellingen . . .* (1700), mildly and cautiously Herman Schijn did so in *Onderzoek op de Rynsburgsche verdraagzaamheid* (1703) and *Ontwerp tot Vereeniging* (1723), one-sidedly and rudely J. Rijsdijk (*q.v.*) did so against Eppo Botterman in *Verdediging van de Regtzinnigheid der ware Mennoniten* (1729) and *Zedige Aanmerkingen* (1735). Besides these, attacks on true or putative Socinianism among the Dutch Mennonites are numerous in (mostly anonymous) pamphlets published by Mennonites, like Jan Theunis' (*q.v.*) *Der Hanssijtsch' Mennoniten Socinianismus* (1627) against Hans de Ries, and *Commonitio* (1655), *Sociniaense Hooftpyn* (*c*1600), and Theodorus van der Meer, *Het Gekraay van een Sociniaanse Haan, onder Doopsgezinde Vederen* (1663), all against Galenus Abrahamsz during the "Lammerenkrijgh" (*q.v.*). The "Socinian" Mennonites were moreover heatedly attacked in a number of books by Calvinist authors like J. Hoornbeek (*q.v.*), J. van den Honert (*q.v.*), and D. Gerdes (*q.v.*).   vDZ.

W. J. Kühler, *Het Socinianisme in Nederland* (Leiden, 1912); W. J. van Douwen, *Socinianen en Doopsgezinden* (Leiden, 1898); N. van der Zijpp, *Geschiedenis der Doopsgezinden in Nederland* (Arnhem, 1952) 99-101, 159-61; H. W. Meihuizen, *Galenus Abrahamsz* (Haarlem, 1954); Kühler, *Geschiedenis* II, 14-29, 79-82, 144-49, 177-82; *Inv. Arch. Amst.* I, Nos. 450 f., 455, 623-28, 644; II, Nos. 2928-39; *DB* 1864, 38 f., 57-60; 1868, 56, 66; 1870, 19-24; 1883, 9-11, 13-18, 72; 1884, 111; 1887, 51-85; 1891, 65 f.; 1896, 149-74; 1900, 25; 1919, 46-62; Earl Morse Wilbur, *A History of Unitarianism:*

Socinianism and Its Antecedents (Cambridge, 1945); which has chapters on "Antitrinitarian Tendencies Among the Early Anabaptists in Germany and Switzerland," "Antitrinitarian Anabaptists in Holland," "The Unitarian Anabaptist Movement in Italy," and "Socinianism Among the Mennonites and Collegiants"; but see Friedmann's critique in "The Encounter of Anabaptists and Mennonites with Anti-Trinitarianism," *MQR* XXII (1948) 139-62; J. C. van Slee, *Geschiedenis van het Socinianisme* (Haarlem, 1914); C. B. Hylkema, *Reformateurs*, 2 vv. (Haarlem, 1900, 1902); Ernst Luckfiel, "Der Socinianismus und seine Entwicklung in Grosspolen," *Ztscht . . . f.d. Provinz Posen* VII, 117-87; Paul Fox, *The Reformation in Poland: Some Social and Economic Aspects* (Baltimore, 1924); Stanislaus Kot, *Socinianism in Poland: The Social and Political Ideas of the Polish Antitrinitarians in the Sixteenth and Seventeenth Centuries* (Boston, 1957).

III. *Socinian (Polish Brethren) Relations with the Hutterites.*

Since the Polish Brethren practiced adult baptism and favored a communal form of living, as the Racovian catechism of 1605 expressly indicates, it was but natural that these Brethren wanted to study the communal way of life in the concrete, in particular the Hutterite way in Moravia. Polish Brethren made at least four extended visits to Moravia in the 16th and early 17th centuries. In one case several young Poles spent a year on a Bruderhof as apprentices, in order to report their experiences later to their church at home. But in spite of friendly words no real rapprochement was possible, due to basic differences in genius and in their understanding of the Scriptures. Stanislaus Kot of Paris has recently published a Polish Brethren document of 1570, which gives a rather unfriendly picture of the Moravian Bruderhofs. At about the same time the Hutterite Chronicle includes the correspondence of the Vorsteher Peter Walpot (*q.v.*) with the Polish elder Simon Ronemberg, apothecary in Cracow (English translation in *MQR* for 1945).

Other contacts between the Polish Brethren and the Anabaptists and Mennonites are connected with the name of Christoph Ostorodt (*q.v.*), a Unitarian minister in Poland before and after 1600. He had tried very hard to establish contacts both in Germany and Holland with the Anabaptists, trying even to convert them to his way; but this endeavor ended with totally negative results. It was not until the later 17th century, when the Polish Brethren were expelled from their home country and were thereupon kindly received in the Netherlands, that closer ties developed between them and Mennonites (see **Socinianism in the Netherlands, Ostorodt**).

A truly rare case was that of Dr. Daniel Zwicker (*q.v.*), a physician and Polish Brother, in Danzig, *c*1650. He had met some Hutterite missionaries from Slovakia, liked their way of life, visited the Bruderhofs in Slovakia which were under Andreas Ehrenpreis, and was so well pleased that he joined the Hutterite brotherhood. With certain mental reservations on both sides he was accepted. But soon he left again for Danzig, only to drift away from all religion. There are also epistles by Ehrenpreis to a Hans Martin and a Jost von Stein, both of Danzig, German-speaking "Polish Brethren." For the interesting exchange of letters, 1591-92, between Ostorodt and the Strasbourg Swiss Brethren, see **Strasbourg Conferences**. R.F.

E. M. Wilbur, *History of Unitarianism, Socinianism and Its Antecedents* (Cambridge, Mass., 1946); Stanislaus Kot, *Socinianism in Poland . . .* (Boston, 1957, originally in Polish at Warsaw, 1932); *idem*, "The Polish Brethren and the Problem of Communism in the 16th Century," in *Transactions of the Unitarian Historical Society* XI (London, 1956); translation of the main source in *Transactions* XII (1957). More literature is given in G. H. Williams, "Studies in the Radical Reformation, a Bibliographical Survey II," *Church History* XXVII (1958) 141-46; see article "Anti-Trinitarianism" for Friedmann's papers on the subject.

Socinus (Sozzini), name of two well-known Unitarian theologians, **Laelius** (Lelio) and **Faustus** (Fausto), Laelius Socinus (b. 1525 at Siena, Italy; d. 1562 at Zürich, Switzerland) was a jurist with a broad theological interest; he turned away from Roman Catholicism, but did not definitively embrace Protestantism. In 1546 he stayed in Venice, where he came into contact with an Evangelical group. He also visited Basel, where he met a number of humanist scholars, including Sebastian Castellio (*q.v.*). He also conferred with some of the great Reformers, visiting Calvin (1548) and Melanchthon (1550). After 1550 he lived mostly at Zürich, but he traveled also in France, England, and Poland. Laelius Socinus, doubting and criticizing the official doctrines of the churches, Catholic as well as Lutheran and Calvinist—he seems not to have been aware of the Mennonites—wrote against the Sacraments and taught a vague anti-Trinitarianism in unclear and covert terms.

Faustus Socinus (b. 1539 at Siena, d. May 31, 1604, near Cracow in Poland) systematically worked out the views of his uncle. He studied at Lyons, France, and other universities. In 1562-74 he lived at Florence, Italy, at the court of Francesco de Medici, a liberal man renowned for his interest in science and arts. In 1574-78 he lived at Basel, devoting himself to the study of theology. In 1578 he came to Transylvania to combat Frans Davidis and his followers, called Nonadorantes, who taught that Jesus was not worthy of worship. In 1579 he moved to Poland, where he remained until his death, building up his doctrine of Unitarianism (see **Socinianism**). He had to combat numerous heterodox groups, Nonadorantes, Arians, Chiliasts, and also Calvinism and Roman Catholicism. After a long and severe struggle his views were fully accepted at the synod of Rakov (Poland) in 1603. Socinus drew up a confession, *Catechesis*, which was not quite finished when he died; it was completed by his closest co-workers and published first in 1605 at Racov, and is therefore called the Racovian catechism. The theological, exegetical, and ethical works of Faustus Socinus were published in *Bibliotheca Fratrum Polonorum* 2 vv. (Amsterdam, 1656). It is interesting to note that Faustus never actually became a member of the Polish Brethren, since he did not accept rebaptism as required, nor was he their founder. vDZ.

David M. Cory, *Faustus Socinus* (Boston, 1932); E. M. Wilbur, *A History of Unitarianism: Socinianism and Its Antecedents* (Cambridge, 1946).

Sodom Road Mennonite Church (MC). Joseph Willich (1808-72) was a deacon (MC), of Reformed background, who came to the Niagara area of Ontario, was employed by John Boyer, married one of his daughters, accepted the Mennonite faith, settled on the Sodom Road south of Niagara Falls and a few miles south of Chippewa. In his home in Willoughby Township, north of Bertie, Ont., services were conducted for several years while he was active. This and the Riverside church afforded the places of worship for Mennonites of this area about the middle of last century. There was no organized work. The ministers in Willoughby were Christian Hershey, Jacob Miller, and John Zavitz.   J.C.F.

Soest, a town in Westphalia, Germany, about 30 miles south of Münster (*q.v.*), was visited in October 1534 by eight apostles sent out by Jan van Leyden (*q.v.*) to convert its citizens. Among the apostles were Johann Dusentschuer (*q.v.*), Hendrik (*q.v.*) Slachtscaep, and Hendrik van Maren (*q.v.*). Soon after their arrival, they were all arrested and, on Oct. 23, 1534, beheaded (not Oct. 21, 1543, as is erroneously stated in *ME* II, 112). Anabaptism could not develop in Soest. (Rembert, *Wiedertäufer,* 308-10; Mellink, *Wederdopers,* 48 f.)   vDZ.

Soet, Jan: see Zoet, Jan.

Soetken Gerrits (Soetken van Roterdamme), d. Dec. 26, 1572, a Mennonite woman of Rotterdam, Holland, who was blind, composed a number of devotional hymns, which were collected by a certain J. C. (unknown) into a hymnbook entitled *Nieu Gheestelijck Liedtboexken,* commonly called Soetken Gerrits' hymnal. This hymnal, containing 102 songs without notes, was published by Gillis Rooman at Haarlem in 1592. The preface contains some biographical material on Soetken Gerrits. A second and a third edition, both containing 98 hymns without notes, appeared in 1618 and 1632, both at Hoorn. The booklet is very rare. Of the second edition there is no extant copy; of the first edition there is only one copy, found in the Amsterdam Mennonite library. Of the third edition, as far as is known, three copies are extant, one in the Amsterdam Mennonite library, one in the library of the University of Gent, and one formerly in the private collection of D. F. Scheurleer at The Hague.

F. C. Wieder, who described the hymnal of Soetken Gerrits, is of the opinion that there was very probably an edition previous to that of 1592, printed shortly after her death. Karel Vos confused Vrou Gerrets van Medenblick with Soetken Gerrits of Rotterdam. The article **Gerrets, Vrou, van Medenblick** (*ME* II, 502) is therefore in error.   vDZ.

F. C. Wieder, *De Schriftuurlijke Liedekens* (The Hague, 1900) 167 f., 173, 174, 175; *ML* II, 84.

Soetken van den Hout(t)e, an Anabaptist martyr, secretly beheaded in the Gravensteen castle at Gent, Belgium, on Nov. 20, 1560 (not Nov. 27, as is stated in *Mart. Mir.* and *ML*), with Martha Baerts and Lynken Pieters. After the execution their corpses were thrown into a pit outside the Muide gate. Soetken van den Houtte, also called Avezoete, was forty years of age and mother of three children, David, Betken, and Tanneken. She was born in Oudenaerde in Flanders. Her husband, Ghislain de Meulenaere, who had died before she was put to death, was also a martyr, as may be seen from Soetken's letter to her

children: "Your father has confessed the truth concerning baptism and the incarnation of Christ, and gave his life for it." Soetken wrote this letter in prison to her children as a "testament." It is often called a "Christelyke kindertucht." In this "testament" she wrote thus: "My dear children, since it pleases the Lord to take me out of this world, I will leave you a memorial, not of silver or gold; for such jewels are perishable: but I should like to write to your heart, which is the word of truth of the Lord . . . . Beware of bad company, and of playing in the streets with bad boys, but learn to read and write." She admonished her children to goodness, kindness, humility, obedience, patience, righteousness, chastity, peacefulness, firmness, mercy, and all Christian virtues.

Soetken also composed a song, "Godt ghy sijt myn Hulper fijn, Verlost my van de eewige pijn" (O God, Thou art my good Helper, Deliver me from eternal torment). This song is found in the *Tweede Liedeboeck* (*q.v.,* Dutch hymnal of 1583). The "testament" and also a letter written in prison to her brother and sister are found in van Braght's *Martyrs' Mirror*. A separate edition of the "testament" was published as early as about 1565; the only copy extant is an incomplete copy, now found in the Royal library at The Hague. A second edition, to which is added Soetken's hymn, was printed in 1579 by Nicolaes Biestkens at Amsterdam. Of this edition also only one copy is extant, found in the city library of Hamburg. There are reprints of the "testament" and the song as follows: Delft 1586; n.p., n.d. (*c*1605); Groningen 1636; Hoorn 1641; Groningen 1664; and Amsterdam 1679. Under the title *Uyterste wille van Soetken van den Houte* it was reprinted at Amsterdam in 1699 and 1748. Copies of a 16th-century German translation, *Ein Testament vonn einer frommen Gott liebhaberin Soecken von Holtz genandt,* are found in the Prussian State Library of Berlin and the city library of Zürich. The "testament" and the other letter by Soetken are also inserted in Thomas von Imbroich's *Confession* of *c*1560 in two editions, one of which is in GCL, and in the well-known devotional book of 1702 (1742 and 1745), *Gueldene Aepfel* (*q.v.*).   vDZ.

Mart. Mir. D 277-82; E 646-51; Verheyden, *Gent,* 26, No. 75; *Bibliographie* I, 171-91, 656-59; Wolkan, *Lieder,* 70; *DB* 1870, 51; *ML* II, 352.

Sol, Johan van: see Jan van Sol.

Solianka (formerly Waltajem), a Mennonite village in Volhynia: see **Waldheim.**

Solothurn is a Swiss canton bordering on Bern (*q.v.*), predominantly Catholic, in which the Anabaptist movement also gained entry, though it was not so strong there as in the canton of Bern.

The council of Bern carried on negotiations with Solothurn repeatedly in the 16th century on the Anabaptist question. On Jan. 10, 1531, it sent a letter to various districts bordering on Solothurn calling attention to the fact that the Anabaptists had recently held a general meeting, at which it had been decided to extend their missionary activity to the canton of Solothurn; "Since their misleading sect and separatistic Pharisaic hypocrisy full of all evil, wickedness, and sedition and contrary to the government instituted by God, are said to teach and to attach the common simple folk to them and deceive them, we therefore command you to watch such people closely and take care especially of the pious that would be influenced thereby" (D. M. R. 467 *Staatsarchiv Bern*). On February 2 Bern called the attention of Solothurn to Anabaptism practiced secretly in the border districts, Wangen, Aarwangen, and Niderbipp, and on May 18 it reminded Solothurn that the "deceiving obstinate Anabaptists" had been staying in Overlinsbach, and that this "sect entirely unworthy of the common Christian status" should be expelled. Solothurn took its time to expel the Anabaptists. From this time on Bern continued to complain about Solothurn's careless attitude whereby the Anabaptist preachers were greatly helped. The Anabaptist movement continued to increase in the Swiss confederacy especially in the Protestant cantons of Zürich, Bern, Basel, and St. Gall. The Anabaptist problem had become a very difficult one for the authorities of the Protestant estates, after all the violent measures for its extermination had proved fruitless. At the parliament in Baden in 1530 it was decided to arrest the Anabaptist leaders and punish them severely in body and property.

On Feb. 5, 1532, Bern complained that Anabaptists were holding secret meetings in the canton of Solothurn. And on March 16 Bern requested Solothurn to report to "my lords" in Bern the names of those who did not come to the preaching service. Bern even found it necessary to send delegates to Solothurn to present its request either to punish the Anabaptists themselves or to permit the Bernese government to reach into Solothurn and punish them. This led to stricter steps by the council of Solothurn; all foreign Anabaptists had to leave the country within two or three days and pay a fine of 10 pounds.

On July 1-9, 1532, the big Anabaptist colloquy of Zofingen (*q.v.*) took place. Bern requested Solothurn to send the Anabaptists from its canton to Zofingen, but it seems that the Solothurn Anabaptists were at first not willing to appear in person, but wished to give a written account, because they "were entirely sure of their faith and therefore needed no colloquy." Bern, however, demanded that Solothurn see to it that at least the Anabaptist preacher Lincki (*q.v.*), whom the Reformed clergy of Bern considered a clever hypocrite, came to the disputation. Lincki was active in Lostorf and Egerkingen in the canton of Solothurn.

In 1533 and 1537 there were again negotiations between Bern and Solothurn on Anabaptist matters since the Anabaptists were meeting on Solothurn soil, holding their meetings in Aetingen and Lüsslinen. In 1545 the council issued a general order to expel the Anabaptists within a week; those who were found after that period were to be tortured. A year later the provost of St. Ursen complained about "non-Christian" meetings. Toward the end of the 16th century the council passed several regulations expelling the Anabaptists and confiscating their property.

The council of Solothurn was also worried by the immigration of Anabaptists from Basel. Since the Anabaptists in the north of the canton of Solothurn in the region of Weinwil fled to Seehof in case of danger, and into the Münster Valley, which was in the bishop's district, the council negotiated on this matter with the Bishop of Basel.

The efforts of Solothurn to gain control of the Anabaptist movement by means of expulsion were only partly successful. In the 17th century it flared up anew. Beginning in 1676 a long line of orders and mandates were published by the council; the magistrates were advised to pay close attention and to institute the sharpest investigations, "so that such weeds can be exterminated before they grow up." In 1697 the homes were searched for dangerous books. In 1707 the pastors were asked what people were neglecting religious services in the churches.

In spite of the mandates the council had to admit in 1710 that the Anabaptist movement was not yet extinguished in Solothurn. In October 1719 a mandate was issued (renewed in November 1725), which imposed a fine of 100 guilders on anyone who would give or sell them any land, lodging, or food.

The Anabaptist movement had apparently become rather strong in Lüterswil; members here were Hans Bandi, Elsbeth Mollet, Urs Stuber, Hans Dick, Peter Mose, Urs Rätz, and in Lüterkofen, Urs Nussbaum, who was found in La Meutte in the Jura. In October 1711 Magistrate Reder reported on his dealings with several Anabaptists who had refused to render the oath of obedience, with the comment that "among them yes and no were as much as an oath, and their conscience did not permit them to give more."

Gotthold Appenzeller wrote the following (*Jahrbuch für Solothurnische Geschichte*): "On April 18, 1757, Johann Karl Grimm reports that he has found out from a dependable man when and in whose home the meetings were held at night. Therefore on the past Saturday night toward 1:00 he had found the people in Stephan Jaggi's house in Gossliwil, and questioned them, taking the names of all the men, had locked up their books, writings, and other effects and had taken Stephan Jaggi and Niklaus Knörr to the authorities. One of them had let a child die unbaptized and had an unbaptized four-year-old." About 20 persons had taken part in the meeting. This was a severe blow for the Anabaptists in the Bucheggberg. To the council this successful coup was very significant. A detailed opinion about it was published, which states among other things: Art. 1: That the Anabaptist sect had been found harmful as early as 1500 by the entire praiseworthy confederacy, they were therefore nowhere tolerated and in short "exterminated from all the villages out of your grace's lands without hesitation and shall be wiped out." The Anabaptists in the Bucheggberg were no longer to have the boldness to hold a meeting on this territory. By rendering an oath they were to desist from their faith, and if they refused, "all these sectarians shall clear the land," in order that "this region all be cleansed, depopulated, and as much as possible untrodden by that kind of people." Art. 2 designated that the Anabaptist property at Bucheggberg be managed by a special magistrate. Art. 3: The two preachers, Stephan Jaggi and Niklaus Knörr, were each to be fined 100 pounds. Furthermore, all who attended the meeting, whether they were really Anabaptists or not, were to pay a fine of 10 pounds. Art. 4 says that the Anabaptists must in addition pay the costs for the soldiers in the inn. Art. 5 gives information on the inventory of the Anabaptists arrested in Bucheggberg. The capital amounted to 8,425 pounds and the "poor" capital of the Anabaptist congregation 2,914 pounds, a total of 11,399 pounds. Their private property was to be left them, but the property of the congregation should be taken from them and used for the benefit of the churches.

On May 16, 1757, the council ordered that the confiscated books be committed to the Capuchin monks. On July 15 the Anabaptists were ordered to leave the canton by September 29. On Aug. 17, 1757, "Altrat" Vogelsand asserted that Jaggi "has lost his mind." The preacher Knörr had to leave his property in Bucheggberg and leave the canton with only 40 crowns. He died in Plagne above Biel (Jura) in July 1773. That was the end of the Anabaptist congregation on Bucheggberg.

In other parts of the canton of Solothurn there are also traces of the Anabaptists in the 17th and 18th centuries. In Kriegstetten, Madle Luterbacher, Caspar Wiedmar, and later Mathis Kaufmann broke out of the prison.

In the district of Falkenstein Franz Fluri and his wife were found, who still "persist in the damned Anabaptist sect." Further it was reported that the Anabaptists detained in prison refused to give up their faith, but at the same time they requested the council to release them to leave the country. But the council decided to have the clergy visit them in prison and "instruct them in our true religion." If they refused to be converted by teaching, other means should be used. The magistrate declared that the persecution of the Anabaptists was difficult to carry out in winter with the great masses of snow and impenetrable mountain roads, for the Anabaptists were meeting at night in the mountains bordering on the bishopric. On March 28, 1731, the council received the report of the magistrate of Falkenstein that Margareth Loosli, Catharin Obersteg, Hans Kaufmann, and others in the district, charged with listening to Anabaptist preaching, were questioned; the main meeting of these people took place in the Münstertal; hence a letter should be written to the bishop in Pruntrut to assist them; if the people were encountered on Solothurn property, they were to be arrested or expelled. Considerable numbers of the Anabaptists were also found in the region of Welscherrohr and Gänsbrunnen close to the border, today in the Bernese Jura. Presumably most of them fled into the bishopric, where they found more toleration. In the powerful changes wrought by the French Revolution the last traces of Anabaptism in the canton of Solothurn died out.

In 1899 Christian Gerber of Bellelay moved to Emmenholz, near Solothurn. A number of families of his descendants have been living here since then. In 1957 monthly meetings of the Mennonite families were still held in the home of Abraham Gerber, preacher, at Brestenberg.   S.G.

Gotthold Appenzeller, "Beiträge zur Geschichte des Solothurner Täufertums," *Jahrbuch f. Solothurner Geschichte*, 1941, pp. 50-89; *idem*, "Solothurner Täufertum im 16. Jahrhundert," in *Festschrift fur Eugen Tatonioff*, 1938, 110-34; Steck and Tobler, *Aktensammlung zur Geschichte der Berner Reformation 1521-1532* (Bern, 1923); Müller, *Berner Täufer;* Samuel Geiser, *Die Taufgesinnten-Gemeinden* (Karlsruhe, 1931); *ML* IV.

Soltau-Uelzen: see **Uelzen.**

Somalia Mennonite Mission (MC) in Somalia (formerly Italian Somaliland), East Africa, was established in 1953 by the Eastern Mennonite Board of Missions and Charities. In 1958 its headquarters was in Mogadiscio, the capital city, with three other stations in Mahaddei Uen, Margherita, and Torda. The staff consisted of four missionary couples, two nurses, three short-term workers, and a Pax unit of three men.   H.S.B.

Somere (Somer, Sommere), **Jaques de,** probably an emigrant from Flanders, Belgium, was a member of the Reformed Church at London, England. In 1575 he wrote a long letter (found in van Braght's *Martyrs' Mirror*) to his mother at Gent, Belgium, in which he tells the story of the Anabaptist martyr Hendrik (*q.v.*) Terwoort and his companions in London. De Somere was apparently on good terms with these Anabaptists, for he wrote very sympathetically about their faith and principles and told his mother that he and a certain Lucas had tried--in vain—to release them from prison. (*Mart. Mir.* D 706-9, E 1019-22.)   vDZ.

Somerghem: see **Zomergem.**

Somerhuys, Catharina and **Lysbeth,** Anabaptist martyrs: see **Catharina Somerhuys.**

Somerset County, Pa., the third county from the west in the southern tier of counties, and Garrett County, Md., at the extreme western end of the state, lie side by side, with the Pennsylvania-Maryland state line running due east and west between the two.

Allegheny Mountain, of the Appalachian mountain range, runs through the two counties, leaving the terrain mountainous and rough with limited areas of arable and productive land. Before the coming of the white man the region was covered with choice timber. Underlying large areas were coal, limestone, fire clay, and other minerals. Mt. Davis, the highest point in Pennsylvania (3,213), is located on Negro Mountain near the southern boundary of Somerset County and the northern edge of the Amish-Mennonite community on the Casselman River. Nearly all of Somerset County lies between 2,000 and 3,000 feet above sea level. The summers are moderate and pleasant, the winters cold with frequent heavy snowfalls. Precipitation is consistently adequate for good crops. Agriculture is probably the backbone of the region's economy, together with a variety of industries springing from natural resources. Somerset County was formed from Bedford in 1795. Garrett County was formed from Allegheny in 1872.

The provincial authorities of Pennsylvania, Maryland, and Virginia had secured the land from the Indians as far west as the Allegheny Mountains by the treaties of 1754-58. However, nearly all of this territory lies west of that boundary. Settlement west of the Allegheny was discouraged and at times

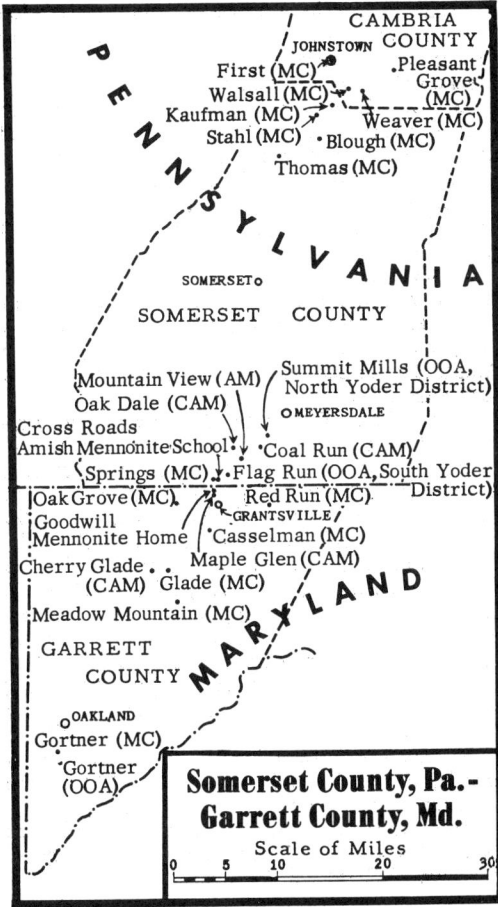

Somerset County, Pa.-
Garrett County, Md.

Scale of Miles

County and the southwestern part of Somerset County, following the general course of the National Highway, U.S. Rt. 40. The Forbes Road, built in 1758 by General Forbes, passed through Somerset County, somewhat north of the present Lincoln Highway, U.S. Rt. 30. Thus nearly all traffic moving west from Virginia, Maryland, and eastern Pennsylvania passed through this region. Many of the early Amish and Mennonite settlements in Ohio, Indiana, Illinois, Iowa, and elsewhere were either founded or largely reinforced by emigrants from these two counties. Nearly all of the Beachy, Peachey, Bontrager, Eash, Gnagey, Schrock, as well as many of the Bender, Yoder, Miller, Keim, and Swartzendruber families in the Amish and Mennonite communities throughout the United States trace their ancestry to this locality.

By 1772 land was being bought in the territory by the Amish, and in 1773 a number of land warrants were issued to them by Pennsylvania. It is almost certain that "Tomahawk Rights" were established before this without any legal recording in the public land office. By 1783 more than thirty Amish and Mennonite names were listed as taxpayers in Brothersvalley Township, which at that time included both the Glades and the Casselman River settlements. By the close of the century the Amish were well established in the two counties, with two distinct settlements: the Glades congregation near the town of Berlin, Somerset County; and the congregation at the "River" (Casselman), located along the Casselman from near Meyersdale, Pa., to beyond Grantsville, Md. Later, about 1800, another settlement was founded in Conemaugh Township, near the northern border of Somerset County, extending north into Cambria County. Still later, about 1849-50, a settlement was effected in the southwestern part of Garrett County, several miles southwest of the town of Oakland, extending west to the village of Aurora, W. Va., in Preston County. This settlement at present surrounds the village of Gortner, Md.

(1) *The Glades,* near Berlin, Pa.—The first land warrants to Amish settlers here were issued in 1773. But some of their names appear on the tax lists prior to the time when they received legal title to their land. The following are some of the earliest dates on the public land records: Christian Zook, warrant 1773; Christian Spiker, taxable 1773; Benedict Leman, war. 1773; John Zook, war. 1773; Christian Yoder, war. 1773; John Yoder, deed 1775; Michael Troyer, tax 1775; John Troyer, tax 1775; Joseph Johns, tax 1775; David Yoder, war. 1777; Jacob Schrock, tax 1779; Peter Leman, tax 1779; John Leman, war. 1785. Christian Blough, who secured his warrant in 1773, had arrived here in 1767. Casper Schrock, warrant dated 1773, had settled on his land in 1772 according to reliable family tradition. Among the ministers who served the congregation were Christian Yoder, the first resident Amish bishop in the Glades who served as bishop 1785-d. 1838. His son Christian Yoder, Jr. (1790-1846), who served first as minister and later as bishop, assisted his father in his old age and continued in his bishop duties until his death. His grandson Abner Yoder also served as minister and then as bishop until he

strictly forbidden, until the land could be legally secured from the Indians. But daring pioneers crossed the mountains and settled here in spite of all protests and dangers. In April 1768 a committee appointed by Governor John Penn found in the region of Pennsylvania west of the Allegheny an estimated 150 illegal white settlers. The Tunkers or Brethren had crossed the mountains and established a small congregation in the "Glades" near Berlin, Brothersvalley Township, in 1762. It is well known that because of similarity in faith and manner of life, the Amish, Mennonites, and Tunkers were companions in pioneer life in many communities in the westward movement. Thus it is probable that the earliest Amish and Mennonite settlers lived in the territory before the land was acquired from the Indians by the treaty of Fort Stanwick in New York in 1768. Local and family traditions support this view.

In 1769 the public land west of Allegheny Mountain was thrown open for settlement. Immediately Somerset and Garrett counties became an important steppingstone in the Amish and Mennonite emigration westward. The Braddock Road, built in 1754 by George Washington's forces, and rebuilt and extended to the Ohio River in 1755 by General Braddock's forces, was the one artery of travel westward from Fort Cumberland, passing through Garrett moved with his family to Johnson County, Iowa, in 1866. Abner was the last resident bishop in the Glades congregation. Jacob Schwartzendruber, ordained a minister in the Amish church at Mengeringhausen, Waldeck, Germany, in 1826, emigrated to America in 1833, and served the Glade congregation until 1840, when he moved about six miles southeast of Grantsville, Md. (New Germany). He served the Casselman River congregation until 1851, when he migrated with his family to Johnson County, Iowa, being the first Amish minister there and the first Amish bishop ordained in Iowa in 1854. Abraham Miller and David Yoder were also ministers here, for they signed their names as such at a ministers' meeting (*Dienerversammlung*) of the three churches in Somerset County on March 18, 1837, along with those already noted above. According to tradition there was also a minister Schrock in later years. Almost certainly other ministers have served the congregation. This congregation figured prominently in Amish history. At least one of the church-wide Amish conferences (*Dienerversammlung*) was held here, Oct. 3, 1830. Some of the ministers were influential throughout the Amish churches. But the congregation is now extinct. The last services were probably held during the 1870's. Jacob B. Schrock, a jurist of Berlin, Pa., recalled in a personal interview in 1950, that as a boy he accompanied his parents on a visit to his grandparents, the Michael Schrocks, about 1879, and saw the old benches stacked on the back porch, left there after the last preaching service of the Amish in that community. The congregation had no meetinghouses. There are practically no church records extant. In the old Amish cemeteries not a single grave bears a legible marker to the writer's knowledge. Fragmentary information must be laboriously secured from family records, local history, and tradition, and from general church history.

A small cemetery 12 x 15 ft. on the old Yoder farmstead marks the resting place of Christian Yoder, Sr., and Christian Yoder, Jr. Another cemetery with about 20 graves is supposed to contain the remains of Yoders and others. Some Lehmans are buried in a small plot containing six or seven graves, on the old Leman farmstead. Another cemetery has been farmed over for some years and all marks obliterated. These are a few of the burial plots of the now extinct settlement.

Why did the Amish leave the Glades? Many emigrated to other communities. Among the early Amish settlers of Holmes and Tuscarawas counties, Ohio; Elkhart County, Ind.; Johnson County, Iowa; Moultrie and Douglas counties, Ill., there were numerous large families who left this congregation in 1830-60. This had a weakening effect. But it appears that unworthy conditions within the church also had their effect. It was said of the congregation, "The people became too ungodly and the church could not stand." Coupled with this is the evident fact that the church lost many members to other denominations, notably to the Church of the Brethren. A few who remained in the community and the Amish Church joined the Casselman River congregation. The last survivor was Benedict Yoder (d. May 20, 1910), grandson of Bishop Christian Yoder,

Sr. The Mennonite Church had no congregation here. Many of the young men accepted military service in the Civil War, and this contributed to the breakup of the Amish community.

(2) *Casselman River*—A few years after the founding of the Glades settlement, the Amish moved on to establish another settlement on the Casselman River. Michael Buechley, Barn Twp., Lancaster Co., Pa., bought two tracts of land some 4 miles southwest of Meyersdale, Pa., in the fall of 1772. In 1773 he bought a third tract and presumably settled here. Peter Livengood, the first family to bring a covered wagon west over the Allegheny Mountain, came in 1775. These two families, along with the John Olinger and Christian Hochstetler families, left the Amish Church and joined the Tunkers or Brethren soon after 1783.

Here, as in the Glades, the Tunkers were very active and gained many members from the Amish. In the town of Meyersdale, the Tunkers or Brethren had at one time more members per square mile than in any other territory in the United States. In 1775 part of the Buechley land passed to Yost Yoder by deed. Public land records show other early dates as follows: John Miller, deed 1775; John Hershberger, taxable 1775; Christian Gnagey, tax. 1775; John Saylor, tax. 1775; Yost Zook, tax. 1773; John Hochstetler, tax. 1779; Andrew Borntreger, tax. 1783; John Borntreger, tax. 1783; Christian Mast, tax. 1783; Jacob Mast, tax. 1783; Jacob Saylor, tax. 1783; Peter Beachey, warrant 1785; Jacob Miller, war. 1793; Joseph Mast, war. 1795. All this land is between Meyersdale, Pa., and the Maryland state line in the northern part of the present Amish-Mennonite community. By the close of the century, the settlement extended south into Garrett County, Md., beyond the town of Grantsville, Md.

This settlement continues to the present time. It has the following congregations: an Old Order Amish congregation dating from the beginning of the settlement and numbering at present 180 members worshiping in two meetinghouses; five Mennonite (MC) congregations with several mission stations, with a total membership of 553, Springs, the oldest, having been organized about 1780 with Jacob Seiler (Saylor) as preacher, who settled south of Meyersdale about this time; a Conservative (Amish) Mennonite congregation formed in 1895, with 260 members and worshiping in three meetinghouses; and a Beachy Amish congregation, numbering 159 members and worshiping in one meetinghouse. Articles covering these congregations will appear under separate heads.

(3) *Conemaugh*—This settlement, located at the northern end of Somerset County, originally included part of the site of the city of Johnstown at its northern end. It appears to have been developed largely by settlers from the Glades settlement near Berlin. Possibly the first land warrant issued to the Amish or Mennonites was to Jacob Blough in 1793. Joseph Johns (Schantz) of the Amish Church moved here from the Glades. He founded the city of Johnstown, beginning to sell city lots from his farm about 1800. Other warrants issued were to David Yoder 1802, Jacob Spiker 1806, Jacob Kime 1806, Tobias Miller 1812, and John Lehman 1835.

John Borntreger, whose warrant was issued in 1803, was evidently seated on his land in 1798. The Amish congregation dates from the beginning of the settlement. The first Amish bishop was probably Jacob Eash (1774-1850), of Berks County. Assisting him for many years was Jacob Miller. John Borntreger, born March 10, 1805, was ordained minister and served here until he moved to Lagrange County, Ind., in April 1844. Joseph Borntreger was ordained deacon in 1839 and moved with his family to Elkhart County, Ind., June 29, 1841. They with three other families were the first Amish to move into Indiana. Other ministers who served the Amish church were Christian (Schmitt) Miller, who died here in 1845; Moses B. Miller, ordained minister 1844 and bishop 1848, shortly before the death of Jacob Eash; Jonathan Hershberger, ordained minister in 1862; and possibly others. The Amish built a meetinghouse northwest of Davidsville in 1875. In 1884 they numbered about 100 members. The congregation gradually declined in numbers until they were finally absorbed by the Mennonite Church. The last Amish services were held in 1916.

The first minister ordained by the Mennonite Church (MC) in this district was Jacob Blough, Jr., in 1803-4. His father was the first landholder noted above. Ordained bishop in 1814, he was the lone minister here until 1830, when he ordained Jacob Blough of another family as minister. In 1842 Samuel Blough was ordained minister and after the death of Bishop Jacob Blough in 1849, Samuel was ordained bishop in 1850. By 1884 the Mennonites had three meetinghouses in Somerset County and one in Cambria County in this district with a total membership of 240. Their membership has increased and today this is the strongest area in the Allegheny Mennonite Conference. The area is generally known as the Johnstown District. A membership of 900 meets for worship in seven meetinghouses, three of them in Cambria County. (See **Kaufman** Amish Church and other articles dealing with the Mennonite church in this area.)

(4) *Gortner*—By 1849-50 the Amish of the Casselman River region moved on to establish another settlement just beyond the Maryland line in Preston County, W. Va., along the Northwestern Turnpike, now U.S. Rt. 50. The location gradually shifted eastward and the settlement now centers on the village of Gortner, Md., three miles southwest of Oakland in the southwestern tip of Garrett County. This region, often called the "Glades," should not be confused with the now extinct Glades settlement near Berlin in Somerset County. Among the first settlers was the Samuel J. Beachy family who moved here from the Casselman River region, to which locality they returned after several years. In 1853 Daniel Beachy with his family moved in. Later he became the first bishop of the congregation. Other early settlers were Petersheim, Miller, Schrock, and Slabaugh. Because of the settlement's central location between the North and South on an important highway, the people suffered much during the Civil War. Raiding parties from both armies took horses, cattle, and other property with them. There were also periods of internal disturbances. Under these discouragements some of the people moved back to the parent congregation on the Casselman River. The settlement grew slowly at first, but has had a healthy growth in recent years. The Amish Church has continued since the founding of the settlement, having a membership at present of 83 and meeting for worship in the Gortner meetinghouse, two miles east of Gortner. In 1899 the Mennonite Church (MC) began services in a union meetinghouse alternately with other groups. This arrangement continues although the group maintains its identity as an unorganized Mennonite mission church.

The Conservative Amish Mennonite Church has several families living in the region who worship with the Casselman River congregation.   I.J.M.

Sommelsdijk, a town on the island of Overflakkee in the Dutch province of South Holland, a center of Anabaptist-Mennonite activity in the 16th century. Paulus (*q.v.*) Harrouts of Sommelsdijk was executed in 1540 at Zierikzee, and Joos (*q.v.*) Jansz of Sommelsdijk died in 1561 as a martyr also at Zierikzee. In 1565 Jan Barentsz and his wife, living at Sommelsdijk, were sought by the police because of their Anabaptist activity, but they had already fled with all their possessions. Sommelsdijk was the birthplace of the noted Dutch elder Leenaert (*q.v.*) Bouwens.

Elder François de Knuyt (*q.v.*) debated with the Reformed pastor Abraham Stamperius on infant baptism at Sommelsdijk in 1617. About this time there was a Mennonite congregation at Sommelsdijk, which had a meetinghouse. Concerning this congregation there is not much information. In the early 18th century it merged with that of the adjacent town of Middelharnis (*q.v.*), but apparently long before, probably by 1664, Sommelsdijk and Middelharnis were more or less one congregation. For the history of this congregation, see **Middelharnis.**   vDZ.

Sommer (Sommers, Summer, Summers), a Mennonite family name of Swiss origin. The early homes of the family were Sumiswald and Lützelflüh in the Emmental, canton of Bern, Switzerland. During the fore part of the 18th century members of the family moved to the Jura, Montbéliard, Alsace, and the Palatinate. The migrations of the early 19th century brought several Sommer families from their European homes to Ohio and Illinois. Isaac Sommer became one of the first settlers in the Sonnenberg settlement in Wayne County, Ohio, coming there in 1819 from the Jura. A brother, Ulrich Sommer, came in 1824. Christian Sommer came in 1819. Christian Sommer (1811-91) was ordained to the ministry in 1838, and bishop of the Sonnenberg congregation in 1862. He preached his farewell sermon Oct. 4, 1891, just two months before his death. Ulrich Sommer (1792-1880) came from Switzerland in 1824 and was ordained a minister of the Sonnenberg congregation in 1827 and bishop in 1842.

In 1836 George Sommers (1801-83) migrated from Alsace to Woodford County, Ill. He was a deacon in the Amish Mennonite church, and one of the pioneer settlers in central Illinois. Peter Sommers, a son, was a minister of the Metamora (MC) church for many years.

Pierre Sommer (*q.v.*, 1874-1952) was the leading minister and elder of the French-speaking congregations in France 1900-50.   D.L.G.

Sommer, Isaac A. (1851-1924), was born near Dalton, Ohio, the son of Abraham and Elizabeth Sommer, on Jan. 17, 1851. He attended the Wadsworth school (*q.v.*) for a total of four years, serving as a schoolteacher 1869-84 when not in school. In the spring of 1884 he worked for the Mennonite Publishing Company at Elkhart, Ind. In the fall of the same year he was appointed editor of the *Christlicher Bundesbote,* the official organ of the General Conference Mennonite Church, serving until 1911. He also edited the *Kinderbote,* beginning in 1887, and *The Mennonite* 1905-11. He was ordained to the ministry in 1887 in his home congregation at Berne, Ind., but he never held a pastorate. He died April 19, 1924.   H.S.B.

Sommer, Pierre (1874-1952), the outstanding leader of the French-speaking Mennonites of France in the 20th century and their historian, was born June 15, 1874, at Herbéviller in Lorraine (Meurthe-et-Moselle), d. April 23, 1952, at Grand-Charmont (Doubs) near Montbéliard, where he had had his home since 1919. After his marriage on May 13, 1909, to Anna Kennel, he made his home on his paternal farm which he operated until into World War I, when he had to leave because it was almost completely destroyed in the fighting.

Sommer's education included two years at the Weierhof Mennonite school in Germany, and the high school (Collège) at Lunéville, France, from which he graduated in 1891. The winter of 1892-93 he spent at the Weierhof school again, where he was much influenced by the teaching of Christian Neff, the local pastor. After four years of military service 1894-98, he spent two years at St. Chrischona, near Basel, having been converted in 1898. He was chosen preacher by the Repaix congregation on Aug. 6, 1899, and ordained as elder May 26, 1901, by Jacob Hege of Reihen, Baden. In the spring of 1927 he was chosen as traveling evangelist by the French Conference, in which capacity he rendered outstanding service, shepherding and reviving the scattered French-speaking groups, which were in a low estate.

Pierre Sommer's service to the Mennonites of France was outstanding in several directions. Unusual intelligence and warmth of personality, combined with a deep and sincere Christian experience and a spirit of aggressive action, aided by a training considerably above the average in his church, plus complete dedication to the cause of the Mennonite brotherhood, enabled him to render exceptionally effective service and exert unusual influence. With his close friend Valentin Pelsy (*q.v.*), of Sarrebourg in Lorraine, and Pierre Kennel, of Montbéliard, his future brother-in-law, he organized the French Mennonite Conference in 1901, and with Pelsy was a dominant leader for the rest of his life. He was the founder and editor (to 1941) of *Christ Seul* (*q.v.*), the French Mennonite paper (preliminaries 1901-7, regular issue 1907-14, 1927-41). He wrote and edited a number of books, producing practically the only French Mennonite literature until 1945: *Formulaire pour les Services du Culte à l'usage des Eglises*

Evangéliques-Mennonites de langue française (appeared as a supplement to *Christ Seul* in 1912; it was a minister's manual); *Manuel d'instruction religieuse,* containing the Zweibrücken (Elbing) catechism, the Dordrecht Confession, a collection of prayers, and a résumé of Mennonite history (Montbéliard, 1922); *Precis d'histoire des Eglises Mennonites* (Montbéliard, 1937, first part written by Valentin Pelsy in 1912). Sommer wrote a series of fifty carefully prepared articles giving congregational histories of all the existing and extinct congregations in France, a total of some 65, to which he prefaced a general introductory account. This valuable series was in effect a history of the Mennonite Church in France, though never collected and published in book form. It is found in *Christ Seul* monthly from April 1929 to February 1933, with two in November 1935 and August 1936, and one in June 1929 on "Our Family Names." Sommer also wrote a number of valuable articles for the *Mennonitisches Lexikon,* and served on the Editorial Council of the MENNONITE ENCYCLOPEDIA until his death. His son-in-law Pierre Widmer has continued in his line, serving as preacher, traveling evangelist, editor of *Christ Seul,* writer, and historian.† H.S.B.

Pierre Widmer, *Pages choisies de Pierre Sommer précédées d'une esquisse biographique* (Grand-Charmont, 1955).

Sommerfeld Colony, one of two colonies (the other was Bergthal, *q.v.*) established in 1948 some 50 miles east of Villarrica in East Paraguay by Sommerfelder Mennonites from Manitoba (West Reserve). In 1953 it had a population of 644 (119 families) in nine villages, occupying *c*93,000 acres. It is located some 15 miles from Bergthal. In the first two years 75 families with 383 persons returned to Canada. The center of the colony is the village of Sommerfeld, where the elder, Isbrandt Friesen, lives and where the co-operative is located.   H.S.B.

Sommerfeld Mennonites, a very conservative body of Manitoba Mennonites of Russian background who originated as a separate group in 1890 when the Bergthal Mennonite Church divided into a minority progressive wing and a majority conservative wing. The issue was acceptance of the Manitoba government requirement of attendance at standard English schools. The Bergthal group had originally all settled in the East Reserve east of the Red River (1874 f.), as a single congregation under one elder, settled in a number of villages, but the half who moved to the West Reserve in the early 1880's were encouraged to elect their own elder, which they did, choosing Johann Funk. Gerhard Wiebe, the original Bergthal elder of the immigration, continued as elder of the East Reserve group. Since Funk took the progressive side in the school issue, and even though his party was in the minority (only 61 families of 300), he and his group considered themselves to be the continuing Bergthal Church, and are so considered and named to this day. The conservative group in the West Reserve, who could not follow the regular elder Funk and elected a new elder for themselves, Abram Doerksen, were considered to have withdrawn and hence no longer entitled to the name Bergthal. They came to be called Sommerfelders because their bishop lived in the village of Sommerfeld, about 6 miles southeast of Altona in the West Reserve. Elder Gerhard Wiebe and the entire membership of the Bergthal group in the East Reserve then threw in their lot with Doerksen and the Sommerfeld group in the West Reserve. Though they could have retained the name Bergthal with full right, or taken on the name Sommerfelder, they came to be called the Chortitz Church because Elder Wiebe lived in the village of Chortitz. Actually the two bodies, Sommerfeld and Chortitz, were identical in position, although because of the parity of the elders and the lack of an over-all organization such as a conference, they remained organizationally as well as geographically distinct. The large Old Colony group in the West Reserve, largely immigrants from the Chortitza (Old Colony) settlement in Russia, with some from the daughter Fürstenland settlement, took the same position on the school question as the Sommerfeld Mennonites, but remained ecclesiastically distinct. Thus there were three conservative groups of pratically identical position bearing—almost accidentally—three different names, Chortitz, Sommerfeld, and Old Colony. The Old Colony group, however, has become and remained distinct, while the Chortitz and Sommerfeld groups have more fellowship and to all practical purposes are one.

The Manitoba conservatives continued to be restless under the threat of the English school system, sincerely believing this would endanger the maintenance of their faith and way of life. Accordingly two large new settlements were established on the frontier in Saskatchewan: (1) Rosthern Reserve in 1893 and (2) Swift Current Reserve in 1900, founded because the Rosthern Reserve was full and overflowing. Actually some went from Rosthern to Swift Current. Most of the settlers in both colonies were Sommerfelders from the West Reserve. In the Rosthern Reserve one Old Colony village was established, while in the Swift Current Reserve a larger percentage was Old Colony. Both colonies were organized as typical Russian colonies with Oberschulze and the village type of settlement. The Swift Current Reserve (south of the city of Swift Current) is an island plateau of rich soil surrounded by an unproductive area; hence it furnished an ideal fulfillment to the Sommerfelder wish for isolation and solidarity, practically uninfluenced by the outside world. The original 30 villages of this settlement are still intact, and the Sommerfelder culture and language of 1900 has been maintained almost unchanged. The Rosthern Reserve with its 15 villages has not been quite as successful in this, since four towns have sprung up in the midst of the reserve, viz., Rosthern, Hague, Osler, and Aberdeen. However, most of the Rosthern villages are still intact, and the greatest proportion of the village people are still Sommerfelders who have maintained their culture substantially unchanged, with some 3,000 members. However, the conservative Old Colony group which settled here calls itself Bergthal and has about 1,000 members. They are not to be confused with the progressive Bergthal group in Manitoba, now a part of the Canadian Conference (GCM).

The next Sommerfelder migration was to Mexico (1922) and Paraguay (1926), the result of the severe pressure, practically persecution, by the Manitoba government in the period of World War I and the strong anti-German feeling of the general populace. Manitoba wanted no cultural pluralism; there was to be only an English culture. The Sommerfelders were right in leaving if their sole goal was to maintain their Low German culture as a supposed necessity to maintaining their faith and way of life. The Old Colony Mennonites (q.v.) of Manitoba (q.v.) led in the move to the South. Most of the new Mexican settlement was Old Colony, with only one Sommerfeld village, whereas in Paraguay all were Sommerfelders. The Sommerfelder Colony in the Chaco of Paraguay was named Menno; hence the name Sommerfelder has disappeared there.

Since only about half of the Sommerfelders went to Mexico or Paraguay, population pressure continued to increase in the four mother Sommerfeld colonies in Manitoba and Saskatchewan. In 1930-38 a continuous migration of Sommerfelders took place to new frontiers west and north. In the early 1930's settlements were established in Sunningdale and Carrot River in Northern Saskatchewan, at that time in forest areas 25 miles beyond the edge of the white settlement. In the late 1930's similar colonies were established at Vanderhoof in central British Columbia, at Peace River in Northern Alberta, and at Gladstone in north-central Manitoba. All these new colonies achieved their aim of avoiding any significant influence from the English school system. English schools are indeed imposed by the provincial governments, but many families live beyond the zone of compulsory attendance, and many build a second home in the bush (forest) where they live in the deep winter, working at logging. Thus the dominant culture is Sommerfeld-Platt and not English Canadian.

In 1948, following World War II, a second migration southward to Mexico and Paraguay occurred, drawing from all four mother settlements. Two settlements were established in southern Paraguay, between Villarrica and the Brazilian border, bearing the name Bergthal and Sommerfeld. In 1950 the population was 1,200, some 500 of the original 1,700 having returned to Canada. Of the original group 1,500 come from Manitoba (both Sommerfeld and Chortitz Mennonites) and 200 from Saskatchewan.

An attempted settlement in Honduras in 1951 by eight Sommerfelder families from Hague, Sask., failed, since the Honduras government refused entry, and the group returned to Hague.

The statement that the Sommerfelder culture has been maintained practically unchanged requires further examination. It is true that most of the outward forms of social organization (colony, village, church, family) have been maintained, as well as the outward forms of religion (simple meetinghouses, absolute authority of the elder and ministers, no ex tempore sermons, but only reading of sermons handed down from the past, old slow tunes in the singing, admission to church membership at adult age by baptism by pouring, usually just before marriage). However, two serious internal consequences are observable: (1) a progressive deterioration in inward spiritual life, and (2) alienation of an increasing percentage of their young people from the church. The complete cut-off from outside cultural influences, except the small amount of English schooling in the elementary schools, has had its inevitable consequence in intellectual and cultural stagnation. The lack of a vital understanding of the Gospel and really creative reading and exposition of the Bible, as well as the suffocation of creativity in the ministry which destroys the possibility of revival and results in a complete bondage to dead tradition, has resulted in serious spiritual stagnation. The focus of all concern on preservation of the Plattdeutsch and the old outward customs has produced regrettable results in many places. This is not true of the Menno Colony in Paraguay, which has made substantial progress in spiritual and cultural respects.

Because the Sommerfelders are very loosely organized as a church, it is possible for variations to develop in attitudes toward the church while remaining ethnically bound to the Sommerfelder body. Three such variational types may be observed: (1) the orthodox, (2) the liberal, (3) the diaspora or scattered. The orthodox, the majority body, consists of those who are baptized and continue a connection with the church. The liberal element, who may or may not once have been baptized and reckoned as members, no longer have any connection with the church. Part of this element continue to live in the villages, sometimes constituting almost the entire population of a village. However, the larger part of the liberal element live in the towns in the vicinity of the main settlements, such as Gretna, Altona, Winkler, and Morden in Manitoba, Hague, Osler, Aberdeen, Rosthern, and Swift Current in Saskatchewan. Most of this group remain unchurched, in fact are generally cold and antipathetic toward all religion. A few have joined other Mennonite congregations or evangelical churches.

The scattered families are to be found in the larger cities throughout Canada. Some have gone to the cities for employment, since the colonies are full and land is hard to get, others to escape the colony life and culture. These generally endeavor to shed their past as rapidly as possible and lose their identity, often anglicizing their names. Some of them react to extremes religiously against their earlier background, joining the Jehovah's Witnesses, Pentecostals, Seventh-Day Adventists, etc. In two cities there are Sommerfelder congregations with meetinghouses, one in Swift Current, and one in Winnipeg of the Chortitz group.

The present total population of the Sommerfelder group in Canada is at least 25,000, with possibly less than one half baptized members. Since no church records are maintained, reliable statistics are difficult to secure. In 1950 the Manitoba Sommerfelders had 4,120 baptized members (with children 7,944) in 14 congregations, and the Chortitz group had 1,684 baptized (with children 3,516) in 8 congregations, making a total population for Manitoba of 11,460, of whom 5,804 were baptized. In Saskatchewan there may be 5,000 baptized members in two northern colonies, 3,000 in Swift Current and 2,000 in Rosthern. The four frontier settlements may have another 1,000. With children there would be probably 10,000 population in Saskatchewan and 2,000

on the frontier. Scattered members with families could total another 2,000. In Mexico the Sommerfelders constitute about 6 per cent of the main Mennonite colony in Chihuahua and might therefore have a population of 1,000 today. The Sommerfeld and Bergthal colonies in Paraguay might today have a population of 2,000 (892 baptized). Menno Colony in the Chaco now has over 4,000 population with 1,359 baptized members; but this group, because of its progressive development in Paraguay, can scarcely be considered Sommerfelder in character today. A small conservative group of possibly 100 souls left the Menno Colony in 1955 to settle in Bolivia. Thus the total population of all Sommerfelder settlements, not counting the scattered families, can be held to be 30,000, of whom probably 12,000 are baptized members.

The Sommerfeld group in Manitoba has suffered two serious schisms. In 1937 the group known as the Rudnerweide Church broke off in the Western Reserve, which in 1957 had a total of 1,700 baptized members, of whom 1,200 (pop. 3,200) were in the original settlement in Southern Manitoba (with 500 scattered unorganized individuals in other places in West Canada). In 1940 a Rudnerweide congregation was organized in Saskatchewan near Hague, which now has 300 baptized members, mostly from the Sommerfeld Mennonites there. The second schism occurred in April 1958, when a conservative faction, numbering about 100 families of the 3,500 existing membership, led however by 12 of the 16 ministers, withdrew ostensibly because of opposition to introducing electric lights into the meetinghouses. The majority group, which calls itself the Reinländer Mennonite Church, elected its own bishop (Cornelius Nickel), since the regular Sommerfeld bishop Johann Friesen stayed with the main body.

H.S.B.

Leo Driedger, "Hague-Osler Settlement," *Menn. Life* XIII (January 1958), and "Saskatchewan Old Colony Mennonites," *Menn. Life* XIII (April 1958); E. K. Francis, *In Search of Utopia* (Altona, 1957); Abraham Schmitt, "The Sommerfelder Mennonites," ms, 1953, GCL.

Sommige andachtighe *ende leerachtige Gheestelicke Liedekens ende Psalmen Davids. . . . Met noch twee Christelicke Sentbrieven geschreven ende ghesonden aen de Ghemeente Godes in Pruyssen* (Amsterdam, 1597) is a Dutch Mennonite hymnal with a preface by G. I. It contains 117 hymns without notes. The two letters added to this hymnbook were written at Amsterdam in April 1595 and on Dec. 19, 1596, by Lubbert Gerritsz (*q.v.*).   vpZ.

Sommige andachtighe *ende leerachtighe Gheestelijcke Liedekens ende Psalmen Davids . . .* (Amsterdam, 1617), a Dutch Mennonite hymnal, not identical with the above. It contains 129 psalms and hymns without notes.   vpZ.

Sommighe leerachtighe geestelijcke Liedekens *uyt den Ouden ende Nieuwen Testaments ghemaeckt, met oock eenighe Psalmen Davids uyt verscheyden boecken, ende oock eenighe die noyt voor desen in druck gheweest zijn, by een vergadert,* is a Dutch Mennonite hymnal (Amsterdam, n.d.-1609). It contains 215 hymns without notes. Herbert Wiebe mentions a Dutch hymnal with the same title, printed at

Haarlem in 1638 and probably used in the Montau congregation in Prussia. This obviously is a later reprint. vDZ.

Herbert Wiebe, *Das Siedlungswerk niederländischer Mennoniten . . .* (Marburg, 1952) 104.

Sommighe Nieuwe Schriftuerelicke Liedekens . . . (Leiden, 1599) is a Dutch Mennonite hymnal containing 77 hymns without notes. The editor was F. vander Straten. vDZ.

Sommige Stichtelyke Liedekens *by diverse personen gemaeckt* is a Dutch Mennonite collection of hymns, of which there were at least two editions, 1618 and 1632, both at Hoorn. vDZ.

M. Schagen, *Naamlijst der Doopsgezinde Schrijveren* (Amsterdam, 1745) 104; Blaupot t. C., *Holland* II, 211.

Song Festivals. Singing has been a favorite tradition and recreation among the Mennonites of Prussia and Russia, which can be traced back to the days when Mennonites lived in secluded and isolated communities where commercial entertainment was scarce and not promoted. The practice of spontaneous singing in the family, church, and community was transplanted to North and South America. The song festivals are a special form of expression of the love of music found among the Mennonites of Russia and now in Canada, the United States, and South America.

Mennonite song festivals became very popular in Russia before World War I. K. G. Neufeld published the magazine *Aufwärts* (*q.v.*), 1909 f., which was originally devoted primarily to music, singing, and song festivals. *Unser Blatt* (1925-28) reported regularly after World War I about the song festivals of the various Mennonite settlements in Russia. No other subject received as much attention and treatment in the paper as the song festivals and the training courses for song leaders. Choirs and song leaders of many villages met at song festivals and inspired each other for better achievements in the art of singing. Even under the Soviets this was one of the activities which was partially tolerated for a while. Small group and family singing continued even during the darkest hour when large meetings and worship services were forbidden.

Well known among the Mennonites (GCM) of Kansas is the Mennonite Song Festival Society which was organized in 1930 at the Alexanderwohl Mennonite Church at Goessel, Kan., during the spring of that year, for church choirs. Smaller song festivals had been held at various places prior to this organization. In 1931 the Eden Mennonite Church of Moundridge, Kan., was the host to the Mennonite Song Festival. Choirs from surrounding Mennonite churches joined in the all-day singing of hymns and choral numbers. The following year at Whitewater a mass women's choir also performed. In 1932 at the Song Festival in Newton it was agreed that the afternoon would be devoted to presentations of songs by various church choirs, while evening programs would be devoted to combined choral singing. After this, with the exception of the years 1935, 1937, 1941, when the Song Festival took place in Lindley Hall in Newton, the choirs performed in the Kidron Park on the Bethel College campus. The number of participating choirs in the early years was

sometimes has high as 30, with a total of 500 to 1,000 singers. The choir groups consisted of 25 to 75 members. Reports indicate that there was a total attendance of 3-5,000. Among the officers of the Mennonite Song Festival Society were Paul Baumgartner, D. C. Wedel, Elizabeth Nickel, and Jacob Bartel. Some of the programs were broadcast. The combined singing was usually under the direction of W. H. Hohmann. As a rule the mass choir rehearsal took place prior to the song festival. The Mennonite Men's Chorus Festival gave its tenth annual presentation on March 23, 1958, at Memorial Hall of Bethel College.

The Mennonite Brethren have similar song festivals. Formerly they took place in various communities and churches. Recently the Mennonite Brethren Central Kansas Choir Festival, as well as the Mennonite Brethren Men's Chorus, are giving their programs in Memorial Hall at Bethel College. In the western part of Kansas there is also an annual song festival, as well as one in Oklahoma and one on the Pacific Coast. H. C. Richert and his Tabor College Choir have had a significant influence on the Mennonite Brethren Song Festival.

Song and music festivals and choir director schools are particularly popular among the Mennonites of Canada both in the General Conference and the Mennonite Brethren churches. The two Bible colleges in Winnipeg and the various schools from coast to coast are centers of these activities. Some of the outstanding leaders were K. H. Neufeld, John Konrad, and Ben Horch. Similar song festivals are held in various places in the western provinces.

C.K.

The April 1948 issue of *Mennonite Life* was devoted primarily to Mennonite music and singing. *Unser Blatt*, published in Russia 1925-28, reports on song festivals, Vol. I, 12, 30, 40, 132, 176, 219, 253, 277 ff., 317; Vol. II, 179, 219, 334, 343, 376; Vol. III, 146, 168, 171; Elizabeth Nickel, "Mennonite Song Festival Society," compiled the minutes 1928-49 (BeCL).

Sonnenberg Mennonite Church, located on a plateau in the Bernese Jura mountain district called Sonnenberg, about six miles from the town of Tramelan, next to Langnau (*q.v.*) the largest and oldest Mennonite congregation in Switzerland, whose members live in a radius of approximately 5 miles from the central meetinghouse which is known as Jeangisboden. The members of the congregation are almost exclusively of Bernese origin and are descendants of the Anabaptists who fled from their homes in the area of Langnau because of persecution.

The beginnings of the Sonnenberg congregation are no longer clear; probably a few families settled here in the 16th century. The scattered and rather isolated farms on the plateaus of the Jura Mountains were a secure place of refuge for persecuted Anabaptists as far back as the time of the Reformation, under the toleration and protection of the Catholic prince-bishop of Basel, who at that time was the ruler of the Jura. Here, however, they had to live in very meager conditions, cultivating stony land which had little water, and here they located their isolated barns as much as possible in secret places. Along with their agricultural work, which was mostly meadow farming, they practiced weaving as a side line. Their simple clothing was thus the product of their own hands.

There is evidence that the first migration on a larger scale from the Bernese area into the Jura, particularly to the Sonnenberg district, began with the severe persecutions of the 1670's and the 1690's; it increased at the beginning of the 18th century, particularly from the Emmental, when the Bernese authorities attempted to drive out all the Anabaptists from their territory. Official reports of 1716 and 1720 indicate that a number of Anabaptist families located in the Sonnenberg district and the region of Soncéboz, Corgémont, and Tramelan at that time. Ernst Müller names numerous Anabaptist families who came into this area at the beginning of the 18th century whose descendants constitute the membership of the Sonnenberg congregation today.

A document of May 24, 1779, and a letter of March 2, 1785, indicate that the elders and ministers of the Swiss congregations met regularly on March 25 for conference. Since these two documents were in the possession of a former deacon of the Sonnenberg congregation it is certain that Sonnenberg was the location of these early conferences. Through these conferences Sonnenberg became the center of the Jura congregations. The Sonnenberg congregation was in close contact with the congregations located at Biderich-Graben, Plagne, etc., in the mountains north of Biel. Niklaus Knörr, who died in Plagne in 1783, was arrested at one o'clock at night on April 18, 1757, in a secret Anabaptist meeting held at Gossliwil in Bucheggberg in the Solothurn district. He later had to flee to the Jura district in a destitute condition.

Among the known ministers and elders of the 18th century Hans Röthlisberger, chosen preacher in 1752 and elder in 1759; Johann Zingg of Corgémontberg and Peter Sommer of Vion near Tavannes were preachers in the Sonnenberg congregation according to a document of Sept. 1, 1850, written at Talvogne requesting military exemption.

At the beginning of the 19th century the congregation had some 200 baptized members. Its alms fund, which goes back at least to 1715, was managed by a deacon. Known deacons were David Tanner of Nidauberg near Soncéboz in 1827, Peter Lehman of Sombevalberg in 1850, and Johannes Zürcher of Talvogne, whose son Peter Zürcher was deacon until late in the 19th century.

In the first half of the 19th century large numbers of Sonnenberg members who found life on the Jura Mountains too difficult emigrated to America, where they settled largely in Ohio and Indiana. The heaviest emigration was in the 1830's, the 1850's, and the 1880's. The congregation founded near Dalton, Ohio, in 1817 took the name Sonnenberg. The large Swiss settlements near Bluffton, Ohio, and Berne, Ind., were also founded by emigrants from the same general area as the one in Sonnenberg, Ohio, although not all came from the same congregation.

Until the end of the 19th century the Sonnenberg congregation met every three weeks for worship in large second-floor rooms of various homes in the congregation, or in the summer in large barns. Those who came on foot from distant farms were given a meal of pea soup and "milk coffee." The meeting lasted several hours. The hymnal used was the *Ausbund* and the Lobwasser Psalmbook of the Reformed Church. For many years Peter Schnegg was the elder of the congregation; David Lerch also served, although he was in the neighboring congregation of Mont-Cortébert.

New life was brought into the congregation from 1876 on through the preaching missions of Jakob Hege (*q.v.*) of Reihen in Baden, the Reiseprediger (*q.v.*) of the South German Mennonites (Verband, *q.v.*), who held numerous Bible conferences. A very fruitful ministry was also rendered by J. A. Sprunger (*q.v.*) of Berne, Ind., who held a number of series of meetings in 1889. Sprunger introduced the songbook of the General Conference Mennonites, called *Gesangbuch mit Noten*.

At the end of the 1880's the congregation established a regular place of meeting, first in the large upper room of a house owned by Niklaus Gerber in Cernil near Tramelan. At the beginning of the 1890's a second location was established at the house of Ulrich Lehman at Brichon. A third meeting place was purchased in 1897 at Fürstenberg, Mont Tramelan. From this time on the meetings were held in rotation every Sunday at one of these places. Since the main meeting at Ulrich Lehman's on the Sonnenberg became too large for the place, the congregation built a meetinghouse on ground furnished by Christian Geiser in Jeangisboden next to his house. This substantial meetinghouse, built largely with volunteer labor from the congregation, was dedicated on Oct. 14, 1900. It has ever since been the meeting place for the conference of the Swiss Mennonite congregations, as well as the central meetinghouse of the Sonnenberg congregation. In 1928 the second story of a house purchased in Les Mottes was rebuilt into a good-sized meeting place to replace the rented room in Cernil.

In 1891, after the death of Elder Peter Schnegg, three ministers were ordained: Samuel Nussbaumer, Christian Habegger, and Jacob Amstutz. Several years later, when Amstutz took over the ministerial work in the Kleintal congregation, Samuel Gerber was ordained preacher. In 1901 Nussbaumer and Gerber were ordained elders. Among the evangelists who served the Sonnenberg congregation repeatedly in the early 19th century were Fritz Schüpbach (1903-8) and later Jacob Vetter.

The Sonnenberg congregation has continued to grow. In 1958 it had a membership of approximately 500 baptized persons, with three ministers, all of whom have been ordained as elders, namely, Samuel Geiser of Fontaines, Daniel Habegger of La Tanne, and Samuel Gerber of Les Reussilles. S.G.

Müller, *Berner Täufer;* Samuel Geiser, *Die Taufgesinnten-Gemeinden* (Karlsruhe, n.d., 1931); *idem*, "The Mennonites of Switzerland and France," *MQR* XI (1937) 44-60; Delbert Gratz, *Bernese Anabaptists and Their American Descendants* (Scottdale, 1953); *ML* IV.

Sonnenberg Mennonite Church (MC), located in Wayne County, Ohio, now a member of the Virginia Conference, was founded by Swiss immigrants from the canton of Bern in the early decades of the 19th century. The first settlers arrived in Wayne County in 1819 in what is now the Sonnenberg neighborhood north of the village of Kidron. The congregation made a steady growth but gradually withdrew, culturally, from its kindred Swiss Mennonite congregations in Allen and Putnam counties, Ohio, Adams County, Ind., and Moniteau County, Mo. After 1878, when the last conference of all the Swiss congregations was held at Sonnenberg, the congregation, under the wise and able leadership of its bishop (or elder) Christian Sommer (ordained preacher in 1844 and elder in 1862), remained independent, but gradually formed cultural and informal organizational ties with the Wayne County Amish Mennonite and Mennonite congregations. In 1886 a few members withdrew, partly under the influence of the "Oberholtzer" Mennonite school at Wadsworth (q.v.), Ohio, to found the Salem Mennonite (GCM) Church (q.v.). In spite of difficulties relating to the transition from German to English and similar matters, chiefly cultural, the congregation continued to grow until in 1935 there were over 500 members. Sonnenberg collaborated more and more with the Amish Mennonite and Mennonite congregations in Bible conferences, Sunday-school meetings, and similar religious activities. In 1935, 330 members withdrew and organized the Kidron Mennonite Church (q.v.) under the Ohio and Eastern Conference. The Sonnenberg congregation suffered a later division which resulted in the organization of the Bethel Mennonite Church (unaffiliated) near Apple Creek, Ohio, with 49 members. The Sonnenberg Church, now a member of the Virginia Conference (q.v.), had a membership of 168 in 1957, with Louis Amstutz as bishop and James Stauffer as minister. J.S.U.

John Umble, "David A. Schneck's Notes on the History of the Sonnenberg (Ohio) Swiss Mennonite Congregation," *MQR* XXIX (1955) 276-99.

Son(n)isten: see **Zonists**.

Sonnius, Franciscus (Frans van der Velde, 1507-76, b. at Son), professor of theology at the University of Leuven, Belgium, thereupon (1560) Roman Catholic bishop, first of 's Hertogenbosch, then of Antwerp, is known in Mennonite history as an inquisitor. In 1545 he was appointed to oversee the extirpation of heresy in the Dutch provinces of Holland and Zeeland, and in 1553 also in Friesland. He also dealt with Anabaptists. The martyrs gave him a good testimony, saying that he was willing to hear them and that he was moderate. The insolence and brutality of many other inquisitors were foreign to Sonnius. He wrote to his instructor that he preferred a certain lenience toward the heretics, trying to save souls and rejecting all kinds of cruelty. vDZ.

N.N.B.Wb. II, 1346 f.; *Inv. Arch. Amst.* I, Nos. 379 f.; I. M. J. Hoog, *De Martelaren der Hervorming* (Schiedam, 1885) 47 f.; L. E. Halkin, *La Réforme en Belgique* (Brussels, 1957) 58.

Sonoy, Dieric (Dirk) (1529-97), a stadholder (governor) of North Holland in the name of William (q.v.) of Orange, protected the Dutch Mennonites against the intolerance of the Reformed, who had asked in 1576 that the Mennonite meetings be prohibited. Sonoy also respected the Mennonite principle of nonresistance, ruling that the Mennonites

should make their contribution in the struggle against the Spaniards not by bearing arms, but by using spades and baskets to dig trenches for defense; he also ordered them to guard duty. (*DB* 1909, 40; 1910, 18.) vDZ.

Sorga, a village about three miles east of Hersfeld in Hesse (q.v.), Germany, which became the center of the Anabaptist movement in this entire region and where a strong Anabaptist congregation existed from about the middle of 1528 to 1533, which had strong connections with the Moravian Anabaptists. Hans Both (q.v.), and later a certain Ilgen, were the leaders or elders of the congregation. Ludwig Spon (q.v.) (or Hans Römer), an active Anabaptist leader in eastern Thuringia and eastern Hesse, testified in 1533 before the court that there were 40-50 persons in the congregation, taught by a minister (*Lehrer*); the Christian life was practiced, and no one suffered need, since there was mutual aid. The greeting of the Lord, "Peace be with you," was the distinguishing mark of the brethren, who celebrated the Lord's Supper according to the ordination of the Lord; for this consisted of nothing more than the partaking of the natural bread, taken with thanksgiving. "Whoever does the will of the Lord has received His body and drunk His blood." Wappler, in reporting the reasons for the strength of the Anabaptist propaganda which proceeded from Sorga into the neighboring Thuringian-Hessian territory, explains that "on the one hand the [tolerant] attitude of Prince Philip of Hesse was responsible, who, due to a certain sympathy for the Anabaptists because of the earnestness of their faith and the boldness of their confessing, always shrank back from severe measures; on the other hand the sermons of the Lutheran preachers all too often failed to produce the fruits of a new life, while their conduct gave much occasion for offense. How strikingly the Anabaptist preachers differed in this respect, who really lived what they preached, and often enough went to their death for the truth of their cause." The Lutheran pastor Raidt in neighboring Hersfeld also had understanding for them. A certain Anabaptist preacher called Alexander (q.v.) testified in July 1533, that he had often been at Sorga, where the brethren held public meetings and preaching ("öffentliche Gemeinde und Predigt").

But the pressure of neighboring Saxony, which demanded the death penalty and strict suppression because of the constant influence of the Sorga Anabaptists in Saxony, as well as the evident increasing strength of the movement, finally moved Philip to drastic action. In September 1533 the entire Sorga congregation was expelled. They, like many other persecuted Anabaptists in Central and Southern Germany, moved to the Hutterites in Moravia, with whom they had intimate connections. George Knobloch testified in September 1534, that "the whole village of Sorga had moved to Moravia, expelled by the Prince." Hans Both went with them. The further history of the Sorga group's failure to find a satisfactory spiritual home with the communal Hutterites, and then partial returns to Hesse is detailed by Wappler partly on the basis of the account in the Hutterite Chronicle (under the year 1533). H.S.B.

P. Wappler, *Die Stellung Kursachsens und des Land-grafen Philipp von Hessen zur Täuferbewegung* (Münster, 1910); *idem, Thüringen*, 73, 103; K. W. H. Hochhuth, "Landgraf Philip und die Wiedertaufer," *Ztscht f. d. hist. Theol.* XXVIII (1858) 538-644; XXIX (1859) 167-234; *ML* IV.

Sorg(h)drager (Zorgdrager), **Kornelis Pietersz** (d. Aug. 9, 1826), was chosen as preacher in 1782 and as elder in 1795 to serve the Janjacobsgezinde (*q.v.*) Mennonite church on the Dutch island of Ameland (*q.v.*). He was untrained, yet very capable and much less conservative than Jacob Jobs (*q.v.*), his coelder until 1804, with whom Sorghdrager could not get along, because Jobs disapproved all innovations and obstructed all proposals and measures which Sorghdrager considered necessary for the sound development of the congregation, such as audible prayer instead of silent prayer, an offering to be held at the end of the services, and the introduction of catechetical instruction for the children. Sorghdrager, who was a man of strong faith and devotion, was a great blessing for the church of Ameland. For his catechetical instruction he published *Vragen aan de Dopelingen met derselver antwoorden* (n.p., n.d.), and during his eldership the Foppe (*q.v.*) Ones congregation merged (1804) with the Janjacobsgezinden. He kept a diary, which contains a large number of interesting particulars concerning the congregation. Some of his descendants served the church as deacons, one of whom was Cornelis Pietersz Sorghdrager, treasurer of the Hollum (*q.v.*) congregation at the close of the 19th century.

Whether the Mennonite Sorghdrager (Zorgdrager) family found at Westzaan, province of North Holland, usually whaling captains, belonged to the same family, could not be ascertained, but they probably did, because most members of the Sorghdrager family of Ameland also were shipmasters. Of the North Holland Sorghdragers, Cornelis Gysbertsz Zorgdrager, commander of a whaling expedition, wrote the book *Bloeyende Opkomst der Aloude en Hedendaagsche Groenlandsche Visscherij* (Amsterdam 1720, repr. The Hague 1727-28), and Dirk Kornelisz Sorgdrager, possibly a son of the former, was a preacher of the Westzaan Frisian congregation in 1746-66.   vDZ.

DB 1889, 1, 19; 1890, 1-13, 29 f., 33; 1898, 67-70; *Naamlijst* 1829, 60; S. Lootsma, *Het Nieuwe Huys* (Zaandam, 1937) 46, 103 f., 190.

Souderton, a town (pop. 4,623) in Montgomery County, Pa., midway between Philadelphia and Allentown, was incorporated as a borough in 1888. Mennonites from the surrounding area, mostly west of town, made up a goodly portion of the earlier inhabitants. There are over 1,400 baptized Mennonites of the M.C. and G.C.M. groups and an unaffiliated church, living in Souderton. Probably 40 per cent of Franconia Conference Mennonites (MC) use Souderton as a shopping center. At least five Mennonite congregations were established in the area in the first half of the 18th century, viz., Franconia, Rockhill, Salford, Line Lexington, and Plains, all 3-5 miles away. Agriculture, marketing, and industry are the principal means of livelihood.   J.M.Mo.

Souderton Mennonite Church (MC), located in Montgomery County, Pa., a member of the Fran-

conia Conference, began in 1879 when families of the Franconia and the Rockhill Mennonite congregations living in Souderton built the first house of worship in Souderton. The congregation was organized in 1891. The first communion was held on April 19, 1891, when 68 members partook. Ministers from established Mennonite congregations accepted appointments to preach at Souderton until 1914, when the first minister there was ordained. Ministers who have served the congregation with the date of ordination were Jacob M. Moyer, minister 1914; bishop 1947; Elmer B. Moyer (d. 1957) minister 1919; Russell B. Musselman, minister 1948. The membership in 1958 was 470; Stanley Shenk was assisting in the ministry. A considerable number have left from here to build mission stations into congregations in the outlying areas.   J.M.Mo.

J. C. Wenger, *History of the Mennonites of the Franconia Conference* (Telford, 1937).

Souterliedekens, a Dutch medieval term for Psalms, were much used in the 16th-century Reformation period. "The *Souterliedekens,* though intended for the use of the Catholics, form the transition to the congregational singing of the Reformed" (Wolkan). A well-known edition was the one published at Antwerp, Belgium, in 1540 under the title *Souterliedekens, Ghemaeckt ter eeren Gods op alle die Psalmen van David: tot stichtinghe ende een gheestelijcke vermakinghe van allen Christen menschen.* This edition was reprinted more than 30 times under a variety of titles, the last reprint having been published in 1652 by Karel de Fleger (Vlieger), a Mennonite printer at Hamburg, Germany.

Though the early Dutch Anabaptists knew the "souterliedekens" and some martyrs are said to have sung a "souterlieken," these Psalms were apparently not popular among the Anabaptists: the reason may have been that the "souterliedekens" had come from Catholicism, with which they wished to make a complete break. They preferred to sing the "liedekens" (songs) written by or in honor of the martyrs, and it was not before the publication of the *Lietboeck* (*q.v.*) of Hans de Ries (*q.v.*) in 1582, which contained some Psalms, that singing of Psalms was introduced in at least a number of Mennonite congregations. (See also **Psalms** and **Hymnology**.)   vDZ.

Wolkan, *Lieder,* 58; F. C. Wieder, *Schriftuurlijke Liedekens* (The Hague, 1900) 129 *et passim.*

South Abbotsford Mennonite Brethren Church, located at Abbotsford, B.C., was organized on May 1, 1932, with 31 members. A. D. Rempel was elected leader of the group, continuing in office until 1945 with the exception of one year. In 1945 Henry H. Nikkel began to serve as leader. The following have been ministers in the congregation: Frank Janzen, Franz C. Thiessen, Jacob F. Redekop, Jacob Wedel, Jacob Bargen, Isaak Janzen, Herman Voth, and John J. Stobbe. In the neighboring districts a number of mission Sunday schools are held among the unchurched. The membership in 1957 was 385, with J. J. Stobbe serving as pastor. In 1950 a section of the congregation was organized separately as the Abbotsford M.B. (*q.v.*) church.   H.H.N.

South America, Mennonites in. The first Mennonites to come to South America were a few individuals from Germany and Russia who came to Brazil before World War I (e.g., a Lichdi from Herrlihof near Augsburg, and a Frederico Arentz from Hamburg, who aided the MCC in its service to the first Russian Mennonite refugees settling in Brazil in 1930 ff.). Some also came to Argentina. The next to enter South America were Mennonite missionaries from North America. The first was the Mennonite Church (MC) with its mission work in central Argentina (1917) and later in the Argentine Chaco (1943), Brazil (1954 in the state of Sao Paulo, and the same year in the Amazon River region by a private board taken over by the general board in 1957), and Uruguay (1954 in Montevideo). Both the General Conference Mennonites and the Mennonite Brethren missionaries entered Colombia (*q.v.*) in 1945, the former in the central part, and the latter in the Choco area on the Pacific Coast. In the same year the M.B. Church began a mission in Curitiba, Brazil. The total number of members in all the missions by 1957 was about 1,000 (Argentina 673, MC; Colombia about 300, GCM and MB; Brazil about 25, MC).

The Mennonite colonization in South America has been by three groups: (1) Russian Mennonites to the Paraguayan Chaco from Manitoba and Saskatchewan (Sommerfeld Mennonites in 1926 and in South Paraguay in 1948); (2) refugees from Russia in 1930 to the state of Santa Catharina, Brazil—later displaced completely to the states of Curitiba and Rio Grande do Sul—and the Paraguayan Chaco (Fernheim Colony), a part going later to East Paraguay (Friesland); (3) refugees from Russia in 1948 to Paraguay (Chaco-Neuland, East Paraguay-Volendam); (4) Danzig and Galician Mennonites to Uruguay in 1948-50 (El Ombu) and 1951 (Gartental) with Delta added in 1955, and a congregation being organized in Montevideo in 1957. About 500 refugees had also finally located in Argentina, largely by transfer from Paraguay. Less than 150 of these have been gathered into a Mennonite congregation in Buenos Aires.

In 1957 the total population of the Mennonite colonies in South America was about 16,500, distributed as follows: Paraguay 11,500, Brazil 3,000, Uruguay 1,500, Argentina 500. The number of baptized members was 7,150, distributed as follows: Paraguay 5,000 (GCM 1,560, MB 1,000, EMB 180, Menno 1,360, Sommerfeld 890), Brazil 1,100 (MB 650, GCM 450), Uruguay 900 (GCM 809, MB 91), Argentina 150 (EMB). By Mennonite bodies this gives: GCM—2,900, MB—1,730, EMB—330.

The total Mennonite immigration to South America according to Fretz has been *c*11,000:

MENNONITE MIGRATIONS TO SOUTH AMERICA
1926-51

From	1926	1930	1931	1932	To Paraguay 1934	1947	1948	1950	1951		Total
Canada	1765	——	——	——	——	——	——	——	———		1765
Russia											
(via Germany)	——	1500	——	——	——	1975	2445	85	15		6020
(via China)	——	——	——	378	——	——	——	——	———		378
(via Holland)	——	——	——	——	——	329	——	——	———		329
Poland	——	——	123	——	——	——	——	——	——		123
										Total,	8615
					To Brazil						
Russia											
(via Germany)	——	1100	——	——	——	——	——	——	——		1100
(via China)	——	——	——	——	100	——	——	——	——		100
										Total,	1200
					To Uruguay						
Germany	——	——	——	——	——	——	467	——	430		897
(via Denmark)	——	——	——	——	——	——	284	——	——		284
										Total,	1181
Total	1765	2600	123	378	100	2304	3196	85	445	Grand Total,	10996

A certain amount of return migration has taken place from Paraguay to Canada from the Sommerfeld colonies—Menno (1926-30), Bergthal, and Sommerfeld (1948-50), but this has ceased. On the other hand, a substantial emigration from the refugee colonies in Paraguay has taken place in recent years and is still going on. From Paraguay some 800 have moved to Canada, and about 150 to Germany. About 100 have also moved from Brazil to Canada.

The Mennonite Central Committee sponsored the refugee colonies in Paraguay and has continued to aid them in various ways to date. It also sponsored the colonies in Uruguay and has been the channel of some aid there. It did not sponsor the colonies in Brazil, which were originally sponsored by the German government.

The MCC has also established and maintained three centers in South America: Asuncion, Paraguay (1935); Sao Paulo, Brazil (1948); and Montevideo, Uruguay (1948).

The Mennonite Biblical Seminary was established in Montevideo in 1956 under an inter-Mennonite international board, supported by the mission boards of the G.C.M. and M.C. North American conferences. There is also an M.B. Bible School in Montevideo, an inter-Mennonite Bible School in Filadelfia, Fernheim Colony, and a Spanish Bible School at Bragado, Argentina.

Two German language Mennonite church papers are published in South America, the *Menno-Blatt* (founded 1930) by the Fernheim Colony administration at Filadelfia, Paraguay, and *Bibel und Pflug* (founded 1954) published privately at Witmarsum,

Brazil. The first Brazil Mennonite paper, *Die Brücke,* was published privately at Witmarsum 1932-37, then for a short time by the Krauel Colony in 1938. The only Spanish language Mennonite periodical has been *La Voz Menonita,* published since 1932 by the Argentine Mennonites (MC). In 1955-58 a settlement of some 260 souls from Menno and Fernheim, Paraguay, was established near Santa Cruz, Bolivia.   H.S.B.

J. W. Fretz, *Pilgrims in Paraguay, The Story of Mennonite Colonization in South America* (Scottdale, 1953); Walter Quiring, *Im Schweisse deines Angesichts; ein mennonitisches Bilderbuch; Paraguay, Brasilien, Argentinien, Uruguay, und Mexico* (Steinbach, 1953).

South Bruderthal Evangelical Mennonite Brethren Church, now in the town of Langham, Sask., was organized in May 1925. The first minister was Jacob R. Doerksen (d. 1940). On Aug. 3, 1929, the original building was destroyed by fire. The basement of a new church was completed, but because of the depression the superstructure could not be finished at that time. Until 1941 this basement served as the place of worship. In 1956 the church was moved to Langham. The membership in 1958 was 85, J. N. Hiebert pastor.   J.N.H.

South Cayuga (Ont.) Mennonite Church (MC), first known as Fry's Corners, is located on the Rainham Road, a mile north of Lake Erie and 8 miles west of the Rainham Mennonite neighborhood. Land was conveyed for worship and school purposes in 1839 and 1843. The present frame meetinghouse was built in 1850. This was a fairly strong fellowship by 1870. The Old Order Mennonite group was the stronger group after the division of 1889. Christian Gayman was an influential bishop here before the division. When John Shirk, the last Old Order minister, moved to Waterloo County, this faction ceased to function. Mennonite ministers in charge have been Moses Hoover of Rainham (*q.v.*) after 1893 and A. Lewis Fretz, also at Rainham since 1931. For several years after 1917 this congregation with under 20 members became the charge of the Rural Mission Board of Ontario. By 1957 the membership had risen to 33.   J.C.F.

South Central Mennonite (MC) Conference, successor to the Kansas-Nebraska Mennonite Conference (*q.v.*), organized in 1921 under the name Missouri-Kansas Conference; it was renamed South Central Conference in 1946 to give more adequate recognition to its congregations in Colorado, Texas, Louisiana, and Mississippi. Beginning in 1921 with 35 reporting congregations with 1,907 baptized members, in 1957 it reported 58 congregations (14 unorganized), with 3,413 members.

The South Central Conference took the lead in the Mennonite Church (MC) in a revision of church polity in 1954-55 by (1) the introduction of the office of regional overseer appointed by the executive committee of conference in conjunction with the ministry of the region, (2) the introduction of a three-year term not only for the overseer but also for the local pastor, and (3) the suspension of further ordination of bishops. The conference has been divided into regions (each with an overseer) as follows: Colorado, Kansas, Missouri, Gulf Coast. (For further statistics, see **Kansas-Nebraska.**)   H.S.B.

South China Mennonite Brethren Mission. The General Conference of the Mennonite Brethren Church in 1909 discussed the matter of opening a mission in China, but the Board of Foreign Missions did not see its way clear to do so at the time. Mr. and Mrs. F. J. Wiens then set out in 1910 to begin an independent M.B. mission in China, receiving their support from friends. On their way they stopped nearly a year in Russia, holding evangelistic meetings in M.B. churches and winning supporters for the intended mission. They arrived at the Baptist Mission, Swatow, South China, in the fall of 1911. In May 1912 they proceeded into the Hakka area 200 miles inland, and opened a mission among the Hakkas at Shanghang (Shonghong), on the Han River, Fukien Province. While procuring or erecting the required buildings, Wiens preached in the city and surrounding villages and opened chapels in strategic centers. Soon a number of Chinese converts were won and baptized and an indigenous church was organized. To supply a pressing need for native evangelists, ministers, and teachers, Wiens opened a Bible institute for training such workers. He also began a school for boys and another for girls, and began medical work. In 1915 the M.B. Conference agreed to give partial support to the mission, and in 1919 it took over the mission and accepted new missionaries for this field.

Mr. and Mrs. J. S. Dick, Helena Heppner, and Tina Kornelsen left for this field in the spring of 1920. Mr. and Mrs. B. F. Wiens followed early in 1921. Their stay and service was short, as less than two years later Mr. Wiens died and Mrs. Wiens returned to the homeland a year later. Maria Richert, Sophia Richert, Paulina Foote, and Adelgunda Priebe entered the work a little later.

The mission prospered for some time, and Mr. and Mrs. Dick began a second station at EngTeng, 40 miles from Shanghang. Schools increased and hospital work expanded. At the 1921 conference F. J. Wiens, who had then returned for his first furlough, reported an indigenous church of 450 members, 11 outstations with ministers, and 17 schools with 30 teachers.

The most serious hindrance for the mission was the continuous political unrest with repeated revolutions and civil wars, which not only interrupted the work, but also endangered the missionaries' lives. In 1927 all the missionaries were obliged to leave the field and were plundered by pirates while proceeding to the coast in river boats.

Several later efforts were made to renew the work of the mission. Mr. and Mrs. Dick returned to China, but were compelled to remain at the coast much of the time. F. J. Wiens returned about 1935 and found the buildings of the mission stations demolished and the native church scattered, but many believers still firm and true in their faith. He did not rebuild the stations but devoted himself to traveling and preaching in the Hakka area. The Conference meanwhile maintained a policy of waiting.

In 1947 the M.B. Conference made another attempt to resume the work of the mission and sent Mr. and Mrs. Roland Wiens there. They still found some believers and an indigenous church again began to rise out of chaos. Some new converts were won and baptized and work in school and hospital was begun. The communistic revolution in China thwarted all further efforts, and all the missionaries were evacuated in 1951.   J.H.L.

F. J. Wiens, *Fifteen Years Among the Hakkas* (n.p., n.d.); *idem, Pionierarbeit unter den Hakkas in Süd-China* (n.p., n.d.-1922?).

South Colon Mennonite Church (MC), Colon, Mich., was established in 1954 by members from Locust Grove (*q.v.*). It had 41 members in 1957, William Wickey serving as minister.   M.G.

South Dakota. Mennonites began to arrive in southern Dakota 16 years before the territory was admitted into the Union. The first group, under the leadership of Daniel Unruh, reached Yankton in October 1873, coming directly from the Crimea in Russia. It was the forerunner of many groups to follow during the 1870's and early 1880's—all from Russia. The great bulk of the immigrants arriving in those years settled in Turner and Hutchinson counties in the southeastern part of the territory. From the very first there were four rather distinct groups even though all came from Russia.

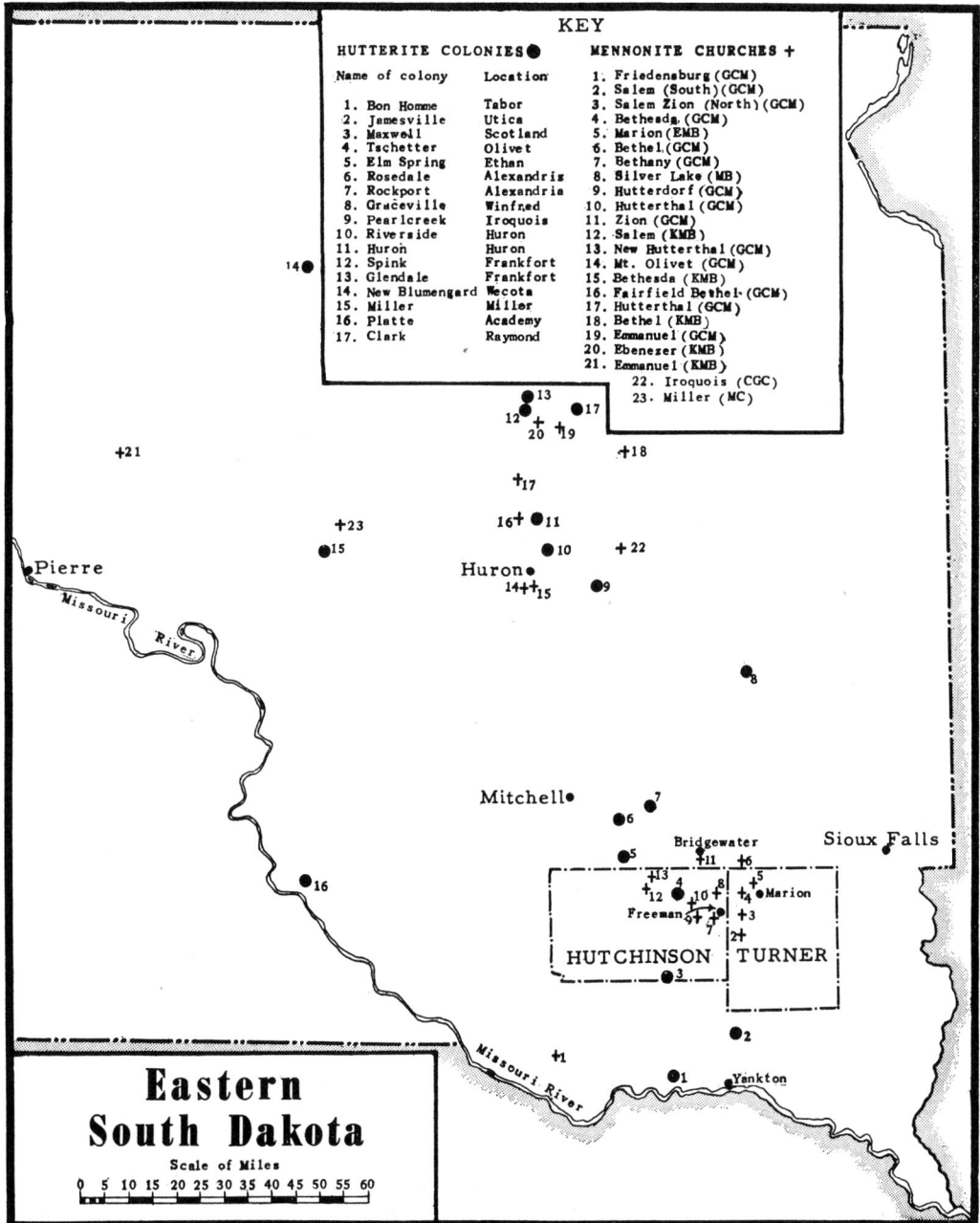

KEY

HUTTERITE COLONIES ●   **MENNONITE CHURCHES** +

Name of colony	Location
1. Bon Homme	Tabor
2. Jamesville	Utica
3. Maxwell	Scotland
4. Tschetter	Olivet
5. Elm Spring	Ethan
6. Rosedale	Alexandria
7. Rockport	Alexandria
8. Graceville	Winfred
9. Pearlcreek	Iroquois
10. Riverside	Huron
11. Huron	Huron
12. Spink	Frankfort
13. Glendale	Frankfort
14. New Blumengard	Wecota
15. Miller	Miller
16. Platte	Academy
17. Clark	Raymond

1. Friedensburg (GCM)
2. Salem (South)(GCM)
3. Salem Zion (North)(GCM)
4. Bethesda (GCM)
5. Marion (EMB)
6. Bethel (GCM)
7. Bethany (GCM)
8. Silver Lake (MB)
9. Hutterdorf (GCM)
10. Hutterthal (GCM)
11. Zion (GCM)
12. Salem (KMB)
13. New Hutterthal (GCM)
14. Mt. Olivet (GCM)
15. Bethesda (KMB)
16. Fairfield Bethel (GCM)
17. Hutterthal (GCM)
18. Bethel (KMB)
19. Emmanuel (GCM)
20. Ebenezer (KMB)
21. Emmanuel (KMB)
22. Iroquois (CGC)
23. Miller (MC)

Eastern South Dakota

Scale of Miles
0 5 10 15 20 25 30 35 40 45 50 55 60

The northern part of the settlement was predominantly Low German with the following family names rather common: Tieszen, Regier, Schmidt, Berg, Goosen, Koehn, Buller, Vogt, Peters, Ratzlaff, Dalke, Becker, Unruh, Ewert, Tiahrt, and Schartner. South of this group were the Swiss settlers who had immigrated from the Province of Volhynia in Russian Poland. Common family names in this group were Albrecht, Fliginger, Gering, Graber, Kaufman, Müller, Preheim, Ries, Schrag, Senner, Stucky, and Schwartz. To the west of these two settlements were the Hutterite Mennonites, whose ethnic background was the same as that of the Hutterian Brethren but who had left communal life long before the movement out of Russia. The more common family names in this group were Hofer, Tschetter, Wipf, Stahl, Gross, Kleinsasser, Mendel, Wollman, Waldner, and Walter. The fourth group represented the Hutterian Brethren. All of the 110 Hutterite colonies now established in the United States and Canada stem from the three original brotherhoods planted in Dakota in the 1870's. The original three were Bon Homme, on the Missouri River, near Tabor; Wolf Creek, on the James River, west of Freeman; and Old Elm Spring, near Milltown. An estimated 1,200-1,500 Mennonites came to Dakota in this early period, not including the approximately 300 Hutterian Brethren who established the original three colonies.

The difficulties pertinent to the establishment of pioneer homes on the western prairies have been repeatedly rehearsed by writers. Suffice it to say that the Mennonite tillers of the soil experienced the whole gamut of pioneering problems. Prairie fires, grasshoppers, Dakota blizzards, spring floods, crop failures, and countless other barriers impeded progress again and again.

That the western states were anxious to get Mennonite settlers is clearly revealed in the editorial policies of the newspapers. The Yankton *Press and Dakotan* was especially anxious to give "this class of immigrants the best chance possible, for we have already seen enough of their thrift and enterprise to convince us that they will make most desirable citizens" (Dec. 4, 1873). The paper pleaded for more united action to secure as much as possible of this "most valuable tide of humanity" (May 28, 1874).

In most instances early church services were held in the homes, and when schools were built these were utilized for worship services. The first meetinghouse was constructed in 1877 in the western part of the settlement by the Hutterthal congregation. The Bethesda congregation in the northern part of the territory erected its first building in 1879. Others followed until by 1900 there were at least a half dozen or more.

At least 80 per cent of the Mennonites in South Dakota are farmers. This dependence on the soil was a contributing factor to the movement of large numbers of Hutterian Mennonites from Hutchinson County to counties in the state farther north and west, notably Beadle, Spink, and Sully. Here cheap marginal land was available which under the stimulus of high prices for farm products brought on by World War I proved tempting for many hundreds of Mennonites. Spurred on by the real-estate men

these people became alarmed lest opportunities for buying land would be curtailed. The dry years in the 1930's brought real hardship to many of these people, since rainfall was considerably less in these counties than in Turner and Hutchinson counties. An increasing number of Mennonite farmers have received recognition at county and state fairs through the exhibition of grain products and purebred livestock and poultry.

Except for the Hutterian Brethren the Mennonites of South Dakota have generally participated in local politics and have quite universally exercised the right of franchise. The only Mennonite ever to hold a major state elective office was David D. Wipf of Freeman, who served two terms as Secretary of State (1905-9). The following Mennonites have represented Hutchinson and Turner counties in the lower house of the state legislature: John J. Wipf, six terms; P. P. Kleinsasser, two terms; Emil J. Waltner, three terms; David J. Mendel, Andrew J. Waltner, J. J. Kleinsasser, J. P. Kleinsasser, John J. Gering, and Joseph K. Schrag, each one term. P. P. Kleinsasser also served two terms in the Senate, and the following have each served one term in the upper house: John J. Wipf, A. A. Wipf, J. C. Graber, and John J. Gering. All of these legislators were affiliated with the Republican Party. On the local level there have been county commissioners, county judges, state's attorneys, township supervisors, mayors, and city councilmen.

The most important institution established by the Mennonites in the state is Freeman Junior College at Freeman, which was incorporated on Dec. 14, 1900, under the name of "South Dakota Mennonite College." The name was changed to Freeman College in 1921, and in 1939 to Freeman Junior College. From the first this institution has been a co-operative endeavor supported by virtually all the Mennonite groups in the state. It has done much to make Freeman the Mennonite center of the state. A more recent institution located at Freeman is the Salem Mennonite Home for the Aged, which first began to operate in 1949. It, too, is co-operatively supported by the Mennonite church groups in the Freeman and Marion communities.   J.D.U.

Statistics—1954

Congregation	Location	Conf.	Mem.
Bethany	Freeman	GCM	306
Bethel	Marion	GCM	63
Bethesda	Marion	GCM	242
Emmanuel	Doland	GCM	88
Fairfield	Hitchcock	GCM	44
Friedensberg	Avon	GCM	99
Hutterdorf	Freeman	GCM	69
Hutterthal	Freeman	GCM	217
Hutterthal	Carpenter	GCM	176
Mt. Olivet	Huron	GCM	75
Neu Hutterthal	Bridgewater	GCM	163
Salem	Freeman	GCM	534
Salem Zion	Freeman	GCM	438
Zion	Bridgewater	GCM	28
Bethel	Carpenter	KMB	315
Ebenezer	Doland	KMB	105
Emmanuel	Onida	KMB	92
Salem	Bridgewater	KMB	222
Silverlake	Freeman	MB	142
Bruderthaler	Marion	EMB	105
Miller	Miller	MC	25
United Missionary Church	Dolton	UMC (MBC)	34
			3582

Hutterian Brethren Colonies

Colony	Location	Population
Bon Homme	Tabor	58
Glendale	Frankfort	97
Graceville	Winfred	71
Huron	Huron	74
Jamesville	Utica	107
Maxwell	Scotland	72
Millerdale	Miller	54
New Elm Spring	Ethan	102
Pearl Creek	Iroquois	94
Platte	Academy	68
Riverside	Huron	48
Rockport	Alexandria	84
Rosedale	Mitchell	92
Spink	Frankfort	94
Tschetter	Olivet	94
		1209

John D. Unruh, "The Mennonites in South Dakota," *South Dakota Historical Review* II (1937) 147-70, taken from his unpublished Ph.D. thesis at the University of Texas; J. J. Gering, *After Fifty Years, A Brief Discussion of the History and Activities of the Swiss-German Mennonites from Russia Who Settled in South Dakota in 1874* (n.p., 1924); Edwin P. Graber, "An Analysis of Social Change in a Swiss-Mennonite Community" (M.A. thesis, University of S. D., 1932).

South End Mennonite Brethren Church, located at Juno and William streets, Winnipeg, Man., was organized on Oct. 4, 1936, under P. J. Kornelsen, who led the church until 1947. At first the meetings were held at the rented Maple Street Mission Church. A year later an old church building on 344 Ross Avenue was bought. In 1940 this church was sold and the present church building, fully equipped, with a seating capacity of 1,200 was bought. The membership in 1957 was 527. J. P. Neufeld was the leading minister. The congregation is a member of the Manitoba Provincial and the Canadian District M.B. conferences. H.Ne.

South Hoffnungsfeld (or South Fairview) Mennonite Brethren Church, now extinct. When the Cherokee strip in Oklahoma was opened for homesteading on Sept. 16, 1893, many members of M.B. church congregations in Kansas and in other states took up homesteads in the vicinity of what is now Fairview, Major Co., Okla. These settlers at first worshiped in houses and sometimes under trees. In the fall of 1895 a church was organized with William Hergert as leader, with a membership of 69. He served in this capacity until November 1900. In 1949 over 100 members of this congregation joined the Fairview City M.B. Church, followed in 1951 by the remaining members. J.C.Gr.

South Holland (Dutch, *Zuid-Holland*), a province of the Netherlands (1,085 sq. miles, pop. 2,400,000 in 1954) in which are found the large cities of The Hague and Rotterdam, has six Mennonite congregations, viz., Leiden, The Hague, Delft, Rotterdam, Dordrecht, and Ouddorp, and "kringen" (circles) at Gouda, Voorburg-Rijswijk, and Gorinchem.

In the 1530's Anabaptism did not spread as much in South Holland as it did in other Dutch provinces like North Holland and Friesland, though there were a number of important Anabaptist centers like Leiden, Brielle, and Schiedam. About 1600 there were probably many Mennonite congregations in this province, most of them small, and usually

founded or increased in membership by Mennonite immigrants from Flanders, Belgium. Most of these Flemish immigrants later moved on to Rotterdam and Haarlem, and thus between 1600 and 1700 more than 20 Mennonite congregations in South Holland died out. Other reasons for the decay were the small membership, the pressure of the Reformed Church, and mixed marriages. By 1700 only Leiden, Gouda, The Hague, Schiedam, Hazerswoude, Rotterdam, Dordrecht, Spijkenisse, and Ouddorp were left, and during the 18th century Gouda, The Hague, Schiedam, Hazerswoude, Dordrecht, and Spijkenisse also dissolved. In 1810 there were only three left—Leiden, Rotterdam, and Ouddorp, with a total of 180 baptized members. Since 1880 there has been considerable growth and new congregations have arisen at The Hague (1881), Dordrecht (1895/6), and Delft (1925), besides the circles mentioned above.

The total number of baptized members in South Holland was 3,307 in 1771; it is now (1958) 4,195, whereas the last census (1947) listed 8,237 persons as Mennonites. vDZ.

South Lawrence Mennonite Church (MC), located 10 miles southeast of Glen Flora, Wis., on state highway 73, and 12 miles east of the Sheldon Mennonite community. In May 1942 J. W. Martin and Sam Helmuth organized a Sunday school in the area and 4 years later Leroy Schrock was called in as pastor. On Dec. 9, 1946, the group of 20 members, of whom 8 were of non-Mennonite background, was organized as a congregation in the North Central Conference. The membership in 1957 was 26, with Leroy Schrock as pastor. L.S.

South Pacific Mission Board, an organization of the South Pacific Mennonite Conference (MC), issues the bimonthly *Southwest Messenger,* first issue January 1956. The board supports the Mennonite Hour, a Spanish Gospel broadcast from Pasadena, sponsors summer camps and Bible schools, as well as mission stations. In 1957 the president of the board was Jacob Shetler and the treasurer Daniel Horst. M.G.

South Peel Old Order Mennonite Church is the strongest of the five O.O.M. churches of Ontario. The frame meetinghouse west of the Conestoga River, west of Wallenstein on the Waterloo-Wellington County line in Peel Township, was erected in 1901, enlarged in 1928, 1932, and again before the middle of the century. Its membership in 1955 was some 400. Those who have ministered at this place are David B. Martin and Henry S. Bauman. Bishop Addison Gingerich (ordained 1942) has present oversight of all five O.O.M. appointments, and the minister at Peel is Abraham Bearinger (1890-   ), ordained 1935. J.C.F.

South Perkasie, a village adjoining Perkasie, Bucks Co., Pa., formerly also known as Bridgetown (for its covered bridge which was still in use in 1958) and Benjamin. In 1866 a Lutheran, Stephen Young, called a meeting in his home of persons interested in building a church. Mennonites, Lutherans, and Reformed worked together in the efforts to provide a church building for the area. The Mennonites purchased the lot on which the building was to be erected. In the final analysis, however, it was the Lutherans and Reformed who used the building. The Mennonites are not known to have ever held regular services there. The site was about midway between the Rockhill and Blooming Glen Mennonite meetinghouses, and only a few miles from each; so there was no particular need for the Mennonites to use the new house of worship.   J.C.W.

South Shafter (Cal.) Mennonite Brethren Church was started in 1957. In 1958 it had a membership of 43, with Jack Williams as temporary pastor.
                                                      H.S.B.

South Side Mennonite Brethren Mission Church, in Minneapolis, Minn., began as a mission on Franklin Avenue in 1907 with Mr. and Mrs. B. F. Wiens as missionaries and Mr. and Mrs. A. A. Schmidt as assistants. Soon the M.B. Conference built a two-story mission building near the Milwaukee Railroad Yards, at 2120 Minnehaha Avenue, in an area where there were many neglected homes with many children. This building provided a chapel seating about 200, and other facilities. When the Wienses left in 1911 the Schmidts took charge of the mission, serving more than 30 years, with a number of assistants. In 1943 Mr. and Mrs. O. W. Dirks were called to the mission. After a year of service, they were replaced by Mr. and Mrs. Melvin Schimnowski. In 1946 Mr. and Mrs. Chester Fast had charge of the mission, with the help of students attending Bible school in the city. This mission has been supported by the M.B. General Conference under the supervision of the Conference City Mission Board. In 1955 it became a congregation with 31 members and Paul G. Hiebert as pastor.   H.E.W.

South Union Mennonite Church (MC), formerly known as the North (Amish) District or the King's Church, located one mile north of West Liberty, Logan Co., Ohio, a member of the Ohio and Eastern Conference, was founded by Amish families from Wayne and Holmes counties, Ohio, and Mifflin County, Pa. In 1840 the Peter Yoder family moved from Wayne County to Union Township, Logan County, and by 1845 enough settlers had arrived to be organized into a congregation by two Holmes County bishops. After a second Amish group had settled in the Kennard-Kingscreek area in Champaign County (now the Oak Grove congregation, *q.v.*), Ohio, the two groups were considered the north and south districts of the same congregation. In 1855 the North District built the first Amish meetinghouse in Ohio one mile west and a half mile north of the present South Union church. Here, also, the first Amish Sunday school was organized in 1863 by the young minister, David Plank (*q.v.*). But for many years the North District held more strictly to some of the old Amish practices than the South and frequent disagreements arose. These differences led to a complete rupture between the two districts during the late 1860's, Bishop-Deacon John P. King, quite conservative, serving the North (Logan County) District and Bishop John Warye the South. David Plank with his father, Samuel Plank, who was a deacon, and a considerable body

of the members of King's congregation sided with Warye and in 1875 built the Walnut Grove church (*q.v.*) several miles west of King's church. In 1876 King's congregation built the South Union meetinghouse at its present location. In 1886 King moved to Coffee County, Kan., leaving the congregation in charge of Christian K. Yoder, brother of John K. Yoder, of Wayne County, Ohio. In 1890 a group of South Union young people refused to unite with the congregation because they were denied an English class in Sunday school. This group was baptized into a Mennonite church at Elida, Ohio, and became the nucleus of the Bethel Mennonite congregation (*q.v.*) at West Liberty, Ohio. In 1895 the South Union and Walnut Grove congregations decided to unite under one bishop. David Plank was chosen by lot and served both congregations until his death in 1912. Then A. I. Yoder (*q.v.*), son of C. K. Yoder, was ordained bishop and served until his death in 1934. S. E. Allgyer (*q.v.*), bishop of the Oak Grove church in Champaign County, then served as bishop of both congregations until his retirement in 1950. In 1953 the congregation completed a large brick church building, and in 1955 a commodious Sunday-school unit. In 1957 the pastor was Bishop Roy S. Koch, and membership 309.   J.S.U.

John Umble, "Early Sunday Schools at West Liberty, Ohio," *Ohio Mennonite Sunday Schools* (Goshen, 1941) 105-58; *idem,* "Early Sunday Schools at West Liberty, Ohio," *MQR* IV (1930) 6-50.

Southern District of the Virginia Mennonite (MC) Conference. The Shenandoah Valley churches were divided into districts in 1837: the Northern (or Lower) District with Broadway as a center, the Central (or Middle) District with Harrisonburg as a center, and the Southern (or Upper) District with Waynesboro in Augusta County as a center. In 1942 the terms "Lower" and "Upper" were discontinued. The Mennonite churches of Augusta County have been known as the Southern District ever since. The Southern District includes six congregations with a total of 522 members as follows: Springdale with 217, Hildebrand with 49 at Waynesboro, Mt. View with 61 at Lyndhurst, Ebenezer with 38 at South Boston, Stuarts Draft with 109, and Greenmonte Rural Mission Church at Greenville with 48 members. The district has traditionally had one bishop, who in 1958 was Franklin Weaver.   H.A.B.

Southern District Conference *of the Mennonite Brethren Church of North America* was organized in 1909, comprising the churches of Kansas, Oklahoma, and California. The California churches, however, withdrew the following year and organized their own conference. The first convention of the Southern District was held in 1910 in the Ebenezer Church near Buhler, Kan., with Johann Foth chairman, M. M. Just vice-chairman, and A. L. Schellenberg secretary.

The purpose for the organization of the district conferences was to stress chiefly the home mission work and evangelism in the churches. At its organization this Conference had a membership of 2,100 with a total of 21 churches. The Colorado and Texas churches soon were added to the Southern District.

A number of leaders made valuable contributions in the early days of the Conference. Among these were Johann Foth, M. M. Just, Heinrich Adrian, and Abr. Schellenberg. Later leaders include H. W. Lohrenz, H. H. Flaming, P. E. Nickel, J. K. Hiebert, P. P. Rempel, J. S. Regier, and P. C. Hiebert. Soon the sphere of labor of this Conference expanded. Home mission work occupied the chief attention and called for the greatest efforts on the part of the Home Missions Committee. A Committee of Reference and Counsel was created and charged with looking after the spiritual welfare of the Conference and assisted the individual churches in the event of difficult problems. The evangelism project for the churches was another important factor to which much emphasis was given. The Home Missions Committee secured qualified evangelists and presented them to the churches for engagement.

A third project of the Conference is extension work. At first this work was confined to the fringe areas of the churches. In 1936 the Conference opened a field of mission work in Texas along the Mexican border with Mr. and Mrs. Harry Neufeld as missionaries. Other stations have been created there since, and also in Arkansas and Wichita missionary projects are carried on with good success.

Although a General Conference project, Tabor College is located in the Southern District, and the Oklahoma churches support a full four-year academy at Corn with a strong Bible department. A church school committee promotes the Sunday-school work as well as the religious education work of this district, and a youth committee has charge of the Christian fellowship work and the youth retreat.

In 1947 a constitution was adopted and in 1948 the Conference was incorporated in Kansas. Thirty-five churches belong to the Conference (1956) with a total membership of 4,763.   P.H.B.

Southern Manitoba Broadcasting Company, operating radio station CFAM at Altona, Man., was organized in 1956 to provide good music, agricultural information, religious services for shut-ins, and an opportunity for ethnic groups to have services in their own languages. First licensed in November 1956 for 1,000 watts, in 1958 the power was increased to 10,000 watts and CFAM could be heard by 95 per cent of all Manitobans, the second most powerful station in Manitoba.   P.Br.

Southwest Messenger, the organ of the South Pacific Mennonite (MC) District Mission Board, an 8-page 6 x 9 inch bimonthly, first issue January 1956, editor Samuel Spicher, place of publication Phoenix, Ariz.   H.S.B.

Southwestern Pennsylvania Conference News. This publication was begun as "Southwestern Pennsylvania Mission News," a bimonthly, on Nov. 23, 1936. The first editors were Sanford G. Shetler and John L. Horst. It began as a mimeographed sheet. With the issue of Jan. 25, 1938, it was changed to a four-page, printed sheet, 6 x 8 in., enlarged in January 1939 to 9 x 12 in. In May 1942, by conference action, the name of the paper was changed to "Southwestern Pennsylvania Conference News," and its contents were adapted to represent the four conference-wide organizations—Church Conference, Mission Board,

Sunday School Conference (now known as the Christian Education Conference), and Associated Sewing Circles. In April 1954 the paper was changed to a monthly and in September 1954 the title was changed to "Allegheny Conference News" after the conference adopted a new constitution which changed its name from Southwestern Pennsylvania to Allegheny. It continues as the official organ of the four conference-wide organizations of Allegheny Conference (MC).   J.L.H.

Southwestern Pennsylvania Mennonite Conference (MC), in 1954 renamed Allegheny Conference with reference to the Allegheny Mountains which run through the district from north to south, was organized in 1876. While Mennonites had settled in the area of the conference much earlier—Somerset County in two areas of Amish (Johnstown in the north and Meyersdale-Springs in the south) 1780-1800, Masontown, Martinsburg, and Scottdale Mennonites all about 1790, Rockton 1839, these being all the settlements at the time of organization, no conference had been formed.

When the Masontown congregation in 1873 called in Bishop Jacob N. Brubacher, of the Lancaster Conference, to conduct the ordination of a bishop—J. N. Durr was ordained—he gave them a cordial invitation to join the Lancaster Conference, having learned in response to his inquiry as to what conference the ministers attended that they sometimes attended the Lancaster Conference and sometimes the Ohio Conference. Bishop Durr did not follow Bishop Brubaker's invitation but took the lead in organizing a conference locally. In April 1876 the Lancaster Conference responded to an appropriate request carried by Bishop Durr and Henry Blauch, a minister, from a meeting of ministers of the area by authorizing the formation of a conference which was to be subject to the Lancaster Conference. The organization meeting was held Sept. 22, 1876, at the Blough meetinghouse near Davidsville, Pa., with the Lancaster moderator, Bishop Benjamin Herr, in charge, but it was not subject to the Lancaster Conference. The first moderator chosen was Bishop Durr, who was for many years the dominant personality in the conference.

In a few years all the Mennonite congregations of the southwestern area of the state were members of the conference. No major new additions occurred until the former Amish Mennonite congregations of Mifflin County, Pa., members of the Eastern A.M. (later Ohio and Eastern A.M.) Conference, joined—Maple Grove at Belleville (1944), and Allensville and Mattawana with mission outposts (1957). In 1957 the Allegheny Conference had 3,177 members in 27 organized and 22 mission congregations. Because of the location of the Mennonite Publishing House in the conference district at Scottdale since 1908, the ordained men on the staff there have been among the outstanding leaders of the conference. These included such men as bishops Aaron Loucks (a native of Scottdale), Daniel Kauffman, J. A. Ressler, John L. Horst, A. J. Metzler (a native of Martinsburg), Paul M. Lederach, and others such as C. F. Yake, Paul Erb, and Ellrose Zook.

A conference mission board, organized in 1913,

and a Sunday-school conference, organized in 1895, now called a Christian Education Conference, have had a strong and wholesome influence. The first permanent Mennonite camp was in this district, located at Laurelville (*q.v.*) in 1944, though not a conference organization; it was preceded by a Young People's Institute organization which held an annual institute at Arbutus Park at Johnstown a number of years earlier. The Arbutus-Laurelville Institute, under a conference organization, has had a wide and wholesome influence. The Johnstown Bible School (*q.v.*), started in 1922, which later became a conference institution, also rendered good service. The Johnstown Mennonite School is not a conference institution.   H.S.B.

History of the Southwestern Pennsylvania Conference (n.p., 1923, not a history but a collection of conference minutes and statistics); *Southwestern Pennsylvania Mission News* (first number Nov. 23, 1936, renamed *Southwestern Pennsylvania Conference News* in May 1942, and *Allegheny Conference News* in November 1954) contains a series of historical sketches of congregations by Ammon Kaufman beginning March 1947, which were largely reprinted in J. L. Horst and Ammon Kaufman, *Seventy-Fifth Anniversary Observance of the Southwestern Pennsylvania Mennonite Conference* (n.p., 1951), and from which came the article "Beginning of the Southwestern Pennsylvania Conference" in *MHB* XII (October 1951).

Soviet Central Asia, region of West Asia bordering in the west on the Caspian Sea, in the north on Siberia, in the south on Persia, Afghanistan, and India, and in the east on China, consists of an area of 1,508,445 sq. mi., with an approximate population of twenty million. At present Soviet Central Asia is composed of the Kazakh SSR, including the former Syr Darya and Dzhetysu regions (1956 pop. 8½ million; capital Alma-Ata), the Uzbek SSR (pop. 7,300,000; capital Tashkent), including the former Bukhara (*q.v.*), southern Khorezm and parts of Samarkand, Amu Darya and Syr Darya, and Turkestan, the Turkmen SSR (1956 pop. 1,400,000; capital Ashkhabad), including the former Turkoman region of Turkestan and the western parts of Bukhaar and Khorezm, the Tadzhik SSR (pop. 1956, 1,800,000; capital Stalinabad), including eastern Turkestan. The largest SSR of all is in the Kazakh SSR with Alma-Ata as its capital and other larger cities like Karaganda, Petropavlovsk, Akmolinsk, Semipalatinsk, Aktyubinsk, and Pavlodar. The Pavlodar Mennonite settlement (*q.v.*) is now a part of it. Other early Mennonite settlements were Auli-Ata (*q.v.*) and Ak-Mechet (*q.v.*). See also **Khiva, Klaas, Epp, Asiatic Russia.**)

The Soviet government has used various methods and experiments since 1917 to transform this vast territory and its primitive population to its basic philosophy and plans. In 1917-24 some independent khanates such as Bukhara and Khiva struggled for their independence. Since 1924 the Soviets have attempted to stamp out the national feelings of the population of these countries and to transform the entire political, economical, and cultural life of the total area to integrate it into the Soviet empire. Stalin stated in 1919 that "owing to its geographical situation, Turkestan is a bridge linking Socialist Russia with the oppressed countries of the east. In view of this, the consolidation of Soviet power in Turkestan may have the greatest revolutionary sig-

nificance for the entire east" (Stackelberg, p. 85). Particularly Khrushchev has pursued the policy of making the vast territory of the Kazakh and Uzbek SSR's an agricultural and industrial stronghold. In the latter, two thirds of the total Soviet cotton crop is raised. The native population is apparently decreasing while the European-Russian population has been moving in in large groups since World War II.

During World War II particularly the Ukrainian population, including many Mennonites and others of German background, were forcibly sent to Soviet Central Asia and other parts of north and east Russia. Later when those who had been taken along with the German army into Germany were repatriated in 1943 by the Soviet army, they were also sent here. Many were sent into the coal mines of the Karaganda region. Klaus Mehnert (189) estimates that one million persons of German background are living in Soviet Asia today.

In the spring of 1954 many hundreds of thousands of people were sent to the Kazakh SSR for agricultural work in the Khrushchev program; some 18,000,000 hectares of land were to be made arable.

The Canadian Mennonite papers contain significant information on the location, life, and activities of the Mennonites in Central Asia. One reporter states that when the German army moved into the Ukraine in 1941, the Mennonites were put into freight cars and sent to the Kustanai region of the Kazakh SSR, arriving there in November 1941. However, the men were drafted in January 1942, and the women and children left to take care of themselves under very primitive conditions (*M.R.*, Sept. 19, 1956, p. 1). The largest concentration of Mennonites in Central Asia is in the Kazakh SSR, the main centers being the region and city of Karaganda. In 1955 the Karaganda Baptist Church had 1,000 members, two thirds of whom were of German background and mostly Mennonites. The Mennonites had previously worshiped separately. The leader of the eight ministers of the church is a Russian Baptist, three are Mennonites, and two are Lutherans. They meet four times a week and have communion services the first Sunday of each month. Every Sunday they have two German sermons. Smaller meetings take place in Mennonite homes. Thirty families had received Bibles from Mennonites in America. The Russian Baptist magazine, *Bratsky Vestnik,* published in Moscow, in its report on the dedication of the Baptist Church of Karaganda on Nov. 18, 1956, says that 133,000 rubles and much voluntary labor had been spent on enlarging and remodeling the church. The Moscow representative, who came by plane to take part in the activities, reports that he visited a Peters family who lived in an attractive home with a nice garden. Peters was working in the mines and earned enough to permit his wife to devote her time to church work.

When H. S. Bender and David Wiens visited Soviet Central Asia a little later, they met some of the Mennonites of this area, particularly of Karaganda and Alma-Ata. The latter also has a large Baptist church in which Mennonites worship. Orie O. Miller, who visited this area in 1958, also made several contacts with the Mennonites. All reports, written and oral, confirm that living conditions, including freedom to move from one place to another, choice of occupation, freedom to worship, have improved considerably. In some instances Mennonites have organized congregations, but these have not been officially registered and approved by the Department of Cults. In some cases, because of local pressure, the meetings have been discontinued. A recent letter reports that a Mennonite baptismal service was stopped when the police arrested the officiating minister. The congregation remained together praying for the minister, and he returned after a few hours (*Bote,* Oct. 8, 1958, p. 4). In general, the Mennonites have suffered with others of German background because of their German culture and language during and after World War II. There are indications that today, at least in some places, there is less discrimination.

Mennonites in this area can be found in almost any occupation, but many of them were originally men and women forced to work in the mines. A letter (*M.R.,* Nov. 9, 1955, pp. 2 & 3) from Stalinabad says that some of the members of a certain family are working in a hospital, one works as a nurse in a clinic, another in a print shop, still another is a railroad engineer, while others are tailors and chaufeurs. They raise two crops a year. They attend the Baptist church of the city, and some sing in the choir. Orie O. Miller visited Stalinabad in 1958 and found these reports confirmed.   C.K.

Klaus Mehnert, *Asien, Moskau und Wir* (Stuttgart, 1957) 174 ff.; Alexander G. Park, *Bolshevism in Turkestan 1917-1927* (New York, 1957); *Bolshaya Sovetskaya Encyclopedia* (Moscow, 1947) 1843 ff., 1895 ff., 1905 ff., 1921 ff., 1883 ff.; G. A. von Stackelberg, *The Sovietisation of Turkestan* (Studies on the Soviet Union I) (Munich, 1957) 74 ff.; "Changes in the Population of the Soviet Union from 1939 to 1956," *Bulletin, Institute for the Study of the USSR* III (November 1956, No. 11) 30 ff.; A. Kravchenko, "Collectivization in the Kirghiz SSR," *Ukrainian Review* (No. 4, Munich, 1957); *Bratsky Vestnik,* 1956-58 (Moscow); Virginia Claassen, Peter Neufeld, Vern Q. Preheim, "Glimpses of the Mennonites in Russia 1948-1957," Mennonite Seminar Study, Bethel College, 1957; H. S. Bender and D. B. Wiens, "Report on the Mission to Russia," Oct. 26-Nov. 16, 1956; Orie O. Miller, "Report on Trip to Soviet Russia, 1958." Regarding "Karaganda" see *Der Bote,* 1955, March 2, p. 8; Nov. 16, p. 7; 1956, Jan. 25, p. 7; Oct. 17, p. 7; Oct. 31, p. 7; Nov. 28, p. 7; *Mennonitische Rundschau,* 1948, June 9, p. 7; 1955, Sept. 21, p. 5; Sept. 28, p. 5; 1956, Jan. 4, p. 2; April 18, p. 8; May 9, p. 5; July 4, p. 8; July 25, p. 5; Dec. 12, p. 3; July 25, p. 15. For "Stalinabad" see *Mennonitische Rundschau,* Nov. 5, 1954, p. 3; Nov. 23, 1955, p. 5. For "Tashkent" see *Mennonitische Rundschau,* July 7, 1954, p. 11. For "Tadzhik SSR" see *Mennonitische Rundschau,* April 27, 1955, p. 6.

Soza, Pedro de, an Anabaptist martyr: see **Peter van Spagnien.**

Sozzini, Lelio and **Fausto:** see **Socinus.**

Spaans, Dutch Mennonite family, since the 17th century found at Barsingerhorn (*q.v.*), where some of its members served as deacons. Simon Spaans (1873-1944), of Barsingerhorn, educated at the university and the Mennonite seminary at Amsterdam, was pastor at Goes-Vlissingen 1899-1907, Enkhuizen 1907-17, and Assen-Stadskanaal 1917-39, in which year he retired. He published some sermons and a paper, *Het Christologische in de Catechese* (Assen, 1927).   vDZ.

Spaar en Hout, a home for the aged at Haarlem, Holland, opened on May 18, 1930. (*DJ* 1931, 104-9.)   vDZ.

Spaargaren, a Mennonite family at Aalsmeer (*q.v.*), Dutch province of North Holland, found there from at least the early 17th century. An Oude Jan Jans Spaargaren, a middle-aged man, is named in 1649. Many members of the Spaargaren family have served the church as deacons, and Jacob Spaargaren was a preacher of the Oude Vermaning (Frisian congregation) on the Uiterweg 1786-1812, while Jan Willems Spaargaren served the same congregation as preacher from 1838 and elder 1850-c60.   vDZ.

W. Tsj. Vleer, *De aloude Aalsmeerse Familiën* (De Kaag, 1954); Dutch *Naamlijst.*

Spaarndam, a hamlet in the Dutch province of North Holland, not far from Haarlem, which was in the 16th century a watery and inaccessible region, was in the period of persecution often a hiding place for dislodged Anabaptists. During a raid in March 1534 at least 105 men and 126 women and a number of children were apprehended at Spaarndam, some of whom were executed at Haarlem.

In December 1534 or in early January 1535 a meeting of 32 Anabaptist leaders was held in the inn "De halve Mane" at Spaarndam. This meeting was called to discuss the matter of revolutionary Anabaptism. Revolutionary Anabaptists such as Meynart (*q.v.*) van Emden instigated an attack on Amsterdam, but most of the leaders refused to consider such rebellion, desiring to hold to peaceful principles. This too was the advice of Jacob van Campen (*q.v.*), the Anabaptist bishop of Amsterdam, who was not present at the Spaarndam meeting. The proceedings of the Spaarndam discussion clearly show that at this moment the majority of the Dutch Anabaptist leaders were averse to violence.   vDZ.

Inv. Arch. Amst. I, Nos. 21b, 24, 27, 66, 79, 217; Grosheide, *Verhooren,* 182 f.; Kühler, *Geschiedenis* I, 141.

Spakenburg, a town in the Dutch province of Utrecht on the Zuiderzee (now IJssel Lake), formerly seat of a Mennonite congregation, which also is called Spakenburg and Bunschoten, or Bunschoten and Spakenburg, and sometimes also Huizen and Spakenburg. For its history see **Bunschoten** and **Huizen.** (*Inv. Arch. Amst.* II, Nos. 2246 f.)   vDZ.

Spanheim Sr., Frederik (Fredericus Spanhemius), b. 1600 at Amberg in Bavaria, Germany, d. 1649 at Leiden, Holland, and his son Frederik Spanheim Jr. (b. Geneva 1632, d. Leiden 1707), both Reformed theologians and professors at the University of Leiden, attacked the Mennonites in their writings. Spanheim Sr. wrote *Variae disputationes antianabaptisticae* (1643-48) and *Diatribe Historica de Origine, Progressu et Sectis Anabaptistarum* (Franeker, 1645; 2d ed. 1656), in which he maintained the old and false theory that the Dutch Mennonites were the descendants of the Münsterite (*q.v.*) Anabaptists. Spanheim Jr. in the second chapter of his book *Controversiarum de Religione Elenchus historico-theologicus* (Leiden, 1687, repr. 1694 and 1757) repeated the assertions of his father. His contentions were opposed by the Mennonites E. A. van

Dooregeest (*q.v.*) in *Brief aan den Heer F. Span-hemius* (Amsterdam, 1693, 2d ed. 1693, 3d ed. augmented with a letter by Herman Schijn, 1700), and Galenus (*q.v.*) Abrahamsz in *Verdediging der Christenen, die Doopsgezinden genaamd worden* (Amsterdam, 1700).   vdZ.

B. Glasius, *Godgeleerd Nederland* III ('s Hertogen-bosch, 1856) 383-86; Schijn-Maatschoen, *Geschiedenis* II, 568, 569.

Spanish Mennonite Church (MC), La Junta, Col., a member of the South Central Conference, was formerly called the Spanish Baptist Church, but was turned over to the Mennonites in 1940, who bought and remodeled the church building, which had been erected in 1921. The present congregation was organized under the leadership of David Castillo, a native of Mexico, in February 1941, when eleven were baptized and six received upon confession of faith. The membership in 1955 was 42, with Castillo as pastor. Since 1944 the congregation has sponsored a Spanish Gospel Program over the local radio station.   E.S.C.

Spat, a Mennonite village in the Crimea. The land for this village, 23,500 acres, was purchased in 1881 by a group of Mennonites from the Molotschna settlement and was located near the station Sarabus. Two villages were established on this land, the larger named Spat and the smaller, about five miles distant, Menlerchik. Spat consisted of 31 settlers, among whom the most influential were Johann Langemann and Cornelius Wall. Economic difficulties were overcome by means of a loan from Molotschna private sources. By 1912 the land, which had been purchased from Anna Semyonova, had been paid for. The villages were established on the usual pattern used by the Mennonites of Russia. Soon Spat became a prosperous center of the Mennonites of the Crimea in agriculture, industry, and education. Langemann had an agricultural implement factory, and there were two large mills owned respectively by Langemann and Janzen and Langemann and Unrau, besides numerous other businesses.   C.K.

H. Goerz, *Die mennonitischen Siedlungen der Krim* (Winnipeg, 1957).

Spat Mennonite Church, Crimea, Russia, was a subsidiary of the Karassan Mennonite Church (*q.v.*) established in 1882. The local meetinghouse was destroyed by fire in 1919. The main place of worship was at Karassan. The village of Spat was also the center of a Mennonite Brethren church. (H. Dirks, *Statistik*, 1905, 63.)   C.K.

Spat Zentralschule was opened in the Spat Mennonite settlement in 1906, when an impressive school building with three teachers' residences was completed. The school differed from other Zentral-schulen in that it was coeducational. The first teachers were Cornelius Janzen, Franz Ediger, and Daniel Enns. Later Cornelius Lehn and Heinrich Ediger taught the school. In addition to this Zentral-schule, the Crimean Mennonites also had the Karassan Zentralschule. Among its teachers were Karl Friedrichsen, K. Bergmann, and J. Loetke-

mann. For a time Karassan also had a girls' school.   C.K.

H. Goerz, *Die mennonitischen Siedlungen der Krim* (Winnipeg, 1957) 47 ff.

Spat-Schöntal Mennonite Brethren Church of Crimea, Russia, was organized as a result of the Mennonite Brethren influences from the Molotschna Mennonite settlement. A group began to meet in private homes where, among other things, Spurgeon's sermons were read and religious experiences were exchanged. Some Mennonite Brethren moved to the Crimea. The first baptism by immersion was conducted there by Elder David Schellenberg on April 28, 1885. Thus a branch of the Rückenau M.B. Church was established at Spat, Crimea. In 1886 Hermann Konrad was ordained minister by David and Abraham Schellenberg. On Oct. 11, 1887, a meetinghouse was dedicated at Spat. In 1891 Kornelius Boschmann, Bernhard Friesen, and Daniel Friesen were ordained by David Schellenberg and Daniel Fast. In 1894 Peter Görzen, Jakob Hiebert, Jr., and Heinrich Janzen were appointed ministers. In 1895 Abraham J. Kröker and in 1897 Jakob Kröker came to Spat. The latter was ordained minister by David Schellenberg on May 25, 1898. Abraham and Jakob Kröker (*q.v.*) began here with the publication of *Christlicher Familienkalender* (1897), *Christlicher Abreisskalender* (1903), and *Friedensstimme* (1903), which efforts later resulted in the founding of "Raduga" (*q.v.*). Heinrich Unruh (*q.v.*) and Cornelius Unruh (*q.v.*) were ordained as missionaries to India at the turn of the century. On May 23, 1899, David Dürksen (*q.v.*) was ordained elder of the Spat M.B. Church, which thus became independent. In 1902 the congregation consisted of 140 families, 330 members, and 810 souls. In 1905 another meetinghouse with a seating capacity of six hundred was established in Schöntal where David Dürksen resided. The Mennonite Brethren had an active part in the establishment of the Zentralschulen in Karassan (1905) and Spat (1906). Some young people did graduate work and made a vital contribution to the spiritual and cultural life of the Mennonites of Russia. Another meetinghouse was established at Annovka. Meetings also took place in Bashlicha and in Tokulchak. David Dürksen died in 1910. It is likely that Hermann Konrad of Spat and Peter Görzen of Schöntal continued as leaders. They officiated at an ordination in 1926 (*Unser Blatt* II, p. 110).   C.K.

H. Dirks, *Statistik* (1905); H. Goerz, *Die mennonitischen Siedlungen der Krim* (Winnipeg, 1957); Friesen, *Brüderschaft*, 465-70; A. H. Unruh, *Die Geschichte der Mennoniten-Brüdergemeinde* (Winnipeg, 1954) 190-95; *Unser Blatt* II (1926) 110, 327 ff.

Spating, Vinzenz, a member of the Great Council of the Swiss canton of Bern, took part in the Anabaptist colloquy of Jan. 22, 1528, on the side of the Anabaptists; he recanted later and was pardoned on Jan. 24. (*Zwingliana* 1933, 409 and 411; *ML* IV.)

Speedwell Mennonite Brethren Church, now extinct, situated 3 miles east and 8 miles north of Fairholme, Sask., a member of the North Saskatchewan M.B. Conference, was organized in 1926 under the leadership of John Kliewer with a membership of 13.

The membership steadily increased to 116 by 1936. Because of heavy emigration to Ontario and British Columbia and because of local farming difficulties, the membership again decreased so that by 1948, when J. A. Enns, who had been leader since 1937, moved away with his family, the few members remaining transferred their membership to other churches. J.H.E.

Sperling (Sparling), a Mennonite family in a number of Prussian congregations as early as 1700, in Montau even before 1700. Tobias Sperling, living in East Prussia, was forced to leave his farm in 1722, moving to West Prussia, where he died. Laurens (Lorenz) Sperling was an elder of the Groningen Old Flemish congregation in the Culmsche Niederung 1757-c80, and Johann Sparling (d. 1799) a preacher and elder (from 1775) of the Klein-Werder (Markushof) congregation. The name is also found among the Mennonites of Russia and America.

The form "Spaarlinck," which is sometimes found, seems to indicate that this family was of Dutch descent. vDZ.

Reimer, *Familiennamen*, 118; Dutch *Naamlijst; Inv. Arch. Amst.* I, 1613, 1627; Max Sperling, *Der Stammbaum der Familie Sperling* (Königsberg, 1910).

Sperling Mennonite Brethren Church of Sperling, Man., a member of the Manitoba Provincial and the Canadian District M.B. conferences, had a membership of 18 in 1957, with D. D. Froese as leading minister. It was organized in 1932 with 20 members out of a group which, meeting earlier with General Conference Mennonites in this area, began to meet separately in May 1928. In January 1954 the Sperling M.B. group temporarily joined the Winkler M.B. congregation, but soon became an independent congregation again. H.Ne.

Speybroeck, M. van, is the author or composer of the Dutch Mennonite hymnal *Syons Wijnberch, inhoudende Verscheyden Schriftuerlijcke Liedekens.* . . . This hymnal is very rare. Copies of a third edition (Vlissingen, 1670), containing 78 hymns without notes on 380 pages, and a later undated edition are found in the Amsterdam Mennonite Library. A sequel or second part of this hymnal was published in 1665 at Vlissingen, entitled *'t Nieuw (q.v.) Geestelijck Kruyt-Hof.* Concerning van Speybroeck no information was available. vDZ.

Speyer, Diet of, 1529, the notorious Imperial Diet at which the first imperial law was passed against the Anabaptists threatening death to anyone who did not recognize infant baptism. Thereby the mandate of Charles V (*q.v.*) of Jan. 4, 1528, acquired the consent of the estates, including the Protestants, who at the same diet protested against compulsion in religious matters. The delegates from the cities (Catholic and Protestant) declared in a petition presented on April 8 to the two estates of princes that they would give their consent to the article on Anabaptism and on April 12 the Protestant princes also expressed their willingness to agree with the majority in the matter of the Anabaptists. Prince Louis V, a Catholic of the Palatinate, suggested a

lightening of the penalty to the effect that only those should be punished with capital punishment who would not desist from Anabaptism. In the session of all the estates of the diet of April 17, a draft of a decision made by the committee, to be included in the mandate against the Anabaptists, was announced to the estates and received the consent of both princely chambers, whereas the cities were for the time being still debating it. The Protestant princes in addition, in their protestation of April 19 and again on April 20, declared their express agreement with the measures to be adopted against the adherents of adult baptism. The imperial law against the Anabaptists was issued April 23, 1529.

The content of the mandate—printed in the *Neue und vollständige Sammlung der Reichsabschiede* (Frankfurt a.M., 1747) II, 284; in J. J. Schmaussens *Corpora juris publici Academ.* III (1755) No. XIX, 141-43; Krohn, 213; and Bossert's *Quellen (TA Württemberg,* 1930) 3*-5*—was about as follows (literally according to Ney, 216, who gives an excerpt): Although the common law forbids upon penalty of death to baptize again an already baptized person and the emperor at the beginning of 1528 has given a new warning against the transgressors of the prohibition, that sect is still increasing. Therefore the regulation is ordered again, that each and every rebaptizer and rebaptized person, man or woman, of an accountable age shall be brought from natural life to death with fire, sword, or the like according to the circumstances of the persons without previous inquisition of spiritual judges. Against the preachers and leaders of the sect as well as those who persisted in the same or fell back into it no mercy shall be exercised but the threatened penalty shall be ruthlessly performed. Those who confess their error, recant, and beg for mercy may be pardoned. Whoever does not have his children baptized shall be considered an Anabaptist. No pardoned person shall be permitted to emigrate, so that the authorities can see to it that he does not backslide. No prince shall receive the subjects of another who have escaped. This mandate shall in all points be most strictly performed by all in order to perform the duties and oaths to the emperor and empire and to avoid the serious displeasure and punishment of the emperor.

The edict of Speyer brought brutal punishment upon the Anabaptists such as was inflicted upon no other religious party of the Holy Roman Empire. The law was repeated at Speyer in 1544, and was finally renewed at the diet of Augsburg in 1551. As late as 1694 the court councillor of Jülich, von Heyden, justified his sudden expulsion of the Mennonites from Rheydt (*q.v.*) by the edict of Speyer.

Hege.

TA Württemberg, 1-3; B. N. Krohn, *Gesch. der Wiedertäufer vornehmlich in Niederdeutschland: Melchior Hofmann und die Sekte der Hofmannianer* (Leipzig, 1785); Ney, "Gesch. des Reichstags zu Speyer 1529," in *Mitteilungen des historischen Vereins der Pfalz* VIII (Speyer, 1879) 130, 175, 189, 215, 234, 254; Rembert, *Wiedertäufer,* 50; *ML IV.*

Spiegel, Kaspar, an Anabaptist martyr of Ostheim, a village in Bavaria, Germany, who was captured early in February 1527 with Beutelhans (*q.v.*) and two other Anabaptists, and as a subject of the bishop of Würzburg was executed with the sword.

Paul Wappler, *Die Stellung Kursachsens und des Landgrafen Philipp von Hessen zur Täuferbewegung* (Münster, 1910) 3 f.; *ML* IV.

Spiegel, Thomas, an Anabaptist martyr, a brother of the above, a carpenter by trade, baptized by Hans Hut (*q.v.*), made an important confession of his faith in his cross-examination on February 19-March 3, 1527. He was executed at Koburg in April 1527. (Wappler, *Thüringen*, 228-33; *ML* IV.)

Spiegel der Taufe, Ein, written by Henry Funck, a Mennonite bishop in the Franconia congregation, and printed by Christopher Saur at Germantown in 1744, was a small-format 94-page book intended to show that pouring is the Scriptural mode of baptism. Evidently the Mennonites of this area were under pressure from the aggressive Tunkers (Church of the Brethren) who insisted that immersion was the only valid mode of baptism. The full title of the book is *Ein Spiegel der Tauffe mit Geist, mit Wasser und mit Blut. Verfasset in neun Theile, Auffs Neue aufgesetzt und ausgezogen aus dem Heiligen Fundament-Buch, des Neuen und Alten Testaments, der Canonischen Bücher. I. Epist. Joh. V. 8.* Saur, being a Tunker immersionist, refused to put his imprint on the title page. Only one complete copy has survived, in the Historical Society of Pennsylvania library in Philadelphia, and a defective copy in GCL.

The author argues from I John 5:8 that Spirit baptism, water baptism, and baptism by blood are one, and must be symbolically identical. Since the baptism of the Holy Spirit was by pouring, and since baptism by blood means going under the blood (by pouring; Jesus poured out His lifeblood for our salvation), hence water baptism must also be by pouring. Other arguments are adduced, such as that the Levitical washings under the Old Covenant were sprinklings. Sprinkling is also acceptable as a mode of baptism; it is certainly not immersion. Funck attributes the error of immersion to too much dependence upon history and the writings of the church fathers, rather than relying exclusively upon the Scriptures. There is other useful material in the book besides the arguments against immersion and for pouring which are sometimes strong and sometimes weak. The author's insistence upon the necessity and value of water baptism in obeying the commandment of Christ suggests that he also had the Quakers in mind who reject water baptism altogether. The book was reprinted four times in German (1834, 1850, 1853, 1861) and three times in English (1851, 1853, 1890) under the title *A Mirror of Baptism with Spirit, with Water, and with Blood. Drawn up in nine parts. Drawn out and enlarged anew out of the Holy Foundation Book, The New and Old Testament, and the Canonical Books. I. Epis. John V, 8.* It evidently served a continuing need, due largely to constant pressure of Brethren teaching. The Brethren won a considerable number of Mennonites to their group in Eastern Pennsylvania, Maryland, and Virginia, where their congregations were often neighbors to Mennonite congregations.　　　　　　　　　　　　　　H.S.B.

Spielmann, Christoph (1861-1917), director of the city archives at Wiesbaden, Germany, and the author of various works on pedagogy and history; e.g., *Sagen und Geschichten aus dem Nassauerland* and *Geschichte von Nassau*, as well as novels, stories, and dramas. In 1894 he published an article in the *Annalen für nassauische Altertumskunde und Geschichtsforschung* (XXVII) with the title "Die Mennoniten und ihre Bedeutung fur die Kultur in Nassau," which aside from a few historical errors is a just evaluation of Mennonitism. (*Menn. Bl.*, 1895, 19 ff.; *ML* IV.)

Spiesheim, a village near Alzey (*q.v.*) in Rheinhessen, Germany, formerly belonging to the Palatinate, in which there have been Mennonites since at least 1661. In that year Wendel Holl of Wolfsheim (*q.v.*) asked permission for the few Mennonites who were living in Bermersheim, Spiesheim, and Aspisheim to hold meetings. The lists of the Generallandesarchiv of Karlsruhe name three Mennonite families living in Spiesheim in 1664: Johann Bliem, Christian Weber, and Wilhelm Ham (Hahn?). In 1685 there were five families: Severin Ham, Matthes Becker, Wilhelm Mäurer, Joh. Bliem, and Heinrich Bliem. In 1738 the lists name the families of Heinrich Hahn, Johannes Weber, Peter Berg ("the young and the old"), Dietrich, Daniel, Heinrich, and Julius Blum, and also Julius and Heinrich Biehn. In 1752 the heads of the families were Peter Berg ("the young and the old"), Julius Biehn, Dietrich and Daniel Bliem, Heinrich Hahn's widow, Johann Jakob Hüthwohl, and Johann Weber. In 1759 there were only Julius Biehn, Johann Weber's widow, Peter Berg, Heinrich Biehn's widow, and as a new name Peter Jansz. The last list of names, 1768, also names five families: Julius Biehn, Hermann Biehn, Peter Jantz, Johann Schmidt's widow, and Peter Berg. A summary of 1773 counts five families with a total of five sons and eight daughters.

In 1732 the Mennonites of Spiesheim still belonged to the Wolfsheim congregation. After the Wolfsheim congregation disbanded, Spiesheim apparently merged with the neighboring Wallertheim. The union existed until at least 1810, for a document left by Johannes Borkholder of Wallertheim shows that he was chosen as preacher of the joint congregation in 1808, and as elder in 1809. The relation of Spiesheim to the neighboring churches is not clear. In the Dutch *Naamlijst* of 1766 Oberflörsheim, Spiesheim, and Griesheim are listed as one congregation with Christian Weber as elder (from 1728) and Wilhelm Krämer, Johannes Schörger, Henrich Müller as preachers. The *Naamlijst* of 1767 lists each of these three congregations as more or less independent, Johann Schörger and Wilhelm Krämer (1748) being the preachers at Spiesheim, while Christian Weber (preacher 1725, elder 1728, d. 1771) of Oberflörsheim still served as elder of the three congregations. The *Naamlijst* of 1775 lists Johann Schörger, Henrich Müller (1759), and Gerhard Berg (1772) as preachers at Spiesheim. Müller and Berg died in 1790 and were followed by Johann Borkholder, the father of the above, and Abraham Hertzler. Shortly after 1775 Johann Schörger died and was followed by his son Andreas Schörger who served until c1783.

In the *Naamlijst* of 1786 and later Spiesheim-Wallertheim is listed together with Erbesbüdisheim and Weierhof, Jacob Galle of Erbesbüdisheim being the elder of this group of congregations. This situation lasted until 1791, when both preachers of Spiesheim-Wallertheim were ordained as elders and this church became independent.

As a contribution for the erection of a new church in Altleiningen (*q.v.*) Hermann Biehn of Spiesheim sent 6 florins and 9 kreutzer from the Schniftenbergerhof congregation and 12 florins from the Spiesheim and Wallertheim congregation to Valentin Krämer in Oberflörsheim. Johann Borkholder signed the resolutions of Ibersheim (*q.v.*) for the Wallertheim (Spiesheim is not named) and Rheingrafenstein (*q.v.*) congregations in 1803.

In the course of an interesting school dispute between the Mennonites and the government of Hesse, which was fought out especially by David Kaege (*q.v.*), of Offstein, other Hessian Mennonite congregations also stated their position. A letter of this kind written to the government of the province of Rheinhessen in December 1828 was signed by the following: for the Spiesheim congregation—Peter Berg and Johannes Berg, preachers; Johannes Schmitt, Vorsteher; and Peter Bien; for the Wallertheim congregation—Christian Hegi, Jakob Schowalter; for the Uffhofen congregation—Jakob Galle, preacher; Jakob Steiner. This seems to indicate that there were three independent congregations. But this can have been the case for only a short time, for in 1829, when a small church was built in Uffhofen (*q.v.*), first Wallertheim and then Spiesheim joined the Mennonite congregation in Uffhofen; the latter are still members there.

Jakob Weber of Spiesheim was the last lay preacher of the congregation. After the Weierhof congregation became responsible for the services at Spiesheim he probably served only on certain occasions. In February 1852 a Mennonite funeral was held in the town church in Spiesheim, which had been built a few years previously with the aid of Mennonite contributions. Since no trained minister was available, a lay preacher, probably Weber, was about to preach the funeral sermon, but was told that he must preach from the altar, and not from the pulpit. On February 27 he wrote a vehement protest to the pastor at Ensisheim, asking either that such restrictions be removed, or that the contributions made by the Mennonites be returned to them. After a correspondence of six months the matter was apparently settled to Weber's satisfaction; the payments made by the Mennonites were not refunded, on the ground that they had used the church six times in the eight years.

An instance of gross intolerance had occurred at Spiesheim about 150 years earlier when the lay preacher Chiles Hahn was fined ten talers for preaching a short funeral sermon in the local Catholic cemetery (see **Burial, Funerals**).

Two instances of the enforcement of the right of redemption (*Jus Retractus, q.v.*) illustrate the lack of protection and legal status of the early Mennonites. In 1732 Johann Weber, a Mennonite, had bought some land at a public auction for 152 florins. A few days later another claimed the right to the land. The Mennonites under the jurisdiction of Alzey made a united appeal to the elector, but to no avail. In 1736 the dispute flared up again in Spiesheim, when a vineyard was claimed in this manner after it had been in Mennonite possession for ten years. This time, however, the elector required the local government to return it to the Mennonites and imposed a fine of 10 talers on the local authorities.

At present there are in Spiesheim five Mennonite families and a few single persons, with the old names of Berg, Schmidt, and Weber. A Beutler family moved in from Sembach in 1875. (*ML* IV.)

P.S.

Spijkenisse, a small town on the island of Putten in the Dutch province of South Holland, formerly the seat of a Mennonite congregation, which is sometimes called "Spijkenis, Heenvliet and Suytlant," and also "Geervliet-Spijkenis." (See also **Geervliet, Heenvliet,** and **Zuidland.**). It is impossible because of lack of sources to ascertain whether and to what extent these congregations were independent of each other. A congregation of Spijkenisse is mentioned before 1600. This congregation, belonging to the Flemish branch, was always small (figures not obtainable). In 1648 its meetinghouse burned down and was rebuilt with financial support by the Rotterdam congregation; also at several other times Rotterdam contributed to the needs of Spijkenisse. After the Lammerenkrijgh (*q.v.*) had divided the Flemish Mennonites into Lamists (*q.v.*) and Zonists (*q.v.*), Spijkenisse, Heenvliet, and Zuidland sided with the conservative Zonists, and in 1664 Huygh Barentsz van der Klok, Leendert Pietersz, and Adriaan Jansz signed the *Verbondt van Eenigheydt* (*q.v.*) for these congregation(s), while in 1674 the congregation rejected liberal Collegiant (*q.v.*) views. It was always served by untrained preachers chosen from the membership; apparently Klaas Cornelissen, who served till about 1721, was the last of them. According to the *Naamlijst* of 1731, 1743, and 1755 the pulpit became vacant and about 1760 the Spijkenisse congregation had ceased to exist. vDZ.

Inv. Arch. Amst. I, No. 896, II, No. 2367; K. Vos, *Geschiedenis der Doopsgezinde gemeente te Rotterdam* (1907), repr., 13.

Spijker, an old Dutch word for warehouse. The Dutch Mennonites in the 16-17th centuries often bought warehouses and adapted them for use as meetinghouses; hence the name "*spijker*" sometimes remained usual for these meetinghouses. In Amsterdam the Groote Spijker near the Jan Rodenpoorts Toren on the Singel Canal was from 1604 the meetinghouse of the Amsterdam Waterlander congregation. It remained in use after the Waterlander merger with the Lamist congregation in 1668. In 1801 after a fusion of Lamists and Zonists in Amsterdam, the pulpit and the organ of the Zon meetinghouse were installed in the Groote Spijker. This meetinghouse was used until 1812, and was razed in 1814. Its organ and pulpit are now in the Leeuwarden church, which bought them in 1812 for 2800 Dutch guilders.

Before the Waterlanders acquired the Groote Spijker, they had held their meetings in the Kleine Spijker in the Teerketelsteeg. This Kleine Spijker

(Oude Spijker) was taken over by a Frisian Mennonite congregation in 1604. (*Inv. Arch. Amst.* II, Nos. 82-99, 1341 f.)   vDZ.

Spink Hutterite Bruderhof, called Spink Hutterian Brethren, Inc., of the Schmiedeleut (*q.v.*) group, located near Frankfort, S.D., was founded in 1905 by members of the Wolf Creek (*q.v.*) Bruderhof. In 1918 they sold this land and moved to Alberta, founding the Stand-Off Colony near Macleod. In 1944 the Bon Homme commune bought this site and rebuilt it; eleven families with Johannes Wipf, who had been chosen to the ministry in 1934, from Bon Homme settled here. Joseph Wipf was chosen preacher in Spink in 1946. In 1958 the commune numbered 152 souls. Land has been bought at Ipswich, S.D., where a new Bruderhof is to be established in the near future by members of Spink.
                    D.D., Jo.W.

Spinniker, Adriaan (Ate), b. March 18, 1676, at Groningen, d. April 28, 1754, at Haarlem, was the son of Preacher Melis Ates Spinniker (*q.v.*). He was baptized in 1695 in the Amsterdam Lamist church, was trained for the ministry by Galenus (*q.v.*) Abrahamsz of Amsterdam, and served as assistant pastor of the Amsterdam Lamist congregation 1700-5. He resigned in 1705 because, as he wrote, "I have not duly guarded against seduction, and have fallen into outrages, by which I feel unworthy not only to continue the holy service of preaching, but also to participate with you in the holy communion of our Lord." He then moved to Haarlem, where he earned his living as a bookkeeper. He was a loyal member of the church, and in 1727 he was asked by the church board of the Peuzelaarsteeg congregation to train young men for the ministry. Spinniker accepted, but resigned in May 1728, feeling that this task could be better undertaken by a minister in active service.

Adriaan Spinniker, who was married to Sara Verduyn of Amsterdam, is known for his poetry. He published several volumes, all very mediocre, including *Lof der Vriendschap* (Amsterdam, 1699; reprinted Rotterdam, 1711), *Morgen en Avondgezangen, Gebedswijze berijmt* (Amsterdam, 1699), *Leerzame Zinnebeelden* (Haarlem, 1714; repr. Haarlem, 1756, Haarlem, 1757), *Gods gerichten op aarde, vertoond in den schrikkelyken storm en hoogen watervloed . . . in't 1717de Jaar voorgevallen* (Haarlem, n.d.–1718), *Vervolg der Leerzame Zinnebeelden,* prefaced by a biography of Spinniker by G. W. van Oosten (Haarlem, 1758). His *De vrijheit op den troon gezet* (Amsterdam, 1743) is a rhymed attack on the heresy-hunters in the Dutch Reformed Church. For the use of the Haarlem Mennonite congregation, Spinniker collaborated in making a new rhymed version of the Psalms. Spinniker also wrote a large amount of topical poetry; such are found in the 1706 edition of J. P. Schabaelje's *Wandelende Ziele,* and Schijn and Maatschoen's *Geschiedenis dier Christenen, welke . . . Mennoniten genaamd worden* I (Amsterdam, 1743). He also wrote the short laudatory poems to each of the portrait engravings in the collection of outstanding Mennonite ministers *Afbeeldingen van Doopsgezinde Leeraren* (Amsterdam, 1743), which pictures

with the same legends are also found in the work by Schijn-Maatschoen.   vDZ.

Inv. Arch. Amst. II, Nos. 908 f., 910 g, 911 f.; *DB* 1863, 162; 1890, 72; 1896, 19; 1918, 61, 62 f.; *N.N.B.Wb.* IV, 1260-62; Chr. Sepp, *Polemische en irenische Theologie* (2d ed. Amsterdam, 1882) 235-39.

Spinniker, Melis Ates, d. Dec. 1681, was a preacher of the Waterlander Mennonite congregation at Groningen, Netherlands, 16 -79. Because of some trouble with the church board here and by the intervention of Galenus (*q.v.*) Abrahamsz, the Schiedam congregation called him as its preacher. Spinniker served at Schiedam from 1669 until his early death in 1681. His widow Grietje Hillebrands with two or three daughters and two sons, one of whom was Adriaan Spinniker (*q.v.*), moved to Amsterdam in 1694. Spinniker had not received special training for the ministry and was a book printer by trade.
                    vDZ.

Inv. Arch. Amst. I, Nos. 796 f., 816, 840; II, Nos. 1833-38, 1862, 1873, 2060, 2207, 2225; *DB* 1909, 160, 166; 1918, 51.

Spinoza, Baruch (Benedictus) de (1632-77), the noted philosopher, was born at Amsterdam on Nov. 24, 1632, of Spanish-Jewish descent. His pantheistic-rationalistic ideas, with an overtone of mysticism, profoundly influenced German and Dutch philosophy. He was expelled from the Jewish community as a heretic and lived in modest retirement, on a friendly footing with the Mennonites and the Collegiants (*q.v.*) in Rijnsburg and The Hague. The Mennonites were instrumental in publishing his writings, when the Dutch Reformed publishers were afraid to do it. One of his greatest benefactors was Joosten de Vries, a Mennonite merchant of Amsterdam. Spinoza died at The Hague on Feb. 21, 1677.
                    NEFF.

W. Meyer and A. Menzel on Spinoza's relations to the Collegiants and to Christendom, *Archiv für Geschichte und Philosophie* XV and XVI (1902); Guido Kolbenheyer, *Amor Dei,* a novel on Spinoza (1905); Ernst Troeltsch, *The Social Teachings of the Christian Churches* (New York, 1912); K. O. Meinsma, *Spinoza en zijn kring* (The Hague 1896); *ML* IV,

Spiritualism, mainly of the 16th century (Rufus M. Jones prefers the term "Spiritual Reformers"), a tendency in the period of the Reformation to emphasize the possession of the Spirit (occasionally called the Holy Spirit, by Anabaptists also called "the Power of God" or the "Heart") over against a literal acceptance of the Scriptures. Actually the conflict between "letter" and "spirit" is as old as the New Testament itself and represents a perennial problem for any honest Christian. In the days of the Reformation two opposing tendencies appear very clearly: a stronger reliance upon the letter of the Scriptures such as with Luther, or a greater emphasis on inner illumination, with its corollary: freedom of decision, centering in man's conscience, and neglect of historical elements in Christianity such as the organized church, the sacraments (as means of salvation), and the historical setting of Christian events: creation, fall, redemption, Last Judgment, etc. While all Scripturally oriented Christians center around some organized form of church life, Spiritualists usually minimize these social aspects of faith, relying on the "invisible" church rather than on any visible one, by this promoting a strong individualistic element within Christianity. In its extremest forms Spiritualism moves even further away from its New Testament matrix, only to become a vague "spiritual religion" of some Neoplatonic character, hence no longer justifiably called "Christian."

It seems that Spiritualism in its different forms of historical expression originated in German and Dutch-speaking areas in the 16th century, while in the 17th century there arose a similar phenomenon in England, i.e., Quakerism. The first to recognize Spiritualism as a particular phenomenon was Hegler (*q.v.*) in his unsurpassed study on Sebastian Franck (1892); his ideas were taken up in part by Troeltsch in his *Social Teachings* (1912, English 1930), in which he made a distinction between (institutional) church, sect (i.e., gathered church or brotherhood), and individualistic Spiritualism. In the latter movement he counts men like Franck, Bünderlin, and Entfelder. Two years later the American Quaker scholar Rufus M. Jones published his *Spiritual Reformers of the 16th and 17th Centuries* (1914) where the term received its final formulation and historic content. Jones sees in men like Denk, Franck, and later Weigel and Boehme, the true forerunners of the Quakers of the 17th century. Actually to pool Denk, Franck, and Schwenckfeld on the one side and Weigel and Boehme (a theosophist) on the other dramatically reveals the vagueness of the term Spiritualism. Karl Holl, another modern church historian concerned with the theme, lumps together all dissidents from the Lutheran way as *Schwärmer* and in another connection also calls them Spiritualists (in conscious opposition to Troeltsch); to him Anabaptists were also a kind of Spiritualists.

A great step forward in the problem of the definition of Spiritualism was achieved by Kühn (*q.v.*) in 1923, who distinguished five types of "Protestants"; besides the "prophetic" type of Luther (believing in the revealed Word of God in the Scriptures), the Spiritualistic type represented by Schwenckfeld in Germany and Roger Williams in America, the "Nachfolge" (discipleship) type such as Anabaptists and Quakers—again a strange fellowship inasmuch as Quakerism is nearer to the Spiritualists than to the Anabaptists, the mystical type (Weigel, Boehme), and the ethical-rational type (Castellio and Arminius, later also Pietism). Köhler (*RGG,* 1931) classified Castellio among the Spiritualists.

Finally, George H. Williams of Harvard presented in his edition of *Spiritual and Anabaptist Writers* (1957) a new classification which seems to come nearer to historical reality than any of the earlier attempts. He distinguished three groups in Spiritualism: revolutionary, evangelical, and rational. For revolutionary Spiritualism Carlstadt and Müntzer are named as typical; for evangelical Spiritualism Schwenckfeld and Gabriel Ascherham are considered as characteristic; for the rational type of Spiritualism Sebastian Franck is named as a representative, but also—strangely—the "pansophist" Paracelsus and the mystic Valentine Weigel. On the other hand, a man like Hans Denk is classified

among the "contemplative Anabaptists," quite in contradistinction to Rufus Jones's opinion.

This survey clearly demonstrates the elusiveness of the concept of Spiritualist as found in the 16th and 17th centuries. Sharper definitions or distinctions are still needed to understand the deeper issues. For instance, for some of these men the doctrine of the "inner word" (see **Bible, Inner and Outer Word**) means a divine impulse to discipleship and a concrete Christianity while to others (e.g., Quakers) it means simply the spiritual equipment in every man, hence a liberating force in life's decisions. It might perhaps be best to distinguish Spiritualism proper (as described by Williams) from spiritualistic tendencies both in general Protestantism and in Anabaptism (this distinction is suggested by Bergsten). In this regard early Anabaptism clearly demonstrates these tendencies without, however, losing its concrete and existential character as the religion of discipleship.

Spiritualism is only in part New Testamental; in part it is Neoplatonic, a teaching which runs like a red thread throughout Western intellectual history (see Lovejoy), and in part is indebted to medieval mysticism (Williams, 87). But beyond that Spiritualists rely either strongly "on that of God in every man" (George Fox's term), i.e., on man's spiritual equipment, or on dreams, visions, revelations, and other inspirations, occasionally called *Eingebungsgeist* (Müntzer, David Joris). The great names in this line are undoubtedly Sebastian Franck (*q.v.*), Johann Bünderlin, Christian Entfelder, and (as a type in itself) Caspar Schwenckfeld, sometimes called the "spiritualistic pietist" of his age. All these men consider the Holy Scripture more as a textbook of Spiritualism than as the one and final revealed Word of God to be unconditionally obeyed. Franck very clearly explains why he could not be an Anabaptist, in spite of all his warm sympathies for these people—it was their discipline, their congregational life, their practical demonstration of discipleship. There was a great controversy between Spiritualism and Anabaptism, even though the delineations are not always clear. Spiritualists are generally individualists, believing in an invisible church rather than in a visible institution or brotherhood, although at times they developed fellowship groups or circles, as around Schwenckfeld. Doctrinally they were not much concerned, inasmuch as the person of Christ is often not absolutely central (for some Christ was only a great teacher). Also sacraments or ordinances were minimized: neither Müntzer nor Joris nor Schwenckfeld cared for baptism or the Lord's Supper, nor did Quakers ever practice these ceremonies. Spiritualists hardly ever speak of the "church under the cross" (see **Martyrdom, Theology of**). Of course, they, too, know of suffering in this world, but it is due to the tension between spirit and flesh and not because the "world" would contradict their teachings and practices. Usually they live a life of withdrawal and inconspicuous conduct, filled with meditation, writing, and a rich correspondence.

At first Spiritualism can be a very strong force in those who actually experience such an immediacy of God's inner light. Later it can and often does develop into two directions: rationalism (Socinianism) and Pietism, sometimes even combining them. This development became particularly obvious in later Dutch Mennonitism—the line from Hans de Ries to Galenus de Haan (see Meihuizen). Thus Kühn's typology can become blurred since there are no pure types. Often Spiritualism ends in religious liberalism, just as Anabaptism at times eventuates into conservatism, fundamentalism, and legalism.

Early Anabaptism, that is, the first generation, 1525/50, bears certain marks of a dynamic spiritual (spiritualistic) character; in fact, this is the very justification for its existence. Inner rebirth and John 3:8 explain the vigor and liveliness of its first representatives anywhere. This has been brought out most impressively in Orley Swartzentruber's analysis of some early documents, Michael Sattler's letter to the congregation in Horb of 1527, and Anneken Jans's farewell letter to her infant son in 1539 (Swartzentruber, 17 ff., 131 ff.). In these analyses it becomes quite clear that to these early martyrs the "inner word" does not mean at all an "antinomian escape" but rather an increased urge for obedience and concrete witnessing to one's faith. Sattler warns his fellow believers of "false brethren," apparently "spiritualizers" (perhaps followers of Hans Denk and Hans Hut; see Kiwiet), and "enthusiasts," but nevertheless he himself uses, as Swartzentruber writes, a "pneumatic language," stressing the inwardness of a dedicated heart. Early Anabaptism represents a unique synthesis of spiritualism, Gospel ethics, and eschatology (ibid., 133); most likely this formula of explanation does not exhaust the phenomenon. Certainly, the idea of a "church without spot and wrinkle" is another aspect of this "Anabaptist spiritualism" which Swartzentruber calls "orthodox spiritualism" (22), something which is very different from the ideas of Spiritualism in the narrower sense of the term used above.

The present writer has discussed the issue of Anabaptism-Spiritualism several times. In his *Mennonite Piety* (79 ff.) he formulated the issue somewhat as follows: "The Spirit can be present only where He can also become flesh" (82). Such a spiritualism is then called a "concrete or Biblical spiritualism" as contrasted to the non-concrete vagueness of Neoplatonic Spiritualism in a Franck or a Campanus. In other words, Anabaptist "spiritualism" requires commitment, *Nachfolge,* obedience, evidencing of faith in life—points little cared for by the Neoplatonists, and hence is probably better not called Spiritualism. But, to be sure, all this is true for the early representatives of the movement (to 1540-55), while later generations show already signs of the "routinization of charisma" (term by Max Weber), that is, a certain formalization of erstwhile spontaneous acts and expressions.

H. W. Meihuizen (*MQR* 1953, 259-304) wrote an important article on the "Spiritualistic Tendencies and Movements Among the Dutch Mennonites of the 16th and 17th Centuries," contrasting the line from Hans de Ries and the Waterlanders up to Galenus Abrahamsz de Haan with the other line from Menno Simons and Dirk Philips to Pieter Jans Twisck and the Hard Frisians, claiming that the spiritualistic line is the very genius of the Dutch Doopsgezinde. To this Friedmann replied in a rather lengthy analysis (*MQR* 1954, 150 f.): It must

be granted that Anabaptism would not be Anabaptism if it did not contain a certain element of spiritualism, i.e., the free working of the Holy Spirit in the understanding of the Scriptures. Without this spiritualism Anabaptism would quickly deteriorate into formalism, legalism, or antinomianism. But it leads rather to emphatic commitments, since it is never an unguided inspirationalism or illuminism (see **Enthusiasts**). Reference was made to Wiswedel's important study on the "Inner and Outer Word" among Anabaptists (see **Bible, Inner and Outer Word**), and in particular to Ulrich Stadler's beautiful tract of 1536 entitled *Vom lebendigen Wort und geschriebenen* (L. Müller, 212-27). But precisely these studies demonstrate convincingly the distance of such thoughts from those of the Spiritualists discussed above, German, Dutch, or English. The question was raised more than once how the Anabaptist brethren could actually know that their "spirit" was the same as the Spirit of the Scriptures and not mere imagination (*Eingebungsgeist*). This was the question of E. Hegenwalt in 1524 (Bender, 122), J. J. Wolleb in 1722 (Friedmann, 42 ff.), and Karl Holl in 1923 (Friedmann, 78). Obviously, no absolute proof can be given but the external results might suggest the answer: the pure church, discipleship, Gospel character of the brotherhood, versus a mildly rationally oriented conventicle or circle of like-minded friends. In the 19th century Ludwig Keller (*q.v.*) was in his own life a dramatic example of this shift: he began as an ardent "Anabaptist" (see **Keller and the Anabaptists**) mainly of the Hans Denk type, only to end as the chairman of the spiritualistic "Comenius-Gesellschaft."

Once more the tension between Anabaptism and Spiritualism becomes an urgent issue in recent studies on Pilgram Marpeck (*q.v.*) and his controversy with Caspar Schwenckfeld. Kiwiet, Bergsten, Klassen, and others put this controversy into the very center of their analyses. For Marpeck the "Word," as revealed in the New Testament, is the carrier of spirit and life, while for Schwenckfeld such ties are nonessential, as one may also receive the inner word without any traditional means (Kiwiet, 111). In other words, the "spirit" of the Spiritualists is not necessarily the Holy Spirit. The difference between Marpeck and Schwenckfeld becomes particularly evident in their ideas concerning the church: visible vs. invisible, discipline vs. no discipline, historical vs. timeless. Bergsten in his Marpeck study (part IV: *Zusammenfassung*) claims that before 1534 Anabaptism and Spiritualism were hard to distinguish (even though the line Grebel-Sattler is different from the line Denk-Hut), but after 1534 the distinction became very clear and sharp, not only sociologically as Troeltsch claimed, but also theologically (no ordinances, etc.). But Klassen holds that the separation of Anabaptism and Spiritualism occurred clearly in 1531.

Still not fully understood is the position of Hans Denk, which might be called a real borderline case. At one time he is nearer Anabaptism, while at another time he appears to be nearer or leaning toward Neoplatonic Spiritualism, although Kiwiet expressly says that he was not a Spiritualist.

The issue of Müntzer and David Joris, both of whom might better be called "inspirationalists" than

Spiritualists, will not be discussed here at any length, in spite of their possible influence upon the early Anabaptists. Anabaptists at all times were cool to the idea of "direct inspiration" (*Eingebungsgeist*) by which these men lived and acted. Of course such a judgment is correct only as long as one adheres to the conventional definition of Anabaptism (see **Anabaptist**, Section 2). In any other case the situation becomes more complicated, and one might then better refer back to G. H. Williams' recent classification (see **Radical Reformation**). Certainly, Spiritualism and Inspirationalism are not identical phenomena (see **Enthusiasts**).

Letter and Spirit represent a basic tension in Christianity from its very beginning (see I Cor. 3:6), and will remain so throughout history: the Word without the Spirit is dead, but the Spirit without the Word is empty of content and without control.

R.F.

Alfred Hegler, *Geist und Schrift bei Sebastian Franck, eine Studie zur Geschichte des Spiritualismus in der Reformationszeit* (Freiburg, 1892); Ernst Troeltsch, *Social Teachings of the Christian Churches* (1912, English N.Y., 1931); Rufus M. Jones, *Spiritual Reformers in the 16th and 17th Centuries* (London, 2nd ed. 1928); Karl Holl, *Luther, Gesammelte Aufsätze zur Kirchengeschichte* I (2nd ed. Tübingen, 1923); R. H. Grützmacher, *Wort und Geist, eine historische und dogmatische Untersuchung* (Leipzig, 1902); Johannes Kühn, *Toleranz und Offenbarung* (Berlin, 1923); Orley Swartzentruber, "The Piety and Theology of the Anabaptist Martyrs in van Braght's Martyrs' Mirror," *MQR* XXVIII (1954) 5-26, 128-42; Robert Friedmann, *Mennonite Piety* (Goshen, 1949); H. W. Meihuizen, "Spiritualistic Tendencies and Movements Among the Dutch Mennonites of the 16th and 17th Centuries," *MQR* XXVII (1953) 259-304; Robert Friedmann, "A Critical Discussion of H. W. Meihuizen's Study," *MQR* XXVIII (1954) 148-54; Jan J. Kiwiet, *Pilgram Marbeck* (Kassel, 1957); T. Bergsten, "Pilgram Marbeck und seine Auseinandersetzung mit Kaspar Schwenckfeld," *Kyrkohistorisk Arsskrift* (Uppsala), 1957-58; G. H. Williams, *Spiritual and Anabaptist Writers* (The Library of Christian Classics, XXV) (Philadelphia, 1925); F. H. Littell, *The Free Church* (Boston, 1957), in particular "The Radical Testimony: the Spiritualizers," 31-37; Walther Köhler, "Spiritualisten, religiöse," *RGG* V (1931) 702-4; Wilhelm Wiswedel, "The Inner and the Outer Word, a Study in an Anabaptist Doctrine of Scripture," *MQR* XXVI (1952) 171-91; Lydia Müller, *Glaubenszeugnisse oberdeutscher Taufgesinnter* (Leipzig, 1938); A. Lovejoy, *The Great Chain of Being* (Baltimore, 1936), dealing with the Neoplatonic trends in Western thought; F. H. Littell, "Spiritualizers, Anabaptists, and the Church," *MQR* XXIX (1955) 34-43; J. J. Kiwiet, "The Life of Hans Denck," *MQR* XXXI (1957) 227-59; *idem*, "The Theology of Hans Denck," *MQR* XXXII (1958) 3-27; H. W. Meihuizen, "Spiritualisme onder de Nederlandse Doopsgezinden," in *DJ* 1953, 25-32; W. Klassen, "Pilgram Marpeck in Recent Research," *MQR* XXXII (1958) 211-28; Walther Köhler, "Die Züricher Täufer," *Gedenkschrift* ((Weierhof, 1925) 59 f.

Spis, Jacob Pietersz, b. in 1725, d. Dec. 13, 1810, at Hoorn, was the last untrained minister of the Mennonite congregation at Hoorn, Dutch province of North Holland. He served 1775-95 and 1802-10. In the period of the French Revolution, Spis was not a Patriot (*q.v.*) as were nearly all the Dutch Mennonites, but a loyal adherent of the Orange party. For this reason he was suspended from his ministry from 1795 to 1802. Spis was also the last conservative leader in Hoorn. (*Naamlijst* 1802, 70; 1806, 73; *DJ* 1941 49-54.)   vDZ.

Spitalhof: see Branchweilerhof.

Spitta, Karl Philipp (1801-59), a German Lutheran pastor and hymn writer, church superintendent at Burghof, Prussia, Germany. His collection of hymns, the *Psalter und Harfe*, is found on the bookshelf of many a Mennonite family. Twenty-two of his hymns were adopted into the hymnal of the South German Mennonites and fourteen into that of the West Prussian Mennonites. (*Gbl.*, 1911, 50, 54; *ML* IV.)   NEFF.

Spittelmaier, Hans, early Anabaptist leader in Moravia, of whom we hear only in the Hutterite Chronicle. Neither his origin nor his end is known. He seems not to have been related to his contemporary Ambrosius Spittelmayr (*q.v.*); the name is Bavarian-Austrian and quite common. In 1527 Hans was ordained minister of the new Anabaptist congregation in Nikolsburg (*q.v.*), Moravia, which was under the leadership of Balthasar Hubmaier and protected by the two manorial lords of Nikolsburg, Hans and (his uncle) Leonhard Liechtenstein (*q.v.*). At the great debate of 1527 between Hubmaier and Hans Hut, Spittelmaier took sides with Hubmaier, mainly by favoring the use of the sword by Christians and the paying of war taxes. When Hubmaier went to Vienna in 1528 (to be martyred eventually), Spittelmaier took his place as the leader of the entire congregation. Soon this congregation grew by newcomers such as Jakob Wideman (*q.v.*), Philipp Plener (*q.v.*), and Gabriel Ascherham (*q.v.*). Spittelmaier preached publicly the Hubmaier doctrine concerning the sword (at least that is what the Chronicle reports). Thereupon, in 1528, a large section under the leadership of Jakob Wideman separated from Spittelmaier and his followers, since they could not possibly tolerate this "principle of the sword." From now on there were two "peoples" in Nikolsburg: the Stäbler (*q.v.*; staff bearers, more correctly bearers of canes), nonresistant and strictly pacifist, who were not willing to support war even in the face of the Turkish danger (the Turks were besieging Vienna in 1529), and the Schwertler (*q.v.*; sword bearers, more correctly those who tolerated the use of the sword), Spittelmaier and Leonhard Liechtenstein. As the latter could not achieve a reconciliation and unification, Lord Liechtenstein expelled them from his territory. Nothing further is known of Spittelmaier.   R.F.

Zieglschmid, *Chronik*; Johann Loserth, *Doctor Balthasar Hubmaier und die Anfänge der Wiedertaufe in Mähren* (Brünn, 1893).

Spittelmayr (Spittelmaier), Ambrosius, an early Anabaptist leader, a citizen of Linz, Upper Austria, and a university student with a good command of Latin, born *c*1497 in Linz where he was baptized and commissioned to preach by Hans Hut on July 25, 1527. He worked as an Anabaptist apostle in the vicinity of Linz for about two weeks after his baptism but then was forced to flee. He traveled through Augsburg, Nuremberg, Schwabach, and Gunzenhausen, preaching and baptizing, until he arrived in Erlangen, where on inquiring after Hans Nadler he was taken prisoner on Sept. 9, 1527. After his first trial he was transferred to Ansbach and on October 2 to Cadolzburg, where he was tortured and tried and finally beheaded on Feb. 6, 1528. He should not be confused with Hans Spittelmaier (*q.v.*), reformer at Nikolsburg, associate of B. Hubmaier.

There are five extant records (*TA,* 25 f.) of his answers to the questions the authorities directed to him at his trial. He wrote out his answer for the trial on October 25, and the 3,000-word document is a moving confession of his Anabaptist faith. It includes a treatment of his view of the knowledge of God, the nature of the covenant in the church, the sharing of goods and property, admonition and discipline, the seven decisions of Scripture, namely, the covenant of God, the kingdom of God, the body of Christ, the end of the world, the judgment, the resurrection, and the eternal verdict; also the person and work of Christ, discipleship and the imitation of Christ, the relationship of the Christian to the state, the significance of the Lord's Supper, the humanity of Mary, the second coming of Christ, and purgatory. A comparison of Hans Hut's answers to the same set of questions (*TA,* 41 f.) makes the similarity between their positions quite obvious. Spittelmayr's confession is particularly significant because it throws light on the teachings of Hut that are not treated as fully in Hut's own tracts and confessions. Hut's seven decisions, for example, are described in greater detail in this confession than anywhere else in the writings of Hut and his followers.

Spittelmayr's view of the essence of the Christian commitment and the nature of the church is illustrated by a set of five questions that penetrate progressively deeper into the implications of the Christian faith which he put to strangers while carrying on his itinerant ministry as an Anabaptist apostle: first he asked whether the individual was a Christian; secondly he inquired about the character of his life and walk as a Christian—was he a disciple? thirdly he asked what his relationship to his Christian brother was like—was he a functioning member of the church? fourthly he asked whether he shared all things with his brothers and they with him—no brother should suffer need of food or clothing; and fifthly he inquired about the practice of brotherly admonition and discipline.

Spittelmayr said of Christ that He was "true God and man, the head of all His members, who has erased with His suffering the eternal wrath of God that was directed against us. He has reconciled us and restored us to peace with God, and as our personal mediator His suffering and death have opened for us the kingdom of heaven from which we had fallen because of Adam." Spittelmayr emphasized in his confession that Christians must live, suffer, and die as Christ died for them if they want to inherit the kingdom of God.

The patient acceptance of suffering is a recurrent theme in the testimonies of Spittelmayr and is presented as an integral part of a life of discipleship. Whoever will not suffer with Christ will not inherit with Christ. Christians must drink the cup that He drank. If men enjoy this world and live according to the lusts of the flesh, they must suffer in the next. Disciples partake of Christ when He is spiritually conceived, born, circumcised, baptized, and preached in them. Spittelmayr's emphasis is on discipleship, the following of Christ, rather than on physical suffering as Thomas Müntzer and some of the earlier mystics maintained.

The covenant consists of brotherly admonition, the sharing of all things, nonresistance to evil men, and participation in baptism and the Lord's Supper. "This covenant is realized in the Spirit, in baptism, and in the drinking of the cup, which Christ has called the baptism of blood. We covenant ourselves to God to remain with Him in one love, one spirit, one faith, and one baptism and on the other hand God covenants to be our Father and to stay with us in tribulation."

Spittelmayr said that he was moved to accept adult baptism because he wanted to be a true and obedient Christian. Christ taught His disciples when He left them saying: Go into all the world and preach the Gospel; whoever believes and is baptized is saved. The preaching of God's Word must come before and not after baptism. Apart from voluntary faith the concept of covenant and baptism are meaningless and the disciple-church an impossibility.

In speaking of the Lord's Supper Spittelmayr accused the priests of a very wooden understanding of Christ's words in John 6: He who eats my flesh and drinks my blood has eternal life. One should not look at these words outwardly but rather put away the letter and seek the spirit. You eat the flesh of Christ by giving yourself here and now as a member of Christ's body. A true Christian must do everything in his spiritual Christ that Christ did visibly in the flesh. It is in this way that the Word becomes flesh and lives in a Christian. The celebration of the supper itself is to remind us of the suffering of Christ and our commitment to follow Him.

Spittelmayr represents a fine example of the early South German position regarding the sharing of goods. "Nobody can inherit the kingdom unless he is poor with Christ, for a Christian has nothing of his own; no place where he can lay his head. A real Christian should not even have enough property on earth to be able to stand on it with one foot. This does not mean that he should go and lie down in the woods and not have a trade, or that he should not have fields and meadows, or that he should not work, but alone that he might not think they are for his own use and be tempted to say: this house is mine, this field is mine, this dollar is mine. Rather he should say it is ours, even as we pray: Our Father. In summary, a Christian should not have anything of his own but should have all things in common with his brother, i.e., not allow him to suffer need. In other words, I will not work that my house be filled, that my larder be supplied with meat, but rather I will see that my brother has enough, for a Christian looks more to his neighbor than to himself. Whoever desires to be rich in this world, who is concerned that he miss nothing when it comes to his person and property, who is honored by men and feared by them, who refuses to prostrate himself at the feet of his Lord . . . will be humbled." This did not mean absolute propertylessness as it did later for the Hutterian Brethren.

Spittelmayr shared Hut's dynamic view of the apostolate. He says of his own role as an apostle:

"It is my desire to preach and baptize and lead men to accept the Christian faith; God instituted this work (the apostolate) by His Son after the resurrection." He refers to Hut as a "commissioned apostle sent from God in these last and most perilous times."

Spittelmayr interprets Christ's command as preaching the Gospel "through" the whole creation. This means that Christ has given men created things that they might use the visible to understand and explain the invisible. Christ did this when He used real water to explain what living water and eternal life are. A man's vocation or trade can become a book through which he learns to know the will of God. This is not understood to be a substitute for the written Word of God. It was through Hans Hut that this interpretation entered the Anabaptist movement.

There is nothing dangerously radical (chiliastic) about Spittelmayr's eschatology. The day and hour of Christ's reappearing is hidden from all men. The end of the world is near, the time when the world and its lusts will pass away. In the future judgment Christ will appear to judge the living and the dead, everybody reaping in eternity what he has sown in time. In the great resurrection the godless will arise to death, for they have lived and lusted here, and the godly will arise to life, for they have been dead here. The eternal verdict will seal the fate of the godless to the eternal fire that does not consume.

Spittelmayr believed that civil authority was originally instituted by God and that it was the duty of government "to judge word and deed that is directed against God." Governments had fallen from this original commission and now resembled Pilate. This does not mean that Spittelmayr advocated resistance to the authorities; on the contrary, he called for obedience. The authorities, however, did not have the right to coerce the Christian's conscience. Besides the principle of nonresistance to evil he said nothing specific about the oath and government office.

Spittelmayr, a disciple of Hans Hut, reflects a position that has much in common with Hans Schlaffer, Leonhard Schiemer, Wolfgang Brandhuber, and also later leaders of the South German Anabaptist movement like Leupold Scharnschlager and Pilgram Marpeck.   H.C.KL.

Alex. Nicoladoni, *Johannes Bünderlin von Linz* (Berlin, 1893) 51-60; *TA Bayern* I; Wiswedel, *Bilder* II, 8-17.

Spoelder, Cornelis (1886-1958), a Dutch Mennonite, professor of Latin and Greek and rector of the Gymnasium at Haarlem, was a man of many interests. He was prominent in sports, was a commander of the Haarlem fire brigade, and member and promoter of many associations, but most of all he was a loyal member of the Mennonite Church. Stemming from a non-Mennonite background he later joined the Haarlem Mennonite congregation, of which he was a deacon from 1945 until his death. He was 1946-55 a trustee of the ADS (*q.v.*) and a curator of its seminary, 1951-55 acting as its moderator. Spoelder was a beloved teacher, a man of strong faith, who sometimes as lay preacher conducted services in Mennonite congregations.   vDZ.

Spoerle, Leonhard, an Anabaptist martyr, a participant in the Martyrs' Synod of Augsburg (*q.v.*), suffered death by martyrdom on Nov. 12, 1527 (place not named).

Spon, Ludwig, of Ershausen, district of Erfurt, was one of the most zealous and successful of the Anabaptist leaders in Thuringia (*q.v.*), Germany, and won many converts for the Anabaptist movement. He was seized in May 1533 and released from prison in November at the request of Philip (*q.v.*) of Hesse. Nothing more is known of him. (Wappler, *Thüringen; ML* IV.)

Spotlight, a booklet including the features of a newspaper and picture book first published by the Winter Bible Term class of 1936 at Hesston College and Bible School, now published annually to record the Winter Bible Term including faculty, students, classes, and activities.   W.E.O.

Spotlight, The, the organ of Western District (GCM) Conference Men, a mimeographed publication appearing usually as a 4-page 8½ x 11 inch quarterly or bimonthly issue, place of publication North Newton, Kan., first issue January 1952.
          H.S.B.

Spring City Mennonite Brethren in Christ Church, located in Spring City, Pa., was organized in 1891 under the leadership of H. B. Musselman. In 1956 the congregation had 67 members with Earl M. Hosler serving as pastor.   P.E.B.

Spring Creek Hutterite Bruderhof, of the Dariusleut (*q.v.*) group, at Lewistown, Mont., was founded in 1945. In 1950 its head preacher was Paul Walter.

Spring Mountain Mennonite Church (MC), located in the village of Spring Mountain within 1½ miles of the town of Schwenksville, Pa., was dedicated on July 17, 1949. On Oct. 17, 1949, Elmer M. Mack, chairman of the Franconia Mennonite Board of Missions and Charities, together with Jacob M. Moyer, bishop of the district, organized the mission group as a congregation of the Franconia Mennonite Conference. In 1955 the baptized membership was 68 with Paul L. Ruth as pastor.   M.D.R.

Spring Valley Mennonite Brethren Church, located 5 miles west and 4½ miles south of Ulysses, Kan., dates back to 1927 when the first services were held in the Spring Valley School. The congregation was organized in 1928. Among the charter members were Harms, Kliewer, Neufeld, Karber, and Buschman families, from Kansas and Oklahoma. The first leader was Isaac Harms. In November 1943 a meetinghouse was moved from Liberal, Kan., and dedicated. A parsonage was added in 1951. The first full-time pastor was Elmer Jantz. In 1958 the membership was 72, and the pastor John H. Flaming.
          J.H.FL.

Spring Valley Mennonite Church (MC), a rural congregation, now extinct, located at Kenmare, Ward Co., N.D. In 1899 D. B. Kauffman moved from Cass Co., Mo., with team and covered wagon and homesteaded, followed in 1900 by four other families. In 1904 a congregation was organized and D. B. Kauffman ordained minister. He served until 1919. In 1905 the church was built and dedicated. In 1921 J. L. Lehman was ordained minister and served until his accidental death in 1928. Archie Kauffman was ordained minister in 1929 and served until 1936. The largest membership was 62 in 1933. Because of dry years all had moved away by 1940, and later the church building was sold. During the 35 years, 90 were baptized and received into the church. Of this number six were ordained ministers and one a bishop.   F.E.K.

Spring Valley Mennonite Church (MC), located 2 miles east and 3 miles south of Canton, McPherson Co., Kan., is a member of the South Central Conference, and the oldest of the four M.C. congregations in central Kansas. It was organized by Bishop Daniel Brundage in 1873, who also organized the three other churches, viz., the Catlin Mennonite Church near Peabody in 1876, the West Liberty Mennonite Church near Inman in 1883, and the Pennsylvania Mennonite Church near Newton in 1885. Brundage also organized the Kansas-Nebraska Mennonite Conference in 1876, which later came to be the Missouri-Kansas Conference but now is called the South Central Conference. In 1957 Charles Diener was pastor, with a membership of 59. C.D.

Spring Valley Mennonite Church (GCM), formerly known as the Newport Mennonite Church, located 8 miles south of Newport, Pend Oreille Co., Wash., began in the 1920's, when Mennonites of Russian-German background settled here having come from Kansas, Oklahoma, and Texas. The church was organized in 1928. Ministers who have served are John W. Kliewer, Peter D. Unruh, Rudolf Schmidt, and Rudolf Toews, who was the pastor in 1959, when the membership was 89.   R.Sc.

Springdale Mennonite Church (MC), also known as Kindig's Church, located at Waynesboro, Va., a member of the Virginia Conference, built its first meetinghouse in 1825, replaced by a larger church in 1941, which seats 450. Mountain View Mennonite Church, built in 1900, and Valley View are congregations started as mission points from Springdale. East Bethel Mennonite Mission, begun in 1952, is a growing mission point. The membership of Springdale in 1957 was 217, with Paul L. Wenger as pastor.   J.R.D.

Springer, Hans, an Anabaptist martyr in Iglau, Moravia. The Anabaptist movement gained adherents here very early; but through the influence of Paul Speratus (*q.v.*) Lutheranism predominated and Anabaptism was suppressed, especially by the Lutheran clergy, as in 1529, 1536, and 1537. The city records and council reports call the Anabaptists

"böse Buben." It was thus impossible for the Anabaptists to organize a congregation. Nevertheless there were occasionally some Anabaptists found in Iglau, and at the end of the century they apparently increased in number. Their leader and preacher was Hans Springer. The city council again took steps to suppress them. In 1592 Hans Springer was surprised in his house and "with great violence was miserably and painfully slain." The erection of the fountain on the market place (1592-94) is attributed to the Anabaptists.   W.W.

A. Altrichter, "Zur Gesch. der Wiedertäufer in Iglau," in *Ztscht des deutschen Vereins für die Geschichte Mährens und Schlesiens*, 1928, 157 f., ML IV.

Springfeld, a Mennonite village name found in the Alexanderwohl settlement near Newton, Kan.; Swift Current, Sask.; and Cuauhtemoc, Mexico. (See Villages.)   C.K.

Springfield Krimmer Mennonite Brethren Church, located in the western part of Marion County, 5 miles southwest of Lehigh, Kan., was organized on April 2, 1902, with David P. Schroeder as elder, ordained on Jan. 24, 1904, by Jacob A. Wiebe, the elder of the Gnadenau K.M.B. Church and founder of the K.M.B. Church. P. A. Wiebe was elected as assistant minister, and later served as elder. The Springfield community was settled in the 1870's by a dozen members of the Gnadenau Church, nine miles east, who in 1878 began to have their own worship services in their homes. As a result of two revivals soon after the organization, about 60 members were added to the church.

The church building was constructed in 1894, and, with additions made later, was still in use in 1949. A small stream fed by an incessant spring, from which the church receives its name, runs across the churchyard; in it the church has practiced immersion by kneeling and dipping forward. Communion is observed with footwashing four times a year. Most members are farmers.

Other ministers and leaders of the church have been Isbrand Harder, H. V. Wiebe, J. T. Krause, J. E. Plett, W. W. Harms, David V. Wiebe, C. F. Plett, and Franklin Wiebe, the present pastor. The membership in 1956 was 77. The first missionaries of the K.M.B. Church, P. V. and H. V. Wiebe, came from this congregation.   P.V.W.

Springfield Township Chapel (MC), located one-half mile southwest of Holland, Ohio, is a mission station established in 1945. It had 40 members in 1957, with Raymond Richer as its pastor.   M.G.

Springfield Mennonite Church (GCM), now extinct, 17 miles south of Hydro, Okla., began in 1898 in the home of J. J. Zerger. The first baptism of thirteen young people was conducted by J. J. Flickner. Attempts to unite with the Bergthal Mennonite Church at Hydro failed. On Sept. 13, 1899, under the leadership of Elder C. Ramseier, the church was organized. On April 19, 1900, J. J. Kaufman and J. T. Albrecht were elected ministers. Later C. P. Stucky was elected minister. The members of the church were primarily Swiss Volhynian Mennonites from Moundridge and Pretty Prairie, Kan. In 1903 a church was built. The last entry of the church record was dated Feb. 2, 1919, stating that Emil Riesen, who had been serving the church, was to issue church letters to the members and care for the few remaining families. It was decided to sell the church and to turn the income over to the Board of Missions. Most of the families had moved away and joined other churches. C.K.

"Geschichte von der Entstehung der Springfeld Gemeinde" (BeCL); H. P. Krehbiel, *Mennonite Churches of North America* (Newton, 1911) 46.

Springfield Mennonite Church (GCM), located in Springfield Twp., Bucks Co., Pa. It is not known when the first meetinghouse was built, but the Mennonite settlers reached the area before the middle of the 18th century; Peter Meyer, the first known preacher, located there in 1741. The letter written by the Franconia bishops to Holland in 1773 seems to call this congregation "Term" (Durham). The second meetinghouse, "in a little grove, delightfully located on high ground, . . . a low stone building," was built in 1824 and is still standing. The names of the ministers who served at Springfield (MC) were Meyer and Moyer, Gehman, and Geisinger. The congregation divided in 1847, the deacon and part of the church following John H. Oberholtzer (*q.v.*) and the two preachers and the other portion of the congregation remaining in the Franconia Conference. The two groups then alternated in the use of the meetinghouse until about 1948, when the Franconia Mennonites discontinued services. In 1888 the Franconia Conference group numbered twenty; in 1936, eleven. The membership of the Eastern District Conference congregation at Springfield (GCM) was 74 in 1895; in 1936 it was 36; and in 1958 it was 44, with Robert M. Landis as pastor. J.C.W.

J. C. Wenger, *History of the Mennonites of the Franconia Conference* (Telford, 1937) 129, 130, 368.

Springs (formerly Tub), a town near Salisbury, Pa., was built on an area originally consisting of two farms, the George Folk farm whose buildings were erected near the present J. J. Otto residence, and the Peter Bitsche farm whose buildings were erected near the present Amos J. Yoder residence. Springs is the home congregation from which all the Mennonite (MC) churches and mission points in the Casselman Valley district have been established. Sunday-school work had its beginning in 1846 in the "Red School House," on the lot now occupied by the F. W. Bender Co. store building. The town has a number of Mennonite-owned industries. It is a community for truck, dairy, and chicken farming, and is known for its good mountain air and its good water, as its name suggests. E.E.B.

Springs Mennonite Church (MC), also known as German Springs, now extinct, was located near Manchester, Okla., in the northwestern part of the state. Organized by S. C. Miller in 1895, it had 22 members in 1905, with George C. Hinkel as its minister. Its meetinghouse was built in 1894. The first minister was Simon Hetrick. It was last listed in the Yearbook of 1919, when it had 22 members, but no minister. M.G.

Springs Mennonite Church (MC), located at Springs, 4 miles west of Salisbury, Pa., a member of the Allegheny Conference, was founded in 1780. Until 1853 the congregation, known as the Society of Mennonites, met in homes for worship under Lancaster Conference. The first minister was Jakob Seiler (later Saylor), an Amishman from Germany, who had been ordained bishop to serve in the Meyersdale area. In 1853, after a period of decline, Henry H. Blauch was ordained to the ministry, and in the half century of his service the church grew from 22 members to about 250 in the Casselman Valley district. In 1859 the Mennonite Union Church, known as Keim's (*q.v.*), was built at St. Paul with the Lutheran and Reformed congregations. In 1874 a meeting was held here to consider the formation of the Southwestern Pennsylvania Conference, now the Allegheny Conference. In 1878 a meetinghouse was built at Springs, known first as the Folk Church. It was remodeled and enlarged in 1916 and 1925, and replaced by a new church in 1954. The product of the missionary outreach of this church are the Oak Grove, Casselman, Glade, Pinto, and Gortner Mennonite churches. Other mission points are Laughlin, turned over to the Brethren; Lageer, turned over to Glade; Bear Hill; Manadier; Fairview; Black Hawk, later called Meadow Mountain; Dry Run; Red Run; Bear Creek, and Meyersdale. The membership of the Springs congregation in 1957 was 291, with Roy Otto as bishop, and Walter Otto as pastor. E.E.B.

Springstein, Man., a town located on the Canadian Pacific railway lines southwest of Winnipeg. Here the "Midwest Properties Co., Ltd." of Minneapolis purchased a tract of land of 2,890 acres. This land was acquired by purchase in 1924 by ten Mennonite families, who had immigrated to Canada from Russia in 1923, for the sum of $240,000, without down payment, but with the obligation of delivering annually half of the harvest to the company as payment on their debt. On Oct. 14, 1923, the families had settled on this farm and helped to thresh out the 1,000 acres of wheat. The school which was opened at Springstein when these families arrived had seven pupils. Today, after 30 years, Springstein is a neat Mennonite village with 18 families. An excellent school of three classes, in which 3 teachers give instruction as far as grade 11, is probably the most valuable possession of Springstein. The teachers and the students are all children of Mennonite parents and the instruction is very closely bound with the Mennonite faith. Opposite the school stands the church (GCM), which has seating space for about 300. One mile southwest of Springstein is the Mennonite Brethren church. Mennonite farmers have bought up most of the land around Springstein.

It has not been easy to develop or even to keep the land at all. It was particularly hard during depression. The "Midwest Properties Company" reduced the purchase price to one half of the original sum, and gave the loan free of interest for 15 years. As the times improved, the financial status of the settlement also improved. W.H.E.

Springstein Mennonite Brethren Church of Springstein, Man., was organized on May 17, 1942, by members of the North End Mennonite Brethren Church of Winnipeg. The church building was erected in 1938 and enlarged in 1948. The church is a member of the Manitoba Provincial and the Canadian District M.B. conferences. In 1957 the membership was 33, with Peter P. Dueck as leading minister. H.NE.

Springstein Mennonite Church (GCM) was organized on Oct. 17, 1938, by the 17 families of the Schoenwiese congregation who were living at Springstein, Man. The meetinghouse, recently built, 50 x 34 ft., seats 300. In 1957 the congregation had 197 baptized members, with William H. Enns as leading minister. W.H.E.

Springtown, Bucks Co., Pa., was a meetinghouse erected by the Lutherans in 1872, with the help of the Reformed and Mennonites, located only a few miles north of the Springfield Mennonite meetinghouse. Fisher (101) reports this joint effort and adds, "The Mennonites discontinued their services and consequently their rights at this point sometime in the past." The Oberholtzer group (Eastern District Conference, GCM) held the important conference meeting of May 1857, at which they acted on the Gehman schism, at Springtown. It is probable that the Mennonites in the joint effort of 1872 were of the Oberholtzer group. H.S.B.

Allen S. Fisher, *Lutheranism in Bucks County 1734-1934* (Tinicum, 1935).

Springvale Hutterite Bruderhof of the Dariusleut (*q.v.*) branch, located near Rockyford, Alberta, was founded in 1918 by the Jamesville Bruderhof in South Dakota. The preachers were Jakob Wurz, chosen in 1913, confirmed in 1915, and Paul Hofer, chosen in 1915 and confirmed in 1921 in Canada. In 1936 the Springvale Bruderhof established Sandhill (*q.v.*), near Beiseker. In 1950 the Bruderhof numbered 77 baptized members. D.D.

Springville Old Order Mennonite Church (Weaverland Conference), located northeast of Lincoln, Lancaster Co., Pa., purchased a German Baptist meetinghouse, which they used until the early 1950's when the new church was built at the crossroads to the east. The membership in 1955 was 235, with the same ministers as the Meadow Valley (*q.v.*) O.O.M. Church. I.D.L.

Spron(c)k, a Dutch Mennonite family, in the 17th century found at Utrecht, Netherlands. Here Abraham Spronck was from about 1620 an elder of the Old Flemish Mennonite congregation, which in 1632 merged with the Flemish, and in 1639 with the High German and Frisian congregation. In all these unifications Abraham Spronck took an active part. In 1632 he signed the Dordrecht (*q.v.*) Confession in the name of the Utrecht congregation. He served until 1652. His son Cornelis Spronk was a deacon of the Utrecht congregation in 1661-63.

The Spronck (Sprunck) family in West and East Prussia was apparently a collateral branch of this same family. It was found in Danzig both in the Flemish and Frisian congregations, from 1678 and 1685 respectively. As early as 1618 a Cornelius Sprungk is named, a farmer at Altebabke, West Prussia. Hans Sprung rented the "Schlossbrennerei" (distillery) at Tiegenhof (*q.v.*) in 1664. Johan Peter Sprunck (*q.v.*) moved from Danzig to Königsberg in East Prussia in 1716. The following members of the family were living in Königsberg in the 18th century: Abraham Jansz, distiller; Bernhard (or Peter Bernhard), distiller; Heinrich, wholesale dealer; and Isaac. Wilhelm Sprunck (1795-1871) was the owner of the famous distillery "Bunte Bock" at Memel, East Prussia. Hermann Sprunck was a preacher of the Heubuden (*q.v.*) congregation in West Prussia in 1869-95(?). vDZ.

H. B. Berghuys, *Geschiedenis der Doopsgezinde gemeente te Utrecht* (n.p., n.d., Utrecht, 1926); Kühler, *Geschiedenis* II, 195, 199; *Inv. Arch. Amst.*, No. 2289; Horst Penner, *Ansiedlung menn. Niederländer im Weichselmündungsgebiet* (Weierhof, 1940) 41, 47, 70; Reimer, *Familiennamen*, 118; *Gesch.-Bl.*, 1956, 29, Nos. 100-6.

Spruce Mountain Mennonite (MC) outpost, located in Pendleton County, on the eastern slope of the Allegheny Mountain six miles southwest of Onego, W. Va. R. H. Benner (MC) responded to a call to preach here in the 1920's. Summer Bible schools and revival meetings were introduced in the 1930's. Since then the membership has declined; the young people have moved out. Only a few small families remain. Services are still held twice a month in a schoolhouse. The membership in 1958 was 5, with Earl J. Hartzler serving as pastor, under the Virginia Mennonite (MC) Conference. H.A.B.

Sprunck (Sprunk, Sprung, Spronck), **Johan Peter** (Jan Pieters) (d. 1753), a resident of Danzig, West Prussia, moved to Königsberg (*q.v.*), East Prussia, in 1716, where he in 1717 obtained a license to distill rye brandy "nach Danziger Art." Sprunck also organized the small group of Mennonite immigrants then living in Königsberg into a Mennonite congregation; he became the elder of this "Clercksche" (*q.v.*) congregation in 1727. He was also watchful of the interests of a group of Mennonite farmers in the Tilsit Niederung (Lowlands), however with little result, because they were expelled by the King of Prussia in 1723. In 1732 the Mennonites of Königsberg were also forced to leave the city; Sprunck and others moved to Danzig, but soon obtained permission to return to Königsberg. This and a number of particulars concerning the Mennonites of Königsberg are found in some letters sent by Sprunck to the Dutch Mennonite Committee of Foreign Needs at Amsterdam. One of these letters contains the information that he personally paid the rent for the room used as a meeting place, and for the purchase of a pulpit, benches, and chairs. This indicates that he was well-to-do. He fell into discord with Jan Bruinvisch (*q.v.*), a Mennonite from Holland who had established a warehouse at Königsberg and who was also an agent of the Dutch Committee of Foreign Needs. Bruinvisch, a member of the Königsberg congregation, was reprimanded by Sprunck for marrying outside the church. Sprunck seems to have been very active, with a great love for the church, but was not free of a certain presumption and ambition; this and a tendency toward the more liberal Collegiant (*q.v.*) views, of which he was accused, caused his dismissal from the eldership in 1743. Peter (Pieter) Sprunck, probably his son, was the elder of the Königsberg congregation 1758-68.   vᴅZ.

Inv. Arch. Amst. I, No. 1622; II, 2, Nos. 771, 776, 787, 794, 796, 799 f.; *Menn. Bl.*, 1857, 25, 27, 55, 62.

Sprunger, a Mennonite family name, the origin of which is not known. Records show that in the 18th century families by the name of Sprunger were citizens of Sarmenstorf in Aargau, and Oberwangen in Thurgau, Switzerland. The Mennonite Sprungers in America trace their ancestry to the Thurgau branch, though when asked they invariably say their forebears came from the canton of Bern. During the religious persecutions one Jacob Sprunger fled from the canton of Thurgau about 1741 and found haven on the Jura Mountains. Jacob had one son, Peter, and three daughters. Though Peter was confirmed in the Reformed Church he eventually joined the Mennonite Church, where later he was elected to the ministry. Peter had four sons and two daughters. In 1852 a group of some 70 left the Jura region and came to America. Most of them were of this Peter Sprunger family and its relation by marriage. It was this group of Sprungers that formed the nucleus of the Mennonite community in Berne, Ind. Some 35 years later S. F. Sprunger (grandson of Peter), wishing to acquaint Peter's descendants with their ancestry, with the help of his cousin Abraham J. Sprunger compiled and edited a genealogy, *Geschlechts- und Namen-Register der Familie Sprunger* (Berne, 1890).   E.S.

Sprunger, John A. (1852-1911), a Mennonite (GCM) evangelist and publisher, was born Aug. 12, 1852, on Münsterberg, Switzerland, a son of Abraham B. and Elizabeth Zürcher-Sprunger. In 1854 the family came to America and settled in Allen County, Ind., in what is now Berne. His formal education consisted of several winter terms in the district school and a short term in the Mennonite school at Wadsworth, Ohio. He was eager to learn and had a good working knowledge of both English and German. As a young man he took active part in church activities, but his interests were rather centered on business affairs. In fact, he became the outstanding early promoter of Berne. He originated or took a prominent part in more business enterprises and built more homes in Berne than any other man, and became wealthy. On Feb. 15, 1880, he married Katharine, a daughter of Peter and Elizabeth Sprunger-Sprunger. In 1888, after the death of his only child, Sprunger resolved to devote his life to Christian work, and devoted his considerable wealth to the cause of Christ. He conducted a few home mission tours in this country. Then he and his wife spent about a year (1889) in Switzerland in successful evangelism, which led to a permanent revival, especially among the Jura Mennonite churches, including Sonnenberg. While there he was ordained to the ministry. Sprunger founded the Light and Hope Missionary Society in 1893, which established the Light and Hope Orphanage (*q.v.*) in Berne on April 1, 1893. Sprunger also established a deaconess training school in connection with the missionary

society, and made the orphanage the headquarters of all these activities. About 1898 he established the Light and Hope Publishing Co. (*q.v.*) at Berne, which published the monthly journal *Licht und Hoffnung* (*q.v.*), started in 1893, and its English counterpart *Light and Hope*. Among the workers in the print shop and orphanage in Berne were William Egle, H. C. Barthel, and John Horsch. Sprunger was strongly influenced by the Christian and Missionary Alliance. Although he worked very closely with the founders of the Missionary Church Association (*q.v.*) for a time, he never fully joined the group.

In 1902 Sprunger moved the orphanage, print shop, and publishing company to Cleveland, Ohio, and soon to Birmingham near Cleveland. Here H. J. Dyck joined the group of workers. Here also Sprunger died Sept. 28, 1911. He was buried at Berne, where his cousin S. F. Sprunger preached the funeral sermon. He was the author of several books, including a 2-volume work, *The Gospel in Types,* and *Outline of Prophecy,* and in German, *Ein Blick in die prophetische Zukunft* (Berne, c1900), *Leben und volle Genüge* (Berne, n.d.), and *Volles Heil* (Berne, n.d.). With H. J. Dyck he edited two hymnals: *Himmels-Harfe für Sonntag-Schulen, Jugendvereine und Evangelisations-Versammlungen* (Birmingham, Ohio, c1907), and *Lieder-Auswahl aus Himmels-Harfe* (Birmingham, c1907).   H.S.B.

Sprunger, Samuel Ferdinand (1848-1923), the son of Abraham and Magdalena (Rüfenacht) Sprunger, was born on the Münsterberg in the Bernese Jura of Switzerland, Oct. 19, 1848. His mother died when he was but fifteen months old leaving him, as the youngest of the family, with two other brothers and three sisters from a previous marriage, to the care of their father. In the spring of 1852 the family crossed the Atlantic and settled in Adams County, Ind. Here "S.F." grew to maturity and on Oct. 2, 1872, married Katherina Luginbill. To them there were born ten children—three sons and seven daughters. He died, after a lingering illness, on Nov. 16, 1923; interment was in the Berne cemetery.

"Sammie," as he was called in the early years, spent only five short terms in country school before the age of twenty. He joined the church by baptism on April 14, 1865, at the age of seventeen. Three years later, on Aug. 23, 1868, one of seventeen candidates, he was chosen by lot for the ministry and immediately ordained. His ordination as elder occurred several years later, on March 5, 1874, Christian Krehbiel officiating. In the meantime he had spent three school years at the new Mennonite educational institute just opened at Wadsworth, Ohio, and was graduated in the first class in the spring of 1871. With the Wadsworth emphasis on Sunday schools, missions, and heartfelt religion, he returned home to resume the ministry and became the center of disagreement and division regarding new methods of work. Through patience and wise conduct and a deeply spiritual ministry, the differing groups were in 15 years brought into a single unified congregation which became the largest in the General Conference Mennonite Church. His 33 years of active leadership of the Berne church (1871-1903) not only brought unity but introduced a new spirit into the congregation's life with a strong emphasis on inner religion, evangelical activities, and practical Christian service. Organizations for Sunday school, missions, higher education, young people's work, and temperance were actively promoted by him in the church and town.

In 1884 Sprunger's name was incorporated in the firm name of Welty and Sprunger, which became the publishing agent for the General Conference Mennonite Book Concern. In this connection he served as Business Manager of the Publication Board of the Conference 1884-90. He also served as editor of the German Sunday School Quarterly 1889-1920, and editor of the *Bundesbote Kalendar* 1886-1922. Upon the organization of the Middle District Conference in 1888 he became its first president, continuing until 1895 and serving again in 1897 and 1898. Sprunger first attended the triennial General Conference as a delegate in 1872, and attended every one thereafter until 1911. He served the General Conference on committees in connection with the Wadsworth school in 1872, 1875, 1876, and in its closing year in 1878. He was a member of the Foreign Mission Board for 25 years (1884-87, 1896-1917), of the Publication Board 10 years (1884-93), of the Home Mission Board 3 years (1893-96), and was one of the General Conference trustees in 1887 and again 1893-1914. He also served as traveling minister (*Reiseprediger*) for the General Conference and was active in visiting churches, assisting in their organization, and, especially among the Swiss churches, in drawing them into conference connection.

Samuel F. Sprunger is described as a man of deep consecration, good judgment, unshakable conviction, remarkable organizing and executive ability, and prodigious memory. He was not too approachable in the intimate personal and pastoral relations, but was unusually strong in the pulpit and as a leader in church and social life. Probably no one was more highly respected in the history of his own congregation nor more influential among the 19th-century Swiss Mennonite immigrants of Ohio and Indiana.

Sprunger edited a collection of Mennonite sermons from Europe and the United States under the title *Festklänge, Predigten von Mennoniten-Predigern aus den Vereinigten Staaten, Russland, Deutschland, Pfalz, Baiern und der Schweiz* (Berne, 1891).

†S.F.P.

Eva F. Sprunger, "Samuel Ferdinand Sprunger, Pastor-Conference Worker," *Menn. Life* VIII (October 1953); idem, *The First Hundred Years* (Berne, 1938); *Mennonite Yearbook and Almanac*, 1925, p. 53; H. P. Krehbiel, *History of the General Conference of the Mennonites of North America* (Canton, 1898) 445; *The Mennonite* (Nov. 29, 1923) 2; *Christlicher Bundesbote* XLII (Nov. 29, 1923) 5.

Spruyt, David, a physician, married to Janneke Bartels, was a preacher of the Lamist congregation at Amsterdam, Holland, in 1648-79. He was a man of liberal opinions, wholeheatedly embracing Collegiant (*q.v.*) views, and a fervent adherent of his co-preacher Galenus (*q.v.*) Abrahamsz. Though he could not measure up to Galenus either in firmness of faith or in intelligence, it was Spruyt who by his perfectionism (*q.v.*; the doctrine that man can completely fulfill the commands of God) initiated the Lammerenkrijgh (*q.v.*), which in 1664 divided the church into the more progressive Lamists (*q.v.*) and the conservative Zonists (*q.v.*). His brother Willem Spruyt became a deacon of the same congregation in 1662.

vDZ.

DB 1900, 1 f., 4, 6, 17, 20; H. W. Meihuizen, *Galenus Abrahamsz* (Haarlem, 1954) 50 and *passim*.

Ssadovoye, an unfortunate Mennonite settlement in the Russian province of Voronesh, east of the Bichug River. In 1909 a company of 50 Mennonites bought for 1,350,000 rubles the estate Ssadovoye with over 13,000 acres of land and a sugar refinery. Forty-three families with about 280 souls settled here in the spring of 1910. Eighteen of them founded the village of Vassilyevka, and the rest settled on individual farms. Poor crops made it impossible to pay more than the interest in the first year, and less than that in the second. The premature winter of 1912 destroyed the entire beet crop. The settlers were bankrupt and had to sell the estate at great sacrifice, losing all they had. In the fall of 1913 all left Ssadovoye.

J.N.

Ssuvorovka, a Mennonite settlement in North Caucasia in the province of Stavropol. It was a daughter colony sponsored by the Zagradovka, Kuban, and other settlements. Two villages were founded, Nikolaifeld in 1894, and Grossfürstental in 1899, a subsidiary of the Mennonite Brethren Church of the Kuban. Later they also built Lavarov and Arrival. At the time of the settlement there were 89 families with about 500 persons and some 100,000 acres of land. The statistics of 1925 indicated a population of 1,000 with an average of about 22 acres each.

TH.B.

Staal, Abraham, b. 1752 at Gouda, d. 18 ? was trained for the ministry at the Amsterdam Mennonite seminary and served as Mennonite pastor at Goes 1779-87, Bolsward 1787-88, and Leeuwarden 1788-98. Particularly after 1795 Staal, an ardent Patriot and admirer of the principles of the French Revolution, engaged in politics and became a member of the provincial government of Friesland in 1796 and soon after a judge in the provincial court. Having been temporarily suspended in 1797 because of his political activity, he resigned in 1798. In 1794 Staal insisted on the establishment of a foundation for pensioning the widows of Mennonite ministers in Friesland; it was, however, not established until 1804.

vDZ.

Inv. Arch. Amst. II, Nos. 1589-92, 1751-54; *Naamlijst* 1796, 62; *Catalogus Amst.*, 293.

Staal, Pieter, a Dutch Mennonite preacher, born at Gouda, who after studying at the Mennonite seminary in Amsterdam served as preacher in the Mennonite congregation of Burtscheid-Vaals and Maastricht 1747-68, living at Burtscheid (*q.v.*). In 1768 he moved to Maastricht (*q.v.*); this was such a disappointment for the members living in Burtscheid and Vaals, that they resolved to dismiss Staal and to call another preacher to serve only in Vaals and

Burtscheid. Staal now served the Maastricht congregation until 1787, in which year he retired because of bad health. The years of birth and death are not known. Apparently he was an uncle of Abraham Staal (*q.v.*). (*Inv. Arch. Amst.* II, Nos. 2077-81.)

vDZ.

Stäbler (bearers of the staff, i.e., instead of the sword), the name given to the completely nonresistant party of Anabaptists at Nikolsburg (*q.v.*), led by Jacob Widemann and Philip Jäger, in contradistinction to the party of Balthasar Hubmaier (*q.v.*) who defended the use of the sword under certain circumstances as well as the payment of war taxes. The Hubmaier party was called the "Schwerdtler" (*q.v.*). The Stäbler became the Hutterites, while the Hubmaier party died out by 1529. As late as 1576 Caspar Franck's *Catalogus Haereticorum* (Ingolstadt) lists the Stäbler as follows: "Stäbler teach that a Christian cannot with a clear conscience and according to the Word of God bear a sword or wage war, but shall let a staff suffice. They are usually reckoned among the Anabaptists, who arose in our time." This does not necessarily mean that they were still in existence in 1576. The Hutterite *Chronik* (Zieglschmid, 86) attributes the name Stäbler to Hans Spittelmaier's (*q.v.*) action.

H.S.B.

Stadler, Ulrich (d. 1540), a Hutterite leader, one of the strongest personalities of the first generation of Anabaptism, next to Riedemann the best theological thinker of the Moravian groups, a man of stern conceptions of true discipleship. He was born in Brixen (*q.v.*), Tirol, and became a mining official in Sterzing (*q.v.*). In the early 1520's he turned Lutheran, but soon joined the Anabaptists of Sterzing. When persecution became unbearable, he moved to Moravia (date not known). At first he became a member of the Austerlitz (*q.v.*) Bruderhof, which (when a group of Tiroleans left it for Auspitz) came under the leadership of Jakob Wideman (*q.v.*) in 1531. In 1535, when persecution also set in in Moravia, Stadler and his co-worker Leonhard Lochmaier (*q.v.*), together with a group of Austerlitz brethren, sought refuge in Poland (*q.v.*). Two Bruderhofs were established there under his supervision in 1535-37: in Ladomir in Podolia (south of Volhynia) near the Galician border and in Krasnikow (in the sources Krasnicktau) in Lodomeria, then a small independent principality in the Volhynian area. A letter "To the Authorities, in Poland" shows that he encountered much tribulation here too, in spite of the renowned tolerance of Polish nobles. In 1537, when persecution in Moravia had ceased, he and Lochmaier returned there with about one hundred persons, surviving many dangers on this return march. In Bucovic (*q.v.*), east of Austerlitz, he established a Bruderhof of his own. At that time Hans Amon (*q.v.*) was the Vorsteher of the Hutterites and their only leader; Stadler visited him and after long talks organically joined the Hutterite brotherhood. He then served as the Vorsteher of the Bucovic Hutterite settlement 1537-d.40.

Stadler's numerous writings can be found in many Hutterite codices both in Europe and in America.

Their numbering is difficult since pieces are put together or separated as the copyist felt moved. Here is the list as complete as possible:

(1) *Vom lebendigen Wort und geschriebenen, ein kurzer Unterschied und Bericht* (Lydia Müller, *Glaubenszeugnisse* I, 212-15). (2) *Eingang ins Christentum*, written in the form of an epistle: "Unsern herzlieben Brüdern und Geschwistrigeten, wo sie seind nach Gottes Willen, zu Handen" (*Glaubenszeugnisse* I, shortened, 227-28; Alker in *ARG* 1955, 233-36, complete). (3) *Was der Tauff sei . . . auch vom Bundt unsres Herrn Jesu Christo mit seiner Braut.* (4) *Gott der gnädige und langmütige Vater . . .* (only in the codex of Vienna, fol. 1-14).

Two church regulations: (5) *Eine liebe Unterrichtung Ulrich Stadlers der Sünden halber, auch des Ausschlusses und wie er darin steht, auch der Gemeinschaft der Güter halber* (*Glaubenszeugnisse* I, 215-27). (The last part of this piece, called "Von der Ordnung der Heiligen in ihrer Gemeinschaft und Leben mit den Gütern ihres Vaters allhie," was published twice: in *Glaubenszeugnisse* I, 222-27, and in Wolkan, *Die Huterer*, 153-60.) (6) *Was die Gemeinschaft Christi heisst in seinem Leib und Blut, eine Ordnung im Haus Gottes* (found only in manuscript copies in Canada). This piece contains also a section: *Vom ehelichen Stande—sechs Artikel* (to be published in *Glaubenszeugnisse* II).

(7) Four epistles "geschrieben von Ladomir in Podolien gen Krasnicktau auf Grenz Polen": (*a*) *An den Bruder Michael, von der Erbsünde, ein kurzer und doch gründlicher Bericht* (*Glaubenszeugnisse* I, 228-32). (*b*) *Ein ander Sendbrief über die Erbsünde, Red und Widerred* (*ibid.*, 233). (*c*) *Ein Sendbrief den Fremdlingen und Bilgramen geen Crasnicktau in Polln, am Lichtmess 1536* (February 2) (*ibid.*, 235 f.). (*d*) *Ein kurzer Mahnbrief* (found only in Canadian copies).

Stadler's Teachings: (A) *Theological Issues:* (1) *Original Sin.* Stadler is one of the very few Anabaptists ever to discuss this doctrine. He knows that the term itself cannot be found in the Scriptures. Although he strongly pleads for a life of purity ("Be pure as newborn babes," I Peter 2:2), he condemns those who think that life without sin is possible. Man, however, can fight the tendencies toward sin, if only he allows the spirit to dominate and to discipline the flesh. Tribulations are the disciple's way to this end. "Whatever does not come out of faith, is sin." (For further details see **Original Sin.**)

(2) *Inner and Outer Word.* Stadler might be called the foremost authority on this central issue of early Anabaptism, having written a special tract on this subject (item 1 above). One might call his position "Biblical Spiritualism," something distinctly different from both "pure" Spiritualism (*q.v.*) and later legalism. Also in his second tract above he stresses the primacy of the inwardness of Christ in the believer (Alker's text, 235). For a full exposition of Stadler's understanding of this point, see **Bible, Inner and Outer Word.**

(B) *The Church:* (1) *Community of Goods.* Stadler's tract "Von der Ordnung der Heiligen" (above 5) might be regarded as the classical expression of this idea of full Christian sharing in the brother-hood-church. It is an original contribution of high spirituality, quite independent of Jacob Hutter's teaching on that point. Stadler's main argument here is the idea of Gelassenheit (*q.v.*), a term more often used by him than by any other Anabaptist (except perhaps Haffner, *q.v.*). Of a true disciple of Christ he expects a "free, detached, resigned heart," which had died to the world and is dedicated alone to the Lord and the brethren (*Glaubenszeugnisse I*, 225 f.). That a life of that kind needs rigid disci-pline he stresses time and again, quite in accord with his idea of purity and fighting sin.

(2) The functions of the "Servant of the Lord" (*Diener des Herren*), Stadler's term for "Vorsteher" or "bishop." The classical exposition of his concept of such a leader and shepherd is found in his para-graph concerning excommunication (*Ausschluss*, in *Glaubenszeugnisse I*, 220-21): "The servant ought to have the power to punish all self-willed, disobedient members." One gets the strong impression that his conception of leadership approximates that of a prior or abbot of a medieval monastery. His ascetic ideals fairly correspond to such a life, with the ex-ception of

(3) *Married Life.* Few Anabaptists have dealt more often and more thoroughly with this theme than Stadler. In his tract *Vom ehelichen Stande*—six articles (to be published in *Glaubenszeugnisse II*) he begins with the motto: "Whoever lacks the gift of chastity [meaning the ability to stand life-long celibacy] ought to marry according to the will of God." Somewhere else he states that "God will wink at our marital work (*Gott aber sihet durch die finger umb unsers zerstörlichen leibs willen im eelichen werk*) . . . for the sake of the children, and He will not count it against us, if it is performed in the fear of the Lord" (*Glaubenszeugnisse I*, 228)— a typically puritanical thought. In two of his epistles he elaborates further on this topic, which certainly was a foremost one in a brotherhood-church as strict as the Hutterites (see **Marriage, Hutterite**).

(4) Finally the over-all ordering of the church, the church discipline or regulation, again a major concern for a leader of Stadler's stature. We know two such Gemeindeordnungen from his pen (items 5 and 6, the latter still unpublished), forerunners of Riedemann's much larger work of 1541 (see **Rechen-schaft**). No details can be offered here; that he sets an ascetic ideal as his model goes almost without saying. A man who wants to discipline his flesh has, of course, not too much appreciation of "Geschleck und gute bissen und trünklein" (delicacies and a good drink, *Glaubenszeugnisse I*, 219). But no work should ever be construed as proof of sinlessness. In all our doings we are always under temptation and must never slacken in our "good fight." If we con-tinue in it, however, we may eventually be saved from "eternal death."

No other Hutterite brother is known to have ex-pressed so radical a viewpoint as Stadler. The nu-merous copies, however, of his writings prove the high regard for teachings of this kind, which later Hutterites called "sharp preaching" (see **Sermons, Hutterite**).   R.F.

Zieglschmid, *Chronik*; 166-70; Lydia Müller, *Glau-benszeugnisse* I (Leipzig, 1938); Lydia Müller and Robert Friedmann, *Glaubenszeugnisse* II (Gütersloh, 1960); Hugo Alker, "Eine Täuferhandschrift des 16. Jahr-hunderts aus der Universitätsbibliothek in Wien," *Archiv Für Ref.-Geschichte* XLVI (1955) 228-43; the Stadler reprint, *ibid.* 233-36; R. Wolkan, *Die Huterer* (Vienna, 1918) 153-60; W. Wiswedel, "The Inner and the Outer Word, a Study in the Anabaptist Doctrine of Scripture," *MQR* XXVI (1952) 171-91, in particular 184-87; Stanislaus Kot, *Socinianism in Poland* (Boston, 1957) 12 f.

Stadnitski, a former Dutch Mennonite family, found from about 1700 particularly at Amsterdam, where they were members of the Lamist congregation, Jan Stadnitski being a deacon in 1734-40 and 1752-57. In the 18th century members of this family conducted a big business under different names (*Handelshuis Stadnitski en Zoon*; later, *Stadnitski en Cuperus*; about 1800, *Stadnitski en van Heukelom*), trading with Germany, Switzerland, Spain, and the Carib-bean islands and equipping ships. They were also bankers.   vDZ.

Stadskanaal, a village in the Dutch province of Gro-ningen, is the seat of a Mennonite congregation founded in 1848 with 13 members. At first it was combined with Veendam (*q.v.*), but by 1850 it was independent. In that year the present meetinghouse was built. An organ was installed in 1904. The baptized membership numbered 32 in 1852, 56 in 1861, 106 in 1900, and 82 in 1958. Its first preacher was L. F. Goteling Vinnis, serving here 1852-55; he was followed by A. S. Hoitsema 1856-98, J. Wuite 1898-1903, and J. J. Heep 1904-13. After a few years of vacancy, it was served in 1917-50 by the pastors of Assen (*q.v.*). Since 1952 Miss H. G. Zijlstra has been the pastor of Stadskanaal. There is a Sunday school for children and a ladies' circle. Some mem-bers of the Panman (*q.v.*) family living at Stads-kanaal have served the congregation well. (*Inv. Arch. Amst.* II, Nos. 2248-51; *DJ* 1850, 55, 60-62.)
                                vDZ.

Staffelstein, Georg von, an Anabaptist elder, active at Heerenhof near Schmalkalden, Germany, in 1530.

Stahelin, Rudolf (1811-1900), a Swiss Protestant his-torian, professor of theology at the University of Basel. His most important work, *Huldreich Zwingli* (1895 and 1897), presents the beginnings of the Anabaptist movement in Zürich and in Switzerland; it is a very valuable book. Other works of particular interest to Mennonites are *Die ersten Märtyrer des evangelischen Glaubens in der Schweiz* (1883), his treatise on *Vadian* in *Beiträge zur vaterländischen Geschichte* (Basel, 1882), *Das theologische Lebens-werk Johann Oekolampads* (Leipzig, 1939), and *Briefe und Akten zum Leben Oekolampads* I and II (Leipzig, 1927-34).   E.T.

Stahl, a Hutterite family name, occurring the first time in 1663, when Johannes Stahl was taken away as a prisoner from Zobelhof, Hungary, by attacking Turks and Tatars; he never returned to the broth-erhood. Since then this name has always been found among the Hutterian Brethren, in Hungary, Tran-sylvania, Rumania, and Russia, from where this family immigrated to America with the Hutterian

Brethren in 1874, and is also found on the Bruderhofs in South Dakota, Montana, Manitoba, and Alberta. D.D.

Stahl, Michael, chosen to the Hutterian Brethren ministry May 8 and confirmed June 22, 1865, in Russia. He was chosen elder on Oct. 21, 1867, and confirmed on the following day by Peter Wedel, an elder from Alexanderwohl. He died Dec. 29, 1900, in the Tschetter Bruderhof in South Dakota, having served in the ministry thirty-five years. D.D.

Stahl Mennonite Church (MC), located 6 miles south of Johnstown, Pa., a member of the Allegheny Conference, had its first meetinghouse erected in 1882, called "Stahl" because the land was donated by John Stahl. Its first minister, Levi A. Blough, was ordained in 1890. The point at which it can be considered a separately organized congregation is difficult to determine. The conference minutes speak of a "Johnstown congregation" as late as 1896, although there were at that time four meetinghouses (Blough-1836, Weaver-1855, Thomas-1874, and Stahl-1882), and not until 1900 was mention made of 5 "congregations" or meetinghouses in the Johnstown district (Elton was added in 1899), with a total membership of 487. The first *Mennonite Yearbook and Directory* (1905) lists Stahl with 176 members and S. G. Shetler (ord. 1897) and S. D. Yoder as ministers. Down to c1940 all the congregations of the Johnstown district had one bishop. Stahl was S. G. Shetler's home congregation, and it was in its meetinghouse that he established (1922) and for many years (1925-35) served as principal of the Johnstown Bible School. Near the church the Johnstown Mennonite School was established in 1944, offering elementary and high-school work. In 1957 the Stahl congregation had a membership of 154, with Sanford G. Shetler as pastor and bishop (ord. 1952). H.S.B.

Ammon Kaufman, "Stahl Mennonite Church," *Southwestern Pennsylvania Conference News* VI (January 1948) 3.

Stähli (Stahly), a Mennonite family of Swiss descent. Heini Stähli, of Seehof, then belonging to the Catholic bishopric of Basel, Switzerland, was imprisoned in 1622 because of his Mennonite convictions. After 1670 some Stählis moved to the Palatinate, Germany, and among the Swiss emigrants moving to the Netherlands in 1711 there was a Jacob Stähly (b. c1676), of Hilterfingen in the area of Thun. His son Jacob Stähly was an elder of the Swiss congregation at Kampen (*q.v.*), Holland, in 1736-57. The Stählis usually belonged to the Amish branch. Apparently the first of this family to emigrate to America were the brothers Johann and Jakob Stähli, of the Palatinate, who went to Ohio in 1829, and ten years later to Elkhart, Ind. vDZ.

D. L. Gratz, *Bernese Anabaptists* (Scottdale, 1953); Müller, *Berner Täufer,* 312.

Stahlville Hutterian Bruderhof, near Rockyford, Alberta, was founded in 1918 by the brotherhood of Lewistown, Mont. Their preachers in 1947 were Johann Stahl, chosen in Montana in 1917 and confirmed in Canada in 1924, David Waldner, chosen in 1933 and confirmed in 1938, and Elias Stahl, chosen in 1944. In 1950 this Bruderhof, belonging to the Dariusleut (*q.v.*), numbered 75 baptized members. D.D.

Stalinabad: see Soviet Central Asia.

Stamperius, Abraham, a Reformed pastor of Sommelsdijk, Dutch province of South Holland, engaged in a public debate with the Mennonite elder François de Knuyt (*q.v.*) in 1617 concerning the Scripturalness of infant baptism. Stamperius published an account of this dispute entitled *Waerachtigh Verhael van't Gespreck ghehouden tot Somelsdijck* .... De Knuyt answered with a refutation *Verantwoordinghe* (1617). (Blaupot t. C., *Holland* I, 194 f.; *DB* 1897, 106; 1908, 106.) vDZ.

Stand-Off Colony, near Macleod in southern Alberta, a Bruderhof of the Hutterite kinship group known as Dariusleut (*q.v.*), was founded in 1918 as the first Hutterite colony in Alberta and in Canada, the land having been bought on May 12, 1918. It was a transfer of the Spink County (S.D.) Bruderhof which had been founded in 1905 from the Wolf Creek (S.D.) Bruderhof. Its founder was the noted Elder Elias Walter, Jr. (*q.v.*), who had been chosen elder (and thus head of the Dariusleut) in 1903 at Wolf Creek Bruderhof, a post which he held till his death on Jan. 1, 1938. Walter's unusual historical sense and great energy led him to edit or sponsor several publications, a number of which after 1923 bore the publication place "Stand-Off Colony bei Macleod Alberta." The first to carry this legend was Rudolf Wolkan's edition of the *Geschicht-Buch,* printed at Vienna in 1923. The first edition of the small hymnal (*Gesangbüchlein*) compiled by Walter was published at Scottdale, Pa., but the second (1930) was published at Stand-Off Colony. Stand-Off Colony operated a bookbindery on behalf of all the colonies, hence was a logical place of publication in addition to the fact that it was the residence of the head of the Dariusleut. It was to the Stand-Off Colony also that Eberhard Arnold, the founder of the New Hutterites (Society of Brethren), came from the Rhönbruderhof in Germany in 1930 to be ordained as a Hutterite minister by Elias Walter. Two daughter colonies have been established by Stand-Off, Granum (Alberta) in 1929, and Riverside (Alberta) in 1939. Elias Walter, Jr., was elected elder of the Dariusleut at Stand-Off in 1928, which office he filled until his death there in 1938. His son Jacob Walter, who follows in his grandfather's steps in historical interest, was elected preacher in 1939 and has since then been the leader of the Bruderhof. In 1958 the population was 88. H.S.B.

Staneke, Johannes Pieter (c1747-Jan. 17, 1808), the son of Reformed parents, reared in the Amsterdam city orphanage, joined the Amsterdam Zonist (*q.v.*) congregation and served as a (untrained) preacher at Middelie 1768-77, Den Burg 1777-90, and Enkhuizen 1790-1806. Descendants of his are still found in the Mennonite Church of Rotterdam. (*Naamlijst* 1808, 67 f.) vDZ.

Stanislaus II, August, the last king of Poland (1764-95), on Dec. 20, 1764, confirmed all former privileges (*q.v.*) to the Mennonites of Elbing, Marienburg, Bärwalde, and Tiegenhof.

W. Mannhardt, *Die Wehrfreiheit der Altpreussischen Mennoniten* (Marienburg, 1863) 91; *ML* IV.

Stanley Old Order Mennonite Church in Huron County, Ont. This area borders the east shore of Lake Huron directly north of Hay Township and Zurich. The Steckle families and a few others living in this area held to the Old Order group following the division of 1889 in Ontario. Worship has been held in the homes. Visiting ministers from Waterloo County have served the worshipers. In 1955 two families remained, one with the Markham Wisler group, the other with the Waterloo Woolwich Old Order congregation. J.C.F.

Stapel, Claes, a Remonstrant (*q.v.*) public notary at Hoorn, Holland, and leader of the "college" (see **Collegiants**) in his home town, compiled a hymnal, *Lusthof der Zielen* (Pleasure Garden of the Soul), of which there were at least seven editions: 1st, Alkmaar 1681; 2d, Harlingen 1686, supplemented by an "Achterhofje" (i.e., Back Garden); 3d, enlarged, Rotterdam 1692; 4th, enlarged, Rotterdam 1697; 5th, Amsterdam 1713; 6th, Amsterdam 1726; 7th, Amsterdam 1743. All editions but one are without notes. It contains 300 hymns in its first edition; the supplement has 80; the 7th edition numbers 461 hymns. The hymns are partly borrowed from older songbooks, but there are also a large number of hymns composed by contemporaries of the editor—12 by Stapel himself, others by Jan Luyken (*q.v.*), Hugo de Groot, Jodocus van Lodensteyn (*q.v.*), and many well-known Collegiants, e.g., Adam Boreel, Barend Joosten Stol, Johannes Bredenburg, and Frans Kuyper. Mennonite authors of hymns found in this hymnal are Menno Simons, the martyr Joos de Tollenaer, Claes Claesz, T. J. van Braght, Pieter Pietersz, Galenus Abrahamsz, and others.

The *Lusthof der Zielen* was undoubtedly the most popular of the numerous Dutch hymnbooks. It was used not only in the Collegiant meetings, but also in many Mennonite congregations; it was used at Grouw, Friesland, until the early 19th century. Marten Schagen listed it among the Mennonite books, but this is wrong. The later Dutch Mennonite hymnals, including the present *Doopsgezinde Bundel* (*q.v.*), contain hymns borrowed from Stapel's *Lusthof.*

In 1672 Stapel wrote a booklet in which he defended the necessity of Christian baptism against the Socinian Frans (de) Kuyper. Though not a Mennonite, Stapel was on friendly terms with many well-known Mennonites of his time. In a letter to him, *Een brief van Dr Galenus Abrahamsz, seer nut en stichtelijck in dese tijdt om gelesen en betracht te werden* (Alkmaar, 1677), Galenus (*q.v.*) Abrahamsz states that salvation rests entirely on the true following of Christ, which was also Stapel's main idea.

H. W. Meihuizen is of the opinion that Stapel may have been the author of the book *Klaar Vertoog* (n.p., 1689), which defended Foecke Floris (*q.v.*)

against the indictments of F. Elgersma, and which was formerly generally ascribed to Galenus Abrahamsz.

Stapel, who always stressed the great importance of Christian morals, particularly of sobriety and of mercy, left behind a fine memorial by founding the Stapelshofje (home for aged women) at Hoorn, in which act of charity he was supported by two other Collegiants, one Mennonite and one Reformed.

vdZ.

J. C. van Slee, *De Rijnsburger Collegianten* (Haarlem, 1895) 191 f., 193, 368; H. W. Meihuizen, *Galenus Abrahamsz* (Haarlem, 1954) 121 f., 162; *DB* 1900, 90-93, 94; Blaupot t. C., *Holland* II, 213; M. Schagen, *Naamlijst der Doopsgezinde Schrijveren* (Amsterdam, 1745) 99.

Stapper, Pieter Jansz (d. 1693), was an elder of the Waterlander congregation of Wormer-Jisp, Dutch province of North Holland. Like many Waterlander ministers in North Holland, Stapper was averse to the progressive Collegiant (*q.v.*) ideas which were at this time very influential among the Dutch Mennonites, affecting both their way of thinking and their practice. He induced his own congregation and some others to join the conservative Zonists (*q.v.*). He tried—and not in vain—to maintain the authority of the old Mennonite confessions of faith in the Waterlander congregations, in this point cooperating with Engel Arents van Dooregeest (*q.v.*), an influential Waterlander leader. He and van Dooregeest, Jacob Jansz Mol (*q.v.*), and others settled a quarrel which had arisen in the Wormerveer Waterlander congregation concerning the authority of the confessions.

Stapper is particularly known for his initiative in drawing up a schedule according to which Waterlander preachers were to conduct regular services in the many vacant Waterlander pulpits. (*Inv. Arch. Amst.* I, Nos. 900-5; *DB* 1872, 55, 67 f.) vdZ.

Staprade (Stapraet), **Hermann,** a "Wassenberg Predikant," born at Mörs, Lower Rhine, Germany, where he was very likely a priest. In 1533 he reached Münster, where he was connected with the St. Lambert Church and joined Henrik Rol and Bernhard Rothmann (*q.v.*). He promoted the Reformation and was one of the first to attack infant baptism, and was criticized for this by the city of Münster. In response to a statement from Marburg in this matter he and his associates gave in writing their reasons for denouncing infant baptism. On Sept. 7, 1533, Staprade refused to baptize children. It is likely that he had to leave the city because of this. However, on Jan. 5, 1534, he was in Münster and was baptized by the Anabaptist leaders. Little is known about his later fate. C.K.

C. A. Cornelius, *Geschichte des Münsterischen Aufruhrs* II (Leipzig, 1860) 345 ff.; *ML* IV.

Star, The, is the official publication of the Students Association of Freeman Junior College, Freeman, S.D. The first issue appeared on Nov. 15, 1919, and with the exception of 1931-34, it has been published every third week of the school year since then.

J.D.U.

Starck, Johann August (1741-1816), chaplain at the court in Darmstadt, Germany, author of the *Geschichte der Taufe und Taufgesinnten* (Leipzig,

1789). Starck wrote his book in 1785 before being attacked by the rationalists as a secret Catholic and Jesuit, but points out that the book itself refutes such an aspersion because it claims to show that the Anabaptists (terrible "Schwärmer") arose because of Catholic errors and abuses.

The contents of the 438 pages fall into four parts: (1) A history of the concepts of baptism from the New Testament to the Reformation, pp. 1-131. (2) A history of the Anabaptists to Münster, pp.132-258, which devotes 23 pages to Müntzer, the Zwickau prophets, and Carlstadt, and claims that Müntzer, transmitted Anabaptist ideas to Hubmaier, Manz, Grebel, and Reublin at Waldshut on his personal visit there, and then treats the Peasants' War. The history of Anabaptism in Switzerland occupies pp. 167-219, followed by the Münsterite story on pp. 219-58. (3) Anabaptism after Münster, pp. 259-391. This last section includes the English Baptists, and the Dutch Remonstrants and Collegiants. (4) A final "Beschluss," pp. 392-438, gives a summary of Anabaptist principles, and a complete(?) list of all Mennonite congregations in Europe and Pennsylvania.

The sources upon which Starck chiefly depends are Bullinger's writings, Ottius' *Annales*, Füssli's *Beyträge*, Meshovius' *Historia*, Jehring's *Historie*, and Arnold's *Kirchen- und Ketzerhistorie*. Starck's attitude is fairer than most other writers on the subject, although he is still quite confused on various points.   H.S.B.

Starewitz (now Steurovice), a village near Auspitz (*q.v.*) in Moravia (*q.v.*). Here the Anabaptists who emigrated from Austerlitz (*q.v.*) with Wilhelm Reublin (*q.v.*) founded a Bruderhof in 1531 on land granted them by Johana of Boscovice. In it lived about fifty members, most of them sick or children.

Stark County (Ohio) Amish Settlement. At least four branches of the Amish Mennonites are found in Stark County—the Old Order Amish, consisting of three districts, with 215 members, the King group (now a district of the Old Order Amish) with 118, the Beachy congregation with 132, the Maple Grove Conservative Mennonite congregation with 126, and the Roman Miller group with some 200 members. The settlement is located in the northwest corner of Stark County and lies mostly within Lake Township, near Hartville. The first Amish settlers came to Stark County in 1905 from Geauga County. They were the families of Joseph D. Coblentz, their first minister, David C. Troyer, and John J. Stutzman. They at once organized a congregation. Daniel J. F. Miller was ordained minister in 1909, joined the Zook group in 1912, then returned to the Old Order, and was installed as bishop in 1918. David Schlabach, from Howard County, Ind., served as bishop of the South District 1918-28, and then returned to Indiana. Seth H. Byler (ord. bishop in 1931) and Henry Sommers have charge of the King group, Jonas J. Coblentz (ord. bishop in 1937) serves the South District, Noah J. Coblentz (ord. 1941) the East District, and Wallace Byler the West District.

The King Amish group was formed in 1907 as an affiliate of the Zook branch of the Amish, found in Mifflin County and in Ontario, by settlers from Lawrence County, Pa., Joshua King being their minister. In 1912 the preachers Daniel J. F. Miller and Phineas V. Yoder led a schism from the O.O.A. and with the assistance of Bishop John P. Zook of Mifflin County organized a new congregation. The withdrawal was due largely to differences on the application of the ban to members who joined other Mennonite branches. After six years, however, Phineas Yoder joined the King group and later the Conservative group. Joshua King (d. 1937), the first minister and organizer of the King church, was ordained bishop in 1909.

The Pleasant View Beachy congregation was formed in 1947. Their ministers in 1957 were Alvin Wittmer, Ely Beachy, and Bishop Samuel Ott. The Maple Grove Conservative Mennonite Church was organized in 1922. In 1957 Roman H. Miller (ordained minister in 1935 and bishop in 1939) withdrew with his followers from the Conservative Conference to start a new unaffiliated congregation at Bethesda, about a mile west of Maple Grove. Until then all of the Amish groups had co-operated in the Lake Center Christian Day School, built in 1947, having an attendance of 129 in grades 1-10 in 1956. Since Miller's new start his group has established a small congregation at New Franklin east of Canton on the Columbiana County border and a mission in Canton.   N.A.K.

Stark (N.D.) Mennonite Brethren Church was a substation of the McClusky M.B. Church, located 28 miles southeast of it. It was organized under the leadership of a deacon, Jacob Sattler. In 1916 a church was built and dedicated. In 1924 it still had 16 members, but when some of these moved away, the meetings were discontinued and the meetinghouse was moved to Goodrich; here the meetings continued for some time, but then the building was sold, and the members joined the McClusky church.   M.A.K.

Starter, Jan Jansz (1594-1626), was born in Amsterdam of English Brownist (*q.v.*) parents. He joined the Waterlander Mennonites, was a bookseller at Leeuwarden in Friesland in 1614-20, back in Amsterdam in 1621, and soon after accepted an administrative office in the army of Ernst von Mansfeld. During a military campaign he met his early death near the Hungarian border in September 1626. Starter was an artist, poet, and engraver. His best-known work is *Friesche Lusthof*, a volume of poems published at Amsterdam in 1621 (reprints 1622, 1624-25, 1627). Concerning his connections with the Mennonite Church there is not much information. They probably were rather loose. Starter's *Menniste Vryage* (Mennonite Courtship) satirizes the "fijne" Mennonites.   vDZ.

G. Kalff, *Gesch. der Nederl. Letterkunde* IV (Groningen, 1909) 172-82; *Algemeen Doopsgez. Weekblad* XII (1957-58), No. 45.

State, Anabaptist-Mennonite Attitude Toward. While it has long been known that the Anabaptists rejected participation in the magistracy, i.e., state office-holding, a comprehensive and systematic analysis of the Anabaptist basic attitude toward the state based upon the sources has been lacking. The resulting unclear and partial understandings have resulted in considerable confusion which has often been compounded by the attempt to include the revolutionary Anabaptists such as the Münsterites and Batenburgers in the general picture and the frequent assumption that the Anabaptist position toward the state was an irresponsible one, the incidental by-product of a Biblical naivete unaware of the complexities of a social order. Recent research, particularly the doctoral dissertation of Hans Hillerbrand, has shown on the contrary that the Anabaptists had a coherent and consistent position toward the state which was deliberately taken and was based upon a thorough, systematic, and basically consistent attitude toward the Scriptures. In short the Anabaptists had a sound theology of the state and a consistent view of the Christians' attitude toward and responsibility to the state based upon a consistent view of the church and the world.

Theology of the State. The beginning of all Anabaptist consideration of the state is the affirmation of its divine origin, an affirmation made specifically, emphatically, and repeatedly. This is true of all governments, whether good or bad. "Even Nero," says H. Schnell, ". . . and Pharaoh . . . and Pilate . . . were servants of God." Ambrosius Spittelmaier said in 1527, "Every government that has existed since the time of Adam and exists today has been instituted by God." This position is grounded in direct Scripture quotations, especially Romans 13. The necessity for the state is human sin, but the ordination of the state expresses both God's wrath against sin and His gracious love. In such a theology of the state the Anabaptists are essentially one with the Reformers. Mennonites have followed their Anabaptist forebears in this position and have always held it.

A major consequence of such an understanding of the nature of the state is that rebellion against the state is impossible for the Christian regardless of how evil it may be in performance. The notion of revolution was of necessity utterly foreign to the Anabaptist mind in general, granting of course the reality of the exceptions in the case of the revolutionary type. Any "left-wing" element in the Reformation which advocated or practiced overthrow of the state at any time and place must therefore be considered non-Anabaptist or deviationist in central character, regardless of any practice of adult baptism or any genetic connection with original peaceful Anabaptism. Among some early Dutch Anabaptists eschatological views and the expectation of the coming of the day of the Lord in the very near future made them consider the state a negligible matter. But this was a question of practical attitude, not of principle.

But the Anabaptist theology of the state went further in concretely defining the tasks of the state and the limitations placed upon it by the divine governance. Its essential function is to maintain order and thus make possible a decent human society. Thus the work of government in punishing the evildoer and protecting the good is proper, good, and necessary, and shows "God's grace and love toward man" (*Aufdeckung*, Bii b). According to a Hessian Anabaptist Confession of 1571, the office and power of the state were ordained for the good of mankind. The Schleitheim Confession of 1527 is very pointed in its sixth article, "On the Sword." "The sword is ordained of God outside the perfection of Christ. It punishes and puts to death the wicked, and guards and protects the good." Menno Simons (Krahn, 165 f.) clearly held that the state is ordained of God with its task assigned by God. This task he understood to be "to punish the evil, to protect the good, to administer a righteous justice, to care for the widows, the orphans, and the poor, and to provide a police force that is not against God and His Word." The government must exercise its office in "pure fear of God . . . and Christian moderation . . . with honorable means . . . without tyranny and blood-shedding." Menno goes so far as to consider capital punishment not allowable.

But the Anabaptists placed a major limitation on the authority of the state: it had no right or jurisdiction to function in the spiritual realm; a government attempting to rule the hearts of men was overstepping its functions and tasks. Several times the martyrs, charged with transgressing the imperial mandates, admitted the charge, but added that the emperor had no right to make such a mandate. Christ alone is the Lord of conscience. Here the Anabaptists and the Reformers parted. For the latter the state was to be the *Defensor fidei*, with the power and duty to maintain religious and ecclesiastical uniformity and suppress dissent. The Anabaptists broke completely with the state-church system with its *corpus christianum*, which the Reformers retained. Hence the Anabaptist concept of religious liberty and religious pluralism, advanced far beyond its time, was in direct clash with both the Catholic and the Protestant concept. It is true that commonly the Reformers' rejection of the Anabaptist position was attached to the concept that religious pluralism would lead to social disorder and ultimate chaos, and that therefore the idea of religious freedom and independence of the church from the state was against God and man, was both blasphemous and seditious. But as early as 1524 the Zürich Anabaptists had replied to Zwingli's charge that rejection of infant baptism would lead to the breakdown of order in society (*Wer ursach gebe zu Aufruhr*) by challenging this fear as groundless (*Protestation*, by Felix Manz)—nothing of the like would happen.

A major consequence of the Anabaptists' positive acceptance of the state as a divine institution with a divinely assigned task to perform was the doctrine of full obedience to the state, except in the spiritual realm. Here obedience is not required, since when the state enters this realm it exceeds the divinely set bounds of its authority. But even here, only passive resistance and suffering are allowed, no active rebellion. That in spite of the repeated affirmations of the Anabaptists of their readiness to obey and promise never to resist, the charge of sedition and rebellion was widespread and persistent even before Münster (1535) is a mystery. That the impact of the latter and the propaganda made of it by the enemies of the Anabaptists would naturally tend to support and intensify the charge is clear. But the coolheaded and objective Sebastian Franck called this fear completely groundless (*Chronica,* 153, 449), saying, "Even if I were the pope, emperor, or Turk, I would have less fear of a rebellion from these people than from any other." In no respect then were the Anabaptists negative toward the state.

In spite of their positive evaluation of the state and their position of obedience toward it, however, the Anabaptists did reject completely all participation in government or holding of government office.

The Anabaptists, as Hillerbrand has shown, had a reasoned and consistent basis for their rejection, and gave four major reasons for their rejection of office holding.

(1) Scripture gives no authorization for it and Scripture was the supreme authority for the Anabaptists. No Christian may use the sword to punish or to kill, "for he has no Scripture for it," as Felix Manz said in 1525.

(2) Christ's example is against taking part in government. "If the governmental authorities wanted to be Christians," says one Anabaptist, "they would actually need to manifest and maintain the nature and manner of the life of Christ." Another says, "Christ Himself says in John 15, If they persecute me they will also persecute you—that is an open testimony that you will not find any government officers among the Christians." A frequently cited example was that Jesus refused to be a judge over the two brothers who had a dispute over their inheritance, hence Christians cannot be judge. Still more frequently cited, Jesus refused to let the people make Him king; He rather fled from them. So we should do likewise and follow Him, says the Schleitheim Confession of 1527. A speaker at the Zofingen debate of 1531 said, "Jesus gave us an example as is stated in I Peter 2, that we should follow His footsteps under the cross." Repeatedly Anabaptist writers refer to the suffering of Christ, whose nature is so different from that of the dominating and proud (*prunkvoll*) authorities. The Schleitheim Confession's article on the sword was frequently quoted by later Anabaptists in rejection of participation in the magistracy.

(3) Indirect teachings against "lording it" over others are given as a ground for rejection of governmental office. The most commonly quoted teaching of Jesus, the locus classicus, is Matt. 20:25-27. "Ye know that the princes of the Gentiles exercise dominion over them, and they that are great exercise authority upon them. But it shall not be so among you; but whosoever will be great among you, let him be your minister; and whosoever will be chief among you, let him be your servant." This passage was taken to prove that there are two diametrically opposed principles in the world which can be stated thus: government rule means might and lordship; to be a Christian means to serve, suffer, and be persecuted. This is a difference that cannot be bridged. When the opponents produced the case of Cornelius as an illustration of a government officer who became a Christian and thus justified Christians holding office, the Anabaptists countered that of course Cornelius was converted to

Christ and thus received new ethical principles for his life and could not have continued as a government officer.

Two other Anabaptist arguments against participation in government fall under the heading of the teaching of Jesus. One was that the government is essentially the bearer of revenge and the pursuit and punishment of the evildoer, whereas the message of Jesus stands diametrically opposed to this: the Christian is not to resist evil or take revenge. In the kingdom of Christ all revenge is forbidden. The second is the Lord's Prayer which indicates that God will forgive us only as we forgive our enemies. If we use revenge, the sword, and prison, what else can we expect from God? If the government officers really love and forgive transgressors, how then can they execute them?

(4) A final basic Anabaptist argument against participation in government is that of the necessary radical separation of the church of Christ from the world. Did not Paul say, "For what have I to do to judge them also that are without" (I Cor. 5:12)? This verse was used to justify the concept that the Christian has no responsibility for maintaining law and order in the world. The world is the "civitas Diaboli"; those who belong to the church of Christ and are concerned to follow Christ dare not have anything to do with it, although of course the Great Commission will lead them out into the world to proclaim the message of Christ. "World" and "kingdom of Christ" are two completely separate realities for the Anabaptist. He was not to be concerned with what goes on in the world.

To the charge of the Reformers that such a denial of responsibility for the social order could mean a disruption of the functions of government and ultimately lead to chaos, the Anabaptists answered that there would always be sufficient available persons to fill the governmental offices. In any case, the state's ministry at this point is not necessary for the Christian, and the Christian does not need to render to the state the oath, nor military service, nor war taxes. The church will discipline its own members for their misdeeds, using only the ban. Of course gross sins are rightly punishable by the state, even if the criminals have been church members.

To the protest of the opponents that the Old Testament saints occupied government offices, that David, for instance, was a king, the Anabaptist answer was simple, the New Testament has replaced the Old. Christ is now the norm, not the Old Testament.

The Anabaptist political ethic with its dualism of holding that God ordained the state with its sword, yet claiming that the state's operation involved non-Christian principles, remained finally unresolved in Anabaptist thinking. The state operates on principles of its own, ordained by God, which parallel the principles of Christ's kingdom, and are not in accord with it. But what of that? Paul Glock's answer to the problem was simply, "Who will quarrel with God's ordination?"

Thus we see that the early Anabaptists faced squarely the issues involved in participation in government, that they took deliberate conclusions based upon Biblical foundations, and that they were consistent in their position. They did not simply yield to the force of circumstances or develop an *ex post facto* justification for what they could not do anyway.

The principle of nonparticipation in government having been established historically at the beginning of the Anabaptist movement, it is necessary to note the record of actual participation in the functions of government (the magistracy) in legislative, executive, or judicial functions, or in subsidiary office holding of a political nature, excluding the welfare functions. In this review we shall omit the revolutionary Anabaptists of Münster who took over the city government in 1534 and established an Old Testament theocracy which was suppressed by military force a year later.

The Anabaptists universally rejected participation in government with one exception. This was the large congregation at Nikolsburg in Moravia, founded by Balthasar Hubmaier in July 1526 and led by him until his arrest and imprisonment at the end of 1527. Hubmaier did not teach nonresistance but found a place for the sword in the hands of the Christian in support of the government; hence his followers were called "Schwerdtler." The local ruler, Lord Leonhard von Liechtenstein, was baptized in 1527 and became a member of Hubmaier's congregation without surrendering his governmental authority. He even used his authority to expel the nonresistant Anabaptist part of the congregation from Nikolsburg in 1528, most of whom later became known as the Hutterites. The Hubmaier congregation was short-lived; no trace of it is found after 1529. The expelled nonresistant part, however, survived in two major groups in Moravia, the Swiss Brethren (found as late as 1615 in this area) and the Hutterites, who continued in Moravia until expelled in 1622.

The first Anabaptists-Mennonites to open the door to participation in government were the Waterlanders, the more open-minded party in Holland. They permitted their members as early as 1570 to hold government offices (van der Zijpp, *Doopsgezinden,* 148), and after that time many of them held such offices, but this was always limited to minor local offices, not involving capital punishment. Often they were semiofficials such as inspectors of the market or trustees of a polder. Only from the early 18th century when the conservative Dutch Mennonites like the Old Frisians still refused to accept any state office did some Waterlanders and progressive Lamists occasionally serve as sheriff or alderman, but only in small towns and in the country where the population was so predominantly Mennonite that scarcely any Reformed could be found to serve in such places. It was not only the duty but also the privilege of the Reformed to govern the country, both in the top offices and in the lower magistracy, and this prerogative was maintained long after the Dutch nation had successfully ended a bitter war with the Spanish for independence. Not until 1795 when complete freedom of religion was achieved in Holland did Mennonites occupy high governmental positions, but after this they entered every level of state offices except that of prime minister, often serving with distinction. Numerous

Dutch Mennonites have entered politics and several have served as cabinet ministers. Among them was C. Lely, who laid the plans for the reclamation of the Zuiderzee. Albertus van Delden of Deventer served for 40 years (1858-98) in governmental functions, both in legislative and executive posts, for a time as minister of finance. The minister of reconstruction after World War II was a Mennonite. Another was minister of the navy in the early 20th century. Several Mennonites held the very high post of governor of the Dutch East Indies. There have been numerous Mennonite burgomasters, including the largest cities of Holland such as Amsterdam, The Hague, and Haarlem. Mennonites have also served frequently as judges of the high courts. There have been Mennonite generals in the army. It is almost two hundred years since any but a small minority of Dutch Mennonites have been opposed to full participation in the life of the state. From 1796 on, the Mennonites used their right of voting, and there never was any hesitation or even religious question about voting, as is sometimes still the case among American Mennonites.

The German Mennonites, both North and South, have followed a pattern similar to that of the Dutch Mennonites, only several decades later. In one case, the city of Friedrichstadt in Holstein, the change came even earlier. This was the earliest city in Europe to give complete toleration to Mennonites. Here from 1711 to 1786 one of the two burgomasters was continuously a Mennonite. In the 19th century Mennonite Jan Jelle Schuett served a half century as burgomaster, receiving knighthood in 1856 from the King of Denmark for his extraordinarily long and meritorious service.

The Mennonite congregations of Crefeld and Emden each furnished a member of the famous first all-German Parliament of 1848 at Frankfurt. One was Hermann von Beckerath of Crefeld, who served a short while as minister of finance in the Prussian cabinet, but retired because of his difference with the politics of the king. He was leader of the Liberal Party in the Prussian parliament 1850-53. The other member of the Frankfurt parliament was Isaac Brons, a deacon of the Emden congregation, who incidentally was an enthusiastic promoter of what is known as Great Germany and one of the founders of the East Frisian Navy League in 1862.

In South Germany it was largely the Palatine Mennonites who entered politics. Peter Eymann, who had been burgomaster of Frankenstein for some years, was elected to the Bavarian parliament in 1848. Much later Heinrich Stauffer, who had been serving in several local government posts, was elected to the German national parliament (Reichstag) in 1903. Jakob Finger, a lifelong member of the Monsheim congregation in Rheinhessen, was an outstanding political leader in Hesse, serving as minister of state for 14 years, 1884-98. He was jokingly referred to as "the little finger by which the Grand Duke of Hesse ruled" his state. The last president of the Berlin Mennonite Church before World War II, a van Dühren, was a judge of the Berlin Supreme Court.

In Russia, apart from the local civil autonomy by which the Mennonite colonies governed themselves under the Fürsorgekomitee at Odessa it should be reported that the noted Johann Cornies (d. 1848), an outstanding agricultural and educational leader in the Molotschna Mennonite settlement, actually was given considerable authority by the Russian governor, which he used effectively, sometimes in almost dictatorial fashion. No Russian representative national parliament was set up until 1905. Very early, however, two Mennonites were elected to serve in that parliament. Abraham Bergmann served in the third and fifth Duma, and Peter Schroeder served in the fourth Duma. When the constitutional assembly was called in 1917 under the Kerensky regime, the Mennonites undertook vigorous organization and joined with other German colonists in a strong but vain attempt to elect a representative. B. H. Unruh, writing in the *Mennonitisches Lexikon* in 1921-22, advocated regular political action by Mennonites working through a political party: "The Mennonites in Russia, remaining true to the principles of their forefathers in this point, will never be in politics for politics' sake, but the life needs of the Mennonite society in Russia and the public welfare in the largest sense, will nevertheless lead them to a moderate political action program." In Siberia the Slavgorod Mennonites sent Franz F. Froese as their representative to the Siberian Duma following the Revolution of 1917, and in the second Siberian Duma they had four representatives—F. F. Froese, Johann Penner, Peter Boldt, and Heinrich Boldt. They also joined the movement to establish an independent German state within an autonomous Siberia.

In Switzerland there was no participation in government until the 20th century. An outstanding case was Elder Samuel Nussbaumer of Basel (d. 1944), long-time president of the Swiss Mennonite Conference, who served many years in the legislature of the half-canton of Baselland.

Thus in the 19th and 20th centuries in Europe the old Anabaptist rejection of participation in the magistracy had completely disappeared among the Mennonites everywhere. Along with the abandonment of the ancient position, the process of assimilation into the national culture meant also the gradual abandonment of nonresistance everywhere except in Russia (and in part in Switzerland).

The history of the attitude and practice of the American Mennonites on participation in government is substantially different from the record in Europe.

The Mennonite immigrants to America came in successive waves from Switzerland-South Germany 1707-56 to Pennsylvania, Amish from Alsace Lorraine, Hesse, and Bavaria 1815-60 to the central states and Ontario, Mennonites from Switzerland and South Germany 1815-60 to the same area, Mennonites from Russia to the western prairie states and provinces 1874-80, and Mennonites from Russia to Canada 1922-25, 1930-31, 1948-53. These groups brought with them attitudes on participation in government reflecting their state of mind and practice in Europe at the time, and naturally perpetuated them in the groups which they constituted in America. The first two immigrant groups later constituted the Mennonite Church (MC), the

Amish, and related conservative groups. Here the attitude of complete nonparticipation was established. It has been fixed in the legislation of the conferences and has been maintained uniformly. The only exceptions have been a few cases of participation in local government. For instance, T. M. Erb, a bishop at Hesston, Kan., and long business manager of Hesston College, served on the Hesston town council, and the mayor of Souderton, Pa., was a lay member of a local Mennonite congregation a generation ago. There have no doubt been other cases of participation in town councils. Many Mennonites and Amish have served on local elected school boards, and some have served as township trustees.

In all the other Mennonite groups established in America, the General Conference, the Mennonite Brethren, etc., there has seemingly never been any tradition or regulation forbidding participation in governmental functions at any level, except participation in the police function. Even here there were in the 20th century two cases where General Conference Mennonites served as sheriff, one a member of the congregation at Deep Run, Bucks Co., Pa.

In many communities where the Mennonite immigrants have constituted a large part of the local population, they have as a matter of course accepted local office and operated the government. A good illustration is Mountain Lake, Minn., where according to the historian of the community, F. P. Schultz, "the Mennonites took over the affairs of the village and township government as soon as they were settled in the community." The following additional statements by Schultz give a more complete picture. "From the time of its separate organization as a municipality in 1886 the village of Mountain Lake was governed by Mennonite officials with the exception of the constable, who was usually an American." "Since 1901 various Mennonites have held different county offices and a few have served as members of the state legislature." John R. Rempel served as Justice of the Peace for 25 years in Mountain Lake (d. 1933). "In recent years, particularly since World War I, village politics rapidly developed into a more typically American setup." In World War II, it might be noted, Mennonites (GCM) also served on local draft boards since the war, at least one at Topeka, Ind., one in Kansas, and one at Mountain Lake, Minn.

Steinbach, Man., is another community which has been almost continuously run by Mennonites in the local government, although the Kleine Gemeinde does not participate. In Goshen, Ind., Frank S. Ebersole, a member of the Eighth Street Mennonite Church (GCM), served a 4-year term as mayor during World War II.

General Conference Mennonites have been elected to provincial and state legislatures. Known cases are Kansas—H. P. Krehbiel, a minister and conference leader, and J. A. Schowalter; Minnesota; Nebraska—Peter Jansen; South Dakota—D. D. Wipf two terms as Secretary of State, J. J. Wipf six terms in the House, P. P. Kleinsasser two terms in the Senate, eight others served in the House and four others in the Senate; Manitoba; and Saskatchewan. Others have entered the political lists only to lose at the ballot box. At least two Mennonites were elected to the United States Congress, E. W. Ramseyer, a member of the church (GCM) at Pulaski, Iowa, who served 18 years in the House of Representatives (1915-33) and then as Commissioner in the U.S. Court of Claims at Washington, D.C., and E. C. Eicher, a member of the Eicher Mennonite Church (GCM) at Wayland, Iowa, who served 6 years in the House of Representatives (1933-39), then for a year as member of the Securities and Exchange Commission, and finally as Chief Justice in the District Court of the District of Columbia at Washington, D.C., where he died in office in 1944. Both men were prominent figures in Congress, the former a Republican, the latter a Democrat.

The most noted politically active Mennonite in America was probably Peter Jansen, born in 1852 in Russia as the son of the noted Cornelius Jansen, who was for a time Prussian Consul in Prussia and South Russia and emigrated to Beatrice, Neb., in 1873. Mr. Jansen began his political career in 1880 as Justice of the Peace. As early as 1884 he was elected an alternate delegate to the National Republican Convention in Chicago. In 1898 he was elected a member of the Nebraska State Legislature, and in 1899 was appointed U.S. Commissioner to the Paris Exposition by President McKinley. In 1910 he was elected to the State Senate of Nebraska. He states in his memoirs that he was frequently urged by friends to become a candidate for governor, but that his pronounced opposition to war and all that was military never permitted him to seek this honor, since as governor of the state he would also be an officer of the militia. He was also conscientiously opposed to the death penalty.

The situation at Germantown, Pa., is unique in American Mennonite history. This settlement was established in 1683 by thirteen families from Crefeld, Germany, who at the time of their arrival were for the most part Quakers, but up to a few years before had been Mennonites. In essence their attitude on political matters therefore was the Mennonite attitude of their home church in Crefeld. During the course of the next 25 years at least 40 or 50 Mennonite families, mostly from the Lower Rhine area, a few from Hamburg-Altona, settled in this Germantown village community. They together with Quakers constituted the corporate members of the Germantown village government. The village had been incorporated in 1691 under the laws of the province of Pennsylvania, receiving a special charter. Since the Mennonites and Quakers who had settled here were the corporate members of this borough which was a closed corporation, they had the exclusive right of franchise, of legislation, and of admitting new members into the corporation. They were therefore under obligation to establish and maintain a local municipal government. So long as the village ordinances and local litigation concerned itself chiefly with stray pigs and line fences, there was little difficulty in securing Quaker and Mennonite officials to serve, but with the building of a jail and the introduction of stocks and a whipping post they lost their desire for office. As early as 1701, Pastorius, the non-Mennonite and non-Quaker civil leader of the village, complained to Penn that for

conscience' sake he found it increasingly difficult to find men who would serve in the general court of Germantown and that he hoped for relief through the arrival of new immigrants. Several men declined to accept offices to which they had been elected. Finally in 1707 the village lost its charter, chiefly because it was unable to carry on the government which its charter required, and it was merged for political purposes with the township of which it was a part. In this interesting Germantown political experiment, we have a situation where the Mennonites and Quakers were in the majority and had the franchise and were unwilling to admit others to the franchise, but at the same time were unwilling to hold the offices necessary to operate the village government.

An altogether different phase of the problem of church and state in Mennonite history, one which has escaped the attention of most Mennonites interested in this problem, occurs in those instances where Mennonite colonies have been granted local political autonomy by the state under whose sovereignty they reside. These cases involve in actual effect the erection of Mennonite states.

The first instance of this in Mennonite history is the autonomy granted to the Mennonite settlements (also to other ethnic immigrant groups) in South Russia by the government 1789 ff. The supervision of affairs in all the settlements was placed in the hands of a Russian governmental committee, with seat in Odessa, placed directly under the national cabinet in Moscow. Within the Mennonite settlements, however, all strictly local village and settlement affairs were given over to the Mennonites themselves. They were given the right to elect their own officials, to establish their own local laws, and thus to govern themselves quite freely. Since all the inhabitants of the Mennonite districts were either baptized members of the Mennonite church or unbaptized members of Mennonite families, and no non-Mennonites were permitted to live in the settlement, this was a purely Mennonite state. (It should be noted that in time the unbaptized proportion of the population became substantial in size but participated fully in civic affairs. To the Russian government the term "Mennonite" was a cultural or racial concept, not necessarily religious.) The actual conduct of government fell largely to the local village assembly and the village magistrate (see **Schulze**). To the Mennonite magistrate fell the lot of administering local discipline, with whipping a common method of punishment.

A closer examination of the situation reveals that actually the government approached a form of theocracy. Even though the elders or bishops were not at the head of civil affairs, yet as heads of the church they exercised great influence over matters of government, especially over the schools. Frequently also the magistrates requested the elders to assist them in many local affairs. Later on the strong influence of the elders in the village government declined. It is needless to say that it was not always easy to carry out the principles of nonresistance and opposition to the use of force which all the Mennonites of Russia firmly believed in, and at the same time maintain the discipline necessary for a stable order. To lead a fellow member to the whipping post required considerable rationalization of the injunction, "Resist not evil." Worst of all was the attempt of certain Mennonite leaders to have the Russian government banish to Siberia some of the leaders of the new (MB) movement of 1860.

When the Russian government in 1870 attempted to cancel most of the privileges of the Mennonites as well as the other German colonists of Russia a large number of them were prepared to leave the country. Under the pressure of the threatened emigration the Russians withdrew part of their proposals, especially that canceling exemption from military service. A compromise was reached, according to which the Mennonite population, through the Mennonite civil organization of their autonomous government, undertook to provide a substitute service for the state in the form of a voluntary forestry service, which was set up in 1880. This furnished the suggestion and inspiration for the American Mennonite proposal for Civilian Public Service in World War II.

The second instance of Mennonite self-government, on a reduced scale to be sure, and of shorter duration, is found in the Russian Mennonite settlements made in Manitoba in the East and West Reserves in 1874-80. The third instance of Mennonite self-government, fully equal to that in Russia, is found in the Mennonite colonies in Paraguay. The autonomy of the Mennonites in the Paraguayan Chaco is greater than that accorded the Mennonites in Russia. As a matter of fact the Mennonites of the Chaco constitute an absolutely independent state. There has never been any application of any of the laws of Paraguay to them in the Chaco, there has never been any police officer or government officer in the colony to exercise any authority on behalf of the national government, except in the case of the suppression of the Nazi movement in 1940(?), the courts of the land have never interfered with the Mennonites of the Chaco, and the army during its occupation of the Chaco never presumed to exercise authority. Since each Mennonite colony in Paraguay is independent, there are 5 Mennonite states: Menno, Fernheim, Friesland, Volendam, and Neuland.

On the whole this form of Mennonite self-government in Paraguay has been very successful to the present date. It has been possible to maintain law and order without using force with the exception of one or two instances where it was necessary to administer corporal punishment to recalcitrant striplings. It is true of course that those who are dissatisfied with the social order in the colony can leave, and are probably under so much social pressure that they voluntarily leave before they become serious problems to the authorities. But in any case, for thirty years these Mennonite states have existed in the heart of South America without the use of force, and have maintained a good degree of law and order, industry, sobriety, and peace.

It is difficult to say whether the former Mennonite settlements in South Russia and the Mennonite colonies in South America present a form of union of church and state or not. It is true that in these colonies the church governed or governs itself without interference or support from the civil government. That is, the Mennonite churches in these colonies have not been subjected to or made a part of the civil government. Nor has the church in its organized form, that is, in its regular meetings or conferences, dictated on the other hand to the government. The functions of church and state have been maintained as completely separate functions, the functions of the state being exercised by the civil assemblies, and the functions of the church being exercised by the ecclesiastical assemblies. Yet the same people are members of both the civil and ecclesiastical assemblies, with the exception of those church members who have been excommunicated or those who have grown up without being baptized and joining the church. However, it is true beyond the shadow of a doubt that the actual leadership of this joint life in the Mennonite colony, both in Russia and South America, has usually been largely in the hands of the elders and ministers. It is inconceivable that anything could be done in these colonies that would be basically contrary to the teachings and wishes of the church leaders. Thus in effect if not in form there is an amalgamation of the church and state. Is this not an ideal solution to the problem? However, this solution seems to be possible only in a state which is not well developed nor prosperous and which has large open spaces in which it is possible to settle blocks of foreign population without interfering with the national life in general. Paraguay is a poor country with a small population and with large unoccupied areas. It is very anxious to secure settlers and it is willing to pay the price of granting practical independence to such foreign groups as the Mennonites in order to secure the benefit of their service in the development of the state, at least in the Gran Chaco territory.

In recent years study conferences have been sponsored in several North American Mennonite groups to deal with the Christian's relation to the state, which have produced valuable series of papers. The Peace Problems Committee (MC) held such a conference at Laurelville, Pa., on Sept. 21-22, 1956, under the title "Nonresistance and Political Responsibility." The MCC Peace Section sponsored an all-Mennonite Conference on "Christian Responsibility to the State" in Chicago on Nov. 15-16, 1957. The Department of Social Science of Bethel College (GCM) sponsors annually (since 1955) a "Conference on Education and Political Responsibility." The essays from *Mennonite Life* listed in the bibliography below were among the papers read at one of these conferences.   H.S.B.

Hans J. Hillerbrand, "The Anabaptist View of the State," *MQR* XXXII (1958) 83-110; *idem*, "Die politische Ethik des Oberdeutschen Täufertums (unpublished dissertation, University of Erlangen, 1957); *idem*, "An Early Anabaptist Treatise on the Christian and the State," *MQR* XXXII (1958) 28-47 (including a photographic reproduction of the complete text of the important tract *Aufdeckung der Babylonischen Hurn und Antichrists (Disclosure of the Harlot of Babylon and of the Antichrist . . . Also About the Victory, Peace, and Reign of the True Christians and How They Are Obedient to the Magistrate, Carrying the Cross of Christ in Patience and Love, Without Rebellion and Resistance*); Robert Kreider, "The Relations of the Anabaptists to the Civil Authorities in Switzerland 1525-1555" (unpublished dissertation, University of Chicago, 1952); *idem*, "The Anabaptist and the State" in *Recovery of the Anabaptist Vision* (Scottdale, 1957) 180-93; L. von

Muralt, *Glaube und Lehre der schweizerischen Wiedertäufer in der Reformationszeit* (Zürich, 1938); Emil Händiges, *Die Lehre der Mennoniten in Geschichte und Gegenwart* (Ludwigshafen, 1921); W. Mannhardt, *Die Wehrfreiheit der Altpreussischen Mennoniten* (Marienburg, 1863); Georg Wünsch, *Evangelische Ethik des Politischen* (Tübingen, 1936); C. Krahn, *Menno Simons* (Karlsruhe, 1936) 164-69; H. S. Bender, "Church and State in Mennonite History," *MQR* XII (1938) 83-103; Edward Yoder, "Christianity and the State," *MQR* XI (1937) 191-95; idem, "The Obligation of the Christian to the State and Community," *MQR* XIII (1939) 104-22; Elmer Neufeld, "Christian Responsibility in the Political Situation," *MQR* (1958) 141-62; H. S. Bender, "The Anabaptists and Religious Liberty in the Sixteenth Century," *MQR* XXIX (1955) 83-100; idem, "The Pacifism of the Sixteenth Century Anabaptists," *MQR* XXX (1956) 5-18; G. F. Hershberger, *Christian Relationship to State and Community* (Akron, 1942); C. K. Lehman, "The Christian and Civil Government" in *Bible Teaching on Nonconformity* (Scottdale, 1940); J. C. Wenger, *Separated unto God* (Scottdale, 1951), chapter, "The Christian and the State," pp. 245-63; Erland Waltner, "An Analysis of the Mennonite Views on the Christian's Relation to the State in the Light of the New Testament" (unpublished doctoral dissertation, Eastern Baptist Theological Seminary, 1948); idem, "The Mennonite View of the Relation of Church and State," *Proceedings of the Fourth Annual Conference on Mennonite Cultural Problems* (N. Newton, 1945); Friesen, *Brüderschaft*, 483 ff.; Gustav E. Reimer and G. R. Gaeddert, *Exiled by the Czar* (Newton, 1956); Samuel Geiser, "Die Wehrlosigkeit in der Schweiz," *Mennonitisches Jahrbuch 1954* (Newton, 1954) 35 ff.; the articles by J. Winfield Fretz, "Should Mennonites Participate in Politics?"; Esko Loewen, "Church and State"; Elmer Ediger, "A Christian's Political Responsibility," in *Menn. Life* XI (July 1956) 139 ff.; John H. Yoder, "Der Staat im Neuen Testament," *Mennonit* X (1957) 84 f., 132 f., 151; N. van der Zijpp, *Geschiedenis der Doopsgezinden in Nederland* (Arnhem, 1952).

* * *

Mennonites in the Netherlands in the early period after 1530 likely still held government office. In so doing they acted in line with the later Menno Simons, who in 1554 still declared, "I should not like to compel a Christian to lay down his office; I would commit him to his own conscience and the guidance of the Holy Spirit" (Kühler, 342). But not long after this Anabaptists are no longer found in office, in the first place because it was no longer possible in the face of the growing persecution, and also because the Mennonites themselves took the position that they must absolutely not hold office. Two confessions of faith, the *Olijftacxken* (1626) and that of Jan Cents (1629), say that government office does not fit into the church. The other old confessions are silent on this point. In the confession of Cornelis Ris (1766) we read, "If such an office should be committed to us, then we should be greatly concerned about it and not prepare to take it, for the will of Christ to rule thus is quite unknown to us." In 1585 the States General released the Mennonites from the duty of holding office, and between 1607 and 1612 there are several resolutions which released them in return for payment, since they were well-to-do. The Waterlanders did not consider an office in government necessarily to be at variance with the Gospel. At the conference of preachers and elders held at Amsterdam in 1581 it was decided that a position on the city council (*vroedschapsambt*) and on the tax commission (*belastingambtenaar*) were permissible. Jan van der Beest, a Mennonite, became a notary at Schiedam on Sept. 29, 1622. He was released from the usual oath of office by the States General, after his petition to this effect had once been refused. Nevertheless many Waterland Mennonites in North Holland until after 1600 frequently refused to hold office and were fined in consequence. This happened, for example, when the Waterlander preacher of Rotterdam, Eduard Nabels (*q.v.*), was appointed sheriff in 1629; he was exempted from this office by paying a "gift" of 25 guilders to the poor of the Reformed Church.

But by degrees the Mennonites frequently accepted office, especially the "lower" ones in which the shedding of blood was not involved. In the course of the 17th and 18th centuries the aversion to public office disappeared among the Mennonites, though the strict group ("fijne") held to the principle until about 1790. Thus in 1719 Pieter Zwart, a deacon in the Frisian congregation of Oude-Niedorp, was nearly excommunicated for accepting the office of *schepen* (alderman). That few public offices were held by Mennonites in the 18th century is also due to the fact that these offices were considered the prerogative of members of the established church; on the whole Mennonites were excluded. Even in places where the Mennonites were in the majority, such as North Holland, they were hardly ever in public office. As soon as this ban was lifted the Mennonites went into the offices, and by the time of the French occupation we find many Mennonites as mayors and as members of city councils. In Hengelo it was, for instance, decided that the city council should consist of three Catholics and two Mennonites. Since 1800 many Mennonites have held important posts in the government, up to the very high positions; thus there was a relatively high number of Mennonite ministers of state; at one time four of the eleven members of the cabinet were Mennonites.

That obedience to the state is an obligation of the Christian is expressly stated in all Dutch Mennonite confessions of faith where the subject is treated at all. The very first one, the Waterlander confession of Hans de Ries (about 1580) says (Article 37): "The temporal power or government is a necessary ordinance of God, ordained and instituted for the preservation of the state and of a good, natural, civil life, to the good for protection, to the evil for punishment. We confess ourselves obliged and bound by God's Word to fear the government, to show it honor and obedience in all things which are not in conflict with the Word of the Lord. We are bound to pray to the Almighty God for it, to thank the Lord for good, honest benevolence, and to give without murmuring the tax, tithe, and fees due it." The other confessions agree with this, especially the Dordrecht Confession and that of Cornelis Ris.

"All the doctrines and confessions of faith of the Mennonites," writes Maatschoen (p. 321), "contain nothing that gives the least appearance or suggestion to sedition or revolt against any princes or governments, or say nothing of inciting men to commit them, but they teach and command the opposite. For their instructions and confessions state clearly, and earnestly instill into the hearts of their pupils and followers, that it is not free to any subject to set up a distinction between the legality or illegality of the supreme authority or to pass judgment on its institutions and laws, but to render complete and faithful obedience to all to protect oneself from threatening evil and money fines, but also and especially for the sake of conscience, as they have learned from the Apostle Paul, Rom. 13:1-7." "No church praises obedience to the supreme authority more emphatically than the Mennonites," a statement that is corroborated by various confessions, in which the author points out the great contrast between them and the fanatics in Germany and the revolt in Münster.   vdZ.

Blaupot t. C., *Holland* I, 211, 213; *idem, Groningen* II, 40; Kühler, *Geschiedenis* I, 342; *DB* 1867, 66; 1873, 163; 1877, 86; 1882, 73; 1899, 181 f.; 1909, 168; *Inv. Arch. Amst.* I, No. 447; Schijn-Maatschoen, *Geschiedenis* I, p. lvii and 2748; *ML* I, 68 f.; III, 289 f.

Statenvertaling is the common title of a Dutch translation of the Bible, thus called because this translation was ordered by the States General of the Netherlands. It was made in 1626-37 by a number of learned men and first appeared in 1637. At first the Mennonites, particularly the more conservatives among them, were opposed to the Statenvertaling, preferring their Biestkens (*q.v.*) Bible; but gradually they introduced the new translation, which was more exact than the Biestkens Bible. Among the Frisian and Flemish Mennonites the Statenvertaling was generally used from about 1650, but not until the 12th edition of T. J. van Braght's *Schole der Deugd* of 1719 were the Bible texts quoted from the Statenvertaling. The Janjacobsgezinden (*q.v.*) and a few other strict groups did not use the Statenvertaling until the 19th century. After World War II the Statvertaling was generally replaced by a new translation published by the Dutch Bible Association (Bijbelgenootschap).   vdZ.

F. Dijkema, "De Doopsgezinden en de Statenvertaling," in *De Statenvertaling 1637-1937* (Haarlem, 1937) 86-91.

Statesburg Amish Mennonite (MC) Church, now extinct, located in Vernon County, Mo., had 18 members in 1905, with C. C. Schrock serving as deacon. The meetinghouse was built in 1894. The congregation was also known as the Katy Church. It is last listed in the Yearbook of 1907.   M.G.

States-General, Dutch: see **Netherlands States-General**.

Staudach(er) (Staudtach), **Hans,** a Hutterite martyr of Kaufbeuren (*q.v.*), Bavaria, Germany, was seized in Austria with Anthoni Keim (*q.v.*), Blasius Beckh (*q.v.*), and Leonhard Schneider (*q.v.*) when they with their wives and children were on their way to Moravia. After a steadfast cross-examination he was beheaded on Nov. 22, 1546, in Vienna. The *Lieder der Hutterischen Brüder* contains two of his songs (pp. 128 ff.), "Hilf Gott, das uns gelinge" and "O Christe rein du bist allein," while a third, "Ich freu mich dein, O Vater mein," is to be found in Pressburg, Codex 236 (according to the *Lieder*, p. 128). Songs were written about him by Hans Gurtzham (*q.v.*), Wolf Sailer (*q.v.*), and Christoff Scheffman. The first of these appears in *Lieder*, p. 136 f.   Hege.

Mart. Mir. D 74, E 475; Wolkan, *Lieder,* 128, 136 f., 179 f.; Zieglschmid, *Chronik,* 265 f.; Wolkan, *Geschicht-Buch,* 257; *ML* IV.

Stauffer, a Mennonite family name, meaning cup-bearer, or perhaps steep hill, comes from the Aar River valley and the Emmental, Switzerland. Christen Stauffer, an "obstinate" Anabaptist preacher, was in prison at Bern in 1644. About 1700 a Swiss Stauffer family settled in Alsace; in the 18th century some Stauffers lived in the Bernese Jura, and c1670 Christian and Ulrich Stauffer emigrated from Eggiswil, canton of Bern, to the Palatinate, Germany. Here some Stauffers were ministers, Christian Stauffer being a deacon or preacher at Gerolsheim (*q.v.*) c1740, Daniel Stauffer, of Guntersblum, serving 1739-c67 as elder of the Altzheim congregation near Oppenheim, and Heinrich Stauffer, a preacher 1758 and elder 1765-1805 of the Ibersheim (*q.v.*) congregation, followed in this office by his relatives Johann Stauffer, preacher from 1787, and Daniel Stauffer, serving until 1842. Hans Stauffer was a Mennonite and was expelled from Switzerland soon after his marriage in 1685 to Kingst Heistand-Risser and settled in the Palatinate. On Nov. 9, 1709, he began his emigration to America. He was in London on Jan. 20, 1710, with his wife and children—Jacob, age 13, Daniel 12, Henry 9, Elisabeth, who was the wife of Paul Friedt, and Maria, ready to sail for America. They came to Colebrookdale, Berks Co., Pa., and were the ancestors of John Stauffer (1762-1822), a preacher of the Franconia Conference (MC), and Bishop John L. Stauffer of Virginia. Ulrich Stowpher and Uldrich Stouper, probably father and son, arrived in America on Sept. 18 and 30, 1727. Vincent Stauffer, probably a son of Ulrich Stowpher, who settled in York County, Pa., qualified on Aug. 24, 1728. Vincent was the ancestor of the preachers Daniel Stauffer (1807-31) and Moses Stauffer (1842-1927) and Bishop Frederick Stauffer (1813-84). Jacob Stauffer (1713-68) arrived in Philadelphia in 1732 and settled in Dauphin County, Pa. Jacob Stofor (b. c1712) arrived in 1732 with his brother Daniel Stiffor. Daniel Stauffer (b. c1708) and his wife Magdalena Hess, of the Pequea Colony, established a mill site on Hammer Creek, four miles north of Lititz. They were the progenitors of the preachers Noah Stauffer (1842-1928) and Norman B. Stauffer (1871-1927), both of Canada. Christian and Johannes Stouper, aged 28 and 20, arrived in 1737. Undoubtedly the last four, Christian, Daniel, Jacob, and John Stauffer, were brothers, the sons of Daniel Stauffer, who died in the Palatinate in 1735. The widow, Veronica, came with Christian and John, traveling on a cart to northern Lancaster County, where both boys settled. Christian Stauffer was the ancestor of Benjamin B. Stauffer (1855-1928), a preacher of the Kaufman church, Benjamin E. Stauffer (1864-1918), the first superintendent of the Old People's Home at Maugansville, Md., and Bishop Elam W. Stauffer, a Mennonite bishop in Africa. Johannes Stauffer was the ancestor of John H. Stauffer (1818-92), a preacher who donated the ground for the Stauffer meetinghouse near Bachmanville. Matthias Stauffer, reputedly an older son of Daniel and Veronica Stauffer, came with his uncle, Hans Stauffer, in 1710, settling at Caernarvon; he was the ancestor of Jacob W. Stauffer (1811-55), the founder of the Stauffer Mennonites (*q.v.*). Christian and Johannes Stauffer, who arrived in America in 1744, were probably brothers of Ulrich and Vincent Stauffer. They settled in Donegal Township, Lancaster County, and Ulrich became the father of Abraham Stauffer (1752-1826), a preacher in Fayette County. Christian Stauffer arrived in 1749, settled in Lampeter, and was the father of Johannes Stauffer (1737-1811), also a preacher. Later arrivals include the preachers Johannes Stauffer (1791-1861) and his son Christian Stauffer (1823-87), who served at Indiantown. Other ordained men were Bishop John Stauffer (1746-1836), of Beaver Creek and Stouffer's church in Washington County, Md., Bishop Michael Stauffer, the first in Augusta County, Va., and Joseph R. Stauffer (1852-1918), of Milford, Neb. Abraham Stauffer (1752-1826) was a pioneer Mennonite bishop in Fayette County, Pa. The Pennsville meetinghouse was near his home. He was the great-grandfather of Henry C. Frick and Abraham O. Tinsman, who were prominent in the coke and iron smelting industry of Western Pennsylvania.

Henry Stauffer (1781-1851) was an early leader in the Columbiana-Mahoning congregation. Born near Hagerstown, Md., he accompanied his parents to Fayette County, Pa., in 1790 and in 1801 he walked through the woods to Mahoning County, Ohio, where he settled. In 1806-9 he served in the Columbiana County militia. He was ordained to the ministry soon after the arrival of Bishop Jacob Nold in 1817, whom he succeeded as bishop after Nold's death in 1834. He was one of the signers of the minutes of a church conference held 1843-44 at the Chester meetinghouse in Wayne County, Ohio.

Jacob Stauffer (1832-99), an early Mennonite preacher of Ohio, was born in York County, Pa., came to Columbiana County, Ohio, with his parents in 1834. He married a daughter of Deacon Jacob Nold. In 1882 he was ordained a minister. He had a concern for small congregations, occasionally preached for the declining congregations at North Georgetown, Columbiana County, Ohio, and Harmony, Butler County, Pa., both of which are now extinct. Rudy L. Stauffer is bishop at Wooster, Ohio, and J. B. Stauffer bishop at Tofield, Alta. (Unless otherwise indicated, the above ordained men are M.C.)

A (non-Mennonite) descendant of this Stauffer family is Ethelbert Stauffer, professor of New Testament at the University of Bonn, Germany.

I.D.L., W.D.S.

Pennsylvania Archives, second series, Vol. XVII; R. B. Strassburger and W. J. Hinke, *Pennsylvania German Pioneers* (Norristown, 1934); *Genealogical Society of Pennsylvania* XV, Nos. 2 and 3 (1947); Martin G. Weaver, *Mennonites of Lancaster County* (Scottdale, 1931); D. Cassel, *Geschichte der Mennoniten* (Philadelphia, 1890); Ezra E. Eby, *Biographical History of Waterloo Township* II (Kitchener, 1895) 501; Daniel Kauffman, *Mennonite Cyclopedic Dictionary* (Scottdale, 1937); Virginia Conference Minutes; files of Amos K. Stauffer; D. L. Gratz, *Bernese Anabaptists* (Scottdale, 1953); *Inv. Arch. Amst.* I, Nos. 1248, 1354, 1356, 1486, 1541; Dutch *Naamlijst*; Müller, *Berner Täufer*, 202 f.; H. S. Bower, *A Genealogical Record of Daniel Stauffer* (Harleysville, 1897); A. J. Fretz, *A Genealogical Record of the Descendants of Henry Stauffer* (Milton, N.J., 1899); Ezra N. Stauffer *Stauffer Genealogy* (Goshen, c1917); David Stauffer, *The Genealogy and Historical Sketch of the Stauffer Family* (Toronto, 1918). *ML* IV, 236.

Stauffer, Jacob W. (1811-55), the founder of the Stauffer Mennonite Church (*q.v.*), was born in Earl Twp., Lancaster Co., Pa., on Sept. 3, 1811, the son of David and Anna Weaver Stauffer. On Nov. 18, 1833, he married Lydia Martin (1817-97). He lived on the home farm between the Linden Grove School and the Pike Mennonite Church. Here they reared their nine children. Of his sons, David M. Stauffer (1834-89) was a bishop, Moses M. Stauffer (1849-99) a preacher, John S. Stauffer (1867- ?) a bishop, and Phares O. Stauffer a bishop, all in Snyder County, Pa., in the Stauffer Mennonite Church. His son Enos had two ordained sons-in-law—John A. Weaver (1881-1954), a bishop, and Peter Weaver, a preacher. Martin S. Weaver, a son of the former, was ordained by the Weaver Mennonites (*q.v.*) at the Pike Mennonite Church. Of the Daniel M. Stauffer line is Bishop Jacob S. Stauffer at the Pike Stauffer Mennonite Church.

Jacob W. Stauffer was ordained to the ministry at Groffdale on Nov. 29, 1840, and served until 1845. Then trouble arose in the congregation, which became a church issue involving the ban. The bishops, with the exception of Jacob Brubaker of Juniata County, sided with the minister Joseph Wenger (1766-1851) and the deacon Benjamin Wenger (1807-84). Thereupon Jacob W. Stauffer and Jacob Weber (1796-1860) withdrew with Bishop Brubaker (above) to form the Stauffer Mennonite Church. He defended his position and tried to show the decline of the old church in a book with the title, *Eine Chronik oder Geschicht-Büchlein* (Lancaster, 1855, 2d ed. 1859). He formulated the principles of discipline and order for the new group. He rejected all attempts to heal the schism.   I.D.L.

Ezra N. Stauffer, *Stauffer Genealogy of America* (Goshen, 1917); M. G. Weaver, *History of Lancaster Conference* (Scottdale, 1937).

Stauffer, John Gehman (1837-1911), Mennonite (GCM) publisher of Quakertown, Pa., was born near Spinnerstown, Milford Twp., Bucks Co., Pa., on Sept. 18, 1837, a direct descendant of the immigrant Hans Stauffer (arrived 1710 at Valley Forge), and the son of Jacob O. and Elizabeth Hiestand Stauffer. In November 1856 he entered the employ of the Mennonitischer Druckverein in Milford Square, soon becoming manager of the small business, as well as compositor, printer, and assistant editor. The chief business of the shop was the publication of *Das Christliche Volks-Blatt* (first issue June 30, 1856). Stauffer continued as an employee in the shop until in 1867 when he apparently bought the shop and continued to print the publications of the Druckverein and its successors on a job basis. In 1881 he moved his shop and family to Quakertown, calling the shop the Quakertown Printing and Publishing House. He printed most of the books, pamphlets, etc., for John Oberholtzer (*q.v.*).

After he bought the print shop in 1867 Stauffer started publishing a German weekly local newspaper, *Independent Reformer,* later changed to *Der Reformer,* then to *Patriot and Reformer,* for a time also apparently as *Der Bucks County Patriot und Reformer und Agriculturist* (see **Reformer und Agriculturist**); it is very difficult at this date to secure a clear idea of these various publications and their relation to each other. In August 1881 he started an English weekly, the *Quakertown Free Press,* which he sold in July 1882.

Stauffer's strong religious interest was expressed in his publication of the German and English monthly Sunday-school papers, *Himmelsmanna* (*q.v.,* 1876-1906) and *Manna* (1879-1908), and the monthly *Die Kirche* (soon changed to *Gemeinde) unterm Kreuz* (*q.v.,* 1885-91). He published the last paper as a staunch Mennonite journal, with a circulation of about 2,000, until about 1889, when he seemingly lost interest in the Mennonite Church. *Die Gemeinde unterm Kreuz* was of course in direct competition with the General Conference Mennonite Church organ, *Christlicher Bundesbote,* and it may be that he found it impossible to secure the necessary Mennonite support to keep it going. An evaluation of Stauffer's work is given in the article *Kirche unterm Kreuz.* Daniel G. Stauffer was a brother. The Uriah S. Stauffer (b. 1859) who took charge of J. G. Stauffer's shop in 1880 and soon bought out the *Quakertown Free Press* and the *Patriot and Reformer* was a son of Enos Stauffer, a relative of J. G. Stauffer. J. G. Stauffer married Sarah Geissinger on June 11, 1870. They had two children, Berend G. and Anna. He died in 1911 at the home of his daughter in California. H.S.B.

J. Battle, *History of Bucks County* (Philadelphia, 1887) 1067 f., contains a biographical sketch of J. G. Stauffer.

Stauffer, Noah (1842-1928), a prominent minister in the Ontario Mennonite (MC) Conference, serving in the Weber congregation near Strasburg, one of the first to advocate evangelism and missions, a leading promoter of the Mennonite General Conference, and probably the first to use English regularly in his preaching of a half century. H.S.B.

Stauffer, Norman B. (1870-1927), the outstanding leader of the Alberta-Saskatchewan Mennonite (MC) Conference, ordained preacher in 1901 and bishop in 1911 at Aldersyde, Alberta. He had moved from Waterloo, Ont., to Alberta in 1900 in the early days of the colonization there. He died Sept. 13, 1927. H.S.B.

Stauffer, Otto, b. 19.. at Obersülzen, Palatinate, Germany, was sent out as a missionary of the Dutch Mennonite Mission Association in 1934; his field was at Kudus (*q.v.*) on the Indonesian island of Java. Here he was a successful missionary until 1940, when he was interned in the course of the war. On Jan. 18, 1942, the ship on which Stauffer and his brother-in-law and fellow missionary Hermann Schmitt (*q.v.*) were transported was torpedoed and both Schmitt and Stauffer found their graves in the waters of the Indian Ocean. Otto Stauffer was married to Martha Klaassen, a daughter of missionary Johann Klaassen (*q.v.*). vDZ.

Stauffer Mennonite Church (MC), a member of the Lancaster Conference, is located near Bachmanville in Conewago Twp., Dauphin Co., Pa. Michael Shenk, Benjamin Longenecker, John Risser, and the Lehmans were in this area in the latter half

of the 18th century. The first meetinghouse was built about 1780. This was a part of the Risser congregation in Lancaster County, sharing its ministry. Before the meetinghouse was built Peter Risser preached for them in private dwellings. It early became a part of the present Noah W. Risser-Clarence E. Lutz Bishop District, with John Mumma as the first resident bishop. The present church was built on the same site in 1918. A well-kept cemetery adjoins the churchyard. The membership (1957) is 163, with J. Frank Zeager as pastor. An outpost at Sand Beach has developed into a permanent Sunday school and mission at East Hanover. I.D.L.

Stauffer Mennonite Church, a small Mennonite branch, began in 1845 as a schism from the Lancaster Mennonite Conference on the question of the treatment of an orphan child adopted by one of the members. Bishop Jacob Brubaker, of Juniata County, and Jacob Stauffer and Jacob Weber, preachers of Groffdale, could not concur in the decision of the bishops of the conference. Stauffer wrote a book of 430 pages of small format in self-defense and as an attack on the bishops of the conference. Its title is *Eine Chronik oder Geschicht-Büchlein von der sogenannten Mennonisten Gemeinde. Zum Dienst und Lehre für alle Liebhaber der Wahrheit, durch die Gnade und Segen Gottes. Aus Geschichten, Vorfällen, Begebenheiten oder Exempeln, und aus heiliger Schrift zusammengezogen* (Lancaster 1855, 1859, Scottdale 1922). Jacob Stauffer and Jacob Weber became the leaders of the new group, their membership being mostly in East and West Earl townships of Lancaster County and in Snyder County, Pa. The Pike meetinghouse (on the Lakes-to-Sea Highway, east of Hinkletown) was granted to the new group. It was later enlarged and is today their chief meetinghouse. Subsequently the following bishops also served: Michael Brubaker, David Stauffer, and John Stauffer, of Snyder County; Samuel Weaver, Moses B. Weaver, Aaron Sensenig, Jesse Bowman, John A. Weaver, and Weaver Zimmerman, the present bishop, from the Pike congregation.

In the spring of 1887 a group from four different Stauffer communities started a utopia near May City, Osceola County, Iowa, with Jesse Bowman, of Ontario, as the leader. This lasted about 27 years, and had 30 members at its peak. Elam C. Martin served as its bishop. In 1916 John A. Weaver led a schism from the Bowman group in Pennsylvania on the extent of shunning, dividing the congregation 101 to 102. In thirty years the old group dwindled to 40 members. Through social contacts of the young people with the young members of the Groffdale Old Order Mennonites many of the Iowa group, who settled near Myerstown, as well as those in Lancaster County, joined the Groffdale O.O.M. group.

Another schism, called the Rissler schism, occurred in 1860-80, because this group believed that all their children should be church members and in the order of the church by the age of twenty-one. This group, by losing their children, is now almost extinct.

In the early 1950's a three-way split occurred in

Snyder County. The smallest group has three members, all Risslers, who meet in the home of the deacon, Moses R. Rissler. A larger group of 60 members uses the German language, prohibits automobiles, and has few conveniences. Their bishop is Weaver Zimmerman, and their minister Martin S. Weaver. This group is known as the Weaver Mennonite Church. The third or Bowman group also worships at the Pike meetinghouse and at Loveville in St. Mary's County, Md. It has 224 members. At the Pike meetinghouse the ministers are Jacob S. Stauffer bishop and Joseph O. Brubaker preacher. At Loveville the ministers are John M. Brubaker and Harry Stauffer. Three additional small groups in the Selinsgrove rural area of Pennsylvania are headed by Phares Stauffer, Aaron S. Martin, and Titus B. Hoover as bishops, and Jacob B. Stauffer, Noah W. Hoover, and Ira S. Martin as ministers. Locally the larger faction worshiping at the Pike meetinghouse are called Weaver Mennonites, the smaller one Stauffer Mennonites, and both are often called Pike Mennonites. All told, the descendants of the 1845 schism, now divided into six groups, number barely 300 members.

The children of this group are dressed plainly from childhood, somewhat like the Old Order Amish, the girls wearing aprons and bonnets, although the bonnets are slightly different.

The boys' clothing resembles that of the Amish, except that it has buttons instead of hooks and eyes. From the age of sixteen to twenty-five the boys often indulge in wild behavior and lose their plainness. Frequently they buy cars and are lost to their own church. The prosperous farms of the group have no tractors nor conveniences. They have no Sunday schools. Their worship services last about three hours.						I.D.L.

Staveren, a small town in the Dutch province of Friesland (pop. 1,166 in 1947, with 112 Mennonites), has been the seat of a Mennonite congregation since early times. Elder Leenaert Bouwens (*q.v.*) baptized 20 persons here in 1551-54, about 9 in 1557-61, and 32 in 1563-65. These numbers indicate that there has been a congregation here since the middle of the 16th century, about whose history, however, there is only very scarce information. In the 17th century it belonged to the Waterlander branch. In 1612 the strict practices of its elder Rijk Jacobs (*q.v.*), who wanted to have all transfers from the Reformed Church rebaptized even if they had been baptized as adults, caused a serious conflict in the congregation. It seems to have led to a division of the congregation, one wing calling itself Frisian (i.e., more conservative) and the other High German (more liberal). When this schism was healed is not known, but it must have taken place before 1647, in which year the congregation was represented at the large Waterlander delegates' conference at Amsterdam. Some old record books (baptisms, death of members, resolutions) go back as far as 1643. In the 16th-18th centuries the congregation was always served by lay ministers chosen from the membership. The last of these was Abraham van der Werff, serving 1764-1807. Because his talents

were very mediocre, and also because he was too conservative for most of the members, a resolution was passed in 1765 to call a second (lay) minister from outside. This was Cornelis de Jongh, a physician, who served at Staveren 1765-84. He was followed by Pieter Klomp 1784-98, J. W. van Douwen 1798-1812, and J. van der Boogh Bleeker 1815-20. In c1822-64 the congregation was served by the pastors of the neighboring church of Warns. In 1866 it obtained a pastor of its own, from 1873 at the same time serving at Molkwerum (*q.v.*), C. Leendertz serving 1866-73, G. Vrijer 1873-75, J. A. Oosterbaan 1876-78, P. K. Bijl 1879-81, A. A. Deenik Mz 1881-99, G. Wuite 1899-1901, H. Hooghiemster 1902-8, J. M. Erkelens 1908-13, J. G. Frerichs 1914-21, H. J. Busé 1922-27, Miss A. J. van den Ban 1927-32, and Miss M. de Boer 1932-39. Miss S. E. Treffers, serving at Staveren 1941-46, also had charge of the Hindeloopen (*q.v.*) congregation from 1942, as did also L. Laurense, pastor of Staveren 1949-53. In 1953-57 the congregation was served by the pastor of Warns. In 1958 the congregations of Staveren, Hindeloopen, and IJlst (*q.v.*) decided to call one minister for the three congregations, and called J. Wieringa, who lives at IJlst.

Concerning the membership the following figures are available: in 1695 about 110 baptized members, in 1764 100, in 1838 25, in 1861 49, in 1900 89, and in 1958 50. The present meetinghouse dates from 1858; an organ was acquired in 1901. The congregation possesses three silver communion cups obtained in 1745. There is a Mennonite ladies' circle, a Sunday school for children, and a youth group.
						vDZ.

Inv. Arch. Amst. I, No. 545; II, Nos. 2252-64; *DJ* 1837, 30; *DB* 1874, 87; 1897, 164; 1901, 215.

Stecklin Mennonite Church (MC), now extinct, located in Whitchurch Twp., York Co., Ont., was founded by several Steckley families living near Bethesda "store corners." Ministers supplied at eight-week intervals in one of the homes from about 1850, alternating with Huber (*q.v.*). It was common among the Tunkers of this county for most of a century to have periodic house services in homes remote from the church, a custom which the Mennonites of the area must also have followed. Stecklin and Huber discontinued after the building of the church at Almira in Markham Township in 1860. (See **Bethesda**).						J.F.C.

Steegen, a village in the Danzig Lowlands, West Prussia, where the Mennonites regularly held meetings in 1920-45, led by a preacher of the Tiegenhagen (*q.v.*) congregation, to which the Steegen Mennonites belonged.						vDZ.

Steeghers, Jozyne, an Anabaptist martyr: see **Sijntgen.**

Steel City Mennonite Church (MC), Bethlehem, Pa., is a mission congregation sponsored by the Franconia Mennonite Conference district mission board. Established in 1951, it had 40 members in 1957.
						M.G.

Steelton Mennonite Gospel Mission (MC) began in 1936, when a club building on South Second Street was rented for Sunday morning services. Tent meeting in the fall of 1936 with Stoner Krady as evangelist resulted in a number of responses. At the first baptismal service five were placed.

Within a year another place for worship was provided in an Episcopal parish house on Pine Street. As the greater part of the growing Sunday school was from the west side of Steelton a store building was purchased on the west side at 304 Myers Street, by the Eastern Mission Board. The superintendents have been Ira Miller, Warren Metzler, Samuel Longenecker, Isaac M. Baer, and Russell J. Baer, who has been serving since 1953. The membership in 1957 was 45.   F.N.H.

Steen (Het Steen, Den Steen), a castle on the Scheldt River at Antwerp, Belgium, was in the 16th century a prison and execution place of a large number of Anabaptist martyrs. At present it is a museum. The old dark cellars in which the martyrs were kept, often in heavy leg irons, may still be seen. (*Antw. Arch.-Blad* VIII, 355, note 1; *DJ* 1952, 21-29.)   vnZ.

Steen, van (von), a Mennonite family of Dutch descent found in West Prussia, Germany, and particularly in Danzig from at least 1678. To this family belonged the Danzig elder Hans von Steen (*q.v.*). Willem van Steen, b. 1698, was expelled from the Tilsit Lowlands, East Prussia, in 1724, and moved to Dannenberg (*q.v.*), from where he was driven away in 1732. With a number of other families he then moved to the Netherlands, living at Wageningen (*q.v.*) in 1733-44, where the Dutch Mennonite Committee of Foreign Needs had established a settlement for twelve East Prussian Mennonite families. Willem van Steen, who administered the houses and the properties of these colonists at Wageningen, earned his living by weaving linen. After all his compatriots had gradually returned to Prussia, Willem van Steen also returned (1744). At Ershorst in the Prussian district of Schardau he wrote two letters to the Committee in Amsterdam.
                                   vnZ.

Reimer, *Familiennamen*, 118; *Inv. Arch. Amst.* I, Nos. 1949, 1978, 1989, 1991, 1994; *DB* 1905, 124, 133, 142, 150, 153, 154 f.

Steen, Hans von (1705-81), a Mennonite minister in West Prussia, was born March 9, 1705, in Neugarten near Danzig, where his parents belonged to the Frisian Mennonite Church. His parents sent him to Amsterdam for business training; he was baptized there in 1726. After his return he joined the Flemish Mennonite Church of Danzig, married Sara Siemens in 1726, and established a small business and a brewery in Danzig. In 1738 von Steen was elected deacon, in 1743 minister, and was ordained as elder by Elder Hans Buhler on June 23, 1754. He did much to defend the legal rights of the Mennonites, who in those days were constantly threatened in various ways. The survival of the church during the difficult years of 1748-60 was due mostly to his efforts. His sermons were popular and attended by non-Mennonites. He was married three

times and had seven children. Only three survived him. His first wife died in 1749 and the second, Elisabeth Tiessen, in 1751, after which he married Christina Loewen. In 1773 he suffered a stroke and in 1779 he was succeeded as elder by Peter Epp (ord. Jan. 30, 1780). On Sept. 21, 1781, he died.

Hans von Steen preached in Dutch and carried on an extensive Dutch and German correspondence. His archives were probably destroyed during World War II. In his later years he instructed the catechetical candidates in the German language. After von Steen the shift from the Dutch to the German language in worship, which he had opposed, made rapid progress. The customary funeral song for Hans von Steen was one of the first to be composed in the German language.   C.K.

H. G. Mannhardt, *Die Danziger Mennonitengemeinde* (Danzig, 1919) 99, 107 ff.; *Inv. Arch. Amst.* I, No. 1647; *DB* 1886, 4 f.; *Gem.-Kal.*, 1927, 58, 75; 1935, 112 f.; Danzig Flemish Church Record (BeCL); *ML* IV.

Steenkiste, van, a former Dutch Mennonite family, whose members came from Belgium to the Dutch province of Zeeland (Aardenburg, Middelburg, Vlissingen) about 1600; some lived at Haarlem, where a Pieter van Steenkiste, apparently a deacon of the Flemish church, was involved in the controversies between Lucas Filips (*q.v.*) and Vincent de Hondt (*q.v.*) about 1600.   vnZ.

Steenwijk, a town (1947 pop. 8,677, with 171 Mennonites) in the Dutch province of Overijssel, the seat of a Mennonite congregation. This congregation had formerly its seat at Zuidveen (*q.v.*), a hamlet about two miles south of Steenwijk. For the early history of this church see **Zuidveen**. In 1848, since most of the members were then living at Steenwijk, a new meetinghouse and parsonage were built at Steenwijk, dedicated on May 4, 1848, by Koenraad Hovens Greve, then the pastor of the congregation. He served until 1862, and was followed by A. J. Bijl 1862-1904, E. Engelkes 1905-13, G. Fopma 1913-42, W. I. Fleischer 1942-46, Miss J. H. van der Slooten 1946-54, and H. J. de Wilde 1954- .

The meetinghouse of 1848 is still in use; in 1896 it was provided with an organ. The membership, which was about 135 in 1848, was 129 in 1861, 190 in 1900, and 167 in 1958. Outstanding families of the Steenwijk congregation were the Rijkmans and Veen families. There is a ladies' circle.

During the 16th century there was some Anabaptist activity at Steenwijk. Elder Leenaert Bouwens (*q.v.*) baptized five persons here in 1552. (*DJ* 1850, 40; *DB* 1878, 1, 37; 1882, 118; 1896, 204.)   vnZ.

Steffen van Halteren, an Anabaptist martyr, a native of the Dutch province of Utrecht, was arrested at Haarlem, Holland, in the house of Lambert Duppijns (*q.v.*), and beheaded at Haarlem on June 2, 1539, with his brother Jan van Halteren and a few others. He apparently was a follower of David Joris (*q.v.*).   vnZ.

Bijdragen en Mededeelingen v. h. Hist. Genootschap Utrecht XLI (1920) 200 f., 208, 210, 217.

Steffens, a Mennonite family, formerly in the congregation of Hamburg-Altona, Germany. Michael Steffens, of Oldesloe, was a preacher at Hamburg

1560-after 1604. According to Gerhard Roosen he was ordained by Menno Simons.   vdZ.

B. C. Roosen, *Geschichte der Menn.-Gemeinde zu Hamburg und Altona* I (Hamburg, 1886) 14, 29.

Steiermark: see Styria.

Steiger, Georg (b. 1814), came to the Emmental (*q.v.*), Switzerland, in early 1835 as an adherent of the revivalistic Samuel Fröhlich (*q.v.*). Steiger was very active among the Emmental Mennonites, who were at this time divided by the work of Fröhlich in 1832. Both Fröhlich and Steiger emphasized baptism by immersion, Steiger saying that "all are spiritually dead as long as they are not baptized by immersion." Among others he rebaptized Christian Baumgartner and Christian Gerber, both preachers of the Langnau Mennonite Church. Steiger worked among the Mennonites and also the Reformed, forming the Neutäufer (*q.v.*) movement.   vdZ.

S. Geiser, *Die Taufgesinnten-Gemeinden* (Karlsruhe, 1932) 467 f.; Delbert L. Gratz, *Bernese Anabaptists* (Scottdale, 1953) 115.

Stein, Diepold von, captain of the Swabian League, seized Eitelhans Langenmantel (*q.v.*) with his servant in Leiterhafen on April 24, 1528, and took them to Weissenborn, where they were put to death. He was thus one of the leaders of the four bands sent out by the League to eradicate the Anabaptists.

Chr. Meyer, "Zur Geschichte der Wiedertäufer in Oberschwaben," *Zeitschrift des historischen Vereins für Schwaben und Neuburg* I (1874) 215; *ML IV.*

Steinabrunn, a village of Lower Austria, not far from Nikolsburg on the Moravian border, the seat of a Hutterite Bruderhof founded in 1537 following the great persecution of 1535. The group immediately chose Mathes Legeder, Gutenhenn Hans, Michel Blauer, and Michel Kramer as deacons. On Dec. 16, 1539, the brotherhood met to discuss the question of union with a group of Swiss Brethren led by Philipp Plener (*q.v.*). But the plan could not be carried out. The royal provost surprised them at night with troops and took 136 persons in chains, men, women, and youths, and imprisoned them in the Falkenstein (*q.v.*) castle, which at that time, together with Steinabrunn, belonged to the barons of Fünfkirchen. After eight days the marshal of Ferdinand appeared with several priests and the executioner and demanded information concerning their faith and the location of their money. They made a confession of their faith. The priests tried in vain to "convert" them. The prisoners were finally told that they would be tolerated if they would live in groups of not more than eight persons; but they refused these terms. At the beginning of the new year the provost returned and again challenged the Brethren to desist from their faith. Those who refused would be delivered to the imperial admiral Andrew Doria to serve as galley slaves on his warships in the Mediterranean in the war against the Turks. Ninety of them, most of them fathers, were taken away chained in pairs; then the sick and the women were released. The men were taken to Trieste; here they managed to escape by making a rope of their chains to let themselves down over the wall facing the sea. On their return journey twelve of them were seized in Lai-

bach in Carinthia and taken back to Trieste; nothing more was ever heard of them. The brotherhood sent Jörg Meyerhofer to Trieste to look for them, but he did not find them. The rest of the fugitives reached Moravia, but three of them died soon after arrival.

The sufferings of the Anabaptists at Steinabrunn are described in several songs: Antoni Erfordter's (*q.v.*) "Geschichte der Verfolgung zu Steinabrunn" (14 stanzas), and Leonhard Roth's similar hymn (15 stanzas), and also in a hymn "To the imprisoned brethren in the Falkenstein" (29 stanzas). (*ML* IV.)   Hege.

Steinbach, a Mennonite village name found in Borozenko, Ukraine; East Reserve of Manitoba; Cuauhtemoc, Mexico; and Menno in the Paraguayan Chaco. (See **Villages.**)   C.K.

Steinbach was the name of a large private estate near the Molotschna Mennonite settlement, Russia, established by Klaas Wiens, the first Oberschulze of the Molotschna settlement. Alexander I visited this estate in 1818 and was impressed by the successful planting of trees on the bare steppes. This was one of the reasons for the founding of the Molotschna Mennonite Agricultural Association (*q.v.*). The nephew of Klaas Wiens, Pieter Schmidt (*q.v.*), was also a successful cultural leader. He established a secondary school on the estate. His son Peter Schmidt continued the tradition. (Friesen, *Brüderschaft,* 158 ff., 167, 615.)   C.K.

Steinbach is a Mennonite town located in the southeastern section of Manitoba. It almost totally occupies section 36 of township 6 and range 6E., with a part of the town outside of the section immediately to the west, and lies in the municipality of Hanover, near its eastern boundary. According to the 1955 census, Steinbach had a population of 2,350, of which 1,837 or some 82.7 per cent are Mennonites. The greater Steinbach area augments this figure to about 3,000. Steinbach was founded in 1874 by Kleine Gemeinde settlers who had just arrived from Russia. Today it has eight Mennonite churches all of Russian Mennonite origin, each with its own house of worship: the Evangelical Mennonite Church (Kleine Gemeinde), the Evangelical Mennonite Brethren, the Mennonite Brethren, the General Conference, Bergthaler, Chortitzer (Steinbach branch), Immanuel Mission Church, and the Church of God in Christ, Mennonite (Holdeman). Three non-Mennonite churches have located in Steinbach in the last few years.

The town was incorporated in 1946. It is now the shopping center of a large community of Mennonites, serving some 10,000 Mennonites in the East Reserve. The town also has a Mennonite hospital (leased to a public hospital administration in 1957), Bible Institute, invalid home, MCC clothing depot, a Bible camp association, and a child welfare home.   A.P.

75. Gedenkfeier der Mennonitischen Einwanderung in Manitoba, Canada (1949); *Facts About Steinbach, An Industrial Survey of the Town of Steinbach,* Given out by the Bureau of Industrial Development, Department of Industry and Commerce, Province of Manitoba (n.d., 1954); "Steinbach, The First Mennonite Settlement in

Western Canada" (unpublished manuscript); *Das 60-jährige Jubiläum der Mennonitischen Ost-Reserve* (Steinbach, 1935); P. J. B. Reimer, "Historical Sketches of Steinbach and District," *Carillon News* VII, Nos. 1-18 and 20 (Steinbach, 1952).

Steinbach Bible Academy, former name of Steinbach Bible Institute (*q.v.*).

Steinbach Bible Academy Bulletin, published by the Steinbach Bible Academy, Man., is a 4-8 page 6 x 9 in. quarterly promotion paper, started in 1945, since 1953 called the *Institute Bulletin.*   C.K.

Steinbach Bible Institute, located at Steinbach, Man., is a school with a three-year course in Bible and a three-year course in secular secondary education accredited by the Department of Education of the Province of Manitoba. Its primary purpose is to prepare Christians for effective Christian service. The Steinbach Bible Institute had its beginning in the fall of 1931 as the Steinbach Bible School with classes, both day and evening, conducted by a Mennonite Brethren minister, Jacob W. Reimer, and a Mennonite Alliance minister, Isaac Ediger. The following year an Evangelical Mennonite Brethren minister, Henry P. Fast, replaced Ediger. Four years later (1936), under the sponsorship of seven men of the M.B. Church, classes were again begun in the local M.B. church under a new staff of two teachers.

In the fall of 1938 a Bible School Association (*Bibelschulverein*) was organized, composed of members of four Mennonite churches of Steinbach and vicinity, which elected a board of directors to operate the school. This meant that the school was now to be interdenominational. The following year the Bible School moved into its own property and classroom building, and by 1942 had some 42 students.

In the fall of 1946 a high-school curriculum was introduced, and the name changed to Steinbach Bible Academy. After a few years the high-school department was dropped, but was reinstated in the fall of 1953, when a new constitution was written and the administration changed from the Verein to a corporation of directors or self-perpetuating board, and the name was changed to Steinbach Bible Institute. The emphasis has also shifted from the building of Christian character and training Sunday-school teachers, to the training of young people for Christian service, especially missions, both home and foreign. As a result a large percentage of students and graduates are entering mission work.

In 1955 the school was moved to a new campus of some thirteen acres just outside Steinbach, with completely new classroom, laboratory, dormitory, dining, and library facilities. The school is now offering a three-year course in Bible and theology, a two-year course in Christian education, and grades ten, eleven, and twelve. Grade twelve is an accredited first-year college course. During the school year 1954-55 the school had 12 teachers, 98 students in the day classes, and 42 in the evening classes. In 1957-58 the day enrollment was 154. More housing has been provided since 1956. B. D. Reimer was long principal, followed by Archie Penner in 1958. †   A.P.

The Star (Annual of the Steinbach Bible Institute) 1947-58; Bible Institute Catalog, 1941-58.

Steinbach (Man.) Church of God in Christ Mennonite Church was organized in 1881 when a large part of the Kleine Gemeinde (*q.v.*) in this area, with the elder and half of the preachers, joined the Church of God in Christ, Mennonite. Worship services were conducted in homes and then in a school building until 1911, when a church building was erected which has a seating capacity of 400. Wilhelm Giesbrecht was in charge of the services from the beginning until his death in 1917. Neighboring ministers then served the congregation until 1921, at which time Gerhard F. Giesbrecht and Jacob F. Barkman were ordained to the ministry. The services, conducted in both German and English, include regular Sunday morning and evening services, Sunday school, midweek Bible study, Christian Endeavor, hospital services, and singing practices. The sewing circle takes an active part in missionary efforts. The membership in 1957 was 160, with A. P. Barkman as minister in charge, assisted by Gerhard F. Giesbrecht and Ronald Wiebe.   J.F.BA.

Steinbach (Man.) Evangelical Mennonite Brethren Church had its beginning in 1897, when four families organized a congregation, three of whom had previously been members of the E.M.B. Church in Minnesota and the fourth, converts from a series of meetings held in 1897 by H. E. Fast of Bingham Lake, Minn. A. F. Friesen was ordained as the first minister. After serious difficulties the very small congregation was reorganized and made a fresh start in 1908, followed by the coming of P. B. Schmidt as pastor in 1909. In 1912 a meetinghouse was built, and H. S. Rempel and P. B. Janz added to the ministry. Internal difficulties again arose and not until 1925 was the congregation on the way to sound prosperity. In 1939 it had risen to 250 members; in 1957 the number was 351. G. S. Rempel served as pastor for many years, being succeeded in 1957 by Sam Epp.   H.S.B.

Steinbach Evangelical (Kleine Gemeinde) Mennonite Church, located at the east end of Steinbach, Man., was erected in 1912. Formerly meetings were held in the school building. The total baptized membership in 1955 was 400. A new church to seat 850 is in process of building near the 1912 church. Services are conducted in both German and English, sometimes concurrently. The baptized membership in 1958 was 490, with Archie Penner as the leading minister, assisted by P. D. Friesen, Jacob P. Dueck, and Benjamin D. Reimer. Heinrich Toews and David Schellenberg are serving in traveling evangelism and missionary work.   D.P.R.

Steinbach Mennonite Brethren Church, located in Steinbach, Man., a member of the Manitoba and Canadian district conferences, was founded by immigrants from Russia in the 1920's. It was organized in 1927 with about 65 members; the first leading minister was G. H. Unruh, assisted by J. W. Reimer (*q.v.*). The first meetinghouse was a remodeled school. Later a church was built, which was enlarged in 1957 to seat about 550. In 1958 the leading minister was H. A. Regehr, assisted by William Schroeder, with a membership of 285. J.WE.

Steinbach Mennonite Church (GCM), located at Hanover St., Steinbach, Man., a member of the Canadian Mennonite Conference, was organized in 1942, composed of 39 members of various congregations, but all of one conference, with 2 preachers. The meetinghouse was built in 1952, 80 x 38 ft., offering 500 seating places. In 1958 the congregation had 5 preachers and a deacon, with 233 baptized members; Henry P. Friesen was the pastor. Most of the older generation of the congregation are immigrants from Russia of the 1922 ff. immigrations. Most of them are farmers, some have trades, and one is the publisher of the *Steinbach Post*.

P.J.R.

Steinbach Post, Steinbach, Man., an 8-page 15 x 32 in. (before 1947, 12 x 18 in.) weekly, published every Tuesday by Derksen Printers Ltd., was started in 1913 by Jacob S. Friesen. In 1924 Arnold (A. B.) Dyck became publisher and editor of the paper. In 1936 G. S. Derksen purchased the paper and became its editor. The *Post* contains world news as well as news from the Mennonite settlements of Manitoba and other provinces, and is read by Mennonites of Canada, Mexico, and Paraguay. The paper claims to be "the oldest Mennonite weekly founded in Canada." Since the death of G. S. Derksen (1957) Jacob H. Block has been the editor. C.K.

Steiner (Stoner), a Mennonite family of Swiss origin, found early in the communes of Signau, Langnau, Trachselwald, and Eggiwil, in the canton of Bern. The first mention of a member of the family as Anabaptist was in 1538 when a Margaret Steiner was brought before the officials at Signau. Members of the family have figured in each of the Swiss Mennonite migrations. Christian Steiner (b. *c*1661), a deacon of Diesbach, was one of the emigrées to the Netherlands in 1711. In the early 18th century some moved to the Jura. By 1750 members of the family were found near Florimont in Alsace. A minister of the Swiss Mennonite congregation there, Hans Steiner, made several trips to the Palatinate with other ministers 1767-80 in an attempt to bring peace to two factions that had arisen in the Mennonite church there (see **Amish Division**).

In the 18th century some Steiners came to Pennsylvania. Most of their descendants have anglicized their name to Stoner. Descendants now live chiefly in Westmoreland, York, and Lancaster counties, Pa., and Virginia and Iowa. In 1825-35 several brothers and cousins, grandchildren of the above Hans Steiner of Florimont, settled near Kitchener, Ont., the Chippewa (now Crown Hill) settlement in northern Wayne County, Ohio, and in Putnam County, Ohio. Daniel Steiner became the first bishop of the Chippewa Swiss Mennonite congregation, and Christian Steiner was the first bishop of the Putnam County Swiss Mennonite congregation.

Christian P. Steiner (1832-1910), minister of the Riley Creek (*q.v.*) (later called Zion) Mennonite Church, Ohio, was one of the early instigators of a general conference in the Mennonite church (MC). Menno S. Steiner (*q.v.*, 1866-1911), a son of Christian P. Steiner, was a Mennonite (MC) evangelist, missionary, leader, author, and first president of the Mennonite Board of Missions and Charities. He lived near Cranberry (now Rockport), Allen County, Ohio, and served with his father as minister of the Zion Mennonite Church. Another son of Christian P. Steiner was Albert Steiner, a bishop (MC) in Columbiana County, Ohio. Two of A. J. Steiner's sons are now serving as bishops, David at North Lima, Ohio, and John at Pleasant View near Goshen, Ind., while a third son, James, is pastor at Wadsworth, Ohio.

Ulrich Steiner (*q.v.*, 1806-77) was an influential Mennonite elder in the Emmental (*q.v.*) Church. He had a glorious vision of heaven and wrote a pamphlet on this entitled *Angenehme Stunden in Zion*. This came into nearly every Swiss Mennonite home in the canton of Bern and America. D.L.G.

Steiner, Ezra Burkholder (1877-1955), a Mennonite (GCM) missionary, was born in Richland Twp., Allen Co., Ohio, on June 8, 1877, the oldest of the seven children (five sons and two daughters) of Sem and Barbara (Burkholder) Steiner. He married Elizabeth Geiger on Aug. 26, 1913. He attended Wheaton College, Wheaton, Ill., and Taylor College, Upland, Ind. He and his wife entered mission service under the General Conference Mennonite Mission Board in India in 1914. They left this mission in 1924 to work in a higher altitude in India which was more suited to his health. They built an independent mission at Dharchula, Almora District, U.P., India, near the Nepal and Tibet borders, supported by friends as well as the churches of their home community, and later by the Evangelical Missionary Association. They appealed especially to the Tibetan and Nepalese traders and residents of the area and built a thriving Christian church. Mrs. Steiner died in 1954 and he died Nov. 4, 1955. Their two children are now missionaries in India; Dr. Bradford Ezra Steiner is the superintendent of the Landour Community Hospital at Landour, and Anita Elizabeth (Mrs. Charles Warren), born 1921, and her husband carry on the work at Dharchula. D.L.G.

Steiner, Georg (also called Goldschmidt, i.e., Goldsmith), a goldsmith of Salzburg (*q.v.*), in whose house the local Anabaptists met in 1527. Hans Hut (*q.v.*) preached here several days and baptized Steiner among others, and lived with Steiner for ten days. Steiner became the treasurer of the congregation. Later Steiner was seized by the authorities of Salzburg. He recanted and was therefore put to death by beheading. His 16-year-old daughter, however, remained steadfast and died as a martyr by drowning. HEGE.

J. Jäkel, *Geschichte der Wiedertäufer in Oberösterreich* (Freistadt, 1889) 57; Chr. Meyer, "Zur Geschichte der Wiedertäufer in Oberschwaben," in *Ztscht des Historischen Vereins für Schwaben und Neuburg* I (1874) 247 f.; F. Gess, *Akten und Briefe zur Kirchenpolitik Herzogs Georgs von Sachsen* III (Leipzig, 1917) 811; *ML* II, 134.

Steiner, Menno Simon (1866-1911), a Mennonite (MC) preacher and leader, was born near Beaverdam, Ohio, on April 30, 1866, a son of Christian Peter Steiner, a farmer-preacher, and Barbara Thut. He graduated from the Bluffton (Ohio) High

School in 1887. Two years previously he had united with his home congregation, the Riley Creek Church (later called Zion), and soon felt a special call to the ministry.

While Steiner was teaching school (1887-90), John F. Funk (*q.v.*) in 1889 persuaded him to work for the Mennonite Publishing Company at Elkhart, Ind. During several summer vacations he traveled for this company among various branches of Mennonites. In letters, diaries, and in numerous articles in the *Herald of Truth* he revealed many of the needs and problems he discovered. In 1889 he became the first secretary of the Mennonite Book and Tract Society. He interrupted his career at Elkhart to attend Oberlin College for theological training (1891-92). In 1892 he helped John S. Coffman (*q.v.*) promote the important first general Sunday-school conference, held near Goshen, Ind. He was chosen moderator of the conference.

Early in 1893 Steiner was ordained to the ministry at Elkhart by Bishop John F. Funk. At the second general Mennonite Sunday-school conference in 1893 he was appointed to establish a mission in Chicago, also to edit a young people's paper. The Home Mission, which he founded in 1893, was the first city mission of the Mennonites in America. On April 8, 1894, he married Clara Daisy Eby. They opened a mission at Canton, Ohio, in January 1895, but remained there for only one year. Meanwhile, he began to hold evangelistic meetings, which occasioned his visits to many states and Canadian provinces. He was also the moving spirit (and sole president) in the organization of the Mennonite Board of Charitable Homes (*q.v.*, 1889), which merged in 1906 with the Mennonite Evangelizing and Benevolent Board (*q.v.*) to become the Mennonite Board of Missions and Charities (*q.v.*), of which he was the first president, serving until his death in 1911. He sought without success to include several smaller Mennonite branches (EMB, Central Conference) in this mission organization.

After 1897 he lived on a small farm east of Columbus Grove, Ohio, where he eked out a modest living, aided by his loyal wife and friends. He helped his father in ministering to the Zion Church, but he was often busy away from home on church work. Here four of his five children were born, namely, Esther A. (Mrs. J. C. Meyer), Luke E., Paul E., and C. Grace (Mrs. Ivan Hostetler). The oldest, Charity E. (Mrs. Lester Hostetler), was born at Canton, Ohio.

Steiner wrote two books, *Pitfalls and Safeguards* (1899), and a biography, *John S. Coffman* (1903). He was the first editor of the *Young People's Paper* (Elkhart, Ind.), serving from January 1894 to March 1895. He carried on a heavy correspondence in his capacity as president of the Mennonite Board of Missions and Charities and two antecedent boards, from 1899 until his death. He helped to organize several charitable institutions, particularly the Mennonite Old People's Home, established in 1901 near Rittman, Ohio.

He died at the Bluffton Sanitarium on March 12, 1911, and was buried in the Zion cemetery, west of Bluffton, Ohio. An obituary was published in the *Gospel Herald* on March 23, 1911.† E.S.M.

John S. Umble, *Mennonite Pioneers* (Scottdale, 1940), Chapter V; *idem, MHB*, 1941; *idem, Ohio Mennonite Sunday Schools* (Goshen, 1941); Daniel Kauffman, *Mennonite Cyclopedic Dictionary* (Scottdale, 1937) (this is useful but contains some errors); J. S. Hartzler and Daniel Kauffman, *Mennonite Church History* (Scottdale, 1905).

Steiner, Ulrich (1806-77), an elder of the Langnau congregation in Emmental, canton of Bern, Switzerland, was born near Trachselwald on Sept. 6, 1806. Later his father, Peter Steiner, bought a farm in the Lauperswil community, which Ulrich took over after his father's death. His ancestors had belonged to the liberal (?) group of Anabaptists in the Emmental while persecution was still raging. His parents did not join until in their later years. Ulrich attended catechetical instruction in the Reformed church at Trachselwald. When his parents joined the Mennonites he also began to attend their meetings, and at the age of nineteen he also joined the Mennonite congregation. Five years later he was chosen as preacher. In 1834 he married Elisabeth Wüthrich of Trub. In the following year he was ordained elder. This was soon after the schism in the Emmental congregation in 1835 caused by the Neutäufer (*q.v.*). He wrote about these difficulties in his booklet *Angenehme Stunden in Zion*. The light of the rising sun with its golden beams seemed to him a symbol of the old church, since it had through all the storms of persecution shone as a bright light, whereas he saw as a symbol of the Neutäufer (or Fröhlichianer) the light of the full moon.

In accord with the Anabaptist regulation of 1823 only the children of Anabaptists were allowed to join the Mennonites, and they were not to make any proselytes. But since others also came to Steiner's baptismal instruction he was accused by the Reformed pastor of proselyting and was imprisoned for several days. On another occasion he was fined on a similar charge. He presented a petition of complaint to the authorities, whereupon he was released.

Steiner's effectiveness in the brotherhood was richly blessed. His preaching was heart-winning, edifying, earnest, but gentle. Through his friendly nature he won many hearts. "Steiner Uli" was respected and loved far beyond the borders of his own brotherhood. He kept up an active correspondence with the Swiss Mennonites in America, especially with the Sonnenberg congregation in Wayne County, Ohio. His booklet *Angenehme Stunden in Zion* was also widely spread in America. A poem of his published in the *Gemeinde-Kalender* (1931) describes the state of those who have finished their course with blessing.

After a prolonged illness, Ulrich Steiner died on July 10, 1877. At his grave the Reformed pastor of Lauperswil recalled how much he had learned and received from this mature father in Christ.† S.G.

S. Geiser, *Die Taufgesinnten-Gemeinden* (Karlsruhe, 1931); *Gem.-Kal.* 1906 and 1931; picture of Ulrich Steiner with his wife, p. 432; picture of him alone in the *Gem.-Kal.* 1906; *ML* IV.

Steinfeld (*Kamenopol*), a Mennonite village name found in the following settlements: Molotschna and Shlachtin, Ukraine; and Neuland, Paraguay. (See **Villages.**) C.K.

Steinfurt: see **Burgsteinfurt.**

Steinman Amish Mennonite Church, located one mile west of the village of Baden on highway 7 and 8, in Waterloo County, Ont., is a member of the Ontario Amish Mennonite Conference, and with the St. Agatha congregation had a combined membership of 520 in 1957. The congregation, first called Wilmot, was organized about 1826.

In 1822 Christian Nafziger, of Bavaria, Germany, purchased land in Wilmot Township for settlement; he returned to Germany and brought his family and others of his congregation to Canada. During his absence a number of families from Pennsylvania moved to Wilmot and a congregation was organized. Most of the settlers however came directly from Europe, mostly Alsace and Lorraine. Names of some early settlers include Fahrni, Roth, Litwiler, Gardner, Miller, Gingerich, Steinman, Wagler, Oesch, Lichti, Gascho, etc.

The congregation worshiped in homes until 1884, when the Steinman meetinghouse was built. A year later another church was built one-half mile west of St. Agatha, and services were held alternately in the two buildings until 1939. Since then services have been held every Sunday in each church. The old Steinman church, a white frame building, was removed and replaced in 1946 by a new brick structure, with a seating capacity of 600. Pennsylvania-Dutch is still spoken at home, but church services are all in English.

The congregation is active in the support of missions, evangelism, and church schools.

The ministers serving the congregation in 1958 were: Moses O. Jantzi and Orland Gingerich, bishops; Peter Nafziger and Elmer Schwartzentruber, ministers.   O.G.

Steinmetz, Georg (Jurriaen Steenmetser in Dutch *Martyrs' Mirror*), a German Anabaptist martyr, was beheaded in 1530 at Pforzheim in Württemberg. He left an effective admonition "for the comfort of all believers," found in the *Martyrs' Mirror*. It is not certain that he is actually the author of the hymn (No. 35 in the *Ausbund*), "Wir danken Gott von Herzen." (*Mart. Mir.* D 31, E 439; Wolkan, *Lieder,* 10; *ML* IV.)   NEFF, W.W.

Stei(n)peck(h), Hanns, an Anabaptist martyr, a master mason, was beheaded and burned with Hans Neumair (*q.v.*) and six other Anabaptists, L. Haslinger and his wife, Jörg Zacherle and his wife, M. Perger, and Jörg Kreutzinger, on July 8, 1528, at Wels, Austria.

Beck, *Geschichts-Bücher,* 280; A. Nicoladoni, *Johannes Bünderlin von Linz und die oberösterreichische Täufergemeinden* (Berlin, 1893) 100, 18 f.; *ML* IV.

Steinreich Mennonite Brethren Church, located near Peabody, Marion Co., Kan., a member of the Southern District Conference, began in 1905 as an extension project of the Ebenfeld M.B. Church. Various ministers from Ebenfeld served the young church, among whom were H. W. Lohrenz and J. W. Lohrenz. The membership in 1957 was 40, mostly rural, with Franz Dick as pastor. The meetinghouse has recently been remodeled.   M.L.W.

Steinsdorf, Hans, a German Anabaptist martyr, a master tailor of Schneeberg, Saxony, who could neither read nor write, was baptized by Peter Reusse (*q.v.*). He parted from his wife and five children who refused to accept his faith, left them the house and settled in another part of Schneeberg, and became the close friend of Hans Hamster (*q.v.*), a peasant with whom he discussed their common faith. In 1538 he was arrested with Heinrich Tritzschel of Saalfeld, his apprentice, who had accepted the Anabaptist faith and attracted the attention of the authorities by his irrational demeanor. They were questioned. The apprentice recanted, and Hans Steinsdorf was led to the castle prison in Zwickau. Here he was frequently visited by the local clergy, who tried in vain to convert him. He asked to be banished from the country, promising never to return. The elector refused to grant this wish, but on Aug. 28, 1538, ordered Wolf Böhm in Zwickau to re-examine Steinsdorf on a number of points on which he had already given specific information. Steinsdorf remained true to his faith. When he was asked where he would go if he were released he replied, "wherever he were commanded by the Heavenly Father, there he would gladly be. If it should be God's will he would stay with his wife and children. But if he was obliged to die for his faith, he would willingly submit." The examination revealed that Steinsdorf thought infant baptism nothing; children, born with a pure spirit, need no baptism. If they die young they are saved. Christ was not baptized as a child. Likewise also all the apostles. Body and blood have a spiritual meaning in the communion service. Elector John Frederick sent this confession of the two Anabaptists, Steinsdorf and Hamster, to the court at Wittenberg for decision. The court was unable to arrive at a decision, but ordered that the Anabaptists be questioned once again. Nothing more is known about the case, but it can be assumed that Steinsdorf and Hamster were beheaded.   NEFF.

Paul Wappler, *Inquisition und Ketzerprozesse zur Reformationszeit* (Leipzig, 1908) 96-117; *ML* IV.

Stemen (Stehmann), **Henry** (1775-1855), one of the first Mennonite settlers to move from Rockingham County, Va., to the Rush Creek region in Richland Twp., Fairfield Co., Ohio, was ordained preacher there in 1809 and bishop in 1820. Christian Stehmann, Henry's father, had moved to Rockingham County from Pennsylvania. Before leaving Rockingham County, Henry Stemen had married Mary Beery, whose brothers were among the charter members of the Dunkard congregation organized in Fairfield County in 1809. Henry and Mary Stemen followed the usual route traveled by Virginia settlers "going West"—up the Potomac and into Pennsylvania along "Braddock's trail," and after stopping for a year or two in Greene County, Pa., arrived in Fairfield County, Ohio, in 1803. The county grew rapidly; the first actual settlers arrived in 1798, and in 1806 the county listed 1,551 taxpayers. In 1841 Stemen moved to Allen County, Ohio, where a Mennonite congregation had been organized several years earlier. For a number of years he seems to have been the only Mennonite bishop in the central, western, and northwestern sections of the state. His ministry was noted for his earnest and expressive sermons. In a very real sense he became an itinerant preacher. Saddling one of his well-kept horses, he would ride through wilderness, mud, and storm from settlement to settlement in Wyandot, Wood, Seneca, Williams, Clark, Logan, Fairfield, and Franklin counties. On these tiring pastoral trips he preached, baptized, held communion services either with an outlying congregation or with a single family living far from a congregation of their own faith. He preached funeral sermons over the graves of those who had been quietly laid away months before because no minister could be called in time for the burial. He ordained bishops, preachers, and deacons and organized congregations on the frontier. In 1843-44 he attended a church conference in the Chester meetinghouse, in Wayne County. On at least one occasion he rode horseback to the Ohio Mennonite Conference in Mahoning County. He made numerous trips to Fairfield County until he ordained John M. Brenneman (*q.v.*) bishop in Franklin County. In 1853 he ordained George Brenneman bishop as his successor, but shortly before his death in 1855 he persuaded John M. Brenneman to move to Allen County and formally installed him as his successor. Most of Henry Stemen's descendants, impatient with the conservative policies of the "unlearned" John M. Brenneman, united with other denominations and rose to prominent positions in the professions in Allen and Van Wert counties. His son Nicholas Stemen (1802-78), however, was a deacon in the Fairfield County Mennonite church.

J.S.U.

History of the Stemen Family (Fort Wayne, 1881); John Umble, "The Fairfield County, Ohio, Background of the Allen County, Ohio, Mennonite Settlement," *MQR* VI (1932) 5-29, *passim.*

Stemen Mennonite (MC) Church (now extinct), located near Pickerington, Franklin Co., Ohio. The meetinghouse was built about 1890 by Benoni Stemen, a wealthy farmer and successful breeder of Galloway cattle. He settled his children on farms around his own and sought to revive the declining interest in the Mennonite faith. But efforts to establish a Sunday school failed; the young people preferred the services in the "English" churches, and the building, falling into disuse, was sold and the benches removed to the Turkey Run Mennonite Church (*q.v.*) in Perry County. J.S.U.

Stemmen uit de Doopsgezinde Broederschap is a 24-page 6 x 8 in. Dutch Mennonite periodical, which appeared in five issues annually 1952-57, and since then in four. Editors are N. van der Zijpp, Th. van der Veer, J. A. Osterbaan, and J. T. Nielsen.

Stenfort (Stenfoort, Stenvoort), a former Dutch Mennonite family, apparently had its origin in (Burg)Steinfurt, Westphalia, Germany. Members of this family lived at Haarlem, Holland, in the 17th-18th centuries, and Salomon Stenfoort was a preacher of Amersfoort and Bunschoten about 1700. (*Inv. Arch. Amst.* II, No. 1522.) vDZ.

Stenvers, a Dutch Mennonite family descended from a family of (Burg)Steinfurt, Westphalia, Germany.

Since the early 17th century a branch lived at Enschedé (*q.v.*) in the textile business, and later textile manufacture; a number of them served as deacons of the Mennonite church. Sometime later its members were also found in other Mennonite congregations. Kl. Stenvers was treasurer of the Deventer (*q.v.*) Mennonite congregation about 1900. In the 17th century the name Stenvers was also spelled Stenforts or Stenvorts. They may have belonged to the same branch as the Stenfort (*q.v.*) family. vDZ.

Stenz, Hans, a Mennonite preacher in Aargau, Switzerland, a native of Setzwyl, but living in Kulm, a peasant, the father of five children, was arrested and sent to Bern, where he was tried with Martin Bruger (*q.v.*) on March 1 and 6, 1645, and March 2, 1646. On Jan. 7, 1648, he had to answer to nine questions which were sent to him: separation, proclamation of the Word through preachers of the established church, the significance of the Old Testament, infant baptism, attitude toward government, holding of government office, interest, tithes, taxes, etc., the right to wage war, the oath, and the punishment of wicked persons. He gave excellent replies, which can be taken as the position of the Mennonites of the time. On Jan. 13, 1648, they were again examined and asked whether they would not return to the church. Then Stenz replied that he could not burden his conscience, but would rather give his blood, if the Lord would give him grace; but he asked the government to be merciful. The council of Bern (*q.v.*) was determined to send them to the galleys as obstinate heretics; but "to spare their souls" they were put into the penitentiary in Zürich. Hans Stenz escaped and was caught; he was expelled and forced to promise that he would never return. He left with his wife and children; nothing more is known of him. NEFF.

Muller, *Berner Täufer*, 106 ff., 182, 216; J. Heiz, *Täufer im Aargau* (Aarau, 1902) 86; *ML* IV.

Sterling Evangelical Mennonite Church (EMC), Sterling, Kan., had its origin in 1880, when members of the Defenseless Mennonite congregations of Ohio, Indiana, and Illinois moved into Kansas. They began meetings in the homes, and in about 1883 organized a church with Jacob Schmucker and John Doetsch as ministers. In 1885 a church was built 11 miles southwest of Sterling, which was used until 1912, when the present church was built. In 1933 the church celebrated Jacob Schmucker's fifty years as pastor of the church. In 1948 the name was changed from Defenseless Mennonite to Evangelical Mennonite Church. The membership in 1955 was 152, with Arthur Enns as pastor. A.Sc.

Sterling Mennonite Church (GCM), Wayne County, Ohio, was founded by Peter Rich and his friends after he had been excommunicated by the Oak Grove Amish Mennonite Church (*q.v.*) in 1869 for refusing to quit his business of brewing beer. After his excommunication Rich attended services in Butler County, Ohio, and between 1896 and 1901 while H. P. Krehbiel was attempting to revive the Canton Mennonite Church as a G.C.M. congregation he attended there. Finally in 1900 the Rich-Krabill group in Sterling was organized as a congregation by G.C.M. ministers and held services in a small church near the Amwell (Sterling) cemetery where Rich and a number of his relatives are buried. When that building was sold and moved away the congregation in 1906 erected a small church at the south edge of Sterling but depended on supply ministers sent by the Home Mission Committee of the Conference or on the ministers of the Wadsworth First Mennonite Church. The congregation is first listed in the 1905 *Mennonite Yearbook and Almanac* as a member of the Middle District Conference. In H. P. Krehbiel's statistical computation of 1911 (*Mennonite Churches of North America*) the congregation appears without a minister but with Peter Krabill as deacon and with 40 members. From that time until 1920 the membership fluctuated between 38 and 43. During the decade following 1920 the congregation disbanded, sold their meetinghouse to a Progressive Brethren congregation, and most of the members united with the Wadsworth Mennonite (GCM) Church. Their strong Swiss-Alsatian Mennonitism brought new emphasis and strength to that congregation.   J.S.U.

John Umble, "The Oak Grove Amish Mennonite Church," *MQR* XXXI (1957) 150-53; Rachel Kreider, "One Hundred Years in Wadsworth," *Menn. Life* VIII (1953) 165-66.

Sterling (Ill.) Reformed Mennonite Church had 52 baptized members in 1958. The first members moved into the area in 1820, but the meetinghouse was not built until 1868.   H.S.B.

Stern, Alfred (1846-1936), a German historian, b. Nov. 22, 1846, professor of history at the University of Bern. He is the author of the article *Dr. Balthasar Hubmaier*, in the *Allgemeine Deutsche Biographie* (XIII, 264), and the book *Ueber die zwölf Artikel der Bauern und einige andere Aktenstücke aus der Bewegung von 1525*, in which he tried to prove that Hubmaier (*q.v.*) was the author of the Twelve Articles. Stern's brother Adolf treated the Anabaptists in a fictional form in his novelle *Die Wiedertäufer* (Leipzig, 1866). (*ML* IV.) NEFF, E.T.

Sterretje, het, a Mennonite congregation at Amsterdam, Holland, which split off from the Kleine Zon (*q.v.*) congregation in 1675. It held its meetings on the Prinsengracht, but in 1692 it merged with the Old Frisian Arke Noach (*q.v.*) congregation. vDZ.

Ster(t)zing, a town in South Tirol (formerly Austria), Italy, was from 1528 a center of Anabaptist activity. Thirty Anabaptists were executed at Sterzing, among whom were Konrad Fichter (*q.v.*) and Lamprecht Gruber (*q.v.*), both in 1532.

Steuber, Hans, of Durlach near Karlsruhe in Baden, Germany, an Anabaptist martyr. In Passau (*q.v.*), where he lay in prison in 1535, he confessed that he had been baptized four years previously by Konrad Lemblin; he would not recant, but remained with the truth. (*ML* IV.) W.W.

Stevele, Nicolas de, an Anabaptist martyr: see **Claes of Armentières.**

Steven Benedictus, an Anabaptist martyr, who was executed at Hoorn, Holland, on June 7, 1535. With him two other men, Sijbrant Jansz and Hendrik Gijsbertsz, and two women, Femmetgen Egberts and Welmoet Jans, were put to death, the three men by beheading, the women by drowning in the Zuiderzee, with heavy stones around their necks. They were arrested in March 1535; all remained steadfast, refusing to yield their faith in spite of the efforts of Catholic clergy. They declared that they did not regret their baptism after the order of Christ, i.e., being baptized unto remission of sins, putting on the Lord Jesus Christ (Rom. 13:14), and obtaining a good conscience toward God (I Pet. 3:21). Their execution shocked the citizens of Hoorn, and even some of the city magistrates, who knew them as good people, were greatly excited. vDZ.

Mart. Mir. D 36 f., E 443; *Inv. Arch. Amst.* I, No. 131; Mellink, *Wederdopers,* 168 f.; *ML* I, 163.

Steven de Graet, whose real name was Steven Segaert, an Anabaptist martyr, a native of Kortrijk (*q.v.*), was executed by burning at the stake at Gent, Belgium, on April 7, 1564, together with his mother Jozyne Steeghers, the widow of Cornelis Segaer(t), commonly called Sijntgen (*q.v.*). Particulars are lacking. Both remained steadfast. Their names are found in the martyr hymn "Als men schreef duyst vijfhondert, ende twee en tsestich mede," found in the *Lietboecken* (see also **Graet, de**). (Offer, 651; *Mart. Mir.* D 301, E 666; Verheyden, *Gent,* 30, No. 99; *ML* II, 154.) vDZ.

Steven Janssen, an Anabaptist martyr, an armorer (*harnaschveger*) and a native of the "lande van den Berch" (near Cologne, Germany), was one of the Naaktlopers (*q.v.*), Anabaptists who ran naked along the streets of Amsterdam on Feb. 10-11, 1535. He was sentenced to death by beheading on Feb. 25 of the same year. (Grosheide, *Verhooren,* 57 f.) vDZ.

Steven van Oudewater, an Anabaptist martyr, was one of the Naaktlopers (*q.v.*), Anabaptists who on Feb. 10-11, 1535, ran naked along the streets of Amsterdam. He was sentenced to death by beheading on Feb. 25, 1535. (Grosheide, *Verhooren,* 57 f.) vDZ.

Steven Pietersz, an Anabaptist martyr, was beheaded at Utrecht, Netherlands, on July 5, 1569. Steven was a native of Bunschoten (*q.v.*) and lived at Amersfoort. He was charged with attending the illegal meetings of the Anabaptists and permitting them to meet in his house. vDZ.

J. Marcus, *Sententiën en indagingen . . . van Alba* (Amsterdam, 1735) 364; I. M. J. Hoog, "Onze Martelaren," in *Ned. Archief v. Kerkgesch.* I (1902) 82 ff., No. 153.

Stevensz, Jan (also called J. S. van Nyeveen), b. May 1634 at Nijeveen, Dutch province of Drente, d. after 1686, a weaver of Kampen. In 1672 he moved to Amsterdam, where he was the city lamplighter. He was always in need, and he was often generously aided by the deacons of the Amsterdam Lamist (*q.v.*) Mennonite congregation, of which he was a member. Stevensz was a difficult and quarrelsome person. For some time he was an ardent follower of the Amsterdam Lamist preacher Galenus (*q.v.*) Abrahamsz, but still greater and more lasting was his veneration of the German theologian and mystic Jakob Böhme. About 1682 Stevensz left the Mennonite Church.

Stevensz wrote some books; e.g., *Apocalypsis ofte Het geopende Boeck met seven segelen* (Amsterdam, 1675), *Fondament-boeck, of Grondigh bewijs van de Kennisse Godts en de Christelijke Godsdienst* (Amsterdam, 1683). In this book Stevensz published two letters of Menno Simons—the one to the brethren in Franeker and the one to the congregation of Emden. In one of the appendices to this book he accused Galenus Abrahamsz of false teachings and unchristian conduct. A third book by Stevensz is *Onderwys door Exempelen ofte Spiegel der lijdsame Heyligen* (Amsterdam, 1686), of which there is a second elarged edition under the revised title *Aenhangsel ofte Vervolg van het Martelaers-boeck van Tieleman van Braght* (Amsterdam, 1686), in which he contributes a number of items on Luther, Menno Simons, and some persons of his own time who met with revilement because of their religious convictions. This book, like its author, is not very important. vdZ.

DB 1902, 87-102; *Inv. Arch. Amst.* II, No. 902; C. B. Hylkema, *Reformateurs* I and II (Haarlem, 1900, 1902) *passim;* H. W. Meihuizen, *Galenus Abrahamsz* (Haarlem, 1954) 152 f., 163.

Stevensville Mennonite Church (MC), now extinct, located 10 miles west of the Niagara River in the northern part of Bertie Twp., Welland Co., Ont., grew out of a settlement of Mennonites early in the 19th century. Among these are the names of Haun, Baker, Barnheart, House, Beam, Danner, Carver, Eberly, Schisler, Learn, Johnson, and Winger. There was a community-built church a few miles west of Stevensville where Mennonites took chief interest. Jacob Krehbiel of Clarence Center came regularly to preach from about 1872 and continued during his more active years. John B. Hershey of the Sherkston congregation about 6 miles south conducted some services; also David Sherk of the United Brethren Church. After Jacob Krehbiel withdrew from the Mennonite Conference (MC) in Ontario to the General Conference Mennonites about 1880, this group organized under him and built a new church in Stevensville. Abram Johnson conducted singing schools in the old log church in the interval before it was dismantled about 1885. The family names may be identified in two cemeteries, one on the Barnheart property (log church), the other in the Haun cemetery on the west outskirts of Stevensville. After Krehbiel discontinued regular services the Church of God congregation took over the use of the church. J.C.F.

Stevensville (Ont.) Reformed Mennonite Church, in Welland County, Ontario. The meetinghouse was built in 1835. The membership was 41 in 1958. H.S.B.

Steyr, a city in Upper Austria, famous as a center of the Austrian steel industry ever since the Middle Ages, with a wealthy and proud citizenship. During the 14th and 15th centuries there existed in this city large and influential Waldensian congregations. Although no recorded ties between Waldensians and Anabaptists can be produced, connections are most probable. It is noteworthy, for instance, that an Anabaptist congregation existed in Steyr as early as 1526, of unknown origin, for when Balthasar Hubmaier (*q.v.*) passed through the city on his way from Zürich to Nikolsburg he found a small congregation shepherded by the chaplain of the "imperial castle," Johann Portner. Portner one year later (1527) introduced Hans Hut to the patricians of this city. Hut had arrived from Nikolsburg and Vienna on his big mission trip (ending in Augsburg in the same year), and immediately began an intensive activity among the well-established burghers of this city. Meetings were held in the house of the respected patrician Veith Pfeffel; another patrician, Leonhard Khoberer, was converted. When Hut was on trial in Augsburg and questioned about his activities, he claimed to have baptized 10 or 12 persons "in Eysenstadt" (Steyr) (Meyer, 226), but the number of converts was certainly far greater than that figure. The city council became disturbed, imprisoned several persons without much ado, and reported the whole situation to Vienna. King Ferdinand I (*q.v.*) was shocked and decided to eradicate the evil. On Oct. 31, 1527, the royal procurator Magister Wolfgang Künigl (*q.v.*) arrived in Steyr and began at once with examinations in an attempt to reverse the trend. Some men remained steadfast; others were willing to recant but were repelled by the brutality of the "Penance of Horb" (*q.v.*), the prescribed ritual of renouncing the Anabaptist faith and all the subsequent penalties connected with it. Even Künigl sensed that this formula was utterly disreputable and petitioned the king not to insist on it; he feared rebellion and foresaw that many would escape only to continue their "heresy" elsewhere.

The court passed the surprisingly mild sentence of several months' imprisonment, deeming this lenience necessary for new attempts at reconversion. Six men yielded not a whit, a few others expressed doubt concerning the deity of Christ, while the majority confessed the simple Apostolic Creed. The king overruled the mild sentence and asked for the names of the jurymen who had not voted for the death penalty. He ordered the execution of all who were obstinate; consequently six men were martyred during Lent and nine more in May 1528, a total of 15 executions. It was expected that this measure had broken the strength of the Steyr Anabaptists.

But ten years later, in 1537-41, Anabaptists were again in Steyr, when the Hutterite chronicle reports the presence of "Philippites" (*q.v.*). Riedemann and other Hutterites visited them now and then, and a few men went to Moravia to discuss a possible merger. Among those mentioned was Wolf Brandhuber, apparently the son of the former leader of the Linz congregation (see **Brandhuber**). Whether or not community of goods was practiced remains undisclosed. Unfortunately these Philippites had no real leader, thus disorder set in and in 1541 the group broke up. Some went to the Hutterites in

Moravia; the majority, however, turned either Catholic or Lutheran. The Chronicle, in its table of martyrs of the year 1542, records for this city of Steyr a total of 30 martyrs, the greatest number in Upper Austria next to Linz.

For some thirty years after this the records are mute concerning Anabaptism. But then, all of a sudden, new troubles arose in this thoroughly Lutheran city. Around 1570 the records mention "subversive" activities, even among members of the city council. The trouble is blamed on missioners from Moravia, though it cannot be proved. There is mention of secret meetings for adult baptism and the celebration of the Lord's Supper, but things remain somewhat obscure. Particularly embarrassing to the city fathers was the case of the two patrician families of Fäbl and Khoberer in 1575. Hans Fäbl, a goldsmith, refused to have his child baptized, and even abused the Lutheran preachers. In this he was supported by his friend Wolf Khoberer, son-in-law of an influential and wealthy council member. It is reasonable to assume that Anabaptist teachings prompted this attitude. The city council felt it necessary to put them into the Tower, primarily to avoid any impression that Lutheranism meant liberty of conscience. Soon, however, influential personalities intervened and the two men were released. Khoberer made his peace with the city fathers, but the more stubborn Fäbl was eventually expelled from the city in 1580. It was the last record in Steyr of Anabaptist ideas or activities.   Gr.M., R.F.

This article is based in the main on research in the archives of Steyr; unfortunately a great number of important records formerly in the archives of the Ministry of Education, Vienna, were destroyed. Grete Mecenseffy, *Geschichte des Protestantismus in Oesterreich* (Graz, 1956) 37; A. Nicoladoni, *Johannes Bünderlin* (Berlin, 1893); J. Jäckel, "Zur Geschichte der Wiedertäufer in Oberösterreich" 47. *Bericht des Museums Francisco-Carolinum* (Linz, 1889); R. Friedmann, "The Philippite Brethren, a Chapter in Anabaptist History," *MQR* XXXII (1958) 278-83; Christian Meyer, "Zur Geschichte der Wiedertäufer in Oberschwaben," *Ztscht des Hist. Vereins für Schwaben und Neuburg* I (1874) 226 (concerning Hans Hut); V. Preuenhuber, *Annales Styrenses* (Nürnberg, 1740) 233-41 and 307; *ML* III, 285 and 318.

Stichting Voor Bijzondere Noden *in de Doopsgezinde Broederschap en Daarbuiten* (Foundation for Special Needs in the Mennonite Brotherhood and Beyond) is a Dutch Mennonite foundation founded on June 3, 1947, upon the instigation of A. P. van de Water, who was its first president. This foundation aims to give relief in special needs, both material and spiritual, which are the result of world conditions; it also continues the work formerly done by the Committee for Foreign Needs (see **Fonds voor Buitenlandsche Nooden**). It is administered by a board (present director is R. de Zeeuw); there are a number of subcommittees for the different branches of the work and contact persons in every Dutch Mennonite congregation. This foundation represents the Dutch Mennonites in the International Mennonite Relief.

Its activities include the Children's Home at Oud-Wulven (*q.v.*) near Houten (1947-58, and now at Schoorl); the care of a number of displaced persons from Eastern Europe; continued care for fatigued housewives, who are temporarily lodged in one of the Mennonite brotherhood homes; since 1958 the care of 30 aged repatriating Dutch Indonesians, lodged in a special house at Baarn. During 1953-54 extensive relief was given to the victims of the flood which struck large areas in Holland on Feb. 1, 1953.

Among the international relief projects are to be mentioned aid to the Mennonite refugees everywhere; material and spiritual aid to the Mennonite congregation of Berlin (*q.v.*) through the Mennoheim; and support to the Mennonites behind the Iron Curtain. The foundation also supports the activities of Mennonite Voluntary Service and cooperates with other churches and groups in the Foundation of Ecumenical Relief to Churches and Refugees operating in Hungary, Greece, Poland, and Italy. It receives its funds from the Pentecost offering held in all the Mennonite congregations (annual proceeds about 60,000 Dutch guilders) and collects food and clothing (processing center at Groningen) regularly for Berlin, and formerly in connection with the Dutch Peace Group also for Emden and Vienna.   R. de Z.

Stichtsche Aenwys: see Stichtsche Presentatie.

Stichtsche Presentatie. During the conflict between the Frisian and Flemish Mennonites in the Netherlands in 1566-68, a group of congregations "in't Sticht van Overyssel," i.e., in the northwestern part of the Dutch province of Overijssel, at first remained neutral, but in September 1568, after Frisians and Flemish had banned each other, they asked to have the whole matter reviewed. This reconsideration took place at a meeting of elders held in the fall of 1568. Thereupon the "Stichtschen" formulated their opinion in an extensive missive, the "Stichtsche Presentatie" (also called "Grote Stichtsche Presentatie," "Stichtsche Aenwys," or "Stichtsche Wtsprake"). This was a well-documented letter of advice of about 260 paragraphs, dated Jan. 3, 1569. The orginal is lost. Extracts are found in J. Outerman, *Onder Verbeteringhe. Verclaringhe met bewijs* (Haarlem, 1634). The Stichtsche congregations, though lamenting the schism, declared in this statement that they chose the side of the Flemish. (*DB* 1893, 72-79.)   vdZ.

Stiens, a village in the Dutch province of Friesland, formerly the seat of a Mennonite congregation, which also was known as the Stiens and Hijum congregation. In 1635 this congregation numbered about 35 baptized members, most of whom, however, lived at Hijum (*q.v.*). These Mennonites of Hijum joined the Hallum (*q.v.*) congregation in the 18th century or even earlier. Then the Stiens congregation, which always was small and which never had a meetinghouse and no preacher after 1704, died out about 1725. Elder Leenaert Bouwens (*q.v.*) baptized one person at Stiens about 1552. Since Nov. 1, 1951, there has been a Mennonite circle (*Kring*) at Stiens, to which 20 Mennonites belong; they hold their meetings every two weeks. The pastors of the neighboring congregations of Oudebildtzijl (*q.v.*) and Hallum take care of the Stiens circle. (Blaupot t. C., *Friesland,* 244, note 95; *DB* 1912, 82.)   vdZ.

Stignitz, a village in the district of Mährisch-Kromau, Moravia, in the domains of Sigmund von Zástrizl, in which there was a Bruderhof of the Hutterian Brethren. The inhabitants were attacked by soldiers and ruffians on Jan. 6 and 7, 1622, soon after the treaty of peace of Nikolsburg, and were severely mistreated. One brother was tortured, another was hanged, but cut down again; a third was set on burning coals and died in consequence, a fourth was cut down, and the women were raped. Finally they turned all the inhabitants, the sick, the aged, and the children out into the cold. Four feeble persons froze to death. The rabble escaped with the plunder and burned the house down. On Jan. 30, 1622, the Brethren were again attacked by troops and plundered. In October 1622 the Brethren were banished from Stignitz, leaving all their possessions behind. They found refuge in Hungary at Dubnitz and Zobelhoff (Soblához). The Zobelhoff Bruderhof was bought of Hieronymus Thaus on Dec. 6, 1622, for 150 talers. (Beck, *Geschichts-Bücher; ML* IV.) HEGE.

Stijl, a Mennonite family formerly found at Harlingen, Dutch province of Friesland. Its members, most of whom were engaged in trade and manufacture, were related by marriage to other Mennonite families of Harlingen like Hannema, Hanekuik, and Oosterbaan. Johannes Stijl, b. 1758 at Harlingen, d. there June 15, 1802, studied at the University of Franeker and the Amsterdam Mennonite seminary and served as pastor in the Mennonite congregations of Emmerich 1786-88 and Makkum 1788-92. The most prominent member of this family was Simon Stijl (1731-1804), a practicing physician at Harlingen, and the author of some important literary and historical works; he did not join the Mennonite Church. vdZ.

Stijntgen van Aken, an Anabaptist martyr, was drowned at the Steen Castle at Antwerp, Belgium, on Dec. 12, 1558, after she had been severely tortured some days before. Stijntgen, whose official name was Stijntgen de Hont (or Honts), was a native of Antwerp. She died valiantly as did the three other women martyrs who were executed at the same time. Their names are found in the hymn "Aenhoort God, hemelsche Vader" (Hear, O God, heavenly Father), found in the *Lietboecxken*. Particulars are lacking. vdZ.

Offer, 566; *Mart. Mir.* D 202, E 583; *Antw. Arch.-Blad* VIII, 456, 466; XIV, 24 f., No. 317; Wolkan, *Lieder*, 63, 72.

Stijntgen Evertsdochter, of Deventer, a Dutch Anabaptist woman, who had also lived at Leiden and Gent, was arrested at Amsterdam in May 1552 together with some 20 other Mennonites. Most of them died as martyrs, but Stijntgen, who had not yet received baptism upon her faith, recanted and was banned from the city. There is no reason to mention her here except for some valuable information she gave the judges concerning the singing of hymns by the Mennonites. She quoted a number of these hymns. vdZ.

Grosheide, *Bijdrage*, 160, 162, 164; Verheyden, "Mennisme in Vlaanderen," MS.

Stijntgen Jan Mickers huysvrou (the wife of Jan Mickers), an Anabaptist martyr, drowned on April 16, 1540, at Alkmaar, Dutch province of North Holland. She had been (re)baptized and rejected the Roman Catholic doctrine of the Mass. Both Stijntgen and her daughter Guert Jansdochter (*q.v.*), executed at Alkmaar on Feb. 6, 1538, are thought to have been adherents of the revolutionary leader Jan van Batenburg (*q.v.*). (*Inv. Arch. Amst.* I, No. 748, 2; *DB* 1909, 24; Mellink, *Wederdopers,* 173.) vdZ.

Stijntgen Jans, of Rotterdam, Holland, was arrested there in 1558. During her trial on Feb. 20 and March 19 she admitted that for about three years she had belonged to the Rotterdam Anabaptist congregation, which met at the Houttuyn. She had been (re)baptized about 1552 at Utrecht by Elder Leenaert Bouwens (*q.v.*). Stijntgen, forty years of age and a native of Maurik in the Dutch province of Gelderland, boldly rejected the Roman Catholic doctrine of the Mass. On March 28, 1558, after Jan (*q.v.*) Hendriks, an Anabaptist martyr, had been put to death before the city hall of Rotterdam, a riot arose among the spectators against the executioner and the city officials; they took the corpse of Jan Hendriks off the scaffold and then attacked the city hall. On this occasion four Anabaptists imprisoned there were liberated by the rebelling crowd; one of the liberated prisoners was Stijntgen Jans, concerning whom there is no further information. (*Mart. Mir.* D. 191-96, E 575-78; *DB* 1903, 3; 1905, 172.) vdZ.

Stijntgen Vercoilgen, an Anabaptist martyr, burned at the stake on April 22, 1569, at Kortrijk (Courtrai) in Flanders, Belgium. Van Braght's *Martyrs' Mirror* erroneously gives March 9, 1569, as the execution date. The official name of this martyr was Josyne Andries (dochter), wife of Rougier van Quoilge. Although she had wanted to join the Mennonite congregation of Kortrijk (*q.v.*) since 1567, she was not baptized until the end of 1568. She was tortured on March 1, 1569, but remained steadfast, and refused to name her fellow members. Though information is scarce, we may conclude that this martyr was well-to-do, since her property was confiscated. During the execution special measures were taken to guard the site, apparently because the magistrates feared intervention from sympathizing spectators. (*Mart. Mir.* D 388, E 740; Verheyden, *Courtrai-Bruxelles,* 38, No. 21.) vdZ.

Stilling: see **Jung-Stilling.**

Stilstaanders, the designation of the Dutch Mennonites who, in 1566-68 during the Frisian-Flemish quarrels and schism, wished "to stand still," i.e., to remain neutral, siding neither with the Frisians nor the Flemish. They were banned by both groups. Most of them soon after joined the Flemish. According to V. P., *Successio Anabaptistica,* Stilstaanders were particularly found in Cleve, Germany, and in the Dutch provinces of South Holland and Friesland. Best known is the attitude of the Zierikzee (*q.v.*) congregation, which was also neutral, and presented its reasons for this position in the book

Een Christelijcke Proeve, of 1570. They accused both parties of a lack of love and brotherliness and exhorted them to singleness of heart, sobriety, contrition, and peace. But this truly Christian admonition had no success at all; both parties were blinded and the schism lasted for nearly a century. vDZ.

BRN VII, 66, 87, 542; Blaupot t. C., *Holland* I, 125 note; *DB* 1872, 56; 1897, 106; H. W. Meihuizen, *Galenus Abrahamsz* (Haarlem, 1954) 8-12.

Stinstra, a former Dutch Mennonite family, now died out. Its origin is at Harlingen, Friesland, where most of them lived and where they were found from at least the early 17th century. Until about 1680 this family bore the family name of Gerlof(s). Symon Johannes (1673-1743) was the first to take the family name of Stinstra. He was born at Harlingen, and conducted an important lumber business there. He was well-to-do, a member and apparently a deacon of the Harlingen Mennonite congregation, and in 1722-39 treasurer of the Mennonite conference of Friesland (FDS). He was married to Trijntje Gooitjens Braam, of an old Harlingen Mennonite family. Among their children were the preacher Johannes Stinstra (*q.v.*) and Gooitjen (Goethius) Stinstra (1705?-64), who was a physician at Harlingen. Their daughter Grietje Stinstra was married to Evert Heeres Oosterbaan and was the mother of the Mennonite professor Heere Oosterbaan (*q.v.*). Simon Stinstra (*c*1735-82), married to Anna Braam, was a son of Gooitjen Stinstra and like his father a physician at Harlingen. Another son of Gooitjen Stinstra was Pieter Stinstra (1747-1819), who studied theology at the University of Franeker and the Amsterdam Mennonite seminary and served as pastor of the Mennonite church of Franeker in 1770-1800. He was a man of great learning. In 1786 he was asked to take a professorship at the Amsterdam Mennonite seminary, but he refused. The Amsterdam archives have a number of handwritten sermons by Pieter Stinstra. In 1800 he retired and settled in Harlingen, where he died.

Other members of this Stinstra family were A. Stinstra, d. 1847, burgomaster of Franeker; both Johannes Stinstra of Franeker, d. 1842, owner of brickworks, and Simon Stinstra, a lawyer at Harlingen, were trustees of the Dutch General Mennonite conference (ADS), in 1840-42 and 1844-63 respectively. Miss Sytske Stinstra, d. Feb. 26, 1900, at Franeker, willed to the congregation of Franeker her stately house and a considerable sum of money.

By marriage the Stinstra family was related with other Mennonite families, particularly of Harlingen, such as Braam, Oosterbaan, Schellingwou, Wybenga, Huidekoper, Fontein, and Yzenbeek.   vDZ.

Inv. Arch. Amst. I, Nos. 1032, 1103, 1161, 1181; II, Nos. 1731-33, 2504; *DJ* 1850, 122; *DB* 1868, 94; 1895, 30; 1900, 225; Blaupot t. C., *Friesland*, 187, 221, 237 f.; G. A. Wumkes, *Stads- en Dorpskroniek van Friesland* (1700-1800) (Leeuwarden, 1930); II (1800-1900) (Leeuwarden, 1934), *passim*; J. W. de Crane, *Hulde aan de Nagedachtenis van P. Stinstra* (n.p., n.d.).

Stinstra, Johannes, b. Aug. 10, 1708, at Harlingen, d. there Jan. 8, 1790, a son of Symon Johannes Stinstra and Trijntje Gooitjens Braam, was a Dutch Mennonite pastor and theologian, studied theology, philosophy, and oriental languages at the University

of Franeker 1726-*c*33. After his study he returned to Harlingen; in the fall of 1733 he was invited by the board of his home church to preach four sermons a year. In 1735 he was appointed full-time pastor of this congregation, serving it until 1785. He rejected two calls by the Amsterdam Lamist congregation and one by the Haarlem Peuzelaarsteeg church. In 1739-40 Stinstra, then the moderator of the Mennonite Conference of Friesland (FDS), presided at the meetings which considered the suspension of two Mennonite preachers, Wytse Jeens (Brouwer) and Pieke Tjommes (*q.v.*), by the Frisian States on the charge of some Reformed pastors that they had taught Socinian (*q.v.*) doctrines. They had refused to sign a formulary drawn up by the States of Friesland, because as a matter of principle they were not willing to sign formularies or confessions, the Scriptures for them as Mennonites being the only source of faith. In behalf of the two preachers and the maintenance of religious freedom Stinstra drew up a defense in the name of the conference, which was published (three editions, all at Leeuwarden, 1741) and presented to the government of Friesland. Its title was *Request (q.v.) met bygevoegde Deductie voor het Regt van Vryheid van Geloove, Godsdienst en Conscientie op den naam van de Doopsgezinde Gemeenten in Friesland ingeleverd aan de E. M. Heeren Staaten der gemelde Provincie* (Request with Following Deduction in Behalf of the Right of Freedom of Religion, Worship and Conscience, in the Name of the Mennonite Congregations of Friesland, Presented to Their Highness, the States of the foresaid Province). This request was opposed and attacked by D. Gerdes (*q.v.*), G. Kulenkamp (*q.v.*), A. Driessen, and some anonymous Reformed authors, whose publications urged the States of Friesland to take measures against the Mennonites of Friesland, since they were infected with the heresies of Socinus.

In the meantime Stinstra, wishing to supplement the *Request* by developing his ideas from the Scriptures, had published five sermons, entitled *De natuure en Gesteldheid van Christus Koninkrijk ...* (Harlingen, 1741, and reprinted) and a separate booklet *Byvoegzel van Aanteekeningen over de vyf Predicatien* (n.p., n.d.-1741). Now the attacks of the Reformed turned directly against Stinstra. A number of Reformed authors, including Gerdes and J. van den Honert (*q.v.*), tried to prove that the author of the "Vijf Predicatien" was a Socinian whose teachings should not be tolerated. Stinstra's book was also discussed in the Reformed synods and in the summer of 1742 an official Reformed charge was made against Stinstra. The government of Friesland ordered that the book by Stinstra be examined by the theological faculties of several Dutch universities. The judgment of all universities was that Stinstra's book did contain Socinian ideas; only Venema of the Franeker University, whose lectures Stinstra had attended while studying at Franeker, declared that the Christian views of his pupil were sound. Thereupon the government of Friesland on Jan. 13, 1742, forbade Stinstra to preach, and not withstanding several petitions by his church board, by the conference of Friesland, and by Stinstra himself, the suspension was not rescinded until 1757. During his enforced rest Stinstra regularly wrote and circulated sermons, which were published in two volumes under the title *Vier en Twintig Leerredenen* (Harlingen, 1746). He also devoted much time to study, his special field being the philosophy of ethics. Stinstra was a man of moderate views and was particularly drawn toward the contemporary liberal theology of English authors like J. Tillotson, James Foster, and particularly Samuel Clarke (*q.v.*), whose sermons Stinstra translated into Dutch: *Predikatien over verscheidene stoffen*, 11 vols., 1739-49. Stinstra also translated into the Dutch three moralistic novels by the English novelist Samuel Richardson (*q.v.*), with whom he kept up a correspondence.

Besides these translations and the *Vier en Twintig Leerredenen*, he also published a few sermons on special occasions, three volumes of sermons, *Oude Voorspelingen aangaande den Messias . . . toegepast op den Heere Jesus . . .* (Harlingen, 1779-86), refutations of the books by J. van den Honert and other opponents, and together with his co-preachers the *Harlinger Vraagenboek* (*q.v.*), a catechism published at Harlingen in 1751. Being opposed to the Moravian Brethren (in the Netherlands usually called Hernhutters, *q.v.*), and their doctrines, he published *Waarschuwinge tegen de Geestdrijverij, vervat in een brief aan de Doopsgezinden in Friesland* (Harlingen, 1750). Of this book a French translation appeared: *Lettre Pastorale contre le Fanatisme* (Leiden, 1752), which also contains an important survey of the origin of the Moravian movement (by an unknown author); a German edition *Warnung vor dem Fanaticismus*, also containing the introduction from the French edition, was published in Berlin, 1752; an English edition, without this introduction, *A Pastoral Letter against Fanaticism Addressed to the Mennonites of Friesland*, appeared in London in 1753.

Stinstra was repeatedly charged with Socinianism, not only by the Reformed theologians, but also by some Mennonites, particularly by the preacher Jacobus Rijsdijk (*q.v.*), a strict Zonist (*q.v.*). Rijsdijk attacked Stinstra in *Godtgeleerde Aanmerkingen . . .*, 2 volumes (Groningen, 1742-44). In general the charge of Socinianism was unfair; Stinstra was not an adherent of Socinus. Nevertheless there was in some points a striking similarity between Socinian concepts and Stinstra's views, particularly his concept of Christianity as a reasonable religious system, the value and truth of which can be recognized and proved by the *ratio* (reason) of man; and the emphasis put on morality, even to the neglect of sentiment and piety, easily makes it understandable that he was taken for a Socinian by many. His sermons, much admired during his lifetime, are for our taste much too prolix, too speculative, too rationalistic, and too moralistic; they are more like treatises or essays than like testimonies. His method of clear rationalistic thinking made him averse to pietism, because of its subjectivism and its overemotionalism. Stinstra, who had great authority among his church members, prevented Johannes Deknatel (*q.v.*), the well-known pietistic preacher of the Amsterdam Lamist Mennonite congregation, from preaching in the Harlingen Mennonite Church. By this partiality he estranged a number of his members who had religious needs that Stinstra could not supply and who began to organize separate meetings, including communion services, in a home. Stinstra was an influential precursor of 19th-century liberalism.   vDZ.

Chr. Sepp, *Johannes Stinstra en zijn tijd* (2 vv., Amsterdam, 1865 and 1866); Blaupot t. C., *Friesland*, 209-15, 236, 327-50; *DB* 1867, 116-41; 1868, 51-84; 1869, 61-63; 1885, 76.

Stirling Avenue Mennonite Church (GCM), located at Kitchener, Ont., was organized in August 1924 with a membership of 115, under the leadership of Urias K. Weber, who had for 17 years been the pastor of the First Mennonite Church (MC), of Kitchener, from which this group separated on a matter of polity. Without conference connection for a number of years, union with the Eastern District Conference in 1946 was followed by union with the General Conference Mennonite Church in 1947. The present church building of brown brick, seating approximately 400, was dedicated on Feb. 1, 1925. Until this time services were conducted in the First Mennonite Church on Sunday afternoons. A parsonage was bought in 1950, and the church enlarged in 1952. The membership is about one fourth rural, the remainder living in Kitchener and surrounding towns. U. K. Weber was succeeded in 1942 by Andrew R. Shelly, of Pennsburg, Pa., who was ordained as elder in 1942. Shelly was succeeded in 1951 by Wilfred D. Ulrich, the present (1957) pastor. Footwashing is optional and there is open communion. The membership in 1958 was 460. E.S.S.

Stirling Mennonite Church (MC), located near Stirling, Alberta. At the annual Alberta-Saskatchewan Mennonite Conference, in session at Creston, Mont., July 1946, Jacob and John Hofer, as representatives of a group who had left the near-by Hutterite settlement a number of years before, made application to the conference for spiritual help. On Nov. 10, 1946, 11 members of the group were received into the Mennonite Church, and on March 16, 1947, organized into a congregation. On the same day John J. Hofer was ordained to the ministry. In 1957 the membership was 26, with John Hofer still serving as pastor. The group continues to practice certain aspects of its former communal way of life.   E.S.

Stobbe, a Mennonite family found since at least 1668 at Danzig and later also in Elbing, Montau, and other West Prussian churches. Some of its members were ministers; e.g., Isaac Stobbe (1712-88), a shoemaker, preacher 1751 and elder 1775 of the Frisian (Neugarten) congregation of Danzig; Erdmann Stobbe, a preacher of the same church 1786-c1808; and Johann Stobbe, of Klein Lunau, preacher 1871 and elder 1875-1906 of the Schönsee (Sosnovka) Mennonite Church.

Peter Stobbe, of Tiegenhof, in the Gross-Werder, was the founder of a famous distillery, still in existence in 1945. From Prussia the name came to Russia and to Canada. (*ML* IV, 246.)   vDZ.

Reimer, *Familiennamen*, 118; Dutch *Naamlijst*; *Inv. Arch. Amst.* I, Nos. 1623, 1716 f., 1719; II, No. 2655.

Stockman(n), a Mennonite family formerly in the congregation of Hamburg (*q.v.*)-Altona, Germany. Its ancestor was Samuel (1) Stockman, who presumably was born at Antwerp, Belgium, and moved from there to Hamburg in the late 16th century. He was married to Louisjen Noë; he was at first a tailor, and later became a prosperous businessman. His son Samuel (2) Stockman, d. Hamburg 1678, a merchant like his father, was for a number of years a deacon of the Hamburg Mennonite Church. A descendant of Samuel (1) was Jan Stockmann, who was chosen preacher of this church in 1711, but served for only two years, dying of the plague in 1713. In the 17th century some members of this family left the Mennonite Church to join the Dompelaar (*q.v.*) congregation at Hamburg, including Isaac Stockmann and his sons Samuel and Jan. Samuel Stockman was a preacher of this Dompelaar church in the 1660's.   vDZ.

B. C. Roosen, *Gesch. der Mennoniten Gemeinde Hamburg und Altona* I (Hamburg, 1886) 9, 13, 31, 32, 34, 36, 43, 47, 66; II (*id.*, 1887) 6, 54.

Stoetenberen (Stutenbernt), a nickname of Bernt (Berend) Rothmann (*q.v.*) in Münster (*q.v.*). *Stoet* means a loaf of bread. He was given this name because he used ordinary bread in the observance of the Lord's Supper, contrary to the Roman Catholic practice of using a wafer. (*DB* 1888, 8 note; 1919, 8.)   vDZ.

Stoffel (Stoffels), a Dutch Mennonite family, formerly at Zaandam, where Gerrit Stoffels was a member of the Old Frisian congregation in 1628, as was his son Pieter Stoffels, a shipbuilder; Jan Stoffelsz, probably Gerrit's grandson, was from 1683 a preacher of the Zaandam Oude Huys (Frisian) congregation. The Stoffels mentioned in the church books as members of the Zaandam Nieuwe Huys congregation may have been descendants. Most members of this family were blacksmiths and carpenters at Zaandam, and later on millwrights, the last of whom was Cornelis Pietersz Stoffel (1776-1836). His son Pieter Corneliszn Stoffel (1818-69) moved to Deventer, where he founded a lumber business. He and some of his descendants were trustees of the Deventer Mennonite Church; his son Pieter Stoffel (1848-1942) was president of the church board. Other sons of Pieter Corneliszn were Willem Stoffel (1859-1945), a lumber dealer and moderator of the Deventer church board, and Cornelis Stoffel (1845-1908), professor of English and Swedish at Amsterdam, later living at Nijmegen, a deacon at Amsterdam and Nijmegen.   vDZ.

S. Lootsma, *Het Nieuwe Huys* (Zaandam, 1937) 80, 114, 190, 192, 199; *De Zondagsbode* XXII (1908-9) No. 4.

Stoltz Plateau, a region in Brazil (*q.v.*) where a number of Mennonite families from Russia settled in 1930. In 1934, however, settlement began to dissolve because of economic difficulties. By 1951 the last Mennonites had left the Stoltz Plateau.   vDZ.

Stoltzfus is an Amish Mennonite family name. Nicholas Stoltzfus and his son Christian (1748-1832; said to have immigrated from Zweibrücken, Germany) arrived at Philadelphia on Oct. 18, 1766. Since they are the only persons by this name to be registered on the 18th-century ship lists, they are presumably the progenitors of all the family in America. Both acquired land in Berks and Lancaster counties by 1770. Nicholas died in 1774 and is buried in King's Cemetery in northern Berks County near Leesport, Pa. Christian, ordained an Amish bishop, moved to Lancaster County about 1800 and was buried in what is now Myers Cemetery in the Mill Creek section in 1832.

The Stoltzfus name has been most common in Eastern Pennsylvania, but it occurs also in Ohio and Iowa, mostly in the Amish Mennonite Church, though in recent years it has become more prevalent in Mennonite (MC) circles. The Fisher family history lists approximately 1400 persons with the name of Stoltzfus who are descendants of Christian Fisher. The 1958 *Mennonite Yearbook* lists 51 ordained men carrying the Stoltzfus name, 30 of whom are Old Order Amish preachers in Pennsylvania. Among the descendants have been Benjamin B. Stoltzfus (1861-1931), a minister and for 16 years superintendent of the Lima, Ohio, Mennonite (MC) Mission; the Christian Stoltzfus mentioned above; Eli B. Stoltzfus (1860-1942), bishop of the Plainview Church at Aurora, Ohio; his son, Elmer Stoltzfus (1896-   ), bishop of the same congregation; the latter's son, Edward Stoltzfus, pastor of the Bethel Mennonite Church at West Liberty, Ohio; and Nicholas M. Stoltzfus (1895-   ), minister in the Manson, Iowa, Mennonite Church. Grant Stoltzfus is a professor at Eastern Mennonite College.   G.M.S.

John M. Fisher, *Descendants and History of Christian Fisher Family* (Ronks, Pa., 1957), with a supplement *Stoltzfus Family,* pp. 601-23.

Stolypin, Peter A. (1862-1911), became prime minister of Russia in 1906 and suppressed the Revolution at that time. He introduced agricultural laws to enable landless peasants and small farmers to acquire crown land. The Mennonites also benefited by this law when they obtained land in the Kulundian Steppes and established the Barnaul-Slavgorod settlement (*q.v.*) in Siberia. On Sept. 10, 1910, Stolypin visited the Slavgorod Mennonite settlement, on which occasion he was received by the Oberschulze Jacob A. Reimer (*q.v.*) and the minister Peter J. Wiebe. Possibly in part as a result of this meeting a post office and a hospital were erected in Orloff and a branch line of the Trans-Siberian Railroad built from Tatarskaya to Slavgorod. In memory of its benefactor, the Slavgorod Mennonites erected a memorial to Peter A. Stolypin in Orloff in 1912. Stolypin was killed by a revolutionary in Kiev in 1911.   C.K.

Der Bote, Aug. 13, 1952, p. 5; Gerhard Fast, *In den Steppen Sibiriens* (Rosthern, 1957) 29 ff.

Stone House, a meetinghouse used by the Mennonites (MC) of Lancaster County, Pa., now replaced by the New Danville (*q.v.*) meetinghouse.   I.D.L.

Stoner Heights Mennonite Church (MC), near Louisville, Ohio, an organized congregation under the Ohio and Eastern Mennonite Conference, was established in 1938. It had 29 members in 1957, with Delvin Nussbaum as pastor.   M.G.

Stonerville Mennonite Church: see **Pennsville.**

Stony Brook Mennonite Church (MC), located on the Lincoln Highway, 4 miles east of York, Pa., had a meetinghouse by 1803, one block southwest of the present site, known as Witmer's. A deed of 1818 states that "David Sprenkle of West Manchester Township sold to David Witmer, Rudolph Forry, both of Spring Garden Township, and Michael Strickler of Hellam Township, Trustees of congregation worshiping at the Mennonist Meetinghouse at the stone ridge in Spring Garden Township 77 P for $72.18, for the Mennist Church, worshiping in and around Spring Garden Township, and for those permitted by said congregation to bury their dead on the Grave Yard, contained on same Lot and for no other purpose whatsoever." This was alongside an earlier family cemetery. The meetinghouse was enlarged several times and in 1884 it was enlarged and considerably renovated. In 1912 the congregation moved into the town, building a brick church, 50 x 75 ft. B. L. Bucher was the pastor in 1957, with a membership of 79. This was a part of the Strickler-Witmer-Liverpool circuit a century ago, but now it is a separate congregation. Winterstown is an outpost of this congregation.

I.D.L.

Stony Brook Old Order Mennonite Church, York County, Pa., worshiped in the same meetinghouse, about 7 miles east of York, as the Lancaster Mennonites (MC) until 1912, when the Mennonites moved to the Highway. Then in 1913 the Old Order congregation built another brick church on the same ground, east of the old, well-kept cemetery. It is still called the Witmer church. The membership in 1955 was 12, with Emanuel Landes, deacon, as the only ordained man. Joseph Hostetter is bishop and the Lancaster County ministers take charge of the fortnightly services.

I.D.L.

Stoppelaar, de, a Dutch Mennonite family, found in the 17th century in Rotterdam, where Daniël de Stoppelaar was a deacon of the High German Mennonite church in 1639. Later members of this family lived in Amsterdam, where Jan (Johannes) de Stoppelaar (d. 1740) was a physician. Both he and his wife Ida de Neufville were members of the Amsterdam Lamist (q.v.) church.

Jan de Stoppelaar (Hengelo 1855-The Hague 1919) studied theology at the Amsterdam Mennonite seminary and served the congregations of St. Anna-Parochie 1880-81 and Krommenie 1881-85. In 1885 he retired because of bad health.

Reinder Jacobus Taekema de Stoppelaar (Ureterp 1873-Enschedé 1948), after studying at the Mennonite seminary and the University of Amsterdam, served as pastor at Oost- and West-Graftdijk 1899-1901 and Warga 1901-38. He is known for a large number of excellent and attractive books of nature description, especially ornithology, particularly of Friesland.

vDZ.

Storch, Nikolaus, one of the "Zwickau Prophets" (see **Thomas Drechsel**), a weaver of Zwickau, Saxony, Germany, a member of a religious sect in Bohemia which held fanatical views concerning the Inner Word, revealed in visions and dreams. Thomas Müntzer (q.v.) was deeply impressed by his unusual knowledge of the Scripture. Storch won a large following among the common people. Summoned before the council of Zwickau to answer for his teaching, he left Zwickau in December 1521 and went to Wittenberg with Drechsel and Marcus Stübner (q.v.) where they had a number of conversations with Melanchthon (q.v.). The Biblical basis they cited for their rejection of infant baptism confused the reformer.

But Storch did not stay in Wittenberg long. He parted from his companions and wandered through Middle Germany, especially Thuringia, preaching everywhere. In September 1522 he had a conversation with Luther in Wittenberg, chiefly on the subject of infant baptism. In 1524 he was for a short time in Strasbourg. In Hof he stayed longer. He may then have turned to South Germany. All trace of him is lost. In 1536 he was reported to be back in Zwickau. At any rate he remained quiet; his role was finished. He advised his followers to have themselves rebaptized. Did they do so? There is no evidence that either he himself or his followers were rebaptized.

NEFF.

Chr. Meyer, "Der Wiedertäufer Nikolaus Storch und seine Anhänger in Hof," in *Ztscht für Kirchengeschichte* XVI (1896) 117-24; *TA Bayern* I, 4 ff.; Paul Wappler, *Thomas Münzer in Zwickau und die 'Zwickauer Propheten'* (Zwickau, 1908); *ML* IV.

Stordeur, Jean, an Anabaptist of Liège (Luik), Belgium, who, because of severe persecution, fled to Geneva, Switzerland, in 1533 with his wife Idelette van Buren (de Bure, q.v.), his father-in-law Lambert van Buren, the book printer Johannes Bomeromanus, and a few other Anabaptists. In Geneva Stordeur and Bomeromanus had two or three disputes with the Reformed pastors Farel and John Calvin (q.v.). On March 30, 1537, both Stordeur and Bomeromanus were banned from the town. In Strasbourg (q.v.) they again met Calvin in 1538, when Calvin was forced to leave Geneva. In 1539 Calvin succeeded in converting Stordeur, who died soon after of the plague. In August 1540 Calvin married his widow.

vDZ.

L. E. Halkin, *La Réforme en Belgique sous Charles-Quint* (Brussels, n.d.-1957) 81, 96; Abr. Hulshof, *Geschiedenis van de Doopsgezinden te Straatsburg . . .* (Amsterdam, 1905) 191 f., 194; *ML* IV.

Storger, Jakob, an Anabaptist martyr of Koburg, who was baptized at Wels in Upper Austria in 1528 by Wolfgang Brandhuber (q.v.), lived at first as a gunsmith in Gittelde im Grund, a valley in the Upper Harz, Germany, but considering his trade sinful he left the region and settled with his family above Zorge near the Spitzenberge. Here he made troughs with other Anabaptists. He was chosen preacher at a meeting of Anabaptists at Langenwiese. In the middle of August he was expelled from Brunswick territory. For six weeks he wandered preaching and baptizing in Thuringia. In October 1537 he settled with his family in a suburb of Mühlhausen. There he was arrested and examined on the rack on Oct. 11. On Nov. 8, 1537, he suffered a martyr's death with three other Anabaptists; he was drowned in the Unstrut between Mühlhausen and Ammern. NEFF.

Wappler, Thüringen, 150, 194; idem, Inquisition und Ketzerprozesse in Zwickau zur Reformationszeit (Leipzig, 1908); ML IV.

Story Friends, the name given to Beams of Light (q.v.) beginning with Vol. 53, No. 1, Jan. 5, 1958.

Story of the Mennonites, The, by C. Henry Smith and revised by Cornelius Krahn, originated when C. Henry Smith (q.v.) published his book under the title The Mennonites, A Brief History of Their Origin and Later Development in Both Europe and America, 340 pp. (Berne, 1920). In 1941 after Smith had written numerous other books The Mennonites appeared in an entirely revised and enlarged edition under the title The Story of the Mennonites, 823 pp. (Newton, Kan.). Of this edition a slightly revised reprint was made in 1945, without taking into consideration the great changes brought about by World War II. The day before C. Henry Smith died, on Oct. 18, 1948, he requested Cornelius Krahn to revise and edit The Story of the Mennonites. This was done in co-operation with the Board of Education and Publication of the General Conference Mennonite Church in the spirit of the author, leaving the book in general as it was conceived by the author. Chapters dealing with contemporary questions were brought up to date. Although the Mennonites of Europe had been most affected by World War II, the settlements of North and South America had also undergone great changes. In order to prevent an increase in size some chapters were reduced. Numerous corrections and changes were made. An index, a bibliography, and illustrations were added. This edition published in 1950 by the Mennonite Publication Office, Newton, Kan., consisted of 856 pages.

In 1957 a fourth edition containing some changes and corrections appeared. Some paragraphs were added to bring chapters up to date dealing with the present. Illustrations were exchanged for charts featuring the origin, spread, and immigration of the Mennonites the world over.

The popularity of C. Henry Smith's Story of the Mennonites is due to the fact that the author had the gift of narrating a very complex, long, and complicated history of a small group of people in an attractive, impressive, and nontechnical way which appeals to the average person not familiar nor interested in detail. This strength reveals at once also the "weakness" of the book, namely, the absence of a detailed presentation of theological questions, partly due to the fact that the author was not a trained theologian but a historian. Thus far the Story of the Mennonites is the most widely used history of the Mennonites produced anywhere in any language. A unique chapter in its history is that it was translated into the German language by A. Esau, a German scientist, while he was in prison in the Netherlands after World War II where P. S. Goerz contacted him and gave him a copy of the book. Esau translated the whole Story, after which Cornelius Krahn edited the manuscript, and the General Conference Board of Education and Pub-

lication in co-operation with D. H. Epp and H. Heese began to publish it in installments in Der Bote with the intention of publishing it in book form. The first half of the book appeared under the title Die Geschichte der Mennoniten Europas (1964). C.K.

Stotzingen, Hans (Henslein) **von,** an Anabaptist martyr, executed about 1528 at Zabern in Alsace. The Martyrs' Mirror contains his address to the spectators at his execution. He is the author of the hymn "Nun heben wir an in Nöten," found in the Ausbund (q.v.). (Mart. Mir. D 17, E 427 f.; Wolkan, Lieder, 141, 146.) NEFF.

Stouffer Mennonite Church (MC), located in the Ringgold District, Washington Co., Md., was organized in the Beaver Creek District, in a building later used by the Brethren Church. In 1828 a stone church was built on the present site. The name was doubtless given in honor of the minister John Stouffer (1746-1836), who later became the bishop. The old building was replaced by a brick church in 1895. This is said to have been the first organized Mennonite congregation in Washington County. The ministers who have served are John Stouffer, Abr. Stouffer, Christian Newcomer, John Martin, John Hoover, David Shank, Denton Martin, and the present (1957) minister, Amos J. Martin. The membership in 1957 was 104. J.D.R.

Straalman (Straelmans), a former Dutch Mennonite family. The origin and genealogy of this family is not clear. Its cradle is Vreden in Westphalia, Germany, where its members, Mennonites, were living in the 16th century. In the early 17th century they were found at Almelo and soon also in Amsterdam and other Dutch towns; in Amsterdam they were wealthy merchants. One of the mightiest merchant princes of 18th-century Amsterdam was Abraham Straalman, d. 1759. His first wife was Catharina Verhamme (1704-37), of an old Mennonite family of Haarlem; his second wife was Suzanna Catharina de Wolf, also a Mennonite. He lived in the stately manor "Vijverhof" on the Vecht River. He was a deacon of the Amsterdam Lamist (q.v.) church 1738-44 and 1755-59. Until the end of the 18th century his relatives and descendants were members of the Amsterdam Mennonite congregation. Some of them served the church as deacons, one of whom was his father, Matthijs Straalman (1693-98, 1703-9). Jan Straalman was a member of the Mennonite committee of Foreign Needs (Relief Committee) about 1730. By marriage the Straalmans were related to other well-known Amsterdam Mennonite families such as van Lennep, de Wolf, de Flines, Seijen, Kops, and van Meekeren.

In the second half of the 18th century some branches of this family died out, and a few of its members joined the Reformed Church. vDZ.

Nederlands Adelsboek XVI (1917) 362; Inv. Arch. Amst. I, No. 1935; II, Nos. 432-35; DB 1905, 126; church records of the Amsterdam Mennonite congregation.

Straatman, Jan Willem (The Hague, Holland, 1824-82), studied at the Mennonite seminary at Amsterdam and became a ministerial candidate in 1849. He served the congregations of Wormerveer-Noord 1849-50 and Groningen 1850-67. Shortly after 1860 he adopted modern (liberal) theology, and soon became a radical exponent of it. From his new viewpoint he wanted to reform his Groningen congregation. Most members of the church board sympathized with the new ideas of their preacher, but a large number of the members of the church did not agree and avoided the church meetings. In 1865 the church board resolved that baptism was not strictly obligatory for those who wished to join the church. In 1867, Straatman and his colleague Cornelis Corver (q.v.), with approval of some members including Samuel van Houten (q.v.), made a number of proposals for a radical reorganization of the church life: (a) baptism to be optional and to be abolished in the future; (b) communion services to be done away with; (c) the preachers to be permitted to omit hymns, prayer, and Scripture reading during the services; (d) preachers to be given freedom to choose the content of their sermons (addresses) from themes outside the Bible; (e) Christian anniversaries such as Good Friday, Easter, Ascension day, Pentecost, and Christmas not to be observed. When these radical proposals were presented in an assembly of members of the church on Nov. 24, 1867, they were rejected by the majority (185 votes against 79) and both Straatman and Corver resigned. Straatman preached his farewell sermon on Dec. 22, 1867, which address was published: *Broeders, ik bid u* (Groningen, 1867). Straatman also published a volume of sermons, *Tiental Leerredenen* (Groningen, 1864). vDZ.

DB 1868, 112-32, 167 f.; 1883, 125; 1901, 28; H. Dassel Sr., *Menno's Volk in Groningen* (Groningen, n.d.-1945) 52, 57.

Strahm: see Strohm.

Stralen, Gottfried, of Geldern, Rhineland, one of the "Wassenberg preachers" (q.v.), was a close friend of Johannes Klopreis (q.v.), and shared his fate. In Münster he was the preacher at the Ueberwasserkirche and took an active part in the religious movement in the city. In October 1533 he was one of the editors of the evangelical *Bekentnisse* (Confession) *van beyden Sacramenten*. With Klopreis he was sent to Warendorf (q.v.) as a Münsterite apostle in 1534 and was burned at the stake with him at Brühl on Feb. 1, 1535. (*ML* IV.)

Strasbourg (pop. 167,149) is a city in Alsace, France, at the junction of the Ill and the Breusch rivers, two miles west of the Rhine. Its strategic location between Switzerland and Wittenberg made it an important center during the time of the Reformation, but its importance derived also from prominent leaders in the city, first of all Jacob Sturm (q.v.), and in the ecclesiastical realm, Bucer (q.v.), Capito (q.v.), and Hedio (q.v.). All of these men were interested in the Anabaptists, and especially in the beginning had personal friends among them; Matthäus Zell (q.v.), and after his death his widow, championed the cause of the Anabaptists. No doubt the close friendship of the Zells with Schwenckfeld contributed to their kindness to the Anabaptists.

Strasbourg was the haven of refuge for Anabaptists from Switzerland, Holland, and North and South Germany. When persecution forced them to leave Augsburg (q.v.) and other localities they came in large numbers to Strasbourg. The Anabaptists called Strasbourg the "City of Hope," and the "Refuge of Righteousness."

Strasbourg responded to the Protestant Reformation as early as 1523 when Matthäus Zell expressed his views on the custom of having godfathers, and left the language of the ceremony of infant baptism as optional, either Latin or German. Through the agitation of Clemens Ziegler (q.v.), a layman, who wrote pamphlets against infant baptism stressing the importance of faith (in which he was greatly indebted to Luther), Bucer wrote to Zwingli on Oct. 31, 1524, to request Scriptural proofs to combat certain false prophets, probably including Carlstadt. That he had the opponents of infant baptism in mind is doubtful, since Anabaptism did not have its real beginning until January 1525. During the same month of October Capito entered the discussion between Luther and Carlstadt on the sacraments, insisting that it was merely a quarrel of words, and that the rites, being purely external, should not be a cause of division among Christians.

Capito at that early date stated the position of Strasbourg: tolerance in external matters. In November 1524 Capito and Bucer wrote to the preachers of Zürich that they had heard that Carlstadt was agitating against the practice of infant baptism, and declared themselves prepared to retain infant baptism as a mere external ceremony with the condition that instruction follow it later. About the same time Nicolaus Gerbel wrote a letter to Luther warning him of Carlstadt's influence on the Strasbourg Reformers, and on Nov. 23, 1524, the Strasbourg Reformers directed a letter to Luther in which they stated that they with Luther had hitherto retained the practice of infant baptism, even though it scarcely corresponded to the practice of the early church and to the Scriptures. In December of that year Strasbourg received communications from both Zwingli and Luther in reply to the Strasbourg statements about the place of infant baptism. In answer Bucer stated his position clearly for the first time, clearly discussing the issues of the ban and infant baptism. He idealized the ban and to some extent longed for it in the church, but thought it impossible in the present situation of the church. As for baptism, his favorite term is that it was an external thing, and hence not bound to any particular age in life. Since there are two baptisms, the inner and the outer, of which only the inner is of decisive importance, one should not overstress the time of baptism. He dealt in this writing with the arguments advanced by Ziegler, but most directly with those of Balthasar Hubmaier. The title of this writing, which is clearly composed by Bucer although it bears the names of all the Strasbourg preachers, is *Grund vnnd vrsach ausz gotlicher schrifft der neüwerung an dem nachtmal des herren . . . , tauff, . . . zu Strassburg fürgenommen* (1525).

In May 1525 the Strasbourg preachers again had to take a stand on the matter of infant baptism and urged their people to place their trust in Christ alone and not in any of the ceremonies which had been done away with. Baptism they defined as a sign of faith and of entrance into the Christian life, by which the parents testify that they will train their child in a Christian manner. Parents were urged not to rush to baptism with weak infants, as though salvation consisted of external washing, and yet they were not to neglect baptism, since it had taken the place of circumcision.

In July 1525 Balthasar Hubmaier (q.v.) published in Strasbourg his important work, *Von dem christlichen tauff der gläubigen*. This book was the Anabaptist reply to Zwingli's book on baptism, and while it was written in Waldshut, Hubmaier himself says that it was published in Strasbourg.

In February 1526 the Strasbourg ministers appeared before the city council to indicate their position on infant baptism. The major point of consideration was that they did not wish to be innovators, and since infant baptism had always been practiced they wished this practice to continue, only that parents ought to wait until a convenient day and not rush their children to be baptized. In March another prominent Anabaptist, Wilhelm Reublin (q.v.), arrived in Strasbourg. When Michael Sattler (q.v.) arrived is not certain, but it was by early 1526 if not late 1525. Hans Denk (q.v.), arriving in November, had an open disputation in December 1526 with the Strasbourg ministers, as a result of which he was dismissed from Strasbourg. As far as is known this is the only open disputation ever held in Strasbourg, for later all requests for public disputations were rejected by the council. Before the close of 1526 other prominent Anabaptists arrived, e.g., Jakob Gross, Jorg Tucher, and Wilhelm Echsel, all of whom engaged in conversation with Bucer about baptism. While the affinities of Capito and Bucer to Anabaptism remained, Michael Sattler (q.v.) at this time (1526-27) wrote a letter to them in which he listed twenty differences between him and them, and requested prayer for the imprisoned Anabaptists. Here the basic difference in the view of the church becomes clear, Sattler insisting on a believer's church and separation between the world and the church. He signed the letter as a "brother in God the heavenly Father." This close relationship is evident also from Capito's letter to the authorities at Horb in 1527 expressing his consternation concerning the martyrdom of Michael Sattler.

In early July 1526 the Strasbourg preachers wrote the *Getrewe Warnung der Prediger des Euangelij zu Strassburg vber die Artickel, so Jacob Kautz Prediger zu Wormbs kürtzlich hat lassen aussgohn . . .*, in which the position of Denk was also attacked.

While these skirmishes were going on, Strasbourg as a city had not taken any official action on the issue of Anabaptism, and not until July 27, 1527, was the first mandate issued against the movement. This mandate indicates that the basic issue of the council against the Anabaptists was that they threatened the absolute right of government and were separatists. As a result they ordered no one to lodge or feed them. This mandate was not enforced very strictly, although in the spring of 1528 Lukas Hackfurt, Fridolin Meiger, and Pilgram Marpeck were all arraigned for giving shelter to the Anabaptists. During these years the Anabaptists worked very closely

with the charities of the city which were directed by Hackfurt, who himself was sympathetic to Anabaptists. The Anabaptist group grew after 1527 because of persecution elsewhere, and their need for temporary material assistance was great.

For the Anabaptist group as a whole these years at Strasbourg were marked by tension. The composition of the group was in constant flux and what it lacked in stability it made up in diversity. There were also those who were on the fringes of Anabaptism, admiring it from afar but unable to bring themselves to shoulder the cross. Such were Ludwig Haetzer (q.v.), Caspar Schwenckfeld (q.v.), Cellarius (q.v.), and Sebastian Franck (q.v.). But there were also some who had joined the Anabaptists but could not integrate their past experience with this new view of the Christian life, and therefore soon left the Anabaptist fold. Such were Kautz (q.v.), Hans Bünderlin (q.v.), and Wilhelm Reublin (q.v.). Both Reublin and Christoph Freisleben (q.v.) differed, however, from Bünderlin and Kautz in that they had made lasting contributions to the Anabaptist cause, while the positions of Kautz and Bünderlin had always been rejected by the majority. Nevertheless the presence of all of these variant personalities in Strasbourg, many of them remaining only a brief period, others like Melchior Hofmann (q.v.) remaining for an extended period of time, caused a leavening to take place which threatened the very existence of Anabaptism. This resulted in a major parting of the ways during these years, from which developed the radical eschatological group with a Valentinian view of the Incarnation represented by Hofmann on the one hand, and on the other hand the quiet spiritualism of Kautz and Bünderlin with its depreciation of historical exegesis and forms. In the center stood what later became the Marpeck brotherhood in other parts of southern Europe, represented by Marpeck himself, Leupold Scharnschlager, Wilhelm Reublin, and probably Fridolin Meiger. It is significant that at this early date Scharnschlager was already opposing Hofmann's Valentinian Christology, and that effective means were used to combat the arguments of spiritualism advanced by Bünderlin as seen in the *Clare verantwurtung* (q.v.), as well as the Zwinglian arguments repeated by Bucer, which stressed the difference between inner and outer participation in the ceremonies of the church. While this central party took over the missionary emphasis of Hans Hut (q.v.) and the tradition left by the Tirolese martyrs (Schiemer and Schlaffer, q.v.), they took over elements from Denk (q.v.) only with extreme selectivity.

After this period of stress and strain Marpeck was expelled from Strasbourg. His exile came about in part because the authorities concentrated their fire on the Anabaptist leadership, and after Reublin's dismissal Marpeck had become the leader of the Strasbourg Anabaptists, but in part also because Bucer exerted pressure upon the council to enforce the mandate of July 1527, which was renewed on Sept. 24, 1530. When Capito, a friend of Marpeck's, left town on Dec. 8, 1531, Bucer immediately started proceedings against Marpeck, which resulted in his expulsion at the end of January 1532. For the next two years Scharnschlager was the leader of the Anabaptists. Just how active the group was at this time is not clear. About a year later, when Thomas Adolf came to be baptized by Scharnschlager, his request was not granted because Scharnschlager had been requested to temporarily suspend baptisms because of some unwholesome elements in the Anabaptist fold. The discussions of the council in 1530-40 were almost entirely occupied with Claus Frey (*q.v.*) and Melchior Hofmann (*q.v.*), who was arrested in May 1533 and died in prison there ten years later, at the end of 1543. On March 3, 1534, "Täuferherren" were installed, constituting a commission for handling Anabaptist matters. Scharnschlager was asked to leave Strasbourg after a hearing on May 27, 1534. At this hearing mention was made of Scharnschlager's desire that the city council as government should not rule over one's faith and decide for the individual what he should believe. He also refused to inform on his fellow Anabaptists, and was therefore imprisoned. On June 16, 1534, he wrote a defense of his faith, stating that since he had not yet fully explicated his position to the council, he would like to develop it further. This defense, found in the Strasbourg archives, is important for a number of reasons. It is one of the clearest extant testimonies to the belief of the Anabaptists that they were actually following in the footsteps of Martin Luther in a number of key points. Scharnschlager discussed Luther's position on the authority of government over matters of faith at some length and insisted that this is exactly what the Anabaptists believe. If government had jurisdiction over faith, said Scharnschlager, Strasbourg would still be under the Roman hierarchy. He stated that he was willing to submit to the council if they were questioning him as elders in the place of Christ, but if they were doing it as government officials he could not allow them to judge his faith. Finally this defense is of importance because it states clearly that Scharnschlager rejected the approach being used at Münster at that very time. Even if there were ten thousand Anabaptists in Strasbourg and only five others, Scharnschlager says that these five would not be compelled to become Anabaptists.

With the departure of Scharnschlager from Strasbourg the Anabaptist movement lost one of its finest leaders. While the movement continued there, the city became more of a meeting place for the series of Strasbourg conferences (*q.v.*) than the location of a strong continuing congregation.

During this decade, however, the influence of Strasbourg was pronounced in other cities of South Germany. Augsburg had as one of its most prominent ministers Wolfgang Musculus (*q.v.*), who had earlier been Bucer's secretary and who had always been more tolerant than Bucer. The relations of Strasbourg to Münster have never been fully clarified, but it is becoming increasingly clear that they were intimate and far-reaching. Rothmann (*q.v.*) had spent some time in Strasbourg in 1531, and had been tremendously impressed with the way in which "Christ and Caesar" were working hand in hand. The Strasbourg clergy received a stenographic report of the disputation between Rothmann and his colleagues in August 1533, and wrote

the *Bericht aus heiliger schrifft* . . . (1534), a 100-page reply to the ministers at Münster. The publication of this *Bericht* at the request of Augsburg indicates that many looked to Strasbourg for help in dealing with the Anabaptists in both the area of theology and practical suppression.

The mandate of March 3, 1534, stating that views not in accord with the Augsburg Confession would not be tolerated, and the synod of 1533 in which all were allowed to present their views to the ministers and a select group of the council, did much to weaken the Anabaptist cause in Strasbourg. On April 28, 1535, compulsory baptism of all infants was ordered. Before this, in 1534, Kilian Aurbacher had written a moving letter from Moravia to Bucer about the danger of compelling people in matters of faith (this letter has been preserved), but its contents were not heeded, and on March 23, 1538, the city council issued a new mandate with four harsh provisions: (1) all Anabaptists were to be banished; (2) in case of return, the offender was to be imprisoned for four weeks on a diet of bread and water, then exiled again; (3) upon a second return he should be punished by cutting off his fingers or by placing him in neck irons and branding his cheek; (4) if he returned a third time, he should be executed by drowning.

On Nov. 23, 1534, Hans Frisch, from Horb, said that there were three groups of Anabaptists in Strasbourg, the factions of Reublin, of Hofmann, and of Kautz, the latter two being somewhat intermingled. At the end of this decade, May 29, 1539, Ruprecht Schwarz, from Mainz, reported to the Strasbourg authorities that there were a number of gatherings in Strasbourg, and said that the Hofmannites and the Swiss Brethren could not attain agreement. The Swiss Brethren, he said, numbered about 100, while the Hofmannites did not exceed five.

It has been estimated that in 1534 the number of Anabaptists in Strasbourg was about 2,000. It is certain that this number did not increase, but rather decreased, for soon the meetings took place outside the city, and the church came to be known as the "Waldskirche." Bucer expressed satisfaction that he could now rest and concentrate on winning Anabaptists for the Reformed cause in Hesse through Peter Tasch (*q.v.*). John Calvin (*q.v.*), the Reformer of Geneva, who stayed at Strasbourg in 1538-41, took great pains to win over the Anabaptists, particularly the French-speaking among them. In a few cases he was successful; one of his converts was Jean Stordeur (*q.v.*).

On April 9, 1540, the Strasbourg Council issued the final mandate against the Anabaptists. Those refusing to take the oath were threatened with loss of life, and those sheltering Anabaptists with corporal punishment and loss of property. This mandate also contained the statement that from time to time large numbers of Anabaptists met in uncustomary places, such as out in the fields.

In later years Marpeck addressed a letter to the people around Strasbourg on the question of Christian liberty, which shows that he felt that they were abusing their Christian freedom and were not taking sufficient precautions to protect the weaker brother. Only he is truly free, who is free in Christ,

42

Marpeck asserts. During that time and later the Strasbourg group was visited by Pilgram Marpeck, as is evident from a reference in one of Scharnschlager's letters to the Strasbourg Anabaptist brotherhood contained in the *Kunstbuch*. This letter is not dated, but possibly belongs in the 1540's. The circular letters No. 3 and No. 35 of the *Kunstbuch,* dated 1544 and 1547, were addressed to those in Alsace. The last known writing of Marpeck, dated Jan. 22, 1555 (No. 15), was sent to a certain Abraham at Langnau in the Kinzig Valley, in which he adds the request to greet certain persons in the Leber Valley, mentioning them by name. The important leader of the Marpeck brotherhood in this area at this time was Sigmund Bosch (*q.v.*). It appears that Marpeck served as liaison for the Moravian, the Swiss, and the Strasbourg Anabaptists. According to court testimony of May 29, 1561, there were three groups of Anabaptists around Strasbourg then—the Bilgramites, the Gabrielites, and the Sattlerites.

An interesting testimony of the faith of the Strasbourg Swiss Brethren is found in a lengthy tract titled *Concerning the Incarnation and Deity of Jesus Christ* (extant in a Dutch print of 1666), written to counter the Socinian wooing of the Strasbourg group begun in 1590 by Voydovsky and continued by Ostorodt (*q.v.*), where particulars are given.

The importance of Strasbourg for Anabaptist history consists in the issues which were resolved there during the early years. Foremost of these were the issues of spiritualism and religious liberty. W.Kl.

* * *

Strasbourg was the scene of at least six important Anabaptist Conferences, 1554, 1555, 1557, 1568, 1592, and 1607. Strasbourg was also represented at the conference in 1591 which drew up the Concept of Cologne (*q.v.*). These conferences are described in the following article, **Strasbourg Conferences**. It is probable that the 16th-century congregation died out. If so, it was renewed by immigration later from other parts of Alsace. In 1796 a conference was held in the neighborhood of Strasbourg, of which little is known. Representatives from the Strasbourg congregation at the Essingen (*q.v.*) Conferences were Hans Rogi for 1759, and Christian Rub for 1779. The general letter of the French Mennonite congregations of 1808 concerning military service was signed for the Strasbourg congregation by Johann Rotacker and Hans Egli. Little is known about the congregation in the 19th century. It must have been small and without influence. Its meetings were held monthly, in places around the city, first at Robertsau, later at Neudorf in the home of an elder. The last known elders were Jacob Egli and his nephew Christian Egli. The latter moved to the region of Chalons-sur-Marne *c*1855; the former died in 1883. After his death the congregation dissolved, some moving away, while the rest joined the Reformed Church. Strangely, Strasbourg does not appear in any of the Dutch *Naamlijsts* or German *Namensverzeichnisse* or yearbooks.

H.S.B.

Abraham Hulshof, *Geschiedenis van de Doopsgezinden te Straatsburg van 1525 tot 1557* (Amsterdam, 1905); Camill Gerbert, *Geschichte der Strassburger Sectenbewegung* (Strassburg, 1889); T. W. Röhrich, "Zur Geschichte der strassburgischen Wiedertäufer in den Jahren 1527 bis 1543," *Zeitschrift für historische Theologie* 1860, 3-121; idem, *Geschichte der Reformation im Elsass* I (1830), II (1832); idem, *Mitteilungen aus der Geschichte der evang. Kirche des Elsasses* (Paris, 1855); P. Sommer, "Assemblée de Strasbourg," *Christ Seul*, April 1932, 5-7; Robert Kreider, "The Anabaptists and the Civil Authorities of Strasbourg, 1525-1555," *Church History* XXIV (1955) 99-118; *ML* IV.

Strasbourg Conferences. Strasbourg in Alsace, a more tolerant city than most places in Europe in the 16th century, was the scene of at least six conferences of Anabaptist ministers in 1554, 1555, 1557, 1568, 1592, and 1607.

1. The conference of 1554 is known solely through a note in the record of the Strasbourg city council meeting of March 9, 1554, reported by Hulshof (p. 218), which reads (in translation): "On the previous Saturday a meeting of Anabaptists was held at the Long Bridge, at which 600 are supposed to have assembled."

2. The conference held Aug. 24, 1555, is known solely through a letter sent to Holland, containing the "Agreement Made by the Brethren and Elders at Strasbourg, Assembled Because of the Question of the Origin of the Flesh of Christ." This document of about 800 words was first published in Hans Alenson's (*q.v.*) *Tegen-Bericht* of 1630 (pages 124 f.) who says he "took it from the copy which had been faithfully translated from the High German into the Netherlands language by I.H.V.P.N. [Carel van Gent?] in Amsterdam, Sept. 1, 1610." A copy of the *Tegen-Bericht* is in the Zürich University Library. The Agreement is also found in the reprint of the *Tegen-Bericht* in BRN VII, occupying pages 226-28. S. Blaupot ten Cate published it from a copy in the Amsterdam Mennonite Library, since lost, in his *Geschiedenis der Doopsgezinden in Groningen, Overijssel en Oost-Friesland* I (Leeuwarden, 1842), pp. 254-57. Hulshof reprinted it from ten Cate in his *Geschiedenis van de Doopsgezinden te Straatsburg van 1525 tot 1557* (Amsterdam, 1905), pp. 220-22. The Agreement clearly states that the meeting was called because the brethren had repeatedly been requested and urged to speak about the Incarnation, and now recently again by the Hofmannites and by the brethren in the Netherlands. They had "gathered from many places." The concern of the Agreement is to bring harmony into the brotherhood by holding to the simple statements of Scripture regarding the Incarnation and going no further. It is more important to keep the commandments of Christ than to press to an understanding of the mysteries of how Christ became flesh. Hulshof assumes that Dutch and High Germans (Swiss Brethren) took part in the meeting. He rightly rejects several statements by Ottius (*Annales Anabaptistici,* 120) who knew about the meeting from the Alenson report, and claims, clearly without foundation, that Moravians (Hutterites) and Germans were together, and that the parties in the dispute excommunicated each other, here basing erroneously on a statement in the *Protocoll* of the Frankenthal disputation of 1571, p. 14, which makes no reference to the Strasbourg Conference of 1555.

3. The conference of 1557 is known solely through a letter written to Menno by two High

German ministers, Zylis and Lemke, on behalf of the Strasbourg conference, giving a report of the conclusions. Hulshof printed the rather lengthy epistle (some 1600 words) in full, because so many incorrect statements about the conference had been made by German historians, who apparently had never seen the text of the letter. He used the reprint by J. G. de Hoop Scheffer, "Opmerkingen en mededeelingen betreffende Menno Simons, VIII," *DB* 1894, 10-70. The letter is reprinted on pp. 47-53 from a handwritten copy (now in the Amsterdam Mennonite Archives) made by J. Cuperus (*q.v.*) in November 1769 from a printed book, *Een gansch duytlic ende bescheyden antwoordt . . . door L.D.W.* According to this letter, some 50 elders and ministers assembled from Moravia, Swabia, Switzerland, Württemberg, Breisgau, and Alsace, as far as 150 miles away, among whom was a preacher in whose house the Schleitheim confession of 1527 had been drawn up. The occasion for the meeting was a controversy between two elders, Theobald of Worms and Farwendel of Kreuznach, over original sin and the sin of the soul and of the flesh, a controversy which had seriously divided the brotherhood. The controversy was overcome at Strasbourg and harmony was restored. The second topic for discussion was the question of the severe application of avoidance or shunning in connection with the ban, including marital avoidance, as advocated by Leenaert Bouwens, who had also won Menno to his view. Bouwens and Menno had called a meeting of Dutch and High German leaders at Cologne in the spring of 1557, at which they had hoped to win the High Germans for their position. But very few High Germans had appeared, and the attempt was a failure. The epistle from the Strasbourg conference, addressed to Menno and the Dutch leaders, was actually a reply to the letter from Menno to the High Germans. It rejected in a kindly spirit the proposals for a strict application of the ban, and expressed the strong hope that differences regarding this matter should not be the cause of a break. Unfortunately their hope was to be disappointed, for this break came in 1559; Menno rejected the proffered hand of reconciliation, and the Dutch elders pronounced the ban on the High Germans at a meeting of delegates of both sides held in that year.

Hulshof reports that the large gathering of Anabaptists at the conferences of 1554 and 1555 led the city council of Strasbourg to renewed action against the brethren, but that the examination of arrested persons by the newly appointed (August 1555) Anabaptist Commission produced no information about the conferences. Petrus Novesianus, a schoolteacher, but not an Anabaptist, reported that there were many Anabaptist sects, naming five, Hutterites, Hofmannites, Swiss, Bilgrammites (Pilgram Marpeck), and Zabites(?).

J. J. Kiwiet, in his *Pilgram Marbeck* (Kassel, 1957), interprets the conference of 1555 as a gathering whose purpose was to unite all the divergent Anabaptist groups, holding that it was really the fruit of Pilgram Marpeck's efforts to unify the groups, and that it succeeded. He offers no documentary proof for his claim, grounding it rather on the evidence of Marpeck's long campaign for unity. It is possible, as he suggests, that Marpeck was present at the conferences of 1554 and 1555. Since he died in 1556 he could not have attended the conference of 1557. The conference of 1557, as the above report shows, was indeed called to bring about unity between the groups in controversy over the doctrine of original sin, and it succeeded. In this sense the conference of 1557 would better fit Kiwiet's thesis than that of 1555, which was called to deal with a theological difference which separated the Dutch and the Hofmannites from the High Germans. However, no unity was achieved at this conference between the disputing parties. It is of interest to note that at this conference it was reported that there were "50 congregations from the Eiffel to Moravia, some of which had 500 to 600 brethren and sisters."

4. The conferences of 1568 and 1607 are known solely through a discipline adopted at the 1568 conference and confirmed at the conference of 1607. It is called "Agreement of the Ministers and Elders of Many Localities in Conference at Strasbourg in the Year 1568, and Reaffirmed at the Strasbourg Conference of 1607." The discipline is known only from handwritten copies handed down from the past, several of which are to be found in the Goshen College and Bethel College Mennonite historical libraries. An edition was printed in 1905 at Elkhart, Ind., together with the disciplines adopted at several later conferences in Europe and America. The oldest manuscript copy extant in America was made in 1836 by Peter Unsicker at Beissenhofen, Germany. H. S. Bender edited and published in German and in English translation a manuscript copy of 1860, "The Discipline Adopted by the Strasbourg Conference of 1568," *MQR* I (1927), pp. 57-66. Here he reports an earlier text in the possession of Peter Kipfer of the Emmental congregation near Langnau, Switzerland, which had been published in paraphrase by Mathias Pohl of Sembach, Palatinate, Germany, in the *Christlicher Gemeinde-Kalender* for 1906, pp. 134-43. Ernst Müller's report in his *Geschichte der bernischen Täufer* (Frauenfeld, 1895), pp. 50-52, apparently was based on the Kipfer copy. The twenty-three articles of the 1568 discipline deal largely with practical questions such as the provisions for traveling ministers to visit the congregations, for selection and ordination of ministers and bishops to fill vacancies, the care for orphans of the brotherhood, moderation in the practice of shunning apostate members, restricting the holy kiss to members, not requiring rebaptism of outsiders who have already been baptized, maintaining simplicity in costume, no rigid uniformity in mode of distributing the communion bread, etc. One article refers to the question of the Incarnation, calling for abiding by the Scripture on this point and avoiding as far as possible all disputing. This is the only known Anabaptist discipline after the Schleitheim discipline of 1527.

5. The conference of 1592 is known solely through a letter written on behalf of the participants of the conference to the Socinians in Poland, in reply to a letter from a Socinian leader, Christian Ostorodt, dated Oct. 20, 1591, found in the City Library of Bern, Switzerland, and published by Theodor Wotschke with an introduction and notes in *Archiv für Reformationsgeschichte* XII (1915)

137-54. The reply of the Strasbourg conference was published under the title (translated), *An Answer of the Swiss Brethren, also Called High Germans, to the Polish, Concerning the Point of the Incarnation and the Deity of Jesus Christ*, in *Handelinge der Vereenigde Vlaemse en Duytse Doopsgesinde Gemeynten Gehouden tot Haerlem Anno 1649* (Vlissingen, 1666). A postscript to the letter adds the note (translated): "Passed at the general gathering of the elders and ministers from many countries, held in the year 1592 at Strasbourg. . . . Translated from the High German into the Low German from Rauf-bits' [Rauf Bitsch] own handwriting." Rauf Bitsch was a leading spokesman of the Brethren in the disputation at Frankenthal in 1571.

The repeated meetings at Strasbourg suggest not only that Strasbourg was tolerant, but that there must have been a continuing Anabaptist congregation at Strasbourg (as indeed we know there was down to at least 1880), that there may have been other congregations in the neighborhood (as we know there were both north and south of Strasbourg in Alsace), and that Strasbourg had an established reputation as a meeting place. Outside of Schleitheim and Augsburg (both in 1527), no other Anabaptist conferences meeting in the 16th century south of Cologne are known. H.S.B.

Abraham Hulshof, *Geschiedenis van de Doopsgezinden te Straatsburg van 1525 tot 1557* (Amsterdam, 1905) particularly Ch. XIII, "Algemeene Vergaderingen door Doopsgezinden uit verschillende Landen in 1554 en volgende Jaaren te Straatsburg gehouden," 218-34; J. H. Ottius, *Annales Anabaptistici* (Basel, 1672); John Horsch, "The Faith of the Swiss Brethren," *MQR* II (1931) 24-27.

Strasbourg Discipline, a set of 23 regulations drawn up in 1568 by the "preachers and elders from many places in the meeting at Strasbourg" and confirmed and renewed in 1607 at the same place by the assembled representatives of the congregations. This *Abrede der Diener und Eltesten* (Agreement of the Preachers and Elders) was expanded at two later conferences, viz., on March 5 (year not given) in Obersülzen in the Palatinate and in 1688 at Ofenstein (Offstein, *q.v.*).

These articles do not constitute an actual confession of faith or dogmatic teachings, but in general discuss practical questions of church life, for the most part dealing with the organization of the congregations, supply of ministers, discipline, ordinances, marriage, care of orphans, etc.

Three manuscript copies of the Strasbourg Discipline recopied and handed down through Amish bishops in Pennsylvania, Iowa, Ohio, and Indiana are now in GCL. One of these was reproduced in German and English translation, "The Discipline Adopted by the Strasbourg Conference of 1568," ed. by H. S. Bender, *MQR* I (1927) 57-66, together with an attached appendix of four articles adopted at Hoffingen in 1630.

William Yoder, an Amish bishop of near Nappanee, Ind., published the Strasbourg Discipline together with additional material in 1905 as *Artikel und Ordnungen der Christlichen Gemeinde in Christo Jesu* (printed at Elkhart, Ind.) as a 16-page booklet (copy in GCL).

The *Gemeinde-Kalender* for 1906 contains an interesting article by Mathias Pohl on the Discipline, in which he presented a paraphrase article by article from an old copy then in the possession of Peter Kipfer of the Emmental congregation near Langnau, Switzerland. Two additional articles appear in this paraphrase, one dealing with tobacco, which could not have been in the 1568 form, hence were likely added in 1607. Also presented by Pohl are four additional articles adopted by a conference at Obersülzen on March 5 (year missing) and another set of five articles adopted by the conference at Ofenstein (Offstein) in March 1688.

Ernst Müller in his *Berner Täufer* (1895) refers to the Strasbourg Discipline with brief characterization and summary (pp. 50-52) stating that the manuscript copy he used was in private possession in Emmental Mennonite hands, possibly the Kipfer copy. He refers to the Obersülzen additions as of March 5, 1668, but does not mention the Ofenstein additions. An interesting and valuable feature of the Kipfer manuscript is a colored drawing on the cover picturing Anabaptist men and women in an assembly. This is reproduced in the Pohl article in black and white.

This is, next to the Schleitheim Confession, the only significant church document of the Swiss Brethren which has been preserved. It is of outstanding significance from the practical point of view, but of no value theologically. H.S.B.

Strasburg Mennonite Church (MC) of Franklin County, Pa., a member of Washington County, Md., and Franklin County, Pa., Conference, began in the early 19th century when a log meetinghouse was built, probably in 1812. A brick building was constructed at a near-by site in 1858 and rebuilt in 1903. In 1942 the United States Government claimed this area for an Ammunition Depot which necessitated securing another, the present, place of worship which was formerly a Brethren Church. Ministers who have served the congregation include John S. Burkholder, Henry Bricker, John Lehman, John Gsell, and Harry H. Witmer, the pastor in 1957, when there were 53 members. S.L.B.

Strasburg Mennonite Church (MC), located 9 miles southeast of Lancaster, Pa., a member of the Lancaster Conference, was from the start a strong Mennonite community. This was the home of Bishop Benedict Brackbill (1665-1720), leader both in Europe and here, his son Ulrich Brackbill (1703-39), also a minister, John Herr (III) (1708-83), and Preacher John Herr (1720-97), who in 1740 built a 2½-story stone house on the Brackbill farm as a dwelling, which was also provided with room for worship services and was used until 1804. (It is now owned by Charles E. Good.) That year John Brackbill, Sr., gave John Brackbill, Jr., John Funk, Henry Breneman, and Jacob Groff the present site of ground on the western edge of the borough, "being willing and desirous to promote the spiritual growth and religious fellowship of the people called Menonists in this neighborhood." This beautiful stone church, 40 x 60 ft., of colonial architecture, was the largest Mennonite meetinghouse of its day. It was enlarged in 1877 and 1887, and razed in 1925 for a new brick church 57 x 103 ft. In 1957 Emory H. Herr was the pastor, with a membership of 348. It formerly was a part of the Brick-Strasburg circuit.

I.D.L.

Strasser, Gottfried (1854-1912), Reformed pastor in Grindelwald in the Bernese Oberland, author of the song which has become the folk song, the *Grindelwaldnerlied* or *Gletscherpfarrer von Grindelwald.* In Langnau (Emmental), where he grew up, Strasser made some observations among the New Amish (*q.v.*), which led him to a closer study of the Anabaptist movement. In 1884 he published a historical treatise, "Der schweizerische Anabaptismus zur Zeit der Reformation," in the *Berner Beiträge zur Geschichte der schweizerischen Reformationskirchen,* which is, however, not entirely objective and does not go beyond the prejudiced position of church historians of an earlier era. As the foundation of his book Strasser used biased sources, especially Bullinger's (*q.v.*) books, and therefore came to the conclusion that the Anabaptists were only fanatics. Even the conversion of Conrad Grebel (*q.v.*) he thought took place from motives of hostility rather than of love for the cause of the Gospel. For the doctrines of the Anabaptists Strasser showed little understanding, although he admitted that their motivation was not mere fanaticism but their wish to be, "after the example of the apostolic time, in the narrower circle of the awakened, a brotherhood of active holiness, the gathering of a truly Christian people which would adhere to the Gospel, live the most blameless lives and not tolerate any grave sin among them." Concerning the strict Biblicism of the Anabaptists Strasser said, "It was not to be avoided that the petrified adherence to the letter of the Bible would soon after the inception of Anabaptism turn into a fanaticism that elevated itself above the Bible." He identifies the Anabaptist movement with the Peasants' Revolt; the reports of fanatical happenings that Strasser gives are taken from Bullinger. On the whole, like his contemporary Emil Egli (*q.v.*), whose works he used, Strasser sought to do justice to the history of the Reformation. (*ML IV.*)

S.G.

Straten (Straeten), **van der,** an Anabaptist-Mennonite family in Flanders, Belgium, three of whose members died as martyrs—Joost (*q.v.*) van der Straten, executed at Antwerp in 1571, and his two sons, Hans (*q.v.*), executed at Brussels in 1571, and Martin (*q.v.*), executed at Gent in 1572. Probably the van der Straten family originally came from Kortrijk (*q.v.*). Among the first Calvinists in Flanders there were also a number of persons bearing the same family name. (Verheyden, *Gent,* 59 f.)

vDZ.

Straub, Hans, the author of the song, "Durch gnad so will ich singen, in Gottes forcht heben an," No. 56 in the *Ausbund.* Nothing else is known of him. (*ML IV.*)

NEFF.

Strawberry Hill (B.C.) Menn. Brethren Church, belonging to the Northern District and Canadian conferences, was organized in November 1944 with 52 members. The meetinghouse is a schoolhouse formerly owned by the Japanese and used for re-

ligious and educational purposes. In 1957 the membership was 105, with Paul J. Wiebe as leading minister, assisted by Abraham H. Toews.

H.D.F.

Strawberry Lake Mission Church (MC), located on the White Earth Indian Reservation, Becker Co., Minn., is a member of the North Central Conference. In 1948 there were ten members, two of whom were Chippewa Indians, and a class of 22 was under instruction for baptism. The work was started by Joe Gingerich of Detroit Lakes, Minn., who conducted Sunday school in a local schoolhouse for a number of years. The meetinghouse was built in 1948 by voluntary labor from several states. In 1957 the membership was 20, with Llewellyn Groff in charge.

L.GR.

Streichenberg, a former Mennonite congregation near Eppingen in Baden, Germany, was settled at the beginning of the 18th century by exiles from the Swiss canton of Bern (Müller, 210, where the name is Streigenberg). At the beginning of the 19th century Martin Frey, a member of the congregation, built a meetinghouse. In 1843 Heinrich Baer of the Dammhof was chosen elder and Samuel Brandt and Daniel Baer deacons. Later the Streichenberg congregation merged with Bockschaft (*q.v.*). In 1731 it numbered ten families. In the Dutch *Naamlijst* of 1766 the congregation is called the Bockschaft, Streichenberg, and Wesingen church. Martin Kräuter was at that time its elder, ordained in 1746. In 1767 the congregation obtained a second elder, Jakob Funck. The *Naamlijst* of 1773 lists Bockschaft and Streichenberg as two separate congregations, each with its own elder and preachers. The elder of the Streichenberg church was Jakob Funck and the preachers were Heinrich Funck (ord. 1772) and Philippus Schneider (1772-after 1801). According to later issues of the *Naamlijst,* Funck was followed in 1773 by Jost Glück, who served until after 1801. Later preachers were Martin Frey 1780-*c* 86, another Heinrich Funk 1783-89, Christian Heer (Herr) 1785-after 1801, and Mathias Bär 1790-after 1801. Neither Streichenberg nor Bockschaft exists any longer under its own name; in 1841 Streichenberg united with Ittlingen (*q.v.*), and since 1913 it has belonged to the Sinsheim (*q.v.*) congregation. (*Menn. Bl.,* 1851, 57; 1855, 70; Müller, *Berner Täufer; ML IV.*)

NEFF, vDZ.

Streigel, Fritz, an Anabaptist martyr, who was beheaded at Baiersdorf in Franconia, Germany, in July 1531 with Hans Schmid (*q.v.*) and Marx Mayer (*q.v.*). (*TA Bayern* I; *ML IV.*)

Streypers, Jan, a Quaker of Kaldekerk, near Crefeld, Germany, probably a Mennonite before 1679 when Quakerism was planted in this area, one of the three promoters of the German settlement along with Jacob Telner (*q.v.*) and Dirck Sipman (*q.v.*). He bought 5,000 acres of land in Pennsylvania from Benjamin Furly, Penn's agent in Rotterdam, which he finally turned over to his younger brother William, one of the first 13 Germantown settler families. He spent a short time in Germantown sometime between 1687 and 1706.

When William Penn came to the Rhineland again in 1686, he visited Wesel, where Jan Streypers and his son-in-law, H. J. van Aaken, met him and accompanied him to Kirchheim and Crefeld. E.H.B.

Fr. Nieper, *Die ersten deutschen Auswanderer aus Krefeld nach Pennsylvanien* (Neukirchen, 1940) 90 ff.; William J. Hull, *William Penn and the Dutch Quaker Migration to Pennsylvania* (Philadelphia, 1935).

Strickler, Hermann: see **Hermann Moded.**

Strickler Mennonite Church (MC), now extinct. Henry Strickler settled southeast of Columbia, Pa., and Jacob and Henry went to Hellman Twp., York Co., early to establish a Mennonite community. About 1790 Jacob sold from his 150-acre farm a three-cornered plot to Henry Strickler, Andrew Garber, and Abraham Flury for a Mennonite meetinghouse. The brick was imported from England for a 30 x 28 ft. building directly south of the Lincoln Highway, about two miles west of Wrightsville. The well-kept Strickler burying ground is about a quarter mile east. The congregation was under Lancaster Conference and was served by Frederick Stauffer as bishop, Daniel Stauffer and David Witmer as ministers, and Michael Strickler as deacon in the late 1880's. Witmer's, now known as Stony Brook (*q.v.*), absorbed this membership and by 1920 the house was razed and plot sold. I.D.L.

Strobel (or Helwig), **Christina,** of Gotha, Germany, an Anabaptist martyr, was drowned with nine other Anabaptists in the Unstrut between Mühlhausen and Ammern, on Nov. 9, 1573. (Wappler, *Thüringen,* 162; *ML* IV.)

Stroe, het, a hamlet on the former island of Wieringen, Dutch province of North Holland, where there was a branch of the Wieringen (*q.v.*) Mennonite congregation, with a meetinghouse of its own. The first meetinghouse, a frame building, was rebuilt in 1738. This curious old-type meetinghouse built like a brick barn burned down on April 2, 1938. (*DB* 1891, 47 ff.; *De Zondagsbode* XVI, 1932-33, No. 24.) vDZ.

Strohm (Strahm), a Mennonite family, formerly living in Switzerland. Ulrich Strohm emigrated to the Palatinate, Germany, in 1671; Martin Strahm (Strohm), of Höchstetten, was in prison at Bern, Switzerland, because of his Mennonite convictions, and was expelled from the country in 1711; he probably also settled in the Palatinate. Here Heinrich Strohm was a preacher of the Oberflörsheim (*q.v.*) and Griesheim congregations 1758-90, and Johannes Strohm was a preacher of the Erpolzheim (*q.v.*) and Friesenheim (*q.v.*) united congregation 1757-80. Another Johannes Strohm (b. 1781 at Kriegsheim, d. 1852 at West Point, Iowa), a preacher of Schway, Bavaria, 1821-47, emigrated to America with some children and many grandchildren. One of these was the preacher Matthias Strahm. vDZ.

Müller, *Berner Täufer,* 202, 307; *Naamlijst; MQR* XXX (1956) 164, No. 62.

Stroink, an old Dutch family for many centuries living in the district of Twente (*q.v.*), province of Overijssel. In the 18th and 19th centuries some members of this Reformed family joined the Mennonites. Stroinks of Enschedé, Gronau, and Zwolle have served the church as deacons. vDZ.

Stroman, a Mennonite family at Norden in East Friesland, Germany, some of whose members have served as deacons. Bernard Johan Hendrik Stroman, b. 1902 at Rotterdam, a printer, published a study on the "wederdopers" in *Vrije Bladen* IX (1932) and some novels, including *Obbe Philipsz Oudste der Dopers* (1935). vDZ.

Struth Mennonite Church near Saverne, Lower Alsace, France, was probably established soon after the end of the Thirty Years' War by emigrants from Switzerland. Its members were increased by refugees who had been driven out of Markirch (*q.v.*) by the decree of 1712. It appears in the Dutch *Naamlijst* of 1768 and following as "Stroeter Gemeente." It was located in the midst of a sympathetic Protestant population, which resulted later in mixed marriages, which may well have accounted in part for the ultimate disappearance of the congregation. Leading names in the community indicate previous Mennonite origin, such as Haury, Zehr, Biehler, Hunzinger, Kempf, Lehmann, Springer, Muller, Maurer, Martin, and Risser. It was represented at the Essingen Conference in 1759 by Uli Sommer, and in 1779 by Christian Nafziger and Hans Schertz. It participated in 1809 in the collection for defraying expenses of the delegates to Paris in the matter of nonresistance. The *Naamlijst* of 1802 lists Christian Naftziger, Jr., as elder. By the middle of the 19th century Struth had died out. H.S.B.

P. Sommer, "Assemblée de Struth," *Christ Seul,* January 1932, 4 f.

Stuartburn (Man.) **Gospel Chapel,** a mission congregation of the Evangelical Mennonite Brethren Church, was started in 1945 subsidized by the conference. In 1957 it had 33 members, with H. P. Wiens as pastor. H.S.B.

Stuarts Draft (Va.) Mennonite Church (MC) was established in 1920 and is a member of the Southern District of the Virginia Mennonite Conference. It had a membership of 109 in 1957 and its preachers were Jason H. Weaver, Paul Barnhart, and Roy D. Kiser. M.G.

Stüblau, northern part of the Danzig Werder in West Prussia, Germany. Here Dutch Mennonites settled at a very early period (c1543) to drain this swampy area. vDZ.

Horst Penner, *Ansiedlung menn. Niederländer im Weichselmündungsgebiet* (Weierhof, 1940) 10, 17 f., 19.

Stübner, Markus Thomae, one of the "Zwickau prophets," the son of the owner of a bathhouse at Elsterberg in Vogtland, therefore called "Stübner" (room owner), studied theology at the University of Wittenberg. He left the university in 1521, met Nikolaus Storch (*q.v.*) and Thomas Müntzer (*q.v.*), and enthusiastically adopted their ideas. He accompanied Müntzer on his third journey to Bohemia. In Zwickau he was a zealous follower of

Storch. With Storch and Thomas Drechsel (*q.v.*) he went to Wittenberg in December 1521 and was the actual spokesman in the discussions with Melanchthon (*q.v.*). He won Martin Cellarius (*q.v.*) and Gerhard von Westerburg (*q.v.*) to their cause. In April 1522 he also had a discussion with Luther, which was, however, fruitless. A letter which he wrote to Luther from the town of Kemberg was answered by Luther with the words, "Farewell, dear Marcus." Nothing is known of Stübner's further fate. NEFF.

Paul Wappler, "Thomas Münzer in Zwickau und die Zwickauer Propheten" (Zwickau, 1908), in *Wissenschaftlicher Beilag zu dem Jahresbericht das Realgymnasiums zu Zwickau* (1908); *ML* IV.

Stuckey (Stucky, Stucki), a Mennonite family of Swiss descent, originally living in the Bernese Oberland. Peter Stucki (*q.v.*) died as a martyr at Bern in 1538. In the 18th and 19th centuries members of this family lived in the Bernese Jura, particularly in the Pruntrut (Porrentruy) district. By the early 18th century some Swiss Stuckis had settled in Alsace; Christen Stucki (b. *c*1687) of Diemtigen in the Bernese Oberland was one of the emigrants to the Netherlands in 1711, and settled with this family near Sappemeer (*q.v.*). His descendants in the 19th century left the Mennonite Church.

The first Stuckeys in America came from Alsace in 1830 (see **Stuckey, Joseph**). They were Amish. Others (see **Stucky, Jacob**) came from Volhynia (*q.v.*) in 1874 to where a Stucki family had emigrated from the canton of Bern in 1740. There are numerous descendants in America. vDZ.

Paul Peachey, *Die soziale Herkunft der Schweizer Täufer* (Karlsruhe, 1956) 140, Nos. 694-96: D. L. Gratz, *Bernese Anabaptists* (Scottdale, 1953) 23, 49, 199; Müller, *Berner Täufer*, 14, 312; *Inv. Arch. Amst.* I, No. 1897.

Stuckey, Joseph (1825-1902), founder and outstanding leader of the Central (Illinois) Conference of Mennonites (*q.v.*), was born in Alsace July 12, 1825, the oldest of the eight children of Peter Stuckey and Elizabeth Sommers, his grandparents having lived in the canton of Bern, Switzerland. He immigrated with his parents in 1830 to Butler County (*q.v.*), Ohio, where he was baptized at the age of eighteen in the Amish congregation. He married Barbara Roth on Dec. 17, 1844; they had two children. In October 1858 he moved to McLean County, Ill., where he was ordained deacon, minister on April 8, 1860, and bishop on April 26, 1864, both times by Bishop Jonathan Yoder, for the Rock Creek (Yoder) A.M. Church, and after Yoder's death became the recognized leader of the Amish Mennonites of Central Illinois. From 1872 to his death on Feb. 5, 1902, he was pastor of the North Danvers congregation. He was in great demand as a preacher and bishop to assist in ordinations, communion services, etc., and traveled widely among the Amish of the central states. He was a regular and influential attendant at the Amish general conferences known as Diener-Versammlungen (*q.v.*) until 1872. In that year, because he refused the request of the conference to excommunicate a member of his congregation who advocated universalism, although Stuckey himself never held this view, he was declared out of fellowship. Most of the

Central Illinois Amish congregations stood with Stuckey, and as a result were out of fellowship with the main body of Amish. Stuckey, however, did not organize his following into a conference until 1899, shortly before his death, when the Central Illinois Conference was established.

He published *Eine Begebenheit die sich in der Mennoniten-Gemeinde in Deutschland und in der Schweiz von 1693 bis 1700 zugetragen hat* (Elkhart, 1883), dealing with the Amish schism.† W.B.W., H.S.B.

W. B. Weaver, *History of the Central Conference Mennonite Church* (Danvers, 1926); Harry Yoder, "Joseph Stuckey and the Central Conference," *Menn. Life* VI (April 1951) 16-19.

Stucki, Peter, an Anabaptist martyr of Wimmis in the Emmental, Swiss canton of Bern, who was executed at Bern on April 16, 1538.

Mart. Mir. E 1129; Adolf Fluri, *Beiträge zur Geschichte der bernischen Täufer* (Bern, 1912) 14; *ML* IV.

Stucky, Jacob (1824-93), pioneer, educator, minister, and elder of the Volhynian Swiss Mennonites in Poland and in America, was born in Volhynia, Russian Poland, on Oct. 25, 1824, the eighth child of Christian and Katharina Mündelheim Stucky. He married Anna Waltner in 1849; eight of their children grew to maturity. His wife died shortly before the trek to America and on May 2, 1879, he married Barbara Kaufmann Voran. His descendants total over 1,335, of whom more than 1,200 are living in the United States and Canada.

Stucky was baptized in 1840 and elected into the ministry on May 29, 1851, and ordained as elder on Sept. 29, 1862. During that year his congregation moved from Eduardsdorf eastward some 160 miles to Kotozufka and Neumannovka, in Russian Poland, where they were permitted to own land on condition that they clear it and build their homes in true pioneering. The Swiss Mennonites established the churches of Zahorez, Horodyszcze, Waldheim, and Kotozufka in Volhynia. Kotozufka, the largest, was known as the Stucky Church. When they were barely established the policies of Russification and militarization dictated another move for conscience' sake. With the assistance of Jacob Goering, Stucky led his entire congregation (except two bachelors) of 73 families from Poland to America. They left their homes on Aug. 6, 1874, and arrived at Peabody, Kan., in approximately one month. They later settled in the region around Moundridge, Kan.

The congregation organized under the name Hoffnungsfeld (GCM). Here Stucky served faithfully until his death. He had a warm personality and was held in high esteem by the Swiss Mennonites of the settlement. He served various kinds of Mennonite groups from Western Kansas to South Dakota. During the first six years in Kansas he baptized 142 persons, 60 of these in his home church, 56 at the Emmanuel Church, then known as the "Cantongemeinde," 20 at Pawnee Rock, and at Hartford in Lyons County, Kan.

Elder Stucky was also concerned with bringing about orderly church life among many groups of Mennonites in Kansas, and played a part in the organization of the Kansas Conference. He promoted the cause of relief and Christian charity, especially regarding widows and orphans. He was also interested in Christian education, and pleaded in the press for a living wage for the instructor so that he could devote his full time to the cause. In 1877 he was elected to a "Committee of Seven" at Alexanderwohl to plan for a "Fortbildungsschule." He served on Kansas (now Western District) Conference committees. He was a member of the Christian Education Committee from 1877 to his death. In 1887 he was one of the thirty-three who signed the Bethel College Corporation Charter. He died at Moundridge on April 25, 1893, and was buried in the Hopefield cemetery. H.J.S.

Jacob M. and Anna J. Goering, *The Rev. Jacob Stucky Family Record 1824-1953* (North Newton, 1954); I. G. Neufeld, "Jacob Stucky—Pioneer of Two Continents," *Menn. Life* IV (January 1949) 46 f.

Studen, Barbeli zur, an Anabaptist martyr, of Sumiswald in Emmental, Swiss canton of Bern, who was executed in Bern in 1537.

Adolf Fluri, *Beiträge zur Geschichte der bernischen Täufer* (Bern, 1912) 14; *Mart. Mir.* E 1129; *ML IV*.

Student Exchange. Beginning in 1946 the Council of Mennonite and Affiliated Colleges in the United States sponsored an international student exchange whereby each Mennonite and Brethren in Christ college provided substantial financial aid to a limited number of select foreign students for a year's study on its campus (in a few cases extended to two years). At first limited to Europe and to Mennonites, this program was later extended to include all countries and all religious backgrounds, although the main emphasis continued to be on Mennonite students. The MCC offices in various countries assisted in the selection of candidates and arrangements for travel. In many of the cases of German students the United States State Department provided substantial travel funds.

In the first ten years (1946-56) a total of 183 students were brought from seven European countries to the United States (Germany 96 began only in 1948—Holland 51, France 16, Italy 10, Waldensians, Switzerland 5, Belgium 3, Greece 2), an average of 18 per year. These were distributed among the American colleges as follows: Goshen 50, Bethel 28, Bluffton 22, Tabor 20, Eastern Mennonite 14, Messiah 14, Freeman 13, Hesston 8, Mennonite Biblical Seminary 4, Upland 3, unspecified 7. The purpose of the program was to enrich the service of these young people to their own churches and communities at home. Most of the 183 remained in their homelands, but 34 later emigrated to the United States or in a few cases (5) to Canada.

A smaller number of Mennonite exchange students were brought from South America to colleges in the United States and Canada, particularly from Paraguay, and a few from Brazil and Argentina. A few Mennonites were also brought from the Mennonite mission fields in India and Japan, and from the National Mennonite Churches in Java. Non-Mennonite students were also brought from Greece, Jordan, Lebanon, South Viet-Nam, Formosa, Hong Kong, Korea, Japan, Jamaica, and Mexico. H.S.B.

Stuhm Lowlands (Stuhmsche Niederung), a district in West Prussia, with the villages and hamlets of Schulwiese, Zwanzigerweide, Montauerweide, Rehhof, Schweinsgrube, Rudnerweide, Gross-Schardau, and Klein-Schardau. In 1744 these villages were predominantly Mennonite. These Mennonites, belonging to the Frisian (in Dutch *Naamlijst* called Waterlander) branch, formed a single congregation, at first called Stuhmsche Niederung, later mostly Tragheimerweide (*q.v.*) or Zwanzigerweide (*q.v.*).

vDZ.

Stumpf, Simon, an ardent follower of Zwingli, who shared Conrad Grebel's (*q.v.*) ideas, a native of Bödigheim, Franconia, came into contact with Zwingli (*q.v.*) at Basel (Simon Stumpf's letter to Zwingli, Basel, July 2, 1519), was given the pastorate at Höngg near Zürich in 1522, was a member of the scholarly circle in Zwingli's home, and an enthusiastic proponent of church reforms. He was a signatory of the petition for the annulment of celibacy of the clergy and soon afterward married. He preached against tithes and interest, and demanded from the pulpit that "idols" in the church be done away with. The result was an outbreak of iconoclasm. At the religious colloquy held at Zürich on Oct. 27, 1523, he objected to leaving the abolition of the Mass to the council, saying that the decision had already been made by the Spirit of God. He became one of Grebel's co-workers and with him demanded that Zwingli establish an apostolic church, but was soon deprived of his parish at Höngg on Nov. 3, 1523, and banished from the canton of Zürich (Dec. 23, 1523). On Nov. 19, 1523, he wrote a penitent letter to Zwingli saying, "I cannot dig ditches and have nothing to dig even if I were able. I have sinned against heaven and against you and am no longer worthy of being called a son, either of God or of men, whom I have offended by my ignorance and stupidity. What is left for me to do? Perhaps: Go and hang yourself? God forbid! Dear Zwingli, graciously pardon Simon, who has seriously erred, so that he might love the more. Lead the stray sheep back to the right way, as you do others every day. Think of the one bowed down. He acknowledges his sickness and is looking for the physician. Consider me as one of your minor day laborers. Do not forget that we are members of Christ, the head. I am, to be sure, an untimely birth, but Christ still lives, who was able to call Lazarus forth from the grave . . . . May He keep your hand and heal me." In April 1527 he was again imprisoned in Zürich, and released with the threat of death if he ever returned. He probably returned to the Catholic Church in Ulm. NEFF.

Emil Egli, *Aktensammlung* (Zürich, 1879) No. 414 (Nov. 3, 1523); 446 (Nov. 14); 463 (Nov. 23); 1167 (Feb. 25, 1527); 326 b supplement; John H. Yoder, "The Turning Point in the Zwinglian Reformation," *MQR* XXXII (1958) 128-40; Egli and Finsler, *Zwinglis Briefwechsel* (Leipzig, 1911); *TA Zürich,* 121 f.; Wirz, *Helvetische Geschichte* (1819) 222 ff.; *Zwingliana* IV, No. 11, p. 321; *ML IV*.

Stumptown Mennonite Church (MC), located near Monterey, 8 miles northeast of Lancaster, Pa., in Upper Leacock Township, a member of the Lancaster Conference, was an outgrowth of the enlarging Mellinger congregation to the northeast. The members used a schoolhouse on the present meetinghouse site until 1846, when a worship center was built. This was enlarged in 1882 and replaced in 1916 by a 48 x 80 ft. brick structure. It was here during the summer of 1868 that John B. Landis and John Stauffer and their wives conducted a small Sunday school before the movement had conference approval. It was a part of the Mellinger-Stumptown circuit until a recent decade. Elmer G. Martin is bishop, Lloyd M. Eby and John G. Oberholtzer ministers. This was the home congregation of Preacher Sanford B. Landis (1868-1926). The membership in 1957 was 310. I.D.L.

Stundism, a religious movement caused by the pietistic revival of the 19th century among the German and Russian population of the Ukraine which resulted in the establishment of a number of Protestant churches in Russia, particularly the Baptists (*q.v.*) and the Evangelical Christians. Stundism can be traced directly to leaders of Pietism who transplanted the practice of private devotional meetings and Bible study from Germany and England to the German settlements in Russia and adherents of the Russian Orthodox Church. The word "Stundism" comes from the German "Stunde," meaning "hour (for worship and fellowship)."

Pietistic influences reached Russian circles in the early 19th century through Jung-Stilling (*q.v.*), Juliane von Krüdener, Alexander I, A. Bengel, and later through numerous individuals who traveled extensively in Russia in the interest of proclaiming the Gospel or who were living in German communities. The Presbyterian John Melville did evangelistic work in Russia after 1823. Through his work Kasha Yagob, who became an effective evangelist, was won for the Gospel. Johann Bonekemper transplanted the method of meeting for an "hour" (*Stunde*) of Bible study, a practice of the Württemberg Pietists, to Russia. These devotional and Bible study meetings conducted in the German settlements were the means of the conversion of Ivan Onyshchenko and Michael Ratushny, from Osnova near the German villages of Rohrbach and Worms of the Odessa area, where Bonekemper conducted pietistic Bible studies. Thus the revival and the method of Bible study were transplanted to the Russian population and "Stundism" originated. Similarly the activities of Eduard Wüst (*q.v.*) c1845 near Berdyansk affected German settlements including the Mennonites, and from them this practice and movement was transplanted to the Russian population.

A. V. Karev strongly emphasizes the significance of the Mennonites, particularly the Mennonite Brethren, in the origin of the Baptist movement in Russia. Gerhard Wieler (*q.v.*), an M.B. preacher of Liebenau, Molotschna settlement, won some followers (Stundists) in the neighboring village of Ostrikove. During the winter of 1863-64 Wieler began to baptize Russian believers by immersion, thus introducing this mode of baptism and the shift among the Russian believers from Stundism to a Baptist organization. In 1869 Abraham Unger

(*q.v.*), also an M.B. preacher, baptized some Russians in Old Danzig (Ukraine), among whom was Ephrim Cimbal, who in turn baptized Michael Ratushny and Alexander Kapustyana. These three became the chief promoters of Stundism and the Baptist movement among the Russian population of the Ukraine. In 1869 J. G. Oncken, a German Baptist, organized the first Baptist church of the Ukraine in Old and New Danzig. The contact between the Mennonite Brethren and the Russian Baptists remained intimate. In 1884 Johann Wieler called the meeting of the Baptists at which a union of Russian Baptists was organized, and served as its chairman until 1886, when he left for Rumania.

Another source of the evangelical movement in Russia was Lord Radstock, an Englishman who started a tract mission in St. Petersburg in 1875, primarily among the aristocracy. Outstanding leaders among them were Pashkov and Korff. Although this movement in Northern Russia originally had little to do with the Mennonites, later contacts were established through such men as Jakob Kroeker. The Mennonite publishing enterprise "Raduga" (*q.v.*) (Rainbow), Halbstadt, South Russia, had a branch in St. Petersburg which distributed Russian Bibles and religious literature. After the Revolution in 1917, Jakob Kroeker established a mission organization in Wernigerode a. H., Germany, "Licht im Osten" (Light in the East), through which thousands of Russian Bibles and other devotional literature were distributed in Soviet Russia and other Slavic countries. In the Bible school of this organization, many young men and women were trained for evangelistic work among the Slavs. Some actually went to Russia. This work was born during World War I when thousands of Russian prisoners of war were reached with the Gospel through evangelism in the prisoner of war camps in Germany. The returning Protestant Christians who had been thus reached strengthened the evangelical movement in Russia. Licht im Osten, operated to some extent by Mennonites, played a very significant role in the promotion of this work until the Iron Curtain closed the contact with the West.

Thus Stundism was the forerunner of the present-day Evangelical-Baptist churches in the Russian area. Under the influence of the Baptist movement through the work of J. G. Oncken and others, Stundism accepted baptism by immersion as the sole form, and by doing so the movement became Baptist and Evangelical Christian, with the exception of some minor Pentecostal groups and the Adventists. Since 1943 they have all been united in the All-Union Council of Evangelical Christian Baptists with headquarters in Moscow. Sectarian groups, such as the Molokans, etc., also played a significant role in the spread of the movement. Jakov Zhidkov, chairman of the All-Union, is of Molokan background. C.K.

Waldemar Gutsche, *Westliche Quellen des russischen Stundismus* (Kassel, 1956); Christophilos, *Ein Blatt aus der Geschichte des Stundismus in Russland* (Berlin, 1904); Johannes Warns, *Russland und das Evangelium. Bilder aus der evangelischen Bewegung des sogenannten Stundismus* (Kassel); Cornelius Krahn, "Russian Baptists and Mennonites," *Menn. Life* XI (July 1956) 99;

A. V. Karev, "The Russian Evangelical-Baptist Movement" (Russian), *Bratsky Vestnik* (Moscow, 1957) No. 3, 5-51; George J. Eisenach, *Pietism and the Russian Germans in the United States* (Berne, 1948); J. G. Kargel, *Zwischen den Enden der Erde* (Wernigerode, 1928); Maria Kroeker, *Ein reiches Leben* (Wüstenrot, 1949); *Menn. Bl.*, 1892, 21; *Gbl.*, 1898, 68 ff.; 1899, 51; *HRE* XVI, 442; *RGG* V, 863; *ML* IV.

Stupman(n), Wilhelm, also called Mottencop (Mottencoup), a glazier, was one of the first Anabaptists in and around Aachen (*q.v.*), Germany. According to a letter of Aug. 16 (not July 16, as stated in *ME* I, 1), 1533, by Duke John III of Jülich to the Catholic bishop of Liége, Stupman, who had been banished from Aachen, had founded at Aachen, Maastricht, and Liége "special sects," which they (i.e., the Anabaptists) called congregations; they called themselves "christliche broeder." About the activity of Stupman, who apparently was very influential, further information is lacking.   vDZ.

W. Bax, *Het Protestantisme in het Bisdom Luik . . . I* (The Hague, 1937) 74 f.

Sturgeon Creek Hutterite Bruderhof of the Schmiedeleut (*q.v.*) branch, located four miles north of Headingly, Man., was founded in 1938 by eleven families with 75 souls who left the Blumengard Bruderhof with their preacher Samuel Kleinsasser, who was chosen a minister in 1933 and ordained in 1942. In 1954, when Sturgeon Creek had a population of 158 with 60 baptized members, a group of 13 families with 73 persons with the minister Jakob Kleinsasser (chosen in 1946 and ordained in 1954) left to found the Crystal Spring Bruderhof, 6 miles southeast of St. Agatha, Man. In 1958 the Sturgeon Creek Bruderhof had 32 baptized members and a population of 98, with Samuel Kleinsasser and Elias Mandel (chosen in 1955) as preachers.   D.D., S.K.

Sturm, Hans, an Anabaptist martyr, a cloth shearer of Steyr (*q.v.*) in Upper Austria, where he escaped prison and death by flight, whereas his wife recanted and his sister was drowned as a martyr in Freistadt. Before long he was arrested for speaking against the prince, but was released after six months. With a copy of a tract on baptism and communion by Wetel of Eibenschitz (*q.v.*) he wandered through Bohemia to Saxony. In Buchholz he met the brother-in-law of Wolf Kratzber, who had heard that his sister in Zwickau was under sentence of exile as an Anabaptist. Sturm went on to Zwickau and was kindly received by Wolf Kratzber and his wife. As a precaution they did not keep him overnight. When he was looking for work it was discovered that he was an Anabaptist and he was imprisoned in a dungeon of the city hall.

On Jan. 26, 1529, Sturm was examined on the rack. His confession revealed that he repudiated infant baptism, for infants could not believe; he had never baptized anyone, for he was too unlearned; the sacrament of the altar he considered mere bread and wine; he rejected community of goods and regarded marriage as sinful. Two additional examinations revealed nothing further. The authorities then inquired of John Frederick (*q.v.*), Duke of Saxony (his father, the elector, was at the diet of Speyer), what should be done with the

prisoner. John replied that the matter should be decided by the court (*Schöffenstuhl*) at Leipzig. The prisoner was then questioned the fourth time. He defended his faith readily and with a remarkable knowledge of the Bible. This time he said that marriage was instituted by God. He vigorously rejected the suspicion of connections with the revolting peasants and said that the state should be obeyed in all matters of the body and property.

On March 15 came the verdict of Leipzig that Sturm was to be burned at the stake. The Zwickau council, however, sent the verdict to the duke, who then ordered that Sturm be brought to Wittenberg for indoctrination. If he then recanted, he would be released; if not, the Wittenberg theologians and jurists should decide what should be done with him.

Under heavy guard Hans Sturm was taken to Wittenberg on April 5. Luther decided that he "was driven by the raging of Satan" and did not look for success in converting him. All of their efforts were in vain; Sturm clung to his convictions. He was therefore condemned by the Wittenberg theologians and jurists to everlasting prison as a "blasphemer and seditionist," and upon the order of the duke was put into the tower at Schweinitz, southeast of Wittenberg, where he remained until his death, *c*1536.   Neff.

Martin Luther's letter to Nikolaus Hausmann of April 8, 1529; *idem, Tischreden.* No. 2032, Erlangen edition; P. Wappler, *Inquisition und Ketzerprozesse in Zwickau zur Reformationszeit* (Leipzig, 1903) 21-39 ff.; *idem, Die Stellung Kursachsens . . .* (Münster, 1910) 22; *ML* IV.

Stuttgart (Ark.) Amish Mennonites: see **Arkansas** and **Arkansas County.**

Stuttgart (Germany) Mennonite Church, a member of the Verband (*q.v.*), was organized in 1933 as an independent congregation; formerly it was a part of the Heilbronn (*q.v.*) congregation. It meets on the first Sunday of each month for worship, and on the third Sunday of each month for a youth Bible class, in rented quarters in Bad Cannstatt at Kreuznacherstrasse 43. The membership in 1958 was 111, with the following ministers: elders, Hermann Funck of Schorndorf and Horst Quiring of Korntal, with Ernst Quapp and Otto Hörr, both of Mühlhausen, as ministers. (*ML* IV, 266 ff.) H.S.B.

Stutzman (Stutsman), a Mennonite family name of Swiss origin. A Swiss Mennonite, Christian Stutzman with his family, arrived in America from Holland in 1711. John Jacob Stutzman arrived in Philadelphia in 1727. His grandson Christian Stutzman married Barbara Hochstedler. The book listing the descendants of this couple contains over 15,000 entries, of whom more than a thousand carry the name Stutzman. Obituaries in the *Herald of Truth* and *Gospel Herald* show the family to be most numerous in Ohio, followed by Nebraska and Indiana. Death notices were carried in these periodicals from at least twelve other states and provinces. Jacob and Paul Stutzman were among the early ministers at Walnut Creek, Ohio, over a century ago. Daniel Stutzman, of Millersburg, Ohio, was the author of the 265-page book, *Der* *schmale Verleugnungsweg, Eine kurze Christliche Vermahnung an meine Kinder* (1917?). In 1937 at least 22 representatives of the Stutzman family were serving in the Mennonite ministry, 11 of whom were in the Old Order Amish Mennonite Church. Among the better-known ministers (MC) was Milo D. Stutzman of Kingman, Alberta.   M.G.

Harvey Hostetler, *Descendants of Barbara Hochstedler and Christian Stutzman* (Scottdale, 1938); Daniel Kauffman, *Mennonite Cyclopedic Dictionary*.

Stuurman, a Dutch family name. There have been three Mennonite ministers by this name. Jan Stuurman was a lay preacher of the Wormerveer Waterlander congregation 1764-68 and of the Frisian congregation at Burg on the island of Texel 1768-*c*76. He seems to have been very conservative and intolerant; about 1776 with a few adherents he separated from the main body of the Burg congregation to found a new congregation, which also had a meetinghouse of its own, but lasted for only a few years. Claes Stuurman, who may have been a son of the former, was a lay preacher at Barsingerhorn-Kolhorn from 1784 until his death in 1827. Hendrik Gerrits Stuurman (1750- Jan. 18, 1790) studied at the Zonist (*q.v.*) Mennonite seminary at Amsterdam and served the Aalsmeer-Uithoorn congregation 1784-90. Until recent times members of this family were found in a number of North Holland Mennonite churches.

Another Stuurman family, apparently not related to the former, is found at Blokzijl, Dutch province of Overijssel. As far as is known its ancestor was Jan Ariaens (*c*1580-*c*1650), a Mennonite who settled at Blokzijl, probably from Giethoorn. In the 17th century his descendants assumed the family name of Stuurman. The early generations, all living at Blokzijl, were helmsmen (hence the name Stuurman), skippers, brewers, and farmers. Since the early 19th century they have spread over the Netherlands; they have been in various occupations and professions—merchants, bakers, physicians, and lawyers.

In Blokzijl (*q.v.*) most of the Stuurmans have been members of the more liberal Noorderkaai church. In the 18th century Arie (Adriaen Hendriks) Stuurman (*c*1686-1763) of Blokzijl, who was a deacon of the Mennonite church 1723-59, as well as a few other members of this family, leaned toward the Hernhutters (Moravian Brethren, *q.v.*), who organized meetings of the group at Blokzijl.
vDZ.

Inv. Arch. Amst. II, No. 1636; *DB* 1873, 146-50; 1885, 77; Dutch *Naamlijst;* F. J. Stuurman, *Het Geslacht Stuurman van Blokzijl* (Zeist, 1948).

Stuyvenberg, Jan Willem van (Amsterdam, Dec. 18, 1868-Baarn, May 30, 1950), a Dutch Mennonite pastor, studied at Amsterdam University and the Mennonite seminary and served at Oost- and West-Graftdijk 1895-97, Blokzijl 1897-1903, Westzaan-Zuid 1903-21, and Amsterdam 1921-36. Van Stuyvenberg was a warm friend of missions; for many years he was on the executive board of the Dutch Mennonite Mission Association, also serving as its secretary. (*DJ* 1951, 14.)   vDZ.

Styria (Steiermark), a province of Austria, capital Graz, in the 16th and 17th centuries administratively closely allied to Carinthia (*q.v.*) as "Inner Austria." Although Lutheranism was eagerly embraced in Styria by both nobility and burghers from its very beginning, Anabaptism never had a strong development there, perhaps in part because of the lack of significant leaders. In the days of the Governor Siegmund of Dietrichstein (*q.v.*), 1515-29, an ardent Lutheran, Protestantism spread quickly across the country in spite of the passionate efforts of King Ferdinand I (*q.v.*) to stem the tide. Not much is known about the origins of Anabaptism in Styria. The preacher Hans Has (Haas) of Windisch-Gräz, who was beheaded in 1527, can hardly be called an Anabaptist even though his fine "Sendbrief an die Auserwählten" (comfort in persecution) is found in the *Kunstbuch* (*q.v.*) of the Marpeck group. It was about this time, 1527-29, that Anabaptism was strongest everywhere. Single Anabaptists are reported in many places such as Rottenmann, Leoben, Bruck an der Mur, Hartberg, and Graz. Although the Lutherans were quite defiant toward the Hapsburg government of Vienna in their own affairs, they eagerly co-operated in the suppression of the Anabaptist "heresy," and Dietrichstein was particularly conspicuous in this regard. The most tragic event was the martyrdom of nine Anabaptist brethren and three sisters in the city of Bruck an der Mur in 1528. The *Lieder der Hutterischen Brüder* (25-27) contains a well-known hymn commemorating this sad event; the hymn is anonymous, but it appears fairly certain that it was composed by Hans Gurtzham (*q.v.*), of whom the *Lieder* brings another almost identical hymn (136 f.) (See also Wackernagel, *Kirchenlied* III, 467 f.) Soon the Anabaptists began the exodus to Moravia, "the promised land."

The next governor of Styria (after 1530), Hans Ungnad von Sonneck, also a Lutheran, stands out as a very lenient and tolerant ruler. To be sure, he had to obey an order by King Ferdinand and tear down the house of Kaspar Maler of Graz, an Anabaptist who had previously arranged meetings in his house but had now gone to Moravia. But Ungnad could boast of having shed no blood; he is reported to have said that he did not want to have anything to do with the Anabaptists, for they were God-fearing, simple people. There was, however, another mass execution in Graz in 1534, the martyrdom of the important Daniel Kropf (*q.v.*), with two other brothers and four sisters. But it seems that it was not Ungnad but his assistant, the Vicedomus Michael Meixner, who passed that sentence. It is quite probable that the events of Münster (*q.v.*) had an unfavorable influence even in Styria. Although records continue to mention Anabaptists here and there, it is quite obvious that no real church life developed at any place; there were rather single individuals, in most cases on their way to Moravia. All in all, the Hutterite Chronicle records (up to 1542) 25 executions for Styria—7 in Graz, 12 in Bruck, one in Unzmarkt, and 5 in Grichsbach.

Toward the end of the 16th century the Hutterite physicians and barber-surgeons were highly appreciated by the nobility (see **Physicians, Hutterite**). Thus, for instance, Elizabeth of Zägl in Friedau "lent" her Anabaptist doctor to her cousin Siegmund of Eibiswald for a fortnight (1590). And as late as 1613 the Abbot Johann of Admont received official permission from the provincial government to call a famous Anabaptist physician of Nikolsburg (see **Goller**) and he issued a passport for his safe conduct. Otherwise, however, Styria played only a marginal role in the history of Anabaptism.

G.Me., R.F.

Zieglschmid, *Chronik; Lieder der Hutterischen Brüder* (Scottdale, 1914) 25-27; Wackernagel, *Kirchenlied* III, 467; Grete Mecenseffy, *Geschichte des Protestantismus in Oesterreich* (Graz, 1956); Loserth, "Wiedertäufer in Steiermark," *Mitt. des Hist. Vereins für Steiermark* XLII (1894) 118-45; *idem, Zur Geschichte der Wiedertäufer in Steiermark," ibid.,* L (1903); *idem,* "Zur Geschichte der Wiedertäufer in der Steiermark" (third installment), in *Ztscht des Hist. Vereins für Steiermark* X (1912) 267-71; *idem,* "Anabaptists in Styria in 1528," in *MQR* VII (1933) 133-41; many more studies by this same author; Paul Dedic, 'Reformation und Gegenreformation in Bruck an der Mur.'' *Jahrbuch der Ges. für die Protest. in Oesterreich* LXIII-IV (1942-43) 15-23; *idem,* "Mährische Wiedertäuferärzte in der Steiermark," *Ztscht des Deutschen Vereins fur die Gesch. von Mähren und Schlesien,* 1938, 22-27.

Suburban Mennonite Mission: see **Cottage City.**

Successio Anabaptistica, Dat is Babel der Wederdopers, is the title of a book published by V. P. in Cologne, 1603; there was a second unaltered edition at Cologne, 1612. This book is very rare; of the first edition only three copies are extant, and four of the second. There was a copy of the second edition in the Danzig Mennonite library; the Amsterdam Mennonite library has a copy of both editions. A reprint with introduction was published by Samuel Cramer in *Bibliotheca Reformatoria Neerlandica* VII (The Hague, 1910). Besides the *Beginsel en voortganck der geschillen* (*q.v.*) written some years later, this book is the only account of 16th-century Dutch Anabaptist history by a comtemporary author who deals especially with various schisms among the Dutch Mennonites; it contains much information about church leaders found in no other source; therefore the book, since it is on the whole very reliable, is a valuable source, though it was written by an opponent of the Mennonites. The author was probably Simon Walraven, who married a granddaughter of Joost Buyck (*q.v.*), burgomaster of Amsterdam, and was later a Roman Catholic priest at Kevendonk near Goch, Germany.

The motive for writing and publishing this book was a publication by the Mennonite author Jacob Pietersz van der Meulen (*q.v.*), who wrote *Successio Apostolica, Dat is Naecominghe ofte Naetredinghe der Apostelen* (Alkmaar, 1600) which attacked the Catholic Church, explaining that a true spiritual apostolic succession is found not among the Catholics but among the Mennonites. Then Walraven tried to show that among the Mennonites there was no apostolic succession but merely a "Babel of confusion." vDZ.

BRN VII, 1-87, 565; K. Vos, *Menno Simons* (Leiden, 1914) 305 f.

Successio Apostolica: see **Apostolic Succession.**

Suderman, a Dutch Mennonite family, apparently not related to the West Prussian Suderman(n) family, was found at Rotterdam, Holland, in the 17th and 18th centuries. Of these Rotterdam Sudermans, all merchants, some were Old Flemish, e.g., Elyas Suderman, who was a deacon of the Old Flemish congregation from 1662, while others belonged to the Waterlander and later to the United Rotterdam Mennonite Church. Willem Suderman (d.1706) was a preacher of the Waterlanders 1675-1700 and of the united church 1700-1. In 1677-84, for some unknown reason, he did not serve. It may have been because of Socinian (*q.v.*) opinions. He was also an ardent Collegiant (*q.v.*). In 1688 he was secretary of the Zuidholland (*q.v.*) Sociëteit. Jan Suderman, a deacon of the united congregation from 1710, who may have been a son of preacher Willem Suderman, was in 1711 a representative of the Rotterdam congregation in the Dutch Committee for Foreign Needs. In 1718 he opposed the resolution of the church board to call pastor Daniel van Heyst (*q.v.*). Concerning this matter Jan Suderman and Aelbert van Meurs (*q.v.*) published *Protest gedaen tegen de maniere van't beroepen van . . . n D. v.H.* (Rotterdam, 1718). Suderman also published *De Godlievende Ziel, vertoont in Zinnebeelden* (Amsterdam, 1724, repr. at Utrecht, 1749).   vDZ.

K. Vos, *Geschiedenis der Doopsgez. gemeente te Rotterdam* (Rotterdam, 1907, repr.) 27, 28, 44, 47; *DB* 1908, 103.

Suderman, Jan, a Mennonite preacher in Amsterdam, published the book, *De Kerkenradt en Gemeente der Doopsgezinden te Amsterdam . . . vertedigt tegen den E. Adriaan van Alcmar* (Amsterdam, 1719). (*Menn. Bl.,* 1890, 100; *DB* 1908, 103, where he is called a deacon in Rotterdam.)

Sudermann (Suderman, Zudermann, Suterman, Soermann), a common name among Mennonites of Danzig in West Prussia, Russia, and some parts of America. The name appeared in Danzig as early as 1671 and was found in Elbing, Heubuden, and Königsberg. The noted author Hermann Sudermann was of Mennonite background, his father having been baptized a Mennonite in Elbing. From this area the name was transplanted to Russia. B. H. Unruh lists 12 different bearers of the name (426). Outstanding in Russia were Leonhard Sudermann (*q.v.*), elder of the Berdyansk Mennonite Church, and in America elder of the Emmaus Mennonite Church, Franz Sudermann, a businessman of Halbstadt, Jakob J. Sudermann, owner of the Apanlee estate, one of the most successful and prosperous Mennonite farmers and cofounder and president of the Halbstadt Kommerzschule. *Who's Who Among the Mennonites* (1943) lists John P. Suderman, former missionary (GCM) to the Hopi Indians, Herman E. Suderman, founder and president of the Midland National Bank, Newton, Kan., John M. Suderman, minister (GCM) and conference worker, Newton, David H. Suderman, professor of music at Bethel College, and Jacob Sudermann, Elkhart, Ind., formerly professor at Goshen College, now on the staff of Indiana University, South Bend branch.

C.K., vDZ.

Bruno Meyer, *Die Sudermanns von Dortmund, ein hansisches Kaufmannsgeschlecht* (Marburg, 1930); Chr. Sepp, *Kerkhistorische Studien* (1885) 238-77; Reimer, *Familiennamen*, 119; Dutch *Naamlijst;* Unruh, *Hintergründe.*

Sudermann, Daniel (1550-1631), a Schwenckfelder (*q.v.*), was born at Liége, France, Feb. 24, 1550, died at Strasbourg, Alsace, in 1631. He was a painter and engraver by profession, as well as a successful poet. One of his 435 hymns, "Elend nit schad, wer tugend hat," is found in Wackernagel, *Kirchenlied* V, No. 827. Many of his hymns are found in Protestant hymnals. Christian Sepp (*q.v.*) published a thorough study of Sudermann in his *Kerkhistorische Studien* (1885) 238-77. (*ML* IV.)

Sudermann, Hermann (1857-1928), a noted German author, was born at Wadziken in East Prussia, Germany, Sept. 30, 1857. His father was a member of the Elbing-Ellerwald Mennonite congregation, but was expelled when he married a Lutheran. Hermann Sudermann's *Frau Sorge* (1887) pictures his unhappy youth in his poverty-stricken home. At an advanced age he wrote *Das Bilderbuch meiner Jugend* (Stuttgart and Berlin, 1922), in which he recalls the unforgettable impressions of the Mennonite services he attended with his aunt, life on the "Hof" of a wealthy Mennonite uncle, picturing the Prussian Mennonites as competent, honest, but gloomy, and the loan of a considerable sum of money by a distant relative in Russia for Hermann's education.

E.H.B.

Elizabeth Bender, "The Mennonites in German Literature" (M.A. thesis, Minnesota, 1943); *ML* IV.

Sudermann, Leonhard (1821-1900), was the elder of the Berdyansk Mennonite Church (*q.v.*), Russia, one of the chief promoters of the Mennonite migration to America, and elder of the Emmaus Mennonite Church (*q.v.*), Whitewater, Kan. He was born at Goldschaar-Heubuden, near Marienburg, West Prussia, on April 21, 1821, the youngest of twelve children, and was baptized in 1838. In 1841, after his father had died, he and his mother migrated to Russia where eight of the children had already gone. On Oct. 23, 1842, he married Marie Sudermann and settled in Berdyansk in 1843. In 1860 he was elected minister and in 1865 elder of the Berdyansk Mennonite Church.

Cornelius Jansen (*q.v.*), a member of Sudermann's congregation, was his close friend. Both men became great promoters of the migration of the Mennonites to America when they found out that certain privileges, particularly those pertaining to military service, were to be withdrawn. Sudermann was one of the delegates sent to St. Petersburg to learn how the new military law would affect the Mennonites. He was sent a second and a third time in 1871. In 1873 he was delegated to go to America with eleven others to investigate settlement possibilities for Mennonites from Russia and Prussia. *Eine Deputationsreise* is Sudermann's detailed report about this journey. After his return to Russia he reported his findings and helped people with their emigration.

In 1876 Sudermann immigrated to America, spending the first six months in Summerfield, Ill.

In 1877 he settled in Butler County, Kan., where some Prussian Mennonites had just organized the Emmaus Mennonite Church. He served this congregation as elder to the end of his life. He was also active in Conference work. He died on Jan. 27, 1900.

Sudermann kept records of all his trips to America and St. Petersburg and kept a diary. This material as well as his letters show that he was a very conscientious and diligent worker. (Most of the materials are found in the BeCL.)† **C.K.**

Ed. Claassen, "Etwas aus dem Leben und Wirken unseres teuren heimgegangenen Aeltesten Leonhard Sudermann," *Christlicher Bundesbote*, Feb. 15, 1900, p 6; H. P. Krehbiel, *History of the General Conference of the Mennonites of North America* (Canton, 1898) 444; Emmaus Mennonite Church, Record Book No. 1; Leonhard Sudermann, *Eine Deputationsreise von Russland nach Amerika vor vierundzwanzig Jahren* (Elkhart, 1897); Leonhard Sudermann, "Bericht über unsere Reise . . . ," *Herold der Wahrheit*, Oct. 15, Nov. 1, and Nov. 15, 1898.

Sugar Creek Mennonite Church (MC), located 1½ miles southeast of Wayland, Iowa, a member of the Iowa-Nebraska Conference, had its beginning in 1843, when Amish Mennonite settlers arrived in the area. When Joseph Goldsmith (*q.v.*), an Amish bishop who had been living in Lee County (*q.v.*), Iowa, moved into the community in 1855, regular church services were instituted, although he may have organized the congregation two years previously. For a period of years there were two places of worship, but in 1862 the northern part of the settlement established a separate congregation, the Eicher Emmanuel Mennonite Church (*q.v.*). The Sugar Creek bishops were influential in the A.M. meeting (Dienerversammlung) and later in the Western District A.M. Conference. Joseph Schlegel (*q.v.*) served as bishop of the church 1868-79, followed by Sebastian Gerig (*q.v.*) 1879-1924, Simon Gingerich 1916-57, and Vernon Gerig 1953- . In 1950 a second meetinghouse for the congregation was dedicated, known as Bethel Mennonite Church (*q.v.*). In 1957 the combined membership was 611, of which number 434 were in the Sugar Creek congregation. Vernon Gerig, upon the retirement of Simon Gingerich in 1957, became the leader of the church. He was assisted by Willard Liechty, minister since 1935. **M.G.**

Sugarcreek, Ohio, is a village of 889 population (1950) in western Tuscarawas County, near the Holmes County line. The Old Order Amish settlement of Holmes County extends several miles eastward past Sugarcreek. The village is the home of *The Budget* (*q.v.*), published here since 1890. The Sugarcreek First Mennonite (GCM) Church (*q.v.*) is located in the village. (See map of Holmes County.) **M.G.**

Sugarcreek First Mennonite Church (GCM) of Sugarcreek, Tuscarawas Co., Ohio, was organized as a congregation in the Middle District Conference in 1926 with 84 charter members under the leadership of Lester Hostetler. The group had withdrawn from the Walnut Creek (MC) congregation of the Ohio and Eastern A.M. Conference. The first meetinghouse here was erected in 1894 as a community church, services being conducted by the

United Brethren and Reformed churches. Later the Church of the Brethren also met here. Additions were built in 1912 and 1928. In 1914 both the United Brethren and the Reformed congregations withdrew to meetinghouses of their own; the Church of the Brethren and the Mennonites used it for services each Sunday until 1956, when the Mennonites purchased the Brethren interest in the building and are now erecting a new church. The membership in 1957 was 250, with Harold D. Thiessen as pastor.   WM.H.S.

Suhner, Rudolf, a young Mennonite, was arrested *c*1643 and imprisoned in the Oethenbach tower at Zürich, Switzerland. After some time he recanted and was released, but soon deplored his apostasy. As a result of this "backsliding" he was arrested again and died in prison. (*Mart. Mir.* D 821, E 1120).   VDZ.

Sumatra, one of the larger islands of Indonesia, former Dutch East Indies. In 1871 the Dutch Mennonite Mission (*q.v.*) Association opened a station at Pakantan among the Battak tribe, where Heinrich Dirks (*q.v.*) was active 1871-80. For lack of Mennonite missionaries his successor was not a Mennonite, but Tillmann Ernst Irle. In 1888, however, a young Mennonite missionary, Gerhard Nikkel (*q.v.*), entered the work here and served until 1901. Other missionaries in this area were Nicolai Wiebe 1890-1900, Johann Thiessen 1901-9, David Dirks 1905-18, Peter Löwen 1912-14, Peter Nachtigal 1912-d.28. After Nachtigal's death the Sumatra mission field was vacant until 1931, when it was transferred to the Rheinische (Rhine) Mission (non-Mennonite). Later converts in this territory joined the Battak inland church. See also **Batta, Hutagodang, Mandailing, Muara-Sipongi, Pakantan,** and **Penjaboengen.**

However there is still a Mennonite Church in Sumatra. In 1952 Zacharias Djz Sahata, a Mennonite preacher appointed by Peter Nachtigal before 1928, living at Poetjoek Pimpinan Perkoempoelan Kristen Penjaboengen (Mandailing) Tapanoeli, Sumatra, wrote to the widow of Peter Nachtigal (living at Lautenbach, near Heilbronn, Germany, d.1958), giving a thorough report of the experiences of the Sumatra Mennonites during and since World War II. He reported small groups or congregations still in existence with a total of 161 souls as follows: Dolok Siantar—13 families (60 persons); Kota-Nopan—2 families (10 persons); Muara-Sipongi—2 families (10 persons); Pakantan—5 families (21 persons). These congregations have not joined the Battak Church but have remained independent as a Mennonite group and are organized as a conference with the name Perkeompoelan Mennonite Protestan Indonesia (Association of Mennonite Protestants in Indonesia). The property of the former Dutch Mission has been destroyed except for small remnants of the building. The five centers of mission work in the Mandailing area were Pakantan, Penjaboengen, Muara-Sipongi, Kota-Nopan, and Bonan-Dolok. There are still churches in these five places.   H.S.B.

Uit Verleden en Heden van de Doopsgezinde Zending (n.p., 1947); *Jaarverslagen* (annual records) of the Dutch Mission Association.

Sumiswald, one of the most beautiful villages (pop. 6,000) of the Emmental, Swiss canton of Bern. Soon after the beginning of the Reformation it became an important center of Anabaptism and added a significant chapter to the story of the martyrdom of the Mennonites of Bern. In 1529 Moritz Kessler (*q.v.*), of Sumiswald, was a martyr in Bern, and in 1537 and 1538 three women of Sumiswald met the same fate. The last Bernese martyr, Hans Haslibacher (*q.v.*), also came from this region. Melchior Aeberli, of Sumiswald, was tortured in Bern in 1569; on the rack he declared that Anabaptist teachings were not sectarian but Scriptural; his uncle Lorentz Aeberli (*q.v.*, executed July 3, 1539) had testified to this doctrine with his blood. Even on the rack he refused to betray any of his brethren. Sumiswald remained an Anabaptist center into the 17th century.   S.G.

S. Geiser, *Die Taufgesinnten-Gemeinden* (Karlsruhe, 1931); *ML* IV.

Summa der Heiligen Schrift, a booklet published at Leipzig in 1520, and in new editions by Eduard Böhmer in 1877 and by Karl Benrath (*q.v.*) in 1880. The author is unknown. Since the booklet maintains that it would be better if no one were baptized until maturity and that war is contrary to the Gospel, it can be assumed that it originated in circles akin to the Anabaptists. (*ML* IV.)

Summer Bible School, sometimes called Vacation Bible School, an auxiliary teaching agency of the Sunday school, operated for 2-4 weeks in the early part of the summer vacation period largely for children of grade-school age, but often including at least the first two years of the high-school age and kindergarten, that is, the age range of 5-16 years. Except for scattered single schools of mixed character the first true summer Bible school was conducted in New York City in 1898, while the first fully organized summer religious day school in which the graded children's school was the main feature was held at Ripon, Wis., in 1908. The Presbyterian Church was the first to promote the vacation Bible school on a church-wide basis through its Board of Home Missions in 1910. In 1911 the Daily Vacation Bible School Association was established to promote such schools in the U.S.A. In 1915 the Northern Baptist Convention became the second denomination to promote the DVBS on a nationwide basis, soon followed by many other Protestant denominations. In 1912 A. L. Lathem, pastor of the First Presbyterian Church at Chester, Pa., in protest against the nonreligious recreation and manual work features of the Daily Vacation Bible School, started an all-Bible school which he named Summer Bible School. His pattern was followed increasingly by the more conservative evangelical groups.

Mennonite Church (MC). The first strictly Mennonite summer Bible school was started in 1923 by Dean Noah Oyer of Hesston College, Hesston, Kan., although Edwin Weaver had conducted a community vacation Bible school in 1922 at Wakarusa, Ind. In 1924 the Prairie Street Mennonite Church at Elkhart started its school. By 1926 there were four such schools in the Mennonite Church, including one at Portland, Ore., and one at Scottdale, Pa., the latter promoted by C. F. Yake, who soon became the outstanding promoter of the cause in the church, and the writer or editor of the earliest summer Bible school manuals. By 1933 there were 40 schools in the Mennonite Church. The Mennonite school, though using the Lathem name, was somewhat different in type from it.

"In the Mennonite summer Bible school there is no shopwork and no unrelated handwork. There is, instead, a properly proportioned amount of activity features, including pupil's workbooks and projects to make the instruction an educative process involving some problem solving, and providing opportunity for informal educational procedures. Integrated memorization of Scripture, missionary emphasis, evangelism, sacred music, and worship, in addition to the transmissive teaching of the Bible, are all essential features of the Mennonite summer Bible school and are designed to bring the child into intimate personal relationship with Jesus, and help him learn to know Jesus as Saviour and Lord."

The need for curriculum materials was sensed from the very beginning. Outlines of courses used by various schools were published in the *Christian Monitor* in the early years of the movement. However, to provide a standardized guide, the General Sunday School Committee appointed a summer Bible school subcommittee which prepared a manual of summer Bible school courses, published by the Mennonite Publishing House at Scottdale in 1928. The committee was composed of Noah Oyer chairman, C. F. Yake editor, and Paul Erb. The manual contained instructions for organizing and conducting a summer Bible school, and provided ten three-week outlines from Kindergarten I and II to Grade VIII. It was designated *Departmental Graded All-Bible Course,* providing ten years' work.

To meet a growing demand, a committee was authorized in 1931 to prepare teachers' manuals, which were published in 1934. This course was designated *A Departmental Graded Summer Bible School Course.* It provided lesson materials for summer Bible schools of three weeks' duration for two preschool ages and eight grades. With the publication of teachers' manuals and promotional work done through the Secretary of Summer Bible Schools of the Mennonite Commission for Christian Education, interest in summer Bible school increased, so that by 1938 there were 150 schools.

The first Mennonite summer Bible school conference was held at the Masontown Mennonite Church, May 18-19, 1933, promoted chiefly by the Southwestern Pennsylvania District Conference; nevertheless it was also general because of churchwide attendance. A general Mennonite Summer Bible School Conference followed, held at the Nappanee Mennonite Church, Ind., May 24-25, 1934. A second one was held at the Metamora Mennonite Church, Ill., June 13-14, 1935; a third at Martinsburg, Pa., May 7-8, 1936; and a fourth at Elida, Ohio, June 10-11, 1937. From these conferences church-wide interest was created; district conferences, institutes, and workshops have been conducted ever since. Many of the district conferences have summer Bible school secretaries, and those conferences which do not, have this office included in the

Sunday-school secretaryship for the promotion of summer Bible schools.

An entirely new course, called the *Herald Summer Bible School Series,* was then prepared with graded materials for thirteen years of Bible school: one nursery, two kindergarten courses, courses for eight grades, and a course each for grades nine and ten. Approximately a dozen writers and artists and an editor were employed to produce these materials which have, since their publication in 1947, become widely used throughout the evangelical Protestant churches of America. Writers were Katherine Royer, Mary Royer, Ida Bontrager, Elizabeth Showalter, Clarence Fretz, and Russell Krabill; the editor was C. F. Yake. The materials are Bible-centered and experience-related. A teacher's manual with a pupil's workbook and supplemental teaching materials are all integral parts of the materials for each course. The work was all done under the Curriculum Committee of the Mennonite Commission for Christian Education, led by Paul Mininger, chairman. The use of these materials has had a most beneficial effect upon the Mennonite Church (MC).

Since the publication of these new materials, summer Bible schools have increased steadily. In 1940 there were 214 schools with 2,086 teachers and an enrollment of 26,635; in 1945, 300 schools with 2,519 teachers and an enrollment of 28,977; in 1954, 722 schools with 7,703 teachers and an enrollment of 84,157. This was the high point, the next three years showing a slight decline.

More than two thirds of the editions of these Scottdale materials are sold to churches other than Mennonite, and more than twice as many pupils from non-Mennonite homes as from Mennonite homes are reached yearly. This does not include the outreach in foreign lands. At the present time a corps of workers is busy in Basel, Switzerland, translating the courses and preparing materials in German and French, and promoting summer Bible camps throughout Europe. This is carried on through the Agape-Verlag created in 1955 as a European agency of the Scottdale publishing house, with co-operation and support from the Mennonite Central Committee. Most of the courses have been translated into Spanish at Scottdale, and are now being sold in Puerto Rico and Latin-American countries, and wherever else Spanish materials are needed.

One of the most interesting aspects of the summer Bible school movement is the missionary education given to the children. Each year the summer Bible school children contribute for missions and relief work more than one third of the total cost of operating all summer Bible schools. In 1954 this was more than $27,000.

Summer Bible schools are enthusiastically promoted in all districts of the Mennonite Church (MC). Lancaster Conference has the largest number of summer Bible schools, many of which are rural and city mission schools. Franconia Conference is next in number. The church has recognized the summer Bible school as a great potential missionary agency for reaching children, establishing new Sunday schools, and founding new churches. This is a major reason for the rapid growth of this movement. Summer Bible schools have become a major feature of the Christian education program in most congregations in almost all branches of the Mennonite brotherhood. For instance, in the G.C.M. Church about 90 per cent of the congregations have it. None of the branches except the M.C. group have produced printed materials for use in their schools; most of them use the publications of the Mennonite Publishing House at Scottdale.   ●   C.F.Y.

C. F. Yake, *The Summer Bible School an Agency for Christian Education, Superintendent's Manual* (Scottdale, 1951).

Summer (Sommer), **Heinrich** (also called Müller), an Anabaptist martyr, was taken prisoner in Zurzach in the Swiss canton of Aargau (*q.v.*) with Jakob Mändl (*q.v.*) and drowned at Baden (Switzerland) on Oct. 9, 1582. He was probably identical with Heinrich Müller of Meisterschwanden (Heiz, 79). Several songs were written in memory of their death.   NEFF, S.G.

Beck, *Geschichts-Bücher*, 275, 281; *Mart. Mir.* D 741, E 1057; Wolkan, *Geschicht-Buch*, 234 f., 408-10; Zieglschmid, *Chronik*, 525, 527 ff.; J. Heiz, *Täufer im Aargau* (Aarau, 1902); *Lieder der Hutterischen Brüder* (Scottdale, 1914) 752; Wolkan, *Lieder*, 234; *ML IV.*

Summerauer (Sumerawer), **Leonhard** (Lienhart), a Hutterite martyr, of the Salzburg area of Austria, was arrested "about eight days before St. Martin's Day" in 1584. While he was in a boat traveling to Tittmoning (*q.v.*), the drunken sailors caused a wreck by colliding with a bridge. He escaped by a ladder put down by spectators. But the sailors cried out that their bad luck was due to the presence of an Anabaptist in the boat, and he was arrested. During his imprisonment of half a year he was severely tortured five times, but remained steadfast. In reply to the demand that he desist from his erroneous faith he said he had twenty years previously desisted from unrighteous living. The Catholic clergy made repeated sincere efforts to convert him; on the very scaffold he was offered freedom if he would recant only two articles of his faith. But he resisted all these attempts, and was beheaded at Burghausen, Bavaria, Germany, on July 5, 1585. His death is the theme of the song "Himmlischer Gott und Herre, lass dich erbarmen schier."   NEFF, E.H.B.

Mart. Mir. D 74, E 1060; *Die Lieder der Hutterischen Brüder* (Scottdale, 1914) 763; Wolkan, *Lieder*, 235; Zieglschmid, *Chronik*, 539-41; Wolkan, *Geschicht-Buch*, 418 f.; *ML IV.*

Summerdale Church of God in Christ Mennonite Church, now extinct, located near Summerdale, Baldwin Co., Ala., was organized in 1934. In 1944 Norman Eicher was ordained as minister and Otto Harms as deacon. The services were conducted in the community hall. The group, composed of settlers from other states, later dissolved, and most of the members formed the Walnut Hill (Fla.) congregation; the most common post-office address is Atmore, Ala.   P.G.H.

Summerfield First Mennonite Church (GCM), at Summerfield, Saint Clair Co., Ill., a member of the Middle District Conference, was founded by immi-

grants who came from the Palatinate, Germany, about the middle of the 19th century. The first regular church service of the group was held at the home of John Kraemer, 4 miles southeast of Summerfield, on Nov. 30, 1856. A church building at the southern outskirts of Summerfield was dedicated on Jan. 23, 1859. Daniel Hege of Lee County, Iowa, became the first pastor of the church. More than a dozen families came with him into the community. The church aligned itself at once with the General Conference Mennonite movement, and in 1863 the third session of the conference was held at Summerfield, in which it was decided to establish the first Mennonite school at Wadsworth, Ohio. In 1910 the congregation bought the abandoned Methodist church in Summerfield, and with some changes and renovations has used it as the place of worship ever since. The membership in 1957 was 92, with Ernest W. Neufeld serving as pastor.   E.B.

Summers Amish Mennonite Church, more generally known as Canton Amish Mennonite Church, now extinct, located about 5 miles southwest of the then limits of Canton, Ohio, near the present village of Richville, was established in 1810-20 by Amish settlers from Pennsylvania. Later settlers were Alsatian Amish Mennonites. An early minister was George Yutzy (*q.v.*). A later minister was Henry Summers, the father of Preacher John Sommers (ord. 1888 at Beech). Other ministers were Daniel Graber, and bishops Christian Klopfenstein and Zehr. After the death of Henry Summers in the late 1870's, ministerial help for the remaining members was supplied by the Oak Grove Mennonite Church at Smithville and the Beech church at Louisville. As late as 1900 the Eastern A.M. Conference appointed someone to serve the congregation. J. S. Gerig and John Sommers served in this way. The members began to move away or to join other M.C. congregations as well as other denominations.

This congregation probably never had a meetinghouse, but used the Mt. Eaton Church of the Brethren for funerals. This Amish congregation had no connection with the Rowland Mennonite Church (*q.v.*), although the two have sometimes been confused.   L.V.C.

Sumner County (Kansas) Old Order Amish settlement dates back to 1916. A congregation of 21 members was located in the west-central part of the county, near Conway Springs and Argonia. The first settlers came from Indiana and included the families of John H. Troyer (minister), Enos Miller (deacon), Amos Miller, and Ben Miller. The congregation met for worship for the first time on Jan. 30, 1916. The first resident bishop was Yost Lehman; he was succeeded by John H. Troyer and Dave D. Nissley. Leander S. Keim of Haven, Kan., was the bishop in charge in 1955.   R.TR.

Sun Valley Evangelical Mennonite Brethren Church, located in Los Angeles, Cal., was organized in 1942. Meetings were at first held in a store building. In 1944 the first church building was erected, enlarged in 1948 and 1955; it now has a seating capacity of 200. In 1958 the membership was 55, with David J. Dirks as pastor.   D.J.D.

Sunbury Mennonite Brethren in Christ Church, Sunbury, Pa., in the Allentown District, had 180 members in 1957, with E. W. Bean as its pastor.
                                                    M.G.

Sundarganj (Dhamtari, India) Mennonite Church (MC). After their arrival in India the first missionaries of this group, Bishop J. A. Ressler and Dr. and Mrs. Page, chose Sundarganj, at the edge of Dhamtari, as the site for their work, and in the autumn of 1899 they struck their tents under mango trees in a lovely grove. Soon the famine of 1899-1900 was upon them. Famine subjects began to pour into Dhamtari and surrounding villages and the missionaries were requested to open a famine relief center. The government officials arranged with the missionaries to give people work on the mission premises where the construction of buildings had been started, the government furnishing the funds and the mission furnishing the material. Thus the first evangelistic opportunity was with the thousands of famine sufferers among whom were nearly a thousand orphans. During 1901-2 Jacob and Mrs. Burkhard and Mahlon C. and Mrs. Lapp arrived, and the work could be organized into orphanage work, medical work, industrial and rehabilitation work, and evangelism through education and special Bible teaching. A number of families who remained in or near Dhamtari after the famine relief became Christian converts and were baptized and received into church fellowship, and many orphans were under special instruction for baptism. This resulted in a very rapid growth of the Christian membership.

Sundarganj became the headquarters of the American Mennonite (MC) Mission. At this station were located the treasurer, the Christian Academy, a large staff of missionaries and Christian teachers, and evangelistic workers.

Shantipur Leper Homes, Rudri, and Balodgahan stations were the natural outgrowth of the work established at Sundarganj. From the lepers fed in separate kitchens near Sundarganj a leper asylum was established near Dhamtari which afterward developed into the Shantipur Leper Homes (*q.v.*). The shifting of the orphan girls to a home separate from the boys gave rise to the mission station of Rudri (*q.v.*). To meet the need for Christian community expansion, especially on the land, the village of Balodgahan was bought in 1906. In 1957 the membership was 589, with D. A. Sonwani and J. H. Flisher serving as ministers in charge. G.J.L.

Sunday School. One of the most characteristic and influential institutions of modern American Christianity is the Sunday school. Like many other good things imported from Europe, it was greatly improved and thoroughly Americanized in the course of its 150 years of history on this continent. First established by Robert Raikes in Gloucester, England, in 1780, it reached Virginia as early as 1786 and passed rapidly from there to the leading cities of the eastern seaboard, including Philadelphia in

1790, and Boston and New York in 1791. In 1811 it reached Canada. By 1815 it had become a powerful, popular movement, and by 1824 a national organization, called the American Sunday School Union, had been organized to promote Sunday schools on a nation-wide scale. In 1830 this organization undertook a great missionary campaign "within two years to establish a Sunday school in every destitute place where it is practicable throughout the valley of the Mississippi," and in 1839 it resolved to establish a Sunday school "in every place in the West."

The first Sunday schools, however, were radically different from the modern Sunday school both in purpose and method. The Sunday school was conceived by Robert Raikes as a school for helping poor factory children of the lower classes to learn something of morals and religion, and to keep them off the street. The first Sunday schools were definitely promoted as private schools with paid teachers to deal with one of the most flagrant evils arising from the newly introduced factory system, the degradation of childhood. Not until 1812, in Philadelphia, was a Sunday school established on a voluntary basis with unpaid teachers with the definite purpose of teaching all children the Bible and leading them into an active religious experience. And not until after 1830 was the idea widespread that children of all classes should have Sunday-school privileges. Not until 1844 did any American denominational body officially and fully recognize the Sunday school as a church agency.

Since, therefore, the early Sunday schools were of private origin and promoted by persons interested in what might be called today "social service among the poor," and since the instruction of the youth of the church was generally carried on by catechetical methods within the ecclesiastical boundaries, there was much opposition to the attempt to make the Sunday school a universal Christian institution. For a generation or more it was promoted by private individuals and private organizations often against the opposition of official church leaders. In some sections of the country widespread bitterness and antagonism were created by the aggressive enterprise of Sunday-school leaders. For instance, in 1830 a Baptist Association in Illinois passed a resolution which is typical of many, saying: "We as an Association do not hesitate to say that we declare an unfellowship with Foreign and Domestic Mission and Bible Societies, Sunday Schools, and Quack Societies, and all other Missionary Institutions." In fact, a large share of the Baptists of the Middle West at that time adopted an anti-mission and anti-Sunday-school position which had an unfortunate effect upon the progress of that denomination in later years.

Along with the Sunday school, other aggressive evangelical methods were used in building up the Christian religion among the masses. The first quarter of the 19th century in America witnessed the organization of several foreign missionary societies, as well as Bible societies, tract societies, temperance societies, anti-Masonic societies, and numerous other organizations. The first foreign mission board, the American Board of Commissioners for Foreign Missions, was established in 1815; the American Bible Society in 1816; the American Sunday School Union in 1824; the American Tract Society in 1825. By 1830 the Bible Society, the Sunday School Union, and the Tract Society were cooperating in a tremendous campaign to Christianize America, and were doing it outside the regular denominational organizations. By 1850 the denominations began to form their own organizations to promote Sunday schools, home missions, and similar enterprises, and by this time great achievements were obtained in establishing the Christian church and Christian morals in the great newly occupied frontier territory. In the forefront of the work were the numerous hard-working, self-sacrificing missionaries of the American Sunday School Union, and the colporteurs of the American Bible Society and the American Tract Society. These men and organizations conquered the frontier for Christ quite as much as did the organized denominational agencies. This tremendous forward movement of evangelical Christianity in America was the result largely of the Great Revival of 1800, which was the most far-reaching in its results of all the revivals which have come to the Christian churches of America.

No doubt the most influential of all these institutions was the Sunday school. It adapted itself to the growing needs of the country, improved its methods, and enlarged its services. Beginning as a school for children from 6 to 12 of the poor classes, it soon sought to provide for all children, and ultimately for all Christians, direct systematic Bible study. In 1825 for the first time, through the American Sunday School Union, uniform lessons and question books were provided. Lesson helps of the modern type were introduced in 1866. In 1872 the modern international series of uniform Sunday-school lessons was set up. Along the way teacher-training courses, Sunday-school institutes, and Sunday-school conventions of various kinds were established to promote enthusiasm and to improve the work. By the fifth national convention of 1872, the American Sunday school had become a thoroughly established, powerful, national institution, recognized by practically all of the churches, and destined to play an increasingly important role in the spiritual history of America and of the world. It was in America, where religious instruction in the public schools is not only practically unknown but forbidden, and where tradition requires complete separation of church and state, that the Sunday school has been able to unfold its true genius and exercise its full power, in contrast to Europe where the state church provides religious instruction in the public schools, and where the Sunday school has never flourished to such a great extent.

It is on this background of American Sunday-school history that the history of the Sunday school among the Mennonites of North America must be understood. The history and development of the Sunday school in the various Mennonite bodies has never been thoroughly studied, except for the Mennonite Church (MC). The following bodies in North America have never accepted the Sunday school: Old Order Amish, Old Order Mennonite,

Reformed Mennonite, Stauffer Mennonite, Old Colony Mennonite, and Sommerfeld Mennonite. The schism of the Wisler (Old Order) Mennonites (*q.v.*) in Indiana in 1872 was occasioned partly by the introduction of the Sunday school. No other schism is directly attributable to the Sunday-school problem.

The Mennonite Church (MC). Probably the first Mennonite Sunday school in North America was established in Waterloo County, Ont., in 1840 in the Wanner and Bechtel (now Hagey) Mennonite meetinghouses. The second Sunday school seems to have been the one held in 1841 by the Kitchener (*q.v.*; then Berlin), Ont., congregation. The third Sunday school apparently was the one established by Bishop Nicholas Johnson in 1842 at Masontown (*q.v.*) in southwestern Pennsylvania. Another early Sunday school was established by Bishop Jacob Gross and Dilman Moyer in 1848 at Moyers (*q.v.*) church near Vineland, Ont. In eastern Pennsylvania in 1847 or earlier, apparently before the G.C.M. schism which he led, John H. Oberholtzer (*q.v.*) introduced a Sunday school into the Swamp (*q.v.*) congregation, near Quakertown, Pa., under the name "Meetings for Instruction of Children," in German "Kinderlehre." The meetings were held on alternate Sunday afternoons and were fairly well attended for a number of years, although a formal Sunday school at West Swamp was not established until 1858. Sunday school was conducted among the Amish of Mifflin County, Pa., before 1850. Most of these Sunday schools were later discontinued.

The first permanent Mennonite (MC) Sunday school in America was started by the South Union congregation near West Liberty, Ohio, by David Plank in May 1863. The record book of this Sunday school contains this statement for May 31, 1863 (translated): "J. C. Kanagy and D. Plank, ministers of the Church of God in this vicinity, have decided with the council of the church to organize a Sunday school in the name of God, for we believe quite confidently that as the fathers and mothers give us their support, much good will arise out of it." In a few years Sunday schools were established in widely scattered sections of the church and gradually became accepted as a part of the ministry of the church to its young people.

The growth of the Sunday school, however, was slow and not without serious opposition. Some of the reasons for opposing it were that it was patterned after that of other churches, was "worldly" and fostered pride, placed teaching responsibility into the hands of the laity, and was unsupported by the Bible. It is an interesting fact that through the Amish churches, which were generally not yet bound together by district conferences, the Sunday-school movement spread among the Mennonites.

In 1863, J. N. Brubacher, then a layman, started a Sunday school in the Pike Schoolhouse in Rapho Twp., Lancaster Co., Pa., having received his inspiration from an Episcopal Sunday school in Philadelphia which he had attended. Upon the ordination of Brubacher as minister in 1865, this Sunday school was discontinued. In 1866 the Washington, Ill., congregation organized a Sunday school. In 1869 the Virginia Conference permitted Sunday schools. The Ohio Conference approved Sunday schools in 1867; Indiana Conference in 1868; and Lancaster Conference in 1871.

In the Lancaster Conference the first permanent Sunday school was organized at Willow Street in 1871, and those at New Providence, Strasburg, Slate Hill, and Churchtown in 1872. Hershey's started one in 1874, Landisville in 1878, and Kraybill's in 1879.

The first permanent Sunday school in the Franconia Conference was started in 1878 at Towamencin, near Lansdale, Pa. However, the majority of the Franconia Conference congregations did not start Sunday schools until after 1880, and many of them not until after 1890, a few even waiting until after 1900.

During the decade 1865-75 Sunday schools were started in every state where there were Mennonite or Amish congregations, and most Mennonite conferences took action approving Sunday schools. In that decade at least 35 permanent Sunday schools were established. By 1875 the victory had been won in substance, and by 1890 in the west it was the exceptional congregation that did not have it. In 1880 J. F. Funk published Sunday-school "question books" authorized by the Lancaster Conference. The victory was sealed in 1890 with the establishment of an English and a German quarterly, published at Elkhart and edited by J. S. Coffman; a General Sunday School Conference was held near Goshen, Ind., in 1892.

Since then the development of Sunday schools in the Mennonite Church has been substantial and progressive. For this no person deserves more credit than I. W. Royer, of Orrville, Ohio, who for many years was Sunday School Secretary of the General Sunday School Committee, which was organized in 1915 to promote Sunday schools, and was displaced in 1937 by the Mennonite Commission for Christian Education. Also through the agency of the summer Bible school many Sunday schools have been begun in rural and city mission stations. In 1932 the Sunday schools had increased to 414 with an enrollment of 62,010; in 1937, 584 schools with 74,654; in 1957, 715 schools with 102,172.

In the Mennonite Church the promotional responsibility for the Sunday school lies with the Commission for Christian Education through its field secretary, and the divisional secretary for Sunday schools. This agency, combined with the extensive graded curriculum materials available through the Herald Uniform Sunday School Series, makes growth in numbers as well as in quality more readily possible.

Sunday-school literature (*q.v.*) as it was developed first at Elkhart by the Mennonite Publishing Company and then at Scottdale by the Mennonite Publishing House, including both the pupil and teacher quarterlies, the Sunday-school papers of several levels (*Beams of Light, Words of Cheer,* and *Youth's Christian Companion*), and the teacher-training materials, has been the most widely read literature in the church and has constituted the backbone of the publication work of the church. Teachers' meetings, formerly held weekly (either on a weekday evening or Sunday morning before

Sunday school), now not so common, have been strong influences for spiritual growth and unity. Teacher-training classes have been prominent in many congregations. Sunday-school conferences (*q.v.*) beginning in 1892 and held annually in most conference districts ever since, although now usually called Christian Workers' Conferences, have been very stimulating to spiritual life and vision. Mission Sunday schools have been the most effective means of church extension in the second quarter of the 20th century and after.

In the long perspective of a century of Sunday-school history, the church of today can better appreciate what the Sunday school has meant for the spiritual life and progress of the Mennonite Church. Without doubt it has been one of the major factors in the revival and forward movement of the last two generations. Amos Herr, one of the most able ministers of the Lancaster Conference in the 19th century, felt in 1880 that it was "the only salvation of the church." While this may be a slight overstatement, yet it is probably true that the Sunday school saved the church from great disaster by the new life, new spirit, new activity, and new vision which it put into the church. Many of the congregations that rejected the Sunday school either have died out or have gradually declined.

Wherein lay the great significance of the Sunday school for the church? A careful study suggests nine major contributions of the Sunday school. This summary is not to imply that the Sunday school was the only source of these improvements, but rather that the Sunday school was in general the initial and most important single factor. (1) The Sunday school was an important factor in holding the young people for the church. (2) It has greatly increased Bible knowledge. (3) It elevated the level of spiritual life. (4) It raised the level of moral life in the church, especially through the teaching of temperance. (5) It provided activity and expression and thus contributed to new life in the church. (6) It created lay leadership. (7) It was largely responsible for the missionary movement. (8) It was a factor in the great awakening of the Mennonite Church which occurred in 1890-1910. (9) It helped to give the Mennonite Church a new vision.

Wherever the North American Mennonites have gone in mission work, at home or abroad, they have taken the Sunday school with them with some adaptations.

Among European Mennonites, the Sunday school was widely accepted during the first quarter of the 20th century as a means of Christian education for children under catechetical age, that is, up to 14 years. It has not, however, taken the American form of a Bible study program for the entire church membership divided into classes before (or after) the regular Sunday morning worship. According to Paul Schowalter the first European Sunday schools were apparently the two introduced in the Palatinate, Germany—in the Deutschhof congregation in 1861, established following the closing of the private elementary school there, and in the Friedelsheim congregation in 1884, begun by the wife of the pastor, Ellenberger, who had learned about the Sunday school at Männedorf in Switzerland. In

Ludwigshafen it was introduced c1918 by the wife of the pastor, Emil Händiges, who came from the Baptists. At present (1958) practically all of the Palatine Mennonite congregations have Sunday schools, many of them introduced in imitation of the children's services in the state church congregations between World Wars I and II. The work of the American Mennonite Pax boys has also stimulated Sunday schools (e.g., Enkenbach). Most of the larger congregations in the Badischer Verband (q.v.) now also have Sunday schools. In Switzerland the Sunday school was introduced at least by 1910 in a number of places, such as Moron and Les Bulles. In West Prussia the Sunday school came in largely between World Wars I and II. (See **West Prussia** and **Russia**.)   H.S.B.

Harold S. Bender, *Mennonite Sunday School Centennial 1840-1940* (Scottdale, 1940) 12-23; Paul M. Lederach, *The History of Religious Education in the Mennonite Church* (doctoral dissertation at Southwestern Baptist Theol. Sem. 1949); John Umble, *Ohio Mennonite Sunday Schools* (Goshen, 1941); idem, "Early Sunday Schools at West Liberty, Ohio," *MQR* IV (1930) 6-50; idem, "Early Mennonite Sunday Schools of Northwestern Ohio," *MQR* V (1931) 100-11, 179-97, 260-71; idem, "Early Mennonite Sunday School Lesson Helps," *MQR* XII (1935) 98-113; Milo Kauffman, "The Rise and Development of Sunday Schools in the Mennonite Church in Indiana" (thesis for the M.A. in R.E., McCormick Theol. Sem. in Chicago, 1931). *ML* IV, 209-11.

General Conference Mennonite Church. The Sunday school came early into the Eastern District Conference of the G.C.M. Church, the oldest component of the conference. Following are the dates of the beginning of the Sunday school in the ten oldest congregations: West Swamp-1858, East Swamp-1859, Flatland-1859, Deep Run-1859, Upper Milford-1860, Germantown-1863, Eden-1867, Philadelphia-1868, Hereford-1870, Springfield-1877. The first Sunday School Convention was held at Philadelphia in 1876; it has been held every year since. (*Historical Booklet and Program of the Diamond Jubilee Sunday School Convention of the Eastern District Conference of the Mennonite Church,* Philadelphia, 1949.)

Prussia and Russia. Among the Mennonites of Prussia and Russia the practice of gathering children for Sunday school to teach them the basic contents of the Bible and the Christian truth is of comparatively recent origin. The Mennonites of the Dutch-Prussian-Russian tradition did this in their parochial elementary schools in Prussia as well as in Russia and during the catechetical instruction before baptism. With the pietistic revival of the 18th and 19th centuries the practice of gathering the children in a Sunday school was introduced. P. M. Friesen (*Brüderschaft,* 1911) makes barely any reference to this practice. This would indicate that the Sunday school had gained little prominence among the Mennonites of Prussia and Russia by the time of World War I. Wherever it was introduced it was primarily in the hands of some young people who felt the need, particularly after the Revolution, of instructing the children in Bible. *Unser Blatt* (1925-28), published for the Mennonites of Russia, hardly mentions such activity. Nevertheless, since religious instruction had been removed from the curriculum of the school, attempts were made in

many settlements to provide this instruction in Sunday school, which was conducted primarily on Sunday afternoons. However, this instruction had to cease completely around 1926-27 when group or public instruction of young people in religion was forbidden.

The Sunday school gradually gained a foothold in the first half of the 20th century among the Mennonites of Prussia and became an accepted practice until the Mennonite churches of that area were dissolved in connection with World War II. However, in all cases these Sunday schools were primarily dependent on the instruction and the abilities of a few individuals without much choice in materials or any preparation for this purpose. Only among those who went to Canada and South America after World War I did this program fully develop. With few exceptions the Sunday school was originally for children of elementary school age and not for adults. In Canada adults are now also attending Sunday school.   C.K.

Netherlands. After Sunday schools for children had been in use in England for more than a century and in a few Dutch towns by individual members of the Reformed Church since 1883, about 1895 Sunday-school work (for children only) was started in some Dutch Mennonite congregations (in Amsterdam as early as 1887). Gradually more and more congregations established Sunday schools for the children (ages about 6 to 12 or 13) of their members and others interested. Now nearly all Dutch Mennonite congregations have Sunday schools. In most churches they are operated according to the West Hill system (used in English Sunday schools since 1903); i.e., the children sit together in small groups on little chairs or benches, divided according to age; the subject matter of teaching and manipulation are adapted to the mental and intellectual grasp of the little ones; an individual approach to each child is aimed at; besides this, the activity of the children is stimulated by reproducing and expressing what has been taught by drawing or modeling in papier-maché or clay. Thus the school-class system is completely abandoned; the meetings are changed into children's religious services. Boys and girls of about 14-17 assist the leaders in these West Hill Sunday schools, to which the children are now admitted in their fourth year.

The high point of the Sunday school is the Christmas holiday, on the occasion of which often a play expressing the meaning of the coming of Jesus Christ is presented by the children.   vdZ.

Sunday School Banner is a weekly magazine, published by the Bethel Publishing Company (q.v.) of the M.B.C. Church since 1911. J. A. Huffman, founder of the firm, was editor of the paper until sometime after 1945. He was succeeded by the present editor, Woodrow I. Goodman. The magazine has varied in size and in number of pages.   N.P.S.

Sunday School Committee, General, of the Mennonite Church (MC) was created in 1915 by the Mennonite General Conference to supervise, coordinate, and strengthen the Sunday-school work of the church. It was discontinued in 1937 when its work was taken over by the newly created Commission for Christian Education and Young People's Work (q.v.). In addition to its general promotional work the committee was given general charge of the editorial work on the Sunday-school literature of the church and for this purpose chose (subject to General Conference approval) a General Sunday School Editor and an Associate Sunday School Editor. It therefore of necessity worked in close relationship with the Mennonite Publication Board. In this connection it also served as the general planning agency and curriculum builder for the Sunday-school literature. For its promotional work it had a General Sunday School Secretary. The committee had six regular members elected for a six-year term, but in addition gradually developed a series of seven subcommittees with co-opted members. I. W. Royer served as General Sunday School Secretary throughout the life of the committee. J. A. Ressler served as General Sunday School Editor from the beginning until his death in 1936. Influential chairmen were Vernon Smucker and Noah Oyer. H.S.B.

Sunday School Literature. In the time before Mennonite Sunday-school literature was available, American Mennonite Sunday schools used the literature in both German and English of the American Sunday School Union (founded in 1817, 1824), the American Tract Society (founded in 1875), and of denominational and interdenominational publishing houses. The David C. Cook publishing house has supplied much literature to Mennonite Sunday schools in various branches. Since in early years the Sunday school served in some Mennonite (MC) and Amish Mennonite congregations as a place to teach the children the German language, John F. Funk published Benjamin Eby's *A B C Buchstabier und Lesebuch* (first published in 1836 in Berlin, Ont., for use in the community day schools) in repeated editions (1869, 1871, 1882, 1896, 1909) for use in Sunday schools.

Funk began the publication of materials for Sunday-school work in May 1873 as a 4-page supplement to the *Herald of Truth* called the *Herald Series of Sunday School Lessons*, but due to opposition ceased publication at the end of the season. In 1880 the Lancaster Mennonite Conference authorized the preparation of Sunday-school *Question Books*, modeled after the American Sunday School Union books. A committee composed of ministers Amos Herr and Jacob N. Brubacher of the Lancaster Conference and Funk, assisted by the Lancaster bishops Isaac Eby and Benjamin Herr, produced the manuscript for the primary and intermediate booklets in 1880, and publication proceeded at once by Funk at Elkhart, followed by the *Infant Lesson Book* and in early 1881 by the fourth in the series, the adult or *Bible Class Question Book*. German editions of all four appeared in 1881-82. J. H. Oberholtzer published at Milford Square, Pa., in 1859, *Das Unparteiische Biblische Fragenbuch. Zum Gebrauch in Sonntagschulen und Familien für Kinder-Unterricht.*

The publication of Sunday-school quarterlies (quarterly lesson help booklets giving the text of the International Series of Sunday-school lessons with editorial helps and commentary by Mennonite writers) was begun by Funk in 1890, with J. S. Coffman as editor, with a German edition also beginning the same year. It was an adult quarterly. Funk never published a primary or a teachers' quarterly. When Funk sold out his periodicals to the Mennonite Publishing House in 1908, the quarterly ceased publication, and was replaced by a new title with the same function.

Funk also published Sunday-school "papers," as they were called, weekly 4-page periodicals largely distributed to the children in the Sunday schools without charge, paid for out of the Sunday-school treasury as were the quarterlies. In 1878 he took over the *Words of Cheer* started by H. A. Mumaw in 1876 as a children's Sunday-school paper. In 1881 he took over the analogous German paper *Der Christliche Jugendfreund,* designed for a slightly older age group, started by S. D. Guengerich of Johnson County, Iowa, in 1878. In 1887 he started a small 4-page weekly tract paper designed largely for Sunday schools, called *Welcome Tidings* (1887-97), also a German edition, *Angenehme Stunden* (1887-93). Neither of these prospered, and both were absorbed into other publications.

Beginning in 1906 the Sunday-school material of Mennonites (MC) consisted of picture rolls and cards and a primary lesson quarterly published by the Gospel Witness Publishing Company at Scottdale, which in 1908 was merged into the Mennonite Publishing House. In 1907 the *Advanced Quarterly* and an *Advanced Teachers' Quarterly* were added. These, based on the international uniform lesson outlines, were published continuously until 1924. The editor of all three for the first years was D. H. Bender. In 1925-36 the uniform lesson materials were increased from three quarterlies to five by the addition of the *Junior-Intermediate Quarterly* and the *Junior Teachers' Quarterly*. The *Primary Quarterly* was revised and improved and the picture rolls and cards continued.

In 1937-50 the lesson materials were increased to seven quarterlies, and new picture rolls and cards adopted. The *Primary Quarterly* was again revised and *Primary Worksheets*, the *Primary Teachers' Quarterly*, and the *Junior Pupil's Quarterly* were started. The *Junior-Intermediate Quarterly* was changed to the *Intermediate Pupil's Quarterly*, and the *Junior-Intermediate Teachers' Quarterly* was added.

In 1951 the Sunday-school materials were designated as "the Herald Uniform Sunday School Series," and at present comprise the following: *Herald Teacher,* helps for teachers of adults, youths, and intermediates, published monthly; *Herald Bible Studies; Herald Youth Bible Studies; Herald Intermediate Bible Studies; Herald Junior Bible Studies* and *Junior Teacher; Herald Primary Bible Studies* with worksheets and *Primary Teacher.*

The Herald Graded Sunday School Series is in preparation. In this series *Kindergarten I* has been in use since 1951; *Nursery* was introduced in 1957, and *Kindergarten II* in 1958. Group graded courses from primary through intermediate are being developed in co-operation with the General Conference Mennonites.

Weekly Sunday-school papers used to supplement the lesson materials are *Words of Cheer* (*q.v.*) since 1876, *Beams of Light* (*q.v.*) since 1906, and *Youth's Christian Companion* (*q.v.*) since 1920.

H.S.B., C.F.Y.

The General Conference Mennonite Church started its Sunday-school quarterlies in 1887 with the German *Sonntagschul-Lektionen für Jung und Alt* which has been in continuous publication to 1958, S. F. Sprunger editor to 1920, followed by C. H. A. van der Smissen. The English *Sunday School Bible Lesson Quarterly*, N. C. Hirschy editor, appeared for only 6 years, 1900-06. In 1937 four new English quarterlies were established, the *Mennonite Adult Quarterly*, the *Mennonite Young People's Quarterly*, the *Mennonite Junior Quarterly*, and the *Mennonite Junior Teacher*, which were replaced by a new series in the fall of 1958, entitled *Adult Bible Study Guide, Youth Bible Study Guide, Junior Bible Study Guide*, and *Junior Bible Study Guide Teacher's Manual*. At the same time the old German quarterly was renamed *Bibel Studien für Erwachsene*. All these use the International Uniform Lessons, and all are published by the Board of Education and Publication, Newton, Kan. The Board also publishes its own imprint edition of the Scottdale *Herald Teacher*. It is publishing jointly with the Herald Press (MC) at Scottdale a new graded series of Sunday-school lessons for various ages of children. It has its own imprint editions of the Herald Press, *Nursery, Home and Church Series, Bible Lessons for Kindergarten Children. Year II*, and *Herald Intermediate Bible Studies*. Two G.C.M. Sunday-school papers are published, the German *Kinderbote* (since 1886), first edited by David Goerz, and the English *Junior Messenger* (since 1939). These are both 4-page papers. The *Kinderbote* was at first a monthly, but is now bimonthly. The *Messenger* is weekly.

The only other Mennonite group publishing its own Sunday-school quarterlies is the Mennonite Brethren, which has had the German *Lektionshefte* since 1904 and the English *Adult Quarterly* since 1958. *Graded Sunday School Lessons* were briefly issued in English (1940-47, senior, intermediate, and primary in one quarterly), and in 1939 for the German, as *Ganze Bibel Graduierte Lektionen*. The *Teachers Manual for Sunday School Lessons* was published 1949-57 (separate quarterlies for primary and junior departments). All these were or are published by the Mennonite Brethren Publishing House at Hillsboro, Kan., and serve both the United States and Canada. On the lower level the United States churches have been using the Scripture Press (Wheaton, Ill.) materials, and the Canadian churches have either translated these into German or produced some of their own.

The smaller Mennonite groups use either the Herald Press materials—e.g., C.G.C., and E.M. (Kleine Gemeinde), the former using the G.C.M. German quarterly since Scottdale dropped the German number—or material from such publishers as the Union Gospel Press (Cleveland, Ohio), Gospel Light Press (California), and the Scripture Press. The Mennonite Brethren in Christ (now UMC) have been publishing their own rather complete Bethel Series since 1910.

An important development in Mennonite Sunday-school literature is the project for joint publication by the Herald Press (MC) and the G.C.M. Board of Education and Publication of a comprehensive graded lesson series. The Canadian M.B. Conference also plans to use this series. H.S.B., W.CL.

H. S. Bender, *Mennonite Sunday School Centennial* (Scottdale, 1940); idem, *Two Centuries;* J. S. Umble, "Early Mennonite Sunday School Lesson Helps," *MQR* XII (1938) 98-113.

Sunny Slope is about 25 miles east of Didsbury, Alberta, on the railway line from Edmonton to Calgary. In 1901-8 a few Mennonites (GCM) settled here. In 1904 Peter Kliewer was elected as minister. A few years later he went as missionary to the Indians in Montana, where he worked many years. A group of Church of God in Christ Mennonites settled here. Since 1940 the Church of New Jerusalem (Swedenborg) has had a small church in Sunny Slope, to which a few families of Mennonite origin belong. Peter Peters of Edmonton serves the latter group as minister. J.G.R.

Sunnyside Conservative Mennonite Church (CM), located a half mile east of Kalona, Iowa, is the third and newest (1957) meetinghouse for the Conservative Mennonite congregation of this area, the other two being Upper Deer Creek (*q.v.*) and Fairview (*q.v.*). In 1959 the membership was 156, with Morris Swartzendruber and Albert Miller as ministers. M.G.

Sunnyside Hutterite Bruderhof, located near Warner, Alberta, was founded in 1932. Their preachers are Jakob Hofer, chosen in 1931, and Andreas Wurz, chosen in 1936. In 1956 the colony had a population of 160, with 64 baptized members.

D.D.

Sunnyside Hutterite Bruderhof, located 5 miles south of Newton Siding, Man., was founded in 1939 by five families from the Milltown Bruderhof and their preacher Joseph Kleinsasser. In 1954 the Bruderhof numbered 93 souls with 37 baptized members. D.D.

Sunnyside Mennonite Church (MC), located 3 miles northeast of Conneaut Lake and 8 miles west of Meadville, Pa., is one of three congregations (with Britton Run, 1931 and Beaverdam, 1940) formed in northwestern Pennsylvania by families moving in from the Middle West, particularly Iowa and Nebraska, in 1925-40 in search of good farming opportunities. The majority of the first families at Sunnyside came in 1937 from Manson, Iowa. Forty-four prospective members, who had been worshiping at the Mennonite mission in Meadville, asked the Ohio and Eastern A.M. Conference for organization, which was effected in October 1937. The meetinghouse was built by stages 1938-44. J. W. Oswald, of Nebraska, served as pastor 1940-47. In

1957 the membership was 95, with Harvey Schrock serving as pastor. **H.S.B.**

Delmer Oswald, "The Planting and Growth of a Community in Northwestern Pennsylvania," *Menn. Community* VI (July 1952) 6-12.

Sunnyside Mennonite Church (MC), in a former suburb of Lancaster, Pa., began as a mission, initiated by David S. High. The first services were held in an abandoned dance hall with 71 from the community present. Through evangelistic sermons and home visitation the work grew until by 1957 the membership was 50, with David S. High, Witmer J. Barge, and Joseph C. Miller, Jr., as ministers. **I.D.L.**

Sunnyside Mennonite Church (MC), located in Dunlap, Ind., between Elkhart and Goshen, a member of the Indiana-Michigan Conference, began in 1946 as a mission of the Goshen College YPCA under the leadership of Paul Mininger (sponsor of the YPCA) and Richard Showalter. A church building was completed in 1948 with the help of the General Mission Board. There were 38 members in 1958, with D. Richard Miller as pastor. **C.A.R.**

Sunnyslope Mennonite Church (MC), located 10 miles north of Phoenix, Ariz., a member of the South Pacific Conference, began on Feb. 20, 1944, when a meeting was called in the home of Harold A. Brooks. In February 1946 an organization was made, with Joe H. Yoder as pastor. He was succeeded in 1948 by Melvin L. Ruth, who was ordained bishop in 1950. The first meetinghouse was built on a donated lot on N. 7th Place in 1946. In 1949 a new church built of pumice block was erected beside it. The older building was then used as a Christian day school and Sunday school. This small group holds a weekly service at a rescue mission in Phoenix. In 1957 the membership was 136, with Melvin L. Ruth as pastor.

In the spring of 1952 the Sunnyslope congregation assumed responsibility of two mission Sunday schools among the colored migrants in the Buckeye community—some 45 miles southwest of Sunnyslope. Later the Sunday schools were combined and a church was erected at Hodge Camp No. 29, 2 miles north of Buckeye. In 1955 Johnwilliam Boyer, a deacon at Sunnyslope since 1950, was ordained to be pastor at Buckeye. Colored people comprise the largest part of attendants, but Spanish and Cocopah Indians are usually also present. Attendance sometimes reaches 90. **M.L.R.**

Sunset Home for the Aged, Geneva, Neb., sponsored by the Mennonite (MC) Board of Missions and Charities, was established in 1951. It has a capacity of twelve guests. Chester Helmick was superintendent in 1958. **M.G.**

Sunshine Mission Home (MB), Buhler, Kan., a home for the aged founded in 1945 and operated by the Buhler Mennonite Brethren Church. It had twenty-one guests in 1958; the superintendent and matron were Mr. and Mrs. John K. Siemens. **M.G.**

Surhuisterveen, a town in the Dutch province of Friesland, mostly rural with some small but growing industry, is the seat of a Mennonite congregation, mention of which is made as early as 1647, but which had obviously been founded some decades before.

The old name of this town is Zuiderhuisterveen. From the origin until the end of the 18th century it was a peat colony. Its first inhabitants, who are said to have been Mennonites, came about 1600 or shortly after to dig the peat, which was shipped out as fuel. About 1700 a number of Menonites from Oldehove and Niehove in the adjacent province of Groningen moved to Surhuisterveen, whose population then largely was Mennonite.

Concerning the history of the Mennonite church of Surhuisterveen there is not much information. Whether there was a High German congregation here as early as 1613, as is mentioned in an old document, is doubtful. About that time there was at least a Waterlander congregation, which in 1695 joined the Sociëteit of Friesland and sent the deacon Gauke Gabes as a delegate to the Waterlander conference meeting at Amsterdam in 1647. Until about 1840 the local Surhuisterveen churchyard had the tombstone of Gabbe Paulus, d. Nov. 13, 1643, aged 72, who had been a preacher of the Mennonite congregation. He may have been one of its first ministers. For more than two centuries the congregation was served by lay preachers. Among these mention should be made of Foecke Floris (*q.v.*), who served in the 1680's, and who was imprisoned in 1687 on the charge of teaching Socinian (*q.v.*) doctrines, and banished from the province of Friesland in 1688; Jan Thomas (*q.v.*), who served here faithfully in 1722-44, likewise of liberal views. The last untrained preachers of Surhuisterveen were Eilert Wynalda 1752-1801, A. A. Venema *c* 1778, Jan Yde Wynalda 1782-1801, and Ynse Ypes Reens 1802-25. The first pastor of this congregation who was educated at the Amsterdam Theological Seminary was Arnoldus de Jong 1826-27, followed by F. E. Wieling 1828-57, A. Broos 1858-64, D. Pekelharing 1864-1908, F. W. W. Braak 1909-17, J. Yntema 1918-22, J. H. van Riemsdijk 1922-29, A. F. L. van Dijk 1932-33, Miss C. Soutendijk 1934-39, R. J. Faber 1940-46, Miss H. A. Leyns 1946-48, Miss W. C. Jolles 1949-53, A. Zwartendijk 1953-57, and J. P. Knipscheer since 1957.

The earliest membership figures date from 1695; the congregation then numbered about 40 baptized members. In 1723 there were 130, in 1828 47, in 1838 68, in 1900 79, and in 1957 131. In 1838, when the Kollum-Buitenpost (*q.v.*) congregation dissolved, the few remaining members joined the Surhuisterveen congregation.

The first meetinghouse was evidently built at a very early time, for in 1685 it was dilapidated and was replaced by another; the present church with adjoining parsonage is the third; it was built in 1859, remodeled in 1877. Surhuisterveen was one of the last Dutch congregations to obtain an organ, singing having been led by precentors. An organ was installed in 1910 and dedicated on July 10 of that year. The congregation has a ladies' circle, a

Sunday school for children, and a youth group. Blaupot ten Cate's statement that in 1711 some Amish Mennonite refugees from Switzerland (see **Swiss Mennonites**) settled at Surhuisterveen is an error.

At Westerveen in the neighborhood of Surhuisterveen a number of Tunkers (see **Brethren Church**) led by Alexander Mack (*q.v.*), having moved from Schwarzenau, Germany, lived in 1720-29; they then emigrated to Germantown, Pa. They apparently had no contacts with the Mennonites of Surhuisterveen.   vDZ.

Blaupot t. C., *Friesland;* J. Huizinga, *Stamboek . . . van Samuel Peter en Barbara Fry* (Groningen, 1890) p. LXXXX; *Inv. Arch. Amst.* II, No. 2265; *DB* 1861, 142; 1878, 131; 1887, 50 ff.; 1896, 150, 165, 171; 1910, 190.

Suspenders (Amish). Various kinds of suspenders and practices related to their wearing have developed among some of the Amish groups. This is true in Mifflin County, Pa., more than in any other region. The following information applies here. The "Old Schoolers" (Nebraska group) maintain a taboo on all suspenders. Trousers are held by a laced-up crotch at the rear of the broadfall trousers. The Byler (next most conservative) group shared this practice but in recent years adopted the practice of the Renno Amish who permit the use of one homemade elastic black suspender, fastened by a single button in front and one in the rear. The Zook group (now belonging to the "Beachy" Amish) permit the use of two suspenders, including plain bought suspenders, which are crossed in the back. Groups permitting one suspender make an exception for boys below school age who may have a wide single suspender split in the middle to allow the head to come through. The Swartzendruber Amish, the most conservative group in Ohio, wear two suspenders that form a "Y" in the back. These forms have given rise to nicknames among the groups: "One Suspender Amish" or sometimes "Swentzli" and "Two Suspender Amish." The various practices provide an excellent example of the slowness of cultural change. They have served as maintenance mechanisms to insure solidarity and consciousness of difference from all other Amish.
                                                      J.A.H.

Surplice Fees (German, **Stolgebühren**) are the fees which had to be paid to the clergy of the state church for the official services rendered. In Prussia the Mennonites were obliged to pay them for weddings and funerals, without having claimed the services of the clergy. After tedious negotiations and all sorts of legal arrangements (edict of July 30, 1789, Mennonite Law of June 12, 1874, and the decision of the imperial court of Oct. 8, 1885) a permanent release from these payments was secured in relatively recent times.

Menn. Bl., 1887, 4 and 11; W. Mannhardt *Die Wehrfreiheit der Altpreussischen Mennoniten* (Marienburg, 1863) 139, 155, and 190; *ML* IV.

Susquehanna Mennonite Church (MC), located a mile west of the Susquehanna River in Snyder County, Pa., worshiped in the Brubaker Schoolhouse until 1890, when the present frame building was furnished. This is a part of the Donald Lauver

Bishop District, with Alvin S. Shafer as pastor. The membership in 1957 was 80.   I.D.L.

Susteren, a village in the Dutch province of Limburg, in the 16th century belonging to the duchy of Jülich (*q.v.*), was a center of Anabaptist activity about 1550. It was then called "The principal point of the (new) religious revival." There is, however, only scarce information about this revival. Fifteen persons were baptized at Susteren by Elder Lemken (*q.v.*), but soon after this all traces of Anabaptists in this area are lost.   vDZ.

Rembert, *Wiedertäufer,* 69, 355, 356; W. Bax, *Het Protestantisme in het Bisdom Luik . . .* I (The Hague, 1937) 73 f., 302, 317.

Suter (Sutter, Suttor, Suder), a Mennonite family name, meaning shoemaker, originating in Kölliken, canton of Aargau, Switzerland. Persons by the name of Suter were known to have been members of the Waldenses in the canton of Bern many years before the beginning of the Anabaptist movement there. In 1538 Jacob Suter is mentioned as having been persecuted for his Anabaptist faith. Members of this family moved to Mennonite communities in Germany and to Florimont and Audincourt, France. Others came to America, settling chiefly in Rockingham County, Va., and Putnam County, Ohio, where a number of them have become leaders in the Mennonite Church (MC). Christian Suter (1791-1874), the second bishop of the Putnam County, Ohio, Swiss Mennonite congregation, helped to organize a Swiss Mennonite congregation in Madison Twp., Polk Co., Iowa, in 1858. Emanuel Suter (1833-1902), an active layman (MC) in Rockingham County, wrote extensively for Mennonite periodicals and served as secretary of the Virginia Conference for about 15 years. His grandson J. Early Suter and the latter's son Daniel B. Suter are ministers in the Virginia Conference, and Daniel is a teacher at Eastern Mennonite College.

An Amish branch of the family can be traced to Bavaria where Sutters owned the large estate near Ingolstadt known as Hellmannsberg during much of the 19th century. At least one Sutter family lived in Dittenfeld near Neuburg about 10 miles west of Ingolstadt. In 1848 a Christian Sutter from this location immigrated to near Morton, Ill., followed by his father John Sutter, an Amish preacher; eight other children, including sons John, Jacob, and Andrew, followed him. From this family apparently all of the numerous Sutters now living in Central Illinois (chiefly at Hopedale), Milford, Neb., and communities in Iowa, Michigan, and at least 9 other states descend. In 1924 this family established a reunion, which in 1945 listed over 1,000 living descendants. (N. P. Springer, "A Brief History of the John and Barbara Sutter Family," manuscript in GCL.)   D.L.G., H.S.B.

Suttere, de (de Sutter, de Zutter, Zutters, de Sitter, de Zitter): see **Sitter, de.**

Sutton (Neb.) Mennonite Brethren Church, now extinct, had its beginning about 1878 and during the 1890's was a flourishing congregation. At that time it built a meetinghouse and Heinrich Schneider became its leader. After that it decreased in membership and dissolved in 1924.   J.H.L.

Suvorovka, a Mennonite settlement in Russia: see **Ssuvorovka.**

Suzanna and Calleken Claes, Anabaptist martyrs: see **Cathalijne and Suzanneken Claes.**

Svistunovo Mennonite Church was located in the Slavgorod Mennonite settlement (*q.v.*) in Siberia, and served the villages of Dolinovka and Tcherneyevka. Worship services were held in the schools.
C.K.

Gerhard Fast, *In den Steppen Sibiriens* (Rosthern, 1957) 72.

Swabian League. On Feb. 14, 1488, the great Swabian League which had been proposed by Emperor Frederick III was constituted at Esslingen for the purpose of preserving the peace against anarchy in Swabia. It embraced the knightly league of St. George and 22 imperial cities, Archduke Sigismund of Austria, and Count Eberhard V of Württemberg. To these were added the Margraves of Brandenburg-Ansbach, Baden, Hessen, and the electors of Mainz and Trier. The first association was to last until 1496 but it was renewed in 1500, 1512, and 1522 until 1533.

The league received an exemplary constitution with a federal council of two sections, a federal court, and a federal army of 12,000 footmen and 1,200 horsemen. Its most significant deeds were the expulsion of Duke Ulrich of Württemberg in 1519, whose land the league sold to Emperor Charles V in 1520, and the cruel subjugation of the rebel peasants in 1525 by Georg Truchsess of Waldburg, the league captain. The league was entirely a tool of Austrian politics and of the Catholic Church; it fought against the spread of the Reformation. For this purpose the council appointed the provost Berthold Aichelin (*q.v.*), who moved about with his horsemen and hanged every adherent of the new faith without benefit of trial "to a dry branch," and thus killed about 1,200 including 40 Protestant preachers. In addition the league had a troop under Diepold von Stein wander through Upper Swabia and oppress Memmingen. They were particularly intent upon catching Anabaptists. Some member princes and cities had joined the Reformation. Therefore the league could no longer be renewed in 1533, especially since now it was opposed by the Smalkaldic League. Austria would have liked to have a replacement for this adaptable tool but none was found.

In many places protests were raised against this procedure; the council of Nürnberg did so, not out of love for the Anabaptists, but because as it said, "The pretense is to hunt the wolves, but they catch the sheep; in this way they will also persecute the confessors and preachers of the Word." The council therefore favored milder measures.

On March 7, 1528, the Swabian League issued an order limiting church fairs and weddings on account of the Anabaptists, "since Anabaptism is breaking in and increasing more and more." They thought the Anabaptists made propaganda at such gatherings.

The chronicles of the Hutterian Brethren report about these bloody deeds by Aichelin (not to be confused with Joseph Lauscher, called Aichelin or Aicheln, who was Land- und Bannrichter of the territory of Lienz in Tirol, and also had much to do with the Anabaptists), "About this time (1528) King Ferdinand sent a wild provost by the name of Aichelin to Swabia and into the land of Württemberg, who then shed much innocent blood, also burned the Mantelhof, nor far from Aalen, with men, youths, women, and maidens, about twenty persons."

The two Anabaptist preachers Griesinger (*q.v.*) and Lochmayer (*q.v.*) were among Aichelin's victims. "But God at last instilled fear into him through the steadfastness of His servants, so that he swore that he would not execute another brother. He was later stabbed in Württemberg and died a shameful death."

On Feb. 2, 1534, the Swabian League came to an end. Its dissolution was urged by Philip of Hesse and Bernhard von Besserer, mayor of Ulm. A number of historians have tried to justify this bloody procedure in the framework of the "dark background of the great social revolution" (Peasants' Revolt). Certainly the decree of the league in an Anabaptist mandate of March 7, 1528, explains "that it can easily be comprehended by every honor-loving Christian ... how Anabaptism ... leads to new revolutions and uprisings" if it is not countered with "painful and serious punishment." But this fear was quite unfounded. It has been proved that not a single Anabaptist leader took part in the Peasants' War. Even in Thuringia the Anabaptist movement proved itself to be entirely peaceful.
G.Bos., W.W.

Beck, *Geschichts-Bücher;* Wolkan, *Geschicht-Buch;* K. Klüpfel, *Urkunden zur Geschichte des Schwäbischen Bundes* II (Stuttgart, 1853); Fr. Thudichum, *Die deutsche Reformation* II (Leipzig, 1909); Wiswedel, *Bilder* II; G. Bossert, "Aichelin," in *Blätter für Württemberg. Kirchengeschichte* VII, 25 ff., 35 ff.; H. Hermelink, *Geschichte der Evangelischen Kirche in Württemberg von der Reformation bis zur Gegenwart* (Stuttgart and Tübingen, 1949) 17 ff., 56; I. Rauscher, "Aichelin," in *Württemberg. Reformationsgeschichte* III; G. A. Will, *Beiträge zur Geschichte des Anabaptismus in Deutschland* (1773) 224-27; K. Klüpfel, "Der Schwäbische Bund," in *Hist. Taschenbuch,* 1853; Zieglschmid, *Chronik;* ML IV.

Swaen Rutgers (Zwaan, Zwaantje, the wife of a certain Rutger, who was living at Emden, East Friesland, Germany, about 1555. Both Rutger and his wife were members of the Mennonite congregation of which Leenaert (*q.v.*) Bouwens was the elder. In 1556 or shortly before, Bouwens banned Rutger for some unknown reason and ordered Swaen to avoid her husband, which she refused to do. Bouwens thereupon threatened also to cut her off from the church, and some time later actually did so. Before Swaen was banned, Menno Simons tried to intervene. He had been informed of the conflict and had been requested to give his opinion on marital avoidance; in response Menno wrote a letter to Emden, dated Nov. 13, 1556, urging moderation and peace. Leenaert Bouwens, however, refused to yield, in spite of the wishes of a large part of the congregation and Menno's kindly advice, and banned Swaen

Rutgers. Dirk Philips (*q.v.*), after Menno the most influential elder of the Mennonites, also championed marital avoidance. Menno Simons received letters not only from Emden, but also from Franeker (*q.v.*) in Friesland, where Joriaen Heyns and Hendrik Naeldeman opposed marital avoidance.

Thus it became necessary for the elders to discuss the question. A meeting for this purpose was held at Harlingen, Friesland, in the spring of 1557. Here Menno was won over to the strict practice of Leenaert Bouwens and Dirk Philips. This issue in the Dutch brotherhood caused the withdrawal of the moderate Waterlanders (*q.v.*) and also the separation of the High Germans (*q.v.*), who were not willing to follow Menno on this point.

Karel Vos's opinion that Swaen Rutgers lived at Franeker is an error, since old writings state explicitly that she lived in Emden.   vDZ.

BRN VII, 54, 58 f., with Menno's letter to the Emden congregation, 449 f.; J. H. Ottius, *Annales Anabaptistici* (Basel, 1672) 118 f.; *DB* 1876, 22; 1894, 35, 40, 43, note 3, 57; Karel Vos, *Menno Simons* (Leiden, 1912) 132 f.; Kühler, *Geschiedenis* I, 317 ff.

Swaene Hermansdochter, an Anabaptist martyr, the widow of Jan Moervinck (Morveldinck? *q.v.*), b. near Coevorden, Dutch province of Drente, was drowned on July 21, 1544, at Utrecht, because she "was an adherent of reprobate sects." She apparently belonged to the revolutionary wing of Dutch Anabaptism, one of its last followers and victims. (Mellink, *Wederdopers*, 240, 410).   vDZ.

Swaerdemaker: see **Zwaardemaker.**

Swalwell (Alberta) M.B. Church: see **Linden** E.M.B. Church.

Swalwell (Alberta) Church of God in Christ Mennonite Church: see **Linden.**

Swamp Mennonite (MC) Church, located in Milford Twp., Bucks Co., Pa., a member of the Franconia Conference, dates back to the early 18th century. Bishop Falentine ("Velte") Clemmer immigrated from Europe to the Swamp area in 1717. The first meetinghouse was built about 1735, a mile west of the present West Swamp Church (GCM). It was torn down and rebuilt on the site of the present West Swamp Church (*q.v.*) in 1790. The East Swamp (GCM) meetinghouse (*q.v.*) was built in 1771, and was later destroyed by fire and rebuilt; the present church was erected in 1850. In the Franconia Conference division of 1847 John H. Oberholtzer and the majority of the Milford Township ministers withdrew from the conference and claimed both meetinghouses. Those who were left, although without a minister, immediately built the Swamp meetinghouse for the group adhering to the Franconia Conference. Soon Jacob Beidler (1809-74) was ordained. In 1863 Abraham Young was ordained to assist him, but was later silenced. Later ministers were John A. Beidler (1840-1912) and the 1958 ministers, John G. Gehman (1875-   ), ordained in 1919, and Abram D. Yoder (1893-   ), ordained in 1935. The member-

ship in 1958 was 75. John H. Oberholtzer (*q.v.*) was ordained preacher at Swamp in 1842. J.C.W.

J. C. Wenger, *History of the Mennonites of the Franconia Conference* (Telford, 1937) 125-28.

Swamp Mennonite Mission, Lancaster Co., Pa.: see **Blainsport.**

Swamp Union Meetinghouse: see **Blainsport** Mennonite Mission.

Swart, a common Dutch family name. A Mennonite Swart family has lived on the Dutch island of Terschelling since the 17th century, many of whose members have served the Terschelling (*q.v.*) congregation as deacons, the last being A. G. Swart and Tjebbe Swart, the latter serving until 1953.

Rindert Swart (Haarlem, 1890-Hindeloopen, 1929) was educated at the Amsterdam University and the Mennonite Seminary and served the congregations of Hindeloopen-Koudum in 1916-19. (*Genealogie van de familie Swart, Terschelling*, n.p., n.d.) vDZ.

Swarte, de, the name of a number of Mennonites in Flanders, Belgium; the martyr books enumerate seven martyrs by this name, and besides them two or three of their wives. Most of them belonged to one family. The information concerning these martyrs is hazy and incomplete. Neither van Braght's *Martyrs' Mirror* nor Froissard's *l'Eglise sous la croix* (Paris, 1857) is complete. Ed Coussemaker, in *Les Troubles Religieuses du XVIe Siècle dans la Flandre Maritime 1560-70* (Brugge, 1876, 4 vols.), names fourteen persons named de Swarte or de Zwarte and some of their wives, viz., Adreaen, Andries, Christiaen, Cornelis, Etienne (Steven), Françoys, Françoys-Anthonis, Gautier (Wouter), Jan, Jacob, Martijn, Mat(t)hieu, Nicolas, and Hans. Of these, the following martyrs are mentioned in this ENCYCLOPEDIA: Christiaen, Claes (i.e., Nicolas), Frans (Françoys), Hans, Jacob, Jan, and Mahieu (Matthieu).   vDZ.

Swartz (Schwartz), Mennonite family found in North America. They descend from the Swiss Schwartz family. Felix Schwartz, of Regensdorf, canton of Zürich, was an Anabaptist in 1527 and Adelheyd Schwartz *c*1530. Mennonites by this name were found in the 17th century in the Emmental (*q.v.*), Switzerland, and in the early 18th century in Alsace (*q.v.*).

In America most Swartz families are descendants of Abraham Schwartz (Swartz), bishop of the Deep Run Mennonite (MC) congregation in Bucks County, Pa., ordained preacher in 1738 and bishop in 1756. Swartz arrived at Philadelphia on the *Friendship* on Oct. 16, 1727. In 1778 he and Bishop Andrew Ziegler of Skippack deposed Bishop Christian Funk for his favorable attitude toward the American Colonies who were in rebellion against England. Early in the 19th century his grandson Christian Swartz moved to Waterloo County, Ont., and became the head of a large family there. Other descendants of the Deep Run pioneer found their way to Virginia and Ohio and points farther west. One of the best-known members of the family was Freeman H. Swartz, General Conference Mennonite pastor at Schwenksville, Pa., 1921-d.57. The Schwartz families among the Amish of Adams County, Ind., are of a different lineage. In the Mennonite Church (MC) in 1958 there were 5 ministers named Swartz, and 9 Schwartzes in the Old Order Amish group, 3 of whom were bishops, practically all in northern Indiana.   J.C.W.

Swartzendruber (Swartzentruber, Swartzendrover, Swartzendruver, Schwartzentruber, Schwartzendruber, Schwarzentruber, Schwarzentruver, Schwarztrauber, Schwarzentraub), a Mennonite family name. It is of Swiss origin and may mean "seller of black grapes." In the early 1700's a family Bible used the spelling Schwarzentraub. This is the earliest occurrence of the name now known. The Schwartzendrubers belonged to the Amish (q.v.) branch of the Mennonites. Among the Swiss Brethren leaving Switzerland for the Netherlands in 1711 there was a Hans Schwartzentrub, of Trub(?), who, however, left the ship at Mannheim. A Christian Schwartztrauben is mentioned in the Dutch *Naamlijst* of 1767-1802 as a preacher of the Weissemheim am Berg congregation (Amish) in the duchy of Leiningen, Germany. Bäntz Schwarztrauben was from 1775 a preacher of the Amish church of Waldeck (q.v.). A Christian Schwarztrauben, by marriage related to the Gingerich family, lived at Mengeringhausen near Kassel and had taken over the "Galgenmühle" from Simon Roth, also Amish.

According to a family tradition the first American Swartzendrubers were immigrants from Waldeck. The first-known immigrations occurred soon after 1800, when settlements were made near Somerset and Berlin, Pa., and in Ontario. Soon, however, migrations to points farther west resulted in comparatively few residents remaining in Pennsylvania; today Ontario, Maryland, Delaware, Ohio, Indiana, and Iowa find the name most prominent. Among the outstanding personalities bearing this name in the past are Jacob J. Schwartzendruber of Waldeck (Germany), Pennsylvania, and Iowa, Jacob Frederick and Joseph Schwartzendruber of Iowa, and Solomon Swartzendruber of Michigan. In 1958 there were seven Mennonite (MC) bishops bearing the name Swartzendruber: A. Lloyd Swartzendruber, John Y. and Morris E. Swartzendruber of Kalona, Iowa, Elmer G. Swartzentruber of Wellman, Iowa, Alva R. Swartzendruber of Hydro, Okla., Amos Swartzentruber of Buenos Aires, Argentina, and Emanuel Swartzendruber of Pigeon, Mich., besides ten preachers. There were also nine Old Order Amish ministers in Ohio, Delaware, Indiana, and Iowa bearing the name. A very conservative group of the Old Order Amish near Dalton, Wayne Co., Ohio, is called the Swartzentruber Amish (q.v.). No outstanding genealogies of the family have been published, although currently one is in process. A booklet, *Documents Relating to Bishop Jacob Schwarzendruber (1800-1868)*, has been printed.   E.G.S., vDZ.

Peter Swartzendruber and Wilmina Eash Genealogy (Westmoreland, N.Y., 1956; Dutch *Naamlijst;* Müller, *Berner Täufer,* 307.

Swartzendruber, Jacob Frederick (1851-1924), an outstanding Amish leader and editor, was born Oct. 17, 1851, in Johnson Co., Iowa, the son of Frederick Schwartzendruber, who had immigrated from Waldeck, Germany. He was married to Elizabeth Bender on Dec. 31, 1871, in Somerset County, Pa. He became a Christian in his youth, uniting with the Amish Mennonite Church. He was ordained to the ministry in March 1878 and served the Lower Deer Creek (also known as the Timber) Church near Kalona, Iowa. He was ordained bishop in the same church Dec. 4, 1887, serving until 1915, when the Lower Deer Creek Church united with the Western Amish Mennonite Conference; then he transferred his membership to the Old Order Amish congregation near Sharon Center in Johnson County. He served one of the districts in this community until his death. He lived for a short time in Lyons County, Kan., and in Oregon, but most of his life was spent in the community of his birth. He served as editor of the *Herold der Wahrheit* for two years and as editor of the Junior Department of this paper until his death. Swartzendruber was an ardent sponsor of social purity and zealous Christian living. Many of his sermons were on separation and a positive expression of the Christian life.

His wide knowledge of Scripture together with his alert mind and wealth of information concerning his day made him quite influential throughout the church. In his possession were many writings of historical value, especially those of his grandfather Jacob Schwartzendruber. Among these is a complete schedule of church services, telling where the service was held, who conducted the devotional service, who delivered the sermon, the date and also other important church business, such as discipline administered to members, approaching marriages announced, etc. Most of the above papers are in the Mennonite Church Archives in the Goshen College Library at Goshen, Ind. Jacob Frederick Swartzendruber died Jan. 17, 1924, and was buried in the Lower Deer Creek Cemetery near Kalona.   A.L.S.

Swartzendruber, Jacob J. (1800-68), the first Old Order Amish Mennonite bishop in Johnson County, Iowa, was born in Waldeck, Germany, in 1800, where he married Barbara Oesch, the widow of Peter Güngerich. He was ordained minister in 1826, emigrated to America in 1833, and lived in Somerset County, Pa., and Garrett County, Md. In 1851 he moved to Iowa and was there ordained bishop two years later. He died June 5, 1868. His son Joseph J. was ordained bishop in 1869 and among Jacob's descendants there have been no less than eight bishops and five ministers who served in Mennonite churches. His Christian ideals and high standards were important in molding the policies of the Amish churches in Iowa.   E.G.S.

Harold S. Bender and John Umble, "Documents Relating to Bishop Jacob Schwarzendruber," 3 articles in *MQR* XX (July 1946) 222-39; Melvin Gingerich, *Mennonites in Iowa* (Iowa City, 1939).

Swartzendruber, Solomon J. (1856-1932), an Amish Mennonite leader and bishop, was born in Allegany (now Garrett) County, Md., on March 27, 1856, the fifth of the eleven children of Joseph J. and Barbara

Brenneman Swartzendruber. When he was about six weeks old his parents moved to Johnson County, Iowa, where his father had purchased a tract of land as one of the first three Mennonite landowners in that community. He united with the Amish Mennonite Church early in life. On Jan. 13, 1881, he was married to Katie Swartzendruber and to them seven children were born. In 1884 they moved to Inman, Kan., where he was ordained to the ministry in 1886 or 1887. Several years later he was ordained bishop. In 1893 he with his family moved to Wright County, Iowa, and helped to organize a church there. In 1902 they moved to Earlham, Madison Co., Iowa. In 1904 they moved to Bay Port, Mich., arriving there on Feb. 18, where he organized and became the first bishop of the Pigeon Conservative (Amish) Mennonite Church which became a large congregation. He was elected moderator of the C.A.M. Conference in 1912, 1914, and 1916. He was assistant moderator in 1913. Three times, in 1914-16, he preached the conference sermon. In 1925-30 he served on its executive committee. In 1919 he moved to Pigeon, Mich., and here he died March 1, 1932.　　　　E.G.S.

History of the Amish Mennonite Conference (Conservative) 1910-1924 (Scottdale, 1925); this report, however, is in error in stating the first conference was held in 1911; *Combined Annual Reports of the Amish Mennonite Conference (Conservative), 1925-1937* (1938).

Sweedlin Valley in Pendleton County, W. Va., is a narrow valley formed by the Sweedlin Mountain and the Shenandoah Mountain. In the center of the South Fork (branch of the Potomac) Valley the Sweedlin Mountain arises at a point three miles north of Oak Flat and extends north for a distance of eight miles. The South Fork Branch flows west of the Mountain; the valley lying east of the Mountain is known as Sweedlin Valley. During the 1880's ministers of the Northern District of the Virginia Conference had not only entered the Brock's Gap country but had extended their witness as far west as the top of the Shenandoah Mountain. It was here that individuals living in Sweedlin Valley learned to know about the Mennonites and invited them to preach for them. Today the Pleasant Grove Mennonite Church is located in the heart of this valley. In 1958 Lloyd Hartzler was pastor, with 55 members.

Wine Spring Schoolhouse, Peru, Pendleton County, W. Va., located in South Fork country several miles north of Sweedlin Valley, has been a preaching place since about 1920 as an extension of the work from the Sweedlin Valley.　　　　H.A.B.

Sweet Home Mennonite Church (MC), located near Sweet Home in Linn County, Ore., on U.S. 20, was organized July 14, 1940, with 43 members under the care of the Pacific Coast Mennonite Conference, and N. A. Lind was given charge as pastor and bishop. The first meetinghouse was dedicated Dec. 14, 1940. Archie Kauffman, a minister, located in the community in 1941, and is the present (1958) pastor, assisted by Willard Stutzman (ordained 1948). In 1952 Wilbert Lind was ordained and with his family sailed for Somalia, Africa, as missionaries under the Eastern Mennonite Board.

Since 1942 the congregation has maintained a mission Sunday school some 13 miles up the Cascade Mts., near Cascadia, where a church was built in 1946. Present attendance is almost equal to that of the home church. The membership in 1958 was 125, with N. M. Birky as bishop.　　　　N.A.L.

Sweet or Bitter Christ, a well-coined phrase set into circulation by Thomas Müntzer (*q.v.*), which caught the imagination of his contemporaries. The idea of the phrase is that divine grace must not be looked at as something to be gained cheaply (Bonhöffer's term) but as precious and costly. In other words, the doctrine of justification by faith alone is not to be interpreted in such a way that man receives this gift without any further personal obligation on his part. "No one is able to believe in Christ," said Müntzer, "unless he tries beforehand to become like Him" (Brandt, 130). In all his writings Müntzer speaks exclusively of the "crucified Christ" and never of the "glorified" one. Such an outlook is usually described as the theology of the cross, for which Müntzer is an outstanding representative if not the originator. It is to be distinguished from the traditional Anabaptist position which might preferably be called "Märtyrertheologie" (see **Martyrdom, Theology of**), in which the idea of a suffering church is central. Nevertheless, the phrase "sweet and bitter Christ" was accepted also by the Anabaptists and became widely used in their polemics against the state churches.

The best references for the use of the idea are to be found in Müntzer's tract of 1524, *Vom gedichteten Glauben* (Brandt, 126 ff.). Item 10 of this tract reads: "Sheep are being poisoned by evil pastures but are fed by salt. To preach to a carnal world a sweet Christ is the greatest poison which has been given to Christ's lambs. For by accepting such a gift, man no longer desires to become like Christ (*christförmig*)" (Brandt, 129). And Item 11 (*ibid.*): "Whoever does not want to accept the bitter Christ will eat himself to death with honey. For whoever does not die with Christ cannot rise with Him either." Obviously behind these words lies an entire theology not completely in agreement with the *sola fide* idea of the official churches.

In the 16th century this idea was accepted primarily by the Anabaptists, and many examples are found in the sources. Thus, for instance, says Hans Schlaffer (*q.v.*), "Everyone wants to have but the sweetest from Christ, but wants to reject the suffering" (Wiswedel, II, 197). Ludwig Haetzer's stanza is likewise well known: "Yes, says the world, there is no need that I should suffer with Christ; since Christ suffered death for me, I may just sin on this account. . . . O brethren mine, it is a sham, the devil has contrived it" (see *MQR 1954*, 35 n). Still clearer is the word of Hans Haffner (*q.v.*) in his tract *Concerning a true soldier of Christ* (*c*1535): "The world accepts Christ as a gift but does not know Him as a suffering Christ" (*MQR 1931*, 92). Pilgram Marpeck's polemic against Schwenckfeld is likewise oriented at least in part to this point. "The crown of thorns precedes the halo of glory," comments Loserth in this connection (Loserth, 160). Elsewhere Marpeck speaks of the lowliness of Christ in contrast to the glorified Redeemer as taught by his opponent.

In our own times Dietrich Bonhöffer knows the same conflict, which he now calls the difference between "cheap grace" and "costly grace." It certainly strikes a central point of theology with practical consequences in life. R.F.

Thomas Müntzer, sein Leben und seine Schriften, ed. Otto H. Brandt (Jena, 1933); D. Bonhöffer, *Cost of Discipleship* (German 1937, Engl. New York, 1952); Wiswedel, *Bilder* II; Pilgram Marpeck, *Verantwortung* . . . ed. Loserth (Vienna, 1929).

Swichtenheuvel (van Swigtenheuvel), a Mennonite family formerly living at Amsterdam and Utrecht. Jan Jansz Swichtenheuvel, of Amsterdam, published *Oprechte Editie, ofte Uytgift van het Geschrift van Doctor Galenus Abrahamsz ende David Spruyt* . . . (Haarlem, 1658), the preface of which, written perhaps by Swichtenheuvel himself, shows him to have been an opponent of Galenus Abrahamsz (*q.v.*), leaning toward the views of the "Ouderen" (Conservatives, later called Zonists).

In Utrecht some members of the Swichtenheuvel family were deacons of the Mennonite congregation: Gillis van Swichtenheuvel 1716-18, Cornelis van Swichtenheuvel four times—1735-37, 1741-44, 1748-50, and 1754-55. Suzanna Swichtenheuvel, who married Jan de Heger, was about 1740 one of the first deaconesses of the Utrecht congregation.

vDZ.

H. W. Meihuizen, *Galenus Abrahamsz* (Haarlem, 1954) 61, 62, 64; C. B. Hylkema, *Reformateurs* I (Haarlem, 1900) 16, 117, 131; H. B. Berghuys, *Geschiedenis der Doopsgezinde gemeente te Utrecht* (n.p., n.d.-1926) 47, 50, 52.

Swift Current (Sask.), city and Mennonite settlement. The city (pop. 10,000) is located in southwest Saskatchewan, 105 miles west of Moose Jaw in a wheat district. Sommerfeld (*q.v.*) and Old Colony (*q.v.*) Mennonites settled south of Swift Current starting in 1900, mostly from the West Reserve in Manitoba, but also from the overflow of the Rosthern settlement. The Old Colony Mennonites settled in villages near the railroad stations of Dunhelm, Wymark, and Blumenhof. In 1914 the following fifteen villages were still in existence: Rosenhof, Rosenfeld, Reinfeld, Rosenbach, Rosenort, Neuendorf, Blumenhof, Schönfeld, Chortitz, Reinland, Schanzenfeld, Blumenort, Schönwiese, Springfeld, and Gnadenthal. In 1911 the total Mennonite population of the Herbert (*q.v.*) and Swift Current area was 4,590. About 1500 of the Old Colony and Sommerfeld Mennonites emigrated to Mexico and Paraguay after World War I. In 1931 the Swift Current Mennonite settlement had a population of 1500. By that time Mennonites from Russia had joined this settlement. In 1950 it was estimated that 3,000 Sommerfelders lived in the settlement.

The Emmaus Mennonite (GCM) Church (*q.v.*) has seven church buildings in this general area, the largest of which is in the city of Swift Current. Other places of worship included Wymark, McMahon, and Reinland. V. E. Nickel is the elder of the church. The total membership in 1956 was 368. There is also an Old Colony Mennonite Church in the Swift Current area. The Mennonite Brethren have a congregation of about 100 in Swift Current, led by F. J. Peters. The Swift Current Bible Institute (*q.v.*) has been functioning since 1936. C.K.

Heinz Lehmann, *Das Deutschtum in Westkanada* (Berlin, 1939) 170; *Jahrbuch der Konferenz der Mennoniten in Canada*, 1956.

Swift Current Bible Institute, located at 510 Cheadle Street east, Swift Current, Sask., was founded in 1936 by N. Banmann through and under the direction of Bishop David Toews for the General Conference of Mennonites of Canada. In 1955 the plant consisted of three buildings—a residence for the principal, a building used for administration, classrooms, girls' dormitory, and kitchen and dining room, and a building for teachers' residence and men's dormitory. The term of the Institute is about 5½ months; the course consists of the regular Evangelical Teacher Training Association subjects and Mennonite history, missions, catechism, etc. There are no educational requirements for admission. It is governed by an executive committee of six members and a board of directors of fourteen members. In 1957 the principal was Werner Zacharias; the staff consisted of three full-time teachers, and the enrollment was 34. W.Z.

Swift Current (Sask.) Mennonite Brethren Church, organized in 1933 with a membership of 26, belongs to the Herbert District Conference. In 1941, with voluntary contribution of work and money by its members, a church was built. The congregation has sent out many workers to home and foreign mission fields. The leader of the congregation 1933-41 was G. A. Warkentin. His successor was Frank J. Peters. The membership in 1957 was 97, with E. J. Lautermilch as pastor. J.I.R.

Swift Current Mennonite Church (Old Colony), located adjacent to the Reinland Mennonite Church, Cuauhtemoc, Chihuahua, Mexico, consists of Old Colony Mennonites who settled here, coming from Swift Current, Sask. The total membership in 1953 was 3,590. (See **Old Colony** Mennonites.) C.K.

Swift Current Mennonite Settlement near Cuauhtemoc, Chihuahua, Mexico, was established in 1926 by approximately 1,000 Old Colony Mennonites from Swift Current, Sask. The settlement consists of some sixteen villages and is located northwest of the larger Manitoba Mennonite settlement (*q.v.*). The land was purchased in the name of two settlers from each village. The settlement has its own civic administration (*Oberschulze, q.v.*) and is an independent ecclesiastical unit with its own elder (Jacob Peters). In 1953 the population was 2,694. C.K.

Swinderen, Hans van: see Schwindern, Hans von.

Swiss Brethren, the oldest and most influential body of German-speaking Anabaptists. The Anabaptist movement had its origin in Zollikon, now a suburb of Zürich, Switzerland, in January 1525 and spread from there in a short time into the surrounding German-speaking area of Switzerland (St. Gall, Appenzell, Aargau, Grisons, Bern, Basel). It spread rapidly beyond the Swiss borders into Tirol, South Germany, and Alsace, and shortly into Middle Germany, down the Rhine as far as Cologne, into Hesse, Thuringia, and Saxony. It is therefore not surprising that the group came to be known as Swiss Brethren, indicating their geographical origin, although the movement was quite indigenous and not a Swiss mission with resident Swiss leaders living in foreign countries.

However, the name soon came to be a designation for a type of Anabaptists differing from other types, first of all distinguished from the Hutterites with their communal living. The Hutterite Chronicle first uses the name in connection with events dated in 1543, where a certain Hans Klöpffer is stated to have "formerly been a minister of the Swiss Brethren." In Moravia a sharp distinction was made between Hutterites and Swiss Brethren, where the former were by far the larger group in number, but the latter nevertheless maintained themselves until at least 1618. The contest between the two groups was sharp also in other places. In Hesse (and elsewhere) Hutterite missioners did not hesitate to "raid" the Swiss Brethren congregations to secure converts for "the Church of God" in Moravia, as a document of 1587 (*TA Hessen*, 494) indicates. Hans Kuchenbecker, called a "Swiss Brethren minister" as late as 1587 (*TA Hessen*, 562), in 1578 insisted in a court hearing (*TA Hessen*, 393) that his group "was not in agreement with those in Bohemia; he and his people were Swiss Brethren." Kuchenbecker submitted an outstanding confession to the court in 1578 which the editor of the *TA Hessen* (404-40) published under the caption, "Confession of the Swiss Brethren." The Hutterite Chronicle consistently refers to Thomas von Imbroich (*q.v.*, executed in 1558) as a "Schweitzerbruder." The first known official use of the name "Swiss Brethren" is found in a decree of the government of Württemberg, issued at Stuttgart in 1559 (published in *TA Württemberg*, 194): "1559. Ducal decree concerning Schwenckfelders and Anabaptists, also other Sects. Item, what kind of a sect and brotherhood [the one is which is] called Swiss Brethren." The published record of the Frankenthal disputation (Heidelberg, 1571) speaks of three major groups among the Anabaptists, "the Hutterites," "the Mennonites," and "you," where "you" quite clearly means the Swiss Brethren who were apparently the leading group and therefore not in need of a label. The first documentary use of the name by the group itself is found in the title of its hymnal, the *Ausbund* (1564-83, 1602, and later), "Some Christian Songs as they were written and sung in the Castle Prison at Passau by the Swiss Brethren." The name "Swiss Brethren" is not a geographical designation, as is clear from the above instances of use. The Swiss Brethren in prison were Philippites en route from Moravia to South Germany. None of them had ever been in Switzerland. The name does, however, connote that this group was later counted as belonging to the Swiss Brethren.

The above usage seems to show that there were only three continuing groups of Anabaptists in the 16th century, the Mennonites of Holland and North Germany, the Hutterites of Moravia and Slovakia, and the Swiss Brethren of Switzerland and South and Middle Germany. Recently several scholars who have studied Marpeck and his work (Jan Kiwiet, William Klassen, Heinold Fast, and Torsten Bergsten) have concluded that there was a fourth major group, the Marpeck brotherhood, led by Marpeck (*q.v.*) and Scharnschlager (*q.v.*), in South Germany which differed somewhat from the Swiss Brethren, though its views were substantially the same, and which owed its origin more to Hans Hut than to the Zürich Swiss Brethren group. They lay much weight on the evidence found in the recently discovered *Kunstbuch* of 1561 (see **Rothenfelder** and **Marpeck**). Here the most striking evidence is supplied by the compiler and copyist, Maler or Rothenfelder, who not only heads two letters of 1541 and 1543 "Pilgrim Marpeck to the Swiss Brethren," but in a marginal note says, "Each church wants to have this power, takes the key, that is of the Holy Spirit, especially the Hutterites, the Swiss, the Bilgisch (= Pilgramites, from Pilgram Marpeck), etc., and no one group has peace with the others in God; each judges the others, and yet all come short in the judgment [of God]" (*Kunstbuch*, folio 42b). Hulshof (*Straatsburg*, 234) quotes from the Strasbourg archives a statement of Petrus Novesianus of *c*1555, which lists the religious groups of that time as "Papists, Zwinglians, Lutherans, Schwenckfelders, Anabaptists, and the latter as Hutterites, Hofmannites, Swiss, Bilgramites, Zabites, etc." And a complaint by certain ministers to the Strasbourg authorities in 1561 lists the Anabaptist groups in Strasbourg as Bilgerer (Pilgramites), Sattlerische (Swiss Brethren), and Gabrielites (*q.v.*).

Evidently the Pilgramites were a distinct group from the Swiss Brethren as late as 1561 (Maler), though Kiwiet holds that the Strasbourg Conference of 1555 united the differing groups. However, the Pilgramites must have been small and localized; the Swiss Brethren extended north as far as Cologne and Hesse. The Pilgramites left no continuing separate congregations, and may well have merged into the Swiss Brethren upon the death of Marpeck and the withdrawal of Scharnschlager to his retreat at Ilanz. The Swiss Brethren continued in the later Swiss, Alsatian, and Palatine Mennonites (including the Amish).

By the last quarter of the 17th century the name "High Germans" or "Upper Germans" was given to the Swiss Brethren, at least in some quarters. For instance, the reply of the Strasbourg Conference of 1592 to the Socinians (see **Strasbourg Conferences** and **Ostorodt**) has the title, *An Answer of the Swiss Brethren, also Called High Germans, to the Polish*, in the form in which it appears in the Dutch Mennonite publication of 1649 entitled *Handelinge der Vereenigde Vlaemse en Duytse Doopsgezinde Gemeynten*. The phrase "Swiss Brethren, also called High Germans" is not in the text of the document but was added by the Dutch editor, and therefore reflects Dutch usage. In the article *High Germans* (*ME* II, 739) van der Zijpp calls the Strasbourg Conferences of 1556 (1555) and 1559 (1557) "meetings of the High Germans." A note by Leenaert

Klock in the Concept of Cologne of 1591 says that this confession was approved by "the ministers and elders and congregations of the regions of Alsace, Breisgau, Strasbourg, Wittenberg [=Weissenburg], Landau, Neustadt, Landesheim, Worms, and Kreuznach," which congregations the beginning of the confession itself calls "High German" in the following words, "we, ministers, elders, and brethren of both sides, whom men have named with two kinds of names, Netherlandish or Frisian, and Upperlandish or High German." The original meaning of "High German" therefore was in effect the Swiss Brethren located in the Palatinate and Strasbourg or along the Upper Rhine.   H.S.B.

Swiss Brethren in Moravia. In Moravia all non-Hutterite Anabaptists were known as Swiss Brethren, hence the term includes such groups as the Philippites (q.v.). There were Swiss Brethren in Nikolsburg (q.v.), where there was a congregation, at Bergen, Polau, Wisternitz, and Voitelsbrunn, and some also in Passwitz, Urbau, Seletitz, and in the mountain town of Jamnitz. In the great persecution of 1535 many of the Swiss Brethren were expelled from Moravia and returned to their old homes in South Germany and Switzerland. A number (now known to have been Philippites) fell prisoner to the Bishop of Passau (q.v.), A number of Swiss Brethren of Jamnitz imprisoned in Passau were released upon the intervention of their baron and protector, Heinrich von Lomnic, through his burgrave in Passau, offering security for damages and payment of costs. When the persecution in Moravia had subsided somewhat, the Brethren again assembled in Polau, Muschau, Znaim, Tasswitz, and other places. The preacher of the Jamnitz congregation, Oswald Glait (q.v.), was drowned as a martyr at Vienna in 1545. About that time the Swiss Brethren gradually began to join the Hutterian Brethren. The first to do so was the preacher Hans Klöpfer (q.v.) at Polau, who united with the Hutterites at Schäckowitz with four other brethren in 1543. Nevertheless there were remnants of the Swiss Brethren congregations in Moravia as late as 1591 at Znaim; in a suburb of Eibenschitz they still had a small congregation in 1618. Erhard's list of sects in Moravia (1589) names Swiss Brethren and Pilgrim Brethren (Marpeckites?). A number of Swiss Brethren families migrated from Moravia to the Danzig area after 1600; a Schellenberger and a Schmidt fled to Przechovka as late as 1634.   HEGE, H.S.B.

Beck, Geschichts-Bücher, 152; G. Bossert, "Aus der nebenkirchlichen religiösen Bewegung der Reformationszeit in Württemberg," in Blätter für württembergische Geschichte XXXIII (1929) 8; ML IV.

Swiss German Dialects. There are many Swiss German dialects, e.g., Basler, Berner, Züricher. Each village and each Alpine valley has its own version. are certain distinctive sounds in the language, such as the guttural ch for k in addition to German ch; the ending li for lein, or a light v sound for l, especially in the Emmental. The Swiss dialects are Alemannic.

The Anabaptists survived the 16th century in only two areas of Switzerland; viz., around Zürich and in the Emmental east of Bern. When they emigrated to non-Germanic lands they retained their Swiss dialect; those who went to German-speaking lands adopted the German dialect of the region. In a single generation in the Palatinate the Zürich and Bernese Anabaptists had completely adopted the speech of the new land. The Emmental Mennonites who found refuge in the French-speaking Bishopric of Basel, in the French-speaking part of the Sundgau, and later in Ohio and Indiana, retained their Swiss dialect. In the Holee and Schänzli congregations in Basel the dialect is not used in services. In the remaining Swiss congregations the services have always been conducted in dialect. The Les Bulles and Pruntrut congregations are, however, changing to French. In the Emmental the current dialect is used. But also in the congregations in the Bernese Jura, whose members are descendants of expellees from the Emmental, the dialect has been almost perfectly preserved. In services the Scripture reading and hymns are in official (High) German, but addresses and prayers in dialect. In the Mennonite schools of the Jura an effort is made to retain the dialect. A drama, Barbara (Bern, 1948), by Heinrich Künzi, dealing with the Anabaptists in the period of persecution, is written in the Bernese dialect.

In Wayne and Putnam counties, Ohio, and in Berne, Ind., services were conducted in Bernese Swiss until well toward the close of the past century. Most of the churches changed from the dialect to standard German before changing to English. Today in the Swiss communities of Ohio and Indiana most persons over 30 years old can carry on at least a limited conversation in their Swiss dialect. The dialect as spoken here contains many old Bernese words nearly extinct in their homeland, and also many Anglicized terms hardly recognizable by either the Swiss or Americans.

The Swiss are proud of their dialects. In the Bern cantonal parliament the Bernese dialect is used. Early school instruction is given in the local dialect. Important dialect authors have been Rudolf von Tavel, Simon Gfeller, Albert Bächtold, and Johann Howald, who translated Matthew, Mark, Luke, and Acts into "Bärndütsch," giving the language a standard orthography and grammar.   D.L.G., S.G.

Swiss Mennonite Church (GCM) was organized Dec. 2, 1904, near Starkweather, N.D., with Christian Kauffman in charge. About 1910, when a number of families moved, the address of the church was changed to Alsen, N.D. The first meetings were then held in the Town Hall. The present meetinghouse was dedicated on Sept. 13, 1919, and is located in Alsen. This church is a member of the Northern District. The membership in 1957 was 79, with Leonard Harder as pastor.   D.G.R.

Swiss Mennonite Church (GCM), located near Whitewater, Kan., was organized by about ten families who left Emmental, canton of Bern, Switzerland, in 1883 and settled in Butler County, Kan. At first the Swiss worshiped in the Emmaus Mennonite Church (q.v.). Other Swiss Mennonites joined this group. Soon separate worship services were started, and in 1890 the Swiss Mennonite

Church joined the Western District Conference and in 1892 the General Conference. D. Gerber was the first minister. In 1921-26 John Roth was the leader. In 1929 the membership was 62 and the Sunday-school attendance 180. Theodore Roth was the leading minister 1930-55. Since 1955 Dan H. Dalke has been the pastor. In 1957 the group had a membership of 141. The change from the German language to the English took place in recent years. After World War II the congregation built a new meetinghouse. **C.K.**

Delbert Gratz, *Bernese Anabaptists* (Scottdale, 1953) 157; *Western District Conference Reports 1890-1957.*

Swiss Mennonites in the Netherlands. During the 16th and early 17th centuries there was hardly any contact between the Dutch and the Swiss Mennonites. About 1640, when the Dutch Mennonites became aware of the bad conditions of the Mennonites in Zürich, Switzerland (see **Hattavier**), and soon after, of the persecutions in the canton of Bern, they tried both directly through one of their members, Adolph de Vreede (*q.v.*), who visited Bern, and especially by the intervention of the Netherlands States-General (*q.v.,* see **François Fagel**) to support their Swiss brethren and to ameliorate their lot. This intervention, however, had only slight effect, and particularly in the canton of Bern conditions gradually grew worse. Bernese authorities had resolved to remove all the Mennonites from their territory because of their refusal to do military service and to unite with the state church. On March 18, 1710, a shipload of Bernese Mennonites who were to be forcibly transported to the English colonies in North America were released by order of the Dutch government when they arrived at Nijmegen (*q.v.*) in the Netherlands. Nearly all of them returned to the Palatinate (*q.v.*), Germany. A small number of Swiss Mennonites seem to have emigrated to the Netherlands as early as 1660, settling in the province of Groningen; Swiss Brethren from the Palatinate are also reported to have settled near the city of Groningen. The Dutch Mennonites, whose delegates had set up a committee for the relief of foreign Mennonites in February 1660 (see **Fonds voor Buitenlandsche Nooden**) and who upon the initiative of Jan van Ranst (*q.v.*) of Rotterdam had made a proposal in 1671 to help the oppressed Mennonites in Switzerland by bringing them all to the Netherlands and settling them there at the expense of the Dutch Mennonites, began a major relief undertaking in 1711, when many Mennonites had to leave Switzerland. Johann Ludwig Runckel (*q.v.*), the "resident" (i.e., ambassador) of the Netherlands in Switzerland, made contact with the Dutch government and the Dutch Mennonites and after much negotiation with the Bernese authorities organized the emigration to the Netherlands. Runckel faced many difficulties. The Bernese Mennonites had just rejected the invitation of King Frederick I to settle in Prussia because they did not like to leave their native country, in spite of all persecution and misery. Also the controversy between the Amish (*q.v.*) and Reist (*q.v.*) groups was unfavorable to the success of the emigration, for often the Reist group refused to sail in the same ships with the

Amish. Besides all this, many Mennonites in the canton of Bern had gone into hiding, although a mandate of amnesty had been proclaimed by the government of Bern. Finally 363 persons, including some non-Mennonites, were more or less voluntarily loaded into four ships and sailed from Basel on July 18, 1711. At Breisach, Germany, thirteen Mennonites left the ships. The others arrived at Amsterdam on Aug. 3, where they were warmly welcomed by the Dutch Mennonites, who attended to their many wants. Provided with many things (including an amazing quantity of hooks and eyes!), they were divided into four groups, and sailed on Aug. 20 from Amsterdam to Harlingen in Friesland (21 persons), to Groningen (126), to Kampen (87), and to Deventer (116). A few remained in Amsterdam. Some of these immigrants were penniless; others had brought their money, even considerable amounts. Some were craftsmen, others farmers. The craftsmen were directed to Groningen and Deventer; the farmers obtained farms near Kampen, Groningen, and Sappemeer. Both the craftsmen and the farmers received ample support from the Dutch Committee. At Groningen Elder Alle Derks (*q.v.*) was very active in behalf of the refugees; at Deventer Steven Cremer (*q.v.*) aided them.

The Swiss emigrant group which was conducted to Harlingen were followers of Hans Reist (all the others were Amish). Only a few stayed at Harlingen; most obtained farms near Gorredijk in Friesland, but they did not feel at home here; in May 1712, with the aid of the Dutch Committee they were settled amidst their coreligionists near Kampen. But because of objection to the Amish views most of them moved to the Palatinate in the next year.

In the following years most of the group which was located at Deventer moved to Kampen or to Groningen and Sappemeer, some emigrated to the Palatinate, and a few soon joined the Deventer Old Flemish Mennonite church. There was no Swiss Mennonite congregation at Deventer as there was at Kampen and at Groningen and Sappemeer.

The Kampen group used the Swiss German language for two or three decades, and then adopted the Dutch in its services. Elders of this group were Daniel Ricken 1712-36, Peter Teune 1736-63, Jacob Stähly 1736-57, Hans Hupster 1769-92, and finally a Dutch Mennonite, Jan Hans Hoosen 1805-22. In 1822 their congregation merged with the Dutch Mennonite church at Kampen.

That there were serious difficulties in the Swiss Amish group (which congregation is not clear) in the Netherlands, so serious as to cause a suspension of all communion, baptism, marriages, and ordinations for at least six years, is revealed by a letter written by Johannes Nafziger, an Amish bishop of Essingen near Landau in the Palatinate in 1781. Nafziger tells of three successive committees of Amish ministers from the Palatinate and Alsace sent to Holland in 1766, 1767(?), and 1770 to settle the dispute and supervise the congregation there, which they successfully did. The letter is published in *MQR* II (1928) 198-204.

The Groningen-Sappemeer group, which was

augmented in the following years by the arrival of some new immigrants from Bern, worshiped both in the town of Groningen and near Sappemeer. Their first elder was Hans Anken (*q.v.*), who seems to have served both in Groningen and Sappemeer as did his successors until about 1760. About 1720 a schism arose among these Swiss Brethren, dividing them into the Oude Zwitsers (Old Swiss) and Nieuwe Zwitsers (New Swiss). The cause of this schism is said to have been the purchase of a house by Elder Anken, which a part of his congregation, composed of very plain people, considered too sumptuous and too worldly. The Oude Zwitsers were the more conservative group, not only in dress, but also in maintaining their native tongue. Their church services also differed from those of the New Swiss, who soon adapted themselves to the Dutch way of living and worshiping, using the Dutch language by about 1750. In the Old Swiss services, after the preacher had finished his sermon other brethren spoke to express their agreement with the sermon or to add a few words from the Bible. They knelt for (silent) prayer and practiced footwashing in their communion services. They had no special confession of faith; the German *Ausbund* was their hymnal.

Both at Groningen (about 1720 in a house "Achter de Muur") and in Sappemeer (in a house on the Kleinemeer) the Swiss Brethren had meetinghouses, which were used in turn both by the Old and the New Swiss. Gradually the ties between the members living in and near Groningen and those in Sappemeer relaxed. In Groningen the Old and New Swiss merged about 1780. Here the Swiss congregation bought the former Waterlander meetinghouse in the Pelsterstraat in 1815. After the death of their last preacher, Christiaan Jacobs Leutscher, who served 1812-d.24, the Swiss congregation merged with the Dutch Mennonite congregation of Groningen.

At Sappemeer the Oude Zwitsers and Nieuwe Zwitsers seem to have merged about 1790. In the meantime some Old Swiss had joined the Sappemeer Old Flemish church, whereas many New Swiss joined the Waterlander congregation. The (united) Swiss congregation of Sappemeer merged with the main Dutch congregation before 1802.

Preachers and elders of the Groningen-Sappemeer Swiss groups (as far as the lists are complete and reliable) were as follows:

New Swiss: Hans Anken, elder 1712-?, Michael Ruysser (Riszer) 1711-59, elder after the death of Anken, Peter Leenders 1711-57, Jan van Ko(o)men, d. 1743, Anthony Kratzer 1740-79, elder 1760, Christiaan Ancken 1754-70, Jan Leenders 1754-59(?), Rudolf Leutscher 1755-61. Then the Groningen New Swiss group was led by Balster Franssen (Wolkammer) 1762-82, Hendrik Cornelis 1768-1808, elder 1794, Rudolf (or Roelof) Jans 1781-d.90, Izaak Jannes Leutscher (1740-1826) 1799, elder 1811, David Jacob de Goed 1811-13, and Christiaan Jacobs Leutscher (1812-24). The last leaders of the Sappemeer group were Isaak van Kalkar (Calcar) 1772-96, Alle Cornelis 1791-1800, and Ties Hansen Top 1791-97. Old Swiss: Abraham Loover (Lauffer), d. 1774, living near Groningen, elder 1726,

Claus Gerber 1739-61, Peter Riegen (Ricken) 1740-72. Jacob Stehle (Stähly), the elder of the Kampen Swiss Mennonite group, also seems to have served the Groningen-Sappemeer group 1736-57. David Righen (d. 1796), preacher 1767, elder 1774, was the last elder of this group.

The Swiss Mennonites in the Netherlands, who at first lived and worshiped rather separately from their Dutch coreligionists both because of their language and their particular views and practices, gradually adjusted themselves to the Dutch Mennonite practices. But not all. A number of them, particularly members of the Kraster (Krätzer), Rijkens (Rich, Ricken), and Stuckje (Stucky) families, joined the Reformed Church in the late 18th and the 19th centuries.

Many descendants of these Swiss Mennonites are still found among the Dutch Mennonites everywhere; particularly the names of Meihuizen (Maihuser), Boer, Rijkens (Rich, Ricken), and Teune.

After 1717 a number of Swiss emigrants moved from the Netherlands to America, receiving financial support from the Dutch Mennonites. (See **Groningen, Kampen, Sappemeer**.) vDZ.

Of the hundreds of letters, documents, and records concerning the Swiss Mennonites found in the Amsterdam Archives, only the most important items are mentioned here:

Inv. Arch. Amst. I, Nos. 1009 f., 1060, 1065, 1151, 1196, 1210-12, 1216, 1225, 1392, 1746 f., 1757-83; 1866-68, 1881; II, 2, Nos. 50 b. 866; J. Huizinga, *Stamboek of Geslachtsregister der Nakomelingen van Samuel Peter (Meihuizen) en Barbara Fry* (Groningen, 1890) I, 1-143; Müller, *Berner Täufer,* 158 f., 164-94, 257-328; Delbert L. Gratz, *Bernese Anabaptists* (Scottdale, 1953) 56-66; H. Dassel Sr, *Menno's Volk in Groningen* (Groningen, n.d.) 21 f., 39-42; M. G. de Boer, "Vom Thunersee zum Sappemeer," in *Berner Zeitschrift f. Gesch. und Heimatkunde,* 1947-I, repr.; *Naamlijst; DB* 1869, 7-11; 1881, 103 f.; 1908, 85-105; 1909, 127-55.

Switzerland, a mountainous country in the center of Europe, area 15,940 square miles, population 4,700,297, with eternally snow-covered Alpine ranges in the southern part, and the blue Jura Mountains in the northwest which extend from Geneva to Basel. Between the Alps and the Jura is the great Swiss plateau, which extends about 240 miles from Geneva to Lake Constance, a rolling terrain broken by smaller plains. Switzerland is a confederation of 22 cantons based on the principles of freedom of the old confederacy. Since the adoption of the new federal constitution in 1848 and its extension in 1874 the nation has become a strongly knit confederacy.

This mountainous land, whose inhabitants loved liberty and were for the most part earnestly religious, is the land of the birth of the Anabaptist movement and the homeland of innumerable refugee and emigrant Anabaptists or Mennonites. In the history of Anabaptism the early decades of the 16th century were of decisive significance. Of all the Anabaptist brotherhoods in Europe at the time of the Reformation, it is generally agreed that the group at Zürich was the first to constitute itself as a brotherhood alongside the prevailing church. The leaders were Conrad Grebel (*q.v.*), Felix Manz (*q.v.*), and George Blaurock (*q.v.*). These men were the friends of Zwingli in the beginning of the Reformation. But as soon as he sponsored the estab-

MENNONITE CONGREGATIONS IN

SWITZERLAND

Cities having Mennonite congregations are underlined
Langnau
For detailed map of canton Bern, see Vol. I, 288.

Scale of Miles

0   5   10   20   30   40

ITALY

AUSTRIA

GERMANY

BAVARIA

VORARLBERG

TYROL

GRISONS (GRAUBÜNDEN)

LIECHTENSTEIN

Bregenz

Maienfeld

Chur

WÜRTTEMBERG

Überlingen

LAKE CONSTANCE

Constance

St. Gall
Appenzell
APPENZELL

ST. GALL

Ilanz

RHINE

THURGAU

SCHAFFHAUSEN
Schleitheim   SCHAFFHAUSEN
Hallau   Schaffhausen
Waldshut

ZURICH

Zurich
Grüningen

Horgen   LAKE ZURICH   LAKE ZUG

LAKE LUCERNE

S W I T Z E R L A N D

Lugano

LAKE LUGANO

Locarno

LAKE MAGGIORE

BADEN

Schopfheim

RHINE

AARGAU

Aarau
Zofingen

BASEL

SOLOTHURN

Solothurn

LUCERNE

Lucerne

Interlaken   Grindelwald

LAKE BRIENZ

Thun   LAKE THUN

RHINE

Zermatt

RHINE

Bienenberg
Liestal
Basel

BERN

Langnau

Bern

Krembach

BERN

ITALY

Mulhouse

ALSACE   Altkirch

Belfort

Montbéliard

BERN

Porrentruy
Courgenay

Tramelan

Biel   LAKE BIEL

La Chaux-de-Fonds

Neuchâtel   LAKE NEUCHÂTEL

F R A N C E

Lausanne

LAKE GENEVA

St. Genis   Geneva

RHONE

RHONE

RHINE

F R A N C E

lishment of a state church, and placed the religious leadership in the hands of the temporal government, they broke with him.

The strict Biblicism of the Zürich Brethren was also soon apparent in their adoption of the baptism of believers and the rejection of infant baptism. In a solemn hour on Jan. 21, 1525, they openly confessed and confirmed their experience of salvation in baptism, although a few days before (Jan. 18) the baptism of infants had been made obligatory by the city council. This was actually the founding of the first Anabaptist congregation. With fiery zeal they promoted the truth they recognized; recognition led to confession, with the result that the movement expanded to such an extent that in a short time there were thriving congregations not only in such Swiss towns as Zürich, St. Gall, Bern, and Basel, but far beyond the Swiss borders, in the Tyrol and South Germany, and adjoining German-speaking lands.

But the consequence was not only a great revival, but also the great tragedy in the history of the Anabaptist movement in the cruel persecution throughout Europe, which lasted more than two centuries in Switzerland. Zürich was first to adopt a policy of violent suppression under the influence of Zwingli. A large number of mandates (q.v.) were issued in the Swiss cities named above for the extermination of the movement. But when no other measures sufficed to crush the movement, the death penalty was adopted. The first death sentence of the new Protestant state church—which had only a short time before been in a severe battle for freedom of religion and conscience—was carried out on Felix Manz in Zürich on Jan. 5, 1527. From then on, we find the Swiss confederacy in a constant struggle with the Anabaptist movement.

The Anabaptist problem was discussed as a federal issue in 1527. On Tuesday, Aug. 2, "the mayor, council and great council of the city of Zürich" sent an invitation to Bern, Basel, Schaffhausen, Chur, Appenzell, and St. Gall to meet in conference in Zürich on account of the Anabaptists, who were steadily increasing in spite of mild and also severe punishment. It was their opinion "that such sect and sinning should not be tolerated within or without our confederacy, since their intent is to destroy not only the true, right, inward faith of Christian hearts, but also external and human order and laws of Christian and orderly government, contrary to brotherly love and good morals." In order to preserve the common Christian peace and to serve the fatherland, the Zürich council proposed that the Protestant estates send a delegation to Zürich on Aug. 12-14 to discuss the matter of punishing seditious Anabaptists.

An agreement (Concordat) was reached by the assembled cantons and a strict mandate issued against the Anabaptists. The document contains first a thorough justification of the mandate. Besides the "eternal and saving Word of God" the "sect and separation" of the Anabaptists had made itself felt, which, to be sure, seeks to defend its principles from the Bible. But it was clear that Anabaptism could not exist according to the Word of God, but must be rejected, and infant baptism be recognized, which had heretofore been practiced generally in Christendom and which is in accord with the Word of God.

Nevertheless the Swiss Brethren continued to increase in Switzerland. At the sessions of the federal parliament in Baden in January 1530, the Anabaptist question was again under discussion. The Protestant towns, Zürich, Bern, Basel, St. Gall, and Constance, united to adopt a common policy against the Anabaptists, because the "confused, miserable sect of the Anabaptists with their rabble and their doctrine are becoming everywhere more numerous and more dangerous, whereby in all true Christian faith great defection and division, much misery, shedding of blood and unrest results."

Much misery and shedding of blood did indeed result from it, but not because of the faith of the Swiss Brethren, but because of the intolerant attitude of the government. It was actually the Protestant estates who insisted on it under the influence of the clergy. The Protestant cantons were very serious in their threat of making Anabaptism a capital crime. The bloody drama begun with Felix Manz in Zürich was continued in other Swiss cities. The Martyrs' Mirror names forty martyrs in Bern alone in 1529-71.

In the course of time there were frequent negotiations between the various cantons concerning the Anabaptists. On July 4, 1585, a conference between the city council of Bern and Zürich was held in Aarau, at which it was decided that those who clung to their faith after friendly instruction should be arrested and led out of the country. A resolution of June 15, 1660, repeated this order of expulsion. But love of country brought many an exile back to the homeland.

This policy of a "Christian government" toward its subjects in the hope of preserving unity of the church, practiced throughout the 16th-18th centuries, did not succeed in wiping out Anabaptism.

There is a vast amount of source material on the faith and life of the Swiss Brethren in the Reformation period. The basic principles are best found in the records of the Zofingen (q.v.) disputation, July 1-9, 1532, and the debate (Täufergespräch) in Bern, March 11-17, 1538. Their doctrines agree exactly with the seven articles of the Schleitheim (q.v.) Confession of 1527. The center of the entire movement lay in the attempt to build their congregational life on the original sources of the Christian church. Their inner and outer life they sought to conform to the teaching of Christ, especially the Sermon on the Mount, and the apostolic teaching of salvation. They defended complete freedom of faith and conscience, the requirement of discipleship, rejection of the oath, and nonresistance, since the Christian should never take revenge, but always practice the love of one's enemy. To realize this New Testament, apostolic church, the first Anabaptists suffered severely. In this bitter contest they were, to be sure, defeated; it remained their only lot to endure injustice.

The causes of the Mennonite emigration from Switzerland were (1) persecution; (2) the military question or nonresistance; (3) an unfavorable economic situation and the restriction of opportunity for development. The large number of emigrations from Switzerland were in general not voluntary withdrawals, but rather expulsions from the country. To expel foreigners on account of religious propaganda in conflict with the state church might be understood; but to banish native citizens, quiet, obedient subjects on account of religious matters is today considered an impossibly severe punishment. Many Mennonites had to emigrate from the cantons of Bern and Zürich involuntarily, especially in the second period of the Zürich Anabaptist movement, the beginning of the 17th century. This wave of emigration removed the last of the Mennonites from the canton of Zürich by about 1700.

The first place of refuge where toleration for extra-church religious movements was found was Moravia. In the south of this margraviate, in the region of Nikolsburg, many Swiss Anabaptists settled. Balthasar Hubmaier (*q.v.*) was one of the first arrivals from Switzerland (1526). Here the Anabaptists were permitted to organize according to their principles, at least for a time. The Swiss Brethren formed an independent branch of the Moravian Anabaptists. At Jamnitz (*q.v.*) and other localities congregations of considerable size gathered. Immigrants from St. Gall and Appenzell joined these congregations.

From Moravia a number of Anabaptist emissaries undertook their dangerous missionary journeys to Switzerland, "to gather the lambs of the Lord." Three of these missionaries were captured in Zurzach (Aargau) in 1582 and executed in the town of Baden. Bern tried to stop the emigration to Moravia, fearing the loss of a large number of its subjects. It seems, however, that this missionary work was successful. The chronicles of the Hutterian Brethren report, "In this year, 1585, so many people came from Switzerland that they could not all be received; but a good part of them were received." And further, "In this 86th year several hundred Swiss came here to the brotherhood . . . who desired to adjust themselves in the faith."

A second major refuge was the Palatinate, especially in the 17th and 18th centuries. The large number of Mennonite family names of Swiss origin now in the Palatinate points to an extensive spread of Anabaptism through the immigration of Swiss Brethren. About 700 persons moved from the canton of Bern to the Palatinate in 1671 and arrived there in the most impoverished condition. The very first arrivals came as early as 1655.

Another place of refuge was the Netherlands (see **Swiss Mennonites in Holland**). The Dutch Mennonites had most generously sympathized with their oppressed brethren. This matter was discussed at the general synod of the Mennonites in Amsterdam on Nov. 5, 1670. The forcible deportation of the Mennonites to the East Indies or to America was thwarted by Dutch intervention. Some Swiss Brethren settled in Holland.

Numerous traces of Swiss emigration are found in Alsace-Lorraine and France. The fact that there are no Mennonites in the interior of France indicates immigration. The almost exclusively Bernese names substantiate their Bernese origin. In 1671-1711 there was a large settlement of Bernese Men-

nonites in Upper Alsace, in the Vosges and the French Jura (Doubs). In the Montbéliard area Count Leopold Eberhard put Mennonites in charge of his estates. These Mennonites thrived.

The later goal of emigrating Swiss Mennonites has been chiefly the United States. There were some Swiss Mennonites among the first Palatine Mennonite immigrants to Pennsylvania in the early 18th century. The emigration of Bernese Mennonites to America was very heavy in the first half of the 19th century. The Mennonites of Pennsylvania are of Swiss origin, nearly all from the canton of Bern, but some from Zürich. Emigration from the Emmental and the Jura was also very strong in 1830-80. These Mennonites settled chiefly in Ohio, Indiana, and Ontario. A glance over the entire emigrant complex of Swiss Mennonites shows that many Mennonites in other lands are related by spiritual as well as blood ties to those of Switzerland.

Concerning the economic conditions of the Swiss Mennonites in the 16th-17th centuries there is little information. Living conditions even after the passing of persecution were extremely simple. These people were very modest in their demands and cultivated a quiet family life, regarding work as a God-given task. In spite of innumerable difficulties the Mennonites have pioneered in new methods of agriculture, which was their principal occupation. In the agricultural history of Switzerland and other adoptive lands the Swiss Mennonites occupy an outstanding place, which has been recognized by objective specialists. An unusual understanding of cattle raising and dairying can be found among the Swiss Mennonites.

Although large blocks of Swiss Mennonites have taken root and contributed to the growth of Mennonitism elsewhere, there has remained in Switzerland a remnant of Mennonite families, who call themselves the "Altevangelische taufgesinnte Gemeinde." The congregations are distributed as follows: Basel-Schänzli (*q.v.*), with a meetinghouse since 1903; west of it close to the French border, Grand Lucelle (*q.v.*), to which belong the Mennonites living on the lonely scattered farms as far as Delsberg. In the extreme north of the Bernese Jura lies Kleintal (*q.v.*), with its center in the Moron chapel, built in 1893, and a meetinghouse in Perceux since 1921 above the cave in the mountain known as the Geisskirchlein, where tradition says the Mennonites used to hold their services during persecution. One of the largest congregations is Sonnenberg (*q.v.*), southwest of Perceux, with its chapel Jeangisboden, built in 1900, and two other meetinghouses at Fürstenberg and Les Mottes. To the south, opposite the Chasseral chain, is the smallest congregation, Mont Cortébert of Cortébert-Matte. On the high plateau of the Jura is the Chaux d'Abel (*q.v.*) congregation, with a school erected in 1863, the gift of David Ummel to the congregation (burned down and rebuilt in 1917). The large chapel built in 1905 belongs to the young people's association, of which several Mennonites are members. Some of the Mennonites on Mt. Chaux d'Abel or Sonvilierberg meet in a hall in the home of the Jungen family. The canton of Neuchatel has only the Chaux de Fonds congregation. Its chapel was built in 1894 outside the town of Les Bulles. The former Locle-Bressels (*q.v.*) congregation is merged with Chaux de Fonds.

The most widely ramified and one of the largest congregations in Switzerland is the Emmental (*q.v.*) congregation with its seat at Langnau, where its organ, *Der Zionspilger,* is published. In Kehr near Langnau stands the first Mennonite chapel built in Switzerland. It was erected in 1888, and was followed by one at Bomatt a.d. Emme and one at Aebnit near Bowil in 1899. Subsidiaries of the Emmental congregation are found at Emmenholz near Solothurn and Pay de Gex (*q.v.*) near Geneva, which was founded early in the present century by Abraham Geiser.

All of these congregations are united into a conference, whose total membership varies from 1800 to 2,000 souls. The Basel congregation with a chapel on Holeestrasse belongs to the Alsatian conference. (See articles on all the Swiss cantons for detailed accounts, e.g. **Bern**).

From 1946 to 1952 the MCC maintained its European headquarters at Basel, and since then has continued to have an office there, including the Agape Verlag established in 1954. In 1951 the European Mennonite Bible School was established in Basel, moved in 1957 to Bienenberg near Liestal, some 10 miles inland. Basel has become the center of international Mennonite exchange and fellowship for Swiss, French, and South German Mennonites. In 1952 the Fifth Mennonite World Conference was held at St. Chrischona, near Basel.

S.G.

E. Egli, *Aktensammlung zur Gesch. der Züricher Reformation* (Zürich, 1879); *Ein Wahrhafftiger Bericht von den Brüdern im Schweizerland in dem Zürcher Gebiet, von dem 1635sten bis in das 1645ste Jahr,* a printed booklet found in the Central Library at Zürich and printed as an appendix to all American editions of the *Ausbund;* Wolkan, *Geschicht-Buch;* Müller, *Berner Täufer;* S. Geiser, *Die Taufgesinnten-Gemeinden* (Karlsruhe, 1931); E. H. Correll, *Das Schweizerische Täufermennonitentum* (Tübingen, 1925); D. L. Gratz, *Bernese Anabaptists and Their American Descendants* (Scottdale, 1953); H. S. Burrage, *A History of the Anabaptists in Switzerland* (Philadelphia, 1882); R. Nitsche, *Geschichte der Wiedertäufer in der Schweiz* (Einsiedeln, 1885); L. von Muralt, *Glaube und Leben der schweizerischen Täufer in der Reformationszeit* (Zürich, 1938); G. Thormann, *Probierstein oder . . . Prüfung des Täuffertums* (Bern, 1693); R. Friedmann, *Mennonite Piety Through the Centuries* (Goshen, 1949); Paul Peachey, *Die soziale Herkunft der Schweizer Täufer* (Karlsruhe, 1954); TA Zürich; ML IV.

Sword and Trumpet, The, a 24-page (plus cover) 8 x 11 quarterly published by a group of interested Mennonites (MC) in Virginia (largely Denbigh, Fentress, and Harrisonburg), first issue January 1929. It announced itself on the masthead as "Devoted to the Defense of a Full Gospel, With Especial Emphasis upon Neglected Truths, and to an Active Opposition of the Various Forms of Error that Contribute to the Religious Drift of the Times," and described itself as "a faith-defending drift-opposing religious quarterly, published under the sanction of the Virginia Conference, . . . intended to supplement every other loyal paper in the Church and supplant none, . . . to be an unmistakable and uncompromising expression of Mennonite Conservatism." Its founder and editor-in-chief until his

death in 1938 was Bishop George R. Brunk of Denbigh, with Ernest G. Gehman of Harrisonburg as office editor, and J. L. Stauffer of Harrisonburg as associate editor from January 1934. Upon Brunk's death publication ceased. It was revived in smaller format (6 x 9), at first 50 pp., then 40 pp., in October 1943, with J. Irvin Lehman as editor (to 1953) and George R. Brunk, Jr., as associate editor. J. Ward Shank has served as editor since January 1954. Ernest G. Gehman has continued without interruption as office editor.

The character of the journal, as stamped upon it by its first editor, has been generally well maintained, although some of its earlier polemic character has been softened. Its chief concerns have been to resist Calvinism (eternal security), Modernism, and popular Fundamentalism, and to support a strong conservative position in church teaching, practice, and discipline. Its circulation in 1959 was *c* 2,000.

H.S.B.

Sybout (Sybrant) Obbes, an Anabaptist martyr, beheaded on Oct. 21, 1536, at Leeuwarden in Friesland, Netherlands. He was baptized in the winter of 1534. When seized because of heresy he recanted, but soon he "again adhered to the sect of the Anabaptists." Caught again he was sentenced to death.

vDZ.

J. Reitsma, *Honderd jaren uit de Geschiedenis der Hervorming . . . in Friesland* (Leeuwarden, 1876) 63.

Sybrandi, a Dutch Mennonite family. (1) Sybren (Sybrand) Sybrandi, b. 1772 at Leeuwarden, d. June 17, 1854, at Haarlem, was educated for the ministry at the Amsterdam Mennonite seminary 1801-5 and served the congregation of Nijmegen 1805-7 and Haarlem 1807-49, in which year he retired. In 1818-45 he was a trustee (1827-28 and 1839-40 moderator) of the A.D.S. (*q.v.*) and during the same period curator of its seminary.

His son (2) Klaas Sybrandi, b. Nov. 18, 1807, at Haarlem, d. there Sept. 5, 1872, was also trained at the Amsterdam seminary and then served as pastor at Nijmegen 1830-34, Groningen 1834-38, and Haarlem 1838-71; then he retired because of illness. He succeeded his father as a delegate in the A.D.S. and curator of the seminary 1845-72, serving as A.D.S. president 1849-50 and 1857-58. Pastor Klaas Sybrandi was a man of great learning. In 1829 he obtained his Ph.D. degree at the University of Leiden with a dissertation on *Plato's Gorgias.* He devoted himself particularly to the study of Greek and Dutch literature, publishing a number of literary studies. Besides these he published many devotional contributions in periodicals, some sermons, and a historical paper in the *Doopsgezinde Bijdragen* of 1867. For many years he was a trustee of the Teyler (*q.v.*) Theological Association at Haarlem. C. Sepp wrote his obituary.

Another son of (1) Sybren Sybrandi was (3) Jacob Sybrandi, b. 1818, at Haarlem, d. Dec. 26, 1895, at Kampen, who after his training at Amsterdam was a Mennonite pastor of Beemster 1844-51 and Kampen 1851-95.

vDZ.

C. Sepp, "Levensbericht" in *Levensberichten van de Maatschappij voor Ned. Letterkunde,* 1873; N.N.B.Wb. IV, 1291 f.; *DB* 1867, 159 ff.; 1873, 193; 1896, 204; 1904, 73.

Sycamore Grove Mennonite Church (MC), located 4 miles northwest of Garden City, Cass Co., Mo., a member of the South Central Conference, was organized in 1868 by Bishop Jacob Kenagy. It was known as the Clearfork Church until 1883, when the present name was adopted. Sunday school was begun in 1871. It was an Amish Mennonite church and a member of the Western A.M. Conference. All services were conducted in German until 1896. In 1885 the Bethel Mennonite Church (*q.v.*) was organized as a more progressive English language group. In 1947, when Bethel was dissolved, the members joined the Sycamore Grove congregation. Missionaries sent out by this congregation were Nellie King and S. Paul Miller. The membership in 1957 was 223, with James D. Yoder as minister.

R.Z.

Symon Fijts, a Mennonite preacher and elder at Texel, an island in the Dutch province of North Holland, in 1569. He visited the martyrs Tijs Juriaensz (*q.v.*), a preacher, and Jan Claesz of Muiden (*q.v.*) in prison and was present at their execution. He was a personal friend of Jan Smit (*q.v.*), who was hanged by the Spaniards in 1572 at Haarlem. He furnished valuable material concerning these martyrs to the editors of the martyrbook, *Historie der warachtighe getuygen Jesu Christi* (1617), which van Braght used in his *Martyrs' Mirror.* (*DB* 1873, 141; 1899, 104, 120; *Mart. Mir.* D 481, 641, E 823, 962; *ML* I, 644.)

K.V., vDZ.

Symon Sieurdtszoon, apparently one of the Anabaptists participating in the assault on the Oldeklooster (*q.v.*), was executed at Leeuwarden in Friesland, Netherlands, on April 10, 1535. (K. Vos, *Menno Simons,* Leiden, 1914, p. 228.)

vDZ.

Symon Symonsz, an Anabaptist martyr, was beheaded on March 17, 1537, at Leeuwarden in Friesland, Netherlands. He was charged with having been rebaptized, "accepting the covenant (*verbond*) of the Anabaptists." He rejected the Mass and spoke disrespectfully of the Catholic Church. His property was confiscated. His place of residence is not stated. The sentence is published in *DB* 1917, 89 f.

vDZ.

Syntgen: see **Sijntgen.**

Syouck Haeyes, a citizen of Leeuwarden in Friesland, Netherlands, was present with Frans Cuyper (*q.v.*) when Menno Simons preached in a field near Leeuwarden in 1542. On Nov. 14, 1542, Syouck was sentenced to banishment from the territory of Leeuwarden. Syouck was probably not a Mennonite. (K. Vos, *Menno Simons,* Leiden, 1914, p. 67, 92, 231.)

vDZ.

Syoucke Metselair, an Anabaptist who had participated in the attack on the Oldeklooster (*q.v.*), was executed at Leeuwarden in Friesland, Netherlands, on April 10, 1535. (K. Vos, *Menno Simons,* Leiden, 1914, p. 228.)

vDZ.

Sytze (Zijtze) **Dirks,** an Anabaptist martyr, was sentenced to death by the Court of Holland on May 16, 1535. He was a native of Gauw, Friesland. In March 1534 he had joined the Anabaptists who sailed from Amsterdam intending to go to Münster (*q.v.*). At Bergklooster (*q.v.*) he was arrested. Sytze is said to have been an Anabaptist preacher. (*Inv. Arch. Amst.* I, No. 745; *DB* 1917, 121, No. 148.)

vDZ.

Syria, including Lebanon, which is now a separate political unit, is a land of historic importance on the eastern coast of the Mediterranean Sea. Damascus, its ancient capital, and Antioch were centers for the beginning and spread of Gentile Christianity. Judaism, Christianity, and Mohammedanism have been the three predominant religions. In modern times both Roman Catholicism and Protestantism have been active in missionary attempts to revive the old churches. Mennonites have been related to this area through the work of the United Orphanage and Mission (*q.v.*), which was begun in 1898 by the Mennonite Brethren in Christ among Armenians at Hadjin, Turkey (*q.v.*), and Near East Relief. During World War I missionaries were forced to leave Turkey; thousands of Armenians lost their lives, while the remainder fled or were deported. Refugee camps were set up in Damascus, Aleppo, and Beirut, from which Armenians were gradually settled in the cities of Syria. To serve these people the United Orphanage and Mission Society returned missionaries for work in Syria. A staff of four to six was maintained in 1923-38; World War II again stopped operations. During this period relief and missionary work was carried on in association with the Spiritual Brotherhood, a group of Armenian Christians under the leadership of Abraham Sefarian. Churches were started in six cities, Alexandretta, Damascus, Kirik Khan, Latakie, Aleppo, and Beirut, with a membership eventually of one thousand. On the departure of the missionaries in 1938 the churches continued independent work. In 1957 the United Missionary Church (formerly MBC) again sent three missionaries to assist in the indigenous work being carried on by Samuel Doctorian in Beirut.

In 1919-21, the Mennonite (MC) Relief Commission for War Sufferers (*q.v.*) co-operated with the Near East Relief (*q.v.*), which had been organized in November 1915, in relief work in Syria, with workers serving at Beirut, Aleppo, Mardin, and other places. (See **Relief Work.**)

In 1957 Menno Travel Service (*q.v.*) opened a Near East office at Beirut, Lebanon.

S.F.P.

Storms, *What Hath God Wrought* (Springfield, Ohio, 1948); *Our Bi-Monthly Letter,* representing the United Missionary Society Operating in Syria.

Syvert Clercq (Stewerdus Clericus) was a Dutch Anabaptist, at first a follower of Melchior Hofmann (*q.v.*), later a Münsterite (see **Münster**). According to the confession of Jan van Batenburg (1537) he was an influential leader, but there is no information concerning his activities. In 1536 he attended the Anabaptist leaders' meeting at Bocholt (*q.v.*) in Westphalia, Germany. (*DB* 1917, 117, No. 81, 120, No. 121; 1919, 193; Mellink, *Wederdopers,* 251 f.)

vDZ.

Tabor Academy began its operations with the opening of Tabor College (*q.v.*), Hillsboro, Kan., in 1908, and was operated under the Tabor College Corporation, which was granted its charter by the State on March 19, 1908. The curriculum provided a standard high-school education with a heavy emphasis on Bible. In its early years it also provided the normal training course for students preparing to teach.

During the early years of the Corporation, the academy dominated the program almost completely. The first-year enrollment of 78 steadily increased until it reached 176 in 1920. From 1916 to 1927 the average was 141. In 1926 the college enrollment surpassed the academy and from that time the academy declined until the college closed for reorganization in 1934-35. During this year the school became a conference institution of the Mennonite Brethren Church.

When the college program was again started under conference operation, the academy continued its program but never regained its earlier enrollment. It was discontinued in 1945 when the conference voted to "leave the operation of the educational program on the secondary school level to local congregations and group organizations." There were several reasons for this decision. (1) Academies which developed in Kansas, Oklahoma, and California relieved the need for conference control of secondary education. (2) As more and more emphasis was placed on college work, it became difficult to operate two schools under one organization. (3) The increasing popularity of public schools kept many students from coming. (4) The cost of operating a dual program became too great.   W.J.P.

Tabor College is a four-year Liberal Arts College located in Hillsboro, Marion Co., Kan., owned and operated by the Conference of the Mennonite Brethren Church of North America through its Board of Education. As early as 1881, three years after the first conference of the Mennonite Brethren Church, the subject of education became a conference issue. The 1884 conference report reveals growing interest in a "Fortbildungsschule" (training school) to retain the German language and to train teachers and mission workers. A School Association was organized in the M.B. Church of Goessel, Kan., which, though it received no direct support from the conference, conducted a Bible school in the small village of Canada, Kan., for two years. In 1886 the school was moved to Lehigh. Lack of leadership and finances forced the Association to discontinue.

Meanwhile another School Association, supported by several Mennonite groups, organized a school near Buhler, Kan., in Reno County. J. F. Duerksen was appointed to direct the school. In 1899 Duerksen was transferred to the head of the German Department of McPherson College in McPherson, Kan., after an agreement was reached that the M.B. Conference would sponsor the German Department.

By this arrangement Duerksen was able to serve as spiritual counselor for Mennonite students. The future educational leadership of the M.B. and K.M.B. conferences received its stimulation under this provisional agreement with McPherson College. This arrangement worked satisfactorily for five years, but soon students began to dream of a conference school. H. W. Lohrenz and P. C. Hiebert, both students of McPherson, became interested in a conference school; and J. K. Hiebert, minister of the Ebenfeld M.B. Church, helped Lohrenz promote the plan and bring the issue before the conference. In 1907 a recommendation for an M.B. college was approved in a special meeting of M.B. and K.M.B. conference representatives. A School Association was formed to carry out the program. Articles of Incorporation were prepared, and a charter was granted by the State of Kansas on March 19, 1908. Hillsboro was chosen as the site when it offered $6,533 in cash, building lots, material, and labor. The management of the corporation was vested in a board of directors composed of nine voting members. J. K. Hiebert was the first board chairman. The school was named Tabor College, and the Society was called the Tabor College Corporation. In the spring of 1908 the building was begun. It was completed at a cost of $13,500. Although the building was not yet completed, classes started on Sept. 14, 1908, in the Church with three teachers—President H. W. Lohrenz, P. C. Hiebert, and P. P. Rempel—and 39 students. Before the year was over the enrollment reached 102, and three more faculty members were added: Z. C. Bartel, Katharina Friesen, and Tina Schultz. By 1910 instruction was offered in seven departments with seven teachers. The academy and the preparatory school dominated the early years of the program.

The early aims of the college as stated by its first president, H. W. Lohrenz, were to offer a liberal arts education in a Christian setting, to prepare young men and women for spiritual leadership in the church, and to provide a program of vocational training. It was the special concern of the Association, of the Board, and of the teachers that the school be a seminary of real Christianity, where the spirit of prayer could prevail and where souls could become better grounded in the spiritual life.

During the first ten years the student enrollment increased to about 200, and the faculty increased to 15 members. The rapid progress, however, was halted temporarily when on April 30, 1918, a fire destroyed the building and practically all of its contents, with a total loss of about $24,000. A new fireproof three-story building, 130 x 90 ft., and a dormitory known as the Mary J. Regier Ladies Home were soon built. Two years after the fire, classes having been housed in temporary quarters throughout the city, Tabor was once more in its own home.

Following the dedication of the new building Sept. 12, 1920, the school enjoyed several years of prosperity and progress. In 1924 a gymnasium was built. Soon, however, the lack of full accreditation for the college division began to be reflected in a decline of enrollment. In 1927 a concerted effort was made to meet the requirements for state accreditation. This goal was achieved. In order to preserve this status, President Lohrenz made the proposal to the conference of 1930 that the college be operated as a conference school. The conference, however, was not ready to accept this responsibility; this left the college with a very uncertain economic foundation. Economic insecurity continued to hamper the college program. The situation was further aggravated by the depression and its aftermath, a decline in student enrollment, the resignation of influential teachers, and hesitant support from the conference. In 1932-33, with less than 100 students and only six full-time teachers, the college lost its state accreditation.

At the General Conference of 1933 the Tabor College Corporation made another official offer to the conference, inviting the church to operate the school. The college then became the property of the M.B. Church. After temporarily closing its doors for reorganization in 1934, the school resumed operation in 1935.

The newly appointed President A. E. Janzen succeeded P. C. Hiebert, who had served as president 1931-33. Janzen introduced the Thousand Friends Plan—each friend giving $10.00 annually—which, together with the church offering, provided a stable financial basis. The board adopted the policy that the institution could not borrow money. The college received a two-year accredited status during the first year as a conference school. The years since 1935 have been characterized by moderate but steady growth in physical facilities plus continuous improvements in the curriculum and in the quality of instruction.

Although the college from its beginning offered a four-year course, in 1942 the Board appointed P. E. Schellenberg as president to expand and strengthen the four-year Liberal Arts course. In 1945 the academy was discontinued. In 1947 a program was set up to meet state requirements for the Secondary Teachers' Certificate. Schellenberg served until 1951, when J. N. C. Hiebert was called to the presidency. Hiebert was inaugurated Feb. 3, 1952, but health conditions forced him to resign in the fall of 1953. Leonard J. Franz then served as acting president until Frank C. Peters was named president-elect in 1954.

At the General Conference of 1954 the conference educational program was reorganized. Under a unified board the U.S. Area Conference was made responsible to operate Tabor College, Pacific Bible Institute (q.v.) and the Mennonite Brethren Biblical Seminary (q.v.). The seminary was moved from Tabor College to Fresno, Cal. The Board then initiated a Budgeted Giving Plan which provided the economic basis for an expansion of the conference educational program. Full accreditation of Tabor College became a major objective. In working toward that goal a long-range building program was inaugurated.

When Frank C. Peters resigned in 1955, Leonard J. Franz was appointed president. Under his leadership the first project, a modern library, was completed in 1957. A completely new science department was developed on the first floor of the administration building in 1957. Dormitory facilities were improved, and on May 25, 1958, ground-breaking ceremonies initiated the building of a new student center and gymnasium, a fitting climax for the fiftieth anniversary.

Since its beginning in 1908 over 4,000 students have attended Tabor College. The maximum enrollment was 422 in 1946-47. The 1958 enrollment was 290. The teaching staff has been increased to 30 members.

Tabor College is a member of the Kansas Foundation for Private Colleges, the Council for the Advancement of Small Colleges, and the Council of Mennonite and Affiliated Colleges. The official publication of the college is the *Tabor College Bulletin*.

Student activities are governed by a student governing body, the Tabor College Associated Students. The religious organizations of the campus are unified in the Christian Fellowship Association, which is the result of a union of the Gospel Team, the Mission Band, the Peace Group, the YMCA, and the YWCA. The *Blue Jay* is the college annual, and the *Tabor College View* is the student paper.

The Annual Bible Conference, running for eight days during the second semester, brings to the community outstanding Bible expositors. The Spiritual Life Emphasis Week, designed primarily for the college family, offers spiritual inspiration during the first semester. Mission and peace conferences are conducted periodically. Chapel services four times a week bring worship into the center of the curriculum. The College Chapel Hour is a weekly radio program, reflecting the testimony of a Christian college. It was started in 1953 and has been carried by 14 stations including HCJB, world-wide missionary station in Quito, Ecuador.

The controlling idealism of the school is well stated in its catalog: "Underlying the philosophy of a Christian Liberal Arts College is the concept that God is the controlling power in the Universe; that Christ is the Divine Mediator and Saviour of man, the fullest revelation of God and the directive in producing a wholesome standard of human conduct. The founders of Tabor College believed that the world and man can best be explained in terms of a Biblical orientation, and they believed that when this concept becomes the integrating force in a college, life becomes meaningful for the student, the faculty, the church, and society."   W.J.P.

Tabor College Herold, a 16-page 6 x 9 in. monthly paper published from January 1912 to 1931, with D. E. Harder as editor, to provide a link between the school and its constituency. It contained news as well as theological, literary, and educational articles. During 1930 a student paper was started under the title *As You Like It.* In 1937 it was changed to the *Tabor Spectator,* and since 1940 it has been called the *Tabor College View.* The *Tabor College Bulletin* is the publication interpreting the college to the constituency.   W.J.P.

Tabor College of Theology. When Tabor College was founded in 1908 by the Tabor College Corporation in Hillsboro, Kan., the study of the Bible was regarded as the core of educational activity. Although the great demand for a liberal arts program resulted in a divisional curriculum, the Bible Department from the first provided unity, direction, and purpose for the entire college program. In addition to offering courses required for academy and college graduation, the Bible Department also offered special courses for students who chose to concentrate on Bible study.

In the early years a Five-Year Bible Course was offered academy and preparatory students. Many of the courses were taught in the German language. This practical course was reduced to a Four-Year Bible Course in 1916. Meanwhile as the college division expanded, a Three-Year Theological Course was added.

During the early years of instruction outstanding teachers like H. W. Lohrenz, P. C. Hiebert, P. P. Rempel, D. E. Harder, and H. F. Toews gave guidance and instruction in the Bible to many students who have become pastors, teachers, and missionaries in the conference program. In more recent years P. R. Lange, Abraham H. Unruh, D. Edmond Hiebert, C. F. Plett, Waldo Hiebert, and Lando Hiebert have helped develop the Bible Department.

The first degree course, the Collegiate Bible Course which led to the degree of Bcaehlor of Theology (Th.B.), was introduced in 1924. During the year 1934-35 the college was closed for reorganization. Shortly after the college was reopened as a conference school of the Mennonite Brethren Church, the Bible Department again expanded. In 1938 the Bachelor of Religious Education (B.R.E.) degree was added. In 1942 the Graduate of Theology (Th.G.) degree was introduced. In 1944 the College of Theology was finally organized as a separate organization. During the same year the Bachelor of Divinity (B.D.) degree was added. This program continued until the conference voted to move the seminary to Fresno, Cal., in 1955. Since then Tabor College has had only a typical college Bible department. W.J.P.

Tabor College View, official biweekly publication of the Associated Students of Tabor College, Hillsboro, Kan., 4 pages, 15 x 11 in., published in cooperation with journalism classes since Sept. 1, 1940, press work by the Mennonite Brethren Publishing House. It is distributed to students, faculty, parents who subscribe, and since 1953 to M.B., K.M.B., and E.M.B. men in I-W service. The circulation is 500. Editors are chosen annually by Student Council. L.J.M.

Tabor Mennonite Brethren Church, now extinct, located in Hamilton County, Kan., was established in 1907. It was disbanded a few years later because of the drought. C.K.

Tabor Mennonite Church (GCM), located 3 miles south and 1½ miles east of Goessel, Marion Co., Kan., a member of the Western District Conference, is a sister church to Alexanderwohl. The church building was dedicated on Oct. 25, 1908. The church

was organized on Jan. 21, 1909, with 115 charter members. H. R. Voth and C. Frey were the pioneer leaders. In the fall of 1909 P. H. Richert was called as pastor and elder, serving until 1946. H. B. Schmidt was pastor 1944-57, followed by James H. Waltner 1958- . In 1938 the church building was enlarged. Several pastors and missionaries have gone out into mission fields. The church has three Christian Endeavor societies, three sewing societies, and a Mennonite men's organization. The membership in 1956 was 422. D.S.T.

Taconis, a Mennonite family at Joure in Friesland, Netherlands, who had a noted nursery in the 19th century. Inne Taconis (b. 1815 at Joure, d. 1865 at Nieuwe Niedorp) was pastor of the Nieuwe and Oude Niedorp Mennonite congregation 1841-65. His wife was Aagtje Ris. Their son Klaas Ris Taconis (b. 1844 at Nieuwe Niedorp, d. 1878 at Joure) was pastor of the Noordeind van Graft congregation 1872-75. In 1875 he retired because of bad health. (*DB* 1865, 167; 1876, 129; 1879, 140.) vDZ.

Tadema, a Dutch family name, originally of the province of Friesland, both Mennonite and non-Mennonite. A Mennonite branch is found in the 18th-19th centuries, members of which were public notaries, among whom was P. Tadema of Akkrum in the early 19th century, who was a deacon of the local congregation. Descendants of this family are Jelte Karel Tadema (Nijkerk in Friesland, 1842-Haarlem, 1899), who was a partner of the F. Bohn printing and publishing company at Haarlem, serving the Haarlem Mennonite congregation as a deacon 1871-99. Both his sons, Jan Cornelis Tadema (Haarlem, 1870-) and Johannes Leendert Tadema (Haarlem, 1874-1949), were partners of the Bohn publishing company. Both joined the Haarlem Mennonite Church and Johannes Leendert served as deacon 1904-49. vDZ.

Tadzhik SSR: see **Soviet Central Asia.**

Taede Ruyerdtszoon (Joncker Kaths), of Hettingahuys, a Dutch Anabaptist martyr, was beheaded at Leeuwarden, the capital of Friesland, on Sept. 30, 1559, because of his Mennonite convictions. Particulars are lacking. vDZ.

Inv. Arch. Amst. I, No. 746; J. Reitsma, *Honderd jaren uit de Gesch. der Hervorming . . . in Friesland* (Leeuwarden, 1876) 64.

Taffin, Jean (1529/30-1602), a Calvinist theologian, who studied at Geneva under Calvin and Beza, French pastor at Metz, Antwerp, and Heidelberg (where he was superintendent of the Reformed church), from 1573 court chaplain of Prince William I of Orange (*q.v.*), and 1584-1602 pastor of the French (Walloon) Reformed church at Amsterdam, attacked the Mennonites in his *Instruction contre les erreurs des Anabaptistes,* 1589, which book also was translated into Dutch: *Onderwysinghe teghens de dwalinghe der Wederdooperen* (Haarlem, 1590), and into German: *Kurtzer Unterricht wider die Irrthumb der Wiedertäuffer* (Amberg, 1597). The book contains four parts: I. Concerning the Incarnation of Christ; II. Concerning the baptism of the infants of Christians; III. Concerning the obligation, authority, and power of the magistracy; IV. Concerning the oath.

G.H., vDZ.

B. Glasius, *Godgeleerd Nederland III* ('s Hertogenbosch, 1856) 411-13; C. Boer, *Hofpredikers van Prins Willem van Oranje* (Assen, 1952); *ML* IV.

Taju, on the Indonesian island of Java, acquired a hospital in 1918, built by the Dutch Mennonite Mission Association (*q.v.*). Dr. Gramberg (*q.v.*) was for a number of years the director of this hospital. It was completely destroyed by a band of fanatical Mohammedans on March 8, 1942. For some time there was also a small Mennonite congregation at Taju, which belonged to the Margoredjo (*q.v.*) district church. (*Jaarverslagen* of the Dutch Mennonite Mission Association.)   vDZ.

Tak (formerly Tack), a widely ramified Dutch Mennonite family, found from the 16th century at Zierikzee, from about 1600 also at Vlissingen, Brouwershaven, and particularly at Middelburg, all in the province of Zeeland. In the course of the 17th century its members moved to Rotterdam and Haarlem. Abraham Jansz Tack, b. 1562 at Zierikzee, moved to Vlissingen about 1590, where he married Maeyken Jan Denysdochter and probably operated a grocery. His grandson Jan Samuels Tack (Vlissingen, 1629-97), a buckwheat miller, was a preacher of the Vlissingen Mennonite congregation from 1673 until his death. His sons and grandsons were grocers. In the early 18th century the Tacks moved from Vlissingen to Middelburg, where they were grocers, grain merchants, and manufacturers of tobacco products and chocolate; one branch owned an ironworks at Middelburg from *c*1740. In the 19th century some Taks were lawyers and government officials. Hemerijk Tak and De Maret Tak are side branches from 1774 and 1805 respectively.

Many of the Taks until recent times served the church as deacons at Vlissingen, Zierikzee, Middelburg, Brouwershaven, Rotterdam, Leiden, Koog-Zaandijk, and Nijmegen. Samuel Adriaansz Tak (1737-1808), of Vlissingen, was trained for the ministry at the Amsterdam Lamist seminary and served from 1765 until his death as the (last) pastor of the Mennonite congregation at Zierikzee. Abraham Tack, who about 1675 was a preacher of the Huiskopers (Danzig Old Flemish) congregation at Haarlem, probably was a member of the same family.   vDZ.

Ned. Patriciaat XLIV (1958) 308-22; *Bijblad Nederl. Leeuw,* 1950, 78-80; *Inv. Arch. Amst.* I, Nos. 2169, 2206; II, Nos. 2382 f., 2389 f., 2520; *DB* 1863, 135; 1868, 93; 1884, 50; 1885, 92, 95; 1907, 169.

Taler (Thaler, Taller), **Hans,** an Anabaptist martyr, was put to death at Stertzing in Tirol (formerly Austria, now Italy) in 1532 with Lambrecht Gruber (*q.v.*), Hans Beck (*q.v.*), Laurenz Schumacher (*q.v.*), Peter Plaver (*q.v.*), and Peter Hungerl (*q.v.*). They were tortured, but still persisted in their faith and were therefore sentenced to death. (Beck, *Geschichts-Bücher,* 105; *Mart. Mir.* D 33, E 440; Zieglschmid, *Chronik,* 103.)

Talma, a village in the Caucasus, where landless Mennonites from the regions of Halbstadt and Gnadenfeld in South Russia organized a Mennonite Brethren congregation in 1901 in the Terek region. It became an independent congregation. (Friesen, *Brüderschaft,* 445, 478.)

Talma Mennonite Brethren Church: see **Terek** Mennonite Brethren Church.

Taming (Dah-ming) (China) Mennonite (GCM) Mission. Taming is the largest city (pop. 50,000) in the southern tip of Hopei Province, and the political, educational, and commercial center of that area, county seat of Taming County (pop. *c*520,000). Missionaries of three Protestant denominations, as well as one independent worker, were located in this city or its suburbs. Those of the General Conference Mennonite Church lived in the city and the south suburb. The Mennonite work had started farther south with center at Kaichow (*q.v.*). In 1920 the mission expanded to the north, occupying Taming as a second center. Two missionary residences and buildings for a primary and junior high school were erected in the south suburb compound of 8½ acres. In this city a large church seating 1,000 and a lower primary school were built. Chinese buildings were remodeled for a missionary residence, a dispensary, and 10 homes for Chinese workers. In a south suburb compound near the city a street chapel and a Young Women's Home Training and Bible School were built. The normal missionary staff was two families and two or three single women. Growing Chinese participation gave rise about 1928 to an indigenous movement known as the "Society to Prepare for Church Independence." It was responsible for starting three churches and several preaching places with local workers and funds. In 1939 the society was absorbed in an all-field church organization. All missionaries left or were interned during World War II and never returned because of Communist occupation, but the Chinese church has continued active.   S.F.P.

Tamme(n)s, Jan, a Dutch Mennonite (Old Flemish), probably a preacher, in the town of Groningen (*q.v.*), who was excommunicated in 1688 because of his Collegiant sympathies and his view that baptism must be by immersion. He held somewhat advanced ideas and could not believe that the Groningen Old Flemish branch was the only true Christian church. He defended Christoffel Wensing (*q.v.*) when Wensing joined the Collegiants. His followers were called the Jan-Tammesvolk (*q.v.*). (*DB* 1883, 75, 78, 81, 85.)   vDZ.

Tampa (Kan.) Mennonite Brethren Church was organized in 1915 with 60 members who had come from Russia. The first leader was Konrad Lepp. In 1958 H. H. Hiebert was pastor, with 30 members.

M.A.K.

Tampa Mennonite (MC) Mission, 1407 Ida Street, Tampa, Fla., operated by the Lancaster Conference, is the outgrowth of the missionary efforts of C. B. Byer and wife, who came to the city in 1927. For a time services were held in a tent on 15th Street;

and in 1929 the present church was built. Work among the Spanish-speaking people (mostly Cubans) was carried on in rented buildings until 1946, when property was bought at 1613 9th Avenue, to serve as a meeting place and as kindergarten and first and second grades of school. The Ida Street mission and work among Latins (the Ybor City Mission) were considered one congregation until 1949. The membership in 1949 was 34. In 1952 the College Hill Mission at 3506 Machado Ave. was begun among the colored people. The membership in the three missions in 1958 was: Ida Street 20, with Martin Lehman as pastor; Ybor City 20, with Isaac Frederick; and College Hill 7, with Alvin Weaver. Ybor City conducts a Christian day school, called Sharon, with John Wenger as principal.

T.H.B.

Tanneken, the name of many Anabaptist martyrs, particularly in Flanders. It is the same name as Anneken (Anna), the "T" before Anneken being an abbreviation of the article "het" (the). vDZ.

Tanneken, an Anabaptist martyr, who by special permission of the council of Flanders, was secretly beheaded in the court of the Gravensteen castle at Gent, Belgium, at three in the afternoon on June 27, 1560, after she had given birth to a child. Miertgen (*q.v.*) was executed at the same time. Their corpses were immediately buried in a pit. Tanneken was born at Kortrijk in Flanders and was the wife of Hans de Smet (*q.v.*), who had died as a martyr on Aug. 7, 1559. Her official name was Anneken Gressy; she was commonly called Tanneken Godtbetert. Tanneken and Miertgen, who were in prison for more than a year, are said to have spoken to the people who passed beneath their windows and to have thrown letters to the street, thus proclaiming their faith. Van Braght's *Martyrs' Mirror* gives only a brief account on these martyrs, erroneously giving the date of execution as 1559. Particulars have been published by A. L. E. Verheyden. Tanneken is one of the martyrs of Gent celebrated in the song "Ic moet een liet beginnen," No. 14 of the *Lietboecxken*. (*Offer,* 348, 556 ff.; *Mart. Mir.* D 246, E 620; Verheyden, *Gent,* 26, No. 73.) vDZ.

Tanneken van Aken, an Anabaptist martyr, is identical with Tanneken van Cluyten (*q.v.*).

Tanneken van den Broucke: see **Tanneken van Mechelen.**

Tanneken (Truyken) van Cluyten, an Anabaptist martyr, was executed by drowning at Antwerp, Belgium, on Dec. 31, 1558. She was born at 's Hertogenbosch, Dutch province of North Brabant. Further particulars are lacking. With many other martyrs executed at Antwerp in 1562 and after, she is celebrated in the hymn "Aenhoort Godt, hemelsche Vader" (Hear, O God, heavenly Father), No. 16 of the *Lietboecxken*. vDZ.

Offer, 566, No. 40; *Mart. Mir.* D 202, E 583; *Antw. Arch.-Bl.* VIII, 456, 466; XIV, 24 f., No. 277; Wolkan, *Lieder,* 63, 72.

Tanneken Delmeere (Tanneken Jans), an Anabaptist martyr, of Oudenaarde in Flanders, the wife of

Jacques Massois, was secretly executed by beheading, together with Lynken Claes (*q.v.*), within the Gravensteen castle at Gent, Belgium, on Aug. 14, 1561. She confessed that she had left the Catholic Church in 1550, and since then had regularly participated in Mennonite meetings. In 1560 she was baptized at Gent by Joos (Joachim Vermeeren, *q.v.*). Both Tanneken and Lynken refused to recant in spite of the unceasing and able endeavors of the inquisitor Titelman (*q.v.*). After several months in prison, weary of all the trials, they sent the warden to the magistrate with the message that all further attempts to "convert" them would be futile. Thereupon the death sentence was pronounced and immediately executed upon these two brave martyrs. (Verheyden, *Gent,* 27, No. 79; *idem,* "Mennisme in Vlaanderen," ms.) vDZ.

Tanneken Janssen, an Anabaptist martyr, burned at the stake at Antwerp, Belgium, on Feb. 17, 1573, with four other victims. She was sentenced to death because she was rebaptized and had attended forbidden meetings. Further particulars are lacking. (*Antw. Arch.-Bl.* XIII, 105, 106, 173; XIV, 90 f., No. 1011.) vDZ.

Tanneken Leonets, an Anabaptist martyr: see **Anneken van Brussel.**

Tanneken van der Leyen (Verleyen), an Anabaptist martyr, was executed at Antwerp, Belgium, on Oct. 5, 1555, by being bound into a sack and drowned in the Scheldt River. The accounts on this martyr in the *Offer des Heeren* and the following martyr books including van Braght's *Martyrs' Mirror* are very concise, mentioning only that Tanneken was a "jonge dochter," i.e., an unmarried woman, of Gent, and that she died steadfast; the exact date of the execution is not given. Génard published a few facts: while still living at Gent Tanneken had joined the Mennonites, but when she was arrested there she recanted. Upon her release she moved to Antwerp and joined the Mennonite congregation there. After her second arrest she was repeatedly tried, first on Jan. 27, 1555. Thus she must have been in prison a relatively long time. She left some property, which was confiscated. Génard also states that before she was executed she had to take off her outer clothing and put on a pair of linen pants. Tanneken is named in the hymn "Aenhoort Godt, hemelsche Vader," No. 16 of the *Lietboecxken*. (She is erroneously called Janneken van der Leyen in *ML* II, 648.) vDZ.

Offer, 564, No. 5; *Mart. Mir.* D 161, E 550; *Antw. Arch.-Bl.* VIII, 426-28, 430, 468; XIV, 20 f., No. 226; Wolkan, *Lieder,* 63, 72.

Tanneken van Mechelen (van den Broucke), the wife of the martyr Hans van der Straeten (*q.v.*), was arrested with her husband at Antwerp, Belgium, in 1571, when she was only 17 years of age, and recanted. As a punishment she was confined in a Catholic convent at Breda, Netherlands, but escaped to Danzig (*q.v.*). Here she made contact with the Mennonite congregation and after repentance was accepted into the church. (*Mart. Mir.* D 540, E 875.) vDZ.

Tanneken van der Meulen, an Anabaptist martyr, was executed at the Vrijdagsmarkt in Gent, Belgium, on Dec. 22, 1569, by burning at the stake after being strangled. Particulars are lacking. Jaecxken van Hussele and Jaecxken Teerlings died with her as martyrs. She is commemorated in the hymn "Alsmen schreef duyst vijfhondert jaer ende twee en tsestich mede," found in the *Lietboecxken*.   vDZ.

Offer, 653, No. 40; *Mart. Mir.* D 407, E 759; Verheyden, *Gent,* 55, No. 184; *ML* III.

Tanneken van Roosbroecke, an Anabaptist martyr: see **Anneken van Roosbroecke.**

Tanneken Vermeeren, an Anabaptist of Antwerp, Belgium, who was in prison there in 1565 because of her convictions. She may have been the same person as Tanneken Wagemans, a Mennonite who escaped from prison at Antwerp during the night of March 13, 1567, with some 60 other prisoners among whom there were eight Mennonites, thereupon moving either to Emden or Cologne. But it is also possible that Tanneken Vermeeren is not identical with Tanneken Wagemans, and that she was executed or died in prison. (Vos, *Antwerpen,* 339 f.)   vDZ.

Tanneken Walraven, an Anabaptist martyr who was burned at the stake at Antwerp, Belgium, on the evening of Pentecost, May 22, 1575. Van Braght's *Martyrs' Mirror* adds that she was executed with her mouth screwed up to prevent speaking to the crowd. She was the wife of Jan Verschelt and the mother of Preacher Jaques Walraven (*q.v.*) of Amsterdam. (See also **Janneken Walraven.**) vDZ.

Mart. Mir. D 693, E 1007; *Antw. Arch.-Bl.* XIII, 193, 201; XIV, 96 f., No. 1085.

Tanowitz (Slavic, *Dunajovice*), a Bruderhof of the Hutterian Brethren, founded in 1591 after they were expelled from Pergen and Voitelsbrunn by Siegmund von Dietrichstein (*q.v.*). On Aug. 10, 1619, the Bruderhof was burned down by soldiers. (Beck, *Geschichts-Bücher,* 206, 374; Zieglschmid, *Chronik,* 07, 002 f., 710.)

Tapper(t), Ruardus (Rieuwert) (1485-1559), a Roman Catholic priest and professor at the University of Louvain, inquisitor in the Netherlands and from 1537 papal head inquisitor. He was active against all kind of "heresy" and also had a hand in many lawsuits against Mennonites. Tapper was narrow-minded, dogmatic, and cunning, and was greatly hated and feared by the people. By his sly methods and his ruthlessness he did great harm to the Reformation cause though he did not succeed in extirpating the Protestant and Anabaptist-Mennonite movements.   vDZ.

N.N.B.Wb. V, 877-79; L. E. Halkin, *La Réforme en Belgique* (Brussels, n.d.-1957) 58, 64; *Inv. Arch. Amst.* I, No. 380, 394a, 394b.

Targier: see Tersier.

Tasch (Tesch), **Peter,** an Anabaptist (Melchiorite) leader, preacher, and author in Hesse, Germany. His work as a missionary extended as far as England (see his letter to Georg Schnabel, *q.v.*). His

tracts, *Von der Taufordnung Christi, Vom Eid,* and *Von der Menschwerdung,* were apparently very influential. In 1536 he was apprehended with a number of other Anabaptists, among whom was Leonhard Fälber. Bucer (*q.v.*) persuaded him in the Marburg colloquy (Oct. 30—Nov. 1, 1538) to join the Reformed Church, and he was frequently used to lead his former associates and brethren to conversion. He is the author of the booklet, *Bekenntnis oder Antwort etlicher Fragstücke oder Artikeln der gefangenen Täufer und Anderer im Land zu Hessen* (Dec. 9, 1538), which was signed by Fälber and eight other Anabaptists, and which was a modified confession of their faith, yielding a number of doctrinal points. (See **Fälber** for particulars.) His later life was by no means above reproach. (See **Bucer** and **England.**)

Rembert, *Wiedertäufer,* 269, 453, 457; Paul Wappler, *Die Stellung Kursachsens und des Landgrafen Philipp von Hessen zur Täuferbewegung* (Münster, 1910) 253; E. Belfort Bax, *Rise and Fall of the Anabaptists* (London, 1903) 336; *ML* IV.

Taschringmaker, an Anabaptist martyr: see **Jasper.**

Tashkent, capital of Uzbek USSR, Soviet Russia, former capital of Turkestan (*q.v.*). This city played a significant role in the history of the Mennonites who migrated to Central Asia (*q.v.*) in 1880 ff. under the leadership of Klaas Epp (*q.v.*) and Abraham Peters (*q.v.*) to find a refuge and establish new settlements. One group resided here temporarily.

Under the Soviet government Tashkent has become a very significant center in Central Asia with a population of about one million. Mennonites who have drifted to this area have thus far not organized a church; some attend the Baptist services. Their number is likely not as large in this area as in Alma Ata, Karaganda, and some other places. (See **Soviet Central Asia.**)   C.K.

Taubenkobel der Hutterischen Wiedertäufer is the title of a violent and scurrilous polemic against the Hutterian Brethren written by Christoph Andreas Fischer (*q.v.*). A copy is in GCL.

Tauber, Caspar, a wealthy and respected citizen of Vienna, the first Lutheran martyr of Austria, whose valiant confession of his faith was praised by the Anabaptists although he was not one of them. Tauber was summoned to the court with two other persons on a charge of spreading heresy and reading Lutheran books. Although he defended himself brilliantly in a public debate Ferdinand had him arrested. The heresy court as well as the clergy tried to lead him to recantation. A supposed recantation by Tauber was actually published, but it was repudiated by his coreligionists. He apparently did consent to withdraw certain "errors." The charges against him were that he denied the real presence of Christ in the communion, rejected all the blessings and ceremonies of the (Catholic) Church, denied the existence of purgatory, repudiated the confessional, denied the intercession of the saints, and believed in the priesthood of all believers. These beliefs he is said to have recanted in a document he signed on Aug. 27, 1524. When however he was brought before the officials to make a public recantation he refused to do so and was consequently executed Sept. 12, 1524. The *Geschichts-Bücher* report his martyrdom as follows: "In the year 1525 (correct to 1524) Kaspar Tauber of Vienna was burned for the sake of the Gospel. He was led out before daybreak, first decapitated, and then burned. A report claimed that he had given the executioner money to pierce him thrice as though he had pierced himself (suicide). He confessed the faith joyfully, regardless of wife, property, and money."

Luther reckoned Tauber among the first martyrs of the Gospel but Ottius rated him as one of the "factious people," while Cochläus rated him several degrees lower. The Anabaptists placed him in their martyrologies. A hymn on Tauber's martyrdom was published in 1525 under the title *Ain christenlich Lied des bewainlichen todes Caspar Taubers genannt, Bürgers zu Wien . . . Gedicht im Jahr 1525*, reprinted in Wackernagel, *Kirchenlied* III, 436-38, with the beginning line, "Nun hört, ich will euch singen aus trauriklichem Müt." Wolkan (*Lieder*, 285) mistakenly lists it as one of the hymns of the German Anabaptists. It does not appear in the *Ausbund* or the *Lieder der Hutterischen Brüder.* Tauber appears in the *Chronik* but before the beginning of the Anabaptist history. The Catholics labeled him as an Anabaptist to discredit him,

LOSERTH, H.S.B.

A. Nicoladoni, *ADB*, vol. 37, 423-29; Georg Loesche, *Geschichte des Protestantismus in Oesterreich* (third ed., Vienna and Leipzig, 1930) 64; Zieglschmid, *Chronik*, 43; *Mart. Mir.* D 2, E 414; *ML* IV.

Tauchnitz, Carl Christian Philipp (1798-1884), a prominent German book dealer, and a warm friend of the German Mennonites. In the winter of 1830 a Baptist preacher in London told him about the German Mennonites, and when he returned to Germany he visited Weierhof, Monsheim, Kindenheim, Spitalhof, and Sembach. In 1831 he became acquainted with several congregations in Baden, where "the Easter days passed very pleasantly and blessedly." On April 17 of that year he preached in Spitalhof on the occasion of the baptism of J. Rothen (*q.v.*). He also preached at the Weierhof and in Oberflorsheim. He frequently took part in the conferences of the Mennonites in the Palatinate and Hesse. He promoted the publication of the first Palatine hymnal (1832) by friendly persuasion of the opponents of the book. He corresponded with most of the Palatine preachers and by word and deed aided in the revival of the brotherhood. He also published several Mennonite works, among them three books by Johannes Molenaar (*Catechismus* 1841 and 1854, *Andenken* 1844, and *Evangelische Stimmen* 1844, a collection of sermons), one by Herman Reeder (*Predigten* 1843), and one by B. K. Roosen (*Menno Symons* 1848). He was especially interested in the founding of a Mennonite theological school, but in vain. He rendered a lasting service to the Mennonites as well as to other free churches. (*Menn. Bl.,* 1884, 38, 43; *Gem.-Kal.,* 1899, 43; *ML* IV.)

NEFF.

Täuferakten and **Täuferakten-Kommission:** see **Quellen.**

Täufergut, the property taken from Swiss Anabaptists by the government at Bern (*q.v.*): see **Confiscation of Property.**

Täuferjäger (Anabaptist-Hunters), a permanent police agency especially created to catch the Mennonites, one of the most infamous institutions of the Bernese state government in the first half of the 18th century. A blind zeal for the preservation of religious uniformity had taken possession of the aristocratic government, and it became the duty of the *Täuferkammer* (*q.v.*) to create its own agency to apprehend the Mennonites, the "Anabaptist-Hunters." It was largely composed of rough brutal men, irresponsible persons who hunted down the Mennonites with ruthless violence and injustice in the service of the government.

For the discovery of a concealed Mennonite the Bernese council offered a reward of 30 crowns on Dec. 28, 1709 (a crown is about equal to a dollar). The "Hunters" were ordered to look especially for Mennonite preachers and keep their eyes open for those who offered their houses and barns for meetings. It was reported that the Mennonites were living in the most remote of the Alpine huts. Everywhere they were to be hunted like game. In the Mennonite homes these men caused tremendous damage, especially if they thought they were on the trail of a preacher.

Among the common people the "Hunters" found little sympathy. Wherever possible people hindered them and protected the Mennonites. Bonfires were lit and bells were rung to warn of the approach of the hated "hunters." Some citizens had to pay heavy fines for helping the victims escape. In the middle of the 18th century this institution was discontinued.

NEFF, S.G.

Samuel Geiser, *Die Taufgesinnten-Gemeinden* (Karlsruhe, 1931); *ML* IV.

Täuferkammer and **Täuferkommission:** see **Commission for Anabaptist Affairs.**

Täufer-Memorial: see **Anabaptist Memorial.**

Täufer-Testamente (Anabaptist Testaments) were 17th and 18th century reprints of the Froschauer (*q.v.*) New Testament, which were widely used by the Swiss Brethren, so named by the Bernese authorities in their anti-Anabaptist decrees because they were printed for and used solely by the Swiss Anabaptists in preference to the authorized Luther version. The appearance of the "Anabaptist Testaments" evoked consternation among the clergy of Bern, Switzerland, and they tried to eliminate these "falsified and dangerous translations." The government issued a mandate against the Mennonites on May 21, 1693, in which one of the orders was that "the proscribed Basel Testaments and other suspicious books of this sect" be confiscated. The Reformed clergy were to explain to the Mennonites the errors in the translation, take the Testaments from their owners, and substitute "the Basel Testament of Luther's version." Exactly what editions of the Froschauer Testament were referred to as *Täufer-Testamente* is not clear. As the article **Froschauer Bibles and Testaments** shows, editions are known of 1588, 1647, 1687, 1702, 1729, 1737, 1790, and 1825. The Pennsylvania Mennonites had an edition reprinted at Ephrata, Pa., in 1787.

S.G., H.S.B.

Täuferurbar, an official Bernese register of Anabaptist property confiscated in the canton, established by a mandate of Feb. 23, 1729, now in the Bernese Staatsarchiv. This register affords insight into the methods by which countless Anabaptist families were practically ruined by the violent measures of the government. One purpose of the register was to give the authorities information as to the spread and development of Anabaptism at this time in order to have help in suppressing it. Another purpose was to give an accounting of what was done with the confiscated property. (Müller, *Berner Täufer; ML* IV.)

S.G.

Tauffers, a castle in the Puster (*q.v.*) Valley, Tirol, Austria (now Italian), where Aendle Sackmann of Ritten, an Anabaptist woman, was put to death for her faith. Elise von Wolkenstein was long imprisoned here. (Beck, *Geschichts-Bücher,* 280; Zieglschmid, *Chronik,* 369 ff.; *ML* IV.)   Hege.

Taufgesinnt, the German counterpart of the Dutch "Doopsgezind" (*q.v.*), was introduced into North Germany under Dutch influence as early as the mid 17th century as an alternate for the name Mennonite. But in Germany, contrary to the development in Holland, it never displaced "Mennonite" and never became part of an official name. In Switzerland, however, it was used by 1810 in a petition by the Langnau Mennonite congregation to the Bernese government, and it ultimately became a part of the official name of the Swiss Mennonite conference (see **Altevangelische Wehrlose Taufgesinnten-Gemeinden**). The name Taufgesinnt appeared in the titles of a considerable number of German books and booklets in the 18th and 19th centuries, but soon disappeared, and is now completely out of use. The first-known printed use of the name was in the 1660 West Prussian Confession, where the expression "Die vereinigte Flämische, Friesische und Hochdeutsche Tauffs-gesinnete oder Mennonisten in Preussen" is used. The first German edition of the Dordrecht Confession (1664), however, used only the name "Mennonisten," as did the 1678 Prussian confession. The standard general Mennonite history by Anna Brons carried the title *Ursprung, Entwickelung und Schicksale der Taufgesinnten oder Mennoniten* in all three editions (1884, 1891, and 1912). The official periodicals did not use Taufgesinnt on their mastheads.   H.S.B.

Taufreden, Hutterite baptismal instructions, since c1560-70 standardized and strictly regulated. Baptism for the brethren has always been a most solemn event, preparing the candidate for his life's pledge to the "narrow path," and thus the instructions preceding this event have always been given much attention (see **Catechetical Instruction**). The procedure of instruction, baptismal examination, and the ritual itself has been preserved to the last detail almost unchanged. The standardized text of these instructions

(see **Sermons, Hutterite**) is also known from old codices and recent copies.

Ever since the "Golden Age" of the Hutterites (1560-90) books had been written containing the baptismal agenda and the instructional sermons or Taufreden, which afford a good insight into the doctrine and Bible exegesis of the Brethren. Very few of the baptismal candidates were newly won converts; most of them had grown up on the Bruderhofs, and were between 20 and 23 years of age, mature enough to weigh the obligation involved in their baptism.

The oldest known codex containing the famous Taufreden is of 1599 (in Bratislava, *q.v.*); since its title page is missing, Beck called it *Codex Ritualis.* Two more or less identical codices containing these Taufreden, written in 1643 and 1652, are in the library of Esztergom (*q.v.*), Hungary; an 18th-century copy was formerly found in the library of the Moravian Brethren, Herrnhut, Saxony. The text of the Taufreden probably goes back to the time of Peter Walpot (*q.v.*), c1570.

Up to recent times it was the custom among the Brethren to assemble the candidates on Friday and Saturday preceding the Sunday of the baptismal ritual, usually two hours before the regular evening prayer meeting for preparatory instruction. On Friday the First Taufrede (described below) was read, which treated Genesis 1-19. Then followed a lengthy prayer by the group, and a sermon (called *Lehr*) dealing with inner rebirth (John 3:3). On Saturday the Second Taufrede was read, followed by a penitential sermon and lengthy prayer, after which came the second Lehr, this time on Romans 6. On Sunday morning came the Third Taufrede, treating the church and its principles. After a prayer the meeting was concluded by the third Lehr on Matt. 28:16-20 (baptism). This ended the worship hour. Then the candidates were examined before the congregation, answering the standardized questions with a simple yes, after which they were baptized. The Hutterites of today follow the same procedure, with the exception that the instruction is now spread over a week.

The text of the Taufreden is of very high order. The first Taufrede is an exposition of the first book of the Bible, especially the first 19 chapters: Creation, fall, and man's very beginnings. The second Rede shows the difference between the Christian way of living and the secular way. The theological elements of this sermon are to a large extent borrowed from Riedemann's *Rechenschaft* (*q.v.*), e.g., such topics as What Sin Is, Concerning Original Sin, and God Punishes Those Who Are Disobedient to His Word. Christians, we read, are not baptized to become poor sinners but to enter a new life (Rom. 6). The third Rede makes it clear that Christ is and ever will be our Mediator, Redeemer, and Reconciliation. "True faith is nothing but an attachment of the heart to God and Christ. He who believes from the heart is assured and sealed by the Holy Spirit [here Ezekiel 36 is quoted as a reference!]. He receives strength from above to do the good which he could not do before, and to hate the evil he could not hate before." The candidate is to become aware of what is expected of him, namely, regret for his former sins, penitence, and readiness for a new, committed life, in which the old Adamic man has died away. All this leads to separation from the world, to Christian resignation (*Gelassenheit, q.v.*), and to full communion of goods.

The text of these three Taufreden, together with the traditional agenda of the ritual, will be published in Vol. II of *Glaubenszeugnisse* as item No. 21. It is a very good illustration of the Hutterite sermon technique and gives an insight into the Anabaptist frame of mind as it reveals itself internally, that is, unobserved by the outside world. R.F.

Lydia Müller and Robert Friedmann, *Glaubenszeugnisse* II (Gütersloh, 1960); W. Wiswedel, "Die alten Täufergemeinden und ihr missionarisches Wirken. III. (a), Die Ausrüstung der Sendboten," *Archiv für Reformationsgeschichte* XLI (1948) 116-18.

Tauler, Johann (*c*1330-61), a noted mystic of the Middle Ages, the son of a well-to-do citizen of Strasbourg, entered the Dominican Order at an early age, probably led to do so by Eckhart. He studied in Cologne under Nikolaus of Basel and Eckhart. For a short time he lived in Strasbourg, preaching and teaching with success. Then he returned to his native town and preached there until his death.

The story told in the *Meisterbuch* of the "Friend of God from the highlands" (Rulman Merswin) does not deal with Tauler, as had been supposed (by Preger and Ludwig Keller, *q.v.*). The books *Buch von der geistlichen Armut* and *Betrachtungen des Leidens und Sterbens Jesu* were not written by him. The hymns formerly attributed to him have also been proved to be spurious. But his sermons, published in various editions, are considered genuinely his. They were much read in certain Mennonite circles, especially in South Germany. The best loved was the "Nachfolge des armen Lebens Jesu," which was, however, falsely attributed to him. NEFF.

H. von Redern, *Der Gottesfreund Johann Tauler* (1923, a popular biography); *RGG* V; J. M. Clark, *The Great German Mystics: Eckhart, Tauler, and Suso* (Oxford, 1949); *ML* IV.

Taurida, a Russian province of the Ukraine bordering to the south on the Black Sea and the Sea of Azov, in the west on the Province of Kherson, and in the northeast on Ekaterinoslav. Originally the Crimea was a part of the province. In 1897 the province had a population of 1,447,790 and an area *c*22,000 square miles. The land consists primarily of rolling steppes. The capital was Simferopol.

Taurida became the second province chosen by the Mennonites for settlement. In 1804 ff. the Molotschna (*q.v.*) settlement was established in the eastern part of the province, which ultimately became the largest Mennonite settlement in Russia, consisting of 56 villages. In 1862 Mennonite settlements in Crimea (*q.v.*) were started (more than 25 villages). Fürstenland (*q.v.*), a daughter colony of the Chortitza settlement, consisting of 6 villages, originated in 1864. Before World War I the total Mennonite population numbered 36,000, distributed over some 90 villages in these settlements and many estates and consisted of 9,234,000 acres. The province of Taurida had a larger Mennonite population than any other province.

During World War II when the German army approached, the Soviet government succeeded in removing most of the population eastward. For this reason fewer Mennonites have come to America from this province since World War II than from Ekaterinoslav, where the Soviets were unable to evacuate the Mennonites west of the Dnepr River when the German army approached. (See also **Molotschna, Ukraine, Russia**.) C.K.

Die Mennoniten-Gemeinden in Russland (Heilbronn, 1921); Jakob Quiring, *Die Mundart von Chortitza in Süd-Russland* (Munich, 1928); Friesen, *Brüderschaft*.

Tavistock (Ont.) Amish Mennonite Church, a branch of the East Zorra A.M. congregation, a member of the Ontario A.M. Conference, was started in 1942, seven years after the first branching out of the East Zorra congregation into the Cassel Church, when the East Zorra meetinghouse became crowded. Since many members were living in Tavistock and vicinity, it was decided that a branch of the church be established there. After several worship services had been held in a public library hall, the board of the local Presbyterian church, owing to a dwindling membership, invited them to use its church. This arrangement was very satisfactory until 1949, when the Presbyterians sold the building. The A.M. group then constructed a new building and dedicated it in July 1951. Until June 1954 Bishop Henry Yantzi was assisted by three ministers, Daniel Wagler, Joel Schwartzentruber, and David Schwartzentruber. Since that time David Schwartzentruber has been the minister in charge. Summer Bible school, young people's meetings, tract packing, and other activities are held in conjunction with the East Zorra and Cassel congregations. The combined membership of the Tavistock, East Zorra, and Cassel congregations was 887 in 1958; the membership at Tavistock alone was approximately 200. R.BE.

Taxation. Special levies or fines were imposed in the 16th century as a milder form of persecution alongside the harsher forms of confiscation of property, exile, imprisonment, and execution, and were continued on down into the 18th century after the harsher forms were abolished. In Zürich in 1525 parents who would not have their children baptized were fined up to five pounds, while in 1526 those who baptized others were given fines of 10-15 pounds. In some cases the Anabaptists had to pay the trial costs. Later those who aided Anabaptists were given fines, while the Anabaptists themselves were fined more heavily. In the mandate of the diet of Augsburg of 1577 lenient judges were threatened with money fines. In most of the mandates of the time similar threats were made against all who would favor the Anabaptists. In the Palatinate those who failed to report Anabaptists were threatened with fines, while in Hesse recanting Anabaptists who returned to their faith were required to pay into the treasury for the poor; Anabaptists leaving their homeland had to pay an emigration fee of 10 gulden.

In the 17th and 18th centuries in the Palatinate all Mennonites were subject to special taxation. A head tax was collected for attendance at their services, which had previously been forbidden. Another special tax was imposed as compensation for exemption from military service. Soon a general tax was imposed. Hutterites living in Mannheim in the mid-17th century were freed from guard duty on payment of two to three gulden per family. Although the Concession of 1664 granted by the Electoral Palatine government mentioned the right of exemption from militia duty, in the course of time a special annual tax was imposed toward the cost of maintaining the militia, at first three gulden per family, later six, and finally twelve gulden. The Mennonites protested this tax, at times on the grounds of poverty, at other times on grounds of conscience since they did not want to contribute toward war in any respect. Frequently special fees were levied for registration of deaths, births, and marriages. The Mennonite settlement of Ibersheim was a special case, since here the settlement paid an annual special tax of 50 gulden in place of head taxes.

The collection of the Mennonite head taxes in the Electoral Palatinate, Baden-Durlach, and other territories often led to quarrels between the local and general authorities; usually the general authorities won out, while the Mennonites paid the bill. With every change of rulers the Mennonites had to petition for a renewal of their privileges and usually had to pay extra "donation money in this connection." At times large sums of money were forced out of Mennonite pockets into the princely treasuries by simple pressure or extortion. In Alsace the Mennonites had a long and hard struggle to secure and maintain the privilege of exemption from military service, in the course of which heavy payments of money had to be made. Sometimes families preferred to emigrate to America rather than keep on paying the severe taxes. It was only toward the end of the 18th century, when the valuable contribution of Mennonite farmers to the improvement of agriculture was recognized, that the levies of special "protection money" finally lessened and later ceased. The French Revolution (1789) in general finally put an end to the special taxation of Mennonites in South Germany and Alsace.

In other parts of Germany as well special levies were imposed upon Anabaptists and Mennonites, in effect in return for limited toleration. In East Friesland (q.v.), for instance, the ruler Rudolf Christian in 1626 introduced the practice of requiring a certain payment per family annually in return for a Schutzbrief (letter of protection), thereby setting a pattern for his successors until East Friesland became Prussian in 1744. But even the Lutheran pastors in this area, particularly in Norden, joined in extorting money by demanding that the Mennonites pay taxes for the upkeep of Lutheran churches and by collecting fees for services, such as funerals, which they did not render. It was only in 1894 that the Mennonites were freed from making contributions to the state church. Similar fees had to be paid by Mennonites in Crefeld to the Reformed Church until they were released from them by the king of Prussia c1720, although in 1721 he required the payment of a fee for the privilege of exemption from military service. In other places also in Germany money payments were required in lieu of military service. In 1814 in West Prussia, when the Landsturm (militia) was established, Mennonites were required to pay a certain sum per acre to support the Landsturm. In Prussia Mennonites were everywhere required to pay the same church taxes (for the support of the state church of course) until into the 20th century. In West Prussia the long legal battle necessary to free the Mennonites from the state church taxes was not victoriously concluded until 1922.

War Taxes. Among the Anabaptists in Moravia the differences regarding payment of special war taxes to support the war against the Turks led to a serious division in 1527. In Nikolsburg Hubmaier led a group ("Schwertler," *q.v.*) who paid the tax and approved the use of the sword in self-defense against the Turks, while the opposing group ("Stäbler," *q.v.*) were negative on both points. In 1511 the "Pikards" in Austerlitz declared they could not pay the war taxes, which were against their conscience. The agreement of Nov. 26, 1556, between the Palatine and Hutterite Anabaptists in the region of Kreuznach stipulated the following regarding the payment of war taxes: "But what is blood money, and serves wars or other unrighteous things or undertakings of the government out of itself and not out of divine orders and thereby attacks the conscience, the God-fearing man is not obliged to pay them, because God demands of him that he love his enemy (Matt. 5; Rom. 12), and the God-fearing man has promised this to God, and he shall not make any weapon that serves only that end (Isa. 2; Mic. 4), that the God-fearing man may not be a partaker in their wickedness or blood guilt."

The Hutterites consistently refused to pay war taxes and special levies. Peter Riedemann's *Rechenschaft* of 1545 says on this point: "For war, killing, and bloodshed (where it is demanded especially for that) we give nothing, but not out of wickedness or arbitrariness, but out of the fear of God (I Tim. 5) that we may not be partakers in strange sins."

In the United States some contemporary pacifists have refused to pay that portion of their federal income taxes which they calculate goes to support the military department and preparation for war, which is now about two thirds of the total; few if any Mennonites have taken this course. However, in the time of the Revolutionary War (1776-83) the Mennonites of the Franconia Conference (*q.v.*) in Pennsylvania divided over their attitude toward the Revolution, including the payment of special war taxes to the rebellious colonies, the majority being opposed to the payment of such taxes. As a consequence Bishop Christian Funk (*q.v.*) and his small group of followers were expelled in 1777. H.S.B.

Taylor, Georg: see Hausrath, Adolf.

Taylor, Thomas, b. 1561/2 in western England, d. at Haarlem, Holland, in 1655. He is said to have been the youngest son of a nobleman. With some other men who did not agree with the doctrines of the English State church he fled to Holland, unable to take along anything but a Bible and a little money. In Haarlem he started a textile business. He married Prijntje (or Proontje) van de(n)

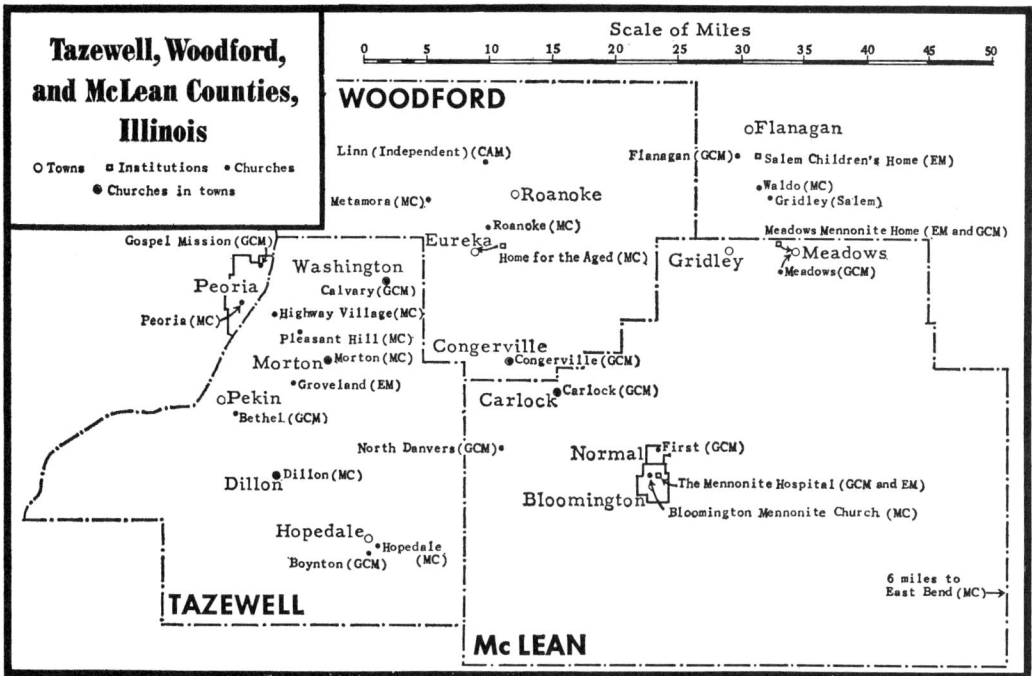

Tazewell, Woodford, and McLean Counties, Illinois

O Towns   □ Institutions   • Churches
● Churches in towns

Scale of Miles

WOODFORD

Linn (Independent) (CAM)

Metamora (MC)●

oRoanoke

●Roanoke (MC)

Gospel Mission (GCM)

Eureka

Home for the Aged (MC)

Washington

Peoria

Calvary (GCM)

Peoria (MC)

●Highway Village (MC)

Pleasant Hill (MC)

Morton● Morton (MC)

●Groveland (EM)

oPekin

●Bethel (GCM)

Congerville

●Congerville (GCM)

Carlock ●Carlock (GCM)

North Danvers (GCM)●

Dillon ●Dillon (MC)

Normal First (GCM)

Bloomington

The Mennonite Hospital (GCM and EM)

Bloomington Mennonite Church (MC)

Hopedale o

●Hopedale

Boynton (GCM) (MC)

TAZEWELL

McLEAN

oFlanagan

Flanagan (GCM)● □ Salem Children's Home (EM)

●Waldo (MC)

●Gridley (Salem)

Meadows Mennonite Home (EM and GCM)

Gridley ▭oMeadows

●Meadows (GCM)

6 miles to
East Bend (MC)→

Kerchhove(n), a Mennonite refugee from Flanders, and joined the Flemish Mennonite church of Haarlem. Throughout his long life his business was prosperous and he died a wealthy man. He is the ancestor of the Dutch Teyler (*q.v.*) family. vDZ.

M. Teyler-van Geleyn, "Stamboek der Teyler's" (manuscript found in the City Library of Haarlem); Blaupot t. C., *Holland* I, 64; *Eigen Haard*, 1885, No. 10.

Tayus, Johannes (d. 1630), a Dutch Reformed pastor, who in 1601, when he was pastor at Brouwershaven in the province of Zeeland, wrote *Proeve van de Leere der Wederdooperen . . . in elf poincten. Daerby een corte weerlegghinge . . .* (Leiden, 1601). The source of Tayus for his opposition to the Mennonites was the *Protocol* (*q.v.*) of the Leeuwarden Disputation of 1596. Tayus referred only to the arguments of the Reformed disputants, neglecting the Mennonite arguments. vDZ.

Tazewell County, Ill. The first Amish Mennonites in Tazewell County settled at Wesley City a few miles southeast of Peoria in 1831. This group met with the Black Partridge congregation in Woodford County until 1837, when Michael Moseman was ordained to lead the Wesley City congregation. This settlement developed into a strong congregation. In 1868 the congregation became a part of the "Egly" movement and is today the Groveland congregation of the Evangelical Mennonite Conference. About 1840 other Amish Mennonite immigrants who had settled along Dillon Creek near Tremont were organized into a congregation under Bishop Andrew Ropp. This congregation was known as Pleasant Grove and today is a part of the Morton congregation.

The first Mennonite church, as distinguished from the Amish, in Illinois was the Union Church organized near Washington. The first settlers came into the area in 1833 but apparently the church was not organized until the early 1840's. A Sunday school was organized in the Union Church around 1865, one of the first in the state. The Union Church no longer exists, most of the members having gone to the Metamora Church with which there had been conjoint services for many years.

In 1958 there were M.C. congregations at Hopedale, Morton, Dillon, Highway Village, and Pleasant Hill; G.C.M. congregations at Hopedale, Pekin, and Washington; and E.M. congregations at Groveland and Morton (organized in 1958). There were approximately 1,700 Mennonites in Tazewell County. T.R.S.

Tchayachy (Chayachy) Mennonite Brethren Church served the villages of Nikolayevka, Alexeyevka, and Tatyanovka of the Slavgorod Mennonite settlement (*q.v.*), Siberia. The leading minister was Wilhelm Giesbrecht, assisted by Heinrich Wiens, Jacob Eck, and Johann Harder. Worship services were originally conducted in school buildings. In 1922 a church was erected which was used conjointly with the Mennonite church of this area. C.K.

Gerhard Fast, *In den Steppen Sibiriens* (Rosthern, 1957) 78.

Tchayachy (Chayachy) Mennonite Church was located in the Slavgorod Mennonite settlement (*q.v.*) in Siberia, and served the following villages: Nikolayevka, Alexeyevka, and Tatyanovka. The leading minister, Heinrich Peters, was assisted by Peter Nickel, Cornelius Fast, and a Görzen. Worship services were conducted together with the Mennonite Brethren of this community in a meetinghouse (erected in 1922) and in schools. (See also **Slavgorod** Mennonite Church.)   C.K.

Gerhard Fast, *In den Steppen Sibiriens* (Rosthern, 1957) 72.

Tchernoglas (Chernoglas), a Mennonite settlement and village, also known as Gerhardstal, located in Novopokrovskaya, province of Ekaterinoslav, Ukraine, Russia, was established by about 25 families or 130 persons in 1860 on a rented estate of 2700 acres. (Friesen, *Brüderschaft*, 676.)   C.K.

Tchongrav (Chongrav) Mennonite Brethren Bible School was established at Tchongrav (Chongrav), Crimea, in 1918 through the efforts of Johann Wiens (*q.v.*) and with the approval of the Mennonite Brethren Conference. He was joined by Abraham H. Unruh, Heinrich J. Braun, and Gerhard Reimer as teachers. In 1924 the government closed the school, which had at that time 50 students and was offering a three-year course. The Winkler, Man., Bible School was in a sense a continuation.   C.K.

Abr. Unruh, *Die mennonitische Bibelschule zu Tschongraw, Krim, in Russland* (Winkler, 1928).

Tchunayev (Chunayev, Tchunaevka) Mennonite Brethren Church, also known as Margenau, was founded in 1899-1900, 15 miles west of Omsk, Siberia, Russia, on the west side of the Irtish River. Approximately 2,700 acres of virgin steppe was purchased from a Kirghiz named Chunayev, by Heinrich and Gerhard Ewert of the Neu-Samara settlement, and Johann F. Matthies, Franz Balzer, and Julius Dick of the Molotschna settlement. These five families are regarded as the Mennonite pioneers of West Siberia.

H. Ewert became the first minister of the congregation and Kornelius Martens the first teacher of a school organized in 1900. During the next four years a number of families from Molotschna, Ignatyevka, and Crimea, including Elder Jacob G. Wiens, joined the Tchunayev church. Under Wiens's leadership branch churches were organized along the Transsiberian Railroad extending approximately 225 miles. Assisting ministers in the early days were Heinrich Ewert, David Janzen, Cornelius Klassen, Johann Friesen, and Wilhelm Giesbrecht. Upon the resignation of Wiens in 1912, Jakob F. Hübert became the elder in June 1913. Headquarters of the congregation now were located in the village of Margenau, Akmolinsk district, 70 miles west of Omsk, where a church building had been erected in 1907. The membership reached 600. Branch congregations were located at Friesenov (*q.v.*) Mikhaylovka, Gorkoya, Kremleva, and several other places. Assisting ministers at this time were Jacob H. Wall, Gerhard P. Reimer, Gerhard J. Wiens, and J. J. Regier.

In 1929, because of Communist pressure, Elder Hübert emigrated to Brazil, where he became the founder and elder of the M.B. Church at Curitiba, Parana. In 1937 the last minister of the Tchunayev congregation was exiled by the Communists and the church was dissolved. Members of the church scattered to various parts of Europe, Canada, the United States, Paraguay, and Brazil.

Another M.B. church in this area, at least in later years, was the Smolyanovka Mennonite Brethren Church, of which Nikolai Siemens was the minister. In 1927 he reported on the life of the church, including a successful evangelistic campaign conducted among the neighboring Russian population in co-operation with the Russian Baptists (*Unser Blatt*, 1927, 42). Johann Heide, an M.B. minister of the Isil'-Kul area, who served as the minister of a Baptist church in the city of Isil'-Kul in the 1920's, reported in 1926 that the church had a membership of 118 and its own meetinghouse (*Unser Blatt*, 1926, 247). Additional reports about the activities of the Mennonite Brethren congregations in the Omsk region are found in *Unser Blatt*. In many instances the Mennonite Brethren worshiped jointly with the Mennonites. In 1930 all organized religious activities had to be discontinued since the ministers were exiled and the church building confiscated. (See also **Friesenov and Gorkoya** Mennonite Brethren Church.) For the latest developments in the religious life in the Omsk settlement, see **Omsk** Mennonite settlement and **Omsk** Mennonite Church.   I.G.N., C.K.

Dirks, *Statistik*, 1905, 56; D. H. Epp, *Adressbüchlein*, 1913; Gerhard Fast, *In den Steppen Sibiriens* (Rosthern, 1957) 142 ff.; A. H. Unruh, *Die Geschichte der Mennoniten-Brüdergemeinde* (Winnipeg, 1954) 205 ff.

Teachers' Association: see **Mennonite Teachers Association** (Lehrerverein), **Mennonite Teachers Association of Kansas**, and the following article.

Teachers Association, The Mennonite (MC), is a semiautonomous organization affiliated with the General Educational Council of the Mennonite Board of Education. It was organized in 1951 with 159 charter members. All members of the church who are actively engaged in teaching or who have qualified for the teaching profession at the elementary, secondary, or collegiate level are eligible for membership; students enrolled in teacher education programs are eligible for associate membership.

The purposes of MTA are (1) to encourage a spirit of fellowship and unity among Mennonite teachers; (2) to assist members in solving ethical problems peculiar to Mennonite teachers; (3) to foster conviction for the promulgation and the preservation of Christian faith and practice; (4) to cultivate the concept that teaching should be an avenue of service; (5) to serve as a clearinghouse for the exchange of valuable experiences and of good teaching techniques; (6) to assist in teacher placement; (7) to encourage teachers to grow professionally; (8) to champion the cause of the Mennonite teacher in every phase of his profession; and (9) to co-operate with the General Educational Council in promoting the educational program of the Mennonite Church.

The annual meeting of MTA is held in conjunction with the annual meeting of the Mennonite Board of Education. The Association seeks to foster some of its purposes through the organization of local Mennonite teachers organizations. In the spring of 1958 the Association published the first issue of the *MTA Bulletin*. In 1958 the officers of MTA were Harold D. Lehman, president; J. Lester Brubaker, vice-president; and E. Grant Herr, secretary-treasurer.   K.L.M.

Teck (Deck), Ulrich, an Anabaptist of Waldshut, was expelled from the canton of Zürich, Switzerland, on Nov. 18, 1525, with Michael Sattler (*q.v.*) and Martin Lingg (*q.v.*) of Schaffhausen. He was evidently very active in the Anabaptist cause in the canton of Zürich. One of the men he baptized there was Hans Künzi of Klingnau.   S.G.

L. von Muralt, *Glaube und Lehre der schweizerischen Wiedertäufer* (Zürich, 1938) 24 f.; *TA Zürich*, 109, 136, 197, 261, 284; *ML* II, 658.

Teenstra, a Dutch Mennonite family, originally from the hamlet of Teerns near Leeuwarden in Friesland, where they were farmers. Later this family is found in the province of Groningen. Some of its members were pioneers in agriculture, as was Marten Dirks Teenstra (Teerns 1742-Zuurdijk 1806). His sons Douwe Teenstra (1768-1823) and Aedsge Teenstra (1776-1813, married to Fokeltje de Waard) in 1795 reclaimed the Ruigezandster polder near Zoutkamp in northwestern Groningen. Douwe is also named for inventing a new way of threshing rape-seed (colza). In the 19th century some of the Teenstras were farmers near Grijpskerk, where they were also deacons of the Mennonite congregation. In this century they traded in grains.   vdZ.

Van der Aa, *Biogr. Wb.* XVII (Haarlem, 1874) 43; S. K. de Waard, *Aanteekeningen uit de Geschiedenis van Doopsgezinden in't Westerkwartier . . .* (Groningen, 1901) 31, 33, 40, 41, 44.

Teere Vriezen (Tender Frisians), a name sometimes given to the Young Frisians. (See **Frisian Mennonites.**)   vdZ.

Teerns, Jelle Sipkes van (1738-March 29, 1823), whose father was a farmer near Leeuwarden in Friesland, Netherlands, and who at first was a farmer himself, thereupon a carpenter, educated himself by reading, particularly on history and theology. In 1768 he was chosen as preacher of the Veenwouden Mennonite congregation and earned his living by continuing his carpentry. He soon established a reputation as an eloquent preacher. In February 1771 he moved to IJlst, where he served the small Waterlander congregation for nearly 50 years, retiring in 1818.

Jelle Sipkes was a clear-headed man; his piety had a strong moralistic tendency; his ideas were rather liberal, both concerning religion and politics. He was always interested in political affairs; as a "patriot" (*q.v.*) he took an active part in the government both of his home town and the provincial government of Friesland in 1795-96. In his private life he had to contend with many sorrows and cares because of illness in his family. Parts of his diary were published by H. J. Busé in *Doopsgezinde Bijdragen* 1909. His son Sipke Jelles van Teerns (1776-1829), a baker by trade, was like his father an untrained minister, serving at Irnsum from 1804 until his death. (*DB* 1870, 151; 1909, 49-103; 1912, 110; *Naamlijst* 1829, 49 f., 54.)   vdZ.

Teickowitz (Takowitz), a castle and village owned by Baron Georg Christoph Teufel, and a Bruderhof of the Hutterian Brethren in Moravia. The baron defended Claus Braidl (*q.v.*) in 1593. The Bruderhof was plundered by troops and partly burned down on Dec. 14, 1620. In October 1622 the Brethren were driven out of Teickowitz, leaving all their property behind. They settled in Hungary. (Beck, *Geschichts-Bücher;* Wolkan, *Geschicht-Buch;* Zieglschmid, *Chronik;* ML IV.)   Hege.

Telner, Jacob, a well-to-do Quaker merchant of Amsterdam, formerly a resident of Crefeld, Germany, was the major liaison between William Penn and his agent Benjamin Furly in Rotterdam, and the thirteen Mennonite-Quaker families of Crefeld who settled Germantown, Pa., in 1683. He was baptized a Mennonite in Amsterdam on March 29, 1665, but became a Quaker there sometime before 1676, possibly as early as 1667. Soon after 1678 he moved to Crefeld and threw himself actively into the promotion of emigration from the Rhineland to Pennsylvania. He is probably as much as any one responsible for the Crefeld colonization of Germantown. In 1678-81 he visited New York and Pennsylvania at least once. On March 9 and 10, 1682, Telner, Dirck Sipman of Crefeld, and Jan Streypers of Kaldenkirchen, each bought 5,000 acres of land in Pennsylvania, securing deeds signed by William Penn personally and executed in London. On June 18, 1683, Telner was with the thirteen emigrant Crefeld families in Rotterdam, at which time he sold 2,000 acres to the three brothers Op den Graeff and 1,000 acres each to three other Crefeld emigrants. He later bought more land there, for he owned a block of land near Skippack which was for a time called Telner's Township. Before Dec. 12, 1684, Telner had arrived in New York and visited Philadelphia and Germantown, but returned to New York to spend the winter there with his family, settling in Germantown in the spring of 1685. Here he lived until 1696, when he returned permanently to Europe. In 1709 ff. he was active in aiding the Palatine and Swiss Mennonites as well as others to get to Pennsylvania. William Penn was so appreciative of his services that he gave him a special grant of 100 acres of "Liberty lands" in Philadelphia's suburbs. Throughout all this time Telner was also active religiously as a Quaker wherever he went. Hull calls him "one of the most useful Quakers of his time."   H.S.B.

William I. Hull, *William Penn and the Dutch Quaker Migration to Pennsylvania* (Swarthmore, 1935), biography of Telner pp. 239-53, from which the above sketch was drawn.

Telugu Mission (MB). *The Field.* The Telugu mission field of the Mennonite Brethren Church of North America is located near the city of Hyderabad, Deccan, India, in the State of Andhra Pradesh, a small section of the field extending into the Madras Presidency. The Muse River forms the northern boundary between the Mennonite Brethren and the American Baptist fields. From here the field extends southward to the Tungabadra and Kisna rivers for a distance of about 120 miles. The maximum width from the east to the west is about 150 miles. The mission field embraces some 10,800 square miles with a population of 1,540,000 scattered in 2,500 villages and Hyderabad City. The field is not a large flat steaming, unhealthy jungle, but is dotted with hills, reaching in some cases to the height of 3,000 feet. Besides, there are some beautiful woods and fertile fields. A railroad traverses the field from north to south and four mission stations, Shamshabad, Jadcherla, Mahbubnagar, and Gadwal, are situated along this railroad. The territory is divided into ten mission fields with a mission center located in each field: Hughestown, Shamshabad, Jadcherla, Kalva-Kurthy, Deverakonda, Nagar-Kurnool, Wanaparty, Mahbubnagar, Narayanpet, Gadwal fields, with a section designated as the "Home Mission," which is being served by the Telugu Mennonite Brethren Convention.

The Founding of the Mission. The mission was founded in 1899 by a group of four missionaries consisting of the N. N. Hieberts, Elizabeth Neufeld, and Anna Suderman. Since the field had formerly been claimed by the American Baptist Mission Union and since it lay between some of their mission stations, credit must be given to the kind co-operation of the Baptist missionaries and to Abraham Friesen, a Mennonite Brethren missionary from South Russia who was serving at Nalgonda, a neighboring Baptist mission station. His help and advice was of great value in securing the field and beginning the work.

On Oct. 10, 1900, the missionaries occupied a very suitable place in Hughestown, three miles south of Secunderabad and just a short distance north of Hyderabad, on an elevated section overlooking both cities, as well as a number of villages. It seemed an ideal location for a mission station. In November of that year they began regular preaching services and opened a school for children.

The new work, however, was not permitted to continue very long. On Jan. 14, 1902, Hiebert became sick and was ordered by the doctor to leave India. In March he and his wife returned to America, never to see India again. Elizabeth Neufeld and Anna Suderman temporarily transferred to the mission of the Mennonite Brethren of Russia and the Baptist Missionary Union. The Hieberts were replaced by John H. Pankratz and his wife, who arrived in India Oct. 20, 1902. Since the original mission station had only been rented, the new missionaries purchased a suitable site for a mission compound in the suburb Mulkapet, taking possession on Nov. 26, 1903. Only four days later they conducted the first service in their home. Abraham Friesen had transferred several national workers to this new work and thus an effective ministry could be begun. In addition to the evangelism, schoolwork was immediately begun, as well as work among the women and the sick. On March 27, 1904, the missionaries, national workers, and a few Christians gathered at the mission station Mulkapet to organize the first Mennonite Brethren Church among the Telugus under the auspices of the Mennonite Brethren Church of North America.

The Growth of the Mission. The Mulkapet mission station was liquidated in 1913 and the work was transferred to Hughestown. Since 1914 the field has been known as the Hughestown mission field.

	Devera-konda	Gadwal	Hughes-town	Jadcherla	Kalva-Kurthy	Mahbub-nagar	Nagar-Kurnool	Shamsha-bad	Wana-party	Nara-yanpet
MISSION STATIONS AND FIELDS										
Square Miles	1,200	1,200	1,100	700	800	1,400	1,200	1,200	1,200	1,000
Population	180,000	170,000	230,000	90,000	100,000	230,000	160,000	120,000	160,000	200,000
Villages	270	250	230	120	130	300	250	150	250	325
Year Founded	1910	1936	1903	1933	1933	1936	1906	1920	1913	1955

Statistical Summary as of 1953. Villages—2,175; stations—9; boarding schools—13 (8 elementary, 3 middle, 1 high, 1 Bible); hospitals—6; staff through the years—59 (20 couples, 19 single women); under appointment—5 (2 couples, 1 single woman); baptized believers—14,000; organized churches—180; church buildings—170; ordained or licensed ministers—113; village evangelists and teachers—175; Bible women—120; villages with Christians—200.

A monthly church paper in the vernacular was begun in 1920, the *Suvarthamani,* which has become the official organ of the indigenous church. The printing press first established at Nagar-Kurnool has been transferred to Mahbubnagar. In 1943 a high school was begun in Shamshabad, which has also been transferred to Mahbubnagar; it offers a three-year course, and had an enrollment of 100 in 1953. The Bethany Bible School, begun in 1920 for the training of indigenous workers, was begun at Nagar-Kurnool, transferred in 1930 to Shamshabad, and in 1946 to Deverakonda. Nearly all of the 300 ministers, evangelists, teachers, Bible women, and other Christian workers have received their training in Bethany.

The advances in recent years have been particularly in strengthening the indigenous church and organizing it on a sound basis. On each of the station fields the churches have formed a field association which has a large annual gathering. All the churches together have formed the Andhra Mennonite Brethren Convention, which is ultimately to take full responsibility for the church in India. A Mission and Church Council, on which the mission has six and the church eight members, handles matters of common concern to both. G.W.P., J.H.L.

G. W. Peters, *The Growth of Foreign Missions in the Mennonite Brethren Church* (Hillsboro, 1952); Mrs. H. T. Esau, *The First Sixty Years of Mennonite Brethren Foreign Missions* (Hillsboro, 1954).

Teminabuan, a mission station on the Dutch part of New Guinea (*q.v.*) operated since 1953 by the Dutch Mennonite Mission Association (*q.v.*). vDZ.

Temmerman, François, an Anabaptist martyr: see **Fransoois de Timmerman.**

Tempel, van den, a former Mennonite family, found at Emden, East Friesland, Germany, and in the Netherlands, particularly at Amsterdam, but also at Leiden. Jan Tonnis (1607-72) was a Mennonite cloth merchant at Emden; he had been trained for this business by his uncle(?) Jacob Theunis(z) (q.v.) at Amsterdam. Jan Tonnis was not only a successful businessman but also a son of the muses, publishing a moralistic-religious play in verse: *Josephs droef en bly-eind Spel* (Groningen, 1639). Since his shop was called "In den Tempel van Salomo" he was commonly called Jan Tempel, and van den Tempel became the family name of his descendants.

Abraham van den Tempel, b. 1622 at Leeuwarden in Friesland, d. Oct. 4, 1672, at Amsterdam, who was a son of the Mennonite preacher and painter Lambert Jacobsz (q.v.), at first applied himself to cloth trade, being trained in Amsterdam and later, c1636-c42, by his relative, the above Jan Tonnis at Emden, whose family name he took. From 1645 he had a cloth shop at Leiden. But he too was not only a businessman, but also a well-known and, in his time, famous painter, particularly painting portraits. His pictures are still found in the Amsterdam Rijksmuseum, the Mauritshuis museum at The Hague, and the city museum of Leiden. One of the well-known Dutch painters who was influenced by van den Tempel was Frans van Mieris, who may have been a Mennonite, and who worked in his studio. Abraham van den Tempel was baptized in 1643 in the Amsterdam Lamist church. He was married to Trijntje Hogemade.   vDZ.

Winkler Prins Encyclopedie (6th ed. Amsterdam) XVII (1953) 373; *idem,* Supplement (1955) 411; *Amstelodamum Yearbook* XXV (1928) 85 f., 108; W. Martin, *Rembrandt en zijn tijd* (*De Holl. Schilderkunst in de XVIIde eeuw* II) 3d ed. (Amsterdam, n.d.,-1944) 154, 220, 227; Thieme-Becker, *Allg. Lexikon der bildenden Künstler* (Leipzig, 1938).

Tempelhof, a village established in 1868 by members of the Temple church or Friends of Jerusalem of Mennonite background from the Molotschna settlement and others from Bessarabia. The settlement was located on the Kuma River in the foothills of the Caucasian Mountains. Tempelhof was a seat of a Temple church. (See also **Temple Church.**)
                    C.K.

Temple (German, *Tempel*) **Church** (*Deutscher Tempel* or *Jerusalemsfreunde*) was organized on June 19, 1861, by Christoph Hoffmann (q.v.), a Lutheran clergyman, at a meeting of the Friends of Jerusalem at Ludwigsburg near Stuttgart, Germany. The movement rooted in Württemberg Pietism. Gottlieb W. Hoffmann, the father of Christoph Hoffmann, had founded the separatist settlement of Korntal near Stuttgart. Philipp M. Hahn (q.v.) influenced Christoph Hoffmann regarding the establishment of the kingdom of God on earth and called all true believers "out of Babel," to which he later added the notion of gathering them in Palestine in order to be enabled to "build the temple of God"

(Eph. 2:21-22; I Pet. 2:51). Already in 1854 Hoffmann had started the paper *Süddeutsche Warte,* an "organ for the gathering of the children of God in Jerusalem."

Germany. First the group established a school at Kirschenhardthof, near Marbach, Württemberg. Close co-workers of Hoffmann were G. H. Hardegg and Christoph Paulus. In 1858 a delegation went to Palestine to investigate settlement possibilities. In 1860 five young men were sent thither as pioneers. In 1866 a settlement was established near Nazareth, and in 1869 the colony of Haifa was established. Jaffa, Sarona, and Rephaim followed. Christoph Hoffmann was the leader of the movement. When he died in 1885 he was succeeded by his son, Christian Hoffmann.

The Pietism of the Temple movement was soon given up and was replaced by a humanistic-rationalistic philosophy. Many of the former friends of Hoffmann turned their backs on him. The rationalism of the University of Tübingen which he had fought in his early days he now embraced. The emphasis on an undenominational, nondoctrinal enlightened Christianity, living a good life, remained with the Templers. They were good business people and promoted cultural endeavors.

Russia. The contact between the Temple movement of Württemberg and the Mennonites of the Ukraine was established through Nikolai Schmidt (q.v.), who had traveled in South Germany and became acquainted with the school at Kirschenhardthof. As a result Johannes Lange (q.v.) of Gnadenfeld (q.v.) attended the school and became a teacher of the Gnadenfeld Bruderschule. His influence as a disciple of Christoph Hoffmann in the school as well as in the community was objected to. A long-drawn-out controversy took place in which the ecclesiastical and civil authorities and the government became involved. Johannes Lange was imprisoned in Halbstadt in 1863. Twenty Mennonites then signed a document organizing the Evangelische Mennonitische Gemeinde of Gnadenfeld which was the beginning of the Temple Church or the Friends of Jerusalem in Russia (1863). In 1866 representatives of this new group obtained permission and established a new settlement in the Kuban (q.v.) area.

In 1868 a delegation rented an estate from Count Orbeliani for thirty years. The Gnadenfeld Templers were joined by those of Württemberg background living in Bessarabia and established the Tempelhof (q.v.) settlement. On the other side of the Kuma River Orbelianovka was established by Württemberg settlers only. In addition two villages were established on the Kuban (q.v.) River named Alexanderfeld (q.v.) and Wohldemfürst (q.v.). With few exceptions all Templers moved to these new settlements. Common names were Lange, Schmidt, Goerzen, Goerz, Arndt, Hausknecht, Rempel, Hübert, and Görke. The pioneer life was difficult, but soon some prosperity was achieved. Great emphasis was placed on education and the development of the cultural life. The two villages on the Kuban River were located adjacent to the Mennonite Brethren settlement. In religious matters the Mennonite Church, the Mennonite Brethren, and the Temple Church, each went its own way, but they co-operated in matters pertaining to the economic and cultural life of the community. When Hoffmann published his five epistles in 1877-82 which attacked the doctrines of the Trinity, pre-existence of Christ, reconciliation, and justification in a rationalistic manner, most of his Mennonite followers deserted him. The periodical of the group, *Die Warte des Tempels,* warmly defended "old evangelical" Mennonitism.

In 1896 the thirty-year lease of Tempelhof and Orbelianovka expired. In 1896-97 the group then started the villages of Olgino (*q.v.*) and Romanovka (*q.v.*) near Sukhaya Padina, consisting of 30 farms with 4,860 acres.

Palestine. Around 1870 some Temple Mennonites moved to Palestine. When in 1902 the Temple settlement Wilhelma near Lydda was established, Mennonites from Wohldemfürst and Alexanderfeld, including Heinrich Sawatzky, Jakob Friesen, Franz Friesen, Johann Friesen, Jakob Goerzen, and Peter Decker, joined this settlement. A photograph of the Temple Council in Palestine in 1935 shows the following members of Mennonite background: Heinrich Sawatzky (Wilhelma), Theodor Fast (Jerusalem), Nikolai Schmidt (Jerusalem), Kurt Lange (Bethlehem), Jacob Decker (Wilhelma). During both World Wars the Templers were interned as German citizens. During World War II the young families were deported to Australia. When the state of Israel was established the remainder had to leave. Of these, 49 persons were sent to Germany, while early in 1949 223 persons landed in Melbourne, Australia, the remainder later going to Germany. In 1953 1,230 Templers were in Australia, living in Victoria, New South Wales, and South Australia. Templers of Mennonite background now live scattered in Germany, Austria, and Canada. Among the latter are particularly those who left Russia before World War I.

Friedrich Lange, the brother of Johannes Lange, was a teacher in Russia and Haifa and wrote *Geschichte des Tempels* (Jerusalem, 1899), a book of 941 pages, relating the early history of the group.

C.K.

Heinrich Sawatzky, *Templer Mennonitischer Herkunft* (Winnipeg, 1955); Franz Isaac, *Die Molotschnaer Mennoniten* (Halbstadt, 1908); H. Görz, *Die Molotschnaer Ansiedlung* (Steinbach, 1951); *Gesellschafts-Vertag und Satzungen . . . der Tempelgesellschaft (The Temple Society Central Fund)* (Jerusalem, 1922); Chr. Hoffman, *Mein Weg nach Jerusalem* (2 vv., 1881-84); E. Rohrer, *Die Tempelgesellschaft* (1920); Friesen, *Brüderschaft,* 87, 727; *Menn. Bl.,* 1888, 139; 1890, 27; 1894, 5; Fritz Grünzweig, *Die Evangelische Brüdergemeinde Korntal* (Metzingen, 1958); *ML IV.*

Temple Hill Mennonite Church (MC), located on Route 33 in Greene Co., Va., 3 miles east of the Skyline drive. The meetinghouse is an unused Methodist church, which was purchased by the Middle District of the Virginia Conference. John Kurtz opened the work on April 13, 1941, and served as pastor for 10 years. The present (1957) membership is 23, with Byard Shank as pastor. N.J.H.

Temple (German, *Tempel*) **Mennonite Churches** were located in Olgino-Tempelhof in the province

of Stavropol at the foothills of the Caucasian Mountains, and at Alexanderfeld (Alexandrodar), Velikoknyazhevsk, Kuban (*q.v.*) district, the latter with Isaak Fast as elder from 1884. Dirks reports a total membership of 148 of whom 49 were active (1905). Johann Lange, Johann Schmidt, Dietrich Dick, and N. Gengenbach served the Olgino-Tempelhof congregation.

The Templers of this area associated closely with those of Palestine. In 1881 Christoph Paulus, his son Franz Paulus, and Friedrich Lange from Palestine visited the Temple congregation in Russia. At this time some guiding principles were agreed upon. Some of the Mennonite Templers joined the settlements in Palestine (see also **Temple Church**).

C.K.

Friesen, *Brüderschaft,* 87, 727; Fr. Lange, *Geschichte des Tempels* (Jerusalem, 1899) 797.

Temperance: see **Alcohol.**

Tennessee, an inland state lying in the east south-central part of the United States, bounded on the west by the Mississippi River. The Unaka Mountain Range of the Blue Ridge traverses the eastern section of the state in a southeasterly direction. The population is largely rural, but during recent years the Tennessee Valley Authority has encouraged the building of large plants by the Aluminum Corporation of America and a rural electrification system that is revolutionizing the state's economy.

The state became the home of an Amish and a Mennonite settlement during the closing decades of the 19th century. In 1872 the Amish bishop, John Stoltzfus, of Lancaster County, Pa., with five of his children and their families, founded a congregation near Concord (*q.v.*) in the southwestern part of Knox County. Another settlement (now extinct) of Amish and Mennonites sprang up about 1890 near McEwen in Dickson County (*q.v.*) about 40 miles west of Nashville. The Concord congregation declined after the death of its founder, several families uniting with the Plymouth Brethren in Knoxville. With a new influx of both Amish and Mennonites after 1884 the membership grew to over 100. A decline set in after the Amish element in the congregation repeatedly voted against conference affiliation. The district mission board of the Virginia Mennonite Conference (*q.v.*) sponsors the present membership of 11. The same board sponsors the Mennonite Gospel Mission (*q.v.*) in Knoxville, membership 37. The Ohio and Eastern Conference (MC) maintains two mission stations in the northeastern corner of the state at Shauns and Indian Springs, and two others just across the border near Lansing and Grayson, N.C.

In 1923-56 the Krimmer Mennonite Brethren maintained a congregation at Shell Creek, Carter County, in the extreme northeastern corner of the state across the North Carolina line, where the conference has a congregation in Watauga County (*q.v.*). About 1934 Robert F. Sherrard, a Defenseless Mennonite (*q.v.*) residing at Gibsonburg, Ohio, founded a mission at Smithville, DeKalb County, near the geographical center of the state. The Evangelical Mennonite Conference (*q.v.*) in 1956 reports 54 members in four congregations in this and adjoining counties served by ministers in Smithville and McMinnville. A growing Old Order Amish congregation near Ethridge, Lawrence County, in the extreme southern part of the state and 140 miles east of Memphis, founded in 1946 by a group including two ministers from Apple Creek, Ohio, now numbers 61 members, with three ministers and two deacons. J.S.U.

Ter Meer (ter Mehr), an outstanding Mennonite family of Crefeld (*q.v.*), Germany, coming originally from München-Gladbach (*q.v.*), where Jan ter Meer (1594-1672) was a Mennonite elder from about 1628. In 1654 he moved to Crefeld (see **Meer, Jan ter**). Mewes (Bartholomäus) ter Meer (1622-92), b. at Deventer, moved to Crefeld in 1654 and became a citizen in 1679. His son Klaas (1650-98) was a lay preacher of the Crefeld congregation, whose daughter Gritgen (1675-1711) was the wife of the Mennonite Jan Crous (preacher 1716-24). Abraham ter Meer (1729-1804), a grandson of Klaas, was a book dealer in Crefeld and publisher and founder of a lending library; he was the center of a group of intellectual clergymen and citizens under the spirit of the Enlightenment. The persons now living who bear the name are descendants of Klaas ter Meer; but the branch of Privy Councillor Edmund ter Meer (1852-1931), founder of the dye factories of Weiler ter Meer in Uerdingen, is no longer Mennonite. E.C.

Beiträge zur Geschichte rheinischer Mennoniten (Weierhof, 1939) 22 f., 81, 118 f., ML IV.

Terek Mennonite Settlement was located in the southeastern corner of European Russia, on the Terek River, which flows into the Caspian Sea in the Eastern Caucasus, bordered on the north by the Aktash River, and situated north of the railroad between Rostov and Petrovsk on the Caspian Sea.

The settlement was established in 1901, on 66,960 acres of land purchased by the Molotschna settlement from the Lvov brothers for about 1,000,000 rubles. The landless families received 108 acres each, while some individuals who had farms were permitted to purchase land in order to make the

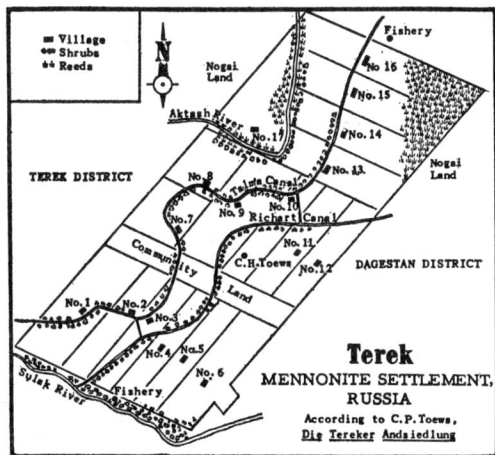

Terek
MENNONITE SETTLEMENT, RUSSIA
According to C.P. Toews,
Die Tereker Ansiedlung

financing of the purchase possible. The total settlement was divided into 17 villages, each village consisting of 24 to 35 farms, each of which had 108 to 216 acres of land. Some land was not distributed and remained community land, and some of it was wasteland. The journey from the Molotschna settlement to the Caucasus took about a week. Each village received a name and a number, as follows: 1, Wanderloo; 2, Khartch; 3, Talma; 4, Konstantinovka; 5, Sulak; 6, Alexandrovka; 7, Maryanovka; 8, Rohrbach; 9, Nikolayevka; 10, Müdelburg; 11, Prätoria; 12, Ostheim; 13, Taranovka; 14, Kameshlak; 15, Kaplan; 16, Agrakhan; 17, Aktash. The latter two villages never materialized. Villages 1-13 were settled at once, and 14 and 15 in 1904. The settlement consisted of 536 families with 3,400 persons. The soil varied greatly and was somewhat sandy. Some of it had a saltpeter content. The land was flat, with some brush. The wells were, as a rule, 15 to 35 feet deep. Some community wells were much deeper. Soon it was discovered that there was oil in the soil. World War I prevented the drilling of wells.

Every village had a Schulze (*q.v.*) and the settlement had an Oberschulze (*q.v.*), the first of whom was Gerhard Schmidt of Nikolayevka, followed by Gerhard Regehr and C. H. Toews. In 1915 a Cossack was put into this office by the government. When the Revolution broke out in 1917 he was succeeded by Cornelius Penner.

The settlement had an organization for the care of orphans (see **Waisenamt**). The first manager of this orphanage was Heinrich Günther, succeeded by C. H. Schmidt. The settlement also had a fire insurance patterned on the Molotschna fire insurance. The mail was originally received in the neighboring town of Khassav-Yurt. In 1908 post office and telegram service were established in the village of Nikolayevka. Nikolayevka was also the seat of the Oberschulze. The "Feldscher" in charge of the health program was M. Freimut. The distributing center (apothecary) was located in Talma. Mrs. Abram Funk, Mrs. G. W. Warkentin, and Margaretha Fast served as midwives and nurses. Cornelius Fast and F. F. Enns also distributed medicines.

During the first years the instruction of children took place in private homes. Most of the teachers had a very poor education. The teachers soon organized a "Lehrerkollegium," of which Cornelius Penner was the chairman. The school board consisted of Franz Enns, Bernard Fast, and Heinrich Sukkau. Regarding the religious life and the churches, see **Terek** Mennonite Church and **Terek** Mennonite Brethren Church.

The settlement made slow economic progress. In 1902 there was a total crop failure. Some soon began to irrigate land. Many, not accustomed to this practice, became discouraged. In 1908 and 1909, after repeated crop failures, many left. On the irrigated land the farmers harvested good crops of winter wheat. A commission consisting of four Tatars, two Russians, and two Mennonites of the Khassav-Yurt district, with the help of the St. Petersburg government, arranged to have irrigation canals established or improved. In addition to the "Talmak Canal" a second one was established known as "Richat-Canal." Irrigation took place in July or August. Two crops a year were harvested. Winter wheat, barley, oats, corn, sugar cane, and vegetables were raised. Great damages were caused by grasshoppers in 1909-10, and by frequent floods recurring in June, July, and August. In 1905, 105 persons died of malaria and typhoid fever, spread by the floods. In 1905 a dike about ten miles in length was constructed along the river in order to prevent floods.

The Mennonites raised cattle, horses, and hogs which they had brought along from the Molotschna settlement. They received good prices for their produce in the markets of Khassav-Yurt and Petrovsk. Because of the distance from markets, stores were opened in various villages, e.g., in Talma (Johann Derksen), Khartch (Daniel Boschman), and Rohrbach (Jacob Rempel). Cornelius and Franz Toews had a lumber and implement store in Nikolayevka. Most of the goods came from Khassav-Yurt and Petrovsk. In 1912 a state bank was opened in Nikolayevka. Johann Nickel established a flour mill in Talma and David Klassen built one in Nikolayevka. Smaller mills were found in various villages. A number of brick factories and carpenter and blacksmith shops were in operation. The governor of the Terek region visited the settlement in 1908 and 1913, and was received with great honors. During the war many of the men served in forestry camps and in hospitals.

With the Revolution of 1917 a new period started. First the settlers were hopeful. But it soon became apparent that the Nogays, Tatars, and Kumeks were now able to exploit the Mennonites without restraint, even driving away their horses during the night. Many Mennonites lost their lives during these attacks. The settlement held prayer meetings and asked the government for help. Finally, when life seemed impossible here, they decided to flee.

On Feb. 8, 1918, a two-mile caravan of settlers moved in the direction of the city of Khassav-Yurt, leaving everything behind that they had built up in seventeen long years. Villages 7, 8, 10, and 11 followed later. Before they left they were attacked again. Many had to flee on foot. On February 18, the larger part of the refugees was transported westward by train. The settlers abandoned 1,600 horses, 2,300 cows, 2,400 sheep, 958 hogs, implements, furniture, and all other property which could not be taken along.

Some of the settlers remained for some time in the Kuban area or outside the danger zone of the native population which had tormented them. In 1920, after the new government had been established, they were invited by the Dagestan administration to return to their settlement. After some negotiations in the capital, Petrovsk, an agreement was reached that they would get their farms back, that the trip to the settlement would be free of charge, that all the items which had been stolen would be returned, etc. In the spring of 1921 sixty families returned, and in the fall of 1921 forty-five more families followed. They settled in the villages 1-5 and 9. Some help was received from American Mennonite Relief. Many homes, churches, and

other property had been destroyed. C. P. Toews became the chairman of the Mennonite administration. Soon theft and murder were repeated and it became obvious that the Mennonites could not stay at the Terek. By 1925 most of them had moved away. Many of them joined the movement to Canada. Others scattered over the various Mennonite settlements in Russia. The Terek Mennonite settlement was the only undertaking of this nature by the Mennonites of Russia which was a complete failure.   C.K.

C. P. Toews, *Die Tereker Ansiedlung* (Steinbach, 1945); D. H. Epp, *Mennonitisches Jahrbuch* No. 10 (Berdyansk, 1913) 121.

Terek Mennonite Brethren Church was established in 1901 in the Terek Mennonite settlement (*q.v.*). In 1905 Jacob Dörksen was leader of the congregation; in 1913 it was Christian Ch. Schmidt. Other ministers were Cornelius Wittenberg, David Wölk, Gerhard Wiens, Gerhard Sukkau, Johann Löpp, and Heinrich Sukkau. In 1910 the congregation became independent. In 1912 it built a meetinghouse in the village of Talma. The congregation was dissolved when the settlers left the settlement in 1923.   C.K.

C. P. Toews, *Die Tereker Ansiedlung* (Steinbach, 1945) 22; H. Dirks, *Statistik der Mennonitengemeinden* (Leipzig, 1906); D. H. Epp, *Adressbüchlein* (Taurien, 1913).

Terek Mennonite Church was established in 1902 in the Terek Mennonite settlement (*q.v.*). Among the first ministers were Wilhelm Sudermann, Dietrich Derksen, Cornelius Fast, Bernhard Fast, and Dietrich Klassen. Later Franz Enns (*q.v.*), who soon became elder, Heinrich Balzer, David Balzer, Gerhard Wiens, Heinrich Regehr, Jacob Bärg, Benjamin Ewert, Cornelius Klassen, and Johann Dück were elected. In 1905 the congregation had a total membership of 1,078, of whom 424 were baptized. A meetinghouse was established in the village of Khartch and a more substantial one in 1908 in the village of Müdelburg. Franz Enns served the congregation as minister in 1903-6 and as elder 1906-18. He was a very talented leader. With the dissolution of the settlement in 1923, the congregation was dissolved.   C.K.

Heinrich Dirks, *Statistik der Mennonitengemeinden* (Leipzig, 1906); D. H. Epp, *Adressbüchlein* (Taurien, 1913); C. P. Toews, *Die Tereker Ansiedlung* (Steinbach, 1945) 22.

Terhorne (in Humsterland): see **Humsterland** and **Noordhoorn.**

Terhorne (in old documents often called Terhorne in Waterland), a village in the Dutch province of Friesland, the seat of a Mennonite congregation, which according to Blaupot ten Cate was founded before 1550; this early date is, however, questionable. Leenaert Bouwens (*q.v.*) baptized 30 persons here in 1561-66, and it is supposed that the letter of Sept. 1, 1557(?), by Menno Simons, *Letter to the Brethren in Waterhorne,* was addressed to the Mennonites of Terhorne.

There is not much information about the Terhorne congregation. About 1713 it joined the Sociëteit of Mennonite congregations in Friesland. The congregation, whose members were mostly farmers and skippers with some fishermen, was until the end of the 18th century rather conservative as to living and dress: in 1765 a woman was not admitted to communion because she wore a gold cap (oorijzer).

The baptized membership, numbering some 110 about 1713 and 125 in 1738, was 119 in 1838, 128 in 1861, 144 in 1901, and 86 in 1958. The present meetinghouse was dedicated on Sept. 24, 1865. An organ was installed in 1907, replaced in 1939. The parsonage, still in use, was a gift of the H. W. van der Velde family in 1855.

Until 1782 the congregation was served by preachers chosen from its own members; then (lay) preachers were called in from outside, one of whom, Oeds Roelofs (q.v.) Dantuma, a baker, served with great blessing from 1791 to 1836. The first pastor of Terhorne educated at the Amsterdam Mennonite Seminary was Jan Hendrik Akkerman, serving 1837-39; he was followed by Pieter Overbeek 1841-67, H. G. Dornseiffen 1867-1902, J. Koster 1902-5, A. Stiel 1905-9, G. A. Hulshoff 1910-13, A. de Vries Mzn 1914-35, J. W. Sipkema 1938-42, J. P. Keuning 1942-45, F. H. Sixma 1945-48, P. Messie 1949-53, and Miss J. Gorter 1954- . Among the church activities are a Sunday school for children and ladies' circle.
vDZ.

Blaupot t. C., *Friesland*, 89, 94, 189, 226, 248, 252, 254, 306; *DB* 1861, 142; *Opera Omnia*, 392; *Writings*, 1055.

Ternaard, a village in the northern part of the Dutch province of Friesland, the seat of a Mennonite congregation since 1849, in which year it split off from the Holwerd-Blija congregation as an independent church. While still a part of the Holwerd (q.v.) congregation the Ternaard group was usually called Vischbuurt, because the meetinghouse was found in Vischbuurt outside of the village of Ternaard. After this group had become independent, a new meetinghouse was built at Ternaard in 1850 and the old Vischbuurt church was sold. The Ternaard church was provided with an organ in 1894. Church activities include a youth group, ages 18-25; a youth group, ages 12-18; Sunday school for children; and a ladies' circle. Outstanding families in the Ternaard congregation are Bierma and Hiddema.

The baptized membership of Ternaard was 31 in 1850, 67 in 1901, 109 in 1958. Pastors serving here have been L. E. Halbertsma 1850, L. Noteboom 1852-58, A. A. Deenik 1860-81, pulpit vacant 1881-97, U. J. Reinders 1897-99, F. W. W. Braak 1900-6, J. G. Frerichs 1906-14, J. H. van Riemsdijk 1914-22, J. Kooiman 1923-30, Jac. Hulshoff 1930-37, K. T. Gorter 1937-39, J. A. A. Meijer 1940-46, Miss H. G. Zijlstra 1946-52, F. R. van der Meulen 1953- . (*DJ* 1850, 45-47; *DB* 1882, 127; 1895, 179; 1900, 230.)
vDZ.

Terneuzen, a town in Dutch Zealand Flanders, where there is a Mennonite Kring (circle), founded in 1942. The pastor of Aardenburg (q.v.) is in charge of this group, now (1958) numbering 19 Mennonites.
vDZ.

Terre Hill Mennonite Brethren in Christ Church located in Lancaster County, Pa., was organized in 1882. In 1957 the congregation had 80 members with Robert W. Smock serving as pastor. R.C.Re.

Terry Civilian Public Service Camp No. 64 was opened near Terry, Mont., Jan. 15, 1943, and was closed June 30, 1946. Under the Bureau of Reclamation and the Farm Security Administration, and operated by the Mennonite Central Committee, Camp Terry helped to develop the Buffalo Rapids irrigation project to improve about 30,000 acres in the level valley of the Yellowstone River. More than 280 men from twenty-two states worked in Camp Terry during its three years of operation. A farm and community school was held in the camp during the winter of 1944-45. An illustrated book, *This Is Our Story,* was produced by the campers in 1944.
M.G.

Melvin Gingerich, *Service for Peace* (Akron, 1949) 169-76.

Terschelling, a Dutch island (1947 pop. 3,544) formerly belonging to the province of North Holland, now to Friesland, with 264 Mennonites. Mennonites have been here since the 16th century. On his visits here Leenaert Bouwens (q.v.) baptized 12 persons in 1563-65, and at least 166 in 1568-82. Shortly after there were two or three congregations of different branches. There may have been a Flemish church, concerning which there is, however, no information. From about 1600 there was a congregation of followers of Elder Jan Jacobsz (q.v.), who made several visits to the island for baptism and communion services. This congregation, whose members were mostly engaged in farming, had its main center in the village of Midsland, while a simple meetinghouse was also found in the village of West-Terschelling. The Janjacobsgezinden (q.v.) often had difficulties with the governors of the island, who refused to acknowledge the marriages performed in their meetinghouses. In 1622 and again in 1679 the governors ordered their marriages to be performed by the magistrates. Finally in 1686 the governor consented to the old practice of having marriages performed in the meetinghouses by the elders. During the 18th century, when the Janjacobsgezinden were less conservative than those in Friesland, the ties with the other Janjacobsgezinden gradually were loosened; the congregation was usually called Old Flemish and later even Zonist (q.v.). Until 1782 this congregation was exclusively led by ministers chosen from the local membership, but in 1782 a preacher was called from outside, viz., A. S. Cuperus (q.v.), who served here 1782-90 and prepared the merger with the Terschelling Lamist church, which came into being in 1790; at this time the baptized membership of the Janjacobsgezinden numbered 73.

The Lamist church was in the 17th century called the Waterlander (q.v.) congregation. In the 18th century it was called United Waterlander and Flemish church, or simply Flemish church, and also Lamist (q.v.) congregation. It was always smaller and less conservative than the Janjacobsgezinden. Its members for a large part were engaged in shipping. In 1713, 70 members of this congregation, which must have been nearly the entire male membership, were commanders of Greenland whalers and other vessels. It had its largest meetinghouse in the village of West-Terschelling and a small one at Midsland. Until the merger it was served by lay preachers, sometimes called from their own members, later mostly from outside. For the salaries of these preachers the congregation was regularly subsidized by those of Amsterdam, Haarlem, and Rotterdam. At the time of the merger with the Janjacobsgezinden (1790) the membership was only 50.

In 1666 a severe blow struck the island; during a raid by the British, then at war with the Dutch, 350 houses of West-Terschelling were reduced to ashes, 180 of which belonged to Mennonites, and two of the Mennonite meetinghouses burned down. A contribution of 11,175 Dutch guilders was raised in several Dutch Mennonite congregations to rebuild these homes and churches. In 1734-36 the two congregations of Terschelling contributed to the relief of the Mennonites in Prussia.

In 1790, when the two congregations merged, neither of the meetinghouses at Midsland was being used; the united congregation used the two meetinghouses of West-Terschelling until 1817, when the former Janjacobsgezinden meetinghouse was sold, only the old Waterlander meetinghouse near the harbor being used henceforth. This church was remodeled in 1850 and installed an organ in 1851. As a gift of the A. C. H. Eschauzier family of The Hague in 1910 it acquired a new organ and stained glass windows, two of them with Biblical figures.

The membership, 123 at the time of the merger in 1790, was 95 in 1830, 125 in 1861, 144 in 1901, 140 in 1958.

After the merger the congregation was at first served by untrained preachers: Eelke Reins van der Werf 1790-d.1818, Dirk Huisman 1818-21, B. P. Boonstra 1822-28, and J. S. Bakker 1830-63. The first pastor educated at the Amsterdam seminary was Karst S. van der Meulen, serving 1863-65, followed by J. H. van der Veen 1866-92, S. D. A. Wartena 1894-97, W. J. Kühler 1897-1902, G. Fopma 1902-8, R. D. Boersma 1908-12, S. I. van der Meulen 1913-16, B. P. de Vries 1916-20, J. D. Dozy 1922-26, O. T. Hylkema 1926-28, W. I. Fleischer 1928-33, J. E. Tuininga 1934-36, G. M. Kosters 1936-41, J. Wieringa 1942-47, Miss T. van der Zijpp 1951-54, and A. P. Goudsbloem 1957-

Church activities include a Sunday school for children and a ladies' circle. Terschelling was one of the first Mennonite congregations in the Netherlands to have a choir (1895). Mennonite families at Terschelling, some of which are still found among the membership, are Swart, Doeksen, Roos, Rotgans, Duyf, Oepkes, Spits, Reedeker, Smit, Schol, Vis, Eschauzier, and Bakker.   vDZ.

Inv. Arch. Amst. I, No. 1180; II, Nos. 361, 1065, 2266-77; II, 2, Nos. 488-91; Blaupot t. C., Holland I, 24; II, 47 f., 196, 203, 205, 233; DJ 1850, 33-35; DB 1861, 88-93, 167 f.; 1895, 181 f.; De Zondagsbode XXIV (1910 f.) No. 10, p. 39; J. Loosjes, "Jan Jacobsz en de Jan-Jacobsgezinden" in Ned. Archief voor Kerkgeschiedenis XI (1914) 235-38 (repr. 51-54); church records of Terschelling.

Tersier (in the 17th century also *Targier,* possibly the original form), a Dutch Mennonite family, probably of Flemish descent, was found at Dordrecht in the 17th century. (1) Abraham Tersier (the name Ferrier, *DB* 1862, 104, is wrong), married to Geertruid Terwen, was chosen in 1691 as elder of the Dordrecht Mennonite congregation. His son (2) Jacob Tersier (Targier) (Dordrecht 1688-1735) was renowned for his poetry in the 18th century; even after he had become blind in 1712 he continued to compose poems, which were written down by his friends. A volume of his verse, *Gedichten,* was published after his death in 1737 at Delft. (3) Joachim Targier, also a poet, may have been his brother. He was a physician and the author of *Medicina Compendiaria* (Leiden, 1698). (4) Abraham Targier, a son of (2) Jacob, obtained his M.D. degree at the University of Leiden in 1739 and practiced medicine in his home town until his death in 1770. His son (5) Bartholomeus Tersier (Dordrecht, 1742 — Haarlem, 1824) obtained his M.D. degree at Leiden in 1769 and practiced medicine at Haarlem for more than fifty years. He was a trustee of the Mennonite Peuzelaarsteeg congregation from 1772 until his death. (6) Abraham Tersier (d. after 1810), probably a son of (3) Joachim, studied theology at the Lamist seminary 1761-68. Though he did not complete the course, he served as the (last) minister of the small congregation at Middelharnis (*q.v.*) 1771-1804. The congregation dissolved in 1805. There are no Tersiers in the Mennonite church at present.   vDZ.

DB 1862, 104; 1868, 92, 95; 1908, 109-13; Van der Aa, Biogr. Woordenboek XVIII (Haarlem, 1874).

Tersteegen, Gerhard (1697-1769), a leading German Pietist, born in Mörs, Germany, lived in Mülheim an der Ruhr and was trained in business. Here he was attracted by mysticism and devoted his life to the promotion of his religious convictions. In 1728 he gave up his business occupation, devoting his full time to helping people with their spiritual and physical needs by leading in devotional meetings, counseling, and practicing medicine as a lay physician. He translated writings by Jean de Labadie, Thomas à Kempis, and others. He published a number of his own writings including *Auserlesene Lebensbeschreibung heiliger Seelen* (3 vv., 1733-53), which included biographies of Catholic and Protestant "saints." In his large correspondence, Mennonites were included. Particularly the von der Leyens and Arnold Goyen of Crefeld were in close touch with him. He even preached in the Crefeld Mennonite church. His writings and songs ("Gott ist gegenwärtig," "Ich bete an die Macht der Liebe") have influenced Mennonite piety in many countries. Tersteegen was the father of Pietism (*q.v.*) along the Lower Rhine.   C.K.

RGG V, 1052; Dirk Cattepoel, "Das religiöse Leben in der Krefelder Mennonitengemeinde des 17. und 18. Jahrhunderts," Beiträge zur Geschichte rheinischer Mennoniten (Weierhof, 1939) 15-17.

Tertullian, Quintus Septimius Florens (*c*160-*c*222), the great Church Father of Carthage, the son of a captain, well educated, familiar with Greek, was converted to Christianity and defended its doctrines in numerous writings. His book *De Baptismo* (Concerning Baptism), in which he attacked infant baptism, is of especial interest to Mennonites. Very earnestly he insisted on faith as the unconditional requirement for a true baptism. This book shows that infant baptism was not yet a universal custom in the church of the second century. The *Martyrs' Mirror* has on its last page an address of encouragement to the martyrs who were confined in prisons at the time of the heathen emperors written by Tertullian. In 1522 Conrad Grebel procured and forwarded to Vadian a copy of the new edition of Tertullian (ed. by Beatus Rhenanus at Basel, 1521). It is probable that he read Tertullian, since he mentions him in the letter to Müntzer (1524). Menno Simons also read Tertullian. It is intriguing, but speculative to think that Tertullian's attack on infant baptism may have influenced the Anabaptists. (*Mart. Mir.* D 838-40, E 1139-41; *ML* IV.)

NEFF, H.S.B.

Terwe(n), a former Dutch Mennonite family, probably stemming from Flanders, Belgium, from where they emigrated because of persecution. It was widely ramified, one branch living at Middelburg, Rotterdam, Amsterdam, and another in Dordrecht, Rotterdam, Haarlem, Utrecht, and Gouda. In the Mennonite congregations of all these towns its members were deacons. The Dordrecht branch was leading in the Mennonite Church of this town from the early 17th century until *c*1725. Jacques Terwen, a preacher or a deacon of the Flemish Dordrecht congregation, signed the Dordrecht Confession in 1632. His father(?), Hendrik Terwen, d. Oct. 2, 1625, was an elder of this congregation; another Hendrik Terwen was an elder of the same congregation from 1658. In Amsterdam the Terwens were found in both the Lamist and the Zonist congregations from *c*1670 until the end of the 18th century. Most members of the Terwen family were well-to-do businessmen and manufacturers. Some of them, e.g., Josine Terwen of Dordrecht, and Laurens Terwen (d. 1705 at Dordrecht), also had poetic interests. Cornelis Terwe, living at Dordrecht in the 17th century, contributed a hymn to the hymnal *Lusthof des Gemoeds* by Claes Stapel (*q.v.*). vDZ.

DB 1862, 103, 104; *N.N.B.Wb.* V, 899; *Inv. Arch. Amst.* II, Nos. 1770, 2099; church records of Middelburg, Rotterdam, Amsterdam, and Utrecht.

Terwey, Jan, b. Oct. 11, 1883, at Amsterdam, who in 1903 was the first Mennonite after many decades to refuse to serve in the army, military service having become compulsory in the Netherlands in 1898. This refusal, then a novelty among the Dutch Mennonites, caused some sensation in the brotherhood. Terwey, who was a painter and etcher, and beautifully illustrated a book for children by Cor Bruyn, shortly after 1920 emigrated to Switzerland. (*DB* 1904, 233; information by Jan Gleysteen, Amsterdam.) vDZ.

Tesch, Peter: see **Tasch, Peter.**

Teschenmacher, Laurenz (Lorenz), a citizen of Aachen (*q.v.*) in Germany, was charged there in 1533 with Lutheranism. Though in a first trial

Teschenmacher refused to give information about his heresy, it was soon proved that he was an Anabaptist and had taught the "new doctrines" in sermons which were attended by his followers. Further particulars are lacking. vDZ.

Testament is the title often given to the letters which the Anabaptist martyrs wrote to their relatives after they had been sentenced to death, particularly to their children. Anneken (*q.v.*) Jans of Rotterdam wrote such a "testament" to her little son, which begins with the words "Isaiah, receive your testament" (*Mart. Mir.* D 48, E 453); Joost (*q.v.*) Verkindert wrote to his children: "Keep this letter for a testament" (*Mart. Mir.* D 526, E 863). The testament of Soetken van den Hout(t)e to her children (found in *Mart. Mir.* D 277, E 646) was separately printed in 1579. vDZ.

Testamenterleütterung (Testament Explanation) *Erleütterung durch auszug aus Heiliger Biblischer schrifft/ tail vnd gegentail/ sampt ains tails angehangen beireden/ zu dienst vnnd fürderung ains klaren urtails/ von wegen vnderschaid Alts vnd News Testaments/ vnnd jre beder Sündtuergebung/ Opffer/ Erlösung/ Gerechtigkait/ Gnad/ Glauben/ Gaist/ Folck unnd anderm so grundtlich/ lautter vnd nutzlich nie ersehen/ genant Testamenterleütterung.*

This book of over 800 pages is one of the fascinating Bible concordances (*q.v.*) which the Anabaptists published. They published topical concordances partly because of their devotion to the Bible and their need for this type of literature, and partly also, no doubt, because an Anabaptist book could not be so easily detected when it was written in the form of a concordance.

The *Testamenterleütterung,* published sometime between the beginning of 1544 and May 6, 1550, at Augsburg by the printing press of the Marpeck brotherhood, is, however, much more than simply a concordance. As the title indicates it consists of a series of excerpts from the Scriptures of the Old and New Testaments (each cited an equal number of times) along with the "tail und gegentail." (These terms are related to debates, and might be translated "affirmative and negative.") In the preface the editor indicates that he will refrain from giving the position of those who insist that the Old and New Testaments are identical and that redemption was present already in the Old Testament. Since that position had received abundant publicity, the *Testamenterleütterung* tried to present the other side of the argument, and to show that there is a real difference. The plan of the book is simply to take a number of key concepts, such as the Holy Spirit, forgiveness, or peace, and amass Scriptural references to them, first under the heading "Yesterday," then under the heading "Today," then finally a section on "Promised Yesterday." Sometimes a section is also added entitled "Longed for Yesterday." This interesting division of history between yesterday and today, yesterday being defined as before the death and resurrection of Christ, today being defined as after these events, is a result of the Marpeck brotherhood's struggle with three opposing ideologies, (1) the Reformed position on the Old Testament, (2) the spiritualistic tendency to relegate everything to the inner man and thus also wipe out all historical progression, and finally (3) the perversion of power which had taken place upon the fringes of Anabaptism at Münster where the Old Testament was made the standard of life.

Four reasons motivated the writing of this book. First, the author wished to refute the commonly held opinion that Christ's suffering worked retroactively into the Old Testament period. To hold such a position is to deny the commonly accepted assertion in the Apostles' Creed that Christ descended into hell, for there would have been no need for Christ to proclaim redemption to the patriarchs if they had already had all the gifts of salvation. Secondly, the suffering and resurrection of Christ is slandered if it is projected into the Old Testament. Thirdly, since the New Testament is clear on the point that redemption came only through Christ, to be vague on the distinction between the Old and New Testaments means to lessen the authority of the Scripture and to imply that it contradicts itself. Fourthly, through a confusion of the relation of the two Testaments earthly power is perverted from its rightful use and used against God's divine purpose.

The abundant use made of this book by the writers of the *Verantwortung* as well as the testimony of Jorg Seifried at Augsburg in May 1550 indicates that the *Testamenterleütterung* was written by Marpeck and his associates. The preface begs the reader not to be too concerned about the author, and if the "Beireden" (explanations) do not suit him, to read only the Scripture passages. Gerhard Hein has suggested that Leupold Scharnschlager (*q.v.*) is primarily responsible for the book.

The influence of the *Testamenterleütterung* is seen by two references in 16th-century literature. Jacob Andreae (*q.v.*) warns his hearers of the Anabaptist book *Today and Yesterday* in his sermons at Esslingen, Württemberg (printed 1568). According to Jan Kiwiet a reference to it also occurs in Andreas Ambergius' *Disputatio contra Anabaptistarum errores* (Wittenberg 1598), folio A 2. Within the Anabaptist brotherhood it is difficult not to see its influence in the Frankenthal Disputation (*q.v.*), where many days were spent on this precise subject of the relation of the Old and New Testaments. The *Testamenterleütterung* represents the finest attempt on the part of the Anabaptists to define the relationship of the Old and New Testaments without injustice to either. It is a monument to a brilliant attempt to arrive at a Biblical theology.

Two copies of this concordance have survived to modern times. One is in the Zürich Zentralbibliothek, the other formerly in the Prussian Staatsbibliothek in Berlin.   W.KL.

Jan J. Kiwiet, *Pilgram Marbeck* ... (Kassel, 1957) 77-80; Wilhelm Wiswedel, "Die Testamentserlaüterung," *Blätter für württembergische Kirchengeschichte* XLI (1937) 64-76; Torsten Bergsten, "Pilgram Marbecks Auseinandersetzung mit Kaspar Schwenckfeld," *Kyrkohistorisk Arsskrift,* 1957 and 1958; John C. Wenger, "The Life and Work of Pilgram Marpeck," *MQR* XII (1938) 160 f.; Johann Loserth, ed. *Quellen und Forschungen zur Geschichte des oberdeutschen Täufertums* (Vienna and Leipzig, 1929) 579-84 (Preface to *Testamenterleütterung*);

Jacob Andrea, *Drey und dreissig Predigen Von den furnemsten Spaltungen in der christlichen Religion* (Tübingen, 1568) Part 4, Sermon 5, p. 101 f.; H. W. Wolff, *Die Einheit des Bundes. Das Verhältnis von Altem und Neuem Testament bei Calvin* (1942).

Testimony. Formerly it was the custom in the congregations of the American Mennonite (MC) and Amish Mennonite groups having the plural ministry to have all the ordained men sit on "the long bench" behind the pulpit on the pulpit platform throughout the service and at the close of the sermon to have each in order of seniority, from a seated position, give a brief "testimony" to the sermon. This consisted normally of a few general comments of appreciation, endorsement, and emphasis. The first to testify concluded with the phrase "further liberty," which was an invitation to the next in order. Sometimes the testimony included a statement of disagreement with the sermon, or it might have been the simple statement "I can say yea and amen to the teaching," or "The message we have heard from the brother is according to the Word of God." The custom is still followed to some extent in the morning services in the Lancaster Conference and the Washington County, Md.-Franklin County, Pa., Conference and in two congregations of the Franconia Conference. It is uniformly followed in the Old Order Amish congregations everywhere. Among the latter it is expected that a senior layman or two will also briefly state his endorsement of the sermon, if he can sincerely do so. In some cases individuals were named by the Amish bishop to give testimony. After the testimonies, the minister who preached the main sermon leads in prayer. The custom was formerly followed also in the Volhynian Swiss churches in Kansas and South Dakota in the G.C.M. group. In Virginia (MC) usually only one minister "testified."

An anecdote is told of an Amish congregation in Johnson County, Iowa, which occurred about 1900, when a layman was called upon who had been sleeping during the sermon and who honestly stated: "I am sorry that I was sleeping and would not want to be responsible for what I did not hear, but what I heard and understood was in accord with God's Word."

The intent of the custom is clearly to (1) give united and strong support to the teaching offered, and (2) furnish a check of the content of the preaching of any one minister by all the others. Information is not available as to the antiquity of the custom or its practice in other groups, but it must have been brought from Europe to America in the earliest times, and probably goes back to the beginning of Anabaptist history, at least in Switzerland and South Germany. In Sappemeer (*q.v.*), Holland, in the Old Swiss congregation "after the preacher had finished his sermon other brethren spoke briefly to express their agreement with the sermon or to add a few words from the Bible."

The universal custom in the Mennonite (MC) conferences of having "testimonies" given to the conference sermon, both in the district conferences and the general conference sessions, by a number of ministers selected by the moderator, is a direct descendant of the testimony in the congregational services. It is strongly maintained in the conference sessions even though it has been dropped in the congregations. H.S.B.

Melvin Gingerich, Chapter XVII, "Church Services," in *The Mennonites in Iowa* (Iowa City, 1939).

Teufel, Eberhard (1884-1957), a Lutheran minister and church historian, was educated in the Württemberg seminaries at Schöntal and Urach in 1898-1902, and at the University of Tübingen 1902-6, as a student of the church historian Karl Müller. In 1910 he studied the Moravian Brethren communities at Herrnhut and Niesky. He served in various rural pastorates in Württemberg, wrote a number of articles on the history of the Herrnhut free church, and published the first scholarly biography of Rothe, the pastor at Berthelsdorf, which position was under the patronage of Zinzendorf, titled "Johann Andreas Rothe (1688-1758): Ein Beitrag zur Kirchengeschichte des sächsischen Oberlausitz im 18. Jahrhundert," in *Beiträge zur sächsischen Kirchengeschichte* XXX (1917) and XXXI (1918), a total of 200 pages. He participated in the *Festschrift* for the 70th anniversary of Karl Müller (1922) with an article, "Luther und Luthertum im Urteil Sebastian Francks." For decades he did research on the Anabaptists and Spiritualists. One result of this was the valuable historiographical report, "Täufertum und Quäkertum im Lichte der neueren Forschung," which appeared in the *Theologische Rundschau* 1941-48: XIII, 21-57, 103-27, 183-97; XIV, 27-52, 124-54; XV, 56-80; XVII, 161-81. He also wrote a number of articles on Anabaptist topics, among them "Der Täuferprozess gegen Pfarrer Hechtlein in Schalkhausen bei Ansbach 1529-30" (*Ztscht f. bayerische Kirchengeschichte*, 1949); "Religiöse Nebenströmungen der Reformation: Wiedertäufer und Schwenckfelder in der Reichsstadt Schwäbischgmünd u. im Remstal," (MS in GCL); "Die Beschlagnahme u. Verwaltung des Täufergutes durch den Fiskus im Herzogtum Württemberg im 16. und 17. Jahrhundert" (*Theologische Ztscht* VIII, 1952, 296-304). His only full-length book was a biography of Sebastian Franck, a favorite of his, *"Landräumig," Sebastian Franck, ein Wanderer an Donau, Rhein und Neckar* (Neustadt an der Aisch, 1954). The task of organizing the papers left by the late Christian Hege, coeditor of the *Mennonitisches Lexikon*, led him into collaboration in the third volume of that work. He was appointed as successor to Walther Köhler after the latter's death in 1946, on the board of the Mennonitischer Geschichtsverein. He was the chief promoter of the renewed publication of the Anabaptist documents (begun in 1930), and was chosen secretary of the Täuferakten-Kommission (*q.v.*) which is composed of representatives of the Geschichtsverein and the Verein für Reformationsgeschichte. He had been assigned the task of editing the second volume of Württemberg *Täuferakten*, begun by G. Bossert, Jr., but died (June 27, 1957) before he could complete the task. He contributed a number of articles to this Encyclopedia. His residence in the last years was Fellbach, a suburb of Stuttgart, Germany. H.S.B.

Ernst Crous, "Eberhard Teufel," *Gesch.-Bl.*, 1955, 32-36.

Teune (Tönnen), a Dutch family descended from the Swiss Thöne family, members of which came to the Netherlands in 1711 because of persecution in Switzerland, settling first at Deventer-Kampen, later also at Sappemeer. The Thöne family in Switzerland was originally not Mennonite, though the Touny mentioned by Peachey, who was an Anabaptist at Bern in 1537, may have belonged to this family. Among the Swiss immigrants to the Netherlands in 1711 was Hans Thönen (Tonnen), a Reformed farmer from Frutigen, b. *c*1661, married to Catherina Ricken (Rich), who was a Mennonite. With their nine children they settled first at Deventer, but soon after near Kampen. Among these immigrants was also Peter Teune (Tönnen), unmarried, aged 25, a shoemaker, who was a preacher of the Swiss congregation at Kampen 1736-63. Descendants of this Teune family were found in the Sappemeer and Kampen Mennonite congregations until recent times, but most of them gradually left the Mennonite Church. About 1900 a descendant, J. Teune, was a deacon of the Hilversum congregation. vDZ.

Paul Peachey, *Soziale Herkunft* (Karlsruhe, 1954) 122, No. 286; *Inv. Arch. Amst.* I, No. 1323; Müller, *Berner Täufer*, 309, 312, 324, 325; D. L. Gratz, *Bernese Anabaptists* (Scottdale, 1953) 49, 65; J. Huizinga, *Stamboek ... van Samuel Peter (Meihuizen) en Barbara Fry* (Groningen, 1890) 25, 32, 67, 114, 115, 117.

Teunis (Tunes), **Abraham,** of Crefeld: see **Tunis.**

Teunis, Jacob, was an elder of the Janjacobsgezinden (*q.v.*), a branch of the Dutch Mennonites. He was ordained with Lourens Jansen by Jan Jacobsz (*q.v.*) himself at Hoorn in 1603. He served until 1618, in which period he was very active in visiting the congregations for baptism and communion. He baptized 670 persons and founded a number of new congregations in Friesland. A song found in the *Nieuwe Gheestelijcke Liedekens* says that he "suffered persecution because of the truth" on the island of Ameland. vDZ.

Blaupot t. C., *Friesland*, 164; J. Loosjes in *Ned. Archief v. Kerkgesch.* XI (1914) 197, 207, 209.

Teunis Jansz, a member of the (Old) Frisian congregation at Alkmaar(?), Holland, published a letter in 1586/7 addressed to the Frisian and the Flemish Mennonites, in which he protested against the Huisko(o)per (*q.v.*) quarrel. Because of his moderate position he was expelled from the church at Alkmaar. (*DB* 1876, 31 f.) vDZ.

Texas, the largest state, area 263,644 sq. miles, in the United States, located in the south-central part of the country, is bounded on the south by Mexico and the Gulf of Mexico. It ranks sixth in population. It ranks first in the number of cattle raised, and first in number of farms, which produce wheat, cotton, rice, sorghum, oats, as well as many vegetables, fruits, and nuts. Petroleum is the leading industrial product. The agricultural opportunities as well as the mild climate of the southern part of the state attracted Mennonite settlers to Texas as early as the first decade of the 20th century. The Mennonite Year-Books of 1905-8 listed a Mennonite preacher Bernard Kroeker of Richmond, near Houston in Ford Bend County. He had 7 members of the Nebraska and Minnesota E.M.B. conference, who held their services in a schoolhouse. By 1905 Mennonite (MC) settlers arrived in the Tuleta area in Bee County, approximately 60 miles northwest of Corpus Christi. The 1907 Year-Book listed Peter Unzicker and D. S. King as preachers of this settlement. In 1957 this church, Tuleta (MC), had 10 members. E. S. Hallman was long pastor and bishop here. In the same general area northwest of Corpus Christi is Calvary Mennonite Church (MC), near Mathis, with a membership of 66 in 1957. This congregation is an outgrowth of mission activity launched in 1946. Forty miles west of Corpus Christi in Alice is a Mennonite mission (MC), started in 1958. A third MC mission, located in Corpus Christi, was started in 1956.

A second center of Mennonite settlement is in the Premont area, approximately 50 miles southwest of Corpus Christi and approximately 100 miles northwest of the extreme southeastern tip of Texas. The Mennonite Brethren moved into this region in 1927 and organized the Premont M.B. Church, which in 1952 had a membership of 53, plus a Mexican chapel with 7 members. Other Mennonites moved into this area in 1928, establishing the Falfurrias congregation (MC), now known as La Gloria, with 25 members in 1957.

Between Laredo and Brownsville along the Rio Grande River the Mennonite Brethren have established a flourishing chain of 7 missions with a total of 271 members as follows: Chihuahua at Mission 72, Grulla 52, La Casita at Garciasville 28, La Joya Chapel at Mission 6, Los Ebanos 74, Lull at Edinburg 15, Mission City Chapel at Mission 24. All the mission churches in southeast Texas work chiefly among the Mexicans.

Two Mennonite churches are located in the northwest part of the state, near the boundary of the Oklahoma panhandle. The Perryton Mennonite Church (MC), which in 1957 had a membership of 50, was begun in 1943. The Bethel Mennonite Church (GCM), in the same county at Waka, had a membership of 18 in 1957. Thus the entire Mennonite membership for Texas in 1957 was 500.

At Texline, in the extreme northwest of Texas on the New Mexico border, a C.G.C. congregation existed 1930-40. M.G.

Texas Mexican Border Mission (MC), carried on in southern Texas with Mathis as a center, where the Mennonite Board of Missions and Charities erected a church in 1955. Mathis is centrally located. This mission is under the direction of the General Mission Board although it is located in the South Central Conference district. In 1945 there were 50 baptized members, scattered over the entire district; in 1957 the membership was 66. This mission was officially organized at Normanna, Tex., on Dec. 11, 1938, when A. H. Kauffman and wife, the first missionaries, became members of the Mexican Mission. On Jan. 1, 1939, Kauffman was ordained to the ministry. During the first few years David Alwine and wife and Arthur Shertz and wife were helpers in the work. On May 12, 1940, the first and only Mennonite Mexican conference was held at Normanna, with representatives present from the mission stations of Falfurrias, Tynan, and Helena. In 1944 the Calvary Mennonite Church was organized at Mathis. In September 1946 the Kauffman family returned to Indiana and the Wm. Lauver family was appointed to take charge of the work in Texas. In 1954 J. Weldon Martin was the superintendent of the mission work until June 1957, when Paul Conrad became the pastor. A voluntary service unit worked at Mathis for several years, assisting in the building of the church and other work.

In August 1958 work was begun at Alice, 35 miles southwest of Mathis, with Sylvester Zapata as licensed pastor. The mission in Corpus Christi, begun in 1956 by Don Brenneman, was continued by J. Weldon Martin. A.H.K.

Texel is the largest of the Dutch North Sea islands (1953 pop. 10,070, with 902 Mennonites); it belongs to the province of North Holland. Means of subsistence are sheep farming, flower growing, agriculture, and tourist trade. On Texel are found the villages of Den Burg (pop. 2,890), Oudeschild (775), Den Hoorn (455), De Koog (515), Oosterend (910), De Waal (275), and De Cocksdorp (345). Anabaptists-Mennonites were found on this island from shortly after 1530. The martyrs Thijs (q.v.) Olbrants and Jan (q.v.) Gerrits, executed in 1543 and 1564, were natives of Texel. Elder Leenaert Bouwens visited the island twice in 1563-82, baptizing 13 persons there. Soon after this the Mennonites of Texel were divided into Waterlanders, Frisians, and Flemish. These branches merged gradually in the 17th-18th centuries. After 1772 there were only two congregations, that of Den Burg, Waal, and Oosterend, and that of Den Hoorn; since 1949 there has been only one congregation, called the Texel Mennonite congregation. For the early history, see **Burg, Hoorn, Oosterend,** and **Waal.**

The Mennonites of Texel, particularly in early times forming an important part of the population, could develop rather undisturbed. Only in 1649 (not 1643 as is stated in ME I, 614) there were difficulties with the Reformed clergy and the magistrates. In this year Claes (q.v.) Arentsz, elder of Nieuwe Zijpe, on the occasion of a baptismal service at De Waal, Texel, slightingly spoke of infant baptism, and was therefore arrested, but soon set free on bail. Soon after he had to return to the island to answer for his opinions to the Reformed clergy. In this dispute he was assisted by Galenus (q.v.) Abrahamsz and two other preachers of the Amsterdam Lamist congregation.

The Texel congregation now (1958) numbers 572 baptized members; meetinghouses are found at Den Burg, Den Hoorn, Oosterend, De Waal, and De Koog, whereas meetings are also organized at Oudeschild in a rented hall. The meetinghouse at De Koog was dedicated Dec. 18, 1955. At present the Texel congregation has two pastors: J. J. J. van Sluys 1954-58, Miss T. van der Zwaag since 1955, and H. van Bilderbeek since 1958. Well-known Mennonite families of Texel are Keyser, Daalder, Eelman, Roeper, and Bakker. (Blaupot t. C., *Holland* I, 195-97; *DJ* 1957, 21-25.) vDZ.

Texline Church of God in Christ Mennonite Church, now extinct, located near Texline, Dallam Co., Tex., was organized in 1930 with 40 members. H. J. Mininger was their pastor, and later Sam L. Fricke was ordained to the ministry. A meetinghouse was built in 1932. Because of the drought and sandstorms, the members soon began to leave, and the congregation became extinct in 1940. H.J.M.

Teyler, a former Dutch Mennonite family. The ancestor of this family was Thomas Taylor (*q.v.*, 1561/2-1655), who moved from England to Haarlem, Holland, where his descendants lived for about two centuries. Like their ancestor they were textile merchants and particularly manufacturers of silk. The Teyler family was very wealthy. A well-known member was Pieter Teyler (*q.v.*) van der Hulst. A branch of this family lived in Amsterdam *c*1660-*c*1780. Most of the Amsterdam Teylers were Zonists (*q.v.*), though some were Lamists (*q.v.*). Both in Haarlem and Amsterdam a number of Teylers were deacons. vDZ.

M. Teyler-van Geleyn, "Stamboek der Teyler's"; W. P. J. Overmeer, *Teyler van der Hulst* (n.p., n.d.); Mennonite church records of Haarlem and Amsterdam.

Teyler Foundation (Dutch, *Teylers Fundatie*) is the name of a foundation at Haarlem, Holland. Pieter Teyler (*q.v.*) van der Hulst willed his house with an important library, many art treasures and valuable rare items, together with a considerable amount of money to found it. The Teyler foundation, which came into being after the death of Teyler in 1778, is governed by five directors; it embraces a "Hofje," i.e., a home for aged women (founded by Teyler in 1756), a museum at Haarlem, in 1885 accommodated in a new building, containing paleontological, mineralogical, and physical sections, a coin and medal room, a collection of graphical art, including a rich collection of etchings by Rembrandt (*q.v.*), pictures, rare books, etc., the publication of a periodical *Teyler's Theologisch Tijdschrift* (1903-11, continued under the name of *Nieuw Theologisch Tijdschrift* 1912-46), and two scholarly associations, each administered by a board of six members. The First Association is for religion and theology, the Second for science, history, literature, and art. Both associations offer annual prizes for the best essay on a specific subject, posited by the trustees of the associations; the manuscripts, which are awarded a prize (a gold medal, or 400 Dutch guilders), are published at the expense of the foundation.

Among the prize winners there have been a rather large number of Mennonites; e.g., for the First Association, Daniel Hovens, Gerrit Hesselink (3 times), Petrus Loosjes, Cornelis de Vries, Jan van Gilse, Jacob Kuiper (3), Jeronimo de Bosch (2), Jan Kops Jac.zn, Hendrik van Voorst (3), Allard Hulshoff (3), Willem de Vos (3), Jan Brouwer (3), Willem Bruin (2), Rinse Koopmans, N. G. van Kampen (2), L. Weydmann, Chr. Sepp, and W. I. Leendertz.

Among the publications of the First Association the following deal with Mennonite history: W. J. Leendertz, *Melchior Hofmann* (1883); F. O. zur Linden, *Melchior Hofmann* (1885); J. C. van Slee, *De Rijnsburger Collegianten* (1896); K. O. Meins-ma, *Spinoza en zijn Kring* (1896); and P. Kawerau, *Melchior Hofmann als religiöser Denker* (1954).

From 1858 to 1892 the directors of the Foundation granted an annual subsidy of 1,000 guilders to the Amsterdam Mennonite Seminary. vDZ.

E. van der Ven, *Origine et but de la Fondation Teyler ... (1881)*; Chr. Sepp, *Proeve eener Pragmatische Gesch. der Theologie in Nederland ...* (Amsterdam, 1868) 48 f. *et passim*; J. Craandijk in *Eigen Haard* 1885, No. 10; *DJ* 1840, 112.

Teyler van der Hulst, Pieter, b. March 25, 1702, at Haarlem, Holland, d. there April 8, 1778, was a descendant of Thomas Taylor (*q.v.*), a son of Isaac Teyler and Maria van der Hulst. Pieter Teyler van der Hulst was married in 1728 to Helena Wijnand Verschaven, of Amsterdam.

He was a loyal Mennonite of somewhat liberal convictions. In 1735, when the Amsterdam Lamist (*q.v.*) congregation on the occasion of starting its theological seminary intended to found a General Dutch Mennonite Conference, Teyler in opposition to the views of his Haarlem co-deacons, promoted this conference ardently but vainly, for the ADS (general conference) was not founded until 1811. He served his home church, the Waterlander Peuzelaarsteeg congregation, as a deacon, and from 1750 he was trustee of the Klein Heiligland orphanage.

He was a silk manufacturer and merchant; through inheritance and through his own prosperous business he became a very wealthy man; yet he is said to have been very sober and even thrifty in his private life, at the same time a benefactor of the poor, liberally contributing to all kinds of charitable associations. In 1756 he founded a home for old women at Klein Heiligland. Being a man of study and scientific interests, Teyler, like many notable persons of this age, collected in his stately house in the Damstraat a large number of books, pictures, physical instruments, and valuable art treasures. After the early death of both his children and his wife (d. 1754) Teyler in 1756 willed his entire property to a foundation which would relieve poverty and promote science and art. (See **Teyler Foundation.**) vDZ.

N.N.B.Wb. V, 903 f.; *DJ* 1917, 21-35 (with portrait); *DB* 1876, 116; *De Zondagsbode* XXVII (1913-14), Nos. 46-47.

Tgahrt (Tjahrt), **Peter,** was elected elder of the Deutsch-Kazun (*q.v.*) Mennonite Church in 1901. In 1912 he left for Germany. (Friesen, *Brüderschaft*, 719.) C.K.

Thaler, Hans: see Taler, Hans.

Thau (Tau) is the last letter of the Hebrew alphabet. The Latin Bible version of the Vulgate reads in Ezek. 9:4 and 6, that a part of the people of Jerusalem were marked with the "sign of tau" on their foreheads, and that these thus marked would be saved in the coming great tribulation. It was apparently Melchior Hofmann who, being acquainted with the Vulgate, introduced this expression in Anabaptism. It then means, as the martyr Anneken Jans (*q.v.*) points out, that "those signed by the Lord, who have received the sign of Tau on their foreheads" are "the chosen, who follow the Lamb"

(*BRN* II, 72, 76). The expression was used by David Joris (*q.v.*) in his *Wonder-Boeck,* but also by Menno Simons (in *Opera Omnia,* 1681, fol. 183a, 282b, 636a; *Writings,* 59, 713, 416). For Menno too it has the meaning of salvation: "So we are marked on our foreheads with the sign of Tau, Ezek. 9. So the kingdom of God is within us." In the same sense the word is used in the booklet *Christelijcke Proeve* (*q.v.*) of 1570, where the Christians are admonished to penitence, that they might be sealed with the sign of Thau in the day of judgment.

vDZ.

BRN II, 72, note 1, 76; *DB* 1917, 156-59; H. W. Mei-huizen, *Galenus Abrahamsz* (Haarlem, 1954) 12.

Theobald, a Mennonite elder at Worms: see **Winter, Diebold.**

Theobald, Zacharias, a Lutheran clergyman, published a book in 1628 with the title, *Warnungs-schreiben vor den alten Wiedertäufern und neuen Schwärmern* (new edition in 1702), in which he sought to prove that the Weigelians and Rosicrucians, etc., were Anabaptists and also to show "what misery and wretchedness they have caused" (Keller, 20 ff.). Calvary mentions this book in his catalog of rare and precious books (Berlin, 1907) on page 61 under the title, *Widertäuferischer Geist . . . das ist: Glaubwürdiger und Historischer Bericht, was Jammer und Elend die alten Wiedertauffer gestiftet und angerichtet* (Nürnberg).　　　NEFF.

Ludwig Keller, *Die Waldenser und die deutschen Bibel-übersetzungen* (Leipzig, 1886) 20 ff.; J. H. Ottius, *Annales Anabaptistici* (Basel, 1672) 4; *ML* IV.

Theologia Deutsch, the original name for the book described in the article **Deutsche Theologie.** The statement of that article that the book was written *c*1500 by Berthold Pirstinger has not been generally accepted by scholars, the majority of whom still hold that it was written *c*1400 by an unknown member of the Teutonic Order at Frankfurt.

The most recent research shows that a number of Anabaptists were familiar with the book and some even quoted from it. According to Kiwiet, Hans Denk took over from the *Theologia Deutsch* the term "Ordnung Gottes," which he discussed extensively in two of his writings: *Was geredt sey* and *Ordnung Gottes und der Creaturen Werk,* although he reinterpreted the content of the concept. It is possible that similarities of phrase and thought found in both Thomas Müntzer and Hans Denk may be due to the use of a common source, i.e., the *Theologia Deutsch,* instead of through direct influence of Müntzer's writings upon Denk.

The 16th-century Hutterites also knew and used the *Theologia Deutsch.* It is quoted under the title *Theologia Germanica* twice in Peter Walpot's article "Concerning True Surrender and True Community of Goods," written about 1577, published in English translation in *MQR* XXXI (1957) 59, 62.

Kiwiet holds that the *Theologia Deutsch,* although first rated highly by Luther (to *c*1523), soon became a book of the "outsiders" (his opponents), i.e., of the Anabaptists, Schwenckfelders, and the later Pietists, and "became a very beloved booklet for many Anabaptists and Anabaptist leaders, espe-

cially among the South Germans and the Hutterites." He says that the *Theologia Deutsch* is not basically a mystical book, but an anti-mystical writing, which insists upon Christian discipleship in life rather than a concentration on inner bliss. The full significance and influence of the *Theologia Deutsch* for Anabaptist doctrine and history remains to be much more fully explored.　　　H.S.B.

G. Baring, "Neues von der 'Theologia Deutsch' und ihrer weltweiten Bedeutung," *Archiv f. Ref.-Gesch.* XLVIII, 2 (1957) 1-10; J. Kiwiet, "Die Theologia Deutsch und ihre Bedeutung während der Zeit der Reformation," *Gesch.-Bl.* XV (1958) 29-35; the latest English edition with introduction is to be found in *Late Medieval Mysticism* (Vol. XIII of the *Library of Christian Classics,* ed. Ray C. Petry, Philadelphia, 1957) 327-51; *Gesch. Bl.,* 23, 1966, 61-73.

Theological Schools and **Seminaries:** see **Seminaries.**

Theology, Anabaptist-Mennonite. An old and almost universal tradition among Mennonites views "theology" with much distrust. It is well expressed in the following statement by van der Zijpp regarding the Dutch Mennonites: "From the very rise of Anabaptism Dutch Mennonites were often very averse to theology, fearing that systematic theology might be a hindrance or even a danger to real Christian piety. This is not only found among many of the martyrs, but for instance also in Galenus (*q.v.*) Abrahamsz and in general among those Mennonites who were influenced by Collegiant (*q.v.*) opinions. The fear that simple pious love for Christ might be depraved and sterilized by theological speculation is still a common phenomenon in present-day Dutch Mennonitism."

This fear of theology had its origin in part in the bitter experience of the Anabaptists (and later Mennonites) that it was the theologians who were their worst enemies, whether Lutheran, Reformed, or Catholic, and who were often responsible for prodding the rulers into harsher measures of persecution; Melanchthon and Bullinger are good examples of this. Anabaptists frequently referred to the theologians as "Schriftgelehrten," i.e., "scribes" (with the New Testament overtone of condemnation as enemies of Christ). Later on in the 17th-19th centuries it was the theologically trained pastors who were the harshest critics of the Mennonites and who attempted, often without success, to prevail upon the princes to refuse to admit Mennonites to their territories, or to expel them after admission, or to forbid their public worship. The princes for their part often favored the Mennonites because of the economic advantage they brought, and were therefore on the whole more tolerant than the "theologians." Theological literature contained much bitter invective and harsh condemnation of the Mennonites.

Another root of the fear of theology was undoubtedly the experience that theological speculation and disputation was often remote from life, a type of rationalistic intellectualizing with little fruit in piety and ethics, whereas the Anabaptist-Mennonite emphasis was on newness of life, holy living, and discipleship. Some scholars hold that the Anabaptists deliberately chose not to write "theology" in the usual sense because of their basic understanding of Christianity in dynamic life terms rather than as a set of intellectual propositions to be integrated into a logically coherent whole. Anabaptist doctrine was, of course, based on a set of implied, though not always explicit, theological assumptions. And in spite of the repression of publication, and other interference with the free expression of their teachings, the writings of men like Pilgram Marpeck (*q.v.*), Menno (*q.v.*) Simons, Dirk (*q.v.*) Philips, Peter Riedemann (*q.v.*), and Peter Walpot (*q.v.*) are couched in coherent theological terms. Nevertheless, the Anabaptist-Mennonite movement has had little philosophical or systematic theology of the type represented by an Aquinas, Melanchthon, Calvin, or Hodge; a major exception was the great Dutch 19th-century liberal theologian Sytse Hoekstra (*q.v.*). But it has had doctrinal expression, in major and minor topical writings, as well as in comprehensive works attempting to cover the entire field of doctrine in systematic form; these expressions have been, however, largely expositions of "Bible doctrine" and not consciously theology in the classical sense. For the Anabaptists doctrinal expression was more often than not occasional, i.e., written to meet specific needs, and therefore usually apologetic or polemic. Sometimes it was in response to attacks by the outside enemy—e.g., Menno Simons against Martin Micron (*q.v.*) or Gellius Faber (*q.v.*), Balthasar Hubmaier (*q.v.*) on Baptism, Pilgram Marpeck against Schwenckfeld (*q.v.*); sometimes it was to combat emerging error within the brotherhood—the Schleitheim Confession, Menno Simons against David Joris (*q.v.*) or Adam Pastor (*q.v.*), Pilgram Marpeck against Johannes Bünderlin and the Spiritualists; sometimes it took the form of testimonies before the magistrates or to accusers in general—the *Rechenschaft* of Peter Riedemann, *Confession* of Thomas von Imbroich, the letters and testimonies of the martyrs in the *Martyrs' Mirror;* sometimes it was simply to strengthen the faith of the brotherhood, such as many of the writings of Menno Simons and the Hutterite writers, and certain early tracts on attitude toward the state, such as Clemens Adler's, and the *Aufdeckung der Babylmischen Hürn und Antichrists.*

What the Anabaptist theological production might have been if the earlier educated leaders of Switzerland and South Germany had not been almost totally wiped out remains a matter of speculation, particularly in view of what a Marpeck, Scharnschlager, Riedemann and Walpot did achieve.

Some of the marginal Anabaptist figures, such as Melchior Hofmann (*q.v.*), wrote speculative eschatological treatises, and others like Christian Entfelder (*q.v.*) and Johannes Bünderlin (*q.v.*) wrote spiritualist tracts. But the main Anabaptist line eschewed these areas and emphases.

A significant amount of theological expression is to be found in the records of the Anabaptist disputations, such as Zofingen 1532, Bern 1538, Frankenthal 1571, Emden 1578, Leeuwarden 1597, at which the Anabaptist participants were compelled to respond to the challenges of the Reformed or Lutheran theologians on various points of theology. John H. Yoder reports over 40 such theological encounters in the first 20 years of Anabaptist history. It is his judgment that the transition from the more

practical questions to "systematic theology" occurred at the Frankenthal debate.

In general, the "theology" of the Anabaptists was a deliberate attempt to understand and express the message of the Bible, particularly of the New Testament as it applies to life. Repeatedly appeals to opponents expressed a willingness to be taught of the Bible, and demanded in turn of the opponents that they teach from the Bible and promise obedience to the Bible. Although Anabaptist Biblicism at times turned into a simplicistic and somewhat over-literalistic or even legalistic handling of the Scriptures, this was by no means general or typical of the movement. The clear distinction, characteristic of Anabaptism, made between the Old and New Testaments and the insistence upon a progressive revelation, with Christ as the norm of all Scriptural truth, is evidence of this.

In the central classic theological points of historic Christian faith the Anabaptists were in basic agreement with the major Protestant bodies. Ulrich Zwingli (*q.v.*) described the early Zürich Anabaptists as differing from him "only in some minor points." Some modern writers have sought to stamp the early Anabaptists as partly anti-Trinitarian. But the Italian and Polish anti-Trinitarians and Socinians (*q.v.*) were not a part of the Anabaptist movement, as recent research (e.g., DeWind) has shown, even though they favored adult baptism. It has likewise been shown that the charge of unitarianism against Hans Denck (*q.v.*), the South German Anabaptist leader, was without basis in fact. Adam Pastor (*q.v.*), who became a unitarian, was expelled by Menno and his coelders. There was a tinge of universalism in Hans Denck. The Christology of Menno Simons and Dirk Philips (derived apparently from Melchior Hofmann) and after them of many of the Dutch Mennonites and their descendants in West Prussia and Russia, manifested an aberration from classic Christology, similar to that of Valentinus, in that it taught that the flesh of Christ was created *de novo* in Mary's womb, and was not of Mary's flesh. Their concern was to secure in this way a sinless Christ, free from the taint of original sin.

Although it is true that the Anabaptists held the basic Reformation emphases of the sole authority of the Bible in matters of faith and life, and justification by faith, the interpretation of Anabaptism by some modern Mennonite historians as basically only Reformation Protestantism with a few added points such as adult baptism, the free church, and ethical earnestness, is an inadequate view. Rather, as more intense research in the documentary sources has shown, Anabaptism is theologically a major type of Protestantism with a theological focus of its own alongside of Lutheranism and Calvinism. It is related to both the latter positions, but through its emphasis on the lordship of Christ, obedient discipleship, and the visible church, it is more closely related to Calvinism.

While most Anabaptists who expressed themselves on the subject of original sin (*q.v.*), did not hold the typical Catholic and Reformation doctrine, they did teach the sinfulness of man, his dependence upon the grace of God and the sacrifice of Christ for forgiveness and redemption, and his need for justification by faith, regeneration by the Holy Spirit, and the continuing work of the Holy Spirit in sanctification, guidance, and strengthening. None of the above topics was the subject of conflict between the Anabaptists and the other Protestants.

In their conception of communion and baptism as symbols, the Anabaptists were Zwinglians, except for Hubmaier who was Lutheran. In their rejection of infant baptism they were not original (most Reformation thinkers at first questioned pedobaptism, often several years before 1525, often as a logical consequence of the emphasis upon justification by faith), but the Anabaptists alone in Reformation times, except for the anti-Trinitarians, adopted believers' baptism as the full consequence of the concept of responsible faith in and obedience to Christ. Baptism was for them rather the symbol of commitment to discipleship and sanctification than of cleansing from past sin.

It was in the doctrines of the church (q.v.) and discipleship (q.v.) that the Anabaptists diverged most emphatically from official Protestant theology, although their stands on certain other points, such as rejection of the oath, refusal to hold governmental office, complete rejection of participation in warfare, insistence upon separation of church and state, and advocacy of freedom of conscience, were also striking divergences which cost them heavily in opposition and persecution. They understood Christianity in terms of discipleship to Christ and acceptance of His full lordship with consequent absolute obedience, rather than chiefly enjoyment of forgiveness and peace with God through justification, although insisting on the latter. They understood salvation not primarily as the attainment of a right status but rather as the production of a right life. They did not teach sinless perfection, but did hold that the Christian can and must live a life of victory over sin, and that it is possible for the church to make measurable progress toward Christ's ideal for her as a body "without spot or wrinkle." The practice of real church discipline as universally demanded among them is evidence both of the absence of perfectionism and of the serious endeavor to attain the highest standards. That this very endeavor has led at times to harshness and schism, as well as tended toward legalism, cannot, on the other hand, be denied.

It was in the doctrine of the church that the divergence from the rest of Christendom, both Catholic and Protestant, was most complete. The Anabaptists broke completely with the medieval concept of the Christian social order (church-state) as expressed in the term "corpus christianum," substituting the "corpus Christianorum." They were the first to insist upon a free church, separate from the state, separated from the world, composed only of committed disciples, who had through personal conversion and dedication accepted Christ as Saviour and Lord. This believers' church they conceived of as a brotherhood, with leaders but without a hierarchy, with responsibility of all the members for the total life and ministry of the church, a disciplined body, a church of order. By their doctrine of the two kingdoms (not the two kingdom doctrine of

Luther), the one the kingdom of Christ, the other the kingdom of this world ruled by Satan, they drew a clear line between the church and the general social order. Since the state was in this general social order "outside the perfection of Christ," although instituted by God and responsible to God, the church could have no part in it nor be subject to it in matters of faith, etc. Finally, the church was understood as a suffering church, bound to suffer in its conflict with the kingdom of this world, as it sought to create the holy community of love within its brotherhood circle, but through victorious steadfastness in suffering demonstrating that it was the body of Christ and would ultimately conquer.

In addition to its distinction from standard Protestantism the Anabaptist theological position must also be distinguished from Spiritualism (q.v.). It was Alfred Hegler of Tübingen who first (c1890) clearly distinguished Spiritualism as a distinct theological position in the Reformation period, and demarcated it from Anabaptism. The Spiritualists were individualists, sometimes bordering on mysticism, yet also rather rationalistic, who minimized external religious forms and ceremonies, in effect denied the necessity for church organization, emphasized the "inner word" of Scripture over against the "outer word," and professed to live from the special presence of the Spirit of God within. Sebastian Franck (q.v.) was the outstanding radical Spiritualist of the Reformation period; Caspar Schwenckfeld (q.v.) was one of a somewhat different type. Among the early Anabaptists there were a number of spiritualistically inclined persons (all of whom soon left the movement), such as Bünderlin, Endtfelder, Jakob Kautz (q.v.) and Obbe (q.v.) Philips. Obbe's individualistic spiritualism stood in contrast to the disciplined church concept of Menno and Dirk Philips, and was a major factor in his withdrawal in 1540. (See his Bekentenisse.)

The struggle with the Spiritualists was the chief theological conflict in the history of early 16th-century Anabaptism, and resulted in the purging of this element. William Klassen has pointed out that this separation took place as early as 1531 in Strasbourg, as is shown by the two Marpeck booklets published there in that year, the Clare Verantwurtung (q.v.), and Ain klarer vast nützlicher unterricht (q.v.), the former directed against Bünderlin, the latter against Schwenckfeld. The battle with Schwenckfeld continued for another twenty years and resulted in the outstanding theological writings of the South German Anabaptists, the Vermanung (1544), the Testamenterleütterung (1544), and the Verantwortung (1545-50), all by Marpeck and his associates, particularly Scharnschlager (q.v.).

A central idea in Marpeck's theology was that of the covenant; according to Klassen it was more significant than the idea of discipleship. The Vermanung was called the "testimony to the covenant," the Testamenterleütterung "the explanation of the covenant." As a regulative theological concept the covenant idea holds together the divine act and man's response, God's proffered grace and man's obedience. This blending of God's part and man's part in redemption and life is a major aspect of the Anabaptist genius, transcending as it does the limitations of the *sola fide* doctrine, and on the other hand avoiding a pure moralism. "Covenant" is basically an Hebraic idea, and as Kiwiet has pointed out the Anabaptists were much nearer to the Hebraic world view than to that of the Greeks.

Anabaptist theology has been held by some scholars to be based largely on the Gospels, with special emphasis on the Sermon on the Mount. The evidence of the documents does not support this conclusion. Rather the Anabaptists drew their views from the entire New Testament, using the Pauline epistles and especially First Peter as well. This was particularly true of Marpeck and his associates, but also of Menno Simons.   H.S.B.

Netherlands. The early Dutch Anabaptists and Mennonites, lacking theological education, were not able to draw up an adequate scholarly theology. Neither Menno (*q.v.*) Simons, nor Dirk (*q.v.*) Philips, nor the other older leaders were real theologians; Adam (*q.v.*) Pastor was an exception. Neither were most Mennonite doctrinal writers of the 17th and 18th centuries scholarly theologians, even when they produced "theological" books. Among Dutch Mennonite authors whose books are theologically important are A. van Eeghem (*q.v.*), Galenus (*q.v.*) Abrahamsz, J. Rijsdijk (*q.v.*), G. de Wind (*q.v.*), J. Stinstra (*q.v.*), Cornelis Ris (*q.v.*), Allard Hulshoff (*q.v.*), and W. de Vos (*q.v.*). The Dutch Mennonite confessions of faith are not to be considered as theological writings in a strict sense. Until the 18th century Mennonites usually occupied themselves with only such theological problems as they felt necessary for combating the views of their Catholic and particularly their Calvinist opponents. In this way, for instance, Jacob Pieters van der Meulen (*q.v.*) wrote about the apostolic succession (*q.v.*), and many authors wrote on believers' baptism. Thus 17th-century Mennonite theology generally was apologetic in character, being mostly engaged in defending the creed. This changed little even after the founding of the Amsterdam Mennonite Seminary in 1735, in which philosophy, science, and the New Testament (especially for the practice of the ministry) were taught rather than systematic theology. About 1700 a few Dutch Mennonite ministers like Douwe Feddriks (*q.v.*) and Jacobus Rijsdijk (*q.v.*), who studied theology, not for the defense of Mennonite doctrines, but for its own sake, were largely influenced by Calvinism, so that their theological systems can hardly be considered Mennonite.

Eighteenth-century Mennonite theology, such as that of J. Stinstra (*q.v.*), took its starting point from the conviction that the human mind as such, and human religious experience, can be the source of knowledge concerning God. These views were developed still more consistently in the modern liberal theology of the 19th century as in the system of S. Hoekstra Bzn (*q.v.*) and his disciples. For Hoekstra, for example, "the piety of the heart" was basic, rather than revelation in the Scriptures; the Bible had no foundational, only illustrative, value. The truth of the Bible is what the human mind (heart) has thought out (experienced) as truth. This liberal theology did not really expound in the strict sense a doctrine concerning God but rather a doctrine of the human understanding of God. It should therefore be called anthropology rather than theology. This type of theology tended strongly toward a psychological understanding of human religious experience, as is seen in the theological works of I. J. le Cosquino de Bussy (*q.v.*).

Though liberal theology is still very common in Dutch Mennonitism, much has changed in recent decades. Recent theological studies such as those by J. E. van Brakel, *Christelijk Geloof* (1934), W. Leendertz, *Dogma* (1917), *Dogma en Existentie* (1933), *Rangorde van Geestelijke Waarden* (1940), and *Gods woord in mensenhanden* (1953), and F. Kuiper, *Leven uit de Hoop* (1958) breathe a different spirit. Among the very few Dutch Mennonite theologians of the 19th century who did not follow Liberalism was Samuel Muller (*q.v.*), who taught at the Amsterdam seminary (1827-56), but who had little influence; his pupils sided largely with Modernism.   vDZ.

Germany, France, and Switzerland. The chief and really only theological writers of the Mennonites of these countries were George Hansen (*q.v.*) of Danzig (d. 1703) and Gerritt Roosen (*q.v.*) of Hamburg (1612-1711), the former writing in the old Anabaptist spirit, the latter already tinged by Pietism. Pietism exerted a significant influence in the 18th century in Hamburg, Crefeld, and the Palatinate (Peter Weber, *q.v.*) and in the 19th and 20th centuries in Switzerland, France, South Germany, and West Prussia. Modern religious liberalism made its inroads into Crefeld and Emden, parallel to that in the Netherlands, and to a lesser extent in Elbing and Danzig.

Russia. The century and a half of Mennonite life in Russia produced no significant theological literature, and brought forth no great changes in Mennonite piety except through the entrance of Pietism through the Mennonite Brethren movement and the introduction of millenarian doctrine in the early 20th century, largely in the M.B. group.

North America. Pietistic influence has been moderately strong in most North American Mennonite groups from the beginning in Colonial Pennsylvania, and millenarian doctrine was imported in the first quarter of the 20th century into considerable sections of all Mennonite groups in both the United States and Canada. The most conservative groups show neither influence. Only a slight touch of modern liberalistic influence was felt in the United States in one or two major groups, now largely overcome. A vigorous revival of interest in the Anabaptist theological heritage marks the middle decade of the 20th century, and there are signs of the emergence of a theology rooted in the distinctive Anabaptist-Mennonite heritage but thoroughly Biblical. A scrutiny of the theological literature produced by North American Mennonites of all branches reveals that apart from short pamphlets and a few brief specialized treatises, only two volumes of any significance have appeared, both by writers in the Mennonite Church (MC)—*Bible Doctrine* (1914) by Daniel Kauffman (1865-1944) and others, on a simple popular level, and *Introduction to Theology* (1954) by J. C. Wenger (1910-   ), on a more advanced level.

The latter volume is the only substantial offering of a comprehensive systematic theology by any Mennonite writer outside of Holland. (See **Baptism, Bible, Church, Communion, Discipleship, Eschatology, Ethics, Free Will, Fundamentalism, Incarnation, Liberalism, Martyrdom (Theology of), Original Sin, Pietism, Sacraments, Spiritualism,** in addition to articles on the various individuals named above.)

H.S.B.

The Recovery of the Anabaptist Vision (Scottdale, 1957) contains several essays bearing on Anabaptist theology: H. S. Bender, "The Anabaptist Vision" (first published in 1944); Fritz Blanke, "Anabaptism and the Reformation"; J. H. Yoder, "The Prophetic Dissent of the Anabaptists"; Robert Friedmann, "The Doctrine of the Two Worlds"; F. H. Littell, "The Anabaptist Concept of the Church"; J. L. Burkholder, "The Anabaptist Vision of Discipleship"; Robert Kreider, "The Anabaptists and the State"; and John Oyer "The Reformers Oppose the Anabaptist Theology"; S. Hoekstra Bzn, *Beginselen en leer der oude Doopsgezinden, vergeleken met die van de overige Protestanten* (Amsterdam, 1863); J. Kühn, *Toleranz und Offenbarung* (Leipzig, 1923); L. von Muralt, *Glaube und Lehre der schweizerischen Wiedertäufer in der Reformationszeit* (Zürich, 1938); Fritz Heyer, *Der Kirchenbegriff der Schwärmer* (Leipzig, 1939); F. H. Littell, *The Anabaptist View of the Church* (n.p., 1952); J. C. Wenger, *The Doctrine of the Mennonites* (Scottdale, 1950); E. Händiges, *Die Lehre der Mennoniten in Geschichte und Gegenwart, nach den Quellen dargestellt* (Kaiserslautern, 1921); Cornelius Krahn, *Menno Simons (1496-1561)* (Karlsruhe, 1936); H. W. Meihuizen, "Spiritualistic Tendencies Among the Dutch Mennonites of the 16th and 17th Centuries," *MQR* XXVII (1953) 259-304; G. D. Kauffman, "Some Theological Emphases of the Early Anabaptists," *MQR* XXV (1951) 75-99; the *MQR* XXIV (January 1950) contains a series of articles on Anabaptist theology reporting the papers of the Anabaptist Theological Seminar held at Goshen College in 1949, including Robert Friedmann's "Anabaptism and Protestantism" and H. S. Bender's "Anabaptist Theology of Discipleship"; D. E. Smucker, "Theological Triumph of the Early Anabaptists," *MQR* XIX (1945) 5-26; Heinold Fast, "The Dependence of the First Anabaptists on Luther, Erasmus, and Zwingli," *MQR* XXX (1956) 104-19; C. J. Dyck, "The Christology of Dirk Philips," *MQR* XXXI (1957) 147-155; H. S. Bender, *Conrad Grebel* (Goshen, 1950); J. J. Kiwiet, *Pilgram Marbeck* (Kassel, 1957), *ML* IV, 305-311.

Theology of Martyrdom, a substantial and significant treatment of certain aspects of early Anabaptist theology, written by Ethelbert Stauffer, in an essay, "Märtyrertheologie und Täufertum." Using original source material drawn largely from the *Martyrs' Mirror,* the *Ausbund* (q.v.), *Lieder der Hutterischen Brüder,* the Hutterite *Geschicht-Buch,* and Menno Simons' works, Stauffer presents an integrated Anabaptist vision of victory for the church and the kingdom of Christ through suffering and martyrdom, in which the Anabaptist martyrs are seen as following in the footsteps of the suffering saints of the Old and New Testaments and most of all in those of Christ Himself. (See **Martyrdom, Theology of.**) H. W. Meihuizen wrote on the theology of the martyrs as found in the *Offer des Heeren.*

H.S.B.

Ethelbert Stauffer, "Märtyrertheologie und Täufertum," in *Ztschf f. Kirchengeschichte* XLII (1933) 545-98; the article appeared in English translation in *MQR* XIX (1945) 179-214; H. W. Meihuizen, "De geloofswereld onzer martelaren, voor zover die af te lezen valt uit het Offer des Heeren," in *Algemeen Doopsgez. Weekblad* V (1951) Nos. 35-50; idem, "De verwachting van de weder komende Christus en het rijk Gods bij de Oude Doops-

gezinden," in *Stemmen uit de Doopsgez. Broederschap* III (1954) No. 3, 42-50.

Thessalonica (Saloniki), a city of Greece which belonged to the Ottoman (Turkish) Empire in the 16th century. Its population is mixed Greek and Macedonian (Slavic). From a hymn in the *Ausbund* (all editions since 1785, pp. 892-95) it has been known that contacts once existed between certain Brethren in this city and Anabaptists in Moravia. Recent research has cleared up the matter, proving that such contact was of a twofold nature. (*a*) Italian anti-Trinitarians (q.v.) around Venice had to flee from the Inquisition in that city soon after 1550; some of them went to Moravia and joined the Hutterites (see **Sega, della**) while others went to Thessalonica where the Moslems granted them asylum. Among the latter was Antonio Rizzetto (q.v.) who, however, after a time became disillusioned with his group in Thessalonica. Having received letters from Francesco della Sega (q.v.) saying that he had found the true church of Christ in Moravia, Rizetto went there c1560. Beck (*Geschichts-Bücher,* 211-12) gives the story in some detail, based on a letter of 1601 by Claus Braidl who vividly remembered the event. Whether Rizzetto came alone or with a group of Brethren from Thessalonica the letter does not say.

(*b*) Another event involving these two groups c1550 is related in the *Martyrs' Mirror* (D 400-2, E 365-67) on the basis of an old Dutch booklet called *Het Brilleken* (1630). Three "Greek Brethren" had undertaken the long journey from Thessalonica to Moravia (Nikolsburg and Pausram, q.v.) to inquire about these spiritually kindred Brethren. The Hutterite communal life did not, however, appeal to them. They went to the Swiss Brethren, likewise at Pausram, whose life and thinking they liked extremely well. Conversation was carried on in the Latin language. The account of their faith given by the "Greek Brethren" was then written down in the form of a "Confession." This document was carefully preserved (in German) and was copied a number of times by later Mennonites (a copy in GCL). This document shows, however, that the visitors came not from Thessalonica but from Larissa in Thessaly, some 120 miles to the south of Thessalonica. When the three Greeks left, one of them, a tailor, left his shears with the Swiss Brethren as a souvenir. From the records it appears unlikely that the Greeks went to other places; Mehrning (q.v.) in 1646 claimed (on hearsay only) that they went as far as the Netherlands.

The character of the Greek visitors is not easy to determine. Their Confession sounds like a Swiss Brethren confession. The most likely conjecture is that they were Greek-Slavic Bogomiles (q.v.). They claimed to have manuscripts from the time of the apostles; but very likely these documents were of more recent origin (though centuries old, written in Old Slavonic). Nothing positive is known about the source of their information about the Anabaptists. The claim of *Het Brilleken* that in the 1530's the Turks had taken an Anabaptist as a prisoner from Moravia to Thessalonica where he spread the news of his Anabaptist church must be taken with much reservation. The Turks did not invade Moravia at that time. The visit of 1550 did not lead to any further contacts.

The *Ausbund* hymn, "O Herr, thue auf die Lefzen mein," seems to be based on the story in the *Martyrs' Mirror,* having been composed sometime before 1695. Unfortunately it is marred by many serious inaccuracies and should not be used as an historical source. R.F.

Beck, *Geschichts-Bücher;* Robert Friedmann, "Christian Sectarians in Thessalonica and Their Relationship to the Anabaptists," *MQR* XXIX (1955) 54-69; H. A. DeWind, "Anabaptists in Thessalonica," *ibid.,* 70-73; *ML* IV.

Theunis (Teunsen), **Jacob,** was an elder of the Janjacobsgezinden (*q.v.*) in the Netherlands. He was ordained at Hoorn on Sept. 20, 1603, by Jan Jacobsz himself. Theunis, who was active until 1618, doing much traveling, baptized 700 persons. He also stayed in Prussia, where he baptized a few persons. (Blaupot t. C., *Friesland,* 164; *DB* 1889, 4.)
VDZ.

Theunis Teeckssen (Anthonis Fredericx), of Naarden, Holland, a Sacramentist (*q.v.*) martyr, executed on Oct. 26, 1529, at The Hague, after he had been in prison for two years. On the way to the scaffold Theunis is said to have sung the hymn "Ick arm schaep aen groener heyde" (I, poor sheep in the green moor), which was a very popular hymn among the early Dutch Mennonites. The martyr Reytse (*q.v.*) Aysesz also sang this hymn. It is inserted in *Veelderhande Liedekens* of 1556 and a number of old Mennonite hymnals. VDZ.

J. G. de Hoop Scheffer, *Geschiedenis der Kerkhervorming in Nederland ... tot* 1531 (Amsterdam, 1873) 587-91.

Theunis Theunisz, a Mennonite preacher either at Vlaardingen or at Dordrecht, preached at Klundert (*q.v.*) in the Dutch province of North Brabant; the meeting, attended by about 50 persons, was surprised by the police and a number of those present were arrested and after trial put to death at Breda (*q.v.*). Theunis and many others, however, were able to escape. (*DB* 1912, 31-33.) VDZ.

Theunis (Theunis, Anthoen) **van Waesten(e),** an Anabaptist martyr, is identical with Anthonis Schoonvelt (*q.v.*). VDZ.

Theunisz (Teunis), **Jacob,** b. *c*1569 at Leer, d. 1625 at Emden, was a cloth merchant at Amsterdam and about 1620 a deacon of the Amsterdam Waterlander Mennonite church. He was married to Pietertgen Lubbertsdochter, the daughter of Elder Lubbert Gerritsz (*q.v.*) and was a loyal and liberal member of the church. All of his children were important leaders. They are Anthoni Jacobsz (*q.v.*), surnamed Roscius, a physician and preacher at Hoorn, Lambert Jacobsz (*q.v.*), a noted painter and preacher at Leeuwarden, Isaak Jacobsz Rooleeuw (*q.v.*), a silk merchant at Amsterdam, and Jacob(us) **Rooleeuw** (*q.v.*), a dyer and preacher at Amsterdam. VDZ.

Theunisz (Tonissen, Anthonisz), **Jan,** who called himself also Joannes Antonides, a Dutch Mennonite,

b. at Alkmaar *c*1569, d. 1637(?) at Amsterdam. This highly gifted but turbulent man is one of the most remarkable personalities among the Dutch Mennonites. With his fiery eyes, his protruding nose, and his long beard reaching to his belt he was a conspicuous figure. He married four times: first to N. N., then to Metgen Claesd., thereupon (1603) to Trijntgen Adriaans van Alckmaer, and finally (1612) to Swaentien Hillebrants of Amsterdam. At first a thread twister, he settled at Leiden as a book printer *c*1599, at the same time operating a bookshop, which was transferred to Amsterdam in 1604, where he soon added his own type foundry. From 1606 he also ran a well-known inn, called "D'os in de Bruyloft," also called "de Menniste Bruiloft" (wedding-party). This inn was an unusual place; it was provided with many curiosities and objects of art; musical performances were given there, attended by the upper ten of Amsterdam; among the regular visitors were Joost van den Vondel (*q.v.*) and the Waterlander preachers Wybrandsz, Hesseling, and Anslo. Another business of this man was the distilling and sale of brandy. But first and foremost Jan Theunisz was a man of learning. Though a self-made man, he knew many languages, not only German and French, and probably also English, but also Latin and Greek, and even Hebrew, Arabic, and Ethiopian. Among the books he printed and published were *Verscheyden Schriftuerlijcke Liedekens* (Scriptural hymns) (1603), a book by the Flemish Elder Claes Claesz (*q.v.*), a number of books by Coornhert (*q.v.*), Coolhaas, and other liberal theologians, a kind of newspaper, but also books which he translated from the Hebrew, the first in this language ever published in the Netherlands. The pamphlets and poems he wrote were usually anonymous, bearing the devices "Jaecht nae't Beste" (Strive for the best) or "een liefhebber der waerheyt" (a friend of the truth). In 1612 he was appointed professor of Arabic at the Leiden University, but already in 1613 he had to give up his professorship because it was considered improper to tolerate a Mennonite in the university; in 1617-26 he taught Hebrew at the "Duytse Academie" at Amsterdam.

Jan Theunisz was a member of the Amsterdam Waterlander congregation, but he was a troublesome member and the church board had much to do with him. In 1612 he was censured for some unknown dissension; again in 1613 because he had offended his brother-in-law contrary to I Cor. 6:4, 6; in 1615 because of a quarrel with his wife. But this was only a prologue to what followed: from 1621, when a conflict arose in the congregation between Nittert Obbes (*q.v.*) and the other preachers, Theunisz sided with Obbes. He published the polemic drawn up by Obbes, gave it the offensive title of *Raeghbesem* (1625, *q.v.*). On Dec. 21, 1625, Jan Theunisz disturbed the communion service in the Waterlander "Groote Spijker" meetinghouse, causing much offense by his foolish conduct; thereupon he was banned (Jan. 25, 1626). He attacked the Amsterdam preachers in a number of pamphlets, and also the Waterlander leader Hans de Ries (*q.v.*), who defended them against Obbes. Among these publications were *Der Hanssijtsche Mennisten*

Socinianismus, and *Der Hanssijtsche Menniste Gheest-drijveren Historie,* both in 1627 at Amsterdam. On Dec. 17, 1634, Theunisz became reconciled with the church, confessing his guilt "in that he had done wrong in word and with writing."   vDZ.

Inv. Arch. Amst. II, Nos. 1206, 1225; H. F. Wijnman, "Jan Theunisz alias Joannes Antonides . . . ," in *Jaarboek Amstelodamum* XXV (1928) 29-123; Kühler, *Geschiedenis* II, *passim.*

Thielemann von Nunkirchen: see **Nunkirchen, Thieleman von,** where the page reference to *Mart. Mir.* D 143 should be corrected to 132. The article **Christian** (*ME* I, 577) requires the correction of Blankenburg, Holland, to Blankenberg in the Duchy of Jülich.   vDZ.

Thielman Naeberchs (Naebrechts), an Anabaptist martyr drowned on Jan. 27, 1560, at Antwerp, Belgium, with three other brethren. In the hymn "Aenhoort God, hemelsche Vader," found in *Offer des Heeren,* this martyr is simply called Thielman. Van Braght's *Martyrs' Mirror* does not name him. Some particulars have been published by P. Génard: Thielman Naeberchs was a native of Milleghen (?) and a tailor by trade. He lived at Antwerp; his furniture was confiscated.   vDZ.

Offer, 567, No. 62; *Bibliographie* II, No. 570; *Antw. Arch.-Bl.* IX, 6, 10, 18; XIV, 28 f., No. 308.

Thielt: see **Tielt.**

Thielt, Paulus van, a Dutch elder: see **Paulus van Meenen.**

Thiensdorf and Preussisch Rosengarth, a former Mennonite congregation situated south of Elbing and east of Marienburg, West Prussia. The origin of the congregation, which was originally called the Kleinwerder congregation since it was not permitted to build a meetinghouse and could therefore not be named for a village, dates back to the Reformation. Dutch Mennonites are mentioned for the first time in Wengeln on the north shore of Lake Drausen in 1531. But they had no doubt been there for some time previously, at least since 1543, when the Anabaptists were expelled from the neighboring Prussian Oberland. The records show that by 1590 the west shore of Lake Drausen with the meadowlands of Kampenau, Markushof, Eschenhorst, and Rosengarth (about 150 hides) was in the hands of the Dutch settlers. (For the settlement of the Lake Drausen Lowlands, see **West Prussia.**) In 1586 Koen Hendrichs, Hans van Mechelen, Jacob Smet, and Long Dirk were representatives of the Kleinwerder congregation.

The congregation seems to have received its stamp from Jan Gerrits van Embden, who came to West Prussia in 1607 because as a Waterlander he did not like the many schisms among the Mennonites in the Netherlands. He was chosen as elder in the Kleinwerder congregation. He was at the same time elder of the United Frisian, Waterlander, and High German congregation in Danzig. As late as 1786 Elder Gerhard Wiebe of Ellerwald called the Kleinwerder congregation "Waterlandish."

Gerrits van Embden traveled to Moravia in 1610 and visited the five High German congregations there (see **West Prussia**). There had been contacts for some years between his congregation in the Kleinwerder and Moravia. In 1604 Josef Hauser, a Hutterite preacher in Moravia, with seven other Hutterites and their wives, came to Prussia. They took a lease for ten years on a farm in the Kleinwerder at Wengeln to establish a Bruderhof for seventy-three persons. Some West Prussian Mennonites were also admitted. But the relations were apparently not the best, for the Hutterite chronicle records that when the Mennonite party was to come to communion Peter von Hasel (Hasselt?) and his wife refused to do so, and were banned for defaming the Bruderhof, accusing it of starving its people.

Since competition with the Elbing craftsmen also created difficulties the Hutterites soon sold their Bruderhof. But there were apparently some Hutterites in the Marienburg Lowlands in after times, perhaps even an independent congregation, for in 1700 Abraham Hartwich wrote in his description of the Werder, "A distinction is made in the Werder between the Manists of two branches, the 'Fine' or Flemish and the 'Coarse' or Frisians. . . . The latter condemn all other sects of the Anabaptists, including the Hutterites, but they gladly receive them when they have been expelled from other Mennonite groups. Therefore they are also called 'Garbage carts'" (Hartwich, 279). Apparently at the beginning of the Thirty Years' War, when the Hutterites were expelled from Bohemia, a considerable number of them came to West Prussia, especially to the Kleinwerder, and were absorbed by the Mennonites.

Worship services were held in homes for a long time. In 1728 the congregation met at Markushof at the home of the elder Melchior Froese. In that year they received permission from the Bishop of Culm to build a meetinghouse. Hitherto a barn had served the purpose, into which benches were carried for the congregation.

The Kleinwerder Mennonites belonged to the Frisian wing. In 1772, when Polish Prussia was incorporated into Prussia, an attempt was made to unite the Flemish and Frisian congregations. The representatives of the Frisians, in order to make a concession to the Flemish, pledged themselves to prohibit mixed marriages with Catholics and Lutherans. On this point conflict arose within the Frisian congregations which in 1791 led to the schism of the minority of the Kleinwerder members under Elder Sperling, who favored the more liberal position. This group built a meetinghouse in Markushof (*q.v.*) and organized a congregation. The original congregation kept the meetinghouse in Thiensdorf. A healing of the schism occurred in 1888 when the dam broke at Jonasdorf and the Nogat River flooded the Kleinwerder. Together they built a new meetinghouse in 1890 at Preussisch Rosengarth. This meetinghouse, contrary to Mennonite custom, had a tower.

The revival movement of New Pietism affected some of the West Prussian Mennonites. Johann Quiering of Preussisch Rosengarth, elder of the Thiensdorf congregation 1848-63, was deeply pietistic. His example was no doubt fruitful in his congregation.

It was especially among the Kleinwerder Mennonites that a new impulse of deepening religious life occurred in the late 19th century, coming from the Gemeinschaftsbewegung (*q.v.*). In their homes they held Bible study meetings and prayer meetings, as well as practicing the customary Mennonite neighborly love. Johann Wieler established several homes for orphans, which were under the management of the institution called Friedenshort.

When the mass exodus of the Mennonites from West Prussia set in in 1945, Cornelius Dirksen remained in the community as the only West Prussian elder, under extreme difficulties serving his people in spite of his own physical weakness. Among the many who died of privation he also buried his wife, who died in 1947. In October 1947 he was expelled from West Prussia.

According to a number of letters written to the Amsterdam Committee for Foreign Needs (May 19, 1767, and Aug. 2, 1767) the Thiensdorf congregation in 1767 then numbered 2,000 souls; the Lord's Supper was attended by 1,200 members. In 1852 the congregation had 808 baptized members, in 1887 766 and 349 children, in 1939 1,124 members. The elders of the last 200 years were Melchior Froese 1728, Johann Peters of Markushof *c*1730, Heinrich Peters of Markushof *c*1730 (lived and died in the church building), Jacob Siebert of Nogathau *c*1758-84, his son Johann Siebert, preacher 1770, elder 1785-98, Wilhelm Martens of Thiergarth 1798-1833, Franz Cornelson of Thörichthof, preacher 1808, elder 1834-48, Johann Quiring of Preussisch Rosengarth, preacher 1823, elder 1848-63, Johann Penner of Thiensdorf 1864-89, Johann Kädtler of Alt-Rosengarth 1889-1912, Johann Cornelson of Thiensdorf 1912-22, Cornelius Dirksen of Markushof 1922-47. **H.P.**

Heinrich Wiehler, "Aus der Geschichte der Vereinigten Mennonitengemeinde Thiensdorf-Markushof," in *Menn. Bl.*, 1928, 92-94, 99 f., 108 f.; Emil Händiges, "Zum 200-Jahrfeier des Baus der ersten Mennonitenkirche in Thiensdorf," *Menn. Bl.*, 1928, 56-58; *Naamlijst* 1793, 58 f.; *Inv. Arch. Amst.* I, Nos. 1571-78, 1703-12; *idem* II, 2, Nos. 735 f., 857; Ernst Crous, "Vom Pietismus bei den altpreussischen Mennoniten im Rahmen ihrer Gesamtgeschichte 1772-1945," *Gesch. Bl.*, 1954, 7-29; "Zwei verdiente Aelteste aus der ehemaligen Gemeinde Thiensdorf-Preussisch Rosengarth, Westpreussen," *Gem.-Kal.*, 1953, 23-26; Abraham Hartwich, *Geogr.-histor. Landesbeschreibung der drei im poln. Preussen liegenden Werder* (Königsberg, 1722); Wolkan, *Geschichts-Buch*, 470 ff.; Hans Alenson, *Tegen-Bericht op de voor-Reden vant groote Martelaar Boek 1630*, BRN VII; ML IV.

Thiers, Barbara von: see Barbara von Thiers.

Thierstein, John R. (1867-1941), a Mennonite (GCM) teacher of modern languages, editor and conference worker, was born in Bowil, Swiss canton of Bern, July 22, 1867. In 1882 the family came to America and settled on a farm near Whitewater, Kan. He attended the Mennonite Seminary at Halstead, graduating in 1892, and secured his A.B. degree in 1896 from the University of Kansas. On Oct. 2, 1895, he married Margaret M. Dirks.

Thierstein had begun his teaching career upon his graduation from the Halstead Seminary. He taught in several Kansas schools 1896-1903, and at Bethel College 1903-4. In 1904 he became president of Freeman Junior College, serving for four years. In 1908 he returned to Switzerland for graduate work, receiving his Ph.D. from the University of Bern in 1910. His dissertation was entitled *Novalis und der Pietismus* (Bern, 1910). For five years he then served as principal of the Atchison County (Kansas) High School. In 1915-21 he served on the faculty of Bluffton College, after which he came to Bethel College where he served until his death in such capacities as professor of education, German, and French, director of the teacher placement bureau, and editor of the *Bethel College Monthly* (*q.v.*).

Thierstein also served many years as a member of the General Conference Board of Publication, being chairman at the time of his death (1941). He had served two terms as secretary of the G.C.M. Church and was a member of the Historical Committee of the General Conference at the time of his death. In 1937-41 he was editor of *The Mennonite* (*q.v.*). As chairman of the Board of Publication he also contributed substantially toward the production of the *Mennonite Hymnary*. While in Switzerland the Thiersteins had adopted a son, Frederic Novalis, who died as a young man in 1926. J.F.S.

Thies (de) Droochscheerder, a follower of the revolutionary Anabaptist leader Jan (*q.v.*) van Geelen, was active at Antwerp, Belgium, in 1535, but like other Münsterites in Belgium he had practically no success. (Vos, *Antwerpen,* 217.) vDZ.

Thiessen (Thiesen, Tiessen, Tyssen, Tieszen), a family name common among Mennonites of Prusso-Russian background, was first entered in the Danzig record in 1685. The name was common in Tiegenhagen, Ladekopp, Rosenort, Fürstenwerder, Heubuden, Elbing, Königsberg. Bernhard Thiessen (*q.v.*) was a minister at Ibersheim, Germany. Dirk Tiessen was a preacher of the Old Flemish Grosswerder congregation, serving as elder of the Petershagen district from 1755, and of the entire Grosswerder congregation 1767-after 1802. Peter Thiessen Sr. and Peter Thiessen Jr. were preachers of the Danzig Flemish church from 1774 and 1800. From Prussia the name was transplanted to Russia. B. H. Unruh lists seventeen bearers of the name who moved to Russia. Outstanding was Johann Thiessen, who owned a flour mill in Ekaterinoslav and was a benefactor of Mennonite causes. He was killed in 1920. Julius J. Thiessen, of the Molotschna, Russia, was an outstanding minister and teacher. Jacob Thiessen, b. 1888 at Olgafeld in Fürstenland, Russia, emigrated to the Netherlands in 1914, and served as minister in the Mennonite congregations of Ouddorp 1939-45 and Blokzijl 1946-53. John Thiessen, of North Newton, Kan., was a missionary in India and is now executive secretary of the Board of Missions of the General Conference Mennonite Church. Jacob J. Thiessen, pastor of the First Mennonite Church of Saskatoon, Sask., has been chairman of the Canadian Mennonite Board of Colonization and president of the Conference of Mennonites in Canada for many years. Franz C.

Thiessen (*q.v.*) was an able educator and minister of the Mennonite Brethren in Canada. Dirk P. Tieszen was a minister (GCM) at Marion, S.D. His son Edward D. Tieszen was the owner of the Tieszen Clinic at Marion.   C.K., vDZ.

Reimer, *Familiennamen,* 119; A. A. Töws, *Mennonitische Märtyrer* I (N. Clearbrook, 1949) 151; Unruh, *Hintergründe.*

Thiessen, Abraham, a Russian Mennonite, expelled from Russia because of his courageous opposition to Russian injustice, fled to Switzerland, arriving in Zürich on May 15, 1876. He published the following writings: *Ein Rätsel, oder die Frage: weshalb war ich vom Jahre 1874-76 in Verbannung?*; *Die Lage der Deutschen Kolonisten in Russland* (Leipzig, 1876); and *Ein Brief, nur für die Mennoniten im berdjanskischen Kreise* (Odessa, 1872).

John Horsch, *Kurzgefasste Gesch. der Mennoniten* (Elkhart, 1890) 126; *Menn. Bl.,* 1876, 95; *ML* IV.

Thiessen, Bernhard (1814-55), a minister of the Ibersheim (*q.v.*) Mennonite Church, was born in Danzig, Germany, studied theology at the universities of Berlin and Bonn, and was the first theologically trained and professional Mennonite minister in Ibersheim (*q.v.*). On June 11, 1843, on a journey, he had preached a sermon in the Ibersheim Mennonite Church, and was thereupon chosen on July 16, 1843, as minister of the congregation. On Sept. 17, 1843, he was ordained as elder by Johannes Risser (*q.v.*), minister of the Sembach Mennonite Church. On June 22, 1845, he married Henriette Sophie Mathilde Schmidt (d. 1849) of Danzig. He performed the functions of his office until May 28, 1855, when he died of a stroke. (*ML* IV.)   A.Br.

Thiessen, Franz C. (1881-1950), a high-school teacher, minister, and musical editor of the Mennonite Brethren Church, was born Aug. 6, 1881, in Rückenau, South Russia, the son of Cornelius and Katharina Nickel Thiessen. He was married twice, first on Aug. 19, 1901, to Lydia Wieler (d. 1908) of Rückenau, and on April 10, 1910, to Margareta Wieler of Rückenau. He had six children. Thiessen received his education in the Ohrloff Zentralschule 1895-97, the normal school at Halbstadt 1898-99, and private studies at Theodosia, Sevastopol, and Kharkov.

Thiessen served for many years in educational work. His work included teaching in the elementary school at Reinfeld, Zagradovka settlement of South Russia 1901-2, the Rückenau Academy 1905, the Alexanderkrone Zentralschule 1906-8, the Davlekanovo Zentralschule 1911-24, the German-English Academy of Rosthern, Sask., 1925-32, the Bible School at Winnipeg, Man., 1932-39, and the Mennonite Brethren Bible School at Abbotsford, B.C.; he was connected with the Mennonite Educational Institute at Abbotsford from 1944 until his death, first as a cofounder and the first principal and later as a teacher. He was ordained to the ministry in 1937 and was pastor of the Northend M.B. Church in Winnipeg 1940-43. In 1924 he was the director of the Mennonite emigration from Russia, in 1924-

25 editor of *Der praktische Landwirt,* and in 1936-40 editor of *Der kleine Afrikabote.*

Franz C. Thiessen was a gifted musician, contributing in both Russia and Canada to choral work. He was rated an authority in this field, and compiled many books of songs for choirs and Sunday schools. He was chairman of the song committee of the M.B. Conference, and his largest and latest work was the new German hymnal for the M.B. Conference. He was also very active in youth work and published several books, *Knospen und Blüten,* with poems and dialogs for youth meetings. He compiled and published textbooks in German and religion for Canadian Mennonite schools, taught Sunday school, preached, and was very active to the day of his death, Feb. 24, 1950.   H.F.K.

Thiessen, Johann, a Mennonite from Russia, was a missionary of the Dutch Mennonite Mission Association on the island of Sumatra (*q.v.*), Indonesia. In July 1901 he took the place of both Nicolai Wiebe (*q.v.*) and Gerhard Nikkel (*q.v.*) at Muara Sipongi (*q.v.*), serving until 1912. The Board of the Association was dissatisfied with Thiessen's work, since he was more Baptist-minded than Mennonite. In 1912 upon his return to Europe he became a Protestant missionary at Brussels, Belgium. (Friesen, *Brüderschaft,* 554 ff.)   vDZ.

Thijmon Hendriksz (Thomas Henriczn), an Anabaptist martyr, beheaded April 12, 1537, at Amsterdam, because he had attended forbidden meetings (of the Anabaptists). He had been rebaptized about three years previously and held heretical views. The sentence in full is published by van Braght. Thijmon was a native of Kampen in the Dutch province of Overijssel. (*Mart. Mir.* D 415, E 766; Grosheide, *Bijdrage,* 140 f., 307.)   vDZ.

Thijs Gerrits: see Gerrits, Thijs.

Thijs Hendriksz (Tijs Hermansz), an Anabaptist martyr, executed at Leeuwarden in Friesland, Netherlands, on May 2, 1553. Thijs, who was paralyzed, was put to death with a young woman, Berendge (*q.v.*), by drowning. They were bound into a sack and thrown from a boat into the town moat. After the sentence was pronounced Thijs protested against the plan of a secret execution and said, "Cats and dogs are thus drowned." They wanted to be executed publicly at the official place of execution, desiring to give a testimony of faith before the bystanders.

There is a song commemorating the firmness of faith of these two martyrs: "Een nieuwe liet heb ic gedicht, van twee schaep wtgekoren." This hymn, found in the hymnal *Veelderhande Liedekens,* is included by Wackernagel. (*Mart. Mir.* D 150, E 539; Wackernagel, *Lieder,* 131.)   vDZ.

Thijs Joriaensz (Jeuriaensz), an Anabaptist martyr, executed at Muiden, Netherlands, in 1569 (exact date unknown), with Jan (*q.v.*) Claesz by burning at the stake "chained together like horses." Van Braght's *Martyrs' Mirror,* following the martyr book of 1626, whose authors obtained data from Simon

Fijts (*q.v.*), a Mennonite preacher of Texel, gives a circumstantial report about these martyrs. Thijs was a native of Rarop (Ransdorp near Amsterdam) and a "dienaer int woord" (preacher). While visiting the congregation of Muiden (*q.v.*) with Jan Claesz, where Thijs was to preach, they were apprehended and imprisoned in the castle of Muiden for about half a year. Thereupon they were conducted to The Hague, where they remained in arrest for half a year, and then returned to the Muiden castle. After another stay there of about three months they were sentenced and executed.

Van Braght includes two letters by Thijs, one written on the 15th day of his imprisonment and addressed to his "brethren and sisters," i.e., the members of his congregation (at Ransdorp?), and one dated at The Hague Feb. 5, 1569, to the congregation of Edam (*q.v.*) in North Holland. Van Braght reports that he chose from the letters written by Thijs Joriaensz which had been published before. Of these the following editions are known (some may have been lost): *Een Christelijcke Sentbrief geschreven wter gevangenisse, van de Sendinghe, Inleydinge ende coemste Jesu Christi*, followed by *Eene hertgrondelijcke en Christelijcke Sentbrief*, and a hymn by Thijs (n.p., 1577; repr. n.p., 1579; Haarlem, 1586), and *Een Christelijcke Sentbrief, van de sendinghe, Inleydinge ende coemste Jesu Christi in deser werelt . . .* (Amsterdam, 1586). Of a booklet by Thijs Joriaensz and Job (*q.v.*) Janze, *Twee brieven . . . met een cleyne voorrede* with four hymns (n.p., 1609) there is only one copy extant, and of this only the first part. It is found in the Amsterdam Mennonite library. These letters by Thijs and Job Janze were addressed to the Frisian leaders Jan (*q.v.*) Willems and Lubbert Gerritsz (*q.v.*).

Unlike most of the martyrs, Thijs took part in the schisms which arose at this time among the Dutch Mennonites, dividing them in several branches. Thijs sided with Dirk (*q.v.*) Philips and the Flemish branch, vehemently asserting that the Frisians were wrong. In his letter he insisted on keeping the congregation "on a solid base and cleansing it from aberrations." These passages in question are not found in van Braght, who shortened the letters. The hymn composed by Thijs, "Ick roep tot u o schepper mijn, waer sal ick zijn?" is included in Wackernagel, *Lieder*. Letters by Thijs Joriaensz in a French translation are found in *Enchiridion ou Manuel de la Réligion Chrestienne . . .* (n.p., 1608), containing works of Dirk Philips, Menno Simons, and others, translated by Virgile de Las.

vDZ.

Mart. Mir. D 480-89, E 833-41; *Bibliographie* I, 205-12, 660 f.; Wackernagel, *Lieder*, 207; Blaupot t. C., *Holland* I, 27; *Biogr. Wb.* IV, 574 f.; *DJ* 1840, 64 f.; *DB* 1870, 51; 1887, 116; 1893, 62; 1899, 78, 90 f., 104, 138.

Thijs Olbrants, an Anabaptist martyr, a native of the Dutch island of Texel, was sentenced to death by the Court of Holland at The Hague on Sept. 15, 1534, and beheaded the same day or the next. Thijs, who had been among the Anabaptists who sailed in March 1534 from Amsterdam in order to go to Münster (*q.v.*) in Westphalia, was arrested near Bergklooster (*q.v.*) but released upon recantation.

But soon after he was again active, reading the Scriptures in Mennonite meetings, and was apprehended a second time and now, remaining steadfast, sentenced to death. (*Inv. Arch. Amst.* I, Nos. 744 f.; *DB* 1873, 140; 1917, 115, No. 47; *ML* III, 297.)

vDZ.

Thijs in die Starre (Mathys Spangemecker), an Anabaptist of Maastricht (*q.v.*) in the Netherlands, who after recanting was beheaded at Maastricht on Feb. 4, 1535. With some 15 or 16 others he had been arrested on Jan. 28, 1535. They were all members of the congregation founded by Henric Rol, and after his martyrdom in September 1534 were led by Jan Smeitgen (*q.v.*). In the trial of Thijs and the others interesting information about the congregational life and views of this Maastricht Anabaptist congregation was given. There was a growing Münsterite (*q.v.*) spirit among these Maastricht Anabaptists. The whole group recanted except Bartholomeus (*q.v.*) van den Berge and Mente (*q.v.*) Jan Heynendochter. Thijs's wife, also a member of the congregation, fled after the execution of her husband; the city board took care of their children.

vDZ.

W. Bax, *Het Protestantisme in het Bisdom Luik . . .* I (The Hague, 1937) 116-18 *et passim*.

T(h)ijs-Gerritsvolk, a branch of the Dutch Mennonites, followers of Elder Thijs Gerrits (*q.v.*), who separated from the main Frisian body in 1589 together with Elder Jan Jacobsz (*q.v.*); but in 1599 he left the Jan Jacobsz group. The Thijs-Gerritsvolk were a branch of the strict Frisians (Harde, or Oude Vriezen). This group, which always was rather small, was dissolved soon after the death of its leader (1601). In later times, when the reason of the schism was forgotten, some strict branches of the Dutch Mennonites, like the Huiskopers (*q.v.*) or Danzig Old Flemish and Ukowallists (*q.v.*) occasionally, though incorrectly, also were called Thijs-Gerritsvolk.

vDZ.

Thirnheim, about two miles southwest of Sinsheim (*q.v.*) in Baden, Germany, formerly the seat of a Mennonite congregation founded c1670 by Swiss immigrants. In 1731 (there is no earlier information) Rudolf Lienhard of Rohrbach was the preacher. The family names were Lienhard, Meyer, Herr, Brand, Plätscher, Wisler, Kratter, and Meili. This information is taken from a letter written to the Dutch Mennonite Committee of Foreign Needs at Amsterdam on Nov. 1, 1731. Soon after 1731 this congregation, called Dürnen or Diernen or Dirnheim in the Dutch *Naamlijst*, was united with that of Immelhausen (*q.v.*). (*Inv. Arch. Amst.* I, Nos. 1471 f.; Müller, *Berner Täufer*, 210; *Naamlijst* 1765 ff.)

vDZ.

Thirty Years' War (1618-48), that terrible war that was so significant to the political and economic position of Germany, was of far-reaching effect on the Mennonites as well, although they took no part at all in this war between Catholicism and Protestantism. To the Mennonites the Thirty Years' War brought one advantage, namely, that the death penalty in religious matters was no longer inflicted on them. The last death sentence passed on an Anabaptist occurred on May 24, 1618, when Jost Wilhelm, "a pious man," was executed for his faith in a village near Bregenz in Voralberg in Austria. Both Catholic and Protestant powers were occupied with other cares than the extermination of the peaceful Anabaptists.

Nevertheless the Mennonites also suffered terribly in the course of events. In Moravia, the only country in which they had been granted toleration and religious freedom at the time, the Catholic leaders, after their victory at the White Mountain near Prague (Nov. 8, 1620), were intent on either converting or expelling them. On Sept. 17, 1622, Emperor Ferdinand II and on Sept. 28 Cardinal Dietrichstein (q.v.) issued mandates banishing the Hutterites out of Moravia. More than 20,000 persons were robbed of their possessions and in spite of the cold were driven into misery with their children and their sick. They sought refuge chiefly in Hungary and Transylvania. The few who remained in Moravia were exiled by further decrees on March 2, 1624, and Dec. 17, 1628.

In the principalities of North Germany the Mennonites were in general spared the confusion of war, though some deep wounds were inflicted here too. The village of Wüstenfelde between Lübeck and Hamburg, where Menno Simons spent the last years of his life and where he was buried, was completely destroyed. In several parts of North Germany the Mennonites were tolerated in the course of the war and were given freedom of religion, for instance in Holstein and East Friesland, as well as in Polish West Prussia, whereas they were still persecuted in Cleve, Jülich, and Berg.

The Peace of Westphalia (Oct. 24, 1648), which concluded the Thirty Years' War, secured religious equality to the great churches in Germany, but no legal status or recognition was granted to the Mennonites. After the suffering of the war years and the moral deterioration in the depopulated country, every government head was glad to have some people with moral standards who would work diligently in rebuilding the devastated country. Thus Charles Louis, the Palatine elector, willingly granted refuge and limited religious liberty in 1664 to Mennonites expelled from Switzerland. They settled on both sides of the Rhine; on the right bank they settled on the devastated land between Wiesloch and Wimpfen, where in the spring of 1622 the two main battles of the Palatinate were fought. Also Mennonite refugees from Flanders were accepted in Crefeld and here laid the foundation of a new industry, the manufacture of silk and velvet; Crefeld is still the German center of this industry. (ML I, 447 f.) HEGE.

Thirty-Fivers: see **Reidenbach** Mennonite Church.

Thoenis (Tönnis, Theunis) **von Hastenraed:** see **Hastenrath, Theunis van.**

Thomae, Markus: see **Stübner.**

Thomae, Nikolaus (Nicolaus Sigelsbach) (1492-?), pastor in Bergzabern, Palatinate, Germany, a close friend of Oecolampadius (q.v.) in Basel and of Johann Bader (q.v.) in Landau. He engaged in a debate with Hans Denk (q.v.), and wrote a detailed report about this encounter in an important letter to Oecolampadius on April 1, 1527. He spent a week in Strasbourg and discussed sixteen difficult points, especially the matter of baptism, with Capito (q.v.) and Bucer (q.v.). He had frequent contacts with Anabaptists, with whom he "associated on a friendly basis, for they are God-fearing and brave people" (Gelbert), as he wrote to his friend Conrad Hubert, Jan 28, 1529. Thomae was not a great scholar. His Latin was not exact. Anabaptists like Hans Denk and Ludwig Haetzer (q.v.) far surpassed Thomae in their mastery of the ancient languages. E.T.

J. P. Gelbert, *Magister Johann Baders Leben und Schriften, Nikolaus Thomae und seine Briefe* (Neustadt, 1868) 159 f.; Christian Hege, *Die Täufer in der Kurpfalz* (Frankfurt, 1908); Ernst Stähelin, *Briefe und Akten zum Leben Oekolampads* I (Leipzig, 1927) 337 and 335 f.; II (1934) 51 ff., 894; idem, *Das theologische Lebenswerk Oekolampads* (Leipzig, 1939); Eberhard Teufel, "Täufertum und Quäkertum," *Theologische Rundschau* XIII (1941) 184; *ML* IV.

Thoman(n), Ruedi, an aged farmer living at Zollikon (q.v.) near Zürich, Switzerland, in whose house Felix Manz (q.v.) and Jörg Blaurock (q.v.) read the Scriptures, baptized, and administered the Lord's Supper on Jan. 25, 1525. The next day in the early morning Marx Bosshart, Ruedi's son-in-law, and Ruedi himself were baptized by Blaurock. A few months later the Zollikon congregation was dissolved by the Zürich magistrates. Ruedi Thoman reported to the government officials of Zürich (end of January, or early February 1525) about the meeting held in his house. His information is very important for knowledge of the practices of baptism and communion in the early Anabaptist period. After this trial there is no further information about Ruedi Thoman; like most of the Zollikon Anabaptists he may have recanted. vDZ.

TA Zürich, Nos. 29-32; Fritz Blanke, *Brüder in Christo* (Zürich, 1955) 27-32.

Thomas (Thomas Pelsser), a Hutterite martyr, a preacher, was burned at the stake in Brno in 1527 with Balthasar (q.v.) and Dominicus (q.v.) after a valiant confession of his faith. According to the Hutterite Chronicle, this execution took place in 1528. (*Mart. Mir.* D 18, E 428; Zieglschmid, *Chronik,* 63; *ML* IV.)

Thomas (Tomes), **Antonius,** is identical with Elder Antonius van Coelen (q.v.).

Thomas (Toenis) **Arentsz,** an Anabaptist martyr burned at the stake with two others June 28, 1553, at Leeuwarden in Friesland, Netherlands. He was (re)baptized, rejected the Catholic doctrine of transubstantiation, and believed "that all that is done in the (Catholic) church is idolatry." He persisted in his heresy, i.e., he died as a loyal member of the Mennonite church. vDZ.

Inv. Arch. Amst. I, No. 746; J. Reitsma, *Honderd jaren uit de geschiedenis der Hervorming ... in Friesland* (Leeuwarden, 1876) 63.

Thomas Drucker is identical with Thomas von Imbroich (*q.v.*).

Thomas Franssen was executed with the sword at The Hague, Netherlands, on Nov. 12, 1536. He was a native of Utrecht and lived at Amsterdam, where he was arrested in the fall of 1536. He was tried at Amsterdam (tortured on Nov. 7) and then taken to The Hague, where the trial was continued. Thomas was charged with crimes of buying and reading heretical books, failing to observe the regulations of the (Catholic) church, eating meat on fast days, and working on holy days. He had not attended (Catholic) church services for three or four years because he did not believe the doctrine of the Mass. In the documents he is said to be a "Lutheran," i.e., heretic, and a Sacramentist (*q.v.*), who taught false doctrines. It is not clear whether he was an Anabaptist, but apparently he was, for he is said to have been rebaptized and to have administered baptism himself. Because he refused to recant and to be instructed by the Catholic theologians, he was sentenced to death. His head was to be put on a pole and his property confiscated. (Grosheide, *Bijdrage*, 99 f.)   vDZ.

Thomas (Tonis) Gerritsz, a Dutch Anabaptist, a native of Lochem, Gelderland, was executed on Jan. 7, 1539, at Delft, Dutch province of South Holland, with Herman van Kelder. They were followers of David (*q.v.*) Joris, and during their trials they gave information concerning the immoral sexual practices of the group which were so severely censured by Menno Simons. (Mellink, *Wederdopers*, 216, 401.)   vDZ.

Thomas Hendricksz, an Anabaptist martyr: see **Thijmon Hendriksz.**

Thomas van Imbroek: see Imbroich, Thomas von.

Thomas Imwald (Thoman im Waldt auff Aldein) of Aldein, an Anabaptist martyr, was put to death at Fill (*q.v.*) in the Adige Valley, Tirol, on Nov. 16, 1529, with Georg Frick (*q.v.*) and two other brethren and four sisters of his faith. In his cross-examination he said he had been baptized by Georg Blaurock (*q.v.*).

Beck, *Geschichts-Bücher,* 89; Zieglschmid, *Chronik,* 74 f.; Wolkan, *Geschicht-Buch,* 53 and 54; *Mart. Mir.* D 27, E 435; *ML* IV.

Thomas (Tomas), Jan, a Dutch Mennonite preacher, b. Jan. 28, 1682, at Oosterlittens, d. July 26, 1744, at Surhuisterveen. He was a farmer, but accepted a call as minister of the Heerenveen-Knijpe congregation, serving here 1714-20 and in the Surhuisterveen congregation 1722-44. His colleague Jan Jogchems of Drachten preached his funeral sermon on Aug. 17, 1744. In 1719 he published at Heerenveen: *Kort Onderwijs voor de Jeugt in de voornaamste Gronden van den Christelijken godsdienst.* The Reformed pastor of Heerenveen discovered in this booklet a number of "Socinian (*q.v.*) errors," and so Thomas was summoned before the Reformed classis and thereupon suspended by the government. Soon after, however, he was active again, baptizing on Jan. 21, 1720. But again he was suspended and the government pressed his dismissal on account of the mandates issued by the States of Friesland in 1662 and 1687 against Socinians, Quakers, and "Dompelaars." The Frisian government, alarmed by Jan Thomas's Socinianism, in 1722 had a confession drawn up which was to be signed by all Mennonite preachers in the province of Friesland, and which emphatically repudiated the doctrines of Socinus. Jan Thomas, who belonged to the liberal wing of the Dutch Mennonites and who had much contact with the Collegiants (*q.v.*), also published his induction sermon at Heerenveen: *Den Wandel der Geloovigen in de vrese Gods* (Heerenveen, 1716), and translated the first Psalm into the Frisian language. (Blaupot t. C., *Friesland,* 205-8; *N.N.B.Wb.* VIII, 1295; *DB* 1896, 149-75.)   vDZ.

Thomas, Jan, an elder of the Flemish Mennonites in Groningen, Netherlands, who together with his coelders Teunis Gerrits and Cornelis Jans wrote a letter (February 1632) to the Flemish (Lamist) congregation of Amsterdam rejecting the invitation to the meeting to be held at Dordrecht, where Flemish and Old Flemish were to be united. They expressed the hope that the Amsterdam congregation would likewise oppose the unification. The merger, however, came about in 1632 on the basis of the Dordrecht (*q.v.*) Confession. Of Jan Thomas there is no further information. (*Inv. Arch. Amst.* I, No. 590.)   vDZ.

Thomas Janszn, of Amsterdam, a Dutch Anabaptist: see **Jan van Delft.**

Thomas Janszoen, a Dutch Anabaptist martyr, sentenced to death on April 10, 1535, by the court of Friesland at Leeuwarden. He was rebaptized and arrested, but pardoned after recanting; afterwards he again joined the Anabaptist "verbondt" (congregation) and was put to death. (*DB* 1917, 90.)   vDZ.

Thomas, Jurjen, a preacher of the Old Flemish Mennonites in the Dutch province of Groningen. As an opponent of Elder Uko Walles (*q.v.*), he was banned on March 4, 1637, by a meeting of elders, because "he was not obedient to the elders." This meeting was probably held in the town of Groningen (not at Noordbroek as stated in *ML* II, 448). After he was censured Thomas is supposed to have lodged a complaint against Walles with the magistrates; in any case Walles soon after was banished forever from the province of Groningen. Afterwards Jurjen Thomas attacked Walles in a booklet, *Vermaninge oft indachtig-makinge in een Nootwendige Verantwoordinge* (1645). Jurjen Thomas had a number of adherents, commonly called Jurjen-Thomasvolk, which for some time formed a separate branch of the Groningen Old Flemish Mennonites, but may soon have dissolved or joined some other group. In the same meeting in which Jurjen Thomas was dismissed, his son Thomas Jurjens had also to answer for his opinions, but he unlike his father conceded and conformed to the views of Uko Walles.   vDZ.

Blaupot t. C., *Friesland,* 161; *idem, Groningen* I, 68-70, 72, note 1, 77; *DB* 1876, 39, note 2; *ML* II, 448.

Thomas Mennonite Church (MC) was the third congregation organized in the Johnstown District of the Allegheny Conference (formerly Southwestern Pennsylvania District Conference). This section had no church building for nearly one hundred years after the first Mennonite settlers came into the vicinity. They attended services a few times a year at the Blough church (erected 1836), which was the original congregation in this area. Prior to 1874 they also occasionally had services in the summer in the Thomasdale Schoolhouse about two miles from Thomas Mills. Names of original settlers in the Thomas church area were Thomas, Croyle, Saylor, Johns, Mishler, Woods, Speigle, Hershberger, Kaufman, Gindelsperger, Alwine, and Lehman. A house of worship (36 x 50 ft.) was erected near Thomas Mills in 1874 on a plot of ground sold by John Thomas, Sr., for $50. In 1916 a new brick building (46 x 70 ft.) was erected to take care of the increasing membership. The church is located about ten miles southwest of Johnstown. The congregation conducts a mission at Headrick just north of Johnstown. Ordained men who have served the congregation have borne the names of Gindelsperger, Hershberger, Saylor, Eash, and Wingard. In 1957 the membership of the congregation was 167, with Aldus Wingard as bishop-pastor.   J.L.H.

Thomas Streck, a Mennonite, a native of Wachtebeke in Flanders, lived at Gent, Belgium, where he was arrested in 1566. Although he was only 18 years of age, he very eloquently and firmly confessed his faith. He is said to have "seduced" many persons, and for his "heresy" he was sentenced to death. For some reason or other the execution was postponed. Thomas, being very frank, requested his release. Verheyden believes that he was not put to death but sent to the galleys (q.v.) after June 10, 1566.   vDZ.
A. L. E. Verheyden, "De Doopsgezinden te Gent 1530-1630," in *Bijdragen tot de Geschiedenis en Oudheidkunde te Gent* (1943) 114 f.

Thomashof, located 2 miles south of Durlach, Baden, Germany, an influential South German Mennonite conference and retreat center, and rest home, called Bibelheim Thomashof, was established by the purchase on March 26, 1924, of the former inn (Kurhaus) by that name with 2 acres of land, lying adjacent to Lamprechtshof, the farm of Elder David Horsch, by a group of men from the Badischer Verband (q.v.), who call themselves the *Bruderrat* (Brother Council) and have owned and operated it. It was dedicated June 29, 1924. On Dec. 27, 1954, an added 30-bed guest building was completed and dedicated. Chr. Schnebele has been the housefather from the beginning. Regular weekly Sunday services are held in the chapel, as are occasional Bible conferences, ministers' weeks, youth conferences, etc. The deaconess work of the Verband also has its headquarters here. Paying guests desiring recreation in a quiet spiritual atmosphere are received at all times. (*ML* IV, 318-20.)   H.S.B.

Thomasz, Jacob, a member of the Waterlander Mennonites, probably at Amsterdam, was opposed to any kind of confession in the Mennonite church. For this reason he attacked Hans de Ries (q.v.), who together with Lubbert Gerritsz (q.v.) had drawn up a confession in 1610. In *Vriendelijcke Aenspraeck* (1613) Thomasz charged de Ries and some of his friends, e.g., Yeme de Ringh (q.v.), with tyrannizing the church. On March 26-28, 1613, Thomasz had to answer before the church board of Amsterdam for his disloyal conduct. The outcome is not known. (*DB* 1864, 45, 49, 52-54.)   vDZ.

Thomme (Tombe, Combe), **Absolon van,** an Anabaptist martyr: see **Absolon de Zanger.**

Thompson Hutterite Bruderhof of the Dariusleut (q.v.) branch, located near Glenwood, Alberta, was founded in 1918. In 1950 the population numbered 76, with Paul J. Tschetter as head preacher. D.D.

Thöne (Tönnen): see **Teune.**

Thonis (Theunis) **van Waesten(e):** see **Anthonis Schoonvelt.**

Thormann, Georg, a Swiss Reformed theologian, wrote a book of 700 pages on the Anabaptists, *Probier-Stein oder Schrifftmässige . . . Prüfung dess Täufferthums, zu allgemeiner Erbauung abgefasset* (Bern, 1693). (See **Probierstein.**)
John Horsch, "Accusations Against the Swiss Brethren," *MQR* VIII (April 1934) 79; *ML* III.

Thorn (Polish *Torun*), a town in Poland situated on the Vistula, where Mennonites lived in 1586. The members may have joined the Obernessau (q.v.) (also called Nieschewski, q.v.) congregation. In 1678 the magistrates of Thorn issued a mandate forbidding the citizens to shelter Arians, Anabaptists, and Mennonites.   vDZ.
Felicia Szper, *Nederl. Nederzettingen in West-Pruisen . . .* (Enkhuizen, 1913) 152, 202 f. *ML* IV, 320-23.

Three Rivers Civilian Public Service Camp No. 107, about 7 miles north of Three Rivers, and about 80 miles southeast of Fresno, Cal., was opened in May 1943 and closed in June 1946. It was operated by the Mennonite Central Committee under the National Park Service. The chief work of the men was fire presuppression and fire fighting. The camp had a capacity of 150 men. *On Sequoia Trails,* an illustrated book produced by the men, presents the activities of the camp.   M.G.
Melvin Gingerich, *Service for Peace* (Akron, 1949) 160-61.

Threshing Stones, used by the Mennonites of Russia and in few cases in the prairie states and provinces, became the emblem of Bethel College and also of agriculture. The threshing stone is a seven-ribbed cone-shaped stone wheel with a round hole through the horizontal axis. It was about thirty inches long and two feet in diameter. Each six-inch rib is tapered from six inches at the base to two and one-half inches at the outer edge. In Kansas such threshing stones were cut according to a wooden model by a stone quarry near Florence, the model having been prepared by the early Mennonite settlers.

The cut grain was spread in two concentric circles on the threshing floor with the heads of the grain facing each other. The threshing stone was pulled by two horses; the ribbed stone rolling over the heads of the grain knocked the grain and chaff from the straw, after which the grain was fanned. Some of these stones are found in the Kauffman Museum in North Newton, Kan., and on Kansas Mennonite farmyards.   J.A.D.

Thudichum, Friedrich (1831-1913), professor of law at the University of Tübingen. In his two-volume work, *Die Deutsche Reformation 1517-1525* (Leipzig, 1907), he gives the Anabaptists a friendly and favorable testimony in these words: "With the most absolute confidence I state as my verdict: to the Brethren is due the credit of having defended in innumerable oppressions a Christianity which alone agrees with the teachings of Jesus and of being among those to whom we owe an enlightened interpretation of philosophy, ethics, and theology, with whose aid in the course of the centuries a humane legislation, nobler international law, and a better organization of the Protestant church have everywhere been achieved" (Vol. II, p. 161). Thudichum was one of the few pupils of Ludwig Keller among German scholars, unique among his fellows, and was ridiculed by the guild. (*ML* IV.)   NEFF, E.T.

Thumb von Neuburg, Hans Konrad (d. 1555), hereditary marshal of Württemberg, a friend of the Anabaptists in Württemberg and of Schwenckfeld, indeed related to him. He and his brother Hans Friedrich (Obervogt in Kirchheim and Teck) accepted the Anabaptists into their villages, viz., in Stetten. There in 1539-44 Hans Konrad sheltered a leader of the Anabaptists, Konrad Sax, employing him as a cooper. For a long time Burkhard Schilling was active as pastor in Stetten and gained adherents there for Schwenckfeld. In 1544 Hans Konrad was removed from his office of hereditary marshal and fell into disfavor with Duke Ulrich. The chief charge against him was his favoring of the Anabaptists and Schwenckfelders, and permitting them to live on his estate Korntal. Until 1544 he constituted an element of unrest in Württemberg; it was impossible to oppose him since he had won the duke to his side. Not until the reform party succeeded in making him disliked at the court could the Reformation be carried out successfully. (*TA Württemberg*, 1167.)   G.Bos.

Thun, a town and district of the canton of Bern, Switzerland, situated on Lake Thun. Moritz Losenegger (*q.v.*) a citizen of Thun, was in prison there as early as 1532. Concerning the spread and development of Anabaptism in the district of Thun there is not much information. In the 17th century and probably even earlier, Anabaptists were found in the villages of Goldenwil, Wattenwil, Hilterfingen, Sigriswil, Diesbach, and a few other hamlets, all mountain villages on the north shore of Lake Thun. Jakob Ammann (*q.v.*), the founder of the Amish (*q.v.*) Mennonites, was of Erlenbach near Thun. In the course of time a number of Anabaptists from the Thun area emigrated; among the emigrants moving in 1711 to the Netherlands were members of the Schneider, Ruff (Rupp), Reuszer (Risser), Richard, Sorg, Schlappach, Eicher, Kienzi, Krähenbühl, and Rüegsegger families from Sigriswil and other villages in the Thun district. Others moved to the Swiss Jura in the 18th century. In 1823 only 85 Mennonites were living in the Thun district (Ritschard, Stähli, Freyenberg, and Winteregg families).   vDZ.

D. L. Gratz, *Bernese Anabaptists* (Scottdale, 1953); Müller, *Berner Täufer*, 310 f.

Thungen, Konrad von, bishop of Würzburg, bloody persecutor of the Anabaptists from 1525 on. (See Eberhard Teufel, "Taufertum und Quäkertum im Lichte der Neueren Forschung," *Theol. Rundschau* XIV, 1942, pp. 145 f.)

Thuringia (Thüringen), a German state (6,022 sq. mi. and 2,927,497 pop. in 1946), located in the heart of Germany and in the heart of the area of the Lutheran Reformation, bounded on the south by Bavaria (Franconia), on the west by Hesse, and on the east and north by Saxony; capital Weimar. Other cities of importance are Erfurt, Gotha, Eisenach, Jena, Mühlhausen. The modern boundaries of Thuringia are not identical with those of the Reformation period, and the territory has suffered many changes in its rulers. In 1946 it was incorporated into the East German state as the westernmost province.

The history of Anabaptism in Thuringia has been exhaustingly treated from the sources by Paul Wappler in his classic work *Die Täuferbewegung in Thüringen von 1526 bis 1584* (Jena, 1913, 540 pp.), in which the first 227 pages give the narrative history, the remaining 300 pages a reproduction *in extenso* of all the archival materials bearing on the subject. Wappler's own summary (pp. 220-27) will be printed immediately following in translation, with slight additions by the writer. Wappler's work is fair, accurate, and thorough and has not been superseded, requiring only some minor revisions. The 1913 volume includes the pertinent material from his two previous works: *Inquisition und Ketzerprozesse in Zwickau zur Reformationszeit* (Leipzig, 1908), and *Die Stellung Kursachsens und des Landgrafen Philipp von Hessen zur Täuferbewegung* (Münster, 1910).   H.S.B.

"Anabaptism in the heart of Germany was a consequence of the great disappointment that had taken possession of broad strata of the people in an increasing measure because of Luther's conservative reformation position and the moral unfruitfulness of his young established church, as well as his position in the Peasants' War, who had shared the mind of Thomas Müntzer both in his mystical and enthusiastic basis and in certain apocalyptic and eschatological expectations. The first center of Anabaptist propaganda (beginning in the summer of 1526) was found in the Saxon enclave of Königsberg in Franconia, where Hans Hut, and with him the cooper Volk Kolerlin, the sexton Kilian Volckaimer (*q.v.*), the peasant Sebastian, and the cabinetmaker Eukarius Kellermann and Joachim Mertz worked for the Anabaptist cause. In their revelations a major role was played by the imminent Turkish invasion and the extermination of the ungodly that was to begin therewith. But this activity was discovered in early February 1527. Beutelhans and Wolf Schominger, citizens of Königsberg, as well as the miller of Aurach and Kaspar Spegel of Ostheim, were put to death, and a number of others escaped with only a penalty of disgrace. At the same time in electoral Saxony a decree was issued permitting only those who had been regularly called to the office of preaching to perform the functions of pastoral care. "Probably from Franconia Anabaptism thereupon pushed up into northern Thuringia in the course of 1527, where Müntzer's social revolutionary ideas had continued to smolder. The leader in the agitation here was the furrier Hans Römer (*q.v.*) of Eisenach. With him were the furrier Christoph Peisker of Quedlinburg, the peasant Volkmar Fischer (*q.v.*) of Rohrborn, and the shoemaker Christoph of Meissen (*q.v.*) or of Mühlhausen. They proclaimed the violent restoration of Jerusalem. Their first goal was an open attack on Erfurt on New Year's Day of 1528. The plot was, however, discovered and twelve of the conspirators were executed. The Anabaptist preachers, however, escaped. Of these, Hans Römer was arrested at Göttingen and Volkmar Fischer at Erfurt in 1534. Fischer was executed. [In the article **Königsberg** Hege challenges the validity of the above charge of revolutionary action. He says, "The death sentence was pronounced on them in spite of a lack of evidence of an intended revolution (all the racked prisoners instead stressed their nonresistance), and in spite of the fact that the burgomaster and council of Königsberg praised their previous conduct, rejected all suspicion of revolutionary plans, and asked their lives to be spared, and that the council of Koburg gave a similar testimonial for Wolf Schreiner."]

"From Franconia and from Hesse about the end of 1526 Anabaptism also penetrated into western Thuringia. Its apostles were Volkmar of Hildburghausen, Michel of Uettingen, the Franconian Georg of Staffelstein, Niklas Schreiber, Hans Both (*q.v.*), and Katharina Valebs. Apocalyptic proclamations constituted the chief theme of their preaching.

"But now Anabaptism progressed along more and more moderate lines. Its principal differences with the established church were now over original sin, infant baptism, and the bodily presence of Christ in the communion. The last of these points came to take on the character of a confession with the Anabaptists. Their ideal was the congregation of saints. Therefore one finds among them also to a greater or lesser degree a withdrawal from the state and its institutions, quiet acceptance of suffering as the cross of Christ, and a simple, devotional religious service by preachers chosen by the congregation. The first arrests in western Thuringia occurred in early 1528. A sexton was executed at Mehlis. Others recanted at Gotha and Georgenthal, but some rejoined the Anabaptists. Six of them were consequently beheaded at Reinhardsbrunn on Jan. 18, 1530. But Anabaptism made most inroads in western Thuringia in the Hausbreitenbach district, to which the lenience of Prince Philip of Hesse, under whose jurisdiction half of the area lay, and the nearness of the Anabaptist congregation of Sorga (*q.v.*) near Hersfeld contributed. Here, besides other apostles, Melchior Rinck (*q.v.*) worked. The basic lines of his system of theology were mysticism and a thoroughly spiritualistic view of the Scriptures. Hence his opposition to all purely external religious customs from which reason is excluded. Called to answer for himself repeatedly, expelled from the country, and punished with imprisonment, Rinck nevertheless continued his Anabaptist activity within Hessian and Thuringian lands.

"To counter the threatening growth of Anabaptism Justus Menius wrote his book in 1530, *Der Widdertauffer lere und geheimnis aus heiliger schrifft widderlegt,* which presents an excellent picture of Anabaptism from the point of view of its opponents. Nevertheless Anabaptism continued to progress in western Thuringia. A number of residents in Hausbreitenbach were arrested in October 1531. An official opinion by the Wittenberg theologians in general favored capital punishment, but upon the intervention of Philip the prisoners were divided, the Saxons beheaded and the Hessians, upon recantation, released. On Nov. 11, 1531, the authorities succeeded in taking Melchior Rinck and eleven of his audience at Vacha. Saxony wanted to have him executed, but he was now sentenced by Philip to life imprisonment.

"Meanwhile Anabaptism was also making progress in the beech forests belonging to the Stift of Fulda. An Anabaptist apostle appeared here as a prophet of God and miracle worker and won a large following. About 40 of them were seized with the apostle on March 25, 1532, at Spahl in the Rockenstuhl district, after valiant self-defense, and taken to Fulda. Overcome in the prison atmosphere by religious madness, most of them remained steadfast and cheerfully submitted to beheading, only the fellow travelers recanted and were then released. But now the places of Melchior Rinck and the executed apostles of Anabaptism had been filled by others, like Georg Zaunring (*q.v.*), Georg Stein, Jakob Schmidt, Christoph of Moravia, the sexton Alexander [*q.v.*, whom Wappler elsewhere calls "one of the noblest figures in the Anabaptist movement" of Middle Germany], the tailor Ilgen, Hans Both, and others. Their center was the Anabaptist congregation at Sorga. From there they developed lively agitation especially in Hausbreitenbach. In early January 1533 arrests were again made here—the peasant Fritz Erbe (*q.v.*) of Herda, and Margaretha Kochs, 'die alte Garköchin.' In July, eighteen more were examined at Berka. But in the end all were released, since Philip continued to oppose the execution demanded by John of Saxony. Only Fritz Erbe and Margaretha were held, Erbe in a city tower of Eisenach, and later in the Wartburg, until his death in 1548. In Gotha the tailor Hans Riemer of Altenbergen was tried in July 1533. He escaped execution by recanting in the last hour.

"Meanwhile Anabaptism had found a new footing in northern Thuringia. The Anabaptist apostles working here were first Volkmar of Hildburghausen, Bernhardus, Georg of Staffelstein, and Katharina Valebs. The chief Anabaptist center here was the area of Frankenhausen. In early 1529 the first examinations were undertaken here. The arrested Anabaptists finally recanted. But in early January 1530 thirteen more were arrested, for the most part stemming from Franconia. Four, who refused to recant, were drowned, and the others expelled from the country. In the middle of 1530 seven more Anabaptists were arrested. Of these, Katharina Valebs, who remained steadfast, was executed, and Erhard Polrus (*q.v.*), who had backslidden, was burned through the cheeks. Now the sexton Alexander began a wide-scale propaganda for Anabaptism throughout northern Thuringia and the southern Harz. With him Jakob Schmiedeknecht was working. They held their secret meetings for a time in Landgrafroda near Allstedt, Frankenhausen, and Sangerhausen. Finally, however, Alexander was seized with the others in the autumn of 1533 and executed in November at Frankenhausen. Meanwhile in the region of Mühlhausen (*q.v.*) Hans Both was continuing the propaganda begun by Alexander. The soul of the movement here was Ludwig Spon. He was arrested in May 1533 with six others and was not released until mid-November by Philip. In September of that year the Anabaptists had been expelled from Sorga. They went to Moravia (*q.v.*), whither, in spite of Hans Both's disappointment there, Anabaptists continued to go until the end of the 16th century.

"In northern Thuringia and in the Harz area Alexander's propaganda was quickly carried on by Peter Reusse of Ruse and Heinz Kraut (*q.v.*) of Esperstedt in its full scope. Especially at Emseloh and Holdenstedt they had numerous followers. They maintained connections with the Hessian Anabaptists, the followers of Melchior Rinck. In early April 1534 Georg Knoblauch (*q.v.*) of Emseloh and his wife were arrested. But he recanted and was released. His wife, however, remaining steadfast, suffered death. Following her, two other Anabaptists were executed. A place of refuge for the Anabaptists of Hesse, who called themselves 'Friends of God,' was the Schneider Mill at Zorge near Ellrich. From here contacts were again established with the Anabaptists of Mühlhausen, who were again working for Anabaptism, e.g., in the area of Neunheiligen. At the end of October 1534 and in January 1535 several residents of Mühlhausen and the vicinity were arrested. But by the middle of 1535 all were released, in spite of the fact that Saxony insisted on capital punishment. They now found a refuge in the Lutter Forest near Lauterberg in the Harz and at Halberstadt, where, following the example of the first Christian church, they led a holy life full of brotherly love in all simplicity. In addition to Peter Reusse and Heinz Kraut, Georg Köhler (*q.v.*) now began to work for the Anabaptist cause. In Riestedt and in the vicinity of Mühlhausen, where Barbara Meissrod's home became a new center for them, they were very successful. In early April 1535 arrests were made in Riestedt. A new hiding place for the followers of Anabaptists was now Schraubenstein between Riestedt and Emseloh. From here they frequently visited their brethren at Halberstadt. On Sept. 2, 1535, two of them, including Georg Köhler, were seized, and soon after beheaded at Sangerhausen with another Anabaptist woman. The same fate soon struck three of the Anabaptists of Halberstadt, who were drowned in the Bode at Gröningen. On Nov. 20, 1535, Heinz Kraut with a number of Anabaptists, including Georg Knoblauch, were at the home of Hans Peissker (*q.v.*) of Kleineuterdorf near Orlamünde, a miller. On the next morning all were arrested, a total of 16 persons, and taken to the Leuchtenburg. The women were detained here, while four of the men, among them Heinz Kraut and Hans Peissker, were taken to Jena, and four others, including Knoblauch, were taken to Neustadt on the Orla, and three to Kahla. The prisoners at Jena, whose trial was conducted by Melanchthon (*q.v.*), were with one exception unreceptive to teaching. They were consequently beheaded on Jan. 26, 1536. Of the other prisoners, at first only Peissker's daughter Margaretha recanted. But after many attempts, in which Melanchthon again participated, both on the Leuchtenburg and at Kahla, all but one were persuaded to recant. The steadfast one was beheaded. A consequence of this Anabaptist trial was that Melanchthon wrote the second Saxon Anabaptist mandate on April 10, 1536, and also the *Verlegung etlicher unchristlicher Artikel, welche die Wiedertäufer fürgeben.* Nevertheless there were further arrests of Anabaptists in eastern Thuringia in 1539 and 1540; the prisoners recanted and were released.

"For the Anabaptists of northern Thuringia and at the Harz Mühlhausen was a center from 1535 on. In the place of Heinz Kraut and Georg Köhler, a certain Matthes was the leader. At the beginning of October 1537 the Mühlhausen city council took steps against these conventicles. Ten of the arrested men and women were drowned in the Unstrut and four expelled from the city. Of the remaining four prisoners, two were drowned on Jan. 17, 1538. About the same time an Anabaptist execution took place at Brücken on the Helme. But still Anabaptism did not disappear from northern Thuringia. In 1544-45 there were again Anabaptist trials at Mühlhausen, but now Philip vigorously opposed their execution.

"In western Thuringia sympathy for Anabaptism was long preserved, especially by the long imprisonment of Fritz Erbe. Two men, who were found in conversation with him in November 1537, were beheaded as blasphemers at the end of January 1538. The excitement caused by this execution was the occasion for the writing of Justus Menius's booklet in 1538, *Wie ein iglicher Christ gegen allerley lere, gut und böse, nach Gottes befelh sich gebürlich halten soll,* a book which denoted a lapse toward Catholic concepts. During Lent of 1539 three Anabaptists were again discovered in the tower with Fritz Erbe. They escaped death by recanting. The same thing recurred in early 1540 in the case of three Anabaptists at Kreuzburg. Meanwhile Anabaptism was gaining the upper hand in Fritz Erbe's home community. On Feb. 7 and 8, 1544, a large Anabaptist cross-examination was held at Berka, but again it took its course without result because of the lenience of Philip.

"In the parish of Gotha the peasant Klaus Ludwig of Tüngeda caused some trouble. Repeatedly examined by Myconius, he always managed to avoid execution by recanting.

"In the gravure of Henneberg Count Wilhelm throughout his life strictly prevented the penetration of Anabaptism into his lands. In 1528, 1529, 1531, 1550, and 1551 there were executions. The last Anabaptist arrested emigrated in 1560.

"After the middle of the 16th century the decline of Anabaptism in Thuringia became increasingly evident." (*ML* IV, 324-27.)   H.S.B.

Thurman Mennonite Church (MC), located one mile north of Thurman, Col. The original settlers came from Nebraska and homesteaded in this area, retaining their conference affiliations with the Kansas-Nebraska and later the Iowa-Nebraska conferences until 1958, when the congregation joined the South Central Conference. The first minister to serve the church here was Joe Schrock, followed by N. M. Birky, Aaron Unternahrer, and Earl Yeackley (the pastor in 1958). On March 22, 1916, the first meetinghouse, built before 1888, was destroyed by a prairie fire; the present frame building was built on the same site. In 1956 the building was moved to its present location in Thurman. Largely because of the drought, the membership, which at one time numbered over 100, had decreased to 14 by 1958.   E.YEA.

Thysken and his wife Mariken (*q.v.*) Vrencken died as Anabaptist martyrs. They were drowned at Stockheim "int Lant van Ludich" (Liege in Belgium?). The year of their execution is unknown; it happened before 1547 according to information given by the martyr Metken (*q.v.*), who was their sister-in-law.   vDZ.

W. Bax, *Het Protestantisme in het bisdom Luik ...* I (The Hague, 1937) 326, 399.

Tiaert Tyercxzoon, of Dokkum, an Anabaptist martyr, beheaded at Leeuwarden in Friesland, Netherlands, on Feb. 8, 1539, because he was rebaptized and harbored "heretical views" concerning the Mass and the doctrines of the (Catholic) church. vDZ.

J. Reitsma, *Honderd jaren uit de Geschiedenis der Hervorming ... in Friesland* (Leeuwarden, 1876) 63.

Tiardus Snekensis (Tjaert van Sneek): see **Tjaert Renicx.**

Tibben, a nickname formerly used for the Mennonites in the Netherlands. In 1549 the name "Tip" was given to the Mennonite woman Hadewych (*q.v.*) in Leeuwarden. In the trial of the martyr Reytse (*q.v.*) Aysesz in 1574 there is a question concerning "Mennonites and Tibben." In a mandate issued in 1612 in the district of Twente (*q.v.*) in the Dutch province of Overijssel is found the phrase "the congregation of the Tibben or Anabaptists." In the same year mention is made of the "Mennonites or Tibben" who are numerous in Westphalia. In the Dutch town of Deventer is found the Tibbensteeg (narrow street). In the province of Groningen the name of Tibben for Mennonites was still common in the 18th century. Thus it can be asserted that the name Tibben was formerly used in Friesland, Groningen, Overijssel, and Westphalia; the name was unknown in Holland and Flanders.

The meaning of the word Tibben is not clear. It is thought to have been derived from a Christian name Tibbe, or the family name Tibma of a person who would have been a follower of Menno Simons, but such a name is unknown. Some are of the opinion that it was derived from a hamlet in Friesland near Dokkum. Broese van Groenou thinks the word is etymologically connected with the Flemish verb *dubben,* Latin *dubitare.* Then a Dibbe or Tibbe would be a dubious person, who cannot be trusted; the word *dubbe* in Flemish also means hypocrite. But this explanation is too farfetched; moreover the name Tibben for Mennonites was unknown in Flanders. Several interpretations of the word Tibben do not satisfy. The most satisfactory one is still the view of de Hoop Scheffer (*DB* 1882, 40) that the Mennonites were sometimes called Tibben after a certain, now unknown, person named Tibbe (or Tjibbe), a corruption of Thiebout.   vDZ.

Blaupot t. C., *Friesland,* 375; *Mart. Mir.* D 682b, E 998; *DB* 1882, 34 ff.; 1888, 49; Friedrich Brune, *Der Kampf um eine evangelische Kirche im Münsterland, 1520-1802* (Witten, 1953) 122 f.; *ME* III, 779.

Tiboel: see **Tieboel.**

Tichelaar, a Dutch family name, very common in the province of Friesland, where tichelaar means owner of a tile factory or maker of brick. There have been many Tichelaar families unrelated to one another. A Mennonite Tichelaar family is still found at Makkum, Friesland. They have been well-to-do owners of tile works and formerly also of sawmills and paper mills. This family is mentioned as early as about 1660, in which year Freerck Jans, a farmer's son, who in 1676 assumed the family name of Tichelaar, bought a tile factory at Makkum. This factory, now N. V. Tichelaars Kleiwarenfabriek (Tichelaar's Clayware Factories, Inc.), is still run by a descendant of the first owner Freerck Jans, the present director being Jan Pieter Tichelaar (b. 1893). This factory now specializes in art pottery; it made the two Mennonite plates pictured among the illustrations of *ME* I, XXV, Nos. 1 and 2. Many members of this Tichelaar family have been deacons of the church and trustees of the conference of Friesland, Pieter Ymes Tichelaar (d. 1808) being treasurer of the Zuiderklasse (*q.v.*) and J. P. Tichelaar in 1941-54 a trustee of the A.D.S. (General Mennonite Conference). Pieter Jans Tichelaar (d. 1890) bequeathed a considerable gift of money to the Makkum congregation.

A member of this Makkum Tichelaar family was Hoito Tichelaar, b. 1743 at Makkum, d. there on March 1, 1818. After studying at the University of Franeker and the Amsterdam Mennonite Seminary he served as pastor at den Hoorn on the island of Texel 1765-66, Bolsward 1766-67, and Amsterdam 1767-1810, until 1801 in the Lamist congregation and from then in the United Mennonite congregation of Amsterdam. He took a keen interest in the merger of the Lamist and Zonist churches (1801). He published only his *Aanspraak aan de kinderen in het Doopsgezinde Weeshuis* (Amsterdam, 1777) and a funeral sermon for his colleague Gerard van Heyningen: *Lykrede* (Amsterdam, 1801). Hoito Tichelaar is said to have been "always eager to oblige"; as a pulpit orator he was not very popular:

his sermons are said to have been "old-fashioned, stiff, and affected."

Other Dutch Mennonite preachers of this name, probably not related to the Makkum Tichelaar family, were Jan Jacobs Tichelaar (c1648-1721), preacher at Stiens until 1704/5 and in the congregation of Oost-Vlieland 1704/5-21, and Douwe Abesz Tichelaar, d. 1746, who was a preacher of the Waterlander congregation on the island of Ameland 1706-46. Nicolaas Tichelaar belongs to the Tigler (q.v.) family.   vDZ.

De Vrije Fries XXVII (Leeuwarden, 1920) 36-40; *Klei, orgaan voor de Klei-verwerkende Industrie* II, No. 2 (June 1952) 136-40; *Menn. Life* VII (1953) 126; XI (1956) 183 f.; *Inv. Arch. Amst.* II, Nos. 710, 915a, 1055, 1474-76, 1480, 1485, 1579-81, 2505; G. A. Wumkes, *Stads- en Dorpskroniek van Friesland,* 2 vv. (Leeuwarden, 1930, 1934) *passim;* Blaupot t. C., *Friesland,* 211, 363, 366; *Naamlijst* 1815, 41; 1829, 23; *DJ* 1850, 123; *DB* 1889, 17, 21; 1898, 12 f., 20, 32; 1899, 211; 1912, 76, 82-86.

Tieboel (Tiboel) (and Tieboel Siegenbeek, a branch of the Tieboel family), an old, originally non-Mennonite family, found as early as c1580 at Emmerich, Germany, who moved to the Netherlands in the early 18th century. Most Tieboels formerly lived in Friesland. Jacobus Tieboel (1760-1830), a physician of Leeuwarden, was married to Christina Lugt (1761-1811), of Amsterdam; both were Mennonites. In the 18th century a Mennonite branch was found at Workum; here Daniel Tieboel was a town clerk; his daughter Geertruida Tieboel was married in 1799 to Matthijs Siegenbeek (q.v., 1774-1854). Their son was Daniel Tieboel Siegenbeek (1806-66), a jurist at Leiden, married to Elisabeth van Heukelom (18..-74). He served many years as a deacon of the Leiden Mennonite congregation and was a trustee of the A.D.S. (General Mennonite Conference) 1851-57 and a curator of the Amsterdam Mennonite Seminary. The last years of his life he was mayor of Leiden.   vDZ.

G. A. Wumkes, *Stads- en Dorpskroniek van Friesland* I (Leeuwarden, 1930) *passim; DB* 1903, 110; 1905, 41; *N.N.B.Wb.* II, 1317.

Tiege, a Prussian Mennonite village name transplanted to the Molotschna and Zagradovka settlements in the Ukraine; Barnaul, Siberia; and Neuland, Paraguay. (See **Villages.**)   C.K.

Tiege, a village of the Molotschna settlement (q.v.), Russia, established in 1805, consisting of 4,503 acres (20 farms), which developed into a significant economic and cultural Mennonite center. In addition to the village school, it had a school for the deaf established by Gerhard Klassen in 1885 (see **Marientaubstummenschule**). Tiege was also the name of an important Mennonite village in the center of the delta of the Vistula and Nogat in West Prussia, near Ladekopp.   C.K.

H. Görz, *Die Molotschnaer Ansiedlung* (Steinbach, 1951) 13, 115; Friesen, *Brüderschaft,* 655.

Tiege Mennonite Brethren Church, of the Zagradovka settlement in Russia. Among the first settlers there were six families who belonged to the M.B. Church, who in 1873 chose Jakob Richert as their first minister. Services were held in private homes until 1881, when a building in Altona was bought

for this purpose. Membership grew rapidly; by 1885 there were 100 members. In 1888 a church was built in Tiege. In 1892 Richert moved away and Isaak Regehr became the leading minister. He retired in 1902. Johann Nikkel was then elected and ordained elder. From this date the church became an independent unit, having formerly been a branch of the Friedensfeld M.B. Church. In 1922 the Tiege church had 427 baptized members; two of their former members were missionaries in foreign fields: Mrs. Abraham Hübert in India and Heinrich Reimer in Kamerun, Africa. In 1929 Elder Nikkel was arrested and starved to death in prison. The other ministers experienced a similar fate. The church building was taken over by the Soviets and converted into a club. All organized church life ceased to exist.   G.L.

Friesen, *Brüderschaft,* 425-27, 462-64; G. Lohrenz, *Sagradowka* (Rosthern, 1947) 79.

Tiegenhagen, a village in the northern part of the lowlands of the Vistula Delta, below sea level, protected from the sea by dikes. The village was founded c1350 by Teutonic knights. When their rule decayed, the village was overtaken by marsh and alders. Not until 1550 were attempts made to resettle the area. By 1640 Tiegenhagen was the Mennonite center of the Tiegenhof Lowlands, where the Mennonites owned over 200 hides of land. Tiegenhagen was also the seat of the Mennonite mutual fire insurance, which was founded in 1623 and covered all the farms and other buildings owned by Mennonites in the Grosswerder. About 1620 Claass Kreker possessed the three "Freihufen" of the village, which his descendants still held in 1750.

The Tiegenhagen Mennonite church belonged to the Flemish branch; until 1639 it was served by the elder of Danzig, but then chose Hans Siemens as its elder and thus became an independent congregation. (See *ML* IV, 518, for a list of the elders of the congregation.) As this Grosswerder congregation continued to grow, it was decided in 1735 to establish four quarters: Elbing Quarter (Rosenort congregation), Tiegenhagen Quarter, Orloff Quarter (Ladekopp congregation), and Bärwald Quarter (Fürstenwerder congregation). All four quarters were to have a single elder, but each was to have its own preachers. Gradually the daughter congregations of the Grosswerder congregation became independent and in the first half of the 19th century chose their own elders, Fürstenwerder being the first to do so in 1809. In 1814 Abraham Wiebe of Tiegenhagen was chosen as elder of the other three quarters. When Wiebe died in 1833, the Tiegenhagen congregation became independent and chose Peter Reimer of Tiegenhagen as its elder. The Ladekopp congregation thereupon chose Jacob Wiebe in the same year, while Rosenort continued to be served by the elder of Tiegenhagen. Finally in 1857 Rosenort chose Nicolaus Fast as its elder.

A special grant by the Bishop of Culm permitted the Mennonites of Tiegenhagen to build a frame church "40 ells long, 22 ells wide, 7 ells high along the walls, with ordinary doors and windows, thatch roof, a chimney extending above the church and an apartment for residence in it" (Driedger). Until 1892 this frame church was in use. In that year the old church was torn down and a new brick church erected on the same site on the bank of the Tiege. The congregation was incorporated in 1882. Between the two World Wars a monthly meeting was held in the northern part of the congregational area in Steegen in the home of Jacob Hamm. The congregation was served by an elder, five preachers, and two deacons. The membership remained rather constant throughout the last century. In 1852 the congregation numbered 591 baptized members. In 1858 there were 754 Mennonites including children, who owned 168 hides of land. In 1887 the baptized membership was 433, with 229 children. In 1940 there were some 800 Mennonites who belonged to the Tiegenhagen congregation and lived in the north of the Grosswerder area and in the Danzig Lowlands.   H.P.

Abraham Driedger, "Aus der Geschichte der Mennonitengemeinde Heubuden," *Menn. Bl.*, 1939, 42; Ernst Regehr, "Zur 300-Jahrfeier der Gemeinde Rosenort," *Menn. Bl.*, 1939, 61 f.; Gustav Reimer, "Ein aufgefundenes Kirchenbuch," *Menn. Bl.*, 1939, 22 f.; Horst Penner, *Ansiedlung menn. Niederländer im Weichselmündungsgebiet von der Mitte des 16. Jh. bis zum Beginn der preussischen Zeit* (Weierhof, 1940); *ML* IV, 329.

Tiegenhof, a town (1939 pop. 3,000) in the Gross-Werder, 20 miles east of Danzig in West Prussia, Germany. In 1562 the Mennonite immigration from the Netherlands to Tiegenhof began, at a time when the region was under the Polish crown. The king had borrowed money from Hans Simon and Steffen Loytzen (*q.v.*), a banking firm of Danzig, and given them the Tiegenhof area as security, whereupon the Loytzen brothers built a Hof on the Dutch pattern (a model farm with Dutch cows). The farm was initially called "the new farm," and later the Loytzenhof. In order to cultivate the region, which was largely marshy and covered with reeds and underbrush to such an extent that it was not arable, the brothers invited Dutch Mennonites to settle there to clear and drain it. After a certain number of free years the Mennonites were to pay for the lands they made arable at the rate of 52 Talers and 13 chickens per hide. In 1581 the Loytzen firm became bankrupt, and Ernst von dem Weiher took over the district. He completed the castle which the Loytzen brothers had begun; the farm was now called the Weiershof. In 1784 the castle was razed and the Protestant church here built of the materials thus secured. About 1760 the name Tiegenhof came into use.

The central location of the town for the Mennonite congregations in the Gross-Werder area made it a convenient meeting place for conferences of the Mennonites of East and West Prussia, which frequently met here, and for Bible conferences.
                                                      E.RE.

E. Regehr, *Geschichts- und Predigertabelle der Mennonitengemeinde Rosenort* (2d ed., Elbing, 1939); Felicia Szper, *Nederlandsche Nederzettingen in West-Pruizen . .* (Enkhuizen, 1919) 95-113, 205, 221, 223; *ML* IV.

Tiegenhof Fire Insurance. In the early 17th century Mennonite farmers in the Tiegenhof area drew up a "Brandordnung" for mutual aid in case of fire.

This arrangement was permitted by the burgomasters of Danzig in 1622. In the next year the Tiegenhöfer Feuerversicherung was founded at Tiegenhagen. It existed until the Mennonites in the Prussian area were expelled from their farms in 1945, and was the model of the Mennonite fire insurance companies in Russia.   vDZ.

Horst Penner, *Ansiedlung Menn. Niederländer im Weichselmündungsgebiet . . .* (Weierhof, 1940) 19, 21.

Tiegerweide, a Prussian Mennonite village name transplanted to the Molotschna settlement, Ukraine, and Omsk, Siberia. (See **Villages.**)

Tiel, a town in the Dutch province of Gelderland (1954 pop. 15,000, with 25 Mennonites) where a *Kring* (group) of Mennonites was founded in 1948, particularly by the activity of H. B. Kossen-van Rhijn, the widow of Pastor D. Kossen (*q.v.*). In 1958 the membership of this group numbered 27; the minister in charge is the pastor of Wageningen (*q.v.*); services are held seven or eight times a year.
                                                      vDZ.

Tieleman, Abraham, b. *c*1733 at Amsterdam, d. there April 26, 1820, was a lay preacher of the Danzig Old Flemish "op de Smallegraft" congregation at Haarlem 1766-86; 1786-88 he served in the Danzig Old Flemish church "bij de Kruikjes" at Amsterdam; in 1788 this small group merged with the Zonists (*q.v.*); in 1790 Tieleman, who had resigned at the merger, became a preacher of this Zonist congregation. In 1801, when the Zonist church merged with the Lamist, Tieleman retired. (*Inv. Arch. Amst.* II, No. 1418; *DB* 1898, 21 f.; *Naamlijst* 1829, 23).)   vDZ.

Tieleman uyt den Nunkerken, an Anabaptist martyr: see **Nunkirchen, Thielemann von.**

Tielen, Tieleman: see **Sittert, Tielen Tielman van.**

Tielt, a town (pop. *c*13,000) in Flanders, Belgium, was the center of an Anabaptist congregation in the 16th century. Their preacher, Paulus (*q.v.*) van Thielt or van Meenen, was an influential elder, who played a large role in the dissensions of the day; he fled to the northern Netherlands. His sister-in-law, Prijntgen Maelbouts (see **Pierijntgen van Male**), the widow of his brother Jacob de Bakker, was beheaded at Gent in 1564. A letter written by him (*BRN* VII, 215) indicates that he was opposed to a strict interpretation of the ban. The martyr Jelis Strings (*q.v.*), who was seized at Werwik with Pieter and Jelis Potvliet, all of them from Tielt, and burned at the stake there in 1562, advised Paulus to flee. In 1568 he baptized the martyr Jan (*q.v.*) van Alckeren outside Halewijn in the presence of 50 members. In 1605 he was a preacher in the congregation at Haarlem, Holland. He was a large, tall man. Elder Jacob (*q.v.*) de Rore also preached in Tielt. In 1573 Anthonis (*q.v.*) Ysbaerts was burned at the stake in Tielt; he had been a servant of the bailiff of Gent and had thus participated in the execution of a number of Anabaptist martyrs. After his conversion he fled to Friesland, but returned to Tielt to help another fugitive from Tielt get some of his possessions. On his visit he was recognized and arrested. A monk, Pieter de Bakker, tried in vain to lead him to recant. By persecution and emigration the Tielt congregation died out probably by 1580, although a few Mennonites were still living in or near the town in 1629. (*ML* IV.)   K.V.

Tiene, Marie, an Anabaptist martyr named acrostically in the song "Met menschlijcke tongen niet." (Wolkan, *Lieder,* 80.)

Tiessen: see **Thiessen.**

Tietes, Jacob: see **Huizinga.**

Tiets Jan Colmerswijff, a Dutch revolutionary Anabaptist arrested on April 7, 1535, when the Oldeklooster (*q.v.*) was recaptured. She was taken to Leeuwarden, the capital of Friesland, and drowned there on April 14, 1535. (K. Vos, *Menno Simons,* Leiden, 1914, 229.)   vDZ.

Tiettye Douwes, an Anabaptist martyr, beheaded on Dec. 7, 1549, at Leeuwarden in Friesland, Netherlands, with Laurens (*q.v.*) Tiettys, who may have been his son. Tiettye had been (re)baptized before the end of March 1535. Further particulars are lacking.   vDZ.

    Inv. Arch. Amst. I, No. 746; J. Reitsma, *Honderd jaren uit de Geschiedenis der Hervorming . . . in Friesland* (Leeuwarden, 1876) 63.

Tiffin Civilian Public Service Unit No. 147 at the Tiffin State Institute, Tiffin, Ohio, opened in June 1945 and closed in November of that year when the place was changed from a home for epileptics to a mental institution. The twenty CPS men engaged in farm and maintenance work. The Mennonite Central Committee operated this unit, composed of men interested in music, who participated in music classes after their working hours.   M.G.

    Melvin Gingerich, *Service for Peace* (Akron, 1949) 246.

Tigler (formerly also Tichelaar), with its lateral Tigler Wybrandi branch, a Mennonite family found in Friesland, Netherlands, as early as 1657. In this year (1) Carst Sickes, probably a native of Stiens near Leeuwarden, had a "tichelwerk" (tilework) at Leeuwarden, from which the family derived its name. Carst and his descendants for many generations were loyal and active members of the Waterlander congregation at Leeuwarden (*q.v.*). His son (2) Claes Karsten Tichelaar (Tigler), d. c1725, was from 1680 a preacher of the congregation and the prosperous owner of the tileworks and other businesses. A sermon of his, *Predicatie* on II Pet. 1:13 f., preached on Aug. 7, 1718, was published at Leeuwarden (n.d. - 1719). He was rather liberalminded: and on Nov. 26, 1719, after a quarrel he and his son (3) Djurre Clases, and his brother Tjerk Karsten (d. 1722), a deacon of the church, were banned on the ground that they worshiped with and participated in a communion service of the Remonstrants at Dokkum. Claes Tigler did not take his excommunication very seriously, considering it invalid because the meeting at which it was decided upon was illegal. Most members of the church sided with him. The city government,

intervening, stated that Jansen's attitude was unchristian. A further meeting of the members nominated new trustees and the ban of the three Tiglers was withdrawn.

(3) Djurre Clases Tigler (Leeuwarden 1688-1760), the owner of the tileworks and of a limekiln, later a wholesale dealer, increased the fortune of the family. He is said to have been one of the wealthiest citizens of his home town. He served the church for many years as a deacon.

His sons were (4) Gerben Djurres (1725-1806) and (5) Klaas Djurres (1724-1811). This Klaas Tigler (also called Nicolaas Tichelaar) studied theology at the University of Franeker and the Amsterdam Mennonite Seminary and served the Mennonite congregation of Huizen (*q.v.*) as preacher for a few months in 1750. He then moved to Leeuwarden, where he accepted a call for half-time service. Until 1752 he was a regular preacher of the Leeuwarden congregation; from then he preached only occasionally. Although after that time he devoted himself mainly to the study of science and literature and the managing of his property, he still remained active in serving the interests of his congregation as well as of the Mennonites in Friesland in general. In Leeuwarden he brought about a merger (1758) of a small congregation meeting at de Zwitserwaltje, usually called the Frisian church, with the large Waterlander congregation. He also was a trustee of the Conference of Friesland. He was married to Hiske Heringa, who died in 1784; they had no children. Klaas Tigler willed most of his wealth (he left over 500,000 Dutch guilders) for a foundation to give financial support to young men of the Tigler family who wished to study at a Dutch university. This foundation is called the Klaas Tigler Leen (*q.v.*).

A lateral branch of the Tigler family is the Tigler Wybrandi family, which descends from Cornelis Wybrandi (b. at Berlikum 1775, d. at Leeuwarden 1839), a merchant and owner of an oil press. Some of the Tigler Wybrandis also served the church as deacons, e.g., Jan Tigler Wybrandi, d. 1912, who was a deacon of the Utrecht congregation in 1897-1903, 1906-8, and 1912. Another member of this family in a side branch was Klaas Overbeek Tigler (1784-1847) of Dokkum, who after studying at the Amsterdam seminary in 1804-10 served the Mennonite congregation of Franeker 1811 - 46. (*DB* 1874, 60-74; Blaupot t. C., *Friesland,* 185, 221; *Inv. Arch. Amst.* II, No. 1955.)

Tijs, an Anabaptist martyr: see **Thijs Hendricksz.**

Tijs van Lind(t) (Thijs de Lind, Thys Hille, Thijs op den Berch, real name Thijs van Lin), an Anabaptist martyr, a pious man who was held in high regard for his benevolence to the poor. Since he could not be persuaded to recant even by the use of torture, he was sentenced to death and burned at the stake at Roermond, then belonging to the duchy of Geldern, now in the Dutch province of Limburg, in July 1551 (not 1550, as van Braght erroneously stated). Van Braght's account in the *Martyrs' Mirror* relates that "shortly after the burning of the pious witness of Jesus Christ" a severe fire broke out in Roermond, which many thought was "a punishment for the innocent blood." This fire did not, however, strike until July 16, 1554.

NEFF.

Mart. Mir. D 98, E 496; W. Bax, *Het Protestantisme in het Bisdom Luik . . .* I (The Hague, 1937) 342, 352, 355; *DB* 1899, 140, 142; *ML* II, 657.

Tijs Rarop: see **Thys Jurriaens.**

Tilsit, a town (pop. *c*60,000) now Russian, in former times Lithuanian, in the 17th and 18th centuries Prussian. In the vicinity of Tilsit (Tilsit Lowlands) Mennonites from West Prussia settled in 1713 ff. Most of them, however, by the order of Frederick William I (*q.v.*), had to leave the country in 1724; they went to the Culm (*q.v.*) area and to Tragheimerweide (*q.v.*) in West Prussia. Shortly after 1740, during the reign of Frederick (*q.v.*) the Great, a new group of immigrants settled in the neighborhood of Tilsit. The Mennonites of the Tilsit Lowland formed the congregation of Plauschwarren (*q.v.*), later called Adlig Pokraken (*q.v.*). In 1776 there were 16 Mennonite families with 77 souls in the Tilsit district, four families living in the town of Tilsit. In 1861, 29 Mennonites were living in the town of Tilsit and 49 in the Tilsit-Ragnit district; in 1910 these figures were 100 and 50 respectively, and in 1925, 85 and 50. (For details see **East Prussia, Gumbinnen, Lithuania,** and **Memelniederung,** and the literature mentioned there.) (*ML* IV, 330-32.)   vDZ.

Timmerman, a common Dutch family name, "timmerman" meaning carpenter. In Mennonite history a number of Timmermans are found, in many cases not related to one another. Herman (*q.v.*)(de) Timmerman was a well-known Mennonite elder in Flanders. Cornelis Jentjes Timmerman was a Mennonite lay preacher at Harlingen in Friesland 1713-d.65, who is said to have possessed a considerable library, which was auctioned after his death. In Prussia and particularly in the towns of Danzig and Königsberg, there lived also a number of Mennonite Timmermans, from the 18th century usually called Zimmerman(n). This Prussian Timmerman-Zimmerman (*q.v.*) family is obviously of Dutch descent.   vDZ.

Timmerman, Herman: see **Herman (de) Timmerman.**

Tinnegieter, Jeronimus (Jeroen): see **Jeroen Tinnegieter.**

Tippecanoe County (Ind.) Swiss Mennonite Settlement: see **Rossville and Buck Creek.**

Tirion, a Dutch Mennonite family whose ancestor, Darther Christoffel Geeraerdtsoon Tierjon (1605-53), moved from Belgium to Rotterdam, Holland, where he died. His son Izaak Tirion (1628-99) lived at Rotterdam and later at Gouda, where he was a deacon in the church. Izaak was married to Suzanna Nieukerck of Amsterdam. His sister Jannetje Tirion was married to Abraham van Loon (*q.v.*) of Gouda. His son Christoffel Tirion (1675-1711) studied medicine, and after obtaining his M.D. degree studied for the ministry under Galenus (*q.v.*) Abrahamsz at Amsterdam, and served as preacher in the Amsterdam Lamist congregation 1700-3. In August 1703 he was censured and excluded from the communion service because of misconduct. In June 1704 he was called as preacher by the Mennonite congregation of Utrecht. Here he was preacher with the conservative Jakob van Griethuyzen, and the majority of the congregation were strongly opposed to Tirion's more liberal views. When a number of his followers severely criticized van Griethuyzen, a schism seemed inevitable, but this was averted by the resignation of Tirion in 1720; he moved to Amsterdam, where he practiced medicine until his death in the next year. Besides his medical thesis of 1695 he published *Predicatie over de Versoekinge onses Heeren Jesu Christi,* a sermon (Amsterdam, 1700), and *Lykreden* (funeral sermon) *over Johannes Andries* (Utrecht, 1706). Christoffel Tirion was married to Dorothea Aldenhove; their son was Izaak Tirion (1708-65), married *c*1730 to Johanna Abrahams Fries (1708-34) of Amsterdam and after her death to Johanna Koster (d. 1793) of Alkmaar. Izaak was also a loyal member of the church and a warm friend of Collegiantism (*q.v.*), serving 1746-51 as a trustee of "De Oranjeappel" (*q.v.*), the Collegiant orphanage. He was a successful printer and publisher of books at Amsterdam. The publishing business was continued by his son and his grandson, both named Izaak Tirion. The latter conducted it until 1811, when he entered into partnership with the Mennonite publisher Johannes Müller (*q.v.*).

Jacob Tirion (1703-68), a son of Christoffel Tirion, moved to Crefeld, Germany, and founded the Crefeld branch of this family; his daughter Hester Tirion (b. 1740) was married to Wopko Molenaar (*q.v.*), a Mennonite pastor of Crefeld. Jan Tirion (Crefeld 1745-Amsterdam 1832) moved back to Amsterdam. His grandson Jan Tirion was a deacon of the Mennonite congregation at The Hague.

In 1585 there was among the Mennonites of Gent, Belgium, a Pieter Tryon, from whom this family may have descended. Risler is, however, of the opinion that the Tirion family originated from the area of Liège, Belgium, the name originally having been Thierry.   vDZ.

Inv. Arch. Amst. II, Nos. 684 f., 1767, 2296; *DB* 1863, 24, 84; 1896, 61, 70; 1918, 64; (H. B. Berghuys), *Geschiedenis der Doopsgezinde gemeente te Utrecht* (n.p., n.d.-1926) 45; Walther Risler, "Ein europäisches Stammbuch vor 150 Jahren: das Tirionsche Freundschaftsalbum," *Die Heimat* XXV (1954) No. 3-4, 137-40.

Tirol, one of the strongest centers of Anabaptism during the 16th century and a fountainhead of great leaders of the movement. After the establishment of the Hutterite (*q.v.*) brotherhood in Moravia practically all Tirolean Anabaptists turned Hutterite, with the exception of a few individuals who followed Pilgram Marpeck (*q.v.*).

Tirol, a province of Austria, named after the Counts of Tirol (near Meran), came into the possession of the Hapsburgs (of Vienna) *c*1360. Its population is German except for the area of the bishopric of Trent where the population is Italian (no Anabaptists lived there). In 1918 South Tirol, i.e., the part of Tirol situated south of the Brenner Pass, was ceded to Italy. Tirol is a mountainous area and the people are sturdy, forceful, and proud of their "liberties." The seat of the provincial government is the city of Innsbruck, situated at the point where the east-west road along the Inn Valley crosses the north-south road over the Brenner Pass, the lowest (4,000 ft.) pass over the Alps. The Inn River flows into Bavaria (border town Kufstein), thence into the Danube at Passau. The main sections of Tirol are the valleys of the Inn, the Eisack, and Adige rivers, and several bishoprics. (1) The Inn Valley (*q.v.*), with the cities Innsbruck, Hall, Schwaz, Rattenberg (*q.v.*), and Kufstein, is rich in ores; its miners represented the most alert social element of Tirol at that time. The old road from Germany to Italy leads through this valley, making it economically well situated and progressive. (2) The Eisack Valley, south of the Brenner Pass, near the bishop's seat at Brixen, is soon joined by the Puster Valley (*q.v.*), the home of Jakob Hutter and Jörg Zaunring. The towns of the Eisack Valley are Klausen (*q.v.*) and Guffidaun (*q.v.*), where Jörg Blaurock (*q.v.*) found his martyr's death in 1529. (3) The Adige (*q.v.*) Valley (German, *Etschtal*) extends through Meran and Bozen down to the border of Italian-speaking Trent. (4) The area of a number of bishoprics such as Brixen (*q.v.*), Salzburg (*q.v.*)—Kitzbühel (*q.v.*) belonged to this bishopric—and Freising (from Rattenburg to Kufstein). In all these ecclesiastical domains the Hapsburg government had less to say and little executive power, although pressure was always exerted.

Anabaptism in Its Struggle with the Hapsburg Government. There is insufficient source material to decide precisely how or when Anabaptism reached Tirol. Very little is known for the time prior to 1527. As everywhere else in German lands, Tirol also experienced a peasant revolt in 1525, under the leadership of a certain Geismaier, which though partly political and economic, was no less a revolt against a decaying Catholicism and a cry for spiritual renewal. Strangely enough, Lutheranism did not have the same appeal here that it had in Germany proper. The first reliable information concerning Anabaptist mission work dates from November 1527. At that time both Leonhard Schiemer (*q.v.*) and Hans Schlaffer (*q.v.*) had entered the Inn Valley from Bavaria. Schiemer was caught at Rattenberg and suffered the first recorded death as a martyr in Tirol in January 1528. Schlaffer was caught about the same time near by in the mining city of Schwaz, where it was said that of 1200 inhabitants 800 were Anabaptists, and was put to death in February 1528. These two executions began the sad spectacle of relentless hunting, torturing, and killing of Anabaptists, which lasted almost to the end of the 16th century. It was carried out mainly upon the stern command of Ferdinand (*q.v.*) of Hapsburg, living in Vienna, who never wearied of insisting upon the harshest measures. But in spite of the pyres and burning fagots all along the Inn Valley Anabaptism only took deeper roots. One chronicler reports one thousand executions up to 1530, although the records of 1539 ac-

count for hardly more than 600, and the Hutterite chronicle speaks of "only" 386 executions up to 1542. Whichever figure is correct, the challenge was severe, but the undaunted spirit of this sturdy mountain folk was ready to meet it. Not Lutheranism but Anabaptism became the answer to the ills of the Catholic Church, from 1527 to 1627. The sharpest of all the numerous mandates (*q.v.*) issued by Ferdinand against the Anabaptists was that of Aug. 20, 1527, proclaimed in Tirol on Nov. 20 of that year. No fewer than 1,200 copies were taken to Innsbruck to be distributed among the clergy and city and county authorities, and to be announced everywhere from pulpits and market places. Actually, however, it had no deterrent effect; judges and jury often felt compassion for the humble victims and hesitated to comply with the orders from Vienna or Innsbruck; only the threat that all sympathizers and Half-Anabaptists (*q.v.*) would be dealt with like Anabaptists achieved the desired effect. That so many Anabaptists escaped the vigilance of the authorities and traveled safely to the "promised land" of Moravia, and that so many missionaries from Switzerland, Bavaria, and Moravia worked here at least for the first 50 to 60 years, holding meetings and building up congregations, proves that no government action could quench the spiritual fire and the serious determination of the population. It was not until the end of the Council of Trent (1563, see **Counter Reformation**) and the internal reforms of the Catholic Church, together with the coming of the Jesuits (*q.v.*), that the vigor of the Anabaptist movement was broken.

In 1527 Schiemer and Schlaffer had come to the Inn Valley from Bavaria, spreading the teachings which they had received from Hans Hut. In May 1529 Jörg Blaurock, who was a refugee from Switzerland, was working ceaselessly in the Adige and Eisack valleys, apparently most successfully. When he was finally caught and executed in Guffidaun (*q.v.*) near Klausen, Sept. 6, 1529, a young boy of eight was watching this weird spectacle: Peter Walpot (*q.v.*), the later outstanding bishop of the Hutterites in Moravia. It is possible that Jakob Hutter (*q.v.*) received his first news of the Anabaptist movement from some brethren in Carinthia (*q.v.*), just east of the Puster Valley. That is about all that is known of outside influences in Tirol. For the greater part Tirolean Anabaptism was an indigenous product. Pilgram Marpeck (*q.v.*) (formerly a Lutheran of Rattenberg) was also converted *c*1527, and likewise Leopold Scharnschlager (*q.v.*), a native of Hopfgarten near Kitzbühel. Members of the Tirolean nobility also now and then turned Anabaptist. Among them were Helene von Freyberg (*q.v.*), mistress of Münichau castle near Kitzbühel, who gave asylum to many an Anabaptist (she was one of the few followers of Pilgram Marpeck); Erhard Zimmermann, the former administrator of Neuhaus; Agnes von Waltenhofen (nee Trautmannsdorf); Christopher Fuchs, captain of the border castle of Kufstein; and Anton and Siegmund Wolkenstein, who belonged to one of the oldest and most highly respected noble families of southern Tirol. Only a recantation at the last moment saved the Wolkenstein brothers from a martyr's death. Helene von Freyberg, however, had to leave the country, bequeathing her estate to her sons.

Johann Loserth (*q.v.*) published in 1892-93 an almost exhaustive account of Anabaptism in Tirol. Recent research by several Innsbruck historians (e.g., Widmoser, Kolb) has added little to the established facts. Widmoser, who in 1951 summarized all this research, comes to the conclusion that Tirol must have produced close to 20,000 Anabaptists during the 16th century (with more than 600 executions all told). Although Widmoser clearly takes the traditional anti-Anabaptist position he has had to admit "that one cannot help getting the impression that the government intentionally exaggerated the danger and perniciousness of Anabaptism in order to get a legal title for its ulterior purpose: the dominance of the state over the church." Previously Widmoser had expressly stated that the persecution was carried out mainly by the Hapsburgs, while the ecclesiastical princes (Brixen, Salzburg, Freising) prior to the Council of Trent (1563) had little power to parallel these activities. Widmoser reveals another motive for the severe persecution, far removed from all spiritual concerns; viz., that Ferdinand needed for his Turkish Wars the money accruing from the confiscation of Anabaptist property. Loserth reports of one peasant who sold his homestead for 1,600 guilders, and another Anabaptist left property behind valued at 12,000 guilders (1555).

Ferdinand was absolutely ruthless. All kinds of tricks were improvised to ferret out the Anabaptists. Special "Anabaptist hunters" (*Täuferjäger*) were organized, and spies appointed to report on secret meetings. The reward for the capture of an Anabaptist, originally 20-40 guilders, was raised to 60-70 guilders, even to 100 in case of a leader. And finally the most severe of all deterrents was applied, the sentencing of these "obstinate heretics" to the galleys of Andrea Doria of Genoa, imperial captain of a navy in the Mediterranean. But this most inhuman measure was even less effective than the pyres of the Inn Valley. Ferdinand attended to every minute detail in the fight against Anabaptism; every case had to be reported to him personally in detail, and the archives of Tirol and Vienna are full of mandates and correspondence in these matters. Hesitant courts were reprimanded and vigilant officials were praised whenever a big catch succeeded. He even prescribed that in case of recantation the offender should be "only" beheaded. Nevertheless the authorities in the various court districts frequently aided the Anabaptists in their flight to Moravia. Since the majority used the waterway down the Inn, a supervision of the boat traffic was enjoined by the king, but in the great majority of cases the emigration nevertheless succeeded.

Two government officials deserve special mention, one more bent on the method of persuasion, the other more on persecution. Dr. Gallus Müller (*q.v.*), Catholic court chaplain in Innsbruck, realizing the shortcomings of his church and having attended a provincial synod at Salzburg in 1537, hoped to exterminate the "error of heresy" by internal improvement, which, however, was never carried out. His work with the imprisoned Anabaptists Leonhard Lochmaier (*q.v.*), and Georg Liebich (*q.v.*) and Ursula Hellriegel (*q.v.*) is discussed in the pertinent articles in this Encyclopedia. No real communication could be achieved between the victims and this Catholic theologian. Soon Dr. Müller changed his mind and aided in drawing up the mandate of November 1539, which calls the Anabaptists not only "falsifiers of the Scriptures" but also outright revolutionaries.

At the same time the notorious Wolfgang Künigl (*q.v.*), imperial court prosecutor and specialist in Anabaptist hunting in Lower and Upper Austria (*q.v.*) in 1527-28, was sent by Ferdinand to Brixen to consult with the prince-bishop as to the best method of halting this "heresy." The result of this conference was a memorandum to the king, dated Oct. 17, 1539, entitled, *Anzaigungen, aus was Ursachen die Wiedertauffer in disem Lande der Fürstlichen Grafschaft Tyroll Iren Fuss dermassen gesetzt und bishero über etlicher Obrigkaiten allem müglichsten Fleiss nit haben mügen ausgereut werden*. The question is asked: Why does the common man adhere to Anabaptism? The answer, somewhat evasive, blames the judges and juries as being too lenient, using the rack too little, allowing the Anabaptists to show the courage of their faith in public. Easing their punishment had done no good. One thing had become clear, namely, that terror did not terrify. In spite of no less than 600 executions (an official figure!) in 1527-39, the expected results were still lacking. The most efficient remedy, i.e., internal church reforms, did not occur to these ecclesiastics and magistrates, who simply wanted to bring these men back into the fold of the Roman Church with a minimum of effort. The king replied with new mandates advising the omission of doctrinal discussion at trials because they merely excited the interest of the public.

The difficulty of finding compliant courts is seen in the trial of Hans Mändl and his two codefendants in 1561, when three of the judges were placed under police surveillance. After 1561 Jesuits came to Innsbruck, and an internal reform was eventually imposed from Rome as the most efficient countermeasure against spreading Protestantism. From now on Anabaptism declined in Tirol. Those who were strong gladly sold their property and emigrated to Moravia, which was then enjoying its Golden Age. Nevertheless the Anabaptist movement in Tirol still had the sympathy of wide circles of the population. Loserth says the Jesuits were no more successful at persuasion than Gallus Müller had been. In the later 16th century (Ferdinand died 1564), the government, better organized than ever before, made more systematic efforts to eradicate any deviation from Catholicism. It became increasingly difficult to evade raids by soldiers, since the majority of both nobles and peasants had now become less disposed to protect these clandestine groups, perhaps an aftereffect of the work of the Jesuits. After 1600 Anabaptism was practically extinct in Tirol, even though the records occasionally mention brethren up to 1627. The Thirty

Years' War, the expulsion of the Anabaptists from Moravia in 1622, and a new spirit of the time had reduced the further growth and spread of Anabaptist teachings. Tirol manifested more or less the same picture as Switzerland, Germany, and Moravia. (See also **Juridical Procedures,** II.)

Development of Anabaptism in Tirol. The story of Anabaptism appears very different when looked at not from the outside, as the official records reflect it, but from the inside where the intrinsic issues are discussed and at stake. For this purpose other source material must be consulted—the writings and chronicles of the Anabaptists themselves. In few countries was the absolute seriousness of life's conduct and the commitment to the way of discipleship more eagerly sought after than in Tirol. Hence few countries produced more and greater leaders than this Austrian province. Jakob Hutter and Hans Amon, Hans Mändl and Peter Walpot, Jeronimus Käls and Hans Kräl, were all outstanding leaders of the Hutterite movement both in Tirol and Moravia. Marpeck and Scharnschlager were equally outstanding leaders of a related Anabaptist movement, different in many ways and yet of the same roots. These men did not produce great doctrinal treatises (except Marpeck and Scharnschlager), but their epistles (*q.v.*) and hymns written in prison, and their farewell words at the place of execution, recorded in the chronicles, as well as their written defenses before the courts (*Urgichten*), are moving witnesses to their spiritual depth and strength.

There can be little doubt that Anabaptism took its start in the lower Inn Valley around Rattenberg and Schwaz, both mining cities. Even though the activities of both Schiemer (*q.v.*) and Schlaffer (*q.v.*) were but short-lived (1527-28), they left a profound impression which was still felt 50 or even 80 years later. The *Kunstbuch* (*q.v.*) of the Marpeck circle, dated 1561, contains their writings as do the numerous Hutterite codices of Moravia and Slovakia. They laid the groundwork, continuing Hans Hut's apostolate, and the Tiroleans remained loyal to it, even though Anabaptism arose independently in other places also, such as Kitzbühel, Brixen, Clausen, Pustertal, etc. The geographic situation—many valleys separated by high, snow-covered mountains— should have worked for independence and particularism; and yet Anabaptism was a fairly uniform movement based on the understanding of the pure Word of the New Testament and obedience to God's commandments (discipleship). Of all places Rattenberg had the highest number of martyrs: 71 by 1542. This is a graphic illustration of the staunchness of the brethren and sisters, in full awareness of the dangers involved. A second wave of new commitments is reported around 1558, due most likely to the work of Hans Mändl (*q.v.*), and as late as 1603 Anabaptists were still passing through Rattenberg.

Of Blaurock and his brief activities south of the Brenner Pass (1529) mention has already been made. But the movement which arose in the nearby Puster Valley and around the city of Bozen (Bolzano) was of more permanent consequence. Here Jörg Zaunring (*q.v.*) was active as early as 1528 in the "Ritten" district, and most likely also Jakob Hutter (*q.v.*), who was born in the Puster Valley. From the Italian-Tirolean border in the south to Kufstein in the north, from the Eisack Valley on the Brenner road to Carinthia in the east, Hutter was active, a true apostle of the new teachings. He must have been an acknowledged leader by 1528-29, for the brotherhoods in the Puster and Eisack valleys decided to send him and Siegmund Schützinger (*q.v.*) to Moravia to inquire whether there was a chance there for a more stable brotherhood life. After a long conversation with Jakob Widemann (*q.v.*) in Austerlitz, Moravia, the two men returned hopefully, and now the first group of emigrants under the leadership of Zaunring went to Moravia. Other trips by Hutter followed in 1531 and 1533. The activities and the success of this man are truly amazing. When persecution (temporarily) became very acute also in Moravia, Hutter was urged to return to Tirol (1535), where he was finally caught and cruelly martyred in February 1536. Also Hans Amon (*q.v.*), bishop in Moravia 1535-42, had spent the years 1530-34 moving all over Tirol. Persecution did not dishearten these people but only speeded the emigration to Moravia. Among these refugees were Jeronimus Käls (*q.v.*), the schoolmaster of Kufstein, a most noble and dedicated representative of Anabaptism, executed in Vienna in 1536.

Ulrich Stadler (*q.v.*), though a Tirolean, did not become an active leader until his emigration to Moravia and thence to Poland (d. 1540). Both Onophrius Griesinger (*q.v.*) and Leonhard Lochmaier (*q.v.*), upon whom Dr. Müller had vainly tried his persuasive arguments, were imprisoned in Brixen and there sealed their faith with their death. It is difficult to imagine the incredible hardships in the dungeons and prisons of that time. Georg Liebich (*q.v.*), who lay in the Vellenburg near Innsbruck for two years (1540-41), experienced haunting visions which drove him nearly mad. Bats, rats, and other vermin made his "dark hole" almost unbearable. The same is told of Hans Kräl (*q.v.*), who in 1557 was captured and thrown into a dungeon of the castle tower of Tauffers (Puster Valley): his clothing rotted from his body and he nearly perished in filth and vermin. In addition to all this, he spent not less than 37 weeks in the block. But he came out to become eventually one of the outstanding leaders of the brotherhood in Moravia where he was bishop 1578-83.

One of the strongest personalities of the Tirolean Hutterites of the mid-16th century was Hans Mändl (*q.v.*), born near Guffidaun in the Eisack Valley, whose activities extended from 1536 to his tragic end in 1561. He was won for the new faith by Griesinger and suffered imprisonment several times. He was one of the finest apostles Anabaptism ever produced, and accordingly his success was simply amazing. But in 1560 he and two fellow Anabaptists were caught in the Inn Valley. His trial and end is well described in the Hutterite chronicle, and his epistles are testimonies of the best Anabaptist spirit known. His readiness to suffer for the sake of his faith has few parallels in the annals of Anabaptism.

One of the last martyrs to be executed in Tirol was Nicholas Geyerspüchler (q.v.), a miller from the neighborhood of Kitzbühel. Though illiterate (an exception; most Anabaptists from Tirol could not only read and write but were extremely skillful in their epistles and other writings), he was most successful in his mission work throughout his home district, whither he had been sent by the Moravian brotherhood. In 1566 he, too, was caught, and after much work by Jesuits and his steadfast defense was first beheaded and then burned, in 1567.

The great church reforms of that time no doubt had some effect, and Anabaptism outside Moravia gradually began to decline. Moreover, the milder regime of Emperor Maximilian II (see **Habsburg**) in 1564-76 soon brought these horrifying executions almost to a conclusion. Two more outstanding Tiroleans became Hutterite leaders, but no longer as apostles or missioners, but as bishops of a well-established brotherhood-church in Moravia. Peter Walpot (q.v.), born 1521 near Klausen, where he had witnessed the death of Blaurock in 1529, seems to have emigrated to Moravia at an early age; in 1542 he was already a preacher, and in 1565-78 a very successful Vorsteher or bishop. He was succeeded by Hans Kräl (q.v., from Kitzbühel), who was bishop in 1578-83 and also continued the great Hutterite chronicle. His previous mission work in Tirol had likewise been of unusual success, as the increasing stream of newcomers from Tirol testifies.

More martyrs were still to come, such as Andreas Pürchner (1584), Georg Wenger, and Jacob Platzer (1591), but in general Anabaptism in Tirol had spent itself by the turn of the century. In the neighboring smaller provinces of Vorarlberg (q.v.), west of Tirol, which by and large played a minor role in this story, the last martyrs were executed in 1618.

Loserth in his classical study of Tirolean Anabaptism also collected some material pertaining to the methods of the missioners in their tireless and dangerous endeavor to reach the widest possible circles. One person deposed at court that he unexpectedly found a notice in his house inviting him to a meeting somewhere in the woods; another heard whispering in the bushes and upon approaching found a group of Anabaptists who brought him special information. Now and then a missioner approached someone who disliked his message, but rarely was he betrayed to the authorities. Many people were indifferent, but it often happened that a young girl or a man servant by chance picked up the words and eventually traveled to Moravia to learn more of that new teaching. When the "good time" set in in Moravia in the second half of the century, the arguments became even more attractive, and people were ready to sell their property and leave their old homes. That the main stock of Hutterites was Tirolean was brought home recently also in an unexpected way: when in 1937 two American Hutterites revisited their old places in Europe, they discovered that their own German language was simply a Tirolean dialect—and this in spite of the fact that they themselves were not of Tirolean extraction.   LOSERTH, R.F.

Hartmann Ammann, *"Die Wiedertäufer im Pustertal und deren Urgichten"* in *Programm des Gymnasiums in Brixen*, 1896-97; Beck, *Geschichtsbücher;* Josef Beck and Johann Loserth, "Georg Blaurock und die Anfänge des Anabaptismus in Graubünden und Tirol," in *Vorträge und Aufsätze der Comenius-Gesellschaft* VII (Berlin, 1899); Ernst Correll, "Anabaptism in Tyrol, a Preview and Discussion," *MQR* I (1927) 49-60; Paul Dedic, "Literaturbericht über den österreichischen Protestantismus von 1918-38," in *ARG* XXXV (1938) 252 ff.; Anton Dörr, *Tiroler Volksgut auf dem Heidenboden* (Eisenstadt, Austria, 1951), who found a miracle play among the Habaners of Burgenland, Austria, which originally was a Christmas play from the lower Inn Valley; Heinold Fast, "Pilgrim Marbeck und das oberdeutsche Täufertum," in *ARG* XLVII (1956) 212-42, particularly 220 note; Hans G. Fischer, *Jakob Huter, Leben, Frömmigkeit, Briefe* (Newton, 1956); R. Friedmann, "Die Briefe der österreichischen Täufer," in *ARG* XXIII, 30-80; bibliography for Tirol, etc., *ibid.*, 161-87 f.; Kirchmaier, *Chronik des Stiftes Neustift bei Brixen, Fontes Rerum Austriacarum* I (Vienna, 1854); Johann von Kripp, "Ein Beitrag zur Geschichte der Wiedertäufer in Tirol," in *Programm des Staatsgymnasiums zu Innsbruck* (Innsbruck, 1897); Loserth, *Anabaptismus; idem, Communismus;* Eduard Widmoser, "Das Tiroler Täufertum," in *Tiroler Heimat* XV, 45-89; XVI, 103-28; (Innsbruck, 1951, 1952) (digests also the recent studies by Kolb, Mayer, Kuppelwieser, and Sinzinger); Adam Wolf, *Geschichtsbilder aus Oesterreich* I (Vienna, 1877); Zieglschmid, *Chronik;* Karl Kuppelwieser, "Die Wiedertäufer im Eisacktal" (unpublished doctoral dissertation at the Univ. of Innsbruck, 1949); Katharina Sinzinger, "Das Täufertum im Pustertal" (unpublished dissertation, Innsbruck, 1950); Franz Kolb, *Die Wiedertäufer im Wipptal* (Innsbruck, 1951); *ML* IV.

Tisen (Tyson), **Reinert:** see **Teissen, Reinert.**

Tiskilwa Mennonite Church (GCM), located in a historic village in the beautiful valley of Bureau County, Ill., was organized in 1911 to serve a small Mennonite group who had withdrawn from the Willow Springs Mennonite (MC) Church (q.v.). The town hall was used until early in 1913, when the present adequate building was erected. The following have served as resident pastors: Eugene Augspurger 1912-20, Ernest Bohn 1925-32, H. E. Nunemaker 1932-41, Henry Toews 1941-43, L. R. Amstutz 1943-47, Emil Sommer 1949-52, and Ben Esch 1952- . The membership in 1957 was 62.

                                             BE.E.

Titelman(s), Pieter (Pierre, Petrus) (1501-72), Roman Catholic dean of Ronse (Renaix) in Flanders, Belgium, and from 1546 official inquisitor of the districts of Flanders and Artois. He was very capable and active and determined to eradicate all heresy: "he was the most hated of all inquisitors, because he was the most hardhearted of this kind of men. His notoriety was due to his intransigence" (Halkin). He was alternately a judge and police dog. Particularly the Mennonites of Flanders encountered his zeal and implacability. As in Halewijn (q.v.) in 1563 and Meenen (q.v.) 1567 he often appeared in various towns to surprise Mennonite meetings and to arrest the attendants. In many of the trials of the martyrs, e.g., those of Jooskint, Claes de Praet, Hans de Vette, and Peter van Wervik, he was the examiner. Claes de Praet frankly charged him with a spirit of persecution. In the discussion with this martyr Titelman admitted that the moral conduct of the Mennonites was irreproachable, and that they were justly praised because of their peace, love, and charity; "but," he said, "what is the good of it . . . if you have not the (right) faith?" This was his settled opinion and he ruthlessly acted in accord with this view.

Not all Catholics approved of Titelman's assiduity and practices. Especially certain magistrates lodged complaints with the governess at Brussels that his rigorous measures were severely injuring the prosperity of many towns. vDZ.

E. Valvekens, *De Inquisitie in de Nederlanden* (1949); L. E. Halkin, *La Réforme en Belgique sous Charles-Quint* (Bruxelles, n.d.-1957) 58; *Mart. Mir.* D 299b, 167b-70a, 170b, *et passim*, E 665, 554-60; *DB* 1906, 68 f.

Tiverton, a town in England, where there was an "Anabaptist" (Baptist) congregation, which together with the other "Anabaptist" churches of London, Coventry, Sarum (Salisbury), and Lincoln, tried to form a union with the Dutch Waterlander (*q.v.*) Mennonites in 1625, which union, however, failed to come about. For details see **Coventry** and **Tookey, Elias.** (*Inv. Arch. Amst.* II, 1368-77.) vDZ.

Tiziano (Titianus or Titiano, first name unknown), Italian "spiritual reformer" and "Anabaptist," appeared briefly upon the historical stage in the mid-16th century. The dates of his birth and death are unknown. He was at one time on the staff of a cardinal in Rome and there he first learned of Lutheran teachings. He then traveled to Geneva and other places where the Reformation had taken hold, including Graubünden (Grisons) and Chiavenna. He made contact with the radical circle surrounding Camillo Renato in 1547 or 1548 and soon became an active proponent of their spiritualizing tenets. His agitations brought him a sizable following and consequent official scrutiny by the authorities at Chur, who had him imprisoned and questioned about his beliefs. He answered in ambiguous language, claiming to be guided only by the Holy Spirit. Fear of capital punishment moved him, however, to sign a confession prepared by Philip Gallicius, pastor at Chur. This confession (which we must remember was intended by Gallicius to constitute a complete recantation and may therefore represent other heresies then current besides Tiziano's own beliefs) implies that Tiziano had denied the Trinity and the divine nature of Christ, had suspected the veracity of Scripture, had placed the authority of the Spirit above that of the Bible, had rejected infant baptism, and had claimed that Christians could not hold magistracies. Tiziano, after signing the statement, was flogged and expelled from Graubünden.

He now returned to Italy and continued to work for his special beliefs. In 1548 or 1549 he met the former priest and current Lutheran Pietro Manelfi (*q.v.*) in Florence and acquainted him with his own views. According to Manelfi's account these included adult baptism; Christians cannot hold magistracies; Scripture only is the basis of Christian doctrine; the Roman Catholic is no true church. There is no mention of anti-Trinitarian teachings. Some months later Tiziano baptized Manelfi at Ferrara. Soon afterwards at Vicenza anti-Trinitarian and Christological questions came to the fore, requiring the calling of a synod at Venice for the establishment of orthodoxy.

Manelfi clearly believed Tiziano responsible for the introduction of "Anabaptist" teachings into Italy and for much of their spread there. He also believed that Tiziano had absorbed the doctrines of the "old Anabaptists." It is at present impossible to disentangle the contributions of Servetus and Camillo Renato (through Tiziano) to the situation that then existed, or to determine what if any part was played by the northern Täufer. Careful study of Manelfi's testimony establishes only the likelihood that Manelfi was postulating connections, which probably did not exist, between the Täufer and his own sect.

Tiziano was present at the Venetian synod in the autumn of 1550, having himself summoned delegates thereto from Switzerland and Graubünden. Of his part in the deliberations we know nothing, but we may assume that he played a leading role, in view both of the anti-Trinitarian character of the conclusions of the synod and of his selection by the group to be an "apostolic bishop" entrusted with the task of carrying tidings of their conclusions to member congregations. Henceforth we lose sight of Tiziano, save for a reference by Manelfi to his apostatizing and subsequent flight from the designs of the podesta and bishop of Padua in Lenten season 1551. We may assume that he was a casualty of the persecution of his sect that followed upon Manelfi's revelations to the Inquisition in the autumn of 1551.

It is, however, possible that Tiziano is identical with one Lorenzo Tizzano (spelling variants are common in the documents) who was involved in the circle of radical reformers surrounding Juan Valdès at Naples. Tizzano recounted his life and activities in a confession prepared for the Inquisition at Venice late in 1553. From it we have the following information: At an early age he entered a monastery of the order of Monte Oliveto and after six years there left, with his superior's permission, to be a secular priest. He served as a chaplain in several localities for a number of years. About ten years after leaving the monastery Tizzano heard about Juan Valdès and his circle in Naples and came under its influence. Members of the circle, including Tizzano, had held opinions which he classified in 1553 as "Lutheran," "Anabaptist," and "diabolical" heresies. In the later 1540's Tizzano moved to Padua and took up the study of medicine while living with his father. Fearful that he might be exposed to the authorities by a man there who had known his views in Naples, Tizzano changed his name to Benedetto Florio. Four or five years after he had arrived in Padua (this would be around 1551) some Lutherans were arrested at the house in which he lived. Fearing a similar fate and troubled in conscience, he traveled to Venice, Ferrara, and Genoa, intending to take ship to Naples. Unable to arrange such passage, he returned to Padua and, overcome by restlessness of spirit, presented himself to the Inquisitor and confessed his identity and his heresies. The Inquisitor arranged for his transfer to Venice in October 1553. There he was imprisoned and ordered to prepare the confession from which we have drawn this information.

Unless Manelfi mistook Tizzano for Tiziano in describing the experience of the latter at Padua in 1551, it is tempting to see an identification between the two figures, for in 1553 Tizzano admitted having begun to doubt his beliefs at Padua two years earlier and having left to avoid arrest. Tizzano's chaplaincy may also have included service with a cardinal. In other respects, however, the two biographies fail to coincide sufficiently to permit a positive identification.

At the time Tizzano was imprisoned at Venice, a request for instructions was sent by the Venetian Inquisitor to Rome. Tizzano was questioned further in 1555 about topics mentioned in the long-delayed reply. They brought to light contacts Tizzano had had with various individuals connected with both the Neapolitan and northern radical-movements but they add nothing to our knowledge of his former views. His later fate is unknown.

DEWIND.

K. Benrath, "Wiedertäufer im Venetianischen um die Mitte des 16. Jahrhunderts," *Theologische Studien und Kritiken* LVIII (1885) 20 ff.; D. Berti, "Di Giovanni Valdès e di taluni suoi discepoli secondo nuovi documenti tolti dall' Archivio Veneto," *Atti della R. Accademia dei Lincei: anno CCLXXV, serie terza, memorie della classe di scienze morali, storiche e filologiche* II (1877-78) 61-81; *Bullingers Korrespondenz mit den Graubündnern*, ed. T. Schiess, Vol. XXIII of *Quellen zur Schweizer Geschichte* (Basel, 1904); E. Comba, *I nostri protestanti* II (Firenze, 1897); E. Comba, "Un sinodo anabattista a Venezia anno 1550," *Rivista cristiana* XIII (1885) 21-24, 83-87; P. D. Rosius de Porta, *Historia Reformationis ecclesiarum Raeticarum*, Vol. I, Part II (Curiae Raetorum, 1771); F. Trechsel, *Die protestantische Antitrinitarier vor Faustus Socin*, Book II, *Lelio Sozzini und die Antitrinitarier seiner Zeit* (Heidelberg, 1844) 82-83; E. M. Wilbur, *A History of Unitarianism: Socinianism and its Antecedents* (Cambridge, Mass., 1947).

Tjaert Geerts, beheaded at Leeuwarden in Friesland, Netherlands, in February 1571 because he had protected some heretics and carried their letters, all contrary to the imperial mandates. Moreover he possessed forbidden heretical books, including twenty copies of Menno Simons. Tjaert probably was a Mennonite.   vDZ.

J. Reitsma, *Honderd jaren uit de Geschiedenis der Hervorming . . . in Friesland* (Leeuwarden, 1876) 159.

Tjaert Renicx, an Anabaptist martyr beheaded with four others at Leeuwarden in Friesland, Netherlands, on Feb. 8, 1539. This martyr is found under different names: Tjaert, Thyaert, Tjard, Tjaar(d)t, Tj. van Kimswerd, Tj. van Witmarsum, Tj. van Sneek (Tiardus Snekensis), Tj. Renicx (Reynersz, Reynerts, Reincx, Reinders). About him there is much mystery. Menno Simons writes about him, "About 1539 a very pious and God-fearing farmer was arrested in the region where I had lived (at Kimswerd near Witmarsum), called Tjard Reynertszoon, because in my misery he had hidden me (in his house), receiving me with pity and love, and was thrown on a wheel . . . a few days later, though he had a good reputation even among his enemies as a blameless and pious man." But Karel Vos, and following him A. F. Mellink, on the contrary state that Tjaert was an outstanding leader of the revolutionary Anabaptists, being identical with Tjaert van Sneek, whom Jan (*q.v.*) van Batenburg ac-

cused of persuading him to join the revolutionary movement. Vos and Mellink say that he was the man who set fire to a cloister in Friesland, who had been among the besiegers of the Oldeklooster (*q.v.*) in March 1535, thereupon fleeing to Groningen, and who in 1536 was present at the Bocholt (*q.v.*) dispute, where he vigorously defended the Münsterite doctrines of polygamy and the temporal kingdom of God.

It will be clear that we have to accept either the account of Menno and to consider Tjaert as a peaceful Anabaptist, or to give credence to the conception of Mellink, who states that Menno Simons perverted historical facts, or to that of Vos, suggesting that after his revolutionary views and practices Tjaert was possibly converted to a better life by Menno.

It is my opinion that Tjaert Renicx of Kimswerd, Menno's friend, is not identical with the revolutionary leader Tjaert van Sneek (Tiardus Snekensis). In the sentence of Tjaert Renicx, published *in extenso* by Vos, he is charged with rebaptism and a derogatory opinion of the Mass; no mention is made of revolutionary activity, and this is very strange if he (leaving other revolutionary practices out of consideration) was the man who had only a few years previously set fire to a cloister in Friesland. There was possibly also a revolutionary Anabaptist by the name of Tjaert van Sneek. vDZ.

Mart. Mir. D. 50, E 454; Menno Simons, *Opera Omnia* 234; *idem, Writings*, 634; K. Vos, *Menno Simons* (Leiden, 1914) 41 f., 66, 230 f.; *DB* 1864, 140; 1906, 3; 1917, 120 (No. 119), 138; 1919, 193; Kühler, *Geschiedenis* I, 201; Mellink, *Wederdopers*, 394 and *passim; ML* III, 486.

Tjaert van Sneek: see **Tjaert Renicx.**

Tjaert Tyercxz, of Dokkum, an Anabaptist martyr, beheaded on Feb. 8, 1539, at Leeuwarden in Friesland, Netherlands, with four other victims. Mellink's suggestion that he and his co-martyrs were revolutionary Anabaptists is without foundation.

vDZ.

K. Vos, *Menno Simons* (Leiden, 1914) 230; Mellink, *Wederdopers*, 252.

Tjaert Tyerczoon, an Anabaptist martyr, burned at the stake on June 1, 1538, at Leeuwarden in Friesland, Netherlands. He had previously been banished from Friesland for six years because of heresy, his heresy consisting in owning forbidden books by Luther and others. After his return to Friesland he joined the Anabaptists, being baptized by a certain Bartholomeus (possibly Bartel, *q.v.*, de Boeckbinder).   vDZ.

J. Reitsma, *Honderd jaren uit de Geschiedenis der Hervorming . . . in Friesland* (Leeuwarden, 1876) 36, 63; Mellink, *Wederdopers*, 252.

Tjahrt (Tjart, Tjardt, Tiart, Tyart, Tgahrt, Tyahrt, Thjardh), a Mennonite family name in West Prussia, particularly in the congregations of Schweingrube, Culmsche Niederung, and Gruppe, after 1830 also found in South Russia, and from 1875 in America. Some of its members were preachers; the Dutch *Naamlijst* names for Prussia: Sievert Tjart until *c*1750, and Steffen Tjart 1781-after 1802, both at Schweingrube, Pieter (Peter) Tjart in the

Stühmsche Niederung before 1734-65. Wilhelm Tyart, of Dragass, was a preacher of the Montau-Gruppe congregation 1897-1932. Johann Tiahrt was ordained as preacher of the Schönsee (*q.v.*) congregation near Culm, and Peter Tgahrt (*q.v.*) was an elder in Deutsch-Kazun. (Reimer, *Familiennamen*, 119; Dutch *Naamlijst*.) vDZ.

Tjalleberd, a village in the Dutch province of Friesland, where according to Blaupot ten Cate, Mennonites were found from the early 17th century, Jacob Theunis (*q.v.*), an elder of the Janjacobsgezinden (*q.v.*), baptizing here 14 persons in 1603-18. Of a Janjacobsgezinde congregation at Tjalleberd, however, nothing is known. If there was one, it had disappeared by 1700.

A new congregation was founded at Tjalleberd in 1817. Shortly after 1800 a number of Mennonite families from Giethoorn (*q.v.*) had moved to Tjalleberd to dig the peat moors here and in the neighboring hamlets of Gersloot and Luinjeberd. Gerrit Bakker, from 1811 pastor of the neighboring congregation of Oldeboorn, took care of the Mennonites in Tjalleberd and its environs; on Feb. 26, 1817, he conducted a service in a barn at Gersloot, which was the beginning of the Tjalleberd congregation. A meetinghouse was built, dedicated on Nov. 15, 1818. The membership then numbered 23; among these were fourteen persons who had moved in from Giethoorn, where they had been baptized. The first preacher of the congregation was Teunis Wolter Schreurs, an untrained minister, from Zwartsluis, who with great blessing served until his death in 1826. He was followed by Wiebe Gosses Hulsinga 1826-*c*29; U. H. Jeepsz, a learned man, Litt. D., though not trained for the ministry, 1830-33; Pieter Willem van Zutphen 1836-40, who was the first pastor of Tjalleberd, trained at the Amsterdam Mennonite seminary; Anthony Winkler Prins 1841-50; F. J. Klaasesz 1851-53; A. S. Hoitsema 1853-56; W. C. van Staveren 1857-d.65; J. U. Uiterwijk 1865-66; H. D. Tjeenk Willink 1868-71; J. Kops 1871-d.72; J. Schippers 1872-80; B. Haga 1881-82; L. van Cleeff IJzn 1882-87; A. van der Wissel 1889-90; F. van der Ploeg 1892-94; A. J. van Loghem Slaterus 1896-99; G. Heeringa 1900-2; U. Y. Veenland 1903-40; Miss C. Boerlage 1941-47; Miss T. van der Zwaag 1947-55; from 1955 Miss T. G. Siccama, then at Bovenknijpe, was temporarily in charge of the Tjalleberd congregation; in 1957 she moved to Wolvega and also serves at Tjalleberd in a more definite union.

The old meetinghouse and parsonage was remodeled in 1847, 1857, and 1867. The present church was built in 1867. A pipe organ was added in 1888.

Only once, in November 1832, the ban was applied and a member cut off from the church. The membership, 23 in 1818, increased to 104 in 1838, 130 in 1861; in 1901 it numbered 101, 115 in 1926, and 96 in 1958. Among the early members were found the following family names, which also are found in Giethoorn: Baas, Petter, Ruiter, Meester, Broers (Broer), Dam, Schreurs, Krikke, Simons, Klaren, and Otter. About 1838 some members of the Wuite (*q.v.*) family came to Tjalleberd from

Giethoorn. Church activities are ladies' circle, youth group, and Sunday school for children. vDZ.

U. Y. Veenland, "Het 100-jarig bestaan der Gemeente te Tjalleberd," in *DJ* 1919, 62-81; *Inv. Arch. Amst.* II, Nos. 2278 f.; II, 2, No. 493; Blaupot t. C., *Friesland*, 164, 245, 248; *Naamlijst* 1829, 52 f.; *DB* 1861, 143; 1872, 4, 191; 1873, 190; 1901, 17.

Tjallingii, Dutch Mennonite family formerly found at Harlingen in Friesland, where from the 17th century until 1910 its members were largely engaged in tileworks and occasionally in lumber and other business. The Tjallingii's brick and stone factory was dissolved in 1910. The Tjallingii were loyal members of the church, some of them being deacons, e.g., Pieter Tjallingii who was moderator of the church board until 1897. vDZ.

De Vrije Fries XVII (Leeuwarden, 1920) 22-27; church records of Harlingen.

Tjallingius, Tjalling, b. 1722, d. May 16, 1804, at Hoorn, was a lay Mennonite preacher at Koudum in Friesland, Netherlands, 1784-1803. Thereupon retiring and moving to Hoorn, he was called to serve the Hoorn congregation 1803, then aged 81, and served one year, until his death. (*Naamlijst* 1804, 67; 1806, 71 f.; *DJ* 1941, 49.) vDZ.

Tjallings, Binnert, a merchant at Grouw in Friesland, Netherlands, was a successful businessman, who, probably through Collegiant (*q.v.*) influence, came to believe that business practices are not compatible with the Christian faith. He gave up his business, studied languages (English, German), history, and theology, and then served the Mennonite congregation at Dokkum as minister 1788-d. 95. This is told by Joost Halbertsma (*q.v.*), whose mother was a sister of Binnert Tjallings. vDZ.

J. H. Halbertsma, *De Doopsgezinden en hunne Herkomst* (Deventer, 1843) 408; *DJ* 1912, 24.

Tjeenk Willink, a Dutch Mennonite family. Wolterus Everhardus Jonas Tjeenk Willink, b. 1816 at Zutphen, d. there 1885, bought the publishing house of H. Asszn Doyer (also a Mennonite) at Zwolle in 1838, which he raised to great prosperity. This publishing house still exists. It specializes in editions of scholarly works. His brother Anne Tjeenk Willink, b. 18.. at Zutphen, d. 1885 at Arnhem, founded a publishing house at Arnhem. His daughter Johanna Margaretha, b. 1883 at Zwolle, was married to Koenraad Kuiper (*q.v.*).

Herman Didericus Tjeenk Willink, b. July 21, 1843, at Zwolle, d. March 8, 1917, at Haarlem, married to Henrietta Berendina van der Goot, a son of the above Wolterus E. J. Tjeenk Willink, studied theology at the Amsterdam Mennonite seminary in 1861-66, obtained his Th.D. degree at the University of Leiden in 1867, and was pastor of the Mennonite congregations of Tjalleberd 1868-71 and Vlissingen 1871-74. In 1874 he retired and became a partner in the bookstore and publishing house of A. C. Kruseman at Haarlem; the firm was then called Kruseman and Tjeenk Willink. In 1878 Tjeenk Willink became the sole owner. His son Herman Didericus Tjeenk Willink (1872-1945) later became his father's partner and was also a trustee of the Haarlem Mennonite congregation 1899-d.1945 and a representative on the A.D.S. board 1927-41. The publishing house is now H. D. Tjeenk Willink and Son, Inc. The director since 1938 has been Ernest Lefebvre, b. 1905, a member and from 1949 a trustee of the congregation of Haarlem. This house has published Mennonite books, e.g., by C. B. Hylkema, W. J. Kühler, and H. W. Meihuizen. vDZ.

N.N.B.Wb. III, 1242 f.; *Winkler Prins Encyclopedie*, 6th ed., XVII (Amsterdam, 1953) 512.

Tjommes, Pieke (d. c1781), a Dutch Mennonite, was a merchant at Heerenveen and a preacher in the Heerenveen-Knijpe Waterlander congregation from 1736. On the charge made by the Reformed pastor of Knijpe, abetted by the Reformed classis of Zevenwolden, accusing him and his co-preachers Wytze Jeens Brouwer (*q.v.*) and Wybe Pieters Zeeman (*q.v.*) of teaching Socinian doctrines, all three had to answer before the district governor of Schoterland. They were asked whether they agreed with the formulary issued by the States of Friesland in 1722. Wybe Pieters declared that he agreed with the articles of the formulary, but Wytze Jeens and Pieke refused to express themselves on this point, because in matters of religion they were not inclined to use other terminology than that used in the Scriptures. Thereupon Wytze and Pieke were suspended (Aug. 23, 1738). Upon an appeal by the congregation to the States of Friesland, the two were examined by some Reformed pastors and judged to be unorthodox on four points (March 13, 1739). The suspension was not revoked and when H. Portier (*q.v.*) presented a petition on their behalf in which he used the term "inquisition" to describe the action of the States, both preachers were deposed (June 5, 1739). Thereupon the Mennonite conference of Friesland deeply concerned itself with the question, though in vain. (See **Stinstra, Johannes.**) Finally on April 15, 1743, Jeens and Tjommes were again permitted to preach and both continued their ministry, Pieke Tjommes however only until 1745, in which year he resigned. The reason is not clear. It may have been because the intolerance of the Frisian States discouraged him, or that his congregation disappointed him. But more likely it was because his religious views had changed. In 1747 he joined the Hernhutters (Moravian Brethren, *q.v.*) and occasionally participated in their communion services at Zeist. vDZ.

P. H. Veen, *De Doopsgezinden in Schoterland* (Leeuwarden, 1869) 35 f., 42, 65-75, 134, 164, 167-172; Blaupot t. C., *Friesland*, 208-10; W. Lütjeharms, *Het Philadelphisch-Oecumenisch streven der Hernhutters . . .* (Zeist, 1935) 65.

Tjum: see Tzum.

Tjummarum, a village in the northwest part of the Dutch province of Friesland, where Elder Leenaert (*q.v.*) Bouwens baptized five persons in 1563-65. At least in 1610 and probably long before, there was a Mennonite congregation here, concerning which information is very scarce. It had a meetinghouse in town and in 1695 it joined the Conference of Friesland, then numbering about 40 members. Throughout the 18th century the pulpit was vacant, services mostly being conducted by the preachers

of Harlingen. In 1762 the few remaining members joined the Franeker (*q.v.*) congregation. vDZ.

H. J. Busé, "De verdwenen Doopsgezinde gemeenten in Friesland," in *De Vrije Fries* XXII, repr. p. 16-18; Blaupot t. C., *Friesland*, 89, 189, 193.

Tobacco. Although the tobacco plant was brought to Europe from America early in the 16th century, it was used only as a medicinal plant throughout that century. Sir Walter Raleigh introduced the smoking of tobacco to England in 1586, from where it gradually spread to Holland and the rest of Europe, although with some initial government resistance. Rotterdam and Amsterdam became centers of the tobacco trade and the Dutch were early among the relatively largest users of tobacco and have remained so. Some Mennonites in Holland became tobacco merchants at an early date in the 17th century. In France and Spain the practice of taking snuff was the first form of using tobacco for pleasure. Pipe-smoking preceded the use of cigars, and the cigarette did not seriously compete with cigars until the beginning of the 20th century. The vast increase in the smoking habit, especially in the form of cigarettes, has been a prominent feature of American culture only since 1910 and is largely due to skillful advertising by cigarette manufacturers. The chewing of tobacco was more prominent in the 19th century, but has now almost disappeared. Antitobacco organizations arose in Europe and America in the latter half of the 19th century somewhat parallel to the temperance and abstinence movements (England 1853, France 1868, Sweden 1886, United States 1901 in the Anti-Cigaret League, Germany 1912).

The first recorded reaction of Mennonites against the use of tobacco was negative. John Horsch, in an article in the *Herold der Wahrheit* (1888, p. 148), quotes article 24 of the *Ordnungsbrief* of the Strasbourg Conference of 1607 as forbidding the use of snuff. "So far as snuff-taking is concerned, it is recognized that public snuff-taking is offensive, hence shall not be permitted. If someone needs it as a medicine he is to do it secretly." Among the articles drawn up in 1639 and read annually, at least until 1716, before the Frisian Conference in North Holland in the 17th-18th centuries, No. 9 is on tobacco; it reads: "No one shall use tobacco because of a bad habit, whereby one wastes time and money and whereby one becomes a burden to others who do not use it, because of a bad odor and spitting. Yea, this evil is becoming so great that instead of getting out the Bible or the hymnbook for mutual edification, the tobacco pipe is brought out for scandal." (The articles were published by Blaupot ten Cate, *Holland* II, 223-28.) Pieter Pietersz (*q.v.*) and other Dutch preachers in the 17th century vehemently opposed the growing use of tobacco (*DB* 1896, 24).

However, the use of tobacco became fairly common among Mennonites in general in Europe, although in recent decades its use has greatly declined in South Germany, Switzerland, and France, and is now almost unknown in some of these areas; this is, however, not the case in Holland.

In Russia smoking never became so widespread among the Mennonites, although there seems to have been no objection to it by the main body. A short-lived attempt by Cornies about 1845 to establish tobacco-raising in the Molotschna settlement failed because other crops were more profitable. The Kleine Gemeinde (founded 1814), the Mennonite Brethren (founded 1860), the Krimmer Mennonite Brethren (founded 1869), and probably the Hutterites, seem to have opposed the use of tobacco from the beginning.

The use of tobacco among the American Mennonites was quite common until the rise of the antialcohol and antitobacco movement in the country, which substantially influenced all groups except the Old Order Amish and Old Order Mennonites. Harley Stucky has shown that some of the Russian Mennonite immigrants of the 1870's who were opposed to the use of tobacco and who came into contact with the American Mennonites and especially John F. Funk of Elkhart, Ind., the publisher of the *Herald of Truth* and the *Mennonitische Rundschau,* probably exerted a wholesome influence against it. The evidence is clear that in the last half of the 19th century smoking and chewing were so common among all the Mennonite groups of Swiss-South German background as to be almost universal. There was also some use of snuff. Chewing was so common at home and even during the church services that spittoons were found behind the pulpits in some of the meetinghouses. A number of the older women smoked pipes (clay or corncob) in the home. An Amish bishop in Iowa complained that some of the ministers said "they cannot preach without a chew of tobacco in their mouths." Daniel Brenneman wrote in the *Herald of Truth* in September 1871, "Who can go into a house of worship and find in almost every nook and corner the filthy stains and noisome stench of tobacco as may be found in some places and feel like justifying the habit, and feel that those do wrong who protest against it?" John F. Funk, the editor, commented in the March 1878 issue, "Here among our American Mennonites the use of tobacco prevails to a very large extent. . . . Some have declared that they would no longer patronize the paper if we should continue to admit articles of this kind [against the use of tobacco]." But there was a growing minority against tobacco and gradually, by education (not legislation) they won the day; by the end of the first quarter of the 19th century its use had practically ceased in the more progressive sections of the Mennonite Church (MC); it went out more slowly in Eastern Pennsylvania and among some of the communities of Amish background in Iowa, Nebraska, and Ontario. The gradual change is well illustrated by tracing the record of antitobacco resolutions in the Virginia Conference. In 1894 the minutes say, "Whereas there is so much chewing tobacco and spitting on the floor in the house of God in time of service, is it not a duty for our members as well as the ministers to speak and protest against such a filthy habit as well as all other bad habits? Decided in the affirmative." Fifty years later (1941) the conference discipline said: "The use of tobacco in any form is not only a filthy habit but its use results in physical injury and is Scripturally inconsistent. Its use is hereby discouraged by both precept and example. Its use shall disqualify any member from ordination. No one shall be received into church membership who does not do all in his power to discontinue its use."

J. W. Fretz, who did careful research in the subject in 1949, summarizes his findings as follows: "(1) By and large, the custom of using tobacco among older Mennonite groups in Europe and America seems to have been similar to the customs of society in general on this point. The custom was at first seemingly opposed, then gradually accepted and finally adopted in a rather widespread fashion. Traditionally, there seems to have been no general conscience against its use. (2) Such groups as the Mennonite Brethren, the Krimmer Mennonite Brethren, the Kleine Gemeinde, the Evangelical Mennonite Brethren, and the Church of God in Christ Mennonite seem to have had a clear and consistent witness against this custom from their origin up to this time. (3) In recent decades there is evidence of a growing conscience against the production and use of tobacco among the Mennonites (MC), the Conservative Amish, and in some cases among the Old Order Amish. (4) An increase in the use of tobacco, especially cigarette smoking, is evident in General Conference and certain Mennonite (MC) churches where the subject is not considered a test of church membership or a matter for discipline. (5) The use of tobacco among Mennonites is definitely related to fashions and fads. Those who have adopted the custom have done so in imitation of those with whom they associated, desiring to conform to the prevailing pattern of social behavior. Those who adopt the cigarette smoking habit are the same ones who are freely adopting changes in society generally. It is an aspect of secularization in that it is a demonstration of individuals accepting for their standards of value and patterns of behavior criteria from secular society rather than from religious faith or the Scriptures. The seeming contradiction between the ethical and moral idealism of the Mennonites on the one hand and the custom of using tobacco on the other is explained in a large measure by the subtle secularization process going on in Mennonite groups."

The growing of tobacco is limited to certain areas where the proper combination of soil and climate makes it profitable. The only extensive tobacco growing areas in Mennonite settlements are in Lancaster County, Pa. (introduced after the middle of the 19th century), and Essex County, Ont. (settled by Mennonites from Russia 1922-25). A growing conscience against producing a crop whose use is prohibited or frowned upon has led to a strong decline in tobacco raising among Mennonites of the Lancaster Conference (MC). No such development has taken place among the Old Order Mennonites or Old Order Amish of this region.

A curiosity is the introduction of a criticism of smoking into the German edition of Menno Simons' works published at Elkhart in 1876. On page 376 in Part I Menno is made to advise parents as follows: "Gestattet ihnen keine Gemeinschaft mit den bösen unnützen Kindern, von denen sie nichts als lügen, fluchen, schwören, rauchen, und Bübereien lernen." The Dutch *Opera Omnia* of 1681 has "vechten" in place of "rauchen," and the German translations of this section usually have "schlagen," although the Peter van Riesen edition of 1834 (Danzig) omits the word. The English translation has "fighting." H.S.B.

J. W. Fretz, "The Growth and Use of Tobacco Among Mennonites," *Proceedings of the Seventh Annual Conference on Mennonite Cultural Problems* (n.p., 1949) 87-100; Harley J. Stucky, "Cultural Interaction Among Mennonites" (unpublished M.A. thesis, Northwestern University, 1947) 40-45.

Tobias Quintincxsz (Questincx), an Anabaptist martyr, burned at the stake on March 20, 1549, at Amsterdam, Netherlands, with seven others. Tobias, a cobbler, was a citizen of Amsterdam (not a native of Linninkhausen as is reported in *ML*). He was charged with the crimes of rebaptism (baptized by Gillis, *q.v.*, van Aken) and persisting in his heresy. On Feb. 14 he was severely tortured. Tobias and his fellow martyrs died valiantly. Van Braght published the sentence from the original records in the *Martyrs' Mirror;* the name of Questincx given here is garbled. Tobias's property was confiscated. He and his co-martyrs are commemorated in the hymn "Tis nu schier al Vervult ons broeders getal," found in *Veelderhande Liedekens* of 1556 and the following editions. (*Mart. Mir.* D 82, E 483; Grosheide, *Bijdrage,* 155 f., 308; *ML* III, 418.) vDZ.

Toe Water, Willem Hendrik, b. May 22, 1885, at Diemen, d. Dec. 12, 1938, at Zwolle, a Dutch Mennonite pastor, who after finishing his theological studies at the university and Mennonite seminary at Amsterdam, served the congregations of Warns 1912-16, St-Anna-Parochie 1916-23, and Zwolle 1923-d.38. He was especially active in the Vereeniging voor Gemeentedagen (now Vereniging voor Doopsgezind Broederschapswerk, *q.v.*), and in 1929-36 served as editor of its periodical *Brieven* (*q.v.*). Toe Water was one of the first Dutch Mennonite ministers who thought it necessary to organize the youth in a special Youth Association (see **Doopsgezinde Jongerenbond**). For many years he was a trustee of the Elspeet (*q.v.*) Brotherhood Home. Toe Water was a pious, poetic, somewhat sensitive spirit; he was a gifted musician, composer of the melody of the Elspeet hymn, a master storyteller. He published a few sermons and a volume of poems, *Kleine Geschenken*. S. H. N. Gorter (*q.v.*), a close friend of Toe Water from 1902, preached his funeral sermon at Zwolle Dec. 15, 1938. vDZ.

Ned. Patriciaat XIII (1923) 415; *Brieven* XXI (1939) No. 12; *De Zondagsbode* LII (1938-39) No. 7; *DJ* 1940, 17-24 with portrait; S. H. N. Gorter, "Ter Herinnering," mimeographed funeral sermon.

Toengen Diruc Jansdochter, an Anabaptist martyr, a native of Breda, was drowned on Jan. 17, 1539, at Delft, Dutch province of South Holland, with four other women, all charged with the crime of rebaptism. Toengen was probably a follower of David (*q.v.*) Joris. (*Inv. Arch. Amst.* I, No. 749.) vDZ.

Toens, a Mennonite family living at Haarlem, Holland. Symon Eduards Toens, married to Geesje Pieters Suiker, of Blokzijl, was from 1696 a preacher and from 1713 an elder of the Danzig Old Flemish congregation at Haarlem. He died there c1758. His son Eduard Toens, like his father the owner of a yarn spinnery, was a preacher of the same congregation 1740-c53. Another son of Symon Eduards was Pieter Toens (Haarlem 1724—Hoogezand shortly after 1800). He was first married to Cornelia Mabé (1716-57) and after her death to Anna Reckmann (1732-after 1800), both of Haarlem. At first he owned a weaving mill and ran a small shop; later he was a partner in a thread factory with his cousin Pieter Loos. About 1765 in a period of economic decline he left this business and started a florist business, which, however, he had to give up in 1776, because it did not pay. Since life was expensive in Haarlem he moved to Hoogezand in the province of Groningen in 1776. In 1753 Pieter Toens had been appointed preacher in the Danzig Old Flemish church of Haarlem, but after four or five years of serving he resigned, and joined the more liberal Peuzelaarsteeg congregation. The reason for this transfer is that he was more progressive than the Danzig Old Flemish Mennonites in general; Toens was particularly averse to banning because of outside marriage, as was still the practice in this group. He then also frequented Collegiant (*q.v.*) meetings and later became interested in politics as a warm Patriot (*q.v.*). At the end of his life he played an important political role: in 1795 he was elected to represent Groningen in the Dutch Second Chamber, of which, being the oldest member, he was the provisional president in 1798. Belonging to the radical Republican party, he was not re-elected in this year. His descendants during the 19th century were found at Hoogezand, some of them being members of the Sappemeer (*q.v.*) Mennonite congregation. (Diary of Pieter Toens, by the courtesy of Prof. Engelbrecht, Pretoria, South Africa; Dutch *Naamlijst*.) vDZ.

Toews (Töws, Toevs, Toeffs, Tewffs, Taevs, Taves), a common family name among Prussian Mennonites of probably Dutch background, derived from Matthew (Mattheus), was found in Tiegenhagen, Ladekopp, Rosenort, Fürstenwerder, Heubuden, Elbing, and Danzig. Isaac Toews and Johann Toews Jr. were preachers of the Ladekopp Old Flemish congregation, from 1762 and 1787 respectively, both serving until after 1802. Abraham Toews was a preacher at Heubuden from 1794, and Johann Toews of Fürstenwerder from 1796. Franz Toews served as preacher in the Fürstenwerder congregation 1822-c50 and Jakob Toews in the same congregation from 1846. Johann Toews was preacher of the Hochzeit congregation from 1796 for more than fifty years. Another Johann was a minister at Ladekopp, preacher from 1832, elder 1853-78. Heinrich Toews served at Pordenau, Russia, as preacher 1839 and as an elder 1842-c79, and his grandson Johann Toews as preacher of the same church from 1876. B. H. Unruh lists fourteen bearers of the name among the immigrants to Russia. Johann Toews (*q.v.*) was elder of the Köppental Mennonite Church of Trakt. Johannes J. Toews, son of Johann Toews, of the Trakt settlement, was a minister of that settlement and died in exile. A. Töws was Oberschulze (1842-48) and co-worker of Johann Cornies. Aron A. Toews (Canada) is the author of *Mennonitische Märtyrer;* Gerhard Toews is the author of *Heimat in Trümmern* and other books; J. B. Toews is the field worker of the M.B. Board of Missions; John A. Toews is the president of the M.B. Bible College at Winnipeg, and Jacob A. Toews is pastor of the M.B. Church in Kitchener, Ont. David Toews (*q.v.*) was a prominent G.C. elder in Canada, with residence in Rosthern, Sask., and was founder and long-time chairman of the Mennonite Board of Colonization (*q.v.*). (See also **Töws.**) C.K., vDZ.

A. A. Toews, *Mennonitische Märtyrer* I (Clearbrook, 1949); H. R. Schröder, *Russlanddeutsche Friesen;* Reimer, *Familiennamen;* Dutch *Naamlijst;* B. H. Unruh, *Hintergründe. ML* IV, 342.

Toews, Cornelius J. (1852-1915), a leading agricultural expert of the Mennonites of Russia, was born in the village of Altenau in the Molotschna Mennonite settlement. In his youth he recognized the value of innovations by Johann Cornies (*q.v.*). As the owner of a large farm at Ebenfeld, near Genichesk, a port on the Sea of Asov, he practiced the culture of grain combined with summer fallow (*Schwarzbrache*), and was one of the pioneers in this profitable method of farming in the Ukraine. His prosperity enabled him both to acquire more and more land and also to give large sums to charitable purposes. He built privately the first telephone in the area of Melitopol (*q.v.*). J.Wi.

Toews, David (1870-1947), an elder (known generally as Bishop Toews in Canadian government and railway circles) and leader in the General Conference Mennonite Church, was born Feb. 9, 1870, at Lysanderhöh near the Volga in Russia, one of the 14 children of Jakob Töws, a minister, who had come to Russia in 1869. When David was 10 years old he accompanied his parents on the ill-fated trek to Turkestan (*q.v.*), experiencing hardships so severe that he later hesitated to talk about them. After four years of disappointment in Turkestan, the Töws family immigrated to Newton, Kan., where Jakob Töws served the Mennonite church as elder for about 30 years. David attended the public school to learn English, then the Zentralschule at Halstead, to prepare to teach. He then taught school at Whitewater, Elbing, and Newton, Kan. In 1888 he was baptized at Newton by his father.

H. H. Ewert, who had been the principal of the Halstead school while Toews attended it, persuaded Toews to accompany him to Gretna, Man., to teach there. In 1895-97 he attended school at Winnipeg. He taught one year in the village of Burwalde near Winkler, and then went to Tiefengrund, Sask., homesteading and teaching school. On Aug. 18, 1901, he was ordained as a minister. On Sept. 20, 1900, Toews married Margaret Friesen. They had one son and eight daughters.

In 1901-4 Toews taught school at Eigenheim, Sask., and then at the German-English Academy (*q.v.*) at Rosthern, which he had helped to establish. He served as principal until 1917, and also as president of the school corporation, which position he held until late in life. In 1913 he was ordained elder of the large Rosenort church, which, together with the chairmanship of the Conference of Mennonites in Canada, 1914-40, required a great deal of time and energy, particularly during World War I. For many years David Toews was a member of the Home Mission Board of the General Conference. In this capacity he was a real assistance particularly to the Mennonite immigrants who came to Canada since 1923.

As chairman of the Canadian Mennonite Board of Colonization 1922-46, David Toews was keenly interested in the well-being of the Mennonites in Russia, who suffered great hardships during the revolution following World War I, and worked unstintingly to aid the Mennonite immigration to Canada. In 1923-30 over 20,000 Mennonites were brought to Canada from Russia under the auspices of the Board.

On Feb. 25, 1947, David Toews died, and was buried in the Rosthern cemetery. J.G.R.

Toews, Henry F. (1879-1942), an M.B. minister, educator, and author, was born in South Russia Feb. 17, 1879, the son of Franz and Agnes (Klassen) Toews. Shortly after his birth the family emigrated to America, settling on a farm southwest of Moundridge, Kan. Toews was converted and baptized at the age of fifteen. After attending Bethel College one summer term, Toews taught in country schools for four years. Then he continued his studies at McPherson College, McPherson, Kan., where he received the A.B. degree. He received his theological training at the Baptist Theological Seminary, Rochester, N.Y., and at the Baptist Theological Seminary, Kansas City, Kan. The latter conferred upon him the B.D. degree. In 1918 McPherson College conferred upon him the D.D. degree.

Toews entered the ministry in 1905 and for several years did evangelistic work; he was ordained in 1914. Toews married Agnes Flaming on Aug. 9, 1908, and established his home at Hillsboro, Kan. Three children were born to them. From 1910 to 1940, except for a period of illness, he was engaged chiefly in teaching, for the greater part of this time at Tabor College in the department of Theology and Bible. One year he taught at the M.B. Bible School, Herbert, Sask.

Toews was very active in the M.B. Church conferences, serving as secretary of the General Conference 1924-27. For some time he edited the Sunday School Quarterly and wrote the Sunday-school lesson helps for the *Zionsbote* and the *Hillsboro Journal.* He was the author of the following books written in German: *Handbuch für Sonntagschularbeiter, Biblische Grundwahrheiten,* and *Jesus kommt wieder.* He also wrote *Topical Outline Studies of Bible Doctrines.* He died in his home at Hillsboro on Jan. 15, 1942. Interment was in the local M.B. cemetery. J.H.L.

Toews, Jacob (1838-1922), an elder of the First Mennonite Church of Newton, Kan., was born at Wotzlaf, West Prussia, June 26, 1838. He attended school at Weisshof and was baptized in 1854. In

1858 he visited his relatives in Russia. On March 15, 1860, he married and in 1864 he was ordained minister by Johann Wiebe. In 1869 he migrated to Russia and took part in the establishment of the Trakt Mennonite settlement (q.v.) in Saratov. In 1880 he joined the group which moved to Central Asia (q.v.) to escape government service and to be prepared to meet the Lord. On Oct. 10, 1884, they arrived in Newton, Kan. In 1886 he was elected elder of the First Mennonite Church and installed by Leonhard Sudermann, which office he held for 31 years. In 1916 he resigned and moved to Aberdeen, Idaho, where he died Jan. 2, 1923. David Toews (q.v.) was his son.   C.K.

"Aeltester Jacob Toews," Bundesbote-Kalender, 1923, p. 24; J. E. Entz, "First Mennonite Church—Newton," Menn. Life VIII (October 1953) 153.

Toews, Jakob (1825-1909), an elder of the congregation of Lichtenau, Petershagen, and Schönsee in the Molotschna Mennonite settlement in South Russia, was born in the village of Fürstenau, Molotschna, two years after his parents had arrived in Russia from Prussia. In 1862 he was elected minister and in 1869 elder of his home congregation. For almost 40 years Toews cared for his large church, which consisted of three subsidiary congregations, Lichtenau, Petershagen, and Schönsee, but which had been organized as a unit. The three meetinghouses of the congregation were located a considerable distance from each other. Godliness, simplicity, and a great firmness of conviction were outstanding features of his character. In 1908 Toews retired from his duties as elder and minister and died one year later. (Der Botschafter, 1909.) H.G.

Toews, Peter (1841-1922), first a Kleine Gemeinde elder, then a Church of God in Christ Mennonite elder, was born July 24, 1841, at Fischau, Molotschna, South Russia, the youngest son of Johann Töws (1793-1873) and Elizabeth Harder. He joined the Kleine Gemeinde in 1861. On Nov. 12, 1863, he was united in marriage with Anna Warkentin. He was ordained as a minister in 1866, and as elder in 1870. He was instrumental in unifying three factions of this denomination. In the early seventies he was sent to St. Petersburg and later to Yalta to interview the Czar, and was prominent in the emigration movement to Canada. With the last 30 families of his group he sailed from Nikopol on May 4, 1875, and on June 29 arrived near Niverville along the Red River in Manitoba. He then settled in Grünfeld.

Endowed with a keen craving for knowledge, Toews read and studied constantly and prayerfully, comparing the Scriptures with the works of earlier writers. With a large part of his flock he joined the Church of God in Christ, Mennonite, in 1882, and was ordained anew to the ministry on Jan. 11, 1882. His sermons were clear and sound, as were also his many articles of Scripture exposition published in the Botschafter der Wahrheit. For many years he was editor of this publication, the official German-language organ of the denomination.

Many of his numerous poems and pamphlet articles were published in periodicals. Many of his hymns are contained in the Liederbuch der Gemeinde Gottes, the first two editions of which he edited. He translated several works from the Dutch into the German language. He corresponded with a number of the leaders of his day. He was a moderator of the general conference.

In 1900-11 he lived at Hochstadt, Man., and on retiring from active service moved to Swalwell, Alberta. Although almost blind during the last years, he continued to study and write. He died on Nov. 2, 1922, at the age of 81 years, after 56 years of consecrated service. He was buried in the Linden cemetery at Swalwell.   P.G.H.

Tofield, Alberta, is a town (pop. 800) located near the center of the province, 35 miles east and 12 miles south of Edmonton. Approximately 530 Mennonites live within shopping distance of the town. These are made up of three groups, including 363 M.C., 185 G.C.M., and 85 M.B. The M.C. Mennonites live in an arc from east around south to southwest, the G.C.M. and M.B. groups in a ¾ circle from east around south to north. About 4 per cent of the M.C., 12 per cent of the G.C.M., and 1 per cent of the M.B. live in Tofield. The M.C. group was first to arrive here, coming in 1910; the other two groups came in 1924. There are three Mennonite churches in the area. The only other institutions are mission Sunday schools and winter Bible schools. The larger part of the original Mennonite settlers came here from Nebraska and Iowa. The General Conference and Mennonite Brethren came from Russia.   M.D.S.

Toger, Frederik, b. c1665 at Amsterdam, d. March 11, 1720, at Leiden, obtained his M.D. degree at the Leiden University in 1699 with a dissertation on "The Plague." He was then a practicing physician and in 1694-1717 also a Mennonite preacher at Leiden, Holland, 1694-1701 in the Waterlander congregation and, after the merger of this church with the Flemish, of the United congregation. Schijn's surmise that he had been a preacher at Brielle 1691-94 has not been substantiated. Toger published De lijdzaamheid en vergelding der Heiligen (Leiden, 1703), an address on I Pet. 3:6, in which he, in a learned manner, describes the meekness and the reward of the righteous; his Bondig Zamenstel der christelyke Godgeleerdheid was edited after his death by his friend Abraham van Loon (q.v.) and published in 1726 at Leiden; reprinted at Leiden in 1738 under the title Samenstel der christelyke godgeleerdheid. It contains six volumes. The first five volumes deal in several chapters with the doctrines of God, man, and Jesus Christ; the sixth in fourteen chapters discusses the Christian faith, regeneration, good works, conversion, justification, baptism, communion, the oath, government, war, death, the resurrection, judgment, bliss, and damnation.   NEFF, vDZ.

Schijn-Maatschoen, Geschiedenis II, 628-46; Blaupot t. C., Holland II, 133 f.; L. G. le Poole, Bijdragen tot . . . het kerkelijk leven onder de Doopsgezinden te Leiden (Leiden, 1905) 64, 87, 99 f., 170, 197; Chr. Sepp, Johannes Stinstra en zijn tijd I (Amsterdam, 1865) 185-88; ML IV.

Tolenaar, Josef: see Zöllner.

Töllinger, Christine, of Penon in Tirol, Austria, an Anabaptist martyr, a widow, was seized with four brethren and three sisters at Fill in the Adige Valley (*q.v.*). They were taken to the castle and cross-examined. Christine confessed that she was baptized in her home by Georg Blaurock (*q.v.*); the bread of the Mass is merely bread; children are saved without rebaptism; with God's help she would die on the confession of her faith. They were all executed on Nov. 18, 1529, at Fill (*q.v.*).

Wolkan, *Geschicht-Buch,* 53 and 55; Zieglschmid, *Chronik,* 74, 76, 78; *Mart. Mir.* D 27, E 435 f.

Tomas, Jan: see **Thomas, Jan.**

Tomkins, David: see **Le Heux, J. W. N.**

Tonawanda, New York, an area on the east side of the Niagara River between Niagara Falls and Buffalo, was once the location of a small Mennonite settlement. The Ebersole name is one of the present indications that Mennonite families formerly lived in this area. The first Mennonites migrating to western New York in the early 1830's were mainly from Lancaster County, Pa. No organized congregation was formed at this place. A few families worshiped in a local church at LaSalle, now a part of the city of Niagara Falls. It was probably after the middle of the century that Jacob Krehbiel preached for these families. It is said that John S. Coffman visited the place while Krehbiel was still living. The work in this place, supported by Jacob Krehbiel, was identified with the conferences under which he served; i.e., M.C. under the Conference of Ontario, and later G.C.M. J.C.F.

Tongeren, Henric van: see **Hendrik Slachtscaep.**

Tongerloo, Van, a Dutch Mennonite family found at Amsterdam from the 16th until the 18th century, when it died out. They were nearly all members of the Flemish, from 1664 of the Lamist (*q.v.*) church. Jasper van Tongerloo was a deacon in the early 17th century and Evert van Tongerloo from 1709. Clara van Tongerloo was married in 1605 to Jacob Haesbaert, who also later was a deacon. Clara was the daughter of a neighbor of Joost van den Vondel (*q.v.*), the famous Dutch poet, who was at this time still a Mennonite and who celebrated her marriage in one of his first poems. The Tongerloo family was related to H. H. van Warendorp (*q.v.*), and from 1632 Jasper van Tongerloo was one of the managers of his estate which included the present Singel Church until 1740. There were at times difficulties between members of the Tongerloo family and the deacons of the Flemish congregation concerning this heritage. (*Inv. Arch. Amst.* I, No. 578; II, Nos. 91, 166, 171-73, 175, 180, 199-200, 209; *DB* 1863, 13, 14, 18, 32, 38, 40, 41.) vDZ.

Tonis Gerrits: see **Thomas Gerritsz.**

Tonnis, Jan: see **Tempel, van den.**

Tookey, Elias, about whose private life and fate there is only scarce information, belonged to a group of Independents at London, England, led by John Murton (*q.v.*). In 1624-25 Tookey and some other members of this church opposed their leader, apparently in part because Murton was rather imperious, and in part because they did not agree with Murton's Calvinistic views, particularly his defense of infant baptism. Tookey and his adherents stressed the freedom of the will and were inclined to believers' baptism. Thereupon Tookey and fifteen other members were banned. This group in March or April 1624 wrote a letter to Reynier Wybrands (*q.v.*), Hans de Ries (*q.v.*), and other Watterlander leaders in Holland. A correspondence followed (letters by Tookey of June 3, 1624, and March 17, 1625, and a letter Nov. 12, 1625, from five "Anabaptist" congregations as Tookey and his group were called). These five "Anabaptist" congregations were Sarum, Coventry, London, Lincoln, and Tyverton. In these letters gradually the idea was developed that the "Anabaptists" would merge with the Dutch Mennonites and particularly the Waterlanders. De Ries answered and sent them the Waterlander confession of faith (by himself and Lubbert Gerritsz, *q.v.*) of 1610 as a basis for negotiations. He wrote that he appreciated their doctrines and admonished them to patience and meekness, but he had scruples regarding some of their practices, e.g., that they had consented to take an oath of allegiance to the British king. Another difference was Tookey's idea that war as such is not a sin, that a righteous war is permissible and military service in special cases permitted to Christians. The negotiations lasted until the end of 1630. The merger did not come about, not only because the Dutch Mennonites did not agree with some of Tookey's ideas, but apparently particularly because de Ries did not wish to risk the adventure. vDZ.

Inv. Arch. Amst. II, Nos. 1367-77; J. G. de Hoop Scheffer and W. E. Griffis, *History of the Free Churchmen* (Ithaca, n.d.-1922) 179 f.

Toorn, Hendrik: see **Toren, Hendrik.**

Toornburg(h) (Torenburg, Toornenburg, also Toorn), **Klaas** (Claes), a physician and preacher of the Waterlander Mennonites in the Netherlands. He is said to have been of delicate health. He was born at Alkmaar *c*1657, studied medicine at Leiden, and settled as a physician in his home town in 1688, where he also was chosen as preacher of the Mennonite Waterlander congregation. From 1696 until 1720, when he retired, he was preacher at De Rijp (*q.v.*), and also practiced medicine. His year of death is unknown. Toornburg published *Schriftuurlijcke Verhandelingh tegens het Eed-zweeren en voor de wraak- en weerloose lijdzaamheyt* (Alkmaar, 1688); *Schriftuurlijcke Verhandeling van de Wraek- en Wereloose Lijdsaemheyt en Volmaeckte Liefde . . .* (Amsterdam, 1688); *Concordantie van gelyk-luydende Plaatsen der Heylige Schrifture* (Alkmaar, 1686); and *Christelijke Overdenkingen des doodts* (Alkmaar, n.d., reprint Amsterdam, 1723). (*N.N.B.Wb.* III, 1244 f.; *DB* 1917, 43 f., 64). vDZ.

Topeka, Ind., a town (pop. 550) located in the northeastern part of the state in Lagrange County. It is situated in what is familiarly known as the Hawpatch, so called because of the many black and red haw bushes that grew among the virgin hardwood timber in the early years. It is located 18 miles southeast of Goshen and 45 miles northwest of Fort Wayne.

Topeka is a thriving trading center for the many Mennonites and Old Order Amish living in this community. The first Mennonites settled in this area in 1846. There are two Mennonite churches in the town: Maple Grove (MC) and the Topeka Mennonite (GCM). The Emma Mennonite (MC) Church is located 5 miles north of Topeka. There are about 500 Mennonites living in and around the town, about 20 per cent of whom live in the town. There are 15 Old Order Amish congregations in the neighborhood of Topeka. The area is a fertile farming community. One of the Mennonite Central Committee cutting centers for the Women's Missionary and Service Auxiliary is operating here.

E.J.Y.

Topeka Mennonite (GCM) Church, located in Topeka, Lagrange Co., Ind., a member of the Central District, began in 1893 when Silver Street (*q.v.*) members and others living near Topeka began to worship together. They purchased the Eden Chapel in 1897, moved it west of Topeka, and used it until the present building was completed in 1927. John Mehl was the first pastor. He was succeeded by John C. Lehman, Ernest Hostetler, Earl Salzman, Wilmer S. Shelly, Esko Loewen, and Orlin F. Frey. The charter membership in 1898 was 21; 90 were added in 1930 when a part of the Maple Grove (MC) congregation merged with this church. The membership in 1959 was 208, with Roy W. Henry as pastor.

O.F.F.

Topeka (Ind.) Mennonite Church (MC): see **Maple Grove.**

Toren, a former meetinghouse at Amsterdam. About 1565 the Waterlander Mennonite church of Amsterdam obtained a warehouse on the Singel Canal between Bergstraat and Torensluis close to the Jan-Rodenburgstoren (dungeon). This building was remodeled and adapted as a meetinghouse and commonly called either "de groote Spijker" (warehouse) or the meetinghouse "by den Toren," also "van den Toren." In 1668, when the Waterlander congregation merged with the Lamists (*q.v.*), both meetinghouses henceforth were used by what was then called the United Flemish and Waterlander church. In 1801, when the Zonist (*q.v.*) congregation of Amsterdam merged with this United church, the Zonist meetinghouse was closed, its pulpit and pipe organ transferred to the Toren church (first used Jan. 17, 1802) from then mostly called the "kleine" (small) church, while the Lamist church, the present Singel church (*q.v.*), was called the "groote" (large) church.

In 1812 the church board resolved to give up the Toren meetinghouse. The last service in the Toren was led by Pastor A. H. van Gelder on April 26, 1812. The organ and pulpit were sold for 2500 Dutch guilders to the Mennonite congregation at Leeuwarden where they are still found in the church at Wirdumerdijk. After 1812 for a few years the former Toren church was used for various pur-

poses until demolished in 1815. (*Inv. Arch. Amst.* II, Nos. 91-99, 265-81; *Naamlijst* 1815, 53 f.)

vdZ.

Toren (Toorn), Hendrik, b. *c*1663 at Rotterdam, Holland, d. *c*1731 in England, married first to Anna Bredenburg (d. 1701) and after her death to Ursula van Alphen (d. 1708), was a Mennonite baker at Rotterdam. In 1687 he was chosen as preacher by the Rotterdam Waterlander congregation. Early in 1691, having given up his bakery, Toren together with Willem Suderman, a member of the same congregation, started an iron trade with England. This firm was dissolved in 1701; Toren, now being the sole owner, went bankrupt and in 1712 presented his bankruptcy petition. In 1713 he entered into a brief partnership with the ex-sheriff Pieter Verbeek. Toren now lived at Delfshaven near Rotterdam, and in 1714 at Delft, from where he moved to England in 1715. In 1716 (?) he settled on the Isle of Man, where he ran some business. In his last years (1720-30) he wrote in English a *History of Holland,* dedicated to the (Anglican) Bishop of Man.

As a preacher of the Rotterdam Mennonite Church he was very active and baptized many persons, among whom was Jan Bisschop (*q.v.*) in 1699, and in 1711-12 he also gave catechetical instruction. In 1696-99 he retired from his ministry, perhaps because he opposed the intended merger of the Waterlanders with the Flemish congregation of Rotterdam, which came about in 1700. When in this union the Waterlander views proved to be predominant, there was no longer any reason for Toren to oppose it, and so he served the united church. During his ministry he published *Timotheus onderwezen in den Christelycken Godsdienst* (Rotterdam, 1709) and *Verdeedigingh van Godts Regtveerdigheid* (Rotterdam, 1710).

Toren had some rather liberal views, as is indicated by his interest in the Collegiants (*q.v.*). In 1693 Toren, Albert van Meurs, a Mennonite deacon, and Jan Suderman, also a Mennonite, had to answer to the magistrates of Rotterdam for Socinian views taught in the "colleges" (meetings of the Collegiants), in which these three men were apparently leaders. When Toren became bankrupt (1712), the preachers and deacons of the Mennonite congregation demanded that he avoid the communion service and "stand still" in his ministry. After this event he retired or was dismissed as a preacher. His name is no longer found in the church records. It is possible or even probable that he left the church.

Toren should be particularly mentioned for his activity in behalf of the persecuted Mennonites of Switzerland. He was a representative of the Rotterdam Mennonites in the Dutch Mennonite Committee of Foreign Needs at Amsterdam from 1709. The Amsterdam Mennonite archives have a copy book of Toren's (*Inv. Arch. Amst.* I, No. 1009) in which he copied a number of letters and gave historical particulars pertaining to the coming of the Swiss Mennonites to the Netherlands in 1710-11. This unique diary is of great value for the study of the Swiss-Palatine emigration.

Toren seems to have had great gifts, but to have been difficult to get along with; not only in 1695-99, but also in 1705 and again in 1711 he temporarily refused to exercise his ministry because he could not have his way. In the meeting of the Foreign Needs Committee at Amsterdam he also created difficulties.

Concerning his family there is little information. Jacob Toren, probably Hendrik's father, was a deacon of the church 1671-73. Some other Torens are mentioned.   vDZ.

H. C. Hazewinkel, "Hendrik Toren," in *Rotterdamsch Jaarboekje* 1949, 223-49; *Inv. Arch. Amst.* I, Nos. 1009 2251 f.; K. Vos. *Geschiedenis der Doopsgezinde gemeente te Rotterdam* (1907, repr.) 25, 28, 44, 47; DB 1908, 85-105, *passim.*

Toronto, Ont., the second largest city of Canada (1956 Greater Toronto population 1,358,028), is a manufacturing and export center on western Lake Ontario. It is known as "a city of churches." Five Mennonite churches and missions, with a total membership of 140, are located in the city. As early as 1907 the Mennonite Church (MC) began mission activity in the city, which resulted in the Danforth Mennonite Church (MC), with 25 members in 1958. Mennonite Brethren and General Conference Mennonites moved into the city later to work and to study. The Mennonite Brethren organized the Willowdale Christian Fellowship in 1957, which had 18 members in 1958. The Toronto United Mennonite Church (GCM), started in 1948, had a membership of 66 in 1958. Warden Park Mennonite Church (MC), organized in 1955, had a membership of 23. Morningside Mennonite Church (MC) was started as a mission in 1948. Ellesmere Mennonite Church (MC), started in 1946, was closed in 1958.   J.H.H.

Toronto United Mennonite Church (GCM), located at 1772 Queen Street East, Toronto, Ont., was organized in 1948 for Mennonites living and studying in the city since 1928. They worshiped in private homes until 1956, when they acquired a meetinghouse. In 1958 the membership was 66, with William Dick as pastor.   M.G.

Torsel, Cuntz, a miller at Bussbach near Bayreuth, Bavaria, Germany, confessed at his cross-examination that Fritz Weigel had convinced him of the truth of Anabaptist teaching. He knew nothing more about him. Further he said that one should believe in none but God and not any saint. He had preached that one should avoid worldly pleasures, not go to taverns, but believe in Christ and serve God. In 1545 he was in prison at Neustadtlein, Kulmbach district of Bavaria. (*TA Bayern* I, 57 ff.; *ML* IV.)   W.W.

Toul, a town in the province of Meurthe et Moselle, France, where there is a Mennonite congregation, organized *c*1885 as the result of a division in the Meuse (*q.v.*) congregation. The original membership consisted largely of Muller families, and the elders have always been Mullers. In 1957 the elders were Joseph Muller of Bois-la-Comte (ord. 1921) and J. B. Muller of Foug, with Raymond Muller and Arsène Zehr as ministers; the member-

ship, including unbaptized children, was some 150. The chief meeting place for worship since about 1920 has been the Reformed church in Toul. Subsidiary meetings were long held at Vaucouleurs and Commercy, but in 1957 at Foug, Pont á Mousson, and Maucourt. The families live widely scattered, chiefly on farms. The membership in 1957 was about 120 souls. (P. Sommer, "Assemblée de Toul," *Christ Seul,* November 1930, 8 f.)   H.S.B.

Towamencin Mennonite (MC) Church, located in Montgomery County, Pa., a member of the Franconia Conference (*q.v.*). Jacob Godshalk, who served as the first bishop for the Mennonites of America from 1708, settled in the present Towamencin Twp., Montgomery Co., Pa., in 1713 or earlier. By 1728 the first Towamencin Mennonite meetinghouse had been built. About 1804 this building burned to the ground. In 1805 a stone building was erected, replaced about sixty years later. The present meetinghouse, the fourth, was built in 1925, 50 x 74 feet. The Towamencin pulpit seems to have been supplied by the Skippack preachers until 1876, when Christian Allebach (1841-1917) was ordained to the ministry. In 1958 the minister was Ellis L. Mack, with a membership of 219.   J.C.W.

J. C. Wenger, *History of the Mennonites of the Franconia Conference* (Telford, 1937) 148-53.

Townline Conservative Mennonite Church, located six miles southwest of Shipshewana, Lagrange Co., Ind., was organized March 25, 1876, with Joseph Yoder as bishop and Joseph Bontrager as minister, and with about 75 charter members, most of whom had belonged to the Forks (*q.v.*) Mennonite congregation (MC). John M. Hostetler was ordained minister in 1876. The church was built in 1877 and is still in use, although remodeled in 1923. Other ministers ordained were Jonathan Troyer 1886, Christian Yoder 1888, Jeptha Troyer 1913, Christian J. Miller 1918, and Noah S. Miller 1920. Jonathan J. Troyer was the most prominent figure in the history of this church, having served as bishop from 1895 until his death in 1930 at the age of 89 years. The Townline congregation in 1957 had a membership of 97, with Eli D. Miller, Calvin Bontrager, and John J. S. Yoder as ministers. The Griner and Pleasant Grove congregations of Elkhart County, Ind., branched off from Townline. S.T.E.

Töws, Aron P. (1887- ?), was born at Fürstenau in the Molotchna Mennonite settlement, Russia, on Jan. 28, 1887. He was graduated from the normal school and served as a teacher in the Nikopol district until 1914. In 1917 he became an enthusiastic co-worker in the establishment of a better Russia. He married Maria Sudermann. In 1923 he was active in the AMRA distributing American relief goods. In 1925 he was elected minister of the Chortitza Mennonite Church and ordained. During these critical years he helped the young men of military age and consequently endured many hardships. On Nov. 28, 1934 (1935), he was arrested and placed in the Zaporozhe prison. Later he was sent to Siberia and to various other places. The family last heard from him in 1941. (A. A. Toews,

Mennonitische Märtyrer I, N. Clearbrook, 1949, 79-85.)   C.K.

Töws, Heinrich (d. 1868), was elected minister of the Mennonite church of Lichtenau, Petershagen, Schönsee, Margenau, and Pordenau in 1839. When the Pordenau Mennonite Church (*q.v.*) was organized in 1842 as one of the three congregations emerging from the one church, Heinrich Töws was ordained as its first elder on Sept. 29, 1842. He died in 1868 and was succeeded by Isaak Peters, who migrated to America in 1874. Little else is known about Heinrich Töws and his work. (Friesen, *Brüderschaft*, 706.)   C.K.

Töws, Johann (1805-89), an elder of the Mennonite congregation at Bröskerfelde (*q.v.*), in West Prussia, then in Ladekopp and Pordenau, rendered his brotherhood meritorious services by his vigorous, sympathetic work. In 1836 he took part in the founding of a school (*Vereinsschule*) in Bröskerfelde, contributing the land for the building and grounds. He corresponded with brethren in other countries, especially in Russia. In the *Mennonitische Blätter* he repeatedly replied to the articles by Christian Schmutz of Rappenau (*q.v.*) on mission work, the proposed ministerial training school, and the monument to Menno Simons. (*Menn. Bl.,* 1866, 29; 1867, 46; 1889, 59; *ML* IV.)   NEFF.

Töws, Johann, ordained minister (1832) and elder (1853) in Prussia, joined the immigrants who established the Köppental-Orloff (Trakt) settlement, Samara, Russia. Since the settlement had an elder in Johann Wall (*q.v.*), he functioned as an honorary coelder. He visited the Mennonites of the Molotschna settlement in the Ukraine repeatedly and advocated the founding of the General Mennonite Conference. (See *Allgemeine Mennonitische Bundeskonferenz.*)   C.K.

Friesen, *Brüderschaft*, 719; H. Ediger, *Beschlüsse* . . . *der Konferenzen* (Berdyansk, 1914) p. 1.

Trachselwald, a village and prefecture in the Emmental (*q.v.*), canton of Bern, Switzerland, was as early as 1534 a center of Anabaptist activity. In the fall of 1535 Moritz Rosenegger (*q.v.*) was baptized here, and in spite of the measures of the Bernese officials Anabaptism flourished. In 1551 the Anabaptists were threatened with confiscation of property and even capital punishment if they refused to renounce their faith; sheltering of Anabaptists was punishable by expulsion. In 1640 Trachselwald is named among the villages where there were many "Täufer." Even the Täuferjäger (*q.v.*) of the 1670's were unable to root out Anabaptism. Benedict Brechbühl (Brechbill, *q.v.*), preacher of the congregation from 1699, lived at Trachselwald. Twice he was banished, fled, and returned. In early January 1709 he was arrested at home, imprisoned at Bern, and on March 18, 1710, deported. This was a severe blow for the Trachselwald group, many of whom in the following years left their homeland, emigrating to the Netherlands or the Palatinate. Yet secretly some Anabaptists remained at Trachselwald. In the second half of the 18th century the Bernese government became more tolerant;

the Mennonites lived and worshiped rather freely; they were members of the Emmental (Langnau) congregation. At the census taken in 1823 the following Mennonite families were living in the prefecture of Trachselwald: Peter Kohler, Christian Kohler, Christen Bichsel, Ulrich Reist, Hans Steiner, Peter Steiner, and Peter Lanz; they numbered 25 persons. Ulrich Steiner (*q.v.*), a strong leader of Swiss Brethren in the 19th century, lived at the Hämlismatt near Trachselwald.   vDZ.

Delbert L. Gratz, *Bernese Anabaptists* (Scottdale, 1953) *passim.*

Tracts. Small printed leaflets (*Flugschriften*) have often played an important role in the course of Christian history. They were much used by all parties in the Reformation from Luther to the Anabaptists. Many Anabaptist hymn pamphlets containing one or more martyr hymns were in effect tracts. Tracts used in modern times in England and America in religious work are however commonly very short leaflets, 2-4 pages in length, seldom longer, and small in format, for cheap production, easy distribution, and quick reading. Almost all types of religious denominations and movements in America have used and do use them. They have most widely been used for evangelistic purposes to reach the unchurched or to win adherents to a new cause.

Organizations have been set up for the specific and sole purpose of preparation and distribution of religious tracts, although these "tract societies" have not always limited themselves to the small tracts. The tract societies arose at the turn of the 18th century concomitantly with foreign mission work and Sunday schools and have been closely related to such enterprises. They also often represent lay interest and have flourished among the free churches in England and pietistic circles on the Continent and religiously aroused lay groups everywhere. Some societies only distribute tracts, while others both publish and distribute.

The first tract societies in Europe were the Tract and Colportage Society of Scotland (1793), the Edinburgh Tract Society (1796), the London Religious Tract Society (1799), the Christlicher Verein im Nördlichen Deutschland (1811), and the Wupperthaler Traktatgesellschaft (1814). The Society for Promoting Christian Knowledge (S.P.-C.K.), founded in England in 1698 as a Christian literature society, has also included an important tract department. In the United States the American Tract Society (1825), though preceded by several local tract societies (1808, 1812, 1814), was the first national agency. It has played a very great role in American religious life especially in the 19th century; much of its literature reached Mennonites, especially in the eastern half of the United States, in both the German and English languages, often largely through the Sunday school. This society and many other tract societies have used colporteurs on a large scale to distribute Christian literature, tracts, and booklets, even books and periodicals.

The only organized Mennonite venture in the tract field has been the Mennonite Book and Tract

Society (q.v.), founded largely by a group of laymen in the M.C. group in 1892 and maintained for 16 years, until its work was taken over in 1908 by the newly organized Mennonite Publishing House at Scottdale. The Mennonite Publishing Company at Elkhart (J. F. Funk) also had a tract series, but its output did not match the (at least) 125-tract series put out by the MBTS. The MBTS attempted the publication of a paper called *Book and Tract Messenger,* but only one issue appeared (September 1899), which contained a history of the society and a list of tracts. The MBTS by no means limited itself to tracts, and was in a sense a competitive Mennonite publisher to the Elkhart Mennonite Publishing Company. Its headquarters were usually the office of the treasurer, which was at Elkhart 1892-99, Scottdale 1898-1902, Spring Grove, Pa., 1902-5, and Scottdale again 1905-8.

Tract publication has been a integral part of the work of the Mennonite Publishing House throughout its history. A total of over 500 tract titles have come from its press. All tracts were distributed free for the first 30 years, subsidized by other House operations and donations. In 1908 the Tract Committee was appointed to supervise and promote this work, which served to 1951. Since 1929 there has been a tract editor giving part time to the work. *The Way,* a 4-page (originally 8-page) monthly paper for free distribution, essentially a tract paper, has been published since 1913, with a very large edition (in 1957 at the average rate of 240,000 monthly). It is estimated that some 40 million copies of this paper have been distributed during its 45-year history. A corresponding paper in Spanish, *El Heraldo Evangelico,* has been published since 1941 (since 1946 by the Scottdale House, subsidized by the Elkhart Mission Board). *The Colporteur,* a promotional paper "to encourage and aid tract distributors," was published 1942-50 for a total of 17 issues. Total tract circulation by the House is vast, averaging more than 3 million copies yearly since 1954, with 6 million in 1953. Since about 1938 the tracts have no longer been given free but sold, although there is a free tract fund supported by donations. The House now has some 4,000 tract customers, most of whom are from non-Mennonite circles.

A number of unofficial private tract publishers (MC) have arisen; e.g., Amos Ogburn of Woodburn, Ore., and J. L. Stauffer of Harrisonburg, Va., the latter operating under the firm name of Tract Press.

Tract distribution is largely the work of individuals although it is promoted by a large number of congregations (MC) in addition to missions. Many Sunday-school classes, local Mennonite Youth Fellowships, and individuals regularly distribute tracts on Sunday afternoons and at other times, often on a house to house basis. Many congregations have racks of tracts on constant display in the lobby of the meetinghouse or elsewhere with a steady supply of current tracts. Ralph Palmer of Denbigh, Va., has devoted most of his time for some years to tract distribution, traveling about the country as a "tract missionary."

Until recently the content of the tracts was usually in the area of Christian nurture with major emphasis on social evils such as strong drink, tobacco, amusements, fashion, as well as distinctive Mennonite doctrines such as nonconformity and separation, although evangelistic materials giving the way of salvation were also included. More recently the emphasis is almost exclusively on evangelistic themes and Christian experience.

Tracts are also used in evangelistic and mission work of other American Mennonite groups, but no organized publication or distribution agencies have been established for this purpose. Many tracts are purchased from non-Mennonite agencies.   H.S.B.

John A. Hostetler, *God Uses Ink* (Scottdale, 1958) 65-71, 147-49.

Trades and Trade Regulations of the Hutterian Brethren: see articles *Gemeindeordnungen* and *Economic History* of the Hutterian Brethren. Attention should also be called to a remarkable passage in Riedemann's *Rechenschaft* of 1541, dealing with "Traders" (English ed., 126 f.): "We allow none of our number to do the work of a trader or merchant, since this is a sinful business; as the wise man saith, 'It is almost impossible for a merchant and trader to keep himself from sin. And as a nail sticks fast between door and hinge, so does also sin stick close between buying and selling' (*Ecclus.* 26:29 and 27:1-2) . . . Therefore we permit this not amongst us, but say with Paul that they should work with their hands what is honest, that they may have to give to him that needs."   R.F.

Peter Rideman, *Account of Our Religion* (Bridgnorth, 1950).

Tragheimerweide, a former Mennonite congregation and settlement in West Prussia, Germany, located between Marienburg and Marienwerder. The last great settlement of Mennonites in West Prussia was made in the Stuhm marshes in 1724. The land was chiefly meadow, which the Mennonites now began to cultivate and on which they lived on their scattered individual farms, with cattle and provisions under one roof with the residence. The occasion for the settlement of these marshes was the return of the Mennonites from Lithuania, who had lived there since 1713, but had to leave the Memel Lowlands in 1724 on account of military service.

On Nov. 10, 1724, representatives of the Grosswerder (q.v.) sold two thirds of Tragheimerweide to Salomon Becher and Jacob Jantzen for 2,200 Prussian guilders for the refugees. In the same year 14 hides of Rudnerweide (q.v.) were transferred to Mennonites coming from the Tilsit (q.v.) marshes who were trying to evade Frederick William's recruiters for the "regiment of giants." Other meadow lands (Schweingrube, Zwanzigerweide, Montauerweide, Zieglershuben, Klein-Schardau, and Gross-Schardau) were sold to Mennonites in these years, with the result that in the second quarter of the 18th century a closed Mennonite settlement came into being. The settlers for the most part came from the Montau (q.v.) and Schönsee (q.v.) congregations. In 1728 the Bishop of Culm permitted them to build a meetinghouse. This chapel was enlarged in 1763 and a cemetery laid out. Whereas this church was built in the style of Mennonite frame churches, the new church, built in 1866 on the site of the old one, was built on a Gothic plan in brick. In 1892 the church acquired a good organ. From 1762 the congregation kept records.

The young congregation, belonging to the Frisian (q.v.) branch (called Waterlander in the Dutch *Naamlijst*) and called the Stuhm (q.v.) Lowlands congregation or Schweingrube, went through a severe crisis in its first years (1733-79). When the Frisian congregations in West Prussia at that time wanted to abolish marriages with Catholics and Lutherans, three members of Tragheimerweide living at Rosenkranz set up violent opposition, and with their followers proceeded to choose their own ministers. A conference of Frisian elders meeting at Schweingrube in 1779 prevented a schism. The Rosenkranz group won; mixed marriages were again tolerated in all the Frisian congregations. The village of Tragheimerweide in 1744 was exclusively Mennonite; by 1772, when less farm lands were obtainable, a number of Mennonites earned their living as weavers. This shortage of farm lands also caused a considerable emigration to South Russia in the early 19th century.

The congregation had two subsidiaries—Marienwerder (q.v.) and Zandersfelde (q.v.). About 1820 the old name of the congregation was gradually replaced by "Tragheimerweide." In 1892-1929 it was called Zwanzigerweide because in 1892 the villages of Tragheimerweide and Zwanzigerweide were merged under the name of the latter; in 1929 the name Tragheimerweide was resumed, when for the purposes of incorporation it was necessary to define the geographic limits of the congregation.

In 1807-8 the Tragheimerweide congregation suffered losses by the emigration of several families to South Russia. In 1852 it had a baptized membership of 336; in 1888, 357; 1928, 550 souls; in 1940, 510 souls. The members, mostly farmers, were scattered over 27 villages and two towns in the areas of Stuhm, Marienwerder, and Mewe. It was served by an elder and five preachers and was a member of the Conference of the Mennonites of East and West Prussia. In 1945, as a result of the flight and expulsion of the Germans from this area, the congregation came to an end.

The Dutch *Naamlijst* records the following elders: Peter Tjart before 1740-c55, Hans Ewert 1750-76, Marten Albrecht 1776-c82, Jakob Ewert, preacher 1776, elder 1788-1800, Julius Adrian, preacher 1795, elder 1800-43. In the last 150 years the elders were Jonas Quiring, preacher 1808, elder 1843-60, David Ewert, preacher 1840, elder 1860-1903, David Pauls 1903-9, Franz Ewert of Gr. Schardau 1913-39, Albert Bartel of Unterberg near Rehhof 1940-45. Albert Bartel was in 1958 the elder of the refugee congregation at Bremen, but lived at Espelkamp.

H.P., vDZ.

Menn. Bl., 1866, 1892, 1928, 1929; B. Ewert, "Geschichtliches aus der Mennonitengemeinde Heubuden-Marienburg," *Gem.-Kal.*, 1940, 48 ff.; Herbert Wiebe, *Das Siedlungswerk niederländischer Mennoniten im Weichseltal ...* (Marburg, 1952) 40, 42, 85; Dutch *Naamlijst*; *Namensverzeichnis* (Elbing, 1843) 23; *Namens-Verzeichnis* 1857 (Danzig, 1857) 14; Mannhardt, *Jahrbuch* 1882, 17, 19; 1888, 14; *ML* IV.

Trail of the Conestoga, The (Toronto, 1924 and 1942), a novel written by B. Mabel Dunham, for many years librarian of the Kitchener (Ont.) Public Library and writer of historical fiction, who was of Mennonite descent. The novel sketches the pioneer trek of Mennonites from Pennsylvania to make the settlement in Waterloo County, Ont., and pictures the motives, the difficulties, and also the rewards of this Mennonite pioneering venture. The leading characters, Benjamin Eby, Joseph Sherk, and Sam Bricker, are well portrayed.

Miss Dunham wrote a sequel to *The Trail of the Conestoga* in *Toward Sodom*, which follows the religious careers of the children of the Horst family in the early Waterloo settlement, as they, all but one, leave the faith of their fathers to join other churches or none at all. All of them, however, make outstanding contributions to church and society. In both novels Mennonite life is sympathetically portrayed. (See **Literature**, ME III, 372.)

E.H.B.

J. Boyd Cressman, Review of *The Trail of the Conestoga* and *Toward Sodom*, *MQR* III (1930); Elizabeth H. Bender, "The Mennonite Theme in Contemporary American Fiction," *Proceedings of the Fourth . . . Conference . . . on Cultural Problems* (North Newton, 1945).

Trakt Mennonite Church, also known as the Köppental-Orloff Mennonite Church, was organized in the Trakt Mennonite settlement (q.v.) in 1853. The first elder was Johann Wall (q.v.), succeeded by David Hamm (q.v.) in 1858, and by Johannes Quiring (q.v.) in 1884. In 1905 the total number of souls in the church was 1,535, of whom 361 did not live within the settlement proper, with 775 baptized members, of whom 200 lived outside the settlement. In addition to the elder, the following served the congregation as ministers: Peter Wiens, Peter Bergmann, Hermann Neufeld, Jakob Bergmann, Johann Toews, and Heinrich Neufeld. P. M. Friesen lists also Cornelius Fröse, J. J. Epp, Isaac Epp, Johannes Janzen, Aron Wiebe, Jakob Quiring. In 1913 Peter J. Dyck was listed as leading minister. Another source states that Peter Wiens succeeded Johannes Quiring when he died in 1912. Elder Hamm was

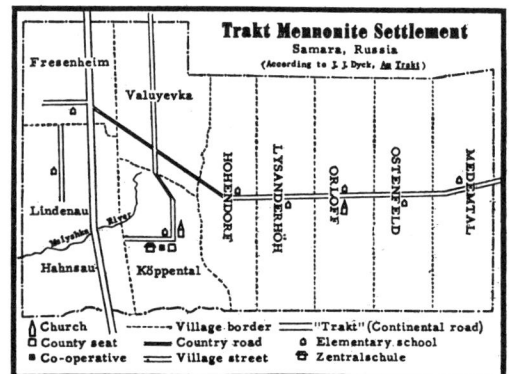

Trakt Mennonite Settlement
Samara, Russia
(According to J. J. Dyck, *Am Trakt*)

Fresenheim
Valuyevka
HOHENDORF
LYSANDERHÖH
ORLOFF
OSTENFELD
MEDENTAL
Lindenau
Hahnsau
Köppental

Church — Village border ═══ "Trakt" (Continental road)
County seat — Country road ⌂ Elementary school
Co-operative ═ Village street ✚ Zentralschule

instrumental in organizing the Allgemeine Bundes-konferenz (*q.v.*).

While Hamm was elder (1880) the congregation went through a crisis caused by Classz Epp Jr. (*q.v.*), who, under the influence of some chiliastic writings and because of the introduction of universal military conscription, sought with a group of followers a place of refuge in Central Asia (*q.v.*). Particularly the village of Hahnsau (*q.v.*) was involved in this movement.

The congregation had two meetinghouses, one in Köppental (erected in 1866) and the other in Orloff. In 1900-12, under the eldership of P. Wiens, Mennonite Brethren evangelists visited the settlement and organized an M.B. congregation, about which little information is available. In the early days there was a Hahnsau and Popovka M.B. Church (*q.v.*), which was discontinued. Under the Soviet government the congregation went through a trying period similar to that of other settlements. During this time Cornelius Nikkel was elder, assisted by the ministers Julius Siebert, Jakob Penner, and Franz Quiring, who was especially successful with the young people. In 1927 Nikkel and Quiring were exiled. The leaders helped the young men of conscription age to be freed from military service. Religious activities were gradually made impossible, and in 1941 when Hitler invaded the Ukraine, all settlers were exiled, primarily to Asiatic Russia.   C.K.

H. Dirks, *Statistik*, 1905, pp. 25, 63; Friesen, *Brüder-schaft*, pp. 129-31, 719; *Am Trakt. Eine mennonitische Kolonie im mittleren Wolgagebiet* (North Kildonan, 1948).

Trakt Mennonite Settlement, formerly located in the province of Samara (*q.v.*) (now Kuibyshev) on the Volga River, Soviet Russia, was established by Mennonites from Prussia in 1853. When, in 1847, Prussia passed a conscription law, Claas Epp Sr. and Johann Wall (*q.v.*) were delegated to investigate settlement possibilities in Russia. The Russian government granted the application for 100 Mennonite families of Prussia to settle in Russia, under the condition that each family make a down payment of 350 talers to the Russian embassy in Berlin, which was to be repaid after settlement, deducting expenses incurred by the government in connection with it. The settlers were to be model farmers for the surrounding population, and were promised free exemption from military service for 20 years, after which time they were expected to pay taxes for the exemption. Every family received 160 acres of land.

The first 22 families under the leadership of Epp and Wall left Prussia in the fall of 1853. They spent some time in the Molotschna settlement until the delegates had located the land for settlement, which was located near the Tarlyka River and its tributary, the Malyshevka, on a tract of land used as a road to haul salt (*Salztrakt*) with sufficient pasture land. In the fall of 1853 the first nine families, coming directly from Prussia, arrived and stayed over winter in the village of Privolynaya. In the spring they established Hahnsau (*q.v.*). Köppental (*q.v.*) was founded in 1855. By 1880 all 10 villages had been established: Hahnsau, Köppental, Lindenau, Fresen-

heim, Hohendorf, Lysanderhöh, Orloff, Valuyevka, Ostenfeld, and Medemtal.

TRAKT MENNONITE SETTLEMENT, 1897

Village	Year of Settlement	No. of Families	Population, 1897
1. Hahnsau	1854		
Settlers moved to Central Asia in 1880-81.			
2. Köppental	1855	36	201
3. Lindenau	1856-59	26	174
4. Fresenheim	1856-59	21	103
5. Hohendorf	1862	18	96
6. Lysanderhöh	1864	22	119
7. Orloff	1871	17	80
8. Valuyevka	1875	8	57
9. Ostenfeld	1872	19	127
10. Medemtal	1872	30	219
		197	1176

The settlement consisted of 37,800 acres. The settlers of Hahnsau and some of the other villages moved to Central Asia (*q.v.*) in 1880-81, under the leadership of Classz Epp Jr. (*q.v.*). The village pattern deviated somewhat from that of the Mennonite villages of the Ukraine. Because the farmers who settled here brought some money, the settlement prospered economically, although the soil was not quite as good as in the Ukraine and in spite of periods of drought. They raised primarily wheat and rye, although barley, oats, and other crops were common. Later they became expert in selecting the most suitable seeds for the territory. Studies of their achievements were made repeatedly by Russian writers even after the Revolution. Their agricultural machinery was in part imported and in part made in local Mennonite factories. Especially well known was the Epp factory of Köppental. The Mennonites also became known for their breeds of horses and cattle.

Culturally the Mennonites of the Trakt settlement developed rapidly. They established elementary schools, and many of their youth attended secondary schools in the Ukraine. Before World War I they established a secondary school at Köppental. They had a mutual aid treasury, fire and theft insurance, as well as accident insurance. The settlement had its own administration. The two outstanding Oberschulzen, Johann D. Dyck (1866-84) and Johann Bergmann (1884-96), made outstanding contributions to the economic and cultural progress, achieved particularly in 1900-14. In 1908 a cheese factory was established. In 1910 an agricultural association was founded which sponsored an agricultural fair in 1913, and the educational system was improved. Five thousand additional acres were purchased for young couples.

At the outbreak of World War I the young Mennonite men were drafted and served in the zemstvo organization in hospital work. The families who lost their breadwinners were remunerated by the settlement. When the Volga Autonomous Soviet Socialist Republic (*q.v.*) was organized in 1924, the Trakt Mennonite settlement became a part of this Republic. D. J. Klassen and J. J. Dyck represented the Mennonites for a time in the legislature. During the period of drought and starvation, the Mennonites of the settlement as well as the population in general were helped by the MCC, represented by C. F. Klassen (*q.v.*) and Peter Fröse (*q.v.*)

After the hardships of the trying years, the agricultural life of the Mennonite settlement was revived during 1923-27. The Malyshevka Agricultural Association was organized in 1923, which specialized in the selection of seeds and making them available far beyond the settlement. The land of the Mennonite settlement was distributed according to the size of the family and the available agricultural machinery. The settlement took an active part in the efforts of the Allrussischer Mennonitischer Landwirtschaftlicher Verein (*q.v.*). Johann L. Penner was the first chairman of the district council after the Revolution; he was succeeded by A. A. Fröse. The young men of military age were at this time freed from military service, after the sincerity of their religious conviction had been examined.

Some Mennonites emigrated to Canada. By 1927 there was a trend toward a more radical Communist program. Around 1929 the settlement had a Mennonite population of about 2,000. Many of the Mennonite leaders were exiled at this time and later just as in the other Mennonite settlements. When Hitler invaded Russia, the Volga Republic was automatically dissolved and most of the population exiled to Asiatic Russia, thus ending the Trakt Mennonite settlement.   C.K.

Am Trakt. Eine mennonitische Kolonie im mittleren Wolgagebiet (North Kildonan, 1948); Lothar König, *Die Deutschtumsinel an der Wolga* (Dülmen, 1938; ML IV, 352.

Transylvania (German, *Siebenbürgen*), a country in Eastern Europe, which from 1621 to 1767 gave asylum to the Hutterian Brethren. Two thirds of the country is surrounded by the crescent of the densely wooded Carpathian Mountains. During the 16th and 17th centuries it was a semi-independent principality, larger than today's Rumanian province of Transylvania, as it then included a large section of Hungary. The population is mainly Rumanian, in religion Greek Orthodox; in the South, however, where the Brethren settled, there existed until 1945 a large German minority, the Transylvanian Saxons, who had since the 16th century been staunch Lutherans. In the North the population is mainly Magyar (Hungarian), traditionally attached to the Calvinist faith, while a certain Hungarian minority, the Szeklers, adopted the strict Socinian (Unitarian) faith. Only after 1691, when the country became part of the Hapsburg empire, did those who were dependent on the Hapsburg dynasty embrace the Catholic faith. Thus there were five very different religions, to which as a sixth religion is to be added the Anabaptist faith of the Hutterites. Until 1919 it belonged to Hungary and thereafter to Rumania.

After 1550 (when the Turks undisputedly dominated Eastern Europe), Transylvania became a principality tributary to Turkey. Both Turks and Hapsburgs tried to have a hand in the politics of that country; only after 1691 Turkey lost its influence there. The Hutterite Chronicle shows a real interest in Transylvania, in the first place because its princes made war against Austria together with the Turks (*c*1600) and thus brought great misery to the Slovakian and Moravian Bruderhofs (see **Böger**). At that time Stephan Bocskay (*q.v.*) was the ruler. He was succeeded by the prince Bethlen Gabor (*q.v.*, Gabriel Bethlem), 1613-29, who ended the war and brought glory and prosperity to his country. It was he—as the Chronicle reports in detail—who brought the Hutterites to Transylvania (to its southern part) to stimulate agriculture. He promised them full religious liberty besides many other privileges. In 1621 a group of 185 Brethren left Slovakia under the leadership of the preacher Franz Walter (see **Walter** family). This exodus is described in great detail in a song in the *Lieder der Hutterischen Brüder* 827-35, called a "Klagelied," of not less than 67 stanzas, the first word of each stanza together forming a remarkable acrostic. In 1622 Prince Bethlen gave the Brethren a charter and in 1625 an even more comprehensive Letter of Protection (or Privilege), published by Zieglschmid in 1940. Had it not been for exposure to a number of Turkish Wars, life would not have been too hard in Transylvania; the land was fertile and persecution was unknown until the time of the Empress Maria Theresa and the work of the Jesuits (after 1750).

The Hutterian Brethren settled first at Alwinz (*q.v.*, Alwinc). The real difficulties there were the lack of effective leadership and their isolation from other Brethren (the Turks, ruling in Hungary, were a block interposed between Slovakia and Transylvania). Johannes Waldner in his *Klein-Geschichtsbuch* lists the Vorstehers of Alvinc in 1621-68 (p. 193); hereafter the community began to decline and by 1690 communal life was being abandoned. In 1694 one of the Hutterite preachers and elders, Georg Geissy, turned Unitarian, a unique case, which brought great distress to the group, for it was now leaderless. The Brethren in Slovakia thereupon dispatched Johann Roth to re-establish the old order, but the former prosperity was gone for good. By 1750 no more than 19 souls had survived (the Kuhr, Zeterle, Stahl, and Wipf families).

See the articles **Carinthia** and **Alwinc** for an account of the nearly miraculous revival of this brotherhood by the Carinthian transmigrants of 1756 ff. Two more Bruderhofs were established in Kreuz and in Stein, two villages not far from Alvinc (1761-67). But the relentless schemes of the Jesuits (above all of Father Delpini) ruined all these hopes. In 1767, when the Brethren could see no chance of living in peace, they risked their great exodus across the mountains into Rumanian Walachia. It was an epic in itself to cross the steep, wooded pass by night, with children, sick, and lame. (See description in the *Klein-Geschichtsbuch*, Waldner himself having been part of the group.) Twenty-two families, however, stayed behind, of which three are still living there today. When, in 1937, two American Hutterites visited the place, they met a certain Joseph Kuhr, who knew all about them by family tradition even though nothing of the old organization had remained. Until World War II certain common patterns had been preserved and the group lived segregated as a unit. The visitors saw also the old church-fortress (Lutheran) where the brethren used to seek refuge in times of war. Also old books were said to be around but could not be seen. As to pottery, some jars, etc., made by their forefathers, were even for sale.

In none of the literature is mention made of another Bruderhof in Transylvania, which existed scarcely more than 17 years, but whose influence was felt long after. This was the Hof in Saros-Patak in the northern Magyar section. Its lot was an unhappy one. After the death of Bethlen Gabor, George I Rakoczy, a Calvinist, became the Prince of Transylvania (1631-48). He also wanted some Hutterite Brethren in his country, and thus sent a message to Slovakia (then belonging to Hapsburg Hungary) demanding such an establishment near his estate and threatening to use force if the Brethren refused to come voluntarily. Then a group of Brethren from Tschäskowitz (Castkovec) very reluctantly moved to the new place (1645) which in the Chronicle is named Bodtok (q.v.; Magyar, Saros-Patak), situated on the river Theiss several miles north of the famous wine estate of Tokay. George II Rakoczy (1648-60) likewise patronized the Brethren, mainly because of their lovely fayence work (see **Ceramics**). The pottery produced in Patak was in great demand among the Hungarian nobles, and exquisite bowls, jars, plates, etc., of this shop are still to be seen in museums and private collections. The next Rakoczy, Francis I, turned Catholic in 1662, and the Bruderhof came to an abrupt end. He called in Jesuits, and most of the Brethren left the Hof, most likely for Slovakia. Some, however, remained and turned Catholic (now called Habaner), and continued their craft for perhaps another century. Some Magyarized their names; at least one former Hutterite by the name of Odler (once Adler) was knighted for his artistic work (see **Habaner**).

The Hutterites left Transylvania, but many of their most precious books had already been confiscated. Today these codices are found in two university libraries: Alba Iulia (formerly Weissenburg; library of the Batthyaneum), holding not less than 18 codices, and Cluj (formerly Klausenburg), with one codex. Two of these codices are extremely old, dated 1587 and 1596; the rest are of the 17th century. Four of these codices contain Hutterite chronicles of varying origin, four are collections of epistles and tracts, two are hymnals, four contain dogmatic tracts, two contain pedagogical writings, and two contain Bible exegesis, probably used for sermons. As far as is known these books have not been studied by any scholar. Nor did the two visiting Hutterites of 1937 succeed in seeing them.

In the 16th century some Transylvanian noblemen gave refuge to learned Unitarians, one of whom was Franz Davidis (d. 1579). He was the leader of a group of left-wing Unitarians called Non-Adorantes because they refused to adore Jesus Christ as God. Davidis found followers among the many dissidents, who were descendants of medieval heretics like the Bogomiles. Some of them rejected infant baptism and practiced adult baptism on confession of faith. In 1567 Fausto Sozzini (q.v.) came

to Transylvania to fight the Davidist group, but was not very successful. In the 18th century Transylvanian Unitarianism was oppressed by the imperial magistrates, but did not disappear.   R.F.

Zieglschmid, *Chronik; idem, Klein-Geschichtsbuch;* E. Nowotny, *Die Transmigration ober- und inner-österreichischer Protestanten nach Siebenbürgen im 18. Jahrhundert* (Schriften des Instituts für Grenz- und Auslandsdeutschtum an der Univ. Marburg VIII, Jena, 1931); R. Friedmann, "Hutterites Revisit Their Old Places in Europe; From the Travel Diary of David Hofer, 1937," *MQR* XXXIII (1959); *idem,* "Anabaptist Pottery Called Haban Fayences," *Menn. Life* XIII (1958); A. J. F. Zieglschmid, "Die ungarischen Wiedertäufer," *Ztscht für Kirchengesch.,* 1940, 363, note 47 (*Schutzbrief Bethlen Gabors,* 1625); *Lieder der Hutterischen Brüder* (Scottdale, 1914) 827-35. The Diaries of the Jesuit P. Delpini, which contain most valuable information about his work in Alvinc, are in the Studienbibliothek of Hermannstadt (Sibiu), but have not yet been published. They would greatly increase our knowledge of those critical years after 1760. For further literature see "Alwinz." The description of the Codices is to be found in remote specialized literature. A complete catalog is in preparation by Robert Friedmann.

Trappe, George von, a Russian government official who under Potemkin (q.v.) and Catherine II of Russia was charged with the responsibility of inviting German settlers to the Ukraine. He was particularly assigned the task of winning and helping the Mennonites of Danzig along these lines and became the director of the Mennonite settlement program. In August 1786 he contacted Peter Epp, elder of the Danzig Mennonite Church, who was very much interested in the invitation. Trappe prepared a leaflet for distribution among the Mennonites of the Danzig Mennonite Church. He was very successful in influencing prospective settlers and made arrangements for a delegation to inspect the Ukraine.

Trappe was interested in the religious unity of the settlers as a prerequisite for the success of his work as director of the Mennonite settlements. On his way to England he stopped in the Netherlands in the summer of 1788 where he visited the Mennonites of Amsterdam, Haarlem, and Harlingen, including H. Oosterbaan, moderator of the Friesland Mennonite Conference (Sociëteit). He presented to them his concern pertaining to the divisions among the Mennonites of Danzig and Prussia into the Flemish and Frisian groups, including the problem of mixed marriages, and found that the Dutch Mennonites had overcome the negative results of this separation. They complied with his request and wrote to their brethren in Danzig, particularly those who were interested in settling in Russia. J. C. Sepp of the Old Flemish Mennonite Church of Amsterdam wrote a letter, dated May 15, 1788, in behalf of the church addressed to the elders and ministers of the Danzig churches. A similar longer letter was written and printed as a result of a conference of Mennonites in Leeuwarden on July 31, 1788, which was entitled *Missive van de Sociëteit der Doopsgezinde gemeenten in Vriesland en Groningen . . . (q.v.).* The concern expressed was that there should be no banning of members marrying from the Frisian into the Flemish group or vice versa. It is an interesting note that von Trappe and the Russian government were vitally interested in the unity of the Mennonite settlers, and shows some of the great difficulties which the settlers would encounter. It is not clear what von Trappe's role was when the pioneer settlers of Chortitza later were actually torn by strife and lacked leadership. (See also **Russia** and **Chortitza**.)   vDZ., C.K.

D. H. Epp, *Die Chortitzer Mennoniten* (Odessa, 1889) pp. 1-63; Blaupot t. C., *Friesland*, 354-63; see also 227 f. and *DB* 1862, 119 f.; *Menn. Life* VI (April 1951) 37.

Trappers, Adriaen Pier, an Anabaptist martyr: see **Adriaen Pietersz.**

Trappstadt, a rural Mennonite congregation located in the northern tip of Bavaria, Germany, near the East Zone border, founded c1800 by families coming from northern Baden, a member of the Verband (*q.v.*) conference. The ministers in 1957 were Emil Heer (ord. 1927), Heinrich Funck (1948), and Kurt Baer (1954); the baptized membership was 49. (*ML* IV, 352.)   H.S.B.

Trechsel, Ulrich (Hans), an Anabaptist of Augsburg, was sent to the Palatinate with Peter Scheppach (*q.v.*) by the Martyrs' Synod (*q.v.*) in 1527. In 1527-28 he was named among the Anabaptists in Strasbourg.   HEGE, G.H.

TA Württemberg; Ludwig Keller, *Die Reformation und die älteren Reformparteien* (Leipzig, 1885); Friedrich Roth, *Augsburger Reformationsgeschichte* I (Munich, 1901) 263, note 70; *ML* IV.

Trementina (New Mexico) Church of God in Christ, Mennonite Spanish Mission, now extinct, was organized in 1944 through the efforts of the Western District Mission Board and other workers. In 1945 it became a General Mission project. Jake Dirksen was its first pastor and superintendent. In 1948 Jaun Estrada was ordained as minister and became the presiding pastor. At that time the membership was 14 and the Sunday-school enrollment 24. Both the Spanish and the English languages were used in the Sunday school and worship services. It became extinct in 1952 when the last members moved to Tucumcari, a city near by. E.F.H.

Trenque Lauquen (Argentina) Mennonite Church (MC). In August 1920 approximately a year and a half after the beginning of mission work in Pehuajó, Argentina, J. W. Shank and T. K. Hershey visited Trenque Lauquen, situated 50 miles southwest of Pehuajó, and about 300 miles southwest of Buenos Aires. The Shank family moved to Trenque Lauquen on Sept. 7, 1920, but illness in the family postponed the formal opening until November 27. At this time Albano Luayza, an experienced Argentine pastor, was secured for evangelistic meetings, and on May 19, 1921, the first four members were received into the church by baptism. By the end of the second year there were about 20 members in this congregation.

Anita Cavadore from Pehuajó arrived in Trenque Lauquen in 1921 as a worker and Bible reader. On Feb. 12-13, 1923, the first conference of the Mennonite Church in Argentina was held in Trenque Lauquen. This gathering, added to the coming of the Orphanage in 1927 and the Printery in 1928, lent stability to the work. Certainly the kinder-

garten played a major role in winning the sympathy and in some cases the active support of the business and professional classes of the city. The economic status of the members has risen; about 85 per cent of the 96 members now own their homes. Carmen Palomeque, a member of the congregation, translated the Bender-Horsch book on Menno Simons into Spanish, which has been published jointly by the Mennonite Printery and the Methodist publishing house at Buenos Aires (1943). This is still the only book in Spanish on Mennonite history.

The T. K. Hershey family was located in Trenque Lauquen 1928-46, followed by the William Hallman family 1946-53, and the Frank Byler family 1953-58.

In 1952 there were significant organizational changes, placing a large number of laymen in all departments of the church activity and the weekly appointments in the neighboring town of Paso. In 1954 the first deacon in the history of the Mennonite Church of Argentina, José Ibarzabal, was elected by the congregation and Pedro Strucchi was consecrated as the assistant pastor.

The institutions located in Trenque Lauquen have included (1) the orphanage 1927-34, with Selena Gamber, Vera Hallman, Elvin Snyder, and Mary F. Snyder; (2) the printery 1928-55, with Juan Battaglia in charge 1928-55; and (3) the campground 1945- . The significance of the campground to the local congregation cannot be overemphasized, since practically all the summer activities of the church as a whole, such as the Annual Conference and Young People's Retreat, are held there. In 1957 the membership was 86, and the pastor was Ernesto Suarez.   W.E.HA.

La Voz Menonita, February 1940; Shank, Hershey, *et al., The Gospel Under the Southern Cross* (Scottdale, 1943).

Tres Lomas (Argentina) Mennonite Church (MC), located at Tres Lomas, F.C.O., province of Buenos Aires, about 325 miles west of the city of Buenos Aires. Work was started in Tres Lomas (pop. 4,000) on May 1, 1925, by Amos Swartzentruber and wife and a congregation was organized by the end of the same year. It was considered a rather receptive town from the very first, probably because there was no Catholic church here. During the first five years 47 were received into the church by baptism and the 1957 membership was 43. The Swartzentrubers lived here from April 1925 until June 1934. The first Roman Catholic church was built here in 1940.   A.Sw.

Tressler Mennonite Church (MC) is located near Greenwood, Del. The settlement of Mennonites in this area was begun in 1914, when a number of Mennonite and Conservative Amish Mennonite families moved into this section from the region of Grantsville, Md. The two groups worshiped together for some time, meeting in homes and barns, under the leadership of the Amish. After some years the Mennonite group began to meet separately under lay leadership. In 1935 the group was organized into a congregation by J. A. Ressler, Scottdale, Pa., a bishop of the Southwestern Pennsylvania (now Allegheny) Mennonite Conference. This seemed to be the logical connection, since most of the people came from this conference area. A school building and ground were donated to the church by the heirs of William Tressler. An addition to this building, bringing the size to 28 x 60 ft., was made in 1954. The first bishop in charge was J. A. Ressler, and the first minister to serve the congregation was W. C. Hershberger, formerly of near Johnstown, Pa. The membership in 1957 was 30 with Walter Campbell as pastor and Paul M. Lederach as bishop.

J.L.H.

Trevose Heights Mennonite Church (MC), a member of the Franconia Conference, is an outpost of the Doylestown Mennonite Church. It is located about 17 miles east of Doylestown, Pa. The work was started with a summer Bible school in 1945; a church building to seat 150 was dedicated on June 16, 1946. Twelve members from the Doylestown congregation made up the worker force. The membership in 1957 was 40, 13 of whom were of non-Mennonite origin. Paul W. Histand was the first appointed superintendent, ordained as minister by lot on April 4, 1948. The next year the congregation was organized and has supported other mission work as well. In 1958 "Heights" was dropped from the name. The Trevose congregation has served as a center for young men in I-W service at the Philadelphia State Hospital; at its height (1957) the I-W group numbered 70. This is a rapidly growing urban area.

P.W.Hı.

Treyer: see also **Dreier** and **Troyer.**

Treyer, Jakob, an Anabaptist of Laufen, Switzerland, near Basel, was put in neck irons in Basel (torture) with Konrad Winkler (q.v.) of Zürich in 1529 because of their steadfastness in the faith. "In the consciousness that they were suffering as martyrs they endured the most degrading corporal punishments . . . cheerfully. Winkler and Treyer stood laughing in the market place in neck irons and one of them preached concerning repentance and the new life to the assembled crowd of spectators. When the executioner then whipped them out of the city, they challenged him to do his duty well, for they gladly suffered for Christ's sake" (Burkhardt). Early in February 1530 Jakob Treyer was sentenced to death by beheading. But in the face of death his steadfastness forsook him; he cast himself at the feet of his judges and begged for mercy, promising to recant and submit to anything. Oecolampadius had assured him in prison that if he recanted he would be shown mercy and promised to intercede for him. He did so, and Treyer was pardoned.

S.G.

Paul Burkhardt, *Die Basler Täufer* (Basel, 1898); *ML* III.

Treytorrens, Nicolas Samuel de, of an outstanding French Swiss family, living in the early 18th century at Eudresin near Neuchâtel, Switzerland, was active in behalf of the oppressed Bernese Mennonites, particularly those who had been deported to serve on the Sicilian galleys (q.v.). The Amsterdam Mennonite archives contain two letters sent by him to the Dutch Mennonite Committee of Foreign Needs at Amsterdam, the first one undated, the other

dated Nov. 15, 1715, and also copies of some of his letters to the preacher Goossen Goyen (q.v.) at Crefeld and to Colonel Hackbrett at Bern, giving information on his efforts to liberate the Mennonite prisoners who were at Palermo, Sicily. He succeeded in having them released and even made a trip to Nice in France to gather these galley slaves. He joyfully paid the considerable expense of their return to Switzerland.

With the Bernese authorities he was at first on good terms and they assisted him in this undertaking by sending letters to the King of Sicily; but in early November 1715, when de Treytorrens visited some 40 Mennonites in prison at Bern and pleaded with the Bernese officials for their release, he was himself arrested, and after a few days released upon paying of a considerable fine. Charged with heresy, he was banished forever from the territory of Bern. (*Inv. Arch. Amst.* I, Nos. 1375-84; Müller, *Berner Täufer,* 228 f.)

vDZ.

Tricht, Jan van, an Anabaptist preacher and martyr: see **Jan Smeitgen.**

Trijn (Tryn), Harmen Thys huysvrouwe, a Dutch Anabaptist arrested April 7, 1535, at the recapture of the Oldeklooster (q.v.). She was drowned at Leeuwarden, Friesland, on April 14, 1535. (K. Vos, *Menno Simons,* Leiden, 1914, 229.)

vDZ.

Trijn Jacobs, an Anabaptist martyr, a widow from Balk in Friesland, was drowned on Nov. 22, 1555, at Leeuwarden, Netherlands, because she "had a low estimation of the sacred sacraments."

vDZ.

J. Reitsma, *Honderd jaren uit de Geschiedenis der Hervorming . . . in Friesland* (Leeuwarden, 1876) 63.

Trijn Jans, an Anabaptist martyr, drowned at Amsterdam, Holland, on May 15, 1535, with nine other victims. She was native of Monnikendam in the Dutch province of North Holland. During the trial on March 1 she related that she had been baptized at Emden, East Friesland, by Melchior (probably Melchior Hofmann, q.v.) and that her husband was executed at Zwolle.

vDZ.

Mart. Mir. D 413, E 764, where the full sentence pronounced on May 15 is found; Grosheide, *Verhooren,* 58; Mellink, *Wederdopers,* 39, 144, 163.

Trijn Jansdochter, an Anabaptist martyr, executed at Amsterdam on May 21, 1535. Trijn was the wife of Jan de Backer and lived on the Pijlsteeg at Amsterdam. In early November 1534 she had been baptized by Jan Matthijs van Middelburg. The rebel Anabaptists who besieged the Amsterdam town hall on May 10-11, 1535, had gathered in her house before going out to attack. Though it is not expressly stated, Trijn may have shared their revolutionary views. She was sentenced to be strangled and to be hanged before her own home.

vDZ.

Grosheide, *Verhooren,* 66; idem, *Bijdrage,* 61, 305; Mellink, *Wederdopers,* 144, 145, 149.

Trijn Pietersdochter, an Anabaptist martyr, drowned at The Hague, Holland, March 18, 1536. She belonged to the revolutionary wing of Anabaptism; on Dec. 31, 1535, she partook in a disturbance at Hazerswoude (q.v.) and during the riot of Poeldijk (q.v.) she was apprehended. (*Inv. Arch. Amst.* I, No. 745; Mellink, *Wederdopers,* 172.)   vDZ.

Trijn(e) (Catharina) **Amkers,** an Anabaptist martyr, who was executed in 1534 (not 1542, as in van Braght, *Mart. Mir.*). Neither the exact date nor the place of execution could be ascertained. Trijn was a native of Krommeniedijk in the Dutch province of North Holland. (*Mart. Mir.* D 62, E 464; *DB* 1917, 170; *ML* I, 56 f.)   vDZ.

Trijnken Keuts (Kuets), an Anabaptist martyr, burned at the stake on March 11, 1559, at Maastricht, Dutch province of Limburg. Her official name was Cathryn Kuesen, wife of Vaes (Servaes) van Kan. She was a God-fearing woman, one of the noblest of the Anabaptist martyrs. About Sept. 16, 1558, she was summoned to appear before the burgomasters of Maastricht. She did not know that a charge of heresy had been lodged against her. Of her own free will—she would probably have been able to escape and to save her life—she entered the Landscroon (seat of the justice of the town). After her frank confession there was no more hope for freedom. At first she was held in the Landscroon, but on Oct. 7 imprisoned in the official prison of Gevangenpoort. Several times she was tried and tortured. She confessed that she had come to the knowledge of truth, which she was eager to serve by a pious life. She had left "the idols of the pope" and thankfully received the baptism on her faith. She rejected the doctrines of the Catholic church: Christ is in heaven, "how could He come into the bread (host)?" The bailiff of the town, Van Eynatten, was unusually kind to her; probably she would have been less severely punished if the imperial chancellor had not insisted on her death.

Catholic priests and theologians tried to make her recant, but in vain. Even the pastor Chimarrheus of Sittard, renowned for his eloquence and especially invited to convert her, had no success. The priests threatened her with everlasting pains in hell. But Trijnken answered, "When you follow me before the judgment seat of God, you will find it to be otherwise!" For 155 days she had to stay in prison, the costs of each day being two pennies, to be paid to the warden for lodging and food. Pastor Chimarrheus received one and a half crowns and a good dinner; the prior of the Dominican cloister also received his remuneration.

On the evening before Palm Sunday Trijnken died. She was conducted to the execution place on the Vrijthof square by soldiers and monks and a large crowd. She was eager to give a testimony, but it was impossible; her mouth was stopped with a gag. Valiantly suffering she joyfully "put off her tabernacle," being burned to ashes.

In her trial she neither spoke of her family nor of the congregation. The sentence reveals that she was a widow. Bax relates that at the moment of her execution the town council deliberated on a boy of twelve years, "being the child of an Anabaptist," who was then imprisoned at the Landscroon. It was decided that the boy should receive ordinary baptism in a Catholic church and then be sent back to his relatives. Was this boy the son of Trijnken?

Bax thinks so. The torture Trijnken had to endure was obviously employed to get information concerning the Maastricht Mennonite congregation, but Trijnken neither named the man who had baptized her nor indicated the members of the church. The Maastricht (*q.v.*) congregation must then have been very small. Half a year after Trijnken's death another member of this congregation, the preacher Jan (*q.v.*) Bosch van (den) Berghe, was put to death.   vDZ.

Mart. Mir. D 244, E 617 f.; W. Bax, *Het Protestantisme in het Bisdom Luik . . .* II (The Hague, 1941) 47-50, 52 note 1; idem, "Twee Doopersche Martelaren in Maastricht 1559," in *DJ* 1939, 53-62; *ML* II, 486.

Trijntgen, the wife of Huybert op der Straeten: see **Huybert.**

Trijntgen (Trijntje, Catharina), the daughter of Lyntgen Joris, an Anabaptist martyr, was one of the twelve persons, six men and six women, executed by the Spaniards in 1571 at Deventer in the Dutch province of Overijssel. They were arrested on March 3, 1571. After a period of imprisonment and trials, two men were executed on May 14, a few days later two men and four women were put to death, and finally on June 16 the remaining two men and Lyntgen and her daughter Trijntgen. They had told Trijntgen that her mother had recanted. Trijntgen had no opportunity to verify this information because in prison they were separated. Now seeing her mother on the scaffold to be burned at the stake, she knew they had told her a lie to make her forsake her faith. She was glad to see her mother firm in the faith and she herself too died faithful. While each was bound to a stake and the servants of the executioner were arranging the firewood around them Trijntgen and her mother cheerfully nodded each to another, and also to the bystanders, among whom there were probably many friends and members of the congregation. (*Mart. Mir.* D 552-54, E 885 ff.; *DB* 1919, 29-37; *ML* II, 435.)   vDZ.

Trijntgen Jan Pannebackersdochter, an Anabaptist martyr, was drowned at Utrecht, Netherlands, on July 1, 1569. She was the wife of Ernst (*q.v.*) Kerstenzoon, who was executed on the same day by burning at the stake.   vDZ.

I. M. J. Hoog, "Onze Martelaren," in *Ned. Archief voor Kerkgeschiedenis* I (1902) No. 174; *DB* 1903, 5.

Trijntje Dircxd., of Dorsten, an Anabaptist martyr, sentenced at Amsterdam on Jan. 15, 1550, to death by drowning. She was the wife of Peter Jansen, and according to her confession had been (re)baptized by Elder Gillis (*q.v.*) van Aken. In the account of the city treasurer of Amsterdam there is the note that on Jan. 17, 1550, Anna van Dorsten and Anna Boens were "executed with water," and also that Floris Engelbrechts was paid 19 schellingen (about two dollars) for converting these two women and for confessing them. If Anna van Dorsten is an error for Trijntje van Dorsten, this woman and Anna Boens (in *ME* I, 125, listed as Anneken Boens) recanted. The matter is not quite clear, however, since it is also possible that the Anna van Dorsten of the treasurer's account is identical with

Anneken Gerytsdochter van Dordrecht, and Anna Boens with Leentgen (or Lysken) Boens who lost her mind in prison. (Grosheide, *Bijdrage,* 157 f., 308.)   vDZ.

Trijntje Jans(sen) van Dulmen, an Anabaptist martyr, drowned on July 7, 1539, at Alkmaar, Dutch province of North Holland, with two other women. She was a native of Dülmen in the bishopric of Münster, Germany. Mellink is of the opinion that she was a Davidjorist (*q.v.*). She was sentenced to death because she had been (re) baptized and rejected the Catholic doctrine of the Mass. (*Inv. Arch. Amst.* I, No. 748; *DB* 1909, 22 f.; Mellink, *Wederdopers,* 173.)   vDZ.

Trijnwouden (Frisian, *Trynwalden*), an area some 8 miles west of Leeuwarden in the Dutch province of Friesland, Netherlands, where there was a Mennonite congregation in the 17th century, and probably already in the 16th, which in 1695 joined the Friesland Sociëteit. After 1698 it is no longer listed in the records of this conference, having probably either died out or merged with a neighboring church.   vDZ.

H. J. Busé, "De verdwenen Doopsgezinde gemeenten in Friesland," in *De Vrije Fries* XXII, repr., p. 18; *DB* 1895, 20.

Trinity Christian Society, the nonsectarian church established in 1854 by the Hunsicker (*q.v.*) group at Freeland, now Collegeville, Pa. In 1888 it was received into the Reformed denomination.   H.S.B.

Tripmaker (Trypmaker): see **Jan Volkertsz.**

Tripp (S.D.) Hutterite Bruderhof, the second Bruderhof of the Schmiedeleut group of the Hutterian Brethren, established in 1878 as a daughter of the Bon Homme Bruderhof near Yankton, located 36 miles northwest of Bon Homme, also called Neudorf and Neuhof. It sold its land in 1883 and bought a tract of land from the Rappites (*q.v.*) or Harmonists at Tidioute, Pa., where a total of 22 families settled in 1883/4. After two years the group moved back to South Dakota in 1886.   H.S.B.

Trissels Mennonite Church (MC), four miles southwest of Broadway, Rockingham Co., Va., is a member of the Virginia Conference. This perhaps was the location of the first Mennonite meetinghouse built in Virginia. The first building, of logs, was built in 1822, and enlarged in 1848. In 1900 it was replaced by a new frame church 40 x 50 ft., built on the opposite side of the cemetery. The third church was built of brick in 1950. Since January 1948 Sunday school and preaching services have been held every Sunday. The first ministers serving this church were Henry Rhodes, Henry Shank, and John Geil. The membership in 1957 was 123, with Norman Yutzy, a licensed minister, as pastor.   T.S.

Tritzschel, Heinrich, an Anabaptist martyr in Saxony. (*Theol. Jahresbericht* XXVIII, 1909, 593.)   HEGE.

Troeltsch, Ernst (1865-1923), professor of church history and sociology of religion, first at the University of Heidelberg, later at the University of Berlin, one of the seminal minds of Germany at the turn of the century. His *Social Teachings of the Christian Churches* (German 1912, English 1930) has become a classic in the area of interpretative church history. Although not too familiar with the history of Anabaptism, Troeltsch was able to describe and evaluate this movement fairly, in fact profoundly. This treatment is particularly surprising in view of the traditional picture of "Old Lutheranism" then still prevalent which identified Anabaptism with *Schwärmertum* (enthusiasm, *q.v.*). The latter term does not appear at all in Troeltsch's writings, which approach the various phenomena exclusively from the point of view of a history of ideas.

Troeltsch dealt with Anabaptism in three of his works: (*a*) *Protestantisches Christentum und Kirche in der Neuzeit* in *Hinnebergs Kultur der Gegenwart* (Leipzig, 1909) 504-16; (*b*) *Die Bedeutung des Protestantismus für die Entstehung der modernen Welt* (1911; English edition, *Protestantism and Progress,* 1912; new edition in a Beacon Paperback #61, 1958); and (*c*) *Soziallehren der christlichen Kirchen und Gruppen* (Tübingen, 1912) 797-815 (English edition, *Social Teachings of the Christian Churches,* N.Y., 1930). In the first-named work Troeltsch used as his source material the writings of C. A. Cornelius (*q.v.*), William Bax, Adolf Hegler (*q.v.*), A. Hulshof (*q.v.*), and Karl Müller's *Church History.* In the *Social Teachings* Troeltsch widened his reading by consulting two of the best sources available: Gottfried Arnold's (*q.v.*) *Kirchen- und Ketzerhistorie* (1699) and Sebastian Franck's *Geschichtsbibel* of 1531 (see **Chronica**). It is mainly from Arnold that he received his basic impression and evaluation—very much in contradistinction to his contemporary Karl Holl, another noted Lutheran church historian of his time and also professor at the University of Berlin, who opposed and criticized Troeltsch, although he actually never studied the history of the evangelical Anabaptists.

Troeltsch facilitated his own evaluation by his well-known classification of church-historical phenomena into *Kirche* (i.e., ecclesiastical or institutional churches, usually state or territorial churches, also *Volkskirchen* or national churches) and *Sekte* (nonconformist free or gathered churches).

Troeltsch recognized in Anabaptism certain traits of the medieval Waldensian movement without, however, claiming direct dependency. The Anabaptists represent to him the best example of a Protestant sect. They find their foundation exclusively in the New Testament, emphasizing the ethical aspect of this book; they oppose the idea of a folk or national church with its uncommitted masses, and they require personal and voluntary decision for Christ. Anabaptism is (according to Troeltsch) a marginal branch of the great Reformation movement of the 16th century, closely connected with this movement's tendencies toward purification of Christendom on the ground of the Scriptures, and showing all the moral earnestness of that great spiritual upheaval. When sectarianism had died out in Catholicism (end of the Middle Ages), it started anew in Protestantism, with all its ethical radicalism and readiness to accept martyrdom. The principle of the Absolute Natural Law, to be obeyed (English ed., p. 696), is then the guiding principle which made Anabaptists stand out over against ecclesiastical Lutheranism and individualistic Spiritualism. As to the radically violent groups (Münsteries, for instance) Troeltsch prefers to use the term "Taboritism," reminiscent of the Hussite Wars in Bohemia. (F. H. Littell uses for this type the term "Maccabeanism.") In no way does Troeltsch lump together these manifold movements of the 16th century; he is most careful to differentiate them intellectually.

In the work *Protestantism and Progress* Anabaptism again receives a very friendly treatment; this time, however, this term means not so much the evangelical Anabaptists of the 16th century as English "Independency," today called Congregationalism, interpenetrated with Baptist elements, which group Troeltsch says "arose from the remnants of the earlier English Anabaptists" (see **England**). "It was now, at last," Troeltsch says in an often repeated statement, "the turn of the stepchildren of the Reformation to have their great hour in the history of the world" (Beacon ed., 124), meaning that in America (New England), where these Nonconformists found their great opportunity of practical demonstration, they carried out three basic Christian principles, namely (1) separation of church and state, (2) voluntarism in the formation of church-bodies, and (3) the inviolability of the inner personal life by the state (liberty of conscience). Even though the reference at this place is mainly to New England Puritanism, the picture itself is certainly even more true for continental Anabaptism. R.F.

Walther Köhler, *Ernst Troeltsch* (Tübingen, 1941); *ML* IV.

Tromp, a Mennonite family, formerly at Woudsend in Friesland, Netherlands, where Age Tromp was from c1760 a ship's carpenter and sailmaker. His son Hylke Ages Tromp founded an insurance business c1760 for bargees and shipowners, which undertaking developed into the "Woudsender Brandassurantie Sociëteit" with Age Hylkes Tromp as secretary; this is now the Woudsend Fire and Life Insurance Company Inc. (headquarters at Sneek). The present director is Hylke Age Tromp, who in 1925-30 was a trustee of the A.D.S.   vDZ.

G. A. Wumkes, *Stads- en Dorpskroniek van Friesland* I (Leeuwarden, 1930) 291, 411; II (1934) 74.

Troyer (Treyer, Treier, Dreier), a Mennonite family name of Swiss origin. Hans Treyer (see **Dreier**), an early Anabaptist leader and one of the first Anabaptists executed in Bern, died on July 8, 1529. Peachey also names a Hans Treyer, a peasant at Laufen, Baselland, active as an Anabaptist 1529-30, and an Anna Dreyer, the wife of a peasant, probably the wife of the former. Jakob Treyer (*q.v.*) was an early Anabaptist of Laufen, near Basel. The name was found among the refugees in the Palatinate after 1664 who later came to Pennsylvania. Beginning c1733 some Treyers (now Troyer) from the canton of Bern, Switzerland, moved to Pennsylvania, settling in Berks County. These were all Amish. By 1752 the brothers Michael and Andreas Troyer were listed as members in the Northkill

Amish congregation in Berks County. The Troyer family spread westward to Somerset County, Pa., and to Ohio and Indiana, in which states by far the heaviest concentrations of the family name are found, although Amish and Mennonite members of the family are also represented in Illinois, Iowa, Nebraska, and Kansas, as well as in Mennonite communities in at least six other states and in Canada. In 1957 at least 53 men bearing the name of Troyer were serving as ministers in Mennonite churches. Of these, 39 were Old Order Amish preachers, 25 of whom were in Ohio. Jonas Troyer (1811-97) was a leading bishop in the Indiana-Michigan A.M. Conference. David A. Treyer (Treier) was an Amish bishop, whose *Hinterlassene Schriften* were published in 1923 (repr. 1925). He also left a manuscript on the dissensions among the Old Order Amish 1850-61 in Ohio. Amos P. Troyer (1856-1935; *q.v.*) was one of the leading Mennonite (MC) bishops in the Pacific Coast conference. D. D. Troyer (1870-1953) of Goshen, Ind., was a well-known bishop and served as president of the Mennonite Publication Board (MC). N. E. Troyer (1879-1954) of West Liberty, Ohio, was a bishop (MC) and an evangelist. Dr. George D. Troyer (1890-   ) served as a medical missionary in India and more recently has been serving in the Puerto Rico Mennonite Mission (MC). His son Dr. Dana Troyer also served as a medical missionary in India. Emanuel Troyer (1871-1942; *q.v.*) was for many years a leading bishop in the Central District Conference. His son Maurice Troyer is vice-president of International Christian University in Tokyo, Japan. Lotus Troyer is a Mennonite (GCM) minister at Meadows, Ill., and has served as president of the Central District Conference. Menno M. Troyer of Conway, Kan., is a minister in the West Liberty (MC) church and is secretary of the South Central Conference.   M.G.

Kate Yoder, *Descendants of Jephtha A. Troyer, 1825-1957* (Berlin, Ohio, 1957); Eli J. Troyer, *Troyer Family Record. Genealogy of David Troyer* (Howe, Ind., 1927); P. Peachey, *Die soziale Herkunft* (Karlsruhe, 1954) 45, 119 (No. 219), 140 (Nos. 707, 708); Samuel Geiser, *Die Taufgesinnten Gemeinden* (Karlsruhe, 1931) 102, 170 f., 181; D. L. Gratz, *Bernese Anabaptists* (Scottdale, 1953) 8, 16, 20, 168; Bender, *Two Centuries*, 60, 84.

Troyer, Amos P. (1856-1935), a prominent Mennonite (MC) bishop of Hubbard, Ore., was born in Wayne County, Ohio, Oct. 23, 1856, the son of Peter and Elizabeth Troyer. He married Delilah Yoder on Jan. 1, 1878, shortly after his baptism in 1877. They had ten children. The family moved to Cass County, Mo., and from there in 1892 to Hubbard. He was ordained deacon in the newly organized Zion Amish Mennonite Church June 18, 1893, and bishop there June 18, 1895, where he served as an able and universally loved pastor until his death on Oct. 23, 1935. He was buried in the Zion Cemetery. He was the outstanding leader in the Amish Mennonite churches in Oregon throughout his 40-year career as bishop, and a leader in the Western District A.M. Conference until its dissolution in 1920.   H.S.B.

Troyer, Emanuel (1871-1942), an outstanding leader in the Central Mennonite Conference, was born Dec. 31, 1871, near Hudson, Ill., son of Manasses and Catherine Salzman Troyer. Baptized in 1888, he was ordained minister in 1899 and bishop in 1911, both times in the East White Oak congregation where he served as assistant pastor and pastor 1892-1928. He served as pastor of the Normal, Ill., congregation 1928-36. He served as conference president for many years, also as conference field secretary 1936-42. He was widely used as an evangelist 1911-20. He was largely responsible for the establishment of the Mennonite Sanitarium (later Mennonite Hospital) at Bloomington, Ill., serving as president of the board from the beginning. He was a leading member of the Foreign Missions Committee of the Conference and the Congo Inland Mission Board. He married Ida Horst Jan. 23, 1895. Maurice Troyer, vice - president of International Christian University, Tokyo, Japan, is a son. He died on June 11, 1942.   H.S.B.

W. B. Weaver, "Biographical and Character Sketch of Rev. E. Troyer," *Central Conference Yearbook* 1943, 3-8.

Trubetskoye, a Mennonite settlement consisting of two villages, Novo-Nikolayevka and Volodyevka, in the district and province of Kherson, established on the rented estate of Trubetskoye in 1904. The population consisted of about 80 families or 400 persons. (Friesen, *Brüderschaft*, 680.)   C.K.

True and Blessed Way, The, *Which Leadeth Beneath the Cross to Heaven or a True Doctrine from the Word of God, for the Benefit of Every Lover of the Truth, and the Encouragement of Their Salvation* (Harrisburg, 1816), pp. 314, a small book by John Herr. This is the English edition of *Der wahre und selige Weg* (Lancaster, 1815), the first and one of the most important works of John Herr, the founder of the Reformed Mennonite Church (1812). It is essentially a defense of the new group, a justification of their breach with the Mennonite Church (MC), and a statement of their principles. Its recurring theme is the apostasy of the Mennonite Church from the teachings of Menno Simons and Dirk Philips. Chapter V (199-284) is headed, "It is explained why we have separated ourselves from the Mennonist Society; and why we cannot find spiritual liberty to hear their teachers." In addition to the reprints in the two editions of Herr's *Complete Works* (1875 and 1890), separate reprints were made in 1874 (German) and 1887 (English).   H.S.B.

Truitje (Truytgen) Gysbertsdochter, an Anabaptist martyr, who with her husband Claes (*q.v.*) Jansz van Oostzanen had joined the exodus of Dutch Anabaptists from Amsterdam to Münster (*q.v.*) in March 1534, sailing over the Zuiderzee. The group was arrested near Bergklooster (*q.v.*). On Aug. 27, 1534, Truitje was sentenced to death by drowning and her husband by beheading. They were probably executed at The Hague. (*Inv. Arch. Amst.* I, Nos. 744 f.; Mellink, *Wederdopers*, 160.)   vDZ.

Trumbull County, Ohio, the next county north of Mahoning County, the location of the third Mennonite settlement in the state, in which the Bristol Mennonite Church was established in Bristol Township, perhaps the first Mennonite congregation in Ohio. William Sager (b. 1772), of Rockingham County, Va., visited Bristol Township in 1802 and purchased land there. In 1804 Sager's brother-in-law Abraham Baughman settled in the township, followed in 1805 by William Sager and William Barb and their families, all Mennonite. Sager's father, Gabriel (1734-1816), emigrated from Germany in 1756, settled first in New Jersey and then in Bucks County, Pa., from where he moved to Rockingham County, Va., and then to Bristol Township in 1808. His son Samuel came to Trumbull County in 1811. The first church in the township was the Mennonite church organized by Gabriel Sager in 1808 at his home. He was a minister, ordained perhaps in Pennsylvania. No meetinghouse was constructed and the church disbanded after Sager's death. Abraham Kagey, a son of the Mennonite minister Jacob Kagey (1760-1815) of New Market, Va., bought land in Bristol Township in 1810 and moved here in 1818 with three brothers and a sister.   W.D.S.

Trustees, Congregational. From the very beginning of the settlement of Mennonites in America, as soon as land was secured for meetinghouses and for schoolhouses, trustees were appointed to hold title to the property of the congregation. Usually two or three trustees were named in the first deed as grantees to receive and hold the property, from whom the title automatically passed to their duly elected or appointed successors, mostly without any additional legal conveyance. However, at times a second conveyance was made, as was the case for the Salford (Pa.) Mennonite congregation in 1763. This conveyance is interesting because of a statement that the names of the trustees were used "by the special nomination and appointment of the Christian Congregation called Menonists (alias Monistoe) who assemble to perform divine worship at a meeting house by them erected on the above described piece of land and that the said Indentures were made for the uses, services, benefit and convenience of the said Congregation and fraternity to a meeting house and school house and a place for them to bury their dead" (Wenger, *Franconia*, 133). The term trustee is not found in the early deeds, but the concept of representatives of the congregation holding property in trust is often clearly stated and always implied. In Colonial America the ministers of the congregations were sometimes designated as the trustees in the property deeds. The congregations were not incorporated as legal entities, and in most cases to this date in North America have not been incorporated. The practice of using trustees is the common form of holding property.

Usually the trustees are also responsible for the maintenance, repair, and servicing of the meetinghouse and grounds. They hire the sexton or janitor, and receive and sometimes hold funds for these purposes, but often all funds are held by the church treasurer. They do not, however, in most congregations of the Mennonite Church (MC) and related groups, hold the alms fund or poor fund, which is received and administered by the deacon. H.S.B.

J. C. Wenger, *History of the Mennonites of the Franconia Conference* (Telford, 1937).

Truyken (Truytgen, also erroneously Ryntgen) **Boens,** an Anabaptist martyr, was burned at the stake with six others on March 20, 1549, at Amsterdam, Holland. She was a native of Antwerp, Belgium, a daughter of Willem Boens and a cousin of the martyr Anneken (*q.v.*) Boens. Elder Gillis (*q.v.*) van Aken had baptized her. This group of martyrs is commemorated in the hymn, "Tis nu schier al vervult ons broeders getal," found in the hymnal *Veelderhande Liedekens* of 1556 and following editions. (*Mart. Mir.* D 82, E 484; Grosheide, *Bijdrage,* 155, 308; *ML* I, 241.)   vᴅZ.

Tryn Rieurtsdochter and **Tryn Willemsdochter** were arrested with many others when the Stadholder of Friesland recaptured the Oldeklooster (*q.v.*) near Bolsward on April 7, 1535. They were taken to Leeuwarden, the capital of Friesland, and executed there on April 14, 1535, by drowning. (K. Vos, *Menno Simons,* Leiden, 1914, 229.)   vᴅZ.

Trynken van Spelle, an Anabaptist martyr, was burned at the stake on May 20, 1573, at Antwerp, Belgium, with three others, because she was rebaptized and frequented forbidden meetings. (*Antw. Arch-Bl.* XIII, 112, 113, 176; XIV, 90 f., No. 1022.)   vᴅZ.

Tryntgen, an Anabaptist martyr, burned at the stake at Maastricht, Dutch province of Limburg, on Jan. 24, 1570. She was a daughter of Neelken (*q.v.*), who suffered martyrdom with her, while Arent (*q.v.*) van Essen and his wife Ursel, also members of the Maastricht congregation, who had been arrested with Neelken and Tryntgen, were put to death two weeks earlier.

Van Braght's *Martyrs' Mirror* relates that when the Duke of Alba (*q.v.*) came to the Netherlands most of the Maastricht congregation fled (probably to Aachen or Burtscheid). These four, however, remained in town. During the night of Nov. 24, 1569, they were arrested. Notwithstanding cruel tortures Tryntgen did not name other members of the church, and she died steadfast. The martyrdom of these four pious Christians is commemorated in the hymn "Nun hoert jhr Freundt ohraamen" (Now listen, ye true friends), apparently composed immediately after their death, for it is found in the hymnal *Ein schon Gesangbüchlein* of 1570 or shortly after. This hymn is also found in the *Ausbund* (*q.v.*).   vᴅZ.

Mart. Mir. D 502, E 844; W. Bax, *Het Protestantisme in het Bisdom Luik . . .* II (The Hague, 1941) 306-10; Wolkan, *Lieder,* 92, 101; *Ausbund,* No. 28.

Tryon, Pieter, a Mennonite of Gent, Belgium, was arrested on March 17, 1585, when he and other brethren were in the home of Jan de Cleercq to divide the money collected from the members for the poor of the church. After much correspondence between the city magistrates and Alexander Farnese, the Spanish governor of Belgium, the whole group was banished for 50 years on Sept. 20, 1585. This event took place during a period of relative toleration of the Mennonites at Gent (*q.v.*). The other persons arrested and banished were Pieter Haesbaert, Jacques de Cleercq, Jacob de Joncheere,

Bauwens Tyncke, Joost Bouckaert, Jan de Backere, Manasses de Bats, and Jacques Houtermans. Some of these names probably are garbled. Jacques Houtermans may be identical with Jacques (*q.v.*) Outerman, who was a Mennonite preacher at Franeker in the Netherlands in the next year, 1586. I venture to surmise that Tryon is a corruption of Tirion and that Pieter Tryon is an ancestor or a relative of the Dutch Mennonite Tirion (*q.v.*) family. (A. L. E. Verheyden, "Mennisme in Vlaanderen," Ms.) vᴅZ.

Trypmaker: see **Jan Volkertsz.**

Tschan(t)z, a family name found among the Mennonites in Switzerland. Hans Tschanz of Kiesen was in prison at Bern in May 1567; after much reluctance he was finally "converted" through torture, admitting that he had erred in rejecting arms-bearing and the oath, and was now willing "to go into the (State) church."

In the 18th century Mennonites by this name are found in the Bernese Jura, from where a certain Amish Tschanz moved to America as early as *c*1733, followed by other members of this family. In 1824 and 1835 members of the Tschantz family from the Sonnenberg (*q.v.*) congregation in the Bernese Jura settled in Wayne County, Ohio. In America the name is usually written Schantz, Schanz, or Shantz (*q.v.*).   vᴅZ.

D. L. Gratz, *Bernese Anabaptists* (Scottdale, 1953); S. Geiser, *Die Mennoniten-Gemeinden* (Karlsruhe, 1932) 193 f.

Tschetter (Czeterle), a Hutterite family name. In 1760 Abraham Tschetter at Sobotiste (*q.v.*), Hungary, vigorously opposed a Jesuit who had been sent by the government to catholicize the Hutterian Brethren and who was preaching in their meeting-house. Tschetter was soon arrested and taken to Erlau, about 50 miles from the Bruderhof, and imprisoned in the Jesuit monastery prison. Here he gave up his faith and became Catholic. Lorenz Tschetter was imprisoned in 1766 at Alwinc (*q.v.*), Hungary, for his faith. Upon his release in 1767 he went to Walachia (*q.v.*) with the rest of the Bruderhof, and from there to Russia (*q.v.*), where the family increased. Paul and Lorentz Tschetter were among the twelve delegates from several Mennonite branches in Russia who came to the United States and Canada in 1873 to look for land and in 1874 led some 40 families to Dakota. Paul Tschetter (*q.v.*) became a leader of the group that joined the K.M.B. Church. His son J. W. Tschetter was long a K.M.B. city missionary in Chicago.

In 1957 five Tschetters were serving as head preachers in Hutterite Bruderhofs of the Dariusleut (*q.v.*), viz., Paul J. Tschetter of the Thompson Bruderhof, Christian Tschetter of the Husher (Rosebud) Bruderhof, Jacob Tschetter of the Howl Ranch (Tschetter) Bruderhof, Lorentz R. Tschetter of the Riverside Bruderhof, and Peter S. Tschetter of the Holt Bruderhof. There were also four Tschetter ministers in the G.C.M. group, among them P. P. Tschetter of Kingman, Kan. D.D., vᴅZ.

"The Diary of Paul Tschetter," *MQR* V (1931) 112-27 and 198-220; C. Henry Smith, *The Coming of the Russian Mennonites* (Berne, 1927) 52, 59, 64, 66, 72-74, 103; Zieglschmid, *Klein-Geschichtbuch,* 234, 254-56.

Tschetter Hutterite Bruderhof, of the Schmiedeleut (*q.v.*) branch, located near Olivet, Hutchinson Co., S.D., was founded in 1890 by members of the Wolf Creek (*q.v.*) colony. In 1918 they sold the property and founded the Rosebud Bruderhof near Redland, Alberta. In 1941 the original (S.D.) site was bought and rebuilt by Brethren from the Barickman commune near Headingly, Man.; fourteen families and David Decker, who was chosen to the ministry in 1931 and confirmed on Dec. 27, 1936, formed the new Tschetter Bruderhof. Jacob Wipf was chosen preacher in 1948; he was the leader of a group of ten families from the Tschetter Bruderhof who established the Gracevale Bruderhof in Winfred, S.D., in 1950, where he was ordained. Paul Decker was chosen as preacher at Tschetter in 1952 and ordained in 1957. In 1958 the Tschetter Bruderhof had 40 baptized members in a population of 142. Gracevale had 30 baptized members. D.D.

Tschetter, Paul (1842-1919), was born in Blumenort, Molotschna, South Russia. He became a member of the Hutterian Brethren in 1860. In that year he was married to Maria Walter. Five sons and five daughters were born to this union, among whom was Joseph W. Tschetter, for many years a minister of the Krimmer Mennonite Brethren in Chicago. In 1866 he was ordained to the ministry and in 1883 to the office of elder. He is buried in the Neuhutterthal cemetery, located 45 miles northwest of Yankton, S.D., on the homestead which he took when he came to America.

In 1873 Tschetter was a member of the delegation sent to St. Petersburg in the matter of continued exemption from military service. Because the answer was not satisfactory a delegation of twelve Mennonites and Hutterites visited the American frontier in 1873 to investigate the possibilities of emigration. Among the twelve were Paul Tschetter and his uncle Lorenz Tschetter, both of Hutterthal. Tschetter appeared before President Grant to plead for exemption from military service for his people who were to settle in America. The diary of his deputation journey to America in 1873 presents a keen analysis of the work and observations of the Russian delegation. In 1874 Tschetter brought his family to America and settled in South Dakota. He never lived in a Bruderhof and thus did not practice the Christian communism of the Hutterian Brethren. He was a leader in the group which joined the Krimmer Mennonite Brethren Conference. ("The Diary of Paul Tschetter, 1873," *MQR* V, 1931, pp. 112-27, 198-220.) M.G.

Tsingfeng (China) Mennonite (GCM) mission. Tsingfeng is a county in southern Hopei Province, with an area of 580 square miles and a population estimated at 344,000. Mission work was begun by the General Conference Mennonite Board of Missions in 1920. A primary school was established and a church organized at the county seat. Later another organized church developed at Kao-Tsun, a market town in the country, and regular services were held in three other preaching places. The staff of nationals consisted of an evangelist at each

organized church, a schoolteacher, and a Bible woman, with other itinerant workers. In 1941 the work was disrupted by the Japanese occupation. Missionary work was not resumed after the war because of Communist control, but the Chinese church continued active. S.F.P.

Tub Mennonite Church: see Springs Mennonite Church.

Tucher, Jörg, an Anabaptist from Wissemburg(?), was arrested at Strasbourg (*q.v.*) together with Jacob Gross (*q.v.*), Matthi(a)s Hiller (*q.v.*), Wilhelm Echsel (*q.v.*), and Jörg Ziegler (*q.v.*). They were among the first Anabaptists in Strasbourg; in August or September 1526 they were probably all banished from the town. vpZ.

Abr. Hulshof, *Geschiedenis van de Doopsgezinden te Straatsburg* (Amsterdam, 1905) 18-23.

Tuchmacher, Hans: see Amon, Hans.

Tuleta Mennonite Church (MC), a member of the South Central Conference located near Tuleta, Bee Co., in southern Texas, between San Antonio and Corpus Christi, was founded in 1905 by Peter Unzicker, a minister from Illinois, who acquired considerable property here and laid out the town site. A few years later other families moved in. Early ministers were J. M. R. Weaver, D. S. King, D. Y. Hooley, C. L. Ressler, and Adolph Nick 1923-25, Daniel Kauffman and Amos S. Horst 1928-29, and E. S. Hallman 1929-d.50. A severe drought in 1917 and other reasons caused most of the families to leave. The highest membership was 104, and the lowest 9, which was the membership in 1957. E.S.H.

Tulsa (Okla.) Mennonite Brethren Church was founded by some members of the Collinsville, Okla., M.B. Church who moved to Tulsa. In 1956 this group organized with Raymond Vogt as pastor. In 1957 the church was accepted into the Southern District Conference. A meetinghouse was built in 1958, when the membership was 25. M.A.K.

Tumbült, Georg, author of the interesting and valuable monograph, *Die Wiedertäufer. Die sozialen und religiösen Bewegungen zur Zeit der Reformation* (Bielefeld and Leipzig, 1899). It contains four art supplements (*Kunstbeilagen*) and 95 authentic illustrations and pictures. It appeared as No. VII in the series *Monographien zur Weltgeschichte* edited by Ed. Heyck and published by Velhagen & Klasing. H.S.B.

Tunes. Like most early Protestant hymnals (many European hymnals continued the pattern), Anabaptist hymnals contained no musical notation, printing the name of the tune to be used at the head of the hymn.

Old Dutch Mennonite hymnals like *Veelderhande Liedekens* (1556 and repr.), *Een Nieu Liedenboeck* (1562), *Lietboecxken van den Offer des Heeren* (1563), Hans de Ries' *Lietboeck* (1582), *Het Twee-de Liedeboeck* (1583), and many others of the 16th and 17th centuries follow this pattern; at the head of each hymn is found at least one and often two tunes of familiar songs, religious as well as secular. Mennonite hymnals outside Holland generally continued this practice until the middle of the 19th century or later. Tunes were in these cases handed down by memory, except when printed in separate books either for the accompanying organ or for voices. The first Palatinate Mennonite hymnal, the *Christliches Gesangbuch* of 1832, did contain many tunes, but Jacob Ellenberger, the editor, also prepared a lithographed book of tunes in four-part harmony for use with the hymnal. The first regularly printed tune book for Mennonites appeared in the mid-19th century. It was *Vierstimmige Melodien* (Dürkheim, 1856), which served the hymnal of the South German Mennonites. Franz's (*q.v.*) *Choralbuch* (Leipzig, 1860) served the hymnal of the Mennonites of South Russia with a four-part harmonized tune book. His 1865 *Choralbuch* was for only one part. A West Prussian *Choralbuch* appeared in 1898. All of these appeared in reprinted editions, the Franz *Choralbuch* of 1865 in the United States and Canada as well. Neither the Dutch nor the American Mennonites produced tune books of their own. An examination of the tunes in these books as well as the titles of the tunes used in all European Mennonite hymnals after the Anabaptist period reveals that they used the tunes prevailing in Protestant hymnals from which the hymns were borrowed.

There has been almost no composition of hymn tunes by European Mennonites. In the 20th century a few hymn compositions by American Mennonites have appeared in American Mennonite hymnals. In the *Church Hymnal, Mennonite* (MC 1927) 27 of the 645 tunes were by 12 different Mennonite composers, all members of the Mennonite Church (MC). Among them were J. D. Brunk, who had 12, A. B. Kolb 3, W. K. Jacobs 2, the rest one each. Since then Walter E. Yoder (MC) has composed a number of tunes, of which three have been used, two in *Life Songs No. 2* and one in *Songs of the Church.* Four tunes by Thersa Hostetler (MC) were used in *Songs of the Church.* A total of 10 Mennonite (MC) tunes were used in this hymnal.

A thorough study of the hymn tunes used in the 52 English hymnals of American Mennonites published 1832-1956, made by Paul Wohlgemuth, revealed that of the 3,860 tunes used only 168 were composed by Mennonites. Wohlgemuth comments: "The Old Mennonites have produced the greatest number of composers and the greatest number of Mennonite hymn tunes. The only Mennonite outside of the Old Mennonite Church who has composed hymn tunes to any extent is Herbert C. Richert, a member of the Mennonite Brethren Church. In the opinion of the writer, Mennonite hymn tunes do not meet the standard of the English or German hymn tunes, yet they are generally better than the standard type of American gospel song. It appears that what is generally called 'Mennonite Hymnody' (the hymn tunes appearing in Mennonite hymnals) is in essence a hymnody borrowed from many different sources." Wohlgemuth's statistics reveal further that only 191, or 5 per cent, of the total of 3,860 tunes used were by German com-

posers, and another 57 from other European countries outside England (which furnished 10 per cent); America furnished 57 per cent, while 23 per cent were of unclassified origin. It is clear that modern American Mennonites are singing predominantly American and English tunes, although those groups using German hymnals such as the Amish, the Old Colony Mennonites, and the Canadian G.C.M. and M.B. groups, of course sing predominantly German tunes. Wohlgemuth makes the following general comment: "The publishing of Mennonite hymnals in the English language began during the birth of the gospel song movement in America. The influence of this movement upon Mennonite hymnals is seen in the use of many American hymn tunes of the refrain type. The gospel song movement has been the greatest single influence upon the Mennonite hymnals published in the English language. The one group of hymnals that has been least affected by this movement is that published by the General Conference Mennonites. In recent years the trend in the larger Mennonite branches has been to use more dignified and more highly qualified hymn tunes."

The first Mennonite hymnal to appear with notes giving the melodies was the 1648 edition of the *Gesang-boeck* by Hans de Ries, although in the 1618 *Het Boeck der Gesangen* the first part containing the Psalms had tunes. In the 18th century all new Mennonite hymnals published in the Netherlands were provided with notes, though many reprints of older hymnals as late as the 1814 reprint of the *Kleyn Hoorns Liet-boeck* were without notes. The first European Mennonite hymnal outside Holland to publish melodies (this time with four-part harmony but not for all hymns) was the 1910 edition of the South German *Gesangbuch,* although the 1832 *Christliches Gesangbuch* for the Palatine Mennonites printed one-part melodies with numerous hymns. No Mennonite hymnals printed in Prussia or Russia ever contained tunes, either four-part or one-part. The first official American Mennonite hymnals to contain tunes (four-part) were the G.C.M. *Gesangbuch mit Noten* (1890) and the M.C. *Hymns and Tunes* (1890), although the latter printed each tune only once accompanied by the several hymns appropriate to be used with it. *The Philharmonia* by M. D. Wenger, published at Elkhart in 1875, describes itself as follows: "A collection of Tunes, Adapted to public and private worship, containing tunes for all the hymns in the English Mennonite Hymn Book, the Gemeinschaftliche, Unparteiische und Allgemeine Liedersammlungen, the Unparteiische Gesangbuch, and the Mennonitische Gesangbuch, with Instructions and Explanations in English and German, also English and German Texts to most of the Tunes, Metrical Indexes, &c., including a greater variety of Metres of Church Music than any other Work of the Kind now Published."

After 1890 all the official hymnals of the major American Mennonite bodies appeared in modern form with tunes and hymns printed together page by page.

The Harmonia Sacra (*q.v.*), which contained tunes with hymns, although printed by a Mennonite (Joseph Funk) and edited or written by him (preceded by *Die Allgemein Nützliche Choral Music* of 1816, and called *A Compilation of Genuine Church Music* in its first four editions 1832-47), was intended for the general public including Mennonites, but was not used in the regular Mennonite worship service.

The sources of the hymn tunes used by the Anabaptists, as indicated in their five 16th-century hymnals, the South German-Swiss *Ausbund* (q.v.), the Lower Rhine *Ein schon Gesangbüchlein* (q.v.) and the four Dutch: *Lietboecxken van den Offer des Heeren* (q.v.), *Veelderhande Liedekens* (q.v.), *Een nieu Liedenboeck* (q.v.), and *Het Tweede Liedeboeck* (q.v.), together with the tunes in the *Lieder der Hutterischen Brüder* first published in 1914 from earlier manuscript materials of 16th-century origin, have been studied carefully by Rosella Duerksen. She had the benefit of George Jackson's study of the origins of the tunes of the *Ausbund*, the results of which appeared in 1945. Jackson concludes from his study of the 36 transcribed *Ausbund* tunes published by J. W. Yoder and a comparison with the tunes found in Erk and Böhme's *Deutscher Liederhort* (2nd ed., Leipzig, 1925) that the *Ausbund* tunes as sung today by the Amish are 16th-century tunes, many of them folk-tunes, some of them, such as the *Hildebrand-ton,* going back to medieval sources. Jackson published a table of "Amish Tunes and Old German Folk Melodies with Which They Show Greater or Lesser Kinship."

Mrs. Duerksen's conclusions are as follows: (1) No original tunes by Anabaptists are extant, and there is no evidence of any dependence upon original melodic compositions by Anabaptists. (2) The tunes in the Anabaptist hymnals were borrowed, chiefly from various Reformation era sources, both sacred and secular, including many folk-tunes, German and Dutch, but including a few French, and including a very few medieval liturgical tunes. Fortunately all hymns carry an indication of the tune to be used, either by a title or by the first line of the song most commonly sung to that tune in the source used. (3) The secular tunes chosen need not come out of secular sources but may come directly out of earlier Lutheran or Reformed [or even Moravian. H.S.B.] hymnals which borrowed secular tunes for sacred hymns. (4) On the whole the Anabaptist tunes were basically a folk-song art. (5) There was considerable duplication of tunes among the various hymnals, just as there was of the hymns.

The three German Anabaptist hymnals, according to Mrs. Duerksen, contained a total of 607 hymns, to which 347 tune indications were given. Of the 73 *Ausbund* tunes 45 were duplicates of the 179 Hutterite tunes, and of the 95 tunes of *Ein schon Gesangbüchlein* 38 were duplicated either in the *Ausbund* or in the Hutterite tune collection. Some tunes were used very often, e.g., in the Hutterite hymnal one was used 32 times, another 30 times. Detailed lists of tunes of various categories are found in Mrs. Duerksen's study. Much less attention is given by Mrs. Duerksen to the Dutch Anabaptist tunes, hence her results for the Dutch hymnals are meager but still worth while.

Transcriptions of a considerable number of Amish hymn tunes have been made. J. W. Yoder published his transcriptions in *Amische Lieder*. Arthur Roth's manuscript transcriptions are deposited in G.C.L. The Library of Congress has recordings of a number of these tunes made by Allen Lomax, and a copy of these is in GCL, besides some recordings by John Umble. H.S.B.

Rosella R. Duerksen, "Anabaptist Hymnody of the Sixteenth Century, a Study of Its Marked Individuality Coupled with a Dependence upon Contemporary Secular and Sacred Musical Style and Form" (unpublished doctoral dissertation at Union Theological Seminary, 1956); Paul W. Wohlgemuth, "Mennonite Hymnals Published in the English Language" (unpublished doctoral dissertation at the University of Southern California, Los Angeles, 1956); John Umble, "Recent Research in Amish Hymn Tunes," MQR XXIV (1950) 91-93; idem, "The Old Order Amish, Their Hymns and Hymn Tunes," Journal of American Folk-Lore LII (1939) 82-95; George P. Jackson, "The American Amish Sing Medieval Folk Tunes Today," Southern Folklore Quarterly X (1945) 151-57; idem, "The Strange Music of the Old Order Amish," Musical Quarterly XXXI (1945) 175-88; Charles Burkhart, "The Church Music of the Old Order Amish and Old Colony Mennonites," MQR XXVII (1953) 34-54; J. W. Yoder, Amische Lieder (Huntingdon, 1942).

Tungming (Dung-ming), one of the southernmost counties of Hopei Province, China, with an area of 690 square miles and a population of about 278,000, formed part of the field of the General Conference Mennonite Mission. Work was begun here by 1911, and a missionary family was assigned for residence in 1915. A church building was erected in the city with workers' homes, and a compound with a primary school and a mission residence developed in the north suburb. Later, dropped as a place of missionary residence, work was continued with Chinese helpers, and an organized church was developed. During the Japanese occupation and the Communist struggle, Tungming, being to the south and separated by the Yellow River, retained missionary contact and freedom in Christian work later than most other parts of the field. Foreign contact with the work was closed by 1950 but the church has continued active. S.F.P.

Tunkers (English, Dippers), until 1933 the official name in Canada for the Brethren in Christ. "Dunkard," often used for the Church of the Brethren, is a corruption of "Tunker."

Turkestan (Turkistan), now divided into a number of republics in Soviet Central Asia, a former Russian gouvernement-general conquered by Russia in 1859-65, with the chief cities Tashkent (q.v.), Bukhara (q.v.), and Samarkand. In 1880 Mennonites from the Molotschna and Trakt Mennonite settlements came to Turkestan to establish settlements at Ak-Mechet (q.v.) in Khiva (q.v.) and Auli-Ata (q.v.), under the leadership of Klaas Epp (q.v.) and Abraham Peters (q.v.). Under the Soviet regime Turkestan was broken up into the Kazakh, Kirghiz, Uzbek, Tadzhik, and Turkmen Soviet Socialist Republics. During and after World War II the former Turkestan has received an influx of population from European Russia which includes many Mennonites. (See **Soviet Central Asia**.) C.K.

Turkey (Ottoman Empire): see **Böger, Salomon,** and **Thessalonica.**

Turkey Red Wheat: see **Wheat.**

Turkey Run Mennonite Church (MC), located south of Bremen, Ohio, a member of the Ohio and Eastern Conference, had its beginning in 1858, when a meetinghouse, 24 x 26 ft., was built to accommodate the members in the southern part of the Fairfield-Perry counties congregation. The building, erected after many had already moved to Allen County, never attracted a large membership. During the Civil War, controversy over the draft caused a further serious decline and toward the close of the century it approached extinction. By 1906 only 8 members remained. The present membership (1957) is 37, with Marion Good as pastor.   J.S.U.

John Umble, "Extinct Ohio Mennonite Churches," *MQR* VI (1932) 23-29 *et passim.*

Turkmen SSR: see **Soviet Central Asia.**

Turmbücher, the records of the court proceedings against the prisoners in Bern, Switzerland, who were held in various prisons (towers). Numerous examinations of the Anabaptists were recorded in these *Turmbücher.* They contain material of primary importance to the history of the Swiss Mennonites of the 16th century. The trials were usually conducted by two members of the city council in the presence of a clergyman and the state's attorney (*Staatsanwalt*). The "obstinate" were examined in the "Marzili," the usual site of torture down on the Aar, used to force them to betray their leaders.

The oldest extant *Turmbuch* begins with 1545. The books containing the records of the executed Anabaptists have disappeared, not only those of the turbulent years before 1543, when so many Swiss Brethren were put to death for their faith, but also those of the time that saw the execution of Wälti Gerber (1566) (*q.v.*) and Hans Haslibacher (1571) (*q.v.*). These gaps cannot be merely accidental. Were consciences burdened by these cruel Anabaptist persecutions?   S.G.

Adolf Fluri, "Täuferhinrichtungen in Bern im 16. Jahrhundert," in *Berner Heim,* 1896; *ML* IV.

Turner's Creek Mennonite Mission (MC), located in Breathitt County, near Talbert, Kentucky, about 20 miles south and west of Jackson, was established in November 1946 under the Conservative (Amish) Mennonite Conference. Alvin Swartz, who opened the work, was ordained as pastor in 1947 and as bishop in 1948; he was still serving in 1958, assisted by Oakley Turner, ordained in 1954. Other workers in 1959 were Mrs. Alvin Swartz, Clara Swartz (on leave), and Mary Elizabeth Miller. The membership in 1959 was 31. A meetinghouse was completed and dedicated in November 1948.   E.R.Sw.

Tuscola County, Mich., the site of an extinct Mennonite settlement about 30 miles southwest of Pigeon in Huron County, where a permanent settlement was made. Among the settlers who moved from Ontario to Tuscola County about 1880 was Daniel Lehman (1834-1919), a preacher who had been ordained Sept. 22, 1861, in the Hay congregation in Ontario. Other settlers included Noah Bechtel, Israel Detweiler, and Abram Lehman. In the course of time most of the Mennonite families moved elsewhere, but Lehman lived at Fairgrove in Tuscola County until his death. Lehman seems not to have maintained any vital connection with any conference of Mennonites; it is likely that his attitudes resembled those of the Wisler (*q.v.*) body rather than either the Ontario or Indiana-Michigan conferences of the Mennonite Church (MC). Peter Ropp, minister at Imlay City, Mich., originally of Ontario, preached Lehman's funeral sermon in the local Presbyterian church in 1919, and his obituary was published in the *Gospel Herald.*   J.C.W.

Tuttle Avenue Mennonite Church (MC), located in Sarasota, Fla., was organized in 1950 by the Virginia Conference with 15 charter members. Truman H. Brunk was appointed bishop, and Myron Augsburger pastor. During two years, while Augsburger was engaged in educational work and tent evangelism, Paul H. Martin served as pastor. The meetinghouse was dedicated on Dec. 31, 1950, and later enlarged. The attendance varies from 50 in summer to 600 or more in winter; the membership in 1957 was 93, with Michael Shenk as pastor. The congregation promotes a home mission outpost, a weekly radio program called "The Voice of Truth," and in co-operation with two other local congregations is promoting the Shekinah Bible School, a four-week school held at the Tuttle Avenue Church. M.S.A.

Tweede Liedeboeck, Het, *van vele diverse Liedekens ghemaeckt wt den ouden ende nieuwen Testamente. Waer af sommighe eertijts in Druck zijn wtghegaen ende sommige noyt in Druck gheweest hebbende daer by ghevoecht, Tot Amsterdam. By Nicolaes Biestkens van Diest . . . Anno 1583,* a Dutch Mennonite hymnbook, is an enlarged edition of the *Nieu* (*q.v.*) *Liedenboeck* of 1562. Whereas the *Nieu Liedenboeck* contained 257 hymns, this *Tweede Liedeboeck* has 294, all without notes. It was called *Tweede* (i.e., second) *Liedeboeck* because it was meant as a sequel and appendix to the hymnal *Veelderhande* (*q.v.*) *Liedekens* of 1582. vDZ.

F. C. Wieder, *De Schriftuurlijke Liedekens* (The Hague, 1900) 163, No. XCV; Wolkan, *Lieder,* 70.

Tweede Pruys Liedtboeksken (Second Prussian Hymnbook), a sequel or second part of the *Pruys* (*q.v.*) *Liedtboeck,* is mentioned in a list of Dutch Mennonite songbooks in *DJ* 1837, 65. It is also mentioned by Blaupot t. C., *Holland* II, 210. The author or editor was S. H. (?); it was printed in 1607 at Alkmaar, Netherlands. Of this hymnal, however, no copy seems to be extant and particulars are unknown.   vDZ.

Twekkelo, a hamlet in the Dutch province of Overijssel a few miles from Hengelo (*q.v.*), where the Mennonites from the district of Twente (*q.v.*) probably already in the 16th century, but certainly in the 17th century, held their meetings on a farm called d'Erve'n Haimer. When after 1625 the Mennonites of Twente could meet more safely the meetings were held in Hengelo, but in 1672, in which year there was temporarily a period of commotion, the center of the congregation again became the barn of Twekkelo. In the early 18th century the records of the Groningen Old Flemish Mennonites still mention "the congregation in Twenthe at Twekkelo." On July 9, 1926, a memorial stone was placed on the wall of the old barn at Twekkelo where the Mennonites had met in times of danger.

vDZ.

Uit het verleden der Doopsgezinden in Twenthe (Borne, n.d.) 11-17; *DJ* 1929, 92 ff.

Twent(h)e, a district in the southeast of the Dutch province of Overijssel, close to the German border. Anabaptists were found here from the 16th century; in 1544 two noblewomen of Beckum (*q.v.*) suffered martyrdom at Delden in Twente. Until 1625 the Mennonites in this area could not live freely and worship without hindrance as they could elsewhere in the Netherlands, for the Spanish domination permitted only Catholicism. Before 1626 there were in Twente several secret Mennonite congregations. Enschedé (*q.v.*) is mentioned in 1580; Almelo (*q.v.*), though there is no literary information about this congregation before 1601, obviously also existed *c*1580; besides these there was the congregation meeting at Twekkelo (*q.v.*), and at Goor (*q.v.*) there were also Mennonites.

Most of the Mennonites in Twente earned their living by farming and weaving; they had probably mostly moved in from elsewhere; many old families in Twente are known to be of Westphalian origin. The idea found in old books and defended by P. Beets that in 1520-30 Anabaptist weavers immigrated from Flanders, Belgium, is not right, though occasionally in a later period of the 16th century a few weavers from Flanders may have settled in Twente. A number of the Mennonite weavers gradually achieved great prosperity and laid the foundations for the big textile industry for which Twente now is known. (Families of ten Cate, *q.v.*, Blijdenstein, *q.v.*, and others.)

Persecutions or at least suppression lasted as long as the Spaniards were in power in Twente. In 1612 a mandate was issued by the governor Unico Ripperda against the "wederdopers oft tibben" (*q.v.*), threatening the Mennonites with disturbing their meetings and arresting their preachers. Thereupon the Mennonites of Twente addressed the (Protestant) magistracy of Deventer (*q.v.*) asking their aid and intercession in the States of Overijssel (letter of Oct. 10, 1612). The difficulties with the governors in Twente, however, lasted until the Spanish troops were forced to leave in 1625. Originally all the Mennonites in Twente formed more or less one congregation, of which there were local groups in the different towns. So this letter to Deventer was a petition of "de gemeente, diemen Manisten noempt, residerende in desen lande van Twenthe."

In the 17th century most Mennonites of Twente belonged to the conservative Groningen Old Flemish branch; only Almelo took a somewhat different point of view, joining the Flemish and later on the Zonist (*q.v.*) conference. Among the Old Flemish leaders in this area are to be mentioned Hendrik Berents Hulshoff (*q.v.*, 1664-1745) and Wolter ten Cate (*q.v.*, 1701-96).

In the course of time independent congregations developed in Almelo, Borne, Enschedé, Goor, and Hengelo. Goor died out in the 18th century; the four others are still existing and together form the Ring (*q.v.*) of Twente. The number of baptized members in Twente stood at *c*350 in 1710, 258 in 1834, 548 in 1901, and 1,219 in 1958. Prominent Mennonite families found in Twente, some of which have died out, having moved elsewhere or having left the church, are Blijdenstein, Busschers, ten Cate, Coster, ter Horst, Jannink, van Lochem, Nieuwenhuis (and Nijhuis), Overbeek, Paschen, Schimmelpenninck, Stenvers, and Warnaars. vDZ.

Inv. Arch. Amst. I, Nos. 270, 1004; Blaupot t. C., *Groningen* I and II, *passim* (the letter to Deventer, II, 187-204); *DJ* 1929, 92-104; *Uit het Verleden der Doopsgezinden in Twenthe* (Borne, n.d.).

Twent(h)e, Ring of, a group of Mennonite congregations in the Dutch district of Twente (*q.v.*), founded July 27, 1856. Like other Rings its purpose was to establish closer contact between the four independent congregations in this area — Almelo, Borne, Enschedé, and Hengelo — and to organize mutual aid in case of vacant pulpits. The history of Ring Twente is found in an address by S. Gosses Gzn, read at the centennial meeting of the Ring on Sept. 14, 1956, which paper was published under the title *De Geschiedenis van een Klavervier* (1957, n.p.). vDZ.

Twijzel-Eestrum, two villages in the Dutch province of Friesland, where the Mennonites have organized a Kring (group). The Kring now (1958) numbers 31 members, partly belonging to the congregation of Veenwouden (*q.v.*), partly to the recently founded congregation of Buitenpost. vDZ.

Twin City Missions (MC), Kansas City, Kan., and Kansas City, Mo., was the name given to the Morris Gospel Hall, R. 2, Kansas City, Kan., and the Mennonite Gospel Center, 1238 Washington, Kansas City, Mo., from 1946 to 1951 when the Morris building was destroyed by the Kansas City flood. The missions were under the superintendency of Edward Yoder, and the membership in 1951 was 38. H.S.B.

Twisck, Pieter Jansz, b. 1565 at Hoorn, d. there Oct. 1, 1636, a Dutch Mennonite elder and prolific author, who lived at Hoorn in the Dutch province of North Holland, where he had a dry goods shop from about 1605 until his death. The belief that he received his family name from Twisk, a town not far from Hoorn, is not correct; the name is derived from a sign on his shop picturing the village of Twisk. Until *c*1609 he called himself simply Pieter Jansz; thereafter he regularly added the name Twisck.

Twisck became a preacher of the Old (or Hard) Frisian Mennonite church at Hoorn in 1592 and soon after an elder. He was a conservative Mennonite; against the Waterlander leader Hans de Ries (*q.v.*), who was more liberal in his views, he emphatically defended the doctrine of Incarnation of Christ as taught by Menno Simons and Dirk Philips. In 1615 de Ries published at Haarlem the *Historie der Martelaren*, with a preface in which he summoned the Dutch Mennonites, divided by schisms, to reunite. Twisck published a second edition of this book, now entitled *Historie der Warachtighe Getuygen Jesu Christi* (Hoorn, 1617), in which he omitted the preface by de Ries but added a confession of faith. Soon after this Twisck and his Old Frisians discovered that de Ries (intentionally, they thought) had omitted the views of the martyrs on the Incarnation, thus falsifying the history of the martyrs. To correct this, Twisck re-edited the martyr book, and thus *Historie van de Vrome Getuygen Jesu Christi* (Hoorn, 1626) appeared. (A new enlarged edition of the 1615 edition by de Ries appeared under the title *Martelaers-Spiegel der Werelose Christenen* at Haarlem, 1631.) For his corrections in the *Historie van de Vrome Getuygen* Twisck was severely attacked by the Waterlander preacher Hans Alenson in *Tegen-Bericht* (Haarlem, 1630).

Twisck as a strict Old Frisian unabatingly maintained the practice of banning, opposed marriage outside the church, and held the view that the other Mennonite groups did not have a good understanding of the church and its basic doctrines. Thus he looked askance at the endeavors for union and merger heard in his day. He declined the invitations of Hans de Ries and the Waterlander leaders in 1604-7, and that of the Flemish brethren of Amsterdam in 1626 (see **Olijftacxken**). In a meeting of different branches of the Dutch Mennonites held at Zaandam Nov. 13-15, 1628, Twisck uttered his grievances against the intended merger and on Jan. 27, 1629, the definite refusal of several Old Frisian churches was sent to the Flemish at Amsterdam. A debate held at Hoorn on April 13, 1622, between Twisck and Jan Luies (*q.v.*) the strong leader of the strictest Flemish, whose standpoint did not much differ from that of Twisck, had no success either.

Twisck was very active as elder. He regularly visited the congregations in North Holland and may have been the founder of the Old Frisian conference in this area. (See **Noordholland**, *Vriesche Doopsgezinde Sociëteit in.*) He also visited the Mennonites elsewhere; before 1620 he was in Holstein and Eiderstedt, and also stayed at Hamburg where there was a Frisian congregation which held the same doctrines as Twisck. His followers in Hamburg and elsewhere were commonly called the Jan-Pietersz-Twisckvolk, or the Twiscken (*q.v.*).

Twisck was a man of little education. He knew no foreign language except a little German. Nevertheless he was a well-read man, who wrote many books. Herman Schijn (*Geschiedenis* II) gives a long list of some 26 titles by him, and there were a few more. Some of Twisck's writings were circulated in manuscript copies during his lifetime; a few of these tracts were printed later. His grandson Pieter Jansz Twisck (*q.v.*) edited some of them. The most important writings of Twisck are (*a*) his *Confession of Faith* of 1617. Twisck himself later denied that he was the author of this confession "first placed before the great martyrs book," claiming that it was drawn up by his co-preacher of Hoorn, Syvaert Pietersz (*q.v.*). Yet we may assume that Twisck had the major part in this con-

fession, which is composed of sentences borrowed from the works of Menno Simons. (*b*) *Concordantie der Heyligher Schrifturen* (Leiden, 1614; Haarlem, 1648) and a sequel to this work, *Bybelsch Naem en Chronyk-boeck* (Hoorn, 1632). (*c*) *Chroniik van den Ondergangh der Tyrannen, Ende de Jaerlijcksche Geschiedenissen in Weereltlijcke ende Kercklijcke Saecken,* 2 vv. (Hoorn, 1617 and 1620). This large book was very popular and much read, also by non-Mennonites. It is a kind of general history, for the first part is largely borrowed from the *Chronica* by Sebastian Franck (*q.v.*) and from many other books, giving a treasury of historical information, including Mennonite history.

Further publications are: *Een Schriftelijck Tracktaet oft Verhandelinghe van Twist* (1604, n.p.; repr. 1626); *Andtwoort ende Wederlegginge . . . op een vrage by Hans de Rijs;* this was written in 1607 and circulated in manuscript copies, but not published until 1614. It appeared at Hoorn with the title *Een corte ghestelijcke verclaringhe van den hoge Priester Aaron* (Hoorn, 1608), and a reprint entitled *Aarons Priesterdom* (Hoorn, 1627); *Religions Vryheyt,* 2 vv. (Hoorn, 1609); *Schriftuerelijcke Vereeniginge* (Hoorn, 1661), which was written by 1613; *Namen ofte Benamingen Christi* (Hoorn, 1615); *Een corte Beschrijvinge van 80. Pausen* (Hoorn, 1616; repr. 1654); *Corte Vertooninghe van den teghen woordighen Staet des Aertbodems* (Leiden, 1623, some reprints); *Een Vaderlijck Geschenk* (Hoorn, 1623; repr.? and ibid., 1646, 1668, 1742); *Ontdeckinge des Pausdoms* (Hoorn, 1624; Haarlem, 1646); *Een lieffelijcke Meditatie . . . op den 85. Psalm* (Hoorn, 1624); *Comeet-Boecxken* (Hoorn, 1624; ibid., 1665); *Rantsoen Christi* (Hoorn, 1624); *Corte Verdedigingh* (Hoorn, 1626; Haarlem, 1646); *Schriftuurlijcke Disputacie aengaende het wesen en de godheyt Christi tusschen S. D. Montanus en* (date of writing unknown: first ed. as far as known at Danzig, 1650); *Pascha of Paeschlam* (Hoorn, 1627); *Rijckdom ende Armoede* (Amsterdam, 1627); *Troost-Brief der Weduwen* (ed. of 1626, at ?; Hoorn, 1630; *idem,* 1636); *Oorloghs-Verstooninghe, ofte Teghen die Krijch en voor de Vrede* (Hoorn, 1631; probably a first edition 1611); *Catechismus* (Haarlem, 1633); *Van de Peste* (. . . 1636; Hoorn, 1636; ibid., 1637); *Tegen de Pauss-lijcke Successie* (Hoorn, 1636); *Kort en Grondigh Bericht van den Val Adams* (Hoorn, 1638); *Tractaet van den Houwelijcken Staet* (Hoorn, 1682); *Verscheyde Artikulen des Geloofs* (Hoorn, 1694; Franeker, 1700).

Twisck also composed a number of hymns, which like his early tracts usually were signed with the device "Na(e) Beter." The following hymnals, some of which were used in the Old Frisian congregations, were published by Twisck: *Eenege Meditations Liedekens . . . genomen wt den XXV. LXXXV. en LXXXVI. Psalm . . .* (n.p., 1603); *Kleyn-Liedtboecxken* (Hoorn, 1633; repr. *ibid.,* 1640; containing 183 hymns); *Fondament oft De Principaelste Liedekens . . .* (Haarlem, 1633) which was added to his *Catechismus.* One of his tracts, which was probably never printed in Dutch, or of which the Dutch copies have been lost, still exists in a German translation, *Das Friedensreich Christi oder Auslegung des 20. Capitels in Offenbarung St. Johannis* (Odessa, 1875; repr. Elkhart, 1888 and 1915); and an English, *The Peaceful Kingdom of Christ* (Elkhart, 1913; n.p., 1940).

Twisck diligently studied the works of Menno Simons and Dirk Philips and was in sympathy with them; the influence of this study is found in many of his writings, particularly in his *Confession of Faith* and in his *Catechism*. Menno's autobiography on "Wtgangh ofte Bekeeringhe" (leaving or conversion) was inserted by Twisck in his *Chronijk van den Ondergangh der Tyrannen* (II, 1067-73). Twisck was well instructed about Menno Simons, for Menno's daughter "more than once" told him personally about her father and how he died. She told him that Menno died "anno 1559, aged 66" (II, 1075); on the same page (also II, 1201) he mentions that, according to another tradition, Menno died on Jan. 13, 1561. These variant dates led historiography astray and for nearly three centuries it was generally accepted that 1559 was the death year of Menno Simons, until Karel Vos proved that it was probably 1561. Menno's letter to the widows, the original of which is now found in the Amsterdam Mennonite Archives, was published by Twisck in his *Troost-Brief der Weduwen* (1626). Of special interest for Mennonite history are the insertions which Twisck and his co-workers made in the martyr book *Historie der Warachtighe Getuygen*, of 1617, adding from the official records (*Sententieboeken*), chronicles, and hymnals a number of accounts on martyrs, among which was the striking history of Dirk (*q.v.*) Willems van Asperen. vDZ.

Inv. Arch. Amst. I, Nos. 501-9, 521, 558-I, 566, 568, 570, 617; II, No. 83; Schijn-Maatschoen, *Geschiedenis* II, 516-34; BRN VII, 144, 155 f., 213-18, 234 f., 242, 251, 259; Kühler, *Geschiedenis* II, 107-14, 128 f., 134, 142, 191 f.; K. Vos, *Menno Simons* (Leiden, 1914) 4, 43 note 1, 68 f., 111, 164, 186 note 1; *DJ* 1837, 96, 97; *DB* 1864, 42 f., 54 f., 125, 127; 1865, 68, 119; 1867, 71; 1870, 69, 72 f.; 1872, 53, 94; 1876, 38 note; 1881, 34 f.; 1882, 41; 1887, 99; 1889, 76; 1892, 26; 1893, 11; 1899, 98 f., 144, 158; Robert Friedmann, *Mennonite Piety Through the Centuries* (Goshen, 1945) 262 f.

Twisck, Pieter Jansz (Pieter Jansz de Jonge), a Dutch Mennonite elder, grandson of the Pieter Jansz Twisck above, served the Old Frisian congregation in Hoorn 1649-after 1690. His stubbornness and strictness in the doctrines on the ban and the mixed marriages caused dissension between Twisck and some followers and the more progressive part of the congregation, of which the preacher Jan Willems Sleutel (*q.v.*) was the leader. When a certain proposal by Twisck was rejected by the church board in April 1688, Twisck protested by retiring from the board. Secretly his group tried to reduce the influence of Sleutel and the progressives; they even proposed to the city magistrates to have the preacher Gerrit Willems Seylemaker removed. Endeavors to heal the rupture failed, and Twisck with a number of adherents held a meeting in his home on Dec. 25, 1689, thus separating from the main body of the church. On Jan. 8, 1690, the schism was completed. With the aid of a gift of 32,000 Dutch guilders received from Immetje Pieters, the widow of the deacon Claes Reyders, Twisck bought a house "De Plemp," which was remodeled as a

meeting place for his group, then usually called "Twiscken" or also "Plempsche Mennoniten." Twisck probably died soon after; the exact year of his death is unknown. In 1743 the "Twiscken" returned to the main body.

Twisck was a man of great power and dominance, not only in the home church, but also elsewhere and particularly in the Frisian conference of North Holland. It was Twisck, for example, who in 1682 dedicated the new meetinghouse of the Frisian congregation at Alkmaar.

As far as is known, Twisck did not publish any writings of his own; he edited a few writings, e.g., *Schriftuurlijke Vereeniging* (1661), of his grandfather's, with whom he was so congenial and whose nature seemed to have passed to his grandson, except his sharp intellect (*DB* 1867, 78-89; 1891, 9). vDZ.

Twisck, Reyner Pietersz (d. 1613 at Hoorn, Holland), a relative, probably an uncle of Pieter Jansz Twisck (*q.v.*), was for many years a sailor and steersman. He invented a number of instruments, including a new kind of compass, which was patented in 1597 by the Dutch States General. (*N.N.-B.Wb.* II, 1458 f.) vDZ.

Twis(c)ken (Twiskers, Pieter-Jansz-Twisckvolk) is a name formerly given to a group of the Dutch Mennonites. It was used (*a*) for the followers of Pieter Jansz Twisck (*q.v.*) Jr. in Hoorn after this elder had separated from the main body; and (*b*) in a more general sense for the Old Frisian (*q.v.*) branch, of which Pieter Jansz Twisck Sr. (*q.v.*) was a leader. In the latter sense the Twisken in Friesland numbered 137 brethren in 1666. The Old Frisian "Arke Noachs" congregation at Amsterdam was also commonly called the Twisck church, as was also at times the Frisian congregation in Hamburg, Germany. vDZ.

Inv. Arch. Amst. I, No. 578; II, No. 83; *DB* 1870, 114; 1874, 114; Blaupot t. C., *Friesland*, 163; B. C. Roosen, *Geschichte der Menn.-Gemeinde zu Hamburg und Altona* I (Hamburg, 1886) 28 f.

Twisk, a village near Hoorn in the Dutch province of North Holland, the seat of a Mennonite congregation since early times. It formerly belonged to the strict branch of the Old Frisians (*q.v.*). Concerning its history there is not much information. It is a clear example of old Frisian strictness, that Jan Jacobsz of Twisk and Jacob Jansz of the neighboring village of Abbekerk refused appointments as magisterial officials. They were exempted on payment of a fine of 25 guilders each, which was given to the Reformed poor of their villages. The Mennonites of Twisk were rather well-to-do, for they made a considerable contribution (more than 4,000 guilders!) in 1672 to help the Netherlands, then at war. They also contributed to collections of money for the Prussian Mennonites. About 1725 the congregation of Abbekerk (*q.v.*) merged with Twisk. No membership figures are known for the early period. The baptized membership numbered 86 in 1793, 107 in 1834, 125 in 1861, 151 in 1901, and 72 in 1958. Since 1919 the pastor of Twisk also serves at Medemblik (*q.v.*).

Until the middle of the 18th century the congregation was served by ministers chosen from its members, the number of preachers usually being three or four. Cornelis de Bleyker (*q.v.*), serving 1770-96, was the first preacher called from outside. He was followed by Atze Wybes van der Hoek 1796-1835. The first minister trained at the Amsterdam Mennonite seminary serving at Twisk was Sjoerd Hoekstra 1835-80, followed by Jan Fopko Bakker 1881-1908, D. Attema 1909-12, S. H. N. Gorter 1912-14, C. C. de Maar 1915-19, A. Keuter 1920-25, H. C. Barthel 1926-35, S. Gosses Gzn 1935-38, R. de Zeeuw 1938-41, Miss A. C. Büch 1941-42, J. Krijtenburg 1942-46, Miss T. G. Siccama 1949-51, and Miss M. G. Stubbe since 1954. There are at present two women's circles in this congregation.

vDZ.

Inv. Arch. Amst. II, Nos. 2280-82; Blaupot t. C., *Holland* I, 212, 251; II, 203, 204, 233; *DB* 1919, 222.

Typhus, a highly contagious and very frequently fatal fever, which often occurs epidemically. It is also called spotted fever or spotted typhus. Body and head lice are the common carriers of the disease. Spotted typhus generally breaks out in epidemic proportions after acute national emergencies such as famine, devastation, etc. The chief occurrence of this plague in the history of the Mennonites was among the Mennonites of the Ukraine in the winter of 1919-20, when the Machno (*q.v.*) hordes brought the epidemic directly into the homes of the Mennonites; they preferred to lodge in Mennonite dwellings. Since the Mennonites had been robbed of their linens and clothes it was impossible for them to observe necessary sanitation. Together with the spotted typhus appeared typhoid fever (paratyphus), which is also carried by lice and bedbugs, but is less serious than typhus.

Very severe suffering was endured from spotted typhus by the Chortitza Mennonite settlement. Several weeks before Christmas of 1919, great numbers began to die; the number gradually decreased toward the spring of 1920. The improvement was due in part to the immunity acquired by the survivors and in part to the possibility, owing to the warm spring weather, of removing the vermin from the houses and people. Of great assistance was also the aid which the villages of the Molotschna settlement rendered in 1920 in supplying linen and nurses to the Chortitza settlement.

The statistics from the village of Nieder-Chortitza (Old Colony) show the following:

	Male	Fem.	Tot.
Mennonite population of the village	441	458	894
Afflicted by illness in the winter of 1919-20	310	327	630
Afflicted by spotted fever	284	286	570
Afflicted by paratyphus	26	41	67
Total deaths	61	33	94

The total deaths amounted to just about 11 per cent of the population. These statistics would apply in the same ratio more or less to the sixteen villages (the island of Chortitza had at this time already been vacated by the Mennonite population) of the Chortitza settlement, bringing the total number of Mennonite deaths from typhus in that winter to *c*1500.

Many also died in the Nikolaipol settlement, and elsewhere wherever the Machno bandits remained for any period of time. As the statistics indicated, there were more deaths among the males than the females, and these were largely men of 40-60 years, the age from which the responsible personalities of society would be drawn. This resulted in great changes in many villages. Thanks to the tenacity and the deeply rooted traditions of the Mennonites (appointing the guardians for the many orphans, the administrators for the widows, regulating the estates through the "Waisenamt") this change was not as painful as it might have been. The villages of the Molotschna settlement also helped in giving many of the orphans homes in their families. The epidemic which afflicted the Menno Colony (*q.v.*) settlers at Puerto Casado, Paraguay, en route to the Chaco interior in 1927 (147 deaths) was typhoid fever and not typhus.

J.G.R.

Die Mennoniten-Gemeinden in Russland während der Kriegs- und Revolutionsjahre 1914 bis 1920 (Heilbronn, 1921); Dietrich Neufeld, *Ein Tagebuch aus dem Reiche des Totentanzes* (Emden, 1921).

Tyverton: see **Tiverton.**

Tzum (Tjum), a village in Friesland, Netherlands, where Elder Leenaert (*q.v.*) Bouwens baptized four persons in 1563-63, and another 15 persons *c*1570. A Mennonite congregation of Tzum is, however, not known; the newly baptized may have joined some neighboring congregations like Blessum or Arum.

vDZ.

U

Ubbens, a Mennonite family at Sappemeer, Netherlands, many of whom have served the local congregation as lay preachers; e.g., Meerten Ubbens (Obbes) (1676-1736), time of serving unknown, his son Ubbo Meertens (1703-82), serving 1733-79, his grandson Meerten Ubbens (Obbes) (1726-86), serving from 1784 until his death. In 1811 their descendants adopted the official family name of Ubbens. vD Z.

J. Huizinga, *Stamboek . . . van Samuel Peter (Meihuizen) en Barbara Fry* (Groningen, 1890) 151, 156; *Dutch Naamlijst.*

Ubbonites, a name sometimes given to the followers of the Anabaptist elder and leader Obbe (*q.v.*) Philips. More usual, however, is the name Obbites (Dutch, *Obbiten*) or Obbenites. Ubbonite delegates were present at the meeting of Anabaptist leaders at Boekholt or Bocholt (*q.v.*) in Westphalia, Germany, in 1536. (*DB* 1864, 137.) vD Z.

Uble Claesz, an Anabaptist martyr beheaded at Leeuwarden, Netherlands, on May 8, 1538. He had left his child unbaptized and had a derogatory opinion of the doctrine of the Mass. Particulars are lacking. vD Z.

Inv. Arch. Amst. I, No. 746; J. Reitsma, *Honderd jaren uit de Geschiedenis der Hervorming . . . in Friesland* (Leeuwarden, 1876) 63.

U(c)kowallists, followers of the Dutch Mennonite elder Uco Walles (*q.v.*), separating with him from the Flemish branch about 1634. At first they seem to have organized separate congregations, particularly in East Friesland, Germany, and in the Dutch provinces of Groningen and Friesland, sometimes calling themselves "'t kleinste hoopjen" (the smallest heap). Concerning these Ukowallists there is not much information. In the first decades of their existence they had much trouble with the government, especially in the province of Groningen, where the magistrates on the advice and the insistence of the Reformed Church were very severe against them; their meetings were forbidden, and a few of their meetinghouses were torn down, in 1640 at Sappemeer, in 1643 at Visvliet. On Jan. 16, 1661, the States of Groningen issued a mandate against "Ucowallists and other new kinds of the Mennonites and 'bigotted fanatics'" (*Swermgeesten*). On April 4, 1657, the city government of Groningen issued such a mandate, reverting to a mandate of Aug. 30, 1637. About 1665 the Ukowallists may have merged with the Groningen Old Flemish Mennonites, but particularly in East Friesland and Groningen the Groningen Old Flemish were sometimes still called Ukowallists in the 18th century. The statement of 1666 that there were 245 male members of the Ukowallists in Friesland refers to the Groningen Old Flemish. Likewise "the ceremony of baptism and communion of the Ukowallists" held at Norden in 1719, described by C. Jehring (mentioned in Blaupot t. C., *Friesland*), relates to the Groningen Old Flemish. vD Z.

Inv. Arch. Amst. I, No. 448; Blaupot t. C., *Friesland,* 161-63, 223, 315-18, 381 f.; *idem, Groningen* I, 193, 210, 227 note 1, 285-87; II, 38, 43-47, 124, 149, 181 f.; G. A. Wumkes, *De Gereformeerde kerk in de Ommelanden . . .* (Groningen, 1904) 34-40; *DB* 1876, 39 note 2; 1879, 87 f.; 1898, 62.

Uco (Uko, Ucko) **Walles:** see **Walles, Uco.**

Udemans, Godefridus, a Reformed pastor at Zierikzee, Dutch province of Zeeland, attacked the Mennonite elder François de Knuyt (*q.v.*). In 1618 Udemans was directed, probably by the Reformed classis of Zierikzee, to inquire into the growth of the Mennonites and the "pestilential influence" of their elder de Knuyt in the province of Zeeland and especially on the island of Schouwen-Duiveland. Thereupon Udemans published *Noodighe Verbeteringhe, dat is Schriftmatighe Aenmerckingen op seker Boecxken van Fr. de Knuyt* (Zierikzee, 1620), a volume of 350 pages. vD Z.

DB 1897, 106, 114 f.; H. W. Meihuizen, *Galenus Abrahamsz* (Haarlem, 1954) 13.

Ueberlingen, a town (pop. *c*8,000) in Baden, Germany, located on the north shore of Lake Constance, is the seat of a Mennonite congregation founded *c*1840. The baptized membership in 1957 was 62, with Ludwig Moser as elder (since 1943). H.S.B.

Uelzen, Germany, the former center of the Hannover Mennonite Church (first called Soltau-Uelzen) composed of Mennonite refugees from the Danzig area, founded in 1948 and renamed Hannover in 1956 since the center of the congregation was moved from the city of Uelzen (21 miles southeast of Lüneburg) to the city of Hannover. Actually in 1955 the 380 registered members were scattered over a wide area. The elder has been Albert Goertz from the beginning, resident in Espelkamp-Mittwald. H.S.B.

Ufa, a province of Russia between the Volga and the Ural Mountains, where a daughter settlement was made about 1894 with its center in Davlekanovo (*q.v.*). Until the Revolution of 1917 the settlement made extraordinary economic and cultural progress. It maintained a secondary school in Davlekanovo (a seven-year course, and later nine) and periodically also a Bible school. In the village there were two small Mennonite congregations, and in the neighborhood there were a number more, among them Berezovka (*q.v.*), Gortchakovo, and Karanbash. Most of the settlers were farmers; in Davlekanovo there were several mill owners and merchants. G.H.

Ufa Mennonite Church: see **Davlekanovo.**

Uffhofen, a village in Rheinhessen, Germany, near Flonheim and Alzey, where there has been a Mennonite congregation since 1829. In the early years of the Anabaptist movement it had also spread into the region of Alzey (*q.v.*), and soon after the Thirty Years' War the first Swiss Mennonite refugees settled here, who met for worship in neighboring

Erbesbüdesheim (*q.v.*) and on the Schniftenberger-hof about 1½ hours distant. In 1828-29 the congregation met in the "Geistermühle" near Uffhofen. In 1829 a handsome church was built in Uffhofen with financial assistance from other congregations. Shortly before this, the Wallertheim congregation had fully united with Uffhofen, and in the early 1830's the Spiesheim (*q.v.*) congregation did likewise. Following the death of the preacher Jakob Galle (*q.v.*) of the Geistermühle in 1835, the pastor of the Weierhof congregation looked after the spiritual needs of the congregation. This arrangement has persisted to the present. The membership was nearly 100 in 1850; in 1957 the number of baptized members was 48, and the minister was Paul Schowalter. Since 1890 the congregation has been incorporated. The congregation belongs to the Vereinigung of the German Mennonites, the South German Mennonite Conference, and the Palatine-Hessian Conference. It also contributes to the *Mennonitische Hilfskasse* (*q.v.*).   NEFF.

J. Galle, "Zur Geschichte der Mennonitengemeinde Uffhofen," in *Gem.-Kal.*, 1957, 52-59; *Der Mennonit* IX (1956) p. 170a; *ML* IV.

Uilke Reitses: see Dijkstra, Uilke Reitses.

Uiterdijk, Menzo, b. 1863 at Grijpskerk, d. 1944(?) at Soestdijk, a Dutch Mennonite pastor, serving at Wolvega 1892-94 and Hoorn 1894-1932, wrote two papers on Mennonite history, one on Pieter Ris published in *Doopsgezind Jaarboekje* in 1940, and one on Jacob Spis in *DJ* 1941.   VDZ.

Uitgeest, a village in the Dutch province of North Holland, formerly the seat of a Mennonite congregation, belonging to the Waterlander (*q.v.*) branch. There is only scarce information about this congregation, which in early times seems to have formed a kind of union with the neighboring churches of Knollendam, Krommeniedijk, and Marken-Binnen. About 1635 Abdias Widmarius (*q.v.*), the Reformed pastor of Uitgeest, was a bitter opponent of the Mennonites. A letter of July 1673 gives the information that the Uitgeest congregation belonged to the stricter wing of the Waterlanders, maintaining the authority of the Confession of Faith (by de Ries, *q.v.*) and opposing the Collegiant (*q.v.*) views and practices. In 1670 the congregation joined the Zonist (*q.v.*) conference. In 1678, 1690, and 1733 the congregation contributed to the needs of the Mennonites in the Palatinate and Prussia. After 1740 the pulpit remained vacant; the last (lay) preacher was Lambert Daniels. In 1787 the congregation united with the Knollendam and Marken-Binnen congregation and in 1813 it is said to have died out. Then the meetinghouse is sold and the funds of the congregation, only 34 Dutch guilders, were given to the Rijper (*q.v.*) Sociëteit, of which the congregation had been a member since c1640. Concerning the membership no figures are available. The elder Engel Arendsz van Dooregeest (*q.v.*) belonged to the Visser family of Uitgeest and was born there. (*Inv. Arch. Amst.* I, No. 892; *DB* 1907, 37, 43, 72-76; *DJ* 1942, 40.)

Uitgezochte Liederen *voor den openbaren en huiselijken Godsdienst* (Selected Hymns for Public and Private Meetings) is a Dutch Mennonite hymnal composed of selections from Mennonite and non-Mennonite hymnbooks, containing 163 hymns with notes, published at West-Zaandam in 1809. The compilers were Jan van Geuns, Matthijs Siegenbeek, P. Beets Pzn, and Jeronimo de Vries. The expectation that this hymnal would be accepted as a general Mennonite hymnal in the Netherlands to be used in all congregations was not realized, though soon after the publication fourteen congregations introduced it in their services. It was also for more than 50 years popular for private use. (*DB* 1865, 76, 88-91; 1900, 110-15, 116, 121.)   VDZ.

Uithoorn, a village near Aalsmeer (*q.v.*) in the Dutch province of North Holland, formerly the seat of a Mennonite congregation called "aan den Uit-hoorn." It belonged to the Waterlander (*q.v.*) branch, though in the 18th century it was usually called Flemish. The congregation of Uithoorn is first mentioned in 1647, but no doubt existed long before. Jan Gerrits Buyser (*q.v.*; d. 1697) was long its preacher. There is very little information on its history and size. It belonged to the Zonist (*q.v.*) Conference, and received regular support from the Amsterdam (de Zon) and Rotterdam congregations. Though small in membership and not very wealthy it contributed liberally to the needs of the Prussian Mennonites in 1733 and 1736. Pieter van Dam, a lay preacher, served here 1743-c76. After the old church had been destroyed by fire a small new meetinghouse was built in 1782; Jacob de Hoop was then its elder. From 1784 Uithoorn was served by the preacher of the Aalsmeer Zijdweg congregation and in 1787 it united with this church for the ministry, but the membership was so small that it was dissolved in 1804, and the meetinghouse sold to a Jewish congregation. The last preacher of Uithoorn was Cornelis Schermer, 1790-1804.   VDZ.

Inv. Arch. Amst. II, Nos. 2283 f.; *Naamlijst* 1806, 64, 76; Blaupot t. C., *Holland* I, 332; II, 45, 232; *DB* 1864, 121; 1907, 78; 1918, 3; *De Zondagsbode* XXIV (1910-11) No. 49, p. 195.

Uithuizen, a village in the Dutch province of Groningen, from the 16th century the seat of a Mennonite congregation, which had to endure many hardships in the last decades of this century after persecution had officially ended. In 1583 Johan Arents, the district governor of Uithuizen, fined all the Mennonites, prevented their meetings, and tried to compel them to attend the Reformed services and have their children baptized. In the 17th century it sided with the Groningen Old Flemish and joined the Old Flemish conference. Until c1820 it was served by lay preachers chosen from the membership; Tjaard Pieters served it 1725-78, more than half a century. An influential elder was Lubbert Egges, preacher from 1739, elder 1755, serving until his death in 1770. After his death the congregation steadily declined. The old doctrines were no longer maintained and the young people did not join the church. In 1710 the baptized membership numbered about 65, in 1733 58, in 1754 37 (a meeting held on June 19 of this year led by Lubbert Jans Kremer was, however, attended by more than 130 persons), in 1767 35, in 1798 25, in 1834 only 15.

The last preacher chosen from the congregation was Hendrik Pieters, serving 1789-c1820. From then the pulpit was vacant until 1842. In 1835 the congregation numbered hardly a dozen members and dissolution seemed inevitable; but Simon Gorter (q.v.), pastor of neighboring Zijldijk, succeeded in infusing new life in the Laodiceanism of the Uithuizen church. By 1840 the membership had risen to nearly 30; in 1842-44 A. J. van Pesch, a retired minister of Rotterdam, served, followed by D. Plantinus 1845-47, H. C. Dronrijp Uges 1847-56, L. van Cleeff 1857-94, M. Honigh 1896-1900, P. Oosterbaan 1901-7, H. Hooghiemster 1908-27; after six years of vacancy M. J. J. Gaaikema 1933-46, Dj. E. W. Siccama 1946-50, Miss N. Klaassen 1954- . The membership, 29 in 1840, was 53 in 1861, 98 in 1900, 102 in 1925, 101 in 1958. A parsonage was built in 1842 and a new meetinghouse in 1868, dedicated Aug. 30 (with organ of 1898). Church activities include a ladies' circle, youth group 18-25, youth group 12-18, and Sunday school for children.   vDZ.

Inv. Arch. Amst. II, Nos. 2285 f.; Blaupot t. C., *Groningen* I, 87, 127, 140, 142, 197 f., 238; *DJ* 1840, 43; 1850, 58 f.; *DB* 1868, 169; 1877, 108; 1879, 6; 1898, 240.

Ukowallisten: see U(c)kowallists.

Ukraine (Russian, *Ukraina*), today Ukrainian Soviet Socialist Republic, a republic of the USSR located in the southwest, on the north shore of the Black Sea (Crimea not included), consisted of 171,770 square miles with a population of 30,960,221 (1939) which was increased during World War II to 213,473 square miles and a population of 40,600,000 (1950). The name Ukraine is popularly believed to mean "borderland," but Ukrainian nationalists interpret it to mean "cut off from something in one's possession" (*Slavonic Encyclopedia*, pp. 1, 325). The story of the Ukraine consists of chapters of nationalism, oppression, heroism, and victory. Kiev (q.v.), the capital of the Ukraine, played a significant role in the early history of Russia. The Cossacks became the protectors and defenders of the Ukraine against the Mongolian occupants and invaders.

In Mennonite history the final subjugation of the Ukraine by Catherine II (Empress 1762-96) played a significant role. She had Potemkin (q.v.) colonize and settle the Ukraine by a transfer of population from central Russia and the invitation of foreign settlers to Russia. This has been presented in greater detail in the article **Russia** (q.v.).

Before World War I the Ukraine had become the chief producer of grains, particularly wheat. The Mennonites of the Ukraine contributed to making the Ukraine the bread basket of Europe by introducing new methods of agriculture (q.v.) and by developing flour industries in various areas. In 1955, however, the Ukraine produced only 14 per cent of the total Soviet output of grain, having become more important in industrial pursuits. The iron located near Krivoi Rog, and manganese at Nikopol, which utilize the coal of the Don Region, are significant for industry. Hydroelectric power is produced at the great Dnieprostroy dam in the region

of the former Mennonite settlement of Chortitza. Some of the major industrial centers and cities are Kiev (q.v.), Kharkov (q.v.), Odessa (q.v.), Dnepropetrovsk (formerly Ekaterinoslav, q.v.), Zaporozhe (formerly Alexandrovsk, q.v.), and Chortitza. The foundation for some of these industrial centers, e.g., the last two, was laid by Mennonites. The reason for the shift from agriculture to industry is the fact that the Soviet Union has opened up vast territories for agriculture east of the Ural Mountains and is industrializing the country rapidly, which results in a greater emphasis on the latter in the Ukraine.

Mennonite Settlements. The Ukraine was a major attraction in 1789-1840 not only for the Mennonites, but also for other foreign settlers, particularly from Germany. Two of the major German settlements were those located in the region of Odessa (q.v.), and in the Molotschna with a center named Prischib (q.v.). The Mennonites were in touch with these settlements and this interchange of cultural ideas and stimulation was of mutual benefit.

The most significant provinces of the Ukraine for the Mennonites were Ekaterinoslav (q.v.), Taurida (q.v.), Kherson (q.v.), and Kharkov (q.v.). In Ekaterinoslav and Taurida the two mother settlements of Chortitza (q.v.) and Molotschna (q.v.) were located. Of the 50 or more Mennonite daughter settlements established in Russia 20 were located in Ekaterinoslav, six in Taurida, four in Kherson, and two in Kharkov, making a total of 32 in the Ukraine, not counting the many large private estates. Of the approximately 120,000 Mennonites located in Russia before World War I, about 75,000 lived in the Ukraine (Ehrt, 153); and of the approximately 3,000,000 acres (see *ME* I, 25) of land owned by the Mennonites of Russia at that time, approximately half (Ehrt, 83) was located in the Ukraine. This does not include the Mennonite population and land located in the Crimea, the Caucasus, the Don Region, along the Volga River, or in central Russia. The major Mennonite industrial and business centers in Russia were located in the Ukraine. This was also true of educational institutions and religious and cultural centers.

As long as there was land available in the Ukraine, the Mennonites aimed to establish daughter settlements in the proximity of the two mother settlements of Chortitza and Molotschna. However, some settlers soon moved beyond the Ukraine. Around 1862 Mennonites of the Ukraine found their way to the Crimea (q.v.), which remained a center of attraction. Here the Mennonites acquired more than 100,000 acres of land located in villages and large estates. Another early settlement was in the Kuban (q.v.) at the foothills of the Caucasian Mountains where the Mennonite Brethren (q.v.) and the Templers (q.v.) received special permission for settlement. Molotschna chiliasts under the leadership of A. Peters (q.v.) went to Central Asia to meet the Lord and established the settlement of Auli-Ata (q.v.) in 1882. Toward the end of the century Mennonites of the Ukraine established themselves at Neu-Samara in 1890; Davlekanovo (q.v.) in 1894; Orenburg (q.v.) in 1894; and Siberia (q.v.) in 1898.

MENNONITE SETTLEMENTS IN
the Ukraine, Russia
(According to K. Beil in: Die Mennoniten-Gemeinden in
Russland, Heilbronn, 1921)

Shaded area and underscored name
are Mennonite Settlements
Province boundaries
● Towns and cities
Railroads

Scale of Miles

0   25   50   75   100

KHARKOV

POLTAVA

KHERSON

BACHMUT
Konstantinovka
Debaltsevo
New York
Ivanovka
Bavenkovo
Naumenko
Petrovka
Borissovo
Margaritovka
Alexandrovka
Baldorf
Ruchenkovo
Volnavacha
Herzenberg
Memrik
Kurachovka
Grunau
Bergtal
Mariupol
Berdyansk
Pavlograd
Chaplino
Voskressenkov
Schönfeld (Brazol)
Orechov
Heidelberg
Alexanderwohl
Gnadenfeld
MOLOTSCHNA
Neu-Stuttgart
Tokmak
Prishib
Halbstadt
Lichtenau Oloff
Butterfeld
Waldheim
Gnadenheim
Rückenau

EKATERINOSLAV
Chernovkas
Nizhnedneprovsk
Verkhnedneprovsk
Vilorodova
Rosenhof
Eichfeld
Schönwiese
Zaporozhe
Neu-Rosengart
Chortitza
Nikolaifeld
Yazekovo Vasilevka
Nikolaipol
Neuhorst
Sofievka
Kronsthal
Kronsweide
Schlachtin
Steinfeld
Sakassy
Grünfeld
Osterwick
Eichenfeld Nikolaifeld
Michaelsburg
Olgafeld
Georgtal
FÜRSTENLAND
Krivoi-Rog
Trubetskoye
Zagradovka
Orloff

DNEPR RIVER

INGULETZ RIVER

Ingul River

TAURIDA

Dornburg
Falk-Lein Estate
Wall Estate
Perekop

NIKOLAYEV

Neu-Danzig
Blumenfeld
Poltava
Steinfeld

ODESSA

BLACK SEA

SEA OF AZOV

KALMIUS RIVER

Taganrog

KUBAN TERRITORY
KUBAN RIVER
EKATERINODAR
Novorossiysk
Achtari
Yeisk
Temryuk

CRIMEA
Simferopol
SEVASTOPOL
Yalta
Feodosia
Sudak
Karasubasar
Zürichtal
Neudorf
Menges
Marienthal
Busau
Meshen
Karalar
Baksan
Tamir Bulat
Kronental
Spat
Menlerchik
Tukulchak
Yevpatoriya

In this program of expansion the mother settlements of the Ukraine, particularly their respective centers, such as Chortitza (*q.v.*), Halbstadt (*q.v.*), Orloff (*q.v.*), and Gnadenfeld (*q.v.*), maintained their importance as economic, cultural, and religious centers. The churches established in many of the new settlements remained subsidiaries of the mother churches in the Ukraine for a generation. In spite of the distance, cultural and religious ties kept the daughter settlements attached to their mother settlements. In many instances the mother settlement financed and supervised the settlement of its landless (*q.v.*) population. As a rule in the layout of the villages, the construction of the homes, and the organization of cultural and religious life in the new settlements, they closely resembled the mother settlement, although an adjustment to geographic, climatic, and other local conditions was noticeable.

The spread of large estate owners, who were particularly numerous in the Ukraine, is a chapter in itself. Johann Cornies (*q.v.*) in the early days, and the Sudermann, Schmidt, and Dyck families in the later days, owned large estates. A total of 384 large estates comprised three tenths of the land owned by Mennonites in Russia. The largest estate in the Ukraine was a ranch of 50,000 acres (*ME I*, 25).

The following is a table of the two mother settlements of the Ukraine, Chortitza and Molotschna, and the daughter settlements of these two which were established in the Ukraine. (For a complete list of all settlements, see the article **Russia**.)

A. *Mother Settlements*

Name	Province	Founded	Villages	Acreage	Population
1. Chortitza	Ekaterinoslav	1789 ff.	19	1789: 89,100	1819: 2,888
				1917:405,000	1941:13,965
2. Molotschna	Taurida	1804 ff.	60	1835:324,000	1835: 6,000
					1926:17,347

B. *Daughter Settlements*

Name	Province	Mother Settlement	Founded	Villages	Acreage	Population
1. Bergthal	Ekaterinoslav	Chortitza	1836–52	5	30,000	1874:3,000
2. Hutterthal	Taurida	Radichev	1843	1		
3. Jewish Settlement (Judenplan)	Kherson	Chortitza	1847	6	5-6 families in each village	
4. Johannesruh	Taurida	Hutterthal	1853	1		
5. Hutterdorf	Taurida	Hutterthal	1857	1		
6. Neu-Hutterthal	Taurida		1857	1		
7. Tchornoglaz	Ekaterinoslav	Chortitza	1860	1	2,700	100
8. Crimea	Taurida	Molotschna	1862 ff.	c25 & estates	1929:108,000	1926:4,817
9. Fürstenland	Taurida	Chortitza	1864–70	7	19,000	1874:1,100
10. Borozenko	Ekaterinoslav	Chortitza	1865–66	6	18,000	1910: 600
11. Friedensfeld (Miropol)	Ekaterinoslav	Molotschna	1867	1	5,400	
12. Brazol (Schönfeld)	Ekaterinoslav	Molotschna	1868	4 & estates	1868: 14,000 1910:187,000	1917:2,000
13. Neu-Schönwiese (Dmitrovka)	Ekaterinoslav	Schönwiese-Chortitza	1868	1	3,788	
14. Yazykovo (Nikolaifeld)	Ekaterinoslav	Chortitza	1869	6	23,315	1930:2,200
15. Nepluyevka	Ekaterinoslav	Chortitza	1870	2	10,800	1910: 550
16. Andreasfeld	Ekaterinoslav	Chortitza	1870	3	10,620	
17. Baratov	Ekaterinoslav	Chortitza	1872	2(4)	1872: 9,800	1905:2,569
18. Zagradovka	Kherson	Molotschna	1871	16	57,445	1922:5,429
19. Schlachtin	Ekaterinoslav	Chortitza	1874	2	10,800	1910:1,000
20. Neu-Rosengart	Ekaterinoslav	Chortitza	1878	2	1,800 23,306	1910: 250
21. Wiesenfeld	Ekaterinoslav	Chortitza	1880	1		
22. Memrik	Ekaterinoslav	Molotschna	1885	10	32,400	1,367
23. Alexandropol	Ekaterinoslav	Molotschna	1888	1		15 families
24. Samoylovka	Kharkov	Molotschna	1888	2		1905: 239
25. Miloradovka	Ekaterinoslav	Chortitza	1889	2	5,670	1910: 200
26. Ignatyevo	Ekaterinoslav	Chortitza	1889-90	7	38,132	1910:1,400
27. Naumenko	Kharkov	Chortitza Molotschna	1890	4(3)	14,350	1905: 700
28. Borissovo	Ekaterinoslav	Chortitza	1892	2	13,770	1910: 400
29. Trubetskoye	Kherson	Molotschna	1904	2	118,800(?)	400
30. Kuzmitsky (Alexandrovka)	Ekaterinoslav	Chortitza		1	1910: 4,860	1910: 200
31. Eugenfeld	Ekaterinoslav	Chortitza		1		
32. Alexeyfeld	Kherson	Molotschna		1		

(Sources: Friesen, *Brüderschaft;* Dirks, *Statistik; Die Mennoniten-Gemeinden in Russland;* J. Quiring, *Die Mundart von Chortitza.*)

Cultural Achievements. The contributions which the Mennonites made in Russia, and their cultural achievement, had their foundation in the settlements of the Ukraine. Here the village settlement and administration as well as the cultural and religious life were developed and transplanted to other areas. The Chortitza and Molotschna settlements developed a pattern of education which spread over Russia and exerted a strong influence on some of the Mennonites in North and South America (see **Education** among the Mennonites of Russia). The agricultural and industrial developments of the Mennonites of the Ukraine were also decisive for all the daughter settlements in the rest of Russia. Outposts of industries such as factories and flour mills were established in Mennonite and non-Mennonite communities, many of which became the attraction of businessmen and workers seeking employment (see articles **Millerovo, New York**). The Ukraine with its fertile black soil (chernozem) gave the Mennonites the extraordinary opportunity of experimenting in agriculture and contributing to the development of hard winter wheat (*q.v.*), one of the most desirable export items. In the 1870's this wheat was transplanted from the steppes of the Ukraine to the prairies of Kansas (*q.v.*). The fact that the Ukraine was agriculturally and industrially an undeveloped territory at the time the Mennonites settled there gave them an excellent opportunity to fulfill a service in this area which they discharged with great success. Again it must be pointed out that they were only a minority among the numerous German settlers of the Ukraine who helped to develop this country in the realm of agriculture and industry. (See also articles **Industry, Business,** and **Agriculture.**)

Religious Life and Migrations. The years 1860-80 were significant and crucial for the Mennonites of the Ukraine. Religious life underwent great changes. A certain integration of the Mennonites coming from various backgrounds had taken place, and the later immigrant groups had transplanted from Germany to the Ukraine elements of Pietism which penetrated the whole like a leaven. The separation of the Kleine Gemeinde, led by Klaas Reimer (*q.v.*) early in the 19th century in the Molotschna settlement, resulted from a protest toward certain adjustments and progress. Gradually, however, pietistic influences such as the support of the St. Petersburg Bible Society, evangelistic efforts, mission festivals, abstinence, got a foothold in the brotherhood although they were promoted only by a minority. The South German Pietist Eduard Wüst (*q.v.*), serving an independent pietistic congregation next to the Molotschna settlement, made a great impact on the Mennonites of the Molotschna. A somewhat similar influence was exerted in the Chortitza settlement by the Baptist J. G. Oncken of Hamburg, Germany. All this not only influenced a large segment of the Mennonites of the Ukraine, but also led to schisms culminating in the establishment of the Mennonite Brethren (*q.v.*), Krimmer Mennonite Brethren (*q.v.*), Templers (*q.v.*) or Friends of Jerusalem, Hermann Peters group (Apostolische Brüdergemeinde, *q.v.*), and the movement of A. Peters (*q.v.*), who led a group to Central Asia

(*q.v.*) to meet the Lord at a specifically designated place. Among these separating groups only the Mennonite Brethren (*q.v.*) secured a significant number of followers among the Mennonites and made an outstanding impact on the total Mennonite brotherhood of Russia and later in South and North America. Only this group spread to nearly all daughter settlements of Russia beyond the Ukraine, while the others remained restricted to certain settlements. The Mennonite Brethren strongly emphasized evangelism, missions, abstinence, and baptism by immersion. Particularly through the former two aspects they served as a leaven in the total brotherhood, while through the last point they established a sharp demarcation line which limited contact with the mother group and others primarily to converts to the Mennonite Brethren. The influence of Pietism, although it caused some schisms, also wholesomely leavened the Mennonite brotherhood. Wüst and other evangelistic and pietistic leaders had many friends and followers among the Mennonite brotherhood of Russia around 1860, some of whom were Johann Harder (*q.v.*), Bernhard Harder (*q.v.*), August Lenzmann (*q.v.*), and Cornelius Jansen (*q.v.*). These felt it to be their duty to remain within the brotherhood and revive and strengthen its spiritual life. An outstanding evangelist, educator, and pioneer writer was Bernhard Harder.

Another significant development among the Mennonites of the Ukraine was the new universal conscription law which became known to the Mennonites around 1870, and resulted in a large emigration to North America 1873-80. One of the chief promoters of this emigration for conscience' sake was Cornelius Jansen (*q.v.*), supported by men like Jacob Buller and Dietrich Gaeddert of Alexanderwohl (*q.v.*), Gerhard Wiebe and Johann Wiebe of Bergthal (*q.v.*) and Fürstenland (*q.v.*), both daughter settlements of Chortitza, and Mennonite representatives form Russian Poland and Prussia. This resulted in the first and up to that time the largest Mennonite migration on record. Some 10,000 Mennonites primarily of the Molotschna settlement, Russian Poland, Galicia, and Prussia, settled in the prairie states of the United States, while some 8,000 Mennonites of Chortitza and its two daughter settlements founded a new home in the East and West Reserves of Manitoba (*q.v.*). Those remaining in Russia accepted the responsibility of doing work in forestry service (*q.v.*) beginning in 1880 and in World War I in hospital service. Once again the threat to the principle of nonresistance had alarmed the Mennonites and caused some to leave the country and others to grow into a more active participation and sense of responsibility in the affairs of the country in which they lived. The challenging alternative service program of the Mennonites of Russia had a wholesome influence on the total brotherhood and also caused a closer co-operation between the main groups which had drifted apart since 1860. Again it was the Ukraine which furnished leadership in this significant program in which Mennonite settlements of the remotest areas benefited.

The Revolution and After (1917-43). With the

outbreak of World War I the decline and the ultimate destruction of Mennonite settlements of the Ukraine was ushered in. A severe anti-German feeling which had been previously active in the Russianization policy of the foreign settlers of Russian now sought to destroy the prosperous settlements by confiscating their property and removing them to uninhabited areas. Only the outbreak of the Revolution in 1917 prevented this act. In a way the Mennonites greeted the new day in which the liberal and democratic government under Kerensky was to establish an era of justice for all. However, the Revolution proved to be another and a more radical step toward the annihilation of all that had been achieved by the Mennonites in more than 100 years. First a civil war, typhoid fever, confiscation of property, starvation, and plundering by irregulars at times led by men like Machno (*q.v.*) or individual bandits caused almost unbearable hardships to the settlements of the Ukraine which suffered much more under them than those located in other parts of Russia. Many of the owners of industries and large estates were put to death by bandits after radical Marxian ideas became prevalent, which ideas were often reinforced by a lingering anti-German feeling.

In March 1917 the Revolution began which was to end World War I for Russia. From March until November of that year the Ukraine was under the temporary government of Kerensky, after which the radical Bolsheviks took over the government, remaining in power in the Ukraine from November 1917 to April 1918 when the German army occupied the Ukraine. In November 1918 the German army withdrew and many of the Mennonite settlements were occupied by Machno's bands (*q.v.*) until July 1919, at which time the army of Denikin took over and occupied the territory until October 1919. From October 1919 until January 1920 Machno and his bands reigned again until the Bolsheviks returned. In June 1920 General Peter Wrangel tried once more, as Denikin had before him, to restore the Czarist government. In the fall of 1920 this dream was shattered forever and the Communist regime took over.

All Ukrainian Mennonite settlements and estates suffered severely during these trying years. Several whole villages were slaughtered by Machno's bandits. Among them were Eichenfeld (*q.v.*) and certain villages of Zagradovka (*q.v.*). In some instances Mennonite young men under the guidance of officers of the German occupation army which withdrew, had organized a "Selbstschutz" (*q.v.*) to protect their settlements and particularly the lives of their family members, during the time when there was no established government and there was imminent danger that roving bandits would molest the settlements. A number of young men also joined the forces of the White army (*q.v.*), which was defeated by the Red army. Some 62 of the surviving young men came to America via Constantinople (*q.v.*). As a rule this self-defense of the Mennonites of the Ukraine was not approved of by the Mennonite authorities of the settlements, and in some cases may have provoked action by the Machno irregulars.

Significant during these years of hardship and trial was the help given to the Mennonites of the Ukraine by the American Mennonites administered through the American Mennonite Relief (*q.v.*), and the Dutch Mennonites through their relief agency. Both agencies sent representatives to Russia. The food and clothing supplied distributed and the agricultural machinery which was made available, as well as the spiritual and moral support, were of great help. The U.S. government relief program, the American Relief Administration (ARA) (*q.v.*) also helped much.

Immediately after the establishment of order by the Communist regime, some hopeful Mennonites anticipated a more or less normal although modified economic and cultural life in the settlements. A gradual adjustment to the new regime became noticeable on the one hand, but also a realization on the other hand that the Communist program was too radical. Hence in 1923-27 and again in 1929-30 many thousands left the Ukraine via Moscow and Riga in order to establish new homes in Canada. Those who were more optimistic formed organizations in order to represent their rights and interests under the new Soviet government. One of the most outstanding organizations was the Verband Bürger Holländischer Herkunft (*q.v.*) (Union of Citizens of Dutch Ancestry). A conference called in Orloff in 1917 during the reign of Kerensky, the Allgemeiner Mennonitischer Kongress (*q.v.*), was designed to regulate the total cultural life of the Mennonites of the Ukraine. However, only two sessions could be held. The last Bundeskonferenz met as an All-Ukrainian Conference at Melitopol (*q.v.*) in 1926. At the risk of imprisonment and loss of life the leaders aimed to find a common platform to solve the problems facing them. Under the NEP (New Economic Policy) this was still possible. After Lenin's death in 1926, Stalin inaugurated a radical program of collectivization (*q.v.*) of all land by exiling the formerly more prosperous farmers (Kulaks, *q.v.*), which affected the Mennonites deeply and caused the disruption and final annihilation of most of their cultural values in the Ukraine. Two main waves of exile, one in 1929-30 and the second in 1937-38, reduced the Mennonite population of the Ukraine considerably, especially the male part. Another wave of evacuation occurred when the German army invaded the Ukraine in 1941. Chortitza is an illustration of what happened to the Mennonite population in 1929-38, when 1,456 people out of a total population of 11,666 (1918) were exiled and 1,281 were evacuated by the Russians eastward when the Germans approached in 1941. This evacuation of the German population was much more successful in the settlements east of the Dniepr, such as the Molotschna and many of the daughter settlements, than those west. The Dniepr formed a natural barrier for the invading German army which prevented the removal of the Chortitza Mennonites and gave the Russians enough time to remove a large portion of the Russo-German population east of the Dniepr. All men between the ages of 16 and 65 had been evacuated previously. However, some of the population of Halbstadt and Stulnevo fell into the hands of the approaching German army. The

Soviet authorities still succeeded in evacuating one third of the remaining Molotschna population to Siberia before the German army reached the villages (G. Fast).

Further statistics of the Chortitza settlement acquired during the German occupation of the Ukraine during World War II reveal that of the Chortitza settlement, 245 individuals were killed by Machno's irregulars, and 30 died of starvation in 1921-22 and 1932-33. About one third of the land formerly owned and farmed by the Mennonites of Chortitza was turned over to the neighboring Russian population. All farming was done collectively. All churches were closed by 1935 and used as theaters, clubhouses, stables, or granaries. Conditions in other settlements were very similar.

During the German occupation of large parts of Russia in 1941-43, the Mennonite settlements of the Ukraine and many others were in the hands of the occupational authorities. Although a large percentage of the population had been evacuated before this to Asiatic and Northern Russia, for those who remained in the Ukraine a revival of some aspects of the cultural and religious life took place for a time. Religious services were introduced, ministers were elected, and baptismal services took place. The old school system was revived. But all of this was of short duration. The German authorities themselves began repressive measures against the church parallel to what was going on in Germany at the time under Hitler.

In the fall of 1943 Germany began to evacuate westward the remaining German, including Mennonite, population of the Ukraine. During the middle of September the Halbstadt district of the Molotschna settlement was evacuated by wagons. In October the Chortitza settlement followed by trains, and in November Zagradovka. The population of other settlements was similarly evacuated. The railroad transports consisted as a rule of 50 freight cars each occupied by approximately 1,200 persons. Many of the evacuees, particularly those traveling by wagons, suffered severely from the attacking Russian army and the partisans. The German government planned to settle the Russo-German population, including the Mennonites, in East Germany, some of them in the Warthegau (q.v.), the territory annexed from Poland along the Vistula River, south of the general area from which the Mennonites had left for Russia 150 years earlier. But many were still in camps, not yet in the area, when the advancing Russian army blasted all such plans. It is estimated that the remaining Mennonite population of the Ukraine transported to Germany was about 35,000. In the Warthegau most Mennonites were made German citizens by a mass decree, and most surviving Mennonite men were drafted into the German army.

When, in January 1945, the Russian army entered this territory on its march westward, the Mennonites tried to flee westward toward the provinces of Saxony, Thuringia, Mecklenburg, Hannover, and Bavaria. Most of those who found themselves in the Russian occupied zone of Germany at the end of the war were forcibly repatriated or sent back to Russia. It has been estimated that this must have been

nearly two thirds of the 35,000 Mennonites who had been transported to Germany, which would be over 20,000. Many family members were again separated. The 12,000-14,000 who escaped to Western Germany found new homes in Canada (q.v.) and South America, with the help of the Mennonite Central Committee, the International Refugee Organization (q.v., IRO), and the Canadian Mennonite Board of Colonization. The full story of those who were sent back is not yet known. Most of them, however, were sent to northern and Asiatic Russia. Recently it has become easier for citizens of the Soviet Union to move about. Some family members from various settlements of the Ukraine scattered during the waves of exile, evacuation, and repatriation have found each other. Some have even visited their home communities in the Ukraine and reported the devastation caused by the scorched earth policy of World War II.

The following information indicates that since the beginning of 1956, a few Mennonites have returned to their home communities in the Ukraine. Marie Schellenberg from Siberia writes, "Since Jan. 13, 1956, we are free to travel" (Bote, Oct. 3, 1956, p. 7). In the same issue of Der Bote, D. and N. Vogt report that they were exiled to the Vologda Region in 1945 and that they returned to their own village of Schönhorst in the Chortitza settlement on April 20, 1956, where they were accepted in the Russian collective farm, although Vogt was 70 years old. They report further that the members of the collective farm were prosperous and that the children of the Vogts also plan to return. Mrs. Paul Neufeld reports that her daughter Marus lives in their home village of Nieder-Chortitza, Chortitza settlement, and that she and her daughter Hilda were also planning to return (Bote, Aug. 29, 1956, p. 7).

More Mennonites may find their way back to the Ukraine and even to their former homes, although a mass reoccupation of Mennonite villages is impossible since the land is all collectivized and the villages resettled. It is also possible that a few families, particularly where one spouse was Russian, remained in the Ukraine when the German army evacuated the Mennonite population in 1943. News has been received that in 1955 a congregation had been begun in the former Memrik colony, with regular services. In spite of this it is very doubtful that there will be a general large-scale return of Mennonite families to their former homes in the Ukraine. Many of the older generation have passed from the scene or do not have the possibility of returning, and for the younger generation the Ukraine is no longer "home."

The former Mennonite population of the Ukraine is today dispersed to many parts of the earth. It found its way to the prairie states and provinces of the United States and Canada in 1874-80 when some 18,000 migrated because of the principle of nonresistance. In 1923-30 some 25,000 left the Soviet Ukraine to find new homes in Canada and South America, and after World War II some 14,000 joined their brethren in Canada and in South America. The remaining former Mennonite population of the Ukraine is today found scattered in Northern

European Russia—Vologda Region (*q.v.*) and Arkhangelsk Region, and particularly in the northeast regions of Molotov, Tyumen, Sverdlovsk, and Chelyabinsk; also the Kazakh SSR in Soviet Central Asia (*q.v.*), Semipalatinsk, Karaganda, and Akmolinsk, and the areas of the older Mennonite settlements and regions of Omsk (*q.v.*), Tomsk (*q.v.*), Novosibirsk (*q.v.*), and Slavgorod (*q.v.*), but also in the far southern area of Tadzhikistan. Many were also sent to the various parts of Eastern Siberia. (See also **Soviet Central Asia.**)

The Ukraine was the cradle of the Mennonite settlements and culture in Russia. For 150 years the Mennonites had a unique opportunity to realize their vision and the contribution they could make in an environment which offered unusual opportunities for economic and cultural pioneering. Slavic and nomadic neighbors learned much through the advanced agricultural methods of the Mennonites. Many thousands of Russian young men and women were trained by working and living with the Mennonites in their homes and villages. The Evangelical movement resulting in the founding of the Evangelical Christians and Baptists (*q.v.*) was greatly influenced by the Mennonites of the Ukraine, which is illustrated by the fact that there is co-operation between the two at this time and that the Mennonites are being paid back in the form of being taken into the congregations and fellowship of these groups wherever they are located close to Baptist churches.   C.K.

Clarence Manning, *The Story of the Ukraine* (New York, 1947); N. D. Polonska-Vasylenko, "The Settlement of the Southern Ukraine (1750-1775)," *The Annals of the Ukrainian Academy of Arts and Sciences in the U.S.* (New York, 1955); John A. Armstrong, *Ukrainian Nationalism 1939-1945* (New York, 1955); B. Yakovlev, *Concentration Camps in the USSR* (Russian) (Münich, 1955); E. Glowinskyj, "Agriculture in the Ukraine"; O. Arkhymovych, "Grain Crops in the Ukraine," *Ukrainian Review* II (Munich, 1956); Shankowsky, "Nazi Occupation in Ukraine," *Ukrainian Review* II (London, 1955); W. C. Wiseley, "The German Settlement of the 'incorporated territory' of the Wartheland and Danzig-West Prussia, 1939-1945" (Ph.D. dissertation, London, 1955).

Mennonites: Franz Isaac, *Die Molotschnaer Mennoniten* (Halbstadt, 1908); Alexander Petzholdt, *Reise im westlichen und südlichen europäischen Russland im Jahre 1855* (Leipzig, 1864); D. H. Epp, *Johann Cornies* (Rosthern, 1946); Jacob Quiring, *Die Mundart von Chortitza in Süd-Russland* (Munich, 1928); Adolf Ehrt, *Das Mennonitentum in Russland* (Berlin, 1932); Gerhard Töws, *Schönfeld* (Winnipeg, 1939); Friesen, *Brüderschaft;* D. H. Epp, *Die Chortitzer Mennoniten* (Odessa, 1889); Gerhard Lohrenz, *Sagradovka* (Rosthern, 1947); H. Goerz, *Memrik* (Rosthern, 1954); H. Goerz, *Die Molotschnaer Ansiedlung* (Steinbach, 1950-51); C. Henry Smith, *The Story of the Mennonites* (Newton, 1957); *idem, The Coming of the Russian Mennonites* (Berne, 1927); Gustav Reimer and G. R. Gaeddert, *Exiled by the Czar* (Newton, 1956); D. G. Rempel, "The Mennonite Colonies in New Russia . . ." (unpubl. doctoral dissertation at Stanford Univ., 1933); P. Hildebrandt, *Erste Auswanderung der Mennoniten aus dem Danziger Gebiet nach Südrussland* (Halbstadt, 1888); A Klaus, *Unsere Kolonien* (Odessa, 1887); Unruh, *Hintergründe;* Leonhard Froese, *Das pädagogische Kultursystem der mennonitischen Siedlungsgruppe in Russland* (Göttingen, 1949); George J. Eisenach, *Pietism and the Russian Germans in the United States* (Berne, 1948); D. Neufeld, *Mennonitentum in der Ukraine Schicksalgeschichte Sagradowkas* (Emden, 1922); *Die Mennoniten-Gemeinden in Russland während der Kriegs- und Revolutionsjahre 1914-1920* (Heilbronn, 1921); A. H. Unruh, *Die Geschichte der Mennoniten-

Brüdergemeinde 1860-1954* (Winnipeg, 1954); K. Stumpp, *Bericht über das Gebiet Chortitza* . . . (Berlin, 1943); *idem, Bericht über das Gebiet Kronau-Orloff* . . . (Berlin, 1943); *Der Bote* (Rosthern); *Mennonitische Rundschau* (Winnipeg); *Mennonite Life* (North Newton); *Mennonitisches Jahrbuch,* ed. Heinrich Dirks (Gross-Tokmak, 1901-14); Cornelius Krahn, "Russian Baptists and Mennonites," *Menn. Life* XI (July 1956) 99.

Ukrainian Mennonite General Conference was held Oct. 5-8, 1926, in the town of Melitopol, Ukraine, Russia, with 84 representatives from the USSR (Ukrainian Soviet Republic), 64 of these from the Mennonite Church and 19 from the Mennonite Brethren and Alliance groups. The total membership of the churches represented was 18,356 in the Mennonite Church and 4,025 in other groups. From other parts of Soviet Russia 14 representatives came, who were given an advisory voice in the conference; of these, two came from the Volga-Trakt area, two from the Caucasus, two from the Crimea, three from Siberia, one from Neu-Samara, two from Orenburg, one from Ufa, and one from Turkestan. This conference was a successor to the General Conference of Mennonites (see **Allgemeine Bundeskonferenz**). The proceedings were conducted in the German language. The sessions were also attended by two representatives of the Ukrainian Soviet government, which had given permission for the meeting. The central business of the conference was establishing an organization for the Mennonite churches in the Ukraine. The organization was built on four levels: first, the autonomous individual congregations; second, the local district union; third, the All-Ukrainian Union; and fourth, the union in the framework of the entire Soviet Union. The projected constitution was accepted by a committee with small changes, to be presented at once for ratification. The first executive committee for the republic was chosen at once, consisting of 11 persons. The second point on the agenda was the Bible school. Not much time was devoted to this subject, since the conference was permited to deal only with the principle of the question. The vote showed that it was the wish of the meeting to have a general Bible school for all the Mennonite branches, to be under the management of the conference.

The improvement of religious and moral conditions in the congregations was discussed, together with suggested means toward achieving this end. Work for the young people was the last matter discussed.

This conference holds an important place in the history of the Russian Mennonite churches in that it was the first conference in the framework of the Ukraine. Unfortunately no further meetings were permitted by the government. (*ML* IV.) D.H.E.

Ulcke Ricoltswiif, a Dutch Anabaptist martyr, drowned on Feb. 4, 1557, at Leeuwarden in Friesland, because "she had received rebaptism and harbored derogatory ideas concerning the sacred sacrament of the mass." Particulars are lacking. vDZ.

Inv. Arch. Amst. I, No. 746; J. Reitsma, *Honderd jaren uit de Geschiedenis der Hervorming . . . in Friesland* (Leeuwarden, 1876) 63.

Uliman, Wolfgang: see **Uolimann, Wolfgang.**

Ulm, a city (pop. 69,941) in Württemberg, Germany, located on the Danube, until 1803 a free city of the empire. Here the Reformation was introduced about 1524-26 by Konrad Sam, and continued by Bucer (q.v.), Oecolampadius (q.v.), Blaurer (q.v.), and Rabus (q.v.). During the first 20 years it was Zwinglian in character, but after a bitter struggle Lutheranism took the upper hand. In consequence of this unpleasant strife, serious, peaceful citizens turned away from the church of Luther and Zwingli and joined the Anabaptists. It may have been Simon Stumpf (q.v.) who transplanted Anabaptist ideas into Ulm, on which Hans Hut (q.v.) built in 1527 and Wilhelm Reublin (q.v.) in 1528. It is reported that Reublin was for a time the leader (Vorsteher) of the congregation. According to the report of the magistrate on Sept. 16, 1527, Hans Denk (q.v.), Ludwig Haetzer (q.v.), and B. Beckenknecht (see Beck, Hans) lived here for a while too. They probably came from Augsburg, where they had attended the Martyrs' Synod (q.v.) on Aug. 20, 1527. But the council saw to it that they soon left the city. Among the prominent converts were the councillors and master goldsmiths Hans Müller and Daniel Hochweher.

On Feb. 14, 1528, the severe imperial mandate (see Mandates) was read to the populace as a deterrent to the movement. From this time on many Anabaptists were called to give an account of themselves before the privy council; among them were Daniel Hochweher and his wife and sister, and also Claus Sporer on July 13. Sporer declared that he was not an Anabaptist (i.e., rebaptizer), for "his first baptism had not been anything; it had given nothing and taken nothing; therefore it was without value." He made a sharp distinction between those who held their wives and all things in common and rejected authority (the Münsterites) and the group in Ulm.

Expulsions from the city now were ordered, especially because Diepold von Stein, the captain of the Swabian League, earnestly admonished the Ulm commander, Philipp von Wenkheim, to pursue the Anabaptists with more rigor. Von Wenkheim replied that he had orders to act rigorously only in case of sedition. In Ulm they were trying to meet the situation first by indoctrination; if this was fruitless, they expelled the obstinate from the city; if they returned, they were put into the tower.

In the villages round about Ulm there were also many Anabaptists. Again and again they were summoned to answer to the religious authorities. In Böhningen they had free entry to the home of the pastor, Martin Karter, since "they liked to hear his sermons." The parson was said to have stated that if he were the ruler of the land he would not expel any Anabaptists.

A courageous, steadfast Anabaptist was Abraham Schneider, also called Brendlin. He defended himself with great ability. He said that if the children had a hidden faith, as was claimed, then they should also have a hidden baptism; an oath was permissible to a Christian in case it was not contrary to God, contrary to the love of one's neighbor, or contrary to the conscience of the person rendering the oath. It is thus evident that the Ulm Anabaptists were

Swiss Brethren. Because they would not accept instruction they had to leave the city territory. Other leading Anabaptists were the physician Nicolas Lauer, Jörg Wernlin (q.v.), and Hans Glaser.

Even if the Ulm congregation never attained the importance of the Augsburg congregation, Ulm was nevertheless an important point on the route of Anabaptist leaders who led to Moravia the converts they had won in Switzerland or along the Rhine. The Anabaptists lodged in the inn "To the Sun" near the bridge over the Danube until the boatmen of Ulm took them further on the Danube. The council decided that it would have to comply with the order of Duke Ernest not to aid the Anabaptists in this way any longer. Thereupon in 1587 the two Anabaptist leaders, Jörg Gutter and Christoph Hirzel, the latter a native of Zürich, were arrested in Ulm. By threats of the rack, the authorities vainly tried to force admissions about their brethren. But the severer measures were not applied; instead, the men were expelled from Ulm and its territory. Although the council of Ulm was relatively lenient in its treatment of the Anabaptists, never for instance confiscating their property, nevertheless under the decisive action of the church superintendent Ludwig Rabus (q.v.; 1556-92) the Anabaptist movement in Ulm died out.

Fritz Friedrich thinks it must be assumed that many of those with Anabaptist inclinations united with the Schwenckfelders (q.v.) in order to avoid persecution, for the latter group was tolerated for a long time in Ulm; and also that Helene Streicher (q.v.), the widow of a merchant, and her daughter Agathe, who later became Schwenckfelders, must originally have been Anabaptists. The latter was a widely known physician; the bishops of Mainz and even Maximilian demanded her services. Friedrich also thinks that in all probability Schwenckfeld (q.v.) spent the last period of his life in the Streicher home on the square in Ulm on Agathe's invitation; he died there on Dec. 10, 1561, and was secretly buried in the basement. After 1589 nothing more is heard of Anabaptists in Ulm. **W.W.**

TA Württemberg; H. Dietrich, D. Konrad Dietrich und sein Briefwechsel (Ulm, 1930) 19; Gottlob Egelhaar, "Geschichte der Reichsstadt Ulm," in Beschreibung des Oberamts Ulm II (Ulm, 1897) 32 ff.; Fritz Friedrich, "Ulmische Kirchengesch. vom Interim bis zum 30-jährigen Krieg 1548-1612," in Blätter für Württemb. Kirchengesch., n.s. I (1933) No. 3-4; Fr. Keidel, "Ulmische Religionsakten 1531-1552," in Württemb. Vierteljahreshefte (1896) 255; K. Th. Keim, Ref.-Gesch. der Reichsstadt Ulm (1851); Fr. Thudichum, Die Deutsche Reformation II (Leipzig, 1909); ML IV.

Ulrich, Duke of Württemberg (1487-1550), was badly reared, became independent too soon, was unhappily married to Sabine of Bavaria, compensated himself by living in splendor, fell into debt that required increased taxes, against which Poor Conrad in the Remstal revolted, and was compelled to accept the terms of the very humiliating treaty of Tübingen. The murder of Hans von Hutten in the forest, the flight of his wife, the violence with which he attached the imperial city of Reutlingen to Württemberg, stirred up the nobility, the dukes of Bavaria, and the Swabian League against him. In 1519 he was driven from his domain by the Swabian

League, who sold it to Charles V, who in turn gave it to his brother Ferdinand. While in Switzerland Ulrich was won to the Reformation by Hartmut von Kronberg and Oecolampadius.

After several attempts to regain his lands, completely impoverished, Ulrich fled to Philip of Hesse, who in the victory of Lauffen on May 13, 1534, restored to him his hereditary lands. But in the treaty of Kaaden, Ulrich had to acknowledge Austria's sovereignty. In gratitude to God Ulrich introduced the Reformation, and to that end called Erhard Schnepf for the region below the Staig, and Ambrose Blarer (q.v.) for the region above the Staig.

The treaty of Kaaden compelled the duke to adopt measures against the Anabaptists. On June 18, 1535, he issued the first Anabaptist decree concerning persons who recanted, and on May 22 a mandate ordering the arrest of native Anabaptists as well as those who came in from the outside. In 1536 he demanded an official opinion of the Tübingen jurists and theologians. The jurists replied that according to canonical law death was the penalty for rebaptism; nevertheless the duke had the right to exercise lenience. The theologians, recognizing the unfeigned simplicity, the zeal, the good appearance of the life of the Anabaptists in contrast to the wild, bold, and wicked life of the populace, earnestly opposed the death penalty and all corporal punishment, and recommended for the leaders and dangerous persons a term in the tower, and after release the wearing of a wooden placard depicting a wolf, a snake, or some other obnoxious beast, exclusion from all meetings, inns, weddings, and as a final punishment, expulsion from the country. Thereupon the duke issued a new regulation requiring the arrest of all Anabaptists and a close cross-examination, and defining the treatment of those who were pardoned. On the whole the Anabaptists were treated with lenience under Ulrich.

Following his defeat in the Smalkaldic War, Ulrich was compelled to humiliate himself before the emperor, pay a severe indemnity, permit his fortresses Asperg, Schorndorf, and Kirchheim to be occupied by Spanish troops, and to submit to the Interim, while Ferdinand threatened him with a court action on a charge of disloyalty as a subject; his death circumvented this misfortune. His difficulties and his return to Protestantism moderated the character of the prince and made him popular. G.Bos.

H. Hermelink, Gesch. der Evangelischen Kirche in Württemberg bis zur Gegenwart (Tübingen, 1949) 60 ff.; L. F. Heyd, Ulrich, Herzog zu Württemberg I-III (Tübingen, 1841-44); B. Kugler, Ulrich, Herzog zu Württemberg (Stuttgart, 1865); D. I. Rauscher, Württembergische Ref.-Gesch. (Stuttgart, 1934) III f.; Ch. F. von Stälin, Württembergische Geschichte IV (Stuttgart, 1873); ML IV.

Ulrich II, Count of East Friesland 1628-47, brother of Rudolf Christian (q.v.), a weak ruler of vacillating character. This trait was evident in his treatment of the Mennonites. He did not renew the letter of protection given by his brother, but continued to collect the protection fee. On Aug. 30, 1631, he issued a new regulation which released the Mennonites from the oath, permitting in its stead the *Mennisten Eid,* the formula of which included a

statement that untruthfulness would carry the same penalty as perjury.

Quite suddenly the count issued an edict on March 10, 1641, which on the basis of complaints raised against the Mennonites (though they were not specifically mentioned), forbade their holding private meetings in which unauthorized persons preached. The edict was enforced. On Feb. 1, 1644, a religious meeting of the Mennonites in Oldeborg was broken up and Johann Siewerds, the preacher, was imprisoned. It was obviously a matter of extorting money from the Mennonites in order to mend Ulrich's financial status, for a note signed by the count on Aug. 23, 1644, shows that the Mennonites gave him 6,000 Reichstaler in exchange for a certain degree of security. This event marked a change in the count's attitude.

Ulrich showed personal favor to Uco Walles (q.v.), granting him and his party a letter of protection made out by him personally on Nov. 26, 1645. About two years later the other Mennonites also received the assurance that the count would henceforth treat them with favor, in return for their making a four-year prepayment of their protection fee of 880 talers, whereas the Ukowallists paid 120 talers. NEFF.

P. Müller, *Die Mennoniten in Ostfriesland vom 16. bis zum 18. Jahrhundert* (Emden and Borkum, 1887) 60, note 35; ML IV.

Ulrich, an Anabaptist martyr executed at Bern, Switzerland, in late 1537 or early 1538. He was a farmer of Rügsau in the canton of Bern. Particulars are lacking. Wolkan mentions an Anabaptist elder Ulrich who about 1535 baptized at Urban in Moravia. This may have been the same person. (*Mart. Mir.* E 1129; Wolkan, *Lieder,* 32.) vDZ.

Ulrich Foundation, Inc., Roanoke, Ill., was incorporated in 1949 as a nonprofit corporation for religious, charitable, and educational work, and scientific and agricultural service and research. In 1958 its officers were R. M. Ulrich, president; Verda Ulrich, vice-president; and Harold A. Zehr, executive secretary. Its planning committee consisted of R. M. Ulrich, Harold A. Zehr, John D. Hartzler, N. D. Kennell, Ivan R. Bachman, and John P. Ulrich. The major activity of the Foundation is the operation of a program near Aibonito, Puerto Rico, which included experimentation in dairying, poultry production, artificial breeding, horticulture, and the operation of a dental service. The program supplements the work of the Mennonite Board of Missions and Charities (q.v.) in the area. The local director was Lawrence Greaser. The organ of the Foundation is *The Foundation Echo.* H.A.Z.

Ulrum, a small village in the northeast of the Dutch province of Groningen, formerly the seat of a Mennonite congregation existing already in the 16th century and later belonging to the Groningen Old Flemish branch. Concerning its history there is little information. At the Old Flemish conference meetings it was represented only in the 18th century. In 1686 and again in 1717 Ulrum was severely struck by a flood of the North Sea; on Nov. 12,

1686, the church lost a member by drowning, and some cattle; much more severe were the losses on Christmas Day of 1717; besides large numbers of cattle (275 cows, 72 horses, 120 sheep, owned by Mennonites), the small congregation of Ulrum lost two men, nine women, and seventeen children. This was the heaviest flood known in history to strike the province of Groningen; it killed no fewer than 2300 persons. According to a circular of the Groningen Old Flemish conference (Sociëteit), which started a relief action in behalf of the Mennonite victims of the flood, Ulrum was the worst hit congregation.

The baptized membership of Ulrum, numbering *c*80 in 1710, rapidly decreased in the 18th century to 45 in 1733, 34 in 1754, and only 8 in 1767, but in the following years there was a considerable increase; in 1792 Ulrum and Houwerzijl (*q.v.*), with which Ulrum united in 1773, together numbered about 60 members. Ulrum was always served by lay preachers chosen from the congregation. From 1783 the pulpit was vacant; an attempt made in 1785 to merge with the Flemish congregation of neighboring den Hoorn failed. In 1791 both Ulrum and Houwerzijl joined the Mennonite conference of Friesland, but this lasted only two years, for in 1793 both were dissolved. Some of the remaining (about 15) members merged with the Den Hoorn (*q.v.*) congregation, but most of them joined the Reformed Church. The meetinghouse was sold. vDZ.

Inv. Arch. Amst. II, No. 2287; Blaupot t. C., *Groningen* I, 127, 140, 142, 202; *Naamlijst* 1792, 59; 1793, 58; old Archives of the congregation of Groningen, No. 146; *DJ* 1840, 43; *DB* 1879, 6; 1906, 46.

Ulus, a pagan tribe in Sumatra (*q.v.*), among whom the Dutch Mennonite missionaries worked. N. D. Schuurmans (*q.v.*) published a thorough report about them in *Mennonitische Blätter* (1891, supplement to No. 11).

Umbitter was a name applied to a deacon (*q.v.*) by the Mennonites of Prussia when he performed special duties in regard to betrothals. Only few references can be found. Mannhardt states (p. 112) that it was the duty of the Umbitter or the minister to go and ask the parents of a girl whether she would be willing to marry a certain young man. He states that on May 5, 1765, it was reported at the brotherhood meeting that the honored tradition that two Umbitters take the marriage proposal to the parents of the girl was falling into disrepute and that some young men were beginning to make their own proposals, even without the knowledge of the parents. It is likely that the Umbitter was also a handy man in taking notices and invitations from home to home or announcing in writing the approaching marriages and funerals. This tradition, no doubt, was transplanted from Holland to Prussia and was perpetuated in Russia and among the Prussian Mennonites of America. Most traces of this practice disappeared during the 19th century. No detailed study of the duties and the practices in connection with the Umbitter has been made. The counterpart of the Umbitter in the Amish congregations was the Steckliman. C.K.

H. G. Mannhardt, *Die Danziger Mennonitengemeinde* (Danzig, 1919) 112-13.

Ummel (in America also Umble), a Mennonite family, whose members originally lived in the Emmental (*q.v.*) area of the Swiss canton of Bern. In 1569 a Barbly (Ummel) Rüsser was examined, and afterwards tortured because of her Anabaptist views. Her daughter Anni Ummel was also tried. On July 23 both women, after recanting, had to confess publicly in the church of Wichtrach, but in 1574 Barbly Ummel was again in prison at Bern because of Anabaptism and again promised henceforth to be a loyal member of the Reformed Church. In the 17th century some of the Ummel family moved to the Bernese Jura; among its descendants was David Ummel (*q.v.*), a prominent elder at La Chaux de Fonds. Other Ummels fled to the Palatinate (*q.v.*) in 1670-71, among whom was Christian Ummel aged 39, with his wife and five children. About the same time or shortly after some Ummels emigrated to Alsace (*q.v.*).

Probably the Ummels were not very numerous in the Palatinate. In Alsace they were found in the early 18th century in the Montbéliard congregation. The first Ummel who emigrated to America was Christian Ummel, an Amishman, who arrived at Philadelphia Oct. 5, 1767, and settled in Lancaster County, Pa. Among the American Umbles are John Umble (b. 1881) and his son Roy Umble, professors at Goshen College.

The family tradition that the Ummels stem from Ireland is not probable. vDZ.

Inv. Arch. Amst. I, No.1248; S. Geiser, *Die Taufgesinnten-Gemeinden* (Karlsruhe, n.d.) 201 f., 203, 478; Müller, *Berner Täufer,* 201; D. L. Gratz, *Bernese Anabaptists* (Scottdale, 1953) 38, 48, 68, 118, 191, 197; C. Henry Smith, *Mennonite Immigration to Pennsylvania* (Norristown, 1929) 239, note 75.

Ummel, David (1797-1896), elder of the Chaux d'Abel (*q.v.*) Mennonite congregation in the Bernese Jura, Switzerland. The patriarch David Ummel was born at Chaux d'Abel on Sept. 14, 1797. He originally belonged to the Amish wing, and was ordained as minister and elder by that group. He was zealously concerned for union between the Amish and the Mennonites in his locality. Though he was zealous "for the law of the fathers," he preached that salvation in Christ is nothing but free grace even for a virtuous Mennonite. He was seriously concerned for the education of the young people, and at considerable sacrifice founded a German school in his village, which later received state recognition. At the age of 90 he made a six-week tour of the Swiss congregations. He died in 1896 at the advanced age of 98 years. S.G.

Samuel Geiser, *Die Taufgesinnten-Gemeinden* (Karlsruhe, 1931) 464, with photograph, and 478; *Menn. Bl.,* 1871, 2; 1872, 21-68; 1878, 75; *ML* IV.

Umstatt, Hans Peter, moved from Crefeld, Germany, to Germantown, Pa., in 1685. His daughter Eva married the immigrant Hendrick (Heinrich) Pannabecker (*q.v.*). His son Johannes (John) Umstatt moved in 1702 or shortly after to Perkiomen Township along the Skippack (*q.v.*). C. Henry Smith assumes that the Umstatts were Mennonites, and this is probable since later descendants called Umstead were to be found in the Mennonite church in Montgomery County, Pa. vDZ.

C. Henry Smith, *The Menn. Immigration to Pennsylvania* (Norristown, 1929) 94, 106, 114, 121, 139 note 23; *MQR* VII (1933) 234 f.

Unger, a Mennonite family found in West Prussia, Germany, from the 17th century until 1945, in the congregations of Thiensdorf, Orlofferfelde (Tiegenhof), Tragheimerweide, Danzig-Neugarten. In 1793 Peter Unger was the first member of this family to emigrate to Russia, settling at Chortitza; after 1800 a number of other Ungers followed. (Reimer, *Familiennamen,* 119; Unruh, *Hintergründe,* 211 *et passim.*) vdZ.

Unger, Abraham (1820-80), elder of the Einlage (*q.v.*) Mennonite congregation, in the Chortitza settlement, Ukraine, in the forefront of the great movement among the Russian Mennonites which led to the formation of the Mennonite Brethren. On March 4, 1862, he was baptized by immersion. On March 11 others followed his example; hence March 11, 1862, is considered the date of the founding of the Einlage Mennonite Brethren Church. Unger was chosen as minister of the congregation. In 1859-60 he corresponded with J. G. Oncken (*q.v.*), the Baptist preacher in Hamburg, and leaned strongly toward Baptist ideas. In 1868 he was chosen elder at a members' meeting conducted by Benzien (*q.v.*), a Baptist preacher; he was ordained Oct. 18, 1869, by Oncken, who made the trip to Russia for the purpose at Unger's request. Under Unger's influence the Mennonite Brethren made baptism by immersion obligatory for their members, refusing to admit anyone to communion who had not thus been baptized. The entire period of his work was a stormy one. The opposing parties were very rigid toward each other. It was impossible to effect a union among the ministers. In the middle 1860's, when it seemed that the "overly-happy" (*Ueberfröhlichen*) would gain the upper hand, they excommunicated him, but were unable to eliminate his influence. He succeeded in averting the danger threatening the brotherhood on the part of this group. In 1876 he resigned his position as elder, but was to the end of his life, in 1880, one of the most influential men of the brotherhood. A.Br.

Union Chapel, located in the northern part of the Middle River District of Augusta County, Va., was built by United Brethren and Mennonites (MC) in the 1870's. Mennonite ministers of the Southern and Middle Districts of the Virginia Conference held services here once a month for many years. No services have been held here by the Mennonites since 1948. H.A.B.

Union County (Pa.) Amish congregation, founded in the Buffalo Valley west of Lewisburg in 1837 by Samuel Lantz and six of his sons-in-law, of Leacock Twp., Lancaster Co., Pa. Several settlers with Amish names had acquired land there fifteen to twenty years earlier. Joining the Lantz family were Hannes and Jacob Beiler, brothers, Solomon Yoder, bishop, and John and Jacob Riehl of Mifflin County, Pa., and several other families from Lancaster and Mifflin counties and from Maryland. Two sons-in-law of Samuel Lantz, Elias Riehl, nephew of Solomon Yoder, and Christian Stoltzfus, were ordained bishop and deacon respectively and worked together harmoniously for many years. During the late 1870's when trouble developed between the bishop's and the deacon's sons, a ministers' committee from Mifflin County silenced the bishop and excommunicated the only two families who supported him. The bishop then united with the Juniata Mennonite congregation. After the death of Christian Stoltzfus in 1883 his sons and daughters and their families moved to Lyon County, Kan., and Lancaster County, Pa. A few of the young people organized a Sunday school but the congregation had suffered a deathblow. The few remaining members who did not move away united with other denominations. Three cemeteries remain: Stoltzfus near Kelley Point, Lantz several miles south, and Beiler at the southern limits of the settlement. Within recent years several reunions of the descendants of the early settlers have aroused interest in caring for the cemeteries. Mennonite families from the Lancaster Mennonite Conference began moving into the valley and in 1948 organized the Buffalo congregation. The membership in 1956 was 85, with Jacob J. Brubaker and John H. Erb as ministers. J.S.U.

John Umble, "The Amish Mennonites of Union County, Pennsylvania," *MQR* VII (July 1933) 162-90.

Union Gospel Printing Company, Cleveland, Ohio (now Union Gospel Press, 2000 Broad Park Road), was established in 1903 by W. B. Musselman, a minister in the Pennsylvania Conference of the M.B.C. Church, who bought the printing plant of the Light and Hope Publishing Co. (*q.v.*) in Cleveland. It has published the *Gospel Herald* for many years, and 1909-16 was the officially authorized publisher of the *Gospel Banner,* the organ of the M.B.C. Church. H.S.B.

Union Mennonite Church, former name of the White Cloud (Mich.) Mennonite Church (MC) (*q.v.*).

Union Mennonite Church (MC), located in Orange County, Va., now extinct. In the 1910's two Shenandoah Valley Mennonite families, Charles Good and John Good, moved east of the Blue Ridge, locating 5 miles east of Gordonville, in Orange County. There was a union or community church near by which Mennonite ministers of the Middle District of the Virginia Conference were permitted to use when they held monthly services for these families. Several native families united with the church. Later Mennonites withdrew from the community and services were discontinued about 1930. H.A.B.

Union Township Mennonite Church: see **Logan County,** Ohio.

Unitarianism. The charge of Unitarianism laid at the door of early Anabaptism by a number of writers is discussed by Robert Friedmann in the article **Anti-Trinitarianism** (*q.v.*), where the later contacts between Hutterites and Dutch Mennonites with the Socinians (*q.v.*), are also discussed. The outstanding cases charged with Unitarianism were Ludwig Haetzer (*q.v.*), Hans Denk (*q.v.*), and Adam Pastor (*q.v.*), although certain writers have attempted to show a wider spread. The latest study on Haetzer (Goeters, 1957) proves that he was not a regular Anabaptist but only a fringe figure in the movement, but that he was a Unitarian in his Christology. The latest study on Hans Denk (Kiwiet, 1957) proves that Denk was not a Unitarian even though Weis and Wilbur, the Unitarian historians, claim him as a forerunner of modern Unitarianism (Wilbur with some limitations). Adam Pastor was, however, an open Unitarian, and as such was excommunicated at the elders' conference at Goch in 1547, a few short years after his ordination as elder by Menno, a sufficient proof that the Anabaptist movement in Holland and Northwest Germany was solidly Trinitarian. Dosker's contention, "There is no question whatever but from the very beginning the Anabaptists had very cloudy ideas concerning the trinity. Menno's view looks strangely like Modalism. And in this connection, it is very significant that Socinianism flourished largely in states like Poland, where the Anabaptists had settled down in force; and also that this same Socinianism, once it was fully established and defined, had a disastrous effect on the later development of the Dutch Anabaptists," is extreme and in error. That the largely untrained and simply Biblicistic early Anabaptists did not formulate precise and refined theological views on the trinity is not to be interpreted as anti-Trinitarianism. The views of the leading Anabaptist writers such as Pilgram Marpeck (*q.v.*), Peter Riedemann (*q.v.*), Menno Simons (*q.v.*), and Dirk Philips (*q.v.*) are clearly Trinitarian.

Most of the discussions of the question of Trinitarianism and anti-Trinitarianism have to do with the question of the relation of Christ the Son to God the Father. The matter of the personality of the Holy Spirit (*q.v.*) is seldom discussed. Here again Dosker's assertions are extreme. He quotes (158) Schijn (giving an incorrect location), "As to the Holy Ghost, He is the power, wisdom, breath of God, but His personality is left in doubt." But again the four major writers mentioned above are completely clear on the personality and deity of the Holy Spirit. Dosker's attempt to taint the whole early Anabaptist movement with at least uncertainty on Trinitarianism if not outright anti-Trinitarianism (*q.v.*) does not stand the test of objective scholarship.

In the 19th century Modernism captured much of Dutch Mennonitism with the result that for some decades in the latter part of the 19th century and on into the early 20th century most Dutch Mennonite ministers were Unitarian in theology. But by midcentury this was largely overcome.   H.S.B.

H. E. Dosker, *The Dutch Anabaptists* (Philadelphia, 1921); Schijn-Maatschoen, *Geschiedenis* III; Jan J. Kiwiet, "The Life of Hans Denk," *MQR* XXXI (1957) 227-59; *idem*, "The Theology of Hans Denk." *MQR* XXXII (1958) 3-27; J. F. Goeters, *Ludwig Hätzer (ca. 1500 bis 1529), Spiritualist und Antitrinitarier, eine Randfigur der frühen Täuferbewegung* (Gütersloh, 1957); E. M. Wilbur, *A History of Unitarianism: Socinianism and its Antecedents* (Cambridge, 1946); F. L. Weis, *The Life and Teachings of Ludwig Hetzer* (n.p., n.d.-1939); *idem, The Life, Teachings and Works of Johannes Denck, 1495-1527* (n.p., n.d.-1925).

United Bethel Conservative Mennonite Church, located near Plain City, in Madison Co., Ohio, a member of the Conservative (Amish) Mennonite Conference, was started by a few Amish families who met for Sunday school, beginning in 1938. Andrew Farmwald was ordained as minister, and Harry Stutzman, of Holmes County, Ohio, was given bishop oversight of the church. Enos Yoder was ordained to the ministry on Jan. 26, 1948, and was still the minister in charge in 1957. The meetinghouse, built in 1948, is a frame structure seating 300 persons. In 1957 the membership was 164, with Ray F. Miller as bishop in charge.   A.D.F.

United Mennonite Bible School, St. Catharines, Ont., of the Canadian Mennonite Conference (GCM), was founded in 1950 and conducted a five-month term each year. In 1955-56, the last year of operation, the enrollment was 17; John W. Neufeld was principal.   M.G.

United Mennonite Educational Institute (GCM), Route 3, Wheatley, Ont., was established in 1944. The 1957-58 enrollment was 86, and its faculty numbered four, with Peter C. Sawatzky as principal. Eleven men were on its board of directors, whose chairman was Ewald Wiebe Staples. The institution has two buildings, a classroom building and an auditorium. With a term of 8½ months the school offers the usual academic subjects but also attempts "to teach and cultivate . . . the fundamentals in Church and Mennonite History and also the German language" for the purpose of "retaining and cultivating" the religious life of the Mennonite congregations of Ontario.   M.G.

United Mennonite Home for the Aged (GCM), Vineland, Ont., was founded Sept. 1, 1955, and serves the United Mennonite churches (GCM) of the Niagara, St. Catharines, Vineland, Waterloo-Kitchener, and Toronto areas. It is financed by gifts and charity collections. A $12,000 grant was received from the Ontario government. Its controlling board is chosen by the constituent churches. In 1958 the home had 47 guests, with John P. Penner as superintendent.   J.P.PE.

United Missionary Church, the new name chosen on Nov. 3, 1947, by the Mennonite Brethren in Christ Church (*q.v.*). At this same time the Pennsylvania Conference withdrew from the main body continuing the former name for itself. Before this withdrawal the church had a total membership of 13,313. Of this number, 4,136 withdrew, leaving 9,177, distributed in seven district conferences as follows: Ontario 2,293, Indiana 2,077, Michigan 2,003, Ohio 1,073, Nebraska 788, Canadian Northwest 513, and Washington 430. In 1955 the total membership of the group was 10,233, in 188 organized congregations and 18 additional "appointments," with 213 ordained ministers. The total value of church property was $5,072,000, and annual per capita giving was $142.07. For the history of the group before 1947 see **Mennonite Brethren in Christ Church.**

The government of the United Missionary

Church functions on three levels, namely, the general conference which meets annually representing the entire denomination, the annual conference which represents a limited area, and the local conference which represents only one congregation. The local conference carries on the work of the local congregation by which it is constituted, and makes recommendations to the annual conference. Its presiding officer is the District Superintendent. The membership of the Annual Conference is made up of "all ordained ministers in good standing, and one lay delegate from each field or local congregation. Probationers who have been assigned work, either by the Annual Conference or by the District Superintendent, are also members of this body. This body appoints pastors, devises means and methods of promoting the general welfare of the church within given areas, and is responsible to the General Conference. The members of the General Conference are the District Superintendents, Editor, Agent of the Bethel Publishing Company, one delegate from every three hundred members and an additional one in case the fraction is two hundred or more." This conference makes rules relative to changes in discipline, procedure of organizations directly responsible to it, and delegates authority to proper personnel, viz., the editor, the agent of the Bethel Publishing Company, and other special representatives. At the general conference session held in Kitchener, Ont., in 1955 certain changes were made in the government and program of the church. The term of members which had been four years was shortened to three years, and provisions were made for the election of a General Superintendent with a term of three years. Kenneth Geiger was elected as the first incumbent of this office.

The headquarters office of the church is at Elkhart, Ind. In Elkhart is also the Bethel Publishing Co. (q.v.), which has been the denominational publishing agency since 1920. The *Gospel Banner* (q.v.) is the denominational organ.

The Ministry. The term of appointment to a pastorate is one year and this may be extended each year by the stationing committee composed of the delegates and the district superintendent. With the election of a general superintendent it is expected that he too will be a member of the stationing group.

Sunday Schools. "Sunday Schools were not general among Mennonites in the days of the organization of the Mennonite Brethren in Christ Church, but began early to be looked upon as an important factor in advancing the Lord's work" (Huffman, 150). Now they are a definite part of the whole church organization.

Camp Meetings. "One of the earliest innovations on Mennonite practice was the institution of the camp meeting" (Huffman, 148). The first one was held in Fetter's Grove, Elkhart Co., Ind., beginning July 30, 1880. These meetings have become permanent fixtures in the denomination, at least one a year being held by each conference.

Youth Work. For a number of years little was done in this area but in the last two decades this aspect of the work has been developed at a rapid pace. The orders from the general conference are now:

"Since the future of the church depends upon the conversion of the rising generation and the enlisting and establishing of these young people in the work of the Lord and the service of the church, young people's work shall be promoted in every church and wherever practicable the work shall be organized. Each conference shall draw up its own plan of organization and give proper supervision to the work" (Discipline 1954). Every conference has a youth director or similar officer. The youth work is not as yet integrated with the general conference program.

Foreign Missions. The earliest missionary from the Mennonite Brethren in Christ Church was Eusebius Hershey, who in 1880 heard the call to foreign service and gave up his life in Liberia, East Africa. Others have heard the call and the fields of China, Africa, India, French Indo-China, Turkey, Palestine, and South America have seen United Missionary Church workers. The United Missionary Society (q.v.), organized in 1920 for the purpose of integrating the work of the whole church in the missionary effort, became an official part of the general conference program. Also the Nigeria and India conferences have been given full status in the general conference setup, and will be represented at the next general conference sessions. The missionary effort has grown until now the church has some 99 missionaries working either under its own or other boards. It supports 17 mission stations, operates 7 day schools, 5 Bible schools, and one teacher training school, 12 medical dispensaries, and one 60-bed hospital. The foreign work sponsors 71 church organizations, supervises 90 national workers, and publishes a paper, *The Missionary Banner.*

Publishing. The United Missionary Church publishes as its official organ the *Gospel Banner.* This is a weekly paper with a departmentalized setup. The editor is elected by the general conference for a term of three years. Besides the *Gospel Banner* the church publishes the Bethel series of Sunday-school literature and a missionary paper, the *Missionary Banner.* The recent general conference created a board of publications, giving it power to enlarge this aspect of the work by installing printing equipment in the headquarters building which houses the Bethel Publishing Company.

Education. The U.M.C. general conference of 1882 entertained a resolution presented by the Ontario group. It read as follows: "We recommend to the General Conference that there be a course of reading adopted for the ministry" (Huffman, 214). From this meager beginning the church has followed the challenge through various Bible school, correspondence school, and evening class efforts, until today there are three established schools in the seven conferences. The Canadian Northwest Conference operates Mountain View Bible School in Didsbury, Alberta. At Kitchener, Ont., the Ontario Conference has Emanuel Bible College; and the Indiana, Michigan, Nebraska, and Ohio conferences together support Bethel College in Mishawaka, Ind., as a four-year coeducational, liberal arts college.

Faith and Practice. The U.M.C. has a definite, evangelical theology of Arminian and Wesleyan character which is officially set forth in *Doctrines and Discipline of the Mennonite Brethren in Christ Church* (1951). In addition to the standard evangelical doctrines it teaches entire sanctification as a second work of grace after justification and regeneration, but also growth in grace and the possibility of sin and restoration after justification. As to ordinances, baptism is by immersion only; open communion is practiced, also washing of the saints' feet. Nonresistance, nonconformity in dress, and the laying aside of needless indulgences are also a part of the teaching. The premillennial position in eschatology is held. In general the church has been much influenced by the Wesleyan type of church polity, doctrinal emphasis, and piety. It belongs to the National Association of Evangelicals.   C.A.N.

J. A. Huffman, *History of the Mennonite Brethren in Christ Church* (New Carlisle, Ohio, 1920); *Doctrine and Discipline of the Mennonite Brethren in Christ Church* (Elkhart, 1951); *The Test of Time, 75th Anniversary of the Indiana Conference* (Elkhart, 1953); *Gospel Banner* containing various reports from year to year; E. R. Storms, *History of the United Missionary Church* (Elkhart, 1958).

United Missionary Society, an organization effected in 1921 by action of the General Conference of 1920. It is composed of representatives of all the annual conferences of the United Missionary Church of the United States and Canada. J. A. Huffman was the first president of the United Missionary Society. The foreign mission work of the church dates back to 1890. It has grown rapidly under the direction of the United Missionary Society. In 1955 there were missions in Africa, India, the Near East, Japan, South America, and Mexico, with about 100 missionaries under this Society. By 1959 the annual budget had reached over $300,000. In 1940 the women's Auxiliary Society of the organization was founded, with organizations in all the annual conferences of the United Missionary Church, and with local organizations in many of the churches, which promote various projects, including hospitals, and maintain a budget of above $50,000. The United Missionary Society is definitely committed to evangelization. It seeks to carry on its work through trained native converts and is developing indigenous churches. The headquarters are at Elkhart, Ind.

J.A.Hu.

United Orphanage and Mission was organized in 1901, for the purpose of promoting and supporting the orphanage work which had been begun among the Armenians in Turkey in 1898 by Rose Lambert of Indiana and Anna Gerber of Ohio. By 1901 scores of Armenian orphans were being supported by friends from America and Europe. In 1911 there were two orpanage institutions, one for boys at Everek and one for girls at Hadjin, Turkey, with 306 orphans.

During World War I the orphanage buildings were burned by the Moslem Turks, and the Armenians scattered, but the successors of the mission continued until 1938 to minister to the Armenian remnant which migrated to Syria. What remains of this good work is now in the charge of the Spiritual Brotherhood, an indigenous Armenian organization whose head is Abraham Sefarian, with headquarters in Aleppo, Syria, and Beirut, Lebanon,

but with groups scattered into various countries, including Africa, Cyprus, the United States, and South America. This movement was really interdenominational, but the board members as well as the missionaries were chiefly of the United Missionary Church from the United States and Canada. In 1932 the United Orphanage was disbanded, and the work was transferred to the United Missionary Society (*q.v.*).   J.A.Hu.

United States of America—General Groups. With a total of *c*152,000 baptized members in all groups, the Mennonites of the United States in 1957 constituted by far the largest national body of Mennonites in the world, the next largest being Canada with 51,000, followed by the Netherlands with 39,000. Of the twelve distinct bodies in the United States (plus several fragmented groups totaling less than 100 members), four are major: the Mennonite Church (MC) with 71,000 (this was the sole body in America until 1812 except for a small group of Amish); the General Conference Mennonite Church with 35,400 (org. in 1860, one section having started by a schism from the MC group in 1847); the Old Order Amish Mennonites with 17,000 (unorganized, but separated from the total Amish Mennonite group in *c*1855-80); and the Mennonite Brethren with 11,600 (est. in Russia by schism in 1860, est. in the United States by immigration 1874-76). Six of the remaining 8 smaller bodies range in size from 4,300 to 1,600; these are (1) the Krimmer Mennonite Brethren with 1,600 (est. in Russia by schism in 1869, immigrated to Kansas in 1874), and five others, all established in the United States by schism, three from the Mennonite Church (MC)—(2) the Church of God in Christ Mennonite (1859) with 4,300, (3) the Evangelical Mennonites (1864) with 2,300, (4) the Old Order or Wisler Mennonites (1871-93) with 4,000—(5) the Beachy Amish by schism from the Old Order Amish (1927 ff.) with 2,400, and (6) the Evangelical Mennonite Brethren by schism from the G.C.M. group in 1889 with 1,600. The two remaining groups, both very small in number and declining in size, originated by schism from the Mennonite Church (MC) in Lancaster County, Pa., i.e., the Reformed Mennonites (1812) with 600, and the Stauffer Mennonites (1845) with 360. Beyond the 12 organized bodies are a number of scattered unaffiliated congregations, most of which are in close relationship with other organized groups, and which for statistical purposes are counted with them. Since the Mennonite Brethren in Christ have changed their name (1947), and wish not to be considered Mennonites, although they had a Mennonite origin (1875 schism from MC), they are omitted from this discussion.

Immigration. The Mennonites of the United States, all of course deriving from Europe by immigration at various times, represent basically two ethnic-culture groups, the Swiss-South German and the Prusso-Russian (largely direct from Russia). The former constitute roughly two thirds, the latter one third, of the total immigrant number. The Swiss-South Germans constitute the entire membership of the Mennonite (MC) and Amish bodies and all branches formed from them (except the CGC group), and about one half of the G.C.M. group.

The Prusso-Russians constitute the entire membership of the M.B., K.M.B., and E.M.B. groups, almost all of the C.G.C. group, and about one half of the G.C.M. group. Geographically, all the Mennonites living east of the prairie states except Minnesota are of Swiss-South German stock, while the Mennonites of the prairie states (North and South Dakota, Nebraska, Kansas, Oklahoma, and Minnesota) are 85 per cent Prusso-Russian, and those in the Mountain and Pacific states are about 60 per cent Prusso-Russian.

Finally it should be noted that of the Swiss-South German group, less than half (c50,000) represent descendants of the 18th-century immigrants from Switzerland and the Palatinate, while the remaining half represent descendants of the 19th-century (first half) largely Amish immigrants from Switzerland, Alsace-Lorraine, Palatinate, Bavaria, and Hesse, plus a substantial group of Swiss background who came in 1874-75 from Volhynia (western Russia) and Galicia (Austria). The Prusso-Russian immigrants practically all came in 1874-80; a very small late arrival group came in 1930 from eastern Russia via Manchuria. The G.C.M. Church is the only group composed of mixed ethnic strains from all European backgrounds and immigration periods.

A very small Lower Rhine element (of Dutch type and connection) constituted the first Mennonite immigration to America in 1683-1702; they have been assimilated completely into the M.C. and G.C.M. Swiss-German groups in the Franconia area.

Although comprehensive immigration statistics were not kept and can be only roughly reconstituted from the available records, the following table of the successive waves of Mennonite immigration to America is approximately correct.

1. Lower Rhine to Germantown 1683-1702	200
2. Swiss and Palatine Mennonites to Eastern Penna. 1707-56	4,000
3. Swiss and Palatine Amish to Eastern Penna. 1738-56	200
4. Alsace-Lorraine, Hessian and Bavarian Amish to Western Penna., Ohio, Illinois, Iowa 1815-60	2,700
5. Swiss Mennonites to Ohio and Indiana 1817-60	500
6. Palatine Mennonites to Ohio, Illinois, and Iowa 1825-60	200
7. Prussian Mennonites to Nebraska and Kansas 1874-80	300
8. Russian Mennonites to the prairie states 1874-80	10,000
9. Russian Mennonites to Reedley, Cal. 1930	200
10. Scattered individuals (second half of 19th century) from Germany, Switzerland, France, and Russia to states west of the Mississippi	200
Total immigrants	18,500

Since the total immigrant group, except for a few in the late 19th century from France, was German-speaking, the Mennonites of the United States long remained German in language and in cultural orientation. The major transition to English began about 1890 east of the Mississippi, but not until after 1900 in the Russian group in the prairie states. By the end of World War I, due in part to repressive measures in many local communities against the German language during the war, the transition was relatively complete. However, the Old Order Amish have never surrendered the German, either in their worship, or in the Pennsylvania-German dialect in their homes.

By internal migration the eastern Pennsylvania Mennonites spread west to Ontario, Ohio, and Indiana, and southward to Maryland and Virginia in the first half of the 19th century. A smaller stream of migrants continued westward to Missouri and Kansas, and finally reached the Pacific Coast in Oregon by the turn of the 20th century. Amish from eastern Pennsylvania moved westward about the same time to central Pennsylvania (Mifflin Co.) and Ohio, with a few going further west. The newer 19th-century Alsatian Amish immigration settled in western Pennsylvania (Somerset Co.), Ontario, Ohio, and Illinois, and moved on in part to Iowa and Nebraska about the middle of the 19th century and later. However, not more than a fifth of the Swiss-South German Mennonite and Amish stock from the Eastern and North Central states finally landed west of the Mississippi. The Swiss and South German Mennonites who came to Ohio in the first half of the 19th century did not join substantially in the westward migration. A small movement to Florida from the Eastern and North Central states developed after World War I but especially after World War II.

The Russian group also joined in the internal westward migration, but not till the 20th century, some going south to Oklahoma when it was opened for settlement in 1892, but many more going to the Pacific Coast, particularly to California (1897 ff.) but also to Oregon, Washington, and Idaho, with a few going north into Montana. None went to Florida.

Thus by immigration from Europe at different times to different areas of the country, and by later internal migration westward, Mennonites have spread across the country from coast to coast, and are now located in 25 states, the only major areas missed being New England and the South and Southwest. Mission expansion has led to a light occupation of even these areas, chiefly by the M.C. group, so that in 1957 forty states out of the 48 (missing Maine, Rhode Island, Massachusetts, Connecticut, New Hampshire, and Utah, Nevada, and Wyoming) and Washington, D.C., had a Mennonite population. The following table lists the distribution of baptized membership throughout the country by states and groups.

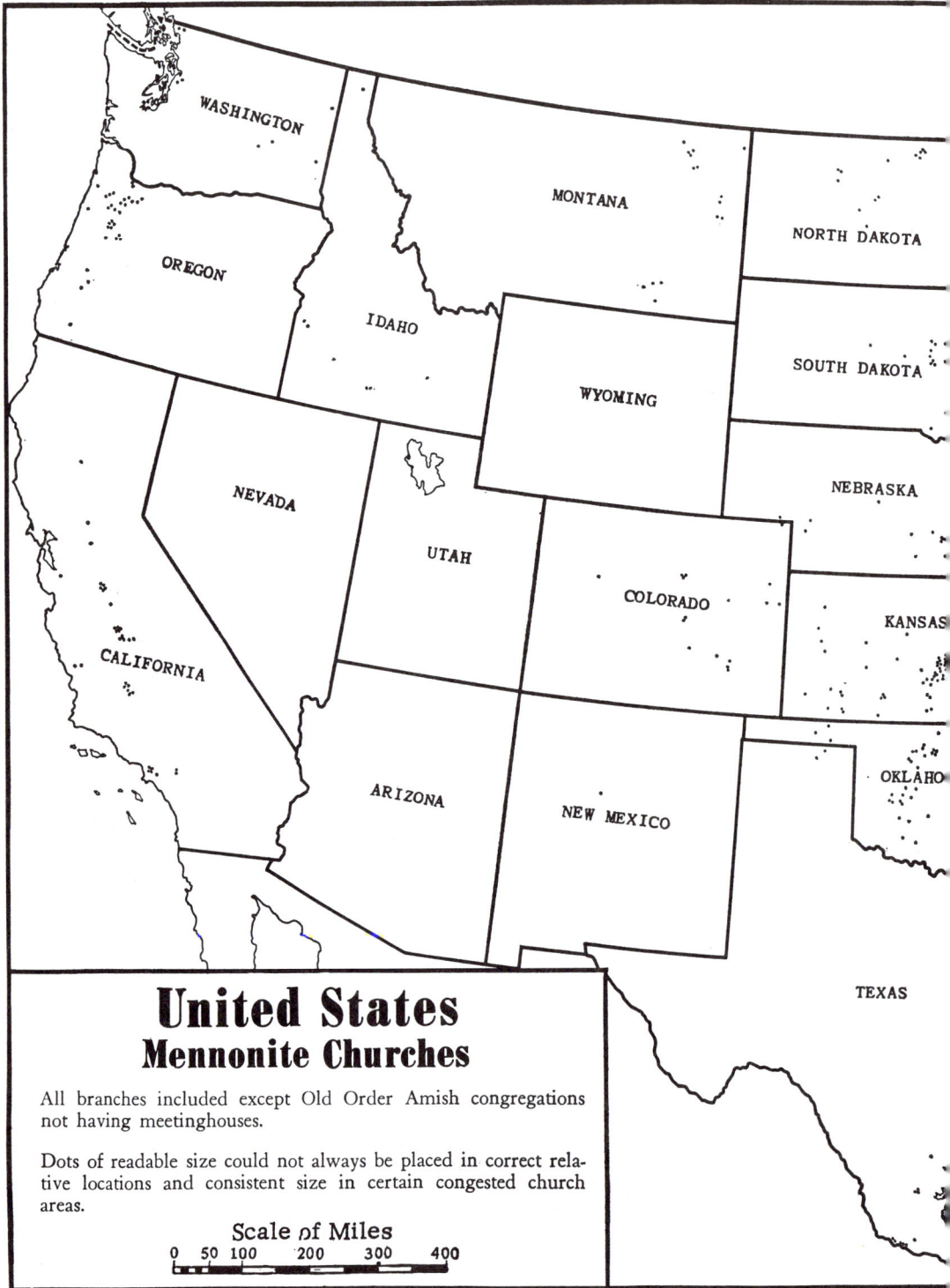

WASHINGTON

MONTANA

NORTH DAKOTA

OREGON

IDAHO

SOUTH DAKOTA

WYOMING

NEBRASKA

NEVADA

UTAH

COLORADO

KANSAS

CALIFORNIA

ARIZONA

NEW MEXICO

OKLAHOMA

TEXAS

United States
Mennonite Churches

All branches included except Old Order Amish congregations not having meetinghouses.

Dots of readable size could not always be placed in correct relative locations and consistent size in certain congested church areas.

Scale of Miles

0   50 100   200   300   400

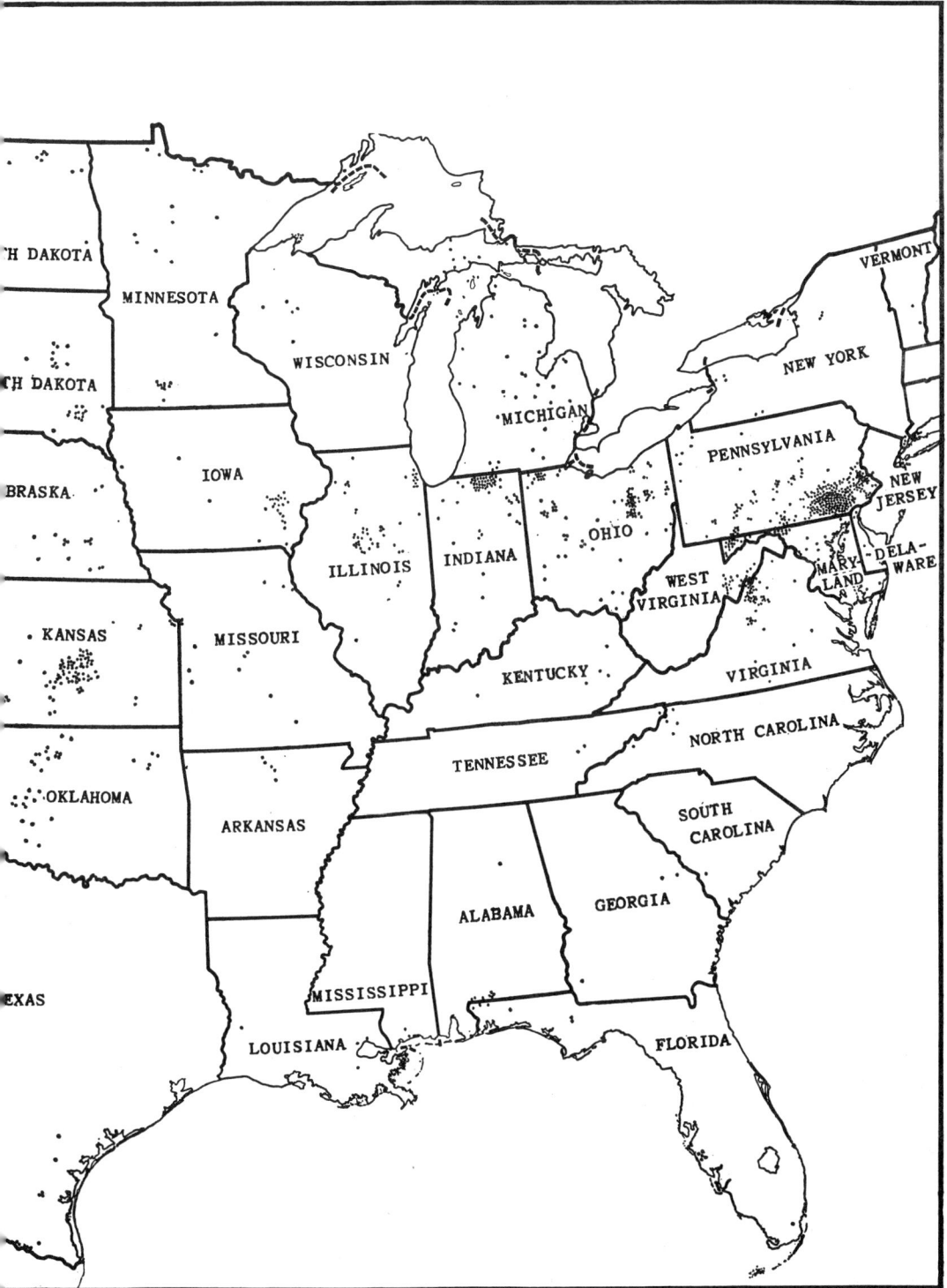

MENNONITE MEMBERSHIP IN THE UNITED STATES BY GROUPS AND STATES

	Mennonite Church (MC)	General Conference Mennonite (GCM)	Mennonite Brethren (MB)	Old Order Amish (OOA)	Beachy Amish	Evangelical Mennonite Brethren (EMB)	Krimmer Mennonite Brethren (KMB)	Church of God in Christ, Mennonite (CGC)	Evangelical Mennonite (EM)	Reformed Mennonite	Old Order Mennonite	
Alabama	87											87
Arizona	163							20				183
Arkansas	85		67	12								164
California	274	1,385	4,376			142	238	521				6,936
Colorado	708	7	153					34				902
Delaware	408			240								648
Florida	528							95				623
Georgia	13				105			97				215
Idaho	293	384						109				786
Illinois	3,443	2,157		730	408	76			434	52		7,300
Indiana	7,905	2,260		3,195	448				739	24	302	14,873
Iowa	3,289	830		794	52	38						5,003
Kansas	1,631	11,141	2,068	350		279	411	2,322	145			18,347
Kentucky	123											123
Louisiana	81							122				203
Maryland	1,793			178	27							1,998
Michigan	2,413	180		244	32	20		347	64	52		3,352
Minnesota	364	1,783	465			306						2,918
Mississippi	87											87
Missouri	514	127		200				96				937
Montana	220	529	203			98						1,050
Nebraska	1,370	1,731	335			157						3,593
New Jersey	15											15
New Mexico	14							13				27
New York	1,332			113						29		1,474
North Carolina	44						170					214
North Dakota	251	313	525	4				25				1,118
Ohio	9,808	2,591		6,586	225			58	853	150	341	20,612
Oklahoma	257	1,857	2,287	160				424				4,985
Oregon	1,860	909	507	28	119	368		13				3,804
Pennsylvania	26,580	4,061		4,168	692					309	3,272	39,082
South Carolina					13							13
South Dakota	26	2,438	140			141	778	33				3,556
Tennessee	48				61				34			143
Texas	151	18	331									500
Vermont	43											43
Virginia	3,820			160	259						225	4,464
Washington		611	187									801
West Virginia	673											673
Wisconsin	130			50				60				240
Wash., D.C.	40											40
Total	70,884	35,315	11,644	17,273	2,380	1,625	1,597	4,389	2,269	616	4,140	152,132

Spiritual Development. In the United States the oppressed Mennonites of Central Europe for the first time had the privilege of full liberty of conscience and unrestricted cultural and economic development, guaranteed first of all by William Penn's Quaker Pennsylvania, to which the 18th-century emigration was exclusively directed. Moreover, the nonresistant Mennonites found in Pennsylvania full sympathy for their position on rejection of warfare and the oath, since the Quakers held the same basic position on these points. Later by constitutional provision in the federal constitution and in most state constitutions these privileges were firmly anchored. The unlimited resources of the new world in fertile land, forests, and minerals, were almost literally free for the taking by the pioneers, and these great economic opportunities continued for two centuries as the frontier moved westward; hence Mennonites of all later immigrant groups also had equal rights to them.

Since all Mennonite immigrants to America were farmers, except the small early Lower Rhine group, and since unoccupied land was plentiful, the typical Mennonite pattern of settlement in America was in fairly compact groups of single farmsteads, though not in exclusive colonies nor in villages. Practically no Mennonite city settlements nor city congregations were founded until the 20th century, with a few exceptions, such as Philadelphia (GCM) in 1865, Elkhart, Ind. (MC) in 1871, Lancaster, Pa. (MC) in 1879. Accordingly the American Mennonites long remained an exclusively rural group, stable, conservative, prosperous; only in the second quarter of the 20th century has any really substantial urbanization set in. Now many have established small businesses and even industries, have entered the professions, or have become laborers. By 1955 the proportion of urban population had passed 50 per cent in practically the entire area east of the Mississippi, and reached 85 per cent in the Franconia area of eastern Pennsylvania. The typical German virtues of thrift, hard work, sobriety, and community solidarity, reinforced by the Mennonite emphasis on nonconformity to the world, mutual aid, simplicity, love, quietness, united in creating a typical American Mennonite character, with a strongly conservative social and religious bent, and a strong group loyalty. This character, coupled with a strong emphasis on tradition, resulted in a notable emphasis on simplicity and nonworldliness which not only developed into a traditional pattern of simplicity in costume, form of worship, and general way of life, but made possible a relative insulation from the surrounding American culture. The absence of a trained ministry, and the general negative attitude toward higher education, meant further that few influences toward change in the traditional pattern entered the group by the educational route. This contributed to a relative stagnation in church life.

As a result of these several factors the great opportunity in America for a free unfolding of the Anabaptist genius was partly lost, and the heritage lay relatively dormant and unfruitful. The carry-over from the long time of persecution in Europe, reinforced by preoccupation with the hardships of pioneering, and by cultural isolation through the retention of the German language in an English environment, contributed much to the loss of a sense of mission. The basic Mennonite heritage of doctrinal and ethical principles was, however, maintained. All Mennonite immigrants of whatever period brought with them a strong commitment to nonresistance, the greater proportion having left Europe to a large extent because of pressure on this very point by the governments and the cultures from which they came. This was particularly true of the 19th-century movements from France, South Germany, Prussia, and Russia, but also to some extent for the earlier 18th-century emigration.

In the second half of the 19th century new influences came to bear on the established Mennonite communities in the East, while the newer immigrants to the midwest from Russia and South Germany brought with them a more vigorous piety and a more aggressive spirit. American revivalism of the Moody type, the Sunday school, outside Protestant literature, the influences from the growing general Protestant emphasis on missions, evangelism, temperance, etc., played their part in breaking through the barriers of isolation and opening up Mennonites in many places to change and progress. But this was not without stress and strain. Formerly large numbers were simply lost to the church, to join other Protestant denominations. Now new life and progress retained many more, but also led to serious divisions in the second half of the 19th century; e.g., Old Order Amish (q.v.), Old Order Mennonite (q.v.), M.B.C. (q.v.), Defenseless Mennonite (q.v.), and Oberholtzer-G.C.M. (q.v.—earlier in the century).

By the beginning of the 20th century a genuine awakening and revival was occurring, with a warmer type of piety, emphasis on Christian experience, activity in evangelism (q.v.), missions (q.v.), education (q.v.), and publication (q.v.), better ministerial service (trained ministry came later), and a recovering sense of mission. This revival has affected all the groups, except the Old Order Amish and Old Order Mennonite, who have resisted all change and remained traditional, a block of at least one eighth of the total United States Mennonite membership. The second quarter of the 20th century has added to the revival a remarkable development in relief work and social service, at first largely under the Mennonite Central Committee, but now spreading into most of the larger groups directly.

Missions have had a remarkable development in all the American Mennonite groups (except the two Old Order groups) in spite of a late start at the turn of the 20th century. By 1957 a total of 638 Mennonite missionaries were at work in 27 foreign countries and Puerto Rico and Alaska, with a total of over 50,000 baptized members on all fields. China, India, East Africa, and the African Congo were the oldest and strongest fields.

Foreign relief work under the Mennonite Central Committee (q.v., org. 1920) had also reached striking proportions, largely after World War II, with operations in a maximum of 20 different countries by over 350 workers at one time in 1948-50, although the famine relief program in Russia in 1920-22 was itself a major effort. The operation of Civilian Public Service by united Mennonite effort under the MCC during World War II reached a maximum of over 4,000 Mennonite conscientious objectors in 1944. After World War II the movement for mental health work resulted in the establishment of three mental hospitals under MCC, and one under the Lancaster Conference (MC). A further outgrowth of the World War II experience was the Voluntary Service program, partly under MCC and partly under the major conferences (MC, GCM, and MB), in which hundreds of Mennonite youth served in a variety of social service and mission-related projects in short summer terms and longer terms of one or two years. Pax Service abroad for conscientious objector men resulted in over 200 serving in reconstruction and other service in Germany, Greece, Korea, and elsewhere, under MCC direction.

Another prominent and highly important development in American Mennonitism in the 20th century has been the forward movement in higher education, with the establishment of colleges and seminaries. Full four-year college programs were established in the three major groups as follows with the year of granting the first B.A. degree: M.C.—Goshen 1910, E.M.C. 1948; G.C.M.—Bethel 1912, Bluffton 1915; M.B.—Tabor 1922. Junior Colleges were also established at Hesston (MC, 1915) and Freeman (GCM, 1923). The following seminaries have been established: Witmarsum (called Mennonite Seminary as part of Bluffton College 1915-21, independent at Bluffton, Ohio 1921-36); Tabor College of Theology (M.B., as part of Tabor College 1924-1955) at Hillsboro, Kan.; Goshen College Biblical Seminary (M.C., as part of Goshen College at Goshen, Ind., 1933-); Mennonite Biblical Seminary (G.C.M., in affiliation with Bethany Biblical Seminary in Chicago 1945-1958, in Elkhart, Ind., 1958-); and Mennonite Brethren Biblical Seminary at Fresno, Cal., in 1955- . The M.B. Bible College (1944-) and the Canadian Mennonite Bible College (G.C.M., 1947-), both Winnipeg, offer theological curriculums, the former Th.B., the latter B.C.E. At least 15 church high schools and 80 elementary schools have also been established, largely since 1945 and chiefly in the MC group, in addition to a number of Bible schools and two Bible Institutes (Grace at Omaha, inter-Mennonite; Fresno, M.B., 1955). These schools, particularly the colleges, have become very influential in the Mennonite brotherhood in the United States, and have contributed much to the strength of church life, witness, and service.

In publication the three major groups have developed publishing houses (MC—Scottdale, Pa., 1908; GCM—Berne, 1884; Newton, 1949; MB— Medford, Okla., 1904, Hillsboro, Kan., 1913); although the Scottdale House with its larger constituency has developed the only major American Mennonite publishing enterprise with substantial books by Mennonite authors. A majority of literary production by American Mennonite writers has been by authors from the Mennonite Church (MC). Outstanding American Mennonite authors have been C. H. Wedel (GCM, d. 1913), Daniel Kauffman (MC, 1865-1944), C. Henry Smith (GCM, 1875-1948), John Horsch (MC, 1867-1941), J. C. Wenger (MC, 1906-), G. F. Hershberger (MC, 1897-). The various Mennonite bodies large and small have almost all established their own periodical organs, of which the chief are the following: M.C.—*Gospel Herald* (circulation 18,500); G.C.M. —*The Mennonite* (circulation 15,000); M.B.—*The Christian Leader* 1937 (circulation 2,500) and *Zionsbote* 1884 (circulation 2,000). Noteworthy other periodicals are the inter-Mennonite *Mennonite Weekly Review* 1923 (circulation 21,000), *Mennonite Life* 1946 (GCM, circulation 2,500), and the *Mennonite Quarterly Review* 1927 (MC, 750).

The growth of awareness of the historic Anabaptist heritage and the attempt to work out its implications theologically and practically, which marked the American Mennonites generally in the second quarter of the 20th century, has helped to awaken most of the groups to the danger of pure traditionalism on the one side, and on the other side the danger of undue influence from outside movements in theology and piety. This has also contributed to the building of a solid foundation for better mutual understanding and co-operation among the various American Mennonite groups.

The striking growth in the number, quality, and significance of inter-Mennonite relationships and co-operative activities, is a marked feature of the mid-20th century in American Mennonitism (see **Inter-Mennonite Relations**). One result of the general drawing together has been a series of group re-unions or mergers, including Mennonite-Amish Mennonite (MC, 1915-25), Mennonite-Conservative Amish (MC, 1955), General Conference-Central Conference (GCM, 1945), Evangelical Mennonite-

E.M.B. (only partially completed) (1953), Mennonite Brethren-Krimmer Mennonite Brethren (MB, 1959).

The Mennonites of the United States in 1957 were basically conservative—evangelical in theology (with some fundamentalist areas), evangelistic, and mission-minded with a strong outreach program, well organized, engaged in many activities of practical and service character, with a vigorous denominational consciousness, a strong program of Christian education in the local congregations and in church colleges, high schools, and seminaries, manifesting a vital piety and sense of mission. The basic historic Anabaptist heritage had been preserved, although the effort to maintain a deep Christian commitment in full discipleship had not been uniformly successful, and the constant battle against worldliness was sometimes lost to looseness and sometimes to legalism.

By virtue of numbers, maintenance of historic heritage, vigor of group life, vitality, and strong participation of the lay membership in the total program of the church, the American Mennonites came to occupy a major place in world Mennonitism. Helped by their size and resources in men and money, and their growing sense of sharing in the life of the Mennonite brotherhood round the world, they were able to render valuable assistance to Mennonites elsewhere, especially in Europe where the suffering and losses due to two world wars have been much more severely felt. (For further information on American Mennonitism, see the articles on the several American bodies, also the several states in which American Mennonites live and treatments of major doctrinal, practical, ecclesiastical, and institutional topics.) H.S.B.

Baptized Membership of Mennonites in the United States by Bodies—1957

Mennonite Church	70,884
General Conference Mennonite Church	35,315
Old Order Amish Mennonite	17,273
Mennonite Brethren	11,644
Church of God in Christ, Mennonite	4,389
Old Order (Wisler) Mennonite	4,140
Beachy Amish Mennonite	2,800
Evangelical Mennonite	2,269
Evangelical Mennonite Brethren	1,625
Evangelical Mennonite (Kleine Gemeinde)	25
Krimmer Mennonite Brethren	1,597
Reformed Mennonite	616
Stauffer Mennonite	362
Weaver Mennonite	60
Total	152,579
Hutterian Brethren	2,720

(Source: *Mennonite Yearbook and Directory 1958*)

C. Henry Smith, *Mennonites of America* (Goshen, 1909); *idem, The Story of the Mennonites* (Berne, 1941, 4th edition revised by C. Krahn, 1957); *idem, The Coming of the Russian Mennonites . . . 1874-1884* (Berne, 1927); *idem, The Mennonite Immigration to Pennsylvania in the Eighteenth Century* (Norristown, 1929); *idem, Mennonites in America* (Akron, 1942); *Proceedings of the Conference on Mennonite Educational and Cultural Problems* I-XI (1942-57); H. S. Bender, "The Mennonites of the United States," *MQR* XI (1937) 68-82; *idem*, "Outside Influences on Mennonite Religious Thought," *Proceedings of the Ninth Conference on Mennonite Educational and Cultural Problems* (1953) 33-41; Don. E. Smucker, "A Critique of Mennonites at Mid-Century," *ibid.*, 99-113.

Universalism, the doctrine that God will ultimately save all men. The adherents of universalism use as a major support Acts 3:21, "Whom the heaven must receive until the times of restitution of all things, which God hath spoken by the mouth of all his holy prophets since the world began." In this passage they find the assertion that everything that God has created will once again be restored to its original state in the creation, whereas most exegetes construe it to refer only to the things foretold by the prophets.

The first proponent of the restoration of all things was Origen. The most important champion of this doctrine in the period of the Reformation was Hans Denck. In his booklet, *Wer die Wahrheit wahrlich lieb hat,* he makes the reference to it in *Gegenschrift* 16, 17, and 28. He mentions it also in other writings, as in *Vom Gesetz Gottes.* His premise is the idea that the nature of God is love and mercy, and that He can therefore not keep His anger forever. His support he took from passages like Isa. 28:21; Jer. 3:21; Rom. 5:18; 11:32; I Cor. 15:22; Eph. 1:10; Col. 1:20; and I Tim. 2:4.

Article 17 of the Augsburg Confession (1530-Lutheran) assumes that all Anabaptists held this doctrine, when it says, "Therefore the Anabaptists are condemned, who teach that the devil and damned persons will not have eternal pain and suffering." But this belief of Denck's was never really accepted in Anabaptist circles. It is found nowhere else except perhaps in Jakob Kautz and Hans Hut. In more recent times, however, some Mennonites in Baden and Württemberg, under the influence of the theologians C. F. Oetinger and Michael Hahn (*q.v.*), accepted the doctrine of the restitution of all things and organized a separate church group, the "Hahnische" Mennonites. But even this movement did not reach any considerable proportions. However, a few Mennonite preachers in the German *Verband* and in Switzerland have occasionally leaned toward this view. (See the polemic written against it by Jakob Vetter, *Warum ich die Wiederbringung aller Dinge ablehne,* 1911.)

In Russia and America, Mennonite bodies have stood firmly against universalism, and the doctrine is practically unknown, although E. F. Stroter's books read by some influenced the Mennonites of Russia, Germany, and the U.S.A. A curiosity is the fact that the refusal of Joseph Stucky to discipline a member in his central Illinois congregation in 1871 for propagating this view was the occasion for the schism which led to the formation of the Central Illinois Conference (*q.v.*). NEFF, H.S.B.

Unparteiische biblische Fragenbuch, Das, *zum Gebrauch in Sonntagschulen und Familien für Kinder-Unterricht,* 1st part (Milford Square, 1859). This 121-page booklet is the first known piece of Sunday-school literature produced by the Mennonites, probably written by John H. Oberholtzer (*q.v.*). It was used in General Conference Mennonite congregations. (Bender, *Two Centuries,* 92.) vDZ.

Unparteiische Kirchen- und Ketzer-Historie by Gottfried Arnold: see **Arnold, Gottfried** and **Ketzer-Historie.**

Unpartheiische Liedersammlung, Eine, *Zum Gebrauch beim Oeffentlichen Gottesdienst und der Häuslichen Erbauung,* the only hymnal except the *Ausbund* used by the Old Order Amish (not for regular Sunday morning worship but only for evening singings and special occasions), and also used by the Old Order Mennonites, first edition 1860 at Lancaster, reprinted there 8 times, twice at Elkhart in 1911 and 1929, and 8 times at Scottdale 1917-54. It is a condensation of 152 hymns from the Lancaster *Unpartheyisches Gesangbuch* (*q.v.*). It is familiarly called by the Amish "das dünne Büchli" (the thin book) in contrast to "das dicke Büchli" (the thick book, i.e., the *Ausbund*). It was published in an enlarged and much revised edition under the same name in 1892 by S. D. Guengerich, an Old Order Amish layman of Amish, Iowa (printed at Elkhart), and reprinted 5 times since (1907-54). H.S.B.

Unpartheyisches Gesangbuch, Ein (*Ein* was dropped after the second edition), first published at Lancaster, Pa., in 1804 as the hymnbook of the Lancaster Mennonite (MC) Conference, the second Mennonite hymnbook to be compiled in America, was long used in this conference (15 editions 1804-87), also in the Ontario, Virginia, and Southwestern Pennsylvania Mennonite (MC) conferences and in the Old Order Mennonite bodies at various places. It is still used in Lancaster County by certain conservative groups (reprints at Lancaster 1923 and 1941 for the Amish congregations). It is noteworthy as the only Mennonite hymnal to borrow substantially from the *Ausbund;* it contains 64 *Ausbund* hymns, which is 45 per cent of the *Ausbund* total, and 17 per cent of the 390 basic hymns in the *Gesangbuch.* The first edition contained 511 pages. (See **Hymnology** for a detailed discussion of the book and the several other hymnals derived from it.) H.S.B.

Unrau: see also Unruh.

Unrau, Abram Abram, a Mennonite leader in the Chortitza settlement of South Russia, was born June 14, 1856, the oldest of the six children of Abram Unrau and Agatha Heese. He married Gertrude Thiessen in August 1876; they had 16 children. His second wife was Maria Hildebrand. He was educated at the Chortitza Zentralschule, ordained as minister on June 8, 1890, and as elder on June 16, 1900. He lived at Chortitza until 1878, Roppow-Gauchur 1878-89, New York (Bachmut district) and Ekaterinovka (near New York village) 1889-1920. He was a wise leader and was well read. He died Aug. 30, 1930, at New York. D.PA.

UNRRA. The United Nations Relief and Rehabilitation Administration was an international organization made up of 47 member governments for the purpose of giving relief and rehabilitation to people in liberated countries in Europe and the Far East. UNRRA was organized in Washington, D.C., on Nov. 9, 1943. Representatives from 44 nations signed the agreement. General councils met in Atlantic City, N.J., on Nov. 11, 1943; Montreal, Quebec, September 1944; and in London, England, in August 1945. The first Director General was Herbert H.

Lehman, former governor of New York. The general headquarters were in Washington, D.C., with regional offices in London, Shanghai, Sydney, and Cairo. Relief and rehabilitation under UNRRA consisted of food, clothing, fuel, medicines, household supplies, seeds, fertilizers, raw materials, machinery, transportation, and public utilities, as well as technical assistance. There were also health and welfare services as well as repatriation of displaced persons. The UNRRA staff was highly specialized and consisted of some 10,000 persons recruited from at least 43 nations. These employees took an oath to adhere to the ideal of international service and agreed to abstain from any act of discrimination on account of race, nationality, creed, or political belief. The purpose of UNRRA was to create a reservoir of emergency supplies and services from which nations could draw who requested assistance and proved their need. Assistance was given only after a thorough investigation by representatives of member nations. The nations given aid were those who did not have adequate foreign exchange to do the relief and rehabilitation job themselves. The original UNRRA budget was over 1¾ billion dollars. Each member nation not occupied by the enemy was asked to contribute at least one per cent of its national income.

In 1943-45 the Mennonite Central Committee, with headquarters at Akron, Pa., loaned a total of 15 workers to UNRRA refugee camps in Egypt. These representatives consisted of five nurses, one doctor, one laboratory technician, one dietitian, and seven welfare workers. In 1945 five of these workers were transferred from Egypt to Italy, where they continued their service in UNRRA-administered refugee camps. From 1944 to 1949 the MCC loaned personnel to UNRRA projects in China. UNRRA furnished tractors and Chinese farmers gave seed and tilled the soil and a number of MCC workers served as field men and mechanics. These men taught the Chinese farmers how to operate the tractors and were charged with the responsibility of keeping the tractors in working order. A third area of co-operation between the MCC and UNRRA was in Poland. UNRRA had shipped to Poland 10,000 American-made farm tractors. These were distributed to 250 tractor stations. In 1947 MCC furnished 23 men to train Polish farmers to operate tractors. These farm-trained technicians served in Poland for a period of 8 months. MCC also co-operated with UNRRA in shipping livestock to European liberated countries. In all a total of over 500 Mennonites served as "seagoing cowboys" (*q.v.*) who cared for livestock on ships. 　　　　　　　　　J.N.B.

Unruh (Unru, Unrau, Onrouw), a widespread family name among the Mennonites of Prussia, Danzig, Russia, and America. Herbert Wiebe found the name first recorded in 1568. It was found in the communities of Schönsee, Przechovka, Jeziorka, Konopath, Kazun, Tragheimerweide, and Thiensdorf. Whether all Unruhs found among Mennonites today have the same ancestor is not known. Some sources trace the first Unruh back to Saxony when a high-ranking military officer joined the Mennonites and became nonresistant. Hendrik Berents

Hulshoff, who visited the Mennonites at Wintersdorf near Culm in 1719, reported that Abram Unrau was elected to the ministry. Among the 35 families who established Brenkenhoffswalde and Franzthal in Mark Brandenburg in 1765 the Unruh family was represented. From here the family was transplanted to Poland, the Molotschna settlement in Russia, and elsewhere. Particularly the Unruhs in Poland spread widely; many migrated to Kansas and Dakota in 1874-75, led by Tobias A. Unruh (*q.v.*). Many of this group joined the Church of God in Christ, Mennonite. Among the Alexanderwohl Mennonites settling near Goessel, Kan., there were also many Unruhs; from here they have spread into many communities. After World War I many Unruhs in Russia migrated to Canada and South America. Heinrich P. Unruh (*q.v.*, d. 1927) was a prominent elder of the Halbstadt Mennonite Church, Molotschna, Russia.

A number of Unruhs served as deacons and preachers in the Prussian churches. Preachers at Montau have been Andreas Unruh (Unrau) of Dragass 1739-d.74; Heinrich Unruh (Unrau) (1740-74) of Montau serving only June-Nov. 23, 1774; Peter Unruh of Dragass 1776-*c*88. The Dutch *Naamlijst* mentions besides these Abraham Unruh, preacher of the Schweingrube Old Flemish congregation *c*1730-*c*65; Heinrich Unruh serving at Konopat-Przechovka *c*1779-*c*1800; Heinrich Unruh serving at Brenkenhoffswalde-Franzthal *c*1782-88.

J. A. Boese, who traced to 1930 the lines of two Unruhs born *c*1740, found that they had 6,500 descendants. The genealogy of the Alexanderwohl Unruh family by P. U. Schmidt lists 251 names.

Outstanding representatives of the family were, in addition to those listed below, Tobias A. Unruh (*q.v.*), P. H. Unruh, late pastor of the Alexanderwohl Mennonite Church, who was an MCC representative during the famine in Russia in 1922; B. H. Unruh, educator and minister who was a member of the Studienkommission (*q.v.*) and traveled in Germany and in America in behalf of the Mennonites of Russia and was instrumental in helping them find new homes in Canada and South America. He is the author of *Die niederländisch-niederdeutschen Hintergründe der mennonitischen Ostwanderungen im 16., 18. und 19. Jahrhundert* (1955). (See biography in *ML* IV, 389.) His brother A. H. Unruh (MB) of Winnipeg is an educator and minister who taught in Russia, Winkler, and Winnipeg and wrote *Die Geschichte der Mennoniten-Brüdergemeinde 1860-1954* (1954). The father of Benjamin and Abraham, Heinrich B. Unruh (*q.v.*), was a prominent elder of the Karassan Mennonite Church in the Crimea, Russia. Heinrich's brother K. B. Unruh (*q.v.*) was a prominent educator in Russia. John D. Unruh, former president of Freeman College, is the author of *In the Name of Christ* (1952). H. T. Unruh (GCM) was a minister at Halstead, Bluffton, and Hillsboro. W. F. Unruh was a missionary in India and secretary of the G.C. Western District Conference. Verney Unruh is a missionary in Japan. Walter F. Unruh was long pastor of the First Mennonite Church in Newton, Kan. In 1957 there were 21 ordained men of the family in U.S. and Canada, 5 Unraus (2 MB, 2

GCM, and an EMB), and 16 Unruhs (5 MB, 5 CGC, and 6 GCM). Of these, 11 were serving in Canada, and 10 in the United States.   A.J.U., vdZ.

B. H. Unruh, "Die Mennoniten in der Neumark," *Gem.-Kal.* 1941, 64; Reimer, *Familiennamen*, 119; P. U. Schmidt, *The Peter Unruh Genealogy* (Goessel, 1941); V. Unruh and A. J. Unruh, *The Tobias A. Unruh Biography, Diary and Family Record, 1819-1950* (Ottumwa, Iowa, 1950); H. B. Koehn, "Minister Tobias A. Unruh Family Relation" (unpublished); Dutch *Naamlijst* 1773 ff.; *Inv. Arch. Amst.* I. Nos. 1678, 1732, 2102, 2134, 2194, 2211, 2216, 2220 f.; II, 2, Nos. 740, 763; L. Stobbe, *Montau-Gruppe, ein Gedenkblatt* (Montau, 1918) 84, 85; Herbert Wiebe, *Das Siedlungswerk niederl. Mennoniten im Weichseltal* (Marburg, 1952) 74-86 *passim*, 95, 97; H. Ch. Hulshoff, "Bezoekreis van Hendrik Berents," in *Bijdragen en Mededeelingen v. h. Hist. Genootschap* LIX (1738) 67 and 74-79; *ML* IV, 369-90.

Unruh, Heinrich Benjamin (1845-82), a Mennonite elder in the Karassan Mennonite Church, Crimea, Russia, was born at Waldheim in the Berdyansk area, on May 24, 1845, the son of Benjamin and Maria Kunkel Unruh. As a child he moved with his parents to the Crimea, settling in the village of Schwestertal. He married Elisabeth Wall, of Schönwiese in the Molotschna settlement, and went to Timir-Bulat in the Eupatoria (Yevpatoriya) district. They raised a family of five sons and four daughters. All of the sons were engaged in religious work. Heinrich and Kornelius Unruh were missionaries in India, Gerhard Unruh a preacher, Abraham Unruh a preacher and teacher (Winnipeg), and Benjamin Unruh a teacher and leader (Karlsruhe).

Heinrich Benjamin Unruh was chosen as minister by the Karassan congregation in 1874, and as elder three years before his death. P. M. Friesen says that he was the first minister in the Crimea to preach without using the traditional written sermons. He stressed personal conversion before baptism. He died in 1882 at the age of 37 years, and was buried at Timir-Bulat.   A.H.U.

H. Goerz, *Die mennonitischen Siedlungen der Krim* (Winnipeg, 1957) 541; Friesen, *Brüderschaft*, 709.

Unruh, Heinrich Peter (1845-1927), a prominent Mennonite educational and church leader in Russia, was born March 23, 1845, in the village of Alexanderwohl, Molotschna settlement, South Russia, the oldest of the seven children of Peter and Sara Schroeder Unruh. Soon the family took up a homestead in the newly founded village of Nicolaidorf, a few miles from Alexanderwohl. He was married twice—first to Helena Löwen (d. 1885), then to Maria Löwen. In school he had an outstanding teacher, H. Richert, who later became a leader in the Alexanderwohl congregation in Kansas. His mastery of German, a good knowledge of Russian, his theology, and a wide range of information Unruh acquired through reading and study. Still quite young, he became a teacher in the village of Muntau near Halbstadt. In 1870 he was elected minister, first of Alexanderwohl, then of the Halbstadt-Ohrloff congregation. In 1885 he gave up teaching and went to America to visit his parents and other close relatives, all of whom had come to Kansas in the 1870's. In 1896 Unruh became elder of the Halbstadt congregation, which at that time separated from Ohrloff and became independent, and from that time he occupied an increasingly important position in school and church affairs, primarily in the Molotschna settlement, although his influence was felt also in other Mennonite settlements in Russia. For 31 years he was a leading member of the Molotschna School Board (*Schulrat*), whose function it was to supervise the teaching of religion and German in the schools, and almost as long he served as chairman of the Molotschna Church Conference (*Kirchenkonvent*). Several times Unruh participated in delegations to St. Petersburg to the highest government officials and also had an audience with the czar.

In all these positions Unruh served his church with great devotion. He was loved and esteemed by all. In 1916, because of age and ill health, he retired as elder of the Halbstadt congregation. Soon after he suffered a stroke which made him an invalid for the rest of his life. He died Nov. 3, 1927, at Muntau, just before religious persecution began in Russia.

Four of H. P. Unruh's children left Russia for Canada in 1924; the widow with some of the other children tried to escape from Russia in 1929, but they were forcibly returned, not to their former home, but to Central Asia.   H.G.

Friesen, *Brüderschaft*; P. U. Schmidt, *The Peter Unruh Genealogy* (Goessel, 1941); H. Goerz, *Die Molotschnaer Ansiedlung* (Steinbach, 1950).

Unruh, Kornelius Benjamin (1849-1910), an educator of the Mennonites of Russia, was born in the village of Waldheim, Molotschna settlement, Russia. His grandfather was a minister of the Brenkenhoffswalde (*q.v.*) church in West Prussia. He received his training in the Halbstadt Zentralschule under Gustav Rempel. At seventeen he started teaching on an estate and later at Blumenort, Molotschna. He had an unusual thirst for knowledge. During his free time and in summer he read and studied privately in Ekaterinoslav, Kiev, and Odessa. He mastered the Russian and French languages and was thoroughly acquainted with modern methods of education. He introduced Russian into the Blumenort elementary school.

In 1870 Unruh accepted the position as teacher at the Halbstadt Zentralschule. After one year he spent three years in Switzerland and Moscow. He studied at the Muristalden (Bern) Protestant normal school and numerous other schools. After his return to Russia he spent one winter in Moscow in private study. In the summer of 1873 he married Maria Epp and became principal of the Ohrloff Zentralschule (*q.v.*), where he taught for 32 years. He was also elected minister of the Orloff Mennonite Church in 1883. In co-operation with others he helped to produce a number of textbooks for Mennonite schools, including the following: *Biblische Geschichten für mennonitische Elementarschulen. Oberstufe* (Halbstadt, 1902); *Leitfaden zur Kirchengeschichte für mennonitische Centralschulen in Russland* (Neuhalbstadt, 1890); *Leitfaden für den Religionsunterricht in den mennonitischen Centralschulen Russlands* (Halbstadt, 1906); *Kratkaya Nemetskaya Grammatika . . .* (a brief German grammar for elementary schools in Russia) (Berdyansk, 1898).

51

In 1905 Unruh resigned from his position and established a secondary school near Novo-Poltavka in the province of Kherson. After two years he established a Bible school in Friedensfeld, Zagradovka settlement. In addition to this he taught Bible and German at the Zagradovka Zentralschule. Because of his extraordinary weight (c400 pounds), his heart suffered severely during the last years of his life. On Aug. 17, 1910, he died. His son, K. K. Unruh, was a lawyer in Ekaterinoslav. B. H. Unruh and A. H. Unruh are his nephews. K. B. Unruh possessed an unusual capacity for work and was an outstanding educator. P. M. Friesen, who was his friend and colleague, ranks him next to Tobias Voth, Hesse, and Franz.   C.K.

Friesen, *Brüderschaft*, 590, 600; H. Görz, *Die Molotschnaer Ansiedlung* (Steinbach, 1951) 162.

Unruh, Peter H. (1881-1943), son of Peter P. and Anna Klassen Unruh, was born in McPherson Co., Kan., Jan. 23, 1881. He was ordained minister of the Alexanderwohl (GCM) congregation in 1900 and elder in 1915. He served as a relief worker in Russia under the MCC 1922-23 and was for some years a member of the MCC and its vice-chairman. He also served for a time on the Conference Peace Committee and as treasurer of the Emergency Relief Board. He was married on Aug. 31, 1905, to Susie Warkentin. He died at Goessel, Kan., July 20, 1943.   H.S.B.

Unruh, Tobias A. (1819-75), a son of Andrew G. and Anna Koehn Unruh, was born at Karolswalde, Polish Russia, May 28, 1819. His schooling was meager, but he had a broad knowledge and a deep understanding of the Bible. He was married to Helena Thomas. On Sept. 27, 1853, he was chosen to the ministry and ordained as elder at Karolswalde on Dec. 15 of the same year. He had oversight of eight villages with two church parishes, Karolswalde (*q.v.*) and Antonofka.

Unruh was sent to St. Petersburg in 1871 to ascertain facts about rumors which reached the villages regarding the Mennonites being placed in the military ranks of Russia. In 1873 he was chosen to accompany the deputies from Russia, Prussia, and Poland sent to locate favorable territory for settling in America. Upon his return after touring the United States and Canada for several months, he worked under many trials and difficulties, remaining in Russia until those of the church who so desired, both with means and without means, were brought to America. He arrived in Philadelphia with the last transport on Jan. 28, 1875. The following spring he settled in Turner County, S.D. He died July 24, 1875, after suffering several weeks from typhoid fever.   A.J.U.

Abe J. Unruh and Verney Unruh, *The Tobias A. Unruh Biography, Diary and Family Record, 1819-1950* (Pulaski, Iowa, 1950).

Unruh, Tobias A. (1851-1947), a minister of the Church of God in Christ, Mennonite, was born on June 18, 1851, at Karolswalde, Poland. He married Elizabeth Jantz on Sept. 27, 1870. They were the parents of five sons and four daughters. In 1876, with several young children, they emigrated to America, settling in McPherson County, Kan. The severe trials of pioneer life in America caused him to search the Scriptures for comfort, and because of his added knowledge of the Word he was chosen for the ministry. Nevertheless his severe spiritual struggles found no release until he acknowledged Christ and experienced the new birth. He was baptized in 1881 by Benjamin Schmidt and became a member of the Church of God in Christ, Mennonite. In 1882, a year later, he was ordained to the ministry by John Holdeman, thus becoming one of the early ministers of the denomination. The glow and fervor of his new experience remained with him throughout his life and ministry. Much of his time was spent in itinerant preaching and intensive evangelism. For many years he served as an elder, and often officiated at ordinations. On Sept. 6, 1947, at the age of 96 years, he was laid to rest in the Lone Tree cemetery, near his home church, the place of his baptism, ordination, and most of his work.

J.J.Ko.

Unschuld und Gegen-Bericht *der Evangelischen Tauff-gesinneten Christen, so Mennonisten genandt werden, über die unverschuldete Beschuldigung, als ob sie von der aufrührischen Münsterschen Rotte entsprossen, und derselben Grund und Lehre führeten, Nebenst Des Menno Simonis Ausgang aus dem Pabstthum, Lebens-Lauff, wie auch Glaubens-Bekäntniss von der heiligen Dreyeinigkeit, Sampt Der also genandten Mennonisten Glaubens-Bekäntniss und Lehre, Wie auch eine Predigt, gehalten in derselben Gemeine, Ausgegeben durch Gerh. Roosen. Hamburg in Verlegung desselben. Ratzeburg, Gedruckt bei Sigismund Hoffmann, 1702.* This important booklet by the pastor of the Hamburg-Altona (Germany) Mennonite Church, Gerrit Roosen (*q.v.*, 1612-1711), published by the author in 1702, was reprinted in a second edition in 1753. The *Unschuld und Gegen-Bericht* section, the first part actually written by the author, covers the first 29 pages, the remaining pages 29-76 constituting translations of three short tracts or sections from Menno Simons' writings. Pages 77-104 contain a brief biography of Menno by Roosen. Two remaining sections of the book, each with separate title page and pagination, contain a confession of faith (40 pp.) written by Roosen, and a sermon (46 pp.) by Roosen. All sections are covered by the general title page and were printed together. The purpose of the book as a whole was to defend the Mennonites from false accusations of Münsterism and heresy, and to prove that the Mennonites are good, pious, and evangelical. The first section, a sketch of the origin of Anabaptism, corrects the history by Sleidanus (*Beschreibung geistlicher and weltlicher Sachen*, 1547 and many later editions), which asserted that Anabaptism was of Münsterite origin.   H.S.B.

Robert Friedmann, *Mennonite Piety Through the Centuries* (Goshen, 1949) 148-51, presents a full discussion of Roosen's volume.

Unser Blatt was published by the *KfK* (Kommission für Kirchenangelegenheiten) of the Allgemeine Bundeskonferenz der Mennonitengemeinden (*q.v.*) of Russia as its monthly organ from November 1925 to June 1928, when it was forbidden by the government. *Unser Blatt* was the first official organ of the conference and made a very significant contribution at a time when there was little contact among the various Mennonite settlements and congregations and when they were going through a severe crisis because of the antireligious propaganda. The paper is today one of the best sources of information on the religious and cultural life of the Mennonites of Russia during that period. It published reports from the various settlements and congregations, statistics, biographies, and Russian laws pertaining to the religious groups and conscientious objectors to war. The editor was Alexander H. Ediger (*q.v.*) and the managing editor K. K. Martens (*q.v.*). Among its regular contributors were David H. Epp and Johann Rempel. The size of the magazine was 9¾ x 6½ in. and the number of pages 16 and later 24. Very few sets of the paper have been preserved in America, but sets are in BeCL and GCL. An almost parallel paper was *Der Praktische Landwirt* (*q.v.*), the organ of the All-Russian Mennonite Agricultural Association (*q.v.*), which appeared monthly from May 1925 to December 1926.

C.K.

Unser Blatt, a four-page semimonthly 8 x 11½ in. (since December 1949, monthly of variable size), published by the MCC through its Gronau (Westphalia), Germany, refugee service headquarters, specifically for the refugees from Russia (and West Prussia) temporarily in Germany en route to North and South America. The first issue was dated Oct. 8, 1947, the last June 15, 1950, when it was merged with *Der Mennonit* (*q.v.*). After Nov. 15, 1949, the appearance and size were irregular; only nine numbers were issued, but several were double numbers. It was named after the *Unser Blatt* published by the Mennonites in South Russia 1925-28. The editor throughout was Siegfried Janzen. The journal was distributed free to refugees, with a circulation of about 1,000. It contained much valuable historical and statistical material on the refugees in Germany, but also several good historical articles on Mennonites in Russia and Poland and numerous illustrations. (Complete file in GCL.)

H.S.B.

Unser Missionsblatt, a German language mission paper published ten times annually by the Mission Sewing Societies of the Canadian Conference of Mennonites since 1946. The first editor was Helena H. Siemens, Altona, Man. Since April 1955 Mrs. Susie Harms, Snowflake, Man., has been the editor.

C.K.

Untere Mennoniten, a name formerly given to a group of Mennonites in Switzerland, Alsace, and the Palatinate who were followers of Hans Reist (*q.v.*), while the Amish (*q.v.*) were sometimes called "Obere Mennoniten." The name was used here and there in Alsace until the middle of the 19th century. (*DB* 1868, 11 f.)

vdZ.

Unzi(c)ker (Hunziker, Huntzicker), a Mennonite family name: see **Hunsicker.**

Unzicker, Christian, an Amish Mennonite preacher in Upper Hesse, Germany, who wrote articles in the *Mennonitische Blätter* sponsoring the training of Mennonite preachers and promoting Mennonite

principles, and who with Joseph Unzicker of Henriettenthal, elder of the Nassau congregation, favored a union of all the Mennonites. On May 20 and 21, 1867, a meeting for the purpose of uniting was held in Offenthal (*q.v.*).

Menn. Bl., 1861, 32; 1862, 52; 1863, 8; 1866, 50 and 77; 1867, 38 and 44; 1868, 7; *ML* IV.

Uolimann (Uollmann, Ulmann, Ulimann), **Wolfgang,** a Swiss Brethren leader in St. Gall (*q.v.*) and Appenzell (*q.v.*). His real name was Wolfgang Schorant. His father, a respected citizen, was a guild master in St. Gall. Uolimann had been a monk in the monastery of St. Lucius in Chur. Obviously the Reformation made a powerful appeal to his religious sensibilities. The evangelical sermons of Johannes Kessler (*q.v.*), though they were private, profoundly affected the populace. In 1524 Uolimann also openly espoused and preached the Gospel in the open air near the Mangen church in St. Gall.

Soon differences of opinion became apparent within the Protestant circles. Lorenz Hochrüttiner (*q.v.*) who had been baptized in Zürich by Conrad Grebel (*q.v.*), sponsored a discussion of baptism on the death of Jesus (Rom. 6) and took a position against infant baptism. Soon afterward, Uolimann met Grebel in Schaffhausen, and was baptized by him by immersion in the Rhine. The founding of the Swiss Brethren congregation in St. Gall followed naturally, and at the same time the break with Zwingli's church occurred. On March 18, Uolimann proclaimed to a large company assembled in the weaver hall (*Weberstube*) that the heavenly Father had revealed to him that he should avoid the church as a place of lies, where the truth had never been proclaimed nor was being proclaimed now.

The two evangelical parties were now clearly defined: the representatives of the Reformed Church with infant baptism, and the representatives of the Brethren with believers' baptism. In the end, however, under the powerful intervention of Vadian (*q.v.*), the Anabaptist movement was suppressed. In April 1525 the Brethren were summoned to the council to answer for their teachings on baptism. Uolimann skillfully defended the Anabaptist position saying that infant baptism was a later institution of the church without Scriptural foundation; that adult baptism implied the obligation to die to vices, live to Christ, and be obedient; their rejection of infant baptism he based on Jesus' command to the disciples to teach, believe, and baptize. This order was maintained about two hundred years, until the time of Cyprian and Tertullian. Formerly baptism had been performed at Easter or Pentecost, then later entirely according to human understanding and not according to the Scripture. Uolimann was at first requested "for the sake of brotherly love to wait with the deed." When he refused, the request was changed to a command with the threat of expulsion in case he did not comply.

The tension continued to mount, leading to two further debates. When the opponents sought to justify infant baptism by reading Zwingli's *Taufbüchlein* (*Vom Tauff, vom Wiedertauff und vom Kindertauff*), Uolimann countered by saying, "If you have Zwingli's word, we want to have God's

Word." In June 1525 the Brethren were forbidden to hold any more meetings in or around the town. Since Uolimann did not comply he was sentenced to banishment on July 17, but was later pardoned upon his oath. His activity in the brotherhood was several times punished by sentence of imprisonment. Although he was a radical innovator, he cannot be held responsible for the excesses that made their appearance in the Anabaptist group at St. Gall.

Little is known of Uolimann's further career. In 1528 he went to Basel in the Anabaptist cause, but was ejected from the city. He led a group of Anabaptists to Moravia, and was leading a second group from Appenzell to Moravia in 1528, when they were seized in Waldsee in Swabia. Uolimann and ten other men were beheaded and the women drowned. Those who recanted were sent home. The chronicle of the Hutterian Brethren records of them, "They testified thus manly and valiantly with their bodies unto death, that their faith and baptism were founded upon divine truth."   S.G.

Emil Egli, *Die St. Galler Täufer* (Zürich, 1887); S. Geiser, *Die Taufgesinnten-Gemeinden* (Karlsruhe, 1931); Wolkan, *Geschicht-Buch;* Zieglschmid, *Chronik,* 48; *Mart. Mir.* D 17, E. 427; Peachey, *Die soziale Herkunft der Schweizer Täufer* (Karlsruhe, 1954) 25 f., 37, 75, 109, No. 19; BRN VII, 26, 516; ML IV.

Upckes, Hendri(c)k, d. 1731 at Workum in Friesland, Netherlands, a wool carder by trade, was from 1708 until his death an untrained and unsalaried Mennonite preacher in his home town, where he served with much blessing. He is said to have written a book on the origin of the Mennonites, but this book is unknown and all information about it is lacking. (*DB* 1903, 86, 88.)   vDZ.

Upland First Mennonite Church (GCM), located in Upland, Cal., in the citrus district of southern California, is affiliated with the Pacific District Conference. The first Mennonite settlers arrived in the early 1890's, attracted for reasons of health. In 1903 they organized a congregation with 18 charter members, with J. J. Voth as the first minister. In 1906 a church was built on Sixth Avenue, replaced in 1925 by a larger one on North Campus Avenue. In 1933 an organ was installed, the gift of Mr. and Mrs. L. M. Ledig. The parsonage was completed in 1940. M. M. Horsch served the congregation 1903-26, except for an interim of three years, 1915-18, when A. S. Shelley served while Horsch filled a term as district evangelist. Albert A. Penner served as pastor in the summers of 1926 and 1927. The ministers thereafter were Lester Hostetler 1927-29, A. J. Neuenschwander 1929-33, Lester Hostetler 1933-41, Earl Salzman 1941-51, Reynold Weinbrenner 1952-53, and Paul L. Goering 1953-   In 1958 the membership was 210.   L.Ho.

Upper Austria: see Austria.

Upper Deer Creek Conservative (Amish) Mennonite Church, located in Iowa County, Iowa, six miles north of Wellman, is a part of the original settlement of Amish Mennonites in this area in 1846. The Upper Deer Creek meetinghouse was built by the Old Order Amish in 1890. Twenty-five years later, in 1915, this congregation was reorganized

under the Conservative Amish Mennonite (now called Conservative Mennonite) Conference, by S. J. Swartzendruber of Bay Port, Mich., and Samuel T. Yoder of Belleville, Pa. Gideon A. Yoder, a son of Bishop Abner Yoder, was the only preacher at that time. Other ministers who have served were Elmer G. Swartzendruber (ord. 1917) and Amos C. Swartzendruber (ord. 1917), Gideon A. Yoder, bishop 1919-31, Elmer G. Swartzendruber, bishop 1931- . In 1917 the meetinghouse was moved about 75 feet southeast and enlarged. The services were usually conducted in German until the transition period of 1925-45; in 1957 possibly 90 per cent of all services were conducted in English. In 1920 evening meetings were started. Sunday school has been held since 1870, although in the earlier years it was discontinued during the winter months. Women's sewing circle, meeting somewhat irregularly since 1918, at present convenes monthly. Midweek prayer meeting is observed. In the molding of policy for the congregation, probably three men stand out most prominently; viz., the first three bishops, Jacob J. Swartzendruber, Abner Yoder, and Joseph J. Swartzendruber. Among the laity Samuel D. Guengerich was outstanding. The total membership of the congregation worshiping in the Upper Deer Creek and the Fairview (*q.v.*) meetinghouses in 1957 was 505. The ministers are Elmer G. Swartzendruber, bishop, Albert S. Miller, Jacob J. Miller, Moses Gingerich, and Morris E. Swartzendruber.   E.G.S.

Upper German Mennonites: see High German Mennonites.

Upper Milford Mennonite Church (GCM), located near Zionsville, 5 miles southwest of Emmaus, Upper Milford Twp., Lehigh Co., Pa., was first affiliated with the Franconia Conference (MC), but since 1847 has been in the Eastern District Conference (GCM). The congregation was established about 1735, and a meetinghouse was built in 1740. In 1816 the original log building, which had been used for both church and school purposes, was displaced by a stone meetinghouse, which was in turn enlarged and renovated in 1843. In the division of 1847 the minister, Joseph Schantz, and almost all the members followed John H. Oberholtzer (*q.v.*) into the new conference. In 1876 the congregation razed the stone building and built a new brick church. William Gehman (*q.v.*), ordained by lot as minister here in 1849, led a division in 1857 and became the founder of the Evangelical Mennonites (*q.v.*). In 1895 the membership was 96; in 1936 it was 164; in 1958 it was 168, with Burton G. Yost as pastor. Other ministers who have served were Uriah Shelly, C. H. A. van der Smissen, A. S. Shelly, W. S. Gottschall, E. S. Shelly, V. B. Boyer, and H. G. Nyce.   B.G.Y.

J. C. Wenger, *History of the Mennonites of the Franconia Conference* (Telford, 1937) 221, 222, 369.

Upper Palatinate (Oberpfalz), one of eight districts of the former kingdom of East Bavaria, Germany, included the river territory of the Regen and the Naab, parts of the Franconian Jura, the several districts south of the Danube near Regensburg. The area of the Upper Palatinate is 3,724 sq. miles, and its population in 1950, 896,520. It is a hilly region, containing the Bohemian Forest and the Fichtelgebirge. Regensburg, its capital, is a historic city and is today an important communication center. With the exception of the section south of the Danube the land of the Upper Palatinate is not very fertile.

For the history of Mennonitism the Upper Palatinate never reached the significance of the Palatinate proper. To be sure, there was in Regensburg (q.v.) an Anabaptist congregation as early as 1527, which reached its peak in 1539. Hermann Nestler gives the number of members as several hundred. But during the period of persecution it disappeared. Not until 260 years later, when the Wittelsbachs inherited the Bavarian lands at the turn of the 18th century, and Maximilian Josef (q.v.), who knew the Mennonites to be competent farmers, called them into the country, was another congregation organized. Some from the region of Zweibrücken and Lorraine settled in the Upper Palatinate, chiefly as renters of the estates of noble landowners. The congregation, belonging to the Amish wing, called its preachers and elders from its own ranks and held its meetings in rotation in the homes of the widely scattered members. About 1890 a minister was employed by the congregation. Since that time the meetings have been held in the Lutheran Bruderhauskirche in Regensburg. They were joined in the course of time by brethren coming from Baden, Württemberg, and the Rheinpfalz. Census figures state the Mennonite population of the Upper Palatinate as 128 in 1875, 178 in 1885, 134 in 1900, and 95 in 1910.   A.S.

Hermann Nestler, *Die Wiedertäuferbewegung in Regensburg* (Regensburg, 1926); *ML* III, 288.

Ureterp, a village in the Dutch province of Friesland. The Mennonites living here were at least from 1695 members of the Drachten (q.v.) congregation, which was officially called the Drachten and Ureterp congregation. Until c1690 Drachten was probably independent, being the nucleus and oldest center from which the present Drachten-Ureterp congregation has developed. The suggestion by Blaupot ten Cate that the Ureterp congregation was founded before 1580 or between 1580 and 1600 is unfounded. The origin of this church is unknown. It existed in the early 17th century, when meetings were held in a barn, probably at Selmien, a hamlet near Ureterp. In November 1661 Michiel Wymmers promised to bequeath a plot of ground "forever" to "the true poor Mennonite followers of Lammert Gaukes" at Ureterp. As late as 1860 the Drachten and Ureterp parts of the congregation were more or less independent of each other, particularly in the care of the poor, for which they each had separate funds. Apparently after the early 18th century (a new meetinghouse was built at Drachten shortly after 1690) no meetings were held at Ureterp. Concerning the meetinghouse in Ureterp there is no information at all.   vDZ.

Blaupot t. C., *Friesland*, 166, 306; G. ten Cate, *Geschiedk. Overzicht van de Doopsgez. gemeente te D. en U.* (Drachten, 1890) 1-17; *DB* 1861, 132; 1890, 93; *DJ* 1942, 45.

Urfehde: see Oath.

Urschitz (Uhrschitz), Hutterite Bruderhof, located near Austerlitz, Moravia, founded about the middle of the 16th century by Hutterites brought in by Ulrich von Kaunitz. The commune was forcibly evacuated, rebuilt in 1569, plundered in 1618. In October 1622 the Brethren had to abandon Urschitz with empty hands; they settled in Hungary (q.v.). This Bruderhof was commonly called Taufarsky. (Zieglschmid, *Chronik; ML* IV.)

Ursel, an Anabaptist martyr, burned at the stake on Jan. 10, 1570, at Maastricht, Netherlands, together with her husband Arent van Essen. (For particulars, see **Trijntgen.**)   vDZ.

Mart. Mir. D 502, E 842 f.; W. Bax, *Het Protestantisme in het Bisdom Luik . . .* II (The Hague, 1941) 306-10.

Ursel (Ursula), an Anabaptist martyr: see **Beckum, Ursula Van.**

Ursenbacherhof in Baden, Germany, former Mennonite congregation: see **Dühren.**

Ursprung, Entwickelung und Schicksale *der altevangelischen Taufgesinnten oder Mennoniten in kurzen Zügen übersichtlich dargestellt,* by Anna Brons (q.v.), was a book of 447 pages, published by the author at Emden in 1884 and in a second edition at the same place in 1891 without changes. The third edition was revised slightly by E. M. ten Cate and published by Johannes Müller at Amsterdam in 1912, with 403 pages. How this book came into being has been related in the article **Anna Brons.** The significance of the book lies in the fact that it was the first detailed German history of the Mennonites of Europe and America. It consists of ten parts. The author treats the Mennonites of Switzerland, South Germany, the Netherlands, Moravia, Prussia, Russia, and North America, and the influence of the Mennonites on other groups. Anna Brons has a pleasant and appealing style without burdening her text with scholarly problems. Her basic convictions were those of the enlightened liberal 19th-century North German and Dutch Mennonites, and she accordingly did not have much interest in the theological problems of the preceding centuries. The book has served as a valuable source of information.   C.K.

Ursula, the title of a Novelle written about the Anabaptists of Zürich, Switzerland, by Gottfried Keller (q.v.).

Ursula, an Anabaptist, probably a martyr. She was the wife of Valentin von Sternenfels, and was one of the Anabaptists imprisoned at Passau (q.v.) in 1535. In her trial she declared that she had been baptized five years previously in the Palatinate by Andreas von Weiss, who had been put to death at Neuburg on the Danube, and that she intended to persist in her faith.   W.W.

Ursula of Kunzensee on the Kocher in Württemberg, Germany, a girl of fifteen who was imprisoned with about 25 other Anabaptists in the castle of Passau in 1535. She confessed that she had been baptized by Blasy (Khumauf) in Auspitz. She also remained loyal to her faith and presumably died a martyr's death.   W.W.

Ursula (Ursel), an Anabaptist martyr, is identical with **Ursula Ochsentreiberin.**

Ursula, the wife of Lienhard Jost (*q.v.*) at Strasbourg, a "prophetess" and like her husband devoted follower of Melchior Hofmann (*q.v.*), who was greatly influenced by her and ranked her prophecies with those of Isaiah and Jeremiah.   vDZ.

BRN VII, 125 f.; A. Hulshof, *Gesch. van de Doopsgezinden te Straatsburg* . . . (Amsterdam, 1905) 117-23.

Ursula von Werdum: see Beckum, Ursula van.

Ursula Corffis (Korffis), of Vuchtenburch(?), an Anabaptist martyr, was drowned at Haarlem, Holland, May 29, 1539. On May 23, 1539, she was apprehended with a number of Anabaptists meeting in the house of Lambrecht Duppijns (*q.v.*). Twice she was tortured on the rack; she confessed that she had been a nun before she joined the Anabaptists. The entire group were followers of David (*q.v.*) Joris.   vDZ.

Uruguay is the smallest independent country in South America. Its 72,000 sq. mi., extending about 350 miles both east to west and north to south, is wedged between the two giants of Latin America, Brazil to the north and Argentina to the west and south. Culturally Uruguay is the most progressive of all South American countries. Its two and one-third million people are mostly of early Spanish and Italian descent, although there are people of German and French immigrant extraction. Montevideo (pop. 700,000), the capital city, is one of the cultural centers of South America. The country's educational program is one of the most progressive and democratic in the world. Attendance is compulsory at its 1500 free public schools. All citizens 18 years old and over are compelled to vote. Although most Uruguayans are Roman Catholic, there is complete religious freedom for all.

The settlement of Mennonites in Uruguay began in 1948 after the Mennonites from West Prussia had been displaced during the gigantic population upheaval there during and following World War II. Most of these Mennonites, who were temporarily stationed in displaced persons camps in Denmark (*q.v.*), were unable to enter Canada and the United States because of their German citizenship. Settlement possibilities in such countries as Brazil, Argentina, and Mexico did not seem favorable, and most of the Danzig Mennonites were opposed to settling in Paraguay. As a last resort they agreed to settle in Eastern Paraguay, in case no other possibilities were open to them. The Mennonite Central Committee, in close touch with these refugees, explored possibilities in Uruguay. Rather unexpectedly opportunity presented itself for entrance and permanent settlement in this country, and on Oct. 27, 1948, the first contingent of 690 Mennonites from Danzig and 60 from Poland arrived in Uruguay. These 20th-century pilgrims had the unusual experience of embarking from Europe for South America without knowing whether they were headed for Paraguay or Uruguay since they had not received official government permission from Uruguay when the ship left Europe. The official assurance was then wired to them on board ship.

With help from the Uruguayan Institute of Colonization and the MCC they were settled in Uruguay. The first contingent was temporarily quartered near the city of Paysandu along the Argentinian border, 250 of them in old army barracks and a vacant warehouse at Colonia, and the remaining 500 in old army barracks at Arapey. Being eager to work, individuals and small groups immediately took whatever jobs they could find—as skilled laborers and factory and farm hands, while others rented small acreages. Many widows and girls found employment as domestics in the cities, especially in Montevideo.

The first permanent settlement was made in April 1950 on a 2,900-acre ranch known locally as El Ombu (*q.v.*), located about 180 miles northwest of Montevideo near the town of Young. This tract was large enough for only about half the total group. The rest continued to find work over widely scattered areas. Some of these were not able to get on land of their own until after the second large land purchase in 1951. The El Ombu ranch was divided into 75 homesteads of varying sizes. The farmers organized an agricultural co-operative in September 1950. The land is owned by the co-operative and cannot be sold without colony permission. The major portion of the credit for the corporate purchase of the land was advanced by the Uruguayan Institue of Colonization. Repayment is arranged over a 30-year period at 5½ per cent interest. Chief crops produced are wheat, peanuts, sunflowers, corn, kaffir, oats, and Sudan grass. Cream and butter also yield substantial cash income.

In October 1951 a second contingent of 431 Danzig refugees landed at Montevideo to boost the total Mennonite population in Uruguay to almost 1,200. Under the leadership of the MCC a subsidiary non-profit corporation known as Uruguay Land Associates was organized by a group of Mennonites, mostly in Kansas and Nebraska, and a sum of $65,000 was raised as a loan to help the new arrivals settle on land. Again with the help of the Uruguayan Institute of Colonization a tract of land was purchased. It was a 4,500-acre ranch known as Brabancia and located near Tres Bocas and now known as the Gartental (*q.v.*) settlement. The land was divided into 139 homesteads of varying size, of which 100 were assigned to the newly arrived settlers, and the rest to the Mennonite settlers of 1948 who, because of lack of land, had not been able to settle at El Ombu.

The third colony in Uruguay, named Delta (*q.v.*) after the Vistula Delta homeland, was established in 1955 on a tract of c3,600 acres in the San José Department about 60 miles northwest of Montevideo, some 150 miles southwest of El Ombu and Gartental. Part of the funds for the land purchased were again furnished by North American Mennonites. The tract was divided into farms of 75 acres, and occupied initially by 40 families, all part of the previously immigrated groups.

Culturally in some respects the Uruguay Mennonites hold more liberal views than other South American Mennonites, especially than those in Paraguay. The main body has organized itself in the Conference of Mennonite churches in Uruguay, and is affiliated with the General Conference Mennonite Church in North America and the Vereinigung der deutschen Mennoniten-Gemeinden in Germany. It had four congregations in 1957: El Ombu 255, Gartental 249, Montevideo 200, and Colonia Delta 120, a total of 809 baptized members. A group of 38 organized a Mennonite Brethren congregation on board ship en route to Uruguay in 1948. All of these came from the Wymysle area in Central Poland. Its total membership in 1957 was 91. The colonies have established their own elementary schools, but teach the nationally approved curriculum.

Because of the generally favorable economic, social, and cultural conditions in Uruguay the Mennonites are rapidly becoming established. It is likely that those who immigrated there will remain permanently, and it is entirely possible that Mennonites from other South American countries may in small groups migrate there too. Generally the colonists are well satisfied with their new home. By comparison with their coreligionists in Brazil and Paraguay their early years have been considerably less difficult.

The MCC has since 1948 maintained a center in Montevideo as a co-ordinating and contact agency with North America, now at Vilardebo 964. In 1956, at the same address, the Mennonite Biblical Seminary (*q.v.*) was established as a bilingual training school operated by a board composed of representatives of all the groups in South America desiring to co-operate (all do except the M.B.), supported by the G.C.M. and M.C. mission boards of North America. The attendance in 1957 was about 36 students.

The Mennonite Church (MC) of North America established a mission in Montevideo in 1954 with two couples, who in 1957 had established a small congregation. The total baptized Mennonite membership in Uruguay in 1957 was about 910, with a total population of some 1300.   J.W.F.

J. W. Fretz, *Pilgrims in Paraguay* (Scottdale, 1953); H. J. Andres, "Colonia Menonite in Uruguay," *Menn. Life* IV (July 1949) 15; Gustav E. Reimer, "Von Danzig nach Uruguay," *Menn. Life* IV (July 1949) 12-14; W. Dück, "Neue Heimat in Uruguay," *Gem.-Kal.* 1952, 56-65; H. Wall, "Drei Jahre in Uruguay," *Gesch.-Bl.* IX (1952) 18-26; *Gem.-Kal.*, 1953, 63-66; 1955, 73-78; 1957, 30-35.

Usquert, a village in the Dutch province of Groningen, in which Anabaptism was found as early as 1533; later there was a Mennonite congregation here belonging to the Flemish branch, not Old Flemish as were most congregations in this province. Of its history there are only a few traces: it was in the 18th century a member of the Humsterlandsche (*q.v.*) Sociëteit; the *Naamlijst* issues of 1731 and 1743 name Jan Jansz as the preacher; he was apparently the last preacher here; according to the issues of 1755-65 the pulpit was vacant, and in those of 1766 ff. the congregation is not named. Yet it seems to have existed until 1784, in which year its property was divided. (Blaupot t. C., *Groningen* I, 15, 149, 201.)   vDZ.

Usury. As used in the Scriptures the term means any kind of interest on money loaned, although in the English language it has come to mean an exorbitant rate of interest, or interest in excess of the legal rate.

The Mosaic code forbade the taking of interest from brethren in the faith, although it might be received from strangers. The prohibition grew out of the agricultural economy of the time when there was little need for productive capital loans for business purposes. The chief purpose of loans was for the assistance of a friend or brother in need. To receive interest under such circumstances was a violation of the law of love which required the Israelite to care for his own. "If you lend money to any of my people with you who is poor, you shall not be to him as a creditor, and you shall not exact interest from him. If ever you take your neighbor's garment in pledge, you shall restore it to him before the sun goes down; for that is his only covering, it is his mantle for his body; in what else shall he sleep" (Ex. 22:25-27, RSV)? This command as well as that of Jesus. "Give to him who begs from you, and do not refuse him who would borrow from you" (Matt. 5:42), are not to be thought of as economic principles or as business procedures. They have to do with the Christian's social responsibility to the poor; they are a statement of the law of love which extends mercy to the brother in need.

In the Middle Ages and the Reformation, as in Biblical times, money was regarded primarily as a medium of exchange, not as productive capital; and money loaned was for the purpose of helping the brother in need, not for investment purposes. For this reason the medieval church, and to some extent Luther, as well as the Anabaptists, opposed the use of interest. This was entirely consistent with the principle of brotherhood espoused by the Anabaptists, as well as with the simple economy of the handicrafts and noncommercial agriculture which characterized their economic life.

The economy of Geneva, on the other hand, was characterized by industry, commerce, and banking in which the borrowing and lending of productive capital and its accompanying payment of interest played an important role. In this setting John Calvin approved the use of interest as an instrument of the business economy, suggesting 5 per cent as a reasonable rate. In the case of noncommercial loans, however, for the aid of the brother in need, he agreed with the Anabaptists that no interest should be paid. Interest in such a case, as well as excessive rates for business loans, he condemned as "usury."

In their later history Mennonites have generally come to accept the practice approved by Calvin, a reasonable rate of interest on business loans, with a low rate or none at all for cases where brother is helping brother in need. Mennonite history reveals many cases where loans with little interest, or none at all, have been made to tide families over difficult financial situations; or where in case the need continued even the payment of the principal was canceled. There have been many cases where loans requiring little or no interest have been extended to assist a poor but worthy young family in getting a start in the purchase of a home or means of livelihood, especially if this could be the means of helping the family to relate its life more constructively to the life and work of the brotherhood.

A recent case was called to the writer's attention where a Mennonite student received a loan to continue his education, with the understanding that upon completion of his education, if he entered into direct church service no interest would be required, and perhaps even part of the loan canceled. But if he entered a business or professional career promising normal financial returns, the normal rate of interest would apply.

During those years of American history when money and credit were scarce and when unscrupulous moneylenders reaped huge profits, Mennonite (MC) conference regulations recognized the temptation of covetousness facing some of the members. The Ohio Conference in 1866 declared the "established rule of the Church" to be "that the brethren should not take more than six per cent interest on money loaned, for the reason that it is unchristian and oppressive. It was further recommended to lend to the honest poor and needy without any interest, yea to lend to the upright in heart, hoping for nothing." Eight years later the Indiana Conference agreed that "In regard to interest it was considered that members of our church should not take more than legal interest and the penalty if a brother transgress in this point shall be he shall pay back the amount exceeding the legal rate and confess his fault." In 1884 the Ohio Conference declared that the "Brethren shall not exact more than legal interest," which position was taken also by the Kansas-Nebraska Conference in 1888 and by the Western District A.M. Conference in 1891.

It was formerly standard practice among the Old Order Amish to make loans for necessary purposes without interest and without notes or mortgages. In recent times this practice has not been fully maintained everywhere.　　　　　　　G.F.H., M.G.

Utenhove, Jan Nicolaesz, a Reformed clergyman, originally from Gent, Belgium, who lived in England for some time and from 1554 at Emden in East Friesland, Germany. In 1556 he moved to Poland to assist John à Lasco (*q.v.*) in promoting the Reformation in the country. He made a new Dutch translation of the New Testament, published at Emden in 1556, reprinted in 1559. Utenhove's hope that this translation would be generally accepted by the Dutch Protestants was not fulfilled; the Calvinists objected to the dialect used by Utenhove, and the Mennonites held to Mattheus Jacobszoon's New Testament and the Liesveldt editions, and from 1560 to the Biestkens (*q.v.*) Bibles.　　　　vDZ.

F. Pijper, *Jan Utenhove* (Leiden, 1883); H. van Druten, *Geschiedenis der Nederl. Bijbelvertaling* (Leiden, 1895) 544-49; *DB* 1879, 16 f.

Utikon, Hans von: see Müller, Hans.

Utrecht, a province of the Netherlands. In this province early Anabaptism had a smaller following than in some other Dutch provinces like North Holland and Friesland. In the southwest part of the province around IJsselstein (*q.v.*) and Benschop (*q.v.*) there was in 1534-44 a live movement of more or less Münsterite character, which was permitted to develop by the tolerant attitude of Ghysbrecht van Baeck (*q.v.*), district governor of IJssel-

stein, whose wife Elsa van Lostadt (*q.v.*) even belonged to the Anabaptists. In the cities of Utrecht (*q.v.*) and Amersfoort (*q.v.*) Anabaptist activity during the 16th century was not very strong. The puzzling information by V. P. in *Successio Anabaptistica* that about 1535 the Anabaptists of Utrecht set up "a king" obviously does not refer to the town of Utrecht but rather to Benschop.

The present province of Utrecht belonged to the territory of the Catholic bishop of Utrecht until 1528, when Emperor Charles V attached it to his dominions. In 1577 Utrecht broke away from Spanish tyranny and joined the United Provinces of the Netherlands, then governed by William (*q.v.*) of Orange. About this time Calvinism became predominant in the province and the Mennonites were no longer persecuted. The relative smallness of the Mennonite congregations in this province may have made the Calvinists of Utrecht more tolerant than they were elsewhere.

In the early 17th century there were in the province, besides Utrecht city, Mennonite congregations at Amersfoort, Bunschoten, Spakenburg, Maarseveen, and Veenendaal, all of which died out in the 17th-18th centuries; from 1754 to 1923 the congregation in the city of Utrecht was the only one in this province.

New congregations arose in the 20th century at Amersfoort in 1923 (circle in 1903) and Zeist in 1931 (circle in 1929); a circle (*kring*) was formed at Bilthoven in 1932.

According to the official census there were in this province 340 Mennonites in 1859, 1,088 in 1899, and 2,912 in 1947. The total number of baptized members of the Mennonite church in the province of Utrecht was 100 in 1847, 553 in 1900, and 1,337 in 1958.　　　　　　　vDZ.

Inv. Arch. Amst. I, Nos. 263, 269, 402, 402a, 408; Mellink, *Wederdopers,* 231-41; *DB* 1863, 94-103.

Utrecht, a city in the Netherlands, capital of the province of Utrecht (*q.v.*), population (1958) 200,-150, with 1,056 Mennonites. In 1568 the States of Utrecht and the magistrates of the city wrote to the Spanish governor Alba (*q.v.*) that until 1566 heresy was unknown in Utrecht and Catholicism flourished. This, however, is not true either of the city or the province.

In the city of Utrecht Anabaptist views were found by 1530, when some persons had to answer for heretical views, among whom was Dirk Weyman who harbored doubt as to the legality of infant baptism. But probably these views were Sacramentist (*q.v.*) rather than Anabaptist. In 1535 a few revolutionary Anabaptists from outside were executed at Utrecht, among whom was Walraven (*q.v.*) Herberts of Middelie, who had been sent to this town to propagate the Münsterite doctrines. Jacob (*q.v.*) Claesz and Govert (*q.v.*) Aertsz, citizens of Utrecht, also executed in 1535, seem to have been peaceful Anabaptists. In 1539 fifteen Anabaptists, probably all followers of David (*q.v.*) Joris and none of them a citizen of Utrecht, were put to death; a number of church robbers executed here in 1540, called Anabaptists in the records, had hardly anything to do with Anabaptism, and the same can be said of a number of followers of Jan Batenburg (*q.v.*) executed at Utrecht in 1544-45, one of whom was the notorious Appelman (*q.v.*).

In general it is true that the early Anabaptist movement had little following in Utrecht before 1550. Yet there was a Mennonite congregation dating from about 1554 which was visited by the elders Leenaert (*q.v.*) Bouwens, Joost (*q.v.*) Verbeek, and Dirk (*q.v.*) Philips. Leenaert stayed at Utrecht several times, baptizing 14 persons in 1554-57, six (or nine) in 1557-61, and 28 in 1563-65. Joost Verbeek administered baptism here in the spring of 1561; among the persons baptized by him were Jan (*q.v.*) Hendriks, Hendrik (*q.v.*) Eemkens, who died as a martyr at Utrecht in 1562, and Willem (*q.v.*) Willemsz. Dirk Philips visited Utrecht about Christmas 1561. In the home of Cornelis van Voordt (*q.v.*) he administered baptism and the Lord's Supper. Shortly after his visit, in early February 1562, a meeting held in this home was surprised by police; some of those present escaped, but others were seized. Their trials give valuable information about the Utrecht congregation: meetings were held in the home of Aeltgen (*q.v.*) van Gent, where Joost Verbeek had baptized in early 1561, or in the stately patrician home of Cornelis van Voordt, who was not a Mennonite, but sympathized with the Mennonites, and whose wife and son Jan had been baptized into the church. Also other members received the congregation in their homes. For the sake of safety they assembled at four in the morning and remained until seven in the evening after night had fallen. The membership is said to have been rather small, not exceeding 30 or 40, including some members living in other towns of the province, e.g., at Vreeland (*q.v.*). A meeting held in 1560 was attended by 14 or 15 persons. In these meetings they read the Scriptures, particularly the New Testament. One of their members possessed a copy of the martyr book *Offer* (*q.v.*) *des Heeren,* which he had bought at Utrecht. A number of those arrested were tortured. The sentences pronounced were rather mild; only Hendrik Eemkens was sentenced to death and executed on June 10, 1562. Others recanted and were banished or sentenced to public penitence. Cornelis van Voordt and his wife Anna were banished forever from the territory of Utrecht, Holland, and Zeeland, and their property was confiscated for the benefit of Philip II.

After this occurrence there is for a long time no clear information about the Mennonites at Utrecht. In 1568-70 six Mennonites were executed at Utrecht but none of them was a native of Utrecht. The congregation persisted in secrecy until the Reformed Church became dominant in Utrecht (1579) and the Mennonites were tolerated and exempted from strict military service (city decrees of May 9, 1581, May 14 and Aug. 14, 1582). In 1592 mention is made of a Mennonite congregation "in which no person is admitted unless baptized by adult baptism, whose behavior is known [to the members] and of whom it is known that he does not use bad language and is not given to drinking, and who does not wrong anybody."

In the early 17th century Utrecht had at least three Mennonite congregations, due to the deplorable schisms among the Dutch Mennonites—Flemish, Frisian, and High German. Among the Flemish, who then seem to have been the largest group, Jan van der Voort (*q.v.*) was ordained as an elder in 1606 by Jacques Outerman (*q.v.*) and Simon (*q.v.*) Fijts. In 1611 van der Voort was still elder, Hans Wijtses the preacher, and Jan Joostes the deacon. The male membership then numbered 73 and the total baptized membership probably some 150. A house in the Jufferstraat (now Springweg) was bought in 1618; it was remodeled into a meetinghouse.

Concerning the Frisians and High Germans nothing is known but that they had united before 1630; on May 19, 1639, this united church merged with the Flemish congregation, which before in 1632 had participated in the general merger of the Flemish and Old Flemish in the Netherlands, accepting the Dordrecht Confession of Faith; Herman Segers, Jan Hendricksen Hooghvelt, and Daniel Lhorens (probably Hovens) signed for the Utrecht congregation.

After the merger of 1632 the Utrecht Mennonite congregation increased in membership; in 1649 it numbered 292 baptized members. It developed in peace until the quarrels of 1661-62. The elders were Abr. Spronck 1639-52, Harmen Segers 1639-63, Daniel Hovens 1640-52, Arent van Heuven 1646-74, Robert J. van Hooghveldt 1646-63, Goris van Aldendorp 1649-72, Jan Andriesz van Aken 1652-1706, Willem van Maurik 1658-73, and Frans Andries 1660-82.

In 1659-64 severe controversies between a conservative part of the congregation led by the preacher van Hooghveldt (*q.v.*) and a more progressive faction led by the preachers van Maurik, van Aldendorp, van Heuven, and van Aken caused unpleasant strife. This conflict described by W. J. Kühler in *DB* 1916, which ran parallel with the dissension at Amsterdam (see **Lammerenkrijgh**), resulted in an initial victory for the conservatives; van Maurik and his group were suspended on July 31, 1661, by 17 elders from outside, among whom were T. J. van Braght (*q.v.*) and Bastiaan van Weenighem (*q.v.*); for nearly three years they abstained from serving. Gradually the authority of the conservative leaders declined, particularly after the death of van Hooghveldt (1663). New preachers chosen after his death were not as aggressive as van Hooghveldt had been. Moreover the majority of the members favored the progressive views. For a number of years the progressives had held separate meetings, but finally peace was restored in 1675. In the meantime van Maurik (*q.v.*) had moved to Amsterdam. During the first years of this conflict a number of writings were published concerning the controversy, including a confession by van Maurik and his friends.

In 1674 the Utrecht congregation joined the Zonist (*q.v.*) Sociëteit, but a number of most strict conservatives left the church and joined the Reformed. The Utrecht congregation was now led by Jacobus van Griethuysen, a rather conservative man, who however was able to satisfy the moderate progressives. Van Griethuysen served 1674-1713. A period of peace and prosperity had dawned, though throughout the 18th century some friction persisted between the more liberal and the more conservative elements of the congregation. The ministers then were A. van Dulken 1681-88, Pieter Noordijk 1685-1704, Christoffel Tirion 1704-10, Teyme van Hilten 1711-15, Isaak Franken 1713-38, G. de Wit 1714-29, Gerardus van Heyningen 1739-58, Marten Schagen 1741-70, Joannes Cuperus 1758-77, Cornelis de Vries 1771-86, Abr. Wijnands 1777-85, and J. A. Hoekstra 1786-1803.

Only half of these men had received a special training for the ministry; Tirion and Franken were trained by Galenus (*q.v.*) Abrahamsz, whereas van Heyningen, Cuperus, and Wijnands studied at the Amsterdam Lamist seminary, and Hoekstra at the Zonist seminary. Since then the Utrecht congregation has been served only by ministers trained at Amsterdam Theological Seminary: Petrus Brouwer 1786-1827, Jan Kops 1816-43 (part-time; he was also a professor of agriculture at the Utrecht University), Wopco Cnoop Koopmans 1823-27, Jan Visscher 1828-61, Jan Hartog 1861-94, Sytze de Waard 1894-1911, P. J. Glasz 1911-34, J. J. G. Wuite 1934- , and C. F. Brüsewitz 1946- .

In the 18th century, doubtless through the influence of liberal ministers like van Heyningen and Cuperus, the congregation began to admit nonmembers to the Lord's Supper and to accept persons into the congregation without (re)baptism. Baptism was then often administered privately in the homes of the candidates.

The old (originally Flemish) meetinghouse on Jufferstraat, a simple building, was equipped with a pipe organ in 1765 (dedicated Aug. 4); this was the first organ placed in a Mennonite church in Holland. This valuable instrument was the gift of four members of the congregation. A new church, still in use, was dedicated on Nov. 7, 1773, by Pastor Cuperus. This was once a beautiful building; some of its beautiful rococo style can still be seen in the interior (pulpit and benches for the church board). The organ from the old meetinghouse was installed in the new one and used until 1870, when a new one was built. The church was remodeled in 1867 and 1922, and enlarged for church activities in 1922.

It is not known which hymnal was first used by the congregation; in 1684 the Psalms *Laus Deo* (*q.v.*) were introduced and used until 1896. Until then the congregation also sang from the *Groote* and *Kleine Bundel* (*q.v.*), introduced in the early 18th century. These hymnals were replaced in 1896 by the *Protestantenbond-bundel,* whereas also the *Leidsch* (*q.v.*) *Bundel* was used. In 1944 these hymnals were replaced by the new Mennonite hymnal.

As to the membership, in 1649 the congregation numbered 292 baptized members, in 1700 about 270; in the 18th-19th centuries the number decreased considerably, in 1836 reaching its lowest point with only 80 members; from then there was a steady and even rapid growth: 102 in 1847, 110 in 1861, 450 in 1895, 553 in 1901, 875 in 1926, reaching its peak with 1,064 in 1941, then decreasing to 752 in 1958. Many old family names found among the membership in former centuries like van (der) Voort, Broekhuizen, van Geleyn, Boogaert, Blank(a)ert, van Heuven, van Aken, Hovens, van Oosterwijk, van Maarseveen, Spronck, Fremery, van Dul(c)ken,

van Hengelaar, van Pesch, van Singel, van Swigtenheuvel, Verbeek, Wijlik, van Arkel, Oortman, van Maurik, etc., are no longer here.

In the 17th-18th centuries the Utrecht church generously supported, both financially and with the service of its ministers, a number of small congregations in the neighborhood like Bunschoten, Spakenburg, Huizen, Veenendaal, Vianen, Gorinchem, Schoonhoven, and Asperen, all now extinct except Huizen (at present called the Hilversum congregation). Liberal help was given not only to its own needy members but also to other Mennonite churches; in 1702, when the Bunschoten meetinghouse was badly damaged by a flood, the Mennonites of Utrecht had it restored, and in the same year gave 832 guilders to the Krommenie congregation, whose meetinghouse had burned down in 1701. To the Prussian Mennonites Utrecht contributed 885 guilders in 1733 and 800 guilders in 1736.

Formerly the Utrecht congregation owned a considerable library of Mennonite books, the gift of its minister Marten Schagen (*q.v.*) in 1777; in 1834 this library was sold for 250 guilders to the A.D.S. to be placed in the Mennonite library of Amsterdam.

Since 1936 the Utrecht and Amsterdam congregations have operated the Brotherhood Home (Broederschapshuis) at Bilthoven (*q.v.*). The Mennonite circle (*kring*) of Bilthoven is in the care of the pastors of Utrecht; this circle organizes religious services every two weeks in the Broederschapshuis as well as other activities. The church activities at Utrecht now (1958) include two ladies' circles, a youth group, and a Sunday school for children.

vDZ.

H. B. Berghuys, *Geschiedenis der Doopsgezinde Gemeente te Utrecht* (n.p., n.d.-1926); Mellink, *Wederdopers,* 231, 232, 234 f., 236 f., 238-40; S. Cramer, "De Doopsgezinde gemeente te Utrecht van 1560 tot 1562," *DB* 1903, 1-53; *Inv. Arch. Amst.* I, Nos. 33 f., 102-4, 106 f., 128, 209 f., 212, 237a, 238, 265, 269, 279, 327, 329, 366, 398a, 402a, 403, 408, 559, 594, 786, 788, 1025, 1071, 1790; II, Nos. 2288-99; II, 2, Nos. 494-96, 645; Kühler, *Geschiedenis* I, 270; II, 199; Blaupot t. C., *Holland* I and II, *passim*; *DB* 1863, 78, 80 f., 83-94, 96-98, 100, 102; 1868, 100-5; 1881, 107 f.; 1888, 124; 1897, 166; 1916, 145-95; 1917, 140.

Utrecht-Gooi, Ring, a Ring (*q.v.,* i.e., district organization) of the Mennonite congregations in the province of Utrecht (*q.v.*) and also those of Het Gooi, the adjacent part of the province of North Holland. This Ring split off from Ring Arnhem (*q.v.*) in 1947. The Ring Utrecht-Gooi embraces the congregations of Utrecht, Amersfoort, Zeist, Baarn, Hilversum, and Bussum. vDZ.

Utrechtsche Vragen (Utrecht Questions), the twelve questions drawn up at Utrecht, probably by the Reformed pastor Cornelis Gentman (*q.v.*), for the examination of Mennonites by the magistrates to establish whether they were orthodox, especially with regard to Socinian (*q.v.*) views, and to be tolerated. These "questions," sometimes cynically called "Geuzenvraagen" by the Mennonites, were applied at Utrecht in 1661, Middleburg 1665, Deventer 1669, and a few other places. They are printed in Blaupot ten Cate, *Groningen* II, 205-13. vDZ.

Utt, Michael, an Anabaptist preacher, a tailor of Stams near Innsbruck, who took part in the disputation of Zofingen (*q.v.*) in 1532. (*Gbl.,* 1913, 50.)

Uutenhove (Utenhove, Wttenhoven), **Anneken,** an Anabaptist martyr: see **Anneken van den Hove.**

Uylenburch (Van), a Dutch family of which there was both a Reformed branch, to which Saskia van Uylenburgh belonged, who was the wife of Rembrandt (*q.v.*), and also a Mennonite branch. Mennonites were (1) Gerrit Uylenburch, who moved from the Netherlands, probably from Leeuwarden in Friesland, to Krakow, Poland, where he was a cabinetmaker for the King of Poland. His son (2) Hendrick Uylenburch, b. at Krakow *c*1587, d. 1661 at Amsterdam, lived at Danzig *c*1612-25 and thereafter at Amsterdam, where he founded an Academy of Art, lodging and stimulating young artists, among whom were Rembrandt, Flinck, and Jacob Backer (*q.v.*). At the same time he operated an art store. A son of (2) Hendrick was (3) Gerrit Uylenburch, b. *c*1625 at Amsterdam, d. *c*1690 in England. He married Elisabeth Just, a Mennonite of Königsberg, and continued his farther's art business, which under his leading became known at home and abroad. Gerrit Uylenburch, who was also an artist and made a self-portrait, was considered the best art connoisseur of his time. In 1645 he was baptized into the Amsterdam Waterlander Mennonite congregation. In 1681 he became bankrupt and moved to England. His brother (4) Abraham Uylenburch, who died at Dublin, Ireland, in 1688 where he was a court painter, was probably not a Mennonite. Another son of (1) Gerrit's was the painter (5) Rombout van Uylenburch, b. *c*1590 at Krakow, d. *c*1628 at ?. From about 1610 he lived at Danzig, Prussia; one of his paintings was a portrait of the Mennonite elder Jan Gerrits (*q.v.*) van Emden.   vD Z.

Thieme-Becker, *Allg. Lexikon der bildenden Künstler* XXXIV (Leipzig, 1940) 16 f.; *Winkler Prins Encyclopedie,* 6th ed., Vol. XVII (Amsterdam, 1953) 810 f.; H. F. Wijman, "Rembrandt en Hendrik Uylenburgh," *Amstelodamum,* June 1956; *ML* III, 242.

Uzbek SSR: see Soviet Central Asia.

V

Vaals, a town in the southeast of the Dutch province of Limburg, close to the German border. Mennonites from Burtscheid (*q.v.*) and Aachen (*q.v.*), Germany, who could not meet there freely, used to meet at Vaals and built a meetinghouse there in the early 17th century. In the 18th century Burtscheid, Vaals, and Aachen formed one single congregation, whose preacher lived at Burtscheid until 1768; he also had charge of the Maastricht congregation. In 1768 Pastor Pieter Staal moved to Maastricht (*q.v.*); the Burtscheid and Vaals sections did not agree with this change and separated from Maastricht, forming the independent congregation of Vaals and Burtscheid, which, however, never had a preacher of its own, died out by *c*1793; it had probably dissolved in 1785. vDZ.

Gedenkboek der Nederl. Herv. Gemeente van Maastricht (Maastricht, 1932) 380-82; *Inv. Arch. Amst.* II, Nos. 2079 f.

Vadian(us) (von Watt), Joachim (1484-1551), humanist scholar, professor, and one-year rector of the University of Vienna 1516-17, physician, burgomaster, and reformer of his home city of St. Gall, Switzerland, some 50 miles east of Zürich in eastern Switzerland, staunch friend and supporter of Ulrich Zwingli, was the friend, teacher, and finally brother-in-law of Conrad Grebel, whose sister Dorothea he married in 1519. He took a strong stand against the emerging Anabaptist movement in St. Gall in 1525 and succeeded in suppressing it in a short time. He was chosen burgomaster first in 1526 and nine times thereafter, but was the real leader of the city continuously from 1526 to his death. Fourteen of the 69 extant personal letters of Conrad Grebel were written to Vadian 1518-25. They have been preserved in the Vadian Letter Collection in the St. Gall City Library, and were published by Arbenz and Wartmann in the *Vadianische Briefsammlung* I-VII (St. Gall, 1888-1913). The very important letter of Grebel and his friends to Thomas Müntzer of September 1524 has miraculously been preserved in the collection, though not published in the *VB*. One letter of Vadian to Grebel, dated Dec. 28, 1524, has been preserved. H.S.B.

H. S. Bender, *Conrad Grebel* (Goshen, 1950); Werner Näf, *Vadian und seine Stadt St. Gallen*, 2 vv. (St. Gall, 1944, 1957); E. Egli, *Die St. Galler Täufer* (Zürich, 1887); *ML* IV.

Vaertgen van Krommenierdyck: see Dirk Vredricx.

Vaille, Anthony del (de la Faille), was a councillor of the court of Friesland, Netherlands, *c*1550. A zealous Roman Catholic, he was a collaborator of the Inquisition in hunting heretics. In September 1557 he sent a friendly invitation to the Mennonite Jacques d'Auchy (*q.v.*) of Harlingen, whom he had met at an earlier date. As soon as Jacques, unaware of danger, arrived he was apprehended, put in prison, tried, and executed on March 14, 1559. Later a few members of the de la Faille family were Mennonites. vDZ.

J. Reitsma, *Honderd jaren uit de Geschiedenis der Hervorming . . . in Friesland* (Leeuwarden, 1876) 89, 96.

Val de Ville, Alsace, formerly called Weilertal (*q.v.*).

Valagin, a village in the Swiss canton of Neuchâtel (*q.v.*), 5 miles north of the town of Neuchâtel, situated on the cantonal highway to Chaux de Fonds (*q.v.*). It is today an ordinary village. Of historical interest is its castle that belonged to the French Counts of Nemours. This family, descended from the house of Savoy, died out in 1659. Duchess Maria Johanna Baptista, the widow of the last Duke of Savoy, inherited the castle as well as the duchy of Valagin. After her death, the graviate passed to the principality of Neuchâtel and in 1707 it became a Prussian province under Frederick I (*q.v.*).

At this point Valagin touches the history of the Mennonites of Bern. The continued oppression by the Bernese government, especially in the mandates of 1693, 1695, 1707, and 1709, caused many Mennonite families to flee from the Jura (*q.v.*), which was a prince-bishopric of Basel (*q.v.*), to the neighboring Neuchâtel (Neuenburg). The Amnesty Proclamation of the Bernese government, Feb. 11, 1711, which permitted the Mennonites to leave with all their possessions, induced many to emigrate. By 1724 seventeen Bernese Mennonite families with 71 persons had settled in the graviate of Valagin, which then belonged to Neuchâtel. Since Neuchâtel and Valagin had made certain agreements with Bern, the mayor of Valagin complained to Bern about this settlement and about the increasing penetration of "sectarians and Anabaptists" from the canton of Bern, on the ground that the religious unity of the canton was threatened; in 1707 Protestantism was made the only legal religion. Bern supported the request of the mayor of Valagin, and both he and the Council of Bern wrote letters to that effect to Frederick William I (*q.v.*) of Prussia on April 17, April 26, May 27, and July 6, 1734, and June 4, 1735. The king replied, "These good people must be tolerated as before, both on account of the good testimonial you give them and also because I consider it wrong to persecute for their religion those who otherwise live as good citizens of their rulers." . . . "All persecution is abhorrent to me, and I do not see why these poor people should be driven from the country, since they do no harm to anyone and commit no acts that could disturb the peace of the state. They seem to me deserving of sympathy, and it would always be more valuable to draw them with kindness and evangelical love besides a good example than to deprive them of a home that they have sought in your land. Therefore it is my will that they should be tolerated until I find it good and necessary to command otherwise." Unfortunately the king found it good in 1735 to command otherwise. On July 16 he ordered that those sectarians who had immigrated into Neuchâtel and Valagin after 1724 should leave the land, but all the others should be tolerated as heretofore. He was obviously politically motivated to take this step, for he wished to win the favor of Neuchâtel and Valagin. But Bern continued to support the mayor of Valagin in trying to have the Swiss Brethren expelled. The governor of Valagin, however, refused point-blank to interfere, because the expulsion was based on private interests rather than religious motivations; indeed, sincere thanks were due the Mennonites in view of their industry and good characteristics. In 1739 the agitation against the Brethren set in anew, with the support of Bern. Apparently none were expelled from Valagin. NEFF, S.G.

Anna Brons, *Ursprung, Entwickelung und Schicksale der . . . Mennoniten* (Emden, 1912) 251; Samuel Geiser, *Die Taufgesinnten-Gemeinden* (Karlsruhe, 1931); Johann Hübner, *Conversations-Lexikon* (Leipzig, 1715); Müller, *Berner Täufer,* 329-33; *ML* IV.

Valckenier, Johan (1617-70), a Reformed theologian in the Netherlands, professor at the universities of Harderwijk 1645-54, Franeker 1654-68, and Leiden 1668-70, among whose theological writings is a book *Anabaptismus confutatus sive controversiarum de religione adversus Anabaptistas succinctum et methodicum syntagma* (Harderwijk, 1652); Chr. Sepp (*q.v.*) wrote a critique of this book (copy in AML). vDZ.

Chr. Sepp, *Het Godgeleerd Onderwijs in Nederland gedurende de 16e en 17e eeuw* II (Amsterdam, 1874) 91 f. and *passim.*

Valdoie, a suburb (pop. 4,000) of the crossroads city of Belfort in eastern France, is the location of the headquarters of the Association Fraternelle Mennonite (*q.v.*) and of the "Villa des Sapins," a Mennonite children's home.

The Valdoie center, a 10.4-acre property overlooking the north end of Valdoie, was acquired in 1950 by the Association Fraternelle Mennonite (AFM), with the help of a loan from the Mennonite Central Committee, for 4,250,000 French francs (approximately $12,150) plus a 25 per cent sales tax. The postwar MCC children's home at Nancy ("Chalet aux Fleurs") was transferred to the large house on the Valdoie site (the "Villa des Sapins") in the same year. The Villa also became the headquarters of the MCC in France.

In 1950-59 the Villa served as a home for underprivileged children under the direction of Mary Ellen Shoup of the MCC and with the support of both French and American Mennonites. About 35 children between the ages of four and twenty-three could be kept in the home at one time; they were kept for an indefinite period of time until a home in a family could be found for them or until they were old enough to find work. During this eight-year period more than 100 children found a home in the Villa. Contacts have been maintained with most of these through regular visits and a small bi-monthly paper, and many of these return to the Villa occasionally for vacations. Since its purchase, the Villa has been used for many meetings of French Mennonite ministers, church workers, and young people.

A second large building on the site, which was remodeled for use as a center for youth camps and other meetings, and has served as headquarters for the AFM, was transferred from John Yoder, the MCC director in France at that time, to a French Mennonite leader. This second building has been the normal meeting place for the spring sessions of the Conference of French-speaking Mennonites (*q.v.*), and on one recent occasion it was used for a regular session of the Conference of the Mennonites of Alsace.

In 1953, a third and smaller building on the site was opened as a home for the aged. This home, with rooms for about twenty elderly people, has always been operated by the AFM.

The responsibility for the management of the children's home was transferred from the MCC to the AFM on Jan. 1, 1959. At present, Ernest Hege is executive secretary of the AFM and director of the home for the aged. Mme. Christiane Gaudry is the present directress of the children's home. A.J.M.

Valebs, Katharina, an Anabaptist martyr, who sealed her loyalty to her faith with a martyr's death at Frankenhausen, Thuringia, in 1530. (Wappler, *Thüringen; ML* IV.)

Valentyne Ryckele, an Anabaptist martyr, burned at the stake at Antwerp, Belgium, in 1568. She was the wife of the martyr Maillart de Grave (*q.v.*). vDZ.

Valerius Schoolmeester, an Anabaptist martyr, executed in 1568 at Brouwershaven on the island of Schouwen, Dutch province of Zeeland. The account on Valerius by van Braght's *Martyrs' Mirror* is rather brief; a number of additional particulars have been published by K. R. Pekelharing. In 1562 Valerius was a teacher at Middelburg, Zeeland, and with some witnesses traveled to Gent, Belgium, "where with the bent knees of my heart I gave myself up to my God," i.e., where he was baptized and accepted into the church. In 1563 he was married. When his school declined he opened a cloth and yarn shop at Middelburg besides his teaching. In October 1564, after two Mennonites had been executed, he fled to Zierikzee where he lived for half a year, thereupon moving to Hoorn (*q.v.*), North Holland, where he earned his living with some business; here he became deathly ill, but recovered. In 1566 he was back in Zeeland, probably at Middelburg; he preached at several places, was arrested at Goes but released on Sept. 5, 1566, without recanting; shortly after this a meeting on the dike near Veere, where he was preaching, was dispersed by the magistrates. Concerning the last eighteen months of his life, his arrest, and execution there is no information except that he was arrested about September 1567 and held in prison for more than 60 weeks. Even the exact date and the manner of his execution are unknown. His widow was remarried to Michiel (*q.v.*) Gerritsz, who died as a martyr at Breda in 1572. The idea (*Bibliographie des Martyrologes*) that he was a relative of the well-known Adriaen Valerius, the author of the Dutch national songbook *Gedenck-clanc* (1626), is probably incorrect.

During his imprisonment Valerius wrote two booklets, (*a*) *Van't afnemen ende 't vervallen der apostelsche ghemeente* (Decline and Decay of the Apostolic Church), in the 60th week of his imprisonment. Of this writing no copy is extant any more. (*b*) A booklet, written in the 14th week of his captivity, entitled *Proba Fidei oft de Proeve des ghe-loofs, waerinne een iegelick mensche . . . hem proeven mach of hy int ghelove recht staet of niet* (Proof of Faith, . . .). Of this book four editions are known—1569; n.d., n.p.; 1590 and 1595 by Biest-kens at Amsterdam; and 1634 by Zacharias Cor-nelisz at Hoorn (printed at Haarlem). The 1634 edition is followed by an autobiographical letter by Valerius, published by Pekelharing. This *Proba Fidei*, the first part of which is reproduced by van Braght in his *Martyrs' Mirror*, is a book of pure and deep piety, an admonition to forsake the world, to bear the cross of Christ, and to practice Christian love. He emphasized personal piety and expected the return of the Lord in the immediate future, i.e., 1568. Would the Lord find faith upon earth? Valerius, who was troubled by the little love of many members of the Hoorn congregation for the church, vigorously refused to take sides in the Frisian-Flemish quarrels which arose in 1565 and which disturbed the Hoorn congregation. His aversion to dogmatic dissensions may have influenced the Zierikzee (*q.v.*) congregation to take their neutralist position in the schism (see Stilstaanders).			vDZ.

Mart. Mir. D 371-77, E 726-31; *Bibliographie* I, 427-46, 673 f.; K. R. Pekelharing, "Bijdragen voor de Geschiedenis der Hervorming in Zeeland," in *Archief uitg. door het Zeeuwsch Genootschap der Wetenschappen* VI (Middelburg, 1866) 60-66; *BRN* VII, 521; *DB* 1870, 51; 1908, 11-14, 62; Blaupot t. C., *Holland* I, 74, 146; Kühler, *Geschiedenis* I, 246, 330, 453; H. W. Meihuizen, *Galenus Abrahamsz* (Haarlem, 1954) 6-12, 127.

Valkkoog: see Koog.

Valley View Hospital, Glenwood Springs, Col., administered by the Mennonite Board of Missions and Charities (MC), was dedicated in 1955. It is a $500,000, 36-bed hospital, with 10 bassinets, serving a large mountain region on the western slope of the Colorado Rocky Mountains, including rural ranching areas as well as a number of small towns. During the 1957-58 fiscal year the hospital had a total of 1,681 inpatients and 2,908 outpatients, with a daily inpatient average of 23 adults. A voluntary service unit has been serving in the hospital as well as in the near-by Mountain View Nursing Home. A Mennonite (MC) congregation was organized in Glenwood Springs in 1956, and its meetinghouse was dedicated in July 1958. Samuel Janzen is administrator of the hospital and Orpha Zimmerman director of nursing service. The hospital was built and is owned by the city.			M.G.

Valley View Mennonite (MC) Church, located 20 miles west of Broadway, Rockingham County, Va., is a member of the Northern District of the Virginia Conference. Rural work was begun in this community about 1880-85 by the Northern District ministers, in schoolhouses and in the Caplingers Chapel (United Brethren) near by. In 1922 a frame church was built to accommodate the growing congregation. Preaching services are held twice a month and Sunday school every Sunday. The 1957 membership was 92. Ray Emswiler was pastor.		T.S.

Valley View Mennonite Church (MC), of the Southern District of the Virginia Conference, is located near Stuarts Draft, 8 miles southwest of Waynesboro, Va. Services were held in a home and then in a store building in 1923; a frame church was built in 1926, replaced in 1955 by a brick structure. Jason Weaver served here first as a deacon, and then as minister. He is assisted by Paul Barnhart. The membership in 1958 was 109.		H.A.B.

Valparaiso (Ind.) Reformed Mennonite Church was founded *c*1860. In 1957 it had 24 members.

Valter, Gerbrand, b. 1740 at Amsterdam (?), d. Dec. 8, 1818, at Purmerend, married to Maria Houttuyn, was a Dutch Mennonite preacher, serving at Langedijk-Koedijk 1771-?, Hoorn until 1778, Edam 1778-80, and Oostzaan-Zuid 1780-1809. Though he did not receive a theological training for the ministry, he was a man of wide knowledge and trained other young men for the ministry. Among his pupils was Nicolaas Messchaert (*q.v.*). Valter published *Vraagen over de Voornaamste Waarheden van den Christelyken Godsdienst* (Amsterdam, 1784). The well-known elder Cornelis Ris (*q.v.*) of Hoorn was his uncle. (*Naamlijst* 1810, 75 f.; 1829, 30; *DB* 1887, 128.)		vDZ.

Vancouver, the great Canadian seaport (1950 pop. 344,833; 1958 metropolitan area *c* 500,000) on the Pacific coast, is situated at the southwest corner of the province of British Columbia. Mennonites have been living in Vancouver since 1930. At present their number is about 3,000, including Vancouver's smaller twin city, New Westminster. Most of the Mennonites live in South Vancouver, where the four churches are located—two G.C.M. and two M.B. There is also a small G.C.M. congregation at New Westminster with a church building. There are 5 Mennonite physicians practicing in Vancouver. Two girls' homes, one G.C.M. and one M.B., care for the girls working in the city. The Mennonite population of Vancouver is rapidly growing.			H.G.

Vancouver First United Mennonite Church (GCM), located at Vancouver, B.C., had its origin in October 1936. Today it is the second largest G.C.M. church in the province of British Columbia, with (December 1957) 353 members. The first meetinghouse, located on 49th Ave., purchased in 1937, was replaced in 1954 by a new spacious church on 52nd Ave., with a seating capacity of 500. Most of the members live in the city and are employed there. About three fourths of the members are immigrants from Europe, mostly Russia, since World War II. The elder (1957) is J. B. Wiens; the ministers are B. B. Friesen, P. Loetkemann, and H. Goerz. Services are conducted in German.			H.G.

Vancouver Mennonite Brethren Church, located at Prince Edward and 43d Ave., B.C., in the city of Vancouver, a member of the M.B. Conference of Canada, was organized on April 25, 1937, with a few dozen members under John Peters. The first meetinghouse was a rented hall. In 1941 the basement of the present church was built. In 1945 the building was completed to accommodate 500 members. The total baptized membership in 1957 was 470, with D. B. Wiens as pastor. In 1952-54 a new church was erected on 59th and Culloden, known as the Fraserview M.B. Church; its membership in 1957 was 449, with P. R. Toews as pastor, assisted by David Vogt. J.F.R.

Varcken, Hendrik Busch, an Anabaptist jurist of Brussels, Belgium, was betrayed by the Davidjorist (q.v.) Reynier Willems and beheaded at Alkmaar on Jan. 23, 1541, although he confessed that he repented having accepted rebaptism. (DB 1909, 26; ML IV.)

Vaser, Jurriaen: see Fasser, Georg.

Vaucouleurs, department of Meuse, France, birthplace of Joan of Arc, the seat of a Mennonite congregation, of which Ligny (q.v.) was the center in 1933. (See also Toul.) vDZ.

Vaughans Schoolhouse Mennonite (MC) Church is a rural mission under the Virginia Conference, located 3 miles west of Lost River, a post office in Hardy County, W. Va. Services were held here for a number of years, probably 1875-1925. At present services are held twice a month in a Brethren church near by. This congregation is a part of the Salem (q.v.) congregation, which is located three miles to the north. T.S.

Vauxhall, Alberta, Mennonite settlement, about 60 miles northeast of Coaldale. In accord with the decision of the Mennonite civic meeting of Coaldale, P. H. Regehr was appointed on Oct. 23, 1929, to investigate possible sites for the settlement of landless persons living in Coaldale. On Nov. 8, 1930, Regehr reported large areas of suitable land available for Mennonite settlement at Medicine Hat and in the Vauxhall district, which would be fertile with irrigation. In 1933-34 both Mennonites (GCM) and Mennonite Brethren from other parts of Alberta moved in. On April 15, 1934, the Vauxhall M.B. Church (q.v.) was organized, which had 86 members in 1959. The Vauxhall-Grantham Mennonite Church (GCM) had 41 members in 1959. In the summer of 1940 of these churches were burned down because of the war spirit, but have been rebuilt. D.J.Th.

Vauxhall (Alta.) Mennonite Brethren Church was organized in 1934 with a membership of 44 when Mennonite settlers came to this area. In 1936 the congregation built a church, which was destroyed by fire in 1940 as a result of arson. In 1941 the basement for a new church building was constructed and used for meetings. The church was completed in January 1949. Peter Langemann was the first presiding minister. In 1959 Henry A. Unruh was

pastor of the congregation, and the membership was 86. A.A.T.

Vauxhall-Grantham Mennonite Church (GCM), Grantham, Alberta, had a membership of 41 in 1959. It had no regular pastor. It began c1934. M.G.

Veelderhande Gheestelicke Liedekens, a Dutch hymnbook, first edition 1558, is a Reformed version of the Veelderhande Liedekens (q.v.). vDZ.

Veelderhande Liedekens (Various Songs), ghemaeckt wyt den Ouden ende Nieuwen Testamente . . . ende op den A.B.C. by den anderen ghevoecht, is a Dutch hymnal. The following editions are known: (1) first, probably 1554, of which no copy is extant; (2) second c1555; (3) third, printed in 1556, probably at Cologne, Germany. The hymns are arranged in alphabetical order. This third edition, which according to Wieder was not printed for the Mennonites but for the Sacramentists (q.v.), includes some hymns by Anabaptist martyrs like Frans (q.v.) van Bolsward. Of this edition a new enlarged edition (4) entitled Veelderhande Liedekens . . . appeared about 1559. The following editions, all containing a number of Mennonite hymns and probably all much used by the Dutch Mennonites, are (5) Veelderhande Liedekens published by Nicolaes Biestkens, n.p., 1560; (6) same title, same publisher, n.p., 1562; (7) same title, 1566, n.p., probably printed by Nicolaes Biestkens at Emden (a specifically Mennonite edition with 257 hymns); (8) an edition of c1566; (9) same title, 1569, n.p.; (10) same title, n.p., 1569, apparently printed by Biestkens at Emden (a somewhat modified reprint of the Nieu, q.v., Liedenboeck of 1562); (11), a reprint of 10, published 1575 under the same title; (12) same title, 1577, n.p.; (13) same title, enlarged edition with an appendix, printed in 1579, n.p., probably by Biestkens, now at Amsterdam; (14) same title, 1570, n.p., exact reprint of 12; (15) same title, 1580, n.p., exact reprint of 13; (16) same title, 1582, n.p., probably printed by Gillis Rooman (q.v.) at Haarlem; (17) same title, 1582; (18) same title, Amsterdam, 1582, containing 321 hymns (according to Wieder this was the first complete Mennonite edition); (19) same title, printed by Rooman at Haarlem, 1589; exact reprint of 17; (20) same title, printed by Rooman, Haarlem, published by Cornelis Claesz at Amsterdam, 1593 (this edition and also Nos. 21, 26, and 28-34 consist of three parts); (21) Amsterdam, 1596, reprint of 20; (22) 1598, n.p., reprint of 4; (23) Amsterdam, 1599; (24) Amsterdam, 1608; (25) Amsterdam, 1608; (26) Amsterdam, 1611; (27) Amsterdam, 1624; (28) Amsterdam, 1630; (29) Amsterdam, 1632; (30) a modified edition printed 1664 for Arent Jansz (q.v.) at Groningen, to be used in the Old Flemish Mennonite congregation on this town (332 hymns on 708 pages), contains an appendix called Sommige Nieuwe Schrijtuerlijcke Liedekens, containing 50 hymns on 146 pages; (31) an edition under the modified title Veelderhande Schrijtuirlijcke Liedekens (Groningen, 1700) in which some of the hymns are slightly changed and the subdivision into three parts has been dropped; (32) reprint of 31 under the same title, Amsterdam, 1724; (33) same title, Amsterdam, 1752. This edition shows considerable modifications as compared with previous editions; it contains 301 hymns. It is also entitled *Geestelyke (q.v.) ofte Nieuwe Herpe Davidts* and was printed for the Flemish congregations in Prussia.

All editions are without notes. The numerous editions of this hymnal clearly show that it was much used, in the Groningen Old Flemish congregations as late as *c*1750.

Copies of 4, 10, 20, 24, 27, 30, and 33 are found in the Amsterdam Mennonite Library.

Non-Mennonite editions of *Veelderhande Liedekens* (besides the above Nos. 1-4) are (34) *Veelderhande Gheestelicke Liedekens,* n.p., 1558, a greatly modified issue of the (3) 1556 edition, a number of hymns by Mennonites being omitted; (35) a reprint of 34, published in 1563, n.p., with a new heading, *Gheestelycke Liedekens;* this edition was reprinted (36) under the title *Veelderhande Gheestelyke Liedekens* in 1580 at ? and (37) under the title *Schriftuerlicke Liedekens* (Dordrecht, 1595).

vdZ.

F. C. Wieder, *De Schriftuurlijke Liedekens* (The Hague, 1900) 135 f., Nos. XXIX and XXXI; 139 f., No. XXXIX; 142, No. XLVI; 145 f., No. XLVII; 149, No. LV; 155, Nos. LXXII-LXVIII; 157 f., Nos. LXXVI-LXXVII; 158 f., Nos. LXXX-LXXXI; 159 f., Nos. LXXXIV-LXXXV; 160, No. LXXXVIII; 161 f., Nos. XC-XCII; 164, No. XCVIII; 168, No. CV; 170, No. CX; 170 f., Nos. CXIII-CXIV; 171 f., Nos. CXIX-CXX; 172, Nos. CXXXII and CXXXV; 176 f., Nos. CXXXVII-CXXXVIII; *Catalogus Amst.,* 260 f., 276; H. Dassel, *Menno's Volk in Groningen* (Groningen, n.d.) 32; Wackernagel, *Lieder;* Rosella Duerksen, "Anabaptist Hymnody of the Sixteenth Century" (Ph.D. thesis, Union Theological Seminary).

Veelderhande Schriftuerlijcke Nieuwe Liedekens by L. K. (i.e., Leenaert Clock, *q.v.*), a Dutch hymnal, was published at Utrecht in 1593 and contains 168 hymns without notes on 514 pages. These *Liedekens* were inserted in an enlarged edition called the *Groote (q.v.) Liedeboeck* by L. C. (1626). The *Veelderhande Schriftuerlijcke Nieuwe Liedekens* of L. K. was also called the *Cleyn Liedeboeck.* (This statement supplements the article **Groote Liedeboeck.**)

vdZ.

Veelderhande Schriftuirlijke Liedekens is the name of a Dutch hymnal which was an edition of *Veelderhande Liedekens* (No. 31). The 1752 edition of this hymnbook (No. 32) was made for the Flemish congregations in Prussia. This hymnal, also called *Geestelyke (q.v.) ofte Nieuwe Herpe Davidts,* contains 284 hymns on 554 pages. vdZ.

Veen, a Dutch Mennonite family, which had its origin in Zuidveen (*q.v.*) between Steenwijk and Giethoorn in the province of Overijssel. Its ancestor as far as known was a certain Luitjen (Luutgen), who came here to dig peat. His son Hendrik Luitjens (Lutes) was a lay preacher *c*1730-d.57 of the Zuidveen congregation of Danzig Old Flemish Mennonites, as were his relatives Wicher Egberts serving until *c*1767 and Reinder Pieters 1764-d.1802. In the 18th century some members of this family moved to Zaandam. This branch adopted Veen as its family name. Willem Veen (1716-95) left

Zuidveen and settled at Purmerend. His son Hendrik (1763-1846) moved to Sneek, where he was a tanner. This Hendrik had four sons: Anthony (1792-1872) was the founder of a large grocery store at Sneek; Willem (1795-1851), who accompanied the Napoleon as a "garde d'honneur" in his campaign to Russia in 1812-13, was later a wine merchant at Sneek, as was his brother Lambertus (1809-99). The other son was Pastor Pieter Hendricsz Veen (*q.v.*).

To this family also belong Lambertus Jacobus Veen (Sneek, 1863-Amsterdam, 1919), a publisher at Amsterdam, Egbertus Veen (Sneek, 1853-Baarn, 1944), a banker at Sneek and for many years a deacon of the Mennonite congregation, and Egbert A. Veen (Sneek, 1870-Zaandam, 1952), a director of the Verkade factories at Zaandam, deacon of the Westzaandam congregation and trustee of the Schoorl Brotherhood Home. Wicher Veen, b. 1920, pastor of IJmuiden 1949-55 and Amsterdam-den Ilp since 1955, also descends from this family. vdZ.

E. A. Veen, *Een Friesch Koopmangeslacht: het geslacht Veen* (Amsterdam, 1947); *Naamlijst* 1806, 82; *DB* 1878, 17-33.

Veen, Pieter Hendriksz, b. April 22, 1804, at Sneek, d. Feb. 19, 1896, at Bovenknijpe, a member of the foregoing Veen family, was trained for the ministry at the Amsterdam Mennonite Seminary and served the congregations of Warns 1832-37 and Bovenknijpe 1832-77. He published *De Doopsgezinden in Schoterland* (Leeuwarden, 1869). His son was Hendrik Veen (1834-1904), a baker at Bolsward, whose son Pieter Veen (1867-1933) was a Mennonite pastor at Bovenknijpe 1893-1907, Middelburg 1907-19, and Monnikendam 1919-33. vdZ.

Veendam-Wildervank, two villages situated close together, both prosperous industrial centers in the Dutch province of Groningen (combined pop. *c*26,000; 273 Mennonites in 1947), is also the name of a Mennonite congregation. The exact date of the founding is not known, but it may be assumed that a congregation arose soon after the peat moors in this area were broken up and Mennonites settled here, *c*1640. The first Mennonites to settle here are thought to have come from the province of Overijssel. At any rate there was a Mennonite congregation here by 1647. In that year the magistrates of Groningen, to which city the peat moors then belonged, watched carefully that no persons "of Uko Walles' opinion" (see **Ukowallists**) settled here. In 1661 all Mennonite meetings were forbidden by the magistrates. Nevertheless the Mennonite congregation developed rather undisturbed. Its first preacher is mentioned in 1672. Meetings were held then and long after in a home, the group being rather small. In 1711 a private room on a farm at the Westerdiep was bought for a meeting place. Whether there were originally two more or less independent churches, one at Veendam and one at Wildervank, could not be ascertained. Originally the congregation was mostly called Wildervank, later Wildervank-Veendam, at present Veendam-Wildervank. In the 17th century the congregation belonged to the progressive Flemish branch. It was also called Waterlander.

About 1752 the preacher Willem Schut bequeathed to the congregation his house, a barn, and some land on the Oosterdiep. Meetings were henceforth held in this house. On this spot a simple meetinghouse was built in 1771, which was used until it burned down in 1849. A new meetinghouse erected on the same place, dedicated Oct. 28, 1849, is still in use, though it was extensively remodeled in 1906, having been seriously damaged by a fire which destroyed eight homes in the neighborhood. The present parsonage was built in 1905.

In the early 19th century the financial situation of the congregation was deplorable and in 1825 even the dissolution of the congregation seemed imminent. Until this time regular subsidies had been received from the congregations of Amsterdam, Rotterdam, Haarlem, Almelo, Hoorn, and Giethoorn and even from Hamburg-Altona in Germany. But in 1825 almost all these churches stopped their subsidies, and a group of prosperous members living at Borger Compagnie left the Veendam-Wildervank congregation to join that of Sappemeer (q.v.). The congregation, which in the 17th and 18th centuries had been served by untrained ministers, was unable to pay the salary of its minister. But in this emergency the members banded together and by considerable financial sacrifice saved the situation. In 1840 a house was bought, which was remodeled as an old people's home, and a pastor was called who was trained at the Amsterdam Seminary. This was P. W. van Zutphen, serving here 1840-50. He was followed by A. Winkler Prins 1850-82, J. van der Ploeg 1883-98, F. van der Ploeg 1898-1906, D. Pottinga 1906-8, B. H. Rudolphi 1908-21, M. A. Hijlkema 1922-26, J. J. G. Wuite 1927-32, S. M. A. Daalder 1933-36, H. W. Meihuizen 1936-38, and Th. van der Veer 1939-42. After a few years of vacancy during which the retired minister M. Onnes Mz 1946-50 acted as pastor, the congregation was served by Miss J. M. Luyt 1950-54 and since 1954 by Miss J. W. Zuidema.

The baptized membership, which in the 17th and 18th centuries never surpassed 50 and in 1808 had dropped to 39, from then increased rapidly: c90 in 1830, 142 in 1850, 160 in 1861, 240 in 1900. Then a sharp decline began: 150 in 1926, 116 in 1958. In 1850 the 13 members then living at Stadskanaal (q.v.) decided to found an independent church. The congregation of Pekela (q.v.), which had merged with Veendam with its few members in 1808, acquired a degree of independence in 1851. A meetinghouse was built at Nieuwe Pekela in 1852, but Veendam-Wildervank and Pekela have always been served by the same preacher.

At first most of the Mennonites of Veendam-Wildervank were peat miners. After the peat had been removed their descendants became farmers; in the 19th and 20th centuries a number of them went into business. Outstanding Mennonites families here are Panman and Nieboer, and formerly also Boer, Boon, and ter Borg.

From c1755 until 1805 the congregation was a member of the Humsterland (q.v.) conference; in 1826 it joined the Groningen Conference. Church activities are now a ladies' circle and Sunday school for children.   vDZ.

M. A. Hijlkema, "Uit de Geschiedenis der Doopsgezinde gemeente te Veendam-Wildervank," in De Zondagsbode XXXVIII (1925-26) No. 52; XXXIX (1926-27) Nos. 1, 4, 8, 17, 53; Inv. Arch. Amst. II, Nos. 2300-9; Blaupot t. C., Groningen I, 149, 209-12, 238; II, 46; DJ 1850, 56; DB 1861, 154; 1903, 191.

Veenendaal, a town in the Dutch province of Utrecht, formerly the seat of a Mennonite congregation, which is found under different names: Veenendaal, Rijns(s)e Veen, Rhenensche Veen, Rijnse (Reense) Veer.

Concerning the founding of this congregation there is no information. It arose in the early 17th century, when the peat moors in this district were opened; many of the miners are said to have been Mennonites. The congregation, which belonged to the Flemish branch and in 1674 joined the Zonist (q.v.) conference, is first mentioned in 1629. Its membership was probably always very small. It was financially supported by the congregations of Utrecht, Amsterdam, Haarlem, Rotterdam, and Leiden. In the 17th century Marten Geurts (q.v.), d. c1685, was its elder. After his death it was served by the preachers of Utrecht and Amersfoort. In c1708-14 Claas Jacobsz was its preacher, and Petrus van Loon 1719-53. In 1754 the congregation ceased holding meetings for lack of members, most of whom had joined the Reformed Church. But though the congregation is not found in the Naamlijst from 1766 on, it was not until May 1802 that the congregation was actually dissolved. vDZ.

Inv. Arch. Amst. I, Nos. 571, 1071, 1953, 1971, 1975, 1982-85; II, Nos. 1619, 2310-36, II, 2, No. 487; DB 1863, 60, 98-101; 1916, 161; 1918, 126.

Veenland, a Dutch Mennonite family of Lippenhuizen in Friesland, Netherlands. Ubele Ymes Veenland (1873-1941), trained at the University of Amsterdam and the Mennonite Seminary, was pastor of the Tjalleberd congregation 1903-40. He published a historical paper about this church in Doopsgezind Jaarboekje 1919. Ubele Veenland served the congregation of Gorredijk-Lippenhuizen as a treasurer 1827-d.67. His son Eesge Ubeles Veenland (b. 1827) was treasurer of the same church 1867-d.1914. Yme Ubeles Veenland, a brother of Eesge, the father of Pastor U. Y. Veenland, also served this congregation as a deacon for a number of years. His son Pieter Ymes Veenland (b. 1875) has been treasurer of the Gorredijk-Lippenhuizen church since 1915.

The tradition that Pieter Ymes, who in 1815 assumed the family name of Van der Woude and was a preacher of the Gorredijk-Lippenhuizen congregation 1782-1805 and of the Oldeboorn Oude Huis congregation 1805-33, and his son Yme Pieters van der Woude, who served at Nes, Ameland, 1821-33 and Oldeboorn Oude Huis 1833-d.36, were members of this family, is doubtful.   vDZ.

Veenstra, a Dutch Mennonite family originating in Veenwouden, Friesland, where (1) Pieter Cornelis was a member and probably a preacher of the Mennonite congregation c1730. His son (2) Fokke Pieters was a preacher at Nieuwe Niedorp 1767-84. Another son of (1) Pieter was (3) Cornelis Pieters Veenstra (1731-77), who was a preacher of the

Oude-Sluis congregation 1763 (or 1767)-77. His son (4) Hendrik Cornelis Veenstra served at Helder Huisduinen 1799-1804, Middelie 1804-6, Ouddorp 1806-14, and Den Burg 1814-43. They were all lay preachers. Only (4) Hendrik had received some theological training from Pastor Sytze H. Hoekstra (*q.v.*). (5) Fokke Veenstra (1812-34), a son of (4) Hendrik, studied at the Amsterdam Mennonite Seminary, but died during his studies.

There have been a number of other Mennonite preachers by this name who were probably not related to this family: Jacob Ruurds Veenstra served at Blokzijl 1786-d.93 and Djurre Sakes Veenstra was a lay preacher at Akkrum 1789-d.1826, "a man of great ability" (Blaupot ten Cate). Neither had theological training.   vdZ.

A. H. Stikker, *Een familie van Galjootschippers, Commandeurs op Groenland en Friese Vermaners: Baske-Hoekstra-Veenstra* (mimeographed,' n.d., 1953); *Naamlijst* 1794, 63; 1804, 66; 1806, 79; 1808, 88; 1829, 57; *DJ* 1850, 32; *DB* 1873, 153-55; Blaupot t. C., *Friesland*, 250.

Veenwouden, a village in the Dutch province of Friesland, the seat of a Mennonite congregation of whose early history nothing is known, church records having been preserved only since 1790. Unlike most congregations in Friesland it did not join the Conference of Friesland when this was founded in 1695, but much later. It contributed a small amount to the needs of the Prussian Mennonites in 1738. Until 1829 it was served by lay preachers chosen from the membership, among whom were Wybe Aukes 1732-70 and Gosse Hulsinga 1781-1829, who was the last lay preacher here. After four years of vacancy U. H. Jeeps was called from outside in 1833, but he died after only a few months. The first minister educated at the Amsterdam Mennonite Seminary to serve here was Hermannus Lambertus Bouman, pastor of Veenwouden 1834-64, followed by H. van Calcar 1865-80, W. I. Leendertz 1881-88, K. R. Schuiling 1889-97, S. D. A. Wartena 1897-1902, G. Heeringa 1902-12, C. Nijdam 1912-26 A. A. Sepp 1926-30, B. H. Rudolphi 1930-35, P. van der Meulen 1935-38, A. J. van der Sluis 1939-46, J. Krijtenburg 1946-51, and J. W. Hilverda 1952-   .

The baptized membership numbered 25 in 1829, 49 in 1861, 136 in 1900, 160 in 1926, 185 in 1958. About 1866 some members left the church because they were dissatisfied with the modernistic (liberal) preaching of Pastor van Calcar. A few of them returned to the church c1880.

Blaupot ten Cate's view that the congregation was founded between 1600 and 1620 is without solid basis. Until 1860 it was usually called Veenwoudsterwal, because its old meetinghouse was found at "de Wal" somewhat east of the present village of Veenwouden. This meetinghouse was remodeled in 1806, but abandoned in 1816, when a new church, still in use, together with a parsonage, was built in town. This church was provided with an organ in 1895.

The pastor of Veenwouden is also in charge of the Kringen (groups) at Bergum, Giekerk, and Twijzel-Eestrum.

Present church activities are a ladies' circle, a youth group 12-18 (Menniste Bouwers Federatie),

youth group 18-25, and a Sunday school for children.   vdZ.

Blaupot t. C., *Friesland*, 189, 248, 306; *DB* 1909, 61 f.; C. Nijdam, *Het Nieuwe Huis* (Bergum, 1916).

Veenwoudsterwal, a former name of the present Veenwouden (*q.v.*) Mennonite congregation. vdZ.

Veer, de (De Fehr, Fehr, Defehr, Devehr, Dever, Devaehr, Du Verre), a widely ramified Mennonite family of Dutch origin found in the Netherlands, Prussia, Russia, and America. The first member of this family of whom there is exact information was (1) Gysbert Jansz de Veer, b. May 14, 1556, at Schiedam, South Holland. He was a grain merchant, who about 1580 may have settled at Danzig, Prussia, thereupon at Amsterdam, where he obtained citizenship in 1601, and finally at Danzig again, where he died on May 17, 1615. One of his sons was (2) Nicolaes (Claes) de Veer (1583-c1650), married to Margaretha Looten, who was a merchant at Amsterdam. Other sons of (1) Gysbert were (3) Abraham de Veer, who lived at Danzig, and (4) Gysbert de Veer (Amsterdam 1600-Danzig 1646), married first to Anna van Buygen (Bergen?), then to Maria van Dijck. (5) Gysbert de Veer, a son of (3) Abraham, was a cloth merchant at Danzig. (6) Cornelis de Veer (Danzig 1636-Neugarten 1699), a son of (4) Gysbert, had a lace business at Danzig. His brother (7) Gysbert is the ancestor of a Mennonite branch in Prussia, Canada, and Mexico. A son of (6) Cornelis was the Mennonite elder of Danzig, Isaac de Veer (*q.v.*). Abraham Gustaf de Veer, b. Aug. 28, 1815, at Danzig, who was a preacher of the Neuwied Mennonite congregation 1843-58, also was a member of this family.

In Amsterdam the de Veer family came to great wealth. Some of its members were deacons of the church and a few served as preachers, e.g. (2) Claes Gysberts de Veer, who from 1632 was a minister of the Danzig Old Flemish congregation at Amsterdam, as was Cornelis Abrahamsz de Veer (d. 1777), who served this church 1737-75. Cornelis de Veer Jr. and Johannes de Veer, both of whom served the Amsterdam congregation as deacons, in 1850-54 and 1855-59, 1865-69 respectively, were among the last male Mennonite members of this family. Of the branch which left the Mennonite Church in the 18th century there are still some descendants living at Amsterdam.

In Prussia the de Veers were found particularly at Danzig, but also at Elbing, Rosenort, and Königsberg. Among the first emigrants from Prussia to Russia was Benjamin de Veer in 1793. He settled at Neuendorf in the Chortitza settlement. An Isaak de Veer is found in 1802 in the village of Chortitz. Members of this family emigrated from Russia to America after 1874. (This article supplements **De-Veer.**)   vdZ.

Nederl. Patriciaat XXV (1939) 270-313; Dutch *Naamlijst;* church records of Amsterdam; *Inv. Arch. Amst.* I, No. 1615; II, 118-21, 128; II, 2, No. 450; Reimer, *Familiennamen,* 119 f.; B. Unruh, *Hintergründe,* 211, 247, 252; *Gesch.-Bl.,* 1956, 29, Nos. 113-15; *Who's Who Among the Mennonites* (North Newton, 1943) 43; *ME* II, 320; *ML* IV, 406 f.

Veer, Isaac de, a descendant of the Dutch de Veer (*q.v.*) family, b. 1673 at Danzig-Neugarten, d. 1745 at Danzig-Alt Schottland, was a lace manufacturer and merchant at Danzig. He was married five times—in 1696 to Sara Siemens (1671-99), in 1700 to Magdalena Suderman (1677-1710), in 1710 to Maria Klemperer (1686-1716), in 1716 to Sara Jantzen (d. 1718), and in 1718 to Maria Danielsen (1697-1756).

After serving as deacon of the Flemish Schladal congregation in Danzig for some years, he was chosen preacher in 1726, and elder in 1737, serving until his death. He was an inspiring leader of the church in a difficult period (Polish civil war, church badly damaged, controversies among the members). He corresponded with the Mennonite leaders at Amsterdam, who at his request contributed financially to the restoration of the church and the old people's home.

Among Isaac's children were Cornelis de Veer (1702-60), who settled at Amsterdam, and Isaac de Veer, many of whose descendants were deacons of the Danzig congregation. Jacob de Veer (b. 1739), Isaac's grandson, was a preacher of the Danzig Flemish congregation 1774 and elder 1790-d. 93. He drew up a new catechism for his church, which was used until 1825. vDZ.

Veere, an old town on the island of Walcheren, Dutch province of Zeeland (pop. *c*1100), was in the 15th and 16th centuries an important seaport. Anabaptism is found here as early as 1534, in which year some Anabaptists fled from the town to evade persecution. A few of them are said to have gone to Münster (*q.v.*) in Westphalia. In 1537 a number of Münsterite Anabaptists, whose names are unknown, were executed at Veere. Adriaen Wouters, of Schiedam, after recanting was executed here in 1539 because of his "bad Anabaptist ideas." In 1561 Mennonites are said to have lived in Veere, but it could not be ascertained for lack of documents whether there was a congregation here at that early date. In 1569 the Mennonite Jan Ysbrants was banished by the magistrates. About 1600 a small Mennonite congregation existed at Veere, of which Laurens Adrianesz de Brie was a preacher in 1614 and Adriaen Vervondel and Maerten Roelants preachers or deacons in 1665. It belonged to the Flemish branch and died out shortly after 1671, the few remaining members joining the neighboring church of Middelburg. vDZ.

Inv. Arch. Amst. I, Nos. 20, 197, 199; II, No. 1267; *DB* 1876, 86; 1883, 89; 1917, 140; Blaupot t. C., *Holland* II, 40 f.; Mellink, *Wederdopers*, 319, 324.

Veerom, Jan Gerritse, of Rotterdam, Netherlands, was a preacher of the Flemish Mennonite congregation here 1641-d. 52. His son Gerrit Jansz Veerom was a preacher of the same church 1653-55, but in 1655, having more liberal convictions than his congregation, he joined the Rotterdam Waterlander congregation. Shortly after he moved to Amsterdam and became a preacher of the Waterlander (Toren) congregation there, and after the merger with the Lamist (*q.v.*) church he served the united congregation until 1671, in which year he was censured for frequenting taverns. With Michiel Co-mans (*q.v.*) he published a booklet in which he attacked the Flemish elder of Rotterdam, Bastiaen van Weenighem (*q.v.*). Gerrit Jansz Veerom, who was a Collegiant (*q.v.*), died at Amsterdam in 1680. vDZ.

Inv. Arch. Amst. II, Nos. 1181, 1184; church records of Rotterdam; *DB* 1891, 4 f.; H. W. Meihuizen, *Galenus Abrahamsz* (Haarlem, 1954) 109, 113.

Veh, Cornelius, an Anabaptist leader concerning whose life few facts are known. His name indicates that he hails from Switzerland, but the circumstances of his affiliation with the Anabaptist movement remain obscure.

The Hutterian Chronicle reports on his activity in connection with its report of Marpeck's attempt to unify the Moravian Anabaptists, 1541, describing Veh's arrival as a threat to the solidarity of the community at Schäckowitz, although he did not win any followers there.

The *Kunstbuch* contains a letter from Veh to the Anabaptist congregation "at Appenzell and around Zürich" (No. 24, fol. 215-27b), dated March 8, 1543, which indicates that Veh was in substantial agreement with the congregation but was critical of the scrupulosity of the Hutterites in certain regulations about work, and especially of their insistence on community of goods. The two major sects, he felt, the Hutterites and the Swiss, were a real danger, both practicing community of goods, the Hutterites more than the Swiss. The tone of the epistle is cordial and warns the readers against giving up their Christian freedom and becoming acclimated to their environment. He mentions false Anabaptists but does not clearly define them.

Another reference to Veh in the *Kunstbuch* indicates an intimate relationship with Pilgram Marpeck. In a letter by Marpeck to the brethren in Moravia and Alsace (No. 3, dated Augsburg, 1544) he calls Cornelius "his beloved son given to him through faith," and admonishes him to watch over the flock of God "and to pay particular heed to freedom among them that all things may be well considered, so that everything may be conducted according to the true redemption of Christ in the church, as God demands it of me and of others" (fol. 8).

The presence of the "Cornelians" on the lists of sects in Moravia compiled by Varotto (1567) and Stredovsky (1600) indicates that the followers of Veh were a separate group of Anabaptists not related to either the Swiss Brethren or the Hutterian Brethren. That they were a part of the Pilgram Marpeck Brotherhood is clear from the absence of their name on Erhard's list, where the Pilgram Brothers are mentioned, as well as from the evidence in the *Kunstbuch*. Veh's group was probably never very large. W.KL.

Heinhold Fast, "Pilgram Marbeck und das oberdeutsche Täufertum," *ARG* 47 (1956) 212-42; Henry A. DeWind, "A Sixteenth Century Description of Religious Sects in Austerlitz, Moravia," *MQR* XXIX (1955) 44-53; Zieglschmid, *Chronik,* 224.

Veit, Melchior, an Anabaptist martyr: see **Vet Melchior.**

Veit tho Pilgrams: see **Fijt Pilgrims.**

Velde, van de (van den Velde, van den Velden, van der Velde), a Dutch family name found among the Mennonites, particularly at Amsterdam. Jan Jansz van de Velde, whose daughter Cathalijne was married to Christiaen van Eeghen (*q.v.*), lived at Cortemarck in Flanders, Belgium, as early as 1550. Karel (*q.v.*) van de(n) Velde, of Gent, died as a Mennonite martyr in 1562 at Hondschoote, Flanders; Raphael (*q.v.*) van de Velde was put to death at Gent in 1576, and Janneken van den Velde(n) (see **Janneken Munstdorp**) suffered martyrdom at Antwerp in 1573.

In Amsterdam Josua van de Velde was appointed as preacher of the Danzig Old Flemish congregation in 1767, but died the same year. Jan van de Velde, of Amsterdam, was trained for the ministry at the Zonist (*q.v.*) seminary at Amsterdam and served as pastor at Wormerveer (Waterlander congregation) 1743-66 and at Ouddorp 1766-d.77. At Amsterdam there were Van de Veldes in both the Zonist and the Lamist congregations. Some of them served as deacons, the last of whom was Lucas Cornelis van de Velde, serving 1908-13, 1919-23, and 1929-34.

Jan van (de) Velde, of Haarlem, made portraits of Menno Simons and Dirk Philips c1630, but it is uncertain whether this van de Velde was a Mennonite.

A Mennonite van der Velde family was formerly found at Terhorne, Friesland. Here H. W. van der Velde presented the church with a new parsonage in 1855.

Certainly all these van de Veldes were not related, though there may have been family relations between the martyrs of Flanders and the Amsterdam branch. (Church records of Amsterdam; Verheyden, *Gent,* 65 f.; *DB* 1890, 69-71; 1916, 38 f., 60-66.)
                    vDZ.

Veldthaler, Michael (d. 158?), a Hutterite Anabaptist, perhaps the only brother coming from the ranks of the South German nobility. He descended from an old Bavarian baronial family, had formerly been a *Pfleger* (i.e., administrator of a county), and was converted to Anabaptism on a visit at Falkenstein (*q.v.*), castle or village, in Austria near the Moravian border, in 1547. Now he cut all his former ties, joined the brotherhood in Moravia, and learned the trade of joinery at Neumühl Bruderhof. Twice thereafter, in 1555 and 1557, he faced grave dangers in work for the brotherhood in South Germany. In 1560 he was made Diener des Wortes (minister), and in 1587 he died at an advanced age in the Bruderhof of Tracht in Moravia.

Veldthaler's first encounter with hostile forces in Bavaria (1555) is related in detail in the Chronicle. A nobleman by the name of Taufkircher of Schloss Gutenberg (Upper Bavaria), who knew Veldthaler from earlier times and apparently wanted to win him back to the Lutheran faith, asked the Brethren to dispatch this brother to him for conversation and counsel. After much hesitation a meeting was arranged in a peasant's house in Bavaria at night. The situation was most unpleasant and aggressive, with the consequence that the authorities were out to catch Veldthaler and his co-workers. It was wintertime and bitter cold; Veldthaler suffered much from lack of shelter, since no one was willing to let him in. Yet he worked on with some success, even though one of his recently won converts had to give his life for this faith. Eventually he returned to the brotherhood.

Two years later, in 1557, he was sent abroad again to visit Brethren in the Rhenish Palatinate. In Swabia, while walking along the road, he met Count Wolf von Oettingen, an old acquaintance, who had learned about the affair with Baron Taufkircher, and who had both Veldthaler and his companion brother arrested. (As a nobleman he could not allow another nobleman to fall so far away from the accepted standards of this rank.) The two men were now put into a dungeon so deep that they could be reached only by a long rope (with knots to hold on) and lighted by a small hole high up. The Brethren suffered much but remained loyal to their faith, not yielding to overtures by former friends. Eventually, out of regard for Veldthaler's father, the two were released and after finishing their assignment returned safely. The story of this Swabian experience is told in an old hymn of 33 stanzas of unknown authorship; the *Lieder der Hutterischen Brüder,* pp. 545-51, prints it after a late copy of 1791, and the Chronicle used it apparently as its only source. The story was not known to Beck.   R.F.

Beck, *Geschichts-Bücher,* 216; Zieglschmid, *Chronik,* 378; *Lieder der Hutterischen Brüder,* 545-51.

Velikoknyazheskoye, a Mennonite settlement in the Kuban, Russia, which in 1926 had 5 villages with 1,374 Mennonites and 1,514 non-Mennonites on 16,700 acres of land. *Praktischer Landwirt,* 1926, No. 5, p. 2; *ML* IV.

Velius: see **Seylemaker.**

Velke Levary (German, *Gross-Schützen*), a village (pop. 2800) in Slovakia on the bank of the Rudava, a tributary on the left side of the March River. The Hutterian Brethren of Moravia were invited to settle here in 1588 by the imperial cupbearer Hans Bernhard von Lembach, who leased them land in return for certain services and payments, and a Bruderhof was established. The Bruderhof at Velke Levary suffered great hardship in the Turkish war of 1605. The troops of General Basta attacked it May 4. Although most of the inhabitants had fled in time, several brothers and sisters were wounded, some of them fatally, and 42, including the housemaster Matthes Pühler, were taken by the Heiducks. Fortunately Hans Zwinkeberger, the barber-surgeon, who had been summoned by the baron, succeeded with the baron's help in releasing the prisoners without paying ransom. But not until 1609 was the new lord, Seifried von Kollonitsch, able to persuade the Brethren to rebuild and resettle the Bruderhof at Velke Levary.

The Thirty Years' War drew Levary into further suffering. On Oct. 23, 1619, the household was robbed twice by the army, and the inmates who fled to the woods were robbed and stripped by the Hussars; on Nov. 3, desperate peasants broke in and carried away all they could find. Scarcely had they set themselves up again, when on July 17, 1620, Polish auxiliaries plundered the brotherhood anew with senseless brutality. On Feb. 6, 1621, the same thing happened again.

When the Anabaptists were expelled from Moravia in 1622 the Slovak Bruderhofs became the places of refuge, although these were also constantly threatened in those restless times. On Oct. 19, 1623, robbers hiding in the ruins of Levary damaged the Bruderhof, and two days later Czober auf Schossberg made a predatory march to Levary and robbed and murdered, until he was prevented by Bethlen's men from worse deeds. Four days later neighbors plundered the Anabaptists and hauled away five wagonloads of booty. On Nov. 9, 1626, about 300 Croats, Walloons, and French broke into the Levary household and plundered, tortured, and raped just as in the neighboring household at St. Johann. Levary fared somewhat better in 1642, when the imperial troops retreating from the Swedish General Torstenson took quarters here, without deeds of violence. On the other hand, three years later in 1645 the Croats fleeing from the Swedes plundered the household in April, and robber peasants plundered it in June, searching for weeks for the supplies buried by the brethren and carrying away what they found.

Scarcely had the brethren with unprecedented energy overcome the consequences of these numerous robberies together with several poor harvests and famine, when another Hungarian war brought new misfortune. In September 1663 Turks and Tatars broke into Protska (q.v.), and the Levary Bruderhof had to be evacuated. The inmates moved into the peasant quarters below the fortress of Blasenstein and remained there nearly nine weeks. On the flight they lost a large part of their goods and cattle, and all their sheep and hogs. On Oct. 11, 1664, German auxiliaries were quartered in the house for a week with 55 horses, and a week later the French, causing several hundred guilders' worth of damage.

The bitterest experience of the Hutterites at Levary occurred in 1685, when their own baron, Ulrich von Kollonitsch, took their goods by violence. He had the wine taken from their cellars, and their plows, harrows, and wagons, and compelled them to do military service. The subordinate authorities exploited this want of order, and took away the products of their crafts. The situation became so unpleasant that no one came to them, and a shortage of working forces ensued, aggravated by excessive forced labor for the landowners. Finally they had to offer cattle in lieu of money, damaging their economy still further.

The Levary brethren abandoned communistic living in 1685, and each one leased his land individually from the barons. They decided that "each should pay for himself." This decision struck the fatal blow to communal living, which had for some time been showing signs of decay in the Hungarian Bruderhofs.

Then there was the additional danger of Catholization, which had long been looming. Intervention by baronial patrons softened the demand in 1733 to having at least the infants baptized. Since some of

the Hutterites had ever since 1688 been complying with this request—not yet compulsory—without being expelled from the brotherhood (a mere reprimand was the penalty), a meeting at Sobotiste (q.v.) decided to obey the command. Also the principle of avoiding the bearing of arms and shedding of blood was violated when in 1741 the Brethren obeyed government orders to furnish two men to serve as Hussars.

The isolation of the Slovakian brotherhoods, who for many years had no contact with their brethren in Transylvania, became their destruction. The barons who had protected the brotherhoods as long as the communal enterprise brought them gain, now treated them like any other taxable subjects, and had no interest in opposing an intolerant government and clergy by defending the Hutterite faith. And finally the pleasure of the brethren in owning personal property and the desire to see it increase overpowered the love for the faith of the fathers; they adapted themselves.

In 1760 came the strict order that they be converted to the Catholic faith, and the Jesuits received the mission to carry it out. Where persuasion was not sufficient, blows and imprisonment helped. A few fled to find their way to the brotherhood in Transylvania; the majority had turned Catholic by 1764. When the Edict of Toleration was passed in 1781, excluding the Anabaptists, about 70 apparent Catholic converts from Sobotiste and Levary emigrated to Russia to join their brethren.

The modern Catholic descendants of the Hutterian Brethren in Levary, Sobotiste, and St. Johann, now called Habaner (q.v.) or Neuhöfler, were living before 1945 in the same places and in the same households, which in Levary comprised forty cabins. They continued to choose an elder and a leader by lot, who managed the (small) capital and the treasury and kept the church records, until recently in German. The ancient handicrafts are forgotten, their books were taken from them, and the memory of the past passed into oblivion. (See **Habaner.**) After 1945 those who had not turned Slovakian but spoke German were summarily expelled.   P.DE.

Beck, *Geschichts-Bücher*, 302; R. Wolkan, *Die Hutterer* (Vienna, 1918); *idem*, *Geschicht-Buch*; Zieglschmid, *Chronik* (552 note 2, with further details); Lydia Müller, *Kommunismus*; Robert Friedmann, "Habaner in der Slovakei," *Wiener Ztscht f. Volkskunde*, 1927 (illustrated); A. J. F. Zieglschmid, "An Unpublished Hausbrief, . . ." in *Germanic Review* XV (1940) 81-97; *ML* II, 44 f.

Vellenberg, a castle four miles southwest of Innsbruck, Austria, today a significant ruin; in the 16th century it had a tower in which Anabaptists were imprisoned. Hans Mändel (q.v.), who lay there in 1561, described it thus: "It is rather deep, I have heard six fathoms; but it has a small window at the top and the sun shines in a while, so that it is light." It was then full of vermin and especially bats. Jörg (Georg) Liebich (q.v.) lay in this dungeon for years (1538-42). Ursula Hellrigl (q.v.), who was arrested for her faith at the age of 18 and spent 5 years in three dungeons, was in the Vellenberg tower for 1½ years. (Zieglschmid, *Chronik;* *ML* IV.)   HEGE.

Velsius, Justus (*c*1505-after 81), a Dutch scholar of The Hague, of whose many-sided life Christian Sepp wrote a long and thorough account, including his relations to Anabaptism. vDZ.

Chr. Sepp, *Kerkhistorische Studiën* (Leiden, 1885) 91-179; *ML* IV.

Veluanus: see Anastasius Veluanus.

Velzen, Gerard van (1697- ?), a Reformed minister at Waaxens in Friesland, Netherlands, in 1741 anonymously published a booklet, *Noodtwendige Voorzorg der Edele mogende Heren Staten der Provincie van Vrieslandt tegen de inkruipende Socinianerye . . .* , attacking the *Deductie* drawn up by J. Stinstra (*q.v.*). Van Velzen exhorted his "brethren in Christ, preachers and members of the Mennonite congregations in Friesland, by whatever names they may be called," to hold to "the God of their fathers, the Trinitarian God, Father, Son and Holy Ghost." vDZ.

Chr. Sepp, *Johannes Stinstra en zijn tijd* I (Amsterdam, 1865) 231-35; II (1866) 90.

Venatorius, Thomas V. (d. 1551), a Protestant theologian and pastor, a friend of Willibald Pirckheimer and Albrecht Dürer, published a booklet against the Anabaptists in 1527.

Kolde, "Thomas Venatorius," in *Beiträge zur bayrischen Kirchengesch.* III (1907) 100 ff.; Ernst Heidrich, *Dürer und die Reformation* (Leipzig, 1909) 29; *ML* IV.

Venema, a Dutch Mennonite family particularly found in Friesland, both Mennonite and non-Mennonite. Arnoldus (Nolle) Abelsz Venema, b. *c*1739 at Buitenpost, d. 1801 at Ameland, married to Sientje Kramer, at first a peddler, later a shopkeeper, was a preacher of the Mennonite congregation of Rottevalle *c*1761-62, the Flemish (Foppe Ones) church on the island of Ameland 1762-68, at Norden in East Friesland, Germany, 1768-74, Aalsmeer 1774-83, Rottevalle 1783-89, Ameland again 1789-d.1801. Returning from Nes, where he had preached on a winter night, he vanished without trace; he probably drowned in the sea in the darkness. Being a self-made man, he was one of those untrained preachers who with great love and no less ability served the church with much blessing. His brother Aldert Abelsz Venema was a preacher at Rottevalle *c*1774-d.88. Another member of this family was Tjebbe Wiegers Venema, b. 1789 at ?, d. Feb. 29, 1856, at Aalsmeer. In 1818 he was appointed ministerial candidate by the Conference of Friesland, serving 1819-d.56 in the Aalsmeer Zijdweg congregation. He was a man of little education; by private study he learned some German, French, and English. But under his leading the congregation flourished. In Gorter's *Doopsgezinde Lectuur* of 1856 he published a paper, "Overzicht van alle Doopsgezinden op aarde."

A Venema was for many years a secretary-treasurer of the Dantumawoude congregation in the early 20th century.

De Zondagsbode XXIV (1910-11) Nos. 49, 51, and 52; *Inv. Arch. Amst.* II, Nos. 1441, 1451, 1486-89, 2214-16, 2265, 2846; *Naamlijst* 1829, 25; Gorter's *Doopsgez. Lectuur (Kerknieuws)* 1856, 29 f.; 1858, 3 f.; *DB* 1872, 38 f.; 1889, 17, 18, 25; 1890, 26; 1895, 81 f., 84; Blaupot t. C., *Friesland*, 233.

Venhuizen, a small village between Hoorn and Enkhuizen in the Dutch province of North Holland, formerly the seat of a Mennonite congregation. Elder Leenaert (*q.v.*) Bouwens baptized five persons here in 1551-54. Probably a congregation was founded soon after, which existed at least in 1567, then belonging to the Old Frisian branch. About this congregation, always small in membership, there is only scant information. It was served by untrained preachers chosen from the membership. In the early 18th century the preachers of Enkhuizen (*q.v.*) usually served at Venhuizen, but from 1740 it again had a preacher of its own, Kiaas Jansz Bakker serving from 1740, and Arent Pietersz Fijn 1775-*c*1810.

In the *Naamlijst* of 1829 this congregation is no longer listed, though it still existed, for its last member did not die until 1848; thereupon the meetinghouse was sold for 493 Dutch guilders and its property, about 6400 guilders, passed to the Rijper Societeit (*q.v.*). vDZ.

De Zondagsbode XLVI (1932-33) Nos. 3-5, 11; *Inv. Arch. Amst.* I, Nos. 411, 1180; *Naamlijst*; *DJ* 1943, 44, 45.

Venice. Through a confusion which was finally cleared up by the work of the American scholar H. A. DeWind, it was long thought that there was an Anabaptist movement in Northern Italy which centered in Venice and flourished about the middle of the 16th century. There was even a report of an "Anabaptist Synod" held at Venice in 1550. DeWind has shown that the group thought to be Anabaptist and even labeled as such by its enemies was a radical evangelical, and finally anti-Trinitarian group, which had nothing to do with true Anabaptism (see Italy). This invalidates much of the work of Karl Benrath (see bibliography).

Antonio Rizzetto (*q.v.*), Giulio Gherlandi (*q.v.*), and Francesco della Saga (*q.v.*), fleeing from Italy, reached Moravia, where they became Hutterite converts, the latter two joining the Hutterite group at Pausram (*q.v.*). Returning to Italy as Anabaptist missionaries, all three were finally imprisoned and executed at Venice, Gherlandi in October 1562, Rizzetto and della Saga in February 1565. The Venetian Archives contain valuable materials on these three Anabaptists and others as well as on the anti-Trinitarian movement as a whole. H.S.B.

"Wiedertäufer im Venetianischen um die Mitte des 16. Jahrhunderts," *Theol. Studien und Kritiken* LVIII (1885) 9-67; Henry A. DeWind, "Italian Hutterite Martyrs," *MQR* XXVIII (1954) 163-85.

Verantwortung, a very important term in Anabaptist thinking. The German word has at least three different meanings: (*a*) moral responsibility for one's acts, presupposing free will; (*b*) accounting or answer to be given if asked; and (*c*) reply or answer, with the connotation of defense, mostly in polemical writings. Generally (*b*) is the major meaning of the term as found in 16th-century Anabaptist literature. The classical locus is I Pet. 3:15; Luther's translation says: "Seid allzeit bereit [originally, 1522, 'erbietig'] zur Verantwortung jedermann, der Grund fordert der Hoffnung die in euch ist." The King James Version has: "Be ready always to give an answer to every man that asketh you a reason of the hope that is in you"; and the Revised Standard Version has: "Always be prepared to make a defense to any one who calls you to account for the hope that is in you." In each instance it means: confess your faith publicly whenever asked, "having a good conscience," as verse 16 continues to say. This is one of the foremost virtues of a disciple of Christ; it made the Hutterite confessions shine in gloomy places, and it was their strength and victory.

Before the rise of Anabaptism, Jörg Haug (q.v.) of Juchsen used this popular quotation as the motto of his widely read tract, *Ordnung eines christlichen Lebens* (1524). Then Peter Riedemann put it on the title page of his great *Rechenschaft* (Verantwortung) of 1541, when he presented to Philip of Hesse "the reason for his hope." This verse is found repeatedly in tracts and records of trials and inquiries by the world. The Brethren were always ready to give an account, and they never tired of explaining the ground of their hope.

(c) The connotation of "Beantwortung" is used often in Anabaptist polemics. Thus, e.g., Pilgram Marpeck (q.v.) replied in 1544 to Schwenkfeld's *Judicium* with a heavy volume called *Verantwortung* (q.v.). Here the term lacks the meaning of (a) altogether.

(a) Only Ulrich Bergfried in a recent study, *Vertantwortung als theologisches Problem im Täufertum des 16. Jahrhunderts* (1938), applies the meaning (a) to a discussion of Anabaptist thought, claiming that this term meaning "responsibility," is the very core of all debates between Anabaptists and Lutherans. He meant to show the implications of the basic decision whether or not man is morally responsible for his acts. Bergfried clearly recognized the exemplary Christian life of the Anabaptists, and then interprets this attempted holy life as emphasizing the problem of "Verantwortung" (responsibility) as the "central norm of all piety and religion." From his strictly Lutheran theological viewpoint Bergfried opposes such an outlook as "anthropocentric" rather than "Christocentric," and thus calls the Anabaptist vision "the myth of the pious man" (201). Bergfried's position is that Christ alone bears our sins and our responsibility, for man is "an enslaved sinner." The ideas of obedience and sanctification of life do not enter his theological system. This interpretation misses the deepest Anabaptist intentions. It is certainly correct that the Anabaptists accepted the idea of Free Will (q.v.), i.e., the possibility of obeying (or disobeying) God's commandments. Hence they never denied that in a certain way man is responsible for his acts, to be sure only after his spiritual rebirth. But to call "responsibility" the key theological problem of Anabaptism is misleading, and rather shows the difficulty which traditional Lutheran theology has in coping adequately with the issue of sanctification and obedience to God's Word. (See also **Sweet and Bitter Christ.**) R.F.

Only for the meaning *a*: Ulrich Bergfried, *Verantwortung als theologisches Problem im Täufertum des 16. Jahrhunderts* (Wuppertal, 1938); Walther Köhler reviewed and criticized Bergfried's book in *Menn. Gesch.-Bl.* (1940) 10 ff.; Hans G. Fischer, "Lutheranism and the Vindication of the Anabaptist Way," *MQR* XXVIII (1954) 27-38.

Verantwortung by Pilgram Marpeck. The word "Verantwortung" appears frequently in Anabaptist book titles and is taken from I Peter 3:15 where the word "defense" (RSV) is thus translated in the Zürich (Froschauer) Bible. This verse is cited more often than any other in the defense or answer of the Anabaptists to their accusers. The word meant "answer" for them, not "responsibility" as it does today.

The most ambitious answer to critics of the Anabaptists was made by the Marpeck (q.v.) brotherhood in the form of the *Verantwortung über Casparn Schwenckfelds Judicium*. This reply circulated only in manuscript and did not appear in print until 1929, when Christian Hege published an edition prepared by Johann Loserth. In this modern edition the first part extends to 113 pages, while the second part contains 389 pages. It consists of 100 *Reden und Antwurten* (Statements and Answers). The Statements are taken verbatim from Schwenckfeld's *Judicium,* and the Answers, which vary considerably in length, constitute the reply to Schwenckfeld's criticism of the *Vermanung* (q.v.). Since the *Vermanung* was a common confession around which the brotherhood was to unite, it is no surprise that Schwenckfeld's *Judicium* was taken with such seriousness, and evoked such an extended reply.

The first part of the book deals with two main themes, baptism and the Lord's Supper, but also treats such matters as the use of the term "sacrament," the covenant, covenant member, dissension among believers, the Incarnation, and testing the spirits. It was written in great haste and hence is more concise than part II. Its main sources are the Scriptures and Schwenckfeld's writings. It was written in a little more than a year and was sent to Schwenckfeld at the beginning of 1544, with the note that if this work brought results the authors would desist from writing the second part; otherwise that would be forthcoming shortly.

The second part was written at greater leisure and makes use of a number of sources, one of the most important being the *Testamenterleütterung* (q.v.), which must have been published soon after the completion of the first part of the *Verantwortung.* The *Testament of the Twelve Patriarchs,* Schwenckfeld's writings, Sebastian Franck's *Paradoxa,* and the *Deutsche Theologie* are also used as sources for the second part. While the first part is pointedly directed against Schwenckfeld, the second part has a much wider frame of reference, even though the starting point continues to be statements appearing in the *Judicium.*

Both the date and authorship of the *Verantwortung* are uncertain. Kiwiet's claim that the second part of the *Verantwortung* was written substantially by Leupold Scharnschlager (q.v.), and that he is solely responsible for the section beginning on page 409 of the printed edition, has not been proved by actual literary analysis; since it is built on slender and inadequate evidence it must remain a conjecture. Since both Marpeck and Scharnschlager worked on the *Vermanung,* the *Verantwortung,* and the *Testamenterleütterung,* it is very difficult to prove who wrote what sections. Individual authorship was not held in high esteem by them, for the brotherhood together studied the Scriptures and their conclusions were always subjected to the scrutiny of the brotherhood. It might be easier to prove that Marpeck wrote the opening section of many of the answers, and that then Scharnschlager furnished a series of Scripture verses connected with the word "Item" at each point to prove the statements made by Marpeck. Scharnschlager's confession to the Strasbourg council in 1534 seems to indicate that he liked to use the concordance style, simply listing a series of Scripture passages, and that he had a predilection for pointing out inconsistencies in the writings of the Reformers (in his confession) and in Schwenckfeld (in the *Verantwortung*). If this could be shown conclusively (and his few extant letters appear to support it), Gerhard Hein's suggestion that Scharnschlager is responsible for the *Testamenterleütterung* would gain some support. He certainly must be considered a coauthor of the *Verantwortung,* for many of the emphases and expressions which occur in his letters are found also there.

The date of the *Verantwortung* is also uncertain. The first part was completed at the end of 1543, and no doubt the Brethren were already working on the second part at that time. In 1546 Schwenckfeld refers to a large book by the Anabaptists in which they treat the faith of the patriarchs, which he has seen. One is inclined to see in this a reference to *Verantwortung* II, since a predominant portion deals with this subject (82 pages). The only question would be whether the time from January 1544 to February 1546 would have allowed Marpeck and Scharnschlager to complete both the *Testamenterleütterung* and *Verantwortung* II. The most probable solution is that *Verantwortung* II was written after 1544 and completed before 1556, the year of Marpeck's death, and that after it had been sent to the various congregations for approval it was copied for a wider use among the brotherhood.

The *Verantwortung* was of limited value since it was directed at a concrete problem, viz., spiritualism. Soon the tension between the Pilgramites and the Schwenckfelders subsided, and the book fell into neglect. (For its later use and influence see **Marpeck.**) The modern Christian who reads it finds that many of the problems to which it is directed are very much with the church today. It is the clearest analysis of spiritualism and its dangers which the Anabaptists produced, and even its repetitious style and verbosity do not minimize its value as a source for the theology of the Marpeck brotherhood.

W.Kl.

Johann Loserth, ed., *Pilgram Marbecks Antwort auf Kaspar Schwenckfelds Beurteilung des Buches der Bundesbezeugung von 1542* (Vienna and Leipzig, 1929); Jan J. Kiwiet, *Pilgram Marbeck* (Kassel, 1957) 74-76; Torsten Bergsten, "Pilgram Marbeck und seine Auseinandersetzung mit Caspar Schwenckfeld," *Kyrkohistorisk Arsskrift,* 1957 and 1958, 56-67.

Verantwurtung, the popular shortened title of *Clare verantwurtung ettlicher Artickel/ so jetz durch jrrige geyster schrifftlich vnnd mündtlich aussschweben/ von wegen der ceremonien dess Newen Testaments/ als Predigen/ Tauffen/ Abendtmal/ Schrifft* etc. This booklet was published in 1531, without indication of its author or locale. Both Camill Ger-

bert and Alexander Nicoladoni, who had never seen the book, erroneously attributed it to Johann Bünderlin (*q.v.*). It was clearly not written by Bünderlin since it attacks Bünderlin's position.

The *Verantwurtung* discusses three points. The first is a reply to the assertion of certain "erring spirits" that the children of God should not use the ceremonies of the New Testament, baptism, Lord's Supper, Scriptures, etc., any longer because of the abuse into which they had fallen. The author's reply is that abuse is not sufficient basis for the cessation of ceremonies, and that length of time does not pervert ceremonies (Bünderlin used this argument), but rather that God even works sometimes to reestablish correct order. To prove this the author somewhat reluctantly adduces evidence from the Old Testament, with the explanation that the erring spirits argue mainly from the Old Testament.

While the first point is discussed in 4½ pages, the second point is given 11½ pages. The author deals here with the assertion by the "erring spirits" that since the apostles are dead there is no longer a command or witness of the Scriptures for the ceremonies, hence they are invalid unless an external command would come that they ought to be continued. The reply to this argument is that then the Lord's Prayer will also need to be discontinued. He rejects the argument that the words of the Bible are not meant for us, and insists that the last days are the days after the life of Christ, and that no special signs are now needed. He criticizes also the excessive individualism of these "spirits" and reminds them that the gifts of the Holy Spirit are given for the common good of the church, and not for individual consumption.

The third argument, 17 pages, deals with the continuity of apostolic authority. The "erring spirits" insist that the apostles were in no position to hand down their authority to their successors; they only called bishops and there it ended. The reply to this objection is an excellent statement on the nature of authority in the church. Christian ministers do not derive their authority from an external act, but from the authority of Christ, who "thrusts His spirit into the bosom of their hearts" as He did to the eleven. In a limited way the author deals also with the accusation that the Anabaptists were making an idol of the ceremonies.

The stress on the order of Christ, the voluntary nature of baptism, footwashing, church leadership, baptism as suffering (sea of tribulation: "meer der trübsal"), all point in the direction of this being an Anabaptist booklet. But where was it published and by whom? The evidence is strong that it is directed against Bünderlin, certain phrases being used which also occur in Bünderlin's writings. If it was directed against him, it likely was written by someone at Strasbourg in 1531. Since Marpeck (*q.v.*) was then in Strasbourg and published two booklets in 1531 it is possible that it was written by him. An argument against his authorship is that the censors reported that one of his two books of 1531 openly asserted Anabaptist doctrine and contained the information that he himself had been baptized. Such information is not contained in the *Clare Verantwurtung,* but is found in the other booklet, *Ain klarer unter-*

richt (see **Unterricht**). One copy is known to exist in the Stuttgart State Library (microfilm in GCL). W.KL.

Camill Gerbert, *Geschichte der Strassburger Secten-bewegung zur Zeit der Reformation 1524-1534* (Strasbourg, 1889) 96; A. Nicoladoni, *Johannes Bünderlin* (Berlin, 1893) 126; W. Klassen, "Pilgram Marpeck's Two Books of 1531," *MQR* XXXIII (1959) 18-30.

Verband badisch-württembergisch-bayrischer Mennonitengemeinden e.V. is the new name given to the Badisch-württembergisch-bayerischer Gemeindeverband (*q.v.*) at the time of its reorganization on March 24, 1949, with legal office at Heilbronn, Württemberg. Christian Landes, Lautenbach, has been the chairman and treasurer since 1949, but the office of chairman is only for legal purposes and has no ecclesiastical significance. The executive officer is Ulrich Hege, Reihen, whose title is secretary. In 1958 the Verband consisted of 21 congregations with 1,585 baptized members, distributed as follows by provinces: Palatinate 2 congregations, 130 members; Baden 7, 486; Württemberg 6, 627, and Bavaria 6, 342. The increase over 1951 was due largely to the inclusion of the refugee congregation at Backnang, Württemberg, with 292 members, chiefly of Galician origin. Eichstock, Bavaria, formerly independent, and Nürnberg, Bavaria, were also taken in. H.S.B.

Verband der Bürger holländischer Herkunft (*Association of Citizens of Dutch Extraction*) was originally known as the *Verband der Gemeinden und Gruppen des Süden Russlands,* the word *Gemeinden* referring to villages rather than to congregations. On Feb. 19, 1921, the church and civil leaders (representatives) of the Molotschna district in South Russia, including about 60 villages (besides three individual farms) covering a Mennonite population of about 28,000, met in the church at Alexanderwohl under the leadership of Elder G. Plett (*q.v.*) of Hierschau, with the purpose of finding some basis on which the young men of the brotherhood in the new Soviet nation could maintain their nonresistant position. A committee consisting of B. B. Janz, chairman, Dietrich Richert, H. Bartel, and A. Fast was chosen to form an organization to deal with the government in carrying out this purpose. The legality of the organization and its civil rights had to be confirmed by a government charter. In Kharkov, the capital of the Ukraine, the word "Mennonite" caused some objection as a religious term, and had to be dropped after a hard struggle. Then the name above was adopted to cover the Mennonites of the Ukraine exclusively with their population of about 60,000, and was chartered in the spring of 1922. The entire constitution was later (about 1924) adopted into the laws of the nation because of a financial loan to the Association from Holland, in the hope of obtaining more such loans from other countries. For religious concerns another committee was later chosen, with Elder Jakob Rempel as chairman. The 30,000-40,000 Mennonites living elsewhere in Russia followed the example of those in the Ukraine and founded the All-Russian Mennonite Agricultural Union (AMLV, *q.v.*), with Peter Froese and C. F. Klassen (*q.v.*) as leaders. Every year a congress of Mennonites was held in

the Ukraine with the permission of the government and in later years with a representative of the government present, to do the business of the Association and to elect the leadership. The most important activities of the Association concerned the economic welfare of the settlements, especially in cattle raising (the German Red cow), the trade of the cooperatives, the elimination of violence on the part of local Soviet officials, securing foreign loans, and also securing permission for the emigration of many Mennonite refugees (which, however, soon became general), at first to Paraguay, then to Canada. Permission for this emigration was secured on April 22, 1922, by the Association. Each Mennonite settlement in the Ukraine formed a local chapter of the central association. The most important of these were in Halbstadt, Gnadenfeld, Chortitza, Zagradovka, and Memrik, with other smaller groups. They were outstandingly successful economically. The first emigrant train with about 700 left Chortitza in June 1923, via Moscow, to Libava for embarkation on a Canadian Pacific steamer.

Not a single communist was a member or an officer in this association. It enjoyed the unquestioned confidence of all the Mennonites. In brief, the Association became the first link in the rescue of the Mennonites from Russia. It was able to function until Feb. 19, 1926, the date of the last congress in Kharkov, where Janz resigned the leadership, and another committee was chosen, consisting of Hermann Dück, Peter Funk, etc., all of whom, with Philipp Cornies, the young assistant of Janz for many years, were sent into exile soon after. Thus the Association was liquidated as a step in the decline of the Mennonite settlements, which were now without legal rights. Janz managed to secure his passage for escape from Russia immediately following the congress of 1926, and in the eleventh hour escaped to Canada in June 1926. B.B.J.

Verbeek (Verbeeck), a rather common Dutch family name both Mennonite and non-Mennonite. Joos(t) (*q.v.*) Verbeeck (Joos de Cruysere), a Mennonite elder, suffered martyrdom at Antwerp, Belgium, in 1561. In the 17th and 18th centuries there were a number of Verbee(c)ks in both the Lamist and Zonist congregations of Amsterdam. They very likely stemmed from Mennonites who had left Flanders because of persecution *c*1580. In Amsterdam the Verbe(c)ks were outstanding businessmen. Some of them served as deacons. Since the early 19th century there have been no Verbeeks among the Amsterdam Mennonites. vDZ.

Verbond (league, covenant), a term much used by the early Dutch Anabaptists, who often called themselves Bondgenoten (*q.v.*), i.e., Covenanters; the expression "van den Verbonde" is frequently found in early Dutch Anabaptist writings. It was especially used by the revolutionary Anabaptists, particularly by the Batenburgers, who were said to be "int verbond van Batenburg." This usage has misled Karel Vos and A. F. Mellink to considering the "Verbond" to mean a social league to overthrow the political order. But this is not right; as Lowell H. Zuck has pointed out in his Yale dissertation, *Anabaptist Revolution Through the Covenant in Six-*

teenth Century Continental Protestantism (New Haven, 1954), "Their motives for revolutionary activity were not nihilistic, but religious. Their purpose was the building of a new society, the kingdom of God on earth, which God would immediately inaugurate eschatologically, after the destruction of the old. Their own revolutionary covenant signaled the end of the Old age and identified those who participate in the New age." The word is derived from the Bible (Jer. 31:31-33; Rom. 11:27, and many other places) and it was also used by the peaceful Anabaptists, among whom "verbond" according to I Peter 3:21, meant a close relation to God, a covenant with God (Christ), as is clearly pointed out by the martyr Jan (*q.v.*) Pauw (Grosheide, *Verhooren,* 50), who said that baptism is a certification or sign of the "verbond," and that all who are in the "verbond" are also baptized, and that the "verbond" is nothing other than that they promise to walk in the ways of God, without deviating from them. (See also **Covenant.**)   vdZ.

Verbond der vier Steden, Het (The League of the Four Towns), also called Ordinantie, is an alliance made about 1560 by the ministers of the Mennonite congregations of Franeker, Harlingen, Leeuwarden, and Dokkum in the Dutch province of Friesland. In this *Ordinantie* of 19 articles they regulated their relations and passed the resolutions that the money for the care of the poor in all four churches would be provided from a common fund, and that the ministers of any of these congregations were also entitled to serve in the other three. The intention of this league was unquestionably laudable, but it was a serious error to conclude it among the ministers without consulting the membership and to keep it secret. Trouble arose when in Franeker Jeroen Tinnegieter (*q.v.*), a Flemish immigrant, was chosen as preacher, who was not accepted by the ministers of Harlingen, Leeuwarden, and Dokkum, where according to the terms of the League Tinnegieter was entitled to preach. Then the secret league came out into the open and particularly the members of Flemish descent in the congregations of Franeker and Harlingen were outraged at the abridgment of their rights. The result was the Flemish-Frisian (*q.v.*) quarrels in 1566-67, which ended with a schism.   vdZ.

DB 1893, 1-90; *Inv. Arch. Amst.* I, No. 464; *BRN* X, 536 ff.; Kühler, *Geschiedenis* I, 397 f., 407-13.

Verbondt van Eenigheydt (Alliance of Unity), an arrangement between a number of Dutch Mennonite churches made at Utrecht on Sept. 9, 1664, and ratified by 98 ministers and deacons, representing 28 churches in a meeting held at Leiden Oct. 1 and 2, 1664. This Alliance meant a concentration of the conservatives after the Dutch Mennonites had been divided by the Lammerenkrijgh (*q.v.*) into a more progressive (Lamist) and a more conservative (Zonist) part. The arrangement is embodied in six articles, which state that the existing and approved confessions of faith that were in harmony with the Scriptures were to be maintained; ministers who opposed these confessions were to be suspended, and newly chosen ministers were to subject themselves to the authority of the confessions. The representa-

tives promised each other to stand together, to maintain the basic creed of the church and to invite other churches to join the Alliance. A booklet containing the minutes of the Utrecht and Leiden meetings and inviting similarly minded churches to join the Alliance was published under the title *Het Oprecht Verbondt van Eenigheydt . . . met minnelijcke aenbiedinge aen alle die soo gesint zijn* (Rotterdam, 1664; reprints Amsterdam 1665, Haarlem 1700, Rotterdam 1739). The Verbondt van Eenigheydt was not a confession of faith as is stated by Herman Schijn, but an agreement to maintain the approved confessions. This Alliance of the conservatives, soon generally called Zonists (*q.v.*), in course of time developed into the Zonist Conference (Sociëteit).   vdZ.

Inv. Arch. Amst. I, Nos. 706, 885-87; *DB* 1863, 60; 1898, 18; Schijn-Maatschoen, *Geschiedenis* II (1744) 212; H. W. Meihuizen, *Galenus Abrahamsz* (Haarlem, 1954) 104-8.

Verbrugge, a former Dutch Mennonite family, descended from Mennonite refugees from Flanders, Belgium, was found in the 17th and 18th centuries at Rotterdam, Haarlem, Amsterdam, and Leiden. Some of its members served as deacons. The Amsterdam branch of this family operated an important trade house. Cornelis Verbrugge, d. 1762 at Leiden, was a physician at Rotterdam from 1736 and for many years a treasurer of the Mennonite congregation.   vdZ.

Verburg, Jan Dionys, d. Oct. 21, 1692, at Rotterdam, Holland, where he was a member of the Waterlander Mennonite congregation. He was, however, more interested in the Collegiant (*q.v.*) movement than in his church, being one of the founders of their "college" in his home town. In the Collegiant movement he played an influential part. He obviously was a man of broad views, who sometimes even preached for the Remonstrant (*q.v.*) congregation of Rotterdam.   vdZ.

J. C. van Slee, *De Rijnsburger Collegianten* (Haarlem, 1895) *passim*; C. B. Hylkema, *Reformateurs,* 2 vv. (Haarlem, 1900-2) *passim.*

Vercolie (Vercolje, Vercoilgen, Verquoilge): see **Verkolje.**

Verdragh der Broeders tot Embden (Agreement of the Brethren at Emden) is the agreement made on April 4, 1579, at Emden in East Friesland, Germany, by Hans de Ries and seven Waterlander leaders, representatives of the Island (i.e., De Rijp), Purmerend, Amsterdam, and Rotterdam on the one hand and the congregation of Emden on the other. This agreement was very important in the development of the Waterlander branch. Though the views of the Emden brethren on the Incarnation differed somewhat from the Waterlander views, the Emden congregation wholeheartedly joined in the union. The original copy of the "Verdragh," signed by the representatives, is found in the Amsterdam Mennonite Archives. It was published by Blaupot ten Cate in *Groningen,* 264-70. (Kühler, *Geschiedenis* I, 365 f.; *DB* 1864, 21; 1917, 14.)   vdZ.

Verduin (Verduyn), a Dutch Mennonite family found in Amsterdam (Lamist church) in the 17th and 18th centuries. A few of them served as deacons. Pieter Adriaens Verduyn (c1625-1700) was a noted physician at Amsterdam, who was called to attend the king of Denmark; he wrote a number of medical works. Another member of this family was Abraham Verduin (q.v.). (N.N.B.Wb. III, 1283 f.; church records of Amsterdam.)   vDZ.

Verduin, Abraham (Amsterdam, Dec. 1, 1668-Koog aan de Zaan, 1756), was trained for the ministry by Galenus (q.v.) Abrahamsz at Amsterdam. He was appointed ministerial candidate by the church board of the Amsterdam Lamist congregation and accepted a call of the Koog-Zaandijk congregation, which caused some trouble with the trustees of the Amsterdam congregation, who wished Verduin to be a preacher of their church. Verduin served at Koog-Zaandijk for nearly sixty years, from 1698 until his death. He was the first formally trained and salaried minister of this congregation. Until 1726 he received a salary of 600 Dutch guilders, but after this year he refused the payment, henceforth serving "for love." He probably practiced some other profession which enabled him to do without the salary. Verduin served with great ability and much blessing. In April 1728 his colleague, Dirk Simonsz Moeriaen(s), a lay preacher, died. Verduin preached his funeral sermon, *Het Heil in den Dood* (Haarlem, n.d.). Besides this sermon he published a large number of books: *Kort Onderwerp van de Voornamste Geloof-zaaken* (Amsterdam, 1707), *Kort onderwys voor Geloofs-leerlingen* (Amsterdam, 1714), *Ootmoedig Gebed van de Hebreeuwse Kerk in de Woestyn*, a sermon (Amsterdam, 1718), *Christelyke Godgeleerheid*, 2 vv. (Haarlem, 1729), *Examen Argumentorum* (Amsterdam, 1729), in which treatise he opposed the Remonstrant professor van Cattenburgh (q.v.), who had attacked the Mennonites because they refused to take an oath, *Geloofsbelydenis volgens de Gronden der Doopsgezinden* (Haarlem, 1729), *Christelyk Onderwys in Geloof en Zeeden* (Haarlem, 1734, 2d ed. Amsterdam, 1739), *Korte Schets van het Christelyk Geloof* (Haarlem, 1734, repr. Amsterdam, 1739, Haarlem, 1741, ibid., 1754), *De Pligt der Barmhertigheid* (Haarlem, 1739), a sermon preached on the occasion of an offering in behalf of the Prussian Mennonites, *Brief aan Koenraad Bremer* (Amsterdam, 1740), *Paulus apostolise vermaaning aan Timotheus* (Haarlem, 1742), *Verhandeling van het Onderscheid tussen de Reden en het Geloof* (Amsterdam, 1746), *Leerredenen* (sermons) *Over de Geboorte, het Lyden, Sterven en Begraaven van onzen Heere en Zaaligmaker Jesus Christus* (Amsterdam, 1752).   vDZ.

Schijn-Maatschoen, *Geschiedenis* III, 497-508 (with portrait); *DB* 1918, 57, 58, 61, 62, 64-67; *Inv. Arch. Amst.* II, Nos. 2033, 2537 f.

Vereeniging tot Handhaving *van Gods onfeilbaar Woord in de Doopsgezinde Gemeente van Amsterdam* was an association of the orthodox members of the Amsterdam Mennonite Church, founded in 1891 when liberal preaching and teaching became predominant in this church. In 1892 this group, which never exceeded 100 members, called C. P. van Eeghen, Jr. (q.v.) as its pastor. It rented a hall where van Eeghen and a few other pastors preached regularly and where they held the Lord's Supper and had a Sunday school for children. In 1912 after the death of van Eeghen, considering that "the association was not as necessary as it had been before," the association was dissolved. (*DB* 1912, 224; annual reports of the Vereeniging.)   vDZ.

Vere(e)niging tot ondersteuning *van Doopsgezinde We(e)zen van onvermogende gemeenten* (Dutch Association for the Relief of Mennonite Orphans of Impecunious congregations) was at first a subdivision of the Haarlemsche Vereeniging (see **Vereeniging van Doopsgezinde Gemeenten**), founded in 1860. Since 1923 the association, to which most Dutch congregations contribute, has acted as an independent body.   vDZ.

Vereeniging van Doopsgezinde Gemeenten (Union of Dutch Mennonite congregations), better known under its common name "Haarlemsche Vereeniging," was founded at Haarlem in 1860. Its objectives were fivefold: (a) to regulate the cases when poor members, financially supported by the church, moved to another congregation; it was agreed that in such circumstances the poor members be supported for ten years by the congregation from which they came, unless the church to which they moved was willing to take over the relief, which was stipulated; (b) to arrange the question of church letters, when a member moved to another congregation; though a Dutch Mennonite can remain a member of a congregation after he has left its territory, it is considered better that he join the church of his residence; (c) the care of Mennonite orphans, particularly in impecunious congregations, by founding an Orphans' Fund; by 1905 this fund amounted to 45,000 Dutch guilders; (d) to consider and promote the founding of new congregations; this project was discussed in the yearly meeting of 1864; (e) to take care of Mennonites living in the Diaspora, first discussed in 1894.

In 1860 69 congregations joined the association, soon followed by others. At first meetings were held each year to discuss the different problems. As its various objectives were gradually committed to subdivisional committees, meetings were held only every fifth year, the last time in July 1925. When the care of members in the Diaspora (see **Verstrooiing**) was assumed by the A.D.S. (q.v.) in 1923, the Vereeniging van Doopsgezinde Gemeenten was dissolved, its subdivision for the care of the orphans becoming an independent association. (*Inv. Arch. Amst.* I, No. 1001; II, 2, pp. 163 f.; *DB* 1861, 94-102; 1876, 69; 1894, 74 f., 79, 110; 1905, 196 f., 200.) vDZ.

Vereeniging van Doopsgezinde Gemeenten *in Gelderland, Overijssel, Utrecht, en de Naburige in het Koninkrijk Pruissen*, founded at Zwolle in 1858: see **Zwolsche Vereeniging.**

Vereeniging van Doopsgezinde Gemeenten *in Zuidholland en Zeeland:* see **Zuidhollands-Zeeuwse Ring.**

Vereeniging voor Gemeentedagen: see **Broederschapswerk.**

Vereinigung der Mennoniten-Gemeinden im Deutschen Reich (since 1934: *der Deutschen Mennonitengemeinden*) was founded in Berlin in 1886 by 18 German Mennonite congregations (12 of North Germany and 6 of the Palatinate), a prior attempt at Friedelsheim in 1874 having failed. Since 1934 all German Mennonite congregations but those of the Badisch-Württembergisch-Bayrischer Gemeindeverband (*q.v.*) have belonged to the Vereinigung; i.e., now about five sixths of the *c*12,000 Mennonites in Germany. The original statutes of 1886 were revised in 1902, 1914, and 1934. In Hamburg in 1897 and 1902 the Vereinigung was incorporated; in 1922, also in Hamburg, it secured the status of a public corporation. An executive committee, a board of directors, and the assembly of representatives of the participating congregations are entrusted with the management. Presidents have been Hinrich van der Smissen of Hamburg 1886-96 and 1902-27; Ernst Weydmann of Crefeld 1896-1902; Hans Müller of Crefeld 1927-32; Emil Händiges of Elbing and later Monsheim 1932-53; Otto Schowalter of Hamburg 1952-58; Abraham Braun of Nierstein/Rhein since **1958.**

The regular triennial assemblies met in Berlin in 1887, 1890, and 1893; Hamburg 1896; Berlin 1899; Hamburg 1902; Berlin 1905; Danzig 1908; Crefeld 1911; Hamburg 1914, 1917, 1920, and 1926 (also an extraordinary assembly in 1927); Berlin 1929, 1932, and 1937; Marienburg 1942; Thomashof 1947; Branchweilerhof 1949; Hamburg 1952; Munich 1955; and Frankfurt/Main 1958.

The liberal city congregations of North Germany had started the Vereinigung and wanted it to follow the model of the Dutch A.D.S. (*q.v.*), but the German Mennonites of 1886 lived under other conditions than the Dutch who had founded the A.D.S. 75 years earlier. The founding German congregations were divided into two types: those under a rationalistic and those under a pietistic influence. So the plan of a Berlin theological professorship failed at the very beginning. The only accomplishment in this field was scholarships for Mennonite students of theology, of which a few were given. But whereas all Dutch Mennonite students had the same teachers and so more or less the same attitudes, since they all attended the Amsterdam Mennonite Seminary (*q.v.*), the German students developed more or less as many attitudes as they had teachers. Even in 1934, when the situation in the Third Reich made unity especially desirable, and in 1951, when the flight to the West resulted in a new situation for North Germany, the differences could not be overcome.

World War I and the subsequent inflation, as well as World War II and the subsequent currency reform, twice ruined the finances of the Vereinigung. The Vereinigung had started to gather an endowment fund. In 1908 alone Bernhard Brons Jr. (*q.v.*) at Emden and his son-in-law Dr. Jan van Delden at Gronau gave M 10,000 each for the Predigerfonds. The assets at the end of 1913, the last year of peace, had reached M 336,173; ten years later only one fourth remained: RM 72,977. And when at the end of 1938, the last year of peace, after some 15 years RM 92,315 had been reached, 10 years later not even one twelfth remained: DM 6,764.

Notwithstanding these handicaps the Vereinigung could do rather valuable work. By means of a "Predigerfonds" (*q.v.*) it raised the salaries of ministers in urgent cases. By means of a "Prediger-Ruhegehaltskasse" and a "Prediger-Witwenkasse" it supplied small pensions for the ministers and their widows. A publications committee provided periodicals for ministers and procured subsidies for printing the *Mennonitische Blätter* (*q.v.*), the *Mennonitisches Lexikon* (*q.v.*), and several books, the latter by a prize competition which produced the *Kurze Geschichte der Mennoniten* by Christine Hege (*q.v.*), published in 1909. The Vereinigung backed the Comeniusgesellschaft (*q.v.*) and the Mennonitischer Geschichtsverein (*q.v.*). It has been connected with the World Alliance for International Friendship through the Churches since 1930, and has been a member of the World Council of Churches since 1948. Delegates are sent to ecumenical meetings, as far as means permit. The Vereinigung was a cofounder of the Arbeitsgemeinschaft der christlichen Kirchen in Deutschland in 1948.

A relief agency, the Hilfswerk der Vereinigung der Deutschen Mennoniten-gemeinden (*q.v., HV-DM*), was started in 1946 for the British and the French Zones while the Christenpflicht (*q.v.*) of the Gemeindeverband was responsible for the American Zone.

The Vereinigung often had to discuss the question of the oath with the authorities. The questions of war and peace, of military service (*q.v.*), and conscientious objectors (*q.v.*) also often led to conversations and negotiations (see **Germany**). E.C.

Reports and proceedings of the Vereinigung, written and printed; H. G. Mannhart, *Jahrbuch*, 1888, 107-33; Abraham Braun, "70 Jahre Vereinigung," in *Der Mennonit* XI (1958) 99-101; Ernst Crous, "70 Jahre Berliner Mennoniten-gemeinde," *Der Mennonit* XI (1958) 102 f.

Vereinsschule: see **Preparatory Schools.**

Vereiniging voor Doopsgezind Broederschapswerk: see **Broederschapswerk.**

Verfalje (Verfailje), a Dutch Mennonite family of Flemish descent, found in the 17th and 18th centuries in the congregations of Haarlem and Amsterdam. Jacob Jacobsz Verfailje (b. 1665 at Haarlem, d. 1738 at Alkmaar) moved with his stepfather Theunis Dirksz Kuyper (*q.v.*) from Haarlem to Alkmaar in 1670, where he learned the trade of shoemaking, and also some Latin. In 1683 he moved with his stepfather to Harlingen, where he became a preacher of the church *c* 1689. In 1694 he was called as preacher to the Lamist (*q.v.*) congregation of Amsterdam (salary 2,000 Dutch guilders!). Here he served until 1727, then moving to Alkmaar, where he served 1727-38 in the Waterlander congregation. A Jacob Jansz Verfalje is mentioned as preacher of Krommenie about 1730. (*Inv. Arch. Amst.* II, Nos. 678-83, 1190, 1192, 1467, 2825; *DB* 1891, 9; 1905, 23 note 1.)   vDZ.

Verhaal der Onderhandeling . . . voorgevallen in Amsterdam 1684 en 1685 (Amsterdam, 1685) is the circumstantial report of the negotiations between the representatives of the Lamist (*q.v.*) and Zonist (*q.v.*) churches of Amsterdam to restore unity in the Amsterdam congregation, which had been severed by the Lammerenkrijgh (*q.v.*) and the schism of 1664. These negotiations, however, failed. The main difference concerned the importance of the confessions of faith. The Zonists thought them indispensable; the Lamists on the contrary did not wish to have fixed confessions of faith. The Lamists were represented in the conferences by Galenus Abrahamsz, Willem van Maurik, and some Amsterdam Lamist deacons; the Zonists by Samuel Apostool and Michiel Fortgens with some Amsterdam Zonist deacons, but also by some Zonist leaders from outside, e.g., Pieter Jansz Stapper, Jan Maartens Mol, E. A. van Dooregeest, and Samuel van Deyl.   vdZ.

Verhaal van't gene verhandelt ende besloten is in de By-eenkomste tot Leyden is the printed report (published at Amsterdam, 1661) of a meeting of a number of Flemish elders, preachers, and deacons, held at Leiden, Holland, on June 18-22, 1660. This meeting was called by the congregations of Rotterdam, Dordrecht, Gouda, and Leiden to discuss the growing liberalism of the Flemish Mennonites, as taught by Galenus (*q.v.*) Abrahamsz of Amsterdam and Willem van Maurik (*q.v.*) at Utrecht. At this meeting of conservative leaders 19 congregations were represented; three others sent a letter of agreement. Tieleman Jansz van Braght (*q.v.*) of Dordrecht was its moderator, Bastiaen van Weenighem (*q.v.*) of Rotterdam its secretary. A survey of the strict Flemish doctrines was presented and a number of congregations, e.g., Schiedam (*q.v.*), were accused of laxity in maintaining the doctrines as formulated in the confessions of faith. Some congregations were reproved for permitting their members to partake in the communion services of Waterlander and Frisian congregations and for admitting Waterlander preachers to their pulpits.

It was resolved to urge Galenus Abrahamsz either to abandon his views or "to stand still" in his ministry; a committee was appointed to admonish him (Galenus refused to receive this committee). It was also resolved to compile a new confession of faith out of the existing confessions, and a committee was appointed to this end (the confession, however, did not materialize).

The Leiden meeting, sometimes ironically called the "Leidsche Synode" by the progressive Mennonites, was actually the beginning of the Lammerenkrijgh (*q.v.*), which led to the Lamist-Zonist schism.   vdZ.

Verhamme, a Dutch Mennonite family, whose ancestor Pieter Verhamme moved from Kortrijk (Courtrai) in Flanders, Belgium, to Haarlem, Holland, in 1567 because of persecution. Here this family was found first in the Flemish, then in the Peuzelaarsteeg Mennonite congregation until it died out in the 18th century. From about 1700 a branch was also found in Amsterdam as members of the Lamist (*q.v.*) church. Here too they died out. Elisabeth Verhamme, one of the last descendants, died unmarried in 1858 and left a legacy to the A.D.S. (*q.v.*).

The Verhammes were prominent businessmen at Haarlem and Amsterdam. Abraham Verhamme

(1639-1727) is said to have been one of the wealthiest citizens of Haarlem. They were faithful members of the church. As far as known, no members of this family served as ministers, but some of them were trustees of the Mennonite orphanage at Haarlem, and a number of them both at Haarlem and Amsterdam served as deacons.   vdZ.

Verhandlungen der Diener-Versammlung, minutes of the Amish Mennonite Ministers' Conferences held annually 1862-78 (except 1877) before district conferences were organized. The minutes for 1862-64 and 1868 were published by John Baer and Son, Lancaster, Pa., and the remainder by John F. Funk and Brother of Chicago (1866) and Elkhart. Among the discussions recorded are the controversy over baptism in a creek, meetinghouses, the function of deacons, teamster service under military control, pensions, singing at funerals, offering a reward for the return of stolen goods, interest rates, investment in government bonds, and the restoration of a bishop who had been guilty of adultery. Names frequently mentioned in the minutes are John K. Yoder (1824-1906, *q.v.*) of Wayne County, Ohio; Samuel Yoder (1824-84, *q.v.*) of Mifflin County, Pa.; and John P. King (1827-87) of Logan County, Ohio, all of whom were born in Mifflin County, Pa. (GCL and BeCL have full sets of minutes.)   J.A.H.

DIENER-VERSAMMLUNGEN 1862-78

Date	Place	Attendance	Pages of Minutes
1862 June 9-12,	Wayne Co., Ohio	72	23
1863 May 25-27,	Mifflin Co., Pa.	42	20
1864 June 16-18,	Goshen, Ind.	71	23
1865 June 5-7,	Wayne Co., Ohio	89	9
1866 May 20-23,	Danvers, Ill.	75	23
1867 June 9-12,	West Liberty, Ohio	42	13
1868 May 21– June 3,	Belleville, Pa.	34	24
1869 May 16-18,	Walnut Creek, Ohio	27	10
1870 June 5-8,	Archbold, Ohio	40	36
1871 May 28-31,	Livingston Co., Ill.	56	30
1872 May 19-22,	Lagrange Co., Ind.	56	39
1873 June 1-4,	Orrville, Ohio	41	47
1874 May 16-19,	Washington Co., Iowa	28	16
1875 May 16-19,	Hopedale, Ill.	38	52
1876 June 4-7,	Archbold, Ohio	30	34
1878 June 9-12,	Eureka, Ill.	43	18

J. A. Hostetler, "Amish Problems at the Dienerversammlungen," *Menn. Life* IV (October 1949) 34-39; J. S. Umble, "The Oak Grove—Pleasant Hill Amish Mennonite Church in Wayne County, Ohio, in the Nineteenth Century (1815-1900)," *MQR* XXXI (July 1957) 3, 156-219.

Verhelle, Pieter, b. *c*1660 at Haarlem, Holland, was a preacher of the Flemish Mennonite congregation at Haarlem until 1693, when he moved to Hamburg, Germany, and served there from 1694 until after 1710. A sermon of his, *Predigt,* is published with Roosen's *Unschuld* (Ratzeburg, 1702). Like his father-in-law, Gerhard Roosen (*q.v.*), he held the conservative Zonist (*q.v.*) doctrines, whereas Jan de Lanoy, also a preacher of the Hamburg-

Altona congregation, was more Lamist (liberal). In his sermons Verhelle often attacked de Lanoy's views. Pieter Verhelle was a member of the Verhelle family that stemmed from Mennonite emigrants from Flanders, Belgium, found at Haarlem from c1600.   vDZ.

B. C. Roosen, *Geschichte der Mennoniten-Gemeinde zu Hamburg und Altona* I (Hamburg, 1886) 55, 65.

Verhogingsfonds: see **Fonds tot Verhoging**. Besides the Fund mentioned there, another Verhogingsfonds existed, established in 1865 by some Mennonites of Amsterdam, whose functions were assumed by the Fund founded in 1911. (*DB* 1865, 150 f.)   vDZ.

Verhuisdenbureau, an office of the Dutch Mennonites which registers the moves of the Mennonites, in order to induce Mennonites moving to a new community to join the congregation in their new residence. The office was started in 1935 and managed by H. C. Barthel 1935-36, G. A. Menalda 1937-42, G. Fopma 1942-51, and F. H. Pasma since Jan. 1, 1952.   vDZ.

Verkade, a Dutch family, found since the 15th century in the province of South Holland, where they were farmers; in the 18th century a few had small businesses such as bakeries and cheese shops. They all belonged to the Reformed Church. Pieter Verkade (Nootdorp, 1767-Vlaardingen, 1848) broke with the family tradition on two points: he left the farm to become a public notary, and he left the Reformed Church to join the Mennonites. His grandson was Ericus Gerhardus Verkade (Vlaardingen, 1935-Hilversum, 1907), who was the founder of the "De Ruyter" bakery at Zaandam. He was a faithful member of the church and served as deacon of the Zaandam-West congregation in 1864-73 and 1875-76; in 1876 he moved to Amsterdam where he was a deacon 1877-81. His nephew Cornelis Pieter Verkade (Harlingen, 1864-Haarlem, 1934), under whose leading the bakery at Zaandam developed into the famous Verkade Factories producing cookies, chocolates, and other confections, was also a deacon of the Zaandam-West congregation, serving 1895-1900 and 1901-10.   vDZ.

Nederl. Patriciaat XL (1954) 373-83; S. Lootsma, *Het Nieuwe Huys* (Zaandam, 1937) 195, 196.

Verkampt, Daniel: see **Daniel van der Campt.**

Verkindert (Ver Kindert, van der Kinderen), a former Dutch Mennonite family. Joost (*q.v.*) Verkindert died as an Anabaptist martyr in 1570 at Antwerp, Belgium. Verkinderts, who may have been Joost's relatives or descendants, shortly after emigrated from Kortrijk (*q.v.*), Flanders, to the Netherlands; some were at Haarlem from c1580. Pieter Ver Kindert, born at Franeker in Friesland, was a cloth merchant at Haarlem and c1620-after 1649 a preacher of the Haarlem Flemish den Blok congregation. In 1649 he was secretary of the Flemish conference held at Haarlem. He published *Een korte en seer grondighe historische Vertellinge belanghende den Twist tot Franicker Anno 1587 . . .* (Haarlem, 1628). This writing, an account of the quarrels which in 1586-87 led to the schism among

the Flemish Mennonites (Huiskopers-Contrahuiskopers), also contains valuable information about the Flemish-Frisian dissensions of 1566-67. His *Brief, dienende om te bewijsen . . .* (Amsterdam, 1634) deals with the same controversies. Verkindert also replied to Petrus Bontemps (*q.v.*), who had attacked the Mennonites, in *Korte Ontschuldinge over d'onbehoorlijcke ende al te sware beschuldinge van Petro Bontemps* (Haarlem, 1643). In addition he published *Korte Verklaeringhe* and *Naerder Verklaeringhe* (both Haarlem, 1634), in which he expounded a number of Scripture texts. Besides these publications, the following are mentioned by Schagen: *Korte verklaringe van de Christelyke Gemeynte ende 't Volck Godts des Nieuwen Testaments* (Haarlem, 1628), *Over de Gemeynte Gods . . . ,* found in the *Huysboeck* of Jan de Buyser (*q.v.*), and *Handelinge der Vereenigde Vlaemse en duytse Doopsgezinde Gemeynten . . .* (Vlissingen, 1666).   vDZ.

Marten Schagen, *Naamlijst der Doopsgezinde Schrijveren* (Amsterdam, 1745); *Biogr. Wb.* IV, 758-60.

Verkolje (Vercoilge, Vercolie), a Mennonite family found in the 17th and 18th centuries at Amsterdam, Holland. They had emigrated from Kortrijk (*q.v.*) in Flanders, Belgium, where Jossine Andries, the wife of Rougier van Quoilge (see **Stijntgen Vercoilgen**), suffered martyrdom in 1567. In Amsterdam they belonged to the Flemish congregation; later they were in both the Lamist and the Zonist churches. Both branches died out in the 18th century.

It could not be ascertained whether Johannes (Jan) Verkolje (Amsterdam, 1650-Delft, 1693) and his son Nicolaas Verkolje, b. 1673 at Delft, from 1700 living at Amsterdam and died there in 1746, both painters, who had some reputation during their lifetime, also were Mennonites, belonging to this same family. The Amsterdam Rijksmuseum has five paintings by Jan Verkolje and one by Nicolaas.   vDZ.

Church records of Amsterdam; Thieme-Becker, *Allg. Lexikon der bildenden Künstler* XXXIV (Leipzig, 1940) 257 f.; *Catalogus Rijksmuseum Amsterdam, 1921.*

Verkruissen (Verkruyssen), a family of Mennonite refugees from Flanders, Belgium, settling at Haarlem, Holland, c1580 and from the 17th century also found at Rotterdam and Amsterdam. Some of its members were deacons of the church. This family died out in the 19th century.   vDZ.

Verlaan, a former Dutch Mennonite family, found in the 17th century at Amsterdam, where Johannes (Jan) Verlaan was a preacher of the Waterlander Toren (*q.v.*) congregation in 1642-45. Nicolaas Verlaan (b. c1690 at Amsterdam, d. c1763 at Haarlem) was trained for the ministry at the Remonstrant (*q.v.*) seminary at Amsterdam, thereupon serving the Amsterdam Lamist congregation 1714-16, Rotterdam 1716-29, and Haarlem Peuzelaarsteeg church 1729-d.c63. During his Rotterdam period he was active in behalf of the suppressed Mennonites of Prussia and occasionally too he supported Mennonites from the Palatinate emigrating to America via Rotterdam.

He was married to Anna van der Hoef; his sons

Jan and Willem Verlaan were both warm Collegiants (*q.v.*) and often addressed the meetings at Rijnsburg (*q.v.*). vDZ.

Verloove (Verlove), a Dutch family of Mennonite refugees, moving from Flanders, Belgium, to Rotterdam and Haarlem, Holland, in the early 17th century or even earlier. An outstanding member of this family was Karel (Carel) Verloove, b. 1633 at Haarlem, d. *c*1700 at Amsterdam, who was a poet, whose verse was highly esteemed during his lifetime. One of his publications was *Uytbreyding over de heylige Lofzangen* (Amsterdam, 1686), a songbook containing some 200 hymns with psalm tunes. He belonged to a group of liberal poets, usually called the circle of Jan Zoet (*q.v.*), all of whom favored Collegiant (*q.v.*) views. Karel Verloove was a friend of Jan Luyken (*q.v.*), who dedicated one of his poems to Verloove, and was well acquainted with Johannes Antonides (*q.v.*) van der Goes and Pieter Cornelisz Plockhoy (*q.v.*). His brother Pieter Verloove also wrote verse. Members of this Verlo(o)ve family are still found in the Rotterdam congregation. vDZ.

N.N.B.Wb. IV, 1380 f.; G. Kalff, *Geschiedenis der Nederl. Letterkunde* IV (Groningen, 1909) 462, 464, 522, 528, 561; V, 133; C. B. Hylkema, *Reformateurs* II (Haarlem, 1902) 103.

Vermande (Vermander, Vermandele, Van (der) Mander), a widely ramified Dutch family, formerly Mennonite. This family is of Flemish descent, emigrating from Flanders, Belgium, to Holland because of persecution. Gerrit (*q.v.*) and Hans (*q.v.*) Vermandele were Anabaptist martyrs, both executed at Antwerp, Belgium, in 1569. Carel Vermander (see **Mander, Carel van**) (1548-1606), a noted poet and painter, moved from Flanders to Haarlem, where he was a member of the Old Flemish congregation. In the early 17th century the Mennonite Vermandeles lived near Aardenburg in Dutch Zeeland Flanders and some Vermanders at Amsterdam. Vermandes were in the 17th century found among the members of the Mennonite congregations in Haarlem, Amsterdam, Rotterdam, and Delft. Some of them were deacons: Lewys Jacobs Vermande served in the Flemish congregation of Rotterdam from 1641; Isaac Jacobs Vermande represented Delft at the Flemish conference at Leiden in 1660, and in 1664 signed the *Verbondt van Eenigheydt* (*q.v.*) for Delft. In Amsterdam they were members of the Zonist (*q.v.*) church. They were all businessmen, some of them, particularly at Amsterdam, very wealthy; e.g., Lodewijk Vermande (1676-1748) of Amsterdam, who in 1716 married Maria Welsingh. They had only one surviving daughter (Maria Alletta 1726-79, married to Hendrik Pieter van Beeck), and this branch died out with her. The Haarlem branch also died out in the 18th century. The members of the Rotterdam and Delft branches, and a side branch at Hoorn, all left the Mennonite Church about 1700. At present there are no Mennonite Vermandes. (Church records of Amsterdam and Rotterdam; family papers of Lodewijk Vermande in the Amsterdam Mennonite archives; *Ned. Patriciaat* XIV, 1924, pp. 348-52.) vDZ.

Vermander, Carel: see **Mander, Carel van.**

Vermaner, a former Dutch Mennonite name for a minister not holding the full office of an elder or bishop (*oudste* and *leeraer* tot den vollen dienst). The vermaner or admonisher was charged to preach and admonish but not to baptize. The Dutch also used the term *prediker* (preacher) for the same office, and in modern times the term *predikant*. That "vermaner" came into use would indicate that the early Dutch Mennonites emphasized strongly that duties of a minister consist not only in preaching the Word of God but also in admonishing the individual members to live a consecrated life. Not by accident did they coin this term; it was deeply anchored in their basic Christian convictions. The term is borrowed from II Peter 1:12 "I will not be negligent to put you always in remembrance of these things" which is read in the Old Dutch Bible versions "to admonish (vermanen) you always about these things." (*DB* 1872, 77.) The title "vermaner" also used by the Danzig Mennonites disappeared during the 17th century in the period of adjustment to the environment. (See also **Ministry,** Netherlands.) C.K.

H. G. Mannhardt, *Die Danziger Mennoniten-Gemeinde* (Danzig, 1919) 106.

Vermaning, a Dutch Mennonite name for meetinghouse in the 17th-19th centuries. Their words *vermaner* (admonisher) and *vermaning* (place of admonishing) indicate the emphasis the Anabaptists placed on practical consecrated Christian living and discipleship. Highly suspicious of the state church ministers and churches, they coined new terms to assure a distinction between their concepts and those of the other churches. The meetinghouse was usually a simple structure, at times barnlike and hidden (*schuilkerk*). The hidden church originated in the days when the Mennonites were not permitted to build meetinghouses, and was also used when they were finally given permission to do so, but under the condition that they would not be on public streets and places but hidden, and that they would have no steeples or bells so that no one would be "misled" to listen to their "admonishings." Today the Dutch refer to their church as *kerk* just as the Reformed Church does. The distinctive name, though sometimes still used in Friesland, mostly disappeared during the 19th century when the Dutch Mennonites adjusted themselves to their environment and culture. (See also **Architecture.**) C.K.

Vermanje, Jan Tjerks (b. *c*1743 at Midlum near Harlingen, d. Dec. 17, 1829, at Den Horn), was an untrained Dutch Mennonite preacher for more than 61 years. His start as a preacher was rather unusual: he was the servant of a farmer at Witveen (*q.v.*) in Friesland, who was a minister of the church; one Sunday when his master was ill, Vermanje preached in his place (a somewhat different account in *DB* 1901, 104, note). His testimony gave such satisfaction that the congregation chose him as preacher in 1762. He served at Witveen until 1782, and though he had a very poor education, being even unable to write, he seems to have been a rather eloquent speaker: in 1782 he was called to the Mildam-Knijpe congregation, where he served for ten years. Here he adopted his family name Vermanje, because he was living in a room of the *vermaning* (*q.v.*, meetinghouse, Frisian *formanje*). On Dec. 27, 1791, he preached the last sermon in the Old Flemish meetinghouse at Beneden-Knijpe, which was then pulled down. Finally he served at Den Horn from 1792 until his death. In his last years, unable to walk, he was carried to the pulpit. (*N.N.B.Wb.* III, 1295; *DJ* 1837, 34; *DB* 1872, 39 f.)

vDZ.

Vermanung, the commonly used short form for a book published in 1542 by Pilgram Marpeck (*q.v.*) and Leupold Scharnschlager (*q.v.*), two leaders in the South German Anabaptist movement. The full title of the book is *Vermanung; auch gantz klarer gründtlicher un(d) unwidersprechlicher bericht zu warer Christlicher . . . pundtssvereynigung allen waren glaubigen frummen und gutthertzigen menschen zu hilff and trost mit grund heyliger schrifft durch bewerung warer Tauff und Abentmals Christi sampt mitlauffung und erklärung irer gegensachen und Argumenten wider alle vermeynte Christliche Pündtnus so sich bissher un(d) noch under dem nammen Christi zutragend*. Our knowledge of it has been greatly enhanced by Schwenckfeld's rather condescending reply to it; the circumstances of its publication are known only from Schwenckfeld's correspondence. Although the book was not directed against Schwenckfeld, he felt attacked by it, and since he had a number of other complaints against Pilgram's brotherhood, he wrote the *Judicium* (see article **Marpeck**) in reply.

About two thirds of the *Vermanung* is an expanded translation of the *Bekentnisse van beyden Sacramenten* published at Münster in 1533 (as discovered by Wray 1954, reported in *ARG* 1956), for which Bernt Rothmann (*q.v.*) is generally given credit, although actually six men signed the introduction. The two main subjects of both books are the sacraments of baptism and communion. First there is a lengthy introduction (not present in the *Bekentnisse*) decrying the splintering of the Anabaptist movement into a variety of sects in the twelve years since 1530, and calling the discouraged to rally around the banner of Christ. Marpeck and Scharnschlager admitted that they used other confessions in the *Vermanung*, but such had first been tested and purified, because they believed that nothing is more dangerous than truth mixed with error. After the introduction there is a discussion of the term "sacrament" (*q.v.*), and then baptism is discussed. While the *Bekentnisse* had brilliant arguments against infant baptism, the logic of adult baptism receives strong support only through the view of the church seen in the *Vermanung*, namely, that it is a suffering community; hence all forms of violence are categorically rejected, with a pointed reference to the outcome of the tragedy at Münster. Marpeck and his co-worker made a much sharper distinction between the Old and New Testaments than did the *Bekentnisse*, and at one point they rejected the typology of the *Bekentnisse*. On original sin, on baptism as pouring as well as immersion, on

remaining faithful unto the end, and finally in the stress on the covenant, the *Vermanung* differs from the *Bekentnisse*. For a full discussion of the content of the *Vermanung* see the article **Marpeck.**

The *Vermanung* is one of the most important books written by the South German Anabaptists in the 16th century. It represents an attempt at unification outside of Switzerland and North Germany, which rejects the Hutterian communism and is aware of what happened at Münster. Further it occasioned the lengthy debates with Caspar Schwenckfeld which forced the Marpeck brotherhood to think through the issues presented by the spiritualists.

In a letter to the Moravian churches in 1553 Marpeck mentioned that he was sending 20 "Bundeszeugnisse" and it is quite possible that this refers to copies of the *Vermanung* since it is also called "Das Buch der Bundesbezeugung." Robert Friedmann found a handwritten copy of the *Vermanung* among Hutterite codices in Austria.

Christian August Salig is the first modern writer to indicate knowledge of the *Vermanung*, and he knew it only through Schwenckfeld's *Judicium*. Two copies are known to exist, one in the British Museum (photocopy in GCL) and the other in the Württemberg Landesbibliothek in Stuttgart, from which the modern edition published in the *Gedenkschrift* was prepared. An English translation has been made (in GCL).   W.Kl.

Christian A. Salig, *Vollständige Historie der Augsburgischen Confession und derselben zugethanen Kirchen* III (Halle, 1735) 1113 ff.; Jan J. Kiwiet, *Pilgram Marbeck* (Kassel, 1957); Torsten Bergsten, "Pilgram Marbeck und seine Auseinandersetzung mit Caspar Schwenckfeld," *Kyrkohistorisk Arsskrift*, 1957 and 1958 (Uppsala); Frank J. Wray, "The 'Vermanung' of 1542 and Rothmann's 'Bekentnisse,' " in *Archiv für Reformationsgeschichte*, 1956, 243-51; Heinold Fast, "Pilgram Marbeck und das oberdeutsche Täufertum," *Archiv für Reformationsgeschichte*, 1956, 232; *Gedenkschrift zum 400-jährigen Jubiläum der Mennoniten . . .* (Karlsruhe, 1925) 185-281.

Vermeer (Vermeeren, Vemeren, Van der Meer), a common Dutch family name. Adriaen (*q.v.*) Vermeer, of Leiden, was an Anabaptist martyr, executed at Haarlem, Holland, in 1537. Joos Vermeeren (Joachim—*q.v.*—de Suickerbacker) of Antwerp, Belgium, was a Mennonite elder in the 1560's. Later there were some Mennonite Vermeers in the Rotterdam congregation and Vermeerens at Haarlem until *c*1900.   vDZ.

Vermeersch (see also **Meersch, van der,** and **Mersch, van der**), a Dutch family of refugees, emigrated from Poperinghe in Flanders, Belgium, for the sake of their faith, moving to Leiden and Haarlem, Holland, in the 1580's. They were probably Mennonites. Among them was Gillis Vermeersch, banished from Poperinghe in 1568. There were Mennonite Vermeersches at Haarlem and Amsterdam in the 17th and 18th centuries. In Haarlem Gillis Vermeersch, married to Maria de Haan, was a trustee of the Waterlander Mennonite orphanage at Haarlem from 1583, and some Vermeersches were deacons of the Mennonite church at Amsterdam during the 17th and 18th centuries.

An outstanding member of this family was Gillis Vermeersch, b. *c*1654 at Amsterdam, d. 1722 at

Harlingen, Friesland, a son of Willem Vermeersch. Gillis moved to Harlingen about 1678 where he was married to Marijke Fontein. At first he was a tinsmith, but later he came to great prosperity as a merchant trading with Prussia and Russia, and shipowner, also participating in the West Indian (Caribbean) Trading company. He was for many years a deacon of the Harlingen congregation and the first treasurer of the Friese Sociëteit, founded in 1695, serving as its treasurer 1696-1721. These families all died out in the 18th century.   vDZ.

Jaarboek van het Centraal Bureau voor Genealogie IX (The Hague, 1955) 179, 186, 188; *DB* 1878, 90; 1895, 30; Blaupot t. C., *Friesland*, 187; G. A. Wumkes, *Stads- en Dorpskroniek van Friesland* I (Leeuwarden, 1930) 1, 2.

Vermeulen (Vermuelen, Vermolen, Vermoelen, Vermule, Van der Meulen), a common Dutch family name, derived from *molen*, i.e., mill, is found among the Mennonites in the Netherlands and formerly in Prussia. Not all the Vermeulen families are related. Some Vermeulens were religious refugees from Flanders, Belgium. Jacob Pietersz Vermeulen (van der Meulen, *q.v.*) was a Mennonite elder at Haarlem, Holland, *c*1600. Krijn Vermeulen (Quirijn van der Meulen, *q.v.*) lived about the same time at Danzig, West Prussia. Ambrosius Vermeulen in 1589 founded at Danzig the well-known distillery "Zum Lachs" in the Breitgasse (*ME* I, 40). A Mennonite Vermeulen family has been living at Rotterdam, Holland, since the early 17th century. Harmen Gillis Vermeulen was a deacon of the Waterlander congregation there from 1666. He had previously been a deacon of the Flemish church, but left this congregation because of its strictness in church discipline. There are still some Vermeulens in the Amsterdam and other Dutch Mennonite congregations.   vDZ.

Vermeulen, Jacob Pietersz: see **Meulen, Jacob Pietersz van der.**

Vermeulen, Krijn (Cryn): see **Meulen, Quirijn van der.**

Vermeulensvolk, a branch of the Dutch Mennonites who sided with Jacob Pieters van der Meulen (*q.v.*), elder at Haarlem, who with his followers left the Old Flemish Mennonites in 1593 (not 1598 as is stated *ME* III, 660). They were also called Bankroetiers (*q.v.*) because the cause of the schism was the failure to apply the ban to a member who became bankrupt (Dutch, *bankroet*).   vDZ.

Vermoser, Jeronimus, city secretary of Laufen, Austria, and an Anabaptist preacher. He was seized by the Salzburg government before Nov. 20, 1527. There is no record of his fate. Very likely he was one of the thirty-eight persons who were locked into a house in Salzburg and burned to death.

Christian Meyer, "Die Anfänge des Wiedertäufertums in Augsburg," in *Zeitschrift des Historischen Vereins für Schwaben und Neuburg* I (1874) 247; Josef Jäkel, *Zur Geschichte der Wiedertäufer in Oberösterreich und speciell in Freistadt (Mus.-Jahr.-Ber. XLVII, 1889) 47; ML* IV.

Verniers, Laurens, a Mennonite elder, at first active in Antwerp, Belgium. In 1567 he was banished

53

from Antwerp by the Duke of Alba (*q.v.*), but he had already escaped to Franeker in Friesland about two years previously. Concerning his work there is not much information. A letter by Elder Hans Busschaert (*q.v.*) to Verniers, published by Vos, says that both Busschaert and Verniers sided with the Flemish during the Flemish-Frisian dissensions. This letter, undated, was probably written shortly after the spring of 1567. In 1570 an elder Laurens of Franeker visited Cleve (*q.v.*), Germany, with Hendrik van Roosevelt (*q.v.*) to settle a quarrel in the Mennonite congregation of this town. After their visit in Cleve they traveled to Cologne to defend themselves against the charge of unorthodoxy made against them by Ameldonck, who then was an elder of Cologne. This Elder Laurens was apparently Verniers. (K. Vos, *Antwerpen*, 338, 382-84; *Inv. Arch. Amst.* I, No. 446; *DB* 1893, 16.)
                vDZ.

Vernon County (Mo.) Amish Mennonite Church was listed by Hartzler and Kauffman (*Mennonite Church History*) in 1905 as a congregation of 18 members in the Amish Mennonite Western District Conference. C. C. Schrock was the deacon as well as the first settler. The date of the first meetinghouse was given as 1894 and the address of the church was Statesburg.   M.G.

Versailles, Mo., the county seat (pop. 1,781) of Morgan County, in the central part of the state. Versailles is the shopping center for about 200 Mennonites living mostly in the farming area northeast of the town. There are two Mennonite churches near Versailles: the Mt. Zion Mennonite Church (MC) 6 miles northeast, and the Bethel Mennonite Church (GCM) 10 miles northeast of Versailles. The first Mennonite settlers located near Versailles in 1868. It was the home of Daniel Kauffman until he moved to Scottdale, Pa., to become editor of the *Gospel Herald.* Very few of the Mennonites live in the town.   L.G.

Verscheyden Schriftuerlijcke Liedekens is a small Dutch hymnal containing 29 hymns, published by Jan Theunisz (*q.v.*). Jan Theunisz, using the motto "Jaecht nae't best," wrote seven of them. (Yearbook *Amstelodamum* XXV, 1928, iii.)   vDZ.

Verschuren (Verschueren, Verschuer, van der Schuere), a former Dutch Mennonite family of Flemish descent, found in Rotterdam, where Joost Verschueren was a deacon of the Old Flemish congregation *c*1631-36, and particularly at Haarlem (Peuzelaarsteeg church), where they are found from *c*1580 until the 18th century, some of them serving as deacons. Dionys van der Schuere (*q.v.*) was a Waterlander preacher at Haarlem and Amsterdam.
                vDZ.

Versluys: see **Sluys** (Sluis) **van der.**

Verspeck (Verspecht), **Albert** (Albrecht), d. 1612 at Amsterdam, was a Dutch Mennonite elder. In 1576 he was an elder of the Waterlander (*q.v.*) Mennonite congregation at Antwerp, Belgium. He was probably engaged in some business, with Hans (*q.v.*) Bret, who suffered martyrdom at Antwerp on Jan. 4, 1577, as his servant. After Bret's death Verspeck moved to the Netherlands. In September 1577, then living at Alkmaar, he was a coauthor with de Ries (q.v.) and some other Waterlander elders of a confession of faith. At the Waterlander conference of 1581 at Amsterdam Verspeck represented the Antwerp congregation, and was sent by the conference, commissioned to visit the church in Gent, Belgium, and the Mennonites in Zeeland every four months. Later he was an elder of the Amsterdam Waterlander congregation until his death.

If the assumption is correct that this Mennonite elder is identical with the Albrecht Verspecks who is mentioned by Wessel as an *ouderling* of the Reformed Church at Antwerp on Nov. 4, 1575, then Verspeck, like de Ries, was Reformed before he joined the Mennonites. vDZ.

K. Vos, *Antwerpen*, 360; J. H. Wessel, *De Leerstellige Strijd* . . . (Assen, 1945) 22 f.; Kühler, *Geschiedenis* I, 335; *BRN* VII, 248; *Inv. Arch. Amst.* I, No. 520; II, Nos. 82b, 834; *DB* 1863, 111 note; 1864, 20; 1872, 57; 1877, 79 f.; 1904, 142, 144 note 2.

Verstrooiing, the Dutch word for Diaspora. The Mennonite congregations are rather thickly scattered in northern and western parts of the Netherlands, but in the east and south they are rather scarce. Mennonites moving to these areas often do not find a Mennonite congregation and remain members of the congregation of their former homes. In order to keep the contact with these "Verstrooiden" (dispersed members), Pastor W. van der Hoek (q.v.) of Kromwal in 1849 asked the A.D.S. (q.v.) to provide care for the Mennonites in the Diaspora, but the A.D.S. did not accept the suggestion at this time, considering this area outside its realm. The Haarlemsche (q.v.) Vereeniging, founded in 1860, discussed this problem in its meeting of 1864, but adopted no special measures. The matter was dropped until the 1892 meeting of the Zwolsche (q.v.) Vereeniging, when Pastor Tj. Kielstra (q.v.) brought up the subject again. Thereupon a committee was appointed to study the matter. The 1894 annual meeting of the Zwolsche Vereeniging resolved to pass the matter to the Haarlemsche Vereeniging. Through the perseverance of Kielstra, a committee was set up by the Haarlemsche Vereeniging. In the summer of 1897 W. J. van Douwen, pastor at Almelo, and F. C. Fleischer, pastor of Broek op Langendijk, visited a large number of scattered Mennonites. They were called *bezoekleraren* (similar to *Reiseprediger* in Germany, Alsace, and Switzerland). This work has been continued until the present time. Especially Kielstra and later Cornelis Vis Jzn (q.v.) should be mentioned as the stimulators of this work. The committee appointed by the Haarlemsche Vereeniging developed in 1905 into an independent association (*Vereeniging ter behartiging van de godsdienstige belangen der Doopsgezinde Broeders en Zusters in de verstrooiing*). In 1925 the A.D.S. took over this activity, and the association was dissolved. At present (1958) ten visiting ministers visit the Mennonites in the Diaspora, who thus receive a pastoral visit at least once a year.

In behalf of these Mennonites the Committee,

the Association, and the A.D.S. have published a number of booklets, No. 1 being published in 1897 and No. 61, the last, in 1941. These *Geschriftjes ten behoeve van de Doopsgezinden in de Verstrooiing* contain reports, sermons, and particularly papers on Mennonite history. vDZ.

DB 1893, 124; 1894, 73-75, 113; 1895, 144; *DJ* 1907, 56-63; annual reports in the *Zondagsbode; Geschriftjes t. b. v. de Doopsgezinden in de Verstrooiing*, Nos. 34 and 42; annual reports of the A.D.S. since 1925.

Verveld (Vervelt, Verrevelt), a former Mennonite family, now extinct, found at Sappemeer, Dutch province of Groningen. Koert Izaks Verveld (1719-1804), a merchant, was a preacher of the Sappemeer Mennonite congregation 1756-d.1804. vDZ.

Vervolg van Christelijke Gezangen (Supplement to Christian Hymns) (Groningen, 1808) is a small Dutch Mennonite hymnal containing 33 hymns with notes, introduced in 1808 in the Zwolle (q.v.) congregation, and for this reason generally called *Zwolsche Bundel* or *Zwolsche Liederen*. (*DB* 1865, 74.) vDZ.

Verwer, a Mennonite family name, found at Zaandam, Amsterdam, Rotterdam, Alkmaar, Graftdijk, and some other congregations in the Dutch province of North Holland (several apparently unrelated branches). Aris Jansz Verwer, d. 1679, was a preacher of the Frisian congregation at Zaandam-West and from about 1649 of the Aris-Janszvolk, a group which had separated from the Zaandam-West Frisian church, and which was dissolved shortly after the death of Aris Jansz. The cause of the schism is not clear.

In the Rotterdam branch there was Adriaan Verwer, a merchant, who later moved to Amsterdam. He was a fervent Collegiant (q.v.), a friend of Joachim Oudaen (q.v.), and the author of a book against the philosopher Spinoza: *De Atheisterye het Mom-aanzigt afgerukt* (1683); he also wrote *Inleiding tot de Christelyke Godsgeleerdheid* (Amsterdam, 1698) and books on the Dutch language (1707) and on the Dutch maritime law (1716, 1730). In Amsterdam (Lamist) and elsewhere some Verwers were deacons. vDZ.

S. Lootsma, *Het Nieuwe Huys* (Zaandam, 1937) 22 f., 101 f., 191; (J. de Lange CJzn), *Beknopte Geschiedenis der Doopsgez. gemeente te Alkmaar* (n.p., n.d.–Alkmaar, 1927) 14, 42, 159; *Inv. Arch. Amst.* I, No. 705; II, Nos. 122; 126; II, 2, No. 378; *DB* 1863, 38; 1912, 106; Marten Schagen, *Naamlijst der Doopsgezinde Schrijveren* (Amsterdam, 1745) 117 f.

Verwer, de, a Dutch Mennonite family name, found at Zaandam and Amsterdam. Abraham de Verwer, b. before 1600, d. August 1650, a member of the Amsterdam Waterlander congregation, was a painter, particularly of naval combats. Two of his works, a naval combat and a view of a sailship, are found at the Amsterdam Rijksmuseum. His drawings have greater merit than his canvasses. In 1639-41 he was in Paris, where he painted and sketched some views of the town. His son Justus de Verwer (c1626-c86), first living at Amsterdam, later at Gouda, of whom it is not known that he was a member of the church, was also a painter.

Jacob de Verwer (1829-71) of Zaandam was

trained for the ministry at the Amsterdam Mennonite Seminary and served as pastor at Baard 1854-56 and De Rijp 1856-d. 71. vDZ.

Thieme-Becker, *Allg. Lexikon der bildenden Künstler* XXXIV (Leipzig, 1940) 306.

Verzaameling van de afbeeldingen *van veele voornaame manen en leeraaren . . . onder de Doopsgezinde Christenen . . .* (Amsterdam, 1743), a collection of pictures which contains the portraits of 30 Mennonite ministers, all Dutch except two, viz., Gerrit Roosen of Hamburg, Germany, and Jan Gerritsz van Emden, of Danzig, Prussia. Each of the copper engravings, reproducing etchings of Rembrandt, Uylenburgh, Mierevelt, T. de Vlieger, and C. van de Pas, is provided with a short laudatory poem by Adriaan Spinniker (*q.v.*). The complete collection of portraits was republished (Amsterdam, 1780) without the verses. The ministers depicted here are Menno Simons, Dirk Philips, Lubbert Gerritsz, Hans de Ries, Jan Gerritsz van Emden, Aldert Volkertsz, Reynier Wybrandsz Wybma, Cornelis Claesz Anslo, Pieter Andries Hesseling, Hans Alenson, Pieter Pietersz, Yeme Jacobsz de Ring, Abraham Dirksz (Bierens), Jan Willemsz, Pieter Gryspeer(t), Tobias Govertsz van den Wyngaard, Bartel Louwer, Anthoni Jacobsz Roscius, Jacob Cornelisz, Gerrit Roosen, Lambert Klaasz Aker, Galenus Abrahamsz, Tieleman van Braght, Lieuwe Willems (de) Graaf, Herman Schijn, Michael Fortgens, Pieter Schrijver, Abraham Verduin, and Joannes Houbakker. vDZ.

Verzaameling van Stichtelyke Gezangen, a songbook published 1705 at Amsterdam. This collection, containing 21 songs with notes, was apparently printed for the Mennonite Zaandam-Oost congregation. It was edited particularly for the young people, who had previously used the *Stichtelijke Rijmen* by Camphuysen (*q.v.*) (Preface). Two of the songs in this *Verzaameling* commemorated the preacher Foe(c)ke Floris (*q.v.*), d. Sept. 28, 1703, who had served at Zaandam-Oost. vDZ.

Vest, Balzer, an Anabaptist martyr, was put to death for his faith in Innsbruck, Austria. Nothing further is known.

Vet, Melchior, an Anabaptist martyr, a friend and traveling companion of Georg (Jörg) Blaurock. He was burned at the stake at Dracha "in the time of Michael Sattler," i.e., in 1527. The Hutterite *Chronik* calls him Veit and says that he was burned at Ettach (Switzerland?). (*Mart. Mir.* D 4, E 416; Zieglschmid, *Chronik,* 48.) vDZ.

Vettre: see **Claudine Levettre.**

Veurne (Furnes), a town in Flanders, Belgium, where an anonymous Anabaptist martyr was executed in 1553. He is celebrated in the song "In bitter-heyt der sielen," No. 10 of the *Lietboecxken.* The hymn speaks of his farewell to his brethren. This seems to indicate the existence of a Mennonite congregation at Veurne, concerning which, however, there is no information; probably this church was the same as that of Leisele near Veurne, of which Maillart (*q.v.*) de Grave and his wife were members

in 1568 and of which Paulus (*q.v.*) van Meenen was the elder. vDZ.

Veyt (Feyt): see **Greyenburger, Veyt.**

Veyt, Peter: see **Voit, Peter.**

Vianen, a small town in the Dutch province of South Holland, formerly the seat of a small Flemish (*q.v.*) Mennonite congregation. In 1649 it had no preacher and was served by the church of Utrecht. Gijsbert Gerritsz of Vianen signed the *Verbondt* (*q.v.*) *van Eenigheydt* for the congregation in 1664. The congregation seems to have died out soon after. At any rate it had dissolved by 1700. (*Inv. Arch. Amst.* II, No. 2337; Blaupot t. C., *Holland* I, 222, 330; II, 43; *DB* 1863, 96, 102.) vDZ.

Viblarre, Andries: see **Andries Meulenaar.**

Victoor (Victor Willemsz), an Anabaptist martyr of Niel? in the territory of Jülich (*q.v.*), was burned at the stake with four others at Antwerp, Belgium, on Jan. 30, 1557. Particulars are lacking. He is celebrated in the song "Aenhoort God, hemelsche Vader," No. 16 of the *Lietboecxken.* (*Offer,* 564; *Mart. Mir.* D 184, E 568; *Antw. Arch.-Bl.* VIII, 433, 437; XIV, 22 f., No. 241.) vDZ.

Vienna, the capital of Austria in both its wider and its narrower sense (see **Austria**), since *c*1300 the seat of the ruling house of Hapsburg (see **Habsburg**), situated on the Danube at the crossroads from East to West and North to South, a strong bulwark against the Turks in 1529 and again in 1683, is a place where many nations and races mingle but has a predominantly German population (1955 *c*1.8 million). Vienna never had an Anabaptist congregation for any length of time but was the scene of execution of at least 23 Anabaptists during the reign of Ferdinand I (*q.v.*). Among the martyrs were Balthasar Hubmaier (*q.v.*) and his wife, executed March 10, 1528; Jacob Wideman (*q.v.*); Hieronymus Käls (*q.v.*), the schoolmaster, martyred with Michel Seifensieder and Hans Oberecker on March 31, 1536; Oswald Glait (*q.v.*) in the autumn of 1546; **Hans** Staudach (*q.v.*) and Anthoni Keim (*q.v.*), executed with two others on Nov. 22, 1546; and finally Hans Gurtzham (*q.v.*) of Carinthia, on June 27, 1550.

The first Anabaptist influence in Vienna was apparently brought by transient brothers on their way to and from Nikolsburg (situated 50 miles north of Vienna), where Anabaptism had shown a vigorous growth ever since Hubmaier and Glait led the movement (*c*1526). Hans Hut (*q.v.*), leaving Nikolsburg with Glait in early 1527, stopped in Vienna and held meetings (well known in Anabaptist history) at a house in the Kärntnerstrasse, where he is said to have baptized not less than fifty persons, among them Leonhard Schiemer (*q.v.*). Discovery of the group by the authorities forced Hut to flee and seems to have led to the final dissolution of this budding congregation. A well-advertised threat of the harshly Catholic Ferdinand to tear down houses which harbored Anabaptists was not carried out, and it is known that the inn "Freisinger Hof" actually had Anabaptist guests after this.

Apparently some of the Austerlitz (*q.v.*) Brethren, led by Jacob Wideman (q.v.), maintained a group in Vienna for a time, but little is known about them. However, Inquisition material shows that booksellers in Vienna were always in contact with Moravia and may have functioned as middlemen (DeWind). Hieronymus Käls, who was arrested with Michel Seifensieder and Hans Oberecker in Vienna on Jan. 8, 1536, while en route to his brethren in Tirol, reported in his second letter from prison, "We have learned that many pious Christian hearts have nobly testified the truth of the Lord here in Vienna, brothers and sisters." Among these was Jacob Wideman, whom Käls mentioned expressly as a martyr (1535). Leonhard Lochmaier (q.v.), likewise en route to Tirol from Moravia, was arrested with Jörg Fasser (q.v.) in Neudorf, south of Vienna, and brought to trial in Mödling near by, but they were soon miraculously freed. Oswald Glait was also arrested in Vienna in the fall of 1546, and having resisted all pressure to recant was drowned in the Danube at night. The last Anabaptist execution in Vienna was that of Hans Gurtzham in 1550.

A milder policy toward nonconformists came with the accession of Emperor Maximilian II in 1564, but this period soon came to an end when Jesuits settled in Vienna and with them the Counter Reformation set in. There is no further record of Anabaptists in Vienna, even not as transients.

After World War II numerous Mennonite refugees from Russia found their way to Austria through Rumania, Hungary, and Czechoslovakia, some of them (c400 at the peak) settling in Vienna, where a few were still living in 1958. The Mennonite Central Committee began relief work in Austria in September 1946, with headquarters in Vienna, ministering to the general population as well as to Mennonite refugees. In 1949 a headquarters house was secured and a spiritual ministry established which ultimately developed into a mission. The mission was fully organized with a pastor in 1957 under the Swiss Mennonite Conference with MCC financial support, and located in the MCC house at Cottagegasse 16, purchased in 1958. In 1959 the mission was transferred to the European Mennonite Evangelization Committee (EMEK).   LOSERTH, R.F.

J. D. Unruh, In the Name of Christ (Scottdale, 1952); Zieglschmid, Chronik; Beck, Geschichts-Bücher; Henry DeWind, "A 16th Century Description of Religious Sects in Austerlitz," MQR XXIX (1955) 45; ML IV.

Vierstra, a Mennonite family found at IJlst in Friesland, Netherlands, where some of its members served as deacons. Sieger Meintes Vierstra (1838-1915) was treasurer of the church for 25 years. Meinte Jans Vierstra (1862-1936), a member of the same family, served the Hindeloopen congregation for many years as a treasurer.   vDZ.

Viet Nam, a country in southeastern Asia formerly known as Indo-China. In 1957 two Mennonite agencies were working in this country. The Viet Nam Mennonite Mission (MC) was founded by the Eastern Mennonite Board of Missions and Charities in 1957. James and Arlene Stauffer and Everett and Margaret Metzler began language study in Saigon in 1957. The Mennonite Central Committee opened relief work in Viet Nam in 1954. The twelve relief workers on the field in 1957 were located at Banmethuot with the Leprosarie de Mission Evangélique and in Saigon.   M.G.

Viglius (Wigle) van Aytta, of Zwichem (1507-77), a learned nobleman of Friesland, Netherlands, a friend of Erasmus (q.v.), a Roman Catholic clergyman, ecclesiastical inspector for the bishop of Utrecht in the Dutch province of Groningen 1534-35, member of the (Spanish) Secret Court of Brussels, several times ambassador of Emperor Charles V, was a bitter opponent of heresy and especially of the Anabaptists. His letters contain some particulars about the Anabaptists after 1534.

A painted portrait which until the early 20th century was supposed to be a picture of Menno Simons (DB 1916, facing p. 33) probably represents Viglius van Aytta.   vDZ.

N.N.B.Wb. II, 46-52; Mellink, Wederdopers, 21, 258, 262, 329; Menn. Life III (1948) No. 3, p. 16; B. H. D. Hermersdorf, Wigle van Aytta van Zwichem (Leiden, 1914).

Vijf geestlicke Liedekens (Five Spiritual Songs) is a small hymnal published (Leiden, 1600) by Jan Theunisz (q.v.). It contains besides the five hymns mentioned in the title a number of other songs, ten of which bear the device "Jaecht nae't best," which was the device of Jan Theunisz himself. Most of these hymns were reprinted in Verscheyden (q.v.) Schriftuerlijcke Liedekens of 1603. (Yearbook Amstelodamum XXV, 1928, p. 109, No. 2.)   vDZ.

Vijg(h), a former Dutch Mennonite family, whose members were found in a number of congregations in the 17th and 18th centuries, e.g., Rotterdam, Brielle, and Amsterdam. A conservative branch of this family at Amsterdam were members of the Zonist (q.v.) church, but most of the Vijghs were rather liberal and frequented Collegiant meetings; Jacques Vijgh, e.g., a flax merchant of Rotterdam, was in 1729 baptized as a Mennonite by immersion. Dirk van Beek, a Mennonite minister of Rotterdam, administered this baptism at Schiedam. In the 18th century some Vijghs left the Mennonite Church, the liberals at Rotterdam and Amsterdam joining the Remonstrants and the conservatives of Amsterdam the Reformed Church.   vDZ.

Church records of Rotterdam and Amsterdam; DB 1909, 161; J. C. van Slee, De Rijnsburger Collegianten (Haarlem, 1895) passim.

Vijnken (Vyntgen) de Jonc(h)eere, an Anabaptist martyr, burned at the stake with her sisters Goudeken (q.v.) and Janneken de Joncheere and two other women on July 21, 1562, at Gent, Belgium. Vijnken, who was unmarried and 30 years of age, was born at Merendree in Flanders. These martyrs are commemorated in the hymn "Als men schreef duyst vijfhondert jaer ende twee en tsestich mede," found in the Lietboecxken. (Mart. Mir. D 289, E 759; Verheyden, Gent, 29, No. 91.)   vDZ.

Vilgard, an Anabaptist martyr: see **Marthin** of Vilgraten.

Vill, a village in the Adige Valley: see **Fill.**

Villa des Sapins: see **Valdoie.**

Villages (*Holländerdörfer*). Nowhere else have Mennonites developed a distinctive village pattern as did the Prusso-Russian group. To be sure, the Swiss Mennonites surviving as religious refugees in remote areas as pioneers on uncultivated land developed a pattern of settlement known as the *Hof*. In the Jura Mountains of Switzerland as well as in Alsace-Lorraine and the southern parts of Germany they became owners or renters of large farms and estates (*Höfe*), on which they established themselves in increasing numbers, developing some of them into small villages and hamlets. Some of the villages still indicate such an origin in the name ending in *hof* or *heim*. Among them are Spitalhof, Friedelsheim, Gerolsheim, Kriegsheim, Weierhof, Ibersheimerhof, and Kohlhof, all located in the Palatinate and Hesse. These places established and occupied originally by Swiss Mennonite refugees have in many instances grown to sizable villages or towns. Some are still primarily occupied by Mennonites, while in others the Mennonite population has become a minority. Today they reveal no peculiar Mennonite characteristics in the total pattern of the surrounding communities.

The Swiss Mennonites settling in Poland, Volhynia, and Galicia established some villages. In Poland they lived in Urszulin and Michelsdorf and in Volhynia in Eduardsdorf, Horodyszcze, Waldheim, Kotozufka, etc. These were the Swiss Volhynian Mennonites who later settled near Moundridge, Kan., and Freeman, S.D. The Swiss Galician Mennonites established the villages of Falkenstein, Einsiedel, Rosenberg, Rosenhof, Kiernica, Horozanna, Ehrenfeld, Dobrovlany, Podusilna, etc. Some of these were not villages in the sense of a closely knit unit. Even the closed villages were not always built according to a specific pattern. The early Galician villages of Falkenstein, Einsiedel, and Neuhof followed a specified plan. The others were mostly cluster villages (*Haufendörfer*). Most of these villages were occupied by the Mennonites for a limited time only. The Hutterite villages are described in the article **Bruderhof.** The Swiss and German Mennonites settling in Pennsylvania, Ohio, Indiana, and other states as a rule lived on individual farms, following the practice of their environment. One exception was Germantown (*q.v.*), Pa., founded in 1683, which was mixed Quaker and Mennonite and soon became a town.

The Mennonites of Prussia and Russia developed a unique pattern of villages during their colonization and settlement efforts, which was also transplanted to Manitoba, Mexico, and Paraguay. This pattern, although of Germanic background, includes some features based on the religio-cultural background and development of the Prusso-Russian Mennonites.

During the first half of the 16th century Dutch religious refugees settled at the mouth of the Vistula River in Prussia, mostly under Polish authorities. Their villages became known as "Holländerdörfer" or "Holländereien." These settlements established by a certain type of settlers under certain contracts with the lords and administered in a certain way became the nucleus or background of the Mennonite villages of Prussia, Poland, and Russia, which were later transplanted to Manitoba. They differed from the type prevailing along the Vistula River. The medieval colony village of the Vistula area was as a rule organized by a "locator" who functioned as Schulze (mayor), through whom a lease was obtained from the royal owners of the land, and who invited settlers from everywhere to till the land on long-term leases. The locator did not pay rent and his office was hereditary. Such a village was established in accordance with the "German right."

The villages established according to the "Dutch right" ("Holländisch Weis' und Gebrauch") functioned on a different basis. A group of settlers entered an agreement with the landowner. The lease agreements differed. The lease was usually for 40 years. The office of the Schulze was not hereditary. He was elected from the village community and had no special privileges; the government was democratic. Originally the occupants of these "Dutch" villages were actually primarily Dutch by background and to a large extent Mennonites. Later on the term "Holländerei" came to mean nothing more than a village and land rented and established on the basis of the "Dutch right." The occupants of such a "Dutch" village could come from any part of Europe and belong to any creed.

By 1772 there were some 400 Holländerdörfer established in the Vistula region, but not nearly all were occupied by Mennonites or by Dutch settlers. Felicia Szper (p. 110) lists for 1676 the following villages as "Holländische Hufen" in the two Werders of Marienburg occupied by Dutch Mennonites: Platenhof, Tiegenhagen, Tiegerweide, Reimerswalde, Orlofferfeld, Pletzgendorf, Orloff, Pietzgendorf, and Petershagenerfeld.

Horst Penner lists for the 18th century the following villages with a predominantly Mennonite population: Altebabke, Altendorf, Beyershorst, Blumen-Ort, Einlage, Freienhuben, Glabitsch, Gross-Plehnendorf, Gross-Walddorf, Halbstadt, Herrenhagen, Heubuden, Klein Mausdorf, Kozelicke, Ladekopp, Marienau, Neuendorf, Neunhuben, Orloff, Orlofferfelde, Petershagen, Pietzkendorf, Poppau, Pordenau, Reimerswalde, Rosenort, Rückenau, Scharfenberg, Schönhorst, Schönsee, Schmerblock, Schönau, Tiege, Tiegenhagen, Tiegerweide, and Wotzlaff.

The villages located on the Vistula were also characterized by being established in swampy areas which had to be drained. Ditches and canals led to the river at the elevated end of the land. Homes were located along the street, which at times followed the windings of the river. Villages established according to the old "German right" did not have the residence, barn, and shed under one roof, as did the Dutch villages, in which the barn was directly connected with the residence and the shed was attached to the barn, the whole in some cases forming a triangle. At some places the dwelling had an addition for the retired parents called *Endenkammer*. The porch added to this structure in many cases was of Prussian and not Dutch background.

In some instances the land of each farmer adjoined his yard. This would indicate that the pattern was related to the "Hufendörfer" practice. E. K. Francis classifies the Russian Mennonite pattern as a "Gewanndorf," which is characterized by the rotation of crops according to an established pattern. This was at times the case in Russia and also Manitoba. However, the Gewanndorf is a cluster of homes and farms, which the Mennonite village never was. The latter always followed a very symmetrical design, the houses being located in a straight line at regular intervals on one side or on both sides of the street. This village therefore more nearly resembled a Hufendorf. However, it developed peculiarities of its own. For this reason it is best to identify this type of village simply as Holländerdorf.

The Holländerdörfer established in the swampy regions of the Vistula Delta by Dutch Mennonites became the pattern not only for other settlers in that area, but were transplanted to entirely new and nonswampy locations in Poland and Russia. Naturally the environment somewhat modified the village pattern and practices. The low countries of the Netherlands and the Vistula areas were exchanged for the steppes of the Ukraine, where there was at times too little rainfall. Although the location of the villages was often chosen along rivers, such as the Dniepr or the Molotschna, the geographic and climatic conditions differed considerably. Hardly any dams had to be built to prevent flooding. The crops differed somewhat. The need for summer fallow made it necessary at times to adhere to an agreed-upon communal pattern of crop rotation.

The great genius and promoter of the uniform establishment of villages was Johann Cornies (q.v.), who as chairman of the Agricultural Association (q.v.) introduced some rigid rules for the layout of villages, exact location of each building in the village, the construction of the buildings, the planting of the shade trees and orchards in the yards, the maintenance of the village street, the location of the school, etc. During the first half of the 19th century a significant feature of the Russian Mennonite village pattern was the communal pasture for all cattle, sheep, and horses. As a rule, the village consisted of a wide unimproved main street with 20 to 40 homes and farmyards on each side. The land of the individual farmer at times adjoined his yard. This was not always the case; if the land surrounding the village was not all of the same quality, it was parceled out to give all the farmers equal shares of both the better and the poorer land. The farm usually consisted of approximately 160 acres. The community had a cowherd who in the early morning drove the cattle and other animals through the village to the community pasture. The village generally had a corral at one end where the horses not needed for farm labor were kept overnight. In the morning they joined the herd. During the hot noon hours the cattle rested at the village pond, creek, or river. The cowherd was usually a native Russian and lived near the corral.

The older villages as a rule consisted of farmers with full-sized farms (Vollwirte) who had originally purchased the land, some owners of half-size farms, and some "Anwohner" (q.v.). The Anwohner lived in a suburb of the village, which had yards and homes for people without land (see Landless). They were as a rule the landless younger generation working for the farmers or in small industry. They were also the candidates for the establishment of a new settlement whenever money and land for this purpose became available. The establishment of new settlements and villages gradually became the responsibility of the Mennonite authorities of the mother settlement. Some of these settlements consisted of only a few villages, while others had nearly as many as the Molotschna settlement, viz., 58 villages. With slight modifications these villages were patterned after those of the mother settlements in the Ukraine. In the early days of the settlement the buildings consisted of a frame of lumber and walls of adobe brick, with a roof of straw and later of shingles. As the settlers became more prosperous they replaced the early buildings with brick structures having a tile or tin roof. The architectural pattern of the house, residence, barn, and shed as a rule remained the same (see Architecture).

The administration of the villages and settlements was similar to that in Prussia, i.e., according to the "Dutch right." The Schulze and other members of the village assembly (Schulteboat) were elected by the voters of the village. Usually the village was administratively a part of the total Mennonite settlement which had an Oberschulze (q.v.) as the mayor. During the early 19th century the Mennonite settlers were not responsible to the local Russian authorities but to the Fürsorgekomitee (q.v.) established by the Russian government to supervise and administer all foreign settlements in Russia. Toward the end of the past century, the Mennonite administrations became responsible to their local Russian administrations (see Government Among Mennonites of Russia).

With few modifications this pattern of village settlement and administration was transplanted to Manitoba by the Old Colony (Chortitza), Fürstenland, and Bergthal Mennonites. The more progressive Bergthal and Kleine Gemeinde groups on the East Reserve provided a disintegrating element when they realized that living on one's own farm had some advantages over the traditional village pattern. Hence many villages were abandoned. The transfer of some of the Bergthal Mennonites to the West Reserve introduced this influence also among the Old Colony and Fürstenland Mennonites. This and the matter of self-administration vs the acceptance of the municipality system and the parochial vs public school system became the vital issues which caused numerous schisms and the ultimate emigration of the more conservative element among the Old Colony, Sommerfeld, and Bergthal Mennonites to Mexico and Paraguay after World Wars I and II. At the turn of the century the Manitoba Mennonites established daughter settlements in the areas of Hague and Swift Current, Sask. Here too, as in Mexico, Menno in the Chaco, and Villarrica in Paraguay, they established villages on the old pattern of Prussia and Russia. Lack of some building materials and adjustment to the Latin-American environment have caused some slight deviations, but basically the layout, architecture, and administration of the village have been maintained.

A very interesting element in the Mennonite practice of establishing villages in various parts of the world is the naming of these villages. As is evident from the village names of the Marienburg Werder, the names were German. The reason for the choice of German names by Dutch settlers may have been that they dealt with authorities and lords who spoke either German or Polish. Some of these German names such as Orloff (although originally very likely Slavic) and Tiege were transplanted to the Ukraine. However, because of the multiplicity of villages established in Russia, most of the names originated there. In the early decades the names were primarily German. Toward the end of the past century they received at times an official Russian name while the settlers themselves gave them German names with a very strong poetic flavor. At the beginning of the 20th century, Russian village names (or even numbers) were used. During the anti-German feeling of World War I many German names were replaced by Russian names. As a result of World War II practically all the names were made Russian.

It was in Russia that the practice of using the same names for villages or daughter settlements flourished, like the repetition of names of grandparents, uncles, and aunts in a newly established family. Certain of these names in the daughter settlements of Russia, Canada, and South America were particularly popular. New combinations appeared. The popularity of names containing "Blume," "Frieden," "Rose," "Schön," or "Wald" reveals that the hard-working Mennonite farmers liked to give their villages poetic names. A new element was added in Russia when they began to name their villages after the czars. Many appendices were added to names such as Alexander and Nicholas (Nikolai). High officials were memorialized in names like Köppental, Konteniusfeld, and Hahnsau. In some instances the villages were named for the Russian noble from whom the land was purchased for the establishment of a daughter settlement.

The Manitoba Mennonites, who were primarily of the Chortitza or Old Colony background in Russia, used a considerable number of names of the villages from which they came, including some found in the Molotschna settlement. It is here that old forms are used to create new names through new combinations. Hardly an English name appears in the 110 villages established in the West and East Reserves. Sometimes the same names are used in both Reserves. The Manitoba names were transplanted to the Swift Current and Hague settlements in Saskatchewan and to the settlements in Mexico and Paraguay. Some of the same names are used in the three (Manitoba, Swift Current, and Durango) settlements of Mexico. It is likely that the village assembly decided on the name. If the majority of the settlers came from one village, they simply agreed to use the same old name. At times the prefix *Neu* (new) was used, e.g., Neu-Schönwiese or Neu-Bergthal.

Some of the Mennonites of the Molotschna settlement who came to the prairie states in and after 1874 made an attempt to perpetuate the village pattern of Russia and Prussia. The Krimmer Men-

nonite Brethren established the village Gnadenau (*q.v.*) at Marion, Kan., and the Alexanderwohl congregation settled originally in seven villages north of Newton. Also the conservative Kleine Gemeinde members of Jansen, Neb., settled in villages. But aside from these hardly any attempts were made to establish villages. The reason for this may be that the Molotschna Mennonites, being more progressive, were inclined to recognize and adopt the good practices of the new country. Although they had asked to have compact areas set aside in order to be able to establish their traditional settlements, they were not granted this privilege. The East and West Reserves were the Canadian answer to this request for the Old Colony Mennonites. As a rule the Mennonites in the prairie states had to be satisfied with the opportunity to purchase alternate sections of land along the railroads such as the Santa Fe and the Burlington. This made it difficult for them to establish compact settlements, and even more so to realize the old traditional village pattern with self-government. The few villages actually established soon disintegrated. However, driving along Highway 15 from Newton to Lehigh or Hillsboro, one can still see remnants of the villages of the Alexanderwohl community near Goessel. To be sure, there are Mennonite towns such as Goessel, Lehigh, Hillsboro, Moundridge, and Elbing in Kansas; Meno in Oklahoma; Henderson and Jansen in Nebraska; Mountain Lake in Minnesota; and Freeman in South Dakota; but they were not established according to the traditional pattern and cannot really be classified as Holländerdörfer. They are typical American towns of the prairie states.

On the following pages a list of Mennonite villages established in Prussia, Russia, Canada, the United States, Mexico, and Paraguay is given. This constitutes the first attempt to list in alphabetical order all Mennonite villages of Prusso-Russian background which could be classified as Holländerdörfer. Only the major Prussian villages of the Marienburg Werder are listed. Various sources were used, some of which conflicted. The list makes, therefore, no claim to completeness or to full accuracy. No attempt has been made to state which villages are still in existence and which have disappeared. The major point is to show how large a number of villages was established and how frequently the names were repeated by pioneers who generation after generation continued their journeys as "pilgrims and strangers."

Not all of the later villages in Russia which were given Russian names are listed. Numerous villages in Russia have doubtless been destroyed and very few are at the present occupied by Mennonites. Of the more than 100 Mennonite villages established on the East and West Reserves of Manitoba, only a small number have survived. This is the case particularly on the East Reserve. The traditional village life continues with a minimum of disturbance from the outside among the Old Colony Mennonites of Mexico and in some of the settlements in Paraguay.

The following list indicates how often the names were repeated in the various settlements. Only those which appear more than five times are listed.

Frequency of Names

13 Chortitza
11 Blumenort, Grünfeld, Orloff, Reinfeld, Schönau
9 Gnadenfeld, Gnadenthal, Hochfeld, Schönthal, Rosenort, Rosenfeld
8 Kleefeld, Neuanlage, Nikolaifeld, Reinland, Rosenthal, Schönfeld
7 Blumenhof, Blumenthal, Grünweide, Grünthal, Halbstadt, Neuhoffnung, Neuhorst, Rosenhof, Schönwiese, Silberfeld, Waldheim
6 Alexandrovka, Blumenfeld, Friedensfeld, Hamburg (Hamberg), Hochstädt, Lichtfelde, Neuendorf, Nikolayevka, Osterwick
5 Altona (Altenau), Bergthal, Blumstein, Kronsthal, Landskrone, Lindenau, Reinthal, Rosengart, Rudnerweide, Sommerfeld, Tiege

In order to identify the settlements in which the villages occurred the key to the symbols, "Mennonite Settlements," which follows the list of villages, should be used.

MENNONITE VILLAGE NAMES
(Holländerdörfer)

In Prussia, Russia, Canada, United States, Mexico, Paraguay

(This is a nearly complete list. Symbols indicate settlements. For key see next section.)

Adelsheim (Dolinovka)—Ch
Ak Metchet (Central Asia)
Aktatch—Te
Alexanderfeld (Grishevka)—Ku
Alexanderkron(e)—Mo, Sl
Alexandertal—Mo, Fü, Al
Alexanderwohl—Mo
Alexandrovka—Me, Te, Sl, Om, Kuz, Da
Alexeyevka—Ig, Om
Alexeyfeld—Sl
Alfneu—MC
Aliesova—Or
Altenau (Altona)—Pr, Mo, Az, MER, MWR
Ananyevka—Sl
Andreasfeld (Ukraine 1870, one village)
Andreyevka: see Gnadenthal
Anna—Sad
Anneskoye—Na
Arrival—Su
Auhagen—PN

Baragan—Cr
Belo Berezevo—A
Berezovka-Udrak—Da
Berezovka—Sl
Bergfeld—MER, MWR, PM
Bergthal—Be, MER, MWR, MC (twice)
Blumenfeld—Bo, Br, KA, Ne, Da, MC
Blumengart—Ch, MER, MWR, PM
Blumenheim—Br, SH, MC
Blumenhof—Bo, MER, MWR, SSC, MC, MD, PFe
Blumenort—Mo, KA, Sl, A, MER, MWR, SSC, NJ, MC, MD, PFe
Blumenstein (Blumstein)—Pr, Mo, MER, MWR, MC
Blumenthal—MWR, Sh, MG (twice), Me, PM, PFe
Bodanovka—A
Bogomazov—NS
Borissopol—Ar
Borissovka—Pa
Brunnenthal—PM
Burwalde (Baburka)—Pr, MFe, MWR, MC

Central (Zentral)—PFr
Choroshoye—Sl
Chortitz(a)—Ch (twice), Ba, Or, Sl, MER, MWR, SH, SSC, MC, PM, PN, PVB

Deyevka—Or
Dmitrovka—Ar
Dobrovka—Or
Dolinovka—Or, Sl
Domninskoye—Pa
Donskoye—NS

Ebenfeld (Rovnopol)—Bo, Sl, Pa, MER
Edenberg—MWR, Sh
Edenthal—MC, PM
Eichenbach—MC
Eichenfeld (Dubovka)—Mill, A
Eichengrund—MWR
Eichenthal—MC
Eigengrund—MER, PM
Eigenhof—MER, PM
Einlage (Kitchkas)—Ch, NWR, MC, PN
Ekaterinovka—Mi, Eg, Sl
Elenovka—Ma, Mill
Elisabettal—Mo
Emmathal—KA
Eugenfeld (near Alexandrovsk, Ukraine, one village)

Felsenbach—Bo
Felsenthal—MC
Feodorovka—Or
Fernheim—MC
Filadelfia—PFe
Fischau—Pr, Mo
Franzfeld (Varvarovka)—Mill
Franzthal—Mo
Fresenheim—At
Friedensdorf—Mo
Friedensfeld—Sl, Om, Mir, A, PM, PFe
Friedensheim—PN, Pv
Friedensruh—Mo, MWR, MC, MFe
Friedrichstal—Be, MER
Fürstenau—Pr, Mo
Fürstenwerder—Pr, Mo, PV

Gelbbrunn—PM
Georgstal—Fü
Gerhardsthal—Tch
Gnadenfeld—Mo, Au, Sl, A, KA, MER, MWR, MC, PM
Gnadenheim—Mo, Sl, Pm, PFe
Gnadenthal—Mo, Ba, Au, Al, KA, MWR, SSC, MC, PN
Gortchakovo—Da
Greenfarm—MWR
Grigoryevka—Na, Sl
Gronau—PN
Grossweide—Pr, Mo, MWR, MC, PM, PN, PFr
Grossfürstental—Su
Grotsfeld (Krotovka)—Al
Grünewald—PV
Grünfeld—Sh, Ba, A, KA, Mer, Sh, MC, (twice), MD, PM
Grünland—MC
Grünthal—MER, MWR, Sh, MC (twice), MD, PM
Grünweide—MWR

Hahnsau—At
Halbstadt—Pr, Mo, Sl, MWR, MC, PM, PN
Hamburg (Hamberg)—Mo, Bo, Om, MER, MWR, MC
Heimstätte—PN
Heuboden—Pr, Be, MER, MWR, NJ, MC, PM
Hierschau—No
Hildesheim—PV
Hochfeld—Mill, KA, MER, MWR, Sh, MC, MD, Pm, PVB
Hochstädt—Sl, MER, Sh, MC, MD, PM
Hochtal—MC
Hoffnungsau—MC
Hoffnungsfeld—MWR, MC
Hoffnungsort—Bo
Hoffnungsthal—MC
Hohenau—PM, PFe
Hohendorf—AT, Au

Ignatyevo—Ig
Insel Chortitza—Ch
Ivangorod—Mill
Ivanovka—Sl, Om

Kalinovo—Me
Kamenka—Or
Kameshevoye—Or
Kameshlak—Te
Kamenets—NS
Kantserovka—Or
Karaguy—Or
Karambash—Da
Karasan—Cr

Karathal—Sl
Karlsruhe—PFe
Karpovka—Me
Kirchheim—PV
Kitchkas—Or
Kleefeld—Mo, Sl, A, MER, MWR, MC, PM, PFe
Kleinstädt—MWR, PM
Klippenfeld—Mo
Klubnikovo—Or
Koltan—NS
Kondratyevka—Bor
Konteniusfeld—Mo
Konstantinovka—Le, Pa
Köppental—AT, Au
Korneyevka—Me
Kornishheim—Pa
Kotlyarevka—Me
Krasnovka—Al
Krassikovo—NS
Kronsfeld—Sh, MWR, MC, PN
Kronsgarten (Kronsgart)—Ch, MER, MWR
Kronsthal (Kolinsk)—Ch, NS, MER, MWR, Sh
Kubanka—Or
Kulikovo—Da
Kuterla—NS

Ladekopp—Pr, Mo
Landskron(e)—Mo, Sl, MER, PFe, PFr
Laubenheim—PM
Lavarov—Su
Leonidovka—Ig, Ar
Lichtenau—Mo, MER, PN
Lichtfelde (Lichterfelde)—Pr, Sl, MWR, MC, Pfe, PV
Lidyevka—Ar
Liebenau—Pr, Mo
Liebental (Lyubimovka)—Al
Lindenau—Pr, Mo, AT, MWR, PM
Lyessovka—Me
Lyubomirovka—Bor
Loshkarevo—Ol
Lugovsk—NS
Lustigstal—Cr
Lystanderhöh—AT

Margenau—Mo, Om
Marianovka (Maryanovka)—Me, Te, Ar
Mariawohl—Mo
Marienthal (Maryevka)—Mo, Al, Pv
Markovka—Sl
Maslyanovka—Om
Medenthal—AT
Memrik—Me, A
Michailovka—Me
Michailsburg—Fu
Miloradovka—Mi, Pa
Miropol—Ol
Montanay—Cr
Morgenthal—MC
Müdelburg—Te
Münsterberg—Mo
Muntau—Pr, Mo
Muravyovka—Al

Nadarovka—Pa
Natashino—Pa
Neuanlage—NJ, MER, MWR, Sh, MC (twice), MD, PM
Neu-Chortitza—Ba (see Chortitza)
Neuenburg (Malashovka)—Ch, MER, MWR, MC
Neuendorf (Neudorf)—Ch, MER, MWR, SSC, MC, PN
Neuheim—Ba, PN
Neuhof—MC, PN
Neuhoffnung (Nadezhdino)—Al, MWR, MER, MC, MD, PM, PVS
Neuhorst—Ch, MER, MWR, Sh, MC, MD, PN
Neukirch—Mo
Neumöln—PM
Neurecht—MC
Neustädt—MC, MD
New York—Ig, A
Nikolaidorf—Mo, Sl
Nikolaifeld—Za, Au, Bor, Su, Sl, Om, Mill, PN
Nikolaithal—Bo
Nikolayevka—Me, Ig, Or, Te, Tr, Sl
Nordthal—MC
Novo-Stepnoye—Sam

Olgafeld—Fü, Sh, MC
Olgino—Ol, Pa
Orbelyanovka—Tem
Orechov—A
Orloff (Ohrloff, Orlovka, Orlovo)—Pr, Mo, AT, Al, Za, Au, Me, Sl, Om, PFe
Ostenfelde—AT
Osterwick—Ch, MER, MWR, Sh, MC, PM
Ostheim—T

Pastwa—Pr, Mo, MER
Paulsheim—Mo
Pessotchnoye—Bez
Petersdorf (Nadezhdovka)—Mill
Petershagen—Pr, Mo
Petrovka—Na, Or
Pleshanovo—NS
Podolsk—NS
Pordenau—Pr, Mo
Prangenau—Pr, Mo
Pretoria—Or, Te
Pribrezhnoye—A
Protessovo—Sl
Putchkovo—Om

Rayevka—Pa
Rebrovka—Pa
Reichenbach—MER, PM
Reinfeld (Rheinfeld)—Pa, Mill, MER, MWR, Sh, SSC, MC, MD, PM, A
Reinland—Pr, MWR, Sh, SSC, MC (twice), PM, PVS
Reinthal—Ch, MWR, MC, PM, PVS
Rio Verde—PM
Rodnitchnoye—Or
Rohrbach—Te
Romanovka—Au, Ig, Or, Ol
Rosenbach—Fü, SSC
Rosenberg—PV
Rosenfeld (Tchistopol)—Sl, MER, MWR, NJ, Sh, SSC, MC, MD, PVB
Rosengart (Novoslobodka)—Ch, NR, MER, MWR, MC
Rosenheim—Da, MC, PM
Rosenhof—Br, Sl, NJ, MWR, SSC, MC, PM
Rosenort—Pr, Mo, NJ, MWR, SSC, MC, MD, PFe, PV
Rosenthal (Kantserovka)—Ch, MER, MWR, NJ, A, MC, MD, PFe
Rosenwald—Sl, OM, MWR
Rovnopol: see Ebenfeld
Rozovka—Min
Rückenau—Pr, PFr
Rudnerweide—Pr, Mo, MWR, MC, PM
Ryskovo—Sam

Samoylovka—Sam
Sandhorst—PN
Saratova—Sl
Sarona—Cr
Schanzenberg—MER
Schanzenfeld—MWR, SSC, MC
Schönau—Pr, Mo, Al, Sl, Min, NER, MWR, MC, PM, PFe
Schönbrunn—PM, PFe
Schöndorf—Bo, MWR, MC
Schöneberg (Smolyanaya)—Ch, MER, MWR
Schönfeld (Krasnopol)—Br, Be, MER, MWR, SSC, MC, MD, PM
Schönhorst (Vodyanaya)—Pr, Ch, MER, MWR
Schönwiese—Ch, MER, MWR, SSC, PM, PFe, PVS
Schönsee—Pr, Mo. Za, MER, Sl, A, PVS
Schönthal—Be, MER, MWR, Sl, MC (twice), MD, PM, PN
Schönwalde—PV
Sergeyevka—Fü, Sl
Shestakovo—Sam
Shumanovka—A
Silberfeld—MER, MWR, MC, MD, PVB, Sl, A
Silberthal—MC
Smolyanovka—Om
Soborovka—Pa
Sofiyevka—Pa
Sommerfeld—MER, MWR, MC, PM, PVS
Sparrau—Pr, Mo
Spat—Cr
Springfeld (Springfield)—KA, SSC
Springstein—MC

Springthal—MC
Steinau (Starozavodskoye)—Bo, Ne
Steinbach—Bo, NER, MC, PM
Steinfeld (Kamenopol)—Mo, Sh, PN
Steinreich—MC
Stepanovka—Or
Strassberg—MER, PN
Sulak—Te
Suvorovka—Or, Sl

Talheim—MC
Talma—Te
Taranovka—Te
Tatyanovka—Sl
Tcherno-Ozernoye—Or
Tchernov—Sl
Tcheryevka—Sl
Tchukreyevka—Om
Tchistopol—Pa
Tempelhof—Tem
Thalbach—MC
Tiefenbrunn—PV
Tiege—Pr, Mo, Az, Sl, PN
Tiegenhagen—Pr, Mo
Tiegerweide—Pr, Mo, Om
Tukulchak—Cr

Valuyevka—AF
Vassilyevka—Na
Vladimirovka—Ar
Vollwerk—MER, PM
Voloyevka—Tr
Vyazemskoye—Ar

Waldeck—PB
Waldheim—Mo, MWR, MC, PM, PFr, PV, PVS
Waldhof—PN
Waldhorst—PV
Waldreich—MC
Waldsruh—PFe, PV
Wanderloh—Te
Weidefeld (Weidenfeld)—MWR, MC, PM, PVB
Wernersdorf—Pr, Mo
Wiesenfeld (single village in Ukraine)—Sl, MC, PFe
Wiesenheim—MC, PM
Wohldemfürst—Ku
Wüstenfelde—PFe

Yurgino—A
Yurmankey—Da

Zabangagul—Or
Zelenoye—Or
Zentral (see Central)

The total number of villages of Prusso-Russian Mennonite settlements following the pattern of the Holländerdörfer is 769. The largest number was located in Russia. The total number of the alphabetical list of "Mennonite Village Names" is 327. The total number of villages including those duplicated in this list is 773. On one hand, this is not a complete list of villages established (the total would probably approach 1,000). On the other hand, not all villages are in existence any more and by far not all villages in existence are occupied by Mennonites today. Nevertheless, this study illustrates a very significant phase of the spread of Mennonites and the socio-economic pattern of their life with a unique religious and cultural background.   C.K.

Gerhard Hein, "The Development of the Mennonite Hof of the 17th Century, Palatinate into the Mennonite Church of Pfalz-Rheinland Today," *MQR* XXIX (1955) 188-96; *idem*, "Wie aus den Mennonitenhöfen der Kurpfalz im 17. Jahrhundert die Mennonitengemeinden in Pfalz-Rheinland von heute wurden," *Der Mennonit* (September 1954) 132; "Dorf," *Der Grosse Brockhaus* (Wiesbaden, 1953) 326; Horst Penner, *Ansiedlung mennonitischer Niederländer im Weichselmündungsgebiet* . . . (Weierhof, 1940); Peter Bachmann, *Mennoniten in Kleinpolen* (Lemberg, 1934); J. W. Fretz, *Pilgrims in Paraguay* (Scottdale, 1953); C. A. Dawson, *Group Settlement, Ethnic Communities in Western Canada* (To-

MENNONITE SETTLEMENTS CONSISTING OF VILLAGES
(Holländerdörfer)

Prussia, Russia, Canada, United States, Mexico, Paraguay

Key to Symbols
(As a rule only the settlements consisting of more than one village are included. Number of villages, year of founding, and abbreviation of name or symbol are given.)

Settlement	Number of Villages	Year of Founding	Symbol
Amur, Siberia	20	1927	A
Alt-Samara (Alexandertal)	8	1861	Al
Am Trakt, Samara	10	1853	AT
Arkadak, Saratov	7	1910	Ar
Auli-Ata, Central Asia	6	1889	Au
Baratov, Ukraine	2	1879	Ba
Barnaul, see Slavgorod			
Bergthal, Ukraine	5	1836	Be
Bezenchuk, Samara	1	1897	Bez
Borozenko, Ukraine	7	1865	Bo
Borrissovo, Ukraine	3	1892	Bor
Brazol (Schönfeld), Ukraine	4	1868	Br
Chortitza, Ukraine	18	1789	Ch
Crimea, Ukraine	25	1862	Cr
Davlekanovo, Ufa	5	1894	Da
Fürstenland, Ukraine	6	1864	Fü
Ignatyevo, Ukraine	7	1889	Ig
Kansas, Alexanderwohl	8	1874	KA
Kuban, Caucasus	2	1863	Ku
Kuzmitsky, Ukraine	1	18?	Kuz
Manitoba, East Reserve	54	1874	MER
Manitoba, West Reserve	56	1875	MWR
Memrik, Ukraine	10	1885	Me
Mexico, Cuauhtemoc	96	1926	MC
Mexico, Durango	16	1927	MD
Millerovo, Don area	5	19?	Mill
Miloradovka, Ukraine	2	1889	Mi
Minusinsk, Siberia	2	1913	Min
Miropol, Ukraine	1	1867	Mir
Molotschna, Ukraine	56	1804	Mo
Naumenko, Ukraine	4	1890	Na
Nebraska, Jansen, U.S.A.	7	1874	NJ
Nepluyevka, Ukraine	2	1870	Ne
Neu-Rosengart, Ukraine	2	1878	NR
Neu-Samara, Samara	12	1890	NS
Olgino, Caucasus	4	1895	Ol
Omsk, Siberia	11	1899	Om
Orenburg (Deyevka)	23	1894	Or
Paraguay, Fernheim	21	1930	PFe
Paraguay, Friesland	9	1937	PFr
Paraguay, Menno	26	1928	PM
Paraguay, Neuland	24	1947	PN
Paraguay, Volendam	16	1947	PV
Paraguay, Villarrica, Bergfeld	7	1948	PVB
Paraguay, Villarrica, Sommerfeld	9	1948	PVS
Pavlodar, Siberia	13	19?	Pa
Prussia, Marienburg Werder		16?	Pr
Rovnopol, Samara	1	1903	Ro
Sadovaya, Voronezh	1	1909	Sad
Samoylovka, Ukraine	4	1888	Sam
Saskatchewan, Hague	17	1894	SH
Saskatchewan, Swift Current	15	1905	SSC
Shlachtin, Ukraine	2	1874	Sh
Slavgorod (Barnaul), Siberia	58	1909	Sl
Suvorovka, Caucasas	4	1894	Su
Terek, Caucasus	13	1901	Te
Tempelhof, Caucasus	2	1868	Tem
Tchornoglas, Ukraine	1	1860	Tch
Trubetskoye, Ukraine	2	1904	Tr
Yazekovo (Nikolaipol), Ukraine	8	1869	Ya
Zagradovka, Ukraine	5	1871	Za
Zentral, Voronezh	1	1909	Ze

769

ronto, 1936); Heinz Lehmann, *Das Deutschtum in West-kanada* (Berlin, 1939); Unruh, *Hintergründe;* E. K. Francis, *In Search of Utopia* (Altona, 1955); Felicia Szper, *Nederlandsche nederzettingen in West-Pruisen gedurende den Poolschen tijd* (Enkhuizen, 1913); E. Keyser, *De Nederlanden en het Weichselland* (Naarden, 1942); H. E. Wolfram, *Die Niederlande und der Deutsche Osten* (Berlin, 1943); "Alexanderwohl Villages in Kansas, 1874," *Menn. Life* IV (October 1949); Walter Schmiedehaus, "Mennonite Life in Mexico," *Menn. Life* II (April 1947); Elisabeth Peters, "Life in a Mennonite Village," *Menn. Life* XI (July 1956); Jacob Quiring, *Die Mundart von Chortitza in Süd-Russland* (Munich, 1928); *Gedenkfeier der Mennonitischen Einwanderung in Manitoba Canada* (Steinbach, 1949); Walter Schmiedehaus, *Ein feste Burg ist unser Gott* (Cuauhtemoc, 1948); Zdzislaw Ludkiewicz, *Osady Holenderskie na nizinie Sartawicko-Nowskiej* (Torun, 1934); *Die Mennoniten-Gemeinden in Russland* (Heilbronn, 1921); Herbert Wiebe, *Das Siedlungswerk niederländischer Mennoniten im Weichseltal . . .* (Marburg, 1952); J. Driediger, "Farming Among the Mennonites in West and East Prussia," *MQR* XXXI (1957) 16-21.

Village Chapel Evangelical Mennonite Brethren Mission, unorganized, was opened in Orange Cove, Cal., with 16 Sunday-school pupils on July 22, 1945. The city then had a population of 2,500. As the population increased to 5,000, attendance increased to 98. Gerhardt T. Thiessen served two years as pastor. In 1949 the population of the town began to decline, and the attendance at the mission with it. In all about 150 professed conversion, but because of constant migration only five were baptized. Leonard Wiebe was the pastor in 1955.   G.T.T.

Villarrica, a Paraguayan town some 120 miles southeast of Asunción, in the area of which Old Colony Mennonites settled in 1948, who like the first Mennonite settlers in Paraguay, i.e., the Menno Colony in the Gran Chaco founded in 1926, also came from Canada. The group at Villarrica numbered 1,644; 740 came from the East Reserve on the Red River in southern Manitoba, 764 came from the West Reserve on the same river, while another 140 came from Saskatchewan. The East Reserve group purchased 27,500 acres, largely of primitive forest land, about 65 miles east of Villarica, and settled in 7 villages with Chortitz as the administrative, trade, and industrial center. The remainder of the group of immigrants founded the colony of Sommerfeld some 15 miles from Bergthal, settling on 85,000 acres of forest land which they purchased at about $3.00 per acre. Here nine villages were built; one of these, also named Sommerfeld, became the trade, industrial, and administrative center.

All the settlers of both these colonies, like the earlier immigrants from Canada, came to Paraguay hoping that it would here be easier for them to preserve their spiritual heritage, the German language (though in everyday life only Plattdeutsch is spoken), and their traditional, rural way of life. All of these they thought were threatened in Canada, with the young people leaving the farms for the city, availing themselves of higher education, and in many instances joining the military forces. The village life, church, and school in the new homeland were arranged according to the traditionally conservative pattern of their forefathers as these settled in Russia in the 1780's and again in Canada in the 1870's. Colony affairs are voted upon by the group,

the ministers are elected from the ranks of the laymen, and teachers for the schools are also laymen able and willing to teach the "three R's." No higher education is provided for, and men rely on reading the Bible which also serves as textbook at school, periodicals—mostly religious journals edited by sister denominations, or farm journals, or the radio for widening their horizons. However, the making of a livelihood in the new homeland calls for considerable adapting. The once proud wheat farmers and "mixed" farmers of the Russian steppes and the Canadian prairies are here truck farmers, gardeners, raising kaffir corn, maize, peanuts, mandioca, and citrus fruits; they become "rancheros" raising the scrub but hardy cattle adapted to the tropics; or they cut, dress, and sell what useful timbers can be found in their forests, mostly lapacho and cedar. Or, lacking the means to start on their own, they are reduced to cowhands and wage earners. Paraguayan conditions, lacking markets and marketing facilities as well as natural resources, do not provide opportunities for much diversification and expansion, nor are economic and political conditions stable enough to encourage it. For this reason about one third of the immigrants that came in 1948 have returned to Canada.   J.W.N.

W. Quiring, *Im Schweisse deines Angesichts* (Steinbach, 1953) 79-102; *Mitteilungen, Inst. für Auslandsbeziehungen,* November-December 1954, 302-3 (Stuttgart, Germany); J. W. Fretz, *Pilgrims in Paraguay* (Scottdale, 1953) 9, 48, 153 ff.

Villegas (Argentina) Mennonite Church (MC) is located in the city of Villegas (pop. 7,000) on the Ferro Carril Oeste (main line of the Western Railroad), seat of the County of Villegas, in the Province of Buenos Aires, Argentina. The evangelical work in this town was begun by the Christian and Missionary Alliance, but because of scarcity of workers they had practically abandoned the town. Because it was near the town of America, where the Mennonites had been working, they exchanged their work established in Maza for this city in February 1941, and in the next month T. H. Brenneman and his family moved there to start the work anew. The congregation was organized in April 1942. The membership in 1957 was 16. The following pastors have served at Villegas: T. H. Brenneman 1941-45; Pedro Lanik, student pastor, 1945-46; Rogelio Perugorría, graduate of the Mennonite Bible Institute of Bragado, 1947-52; Alberto Ens 1953-54; Heriberto Palomeque 1954-55; Lawrence Brunk 1956-58; and Aladino Scorza 1959-.   E.V.S.

J. W. Shank et al., *The Gospel Under the Southern Cross* (Scottdale, 1943) 74 f., 195; *Minutes of the Twenty-first Convention of the Argentine Mennonite Church* (1947).

Villers-le-Château, a former Mennonite congregation near Châlons-sur-Marne, France, which died out in the 19th century. (*Almanach Menn. du Cinquantenaire* 1901-1951, 35.)

Villgraten: see **Mart(h)in** of Vilgraten.

Vilna: see **Wilna.**

Vincent Dircxzoon, an Anabaptist martyr, executed on Nov. 29, 1555, at Leeuwarden in Friesland, Netherlands. He was a tailor of IJlst (*q.v.*). Further particulars are lacking. His name and the date of his execution are found on a memorial table in the Mennonite church of IJlst.	vdZ.

Vincent van der Hoeve: see **Hoeve, van der.**

Vincent de Hondtsvolk, followers of Vincent de Hondt (*q.v.*), an elder of Haarlem, also called Dantzigers, who separated from the Flemish Mennonites and from c1620 assembled in the meetinghouse "Het Goudgrendeltje" on the Smallegracht, Haarlem, until they merged with the Heiligland (Flemish) congregation c1782. An attempt in 1633 to merge with the Old Flemish church miscarried. (Kühler, *Geschiedenis* II, 197.)	vdZ.

Vincent Mennonite Church (MC), located in East Vincent Twp., Chester Co., Pa., a member of the Franconia Conference, was probably established in 1735. In 1798 John and Catherine Rhoades conveyed two acres of land to representatives of the congregation, and for a long time the meetinghouse was called the Rhoades Church. This meetinghouse was remodeled in 1858, and razed in 1889 when a new church, 35 x 55 ft., was built. The Vincent congregation was small. It is claimed that the steep-pitched roof (making it appear more churchlike than most Mennonite meetinghouses) was built to facilitate the sale of the church in case the congregation died out. Sunday school and the English language were both adopted well in advance of the rest of the Franconia Conference congregations, and these two changes probably prevented the death of the church. The ministers of the congregation in 1958 were Amos Kolb, bishop, and Matthew Kolb and Jacob F. Kolb, preachers, with a membership of 152.	J.C.W.

J. C. Wenger, *History of the Mennonites of the Franconia Conference* (Telford, 1937) 112-16.

Vincente Adriaensdochter, an Anabaptist martyr, drowned at Delft, Holland, on Jan. 24, 1539, with three other women. She is probably the same person as the Vincente Adriaens from Naaldwijk, who had attended a meeting held in her home town in 1536. Vincente was apparently an adherent of David (*q.v.*) Joris. (*Inv. Arch. Amst.* I, No. 749; Mellink, *Wederdopers*, 204, 220 f.)	vdZ.

Vinck, Otto, an estate steward at Wesel (*q.v.*) in Rhineland, Germany, in whose house Henric (*q.v.*) Rol administered baptism in February or early March 1534; among the persons then baptized was Vinck himself. Jan (*q.v.*) van Geelen visited him in December 1534 or January 1535. On Jan. 18, 1535, Vinck, who was an instrument of the revolutionary leaders at Münster (*q.v.*), was arrested, being charged with an attempt to create a revolt at Wesel. On April 13, 1535, he was beheaded. The question whether his activity was connected with the expectation of many Dutch Anabaptists that Wesel would be "the new Zion," is still to be studied. (Mellink, *Wederdopers.*)	vdZ.

Vine Press was a printed, bimonthly, four-page 7 x 8½ in. paper sponsored by the Middle District Conference (GCM) Young People's Union begun in December 1936 by Inda Sprunger. This English periodical, circulation 650 copies, was sent to churches and Bluffton College for distribution. It was discontinued in 1957 in favor of the Youth Page in the *Central District Reporter* after the merger of the Middle and Central district conferences.	O.A.K.

Vineland, a village in Lincoln County, Ont., the heart of the fruit-growing belt of the Niagara Peninsula, the site of the oldest existing (not the first) settlement of Mennonites in Ontario, and the first organized Mennonite church, founded in 1801. The settlement is historically known as the Twenty, taking its name from the Twenty Mile Creek, about 20 miles from Niagara Falls. The first settlers arrived about 1786 from Pennsylvania, with a large number coming from Bucks County, Pa., in 1800-1. The church here suffered three serious schisms during the latter half of the century, giving birth to the Mennonite Brethren in Christ congregation about 1875, and the Wisler Church, now extinct, in 1889. The membership in 1959 was 68; it is an M.C. congregation.

Two congregations of Russian Mennonites have been established in the village following the immigration of 1922-23. The United Mennonite Church, organized in 1936, has a membership of over 340, and the Mennonite Brethren, organized in 1935, a membership of 270. A large percentage of the members are fruit-growers, with an increasing number finding employment in near-by cities. Bethesda Home, a mental hospital operated by the Mennonite Brethren Conference, is located about two miles southwest of the village. A home for the aged was erected in the village in 1955 by the United Mennonite churches of the area. (See **Twenty.**)	B.C.

Vineland (Ont.) **First** Mennonite Church (MC), until 1956 known as the Moyer Mennonite Church (*q.v.*).

Vineland (Ont.) Mennonite Brethren Church, a member of the Canadian M.B. Conference, was organized on Nov. 20, 1932, under the leadership of D. Klassen. The first meeting place was a rented implement shed, where services were held with the members of the United Mennonite Church. All of the original members were immigrants from Russia. Later the building was bought by the Mennonite Brethren Church and converted into an attractive church building, like a tabernacle in appearance. Ministers who have served the congregation are D. Klassen, J. F. Dick, G. Matthies, B. B. Boldt, I. Ewert, P. F. Goertzen, J. K. Janzen, D. M. Thielman, A. A. Froese, Peter Mandtler, Henry Wiebe, and A. G. Wall who is still (1957) serving as pastor, with a membership of 250.	H.H.J.

Vineland (N.J.) **Training School** was the location of Civilian Public Service Unit No. 92 from March 28, 1943, to June 14, 1946. The unit, operated by the Mennonite Central Committee, consisted of 16 men in 1945, who did maintenance and farm work as well as serving as orderlies and attendants. The school had a population of 550 mentally deficient children. (M. Gingerich, *Service for Peace*, Akron, 1949, pp. 237 f.)	M.G.

Vineland (Ont.) United Mennonite Church (GCM), a member of the Conference of Mennonites in Canada, was formed by Mennonites who arrived from Russia in 1924-26 and later, who at first worshiped in an old abandoned sawmill. In 1927 they joined the United Mennonite Church in Ontario under the leadership of Bishop J. H. Janzen of Waterloo. The first ministers to serve this group were John Wichert, elected by the group in 1927, and Cornelius Neufeld and Nicholas Fransen, elected in 1929. Until that time sermons were read from books by someone in the congregation. On Dec. 24, 1935, a new meetinghouse was ready for occupation, built mostly by voluntary labor. On April 13, 1936, the congregation resolved to separate from the Waterloo United Mennonite Church and organize as an independent congregation under the leadership of Bishop Dietrich H. Koop. By 1942 the congregation had grown to such an extent that the church had to be enlarged. In 1944 Koop died and John J. Wichert was elected to this office. Other ministers serving the congregation are Nicholas Fransen, Abram H. Harder, and John W. Neufeld (ordained 1954). In 1957 a larger church was built of brick. The membership in 1958 was 348; John J. Wichert was the pastor.   J.J.W.

Vinne, van der, a Dutch Mennonite family, probably of Flemish descent, living at Harlingen in Friesland c1600, from where Laurens van de Vinne moved to Haarlem c1610. Since then van der Vinnes have been members of the Haarlem Mennonite congregation.

Many members of this family were artists. (1) Vincent Laurensz (Haarlem, 1629-1702) was a physician and a talented painter; in 1649-52 he traveled in Germany, writing a diary of this trip. He also published a list of painters whom he knew at Haarlem. His sons were (2) Isaac (Haarlem, 1655-1740), who operated a printing house and a bookshop, and in his leisure hours made meritorious etchings; (3) Laurens (Haarlem, 1658-1729), who managed a cotton factory and was also a painter; and (4) Jan (Haarlem, 1663-1721), a painter and etcher and the owner of a silk mill. Sons of (3) Laurens were (5) Vincent (Haarlem, 1686-1742), painter and etcher, (6) Jacob (Haarlem, 1688-1737), painter and etcher, deacon of the Mennonite congregation, and (7) Jan (Haarlem, 1699-1753), also a painter. (8) Laurens (Haarlem, 1712-42), a son of (6) Jacob, also made some paintings. Sons of (7) Jan were (9) Vincent (Haarlem, 1732-?), a painter and etcher, and (10) Jan (Haarlem, 1734-1805), an etcher.

Their art, though not without merit, seldom surpasses mediocrity. Most important is the work of (1) Vincent, who specialized in still life; a self portrait by him is found in the Frans Hals museum at Haarlem. Etchings and drawings of several members of this family are found in the Teyler museum at Haarlem.

The van der Vinnes were loyal members of the church. In addition to (6) Jacob, other members of this family served as deacons at Haarlem—Izaak van der Vinne, d. 1801, serving for 45 years, Vincent van der Vinne, d. 1811, serving for 46 years, Fran-çois Huurkamp van der Vinne, d. 1815, 38 years, Vincent van der Vinne (1798-1856, a great-grandson of [6] Jacob), who is also known for his etchings and woodcuts, deacon from 1837 until his death, representative of Haarlem on the board of the A.D.S. (q.v.) from 1854. Some members of this family also served as trustees of the Haarlem Mennonite orphanage.   vdZ.

Church records of Haarlem; Thieme-Becker, *Allg. Lexikon der bildenden Künstler* XXXIV (Leipzig, 1940) 392-94.

Vinne, Dionysius, one of the Wassenberg preachers (q.v.), b. at Diest in Brabant, was won to Lutheranism by 1523 in Antwerp, later betook himself to Jülich. With brief interruptions he zealously preached the new doctrine in Wassenberg, Höngen, and especially Süstern. On Sept. 17, 1532, he went to Münster in Westphalia, was baptized there on Jan. 5, 1534, and appointed to the office of apostle. On Oct. 13, 1534, he was sent as an apostle to Osnabrück, where he was immediately arrested. Vinne and four other apostles were executed at Iburg, one died in prison, and one, i.e., Graess (q.v.), was pardoned.   NEFF.

Rembert, *Wiedertäufer*, 302 ff.; W. Bax, *Het Protestantisme in het Bisdom Luik* I (The Hague, 1937) 48-50 and *passim;* Mellink, *Wederdopers*, 48 f. and *passim; ML* IV.

Virgil Mennonite Brethren Church, also called the Niagara congregation, located near Virgil, Lincoln Co., Ont., a member of the Canadian M.B. Conference, was organized Nov. 6, 1937, under the leadership of John F. Dick. The membership in 1957 was 477, most of whom are rural people. The first meeting place was a rented hall in Niagara-on-the-Lake. Then a church was built near the village of Virgil. The congregation in the beginning consisted of only a few members, but grew very quickly because of a strong influx of Mennonite Brethren families from Western Canada after a series of droughts and crop failures. Ministers who have served the congregation are J. F. Dick, D. Klassen, A. Block, J. Derksen, P. Friesen, F. Wiens, P. Esau, F. F. Kroeker, I. Ewert, and John D. Penner. The pastor in 1957 was F. J. Wiens.   H.H.J.

Virginia, known since the adoption of the first state constitution in 1776 as the Commonwealth of Virginia, area 40,815 square miles, population 3,318,680, the oldest of the 13 original colonies, founded in 1607. West Virginia (q.v.) was a part of the state until 1863. Geographically present-day Virginia is divided into three areas—the coastal plain or tidewater Virginia, the Piedmont Plateau, and the Great Valley area between the Blue Ridge Mountains on the east and the Alleghenies on the west. Distinction should be made between the Valley of Virginia and the Shenandoah Valley. The latter is only that part of the Valley which is drained by the Shenandoah rivers, tributaries of the Potomac, at Harpers Ferry. The Shenandoah Valley consists of about two thirds of the northern part of the Valley.

Not all the land of colonial Virginia was used for farming; much of it was used for grazing. Here the first roundups and corrals in American history took place. The plantation system did not come to

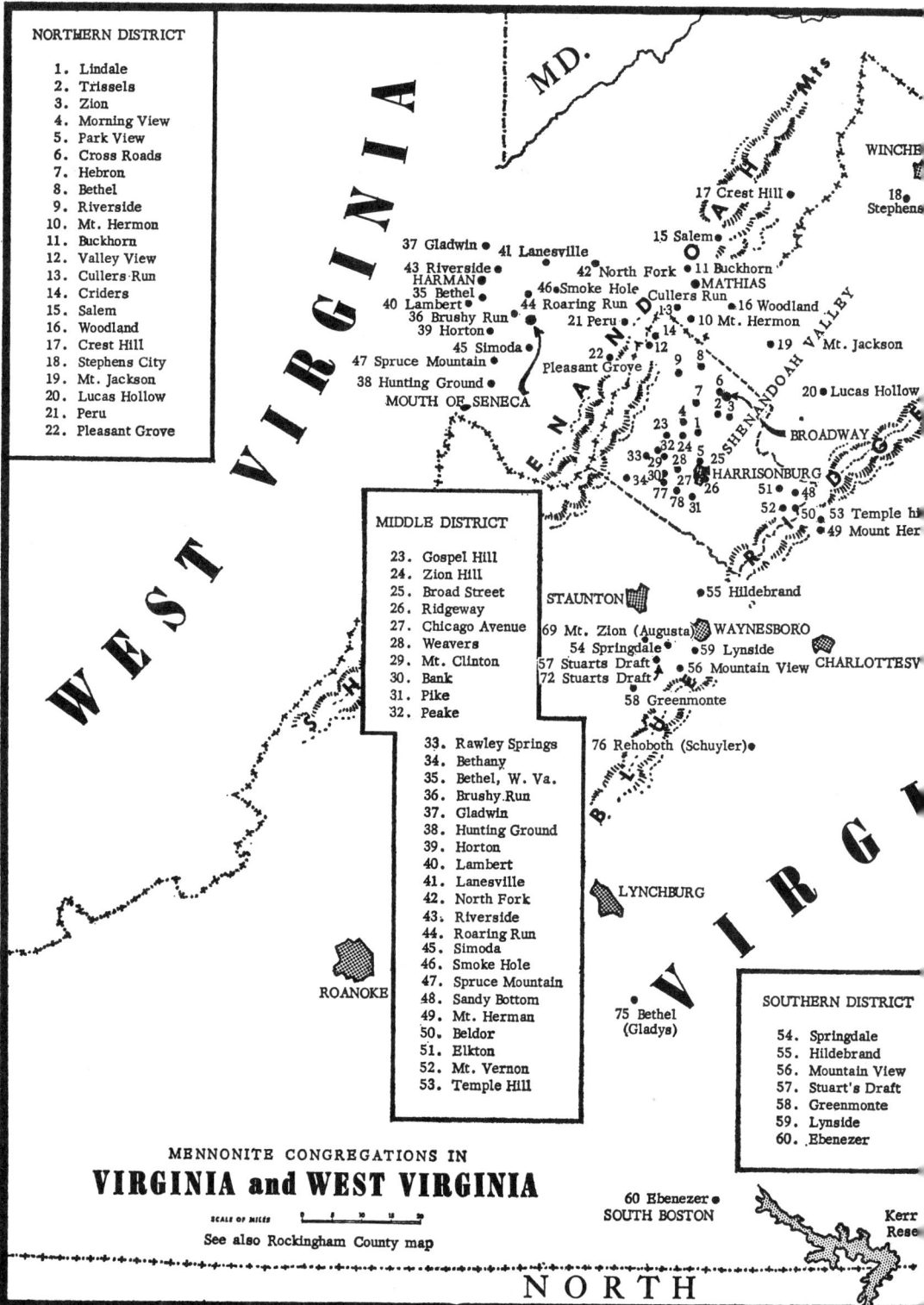

NORTHERN DISTRICT

1. Lindale
2. Trissels
3. Zion
4. Morning View
5. Park View
6. Cross Roads
7. Hebron
8. Bethel
9. Riverside
10. Mt. Hermon
11. Buckhorn
12. Valley View
13. Cullers Run
14. Criders
15. Salem
16. Woodland
17. Crest Hill
18. Stephens City
19. Mt. Jackson
20. Lucas Hollow
21. Peru
22. Pleasant Grove

MIDDLE DISTRICT

23. Gospel Hill
24. Zion Hill
25. Broad Street
26. Ridgeway
27. Chicago Avenue
28. Weavers
29. Mt. Clinton
30. Bank
31. Pike
32. Peake

33. Rawley Springs
34. Bethany
35. Bethel, W. Va.
36. Brushy Run
37. Gladwin
38. Hunting Ground
39. Horton
40. Lambert
41. Lanesville
42. North Fork
43. Riverside
44. Roaring Run
45. Simoda
46. Smoke Hole
47. Spruce Mountain
48. Sandy Bottom
49. Mt. Herman
50. Beldor
51. Elkton
52. Mt. Vernon
53. Temple Hill

SOUTHERN DISTRICT

54. Springdale
55. Hildebrand
56. Mountain View
57. Stuart's Draft
58. Greenmonte
59. Lynside
60. Ebenezer

MD.

WINCHE

17 Crest Hill
18
Stephens
15 Salem

37 Gladwin   41 Lanesville
43 Riverside   42 North Fork   11 Buckhorn
HARMAN   MATHIAS
35 Bethel   46 Smoke Hole   Cullers Run   16 Woodland
40 Lambert   44 Roaring Run   1-3   10 Mt. Hermon
36 Brushy Run   21 Peru   19 Mt. Jackson
39 Horton   14
45 Simoda   22   12   8
47 Spruce Mountain   Pleasant Grove   7   6   20 Lucas Hollow
38 Hunting Ground   4 1   2 3   BROADWAY
MOUTH OF SENECA   23   5
          32 24   25   HARRISONBURG
33   29 28   27   26   51   48
34 30   77   78 31   52   50   53 Temple hi
            49 Mount Her

STAUNTON   55 Hildebrand

69 Mt. Zion (Augusta)   WAYNESBORO
54 Springdale   59 Lynside
57 Stuarts Draft   56 Mountain View   CHARLOTTESV
72 Stuarts Draft
58 Greenmonte

76 Rehoboth (Schuyler)

LYNCHBURG

ROANOKE

75 Bethel
(Gladys)

60 Ebenezer
SOUTH BOSTON

Kerr
Rese

VIRGI

WEST VIRGINIA

MENNONITE CONGREGATIONS IN
VIRGINIA and WEST VIRGINIA

SCALE OF MILES

See also Rockingham County map

NORTH

HARPERS FERRY

WINCHESTER

18 ·
Stephens City

BALTIMORE

DELAWARE

M A R Y L A N D

WASHINGTON

BEACHY AMISH

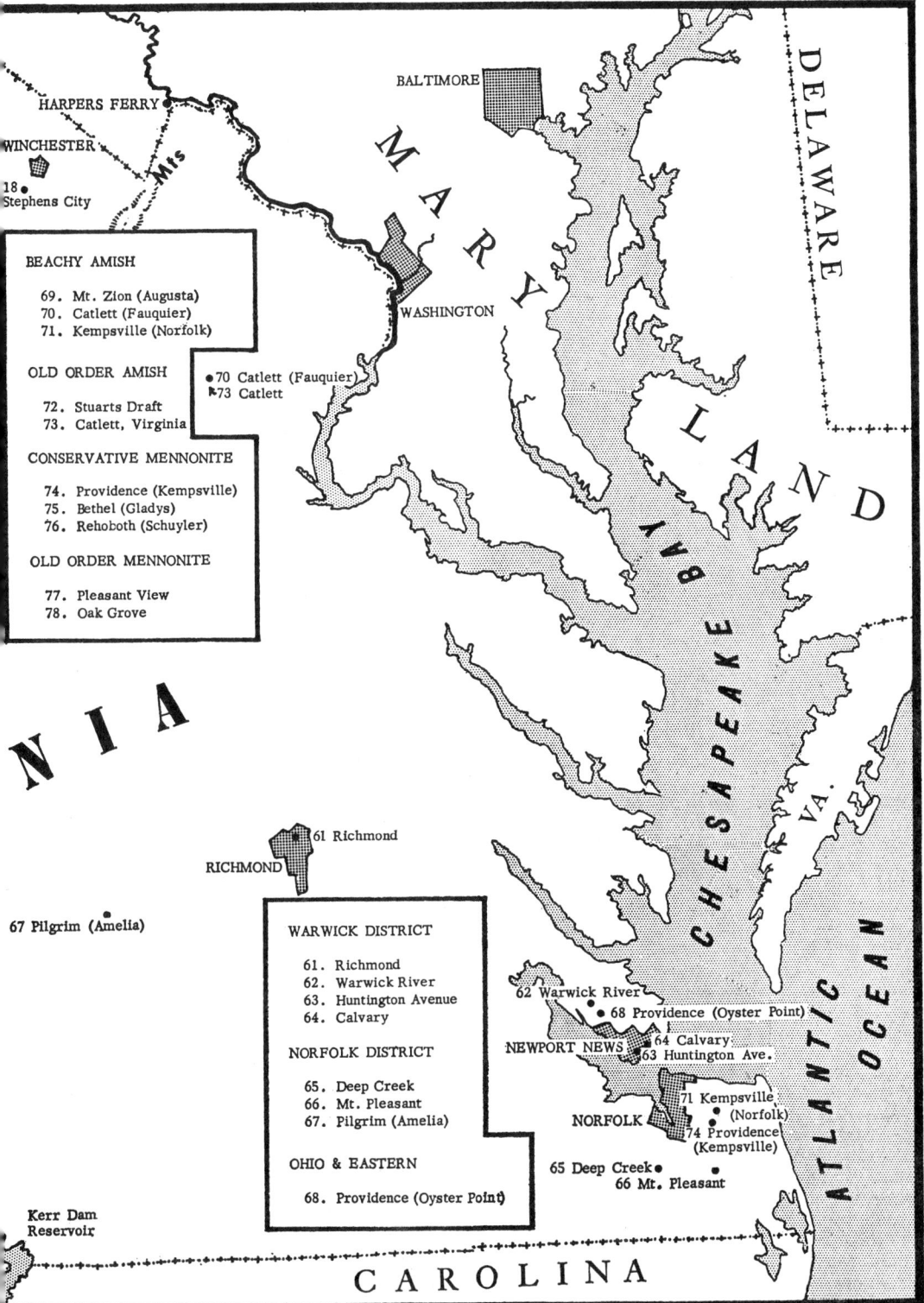

69. Mt. Zion (Augusta)
70. Catlett (Fauquier)
71. Kempsville (Norfolk)

OLD ORDER AMISH

72. Stuarts Draft
73. Catlett, Virginia

● 70 Catlett (Fauquier)
▶73 Catlett

CONSERVATIVE MENNONITE

74. Providence (Kempsville)
75. Bethel (Gladys)
76. Rehoboth (Schuyler)

OLD ORDER MENNONITE

77. Pleasant View
78. Oak Grove

C H E S A P E A K E   B A Y

VA.

N I A

● 61 Richmond

RICHMOND

67 Pilgrim (Amelia) ·

WARWICK DISTRICT

61. Richmond
62. Warwick River
63. Huntington Avenue
64. Calvary

NORFOLK DISTRICT

65. Deep Creek
66. Mt. Pleasant
67. Pilgrim (Amelia)

OHIO & EASTERN

68. Providence (Oyster Point)

62 Warwick River
● 68 Providence (Oyster Point)
64 Calvary
NEWPORT NEWS · 63 Huntington Ave.

71 Kempsville
(Norfolk)
NORFOLK · 74 Providence
(Kempsville)

65 Deep Creek ●
66 Mt. Pleasant

ATLANTIC OCEAN

Kerr Dam
Reservoir

C A R O L I N A

Virginia until after the Revolution, when the price of tobacco was so low that the small farmer was unable to carry on and sold his land to the larger landowner. The result was the plantation system. The exception to the above rule was the Shenandoah Valley of Virginia. This area was settled by the Pennsylvania Germans, who proved to be better farmers than the English, preserving and conserving the native fertility of soil. Even today Pennsylvania German farms can be recognized.

In religion in many respects local government and church organization in Virginia was a replica of the mother country of England. The county board or bench ruled the county and the vestry board organized on the same pattern was responsible for the religious life of the people. These agencies were self-perpetuating. On the state level, until 1787 Virginia had the state church, the Anglican Church. This meant that everyone in Virginia was expected to join this church. The sumptuary laws of early Virginia were almost as strict as those in Massachusetts. Quakers were banned in 1660; they were not to hold conventicles. In the 18th century dissenters were permitted in the Valley of Virginia. Their coming was the beginning of the breakdown in the state church system. Mennonites, Quakers, Lutherans, and other groups came, followed by the Baptists just before the American Revolution.

These groups in time became champions of religious freedom in the state. The Enlightenment of the 18th century had its influence too. Thomas Jefferson became one of the leaders of the movement. He became a champion for religious freedom and for the disestablishment of the state church in Virginia. Jefferson believed that there should be no compulsion in matters of religion. He was aided in his cause by the dissenters. Some of these, particularly the Baptists, had wholeheartedly participated in the American Revolution. Should they not be free to worship God as they pleased? They naturally thought so and used their participation in the war as a lever to obtain freedom in religion. The Pennsylvania Germans worked with and for Jefferson too. It is said that the Pennsylvania Germans came "down in shoals" to vote for Thomas Jefferson. It was in 1787 that the state church of Virginia was disestablished. Mr. Jefferson considered this as one of three outstanding achievements of his life.

Of the 100 counties in Virginia, Mennonites have lived in 15; viz., Page, Frederick, Shenandoah, Rockingham, and Augusta in the Shenandoah Valley; Fauquier, Orange, Fairfax, Greene, Nelson, and Albemarle, just east of the Blue Ridge; Amelia and Halifax in the center; and Warwick, Norfolk, and Princess Anne on the Atlantic Coast. The most populous Mennonite settlements in the Valley are found in Rockingham and Augusta counties, and in the southeastern part of the state at Denbigh and Fentress in Warwick and Norfolk counties.

The original settlements made in Page, Frederick, and Shenandoah counties in 1728 were nearly wiped out by an Indian raid in 1758. Page County (*q.v.*) was also the scene of the Rhodes massacre when John Rhodes and members of his family were killed near Luray in 1764. The next two settlements were made in Rockingham County, the first and largest

in the Linville Creek, Cedar Run, and Brock's Creek area extending from Edom and Broadway on the east to Turleytown and Cootes Store on the west. In 1773 this area was occupied by the Stovers, Shanks, Brennemans, Brunks, Coffmans, Beerys, and Geils. The above settlement in the northern part of the county soon overflowed to help establish a new and second settlement in the vicinity of Harrisonburg. A third settlement was made soon after the Revolution in Augusta County near Waynesboro.

Most of the Virginia Mennonites who came in 1773-1820 came from Montgomery, Lancaster, and York counties in Pennsylvania. The period 1820-30 was the time of organization of the oldest existing continuous congregations in Rockingham and Augusta counties. A settlement made in Frederick County (Winchester) (*q.v.*) in the 1870's died out by 1900-10. The coastal settlements in Warwick (Denbigh) and Norfolk (Fentress) counties were begun in 1897 and 1900 respectively of different stock, mostly from Allen County, Ohio. The small settlement in Halifax County, near South Boston, was started in 1900. In recent years Old Order Amish settlements were made in the Stuarts Draft (Augusta County) and Catlett (Fauquier County) areas. In both areas Beachy Amish congregations have emerged. Near Kempsville, in Princess Anne County on the coast, an Old Order Amish settlement was established in 1903. In the 1940's the Old Order Amish of Kempsville withdrew to re-establish themselves in the Shenandoah Valley at Stuarts Draft, Augusta County. In the 1950's a Beachy Amish Mennonite church and a Conservative Mennonite church were formed in the Kempsville area. The Conservative Mennonites have two other congregations in the state—one at Gladys, the other at Schuyler, Va.

The only division among the Virginia Mennonites occurred about 1900 when a small group of Old Order Mennonites (*q.v.*) separated from the main Virginia Conference body in Rockingham County. Today this group has two congregations near Dayton.

Thus in 1957 the total Mennonite and Amish baptized membership in Virginia was 4,304, distributed as follows:

VIRGINIA MENNONITES BY BRANCHES

Name	Congregations	Members
Virginia Conference (MC)	43	3,514
Ohio and Eastern Conference (MC)	1	31
Conservative Conference (MC)	3	115
Old Order Mennonites	2	350
Beachy Amish	3	259
Old Order Amish	2	160
Six groups Total	54	4,429

Of this number the 31 congregations of the Virginia Mennonite Conference (MC) in the Shenandoah Valley with their 2,838 members constitute the heart of Virginia Mennonitism, with the Eastern Mennonite College at Harrisonburg as a strong asset. At Harrisonburg also is the headquarters of Mennonite Broadcasts (*q.v.*) and the Virginia Mennonite Home for the Aged (*q.v.*). A second center is the Denbigh-Fentress area around Norfolk, where there are 9 congregations affiliated with the Mennonite General Conference, with 731 members.

H.A.B.

Virginia Conference of the Mennonite Church (MC). The Lancaster Conference had supervision over the Virginia Mennonites in the 18th and early 19th centuries, although very little is known about this arrangement. Apparently in times of crisis at least, and probably also for the ordination of ministers, the Virginia members called in Lancaster leaders for assistance.

It was not until 1835 that the more progressive leaders of the Virginia Mennonites took steps to establish a conference of their own. The first meeting was held at the Weavers church (*q.v.*) in that year. The minutes of this first Virginia conference in German have been preserved and have been published in English translation in the *Minutes of the Virginia Mennonite Conference.* The conference was divided into three bishop districts in 1837, which now have the names Northern (for northern Rockingham County), Middle (for western Rockingham County), and Southern (for the churches in Augusta County). With the expansion of the Virginia Conference in the late 19th and 20th centuries other districts have been added, the principal ones being Warwick, Norfolk, Tennessee, and Sonnenberg in Ohio.

No records of the Virginia Conference were kept 1836-59. Informal meetings of the Virginia church leaders were likely held during this period. The so-called Burkholder Confession of Faith was translated into English and published in 1837. A committee was appointed to select hymns for an English hymnbook, which was published in 1847 under the title *A Selection of Psalms, Hymns, and Spiritual Songs* as the first English Mennonite hymnal in America.

The first attempt to compile the minutes of the Virginia Conference was made in 1883 when a committee of five was appointed, who published their work in 1884 under the title *Proceedings of the Mennonite Conferences in the Valley of Virginia.* It was also decided by the conference at that time to print the minutes of each successive conference. A second compiling committee was appointed in 1910 when a summary of all the minutes of the Virginia Conference was published in booklet form, together with some biographical sketches of early leaders, under the title *A History of the Mennonite Conference of Virginia and Its Work.* A third compilation was issued in 1939, when all the minutes of the conference were published under the title *Minutes of the Virginia Mennonite Conference, Including Some Historical Data, A Brief Biographical Sketch of Its Founders and Organizers, and Her Official Statement of Christian Fundamentals, Constitution, and Rules and Discipline.*

The records show that district meetings were held following the semiannual state conference, at which meetings the resolutions of conference were presented to and ratified by the congregations. In 1884 it was decided that resolutions of conference should not be published as being accepted until they were ratified by the congregations. How general these

district meetings were is not known. For the Middle District numerous references to these meetings have been preserved. No records are extant for the Northern and Southern districts, but it can be assumed that they were also held. It was thought that these meetings helped the officials of the church apply the resolutions of conference. These district meetings to ratify conference resolutions were discontinued in the 1920's; the reasons for this are not clear. In time the resolutions passed by the conference were simply regarded as decrees "for to keep," not needing ratification by the membership.

The organization of the Virginia Conference was very simple at first. The offices were moderator and secretary. The moderators were usually ministers, but in recent years bishops have served in this capacity. The list includes Michael Shank, Joseph N. Driver, Samuel Shank, Christian Good, L. J. Heatwole, A. B. Burkholder, J. S. Martin, John L. Stauffer, and Truman Brunk. For many years lay brethren served as secretaries. This practice was discontinued in the 1930's. It was thought advisable at that time to have members of conference act in this capacity. A roster of the secretaries includes David H. Landes, Emanuel Suter, C. H. Brunk, S. M. Burkholder, C. D. Wenger, E. J. Berkey, H. D. Weaver, J. R. Mumaw, Ward Shank, and Linden Wenger.

At first the lay members did not attend the conference sessions. It was just a matter of the Virginia ministers meeting semiannually to talk over their common problems with the subsequent passing of resolutions that might be helpful. Somewhat later the lay members of the church were invited, and now a certain number attend. All the bishops occupied the bench behind the long pulpit; they took turns addressing the opening session of the conference. Then there were testimonies from all the ministers and deacons. Following this the regular business of the conference was considered.

A number of changes have been made in the organization and procedure in recent decades. The bishops discontinued the use of the pulpit; their opening admonitions were replaced by a conference sermon; the testimonies were limited to a few visitors. Bishops served as moderators. Closed or preliminary sessions of conference were held in which problems facing the conference were discussed. This body then decided what subjects should be presented to the open conference for discussion and possible action. Since 1911 the semiannual conferences have been replaced by annual conferences.

Resolutions, some conservative, others progressive, have been formed and adopted. A number of conference actions have dealt with the subject of pride and the drift toward worldliness. To check or to prevent the entrance of doctrinally liberal thought into the church doctrinal statements were drawn up by the conference which were accepted almost without change by the Mennonite General Conference in 1921. In keeping with the conservative emphasis resolutions were passed which asked the members of conference to discontinue the use of musical instruments in their homes, and the use of the radio was made a test of membership for a number of years.

One Virginia bishop advocated the establishment

of a General Conference fifty years before it was organized. Then when General Conference did come in 1898 the Virginia Conference held aloof from it until 1911. Sunday schools were permitted in 1869. The conference was slow in working with the Mennonite Board of Missions and Charities, but it sanctioned the establishment of a local mission board which continues to function. One illustration of change in the history of the conference was the removal of the ban on the use of radios and musical instruments. As a result of this and subsequent actions, the Virginia Conference has become the home of Mennonite Broadcasts, Incorporated (*q.v.*).

The work and organization of the Virginia Conference has been greatly increased in the last 50 years. Illustrations of this would include the Virginia Mennonite Board of Missions and Charities for city, rural, and even foreign work, the Property Aid Plan, the Automobile Aid Plan, the organization and supervision of highland churches, and the establishment of Eastern Mennonite College (*q.v.*) as a conference school. In 1958 the Virginia Conference had a baptized membership of 4,741, with 32 organized congregations and 52 unorganized mission congregations. There were 9 bishops, 90 ministers, and 20 deacons. H.A.B.

Virginia Mennonite Automobile Aid Plan, Harrisonburg, Va., was organized in 1933 under the Virginia (MC) Conference to provide insurance coverage for damage to automobiles and hospital and surgical care to owners and dependents. In 1958, 1,252 vehicles were listed. H.S.B.

Virginia Mennonite Property Aid Plan was authorized by the Virginia Mennonite Conference (MC) in 1911. The Aid Plan covers loss by fire, lightning, and windstorm, to dwellings, farm and commercial buildings, and churches. Membership is limited to members of the Mennonite Church and serves in addition to Virginia parts of West Virginia, Tennessee, Ohio, Florida, and Georgia which have some connection with Virginia Conference. Offices are at Harrisonburg, Va. In 1958 listings numbered 1,497, covering $21,164,868 in property holdings. L.M.W.

Vis, a common Dutch family name found in many parts of the Netherlands, both Mennonite and non-Mennonite. A widely ramified Mennonite family, the interrelationships of which have not yet been cleared up, was found in the Zaan district in the province of North Holland in the 17th century. A Mennonite branch at first seems to have lived in Zaandijk, but in the early 17th century was also found at Zaandam; its members spread all over Holland in the 19th century.

Gerrit Jansz Vis, of Zaandijk, was a well-to-do merchant and shipowner. In 1728 he was appointed one of the directors (surveyors) of the Dutch Greenland Whaling; though a Mennonite he was chosen as a burgomaster of Zaandijk in 1740.

Waligh Gerrits Vis, d. April 1767, of Zaandam, was a lay preacher of the Frisian congregation (Oude Huys) at West-Zaandam 1714-66. Among his descendants was Heyme Vis Jr (1826-1914), a factory owner at Zaandam, trustee of the A.D.S. in 1895-1902 and member of the church board of Zaandam-Oost for many years. Numerous members of

the Vis family have served as deacons at Zaandam, in both the West and Oost congregations, Koog-Zaandijk, Wormerveen, Utrecht, and other places.

The following Vises were all educated at the Amsterdam Mennonite Seminary and served the church as pastors: Abraham Vis (Zaandam, 1837-Heerenveen, 1911), serving at Mensingeweer 1861-63, Zwolle 1863-66, and Heerenveen 1866-1901. He was a trustee of the A.D.S. 1886-1905. Pieter Albert Vis (Workum, 1865-Heelsum, 1940) served at Witmarsum-Pingjum 1890-91, Beemster 1891-1914, Edam 1914-18, and Irnsum-Poppingewier 1918-30. He championed state pensions for the aged (actualized in the Netherlands in 1957) and for many years delivered addresses and propaganda speeches on the subject. His sermon commemorating his 25 years in the ministry, *Gadachtenispreek,* was published (n.p., n.d.-1915). Both his sons Pieter and Albert Vis went into the ministry. Pieter Vis (de Beemster, 1893-The Hague, 1942) served at Mensingeweer 1917-20, Drachten 1920-26, Arnhem 1926-38, and The Hague 1938-42. He was one of the first Dutch Mennonite ministers to promote youth associations and a founder and the first president of the Friese (*q.v.*) Doopsgezinde Jongeren Bond (1924) and also the first president (1928) of the (general) Doopsgezinde (*q.v.*) Jongeren Bond. He promoted the forming of groups of catechism classes. He published some sermons and papers, e.g., his address on "Verschuivingen in het Oorlogsvraagstuk" (*DJ* 1940). His brother Albert Vis (b. 1894 at de Beemster) served at Witmarsum-Pingjum 1919-22, Heerenveen 1922-25, Den Burg 1925-39, and since 1939 at Beverwijk. He obtained his Th.D. degree in 1936 at the University of Amsterdam on the dissertation (in English) *The Messianic Psalm Quotations in the New Testament* (Amsterdam, 1936).

Cornelis Vis Jzn (Oudkarspel, 1872-Winschoten, 1952) was a pastor of the congregations of Noordeind van Graft 1896-99, Warga 1899-1906, Noord- and Zuid-Zijpe 1906-9, Kampen 1909-30, and Winschoten 1930-39. For many years he was the stimulating secretary of the Association for the Mennonites in the Diaspora (see **Verstrooiing**). Jan Mari Vis (Amsterdam, 1880-Noordbroek, 1956) served at Noordbroek 1906-45. In 1924-45 he also served the congregation of Mensingeweer and 1928-45 of Middelstum. Besides his ministry he was a practicing lawyer.

Not related to the former branch is the Mennonite Vis family on the island of Terschelling, some of whom have been deacons of the church, Pieter Vis, d. 1927, serving for 40 years, and a Vis family, originally found at Venhuizen (*q.v.*), of which Suffridus A. Vis (b. Amsterdam, 1927), serving as pastor at Aardenburg since 1952, is a descendant.

G. J. Honig and J. C. Vis, *Geschiedenis en Handboek der Familie Vis* (1899); S. Lootsma, *Het Nieuwe Huys* (Zaandam, 1937) 190, 192; *Inv. Arch. Amst.* II, 2, No. 675; *DB* 1894, 154; 1901, 213; 1902, 243; *De Zondagsbode* XXIV (1910-11) No. 26 f.; XXVIII (1914-15) No. 16; *DJ* 1943, 26-32; 1953, 13.

Vis(ch)buurt: see **Ternaard.**

Vischer, Andreas, is mentioned in Wolkan, *Lieder,* 32. He was an elder at Auspitz (*q.v.*), Moravia, about 1535. vDZ.

Vischer, Gall: see Fischer, Gall.

Vischer, Laux, a potter, guildmaster of the carpenters in Augsburg, united with the Anabaptists and was taken prisoner, put in chains, and expelled from the city on Oct. 18, 1527, together with Eitelhans Langenmantel (*q.v.*), Endres Widholz, Gall Fischer (*q.v.*), Peter Schleppach, Hans Kissling, and Ulrich Eckart. Vischer was also made to pay a fine, which was put into the alms fund. He is designated as "one of the chief adherents and promoters of Anabaptism." His son, the potter Laux Vischer, had likewise joined the Anabaptists and was baptized in the summer of 1527 by Jörg of Passau (*q.v.*). Laux Vischer the younger was arrested in April 1528 and recanted. Also his mother Anna, who had been baptized by Salminger (*q.v.*) and recanted on Oct. 3, 1527, was arrested in April 1528, put in irons, and expelled from the city. HEGE.

Fr. Roth, "Der Höhepunkt der wiedertäuferischen Bewegung in Augsburg und ihr Niedergang im Jahre 1528," *passim, Ztscht des hist. Vereins f. Schwaben u. Neuburg* XXVIII, Augsburg, 1901); *ML* IV.

Vischer, Lienhard, a Mennonite elder of Moravia, who was active in Bavaria (*q.v.*) c1584-87. (*ME* I, 252.).

Vishenau, a principality in Moravia, where the Hutterian Brethren established two Bruderhofs. The Brethren here became noted for their production of beautiful ceramics (*q.v.*). The Bruderhofs were burned down on June 20, 1605, by soldiers. In October 1622, the Brethren were expelled from Vishenau, leaving all their possessions behind. They settled in Hungary. HEGE.

F. Hruby, "Die Wiedertäufer in Mahren," in *Archiv für Ref.-Gesch.* XXX (1933) 197; K. Cernohorsky (in Czech), *The Production of Vishenau Fayence* (Vishenau, 1928); Beck, *Geschichts-Bücher*, 351, 408; *ML* IV.

Visscher, a common Dutch family name, Mennonite as well as non-Mennonite. Jan Visscher (b. 1801 at Blokzijl, d. Aug. 14, 1882, at Utrecht) was a Mennonite minister, educated at the Amsterdam seminary and pastor of Hengelo 1824-28 and Utrecht from 1828-61. He wrote a paper against the modern (liberal) theology of J. H. Scholten, professor at Leiden, found in *Jaarboeken voor Wetenschappelijke Theologie* VIII, 1850, separately reprinted under the title *Brief aan een' Doopsgezinden broeder over den Heiligen Doop* (Utrecht, 1851); with his colleague D. S. Gorter (*q.v.*) he had a debate on the same question. He also published *Een woord van Troost*, a sermon (Haarlem, 1859), *Tweetal Leerredenen* (Haarlem, 1859), and a few other sermons. In the *Doopsgezinde Bijdragen* of 1876 he published a paper on the question whether persons who had been admitted into Mennonite congregations without baptism should be accepted by other Mennonite congregations. In an era of growing liberalism among the Dutch Mennonites Visscher was a champion of the conservative suprarationalist views. His son Jan Visscher (b. 1829 at Utrecht, d. April 27, 1885, at Akkrum) was a Mennonite pastor at Akkrum 1855-d.85. Both father and son Jan Visscher were trustees of the A.D.S. (*q.v.*). Alle Visscher (*q.v.*) was not related to them. vDZ.

H. B. Berghuys, *Geschiedenis der Doopsgezinde gemeente te Utrecht* (n.p., n.d.-1926) 80 f., 84.

Visscher, Alle, a native of Bolsward in Friesland, Netherlands, was a friend of Menno Simons, whom he visited at Wüstenfelde (*q.v.*) a few days before his death. Alenson reports that Menno said to Alle, "Do not be a servant of men as I have been." (*Tegenbericht, BRN* VII, 258.) vDZ.

Visscher, Jan Cornelisz, a member and probably a deacon of the Waterlander congregation of Amsterdam, who with Anslo (*q.v.*) and other church leaders attended a meeting held 1614 at Baambrugge to settle a dispute between Rijk Jacobs (*q.v.*) and Hans de Ries (*q.v.*). (*Inv. Arch. Amst.* I, No. 548.) vDZ.

Visschersweert, a hamlet on the Maas River in the present Dutch province of Limburg, in the 16th century belonging to the territory of Valkenburg, was, like the neighboring hamlet of Illikhoven (*q.v.*), a center of Mennonite activity c1545-47. On a pasture near Visschersweert Menno Simons preached in 1545, and from Visschersweert he went by boat to Roermond. Theunis van Hastenrath (*q.v.*) also preached and baptized here. Among the Mennonites of Visschersweert were Jan (*q.v.*) Neulen, Eeren Neuten, and the martyrs Metken (*q.v.*) and her husband Jacob Vrancken. vDZ.

W. Bax, *Het Protestantisme in het Bisdom Luik* I (The Hague, 1937) 330 f. and *passim*; Ernst Crous, "Auf Mennos Spuren am Niederrhein," in *Der Mennonit* VIII (1955) 155; *DB* 1864, 151 f.; 1890, 54-56, 60 f.

Visser, a Dutch family name, Mennonite as well as non-Mennonite; the name is still very common, and means "fisherman." Many of the numerous Mennonite Visser families are not interrelated. The following persons by this name have served as Mennonite ministers: Jan Visser, d. c1762, serving at Schiedam 1728-31 and at Haarlem (Peuzelaarsteeg congregation) 1731-57. He published *Redenvoering* (Sermon) *over Matt. 24 vers 6-8 op den Beededag des Jaars 1741* (Haarlem, 1742).

Pieter Jans Visser, d. Oct. 30, 1789, was a lay preacher of Twisk 1743-46 and Hoorn 1746-d.89. His son (?) Jan Visser, d. Nov. 29, 1831, also a lay preacher, served at Medemblik 1780-83 and Koog-Zaandijk 1783-d.1831. A *Leerrede* (Sermon) of his was published at Purmerend in 1808. Dirk Gerbens Visser, d. July 1836, was a lay preacher at Gorredijk-Lippenhuizen 1806-29 and at Irnsum 1829-d.36. Haitje Hantjes Visser was a lay preacher and later elder of the congregation of Balk 1828-54.

Cornelis Visser, d. 1944, of Haarlem, a deacon from 1900 until his death, was for many years the secretary of the Dienstjarenfonds (*q.v.*). vDZ.

Vissering, a Mennonite family found since the 17th century at Leer in East Friesland, Germany. David Joosten, who died in 1709, did not yet bear this family name; his descendants, usually businessmen and wholesalers, were among the pillars of the Mennonite congregation of Leer. His sons adopted the family name of Vissering (at first also Visring). In the course of the 17th century there were branches of this family at Leer, Emden, and Amsterdam. The branch at Leer died out in the 19th century.

The Emden branch left the Mennonites and joined the Reformed Church. The branch at Amsterdam, founded by Coenraad Vissering (1746-1810, a grandson of David Joosten), who became a banker at Amsterdam, at first belonged to the Zonist congregation and after the merger of this church with the Lamists in 1801 to the United Mennonite church. Some of them were deacons at Amsterdam.

This family furnished two Mennonite preachers, e.g., Jacobus David Vissering (q.v.) and his son Gerbrand Vissering (q.v.).

Prominent members were Simon Vissering (q.v.) and his son Gerard Vissering (1865-1937), a financial expert, director of the Dutch National Bank, financial adviser to the former League of Nations, who was called by the governments of China, South Africa, and Turkey to organize or reform their monetary systems. Both were of the Dutch branch. Willem Vissering (1802-60), living on the estate Lintel near Norden, East Friesland, was a "Landrat"; his son Friedrich Bodewin Vissering (1826-85), living on an estate near Dornum in East Friesland, was an "Oekonomienrat" and a member of the German Parliament.　　　　　　　　　vDZ.

Ned. Patriciaat XXIV (1938) 300-18; G. ten Cate, Geslachtlijst van de familie Vissering (n.p., 1903); DB 1904, 241; MQR XXV, 249.

Vissering, Gerbrand, b. June 2, 1813, at Groningen, d. June 27, 1869, at Jisp, unmarried, was a son of Jacobus David Vissering (q.v.) and his second wife Baudina Cnoop. He studied theology at the University of Groningen and the Mennonite Seminary at Amsterdam, thereupon serving as pastor at Zuid-Zijpe 1837-42 and Wormer-Jisp 1842-d.69. Vissering was a somewhat solitary man and a Greek scholar; his sermons were not very popular. In 1854 he published a new translation of the New Testament from the original Greek (Amsterdam, 1854, repr. 1859). For this scholarly work he received in 1860 an honorary Th.D. degree from the Groningen University. His New Testament translation was also much appreciated by the Synod of the Dutch Reformed Church, who recommended his version and appointed him on a committee to prepare a new Dutch Bible to replace the antiquated Statenvertaling (q.v.).　　　　　　　　　vDZ.

D. Harting, Levensbericht van Dr. G. Vissering (Leiden, 1870).

Vissering, Jacobus David, b. Oct. 24, 1774, at Leer in East Friesland, Germany, d. Dec. 17, 1846, at Groningen, Netherlands, married first to Trijntje Kool (1772-1803) of Beverwijk, then to Baudina Cnoop (1779-1849) of Bolsward, was a Dutch Mennonite pastor. After studying theology at the University of Groningen, he was trained for the ministry by Pieter Beets (q.v.), pastor at Westzaandam, and appointed ministerial candidate by the church board of Westzaandam on March 12, 1798. He served at Alkmaar 1798-1809 and at Groningen 1809-46, retiring on Nov. 29 of this year, after he had served for 47 years. Particularly in Groningen he worked with great blessing. During his pastorate Vissering, who was the preacher of the united Flemish and Waterlander Pelsterstraat church, and his colleague Pieter Klomp (q.v.) of the Old Flemish congregation in the Boteringestraat succeeded in bringing about a merger of these two congregations in 1809. In 1815 Vissering dedicated the new meetinghouse in the Boteringestraat. As far as is known he did not publish any writings.　　　　　　　　　vDZ.

Naamlijst 1798, 63; H. Dassel Sr, Menno's Volk in Groningen (Groningen, n.d.-1953) 39, 41, 43, 48 f.; DB 1882, 87 f.; 1883, 41.

Vissering, Simon, b. June 23, 1818, at Amsterdam, d. Aug. 27, 1888, at Ellecom, was a descendant of the Vissering (q.v.) family of Leer. He was married to Geertje Corver (1825-98) of Amsterdam. Vissering studied law and was at first a lawyer at Amsterdam. In 1850-79 he was professor of politics at the University of Leiden. In 1879 he became Minister of Finance of the Netherlands. He was a loyal member of the church. During his Leiden period he was on the board of the Leiden congregation 1859-79. He was also interested in the founding of the Mennonite congregation at The Hague in 1881. In 1866-73 he was a trustee of the A.D.S. (q.v.); in 1867 he took the initiative for a better constitution for the A.D.S. Besides being a brilliant jurist and financial expert, he took a keen interest in literature, serving as coeditor of the leading Dutch periodical (monthly) De Gids 1849-88, and for a few years he was editor of the Amsterdamsche Courant. He published papers on juridical, economic, statistical, financial, and literary subjects. A large number of these papers were published in Herinneringen (3 vv.) and Verspreide Geschriften (Leiden, 1889). (N.N.B.Wb. X, 119-22; Buys, "In Memoriam" in De Gids 1888.)　　　　　　　　　vDZ.

Visvliet, a village in the Dutch province of Groningen, where there was formerly a Mennonite congregation, usually called Kollum (q.v.) and Visvliet. It was probably Leenaert (q.v.) Bouwens who laid the foundation of this congregation by baptizing seven persons at Visvliet in 1551-54, five in 1554-56, and six in 1563-65. Concerning the Mennonites of Visvliet there is only scarce information. In 1643 it is reported that some Visvliet Mennonites had the "insolence to buy a house, which they provided with benches for use as their church." In the next year on the orders of the States of Groningen this meetinghouse was demolished, but the Mennonites continued to hold their meetings. At this time the Mennonites of Visvliet were very likely Ukowallists (q.v.). Later their congregation belonged to the Groningen Old Flemish conference and was represented at its meetings in 1681 and 1683. By 1700 the congregation had died out.　　　　　　　　　vDZ.

G. A. Wumkes, De Gereformeerde Kerk in de Ommelanden (Groningen, 1904) 38; DB 1879, 3.

Vit tho Pilgram: see **Fijt Pilgrims.**

Vlaanderen, Oost and **West,** two provinces of Belgium: see **Flanders.**

Vlaardingen, a town in the Dutch province of South Holland, some 8 miles west of Rotterdam, formerly the seat of a Mennonite congregation. Anabaptism was found here as early as 1535, for on Dec. 15, 1535, Brunt, the attorney general, wrote to the Stadholder van Hoogstraten that the Anabaptists of

Vlaardingen could not be arrested because they had all fled. In 1539 Anabaptists were again mentioned here. Later there was a congregation, of which Theunis Theunisz was a preacher in 1571. Still later there were an Old Flemish and a Flemish congregation, which may have merged in 1632 or shortly after. In 1651 a (new?) meetinghouse was built on the Fransenstraat, but in 1681 this house was sold, the congregation then having dissolved.   vDZ.

Inv. Arch. Amst. I, Nos. 143, 213, 593; *DB* 1912, 31, 38, 42; information from M. C. Sigal, former archivist of Vlaardingen; *De Zondagsbode* LII (1928-29) No. 32; *Algemeen Doopsgez. Weekblad* IV (1949-50) No. 16.

Vlaming (Vlamingh, Flaming, Flaminck, Fleming, Flemming, Flämmig, Flamig), a Mennonite family name. There was formerly a Vlaming(h) Mennonite family at Amsterdam, now extinct, of which Hans Vlamingh (*q.v.*) was a member. Cornelis (*q.v.*) de Vlaminck (Cornelis Jansz), according to Mellink a revolutionary Anabaptist, executed at Zwolle in 1535, was an Anabaptist at Amsterdam. Hans Hendricksen van Linth, called Hans Vleminck, and his wife Linken, who had both fled, were banished Oct. 12, 1575, because of Anabaptism. These Vlamings are apparently unrelated; the name simply means that they stemmed from Flanders (modern Belgium). A Vlaming (Flemming) family is also found among the West Prussian Mennonites, at Montau as early as 1636. Hans Vlaming was preacher of the Nieschewski (*q.v.*) church from 1737; he later moved to Deutsch Kazun (*q.v.*), where he also was a minister, serving until c1795. Heinrich Flaming moved from Franztal, West Prussia, to Molotschna, Russia, in 1825. There are also some Flamings in America.   vDZ.

Vlamingen (Vlaamschen, Vlaamsche Doopsgezinden), a branch of the Dutch Mennonites: see **Flemish Mennonites.**

Vlamingen, Dan(t)ziger Oude: see **Danzig Old Flemish Mennonites.**

Vlamingen, Groninger Oude: see **Groningen Old Flemish Mennonites** and **Groninger Doopsgezinde Sociëteit**(1).

Vlamingh, Hans (d. c1672 at Amsterdam), a Mennonite merchant in Amsterdam who took a warm interest in the oppressed and persecuted Swiss Brethren in the canton of Bern (*q.v.*). He sent several letters to the authorities at Bern, two of them dated Oct. 24, 1659, and April 16, 1660, which were published by Ernst Müller. Vlamingh presents a lengthy declaration of the innocence of the Swiss Brethren and the obligation of the state to grant them the free exercise of their religion. Besides his intervention Vlamingh started a relief action in the Amsterdam Zonist (*q.v.*) congregation, in which also the Lamist (*q.v.*) congregation participated. A Commission for Swiss Matters was appointed (which later developed into the general Mennonite Committee for Foreign Needs), on which Vlamingh served as secretary and treasurer. In 1671 he corresponded with Swiss leaders who had recently emigrated to the Palatinate, e.g., Valentin Huthwohl, Johann Clemens, and Jacob Everlinck. From the Palatine

Mennonites he received a letter of thanks with a list of the Mennonites who had immigrated into the Palatinate from Switzerland. Vlamingh, whom Ottius called "Hans Flamming, a Mennonite, a merchant of Amsterdam, an honest and reliable man," was a loyal Mennonite. In 1639 he was active in the merger of the Frisian-High German congregation of Amsterdam with the Flemish "bij't Lam" church. In the same year he was at Utrecht to bring about a similar union between the Frisian and Flemish congregations. In 1639 and from 1656 he was a deacon of the Lamist church. In the schism of 1664 (see **Lammerenkrijgh**) Vlamingh sided with the conservative Zonists and served as a deacon in the Zonist church as well as treasurer from the beginning. In this capacity he asked the Lamists for a division of the church property.   NEFF, vDZ.

Ottius, *Annales Anabaptistici* (Basel, 1672) 329 f., 335 f., 348, 350 f.; *Mart. Mir.* D 805, E 1104; Müller, *Berner Täufer,* 173-79, 186; *Inv. Arch. Amst.* I, Nos. 1194, 1248, 1405; *DB* 1863, 32, 80; Kühler, *Geschiedenis* II, 199; *ML* III.

Vliedorp, a hamlet in the northeast of the Dutch province of Groningen, where there was a Mennonite congregation in the 17th century which belonged to the Groningen Old Flemish branch. This congregation, mentioned in a letter of 1626, was represented at the conferences of the Old Flemish held in 1679, 1681, and 1683, in 1679 by its elder Walle Luitjes, who died in that year. The congregation, which was probably small, had merged with the neighboring church of Kloosterburen (*q.v.*) before 1710 and together with this church with that of Rasquert (*q.v.*). (*Inv. Arch. Amst.* I, No. 562; Kühler, *Geschiedenis* II, 138; *DB* 1879, 6.)   vDZ.

Vlieger, de, a Mennonite family in Hamburg, Germany, where this family is found at least from the early 17th century: in 1611 the Mennonite Symon de Vlieger was married to Maria Koen(en). A man of importance was Carl de Vlieger, d. about 1702, married in 1666 to the widow of the preacher Werner Jansz Colombier and in 1681 to a daughter of Elder Gerhard Roosen (*q.v.*). Carl de Vlieger took part in Greenland whaling from 1674 on by equipping his own ships, as did also his sons and his grandsons. The de Vlieger family became very wealthy. Carl de Vlieger contributed liberally to the building of the meetinghouse at Altona in 1674, as did his widow in 1716, when a new church was to be built to replace the former, which was burned down during the war in 1713. Many members of the de Vlieger family were deacons, and some served as preachers; one of these was Gerrit Vlieger from 1765.

It could not be ascertained whether Karl de Fleger (Vlieger), who in 1652 published a Mennonite hymnal with a confession of faith (see **Psalmen, de CL**), belonged to this family. Some members of the de Vlieger family, temporarily living at Amsterdam, were members of the Zonist (*q.v.*) church. The Hamburg de Vlieger family died out in the early 19th century.

A Mennonite de Vlieger family, emigrants from Waarschoot in Flanders, Belgium, was living at Aardenburg (*q.v.*) in Dutch Zeeland Flanders in the 17th century. One Jan de Vlieger (1700-32), apparently a descendant of this branch, lived at Zierik-zee. Some de Vliegers were members of the Amsterdam Lamist church in the 18th century. The relationship between this family and de Vliegers of Hamburg and Aardenburg could not be determined.

vDZ.

B. C. Roosen, *Geschichte der Mennoniten-Gemeinde zu Hamburg und Altona* I (Hamburg, 1886) 37, 39, 46, 48, 57, 58, 61, 64; II (Hamburg, 1887) 6, 16, 49, 55, 82, 84; Wanda Oesau, *Hamburgs Grönlandfahrt* (Glückstadt-Hamburg, 1955) 143-45; church records of Aardenburg and Amsterdam; Robert Dollinger, *Geschichte der Mennoniten in Schleswig-Holstein, Hamburg und Lübeck* (Neumünster, 1930).

Vlieland, one of the Dutch North Sea islands, where there was formerly a Mennonite congregation. In the 17th century Westvlieland was a Mennonite center, with two meetinghouses; but this western part was gradually swallowed up by the sea, and the population moved to Oostvlieland in the early 18th century; the Mennonite congregation was then usually known as Oostvlieland (or Oosterend op't Vlie). There was a Mennonite congregation on Vlieland by c1560. In 1563-65 Leenaert (*q.v.*) Bouwens baptized 45 persons here and later nine; the martyr Jan (*q.v.*) Geertsz, of the neighboring island of Texel, executed in 1564, greeted the brethren of Vlieland in his "Testament."

About 1600 there were two congregations on Vlieland, one Waterlander (*q.v.*) and one Janjacobsgezinden (*q.v.*), to the members of which Jan (*q.v.*) Jacobsz dedicated the hymn "Aen die Vlielanders," found in *Eenighe Gheestelijcke Liedekens* (Amsterdam, 1612). The Janjacobsgezinde congregation had a meetinghouse in Westvlieland, and died out before 1705. The Waterlander congregation, though at first larger in membership (129 baptized members in 1705), was rather poor, and was subsidized by the Rijper (*q.v.*) Sociëteit, of which it was a member from 1703, and also by the Lamist congregation of Amsterdam. Most Mennonites of Vlieland were sailors and captains on the large vessels sailing from Amsterdam and other Zuiderzee ports as far as Denmark, Danzig, and Russia, and in the church books numerous notices are found concerning members having died at Kopenhagen, Danzig, Saint Petersburg, and other distant cities or at sea. Other members of the Vlieland congregation were engaged in coastal navigation and herring fishery. During a large part of the year the church meetings were attended largely by women and children, the male members being abroad. As elsewhere in seaports the moral level of the church members was low and discipline more necessary than in most Dutch churches. It was very difficult to find deacons and preachers from their own membership, most of the men being absent for months. Consequently the old men had to serve as deacons and at a rather early date preachers, all untrained, were called from outside: Jan Jacobs Tichelaar, called from Stiens, served 1704/5-d.21, followed by Jelte Jeltes Postums 1721-49, Dirk Jansz Bogert 1751-61, Aris Dirksz Baas 1762-69, Hendrik Tijmens 1770-78, and Adriaan Vrijer 1778-98. Then the pulpit remained vacant. The membership had rapidly decreased: 129 baptized members in 1705, about 80 in 1750, 20 in 1778, and only four in 1808. In 1813 the congregation was

dissolved; the property, about 1500 Dutch guilders, was transferred to the Rijper Sociëteit, which also sold the meetinghouse (for 500 guilders) and supported the last member, who died in 1819. At present the pastor of the neighboring island of Terschelling (*q.v.*) is in charge of the few Mennonites living on Vlieland.

J. Loosjes, "De Doopsgezinde gemeente op Vlieland," in *DB* 1912, 76-93; *Inv. Arch. Amst.* I, No. 726; II, Nos. 915, 1055, 2338 f.; II, 2, Nos. 498a, 498b; *DB* 1861, 92 f.; *DJ* 1942, 40; 1943, 45 f.

Vliermaal, a village near Hasselt in the Belgian province of Limburg, where in 1538 a number of Anabaptists were sentenced to death. Some Anabaptists from Aachen, Germany, and from England had recently settled in the region of Hasselt. According to somewhat inexact information nine men were burned at the stake and ten women executed by drowning. These victims were apparently Anabaptists. Their names are not given, with one exception: Jannes (*q.v.*) van Rommerswael, who was executed at Curingen near Hasselt, June 14, 1538.

vDZ.

W. Bax, *Het Protestantisme in het Bisdom Luik* I (The Hague, 1937) 161.

Vliet, van der, a Dutch Mennonite family, whose progenitor was (1) Lucas (Luitje) Heeres van der Vliet (before 1600-after 1645), a merchant at Appingedam (*q.v.*) in the province of Groningen, and a preacher of the local Mennonite church. His son (2) Lucas Lucasz van der Vliet (1624-98), also a merchant, moved to Amsterdam, where his son (3) Dirk van der Vliet (1651-79) was a gold and silver smith. (4) Jan van der Vliet (1678-1723), a son of (3) Dirk, had a prosperous cloth shop, but it was (5) Cornelis van der Vliet (1705-80) and his brother (6) Jan van der Vliet (1717-85), sons of (4) Jan, who made the fortune of this family by the ironworks they founded at Amsterdam. The firm still exists, since 1906 under the name Van der Vliet and de Jonge. At the same time Cornelis and his descendants operated an important wholesale business.

The first members of this family at Amsterdam were all Lamists. From 1730, however, one branch belonged to the Zonists. In both Amsterdam churches some of the van der Vliets were deacons. (6) Jan van der Vliet and his sister Cornelia (1720-93), married to Pieter Verbeek, were friends of Zinzendorf (*q.v.*) and benefactors of the Moravian Brethren (Hernhutters, *q.v.*) in Holland. Until 1807 all the members of this family married Mennonites with only one exception in 1781; in the 19th century they all married non-Mennonites.

vDZ.

Nederl. Patriciaat XI (1920) 320-31; W. J. J. C. Bijleveld, *Genealogie van het Geslacht van der Vliet* (The Hague, 1924); W. Lütjeharms, *Het Oecumenisch-Philadelphisch Streven der Hernhutters* (Zeist, 1935) 143, 167; Amsterdam church records.

Vlissingen, a seaport on the island of Walcheren (*q.v.*) in the Dutch province of Zeeland (1955 pop. 26,000; 200 Mennonites). Anabaptism seems to have arisen here somewhat later than in the other towns of Walcheren like Middelburg and Veere; not until 1567 is there information about it. In 1567 Hendrick (*q.v.*) Alewijnsz, of Vlissingen, traveled about preaching; arrested in 1568, he died as a martyr at Middelburg in 1569. He also preached in the neighborhood of Vlissingen. That there was then a congregation at Vlissingen may be concluded from a letter written by the martyr Hans (*q.v.*) Marijnsz van Oosten, of Vlissingen, who was executed with Hendrik Alewijnsz in 1569. On the same day another martyr, Gerrit (*q.v.*) Duynherder, probably also from Vlissingen, was put to death. Dirk (*q.v.*) Meeuwesz, of Vlissingen, was apprehended in 1570 and burned at the stake there in 1571. He is the only martyr who died in Vlissingen. From *c*1575 Mennonites of Flanders, Belgium, came to Vlissingen, where it was safer, for baptism. One of the elders from Flanders who performed baptisms at Vlissingen was Hans (*q.v.*) Busschaert, *c*1587. About this time or shortly before, the congregation was greatly increased by the arrival of Mennonite refugees from Flanders. Thus the congregation was mostly of Flemish descent, and consequently sided with the Flemish branch. According to Faukelius (*q.v.*) there was *c*1600 also a congregation of the Naeldemansvolk (*q.v.*), of which Cornelis (de) Compas(maker) was the leader; they were also called "Compasmennisten." This account obviously refers to a Waterlander congregation at Vlissingen, concerning which there is no further information.

The Flemish church was always small (exact figures before *c*1638 not available); in the 17th century the following families, all descendants of refugees from Flanders, are found among the members: van Daelle (Dale), Fa(c)k, Geleynsz, van Houteryve (Outrijve), Ta(c)k, and Willeboorts. Besides the Waterlander and Flemish congregations in the early 17th century there was at Vlissingen also an Old Flemish congregation which in 1602 separated from the Flemish church; it is also called the Huiskopers (*q.v.*) or Voetwasschers church. This small group disappeared shortly after 1640, probably by merging with the Flemish.

About 1620 the number of Mennonites at Vlissingen can be estimated at *c*400. They seem not to have encountered special difficulties from the Reformed magistrates: in 1589 an agreement was made to exempt the Mennonites from military service upon payment of a certain sum by the congregation. During the 17th century Mennonites had to have their marriages performed by the city officials after announcement in the Reformed church, but from 1638 their marriages could be performed in their own meetinghouse. The Mennonites of Vlissingen could meet rather freely. At first meetings were held in private homes; when the membership increased in the early 17th century a house near the Reformed church was used as a meetinghouse. In 1641 a house on the Peperdijk was remodeled into a church (the "new church" mentioned in 1668 probably refers to some alteration of the Peperdijk meetinghouse). This meetinghouse was very plain, with backless benches and without a pulpit. It was remodeled in 1723, 1744, 1848, and 1859. In 1744 it obtained a pulpit; in 1848 a parlor organ. In 1859 the pulpit was replaced by a simple platform. This meetinghouse was used until 1889.

In 1632 the preacher Oillaert Willeboorts and the deacons Per Jacob Pennen (the name obviously mutilated) and Lieven Marijnsz signed the Dordrecht (*q.v.*) confession for Vlissingen. During the Lammerenkrijgh (*q.v.*) after the Lamist-Zonist schism Vlissingen, influenced by its elder Pieter Baert, sided with the progressive Lamists.

The congregation of Vlissingen like that of Middelburg has an important and considerable archives, now found in the Provincial Zeeland Archives at Middelburg. Records of members and other Vlissingen church books are preserved since 1665. The congregation contributed liberally to the Committee for Foreign Needs and to other needs also of non-Mennonites.

There is a complete list of ministers since 1628. Until 1689 they served without remuneration; in this year it was decided to pay the preacher a salary of 300 Dutch guilders, soon considerably raised. The list of ministers reads as follows: Oillaert Willeboorts 1628-after 1648, Gillis Anthonissen Timmermans 1638, Cornelis Remeusz Elinck 1642, Joost van Outrijve 1649-72, Frans Claesz 1649, Frans Cornelisz 1650, Adriaen van Nispen 1650, Antheunis de Niel 1659, Pieter Baert 1659- after 1673, Jan Pietersz van Nes 1660, Pieter de Jager 1663-71, Maurits Arents 1663, Frans Theunissen Hugemans 1667, Leendert Lievens 1670, Jan Samuelsz Tack 1673-d.97, Lieven van Outrijve 1675-d.82, Anthony van Stein 1676, Christiaen van Nispen 1683, Joost van Outrijve 1686-93, Paulus de Wind 1691, Joannes Nettis 1700, Jan van de Voorde 1701, Gerbrand Voor(e)n 1701-*c*25, Abbe Cornelisz Oosterling 1704, Jan Cornelisz Wit 1718, Gerardus Pauli 1722, Frederik Jaarsma 1726-50, Jacobus Hesseling 1750-53, Joannes Cuperus 1753-58, Gerlof Rekker 1759-1809. After the death of Rekker (1809) the membership being rather small and finances insufficient, the congregation of Vlissingen was served by the ministers of Middelburg until 1871. In this year Vlissingen again had a pastor of its own, H. D. Tjeenk Willink, serving 1871-73, followed by A. Snellen 1874-78 and J. Dyserinck 1879-84; when Dyserinck left a union was again made with Middelburg, whose pastor served until 1899; then a union was made with Goes, which lasted until 1919, pastor T. H. Siemelink, who served in the combination Goes-Vlissingen 1908-19, from 1919 serving only at Vlissingen until he retired in 1927. He was followed by O. L. van der Veen 1929-31, Miss A. J. van den Ban 1932-39, and Miss M. de Boer since 1939.

The baptized membership was about 165 in 1665 and *c*285 in 1673. From then it decreased, many Mennonites moving to Middelburg and Amsterdam. In 1730 the baptized membership stood at 125, in 1757 at 99, in 1773 at 74, in 1834 at 22, and in 1838 at only 18. From then there was a considerable increase: 32 in 1861, 49 in 1888, 98 in 1901, 115 in 1926, and 183 in 1958.

The old meetinghouse of 1641 on the Peperdijk was sold in 1889 to a Reformed group: a new church was dedicated on July 6, 1890, by Pastor Tj. Kielstra of Middelburg. This church, furnished with a new organ in 1908, was destroyed during World War II on April 24, 1942. On Feb. 20, 1949, a new meetinghouse on Vrijdomsweg 1 (architect P. Feenstra) was dedicated by Miss de Boer, pastor of the congregation. Church activities are now (1958): a ladies' circle, youth groups, Sunday school for children.　　　　　　　　　　　　　　　　vDZ.

Inv. Arch. Amst. I, Nos. 559, 580 f., 1167, 1996; II, Nos. 1266, 1270 f., 2340 f.; II, 2, Nos. 499-642; J. Cuperus and J. de Loos, "History of the Congregation," manuscript in the Archives of the congregation; H. P. Winkelman. "De Doopsgezinde Gemeente te Vlissingen," *DB* 1875, 32-42; K. R. Pekelharing, "Bijdragen voor de Geschiedenis der Hervorming in Zeeland 1524-72," in *Archief VI* of the Zeeuwsch Genootschap van Wetenschappen (Middelburg, 1866) 293 f., 296 f., 303, 305, 306; *Mart. Mir.* D 405 f., E 757 f; *DJ* 1837, 6; 1850, 43; *DB* 1861, 176; 1872, 196; 1877, 5; 1883, 101 f.; 1884, 111 f.; 1885, 131 f.; 1890, 143; 1899, 212; 1907, 168; *DJ* 1950, 33-38; *Algemeen Doopsgez. Weekblad* XI (1956-57) No. 51.

Vlugt, van der, a Mennonite family of bankers at Haarlem, Holland, six of whom served as deacons of the Haarlem Mennonite congregation since 1762, and some of whom were trustees of the A.D.S. (*q.v.*). An outstanding member of this family was Willem van der Vlugt (b. 1853 at Haarlem, d. 19— at Leiden), who studied law and from 1880 was professor of law at Leiden University; he also was a member of the Dutch Second Chamber. From 1885 he was a deacon at Leiden, and 1887-1921 a trustee of the A.D.S., its moderator 1895-96, and curator of the Mennonite seminary 1890-1921. Jan van der Vlugt of Haarlem was treasurer of the Committee for Foreign Needs from 1921, acting in behalf of the Russian refugees. Abraham Jan Theodoor van der Vlugt (1894-1954) was active in the relief of the Mennonite refugees from Russia in 1923. In 1929-38 he was a trustee (also treasurer and moderator) of the Hague congregation; in 1945 he was appointed Minister of State and ambassador of the Netherlands to Finland, where he suddenly died at Helsinki on Jan. 8, 1954.　　　　　　　　　　　　vDZ.

Vöcklabruck, a town in Upper Austria, the home of Leonhard Schiemer (*q.v.*), the first elder of the Anabaptists in Upper Austria. About Pentecost of 1528, eight Anabaptists, among them Hans Tischler, a preacher, and Lienhart Laitschneider of Salzburg, were put to death here. These executions, performed on the grounds of the church, led to a trial, because Ciriac, Baron of Polheim (owner of Puchheim), who as Vogt of the parish of St. Gilgen saw in this deed an interference into his jurisdiction, demanded the sum of 1,000 florins as compensation. The city was summoned to answer this charge.　　　HEGE.

Josef Jäkel, "Zur Geschichte der Wiedertäufer in Oberösterreich und speziell in Freistadt," in *47. Bericht des Museums Franciscus Carolius* (Linz, 1889); *ML* IV.

Voet (Voth), a Mennonite family in Prussia: see **Foth.**

Voet (Foth), **Hans,** was a preacher of the Groningen Old Flemish congregation in Lithuania (*q.v.*), and after his expulsion from there, until 1760 in the Groningen Old Flemish congregation at Schönsee in the territory of Culm, West Prussia. In 1727 and again in 1732 he wrote a letter to the Mennonites at Amsterdam complaining that the Catholic bishop of Culm was severely oppressing them so that they needed much money to satisfy the bishop and his officials. (*Inv. Arch. Amst.* II, 2, Nos. 738, 763.)　　　　　　　　　　　　　　　　　vDZ.

Voetwasschers (Footwashers), a name given to some Dutch Mennonites in the 16th century, found *c*1576 at Middelburg and other places in the province of Zeeland. This group soon disappeared by merging with the Waterlanders (*q.v.*). (*Inv. Arch. Amst.* II, 2, Nos. 280, 282; *DB* 1863, 112 f.)　　　vDZ.

Vogel, a former Mennonite family at Edam, Dutch province of North Holland, where Claas Dirkse Vogel, d. Sept. 21, 1741, was a preacher of the Frisian congregation. A Hans Vogel is mentioned in Prussia.　　　　　　　　　　　　　　　　　vDZ.

DB 1887, 117, 119, 120, 128, 130, 131; F. Szper, *Nederl. Nederzettingen in West Pruisen* (Enkhuizen, 1913) 47.

Vogel, de, a Dutch Mennonite family, died out at the end of the 18th century. Members of this family were found at Leiden until 1710 and particularly in the Amsterdam Lamist church; as early as 1622 Salomon de Vogel (*q.v.*) was a member of this church. He was one of the deacons of six Dutch Mennonite congregations, who on May 20, 1661, petitioned the magistrates of Bern in behalf of their Swiss co-religionists, who were being persecuted.

They were loyal members of the church. Some of them left property to the church. Many of them served as deacons at Leiden, Jan de Vogel serving in the Flemish congregation until 1664; his son Willem de Vogel 1679-84. A Thomas de Vogel was a deacon of the Leiden Waterlander congregation until 1672 and Willem de Vogel from 1676 in the same church. Deacons at Amsterdam were Jan de Vogel Thomasz 1709-15 and 1721-26, and his son Thomas de Vogel 1731-37, 1741-47, and 1755-60. Cornelis de Vogel Leonardsz (*q.v.*) at Danzig and Leonard Thomas de Vogel (*q.v.*) belonged to this family.　　vDZ.

Church records of Amsterdam; L. G. le Poole, *Bijdragen tot de kennis van het kerkelijk leven onder de Doopsgezinden . . . te Leiden* (Leiden, 1905) 10 f., 12, 15-17, 65, 66, 196; Müller, *Berner Täufer,* 192.

Vogel, Cornelis de (Cornelis Leonardsz), a member of the Lamist Mennonite congregation at Amsterdam, Holland, who moved to Danzig, Prussia, in 1726 for his banking business. He presented a letter of membership to the Danzig Mennonite Schladall congregation, but he was refused in 1727 because he wore a periwig. Thereupon de Vogel asked admission to the Markushof (*q.v.*) congregation in 1728, but was rejected there too. These refusals, which were particularly due to the conservatism of the Danzig elder Hendrik (Heinrich) van Dühren (*q.v.*), caused much trouble in the Danzig congregation. In 1735 de Vogel had not yet been admitted as a member.

Cornelis de Vogel Leonardsz, as well as his father-in-law Jan van Hoek (*q.v.*) and his brother-in-law Jan van Hoek, both of whom were Danzig bankers, served as mediators between the Prussian Mennonites and the Dutch Mennonite Committee for Foreign Needs. (*Inv. Arch. Amst.* I, Nos. 1235, 1624, 1628, 1632, 1639, 1642, 1648, 1650; II, 2, Nos. 2634 f., 2640 f.)　　　　　　　　　　　　　　　vDZ.

Vogel, Huizen de, three houses on Kerkstraat 316-20 at Amsterdam, bequeathed to the Lamist Mennonite congregation at Amsterdam in 1794 by Leonard Thomas de Vogel (*q.v.*). The houses at first were used to lodge the orphans of the church, but since 1800 they have been used for aged married couples. (*Inv. Arch. Amst.* II, 533-37.)   vDZ.

Vogel, Leonhard Thomas de, b. at Amsterdam *c*1725, d. 1794 at his stately country home, "Vijverburg" on the Vecht River, of which he had been the owner since 1770, a son of Thomas de Vogel and Elisabeth Bosch, married 1756 to Catharine van Lennep (1726-), died childless. From his great fortune he bequeathed to the congregation *bij't Lam* at Amsterdam, into which he was baptized in 1745, three houses on the Kerkstraat (see **Vogel, Huizen de**) and a sum of money to be administered by the trustees of the congregation as "Fonds de Vogel," for the expenses of the Mennonite theological seminary, which was then an activity of the Amsterdam Lamist congregation. Since the founding of the A.D.S. (*q.v.*) in 1811, which took over the seminary, this fund has always been represented among the trustees of the A.D.S. (*Inv. Arch. Amst.* II, Nos. 310, 2476, 2499, 2559, 2568 f.; *DJ* 1850, 138, 140; *Verslagen* of the A.D.S.)   vDZ.

Vogel, Wolfgang (*c*1500-27), an Anabaptist martyr, born in Reutlingen, Swabia; he joined the reform movement of Nürnberg at an early age. Around 1523-24 there was in this city a group of "evangelical-minded men" who found themselves in open conflict with the budding Lutheran movement. The poet Hans Sachs is said to have belonged to this group, and Vogel apparently shared its "radical" outlook. In 1524 as pastor in Bopfingen and in 1525 as pastor in Eltersdorf, he tried to introduce the Reformation. In early 1526 he also became acquainted with Hans Hut, who was then a bookseller in Nürnberg, and it is probable that Hut won him for the new, still more radical ideas of Anabaptism.

Hearing that Bopfingen had dismissed his successor (a like-minded preacher), Vogel addressed a missive to the citizens of that city, called *Tröstlicher Sendbrief und christliche Ermahnung zum Evangelio, an den ehrbaren Rat und die ganze Gemeinde zu Bopfingen* (1526), a pamphlet, printed without naming the printer or the place of publication. (Today only two copies of it are known: one in the Mennonite library at Amsterdam, and the other in the archives of Nürnberg.) The Bopfingen council was embarrassed and offended by this somewhat aggressively prophetic pamphlet, a true penitential sermon, and decided to forward it to the Nürnberg council for advice and action. Lazarus Spengler, a leading councilman and censor of Nürnberg, called Vogel from Eltersdorf to account for this tract, and warned him not to indulge further in such "liberties." Although it dismissed him, the council soon discovered that Vogel was an Anabaptist. Upon examination he admitted having been baptized by Hut and also having baptized others. Since there was as yet no Anabaptist church organization Vogel seems to have acted as an isolated individual. Vogel, under the jurisdiction of the Nürnberg council, was imprisoned and the case reported to Kasimir, Margrave of Brandenburg (Bayreuth-Ansbach); but before it could receive an answer it decided to make an example of Vogel. Thus a sham trial was held, complete with torture, and an argument was trumped up that Vogel intended rebellion. On March 26, 1527, he was beheaded without opportunity to defend himself. The trial records no longer exist and may have been destroyed to obscure the situation.

The most important aspect of this story (a first in the long epic of Anabaptist persecutions) is the *Sendbrief* of 1526, which profoundly reflects the spirit of this first decade of both the Reformation and Anabaptism. Wiswedel gives an elaborate summary of its contents (pp. 162-69). Not unlike Haug's (*q.v.*) *Christliche Ordnung* of 1524, this *Sendbrief* is less typically Anabaptist than non-Lutheran. It is a forceful call to repentance addressed to the citizenry of Bopfingen and to authorities in general, "kings, princes, and lords." The old theme of "reason and obedience" (*q.v.*) occupies a central place in his arguments. The cross is inevitable for those who obey God's Word: like gold in fire so also must man be tried by tribulation and persecution. One can easily understand that the council members of both Bopfingen and Nürnberg were baffled by this letter; they simply interpreted it as a voice of rebellion.

In 1717, two hundred years later, in the days of flowering Pietism (*q.v.*), Dr. J. D. Herrnschmidt, professor of theology in Halle, by chance discovered a copy of this *Sendbrief,* perhaps in the archives of Bopfingen, where he had been a superintendent, and re-edited it in 1717 as a devotional tract for his congregation in Halle. What once had caused martyrdom for its author was now welcomed and applauded, even though there is good reason to assume that the pamphlet was reinterpreted in the mild and rather harmless way of 18th-century Pietism. R.F.

J. H. Ottius, *Annales Anabaptistici* (Basel, 1672); Wiswedel, *Bilder* I, 152-69; Wappler, *Thüringen*, 245; *TA Bayern* I; R. Friedmann, *Mennonite Piety Through the Centuries* (Goshen, 1949) 26 f.

Vogelsberg: see Mont des Oiseaux.

Vogelstock, near Landau in the Palatinate, Germany. A Mennonite congregation of Bächlingen-Vogelstock is mentioned in the Dutch *Naamlijst* from 1767. Its preachers were Johannes Ellenberger 1754-d.*c*85, Philip Sties until *c*1769, Johann Berg serving 1763-after 1802, Jacob Sties(s) from 1769, Daniel van Huben (?) 1782-*c*88, and Jacob Sautor 1787-after 1802. Elders of this congregation were Daniel Hirschler, living at the Geisberg, until 1769, at the same time elder of the Schafbusch (*q.v.*) congregation, and 1769-85 Christian Hege of the Branchweilerhof. In 1785 preacher Stiess was chosen as elder, serving until after 1802. In the *Naamlijst* of 1784 and following editions this congregation is listed as Bächlingen-Vogelstock-Sankt Johanneskirchen. In the 19th century it was called Sankt Johann or Johanniskirchen. The *Namensverzeichnis* (Danzig, 1857, p. 37) mentions preachers Jacob Zörger and Jacob Res serving from 1851, and Jacob Riess, also serving from 1859. The congregation then numbered 70 baptized members. In 1887 (Mannhardt, *Jahrbuch* 1888, p. 28, No. 14) it numbered 40 souls, with Jacob Zörger as preacher. (See also **Sankt Johann.**)   vDZ.

Vogt, a Mennonite family name: see **Voth.**

Voit (Veyt), **Peter,** a Hutterite missioner and co-worker with Jakob Hutter. Hutter mentions him twice in his letters, once saying that Voit had brought a group of converts from Tirol to Moravia. Voit was seized in Austria in 1534 and imprisoned in a dark dungeon in Egenburg, and his ankles were so tightly bound in irons that gangrene set in and his feet decayed. Helplessly he had to suffer having the mice eat his toes. He was later released. He was received by the exiled Moravian Anabaptists, who were themselves in dire need (1538) and lodging in the open field. Both of his feet had to be amputated. He died in 1570. (Zieglschmid, *Chronik,* 121, 138, 143; *ML* IV.)   HEGE.

Voitelsbrunn (Veutlasprun, Voitlsbrunn, Slovakian *Selec*), a village in Moravia near the Thaya marshes between Nikolsburg and Feldsberg, was the site of two Hutterite Bruderhofs, the first established in 1557, the other in 1561. The Brethren had a noted bathhouse here. They were expelled from Voitelsbrunn by Sigmund von Dietrichstein (*q.v.*) in 1591. (Zieglschmid, *Chronik,* 368; Wolkan, *Geschicht-Buch,* 279, 432; *ML* IV.)

Vola-Vodzinska Mennonite Church, located near Plonsk, northwest of Warsaw, Poland, was a subsidiary of the Deutsch-Kazun Mennonite Church (*q.v.*). The *Namens-Verzeichnis* of Prussian Mennonites mentions this congregation for the first time in 1843 (p. 34), when the following ministers were listed: Franz Ewert (1818), Benjamin Foth (1837), Jacob Köthler (1842), and Heinrich Kliewer (1842). Heinrich Kerber and Heinrich Kliewer, both elected in 1842, were deacons. The fact that 1842 is given four times as the year of the election of the church officials could indicate that this was the year of the organization of the church.

In 1857, in addition to Jacob Köthler and Heinrich Kliewer, Peter Froms was listed as minister. The deacons were the same. In 1881 Cornelius Balzer, Julius Balzer, and Peter Pauls are listed as ministers, all elected in 1880. Heinrich Bartel served as deacon. At this time the congregation, although still a subsidiary of Deutsch-Kazun, had its own meetinghouse at Vola-Vodzinska. Together the congregations had a membership of 597. Kupsch reports that many of the Mennonites of this group joined the Baptists around 1860. Many others no doubt joined the emigration to the United States around 1874. By the outbreak of World War I there were only eight families or 35 persons left at Vola-Vodzinska (see Deutsch-Kazun).

Kupsch has given an account of a revival among the Mennonites of this area in the villages of Adamov, Kicin, and Vola-Vodzinska. Above all, Peter Ewert (*q.v.*) and Johann Penner (*q.v.*) were instrumental in promoting the revival and introducing baptism by immersion, which ultimately took a large part of the congregation to the Baptist Church. In 1858 Johann Penner, of Adamov, on a visit to his relatives at Vola-Vodzinska, testified for his renewed faith and was imprisoned for ten days. A revival occurred. The first baptism by immersion took place at Kicin on Aug. 25, 1860. Soon there was

disunity between the Baptists of Mennonite background and those of Lutheran tradition. The Baptists did not share the Mennonite principle of nonresistance and the practice of footwashing. For a while Penner and Ewert separated from the Baptists. However, "Ewert recognized his error, repented, and came back to the Baptists, and became a missionary. Penner also returned to the Baptists in 1863."

In 1862 the Baptists in Vola-Vodzinska had a following of about 20 among the Mennonites. The Baptist missionary Alf (*q.v.*) was quite active among them. He and Ewert also corresponded with the Mennonite Brethren of the Ukraine. The Mennonites of Poland who were revived and testified for their new Baptist faith shared in the persecution which came over this new movement. They were pioneers of the revival which spread through Poland and gave rise to the Baptist movement and at the same time they speeded up the disintegration of small struggling Mennonite groups and churches.
                                                     C.K.

Kupsch, *Gesch. der Baptisten in Polen* (Lodz, 1932); Friesen, *Brüderschaft,* 244 ff.; *Namens-Verzeichnis* (1843, 1857, 1881).

Volbot (Volboet), **Abraham Davidsz,** was a member of the Flemish Mennonite congregation "in den Blok" (*q.v.*) at Haarlem. After the Reformed pastor of Haarlem, Petrus Bontemps (*q.v.*), had attacked the Mennonites and had been replied to by the Mennonite deacon Joost Hendricks (*q.v.*) of Amsterdam, Volbot also entered into the polemics by publishing (under the pseudonym of Gerard van Vryburgh) two pamphlets with curious titles: *Hollandsche Zeep tegen Uytheemsche Vlecken* . . . (Amsterdam, 1643, repr. 1644) and, after the reply of Bontemps, *Loogh-Water op de Laster-Vlecken van P.B.* . . . (Amsterdam, 1664, should be 1644). A. D. Volbot was a strict Flemish Mennonite, an opponent of Galenus (*q.v.*) Abrahamsz and of Collegiantism (*q.v.*) in 1655. About his private life nothing is known.   vDZ.

DB 1863, 134, 136; J. C. van Slee, *De Rijnsburger Collegianten* (Haarlem, 1895) 146.

Volder (de), a Mennonite family at Alkmaar, Netherlands. Pieter de Volder was a preacher of the local Flemish congregation in 1621 and Grietje Jacobs Volder the mother of Marten Schagen (*q.v.*). vDZ.

Volendam, a steamer of the (Dutch) Holland-America Line of 15,434 tons gross, built in 1922, scrapped in 1952, named after the small Dutch town of Volendam in North Holland, was used for the transport of Mennonite refugees, and is particularly known for its transport of Mennonites from Europe to Buenos Aires in 1947. C. F. Klassen (*q.v.*), then the MCC representative in Europe, who organized the journey, chartered the ship. Some 650 Mennonite refugees embarked at Rotterdam, Netherlands, on Jan. 28, 1947; in Bremerhaven some 450 others from a refugee camp at Gronau, Germany, joined them. Then they waited for a large group from Berlin. Because Klassen gave a financial guarantee to the Holland-America Line for a possible delay in sailing and this warrant was accepted without the usual bail, the ship waited for the Berlin group. This was a group of some 1,100 Mennonite refugees from Russia who after much trouble and danger of life had reached Berlin and even in Berlin had a narrow escape, for only at the last moment did the Russian authorities give the necessary permission to travel through the Eastern Zone of Germany, occupied by the Russians. Packed into railway freight cars they were transported to Bremerhaven, from where the *Volendam* sailed on Feb. 1, 1947, with the 2,306 Mennonites. The emigrants were led by Peter and Elfrieda Dyck, who had come with the Berlin group. During the train journey a woman died, and a baby during embarkation. Two aged persons and a baby died at sea, and four children were born on the boat: one was named Peter Volendam (after Peter Dyck and the ship), and one Elfrieda (after Mrs. Dyck). Upon arrival at Buenos Aires further transportation was difficult, and for a large number of these immigrants impossible until October 1948, because a revolution had broken out in Paraguay. About 1,200 of the passengers of the *Volendam* settled in Eastern Paraguay, giving to their new colony the name of Volendam after the ship which had brought them to the new world and to liberty. Of the remaining 1,100, 870 founded the Neuland (*q.v.*) Colony in the Paraguayan Chaco (*q.v.*), 162 remained in Buenos Aires, and the rest joined their relatives in the Fernheim or Friesland colonies or settled in Asunción, the capital of Paraguay.

A second Mennonite transport of the *Volendam* was that in 1947 of 1,640 (including 635 infants) Old Colonists (*q.v.*) from Quebec to Buenos Aires, who were also to settle in Paraguay, and a third transport by the *Volendam* was in October 1948, that of a group of 751 West Prussian and Galician Mennonites for Montevideo, Uruguay, and a number of Mennonites from Russia, who intended to go to Paraguay, and who disembarked in Buenos Aires. The International Refugee Organization (*q.v.*) paid about $160,000 for the cost of the first chartering of the *Volendam* and assumed the full cost of the third transport as far as Asunción.

Thus the name of the *Volendam* is well known in Mennonite history.   C.A.W.B.

Logbooks of the *Volendam*; J. W. Fretz, *Pilgrims in Paraguay* (Scottdale, n.d., 1953) 39-41; "Peter Dyck's Story," *Menn. Life* III (1948) No. 1, 8-11; Gustav E. Reimer, "Von Danzig nach Uruguay," *Menn. Life* IV (1949) No. 3, 12-14.

Volendam Agricultural Co-operative (*Cooperative Agricola de Volendam*), located in Colony Volendam in Alto-Paraguay near the port of Mbopicua, was organized on July 2, 1947, under the Paraguayan law No. 13635 of 1942, with a membership of 295, which included all family heads of the colony. The Co-operative was founded upon the advice of the colony leaders and MCC representatives to facilitate adequate distribution of funds made available by the MCC, to enable the economical provision of supplies to the settlers and profitable sale of their produce, and to establish small basic industries which would meet the daily needs of the immigrants. The first year its only capital was maintenance funds and loans made available by the MCC.

Its shares are valued at 20,000 guaranies, payable by dividends, and its 1949 turnover was 460,000 guaranies; profits are either used for the expansion of the Co-operative or paid to the members in the form of new shares. The Co-operative and its president are responsible to the administration of the colony (Amt) for all its activities (see **Volendam Colony**) and acts as the financial arm of the colony in all matters. Besides a shortage of operating capital, considerable difficulties were at first encountered through the armed raids of Paraguayan bandits at repeated intervals, who took advantage of the unarmed Mennonite watchmen.   P.K.

Volendam Colony, Paraguay, was founded July 1, 1947, when the 57,000-acre tract of land occupied by the colony at Mbopicua on the east side of the Paraguay River near the Friesland Colony (*q.v.*), 8 miles north of Rosario, was purchased. The 1,135 settlers (295 families) were part of the contingent which had been brought to South America by the *Volendam*, having been rescued out of Berlin. Another large group of the *Volendam*, passengers settled contemporaneously in the Neuland Colony (*q.v.*) near Fernheim Colony. C. A. Defehr of Winnipeg, the MCC representative for this purpose in Paraguay, had chosen the location and arranged the land purchase. Two additional small groups of immigrants arrived in Volendam from Europe in 1948. A group of some 50 came on the *Stuart Heinzelman* to Buenos Aires in July 1948. In November 1948 a larger group of 447 for Volendam arrived in Buenos Aires on the second voyage of the *Volendam*. Thus the total immigrant group of settlers in Volendam in 1948 was almost 1,723. The first 1,135 settlers established 12 villages, with a co-operative and a "Waisenamt" (*q.v.*). The river harbor was named Puerto Menno. In 1950 Volendam had 15 villages with a total population of 1,810 in 441 families on 441 farms, and 8 elementary schools. Most of the land was heavily wooded, though fertile, and had to be cleared by hand. The economic progress of the colony was slow, and a considerable number of persons have migrated to Canada, so that in 1959 the total Volendam population was only c1200. In 1950 the total church membership was 938—800 in the Mennonite Church and 138 in the Mennonite Brethren Church.   H.S.B.

J. W. Fretz, *Pilgrims in Paraguay* (Scottdale, 1953); W. Quiring, *Im Schweisse Deines Angesichts* (Steinbach, 1953).

Volendam Mennonite Brethren Church, located in Colony Volendam near Puerto Mbopicua, Alto-Paraguay, is a branch of the Friesland M.B. Church and hence of the General Conference of the M.B. Church of North America. Upon the arrival of the first immigrants from Russia via Germany after World War II in 1947-1948, services for the church group were sponsored and conducted largely by the Friesland M.B. Church under the leadership of Kornelius Voth. In late 1948 another group of immigrants joined them including their minister, Franz Janzen. Services continued as before until the Volendam M.B. Church was formally organized on Nov. 9, 1949, under the leadership of Franz Janzen assisted by Kornelius Voth of Friesland, with a membership of 138. Later Johann Barwich was ordained deacon. Services are held regularly in co-operation with the Mennonite Church, except on the first Sunday of each month, when they are held separately in the village schools. A new brick church with seating capacity of 400 was built in the village of Mariental in 1950. Choir and youth work are largely in co-operation with the local Mennonite church. Church discipline is practiced according to Biblical teachings and other church practices are similar to those observed and followed in the Friesland M.B. Church. In 1957 the membership was 112, with Aron Reimer as pastor. J.Fu.

Volendam Mennonite Church (GCM), located in Colony Volendam near Puerto Mbopicua, Alto-Paraguay, a member of the South American District Conference and also of the General Conference Mennonite Church, was organized temporarily in 1947 and fully approved on April 15, 1948, under the leadership of Hans Epp, with a membership of 599, all of whom were immigrants from Russia via Germany through the Mennonite Central Committee during 1947-48. The current membership is 800 and is served by two ordained ministers, Hans Epp and Jakob Priess, and nine young unordained ministers, none of whom have had special ministerial training. The ordained ministers receive financial support from the G.C.M. Church of North America. Church services are held regularly together with the Mennonite Brethren, except on the first Sunday of every month, when only members attend, in 12 school buildings in various villages. A new brick church was built near the village of Tiefenbrunn in 1950. Saturday services known as "Wochenschluss," young people's instruction in Mennonite history and Bible, and Sunday school are held regularly. The church has four choirs. Church discipline is attempted but difficult to enforce at this early stage. Communion services are held six times each year. H.P.E.

Volga German Autonomous Soviet Socialist Republic, also known as German Volga Republic, was established as a settlement in southeastern European Russia consisting of 10,885 square miles, had a population of 605,542, and was located mostly on the east bank of the Volga, adjacent to the Saratov and Stalingrad regions. The Germans constituting the Republic, largely Lutherans, had come to Russia c1760, having been invited by Catherine II. They lost their special privileges and autonomy c1870. Many migrated to North and South America at that time. The Revolution of 1917 prevented a transfer of the population to Siberia, which had been ordered in 1915. In 1918 the region was organized as a German district and in 1924 as an Autonomous Republic. The Republic suffered severely in the famine of 1921-22. The capital of the Republic was Engels, formerly Pokrovsk. The Trakt Mennonite settlement (*q.v.*) was located in this Republic. On Sept. 24, 1941, after Hitler had invaded Russia, the Republic was dissolved and the German population, which comprised 67 per cent of the total, was exiled to Asiatic Russia. This included the Mennonites. C.K.

Am Trakt. Eine mennonitische Kolonie im mittleren Wolgagebiet (North Kildonan, 1948); Lothar König, *Die Deutschtumsinsel an der Wolga* (Dülmen, 1938); Johannes Schleuning, *Die deutschen Kolonien im Wolgagebiet* (n.d., n.p.); Gerhard Bonwetsch, *Geschichte der deutschen Kolonien an der Wolga* (Stuttgart, 1919).

Volhynia, a province of western Russia before 1917, the location of several Mennonite settlements 1800-74. The Mennonite pioneers coming to Volhynia, some of Dutch and some of Swiss ethnic origin, were among the first German colonists to penetrate western Russia, a movement sponsored by Polish and Russian noblemen to aid the economic development of the country.

On the basis of the accentuated discriminatory policy of the militaristic Prussian government against the ethnically Dutch Mennonites of the Vistula Delta area (which also generated the larger migration to the southern Ukraine) and because of the liberal offer of the Polish Count Potocki, a small group of Mennonites from the Graudenz (*q.v.*) area moved to Potocki's land in 1791, settling in the village of Michalin, near Machnovka, southwest of Kiev. When the Michalin area passed under Russian control at the second partitioning of Poland, in 1793, an effort was made by the Russian authorities to impose additional taxes on the Mennonites, i.e., the taxes normally wrested from all Russian serfs. The Mennonites insisted on their privileged status (as German colonists and Mennonites) and finally in 1804 secured a ruling in their favor. Meanwhile, however, a large number of the Michalin settlers accepted the good offer of Prince Edward Lubanirsky and in 1801-12 settled in villages near Ostrog in Volhynia. A few families from Zabara joined them soon after. Those who remained in Michalin were reinforced by other Dutch-Prussian Mennonites and the community continued until 1874.

The first and leading village inhabited was Karolswalde (*q.v.*), situated four miles south of Ostrog. In 1821 the Mennonites were located in two villages, Karolswalde and Antonovka, with 38 families. Further expansion occurred in 1828 with the settling of the neighboring village of Karolsberge. In a listing of 1857, in addition to the three villages mentioned above, Jadvinin and Dossidorf were named. In 1874 Fürstendorf, Gnadenthal, and Waldheim were added, but Dossidorf was not mentioned. An additional village associated with the group was Fürstenthal. All of the villages were located in the vicinity of Ostrog, most of them south of that center. The most common family names were Unruh, Dirks, Schartner, Koehn, and Youtz. The Mennonites living in these villages were organized into one congregation. There is evidence that in 1857 and after, they met in two groups. Benjamin Dircks was ordained to the eldership in 1817 and Tobias Unruh in 1853. Economic progress was slow. Virtually the entire group, under the leadership of Elder Tobias Unruh, migrated to America in 1874 to find new homes near Canton and Pawnee Rock, Kan., and Avon, S.D.

Additional Dutch-Prussian Mennonites came to Volhynia in 1806-18 and possibly later. Although some of the details of the movements of these later groups are lacking, it is known that some came from the Schwetz-Graudenz area on the Vistula River, and others from the Netzebruch near Driesen in

Neumark, province of Brandenburg, Germany. The best known of these migrations was that of a group of 21 Mennonite families with the names of Beyer, Böse, Dirks, Voth, Nachtigall, Nickel, Pankratz, Richard, Sperling, Unruh, and Ziekle, who in 1811 entered into a contract with the nobleman Waclav Borejko, settling on his land and founding the village of Zofyovka located north of the town of Wysock on the Horyn River. The terms of the contract were very good, as will be suggested below, but the land on which they located was marshy. The group left Zofyovka in 1828 and established "Ostrova" which is identical with Jozefin, 20 miles northeast of Luck, Volhynia. They also settled in the neighboring village which they again named Zofyovka. Here they were on the land of Count Michael Bichkovski.

The second group coming in 1806-18 settled near the town of Rafalovka on the Styr River some distance north of Luck, on the land of Count Olisarov. Later this group moved to the colony of "Vola" in Volhynia but neither the time of the move nor the location of the colony is known. A third group coming to Volhynia, some of which may have come as late as 1823, settled in two villages 20 miles southwest of Novograd Volynski, named Waldheim (Waltajem) and Zabara (Dossidorf). There is evidence that in this period some Dutch-Prussian Mennonites located at the villages of Horodyszcze, Bereza, and Melanienwald, all three approximately 25 miles northwest of Novograd Volynski.

In 1836 (some writers suggest 1838) the Mennonites living in the above villages of Jozefin-Zofyovka, Waldheim-Zabara, and Horodyszcze-Bereza, 40 families in all, left Volhynia, and settled in the south Ukrainian Molotschna Mennonite settlement, where they founded the village of Waldheim, a name carried with them from Volhynia. The move was fostered by the fact that the Netzebruch Mennonites, who were related to some of them, had gone to the Molotschna settlement in 1834, and also because it was felt that Mennonite privileges were better and more secure in the Ukraine.

Not all were satisfied with their new home, Waldheim, in the Molotschna settlement. Religious and economic misunderstandings arose between the older settlers and the newcomers. The dissatisfied members secured permission from the Russian government to return to Volhynia, and accordingly in 1848 they trekked back to Volhynia and founded the village of Heinrichsdorf some miles north of Berdichev in Eastern Volhynia. Here the group lived until 1874 when they left for America. During at least the latter years of their stay the group acknowledged the eldership of Tobias Unruh of the Ostrog Mennonite settlement and accepted his supervision.

Mention should also be made of a village of Dutch-Prussian Mennonites, Lindenthal, located approximately 10 or 15 miles northwest of Zhitomir. The source of this settlement and the time of origin is unknown.

Two groups of ethnically Swiss Mennonites also proceeded to Volhynia, and met and merged there into a larger community. One group from South Germany, coming as part of the Mennonite movement to Galicia in 1784-86, consisting of nine families (prominent were Krehbiel, Miller, Schrag, and Zerger), left the Galician Mennonite settlement in 1796 and attempted unsuccessfully to integrate themselves into the Hutterite Bruderhof located in the northern Ukraine on the River Desna at Vishenka. The actual involvement in communal living, demanding economic and some religious reorientation, was not as satisfactory as anticipated, and therefore in the spring of 1797 the party left the Hutterites. Most of them settled near or joined the Dutch-Prussian colony of Michalin, referred to above. A few families went to Michelsdorf, a village to be mentioned below. Those who dropped anchor at Michalin stayed there until the disagreement with the government regarding taxes became acute; then when some of the Dutch-Prussian Mennonites went to Ostrog the Swiss families likewise moved to Volhynia, going northwest a bit farther, however, to the Dubno area. On the lands of Prince Lubanirsky they inhabited the village of Berezina, possibly situated a mile or two south of Dubno. The stay at Berezina was short because the dam proposed by the prince was to flood the village. On the recommendation of Lubanirsky the group resettled at Vignanka, a mile north of Dubno. Here the group lived for some years, and as the number enlarged some probably moved to the near-by villages of Futtor and Zahoriz, both known to have had Swiss Mennonites. When the second group of Swiss Mennonites came from Michelsdorf to Eduardsdorf, the Vignanka group in the course of time became a part of the Eduardsdorf settlement, some moving to that village and all becoming ecclesiastically related to the Eduardsdorf congregation. In 1874, however, Vignanka was no longer inhabited by Mennonites.

The second group of Swiss Mennonites to find their way to Volhynia left Montbéliard, France, in 1791; it consisted of six or more Amish families with the names of Gering, Graber, Kaufman, Stucky, Lichti, and Roth. Although the group may have proceeded directly to Poland, there is some evidence they spent a few years in the Russian province of Podolia. Sometime between 1795 and 1800 the party settled in the Polish villages of Urzulin and Michelsdorf, both located 30 miles northeast of Lublin. Joseph Mündlein of the Galician Mennonites joined the group after their arrival and is known to have been their elder in 1802. The group was further reinforced by a few families who had been a part of the ill-fated attempt to join the Hutterite colony.

Never fully satisfied with the productivity of their marshy land and because of better prospects in Volhynia, the larger part of the Michelsdorf-Urzulin colony accepted the offer of Prince Lubanirsky and under his sponsorship founded the village of Eduardsdorf about 1807, 15 miles west-southwest of Dubno. It became the leading village of the Swiss Mennonites until 1861, and from it the Mennonites found their way into the neighboring villages of Zahoriz, Futtor, Hecker, Goritt (Koryto), Lisseberg, and possibly others.

The remaining Swiss Mennonites left Michelsdorf and Urzulin in 1837, proceeding to Horodyszcze, apparently 25 miles northeast of Rovno. In the same year, or soon thereafter, a few families from Horo-

dyszcze moved to Dossidorf (Zabara) and Waldheim. There is some evidence that all three of these
villages were taken over from the Prussian Mennonites who had left for the Molotschna in 1836. Bereza
and Alt-Kolowert were Swiss Mennonite villages
near Horodyszcze.

With the increasing scarcity of land near Dubno
and the opening of considerable land for ownership
in eastern Volhynia, the larger portion of the people
of the Eduardsdorf settlement moved in 1861 to two
villages, Kutusovka and Neumannovka (q.v.), 30
miles northwest of Zhitomir. Those remaining in
the Dubno area lived in the villages of Futtor, Zahoriz, Hecker, and Goritt. Church services were
held alternately at the first two mentioned villages.

Kutusovka (q.v.) and Neumannovka were located
3 miles apart. In time dwellings were built along the
road between the two villages. The church was built
between the two villages and gradually the entire
complex was known as Kutusovka. Economic conditions were good, with a good market for surplus
products in Zhitomir and Kiev.

Many of the Swiss Mennonites were Amish during much of their stay in Volhynia, losing however
some of the distinctive characteristics in the years
prior to their emigration to America. In the early
years in Volhynia the group subscribed to the Amish
Discipline signed at Essingen (q.v.) in 1779. There
is evidence that Pietism was influential in their later
changing orientation. At the time of the migration
to America the Swiss Mennonites were organized
into four congregations, Zahoriz-Futtor, Waldheim,
Horodyszcze, and Kutusovka, with meetinghouses
at the latter two locations. Through intermarriage
with other Mennonites and non-Mennonite German
colonists, there were added to the already present
Swiss-German family names of Albrecht, Flickinger,
Gering, Graber, Kaufman, Krehbiel, Miller, Schrag,
Schwartz, Stucky, Sutter, and Zerger, such names as
Dirks, Ortmann, Prieheim, Ries, Senner, Straus,
Wedel, Voran, and Waltner. The group spoke a
South German dialect.

A total of 159 families left Volhynia in 1874 for
America, and settled in Hutchinson and Turner
counties, S.D., and McPherson and Harvey counties,
Kan. The first group left Russia from the villages of
Zahoriz and Futtor, the second group from Goritt
and Hecker, the third group from Horodyszcze and
Waldheim, and the last group from Kutusovka. By
and large the first three groups settled in South
Dakota and the fourth in Kansas.

The Mennonites, both Dutch and Swiss, were
brought to Volhynia primarily through the liberal
offers of progressive noblemen. Although the details of the privileges given the Mennonites are in
general not known, there is evidence that they were
superior to those normally given to German colonists but inferior to the sweeping concessions granted by Empress Catherine to the south Ukrainian
Mennonites. The only extant contract is the one
entered into by Count Boreyko and the 21 families
who settled at Zofyovka near Wysock. Some of the
conditions in the contract were as follows. With the
exception of a land tax of 120 gulden per hide (per
year; they rented a total of 33 hides) to be paid
after the initial three years, the colonists were to be
free of all other state taxes, dues, and responsibilities.
They were given complete freedom as to vocation,
engaging in skills without responsibility to any
guild, and were given a free hand in disposing of
their products. They were given complete religious
freedom with the encouragement of a grant of half
a hide of land for the erection of a school and
cemetery. Every household was given 200 gulden
as a loan to enable it to begin farming.

Although conditions were favorable for that time,
the repeated moving, the sometimes poor land, and
the economic disadvantages of peasantry resulted in
limited economic progress for the Mennonites of
Volhynia. Much of the gain was lost when land and
goods had to be sold at great loss at the time of their
emigration to America. With some exceptions such
as the later years in Waldheim and Kutusovka, the
land was rented, not owned. In northern Volhynia
greater attention was given to cattle raising, whereas
in southern Volhynia more small grain crops were
raised. Although the majority of the Mennonites
were farmers, others, especially in Ostrog and Heinrichsdorf, were blacksmiths, carpenters, wagon-
makers, cabinetmakers, weavers, millers, stone-
masons, and bricklayers. Farming was primitive, the
implements consisting of the plow, harrow, wagon,
scythe, and sickle; the main crops were rye, wheat,
buckwheat, oats, millet, flax, peas, and potatoes.
Cereal crops were scythed by hand, stored in the
shed, and threshed by flail during the winter
months. Pasture land was often held in common.

In apparently all instances the Mennonites in Volhynia had religious freedom. The ministry was
threefold, consisting of elder, minister, and deacon.
The Swiss Mennonites usually had an elder for each
congregation, but the Prussians often had one elder
supervising several congregations. Services lasted
two to three hours; sermons were often read from a
book of sermons. Church discipline was severe, including the use of the ban. Officials of the various
congregations had considerable contact with one
another. There was a strong stress on tradition.

The schools were elementary and were administered by the church. School days were ended when
an individual was mature enough to work. Thus
educational advancement, at least in part, was limited by economic considerations. Sometimes the minister was also the schoolteacher. Both the religious
and educational life of the Mennonites in Volhynia
lacked the stimulation and challenge of outside contact.

There was considerable inter-colony visitation
among the Mennonites in Volhynia, especially within either the Swiss or Prussian groups; there also
was some moving of individual families from one
village to another. However, very little if any of this
took place between the Prussian and the Swiss.
Since the Mennonites were few in number and scattered among the Slavs, the influence of Russian culture was marked, especially in the later years.

Although the great majority of Volhynian Mennonites emigrated to America in 1874, a few stayed
on. Seven families, in part or whole of the Swiss
Volhynian Mennonites, are known to have remained
in Volhynia. Some of these came to America within
ten years after the main groups had left. During

World War I a Benjamin Schrag moved from Eduardsdorf to the Galician Mennonite settlement near Lemberg. Even in World War II a German Mennonite soldier fighting on the Russian front found evidences of the Swiss Mennonite stay in Volhynia. Before World War I there still were 15 families (Prussian) living in Lindenthal, two near Ostrog, eight near Luck, and seven in the Minsk area.   M.H.S.

Walter Kuhn, "Deutsche Täufersiedlungen im westukrainischen Raume," *Zeitschrift für Ostforschung* IV (1955); Ernst Crous, "Mennoniten in Wolhynien," *Gesch.-Bl.* XIII (1956) 2-10; M. Woltner, *Die Gemeindeberichte von 1848 der deutschen Siedlungen am Schwarzen Meer* (Sammlung Leibbrant); J. A. Schmidt, *Schmidt Family Record* (Vermillion, 1948); J. A. Boese, *Loretta's Settlement* (Tyndall, S.D., 1950); C. Henry Smith, *The Coming of the Russian Mennonites* (Berne, 1927); Karasek-Luck, *Die deutschen Siedlungen in Wolhynien* (Leipzig, 1931); P. P. Wedel, *Kurze Geschichte der aus Wolhynien, Russland nach Kansas ausgewanderten Schweizer-Mennoniten* (Moundridge, 1929); P. R. Kaufman, *Unser Volk und seine Geschichte* (Basil, Kan., 1931); Martin H. Schrag, "European History of the Swiss-Volhynian Mennonite Ancestors of Mennonites Now Living in Kansas and South Dakota" (unpublished master's thesis, Eastern Baptist Theological Seminary, 1956); idem, "The Swiss-Volhynian Mennonite Background." *Menn. Life* X (October 1954); *ML* IV, 555 f.

Volk, Jörg, a radical Anabaptist of Franconia, was in Augsburg at the time of the Martyr Synod in August 1527. He was executed in Bamberg in January 1528. He was accused in 1530 by Marx Mayr, at the latter's trial, of having advocated community of wives at a meeting in Thuringia in 1527.

J. E. Jörg, *Deutschland in der Revolutionsperiode von 1522 bis 1526* (Freiburg i.B., 1851) 682, 287; Fr. Roth, *Augsburgs Ref.-Gesch.* (Munich, 1889) 232; *ML* III.

Volkert, Jansz, b. c1610 at Hoorn, d. there 1681, a well-to-do cloth merchant on the Nieuwedijk at Amsterdam, was a syndic of the Cloth Guild. As such he was depicted in 1661 by Rembrandt (*q.v.*) in the famous painting "De Staalmeesters" (the Cloth Syndics) now found in the Amsterdam Rijksmuseum (Jansz is the second person to the left, standing). He was also the owner of an art cabinet in which he collected paintings, books, and curiosities, and was a member and probably a deacon of the Old Frisian Mennonite church (Bloemstraat congregation) at Amsterdam. His last years he spent in the home of Jacob Fransz Sleutel (*q.v.*), who was married to his sister Aaltje Jans. (Yearbook *Amstelodamum*, 1957; *Algemeen Doopsgez. Weekblad* XII, 1957-58, No. 41, p. 5.)   vdZ.

Volkertsz, Aldert, b. 1569 at Amsterdam, Netherlands, d. there Aug. 26, 1645, was a preacher of the Old Frisian (Bloemstraat) congregation for more than 40 years. Schijn-Maatschoen inserts a laudatory poem on him. Under the enigmatic motto, "Soo Gode wil my ga," he wrote a songbook entitled *Nieu Geestelijck Liet-Boeck, ghenaempt den Bloempot* (Amsterdam, 1626), which contains 56 hymns without notes. A copy of this hymnal is found in the Amsterdam Mennonite library. (Schijn-Maatschoen, *Geschiedenis* III, 77-80, with portrait.)
                                                vdZ.

Volkertsz, Jan: see **Jan Volkertsz Trypmaker.**

Vollenhoven, a Dutch Mennonite family, whose progenitor was (1) Jan Hendricksz (de) Hertoghe (Amsterdam, 1657-1727), who took the family name of Vollenhove(n). Both he and his wife Lysbeth Rombouts as well as his descendants were members of the Amsterdam Mennonite Lamist (*q.v.*) congregation. His grandson (2) Cornelis Vollenhoven (1723-89) was a merchant at Amsterdam. A son of (2) Cornelis was (3) Hendrik Vollenhoven (1753-1826), married to Catharina Johanna van Bee(c)k, who obtained his D. Jur. degree at Leiden in 1774 and after the Napoleonic Wars was a high official in the Dutch state. He served as a deacon in the Amsterdam congregation and was also a trustee of the Amsterdam Mennonite seminary. A son of his was (4) Jacob van Beeck Vollenhoven (1780-1834), a businessman at Amsterdam, partner in the trading company of Ten Cate and Vollenhoven, consul of Prussia, cofounder and trustee of the A.D.S. (*q.v.*) and curator of its seminary, both 1811-d.34. (5) Hendrik van Beeck Vollenhoven (1811-71), a son of (4) Jacob, was a physician at Amsterdam until 1840; he then gave up his practice because of poor health, to become a member of the van Heukelom and Vollenhoven firm of grain merchants. He was a member of the Dutch First Chamber 1849-71 and its president 1870-71. He served the Mennonite church as a trustee of the A.D.S. (moderator 1856-57) and seminary curator. Like his father and other members of the family he was a deacon of the Amsterdam congregation. His grandson Hendrik **van** Beeck Vollenhoven (1877-1943) was a physician at Haarlem and a deacon of the Haarlem Mennonite congregation 1924-d.43.   vdZ.

Nederl. Patriciaat XI (1920) 332-37; church records of Amsterdam; *DJ* 1850, 143; *Inv. Arch. Amst.* II, No. 2495; *DB* 1863, 24; 1868, 100; 1898, 32; 1907, 196; *N.N.B.Wb.* IX, 1222 f., 1224 f.

Vollenhoven, van, an outstanding and widely ramified Dutch family, Mennonite until the 19th century. By its faithfulness and its contributions, both spiritual and financial, this family has given the Mennonite church in Holland meritorious service. Its ancestor was (1) Lubbert Wolfertsz (1578-1663), at first a bargeman, who took the family name of van Vollenhoven, probably after the town of Vollenhove (province of Overijssel), from which he may have stemmed. From about 1610 he lived at Schiedam (*q.v.*) near Rotterdam, where he operated a cloth business, and was also a shipowner. He was a deacon and probably a preacher of the Schiedam Flemish Mennonite congregation from 1630. His son was (2) Coenraad Lubbertsz, called Koenraad van Vollenhoven (*q.v.*), who was a Mennonite preacher at Schiedam and at Haarlem. Another son of (1) Lubbert Wolfertsz was (3) Jan Lubbertsz van Vollenhoven (Schiedam, 1624-Amsterdam, c1670), founder of the Amsterdam branch of this family. (4) Anthoni Lubberts (1617-1707), another son of (1) Lubbert, was an important owner of herring boats at Schiedam and a founder of the large herring fishery of Vlaardingen. (5) Cornelis van Vollenhoven (Schiedam, 1690-Rotterdam, 1768), a grandson of (4) Anthoni, was a flax merchant at Rotterdam and the founder of the Rotterdam branch. He was a deacon of the church at Rotterdam, as were nine of his descendants between 1721 and 1840. In the 19th century this branch joined the Remonstrants (*q.v.*). Other prominent members of this family were (6) Coenraad van Vollenhoven (Schiedam, 1682-1743), a son of (4) Anthoni, an owner of herring boats, director of the relief of the poor and of the town orphanage, deacon of the Schiedam Mennonite Church, (7) Willem van Vollenhoven (1707-79), a merchant and wholesale dealer at Amsterdam, who later lived at Haarlem, where he was a deacon and a trustee of the Mennonite orphanage. He is the founder of the Haarlem branch. (8) Jan Messchert van Vollenhoven (Rotterdam, 1748-Bloemendaal, 1814), owner of a brewery at Amsterdam, director of the Dutch Levant trade, shipowner, and writer. His son Jan Messchert van Vollenhoven (1812-81) in many respects broke the traditions of his family: he studied law, was not engaged in business but in politics, left the liberal political views of his ancestors to side with the "Anti-Revolutionaries," for which political party he was a member both of the Second and the First Chamber. He was a burgomaster of Amsterdam 1858-66. His descendants were Reformed. (9) Aelbert van Meurs van Vollenhoven (Rotterdam, 1749-Utrecht, 1817) was a wholesale dealer and banker at Rotterdam and a deacon of the Rotterdam congregation. His widow Alida (Hesselink) van Vollenhoven (Heerenveen, 1754-Utrecht, 1829) left a considerable sum to the congregation of Knijpe (*q.v.*) into which she had been baptized. (10) Maria Elisabeth van Vollenhove (1730-1811), a great-granddaughter of (4) Anthoni, was first married to the Remonstrant pastor Jan Verbeek and then (1797) to the Mennonite pastor Cornelis de Vries (*q.v.*) at Haarlem. After 1881 there are no Mennonite van Vollenhovens. Some branches died out; others joined the Remonstrants and the Reformed church. An outstanding non-Mennonite descendant of this family was Cornelis van Vollenhoven (1874-1933), from 1901 professor of international law at the University of Leiden.   vDZ.

Nederl. Patriciaat XVI (1926) 278-340; *DB* 1863, 22, 24; 1909, 164, 166, 167; P. Veen, *De Doopsgezinden in Schoterland* (Leeuwarden, 1869) 118 f.; K. Vos, *Geschiedenis der Doopsgezinde gemeente te Rotterdam* (repr. Rotterdam, 1907) 47 f.; J. Rogge, *Het Handelshuis van Eeghen* (Amsterdam, 1948) 52, 97, 109; *N.N.B.Wb.* III, 1333 f.

Vollenhoven, Koenraad van (Coenraad Lubbertsz), b. Jan. 9, 1611, at Schiedam, d. Oct. 21, 1679, at Haarlem, was married three times, in 1631 to Marytge van Bergum, in 1638 to Magteld Strick, and in 1669 to Gertruy Wybrandsdochter. He was a cloth merchant and a Mennonite preacher and elder, 1634-40 at Schiedam and 1640-d.79 in the Flemish den Blok congregation of Haarlem (it is not clear how he could sign a contract in Haarlem as early as September 1635, as is stated in *DB* 1865, 19). During his ministry at Haarlem this congregation also became involved in the differences between a more progressive and a more strictly conservative part, which had in Amsterdam led to the Lamist-Zonist schism (see **Lammerenkrijgh**). Van Vollenhoven sided with the liberal Lamists or Galenists, followers of Galenus (*q.v.*) Abrahamsz, supported by the preacher Jan des Rameaux, while the Haarlem conservative Flemish Mennonites were led by preacher

Isaac Snep (*q.v.*). The dissensions ended with a schism in 1665 as in Amsterdam; even the intervention of the magistrates of Haarlem could not prevent the split. In 1670 a wall was built in the Blok meetinghouse to separate it into two meetinghouses, one for the Lamists, led by van Vollenhoven, and one for the Zonists, led by Snep. Like most Lamists van Vollenhoven was a Collegiant (*q.v.*).   vDZ.

DB 1863, 130, 137-43, 156 f.; 1865, 19-21; 1909, 166; W. J. Kühler, *Het Socinianisme in Nederland* (Leiden, 1912) 174 f.; J. C. van Slee, *De Rijnsburger Collegianten* (Haarlem, 1895) 184.

Vologda Region, located in north central European Soviet Russia, consists of 57,514 square miles, with a population of nearly two million. The region consists of many marshes, lakes, streams, and extensive forests, and has long winters and poor soil. The chief towns are Vologda, the capital, Cherepovets, and Veliki Ustyug. Because of the many forests and the severe winters, which make settlement in the region unpopular, this territory has been used extensively for exile by the Soviets. Thousands of Mennonites were exiled to this region 1925-40 and many perished. During the last years some moved from here to warmer climates.   C.K.

The most vivid description of the fate of those exiled has been presented by Hans Harder in his novel *In Wologdas weissen Wäldern* (Altona, n.d.-c1930); J. Rempel, *Der Sowjethölle entronnen* (Kassel, 1935), and G. Fast, *Im Schatten des Todes* (2nd ed., Winnipeg, 1956).

Volost, the Russian word for county and county government, also used by the Mennonites of Russia, although the German word *Gebietsamt* was more commonly used. (See also **Government** of Mennonites in Russia.)   C.K.

Voluntary Service, the name given to a program of practical service "In the name of Christ" for young people, primarily in Mennonite and affiliated groups, which arose in the latter part of World War II and has been sponsored and administered largely by the Mennonite Central Committee and several of the larger Mennonite groups, especially the Mennonite Church (MC) and the General Conference Mennonite Church. Voluntary Service arose initially early in 1943 in the Mennonite Church (MC) as the result of a request from the Virginia Conference to the Peace Problems Committee in late 1942 to provide some type of service as an alternate to civil defense work which was at that time being pressed upon Virginia Mennonites by the Government Civil Defense Agency. The Peace Problems Committee in turn requested the Relief Committee at a conjoint meeting Feb. 12, 1943, to undertake setting up a program for Mennonite service units. The proposal was described in a memorandum of that date as follows: (1) We believe that in addition to meeting the present emergency situation, we should think in terms of a long-range program of Christian testimony through our units. (2) We believe it will be practical to organize Mennonite service units which shall be distinctly Mennonite in their personnel, work, and practice. (3) The service should be put on a voluntary and nonremunerative basis. (4) The service units should be a particular avenue for youth expression of our Christian faith and Mennonite practice. (5) The service units should be initiated through our church schools and through other church organizations where there is sufficient interest and personnel to undertake it. (6) The service units should include the particular skills existing within our Mennonite constituency as well as the trained abilities of those who are preparing for the work of teaching and evangelism in the church. (7) The service units should be integrated into our whole church and missionary program.

Voluntary Service was first undertaken as a summer service program. The first unit of four worked in Chicago May 2 to July 2, 1944, in connection with the Mennonite (MC) Mission work there, doing a religious survey, conducting a summer Bible school, and renovating mission buildings. In 1945 three units were set up in connection with the Canton and Detroit city missions, the West Liberty (Ohio) Children's Home, and the rural mission work at Culp, Ark. The program of summer service units developed rapidly thereafter. The Peace Problems Committee brought to the Mennonite General Conference session of August 1946 a proposal for a permanent long-range service program under the Mennonite Relief Committee including year-round service, which was approved by the Conference. A General Council (MC General Conference) policy resolution adopted Oct. 18, 1950, urged vigorous development of a broad Voluntary Service program. A full-time director of VS under the MRC was appointed, beginning June 1, 1949, and a year-round VS program in addition to the summer program was set up, beginning Sept. 1, 1949. This program has grown until on Feb. 1, 1958, the year-round service had 165 workers in 28 projects on the continental United States, Puerto Rico, Alberta and Ontario, Canada, and Algeria, while the summer service program in 1958 had 150 workers in 17 widely scattered units. Meanwhile the Lancaster Conference had established a vigorous summer service program and several other conferences had started limited programs. In all of these programs the original connection of church- and mission-related projects was maintained.

Meanwhile the MCC had inaugurated a VS program, which arose in part out of the summer service projects established during World War II for girls in connection with CPS (1944, 1945, 1946), and in part under the influence of the example of the Quaker summer work camps which had been operated as early as 1935. The first regular MCC summer service units (6), including one at Cuauhtemoc, Mexico, were operated in 1947 after CPS had closed. Year-round VS was inaugurated in 1947-48 at Gulfport, Miss. The MCC program developed rapidly and by 1957-58 had 193 workers in summer service units and 112 in year-round service. The General Conference Mennonite Church has operated a program since 1946 including both summer units and year-round service projects. In 1958 it had 35 participants in 8 year-round units and 81 in 16 summer units. MCC summer service began in Canada in 1948, and year-round service in 1953. During recent years Canadian Summer Service had 80-90 workers each summer. The year-round program is now concentrated in Newfoundland, where there were 33 workers in 1958.

The Mennonite Brethren Church does not currently operate a VS program of its own, although some district conferences did so in the early 1950's. A number of its young people are serving in the VS program of the MCC. The 1957 M.B. General Conference approved VS in the following resolution: (a) "That we stand in approval of Voluntary Service whenever and wherever it remains in line with the evangelical policies of the church. (b) That mature young people from our churches who are members in good standing, are well established in faith, and who have a missionary motive for service be encouraged to enter voluntary service."

It has been agreed that MCC operate VS for those Mennonite bodies which do not operate their own programs and in addition operate pioneer and experimental types of projects and furnish general leadership. A Voluntary Service section was set up in MCC administration at Akron in 1947; Elmer Ediger served as first director until 1951. In 1957 this section was combined with the I-W Service section.

The Voluntary Service concept has spread to Europe and South America through MCC. In 1952 European VS was established as "Mennonitischer freiwilliger Dienst," under the direction of a board composed of representatives of the European Mennonite churches of Holland, Switzerland, France, and Germany, and the MCC. The MFD operates only summer service projects, with headquarters in Kaiserslautern, Germany. Already in 1948-51, American Mennonite college students who came in summer tours to Europe, had spent several weeks each summer in VS in summer work camps under MCC sponsorship. In 1957 a Mennonite VS program was begun in South America under MCC sponsorship, with Martin Duerksen of Buenos Aires as director, called Christlicher Dienst.

Related to Voluntary Service but actually an alternative to I-W Service (q.v.) is Pax Service (q.v.), a program for overseas service by young men serving as conscientious objectors under the United States Selective Service Act (draft), who volunteer for service abroad under MCC. Pax (i.e., Peace) was begun in 1950 and has operated largely in Germany, although also in Greece, Korea, Peru, and Paraguay. The Pax period of service is two years, the terms are the same as for VS, i.e., maintenance and $10.00 per month pocket money, and the cost is borne largely by the church. In 1958 110 men were serving in Pax.

In the short space of twelve years the VS idea has become widely accepted throughout American Mennonitism, particularly for mature young people. It has promoted the spirit of Christian service in the name of Christ, and particularly in those cases where it is kept in close connection with the missionary and evangelistic outreach of the church it has brought an added new approach to evangelism. It has also opened up an avenue for dedicated and sacrificial short-term service for many who might not be able or qualified to do regular full-time Christian work on a lifetime basis.　　　　H.S.B.

VS 1958, Relief and Service Office of the Mennonite

Board of Missions and Charities, Elkhart, Ind.; *Agape,* a monthly VS periodical published by the Mennonite Relief and Service Committee, Elkhart, 1955-; J. D. Unruh, *In the Name of Christ* (Scottdale, 1952) Chapter **XVI,** "Voluntary Service," 294-309.

Von dem unverschampten frävel, *ergerlichen verwyrren unnd unwarhafftem leeren der selbsgesandten Widertöuffern, vier gespräch Bücher, zu verwarnenn den einfalten, Durch Heinrychen Bullinger geschrieben. Ein guter bericht vonn Zinsen. Ouch ein schöne underwysung von Zähenden* (Zürich, 1531, 178 leaves), is the title of the first of the two books against the Anabaptists written by Heinrich Bullinger (*q.v.*), which appeared in print in February 1531 in Zürich, though written in 1530. The occasion was the activity of the Anabaptist preacher Hans Pfistermeyer (*q.v.*) in the "Free Counties" between Zürich and Aarau (*q.v.*). The young Bullinger was at that time a minister in his home town of Bremgarten, the principal town of this region. Here he had helped the Reformation to break through and had gathered a lively congregation. Pfistermeyer's preaching stirred up large crowds. They were fascinated by his main theme, the question of tithes and interest. The official ministers had much trouble and sought help; this was the occasion for Bullinger's book. For some years already he had discussed Anabaptist ideas in his private writings and letters. Now his friends urged him to summarize his experience with the Anabaptists and give guidance to refute them. The book was begun in April 1530 and finished toward the end of the year. When Bullinger discussed the question of the interest with some Anabaptists in January 1531, his manuscript must have been already in print.

The book has four sections ("books") and two appendices. Except for the appendices it is written as a dialogue (*gespräch Bücher*) between Simon, who sympathizes with the Anabaptists, and Jojada, who defends "the truth." During the process of the discussion Simon is convinced by Jojada. The argumentation tends to popularize the problems and their orthodox solution. There is no interest in the history of Anabaptism, only in its refutation.

A list of twenty Anabaptist errors covers the themes discussed: (1) spirit and Scripture, (2) the right to preach, (3) the unity of the church and separation, (4) justification and sanctification, (5) the sleep of the soul, (6) rebaptism, (7) baptism of infants, (8) community of goods, (9) the vagrancy of the Anabaptists, (10) preachers and education, (11-16) the Christian and the magistracy, nonresistance, oath, death penalty and war: the whole of the third book, (17-20) spiritual and material freedom (tithes, interest, and usury: the whole of the fourth book). The appendices continue to discuss the last question in a different literary form: the first is a tract on interests and usury, the second a letter to Bullinger's brother on tithes.

The picture of the Anabaptists drawn by Bullinger is a vivid one. Scholars, therefore, have been tempted to follow him in delineating the life and piety of Anabaptism. A comparison, however, shows that it contains scarcely any traits that had not been attributed to the Anabaptists by Bullinger's teacher Zwingli (*q.v.*). For both men the main accusation was one of separatism and sedition, and this disqualified the Anabaptists morally. Theologically the Anabaptist error was the ideal of a pure and stainless church, and accordingly the postulation of a "sinless" life. That in contrast to this demand their way of living was full of the most reprehensible conduct was stressed indefatigably by both Zwingli and Bullinger. The dependence of Bullinger on Zwingli goes so far that one could almost imagine a similarly vivid picture of the Anabaptists even if Bullinger never had seen any but had only read the anti-Anabaptist writings of Zwingli.

Also Bullinger's refutation of the Anabaptist position kept chiefly to Zwingli's arguments. His main interest was to defend the integrity of the "Volkskirche" against all divisive tendencies. It was only within such an over-all organization that he saw any guarantee of a possibility to preach the Gospel to all men, believers and nonbelievers. A small community consisting only of confessing Christians could not be a tool of the Almighty God who wanted to save all the world. To Bullinger's eyes it was hypocrisy. He supported his arguments by two fundamental ideas. The first was the invisibility of the true church: because all true believers are known only to God, all outward things, including church organization and discipline, can be delegated to the magistracy. The second idea was the incapability even of the Christian to obey the divine commands: lacking this prerequisite of all Christian ethics man nevertheless can do the will of God by following the less difficult Golden Rule or law of charity (neighborly love), a civic virtue sufficient to justify the name of "Christian." Especially this concept of a second, less rigorous, will of God was a key to refute all Anabaptist demands for a serious obedience to New Testament commands.

The influence of Bullinger's book reached far. In April 1531 it was used in dealing with Hans Pfistermeyer in Bern. Sebastian Franck (*q.v.*) published extracts in his Chronicle which appeared in September of the same year. Menno Simons knew Bullinger through Franck. In many letters Bullinger was asked to send the book to his friends. In 1535 it was translated into Latin and slightly supplemented by Bullinger's colleague Leo Jud: *Adversus omnia Catabaptistarum prava dogmata . . . libri IIII per Leonem Judae aucti . . .* and published in Zürich. In 1548 and 1551 three English translations (partly extracts?) appeared by the French refugee Jean Veron: (1) *An Holesome Antidotus or Counterpoysen agaynst the pestylent heresye and secte of the Anabaptistes . . .* (London, 1548); (2) *A most necessary and fruteful Dialogue, betweene ye Seditious Libertin or rebel Anabaptist, and the true obedient Christian . . .* (Worcester, 1551); (3) *A most sure and strong defence of the baptisme of children, against ye pestiferous secte of the Anabaptystes* (Worcester, 1551). A Dutch edition did not appear, but the necessity of such a translation was one of the occasions for Bullinger's second book against the Anabaptists (*Der Widertoufferen ursprung, q.v.*).

H.F.

Vondel, van den (van Vondel, van Vondelen, van den Vondellen), a Dutch family, originally from

Antwerp, Belgium, where Joost van den Vondel joined the Mennonites. Because of persecution Joost like many others left Antwerp in 1582 with his wife, moving to Cologne, Germany, where at this time the Mennonites could live rather unmolested. Joost van den Vondel's wife died soon after and in 1585 he married Sara Cranen (Kraen, *q.v.*), also a Mennonite refugee from Antwerp who was living at Cologne. Joost and Sara had seven children; among them were Clementia, b. 1586, in 1607 married the widower Hans de Wolff of the Mennonite de Wolff (*q.v.*) family at Amsterdam; Joost (*q.v.*), b. 1587; Sara, b. 1595, in 1614 married the Mennonite grain merchant Joost Willemsz van Nijkercke (Nieukerck, *q.v.*) at Amsterdam; and Catharina, b. 1602, in 1624 married Jan Arisz Bruyninck of Amsterdam; Catharina joined the Catholic Church in 1644.

Joost van den Vondel and Sara Cranen lived at Cologne until 1595. Gradually conditions there had grown worse for the Mennonites and after Joost had been fined for "heresy" in 1595, he and his family left the town. Via Frankfort and Bremen, Germany, they moved to Utrecht, Netherlands, where they lived for nearly a year, settling at Amsterdam in 1596, where they started a silk shop in Warmoesstraat. Joost died in 1608. He may have been a member of the Amsterdam Flemish congregation; his wife Sara, d. 1637, was a faithful member of this congregation.

The suggestion has been made (A. J. Barnouw, *Vondel,* Haarlem, 1926, p. 3) that the Anabaptist martyr Joost (*q.v.*) de Hoedemaker, who suffered martyrdom at Antwerp in 1569, belonged to the same family, since both he and Joost van den Vondel (at Antwerp and Cologne) were hatters. Adriaen Vondel (Vervondel) was a preacher of the Mennonite church at Veere, Zeeland, in 1665. (For literature, see **Vondel, Joost van den.**)   vDZ.

Vondel, Joost van den, b. Nov. 17, 1587, at Cologne, Germany, d. Feb. 5, 1679, at Amsterdam, Netherlands, the son of Joost van den Vondel of Antwerp and Sara Cranen (Kraen), operated a silk business at Amsterdam, at first with his mother, then independently until this business failed. In his old age he was a clerk in the city pawnshop of Amsterdam. In 1610 he married Maeyken de Wolff; they had four children, Joost (b. 1612), Anna (1613-72), Constantijn, and Saartje (the last two died at an early age). In 1641 Joost Jr. joined the Catholic Church with his father, and Anna also became a Catholic.

Joost van den Vondel is the greatest Dutch poet. His literary works, among which were a number of Biblical and historical plays in verse, are among the treasures of the Dutch literature.

Like his parents he was a Mennonite. He, however, did not join the Flemish church as they did, but the Waterlander congregation of Amsterdam. It is not clear why he preferred this branch of Mennonites, but it was probably because the Waterlanders were more open to culture and the arts than the Flemish. In 1616 he was chosen (by lot) as a deacon of the Amsterdam Waterlander congregation, serving until 1620, in this year taking leave because of "great unfitness because of his depression," as is said in the *Memoriael* by the Waterlander preacher Reynier Wybrands. It is not clear what this meant. Probably he was ill, suffering a depression of spirits; but it is also possible that the church did not approve of his connections with the literary clubs of that time (*Rederijkers*) or his Remonstrant (*q.v.*) leanings. In 1624 he wrote a sonnet for Anthoni Jacobsz Roscius (*q.v.*), a Waterlander preacher of Hoorn, who had suffered a tragic death. In 1626 during a conflict in the Amsterdam Waterlander congregation between Nittert Obbes (*q.v.*) and the other preachers of the church Vondel took the side of Obbes in his poem *Antidotum, Tegen het vergift der Geestdryvers, Tot verdedigingh van't beschreven woord Gods.* About 1638 he composed the familiar laudatory inscription to Rembrandt's etching of Preacher Cornelis Claesz Anslo (*q.v.*). But after 1620 he had no special connections with the congregation and was gradually estranged from it. About 1641 he joined the Roman Catholic Church. The reason for this step is still a matter of discussion. A number of reasons may have co-operated in inducing him to this step. Among these reasons there certainly were a feeling of discomfort in the "divided church" and a longing for the unity of all Christians, the sparse furnishings of the Mennonite meetinghouses, and their sober worship services. Other factors were the influence of ecumenists like Hugo de Groot, and particularly of Catholic friends such as Plemp, and finally the propaganda of the Jesuits at Amsterdam, who in this period made a large number of converts including some Mennonites.

As there is no agreement as to the year in which Vondel actually joined the Catholic Church (Catholic authors usually assume it to have been 1639, but it was probably not until 1641), there is no agreement as to Vondel's Catholic mentality. Whereas Brom boldly claims that even as a Mennonite Vondel was "as Roman Catholic as an altar," Smit says, "His Mennonite conviction during his whole life remains the kernel of his religious attitude. Much that has been called pure Catholic in him is basically pure Mennonite. His famous tragedies show strong Mennonite characteristics." It is, according to Smit, notably the Waterlander piety which was continued, and which can be clearly shown in his later tragedies.

After Vondel had left the Mennonite Church he remained in contact with a number of them. For some Mennonite couples he composed nuptial hymns (this, however, was mostly hack work). Laudatory poems, nuptial poems, and poems of mourning were written by Vondel for members of the following Mennonite families: Anslo, Block, de Flines, Linnich, de Wolff, Leeuw, Looten, de Neufville, van Tongerlo(o), and de Vries. Among his Mennonite friends until his death were the Blocks, and especially Agnes Block, who was married first to Vondel's relative Joan de Wolff and then to Sybrand de Flines, both members of the Mennonite church. She visited him regularly, she contributed to his material needs, she comforted him in the loneliness of his old age; on a last visit shortly before his death, she spoke with him on death and eternity.

There are a number of editions of Vondel's literary works. At first the tragedies and other works were printed separately and some poems even on loose sheets. The last edition of his complete writings is an edition in ten volumes with an index, published at Amsterdam 1927-37. vdZ.

Of the numerous books and papers concerning Joost van den Vondel we mention only P. Leendertz Jr., *Het leven van Vondel* (Amsterdam, 1910); A. J. Barnouw, *Vondel* (Haarlem, 1926); J. M. F. Sterck, *Het leven van Joost van den Vondel* (Haarlem, 1926); G. Brom, *Vondel's Bekering* (Amsterdam, 1907); B. H. Molkenboer, "Wanneer werd Vondel Katholiek?" in *Vondelkroniek* III, 1932; W. A. P. Smit, "Vondel en zijn Bekering," in *Nieuwe Taalgids* XXIX (Groningen, 1935); G. Brom, "Vondel en Rembrandt," in *Jaarboek van de Maatschappij voor Nederl. Letterkunde* 1955-56 (Leiden, 1956); G. Brom, *Vondels Geloof* (Amsterdam, 1935).

Voogt (Voogd, Voocht), a Dutch family name. Jacob Jansen Voogt was a preacher of the Waterlander Mennonites at Leeuwarden in Friesland; in 1687 he was banished from the town under suspicion of Socinianism (*q.v.*), but this sentence was mitigated and Voogt was allowed to preach again on condition that his sermons be examined by a Reformed pastor before he preached them. This man is probably identical with the Jacob Janse Voocht who was a weaver at Amsterdam 1671-*c*82 and was a leader of the "College" (see **Collegiants**) there.

The West Prussian Mennonite Vogt (*q.v.*) family is apparently not related to the Dutch Voogt family. Nor is there any connection between the Swiss, South German, and American Vogt family name and this Dutch name. vdZ.

Blaupot t. C., *Friesland*, 205; *DB* 1860, 60 f.; J. v. van Slee, *De Rijnsburger Collegianten* (Haarlem, 1895) 165, 260, 357 f.; Reimer, *Familiennamen*, 120.

Voorburg-Rijswijk, two suburbs of The Hague, Netherlands, where there is a Mennonite Kring (circle), founded in 1948 as a part of the Hague congregation. Services are held monthly in the church of the Dutch Protestant Association at Voorburg. vdZ.

Voordt, van, a patrician family at Utrecht, Netherlands, members of which were Mennonites *c*1561. Mennonite meetings were held in the home of Cornelis van Voordt. Probably Cornelis was not a member of the church, though he was in sympathy with it. Anna, his wife, and Jan, his son, were baptized by Elder Dirk (*q.v.*) Philips shortly before Christmas of 1561 in a meeting held in his home. In February or March 1562 a meeting here was surprised by the police and a number of Mennonites were arrested and tried. Cornelis and his wife, who were not present when the meeting was surprised, were forever banished from Utrecht, Holland, and Zeeland, and their property was confiscated. Jan van der Voordt, who was apprehended, recanted and was probably released. Berghuys is of the opinion that the Jan van der Voort who was ordained as a preacher or elder of the Utrecht Mennonite congregation was identical with this Jan van Voordt. This is, however, doubtful, for he would have been about 75 years old in 1606. vdZ.

DB 1874, 7 f., 18-20, 24 f. et *passim*; (H. B. Berghuys), *Geschiedenis der Doopsgez. gemeente te Utrecht* (n.p., n.d.-1926) 26.

Voorhelm and its lateral branch **Voorhelm Schneevo(o)gt,** a Mennonite family at Haarlem in the 17th-19th centuries, now extinct. Dirk Voorhelm was a preacher of the Jan-Evertsvolk (*q.v.*) or Kruisstraat congregation, which had separated from the main Flemish body in 1680. In 1690 he was present at Nijmegen when Elder Jan ter Mehr (*q.v.*), of Crefeld, ordained some preachers and deacons. The years of Dirk Voorhelm's service are unknown. He published a funeral sermon for his co-preacher Matthijs van Dalen, *Lyck-Reden* ... (Haarlem, n.d.-1707). Two of his sons, Dirk Voorhelm, d. 1764, and Pieter Voorhelm, served the same church as preachers from 1711 and 1715 respectively until 1747 when this congregation merged with the Vlaamsche Blok (*q.v.*) congregation on the Klein Heiligland, and then served the united congregation until 1764 and *c*1755. Both Dirk and Pieter were trustees of the Flemish Mennonite orphanage from 1732 and 1707. The Voorhelms at Haarlem were businessmen; in the 18th century they specialized in bulb raising.

A member of this family was Maria Voorhelm, of Haarlem. She was baptized in 1740 at a private meeting in the home of her parents by Pastor Johannes Deknatel (*q.v.*) of Amsterdam, into "the general Christian Church," i.e., not into a special branch or congregation. At first she worshiped with the Moravian Brethren (*q.v.*, Herrnhuter) at Amsterdam; later she joined the Klein Heiligland Mennonite congregation at Haarlem. In 1742 she was married to J. H. Schneevogt, who was a partner in the bulb nursery of the Voorhelm family. Their descendants took the family name of Voorhelm Schneevoogt. George Voorhelm Schneevoogt, d. 1850, was a deacon at Haarlem 1808-d.50 and a trustee of the Haarlem Mennonite orphanage until 1837; his son Carel Godfried Voorhelm Schneevogt, d. Oct. 24, 1877, at Haarlem, bequeathed 1,000 guilders to the A.D.S., of which he had been a trustee 1856-77; this donation is still administered as the Schneevoogt Fund. He was a deacon at Haarlem 1836-d.77. His brother Gustaaf Eduard Voorhelm Schneevoogt (1814-71), who in his youth was educated in the Herrnhut school at Neuwied, was a physician and a pioneer for a better medical and social treatment of the insane. From 1851 he was a medical professor at the University of Amsterdam. vdZ.

Church records of Haarlem; *De weeshuizen der Doopsgezinden te Haarlem 1634-1934* (Haarlem, 1934) 24, 31, 32, 90; *DB* 1863, 145; 1874, 16; *Inv. Arch. Amst.* II, 2, Nos. 72 f.; J. W. Lütjeharms, *Het Oecumenisch-philadelphisch streven der Hernhutters* (Zeist, 1935) 59, 143 f.; annual report of the A.D.S. 1878, 9, 14; *N.N.B.Wb.* IV, 1234 f.

Voornaemste Hooft-Ketteren, De: see **Greuwel der vornahmsten Haupt-Ketzeren.**

Voorst, van, a Mennonite family, originally found at Emmerich, Germany, and from *c*1670 at Amsterdam, Holland. At Emmerich Hendrik van Voorst, a shopkeeper, was a preacher of the Mennonite church in the 17th century. On June 17-18, 1672, he was interrogated by Femundus Formantin (*q.v.*), a French Catholic theologian, who accompanied the French armies invading the Netherlands. The interesting discussion dealt with the Mennonite views on the Scriptures, baptism, marriage, adoration of the saints, the Incarnation, and the Holy Spirit. Van Voorst ably defended the Mennonite doctrines and Formantin was impressed by his answers. The result was that the Mennonites were not molested. In 1690 van Voorst was active in behalf of the Mennonite refugees from the Palatinate.

The first member of this family at Amsterdam was Ameldonck van Voorst, a native of Emmerich, who settled at Amsterdam as a medical doctor c1680. He was married in 1682 to Cecelia Verkolje, and a member of the Lamist Mennonite congregation. Paulus van Voorst, married to Christina Roeters, a member of the Lamist church and its deacon 1706-12 and 1718-24, and a trustee of the Collegiant (*q.v.*) Oranjeappel orphanage 1694-1706, was the treasurer of the Dutch Mennonite Committee for Foreign Needs c1715-35. Most members of this family at Amsterdam were Lamists; some, however, in the 18th century were Zonists (*q.v.*). The van Voorst family is found in Amsterdam until c1820. Hendrik van Voorst (*q.v.*) belonged to this family.

vDZ.

Inv. Arch. Amst. I, Nos. 1372, 1380, 1424, 1607, 1622, 2115, 2117, 2329, 2331; II, No. 2701; II, 2, Nos. 793, 861; *DB* 1873, 58-71; J. Rogge, *Het Handelshuis van Eeghen* (Amsterdam, 1948) 264 note.

Voorst, Hendrik van, b. 1750 at Amsterdam, d. Oct. 2, 1808, at Zaandam, a Dutch Mennonite pastor, trained for the ministry at the Amsterdam Lamist Mennonite seminary in 1774-78, serving in the Zaandam-Oost congregation 1779-d.1808. He was a man of learning, particularly in philosophy. Three of his papers were given awards by the Teyler (*q.v.*) Foundation at Haarlem and published in the *Verhandelingen* (essays) of this association. His descendants in the 19th century produced ship biscuits, flour, and rice at Zaandam. (*Naamlijst* 1808, 74.)

vDZ.

Voort, van der (van Voort), a former Mennonite family at Utrecht, Netherlands; Jan van der Voort, who was ordained as a preacher or elder of the Utrecht Mennonite congregation in 1606, is thought to be identical with Jan van Voordt (*q.v.*), who was baptized at Utrecht in 1561 by Dirk Philips (*q.v.*). In 1618 he was still serving, in this year buying a house in the Jufferstraat (later called Springweg), which was remodeled into a meetinghouse.

vDZ.

(H. B. Berghuys), *Geschiedenis der Doopsgez. gemeente te Utrecht* (n.p., n.d.-1926) 26 f.

Vorarlberg, the westernmost province of Austria, situated between the upper Rhine and the Arlberg Pass, with Bregenz on Lake Constance as capital. The population is Alamannic, hence akin to the Swiss and the Swabians. In the 16th century the country was composed of four manorial jurisdictional districts (*Herrschaften*), and was administered politically by the provincial government in Tirol. It had, however, a top magistrate (*Oberster Hauptmann*) as local authority. Around 1580 this was Count Hannibal of Hohenembs, who played a role in Anabaptist history. In spite of the openness of the country to Switzerland and Swabia and its proximity to Tirol in the east, Anabaptism was never very active here, except for the brief period of 1577-90. Only three death sentences of Anabaptists are known: Melchior Platzer (*q.v.*) in 1583 and two cases as late as 1618, Jost Wilhelm and Christine Brünnerin, neither of whom had yet received adult baptism but declared themselves as Anabaptists nevertheless.

The center of Anabaptist activities was the area of the "Farther (Hinterer) Bregenzerwald" (*q.v.*), a rather remote district with the parish of Au on the Eck River as its main place. The local authorities were inclined by and large to leniency. In spite of the fact that some Anabaptists had several times broken their "oath" never to return, they did not suffer the ultimate penalty, even though the Innsbruck government urged greater harshness. But the Vorarlbergers more or less resented these Tirolean interferences and in most cases disregarded them.

A number of family names appear both in the court records of the time and in the Hutterite chronicle, such as Seyfried (or Seiffert), Mosbrugger (Mosbrucker), Sailer, Wilhelm, Albrecht, Rusch (Ruesch), Berwig, and Beer. A certain Jacob Seyfried was apparently the first to have been active as a "street corner preacher" and promoter of Anabaptist ideas (c1577). In spite of his "promise" to stay away he returned no less than three times to the Bregenzerwald district. In 1579 Archduke Ferdinand of Tirol ordered that he should be sentenced to death if he returned once more. (This was the rather short period when Hapsburgs were slightly more lenient in religious matters than ever before. Emperor Maximilian II, *q.v.*, is said to have shown leanings toward Protestantism; he died 1576, and soon afterwards the full sway of the Counter Reformation came into play.) In 1580 Anabaptist books were confiscated and one year later publicly burned; their list was sent to Innsbruck.

Between 1580 and 1585 a lively emigration to Moravia set in, mainly from the parish of Au; the County Council of the "Hinterer Bregenzerwald" reported in 1581 that forty persons had already left and more were preparing for this transfer, selling their property as best they could. Time and again one reads in archive records of "suspect people," their secret meetings, and of sectarian books all over this district. Now and then one hears also of a few returnees who had been dissatisfied in Moravia "with food and drink," but they represent a small minority. Often it happens that Anabaptists are even supported by the lower magistrates of the "Herrschaft" as was also often the case in Tirol. Loserth names in particular a certain councilman Philipp Koler (of the Bregenzerwald court district) as such a sympathizer and helper.

The climax of Anabaptism in Vorarlberg happened around 1583; in this year the former apothecary of Rankweil, Vorarlberg, Melchior Platzer (*q.v.*), who had become a schoolmaster at a Bruderhof in Moravia, returned as a missioner and was said to have been most successful in winning new converts to the Anabaptist way. Eventually he was caught, imprisoned, and treated in the traditional way (tortured). Still, the authorities would have released him also if he had been willing to pledge never to return to country and county. As he refused to do so he was handed over to Count Hannibal of Hohenembs, who apparently wanted to please the Innsbruck authorities and approved the death sentence. After 26 weeks of imprisonment in chains he was executed by the sword in Rankweil, Nov. 6, 1583. He met his fate with the traditional Anabaptist attitude, singing and admonishing the assembled people to repentance. Hans Kräl, the bishop of the Hutterites in Moravia and himself a Tirolean, had previously sent him a very fine epistle of comfort and encouragement. An anonymous hymn of 29 stanzas tells the story of his martyrdom (*Lieder der Hutterischen Brüder*, 756-60).

After this period of 1577-90 we hear only now and then of new happenings in this area concerning Anabaptism and migration to Moravia. The Seyfried (or Seiffert) family was the most active of all over a period of 36 years (1577-1613). Also the Wilhelm family deserves mention. Thomas Wilhelm of Au had become a Diener des Wortes (preacher) with the Hutterites in Moravia 1617, but somehow came into conflict with the brotherhood, moved to Alwinz (*q.v.*) in Transylvania, and finally was said to have ended somewhere in Switzerland. The records of 1613, 1617, and 1618 contain references to several men and women who recanted from their Anabaptist faith, admitting that their children or other members of their household had gone to Moravia to join the Hutterite brotherhood. (During all these years one hears of only one case where a brother went to Switzerland to join a congregation there.)

The year 1618, finally, saw the two last cases mentioned above: Christine Brünnerin (in court records named Brenner) of the village of Au wanted to join her daughter in Moravia, but was caught while preparing to emigrate. She was badly tortured yet remained steadfast. Contrary to the usual practice in Vorarlberg, she was sentenced to death and executed by the sword Aug. 8, 1618. "Although she had not yet received water baptism and had not yet come to the brotherhood, God gave her the strength to acquire the baptism of the Spirit and of blood which is more important" (Beck, 370).

The other case is that of Joss Wilhelm and his wife Elsa (nee Moshrugger), "pious, God-fearing, and well-to-do people" (Beck, 368). Their son (was this the above-mentioned Thomas?) had been in Moravia long before and had told them of the true Christian life in the brotherhood, and also that life in the world was wrong and sinful. Thereupon the two prepared likewise to migrate from Vorarlberg to Moravia but were caught and kept in prison for more than one year. The Innsbruck government insisted on a trial at the court of Bregenz. Joss was severely racked but betrayed no one. Finally, on May 14, 1618, he, too, was executed by the sword. The Hutterite Chronicle reports that the question was raised at which place his body should be buried. The Catholic priest of Au is said to have decided, "Bury him in my churchyard; I have no more pious man in it" (Beck, 369). His wife was sentenced to life imprisonment and loss of all property. The *Lieder der Hutterischen Brüder* contains a hymn of

24 stanzas commemorating the martyrdom of these two witnesses to the faith (817-21).

The last name recorded is that of Hans Mosbrugger (possibly a brother of Elsa Wilhelm) who lived in Moravia in 1621. (See **Bregenzerwald**.)

LOSERTH, R.F.

Beck, *Geschichts-Bücher*, in particular the long footnote 283-86; Joseph Bergmann, "Die Wiedertäufer in Au im Bregenzerwald und ihre Auswanderung nach Mähren im Jahre 1585," in *Sitzungsberichte der kaiserlichen Akademie der Wissenschaften* I (Vienna, 1843); John Horsch, "Ein Geisteszeugnis aus den wehrlosen Gemeinden des sechzehnten Jahrhunderts," *Menn. Fam.-Kal.* (Scottdale) 1928, pp. 20-26; *idem*, "Ein Sendschreiben Hans Kräls an einen Märtyrer," *ibid.*, 1914, 32-35; *Lieder der Hutterischen Brüder* (Scottdale, 1914); J. Loserth, "Die letzten Züge der Wiedertäufer nach Mähren," *Zeitschrift des Deutschen Vereins f.d. Gesch. von Mähren und Schlesien*, 1922; ML IV.

Vorbereitungsschule: see **Preparatory Schools.**

Vormoser: see **Vermoser.**

Vorsänger, a title commonly used in German-speaking Mennonite churches in Europe and America to designate the leader of congregational singing: see **Chorister.**

Vorsterman, a former Mennonite family at Amsterdam, Holland, from *c*1620 until the 18th century, when it died out. A well-known member of this family was Jacob Vorsterman, d.1729, who was very active as a trustee and secretary and treasurer of the Dutch Mennonite Committee for Foreign Needs. With Herman Schijn (*q.v.*) and five other brethren he presented a petition in the name of the Dutch Mennonites to the Bernese government in behalf of the suppressed Swiss Mennonites in 1710. The great relief action for the Swiss refugees in 1710-13 was described by Vorsterman in his *Relaas wegens het afvoeren der Doopsgezinden uit Zwitserland en het overbrengen van velen hunner in Nederland*, which account is found in manuscript in the Amsterdam Mennonite archives. Jacob Vorsterman was four times a deacon of the Amsterdam Zonist (*q.v.*) congregation. His father Abraham Vorsterman had also been a deacon of this church. His son Abraham joined the Amsterdam Lamist congregation, of which he was a deacon 1743-49. vDZ.

Inv. Arch. Amst. I, Nos. 1211, 1272, 1275, 1294, 1348, 1860, 1864, 1866, 1892, 1432, 1885, 2251; Müller, *Berner Täufer*, 194; *DB* 1909, 136 note 7.

Vorwärts was a weekly eight-page periodical, published as a community German language newspaper at Hillsboro, Kan., 1910-40. The newspaper had its background in the *Hillsboro Presse* published by the Central Publishing Company, beginning in 1900, later called *Hillsboro Journal* (German). Under the editorship of Jacob G. Ewert (*q.v.*) the name of the periodical was changed to *Vorwärts* in 1910 and to *Hillsboro Vorwärts* in 1932. In 1913 the publishing interests of the Mennonite Brethren were moved from McPherson to Hillsboro. With the move A. L. Schellenberg (*q.v.*), editor of *Zionsbote* (*q.v.*) and *Der Deutsche Westen* (*q.v.*), took over the editorship of *Vorwärts*, continuing until August 1919 and again 1922-30. By 1919 the periodical had 5,500 subscribers in and around Hillsboro as well as among

Mennonite Brethren generally. J. D. Fast served as editor 1919-22, and during the final ten years P. H. Berg took over editorial duties. In the latter thirties an increasing amount of space was given to the English language and early in 1940 the name was changed to *Hillsboro Journal* (*q.v.*).   J.F.S.

T. R. Schellenberg, "Editor Abraham L. Schellenberg," *Menn. Life* IX (January 1954).

Vorwärts-Kalender, a German yearly almanac, 64-160 pages of informative articles, poetry, and advertising, was issued by the Mennonite Brethren Publishing House 1925-42. It was offered as a premium to *Vorwärts* subscribers and was sold for 25 cents per issue.   O.HA.

Vos, a common Dutch family name, both Mennonite and non-Mennonite; in a number of congregations there are members by this name belonging to several unrelated families. Mennonite ministers by this name were Willem Vos, preacher of the Haarlem Peuzelaarsteeg congregation 1705-c50, Klaas Pietersz Vos, preacher at Monnikendam in the early 18th century, Marcus Vos, preacher of the Groningen Old Flemish congregation at Zaandam 1757-74, and Karel Vos (*q.v.*).   vDZ.

Vos, de, a common Dutch family name. Mennonites by this name were formerly found at Rotterdam, Amsterdam, Haarlem, and Hamburg-Altona. The relationship between these families could not be ascertained. At Rotterdam Anthoni de Vos was a deacon of the Flemish congregation in 1688-90. Aplonie de Vos was a preacher of the Lamist (*q.v.*) congregation of Amsterdam in 1687-95. There was a de Vos family in the Amsterdam Zonist (*q.v.*) congregation in the 17th and 18th centuries. Not related to this Zonist family was a Lamist de Vos family at Amsterdam, of which Jacobus de Vos, of Haarlem, married there c1690 to Catharina van de Rijp, was probably a member. Among these de Voses some living at Amsterdam were important in the Mennonite church as well as in the Dutch business and cultural life. (1) Jacob(us) de Vos, who conducted an insurance business (first De Vos en Sanders, now De Vos en Zoonen); his son (2) Jacob de Vos (1735-1833), unmarried, manager of the insurance business, noted connoisseur of art, proprietor of an art collection, which after his death was sold for 121,500 guilders; (3) Willem de Vos (*q.v.*), also a son of (1), a Mennonite pastor (4) Jacob de Vos, son of (3), Amsterdam, 1774-Bloemendaal, 1844, who studied Latin and Greek, but later became a partner in the insurance company of his uncle (2) Jacob; he was interested in the arts (he designed the commemorative medal issued by the A.D.S. in 1835 for the centennial of the Amsterdam Mennonite Seminary), a trustee of the A.D.S., and in 1815-19 a deacon of the Amsterdam congregation, as were some of his descendants. At Haarlem the Mennonite Willem de Vos promoted Collegiant (*q.v.*) principles; in 1710-43 he often addressed the yearly Collegiant meetings held at Rijnsburg (*q.v.*).

For the Hamburg de Vos family see **Voss, de.**
        vDZ.

Church records of Amsterdam; *N.N.B.Wb.* X, 1137; *DJ* 1850, 170 note; J. C. van Slee, *De Rijnsburger Collegianten* (Haarlem, 1895) 187.

Vos, Karel, b. Aug. 22, 1874, at Rotterdam, d. May 30, 1926, at Middelstum, a Dutch Mennonite pastor and outstanding historian. He was a son of Jan M. Vos, a (non-Mennonite) schoolteacher at Rotterdam, and Wilhemina Wijbrands (Mennonite). The pastors and historians Aem. W. Wijbrands (*q.v.*) and C. N. Wijbrands (*q.v.*) were his uncles, and W. J. Kühler (*q.v.*) was his cousin.

Vos was trained for the ministry at the Amsterdam University and the Mennonite seminary. He only served two small congregations—Woudsend 1903-11 and Middelstum 1911-d.26. This enabled him to devote himself to the study of theological problems and particularly to the study of the history of the Dutch Mennonites, to which he was stimulated by S. Cramer, his professor in Mennonite history in Amsterdam. His most important work in this field is his book *Menno Simons 1496-1561. Zijn leven en werken en zijne Reformatorische Denkbeelden* (Leiden, 1914). For this book, the first up-to-date biography of this great leader, he did painstaking work. One of the results was that the years of birth and death of Menno could with great probability be fixed at 1496 and 1561.

Besides this book Vos published a large number of papers in *De Zondagsbode* and *Doopsgezinde Bijdragen:* "Jan Jansz Schot" (1905), "De Doopsgezinden te Ouddorp-Goedereede" (1907), "De Doopsgezinden te Middelharnis-Sommelsdijk" (1908), "De Doopsgezinden te Schiedam" (1909), "De doop bij overstorting" (1911), "Jaartallen uit het leven van Menno Simons" (1912), "Kleine bijdragen over de Doopersche beweging in Nederland tot het optreden van Menno Simons" (1917); in *De Gids* he published "Reyer Anslo's Overgang" (1906), "Rembrandt's Geloof" (1909), and "Revolutionnaire Hervorming" (1920); some of his publications in *Nederlandsch Archief voor Kerkgeschiedenis* were "De copia der Outsten" (1911), "Meyndert van Emden" (also 1911), "Anabaptisten te Ahaus" (1914), "De Avondmaalsbediening bij de Doopsgezinden" (1915); in *Groningsche Volksalmanak* are found "Menno Simons in Groningen" and "Claas Ganglofs" (both 1919), "Brief over den watersnood in 1717" and "Doopsgezinde families onder Middelstum" (both 1921); "De Dooplijst van Leenaert Bouwens" is found in *Bijdr. en Mededeelingen v. h. Hist. Genootschap* (XXXVI, 1915), "De Doopsgezinden te Antwerpen" in *Bulletin de la Commission Royale d'Histoire de Belgique* (vol. LXXXIV, 1920). In the great historical survey (2 vols.) *Rotterdam in den loop der Eeuwen* (Rotterdam, 1907) he published in Vol. II a chapter on "De Geschiedenis der Doopsgezinde Gemeente te Rotterdam" (also separate edition). For the "Geschriftjes t. b. v. de Doopsgezinden in de Verstrooiing" he wrote Nos. 28, *Onze Doopsgezinde Sociëteiten;* 29, *Oranje en de Doopsgezinden;* 33, *Adam Pastor;* 43, *Twee brieven van Menno Simons;* 44, *Balthasar Hubmaier;* and 47, *De Avondmaalsbediening bij de Doopsgezinden.* His last work was an address for the Centennial of the Groningen Conference, but because of bad health he could not attend the meeting; the paper was read by N. van der Zijpp and after Vos's death a few days later, edited by him under the title *Het Honderdjarig bestaan der Sociëteit van Doopsgezinde Ge-*

meenten in Groningen en Oost-Friesland (Groningen, 1926).

Vos also published *Levensbericht van C. N. Wijbrands* (Leiden, 1914), *Aanteekeningen voor de Doop-catechisatie* (n.p., n.d.), a number of pamphlets on theological and social subjects, and a few sermons. Outstanding Dutch newspapers like the *Handelsblad* and the *Nieuwe Rotterdammer Courant* published articles of his. Vos also made the index for both the *Bibliotheca* (*q.v.*) *Reformatoria Neërlandica* (1910) and *Doopsgezinde* (*q.v.*) *Bijdragen* (1912).

Vos was a man of radical liberal conviction; this view also influenced his conception of the history of the Mennonites. He was of the opinion that the revolutionary principles as found among the Münsterites (*q.v.*) were dominant among the Dutch Anabaptists at least until 1540 and that peaceful views and practices were very scarce in Dutch Anabaptism until that date. This conception was opposed by W. J. Kühler, John Horsch, Cornelius Krahn, and N. van der Zijpp. A. F. Mellink, however, in *De Wederdopers in de Noordelijke Nederlanden 1531-44* (Groningen, 1954) carried forward Vos's theory.

Vos's scholarly qualities are great. During his lifetime his merits were highly esteemed, and he was appointed member of a number of Dutch historical societies and associations. After his death he was commemorated in the *Zondagsbode*, in *Doopsgezinde Jaarboekje* 1927, 21-23 (with portrait), in *Groningsche Volksalmanak* 1927, and in *Levensberichten van de Maatschappij voor Nederl. Letterkunde* 1928.   vᴅZ.

Vos, Willem de, b. 1737 at Amsterdam, d. there Jan. 8, 1823, married to Elizabeth Kops in 1766, a member of the above de Vos family, was a Dutch Mennonite pastor. It is not known how or where he was trained for the ministry, but it is certain that he received a good education, including a Th.D. degree. In 1759-62 he was pastor of the Mennonite congregation of Haarlem and from 1762 of the Lamist church, and after the merger (1801), of the United Mennonite congregation at Amsterdam, until he retired in 1814. He was a cofounder of the A.D.S. (*q.v.*) in 1811, and its first moderator 1811-12. He also acted as curator of its seminary. He promoted the merger of the Amsterdam Lamist and Zonist churches, which came about in 1801. Willem de Vos was a man of great learning, specializing in philosophy. His studies on (*a*) "De Grondregel der Protestanten . . . om in zaken van den godsdienst voor zich zelven te oordeelen," (*b*) "In hoeverre Jezus en zijne apostelen . . . zich naar de toen heerschende volksbegrippen hebben geschikt," and (*c*) "De genoegzaamheid van het inwendig bewijs voor de goddelijkheid der Evangelie-leer" (these essays are also known under somewhat modified titles) were given awards by the Teyler (*q.v.*) Foundation at Haarlem and published in its *Verhandelingen*, vols. IX (1789), XI (1791), and XV (1795). De Vos wrote an appreciative sketch of his colleague Allard Hulshoff (*q.v.*), d.1795, in *Leven en Character van A. H.* (Amsterdam, 1795). In 1786 he taught philosophy and religion in the Mennonite seminary.

He was a member of a number of learned societies, for which he sometimes delivered addresses on religious and timely subjects.   vᴅZ.

N.N.B.Wb. X, 1137 f.; *Naamlijst* 1829, 24; *Inv. Arch. Amst.* II, Nos. 692, 697, 2505 f.; *DJ* 1840, 112; 1850, 113, 122, 143, 170, note 1; *DB* 1863, 16; 1898, 13, 20, 26, 32.

Vosges (France) Mennonite Church (called Darney, *q.v.*, 1933-41) is one of the oldest Mennonite congregations in the French-speaking part of France, having always consisted of widely scattered farm families living west of the Vosges Mts., with the city of Epinal as the approximate center. During most of its history the meetings have been held in rotation in the homes. Before 1766 Mennonites were living in the mountainous area around Donon in the northeast of the Vosges Department. From here they moved westward, being joined by some families from the Markirch (*q.v.*, Ste-Marie-aux-Mines) area. Others came later from the region of Zweibrücken and Saarguemines. The original families all spoke German, but by 1869 the language had become French. One of the alert elders, named Schweitzer of Goncourt, joined with the elder André Rediger of the Haute Marne congregation in 1869 in providing a French translation of the Zweibrücken (Elbing-Waldeck) catechism.

Because of intermarriage with Catholics, emigration to America, and moving westward in France into the Haute Marne area the congregation gradually grew smaller, so that in the 1930's the baptized membership was not more than 15, and the congregation held no services during the winter from November to March. Among the known elders' names were Hans Roger c1820-68, Joseph Schweitzer 1843-96, Jean Kremer 1894-1909, Nicholas Kremer 1898- , Joseph Kislig 1914- . In 1957 the congregation had some 45 members including unbaptized children, and met only once a month in private homes. Elder Kislig had retired, and the active minister was Jean Abresol.   H.S.B.

P. Sommer, "Assemblée des Vosges (Darney)," *Christ Seul*, August 1930, 5-9.

Voss, de, a former Mennonite family at Hamburg-Altona, Germany. In the 16th and 17th centuries the name was usually de Vos, like that of the Dutch de Vos family. In Hamburg a Willem de Vos is found as early as 1569. Gysbert and Gilbert de Vos, probably his sons, lived here in 1605. They certainly were immigrants from Flanders, Belgium, and relatives of Jan de Vos, b. c1550, who was burgomaster of Hondschooten in Flanders, and whose son Pieter de Vos, b. c1590, joined the Reformed and emigrated to Colchester, England. In 1627 Pieter (or Peter) de Vos was at Amsterdam and soon after he lived at Hamburg; by a privilege granted c1639 by Otto, Count of Schauenburg, he became the founder of Hamburg's big industry and of the considerable wealth of the de Voss family. He conducted a number of businesses at the same time, among which was a brewery operated for two centuries by members of the de Voss family; he and his descendants were also engaged in Greenland whaling. His son Abraham de Vos (1627-82), a merchant and businessman like his father, who apparently was baptized into the Baptist Church at Colchester, joined the Dompelaars (*q.v.*) at Hamburg in 1656 and became a preacher for this group. A few other de Vosses left the Mennonite congregation to join this group with him. Most of the family, however, remained Mennonite and until the 19th century many served as deacons. Jan Janssen de Voss, d. 1716, a deacon from 1706, was a preacher of the Hamburg Mennonite congregation 1712-d.16. Pieter de Vos Pz was an assistant pastor in 1727. Adriana de Voss, who emigrated to Germantown in 1700 with her husband, Harmen Karsdorp, and their children, may have been a member of this family.   vDZ.

"*Geslachtsregister der de Vossen,*" manuscript, by Gysbert van der Smissen in the 18th century; B. C. Roosen, *Geschichte der Mennoniten-Gemeinde zu Hamburg und Altona* I (Hamburg, 1886) 8, 9, 31, 40, 43, 47, 63, 66, 72; II (Hamburg, 1887) 6, 7, 8, 11, 84, 85; *MQR* VII (1933) 236.

Vossen, Arnold van (d. after 1708), a Mennonite immigrant from Hamburg, Germany, who arrived at Philadelphia, Pa., in 1700, joined the Germantown Mennonite Church. After some difficulty with van Vossen, Hans Neuss (Nice), the preacher of this congregation, left the church. Van Vossen may have been a member of the de Voss (*q.v.*) family of Hamburg-Altona. In 1702 he gave the land for the building of the Germantown meetinghouse. vDZ.

C. Henry Smith, *The Mennonite Immigration in Pennsylvania* (Norristown, Pa., 1929) 95, 96, 97, 104, 115; *MQR* VII (1933) 236; *ML* III, 424.

Vossenholius, Adrianus, a theologian and an opponent of the Mennonites whom he attacked in *Dialogus. Ein Göttlich und Christlich Gespreck mit den Wedderdöperen . . . geholden* (Hamburg, 1575). This book, translated from Dutch into German, does not contain any valuable information. (*Catalogus Amst.*, 101.)   vDZ.

Voth (also Vooth, Voodt, Vodt, Voht, Voet, Vogt, Foht, Foth, Fogt, Fodt, Foot, a Mennonite family name, rather common among the former Prussian Mennonites, found there by 1630, in Danzig by 1677, but chiefly in the congregations of Montau-Gruppe, Schönsee, Jeziorka, Tragheimerweide, and Danzig. Hans Voth (Voet), a deacon or a preacher in Lithuania (*q.v.*), was expelled from there and emigrated to Walcheren (*q.v.*) in the Netherlands in 1733. Returning *c*1738 he again settled in Lithuania, for in the *Naamlijst* of 1743 he is mentioned as an elder of the Waterlanders (this means Frisians) in Lithuania. He died about 1753. Gillis and his brother Heinrich Voet were also expelled from Lithuania and living at Walcheren about the same time as Hans Voet. Not identical with the former Hans is the Hans Voet of Schönsee, who was before 1719 a preacher of the Groningen Old Flemish congregation at Przechovka-Konopat in West Prussia, and who visited Holland in 1726 to inform the Dutch Committee for Foreign Needs at Amsterdam concerning the situation in the territory of Culm (*q.v.*). In his letters of July 24 and Sept. 9, 1732, and March 16, 1735, he reported about the harsh measures of the Catholic bishop of Culm against the Mennonites. He was still serving in 1758, but by 1760 he had died.

Andreas Voth was a preacher of Jeziorka 1754-*c*88 and from 1765 of Brenkenhoffswalde (*q.v.*), as were Ernst Voth from 1762 and Cornelius Voth 1792, both serving until after 1802. The following ministers are named in the German *Namensverzeichnisse* and the *Jahrbuch* by Mannhardt: Peter Voth (1795-1850), of Komrau, 1826 preacher, 1830-d.50 elder of Montau-Gruppe, Heinrich Voth, preacher of Obernessau from 1875, and another Heinrich Voth, elder of the Lithuania congregation from 1882.

Whether the Prussian Voth-Foth family descended from a Dutch-Flemish Voogt family, or from a Swiss Vogt family, is doubtful. Vogt was a family name found among the early Swiss Anabaptists. Hans Vogt, of Villingen, canton of Aargau, attended the third Anabaptist disputation at Bern.

A number of Voths (also Vogt) emigrated from Prussia to Russia. Here David Voth was a deacon of the Gnadenfeld congregation as early as 1814, and Peter Voth a preacher of the Alexanderwohl church from 1848. Andreas Voth (*q.v.*), born in West Prussia, was a prominent M.B. educator in the Molotschna. Elder Heinrich Voth was ordained in 1925 to serve the Zagradovka Mennonite Church, and was the only Mennonite elder known to have survived the tribulation of the years since then and has been active in the post-Stalin period in ministering to the scattered Mennonite groups all over Russia. From Russia and Poland the name was transplanted to North and South America. H. R. Voth (*q.v.*) was a prominent missionary (GCM) to the Indians. Heinrich Voth (*q.v.*) and his two sons John and Henry S. Voth (*q.v.*) were prominent M.B. ministers and leaders. J. W. Vogt was for many years pastor of the Hillsboro Mennonite Brethren Church, then principal of the Corn (Okla.) Bible Academy, and more recently pastor of the M.B. Church at Neuwied, Germany. Other M.B. ministers bearing the name are Herman Voth, leader of the East Aldergrove (B.C.) Church, and D. Vogt, assistant leader at Fraserview, Vancouver, B.C. John J. Voth has served Bethel College and other institutions. Dr. Harold Vogt is on the staff of Prairie View Hospital.   vDZ.

A. A. Toews, *Mennonitische Märtyrer* I (N. Clearbrook, 1949); Reimer, *Familiennamen;* Unruh, *Hintergründe; Inv. Arch. Amst.* I, Nos. 1114, 1596, 1621, 1661, 2012, 2033, 2061, 2108; II, No. 2636; II, 2, Nos. 738, 763, 779, 784; "Bezoekreis van H. B. Hulshoff," in *Bijdr. en Mededeelingen v.h. hist. genootschap* LIX (1938).

Voth, Andreas (1821-85), an M.B. educator in Russia, was born at Brenkenhoffswalde, West Prussia, Germany, emigrated to Russia with his parents in 1834 and settled in Gnadenfeld in the Molotschna Mennonite settlement. Voth had a better than ordinary education, with Wilhelm and Friedrich Lange (*q.v.*) and Heinrich Franz (*q.v.*) as his teachers. He served as a village teacher at Pastwa and Halbstadt. In 1853 he left teaching to enter business, but though he was not very successful in business and was burdened by it, he still spent much of his time and energy sacrificially. He rejected the office of minister, feeling himself unworthy of it, but served as a deacon. Voth possessed special gifts for mediation. He mediated between the ministers and teachers, between teachers and Russian officials, and between the Mennonite body and the Russian government. In all circles he enjoyed respect and confidence. His service as chairman of the Molotschna school board 1871-83 was very fruitful. He created a fund of 2,000 rubles for promising young men who wanted to prepare for teaching. Under his leadership the entire school system was reformed. The Halbstadt Zentralschule added a two-year pedagogical course for village teachers, followed later by other Zentralschulen. Voth founded the first secondary school for girls in his own home and at his own risk. He also played an essential role in revitalizing the teachers' conferences. When he retired from the board the Molotschna settlement and its subsidiaries had a unified program of instruction. In 1877 the Russian government gave him a medal in recognition of his educational work. Unfortunately, in his good nature, Voth allowed himself to be used as a tool by the wealthier landowners to try to secure special favors for them from the government at St. Petersburg. For this he was severely censured by the government minister. He vowed that he would never again act in that capacity. In consequence these men abandoned him, disregarding the great sacrifices he had made. He died on June 17, 1885, an economically ruined man. He had laid the foundations upon which Klett (*q.v.*) and Heese (*q.v.*) were able to build the educational system to new heights.   A.B.

Peter Braun, "Der Molotschnaer Mennoniten Schulrat"; Friesen, *Brüderschaft*, 494, 646, 648; *ML* IV.

Voth, Heinrich (1851-1918), an elder and outstanding leader of the Mennonite Brethren Church, was born in the village of Gnadenheim, province of Taurida, South Russia, on Feb. 19, 1851, the third of the seven children of Heinrich and Helena (Fast) Voth. On June 12, 1873, he married Sarah Kornelsen. Nine children grew to adulthood. He taught in the Mennonite village school at Klippenfeld two years. During this time Voth was converted and had a deep religious experience, and a remarkable revival also occurred in his school. In 1876 the family emigrated to America, establishing a home on a farm near Bingham Lake, Minn. In June 1877 he joined the M.B. Church and immediately became an active member. At first he led the Sunday school, then he was elected to the ministry and in 1885 was ordained elder. He served as minister and pastor of the Bingham Lake M.B. Church about 40 years. During this time the congregation grew into one of the largest and most influential of the M.B. Church.

Elder Voth was active in the Mennonite Brethren Conference in many ways, attending every general conference from its beginning until his death. He traveled much as an evangelist and as itinerating preacher, holding meetings in all the M.B. churches. He had a thorough knowledge of the Scriptures and gave valuable Bible addresses. He served the M.B. General Conference on various committees; he was chairman of the Board of Foreign Missions in 1909-18. He served as moderator of the General Conference 14 years and as moderator of the Central District Conference 15 years. His oldest son, Henry S. Voth (*q.v.*), became a noted evangelist

and pastor of the M.B. Church and a leading man in its conference activities, and his son John H. Voth served as an M.B. missionary to India for 34 years. In March 1918, the Voths moved to Vanderhuf, B.C., where he died Nov. 26, 1918. Interment was at Winkler, Man.   J.H.L.

Voth, Heinrich S. (1878-1953), an outstanding Mennonite Brethren evangelist and leader, was born Jan. 28, 1878, near Bingham Lake, Cottonwood Co., Minn., the oldest son of Elder Heinrich Voth. His father was the leader of the local M.B. church and also a teacher. Heinrich S. Voth completed his secondary education in 1896. He taught public school in 1899 at Langdon, N.D. In 1900-1 he was engaged in colportage; he attended McPherson College, McPherson, Kan., in 1901-2, and in 1902 he was designated by the M.B. Church of North America to serve as evangelist, which position he held until 1908. On Aug. 28, 1904, he was married to Susie Warkentin, daughter of Johann Warkentin of Winkler, Man. On Dec. 5, 1908, he was ordained as minister in the M.B. Church of Winkler. He then served as pastor of the M.B. churches of Dallas and Portland, Ore., during 1909-16. He resumed his position as evangelist in 1916-20, following which he settled on a farm near Winkler and served as minister to this church. In 1931 he accepted the pastorate of the M.B. Church of Winkler, Man., and served in this capacity for 20 years.

Voth served on numerous committees during his most active life, a few of which will be mentioned here. He was vice-chairman of the M.B. General Conference in 1924-36, 1939, 1943, 1945-48. He was a member of the Board of Foreign Missions 1927-53, serving either as vice-president or secretary. He was a member of the General Conference Board of Education 1930-36 and member of the Board of Welfare of the General Conference 1930-43. He also served as Board chairman of the South Side Mission in Minneapolis, Minn., 1921-36. He served as chairman of the annual Northern District (Canadian) Conference for 18 years.

H. S. Voth was a man of breadth and force, with keen insight and tact in dealing with social problems. A characteristic phrase, "O Herr hilf, O Herr lass wohlgelingen," will linger long in the ears of those who knew him well. He died on Oct. 23, 1953.   A.V.

Voth, Henry R. (1855-1931), a Mennonite (GCM) minister, missionary, anthropologist, and home mission worker, was born April 15, 1855, in South Russia. He came to America in 1874 and after teaching school the first winter entered the Wadsworth School (*q.v.*) in Ohio in preparation for mission work. He later attended the theological seminary of the Evangelical Synod of North America at Marthasville, Mo. After a short medical course in St. Louis he was sent to Darlington (*q.v.*), Indian Territory, to work among the Cheyenne (*q.v.*) and Arapaho (*q.v.*) Indians. His wife, Barbara Baer, whom he married in 1884, died there in 1889. In 1892 he was sent to Arizona (*q.v.*), to open a new mission field among the Hopi (*q.v.*) Indians. His second wife, Martha Moser of Dalton, Ohio, died in Arizona in 1901.

During his nine years in Arizona, Voth developed an intimate acquaintance with the Hopi Indians, collecting much original material relative to Indian religious life and folklore which was later displayed in the Field Museum, Chicago. He collaborated with George A. Dorsey in certain studies of the Hopis. He also wrote a number of original monographs published in the Anthropological Series of the Field Columbian Museum. Ed. G. Kaufman lists the following publications written by Voth and published in this series: (1) *Brief Miscellaneous Hopi Papers*, 1912, vol. XI, No. 2; (2) *Hopi Proper Names*, 1905, vol. VI, No. 3; (3) *The Oraibi Marau Ceremony*, 1912, vol. XI, No. 1; (4) *Oraibi Natal Customs and Ceremonies*, 1905, vol. VI, No. 2; (5) *The Oraibi Oaquoel Ceremony*, 1903, vol. VI, No. 1; (6) *The Oraibi Powamu Ceremony*, 1901, vol. III, No. 2; (7) *The Oraibi Summer Snake Ceremony*, 1903, vol. III, No. 4; (8) *The Traditions of the Hopi*, 1915, vol. VIII; (9) H. R. Voth joint author with G. A. Dorsey, *The Mishongnovi Ceremonies of Snake and Antelope Fraternities*, 1901, vol. III, No. 3; (10) Voth & Dorsey, *The Oraibi Soyal Ceremony*, 1901, vol. III, No. 1.

On leaving Arizona Voth served as home mission worker in the Western District Conference, giving much of his time to new congregations in Oklahoma. In 1906 he married Katie Herschler of Perry, Okla. In 1914-27 he served the congregations of Goltry and Gotebo, Okla. In 1927 he retired to Newton, where he died June 2, 1931.

Voth was president of the Mennonite Historical Association (*q.v.*) 1914-30. His interest in collecting historical items and in studying Indian language and folklore is reflected in the extensive H. R. Voth Collection in the Bethel College Historical Library. This collection contains his manuscript studies in the Arapaho language, and studies in Hopi ceremonial rites and folklore, in addition to a Hopi dictionary.   J.F.S.

Ed. G. Kaufman, *The Development of the Missionary and Philanthropic Interest Among the Mennonites of North America* (Berne, 1931); *The Mennonite*, June 25, 1931.

Voth, Johann W., was born Jan. 27, 1863, the son of Elder W. Voth. He was a farmer. In 1907 he was elected minister of the Nikolaifeld Church in Zagradovka (*q.v.*), South Russia, and as elder upon Martens' resignation in 1908. He was well-intentioned but not a leader. In 1921 he had to resign as elder and minister, and lived quietly in retirement. Nothing is known of the end of his life. (G. J. Lohrenz, *Sagradowka*, Rosthern, 1947, p. 76.)   G.L.

Voth, John Homer (1879-1943), an evangelist and foreign missionary of the Mennonite Brethren Church, was born on a farm near Bingham Lake, Minn., Dec. 23, 1879, the third of the nine children of Heinrich and Sarah (Kornelsen) Voth. At attended high school at Windom, Minn. At 15 he was converted and baptized and joined the Bingham Lake M.B. Church of which his father was elder. Voth began to teach in rural schools at 17 and continued this several years. In 1901 he came to McPherson, Kan., where for a number of years he attended the German Department School of the

M.B. Church. For three years he studied at the German Baptist Theological Seminary, Rochester, N.Y., where he was graduated. In 1918 Tabor College conferred on him the A.B. degree. On Aug. 18, 1907, Voth married Maria Epp. Of their eight children, two sons died in infancy and one while in service during World War II. In 1905-7 Voth did considerable evangelistic work in the M.B. Conference. He was ordained as a missionary to India by the M.B. Foreign Mission Board and left for this field in 1908.

Voth rendered valuable and effective services as itinerating missionary of the M.B. Mission among the Telugus in the Hyderabad State of India. He erected most of the buildings on the Devarakonda Station. He was successful in winning converts, training indigenous workers, and establishing churches. He began the monthly Telugu paper, "Suvarthamani," in 1920, which became the organ of the Andhra M.B. Church. When he finally left India in 1942 after a period of 34 years' service, there were 17 M.B. churches with a total of more than 3,000 members in the Devarakonda field.

Through his extensive writing for the *Zionsbote* and through his aggressive itineraries while on furlough, he created much interest for the cause of foreign missions in the M.B. Conference. In the summer of 1942 he and his wife returned to America and established their home at Tulsa, Okla. Here he died July 29, 1943. Interment was at Mountain Lake, Minn.   J.H.L.

Voth, Tobias (1791-?), a pioneer educator among the Mennonites of Russia, was born July 16, 1791, at Brenkenhoffswalde (*q.v.*) near Driesen, Mark Brandenburg, Germany, where his father was a minister. He attended the local school under teachers who had studied in Leipzig and Berlin. At the age of sixteen he became a teacher of the local school, which position he held for five years. After passing a teachers' examination he taught at Soldin, where he married a Lutheran girl. In 1812 he accepted a school in Königsberg in Neumark. In 1818 he reported in his diary that he and his wife were converted through Jung-Stilling's writings, and then had fellowship with other Pietists. For two years he taught at Graudenz. In 1822 he went to the Molotschna to teach in the Ohrloff (*q.v.*) Zentralschule, where he also sponsored reading and mission circles. This school was sponsored by the Agricultural Association (*q.v.*), of which Johann Cornies (*q.v.*) was the chairman. Because of a disagreement with Cornies, Voth resigned after seven years of teaching and went to Schönwiese near Chortitza, where he taught for a number of years in a private secondary school. After this he taught in a secondary school at Steinbach, Molotschna. He died in Berdyansk. He was a gifted pioneer educator but did not find enough response and appreciation for his talents and as a result suffered many privations.   C.K.

Friesen, *Brüderschaft*, 78-79, 569-77; H. Görz, *Die Molotschnaer Ansiedlung* (Steinbach, 1950) 102-3.

Voth, Wilhelm (1832-1914), a Russian Mennonite elder, was born Dec. 23, 1832, in the Molotschna Mennonite settlement in South Russia, and moved to Zagradovka in 1872. Voth was poor, sickly, had a large family, was meagerly educated, but was a great reader, keen observer, and possessed great will power; he took a keen interest in all that took place in Mennonite circles. The new settlement at Zagradovka, comprising several thousand souls, had no ordained minister. In 1872 Voth and a few others were elected to preach. On June 2, 1874, the new congregation was formally organized; Voth was elected and ordained on the same day to serve as elder. It required leadership, courage, and wisdom to form this heterogeneous mass into a congregation. A meetinghouse, costing 7,000 rubles, was built in the village of Nikolaifeld and dedicated on May 5, 1891. With the organization of the large congregation and the construction of the church Voth's main work was done. His failing health forced him to resign as elder in May 1895. He died Aug. 20, 1914.

G.L.

G. J. Lohrenz, *Sagradowka* (Rosthern, 1947) 64; Friesen, *Brüderschaft*, 720.

Voting in governmental elections was long restricted by property qualifications and other requirements, so that full universal and democratic male suffrage was a late development in the Western World. In the United States it came into general acceptance *c*1825-40, in western continental Europe somewhat later, and in eastern Europe much later. Anabaptists as a nontolerated group or as refugee noncitizens would scarcely ever have had the privilege of voting. Most Mennonites in Europe, by the time they legally had the right to vote, were sufficiently assimilated into the prevailing culture, or had dropped the original Anabaptist doctrines of nonparticipation in the magistracy and nonresistance, to the extent that they felt no obstacle in their faith or principles to voting. In some other places full citizenship, including the right to hold office, was not granted Mennonites until quite late, in West Prussia not until 1867, and here it was conditioned upon acceptance of military service as a universal obligation.

In the New World with its freedoms, Mennonites from the outset have had the right to vote, subject to the same qualifications required of others. The only exception was when temporarily during World War I the Canadian government suspended the right to vote for all groups officially standing for nonresistance. This action was quickly rescinded at the end of the war.

American Mennonites themselves have generally exercised their right of suffrage, including even very conservative groups like the Old Order Amish. It is claimed that the Mennonites in Colonial Pennsylvania, along with other nonresistant German groups, helped to keep the Quaker Assembly in power years after it would otherwise have lost at the polls. Only in recent times have some more conservative individuals concluded that they should not vote because it presumably involved them in the support of men in offices which they themselves could not occupy. Some have also felt that the doctrine of separation of church and state, or even of separation from the world, required abstinence from voting. However, there is no record of any group or conference action prohibiting voting, al-

though sentiment in some areas has become so strong on the point, especially in the Mennonite Church (MC), as to greatly reduce the number of Mennonite voters. Resolutions have been passed, however, discouraging or forbidding "electioneering," or "taking part in politics." It must be remembered of course that the percentage of voting in general in America is relatively low, often less than half of the qualified voters, and even in presidential elections seldom more than 50 per cent. Sentiment against voting becomes particularly strong in times of national stress and war or danger of war.

In areas of concentrated Mennonite population, Mennonite votes have been important, and Mennonites have been traditionally attached to one political party. In Canada most Mennonites were long thought to be supporters of the Liberal Party. In some areas, Iowa for instance, the Amish usually voted democratic. In other areas such as eastern Pennsylvania, Mennonites were traditionally thought to be **Republican.**

Even Mennonites who did not vote in political elections usually voted in "local option" elections in favor of the prohibition of the sale of alcoholic liquor. George R. Brunk, a bishop (MC) of Denbigh, Va., in one such election publicly urged his members to "vote out the saloon." On the other hand, some held that legislation was ineffective against liquor sale and consumption and that the Christian's method to work against such evils was not by political methods but by spiritual methods and education.

Occasionally pamphlets have been published against voting, as well as articles in such church papers as the *Gospel Herald*. Among the pamphlets were one by S. D. Mast, an Old Order Amish minister, *Das Christenthum und der Stimmkasten oder die Ursache warum ich nicht an die weltliche Wahl gehe* (*c*1875, 10 pp.), and J. L. Stauffer's tract of about 1915, *Questions for the Christian Professor Who Votes* (12 pp.).   H.S.B.

Voz Menonita, La, the monthly 24-page (with cover) 6 x 9 in. organ of the Mennonite Church (MC, Iglesia Evangelica Menonita en la Argentina) in Argentina, first number March 1932. It was varied somewhat in number of pages and in page size. In 1932-35 it was 5½ x 7½; 1936-53, 6½ x 9½; 1953- , 6½ x 8½. Editors have been Albano Luayza 1932-48, Ernesto Suárez Vilela 1949-56, Pedro Lanik 1956-58, and Marta de Alvarez beginning with March 1958. The place of publication has varied but in 1958 was Buenos Aires.   H.S.B.

V. P., the author of *Successio Anabaptistica:* see **Walrave, Simon.**

Vrank Willemsz (Winsen), of Amsterdam, was one of the first nine Dutch Anabaptists executed for their Anabaptist views. They all recanted, but nevertheless they were put to death at The Hague on Dec. 5, 1531. For particulars see **Jan van Delft.**

vDZ.

Vrede-bode *aen onse lieve Vrienden, den Broederen met Haeren Dienaren ende Oudsten Vincent de Hondt* is an invitation of the Old Flemish Mennonites meeting at Utrecht in 1633 which offered peace and union to the Vincent de Hondtsvolk (*q.v.*), which was, however, not accepted. (Kühler, *Geschiedenis* II, 197.) vDZ.

Vrede-handeling is the title of a booklet published at Rotterdam, Netherlands, in 1671, containing an account of the negotiations between the Waterlander Mennonites of Rotterdam and the Remonstrant (*q.v.*) church in this city concerning a union, which union, however, did not come about. vDZ.

Vredehandelingen, *openbaar ghehouden tot Amsterdam den 3, 4, en 5 October 1630, tusschen de Dienaren der Vlaemsche Ghemeente ter eender ende de Vereenigde Hoogduytschen en Vriesen ter ander zyde* (Amsterdam, 1630), and the same booklet followed by *Een korte Vertooninge van het gene . . . vorder gehandelt is in de Vergaderinghe . . . 1636* (Haarlem, 1636), are two books mentioned by Schagen, now apparently lost, which give the negotiations leading in 1639 to the merger of the Flemish congregation of Amsterdam with the High German and Frisian group. The most important facts of these negotiations are also found in *Kort Verhael van de Vereeniginghe tusschen de Doopsgesinde Ghemeynten* (1639). vDZ.

M. Schagen, *Naamlijst der Doopsgezinde Schryveren* (Amsterdam, 1745) 126 f.

Vreden, a town in Westphalia, Germany, where there was some revolutionary Anabaptist activity in 1534-35. A number of Mennonites lived here *c*1600. In 1593 the Catholic priest of Vreden complained that some of the children were unbaptized and that a few persons neglected to have their marriages solemnized in the (Catholic) church. There is an old Mennonite song addressed "aen de vrienden ter stede/ tot Boeckholt en tot Vrede/ tot Almelo oock mede"; this seems to indicate the existence of a congregation at Vreden. Shortly after 1600 all Mennonites were banished from the town, and though this sentence was never carried out rigorously, most Mennonites had left the town before 1615. Members of the following families are named as Mennonites here *c*1600: Straalman, Hofkes, Hölscher, Brommel (Brummel), Willink, Degenehr (Degenaar), Swerink, Budde(n), Portener, Walien. Some of these are found among the Dutch Mennonites at other places, particularly at Enschedé, about the same time or later. The Mennonite elder Hendrik (*q.v.*) van Vreeden and the Dutch Mennonite van Vre(e)den family found at Amsterdam in the 17th and 18th centuries may originally have been natives of Vreden. vDZ.

Vredesgroep: see **Doopsgezinde Vredesgroep.**

Vreede, a former Dutch Mennonite family, whose ancestor Dirck Pietersz Vreede, a native of Opspringen in the territory of Jülich (*q.v.*), Germany, moved to Leiden, Holland, *c*1655, because of persecution. In Leiden he was a tinsmith. He died in 1687, and must have been well-to-do, for he left a considerable legacy to the Leiden Waterlander Mennonite congregation, of which he had been a deacon since 1670. Most of his descendants were textile

merchants or manufacturers; they were nearly all deacons of the church at Leiden, and some of them were trustees of the Bethlehems Hofje (old people's home). An outstanding member of this family was Pieter Vreede (1750-1837), manufacturer of cloth and woolen blankets, a fervent Patriot (*q.v.*), who played an important part in the Dutch political situation of about 1790 and shortly after. In 1798 he attained great political authority as a member of the *Uitvoerend Bewind* (executive government) of the Dutch Republic, sharing this power with two others, one of whom was the Mennonite Wybo Fijnje (*q.v.*). This office, however, lasted only for a short time, for Vreede and his group were too radical. He retired from politics, devoting his attention to his business, then at Tilburg. He was a close friend of F. A. van der Kemp (*q.v.*), once also a Patriot; in 1828 van der Kemp wrote him a letter from America. Though a member of the church Pieter Vreede, unlike his ancestors, was not interested in congregational life. His descendants, among whom was the famous professor of law G. W. Vreede (1809-80) at Utrecht, did not join the church. vDZ.

Nederl. Patriciaat XLI (1955) 341-70; L. G. le Poole, *Bijdragen tot de kennis van . . . de Doopsgezinden . . . te Leiden* (Leiden, 1905) *passim;* J. van der Poel, "Leven en Bedrijf van Pieter Vreede," in *Verslag Historisch Genootschap,* 1951, 30 ff.; *DB* 1907, 124, 145; *N.N.B.Wb.* IX, 1245-54.

Vreede, Adolf de, in 1660 presented three petitions to Bern, Switzerland, in behalf of the Bernese Mennonites, drawn up respectively by the Dutch States General and the cities of Amsterdam and Rotterdam. De Vreede, who arrived at Bern on June 11, was permitted to converse with the Swiss brethren who were in prison. This conversation, held in the presence of the Bernese *Oberschultheis,* had little success; the Swiss Mennonites were stubborn and perhaps somewhat embarrassed by the worldly figure of Vreede and the annoying presence of the Bernese official. They accused the Dutch Mennonites of worldliness and refused to consider the Dutch proposal to leave Switzerland and settle in the Netherlands. Nevertheless as a result of this visit a small number of the Swiss Brethren soon moved to the Netherlands. Concerning de Vreede there is no further information. He is said to have been a Mennonite, but he could not be identified as such. (Müller, *Berner Täufer,* 185-91.) vDZ.

Vreede (Vreeden, Vrede, Vreden), **Isaac van,** d. 1682, was chosen in March 1662 as a preacher of the Flemish Mennonite congregation (*bij't Lam*) at Amsterdam, Holland. After the schism in this church (see **Lammerenkrijgh**), van Vreede sided against Galenus (*q.v.*) Abrahamsz with the conservative leaders like Samuel Apostool (*q.v.*) and in June 1664 became a preacher in the Zonist (*q.v.*) church at Amsterdam. But here he did not feel at home. In 1670 he left the congregation with his co-preacher Pieter van Eyssen and founded the "Kleine Zon" congregation. In 1675 van Vreede left this group, founding the small congregation of "Het Sterretje." Being dismissed because of his quarrelsome intolerance he moved to Gouda, where he was called as preacher (1677) of the (Lamist) Mennonite congregation. It is one of the curiosities of history that this man, who had been a champion of the utmost strictness and had sharply attacked Galenus Abrahamsz and his ideas in *Vrede-Presentatie aan Galenus Abrahamsz en zijne Mede-stemmers* (Amsterdam, 1664), in 1679 invited his former opponent to perform baptism and administer the Lord's Supper at Gouda.   vdZ.

H. W. Meihuizen, *Galenus Abrahamsz* (Haarlem, 1954) 79 f., 86, 98, 113 f.; *Inv. Arch. Amst.* II, Nos. 1404, 1762 2207, 2224 f.; *DB* 1900, 20, 32; 1918, 52.

Vreeden, Hendrik van, a Dutch Mennonite elder: see **Hendrik van Vre(e)den.**

Vreeken (formerly also Vreeke), a Mennonite family found at Aalsmeer, Netherlands, from at least the early 17th century. Most of them were fishermen in the 17th-19th centuries. They belonged to the Frisian Mennonites and in the 19th century to the "Nieuwe Vermaning." Many of them served as deacons and (lay) preachers. Ministers were Claes Fredriks, preacher 1732, elder 1742-d.89, Willem Arends Vreeke 1788-c1812, his brother Vreek Arends Vreeke 1788-d.1814, Cornelis Pietersz Vreeke 1801-c32, Klaas Vreeksz Vreeken 1832, elder until 1866, Willem Arends Vreeken 1849, elder 1850-66, Dirk Vreeken c1858-66. In 1866 when the "Nieuwe Vermaning" merged with the Zijdweg congregation, Cornelis, Klaas, and Willem Vreeken retired.   vdZ.

W. Tsj. Vleer, *De Aloude Aalsmeerse Familiën* (De Kaag, 1954) 43; Dutch *Naamlijst;* Gorter's *Doopsgez. Lectuur,* 1856, 58.

Vreeland, a village in the Dutch province of Utrecht, where there were Mennonites in the 16th century. About 1560 Wouter de Vries was the preacher of a small congregation at Vreeland, which met in the home of a certain Neeltgen where the members read from the New Testament and "by bad, false, and heretical teaching had seduced some persons." Three of them were arrested in early 1562 and tried in Utrecht: Neeltgen (Neeltje Claesdochter) and Gysbert Joosten and his wife. They confessed that they had attended a meeting at Utrecht in December 1561, in which Dirk (*q.v.*) Philips had preached and baptized. After renouncing their faith they were released. Nothing more is known of a Mennonite congregation at Vreeland. (*DB* 1903, 5 f., 19, 26.)   vdZ.

Vries, de, a common Dutch family name, both Mennonite and non-Mennonite, found in nearly every Mennonite congregation, and in several unrelated families.

A prominent and widely ramified Mennonite de Vries family is found in Amsterdam. Its ancestor Wouter Takes (c1650-1728) settled as a butter merchant at Amsterdam c1689. He came from IJlst in Friesland and for this reason he was called de Vries, i.e., the Frisian. His son Gerrit de Vries (1691-1754) was an important merchant as were his sons and his grandsons. Among his descendants were the Mennonite pastors Abraham de Vries (1773-1862, *q.v.*) and Jeronimo de Vries (1838-1915, *q.v.*). Outstanding members of this family were Gerrit de Vries (1818-1900), a son of Pastor Abraham de Vries),

who was a lawyer at Haarlem and in 1872-74 Prime Minister and Minister of Justice, later Privy Councillor of the Netherlands. He was a deacon of the Haarlem congregation from 1842 until he moved to The Hague in 1882. His son was the famous botanist Hugo de Vries (1848-1935). Matthias de Vries (1820-92, also a son of Pastor Abraham de Vries) was professor of Dutch literature at the universities of Groningen (1849-53) and Leiden (1853-90); Jeronimo de Vries (1776-1853), during his life noted as a literary man, editor of Vondel's (*q.v.*) works, numismatist and art connoisseur, deacon at Amsterdam and trustee of the A.D.S. (*q.v.*) in 1827-52, moderator 1842-43, and curator of its seminary, and his sons Jeronimo de Vries (1808-80), district judge at Amsterdam, author of juridical works, and Abraham de Vries (1817-79), justice in the court of Amsterdam, both of whom served the Amsterdam congregation as deacons, Jeronimo also as a trustee of the A.D.S. Also a number of other members of this family were deacons; until recent times a total of 14 at Amsterdam.

Another Mennonite family by this name was found at Amsterdam in the 17th century. Its members were, however, usually more interested in the Collegiant (*q.v.*) movement than in the Lamist (*q.v.*) church, of which they were members. They are known for their interest in Spinoza, whom they supported financially. They were well-to-do merchants. Among them were Joost Fransen de Vries, d. before 1654, married to Maria de Wolf, and their sons Isaack Joosten (b. 1632), Simon Joosten (1633/4-67), and Frans Joosten (1635-64).

Mennonite ministers by the name of de Vries (mostly not related) have been: Abraham de Vries (*q.v.*); Anthoni de Vries Mz (b. 1870), of Grijpskerk, pastor at Zwartsluis 1898, Zijldijk 1903, Ytens 1906, Terhorne 1914-35; Anthony de Vries (Amsterdam, c1745-Emmerich, Aug. 26, 1817), preacher of De Rijp 1770-71, Zaandam Oude Huys 1771-91 and after seven years of retirement, served at Emmerich, Germany, 1798-1817; Bouwe Pieter de Vries (b. 1893), pastor of Terschelling 1917, Hindeloopen-Koudum 1920, Balk-Woudsend 1923, Hoorn-Enkhuizen 1933, retired in 1948; Cornelis de Vries (*q.v.*); Derk de Vries (d. c1778), who was an untrained preacher at Langedijk-Koedijk 1727-c68; Hendrik Wiebes de Vries, of Heerenveen, d. there 1807 at an advanced age, lay preacher at Heerenveen 1760-65 and Blokzijl 1765-82; Jacob de Vries, until at least 1719 an untrained preacher of the Waterlander congregation at Alkmaar, author of *De Jeugd ondervraagd Tot Doop en Avondmaal* (Alkmaar, 1714); Jan Simons de Vries (b. 1742, d. July 31, 1822), an untrained preacher at Veendam 1771 and den Ilp-Landsmeer 1781-1820; Jeronimo de Vries (*q.v.*); Klaas de Vries (*q.v.*); Paulus Simons de Vries (d.1808), lay preacher at Sloten 1765-69, and of the Ameland Waterlander congregation 1769-1804; Reitze de Vries (d.1860), pastor of Monnikendam 1809, Makkum 1814, and again Monnikendam 1818-59; Remmert Jacobsz de Vries (1643-1721), an untrained preacher and elder of the Zaandam Nieuwe Huys congregation 1673-c1721; Uilke Wytzes de Vries (d. c1781), an untrained preacher at Leeuwarden 1726-62; Wytze de Vries (d.1727), father of the former Uilke, an untrained preacher at Leeuwarden and Emden; he delivered a funeral sermon for his colleague N. J. Ley of Emden, which was published: *Lyk-reeden* (Amsterdam, 1728).

vDZ.

Nederl. Patriciaat V (1914) 439-49; XXVII (1941) 370-92; J. H. de Vries, *De Amsterdamsche Doopsgezinde Familie de Vries* (Zutphen, 1911); *N.N.B.Wb.* I, 1525-27; III, 1358-61; IV, 1428 f.; IX, 1255-58; Dutch *Naamlijst*, particularly 1792, 58; 1808, 76; 1829, 26, 70; *DB* 1889, 17, 25 f.; 1890, 14; 1891, 7, 9; 1896, 64, 69 f.; K. O. Meinsma, *Spinoza en zijn Kring* (The Hague, 1896) 103 *et passim.*

Vries, Abraham de, b. April 20, 1773, at Amsterdam, d. Nov. 3, 1862, at Haarlem, a Dutch Mennonite minister. He was a son of Gerrit de Vries and Catharina de Bosch. In 1814 he married Hillegonda van Geuns, d. 1866, the widow of Jacob Veen. Abraham de Vries, who was in his youth greatly interested in politics (like most Mennonites he was a Patriot, *q.v.*), and who in his student years at the Amsterdam seminary was even a captain of the *Landstorm* (army reserves), was appointed ministerial candidate in 1799. Thereupon he served the congregations of Nijmegen 1799-1801, Leiden 1801-3, and Haarlem 1803-38, in which year he retired. He was a man of great authority both in his own congregations and in the A.D.S. (*q.v.*), of which he was a cofounder in 1811, a member of its board 1811-39, and an honorary member 1839-57, when he resigned; he also was a curator of its seminary.

De Vries did not leave any theological writings. More than a theologian he was a literary man, well versed in several languages. In 1820 he refused a professorship in Greek and Latin at the University of Leiden. This university granted him an honorary Dr. Lit. Hum. degree in 1822. For more than 40 years he was also the city librarian and archivist of Haarlem. One of his sons was the well-known professor of Dutch literature Matthias de Vries (1820-92); another son was Gerrit de Vries (1818-1900), a lawyer and in 1872-74 Dutch Prime Minister.

Abraham de Vries was a member of several literary societies, including the Association for Dutch Literature; in the *Levensberichten* of this Association Chr. Sepp (*q.v.*) published an appreciative biography of de Vries (Leiden, 1863). (*Naamlijst* 1800, 58; *DJ* 1850, 143; *N.N.B.Wb.* V, 1078-80.) vDZ.

Vries, Cornelis de (1755-1811), a deacon of the Zaandam-Oost Mennonite congregation, who was the center of the preparation for the founding of the A.D.S. (*q.v.*) in 1811, not only serving as secretary of the preparatory committee, but also as the projector of its regulations and rules. He died just after the first meeting of the A.D.S. (*DJ* 1850, 144.)

vDZ.

Vries, Cornelis (Kornelis) de, b. Aug. 16, 1740, at Koog aan de Zaan, d. Nov. 21, 1812, at Haarlem, married first to Alida Reesen, later to Maria Elisabeth van Vollenhoven, a Dutch Mennonite minister, who studied at the Zonist (*q.v.*) seminary and served the congregations of Enschedé 1763-71 and Utrecht 1771-86. In 1786 he retired to devote himself to study and literature. Moving to Haarlem in

1788, he established the *Algemeene Konst- en Letterbode,* a newspaper on art and literature, of which he was the editor until 1809. Besides articles in this periodical he published some doctrinal studies. On Nov. 7, 1773, on the occasion of the dedication of the new meetinghouse at Utrecht, he delivered a sermon which some members of the Reformed Church considered an offense to "the public (i.e., Reformed) church." Even the magistrates of Utrecht discussed the matter, but did not take action. This sermon was published under the title *De Verdraagzame Begrippen der Doopsgezinden niet onbestaanbaar met hunne aanhoudende afzondering van de overige Kristenheid* (Utrecht, 1773). De Vries further published *Inwydingsreden over de tempels . . .* (Amsterdam, 1769), a sermon preached at Enschedé at the dedication of the new meetinghouse; *De onderscheidene en uitstekender Gelukzaligheid . . . ,* a funeral sermon for his colleague Joh. Cuperus (Utrecht, 1777); *Geschiedenis van de eerste zonde der menschen . . .* (Amsterdam, 1781); *Katechismus der H. Schriftuur* (Rotterdam, 1782); *Kleine Katechismus* (Haarlem, 1786); and *Godsdienstig Leerboek voor Kristelijke Aankomelingen* (Haarlem, 1802). De Vries was also interested in Mennonite history and possessed a good collection of about 1500 Mennonite books, which he contributed to the Enschedé congregation; this collection was destroyed in 1862 when the church burned down. A number of learned societies invited him to join. During his Utrecht period he was the editor of the *Utrechtsche Courant* 1782-87. vDZ.

J. van Geuns, *Levensbericht* (Obituary) in the *Konsten Letterbode* (1813) No. 15; (H. B. Berghuys), *Geschiedenis der Doopsgez. gemeente te Utrecht* (n.p., n.d.-1926) 60-62, 64 f.; *Naamlijst* 1815, 71 f.; *DB* 1863, 92 f.; 1868, 88; *Inv. Arch. Amst.* I, Nos. 761, 2332.

Vries, Henri Marie de (1836-1910), whose father was not a Mennonite, but whose mother was a Mennonite, a daughter of Jeronimo de Vries (1808-80) of Amsterdam, lived from 1871 at The Hague, where he was a director of the Dutch State Bank and a member of the city council. When he came to The Hague there was no Mennonite congregation there. De Vries was the chief promoter in the founding of a congregation in The Hague. For many years he was a trustee and moderator of this new congregation and in 1887-1905 he was a trustee of the A.D.S. (*q.v.*). vDZ.

A commemorative biographical sketch (with portrait) is found in *DB* 1910, 219-29; see also "De Zondagsbode" XXIII (1909-10) No. 19.

Vries, Jeronimo de, b. June 17, 1838, at Amsterdam, d. April 29, 1915, at Haarlem, a Dutch Mennonite minister, a son of Gerrit de Vries Jzn. He married A. M. Jarman, d. 1902. He was educated at the Athenaeum at Amsterdam, where he studied classical languages and Dutch literature, and at the Amsterdam Mennonite Seminary. He served in the congregations of Noordeind van Graft 1862-65, Krommenie 1865-70, Wormerveer 1870-72, and Haarlem 1872-1908, retiring in this year. Particularly in the Haarlem congregation he developed his great gifts of intellect and heart. His health was poor; but he was a popular pulpit orator, a man of liberal convictions who stressed the ethical meaning of Christianity. Yet he was not a cold moralizer; his sermons overflowed with genuine piety and are at the same time stylistic masterpieces.

He published four volumes of *preeken* (sermons): *Een Bundel Preeken* (Haarlem, 1891, two reprints), *Tweede Bundel Preeken* (Haarlem, 1897), *Twaalf Preeken* (Haarlem, 1908), *Twaalf Preeken, Nieuwe Bundel* (Haarlem 1909-10). Besides these sermons he published *Zedekundige Schetsen en Omtrekken voor de Jeugd* (Haarlem, 1898); *Karakterschetsen,* an anthology, was published after his death by H. Britzel (Haarlem, 1915).

His colleagues, Simon Gorter, d.1871, and Jacobus Craandijk, d.1912, were commemorated by de Vries in the *Levensberichten* of the Association for Dutch Literature. In *Eigen Haard,* of which very popular weekly he was the editor for many years, he published numerous articles, a few of them concerning Dutch Mennonite history.

Jeronimo de Vries was a trustee of the A.D.S. (*q.v.*) 1886-1911, curator of its seminary, secretary of the Haarlemsche (*q.v.*) Vereeniging, and on the board of a number of non-Mennonite associations; e.g., codirector of the Teyler (*q.v.*) Foundation and trustee of the Nederlandsche Protestantenbond (*q.v.,* Dutch liberal Protestant union), being a coeditor of its hymnal in 1882.

He was honored by S. Cramer (*q.v.*) in *Doopsgezinde Bijdragen* 1902, 172-86, and after his death by B. ter Haar in *Levensberichten* of the Association for Dutch Literature (Leiden, 1916, 255-90), by A. Binnerts Szn in *Doopsgezind Jaarboekje* 1916, 23-35 (with portrait) and in *De Zondagsbode* XXVIII (1914-15) No. 28.   vdZ.

Vries, Klaas de, b. March 1716 at Emden, d. July 23, 1766, at Amsterdam, a son of Preacher Wytze de Vries and Grietje Wessels, was a Dutch Mennonite minister. He was educated at the University of Franeker and the Amsterdam Mennonite Seminary. He served as pastor at Emmerich (Germany) 1741-44 and Amsterdam (Lamist church) 1744-d.66. In spite of poor health he was very active. He is said to have carefully prepared his sermons, which, however, were learned essays on religion and morals rather than direct Christian testimonies. In a commemorative poem he is called a preacher of penitence, but this is a somewhat rhetorical epithet for this rationalistically minded man. He opposed catechetical instruction by the church, believing that this was the task of the parents. Though he did not publish much, he was a man of great learning. After the death of Professor Tjerk Nieuwenhuis (*q.v.*) in 1759 he taught philosophy and physics at the Seminary for some time. His colleague Allard Hulshoff preached his funeral sermon: *Klaas de Vries . . . geschetst in eene Lykrede* (Amsterdam, 1766). His brother Uilke Wytzes de Vries (d. 1781) was an untrained minister of the Leeuwarden Mennonite congregation 1726-62. (*DJ* 1850, 112; *DB* 1918, 50, note 1.)   vdZ.

Vries, Simon Sakes de, b. c1723 at Deventer, Netherlands, d. there 1793, apparently a Mennonite, made a legacy to the Deventer Mennonite congregation. He was educated at the Athenaeum Illustre at Deventer, Utrecht University, obtaining his Ph.D. degree in 1744 from Leiden University. Oxford University granted him an honorary Ph.D. degree. De Vries, who was unmarried, and obviously a man of means, then returned to Deventer and divided his time between his brewery and his learned studies and writings. (*N.N.B.Wb.* I, 1527 f.; Blaupot t. C., *Holland* II, 157 f.; *DB* 1868, 99.)   vdZ.

Vriesche Sociëteit in Noordholland (Frisian Conference in North Holland): see **Friesche Sociëteit.**

Vrieze (Vreese, Vreeze, Vries, Vriesse), **de,** a former Dutch Mennonite family, in the 17th century living at Aardenburg (*q.v.*) in Dutch Zeeland Flanders, whither they had emigrated from Flanders, Belgium. In the 18th century (some even earlier) they left the Mennonites and joined the Reformed Church. (*De Nederl. Leeuw* 1918; *DB* 1877, 11, 12.)   vdZ.

Vriezen (Vriesche Doopsgezinden): see **Frisian Mennonites.**

Vrijburg(h), Geert van: see **Volbot, A. D.**

Vrijer, a former Mennonite family in the Dutch province of North Holland. Four of its members served as pastors: (1) Frans Albertsz Vrijer was preacher in the Frisian congregation of Barsingerhorn-Kolhorn 1723-c55. Though he had not received a special training for the ministry, he later trained some Mennonite preachers. His son was (2) Albert Fransz Vrijer, trained by his father, serving at Barsingerhorn-Kolhorn 1741-55, Den Ilp-Landsmeer 1755-70, and Wormerveer-Noord 1770-98. He published *Leerreden . . .* (Amsterdam, n.d.-1791) (*Naamlijst* 1792, 57 f.). (3) Adriaan Vrijer, a son of (2) Albert, was preacher of Oosterend on the island of Vlieland 1778-98 (*DB* 1912, 89 f.). (4) Gerrit Vrijer Az (1842-96), a grandson of (2) Albert, was a pastor of the congregations at Mensingeweer 1868-73, Staveren-Molkwerum 1873-75, Poppingewier 1875-79, Noordeinde van Graft 1879-82, Den Horn 1882-84, and Broek op Langendijk 1884-96. He was educated at the Amsterdam Mennonite Seminary.   vdZ.

Vrou Gerits: see Gerrets.

Vught, a village in the Dutch province of North Brabant, about five miles south of 's Hertogenbosch (*q.v.*). In 1533 a Sacramentist (*q.v.*) meeting was held near Vught attended by 200 persons; this shows that the new ideas had some adherents there. On Sept. 9 and 11, 1538, eight Anabaptists, including Paulus (*q.v.*) van Drunen, were burned at the stake at Vught. They probably lived at 's Hertogenbosch, where Paulus van Drunen was the elder of the congregation. In 1544 Magdalena (*q.v.*) of Waterland, a Davidjorist (*q.v.*), was executed here. Thereafter there are no traces of Anabaptists and Mennonites at Vught. In 1947 a *Kring* (circle) of Mennonites living at 's Hertogenbosch-Vught was founded, served at first by the pastor of Eindhoven, and since 1956 by the pastor of Nijmegen.   vdZ.

Mart. Mir. D 41 f., E 447 f.; *DB* 1917, 184-94; Mellink, *Wederdopers,* 314 f., 337 f., 414; *Inv. Arch. Amst.* I, No. 287.

W

Waal, De, a village on the Dutch island of Texel (*q.v.*), where there were three Mennonite meetinghouses in the 17th century—Waterlander, Frisian, and Flemish; the groups at De Waal using these meetinghouses were not independent congregations, but each more or less united with their respective congregations at Den Burg (*q.v.*). In 1772 all the Mennonite congregations of Texel except Den Hoorn (*q.v.*) merged into one single congregation called the Burg-Waal-Oosterend congregation. Thereupon the Frisian meetinghouse at De Waal was torn down (the Flemish meetinghouse had been abandoned at an earlier date) and the Waterlander meetinghouse only was left. It was remodeled in 1842 and is still in use. In the 19th century sometimes one of the preachers of the united congregation lived at De Waal. At present the Mennonites of De Waal belong to the Texel congregation, embracing all Mennonites on the island, including those of Den Hoorn. At De Waal there is a separate ladies' circle, a Sunday school for children, and a boys' club.

In 1649 (not 1648; see *ME* I, 614) Elder Claes (*q.v.*) Arentsz, of Nieuwe Zijpe, irritated the Reformed in his baptismal sermon at De Waal, which led to a religious disputation. (*DB* 1872, 195; 1873, 142, 143, 149; Blaupot t. C., *Holland* I, 195.) vDZ.

Waard, de, a Dutch Mennonite family originating on a polder near Pieterzijl in the province of Groningen, called the Waarden, from which this family has derived its name. Until *c*1850 they were nearly all farmers. Many of them served as deacons in the Pieterzijl (*q.v.*) (since 1892 called Grijpskerk, *q.v.*) Mennonite congregation, and Jacob Symons, a farmer at Ruigewaard, was 1726-d. *c*60 a lay preacher of this congregation, as was his son Jan Jacobs de Waard, who served 1753-d. *c*90.

Sytze Klazes de Waard (Pieterzijl, 1796-Haarlem, 1856), married to W. J. Krythe, was trained for the ministry at the Amsterdam Mennonite Seminary and served at Mensingeweer 1821-26, Akkrum 1826-28, and Haarlem 1828-d.56. He published, as far as is known, only three addresses on religious subjects held before the Haarlem Department of the Maatschappij (*q.v.*) tot Nut van 't Algemeen.

His grandson Sytze Klazes de Waard (Groningen, 1849-Alassio, Italy, 1915), married to M. E. Backer, at first studied mathematics and physics, thereupon literature and theology, and after finishing his study at the Amsterdam seminary served as Mennonite pastor at Westzaan-Zuid 1879-83, The Hague 1883-94, and Utrecht 1894-1911, in which year he retired because of poor health. He published the dedication sermon, *Tempelwijding* (The Hague, 1886, reprinted 1886), delivered in September 1886, when the young congregation of The Hague acquired a meetinghouse. He also published a volume of sermons, *Overdenkingen* (Amsterdam, 1915), and a number of sermons preached on special occasions.

Another Sytze Klazes de Waard (1821-1911) obtained his M.D. degree at Groningen and practiced medicine for more than fifty years in his home town. He was for about the same time a treasurer of the Pieterzijl (Grijpskerk) congregation and published a booklet on the Mennonite history of the area in which he lived: *Aanteekeningen uit de Geschiedenis der Doopsgezinden in 't Westerkwartier* (Groningen, 1901), which contains many particulars on the De Waard family. vDZ.

De Waarden en het Geslacht de Waard (Groningen, 1937); *Naamlijst* 1829, 25, 66; Gorter's *Doopsgez. Lectuur* 1858, "Kerknieuws" 1, 17 f.; (H. B. Berghuys), *Geschiedenis van de Doopsgez. gemeente te Utrecht* (n.p., n.d.-1926) 89-94; *De Zondagsbode* XXIV (1910-11) No. 34.

Waasten(e) (Warneton), a town in the province of West Flanders, Belgium, where there was a Mennonite congregation about the middle of the 16th century, of which, however, there is no further information. Waasten was one of the congregations in whose name Adriaan van Kortrijk (*q.v.*) wrote to the congregation of Antwerp *c*1545. Like most congregations in Flanders it was probably soon wiped out by persecution. Hans (*q.v.*) Vermeersch was an Anabaptist martyr in Waastene in 1559. (Verheyden, "Mennisme in Vlaanderen," ms.) vDZ.

Wabbe Lysbethsdochter, of Pingjum in Friesland, Netherlands, was among the Anabaptists arrested at Oldeklooster (*q.v.*) in Friesland in 1535, and executed at Leeuwarden on March 14 of that year. (Vos, *Menno Simons,* 229.) vDZ.

Wäbl, Johann: see **Waibl, Johannes.**

Wackernagel, Philipp (1800-77), a German hymnologist, author of *Das deutsche Kirchenlied von der ältesten Zeit bis zu Anfang des XVII. Jahrhunderts,* 5 vv. (Leipzig, 1864-77), and *Lieder der niederländischen Reformierten aus der Zeit der Verfolgung im 16. Jahrhundert* (Frankfurt, 1867), both containing considerable numbers of Anabaptist hymns. (See **Hymnology,** *ME* II, p. 871, for details.) vDZ.

Wädenswil (Wädenswyl, Wädiswill), a village in the canton of Zürich, Switzerland, was the scene of a disputation by the Reformed clergy with the Anabaptists on Jan. 26, 1613, whose purpose was to secure the return of the Anabaptist dissenters to the Reformed Church. Fifteen Anabaptists appeared, led by Elder Hans Landis (*q.v.*) of Horgerberg, supported by Galli Fuchs, a schoolteacher, and Bachmann, a blacksmith. The representatives of the authorities were Zürich burgomaster Rudolf Rhaan, Landvogt Konrad Grebel, Pastor Hans Jacob Breitinger of St. Peter's Church in Zürich, and the parish pastors of Horgen, Wädenswyl, and Richterswyl. The protocol of the disputation is to be found in the Zürich Staatsarchiv II. 44, under the title "Action mit den Wiedertauffern in Schloss der

Herrschaft Wädiswil 26. I. anno 1613 gehalten."

Breitinger, the chief Reformed speaker, sought the reason for the separation of the Anabaptists from the state church. The repeated answer of the Anabaptists was that the life of the members of the state church manifested gross sin, and that sinners were admitted to the communion along with the godly. When Breitinger argued from the parable of the tares that the church should not attempt to root out the sinners but leave that to God, the Anabaptists only felt their view confirmed. The appeal of the burgomaster that they submit to the authorities and return to the church, that the authorities would appreciate their holy living, "the holier the better," fell on deaf ears. The Anabaptists steadfastly refused to yield and said unitedly, "We are ready to sacrifice life, body, property, and blood." They pleaded for toleration.

A second disputation in March 1613 had no better results. Landis refused all compromises, including the offer of emigration, saying, "The earth is the Lord's and no one has the authority to expel them from the country."

Thereupon the authorities invoked upon Anabaptists the heavy penalty of six years of service as galley slaves in the French or Venetian navies, a severe punishment usually reserved for criminals. Three recanted. The other three, Landis, Galli, and Stephan Zehender (*q.v.*), were sent in chains to Solothurn en route to the French galley, where they fortunately escaped. When Landis returned to Zürich the next year to serve his flock, he was arrested, tried, and executed on Sept. 29, 1614, as the last Anabaptist martyr (by direct execution) in Switzerland. (See also **Horgen** and **Zürich**.)

H.S.B.

Samuel Geiser, *Die Taufgesinnten-Gemeinden* (Karlsruhe, 1931) 377-89; Cornelius Bergmann, *Die Täuferbewegung im Kanton Zürich bis 1660* (Leipzig, 1916) 82-88; Paul Kläui, "Hans Landis of Zurich," *MQR* XXII (1948) 203-11.

Wadsworth, Ohio, the site of the first Mennonite higher school in America (1867-78) and the first Mennonite Sunday school in Ohio (1854), is located 30 miles south of Cleveland in southeastern Medina County. Once an agricultural center and then a coal-mining town, it is now an industrial city of 10,000, known for the production of matches, valves, rubber soles, brick and tile, and iron castings.

The Mennonite community is located for the most part west of town, where they settled north and south along the River Styx as early as 1828. The Wisler Mennonite Church stands on the site of the original church (three miles southwest). Almost all of its 30 members are rural, half of them living in the Wadsworth area. Near by is the Bethel Mennonite (MC) Church (132 members), organized after the division of 1872. Of its 40 families, 33 consider Wadsworth their shopping center, and 40 per cent earn the major portion of their incomes in town. The General Conference Mennonite Church, founded on the outskirts in 1852 and moved into town forty years later, is over 80 per cent urban, but 22 per cent of its 250 members are identified with other communities. R.W.K.

Rachel Kreider, "One Hundred Years in Wadsworth," *Menn. Life* VIII (October 1953).

Wadsworth First Mennonite Church (GCM), located in Wadsworth, Medina Co., Ohio, 12 miles west of Akron, was organized by Ephraim Hunsberger in 1852, who came to Wadsworth from Berks County, Pa. The first members were three families from the Bally Mennonite (GCM) Church at Hereford, Pa., who came in 1851. At the dedication of the first meetinghouse on Oct. 9, 1853, twelve were baptized to be added to the charter membership of 10. Hunsberger was ordained Oct. 10, 1852, in Pennsylvania for the new congregation at Wadsworth, and began preaching at Wadsworth the same month. The first deacon was ordained in 1853. In 1892 the congregation purchased its present meetinghouse, a former Congregational church on the corner of College and Pardee streets. The membership in 1957 was 264; A. J. Neuenschwander was the pastor. R.L.M.

Wadsworth Mennonite School, or simply the Wadsworth Institute, was the common designation in English for an institution which operated from Jan. 2, 1868, until Dec. 31, 1878, at Wadsworth, Ohio, and which was officially the *Christliche Bildungs-Anstalt der Mennoniten Gemeinschaft.* This was one of the very first attempts of the Mennonites in higher education, preceded only by the seminary in Amsterdam, started in 1735, and contemporary with the Weierhof (German) institution of 1867 and certain normal schools of the Mennonites in Russia. It grew out of the movement for union among Mennonites in America which resulted in the General Conference Mennonite Church (*q.v.*) organized in 1860. In this connection more adequate training was felt necessary for ministers and church workers. A program of systematic explanation and solicitation was inaugurated with the result that the General Conference was able to authorize the school in 1863 and complete the building for dedication in 1866. The school as planned was to provide three years of instruction primarily in Biblical subjects and largely in the German language. Carl Justus van der Smissen (*q.v.*), a university-trained Mennonite pastor in Germany, was induced to undertake pioneering service in the school and arrived in December 1868. In the meantime the school had been started under temporary supervision of Christian Schowalter with an assistant teacher and 24 students.

The program at Wadsworth was a combination of study and work. Rising at five o'clock and washing was followed by cleaning rooms, with morning devotions and breakfast at 7:30. The morning was given to study and instruction and the afternoon to work, each student being assigned projects in the yard, garden, or field. Supper at six was preceded by an hour of study and followed by another study period, with devotions again at nine. The school bulletin for 1876 lists a faculty of seven persons and three departments of instruction with courses as follows: *Theological Department*—Biblical History, Bible Knowledge, Exegesis, Doctrine Symbolics, Church History, History of the Bible, Catechism Instruction, Homiletics; *German Department*—Reading, Writing, Grammar, Spelling, Composition; *English Department*—Reading, Writing, Orthography, Grammar, Geography, Natural Philosophy, Logic, Algebra, Geometry, Trigonometry, and any of the branches usually taught in academies and colleges.

The influence of the van der Smissen family in the Wadsworth school was strongly felt. The father, mother, and two daughters were from a European culture with a background of books, music, wealth, yet withal deeply spiritual and keenly interested in mission work, evangelism, and young people. They exerted a deep influence on the young men from the rougher American communities. Yet, because of conditions inherent in the situation, difficulties began to arise early in the life of the school. Friction developed within the faculty between those of European and American culture; misunderstandings arose between the supporting constituency of the East and West; and enrollment decreased. Debts were incurred and the total indebtedness increased year by year, amounting in 1876 to over $9,000.00. In 1877 a serious attempt was made to erase the indebtedness and eliminate friction. The school was divided into two separate departments, German and English; the former was the theological work under the German teacher, and the latter the English and normal school work under the English teacher. Women also were allowed to enroll. The number of theological students increased to 16 while the normal school operated profitably with 30 or more students, and after 1878 was called the "Excelsior Normal School." Better feeling resulted in these two years and the indebtedness was reduced, but it was apparently too late. The General Conference in 1878 was thoroughly discouraged. A special committee found the double arrangement of the school unsatisfactory and the location unsuited for a school in which the German language dominated. The theological department consequently was closed in December 1878, and the normal school department, which operated independently, closed in May 1879. The total enrollment for the first nine years was 310, or an average yearly attendance of 34. Some 209 different persons attended the school, of whom not less than 130 were from Mennonite families.

The Wadsworth school made significant contributions to the church in spite of its relatively brief period of existence. It promoted unification by challenging the congregations to work together and by developing friendships between students from widely separated areas. It showed, in spite of opposition, that higher education was not incompatible with humility and evangelical zeal. It developed over the decade a generation of trained ministers who in general marked the beginning of the change from the lay ministry to the trained ministry. It promoted certain forms of evangelical work which introduced a new spirit in many of the churches. This is particularly true in the cause of missions, which was deeply woven into the Wadsworth program. Though the school was closed it confirmed the sentiment for education and blazed the way for the institutions of the next century.   S.F.P.

Verhandlungen der Allgemeinen Konferenz der Mennoniten . . . Erste bis Elfte Sitzungen (Berne); H. P. Krehbiel, *History of the General Conference . . .* (Canton, 1898); *Christliche Bildungs-Anstalt der Mennoniten Gemeinschaft, Wadsworth, Ohio;* J. E. Hartzler, *Education Among the Mennonites of America* (Danvers, Ill., 1925); Hillegonda van der Smissen, *Sketches from My Life* (Newton, n.d.); Anna Kreider, "Beginning of Theological Training Among the Mennonites of America," *Menn. Life* XIV (April 1959); Records of the school, BeCL.

Wadzeck, Friedrich (1762-1823), coauthor of *Beiträge zur Kenntnis der Mennoniten-Gemeinden in Europa und Amerika,* stemmed from the Moravian Brethren congregation in Berlin, of which his father was a sexton. He was professor of literature, physics, and natural history in the royal cadet corps in Berlin, founding its library and serving as librarian. After 31 years of service he was retired, principally because of his opposition to the athletic program. Thereupon he devoted himself to establishing homes in Berlin for neglected children, which opened in 1819 and at the time of his death four years later were sheltering 400 children of the poorest families of Berlin. Wadzeck also left a large collection of copper etchings, containing the portraits of about 50,000 famous men and women. In co-operation with the Baron von Reiswitz (*q.v.*) he wrote a book on the Mennonites, which was published in Berlin (1821) with the title *Beiträge zur Kenntnis der Mennoniten-Gemeinden in Europa und Amerika, statistischen, historischen und religiösen Inhalts,* the income from which he applied to his charities.

A second volume with almost the same title as the 1821 volume, published by Baron Reiswitz as sole author under the title *Beiträge zur Kenntniss der taufgesinnten Gemeinden oder der Mennoniten, statistischen, historischen und religiösen, auch juristischen Inhalts, Zweiter Theil* (Breslau, 1829), gives the impression that Reiswitz did most of the work on the first volume, and reports that Wadzeck was too busy caring for poor children to even use for the benefit of the children the 500 free copies which he had received.

Friedrich August Schmidt's *Neuer Nekrolog der Deutschen* I (1823) No. 1, 272-94, contains a portrait of Wadzeck. There may be other articles on the Mennonites in the periodical published by Wadzeck from 1809 with the title *Nützliches und Unterhaltendes Wochenblatt für den gebildeten Bürger und denkenden Landmann,* which continued after his death in the interests of the institutions he founded. (*ML* III.)   HEGE, H.S.B.

Waechlink (Waeckling) **Dirks** (also *Walig* [Walich, Walrius] *Dirck Luytgens*) of Winkel in the Dutch province of North Holland, an Anabaptist martyr, was burned at the stake on July 7, 1558, at The Hague together with Adriaen Pieters and Maerten Cornelisz. Waechlink was (re)baptized in 1538, arrested shortly after, but pardoned. Shortly before his arrest in 1558 he had publicly opposed the Catholic priest of Winkel, saying that the Mass was idolatry, and that in the Lord's Supper they should take "common bread of the table" as the apostles received from the hands of Christ and as is the practice of Sacramentists (*q.v.*) and Anabaptists. (*Mart. Mir.* D 202, E 583; *Inv. Arch. Amst.* I, No. 390; *ML* I, 451.)   vDZ.

Wael, Burgert van der, author or composer of the Mennonite hymnal *Eeuwig Geluyt-makende Vreugt-Basuyn geblazen ter Gedachtenisse van de Geboorte, 't Leven, Lyden, Sterven, Verryzen en Hemelvaart onzes Heilands en Zaligmakers* . . . (Dordrecht, 1670; Edam, 1699; Amsterdam, 1703, 1734, and 1736). No copy seems to be extant. About van der Wael all information is lacking.   vDZ.

M. Schagen, *Naamlijst der Doopsgezinde Schrijveren* (Amsterdam, 1745) 128; *DJ* 1837, 65.

Waelty (Wälti), **Bernhard,** an Anabaptist martyr, a peasant of Rüderswil, Switzerland, was put to death for his faith at Bern on July 7, 1537.

Mart. Mir. E 1129; Adolf Fluri, *Beiträge zur Geschichte der bernischen Täufer* (Bern, 1912) 14.

Waerma, Meindert, Hendrik, and **Jacob,** Mennonite ministers. Meindert Waerma was from 1715 a preacher of the Groningen Old Flemish congregation at Emden in East Friesland, Germany. His son, Hendrik Waerma, b. 1711 at Emden, d. July 26, 1771, at Deventer, married to Hester Saaxuma, of Groningen, was a preacher in his father's church at Emden 1741-61 and at Deventer, Netherlands, 1761-d.71. Though belonging to the Groningen Old Flemish branch, Hendrik Waerma was a man of tolerant and rather liberal views, as may be seen from the fact that he sent his son to the Amsterdam Lamist seminary. His many writings breathe a spirit of toleration. He published *Beknopt Ontwerp van de Voornaamste Geloof-zaaken der Christelyke Godsdienst volgens de H. Schriftuur en de Belydenissen der Doopsgezinden* (Emden, 1744); *De Waare Weg des Heyls,* twelve sermons (Groningen, 1751); *Lijk-Predikacie. Op H.B. Alringh* (1757); *Afscheydspredikacie Embden 1761* (Deventer, 1762); *Historisch Verhael wegens de oudheid en schriftmatigheid van het Geloof of de Leere der Doopsgezinden* (Groningen, 1767); *De Evangelische Geloofsleer der Doopsgezinde Christenen, die ook Mennonisten genaamt worden,* followed by *Beknopt Historisch Verhaal wegens de Leere der Doopsgezinden* (Groningen, 1768), and *Nodige Beantwoording* (Groningen, 1768). The Mennonite Archives at Amsterdam contain a manuscript by H. Waerma, "Annotatie van de merkwaardigste voorvallen myns leevens," of 1747.

Jacobus Waerma (the son of Hendrik), b. 1753 at Emden, d. 1782 at Makkum, was trained for the ministry at the Amsterdam Lamist seminary and served at Makkum from 1777-d.82.   vDZ.

Inv. Arch. Amst. I, No. 682; II, 2, No. 685; Van der Aa, *Biogr. Wb.;* Blaupot t. C., *Groningen* II, 116, 124, 137, 226; *DB* 1881, 97; 1898, 64; 1919, 93 f.

Waffenlose Wächter, Der (*The Weaponless Watchman*), first issue apparently January 1871, an 8-page (sometimes 4-page) 10½ x 13½ in. (later 12 x 19) monthly, later bimonthly 1878-79, monthly 1880-81, 24-page quarterly 1882-88, published by Samuel Ernst (1825-1909) at Millwood and Gap, Pa., transferred 1873-77 to Lancaster, Pa., and back again to Gap (Millwood) 1877-83, moved to Olathe, Kan., 1884-88. Published as a bilingual religious paper (German, English), successor to *Acorn & Germ* which had been published at Millwood by S. Ernst

and E. Z. Ernst as a trilingual paper (German, English, and Pennsylvania-Dutch) as follows: July 6, 1870, Sept. 14, 1870, and thereafter weekly to Dec. 7, 1870. In an autobiographical statement Ernst states that he published the journal "for nearly 18 years." In a family history, a son of Samuel, E. Z. Ernst states: "He [E. Z.] was a publisher and printer by trade beginning the business in 1870, . . . publishing the 'Acorn & Germ' and the 'Waffenlose Waechter' with his father near Gap, Lancaster County, Pa. In March 1877, he established the 'Sunbeam' of Lititz, Pa., in partnership with his brother-in-law, John G. Zook, but sold out and left for Kansas in 1879." About his father, E. Z. Ernst states, "They belonged to the Old Mennonites, organized and conducted a singing school at Millwood school district north of Gap, Pa., in 1870 and soon began publishing 'Waffenlose Waechter' for nearly 20 years." Ernst moved to Olathe, Kan., in 1884, bringing the paper with him and continuing its publication for several years. Inconclusive data does not permit an exact report concerning the paper, and only a few copies have been preserved in GCL and BeCL. The publisher states the paper's policy as "neutral in politics and non-sectarian," although it quite clearly was directed primarily to Mennonites as the name would indicate. It carried some articles on Mennonite history.   H.S.B.

E. Z. Ernst, *A Condensed Genealogical Record of the Descendants of Sebastian Ernst* (Los Angeles, 1927); Samuel Ernst, *The 50th Anniversary* (n.p., n.d.-1898).

Wagenaar, Jan (Amsterdam, 1709-73), outstanding Dutch historian, author of *Vaderlandsche Historie* (21 vv., 1749-59) and a famous history of Amsterdam, at first belonged to the Reformed Church, but in 1730 joined the Mennonites, whom he however soon had left to participate in the Collegiant (*q.v.*) movement. He was also the author of some theological writings. When the Remonstrant (*q.v.*) minister K. Bremer (*q.v.*) attacked the Mennonites because of rejecting infant baptism, Wagenaar came to their defense, publishing *Onderzoek over de oudheid en schriftmatigheid van den Kinderdoop* (Leiden, 1740, 2d ed. Amsterdam, 1776).   vDZ.

Winkler Prins Encyclopedie, 6th ed., vol. XVIII (Amsterdam, 1954) 324; Blaupot t. C., *Holland* II, 26, 30, 31; *DJ* 1850, 128; *DB* 1912, 106.

Wageningen, a town in the Dutch province of Gelderland (1958 pop. *c*20,000; *c*200 Mennonites), the seat of the Dutch Agricultural University, also the seat of a Mennonite congregation. In 1892 C. Honigh began to work toward the founding of a congregation, soon assisted by B. D. van der Laag, d.1901, and P. Hoekstra, but it was not until Feb. 10, 1895, that a meeting of some 30 Mennonites living at Wageningen and surrounding villages decided to appoint a committee to arrange the founding; the result was the founding of an association for the promotion of the interests of Mennonites in Wageningen and surroundings in early February 1896; in 1905 this association was converted into a Mennonite congregation. On Good Friday of 1896 ten persons were baptized at Wageningen; this baptismal service was followed by a communion service, both led by B. Cuperus, retired Mennonite pastor of Zutphen, who had conducted a worship service at Wageningen on Oct. 9, 1895, and who henceforth preached there regularly, also giving catechetical instruction, and who by his liberal financial contributions made it possible for the small young congregation to build a meetinghouse, which was dedicated by Cuperus on Ascension Day May 24, 1901. Cuperus served until 1903, then resigning because of bad health; he was followed by S. D. A. Wartena of Zutphen. On Nov. 22, 1908, A. J. van Loghum Slaterus preached his entrance sermon as Wageningen's first regular minister. He served until 1917, followed by F. W. W. Braak 1918-20, P. G. van Slogteren 1922-26, M. van der Vegte Jr. 1927-40, and B. Dufour 1940- .

During World War II the meetinghouse was completely destroyed on May 10, 1940. A new church could not be acquired before 1951, planned by architect W. Gerretsen, and dedicated April 29, 1951, by Pastor Dufour.

The baptized membership was 32 in 1896, 55 in 1901, 73 in 1925, 108 in 1940, and 275 in 1958; church activities are a ladies' circle, and Sunday school for children.

In December 1732 the Mennonite Committee for Foreign Needs settled fifteen Mennonite refugee families from Lithuania (q.v.) in the neighborhood of Wageningen, forming a hamlet then called Mennonietenbuurt. This settlement failed; some of these colonists had moved to Walcheren (q.v.) by 1736, where another group of Lithuanian refugees had settled. By 1738 the colony was dissolved and the houses were sold. A detailed account on this colonization was published by A. van Gulik in *Doopsgezinde Bijdragen* of 1905 and 1906 under the title "De mislukte kolonizatie te Wageningen." vDZ.

P. Hoekstra, "Hoe de gemeente Wageningen e.o. tot stand kwam," in *DJ* 1927, 55-71; *DB* 1895, 183; 1896, 209; 1900, 230; 1901, 215; 1905, 112-68; 1906, 93-115; 1909, 186; *Inv. Arch. Amst.* I, Nos. 1173, 1237, 1921-94; *DJ* 1942, 45; 1952, 46-50.

Wagenmaker, a Mennonite family on the former Dutch island of Wieringen (q.v.), where many of its members have served the church as deacons since the 17th century. Cornelis Wagen(n)maker was from 1740 a preacher and 1743-d.84 an elder of the Wieringen congregation. He published *Onderwyzing aangaande het Christelyk Geloof,* a catechism (Amsterdam, 1759, repr. 1776). (*DJ* 1837, 117; *DB* 1891, 49, 50, 51, 57-59.) vDZ.

Wagmann, Ully, a Mennonite minister in the canton of Zürich, Switzerland, was arrested and imprisoned in the monastery of Oethenbach (q.v.), where he had to endure many hardships, from which he died in prison in 1654. (*Mart. Mir.* D 824, E 1122; see also **Zürich.**) vDZ.

Wagner, a family name found among the early Swiss Brethren; in 1529 there was a Marti Wagner in Therwil, Basselland, and a Hans Wagner in the Regensberg district. Bernhard Wagner (d. 1716/7), who was from 1712 an assistant of the Dutch ambassador Runckel (q.v.) and who settled the finances of the Mennonite emigrants to the Netherlands, was probably not a Mennonite. The martyr Georg

(Jörg) Wagner (q.v.) was apparently not related to the former. Among the Hutterites in Moravia Georg Wagner (Wiser or Rader) was a preacher, who died in 1591 after having served for 31 years. In the 18th century some Wagners emigrated to America. Richard Wagner is elder of the Mennonite congregation at Frankfurt, Germany. vDZ.

Paul Peachey, *Die soziale Herkunft der Schweizer Täufer* (Karlsruhe, 1954) 141, No. 719; *TA Zürich,* 297, 298; *Inv. Arch. Amst.* I, Nos. 1359, 1363, 1369, 1373, 1388, 1390; Zieglschmid, *Chronik,* 420, 458, 592.

Wagner, Georg, one of the strong men of faith of the Reformation era, a martyr who is claimed by both the Lutherans and the Anabaptists. The Hutterite *Chronik* devotes two pages to his martyrdom (pp. 69-71). He stemmed, according to the account in the Hutterite chronicle, from Emering in Bayerland (Bavaria?). The date of his birth is unknown. He was seized in Munich, and was severely tortured in the Falkenturm. He persisted in four articles of faith: (1) the priests cannot forgive sin; (2) God or Christ is not bodily in the bread; (3) a human being cannot bring God from heaven; and (4) the water of baptism does not save. The greatest efforts were made to convert him. "Even the prince had pity upon him and is said to have most urgently admonished him and offered him a prebendary for his lifetime if he would recant." When the sad fate of his wife and child was presented to him, he said the two were so dear to him that he would not give them up for all of Bavaria; nevertheless for the sake of the Lord and God he would give them up. Nor was his wife able to persuade him. He died on Feb. 8, 1527. He was not Anabaptist. LOSERTH, H.S.B.

Wahli, Bendicht (c1720-95), a Swiss Mennonite elder, was born in Bolligen, Swiss canton of Bern. He married Katherina Oberli (d. 1771) of Lützelflüh c1742, and rented the Berghaus (also called Maison Blanche) near Magglingen, on the mountain above Biel, in 1744. It was here that their four daughters and one son were born and raised. He was chosen as a minister of the Mennonites in the Jura in 1760 and became a highly respected leader. In 1782 he went with Peter Ramseyer, Hans Lehman, Hans Steiner, and David Baumgartner to Himmelshäuserhof, Palatinate, to help restore peace among the brethren there.

C. H. Meiners, Professors of Philosophy at the University of Göttingen, visited Bendicht Wahli while on a tour of Switzerland in the summer of 1782. In his printed report Meiners gives him the nickname "Täufer-Benz." He speaks of Wahli's industry in wresting a beautiful farm from a stony upland, walking for many miles over hill and valley to preach for several hours to a gathering of Anabaptists, earning his living by weaving; Meiners describes him as very intelligent and, though he had little schooling, able to speak with great knowledge on theological topics.

The Anabaptists have become well known in the canton of Bern because of an anecdote about "Täufer-Benz" that appeared in the obligatory reader for the fifth grade of the Bernese primary school in 1896-1920. The story relates that on a trip Täufer-Benz found a man weeping because he had been robbed of his money. Benz asked if he had been robbed of his God also. Receiving a negative reply, Benz said that then he had not been robbed of everything. Benz handed the astonished traveler his own filled purse saying that God had directed him to do this in His name. Before the traveler could recover from his astonishment Benz had proceeded on his way.   D.L.G.

Jakob Wyss, "Das Weisshaus (La Maison Blanche) in Leubringen," *Bieler Jahrbuch* 1933, 34-63; Heinrich Ludwig Lehmann, *Das Bisthum Basel* (1798) 101-3; A. Jakob Amstutz, "Die Wiedertäufer," *Gem.-Kal.,* 1924, p. 48; C. H. Meiners, *Briefe über die Schweiz* I (1784) 147; *ML IV.*

Wahrheitsfreund, Der (1915-47), the German organ of the Krimmer Mennonite Brethren Church, was first published July 28, 1915. From that date to Oct. 25, 1933, it was published by the K.M.B. Publishing House, Chicago, Ill. In November 1933 the Krimmer Mennonite Publishing Committee became the publisher, with the office of publication at Hillsboro, Kan., for one year, and thereafter at Inman, Kan. The editors were M. B. Fast, July 28, 1915, to Dec. 26, 1917; D. M. Hofer, Jan. 2, 1918, to Oct. 25, 1933; J. G. Barkman during the one year at Hillsboro; J. H. Klassen from Nov. 7, 1935, until Dec. 12, 1945; and W. W. Harms from Dec. 9, 1945, until publication ceased. It appeared weekly, except for the first ten months of 1934, when it became biweekly. Each issue contained sixteen 12¼ x 9¼ in. pages regularly from 1915 to July 5, 1933, and again from Nov. 21, 1934, until Jan. 1, 1941, having only 8 pages during the remainder of its history. The contents were typical of a denominational organ, with special features for young people and children. Articles in the English language appeared in the children's section as early as the second year of publication. By 1940 half of each issue was in the English language. Decline in the list of subscribers led the K.M.B. Conference in its October 1947 meeting to a decision to discontinue *Der Wahrheitsfreund* and to increase the size of its English counterpart, *The Christian Witness. Der Wahrheitsfreund* ceased publication with a special farewell number Nov. 5, 1947. (Nearly complete files in BeCl and GCL.) In September 1934 J. W. Tschetter, who had been associate editor of *Der Wahrheitsfreund* 1918-33 and an intimate colleague of D. M. Hofer in the K.M.B. Chicago Mission, started a rival paper called *The Friend of Truth (q.v.),* which was discontinued in April 1939.   N.P.S.

Waibl, Johannes, a Hutterite, d. March 2, 1661, at Velké Levary, Czechoslovakia. He is the author of the song, "In meinem letzten endte rueff ich, o, Herr, zu dir," found in Wolkan, *Lieder,* 242 f., but not found in the *Lieder der Hutterischen Brüder.* (Beck, *Geschichts-Bücher,* 499; ML IV.)

Waisenamt (Orphans Office), an extraordinarily useful and important mutual aid church institution developed by the Mennonites in Russia for the administration of the estates of orphans, later used for a similar service to widows and elderly people or anyone needing help in the investment, care, and administration of funds. In effect the Waisenamt became a trust institution and almost a bank, rendering many services which modern trust companies and commercial banks perform on a business basis. The Waisenamt was actually a committee of usually two or three men called "Waisenmänner" (the chairman being called "Waisenältester," i.e., Orphan Elder), competent and experienced in handling financial matters, who served without pay (later the chairman was paid) in the spirit of Christian brotherly love. Since the capital accumulated during the operations of the trust committee soon attained considerable size and often had to be held for a period of years, it became necessary to invest the trust funds to secure returns in the form of interest; hence an investment business naturally developed. Persons seeking credit likewise naturally turned to the Waisenamt for loans. Inevitably a type of banking business developed.

Such an institution could develop only in a group or society set up in relative isolation from the surrounding culture and legally given a considerable degree of autonomy, as was the case in the Mennonite settlements established in Russia in 1789 f. and 1803 f. In a sense the Waisenamt was a necessity, particularly in the absence of adequate Russian governmental provisions in this field, as well as because of the wide variation between local Russian customs relating to inheritance and those brought along from West Prussia. A similar situation prevailed in Manitoba and Paraguay when immigrants from Russia reached these lands, although in Manitoba the legal arrangements were much more adequate. In Manitoba also, as the state came more and more to regulate private financial and lending institutions, compulsory regulation and finally incorporation was forced upon several of the Waisenamt organizations there. With the exception of this one region the Mennonite Waisenamt institution developed autonomously in the 19th century and remained so to the Revolution in Russia. It is still completely free in Mexico and Paraguay to operate autonomously in accord with the long-established customs and experience of the group. Numbers of men have rendered outstanding service to their people through their Waisenamt service, particularly in Russia and Manitoba. Fortunately a brief history and description of the Waisenamt as it developed in Russia is available from the pen of Johann Riediger, the last Orphan Elder of the Halbstadt district in the Molotschna settlement of South Russia, written in 1930 at Mölln, Germany, where Riediger was a refugee at the time. It was published as the introduction to a booklet called *Teilungsordnung der in Süd-Russland angesiedelten Mennoniten, auf Anregung der mennonitischen Flüchtlinge in Deutschland neu herausgegeben* (Karlsruhe, 1930). This account is presented in translation in the immediately following paragraphs.

"Since there is a danger that children will squander what the parents have saved through their labor, and also that inherited property may be administered poorly or in bad faith by relatives or friends, it becomes necessary to protect the interests of minor heirs, both in their personal life and in their finances, by means of special regulations. This was clearly recognized by the Mennonites in Russia when in 1807 they wrote down in 17 points the traditional practices regarding rights of inheritance and division of estates which they had brought along from the old homeland. This was simply the customary practice, quite simple practical rules which had proved their value in the course of the years. In 1814 these inheritance regulations (*Teilungsordnung*) were enlarged to 27 points. Later they were repeatedly revised in 1824, 1826, 1843, 1850; in 1894 the regulations were thoroughly reviewed and published in a small booklet in German and Russian by the publishing firm of H. A. Ediger in Berdyansk [called *Teilungsordnung*].

"In 1904 all the village communes of the Halbstadt district decided to reorganize the management of Waisenamt funds by establishing the Halbstadt Orphans Fund (*Waisenkasse*). The writer had had sufficient experience in the management of the previous system to learn its shortcomings and to help correct them in the new plan. He can highly recommend the new system in the form in which it existed in Halbstadt from that day on to the end.

"The Orphan Elders [managers] met weekly in Halbstadt to execute the necessary deposits and withdrawals of all trust monies. It should be inserted here that one should not give one man [elder] the responsibility for more than 8-10 villages (200-50 families) and that in any case a sort of Orphans Court should be established for the arbitration of disputes. Each village had its own record book in the Orphans Fund, in which all transactions were entered. For each ward of the trust one page was reserved. . . . The investment capital for each ward was paid into the Fund by his guardian and loaned out at 6 per cent, of which 5 per cent was credited annually to the ward, one per cent being used for overhead and to build up a reserve. The non-investment capital of a ward was only deposited but could be loaned out under certain conditions by the administrator of the Fund. The Orphan Elder received an annual allowance. The management costs were covered by a one-half per cent levy on participating capital deposits.

"The funds of aged widows and widowers, and in fact of all persons who were unable to manage their affairs themselves, were administered under the same terms. The money deposited for investment could be loaned out only in the Halbstadt district and for a maximum period of five years. Each borrower had to furnish two bondsmen whose signatures were to be attested by the elder for the village, whereby the village assumed a certain degree of guarantee for the loaned money of the ward. Guardians and caretakers [curators] had to be approved by the Waisenant administration after their elections."

The published *Teilungsordnung* of 1930 contained two parts: (I) *Teilungs-Ordnung der Molotschnaer Mennoniten-Gemeinde und deren Tochter-Kolonien* in 25 paragraphs, and (II) *Teilungs-Ordnung der Chortitzaer Mennoniten-Gemeinden und deren Tochterkolonien* in 61 paragraphs, a total of 64 pages. Authentic printed copies of the original booklets were brought along from Russia and edited for publication by Benjamin H. Unruh. The publication was financed by the MCC, and several hundred copies were sent with the refugees to Brazil and Paraguay, where apparently each Mennonite colony set up a Waisenamt.

The Bergthal Waisenamt in Russia was used as the institution to finance the emigration of that group to Manitoba, although numbers of families also secured private loans. This Waisenamt had about $100,000 of capital at the time (1874). A flat levy of 25 per cent was made on all deposits to aid the penniless among the emigrants. This entire Waisenamt was simply transferred to Manitoba where it kept on functioning, as was the case with all the separate immigrant groups. After the division of the Bergthal church in Manitoba into three bodies, there were five Waisenamt institutions at the same time in Manitoba: (1) Old Colony and the Fürstenland group; (2) Kleine Gemeinde; (3) Chortitz of the Bergthal group in the East Reserve; (4) Bergthal of the liberal Bergthal group in the West Reserve; and (5) Sommerfeld of the conservative Bergthal group in the West Reserve.

"In Russia-Manitoba Waisenamt was not only a trust company, but an institution whose rules represented a body of laws regulating the transfer of property from one generation to another. Finally it served as a savings bank and finance institution. Historically the principles under which it operated reflected ancient concepts of farm property and inheritance which once had been widespread among the German colonists in Eastern Europe" (Francis, *Utopia*, p. 125, where the basic principles of inheritance and the operating regulations are described in detail).

The Waisenamt regulations were not only social rules but were grounded in Bible passages and hence had religious sanctions. The church elder had to sign every inheritance transfer contract. Even though the regulations in Manitoba had to be approved by the provincial government (they were always approved because not considered legally binding or in conflict with Manitoba law), they were still considered by the people as church regulations.

The Waisenamts in Manitoba served the people well until the time of the depression in the 1920's. The two which had been incorporated in Manitoba under government pressure went bankrupt, since borrowers were unable to repay loans, and depositors therefore could not secure repayments. To date the two bankrupt institutions have not been fully reorganized and are therefore not functioning. However there are still (1958) six Canadian Waisenamts in existence, four in Manitoba (three in the West Reserve and one in the East Reserve) and at least two in Saskatchewan where they are simply called "Mennonite Waisenamt." In Manitoba the four are called Sommerfelder, Bergthaler, Rosengart, and Chortitz.

The Waisenamts established in the Mennonite settlements in Mexico and Paraguay, 1922-30, have functioned effectively, although in Paraguay the co-operatives have taken over much of the function of providing credit to borrowers.

The basic decree-law (*Privilegium*) governing the settlement of Mennonites in Paraguay, adopted in 1927, contains in Article Two the following provision: "To administer the inheritances and especially the properties of widows and orphans by means of their special system of trust committees known as *Waisenamt* and in accordance with the particular rules of the community without any kind of restriction." Article Six specifies that there must be a report to the government by "the recognized authorities of the colonists" of "the names, authorities, and regulations of the trust committees (*Waisenamt*) in order that these may be approved by Congress." H.S.B.

J. W. Fretz, *Mennonite Colonization in Mexico* (Akron, 1945) 28 f.; *idem, Pilgrims in Paraguay* (Scottdale, 1953) 105, 230; E. K. Francis, *In Search of Utopia* (Altona, 1955) 125-30; *idem,* "Mennonite Institutions in Early Manitoba, A Study of Their Origins," *Agricultural History* XXII (1948) 147 f., 150.

Waisenhaus (Orphanage), a prison in Bern, Switzerland, was built in 1657 as a dual purpose building: (1) as a reformatory and (2) as a training school for orphan children. It was located on the north side of the French Church (then the Predigerkirche). From the beginning it was also used as a prison for Anabaptists, and the very first instruction (July 13, 1657) to the board of managers specified that provision be made for "Widerteufer." Then on Dec. 20, 1658, the city council ordered the magistrates of Thun, Burgdorf, Langenthal, and Brugg to arrest the Anabaptist ministers and send them to Bern, and decreed that "a directorium of civil and clerical persons be established to see that this intent against the Anabaptist sect be diligently pursued and execution accomplished." This was the origin of the notorious "Täuferkammer" (Anabaptist Bureau; see **Bern**, ME I, 295) set up later. A subcommission of six was then set up on Jan. 4, 1659, called "Committeerten zum Teufferischen geschefft," which had direct charge of Anabaptist matters under the Waisenhaus board. The first Anabaptist minister to be imprisoned in the Waisenhaus was Anthoni Himmelberg (*q.v.*), incarcerated on June 24, 1658, who died in prison on Oct. 25, 1660. The Waisenhaus served for many years as the Anabaptist incarceration house. H.S.B.

Adolf Fluri, "Das Waisenhaus als Täufer-Gefängnis," *Beiträge zur Geschichte der Bernischen Täufer* (Bern, 1912) 22 pp. of a reprint from *Blätter für bernische Geschichte, Kunst und Altertumskunde.*

Wakarusa, a town (pop. 1200) located in Olive Twp., Elkhart Co., Ind. Mennonite pioneers had settled in the vicinity before 1852, when the town was platted, and the Holdeman Mennonite (MC) Church had been built the year before. Approximately 60 Mennonite families live in the town, and about 10 business establishments are operated or managed by Mennonites. The town is a shopping center for some 750 Mennonites. The six Mennonite churches in the vicinity include Holdeman (MC), Salem (MC), Olive (MC), Yellow Creek (MC), Yellow Creek (Wisler), and Blossers (Wisler). The County Line (Wisler) church, 2 miles west and 1½ miles north of Wakarusa, was used for a number of years as an alternate place of worship for the Yellow Creek-Blossers group. The first Mennonite settlers in the Wakarusa community were Holdeman, Weldy, Davidhizar, Smeltzer, Lechlitner, Loucks, and Hartman families. L.V.C.

Walch, Johannes (b. 1551), of Schorndorf, Württemberg, an Anabaptist, in some way related to Heinrich and Hans Walch, who in 1542 were named in the "Turkish tax list," but are missing in the list of 1545. Heinrich was mayor of Schorndorf, but had committed some wrong and was expelled in 1545; likewise his brother Hans, a cooper, fled to Stetten, the refuge of the Anabaptists and Schwenckfelders under Hans Konrad Thumb (*q.v.*) in 1545. Possibly Heinrich and Hans were brothers, the former aiding the latter to escape. On Nov. 14, 1571, the retired mayor of Schorndorf, Hans Ulrich Walch, was a cosignatory of the will of a tanner, Hans Heutlin, whose wife emigrated after his death as an Anabaptist. A close relationship has not been established.

Johann Walch studied at the University of Tübingen, received the Master's degree in 1573, and then a musical degree (Repetens musicus). In 1578 he became deacon in Nürtingen. On December 4, he made a note in the Nürtingen baptismal record that before he performed a baptism he asked the sponsors questions about the power, benefit, comfort, and necessity of baptism, its originator, and the duties of the sponsors. In 1579 seven such tests were listed in the baptismal record. His seriousness as a pastor is evident. But this did not add to his popularity. There were also disputes with the priest Elias Benignus, as recorded in the Stuttgart *Synodalprotokoll* of March 11, 1581. Walch as deacon insisted among other things that the impenitent be excluded, which the priest would have the official right to do, and discussed this question among his confidential friends. But the congregation wished to have him transferred.

In January 1582 the authorities suspected Johann Walch of Anabaptist ideas. On January 20 he made the last entry into the baptismal record. Walch asked for release from his position, saying that he could not officiate any longer in view of the abuse of absolution and communion. During his examination he was recognized as an Anabaptist, though he tried to talk himself out of it. Finally he admitted that he had no faith either in Anabaptism or in the presence of Christ in the emblems of communion. The discussions lasted from Jan. 21 to Feb. 9, 1582; he refused to be instructed thereby.

The duke directed that he be put into the monastery at Bebenhausen. He was held there four months. The abbot, who was Eberhard Bidembach, the son-in-law of Johannes Brenz (*q.v.*), was assisted by Jacob Andreae, Heerbrand, Dietrich Schnepf, and other Tübingen theologians in trying to convert Walch. Walch finally signed a recantation on July 12, 1582. He now went to Stuttgart to the home of his father-in-law Ludwig Daser, the ducal director of music, who was to keep an eye on him. But in a short time he secretly went to Moravia with his wife Marie, his sons Severus and Secundus, and his sister Maria. From Pausram, which he reached by way of Vienna, he wrote to a citizen of Nürtingen, inviting him to follow them to Moravia. After his sister's death he returned. That was not later than 1587, for on Nov. 17, 1587, her estate was divided among the heirs.

Walch next went to Rod on the Rieberg, across the Rhine, three miles from Speyer. He lived on the Remberg estate of the Count of Löwenstein, serving as a cattle supervisor and physician (*Arzneikundiger*), as Veltin Rod (Wendel), an Anabaptist living in Rod, wrote to the inspecting abbot of Maulbronn. He must have won some adherents not only in chemistry (alchemy), but also in Anabaptism. The physician Hieronymus Walch and his son by the same name later appearing in Württemberg were perhaps his descendants.

Walch wrote scientific and philosophical tracts, which he published in Strasbourg in 1609 and 1618. In 1609 his *Decas fabularum humani generis* appeared, which contains some information about Marpeck. The foreword he wrote in his museum in Meistratzheim in Lower Alsace as the guest of the lords of Landsberg. On May 2, 1608, he dedicated the pamphlet to his students, Günther von Landsberg and Johann Reichard Wurmser von Wendenheim. In 1619 his tract of philosophical and chemical content appeared, called *Der kleine Bauer, sampt beygefugten commentariis,* dedicated to Count Johann Reinhard von Hanna und Zweibrücken on July 25, 1618. In the home of the canon Johann Gessler he wrote to Jung S. Peter about the silver mine in Ste-Marie-aux-Mines (Alsace). When and where Walch died is not known. Walch was one of the Swiss Brethren, and was thereby opposed to the Hutterite doctrine of community of goods. Thomas Hägen, an Anabaptist refugee from Göppingen to Moravia, sent him a greeting on July 25, 1597, by way of David Laister. At that time Walch was in Strasbourg. (*ML* IV.)   G.Bos.

Walcheren, an island belonging to the Dutch province of Zeeland (*q.v.*); Middelburg, the capital of Zeeland, is located on this island. Anabaptists were found at Walcheren by 1534, and later there were Mennonite congregations at Middelburg, Vlissingen, both of which still exist, and Veere, which died out shortly after 1671. In the early 17th century the Reformed classis of Walcheren, which was very strict and intolerant, acted against the Mennonites, but nevertheless the Mennonite congregations on Walcheren could develop.

In the early 18th century Walcheren for some years was the refuge for a number of Mennonite families who had been expelled from Lithuania (*q.v.*). They came to the Netherlands in December 1732 and were settled partly at Wageningen (*q.v.*) and partly on the island of Walcheren, where the Mennonite Committee for Foreign Needs bought farms for them in several villages. The church board of Middelburg (*q.v.*) administered the farms and aided the refugees in their many needs and difficulties. At first (December 1732) 15 families settled at Walcheren, in the following years some of the refugees from Wageningen also moved to Walcheren, but by 1736 some of them returned to Prussia, followed by the others. Most of them had left Walcheren by 1739; the last of these settlers left in 1744. The settlers did not feel at home and complained of the interference of the Middelburg deacons and the "big bosses" of the Amsterdam committee. The colonization was a failure.

The Dutch Mennonites spent about 80,000 Dutch guilders for this adventure.

During World War II Walcheren was badly damaged; the town of Vlissingen (*q.v.*) was largely destroyed; its Mennonite church was bombed. And in September 1944 nearly the whole island was flooded and the population had to flee. An MCC reconstruction unit of 11 men served on Walcheren from May 28, 1946, to Dec. 22, 1947. After the flood disaster of Feb. 1, 1953, a Mennonite voluntary service group worked on Walcheren.   vDZ.

Inv. Arch. Amst. I, Nos. 1995-2243; *DB* 1883, 88 ff.; 1884, 104 ff.; 1897, 163; 1908, 3 ff., 29; *Menn. Life* I (January 1946) 33-37; J. D. Unruh, *In the Name of Christ* (Scottdale, 1952) 115-17.

Walchers Liedboeck (Vlissingen, 1613) is a Dutch songbook composed by Jan Philipsz Schabaelje (*q.v.*) and his brother Dirk Schabaelje.   vDZ.

Waldeck, formerly a small principality between Westphalia on the north and west and Hesse-Nassau on the south and east, capital Arolsen. It remained independent until 1867 when the administration of government was turned over to Prussia. The prince, however, remained on the throne until Nov. 13, 1918, when Waldeck became a Free State. In 1929 it was completely merged with Prussia. The village of Waldeck (pop. 900) lies in the province of Hesse-Nassau.

An Amish community existed in Waldeck and the neighboring territories of Wittgenstein, Berleburg, and Hesse for at least a century. In all the issues of the Dutch *Naamlijst* that reported German congregations, 1766-1810, Waldeck, Wittgenstein, and Berleburg all appear as congregations with separate ministerial lists. In 1766 Berleburg is described as 10 (2 German miles) miles from Wittgenstein and Wittgenstein as 18 (4 German miles) miles from Marburg (Hesse). The introduction to the 1797 edition of the Elbing Catechism states, "We elders and ministers of the Mennonite Church, who live in Hesse and Waldeck, have united to publish anew this catechism," but the title page says the booklet is published by "die Christliche Gemeine im Waldeckischen welche Mennonisten benennet werden." The *Naamlijst* calls all three congregations "Zwitzers." Apparently the scattered families lived not too far apart to think of themselves as one church, and it is known that the families were interrelated.

The *Naamlijst* reports as ministers for the Waldeck congregations: 1766, Michael Güngerich, Johannes Schänebeck, Christian Güngerich, Hans König, Christian Jungerich Jr.; 1769, the same except Schänebeck; 1780, Hans König as elder (ord. 1770), Christian Güngerich as elder (ord. 1773), and Bäntz Schwartztrauben (ord. 1775); 1784, the same two elders plus Peter Güngerich and Christian Güngerich Jr.; 1786, 1793, 1802, and 1810, the same. For Wittgenstein only one appears, always David Ekker 1766-1810 (ord. c1760). For Berleburg likewise only one appears 1766-1810, always Michael Güngerich (ord. 1775), in 1766 called Jr.

The meetings were certainly held in rotation in the homes. The meeting which decided on publishing the catechism is stated in the introduction to have been held on a farm called Mittelhof in Nieder-hessen Dec. 11, 1796. From information secured from descendants who migrated to America c1831-35, two locations in Waldeck are known as places of residence; Mengeringhausen in Waldeck, where Christian Schwartzentruber was born in 1765, and where he operated a mill at the edge of town called the Galgenmühle; Hüninghausen, an estate near Helsen in Waldeck, where Christian Güngerich rented a dairy farm in 1743. (These two places are about 1½ miles apart, some 20 miles west of Kassel. Reinhardtshausen in Waldeck is also named as an Amish address in 1818.)

Among the family names known to have been found among the Amish in this general area including Hesse-Nassau, were Güngerich, Schwartzentruber, Schönbeck, Otto, Brenneman, Bender, Roth, Schöttler(?). The John Bender family emigrated to Somerset County, Pa., in 1851 from Oberweimar near Marburg in Hesse. The source of these families is not certain, but it was probably Alsace. In 1738 a Christian Güngerich formerly living on the Fleckstein Hof willed to Christian Güngerich the estate of Rödern in Northern Alsace.

Most of the Amish families of Waldeck and Hesse emigrated to Canada and the United States in the period 1830-60. The first location was Somerset County, Pa., near Springs, and Grantsville, Garrett Co., Md. Another was west of Kitchener, Ont. A third was Kalona, Iowa, although most of the settlers came to this region from Somerset County or its daughter settlement in Holmes County, Ohio. A few families, among them the Güngerich family, came first to Fairfield County, Ohio, then to Kalona. A considerable number of 20th-century Mennonite (MC) and Amish ministers and teachers descend directly from the Waldeck-Hesse group, among them S. C. Yoder, Simon Gingerich, Amos Gingerich, Paul Guengerich, Orland Gingerich, Melvin Gingerich, A. Lloyd Swartzendruber, Elmer Swatrzendruber, D. H. Bender, H. S. Bender, Paul Bender, Ezra Bender. A majority of the Springs-Grantsville Mennonite and Amish membership of today, as well as about half of the Johnson County, Iowa, Mennonite and Amish groups, descend from the Waldeck-Hesse Amish.

The group who remained in Waldeck-Hesse gradually died out, and by the late 19th century had completely disappeared. A Paul Güngerich of Plettenburg, Westphalia, in 1957 reported that his parents were Mennonites and that he had been reared a Mennonite. The complaint of Christian Gingerich, a tenant of the Fiddemühlen farm in 1859, may be indicative of conditions: "He has for some time been unable to satisfy his religious needs in the Mennonite society because the sermons of the Mennonite preachers annoy rather than edify and even cause merriment. Also the celebration of the sacraments, especially that of the Holy Lord's Supper, were conducted without sanctity and the preceding ordinance of footwashing takes place with gross joking." In the absence of any representation of the Waldeck-Niederhesse congregation at the Offental (near St. Goarshausen) Amish Conference of May 20-21, 1867, it may be assumed that the congregation had died out by that time. The congregation had been represented in the notable Essingen (q.v.) Amish Conference of 1779 in the Palatinate by Christian Güngerich and Hans Schwartzentruber. Many of the descendants of the now extinct congregation joined the state church in Hesse and Waldeck. One of them, a Brenneman, is now serving as a Lutheran district superintendent in Hesse. The Hüninghausen estate was in the possession of the Güngerich family until World War I.   H.S.B.

Waldenses, the most important sectarian religious movement of the later Middle Ages, descendants of which still exist, known since 1532 as the Waldensian Church of Italy, a Protestant evangelical body, Reformed-Calvinistic in theology and polity. About the earlier history of the Waldenses considerable uncertainty exists because of the lack of adequate sources. Even the name is in doubt, although it was probably given because of Peter Waldo of Lyons, France, the founder of at least the French wing of the movement, a rich merchant who c1177 gave away his property and began a movement for Bible study and preaching, sending out his followers two by two. His followers were called the Poor Men of Lyons, since they took a vow of poverty. A similar movement about the same time in northern Italy, called the Poor Men of Lombardy, was probably a continuation of the Humiliati or followers of Arnold of Brescia. An attempted alliance of the two movements in 1184 was only partially successful. Their disregard of the prohibition of preaching by laymen issued in 1179 by the pope led to their persecution in many places for centuries, but did not result in their formal withdrawal from the Catholic Church. Most of them continued to observe the Mass and baptize their infants in the church. Although they suffered greatly they were never totally wiped out except in certain regions. Numerous martyrdoms were recorded; e.g., in Strasbourg some 80 were burned at the stake in 1211. Religious colloquies held to win them back to the church (e.g., in 1191 and 1206) were futile.

Various accounts have been given of their rapid growth and extensive spread geographically and in numbers, some of which are perhaps exaggerated. They spread early (1231-33) into South Germany, especially in Württemberg and Bavaria. In Austria about the same time the number was reported at 80,000. In South Germany they won many converts among the wool weavers. Nobles were among their patrons and even members. The Saxon nobleman, Johannes Drandorf, was martyred at Worms in 1423. Two of their most prominent martyrs were their bishops Friedrich Reiser (Strasbourg, 1450) and Stephen (Vienna, 1471). The last persecution in Germany was in 1479, ordered by Elector Albrecht Achilles of Prussia.

The Waldenses spread northward down the Rhine and into the Low Countries, as well as eastward into Bohemia, Moravia, Silesia, and Poland. As early as the 13th century they found refuge in the Alpine valleys of Piedmont west of Turin, and it is here that the remnant survived from which the modern Waldensian Church has sprung. Everywhere else they finally died out, largely before the

Reformation, though not everywhere by that time. By 1719 the total number of Waldenses was c4,000 including children. Civic rights and a certain amount of religious freedom was granted by the Italian government on Feb. 17, 1848.

Romantic hero worship has often been inclined to make the medieval Waldenses full evangelicals of Protestant character, but this was not the case. They did emphasize the authority of the Bible as the only guide for faith and life, and laid particular stress on the words and example of Jesus, especially the Sermon on the Mount. They at first rejected all killing including capital punishment and war, and were nonresistant, although in the 17th century they defended themselves by arms, having dropped nonresistance and other earlier principles, including rejection of the oath and government office, when they became Reformed in 1532. Originally they formed an association of men and women who had rejected the world and had obligated themselves to apostolic poverty and a life of discipleship to Jesus through a formal vow. Some expressed doubts about infant baptism, but it was never rejected by the group. They rejected the hierarchy of priests and insisted upon the right of laymen to preach. Their preaching consisted usually of simple admonition to repentance, faith, and obedience in following the commands of Christ. Though not formally withdrawing from the Catholic Church, they set up at least later their own organization with a threefold ministry of bishop, presbyter, and deacon, with formal ordination. The preacher was called "uncle."

In modern times, about the middle of the 19th century, they experienced a spiritual revival, largely under influence from England, which ultimately turned them into an aggressive evangelistic group. The number of congregations and members in the new congregations in the cities such as Tunis, Milan, Venice, Rome, Bologna, Florence, and Naples has for some time been larger than at the home base congregations in the Piedmont valleys. In 1930 there were some 80 congregations with 22,907 members, including a considerable emigrant colony in Uruguay and a few congregations in the Eastern United States.

Mennonites have had little contact with the Waldenses. Dutch Mennonites gave them some support in the 19th century, and Anna Brons (q.v.) of Emden raised a bicentennial offering for them in 1889, amounting to 880 marks. From the late summer of 1946 to 1949 the MCC carried on relief work in the Waldensian valleys for the population there which had suffered heavily during the war. Headquarters were maintained in Torre Pellice, the Waldensian capital. This was followed by a student exchange program whereby a number of young Waldenses studied in American Mennonite colleges. A warm feeling of fellowship developed between the Mennonite workers and the Waldensian Church and H. S. Bender served as a fraternal delegate at the Waldensian Synod in 1948 and also lectured at the Waldensian Theological Seminary in that same year. In 1950 Waldensian preachers in Uruguay were helpful in establishing the Mennonite settlement at El Ombu (q.v.).

The theory of Waldensian origin of the Anabaptists was popular among Dutch and German Mennonites in the 17th-19th centuries, though never proposed by the 16th-century Anabaptists themselves. It was held by such writers as van Braght (*Martyrs' Mirror* of 1660), who seemingly took it over from the earlier martyr books (e.g., the 1631 Haarlem book), Herman Schijn, and Galenus Abrahamsz, and from them was passed on to others. Apparently the Mennonite writers ultimately derived their authority for the theory from Sebastian Franck (*Chronica*, p. 483) or from a supposed similarity of teachings. It was also a convenient apologetic weapon to counter those enemies who attributed Anabaptist origins to the Münsterites. It was, however, approved by Carel van Gent (1615), and such writers as Brandt, Meshovius, and Gottfried Arnold. Modern historians all reject the theory, such as Kühler and van der Zijpp in Holland, Crous, Hege, and Neff in Germany, and Horsch and Smith in America. No actual case of a Waldensian becoming an Anabaptist has ever been adduced, and the early leaders in Switzerland, Holland, South Germany, and Austria can all be identified as either Catholic or Protestant in background. No Waldensian congregation was demonstrably in existence in German Switzerland for c100 years before the Anabaptist beginning in 1525. The same is true for Holland and South Germany.

A different situation obtained in Bohemia and Moravia. It is known that the Waldenses had great success in this area in the 14th-15th centuries; over 300 congregations are reported to have been in existence at one time. A. H. Newman held that Waldensian views were communicated to the Bohemian Brethren, and that from both groups members joined the Moravian Anabaptists in the 16th century. This still does not prove a Waldensian or Bohemian Brethren origin for the Moravian Anabaptists, since it is known that Hubmaier, Reublin, and refugees from Tirol introduced Anabaptism at Nikolsburg in 1526 ff. However, the similarity of teachings of the strict group of the Bohemian Brethren and those of the Anabaptists is sufficient ground for more careful study of the relation of the two groups, and with them of the Waldenses in this area. It is well known that a bishop of the Waldenses ordained the first bishop of the Bohemian Brethren c1460.

The tempting and romantic theory of apostolic succession from the apostles down to the Anabaptists through successive Old Evangelical groups, which has been very popular with those among Mennonites and Baptists who feel the need of such an apostolic succession, always includes the Waldenses as the last link before the Anabaptists. It has, also, no basis in fact.   NEFF, H.S.B.

Ludwig Keller, *Reformation*; idem, *Johann Staupitz und die Anfänge der Reformation* (Leipzig, 1885); K. Müller, *Die Waldenser und ihre einzelnen Gruppen bis zum Anfang des 14. Jahrhunderts* (Gotha, 1886); idem, *Die Waldenser und die Deutschen Bibelübersetzungen. Nebst Beiträgen zur Geschichte der Reformation* (Leipzig, 1886); Ignaz von Döllinger, *Dokumente vornehmlich zur Geschichte der Waldensier und Katharer* (Munich, 1890); James Gibson, *The Waldenses*, 3rd ed. (London, 1909); Emile Comba, *Storia dei Valdesi* (1934); *Menn. Life* V (April 1950) contains the following articles: Bertha Fast, "Waldensians After World War II"; Albert Roland, "Waldensians—Their Heroic Story"; and Sandro Sarti, "Waldensians and the Mennonites"; Blaupot t. C., *Geschiedkundig onderzoek naar den Waldenzischen oorsprong van de Nederlandsche Doopsgezinden* (Amsterdam, 1844); Marten Schagen, *Historie der Christenen, die men gemennlyk Waldensen noemt* (Haarlem, 1765); *ML* IV.

Waldhauser, Thomas (Thoman Waldhauser, or "Tall Thoman"), played an important role among the Anabaptists in Upper Austria. After he had become a Protestant he gave up his position as Catholic chaplain in Grein—he is often called Thoman von Grein—and accepted a position with the Lutheran barons of Hardegg in the village of Krauz. Since he was not satisfied with the Lutheranism adopted by his baron, he joined the brotherhood of the Anabaptists in Styria in 1527. From Styria he went to Bavaria with the schoolmaster of Wels (*q.v.*) and in Regensburg associated with Ludwig Haetzer. From Bavaria he went to Moravia. At the beginning of the next year he was in prison at Brno. In the spring of 1528 Hans Kuhn of Passau wrote that Brother Thoman von Grein was in prison. After a long imprisonment and trial he was sentenced to death with two other Brethren, called Balthasar and Dominicus in both the Hutterite Chronicle and van Braght's *Martyrs' Mirror;* all three died at the stake on the Friday before Easter, April 10, 1528, at Brno. A letter by Johannes of Zwola to Johannes Hess, from Tobichau, dated April 15, 1528, indicates that one of these two men was the Bohemian Brother Johann Cizek (Zeising, *q.v.*). Waldhauser wrote an epistle of farewell, which is found in manuscripts 163 and 190 at Pressburg, with the title, "Ein Sendbrieff Thoman Waldhausers an die so Brüder gewesen sein—zu Brünn. Im 1528. Jahr gesandt aus der Gefangnus zu Brünn am Samstag vorm Palmtag genannten Jahrs."

Before they were sentenced the three warned the council against the shedding of innocent blood, for God would not leave it unpunished. One of the councillors mocked at this idea and acted as if he were washing his hands (in innocence). "But God gave him his washing," says the Chronicle. He died suddenly even before the Brethren were executed. In prison Thomas wrote a brief, moving letter of consolation to the Brethren at Brno. The report had reached him that several of the Brethren had recanted in the face of the raging dragon, which greatly grieved him and led him to write to them, reminding them that God in His great love had sent His own Son to redeem them from sin and to bring them eternal life, and urging watchfulness and steadfastness. In conclusion he besought them to pray for him, because he felt that God would soon release him from his suffering. It was his only wish that his death might bring honor to God. To all who were serving God with a pure heart he sent a sincere parting greeting. (*Moravian* national archives at Brno, Beck collection no. 56, pp. 1-4; Beck, *Geschichts-Bücher,* 65; *Mart. Mir.* D 42, E 428; see also **Thomas;** *ML* IV.)   W.W.

Waldheim, a Mennonite village name found in the Molotschna settlement in the Ukraine, the West Reserve of Manitoba, Saskatchewan, Cuauh-temoc in Mexico, and in Menno, Friesland, Volendam, and Villarrica in Paraguay. (See **Villages.**)
                                                        C.K.

Waldheim (Russian, *Waltajem,* later *Solianka*) and **Dosidorf** (*Zabara*). About 1837 twelve Swiss-Volhynian Mennonite families from Horodyszcze (*q.v.*), Volhynia, settled the two villages, Waldheim and Dosidorf, which were located approximately 20 miles southwest of Novograd-Volynsk. In 1843 this congregation was called the "Gemeinde in der Colonie Dosidorf," but later Waldheim became the leading village. The land was owned by the settlers, this being the first instance of ownership among the Swiss-Volhynian Mennonites. The church was served by elders Joseph and Johan Schrag and minister Christian Graber. A few families left the two villages in 1861 and joined the new settlement at Neumannovka-Kutusovka (*q.v.*) in eastern Volhynia. The entire Waldheim-Dosidorf group emigrated to Hutchinson and Turner counties in South Dakota in 1874.   M.H.S.

Waldheim, Sask., is a town (pop. 462) situated in a Mennonite district about 35 miles north of Saskatoon. The two main churches of the town are the Canadian Conference (GCM) Church with 209 members (1957) and J. L. Zacharias as leading minister, and the Mennonite Brethren Church with 87 members and J. H. Jantzen as the leader and deacon. The town also has a Seventh-Day Adventist Church, whose members come mostly from Mennonites. There is also a hospital in the town.
                                                        J.G.R.

Waldheim Mennonite Brethren Church, located in the town of Waldheim in northern Saskatchewan, a member of the Canadian M.B. Conference, was organized in 1918 with 88 members under the leadership of Elder David Dyck. Since its organization 150 members have been baptized. Following the revival under F. J. Wiens in 1930 thirty-four were baptized and after a revival in 1947 thirty-three. A church was built in 1919. The membership in 1957 was 89. Presiding ministers of the church have been Elder David Dyck, Jacob T. Ediger, G. A. Willems, and the present (1957) leader, John H. Jantzen.   J.H.E.

Waldner (Waltner), a Hutterite family name stemming from Aemlach, Carinthia, Austria. Jörg Waldner was one of the Lutheran Carinthian exiles who were expelled to Hungary in 1755 because they refused to accept Catholicism. He was sent to Transylvania, and there united with the Hutterian Brethren at Alwinz (*q.v.*). His son Johannes Waldner, a preacher, was the chronicler of the *Klein-Geschichtsbuch.* He died in Russia on Dec. 14, 1824. During this time the Hutterites abandoned their practice of community (*q.v.*) of goods. Michael Waldner, also a preacher, reinstituted community of goods in 1859, and joined the emigration to the United States in 1874, where they established the first American Bruderhof at Bon Homme, 20 miles west of Yankton, S.D. The name is now found in the Hutterite communities in South Dakota, Montana, Alberta, and Manitoba. There are 34

Hutterite ministers with this name. The name as found in the General Conference Mennonite Church (Waltner) is of Hutterite origin. Erland Waltner is president of Mennonite Biblical Seminary, Elkhart, Ind., and Lena Waltner is instructor in art at Bethel College. Harris Waltner and James Waltner are G.C.M. pastors in Kansas. (Zieglschmid, *Klein-Geschichtsbuch*, 269.) **D.D.**

Waldner, Christian, chosen to the Hutterian Brethren ministry June 26, 1898, and confirmed by Darius Walter in Canada. After the death of Elias Walter he became the elder of the Dariusleut (*q.v.*), living in the West Raley Bruderhof in Canada. He died Feb. 23, 1937. **D.D.**

Waldner, Jakob, a minister of the Hutterian Brethren, chosen in 1875 by the Bruderhof in Bon Homme, S.D., was confirmed July 7, 1877. He died Aug. 11, 1897, at the age of 59 years, having served in the ministry for 22. By trade he was a smith and was one of the first to join the Schmiedeleut (*q.v.*) wing of the Hutterian Brethren, of which Michael Waldner and Jakob Hofer were ministers. Both of these men were blacksmiths in Russia. Jakob Waldner also served as a teacher for 14 years. **D.D.**

Waldner, Johannes (1749-1824), born near Villach, Carinthia, of Lutheran parents, with whom he migrated on the order of Empress Maria Theresa to Transylvania in 1755, along with other Lutherans. Here the entire Carinthian exile group turned Hutterite and became the very soul of a revitalization of the brotherhood. In his later years he wrote his recollections, called *Denkwürdigkeiten,* as a sort of continuation of the old Hutterite chronicle, the *Geschicht-Buch.* Thus grew a remarkable new book, the *Klein-Geschichtsbuch der Hutterischen Brüder* (first printed in 1947). Waldner wrote the story only to the year 1802; the remainder to 1947 was done by other writers. In this work he mentioned his own experiences at different places.

In 1767 Waldner shared the dramatic flight of the brotherhood across the mountains into Rumania (Walachia) and all their subsequent hardships until the Brethren found a new home in Ukraine, first in Vishenka (*q.v.*), later in Radichev (*q.v.*). In 1782 he was elected preacher, and in 1794 bishop of the entire brotherhood. In 1818 an unfortunate conflict arose as one group wished to give up the principle of community of goods. Waldner insisted on continuing this time-honored principle in spite of all external difficulties. "I would rather die at the stake than to abandon the old practice" (423). Thus a split occurred and Waldner moved to a new place near by called Neudorf. In 1824 he died at the age of 75.

Waldner began writing his *Denkwürdigkeiten* in 1793, but he prefaced this personal story by a brief recapitulation of Hutterite history as found in the larger chronicle and amplified it by records otherwise unknown. This resulted in a brilliant history of the Hutterites, more condensed than the older (Braitmichel) chronicle, and yet full and rich. Johann Loserth, who read this work for the first time

c1930, considered Waldner an outstanding history writer, with a unique skill in making events live.

But this revival of the interest in history was only secondary to Waldner's more central achievements. His main concern was the revival of the old and genuine spirit of the Hutterites as it had been at the time of the great bishop Andreas Ehrenpreis (*q.v.*; d.1662). A major avenue to this end was the collection and rewriting of the old sermons (*q.v.*) which at Waldner's time had almost been forgotten. New sermon books were produced by Waldner and his co-workers, taken from old sermon notebooks. Waldner also incorporated excerpts from these sermons into the *Klein-Geschichtsbuch* (204-21). This made an invaluable inheritance for the brethren, which has continued alive to this day, and which is the very center of all their piety. Waldner also renewed the old Gemeindeordnungen (*q.v.*) and insisted on their observance. In short, he became the rejuvenator of the brotherhood at a time when it was particularly difficult to continue the tradition. That the Hutterites could survive so strongly through the ages (after the conclusion of the heroic first century) is due mainly to the work of three outstanding men: Ehrenpreis, Waldner, and Elias Walter.

R.F.

J. Loserth, "Decline and Revival of the Hutterites," *MQR* IV (1930) 93-112; R. Friedmann, *Mennonite Piety Through the Centuries* (Goshen, 1949) 113-15.

Waldner, Michael, a Hutterian Brethren minister, chosen in 1856 in Russia, and confirmed in office in 1858. With Jakob Hofer he re-established community of goods in 1859. He died Oct. 13, 1889, in the Bon Homme Bruderhof in South Dakota, at the age of 55 years, having served in the ministry 33 years. **D.D.**

Waldo Mennonite Church (MC), located 4 miles south of Flanagan, Ill., a member of the Illinois Conference, dates back to 1855, when the first settlers, who were all Amish, came from France and Germany. In 1860-67 the ministers were Christian Slagell, J. P. Smith, Jacob Rediger, and an Oyer, who held services in homes of members. Daniel Steinmann (ordained preacher in 1867) was bishop 1886-1908, and J. D. Hartzler (ordained preacher in 1920) was bishop 1927-59. In 1867 a meetinghouse was built, replaced in 1906 by a new building, which was destroyed by fire in 1933; the present building, still on the original site, was erected in the same year, seating capacity 300.

The first Sunday school was started in 1868. Church services and Sunday school were held on alternate Sundays until 1875, when they were joined into one service. The Waldo church was one of the first in the state to take this step. In 1957 the membership was 254, with Edwin J. Stalter as minister.

J.D.H.

Waliën (Walyen, Walijen), a Dutch Mennonite family found from the early 17th century until about 1830 among the members of the congregation of Winterswijk, where some of them served as deacons and where shortly after 1600 Mennonite meetings were held in the rear of the house of Hindrick Walien. Occasionally they are also found in the congregation at Almelo and elsewhere. There was a branch of this family at Amsterdam (Lamist church) c1700-60; here too some Waliens were deacons. At Winterswijk they were textile merchants and manufacturers.

According to a family tradition the Waliëns, who are found at Bocholt, Westphalia, Germany, from the 10th century, were expelled from there in 1611 and then with other Mennonites moved to Winterswijk. According to another tradition, they received their family name from the old farm named Waljen near Winterswijk. Mennonite members of this family were also found c1600 at Vreden (q.v.) in Westphalia.   vdZ.

F. C. Fleischer, *De Doopsgez. gemeente te Winterswijk* (1911) 10, 18, 30 *et passim;* church records of Amsterdam.

Walig, a Dutch Mennonite family, found since the 16th century in the Zaan district, province of North Holland. Deacons by this name are found in the Mennonite congregations of Zaandam and Krommenie. Jan Walig (1796-1868), of Zaandam, was trained for the ministry at the Amsterdam seminary and served as pastor at Krommenie 1821-64.
                                              vdZ.

Walig Dirck Luytgens, an Anabaptist martyr: see Waechlink Dirks.

Walker (Mo.) Mennonite Church (MC) had 12 members in 1958. George W. Holderman was its pastor.

Wall (de Wael, de Wale, Wahl, Waalde, Walde, van de Walle), a Mennonite family name of Prussian background. The name appeared in Danzig in 1586 and also in Tiegenhagen, Rosenort, Ladekopp, and Heubuden and was transplanted to Russia and America. It is likely that the name is of Dutch origin. In Holland the name usually appears as de Wale. Uco Walles was a Dutch Mennonite leader. A. Wall was a physician in Halbstadt, Molotschna. Aaron Wall of Mountain Lake, Minn., was one of the founders of the E.M.B. Church. Heinrich Wall is teaching at the Canadian Mennonite Bible College. His brother Cornelius Wall has been teacher at Mountain Lake, Hesston, Winnipeg, and Basel. In 1958 there were 17 ministers bearing the name Wall, all but one in the United States, and mostly in California: E.M.B. five, M.B. ten, G.C.M. two. (Reimer, *Familiennamen,* 120.)   C.K.

Wall, Aaron (1834-1905), a minister and cofounder of the Evangelical Mennonite Brethren, was born Jan. 1, 1834, at Pordenau, South Russia. On Jan. 30, 1858, he married Aganetha Dick. They had 5 sons and 4 daughters. They made their home in the village of Hamberg. On Feb. 20, 1871, Wall was elected as a minister and preached his first sermon on I John 4:18. In 1875 they moved with their family to North America and settled on a farm north of Mountain Lake, Minn. In 1876 he was elected as elder of the Bergfelder Church. Stressing regeneration and the new walk in Christ, he with others of like conviction separated from the church and founded the Bruderthaler Church in 1889. He was also instrumental in founding the Conference

of the United Mennonite Brethren in North America (later Defenseless), now known as the Evangelical Mennonite Brethren. He had a congenial and pleasing personality. He was an earnest but loving shepherd of his flock. In his work of setting dislocated and broken bones he had many an opportunity to speak with his patients about their salvation.

Shortly before his death Wall conducted the church election in which Henry I. Dick was elected elder, and on July 18 ordained him. He died on Aug. 6, 1905.   H.H.Di.

Wall, Franz (d. 1906), a Mennonite minister and founder of the Muntau Hospital (q.v.). Influenced by George Muller of Bristol, England, he started the hospital in 1889 in order to relieve suffering. After his death his son Franz Fr. Wall (b. 1882) continued as manager, assisted by his sisters, who had received special training in the field. The building was enlarged into a two-story building, and significant doctors, e.g., E. Tavonius, were won for it. In 1930 Wall had to give up his position and the hospital was taken over by the Soviet government. He was exiled in 1936 and nothing is known about him since 1939.   C.K.

A. A. Toews, *Mennonitische Märtyrer* I (N. Clearbrook, 1949) 318; Reimer, *Familiennamen,* 120.

Wall, Jacob A. (1864-1954), son of Aaron (q.v.) and Aganetha Wall, was born Sept. 24, 1864, in the village of Hamberg, South Russia. In 1875 he came with his parents to Mountain Lake, Minn. On May 31, 1885, he was married to Elizabeth Fast. They had 9 children, of whom 3 died in their childhood. In 1906 his wife died and on June 14, 1907, he was married to Katherina Flaming, who had 4 children.

Wall was ordained as a minister of the E.M.B. Church on July 20, 1902. In 1916 he moved with his family and with others to the community northwest of Wolf Point, Mont., and organized the Evangelical Mennonite Brethren Church there, of which he was the leading pastor for many years. In 1938 he came to Dallas, Ore. He served as a member of the Board of Foreign Missions of the Evangelical Mennonite Brethren for a period of 21 years, and 9 years on the publication committee, during which time he had a large share in making the constitution of the Defenseless Mennonite Brethren in Christ of North America, now known as the Evangelical Mennonite Brethren. He died on Oct. 7, 1954, over 90 years of age.   H.H.Di.

Wall, Johann, first elder of Köppental-Orloff Mennonite Church, Trakt, Samara, Russia. When the threat of loss of military exemption faced the Mennonites of Prussia, Johann Wall and Claas Epp, Sr., were sent to Russia in 1853 to locate a place for settlement. With the help of Philip Wiebe and von Köppen they located land for 100 families on the "Trakt" (q.v.), Samara. The settlement was established in 1854.

Johann Wall and the Prussian Mennonites that joined him and Claas Epp, Sr., to settle in Samara not only had very strong convictions regarding nonresistance, but also adhered to some pietistic-chiliastic views regarding the second coming of Christ and the role which the children of God would play at that time. They were strongly influenced by Jung-Stilling (*q.v.*) and Clöter.

When Wall visited the Molotschna Mennonites in 1853 he was ordained elder in Orloff by B. Fast. His report of conditions found in the Molotschna settlement is interesting. He comments, "Extraordinary privileges obligate to extraordinary contributions;" and speaking of divisions among the Mennonites he paraphrases Paul's admonition to the Galatians (3:1), "Oh, foolish Mennonites, who hath bewitched you . . . ?" Wall was succeeded as elder by David Hamm (*q.v.*), who continued the struggle with the radical chiliastic element of the settlement. C.K.

Friesen, *Brüderschaft*, 129; H. Dirks, *Mennonitisches Jahrbuch* 1907, 73; F. Bartsch, *Unser Auszug nach Mittel-Asien* (Halbstadt, 1907) 80.

Wallace Mennonite Church (MC), located in Wallace Twp., Perth Co., Ont. About 1860 Mennonite families began to move into this neighborhood some 30 miles northwest of Waterloo County, where homes were available at low costs. Some 15 families lived here until 1899. At first meetings were held in their homes by ministers from the organized churches. In 1871 a meetinghouse was erected on the Sixth Concession road. Isaac Weber served as minister 1869-92, and Isaac Hallman became minister in 1884. From 1876 communion was served regularly twice a year. The M.B.C. division organized a congregation in this settlement with its beginnings in 1875. At first services were alternated in the church, then the M.B.C. group came in possession of the building. The M.C. group built another church, but soon began to return to the Waterloo communities. A tidy cemetery still exists. The Evangelical Association has use of the church. J.C.F.

Walle, van de, Mennonite family name. Jan (*q.v.*), Joos (*q.v.*), Laurens (*q.v.*), and Lieven (*q.v.*) van de Walle were Anabaptist martyrs; Willem van de Walle was banished from Gent, Belgium, in 1535 because of his Anabaptist views; Geeraerdt van de Walle, of Hansbeke, who lived at Gent, was baptized by Elder Hans Busschaert (*q.v.*) at Vlissingen in 1587. Later a van de Walle family is found at Rotterdam, where Jan Jacobs van de Walle was a deacon of the Flemish church 1647-50, later joining the Waterlanders; in this congregation his son Jacob van de Walle, a well-to-do flax merchant, was a preacher 1670-d.78. At Amsterdam Christoffel van de Walle was a preacher of the Lamist (*q.v.*) congregation 1683-d.1711. Jacob van de Walle, a Mennonite, probably of Rotterdam, was worshiping with the pietistic adherents of Philipp Jakob Spener at Frankfurt. (Verheyden, *Gent*, 2, No. 5; *idem*, "Mennisme in Vlaanderen," ms.; *DB* 1884, 72; see also **Wall.**) vdZ.

Wallenstein is a "country corners" 7 miles west of Elmira, in the west Woolwich area of Waterloo County, Ont., where for a few years about 1933 the Mennonite (MC) Conference of Ontario supplied ministerial and Sunday-school assistance in a small church. No organized work followed. J.C.F.

Wallertheim, a village in the Palatinate, Germany. The Wallertheim Mennonite congregation merged with Spiesheim (*q.v.*) in the 18th century. vdZ.

Walles, Uco (Uko, Ucke), b. 1583 at Noordbroek, d. February 1653 at Sylmönken in East Friesland, a farmer and wood dealer at Noordbroek, Dutch province of Groningen, was a Mennonite elder. He was an adherent of the very strict elder Jan Luies (*q.v.*), and with a great number of followers, he left the main Flemish branch in 1634; he henceforth banned all the moderate Flemish, and soon was the leader of the Ukowallists (*q.v.*), who had congregations in many towns of Groningen and Friesland and in East Friesland. Walles not only rejected all other Mennonite branches, but also attacked the Reformed; in 1635 he had a dispute with the Reformed pastor à Hengel at Godlinze. This debate and his intolerance drew the attention of the magistrates to him, particularly after the sensational meeting in the spring of 1637 in which Jurjen Thomas (*q.v.*) was banned. On April 8, 1637, Walles was permanently banished from the province of Groningen; thereupon he moved to East Friesland, Germany. In vain he asked that the sentence of banishment be revoked: he was only allowed to return long enough to arrange his affairs. But in 1642 he ventured to settle again on a farm at Noordbroek; when this became known he was arrested and conducted across the German border. He then lived in Neustadt-Gödens and other towns of East Friesland, where he had a large following, e.g., at Norden (*q.v.*).

Walles was "a forceful personality, a man of irreproachable conduct and strong conviction, with an excellent knowledge of the Bible, and a good speaker" (Wumkes). His allegorical interpretations of the death of Christ deeply impressed his contemporaries. He annoyed his Reformed opponents especially by his belief that Judas was not forever lost, but through the blood of Christ entered upon the joys of heaven.

Walles was attacked in books by the following Reformed theologians: L. Pimperlingh, L. Alphusius, Johannes Lubbertus, J. Barchman, and Adolf Sibelius. He published a number of writings, mostly polemical defenses of his views against his opponents *Noodwendighe Verantwoordinghe . . .* (n.p., 1637), *Een Weemoedige Klaghende Supplicatie aan alle menschen . . .* (n.p., 1645), *Twee Brieven aan Laurens Pimperlingh* (n.p., 1645), and *Een corte leerachtige verklaringe uyt de H. Schrifture vervatet, hoe men de tijdt verstaen sal, doe Christus . . . op aerden was* (n.p., 1645). In the Dutch State Archives at Groningen are found five treatises by Walles in manuscript.

His followers, the Ukowallists (*q.v.*), in the province of Groningen had to endure many hardships, for a few decades not even being permitted to hold meetings. But the measures of the magistrates ceased c1665; about the same time or shortly after the Ukowallists everywhere merged with the Groningen Old Flemish Mennonites. vdZ.

N.N.B.Wb. III, 1383-87; Blaupot t. C., *Friesland*, 139, 160 f.; *idem, Groningen* I, 66-80, 121, 283 ff.; II, 222 f.; *Inv. Arch. Amst.* I, No. 610; *DB* 1870, 114; 1876, 39 note 2; 1879, 8, 86-88.

Wallmann (Woleman, Wullman), a name which occurs among the Mennonites of Russia and among the Hutterites. Hans Woleman is mentioned in the *Klein-Geschichtsbuch* (p. 138) among the Hutterites during the Thirty Years' War. Among those who went to Russia in 1784 Jacob Waleman and Katherina Walemanin (p. 373) are mentioned. During the early 19th century Andreas Wallmann left the Hutterite group of Russia and joined the Mennonites of the Chortitza settlement. He married Katharina Lepp and worked for the well-known industrialist Peter Lepp (*q.v.*), later becoming a shareholder in the factories at both Chortitza and Alexandrovsk. His son became the manager of the Chortitza factory. The factories known as "Lepp and Wallmann" were renamed by the Soviets as "Fabrika No. 2." Through Andreas Wallmann this Hutterite name was transplanted to the Low German Mennonites of Russia and America. There are no Mennonite ministers by this name in the United States or Canada.   C.K.

Walnut Creek Mennonite Church (MC), a member of the Ohio and Eastern Conference, is located less than a mile southeast of Walnut Creek, Holmes Co., Ohio. The first settlers were Jonas Stutzman and four young Amish couples from Somerset, Pa., in 1809-10. Church services were held in the homes, and by 1850 there were four Amish church districts in this spreading settlement. One of these suffered a division, and the liberal segment led by Bishop "Gross" Mose Miller became the nucleus of the Walnut Creek A.M. Church. In 1862 the first meetinghouse was built, replaced in 1896 by the present building, which was enlarged in 1908 and 1950. The membership in 1957 was 598. Paul R. Miller, a great-great-grandson of the founder, is the present bishop and pastor.   P.R.M.

Nettie Glick, *Historical Sketch of the Walnutcreek A.M. Church* (Scottdale, 1933).

Walnut Grove Amish Mennonite Church (now extinct) was formed in Logan County, Ohio, by that part of the Logan County Mennonites who adhered to the more progressive discipline of John Warye, bishop at Oak Grove (*q.v.*) in Champaign County, and David Plank (*q.v.*), preacher at Walnut Grove. They built a meetinghouse about three miles west of the South Union Mennonite Church (*q.v.*). David S. Yoder, farmer-schoolteacher and prominent Sunday-school worker and mission committeeman, was a member of this congregation. In 1885, when John P. King, bishop at South Union, moved to Hartford, Kan., it was decided to place both David Plank and Christian K. Yoder, preacher at South Union, in the lot and that whichever was chosen was to be bishop of both congregations. David Plank was chosen and ordained. Then for several years services alternated at the two churches, but in 1929 services were discontinued at Walnut Grove and the plot reverted to the original owners. The former church building is now an implement shed.   J.S.U.

John Umble, "Early Sunday Schools at West Liberty, Ohio," *MQR* IV (1930) 6-50, *passim*.

Walnut Hill Church of God in Christ Mennonite Church, located at Walnut Hill, Escambia Co., Fla., was organized in 1946 by several young homeseekers. It has had a continual growth by others moving in and by additions through baptism. The membership in 1959 was 105. The meetinghouse, which seats 180, was built in 1950. The congregation has an active sewing circle. Francis Peters and Harry Harms are the ministers, assisted by P. G. Hiebert and the newly ordained Wilbert Peters.   F.P.

Walpot (Walbot), **Peter** (1521-78), bishop of the Hutterian Brethren in Moravia during their Golden Age, one of the outstanding leaders of the brotherhood, a creative writer and organizer, a stern and upright character, who did much to bring the brotherhood to that spiritual and moral height which attracted many converts during the second half of the 16th century. He was a Tirolean, born near Klausen, south of the Brenner Pass; when eight years old he was present when George Blaurock (*q.v.*) was executed for his faith in Guffidaun near Klausen. He seems to have turned Anabaptist at an early age (like many other Tiroleans), for in 1542 he was already a minister (*Diener des Worts*) in Moravia. By profession he was a cloth-shearer (*Tuchscherer*), whence he was often called "Peter Scherer." From now on he participated in all the major activities of the brotherhood; e.g., in the important debate between the Gabrielites (*q.v.*) and the Hutterites in 1545 (*Chronik*, 252-56). It appears that Walpot was particularly well-read, not only in the Scriptures, but also in church history and in contemporary polemics and apologetics. He is probably the author of the remarkable "Fünf Artikel des grössten Streites zwischen uns und der Welt" (*Chronik* at the year 1547, pp. 269-316; reprinted in *Glaubenszeugnisse* I, 237-57), a summary of the most significant theological and practical positions of the Hutterites in which they differ from the "world," a tract apparently derived from the earlier debate with the Gabrielites. From now on the Hutterites had not only Riedemann's *Rechenschaft* (*q.v.*) but also these *Fünf Artikel* to give an account of their faith and life.

In 1546 Walpot and his wife were active in Silesia "in the work of the Lord," apparently among the remnants of the Gabrielites, once going as far as Danzig. After Riedemann's death (1556) Walpot was the uncontested spiritual leader of the brotherhood. When, in 1557, Lutheran theologians at Worms published their condemnation of Anabaptism in the *Prozess wie es soll gehalten werden* (also called *Bedenken, q.v.*), only the Hutterites replied (even though they were more remote from the controversy than any other Anabaptist group), and this reply became known as *Handbüchlein wider den Prozess . . .* (*q.v.*, to be published in *Glaubenszeugnisse* II). It is a fine and highly spiritual apology of Anabaptism. To be sure, it was circulated anonymously and was approved by the entire brotherhood, but there can be no doubt that it was Walpot who formulated the points of defense and of emphasis.

In 1565 when the bishop of the brotherhood, Leonhard Lanzenstiel, died, Walpot was elected the new bishop, both of Moravia and adjacent Slovakia. This office he filled for the next 13 years (1565-78) with much energy and wisdom. While he had seen great hardship in Moravia during the 1540's, now a time of peaceful development had set in. There was no longer any persecution in Moravia (the Counter Reformation did not come to that country until the end of the century) and the brotherhood spread and flourished, numbering at that time 30,000 baptized souls. The administrative center was the Bruderhof of Neumühl (*q.v.*), where the bishop resided. The Brethren could now afford to have one of their most precious books printed, Riedemann's *Rechenschaft,* most likely by an itinerant journeyman printer by the name of Vollandt at the Neumühl Hof (see **Rechenschaft**), where Walpot was instrumental in this enterprise.

The activities of this excellent man must have been manifold indeed. Missioners were sent out into all German lands (as far as Denmark) and into Switzerland. Many newcomers had to be assimilated, and the discipline at home had to be carefully watched and regulated lest the community deteriorate. A wealth of epistles from this period have survived, written to the missioners abroad "in the name of the entire brotherhood," encouraging and comforting them in their hard work. No doubt most of these were drafted by the bishop himself. Kaspar Braitmichel (*q.v.*) now began the first draft of what gradually became *Das grosse Geschicht-Buch* (greater Chronicle), assisted by Walpot. An enormous correspondence was brought in almost daily by returning Brethren (no other mail was ever used), and had to be read before the assembled Brethren and answered. Economic and social questions both in Moravia and Slovakia had to be solved; e.g., the relationship to the manorial lords and to the larger cities (many a farmer in Moravia noted with envy the thriving colonies and their enterprise). There were also the schools of the brotherhood to be managed, and on inspection Walpot found many things that needed attention. A model "school regulation" and a fine "address to the schoolmasters," Nov. 15, 1568 (see **Education, Hutterite**), remarkably modern for the 16th century, both by Walpot, have been preserved.

In the late 1560's and early 1570's, Polish Unitarians visited the Moravian Bruderhofs several times, in fact at one time (1569?) a number of young Poles volunteered to live for one whole year in the Bruderhofs in order to learn how to run such a collective large-scale enterprise. (They were disappointed and became severely critical, since such a Bruderhof is possible only on the basis of a specific attitude, foreign to the Poles.) These visits resulted in an exchange of letters of unusual interest; Walpot's epistles to the Poles were inserted into the Chronicle (*Chronik,* 443-58).

The Protocol of the Frankenthal Colloquy of 1571 claims that a certain Peter Scherer and two other Brothers attended this occasion; Wolkan and Hege assumed that this was Peter Walpot. Yet neither a Scherer nor a Walpot is listed as participating in the debate in any conspicuous way, and Walpot did not even respond when Dathenus (*q.v.*) asked whether Hutterites were present.

57

During the 1570's Walpot also drew up a catechism for the children (still in use today, to be published in part in *Glaubenszeugnisse* II), several prayers for children, and also some hymns to be learned in school.

With Swiss Brethren of the Rhine area a lively correspondence developed (see **Schmidt, Hans**), the most important epistle being the letter addressed to the Swiss Brethren of Modenbach on the Rhine in 1577, in which the distinguishing points between Hutterites and Swiss Brethren were again formulated and defended. In an earlier paper by this writer also the anonymous tract "Anschlag and Fürwenden" was attributed to Walpot, but more recent research has shown that it was drawn up by Leonhard Dax (*q.v.*, d. 1574), doubtless with Walpot's full approval. Dax, a former Catholic priest and versed in the Latin language, soon became an important assistant to Walpot in all matters of theology and literary polemics.

The most important contribution of this busy man was still to come: the elaboration of the Hutterite program of 1545-47, i.e., the "Five Articles." Now in more peaceful times Walpot could develop the ideas of this program by adding ample Biblical and church historical references, and by elaborating on each point. Thus there developed a large work (far larger than the *Rechenschaft*) of basic nature, the anonymously written *Ein schön lustig Büchlein etliche Hauptartikel unseres christlichen Glaubens,* etc., briefly called *Das grosse Artikelbuch* (see **Article Book**), dated 1577. That it was authored by Walpot is beyond doubt; in fact one 18th-century copy (now in Montana) expressly names him as the writer. And yet it was more the result of the work of the brotherhood as a whole than was, e.g., Riedemann's *Rechenschaft,* which was written in a lonely prison in Hesse. Some 23 old copies of the 16th and 17th centuries still extant, and many new ones give evidence of the continued interest of the brotherhood in this work (to be published in its entirety in *Glaubenszeugnisse* II; one article was also published in English translation in *MQR,* 1957).

On Jan. 30, 1578, Walpot died, not without having first addressed all the elders of his church assembled around his bed. The Chronicle contains this last address, and then adds a special paragraph of praise and gratitude. "He was a loyal shepherd," the Chronicle says, "an outstanding teacher (i.e., preacher), and a godly ruler, etc."

Besides the tracts and epistles mentioned above, Walpot also composed two hymns (*Lieder der Hutterischen Brüder,* 737-39). He was probably the author of the earliest known sermons of the brotherhood (see **Sermons, Hutterite**). Although these early sermons are anonymous, the dates indicate that this bishop was the author.

Walpot's richly filled life gave new strength and direction to the brotherhood. He was perhaps less "spiritual" (pneumatic) than Riedemann, but he was nevertheless the true continuer of the ideas of Jakob Hutter. Obedience to the Word of God, resignation (*Gelassenheit*) in all things secular, and loyalty to the great cause of Anabaptism—these are the forces which moved the life and activities of this outstanding Anabaptist brother.   **R.F.**

R. Friedmann, "Eine dogmatische Hauptschrift . . . ,"
Archiv für Ref.-Gesch. XXVIII (1931) 102-11 and 217-
18; for the individual works see also the bibliographies
of the articles mentioned above; Lydia Müller, *Glaubenszeugnisse oberdeutscher Taufgesinnter* I (Leipzig, 1938);
idem and R. Friedmann, *Glaubenszeugnisse* II (Gütersloh, 1960); *ML* IV.

Walrave, Simon, b. *c*1570 at Alkmaar, Netherlands,
licentiate of law, who after the death of his wife became a Catholic priest, serving at Kervendonk, near
Goch, Germany, presumably is the author (under the
initials V.P.) of *Successio* (*q.v.*) *Anabaptistica, Dat
is Babel der Wederdopers,* printed in 1603 at Cologne. A reprint is found in *Bibliotheca Reformatoria Neerlandica* VII. (*BRN* VII, 4-87.)   vDZ.

Walraven Herberts, of Middelie(?), at first a Catholic priest at Deventer, Netherlands, in 1533 joined
the Dutch Anabaptists and moved to Münster (*q.v.*)
in Westphalia, and in 1534 became a follower of Jan
van Leyden (*q.v.*). In early 1535 he was sent out
from Münster to propagate the Münsterite doctrines
and to solicit soldiers for Jan van Leyden. He
worked at Deventer, Zwolle, Amsterdam, North
Holland, and Utrecht. To earn his living in the
meantime he did not hesitate to pass as a Catholic
priest and even celebrated masses. Notwithstanding
his slyness he was apprehended at Utrecht and
burned at the stake there on March 11, 1535. vDZ.

Inv. Arch. Amst. I, No. 102; *DB* 1892, 11; 1917, 117.
No. 68; Mellink, *Wederdopers, passim.*

Walraven, Tanneken, an Anabaptist martyr: see
Janneken Walraven.

Walsall Mennonite Church (MC), located near
Johnstown, Pa., began as a mission Sunday-school
outpost of the Stahl (*q.v.*) congregation in the Walsall school building in 1938. In 1941 a small chapel,
with a seating capacity of 60, was erected by the
Stahl congregation. It was organized as a congregation under the Allegheny Mennonite Conference in
1951. The membership in 1958 was 35, with David
C. Alwine in charge. The community in which the
church is located and from which the membership
is drawn is of varied background. The congregation
had a very rapid increase at the time of its organization, but since that time there has been a gradual
decrease, due to the changing population and other
reasons. In 1959 there were 32 members.   D.C.A.

Walsh Church of God in Christ Mennonite Church,
now extinct, located 8 miles south of Walsh, Baca
Co., Col., was organized in 1930 with A. T. Koehn
as minister and Jonas W. Koehn as deacon, and a
membership of 40. It reached a membership of 80.
Worship services were held in schools. Since additional members moved in, a second congregation of
80 members was organized 5 miles north of Bartlett.
Albert Dirks and Jesse H. Jantz were ordained to
the ministry and Simon Unruh as deacon. Because
of the drought and dust storms the members moved
to other locations about 1936.   J.J.

Waltajem, a Mennonite village in Volhynia: see
Waldheim.

Walter (Walther), a Hutterite family name, the
oldest such name still in existence. The earliest

Anabaptist member of this family was one Franz
Walter, a barber-surgeon from Oetisheim near
Maulbronn, Württemberg, who emigrated to Mo-
ravia in the 1580's to join the Hutterites. In 1597
he was made preacher at the Pribitz Bruderhof in
Moravia. In 1621, at the height of the Thirty Years'
War and the Hapsburg persecutions, he left Moravia,
first for Slovakia; then in the same year he with
183 other persons crossed through Hungary to
Transylvania (*q.v.*), obeying an urgent invitation by
Prince Bethlen Gabor. Franz Walter became the
Vorsteher or bishop of the group which now settled
at Alwinz (*q.v.*), but did not enjoy the newly found
peace very long, dying in the same year (1621).
Nothing more about the Walters is reported in the
Hutterite Chronicle, and the Smaller Chronicle reports nothing until 1746, when a Zacharias Walter
(*q.v.*) was made elder in Sobotiste, Slovakia, but
eventually turned Catholic (1763). Of this Zacharias
only one son, Jacob (1740-85), emigrated to the
Ukraine in 1784, and it is from this man that all
later Hutterite Walters descend. (There are still
some Walters in Slovakia among the Catholic
Habaners, *q.v.*) This Jacob had a son Jacob (1770-
1855), who in 1818 changed from communal living
to private property in Radichev, Ukraine. His
grandson Darius Walter (1835-1903), however, was
one of the few men who re-established the community of goods in Russia in 1860. In 1874 this family
came to America and established the Wolf Creek
Bruderhof near Freeman, S.D. In recognition of
their leader this group adopted the name "Dariusleut" (*q.v.*). The nephew of Darius was Elias Walter Jr. (*q.v.*), the revitalizer of the entire brotherhood. Today the Walter family is widespread and
numerous among the Hutterites, almost a clan in
itself.   R.F.

Beck, *Geschichtsbücher;* Zieglschmid, *Klein-Geschichtsbuch; TA Württemberg; ML* IV.

Walter, Darius (1835-1903), a Hutterite preacher,
the founder of the Dariusleut (*q.v.*) kinship group,
was born in South Russia, where he was chosen
preacher in 1858. In 1860 he began to re-establish
communal life after it had been discontinued among
the Hutterites since 1818. This was achieved in the
village of Hutterdorf in the Molotschna district; Jörg Hofer, also a preacher, immediately
joined this new Bruderhof enterprise and the two
men now successfully carried through the principle
of community of goods against strong odds. When
the great exodus from Russia began in 1874, Walter
and Hofer led their group to America. Near Yankton, S.D., the farm Wolf Creek was bought in the
same year, and the next spring communal life was
started there again as it had been in Russia. Thus
began what is now known as the Dariusleut, one of
the three kinship groups of the Hutterites. Darius
Walter died July 21, 1903, at the Wolf Creek Bruderhof, having been in office 45 years. Only one daughter survived him. (Zieglschmid, *Klein-Geschichtsbuch.*)   D.D., R.F.

Walter, Elias, Jr. (1862-1938), Hutterite bishop of
the Dariusleut. He was born in Russia and came to
America in 1874 as a boy of 12 when the **family of**

Darius Walter (*q.v.*) settled at the Wolf Creek colony in South Dakota. He was ordained preacher in 1898, and served in this capacity for forty years; in 1928 he was elected bishop of the Dariusleut. He was among the first to establish a Bruderhof in Canada (1897-1905), and he migrated as the first Hutterite minister to Canada in 1918, when the harshness of the United States government during World War I drove the Brethren away from South Dakota. He then settled in the Stand-Off Colony in southern Alberta, near Lethbridge, where some of his descendants still live.

In 1888 Elias Walter came into contact with John Horsch (*q.v.*), forming a friendship which proved most profitable to both. It was through Horsch that the European world (see **Wolkan**) first learned of the existence of the Hutterites in America. In 1889 Walter discovered the original Hutterite Chronicle (*Geschich-Buch*) at a neighboring colony of Hutterian Brethren who had come from Russia. This Chronicle he copied not less than three times; one copy he sent later to Rudolf Wolkan in Vienna, who published the book in 1923. The title page bears as publication place Vienna and Stand-Off Colony.

Walter was a man of the greatest dedication to a revival of the old, genuine Hutterite spirit. Not since Johannes Waldner (*q.v.*), who died in 1824, had the brotherhood had a leader like Elias Walter. Without Andreas Ehrenpreis (*q.v.*) in the 17th century, Waldner in the 18th, and Walter in the 19th and 20th centuries, modern Hutteritism would be almost unthinkable. Walter was a man of indefatigable activity, a bishop in the true sense of the word, concerned at all times for the spiritual needs not only of the Dariusleut but of all Hutterites in both good and bad days. In his lifetime he copied innumerable volumes of Hutterite literature: 21 sermon books, 12 epistle books, the *Handbüchlein wider den Prozess* (*q.v.*), a commentary on the Book of Revelation (see **Olivi**), the Article Book (*q.v.*), and many more. He also began the compilation of a fairly comprehensive catalog of all Hutterite writings, which is of inestimable value for present-day scholarship.

In 1902 Walter published Riedemann's great *Rechenschaft* (*q.v.*) at Berne, Ind., using the rare copy of the library of the University of Chicago as his source. In 1914 he established a real precedent when he published the *Lieder der Hutterischen Brüder* (*q.v.*) at Scottdale, Pa., since then the generally accepted hymnal of all Hutterites. This work is based on the compilation of three old hymn codices of the 16th and 17th centuries. In 1919 he published the *Gesangbüchlein . . . meistens aus alten Handschriften gesammelt* (Scottdale), containing other hymns than the 1914 edition, but smaller in size. In 1920 he published Andreas Ehrenpreis' *Sendbrief . . . brüderliche Gemeinschaft, das höchste Gebot der Liebe, betreffend* at Scottdale. In 1923 the great chronicle or *Geschicht-Buch* (see above) appeared, in 1925 also the *Geschichte der zwölf Patriarchen*, a smaller volume also edited by Walter.

In 1930 Eberhard Arnold (*q.v.*), who made his first contact with him in 1926, came to America, visited all colonies, and was finally ordained preacher by Elias Walter at Stand-Off Colony. Arnold

then also received from Walter a number of most valuable old codices of former centuries as well as a number of sermon books.

One special aspect of Walter's activities was his bookbindery at Stand-Off Colony. Here he bound for practically all the Hutterite preachers their (handwritten) sermon books. He bound also the Chronicle in innumerable copies, as well as hymnbooks, tracts, etc., all with great skill and care. His son continues this activity.

Elias Walter was married to Elizabeth Hofer (1886). They were blessed with a large family, 7 daughters and 3 sons. The youngest son, Jacob (b. 1910), was elected preacher after his father's death in 1938, and is still serving in this capacity (see **Walter** Family).

John Horsch and Elias Walter carried on a long and fruitful correspondence until Walter's death. Horsch was the actual editor of all the manuscripts which were printed at Berne and Scottdale. A long list of titles of the (hitherto unknown) codices is published in Horsch's *Kurzgefasste Geschichte der Mennoniten Gemeinden, sowie einem Verzeichnis der Literatur der Taufgesinnten* (Elkhart, 1890). Horsch was also the liaison with Wolkan in Vienna. When the United States draft laws during World War I caused difficulties for the Hutterites, it was Elias Walter who represented the Hutterites in negotiations in Washington, and it was John Horsch who served as a go-between. A considerable file of Walter-Horsch correspondence has been preserved in the Goshen College Historical Library. The oldest Hutterite Epistle Book, a codex of 1566, existing at one Hutterite Bruderhof, was sent to Horsch in Elkhart in 1888, who published a considerable number of epistles from it in the *Herold der Wahrheit* (1888-89).

A series of articles by Elias Walter under the title, "Wie kamen die Hutterischen Brüder nach Amerika?" appeared in the *Mennonitische Blätter* for 1908, pp. 49 f., 53-55, 61-63, 70, and 87-89; Zieglschmid, Klein-Geschichtsbuch, 494.   R.F., H.S.B.

Walter, Hans, is named by Wolkan as an Anabaptist song writer. This is an error, in so far as he refers to No. 64 in the *Ausbund*, "Herzlich tut mich erfreuen die liebe Sommerzeit," which was written by Johannes Walther, a Lutheran poet. (Wolkan, *Lieder*, 148.)   NEFF.

Walter, Jakob, a bishop of the Hutterian Brethren in Moravia, who under the pressure of the government migrated to Little Russia in 1784, where he lived for 58 years, and then went to Russia, founding the Bruderhof Radichev (*q.v.*) and later also Hutterthal.   NEFF.

Beck, *Geschichts-Bücher*, 640, 1642; Anna Brons, *Ursprung, Entwickelung und Schicksale der . . . Mennoniten* (Norden, 1891) 173, 295.

Walter, Zacharias, bishop of the Hutterites in Slovakia 1746-61, a tailor by trade. He was made preacher in Sobotiste (*q.v.*) in 1736, and was chosen bishop of all Hutterites in Slovakia in 1746, the last one prior to their acceptance of Catholicism (see **Habaner**). In 1748 Walter carried on correspondence with the Dutch Mennonites and received devotional literature from them (his letters are in the Mennonite Archives in Amsterdam). When the government of Maria Theresa undertook the forcible conversion of the Brethren, Walter and other elders were seized at Sobotiste on March 21, 1761, and soon thereafter turned over to the Jesuits in Budapest. Meanwhile the work of conversion by duress went on in the different Bruderhofs (see **Slovakia**), mainly by taking children away. A Jesuit report of Sept. 18, 1763, claims that all attempts to convert Zacharias had failed. But eventually he, too, succumbed to the unbelievable pressure and promised to accept the Catholic faith, whereupon he was released from the monastery (1763). Of course this ended all his functions in the church. After his return he fell into such dire poverty that he appealed to the Empress for support, which the archbishop of Esztergom had to award him.

His son Jacob Walter secretly emigrated to Russia in 1784 but died the following year by drowning. Another Zacharias Walter in Russia became assistant to the Elder George Waldner in 1857.

HEGE, R.F.

Beck, *Geschichts-Bücher*, 572, 3, 591, 5, 610, 7; *Inv. Arch. Amst.* II, 419 f.; Zieglschmid, *Klein-Geschichtsbuch*, 230, 5, 8; 244, 263 (pp. 443 f. and 566 pertain to the other Zacharias Walter); *ML* IV.

Wälti: see **Welty.**

Waltner: see **Waldner.**

Walton Mennonite Church (GCM), located in Walton Twp., Harvey Co., Kan., a member of the Western District Conference, was organized on June 7, 1942, with 49 charter members. The members met in 1939-43 in the Walton School. The present church, seating 240, was built in 1943. The membership in 1957 was 154, with C. D. Boese as pastor.

C.D.B.

Waltonville, a rural hamlet on the meandering road from Hummelstown to Middletown, Lancaster Co., Pa., where in 1933 some members of the Strickler-Shope congregation held Sunday school in a member's yard. The congregation took over the work thus opened. A deserted red school, abandoned through the Derry Township consolidation, was leased for their services, and opened Oct. 15, 1933. The general attendance was 62. In 1935 it was decided to transport the children to the Strickler-Shope Sunday school and discontinue Waltonville. I.D.L.

Wanaparty Mennonite Brethren Mission station, India, located in the Wanaparty Samistan, 95 miles southwest of Hyderabad, was begun by F. A. Janzen and his wife in 1915, who erected most of the buildings. These include a mission bungalow, a church, a school, a hospital, hostels for school children, and living quarters for indigenous workers. Besides the Janzens the following missionaries have worked here: Mr. and Mrs. P. V. Balzer, Mr. and Mrs. J. N. C. Hiebert, Mr. and Mrs. J. J. Dick, Margaret Suderman, and Anna Suderman. In 1954 the station was supervised by J. J. Kasper of Nagar Kurnool. The activities on the station include the regular church worship services, a school, which has developed from a primary into a middle school; and a

hospital, which is patronized by many from the surrounding villages. The Wanaparty Station Field with an area of 1200 square miles and a population of 180,000 has been a responsive field for evangelism; the indigenous M.B. Church of the Telugus numbers over 1,000 members. J.H.L.

Wandering Soul, the English (German, *Wandelnde* or *Wandlende Seele*) title of a popular devotional book, originally written in Dutch by Jan Philips Schabaelje (*q.v.*), a Waterlander Mennonite, and published in 1635 at Alkmaar in the Netherlands. At present the work is little known, although it remains in print in German (Berne, 1952) and in English (Scottdale, 1958) editions, but a large number of editions in Dutch as well as in German and English translation give evidence that it appealed widely until the end of the 19th century. In the Dutch editions it is appended to *Lusthof des Gemoeds,* a brief devotional work by the same author, with which it had a common title page and pagination. The composite title of the 1638 edition, the earliest edition which is extant, is *Lust Hof des Gemoets inhoudende verscheijden Geestelicke Oeffeningen. Met noch drie Collatien der wandelende ziele met Adam, Noah, ende Symeon Cleophas.* It was printed by Thomas Fonteyn at Haarlem for Claes Jacobsz at De Rijp. In this early edition, probably the second, a third dialogue had been added. The earlier edition(s) contained two dialogues, those with Adam and Noah. The new dialogue, a lengthy one with Simon Cleophas, extended the book in the 12mo format to 603 pages. Some of the later Dutch editions reprinted only the two original dialogues but most contained the three, as was the case with all the German and English editions. A 1656 Dutch edition added dialogues with Jacob and Joseph, written by Schabaelje, but these were never reprinted. The number of Dutch editions is not known exactly. Maatschoen, in a footnote in Schijn (1744), estimates it "was printed at least forty or fifty times." Currently it is possible to locate 48 editions. The last known Dutch reprint appeared in 1768. All the Dutch editions contained illustrations, usually very simple woodcuts by unidentified artists, but in 1706 the book was enlarged to octavo format and enhanced by the addition of 25 etchings done by Jan Luyken (*q.v.*) with accompanying verses, and the title was changed to *De vermeerderde Lusthof.* In this form it was reprinted in 1724, 1742, and 1768.

In translation the book gained an independent character. In both German and English it was separated from the *Lusthof* and published as a distinct work. The earliest known German edition was 1741, *Die wandlende Seel, das ist: Gespräch der wandlenden Seelen mit Adam, Noah und Simon Cleophas,* printed at Basel by von Mechel (*q.v.*). This edition, however, is indicated as the fourth, which points to evidence that it was translated and published much earlier in the 18th century. The translator was B.B.B., possibly Benedict Brechbill (*q.v.*). Two further editions, 1770 and 1811, came from the von Mechel press, and at least three editions appeared in Germany during the same period, at Frankfurt and Leipzig in 1758 and 1770 and at Stuttgart in 1860. In America Saur reprinted the same German translation at Germantown, in 1768 and 1771. Other Germantown imprints are 1794 and 1805, which were followed by 12 known editions in the 19th century at Philadelphia and Harrisburg, Pa. In 1919 the Mennonite Publishing House at Scottdale, Pa., published a new edition to meet the demand for it among the Amish, and in 1952 the Amish publisher J. A. Raber of Baltic, Ohio, repeated. A study of the publishers of these many editions indicates that the book had an appeal beyond Mennonite circles. The English translation was made from the German translation rather than the original Dutch, by I. Daniel Rupp (q.v.), and was printed in 1834 as *The Wandering Soul: Dialogues between the Wandering Soul and Adam, Noah, and Simon Cleophas*. It was published by the translator and John Winebrenner at Harrisburg, Pa., and was illustrated. In 1838 Johnson and Stockton at Pittsburgh published a new edition with the title changed to *The Pilgrim Soul*. Two English editions came out in Virginia, at Woodstock in 1840 and at Winchester in 1841. Rupp reprinted the book in 1834 and 1840, an edition appeared at Harrisburg in 1857, John Baer's Sons at Lancaster published one in 1874, and the Light (q.v.) and Hope Press, of Berne, Ind., the last in 1958. In all at least 84 editions have appeared, 48 Dutch, 9 German in Europe, 18 German in the United States, and 9 English in the United States. It is probably the most widely read book by a Mennonite ever published.

The subject matter of the book pertains chiefly to historical events, both Biblical and secular, from the Creation to about the end of the first century after Christ. Simon Cleophas, a character taken from Eusebius, is said to have witnessed the fall of Jerusalem. Schabaelje lists the sources of his information as the Bible, Josephus, Augustine, Erasmus, and others. The work is a popular treatment and accurate for its time of composition, although there is a tendency to speculate about the origin of races and nations. Rather than a historical work, it is cast in literary form, that of the dialogue, which was prevalent and popular for a long time after the Middle Ages. The Wandering Soul, an earnest Christian desiring to finish the course of his pilgrimage, seeks admonition from Adam, Noah, and Simon Cleophas. The skillful handling of the conversation breaks the monotony of what would otherwise be an extended historical account with admonition. Some of the characters come to life and reflect a genial piety. In both conception and execution the book has some literary merit, which likely accounts in part for its wide appeal. In purpose, however, it is a devotional book, a work of spiritual edification in a practical sense. It was intended, as the German translator notes, to incite its readers to become pilgrims. The book reflects the particular piety characteristic of many Waterlander Mennonites in Holland in the 17th century, a spiritualistic fervor with a strong moral note. The concern with practical piety, however, and the concept of the Christian life as a pilgrimage, are reminiscent of the larger Anabaptist movement. I.B.H.

Schijn-Maatschoen, *Geschiedenis* II, 584-86; Robert Friedmann, *Mennonite Piety Through the Centuries* (Goshen, 1949) 111-15; Irvin B. Horst, "*The Wandering* Soul, a Remarkable Book of Devotion," *MHB*, October 1957. For a partial list of Dutch editions, see *Catalogus Amst.*, 224-26, 355; for a list of American editions, see Bender, *Two Centuries*; and Horst, op. cit.

Wanger, Georg, an Anabaptist martyr: see **Wagner, Georg** and **Wenger, Geörg.**

Wanner, Albrecht, an Anabaptist at Schlettstadt (Selestat) in Alsace, from where he was expelled because of Anabaptist activity, came to Strasbourg (q.v.) in 1525/6, where he was arrested with a number of other Anabaptists in 1527 and after trial banished from the city. vDZ.

A. Hulshof, *Geschiedenis van de Doopsgezinde te Straatsburg* (Amsterdam, 1905) 59 f.

Wanner Mennonite Church (MC), located one mile west of Hespeler, Ont., a member of the Ontario Conference, was one of the earliest Mennonite congregations of Ontario, closely associated with the Hagey (now Preston) congregation, the ministers alternating in serving the two congregations. Joseph Bechtel, who came from Pennsylvania in 1802, the first Mennonite minister in Ontario, served here; he was probably a member at Hageys, while Martin Baer (ordained preacher 1808) was a member at Wanners church. The first meetinghouse, erected in 1829, had two Mennonnite and two Tunker (Brethren in Christ) trustees, and was also used as a school 1829-48. The brick meetinghouse was built in 1837, replaced by a new building in 1938. John Baer, a son of Martin Baer (ordained 1838), left the church in 1874 to follow Solomon Eby into the M.B.C. Church. David Sherk, a leading Ontario minister, served here 1838-82. Later ministers were Absalom B. Snyder 1892-1936 and S. M. Kanagy 1932-41. Merle Shantz has been pastor since 1949. In 1958 the membership was 116. Me.S.

Wanty, Sara (*Mart. Mir.* has "Wanrij"), the wife of Hans Pfister, was imprisoned at Zürich, Switzerland, in 1643 with two other women because of Mennonite convictions; she suffered many hardships and finally died in prison. (*Mart. Mir.* D 822, E 1120 f.) vDZ.

War Sufferers' Relief. American Mennonites have been particularly concerned, because of their nonresistant principles, to relieve suffering caused by war. Hence one of the major groups, the Mennonite Church (MC), gave its official relief organization, founded in 1917, the name "Mennonite Relief Commission for War Sufferers," which was changed in 1926 to "Mennonite Relief Committee" (q.v.). H.S.B.

War Sufferers' Relief Bulletin began publication in March 1945 and continued monthly for two years (two volumes with 12 issues each), published by the MCC headquarters at Akron, Pa., 6½ x 9 in., with 8 pages. The editors were Irvin B. Horst, Daniel B. Suter, John A. Hostetler, and Ernest W. Lehman. The *Bulletin* was intended to make MCC foreign relief news available to the constituency by publishing current news as well as detailed reports from foreign workers. In addition to disseminating relief news, the publication also gave something of the concern and spirit in which the foreign relief program was carried on. This is evident from the quotation, "Not to be ministered unto, but to minister," which appeared under the banner of each issue. In 1947 the *War Sufferers' Relief Bulletin* was enlarged and published under the name *MCC Services Bulletin* (*q.v.*).   J.N.B.

Warden Park Mennonite Church (MC), 46 Scotia Ave., Toronto, Ont., was organized in 1955 as a result of mission work begun here in 1937. In 1958 the membership of 23 was served by John H. Hess.
                                                        J.H.H.

Warden Mennonite Church (GCM), located at Warden, Wash., is a member of the Pacific District Mennonite Conference but not of the General Conference. It was first listed in the 1957-58 *Handbook of Information*. In 1958 it had a membership of 20.
                                                        J.U.

Warendorf, a town in the district of Münster, Westphalia, Germany. In this town Bernhard Rothmann (*q.v.*) was rector of the Latin school 1521-23, and after leaving the town maintained contact with the mayor. An intimate friend of Rothmann's was Hermann Regewordt, pastor of the New Church and a member of a respected family of Warendorf. Beginning in March 1533, Regewordt preached Protestant sermons with the support of the city council. Francis, Count of Waldeck, bishop of Münster (*q.v.*), warned the town. In December 1533, Heinrich Waren came to Warendorf. As the Anabaptists gained the upper hand in Münster, he openly confessed himself as one of them. One of the converts he baptized was Pastor Regewordt. When the bishop, residing in the near-by Sassenberg, demanded the unconditional surrender of the city and the removal of the preachers, Waren and Regewordt went to Münster, arriving there on Feb. 17, 1534, with many followers, including Dusentschuer, who later became a "prophet." Dusentschuer became the willing tool of Jan van Leyden (*q.v.*), and promoted his elevation to the kingship as God's will. After the brilliant repulse of the attack against Münster on Aug. 31, 1534, Dusentschuer proposed that 28 apostles be sent out two by two to spread the ideas found in Rothmann's *Restitution*. To Warendorf were sent Johann Klopreis (*q.v.*), Gottfried Straelen, Theodor von Alffen, Anton Prumeren, and Anton Ummegrove. Waren and Dusentschuer were sent to Soest. Regewordt was in the group sent to Coesfeld, all of whom were beheaded on Oct. 23, 1534, upon orders of the bishop. The five sent to Warendorf arrived there on Oct. 14, 1534. Klopreis had for years worked as a chaplain in Wassenberg (*q.v.*) under the protection of the magistrate and had come to Münster in 1533. In Warendorf the apostles loudly called upon the city to repent. They were hospitably received by Erpo Holland, a councilor, in whose home baptisms were performed. Under Erpo Holland's influence the council refused to turn the apostles over to the bishop, but protected them to the uttermost. The council and most of the citizenry joined the Anabaptists, though not many baptisms were performed for the time being. When his threatening letters were disregarded, the bishop made a sudden attack on the town. The city, realiz-ing the hopelessness of resistance, opened its doors. On October 24 three Warendorf citizens, Erpo Holland, Johann Stopenberg, and Bernd Butermann, were put to death on the market square together with the apostles Straelen, Ummegrove, Prumeren, and von Alffen. Alffen might have escaped, for he had influential friends, but he refused to do so, rejecting all offers of clemency. The *Newe Zeitung* reported that they thanked God the Father for making them worthy of suffering for His sake. Klopreis (*q.v.*) was taken to the Iburg, then sent to the Archbishop of Cologne, and burned at the stake on Feb. 1, 1535. His last words were, "Father, into Thy hands I commend my spirit."

On the day after the execution Catholic worship was reinstated in Warendorf. All the freedoms and rights, all documents and seals, city books, and arms were taken from the city. A fortification was erected and constant surveillance by occupying troops instituted. The privileges were gradually returned in 1542-46. But a congregation of quiet Anabaptists remained in the city and the neighboring villages. It took decades to lead the people back to the Catholic Church even outwardly. The missionary work of the Jesuits and Franciscans then gradually achieved the objectives of the Counter Reformation.

Warendorf was the home town of Hermann (Harmen) Heilinck, the wealthy cloth merchant who equipped a warehouse as a meeting place for the Flemish Mennonite congregation in Amsterdam (*ML* I, 60), and gave it to the Mennonites as a gift.
                                                        J.WA.

Warendorf Blätter (1902-10); L. Keller, *Geschichte der Wiedertäufer und ihres Reiches zu Münster* (Münster, 1889); Rembert, *Wiedertäufer*; W. Zuhorn, *Kirchengeschichte der Stadt Warendorf* (Warendorf, 1918); Friedrich Brune, *Der Kampf um eine evangelische Kirche im Münsterland, 1520-1802* (Witten, 1953); *ML* IV.

Warendorp, Harmen Hendriksz van (d. April 1632, a son of Hendrik He(i)linck Seelslager, a shoemaker at Warendorp in Westphalia, Germany, and Elsgen Heyteman, was born about 1560 at Warendorp. He started a cloth shop at Aachen, Germany, probably living at Burtscheid (*q.v.*) where there was a Mennonite congregation. In 1593 he married Christine Rasselaers of Cologne (d. May 11, 1632). Their three daughters died at an early age. In 1607 van Warendorp, who had become wealthy, moved to Amsterdam, Netherlands, where he joined the Flemish Mennonite congregation. On June 28, 1607, he bought a plot of ground on the Singel canal, near the brewery "Het Lam," on which he had built a meetinghouse for the Flemish congregation. He also bought two houses on the Heerengracht and two on the Singel, and lived at the house called "Aken" (i.e., Aachen), which now is the office of the A.D.S. and the living quarters of the sexton of the church (Singel 454). He let the congregation use the meetinghouse rent free, but made some strange stipulations, e.g., that no hymns should be sung but the Psalms of David; whenever another hymn was sung the preacher was to be fined. After the death of van Warendorp April 1632 his heirs for more than a century remained the owners of the meetinghouse, which occasionally led to difficulties. In 1740 the

Lamist Mennonite congregation, after a lawsuit, became the owner of the church and the adjacent houses. K.V.

F. Muller, "Omstandig verhaal van de stichting der tegenwoordige vergaderplaats van de Vereenigde Doopsgez. Gemeente te Amsterdam," *DB* 1863, 1-42; 1900, 85; *N.N.B.Wb.* III, 1393; *Inv. Arch. Amst.* I, No. 703; II, Nos. 131-34, 162-209; Kühler, *Geschiedenis* II, 185 f.; F. Kuiper and N. van der Zijpp, *Bij 't Lam 1608-1958* (Amsterdam, 1959) 12, 25-30.

Warffum, a village in the Dutch province of Groningen, where in early 1535 the cloister of the knights of St. John was attacked by a group of 70 revolutionary Anabaptists, led by Jacob (*q.v.*) Cremer. The attack, however, was repulsed and the Anabaptists put to flight by the soldiers of stadholder Karel van Gelre. (*BRN* VII, 369; Kühler, *Geschiedenis* I, 169 f.) vDZ.

Warga, a village in Friesland, where Leenaert (*q.v.*) Bouwens baptized 21 persons in 1563-65 and 39 in 1568-82. The founding of the Warga Mennonite congregation may date from this time. About its history there is not much information, though church records have been preserved since 1732. In 1695 it joined the conference (Sociëteit) of Friesland, founded in that year. Until 1826 it was served by ministers chosen from their own members. The first minister serving here who was educated at the Amsterdam seminary was Sine J. van der Goot, 1826-33, followed by C. Cardinaal Jr. 1834-38, Joh. Pol 1839-47, D. Plantinus 1847-49, Taco Kuiper 1850-52, R. J. Bakker 1853-57, F. J. Klaasesz 1858-d.65, J. H. Uiterwijk 1866-67, J. P. van der Vegte 1868-74, B. Haga 1875-81, R. Kuiken 1882-91, P. Sybolts 1892-94, A. K. Kuiper 1895-99, Corn. Vis Jr. 1899-1905, F. W. W. Braak 1906-9, M. Onnes Mzn 1909-11, R. J. de Stoppelaar 1911-38, Miss S. E. Doyer 1943-46. After the resignation of Miss Doyer the pulpit remained vacant; Pastor F. H. Sixma, first at Terhorne, then at Giethoorn, took care of the Mennonites in Warga until August 1954, when it made an arrangement with the congregations of Irnsum-Poppingewier to be served by the preacher of these congregations.

The baptized membership of the Warga congregation numbered about 65 in 1695; 55 in 1779, increasing to 159 by 1838; 186 in 1861; from then a decrease: 183 in 1901; 180 in 1926; 160 in 1930; 102 in 1940, and 75 in 1958.

Of the first meetinghouse nothing is known except that it was replaced c1865. When this church became too large for the diminishing membership and moreover was dilapidated, a new meetinghouse was erected with the help of a Mennonite voluntary service group, dedicated on Nov. 18, 1956. Church activities now include a ladies' circle. vDZ.

Blaupot t. C., *Friesland*, 89, 93 note 72, 189, 248, 254, 306; *DB* 1890, 84; 1900, 93; *DJ* 1958, 36-39.

Warkentin (Warckentien, Warckentyn, Workentyn), a common Mennonite name of Prussian background found in Tiegenhagen, Ladekopp, Rosenort, Fürstenwerder, Heubuden, Danzig, and Königsberg as early as 1667. From Prussia the name spread to Russia and America. Cornelius Warkentin (*q.v.*) helped the early Russian Mennonites in their religious problems. Bernhard Warkentin (*q.v.*) was instrumental in the settlement of the Mennonites from Russia in Kansas and the introduction of hard winter wheat. Abraham Warkentin (*q.v.*) taught at Bethel College and was the first president of Mennonite Biblical Seminary. John W. Warkentin of Hillsboro, Kan., is active in M.B. church and college work. Cornelius J. Warkentin is an elder at Waldheim (GCM), Sask., and active in conference work. There was a total of 25 Warkentin ministers in North America in 1957, 15 M.B. (all but five in Canada) and 10 G.C.M. (all in Canada). (Reimer, *Familiennamen,* 120; *Who's Who Among the Mennonites,* 1943.) C.K.

Warkentin, Abraham (1885-1947), a Mennonite (GCM) minister and educator, was born in Ladekopp in the Molotschna Mennonite settlement of South Russia, on Aug. 22, 1885, the son of Gerhard Warkentin. After attending the Zentralschule at Ohrloff 1899-1900 and at Halbstadt 1900-2 and the normal school at Halbstadt until 1904, he taught in the Alexanderwohl school until 1912. In 1912-15 he attended the Baptist Theological Seminary at Hamburg, Germany, then taught at the Realschule at Wilhelmsdorf, Württemberg, Germany, 1916-20. He served as secretary of the Deutsche Mennonitenhilfe (*q.v.*) in Germany 1920-23. In Russia Warkentin was a member of the Lichtfelde Evangelical Mennonite Church. He married Elizabeth Unger of Alexanderwohl, Aug. 24, 1912. Four children were born to them. In 1920 Abraham Warkentin was ordained minister and elder by the Conference of South German Mennonites. In 1923 the family emigrated to the United States. After a brief stay in Hillsboro, Kan., they moved to Newton, Kan., where he became assistant pastor of the First Mennonite Church and instructor in languages and Bible at Bethel College. During 1927-29 he earned his A.B. and A.M. degrees at the University of Kansas, then returned to teach at Bethel College. In 1933 he entered the University of Chicago where he received the Ph.D. degree in 1935. His dissertation, *Die Gestalt des Teufels in der deutschen Volkssage,* was published in 1937.

From 1935 until 1943 Warkentin continued as professor of Bible and German at Bethel College. He was also principal of the Bethel College Mennonite Bible Academy and coeditor of the *Bethel College Monthly* (1925-27). In addition he was editor in chief of the G.C.M. Sunday-school quarterly 1937-42, a member of the MCC 1933-40, secretary of the G.C.M. Placement Committee 1941-43, and member of the G.C.M. Historical Committee 1941-47.

Among Warkentin's significant achievements was the revitalizing of the Mennonite Historical collection at Bethel College. He laid the foundation for the present Bethel College Historical Library (see **Mennonite Historical Library** of Bethel College). In 1943 he suffered a stroke and was forced to resign from his duties in connection with Bethel College and the First Mennonite Church. After his health was sufficiently restored he accepted the assignment of establishing the Mennonite Biblical Seminary (*q.v.*) in Chicago which started functioning in 1945 and of which he was the first president. He died on

Aug. 30, 1947. Warkentin's contribution in education, in strengthening basic Mennonite and Christian convictions within the church, in the production of Christian literature, relief work, and the training of the ministry was of great significance. He also wrote *Who's Who Among the Mennonites* (N. Newton, 1937, 1943) (with Melvin Gingerich); *Der Eid* (G.C.M. Committee on Doctrine and Conduct, n.d.); *Extracts from Mennonite History in Outline Form* (n.p., n.d.); *A Harmony of the Kings* (North Newton, 1939 and 1942); *The Oath* (G.C.M. Committee on Doctrine and Conduct, 1937). He was also a regular contributor to various periodicals and an appreciated Bible and conference lecturer.

C.K.

Cornelius Krahn, "Dr. A. Warkentin," *The Mennonite*, Sept. 16, 1947, p. 3.

Warkentin, Bernhard (1847-1908), a General Conference Mennonite leader, was born in the village of Altonau, Molotschna Mennonite settlement of Russia, on June 18, 1847. He attended the secondary school in Halbstadt and a business college in Odessa. His father was a miller and had made a trip to Siberia to investigate settlement possibilities there. When the Mennonites of Russia became restless around 1870 about the prospective loss of certain privileges, America became a favorite topic of conversation. Bernhard Warkentin, Philip Wiebe, Peter Dick, and Jacob Bähr, all young men with well-to-do parents, made a trip to America in 1872. In 1872 they arrived at Summerfield, Ill., where Warkentin made his headquarters at the home of Christian Krehbiel. He was in constant touch with his friend David Goerz (*q.v.*) back in Russia. He traveled extensively, investigating Manitoba, Minnesota, the Dakota territory, Kansas, and Texas, always reporting his findings. Railroad agents contacted him as soon as it became known that a considerable number of Mennonites were considering coming to America. He settled in Halstead, Kan., in 1873 with the Summerfield Mennonites under the leadership of Christian Krehbiel, after attending McKendrie College of Lebanon, Ill., for one year.

In 1875 Warkentin married Wilhelmina Eisenmayer. His father came from Russia to attend the wedding. In 1873 he built a gristmill at Halstead on the Little Arkansas River. In 1878 the Halstead Mill and Elevator Company was organized, of which his father-in-law was principal stockholder and president. In 1885 Warkentin made a trip to Europe, particularly South Russia, and after his return moved to Newton in 1886 and established the Newton Milling and Elevator Company. In 1900 he established the Blackwell (Okla.) Milling and Elevator Company. The milling industry which he started with a daily capacity of 10 barrels grew to a capacity of 1700 barrels, the flour being sold throughout the United States and Europe.

Warkentin's greatest public service was probably the introduction of the hard winter wheat to Kansas. Hard winter wheat or red Turkey wheat had been sown by the Mennonites immediately after their arrival in Kansas. It was Warkentin, however, who experimented with the various varieties of wheat in co-operation with Mark A. Carleton, a rep-

resentative of the U.S. Department of Agriculture. In 1885 Warkentin made arrangements in South Russia for a large shipment of hard winter wheat to Kansas for distribution among the farmers. He was assisted by his brother-in-law Johann Philipp Wiebe and his nephew Bernhard Enns. In 1900 the Kansas State Millers Association and the Kansas State Dealers Association asked Warkentin to arrange for a large-scale importation of seed wheat. About 15,000 bushels were imported as a result. Carleton went to the Ukraine in 1898 to study the red Turkey wheat in its native country and experimented with some 300 varieties of wheat near Halstead (see **Wheat**).

Warkentin organized the Halstead State Bank and the Kansas State Bank of Newton, of which he was director and president. He held numerous other public offices and was active in the founding of Bethel College, the Bethel Deaconess Hospital, and the Mennonite Mutual Fire Insurance Co. at Newton.

Death came to Warkentin on April 1, 1908, in Beirut, Syria. While he and Mrs. Warkentin were traveling from Damascus to Beirut, a pistol accidentally discharged in the adjoining compartment killing Warkentin. He was buried in the Greenwood cemetery at Newton. Bernhard Warkentin's significance goes far beyond his instrumentality in bringing Mennonites to America. He was a pioneer of Kansas in helping to establish numerous institutions and businesses and making Kansas a "bread basket."

C.K.

Kansas (Chicago, 1912) Part II, 1098 f.; William E. Connelley, *A Standard History of Kansas and Kansans* V (New York, 1918) 2291 f.; Cornelius Krahn, "Some Letters of Bernhard Warkentin Pertaining to the Migration of 1873-1875," *MQR* (1950) 248-63; idem, ed., *From the Steppes to the Prairies (1874-1949)* (Newton, 1949) 8-12; "Milling Industry—A Monument to Bernhard Warkentin, Founder," *The Newton Kansan* (Aug. 22, 1922) 100 f.; "Bernhard Warkentin," *Mennonite Year Book and Almanac* (1909) 24-26; "Ueber den Heimgang unseres früheren Direktors Bernhard Warkentin," *Monatsblätter aus Bethel College* (Newton, May 1908) 54-57; Letters of Bernhard Warkentin to David Görz and Mark A. Carleton and his "Diary" are in the Bernhard Warkentin Collection, BeCL.

Warkentin, Cornelius (1740-1809), an elder (ordained preacher Jan. 6, 1775, elder Oct. 11, 1795) of the Rosenort Mennonite Church (*q.v.*), West Prussia, Germany, and one of the most outstanding men of his time in the West Prussian brotherhood, played a significant role in the organization and establishment of the Chortitza Mennonite Church (*q.v.*) in Russia. He and Cornelius Regier, elder of the Heubuden Mennonite Church (*q.v.*), made a trip to Chortitza in 1795 upon invitation of the congregation to settle a difficulty which had arisen during the early years and because of the death of the elder, Behrendt Penner (*q.v.*). The two worked with great success, but before the task was accomplished Cornelius Regier died after ordaining Cornelius Warkentin to the office of elder. Warkentin continued the work and returned to his church, stopping on the way at various places. He received from the Czar a gold medal accompanied by a letter dated 1804, in recognition of the service he had rendered to the Mennonites. Warkentin's account of the trip was published in the *Mennonitische Rundschau*

(No. 4, 1897) and by P. M. Friesen (134). He and Regier did much to help the settlers to overcome their early difficulties. He kept a detailed diary of the trip, which has been preserved. Friesen describes the man and his work in Russia as follows (p. 47): "He was an impressive and heart-winning personality. . . . He writes, speaks, functions in office, and acts before the high or the lowly like a man with a good general theological training. The Mennonites as well as the Lutheran and Catholic clergy, imperial Russian colonial officials, governors, and highly placed persons treat him with honor and affection. His visit to the Chortitza Mennonite settlement is a continuous Pentecost for the orphaned settlers, his departure a heartbreaking grief." C.K.

D. H. Epp, *Die Chortitzer Mennoniten* (Odessa, 1889) 85; Peter Hildebrand, *Erste Auswanderung der Mennoniten aus dem Danziger Gebiet nach Südrussland* (Halbstadt, 1888) 67; Ernst Regehr, *Geschichts- und Predigertabelle der Mennoniten-gemeinde Rosenort* (2d ed., Elbing, 1939); Friesen, *Brüderschaft*, 134; *ML* IV.

Warkentin, Dirk (d. 1869), was chosen minister of the Lichtenau-Petershagen Mennonite Church (*q.v.*), Molotschna, South Russia, in 1841, and succeeded Jacob Warkentin as elder in 1842 when Jacob Warkentin was forced to resign. C.K.

Friesen, *Brüderschaft*, 113, 119, 704; H. Görz, *Die Molotschnaer Ansiedlung* (Steinbach, 1951) 58 ff.

Warkentin, Gerhard (1837-1902), was born in Tiegenhagen, Molotschna, South Russia. He came to Zagradovka in 1873, farming in the village of Blumenort; he then taught school for a number of years. He was elected minister by the Nikolaifeld Mennonite Church in 1873, and became the assistant of Elder Voth; upon Voth's retirement in 1895, Warkentin succeeded him in that office. He died May 28, 1902. G.L.

Friesen, *Brüderschaft*, 710; G. Lohrenz, *Sagradowka* (Rosthern, 1947) 70.

Warkentin, Jacob, was elected minister of the Ohrloff-Petershagen (*q.v.*) Mennonite Church, Molotschna, South Russia, and became elder of the Lichtenau-Petershagen congregation when a group separated under his leadership in 1824. Bernhard Fast (*q.v.*) was the more progressive elder of the smaller remaining Ohrloff congregation. The controversy about this division has been related in the articles under the respective churches. Warkentin was extremely conservative and objected to higher education, to supporting Bible societies, and to sitting around the table at the Lord's Supper. Later Warkentin encountered difficulties with the progressive Johann Cornies (*q.v.*), and the Fürsorgekommite (*q.v.*) forced him to resign from his office in 1842. The large congregation was now broken up. Heinrich Wiens (*q.v.*) became elder of the Margenau-Schönsee Church, Dirk Warkentin (*q.v.*) became elder of the Petershagen Church, and Heinrich Töws elder of the Pordenau Church. C.K.

Friesen, *Brüderschaft*, 113, 119, 704; H. Görz, *Die Molotschnaer Ansiedlung* (Steinbach, 1951) 58 ff.

Warkentin, Johann (1859-1948), minister of the Mennonite Brethren Church, son of Jacob and Helena (Dyck) Warkentin, was born at Nieder-Chortitza, South Russia, on Sept. 29, 1859. In 1879 the family emigrated to Canada, settling on a farm southwest of Winkler, Man. Through private study he gained a fair education and for eight years he taught school in the new Mennonite settlements. On Oct. 23, 1881, Warkentin married Sarah Loewen and established a farm home. They had ten children. In 1890 he was converted, baptized, and joined the M.B. Church. He soon became an active Sunday-school worker and director in singing. The Winkler M.B. Church elected him to the ministry and ordained him in 1895. In 1906 he was entrusted with the pastoral leadership of the church, a work he fulfilled until 1930. In addition he also frequently ministered in surrounding churches. Warkentin was active in the M.B. Conference, serving for some time on the Board of Directors for Foreign Missions. His daughter Helen became a missionary to India. After the death of his first wife he married Mrs. Elizabeth (Hooge) Dyck. He died at his home at Winkler on May 18, 1948, and was buried in the local M.B. cemetery. J.H.L.

Warmen Mennonite Brethren Mission, located at Warmen, a village approximately 16 miles northeast of Saskatoon, Sask., began in 1939, and has been under the guidance of the M.B. Missions of Saskatchewan since 1944. The Mission Church was organized in 1953 with Norman Fehr as the pastor. In 1939 the M.B. District Conference was asked to assume the responsibility of serving the group and in 1940 built a church. The membership in 1957 was 18. J.H.E.

Warnaars (Warnaers, Warners, Warnaer, Warner, Werner, Warnaertsen), a Dutch family, originally living in the district of Twente (*q.v.*), province of Overijssel, where some of its members by marriage became Mennonites *c*1640. Until *c*1875 some were members of the Mennonite congregation of Almelo (*q.v.*), and some also of Enschedé. At first they were weavers and lumber and linen merchants; later some were wholesale dealers. Many of them served the church of Almelo as deacons, and Gerrit Warnaars (1663-*c*1728) was a lay preacher, serving at Almelo until 1697 and 1697-1728(?) at Haarlem. Lourens Warners, a preacher of the Groningen Old Flemish church at Emden, East Friesland, 1721-60, may also have been a member of this family. A side branch of this family, found at Amsterdam from *c*1670, was engaged in business, banking, and insurance, and furnished some deacons, while two of them were trustees of the A.D.S. (*q.v.*). vDZ.

Nederl. Patriciaat IV (1913) 431-35; J. H. Warnaars, *Het Geslacht Warnaars* (Amsterdam, n.d.,—1920).

Warneke Chapel (MC), Pedro, Ohio, was established in 1952 under the Ohio Mennonite Mission Board. In 1958 it had 25 members. Chauncey Grieser was its pastor. M.G.

Warner Tute, a Dutch Anabaptist, baptized *c*1535 at Deventer by Hendrick Kistemecker (*q.v.*) of Zutphen, and beheaded at Kampen, is a typical example of early Dutch Anabaptist chiliasm, declaring that one Johan had told him "there would be an assembling [of the elect Anabaptists], at a place unknown to him [Warner] but provided by God, and then the trumpets from heaven would blow and at this moment everyone should be prepared." He obviously belonged to the revolutionary wing of Anabaptists. (*DB* 1875, 62 f.) vDZ.

Warns, a village in the southwest of the Dutch province of Friesland, the seat of a Mennonite congregation, of which—unlike most Dutch rural congregations—there is good information, at least since *c*1650. The congregation has a rather well preserved archives, containing cash books from 1652, which minutely mention the amounts paid out to the poor members of the church, a baptismal and disciplinary book from 1655, and a number of old documents. From these materials G. E. Frerichs (*q.v.*) published a short history of the congregation in *Doopsgezinde Bijdragen* of 1874, and H. Bakels (*q.v.*) published interesting particulars in a somewhat novelistic form in *Doopsgezinde Bijdragen* of 1900, 1901, 1902, and 1904, and later separately in *Het Volk van Menno* (Leiden, 1908).

Concerning the founding of the Warns congregation accounts are lacking. According to an old tradition it existed already in 1570, meetings then for safety's sake being held at night on a small island in the swamps about two miles north of the village. About 1600 there seems to have been a High German congregation whose members were scattered over the villages of Warns, Hemelum, and Bakhuizen. This congregation, however, had dissolved (or merged) by 1647. In this year there was at Warns only one congregation, belonging to the Waterlander (*q.v.*) branch, which had a simple meetinghouse, a former barn, standing alone in a field. It became too small for the growing congregation and in the winter was difficult to reach because of the high level of the water from the adjacent lakes, and so, with the consent of the magistrates, a new meetinghouse was built in the town in 1664-76. This was replaced by the present church, dedicated Nov. 18, 1877 (organ of 1896; front of the church renovated in 1950). A parsonage was built in 1826, replaced in 1932.

The baptized membership numbered 232 in 1654, about 210 in 1710, 90 in 1792, 108 in 1838, 147 in 1861, 149 in 1900, 106 in 1926, and 100 in 1958.

Until the 18th century the village of Warns did not subsist on farming, as it does for the most part now, but largely on navigation. Particularly among the Warns Mennonites of the 17th and 18th centuries there were many skippers and sailors, concerning many of whom the church records note that they drowned or died as far away as Sweden and Russia. This sociological structure of the congregation influenced church life in three points: (*a*) The seamen usually being absent from the end of February until October or November, baptism and communion services, preceded by church discipline, were not held shortly before Easter as was usual in Dutch Mennonite congregations, but in January or early February. (*b*) The number of widows and orphans in the 17th and 18th centuries was extremely large, and consequently high demands were made upon the funds of the deacons; in 1695, for example, about 50 members, one fourth of the total membership, received more or less of

their livelihood from the church, in 1709 even 95 of the 215 members. This financial support was given liberally. (*c*) Through the decline of navigation because of wars, particularly in 1665-85 and in the early 18th century, many towns on the former Zuiderzee (now IJssel Lake) lost their wealth; this, for example, was ruinous for the Mennonite congregations of Molkwerum (*q.v.*) and Hindeloopen (*q.v.*). Warns also declined; many who had been engaged in navigation moved elsewhere. This accounts for the rapid decrease of the membership in the 18th century.

The congregation of Warns formerly was rather conservative. Church discipline was strictly maintained. Plain dress was found until the early 19th century.

Though the finances of the church were continuously saddled with considerable amounts for the needs of its own members, the congregation contributed liberally to many needs, both Mennonite and non-Mennonite. In 1727 and 1733 offerings were taken for the needs of the Prussian Mennonites, in 1736 for the Swiss Brethren.

In former times the church was led by the deacons, usually seven, from whom were chosen the preachers and the elder. A striking practice of the 18th century was to call elders from outside to perform baptism and administer the Lord's Supper and to exercise the church discipline, obviously because an outsider had more authority than their own elder, who was related by ties of blood and often by financial dealings to many of the members. Until 1700 the ministers served without remuneration. When the elder Ruurd Dirks in this year was granted a "liberal gift" by members of the congregation, the aged preacher Auke Feltjers was greatly incensed by this innovation; the dissension was stilled when Ruurd Dirks gave his "gift" to the poor of the church. But gradually a salary for the ministers became usual. The last of the lay ministers were Jan Cornelisz (*q.v.*), elder at Warns 1716-50, noted for his eloquence, who received an annual salary of 150 Dutch guilders, Atse Wytses (van der Zijpp), serving 1750-1808, and Wolter Maakal (*q.v.*), serving 1810-16. After his resignation N. Pott, who also was a lay preacher, was called in from outside. He served 1816-25, followed by H. J. Smit 1825-30, Pieter Veen, who was the first pastor trained at the Amsterdam Mennonite seminary, serving here 1830-35, Douwe S. Gorter 1835-50, L. van Cleeff 1854-57, P. Brouwer 1857-63, G. E. Frerichs 1863-78, A. C. Leendertz 1879-82, A. H. ten Cate 1883-93, H. Bakels 1896-1901, J. D. van Calcar 1902-6, P. M. Heringa 1906-12, W. H. toe Water 1912-16, P. Ens 1916-41, W. Broer 1941-49, J. Nielsen 1953-57, and J. S. Postma 1957- .

In 1830-64 and 1953-57 the pastors of Warns also served at Staveren (*q.v.*). The small congregation of Hemelum (*q.v.*) merged with Warns *c*1700, Bakhuizen in 1799, Molkwerum (*q.v.*) in 1948. Until about 1915 and again since 1958 services have also been held in the neighboring village of Hemelum.

Church activities at present (1958) include two ladies' circles, a youth circle, ages 18-25, and a Sunday school for children. vDZ.

Blaupot t. C., *Friesland*, 168, 169, 185, 188, 248, 254, 306, 324, 325; *Naamlijst* 1829, 59; *DB* 1874, 85-114; 1900, 38-70; 1901, 57-126; 1902, 29-86; 1903, 81, 90 f.; 1904. 30-65; H. Bakels, *Het Volk van Menno* (Leiden, 1908).

Warns, Johannes (1874-1937), founder of the Wiedenest Baptist Bible School, was the son of a clergyman in East Friesland, Germany, studied Protestant theology in the universities of Greifswald, Halle, Berlin, and Bonn, but did not accept a pastorate, preferring to serve the Lord in his own way. He joined the Baptists and in 1905 founded in Berlin the Bible School for home and foreign missions, which was transferred to Wiedenest, Rhineland, in 1919. Warns made twenty-five extended journeys, visiting many countries. He was especially closely attached to English circles. But the Mennonites of Russia also received his warm interest. Many refugees found shelter for a longer or shorter time with him. Warns wrote the book, *Die Taufe. Gedanken über die urchristliche Taufe, ihre Geschichte und ihre Bedeutung für die Gegenwart* (Bad Homburg, 1913; second ed. Cassel, 1922). In 1920 he wrote the book, *Russland und das Evangelium;* in 1919, *Staatskirche? Volkskirche? Freikirche?* in 1909 he published the missionary magazine *Offene Türen;* in 1920 *Mitteilungen der Bibelschule;* in 1926, the evangelization paper *Der Wegweiser.* He died at Wiedenest, Jan. 27, 1937. He is the author of the article **Kindertaufe** in the *Mennonitisches Lexikon* II, 487-94, and also the article **Warendorf** in this ENCYCLOPEDIA. K.RA.

Dein Reich Komme (1937) 62-64; *Nach dem Gesetz und Zeugnis* (1935) 70.

Warren Street Mennonite Church (GCM), located in Middlebury, Ind., a member of the Central Conference, had its origin in 1923, when Simon S. Yoder, a minister, withdrew from the Indiana-Michigan Mennonite Conference (MC), taking about 100 members with him. The congregation remained independent of any conference affiliation until 1926, when it was received into the fellowship of the Central Conference of Mennonites. In 1957 the membership was 59, with Elmer A. Wall as minister. For a meetinghouse the congregation in 1923 bought from the town the former "opera house" and remodeled it. J.C.W.

Warte-Jahrbuch *für die Mennonitische Gemeinschaft in Canada* (2 issues, 1943 and 1944), edited and published by Arnold Dyck, Steinbach, Man., was the continuation, after a 5-year gap, of *Mennonitische Volkswarte* (*q.v.*), portraying the culture of the Mennonites of Prusso-German background in Canada. Historical articles and original fiction and poetry by Mennonite contributors appeared on its pages. Lack of support and small circulation forced it to discontinue. C.K.

Wartena, a Dutch family name, originally of Friesland. In its Mennonite branch the following were ministers: Abe Ruurds Wartena, a preacher of the Wieringen congregation 1807-d.9 (*DB* 1891, 53 f., 57), Sjoerd Wartena (Grouw, 1843-Lochem, 1917), educated at the Amsterdam seminary, served as pastor at Wolvega 1868-73, Rottevalle 1873-80, Bovenknijpe 1880-84, Workum 1884-86, and Hallum from

1886 until he retired in 1908. His son Sjoerd Dirk August Wartena (Wolvega, 1871-Doorwerth, 1953), educated at the university and the seminary at Amsterdam, served at Terschelling 1894-97, Veenwouden 1897-1902, Zutphen 1902-9, Heerenveen 1909-22, and Hallum from 1922 until he retired in 1936. He is the author of a paper on "Jan Thomas," *DB* 1896.

Johannes Aeschinus Wartena (b. 1869 at Grouw) was a pastor of the Midwolda-Beerta-Meeden congregation in 1891-1901, when he resigned. Sjoerd Wartena, a loyal member of the church, was a physician at Hindeloopen in 1839-89. Another Sjoerd Wartena, b. 1897 at Nijland, rector of the Gymnasium at Leeuwarden since 1931, was a member and moderator of the board of the Leeuwarden Mennonite congregation 1935-38. vDZ.

Wartenberg in the Palatinate, Germany. Until *c*1780 the present congregation of Sembach (*q.v.*) was sometimes—as in the Dutch *Naamlijst*—called either simply Wartenberg or Wartenberg-Sembach, since some of the elders and preachers lived at Wartenberg. vDZ.

Warwick, Va. Warwick County was incorporated as the City of Warwick in 1953, and in 1958 the city of Warwick and Newport News consolidated to become Newport News. The city of Warwick had a population of nearly 40,000 in 1956. It is located on the southwestern shore of the Virginia peninsula along the James River. Two Mennonite churches, the Warwick River (*q.v.*) Mennonite Church (MC) and the Providence (*q.v.*) Amish Mennonite Church (MC), with a total membership of 371, are located within its limits. The first Mennonite settlers came to this area in 1897. (See **Denbigh**.) C.N.K.

Warwick River Mennonite Church (MC), located on the Virginia peninsula 12 miles north of Newport News in the City of Warwick (*q.v.*) near Denbigh. In 1897 Isaac D. Hertzler of Long Green, Md., and David Z. Yoder of Smithville, Ohio, purchased a tract of 1,200 acres from the Young plantation, and five families moved into the area, purchasing plots from this original tract. The early settlers came from Michigan, Ohio, Rockingham County, Va., Tennessee, and Maryland. The community is predominantly rural.

The congregation, including both Mennonites and Amish, was organized in the spring of 1898 under the leadership of the original settlers, I. D. Hertzler (1852-1936), Jacob Hahn (1839-1926), and D. Z. Yoder (1849-1929), all of whom were ministers. In 1900 D. Z. Yoder withdrew with several Amish families and organized the Providence congregation (*q.v.*). Daniel Shenk (1853-1943) of Allen County, Ohio, was then ordained minister of the new congregation. George R. Brunk (1871-1938), who moved into the community from Kansas in 1910, was the first resident bishop. He was succeeded by his son Truman H. Brunk (b. 1902) in 1940. The other ministers in 1957 were George R. Brunk (b. 1911) and John H. Shenk (b. 1911). The membership in 1957 was 277. It has been affiliated with the Virginia Conference since 1904.

In 1899 a frame building 20 x 30 ft. was erected to serve as a schoolhouse and meetinghouse. In 1908 it was replaced by a larger building, which has been remodeled and enlarged to seat 350. A mission outpost was established in Newport News in 1928, which is now the Huntington Avenue (*q.v.*) Mennonite Church. In 1952 the Madison Avenue Chapel (*q.v.*) was organized as a mission among the Negroes of Newport News. In 1951 the Rock of Ages Broadcast, presently heard over stations in Richmond, Va., and Tangier, Africa, was organized as a congregational project. An elementary school was opened in 1942, and a four-room tile schoolhouse was built in 1949. The *Warwick River Tide,* a biweekly community paper, has been published since 1945 as an adjunct to the school. C.N.K.

The *Warwick River Tide,* Phebe Kraus and Eva Carper, editors, 1945- ; J. H. Yoder, *Fifty Years Building on the Warwick* (Denbigh, c1947).

Wasen, one of the larger villages in the Emmental, Switzerland, to which the Anabaptist movement found early entry. In the 16th century there was a considerable congregation there, which held its meetings in a lonely spot in the forest known as the Täuferloch (Anabaptist Hollow), back in the valley of the Kurzenri, between cliffs. Their leader, Hans Meister, a close friend of Hans Haslibacher (*q.v.*), for many years evaded his captors in a hiding place in his own house. He was buried in his house; for when the house was rebuilt in the 19th century his skeleton was found there. A mason, Peter Ritter, who made fun of the skull, was immediately stricken with violent pains and died soon after. (The *Zionspilger* of 1890, No. 18, p. 3, reprints an article on Wasen from the *Berner Tagblatt* of Sept. 1, 1890.) S.G.

Washington, a state in the northwest corner of the United States, with an estimated population of 2,600,000 and an area of 61,192 square miles. Its Puget Sound area is a great commercial center and the nearest American gateway to the ports of Asia. The state produces much wheat, fruit, and forest products. The first Mennonites to settle in Washington came to Whiteman County in 1886, from Pulaski, Iowa. In 1893 these early settlers organized what is now the Onecho Mennonite Church (*q.v.*). In 1900 a congregation, formerly from Freeman, S.D., moved to Adams County from Lane County, Ore., and is now the Menno Mennonite Church (*q.v.*). In 1918 the First Mennonite Church of Monroe (*q.v.*) was organized by settlers from Pretty Prairie, Kan., and Corn, Okla. The Newport Mennonite Church, known as Spring Valley (*q.v.*), was organized in 1928 by settlers who began coming to this area in 1922. In 1944 the Mennonite Country Church east of Monroe was organized, and in 1945 the Glendale Mennonite Church (*q.v.*) of Lynden. The latest congregation to be established was Warden. There are thus seven G.C.M. churches in the state. The one Mennonite Brethren church in Washington is the Whitehorn M.B. Church, near Blaine (*q.v.*), which was organized in 1937. Of the eight churches, one is in the northeast, one in the southeast, two in the east central, two near Seattle, and

two not far from Vancouver. Total membership in 1957 was 752—M.B. 187, G.C.M. 565. W.W.W.

H. D. Burkholder, *The Story of Our Conference and Churches* (North Newton, 1951).

Washington County, Iowa, in the southeastern part of the state, has Mennonite settlements in two areas, i.e., in the northern and the southern tiers of townships. The Johnson County (*q.v.*) settlement to the north has spread south into the northern Washington County townships of Lime Creek, English River, and Iowa. In Lime Creek are Wellman (*q.v.*) and Daytonville, each with a Mennonite church. Kalona (*q.v.*) is in English River and the location of the Kalona Mennonite Church and the Pleasant View Home for the Aged (*q.v.*). A short distance east of Kalona is the Sunnyside Conservative Mennonite Church (*q.v.*). The Old Order Amish settlement of Johnson County has also expanded into the northern part of Washington County. Near the center of the county is the county seat of Washington, in which a number of Mennonite families reside. The Mennonites in Marion Township in the southern tier of counties are a part of the Henry County (*q.v.*) settlement bordering Washington County on the south. In Marion Township are the Bethel Mennonite Church (*q.v.*) and the Eicher Emanuel Mennonite Church (*q.v.*). In 1958 Mennonites began to hold services in the Eureka church in Marion Township. The Eicher church is a G.C.M. congregation, while the others in the country are M.C. and C.M. The total Mennonite and Amish membership living in the county is c600. (See map of Johnson County, Vol. III, 116.) M.G.

Washington County, Md., is the third county from the western end of the state. The Mennonite community is located in the vicinity of Hagerstown, the county seat, where Mennonites had settled as early as 1776. They now number about 850, all members of the Mennonite Church (MC). This includes those who are members of the Washington Co., Md., and Franklin Co., Pa., Conference, together with a small group who have united with the Ohio and Eastern Conference. Most are descendants of settlers from Lancaster County, Pa.; there are also some converts resulting from missionary efforts. There are six churches in the district, three mission projects in the county, and one at Flintstone in Allegany County, Md.; the Old People's Home is located at Maugansville. M.K.H.

Washington County Mennonite Mutual Association of Wayland, Iowa, is a subsidiary of the Mennonite Aid Plan (*q.v.*) of Freeman, S.D., organized in 1950 to comply with the insurance laws of Iowa. Reinsurance is carried with the Freeman parent organization. It serves all Mennonites of Washington County and bordering counties with mutual fire and storm insurance. In 1953 it had 130 members, with a property coverage of $1,580,000. H.S.B.

Washington County (Maryland) **and Franklin County** (Pennsylvania) **Mennonite Conference** (MC). The earliest reference to this conference is found in the November 1864 issue of the *Herald of Truth,*

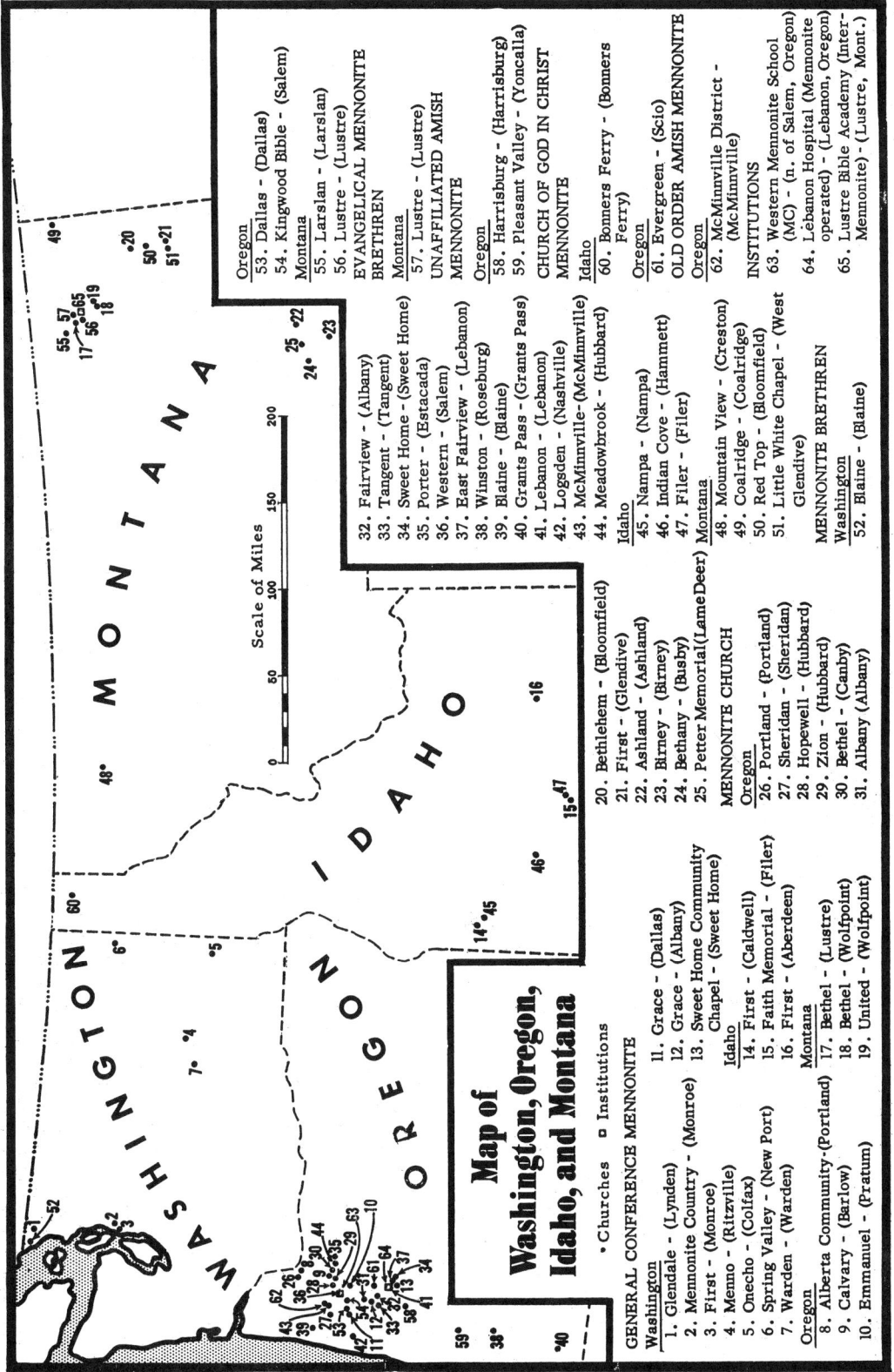

Map of Washington, Oregon, Idaho, and Montana

• Churches □ Institutions

GENERAL CONFERENCE MENNONITE

Washington
1. Glendale - (Lynden)
2. Mennonite Country - (Monroe)
3. First - (Monroe)
4. Menno - (Ritzville)
5. Onecho - (Colfax)
6. Spring Valley - (New Port)
7. Warden - (Warden)

Oregon
8. Alberta Community - (Portland)
9. Calvary - (Barlow)
10. Emmanuel - (Pratum)

11. Grace - (Dallas)
12. Grace - (Albany)
13. Sweet Home Community Chapel - (Sweet Home)

Idaho
14. First - (Caldwell)
15. Faith Memorial - (Filer)
16. First - (Aberdeen)

Montana
17. Bethel - (Lustre)
18. Bethel - (Wolfpoint)
19. United - (Wolfpoint)

20. Bethlehem - (Bloomfield)
21. First - (Glendive)
22. Ashland - (Ashland)
23. Birney - (Birney)
24. Bethany - (Busby)
25. Petter Memorial(LameDeer)

MENNONITE CHURCH

Oregon
26. Portland - (Portland)
27. Sheridan - (Sheridan)
28. Hopewell - (Hubbard)
29. Zion - (Hubbard)
30. Bethel - (Canby)
31. Albany (Albany)

32. Fairview - (Albany)
33. Tangent - (Tangent)
34. Sweet Home - (Sweet Home)
35. Porter - (Estacada)
36. Western - (Salem)
37. East Fairview - (Lebanon)
38. Winston - (Roseburg)
39. Blaine - (Blaine)
40. Grants Pass - (Grants Pass)
41. Lebanon - (Lebanon)
42. Logsden - (Nashville)
43. McMinnville- (McMinnville)
44. Meadowbrook - (Hubbard)

Idaho
45. Nampa - (Nampa)
46. Indian Cove - (Hammett)
47. Filer - (Filer)

Montana
48. Mountain View - (Creston)
49. Coalridge - (Coalridge)
50. Red Top - (Bloomfield)
51. Little White Chapel - (West Glendive)

MENNONITE BRETHREN

Washington
52. Blaine - (Blaine)

Oregon
53. Dallas - (Dallas)
54. Kingwood Bible - (Salem)

Montana
55. Larslan - (Larslan)
56. Lustre - (Lustre)

EVANGELICAL MENNONITE BRETHREN

Montana
57. Lustre - (Lustre)

UNAFFILIATED AMISH MENNONITE

Oregon
58. Harrisburg - (Harrisburg)
59. Pleasant Valley - (Yoncalla)

CHURCH OF GOD IN CHRIST MENNONITE

Idaho
60. Bonners Ferry - (Bonners Ferry)

Oregon
61. Evergreen - (Scio)

OLD ORDER AMISH MENNONITE

Oregon
62. McMinnville District - (McMinnville)

INSTITUTIONS

63. Western Mennonite School (MC) - (n. of Salem, Oregon)
64. Lebanon Hospital (Mennonite operated) - (Lebanon, Oregon)
65. Lustre Bible Academy (Inter-Mennonite) - (Lustre, Mont.)

WASHINGTON

MONTANA

IDAHO

OREGON

Scale of Miles

0   50   100   150   200

where it is called semiannual; however, only annual sessions are known to have been held.

By earliest reports the moderator of Lancaster Conference served here also, and the Lancaster discipline and actions were used without change until 1915. However, beginning in 1912 additional actions were passed by the Washington County, Md., and Franklin County, Pa., Conference. Separate rules and discipline were adopted in 1922, revised in 1930 and 1957. About 1909, 9 congregations and 732 members were reported. Its congregations are all located in the two counties included in its name. Mission outposts are also conducted in Allegany County, Md., and Fulton County, Pa.

The Conference operates nine mission stations and through its District Mission Board the Maugansville Home for the Aged. Its Brotherly Aid Plan is very simply organized but functions efficiently in case of loss by fire or storm.

The Confession of Dordrecht of 1632 and the Doctrinal Statement of the Mennonite General Conference (MC) have been accepted as the basic doctrinal statements. In practice it is among the most conservative of the Mennonite conferences, with most of the men wearing the "plain" coat, and women the "cape" dress. The woman's veiling is worn at all times. Life insurance, lodge membership, attendance at farm shows, and possession of television are not allowed. A strong home life without radio is encouraged.

This conference belongs to the group related to the Mennonite (MC) General Conference, but has never been organizationally connected with it, though it supports many of its projects, and proportionately has contributed largely to the medical, teaching, missionary, and preaching personnel of the church. Since the adoption of the English language at the turn of the century and the use of more aggressive methods the conference has grown. Today (1959) there are 14 congregations, 9 mission congregations, 4 resident bishops, 20 ministers, and 1,645 members.　　　　　　　　　　J.I.L.

Washington, D.C., capital of the United States, 1950 pop. 802,178, located in and identical in territory with the small federal district known as the District of Columbia with 69 sq. mi., although the metropolitan area extends into the neighboring states of Maryland and Virginia on both sides of the Potomac. The area is the home of two small Mennonite congregations. The one inside the city limits is Woodridge Mennonite Church (MC) with 40 members belonging to the Allegheny Conference, founded in 1945, and the other just outside, in Maryland, is the Cottage City Mennonite Church with 36 members founded in 1922, belonging to the Lancaster Conference. It has also been the location of the office of the National Service Board for Religious Objectors (q.v.) since its creation in 1940.　　H.S.B.

Washita Arapaho Mennonite (GCM) Mission Station, Okla., located 5 miles west and 2 south of Corn (q.v.) on the Washita River, was started among Arapaho Indians in July 1889 by J. J. Kliewer. Washita was originally called Shelly. When a large Mennonite settlement originated in this area the Indians gradually moved away. J. J. Kliewer became a minister of the Bergthal Mennonite Church which arose here, and the General Conference Mission Board discontinued this station around 1900.
　　　　　　　　　　　　　　　　　C.K.

Marvin Kroeker, "Mennonites in the Oklahoma 'Runs,' " *Menn. Life* X (July 1955) 115; H. P. Krehbiel, *The History of the General Conference* (Canton, 1898) I, 3, 10; II, 14.

Washita County, located in the southwestern part of Oklahoma, is bisected by the Washita River. There are about 1,300 Mennonites living in the northeast section of Washita County, and a few families in adjacent Custer County. Of these about 900 are Mennonite Brethren and about 400 General Conference Mennonites. Washita County, a part of the Arapaho-Cheyenne Reservation, was opened to settlement in 1892. The first Mennonite settlers came in the latter part of 1892, filing for land with the intention of moving here the following year. In the spring of 1893 the first families moved into the county from Kansas. There are four Mennonite churches in the county, two each of M.B. and G.C.M. A number of Mennonite Brethren families and a few Mennonites started the Calvary Baptist Church a few years ago. The M.B. Church has a four-year accredited academy, located in Corn (q.v.), which draws students from all over Oklahoma and beyond.　　　　　　　　　　H.H.

Washita Gemeinschule: see Corn Bible Academy.

Wassenberger Prädikanten, the intellectual leaders of the district of Wassenberg in the duchy of Jülich 1528-32, under the protection of the bailiff (*Drost*) Werner von Pallant (q.v.), who zealously worked for the Reformation. They did not have a unified system of thought, but were quite independent of each other. The unifying factor was their antipathy to the Catholic Church. Most of them rejected infant baptism and were in many respects akin to Anabaptism. When Werner von Pallant was threatened with loss of his position—the threat became fact in 1533—most of them betook themselves to Münster, where they joined the Anabaptists and found an early death. Rembert, who gives the most detailed and reliable account of them (*Wiedertäufer*, 149 f.), describes them as follows: "Prädikanten was what they called those 'heretical' preachers who streamed together there [at Wassenberg], Joh. Campanus, Klopreis, Dionysius Vinne, Slachtscaep, Roll, and others. They preached busily in the neighborhood and won a considerable following, especially in Dremmen, Hückelhofen, Breeberen, also in Süstern and Höngen. . . . Since the preachers concentrated their work in northwestern Jülich, but especially in Wassenberg as their center, they were commonly called 'the Wassenberger Prädikanten.' For more than three years most of them could continue their work undisturbed before the government took action against them. During this time significant and dubious changes took place in the theology of these men." (See **Henric Rol, Johannes Campanus, Johann Klopreis, Hendrik Slachtscaep, Dionysius Vinne.**) (Rembert, *Wiedertäufer*; ML IV.)
　　　　　　　　　　　　　　　　HEGE, H.S.B.

Watchful Pilgrim, a "Religious Monthly Journal Devoted to the Interest of the Mennonite Church, the Exposition of Gospel Truth, and the Promotion of Practical Piety among all classes," published by Abraham Blosser (MC) at Dale Enterprise, Va., first issue August 1881, as a 24-page 8½ x 11½ in. paper. At least by September 1884 it was appearing as an 8-page semimonthly. GCL has scattered numbers, the last being March 1, 1888. An interesting feature of the last years was the "Meeting Calendar" for the Virginia Mennonite congregations.   H.S.B.

Water, Adrianus Pieter van de (1896-1951), a Mennonite minister, serving the congregations of Leermens-Loppersum 1925-27 (1927-35 pastor of the Dutch Protestant Union at Baarn and active with the International School of Philosophy at Amersfoort), Oldeboorn 1935-39, Zwolle 1939-42, Apeldoorn 1942-45, Hallum 1945-48, and St. Anna-Parochie 1948-50, was appointed in June 1950 by the trustees of the A.D.S. (*q.v.*) as a minister at large among the Dutch Mennonites, particularly to build up the work of "special needs" (see **Stichting voor Bizondere Noden**). He could devote his great intelligence and organizational ability to this work for only one year, dying on June 7, 1951. Van de Water also was a promoter of the children's home Oud Wulven (*q.v.*) at Houten (since 1958 at Schoorl), was active in the care of Jewish refugees from Germany in the Nazi period shortly before World War II and of the displaced persons from Eastern Europe after the war. He published two papers in *Doopsgezind Jaarboekje:* "Het Protestantsch - Joodsche Vluchtelingenwerk" (1940) and "Moeilijkheden en mogelijkheden voor de financiën in onze Broederschap" (1950). His address given at the fifth Mennonite World Conference is found in the Proceedings of this conference (Akron, 1950). (*Algemeen Doopsgez. Weekblad* of June 16, 1951; *DJ* 1952, 13 f.)
                                                          vɒZ.

Water, W. H. toe: see **Toe Water.**

Watergang, a hamlet in the Dutch province of North Holland, where Elder Leenaert (*q.v.*) Bouwens baptized 14 persons in 1563-65; they may have joined or founded a congregation in the neighborhood such as Uitgeest (*q.v.*), for there was never a congregation at Watergang.   vɒZ.

Waterhorne. Menno Simons wrote a letter *c*1558 to the brethren in the Waterhorne; this probably means Terhorne (*q.v.*) in the Dutch province of Friesland. The letter is found in *Opera Omnia*, 399, *Writings*, 1055.   vɒZ.

Waterland is called a district in the Dutch province of North Holland, approximately bounded by the Zaan River on the south and the west, by the Zuiderzee (now IJssel Lake) on the east, and on the north by the former lakes south of the line Alkmaar-Hoorn. In this territory as early as 1534 there were numerous Anabaptists, and after *c*1555 because of their progressiveness "Waterlander" became the name of a branch of the Dutch Mennonites. (See **Waterlanders.**)   vɒZ.

Waterlanders, a branch of the Dutch Mennonites, deriving their name from Waterland, a region in the province of North Holland.

After most of the Mennonite elders, e.g., Dirk Philipsz, Menno Simons, and particularly Leenaert (*q.v.*) Bouwens, in 1555-57 proceeded to a more strict practice concerning the ban (*q.v.*) and avoidance (*q.v.;* see also **Swaen Rutgers**), some less strict Mennonites protested, and a conference of South German Anabaptists held at Strasbourg in 1557 condemned this rigorism and turned from Menno and his coelders. Before this some groups of moderates at Emden, Franeker, in Waterland, and elsewhere, had separated from the main body. Fortunately this controversy, unlike the later schisms among the Dutch Mennonites, did not include the ban of the separated, but for two centuries or more the more liberal took their own course. By Leenaert Bouwens and his adherents they were called "Scheedemakers" (after Elder Jacob—*q.v.*—Jans Scheedemaker; the word "scheedemaker," however, also has the derogatory meaning of schismatic), or "De Drekwagen" (*q.v.,* garbage wagon). At first they are found under different names like Franekers, or Franekeraars (after the town of Franeker, *q.v.,* where they had many followers), Joriaen-Heynsvolk, or Naeldemansvolk (*q.v.*), but soon they were generally known as Waterlanders.

Among the Dutch Mennonites until *c*1665 they were the least strict and most progressive and liberal branch. From the very beginning they were not as averse to contacts with "the world" as the strict Mennonites. Intermarriage with non-Mennonites, though denounced in the conference meetings as "evil and impure," was practiced and tolerated. They soon permitted their members to hold some lower magisterial offices. Though the principle of nonresistance was emphatically taught, two Waterlander brethren (see **Bogaert, P. W.**) in 1568 visited the Prince of Orange in his army camp to offer him a considerable sum of money which they had collected in their congregations to enable him to fight the Spaniards then dominating the Netherlands, and from *c*1630 church discipline slackened against members who served on armed ships. They did not use the name "Mennisten," thinking it inappropriate to be named for a man, preferring to be called "Doopsgezinden" (*q.v.*). They rejected the doctrine of the Incarnation (*q.v.*) as taught by Menno Simons and Dirk Philipsz and by *c*1620 they are said not to have rebaptized members of the Reformed Church (who had been baptized in infancy) who joined a Waterlander congregation. They admitted to the Lord's table members of other Mennonite branches and even of other churches, and were on friendly terms with kindred spirits like Coornhert (*q.v.*). Yet they were not the garbage wagon as Leenaert Bouwens had decried them: they decidedly refused to accept the Socinian (*q.v.*) teachings of the Polish Brethren Ostorodt (*q.v.*) and Voydovsky shortly after 1600, and their Prussian congregations firmly resisted Socinian infiltration (see **Moscorovius**). They were not so liberal as to enter into a union with some English nonconformists who taught believers' baptism and who wanted to merge with them; the fact that these English "Anabaptists" had no objections to swearing an oath prevented the union (see **Coventry**, and **Tookey, Elias**).

At first the local church among the Waterlanders had great authority and was entitled to choose its own ministers, "leeraers tot den vollen dienst" (elders) and "vermaners" (preachers) as well as "armendienaers" (deacons), but by 1581 it was usual for the elders and often the preachers to be appointed by the leaders, i.e., by Hans de Ries (*q.v.*), who was a powerful leader of the Waterlanders from 1577 until his death in 1638. By his authority the Waterlanders, unlike all other Mennonite branches, held their communion services seated around a table. De Ries also introduced the singing of Psalms, and undoubtedly it was also due to him that after *c*1580 silent prayer was gradually replaced by a prayer spoken by the minister, though silent prayer was still found in a few Waterlander churches as late as 1660.

It is hard to imagine that these individualistic, partly spiritualistic Waterlanders wanted a common confession; yet the Waterlanders were the first Dutch Mennonites to have a confession of faith. It was drawn up in 1577 by Scheedemaker and a few other ministers, including de Ries, and contains 25 articles (it was reprinted in *DB* 1904).

The Waterlanders were also the first to hold a kind of more or less regular conference meeting, the first of which was held at Emden, East Friesland, in September 1568 (the interesting minutes are published in *DB* 1877, 69-75). A following delegates' meeting was held March 4-7, 1581, at Amsterdam (minutes in *DB* 1877, 80-87). Twelve congregations were represented—Gent and Antwerp in Belgium, Amsterdam, Rotterdam, Purmerend, Zaandam, Jisp, Schermerhorn, Graft, De Rijp, Westzaan, and Wormer. As in 1568, a number of practical church matters were regulated, "not as new laws, but as good advice," as the final clause states.

Apart from de Ries outstanding leaders were the elder Scheedemaker, Lubbert Gerritsz (*q.v.*) at Amsterdam and Jan Gerritz (*q.v.*) van Emden at Danzig.

After the High German and (Mild) Frisian Mennonites had merged shortly after 1591 on the basis of the Concept (*q.v.*) of Cologne, a number of Waterlander congregations joined this union *c*1600, henceforth called "Bevredigde Broederschap" (*q.v.*). But since the Waterlanders in this union proved to be more liberal in church matters than particularly the High Germans, a number of High Germans and some Frisians withdrew from the Bevredigde Broederschap in 1613 (see **Afgedeelden**). Some Bevredigden thereupon were absorbed by the Waterlanders.

The Waterlanders were very active in collecting accounts of martyrs; shortly after 1600 they even sent a brother to Germany, Austria, and Moravia, to make inquiries; de Ries in 1615 published a new martyr book, entitled *Historie der Martelaren . . .* with a Preface which is typically Waterlander.

Though exact figures of the number of their congregations and membership are not available, the Waterlanders in the early 17th century had a considerable following. In Friesland the number of their brethren in 1666 was 882, somewhat more than one sixth of all the Mennonites. In North Holland,

where they had their own conferece (see **Rijper Societeit**), the Waterlanders *c*1650 outnumbered all other branches; in Amsterdam the baptized membership in 1615 numbered more than 1,000. At a conference held in September 1647 at Amsterdam 58 delegates were present, representing 41 churches, 22 of them from towns in the present province of North Holland, 6 from South Holland, 10 from Friesland, 2 from Groningen, and Emden in East Friesland. At this meeting it was resolved "to offer peace" to (i.e., to propose a merger with) the united Flemish, High German, and Frisian group.

It is noteworthy that the Waterlanders, who, unlike the strict groups, did not consider their own church as the (only) true Mennonite church, which, as is pointed out by de Ries in the preface to the martyr book, fervently hoped for and ardently acted in behalf of a general union of all Mennonites, were not involved in several endeavors "to make peace"; the forementioned request of 1647 to the Flemish was dropped. Obviously the other branches did not appreciate the liberal views of the Waterlanders. A meeting of Flemish delegates at Leiden in 1660 (see **Leidsche Synode**) emphatically disapproved their lax church discipline, their marriage with non-Mennonites, their acceptance of Reformed and even unbaptized persons in their communion services, and their neglect of proper ordination for the ministers, not clearly distinguishing between the offices of elder and preacher. Moreover they were censured for their friendly interest in the Collegiants (*q.v.*).

It was not until the Lammerenkrijgh (*q.v.*) had in 1664 regrouped the Dutch Mennonites into two new branches—the progressive Lamists (*q.v.*) and the conservative Zonists (*q.v.*)—that in many towns the Waterlanders merged with the Lamists—at Amsterdam in 1668, at Haarlem in 1672, at Rotterdam in 1700, and at Leiden in 1701. But on the other hand a number of rural Waterlander churches in North Holland joined the Zonist conference (Societeit) in 1674. This was due to the influence of some of their elders like E. A. van Dooregeest (*q.v.*), P. J. Stapper (*q.v.*), D. S. Moeriaen(s), and Jan Maertensz Mol, who strongly emphasized maintaining the confession of faith drawn up in 1610 by Ries and Lubbert Gerritsz, and who rejected the "unlimited toleration" of the Collegiants. As a consequence of this influence some Waterlander churches like De Rijp, Oostzaandam, Westzaan, and others resolved to maintain the confession, to admit to communion services only those who were baptized upon the confession of faith, and to refuse the pulpit to those ministers who worshiped with the Collegiants at Rijnsburg (*q.v.*). This meant the dissolving of the Waterlander branch, their churches partly merging with the Lamists, partly with the Zonists. The (Waterlander) Rijper Conference however continued its activities, and many of the congregations retained the name of Waterlander until the 19th century.   vDZ.

Inv. Arch. Amst. I, Nos. 465, 471-76, 478-91, 507, 510-14, 517, 524, 526-33, 537 f., 540-43, 546-54, 556, 575, 579, 774, 776 f., 890-96, 899-911; II, No. 2626; *DB* 1872, 55, 57-59, 67 f.; 1876, 21-25; 1877, 66-93; 1892, 99-101; 1894, 34; 1897, 91 f., 97-105, 109 f., 113, 119; 1898, 55; 1903, 57-77, 80-85; 1904, 138-59; Blaupot t. C., *Friesland*, 163 *et passim*; Kühler, *Geschiedenis* I, *passim*; II, *passim*; III, 9, 17-20, 44.

Waterlandsche Sociëteit (Conference) **in Noordholland**: see **Rijper Sociëteit.**

Waterlandsche Sociëteit (Conference) **in Zuidholland**: see **Zuidhollandsche Sociëteit.**

Waterloo, a city (pop. 14,000) located in the southern part of Ontario, has two Mennonite churches, the Erb Street Mennonite Church (MC) founded in 1851, with 276 members in 1957, and the United Mennonite Church (GCM) whose members are mostly immigrants from Russia, founded in 1925, with 407 members in 1957. Waterloo and Kitchener (*q.v.*) are built together, hence are often called the "Twin Cities." Together they constitute an urban community of more than 60,000 (1958). There are numerous Mennonite congregations around Waterloo. (See **Waterloo County.**)   J.B.M.

Waterloo County, Ont., Mennonite settlement began in Waterloo County in the spring of 1800 when Joseph Schoerg and Samuel Betzner, with their families, arrived on the banks of the Grand River in what was then Upper Canada, from Franklin County, Pa. They were the first white settlers in this county. The settlement grew steadily until by 1828 there were 1,000 Mennonite members and 2,000 hearers. The land was taken from the Beasley Tract, this being 94,012 acres of Six Nations Indians' lands in the Grand River Basin purchased from them by one Richard Beasley through the government of Upper Canada which acted as trustee. In November 1803 an agreement was signed between the German Company on the one hand, representing the Mennonites, and Beasley, on the other hand, for the purchase of 60,000 acres of his land for the sum of 10,000 pounds. On this land there was a mortgage of $20,000. Precisely when this fact was discovered is a matter of some doubt. Suffice it to say that Joseph Sherk and Samuel Bricker went to Pennsylvania to procure this money. In April 1803 a joint stock company was organized in the home of "Hannes" Eby in Lancaster County to raise the mortgage

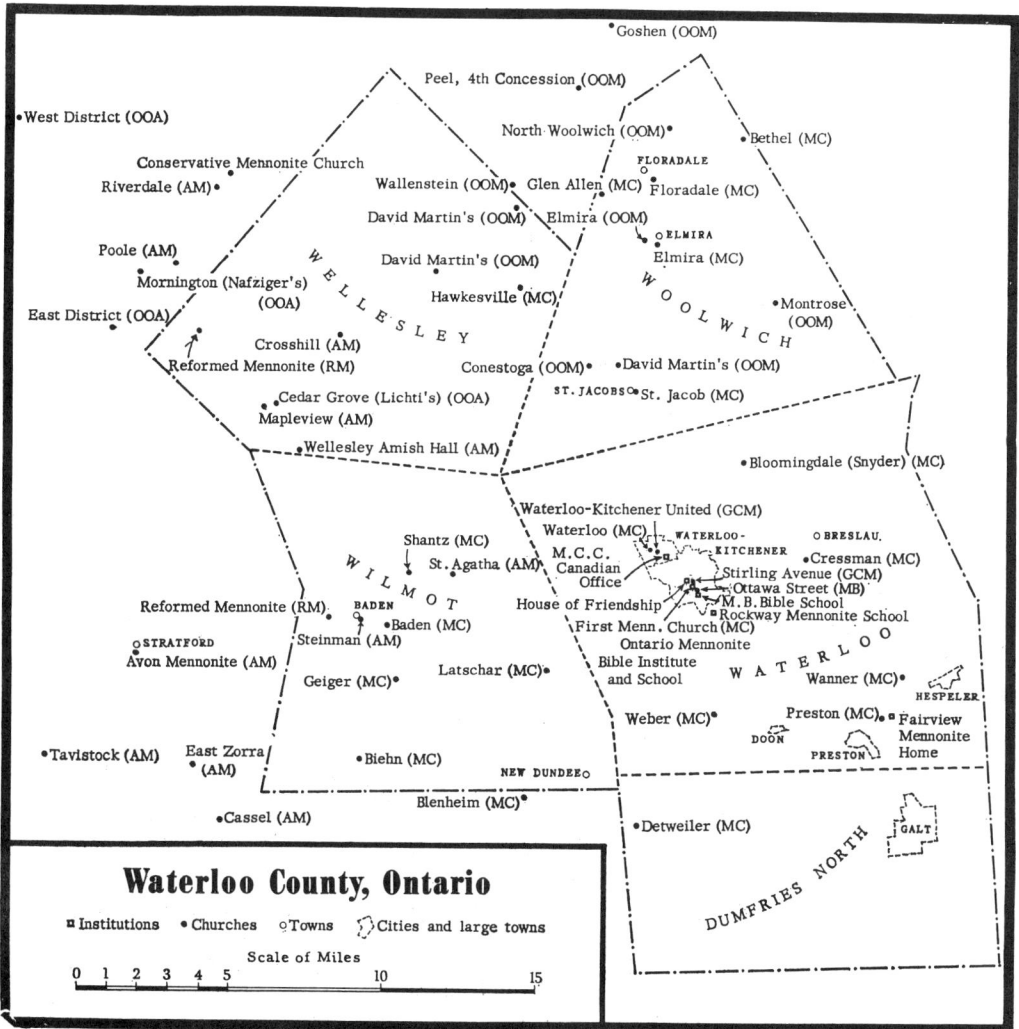

Waterloo County, Ontario

◻ Institutions   • Churches   ○ Towns   ⬙ Cities and large towns

Scale of Miles

0 1 2 3 4 5   10   15

money. This was done within two years, for on June 29, 1805, the deed for the 60,000 acres was executed in the Registry at Berlin, Ont. Mutual faith and co-operation motivated this transaction. Most likely it was "Hannes" Eby who persuaded his brethren in Lancaster to aid their brethren in Waterloo. Most of the early settlers came from Lancaster County, Pa., and some from the Franconia area—Bucks, Montgomery, and (a few) Franklin counties. In 1957 there were 18 active M.C. congregations in the county with a membership of 2,899. Dates given are those of the erection of church buildings, as closely as can be determined, although in many cases services were held in homes prior to the building of a church. Names of congregations are listed as in the *Mennonite Yearbook*, being both family and place names. The former are the survival of the pioneer custom of naming a church after the family from whose land the property was secured, either by purchase or donation. These congregations are First Mennonite, 1813; Snyder (Bloomingdale), 1826; Wanner (Hespeler), 1829; Detweiler (Roseville), 1830; Geiger (New Hamburg), 1831; Cressman (Breslau), 1834; Latschar (Mannheim), 1839; Blenheim (New Dundee), 1839; Weber (Strasburg), 1840; Shantz (Baden), 1840; Hagey, now called Preston, 1842; St. Jacobs, 1844; Waterloo (David Eby), 1851; Biehn (New Hamburg), 1865; Floradale, 1896; Baden, 1913; Elmira, 1924; Hawkesville, 1950. With the exception of Kitchener, which is 70 per cent urban and 30 per cent rural, and Waterloo, which is 50 per cent of each, these are all rural congregations. Each of these churches, except Hawkesville, has its own cemetery. Following are some of the most typical family names in these congregations, although many of these have disappeared from the rolls of active memberships: Betzner, Schoerg (Sherk), Reichert, Gingerich, Bechtel, Kinsey, Rosenberger, Biehn, Clemens, Bear, Sararas, Shupe, Livergood, Wismer, Ringler, Correll, Saltzberger, Bricker, Erb, Groh, Stauffer, Kraft, Hammacher, Bergey, Scheirich (Shiry), Bauman, Eby, Schneider, Cress, Brech, Bliehm, Shantz, Rotharmel, Strohm, Cressman, Bretz, Brubacher, Weber, Eckert, Pannebecker, Eschelman, Springer, Herner, Bock, Bowman, Martin, Burkholder, Good, Burkhard, Musselman, Shoemaker, Detweiler, Hallman, Huber, Lichty, Schlichter, Wanner, Hagey, Risser, Clemmer, Groff, Shuh, Wenger, Hurst, Hoffman, Moyer, Bingeman, Fried, Kolb, Gehman, Schiedel.

Three schisms resulted in the formation of other Mennonite groups. The first was that of the Mennonite Brethren in Christ (*q.v.*) in the early 1870's. This was a division on the progressive side, the points at issue being mainly the conducting of prayer and revival meetings and Sunday schools. In 1953 this group had 5 congregations in the county with a total of 666 members. In 1948 they changed their name to United Missionary Church (*q.v.*), thus abandoning entirely the name Mennonite. In the late 1880's occurred the second division, this time on the conservative side, when the Old Order (Wisler) Mennonites seceded. They are now subdivided into three groups, namely, the original Old Order, the Waterloo-Markham conference,

and the David Martin group. The difference in these factions concerns the ownership and use of modern inventions, together with some points of attire. No points of faith are involved since all adhere to the Dordrecht Confession (*q.v.*) of 1632. Of these three factions the first has five congregations with a total of 1,061 members, the second five congregations and 630 members, and the third three congregations with 116 members, a total of 1,807. None of these factions hold revival meetings. Instead a public invitation is given each year from their pulpits. Those accepting the invitation are then instructed in the Dordrecht Confession and in their own group discipline. The third division occurred in the First Mennonite Church (*q.v.*) of Kitchener in 1924 and resulted in the formation of the Stirling Avenue (*q.v.*) G.C.M. Church, which in 1957 had 476 members.

The remaining Mennonite groups in the county are the Amish Mennonites, Reformed Mennonites, and the "Russian" Mennonites. The Amish Mennonite settlement is located in Wilmot Township. It was begun in 1824 by Christian Nafziger (*q.v.*), who came from Bavaria to America and arranged with Governor Maitland of Upper Canada for the purchase of lands in this township. In 1826 the Ropp family emigrated from Alsace and settled in Wilmot Township. Thus the Amish Mennonites are of both Bavarian and Alsatian origin. Reasons for emigration were desire for new land and exemption from military service. Typical family names among them are Nafziger, Steinman, Bender, Ropp, Lichty, Jantzi, Schwarzendruber, Roth, Jutzi, Mayer, Schultz, Wagler, Gascho, Miller, and Brenneman. In 1957 there were five congregations of this group in Waterloo County and five just outside in Perth and Oxford, all those in Waterloo County being in the Ontario A.M. Conference. The total membership in the county is 1,103. The main difference between them and the M.C. group is in social customs. In addition to this main group of Amish Mennonites there is a small congregation of Old Order Amish (*q.v.*) in the county with 140 members. They worship only in private homes. In 1956 a schismatic group at Milverton under Valentine Nafziger withdrew from the Ontario A.M. conference.

The Reformed Mennonites are a small, closely knit group with two meetinghouses (Hostetters near New Hamburg, 1844, and Kingwood near Wellesley, 1850) and 77 members in the county.

Two Mennonite churches were formed in Waterloo County by emigrants from Russia (*q.v.*) in 1922-25, the United Mennonite (GCM) with 407 members, in the city of Waterloo, and the Mennonite Brethren, with 405 members, in Kitchener. In both, services are still conducted in German. The other emigration from Russia, that of the 1870's, left no churches in Waterloo County, but Jacob Y. Shantz (*q.v.*), then a leading member of the Mennonite Brethren in Christ, was the guiding spirit in settling these people in the Red River Valley in Manitoba, and the whole movement received solid financial support from the Mennonites of Waterloo County.

The Mennonites have the following institutions in

Waterloo County: Rockway Mennonite School (MC, 1945) and Golden Rule Bookstore (MC, 1938), both in Kitchener, Fairview Mennonite Home (MC, 1943, 1956) in Preston, and the Mennonite Brethren Bible School in Kitchener. The MCC Canadian headquarters office has been in Waterloo since 1948 (1944-48 in Kitchener). The United Missionary Church established Emmanuel Bible College here in 1940.

The Mennonites of Waterloo County are chiefly an agricultural people. There is, however, no communal organization to aid in the purchase of land. Most Mennonites who come to the cities of Kitchener and Waterloo are industrial workers. The percentage of business and professional people is small. The Mennonites (MC) have a fire insurance organization called the Mennonite Aid Union (q.v.), founded in 1867. Rates are low and membership is limited to adherents of this branch of Mennonites and their families. Waterloo County was the first Mennonite community of any real size in Canada, and contains more Mennonites than any other county in the Dominion, 7,836 members (not counting the UMC), and has had and continues to exert a marked influence on Mennonite religious and cultural life.   J.B.C.

L. J. Burkholder, *A Brief History of the Mennonites in Ontario* (n.p., 1935); Ezra E. Eby, *A Biographical History of Waterloo Township and Other Townships of the County, Being a History of the Early Settlers and Their Descendants Mostly all of Pennsylvania Dutch Origin, and also Other Unpublished Historical Information Chiefly of a Local Character*, 2 vv. (Berlin, Ont., 1895-96); G. Elmore Reaman, *The Trail of the Black Walnut* (n.p., 1957); *Waterloo Historical Society Annual Report*, 1912.

Waterloo (Ont.) Mennonite Church (MC): see **Erb Street** Mennonite Church.

Waterloo-Kitchener United Mennonite Church (GCM), 15 George St., Waterloo, Ont., a member of the Canadian District Conference, was organized in 1925 under the name "Die mennonitische Flüchtlingsgemeinde in Ontario." In 1926 this name was changed to Waterloo-Kitchener Mennonite Church, and the word "United" was placed before Mennonite in 1927. The 52 charter members had come to Canada from Russia in 1924. Because of the influx of immigrants the membership rose to 302 within six months. The leadership was entrusted to J. H. Janzen. At first the congregation met in a rented hall. In 1927 a church building was rented, which was purchased in 1932, constructed in 1888 of stone and brick. An addition of similar building material was made to the church in 1952, doubling its size and providing seating accommodation for 375. Since World War II many Mennonite immigrants who came to Waterloo have joined the fellowship of this group.

This congregation was the first one to be organized in Ontario by the immigrants of 1924. From here the groups at Essex, Vineland, Port Rowan, and Virgil have originated. The first missionary to be sent to the foreign field by the Ontario G.C.M. churches came from this congregation, viz., Rudolph Martens and his wife Dr. Elvina Martens. The congregation is predominantly urban. In 1957 the minister was Henry H. Epp, and the membership was 407.   H.P.E.

Waterloo-Markham Conference of Old Order Mennonites was formed in 1939 by the more progressive faction of the O.O.M. in the Wisler communities of Ontario. They use the same meetinghouses as the Old Order at Martins (St. Jacobs), in North Woolwich (Floradale), and in West Woolwich (Elmira). They have purchased the Goshen church in Peel Township and have built a new church in East Woolwich near West Montrose. Their bishop is Amsey M. Martin for the Waterloo section, with ministers Urias Martin, Noah B. Martin, Ira S. Brubacher, and George Brubacher. In the Markham section they worship at Altona, Almira, and the Reesor church, with Bishop Abram Smith and ministers Fred Nighswander and Cecil Reesor. They have a few members at Rainham and at Zurich. This conference takes an active part in the relief program and the peace testimony and has an awakening interest in evangelism and in missions. In 1957 there were 638 members, of whom 530 were in Waterloo County in two major congregations, 105 in Markham in two major congregations, and three at Rainham.   J.C.F.

Watonwan County is located in the southern part of Minnesota. It is the fourth county east of the South Dakota line in the second tier of counties above the Iowa border. Most of the Mennonites are found in the western and northwestern parts of the county. Four hundred Mennonites, members of seven congregations, five of which are, however, centered in Cottonwood County (q.v.), live in Watonwan County. The Mennonite settlement extends solidly westward into Cottonwood County, with a few living in surrounding counties. There are 403 G.C.M., seven E.M.B., and four M.B. members living in Watonwan County. The first Russian Mennonites in the county settled in Butterfield Township in 1875; the first Galician Mennonites came in 1881. The two Mennonite churches in Watonwan County are the Mennonite Church (GCM) of Butterfield and the First Mennonite Church (GCM) north of Butterfield. There are no other Mennonite institutions in the county.   W.L.

Watrous (or Philadelphia) Mennonite Brethren Church, located northeast of Watrous in north Saskatchewan, was organized under the leadership of P. D. Janzen as an Evangelical Mennonite Brethren Church in 1927 with 40 members. In 1935 the church, with a membership of 150, joined the Canadian M.B. Conference. As elsewhere in Saskatchewan, large numbers moved out of the province, so that the membership in 1957 was 68. In 1948 a new church building was erected. Leading ministers who have served the church are P. D. Janzen, Frank Wiens, Jacob D. Dick, and Dan Klassen, who was the pastor in 1957.   J.H.E.

Watt, Joachim von: see **Vadian(us)**.

Wauseon (Ohio) Evangelical Mennonite Church was organized in December 1948 by 106 charter members who transferred from the Archbold

(Ohio) E.M.C. congregation, which had helped finance the building project and authorized the new congregation. Gordon G. Zimmerman was the first pastor. Its meetinghouse was dedicated Jan. 29, 1949. On Dec. 31, 1958, the congregation had 278 members, with Arthur Enns as pastor.

H.A.Dr.

Wawasee Lakeside Chapel Mennonite Church (MC), Syracuse, Ind., founded in 1947, is a mission church under the Indiana-Michigan Mennonite Mission Board and is located on the east side of Lake Wawasee. In 1958 it had 15 members, with Herbert L. Yoder serving as pastor.   M.G.

Way, The, first published in January 1913 by the Mennonite Publishing House, Scottdale, Pa., began as an 8-page, 6 x 9 in., illustrated monthly. The paper was intended to be purchased by individuals, organizations, or congregations of the Mennonite Church (MC) for free distribution as a missionary project. Editors (until 1938 there were two co-editors) of the *Way* have been John H. Mosemann, Sr., and J. A. Ressler 1913-23, Mosemann and John L. Horst 1923-38, Horst alone 1938-48, Harold Brenneman 1948-57, and Urie Bender 1957- . In July 1943 the size was changed to 4 pages and somewhat later to 5½ x 8 in. Since its beginning most of the articles, stories, and poems have been selected from other papers and have constantly maintained a strong emphasis on evangelism. The monthly circulation in 1957 was 240,000.   E.D.Z.

Way to the City of Peace, *in Which Is Shown How to Obtain Peace,* by Pieter Pietersz (1574-1651), a book of considerable popularity first published about 1625, 5th edition 1642, at least eight editions in Dutch, in addition to at least three editions in his *Opera Omnia* (two 1715 and one n.d. in GCL), a German edition (1790 alone), and two editions of his *Ausgewählte Schriften* (1865 at Stuttgart and 1901 at Elkhart, both in GCL). The book depicts the Christian's journey to the heavenly Jerusalem, the city of peace. Its remarkable similarity to Bunyan's *Pilgrim's Progress from This World to That Which Is to Come* (1678) suggests dependency of Bunyan on Pietersz, which however has not been proved. (See **Pieter Pietersz** for fuller discussion.)

H.S.B.

A detailed account is given by J. J. Honig in "Reizen naar de Eeuwigheid," *DB* 1896, 1-35, esp. 18-26; see also R. Friedmann, *Mennonite Piety Through the Centuries* (Goshen, 1949) 106-9.

Wayland, Iowa, a town in northwestern Henry County, near the Washington County line, is located in the southeastern part of the state. It was at first known as Marshall. Mennonites have lived in its vicinity since the late 1840's. Its estimated population in 1958 was 660, when approximately 115 Mennonite families lived in the town. Mennonites operated 22 businesses within Wayland, and among the professional men were a Mennonite doctor, a veterinarian, and a dentist. The Wayland Mennonite (GCM) Church (*q.v.*), with 345 members, is located in the town, while the Sugar Creek Mennonite (MC) Church is situated 2 miles southeast of town.

The Eicher Emmanuel (GCM) Mennonite Church (*q.v.*), 4 miles northeast of Wayland, is in Washington County, as is also the Bethel Mennonite (MC) Church (*q.v.*), 3 miles north of the town.

M.G.

Wayland (Iowa) Mennonite Church (GCM), a member of the Middle District, is largely an outgrowth of the Eicher Emmanuel Mennonite Church (*q.v.*) near Wayland. The present wood structure, dedicated in 1900, was enlarged in 1911 to seat about 250. The church was organized with 56 charter members on March 8, 1900, with Peter E. Stuckey as the first pastor. Loris A. Habegger has been the pastor since June 5, 1954. The membership in 1957 was 345. The members are largely of Swiss, Alsatian, and French background, but have intermarried with other ethnic groups. Secret orders and military participation are no longer deterrent to membership.   L.A.H.

Wayne County, Ohio, established in 1796, was the third county formed from the original Northwest Territory and originally included parts of Ohio, Indiana, Illinois, Wisconsin, and all of Michigan. It now contains an area of 540 square miles, lying 30 miles south of Cleveland and 50 west of the Pennsylvania boundary. The soil, a deep clayey loam, is well adapted for growing wheat. The surface is mostly rolling, and formerly was heavily forested.

The earliest trail from east to west led from Pittsburgh, Pa., south of Wooster to Sandusky, Ohio. This may account for the early settlement of the area east of Wooster in Green Township and in Chester Township west-northwest. Although a few Amish ventured into Holmes County to the south as early as 1809 and Mennonites settled farther east in the state about the same time, neither Amish nor Mennonites attempted settlement in Wayne until the end of the War of 1812-14 had made the region relatively free from the danger of Indian raids. Amish from Somerset and Mifflin counties, Pa., arrived first and founded, in the townships lying east and northeast of Wooster, what later developed into the Oak Grove and Pleasant Hill Amish Mennonite congregation (*q.v.*). Swiss Mennonites from the Bernese Jura founded Sonnenberg (*q.v.*) in 1819 and Chippeway (now Crown Hill, *q.v.*) in 1825. Mennonites from Lancaster County, Pa., founded Martins (*q.v.*) southeast of Orrville in 1824. Another group of Mennonites from Bucks County, Pa., settled in Chester Township during the late 1820's and early 1830's. They were akin to some of the Mennonites who founded the Guilford congregation (*q.v.*) in Medina County (*q.v.*).

Several Wayne County congregations have become extinct or the members have moved away. The original Amish settlement in Green and Milton townships gradually became Amish Mennonite (*q.v.*) during the second half of the 19th century and are known as the Oak Grove (*q.v.*) and Pleasant Hill (*q.v.*) congregations. The small group who withdrew before the middle of the century to maintain an Old Order Amish congregation disappeared soon after the death of their bishop, Hannes Yoder. The present Old Order Amish in the coun-

MENNONITE CHURCHES IN
Wayne County, Ohio

———— Names of congregations underlined
▲ Institutions
🗻 Boundary of Old Order Amish settlements

Scale of Miles
0 1 2 3 4 5 6 7 8 9 10

CONGRESS Creston MILTON Rittman CHIPPEWA

Sterling ▫location of
Peter Rich Church
(GCM)

CANAAN

Crown Hill (MC) ▫Home for the Aged, Rittman (MC)

Pleasant Hill (MC)(1880-1959) ▫Marshallville

GREEN BAUGHMAN

Smithville ▫Smithville(MC) ▫Marshallville
Reformed Mennonite Church

Oak Grove (Independent- MC)
Orrville

CHESTER WAYNE Orrville (MC) County Line Wisler
(Wayne Co.Wislers also
use this house) (OOM)

Eight Square Wisler (Also called
Chester) (OOM)
▫site of first
Holdeman church
(CGCM)

Wooster (MC) Salem(MC) Chestnut Ridge (MC)
Martins (MC)

Wooster East Union (CAM)

PLAIN Camp Luz (MC) Dalton

Bethel, Kidron (Independent)
SUGAR CREEK
Salem (GCM)
WOOSTER EAST UNION Sonnenberg (MC)
Kidron(MC) Kidron

Apple Creek

CLINTON FRANKLIN SALT CREEK Maysville (CAM) Mt. Eaton
PAINT

OLD ORDER AMISH SETTLEMENT
Fredericksburg

ty have within recent decades been moving into the southeastern townships from the expanding congregations in Holmes County to the south. They now number 11 districts with 823 members. (See **Wayne County, Ohio, Amish.**) The Rich and Krabill families who left the Oak Grove congregation in 1869 and who later founded the Sterling, Ohio, Mennonite Church (*q.v.,* GCM) united with the Wadsworth Mennonite Church (*q.v.,* GCM) about 1920. A small Brethren in Christ congregation, proselyted from the Amish and Mennonites in the county about the middle of the century, and though served by the highly respected elder Elias Schrock, became extinct before the end of the century. The John Holdeman Church, later called Church of God in Christ, Mennonite (*q.v.*), was founded in Chester Township in 1859 and erected a meetinghouse there, but moved west about 1883. The city congregations in Orrville (founded 1909) and Wooster (founded 1942) are composed of families with varying background. The Conservative congregations at Maysville and East Union are of recent origin out of the Old Order Amish.

All but one of the original Mennonite congregations (Martin's, *q.v.*) became Old Order Mennonite

(*q.v.*) during the Wisler (*q.v.*) controversy in Elkhart County, Ind., about 1871-72. Some of these are nearing extinction. A few Milton Township Swiss Mennonites helped to found the Apostolic Christian Church in that township about 1855. The Sonnenberg Swiss Mennonite congregation has suffered considerable loss: first, in 1886 to the Salem congregation (*q.v.,* GCM); in 1893-94 several members to the "Russelites," i.e., Jehovah's Witnesses; in 1917-19 to the Kidron Tabernacle, which is now losing most of its young people to the Missionary Church in Dalton; in 1935 to the Kidron congregation (*q.v.,* MC); and within the past few years 40 members to a new independent Bethel congregation near Apple Creek, formerly meeting in the Frog Pond schoolhouse.

Of the Mennonite congregations active in the county at present the following have an Amish (Amish Mennonite) background: Oak Grove (MC), 398 members; Pleasant Hill (MC), 180; Salem (MC), 45; Orrville (MC), 265; Wooster (MC), 115; Maysville (CAM), 180; East Union (CAM), 90. The following were originally Mennonite: Martins (MC), 186; Wayne County (OOM), 3; Eight Square (OOM), 5; Chester (OOM), 40; County Line

(OOM), 160; Chestnut Ridge (MC), 44. Those with a Swiss Mennonite background are Sonnenberg (MC), 168; Crown Hill (MC), 144; Salem (GCM), 204; Kidron (MC), 509; Bethel (MC), 50; Marshallville, Reformed Mennonite, 24.

All of the M.C. congregations are members of the Ohio and Eastern Conference except Oak Grove and Bethel which are independent, and Sonnenberg, a member of the Virginia Conference. Chestnut Ridge also is a member of the Virginia Conference.

The total membership of all branches in the county in 1957 was 3,393, distributed as follows: Mennonite Church (MC), 12 congregations with 2,134 members; Old Order Amish, 14 with 1,061; Old Order Mennonites, 4 with 208; General Conference Mennonite, 1 with 204; Reformed Mennonite, 1 with 24.   J.S.U.

Wayne County (Ohio) Amish congregation, founded in Green Township in 1818 by David Stutzman, Henry Yoder, and Peter, Abraham, and Jacob Schrock from Somerset County, Pa., and by David Zook, Christian Lantz, Jacob Yoder, and Christian Brandt from Mifflin County, Pa. Plank families were also prominent in the settlement at an early date. In 1834 David Zook moved to Fairfield County, Ohio (q.v.), leaving the congregation in charge of Jacob Yoder and Hannes Yoder, bishops. The settlement grew rapidly. Before 1850 the 300 members organized a northern and a southern district and soon after that date began to adopt a more liberal discipline later known as Amish Mennonite. In protest Hannes Yoder, bishop, and Emanuel Hochstetler, preacher, with a small following withdrew to maintain the strict Old Order until the former's death about 1860. After 1855 a large majority of the congregation followed the more progressive leadership of John K. Yoder, bishop (q.v.), to found what eventually became the Oak Grove Amish Mennonite Church (q.v.). When the Oak Grove congregation built a meetinghouse in 1862, a small number under the leadership of Emanuel Hochstetler again withdrew, but the little band became extinct even before his death.

During the early years of the present century Amish from the overcrowded Amish settlement in Holmes and Tuscarawas counties began to move into southeastern Wayne County. The first year in which the *Mennonite Yearbook* lists Amish preachers with a Wayne County address is 1913. In that year Samuel E. Yoder, formerly a preacher in Tuscarawas County but ordained bishop before 1906, and Daniel Wengerd and B. J. Yoder, preachers, give Fredericksburg, Wayne County, as their address. This is the first year that either Wengerd or B. J. Yoder is listed as a minister. Within recent years the expansion from Holmes and Tuscarawas continues northward and northeastward into Wayne and southward into Coshocton County. At present (1957) Wayne County has fourteen "districts" or congregations with a total baptized membership of 1,061 in seven districts around Fredericksburg, one each near Dalton and Mt. Eaton, three at Apple Creek, and one north, one south of Orrville. Eleven bishops, thirty ministers, and ten deacons serve the fourteen Wayne County Amish districts.   J.S.U.

John Umble, "The Oak Grove . . . Mennonite Church," *MQR* XXXI (July 1957) 156-73.

Wayne County (Ohio) Old Order Mennonites. In the division of 1872 between the Mennonites who remained with the Ohio Conference (MC) and those who followed Jacob Wisler (q.v.), two congregations of Wisler Mennonites were formed in Wayne County: (1) Chester (q.v.), northwest of Wooster, which worshiped in the meetinghouse in the center of Chester Township in Section 16, and which simply left the Ohio Conference as an entire congregation, and (2) Orrville, which worshiped in two meetinghouses east of Orrville, viz., Chestnut Ridge (q.v.) in Section 32, and County Line (q.v.) in Section 36, which borders on Stark County. (1) In 1872 the leading ministers in the Chester congregation were Bishop John Shaum (1797-1882) and Preacher Peter Troxel (1804-95). The group built a new house of worship in 1873, but this was not an internal schismatic move, for the entire congregation became Wisler Mennonite. The division within the Wisler Conference in 1907 involved the Chester congregation, the progressive group becoming increasingly strong numerically in the following decades, while the Old Order group almost died out. The latter, known as the Eight Square (q.v.) congregation, had only 5 members in 1958, served by William H. Brubacher, 66, while the Wisler congregation numbered 50 members. The Wisler ministry consisted of Bishop Carl J. Good and Deacon Amos Martin. (2) The County Line meetinghouse was built in 1891 by the Wisler Mennonites who had withdrawn in 1872 from the Pleasant View (MC) congregation. The Chestnut Ridge meetinghouse was built in 1908 by the Wisler Mennonites who had withdrawn in 1872 from the Martins (MC) congregation. Both Wisler groups had alternated in the use of old meetinghouses with the congregations from which they withdrew, until the building of the two Wisler houses of worship. The two groups of Wisler Mennonites at Orrville, however, composed but one congregation. The strong leader of this congregation was Bishop Henry Hursh (1839-1916), ordained preacher in 1873 and bishop in 1878. He led the progressive portion of the Ohio and Indiana Wisler Conference in 1907, while Bishop John W. Martin (1852-1940) of Elkhart County, Ind., led the more conservative portion of the conference. Almost the entire Orrville congregation followed Hursh in the 1907 division. In 1953 Deacon Harry A. Landis and about 40 former members of the Orrville Wisler congregation affiliated themselves with the Virginia Conference (MC), and were granted the ownership of the Chestnut Ridge meetinghouse by the Wisler congregation. Frank E. Nice of the Franconia Conference was ordained preacher to serve the group. The remaining Orrville Wisler congregation worships in the County Line meetinghouse and has a membership of 160. It was served in 1958 by preachers Elmer Good, Cleophas Steiner, and Jacob Neuenschwander (who transferred as a preacher to the Wisler Mennonites in 1954 when his Sonnenberg congregation united with the Virginia Conference, (MC). The tiny Old Order group of Wisler Mennonites in Wayne County has but three members, served by Daniel Brubaker (1873-), who was ordained in 1905. J.C.W.

Waynesboro, a city (pop. 12,357) in Augusta County, Va., is the trading center for an Amish and Mennonite population of 788 members. There are six congregations of the Southern District (*q.v.*) of the Virginia Conference (MC) with a total of 602 members in the neighborhood: Springdale 5 miles south, Hildebrands 5 miles north, Mt. View 15 miles south, Stuarts Draft 15 miles southwest, Greenmonte 20 miles southwest, and Lynside 6 miles south. The Mt. Zion Beachy Amish church with 81 members is located 12 miles west, and an Old Order Amish group with 105 members 10 miles west near Stuarts Draft. H.S.B.

Waynesboro (Ga.) Mennonite Church (MC), a member of the Lancaster Conference, was established in 1957 and had 7 members in 1958, with Noah H. Hege as pastor. M.G.

Waynesboro (Pa.) Reformed Mennonite Church began in 1827 at Ringgold, Md., but when many members moved to Waynesboro, Pa., the congregation was transferred and built a meetinghouse there in 1876, which was replaced by a new house in 1900. In 1957 the membership was 24. H.S.B.

Wayside Mennonite Church (MC), since 1957 called the Crossroads Bible Church, 4 miles north of Gulfport, Miss., is a member of the South Central Conference. The congregation was organized May 13, 1948, with Edward J. Miller as pastor, who was still serving in 1958. The members are largely natives of South Mississippi. In the spring of 1945 a CPS camp was established in the area of Gulfport, the men of which assisted in a union Sunday school in the camp church. In the fall of 1947 J. W. Hess held revival meetings at the Gulfhaven church. In just a little more than a year from the time the first members were baptized, a building was erected and a pastor placed in charge of a growing congregation, which in 1958 numbered 25 members. P.H.

Wayside Mennonite Church (MC), near Brimley, Mich., is located 15 miles southwest of Sault Sainte Marie. It was established in 1948 as a mission station under the Indiana-Michigan Mennonite Mission Board. It had 32 members in 1958, with Ralph Birkey as pastor. M.G.

Weatherford (Okla.) Mennonite Brethren Church, organized Jan. 17, 1954, located at 712 North Broadway. It had 61 members in 1957, with B. W. Vogt as its pastor. M.G.

Weaver (Weber), an old Mennonite family of Swiss origin. As early as 1664 the Palatine Mennonite Census Lists reported two Webers, Peter at Oberflörsheim and Christian at Spiesheim; in 1685 Peter Weber was still living at Oberflörsheim (6 sons and a daughter), a second Peter Weber at Waltzheim, Johannes Weber at Osthofen, and Heinrich Weber and Dietrich Weber at Gundersheim. In 1732 Peter Weber was a minister at Oberflörsheim. In 1738 in addition to the Weber families at Oberflörsheim

(Peter Sr., Peter Jr., Dietrich, and Christian), Gundersheim (Peter), Spiesheim (Johannes), Wolfsheim (Mathias, Johannes), there were at Heppenheim near Alzey four Weber families (Johannes, Heinrich, Martin, and Matthäus). All of these locations were in the Palatinate west of the Rhine. The Webers have ever since been well established in this region. In 1940, according to the Franz Crous lists, there were 67 Mennonite Webers (including children) in the South German Mennonite churches (only one elsewhere in Germany, at Crefeld), of whom 46 were in the Palatinate (Monsheim congregation leading with 22, Kühbörncheshof 8, Neudorferhof 7, Uffhofen 5, three other congregations 4), plus one in Frankfurt and two in the Ingolstadt congregation in Bavaria. Outstanding among the Webers in the 18th century was Peter Weber of Kindenheim (*q.v.*, 1731-81), a very influential preacher and a strong Pietist.

Several Webers emigrated from the Palatinate to Lancaster County, Pa., in the early 18th century. At least four are known to have arrived before 1718, all brothers—Jacob, Henry, George, and John. The first three established a settlement in the rich bottom land between Blue Ball and Conestoga, which came to be known as Weberthal or Weaverland, and from which the present Weaverland (*q.v.*) Mennonite Church (MC) takes its name. Among their descendants were two bishops serving the Weaverland-Groffdale district (George, served 1854-83, and Benjamin 1902-8) and a host of ministers serving both in the Weaverland district (MC) and elsewhere, chiefly Virginia, Indiana, and Kansas, as well as in the Old Order Mennonite group in the Blue Ball-New Holland area. M. G. Weaver, himself a descendant, listed in his *Mennonites of Lancaster Conference* in 1931 a total of 32 ordained (10 being deacons) men bearing the name (3 Weber, 39 Weaver), of whom 31 were serving in the Mennonite Church (MC) including four bishops, mostly in the Lancaster Conference and the Virginia Conference. In addition there were four O.O.M. ministers with the name Weaver, and seven O.O.A. ministers, and one G.C.M. minister. J. W. Weaver (d. 1944) was a prominent Lancaster Conference evangelist and founder and manager of the Weaver Book Store at New Holland, Pa. Edwin Weaver was a missionary bishop in India. U. K. Weber was long pastor of the First Mennonite and Stirling Avenue Mennonite churches in Kitchener, Ont. H.S.B.

Ezra N. Stauffer, *Weber or Weaver Family History* (Nappanee, 1953); Esther Weaver, *Descendants of Henry B. Weaver* (Ephrata?, 1953); M. G. Weaver, *Mennonites of Lancaster Conference* (Scottdale, 1931); Franz Crous, "Mennonitenfamilien in Zahlen," *Gesch.-Bl.* V (1940) 26-44; Paul Peachey, *Die soziale Herkunft der Schweizer Täufer* (Karlsruhe, 1954); Delbert Gratz, *Bernese Anabaptists* (Scottdale, 1953); *ML* IV.

Weaver, Benjamin (Nov. 27, 1853-Sept. 3, 1928), the second child and oldest son of Isaac Weaver and Catherine Witwer, was a direct descendant of both Henry Weaver and Deacon Michael Witwer, Weaverland, Lancaster Co., Pa., Swiss pioneers. Benjamin Weaver's brother, John Weaver, was a Mennonite evangelist-pastor, and both George Weaver and David Weaver were elders in the Church of the Brethren. Benjamin married Barbara Sauder (1851-1916). They had seven children; Benjamin Weaver, a preacher of Bowmansville, is a grandson. Four children, 32 grandchildren, and 15 great-grand-children survived him.

In 1882 Benjamin Weaver bought the Upper Windsor gristmill from his father and successfully operated it for many years. His integrity was unquestioned, and his wit in crises was quite medicinal. He retired near Union Grove, then to Terre Hill, and spent his last days in Goodville.

Benjamin Weaver's first active church work was as the first Sunday-school superintendent in the Churchtown congregation in 1894. In 1898 he was appointed to the board of the Welsh Mountain Mission. In 1899 he was ordained as minister of the Weaverland circuit, and on Jan. 23, 1903, as bishop for the district from Groffdale to Allegheny. He became familiar with the Bible as a boy; in fact he memorized many stories before his eighteenth birthday. With his genial disposition, warm hand-shake, and oratorical ability in both the German and the English, he held a large circle of friends, both within and without the church, gaining most of the children of members and also many whose fathers and grandfathers had left with the schism of 1893. Entering the Bishop Board when Jacob N. Brubacher, Isaac Eby, and Martin Rutt were the influential trio, he soon became a valuable asset. He was an organizer of both the Oreville Old People's Home and the Millersville Children's Home. He served as moderator of the Conference 1922-28. Noah H. Mack was his assistant bishop 1919-26, and John M. Sauder from 1926, who succeeded him when he died in 1928.   I.D.L.

Weaver, John W. (July 4, 1870-Feb. 18, 1944), was the ninth of the eleven children of Isaac Weaver and Catherine Witwer, east of Union Grove, Lancaster Co., Pa. Bishop Benjamin Weaver (*q.v.*) was a brother. He was reared in a godly home, was well acquainted with the Bible, and able to quote much from it as a young man. He was very modest. His home was not affected by the division of 1893, even though he had been baptized by Jonas Martin in 1888. On Nov. 15, 1891, he married Anna M. Nolt (1868-1946). He became a saddler in Union Grove and in 1895 started a bookstore. In 1897 he became a member of the Mennonite Book and Tract Society and two years later secretary-treasurer. In 1915 he was coauthor of a book on the ministry and in 1940 of *Talks with Young People*. He also wrote the tracts, *A Letter to Young Church Members* and *A Message to Young People*. His greatest work was the Conference Meeting Calendar, which he published for forty years. John W. Weaver's son David is also a minister.

John W. Weaver, the first chairman of the Conference Library Committee, the first Sunday-school superintendent at Lichty in 1897, a member of the Weaverland Missions Committee in 1907, was ordained to the ministry by his brother Benjamin on Aug. 19, 1909. That fall he held revival meetings at Red Well. He was a promoter of the Millersville Children's Home, a charter member of the Eastern Board of Missions and Charities, and became its first field worker. As such he nurtured many new missions, especially Diamond Rock and Miners Village. He was a very successful evangelist throughout the Lancaster Conference and beyond. His extensive evangelistic effort practically closed in 1926, when he collapsed in the pulpit at East Petersburg.
                                                        I.D.L.

Weaver Mennonite Church (MC), located on State Route 56, two miles east of Johnstown, Pa., in Cambria County just across the border from Somerset County, a member of the Allegheny Conference, had its beginning before 1800 when the Weaver, Baumgardner, Keim, Blough, and other families, including some Amish and some Dunkers, settled in this fertile region underlaid with good coal. The first services were held (date unknown) in a log schoolhouse deeded on May 7, 1817, to Christian Lehman and Jacob Whetstone as trustees. In 1855 a log meetinghouse (30 x 36 ft.) was erected beside the schoolhouse, replaced in 1878 by the present frame meetinghouse (40 x 50 ft.), which has been remodeled twice. For many years the congregation had no resident minister, and was served once in four weeks by a minister from the Blough (*q.v.*) church in Somerset County, 10 miles to the south. In 1854 Samuel Blough was ordained as the first resident minister, who also served as bishop 1878-83. In 1879-80 Sunday school was begun. The first sewing circle in the Johnstown district was established here in 1910. Alexander Weaver was long a minister here, 1893-1952. In 1957 the membership was 51, with Harold E. Thomas as pastor and Hiram Wingard (1914-   ) as assistant.   H.S.B.

Ammon Kaufman, "Weaver Church," *Southwestern Pennsylvania Conference News* VI (November-December 1947) 3.

Weaver Mennonites. In the spring of 1916, when Bishop Aaron Sensenig was physically handicapped, the Stauffer members of the Pike (*q.v.*) congregation, near Hinkletown, Pa., wanted other leadership and favored a stricter observance of shunning. After his death that fall John A. Weaver, a preacher, tried to restore peace, but failed, and the resultant schism divided the congregation into equal parts, 101 and 102. Following the Stauffer (*q.v.*) division of 1846 there had been peace until about 1870, when Samuel Bowman, Jacob Weber, and Philip Rissler led a small schismatic group who felt that children who were not in the church and its order should be obliged to leave the parental home. After the division of 1916 this Rissler group joined the Stauffer group again for five years, then separated and divided again, so that today the only remaining members of the Bowman-Rissler group are three men and the wife of one of them. Jesse Bowman, of the Iowa (*q.v.*) Experiment, came to Lebanon County, Pa., and was given the bishop oversight of the new Lebanon County group and the Pike congregation. (He with his group joined the Old Order Mennonites, *q.v.*) Then Elam C. Martin, of Michigan, was ordained bishop at the Pike church. After his death in 1928 John A. Weaver served until his death on March 25, 1953. Thereupon Weaver W. Zimmerman was chosen bishop. Peter L. Weaver and Martin S. Weaver are the ministers. Membership of the Weaver group meeting in the Pike church (exclusively) is 60 (including the four Risslers). Services are conducted in German and last two hours; they have no evangelistic meetings, Sunday schools, or youth activities. They use only horses for transportation and farming. In the 1916 division Deacon Levi Zimmerman went with the Stauffers. Bishop John Stauffer, of Snyder County, then ordained David Stauffer and Jacob Stauffer and later Joseph O. Brubaker. The Stauffers in Snyder County had numerous divisions. In addition to these two places of worship, they also have a con-congregation near Loveville, Md. At the Pike church where they are strongest, Jacob S. Stauffer is bishop and Joseph O. Brubaker minister. At the three places, inclusive of all the splinter groups, the Stauffer Mennonites have a total membership of 223.

I.D.L.

Weaverland Mennonite Church (MC), in eastern Lancaster County, Pa., has been a strong Mennonite center since the days of David Martin and the coming of George, Henry, and Jacob Weaver from West Lampeter Township in c1723. A congregation was organized by 1733. Peter Shirk (d. 1770), one of the first ministers, mentions Henry Martin (later bishop), John Witwer, Martin Huber, and John Sensenig as "elders of the Mennonite meeting." A church-schoolhouse may have been built, but by 1766 there was a 34 x 50 ft. stone church with a seating capacity of about 240. The sexton lived on the west end. The new addition in 1853, with its two ten-plate stoves in the central aisle, seated about 400. In 1883 a new stone church, 50 x 78 ft., seated 600. The present brick church, 60 x 120 ft., was erected in 1926.

This was the home congregation of bishops Henry Martin (1741-1825), Jonas H. Martin (1839-1925), John M. Sauder (1864-1939), and J. Paul Graybill; preachers Peter Shirk (d. 1770), Daniel Witwer (1767-1819), Tobias Wanner (1813-87), Samuel B. Witmer (1861-1909), I. B. Good (1861-1946). It has been the central church for a circuit which includes Martindale, Lichty, Goodville, and Churchtown. The three Mennonites arrested for sheltering Hessian soldiers overnight were from this congregation. Deacon John Weber (1786-1854), Abraham Weber (1787-1867), Peter Martin (1769-1831) and fourteen of his children, Daniel Weber (1797-1864), and others from this congregation helped to settle Ontario in 1809-19. The first Sunday school, organized by Samuel H. Musselman and Isaac W. Martin in the spring of 1893, precipitated the O.O.M. schism in the fall of that year. The Weaverland Missions Committee (1906-28) founded permanent work at Diamond Rock (now Frazer) and Red Run. In 1912 I. B. Good promoted the Weaverland Young People's Meeting "distinctly for young people." This congregation, long the largest in the Lancaster Conference (now second), listed 575 members in 1957, with J. Paul Graybill as resident bishop and D. N. Weaver, Alvin G. Martin, and A. H. Hollinger as ministers.

I.D.L.

Weaverland Old Order Mennonite Church was organized by Bishop Jonas Martin in 1893. The following summer they built a stone meetinghouse

50 x 78 ft., an exact replica of the one built by the united church in 1883 and reserved by the Lancaster Mennonite (MC) Conference. Since the division into the Groffdale and Weaverland groups in 1926, both have been using this meetinghouse. The Groffdale group, with Aaron Z. Sensenig as bishop, and George G. Horst and Harry H. Martin as ministers, serves a membership of 275. Their preaching is exclusively in German, with no night services; for transportation they use horse and buggy. It is a part of the Martindale-Weaverland circuit. The Weaverland Conference, meeting on the alternate Sundays, have Joseph O. Weaver as bishop and John B. Weaver as minister, with a membership of 280. They are in the German-English transition, have no Sunday school nor official church activities, and travel mostly in automobiles with the bumpers painted black. Both groups are growing in this area.

I.D.L.

Weavers Mennonite Church (MC), located 2½ miles west of Harrisonburg, Va., on the Rawley Pike in the Middle District of the Virginia Conference, is the largest congregation in the conference. The congregation was first known as the Burkholder church because of the part played by Bishop Peter Burkholder in the early 19th century in building the meetinghouse. Later Samuel Weaver bought and occupied land west of the church. He became its lifelong sexton and in time the church was called Weavers after him. The first meetinghouse, built in 1827, was a small log church covered with weatherboards, which stood broadside to the highway. It was replaced in 1881 and again in 1941, this time on the south side of Rawley Pike, built of native limestone. The first church was used by Union soldiers in the Civil War as a camping place. Cuts or scars made by the spurs worn by the soldiers on the long open pulpit indicated that it was used as a sleeping bunk.

Two schoolhouses have stood on the church grounds; one was built by the Mennonites, the other later by the county.

The first session of the Virginia Conference was held here in 1835. John S. Coffman (q.v.) held the first series of revival meetings in the Virginia Conference at Weavers in 1888.

Since 1900 the Weavers church has served as the center of the *Harmonia Sacra* singing movement in the Shenandoah Valley; more than fifty annual singings have been held here on New Year's Day.

In 1958 Oliver Keener and Isaac Risser were serving as pastors of the church, with D. W. Lehman as bishop and a membership of 302. H.A.B.

Weavertown Amish Church (Beachy Amish), located in central and east-central Lancaster County, Pa., was organized in 1910 with about 35 families by John P. Zook and Samuel Beachey of the Kishacoquillas Valley. The main issue was on avoidance and the ban. Christian L. King was the first bishop, followed by John A. Stoltzfus and George W. Beiler. Elam L. Kauffman and Aaron S. Glick were the ministers in 1957. In 1928 the group acquired the Molasses Hill Brethren meetinghouse near Bird-in-Hand on Route 1, and remodeled it for their own use. The services are mostly German. Sunday school without helps is held all forenoon on every second Sunday. Young people's meeting is held Sunday evenings once a month. On Ascension Day in 1958 the Beachy Amish young people of the United States held an all-day conference with Weavertown as the host. In conjunction with the Norfolk (Va.) Beachy Amish, Elam L. Kauffman, as the Weavertown representative, opened a mission in Berlin, Germany. Kauffman also is the conferee on the Mennonite Central Committee. The membership in 1958 was 275.   I.D.L.

Webb School, in Pickering Twp., Ontario Co., Ont., was an outpost of the Mennonites of York County (MC), begun as a Sunday school in 1939. This outpost was a short-lived summer venture when World War II broke out. Altona and Markham families helped to befriend this neglected neighborhood for a few years, and then later at Coronation Gardens, several miles farther east, by Sunday school and summer Bible school for about five years. The work was closed for want of suitable housing.
                                                        J.C.F.

Weber: see **Weaver.**

Weber, Gregor, of Pflaurenz in the Puster Valley, Tirol, a friend and teacher of Jakob Hutter (*q.v.*), died a martyr's death at Michelsburg (*q.v.*) in 1529. (*ML IV.*)

Weber, Hans (also called Distler), an Anabaptist of Iphofen in Franconia, Germany. Because he had sheltered Jörg von Passau (see **Nespitzer, Georg**), an Anabaptist preacher, and been baptized by him (*c*1527), he was punished with a fine and the loss of two fingers. In addition he was obliged to remain in the region the rest of his life, without freedom to dispose of his property.   W.W.
Ztscht für bayrische Kirchengeschichte XVI (1910) 172; *ML* IV.

Weber, Peter (1731-81), a Mennonite preacher of the Palatinate, Germany, who played a leading role in German pietistic circles, was born probably at Hardenberg near Dürkheim a.d.H. He experienced an early conversion through reading the writings of Johannes Deknatel (*q.v.*). About 1750 he married Katharina Schmidt, establishing himself in Hardenberg as a weaver. In 1757/8 he was chosen preacher in the congregation at Höningen. His influence began to widen, having a marked almost revivalistic effect, but also meeting opposition. On Dec. 30, 1758, Weber and three other preachers were removed from their office. Soon Adam Krehbiel (*q.v.*) was also removed from office. Serious division threatened the Palatinate congregations on the issue of Pietism. From the Deknatel group in Holland came support and encouragement for Weber, who had visited Amsterdam in 1757. The division was deepened by Weber's publication of a sharply polemic tract, *Vermahnendes Bekenntnis, wie die Lehrer nach der Schrift geartet sein müssen, aus Menno gezogen und in den Druck gegeben von einem Freund der Wahrheit.* Weber continued to hold private Bible study meetings and even public meetings, which led to the fear he would start a new Mennonite group. A second "silencing" of Weber by the churches resulted in complete cessation of all his activities. In 1763 peace was finally restored, partly through the efforts of Lorenz Friedenreich (*q.v.*), the influential elder of Neuwied. In 1778 Weber moved to Kindenheim, where he died Sept. 8, 1781. He shared in the publication of the 1780 edition of the *Martyrs' Mirror* at Pirmasens.

Peter Weber was an unusually powerful preacher, widely used in the Palatinate Mennonite churches and beyond, with an extensive acquaintance and wide correspondence with Pietist leaders.   H.S.B.
Christian Neff published a very appreciative biographical sketch of Weber, with extensive extracts from his letters in *Gem.-Kal.* 1930, 61-102; *ML* IV.

Weber, Philipp, the name of two early Anabaptists, both named for their profession. One was Philipp Plener (also called Blauärmel), the founder of the Philippite brotherhood (*q.v.*) in Moravia. The other was Philipp Jäger, the assistant of Jacob Wiedeman (*q.v.*), leader of the Stäbler (*q.v.*) in Moravia 1528-35. Of this Philipp Jäger we learn only, through the Hutterite chronicle, that he helped Wiedeman establish the new Bruderhof in Austerlitz.   R.F.

Weber Mennonite Church (MC), located 4 miles southwest of Kitchener, Ont., a member of the Ontario Mennonite Conference, was organized in 1838. The first meetinghouse was built in 1842; it was replaced by a brick building in 1895, seating capacity 150. Simon Martin served as pastor 1931-58 and in 1958 was still serving as bishop, with Lester Bauman as pastor since May 25, 1958. The membership was 73.   S.B.M.

Weckh, Hans, a Hutterite martyr, was executed with his brother-in-law Heinrich Adam (see **Adams, Heinrich**) at Aachen on Oct. 21, 1558. (In *ML* I, 148, and *ME* I, 11, he is erroneously called Hans Beck.) Weckh was one of a company of twelve, six brethren and six sisters, led by Han Schmid (*q.v.*, Raiffer), who were sent on a missionary tour to the Netherlands and were all arrested in Aachen on Jan. 9, 1558, when a meeting was surprised by the authorities. Five of the men were executed, Schmid on Oct. 19, 1558, Matthias Schmidt and Tillman Schneider on Jan. 4, 1559, and Weckh and Heinrich Adam(s) on Oct. 21, 1558. The sixth brother apostatized and was released, but later repented and joined the church again. The six women were severely scourged and released. (*Mart. Mir* D. 209-11, E 588-90.)   H.S.B.

Wedel, a city and Mennonite settlement near Hamburg, Schleswig-Holstein, Germany. Mennonite refugees from Danzig and West Prussia have been settled here in 12 homes which in 1958 housed 133 persons. The building was done primarily by Pax boys. A church was built and dedicated in 1958. The minister of this group and others is Arthur Goetzke.   C.K.
Otto Regier, "Neue Heimat in Schleswig-Holstein," *Gem.-Kal.,* 1957, 39-43; *ML* IV.

Wedel (Wedell, Weedel, Wedler, Wiedel, Wadel), a family name which was found among the Mennonites of Prussia particularly at Schönsee, Przechovka, and Konopat, and also occurring in Thiensdorf and Montau-Gruppe. Schroeder assumes that the ancestor of this family came from East Friesland. According to the Alexanderwohl church record the first representative of the Przechovka or Alexanderwohl church in Prussia was Frantz Wedel, who was present when the village was leased in 1640. Some early members of the group were Benjamin Wedel (1766-1813) and Peter Wedel (1792-1871). Jacob Wedel (1754-91) was elected elder in 1785. He started the Alexanderwohl Mennonite Church record, probably the oldest American Mennonite church record, entitled *Die Erste stamm Nahmen Unserer Bisher so genante Oude Vlamingen oder Groningersche Mennonisten Sozietaets alhier in Preusen* and going back to 1669.

From Prussia the name Wedel was transplanted to Russia where it was found primarily in the Alexanderwohl church, and from there to the Alexanderwohl (*q.v.*) church at Goessel, Kan. C. H. Wedel (*q.v.*, 1862-1911), the first president of Bethel College, was born in this community. Theodore O. Wedel, an Episcopal clergyman in Washington, D.C., is his son. In this group are Cornelius C. Wedel, minister of the Alexanderwohl Mennonite Church (1898-1957); his son, David C. Wedel, president of Bethel College since 1952; Frank F. Wedel, former manager of Salem Deaconess Hospital (*q.v.*).

In Prussia a Low-German-speaking Wedel of the Przechovka group married into the Swiss Volhynian group which later settled near Moundridge, Kan. Of this line of Wedels are Peter J. Wedel (1871-1951), professor of Bethel College; his son Waldo Rudolph Wedel, archaeologist; Philip Arnold Wedel, minister of the Alexanderwohl Mennonite Church; the late Edward B. Wedel, professor of the University of Wichita; and his son Arnold Wedel, professor at Bethel College, all of the G.C.M. group. In the M.B. group there are Herbert Wedel of Fresno, Cal., and J. Wedel at Abbotsford, B.C., and Ruben Wedel at Premont, Tex., all ministers. C.K.

Reimer, *Familiennamen*, 120; H. H. Schroeder, *Russlanddeutsche Friesen* (Döllstädt, 1936) 99; J. A. Duerksen, "Przechowka and Alexanderwohl," *Menn. Life* X (April 1955) 76-82.

Wedel, Benjamin (*c*1700-59), was born near Schwetz, West Prussia, Germany, and lived in the village of Terespolna. His second wife was Sarcke Pankratz of Konopat. He was a second known elder of the Przechovka Mennonite Church near Schwetz. He was likely the host of Hendrick Berends Hulshoff of Holland, who visited the congregation in 1719. Wedel died in November 1759. J.A.D.

J. A. Duerksen, "Przechowka and Alexanderwohl," *Menn. Life* X (April 1955) 76.

Wedel, Benjamin (1742-85), was born Oct. 27, 1742, the son of Peter Wedel and Maricke Richert, and lived in the village of Przechovka, West Prussia. He was baptized at the age of 17 and on Nov. 4, 1760, married Trincke Schmidt of Konopat. He was minister and elder of the Przechovka Mennonite

Church near Schwetz. Two of his sons, Benjamin and Peter, were also elders of the same church. He died Jan. 4, 1785. J.A.D.

J. A. Duerksen, "Przechowka and Alexanderwohl," *Menn. Life* X (April 1955) 76.

Wedel, Benjamin (1766-1813), was born Aug. 7, 1766, the son of Benjamin Wedel (1742-85) and Trincke Schmidt. He was baptized at the age of 17 and on Nov. 13, 1785, was married to Sarcke Ratzlaff. He served the Przechovka Mennonite Church as minister from 1791 and as elder 1794-1809. He died in September 1813. J.A.D.

J. A. Duerksen, "Przechowka and Alexanderwohl," *Menn. Life* X (April 1955) 76.

Wedel, Cornelius Heinrich (1860-1910), a Mennonite (GCM) minister, educator, historian, and first president of Bethel College, was born at Margenau, Molotschna Mennonite settlement, May 12, 1860, the son of Cornelius P. Wedel, who was a teacher. He lost his mother at the age of six. His father taught first at Margenau, then at Alexanderwohl, where Cornelius received his first education. In 1874 the family migrated to the present Goessel, Kan., with the Alexanderwohl group. In 1876-80 he taught school in this community. During some summers he attended schools in Marion Centre and in Hillsboro to learn English and to acquire a teacher's certificate. At the age of eighteen he was baptized in the Alexanderwohl church where he organized and taught Sunday school and mission studies. In 1881 he received a call to the Darlington, Okla., mission. In 1882 he gave up the work because of eye trouble.

In 1883 he attended McKendry College, Lebanon, Ill., and the following years Bloomfield Theological Seminary, N.J., where he particularly studied under George Seibert and taught 1898-1900. Numerous class notebooks kept by Wedel give an insight into the instruction he received and into his studies. Here he was also in close touch with N. B. Grubb. In 1890 he accepted the call to the Halstead School, Halstead, Kan., where he taught for three years. On Aug. 17, 1890, he was ordained minister in the Alexanderwohl Mennonite Church. On March 30, 1891, he married Susanna Richert. He continued his study for two more years at Ursinus College, Collegeville, Pa., where he received his M.A. degree. In 1893 he became president of Bethel College and professor of Bible, which position he held until his death in 1910.

In 1896 and 1898 Wedel made extensive trips to Germany, the Netherlands, Switzerland, and Russia for research in Mennonite history. His notebooks ("Reise nach Europa") and his printed reports give good insights as to what he looked for and what he found. He became a close friend of Samuel Cramer of Amsterdam and many other leading Mennonites. After his return he published "Aus der Reisemappe" and "Reiseskizzen und Randglossen," which were reports about his trip (*School and College Journal*, 1897 and 1899). In 1898 he published his first book, entitled *Bilder aus der Kirchengeschichte für mennonitische Gemeindeschulen* (*q.v.*), which has been reprinted many times and also appeared in English in 1920 as "Sketches from Church History for Mennonite Schools."

As an educator Wedel made an outstanding contribution among the Mennnonites of America. He taught Bible, church history, Mennonite history, and German literature. The numerous notebooks which originated in his classrooms and have become a part of a C. H. Wedel Collection mirror his achievements. He was president of Bethel College 1893-1910 and served repeatedly at Bethel College Mennonite Church as pastor 1897-1910. In the *Monatsblätter aus Bethel College,* of which he was coeditor, and the *School and College Journal,* he published 182 articles on Mennonite history, literature, and other areas, besides his articles for other periodicals. A most outstanding work is the four-volume set, *Abriss der Geschichte der Mennoniten* (Newton, 1900-4), which constitutes the first general and comprehensive history of the Mennonites written and published in America. Other books are as follows: *Randzeichnungen zu den Geschichten des Alten Testaments* (1899); *Randzeichnungen zu den Geschichten des Neuen Testaments* (1900); *Geleitworte an junge Christen zunächst in unsern mennonitischen Kreisen* (1903); *Kurzgefasste Kirchengeschichte* (1905); *Briefliche Blätter an einen Lernenden über Bildung, Gesellschafts- und Heiratsfragen* (1906); *Meditationen zu den Fragen und Antworten unseres Katechismus* (1910). All of these books except *Meditationen* were published by Bethel College. Wedel died March 28, 1910, and was buried in the Greenwood Cemetery, Newton.   C.K.

C. H. Wedel, *Tagebuch,* 2 vv., 1885-1910; C. H. Wedel, "Reise nach Europa," 1898; H. R. Voth, "Prof. C. H. Wedel," *Christlicher Bundesbote* (April 21 and 28, 1910) 5; H. R. Voth, "Prof. C. H. Wedel. Kurze Lebensskizze," *Bethel College Monthly* (May and June, 1910) 6 and 1; Peter J. Wedel, *The Story of Bethel College* (North Newton, 1954); David C. Wedel, "The Contribution of C. H. Wedel to the Mennonite Church Through Education" (Th.D. dissertation, Iliff School of Theology, Denver, 1952); C. H. Wedel, "Mein Lebenslauf" (1881); term papers by Richard Schmidt, John P. Loewen, and Dorothea Franzen.

Wedel, Jacob, was born Jan. 20, 1754, the son of Peter Wedel and Sarcke Ratzlaff. He lived in the village of Przechovka. At the age of 18 he was baptized, and on Feb. 21, 1779, married Lencke Ratzlaff. At the age of 21 he was elected minister and in 1785 he succeeded Benjamin Wedel (c1742-85) as elder. Jacob Wedel is the originator of the Przechovka-Alexanderwohl church record. He endeavored to trace every family back to the place of origin. He died on Sept. 5, 1791.   J.A.D.

J. A. Duerksen, "Przechowka and Alexanderwohl," *Menn. Life* X (April 1955) 76; *ML* IV.

Wedel, Peter (1769- ?), was born Feb. 4, 1769, the son of Benjamin Wedel (1742-85) and Trincke Schmidt, and a brother of Benjamin Wedel (1766-1813). At the age of 16 he was baptized and in 1791 married Maricke Bethcken, of Neu-Dessau near Driesen. At the age of 30 he was elected minister and in 1809 elder of the Przechovka Mennonite Church near Schwetz. He lived at Konopat.
                                                    J.A.D.
J. A. Duerksen, "Przechowka and Alexanderwohl," *Menn. Life* X (April 1955) 76.

Wedel, Peter (1792-1871), was born at Przechovka, Prussia, on May 26, 1792, to Benjamin Wedel (1766-1813). He was chosen minister in his home congregation in 1813 and elder in 1814. On Sept. 21, 1817, he married Elscke Buller (d. 1832). In 1820 Wedel led his congregation from Prussia to the Molotschna settlement, where they established the village and congregation of Alexanderwohl in 1821. On Jan. 24, 1833, he married Anna Richert (b. 1811). Six children were born of the first marriage and eleven of the second. In 1832 he made a trip to Poland to visit Mennonite congregations and serve as minister. Peter Wedel preached his last sermon on June 22, 1871 (John 3:16), and died July 8, 1871. He was succeeded by Jakob Buller (*q.v.*), who led the Alexanderwohl church (*q.v.*) to America.

The letters of elder Wilhelm Lange (*q.v.*) of Brenckenhoffswalde, Prussia, to Peter Wedel in 1817-20 (preserved in BeCL) are of great significance regarding the spiritual and social conditions of the Mennonites of that time, the contacts of the group with pietistic circles, as well as their migration to Russia. Wedel was the leader of a moderately progressive group during the days of the Klaas Reimer (*q.v.*) and Bible society controversies, the revival and the founding of various Mennonite groups. He was in contact with Moravians and promoted missions.   C.K.

Jakob Brandt, "Kurze Notizen aus dem Lebenslauf des verstorbenen Aeltesten Peter Wedel" (BeCL); Friesen, *Brüderschaft,* 75, 108 f., 117, 167, 305; J. A. Duerksen, "Przechowka and Alexanderwohl," *Menn. Life* X (April 1955) 76.

Wedel, Peter H. (c1865-97), an evangelist and missionary of the Mennonite Brethren Church, was born in Alexanderwohl, Molotschna Mennonite settlement, South Russia, about 1865, the son of Cornelius P. Wedel, who emigrated to America in 1874 with his family, settling near Goessel, Marion Co., Kan. Cornelius Wedel became elder of the M.B. Church there in 1886. Their son Peter, a very gifted boy, received his education partly in Russia and partly in America and became a country schoolteacher.

Wedel was converted at an early age and joined the M.B. Church through baptism and became an active member. The Mennonitischer Schulverein (*q.v.*) supported Wedel at the Baptist Theological Seminary, Rochester, N.Y., for some time, hoping that he would later establish a Mennonite Brethren church school.

Upon the completion of his course Wedel, however, decided to enter evangelistic work. In 1888-95 he was exceedingly active and effective in conducting evangelistic campaigns in the M.B. congregations of Kansas, Nebraska, South Dakota, and Minnesota.

Wedel felt called to serve as a foreign missionary. Since the M.B. Church at that time had no foreign mission field, he decided to go under the German Baptist Missionary Society. After his marriage to Martha Liebig he left for Cameroons, Africa, stopping in Germany and also making a visit to the Mennonite settlements of South Russia, in both countries conducting very effective evangelistic campaigns. After two years of effective service on the mission field his health required him to leave. He died on the voyage to Europe on Aug. 10, 1897, and was buried at sea. His short service and early death had a profound effect upon the Mennonite Brethren Church and was a powerful influence in beginning its own foreign mission work   J.H.L.

Wederdo(o)pers (German, *Wiedertäufer*) is the name formerly often given to the Mennonites in Holland, e.g., by Guy de Brez (*q.v.*) and Calvinist opponents of the Dutch Mennonites until the 18th century. Mennonite authors used the word "Wederdopers" only to denote the revolutionary Anabaptists, particularly those of Münster (*q.v.*) (See **Anabaptist.**)   vDZ.

Weduwfonds van Doopsgezinde Predikanten in de Provincie Groningen (Fund for pensioning widows of Mennonite ministers in the Dutch province of Groningen) was founded in 1835. (*DJ* 1837, 31 f.)
                                                  vDZ.

Weduwfonds voor Noord- en Zuid-Holland: see **Fonds tot Ondersteuning.**

Weduwenfonds voor Doopsgezinde Predikanten: see **Zwolsche Weduwenfonds.**

Weekday Bible School, a name given to an arrangement whereby the public schools, especially high schools, in some American communities have at times permitted or invited representatives of the local churches to teach Bible to volunteer classes in the school building, either at a regular period in the daily class schedule, after the last period of the regular schedule, or during a noon or recess period. At times pupils have been released to attend classes conducted at near-by churches. Sometimes teachers have been provided by single churches, at other times by co-operating churches, at times by colleges or seminaries near by. Often the salary of the Bible teacher is paid by the church or churches, at times even by the school. Not often have Mennonites taken up this type of religious instruction because of lack of teachers or distance from the school. A notable exception has been Elkhart and Lagrange counties in Northern Indiana, especially Goshen, Topeka, Nappanee, Wakarusa, and Millersburg, where Mennonite churches have shared in supporting such a program and some Mennonite teachers have served, and where a number of students of the Goshen College Biblical Seminary have taught in the high schools on practical work assignments from the seminary. This program has been discontinued.

Another meaning of the weekday Bible school refers to a congregational evening Bible study meeting not connected with the public school. The first appearance of this weekday Bible school in the Mennonite Church (MC) was c1930, when J. D. Mininger established a school at the Kansas City Mennonite Mission, which was one of a large number of such schools co-operating in an interdenominational community school planned to serve the children of school age. Weekday Bible schools found sufficient interest also in the Lancaster Mennonite Conference that a weekday Bible school course was prepared by a Conference committee to meet local needs. In

1940 the Curriculum Committee of the General Sunday School Committee built an enlarged curriculum based on the Lancaster course. In the next decade a considerable number of congregations introduced the weekday Bible school, but attached it to the Wednesday evening congregational meeting. This was something quite different from work in the public schools. The greatest flourishing of this movement was in the Franconia Conference, where for a decade large numbers enrolled in the Wednesday evening Bible study classes.

Between 1946 and 1954 little work was done in preparation of a weekday Bible school curriculum. The Lancaster materials for twelve grades (two preschool, grades 1-10) continue to be available and have gone through several editions. During the summer of 1954, however, outlines for a weekday Bible curriculum were prepared to supplement the projected graded Sunday-school curriculum. Weekday Bible school promotion has been carried on by the Mennonite Commission for Christian Education through its Weekday Bible School Secretary, Noah G. Good, Lancaster, Pa.

                                          H.S.B., P.M.L.

Paul Lederach, "History of Religious Education in the Mennonite Church" (unpublished doctoral dissertation at Southwestern Baptist Theological Seminary, 1949) 257-60.

Weekly Echo, edited and published by D. G. Gehman, Bally, Pa., was an 8-column, 4-page newspaper, 22 x 15½ in., with the stated purpose of supplementing the *Herald of Truth* by reporting news of particular interest to every Mennonite family and more particularly to Mennonites in Eastern Pennsylvania and Washington County, Md. The first issue appeared April 24, 1902. Publication ceased with the ninth issue, June 19, 1902, the paper having failed to receive the expected support and encouragement from "the Mennonite people at large." In addition to purely personal items from Mennonite communities in eastern Pennsylvania, it contained inspirational articles, home and farm features, a weekly discussion of the Sunday-school lesson by D. M. Stearns, articles on Mennonite history, and a few advertisements. The last five issues included the "Calendar of Meetings at all the Mennonite Congregations in Eastern Pa." for the following Sunday. The Goshen College Library has issues 5, 6, 8, and 9.   N.P.S.

Weenig(h)em, Bastiaan (Sebastiaan) **van,** b. c1625, d. March 24, 1697, was a merchant at Rotterdam, Holland, and a minister of the local Flemish Mennonite church from 1655 and elder from 1659. He was a man of great power and authority, somewhat imperious, prompted by great love for the church and the desire to maintain its strictly basic principles, a fervid opponent of Collegiantism (*q.v.*) and other liberal movements in the Dutch brotherhood which he often fought with more vigor and ability than courtesy. In 1659 and again in 1668 he dropped the proposal of the Rotterdam Waterlanders (*q.v.*) to merge with the Flemish. In 1660 he was the instigator and secretary of a conference of conservative Flemish leaders held at Leiden (see **Leidsche Synode**) to take measures against Galenus (q.v.) Abrahamsz and his progressive adherents. In July and August 1661 he was one of the seventeen ministers called in to mediate in the dissensions in the Utrecht Flemish congregation between a strict and a moderate group. They solved the matter by suspending the progressive preachers (see **Maurik, W. van**). Van Weenigem led the Flemish congregation of Schiedam (q.v.) in 1674 to a stricter church discipline, excluding from the pulpit preachers who did not agree with the confessions of faith, and refusing the Lord's Supper to such members as worshiped with the Collegiants or the Remonstrants (q.v.). After the great schism among the Dutch Mennonites in 1664 when the Lammerenkrijgh (q.v.) divided them into liberal Lamists (q.v.) and strict Zonists (q.v.), van Weenigem visited many churches persuading them to side with the Zonists, in this way preparing the Zonist conference called the Verbondt (q.v.) van Eenigheydt.

He often served in other Mennonite congregations and was very active in supporting a number of small churches in the neighborhood of Rotterdam like Zevenhoven and Sommelsdijk (q.v.); in Sommelsdijk he settled a quarrel in 1676. Several times he preached and administered baptism and communion at Hamburg and in 1663 he ordained Gerrit Roosen (q.v.) as an elder of the Hamburg-Altona congregation.

In the struggle against the growing liberalism van Weenigem was supported by the well-known elder of Dordrecht and composer of the great Martyrs' Mirror, T. J. van Braght (q.v.). Together they drew up a new confession of faith in 1661, which was, however, never officially approved, but became the basis of the Verbondt van Eenigheydt. The Amsterdam Library has a copy of Bastiaan van Weynich —Om uyt last van Tieleman van Bracht, Bisschop van Dort. Copia van een ernstige Vermaen-Brief, geschreven aen Samuel Apostool (q.v.) cum Sociis. Dordrecht den 20 Jan. 1664 (n.p., n.d.), an anonymous booklet which severely critcizes van Weenighem's conservatism.

When gradually a less strict and more tolerant attitude arose in the Rotterdam Flemish congregation, van Weenigem was deeply disappointed; he then resigned as elder on Jan. 13, 1686.

In July 1663, when in Hamburg, he met with representatives of the Hamburg Dompelaars (q.v.) church, who had separated from the Mennonites. This conversation was followed by a correspondence which lasted until 1667 and by the publication of a number of books on baptism. Van Weenigem published Nootwendige Verantwoording van zeventien Redenen (Rotterdam, 1666), and De Maniere van Doop, Voetwasschinge en Avontmael, soo by de Dompelaars tot Hamborg gebruyckt wert, wederleyt (Rotterdam, 1666). He was opposed by the Hamburg Dompelaar preacher Jan Arents in Eindelijcke Verklaringe der gedoopte Christenen . . . (n.p., 1668), then wrote Antidotum ofte Tegengif op eenen Brief, geschr. uyt Hamborgh, van Samuel Stockmann Isaacksz. . . . En op seker Boeckjen genaemt: Eyndelijcke Verklaringe . . . (Rotterdam, 1669). This latter book by van Weenigem was refuted by W. D. Redoch, Antidoti Wenigani Vanitas, of Ydelheydt van Bastiaans van W.'s laatste uyt-

gegevene Tracktaatje . . . , 2 vv. (Haarlem, 1672 and 1673).

Besides these polemics van Weenigem published Kruys-poorte of Lydens-schoole (Rotterdam, 1664), Gansche Natuere des Doops (Rotterdam, 1668), 't Gelukkig Afsterven der Rechtveerdige (Rotterdam, 1684), a catechetical booklet, called Catechisatie ofte Vragen en Antwoorden over het . . . heyligh Euangelium van Mattheus (Rotterdam, 1684), and his farewell sermon Afscheyds-Reden gedaen tot Rotterdam (n.p., 1686).

In his old age (June 1694) van Weenigem was temporarily excluded from the communion service because as a minor public official he had sworn an oath. Though he was somewhat disappointed, he remained a loyal member of the church. At his death he left the Rotterdam congregation a large legacy.

Van Weenigem, who (judging by his family name) stemmed from Flanders, married Liesbet van Hemelcours. Both he and his wife were baptized in in 1649 into the Rotterdam Flemish congregation. They had two daughters, one of whom was Elizabeth Catharine, b. in 1647, who in 1674 was married to Pieter van Beeck, a wealthy Mennonite merchant in Amsterdam.

In Amsterdam (Zonist church) there were also some van Weenigems. A Sebastiaan van Weenigem was baptized there in 1713.   vDZ.

N.N.B.Wb. III, 1397; K. Vos, Geschiedenis der Doopsgez. gemeente te Rotterdam (1907, repr.) 18-20, 42; DB 1896, 55, 58; 1900, 188; 1908, 107; 1909, 159; 1916, 150 f., 170, 172, 181; B. C. Roosen, Gesch. der Mennoniten-Gemeinde zu Hamburg und Altona I (Hamburg, 1886) 43, 46 f., 60; K. Vos, "Sebastiaan van Weenigem en het Eedsvraagstuk," in Ned. Archief v. Kerkgeschiedenis II (1908) 137 f. (1909).

Weeping Water, Neb., Civilian Public Service Camp No. 25, located 35 miles east of Lincoln, was opened in April 1942 and closed in April 1943. It was a soil conservation camp operated by the Mennonite Central Committee.   M.G.

Melvin Gingerich, Service for Peace (Akron, 1949) 121.

Weesp, a town in the Dutch province of North Holland, some ten miles east of Amsterdam, formerly the seat of a Mennonite congregation, concerning which there is only scant information. The year of founding is not known. Elder Leenaert (q.v.) Bouwens baptized seven persons c1575 at Weesp (not 55 as is stated by Blaupot ten Cate). Originally the congregation of Weesp was more or less connected with that of neighboring Muiden (q.v.). In the 17th century there were two congregations at Weesp, one Flemish and one Waterlander; the latter, which was represented in 1647 at the Waterlander conference at Amsterdam by Johannes Verlaen, merged before 1675 with the Flemish congregation, which was then also called Weesp and Overmeer (q.v.). In 1655 it contributed liberally to the needs of the congregation of De Rijp (q.v.), which had suffered considerable damage by a great fire. In 1675 Weesp joined the (Lamist) Conference of South Holland. Since the pulpit was from this time on mostly vacant, the congregation was supported by the Lamist congregation of Amsterdam, both financially and with ministerial service. The membership was very small, in 1686 numbering hardly a dozen baptized members. The church books of the Weesp congregation, which are now in the Amsterdam Mennonite archives, cover the years 1692-1761. From these it is known that the congregation had died out by 1760, but it is not mentioned in the *Naamlijsts* of 1743 and later. vDZ.

Inv. Arch. Amst. I, No. 814; II, Nos. 2288, 2342 f.; II, 2, Nos. 376, 643-50; *DB* 1872, 61, 67; 1892, 124, 125, 126; 1918, 3, 50, 52; Blaupot t. C., *Holland* I, 24, 222, 330; II, 45.

Weetdoener was the name of the man who during the 16th-century period of persecution of the Anabaptists-Mennonites announced to the members of the church the place and hour of meetings, which varied because of danger of being surprised. Weetdoeners who thus made the rounds of the entire congregation are known in Amsterdam and Antwerp, and probably also functioned in other larger towns. At Strasbourg in 1540 a "Büttel" performed these services. vDZ.

Wegh na Vreden-stadt: see **Way to the City of Peace.**

Wehrfreiheit der Altpreussischen Mennoniten, Die. *Eine geschichtliche Erörterung* (Marienburg, 1863), by Wilhelm Mannhardt (*q.v.*), was the first comprehensive documented history of the Mennonite principle of nonresistance. The book consists of 202 pages and 95 pages of appendices. In the first chapter the author treats the "dogma" of nonresistance among the various Mennonite groups; in the second chapter, the major part of the book, he presents the relation of the Mennonites of Prussia to the state. In an appendix he quotes from the writings of Menno Simons and from Mennonite confessions of faith, catechisms, and official documents by the governments to prove that the Mennonites traditionally have adhered to the principle of nonresistance and that this has been honored by rulers and governments.

The reason for the writing of this book was a Prussian cabinet order in preparation according to which the Mennonites of Prussia, who had enjoyed complete exemption from military service, were now expected to do alternative service. In spite of the book the cabinet order was passed March 3, 1868. This book designates the last definite stand on nonresistance by a large group of Prussian Mennonites. Those who were not willing to accept alternative noncombatant service migrated to Russia and America. The majority, however, stayed and accepted this service and gradually also full military service. By 1933 no German Mennonites claimed exemption from full military service. Mannhardt also wrote the Danzig *Gedenkbuch der Gemeinde,* vol. III, in which he relates this development in great detail. Later he somewhat modified his position on nonresistance, and wrote a series of articles in *Mennonitische Blätter,* "Zur Wehrfrage," 1868, 75 f., and 1869, 5-8, 12-15, 31-34, 37-41, 48-50. (See also **Nonresistance** and **Mannhardt, Johann Wilhelm.**) C.K.

H. G. Mannhardt, *Die Danziger Mennonitengemeinde* (Danzig, 1919) 124 ff., 175 ff.; *ML* IV.

Weierhof, a hamlet at the foot of the Donnersberg (*q.v.*) near Marnheim, Palatinate, Germany, the center of a Mennonite congregation. It was originally (from 835) the property of a monastery, was secularized in 1564, destroyed in the Thirty Years' War, and in 1682 given in hereditary lease to the "Mennonist" Peter Crayenbühl (Krehbiel). In his letter to the elector negotiating for the estate, Crayenbühl requested that he and his family be permitted to perform their worship unmolested. The position taken by the Protestant state church council to this request states, "The church council is of the opinion . . . that what the petitioner wants to read and pray in his house with his children cannot be refused him, but it would have to be done with the express restriction that he will not take on any Anabaptist help or admit any other persons of the Anabaptist sect and under any pretext or appearance form a congregation of them. Otherwise he shall lose even this particular concession and be expelled." This was in principle the attitude of the time toward the Mennonites who were settling in the region. According to the lists of Mennonites in the Generallandesarchiv in Karlsruhe the following are named in 1685 in the territory now included in the Weierhof congregation: Elbisheimerhöfe, Braun Herbach with five children, and Christoffel Gohl with three children; in Marnheim, Martin Tempel's widow and seven children; in Weierhof, Peter Creyenbühl with nine children, six of them sons; two were married and living on the home place, viz., Ulrich with three children and Peter with one child; on Heyerhof, Ulrich Burkard with one daughter, Jacob Trinkener with two sons and a daughter, Felix Berky with two sons; Peter Brubacher, no children; in Immesheim, one family; in 1686 in the Bolanden district 10 families with 32 children; in 1687 at Marnheim and Elbisheimerhof, one family. But very soon a decided change took place. In 1706 the Weierhof with other estates and villages passed into the jurisdiction of Nassau-Weilburg, whose rulers were less intolerant toward the Mennonites than the Catholic electors of the Palatinate. It is probable that a congregation was organized at this time, though the contract as late as 1770 stipulated that the lessee was permitted to worship with his own family, but not to admit anybody else. An almsbook, which goes back to 1716, indicates that the congregations of Weierhof and Erbesbüdesheim (*q.v.*) held their services together, alternating between the two places. Christel Krehbiel was the deacon. As far as is known there were many Mennonites living in the villages and farms of the vicinity, as in Albisheim, Bennhausen, Bolanderhof, Donnersbergerhof (*q.v.*), Froschauerhof, Gundheimerhof, Marnheim, Münsterhof, Neuhof, Niederwiesen, Rosenthalerhof, and Rüssingen. In 1748 the Erbesbüdesheim congregation became independent. In 1835 it resumed the former bonds with Weierhof, but was then known as the Uffhofen congregation; the two congregations jointly engaged Weierhof's first professional minister, Hermann Reeder (*q.v.*), and have continued this practice ever since.

A list of Mennonites left of the Rhine drawn up in 1732 names twenty families on the Weierhof. The preachers were Rudolf Kägy at Niederwiesen and Hans Ellenberger; Jakob Hagmann was the deacon. A list of 1762 gives Ulrich Ellenberger, Hans Bürcky, Abraham Künzi, and Jakob Haury as elders and preachers.

The Dutch *Naamlijst* (*q.v.*) of 1766 for "Rheingrafenstein, Erbesbüdesheim, and Weierhof" lists Ulrich Ellenberger, elder 1743; Christian Moser (1787 mentioned in the Rheingrafenstein congregation), Jakob Galle (in 1787 in the Erbesbüdesheim congregation, from Uffhofen), Jakob Herr (?), Adam Krehbiel, Christian Krehbiel. The 1787 list (partly in contradiction with the above, based on Reeder's report) names for the now independent congregation of Weierhof "bei Kirchheimbolanden": Adam Krehbiel 1758, Michael Krehbiel 1762, Rudolf Ellenberger 1766, Ulrich Krehbiel 1783.

After the death of Ulrich Ellenberger (c1765), Jost's son Adam Krehbiel took charge of the congregation. His faithful service and the love and devotion with which he always performed the duties of his office are attested again and again. Even today his name "Adamvetter" lives on in tradition. He was a friend of Peter Weber (*q.v.*) of Hardenberg and shared his experience. It is possible that the petition of 1767 to the authorities of Nassau-Weilburg, requesting permission to hold services in their homes, originated with him. This request was apparently granted, for on Sept. 4, 1769, another request was addressed to the prince by Heinrich, Adam, and Christian Krehbiel and Jakob Kägy, requesting permission to build a dwelling house with a room large enough for their services. This request apparently received no answer. Nevertheless they began to build the following spring, but had to stop upon government orders. Through the intervention of La Poitrie they, however, soon received the desired permission upon payment of a fee. In the same year, perhaps in October 1770, the meetinghouse, known as "Die Lehr" was put into use, with the assistance of Jakob Galle of Uffhofen and Johannes Krehbiel of Wartenberg. In 1777 Christian Krehbiel took over the function of the deacon and treasurer.

To support Adam Krehbiel, Michael Krehbiel of Donnersberg was ordained to the ministry in 1781 and Rudolf Ellenberger of Rüssingen in 1783. But in the 1790's they died, leaving Adam alone again. In consequence of the French Revolution the chapel was used as a soldiers' barracks, and was badly damaged. During this time the congregation again met in the home of Adam Krehbiel. The aged "Adamvetter" had by this time become quite feeble. Assistants chosen to support him were Johannes Krehbiel, his son-in-law, Johannes Stauffer of Bolanderhof (he died after preaching only two sermons), Jakob Brubacher of Albisheim, and Jakob Krehbiel, a grandson of Adam. Adamvetter died in 1794, mourned by the entire congregation as well as others who had a high regard for him. Now Johannes Bürcky of Albisheim and Michael Krehbiel II of Donnersberg were chosen as preachers; but Jakob had the burden of the responsibility.

The Ibersheim conferences of 1793 and 1795 were attended by Jakob Krehbiel and his father Johannes representing Weierhof.

In 1812-13 the congregation acquired a cemetery.

A plague-like epidemic carried by the soldiers fleeing from Russia struck many people, including Jakob Krehbiel and Johannes Bürcky. The congregation was then in a rather orphaned state. For a time the preachers of the neighboring congregations, especially Jakob Neff of Kriegsheim, looked after the elder's work, until a new election was held in 1816. Jakob Krehbiel of Pfrimmerhof and Georg Neukumeter of Bennhausen were chosen. The former in particular worked with devotion and fluency until he emigrated to America in 1827. As is shown in a booklet, he had drawn a small salary. The preachers then chosen had difficulty in consenting to take upon themselves the entire duty; also some dissensions had arisen within the congregation.

Hermann Reeder (*q.v.*), the preacher of the Neuwied congregation, made a visit at Weierhof and was chosen the first professional minister of the Weierhof congregation in 1835. He had received some training with the English Baptists and was therefore considered an educated man. The religious life of the congregation grew under his care. Church attendance increased to such an extent that a new church had to be built. On Nov. 1, 1837, the new church, built on the plans of a Baptist chapel in Tottenham, England, was dedicated by Risser of Sembach (*q.v.*), Jakob Ellenberger of Friedelsheim (*q.v.*), and Molenaar of Monsheim. The entire cost was met by voluntary contributions. The contractor or supervisor of the erection was Jakob Krehbiel, a miller. In 1848 Reeder returned to Neuwied.

Reeder's successor was Michael Löwenberg (*q.v.*), who was in addition a teacher in the village. Upon his death in 1874 his son Thomas was chosen, who made a contribution especially in choral work. He served the congregation until 1882, when he accepted a call to Ibersheim (*q.v.*). Shortly before he left he had begun a parsonage according to plans of his own. It was completed after his departure and acquired by the congregation. Until Johannes Krehbiel of Weierhof could complete his education, S. Blickensdörfer of Sembach looked after the congregation. In 1886 Johannes Krehbiel took over his work. But soon afterward he succumbed to a mysterious disease. The new choice fell upon Christian Neff of Ludwigshafen, who was ordained in the winter of 1887. He served the congregation without intermission until 1938, when his assistant, Paul Schowalter of the Kaplaneihof of the Deutschhof-Geisberg congregation (*q.v.*), became his successor. During World War II Neff had to take charge of the Weierhof congregation once more until Schowalter's discharge from the army.

During the long and blessed service of Christian Neff the Weierhof parsonage was a frequent center for visits by brethren from Germany and other countries. Americans, French, Dutch, Russian, and Swiss brethren came here to visit or to study. As preacher and pastor of his congregation, for decades as chairman of the Conference of South German Mennonites (*q.v.*) and many other Mennonite associations, as a competent scholar in Mennonite history, as a pillar of all German Mennonitism and beyond its borders, he will not be forgotten. He died on Dec. 30, 1946, at the Weierhof.

Weierhof very early (c1800) had its own school,

a sort of ministerial training school, which was after a period of interruptions built up by Michael Löwenberg and was finally to be developed into a secondary school with a boarding school. Known as the "Realanstalt am Donnersberg" (q.v.), under the leadership of Ernst and Gustav Göbel, it became known far beyond the Palatinate among Mennonites and non-Mennonites. Its music teacher, Lorenz Wettschureck, edited the musical part of the hymnal of the Conference of the South German Mennonites in 1910 and added four-part harmonization.

Conferences of the Palatine and Hessian Mennonites were held at the Weierhof in 1830, 1873, 1882, 1890, 1900, 1911, 1925, 1933, and 1940. On April 3 and 4, 1918, there was a conference of Russian Mennonites, attended by about 20 persons, at which the question of the resettlement of Russian Mennonites was discussed in the light of the Revolution. Also the conferences of the leaders and ministers of the Palatinate and Rhenish Hesse were held annually in near-by Marnheim.

Of special value to the religious life of the brotherhood were the Bible courses held at the Weierhof 1907-14 by Jakob Vetter. After World War I they were resumed (with a few intermissions) by Jakob Kroeker (q.v.), with the co-operation of the preachers of the Palatine-Hessian congregations as well as those of Switzerland. There were often visitors from many German congregations present.

The Weierhof congregation is a member of the *Konferenz der pfälzisch-hessischen Mennonitengemeinden*, the *Konferenz der süddeutschen Mennoniten*, the *Vereinigung der Deutschen Mennonitengemeinden*, and the "funds" connected with this *Vereinigung*, and also of the *Vereinigung der bairischen Mennonitengemeinden*.

The membership of the Weierhof congregation varies in number between 350 and 400, inclusive of unbaptized children. The baptized membership in 1957 was about 450 adults, besides 85 children. The members live in 50 different villages. Of these, 107 adults and 57 children are refugees, most of them from West Prussia, who moved into the area in 1948-49. Neff, C.G.

Christian Galle, "Der Weierhof im Wandel der Zeit," *Menn. Jahrbuch* (Newton, 1955) 9-16; *Gem.-Kal.* 1958, 47-60; *ML* IV.

Weigel, Valentin (1533-88), a Protestant pastor in Zschoppau, Saxony, Germany. His important writings, which did not become generally known until after his death, reveal a remarkable similarity in spirit to Tauler (q.v.) and Sebastian Franck (q.v.). They had a strong influence upon Jakob Böhme, Gottfried Arnold (q.v.), and Johannes Arndt. His ideas are closely related to those of the Anabaptists and he is therefore often erroneously reckoned among them. (See **Spiritualists**.) (*ML* IV.) Neff

Weil, Alexander, author of *Histoire de la guerre des Anabaptistes* (Paris, 1875). The author presents Anabaptism as a war similar to the Peasants' War, the political and social aspects of the latter corresponding to the religious and social aspects of the other. He shows little understanding for the essence of Anabaptism. Though he makes an (unsuccessful) attempt to distinguish the radical Anabaptists from

the peaceful ones, he sees in the former only the logical outcome of the latter. In the introduction he tries to present the fundamental principles of Anabaptism. The chapter headings indicate the nature of the book. Part I: (1) The Anabaptists in Zwickau and Wittenberg; (2) The Anabaptists at the Head of the Revolting Peasants; (3) The Anabaptists in Switzerland; (4) The Anabaptists in Sweden; (5) Persecutions and Martyrs. Part II: Peaceful Attempts: (1) The Hutterian Brethren; (2) The Gabrielites; (3) Hutterite Customs. Gabriel's Death; (4) Confession of Faith of the Anabaptists After the Reaction and Persecution; (5) Melchior Hofmann and Matthijssen. Part III: (1) Münster; (2) The First Conflicts with the Bishopric; (3) Knipperdolling; The English Plague; (4) Rottmann; (5) Struggle Between Rottmann and the Bishop of Waldeck; (6) Consequences of the Conflict and the Beginning of Hostility; (7) Letters of Luther and Melanchthon; (8) Repressalien and the Treaty of Peace; (9) Rottmann, Anabaptist; (10) Jan Bockelson van Leiden. (*ML* IV.) Neff

Weilertal (Val-de-Ville) in Alsace, a valley where the Mennonite congregation of Markirch (q.v.), also called Chatenois (q.v.) or Kestenholtz, held its meetings in the early 20th century. In 1941 the baptized membership numbered about 20. During World War II this congregation was dissolved, the few remaining members joining the Le Hang (q.v.) church. vDZ.

Weischenfelder, Hans, an Anabaptist martyr, burned at the stake at Bamberg (q.v.), Bavaria, on Jan. 30, 1528, with Endres Weiss, Else Koch, Margaret Petz, and Katharina Rosner. Weischenfelder was a miller of Uetzing, Upper Franconia, Germany. In his cross-examination he said that he was on his way to Moravia to join the Hutterites, that he was baptized by Hans Hut (q.v.), and made brief statements on some points of doctrine, such as the sacraments. But instead of going to Moravia he stayed behind at Passau "to tend the flock" there. In March 1527, under pressure, he turned against Hut and testified that Hut had been guilty of revolutionary teachings, although Mertain Weischenfelder (q.v.) and others denied this. H.S.B.

Wappler, *Thüringen,* 273-82; Herbert Klassen, "Some Aspects of the Teaching of Hans Hut" (M.A. thesis, University of British Columbia, 1958); *ML* IV.

Weischenfelder, Mertain and **Veit,** Anabaptists of Uetzing, Upper Franconia, Germany, were baptized by Hans Hut in October 1526. Their three cross-examinations, March 16-18, 1527, are of importance to the history of the Anabaptists of Franconia and the work of Hans Hut (q.v.). Mertain testified that Hut never preached revolutionary doctrine. (Wappler, *Thüringen,* 236-43; *ML* IV.) Neff

Weiss, Endres, an Anabaptist martyr, burned at the stake on Jan. 30, 1528, at Bamberg, Germany, with four other Anabaptists. (See **Weischenfelder, Hans.**)

Weisse, Michael, a native of Silesia, Germany. He was a Roman Catholic priest who in 1531 became a minister of the Moravian Brethren in Moravia. He occupies a position of honor in the history of German hymnology by his hymnal, *Ein New Gesangbuchlen*. Five hymns of this hymnal also appear in the second part of the *Ausbund* (*q.v.*), first printed in 1583, where four of them are attributed to Anabaptists and one to John Hus. These five hymns are: "Als Christus mit seinr waren lehr," by Michael Sattler (*q.v.*) (*Ausbund*, No. 46); "Du glaubigs hertz, so benedey," by Walpurga von Pappenheim (*q.v.*) (*Ausbund*, No. 409); "O Jesu, der du sehlig machst," by Lorentz Ringmacher (*q.v.*) (*Ausbund*, No. 407); "O Gott Schöpffer, Heilger Geist," by Christof Bifel (*Ausbund*, No. 274); and "Jesus Christus Gottes Sohn," by John Hus (*Ausbund*, No. 216). Wolkan, however, considers all these attributions erroneous, and says that all five of these hymns were written by Weisse. These songs are also found in Wackernagel, *Kirchenlied* III, Nos. 405, 334, 386, 320, 318.   W.W.

J. Theodor Müller, *Geschichte der Böhmischen Brüder* II (Herrnhut, 1931) 28-30; *ML* IV.

Weissenheim am Berg, in the duchy of Leiningen, Palatinate, Germany, is mentioned in the Dutch *Naamlijst* of 1767 as the seat of a Mennonite congregation of Swiss refugees, with Christian Jotter (Yoder) (later elder until *c*1785) and Christian Schwartstrauben (until *c*1785) as preachers. The Mennonites of Weissenheim, who under the counts of Leiningen (*q.v.*) worshiped undisturbed, later formed the congregation of Altleiningen (*q.v.*).

vDZ.

Welcome Tidings, a weekly 4-page 6½ x 10½ inch tract paper for use in Sunday schools, published by the Mennonite Publishing Company at Elkhart, Ind. The first issue was about April 1, 1887, the last December 1895, when the *Words of Cheer* became a weekly (January 1896) taking its place. GCL has an almost complete file. (The German issue was *Angenehme Stunden; q.v.*) In the first period it suspended publication during the winter months since few Sunday schools operated "evergreen."   H.S.B.

Weldy: see Welty.

Wellesley, Ont. The Mennonite Conference (MC) of Ontario in 1865 provided preaching services every four weeks for scattered families of Wellesley Township northwest of Waterloo County. Regular appointments were listed for twenty years. No communion service was reported. Since 1900 only a cemetery remains. The nearer Mennonite churches now are Shantz north of Baden, Hawkesville to the east, and Maple View A.M. westward.   J.C.F.

Wellesley Maple View Amish Mennonite Church: see **Maple View.**

Wellesley Old Order Amish congregation had its origin in 1886 as a schism of five families from the Maple View A.M. (*q.v.*) congregation in opposition to the use of a meetinghouse for worship. They were under bishop oversight from Holmes County, Ohio, until 1891, when they became an organized separate congregation, but they alternate services in close fellowship with the Mornington (*q.v.*) O.O.A.

group. The Lichti A.M. Church (*q.v.*), located a mile north of the village of Wellesley, broke off in 1912; it has a meetinghouse. The Mornington O.O.A. group in the same neighborhood was formed by a schism from the Poole A.M. (*q.v.*) congregation in 1886, also because of objections to a meetinghouse. The Poole A.M. group suffered a second schism in 1904, when the Nafziger O.O.A. congregation separated, which is now parallel to the Lichti A.M. congregation, having its own meetinghouse.

In 1958 the Wellesley O.O.A. congregation had 48 families with 140 members. The ministers were Amos Z. Albrecht bishop, and Menno Lichti, J. K. Jantzi, and J. N. Jantzi as preachers.   J.C.F.

Wellesley (Ont.) Reformed Mennonite Church: see **Kingwood** Meetinghouse.

Wellington County, Ont., borders Waterloo County on the east and on the north. In Puslinch Township reside a few families of the Wanner Mennonite Church. Puslinch Center was a Mennonite outpost (MC) about a century ago. There are some families of the Bethel (Elora) Mennonite (MC) Church and of the O.O.M. Church of West Montrose, an active Mennonite (MC) congregation at Glen Allen, and an O.O.M. congregation at Goshen. An M.C. congregation in Maryborough Township has died out. Other M.C. congregations with meetinghouses are located at Moorefield and at Berea (Bosworth Corners) west of Parker and 7 miles west of Alma. Guelph is the principal urban center of Wellington County.   J.C.F.

Wellman, Iowa, in northwestern Washington County (*q.v.*), had a population of 1,126 in 1958, among whom were at least 40 Mennonite families. Twelve Mennonite families lived in adjoining Daytonville. Nine Mennonite businesses are operated in the town. Although not exclusively Mennonite, the widely known Maplecrest Turkey Farms, long the largest independent turkey processing corporation in the world, was established by a local Mennonite, A. C. Gingerich. This organization has created many economic opportunities and considerable employment for the town and community. In 1953, for instance, 125 farmers were raising turkeys for processing in the Maplecrest plant. The Wellman Mennonite Church in the northern part of the town had a membership of 330 in 1957, and the near-by Daytonville Mennonite Church had 81. Wellman is a shopping center for a large Mennonite population living mostly north of the town. (See map of Johnson County.)

M.G.

Wellman Mennonite Church (MC), formerly called the Daytonville Mission, located in Wellman, Iowa, a member of the Iowa-Nebraska Conference, began in 1906 as a Sunday school in Daytonville Schoolhouse conducted by members of West Union congregation. The meetinghouse was acquired in 1911. W. S. Guengerich was first resident minister, ordained in 1925, followed by Edward Diener in 1926. The congregation was organized May 6, 1935. A new church with seating capacity of 650 at the north edge of Wellman was dedicated Nov. 10, 1940. The ministers in 1957 were George S. Miller and J. Max Yoder; the bishop was Simon Gingerich. The membership was 335. G.S.M.

Wells Tannery, Pa., Civilian Public Service Camp: see **Sideling Hill**.

Welmoet (Welmoed, Welmut, Weynken) **Jans** (dochter), an Anabaptist martyr, executed on June 7, 1535, at Hoorn, Dutch province of North Holland, together with four other victims, three men and one woman. They had been arrested in March 1535; apparently the city magistrates of Hoorn (*q.v.*) hesitated to sentence these five persons, who had a good reputation with their fellow citizens, and it was not until the Court of Holland at The Hague insisted on immediate and rigorous punishment that they were sentenced to death. They all died steadfast. The men were decapitated and the women "were led to the sea, where heavy stones were tied to their necks, and they were cast in, and drowned. Their bodies were ignominiously left to float about for a long time until the rulers were moved to have them taken out and buried." vDZ.

Mart. Mir. D 36 f., E 443 f.; *Inv. Arch. Amst.* I, No. 131; Mellink, *Wederdopers*, 168 f.

Wels, a town in Upper Austria, the seat of an Anabaptist congregation in 1528, which was, however, soon violently suppressed by the government. A number of members fled from the town when persecution set in. In 1528 Luther sent a warning concerning them to Wenzel Link, a clergyman in Nürnberg. Those who remained were arrested and those who did not recant were executed. At least twelve suffered martyrdom. (See **Haslinger, Leonhard** for an account of the trial and other particulars.) The captain's report, dated June 8, 1528, gives their names as Hans Neumair (*q.v.*), Leonhard Haslinger (*q.v.*), Hans Steinpeckh, Jörg Zacherle, Ulrich Perger, Jörg Kneuzinger, Peckenknecht, and two shoemaker's apprentices, both named Sebastian (Wastl). On the following Monday the wives of Haslinger and Zacherle, both named Barbara, were drowned. Madlen, the wife of Steinpeckh, was pregnant and was not executed until after the birth of her child. Six persons proffered the required oath and were released. HEGE.

J. Jäkel, *Zur Geschichte der Wiedertäufer in Oberösterreich* . . . (1889) 43 f.; Bernhard Raupach, *Evangelisches Oesterreich* . . . (Hamburg, 1772) 51; Beck, *Geschichts-Bücher*, 280; *ML* IV.

Welsh (Wälsch), **Antonius**: see **Rizzetto, Antonio**.

Welsh Mountain Industrial Mission (MC), near New Holland, Pa., grew out of an effort to help the Negroes who had settled on the Welsh Mountain. Because of low moral standards they had become shiftless and many of them outlaws. The Lancaster County Sunday School Mission held at Kinzers, in 1898 appointed twelve directors to establish an industrial mission. Samuel H. Musselman was the first chairman and Noah H. Mack secretary. Mack also served as superintendent until 1910. People were given an opportunity to work and were paid in provisions. The scope of activities included a store, school, truck and general farming, a shirt factory, broom making, carpet weaving, and, above all, preaching the Gospel. On Jan. 24, 1924, Arthur T. Moyer, who had served as superintendent from April 1, 1913, was fatally shot by a resident of the community who was caught stealing corn. The mission has been sponsored by the Eastern Mennonite Board of Missions and Charities since 1917.

The industrial phase was gradually discontinued and was closed *c*1924 and the property was converted into the Welsh Mountain Samaritan Home. The spiritual ministry was continued by the home staff until 1938, when the Welsh Mountain Mission was organized. A stone building 24 x 40 ft., originally built as a shirt factory, is used for meetings.

The program continues on an interracial basis. This was probably the first organized effort in the Mennonite church on behalf of the colored race. The total membership in 1957, including some workers, was 38, with Ira J. Buckwalter as superintendent and pastor. I.J.B.

Welsh Mountain Samaritan Home, located near New Holland, Pa., and sponsored by the Eastern Mennonite Board of Missions and Charities (MC), is the successor of the Welsh Mountain Industrial Mission (*q.v.*), which was converted into an old people's home and the name changed in 1924. The first guests were received soon afterward. Benjamin Buckwalter and wife of Newton, Kan., were assigned as the first superintendent and matron in charge. Extensions to the building were built in 1929 and again in 1940. The guest capacity is 32, with a staff of about 10. The location is healthful and many have found this a pleasant retreat to spend their closing days. Jesse Yoder and wife of Belleville, Pa., are the present superintendent and matron. I.J.B.

Welsing (Welsingh, Welsinck, Welzing), a Dutch Mennonite family, originally from Rees (*q.v.*) in the Rhineland, Germany, living there until the 18th century. Jakob Welsing, of Rees, was married in 1680 to Helena, a daughter of preacher Hendrik van Voorst, of Emmerich, and was a preacher of the Rees Mennonite congregation, as was his son (?) Isaack Welsink 1727-*c*35. Hendrik Welsing served the Rees congregation 1735-61/2 as its last preacher.

In 1657 a certain Jan Wolsingh (Welsinck) became a citizen of Nijmegen, Netherlands, and was soon after chosen as deacon or preacher of the Mennonite congregation, for in 1664 he was among the representatives of the Nijmegen congregation to sign the *Verbondt van Eenigheydt* (*q.v.*). Though it is not stated where he came from in 1657, it may be surmised that like most immigrants of Nijmegen in this period, he had moved in from the duchy of Jülich (*q.v.*), in which the Mennonites were not tolerated at that time.

About the same time some Welsings, probably from Rees, settled in Amsterdam, Holland, where they were members of the Lamist (*q.v.*) congregation, of which church Jan Welsing Is.zn was a deacon 1691-96, 1701-7, and 1713-18, and François Welsing 1734-40 and 1744-50. Their descendants are still found in the Rotterdam congregation.

Abraham Welsing, of Rees, moved to Cleve (*q.v.*) where he obtained citizenship in 1671 and started a linen weaving business, which had by 1716 grown into a considerable enterprise.   vDZ.

Dutch *Naamlijst;* church records of Amsterdam and Rotterdam; P. C. G. Guyot, *Bijdragen tot de Gesch. der Doopsgezinden te Nijmegen* (Nijmegen, 1845) 75; *MQR* XXV (1951) 250 f.; *ML* III, 440.

Welty (Wälti, Weldy, Welti), a Mennonite family name of Swiss origin meaning Walter, i.e., Ruler. The family originated in the communes of Rüderswil and Lauperswil in the canton of Bern. As early as 1534 a member of the family, Stoffel Wälti, was brought before the Bernese authorities for listening to Anabaptist sermons. Bernhard Wälti of Rüderswil met a martyr's death in Bern on July 7, 1537, for his Anabaptist faith. In 1672 the records reveal that a Hans Wälti was imprisoned in Bern and flogged for being an Anabaptist. He is probably the Hans Wälti listed in the Palatinate as a refugee a short time later. In 1703 Hans Wälti (called "Rot Hans") and others were imprisoned and sent to Bern. As early as 1738 an Uli Wälti and family of Rüderswyl were living in the Jura in Chaluet, near Moutier, having fled the intolerance of their Emmental home. Ulrich Weldy was listed in 1762 as a minister in the Palatinate. Niklaus Wälti of Lauperswil (1764-1834) and his family lived at Wintersingen, canton of Basel. His son John (1787-1855) became the progenitor of the family that settled in Putnam County, Ohio.

The ancestors of the Wälti families who settled in Wayne County, Ohio, in the 1830's and 1840's were Ulrich (1750-1834) of Rüderswyl and Christian (1767-?) of Lauperswil. Their descendants are also found at present in Moniteau County, Mo., as well as other Mennonite communities.

Another family of Wältis came to America in the fore part of the 19th century and settled in Westmoreland County, Pa. In 1851 they moved to northern Indiana where they changed their name to Weldy. Abraham Welty (   ) was the first Mennonite (MC) minister and bishop in Tuscarawas County, Ohio. Henry Weldy (1862-1934) served as a minister in the Holdeman Mennonite Church (MC), Elkhart County, Ind., as did also Silas L. Weldy (1877-1955). Dwight E. Weldy (1918-   ) joined the Goshen College faculty in 1948.

D.L.G.

Samuel H. Baumgartner, *Brief Sketches of Eight Generations. Descendants of Ulrich Welty born 1728* (Indianapolis, 1926); Daniel Kauffman, *Mennonite Cyclopedic Dictionary,* 392.

Welty and Sprunger, a bookstore and later a publishing agency, at Berne, Ind., the forerunner of the Mennonite Book Concern (*q.v.*), was organized as a partnership in 1884, named for the brothers Joel and Daniel Welty, and S. F. Sprunger, the pastor of the Berne (*q.v.*) Mennonite Church. The Welty brothers had opened the bookstore on May 9, 1882, with chief emphasis on religious books. In the fall of 1884 the General Conference (GCM) established a conference publication agency, called the "Christliche Central-Buchhandlung der Allgemeinen Conferenz der Mennoniten." It used several bookstores as outlets, among them the firm of Welty and Sprunger, and the firm name continued to appear on the title page of some publications immediately

following the conference publishing agency name. In 1893 the name was changed to Mennonite Book Concern and Welty and Sprunger disappeared. Joel Welty was the manager from 1884 on. In the fall of 1884 Welty and Sprunger loaned the conference $1,000 for three years as a capital fund with which to establish the conference publishing agency. In 1889 Welty and Sprunger appeared without the conference publishing agency as the publishers of the *Sonntagschul-Lektionen.*   H.S.B.

Wendel Ravens, an Anabaptist martyr: see **Ravens, Wendel.**

Wendelmoet Claesdochter, a Sacramentist martyr: see **Weynken Claes.**

Wengeln, a village in Prussia. In 1604 some Hutterian Brethren of Moravia sought permission to settle in Elbing (*q.v.*), West Prussia (*q.v.*). They had a lengthy talk with the mayor and the councillors, but in spite of the intercession of the Mennonites their petition was refused. They then settled in Wengeln, rented nine hides of land, and lived there under the protection of the Polish government according to the dictates of their conscience. In spite of protest by the Elbing city council, they were not molested. In the course of time this settlement was absorbed into the Mennonite settlement.   W.W.

L. Neubaur, "Mährische [Hutterite] Brüder in Elbing," *Ztscht für Kirchengeschichte,* 1912, 447-55; *ML* IV.

Wenger (Wanger, Winger), a Swiss Mennonite family name occurring among the Swiss and American Mennonites, especially in the M.C. branch. The progenitor of large numbers of American Wengers was Christian Wenger, who came to Philadelphia in 1727 and located in Lancaster County, where he married Eva Grabill. Two of his sons settled in the Shenandoah Valley of Virginia; from this branch of the family came the well-known evangelist and college president Amos D. Wenger (1867-1935) and Old Order Mennonite bishop John Dan Wenger, son-in-law of Bishop John Geil (1799-1899). In the Pennsylvania branch of the family a rather large number of ministers and deacons have served, almost all of them in the Lancaster Conference. Jonas G. Wenger (1840-1922), of Lancaster County, Pa., was a superintendent of the Old People's Home at Marshallville, Ohio. Martin D. Wenger (1841-1901), of Lancaster county, did his lifework at Elkhart, Ind., working for John F. Funk's Mennonite Publishing Company. John C. Wenger has taught in Goshen College Biblical Seminary since 1938, and served as deacon, preacher, and bishop in the Indiana-Michigan Conference (MC). His great-uncle, blind John S. Wenger (1843-1916), of Weaverland, Lancaster County, was widely known for his mechanical ability and for his devotion to the church; his biography is included in the booklet *Overcoming Handicaps.* Samuel S. Wenger (1903-) is an attorney at Lancaster, Pa. Paul A. Wenger (1889-   ) is a missionary in India. Frank and Harry Wenger are leaders in the C.G.C. Church.   J.C.W.

J. G. Wenger *et al., Descendants of Christian Wenger* (Elkhart, 1903); Delbert Gratz, *Bernese Anabaptists* (Scottdale, 1953).

Wenger, Amos Daniel (1867-1935), a Mennonite (MC) educator and leader, was born Nov. 25, 1867, in Rockingham County, not far from Edom, Va., the eighth of the eleven children of Jacob and Hannah Brenneman Wenger.

The summer he was eighteen he took a three weeks' normal course at Broadway, Va., and secured a teacher's certificate. In 1890-91 he taught the Perry School near South English, Iowa. In 1894 he was graduated from the Warrensburg Normal, Warrensburg, Mo. In the summer of 1894 he attended Moody Bible Insititute. After teaching the Sugar Creek School in Cass County, Mo., during which year he was ordained to the ministry by Bishop David Kauffman, he attended Penn College at Oskaloosa, Iowa, during the winter of 1895-96. Plans for more education were canceled as he became engaged in evangelistic work. The years 1894-1908 marked his greatest evangelistic effort.

After his trip around the world in 1899-1900, he published his book, *Six Months in Bible Lands*. Among the tracts he wrote as tract editor are: "Jesus Christ Is Coming," "Why I Do Not Join the Lodge," "Buried with Him in Baptism." His pamphlet, "Who Should Educate Our Children," was published in 1926. He also wrote the articles "Baptism" and "Temptation" for the first Bible Doctrine book (1914).

Wenger was pastor at Bethel, Cass Co., Mo., 1894-95, Keokuk Co., Iowa, 1896, Millersville, Pa., 1897-1908, Fentress, Va., 1908-22, and Harrisonburg, Va., 1922-35. He served on the Mennonite Publishing Committee and for several years was contributing editor to the *Gospel Herald*. In 1901-15 he was a member of the board of Elkhart Institute. He was tract editor for the Mennonite Publishing House, secretary of the General Mission Committee, a member of the Mennonite Board of Education. He served as a teacher and as president at Eastern Mennonite School (now E.M. College) 1922-d.35. He was also treasurer of its Board of Trustees.

He married Mary Hostetter (d. 1898) of Millersville, Pa., July 1, 1897. On Sept. 27, 1900, he married Anna May Lehman, also of Millersville, who was the mother of his eight children, one son of whom died in infancy. His three sons, Amos D. Wenger of Fentress, Paul L. Wenger of Waynesboro, Va., and Chester L. Wenger of Ethiopia, Africa, are (MC) ministers. Two daughters are ministers' wives, one a deacon's wife, and the fourth daughter is Rhoda Wenger, a missionary in Tanganyika (*q.v.*), Africa.

A. D. Wenger died Oct. 5, 1935, at Harrisonburg, Va., and was buried at the Mt. Pleasant Mennonite Church, Fentress, Va.   M.W.K.

Wenger, Geörg (George Wagner in van Braght, *Martyrs' Mirror*), an Anabaptist martyr, who was beheaded in 1591 at Lorentz in the Puster Valley in Tirol, Austria, after he had been imprisoned more than a year. In spite of torture he refused to betray his brethren, and all attempts to convert him to the Catholic faith failed. He was sentenced to death for leaving the Catholic Church, practicing a different baptism, and leading others to his heretical sect. When the sentence was read he replied that it was not a heretical sect that he belonged to, but the divine truth and the right way to the kingdom of God. Many followed to the site of execution, and many wept. He asked that his hands be untied that he might raise them in praise to God and to pray for strength to the end. Wolkan includes a song written in commemoration of his death and that of Jacob Platzer (*q.v.*), "Ihr Liebhaber der Wahrheit guet, lassts euch erzählen mit freiem Muet." John Horsch mentions three epistles written by him.   NEFF.

Beck, *Geschichts-Bücher*, 308; John Horsch, *The Hutterian Brethren* . . . (Scottdale, 1928) 133; Wolkan, *Lieder*, 236; *Mart. Mir.* D 778 f., E 1080-82, with picture; *ML* IV.

Wenger Mennonites. At first, after their organization in Lancaster County in 1893, the Old Order Mennonites under J. H. Martin prospered. But by 1926 Joseph Wenger and his element disagreed and some formed a separate unit. This separate unit, the Groffdale Conference, has no evening services, uses horses and carriages, and the same type of agricultural practices. Their language is German exclusively in the pulpit and considerably in the homes. They advised their boys in World War II days to go to jail rather than accept the CPS alternative. They use the singing table and the German hymnal. They number over 1200, mostly in eastern Lancaster County, Pa. They co-operate with the Addison Gingrich group at St. Jacobs, Ont., and some Wisler Mennonites in Indiana.   I.D.L.

Weniger, Martin, one of the chief spokesmen for the Anabaptists at the Zofingen (*q.v.*) disputation.

Wensing (Wenzing), **Christoffel Alberts,** of Groningen, Netherlands, d. there Aug. 23, 1703, married in 1682 to Antje Mennes of Appingedam, was a member of the local Groningen Old Flemish congregation. When he began to attend Collegiant (*q.v.*) meetings he had to answer before the elders of the church (Feb. 15, May, June 2, 1685, Jan. 17, July 25-28, Oct. 24, 1686). In several meetings Wensing defended Collegiant views, particularly on baptism by immersion, denying that the Old Flemish were the only true church, objecting to marital avoidance as practiced by the Old Flemish and the ban in case of marriage with a nonmember. Gradually other members of his congregation also began to worship with the Collegiants. Finally Wensing was banned on May 30, 1687, and the other adherents of Collegiantism soon after. Wensing, who is said to have been highly esteemed by his friends, wrote an account of his relations with the Collegiants and his banning by the Old Flemish; this manuscript is found in the Amsterdam Mennonite Archives.   vDZ.

Inv. Arch. Amst. II, No. 2945; *DB* 1879, 12 f.; 1883, 73-86; 1891, 25 ff.; J. C. van Slee, *De Rijnsburger Collegianten* (Haarlem, 1895) 222-28.

Werder (Danzig Werder, Grosses or Marienburg Werder, Elbing Werder, Grosswerder): see **Marienburg Werder.**

Werner, Valentin, one of the Swiss Brethren to whom Pilgram Marpeck's *Verantwortung* was given for criticism. On Aug. 26, 1559, he wrote a letter in Augsburg to Leupold Scharnschlager, the leader (*Vorsteher*) of the Grisons brotherhood, thanking him for all his trouble and effort in connection with Werner's epistle concerning the Judgment (*Gericht*). The rest of the letter deals with the joy and blessedness of being permitted to belong to the church of the elect and of being separated from the evil world.   W.W.

Ztscht des Vereins f. d. Gesch. Mährens u. Schlesiens, 1925, Nos. 3 and 4, 48-50; *Zwingliana*, 1926, 332-337; *ML* IV.

Wernersville, Pa., the location of Western State Hospital, a mental hospital in which Civilian Public Service Unit No. 118 served from November 1943 to June 1946, with the Mennonite Central Committee as the operating organization. The unit consisted of 30 men.   M.G.

Melvin Gingerich, *Service for Peace* (Akron, 1949) 239.

Wernlin (Wern, Werlin, Werner), **Jörg** (d. *c*1559), called Scherer, the son of Georg Wernlin of Esslingen (*q.v.*), who was a student at the University of Heidelberg in 1483 and was in 1523 the notary and secretary of the monastery at Adelberg. Jörg Wernlin studied the profession of barber-surgeon in Ulm, presumably with Nikolaus Launer, a physician suspected of Anabaptist sympathies. In 1530 Wernlin was arrested as an Anabaptist and chained in the hospital; then he was transferred to the prison as a dangerous preacher who led many astray; and finally, in spite of the pleas of his pregnant wife, he was expelled from the town because he refused to render the required oath. As Jörg Werlin Gunzenhofen (?), probably from Gunzenhausen, he tried to return to Ulm in 1531-32; he probably succeeded. He then became the doctor of the poor in the hospital and almshouse. In 1533 he apparently went to Moravia, but finding himself in disagreement with the Hutterites he returned to Ulm. In 1537 he was again expelled because of his Anabaptism. He betook himself to the Remstal, lived in the hamlet Wieler zum Stein, district of Marbach, in 1539, and as Jörg Schere served as a wound doctor. In 1540 he was in Esslingen and Stetten in the Remstal, which belonged to Hans Konrad Thumb of Neuburg, who sheltered Anabaptists and Schwenckfelders. In 1544 Wernlin became acquainted with Pilgram Marpeck and Schwenckfeld. He worked zealously in the Anabaptist cause. He was in Kirchenkirnberg in 1552. As Vorsteher of the Swiss Brethren he gathered from 70 to 100 people once a month for religious services in the woods around Esslingen, baptized, and in isolated homes served communion as late as 1557. He joined Pilgram Marpeck in resisting Schwenckfeld's attacks on the Anabaptists.   G.Bos.

City Archives of Ulm, *Rats- und Religionsprotokoll; Blätter für Württembergische Kirchengesch. 1897*, 118; *TA Württemberg; ML* IV.

Wervik, a town in the Belgian province of West Flanders close to the French boundary, is known in Mennonite history as the birthplace of the martyr Peter (*q.v.*) van Olmen (van Wervick). Here the martyrs Jelis (*q.v.*) Strings and Jelis (*q.v.*) and Pieter (*q.v.*) Potvliet were executed in 1562. The

inquisitor Titelman (*q.v.*) listed Wervik among the Flemish towns in which there was strong Anabaptist activity in 1561. Whether there was a congregation or not is unknown. About 1558 elder Jacob (*q.v.*) de Rore preached and baptized here.
vDZ.

Wesbus(ch), van, a former Mennonite family at Haarlem, Holland. Passchier van Wesbus (d. *c*1630), his son Hans Passchiers, his grandsons Jan (d. 1704) and Isaac, and his great-grandson Frans (b. 1700) were publishers and book printers at Haarlem, from whose presses appeared more than forty Mennonite books in 1601-72, including the *Martelaers-Spiegel* of 1631, writings of Dirk Philips, Hans de Ries, Jacques Outerman, Vincent de Hondt, Pieter Pietersz, Pieter Jansz Twisck, Pieter Verkindert, and others, and also some Mennonite hymnals. Hans Passchiers van Wesbus also published about 1630 a portrait of Menno Simons engraved by J. van (der) Velde.   vDZ.

Wesel, a town (1953 pop. 22,000) on the Lower Rhine in Germany, in the 16th century belonging to the duchy of Cleve (*q.v.*). Adolf Clarenbach (*q.v.*) was active here in 1524. In 1534, when Anabaptists from the Netherlands and from Cleve streamed into Münster, active contacts were maintained between Wesel and Münster. Heinrich Santes, a coppersmith of Wesel, was made a duke by Jan Bockelson. There were rumors that there were large numbers of Anabaptists in Wesel. The council arrested suspect wanderers. Heinrich Graess, one of the "prophets" sent out by Münster, was imprisoned and confessed his mission in Wesel and also betrayed his brethren in the town. Eighteen persons were imprisoned in 1535, whose names are given in the records. Some of them had been expelled from other places and had come to Wesel as refugees, e.g., Karl of Süstern, a cobbler, who was banished from Liége in 1534. Wolter Teschemacher, a native of Kuilenborgh, had reputedly just arrived from Münster to gain adherents and procure food for the besieged town. There were Wesel citizens among these Anabaptists: Otto Vink and his wife, Wilhelm Schlebusch and his wife, and Lijntgen Bottermanns. They were also arrested, although they belonged to the first families of the city and had been on the city council. The names of the prisoners, to whom 16 were added later, show that they came from all classes. Vink, Schlebusch, their wives, and four others were executed on Mt. Calvary and buried there in the presence of the Duke of Cleve. One woman was drowned, some were banished, and others pardoned. Several years later, when quiet Anabaptist groups were found in the city, the city council was less severe. But the radical wing of Anabaptists was not yet eradicated. In the early years of the Dutch War of Liberation the cobbler "King" Jan (*q.v.*) Willemsz, of Roermond, wandered through the country with a band of 300 companions, robbing and plundering in the region of Emmerich, Wesel, and Kalkar. No wonder that the Mennonites as late as 1700 were haunted by the specter of the Münster atrocities.

When the Reformed creed became dominant in Wesel, the Mennonites could maintain themselves only in smaller numbers in near-by Cleve and were not able to organize a congregation. The city council prevented any Mennonites from the outside from settling in the city. On Jan. 12, 1638, Johann Rebber, a Mennonite from Hamm, who had settled in Wesel without knowledge of the city council, was permitted to remain until Easter. The Reesen and Crämer families stayed longer. Maurice of Orange, the Stadholder in Cleve, requested of Frederick William, Elector of Brandenburg, that the Mennonites be tolerated and not be burdened with the oath. Nevertheless Jan Reesen and his brother had to obtain permission to retain the rights which they as citizens had enjoyed for 40 years. In 1694, when the Mennonites were expelled from Rheydt, Gottschalk Dietrichs of Elten came to Wesel with his family. He died here in 1701, and his wife in 1710. His three daughters remained in Wesel. After this nothing more is heard of Mennonites in Wesel.

HEGE.

K. W. Bouterwek, "Bekäntnus einiger persohnen, so der Widdertauff und des Munsterischen Unwesens halben alhie zu Wesel im Jahr 1535 eingezogen worden," *Drey Stück aus den Weselischen Wiedertäuffer-Acten* (Fortges. Sammlung v. alten u. neuen theolog. Sachen, n.p., 1739) 409-24; *Ztscht des Bergischen Gesch.-Vereins* I, 360-84; Rembert, *Wiedertäufer*; ML IV.

Wesley Chapel Mennonite Church (MC), Newark, Del., was founded in 1950. In 1957 it had 52 members, with Herman N. Glick as pastor. The congregation is a member of the Ohio and Eastern Mennonite Conference. M.G.

Wessenmiller (Wyssmüller?), **Peter,** from Wimmis, an Anabaptist martyr, executed on Sept. 17, 1538, at Bern, Switzerland. vDZ.

Delbert Gratz, *Bernese Anabaptists* (Scottdale, 1954) 23, No. 28.

West Abbotsford Mennonite Church (GCM), King Road, Abbotsford, B.C., had 395 members in 1958, with A. A. Harder as elder. Peter Derksen, a Mennonite missionary in Japan, is a member of this church. M.G.

West Chester Mennonite Church (MC), in West Chester, Pa., was established in 1953. A mission station of the Lancaster Conference, it had 30 members in 1957, with Joseph M. Kennel as pastor. M.G.

West China Mennonite Brethren Mission. H. C. Bartel and his wife, members of the Krimmer Mennonite Brethren Church and founders of the China Mennonite Mission in Shantung and Honan provinces, left this field in 1941 and went to West China. Here they began to do mission work in the rugged and mountainous area of Shensi and Kansu provinces. Some time later Paulina Foote, who had formerly worked with the Bartels, escaped from the Japanese occupied area in China and joined them. Through these events many in the M.B. Church became interested in this part of China, sent contributions for these workers, and created a sentiment to begin an M.B. Mission in West China.

Through co-operating with H. C. Bartel the M.B. Board of Foreign Missions found a way to begin a mission in West China and presented a plan to the 1945 M.B. General Conference. With the approval of the Conference a field lying partly in Shensi Province and partly in Kansu Province was taken over. Provision was also made for collaboration with the Krimmer M.B. Church, so that each church would work a part of the field.

To this field the M.B. Board of Foreign Missions sent the following missionaries: Mr. and Mrs. P. D. Kiehn, Bena and Emma Bartel in 1946; Mr. and Mrs. P. P. Baltzer and Mr. and Mrs. Harold Baltzer in 1947. These workers occupied the field with headquarters at Shuang Shih Pu and a second station at Huei Hsien. Several Chinese were converted and baptized and an indigenous church was organized.

Due to ill health the P. D. Kiehns returned to America in 1948. The two Baltzer families returned in the summer of 1949 when the onslaught of Communism began to threaten this area, and the others followed when the work had to be closed. J.H.L.

West Clinton Mennonite Church (MC), located 2 miles southeast of Pettisville, Fulton Co., Ohio, began as an outgrowth of the Central congregation, and until 1943 operated with Central and Lockport as one congregation under a common ministry with circuit preaching. The meetinghouse was enlarged in 1935, and seats about 500. The congregation was separately organized in 1943 under the leadership of Edward B. Frey, who was ordained minister in 1925 and bishop in 1933.

On Oct. 22, 1944, D. L. Sommers, who moved in from Oklahoma, was installed as minister. The congregation opened the Holland Mission in 1945 and also supported the missions at Bancroft, Toledo, and Cloverdale, Ohio. In 1947 Olen Nofziger was ordained minister, and in 1950 Raymond Richer was ordained minister with special charge at Holland. The congregation has three foreign missionaries, Vesta (Nafziger) Miller in India and Carl Beck and Ruth (Frey) Shenk in Japan. In 1956 the congregation built the North Clinton meetinghouse, where about one third of the members began to meet for services in January 1957. Later in the year Olen Nofziger was made minister in charge. In 1958 William Nofziger was ordained as minister at West Clinton. The membership in 1957 was 440; the ministers were Edward B. Frey, bishop, and D. L. Sommers and Olen Nofziger. E.B.F.

West Fairview Mennonite Church (MC), located near Beaver Crossing, Seward Co., Neb., is a member of the Iowa-Nebraska Conference. It began as an extension Sunday school of the East Fairview Mennonite Church prior to 1904, for the benefit of members who lived too far away from the church. These members met in various schools until 1905, when a meetinghouse was built about five miles from the East Fairview meetinghouse. Joe Whitaker from Parnell, Iowa, became the first minister. Other ministers who have served are John Steckley, Chris Steckley, Fred Gingerich, Jacob Oswald, John R. Troyer, Ezra Roth, Lloyal Burkey, Dale Oswald, and William R. Eicher (ordained as minister in 1916 and as bishop in 1932), the bishop-pastor in 1959. The membership in 1959 was 110. A new church, 72 x 42 ft., was dedicated in 1956. W.R.E.

West Friesland is (*a*) a district in the present Dutch province of North Holland, in which are found the Mennonite congregations of Enkhuizen, Hoorn, Twisk-Abbekerk, and Medemblik, and the former congregations of Bovenkarspel and Venhuizen, now extinct; (*b*) in German literature the present Dutch province of Friesland, to distinguish it from the German province of East Friesland.   vDZ.

West Liberty, Ohio, a village of *c*1400, located almost on the boundary between Logan and Champaign counties, is the center of a Mennonite (MC) community of three congregations with a total of some 700 baptized members: Bethel in town, Oak Grove to the southeast, and South Union to the north. In the village is the Adriel School for retarded children, formerly the Mennonite Children's Home. The community was settled *c*1850 and has grown steadily.   H.S.B.

West Liberty Mennonite Church (MC), located in southwestern McPherson County, Kan., 4 miles west and 4 north of Inman, Kan., a member of the South Central Conference, the third oldest M.C. congregation in Kansas, was organized in 1883 by Daniel Brundage with nine charter members, who had come from Indiana and Illinois. They purchased the Liberty School in 1884 and moved it to the present building site. The church was first officially named the West Liberty Mennonite Association. In 1892 when a new building was erected the present name was adopted. This meetinghouse was replaced by a new one in 1949.

When the first settlers arrived they attended the Union Sunday School at the Liberty schoolhouse. The Sunday school has continued to serve the people of the community. By 1900 the membership reached 87, and has since then always been around 100.

The following bishops have served this congregation: Daniel Brundage, Daniel Wismer, B. F. Hamilton 1883-1900, S. C. Miller 1900-10, T. M. Erb and D. H. Bender 1911-23, Harry A. Diener 1923-25, and J. G. Hartzler 1925-55; among the ministers were George R. Brunk 1893-1907, Charles D. Yoder 1895-1923, and Menno M. Troyer 1927- , pastor since 1955. The membership in 1957 was 91.   M.M.T.

West New Hopedale Mennonite Church (GCM), located 4 miles north of Ringwood, Okla., is a member of the Western District Conference. In 1958 it had 63 members, with Edward J. Wiebe as pastor. This congregation is a neighbor to the New Hopedale Mennonite Church (*q.v.*), of Meno, Okla., having separated from it with over 50 members. It organized in 1947 as a fully separate congregation.   M.G.

West Park Mennonite Brethren Church is located at 3279 West Jensen Street, Fresno, Cal. In 1957 it had a membership of 43, with J. K. Isaak as pastor.   M.G.

West Point (Iowa) Mennonite (GCM) Church, now extinct, in Lee County (*q.v.*), was organized in December 1849, by immigrants from the Palatinate and other points in Germany, when John C. Krehbiel and Jacob Ellenberger were chosen preachers.

Their first building, a log structure, was located 1½ miles east of the present village of Franklin and 4 miles from West Point. The first service in the new church was held on Pentecost of 1850 and on the next Pentecost they observed their first communion service. In 1855 services were alternated between the log structure and buildings in West Point. Finally on July 26, 1863, the new Mennonite church in West Point was dedicated. In 1879 its membership was 59, whereas it had been as high as 79. John C. Krehbiel, who died in 1886, was the last preacher, but one of the deacons, Henry Weber, conducted services by reading sermons for perhaps 10 years after Krehbiel's death. In a meeting of the West Point church and the near-by Zion Mennonite Church on March 21, 1859, the two congregations decided to work for a union of all Mennonites in America and agreed to invite other Mennonite churches to join their union and meet with them at West Point on the second day of Pentecost 1860. The meeting, which marks the beginning of the General Conference of Mennonites, was largely the result of the leadership of Daniel Krehbiel, a member of the West Point church.   M.G.

M. Gingerich, *The Mennonites in Iowa* (Iowa City, 1939) 67-92; H. P. Krehbiel, *The History of the General Conference of the Mennonites of North America* (Canton, Ohio, 1898) 30-77.

West Prussia was the region on both sides of the lower Vistula between Danzig and Thorn. As the western part of the possessions of the Teutonic Knights it was ceded to Poland in 1466, where it remained until it was made a part of rapidly expanding Prussia in 1772. The Mennonite population of this province probably never exceeded 15,000 souls. Nevertheless West Prussian Mennonitism is the mother soil from which nearly half the Mennonites of the entire world were transplanted to Russia, Asia, and North and South America. East Prussia, the territory immediately to the east of West Prussia, consisting largely of the eastern part of the former territory of the Teutonic Knights, was made a secular duchy in 1525 by Duke Albrecht. The history of the Anabaptists and Mennonites in this area is given in the article **East Prussia**. The city of Danzig (*q.v.*) was a free city, under Polish suzerainty 1466-1722, and from 1722 under Prussian suzerainty, and was never actually a part of West Prussia. (See **Danzig** for the history of the Mennonites in this area.)

The West Prussian congregations were built largely by refugees from the Netherlands. Since the Reformation in that country took on an Anabaptist character after the appearance of Melchior Hofmann (*c*1530), the opposition of the authorities was directed principally against the Anabaptists. Charles V refused to tolerate any heretics in his hereditary lands, Holland, Zeeland, and the southern Netherlands. In the territories later added east and south of the Zuiderzee (Utrecht in 1527, Overijssel 1528, Friesland 1534, Groningen 1536, Drenthe 1537, and Gelderland 1543), persecution never reached such excesses and did not become severe until the rule of the Duke of Alva.

In 1535 a proclamation was issued against the Anabaptists in the Netherlands, because some radi-

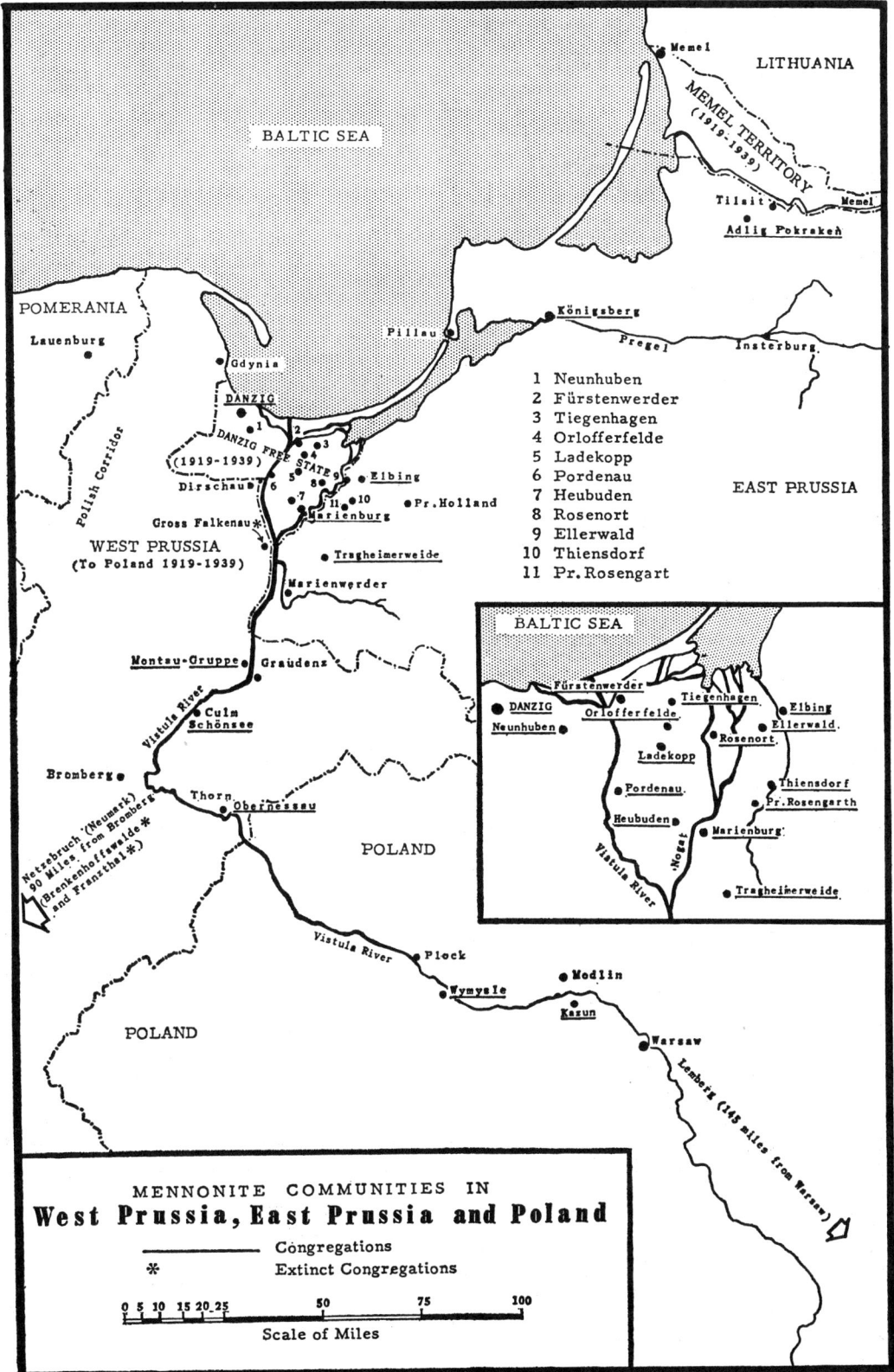

BALTIC SEA

LITHUANIA

Memel

MEMEL TERRITORY
(1919-1939)

POMERANIA

Lauenburg

Pillau

Königsberg

Pregel

Insterburg

Gdynia

DANZIG

DANZIG FREE STATE
(1919-1939)

Dirschau

Gross Falkenau *

WEST PRUSSIA
(To Poland 1919-1939)

Elbing

Marienburg

Pr.Holland

EAST PRUSSIA

Tragheimerweide

Marienwerder

1 Neunhuben
2 Fürstenwerder
3 Tiegenhagen
4 Orlofferfelde
5 Ladekopp
6 Pordenau
7 Heubuden
8 Rosenort
9 Ellerwald
10 Thiensdorf
11 Pr. Rosengart

Tilsit
Adlig Pokraken

BALTIC SEA

Fürstenwerder
DANZIG
Neunhuben
Orlofferfelde
Tiegenhagen
Elbing
Ellerwald
Rosenort
Ladekopp
Thiensdorf
Pr.Rosengarth
Pordenau
Marienburg
Heubuden
Vistula River
Nogat
Tragheimerweide

Montau-Gruppe   Graudenz

Vistula River

Culm
Schönsee

Bromberg

Thorn   Obernessau

POLAND

Netzebruch (Neumark)
90 Miles from Bromberg
(Brenkenhoffswalde *
and Franzthal *)

Vistula River   Plock
Modlin
Wymysle
Kasun
Warsaw

POLAND

Lenberg (165 miles from Warsaw)

MENNONITE COMMUNITIES IN
West Prussia, East Prussia and Poland

———————   Congregations
*   Extinct Congregations

0 5 10 15 20 25   50   75   100

Scale of Miles

cal elements among them, incited by the example of Münster, had made an attack on the Oldeklooster (*q.v.*) in Friesland and on the city hall of Amsterdam. Revolutionary or peaceful, the Anabaptists were henceforth without discrimination subject to severe persecution with fire and sword. Some Anabaptists escaped to Prussia via the North Sea and Baltic Sea routes. In 1534 the Danzig city council wrote the harbor cities of Amsterdam, Antwerp, zur Fähre, Enkhuizen, and Emden, requesting that no Anabaptists be permitted to board the boats to Danzig. Especially from the crown lands Anabaptists came to Prussia in the first fifteen years after Melchior Hofmann's activity; the Duchy of Albrecht of Hohenzollern (East Prussia), Protestant since 1525, offered them refuge. In Polish Prussia (West Prussia) the Reformation was violently suppressed in the early years; in 1526 several citizens of Danzig were put to death as Protestants on royal orders. But after 1543 the Protestant creeds enjoyed a certain measure of freedom, since otherwise the possession of West Prussia would have become uncertain for the kings of Poland, for the estates of West Prussia would not have submitted to religious suppression. This freedom also benefited the Anabaptists, though they were, to be sure, merely tolerated.

On Feb. 1, 1539, the first Mennonite (Anabaptist) settlement in the general area of Prussia was begun by two preachers from the Netherlands—Hermann Sachs and Hugo Mattheissen (*q.v.*)—in Schönberg in the Oberland of East Prussia, where 4,250 acres were made available for settlers. Hugo was a preacher of the Danzig Mennonites during the years when Menno (*q.v.*) Simons and Dirk (*q.v.*) Philips organized the West Prussian congregations. Herman van Bommel (*q.v.*) also became a preacher of the Danzig Anabaptists. It was rumored that young Stadholder Karl was favorably inclined to the Anabaptists. Before 1549 Thonis Barbier of Emden and Michel Janszoon of Oisterhout, Brabant, served as deacons in the Danzig congregation. Apparently the only Anabaptist congregation before Menno's (he visited Prussia not later than 1549) time was that at Danzig, though some of the members lived in and around Elbing. Scattered Anabaptists must have settled in Danzig and Elbing in the early 1530's.

When it was discovered that the Dutch settlers differed from the Prussian church constitution in the matter of baptism and the Lord's Supper, the unofficial toleration was annulled, and the great majority of the settlers were expelled. Thus the first Anabaptist settlement in the duchy of Prussia was destroyed. The settlers found new homes in West Prussia, and in the free cities of Elbing (*q.v.*) and Danzig (*q.v.*), where the Polish authorities had to give religious toleration to their German subjects, who for the most part had accepted the Reformation. The Anabaptists who settled in the Vistula Delta before 1547 were almost exclusively from the crown lands of the Netherlands, especially from the provinces of Holland, Zeeland, and Brabant. Although all these immigrants were settled as farmers, some of them had previously been in other trades or professions. From the regions acquired after 1524, in which the imperial edicts were laxly executed,

there were few emigrants to Prussia until 1547. About 1570 Johann de Mepschop den Ham of Ommelanden (Groningen) united with the Danzig congregation. The Epp, Ens, and Tgahrt families very likely came from the province of Groningen, and the Wiebes from West Friesland. The Janszoon, Rosenfeld, and Momber families came from Flanders, and the Sudermanns from Rotterdam.

In the case of many of the immigrants of the first 100 years the country of origin is given. Thirty-six persons, perhaps with their families, came from the present Netherlands (from Limburg 1, Gelderland 2, Utrecht 3, Friesland 10, Groningen 3, Drenthe 1, Overijssel 2, North Holland 8, South Holland 5, North Brabant 1). From what is now Belgium there were 18 persons by 1640 (from Brabant 10, Antwerp province 4, Flanders 2, and elsewhere 2). From Germany there were nine (Emden 4, Oldenburg 1, Holstein 2, Westphalia 1, Rhineland 1), from Luxembourg one, and from the High German congregation in Moravia two. Most of the immigrants had come from the cities. Later investigation may show a greater participation by Westphalia and the northern Rhineland. But there were also scattered instances of immigration from all the North German regions as far as Mecklenburg. It is not yet known how strong the immigration from South Germany or Moravia was.

In the spring of 1535, 200 Anabaptists (60 families) expelled from Moravia, in part of Silesian origin, came to the region of Thorn, Graudenz, and the Duchy of Prussia. They constituted the initial core of the Anabaptist congregations in the lowlands of the Vistula near Culm (*q.v.*) and Graudenz (*q.v.*).

A new phase in the West Prussian Anabaptist movement now developed in 1547-50, which was to make it permanent. The great drainage enterprise was initiated to drain the Vistula Delta, which covered an area forty miles in width from Drausen Lake to Ellerwald and included the two great delta areas east of Danzig, an undertaking which was to require three to four generations. About 1550 the Anabaptists began their work at two points: at Wengeln on Drausen Lake and near Elbing in the Ellerwald (*q.v.*) area. In 1547 the territory of Tiegenhof, commonly called the "Unterwerder" (Lower Delta), was acquired by the Danzig banker Loysen, who used Mennonite settlers from Holland in the following years for the work of drainage. In the same year two prominent Anabaptists who had been living in the duchy, Herman van Bommel (*q.v.*) and Tönnis Florissen, acquired large areas in the Danzig Werder (lowlands) for settlement.

For these extensive undertakings the number of Anabaptists already living in Prussia was quite inadequate. Accordingly, Philip Edzema, a Frisian, went to Holland with a letter of recommendation from the Danzig council to enlist "people of his nation." Somewhat earlier similar enterprises were begun by the Anabaptists in the Vistula Valley at Culm, Graudenz, and Thorn.

From the religious point of view the years 1547-50 were also a turning point. It is only from this time on that one can really speak of Mennonites in West Prussia. By 1550 a large Anabaptist congregation had been established in West Prussia, with its center in Schottland just outside the walls of Danzig, since the Anabaptists were not permitted to settle in the city proper. Here they had their worship and established their shops for the manufacture of fine textiles and brandy. Hugo Mattheissen and Herman van Bommel were the ministers of the Danzig Anabaptist congregation c1550. The church also had two deacons, Tonas Barbier, a native of Emden, and Michel Janszoon of Oisterhout in Brabant.

In the summer of 1549 Menno Simons came to Prussia with Dirk Philips to establish the church in Prussia in permanent form. It was no doubt at this time that the influence of the Sacramentists, which was being felt among the Anabaptists in Prussia, was rooted out. Menno Simons' loving concern for the "brethren in Prussia" is evidenced by a letter he wrote to them on Oct. 7, 1549, from his home in the west, closely following his visit to them.

The significance of the refugee group here was so great that Menno's most intimate co-worker, Dirk Philips (q.v.), assumed the leadership of the congregation in Danzig for the rest of his life. In 1567 he made a trip to Emden to mediate in a controversy between the Flemish and the Frisian Mennonites in Holland. He died in Emden.

From this time on there were both Flemish (q.v.) and Frisian (q.v.) congregations in West Prussia. It is due to the influence of Dirk Philips that the stricter Flemish party won the upper hand, both in Danzig and in the northern coastal area near Elbing, particularly in what is known as the "Grosswerder," i.e., the Great Delta. In the Kleinwerder and in the valley of the Vistula the Frisian party was dominant. In Danzig also there was a small congregation of the United Frisian, Waterlander (q.v.), and High German (q.v.) groups in addition to the large Flemish group. The Frisian congregations had an able leader in Jan Gerritsz, who came from the Netherlands in 1607. Since in that year the ruthless destruction of the great Anabaptist congregations in Moravia also began, he, as elder of the United Church in Danzig, which included the High German group, visited the High German congregations in Moravia and brought back with him to Danzig a preacher by the name of Wall. In 1604 the Swiss Anabaptist preacher Joseph Hauser with seven other brethren and their families, a total of 37 persons, had already emigrated from Moravia to Prussia. After an unsuccessful attempt to settle in Elbing, they finally located in the Mennonite settlement in Wengeln on Drausen Lake. At this time also apparently a number of Anabaptist families of Swiss Brethren origin settled in the Vistula Valley.

In the first decades of the 17th century the dominant position of the Danzig city church in West Prussian Mennonitism gradually declined, and the rural Mennonites began to develop both ecclesiastically and economically into strong groups. In 1613 the Mennonites of the Danzig Werder refused on conscientious grounds to obey the demand of the city council for military service, and received exemption from this service on the basis of a money payment. This is the first appearance of the problem of nonresistance (q.v.) in the history of the

West Prussian Mennonites, a problem which was to be so important in their later history. In 1622 there occurred another significant development, namely, the formation of a fire insurance organization covering all the Mennonite farmers in the Danzig Werder and the Grosswerder. Through this co-operative organization a farmer who had lost his buildings by fire recovered his loss by money payments from the other farmers by a prorated charge on their acreage. The near neighbors also helped in the work of clearing away the ruins and erecting new buildings.

During this time the Mennonites suffered grievously under the attacks of a hostile environment. Their "defenselessness" was exploited, and enormous sums of money were extracted from them, until finally King Wladislaus IV granted them a "privilegium" or charter in 1642, which promised them a large measure of toleration as well as protection and a guarantee of their old privileges for all time. (This was granted naturally also on the basis of a money payment.) This charter refers with high praise to their great services to the country in the matter of drainage and recovery of land in the Werder. It was repeatedly confirmed and renewed by the later kings.

About this time, that is, one hundred years after the beginning, the basic work in the drainage of the three Werders had been completed, with windmills, dikes, sluices, and countless drainage ditches. Fat cattle pastured on the fertile meadows. The extensive polders of the three Werders were completed. However, this tremendous achievement was accomplished at a very high cost in human life. Eighty per cent of the settlers are said to have died of marsh fever.

The newly settled area in the Grosswerder was included in the territory of the Flemish congregation, since the unity in colonization work was accompanied by unity in church work. The center of this congregation, the congregation of the "Niederung," later became the Rosenort (q.v.) congregation. In 1639 Jan Siemens was chosen as the first elder of this congregation. Up until this time the elder of the Danzig church had served the group in the ordinances of baptism and the Lord's Supper. A smaller Frisian congregation was organized in the neighborhood with the name Orlofferfelde (q.v.). Other Frisian congregations were organized at Markushof (q.v.), Montau (q.v.), and Schönsee (q.v.), while a smaller Flemish congregation was organized at Culm and a larger one in Elbing-Ellerwald.

In 1638 Johann Jakobsen van Geltema, who was in close contact with the settlers, at least through the marriage of his daughter to a Mennonite, took possession of the Tiegenhof area through mortgage. Thereby the position of the Mennonite settlers was made more secure, and in the following decades there was further immigration into the Grosswerder from the Danzig region. The causes of this immigration were not only the unfriendly attitude of the Danzig council toward the Mennonites, who had a difficult time during the period when the shoemaker Georg Hansen (q.v.) was their elder, but also the inundation of the Danzig Werder in 1656 at the time of the war between Sweden and Poland. After 1700, however, there was no more room for the surplus population of the growing Mennonite settlement. Consequently, when the great plague of 1709 in the eastern part of East Prussia wiped out the greater part of the population there, the Prussian government offered the Mennonites land for settlement in the delta of the Memel River. But in 1724 the militaristic king of Prussia, Frederick William I, ordered the nonresistant Mennonites expelled, since they refused to take up arms. The returning settlers from the Memel territory naturally increased the already excessive population in the West Prussian area.

Two possibilities now offered themselves for the acquisition of new land for settlement by the Mennonites. One was the purchase of scattered surplus parcels of land belonging to the villages of the former Teutonic Knights. By this method a considerable number of individual farms were secured, on each of which a single family was settled, living on its acreage under one roof with the cattle and the produce from the fields. The stables were attached next to the dwelling and the barn to the stable. The barnyard was usually surrounded by high trees and gardens were filled with flowers; all was kept scrupulously clean. The people observed the most conscientious cleanliness and simplicity in clothing and in their furniture.

The second possibility of land purchase arose when the distribution of the scattered farms and meadows which formerly belonged to the Teutonic Knights in the Marienwerder region and in the "Oberwerder" were offered for sale. A small group of Mennonites had settled as early as 1554 in the Oberwerder in and around Heubuden. Now Heubüden (q.v.) became a very large congregation, whose members were settled on the extensive grazing lands which had formerly been used for the enormous number of horses required by the knights. This new area extended from the former Order estates of Kalthof and Warnau near Marienburg through Heubuden to Leske. As a result the membership of the Heubuden congregation increased greatly during the first half of the 18th century. In 1711 there were only eleven candidates for baptism, but in 1743 three times as many. In 1728 the congregation, which for 60 years previously had had no ministers of its own, now chose Jakob Dyck as its first elder. Another Frisian congregation was established on the grazing lands of the Marienwerder area south of Marienburg, called Tragheimerweide (q.v.), chiefly by returning settlers expelled from the Memel district.

Meanwhile, growth in membership finally compelled the Grosswerder congregation to subdivide into four new congregations. In 1735 Tiegenhagen (q.v.), Fürstenwerder (q.v.), and Ladekopp (q.v.) were organized, Rosenort remaining as the central congregation. Church buildings were permitted by the authorities in the Vistula Delta only after a long delay. The dates of the first two churches are 1728 at Thiensdorf (q.v.) and 1754 at Rosenort. The other congregations built their churches in 1768. The services had previously been conducted in barns.

The church records give evidence of active spiritual life in the Grosswerder congregation. In July 1741, in the stable of the widow Suckau in Mausdorferfeld, baptism was administered to 51 candidates in the presence of 1,000 people. On March 2, 1775, the Lord's Supper was celebrated in the new church at Rosenort with 1,566 participants. On July 6, 1755, the newly elected elder, Abraham Penner, was ordained by a Danzig elder, Hans van Steen (q.v.), in the presence of a crowd of 2,500-3,000. "The floor of the building was removed, some sat in the balcony, others stood on ladders which were placed against the windows from the outside, while others stood on carriages" (Regehr).

Hans van Steen was the last elder who strongly urged the use of the Dutch. From 1600 to 1750 there was frequent contact between Danzig and Holland, not only correspondence (the Amsterdam Mennonite Archives contain a large number of such letters), but also by personal visits. The wealthy members, especially those in Danzig, preferred to send their sons to Amsterdam to complete their schooling and learn commercial practice. Marriages back and forth were also not uncommon. The country congregations, however, could not continue this regular personal contact with Holland, since they had adopted the Low German dialect known as "Werderplatt" much earlier than in Danzig for use in everyday life, and even in preaching introduced the High German one to two decades earlier than in the city. Previous to this apparently all Anabaptist-Mennonites had used only Dutch in home and in church.

As to education, the Mennonite farmers had their own schools even in the 16th century. From 1700 on the charters almost universally mentioned the right of the Mennonites to have their children educated by their own teachers. Another important feature of the West Prussian Mennonite church life in earlier times was the hospital or old people's home which each congregation erected beside the church. Brotherly aid in various forms was considered to be a chief duty of the Mennonites.

The last years of the Polish period were marked by a considerable loss of legal protection. In 1765 two hundred Mennonites, forced to emigrate from the Vistula Valley for religious reasons, settled in the Neumark (q.v.). The first partition of Poland in 1772, by which West Prussia became a part of the Kingdom of Prussia, meant at first an advantage for the Mennonites, since Frederick the Great had a high regard for superior farmers. Accordingly, when the ceremonial honoring of the new king was to take place in the autumn of 1772 in the mighty old castle of the Teutonic Knights in Marienburg, the Mennonites of the region delivered for the festival meal two fat oxen, 400 pounds of butter, 100 ducks and hens, and 20 cheeses. At the same time they showed the king their Polish charters with privileges, and requested him to give them a similar charter, which they actually received in 1780. In this charter, among other things, their exemption from military service was confirmed.

But it soon became clear that the Mennonites were now subjects of a military state. According to the Prussian army code the obligation of military service derived from the ownership of property. Accordingly, the purchase of property by Mennonites, whose number was constantly increasing, would reduce the number of men available for military service, and could not be in the interest of the state. But Frederick the Great was generous in this point, and in 1781-84 alone granted permission for the purchase by Mennonites of 296 new tracts of land never held by Mennonites before. However, all Mennonites in West Prussia and East Prussia had to pay for military exemption by contributing annually (from 1773) a total of 5,500 talers to the support of the military academy in Culm.

Outside Danzig and Thorn the Mennonites at that time numbered 13,500 souls and owned approximately 150,000 Prussian "Morgen" of the best lowlands in the Delta of the Vistula. After Frederick's death the generosity of the government came to an end. The Lutheran pastors of the Werder, concerned for the future of their congregations, as well as the government officials responsible for providing recruits for military service, urged the king to prohibit further extension of Mennonite landholdings. For this reason Frederick William II issued a special decree in 1789 bearing the title "Edict Concerning the Future of Mennonitism," which guaranteed freedom of conscience in regard to military service but restricted sharply the opportunity to purchase land and obliged the Mennonite landowners to pay the regular church tax required of members of the Lutheran churches. Thus began an eighty-year struggle by the West Prussian Mennonites to maintain their practice of nonresistance. In 1801 the edict of 1789 was further sharpened to make the purchase of any further land impossible.

Under these conditions the surplus Mennonite rural population had only one outlet—emigration. This emigration was now undertaken in the form of a large-scale movement to South Russia. The ancient migration route up the Vistula to the broad steppes of the Black Sea area, which the Goths had once traveled, was now again traveled by countless farm wagons loaded high with furniture, beds and household goods. But it was not only the landless and poorer Mennonites who sought a new home in the Ukraine. Many others who were not satisfied with the new conditions in West Prussia sold their farms and joined the migrants. In 1787-1866 the surplus population of the West Prussian Mennonites migrated to Russia, as is evidenced by the fact that the population figure in the homeland remained static at about 13,000 souls. A considerable number emigrated to the Samara region of Russia in 1859 to found the Alexandertal (*q.v.*) settlement.

In the time of Prussia's distress during the Napoleonic Wars (1806-14) the Mennonites who remained in West Prussia gave their loyal support to the government, but nevertheless were subjected to a renewed and vigorous attack on their freedom from military service. In 1806 the Mennonites made a voluntary grant of 30,000 talers to Frederick William III on the occasion of his visit to Königsberg. In 1810 they added another voluntary contribution of 10,000 talers to the compulsory war tax which all Prussians had to pay. When the king issued his famous "appeal to my people" in 1813, love for the enslaved homeland was strong in the hearts of the Mennonites, but their spiritual duty to God, which forbade military service for them, still held first

place in their consciences. Accordingly, they did not furnish any soldiers, but delivered 500 horses and paid 25,000 talers tax. In addition they made a voluntary contribution of 60,000 guilders and 6,000 ells of linen. All attempts to force them into active military service, however, met a stubbornly successful resistance which was expressed in the following statement: "Although we are prepared to support in every way possible the state which protects and tolerates us, it is impossible for us to have any part in military service as long as we are Mennonites and remain so." A number of their young men, to be sure, accepted military service, who were then excommunicated. Although official pressure was brought occasionally to force the churches to receive these young men back into fellowship after their return from the front, the churches held their position and refused. Again, when the military reserve corps (Landsturm) was established by the army and universal military service was introduced in September 1814, new attempts were made to persuade the Mennonites to accept military service. All such attempts failed. As a substitute the Mennonites paid a certain sum per acre into the military treasury to support the Landsturm. The Alexandertal (Russia) settlement was founded in 1859 by a group who wanted to maintain full nonresistance.

A crucial time for the congregations came when the North German Confederacy passed a law on Nov. 9, 1867, which annulled the Mennonite privilege of exemption from military service. The crisis was alleviated somewhat by a modification of the law by an Order of Cabinet dated March 3, 1868, which authorized noncombatant service by those Mennonites who could not conscientiously serve with arms, offering service as hospital orderlies, clerks, and in transportation. They were also released from the military oath of loyalty and permitted to substitute a simple handclasp. However, a great number of Mennonites could not conscientiously accept even noncombatant military service. The elders of the congregations at Heubuden, Elbing, and Obernessau emigrated soon thereafter with a part of their congregations to Kansas (*q.v.*) and Nebraska (*q.v.*).

For those who remained behind the previous restrictions in the purchase of land naturally fell away. Mixed marriages with other faiths became more frequent. Mennonites now became better citizens. To achieve this position, however, they had to surrender one of the two fundamental articles of faith. This meant that their separation from the world and their peculiar character as Mennonites was in part eliminated. Until World War I something of this typical Mennonite character as different from the surrounding world remained in the sense that a large percentage of the Mennonite men still took noncombatant service. The Versailles treaty of 1920, following World War I, imposed considerable difficulties upon the Mennonites of this region, who were divided by the new boundaries into three almost equal blocks, Danzig Free State, Poland, and East Prussia.

In World War II the Mennonites of West Prussia took regular military service along with other Germans. The Bolshevik flood from the East now took from them their homeland and their existence as a settlement. When the Russian army in 1945 marched into the Vistula Delta, where the great majority of the Mennonites of West Prussia lived, the great emigration began. On Jan. 24, 1945, the endless columns of wagons and trucks began to move the Mennonites out of the Werder territory which had been their home for 400 years. This was no organized movement. Part of the group succeeded in getting across the Oder River before the Russsian army encircled Danzig. The remainder finally fled by sea to save their bare lives, and many of these finally reached Denmark. A large part of those who remained behind were transported into the interior of Russia, or suffered severely in their old home territory. Some 1,800 were finally located in camps in Denmark, where elders Bruno Ewert of Heubuden and Bruno Enss of Orlofferfeld took charge of the group. In September 1945 a commissioner of the Mennonite Central Committee, C. F. Klassen (*q.v.*), visited the group in Denmark and initiated the relief work of the American Mennonites for them. Some 691 persons of this group were settled in Uruguay, Oct. 7, 1948, by the MCC. In October 1951 another group of 431 was settled there. In Germany Gustav Reimer, a former deacon of Heubuden, secretary of the conference of the former West and East Prussian congregations, was assigned the task of re-establishing contact among the widely scattered members in Germany and aiding them in their attempt to find a new homeland elsewhere.

At the present time some 5,500 West Prussian Mennonites are living as refugees in the northern and Rhine provinces of Germany and another 1,000 in Württemberg, Baden, and a large number in the Palatinate. The number in the Russian Zone is not known, but is probably also nearly 1,000. The largest concentration in any one area in Germany is in Schleswig-Holstein and around Hamburg, where *c*2,700 are located. In 1959 the baptized membership of the former West Prussian (including Danzig and East Prussia) congregations was distributed as follows: North Germany—*c*4,000, of whom *c*2,100 are in nine new refugee congregations widely scattered and an equal number in the eight established congregations; South Germany—*c*600, of whom two thirds are in the Palatinate. Only two new refugee congregations have been established in the South—Enkenbach in the Palatinate and Backnang near Stuttgart. In Uruguay (*q.v.*) there were in 1957 four congregations with a total of 809 members—El Ombu (*q.v.*), Gartental (*q.v.*), Montevideo, and Colonia Delta. The nine congregations in North Germany are organized under a conference committee called "Aeltestenausschuss der Konferenz der west- und ostpreussischen Gemeinden." In Uruguay the four congregations form a conference which is affiliated with the General Conference Mennonite Church in North America.   H.P.

M. Beheim-Schwarzbach, *Hohenzollernsche Kolonisation* (Leipzig, 1874); Hans Alenson, *Tegen-Bericht op de voor-Reden vant groote Martelaer Boek* (1630, in BRN VII, 1910); Blaupot t. C., *Groningen;* Erich Keyser, "Die Niederlande und das Weichselland," in *Deutsches Archiv für Landes- und Volksforschung* VII (1942); Emil Händiges, *Beiträge zur Geschichte der Mennonitengemeinde Elbing-Ellerwald* (Weierhof, 1938); H. G. Mannhardt, *Die Danziger Mennonitengemeinde* (Danzig, 1919); H. Wiehler, "Aus der Geschichte der Vereinigten Mennonitengemeinde Thiensdorf - Markushof," in *Menn. Bl.,* 1928, 92-94, 99 f., 108 f.; Wilhelm Mannhardt, *Die Wehrfreiheit der Altpreussischen Mennoniten* (Marienburg, 1863); Kurt Kauenhowen, ed , *Mitteilungen des Sippenverbandes der Danziger Mennonitenfamilien Epp-Kauenhowen-Zimmermann* (Göttingen, 1935-43); H. Nottarp, *Die Mennoniten in den Marienburger Werdern* (Halle, 1929); Horst Penner, *Ansiedlung Menn. Niederländer im Weichselmündungsgebiet von der Mitte des 16. Jahrhunderts bis zum Beginn der preussischen Zeit* (Weierhof, 1940); Horst Quiring, "Die Beziehungen zwischen holländischen und westpreussischen Mennoniten," in *Menn. Bl.,* 1936, 39-41; idem, "Aus den ersten Jahrzehnten der Mennoniten in Westpreussen," in *Gesch. Bl.,* 1937, 32-35; Reimer, *Familiennamen;* Ernst Regehr, *Geschichts- und Predigertabelle der Mennonitengemeinde Rosenort* (Elbing, 1939); A. Driedger, "Aus der Geschichte der Mennonitengemeinde Heubuden," in *Menn. Bl.,* 1939; Ernst Crous, "Vom Pietismus bei den altpreussischen Mennoniten im Rahmen ihrer Gesamtgeschichte 1772-1945," in *Gesch.-Bl.,* 1954, 7-29; Felicia Szper, *Nederlandsche Nederzettingen in West-Pruisen gedurende de Poolschen tijd* (Enkhuizen, 1913); B. Schumacher, *Niederländische Ansiedlungen im Herzogtum Preussen zur Zeit Herzog Albrechts* (Leipzig, 1913); Unruh, *Hintergründe;* Reiswitz und Wadzeck, *Beiträge zur Kenntnis der Mennonitengemeinden in Europa und Amerika* (Berlin, 1821); idem, *Beiträge zur Kenntnis der Taufgesinnten Gemeinden oder der Mennoniten . . .* (Breslau, 1829); Max Schön, *Das Mennonitenthum in Westpreussen* (Berlin, 1886); Herbert Wiebe, *Das Siedlungswerk niederländischer Mennoniten im Weichseltal zwischen Fordon und Weissenberg bis zum Ausgang des 18. Jahrhunderts* (Marburg, 1952); B. Schumacher, *Geschichte Ost- und Westpreussens,* 3d ed. (Würzburg, 1958); Hermann Epp, "Die westpreussischen Mennoniten von 1933 bis zum Untergang," *Der Mennonit,* 1948, 4 f., 20; Horst Penner, "Anabaptists and Mennonites of East Prussia," *MQR* XXII (1948) 212-25; idem, "West Prussian Mennonites Through Four Centuries," *MQR* XXIV (1950) 124-29; B. H. Unruh, "Dutch Backgrounds of Mennonite Migration of the 16th Century to Prussia," *MQR* X (1936) 173-81; Robert Friedmann, "Devotional Literature of the Mennonites in Danzig and Prussia to 1800," *MQR* XVIII (1944) 162-73; Ernst Crous, "Mennonites in Germany Since the Thirty Years' War," *MQR* XXV (1951) 235-62; Bruno Ewert, "Four Centuries of Prussian Mennonites," *Menn. Life* III (April 1948) 10-18; Horst Penner, *Weltweite Bruderschaft* (Karlsruhe, 1955); Horst Quiring, "Die Auswanderung der Mennoniten aus Preussen 1788-1879," *Menn. Life* VI (April 1951) 37; Bruno Ewert, "Four Centuries of Prussian Mennonites," *Menn. Life* III (April 1948) 11; Hermann Epp, "From the Vistula to the Dnieper," *Menn. Life* VI (October 1951) 14; Kurt Kauenhoven, "Mennonite Artists—Danzig and Koenigsberg," *Menn. Life* IV (July 1949) 17; Zdzislay Ludkiewicz, *Osady Holenderskie na nizinie Sartawickp-Nowskiej* (Thorn, 1934); B. H. Unruh, *Hintergründe;* Peter J. Dyck, "Only Memory and Monuments," *Menn. Life* XIV (January 1959); *ML* IV.

West Raley Hutterite Bruderhof of the Dariusleut (*q.v.*) near Cardston, Alberta, had a population of 117 in 1950, with Christian C. Waldner as minister.   vDZ.

West Reserve, Man., located west of the Red River and north of the United States border, was set aside like the East Reserve (*q.v.*) for a Mennonite settlement. When Mennonite delegates inspected the land of Manitoba, the Bergthal and the Kleine Gemeinde delegates, Jacob Peters, Heinrich Wiebe, David Classen, and Cornelius Toews, who had chosen Manitoba for their constituency, investigated this land with the other Mennonite delegates in 1873. All twelve delegates went first to the East Reserve; in 1874 the four delegates of the Bergthal and the Kleine Gemeinde immigrants came to Winnipeg and chose the East Reserve for settlement. Thus the East Reserve became the settlement of the Bergthal Mennonites (*q.v.*). Bergthal in Russia was a daughter colony of the Chortitza or Old Colony Mennonite settlement.

In 1875, when the first Mennonites of the Chortitza settlement and its daughter settlement Fürstenland under the leadership of Elder Johann Wiebe arrived in Manitoba, they settled on the West Reserve. A total of 580 families or 3,240 persons left the Chortitza and Fürstenland settlements. With few exceptions, all of them settled on the West Reserve. Of this total, about two thirds came from Chortitza and one third from Fürstenland (Epp, *Chortitzer Mennoniten*). By 1877 they had established the following villages: Hoffnungsfeld, Eichenfeld, Schantzenfeld, Grünfeld, Ebenfeld, Reinland, Hochfeld, Rosengart, Waldheim, Neuendorf, Neuenburg, Blumengart, Blumenstein, Kronsthal, Chortitza, Osterwick, Schönfeld, Schönwiese, Rosenort, Rosenhof, Schöndorf, Rosenfeld, Neuhorst, Blumenhorst, and Blumenfeld.

The West Reserve, located between Emerson and Mountain City, and eighteen miles north of the United States boundary, was (according to E. K. Francis) the first permanent agricultural settlement in the open prairies of Western Canada without direct access to a major body of water. This turned out to be some of the best farm land in Manitoba. It was set aside for the "exclusive use of the Mennonites from Russia" by Order-in-Council of April 25, 1876. At that time the East and West Reserves included 25 townships consisting of over half a million acres. The West Reserve consisted of 17 townships. The land was extremely level and trees for fuel and lumber had to be hauled from the Pembina Mountains. During the summer and fall of 1875, while the settlers were living in immigration houses, they staked out their villages and homesteads and began to construct their primitive, tentative shelters. In the spring of the following year they planted 1,475 acres of wheat and potatoes. In 1876 over 800 persons joined the settlers of the West Reserve. In the next four years the number of families coming directly from Russia gradually decreased.

Barely had the Chortitza-Fürstenland Mennonites established themselves when a movement of the Bergthal Mennonites from the East Reserve to the West Reserve set in. Around 1880 Hespeler reported that some 300 families had moved to the West Reserve, leaving some 400 on the East Reserve. The reason given was primarily that the East Reserve suffered more during the wet years. In addition to this, it was discovered that the land of the West Reserve was better. Some of the villages established by the Bergthal people on the West Reserve were Gnadenfeld, Schönhorst, Sommerfeld, Halbstadt, Altona, Bergfeld, and Schönthal. The Dominion Land's Act made it possible for those from the East Reserve to acquire a second homestead in the West Reserve. They settled mostly on the fringes of the area occupied by those who had come directly from Russia to the West Reserve.

The Bergthal Mennonites moving in and establishing homes for the second time in Manitoba were inclined to give up some old practices brought along from Russia and to adjust themselves more fully to the Canadian environment. Thus they introduced a disrupting element into the fixed pattern and way of life of the Old Colony Mennonites of the West Reserve. Some of them discarded the practice of living in closed villages from which each farmer would work his narrow strip of land adjacent to the village and by which they would share the community pasture. This village plan constituted a closely knit civic entity which was the nucleus and foundation for the self-government, parochial schools and the traditional, total way of life. Many felt that deviation from this pattern would introduce a breakdown of the cultural and religious life cherished for generations.

In 1880, when the Canadian provincial government replaced the Mennonite self-government of the Schulze and Oberschulze by the regular civic government, the Bergthal Mennonites of the West Reserve were ready to accept this, while the Old Colony-Fürstenland Mennonites were determined to retain their system of self-government. The Bergthal Mennonites were mostly located in the Douglas municipality (now Rhineland) and the Old Colony Mennonites in the Rhineland municipality (now Stanley). From now on among the Old Colony Mennonites the unofficial Oberschulze functioned beside the official reeve of the municipality. The Old Colony Mennonites also became guardians of the old school system which they wanted to keep in their own hands when some Mennonites started to campaign for improvement of educational facilities and standards and were willing to accept aid from the government and thereby exchange their parochial schools for public schools. The school question became one of the chief reasons why the Old Colony Mennonites of the West Reserve later moved to Mexico.

These differences were some of the factors that made it impossible for the original Mennonite settlers of the West Reserve who had come from Chortitza and Fürstenland under the leadership of Elder Johann Wiebe to have full fellowship with the Bergthal Mennonites who moved in later. The former had organized as the Reinland Mennonite Church, which later became known as the Old Colony Mennonite Church, while the newcomers, under the leadership of Elder Gerhard Wiebe of the Bergthal Mennonite Church (*q.v.*) of the East Reserve, founded the Bergthal Mennonite Church of the West Reserve, with Johann Funk as elder. The latter group retained the name Bergthal Mennonite Church, while the one on the East Reserve became known as the Chortitza Mennonite Church, since its elder resided in the village of Chortitz. In 1890 the larger part of the Bergthal Mennonites started a new church, which became known as the Sommerfeld Mennonite Church (*q.v.*), since its elder Abraham Dörksen lived in the village of Sommerfeld. The progressive minority, under the leadership of Elder Johann Funk, retained the name Bergthal Mennonite Church (*q.v.*).

In the beginning the Mennonite villages covered only part of the West Reserve, gradually expanding within the limits of the reserve actually set aside. In the course of time they yielded portions of re-

ORIGINAL SETTLEMENT OF
West Reserve, Manitoba

Prepared by E. K. Francis

Legend

- ∿ River — ∿ Slough
- ••••• Dredge canal
- Main trail (Post Road)
- ▦ Railroad
- Beginning of slope of Pembina Mountains
- Hudson's Bay Company or school sections
- Boundary of Reserve (original grant)
- ▫ House row – village — □ Towns

- ---------- Limits of village area (where exact boundaries could be established)
- CAPITALIZED VILLAGE NAMES — F Fürstenland village; B Bergthal village
- Other Names: Mixed population
- UNDERLINED: LARGE CAPITALS UNDERLINED Railroad towns

Place names having no symbol for village site indicate scattered habitat or that site could not be located.

Scale of Miles
0 1 2 3 4 5 6 7 8 9 10

A township is six miles square.

Rosenhof-Rosenort (Kleine Gemeinde)

MORRIS • RED RIVER • EMERSON

DRAINAGE · DRAINAGE

Kronsweide · Rose Farm · Grossweide · HAMBURG

ROSENFELD · Kleinstadt · Blumenthal · Halbstadt

ALTONA · GRETNA · Eigenfund · Neubergthal · Schönwiese · Edenburg

Rosenheim · Rosenthal · Rosenfeld · BUFFALO · Schönthal · Grünthal

HORNDEAN · Bergthal · Reinthal · Rosenort · Schönhorst

Heubeden · Neuhoffnung · Lichtenau · Altbergthal · Eigenhof

Neuenburg · Radiowweide · GNADEN-THAL · ROSENORT · KRONSTHAL · KRONSGART · NEUBERGST

PLUM COULÉE · C.P.R. · KLEEFELD · BLUMENGART · NEUANLAGE · Schönwiese Land · Brown's Inn · ROSEN-GART

NEUENFELD · GREINFELD · NEUREIN-LAND · FRIEDENSRUH · EIGENFELD · NEUENBURG · FREINLAND

Kronsgart · Green Farm · Rosenbach · SCHANZEN-FELD · ROSENTHAL · BLUMENFELD · HOCHFELD

WINKLER · HOFFNUNGSFELD · GREINFELD · REICHENBACH · GREINFELD

Burnside · SCHÖNFELD · BLUMSTEIN · CRONITZ · OSTERWICK · EICHENFELD · KRONSFELD · Haskett

MORDEN · SCHÖNDORF · POST ROAD · Eidhelm · EDENHAGE · REINLAND · PEMBINA HILLS

Mountain City · PEMBINA HILLS

UNITED STATES

Range 1 East of Principal Meridian · Range 1 West of Principal Meridian · Range 2 · Range 3 · Range 4 · Range 5 · Range 6

Principal Meridian

TOWNSHIP 5   TOWNSHIP 4   TOWNSHIP 3   TOWNSHIP 2   TOWNSHIP 1 served land to non-Mennonites and acquired other parcels outside their boundaries. The word "Reserve" eventually became attached to land actually occupied by the Mennonites, particularly after the original grants had expired. At the time when the municipalities of Rhineland and Douglas were incorporated only a few non-Mennonites lived within the Reserve. As time went on more and more of the villages were abandoned. In some instances today only a grove of trees indicates the site of a former village. Some of the villages have become significant communities and business centers. Other places originally established by non-Mennonites have grown into towns primarily occupied by Mennonites today. Among the Mennonite villages which have become trade centers are Reinland, Sommerfeld, Neubergthal, Kronsgart, and Rosenfeld. Among those started by non-Mennonites after 1890 the following have become railroad and trade centers: Altona, Winkler, Gretna, Plum Coulee, Horndean, and Lowe Farm. Of particular significance as industrial centers are Altona (*q.v.*), Winkler (*q.v.*), and Gretna (*q.v.*). (For a complete history of the West Reserve see articles **Manitoba**, **Old Colony Mennonites**, and the towns mentioned.) C.K.

E. K. Francis, *In Search of Utopia* (Altona, 1955); Cornelius Krahn, "Adventure in Conviction. Russia, Canada, and Mexico" (manuscript); C. A. Dawson, *Group Settlement; Ethnic Communities in Western Canada* (Toronto, 1936); D. H. Epp, *Die Chortitzer Mennoniten* (Odessa, 1889); C. Henry Smith, *The Coming of the Russian Mennonites* (Berne, 1927); *ML* IV.

West Richwoods (CAM) Conservative Mennonite Church, Mountain View, Ark., was established in 1954. Valentine J. Headings was the bishop of the 12 members in 1957. M.G.

West Salem Mennonite Brethren Church: see **Kingwood Bible Church.**

West Sterling Mennonite Church (MC), Sterling, Ill., was established in 1928. It had 57 members in 1957, with Vernon Schertz as pastor, and was a mission congregation sponsored by the Science Ridge Mennonite Church. M.G.

West Swamp Mennonite Church (GCM), located between Milford Square and Steinsburg in Milford Twp., Bucks Co., Pa., about 4 miles northwest of Quakertown, a member of the Eastern District Conference, was organized before 1727. It is possible that it was organized in 1717, when Felty (Valentine) Clemmer, the first minister, arrived in America. According to tradition, the first meetinghouse was erected in 1735 on land owned by William Allen. A marker was erected in 1944 at a spot which is thought to be the site of this meetinghouse, about midway between the present East and West Swamp churches. In 1771 a meetinghouse was erected a mile east of the first building. This is the site of the present East Swamp church. Services were held alternately in both buildings. In 1790 another building was erected about one-half mile west of the original meetinghouse on the site of the present West Swamp church. It was replaced in 1819 and again in 1873.

In 1847 John H. Oberholtzer began to organize Bible instruction classes in this church. In the Oberholtzer division of that year the congregation joined the new movement, later joining the Eastern District Conference (GCM). As the number of members increased separate congregations were organized (1877), which are known as East Swamp (*q.v.*) and West Swamp; they continued to be served by the same minister until 1921. West Swamp is largely a rural church, though there are quite a few who live in near-by towns. The present (1958) minister is Arthur S. Rosenberger, and the membership is 281. A.S.R.

J. C. Wenger, *History of the Mennonites of the Franconia Conference* (Telford, 1937); *Menn. Life* II (1947) 33-37.

West Terschelling: see **Terschelling.**

West Union Mennonite Church (MC), a member of the Iowa-Nebraska Conference, located at Parnell, 9 miles north of Wellman, Iowa, was organized Dec. 11, 1897, by part of the group which worshiped at the Union Meetinghouse northwest of Kalona and which had left the Old Order Amish in 1884 with Christian Warey as minister. They worshiped at the Greene Center Schoolhouse until their church was completed and dedicated June 5, 1898. In 1917 the present building with a seating capacity of 400-500 was erected. Approximately 50 members worship at the Parnell Mission Church, which was started by West Union in 1948. In 1906 West Union started a mission Sunday school near Wellman, which became the Wellman Mennonite Church in 1935. The membership in 1957 was 386, with Herman Ropp as bishop and Paul T. Guengerich and Amos Gingerich as ministers. Bishops Christian Warey, A. I. Yoder, J. K. Yoder, A. G. Yoder, and John Y. Swartzendruber have served this congregation. P.T.G.

West Union Mennonite Church (MC), Rexville, N.Y., was established in 1954 under the Lancaster Mennonite Conference. It had 17 members in 1957, with Carl E. Christman as pastor. M.G.

West Virginia. The territory of this state, located west of Virginia, was a part of Virginia until April 20, 1863. On that date West Virginia was declared a separate state by President Lincoln. This action was the result of the refusal of the northwestern counties of Virginia to accept the secession from the union decreed by the majority of the counties.

A few Mennonite (MC) families settled within the bounds of West Virginia near the close of the 18th century. These early settlements were made in Greenbrier and Rockbridge counties. Since the formation of the new state in 1863 the witness of the Shenandoah Valley Mennonite churches has been effectually brought to the people of Pendleton, Randolph, Tucker, and Hardy counties of West Virginia, which are over the mountains just across the Virginia border. In these areas there were in 1957 a total of 21 congregations, missions, or preaching points, with a total of 533 baptized members. The oldest of these was Salem at Needmore, started in 1868, now with 113 members. These congregations are all Virginia Conference and are served by the bishops of two of the Shenandoah Valley districts.   H.A.B.

West Woolwich Old Order Mennonite Church, situated just on the western limits of the town of Elmira, Waterloo Co., Ont. In 1854 land was acquired and a frame building erected, enlarged in 1880 and again in 1908, and land added in 1908 and in 1919. The ministers who served at this place are Peter Martin, David B. Martin, Amos Gingerich, and Jesse Bauman. Those responsible in 1955 were Edward Martin (1903-), minister, ordained 1940; and Clarence Martin (1907-), deacon, ordained 1954. The membership was approximately 250.

In 1939 a part of this group separated and affiliated with the Markham-Waterloo Conference of Mennonites. In 1954 these held a membership of 217, served by George Brubacher (1897-), minister, ordained 1942, and Ivan S. Martin (1907-), deacon, ordained 1942. Both groups use this same church.   J.C.F.

West Zion Mennonite Church (GCM), located in Moundridge, McPherson Co., Kan., a member of the Western District, was organized on March 4, 1888, by members from the First Mennonite Church of Christian (now Moundridge). Most of these first members had moved to Kansas from Lee County, Iowa, in the 1870's and named the new congregation after the mother church, the Zion Mennonite Church of Donnellson, Iowa. The names of the charter members were Galle, Rupp, Eymann, Ruth, Schowalter, and Krehbiel. William Galle was elected the first elder and served until his death in 1920, although he was assisted after 1909. The congregation first met in a schoolhouse, which was remodeled and enlarged in 1896. In 1907 a new church building was dedicated. A basement was added to this in 1937. That same meetinghouse, seating approximately 350, is used today.

In 1957 the congregation had 266 members, approximately one third of whom live on farms. The first families were mostly of South German ancestry. Today the congregation is heterogeneous in background, including members from various Mennonite and non-Mennonite groups. Men who have served as pastors of this congregation are William Galle, J. M. Suderman, J. P. Baehr, D. J. Brand, P. K. Regier, W. F. Unruh, John B. Graber, and Harris Waltner.   H.WAL.

West Zion Mennonite Church (MC), located near Carstairs, Alberta, approximately 40 miles north of Calgary, a member of the Alberta-Saskatchewan Conference, was organized in 1901. The first Mennonite to settle in the Carstairs-Didsbury district was Andrew Weber, who came west from Ontario in 1894. A few others came later, but the main settlement was made in April 1901. A meetinghouse was built in the fall of 1901. It was replaced by a new church in 1932. This congregation is unique in that approximately half of the membership is of British origin. Ordained men who have served or are serving the West Zion Church are the following: Israel R. Shantz, Amos Weber, Moses H. Schmitt, Noah R. Weber, Henry Weber, Allan Good,

Norman Buschert, Alvin Steckly, Abe Reist, Ezra Stauffer, Linford Hackman, Henry J. Harder, and Gordon Buschert, the last two of whom were the ministers in 1957; the membership was 78.   E.S.

Westerburg, Gerhard (d. 1558), for a short time an Anabaptist leader in the region of Cologne, Germany. He attached himself to various movements at different places, always however in the sincere desire to improve religious, political, and social conditions. He was the son of a patrician family, born probably at the end of the 15th century, studied at the University of Cologne (in the Bursa Montana) 1514-15 and at the University of Bologna 1515-17, devoting himself to general cultural as well as legal studies. At Cologne he secured the M.A. degree, and at Bologna the degree of doctor in both civil and ecclesiastical law. A trip to Rome introduced him to the evil conditions of the church at the top.

Westerburg was introduced to the Reformation by Nikolaus Storch (*q.v.*) of Zwickau, whom he entertained in his home and whom he then accompanied to Wittenberg, where he met Luther and Cellarius (*q.v.*) in 1522. Through Storch he became acquainted with the emerging opposition to infant baptism. Soon he was attracted to Andreas Carlstadt (*q.v.*) in Wittenberg and then in Orlamünde, whose teachings concerning the Lord's Supper he adopted, and whose sister he married. He even moved to Jena in the neighborhood of Orlamünde in 1523-24 to be nearer to him. He began his literary career as an enthusiastic advocate of Carlstadt's views in 1523 with an eight-page pamphlet entitled *Vom Fegfeuer,* which was the occasion for his nickname "Dr. Fegfeuer." He was expelled from Saxony along with Carlstadt in the autumn of 1524, and in October of that year he appeared in Zürich and Basel, bringing several pamphlets written by Carlstadt on the Lord's Supper, baptism, etc., which he gave to a printer in Basel for publication. All were printed, except the pamphlet against infant baptism. At this time Westerburg became acquainted with Conrad Grebel and his circle in Zürich, and Felix Manz is known to have secured a quantity of the Carlstadt pamphlets in Basel and distributed them in Zürich.

In the spring of 1525, when Carlstadt was becoming involved in the Peasants' War during his stay in Rothenburg ob der Tauber, Westerburg appeared in Frankfurt am Main as the leader both of a Reformation group and of a little civil rebellion, the latter in assistance to the peasants who were at that time moving to the north and were seeking sympathy in the cities. The forty-two "Frankfurt Articles" were based on a brief draft of eleven articles which had probably been prepared a week earlier (April 13) by "several Christian brethren of the city of Frankfurt and Sachsenhausen," which means a group led by Westerburg. The forty-two articles, which included religious, political, and social demands and represented the desire of the lower classes in the city and its suburbs to improve their economic and political lot, were focused on a program of improving the entire life of the city on the basis of the Gospel. They were moderate demands, and in no sense radically revolutionary. For the general forward movement in the cities of West Germany, their significance is comparable to that of the Twelve Articles for the Peasants' War. Except for these Twelve Articles, they were the only set of articles of this sort printed and they became the model for similar statements in various other towns and cities. In this manner they promoted the spread of the movement as far south as Speyer and as far north as Münster and Osnabrück. The articles were accepted by the Frankfurt city council, although they were the occasion of much confusion and many difficulties in the city. It must, however, not be forgotten, as Steitz (p. 95) says, that these articles revived the Reformation movement in Frankfurt which had been begun in 1522 through the sermons of the preacher Ibach, but which had come to a stand-still because of the defeat of the Imperial Knights, who had assumed the protectorate of the movement.

At this time Westerburg lived in Frankfurt with his wife and child in the home of Hans Brommen in Gallengasse. After the defeat of the peasants he was expelled from the city in the middle of May on the very day of the battle at Zabern. He thereupon returned to Cologne, but again ran into difficulties. He reports his experiences of this time in a booklet of 56 pages, printed at Marburg in 1533 by Franz Rhode, in which he describes "how the learned men of Cologne, doctors of divinity and heresy hunters, in March 1526 condemned and damned as an unbeliever Dr. Gerhard Westerburg on account of his teaching regarding purgatory." But the lawyer Westerburg succeeded in securing for himself such a favorable decision by the imperial governmental office in Esslingen in the same month that in spite of published attacks against him, among others by Johannes Cochlaeus (q.v.), his university comrade in Italy, he could continue his residence seven years longer in Cologne. He was not spared attacks by the city council and the Elector, and he could not take part in the trial of Adolf Clarenbach (q.v.) and Peter Fliesteden and could only witness their execution on Sept. 28, 1529.

Now Westerburg, his brother Arnold, and their two wives became Anabaptists, and in a short time Westerburg became the very soul of the Anabaptist movement in Cologne. Enthusiastically he watched the development of the left wing of the Reformation, in which he had years before become deeply interested. He was immediately drawn by the "New Jerusalem" arising in Münster, with its professed purpose to create a new social order based on the pure teaching of the Gospel. In Münster as well as in Cologne several Anabaptists testified, after they had been condemned to death, that the two Westerburg brothers were intimately connected with the Anabaptist movement in Cologne and Münster, Gerhard and Arnold having gone to Münster in the winter of 1534, where they were rebaptized by Heinrich Roll in Knipperdolling's home. Westerburg did not remain long; by Fastnacht he was back again in Cologne diligently promoting the Anabaptist movement. On Feb. 15, 1534, in his house in the Herzogstrasse, he baptized the glazier Richard von Richrath, as well as his own wife. Later he baptized Michael, the servant of a canon of Aachen (born in Brabant), also Peter, the brother of Richard von Richrath. Accompanied by Richard he went to Mörs, where he sought to win converts for the new way. But when he was notified by the bailiff that he would not be tolerated in the district of Mörs he returned to Cologne without having baptized a single person.

The Anabaptist congregation in Cologne at first developed vigorously, but Gerhard Westerburg soon fled the city, although his brother Arnold continued steadfast and suffered both in Cologne and in exile for the Anabaptist cause. A minute in the record of the city council of Strasbourg dated April 22, 1534, states that Roll in the company of Westerburg preached and baptized in the house 'zum gerten fisch." In Cologne, however, on Nov. 7, 1534, Richard von Richrath, a second glazier named Gothard, and Johann Mey, a blacksmith, were executed, the first burned at the stake at Galgenberge, the last two beheaded in the Junkern churchyard.

Although no information is available concerning Westerburg during the years 1535-41, he apparently left the Anabaptists to join the Reformed Church at this time. Later he did not like to remember this Anabaptist interlude. In 1542-43 he appeared in Königsberg at the court of Albrecht, Duke of Prussia, and later in Emden. He also spent some time in East Friesland under the protection of Countess Anna. According to a report which is probably not altogether reliable, which appears in the "Ostfriesisches Predigerdenkmal" of Reershemius, he served in his last years as preacher in Neustadt-Goedens and died there in 1558.   E.C.

Biography by Adolf Brecher in ADB 42 (1897, 182-84); H. S. Bender, Conrad Grebel (Goshen, 1950) 180 f., 122 f., 123, 192, 258 f., 273; Corpus Reform., Opera Melanchthoni V, 41; Leonhard Ennen, Geschichte der Stadt Köln IV (Cologne and Neuss, 1875) 337-53; Günther Franz, Der deutsche Bauernkreig, 4th ed. (Darmstadt, 1956) 228-30; Abraham Hulshof, Geschiedenis van de Doopsgezinden te Straatsburg van 1527 tot 1557 (Amsterdam, 1905); Friedrich Nippold, review on Gerhard Westerburg in Jenaer Literaturzeitung III (Jena, 1876) 385-90; Rembert, Wiedertaufer, 18, 33 ff., 45, 62, 65, 81, 114, 116, 137 f., 216 f., 232, 265, 319, 332, 381, 475, 476; Georg Eduard Steitz, Dr. Gerhard Westerburg, der Leiter des Bürgeraufstandes zu Frankfurt a. M. im Jahre 1525; Archiv für Frankfurts Gesch. u. Kunst V (Frankfurt, 1872) 1-215; Paul Tschackert, Urkundenbuch zur Reformationsgesch. des Herzogthums Preussen III (Leipzig, 1890) 17 et passim; ML IV.

Westerdijk, Pieter Bernard (Assen 1869-Amsterdam 1954), a Dutch Mennonite pastor. After completing his studies at the university and the Mennonite seminary at Amsterdam, he served the congregations of Dantumawoude 1892-99, Enschedé 1899-1911, and Amsterdam 1911-35, in which year he retired. In 1914-41 he was a trustee of the A.D.S., its secretary 1914-21, and its moderator 1929-35. He published a number of theological articles in Tijdspiegel and Nieuw Theologisch Tijdschrift, some sermons, including his sermon of dedication of the Gronau (q.v.) church (Enschedé, n.d.), some booklets like Ons godsdienstig zedelijk leven (Assen, 1903), Waarom wij aan persoonlijke onsterfelijkheid gelooven (Assen, 1906), and De Doopsgezinden

(Lochem, n.d.), and a book *Bijbelsche Gestalten* (Amsterdam, 1935). (*DJ* 1955, 11 f.) vDZ.

Westeremden, in the Dutch province of Groningen, formerly the seat of a Mennonite congregation belonging to the Groningen Old Flemish and in the 17th century temporarily to the very strict Ukowallists (*q.v.*). The congregation existed from the early 16th century; by the early 17th century it was more or less united with that of Middelstum. The relations to Middelstum, however, are not quite clear; in the 18th century Westeremden was independent again until it merged in 1783 with Huizinge (*q.v.*), the name of the congregation then being Huizinge and Westeremden. There was a small meetinghouse at Westeremden, but after a new meetinghouse was built in Huizinge in 1815 no meetings were held at Westeremden. The membership at Westeremden was always very small, in 1800 only seven. The Groningen Old Flemish elder Luirt Luirts (*q.v.*), who was very influential *c*1655-74, was a farmer at Westeremden. vDZ.

Blaupot t. C., *Groningen* I, 52, 149, 199-201; *DB* 1872, 2; 1879, 5; *Groningsche Volksalmanak* 1921, 97 ff.

Westergeest, a hamlet in the northeastern part of the Dutch province of Friesland, where Leenaert (*q.v.*) Bouwens baptized five persons in 1563-65, and ten in 1568-82. Since there was never a congregation at Westergeest, the converts may have joined a neighboring congregation like Dokkum or Dantumawoude. vDZ.

Westerhove(n), van, a former Mennonite family at Haarlem, Holland. Some of its members served as deacons and as trustees of the Mennonite orphanages. Jan van Westerhoven, a deacon of the Flemish Den Blok (*q.v.*) congregation, was banned from this church in 1662 because he had taken the Lord's Supper in the Waterlander church. He thereupon joined the Haarlem Waterlander Peuzelaarsteeg congregation, which he also served as a deacon and soon after as a preacher. When this congregation in 1672 merged with the moderate Flemish (Lamists, *q.v.*), he became an elder of the united church. On March 7, 1683, he dedicated the new Peuzelaarsteeg meetinghouse. He published *De Schepper verheerlijkt door de Schepselen* (1700), a devotional book, which was popular for three generations. Jan van Westerhoven had Collegiant (*q.v.*) leanings as did also his son Jacob. vDZ.

DB 1863, 139, 141, 148; 1892, 108 note 2; Blaupot t. C., *Holland* I, 346.

Westerkwartier is the southwest district of the present Dutch province of Groningen (*q.v.*), in which are found the congregations of Grijpskerk (formerly Pieterzijl), Den Horn (formerly Zuidhorn), and Noordhorn (formerly Humsterland) and the extinct congregation of Visvliet. A short history, particularly on the southern part of the Westerkwartier, is found in S. K. de Waard, *Aanteekeningen uit de Geschiedenis van Doopsgezinden in 't Westerkwartier* (Groningen, 1901). vDZ.

Westermaier, Veit, a member of the Augsburg (*q.v.*) Anabaptist congregation, was baptized in the home of Scolastica Stierpeurin, and on Jan. 28,

1528, was burned through both cheeks and expelled from the city on account of various "misdemeanors" as an Anabaptist. HEGE.

F. Roth, "Zur Geschichte der Wiedertäufer in Oberschwaben," in *Ztscht des hist. Vereins f. Schwaben u. Neuburg* XXVIII (1901) 51; *ML* IV.

Western Book and Publishing Company was organized by H. P. Krehbiel when he moved the *Review* (*q.v.*) to Newton, Kan., from Canton, Ohio, in December 1900 and bought the rights to *Das Kansas Volksblatt* from the Kansan Company which had acquired this periodical from W. J. Krehbiel and David Goerz in 1899.

H. P. Krehbiel, manager, was joined by C. E. Krehbiel in 1901, who served as secretary of the company. The *Review* was continued through 1904. The *Post und Volksblatt* began publication in 1904 with H. P. and C. E. Krehbiel as editors. In 1909 the *Post und Volksblatt* was discontinued and the Western Book and Publishing Company reorganized as the Herold Book and Publishing Company (*q.v.*). J.F.S.

Newton Kansan, Fiftieth Anniversary Number, 1922; *Post und Volksblatt,* 1904-9; *The Review,* 1899-1904.

Western Children's Mission was established and incorporated *c*1935 by an interdenominational group, including members of the Mennonite Brethren Church in Saskatchewan, as an evangelistic agency to reach unchurched children, operating in the three western Canadian provinces of British Columbia, Alberta, and Saskatchewan. In 1952 the Western Children's Mission was broken up into three provincial agencies. The West Coast Children's Mission took over the work in British Columbia; the Rand Mission, which was taken over by the M.B. Alberta Conference, continued the work in Alberta; and the Saskatchewan work was taken over by the M.B. conference of that province under the name Mennonite Brethren Mission of Saskatchewan, with headquarters at Hepburn, Sask. J.S.AD.

Western District Amish Mennonite Conference was the counterpart of the Eastern Amish Mennonite Conference (*q.v.*) and included Illinois, Iowa, Missouri, Arkansas, Kansas, Oklahoma, Nebraska, Colorado, and Oregon. Following the discontinuance of the Amish ministers' meetings of 1862-78 (*Diener-Versammlungen, q.v.*), the more progressive Amish leaders met occasionally for counsel and fellowship. One such informal meeting was held in Illinois around 1882 and another one in the Sycamore Grove church in Cass County, Mo., in 1883. In 1884 these western Amish ministers held a conference in Henry County, Iowa, at which time it was agreed to hold annual conferences, a plan which was followed from that date on. The earliest complete list of congregations belonging to the conference is the 1905 summary, which names 32 churches. A booklet entitled *Western District A.M. Conference. Record of Conference Proceedings from the Date of its Organization* begins with a report of the conference of 1890 held in the Sycamore Grove church, and ends with the conference of 1912, near Wayland, Iowa. Although conferences were held before 1890, evidently it was in 1890 that the conference became completely organized. Subsequent annual reports end with 1920, the year in which a merger was effected between the Mennonite (MC) conferences west of Indiana and the Western A.M. Conference. (This latter term was used interchangeably with "Western District A.M. Conference.") The five conferences affected by the merger were the Western A.M., Pacific Coast (MC), Illinois (MC), Missouri-Iowa (MC), and Kansas-Nebraska (MC). As a result of the merger the following five new Mennonite conferences appeared: Illinois, Iowa - Nebraska, Missouri-Kansas, Dakota-Montana, and Pacific Coast.

At the time of the dissolution of the Western A.M. Conference in 1920 the membership of that body was 4,388, in the following 32 congregations: Illinois (9)—Hopedale, Goodfield, Roanoke, Metamora, East Bend, Willow Springs, Ohio Station, Waldo, Pleasant Grove; Iowa (6)—Sugar Creek, Lower Deer Creek, West Union, Daytonville, East Union, Cedar Creek; Missouri (2) — Sycamore Grove, Fairview; Arkansas—Stuttgart; Nebraska (7)—East Fairview, Salem, Plum Creek, Wood River, West Fairview, East Fairview (Chappell), Slocum; Kansas—Crystal Springs; Oklahoma (2)—Pleasant View, A.M. of the Center Township at Pryor; Colorado—Thurman; Oregon (3)—Fairview, Zion, Bethel.

Ten outstanding leaders of the Western District A.M. Conference were Joseph Schlegel of Nebraska (1837-1913), in Iowa Sebastian Gerig (1838-1934) and Daniel Graber (1858-1930), in Missouri John J. Hartzler (1845-1936), and in Illinois John Smith (1843-1906), John C. Birky (1849-1920), Daniel Orendorff (1838-1918), Samuel Gerber (1863-1929), Andrew A. Schrock (1863-1939), and Chauncy A. Hartzler (1876-1947).   M.G.

M. Gingerich, "Ten Leaders of the Western District Amish Mennonite Conference," *MHB*, October 1940, pp. 1, 2, 3; J. S. Hartzler and Daniel Kauffman, *Mennonite Church History* (Scottdale, 1905).

Western District Conference of the General Conference Mennonite Church in 1957 comprised 67 churches with a membership of 13,561 located in Colorado, Kansas, Nebraska, Oklahoma, and Mexico. The name "Western District" was formerly applied to what later became the Middle District Conference (*q.v.*). Since Kansas was somewhat remote from the Middle District area of Iowa, Illinois, and Ohio, Mennonites of Kansas organized themselves into a local conference called the Kansas Conference (*q.v.*). With the realignment and renaming of district conferences as recommended by the General Conference the Western District became the Middle District and the Kansas Conference became the Western District. The last session of the Kansas Conference and the first session of the Western District Conference were held at Newton on successive days, Oct. 26-28, 1892.

Nineteen churches were represented at the first session of the Western District. First elected officers of the Conference were David Goerz, president; W. J. Ewert, secretary; and Andreas Wiebe, treasurer. Early concerns of the Conference dealt with the Halstead Preparatory School (*q.v.*), home missions, especially as it involved the visitation of smaller

groups in outlying areas, and the promotion of orderly and fruitful activity within the churches.

The Committee for Church Affairs exercised a pastoral concern over the churches, arbitrating differences, counseling with leaders, and exercising disciplinary measures. The Committee on School and Educational Concerns promoted Sunday-school work, parochial and daily vacation Bible schools, and encouraged the Mennonite or German Teachers' Association (*q.v.*) and the German Teachers' Institute (*q.v.*).

In 1893 a committee for relief of the poor, later known as the Charity Committee (*q.v.*), was established to give financial assistance to needy members. A Deaconess Committee was added in 1905 to promote the deaconess cause among the churches of the Conference.

Auxiliaries of the Conference, sometimes reporting directly to the Conference and later through established committees, are the Sunday School Convention, the Christian Endeavor Convention, the Youth Fellowship, the Women's Missionary Association, the Ministers' Conference, the Oklahoma Convention, the Men's Brotherhood, the Oklahoma Bible Academy, and some of the hospitals.

Upon the establishment of Bethel College it reported to the Conference, and after 1920 the Conference named a majority of the College corporation.

The entry of the United States into World War I gave rise to the creation of the Exemption Committee, which later became the Peace and Service Committee. Its primary concern was the status of men drafted for military service, while later it was concerned with all phases of peace education and promotion.

The Education Committee continues to promote daily vacation Bible schools, sponsors Sunday school and youth workers' institutes, and the Western District Loan Library and submits reports of Bible schools and Conference auxiliaries.

Home mission projects have included such churches as the Grace Mennonite Church, Enid; the Meadow Mennonite Church, Colby; the Lorraine Avenue Mennonite Church, Wichita; and more recently churches in Topeka, Kansas City, and Denver.
                                        J.F.S.

Western District Tidings was a quarterly 8½ x 12 in. periodical varying from 4 to 8 pages, published by the Western District Christian Endeavor Convention (GCM) to provide a medium of exchange for ideas of local C.E. Societies, to promote the projects of the Western District C.E. Convention, particularly the various retreats for young people, and to provide the young people with inspirational reading material. It was begun in 1939 under the editorship of William Juhnke who was succeeded toward the end of 1944 by Rosella Reimer (Mrs. Harold Duerksen). It discontinued publication after the June 1946 issue.   J.F.S.

Western Gospel Mission, an interdenominational undertaking, was organized in early 1944 by members of the Prairie Rose Evangelical Mennonite Church (Kleine Gemeinde) near Steinbach, Man. In June 1946 it was reorganized when three congregations of the E.M. Church—Steinbach, Kleefeld, and Prairie Rose—united in the project. Four years later, because of the great needs and many open doors, other groups of evangelical Christians were invited to take part. Incorporated in 1956, with a federal charter, it now operates in three of the ten Canadian provinces—Manitoba, Saskatchewan, and Ontario, with headquarters in Steinbach, Man. The work is carried on from seven main stations, from which resident missionaries operate the outstations. The main stations at Weekes, Canora, Kamsack, Wynyard, Pelly, and Danbury in Saskatchewan also serve Mozart, Neely Lake, Haglof, Veregin, White Beech, Stenen, and Arabella. In Manitoba, Dominion City, Grand Marais, and Mafeking are main stations serving also Victoria Beach, Beaconia, Falcon Beach, Roseau Indian Reserve, Balsam Bay, Baden, Bellsite, and Noora. In Ontario a work was started early in 1958 at Kenora. The purpose of the mission is to bring the Gospel into the neglected areas of Canada. The aim is to establish indigenous Sunday schools and churches as soon as possible. The board of directors of eleven members, three from the Rudnerweide Mennonite Church and eight from the Evangelical Mennonite Church, are chosen by the board themselves, except for the three founding churches which elect their own representatives. Since 1957 the mission has published a 6-page *Bulletin*.   B.D.R.

Western Mennonite Church (MC), Salem, Ore., was established in 1948. It meets in the chapel of the Western Mennonite School. It had 78 members in 1957, with Marcus Lind as its pastor and bishop. It is a member of the Pacific Coast Conference.
                                                                         M.G.

Western Mennonite School is a standard high school committed to the cause of training the youth of the Pacific Coast Conference District (MC). A Committee appointed by the Conference in 1944 and composed of Milton R. Martin, Marcus Lind, and Gabriel D. Shenk, proposed that the Conference take necessary steps for opening and operating such a school. This proposal was accepted by Conference June 21-22, 1945. At this same time, Oregon passed the School Attendance Law which raised compulsory school age to sixteen, a circumstance that created much pressure in favor of a church high school. In September 1945 classes were held in the Bellevue school building located between Sheridan and McMinnville, Ore. In the second year school opened on the permanent campus located 10 miles north of Salem on the Wallace Road, Route 221. F. J. Gingerich of Canby, Ore., was the first president of the school board, serving for six years. He donated 12 acres of land which comprise the immediate campus: Later the board purchased an additional 32 acres.

Marcus Lind of Salem, Ore., served as its first principal 1945-52, followed by Clayton Swartzentruber 1952-57, C. J. Ramer 1957-58, and E. L. Keener 1958-59. At present the physical plant includes an administration building with classrooms, boys' dormitory, dining hall, and chapel; girls' dormitory; auditorium-gymnasium; industrial arts building; and

a new administration building. The enrollment in 1959-60 was 129, with Paul E. Yoder as principal.
                                                                         CL.S.

Western Publishing Co., at Halstead, Kan., was organized in 1875 and chartered under the laws of Kansas with 1,000 shares of stock. Its purpose was to publish and distribute Christian literature among Mennonites. Thus it took over the publication of *Zur Heimath* (*q.v.*) from the Mennonite Board of Guardians in January 1876 and continued its publication with David Goerz as editor.

Members of the first board of directors were Wilhelm Ewert, David Goerz, John Lehmann, Peter Wiebe, and Bernhard Warkentin. In addition to these Christian Krehbiel, Heinrich Richert, and Hermann Sudermann served at various times until the company was dissolved in 1882.

In addition to *Zur Heimath* (*q.v.*) the Western Publishing Co. also published *Nachrichten aus der Heidenwelt* (*q.v.*) for the General Conference 1877-81. It also published some books, and operated a bookbindery and bookstore. David Goerz, secretary of the company throughout its existence, was the moving spirit of the organization. In its last year (1882) there were stockholders in eight states, Indian Territory, Germany, and Russia. The General Conference, the Western District Conference, and the Kansas Conference also were shareholders. (*Zur Heimath*, 1875-81.)   J.F.S.

Westfield (Tex.) Mennonite Brethren Church, located 15 miles north of Houston, was started in 1897 when nine families from Kirk, Col., and some from Kansas organized a small M.B. church here under the leadership of H. Berchtold. They had a very prosperous beginning, starting also a Christian day school. The unhealthy climate, however, forced them to leave this place in 1900. Most of the families moved to Corn and Enid, Okla.   M.A.K.

West-Graftdijk: see Graftdijk.

Westheimer Mennonite Church (GCM), located near Rosemary, Alberta, was established in an abandoned, weedy irrigation area in the fall of 1928, when four families settled there. The land in the area was owned by the Canadian Pacific Railroad, which had spent millions of dollars to develop the Eastern Irrigation District. When the Mennonites, like earlier settlers in the district, were unable to make a living on this land, the railroad in 1935 gave the land to a corporation of farmers, to which the farmers made yearly payments. Under this arrangement the farmers of the area have prospered.

On Feb. 6, 1930, the Mennonites living at Rosemary, Countess, and Gem organized the Westheimer Mennonite Church. In February 1935 the congregation built a church in Rosemary. The building was enlarged in 1947 and in 1949 when the Mennonites in the Clemenceau school district united with the Westheimer congregation. In June 1957, 51 members at Gem, Alberta, organized the independent Gem Mennonite Church. In February 1959 the Westheimer congregation was renamed the Rosemary Mennonite Church. In 1959 its membership was 278, with J. D. Nickel as elder. P.P.D., J.D.N.

Westhofen, a market town in the Worms district in Germany. Before Lutheranism found entry into Westhofen in 1540, Anabaptism was represented here in the 1520's by Wolf Fuchs. The priest Jakob Ebersmann states that according to the court records Wolf Fuchs was charged with Anabaptism and heresy before the court of the Inquisition at Alzey, and was excommunicated. He had been baptized by "Master Jacobus in Worms." E.H.C.

Jakob Ebersmann, *Geschichte von Westhofen, Monzernheim und Blödesheim* (Worms, 1909) 27; *ML* IV.

Westland, a district in the Dutch province of South Holland, south of The Hague, where in the fall of 1535 and early 1536 fanatical Anabaptism was active in the villages of Terheide, Naaldwijk, and Poeldijk. At the end of February 1536 a meeting of these revolutionary chiliasts in the house of Jutte Eeuwouts at Poeldijk was surprised by the police. For particulars see **Jutte Eeuwouts** and **Poeldijk.** After this there are no traces of Anabaptism in the Westland. vDZ.

E. van Bergen, "De Wederdoopers in het Westland," in *Bijdragen voor de Geschiedenis van het Bisdom Haarlem* XXVIII (Haarlem, 1903) 269-88.

Westmoreland County, a large county in Southwestern Pennsylvania, with an area of 1,025 square miles and a population of over 300,000, was organized in 1773. At that time it embraced about one fourth of the state. It was later divided into fourteen additional counties or parts of counties. Mennonite settlers came into this county in the last decade of the 18th century from Bucks, Chester, Berks, Lancaster, Northampton, Bedford, and perhaps other counties. The first-known Mennonite settler was George Mumma, who purchased land near Scottdale in 1794. Other early settlers bore the names of Fox, Overholt, Funk, Welty, Rosenberger, Tintsman, Yothers, Stoner, Fretz, and Loucks. Mennonite settlers had located in the part of Fayette County adjacent to the Scottdale area a few years earlier. A log church was erected at Stonerville, now Alverton, about 1799, and a similar building at Pennsville, Fayette County, which provided places of worship for the fairly large Mennonite community in this area in the first half of the 19th century. These churches were merged into one congregation at Scottdale when that church was built in 1893. Two additional organized congregations have grown out of the Scottdale Church, one at North Scottdale in East Huntingdon Township, about a mile north, and another at Kingview, about a mile east in Fayette County. J.L.H.

J. W. Jordan, *History of Westmoreland County, Pa.* (1906).

Westphalia (Westfalen), a former province (area 7,806 sq. miles, 1939 pop. 5,200,000) of Prussia, Germany, of which the chief cities are Münster, Bielefeld, Hamm, Bocholt, Paderborn, and those of the Ruhr Valley. The geographic boundaries of the territory called Westphalia have in the past been flexible and often changed according to the political and religious constellations of the day. Anabaptism in Westphalia has primarily become known in connection with the radical Münsterite Anabaptism (*q.v.*). Less known is the fact that after the end of the Münsterite movement in 1535 Anabaptism survived in various cities and communities in Westphalia. These Anabaptists, commonly known as "Mennisten" or "Tibben" (*q.v.*), had very little or nothing in common with the radical Münsterites. At the time of the Reformation Westphalia had three bishoprics, Münster, Minden, and Paderborn, and the abbeys Korvey and Herford, which were religious territories subject directly to the emperor. Secular entities were Cleve and the Duchy of Westphalia. Many of the cities of the province enjoyed great freedom. These territorial conditions determined to a large extent the outcome of the denominational lines of the province, in accordance with the principal *cuius regio eius religio.* In 1947 the province of North Rhine-Westphalia was formed.

The Lutheran reform movement reached Westphalia, particularly the eastern parts, in the early days of the Reformation. In the western part in places like Jülich and Cleve the Reformed influences became more noticeable. In the Duchy of Westphalia the Reformation came to a stop when Hermann von Wied, Bishop of Cologne, abdicated in 1547. Philip of Hesse exerted considerable influence in some parts. In the city of Münster (*q.v.*) various forces paved the way for the Reformation, some coming from Luther, others from the Lower Rhine and the Netherlands until the city was converted into a radical Anabaptist "New Jerusalem" which was liquidated in 1535 by the Bishop of Münster, Franz von Waldeck. All Anabaptism, everywhere, even if it had nothing to do with the "New Jerusalem," had received a setback from which it never recuperated, particularly in Westphalia. Keller's three-volume work, *Die Gegenreformation in Westfalen und am Niederrhein,* is to a considerable extent a record of the heroic struggle for survival by peaceful Anabaptism in the province of Westphalia. The Reformed and the Lutheran churches were, of course, witnessing in a similar way. Yet in his presentation of *Der Kampf um eine evangelische Kirche im Münsterland 1520-1802,* Friedrich Brune finds the evangelical movement closely interwoven with Anabaptism, particularly in the beginning, and his book is therefore also to some extent a history of Anabaptism in the rural areas of Münster seen from a Lutheran point of view.

(1) *After "Münster."* In the city of Münster, Catholicism was fully restored after 1535, but Philip of Hesse insisted that at least one or two evangelical ministers be permitted to preach. Anabaptists, of course, were not permitted in the city. Münster, however, had lost the political, intellectual, and religious liberties it had enjoyed under the guilds which were now forbidden. In the surrounding towns and communities of Ahlen, Warendorf, Dülmen, Coesfeld, Ahaus, Vreden, Bocholt, Borken, and Freckenhorst, not only Protestantism but also Anabaptist congregations survived at places for a century.

In Warendorf (*q.v.*), where Anabaptism found entry in 1534, one of the Anabaptist preachers was Johann Klopreis (*q.v.*). More than fifty persons were baptized here. The city council was sympathetic toward Anabaptism until Franz von Waldeck interfered. The monastery Freckenhorst (*q.v.*) near Warendorf, which became Protestant in 1532, was an Anabaptist stronghold. In Coesfeld Anabaptism was established in 1534. Some followers went to Münster. In Dülmen the evangelical movement and Anabaptism were started through the preaching of Bernhard Rothmann. Two ministers from Münster were invited to promote the preaching of the Gospel there but were stopped by the bishop. In Vreden there were "several sects" who met outside the city in the barns and groves and practiced "their unusual baptism" (Brune).

Bocholt also had special significance for the Anabaptists: a meeting of the surviving groups took place in 1536 in which David Joris (*q.v.*) seems to have been dominant. Adam Pastor (*q.v.*), for a while a co-worker of Menno Simons, came from "Dorpen" in Westphalia, evidently the village of Dörpen on the Ems in the northern part in the bishopric of Münster. On Menno Simons' journey from East Friesland to Cologne in 1545 and also when he returned to Lübeck in 1546 he may have passed through Westphalia.

(2) *Cleve-Mark.* The persistence of the Anabaptists in Cleve and Mark is verified by the edicts issued by Count Wilhelm to his officers. On March 9, 1560, he gave detailed instructions as to the techniques to be used to win them back to the church. On June 10, 1560, the circulation of Anabaptist books was forbidden. On Jan. 23, 1565, he addressed the mayor and the city council of Soest demanding that they proclaim nontolerance of the Anabaptists. On July 28, 1576, he again issued an edict against the Anabaptists of Cleve-Mark, and on Aug. 16, 1576, another for the city of Soest. Again on Sept. 24, 1580, he decreed "that Anabaptists, Calvinists, and other sects" should be forbidden and that their ministers should be imprisoned; strangers were to carry passports. On Oct. 1, 1585, he again issued an edict against "Corner-baptists and Anabaptists, Sacramentists," and other sects, calling attention to the previously published edicts.

The third synod of Berg, Jan. 3, 1590, states that Anabaptists were forbidden in the city of Elberfeld. On Feb. 25, 1619, it was reported that the city of Sittard had a number of citizens who were Anabaptists, and on April 9, 1619, it was reported that "the Anabaptists are increasing" in the country of Löwenberg (the only place that has thus far been fully investigated). (Keller I, 90, 92, 119, 245, 247, 259; II, 75, 102; III, 253 f.)

(3) *Bishopric of Münster.* The minutes of the Cathedral Chapter of Münster of 1596-97 deal extensively with the Anabaptists at such places as Wüllen, Borken, and Vreden. Special attention was to be paid to the "Tibben" or Anabaptists who were penetrating cities here and there.

The Anabaptists of Bocholt (*q.v.*), it was reported to the council of Münster on Dec. 18, 1599, had not left the city on the specified date. On June 6, 1607, the council of Münster asked the officers of Bocholt, Ahaus, and other places to expel the Anabaptists immediately. On July 18, 1607, the Anabaptists writing "to the Council of Münster" referred to themselves as "All fellow believers, commonly known as Mennisten." They declared that they had nothing in common with the Münsterites of 1533; everybody could testify that they were quiet citizens; for this reason they requested that the edicts against them be annulled. A similar petition was sent to the Elector Ernst on Aug. 18, 1607, and also on Sept. 12, 1607, by citizens of Vreden. The negotiations concerning the exile of the Anabaptists at Ahaus, Bocholt, Vreden, and Borken continued.

In an edict of Oct. 20, 1611, Anabaptists of Horstmar, Borkelo, Bevergern, Kloppenburg, Dülmen, Werne, Wolbeck, Sassenberg, and Stromberg are mentioned. From that date until June 19, 1612, numerous reports were issued on the subject. Places like Freckenhorst and Harsewinkel still had Anabaptists. A list of Anabaptists at Vreden and Ahaus was submitted on June 6, 20, and 22, 1612. On Sept. 2, 1614, it was reported that the Anabaptists who had been exiled from Borken, Vreden, Bocholt, and Ahaus had returned. Negotiations concerning the Borken Anabaptists continued through Oct. 24, 1622.

In 1612 Warendorf, Freckenhorst, Harsewinkel, Beelen, Bocholt, Ahaus, Ottenstein, Wessum, Wüllen, Vreden, and other places still had some Anabaptists, particularly Vreden. Gradually, however, they had to leave these places, moving to Gronau, Hamm, Emmerich, Emden, Winterswijk, and Zutphen. However, during the official Catholic Church inspection of 1613-16 numerous Anabaptists were still found in various places. Borken still had six or seven members who met regularly. (Keller II, 334 ff., 345, 354, 389, 407 ff.; III, 398, 404 ff., 429 ff., 491 ff., 512, 527, 535, 570 ff., 581 ff.)

The various records give impressive information on the number and the steadfastness of the Anabaptists in Westphalia. However, they reveal little regarding their basic beliefs and practices. There is no trace of revolutionary activities. Brune, a Lutheran author, speaks very highly of them in his study of the Lutheran church, designating them as pious, industrious, and reliable citizens, highly honored by their neighbors. In Warendorf even a Catholic priest, Boethorn, is said to have sympathized with the Anabaptists in the early 17th century.

(4) *Other Areas.* The *Martyrs' Mirror* reports under the year 1601 that Johann von Stein, Count of Wittgenstein, Lord of Homburg, executed four Anabaptists, Hybert op der Straaten, his wife Trynken, Pieter ten Hove, and Lysken van Linschoten. At the beginning of the 18th century there was a small Mennonite church in Hamm, gravure of Mark, and at the end of the century there was a small Amish Mennonite church at Petershagen (*q.v.*) near Minden.

(5) *Later Period.* To what an extent, if any, the membership of the Mennonite Church of Gronau (*q.v.*) is of old Westphalia Anabaptist stock is not known. In any event this is the oldest Mennonite church in Westphalia. It was organized Feb. 4, 1888, in Gronau, 32 miles northwest of Münster, by about 20 Mennonite families living in Gronau and Ahaus, where a large Mennonite industrial center has since

developed. After World War II a number of Mennonite refugees joined the congregation. It was also the gateway for thousands of others who went to Canada.

After World War II numerous Mennonites from Eastern Germany and some from Poland and Russia settled in Westphalia, and have organized churches in several places. The Bergisches Land (*q.v.*) congregation was organized in 1948 in Niederar-Ahe; it includes also the Sauerland area and has a baptized membership of 199. The elder of the church is Fritz Marienfeld. The congregation at Espelkamp (*q.v.*), organized in 1952, has its own meetinghouse and a baptized membership of 150.

Another congregation, the Mennonite Church of Westphalia, meets at various places, such as Osnabrück, Münster, Recklinghausen, Bielefeld, Brakel, and Detmold, and has a membership of 600. C.K.

For the literature on the Münster Anabaptists see that article. "Westfalen," *RGG* V (Tübingen, 1931) 1883; Friedrich Brune, *Der Kampf um eine evangelische Kirche im Münsterland 1520-1802* (Witten, 1953); Robert Stuperich, *Das Münsterische Täufertum* (Münster, 1958); Ludwig Keller, *Die Gegenreformation in Westfalen und am Niederrhein*, 3 vv. (Leipzig, 1881-95); *Gem.-Kal.*, 1958, 82-85; W. Risler, "Täufer im bergischen Amt Löwenburg, Siebengebirge," *Gesch.-Bl.*, 1955; in "Mennoniten in Duisburg," *Gesch.-Bl.*, May 1951, Risler presents an introduction and list of Mennonites of Duisburg; Ernst Crous, "Auf Mennos Spuren am Niederrhein," *Der Mennonit* VIII (1955) 187; *idem*, "Die rechtliche Lage der Krefelder Mennonitengemeinde im 17. u. 18. Jh.," *Beiträge zur Gesch. rhein. Mennoniten* (Weierhof, 1939) 40; *ML* IV.

Westzaan, a village in the Dutch province of North Holland (1947 pop. 3,318; 204 Mennonites), was at a very early date an important center of Anabaptism. During the winter of 1533-34 no less than some 200 are said to have been (re)baptized here. This early congregation had a strong tendency toward radical chiliasm; many of its members were among the Anabaptists who sailed from Amsterdam for Münster (*q.v.*) in March 1534, some of whom were pronounced revolutionary and were executed. After the Münsterite period a peaceful Anabaptism developed clandestinely in Westzaan. Concerning this period there is not much information. At the end of the 16th century there were two Mennonite congregations here, a Waterlander (*q.v.*) in the northern part of the village, and a Frisian (*q.v.*) in the southern part; they did not merge until 1949.

The Waterlander congregation, later usually called Westzaan-(op het) Noord, was represented at a Waterlander conference at Amsterdam in 1581. Of its history there is only scanty information. Shortly after 1600 it obtained a meetinghouse, which was remodeled several times. Though the Dutch Waterlanders were in general rather liberal, Waterlander churches in North Holland in the later 17th century took a more conservative attitude, rejecting Collegiantism (*q.v.*) and strictly maintaining the confession of faith by Hans de Ries (*q.v.*), also refusing to hold government offices (mentioned in 1628). The membership numbered 150 in 1760, 70 in 1827, 114 in 1861, 146 in 1900, 156 in 1929, and 134 in 1949. Until 1876 this church was served by untrained preachers, some of whom were outstanding;

e.g., Willem Bruin 1786-1826 and Jacob Hartog Jansz 1828-76. The first minister trained at the Mennonite seminary was C. R. van Dokkum, serving in the Westzaan-Noord congregation 1877-1902; he was followed by R. Schuursma 1903-10 and M. Onnes Mzn 1911-29. In 1930, both churches of Westzaan being vacant, they called A. A. Sepp as a pastor for both congregations. He served here 1930-34, followed by M. A. Hijlkema 1935-47, E. Daalder 1947-51, J. Wieringa 1952-58, and A. H. Swerms 1958-. In 1949 a complete merger was made by the two churches.

The Westzaan-(op het) Zuid church was the mother congregation of the Frisian church of Zaandam (*q.v.*), which became an independent congregation *c*1700. Until then the preachers of the Westzaan-Zuid congregation often lived at Zaandam. Westzaan-Zuid has a fine old meetinghouse built in 1695; it is one of the few remaining frame churches, which were formerly rather common in North Holland. This building, well preserved, acquired a pipe organ in 1881. The membership, though exact figures are missing, was presumably rather large in the 17th century, but since *c*1780 there has been a considerable decrease, mostly because many members moved from Westzaan to Zaandam. In 1725 the baptized membership numbered 210, 252 in 1769, only 75 in 1830, 144 in 1861, 116 in 1900, 98 in 1929, and 81 in 1949. Until 1843 the Westzaan-Zuid congregation was served by lay preachers. In that year Chr. Sepp, who had been educated at the Amsterdam Seminary, was called, serving here 1843-48. He was followed by J. A. J. Verstege 1848-58, A. Ballot 1860-64, H. Cremer 1866, S. Kutsch Lojenga 1866-72, A. G. van Gilse 1872-78, S. K. de Waard 1878-84, C. N. Wybrands 1884-86. After the pulpit had been vacant for three years, Pastor van Dokkum of the Westzaan-Noord congregation was asked to take on the congregation "op't Zuid"; he served here 1889-1902. After his retirement both Westzaan-Noord and Westzaan-Zuid again called pastors of their own; in Zuid this was J. W. van Stuyvenberg, serving here 1903-21, followed by W. Mesdag 1924-29. In the next year (as mentioned above) both churches called Pastor Sepp, and finally in 1949, then together numbering 215 baptized members, they completely merged.

The Westzaan-Zuid congregation formerly operated an orphanage, which was closed about 1890 for lack of orphans. At present there are ladies' circles in both northern and southern parts of Westzaan, and a Sunday school for children. The present baptized membership is 170. vdZ.

Inv. Arch. Amst. I, Nos. 14, 110, 413, 865, 892, 896; *DB* 1861, 163; 1872, 57; 1877, 80; 1889, 134; Blaupot t. C., *Holland* I and II, *passim*; Kühler, *Geschiedenis* I, 87, 92; S. Lootsma, *Het Nieuwe Huys* (Zaandam, 1937) 188 ff.

Westzaandam: see Zaandam.

Weydmann, Ernst (1837-1903), a Mennonite preacher of Crefeld. He was the son of Leonhard Weydmann, and like his father he studied at the University and Mennonite Seminary of Amsterdam, where at this time the professors were Samuel Muller (*q.v.*), conservative and a powerful personality; Sytse Hoekstra (*q.v.*), a prominent Dutch Modernist; Jan van Gilse (*q.v.*), and J. G. de Hoop Scheffer. Ernst Weydmann succeeded his father and served his home congregation from 1866 to 1903. Like the former ministers, he worked in close co-operation with his Protestant colleagues; sometimes they exchanged pulpits. He was seriously interested in a union of the German Mennonites. In Ebensheim in 1874 an attempt at union failed, but in Berlin in 1886 the Vereinigung (*q.v.*) was organized. In that year Weydmann became the Crefeld representative of the Vereinigung and in 1896-1902 he served as chairman of its Consistorium. Weydmann published a new edition of the *Christliche Lehre* written by his father (see **Weydmann, Leonhard**). Ernst Weydmann's *Geschichte der Mennoniten bis zum 18. Jahrhundert* was published posthumously in 1905.   E.C.

Dirk Cattepoel, *Die akademisch vorgebildeten Prediger der Krefelder Mennonitengemeinde* (Weierhof, 1939); F. C. Fleischer, in *Zondagsbode*, Aug. 16, 1903; *Gem.-Kal.*, 1906, 115-18; *ML* IV.

Weydmann, Leonhard, a Mennonite preacher in Monsheim and Crefeld, b. March 15, 1793, at Crefeld, d. April 13, 1868, at Crefeld, the son of a Reformed father and a Mennonite mother. He was educated in Basel. In Amsterdam he witnessed the establishment of the A.D.S. (1811). The Mennonite professors at Amsterdam at that time were Gerrit Hesselink (*q.v.*), who was a natural scientist rather than a theologian, and Rinse Koopmans (*q.v.*), who stressed the divine authority of revealed doctrine. In 1812 Weydmann wrote a paper on the "Excellence of Mathematics," in 1814 a paper on "Baptism, as It Was Practiced by the Apostles and the Superstitious Practices That Were Later Connected with It," and another work about the "Authenticity of the Books of the New Testament." He studied briefly then at the University of Berlin and in 1816 became the minister in Zutphen and after that in Friedrichstadt.

After several months in Crefeld he received a call to the Kriegsheim congregation and then in 1820 a call to Monsheim. Here he witnessed the establishment of the Palatine-Hessian Conference (1824), which was accompanied by an increased interest in missions. He was the first trained minister in the Palatinate and rendered valuable service there in the matter of their hymnal (1832) and their catechism (1836).

In 1836-66 he served in his home congregation of Crefeld. Here too he did some literary work. In 1850 he published the book *Luther, ein Charakter- und Spiegelbild für unsere Zeit,* and in 1852 *Christliche Lehre, zunächst zum Gebrauch der Taufgesinnten in Deutschland.*   E.C.

Weyneken (Wyneken, Wijnken) **Jans,** a revolutionary Anabaptist of Friesland. She sailed with an Amsterdam group in March 1534 en route to Münster (*q.v.*), but was apprehended at Bergklooster (*q.v.*) in the Dutch province of Overijssel. On May 11, 1534, the Court of Holland sentenced her to be burned at the stake. The sentence was apparently executed at The Hague. (*Inv. Arch. Amst.* I, No. 745; *DB* 1917, 121, No. 143; Mellink, *Wederdopers,* 245.)   vDZ.

Weynken Claes (Wendelmoet Claesdochter), a martyr of Monnikendam in the Dutch province of North Holland, burned at the stake at The Hague on Nov. 20, 1527, after she had been in prison for half a year. On Nov. 15, 1527, she was conducted from the castle of Woerden to The Hague to be tried before the stadholder and the Court of Holland. Weynken Claes was not an Anabaptist in the strict sense, since Anabaptism did not arise in Holland before the fall of 1530, but a Sacramentist (*q.v.*). The ideas she defended in her trial were the Sacramentist views—rejecting and attacking the Catholic doctrine of transubstantiation, the power claimed by the Catholic Church to forgive sins, and the seven Catholic sacraments, but not infant baptism. This explains why she is listed in the Lutheran (Rabus, *q.v.*) and the Reformed (van Haemstede, *q.v.*) as well as in the Mennonite martyr books from the *Offer des Heeren* to van Braght's *Martyrs' Mirror.* That she was not an Anabaptist is also shown by the fact that though she was executed in 1527, she was not listed in the first three editions of *Offer des Heeren,* but was first inserted in the appendix of the 1570 edition.

Yet there was adequate reason to list her among the Anabaptist martyrs. First, Monnikendam was by 1534 predominantly Anabaptist, and later a considerable Mennonite congregation was found here, among whose members there may have been descendants of Weynken or relatives or friends. Secondly, the objections of later Anabaptism to the doctrines and practices of the Catholic Church are identical with those of Weynken Claes, Anabaptist martyrs again and again expressing their rejection of transubstantiation, etc., with Weynken's very words. She valiantly, freely, and ably defended her views; her somewhat crude expressions show that she was of the common people. Concerning the sacred host, she said that it is merely bread and water; concerning the extreme unction she answered, "Oil is good for salad or to oil your shoes with"; and when a monk showed her a wooden crucifix, saying, "See, here is your Lord and your God," she answered, "This is not my God; the cross by which I am redeemed is a different one. This is a wooden god; throw him into the fire, and warm yourselves with him." She firmly confessed her faith in Christ as her only Saviour; she confidently believed in the grace of God; the glow of the burning pile near the stake did not frighten her, and she died steadfast.

The source for the trial and death of Weynken Claes used by several martyr books was a pamphlet printed at Antwerp in 1528 (no copy has survived). An account in German, entitled *Ein wunderliche geschycht, newlich geschehen in dem Hag in Holland im iar MDXXVII den XX tag Novembris, von einr frawen geheissen Wendelmut Clausen dochter, einr witwe, die do verprendt ist* (copies in the libraries of Munich and Vienna), obviously a translation of the Dutch pamphlet of 1528, was used by Rabus.

In the *Offer des Heeren* this account is followed by a hymn on Weynken, beginning "De Heer moet zijn ghepresen/Van zijn goedertierenheit."   vDZ.

BRN II, 422-29; *Mart. Mir.* D 11-13, E 422-24; *Inv.*

Arch. Amst. I, No. la-d; *Bibliographie* I, 82-91, 651 f.; II, 671, No. 135; Wolkan, *Lieder*, 68; *ML* I, 358.

Wheat has been raised by Mennonites in Russia and America in large quantities. In the pioneer days in the Ukraine (*q.v.*) the Mennonites engaged in small-scale diversified farming, and wheat production played no significant role. (See **Agriculture.**) Gradually the Mennonites concentrated on wheat raising. Originally they primarily raised summer wheat. Gradually they shifted to hard winter wheat, which was grown in the Black Sea and Mediterranean areas, which was known as Red Turkey, Crimean, Odessa, Bulgarian, Hungarian, Russian, and Mennonite wheat. That this variety was introduced into the Ukraine by the father of Bernhard Warkentin (*q.v.*) is not likely. It was generally sown by German and Greek settlers and Russian farmers in that area, and it is likely that he promoted it. Around 1850 the London wheat market began to appreciate this hard wheat. The increased production of wheat went hand in hand with the development of improved machinery and the opening of ports along the Black Sea and Sea of Azov, which made the Ukraine the granary of Europe. The ports of Berdyansk and Mariupol near the Mennonite settlement shipped the best quality of wheat. Cornelius Jansen stated that the Mennonites of the Molotschna produced nearly half a million bushels of wheat in 1855. In 1874 Senator Windom, of Minnesota, urged Congress to promote the immigration of Mennonites to the prairie states to enable America to meet the competition of wheat shipments from Russia and Canada on the world market.

When the Mennonites arrived in the prairie states and provinces, they brought with them, along with household goods and furniture, various seeds they had been planting in the steppes of the Ukraine, including smaller quantities of varieties of wheat. The various stories in circulation about how this wheat was selected and who brought it cannot be taken too seriously. It is possible that Kansas raised some hard winter wheat varieties prior to the coming of the Mennonites. However, the fact remains (even Malin, who has questioned many claims, confirms it) that the counties in which the Mennonites lived and those in the immediate surroundings were the first to raise the hard winter wheat varieties on a larger scale (162-78).

Bernhard Warkentin, whose father was a miller in Russia and who was among the first to come to America in 1872, immediately saw the agricultural and milling possibilities in the prairie states and built a mill in Halstead with his father-in-law. He demonstrated on his farm and in his mill the great superiority of winter wheat over the soft varieties still in use. He imported a large shipment of winter wheat from the Crimea in 1885-86 for distribution among the farmers. Soon after this Mark A. Carleton, the noted cerealist, probably became acquainted with Warkentin and the Mennonites when he was teaching at Garfield University at Wichita (1889-91). In 1896 when he experimented with wheat and oats in Salina, he called on Warkentin, and in 1899 he secured through Warkentin a plot of land for further experiments in some 300 varieties. The correspondence between Warkentin and Carleton (copies in BeCL) reveals clearly the role of the Mennonites in introducing the hard winter wheat to the prairie states. Carleton states in an article in the *Yearbook* (1914) that each Mennonite "family brought over a bushel or more of Crimean wheat for seed, and from this seed was grown the first crop of Kansas hard winter wheat" (399), and that the "good qualities of Turkey wheat were not generally appreciated much before the close of the last century, 25 years after its introduction into Kansas by the Mennonites" (401). In 1898 Carleton, with the help of Warkentin, went to the Ukraine to get some hard winter wheat varieties. In 1901, upon the request of the Kansas State Millers Association, Warkentin had about 15,000 bushels imported and distributed. Among the hard winter wheat varieties which have been developed from this original hard wheat, the best known are Kanred, Black Hull, and Tenmarq.

Although the hard winter wheat is limited to the states of Oklahoma, Kansas, and Nebraska, the Mennonites of other areas have made a similar contribution in other kinds of wheat, especially in Manitoba.

Malin's book, *Winter Wheat,* is a valuable source of information, but needs to be checked and brought up to date. He did not make use of some of the valuable sources such as the Carleton-Warkentin correspondence and the notices which regularly appeared in the *Weekly Kansan* of Newton. The study of the contribution of the Mennonites in the promotion of winter wheat is still to be made.

C.K.

T. R. Schellenberg, "Correspondence Between Mark A. Carleton and Bernhard Warkentin Regarding Turkey Wheat," excerpts from the National Archives and the Department of Agriculture (BeCL); James C. Malin, *Winter Wheat in the Golden Belt of Kansas* (Lawrence, 1944); Mark A. Carleton, "Successful Wheat Growing in Semiarid Districts" and "Hard Wheats Winning Their Way," *Yearbook of the Department of Agriculture,* 1900, pp. 529-42; 1914, pp. 391-420; Cornelius Krahn, ed., *From the Steppes to the Prairies* (Newton, 1949); William E. Connelley, "Bernhard Warkentin," in *A Standard History of Kansas and Kansans* V (Chicago-New York, 1918) 2291; H. D. Seymour, *Russia on the Black Sea and Sea of Azof . . .* (London, 1855) 315 ff.; A. Ehrt, *Das Mennonitentum in Russland von seiner Einwanderung bis zur Gegenwart* (Berlin, 1932); D. G. Rempel, "The Mennonite Colonies in New Russia . . . 1789-1914" (unpublished doctoral dissertation at Stanford University, 1933); S. P. Sorokin, *Semenovodstvo v semennykh tovarishestvakh Vserossiyskovo Mennonitskovo Selsko-Khozyaystvennovo Obshestva* (Moscow, 1926).

White Cloud Mennonite (MC) Church, located one mile southeast of White Cloud, Mich., is in the Indiana-Michigan Conference. Mennonite families from the Shore congregation in Lagrange County, Ind., began moving into the area in 1896. Regular Sunday-school services were started in a schoolhouse in 1898 and the next year Bishop P. Y. Lehman of Indiana organized a congregation of 22 charter members. In 1900, when the congregation had grown to 35 members, Bishop John F. Funk (*q.v.*) ordained Jacob P. Miller (1850-1927) to the ministry. On May 1, 1901, P. Y. Lehman ordained him as bishop. In 1903 the congregation began to worship in a building known as the Union Church, and for a time was known by this name. After 1910 J. P. Miller was no longer located at White Cloud, and T. U. Nelson (1870-1950) became the long-time preacher, having been ordained by Miller on Dec. 5, 1910. The pastor of the church in 1958 was Edward D. Jones, and the membership was 54.   J.C.W.

Winifred Nelson Beechy, "History of the White Cloud Mennonite Church," *MHB*, July 1952, 1-4.

White Hall Mennonite (MC) Church, now extinct, near Oronogo in Jasper County, Mo., was last listed in the 1953 *Mennonite Yearbook,* with 15 members. In 1936 the church had its largest membership of 69. Joseph Blosser and family of Virginia, who arrived in Jasper County in 1867, were the first Mennonites in the area; by 1892 the church had grown to some 20 members. The congregation worshiped in the White Hall school until 1897, when it built a church across the road from the school. The first minister was Joseph Weaver, from Virginia, who was ordained in Missouri. Andrew Shenk, from Ohio, became the minister of the church in 1895. Another well-known preacher of the congregation was E. J. Berkey.   M.G.

Whitehorn Mennonite Brethren Church, Blaine, Wash.: see **Blaine** Mennonite Brethren Church.

Whitehouse (Ohio) Reformed Mennonite Church at Whitehouse, Lucas Co., Ohio, was established in 1852. In 1957 it had 6 members.   H.S.B.

Whitemouth Church of God in Christ Mennonite Church is located 3 miles northwest of Elma, Man. In 1959 it had 45 members, with M. P. Barkman as minister. The congregation was first listed in the Yearbook (CGC) for 1950.   M.G.

Whitewater, Kan., is located in Butler County southeast of the center of the state. Established in 1878, it had a population in 1957 of 510. In the town is found the Swiss Mennonite Church (GCM); three more churches (all GCM), Emmaus, Grace Hill (Gnadenberg), and Zion at Elbing, are within a ten-mile radius of Whitewater.

The first settlement of Mennonites in this area was made in the Grace Hill community in the winter of 1874-75, by Mennonites coming from Michalin (*q.v.*), Polish Russia. This church had a membership of 210 in 1957. The postal center of the community in 1875 was Sheldon, half a mile east and one mile south of the Grace Hill church. After a few years it ceased to exist. In 1876 a group from the Heubuden congregation in Prussia arrived, founding the Emmaus church, located southeast of Whitewater. In 1957 this church had a membership of 367. Seven miles north of Whitewater another group from Prussia organized a church in 1883. Later the Rock Island Railroad was built and the village here was called Elbing, after Elbing in Prussia. The Zion Mennonite Church in Elbing had a membership of 155 in 1957. Elbing became the location of Berean Academy, an independent Christian high school opened in September 1946. The Swiss Mennonite group settled in the

area immediately north of Whitewater in 1883. Until 1953 the church was located north of Whitewater, but is now in the town. In 1957 it had a membership of 146.   J.F.S.

Whitewater (Man.) Mennonite Church (GCM) was organized April 18, 1927, by Mennonite families from Russia who had settled in that community starting in 1924. The first elder was Franz F. Enns (*q.v.*), of Lena, Man., who had been elder of the Terek Mennonite Church in Russia. On June 16, 1938, the present elder, G. G. Neufeld, succeeded him.

In 1958 the congregation had 565 members and a total population of 1,209 in 257 families; it had six branch congregations: Whitewater 162, Rivers 96, Ninga 63, Lena 80, Crystal City 135, Manitou 29. Five of these groups have their own meetinghouses in which they worship every Sunday. Worship is conducted in German. All branches have Sunday school, choirs, youth groups, evangelistic services, and women's mission groups. There is an annual conference for the 24 ministers and deacons. The elder baptizes and observes the Lord's Supper four times annually with all groups. Footwashing has been dropped.   G.G.N.

Wichita, county seat (pop. 250,000) of Sedgwick County, Kan., lies near the eastern end of the Great Bend Prairie, in the south-central section of Kansas, 25 miles south of Newton. Most of the strong Mennonite communities of central Kansas lie within shopping distance. There are two Mennonite Brethren churches (128 members), two Mennonite (MC) (one with 23 members, the other a Negro mission, not yet organized, but with church dedicated in 1959), and one General Conference Mennonite Church (410) within the area of Greater Wichita, with a total membership of 561. The Mennonites are scattered over all areas of the city and the suburban fringe outside the city limits. Wichita schools hire many Mennonite teachers. Some Mennonite students take graduate work at the University of Wichita. Nurses and doctors study and intern in the city's hospitals. Wealthy homes desire the domestic services of Mennonite girls. The varied industries, including the large airplane factories, offer employment for both men and women.   G.S.S.

J. H. Langenwalter, "From Whence Came the Mennonites of Wichita"; G. S. Stoneback, "Mennonites of Wichita Live and Work"; Orlando Harms, "Mennonites of Wichita Worship"; all in *Mennonite Life* VIII (January 1953).

Wichita (Kan.) **First** Mennonite Brethren Church, a member of the Southern District Conference, had its beginning in 1942. A church at 1702 West Second Street was purchased and on May 16, 1943, the congregation was organized with 19 charter members, mainly from the M.B. and K.M.B. conferences. In 1958 the membership was 96. In addition to considerable renovating and remodeling of the church, a new parsonage was built in 1950. In 1958 plans were in progress for the construction of a church in another area of the city. Serving the church as pastors have been Estil Schale 1943-46,

Orlando Harms 1946-53, George A. Vogt 1954-56, and Victor E. Becker, the pastor in 1958. O.HA.

Wickersham Schoolhouse, located in West Donegal Twp., Lancaster Co., Pa., is a two-story brick building which was used as a union Sunday school with Mennonite personnel intermittently in 1892-1915; then most of the pupils were moved to Bossler's, a few miles away. In 1935 it was reopened as an outpost of Bossler's; in 1951 it was taken over by an independent group. I.D.L.

Wickrath, an imperial district on the Niers River, south of Rheydt, Rheinland, Germany. The baron of Quadt-Wickrath accepted in his domain the Mennonites who had been expelled from Holland in 1652. In September 1663 he received an imperial demand to "deliver the Anabaptists taken in by him who had been expelled from other territories, of whom there were about 50 in the Wickrath domain," in the space of three months, because "this forbidden sect was everywhere making inroads into the empire." At first this command was disregarded, but ten years later the Mennonites had to leave Wickrath. Most of them went to adjacent Rheydt, where until 1694 they enjoyed the protection of the barons of Rylandt-Rheydt and then were expelled by John William, the Palatine Elector. (*ML* IV.) W.N.

Wideman (Wiedemann, Widman), **Jakob** (d. 1535/6), an early Moravian Anabaptist leader, often called the "one-eyed Jakob," was born in Memmingen (*q.v.*), Swabia, and seems to have been converted to Anabaptism in 1527, probably in Augsburg. From here he went to Nikolsburg, where at that time the conflict between the Schwertler (*q.v.*) and Stäbler (*q.v.*) was becoming more and more acute. In 1528 Wideman separated from the Schwertler (the former Hubmaier group, now headed by Hans Spittelmaier, *q.v.*, and supported by the lords of Liechtenstein), rallying, together with Philipp Jäger (or Weber, *q.v.*), the nonresistant Stäbler around him. When this group was no longer permitted to live on the Liechtenstein territory at Nikolsburg, the Brethren moved away in great poverty, not knowing where to turn. It was a group of about 200 adults and many children. In this predicament several men laid a cloak on the ground upon which everyone voluntarily put whatever he possessed of money or goods, in order to support the needy according to the teachings of the Book of Acts. Fortunately the manorial lords of Austerlitz (*q.v.*), viz., the four Kaunitz brothers, were willing to accept this group on their estates. Thus began the first fully communal Anabaptist settlement. Since they lived in Austerlitz, they became known all over the country as the "Austerlitz Brethren." Wideman was the Vorsteher (elder) of the group, which from now on grew steadily by new accessions from South Germany and Tirol. In 1531 another split took place; the Tiroleans under Jörg Zaunring (*q.v.*), a co-worker of Jakob Hutter, moved away to Auspitz, where they started their own communal Bruderhof, leaving Wideman with the Austerlitz group.

Unfortunately the Hutterite Chronicle shows little interest in the Austerlitz group and other sources are scanty. The Philippites (*q.v.*) also settled in Austerlitz on the same estate, but as a separate people under Plener. There were now four groups in Moravia living in community: in Austerlitz the Wideman group and the Philippites, the Gabrielites in Rossitz, and the Tiroleans (under Zaunring and later Schützinger) in Auspitz. Unfortunately they did not always live in brotherly peace. Jakob Hutter wrote in 1533: "I know these Austerlitzers very well, they do not walk according to the rule of Christ; nevertheless I believe that there are good, God-fearing people among them." When Ulrich Stadler (*q.v.*) came from Tirol to Moravia, he joined the Wideman group and remained with it until the hardship year of 1535. Whether or not Wideman was always their bishop cannot be stated with certainty. Beck (50) claims that in 1530-31 Wideman was in Strasbourg, then a center of Anabaptism, but was expelled from that city, and very likely returned to Austerlitz.

In 1535 King Ferdinand of Hapsburg ordered all the nobles to expel the Brethren from Moravian soil (see **Moravia**). The lords had to comply, and thus also the Austerlitz group was dispersed as the Philippites had been. Ulrich Stadler and his group went to Poland; others went back to Germany; Wideman, however, together with several Brethren, apparently went to Vienna in Austria. Here the group was caught, tortured, and eventually martyred (1535 or 1536). This we learn, almost incidentally, from a letter of Jeremy Käls (*q.v.*), himself a prisoner in Vienna and soon to be a martyr. In his cell he learned of the fate of his fellow believers, but gives no particulars. No writings and no hymns by Wideman seem to have been preserved. R.F.

Zieglschmid, *Chronik;* Beck, *Geschichts-Bücher,* 50; F. Roth, *Augsburgs Reformationsgeschichte* II (Munich, 1901) 232; *ML* IV.

Wideman Mennonite Church (MC), located 3 miles north of Markham, York Co., Ont., is named after its first minister, Henry Wideman (d. 1810), of Bucks County, Pa., who arrived in 1803, and across from whose homestead the first meetinghouse was erected c1812. The first log church was replaced by a brick structure c1857 and again in 1928 by a 38 x 65 ft. brick building. Among the early families were Hoovers, Stouffers, Reesors, and Sherks. The second minister, Martin Hoover, arrived in 1804. Bishop Abraham Grove (d. 1836), who had been ordained in Pennsylvania prior to coming to Markham, arrived in 1808. Jacob Grove (d. 1863), son of Abraham, was ordained minister in 1836 and bishop in 1837. Christian Reesor (d. 1915) was ordained bishop in 1887; he withdrew with the Old Order (Wisler) schism in 1889. Other ministers were Joseph Barkley (ord. 1864), S. R. Hoover 1888), L. W. Hoover (1914), A. L. Fretz (1920, moved to Rainham in 1931), A. D. Grove (1932), Elmer H. Burkholder (1947). Sunday school was begun c1876, closed in the eighties, permanently opened in 1892. Wideman's was the center and largest congregation of the York County settlement. A substantial part of the congregation followed its bishop, Christian Reesor, into the Old Order (Wisler) movement in 1889 or soon thereafter. The Mennonite Brethren in Christ (*q.v.*) movement (1875 ff.) also drew away a number of members and led to the establishment of substantial M.B.C. congregations in Markham and Stouffville. In 1958 the congregation had 151 members, with Aaron Grove and Elmer Burkholder as ministers.

H.S.B.

Widemann, Michael (or Beck), an Anabaptist martyr, who was seized at Ried in Allgäu, Bavaria, Germany, with a group of followers in 1538. The others were released. When he was admonished to recant, he replied, "I have become converted once and have renounced all unrighteousness, and in this conversion I will persevere unto the end." After six months in prison he was beheaded and burned. (Beck, *Geschichts-Bücher*, 141; *Mart. Mir.* D 43, E 449; *ML* IV.)   NEFF.

Widertoufferen vrsprung (Der), *fürgang, secten, wäsen, fürnemme vnd gemeine jrer leer artickel, ouch jre gründ und warumb sy sich absünderind, vnnd ein eigne kirchen anrichtind, mit widerlegung vnd antwort vff alle vnd yede jre gründ und artickel, sampt Christenlichem bericht vnd vermanen, dass sy jres irrthumbs vnd absünderens abstandind, und sich mit der kirchen Christi vereinigind, abgeteilt in VI Bücher, und beschriben durch Heynrichen Bullingern dienern der kirchen zu Zürych. Was in disen Büchern gehandlet sye, wirst hienach in einem kurzen Register vff die Vorred finden. So ist zum end gethon der Töuffern Büchli, mit dem sy vrsach anzeigend, warumb sy nit zur kirchen gon wöllind* (2nd ed., Zürich, 1561), pp. 28, 231. The last section mentioned in the title covers pp. 214-31, under the title *Verantwortung etlicher die man Töuffer nennt, vff die fragen warumb sy nit zuo kirchen gangind,* though the folio lines read *Der Töufferen verantwortung Irer von der kirchen absünderung.* This is the title of the second book against the Anabaptists by Heinrich Bullinger (*q.v.*), written between Nov. 24, 1559, and March 8, 1560, in print (first edition) in March 1560, introduction signed March 15. The history of its beginnings is a rather long one.

After the first book, *Von dem unverschampten fräfel* (*q.v.*), had been so great a success, Bullinger planned to write a new version dealing with the further development of the Anabaptist movement. He took the first step in 1542. For some years he had corresponded with the preacher Hermann Aquilomontanus in Oldersum, East Friesland (*q.v.*), who twice a year traveled to the book fair in Frankfurt and served as a messenger between North Germany and Switzerland. Urged by the North German friends Bullinger in 1542 wrote the Latin draft of a systematic refutation of Anabaptism entitled *Contra anabaptistas consignata quaedam.* It was never published; the manuscript lies in the Central Library in Zürich. It is not known why he discontinued the work for 17 years, but when he took it up again in 1559 his experiences, his interests, and the occasion, had changed. With great sorrow Bullinger saw the disunion between the Lutheran and the Zwinglian churches. Not only was it in his eyes un-Biblical, it was also politically a great disadvantage to the Reformation. Bullinger was particularly incensed by the Lutheran charge identifying the Swiss churches with the Anabaptists and calling them "Schwärmer" or sacramentists. Indefatigably he affirmed that the Zwinglian church had nothing to do with such "heresies," that it was orthodox and could never be looked upon as a sect. This was the purpose of his second book against the Anabaptists.

The volume has more than 500 pages and is divided into six "books" and an appendix. However, the following outline is more helpful. (A) The origins of Anabaptism in Saxony, and its rise and history in Switzerland to 1532 (f. 1-17a); (B) The Anabaptist groups—(1) the "general Anabaptists," and (2) the "special Anabaptists" (f. 17a-75); (C) The refutation of the "general Anabaptists" (f. 76-236); (D) Appendix, with comments on an Anabaptist tract on separation from the state church (f. 237-56; *Verantwortung etlicher, die man Töuffer nennt*).

Though parts (C) and (D) comprise most of the book they are the least important, because they are largely repetitive of his first book The historical parts (A) and (B), however, are new and of great significance. Bullinger here claims that the origin of Anabaptism was due to the activity of Nicolaus Storch (*q.v.*) and Thomas Müntzer (*q.v.*) in Saxony (*q.v.*), and that Zürich Anabaptism was only an offspring of the Middle German radical movement. Its rise in Zürich was the result of some rebellious elements whom Zwingli had tried in vain to pacify. On this view and on many other historical details Bullinger was soon considered the authoritative witness, and, though he was not the first to advocate the theory mentioned, he was the most influential one.

Bullinger intended his historical portrayal of Anabaptism to prove the main thesis of the book, that the Zwinglian Reformation originally had nothing to do with Anabaptism. This very intent casts doubt on the historical construction. Bullinger's trustworthiness must be seriously called into question for another reason. He did not record the beginnings of Anabaptism as an eyewitness, although he had seen many things himself. Instead he rather uncritically depended on what other authors had written on the subject before him, deviating only where he could underline his main theory. In most cases not Bullinger, therefore, but his sources must be examined and evaluated. Where, however, firsthand sources contradict Bullinger's account neither he nor his predecessors can claim reliability. Such is the case with his theory on the dependence of Zürich Anabaptism on Müntzer.

The first edition of the book was sold within a few months. Bullinger himself sent it to 98 persons, of whom the most prominent were Duke Christoph of Württemberg, Elector Frederik III of the Palatinate, Prince Philipp of Hesse, King Maximilian II of Bohemia, and Queen Elizabeth of England. In his still extant letters of dedication he recommends the Swiss churches as being orthodox and peaceful followers of the Gospel and supporters of the magistracy. The second German edition appeared with hardly any alterations in January 1561. By August 1560 a Latin translation by Josias Simler had been printed in Zürich: *H. Bullingeri adversus anabaptistas libri VI.* . . . During the same year also a Dutch translation was begun; it did not, however, appear until 1569, in Emden (*q.v.*); *Teghens de Wederdoopers, ses Boecken Henrici Bullingeri.* . . . The translator was Gerard Nicolai (*q.v.*), a Reformed preacher in Emden and Norden (*q.v.*), who also inserted valuable comments on the history of Anabaptism in the Netherlands and Northern Germany (see *BRN* VII, where Nicolai's *Inlasschingen* are reprinted). This translation was issued a second time in 1617 in Amsterdam. In 1665 the appendix appeared as a separate print at the same place. Plans even were made to translate the book into French, but nothing is known of such an edition.

H. S. Bender has made a careful study of Bullinger's deliberate and false reconstruction of the history of the origins of Anabaptism in *Conrad Grebel* (Goshen, 1950).　　　　　　　　H.F.

E. H. Correll, *Das schweizerische Täufermennonitentum* (Tübingen, 1925); A. Bucher, *Die Reformation in den Freien Aemtern und in der Stadt Bremgarten (bis 1531), Supplement of the Jahresbericht der Kantonalen Lehranstalten Sarnen* (1949/50 dissertation at the University of Freiburg, Switzerland, pp. 136-42, "Die Täufer in den Freien Aemtern"); H. S. Bender, "Die Zwickauer Propheten, Thomas Müntzer und die Täufer," *Theol. Zeitschrift* VIII (Basel, 1952) 262-78; H. Fast, *Heinrich Bullinger und die Täufer, Ein Beitrag zur Historiographie und Theologie im 16. Jhdt.* (Weierhof, 1959); J. H. Yoder, *Täufertum und Reformation in der Schweiz* I (Weierhof, 1959); W. A. Schulze, "Die Lehre Bullingers vom Zins," *Archiv für Reformationsgeschichte* XLVIII (1957) 225-29; *ML* I, 291-94.

Widholz, Endres (Andreas), an Anabaptist of Augsburg, Germany, was arrested in September 1527 and expelled from the city on Oct. 17, 1527, with Hans Langenmantel (*q.v.*), Hans Kiessling (*q.v.*), and Gall Fischer (*q.v.*). Widholz was a master in the guild of grocers. After his banishment his wife put their home at the disposal of the congregation for meetings.　　　　　　　　HEGE.

Fr. Roth, *Augsburgs Reformationsgeschichte* II (Augsburg, 1901) 229, 234; *TA Württemberg; ML* IV.

Widlingmaier, Anna (Stixanna), of Hohrain, Württemberg, wife of Michael Widlingmaier (Billinger), was an "obstinate Anabaptist" of Stauffen. After joining the group she was taught to read by a young boy. She was arrested several times. At her last examination, Sept. 23, 1597, she was charged with having been an Anabaptist 23 years, during which she had not attended (the established) church or communion, but instead had run to meetings in the woods. She had already been imprisoned and expelled from the country (1576), but had returned contrary to the strict prohibition to do so. Now she was 60 years old and had been blind for six years, and had misled two young girls to join her group. Johann Fabri argued with her for five hours, refuting 32 Anabaptist errors. She replied that she could of course not answer all those articles, but she would nevertheless not be converted to his opinion. She had made the covenant of a good conscience with God, and would abide by it

even if she had to give her life. Her husband asked the magistrate to let her leave the country, but was refused. She died 10 days later, apparently in prison. (*TA Württemberg; ML* IV.)　　　　W.W.

Widmarius, Abdias, a Reformed clergyman (1591-1668), educated at the universities of Heidelberg and Marburg, was preacher at Altdorf near Speyer and Neuhausen near Worms, Germany. During the Thirty Years' War he found refuge in Holland. He preached at Uitgeest, Gouda, and taught in the universities of Harderwijk and Groningen. The records he kept in Uitgeest are of value to Anabaptist history, especially his information on discussions with the Mennonites and his account of the debate at Alkmaar in 1597. (*DB* 1907, 36-77; *ML* IV.)
　　　　　　　　　　　　　　　　　NEFF.

Widmer: see also **Witmer.**

Widmer, Christian, b. Dec. 24, 1796, the son of Hans Widmer (*q.v.*), is one of the genuine Mennonite patriarchs. He lived in Epiquerez, Clos du Doubs, in the Bernese Jura, close to the French border. His wife was Verena Eicher of Buchholterberg (Emmental), married at Montbéliard on Sept. 25, 1821. The patriarchal figures of Christian Widmer and his wife, who with their ancient costumes and simplicity are a monument of a former time, represent the customs, the piety, and the industry of the old Mennonites. The numerous descendants of this Widmer family are now competent farmers in the region of Montbéliard and in Alsace. Several of these descendants have been successful preachers and elders.　　　　　　　　S.G.

Widmer, Hans, the son of Johann Jakob of Sumiswald in the Emmental, Switzerland, fled during the persecution of the 18th century to Voverence near Vaufrey, Doubs, in France. His wife was Katharina Graber of Huttwil. Hans Widmer was the progenitor of the widely ramified Mennonite Widmer families. Five sons and two daughters left numerous progeny, some of whom emigrated to America. His oldest son, Johannes, had 8 children; Peter 11, Christian 14, Daniel 13, and Jakob 8. Hans Widmer died at the age of 103.　　　　S.G.

Widmer, Joseph, a Mennonite preacher in the Emmental (*q.v.*), Switzerland, was seized in February 1649 in the territory of Signau, sent to Bern upon government order, and there placed in solitary confinement. On account of his advanced age, Widmer was soon released upon the promise to refrain from preaching and to attend church services regularly. The Signau magistrate was to keep a close watch over him. It has not yet been shown whether or not the Widmers who settled in France are descendants of this Joseph Widmer. (Bern Archives, *Ratsmanual* 1649, 102:119; 102:131; 102:210).　　S.G.

Widow of Thomase de Schrijnwerckere, an Anabaptist martyr, was executed about 1538 at Utrecht, Netherlands, because of Anabaptism. Particulars are lacking. (*Antw. Arch.-Blad* VIII, 444; XIV, 16 f., No. 168.)　　　　　　　　　　　VDZ.

Wiebe (Wieb), a Mennonite family name of Dutch origin derived from the Christian name Wiebe or

Wiebke, which spread to Prussia, Poland, Russia, and America. In 1616 Adam Wiebe came to Danzig from Harlingen, Holland. The name was found in Tiegenhagen, Ladekopp, Rosenort, Fürstenwerder, Heubuden, Elbing, Neunhuben, and Königsberg. Horst Penner has written a detailed account of the early history of this family. According to Franz Crous the name Wiebe ranked second to Penner in frequency among the Prussian Mennonites (366 bearers) before World War II. Herbert Wiebe was the author of *Das Siedlungswerk niederländischer Mennoniten im Weichseltal* . . . (Marburg, 1952). The name was also very common in all the Mennonite settlements of Russia and is so today among the Mennonites of Canada, and United States, and South America. Dietrich Wiebe was a well-known bonesetter of Lichtfelde, Molotschna, Russia.

Who's Who Among the Mennonites (1943) listed 14 ministers by this name in the United States and Canada, among whom were D. V. Wiebe, K.M.B. minister and educator; Frank V. Wiebe, late pastor of the Gnadenau K.M.B. Church and missionary in China; Henry D. Wiebe, late M.B. pastor at Shafter, Cal., J. F. D. Wiebe, late K.M.B. minister, Herbert, Sask., and John A. Wiebe, M.B. missionary in India. A. J. Wiebe was a pioneer G.C.M. minister at Paso Robles, Cal. Peter Wiebe is a bishop (MC) near Goshen, Ind.; Orlando Wiebe (EMB), a teacher at Grace Bible Institute; Arno Wiebe, an E.M.B. pastor at Dallas, Ore.; and H. P. Wiebe an E.M.B. pastor at Abbotsford, B.C. G.C.M. pastors include Abe Wiebe at Freeman, S.D., Willard Wiebe at Mt. Lake, Minn., and Ed Wiebe at Ringwood, Okla.; and M.B. pastors are J. J. Wiebe at Kelowna, B.C., W. J. Wiebe at Morden, Man., Anton Wiebe at Niverville, Man., H. G. Wiebe at Leamington, Ont., and J. P. Wiebe at Hepburn, Sask. In 1957 there were 40 active ministers in North America bearing the name, 23 in Canada and 17 in the United States distributed as follows: British Columbia 7, Saskatchewan 5, Manitoba 9, Ontario 2, California 8, Oregon 2, Kansas 2, and one each in Indiana, Oklahoma, Nebraska, Minnesota, and South Dakota. The M.B. conference had 24 ministers with this name, G.C.M. 7, E.M.B. 4, K.M.B. 1, M.C. 1, and C.G.C. 3.   C.K.

Reimer, *Familiennamen*, 120; H. H. Schröder, *Russlanddeutsche Friesen* (Döllstädt, 1936) 99; Franz Crous, "Mennonitenfamilien in Zahlen," *Gesch.-Bl.* (August 1940) 41; A. A. Töws, *Mennonitische Märtyrer* I (N. Clearbrook, 1954) 86-89; Horst Penner, "Die Wiebes," *Menn. Jahrbuch 1951* (Newton, 1951)14-20; *ML IV*, **528**.

Wiebe, Gerhard (1827-1900), elder of the Bergthal Mennonite Church (*q.v.*) in South Russia, was born July 25, 1827, in the village of Heuboden, one of the five comprising the Bergthal settlement (a daughter colony of Chortitza) in the Mariupol district of the province of Ekaterinoslav in the Ukraine. He was the oldest of the six children of Gerhard (1800-58) and Agatha Wiebe. On May 26, 1846, he was baptized. He married Elisabeth Dyck on June 12, 1847. Ten children were born to them. He became deacon in 1854, minister in 1861, and elder on March 29, 1866, which office he held until 1882.

Wiebe was a leader during the emigration of the entire Bergthal settlement to Manitoba in 1874-76 and played a significant role in negotiating permission for the emigration. He and his family came over in 1875, settling in the village of Chortitz in the East Reserve (*q.v.*) in Manitoba, where he lived until his death on May 5, 1900.

In his book *Ursachen und Geschichte der Auswanderung der Mennoniten aus Russland nach Amerika* (n.d.) Wiebe not only gives an account of the coming of the Bergthal group to Manitoba, but also presents the extremely conservative religious and cultural views of the Mennonites of his day. In minor details he was less conservative than his cousin Johann Wiebe (*q.v.*), elder of the Old Colony Mennonites (*q.v.*) of the West Reserve (*q.v.*), but basically the two men were of the same spirit. The traditional cultural patterns, such as the closed village community, the independent parochial village school, and the autonomy of the Mennonite communities, were as dear to him as to Johann Wiebe, although these disintegrated more rapidly among his followers than among the Old Colony Mennonites led by Johann Wiebe. His conservative attitude was noticeable when Johann K. Funk, who was more progressive, became leader of a group which favored among other things better education. This minority group is known to this day as the Bergthal Mennonite Church (*q.v.*), while the larger following of Gerhard Wiebe is known as the Chortitz and Sommerfeld Mennonite Church (*q.v.*). Gerhard Wiebe took a course between the extremely conservative Old Colony Mennonites, led by Johann Wiebe, and the more progressive Bergthal Mennonites.

T.E.F., C.K.

Wiebe, Henry Dietrich (1889-1949), educator, evangelist, pastor, and a leading worker of the Mennonite Brethren Church, the son of Dietrich and Elizabeth Heidebrecht Wiebe, was born at Hillsboro, Kan., Dec. 12, 1889. He was educated at the Hillsboro Academy, Tabor College, Teacher's College at Weatherford, Okla., and the University of Oklahoma, earning the degrees B.A., M.A., and Th.B., and later having the honorary degree of D.D. conferred upon him. During his student days Wiebe was converted and joined the M.B. Church. He married Gertrude Klaassen at Turnhill, Sask., Aug. 7, 1919. They had three sons and one daughter.

Wiebe taught the Hope Valley School near Hillsboro, Kan., 1914-18, served as principal and instructor at the M.B. Bible Academy, Corn, Okla., 1919-36, and as instructor of Bible and German at Tabor College, 1937-39. The M.B. Church ordained Wiebe to the ministry in 1917. Until 1936 he was a traveling evangelist much of the time and conducted many evangelistic meetings in all the district conferences of the M.B. Church.

The ministry of Wiebe included services as assistant pastor of the M.B. Church, Corn, Okla., minister of several community churches in southern Oklahoma, and pastorates at the M.B. churches at Shafter, Rosedale, and Lodi, Cal. In the Southern District Conference he served as moderator and as secretary of its Home Mission Committee. He was a member of the Board of Directors of Tabor College 1933-36. In the Pacific District Conference he was moderator 1940-42 and secretary of its Home Mission Board 1942-49, and for some time chairman of the Educational Board for Pacific Bible Institute. In the General Conference of the M.B. Church he filled the post of moderator in 1945-48. Wiebe died at his home in Reedley, Cal., July 10, 1949. J.H.L.

Wiebe, Jakob (d. 1880), an educator and elder, brother of Philipp Wiebe (*q.v.*), was a teacher of the Halbstadt Zentralschule of Molotschna, Russia, and became the first elder of the Karassan Mennonite Church (*q.v.*) when the church was organized in 1862. Little is known about his life and work, with the exception of a letter which he wrote to Johann Wiebe (*q.v.*) of Alexandertal concerning the nonresistance and migration of the Mennonites to America (dated Feb. 27, 1876). He rejected the reasons given for the migration, claiming that Russia was giving full guarantees to those who wanted to maintain the doctrine of nonresistance and that it was the duty of Mennonites to stay in Russia and make a positive contribution. "We are supposed to be the salt of the earth and Russia is a part of this earth where the salt is needed as much as anywhere else." He charged that although the original motive for the migration to America was religious, the reasons now were the relatives, luring mountains of gold, curiosity, and the fear that the sons would have to serve in some form; many were going to America who had absolutely no concept of nonresistance or true Christianity. (Friesen, *Brüderschaft*, 511-13, 599, 709.)   C.K.

Wiebe, Jakob Abram (1836-1921), a cofounder of the Krimmer Mennonite Brethren Church, was born Aug. 6, 1836, in Margenau, South Russia, the oldest of the eight children of Jacob and Anna Wiebe, who were Mennonite immigrants from Prussia. Through private study he acquired a practical education. In his early youth he was employed as driver for the Oberschulze and thus came in contact with the leading persons of the settlement and learned to draw conclusions and make his own decisions. This was the beginning of the reforms he later instituted.

Wiebe was baptized on Pentecost of 1856 and became a member of the Lichtenau Mennonite Church at Petershagen. On April 11, 1857, he married Justina Friesen (d. 1916) from Halbstadt, and bought a small farm with an oil press in Orloff. In 1861 he moved to the Crimea, a new Mennonite settlement, and founded a home in the village of Annenfeld. Serious disappointments and even failures met them; but with courage, economy, and hard work they overcame them. In 1864 both joined the Kleine Gemeinde, the most conservative Mennonite group. On Dec. 4, 1867, he was elected minister of this church and on Easter Day of 1869 he was ordained elder. But since even in this group he was unable to carry out the reforms he considered fundamental to Christian living, he with twelve others withdrew from the Kleine Gemeinde on Sept. 21, 1869, and organized the "Krimmer Mennoniten - Brüdergemeinde" (Crimean Mennonite Brethren Church), baptizing by immersion, kneeling and dipping forward. Their aim was to live a fuller, more consecrated Christian life. A change in the Russian military law persuaded them to

emigrate to America, and this group, about 40 families, found a new home in Marion County, Kan., under Jacob A. Wiebe's leadership, arriving there on Aug. 17, 1874. They settled in a village which they named "Gnadenau," and which became one of the first rural districts of European Mennonites in Kansas.

In spiritual difficulties Wiebe proved a dependable leader. He had acquired the art of setting broken bones and sprains; this was a special boon in a country where doctors were scarce. Both the new church and the village prospered and in a few years a church was built as a home center while groups were organized in the neighboring counties and states. On Sept. 10, 1900, he ordained his younger brother Heinrich Wiebe as elder in his place and retired for reasons of health, having served a total of 34 years. He died June 23, 1921, at Hillsboro, and is buried in the Gnadenau cemetery. His character was deeply religious. He was confident of the correctness of his organizing the Krimmer Mennonite Brethren Church; he was a Mennonite to the innermost part of his heart. He was not a Calvinist, nor a millennialist; he was thoroughly saturated with principles of Menno Simons, even to the extreme. His private and family life was ideal and he had many friends. His death marked the passing of a departing age and the opening of a new era for the K.M.B. Church.   J.Z.W.

P. A. Wiebe, *Kurze Biographie des Bruders Jakob A. Wiebe, seine Jugend, seine Bekehrung, & wie die Krimmer Mennoniten Brüdergemeinde gegründet wurde* (n.p., 1924).

Wiebe, Jakob Abram (1853-1907), an elder of the Kronsweide Mennonite Church near Chortitza, South Russia, was born Aug. 14, 1853, at Einlage, Chortitza Mennonite settlement, the oldest of the six children of Abram Heinrich and Margarete Epp Wiebe. In 1877 he married Elizabeth Janzen. Three of his twelve children are still living. One of his sons was a teacher in the Nikolai Zentralschule at Yazykovo (*q.v.*), and another was a Mennonite minister. He received his education at the Zentralschule and Teacher's Seminary at Chortitza, and then taught school for 28 years. He was ordained minister of the Kronsweide Mennonite Church in 1881, and elder in 1902. He lived in Kronsweide 1875-80, Bergmannsthal 1880-1905, and Einlage 1905-7. J. A. Wiebe died Jan. 5, 1907, at Einlage, in the Chortitza settlement. (A biographical sketch in *Mennonitisches Jahrbuch*, Berdyansk, 1908.)   H.J.W.

Wiebe, Johann (1766-1823), the second elder of the Mennonite church in the Chortitza settlement in South Russia, had been chosen as coelder in 1791 to serve with Bernhard Penner (*q.v.*) during the first year of the settlement, but had declined because he felt himself too young (he was only twenty-five years of age) and too inexperienced. But soon after, when Penner died, he accepted the office, the church having given him an assistant elder in David Epp (b. 1748). He was sent to Prussia to get some help in 1794 and brought Cornelius Warkentin (*q.v.*) and Cornelius Regier (*q.v.*) along to set the church life in the Chortitza settlement

61

in order. Warkentin confirmed both Wiebe and Epp in their office in 1794 and succeeded in establishing peace in the congregation. Epp died in 1802. He was succeeded by the following elders who served as assistants to Wiebe: Bernhard Bergen, chosen 1806, d. 1809, and Jakob Dyck, chosen 1812, d. 1823. In 1805 Wiebe made a trip to the Molotschna to settle some difficulties, where he ordained Jakob Enns (*q.v.*) of Tiegenhagen elder. He died March 31, 1823. (Friesen, *Brüderschaft*, 74, 107, 135, 699.)   B.J.S., C.K.

Wiebe, Johann (1837-1906), an elder of the Fürstenland Mennonite Church (*q.v.*), Russia, and promoter of the Mennonite migration to America. He was born March 23, 1837, in the Fürstenland settlement and married Judith Wall on Dec. 4, 1856. He was ordained minister in 1865 and elder 1870. He left Russia in 1875 with 1,100 Mennonites, some of them preceding and some following him, to settle in the West Reserve (*q.v.*), Man.; they were followed by Mennonites coming from the Chortitza (*q.v.*) and Bergthal (*q.v.*) settlements under the leadership of his cousin, Elder Gerhard Wiebe (*q.v.*), who settled in the East Reserve (*q.v.*). Soon some Mennonites of the East Reserve crossed the Red River and joined those on the West Reserve, introducing some new patterns of culture and economic and religious life to which Johann Wiebe objected more than any of his coministers.

Before the migration of the Mennonites to Manitoba some progressive communities, including Fürstenland, had introduced the use of the *Choralbuch* (*q.v.*) to improve the singing. Bergthal (*q.v.*) had not done so. In Manitoba Johann Wiebe returned to the traditional singing, discarding the *Choralbuch*, which is typical of the Old Colony Mennonites to this day, while Gerhard Wiebe, the elder of the Bergthal group, introduced the *Choralbuch* in Manitoba and thus broke away from the traditional singing.

On Oct. 5, 1880, a "Bruderschaft" (*q.v.*) called by Elder Johann Wiebe of the Reinland or Old Colony Mennonite Church decided that those who were willing to adhere to the traditional principles and practices of the church should renew their membership. Those who refused were not considered members. This was the official parting of the ways between the Old Colony Mennonites under the leadership of Johann Wiebe and the Bergthal Mennonites under the leadership of Johann K. Funk. When Johann Wiebe died he was succeeded as elder by Johann Friesen, under whom a large number of the Old Colony Mennonites of Manitoba and Saskatchewan migrated to Mexico (*q.v.*) in 1922-26.

Johann Wiebe possibly did more than anyone else to develop and maintain the consistently conservative attitude which characterizes the Old Colony Mennonites today. He died in the village of Rosengart, Man., on Feb. 21, 1906. During his service he preached 1,544 times and baptized 2,228 persons. He wrote a short account of the emigration of his congregation from Russia to Canada, *Unsere Reise von Russland nach Amerika aufgezeichnet*, published in Blumenthal, Hague, Sask.

(n.d.) (10 pp.). (See **Old Colony Mennonites, Bergthal** Mennonite Church, and **Manitoba**.)   C.K.

Friesen, *Brüderschaft*, 700; G. Wiebe, *Ursachen und Geschichte der Answanderung der Mennoniten aus Russland nach Amerika* (n.p., n.d.).

Wiebe, Johann, of the Alexandertal Mennonite Church (*q.v.*), Samara, Russia, was ordained minister in 1873 and elder 1874. In 1876 he corresponded with Jakob Wiebe (*q.v.*), elder of the Karassan Mennonite Church (*q.v.*), Crimea, regarding nonresistance, alternative service, and the migration to America. Jakob Wiebe was strongly opposed to the latter and likely influenced Johann Wiebe. After the Mennonite Brethren Church had been transplanted to Alexandertal, Wiebe aimed to introduce some of its practices in his congregation. In 1897 he joined the local Mariental M.B. Church (*q.v.*) and became the elder of this small group. He was still serving in 1910. (Friesen, *Brüderschaft*, 480, 719 f.)   C.K.

Wiebe, Peter A. (1847-1926), a Krimmer Mennonite Brethren minister and elder, was born at Margenau, South Russia, Nov. 27, 1847, the sixth son of Jacob Wiebe and Anna Wiens Wiebe, and the brother of Jacob A. Wiebe, K.M.B. founder. He married Sarah Voth on March 20, 1870, to which union were born eleven children. Immigrating to Kansas in the fall of 1874, they settled at Springfield, near Lehigh, in 1875. They were baptized April 21, 1878, and joined the Gnadenau K.M.B. Church near Hillsboro, Kan. He was elected deacon in 1884, minister in 1891, and elder in 1912. He was a pioneer in Sunday-school work in his church; he served as board member and chairman of the Home for the Friendless, as chairman of the Bethesda Hospital board, as board member of the Salem Home and Hospital, and as executive board member of the K.M.B. Conference and as a member of various conference committees. From 1892 to 1909 he engaged in evangelistic work in Nebraska, South Dakota, California, and Canada, and was deeply interested in home and foreign missionary work. He was a successful farmer; in 1904 he was awarded a Gold Medal by the St. Louis World Fair for Turkey Red wheat raised on his farm.

Peter A. Wiebe was the author of numerous articles on nonresistance. His autobiography was published in 1921 in the *Genealogy Record of the Groening and Wiebe Families*. In 1924 he wrote *A Brief Biography of Jacob A. Wiebe and the Organization of the Krimmer Mennonite Brethren Church*, and in 1925 *The Way to Eternal Life*.

Wiebe died June 26, 1926, at Hillsboro and is interred at the Springfield cemetery. His biography was published in 1955 as a booklet, *My Parents*.   D.V.W.

Wiebe, Philipp (d. 1870), chairman of the Agricultural Association (*q.v.*) of the Molotschna Mennonite settlement, made a significant contribution as a successor of Johann Cornies (*q.v.*). With this office he inherited the supervision of the agricultural or economic and the cultural or educational aspects of the settlement, including the many religious problems of the time. When Cornies died in 1848,

Wiebe continued to promote a higher level of education, regular attendance at school, higher salaries for teachers, better school buildings, and regular teachers' conferences. The school age was determined to be from six to fourteen, and teachers' conferences became obligatory in 1850. Because of ill health, he had to resign as chairman of the Agricultural Association. In 1869 he became the first chairman of the "Molotschnaer Mennonitischer Schulrat" (q.v.). In 1870 he died.

Wiebe, as a son-in-law of Johann Cornies, inherited some of his large estates, Yushanlee and a part of Tashchenak. He acquired an estate north of the Sea of Azov from a certain Kampenhausen. He had to cope with the general problems of land distribution to the landless (q.v.) and the founding of new groups such as the Mennonite Brethren and the Templers (q.v.). His son, Johann Philipp Wiebe, born Oct. 14, 1849, continued in the footsteps of his father and grandfather; he married the sister of Bernhard Warkentin (q.v.) in 1871 and became instrumental in the transplanting of hard winter wheat from his estates to the prairies of Kansas.   C.K.

H. Görz, *Die Molotschnaer Ansiedlung* (Steinbach, 1950) 101; Friesen, *Brüderschaft*, 644 f.; Nikolai Regehr, *Johann Philipp Wiebe* (Steinbach, 1952) 42 ff.; Franz Isaac, *Die Molotschnaer Mennoniten* (Halbstadt, 1908) 33-35, 145 ff.

Wied, Herman von (1477-1552), was the Catholic Archbishop and Elector of Cologne, Germany, in 1532-46. By his favorable inclination toward the Reformation he differed from other Catholic bishops, opposed the general practice of the Catholic church and the policy of Emperor Charles V (q.v.), and refused to suppress the Lutherans in his bishopric. In general he rejected capital punishment for heretics. In 1542 he called Martin Bucer (q.v.) to his court to reform the bishopric. Because of his tolerance it was possible for Menno Simons to live undisturbed in the bishopric of Cologne from July 1544 until 1546, when von Wied was dismissed. Menno gives him a good testimonial. His brother Friedrich von Wied was about the same time the bishop of Münster (q.v.). (Menno Simons, *Opera*, 235a; *Writings*, 635.)   vDZ.

Wieder, F. C., librarian of the Dutch Royal Library at The Hague, is the author of *De Schriftuurlijke Liedekens* (The Hague, 1900), which gives a thorough account of 16th-century Dutch hymnbooks, including all Mennonite hymnals.   vDZ.

Wiedertäufer: see Wederdo(o)pers and Anabaptist.

Wiedertäufer Ordnung (Anabaptist Regulation), issued Feb. 27, 1695, by the cantonal government of Bern, Switzerland, after previous regulations had failed to eliminate the Swiss Brethren. The government was determined "with God's aid and support to uproot this weed from our lands." The Ordnung decreed that Swiss Brethren who returned after being banished should be forged to chains in Bern. For any preacher delivered to the authorities a reward of 100 talers was offered. A fine of 50 pounds was imposed upon any who employed a

servant or rented any land to anyone who did not have a certificate from his home community showing that he was an honorable and obedient citizen. Since the women were not included in the required oath of loyalty, an annual inspection should be made in the homes and a written account kept of all the members of each family, "whether they attend the sermons, children's instruction and instruction of the old, and also whether they attend the holy sacraments fittingly and zealously, and have their children baptized at the right time or not at all. . . . But the very aged feeble women, if temporary admonition and warning do not take effect, shall be taken hither to our island to the place prepared, and kept in eternal prison at their own expense, and not released until they promise obedience. . . . We will have the imprisonment so arranged that nobody can speak to them or free them."

The embittered government continued its persecution beyond life itself. The regulation stipulated: since these people hesitated to attend church with the other subjects and deliberately separated themselves, "we will have them excluded from the church and ordain herewith: That no men or women in this land dying in this error and obstinacy shall be buried in a cemetery or other usual burial place." In Kurzenei near Wasen there is a hidden place called the "Täuferloch," where the Anabaptists met and buried their dead in the period of persecution.

The ordinance was to be read from all the pulpits on Sunday, March 10. On March 28, 1695, all officials received a supplementary order to send in an exact list of those who absented themselves from the Easter communion service.   S.G.

The library of the university and city of Bern, *Alte Drucke*, No. 139: State archives of Bern, *Mandatenbuch* 10, pp. 130, 141, 144, 164; see also "Mandates"; *ML IV*.

Wiehler (Wieler, Willer), a family name found among the Mennonites of Danzig and Prussia. It appeared in Orlofferfeld (1601), Elbing, Tiegenhagen, Ladekopp, Rosenort, Heubuden, Königsberg, and Danzig (1718). Before World War II there were 120 representatives of the name in West Prussia. The name spread to Russia and North and South America. Johann Wieler (q.v.) and Gerhard Wieler (q.v.) were among the founders of the Mennonite Brethren Church in Russia; Johann J. Wieler was a teacher of the Halbstadt Zentralschule; Johann J. Wieler, of Winnipeg and Saskatoon, was a special representative of the Department of Colonization and Agriculture of the Canadian National Railways and helped many Mennonite and other immigrants after both world wars.   C.K.

Reimer, *Familiennamen*, 120; H. H. Schroeder, *Russlanddeutsche Friesen* (Döllstadt-Langensalza, 1936) 99; Franz Crous, "Mennonitische Familien in Zahlen," *Gesch.-Bl.* (August 1940)|41; *ML IV*, 534.

Wieler, Gerhard, an early lay leader in the Mennonite Brethren Church in Russia, an older brother of Johann Wieler (q.v.), was born in Chortitza, South Russia, a son of J. Wieler. He and his brother had the best formal training of the group and mastered the Russian language as well as German

(Friesen, 236). He was active in St. Petersburg for some time, seeking to obtain recognition of the newly founded M.B. Church. For a while he was a teacher in Liebenau, Molotschna, but lost his position in 1861 because of his views. Because he baptized some native Russians he was imprisoned. After his release he returned to the Einlage M.B. Church, promoting extreme views. He and others promoted the expression of joy in the newly found faith and peace by means of shouting, jumping, and the use of various musical instruments. He was opposed to the use of pictures and the printed devotional aids in use at that time by the Mennonites, written by Hofacker, Arndt, and others. Benjamin Bekker (*q.v.*) of the Molotschna settlement supported these views for a while. Wieler and Bekker as "apostles" used the ban arbitrarily, excommunicating even Wieler's father and brother. Gradually, as the more disciplined and saner element gained the upper hand, Wieler's and Bekker's influence waned. In 1867 Gerhard Wieler is supposed to have returned to the Mennonite Church of Chortitza and later gone to North America, where he became a member of the United Brethren in Christ. Unfortunately all reports about him have come from his opponents and he has left no records to justify his actions.   C.K.

Friesen, *Brüderschaft*, 209, 233, 236, 245 f., 267 f., 280, 315, 320, 332, 337, 344, 349 f., 355, 360 f., 368, 371, 375, 378.

Wieler, Johann (1839-89), a Mennonite Brethren evangelist, was born Nov. 22, 1839, in Chortitza, South Russia, the son of a teacher, Johann Wieler. He pursued a vigorous course of studies, thus qualifying himself as a teacher, and was particularly interested in the Russian language. He taught in the secondary school in Halbstadt. As a young man he was converted and joined the M.B. Church; as a minister he showed particular gifts for evangelistic work. He was deeply interested in evangelizing the Russians and even proposed to the M.B. Conference that it engage in missionary activities in this field in spite of the fact that such work was strictly prohibited by the Russian government. When the M.B. Conference rejected his proposal, he launched out on his own. This course brought him under suspicion with government officials, and when he baptized a Russian woman he was forced to flee, and remained in seclusion for some time. He finally emigrated to Germany, where he joined the Baptists. His family followed. He was, however, soon ordered to leave Germany and thus came to Roumania, where he ministered in a Russian Baptist Church in the town of Tultcha for approximately two years. When a new church building was under construction, he fell from a ladder and thus received fatal injuries; he died in 1889 at the age of 50.   J.J.T.

Waldemar Gutsche, *Westliche Quellen des russischen Stundismus. Anfänger der evangelischen Bewegung in Russland* (Kassel, 1956); A. H. Unruh, *Die Geschichte der Mennoniten-Bruedergemeinde 1860-1954* (Hillsboro, 1954).

Wieling, Sjoerd Ebeles, b. 1772 at Drachten, d. 1835 at Zaandam, a Dutch Mennonite pastor, was educated at the Amsterdam Seminary and served the congregations of Oldeboorn (Nieuwe Huis) 1805-8, Midwolda-Beerta 1808-22, and Zaandam-Oost 1822-35. He was a curator of the Amsterdam Seminary 1825-35. On April 4, 1819, he preached the dedicatory sermon in the new Mensingeweer (*q.v.*) meetinghouse, which as *Inwijding* was published (Groningen, 1819). Another publication of his is a sermon *Opwekking* (Zaandam, 1825), preached at Zaandam after the disastrous flood of February 1825.

His brother Foppe Ebeles Wieling, d. 1871, a lay preacher, served the small congregation at Huizinge 1815-28 and the one at Surhuisterveen 1828-57. (*N.N.B.Wb.* X, 1202 f.)   vDZ.

Wielmacker, John, an Anabaptist martyr: see **Jan Pietersz.**

Wiens (Wienss, Wientz, Winantz, Wynes), a family name likely of Dutch origin found among the Mennonites of Danzig and Prussia as early as 1568. The name occurred in Tiegenhagen, Ladekopp, Rosenort, Fürstenwerder, Heubuden, and Danzig (1607). Before World War II the name ranked third among the Mennonites of Prussia, having 355 representatives. Peter Wiens was director of the Halbstadt School of Commerce in Russia; Kornelius A. Wiens was teacher of the Halbstadt Zentralschule and suffered under Soviet persecution; P. G. Wiens was a missionary in India; Jacob W. Wiens was the elder of the Ebenfeld Mennonite Church (GCM) in Saskatchewan; F. B. Wiens (GCM) was an educator in Russia and his son Jacob B. Wiens is the elder of the First United Mennonite (GCM) Church of Vancouver.   C.K.

Reimer, *Familiennamen*, 120; H. H. Schroeder, *Russlanddeutsche Friesen* (Döllstadt-Langensalza, 1936) 99; Franz Crous, "Mennonitische Familien in Zahlen," *Gesch.-Bl.* (August 1940) 41; *ML* IV, 536.

Wiens, Cornelius Abraham, an elder of the Kuban Mennonite Brethren Church (*q.v.*), a teacher, was ordained minister in 1895. In 1905 he was ordained elder by David Schellenberg.   C.K.

Friesen, *Brüderschaft*, 457 ff.; D. H. Epp, *Adressbüchlein* (Berdyansk, 1913) 11.

Wiens, Franz (1810-53), an elder in the Chortitza Mennonite Church in South Russia, a preacher from 1843, coelder with Jakob Dyck from 1851, died Nov. 16, 1853. Dyck survived him by one year.   B.J.S.

Wiens, Franz J. (1880-1942), an evangelist and foreign missionary of the Mennonite Brethren Church, son of Jacob and Maria (Friesen) Wiens, was born on a farm near Henderson, Nebr., on June 30, 1880. Converted at an early age, he joined the Henderson M.B. Church through baptism. Feeling a call to foreign mission work, Wiens studied at the following schools: the German Department School of the M.B. Church at McPherson, Kan.; McPherson College at McPherson, Kan.; York (Neb.) College; and the German Baptist Theological Seminary, Rochester, N.Y., where he was graduated in 1906. He later received the A.B. degree from Tabor College, Hillsboro, Kan.

In 1902 he married Agnes Harder. To them five children were born. In 1906-9 Wiens was employed as evangelist by the M.B. Conference. In 1910 he was ordained as a missionary and left for China, stopping in Russia for several months, where he conducted remarkable revival meetings in Mennonite circles. Upon arrival in South China in 1911 he spent some time at Swatow studying the Chinese language. The Wienses then proceeded about 200 miles inland and opened a mission among the Hakkas at Shanghang, Fukien Province. They erected the required buildings, made extensive tours into the field, opened a school for children, established a Bible school for training indigenous workers, and began a hospital. Several Chinese churches were established in the surrounding territory.

In 1919 the M.B. General Conference took over the support and supervision of this mission, and sent new missionaries. The work expanded remarkably in spite of civil war and revolutions. At times the missionaries were in great danger and on one occasion had to flee to the coast. The mission station was destroyed during their absence, but the work continued. Mrs. Wiens died in China in 1935. Some time later Wiens married Agnes Koop. In the summer of 1940 they returned to America, making their home at Reedley, Cal. Wiens wrote many reports for his church paper, the *Zionsbote*. His two longer publications are *Pionierarbeit unter den Hakkas in Süd-China* and *Fifteen Years Among the Hakkas of South China*. He died in Reedley, on Sept. 28, 1942, and was buried in the local cemetery. (*ML* IV, 536.)   J.H.L.

Wiens, Heinrich, was elected minister of the Ohrloff Mennonite Church, Molotschna, South Russia, in 1825 and became elder of the Margenau-Landskrone church (*q.v.*) in 1842. He was deprived of his office in 1846 and expelled from the country because of differences he had with Johann Cornies (*q.v.*) and the Fürsorgekomitee (*q.v.*). His case was similar to that of Jakob Warkentin (*q.v.*). Both cases are illustrations of the problems that can confront a Mennonite community when its civil and religious authorities feel that one is interfering with the duties of the other. This case has been dealt with at length by P. M. Friesen, Franz Isaac, and others. A unique side line is that Wiens became the martyr hero for the conservative Mennonites, who published his account in Manitoba, whence it was taken to Mexico and there is cherished as an item of classic martyr literature.

After Wiens's exile had been announced he wrote a farewell sermon which was read to the congregation. He went to Prussia in 1847 and later returned to Russia where he lived as private citizen unmolested, preaching only on special occasions such as funerals.   C.K.

Friesen, *Brüderschaft*, 76; *Ein Abschied und Bericht wie es in der Molotschnerkolonie in d. früh. Jahre zugegangen ist, und wie die Vorgesetzten den ehr. Aeltesten Heinrich Wiens von Gnadenheim aus dem Lande verwiesen haben. Seine Rückkehr nebst Beschreibung der ganzen Reise* (Manitoba, 1903).

Wiens, Jakob B., b. Oct. 1870, Crimea, Russia; d. May 22, 1939, Saskatoon, Sask. He received his education at Rückenau and the Zentralschule of Halbstadt and was a teacher at Tiegerweide, Molotschna

Mennonite settlement, South Russia. He taught for twenty years. On May 23, 1893, he married Helena Wiens; in 1901 he was elected minister; and in 1911 he succeeded Abram Görz as elder of Orloff-Neukirch Mennonite Church. In 1924 he left Russia and arrived at Waterloo, Ont., on Aug. 16, proceeded to Herschel, Sask., and there founded the Ebenfeld Mennonite Church (GCM). He served also in the surrounding communities of Luseland, Superb, and Kindersley-Glydden, which were subsidiaries of the Ebenfeld church.   C.K.

J. G. Rempel, *Fünfzig Jahre Konferenzbestrebungen 1902-1952* I (Steinbach, n.d.) 198.

Wiens, Kornelius Abraham, a teacher, graduated from the Ohrloff (*q.v.*) Zentralschule and the Halbstadt Normal School and was for a number of years an elementary teacher in the Molotschna settlement, Russia. He attended the Theological Seminary (Predigerschule) at Basel and taught Bible and German at the Halbstadt Mädchenschule. In 1907 he became teacher of the Halbstadt Zentralschule where he was also elected minister of the Halbstadt Mennonite Church. He is likely the coauthor of *Biblische Geschichten für mennonitische Elementarschulen* (Halbstadt, 1902), prepared by K. Unruh, W. Neufeld, and K. Wiens. He received a medal from the Russian government in recognition of his educational achievements.   C.K.

Friesen, *Brüderschaft*, 604, 626; H. Görz, *Die Molotschnaer Ansiedlung* (Steinbach, 1951) 165.

Wiens, Peter Johann, a teacher, educated at the Gnadenfeld Zentralschule (Molotschna, Russia) and the universities of Kharkov and Dorpat, where he studied mathematics. After this he taught at the Ohrloff Zentralschule for three years. In 1909 he became the director of the Halbstadt Kommerzschule (*q.v.*). (Friesen, *Brüderschaft*, 595, 628.)
                    C.K.

Wieringen: see **Hippolytushoef.**

Wieringermeer, a Dutch polder reclaimed in 1936 in the former Zuiderzee (now IJssel Lake). At first the pastor of Hippolytushoef (*q.v.*) was in charge of the Mennonites living on this polder, who organized into an independent congregation on Oct. 18, 1942, served by the pastor of Twisk (*q.v.*). In 1958 the baptized membership numbered 52.   vDZ.

Wieringerwaard, an old polder reclaimed in 1610 in the Dutch province of North Holland; the Mennonites living here did not form a congregation but belonged to the Barsingerhorn (*q.v.*) Waterlander congregation. They, however, had a meetinghouse of their own in the hamlet of Kreil, which was renovated in 1859 and used until 1923. Wieringerwaard is sometimes inaccurately called Nieuwe Zijpe. (*DB* 1861, 156 f.)   vDZ.

Wiersema, a Mennonite family found in the Dutch province of Groningen since the 17th century. Luitjen Olferts (Wiersema, or Wiersum), d. 1784 at Eenrum, was a lay preacher of the Rasquert (Baflo) congregation 1757-84. Enno Wiersema (*c*1720-85), who was trained for the ministry by one of the ministers in the town of Groningen, served 1744-45 at Ouddorp and 1745-85 at Winterswijk, also taking charge of the Zutphen congregation, whose pulpit was mostly vacant. He was married in 1747 to Magtelt Waliën of Winterswijk. At present there are still a number of Wiersemas in the province of Groningen. vDZ.

Wiersma, common family name in Friesland. Mennonite families by this name furnished deacons in the congregations of Holwerd-Blija, Ternaard, Ytens, and Hindeloopen. vDZ.

Wiersum, an old Mennonite family in the Dutch province of Groningen, which is derived from the same ancestor as the Wiersema (*q.v.*) family. Until recent times the Wiersums were nearly all farmers, and often deacons of the Mennonite church. Eppe (Tonnisz) Wiersum (Uithuizen 1869-Rotterdam 1955) was city archivist of Rotterdam from 1904. He did not join the church, but was much interested in Mennonite history. In the *Rotterdamsch Jaarboekje* of 1910 he published a paper on Jan Bisschop (*q.v.*). He rendered a real service to the Rotterdam Mennonite congregation by arranging and describing its rich archives (printed catalogue). An address by Wiersum, "De Doopsgezinde Gemeente in het Rotterdam van omstreeks 1775," was published in *Na Hondertvijftig Jaar* (Rotterdam, 1925). vDZ.

Wierum, a small village in the northeast of the Dutch province of Friesland, where Jacob Teunis, elder of the Jan-Jacobszgezinden (*q.v.*), baptized at least 34 persons in 1603-18, was probably the seat of a Jan-Jacobszgezinde congregation, concerning which there is, however, no further information. (Blaupot t. C., *Friesland*, 164.) vDZ.

Wiesenfeld, a common Mennonite village name. The first village by this name was Wiesenfeld established in 1880 near Pavlograd, Ukraine. From here the name was transplanted to Slavgorod (Barnaul), Siberia; Cuauhtemoc, Mexico; and Fernheim, Paraguay. (See **Villages.**) C.K.

Wiesenfeld Mennonite Brethren Church. The village of Wiesenfeld, about 10 miles from the railroad station of Zaitsevo, Pavlograd (*q.v.*) district of the province of Ekaterinoslav, South Russia, was founded by members of the Gnadenfeld M.B. Church in the Molotschna settlement, most of them from the Andreasfeld area, and the church became an affiliate of the Gnadenfeld church. When the Einlage M.B. Church became better established and more members arrived from this church, the congregation here affiliated itself with Einlage. The first minister of this group was Peter Friesen, a blacksmith and bonesetter. Later Jacob D. Reimer and Cornelius Reimer served as ministers. The congregation had at one time 107 members. Because of a misunderstanding the church was closed for some time during World War I, but the right of public worship was later reinstated. In 1919 during the Revolution the entire village was destroyed by Machno bands and the church ceased to exist. Its last minister was Cornelius Reimer, the father of Jacob Reimer of Sardis, B.C. P.H.B.

Wife of Jan (Hans) Collen, an Anabaptist martyr, executed at Antwerp, Belgium, in 1559, exact date unknown, probably in May of that year. (*Antw. Arch.-Blad* VIII, 470; XIV, 26 f., No. 290.) vDZ.

Wijbrandi: see **Wybrandi.**

Wijbrands: see **Wybrands.**

Wijbrands(z), Reinier: see **Wybma, R. W.**

Wijnalda: see **Wynalda.**

Wijnands (Wynands, Wynants, Wynanz), a family name formerly rather common in the Netherlands. Mennonite branches, some of which could not be traced back to a common ancestor, formerly lived at Haarlem, Rotterdam, Utrecht, Harlingen, and other places. A Wynands Mennonite family living at Hamburg, Germany, from the 17th century was of Dutch descent. At Haarlem some Wijnands were deacons in the 17th-19th centuries, in Rotterdam in the 19th century. There have also been some Mennonite ministers by this name. Jan Wynants, b. c1596, was a preacher(?) of the Haarlem Flemish congregation in the early 17th century. Willem Wynands (*q.v.*, 1630-58) was a preacher at Hamburg-Altona.

Abraham Wynands, b. Dec. 1703, at Altona, d. there Aug. 29, 1790, was a preacher from 1727, and an elder c1750 of the Hamburg-Altona congregation. He had been trained for the ministry by Abraham Verduin (*q.v.*), pastor of Koog aan de Zaan. Gerrit Karsdorp (*q.v.*) published a funeral sermon on his death, *Stand- en Gedagtenis-Rede over Abr. Wynands* (Altona, 1790).

Another Abraham Wijnands, of Harlingen in Friesland, was trained for the ministry 1767-72 at the Amsterdam Lamist seminary. He served as pastor at Middelburg 1773-77 and Utrecht 1777-83, in which year he retired. His farewell sermon, *Leerreden, waarin de Godsdienst wordt aangeprezen,* was published at Haarlem, 1785.

Wijnand Peters Wijnands (Winands, Wynantz), d. 1777 at Crefeld, Germany, was the last unsalaried preacher of the Crefeld (*q.v.*) Mennonite church, serving 1729-73, in which year he retired. vDZ.

Inv. Arch. Amst. II, Nos. 1584-86; II, 2, Nos. 78, 80; *Naamlijst* 1791, 62 f.; *DB* 1892, 75; *N.N.B.Wb.* III, 1503; B. K. Roosen, *Geschichte der Mennoniten-Gemeinde zu Hamburg und Altona* I (Hamburg, 1886) 29, 44 f.; II (*ibid.* 1887) 11 f., 16, 32, 48, 49, 52 f.; Schijn-Maatschoen, *Geschiedenis* II, 648 f.; Bender, *Two Centuries,* 13.

Wijngaard (Wyngaert), **Govaert Tobiasz van den,** a son of Elder Tobias van den Wijngaard (see below), was a preacher of the Lamist (*q.v.*) Mennonite congregation at Amsterdam 1654-70. Unlike his father, he was an adherent of Galenus (*q.v.*) Abrahamsz. He published ten sermons, added to LVII] *Stichtelycke Predicatiën* (Amsterdam, 1660), a volume of sermons by Willem Wynands (*q.v.*). His son Tobias van den Wijngaard was a deacon of the Amsterdam Lamist congregation 1707-12. vDZ.

Schijn-Maatschoen, *Geschiedenis* II, 649; H. W. Meihuizen, *Galenus Abrahamsz* (Haarlem, 1954) 35, 106.

Wijngaard (Wyngaert), **Tobias Govertsen van den,** b. 1587 at Amsterdam, d. there in 1669, was from 1617 a preacher and soon after an elder of the Amsterdam Flemish Mennonite congregation. In this church he was an influential leader. Outside his home church he also had great authority. He often preached in other congregations as far as Hamburg, Germany. In 1659 van den Wijngaard ordained Bastiaen van Weenigem (*q.v.*) at Rotterdam. At first van den Wijngaard was a man of broad views. He wholeheartedly co-operated with his fellow ministers in 1626 in drawing up the Olijftack (*q.v.*) confession with the preceding *Brief tot Vreed-Bereydinge* (letter to prepare for the union of the Dutch Mennonites). In 1632 he was active in bringing about the merger of the Flemish Mennonites with the Old Flemish on the basis of the Dordrecht (*q.v.*) confession, and he sincerely rejoiced over the merger of his own congregation with the High German-Frisian congregation in 1639. But he gradually grew more conservative, and from 1663 he was the leader of the opposition to Galenus (*q.v.*) Abrahamsz, who was a minister of the same congregation, and insisted on separation from the Galenists. He withdrew from the Lamist church in June 1664 with Samuel Apostool and some 500 members to found the Amsterdam Zonist (*q.v.*) congregation, of which he served as elder until 1667, when he retired after having served for fifty years. At an advanced age he also took an active part in organizing the conservative Mennonites into the *Verbondt van Eenigheydt (q.v.).*

Van den Wijngaard published *Vrede-Presentatie . . . aen Galenus Abrahamsz* (1663); *Compromis tusschen D. Galenus Abrahamsz nevens sijne medestanders en Tobias Govertsz en sijne medestanders* (Amsterdam, 1665), and probably also a letter to the congregations in Friesland, printed at Amsterdam in 1664. The original of this letter is found in the Amsterdam Mennonite archives.   vDZ.

H. W. Meihuizen, *Galenus Abrahamsz* (Haarlem, 1954); Schijn-Maatschoen, *Geschiedenis* III, 237-49 (with portrait); *Inv. Arch. Amst.* I, Nos. 566, 598, 609; II, Nos. 1232-34, 1270-72, 1387; *DB* 1881, 38; 1896, 46 f., 48; 1900, 20, 26, 29, 31, 36.

Wijns, a village in the Dutch province of Friesland, where Leenaert (*q.v.*) Bouwens baptized 21 persons in 1568-82. Since nothing is known concerning a Mennonite congregation at Wijns, it is assumed that the newly baptized joined a neighboring church.   vDZ.

Wijnssem (Wynssem) **van,** a patrician family at Deventer, Dutch province of Overijssel, some of whose members joined the early Anabaptist movement. Miss Lubbe van Wijnssem lived at Münster (*q.v.*) as early as 1533 and again in 1534 with Hylle, the widow of Lubbert van Renssen, who was the mother-in-law of her brother Jacob. Jacob **van** Wijnssem, a burgomaster of Deventer, also took the side of the Münsterite Anabaptists. He and his brother Johan were baptized in Münster by Jan van Leyden (*q.v.*) in February 1534. Their parents, Jan (Johan) van Wijnssem and Beatrix, were also baptized and received into the Anabaptist congre-

gation in their home at Deventer. It was intolerable that high officials like Jacob van Wijnssem should be revolutionary Anabaptists with many followers at Deventer, and when it was reported that the Anabaptists intended to seize the town, a number of them were arrested in January 1535, including Johan van Wijnssem, who was beheaded at Deventer on Feb. 6, 1535. About the fate of Lubbe van Wijnssem is no further information. Jan (Johan) van Wijnssem and his wife were pardoned because of their age and only banished from the town. Jacob van Wijnssem escaped arrest by flight. Later on, having renounced Anabaptism, he returned to Deventer and served as burgomaster again in 1539. (*DB* 1919, 2-8, 12, 14; Mellink, *Wederdopers.*)   vDZ.

Wijtses, Atse: see Zijpp, van der.

Wildcat (Ken.) Mennonite Mission (MC), Wildcat, established in 1949, is sponsored by the Pike Mennonite Church (*q.v.*), Elida, Ohio. In 1957 it had 35 members, with Merlin Good serving as pastor.   M.G.

Wilde, W., a Dutch Roman Catholic, published two papers, "De Geloofsvervolging der 16de eeuw" and "Merkwaardige cijfers betreffende de geloofsvervolging," in *Studiën,* 1877 and 1894. In these papers he accused T. J. van Braght of partiality and inexactness in his *Martyrs' Mirror.* Wilde was opposed by Samuel Cramer (*q.v.*) in *Doopsgezinde Bijdragen* 1899, 70 ff. Thereupon Wilde published *Zonderlinge Critiek* (Amsterdam, 1900), and Cramer replied in *De Zondagsbode* and in *Doopsgezinde Bijdragen* 1900, 191-210.   vDZ.

Wildenbruch, Ernst von (1845-1909), a German dramatist, author of *Der Menonit,* in which the Mennonites play an extremely unfavorable role on account of lack of patriotism. It is a caricature with propagandist intentions. In 1882 it was repeatedly presented on the German stage, and was considered a great success for the author.

The executive committee of the Vereiningung (*q.v.*) wrote a letter to Wildenbruch in May 1888, explaining the offending import of the drama. Wildenbruch's reply referred to the account by Bishop Eylert (*q.v.*) on Frederick William III, from which he had taken the material. He admitted that his picture might seem unjust, but thought that he was justified in the light of the moral effect of the play and his freedom as a poet. On May 26, 1888, the Mennonite congregation of Emden presented a petition to the theater in Berlin to prevent the presentation of the play there. The petition was answered negatively. Also the editor of the *Mennonitische Blätter* wrote a protest to the author on May 29, 1888. On Aug. 16, 1888, the drama was presented in Berlin. The Curatorium of the Vereinigung had a protest composed by Pastor Weydmann and H. G. Mannhardt sent to all the Berlin newspapers. It was accepted by all the papers. At the outbreak of World War I the play was to be used to rouse public enthusiasm; but upon objection by the Mennonites, including the Conference of South

German Mennonites, it was removed from the program.   NEFF.

Elizabeth H. Bender, "Ernst von Wildenbruch's Drama *Der Menonit*," *MQR* XVIII (1944) 22-35; *ML* IV.

Wildervank, a village in the Dutch province of Groningen, seat of a Mennonite congregation united with that of Veendam (*q.v.*). It is not certain whether there was an independent congregation in Wildervank in the 17th century.   VDZ.

Wildwood Mennonite Church (MC), located at Curtis, Mich., began in 1939 as a mission under the Indiana-Michigan board until 1956, when it became an independent congregation, with a summer Bible school conducted by Chester Osborne. Clarence Troyer, a minister, came in the spring of 1940. The Beulah School was purchased in 1945 and converted into a meetinghouse. From this congregation the work at Naubinway and Brimley was started. Clarence Troyer was ordained bishop in 1948; in 1952 Lloyd Miller was ordained as assistant pastor of the congregation. They were still serving in 1959, when the membership was 32.   W.I.T.

Will, Georg Andreae, a church historian of Nürnberg, Germany, who published in 1770 a history of the Anabaptist movement in Franconia titled, *Beyträge zur Fränkischen Kirchen-Historie in einer Geschichte der Wiedertäufer, welche um die Zeit der gesegneten Kirchenreinigung Frankenland und besonders die Stadt Nürnberg beunruhigt haben* (Nürnberg, 1770). In 1773 a stereotyped edition appeared with the title *Beiträge zur Geschichte des Anabaptismus in Deutschland.* The book is, as the title of the first edition indicates, written entirely in the spirit of the old Lutheran historiography and sees in the Anabaptist movement only "disorder" and "false doctrine." Will, however, deals for the most part with Thomas Müntzer, whom the Anabaptists had rejected. He makes the interesting concession that there had been cases in Franconia where innocent persons had been taken for Anabaptists and been punished with loss of life (106). (*ML* IV.)   HEGE.

Willeboort Cornelisz, an Anabaptist martyr, beheaded on Oct. 26, 1564, at Middelburg, the capital of the Dutch province of Zeeland. Willeboort, who was a native of Oostkapelle on the Zeeland island of Walcheren (*q.v.*), was arrested with his wife, Maeyken (*q.v.*) Pieters, in the night of Jan. 19, 1561, and imprisoned at Middelburg for three years and nine months. He was tried by the Catholic bishop of Middelburg and tortured several times. Remaining steadfast, he was sentenced to death, but the execution was delayed again and again until it finally took place secretly within the Gravensteen castle for fear of a popular uprising. Maeyken, who gave birth to a child in prison on Sept. 17, 1561, escaped with a number of other prisoners.

From prison Willeboort wrote a letter to his wife, which was first published in the Great Martyrs' book of 1615, and was also included in van Braght's *Martyrs' Mirror.* The date of Willeboort's death as given by van Braght (Sept. 14, 1564, repeated in *ML*) is incorrect.   VDZ.

Offer, 463 note 1, 469; *Mart. Mir.* D 305, E 677; K. R. Pekelharing, "Geschiedenis der Hervorming in Zeeland," in *Archief Zeeuwsch Genootschap* VI (1866) 44-47; *ML* I, 372.

Willeboorts, a former Dutch Mennonite family, at first at Vlissingen in Zeeland, later particularly at Amsterdam. This family may have descended from the martyr Willeboort (*q.v.*) Cornelisz. Oillaert Willeboort(s) was the elder of the Vlissingen Mennonite congregation *c*1628-after 65. In 1632 he signed the Dordrecht (*q.v.*) Confession in the name of the Vlissingen congregation. In 1665 he sided with the Galenist (*q.v.*) party against Tobias Govertsz (van den Wijngaard, *q.v.*) and the Zonists. In Amsterdam, some of the family were deacons of the Lamist congregation. Daniel and Jacob Willeboorts moved to Königsberg, East Prussia, in 1752 and joined the Mennonite Church. In Amsterdam this family died out in the 18th century. (*Inv. Arch. Amst.* II, Nos. 1270-72; *DB* 1875, 35; church records of Amsterdam.)   VDZ.

Willem, the husband of Aecht (*q.v.*) Melis, an Anabaptist martyr, arrested at Krommenieërdijk in Waterland, Dutch province of North Holland, was executed, probably in 1534 (1542, as in the *Martyrs' Mirror,* is wrong), with nine others. (*Mart. Mir.* D 62, E 464 f.; *DB* 1917, 170.)   VDZ.

Willem van Ackere (Guillaume de Camp), an Anabaptist martyr, a native of Kortrijk in Flanders, baptized by Gillis (*q.v.*) van Aken, was burned at the stake at Merelbeke near Gent, Belgium, on July 11, 1551. (Verheyden, *Gent,* 15 f., No. 29.)   VDZ.

Willem Aelbrechts, an Anabaptist martyr, a cabinetmaker of Utrecht, was sentenced to death by the sword at Delft, Holland, on Jan. 7, 1539. Ten others, all like Willem adherents of David (*q.v.*) Joris, were executed there at the same time. (*Inv. Arch. Amst.* I, No. 479.)   VDZ.

Willem Aertsz (Willem de Hoedemaker), a Dutch Anabaptist martyr, b. at Driel in Gelderland, a young man living at Ieper in Flanders, was captured at Zwevegem and burned at the stake on the market place of Kortrijk, Belgium, on Nov. 8, 1567. His property was confiscated. Willem, who had been a member of the church since 1563, was a son or brother of Hendrik (*q.v.*) Aertsen and Janneken (*q.v.*) Cabiljaus, both of whom died as martyrs. (*Mart. Mir.* D 358, E 715; Verheyden, *Courtrai-Bruxelles,* 37, No. 19; *ML* I, 86.)   VDZ.

Willem de Cle(e)rck (Guilliame van Poperinghe, also called Jan, and in the *Martyrs' Mirror* Willem van Poperinge), an Anabaptist martyr, executed on March 30, 1569, at Antwerp, Belgium. Before the judges he declared that he was born at Meenen in Flanders and lived at Dambrugge. He had been married to Maeyken (*q.v.*) Christiaens "before the congregation" eight years previously at Nijpkerke (Nieppe); they had four children, who had not been baptized into the Catholic Church, "because baptism is the prerogative of adults." He himself had been (re)baptized in 1557 at Meenen by Joachim (*q.v.*) Vermeeren. Willem was arrested during a meeting of the Antwerp congregation in the house of Jan (*q.v.*) Poote. His wife suffered martyrdom on April 4, 1569. vDZ.

Mart. Mir. D 415, E 766; *Antw. Arch.-Blad* XII, 348, 369, 399, 439; XIV, 64 f., No. 716; *ML* III, 383.

Willem de Cleermaker (Willem Enckus or Enchus), an Anabaptist martyr, executed Oct. 5, 1560, at Antwerp, Belgium, by being drowned secretly within the Steen castle. Van Braght's information that he was burned at the stake on the market place early in the morning is incorrect. Van Braght gives only the year 1560, not the exact date. Willem was a native of Berg in the district of Cologne, Germany. He died after a frank and valiant confession of faith, and is commemorated in the hymn "Een nieuwe liedt" (a new song), No. 10 of the *Lietboecxḵen*. vDZ.

Offer, 544-47; *Mart. Mir.* D 275, E 645; *Antw. Arch.-Blad* IX, 114, 121; XIV, 30 f., No. 332; Wolkan, *Lieder,* 62, 71.

Willem Cornelisz, of Hazerswoude, an Anabaptist martyr, burned at the stake at The Hague, Holland, on April 15, 1534. Willem had been among the Anabaptists who sailed from Amsterdam for Münster (*q.v.*) in March 1534. He is identical with the anonymous martyr listed in the *Martyrs' Mirror* as having been executed in 1532. (*Mart. Mir.* D 34, E 441; *DB* 1917, 121, No. 124, 171; Mellink, *Wederdopers,* 190.) vDZ.

Willem de Cuyper (Willem de Propheet), an Anabaptist martyr, beheaded on March 26, 1534, at The Hague, Holland (not at Haarlem, as is sometimes stated). Willem was a native of Heusden in the Dutch province of North Brabant. He was particularly active in Brabant and at Amsterdam. On Jan. 5, 1534, he arrived at Münster (*q.v.*), Westphalia, as an apostle of Jan (*q.v.*) Matthijsz of Haarlem. Soon after, he was back in Amsterdam, where he and others ran through the streets on March 22 with a naked sword to announce the wrath of God to the city, on which occasion he and his companions were arrested. Willem de Cuyper, whom Vos and Mellink list as a thoroughly revolutionary Anabaptist, was rather, as has been explained by Kühler, a true and radical disciple of Melchior Hofmann (*q.v.*), whose chiliastic views were easily and involuntarily adapted to revolutionary ideas. Willem de Cuyper was a dangerous and influential leader, not because of revolutionary ideas, but because of his prophecies.

Willem was married by Jan (*q.v.*) Volkertsz Trypmaker in 1531 to Margriete (*q.v.*) Willems uyt Hitlant, who after the death of her husband continued his Anabaptist activities and was executed by hanging on July 10, 1535. vDZ.

Inv. Arch. Amst. I, Nos. 24, 27, 745; *DB* 1917, 100 f., 103, 111, No. 19, 151 f.; Kühler, *Geschiedenis* I, 73, 75, 105 f.; Mellink, *Wederdopers.*

Willem van (den) Daele, an Anabaptist martyr: see Guillaume van Dale.

Willem Dirks: see Willem Zeylmaker.

Willem Dirksz Bijstervelt (Willem Cuper) and his wife Aecht Matthijsdochter were sentenced to death on March 16, 1535, by the Court of Holland. Aecht recanted and was pardoned on June 12, 1535, but Willem was probably executed. Particulars are lacking. (*Inv. Arch. Amst.* I, No. 745.) vDZ.

Willem Droochscheerder (Willem van Thye), an Anabaptist martyr, burned at the stake at Antwerp, Belgium, on Jan. 30, 1557. The sentence was executed in a particularly cruel way, the victim being burned alive without having been strangled before as was usual. Van Braght's *Martyrs' Mirror* does not mention the exact date of execution. Willem, who was a native of Nere (Neeritter) near Roermond in the present Dutch province of Limburg, wrote a letter from prison to his brother N. and his sister N. In this letter he thankfully writes that prison and torture did not vanquish his faith: "They (the persecutors) cannot harm a hair without the will of our Father; the more we are oppressed, the more we are comforted." In prison he also wrote the song "Christen broeders, weest nu al verblijt" (Christian brethren, now all rejoice). Both the letter and the hymn are found in *Offer des Heeren,* the letter also in the *Martyrs' Mirror.* Willem is commemorated in the hymn "Aenhoort God, hemelsche Vader," No. 16 of the *Lietboecxḵen.* vDZ.

Offer, 443-47, 564, No. 12; *Mart. Mir.* D 184 f., E 568 f.; *Antw. Arch.-Blad* VIII, 433, 437; XIV, 22 f., No. 238; Kühler, *Geschiedenis* I, 255; Wolkan, *Lieder,* 68; *ML* I, 478.

Willem de(n) Duy(c)k, an Anabaptist martyr, executed in 1565 (exact date unknown) at Gent, Belgium. Particulars are lacking. He is commemorated in the hymn "Als men schreef duyst vijfhondert jaer, ende twee en tesestich mede," found in the *Lietboecxḵen.* (*Offer,* 652, No. 21; *Mart. Mir.* D. 324, E 686; Verheyden, *Gent,* 31, No. 105; *ML* I, 497.) vDZ.

Willem Eynoutsz, of Barsingerhorn, an Anabaptist martyr, beheaded on Dec. 20, 1539, at Leiden, Holland, together with Claes Claesz of Schiedam. Particulars are lacking. (Mellink, *Wederdopers,* 204.) vDZ.

Willem Glaesmaker, an Anabaptist martyr, of Deventer, Holland, executed there Feb. 6, 1535. He was a Münsterite (*q.v.*) Anabaptist; a few weeks before his arrest (Jan. 28, 1535) Hendrik Cramer had delivered to his house at Deventer a number of copies of Rothmann's revolutionary booklet *Van der Wrake* (*q.v.*). (*DB* 1919, 7 f.; Mellink, *Wederdopers.*) vDZ.

Willem van Haverbeke (Guillaume van Hamerbele), an Anabaptist martyr, was burned at the stake on Nov. 20, 1561, at Kortrijk, Belgium, together with Absolon (*q.v.*) de Zanger. Willem, who was born at Gulleghem, a weaver by trade, lived at Meenen, Flanders. His property was confiscated. He is said to have been a preacher; in his home were found a number of heretical books and letters by Anabaptist leaders. (Van Braght's *Martyrs' Mirror* states wrong-

ly that he was executed in 1558.) (*Mart. Mir.* D 201, E 582; Verheyden, *Courtrai-Bruxelles,* 35, No. 13.)
vDZ.

Willem Hoedemaker (hatmaker), an Anabaptist martyr, was arrested during a meeting near Doornik (*q.v.*), Belgium. He was first brought to Doornik, thereupon to Bergen (Mons), where he was tried, and finally burned at the stake at Obignies near Doornik in 1558 (exact date unknown) with five other brethren, all of whom remained steadfast. (*Mart. Mir.* D 203, E 584.)
vDZ.

Willem Huyberts (Hubrechts), an Anabaptist martyr, burned at the stake on Feb. 21, 1573, at Antwerp, Belgium, together with Lynken Ghyselleers and Lysken Pennaerts. Willem, apparently a young man, was not yet a member of the church; during his trial he confessed that he was not yet (re)baptized, but was eager to receive baptism. The authorities, assisted by the clergy, sought fanatically "to convert him," but in vain. Willem remained steadfast. (*Antw. Arch.-Blad* XIII, 106, 107, 174; XIV, 90 f., No. 1013.)
vDZ.

Willem Huygen (Hugesz), an Anabaptist martyr who participated in the riot of Poeldijk (*q.v.*), Holland, was beheaded at The Hague on March 14, 1536. He was an adherent of the revolutionary wing of Anabaptism.
vDZ.

E. van Bergen, "De Wederdoopers in het Westland," in *Bijdragen voor de Gesch. van het bisdom Haarlem* XXVIII (1903) 275 ff.

Willem Jansen, a Mennonite elder at Emden, East Friesland, Germany, whom K. Vos considers to have been the secretary of the disputation held at Emden in 1578 between some Flemish Mennonite leaders and a number of Calvinist theologians. If this surmise is correct, Willem Jansen and not Carel van Gent (Ghendt), under the pseudonym of I.H.V.P.N., is the author of *Beginsel* (*q.v.*) *en Voortganck der Geschillen.* (Vos, *Menno Simons,* 306 f.; *ML* IV.)
vDZ.

Willem Jansz (Janssen), also called "Spaansche Willem van Doornickendam," an Anabaptist martyr, burned at the stake at Amsterdam, on March 12, 1569, together with Jan (*q.v.*) Quirijnsz and Cornelis (*q.v.*) Jansz. Willem was burned alive, without having been previously strangled as was usual.

The story of Willem's brotherly love, his loyalty, and his frankness is very striking; having heard that his coreligionist and friend Pieter (*q.v.*) Pietersz Beckjen was to die for his faith, Willem, who lived in Waterland, probably at Durgerdam, hastened to Amsterdam to comfort him. Standing near the place of execution he loudly called to Pieter: "Fight valiantly, my dear brother." Immediately afterwards he was arrested, put in prison, and tried on Feb. 26 and 28, and March 9, 1569. During these trials he confessed that he had been (re)baptized about eight years before. He also admitted that he had sometimes preached "in the manner of the Mennonites." During the torture he did not betray his brethren, refusing to name them. He gave some information on the dissensions which had arisen

among the Mennonites, a question which was only rarely raised in the trials of the martyrs. Willem informed the inquisitors that he had been banned by the party of Dirk (*q.v.*) Philipsz, i.e., the Flemish branch, because he had sided with the Frisians.

Because of his heresy, his frankness, and his unwillingness to be converted by the Catholic clergymen, he was sentenced to death. The sentence is published in full by van Braght in the *Martyrs' Mirror.* His property was confiscated. (*Mart. Mir.* D 490-92, E missing; Grosheide, *Bijdrage,* 180 f.; *DB* 1899, 128; *ML* I, 493.)
vDZ.

Willem Jansz, of Utrecht, Netherlands, a cloth shearer or cloth merchant, in early 1562 sold for six pennies a copy of the martyr book *Offer* (*q.v.*) *des Heeren* (first ed. 1562) to his fellow citizen Willem Willemz. Willem Jansz was a Mennonite; he and his wife Maria regularly attended the secret meetings of the small group of Mennonites at Utrecht. When a meeting was surprised by the officials in the spring of 1562, Willem Jansz was not present. Nothing more is heard about him. (*DB* 1903, 10, 12, 19, 35, 40, 42.)
vDZ.

Willem van Keppel: see Keppel, Wilhelm von.

Willem de Kistemaker (Wilhelm Kistenmacker), an Anabaptist martyr, executed in 1551 at Cleve in the Rhineland, Germany, together with Wendel Ravens. Van Braght gives the information that Willem had left his native country, probably Holland, and was living at Weess(?) near Cleve. He is said to have written some letters from prison, concerning which there is, however, no further information. (*Mart. Mir.* D 131, E 525; *ML* II, 501.)
vDZ.

Willem Koussenmacher, an Anabaptist martyr of Antwerp, was executed in 1535 at Wesel. At his cross-examination he said, "What one cannot grasp from Scripture is human work." The one who baptized him directed him to yield himself entirely to God.

Albrecht Wolters, *Reformationsgeschichte der Stadt Wesel* (Bonn, 1868); Rembert, *Wiedertäufer,* 400.

Willem van Leuven(e), an Anabaptist martyr, burned at the stake on Feb. 17, 1553, at the Vrijdagsmarkt at Gent, Belgium. (Van Braght gives the date as 1554.) Willem, who was a shoemaker or a cobbler, was an outstanding member in the Mennonite congregation of Gent. His wife, Levina (*q.v.*) Ghyselins, suffered martyrdom at Gent, Feb. 14, 1554. Their son Frans (*q.v.*) van Leuvene was executed at Gent in 1573. Willem van Leuven was the grandfather of Jan Doom, who in the early 17th century was a preacher of the Flemish Mennonite congregation at Haarlem, Holland. (*Mart. Mir.* D 160, E 549 f.; Verheyden, *Gent,* 18, No. 36; *DB* 1899, 67; *ML* II, 643.)
vDZ.

Willem Matthijsz (in *Offer* and *Martyrs' Mirror* simply called Willem), an Anabaptist martyr, sentenced to death by strangling and then burning at the stake. He was sentenced on Aug. 21, 1552, and the execution took place at Leiden, Holland, that very day or soon after. Three women, Maritgen,

Dieuwertgen, and Maritgen, were arrested and sentenced to death with him. There is no further information except the fact that he was a young man and that he valiantly confessed his faith. (Van Bracht erroneously gives 1550 as the year of his death.) Willem is commemorated in a hymn by Adriaen (*q.v.*) Cornelis, "Eylaes ick mach wel suchten," hymn No. 18 of the *Lietboecxken*. (*Offer,* 578-80, note 1; *Mart. Mir.* D 97, E 495; Wolkan, *Lieder,* 63, 70). vDZ.

Willem Mulaer (Mulier), an Anabaptist martyr, beheaded on July 15, 1535, at Gent, Belgium. He was the first Anabaptist martyr to die at Gent. Further particulars are lacking. (Verheyden, *Gent,* 1, No. 2.) vDZ.

Willem van Poperinge, an Anabaptist martyr: see **Willem de Cle(e)rck.**

Willem (de) Rijke(n) (Willem de Rijker, or de Rickere, Guillaume de Riche), an Anabaptist martyr, burned at the stake at Meenen in Flanders, Belgium, on Dec. 5, 1572, with Christoffel Fierens. (For particulars see **Christoffel Fierens.**) Willem was probably a relative of the martyr Christiaen (*q.v.*) de Rijcke. vDZ.

Mart. Mir. D 640, E 961 f.; *DB* 1899, 111 note, where the date of his execution is incorrectly given as Aug. 18, 1575; *ML* I, 643.

Willem (Guillame) van Roosendaele, an Anabaptist martyr, burned alive at Antwerp, Belgium, on Sept. 23, 1552. Particulars are lacking. (*Antw. Arch.-Blad* XIII, 420, 422, 424; XIV, 20 f., No. 220.) vDZ.

Willem de Snyder (Willem Snyders), an Anabaptist martyr, burned at the stake on May 18, 1570 (Van Bracht's *Martyrs' Mirror* has May 3, 1568), near Brugge, Belgium. Verheyden has published a number of particulars on a group of Anabaptists captured while holding a meeting on Ascension Day, May 4, 1570, in the woods of Tillegem near Brugge. Among those arrested were Willem de Snyder and his wife Christijntgen (*q.v.*). Willem, whose official name was Willem Vernon, was born at Dixmuiden and was a citizen of Brugge. He was a wood carver. Before the judges he declared that he had been a member of the church for six years. Though he was cruelly tortured, he refused to recant or to name other members of the Brugge congregation. He was executed with Karel (*q.v.*) (Kaerle de Raed) and Hansken (*q.v.*) in't Schaeck at Tillegem. His wife suffered martyrdom a few days later. (*Mart. Mir.* D 369, E 725 f.; Verheyden, *Brugge,* 61, No. 65.) vDZ.

Willem Timmerman (i.e., carpenter), an Anabaptist martyr, was arrested at Antwerp, Belgium, in 1567 because of Anabaptism and imprisoned in the Steen castle. Having escaped in April of that year he was banished from the Antwerp territory forever; upon his return to Antwerp he was captured and burned at the stake on Oct. 12, 1569. Particulars are lacking. (*Antw. Arch.-Blad* IX, 351, 469; XIV, 42 f., No. 495.) vDZ.

Willem van Utrecht participated in the Anabaptist uprising at Amsterdam, Holland, on May 10-11, 1535, was captured in the siege of the town hall and executed with bestial cruelty. It is not clear whether he was an Anabaptist. (Grosheide, *Verhooren,* 60, 64.) vDZ.

Willem de Vileers (Vylers), an Anabaptist martyr, was burned at the stake on April 3, 1557, on the Vrijdagsmarkt at Gent, Belgium. He was a miller. His "heresy" was reported to the magistrates by a man who pretended he wanted to join the church. (Verheyden, *Gent,* 23, No. 50.) vDZ.

Willem Wiggersz, an Anabaptist martyr, captured at Barsingerhorn in the Dutch province of North Holland, was after eight days of arrest and trial beheaded at Schagen in 1534. (*Mart. Mir.* D 35, E 442; *DB* 1917, 171.) vDZ.

Willem Willemsz Schaerslyper, a Dutch Anabaptist martyr, who participated in the journey to Münster (*q.v.*), Westphalia; being arrested at Bergklooster (*q.v.*) he was sentenced to death by the Court of Holland on July 28, 1534. He was probably beheaded at The Hague. (*Inv. Arch. Amst.* I, No. 745.) vDZ.

Willem Willemsz, a tailor of Utrecht, Netherlands, a member of the Utrecht congregation, was arrested there in 1562. He declared that he had not attended the Catholic church since 1559, in which year he had bought a New Testament. Since 1560 he had attended Mennonite meetings, and was baptized in early 1561 by Elder Joost Verbeeck of Antwerp. Besides a New Testament he also possessed a copy of the first Dutch martyr book, *Offer des Heeren* (first ed. 1562). After being tortured two or three times Willem recanted and was banished from the town on May 12, 1562, and sentenced to the galleys. vDZ.

Inv. Arch. Amst. I, Nos. 47c, 398a; *DB* 1903, 6, 7, 8 f., 11, 12, 13, 15, 16, 20, 25, 36; 1908, 126; Kühler, *Geschiedenis* I, 294.

Willem Willemzoon van der Leye, an Anabaptist martyr, was arrested at the Oldeklooster (*q.v.*) siege and beheaded on April 10, 1535, at Leeuwarden in Friesland, Netherlands. (Vos, *Menno Simons,* 228.) vDZ.

Willem de Zager, an Anabaptist martyr, was burned at the stake with Dirk (*q.v.*) Anoot in 1569 at Ieper (Ypres) in Flanders, Belgium. Particulars are lacking. (*Mart. Mir.* D 406, E 758.) vDZ.

Willem Zeylmaker (Willem Dirksz), of Amsterdam, was a notorious Dutch Anabaptist leader of the revolutionary Batenburger (*q.v.*) group. He is said to have had many adherents at Alkmaar and other places. Arrested at Utrecht, Netherlands, in May 1544, he was burned at the stake on Feb. 7, 1545, together with Cornelis (*q.v.*) Appelman, another revolutionary leader. (*Inv. Arch. Amst.* I, Nos. 265, 301, 307, 310; *DB* 1909, 17, 21, 29 f.; 1917, 140; Mellink, *Wederdopers*.) vDZ.

Willemken Willem Claesdochter, of IJsselstein, an Anabaptist martyr, drowned on July 21, 1544, at Utrecht, Netherlands. She is charged with belonging to "reprobate sects." Some years previously she had been arrested because of Anabaptist activity, but then after recanting was set free. She was probably an adherent of revolutionary Anabaptism, whose last adherents were executed in 1545. (Mellink, *Wederdopers,* 240, 410.)   vDZ.

Willems: see **Willms.**

Willems(z), Jan, an elder and leader of the Frisian Mennonites: see **Jan Willemsz.**

Willemsz, Jan, b. May 9, 1583, at Cologne, Germany, d. 1660 at De Rijp in North Holland, Netherlands, a physician and in 1610-60 a Mennonite minister, at first a preacher, soon an elder of the Waterlander Mennonite congregation at De Rijp. He was educated for the Catholic priesthood, but he ran away from school and became a soldier. On a Sunday morning at Haarlem, Holland, he accidentally arrived in the Waterlander meetinghouse and was converted; he wanted to be a member of the church. The Haarlem Waterlander congregation bought off his military obligations and thereupon he was baptized upon his confession of faith. His marriage to a well-to-do lady of De Rijp enabled him to study medicine. After finishing his study he settled at De Rijp to practice medicine; soon after this he was chosen as a preacher of the congregation. His long service seems to have been blessed, though it is said that he was somewhat stubborn and quarreled with other leaders, including his colleague Pieter Pietersz (*q.v.*). Willemz seems to have sympathized with Nittert Obbes (*q.v.*) in the latter's conflict with the Waterlander leader Hans de Ries (*q.v.*); a booklet by Jan Willemsz, *Raegh-Stock voor Nittert Obbes Reaghbesem,* in which Willemsz defended Obbes against de Ries, exists only as a résumé by Jan Theunisz (*q.v.*). Of special interest is Willemsz' *Grondich Ondersoeck,* in which he attacked the practice of ordaining deacons with the laying on of hands.   vDZ.

Schijn-Maatschoen, *Geschiedenis* II, 651, 683 (with portrait); *N.N.B.Wb.* I, 1578; *DB* 1917, 30-32; Kühler, *Geschiedenis* II, 170 ff.; Yearbook *Amstelodamum* XXV (1928) 98, 118.

Willemszen, Louwerens (Lourens Willems, L. W. van Alckmaer), a deacon of the Rotterdam Old Flemish congregation, was vigorously opposed to the conciliatory *Olyftack* (*q.v.*) confession (1626) inasmuch as this confession was intended to unite several branches of Dutch Mennonites, and also to the merger of the Flemish and Old Flemish branches in 1632. Willemszen and a few other conservatives tried, but in vain, to retain the Rotterdam Old Flemish meetinghouse for their small group, which did not share in the merger. During these quarrels Willemszen published some booklets: *Een korte onderscheydelycke vertooninghe aan onze Medeghenoten des Gheloofs* (Rotterdam, 1629), *Aarons Roede Vertoond . . . aan onze Medeghenooten des Gheloofs* (Amsterdam, 1630, 3d ed. Rotterdam,

1633), *Ezelinnen Zoon* (Rotterdam, 1633), and *Kakebeen, of Ezels Kinnebakken* (Rotterdam, 1636).
                      vDZ.

Inv. Arch. Amst. II, 2, Nos. 424-26, 428, 431, 434; K. Vos, *Geschiedenis der Doopsgez. Gemeente te Rotterdam* (1907), repr., 11, 45; Kühler, *Geschiedenis* II, 194 f.; M. Schagen, *Naamlijst der Doopsgezinde Schrijveren* (Amsterdam, 1745) 4 f.

Willenbach, a large farm estate near Jagstfeld, which gave its name to a Mennonite congregation c1780-1810, which later became the Heilbronn (*q.v.*) congregation, Württemberg, Germany.   vDZ.

Willer (Willher), **Barbeli** and **Hans,** Anabaptist martyrs; Barbeli (Barbara) Willher, who may have been the same person as "Barbli with the wooden leg" a native of Hasli, was drowned at Bern, Switzerland, in late 1537 or early 1538, and Hans Willer was executed there in August 1538.   vDZ.

D. L. Gratz, *Bernese Anabaptists* (Scottdale, 1953) 22, 23.

William I of Orange (1533-84) was born at Dillenburg in Hesse-Nassau, Germany, on April 11, 1533. He was assassinated on July 10, 1584, at Delft, Netherlands. In 1566, while serving Philipp II of Spain as governor of Antwerp, he still insisted on the execution of the Mennonites. Two years later William led the revolt (War of Liberation) of the Netherlands against Spain. Then being appointed stadholder of Holland and Zeeland, his views completely changed. He now tried to unite all forces in the war against Spain. He left the Catholic Church to become a Calvinist, and practiced tolerance even toward the Mennonites. Whereas some of his counselors (e.g., Marnix van St. Aldegonde, *q.v.*) insisted on the persecution of the Mennonites, William defended them. On April 20, 1572, he wrote a letter to his governor in North Holland ordering that nobody should be hindered in preaching the Word of God. On July 15, of that year, in the meeting of the Dutch States-General, he proposed religious freedom. The States, however (particularly in 1583), resolved that in the United Netherlands only the Reformed Church should be allowed to meet publicly, all others being simply tolerated. In 1577, and again in 1578, 1580, and 1582, he defended the Mennonites of Middelburg, capital of Zeeland, against the local authorities, releasing them from swearing oaths and bearing arms, which privileges soon became valid throughout the Netherlands. It seems somewhat contrary to this policy of toleration that in 1581 William issued a mandate in accord with the views of the States-General, ordering that no other religion but the Reformed be granted the public exercise of its faith. But this mandate was meant to break the influence and power of the Catholic Church, whose members often were pro-Spanish, though it was later often used against the Mennonites.

The Mennonites on their part were grateful to William for his protection and the granted privileges. As early as July 29, 1572, two Waterlander leaders (see **Bogaert, P. W.** and **Cortenbosch, D. J.**) brought to the Prince of Orange 1060 guilders in the name of the Dutch Mennonites, to be used for the welfare of the country. NEFF, VDZ.

A. A. van Schelven, *Willem van Oranje* (Haarlem, 1933); K. Vos, *Oranje en de Doopsgezinden* (Amsterdam, n.d.-1911) 5-11; *DJ* 1930, 115-41; *Inv. Arch. Amst.* I, Nos. 409, 421 f., 426, 428 f., 431; Kühler, *Geschiedenis* 1; *DB* 1873, 3-11; 1875, 99; 1882, 7; 1883, 19; 1895, 5; 1896, 156; 1908, 42, 45 f.; N. Japikse, "Die Oranier, Statthalter und Könige in den Niederlanden," in *Archiv für Ref.-Gesch.*, 1941; A. L. E. Verheyden, "Mennisme in Vlaanderen" (manuscript); *ML* III, 307.

William III of Orange (1650-1702), from 1672 stadholder of the Netherlands except Friesland, and by his marriage to Mary Stuart in 1689 also king of England, a haughty, reticent man, energetic politician, and capable general, paladin of Protestantism, often defended the Mennonites in the Netherlands and elsewhere against oppression. On May 15, 1673, he issued a mandate by which the Mennonites in North Holland were exempted from military service. On Nov. 11, 1688, he suspended the suit against the Mennonite preacher Foecke Floris (*q.v.*), who was charged with Socinianism. On Aug. 11, 1694, and again on July 14, 1697, he wrote a letter to John William, Elector of the Palatinate (*q.v.*), in favor of the Mennonites who were suppressed in his territory and particularly in the Duchy of Jülich (*q.v.*). VDZ.

J. K. Oudendijk, *Willem III* (1953); *Inv. Arch. Amst.* I, Nos. 454, 456, 1749, 1755; *DB* 1887, 71 ff.; 1895, 5 f.; *ML* III, 308.

Williams County (Ohio) Mennonite Church (MC), also known as Hoffers (now extinct), located northwest of West Unity, Ohio, was founded in 1842-43 by settlers from Canada and from Lebanon and Lancaster counties in Pennsylvania. Located in the "Black Swamp" area of northwestern Ohio, the county offered cheap land for easterners who had become bankrupt during the financial panic of Martin Van Buren's administration. Daniel Lehman, Peter Borkholder, and Isaac Hoffer, a preacher and later a bishop, were the first settlers. Others who followed a little later were Joseph Borkholder, Jacob Eberly, Samuel and Solomon Lehman, Jacob Delp, Menno Naragang (?), John Detweiler, Abraham Metzler, Moses Koch, John Dill, Martin Myers, William Rhodes, Levi H. Eberly, and a Kilmer family who had moved from Crawford County, Ohio. Ministers ordained from the congregation were Levi H. Eberly, Martin Myers, and Joseph Borkholder. For the first few decades the congregation gave promise of growth and built a small meetinghouse on the northeast corner of Hoffer's farm. After the bishop's death in 1880 the congregation declined. His successor, Abraham Lehman, following the lead of Jacob Wisler (*q.v.*) of Indiana, prohibited Sunday school and other young people's religious activities. Some members moved to Elkhart County, Ind., or united with the local Church of the Brethren or other denominations in the neighborhood. The small well-kept cemetery plot back of the barn on the late Bishop Hoffer's farm provides the last resting place for the older members of the congregation. J.S.U.

John Umble, "Extinct Ohio Mennonite Churches," *MQR* XVIII (1944) 36-48.

Williams, Jan (1533-88), married Aagt Pieters in 1589, the father of 4 sons and 5 daughters. In 1557 after the separation of the Waterlanders he was chosen elder by the stricter party and ordained by Dirk Philips. He lived in Hoorn, where he and Lubbert Gerrits (after 1559) were influential leaders. He was one of the arbitrators of the dissension in Franeker in 1567, which led to the division between the Frisians and the Flemish. As a member of the Frisian group he continually strove for peace, one result of his efforts being the agreement of Humster in 1574. He was the progenitor of the Sleutel family. (G. J. de Hoop Scheffer, "Het geslacht Sleutel," in *DB* 1861, 50-65.) VDZ.

Williamson Mennonite Church (MC), located one mile west of Williamson in Franklin County, Pa., a member of the Washington County, Md., and Franklin County, Pa., Conference, had a joint ministerial body with the Marion congregation until March 23, 1948, when Mahlon Eshleman was ordained exclusively for this congregation (Williamson). Previous to 1869, when the meetinghouse was built, the members worshiped jointly with what is now the Marion congregation, the meetinghouse then being located at Brown's Mill. By 1924 the membership had dwindled to 5, but by 1954 had risen to 65. In 1957 the minister was Mahlon D. Eshleman, and the membership was 49. C.S.

Williamsville (N.Y.) Reformed Mennonite Church, in Erie County near Buffalo, was founded about 1833 by John Herr (*q.v.*), the first leader of the Reformed Mennonites. In 1957 the membership was 34. H.S.B.

Willink, a widely ramified Dutch Mennonite family which took its name from the farm "Het Willink" near Winterswijk in the Dutch province of Gelderland, where they were living in the 16th century; but originally this family probably stemmed from Westphalia, Germany, where it was found in the towns of Vreden, Bocholt, and Burgsteinfurt until the 17th century. In the 16th and 17th centuries there were both a Mennonite and a Reformed branch.

Jan Willink, b. c1561, married in 1591 to Judith Busschers (both probably Mennonites), lived at Groenlo in Gelderland. They died in 1636 of the plague. Soon afterward the Willinks, who were textile manufacturers, were members of the Winterswijk (*q.v.*) Mennonite congregation, where many of them have been deacons; Berend Willink was an untrained preacher of this church 1693-1700. In the 17th and 18th centuries some Willinks lived at Deventer, where Ananias Willink was a lay preacher c1670, and in Enschedé and other Dutch towns. A branch of this family is found at Amsterdam from c1650, engaged as linen merchants and later as bankers. Another branch is found in Hamburg, Germany, from 1734; Lucas Willink was a deacon of the Mennonite congregation here in the early 19th century. Later this Hamburg branch joined the Lutherans. In Amsterdam the Willinks were mostly members and often deacons of the Lamist (*q.v.*) congregation; the first of these deacons was the merchant Gerrit Willink (1618-79), serving from 1656. Jan Willink was a lay preacher in this church 1675-d. 1725. A few Willinks at Amsterdam were members of the Zonist (*q.v.*) congregation.

Jan Ananiasz Willink (Amsterdam, 1751-1827), a deacon of the Lamist and later of the United congregation, was a cofounder of the A.D.S. and a trustee 1811-27. His cousins Willem Willink (1750-1841) and Jan Willink (1778-1827) were trustees of the A.D.S., in 1811-18 and 1819-27. Ananias Willink Jansz (Amsterdam, 1778-1863), director of the Dutch State Bank, was treasurer of the A.D.S. and curator of its seminary 1827-47.

Jan Jansz Willink (1676-1722), a wine merchant of Amsterdam and deacon of the Lamist church, was an active member and secretary of the Dutch Mennonite Committee for Foreign Needs. In December 1710 he and Cornelis Beets contacted François Fagel (*q.v.*) and the Dutch States-General in behalf of the oppressed Swiss Mennonites. He was also a poet, highly esteemed during his lifetime, now forgotten, who published a number of volumes of poetry, e.g., *Bloemkrans van christelijke liefde- en zeededichten* (Amsterdam, 1714, repr. *ibid.* 1723), *Lusthof van christelijke dank- en beedezangen* (2 vv., Amsterdam, 1714, repr. n.d.-1720, 1726), and *Christelijke Gebeden* (Amsterdam, 1718, many reprints). Anthony François Willink (Amsterdam, 1825-92), also a trustee of the A.D.S., was for many years the president of the Dutch Mennonite Mission Association. (See also **Tjeenk Willink.**)

At present there are only a few Mennonite Willinks in Holland.   vDZ.

F. Willink, *Stamboek der Willingen . . .* (Amsterdam, 1721); P. Beets, *Stamboek der Willingen* (Deventer, 1767); *Ned. Patriciaat* XXVIII (1942) 349-64; *ibid.* XXXVI (1950) 368-78; F. C. Fleischer, *De Doopsgezinde Gemeente te Winterswijk* (Winterswijk, 1911) 7, 8, 20, 21, 29, 30 *et passim*; *Inv. Arch. Amst.* I, Nos. 1294, 1327; *DJ* 1850, 143; *DB* 1893, 107; 1897, 41 f.; 1909, 139, 144; 1912, 111 f.; 1919, 65; B. C. Roosen, *Gesch. der Mennoniten-Gemeinde zu Hamburg und Altona* II (Hamburg, 1887) 81, 85; *N.N.B.Wb.*, 1463-65.

Willms (Willems, Willm, Willmsen, Wilms, Willemsen, Wilhelm), a family name among the Mennonites of Prussian background derived from the Dutch Christian name Willem (William), found in the church records of Danzig (1690), Tiegenhagen, Ladekopp, Rosenort, Fürstenwerder, Heubuden, Elbing, Montau-Gruppe, Schönsee, Tragheimerweide, and Kazun. From Danzig and Prussia the name spread to Russia and North and South America. The name is also found in the Netherlands but is not common among Mennonites. In 1723 Albert Willems from Holland, with Alle Derks, visited the Prussian Mennonites. Among the Mennonites in Russia bearing the name were Peter Willms of Halbstadt, Molotschna, the owner of a starch factory, and Heinrich Willms of Halbstadt, Molotschna, the owner of three large flour mills with an annual turnover of $500,000. H. J. Willms was in the administration of Concordia Hospital, Winnipeg; Gerhard H. Willms is manager of the Herald Book and Printing Co., Newton, Kan.

C.K.

Reimer, *Familiennamen*, 120; H. H. Schröder, *Russlanddeutsche Friesen* (Döllstadt, 1936) 99.

Willow Creek, a Hutterite Bruderhof of the Dariusleut (*q.v.*) branch, near Stettler, in Alberta. The population in 1950 was 89, with Jacob S. Stahl as head preacher.   vDZ.

Willow Creek Mennonite Church (GCM): see **San Marcos.**

Willow Springs Mennonite Church (MC), located 4 miles south of Tiskilwa, Bureau Co., Ill., a member of the Illinois Conference, was organized in 1836 as an Amish Mennonite congregation, the settlers having come mostly from Bavaria, Germany, plus a few from Butler County, Ohio. The Bavarians had first settled in 1835 in the Hennepin and Granville neighborhood in Putnam County. After meeting in homes for 35 years the congregation built its first meetinghouse in 1873. This was destroyed by lightning in 1896, but was immediately rebuilt, and later enlarged several times.

Three subsidiary groups have been formed from Willow Springs: Ohio Station in the north central part of the county 1840-1915, which never developed into a congregation; Sheffield in the western part of the county 1943-50; and the Tiskilwa Mennonite Church (GCM; *q.v.*), which was formed in 1911 when a group withdrew to join the Central Illinois Conference (*q.v.*).

The first minister in the Hennepin community was Jacob Burkey of Hesse, Germany, who never lived in the Tiskilwa neighborhood. The Willow Springs congregation suffered for many years from inadequate and even absentee ministerial leadership and was not established on a sound basis until 1868, when Joseph Burkey, a minister at Tremont, Ill., moved in and was ordained bishop a year later. His successor was C. A. Hartzler, a minister from Garden City, Mo., who came in 1913 and was ordained bishop a year later. C. W. Long was pastor in 1957, with a membership of 142.   H.S.B.

H. F. Weber, *Centennial History of the Mennonites of Illinois* (Goshen, 1931) 222-36.

Willow Street Mennonite Church: see **Brick Mennonite Church.**

Willowdale Christian Fellowship, 10 Burke Street (Willowdale), Toronto, Ont., was organized in August 1957. Its members are Mennonite Brethren who come to the city to study or work. A center was dedicated in January 1958. Henry Voth was the minister for the 18 members.   J.H.H.

Wilmington (Del.) Mennonite Church (CAM) meets at 10th and Harrison streets. This mission station was established in 1948 and by 1957 had 22 members, with Amos Bontrager serving as pastor.
M.G.

Wilmot (Ont.) Reformed Mennonite Church: see **Hostetlers Meetinghouse.**

Wilmsen, Johann: see **Jan Willems(z).**

Wilson Bend Mennonite Church: see **Providence Mennonite Church.**

Wilson Siding, a Hutterite Bruderhof of the Dariusleut (*q.v.*) branch, at Lethbridge, in Alberta. The population in 1950 was 140, with John M. Wurz as head preacher.

Wimmer (Winter), **Wolfgang**, an Anabaptist martyr of Steyr, Austria, a tailor of Nistelbach and an Anabaptist preacher, who was burned to death with his wife Martha on Oct. 27, 1527, in a group of 37 Anabaptists (including Eucharius Binder, *q.v.*) who were locked in a house which was then burned down. (Beck, *Geschichts-Bücher,* 27.)

Winchester (Va.) Mennonite Church (MC), now extinct, was in existence about 1870-1900. Following the Civil War a number of farms in the vicinity of Winchester, Kernstown, and Stephens City in Frederick County, Va., were purchased by Mennonites who came here from Lancaster County, Pa., Maryland, and the upper (southern) part of the Shenandoah Valley, attracted by cheap land. At the height of the movement there were four Mennonite preaching appointments. (One of these was the Kernstown—*q.v.*—congregation.) Two sessions of the Virginia Conference were held here before 1900. The most important leader of the church in this area was Christley Brunk, from near Broadway, Va.

The congregation entered a period of decline in the 1890's. Successful leadership was not perpetuated. The young people did not become members of the church. A number of Mennonites joined other denominations, while others moved away. The Kernstown meetinghouse was sold in 1907.

H.A.B.

Wind, de, a former Dutch Mennonite family, now extinct. The idea, found in older books, that this family stemmed from Germany is wrong. About 1566 two brothers, Pieter and Jan de Wind, fled because of persecution from Flanders, Belgium, to Vlissingen (*q.v.*) in the Dutch province of Zeeland. Jan joined the Reformed Church. (1) Pieter became a Mennonite, and his descendants gave the Mennonite church in the Netherlands meritorious service. (2) Paulus de Wind, a weaver, son of (1) Pieter, moved from Vlissingen to Middelburg. (3) Gerard de Wind, a son of (2) Paulus, was a cloth shearer. (4) Paulus de Wind (1655-1728), a son of (3) Gerard, married to Jacomyntje Frans, was a cheese and butter merchant at Vlissingen and an elder of the Vlissingen congregation 1691-1704, then moved to Zwolle, where he died. After this, most of the de Winds were practicing physicians in Middelburg (*q.v.*), where nearly all served the church as deacons. (5) Gerard de Wind (*q.v.*) was a son of (4) Paulus. His sons were (6) Jan van Beekhoven de Wind (Middelburg *c*1710-Haarlem?), physician and preacher at Gouda 1734-37 and of the Haarlem Peuzelaarsteeg congregation 1737-*c*70, (7) Paulus de Wind (1714-71) (Nos. (7) to (11) were born and died at Middelburg and practiced medicine there unless otherwise noted), (7) Paulus de Wind, married to Berdina Tak and later to Cornelia Dobbelaers, and (8) Gerard de Wind (1730-1800), married to Suzanna van Hoorn, professor of anatomy at Middelburg. A son of (7) Paulus was (9) Samuel de Wind (1742-1803), married to Cornelia Dobbelaer, known for his benefi-

cence, as was his son (10) Paulus de Wind (1767-97), married to his cousin Elizabeth de Wind. Another son of (9) Samuel was (11) Boudewijn Dobbelaer de Wind (1775-1818), married to Petronella Tak, a pillar of the church and a very popular man in his home town. (12) Samuel de Wind (1793-1856), married to his cousin Cornelia Dobbelaer, a son of (10) Paulus, was a well-known lawyer in Middelburg. He published also a number of studies on the history of Vlissingen and was very active in the church. His son (13) Samuel Dobbelaer de Wind (1817-89) was a physician at Middelburg. With him the family died out in the male line. In the 18th century a branch of this family, now also extinct, was found at Amsterdam.   vDZ.

F. Nagtglas, *Levensberichten van Zeeuwen* II (Middelburg, 1893) 974-84; *Inv. Arch. Amst.* II, Nos. 985, 1790, 1792, 1877, 2236; *N.N.B.Wb.* IV, 1466; V, 1138-40; *DB* 1868, 92, 93, 95; 1875, 35.

Wind, Gerard (Gerardus) **de,** b. 1685 at Vlissingen, d. 1752 at Middelburg, married to Elisabeth Beekhoven. He was trained for the ministry by Adriaan van Eeghem (*q.v.*) at Middelburg and by Galenus (*q.v.*) Abrahamsz and the Remonstrant seminary at Amsterdam. He also studied medicine in Utrecht. Returning to Middelburg, where he practiced medicine, he became also a preacher of the Middelburg Mennonite congregation in 1705, serving until his death. He published *Lijkreden over het Afsterven van A. van Eeghem* (Vlissingen, 1709), *Johannes Kiens redenen des geloofs onderzocht* (Middelburg, 1711), *Verhandeling over de bijzondere genade Gods* (Amsterdam, 1725), and *Verhandeling van Gods algemeene genade* (Amsterdam, 1728). He also edited the theological writings of van Eeghem: *De Christelijke Godgeleerdheid van A.v.E.* (Vlissingen, 1710). De Wind was attacked by G. van Hemert (*q.v.*), his Reformed colleague at Middelburg, in *G. de Wind uit ziyne verhandeling van Godts algemeene Genade ontmaskert* (Middelburg, 1730).

vDZ.

Blaupot t. C., *Holland* II, 131 f.; *N.N.B.Wb.* V, 1138 f.; *Inv. Arch. Amst.* I, Nos. 1806, 2020.

Windesheim, a village in the Dutch province of Overijssel, where a monastery was founded in 1385, which was the center of the Windesheim monastic order issuing from the Brethren (*q.v.*) of the Common Life movement. This monastic order stressed knowledge of the Bible and reading of the Bible in the vernacular and cultivated evangelical piety. According to Kühler, it prepared the soil for Sacramentism (*q.v.*) and Anabaptism.   vDZ.

J. G. R. Acquoy, *Het Klooster van Windesheim* (3 vv., Utrecht, 1875-80); Kühler, *Geschiedenis* I, 28.

Winding Mill (Pa.) Reformed Mennonite Church, near Mechanicsburg, Cumberland Co., Pa., was organized in 1870. In 1948 it had eight members. By 1957 it had been combined with the Middlesex Reformed Mennonite Church near Carlisle, Pa.

H.S.B.

Wine Spring Schoolhouse, Peru, Pendleton Co., W. Va., is located in South Fork (Branch of the Potomac) country several miles north of Sweedlin Valley. The Mennonites (MC) began preaching here *c*1920. It was an extension of the work from the Sweedlin Valley by the Northern District council. At the present time the pastor of the Pleasant Grove church in Sweedlin Valley is responsible for the services here. Wine Spring is listed as Peru in the *Mennonite Yearbook*.   H.A.B.

Winkel, a small village in the Dutch province of North Holland, about four miles from Barsingerhorn (*q.v.*), was in 1533-34 a center of Anabaptist activity, nearly the whole population being Anabaptist. Anabaptism was not rooted out here in the campaign of Reinier Brunt in early 1534; in 1540-41 mention is made of Anabaptism in Winkel, and still in 1558 Mennonite meetings were held here. After this Mennonites are not mentioned. L. Nannings Smit, Waechlink Dirks, Maerten Cornelisz, and Adriaen Pietersz, all of Winkel, died as martyrs, Smit in 1540, the other three in 1558. (*Inv. Arch. Amst.* I, Nos. 234, 240, 390-92.)   vDZ.

Winkelman, a Dutch Mennonite family stemming from Mennonites from Flanders, Belgium. Pieter Janse Wynckelman (Winkelman) was from 1625 a deacon of the Flemish congregation at Rotterdam; there were also Winkelmans at Vlissingen, where some of them were deacons in the 19th and 20th centuries. One of them, Henrik Pierre Winkelman (Vlissingen, 1813-78), an apothecary and for many years the chairman of the local congregation, published a paper on the history of the Vlissingen congregation in *Doopsgezinde Bijdragen* of 1875. B. J. Winkelman was moderator of the Mennonite Kring (circle), later congregation, of Eindhoven (*q.v.*) 1928-42.   vDZ.

Winkler, a town (pop. 2,500) in southern Manitoba, 80 miles southwest of Winnipeg, 12 miles north of the United States boundary, in an area where grains, fruits, sugar beets, sunflowers, corn, and canning crops are grown, was founded in 1892. It is the business, educational, and religious center for a 6,000 Mennonite population in the rural municipalities of Stanley and Rhineland, which were settled village-style in 1875. It has an M.B. Bible school, organized in 1925, with 4 teachers and 80 students; a public high school, largely Mennonite in teachers and student body, with 9 teachers and 225 students; and four Mennonite churches: Bergthal, Mennonite Brethren, Rudnerweide, and Sommerfeld, with a total membership of over 1,000. The Winkler M.B. Church (*q.v.*), organized in Burwalde in 1886, was the first M.B. church in Canada.   Pe.B.

Frank Brown, "Winkler, Manitoba," *Menn. Life* XI (July 1956).

Winkler Bible School, located in Winkler, Man., was founded in the fall of 1925 by A. H. Unruh. It was patterned after Tchongrav (*q.v.*) in South Russia, and was organized by three former teachers of that school. Unruh was the first of them to emigrate, followed by G. J. Reimer in 1926 and by J. G. Wiens. The school was erected for the purpose of teaching the Bible, especially to young people, to prepare them for missionary work as well as pastoral service. Its name is Peniel (Gen. 32:30), and its motto is, "I will not let thee go, except thou

bless me" (v. 26). The school has had 22 teachers in 34 years, and has operated in three-, four-, and five-year courses.   H.H.R.

Winkler, Konrad, an Anabaptist martyr of Wasserberg in the canton of Zürich, is the fourth martyr of the Zürich Swiss Brethren group. At a cross-examination in June 1525 he asserted that he had not baptized and promised to be obedient, but was nevertheless fined because he had contradicted the preacher in his sermon. Later Winkler appeared in the Zürich lowlands as an Anabaptist preacher. In Basel he also sought to promote the Anabaptist cause, but was arrested and placed in stocks with Treyer (*q.v.*). On Jan. 20, 1530, he was condemned to death at Zürich as "a real leader and mobster of this affair," who had for several months preached for large crowds and baptized many men and women. He was drowned in the Limmat bound as Felix Manz (*q.v.*) had been. His property was confiscated.   S.G.

Emil Egli, *Die Züricher Wiedertäufer zur Reformationszeit* (Zürich, 1878) 89; *TA Zürich,* 332 f., where Winkler's importance is indicated by the length of the verdict; *ML* IV.

Winkler Mennonite Brethren Church at Winkler, Man., the oldest M.B. Church in Canada, began as the result of home mission effort of the Conference of the M.B. Church. In 1883 the Conference sent Heinrich Voth and David Dyck as evangelists to Manitoba. On May 30, 1886, the first baptismal service was held, when six members were received into church membership.

Gerhard Wiebe, an immigrant from Russia, organized the group into a congregation of 16 members. In 1889 the first church building was erected 6 miles northwest of Winkler, in the village of Burwalde. In 1895 David Dyck, a minister from Colorado, became leader of this church, which at that time numbered 84 members. Affiliated stations were opened at Kronsgart and Grossweide, which developed into new churches. Since 1898 there have been quarterly meetings in which all three congregations participated. In 1898 the church building was moved from Burwalde to just outside Winkler. Shortly after, a new one was erected on the same site; it was enlarged twice. In 1947 the building and lot were sold, and a new building was erected in Winkler, 60 x 102 ft., seating capacity 1,000.

In 1895 John Warkentin was ordained as minister and in 1906 he became the presiding minister of the church, a position he held 25 years. In 1898 the Conference of the M.B. Church was held at Winkler. This was the first time that it convened in Canada.

In 1906 P. H. Neufeld was ordained to the ministry. In 1931 H. S. Voth became leader and pastor of the church, followed by G. D. Pries. In 1959 the leader was J. H. Quiring, with a membership of 374.   H.H.R.

Winkler Prins, Anthony, b. Jan. 31, 1817, at Voorst, Netherlands, d. Jan. 4, 1908, at Voorburg, studied theology at the University of Utrecht and the Amsterdam Mennonite seminary and was a pastor at Tjalleberd 1841-50 and Veendam 1850-82, retiring in this year. He published a volume of sermons, *Leerredenen* (Heerenveen, 1851), and his farewell sermon, *Afscheidsrede,* from Veendam (Wildervank, 1882). But more than a theologian, Winkler Prins was a literary man; during his student years in Amsterdam, he—with H. C. Dronrijp Uges, D. Harting, P. Leendertz, and J. G. de Hoop Scheffer—was a cofounder of the literary club N.E.K. (*q.v.*), and in 1842-44 he published the periodical *Braga,* in which he and his friends sharply criticized the low level of contemporary Dutch literature. From 1838 Prins published articles in many Dutch literary periodicals and newspapers. He also published poems. The complete, long list of his writings is found in the *Levensbericht* (obituary) of the Dutch Association for Literature, of which he was a member. His chief publication is the Dutch illustrated encyclopedia (*Winkler Prins Encyclopedie*) in 16 vv. (Amsterdam, 1869-82; 6th revised edition at Amsterdam 1947-55), for which he did painstaking work.

Winkler Prins was a versatile man. Particularly during his Veendam period he was "the intellectual pioneer" of this area, successfully promoting better schools in Veendam, the improvement of agricultural methods, and many other public interests. In 1864 he was chosen as a member of the Second Chamber of Parliament, but declined.

Anthony Winkler Prins was the son of (M.D.) Jacob Prins and Johanna van Marle Winkler. In 1847 he was married to H. R. Klijnsma. H. A. Lunshof wrote a biographical novel on the life of Winkler Prins, entitled *Leven zonder demon* (Amsterdam, 1950). vDZ.

J. Dyserinck, *Levensbericht van A. Winkler Prins* (Leiden, 1909); *N.N.B.Wb.* V, 538-40; *DB* 1864, 170; 1908, 207; *DJ* 1909, 21-33 (with portrait).

Winnebago (Wis.) **State Hospital** was the location of Civilian Public Service Unit No. 122, which was operated by the Mennonite Central Committee from November 1943 to February 1946. The unit of 15 men worked as attendants in this 500-bed hospital, which treated acute psychiatric patients. M.G.

Melvin Gingerich, *Service for Peace* (Akron, 1949) 240-44.

Winnipeg, the capital (pop. 243,287) of the province of Manitoba, incorporated in 1873 with a population of 1,869, is situated at the confluence of the Red and Assiniboine rivers, 40 miles south of Lake Winnipeg, and 60 miles north of the United States border, almost midway between the Atlantic and Pacific oceans. The metropolitan area of Greater Winnipeg has a population of 354,069 out of a provincial total of 776,541. The total Mennonite population of Manitoba, including Hutterites, was 44,667 in 1957, the majority of whom are descendants of the immigrants from Russia of 1874-80, although a considerable number are from the immigrations of 1922-25 and 1948-53. The Mennonite population of Greater Winnipeg was over 7,000 in 1957, constituting the largest Mennonite city population in the world.

Mennonite church work in Winnipeg began in 1907 when the Winkler M.B. Church began a mission there. The second work was a G.C.M. mission begun in 1921. Other missions have been established

by the older Manitoba groups in later years as follows: E.M.B. in 1949, Chortitz in 1952, Evangelical (Kleine Gemeinde) in 1954, and the Church of God in Christ Mennonites (discontinued). The first three missions have developed into regular congregations for Mennonites, while the latter two serve as unorganized Mennonite fellowship groups; the missions have as a whole not won many non-Mennonites, and would have remained small had it not been for the immigration from Russia beginning in 1922. This latter movement was intended to go to the farming territory of southern Manitoba, but only a part of the immigrants have remained on the land. Large numbers, lacking capital, moved to the city to secure work. The later immigration after World War II (1948 ff.) went largely directly to the city. Of the present Winnipeg Mennonite population of over 7,000, at least 90 per cent is composed of immigrants since 1922.

In 1957 Greater Winnipeg had c4,000 baptized Mennonites distributed as follows: G.C.M.—2,215 in 4 congregations (First or Schoenwiese founded in 1926, 1,291; Sargent Avenue in 1928, 323; Bethel in 1938, 379; Bergthal Winnipeg Mission in 1950, 222); M.B.—1,521 in 4 congregations (Elmwood, formerly North End founded in 1913, new building in 1954, 460; North Kildonan in 1928, 499; South End in 1936, 521; Gospel Light, 41); E.M.B.—71 in one congregation, the Christian Fellowship Chapel (founded in 1949), plus a mission; and four missions (a total of 180 members) as follows: Chortitz (1952, 43), Evangelical (Kleine Gemeinde 1954, 50), C.G.C. (15), and Rudnerweide. The G.C.M. group also operates the St. Vital Mission in North Winnipeg, begun as a Sunday school in 1947.

The Mennonite Brethren and General Conference Mennonites have both developed educational institutions in Winnipeg. The M.B. have the M.B. Bible College (est. 1944 on the north side at 77 Kelvin St.) and the near-by M.B. Collegiate Institute (1945). The G.C.M. have the Canadian Mennonite Bible College (est. 1947) on the far south side in Tuxedo at 600 University Boulevard East, and Mennonite Educational Institute (1958). Other charitable institutions (all GCM) include Concordia Hospital (est. 1929), an 80-bed institution, Bethania Home for the Aged and Infirm with 84 beds (est. 1946 on 108 acres 11 miles north of Winnipeg), Ebenezer Girls' Home (est. 1926). The Christian Press, an M.B. publishing agency, publisher of the *Mennonitische Rundschau,* with a bookstore, was established by Herman Neufeld in 1923, and taken over in 1945 by a board which is partly conference controlled.

Mennonites also own and operate many private business institutions, a few of which follow. The Konrad Conservatory of Music, operating under this name since 1950, employs 17 teachers and has about 300 students in instrumental and vocal music and music theory, of whom about 65 are Mennonites. C. A. DeFehr and Sons, Ltd. (est. 1925), with a branch of equal size in Edmonton, Alberta, is a wholesale distributor for larger appliances, small implements, heating units, and fuel, with about 2,000 dealers. Monarch Machinery Co., Ltd. (est. by J. J. Klassen in 1935) has a turnover of over $1,000,000, and engages over 100 employees in the manufacture of pumps and farm equipment. John Martens & Co., Ltd. (est. in 1947), a wholesale sporting goods company, has 11 employees and a turnover of about $500,000. C. Huebert Lumber Co., Ltd., reached a peak turnover of about $900,000, but since 1952 the owner has gone over into the fiberboard manufacturing business.   D. JA.

G. Lohrenz, "The Mennonites in Winnipeg," *Menn. Life* VI (1951) 16-25; J. H. Enns, "Winnipeg, Manitoba," *Menn. Life* XI (July 1956).

Winnipeg City Mission of the Mennonite Brethren Church had its beginning when John Warkentin of Winkler, Man., presented a report to the Canadian M.B. Conference about the Mennonite Brethren and Baptists residing in Winnipeg who had no church affiliation. In 1913 the Conference stationed W. J. Bestvater as its first city missionary in Winnipeg. A small church building was purchased, but as the work grew, larger meeting places were provided. After Bestvater, the following served as missionaries: E. H. Nickel 1921-25; C. N. Hiebert 1925-41, and William Falk 1941- . The work has reached every section of the city. The Mary-Martha Home (*q.v.*) is also a branch of this mission.   G.D.H.

Winnipeg (Man.) E.M.B. Church, called Christian Fellowship Chapel, was started in 1943. In 1957 it had 76 members, with John Eveland as pastor. Its meetinghouse was built in 1945.   H.S.B.

Winnipeg (Man.) German Bible School was conducted in the basement of the North End Mennonite Brethren Church (now called Elmwood M.B. Church) 1931-44. It was an evening school conducted for Mennonites working in the city. No academic subjects were taught. The student body, mostly girls, varied from 12 to 30. The chief teachers were A. B. Peters and F. C. Thiessen.   F.C.P.

Winnipeg South End Mennonite Brethren Church, Winnipeg, Man., was organized in 1936 with 90 members, under the leadership of P. Kornelsen, to serve members living in the south part of the city. The present meetinghouse was purchased from another denomination. In 1958 the congregation had 554 members, with J. P. Neufeld as leader and minister. A former minister was H. H. Janzen, widely known in American and European Mennonite circles.   H.H.R.

Winnoxbergen, (Sint), a village in West Flanders, Belgium, where there was some Anabaptist activity *c*1565. Jan (*q.v.*) Portier preached here for a large number of Anabaptists and once administered baptism. Of a congregation in this village, however, nothing is known. Wouter Wychelssone, an otherwise unknown Mennonite, was arrested here in May 1591. (Verheyden, "Mennisme in Vlaanderen," ms.)   vDZ.

Winschoten: see Midwolda, also **Winschoten** in Supplement.

Winston Mennonite Church (MC), Roseburg, Ore., established in 1955, had 18 members in 1957, with Roy E. Hostetler as pastor.   M.G.

Winsum, a village in the Dutch province of Groningen. Leenaert (*q.v.*) Bouwens baptized 7 persons

here in 1554-56. At this time or soon after a Mennonite congregation may have been founded, which later belonged to the Flemish branch. For further particulars see **Obergum,** a twin town of Winsum. The congregation was sometimes called Winsum and sometimes Obergum. (*Inv. Arch. Amst.* II, Nos. 1841, 1843.)   vDZ.

Winter, Diebold, an Anabaptist preacher of Wissembourg in Alsace, an outstanding participant in the disputation of Pfeddersheim (*q.v.*) in 1557 and at Frankenthal (*q.v.*) 14 years later. He is apparently identical with Elder Theobald, who argued with Farwendel (*q.v.*) on the question of original sin.

Beck, *Geschichts-Bücher,* 226; A. Brons, *Ursprung, Entwicklung und Schicksale der . . . Mennoniten* (Emden, 1912) 180; Chr. Hege, *Die Täufer in der Kurpfalz* (Frankfurt, 1908) III; *ML* IV.

Winter, Hendrik de (Amsterdam, 1717-after 1782), artist and art dealer, made the etchings of baptism, communion, and footwashing found in Schijn-Maatschoen, *Geschiedenis* I (Amsterdam, 1743). vDZ.

Thieme-Becker, *Allg. Lexikon für bildenden Künstler* XXXVI (1947) 76.

Winter, Valentin, leader (*Vorsteher*) of the Hutterian Brethren, chosen to the office on Feb. 22, 1622, at Pausram, d. Nov. 29, 1631, having led the brotherhood with skill and faithfulness for ten years. He is the author of the song, "Von Gottes Lieb und Fürsorg viel." (Wolkan, *Geschicht-Buch,* 601 f.; Wolkan, *Lieder,* 242; *ML* IV.)

Winter, Vitus Anton, pastor of the St. Jacobs church and professor in the Ludwigs Maximilian University at Landshut, Bavaria, Germany, author of *Geschichte der bairischen Wiedertäufer im 16. Jahrhundert* (Munich, 1809). This book attempts a treatment of Bavarian Anabaptist history on the basis of the sources, but actually offers little. Of value is only some information on Anabaptist leaders like Augustin Würzelburger and Georg Wagner and on the terrible persecution and suppression of the Anabaptist movement by the Bavarian dukes. The documents given at the end of the book are also valuable. (*ML* IV.)   NEFF.

Winter, Wolfgang: see **Wimmer, Wolfgang.**

Winter Bible Schools, formerly called "short term" or "special term Bible schools," are organized adult education programs of two to six weeks' duration held on the campus of church high schools or colleges, or in local congregations at the meetinghouse, and relatively unique to the Mennonite Church (MC) in North America. The schools usually have no educational requirements for admission, and credits are not usually transferable, although sometimes credit is given by church high schools. These schools flourished largely in 1920-40, at a time when the Mennonite population was still predominantly rural, and when many young people did not go to high school or college. At the peak, in 1939, the combined attendance was about 2,000. Since then attendance has declined greatly.

The first Winter Bible School was held at Elkhart Institute (later Goshen College) in 1900 for a

4-weeks' term. It soon became a 6-weeks' school, held in January-February, and was not finally discontinued until 1954. The second school was the Ontario Mennonite Bible School (q.v.), established in 1907 at the First Mennonite Church in Kitchener, Ont., and still in operation. In 1929 the term was lengthened to 12 weeks, and in 1951 an additional 5-months' course was established under a separate board but in the same quarters, called the Ontario Mennonite Bible Institute (q.v.). The third school, established at Hesston College, Hesston, Kan., in 1909, and the fourth, established at Eastern Mennonite College, Harrisonburg, Va., in 1917 (preliminary terms in 1915 at Alexandria, Va., and in 1916 at Harrisonburg) are still operating. The Johnstown (Pa.) Bible School operated 1922-56, and the Canton (Ohio) Bible School 1913-55 (with omissions). The Alberta-Saskatchewan school at Carstairs, Alberta, begun in 1935, is still operating.

In conference districts in which the constituency is scattered, migratory winter Bible schools were developed which held sessions at various places in the conference district, either from year to year or within the same year. Four conference districts developed such migratory winter Bible schools— Dakota-Montana, now North Central; Pacific Coast; Ontario Amish Mennonite; and Alberta-Saskatchewan.

Many local congregations began to sponsor winter Bible schools. These were usually not held longer than 2 or 3 weeks. Attempts at this type of school were made as early as 1914, but it was not until 1930 that these schools became successful. The Amish Mennonite Church near Allensville, Pa., conducted a 3-week school, Feb. 2-20, 1914, under the name of Big Valley Bible School. The next session was held in 1924. Another session was in 1927. The work was revived in 1933 and continued without interruption to 1948. Similar schools were conducted in 1930-36 in the churches around Kalona and Wayland, Iowa. Winter Bible schools have been held at various times since 1930 at the Central church near Archbold, Ohio; Bowne church, Clarksville, Mich.; Midland church, Midland, Mich.; Leo church, Leo, Ind.; Creston church, Creston, Mont.; Maple Grove Amish Mennonite church near Atglen, Pa.; Howard-Miami church, Kokomo, Ind.; Fairview church, Fairview, Mich.; Zion church, Hubbard, Ore.; Berea church, Montgomery, Ind.; Shore church near Shipshewana, Ind., and others.

In 1939 winter Bible schools were begun in the Lancaster Conference District in Eastern Pennsylvania. An evening version of the winter Bible school became quite successful in the Franconia Conference District; although it originated in Franconia as early as 1932, it did not begin to reach its greatest strength until 1940-41, when the evening winter Bible school classes in seven Franconia churches had a combined enrollment of over 1,000.

Most of the 6-weeks' winter Bible schools added special courses for ministers, and a number established a Ministers' Week. In 1940 the Winter Bible School Council was established under the General Educational Council of the Mennonite Board of Education to aid in strengthening and promoting the winter Bible school work.

Without doubt the winter Bible schools have been of great value in Bible teaching and spiritual edification and inspiration; in a sense they took over the function which the congregational Bible conferences had earlier filled. In the 1950's it was becoming clear that their day was past in many parts of the church, although they were still filling a need in some areas. P.M.L., H.S.B.

Clarence Fretz, "A History of Winter Bible Schools in the Mennonite Church," MQR XVI (1942) 51-81, and 178-95; P. M. Lederach, "A History of Religious Education in the Mennonite Church" (unpublished doctoral dissertation, Southwestern Baptist Theological Seminary, 1949).

Winterfeld, Karl von (1784-1852), a jurist who distinguished himself by several works on church music, including *Zur Geschichte heiliger Tonkunst,* a series of articles published in two volumes (Leipzig, 1850-52). In the second volume he devotes a very interesting chapter to the hymns of the Anabaptists in the 16th century, analyzing with complete objectivity a hymnbook of 1570 which came into his hands in the Royal Library in Munich, titled, *Ein schon Gesangbüchlein geistlicher Lieder* (see **Hymnology**). Historically this work has been superseded by Rudolf Wolkan's *Lieder der Wiedertäufer* (Berlin, 1903). It nevertheless is to Winterfeld's credit that he pointed out the uniqueness and significance of Anabaptist songs 50 years earlier than Wolkan. (*ML IV.*) NEFF.

Winterswijk, a town in the Dutch province of Gelderland (pop. *c*23,000 with *c*120 Mennonites), seat of a Mennonite congregation, concerning whose origin there is no exact information. F. C. Fleischer suggests that Mennonites living at Winterswijk and surroundings because of persecution crossed the border to adjacent Westphalia, Germany, as early as 1543, and settled in Bocholt (q.v.) and other Westphalian towns until they were expelled by a mandate of the bishop of Münster *c*1610. Then some Mennonites, including the Waliën (q.v.) and Willink (q.v.) families, settled in Winterswijk. A note in the old Winterswijk church book says that Mennonite meetings started in 1611 in the home of Hindrick Waliën at Winterswijk. At least in 1638 there was a Mennonite congregation here, whose membership until the middle of the 19th century was very small, seldom surpassing 30 members. This congregation in the 17th and 18th centuries was called Waterlander, which means simply that it was rather liberal. Whether there was also a second (Flemish?) church at Winterswijk is questionable. A meetinghouse, still in use, was built in 1711 after meetings had been held for a century in the Waliën home.

Mennonite families found at Winterswijk in the 18th century were ten Broeke, ten Cate, Coenders, Coster, Dekkers, Eppenhof(f), Hoedemaker, Hofkes, Nieuwenhuys, Waliën (Walyen), Wenkelaar, and Willink, soon after also van Lochem and Paschen. Nearly all these families died out or moved elsewhere in the 19th century or earlier, only the Paschen and Willink families being found here until recent times. Most members of the Winterswijk congregation, nearly all engaged in business and manufacturing, particularly textiles, iron, and brickyards, were well-to-do in the 18th century. In 1733 and 1736 they contributed 150 and 95 guilders for relief of the Prussian Mennonites.

At first the congregation was served by a preacher chosen from the membership. Harmen Eppenhof, the last of these untrained and unsalaried ministers, served until d.1693. From 1700 the church was served by preachers who received some salary and had some training for the ministry, but had no university or seminary education. The first pastor of Winterswijk trained at the Amsterdam seminary was Pieter van Delden, serving 1786-1800. He was succeeded by A. R. Fink, a former Lutheran pastor, 1802-34, G. H. van Velsen Coster 1836-65, A. Snellen 1867-74, S. Lulofs 1875-77, P. E. Lugt 1878-1908, F. C. Fleischer 1909-24, C. C. de Maar 1925-40, and Miss J. M. Eelman 1942-55. Since 1956 the congregation has been served by the pastor of Zutphen (*q.v.*). The baptized membership, numbering 24 in 1746, was *c*40 in 1800, 13 in 1847, 19 in 1861, 45 in 1900, 63 in 1926, 76 in 1940, and 150 in 1958. The members live at Winterswijk and surrounding towns.

Until 1786 the deacons, sometimes called directors, always two, were chosen from the married men. After 1786 unmarried men were also eligible. From 1825 until *c*1920 there was usually only one deacon, who served for many years. Church activities now (1958) are a ladies' circle and a Sunday school for children.   vDZ.

F. C. Fleischer, *De Doopsgezinde gemeente te Winterswijk* (n.p., 1911); *Inv. Arch. Amst.* II, Nos 2344-46; *Naamlijst* 1804, 69; *DB* 1909, 172; Blaupot t. C., *Holland* II, 49, 205, 233.

Winton Church of God in Christ Mennonite Church, located just east of Winton, Cal., had its beginning in 1911, when the first 12 members assembled in a barn for worship services. The first church building was erected in 1912. It was replaced by larger buildings in 1917, 1926, and 1945. The present building has a seating capacity of 800. The ministers in 1957 were Edward Jantz, John Wiens, D. H. Dyck, John Esau, and A. T. Koehn; the membership was 290.
                                                  N.K.

Winton Mennonite Brethren Church, located at Winton, Cal., was organized in 1922 under the leadership of J. M. Enns. The membership in 1957 was 51, with Menno A. Shellenberg as pastor. In 1958 the church moved to Atwater.   M.A.S.

Winton Mennonite Church (MC): see **Sharon** Mennonite Church.

Wipf, an old Hutterite family, probably of Swiss origin. We do not know when the Wipfs joined the brotherhood and how they happened to settle in Alwinz (*q.v.*), Transylvania. Perhaps they went there with the first settlers in 1621. In any case in 1694 one Michael Wipf was made Vorsteher (bishop) in Alwinz, though he was not particularly successful. The Wipfs of today are probably not descended from this man but from another Wipf, whose widow Annele together with her five children belonged to the few surviving "old Hutterites" in Transylvania prior to the coming of the Carinthians in 1756. She is expressly named by Johannes Waldner, the author of the *Klein-Geschichtsbuch*.

She and the children then went to Russia with the rest of the group. A Jakob Wipf was "the teacher" *c*1853. At that time a group of Hutterites led by Peter Hofer (see **Hofer**) and Jakob Wipf separated from the Hutterthal colony to start a new settlement, Johannesruh, named after Johann Cornies (*q.v.*). Jakob Wipf must have been a very alert and intelligent leader; he had attended the Mennonite Zentralschule at Halbstadt, Molotschna, and received a teacher's license. In 1864, when this group experimented for a few years with the re-establishment of communal living, it became known as the "Lehrerleut" (*q.v.*), since Wipf was a teacher and was generally known as Jakob Lehrer. In 1874 the great exodus from Russia began, but at first only the Dariusleut (*q.v.*) and the Schmiedeleut (*q.v.*) went to America, settling in South Dakota. In 1875-76 two Brethren from the Bon Homme colony, S.D., went back to Russia to encourage the Lehrerleut, led by Jakob Wipf and Peter Hofer, to come to America and to re-establish there their former community of goods. This they did. In 1877 Wipf, Hofer, and 13 other families migrated and established a colony at Old Elmspring, near Alexandria, S.D., (later near Parkston), thus establishing the third Hutterite Bruderhof in America. Jakob Wipf was its Vorsteher until his death in 1896. A number of Wipfs, however, broke away from this communal living and settled in and around Freeman, S.D., becoming known as the "Prairie Leut." They joined other Mennonite groups. (Zieglschmid, *Klein-Geschichtsbuch,* 228, 257.)   R.F.

Wirdum, a hamlet in East Friesland, Germany. Leenaert (*q.v.*) Bouwens baptized three persons here in 1551-54 and 28 in 1563-65. It is not known that there was a congregation at Wirdum; they may have joined the congregation soon after called Emsigerland (*q.v.*).

Wirdum, a village six miles south of Leeuwarden in the Dutch province of Friesland, where Leenaert (*q.v.*) Bouwens baptized at least 365 persons in 1551-82. There was, however, no Mennonite congregation at Wirdum. The converts probably joined the church of Leeuwarden (*q.v.*) or some other neighboring congregation.   vDZ.

Wisconsin, a midwestern state north of Illinois, has an area of 56,154 sq. mi. and in 1956 had a population of 3,764,000. It is the leading dairy state, ranking first in the nation in the production of milk and cheese and second in butter. The first Mennonites in the state were several Amish families who moved into Sawyer County (*q.v.*), in the northwestern part of the state, in 1909, the Bontreger family in the following year, and later 15 other families, settling near Exeland. The congregation, now extinct, was last listed in the 1927 *Mennonite Yearbook.* A second O.O.A. settlement in near-by Rusk County was listed in the Yearbook 1922-34, under the addresses of Glen Flora and Ingram. A third O.O.A. settlement was listed for the first time in 1934 at Medford, Taylor Co., a town about 35 miles southeast of Glen Flora. William M. Miller, an Amish bishop from Haven, Kan., was living here by 1925, and Joseph Y. Lehman, a minister, by 1930 or earlier. In 1950 the membership of this group had reached 94, and the settlement was divided into two districts, the North Side and the South Side, very likely in 1951. The South Side spills over into Clark County and has Curtiss for its address.

The Mennonite Church (MC) has three organized and two unorganized congregations in Wisconsin. Mission activity began in the area southeast of Exeland (q.v.) in 1929, but a congregation was not organized until 1954. The membership in 1957 was 24. The largest of the five congregations is Sheldon (q.v.) in Rusk County. Mission activity was started in the area in 1932 and a church organized in 1936. Its 1957 membership was 73. South Lawrence (q.v.) at Glen Flora was started in 1946 and in 1957 had a membership of 26. The two unorganized congregations are at Loyal and Hayward, both in northwestern Wisconsin. The total Amish and Mennonite membership for Wisconsin in 1958 was approximately 225.

During the years of Civilian Public Service Mennonite young men served in dairy units in the southern half of Wisconsin. By the summer of 1943 Dodge, Fond du Lac, Green, Dane, and Outagamie counties had 20 assignees each. Other Mennonite CO's served in the Southern Wisconsin Colony and Training School for the feeble-minded, at Union Grove (q.v.), and in the Winnebago (q.v.) State Hospital, a phychiatric hospital. M.G.

Wisler (Whisler, Whistler), a Mennonite family, found in the Emmental, Switzerland. Some emigrated to the Palatinate, Germany, where Heinrich Wissler was a preacher of the Erpolzheim-Friedelsheim congregation 1762-c90, and Johann Wissler (Wiesler) preacher of the Ruchheim congregation from 1775, elder 1790-after 1802. From Switzerland or the Palatinate the family came to America, now occurring most frequently in the Deep Run area of Bucks County, Pa., in Mahoning-Columbiana counties of eastern Ohio, and in Elkhart County, Ind. For Mennonite history the most significant branch of the family goes back to Christian Wisler (d. 1830), who did service in the Revolutionary War and married Susan Holdeman (1774-1838) of Bucks County. They were probably affiliated with the Deep Run Mennonite Church after marriage. Christian and Susan were the parents of eleven children. About 1820 the family removed to Columbiana County, Ohio, settling in the portion that became Mahoning County in 1846. Susan is buried in the Midway cemetery. Three of the children moved to Elkhart County: John Wisler (1800-90), Jacob Wisler (1808-89), ordained preacher at the Oberholtzer church (now Midway) in 1833, and bishop at the Yellow Creek church in Elkhart County in 1851; and Susanna Wisler (b. 1813), who married Henry Yoder. Bishop Jacob Wisler (q.v.) founded the Old Order Mennonite Church in Indiana and Ohio in 1872. Contrary to the beliefs of the family in Elkhart County, there seems to be no close connection between this family and that of the Quaker artist, James Whistler (1834-1903), who was born in Massachusetts, the son of Major George Washington Whistler. One of Bishop Jacob Wisler's sons, John

H., changed his name to Whisler; he was the father of Jonas L. Whisler (b. 1872), proprietor of Whisler Brand Meat Products, Goshen, Ind. J.C.W.

Wisler, Jacob (1808-89), founder of the Old Order Mennonites (q.v.), was born in Bucks County, Pa., on Oct. 31, 1808, the eighth child of Christian Wisler and Susan Holdeman. He moved with his parents to Columbiana County, Ohio, about 1820. There on Nov. 19, 1827, he married Mary Hoover (1808-60). To this union were born at least seven children, including David (1830-1902), a deacon. In 1833 Jacob was ordained to the ministry in the Midway Mennonite (MC) Church (q.v.) near North Lima, Ohio, almost certainly by Bishop Jacob Nold. In 1848 he and his family moved to Elkhart County, Ind., and settled on a farm one mile north of the present Yellow Creek church (q.v.) and two and three-fourths miles west. His second wife was Catherine Knopp; this union was childless. In 1851 Abraham Rohrer, a bishop of Medina County, Ohio, who had ordained Martin Hoover (d. 1850 at the age of 89) bishop just before he came to Elkhart County in 1845, came to Yellow Creek and ordained Wisler as his successor. Wisler's conservative attitudes caused Joseph Rohrer, a fellow minister, to leave the Mennonite Church and unite with the Evangelical Church. Wisler also had difficulty with Joseph Holdeman, a deacon of the near-by Holdeman (q.v.) congregation. Much more serious were his differences with Daniel Brenneman (q.v.), a preacher of Fairfield County, Ohio, who settled in Elkhart County in 1864. Vain efforts were made annually in 1867-71 to effect permanent peace among the ministers of western Elkhart County (considered as one bishop district west of Goshen), but Wisler was unwilling to accept the Sunday school and similar new institutions and practices. Following a decision against Wisler by an outside committee of six bishops to suspend his bishop office, John F. Funk (q.v.), on behalf of the majority of the ministers, on Jan. 6, 1872, announced that Wisler and his followers were no longer members of the church. Thereupon Wisler led a schism, establishing a continuing Yellow Creek congregation which came to be called the Old Order Mennonite Church. He was followed by similarly minded "old order" groups near Wadsworth, Orrville, and North Lima, Ohio. Wisler died on May 1, 1889, and was buried in the old Mennonite cemetery across the road from the Wisler Yellow Creek (frame) meetinghouse. Christian Shaum, Wisler's assistant bishop, and Martin A. Hoover preached at his funeral service.

A number of efforts toward healing the Wisler schism were made in 1872-89, but Wisler always felt that he and his group were a happy fellowship, much closer to the old Mennonite practices and attitudes than were the "Funk" Mennonites (MC), and that therefore there was no reason to attempt a reunion. If the more progressive group wished to return to the old ways and drop the Sunday school, they could join the congregation in which he had been a preacher since 1848 and a bishop since 1851. J.C.W.

Wisler Mennonites in Ontario. In 1917 the ultra-conservative element of Old Order Mennonites (*q.v.*) in Ontario (*q.v.*), located in Woolwich and Wellesley townships, Waterloo County, separated from the main body under the leadership of Deacon David W. Martin. They have practiced very exacting conservative methods. From a small number of families at first the group has grown to a membership of 116, in 1954, with three churches—Wellesley near Wallenstein, Martins near Hawkesville, and Conestoga near St. Jacobs. The group is not affiliated with any conference. At first they chose Daniel M. Brubacher as bishop. In 1920 a schism on the question of the ban gave rise to the Brubacher group and the Martin group. In 1921 Enoch Horst was chosen bishop of the Martin group. In 1924 Horst left the Martin group and has stood alone. In 1925 David W. Martin became bishop of the Martin group. The Brubacher group has practically lost out. In 1957 the ministers were Manasseh M. Frey, Martin B. Frey, and Elam Martin.   J.C.F.

L. J. Burkholder, *Brief History of Mennonites in Ontario* (Toronto, 1935) 200, 208-9.

Wislerites: see Old Order Mennonites.

Wismar Resolutions, called in Dutch *Besluyt tot Wismar,* also *Bespreck van Wismar,* were the result of a conference of Mennonite elders held in 1554 at Wismar in Mecklenburg, Germany. Present were (according to Vos) Menno (*q.v.*) Simons, who was then living in Wismar, Dirk (*q.v.*) Philips, Leenaert (*q.v.*) Bouwens, Gillis van Aken (*q.v.*), Herman (*q.v.*) van Tielt, Hans Busschaert (*q.v.*), and Hoyte (*q.v.*) Riencx. The *Besluyt tot Wismar* contains nine articles. The first five articles deal with shunning or avoidance (ban). Article 6 deals with the question of young believers needing the approbation of their elders for getting married. Article 7, which is not quite clear, deals with the right of believers to invoke the aid of a worldly court. Article 8 treats the subject of bearing arms; this article also is not very clear but it seems that the elders at Wismar did not profess absolute nonresistance. Article 9 states that only a person who is ordained by a congregation or an elder may teach and admonish, i.e., function as a preacher in a congregation.

The *Besluyt tot Wismar* was printed several times. It appears at the end of Menno's *Een lieffelijcke vermaninghe van dat schouwen der valscher broederen* (Harlingen, likely 1576), in the *Successio Anabaptistica* of 1603 (reprinted *BRN* VII, 51-53), and in *Grouwelen der Hooft-ketteren* (Leiden, 1623). It is also found in Blaupot t. C., *Groningen* I, 252-54, and Vos, *Menno Simons* (Leiden, 1914) 123-27. The first three articles are in *Het Brilleken* (Haarlem, 1630). (*ML* IV, 548-50.)   vnZ.

Wissel, van der, a Dutch Mennonite family at least from the 17th century found in the Lamist (*q.v.*) church at Amsterdam, from the 18th century at Vlissingen, Zierikzee and other congregations, in the first generations all businessmen, from the 19th century also physicians. Two members of this family went into the ministry. Anthonie van der Wissel (b.1862 at Amsterdam, d.1951 at Bilthoven) studied theology at the Amsterdam university and Mennonite seminary and was a Mennonite pastor of Tjalleberd 1889-90 and Drachten-Ureterp 1890-1903. From 1903 until 1925 he served as pastor of a group of liberal Reformed at Leiden.

His son Felix van der Wissel, b. 1892 at Amsterdam, studied theology at the Amsterdam university and the Mennonite seminary, was afterwards a teacher in primary schools and served as a pastor at Aardenburg 1927-32, Kampen 1932-37, and Leeuwarden 1937-57. He was the chairman of the Dutch Mennonite Peace Group (Doopsgezinde—*q.v.*—Vredesgroep) 1947-56. He published *Verlossing* (Assen, 1936), *Evangelie en Oorlog,* three sermons (Leeuwarden, 1945), *Perspectief,* seven sermons (Leeuwarden, 1956), *Ondogmatische Geloofsbeschouwingen* (Lochem, 1958), and a number of papers in *Nieuw Theologisch Tijdschrift, Algemeen Doopsgezind Weekblad,* and *Stemmen uit de Doopsgezinde Broederschap.*   vnZ.

Wis(s)mer, a Mennonite family of German descent in America. The first of them to emigrate to America was Jacob Wismer (1684-1787), who moved to Carolina in 1710, where he nearly lost his life in an Indian raid. Shortly after 1720 he settled as the first Mennonite in Bucks County, Pa., living in what is now Bedminster Township, where he died at the age of 102. There have been a large number of Wismer leaders of the church: Wenger lists for the Franconia (*q.v.*) Conference one bishop: Abraham Wismer (1797-1877), ordained preacher at Skippack 1838, bishop in 1852; three preachers: Abraham Wismer (1746-1823) at Deep Run, Henry K. Wismer (1823-1910) in the Skippack church, and Enos Wismer (1868-1951), of Deep Run; and two deacons: Abraham Wismer (1791-1859) of Plumstead Township, who also left some historical papers, and Benjamin Wismer (1856-1934) of the Skippack congregation. After 1800 some Wismers moved from the Franconia region to Waterloo in Ontario, among them Daniel Wismer (1820-1909), a bishop in the Waterloo congregation (MC) and in Marion County, Kan. Henry and Christian Wismer joined the Brethren (*q.v.*) in Christ (River Brethren), the latter *c*1860.   vnZ.

A. J. Fretz, *A Brief History of Jacob Wismer and a Complete Genealogical Family Register* (Elkhart, 1893) 294 *et passim;* Daniel Kauffman, *Menn. Cyclopedic Dictionary,* 397 f.

Wiszowaty, Andreas (1608-78), a Unitarian theologian, great-grandson of Fausto Sozzini (*q.v.*), studied in Leiden, Holland, in 1631, served the Unitarian church in Poland until he was expelled in 1658, traveled in Hungary, lived at Mannheim, Germany, 1663-66, and from then until his death in Amsterdam. He is said to have published 62 writings, some of which influenced the Dutch Mennonites. Wiszowaty also co-operated in the revision of the Rakow (*q.v.*) catechism.

In the early 18th century a Wiszowaty family, four sisters, probably great-granddaughters of Andreas, were baptized into the Amsterdam Zonist (*q.v.*) congregation, in 1713, 1716(?), 1718, and 1721.   vnZ.

W. J. Kühler, *Het Socinianisme in Nederland* (Leiden, 1912) 229 f., 236 ff.; church records of Amsterdam.

Wit, de, a common Dutch Mennonite family name, with a number of unrelated branches. A Mennonite de Wit family is found at Wieringen, where Jan Jansz de Wit was a lay preacher in the Frisian congregation 1736-40(?) and his brother Simon Jansz de Wit 1736-43; in 1743 he resigned, serving from then until his death in 1784 as a deacon. Many of their descendants were deacons at Wieringen until recent times. Willem de Wit, concerning whom there is no information except that he was a man of great ability and eloquence, was a preacher of the Waterlander congregation at Haarlem c1660. G. de Wit was a preacher at Utrecht 1714-29. In Alkmaar a de Wit family is mentioned from 1682. Jan Jansz de Wit was a minister of the Alkmaar Frisian congregation 1715-d.29. Some de Wits also served here as deacons, among whom was Jan de Wit Dzn, 1898-1927. Jan Cornelisz de Wit (de Witte) was an untrained preacher at Oostgraftdijk at least 1714-16, at Texel 1716-18, and Vlissingen 1718-c26. In Enkhuizen, den Helder, Zaandam, and Hoorn there were also deacons by the name of de Wit. vDZ.

Inv. Arch. Amst. II, 1612, 1625-28; *DB* 1863, 138; 1875, 35; 1891, 9, 10, 47, 49, 57 ff.; 1910, 119; (J. de Lange CJzn), *Beknopte Geschiedenis der Doopsgez. gemeente te Alkmaar* (n.p., n.d.-1927) 39, 70, 91, 157, 160, 161, 163; (H. B. Berghuys), *Geschiedenis der Doopsgez. gemeente te Utrecht* (n.p., n.d.-1926) 47; Blaupot t. C., *Holland* I, 38; *De Zondagsbode* XL (1926-27) No. 3.

Witmarsum, a village in the Dutch province of Friesland, the birthplace of Menno Simons. (*q.v.*). Menno was a Catholic pastor here from 1531 until he withdrew from the Catholic Church, probably on Jan. 30, 1536. According to a local tradition, Menno lived at Witmarsum for some time after his withdrawal, preaching the Gospel to his adherents in a house outside the town. This tradition is, however, probably in error, for the Court of Friesland and the Stadholder were very alert for heresy: as early as 1527, before Menno was in Witmarsum, a search for heretical books was made in the parsonage. And in the fall of 1536, when Menno secretly visited Witmarsum, the Stadholder of Friesland immediately had his hosts arrested. Thus it must be assumed that after leaving the Catholic Church Menno left Witmarsum at once.

Whether Menno left a Mennonite congregation at Witmarsum or not is an open question. At any rate, there was such a congregation here by 1560. Leenaert (*q.v.*) Bouwens baptized five (possibly eight) persons at Witmarsum in 1557-61 and another five in 1563-65. Concerning the early history of the congregation there is only one bit of information. It was more or less united (complete union not before 1823) with the neighboring Pingjum (*q.v.*) congregation, and in the 17th century Pingjum seems to have been the more important part of the union. In the 17th and 18th centuries the church was called Waterlander and Flemish, but this obviously does not mean that it was formed by a Waterlander and a Flemish congregation, but simply that it held the progressive Lamist (*q.v.*) views of the united Flemish-Waterlander church of Amsterdam. In 1695 Witmarsum joined the newly founded Sociëteit (conference) of Friesland; at this time it numbered

about 25 baptized members. Membership figures of the 18th century are not available; in 1828 there were less than 20 members; from then the figures are always those of Pingjum and Witmarsum together: 54 in 1861, 80 in 1900, 48 in 1958.

Until 1877 services at Witmarsum were held in a very simple meetinghouse called the Menno Simons House, because according to the (incorrect) tradition Menno lived or preached here. This meetinghouse was remodeled in 1828 (engraving of this old meetinghouse by Dirk Sluyter c1828). The last service was held here on Dec. 9, 1877, and the next Sunday a new church in town was dedicated, which is still in use. It was equipped with an organ in 1881 and thoroughly renovated in 1887.

Until 1794 the congregation was served by untrained and unsalaried ministers, chosen from the membership, and later by untrained ministers from abroad who received some salary. The first minister educated at the Amsterdam Theological Seminary to serve the Witmarsum-Pingjum congregations was C. Corver 1859-63, followed by S. G. Binnerts 1863-70, J. Sepp 1871-73, P. Feenstra Jr. 1873-81, B. Haga 1882-88, P. A. Vis 1889-91, P. Ens 1899-1903, H. Westra 1904-7, J. E. van Brakel 1908-14, A. A. Sepp 1914-18, Alb. Vis 1919-22, P. J. Smidts 1923-27, W. F. Golterman 1933-36, H. P. Tulner 1936-39, A. H. van Drooge 1940-46, and Miss S. E. Doyer 1946-57. Since 1933 the pastor also served the Makkum congregation (the pastors Golterman and van Drooge lived at Makkum, Tulner and Doyer at Witmarsum). Since 1957 the Makkum, Witmarsum, and Pingjum congregations are served together by the pastor of Bolsward (*q.v.*).

Church activities are a ladies' circle and youth group "Menniste Bouwers." On the site of the old meetinghouse a monument was erected to Menno Simons, dedicated on Sept. 11, 1879, by P. Cool, retired pastor of Harlingen. vDZ.

Inv. Arch. Amst. I, No. 2; II, No. 2347; II, 2, No. 651; K. Vos, *Menno Simons* (Leiden, 1914) 52, 230; Blaupot t. C., *Friesland*, 56, 89, 188, 205, 245, 254, 306; *Naamlijst* 1829, 46; *DB* 1878, 132; 1880, 164; 1888, 148; 1916, 81 f.; P. Cool and P. Feenstra Jr., *Gedenkschrift van het Menno-Simons-Monument* (Zwolle, 1879).

Witmarsum, the central one of the three (the other two Gnadenthal and Waldheim) civil districts (villages) into which the Krauel (*q.v.*) Mennonite Colony in the state of Santa Catarina, Brazil (*q.v.*), founded in February 1930, was divided. Witmarsum can be considered the capital of the Krauel Colony since it was the seat of the co-operative store (Cooperacion Agricola Witmarsum), the Zentralschule (each village had an elementary school), the hospital (est. 1935, new building 1937), the creamery, and the starch factory; there was, however, no central seat of government. Each village had its own Schulze, while the Oberschulze or mayor of the entire settlement continued to live on his own farm in his home village. David Nikkel, the Oberschulze during most of the Krauel Colony history, did not live in Witmarsum. The two churches in the Krauel Colony, the Witmarsum Mennonite Church and Witmarsum Mennonite Brethren Church, first worshiped in the school buildings. In 1948 the M.B.

meetinghouse was built in Witmarsum; of the two Mennonite meetinghouses, the main one was built in Witmarsum in 1950.

The economic enterprises in Witmarsum consisted of two milk assembly and separating plants, a slaughterhouse and equipment, a large starch factory, two sawmills, a feed and flour mill, an electric generating plant, the colony co-operative store and all equipment. There were in addition a number of individually owned services, such as saddlers, shoemakers, blacksmiths, woodworking shops, and a small leather goods factory.

Witmarsum originally had 70 of the 150 Krauel families. By 1934, the high point in Krauel population, Witmarsum had 341 of the 846 in the entire colony. There was little concentration of Krauel population, since families occupied farm tracts of 40-100 acres scattered along a 12-mile stretch of the 1½ to 2 mile wide Rio Alto Krauel Valley. When the Krauel Colony was dissolved in 1952, Witmarsum also disappeared as a Mennonite settlement. Other settlers moved in, but it is not known whether the name was retained.   H.S.B., H.L.B.

Witmarsum, The, the Bluffton College student news publication, continued from *The College Record* (April 1902-June 1913), first issue October 1913. It has varied in size, format, and periodicity from 6 x 8 in. to 13 x 19 in. and in 1958 to 10¼ x 13½, from 16 to 4 pages (1958), and from biweekly to bimonthly (in 1958 weekly).   D.L.G.

Witmarsum Theological Seminary Bulletin was the organ of the seminary, issued quarterly, 6 x 9 in., variable in length, first issue March 1922, last issue apparently March 1931 (Vol. X, No. 1). The March issue was the annual (or biennial) catalog. For some years the May issue was in the form of a student annual, called *Witmarsum Spirit*. The *Bulletin of the Mennonite Biblical Seminary* in Chicago (first issue October 1945) was intended as a successor to the *Witmarsum Bulletin*, but was erroneously numbered Volume IX.   H.S.B.

Witmarsum Theological Seminary was located at Bluffton, Ohio, 1921-31. It had its beginning in the fall of 1914 as a department of Bluffton College and was known as Mennonite Seminary, but to better serve its constituency it was made an independent institution, and on July 6, 1921, it was reorganized under its own charter, board of trustees, faculty and administrative management, taking the name Witmarsum Theological Seminary.

The board of trustees of the Seminary was made up of two representatives each from six different Mennonite branches in the United States and two representatives of the alumni of the Seminary. This was designed to make the Seminary a unifying agency among the Mennonites in America. The faculty was also made up of men from different branches. The Seminary had students from all these six branches. The groups intended to be represented were the following: G.C.M., M.B., M.C., E.M., M.B.C., and Central Conference. Actually the support was limited largely to the G.C.M. and Central Conference groups.

The faculty consisted of four full-time professors:

J. E. Hartzler, President; Paul Whitmer, Dean; Jacob Quiring, Old Testament; J. A. Huffman, New Testament. The part-time men were N. E. Byers, S. M. Musselman, and others. The part-time professors were either pastors of churches or teachers in Bluffton College. The work of the Seminary was divided into two schools. The Graduate Seminary, open to men and women who had completed the regular college course with the A.B. or equivalent degree, offered a 3-year B.D. course. The second school was the Theological College which required high-school graduation for admission and offered a 4-year Th.B. course. Students came mostly from Bethel and Bluffton colleges, with a few from Goshen and Tabor.

In the Graduate Seminary the work was arranged under nine departments: Old Testament, New Testament, Church History, Systematic Theology, Philosophy of Religion and Religious Education, Homiletics and Practical Theology, History of Religions and Missions, Public Speaking, and Church Music. The Biblical departments had each the services of a full-time professor. In the Theological College the work was a combination of collegiate and theological courses. The Seminary graduated a total of 26 men and 3 women in its 11-year history. The total number of degrees granted from the beginning of the Mennonite Seminary in 1914 was 56, mostly B.D. Some M.A. degrees were granted by Bluffton College for work done in the Seminary. A two-year lower level English Bible course was offered for a time, but enjoyed only a small attendance.

The Seminary had a small endowment of $25,000, but the main support came from five conferences, each of which assumed the support of one chair.

With the coming of the movement for standard theological seminaries and the resulting mergers and affiliations of seminaries to qualify for that rating, Witmarsum Seminary became conscious of the need for changes in its setup. Letters were addressed to a number of well-established seminaries inquiring what opportunity there might be for an affiliation with them. The responses from all the seminaries contacted were generous and eager to enter such a relationship. This was a difficult decision to make. Location, type of teaching, cultural and social differences in these seminaries varied widely. On these points the seminary family differed. No agreement seemed possible; consequently the Witmarsum organization disintegrated and the Seminary closed in May 1931. After 14 years the Seminary reopened in Chicago under a new name and organization but with the help of $11,000 in liquid assets and the library and equipment of Witmarsum Seminary.   P.E.W.

J. E. Hartzler, *Education Among the Mennonites of America* (Danvers, Ill., 1935) 174-79.

Witmer (Widmer, Whitmer), a Mennonite family name found among the Swiss Brethren since 1531. Some bearers fled to the Palatinate c1670 and to France (see **Widmer, Hans,** and **Widmer, Christian**). Among the immigrants of 1717 to Lancaster County, Pa., were Benjamin Witmer and his son Abraham, who four years later bought 265 acres from the London Company. Benjamin's son John had a family of seven children, and his son Benjamin inherited his uncle Abraham's lands; another Abraham built the Bridgeport Bridge at the end of East King Street, Lancaster, in 1798. Included in the Mennonite ministry were the two Abraham Witmers of the Manor, Samuel B. Witmer (1767-1819) of Weaverland, David Witmer (1800-76) of Mellingers congregation, David Witmer of York County, Esaias Witmer (1856-1937) of the Metzler congregation, and Mahlon Witmer, bishop of the New Holland congregation. A branch of the family settled in Columbiana County, Ohio, where I. B. Witmer was long minister (MC) at Leetonia, and from which place Paul E. Whitmer came, who was a teacher and dean at Goshen College, later teacher and dean at Witmarsum Theological Seminary, and G.C.M. minister near Bluffton, Ohio. A branch in Ontario furnished ministers (MC) J. Wesley Witmer at Hespeler, Leslie H. Witmer at Baden, and Robert Witmer, a missionary in Paris, France.   I.D.L.

Paul Peachey, *Die soziale Herkunft der Schweizer Täufer* (Karlsruhe, 1954); D. L. Gratz, *Bernese Anabaptists* (Scottdale, 1953).

Witness of the Word: see Zeugnis der Schrift.

Witte, Jan de, author of *Vrede-schrift daer inne gehandelt wort van de voornaamste verschillen in de Leere en verstanden onder de Doopsghesinde Gemeenten* . . . (Amsterdam, 1638). This writing, dealing with the differences between several branches of the Dutch Mennonites, was published by "a friend of the truth," apparently after the death of de Witte. De Witte also wrote *Sommige Spreucken oft Redenen wt der H. Schrift, Fonteynewijs by een vergadert* . . . (Amsterdam, 1605). Concerning de Witte nothing is known except that he belonged to the Waterlander (*q.v.*) branch. (Kühler, *Geschiedenis* II, 3 f., 33 f., 39, 76.)   vDZ.

Wittenoom, C., a Dutch Mennonite, published *In't rym de twee Sentbrieven Pauli, geschreeven aan die van Romen en d'eerste Sentbrief aan die van Corinthen* . . . (Amsterdam, 1692). He also composed a number of hymns.   vDZ.

Wittgenstein, now a county (pop. 29,264) in the province of North Rhine-Westphalia, in the 18th and 19th centuries a principality ruled by the counts of Sayn-Wittgenstein. For the small Amish Mennonite congregation here, see **Waldeck.**

Witveen, a hamlet in the Dutch province of Friesland, the seat of a Mennonite congregation now called Rottevalle (*q.v.*). The congregation at Witveen was probably founded c1620, when the peat fens (Dutch, *veen*) in this area were broken up. The first peat diggers were mostly Mennonites; at first meetings were held in a peat digger's hut, but in 1671 a plain meetinghouse was erected, which was considerably remodeled and enlarged in 1712. This church had some windows painted with Bible texts and the names of members of the congregation, presumably those who had financed this church. In 1714 Witveen joined the Mennonite conference of Friesland (FDS). It then numbered about 60 baptized members, 108 in 1751, and 120 in 1760. At this time some of the members lived at neighboring Rottevalle, and the congregation, at

first also called Witveen and Oostermeer, was then mostly called Witveen and Rottevalle, or even Rottevalle and Witveen. More and more Rottevalle became the center of the congregation, particularly after a meetinghouse was built here c1770. In 1810 only a small part of the membership lived at Witveen, and in 1830 the Witveen church was put out of use. For further history of the congregation see **Rottevalle.** (*DB* 1872, 33 ff.; Blaupot t. C., *Friesland,* 189, note 9; *DJ* 1840, 22.)   vDZ.

W.M.S.A.: see **Women's Missionary and Service Auxiliary.**

Woerden, a town in the Dutch province of South Holland, formerly the seat of a Waterlander Mennonite congregation. There is no information on the origin of this church and only a few accounts on its history. In 1647 it was represented at the Waterlander delegates' meeting at Amsterdam by the deacon Louris Diricxsz. It disappeared between 1700 and 1730. (Blaupot t. C., *Holland* I, 332; II, 43; *DB* 1907, 78.)   vDZ.

Wohl (Uohll), Wolf, was a Mennonite preacher in Moravia (*q.v.*), who after a visit of Jan Gerrits (*q.v.*) van Emden accompanied him to Danzig and became a preacher of the Danzig congregation, of which Krijn Vermeulen (van der Meulen, *q.v.*) was at this time also a preacher. Vermeulen and Wohl disputed on the doctrine of Incarnation, Vermeulen defending the views of Menno Simons and Dirk Philips, and Wohl rejecting them. Further particulars are lacking. (*BRN* VII, 190 f.)   vDZ.

Wohlgemuth, Daniel (1876—), a son of Johannes Wohlgemuth of Albisheim a.d. Pfrim and Katharina Krehbiel of Weierhof, was born at Albisheim April 17, 1876, but reared by his uncle Johannes Krehbiel of Weierhof, studied art at Frankfurt and Strasbourg, and finally at the Art Academy in Munich under Franz von Stuck. His travels in Italy, Palestine, and Russia contributed to his development. His artistic work was done chiefly in his native Rhenish Hesse and the Palatinate (for a time living at Weierhof, later at Gundersheim near Worms), but also for a time in Munich and Berlin. His chief medium is black and white drawing, including charcoal (often lithographs) but also water colors and oils. His themes are largely landscapes, often of his native land, with a fine series on Palestine. He has also done many portraits, including an excellent one of Albert Schweitzer. His works are found in all the leading German galleries, such as Munich, Stuttgart, Karlsruhe, Mannheim, Frankfurt, Dresden, Berlin, Homburg, and Leipzig. He has received acclaim by leading art critics. C.K.

Martha Händiges, "Palästinabilder eines mennonitischen Malers," *Menn. Jugendwarte* (Ludwigshafen, Germany) 1921, No. 4, 18-23; 1823. C. Krahn, "Daniel Wohlgemuth—An Artist of Bible Lands," *Menn. Life* IX (1954) 4-6; Friedrich M. Illert, *Daniel Wohlgemuth: An seinem 80. Geburtstag* (Worms, 1956).

Wola Wodzinska Mennonite Church: see Vola Vodzinska Mennonite Church.

Woldampt, a district in the Dutch province of Groningen; the Mennonite congregation in this region in the 17th and 18th centuries was sometimes called Woldampt. This obviously meant Midwolda (*q.v.*). (See also **Oldampt**.)   vDZ.

Wolf Creek, a Hutterite Bruderhof, located on the James River, Hutchinson Co., S.D., some 40 miles northeast of the first Bruderhof at Bon Homme, was founded in the spring of 1875 by preachers George Hofer and Darius Walter, who were both chosen and confirmed in Russia. Preacher Michael Stahl, who was also chosen in Russia, was confirmed by Peter Wedel, the elder in Alexanderwhol in 1865, and died in the Tschetter commune (South Dakota) in 1900. Elias Walter, Sr. (*q.v.*) was chosen preacher here in 1889. This was the mother Bruderhof of the Dariusleut (*q.v.*), one of the three Hutterite kinship groups in America, named after Darius Walter. The group arrived in South Dakota Aug. 10, 1874, and settled first at Silver Lake where they wintered until they could occupy the 5,400-acre tract at Wolf Creek which they had purchased the previous summer. In 1930 the Bruderhof was sold and the Brethren founded the Wolf Creek Bruderhof in Alberta, which in 1950 numbered 76 souls, with 35 baptized members.   D.D.

Wolf Point (Mont.) **Gospel Fellowship** Mennonite Brethren Church is located 23 miles north and 13 miles west of Wolf Point. The congregation was organized in 1956. In 1957 it had 37 members, with Karl Dick as pastor.   K.D.

Wolf(f), de, a former Mennonite family of Amsterdam, Holland, found there *c*1595-*c*1840. They were members of the Flemish congregation and from 1664 sided with the Lamists (*q.v.*). Some de Wolffs were deacons of this church. The de Wolffs originally were Mennonites from Antwerp, Belgium, who in the 1580's fled to Cologne, Germany, and soon after moved to Amsterdam. Maeyken de Wolf (1586-1635) was married to the Dutch poet Joost van den Vondel (*q.v.*); her brother Hans de Wolf (d. before 1625) was married to Joost's sister Clementia van den Vondel. In Amsterdam the de Wolffs were businessmen, particularly silk merchants. Among them were Hans de Wolff (1614-*c*70), married first to Cornelia Block and in 1643 to Agnes Block (he left a considerable legacy to the Lamist congregation for the founding of an orphanage), and Pieter de Wolff (1646-91), married to Clementia van der Vecht, a very wealthy silk merchant with great interest in the church. A side branch of this family lived at Haarlem in the 17th and 18th centuries, which was, however, more conservative than the Amsterdam de Wolffs. Olivier de Wolff, from 1653 a trustee of the Haarlem Flemish Mennonite orphanage, also a deacon, represented the Haarlem Flemish congregation at the conservative conference (see **Leidsche Synode**) held at Leiden 1660.   vDZ.

J. F. M. Sterck, *Het Leven van Joost van den Vondel* (Haarlem, 1926) 4, 12, 127 *et passim; Inv. Arch. Amst.* II, No. 553; *DB* 1863, 23; church records of Amsterdam.

Wolf(f), Hans, a weaver of Beufeld near Strasbourg (*q.v.*), a fanatical Anabaptist, who preached and baptized at Strasbourg in early 1526. He proph-

esied that the world would be destroyed on the stroke of twelve in 1533. Capito (*q.v.*) tried to change his views, but in vain. Thereupon Wolf, who sharply attacked the Reformed pastors of Strasbourg, was arrested and banished on July 30, 1526.   vDZ.

Abr. Hulshof, *Geschiedenis van de Doopsgezinden te Straatsburg* (Amsterdam, 1905) 11-17, 116.

Wolfgang of Mos: see **Mos, Wolfgang von.**

Wolfganzen, a village in Alsace, located about one mile northwest of Neuf-Brisach and 8 miles southeast of Colmar; in 1909-23 it was the seat of the Mennonite congregation which had earlier been called by various names (including Colmar and Muntzenheim, *q.v.*) and which furnished the members for the two modern congregations of Colmar (*q.v.*), formed 1920-22, and Neuf-Brisach (*q.v.*), formed about the same time. The congregation met in an unoccupied school in the village until World War I, when the building was taken over for military purposes and the village made the town hall available. The elder was Benjamin Peterschmitt, who served 1891-1932, continuing at Neuf-Brisach after the congregation was formed. The membership of Wolfganzen was some 130. (See **Colmar.**)   H.S.B.

Wölfl of Götzenberg (a hill near Nider-Vintel in the district of Bruneck belonging to the jurisdiction of Schöneck), Austria, an Anabaptist martyr, was executed in 1533 with six fellow believers (see **Alseider** for names and details) in the Guifidaun castle in the Adige Valley, Tirol.   HEGE.

Zieglschmid, *Chronik; Mart. Mir.* D 36, E 444 (where he is called Wolfert); *ML* IV.

Wolfsheim, a village some 6 miles from Alzey, Rhenish Hesse, Germany, was the seat of a Mennonite congregation *c*1660-1800, the members of which very likely emigrated from Switzerland. In the Mennonite census lists of the Karlsruhe archives the name Wolfsheim occurs in the 1660's with the Mennonite families of Wendell Holl, Thomas Holl, Thomas Rohr, and Stephen von Niederdahlheim. In 1680 the names are Peter Damm, Thomas Rohr, Johannes Schuhmacher, Abraham Holl, Wendel Holl, Rupprecht Rohr, Thillmann Kolb, and Heinrich (last name not legible). In 1685 Tillman Kolb appears with a wife and 7 children, among them 5 sons. Four sons and a daughter emigrated to Germantown, Pa., in 1707. The lists of 1738-73 name Matthias Weber, Johannes Weber, Peter Böhmer, Hermann Janson, Wendel Janson, and Johannes Kaegy.

On Aug. 11, 1661, the elector gave orders that the Mennonites should not hold any religious meetings in Wolfsheim on penalty of a 50 reichstaler fine because the church inspector of Odernheim reported that they were meeting in groups of 200 and holding their religious services in great crowds and were seeking to mislead others, Reformed Christians, to their hypocrisy. Thereupon Wendel Holl "together with his fellow servants" presented a petition to the elector with the comment that they had never increased their number in the country and had been conducting their meetings very quietly; some Mennonites who had been expelled from the Bernese country had been accepted in the Palatinate; he closed with the petition that "the few Mennonites that meet at Wolfsheim, Germersheim, Spiesheim, and Aspisheim, should graciously be allowed to hold our meetings in all quietness." It was decided by the electoral government on Oct. 23, 1661, that as often as they met, the office at Alzey should take a tax from every person, old or young.

On July 13, 1661, Wendel Holl at Wolfsheim and Peter Damm at Weinsheim presented a petition to the office at Alzey that two Mennonites who wanted to settle and buy a ruined estate and pay cash for it might be excused from the tax mentioned above. This petition was refused. Ernest Müller reports (212) that in 1732 there were 18 families in the Wolfsheim congregation; the preachers were Gotthilf Holl and Johannes Schmitt, with Peter Berg as deacon. Toward the end of the 18th century the congregation was dissolved. The remaining members joined the Uffhofen (q.v.) congregation.

Wilhelm Niepoth's recent research has shown that some of the Palatine Mennonites stem, not from Switzerland, but from the district of Löwenberg in the Siebengebirge not far from Bad Godesberg. Three of these families settled in Wolfsheim c1655-80: Thomas Rohr from Niederdollendorf, a Shumacher family, and a Stephen from Niederdollendorf. NEFF, H.S.B.

Müller, *Berner Täufer;* W. Niepoth, "Migrations and Change of the Mennonite Schumacher Family," *MQR* XXXII (1959); *ML* IV.

Wolkan, Rudolf (1860-1927), Professor of German Literature at the University of Vienna, a cofounder with Beck (q.v.) and Loserth (q.v.) of the Austrian school of Anabaptist historiography around the turn of the 20th century. Wolkan did a great deal to secure a fairer treatment for Anabaptism in academic circles and greatly advanced research in this field. In 1903, as an instructor he published (in Berlin) his epoch-making *Lieder der Wiedertäufer,* a basic and as yet unsurpassed study in which for the first time the chaotic mass of Anabaptist hymns received a systematic organization and friendly interpretation. Wolkan was the first to differentiate clearly between three distinct groups of Anabaptists: the Swiss Brethren, the Dutch and North German Mennonites, and the Hutterites. Of particular value was Wolkan's research concerning the origin of the *Ausbund* (q.v.). His oldest copy was of 1583, but he knew that an earlier one had existed. He studied the Passau records of the Munich "Reichsarchiv" and discovered there the trial records of 1535 which threw light on the background of the oldest section of this famous hymnal. He also utilized for the first time the *Protocoll* of the Frankenthal Colloquy in order to clarify the doctrinal position of the groups involved. His book came to America, where John Horsch (q.v.) gladly welcomed it. Through Horsch, Wolkan learned for the first time that the Hutterian Brethren were still in existence in South Dakota (neither Beck nor Loserth had any knowledge of this kind), and soon a lively correspondence between Wolkan and Elias Walter (q.v.), a bishop

of the Brethren in America, ensued. In 1908 Wolkan published a brief article in the *Oesterreichische Rundschau* ("Oesterreichische Wiedertäufer in Amerika"), informing the scholarly world of the modern Hutterites. The fruit of further studies and correspondence with Canadian Hutterites was another book, *Die Huterer,* published in Vienna 1918 under very difficult conditions. It contains not only a brief history of the Hutterites and a description of their form of life, both past and present, but also a brief and highly interesting Hutterite tract concerning community living written by Ulrich Stadler c1536, and found by Wolkan in an original Hutterite codex at the library of the University of Vienna (Viennese codex). This tract (in Wolkan's book pp. 153-60) was published once more by Lydia Müller (*Glaubenszeugnisse* I, 222-27). Elias Walter, glad to have come into contact with a real scholar and friend of the Anabaptists, suggested that Wolkan undertake the gigantic task of the first publication of the Hutterite "greater" chronicle, a book thought lost by all earlier scholars, but well preserved by the Brethren in Canada. Walter meticulously copied this huge codex and sent this copy to Vienna. Wolkan then began to edit the work, mainly by adding significant excerpts from other Hutterite sources in footnotes. In 1923 this *Geschicht-Buch der Hutterischen Brüder* came out as a volume of nearly 700 pages, a tremendous gain for all future research and indispensable to every scholar. (When the stock was sold out, the Hutterites in Canada asked Professor Zieglschmid, q.v., to produce another edition of the same book, which in 1943 in part replaced the older, modernized edition by Wolkan.) Wolkan accomplished this work with great personal sympathy for the Brethren, championing their recognition in the German scholarly world.

A last personal note should be added by the writer of this article. It was in 1923 that Wolkan suggested to him (then a student at the University of Vienna) that he undertake a dissertation on the hitherto overlooked epistles of the Hutterites, thus starting him on the road to continued Anabaptist research. Wolkan made available to him not only the Viennese codex but also other codices from Bratislava and Esztergom as well, and guided this work by his kind counsel. Through Wolkan the writer came into contact not only with Christian Neff and the *Mennonitisches Lexikon,* but also with John Horsch and Elias Walter in America. Finally he also encouraged a research trip to Slovakia, to visit and study the remnants of former Bruderhofs (Habaner). Wolkan himself contributed to the first volume of the *Mennonitisches Lexikon* and would have continued to do so had he not passed away unexpectedly in 1927, aged 67. R.F.

Wolleb, Johann Jacob, pietistic Reformed minister in Thenniken, canton of Basel, Switzerland, during the first half of the 18th century. He was the author of the remarkable book, *Gespräch zwischen einem Pietisten und einem Wiedertäufer* (Basel, 1722). In his later years he became an enthusiastic follower of Count Zinzendorf (q.v.), who visited him in 1740. The *Gespräch* was written apparently in a missionary spirit, with the hope of winning the Anabaptists (of the Jura area) to the new trend of Pietism (*q.v.*). For details see **Gespräch.** R.F.

R. Friedmann, *Mennonite Piety Through the Centuries* (Goshen, 1949) 40; P. Wernle, *Geschichte des Schweizer Protestantismus im 18. Jahrhundert* I (Tübingen, 1923); Jöcher, *Gelehrten Lexicon* (1756).

Wollmann, Jakob, an elder of the Hutterian Brethren, was chosen in 1724 as successor of Matthias Helm and confirmed by him as the chief leader of the Hutterite congregations in Hungary at the age of only 31. Under his leadership the brotherhood was exposed to great oppressions by the renewed effort to Catholicize them. The elders and preachers yielded under government compulsion in 1733 to having their children baptized by Catholic priests, although the children were later usually baptized once more by their own elders. Wollmann died in 1734, and was succeeded by Georg Frank. (Beck, *Geschichts-Bücher; ML* IV.) HEGE.

Wolvega, a town in the Dutch province of Friesland, where a Mennonite congregation was founded in 1861. A hall was bought and adapted into a meetinghouse (remodeled in 1875) and furnished with a pipe organ in 1901. The baptized membership then numbered 36; this number was 92 in 1900, 90 in 1926, and 107 in 1958. At first services were conducted and catechetical instruction given by pastors of neighboring congregations. The first resident pastor of Wolvega was J. S. S. Ballot, serving 1863-66, followed by C. J. Bakker 1866-68, S. Wartena Jr. 1868-73, J. Hoekstra 1874-79, A. Blaauw Kz 1881-82, G. ten Cate 1883-91, M. Uiterdijk 1892-94, F. van der Ploeg 1894-98, M. van der Vegte Jr. 1899-1913, W. Banga 1914-30, vacant 1930-33, the pastor of Heerenveen (*q.v.*) 1933-42, vacant 1942-47, Miss C. Boerlage 1947-57. In 1957 the pastoral responsibility was given to Miss T. G. Siccama, who, living at Wolvega, at the same time serves the Tjalleberd (*q.v.*) congregation.

Church activities are a ladies' circle, two Menniste Bouwers clubs, and a Sunday school for children. (*DB* 1862, 142 f.; 1864, 168; 1902, 247.) vDZ.

Women in Church Vocations (WCV), an organization of the General Conference Mennonite Church replacing the former deaconess (*q.v.*) program. However, it seeks to foster this spirit in a broader, fresher, and more adaptable form for our day. In the early 1950's, a study and re-evaluation of this deaconess movement, authorized by the Conference and by the deaconesses themselves, resulted in the conclusion that, like other church groups, the General Conference would need to find a new form or pattern of service for the women in church vocations.

Eight representative young women met with a special committee of the Board of Christian Service in St. Louis in July 1956 and, after a study of other denominational deaconess programs, formulated recommendations which were adopted by the Conference in 1956. The new program offers avenues for recruiting young women, helping provide adequate spiritual and specialized training, assisting with counseling and placement, and continuing to provide opportunities for further inspiration and fellowship. Each enrolled member shall have been led to devote herself to Christlike service within the framework of the church. She shall possess emotional and physical health, have a wholesome personality, be under 36 years of age when accepted, and be desirous of growing spiritually and in her chosen vocation. She will be considered an active member as long as she is giving full-time service to the church, whether married or not.

Initially it was urged that each member earn her A.B. degree and then complete a year of training at Mennonite Biblical Seminary in order to equip her for spiritually effective service, a five-year program in possible addition to specialized and technical preparation such as nurse's training. Some revision of this requirement is now in process. Early in 1957 Marion Keeney was asked by the Committee on Women in Church Vocations to serve as promotional secretary. In September 1957, six young women were enrolled in the program—four of them at the Seminary for their year of study, and one each at Bethel and Bluffton completing the B.A. degree. This program is related to the Conference through the Board of Christian Service. Scholarship aid is provided by the Board, by the Women's Missionary Association, and by the colleges, all of which organizations are represented on the Committee of Women in Church Vocations. E.C.G.

Elmer Ediger, "Women and Church Vocational Service," *The Mennonite,* 1956, June 27 and December 4; Marion Keeney, "Women in Church Vocations," *The Mennonite,* 1958, June 3 and June 10; Doreen Harms, "New Avenues of Service for Women," *Menn. Life* XII (January 1957).

Women, Status of: *Anabaptism.* In the early Anabaptist movement women played an important role. The Anabaptist emphasis upon voluntary membership, adult baptism, and personal commitment inevitably opened up new perspectives for women. The court records in the Swiss-South German areas as well as in Holland show that they could and did give vigorous and intelligent independent testimonies of their own to their faith, and shared martyrdom unflinchingly with the men, although the number of male martyrs reported generally outnumbered the women two to one; the women were often given milder penalties than the men. "Brothers and Sisters" are often mentioned together in the Hutterite Chronicle. The Anabaptist basic position elevated marriage to a more spiritual relationship (see **Marriage**) than in the Catholic and Protestant culture of the time. At times the Hutterite men spoke of their wives as "married sister." But no women are known to have been chosen as preachers or deacons. Later, after the creative period of Anabaptism was past, the settled communities and congregations reverted more to the typical patriarchal attitude of European culture.

A few noblewomen were prominent in South German and Tirolean-Austrian Anabaptism, such as Helene von Freyberg (*q.v.*) of Münichau, Tirol, Walpurga Marschalkin von Pappenheim (*q.v.*) of Kalden, Bavaria, and Agnes von Waldenhofen of Trautmannsdorf, Tirol. H.S.B.

Netherlands. Women played an important role in early Dutch Anabaptism and Mennonitism. Although among the martyrs women were outnumbered by men (in Amsterdam, for example, 106 male and 33 female Anabaptists were executed), there were many women who suffered martyrdom for their faith. Some women are said to have taught in Anabaptist meetings, for example, Aeffgen (*q.v.*) Lystyncx; the martyr Elisabeth (*q.v.*) Dirks is even called a "leeraresse" (preacher). Only a few women among the early Dutch Anabaptists composed hymns; Soetken (*q.v.*) Gerrits of Rotterdam, and Vrou Gerrets (*q.v.*) of Medemblik published hymnals. Soon after persecution was ended, *c*1570, women are named as deaconesses (*q.v.*), and from the early 17th century also as trustees of orphanages and old people's homes.

In the 17th-19th centuries women had no voting power and were not eligible as members of the church boards. In some congregations women have voted in the choosing of a pastor since *c*1865. Soon after this a number of congregations granted suffrage to women members also in other cases (*DB* 1879, 117 f.). In 1900, in 113 congregations the women had full suffrage, in 30 only in the case of calling a pastor, and in 12 no suffrage at all (*DB* 1900). At present in nearly all the congregations women have complete right of voting and in nearly all they are now eligible as members of the church boards. Such women trustees were first found in 1905 at Middelburg, and about the same time at Dordrecht and Leiden. At present all but a few congregations have women trustees. The office of deaconess (*q.v.*) developed among the Dutch Anabaptists.

Women have been pastors of Dutch Mennonite congregations since 1911. At present (1959), of a total of 109 pastors 25 are women. Ladies' circles, now usual in all Dutch congregations, and organized in the central Federatie van *Zusterkringen* (*q.v.*) since 1949, date from about 1910. vDZ.

* * *

Prussian-Russian Background. The status of women among the Mennonites of this background does not differ greatly from that of other Mennonite groups under similar conditions nor from that of other Protestant groups, depending to a large extent on the sociological and cultural development of the particular group and ancient traditions and particularly the interpretation of Biblical references to women.

However, once the Mennonites had settled in isolated areas of Prussia and Russia they seemed to fall back into the patterns of tradition and environment. The wife was busy rearing the large family and fulfilling her obligations on the farm. In business transactions and in church and community the responsibility rested entirely on the husband. The congregational meetings were typically referred to as "Bruderschaft," implying that the brethren alone attended such meetings and voted. In general, development proceeded along the following steps: At first, church matters were primarily disposed of by the elder, ministers, and deacons; later responsibility was extended to include all male

members; then (under the influence of the 19th-century emancipation movement) further extended to include the women. This stage had not been developed among the Mennonites of Prussia and Russia, and came later in America. Pietism (*q.v.*), which reached most Mennonite settlements during the 19th century, also had its effect. The emphasis on spontaneous conversion and antipathy toward tradition broke barriers and promoted equality in general, and also between the sexes. Paul's admonition, "Let the women be silent in the churches" (I Cor. 14:34), was interpreted to mean only that women should not preach. With the introduction of Bible study, prayer meeting, Sunday school, and mission societies, a wide field was opened for Mennonite women. Now they could express their views in Bible studies, they participated audibly in prayer meetings, they taught Sunday-school classes, discussed missionary affairs in sewing circles and many other organizations, and as mission workers engaged in direct evangelism and teaching.

With the teaching of Sunday-school classes and active participation in the affairs of the church the "Bruderschaft" meetings were gradually "invaded" by the women. If the women were teaching Sunday-school classes, they could perhaps also participate in the election of Sunday-school teachers. If they were actively engaged in mission work, could they not also vote in matters pertaining to missions? If they were active in most of the phases of church work, should they not also express their views publicly and by voting? Gradually this change took place in the early 20th century, particularly in the Mennonite churches of the prairie states and provinces under prevalent democratic influences. Most of the modern constitutions of the General Conference, Mennonite Brethren, Evangelical Mennonite Brethren, Krimmer Mennonite Brethren, and other groups made provision for this change. In many of the churches women filled church offices. There still seems to be some hesitation about installing women as deacons, although this was an ancient tradition in the Mennonite churches of the Netherlands.

In Canada this development has not been as rapid as in the United States, even among the more progressive G.C.M. and M.B. churches. Among the more conservative groups, such as the Sommerfeld and Old Colony Mennonites, the old pattern has been preserved; officially and outwardly women have no vote in the affairs of the church and community life.

The great change that has taken place among most Mennonites is due partly to the change in their socio-economic structure. With a move from the farm to the city many Mennonite women find work outside their homes. Among the first vocations chosen by Mennonite women were teaching, nursing, and office work. The quite general acceptance of secondary and college education also has promoted equalization. Mennonites, however, do not elect women as ministers, as has been the practice of the Dutch Mennonites for half a century.

Women's stepping out of their homes into public life has brought many changes. The former nonconformity patterns adhered to by conservative groups have been given up to a large extent. While the men adjusted themselves to their environment in styles, they often expected the women to maintain the older traditions. This total development again has had an influence on the Mennonite family (q.v.) and the number of children in the family.

The traditional seating arrangement in the church, with the women on one side and the men on the other, is simply the old Protestant pattern preserved most consistently in conservative rural settings, and disappears as greater equality and participation by the women in the affairs of the church and community takes place.

The number of Mennonite women's organizations is growing steadily. Most common are the mission circles, societies, or associations (q.v.). Well known are the Mennonite deaconesses (q.v.), who have done a great work in connection with hospitals in Russia and America. However, this vocation no longer attracts the young women of today and is probably on the way out. One of the most recent G.C.M. organizations is Women in Church Vocations (q.v.).   C.K.

Leonhard Froese, "Das pädagogische Kultursystem der mennonitischen Siedlungsgruppe in Russland" (unpublished doctoral dissertation at Göttingen, 1949); Eva Geiger Harshbarger, "The Status of Mennonite Women in Kansas in Their Church and Home Relationships" (M.Sc. thesis, Kansas State College, 1945).

* * *

Swiss-South German Background. The status of women in the Swiss-South German Mennonite churches in Europe and America after the Anabaptist era has remained relatively stable and conservative throughout until modern times. In general the patriarchal type of family life has prevailed, with women in a respected, responsible position in the home, but "silent" in church life in participation both in public address and in ecclesiastical government and church work. However, where Mennonite families occupied larger farm estates, whether as renters or owners, the wives occupied an important place as chatelaines or managers of the extensive households with numerous servants, a position as different from that of an ordinary peasant farmer's wife as the position of the Mennonite estate manager differed from the ordinary peasant or small farmer. In the past half century and more the daughters in such families usually received wide experience in household management both in apprenticeships and in formal schooling before marriage. In Europe women did not enjoy (and have not enjoyed to date) the privilege of voting in church congregational meetings except in the election of ministers, nor do they hold any sort of office, certainly not as ministers. The deaconess work was introduced in South Germany (Badischer Verband, q.v., in 1904).

In North America, churches of Swiss-South German background have followed two courses in modern times. The very conservative groups have maintained the patriarchal type of family life with a corresponding place for women. In the progressive bodies (MC, EMC, GCM Swiss) since 1900 women have gradually moved into full participation in all aspects of church life and service, except in the ministry and in office-holding in general congregational life. However, voting for candidates for the ministry and for regular offices in the congregation has always been open to women in these groups, even though they have not always exercised their privileges. Women's work in the form of sewing circles (q.v.) and missionary organizations (see W.M.S.A.) arose in the M.C. congregations c1910, and is now in a flourishing state. The service of women as missionaries and Sunday-school teachers, in which they were often asked to speak at regular or special congregational or general meetings, broke down the prohibition of women speaking from the pulpit (laymen had also been denied this right), although in many of the more conservative areas, especially in Pennsylvania, Maryland, and Virginia, neither women nor laymen are as yet permitted to speak from behind the pulpit.

The custom of seating the women separately from the men in the meetinghouse, whether in the center (with the men seated around the outside) or on one side, is deeply ingrained and remains unchanged in the conservative congregations. In other areas it is being displaced by family seating.   H.S.B.

Women's Missionary and Service Auxiliary is an auxiliary organization of the Mennonite Board of Missions and Charities (MC), Elkhart, Ind. It grew out of the sewing circle (q.v.) and women's missionary organizations which developed during the first half of the 20th century in the M.C. congregations in the United States and Canada. As early as 1895 Mennonite women in eastern Pennsylvania were sewing garments for the poor. As a result of the work of Mary A. Mellinger in Lancaster County, Pa., the Paradise Sewing Circle was organized in 1897. The Associated Sewing Circles (q.v.) was organized in Lancaster County in 1911. As early as 1900 a Sisters' Sewing Circle was organized in the Science Ridge Mennonite Church, Sterling, Ill. During that decade other circles were organized in Illinois, Pennsylvania, Indiana, Ontario, Minnesota, Ohio, and Ontario. As early as 1911 Mennonite (MC) women, under the leadership of Clara Eby Steiner (1873-1929) of Columbus Grove, Ohio, began to promote a general society of sewing circles. With the formation of a general organization, Mary Burkhard became its president, serving 1916-23. She was followed by Mary Ann Cressman 1923-30, Lina Z. Ressler 1930-37, Cora Buzzard 1937-44, Ruth B. Miller 1944-50, and Minnie Graber 1950- . Clara Eby Steiner became the first secretary of the organization, serving 1916-26, during which time she wrote many letters to promote sewing circles. A third pioneer was Ruth A. Yoder, who served as treasurer of the organization 1916-29. Mary Ann Cressman, Crissie Y. Shank, Mary Ann Gerig, and Stella S. Kreider were additional members of the general committee in the 1920's. In 1917 the women's organization became church-wide, when general officers and branch secretaries to cover the entire church were elected, and in 1924 its permanent constitution was adopted. In her second annual newsletter, secretary Clara Eby Steiner reported that for the year ending March 31, 1919, thirteen branch secretaries had reported total receipts of $13,763.58. In addition they had reported 11,957 garments made and at the same time the Friends reported 27,189 garments given to them for war relief by Mennonite women. By March 1920, the organization had 13 branches, 124 circles, and 2,262 members.

Beginning in 1922 the organization operated under the name Mennonite Women's Missionary Society. Because of a lack of good co-ordination between this society and the Mennonite Board of Missions and Charities, in 1928 the Board accepted a report providing for a "Woman's Mission Committee" to operate under the Mission Board. In its printed constitution of 1933 the name adopted for the committee was "The General Sewing Circle Committee of the Mennonite Board of Missions and Charities." Misunderstandings arose during this time of the transition of the women's society from an independent status to one of dependency on the Mission Board, and consequently for a time the membership in the new organization was less than half of what it had been in the former society. Eventually membership in the new organization surpassed the highest membership obtained by the old and is now widely accepted. The WMSA meets annually in connection with the annual meeting of the Mission Board.

In 1947 the committee was again reorganized, its name was changed to Women's Missionary Sewing Circle Organization, and from that time it was regarded as an "auxiliary of the Mennonite Board of Missions and Charities." In January 1954 its first full-time secretary was appointed. With the rapid growth of the organization and the extension of its activities into areas beyond sewing, the name was changed to Women's Missionary and Service Auxiliary in its 1955 annual meeting. President Minnie Graber reported, "We strive toward the vision of concerting the efforts of every Mennonite woman and girl to the total program of the Mennonite Church so that wherever the church is found, in city or country, at home or abroad, in charitable or educational institutions, in community efforts, in relief to the ends of the world, there we may be found enhancing the attractiveness of the Gospel and giving expression to the love of Jesus."

The 1958 secretary's report listed 826 auxiliaries or local units, of which 236 were girls' auxiliaries, with a total membership of 15,690. Cash receipts during the year totaled over $175,000 and other contributions amounted to a value of more than $121,000. More than 71,000 garments were received besides large amounts of bedding and linens, baby garments, Christmas bundles, and other material aid gifts. Between the local groups and the general organization were the district organizations through which the national officers worked. Emphasis was given to women's fellowship meetings, in which mission and home interests were discussed and prayers offered for the work of the church. A literature secretary is responsible for producing the *Daily Prayer Guide* (*q.v.*, 1951-), of which 12,000 copies were printed for 1958, and the WMSA *Monthly* (begun in 1930 as *Missionary Sewing Circle Letters, q.v.*), which had a circulation of 11,800. A suggested reading list (twelve books) in flyer form was printed and distributed in 1957. The general committee had begun work on *A Handbook*

for the use of its local and district officers. The executive secretary carries out the assignments of the general committee, prepares the *Program Guide* for the use of the local auxiliaries, prepares publicity, and informs the auxiliaries of the mission needs of the church. A secretary of home and special interests promotes prayer fellowships, homemakers' organizations, and mission study groups. The secretary of girls' activities promotes girls' missionary and service auxiliaries, supplies materials for a page on "With Our Girls" in the *Monthly,* and serves as assistant Junior Activities Secretary on the Commission for Christian Education.   M.G.

Women's Missionary and Service Monthly is an eight-page magazine, 6 x 9 in., published by the Women's Missionary and Service Auxiliary of the Mennonite Board of Missions and Charities (MC) to promote interest in missions and relief. It is printed by the Mennonite Publishing House, Scottdale, Pa., and has a circulation of approximately 12,000. Mrs. Fred Gingerich is the editor. As in the first copy, published in 1919, the magazine reports work done, gives information of work to be done, tells of places where money and personnel are needed, and offers spiritual messages witnessing to God's faithfulness and love.   L.S.S.

Women's Missionary Association of the General Conference Mennonite Church, an auxiliary to the G.C.M. Church, meets in a delegated session once every three years, at the time of the General Conference. It was organized in 1917 at Reedley, Cal. Before that, women's meetings and inspirational missionary programs sponsored by women had been held at General Conference sessions. The first recorded business meeting was held at Berne, Ind., on Oct. 16, 1902, with Sister Hillegonda van der Smissen as president and Sara Sprunger as secretary. Between conference sessions the work of the Association is carried on by the Executive Council, which is composed of president, first and second vice-presidents, secretary, chairmen of Literature Committee, Committee of Advisers, and Committee of Young Mission Workers. Each member of the Council serves for six years, except the chairman of the Literature Committee, whose members serve nine years each. The treasurer for the Women's Missionary Association and the editor of the monthly periodical, *Missionary News and Notes,* are appointed by the Executive Council. *Unser Missionsblatt* is the Canadian sister publication provided in the German language. The current annual budget totals $70,288.

The purpose of the organization, as stated in the first constitution, adopted at Hutchinson, Kan., Aug. 23, 1929, is to glorify God and serve the Conference and its missionary representatives (1) in the support of home and foreign missions; (2) in the spread of mission interests; (3) in the promotion of co-operation between mission societies and missions; and (4) in the production and dissemination of missionary literature.

Those who have served as president are Sister Hillegonda van der Smissen, Mrs. S. S. Haury, Mrs. J. E. Kaufman, Mrs. A. M. Lohrentz, Mrs. D. P. Ewert, and Mrs. Olin A. Krehbiel. Others who served in varied capacities for many years are Mrs. P. R. Schroeder, Mrs. R. A. Goerz, Mrs. Frieda Regier Entz, and Mrs. W. C. Voth.   E.C.L.

Wood County (Ohio) Mennonite Church (MC), founded *c*1835-45, became extinct 1882-85 when several groups of families left for Elkhart County,. Ind., and ten families moved to Alanson, Mich., leaving only six members. The last minister had moved to Wayne County, Ohio, in 1884. The meetinghouse built of hewn logs and ceiled with poplar boards before 1856 was razed in 1885, and in 1910 Lewis P. Risser and George Milner, "trustees of the Mennonite Cemetery Association," deeded the cemetery plot on the northeast banks of the South Branch of the Portage River to "the trustees of Perry township." Some of the early settlers were from the Franconia district in southeastern Pennsylvania. Names of members included Tyson, Landis, Pletcher, Risser, Legron (Lechrone), Bachman, Brandt, and Boyer. Ministers of the congregation were Jacob Kaempfer, Henry Pletcher, and Jacob Tyson. Jacob Kaempfer preached only in German; his wife, a member of the Winebrennerians (Church of God), never attended services with him. Henry Pletcher could preach in both English and German, preferred English, favored Sunday school, and was silenced as too "liberal," before he and his friends moved to Indiana and united with the Yellow Creek (*q.v.*) congregation. His successor, Jacob Tyson, sided with the Wisler (*q.v.*) faction. The congregation never had a resident bishop, but was served by Bishop John M. Brenneman until his retirement and then by Peter Imhoff, bishop of the Wisler congregations in Ashland and western Wayne counties. Unsatisfactory health conditions in the "Black Swamp" area may have been a determining factor in the reremoval of a large part of the congregation to Michigan. Typhoid and malaria took a heavy toll. The church was near Jersey City.   J.S.U.

John Umble, "Extinct Mennonite Churches in Ohio," *MQR* XVIII (1944) 89-116.

Wood River Mennonite Church (MC), located in Wood River, Hall Co., Neb., a member of the Iowa-Nebraska Conference, had its beginning in 1904-5 when a group of Mennonites from Milford, Neb., about 100 miles east of Wood River, settled in this neighborhood. Among the group were the John B. Jantzi, David D. Stutzman, Peter Zehr, Mose Zehr, and Ruel Riley families. In the fall of 1905 they organized a Sunday school and soon afterward a congregation. Their first meeting place was in a rented building located 1½ miles east and 5 miles north of Wood River. In the fall and winter of 1908-9 a plot of land was obtained 4½ miles north and 1 mile west of Wood River, on which a frame building, with seating capacity of about 200, was erected.

Joseph E. Zimmerman was ordained the first minister in 1906. The present ministers are William R. Eicher bishop and Alvin Gascho minister. The membership was 49 in 1958.   A.GA.

Woodburn (Ind.) Evangelical Mennonite Church was organized in 1893. Its meetinghouse was constructed in 1896. Among the early ministers who served the church were Andrew Gerig, J. K. Gerig,

E. J. Oyer, Harold Froker, and Emanuel M. Rocke. In 1957 the congregation had 154 members, with Alvin G. Becker serving as pastor.   E.M.R.

Woodcrest, one of eleven communities operated by and comprising the Society of Brothers (*q.v.*), is located near the junction of New York State Highways 32 and 213, three miles west of Rifton, about 70 miles north of New York City. It was established early in the summer of 1954 on a woodland tract of 96 acres with about a dozen buildings available for use, to which have been added three apartment dwellings, a nursery, and a Center House to replace the Carriage House which burned in 1957. Other buildings serve as schoolhouse, a shop, sewing room, laundry, or other maintenance functions. The household, including resident guests and children, comprises about 230, of whom 70 are full members; about half of the household are children. Living expenses are met from the sale of quality, educational toys made of wood, sales being primarily to schools and churches.   B.B.

Woodford County, Ill. The first body of Amish Mennonite settlers in Woodford County came as immigrants from Alsace in 1831 and settled in Worth Township along the Black Partridge Creek northwest of the present town of Metamora. In 1833 Christian Engle, a bishop ordained in Europe, organized this body of believers into a congregation. The members. met in homes until 1854, when a brick meetinghouse was constructed, called the Partridge Church. Most of the settlers later moved to the prairies east of Metamora and formed the Metamora congregation. The Partridge Church was the first German church west of Ohio and the second of any denomination in Woodford County; it was for years the church home for all Mennonite immigrants, although they may have settled at some distance. In 1834 a settlement was made near Congerville, known as the Mackinaw Settlement. This later developed into three congregations: Roanoke, Goodfield in Woodford County, and North Danvers in McLean County. Goodfield later merged with the Tremont congregation to form the Morton Mennonite Church.

At present there are two Mennonite (MC) congregations in Woodford County—Metamora and Roanoke, with a total membership of 722. The General Conference has a congregation at Congerville with 117 members. Many other Woodford County residents are members of the Calvary Mennonite Church (GCM) at Washington. An independent Conservative Amish Mennonite congregation is located in Linn Township, about five miles northwest of Roanoke. This group had its origin in the "Sleeping Preacher" (*q.v.*) movement in the early part of the century. In 1958 it had 172 members.

There are approximately 1,500 Mennonites living in Woodford County today, about 7 per cent of the total population. In addition there is approximately the same number of the Apostolic Christian (*q.v.*) faith sometimes called the "New Amish," who have much in common with the Mennonites in their origin and doctrine. The Mennonite Home for the Aged at Eureka is operated by the Mennonite Board of Missions and Charities (MC) through a local board. T.R.S.

Woodlake (Cal.) Mennonite Settlement (GCM) and Church, now extinct, was established in the eastern part of the San Joaquin Valley of central California. Before World War I numerous Mennonites became stockholders of the Woodlake Citrus Development Company, some of whom never moved to Woodlake. The virgin land of the Woodlake area was gradually transformed into orange groves. Some of the families who founded the town of Woodlake came from Reedley and Upland. The spiritual needs were taken care of by visiting ministers from Mennonite communities in California.

In 1915 H. A. Bachmann came to Woodlake and on June 13, 1915, the First Mennonite Church was organized with 18 members who met in the local school. In 1916-18 F. J. Isaac served as minister, followed in 1918-19 by J. J. Engbrecht. After this the Reedley Mennonite Church provided for occasional services. In 1926 some young people were baptized. The last meeting of the congregation was held on Jan. 20, 1929, attended by three families. In 1953 there were only three families living at Woodlake who had once belonged to the Mennonite Church of that place. C.K.

Woodland Mennonite Mission (MC) was opened in a small community of fourteen homes located 2 miles west of Milroy, Mifflin Co., Pa., in the summer of 1940 by John L. Mast, senior bishop of the Locust Grove Conservative Mennonite Church, in the township schoolhouse. On Aug. 25, 1951, the schoolhouse was purchased by the church and remodeled for use as a church. In 1957 there were six members, with Ivan Yoder as pastor. J.P.Y.

Woodland Mennonite Church (GCM), located in Warroad, Roseau Co., Minn., a member of the Northern District, was organized on March 3, 1939, with 30 charter members, by families who had arrived a few years before. The meetinghouse was built in 1950, with a seating capacity of 150. The members are mostly descendants of the 1874 ff. immigration from Russia. The pastor is Arthur F. Ortmann, who organized the church. The membership is now 86. A.F.O.

Woodland Mennonite Church (MC), located at 1837 Woodland Ave., Wichita, Kan., now extinct, started as Mennonite Gospel Mission in a rented building at 1202 South Pattie Ave., April 17, 1921. Vernon Shellenberger was the first superintendent, with Paul Erb as nonresident minister and T. M. Erb as bishop. In 1924 a new building was erected on Woodland Avenue in the northwestern part of the city. The mission character of the work had to make room for a church home for Mennonite families living in the city, and for an increasing number of working girls. Resident pastors were Henry J. King 1924-27, Leroy Thayer 1927-36, I. Mark Ross 1940-45, Glen Whitaker 1948-51, Edward Kauffman 1951-52. The last service was held Sept. 28, 1952, and the property was sold soon after. Mission work by the Mennonite Church (MC) is now carried on

in a section called Eureka Gardens (q.v.), and at a Negro church at 10th and Piatt erected in 1959. E.Bu.

Woodland Tabernacle is a Mennonite (MC) rural mission church 4 miles north of Orkney Springs, near Jerome, Shenandoah Co., Va., under the Virginia Conference. An inexpensive building was erected here in 1944 to care for the work that was formerly carried on at the Lindamood schoolhouse. The membership here is the outgrowth and remnant of the Powder Spring (q.v.) congregation, which was located several miles south of this place. The membership in 1958 was 22, with James E. Gross in charge. T.S.

Woodlawn Mennonite Church (GCM), Chicago, Ill., located at 1143 East 46th Street, was organized as a congregation in 1951. It grew out of a Sunday school which had been operated several years before that by the staff and students of the Mennonite Biblical Seminary. J. N. Smucker came as the first pastor in 1952. It is a member of the Central District Conference. It is an interracial church in an area of growing Negro population. In 1959 it had 51 members, with Delton W. Franz as its pastor and Vincent G. Harding the associate pastor. M.G.

Woodridge Mennonite Church (MC), Washington, D.C., is a member of the Allegheny Conference. In 1957 it had 40 members, with John R. Martin as pastor. The congregation was organized in 1952 as "Georgetown," with 23 members, but changed its name to Woodridge the next year. Nevin Miller served as pastor from the beginning to 1956, at first commuting from Harrisonburg, Va., where he was a teacher. The congregation worshiped in a rented church building in the city of Washington, D.C., until its own meetinghouse was built in 1959 at Hyattsville, Md., just outside the District of Columbia to the northeast. M.G.

Woodrow Mennonite Brethren Church, located 6 miles north of Woodrow, Sask., formerly known as Hoffnungsfeld, a member of the Herbert District Conference, was organized in 1910 under the leadership of George Reimche. The initial membership of 28 increased to 75 by 1957. George Reimche was succeeded by John Ollenberger, Ludwig Seibel, John Ollenberger again, E. J. Lautermilch, and Samuel Sutter, the leader in 1957. J.I.R.

Woodson County (Kan.) Mennonite Brethren Church, now extinct, was founded in 1876 by a number of M.B. families who emigrated from the Chortitza settlement in Russia to America. In the fall of 1878 Bernard Pauls and David Dick were elected as ministers; they were ordained in 1881. Soon both moved away, and the church elected Cornelius Nickel and Peter Nickel as ministers. In 1888 the congregation had 52 members. Most of these, however, moved away in 1892, and the church was discontinued. M.A.K.

Woodville Conservative Mennonite Church, located at Woodville, Jefferson Co., N.Y., a member of the Conservative Mennonite Conference, organized in May 1947 with 22 members under the leadership of

Lloyd Boshart. The membership in 1957 was 66, all of whom are rural people. The meetinghouse is a rural school building which was purchased in April 1948. The bishop is Andrew Gingerich.　　A.Gɪ.

Woolwich Mennonites: see Old Order Mennonites in Ontario.

Wooster Mennonite Church (MC), formerly known as the Wooster Mennonite Mission, located in the city of Wooster, Wayne Co., Ohio, is a member of the Ohio and Eastern Conference. It was started by the Salem Mennonite Church of Wayne County as a mission with Rudy Stauffer as pastor, and was organized in November 1944 under the Ohio Mennonite Mission Board, with eight charter members. The congregation worshiped in a house on Gasche Street until 1951, became an independent congregation, and built a new brick church in 1954 with a seating capacity of 300. The 144 members (1959) represent ten denominational backgrounds, a mixed character of urban and rural. Paul Brunner is pastor.　　D.W.M.

Wopkens, Thomas (b. 1700 at Leeuwarden, d. 1775 at Harlingen), was trained for the ministry at the Remonstrant (*q.v.*) seminary at Amsterdam. He served in the Amsterdam Lamist congregation 1726-29 and at Harlingen 1729-46. Wopkens was a man of great knowledge and learning; he published a critical edition in Latin of the works of Cicero, entitled *Lectionum Tulliarum . . . Libri tres* (Amsterdam, 1730) and Dutch translations of some Latin works on theology. He was a man of liberal views and co-operated closely with his Harlingen copastor Johannes Stinstra (*q.v.*). His poor health forced him to resign at a rather early age.　　vᴅZ.

Chr. Sepp, *Johannes Stinstra en zijn tijd* (Amsterdam, 1865-66) I, 210 f.; II, 141, 147; Blaupot t. C., *Friesland*, 237; *Inv. Arch. Amst.* I, No. 669; *DJ* 1840, 113.

Worcester Mennonite Church (MC), known also in the past as Methacton, is located in Worcester Township near Fairview, Montgomery Co., Pa., and is a member of the Franconia Conference. The date of organization is uncertain. According to Joseph Heebner, a historian of Worcester, the church was started by the Henry Rittenhouse family (grandson of William Rittenhouse) and it is presumed that the first meetinghouse was built a few years after eight trustees in 1739 acquired a burial ground for a union cemetery. Five of these trustees were Mennonites: Henry Rittenhouse, Christopher Zimmerman, Conrad Stem, Peter Keyser, and Peter Custard. It is known that the meetinghouse was there by 1771. In 1873 the third and present meetinghouse was erected. It has never been a large congregation. There were about 50 members in 1890. Sunday school with an attendance of 125 was started in 1898 but by 1920 it was discontinued and the congregation dwindled. Extreme reluctance to adopt progressive methods and the long continuance of the "circuit system" of ministerial leadership are some reasons given for the decline in interest. In 1943 there was one communicant member and the Franconia Mission Board made Worcester a mission station. An annex was added to the church building in 1948 to provide

space for Sunday school and for summer Bible school, in which the enrollment had reached several hundred. On Jan. 22, 1950, Paul R. Clemens was ordained minister and Worcester again became an organized congregation, with 80 members in 1958.　　P.R.C.

Beulah Clemens, "History of Worcester Church," *Mission News* (Franconia) May-June, 1958, p. 2.

Word of Testimony was a quarterly publication of the China Mennonite Mission Society (MB), 7¼ x 10 in., at Tsaohsien, Shantung, China, first issue probably 1929. During the latter period of its publication it was edited by Loyal H. Bartel. It had 4-12 pages and presented reports and articles by the M.B. missionaries in the Shantung area.　　J.F.S.

Words of Cheer, a Mennonite (MC) periodical for children, ages 9-11, was first published in April 1876, at Orrville, Ohio, by Dr. Henry A. Mumaw, editor and founder. It appeared as an 8-page monthly and was intended to reach boys and girls for reading at home. In 1878 the paper was sold to the Mennonite Publishing Company at Elkhart, Ind., and was edited by Joseph Summers. In August 1892 Abram B. Kolb was appointed as editor. Other editors were as follows: D. H. Bender 1904-8, A. D. Martin 1908-9, H. Frank Reist 1909-12, J. A. Ressler 1912-36, Ellrose D. Zook 1936-49, Elizabeth A. Showalter 1949- . In 1908 the paper was sold to the Mennonite Publishing House, Scottdale, Pa., the first issue of the new owner appearing April 26, 1908. In 1892 the format was enlarged but the pages were reduced from eight to four. The paper contains stories, articles, poems, puzzles, and children's letters. It is illustrated and occasionally appears in two colors. Beginning in 1951 the paper was enlarged to 8 pages and reduced in size to 8 x 10¾ in. Its circulation in 1958 was 26,750.　　E.D.Z.

Worker's Exchange, the periodical of the Pacific District of the General Conference Mennonite Church, was begun by Emma Ruth in 1930 in her capacity as field secretary of the conference. Since then the *Worker's Exchange* was usually published every month with the exception of July, August, and sometimes September. Its format and method of printing have varied. Editors have been Emma Ruth, Reedley, Cal., 1930-43; Mrs. E. J. Muller, Lind, Wash., 1943-46; Henry B. Dirks, Los Angeles, Cal., 1946-48; Willard Wiebe, Lind, Wash., 1948-50; Clyde H. Dirks, Portland, Ore., 1950-53; and George A. Fast, Milwaukie, Ore., 1953- . The place of publication has always been the home of the editor.　　J.F.S.

Workum, a town in the Dutch province of Friesland (1953 pop. 4,080, with 190 Mennonites), with a Mennonite congregation. The year of the origin of this congregation is unknown, but Anabaptists were found here at an early date. The martyr Claesken (*q.v.*) Gaeledochter was baptized "near Workum in the fields" in 1549. Both she and her husband Hendrik (*q.v.*) Eeuwesz were executed at Leeuwarden in 1559. Leenaert (*q.v.*) Bouwens baptized 23 persons at Workum in 1551-54, one in 1557, and 25 in 1563-65. In 1574 Hendrik (*q.v.*) Pruyt died at the hands of Spanish soldiers. At this time or shortly after, the Mennonites must have been rather numerous at Workum and soon they were leading in trade and shipping, then an important means of livelihood in this town. In 1578 when the town was liberated from the Spanish yoke, a Mennonite, Hemme (*q.v.*) Haucx (b. 1511), became a burgomaster of Workum, and three other Mennonites were in the town council; they were exempted from the oath. But as early as 1600 Calvinism became predominant at Workum, which was somewhat intolerant toward Mennonitism. In 1605 the Reformed pastor Johannes Bilt (*q.v.*) sharply attacked the Mennonites, and in 1608 the remodeling of the meetinghouse was forbidden. But soon relations between the magistrates and the Mennonites seem to have improved; no further trouble occurred.

There is some unclear information that there were three congregations at Workum *c*1580, one High German, one Frisian, and one Waterlander, but only of the Waterlander church is there anything definitely known. This congregation, which in 1647 was represented at the Waterlander conference at Amsterdam, was divided by a schism, probably before 1600. A more conservative part of the congregation separated from the main, rather progressive body. This conservative group may have assumed the name of Frisian or High German. Each group had a meetinghouse; the progressives met at de Keet, a former salt works located on the site of the present meetinghouse, whereas the conservatives met in a private home, not far from de Keet. It is not known when and how this division ended, but the conservative group had disappeared at least by 1620. The preacher of the Keet congregation was a certain Eenke from about 1580; his son Rippert Eenkes (*q.v.*) was a preacher from *c*1600 and soon after an elder, serving until after 1627. He was an influential Waterlander leader, who conducted services in a number of congregations as far away as Amsterdam, Haarlem, and Emden, and even in Danzig in Prussia. But in his home church his advanced ideas evoked much opposition and in 1618 he was suspended on a charge of misconduct, which was used to eliminate the powerful elder, beloved by many but undesirable for more. Many conferences were held to restore peace; in the meantime it became clear that the charge was false. Finally the Waterlander leader Hans de Ries (*q.v.*), who visited Workum more than once, succeeded in 1620 in settling the dissensions. After the death of Eenkes the congregation continued until 1738 to choose their ministers from their own members. Usually there were three or four preachers, whereas baptism and communion services were led by elders from elsewhere.

In 1695 the Workum congregation was one of the founders of the Mennonite conference of Friesland (FDS). The ties with the Waterlanders in North Holland, which had been very strong in the early 17th century, were loosened. Workum was always a loyal and even leading member in the FDS, except in 1817, when it withdrew for a few months because it was dissatisfied with the subsidy policy of the conference, Workum also played an important role in the Zuiderklasse (*q.v.*).

A new meetinghouse, spacious and well-built, was erected in 1695. This meetinghouse is still in use; in 1956-57 it was renovated, and rededicated April 11, 1957. The cost of the 1695 church had been about 5,100 Dutch guilders. Many members of the church were well-to-do businessmen in shipping, shipbuilding, lumbering, or lime-burning. The wealthiest citizens of Workum in the 17th and early 18th centuries, members of the Hinlopen, Roos, Molenaar, and de Hoop families, were Mennonites. These families all died out or had left Workum by the 19th century. In the 18th century the prosperity of the town declined, particularly because of the decline of Baltic Sea shipping. At the same time the prosperity and the membership of the Workum Mennonite congregation declined. The baptized membership, which is estimated at more than 400 *c*1650, stood at 417 in 1692, 434 in 1703, 399 in 1715, and 325 in 1748, but from then there was a catastrophic decay: about 230 in 1762, *c*190 in 1791, 74 in 1838, 70 in 1861; from then there was some increase: 97 in 1900, 114 in 1926, 112 in 1940, followed by a slight decrease in the last years. In 1958 the membership numbered 89.

In 1738 the first salaried minister, coming from outside, was Jan Cornelis Dam, who served at Workum 1738-82. He was followed by Sybren Hofstra 1782-1811, J. van Douwen 1811-25, S. J. van der Goot 1826, who was the first pastor of Workum educated at the Amsterdam Mennonite seminary, Jacob Oosterbaan 1827-39, J. H. Akkeringa 1839-73, J. Westerman Holstijn 1874-83, S. Wartena Jr. 1884-86, four years of vacancy, T. H. Siemelink 1890-1908, H. Westra 1908-11, J. Kooiman 1911-14, I. Hulshoff 1914-35, J. P. H. Grootes 1935-39, D. Richards 1940-44, G. de Groot 1944-48, R. Hofman 1950-54, and Miss M. J. van Hamel from 1954. Since 1942 the pastors of Workum have also been in charge of the small congregation of Koudum (*q.v.*).

At the close of the 18th century peace was greatly disturbed in the Workum church by differing political views. Whereas the deacon Ruurd Wopkes sided with the Orangists (political party favoring the Prince of Orange and the established political order), many members, e.g., the merchant Jan Douwes de Hoop and particularly the pastor Sybren Hofstra, were Patriots (*q.v.*); abandoning the principle of nonbearing of arms, they together with the non-Mennonite citizens organized a voluntary militia in 1785, and in 1787 tried (but in vain) to take possession of the city government. Thereupon Jan de Hoop's home was plundered and pastor Hofstra was suspended from his office 1787-95 by the city magistrates. In 1797 peace, both political and congregational, was restored. By the Napoleonic occupation and the financial measures of Napoleon the Mennonite congregation of Workum, formerly rather well-to-do, was greatly impoverished. The considerable legacy willed to the church by Simen Durk Hinlopen in 1795 was nearly all claimed as a compulsory state loan; in 1811 there were no funds to pay the pastor's salary. The financial situation was improved after 1815 by the generous gifts of its treasurer, J. J. Stelwagen, and a regular subsidy from the A.D.S. from 1818.

Church activities in 1959 are: ladies' circle, youth group 18-25, and a Sunday school for children. vDZ.

T. H. Siemelink, "Geschiedenis van de Doopsgezinde gemeente te Workum," in *DB* 1899, 1903, and 1905; *idem, Toespraak* to commemorate the second centennial of the meetinghouse (n.p., n.d.-1895); *Inv. Arch. Amst.* I, No. 663; II, Nos. 2348-51; II, 2, Nos. 652-71; Blaupot t. C., *Friesland,* 89, 157, 169, 187, 188, 246, 248, 252, 306; *DB* 1861, 144; 1873, 83, 90-103; 1888, 116; 1895, 179.

World Conference: see **Mennonite World Conference.**

World Mennonite Membership Distribution. Beginning as a Reformation movement in Switzerland (1525) and Holland (1530), Anabaptism spread from the first center immediately into South and Middle Germany and Austria, Tirol, and Moravia (1525-28), and from the second to Flanders, the Lower Rhine area, and Northwest Germany (1530-50), and on to West and East Prussia, Danzig, and the Vistula Delta in Poland (1540-60). No information is available on the early membership totals, but there is sufficient evidence to believe that there were at least 5,000 martyrs in the first generation, 1525-55. The Hutterite population reached at least 15-20,000 by 1555 in Moravia.

By 1700 the distribution of baptized members was probably as follows: Holland 80,000, Switzerland 500, Palatinate 500, Northwest Germany with Holstein 1,000, West Prussia and associated areas 7,500, Hungary and Slovakia 500, making a total of 90,000 in Europe, plus a small handful of 25 in the newly established Germantown settlement in Pennsylvania.

By 1850 world membership had declined by one fourth, due exclusively to the formidable decline in Holland. The distribution can be calculated roughly as follows: Holland 25,000, Switzerland 500, France 500, South Germany 1,000, Northwest Germany 1,500, West Prussia etc. 7,500, South Russia 10,000, Eastern United States 20,000, Ontario 1,500; total 67,500.

Fifty years later, by 1900, with the strong expansion in Russia to 40,000, in the United States (now including the Midwest) to 50,000, and in Canada (now including Manitoba) to 25,000, while the rest of Europe remained largely static, the total more than doubled, reaching 150,000. By this time the North American continent had become the home of half of world Mennonitism.

By 1959 Mennonitism had expanded by migration into the Latin American countries of Mexico, Paraguay, Brazil, Uruguay, Argentina, and Honduras (total 25,000 members). By missionary outreach it expanded into three continents: beginning in 1851 to Asia (Java), in 1899 to India, in 1905 to China, and in 1949 to Japan (Formosa and Viet-Nam later); in 1910 to Africa (Belgian Congo, 1934 to East Africa, Tanganyika), and in 1917 to South America (Argentina, 1945 to Colombia). In 1958 the total membership in these younger churches was 65,000, distributed by continents as follows: Africa 28,000, Asia 36,000, and South America 1,000. Meanwhile Mennonitism had been wiped out in West Prussia in 1945, and decimated in Russia 1917-30 and 1940-55, but had grown substantially again in Holland, and very substantially in North America by immigration from Russia (1922-30, 1947-50), as well as by natural growth. The total world membership had again more than doubled in the base countries, in 1958 reaching 325,000, and together with the young churches in Asia and Africa had approached 400,000, of which total half was in the United States-Canada block.

The following world membership distribution in 1958 by continents and countries is taken from the *Mennonite Yearbook and Directory* for 1959 and represents the best available information, based largely on official reports except as indicated by *, which is an estimate.

Europe		95,764
Russia	40,000*	
Holland	39,000	
Germany	12,078	
France	2,700	
Switzerland	1,900	
Sicily	90	
Luxembourg	50	
Belgium	24	
Austria	12	
	95,764	
North America		220,272
United States	159,445	
Canada	52,987	
Mexico	7,348	
Honduras	50	
Puerto Rico	365	
Jamaica	64	
Cuba	13	
	219,771	
Asia		36,013
India	28,086	
China	4,000*	
Java	3,343	
Japan	494	
Formosa	90	
	36,013	
Africa		27,809
Belgian Congo	26,000	
Tanganyika	1,632	
Ethiopia	150	
Ghana	27	
	27,809	
South America		10,639
Paraguay	6,189	
Uruguay	1,768	
Brazil	1,632	
Argentina	738	
Colombia	300	
Bolivia	12	
	10,639	
Total world Mennonite membership		390,497
Including children in the total population		520,000*
Hutterian Brethren population		
Canada	8,590	
United States	2,940	
Total	11,530	

For a review of the history of world Mennonitism by larger areas see *Asia, Africa, Canada, Europe, Germany, Netherlands, Russia, South America, United States.*

The distribution of world Mennonite membership by ethnic groups descending from the original (1) Swiss-South German and (2) Dutch-North German sources is estimated as follows by continents:

World Mennonite Distribution by Historic Ethnic Groups

(Rounded figures)

	Dutch-North German	Swiss-South German
Europe		
Russia	40,000	
Holland	39,000	
Germany	9,500	2,500
France		2,700
Switzerland		1,900
	88,500	7,100
North America		
United States	33,800	126,000
Canada	43,000	10,000
Mexico	6,800	
	83,600	136,000
South America		
Paraguay	6,200	
Uruguay	1,750	
Brazil	1,600	
Argentina	150	
	9,700	
Grand Total	181,800	143,100

Mennonite Yearbook and Directory 1959 (Scottdale, Pa.)   H.S.B.

Worldliness, a term not unique to Mennonites, but very common among them, used to designate attitudes, tendencies, and behavior influenced by the "world," thought of as the evil system of life and conduct opposed to Christ. "World" is used frequently in this sense in the New Testament. Paul (Gal. 1:4) described Christ's saving work as a deliverance "from this present evil world." Jesus said (John 17:16) that His disciples "are not of the world, even as I am not of the world," whence comes the expression, "in the world but not of the world." James (1:27) defines pure religion as including "to keep . . . [oneself] unspotted from the world." John (I John 5:19) speaks of the "whole world . . . [lying] in wickedness" and promises Christians that they will overcome the world. The two most common passages used in regard to worldliness are Rom. 12:2, "Be not conformed to this world," and I John 2:15, "Love not the world, neither the things that are in the world. If any man love the world, the love of the Father is not in him." A major difficulty has been that of identifying precisely what "world" is, and therefore what "worldliness" is. The temptation, not always avoided, has been to emphasize aspects of culture as worldly because easily identified, while overlooking the deeper aspects of worldliness such as materialism. Nevertheless the problem of worldliness has been and remains a major concern for all earnest Christians who endeavor to follow their Lord closely in true discipleship, and requires all the resources of grace and insight to master it. (See **Nonconformity.**)
                                                    H.S.B.

Wormer, a village in the Dutch province of North Holland on the Zaan River (1953 pop. 5400, with 120 Mennonites), the seat of a Mennonite congregation. Early Anabaptism, found here from 1533, was somewhat revolutionary; in March 1534 there were some 30 inhabitants of Wormer among the Anabaptists who sailed from Amsterdam en route to Münster (*q.v.*) in Westphalia. Pieter (*q.v.*) Pietersz, of Wormer, who was among them, was executed in 1534. Anabaptists of Wormer in December 1534 tore the sacrament from the hands of the Catholic priest Duncanus (*q.v.*) (see **Dirck van Wormer**). In early 1535, during a raid in the Waterland district of North Holland, only a few persons were apprehended at Wormer, the others having fled until autumn. A bit of information dated March 4, 1535, seems to indicate that a house at Wormer in which the Anabaptists had held meetings was destroyed. In 1536 Frans (*q.v.*) Dirksz Quintijn (Frans van Wormer), who had promulgated a plan to seize the city of Alkmaar, was executed there. In 1543 a new raid was made in the villages of Wormer and neighboring Jisp, without success however; all the Anabaptists had fled. Cecilia (*q.v.*) Jheronimusdochter, a native of Wormer, died as a martyr in 1549.

Soon after this there was a congregation at Wormer, which in the 1550's joined the Waterlanders. To the Waterlander conferences of 1581 and 1647, both held at Amsterdam, the Wormer congregation sent a representative. Like most Waterlander congregations in North Holland, that of Wormer was in the 17th century rather conservative, strictly maintaining the confession of de Ries (*q.v.*) and opposed to Collegiant (*q.v.*) views. About 1674 both the congregations of Wormer and Jisp (*q.v.*) joined the Zonist (*q.v.*) Sociëteit. By this time Wormer and Jisp seem to have partly united (complete union not before 1834). They were led by very conservative ministers like Pieter Jans Stapper (*q.v.*) and some members of the Mol (*q.v.*) family. In 1698 Jacob Pieters Banning, a more liberal preacher at Wormer, was dismissed by a council of Zonist leaders, including Herman Schijn, E. A. van Dooregeest, and D. S. Moeriaen.

The town of Wormer in the second half of the 16th century became very prosperous, its inhabitants being engaged in herring fishing and in the 17th century also in whaling and industries connected with fishery: shipbuilding, baking ship biscuit, etc. In 1673, 800 guilders were collected in the Mennonite congregation as a contribution to the expenses of war. But in the early 18th century a great economic decline began, which cast its shadow on the Mennonite congregation. Though exact figures of membership are not available, there was a considerable decrease about 1720, the membership dropping to about one third of that of 100 years earlier. The amounts collected for the Mennonites of Poland and Prussia in 1727 and 1733 were therefore rather small: 60 and 75 guilders, respectively.

Until 1831 the congregation of Wormer-Jisp was served by lay preachers, usually chosen from its own membership; one of them was Klaas Yp, who served 1743-d.95, more than half a century. In 1831 the congregation called its first minister trained at the Amsterdam Mennonite seminary—C. Cardinaal, who served here until 1834. He was followed by G. L. Bavink, serving 1834-36, W. A. van Kampen 1836-41, P. van der Goot 1842-43, G. Vissering 1843-69, E. M. Mulder 1869-71, A. G. van Gilse 1871-72, A. Mulder 1873-74, W. I. Leendertz 1875-78, J. G. Boekenoogen 1881-84, and W. P. J. van Haarst 1884-1921. After the departure of van Haarst the pulpit was vacant for nearly two years. Since Feb. 11, 1923, the pastor of neighboring Krommenie (q.v.) has also been serving at Wormer-Jisp.

The baptized membership of the congregation numbered 58 in 1847, 62 in 1861, 96 in 1900, 123 in 1926, and 80 in 1958 (about 50 living in Wormer). The old meetinghouse, a frame building of c1755, was replaced by a brick church in 1851. Church activities are a ladies' circle, a circle of young members, and a Sunday school for children.   vDZ.

Inv. Arch. Amst. I, Nos. 10, 62b, 83, 85c, 98, 131, 137, 159, 159a, 253, 357, 896, 904; II, Nos. 2352-56; Kühler, *Geschiedenis* I, 87, 92, 366; Blaupot t. C., *Holland* I, 45, 251, 348; *idem* II, 204, 234; *DJ* 1837, 17 f.; 1850, 22-24; *DB* 1861, 164; 1872, 57; 1877, 80; 1898, 78-106; 1909, 18; 1917, 173.

Wormerveer, an industrial town in the Dutch province of North Holland on the Zaan River (pop. c12,000, with c500 Mennonites), the seat of a Mennonite congregation, concerning the origin of which there is no information. At the end of the 16th century there were at Wormerveer two Mennonite congregations, a Waterlander, generally called Wormerveer *op't Noord,* and a Frisian, usually called Wormerveer *op't Zuid.*

1. Concerning the early history of the North congregation (*op't Noord*) there is only sparse information. It was represented at the Waterlander conference at Amsterdam in 1647. It was a member of the Waterlander (Rijper, *q.v.*) Sociëteit and joined the Zonist (*q.v.*) conference c1674. At this time a severe dispute arose in this church between a more conservative part which stressed the confession of faith and opposing Collegiantism (*q.v.*), and a more progressive part which favored Collegiant views and practices. This dispute lasted from c1669 for more than ten years; even the intervention of the Court of Holland in 1674 and 1678 did not clear away the dissensions. Finally Galenus (*q.v.*) Abrahamsz in 1681 succeeded in restoring peace. The booklet *De Quynende Kercke der Waterlandse Doopsgesinde tot Wormer-veer* (Amsterdam, 1677), though somewhat partial, relates the background of this conflict. After the quarrel was settled, the North congregation, or at least its ministers, remained rather conservative; this was the hotbed of new dissensions in the following three decades. At first the membership must have been very numerous; in 1675 it still numbered 300. But gradually a number of more progressive members joined the Wormerveer Frisian church.

The North congregation was served by lay preachers, at first chosen from the membership, later called

from outside, the last of whom were Albert Vrijer, serving 1770-98, and Klaas Schermer 1800-49. The first salaried minister educated at the Amsterdam seminary to serve here was J. W. Straatman, serving 1849-50, followed by G. ten Cate 1851-58, A. J. Bijl 1861-62, J. H. van der Veen 1863-66, and G. Kool 1866-99. In 1899, the pulpit being vacant, it was resolved to merge with the Wormerveer South (*op't Zuid*) congregation, then also vacant. On Sunday, Aug. 22, 1899, the last service was held in the meetinghouse of the North congregation. At this time the membership was 56 (78 in 1847, 70 in 1861). Previous attempts at unification of the two congregations in 1725, 1789, and 1863 had failed.

2. The South congregation (*op't Zuid;* Frisian), a member of the Frisian Conference of North Holland, was in the 17th century much smaller in membership than the Waterlander congregation. In the late 16th and the early 17th centuries it was more conservative than the North church. The ban was maintained more strictly, outside marriages were unknown, and its members were opposed to serving in public offices; for example, in 1626 Pieter Jansen was fined for refusing to accept the office of sheriff; in 1628 two other brethren of the church refused to be members of the town council. But in course of time the congregation, which consisted largely of rather well-to-do businessmen, and which was led by capable ministers and deacons, grew more progressive and more liberal than the North church, though no member of the South congregation held a public office before 1796. Whereas in the Waterlander congregation only a few members participated in the Collegiant (*q.v.*) meetings, many outstanding members of the South church were ardent Collegiants, including the preacher Dirck Jacobs Kipper (1655-1734) and particularly Jan Gerritsz Schenk (d. 1760), who from 1726 often performed baptism at the Collegiant center at Rijnsburg (*q.v.*), and made a bequest of 40,000 guilders to the Collegiants. He also had the large masonry baptismal tub at Rijnsburg made at his expense. The gift of 2,305 guilders collected in 1673 for the national needs during wartime bears testimony to the importance of the congregation and the wealth of its members, who in 1727, 1733, and 1736 contributed 184 guilders, 337 guilders, and 1,650 guilders to the needs of the Prussian Mennonites.

Until 1764 the congregation was served by unsalaried and untrained preachers, including some capable and influential men like Dirck Gerritsz (1565-1626), founder of the paper industry on the Zaan, his son Jacob Dirks (*q.v.,* 1615-89), and his grandson Dirk Jacobsz Kipper (1655-1734), cheese merchants, Pieter Jansz (*q.v.*) van den Busch (d.1698), and Gerrit Blaauw, serving 1726-80. The first salaried minister was Bernardus Doornbosch (*q.v.*), serving 1764-80; he was a beloved preacher, but his moral conduct was not above reproach and so he was dismissed. He was followed by Arent van Groenou 1780-91, Leendert Klein, who was the first pastor in this congregation trained at the Amsterdam seminary, serving at Wormerveer 1791-1826, followed by Jan Gerrit Boekenoogen 1827-63, Simon Gorter 1863-70, Jer. de Vries 1870-72, I. J. le Cosquino de Bussy 1872-78, I. H. Boeke 1878-84, P. K.

Bijl 1886-88, H. van Cleeff 1889-96, and B. P. Plantinga 1897-98.

The membership of the South congregation was 167 in 1761, 229 in 1794, 193 in 1847, 223 in 1861, and 360 in 1898.

3. The (united) Mennonite congregation of Wormerveer started in September 1899 with 460 baptized members. The membership numbered 475 in 1933, 355 in 1958. Pastors were A. K. Kuiper 1899-1901, H. Britzel 1902-38, P. van der Meulen 1938-47, and P. J. Smidts since 1947. The present meetinghouse is that of the former South congregation, built in 1831 (organ of 1855). The Wormerveer congregation is the only Dutch congregation which published a weekly paper: *Ons Doopsgezind Krantje* appeared from Sept. 6, 1913, until World War II. Church activities are a church choir, ladies' circle, youth group 18-25, youth group Elfregi, Sunday school for children. From Sept. 1, 1934, until 1947 the pastor of Wormerveer was also in charge of the congregation of Knollendam (*q.v.*).

The Mennonites have played an important part in the life and economic growth of the town. In the 16th century Wormerveer was but a small hamlet. In 1613 the population numbered only about 450 souls, in 1638 about 800, and only a small percentage of them were not Mennonites. At present Wormerveer has a considerable industry (oil, soap, oats, flour, rice, cocoa, paper, dyes, chlorine; shipbuilding). In most of these industries the Mennonites until recent times were leading. Many old families which were formerly found among the Wormerveer Mennonites, such as Blaaum, Schenk, Laan, Prins, Keen, Vas, Ris, Boekenoogen, Koekebakker, van Gelder, Groot, Lely, and Volger, have died out or left the town. Of the old Mennonite families at present only Aten, Dekker, and Vis are found among the members of Wormerveer.   vdZ.

Inv. Arch. Amst. I, Nos. 447, 900-5; II, Nos. 2357 f., 2359; II, 2, No. 672; Blaupot t. C., *Holland* I, 212, 251, 271, 348; II, 194, 197, 201, 204, 232; J. C. van Slee, *De Rijnsburger Collegianten* (The Hague, 1896) 196-200; *DJ* 1837, 18; *DB* 1861, 164 f.; 1882, 114; 1883, 72; 1899, 213; 1901, 15; 1918, 146; *De Zondagsbode* XLIV (1930-31) No. 52.

Worms, a town on the Rhine in the Palatinate, Germany (pop. 56,500 in 1953), was in 1527 a center of Anabaptist activity. In January 1527 both Hans Denk (*q.v.*) and Ludwig Haetzer (*q.v.*) came to Worms, where they completed and published their translation of the Old Testament Prophets (see **Worms Prophets**). There was probably no Anabaptist congregation in this town before 1527. The rise of the Worms Anabaptist movement may have been the result of the work of Melchior Rinck (*q.v.*), Haetzer, and particularly Denk, though Fellmann is of the opinion that Denk was not especially active here, leading a retired life. In any case it is clear that Denk deeply influenced Jacob Kautz (*q.v.*), one of the Reformed preachers at Worms, who even before the coming of Denk and Haetzer opposed infant baptism. Kautz was won over for the Anabaptist principles; among his converts was his co-preacher Hilarius (*q.v.*), who in turn converted many others. The clergy and the city government at this time lived in a kind of vacuum

between Catholicism and Reformation and did not seriously counteract Anabaptist activity.

On June 9, 1527, Kautz attached seven Anabaptist theses on the door of the Dominican Church, inviting to a public debate on June 13. Whereas Hege held that these theses differed from the views of Denk, Goeters states that Denk was the very father of Kautz's theses. The disputation was not held in the way Kautz wished, because the Reformed (Lutheran) pastors, either for the safety of their church or for political reasons, were not inclined to participate. The result was that on June 13 Kautz and other preachers gave a free testimony and broad explanation of their Anabaptist views to a large attendance. Thereupon both the Lutheran pastors and the Catholics tried to stop the movement. The Catholics denounced the theses to the Palatine Elector, saying that Kautz's ideas concerning baptism and communion were a horror for all true Christians. The Lutheran preachers of Worms, Ulrich Preu and Johann Freiherr, replied to Kautz's theses with "seven articles," which had been promulgated by the press. In July 1 the city council of Worms resolved to banish Kautz and Hilarius from the town. The next day the Reformed preachers of Strasbourg, who had anxiously followed developments at Worms, published *Getrewe Warnung der Prediger des Evangely zu Strassburg über die Artickel, so Jakob Kautz, Prediger zu Wormbs, kürzlich hat lassen ausgehen.* About the same time Denk and Haetzer also left the city. Rinck had already been banished. After the Anabaptist leaders had been removed from the stage, Anabaptism in Worms soon declined, though a congregation still seems to have existed for a short while.   vdZ.

Chr. Hege, *Die Täufer in der Kurpfalz* (Frankfurt, 1908) 34 ff.; *TA Baden-Pfalz,* No. 129; J. F. Gerhard Goeters, *Ludwig Hätzer* (Gütersloh, 1957) 97-99, 104-9; W. Fellmann, *Hans Denck, Schriften, 2. Teil* (Gütersloh, 1956) 13 f.

Worms Prophets, a translation of the Old Testament Prophets by Ludwig Haetzer with some assistance from Hans Denk, named after the city of Worms in which the first two editions appeared. The exact title of the first edition is *Alle Propheten nach Hebräischer sprach verteutscht* (Worms, Peter Schöffer, 1527). A total of 12 separate editions appeared 1527-31, as follows: (1) and (2) at Worms April 13, 1527, in octavo and folio; (3) Augsburg June 1527 in folio; (4) Worms Sept. 7, 1527, in octavo; (5) Augsburg Dec. 14, 1527, in octavo; (6) Hagenau (Alsace) Feb. 12, 1528, in folio; (7) Augsburg Feb. 24, 1528, in folio; (8) Augsburg March 7, 1528, in folio; (9) Worms June 19, 1528, in octavo; (10, 11, and 12) Augsburg June 25, 1528, May 19, 1528, and Nov. 4, 1528, all in octavo. A part of the translation appeared in three editions of the complete Bible published at Strasbourg 1529/30, 1530/32, and 1535/36, although only a few copies of the last edition used the Worms translation, most using Luther's text. Two concordances cite the Worms translation—(1) Leonhard Brunner's (Worms, 1529), and (2) one published by Köpfl at Strasbourg in 1530. Denk's own commentary on Micah of 1532 also uses it.

The Worms translation of the Prophets was the first Protestant translation of this part of the Bible, and as such served a real need and was in great demand; particularly since it was a fairly good translation directly from the Hebrew. Luther had a copy by May 4, 1527, Franz Kolb in Bern one by May 5. It was certainly on the market for the Frankfurt spring book fair in 1527. By early May the city council of Nürnberg had forbidden its sale in the city. The ultimate reaction of both Lutheran and Zwinglian leaders was negative, not because of poor literary quality or accuracy (Luther recognized its good points), but because its authors came from "the Anabaptist sect," who were guilty of certain heresies, and also because they cited some Jewish authorities in their translation. Goeters believes that both Luther and Leo Jud felt pressed to proceed with their translations because of the popularity of the Worms translation. In 1529 the Zürich translation appeared (Froschauer edition). The same Worms printer (Peter Schöffer) who had printed the Haetzer-Denk Prophets adopted the Zürich translation at once for his 1529 full Bible. With the appearance of Luther's full Bible in 1532 the Worms translation was completely overshadowed and disappeared. According to Baring some 80 copies of the various editions have survived, largely in European libraries, to testify to its early popularity.

Recent research, especially that of Goeters, has corrected some long-standing misconceptions about the Worms translation. (1) The prime author was Haetzer, with Denk as a useful assistant but not as a prime author. (2) The claim of Christian Hege (ML I, 408) that Luther and the Zürich translators depended heavily upon the work of Haetzer and Denk, and the claim of Ludwig Keller that the two other translations are based on the Worms translation, are much exaggerated, although both profited from it. Goeters' judgment is sound: "Next to the Bible text itself, the Worms Prophets were the most important literary material for the Lutheran and Zürich translations." (3) There is evidence that the Worms translation of Habakkuk is dependent upon Luther's 1526 translation of the same book.

In the light of Goeters' demonstration that Haetzer was only a fringe figure in the Anabaptist movement, and that in Strasbourg in December 1526 he vigorously repudiated Anabaptist views and connections just when he was beginning the translation, the "Anabaptist" character of the Worms translation might need to be questioned. On the other hand, Denk was clearly an Anabaptist at this time, and Haetzer was definitely under his influence during their joint work on the translation while they were together in Worms February-July 1527, after which their paths separated, never to cross again. H.S.B.

G. Baring, "Die Wormser Propheten," in Beilage zum dritten Bericht des deutschen Bibelarchivs (Hamburg, 1933) and in Archiv für Reformationsgeschichte XXXI (1934) 23-41; E. Stähelin, Das theologische Lebenswerk Johannes Oekolampads (Leipzig, 1939); Chr. Hege, Die Täufer in der Kurpfalz (Frankfurt, 1908); E. Teufel, in Theologische Rundschau XV (1943) 58-62; Ernst Crous, "Zu den Bibelübersetzungen von Hätzer und Denk," in Beiträge zur Geschichte der Mennoniten (Weierhof, 1938) 72-83; G. Baring, Hans Denck Schriften I. Teil: Bibliographie (Gütersloh, 1955); J. F. G. Goeters, Ludwig Hätzer (Gütersloh, 1957), esp. "Die Wormser Ueber-

setzung der Propheten," 99-104; G. Haake, "Studien über die Wormser Uebersetzung der Propheten," Menn. Bl., 1898, 27-29; W. Fellmann, "Fünf alte Wormser Täuferdrucke," Gesch.-Bl., 1937, 25-31; F. W. E. Roth, Die Mainzer Buchdruckerfamilie Schöffer während des 16. Jahrhunderts (Leipzig, 1892) 133 ff.; idem, Die Buchdruckereien zu Worms a. Rhein im XVI. Jahrhundert (Worms, 1892) 18 ff.; Ludwig Keller, Ein Apostel der Wiedertäufer (Leipzig, 1882) 210-14; ML IV.

Worship, Public. *Anabaptist.* In contrast to the general Reformation doctrine that the church comes to expression when the Word is preached and the sacraments properly observed, the Anabaptists believed that the "true church is raised up" where "faith, spirit, and power" result in "repentance and change of life" and obedience to the truth. Hence the Anabaptists placed little emphasis in formal public worship or ceremonies, and rejected all liturgy. Persecution, which made meetings difficult and often dangerous, gave added support to this basic attitude. The Anabaptists did not come from a week of irreligious, worldly living and expect a beautiful building and attractive liturgy to draw them to God. They insisted that the Christian walks with God constantly in holy obedience and expected their daily life to come naturally to a climax in the fellowship of the gathered community of disciples, where a major concern was to seek the will of God from His Word and to help one another to higher levels of discipleship.

In such worship a common searching of life was involved, and discipline naturally resulted, often carried through as a supplement to the regular worship. The fact that several ministers served the group in Bible reading, admonition, and prayer, and that services were not held in large church buildings but in homes or barns, in forest retreats, or even caves, in addition to the understanding that every member was a responsible adult who had chosen to follow Christ and shared fully in the life of the brotherhood, added to the intense sense of participation by all. Hence, Anabaptist congregations were not "audiences" in attendance upon a worship service furnished by a clergyman in a building belonging to the state and used for nothing else, but a genuine brotherhood sharing in Bible study, prayer, and mutual admonition. The high authority of the Bible of course placed it in the very center of the service, and the reading and exposition of it, or admonition from it, was the most important element. In a sense life was more important than worship.

One of the results of this attitude was that Anabaptists steadfastly refused to attend the worship of the state church, even though as a consequence they were often punished and imprisoned. In fact, one of the ways that Anabaptists were detected was by nonattendance at the public preaching and communion services. The court records contain many cases of attempted compulsory attendance and penalties. Bullinger's Der Widertoufferen Ursprung (1560) contains as an appendix a reprint of an Anabaptist "booklet" giving the reasons why they did not attend "church."

There is no evidence of any Anabaptist meetinghouse built in the 16th century, except the one in Elbing-Ellerwald in West Prussia, built in 1590. However, before 1600 buildings such as warehouses were purchased in Holland and East Friesland and converted into meetinghouses (external remodeling to look like a church was forbidden). In Rotterdam such a building was in possession of the old Flemish at least by 1580. During the period of persecution the Anabaptists did not even have regular meeting places. A martyr of 1556 at Antwerp, Claes de Praet, testified that they met "there where Christ and His apostles held their meetings, in the woods, in the fields, on the seashore, and sometimes in homes." In larger towns such as Amsterdam meetings were held in private homes from the beginning. For the sake of safety, meeting places were constantly changed and messengers visited the members or sent notes to them to announce the place and the hour of the next meeting. This was true not only in the Netherlands and North Germany, but also in the South. A document of 1539 in the Strasbourg archives gives the exact wording of such a note which has been preserved: "Grace and peace from God the Father through Jesus Christ, our Lord and Savior. Amen. Beloved Jacob and dear Elsbeth, I am letting you know that on the coming Tuesday a meeting will be held at Schilken in the house where we were the last time. And don't come so late as the last time, and let the old man in Westhoffen also know. With this I commend you to God, peace be with you all who love God from the heart. Amen." Ruprecht Schwarz is named as one of the notifiers for the Strasbourg Anabaptists. His testimony (1539) describes the meeting places in or near Strasbourg as follows: "Says: They assembled in Schwabenloch and behind the Guten Leuten, also on the Illkirchen Nachtweid and in the Siegelsheimer Forest. Says, the Swiss Brethren and the Hofmannites were not united; the former were about 100, the latter not more than 5. They no longer attended the preaching [of the state church], because the preachers did not practice the ban, allowed good and bad go, that is abominable." In the Low Countries the man who notified the members of the time and place of meeting was called the "Weetdoener" (q.v.).

Little direct description of Anabaptist worship is available. There can be little doubt, however, about its simplicity, and that it included basically, at least after the very earliest days, Scripture reading, prayer, preaching, and singing. An early discipline found in the Berne archives says: "The brethren and sisters should meet at least three or four times each week to study the teachings of Christ and His apostles and admonish each other in the Lord. When they meet they should read something they understand which God has laid on their heart. The others should be quiet and listen so that two or three are not speaking at the same time and hindering the others from hearing. The psalter should be read daily by all. . . . The food for meals during times of meeting should be furnished by the brethren at whose home the meeting is held. . . . The Lord's Supper should be observed as often as the brethren come together." Peter Riedemann's Confession (c1540) describes a Hutterite worship service as follows: "When we come together, we do so with the desire to encourage and awaken our hearts in the grace of God, to walk in the Lord's sight with great-

er diligence and attention. Therefore, the people are first encouraged to mark diligently and to consider why we have met and come together, that they may prepare their hearts for prayer, so that they may come worthily before the Lord and pray for what concerns the church and all her members. After this we give thanks to God for all the good that He has given us through Christ, and for accepting us into His grace and revealing to us His truth. This is followed by an earnest prayer that He keep us faithful and devout therein to the end, and supply all our desires and needs, and open our hearts that we may use His Word with profit, hear, accept, and keep it. When this is done, one proceeds to proclaim the Lord's Word faithfully, according to the grace given by God, encouraging the heart to fear the Lord and to remain in His fear. When all this is completed the minister commends the church to God the Lord and lets them depart one from another, each to his place. When, however, we come together to keep the Lord's Memory or Supper the people are encouraged and taught for one, two, or three days and told vividly what the Lord's Supper is, what happens there and what one does thereby, and how one should prepare himself worthily to receive the same. Every day, however, has also its thanksgiving and prayer. When all this has taken place, and the Lord's Supper has been kept, a hymn of praise is sung to the Lord. Then the people are admonished to walk in accordance with what they have shown to be in their hearts, and then they are commended to the Lord and allowed to separate" (Riedemann's Confession, 129 f.).

Singing was certainly a part of Anabaptist worship, both in the North and the South, although at times it was suppressed because of danger. By the 1560's at least five distinct Anabaptist hymnals had been printed, besides earlier hymn leaflets and pamphlets. One hymnal was Swiss, one Lower Rhine, and three Dutch. The first part of the *Ausbund* is composed of hymns written in 1535 in Passau, "composed and sung" by imprisoned Swiss Brethren, as the title page says. Over 130 Anabaptist hymn writers are known. Songs were used in evangelism. Christian Neff says, "A flood of religious songs poured over the young brotherhood like a vivifying and refreshing stream." (See **Music, Church; Hymnology; Tunes.**) This was in spite of the fact that Conrad Grebel, in line with Zwingli, opposed all music, including singing in worship. Riedemann's Confession contains an article "Concerning Singing" (123), which says among other things, "To sing spiritual songs is pleasing to God, if we sing in the right way, that is, attentively, in the fear of God and are inspired by the Spirit of Christ. . . . Among us we do not allow other than spiritual songs to be sung."

Anabaptist worship traditions were long perpetuated in the worship of their descendants, in many cases down to the present day, as will be seen in the following sections of this article. H.S.B.

Paul M. Miller, "Worship Among the Early Anabaptists," *MQR* XXX (1956) 235-46; Peter Rideman, *Account of Our Religion, Doctrine and Faith* (Bridgnorth, England, 1950, translated from the German *Rechenschaft* of 1565).

Dutch Tradition and Practice. During the persecution period public worship of the Mennonites in the Netherlands was, of course, impossible; meetings then could be held only secretly. But by c1575 church services were held publicly, though until 1795 a number of restrictions were made by the magistrates concerning Mennonite meetings; particularly in the 17th century these restrictions often were rather rigorous. Mennonite meetinghouses then were not permitted on main streets and were not allowed to look like churches; hence a number of hidden and barnlike meetinghouses. At Aardenburg, Leiden, and other towns the public services of the Mennonites were not permitted to begin until the Reformed services had finished. But gradually these restrictions were dropped. In the 17th and 18th centuries religious services at Amsterdam, Haarlem, Rotterdam, and other larger towns were usually held twice each Sunday, and during the winter months also on a weekday, usually on Wednesday. In the country there was mostly one meeting on Sunday morning and in small congregations sometimes only each fortnight. Afternoon or evening services are now rather seldom.

Concerning the order of service in early times and in the 17th century there is only scarce information. Simon Rues gave circumstantial information on Mennonite public worship in 1742 in his book *Tegenwoordige Staet der Doopsgezinden* (Amsterdam, 1745). At this time there was a considerable difference between the worship services of the Lamists (*q.v.*) and the Zonists (*q.v.*) on the one hand and the Fijne (*q.v.*) Mennonites on the other hand. The order of service among the Fijne was usually as follows: hymn by the congregation, opening address by the minister, prayer, sermon, another prayer, closing hymn by the congregation; the benediction by the preacher dates from the early 18th century; before this time the closing hymn ended the service. For the prayers, always silent, the congregation knelt. No offering was taken, not even at the exit. The minister read his sermon from manuscript while seated on a chair. He wore no special garb. The order used by the Lamists and Zonists was largely influenced by that of the Calvinists: invocation by the minister, singing of a Psalm, a long prayer by the minister, then mostly, but not always, Scripture reading, sermon, from the early 18th century interrupted by congregational singing, during which an offering was usually taken, prayer after the sermon, another Psalm, benediction, and offering at the exit. In some churches, as the Amsterdam Lamist Church, there was Scripture reading before the minister mounted the pulpit. The minister stood while praying and preaching. In the 17th and 18th centuries the minister wore a robe with bands and a *steek* (three-cornered hat). Baptism and communion services, of course, had a somewhat different order. Among the Dutch Mennonite congregations of Flemish or Frisian background the worshipers remained seated throughout the service; the pastor or the deacons distributed bread and wine. This practice is still observed. In the congregations of Waterlander descent the attendants gather around one or more communion tables. (This practice, introduced by Hans de Ries, *q.v.*, was borrowed from the Calvinists.)

At present the ordinary Sunday service, varying slightly from congregation to congregation, takes place as follows: invocation, congregational singing, Scripture reading, prayer, hymn, sermon, organ, prayer (often the Lord's Prayer), hymn, and benediction. In most churches the offering is taken only at the exit. In 1948 a subcommittee of the A.D.S. compiled a *Kanselboek* (*q.v.;* book for the pulpit), containing suggestions for the order of the regular services as well as for a number of special meetings, like baptism and communion services.

Organs, the first of which was adopted in a Mennonite church in 1762, were until c1890 used only to accompany congregational singing, but since that time the organs, now found in all Dutch Mennonite meetinghouses, have a special function in the worship service. Choir (*q.v.*) singing is practiced in only a few churches and never regularly; solo singing and the use of other instruments than organs are practically unknown.   vDZ.

* * *

Prussian-Russian Tradition. Early Mennonite practices in Danzig, Prussia, Poland, and Russia were very similar to those of the early Dutch Mennonites. The meetings during the 16th-17th centuries took place mostly in private homes, barns, or sheds, partly because of pioneer conditions, but also because Mennonites were not permitted to worship in conspicuous public buildings. The Frisian Mennonite Church of Danzig was permitted to erect a meetinghouse in 1638, located in a garden and not distinguished from a residence. Most of the early buildings were in the name of some church member and not of the congregation. After the song leader had announced and led the hymn the sermon followed. The chairs for the ministers and deacons were located along the longer side of the wall on an elevation. There was no pulpit, but the central chair was a little higher. The minister presented his sermon while seated, and without notes. Gradually the practice of the minister delivering his sermon standing behind a pulpit, making use of outlines or notes, was introduced. Hans von Steen (*q.v.*) deeply deplored this innovation, fearing that "the beautiful simplicity of Menno's church was more and more disappearing."

Gradually the Prussian Mennonite churches adjusted themselves to their environment in their worship services by introducing some more elaborate elements of worship. The city churches, which had trained ministers, depended more or less on the taste of the individual minister, while the rural churches retained old practices for a longer period. A handbook for the minister and worship services was introduced quite early in some churches (see **Ministers' Manuals**). In some city churches communion tables were introduced and the ministers accepted the traditional clerical garb of the surrounding Lutheran Church during the worship service.

After the earliest practice, in which the sermons and exhortations were delivered extempore, the written sermon was introduced by the ministers of Holland and Prussia. Large collections of written sermons (*q.v.*) have been preserved. In Russia the tradition of reading the sermons was continued. In many instances, but not always, these sermons were prepared and written by the minister delivering them. He would repeat the sermon, stating on the first page on what occasions the sermon had been delivered. Many sermons were handed down from generation to generation, as is still the case among the conservative Mennonites of Manitoba and Mexico. In Russia, through revivalistic influences, this practice was gradually given up. One of the pioneers in free preaching was Bernhard Harder (*q.v.*), who began to preach heart-warming evangelistic sermons. Today among the Mennonites of Russian background in North and South America, with the exception of the very conservative groups, sermons are as a rule composed and delivered by the minister himself and delivered extempore—possibly with notes. Some ministers write their sermons out, but commit them to memory before delivering them.

In Russia the simple worship service of the early Dutch and Prussian tradition was perpetuated. But in the middle of the 19th century new and more spontaneous patterns of worship developed under the influence of the Pietists and Baptists, and were introduced first among the newly organized (1860) Mennonite Brethren. Some of the characteristics were the introduction of lighter hymns (Paul Gerhardt) and a prayer meeting before the preaching during the Sunday morning worship, preceded by Scripture reading and admonishing to prayer by one of the brethren of the congregation. The prayers were pronounced audibly by brothers and sisters in the congregation, young and old.

The worship service among the Mennonites who came from Prussia and Russia to America in 1874 ff. resembled that of the congregations from which they had come. Only gradually adjustments were made. This was first noticeable when the members of a congregation and the ministers came from various backgrounds in Russia and Prussia and adjustment to one pattern became necessary. Additional changes took place when the ministers received special training and changed from the German language to English. The worship practices of a congregation in a rural setting with a minister who has had no special training usually differ from those of a city church with a minister who has had theological training and especially if he has attended a non-Mennonite theological institution with liturgical leanings. Again a congregation with a minister who has received his training in a Bible institute will likely promote spontaneous forms of worship. In general, however, the colleges and the conference seminaries as well as the handbooks produced for this purpose do and will continue to promote uniformity along these lines. An innovation which is almost universal is the mimeographing or printing of worship bulletins (*q.v.*) which include the order of worship and the announcements for the week.

Hesitancy to collect money during the services for causes of the congregation or conference for a time hindered the introduction of this practice in some places, but it has become an integral part of every worship service. This practice is increasing among Mennonites who have come from Europe more recently, and is gradually being accepted by even the more conservative groups.

In the early days singing was not necessarily an integral part of the congregational worship, but later became a very essential part. During the latter part of the 18th century, organs (*q.v.*) were introduced in Holland and Germany, but in Russia and America not until the early 20th century. In Russia and America also choirs were introduced during the beginning of the 20th century and have become an integral part in many worship services, but not in Germany and Holland. The most conservative groups have neither organs nor choirs.

As a rule the worship order in General Conference Mennonite churches is as follows: Organ prelude, invocation, hymn, responsive reading or Scripture reading, prayer, choir, offering, hymn, sermon, hymn, benediction, organ postlude; or organ prelude, hymn, call to worship, invocation and Lord's Prayer, hymn, responsive reading, Scripture reading, prayer, offering, hymn, sermon, prayer and benediction, hymn, organ postlude.

As a rule, worship services formerly lasted up to two or three hours. Today a worship service hardly ever exceeds an hour, of which about half is devoted to the sermon and the other half to singing, Scripture reading, responsive reading, prayer, and offering. Formerly announcements were made from the pulpit in connection with the worship service. Today they have been eliminated in those congregations that use church bulletins. Most of the churches have ushers, who greet the worshiper at the door and help him locate a seat, and pass the collection plates.

Seating of the sexes in worship services was formerly universally separate. The most common form earlier was to have the women seated in the central part of the meetinghouse, with the men seated around them on the outside on benches facing inward, although in Russia and America the more common practice was to have the men on the right and the women on the left side of a central aisle. (See also **Architecture, Music, Hymnology, Organs, Sermons, Ministers' Handbooks, Singing, Choirs**.)

C.K., vDZ.

S. F. Rues, *Aufrichtige Nachrichten von dem gegenwärtigen Zustande der Mennoniten oder Taufgesinnten* (Jena, 1743) 46, 67, 128; N. van der Zijpp, *Geschiedenis der Doopsgezinden in Nederland* (Arnhem, 1952) 110; H. G. Mannhardt, *Die Danziger Mennonitengemeinde* (Danzig, 1919) 104; James Bixel, "Music in Worship," *Menn. Life* XIII (July 1958).

• • •

Swiss-South German Tradition. The worship of the Mennonites of Switzerland and South Germany was marked by simplicity, sincerity, and directness. Regular meetings for worship, prayer, preaching, and admonition, led by an elder or minister, were held in forests (e.g., at Immelhausen in Baden, as late as 1654), in remote farmhouses or barns, or in rooms in homes (sometimes especially built for such purposes). Meetinghouses (*q.v.*), at first forbidden by intolerant authorities, came late. The earliest were built in the Palatinate, e.g., Weierhof 1770, but most of them after 1800; Montbéliard 1832; in Alsace the first was Birkenhof 1845; in Switzerland, Basel-Binningen 1841; but most at the end of the

19th century, e.g., Langnau 1888. These meeting-houses were simple, unadorned, without tower or bell (except Ibersheim 1836), but usually with pulpits in the middle of one end which were sometimes somewhat elevated in imitation of the typical Protestant pulpit, but without organs (harmoniums were introduced later), men and women sitting separate.

In America simple meetinghouses were built from the beginning, probably in part modeled after the Quaker meetinghouse since the early immigrants had had no experience in Europe in building them. In some instances instead of a pulpit a table was placed in the middle of the long side, replaced later by a long pulpit, and in the first quarter of the 20th century by a small one-man type of pulpit. The pulpit still remained in the central location, symbolic of the central place of preaching in the worship. Special communion tables were not and are still not used. All the ministers sat on a long bench behind the table or pulpit. Song leaders sat around a table placed in front of the pulpit, from which they led the singing, seated; after the table disappeared they sat usually on the first or second bench. Standing to lead the singing came in only in the 20th century. The Amish never adopted meetinghouses, and to this day meet in homes, which customarily have a large room built for worship purposes, backless benches being hauled by wagon from place to place.

In Europe and America in earlier times meetings were customarily held once every two weeks in the morning, although neighboring congregations usually alternated, making it possible to attend services every week. Most families "went visiting" neighbors and friends for Sunday dinner on the open Sunday. Some conservative congregations in the East maintained the custom of biweekly services until far into the 20th century.

The order of service and manner of worship in both Europe and America was always simple, sober, and nonliturgical, with emphasis on the sermon, which was usually admonitory, didactic, and practical. Singing was always included, usually one or two hymns at the beginning, one after the Scripture reading and prayer, and one after the sermon. One minister "made the opening," i.e., read a Scripture selection (in Amish congregations determined by a traditional list of pericopes for each Sunday, since 1916 available in printed form), followed by kneeling silent prayer (replaced by audible prayer at various dates, but still silent in traditional congregations of certain sections such as Franconia and Lancaster). The sermon, delivered extempore by a second minister, was usually quite long (now reduced to 30-40 minutes), followed by kneeling prayer always closed by the Lord's Prayer. The latter is now widely dropped, but still practiced in parts of Lancaster and Franconia. The benediction, formerly given seated without the preacher's hand raised, was preceded by a closing hymn. The announcements were formerly made only just before or after the benediction. The offering was placed in boxes at the exits, but is now in America taken by passing collection plates through the congregation. Ushers were unknown, and still are not used in Europe. Offerings were not taken regularly until modern times, earlier only for special needs. Ordinary expenses were met by assessments or payments to the deacon. The Sunday school brought with it offerings (at first for children "penny" offerings) for expenses, still customary, but church offerings were held at first once monthly for missions; now the common practice is to take them every Sunday, in some places even on Sunday evenings. The custom of worshipers standing silently in prayer before sitting down in the pew, or of bowing the head in prayer in the pew, which has become common in Europe, has not been adopted in America.

Musical instruments are still strictly banned (a few exceptions in Latin American churches) from all services of the Mennonite Church (MC) and all related and conservative groups. Even in the worship of the Swiss congregations in Ohio and Indiana who later joined the General Conference Mennonite Church, and in the descendant groups from the Amish such as the Evangelical Mennonites and the Central Conference, they were admitted only late in the 19th or early in the 20th century (see Organs). The Brethren in Christ did not permit them until 1955, when approving conference action was taken. Choirs (q.v.) are still unknown in the Mennonite Church (MC) and related conservative groups, the emphasis being strongly on congregational singing only. Lighter Gospel hymns were introduced through revivalistic influences about the turn of the 20th century in the American churches of Swiss-South German descent, as was the case also in Switzerland and France (not in South Germany, where the chorale type hymn was retained in the Mennonite hymnals), although worship remained sober and traditional. Only rarely in the regular worship did lay members participate by prayer or testimony, and "Amens" or similar ejaculations from the congregation during the sermon were and are unknown.

In America (not in Europe) the custom of bringing even very small children along to the morning worship has been and still is widespread. Sunday school, which usually precedes the preaching service (in Europe parallel to the preaching service), provides special classes for small children, but their presence in the second service often interferes with a reverential atmosphere. Many modern meetinghouses now provide special separate rooms in the rear or in balconies for mothers with small children, with glass partitions from the main room. Church bulletins, mimeographed or printed, giving the order of service and announcements for the week, have come into use in the Mennonite Church (MC) since about 1940, but are not found in the more conservative groups.

Sunday evening services in America were not introduced until late in the 19th century or even later in the Mennonite Church (MC) (not at all in the Amish congregations). This forced the introduction of lights into the meetinghouses, which at times was the cause of much controversy. The evening service was introduced in part to provide "Young People's Meetings" (q.v.), in part to make evening services possible during the week of evangelistic meetings.   H.S.B.

Wössingen (Baden) Mennonite Church, originating about 1700, a member of the Verband (*q.v.*) conference, in 1959 had a membership of 49 and 17 unbaptized children, with Rudolf Funck as elder (1948) and Helmut Kreiter as preacher. The village of Wössingen lies about 10 miles east-northeast of Karlsruhe. Wössingen is one of the oldest Mennonite congregations east of the Rhine. The Swiss Mennonites who fled from their homeland in Bern and Zürich from 1650 on, first came into the Palatinate, but from about 1700 on also into the territory of the Margrave of Baden-Durlach. The tolerant Charles William (1709-18), founder of Karlsruhe, in 1715 offered religious freedom to all who would settle in the vicinity of his castle Karlsruhe. The Mennonites who came here became tenant farmers on the baronial estates where they were highly valued, and they have remained largely of this type. The descendants of the original families who settled in this neighborhood are now largely members of the Wössingen and Durlach congregations. In 1731 Wössingen appears in Ernst Müller's list of 13 Swiss congregations in the "Upper Palatinate." The *Naamlijst* for 1766 lists "Wesingen" as part of a congregation called "Boekschaft, Streichenberg en Wesingen," with Martin Krauter as elder, ordained 1746. It was listed further in the *Naamlijst* for 1786, 1793, and 1802, with Jost Glück as elder throughout, ordained preacher in 1756 and elder in 1773. In the 1857 *Namensverzeichnis* Heinrich Funk and Martin Funk appear as elders, ordained in 1835 and 1839 respectively, with a baptized membership of 55. In the Mannhardt *Jahrbuch* of 1881 the elders were listed as Philipp Schneider (1859) and Christian Funk (1872), membership 40.   H.S.B.

Wostitz (Wastitz; Czech, *Wostice*), a market village northwest of Nikolsburg (*q.v.*), the seat of a Hutterite Bruderhof which was built in 1557 with the consent of Albrecht Boskowice. In 1574-1622 the areas of Wostitz and Purschitz belonged to the dukes of Thurn-Valsassina. The archives of Liechtenstein (located in Vienna) of the years 1569 and 1571 contain a series of letters by Albrecht of Boskowice which give special recognition to the capabilities of the Hutterian Brethren in agriculture and the crafts. They apparently built the castle in Wostitz, for Albrecht gave his official the commission to make a better proposition with the Brethren for the "new building" in Wostitz. The achievements of the Brethren at Wostitz were very highly valued, as was also their medical skill. Duke Francis Thurn took his son John Jacob Thurn, who had been injured in battle in 1583, from the hospital in Vienna to Wostitz where he could have the benefit of the healing skill of the Hutterite physician. On Sept. 24, 1583, he wrote that the Anabaptist doctor in Wostitz had successfully treated his son. He had expelled the Hutterian Brethren from Wostitz two years previously, because the Hutterite servants in the duke's family refused to serve in the merriment on the occasion of a wedding. The Chronicle reports that shortly after the Brethren had moved away the duke's wife became very ill and died after three weeks.

In 1591 the Bruderhof in Wostitz was occupied by Hutterian Brethren who had had to leave Pergen and Veitelsbrunn. In 1617 they (50 persons) were violently expelled by Duke Veit Heinrich von Thurn, with the loss of all their property. HEGE.

Archiv für Reformationsgeschichte, 1933; Zieglschmid, Chronik; Beck, Geschichts-Bücher; ML IV.

Woudsend, a town in the Dutch province of Friesland, the seat of a Mennonite congregation, which, according to Blaupot ten Cate, was founded in 1600-20. This congregation was called Waterlander; in the 17th century there was at Woudsend also a small Janjacobsgezinden (*q.v.*) church, which may have been somewhat older than the Waterlander congregation. Concerning the Janjacobsgezinden, however, there is no further information; this congregation may have dissolved by 1630. In 1695 the Waterlander church joined the Mennonite conference of Friesland (FDS), then numbering about 40 baptized members; Arjen Clasen was its preacher from 1682 until 1727. A meetinghouse erected in 1722 had some stained glass windows. It was replaced by a new church, dedicated Feb. 13, 1859.

The membership was always small: *c*40 in 1695, *c*30 in 1761, 34 in 1838, 39 in 1861, 50 in 1900, 29 in 1958. The baptism book of the congregation dates from 1682. Until 1819 the congregation was served by untrained and unsalaried preachers, chosen from their own members, of whom Uilke Johannes Stinne, serving 1769-1800, and Foeke Ymes Postma 1800-19 were the last ones. In 1819 J. Oosterbaan, educated at the Amsterdam seminary, was called to serve in Woudsend (until 1824); he was followed by H. W. Woudstra 1826-27, J. S. Bakker 1828-30, G. J. Boetje 1831-37, J. de Liefde 1837-39, P. Douwes Dekker 1839-40, P. Leendertz Wz 1840-55, J. D. van der Plaats 1856-83, S. J. Andriessen 1890-97, J. Koster 1897-1902, K. Vos 1903-11, H. G. Berg 1912-15, R. C. de Lange 1915-19. Since 1920 the pastor of neighboring Balk (*q.v.*) has also been the pastor of the Woudsend congregation.   vDZ.

Inv. Arch. Amst. II, No. 2360; Blaupot t. C., Friesland, 164, 188, 248, 306; DB 1861, 144 f.; 1895, 12; 1901, 145 f.; Naamlijst 1829, 53 f.; De Zondagsbode IV (1890-91) No. 25; XXII (1908-9) Nos. 25-27.

Wouter, a Dominican monk, as early as 1510 in Utrecht, Netherlands, sharply criticized Roman Catholic practices; he was, however, forced to recant. But again in 1517 he attacked the Catholic Church, discarded his monastic dress, and traveled through Holland preaching "the truth of the Gospel" in a number of Dutch towns. This "Lutheran monk," who fled to Strasbourg (*q.v.*) *c*1521, awakened a true evangelical spirit in many of his adherents, among whom were Cornelis Hoen (*q.v.*) and Guilhelmus Gnapheus (*q.v.*), and largely opened the way for Sacramentism (*q.v.*) and Anabaptism. At Delp (*q.v.*), where Wouter lived for a time, David Joris became his follower *c*1520.   vDZ.

L. Knappert, Het ontstaan en de vestiging van het Protestantisme in de Nederlanden (Utrecht, 1924) 115 f., 137, 142; Kühler, Geschiedenis I, 196; Mellink, Wederdopers, 331, 334.

Wouter of Capelle, an Anabaptist martyr, was executed at Dixmuiden (*q.v.*) in Flanders, Belgium, in 1553. Particulars are lacking, except that Wouter was a weaver of serge. (*Mart. Mir. D.*, 150, 795, E 539, 1086.)   vDZ.

Wouter of Hondschoten, an Anabaptist martyr, was drowned at Hondschoote in Flanders, Belgium, in 1558. Particulars are lacking. (*Mart. Mir.* D 202, E 583.)   vDZ.

Wouter Denys, an Anabaptist martyr, who was seized at Meenen in Belgium with five companions and after cruel torture burned at the stake in Courtrai on April 30, 1569. "With metal cut from a coin and with ink made of chalk" he wrote several letters, three of which are given in the *Martyrs' Mirror.* The first was written to his wife, admonishing her to walk in the fear of the Lord and to seek her salvation more earnestly than heretofore; the third letter, more general in character, requested the intercession of friends for the prisoners. He was a native of Courtrai (Kortrijk) and had been (re)baptized in 1569. (*Mart. Mir.* D 408 f., E 759-61; Verheyden, *Courtrai-Bruxelles,* 39, No. 27; *ML* IV.)   NEFF.

Wouter van Stoelwij(c)k (of Stolwijk in the Dutch province of South Holland?), an Anabaptist martyr, was burned at the stake at Brussels, Belgium, on March 24, 1541. Van Braght says he was executed at Vilvoorde, but this is a mistake. Van Braght also relates that he was arrested in 1541, but this too is wrong: he was captured on Feb. 11, 1538, and imprisoned at the castle of Vilvoorde for more than three years. Particulars are lacking. In prison Wouter wrote a long letter which was published under the title *Een trostelycke Vermaninghe* (n.p., 1558) and which is found in the *Martyrs' Mirror.*
                                                          vDZ.

Mart. Mir. D. 51-61, E 455; Verheyden, *Courtrai-Bruxelles,* 62, No. 10; *DB* 1870, 51; *Bibliographie* I, 377 f., 669 f.

Wouter Thonisz (Thomasz), of Woerden, an Anabaptist martyr, was sentenced to death by beheading by the Court of Holland on May 16, 1534. He probably died at The Hague. Wouter was one of the Anabaptists who had sailed from Amsterdam on March 24, 1534, en route to Münster (*q.v.*), and were arrested at Bergklooster (*q.v.*). (*Inv. Arch. Amst.* I, No. 744 f.; *DB* 1917, 122, No. 149.)   vDZ.

Wouter de Vries was a Mennonite preacher at Vreeland (*q.v.*) in the Dutch province of Utrecht c1560. Nothing more is known about him. (*Inv. Arch. Amst.* I, No. 402; *DB* 1903, 6, 19.)   vDZ.

Wouters, a former Dutch Mennonite family. A Be-(e)rent Wolters (Wouters) moved c1670 from Munsterland, Westphalia, Germany, to Knijpe (*q.v.*) in the Dutch province of Friesland, where he was converted from Catholicism and joined the Groningen Old Flemish Mennonite congregation. His son Wouter Berends, b. at Knijpe in 1671 (perhaps 1677), d. at Sneek in 1760, moved to Sneek c1693, where he opened a brush shop and soon became well-to-do. Then he bought two oil presses, a soap factory, and was the owner of boats shipping freight from Sneek as far as Rotterdam. He was a conservative Mennonite, not joining the rather liberal congregation at Sneek, but the Old Flemish

church of neighboring IJlst (*q.v.*). In 1746, at the age of c70, he founded a Groningen Old Flemish congregation at Sneek (*q.v.*), which he financed and to which he gave the use of one of his warehouses on the Kleinzand, adapted into a plain meetinghouse. Of this congregation, starting with 17 baptized members, his son Andries, who took the family name of Wouters (1714-81), was a deacon from 1746 until his death. Andries Wouters, a well-to-do merchant at Sneek, was secretary of the Groningen Old Flemish Conference and was one of the delegates of this conference who in 1766 negotiated with the Zonists (*q.v.*) to merge the two groups; this merger, however, failed to come about. Andries Wouters was also diligent in behalf of the Mennonites in West Prussia. His brother Wybe Wouters (Sneek 1704-69) also acted as secretary of the same conference, as did his grandson Wybe Wouters (1762-1826), a bookseller and publisher at Groningen, who was the last secretary of the conference before it was dissolved in 1815. In the 19th century most members of the Wouters family held high military offices, usually leaving the Mennonite Church. Julia Wouters (Sneek 1829-Oudeschoot 1892) bequeathed her stately country house "Veenlust" at Oudeschoot, Friesland, as a home for old ladies of the higher classes, called Julia Jan Woutersstichting.   vDZ.

A. Haga, "Bijdrage tot de genealogie van het Doopsgezinde Sneeksche geslacht Wouters," in *De Nederlandsche Leeuw,* 1941 (repr.); *DB* 1890, 94-100, 102-4, 108, 110; 1892, 91 f., 95, 96; *Inv. Arch. Amst.* I, Nos. 1112, 1714, 1721; Blaupot t. C., *Friesland,* 195, 224, 225; idem, *Groningen* I, 136, 148, 150.

Wrake, Van de, a booklet by Bernhard Rothmann (*q.v.*) in Münster (*q.v.*), entitled *Eyn gantz troestlick bericht vande Wrake . . . an alle ware Israeliten unnd Bundtgeneten Christi . . . durch de gemeinte Christi tho Munster* (Münster, 1534), was a writing in which the Anabaptists of Holland were summoned to abandon their peaceful attitude and to support the "kingdom of God" at Münster with weapons. Four men distributed the booklet among the Dutch Anabaptists; at Maastricht (*q.v.*) and elsewhere it was eagerly read. It had a baleful influence, moving many Anabaptists to take up arms and join the Münsterites. *Van de Wrake* was refuted by Menno Simons in *Gantsch duydtlijck bewys tegens . . . Jan van Leyden. Van de Wrake* was re-edited by K. W. Bouterwek in *Zur Literatur und Geschichte der Wiedertäufer* I (Bonn, n.d.-1864) 66-80.   vDZ.

Kühler, *Geschiedenis* I, 129 f., 140, 146, 165; Mellink, *Wederdopers,* 371 ff.; *DB* 1884, 11, 13; 1889, 67-72; 1905, 86 f.

Wright County (Iowa) Amish Mennonite Church, now extinct, located one mile east of the Dayton Center Schoolhouse, was founded in 1893 when five families from Johnson County, Iowa, led by Solomon Swartzendruber from McPherson County, Kan., settled near Clarion, joined in the following years by more families. From the beginning church services were held the Gilette Schoolhouse in Dayton Township. In 1898 a meetinghouse was built on a plot of land donated by Joel Swartzendruber. Early in its history some contention arose over the observance of Amish traditions and practices and later over the use of the German language in church services. In the spring of 1901 Solomon Swartzendruber and his brother-in-law John Gunden moved away from the colony. The remaining members tried to maintain their church life, but unrest continued and more moved away. In 1911 the last families left the community and a promising congregation in one of the finest farming communities in the United States became extinct. A few years later the church building was dismantled and rebuilt in Daytonville, Iowa, for the Daytonville Mission. Later it was sold. The cemetery, which contained the remains of some half-dozen members of the congregation or their children, was discontinued in 1941, when the bodies were exhumed and shipped to the settlements where the former residents of this church now live, and laid away in the family burial plots.   S.C.Y.

Wucherer, Hans, an Anabaptist martyr who, after brutal torture, was burned at the stake at Burkhausen, Bavaria, in 1537 together with Hans Bartel (*q.v.*), who is also known as Bärtel Synbeck, a weaver of Kaufbeuren. In prison he wrote a moving letter to his wife, which is reprinted in the Hutterite Chronicle, bidding her farewell and admonishing her "to remain true to the brotherhood and to God." (Zieglschmid, *Chronik*, 185 f.; *Mart. Mir.* D 41, where the name is Woekeraar, E 447; *ML* IV.)
                                        NEFF.

Wuite, a Dutch Mennonite family, originally at Giethoorn (*q.v.*), Dutch province of Overijssel, where Harm Roelofs (Wuite) was a Mennonite preacher in the Giethoorn-Zuid congregation 1739-d. 92. His son Roelof Harms Wuite was a preacher of the same church 1783-d. 93. Roelof Roelofs Wuite moved *c*1830 from Giethoorn to Tjalleberd (*q.v.*) in Friesland, where he engaged in peat-digging and later in farming. His cousins(?) Jacob Jansz Wuite and Jan Jansz Wuite settled about the same time as farmers on the neighboring hamlet of Luinjeberd. Jan Jacobs Wuite (1845-1908), a son of the above Jacob Jansz Wuite, was for 35 years a trustee of the Tjalleberd congregation. His son was Jan Wuite (Luinjeberd, May 2, 1874-Haarlem, July 5, 1931), who after studying at the university and the Mennonite seminary of Amsterdam served as pastor at Stadskanaal 1898-1904, Drachten-Ureterp 1904-12, Leiden 1912-25, and Bovenknijpe 1925-30. He was editor of *De Zondagsbode* (*q.v.*) from 1916 until November 1930, and of the *Doopsgezind Jaarboekje* (*q.v.*) 1927-30. He published a paper. "De Scheurin tusschen het Lam en de Zon," in *DB* 1900, and in *DB* 1904 a Dutch translation of S. Cramer's article on Menno Simons from *Herzog's Realencyclopädie* XII under the new title "Menno's Leven." In *DJ* 1914 he commemorated his professor Samuel Cramer (*q.v.*). An address of his, "De taak van de predikant in onze gemeente," given before the ANDPV (Dutch Mennonite ministers' association), was published in *DJ* 1928. *Gods Wegen, godsdienstige schetsen* (Schagen n.d.-1933,) came from the press after his death.
Geert Wuite Janszoon (Luinjeberd, July 16, 1874-

The Hague, Feb. 21, 1940) also studied theology at the university and the Amsterdam seminary and served as pastor of the Mennonite congregations at Staveren-Molkwerum 1899-1902, Arnhem 1902-10, and The Hague 1910-39. Particularly at The Hague he was a popular preacher and an influential leader of the church. The Wuite House of the congregation at The Hague is named after him. He was a trustee of the A.D.S. 1931-39. He published a number of sermons, and a volume of sermons entitled *Soli Deo Gloria* (Busonn, 1939) was published when he retired. His son Jan Johan Gerard Wuite (b. at Staveren 1900) after studying at Leiden and Amsterdam was a pastor at Veendam 1927-32, Zaandam-Oost 1932-34, and Utrecht 1934- . He was a trustee of the A.D.S. 1933-34 and 1943- , and a curator of its seminary 1946- , acting as its moderator 1955- .
Many members of this family have served as deacons at Giethoorn, Tjalleberd, Zwolle, Leeuwarden, Amsterdam, and The Hague.   vDZ.

Naamlijst 1793, 63; DB 1878, 23; DJ 1919, 66, 68, 71, 72; 1928, 96; 1932, 23-37; 1941, 17-24; De Zondagsbode XXII (1908-9) Nos. 8, 10; XLIV (1930-31) Nos. 37 f.

Wullenwewer, Jürgen (1492-1537), a Hanseatic statesman, a native of Hamburg, was elected as a member of the council of Lübeck in 1533, and 14 days later as mayor. He strove to re-establish the political supremacy of Lübeck on the Baltic Sea; but after the Danish victory in the Battle of Assens (June 11, 1535), when the rule of the democracy in Lübeck collapsed, Wullenwewer resigned in August 1535, but continued to be interested in Nordic politics. The Lutheran superintendent Bonnuns demanded Wollenwewer's expulsion on the ground of his supposed intention of introducing Anabaptism in Lübeck; Wullenwewer was accordingly arrested in November 1535 and consigned to the zealously Catholic Duke Henry the Younger. Under torture Wullenwewer "confessed" that he had had connections with the Anabaptists. How far these "confessions," which are still extant, correspond with reality must be the subject of further investigation. He was sentenced to death and beheaded on Sept. 29, 1537. Wullenwewer's fate has been treated by Köhler in a novel and by Gotzkow and Heinrich Kruse in dramas.   HEGE.

Heinrich Handelmann, *Die letzten Zeiten hansischer Uebermacht im Skandinavischen Norden* (Kiel, 1853); Caspar Paludan-Müller, *Grevens Feide* I and II (Copenhagen, 1853-54); Georg Waitz, *Lübeck unter Jürgen Wullenwewer und die europäische Politik* (3 vv., Berlin, 1855-56); K. Kupisch in *Furche* No. 24, 1938, presents a brief sketch of Jürgen Wullenwewer, seeing tragedy in the entanglement of religion and politics; J. Wipf, *Ref.-Gesch. der Stadt und Landschaft Schaffhausen* (Zürich and Leipzig, 1929) 175 f.; W. Stolze, "Ueber die Bedeutung des Bauernkrieges für die deutsche Geschichte," in *Ztscht für Kirchengesch.* XLIX (1930) 189-97; *ML* IV.

Wunderl, Johann: *see* **Bünderlin, Hans.**

Württemberg, one of the larger states of Germany (1939, 7,532 sq. mi., and pop. 2,896,820), is located between Baden and Bavaria. (Since 1945 it is united with Baden into one political unit.) Württemberg is composed of the former duchy of Württemberg, the gravures of Hohenberg, Hohenlohe, Limpurg,

Löwenstein, part of the margravure of Ansbach-Bayreuth, the Landvogtei of Swabia, the realm of the counts of Thurn and Taxis, 18 imperial cities, and numerous knightly estates and monasteries. In the time of the Reformation these were still independent. After the time of Napoleon, that is, after 1801, the Mennonites of all Württemberg are included here.

(I) *The Duchy*. In 1520-34 it was under the domination of Austria, since the Swabian League had expelled Duke Ulrich because of a murder and had sold the country to Austria. The Anabaptists had been active here since the execution of Michael Sattler (*q.v.*) in May 1527. The government had become attentive to this movement proceeding from Horb and Rottenberg, and from Esslingen and Gmünd. On Jan. 26, 1528, King Ferdinand gave orders to the Württemberg government as to procedure with the Anabaptists. The Anabaptists were classed with murderers, arsonists, and vagabonds. The provost of the Swabian League, Berthold Aichelin, also carried on his nefarious work in this duchy and here came to an infamous end. The trial of Augustin Bader (*q.v.*) took place in Stuttgart. With his execution the very small chiliastic revolutionary group in Württemberg had come to an end. But the regular peaceful Anabaptists were active here continuously from 1526. The Hutterian Brethren also were active and sent emissaries from Moravia, who won more and more new followers in this country which had meanwhile been subject to a famine. The Swiss Brethren found the greatest response. After Michael Sattler had gathered these quiet Anabaptists, who were entirely bent upon living a holy life quite in accord with the Scripture like the first Anabaptists in Zürich, this group established itself firmly in Württemberg. Not until the Thirty Years' War did this type of Anabaptism die out. The Anabaptist striving for sanctification, however, continued later in Pietism which was connected with the established church.

The Anabaptist literature was feared. All booksellers' wares were checked. The Anabaptists were not only accused of murder and arson but they were also blamed for the increase in divorces. Indeed, continuance of marriage with an unbeliever was a very serious question for an Anabaptist.

The Austrian government condemned Aichelin's brutal proceedings and tried to hold strictly to legal process. But this process provided for capital punishment for Anabaptists. The Swabian spirit rebelled against such measures. Even though the government might have the imperial mandates solemnly read in the churches, an effort was still made to convert the Anabaptists by having preachers and university professors debate with them. Only the most obstinate were punished with death. A Hutterite martyr catalog of 1531 names 55 from Württemberg out of a total of 410. A later catalog of 1581 counts 67 from Württemberg among a total of 2,169 blood witnesses. But these figures are not exact. There were more victims in Württemberg than these, since it has been shown that there are more places in which capital punishment was applied than those named in these sketches.

When Duke Ulrich returned to his country in 1534-50, Anabaptist executions ceased. To be sure, the Strasbourg Reformers Capito (*q.v.*) and Bucer (*q.v.*) warned the Duke against the Anabaptists and against Schwenckfeld (*q.v.*). In the Peace of Kaaden (*q.v.*) Ulrich obligated himself to punish them. But the treatment grew more lenient. On June 18, 1535, Ulrich's first Anabaptist mandate concerning the treatment of recanting Anabaptists was published. These recanters were to give up all connections with Anabaptists and to obey the government in all things, hence also to attend the established religious services and communion; "corner preachers" traveling through were to be reported like vagabonds; backsliders were to be punished with death. At first the horror of the events in Münster in 1534-35 affected the Duke's judgment. But after its fall Ulrich sought advice of the jurists at the University of Tübingen. Their answer of June 9, 1536, to be sure, pointed to the imperial law requiring the death of such Anabaptists, but it recommended lenience. The theologians advised lenience because these simple people "see in these mild spirits such a fine appearance of life and, on the other hand, with us and the great crowd of our people unfortunately such a wild, bold, and degraded life." The death penalty, they said, would deprive the victim of the possibility of conversion. Arrest would prevent infection and would give opportunity for a change of mind. Expulsion from the country, they said, is unbrotherly since in that way ruin goes to the other countries. Here they were expressing the ideas of Johannes Brenz, the Reformer of Nürnberg.

The ducal regulation of 1536 emanates from these views of the theologians and jurists. Anabaptists were arrested and under the threat of the rack were questioned (1) regarding any possible participation in the Peasants' War; (2) concerning the time, place, participants, leaders, and the reason of Anabaptism; (3) concerning infant baptism, communion, the oath, the Christian character of the government, and participation in war; (4) concerning the restoration of all things, concerning the sonship of Christ and His sufficient atonement; (5) concerning possible recantation. If they recanted they had to give up all Anabaptist living and under oath vow obedience to the temporal and to the spiritual authorities. Backsliding would be punished by death. The leaders were questioned more strictly, probably under torture, concerning their adherents, their peculiar doctrine, whether they had anything to do with Münster or Moravia, concerning their signs of recognition, whether they had any plans for violence. The authorities feared the overthrow of all social order. As a punishment banishment was provided as well as confiscation of property, and death in the case of illegal return. Skilled clergymen were engaged to instruct the prisoners.

An Anabaptist by the name of Hans Fritz of Dettingen said in 1565 that he had previously been questioned by Erhard Schnepf and others but that he had been permitted to keep his faith. Proceedings were thus apparently not violent.

The Anabaptists preferably stayed near the state borders. They held their meetings in secluded places. Popular with them was the song written by Jörg Wagner, who was burned at the stake at Munich in

1527. They recognized each other by the greeting, "The grace of the Lord be with us all."

A number of noblemen gave them protection and lodging in their villages; for example, the Weittershausens at Bromberg near Hohenhaslach, the Nippenburgs in Schwieberdingen and Hemmingen, the Thumbs in Köngen and Stetten. The Anabaptist economic capability and honesty stood them in good stead. Their nonresistance made them adaptable.

The interim government of Charles V brought the Anabaptists a certain lessening of danger; the attention of the authorities was diverted. Since the Moravian Landtag of 1547 decided not to tolerate more than 5 to 7 persons living in one house, the Bruderhofs of the Hutterian Brethren had consequently become impossible there, and some of them returned to their old homes. A more careful distinction was now made in Württemberg between the Hutterian Brethren, the Swiss Brethren, and the Schwenckfelders. The earnestness of the Anabaptists was recognized; but the fear of possible revolutionary efforts continued for a long time and accounts for Ulrich's serious doubts even about the peaceful Anabaptists.

Under Duke Christoph, 1550-68, the Anabaptist movement increased, probably in consequence of the work of the Hutterian Brethren in the country. The Treaty of Passau gave the Duke a free hand. In 1553 the church inspection regulation stipulated that the superintendents and the church councils should consult together four times a year concerning the Anabaptists and the Schwenckfelders. Thus the Württemberg synod owes its creation to the struggle with the "sects." On June 14, 1554, an order was issued not only against "Kaspar Schwenckfeld's own accursed person," but also against the Anabaptists. Jacob Andreae (q.v.) no doubt incited the Duke to this measure; he had had to deal with Anabaptists from Stauffen in his parish at Göppingen. The order required church attendance, forbade all meetings of Anabaptists, and required immediate reports about everything. The trial in 1557 of the Rapp brothers reveals the Duke's zeal for pure doctrine. Brenz and the court chaplain Bidembach took the greatest pains to convert the two brothers. With the younger one they succeeded, but the older one remained stiff-necked and was expelled from the country. At the disputation at Pfeddersheim on Aug. 24, 1557, Andreae won to his side the magistrate (Vogt) of Alzey who had favored the Anabaptists.

In Worms Brenz and Andreae in 1557 took part in composing the *Prozess (q.v.) wie es soll gehalten werden mit den Wiedertäufern.* Brenz was a signatory. But it is somewhat remarkable that the recommendation of the death penalty and the reference to Servetus' execution is crossed out. Who did this can no longer be ascertained, whether Brenz or the Duke. But the crossing is clear evidence of the strong feeling in Württemberg against the shedding of blood in spite of Lev. 24:16, "He that blasphemeth . . . shall surely be put to death."

On June 25, 1558, Duke Christoph issued the mandate that remained authoritative for dealing with all sectarians, including the Anabaptists. It gives the exact questions by which the Anabaptists

were to be cross-examined. If the leaders did not give adequate answers they were to be tortured. Repentant ones were to recant before the assembled congregation. Obstinate ones were to be kept in prison. Property confiscated from the Anabaptists was to be used for the expenses of the prisoners and for their innocent dependents. One of the questions asked was whether a Christian may dismiss his wife for confessional reasons, and how many wives one may have.

The Duke's zeal induced the people of Esslingen on July 5, 1562, to arrest some Swiss Brethren who were at a meeting in the Heinbachtal and to examine them. The prisoners were all from Württemberg. They were dismissed after a few weeks upon their promise to avoid the city. In 1563 an Anabaptist, Barbara Löffler of Stuttgart, was branded because she had backslidden into Anabaptism. In 1557 began the 19-year imprisonment of the Hutterite Paul Glock in Hohenwittlingen.

The verdict of popular opinion concerning the Duke's zeal to preserve the pure doctrine was, "The pope compelled us to attend communion with the ban, but you with the tower [prison]," as an Anabaptist said in 1565. Everywhere the Anabaptists sought earnestly for sanctification. In 1569 an Anabaptist exile wrote to the government: "It gave me offense to see that so many go to the Lord's Supper heedlessly out of old habit; they are this year like last year and last year like this year and I have not seen any change in them nor any laying aside of the old Adam."

The Lutheran state church was established under Duke Christoph. Brenz's idea that heretics should be attacked only with the Word disappeared. In 1557 Andreae still preached his 33 sermons against all sectarians including the Anabaptists, but without success. Nevertheless for the sake of their clarity they are worth reading.

The bad life of many an official under Duke Louis, 1568-93, and a number of famines induced many Württembergers to follow the call to Moravia as the promised land of all Anabaptists. Twice a year their missioners appeared in the country. But the Swiss Brethren were also at work, though very quietly. The period of the developing Formula of Concord, to which Jacob Andreae was giving his attention, was a time of strong increase of Anabaptism in Moravia as well as in Württemberg. The tone of the records becomes harder. A marginal note, "Just deal harshly with this little rabble of rogues," may have come from the Duke. The Anabaptist leaders are now called "work devils" and their preaching a "chattering." The Anabaptist regulation was revised and expanded in 1570-71. A clear distinction was made now between leaders and the simple Anabaptists. The rack was used more frequently; the introduction of capital punishment was considered but rejected. In the period of the Duke's minority outstanding officials and theologians paid close attention to the Anabaptists. The witch trials compelled everyone everywhere to make a clear statement of faith. What was one to say about divorce for reasons of faith? How should one deal with people who secretly lodged their Anabaptist relatives? Should one leave Anabaptist wives in the country or expel them if their families remained true to the church? What should one do with children of Anabaptists? Should they be baptized and taken from their parents, or should they be permitted to leave the country with their parents? What should become of the lords who have taken Anabaptists on their estates? A number of questions had to be discussed and newly regulated. In 1584 the regulation was again reviewed and sharpened.

The theologians expressed themselves as opposed to the death penalty which had been advised by the jurists, Biedenbach in 1570 and more especially Lukas Osiander (*q.v.*) in 1584. One of Osiander's main arguments was that the Papists might likewise apply the death penalty against Protestants if one used it against Anabaptists. The Duke decided to wait and to follow the milder way. The numerous church inspections occurring twice annually after 1573 brought much difficulty and annoyance but little success. When an Anabaptist escaped out of the country there was occasionally a note in the margin of the records, "Is probably outside." If the inspection brought an Anabaptist to the preaching or communion service, a "thank God" shows the mind of the church council. Often, however, one reads: "One must commit it to God."

Duke Frederick, 1593-1608, who was always in need of money, had the land procurator Esslinger ascertain the exact amount of the Anabaptist estates, and rent them out. The proceeds were to go directly to the Duke instead of to the church treasury. He wanted to use the money for the church in his newly founded Freudenstadt. Thus the question of faith became one of finances. The most dubious thing was that even the young theologians began to occupy themselves with the books of the Anabaptists. Menno's *Foundation Book* and the hymns of the Swiss Brethren were found among them now and then.

The property of the Anabaptists was reckoned after 1604 at some 55,293 guilders. In 1630 there were still 24,000 guilders. After this there is no official estimate concerning the Anabaptists and their property.

In the Thirty Years' War the Anabaptists finally died out in Württemberg. Individual Anabaptists found there later were only temporarily in the country.

The Anabaptists of Württemberg were usually peasants and vinedressers. But occasionally there were also other vocations represented among them, particularly physicians. For example, Jörg Wernlin (*q.v.*) called Scherer, who died *c*1559 in Kirchenkirnberg and is often named as a zealous leader of the Swiss Brethren, remained in the country for a long time; he had once vainly sought connections with the Hutterian Brethren in Moravia. Indeed, even a Lutheran deacon, M. Johann Walch (*q.v.*), had to be dismissed in 1582, who at first emigrated to Moravia, but later went to Strasbourg and from there kept in contact with the Swiss Brethren in Württemberg.

According to the Anabaptist census of Dec. 4, 1570, there were 129 Anabaptists in the duchy; in the district of Lorch alone there were 109. In official circles the number of stiff-necked ones was reckoned at least 100, who were to be kept in permanent imprisonment and which would cause an expense of 5,000 guilders annually.

In Moravia many "Swabians" (Anabaptists who stemmed from Württemberg) occupied outstanding positions among the Hutterian Brethren. Among their bishops was Sebastian Dietrich of Markgröningen, a widely renowned physician, 1611-19. His successors, Ulrich Jaussling (Jaussle, Jausel) 1619-21, Valentin Winter 1622-31, and Heinrich Hartman 1631-39, were probably also Swabians. Andreas Ehrenpreis 1639-62, stemmed from Illingen. He was the object of a written attack by the Stuttgart provost Melchior Nicolai in 1650. His successor, Johann Rieger (Rinker, Rükker), 1662-87, was probably from Hohenstaufen. He was replaced by Johann Milter, 1687-88, of Dettingen near Kirchheim; then followed Caspar Eglauch of Bartenbach 1688-93; Tobias Bertsch 1694-1701 was from the Maulbronn district; Zacharias Walter, the grandson of the founder of the Anabaptist settlement in Alwinz in Transylvania, who had come from Oetisheim, was their last bishop, 1746-61. Also among the Hutterite preachers and managers there was a series of Swabians—Hasel (*q.v.*), Glock (*q.v.*), Binder, Hans Schmidt, and Wernlin (*q.v.*).

By 1570 the various forms of Anabaptism were well recognized in Württemberg; distinctions were made between the Hutterites, the Moserites, the Hofer Brethren, in contradistinction to the Davidjorists, the Münsterites, and the followers of Servetus. The Hofer group were an offshoot of the Hutterites; the Moser group must have been Swiss Brethren. The difference between the Hutterites and the Swiss Brethren lay not only in the question of private or communal property but also in doctrine. But in common to both was the striving for holiness, which always made an impression on the churchmen. One found among them, the "poor erroneous but not bad-hearted people, a great, ardent, but unintelligent zeal," whereas the people of the Black Forest thought: "He who does not carry a sword and leads an inoffensive life is an Anabaptist." In 1574 it was said in Rosenfeld, "If one does not curse or go into the tavern, one is an Anabaptist." The magistrates, however, said from their experience that they had never yet heard of a Hutterite who had denied his faith. Life and doctrine were in their case integrated, as was said in Gündelbach. The Junker of Hemmingen had an Anabaptist buried honorably in the cemetery, saying that he considered him a saved man; if he were to die today or tomorrow he would not want to get into any other heaven but the one into which this Anabaptist had gone. Such voices testify to the impression made by the quiet walk of the Swiss Brethren as well as by the steadfastness of the Hutterian Brethren. The Anabaptists differed sharply from Schwenckfeld, as is clearly shown in the dispute between Schwenckfeld and Pilgram Marpeck, but a quiet life and striving for holiness was characteristic of both groups. Conspicuous in the Anabaptist testimonies is the frequent use of the fourth book of

Ezra (*q.v.*) and the preference for the Epistle of James. Besides their greeting, another common point of distinction was their homemade, simple clothing.

After 1571 obstinate Anabaptist women were forged to chains. A church funeral was denied Anabaptists, and many were branded. The leaders were often held in prison for many years. Paul Glock was released only because the Duke pardoned him for his outstanding work in extinguishing a fire.

The same villages in which Anabaptists had once appeared later had a great inclination to Pietism. The church managed to keep the latter in the church, especially through the influence of J. A. Bengel in the Pietist Edict of 1743, since the leaders recognized that these Pietists were striving for quiet conduct, for holiness, and for edification; indeed the church often won them as energetic promoters of the church life. This it had failed to do in the case of the Anabaptists.

A part of the Anabaptists in South Germany, the immediate followers of Pilgram Marpeck and Leupold Scharnschlager, *c*1530-55, seem to have formed a group somewhat distinct from the Swiss Brethren, although the differences were not great. They were sometimes called "Pilgramites." J. J. Kiwiet considers this group to have originated as followers of Hans Denk (*q.v.*) and Hans Hut (*q.v.*), rather than Michael Sattler and his associates, and thus to have had a distinct origin from the Swiss Brethren proper. (See Kiwiet's *Pilgram Marbeck* and the article **Marpeck**.) He holds that Marpeck succeeded in bringing together his group and the Swiss Brethren by about 1555, as well as the remnants of the Hofmannites. No doubt there were *Pilgramites* in Württemberg, although *TA Württemberg* contains no references to this group, and the only group name that appears i the official records is Swiss Brethren.

(II) *Württemberg after 1801.* In 1763-65 Mennonites are named in Bonfeld and Fürfeld in (what was later) northwestern Württemberg as renters on the Gemmingen estates: Heinrich Beer and Jakob Ebe. These villages were then not yet politically a part of Württemberg. In 1801 Duke Frederick granted the Mennonite renters of the estate of Lautenbach near Neckarsulm, after it had become a part of Württemberg, the privilege to take over in lease some of the estates in his land. In return they were to pay a fee for protection. They could not acquire the right of citizenship but they received the right to hold worship in their homes and complete toleration of their religious opinions and their religious usages as far as to instruct their children in their religious concepts. A vow was permitted to take the place of the oath. In accord with the decree of the minister of justice of April 30, 1845, the formula of affirmation for the Mennonites read: "With a solemn reference to Matthew 5:37 I assure the government instituted by God, that in the matter in which I am being heard in a legal matter I will tell all that is known to me about it in a pure, unfalsified truth, and will conceal nothing, with 'yes,'" which words were to be fortified by a handclasp of the one obligated to the oath.

According to the decree of June 20, 1807, the Mennonites were to be tolerated and permitted to stay in that kingdom as long as they behaved well; but they should by no means be granted the right of citizenship if they would not personally serve in the army.

According to the regulation of military conscription of August 20, Section 13, the Mennonites could choose to pay a certain amount of redemption money in place of military service. On Feb. 18, 1810, King Frederick commanded that the funds of the Anabaptists who were subject to military duty should be treated like the funds of the Jews.

With the introduction of general military duty the right of exemption by redemption payment ended. On the basis of the standardization of the Württemberg military service regulations with those of Prussia in the formation of an imperial army, the Prussian Order of Cabinet of Jan. 31, 1868, was authoritative also for the Mennonites in Württemberg. It specified that Mennonites subject to military duty could render noncombatant service in the hospital corps, or as secretaries in the army, as well as craftsmen and with the transportation corps.

The first Mennonites came to Württemberg about 1801. Soon after some came as renters on the estates of the Imperial Knights which had passed to the realm of Württemberg, such as Willenbach, Hösselinshof, Seehof, Sülzhof near Neckarsulm, Breitenau near Weinsberg, Liebenstein near Besigheim, Mühlhausen near Cannstadt. Some of these estates are now leased to sugar factories and therefore the Mennonites have disappeared from them. But many are still living on estates scattered largely in the northern half of the country and are highly valued for their farming capability. Lautenbach, Willenbach, Liebenstein, Breitenau are among those still or again in Mennonite hands. Others have moved to the cities and have opened businesses or have adopted other vocations. The Lichdi chain of grocery stores is owned and operated by a Mennonite preacher, with office in Heilbronn. According to the census of 1868 Mennonites in Württemberg were distributed as follows:

Name of Township (Oberamt)	Male	Female
Brackenheim	9	3
Neckarsulm	27	24
Vaihingen (Rieth)	8	11
Elsewhere	4	11
Total for the Neckar district	48	49
		Total 97
Künzelsau	32	23
Mergentheim	4	5
Oehringen	2	2
Elsewhere	11	6
Total in the Jagst district	49	36
		Total 85

There were therefore in Württemberg 182, of whom 141 were adults.

In the later census lists the Mennonites are often grouped together with the Baptists and other religious parties under the heading "Of other confession," so that it is impossible to set up a list of places where the Mennonites of Württemberg lived as can be done for Baden and Bavaria. But the total Mennonite population in 1905 was 272, and in 1925 was 729, a remarkable growth. Of the 729 in 1925, 173 were in cities of over 10,000 population; 37 in cities over 5,000 population, a total of 210 in the cities; the other 519 were in the country. In agriculture there were 282, in crafts and industry 83, in trade and transportation 56, in offices and schools 44, in the public health and welfare departments 22, in domestic service 13, and with unnamed work 98. One sees how predominant agriculture was, but how more and more the Mennonites have been turning to city vocations.

Familiar names among the Mennonites in Württemberg are Baer, Fellmann, Funck, Hege, Horsch, Landes, Schmutz, and Schneider. Most of these families are engaged in agriculture.

In 1958 Württemberg had the following six congregations, all members of the Badisch-Württembergisch-Bayrisch Gemeinde-Verband (q.v.): Heilbronn (q.v., org. 1890, 120 members), Nesselbach (q.v., 1890, 28), Möckmühl (q.v., 1914, 23), Stuttgart (1933, 111), Reutlingen (1948, 53), and Backnang (1947, 292), a total of 627 baptized members. The Backnang congregation consists wholly of refugees from Poland and Russia now settled in the Sachsenweiler Siedlung at the edge of Backnang. All the other congregations consist of descendants of the original Swiss immigrant stock of 1650-1750, which first came to the Karlsruhe-Durlach and Heidelberg-Sinsheim areas (the latter formerly Palatinate). Only Heilbronn and Backnang have meetinghouses of their own; the other congregations use rented meeting rooms. (*Gem.-Kal.,* 1959, 89 f.)

G.Bos., H.S.B.

TA Württemberg; Gustav Bossert, "Aus der nebenkirchlichen religiösen Bewegung der Reformationszeit in Württemberg (Wiedertäufer und Schwenckfelder)" in *Blätter für württemberg. Kirchengesch.* XXXIII (1929) 1-41; *idem,* "Wiedertäuferbischöfe aus Württemberg und Schwaben ausserhalb Schwabens," in *Schwäbischer Merkur,* June 9, 1930, and Feb. 8, 1923; Reyscher, *Sammlung der württembergischen Gesetze* IX, 101; Stälin, *Die Rechtsverhältnisse der religiösen Gemeinschaften und fremden Religionsverwandten in Württemberg,* in *Württemberg. Jahrb. für Statistik u. Landeskunde* (1868) 214; *Ztscht für Gesch. des Oberrheins* 1914, 57; Julius Rauscher, *Württembergische Reformationsgeschichte* (Stuttgart, 1934); Karl Grüneisen, "Abriss einer Geschichte der religiösen Gemeinschaften in Württemberg mit besonderer Rücksicht," *Ztscht f.d. hist. Theol.* (1841) 63-142, which also appeared as *Geschichte der neuen Taufgesinnten in Württemberg,* and was translated into Dutch as *Mennonieten en Doopsgezinden in Württemberg* (Amsterdam, 1848); Hans Hillerbrand, *Die politische Ethik des oberdeutschen Täufertums* (Gütersloh, 1959); H. W. Schraepler, *Die rechtliche Behandlung der Täufer in der deutschen Schweiz, Südwestdeutschland und Hessen* (Weierhof and Tübingen, 1957); Eberhard Teufel, "Die Beschlagnahme und Verwaltung des Täufergutes durch den Fiskus im Herzogtum Württemberg im 16. und 17. Jahrhundert," *Theologische Zeitschrift* (Basel) VIII (1952) 296-304; Jan J. Kiwiet, *Pilgram Marbeck* (Kassel, 1957); Christian Schmutz, "Die Mennonitengemeinden in Baden (und Württemberg) vor 100 Jahren," *Gem.-Kal.* 1955, 60-68; *ML* IV.

Würtzlburger (Wirtzlburger, Wiesslburger, Wieslberger), **Augustin,** a schoolteacher of Regensburg, Bavaria, born at Würzelburg near Landshut, an Anabaptist minister baptized by Leonhard Friesleben (q.v.) on Nov. 18, 1527, and thus made a member of the newly established Regensburg Anabaptist

congregation. In Passion Week, 1528, a certain Hans, delegate from the Augsburg Anabaptist congregation, came to Würtzlburger with the message that the two men had been commissioned as apostles for Bavaria. Since neither wanted at first to accept the dangerous commission, they cast lots, the lot falling on Würtzlburger. The latter at once undertook his work, which was to preach, teach, and baptize. His first attempt in his home neighborhood at Würzelburg was not very fruitful, but at Süssbach near he baptized nine. An attendant at one of his meetings here betrayed him, whereupon he was arrested, but released. Again betrayed by one of those whom he had baptized who was executed, he was again arrested on May 21, 1528, and after a five months' imprisonment in Regensburg executed on Oct. 10, 1528. The record of his three examinations in May and his "Urgicht" on the day of his death contain valuable evidence concerning the beliefs and attitudes of the early Anabaptists in Regensburg. Würtzlburger manfully confessed his faith, declaring that his religious convictions were grounded in Holy Scripture, and that he would be ready to change if he could be taught something better from Scripture. Under torture he cried out that "it was a miserable and grievous thing that they were not willing to let him stand by the truth; he wanted nothing else than to live as a true Christian." Würtzlburger's wife was also baptized.   H.S.B.

Herman Nestler, *Die Wiedertäuferbewegung in Regensburg* (Regensburg, 1926), which prints 19 documents on the Würtzlburger case, which are also printed in *TA Bayern* II.

Würz (Wurz), a Hutterite family name. Joseph Würz was chosen as preacher in 1611 at Neumühl, Moravia. In 1650 Moses Würz was chosen as preacher at Sobotiste in Hungary. In 1792 Andreas Würz was chosen preacher in Russia. In 1874, when the Hutterian Brethren emigrated from Russia to America, there were among them some members of this family. The name is still found in the Bruderhofs of the United States and Canada. (Zieglschmid, *Kleingeschichtbuch,* 389; *ML* IV.)   D.D.

Würzburg. There were many Anabaptists in the bishopric of Würzburg in 1527-28. Hans Hut (q.v.) and Georg Nespitzer (q.v.) were extremely active here, but the bloodthirsty Bishop Konrad also immediately went into action against them in measures which exceeded any imaginable forms of punishment at the disposal of temporal governments. Duke Wilhelm von Hennenberg, who in spite of the Imperial Edict of April 23, 1529, did not share the attitude of the Würzburg bishop in considering Anabaptism a capital crime but punished the prisoners with more lenient measures, was therefore accused at the Imperial court. This lawsuit lasted beyond the Anabaptist period in the Würzburg area and did not come to a conclusion until about 1540. Bishop Konrad treated all "sectarians" in summary fashion. There is very little to be found in the documents of the former bishopric of Würzburg by way of records of trials, cross-examinations, or statements of imprisoned Anabaptists such as one finds in other places, but a contemporary, Lorenz Fries, reports in his Chronicle that at the beginning of 1528 four men and two women from Ipshoven were brought as prisoners to Würzburg. On February 4 the men were beheaded, the women burned at the stake, and the next day two women, a mother and daughter, were drowned in the Main River. A number recanted; many of these had a hand cut off. Others fled to Moravia, and so it is understandable that the policy of the stake which the bishop applied against the Anabaptists in his country soon cleansed his area of this "sectarianism." W.W.

Beiträge zur bayrischen Kirchengesch. XVI (1910) 170-77; Wiswedel, *Bilder* I, 131; *ML* IV.

Würzburg-Giebelstadt, a Mennonite congregation with a meeting place in the city of Würzburg (1939 pop. 107,915) in northern Bavaria, and until 1955 having a subsidiary meeting place in the town of Giebelstadt about 7 miles south of Würzburg. In 1957 it had 75 baptized members, with Johannes Schmutz as elder (1933) and Ulrich Hirschler as preacher. Before 1950 the congregation was called Giebelstadt-Würzburg. The meetings in Würzburg were begun *c*1927, and the congregation was really the Giebelstadt (*q.v.*) congregation which had its organized beginning in 1810 as the Rottenbauer congregation. H.S.B.

Wüst, Eduard (1818-59), a Lutheran pietistic evangelist in Germany and Russia, was born at Murrhardt, Württemberg, Germany, Feb. 23, 1818, the son of Johann J. Wüst, an innkeeper and baker. In 1832 he attended the Gymnasium of Stuttgart. From his early youth he was torn between study and prayer and wasting his time in bad company. In 1835 he entered the University of Tübingen. Because he could not give up associating with bad influences, his brother, a minister at Mergentheim, took him into his home after two and one-half years. A year later he returned to Tübingen to continue his studies. After this had been repeated a number of times he finally passed his theological examination in Tübingen and in the fall of 1841 became assistant pastor at Neuenkirchen. Now a complete change took place. He devoted his time to serious study and the preparation of sermons. In the fall of 1843 he became assistant in Murrhardt, where he began to associate with the Württemberg Pietists (*q.v.*). A succession of religious experiences deepened his convictions. In 1844 he became assistant minister at Riedenau near Backnang. By now he had developed into a fiery preacher of repentance, opposing the amusements which had done so much harm to his own life. His pietistic zeal, in opposition to some of the practices in the church, made it impossible for him to continue his service. He was dismissed, and moved to his mother's home in Stuttgart. All attempts to have him reinstated failed. He now occasionally served pietistic circles in the vicinity, whereby he met Wilhelm Nast, a Methodist minister of Cincinnati, Ohio.

For a while Wüst worked among the Pietists of Württemberg who had separated from the state church. Some of them had moved to the Ukraine in 1816-22, settling along the Berda River near the Sea of Azov and establishing the villages of Neuhoffnung, Neuhoffnungstal, Neu-Stuttgart, and Rosenfeld. This migration to Russia was due partly to

religious oppression and partly to their expectation that the second coming of the Lord was at hand, based on the teachings of Bengel and Oetinger. Neuhoffnung extended a call to Wüst in January 1845, which he accepted. From his first to his last sermon he preached repentance and caused a revival. Soon not only his congregation, but also the neighboring churches, including Mennonites, came to listen. He introduced rigid church discipline but maintained the confidence and loyalty of his church members. Wüst's direct influence on the Mennonites was exercised in two ways. One was through addresses given at the missionary meetings at Gnadenfeld in the Molotschna. He spoke by invitation at such a meeting in 1846. Another was through his devotional addresses and Bible expositions given at the Saturday evening meetings held by the Mennonites of Berdyansk in their homes. Two preachers in the Berdyansk Mennonite congregation, Jacob Buhler and Leonhard Sudermann, were close friends of Wüst's and greatly influenced by him. Unruh (p. 29) attributes to Wüst "a mighty stimulus to new life in Mennonite circles," but states also that "opposition to the new movement was caused by his activity."

The great revival, in which the free grace of God was emphasized, caused a group of brethren to express the newly found, emotionally experienced salvation in great joy similar to the manner of the later Pentecostal groups. Kappes became the leader of this wing, which separated from Wüst in the fall of 1858. Unfortunately Wüst died at this crucial moment, on July 13, 1859. This was also the time when some of the Mennonites under his influence were promoting views which were not accepted by the elders, and caused the founding of the Mennonite Brethren Church (*q.v.*) and the Templer Church (*q.v.*). Wüst had a considerable influence in this matter, although he cannot be held responsible for all the positive and negative aspects which resulted from his work. He remained a friend of such Mennonite leaders as August Lenzmann and Cornelius Jansen. People who came in touch with Wüst either accepted his views or became his opponents. A more gentle spirit with the same positive influence might have prevented the splits which took place in the Mennonite brotherhood as a result of his preaching. C.K.

A. Kröker, *Pfarrer Eduard Wüst, der grosse Erweckungsprediger in den deutschen Kolonien Südrusslands* (1903); Friesen, *Brüderschaft,* 168-86; George Eisenach, *Pietism and the Russian Germans in the United States* (Berne, 1948); A. H. Unruh, *Die Geschichte der Mennoniten-Brüdergemeinde* (Winnipeg, 1954) 28-32; Eduard Wüst, *Antritts-Predigt des Eduard Hugo Otto Wüst* (Moscow, 1850); idem, *Die Herzen überwältigende Liebe* (Moscow, 1851); idem, *Zehn Passions-Predigten* (Reval, 1853).

Wüstenfelde, a village near Oldesloe in the German province of Holstein, was the place where Menno (*q.v.*) Simons could live and work quietly during his last years. Wüstenfelde was a territory belonging to the nobleman Bartholomeus von Ahlefeldt (*q.v.*), who permitted persecuted Mennonites to settle here. Menno moved to Wüstenfelde in the late summer of 1554 and died here on Jan. 31, 1561. The village was wiped out in the Thirty Years' War.

A monument to Menno Simons was erected on the presumed location of the village by the Hamburg-Altona Mennonite Church in 1906. vDZ.

Wüthrich, Peter, an Anabaptist preacher in the Emmental, Switzerland, was compelled to emigrate in accord with a regulation of the Bernese cantonal government of Feb. 11, 1711. Many of the exiles returned, including Peter Wüthrich. A regulation of Dec. 11, 1711, stipulated that the Anabaptists who returned were to be put into prison, some in chains, the others without chains and to be held there until they should die or conform to the church regulations (*Ratsmanual* 49, 431).

As in 1571, again six of the outstanding Anabaptist leaders were to be condemned to galley slavery (*q.v.*), concerning whom an Anabaptist hymn says, "They have taken six Brethren, have forged chains upon them, are sending them to the sea; may God be the captain of their souls."

These six men were to be put for safer keeping into the Titliger tower. On the next day a note was sent to the Täuferkammer (*q.v.*) which gave the information that on account of the feebleness of old age not more than four were found fit for galley service. These were Hans Luthi, the preacher of Schaufel Bühl, 54 years old; Nikolaus Baumgartner of Trub, 40; Peter Wüthrich of Trub, 50; and Joseph Probst of Trub, 50. A fifth man, Christian Liebe of the Palatinate, who was seized in the canton of Bern, was sent to the galleys with the others. These five men were delivered to Captain Hackbrett, who conducted them to Sicily where they were forged to the oars of a galley.

According to a letter, Baumgartner died in Turin and Hans Luthi died on the galley. Concerning the other three, one of whom was Peter Wüthrich, a letter was sent from Palermo to the Dutch Mennonites (*Inv. Arch. Amst.,* reprinted in Müller). The Dutch Mennonites intervened and they were released in January 1716. They arrived in Neuenburg by way of Turin and Geneva in a very wretched condition. Wüthrich and Probst are said to have moved into the Bernese Jura. **S.G.**

S. Geiser, *Die Taufgesinnten-Gemeinden* (Karlsruhe, 1931); Müller, *Berner Täufer; ML* IV.

Wybma, Reynier Wybrands, b. 1573, d. 1645 at Amsterdam, was from about 1605 a preacher and from 1612 an elder of the Waterlander congregation of Amsterdam, where he lived from 1605. He was ordained to the eldership by Elder Lubbert Gerritsz (*q.v.*) on his deathbed, Jan. 17, 1612. At first Reynier Wybrands, as he is mostly called, was a glazier, later he had a business. He was engaged in many problems and quarrels of his age: in 1607-8 and again in 1618 he tried to settle the difficulties concerning Nittert Obbes (*q.v.*) in his Amsterdam home church, in 1634 he mediated in a conflict at Rotterdam concerning Elder Eduard Nabels (*q.v.*). His *Memoriael,* a book in which he wrote all that happened in his Amsterdam congregation, is found in the Amsterdam Archives. During his eldership the union of an Anabaptist-Brownist group of English refugees at Amsterdam (see **Smyth, John**) and his Waterlander congregation came about in 1615.

In the same year he carried on a correspondence with some Waterlander (also called Frisian) churches in Prussia.

Apart from an undated manuscript concerning exclusion from the Lord's table, now found in the Amsterdam Archives Reynier Wybrands wrote *Catechesis, Dat is, onderwijsinghe in de Christelijcke Religie* (Amsterdam, 1640; repr. 1640 and 1672 at Amsterdam). In 1626 he and his co-ministers P. A. Hesseling and Cornelis Claesz Anslo published *Apologia oft Verantwoordinghe* against Nittert Obbes. vDZ.

Inv. Arch. Amst. I, Nos. 663, 909; II, Nos. 834 f., 1179 f., 1198, 1200, 1203 f., 1226, 1345, 1359, 1366, 1372, 2626, 2930 f.; II, 2, Nos. 332-45, 347-49, 351, 364, 652 f., 658-63; Schijn-Maatschoen, *Geschiedenis* II, 494-516 (with portrait); Kühler, *Geschiedenis* II, *passim; DB* 1864, 3, 49, 51, 62 ff., 71; 1897, 87, 119; 1903, 62 ff., 79; 1906, 140-44.

Wybrandi, a Dutch Mennonite family, formerly found in Friesland, usually butter merchants, and owners of tileworks at Leeuwarden, where they lived from the 17th century. Gentius Wybrandi, b. *c*1735 at Leeuwarden, d. there *c*1810, studied at the Zonist (*q.v.*) seminary at Amsterdam and was a pastor at Berlikum 1761-82 and Heerenveen 1782-88, in which year he retired, devoting himself to farming and business. A side branch by marriage with the Tigler (*q.v.*) family is the Tigler Wybrandi family. vDZ.

Wybrands (Wijbrands), **Aemilius Willem,** b. Oct. 1, 1838, at Amsterdam, d. Sept. 22, 1886, at Leiden, was educated at the Athenaeum and Mennonite seminary at Amsterdam and served as pastor of the Mennonite congregations of Edam 1862-70, Hoorn 1870-82, and Leiden 1882-86. Though he died before the age of 48, he left a large number of writings, particularly dealing with medieval history and literature. Among his best works are *Het kerkelijk drama in de Middeleeuwen* (1861), *De Dialogus Miraculorum van Ceasarius van Heisterbach* (1873), and *De Abdij Bloemhof te Wittewierum* (1883). (*N.N.B.Wb.* IV, 1486 f.) vDZ.

Wybrands (Wijbrans), **Christiaan Nicolaas,** b. March 24, 1852, at Amsterdam, d. there Aug. 16, 1913, educated at the Amsterdam Mennonite seminary, served the congregations of Noordeind van Graft 1877-78, Edam 1878-81, IJlst 1881-84, Westzaan-Zuid 1884-86, and Enschedé 1886-98. In 1898 he retired because of his health. Particularly at Enschedé he was very active. He was the promoter of the founding of the Mennonite congregation of Gronau (*q.v.*), which formerly belonged to the Enschedé congregation. Through his initiative the weak Zwolsche (*q.v.*) Fonds (fund for the pensioning of widows of Mennonite pastors) was united in 1897 with the Fonds (*q.v.*) tot Ondersteuning.

Among the many publications of C. N. Wybrands are a few papers in the *Doopsgezinde Bijdragen,* e.g., a study on the congregation of Noordeind van Graft (1878), and one on the congregation of Edam (1887). In *De Zondagsbode* he published articles on the Anslo (*q.v.*) family (XII, Nos. 16-21), on Rembrandt (*q.v.*) (XIX, Nos. 35-41), and particularly on "Het Menniste Zusje" (XV, Nos. 42-52, and

XVI, Nos. 1-10). Of this "Het Menniste Zusje" an enlarged and illustrated edition was published in *Verslag Koninklijke Oudheidkundig Genootschap*, 1913.   vDZ.

K. Vos, *Levensbericht van C. N. Wybrands* (Leiden, 1914).

Wybrands (Wijbrands), Karel (d. 1852), a teacher at Amsterdam, married to Petronella Veerman, was the father of seven children, two of whom, Aemilius Willem and Christiaan Nicolaas, were Mennonite pastors; his daughter Karolina Petronella was married to Paulus Frans Kühler, and was the mother of Professor W. J. Kühler (*q.v.*); Wilhemina, married to the teacher Jan M. Vos, was the mother of Pastor Karel Vos (*q.v.*).   vDZ.

Wybrands(z), Reynier: see **Wybma, R. W.**

Wybrandt Jans, of Hartwerd near Bolsward in the Dutch province of Friesland, was burned at the stake at Leeuwarden on June 28, 1530, because he held heretical views on the doctrines of the Incarnation of Christ and His two natures. Although Karel Vos thought that this had reference to the doctrine of the Incarnation as taught by Melchior Hofmann (*q.v.*) and later also by Menno Simons, Wybrandt Jans was probably not an Anabaptist, but a Sacramentist (*q.v.*).   vDZ.

W. J. Kühler, *Het Socinianisme in Nederland* (Leiden, 1912) 28; K. Vos, "Wijbrant Jans van Hartwerd," in *Ned. Archief voor Kirkgesch.*, 1915, 202 ff.; *DB* 1899, 36, note 1; 1917, 81; *ML* II, 259.

Wynalda, a Mennonite family found from the 17th century in the Dutch province of Friesland. There were a number of Mennonite preachers by this name: Eilert and his son Yde Wynalda were untrained preachers at Surhuisterveen from 1750 and 1772 respectively, both of whom died in 1801-2. Tjebbe Wynalda, d. *c*1797 at Pingjum, was a lay preacher of the Witmarsum congregation 1750-94. Jan Evertsz Wynalda, educated at the Zonist (*q.v.*) seminary, served at Enkhuizen 1785-86 and Blokzijl 1786-d. 95.

Agge (Aggeus) Wynalda, b. Oct. 17, 1712, at Dokkum, d. Oct. 19, 1792, at Haarlem, received his training at the Remonstrant seminary at Amsterdam, thereupon serving at Emden *c*1733-36 and Haarlem 1736-d.92. In 1742 he dedicated the new Buitenpost (*q.v.*) meetinghouse with a sermon which was published under the title *Davids Liefde tot Gods Huis* (Amsterdam, 1743).   vDZ.

Wynands (Wynandsz, Wynants): see **Wijnandsz.**

Wynands (Wynantz), Willem (Wilhelm), b. March 28, 1630, at Altona, d. there Dec. 21, 1658, a son of Pieter Wynands and Perina Noë, was a preacher of the Hamburg-Altona church from June 17, 1655, until his death three years later. His sermons were published after his death, entitled *LVIIJ Stichtelycke Predicatiën* (Amsterdam, 1660). Of these sermons, 57 were composed by Wynands, and one by Barend Roelofsz, also a preacher of Hamburg, and written from memory by Wynands. This book of sermons

was very popular among the more conservative Mennonites; in the Balk (*q.v.*) congregation it was used until the early 19th century. According to a letter of 1773, the Mennonites in America liked Wynands' sermons. David Zug translated a number of them into German, published as *Predigten über höchst wichtige Gegenstände des Christenthums*, with a tract by Menno Simons (Lancaster 1830; reprints Lancaster 1871, Scottdale 1926). (See also **Wijnands.**)   vDZ.

Wyngaert, Govert and Tobias Govertsen van den: see **Wijngaard, van den.**

Wyntgens van Westbrouck, Philips, a weaver at Amsterdam, an Anabaptist martyr, was executed on March 10, 1533, probably at Amsterdam. His head was to be put on a stake as a deterrent example. His property was confiscated. (Grosheide, *Bijdrage*, 36, 50, 302.)   vDZ.

Wyse (Wyss, Weis, Weiss, Weisse, Weisz, Weyss, Wise), a Swiss Mennonite name found in South Germany, France, and the United States. In 1940, nine persons with the name were members of two Mennonite congregations in South Germany, and in 1951 four in the French Mennonite Conference. Endres Weiss (*q.v.*), an Anabaptist martyr, was burned at the stake in 1528. The first known Weiss in the Palatinate was Hans Weiss, who had three sons, one of whom, Christian, became the ancestor of the Weiss families in Wartenberg as well as many Weiss families in America. In 1717 Hans Weyss was named in a Palatine Mennonite census list, while in 1743 Michael Weiss and Jacob Weiss were named in a similar list. These last two were listed again in 1744 as being from Osthoffen. Jacob Weis, probably a Mennonite, was among the immigrants landing in Philadelphia in 1728; one of the settlers in Upper Milford Twp., Lehigh Co., Pa., was Jacob Weisz. Among the early members of the Mennonite church in this township were George Weiss and Rudolph Weiss. The name Weiss is found in the old Hereford and Boyertown cemeteries in Berks County, Pa.

Most of the American Wyse Mennonites now live in Fulton County, Ohio, and Henry County, Iowa. Their ancestors were Peter Wyss (1800-56), whose passport is dated April 1824, and who had been a resident of Burgdorf, canton of Bern, Switzerland, and his nephew John Wyse (1821-84). In Fulton County, Ohio, Peter was one of the first ministers in the Amish Mennonite church. In the same county his son Jephtha Wyse (1838-87) was ordained as minister there in 1866. John Wyse (1821-84) was ordained deacon *c*1864, and his son Daniel J. Wyse (1847-1925) as minister in 1888. In 1958 five ordained members of the Wyse family were serving the Mennonite Church (MC). Olive G. Wyse has for many years been a member of the Goshen College faculty.   M.G.

M. Pohl, "Geschichtliche Beiträge aus den Pfälzer Mennonitengemeinden," *Gem.-Kal.*, 1905, 133-47, especially 145.

Wytses, Atse: see **Zijpp, van der.**

Y

Yamhill County (Ore.) Old Order Amish settlement: see McMinnville O.O. Amish.

Yarrow, British Columbia, a farming village 11 miles southwest of Chilliwack, is wedged in by the Vedder Mountain to the south and the Vedder River to the north. The oldest Mennonite settlement in the Fraser Valley was founded by a non-Mennonite farmer, Chauncy Eckert, who purchased 1,640 acres of fertile land along the British Columbia Electric Railway for the Mennonites whom he admired because of their honesty and farming ability. In February 1928 the first families arrived from other parts of B.C. or the prairie provinces. After much experimentation with various crops, Yarrow specialized in raising raspberries, becoming the berry center of the province. In 1954, 1,500 tons of berries were shipped, mostly to the United States, grossing approximately $300,000. Two dozen business establishments, including a sawmill, box factory, and four berry-processing plants, serve the trading area. The General Conference and the Mennonite Brethren each have a church in the village, the latter being the largest M.B. congregation in Canada. A Bible school and a Christian high school, valued at $75,000, are operated here by the M.B. Church. The Elementary-Junior High School, valued at $200,000, founded by four M.B. churches in the district, is now owned and operated by the municipality. A privately owned home for the aged is providing a place of rest for many people who move to Yarrow because of the mild climate and the opportunities for Mennonite fellowship. The population (1955) is 2,000, of which 99 per cent are Mennonites, with an additional 2,000 Mennonites living in the immediate shopping area, extending approximately three miles east and west.   I.G.N.

B. B. Wiens, "Pioneering in British Columbia," *Menn. Life* I (July 1945).

Yarrow Bible School, located in Yarrow, B.C., was opened in September 1930 by members of the Yarrow Mennonite Brethren Church. P. D. Loewen was engaged as the first teacher. Until 1934 the school functioned as a day or evening school, with one or two classes, but with a small enrollment. J. A. Harder assisted at intervals. A. Nachtigal continued the school in 1935-37, and J. A. Harder in 1937-41. In 1940 a four-class schedule was introduced, with four instructors, and the school became a member of the ETTA. In 1942 the school had its record enrollment of 155 students, but subsequently the attendance declined because of World War II. Other principals were C. C. Peters 1941-47, G. H. Sukkau 1947-52, and H. Warkentin 1952-55. In 1946 the Yarrow M.B. Church assumed full responsibility for the school. The presence of other schools in the province and the trend toward secular education caused the Bible School to be closed in 1955. About 135 students graduated from the four-year course.   H.Wa.

Yarrow Mennonite Brethren Church, located at Chilliwack, B.C., a member of the Canadian District Conference, was organized under the leadership of P. Dyck on Feb. 3, 1929, with 94 members. The meetings were held in the public school until 1930. That year the first church building was started, but was never finished. In 1933 a building for Sunday school and Bible school classes was erected. On account of the rapid growth of the church membership, it became necessary in 1938 to dismantle the church building and erect the present enlarged building, 90 x 60 ft. In 1946 a new spacious Bible school building was constructed. The early ministers of the church were P. J. Reimer, K. A. Klassen, P. H. Neufeld, P. Duke, J. Abrahams, and J. Epp. In 1957 Herman Lenzmann was pastor, with a membership of 708. The congregation has 13 missionaries on the foreign field.   J.A.Ha.

Yarrow United Mennonite Church located near Chilliwack, B.C., originally a subsidiary of the First Mennonite Church (GCM) at Sardis, was organized as an independent congregation on Oct. 25, 1938, when the present frame church was built to seat 175. The members are exclusively Mennonite immigrants from Russia and their descendants, many of whom had settled first in the prairie states. They are chiefly engaged in berry farming and dairying. Services are conducted in German. At home Low German and English are spoken. In 1957 the membership was 175. The leading minister was John J. Klassen, assisted by Isaak Penner.   J.J.Kl.

Yazykovo, a Mennonite settlement located approximately 15 miles from the village of Chortitza, Russia, consisted of 6 villages, 4 of which were established in 1869: Nikolaifeld (Nikolaipol), Franzfeld (Varvarovka), Eichenfeld (Dubovka), and Adelsheim (Dolinovka); Hochfeld (Morozovo) followed. Petersdorf (Petershivka), which had been previously settled, was also a part of this settlement. The name Yazykovo was derived from the name of the nobleman from whom the land was bought. The administration of the settlement (volost) was located in Nikolaipol. The land, consisting of 19,800 acres (Friesen, p. 677, 23,300 acres), was purchased by the Chortitza settlement for 240,000 rubles and divided into 147 farms consisting of 135 acres each. An additional 2600 acres was purchased privately (Friesen). At the beginning of the century there were 440 families with a total population of 2200 (Friesen; according to D. H. Epp, *Statistik*, 61, the figure was lower). Soon the settlement achieved prosperity.

Being located on the edge of the larger Chortitza settlement, some of the villages suffered severely during the Revolution and civil war. In Eichenfeld in a single night 82 people were killed. Eichenfeld and Petersdorf were completely destroyed. The other villages suffered severely under the Soviets. Many were exiled. During the German occupation of the Ukraine the remaining inhabitants were taken to Germany in 1943, whence some were later returned to Russia by the Red army and others came to America (for details see articles under respective village names). Most of the inhabitants were members of the Nikolaifeld (Yazykovo) Mennonite Church (*q.v.*), which was a subsidiary of the Chortitza Mennonite Church. There was also a branch of the Einlage Mennonite Brethren Church (*q.v.*) in the villages. During the German occupation, 1941-43, Adelsheim, Hochfeld, and Nikolaifeld had churches and choirs. C.K.

ML II, 394; K. Stumpp, *Bericht über das Gebiet Chortitza* (Berlin, 1943).

Yazykovo Mennonite Brethren Church at Yazykovo-Nikolaipol, province of Ekaterinoslav, South Russia, was organized in 1875-80 at Nikolaipol, perhaps the largest of the villages in the Mennonite settlement. Peter Peters, Cornelius Fehr, and Martin Koslowsky were the first ministers of the church. It was at first affiliated with the Einlage M.B. Church (*q.v.*) about 15 miles to the south, but later became an independent congregation. The later ministers were Gerhard Regehr, Peter Toews, Joh. Peters, and Johann Schellenberg. The M.B. Church at Nikolaipol after a period of struggle became well established spiritually. The Alliance movement made itself felt quite strongly, strengthening rather than impeding the spiritual life of the church. During the Russian Revolution of 1917-20 some of the villages were utterly destroyed by Machno bandits and the church probably ceased to exist. Elder Gerhard Regehr, who lived at Reinfeld near Nikolaipol, managed to escape and in 1952 lived at Seattle, Wash. Johann Schellenberg was executed by the Machno bandits during the Dubovka massacre. P.H.B.

Ybor Mennonite Mission (MC) among the Spanish-speaking people in Ybor City, Fla.: see **Tampa** Mennonite Mission.

Ydewons, of Langweer in the Dutch province of Friesland, a revolutionary Anabaptist, beheaded on May 11, 1534, probably at Amsterdam. (*DB* 1917, 121, No. 144; Mellink, *Wederdopers,* 245.) vdZ.

Ydse Gaukes, an Anabaptist martyr, who after much torture was burned at the stake at Deventer, Netherlands, on June 16, 1571 (not July 16, as stated in *Martyrs' Mirror* and *Mennonitisches Lexikon*). He was arrested by the Spanish soldiers at Deventer on March 11, 1571, with his wife Anneken and ten other Mennonites. (For detailed information, see **Anneken.**) Ydse Gaukes wrote three letters from prison. His first letter, dated March 31, addressed to his brother and his friends, contains moving particulars about the tortures of the prisoners. In his second letter, undated, he sends greetings to W. and L. J. at Molkwerum (*q.v.*) in Friesland, where he probably came from. He was a boatman. His third letter, written only two days before his death, is a farewell letter to his brothers Bauke, Simon, and Pieter. When he wrote this letter most of his fellow prisoners had already been executed. (*Mart. Mir.* D 552-60, E 885-88; *DB* 1919, 29-37; *ML* II, 36). vdZ.

Year Book of the General Conference of the Mennonite Brethren Church of North America was first published in 1883 and since then has been published following each convention of the General Conference, which met annually until 1909 and triennially since then. The *Year Book* contains the minutes, reports, and resolutions of the particular session of the Conference and a directory of ministers and church workers listed by churches. Until 1936 it was issued entirely in German. In 1939 an English synopsis of the Conference decisions was issued in addition to the *Year Book*. In 1943 the *Year Book* was issued in two editions, one German and one English. Since 1946 (November 1945) it has been issued in English with a German synopsis as part of the book. The *Year Book* has varied in number of pages from 16 to 224. Each district issues a yearbook after each annual district conference, containing the same information for the district as the General Conference *Year Book* contains for the General Conference. O.H.

Year Book of the Krimmer Mennonite Brethren Church was first published in 1905, reporting the 26th Conference Session held at the Salem K.M.B. Church, Bridgewater, S.D. The 500 copies of this first pamphlet of 8 pages, 3⅝ x 6 inches, were printed entirely in German by the *Rundschau*, Elkhart, Ind. It is published annually for the purpose of distributing information of its activities among its churches, and to preserve an official record. The pamphlet contains reports of the work carried on by the Conference during that year through its committees and its churches, as well as the recommendations and resolutions adopted by the delegates for the new year. Until 1938 it was published in German; 1939-44 it contained reports in both languages; since 1945 it has been published in English. The pamphlet has been enlarged to 85-95 pages, 5¼ x 8 inches. The Fifty-third Year Book, submitting the report of the 78th Session, was published in 1957. C.F.P.

Yearbook of the Central Conference of Mennonites, generally a 40-page issue, was first published in 1922, and appeared regularly 1922-56. Special events of the year, conference minutes and reports, and a directory of conference organizations with names and addresses of officers were the principal contents. Editors were W. H. Grubb 1922-25, H. E. Nunemaker 1926, W. B. Weaver 1927-37, and R. L. Hartzler 1938-56. R.L.H.

Yearbook of the General Conference Mennonite Church, from 1895 to 1930 published as *Mennonite Yearbook and Almanac,* publisher Eastern District Mennonite Conference at Quakertown, Pa., to 1924, and the General Conference Mennonite Publication Board through the Mennonite Book Concern at Berne, Ind., 1924-30. Up to 1928 it contained historical material, in addition to church statistics and the annual almanac material prepared by L. J. Heatwole, which later was discontinued in 1930. In 1895-1952 it was usually a 48-page issue (first issues 40 pp.), thereafter increasing in size because of a much enlarged statistical section, the 1958 number having 92 pages; with 1946, however, the title was changed to *Handbook of Information of the General Conference of the Mennonite Church of North America.* The format has been approximately 6½ x 9 throughout its history, with minor variations.

H.S.B.

Yearbooks (*Jahrbücher*), Mennonite, annuals published by Mennonite conferences or individuals, have been of five types: (1) almanacs (*q.v.*) with some popular religious, literary, educational, historical, or practical material; (2) statistical handbooks giving primarily a directory of congregations, ministers, institutions, and conference organizations and officers, with membership (and financial statistics) with or without some summary reports of the year's church occurrences and activities, sometimes combined with (1); (3) minutes of annual or other conferences (may be called yearbook even though the period covered may be several years), plus ministerial and missionary directory; (4) purely a directory of congregations with membership and ministerial listings; (5) purely literary or historical annuals. Some yearbooks are very small and some large, both in pages and format. Some are distributed free and some sell for substantial prices, and one or two have large editions. One, the *Mennonite Yearbook and Directory,* attempts a world-wide coverage of Mennonite ministerial lists and group membership, and has an edition of 12,000. The following list is chronological and not descriptive nor bibliographically complete. (See the articles for the more important ones as indicated by *q.v.*) The titles of the yearbooks have in some cases changed erratically, as well as has the scope of the coverage geographically, the type of content, size, and place of publication.

1. EUROPE—*Naamlijst (q.v.) der tegenwoordig in dienst zijnde predikanten der Mennoniten in de Vereenigde Nederlande,* irregularly 1731-1829; *Namensverzeichnis der Aeltesten und Lehrer der mennonitischen Gemeinen in Süd-, Ost-, Westpreussen, Lithauen und Polen (q.v.),* occasional, 1823, 1835, 1843, 1857, 1881; *Jaarboekje voor de Doopsgezinde gemeenten in de Nederlanden (q.v.),* published by Samuel Muller, occasional, 1837, 1840, 1850; *Jahrbuch der Mennoniten-Gemeinden (q.v.),* published by H. G. Mannhardt, twice only, 1884, 1888; *Christlicher Gemeinde-Kalender (q.v.)* 1892-1941, called *Mennonitischer Gemeinde-Kalender* 1951- , published by the South German Conference; *Christlicher Familienkalender (q.v.),* published in Russia by A. Kroeker and later by Raduga (*q.v.*) 1897-1915, 1918-19; *Doopsgezind Jaarboekje (q.v.),* Netherlands, 1902-42, 1949- ; *Mennonitisches Jahrbuch (q.v.)* 1904-14, published in Russia by H. Dirks 1904-11 and D. H. Epp 1912-14.

2. NORTH AMERICA—*Mennonite Family Almanac,* later *Family Almanac (q.v.)* at Elkhart, Ind., 1870-1908, at Scottdale, Pa., 1909-55; *Familien-Kalender (q.v.)* at Elkhart 1870-1908, at Scottdale 1909-40; *Christlicher Familien-Kalender (q.v.),* published by David Goerz at Halstead, Kan., 1885, becoming *Bundesbote-Kalender (q.v.)* in 1886, published by GCM Conference 1886-1947; *Mennonite Yearbook and Almanac* (GCM) 1895-1930, changed to *Yearbook of the General Conference of the Mennonite Church of North America* 1931-45, then to *Handbook of Information of the General Conference of the Mennonite Church of North America,* 1946- ; *Mennonite Yearbook and Directory (q.v.)* (MC), Scottdale, 1905-8, 1913- ; *Yearbook of the Central Conference of Mennonites (q.v.)* 1922-46; *Vorwärts-Kalender (q.v.),* published by the M.B. Publishing House at Hillsboro, Kan., 1925-43; *Der Neue Amerikanische Calender (q.v.)* 1930- , published by J. A. Raber, Baltic, Ohio, for the Old Order Amish, containing a complete directory of Amish ministers; *Yearbook, Church of God in Christ,* 1945- ; *Mennonitisches Jahrbuch (q.v.)* (GCM), 1948- , published primarily for Canadians, described as a successor to *Bundesbote-Kalender,* but quite different in character; *Warte-Jahrbuch,* published by Arnold Dyck at Steinbach, Man., 1943-44. *The Ohio Amish Directory,* published by Ervin Gingerich, Millersburg, Ohio, 1954- , is unique in including a complete name list of heads of families along with a congregational directory.

The remaining yearbooks to be listed are essentially conference reports, sometimes with statistics, and it is not easy to determine the year of first issue, the language formerly used, whether German or English or both, or the frequency of appearance. Nor do they always bear the same name. Those still appearing in 1958 were the following: *Jahrbuch der Konferenz der Mennoniten in Canada; K.M.B. Conference Yearbook; Annual Report of the Evangelical Mennonite Brethren; Annual Report of the Conference of the Evangelical Mennonite Church; Yearbook of the General Conference, Mennonite Brethren Church of North America (q.v.),* triennial, first published in 1883; *Yearbook* published by each of the M.B. district conferences, containing besides conference proceedings a directory of congregations and ministers. The M.B.C. and U.M.C. general conference proceedings and district conference proceedings were also published as yearbooks containing much statistical material, often called *Conference Journal* or *Proceedings of the Conference.* The U.M.C. has published an annual *United Missionary Church Yearbook* at Kitchener, Ont., 1946- .

H.S.B.

J. C. Wenger, "Mennonite Yearbooks," *MQR* XIV (1940) 59-63; Melvin Gingerich and H. S. Bender, "Mennonite Yearbooks and Almanacs," *MQR* XXIV (1950).

Yellow Creek Mennonite (MC) Church, located in Harrison Twp., Elkhart Co., Ind., is a member of the Indiana-Michigan Conference. The first meetinghouse used by the settlers who began coming into the area in 1845, led by the aged Bishop Martin Hoover (*c*1761-1850) of Medina County, Ohio, was a log building one-half mile north of the village of South West, a short distance south of the present Yellow Creek Church of the Brethren. In 1849 the Yellow Creek Mennonites built a log meetinghouse 26 feet square on the plot where the old cemetery now is located on the east side of the road. This was later enlarged. In 1861 Andrew and Lydia Bigler sold two acres to the "Old Mennonite Church" for $200.00. This is the site of the present Wisler meetinghouse across the road from the 1849 meetinghouse. On this lot the congregation built a frame meetinghouse 40 x 60 ft. When John F. Funk (*q.v.*) attended the annual fall conference at Yellow Creek in 1862 he estimated the Elkhart County Mennonite membership at 400-500. A visitor, Deacon Frederick A. Rodes of Virginia, estimated the capacity of the meetinghouse at 500-600, but Bishop John M. Brenneman, who served as moderator of the conference, estimated the number of the communicants at 300-400. On this occasion in 1862, 46 members were baptized. After the new meetinghouse was built in 1861 the 1849 meetinghouse was moved to the northwest corner of Sec. 16 of Union Township, where it came to be known as Blossers Church and served as a sort of outpost of the Yellow Creek congregation, along with Shaums (Olive), Holdeman, and Christophels. After the Wisler division (1872) the Wisler and Funk groups alternated in the use of the Yellow Creek, Blossers, and Shaums meetinghouses. In 1907 the Wisler group split into two groups, which together bought the meetinghouse of the "Funk Congregation" (MC) at Yellow Creek in 1912. The Funk group then built the present brick meetinghouse a short distance to the north of the frame meetinghouse, and enlarged it in 1948. In 1874 the Brenneman (MBC) schism occurred when Daniel Brenneman, a progressive younger minister, was discharged, and his wing organized the Bethel Church 1½ miles northwest of the Yellow Creek meetinghouse. The membership of the Yellow Creek congregation (MC) was reported as only 80 in 1890 (J. F. Funk) and 129 in 1896 (deacon Jacob G. Long). These low figures are accounted for by the schisms of Jacob Wisler (*q.v.*) and Daniel Brenneman (*q.v.*) in 1872 and 1874 as well as by the full congregational organization of what had originally been Yellow Creek outposts: Shaums (Olive), Holdeman, Salem (merger of Blossers and Christophels), and the Prairie Street Church in Elkhart. In 1958 the membership at Yellow Creek had grown to 326, and the bishop-pastor was Peter Wiebe. Yellow Creek is the center of the large Mennonite (as contrasted with Amish Mennonite east of Goshen) settlement west of Goshen. (Files of the *Herald of Truth;* John F. Funk diaries and private papers.)   J.C.W.

Yellow Creek Old Order and Wisler (*q.v.*) Mennonite meetinghouse, located slightly south of the Yellow Creek Mennonite (MC) Church (*q.v.*), in Elkhart County, Ind., was built in 1861 and enlarged in 1954. After the Wisler schism in 1872, the Wisler and M.C. groups alternated in the use of the building until 1912, when the M.C. congregation built its new meetinghouse. In 1907 the Wisler Mennonites divided into two groups, the more conservative Old Order or Martin Mennonites (*q.v.*) who do not permit telephones or automobiles, and the Wisler or Ramer Mennonites (*q.v.*), and these two groups now alternate in the use of the old Yellow Creek meetinghouse and the Blosser meetinghouse (built 1891). The ministers in the Ramer group, which in 1958 had 200 members, were William Ramer bishop, and Paul Hoover and Joseph E. Martin (formerly the bishop in the Martin group) preachers; the ministers in the Martin group were William G. Weaver bishop, and

Enos Martin, Henry E. Martin, and Harvey Horst preachers, with a membership of 100.   J.C.W.

Yenisei Province (now Krasnoyarsk Territory, Siberia), Russia, on the left bank of the Yenisei River, had a Mennonite settlement for a time. In 1913 some 32 families from the Ignatyevo (*q.v.*) Mennonite settlement in the Ukraine established two villages, Rozovka and Krasnovka, about 40 miles south of the city of Minusinsk. During the Revolution this settlement suffered severely. In 1926 there were only 10 families left. When G. Rosenfeld and J. Pätkau visited the Mennonites here in 1927, they reported that the settlement had been dissolved because of unfavorable conditions and that the few remaining families were too poor to move elsewhere.   C.K.

Jakob Quiring, *Die Mundart von Chortitza in Süd-Russland* (Munich, 1928) 41; *Unser Blatt* III (1927) 11.

Yetelhauser (Yedelhauser, Jedelhaus), **Michael**, a tailor of Weyl (Weil(?)) der Stadt in Württemberg), was imprisoned in the Upper House Prison in Passau (*q.v.*) with about 60 fellow believers. In September 1538, the fourth year of his imprisonment, he recanted. The record of his cross-examination says that Michael would follow the church in the expectation that the church would reform according to the word and command of God and do away with the abuses. The confession of Hans Pfeiffer (Mosheim calls him Hans Beck; this is surely an error; see *ML* I, 149 f.; Wiswedel I, 29) is said to have had the same general content. But since these two men did not accept the Catholic doctrine of the sacrament in one form, the ruler and administrator were unwilling to release them. But Pfeiffer and Yetelhauser escaped from prison. Mosheim, the recorder, who had taken great pains for the "conversion" of these two Anabaptists and did not agree with the administrator with respect to several "articles," was at Nürnberg a year later. Here the two Anabaptists looked him up. For that reason Mosheim was suspected of Anabaptism, and so there developed a "right spiritual struggle" between him and the Nürnberg clergy. Mosheim was apparently a wavering character who, though no longer completely in the old church, wanted to clear his name of any suspicion of Anabaptism. He declared that he had induced Yetelhauser and Pfeiffer to recant and had earnestly prayed for their release and God had heard him. Now they had come to him in Nürnberg; it would be better to listen to them in person. His suggestion was accepted. The two Anabaptists in the presence of two clergymen, two councillors, and a secretary were examined at the Rathaus. "The people of Nürnberg found pleasure in the confession of the two," comments Mosheim in his document.

Michael Yetelhauser answered the question how man is justified before God and saved: "Alone through the recognition that Christ died for us, has paid the price of sin, and done satisfaction, and thus the heart of man is struck and illuminated to such an extent through the power of God that he recognizes such a kindness which has happened in his favor, and is sincerely happy and comforted." In reply to the question whether works have nothing to do with this justification he declared: "He who has a true Christian faith must also do Christian good works; such good works cannot be separated from the faith. However, justification and salvation are not ascribed to the works, but alone to faith. For that which Christ acquired for man even before he is born cannot be achieved with any work." In answer to the question whether his Brethren held the same view of justification he replied: "Yes, and he has been with them. They urgently insist on good works." Nothing is known concerning Yetelhauser's later fate.   W.W.

Ruprecht von Mosheim, *Eine Christliche wahrhaftige gründliche entschuldung* (Kirchen-Bibliothek Neustadt, collection 447): W. Wiswedel, *Bilder* II, 29.

Ylst: see **IJlst.**

Ymuiden: see **IJmuiden.**

Yntema: see **IJntema.**

Yoder, Kan., a village (pop. *c*100), the center of a large Amish and Mennonite community, named after Eli M. Yoder, the son of an Old Order Amish Mennonite bishop of Maryland, who in 1870 homesteaded in Reno County, Kan., about 12 miles southeast of Hutchinson. In 1886 the Missouri Pacific R.R. Company built a track connecting Hutchinson and Wichita, which crossed the northeast corner of the Yoder farm, separating about 5 acres from the rest of the farm. On this corner plot Yoder built a general store and a post office. This was the origin of the village. In 1883 Christian Miller of Shelby County, Ill., bought a farm about 2 miles east of Yoder; in the following years other families arrived, making Yoder the center of the Amish community. Jonas D. Bontrager was chosen as preacher in 1885, and as bishop in 1887. By 1918 there were four Amish congregations with perhaps 80 to 90 families. In 1943 a naval air base established one mile west of Yoder, covering four sections of land, caused a number of Amish and Mennonite families to move away. There were in 1955 about 50 Amish families in the community, making two congregations.

On April 18, 1919, the Yoder Mennonite Church (MC) was organized with 65 charter members, almost all of Old Order Amish background, and L. O. King as pastor. In the same year a meetinghouse 40 x 60 ft. was built one mile north of Yoder, which was enlarged and remodeled in 1952.   H.A.D.

Yoder (Ioder, Joder, Jodter, Jotter, Yoeder, Yother, Yothers, Yotter), a Mennonite family name of Swiss origin. The Swiss encyclopedia (*Historisch-biographisches Lexikon der Schweiz*) locates this "ancient family" in the village of Steffisberg on the edge of the Oberland in the canton of Bern, while another authority on Swiss families traces them to the village of Muri, nearer Bern. A history of the Emmental lists Joders among the early residents. The name Yoder evidently is derived from the Christian name "Theodore." For example, Saint Theodore, a missionary in the Swiss Alps in the Middle Ages, was abbreviated to "St. Joder." August 16 is still listed as "St. Joder's Day" in the Swiss Reformed church almanacs. Joder first appears as a family name in the canton of Bern in the 14th century. At Steffisberg the Joders began to appear in the records as early as 1529 and at Muri slightly later.

Although some of the Swiss Joders became members of the Reformed Church and eventually brought this faith with them to America, others became Anabaptists. Heini Joder was imprisoned at Basel in 1531 for spreading the Anabaptist faith. The Bern records show that other Joders became Anabaptists in the 17th century. In the same century members of the Joder family migrated to the Palatinate. Among the Palatinate estates on which Joders lived were Branchweilerhof near Neustadt and Vogelstockerhof near Annweiler. In 1717 a Mennonite Jost Jodter lived in Lachen. The Palatine Mennonite census list of 1724 names a Johannes Joder at Mussbach, while the 1738 census named a Jost Jother in Oggersheim. A Johannes Yother lived at Mussbach in 1759. The 1940 list of Mennonite family names in South Germany shows 34 Jothers in 6 congregations. In 1951, seven persons with the name Yoder, Ioder, or Jother were members in three churches of the French Mennonite Conference.

Yoders of the Reformed Church came to Pennsylvania as early as 1710, settling in Berks County. In 1742 Christian Jother, Christian Jotter, Jr., and Jacob Yoder, all apparently Amish Mennonites, arrived in Pennsylvania. There is considerable doubt that the widow Barbara Yoder, who supposedly arrived in 1714 and who is often mentioned among Amish immigrants, was actually one of the early Amish settlers in Pennsylvania. Jacob Yoder, who arrived in America in 1742, is generally referred to as "Strong Jacob Yoder," many legends having developed concerning the feats of this early Amish ancestor of a large number of Amish and Mennonite descendants. Christian Yoder, Jr., is likewise the ancestor of many Amish and Mennonites. Yoders continued to emigrate to America, some arriving in the first half of the 19th century.

From Eastern Pennsylvania the Amish Yoders migrated westward to Somerset and Mifflin counties, and from there to Ohio, Indiana, Iowa, and other midwestern and western states. A file of Yoder obituaries in Mennonite church papers (1864-1951) has the following number from these leading states: Ohio, 200; Indiana, 180; Pennsylvania, 176; Iowa, 53; Missouri, 38; Kansas, 28; Oregon, 22; and Illinois, 17. Sixteen additional states and provinces are included in this list. The family name is also widely represented among the Church of the Brethren. In 1957 the more than 180 ordained Yoders serving in Amish and Mennonite churches were represented in these groups: O.O.A. 99, M.C. 58, C.A.M. 14, Beachy Amish 11, and G.C.M. 3. Thus the Yoder family is the second most widely represented family in the ministry of the American Mennonite churches, being surpassed only by the Millers, who have 237 ordained men. These two family names are also the most numerous in the Goshen College student body. Among the Mennonite (MC) leaders have been Abner G. Yoder (*q.v.*), A. I. Yoder (*q.v.*), C. Z. Yoder (*q.v.*), David S. Yoder (*q.v.*), Edward Yoder (*q.v.*), John K. Yoder (*q.v.*), Joseph W. Yoder (*q.v.*), and A. B. Yoder (*q.v.*), long a leading elder in the M.B.C. Church. Among the better-known representatives of the family in 1958 were Allen Yoder (GCM), retired minister in the Central District Conference, his son Harry Yoder of the Bluffton College faculty, Sanford C. Yoder, president emeritus of Goshen College and former secretary of the Mennonite Board of Missions and Charities as well as a bishop in the Mennonite Church (MC), Walter Yoder, former professor of music at Goshen College, Jonathan G. Yoder (MC), former medical missionary in India, Samuel A. Yoder (MC), Goshen College professor, Bishop D. A. Yoder (MC), former president of the Mennonite Board of Education, Edwin J. Yoder (MC), Mennonite bishop in Indiana, J. Otis Yoder, Eastern Mennonite College faculty member, Gideon G. Yoder, bishop and Hesston College faculty member, and bishops Ray F. Yoder in Indiana and Elmer E. Yoder, Paul Yoder, and Stephen A. Yoder of Ohio.

Contrary to the common understanding not all the Yoders are of Amish descent. Of those listed above, the following are of the Mennonite Yoders: D. A. Yoder, Paul Yoder, Stephen Yoder, R. F. Yoder, and A. B. Yoder. Yoders are still to be found in the Franconia Conference (MC) area. When the first Mennonite Yoders arrived has not been determined. M.G.

Don Yoder, "Origins of the Pennsylvania Yoders," in *The Yoder Family Reunion Book* (n.p., 1954); C. Z. Mast and Robert E. Simpson, *Annals of the Conestoga Valley* (Elverson, Pa., 1942) 267-74.

Yoder, Abner G. (1879-1942), a Mennonite (MC) bishop and leader, was born Oct. 4, 1879, in Johnson County, Iowa, the oldest son of Bishop (Conservative Amish) Gideon A. and Mattie (Miller) Yoder. His ancestors emigrated from Switzerland in 1742 and settled in Berks County, Pa. On Dec. 4, 1902, he married Mary G. Gingerich. There were four children: Edwin, Oren, and Katie of Parnell, Iowa, and Gideon of Hesston, Kan. In his early twenties he became a member of the West Union congregation. In 1906 he became the first superintendent of the Daytonville mission Sunday school.

On May 2, 1909, he was ordained to the office of deacon and commissioned to preach in the West Union congregation. On Dec. 21, 1924, he was chosen bishop, continuing in office until death. He served in the church in many different channels. In addition to local service he took an active part in evangelistic work. For many years he was chairman of the board of the Mennonite Children's Home at Kansas City, Kan., and treasurer of the General Sunday School Committee. He also served on various boards and committees. In 1937 he preached the General Conference sermon at Turner, Ore., and in 1939 served as moderator of General Conference at Allensville, Pa. At the time of his death he was moderator of the Iowa-Nebraska Conference as well as a member of the General Problems Committee of General Conference (MC). He died July 6, 1942. E.Yo.

Yoder, Abraham B. (1867-1953), a leader in the United Missionary Church, was born in Elkhart County, Ind., the son of Henry B. and Elizabeth (Bixler) Yoder, taught grade school for sixteen years. He was converted at the age of twenty-three, entered the ministry in 1896, and was ordained in 1899. He married Mary M. Myers on Aug. 31, 1899. They had one child, Ray O. Yoder. He held pastorates at Shambaugh and New Market, Iowa, and at Elkhart, Bethel, Wakarusa, South West, Pleasant Hill, and Goshen in the Indiana Conference. He served as Presiding Elder in the Indiana Conference for twelve years; was delegate to a number of general conferences, and served as Chairman of General Conference in 1920. He was a member of the Board of Directors of the United Missionary Society for many years, a member of the Executive Board of the United Missionary Church, and editor of the *Gospel Banner* 1924-37. He died Oct. 19, 1953.† J.A.Hu.

Yoder, Christian Z. (1845-1939), a leading Ohio Mennonite (MC) minister, a son of John K. and Lydia Zook Yoder, was born in Mifflin County, Pa., moved to Wayne County, Ohio, with his parents in 1855, and resided there until his death. He was known church-wide as "C. Z. Yoder" or simply as "C. Z." He served the Oak Grove Amish Mennonite congregation (*q.v.*) as deacon (1890-1904) and as minister (1904-39). At an early age he began his service to his home community. He was a successful farmer from 1865 until his retirement in 1895, and introduced new agricultural practices into the community, especially in the culture of vegetables and berries and in the use of the greenhouse. He was an organizer of the speakers at farm institutes, and a contributor to farm papers. For many years during the period when the one-room schoolhouses were being built he was a member of the township school board. At his suggestion, each received its artistic planting of pine trees. As early as 1866 he organized and led a singing school at the Center Schoolhouse, Wayne County. He helped to organize the first Sunday school in the Oak Grove church in 1871 and served as superintendent for 22 years. By the organization of the first Young People's Bible Meeting in 1889 he helped to raise the intellectual, cultural, and spiritual level of the congregation and the community. In 1890 he served as chairman of the committee which drew up and secured the adoption by the congregation of a "new order" which provided for buttons instead of hooks and eyes on men's clothing and made possible the ingathering of a large group of young people who had refused to unite with the congregation. His interest in missions, as indicated by the early missionary collections in the Sunday school and the young people's meeting, probably led to his appointment as a director of the Mennonite Evangelizing and Benevolent Board of America when that organization replaced the Mennonite Evangelizing Committee (*q.v.*) in 1892 in order to make room on the board for Amish Mennonites. He assisted in organizing the Ohio Mennonite Sunday School Conference (*q.v.*) in 1895. For many years he served as an evangelist, his preaching and singing ministry taking him to Amish and Mennonite communities in all sections of the country. Following is a partial list of the positions which he held in the Mennonite Church: 1899-1906 vice-president, Mennonite Board of Charitable Homes and Missions; 1906-11 vice-president, and

1911-20 president, Mennonite Board of Missions and Charities; 1920-28 chairman of the Missions Committee of the Board; after 1928, honorary member of the Board. He served on the Music Committee of General Conference (MC) 1909-35 and assisted in the compilation of the German and English hymnals published in 1894-1927. Never an outstanding preacher, his varied talents made a large place for him in the counsels of the church. A son John (now deceased), a grandson Howard, and a great-grandson John Howard are continuing C. Z. Yoder's interest in the life and work of the Mennonite Church.　　　　　　　J.S.U.

Yoder, David S., a Mennonite (MC) lay leader, was born near Spruce Hill, Juniata Co., Pa., on Feb. 24, 1852, the sixth of nine children of Joseph and Hannah Sharp Yoder, of whom only four grew to adulthood. His father was a brother-in-law of Shem Zook, publisher of the German edition of the *Martyrs' Mirror* in 1849. His mother was the oldest sister of Solomon Z. Sharp, pioneer educator in the Church of the Brethren. He went to Academia Seminary near his home, and to Kishacoquillas Seminary not far from Belleville, Pa. He then taught in the schools of Huntingdon County.

In the late 1870's he went to Logan County, Ohio, where he taught schools near West Liberty for five years and became a member of the South Union congregation. He was married to Armenon Yoder on March 1, 1881. They had five children: Mamie M. (Mrs. J. E. Hartzler), Ruth A., John L., Nellie A., and Joe H. With David Plank, a minister, and S. E. Allgyer he was a pioneer in Mennonite Sunday-school work in Logan and Champaign counties, Ohio, served as superintendent for many years and as a teacher until he was incapacitated by old age. He served his church in its then broadening program in a number of official capacities. In 1905 he was elected to the Mennonite Evangelizing and Benevolent Board, and helped to form the Mennonite Board of Missions and Charities, which organization was completed May 2, 1906. He was a member of this Board 1906-18, and served on the Executive Committee 1910-17. He was elected to the Board of the Elkhart Institute Association in 1901 for a term of three years. Secretarial records give his name on the Board as of 1905. He was a member of the Mennonite Board of Education to 1918, and was treasurer in 1918. He was active in the Ohio Mennonite Sunday-school conference movement. He was treasurer of the Ohio Sunday School and Young People's Conference 1912-15, and treasurer of the Ohio Mennonite Sunday School Conference 1916-24, a member of its Executive Committee 1924-30. He was also active in the organization of the Mennonite Aid Plan, a mutual insurance organization for members of the Mennonite Church of Logan and Champaign counties, and served as its secretary for many years.

From the late 1870's to 1899 he lived near West Liberty, Ohio, and 1899-1945 near Bellefontaine, Ohio. He died at his home May 4, 1945. Interment was in Fair View Cemetery at West Liberty.

　　　　　　　J.L.Y.

Yoder, Edward (1893-1945), Mennonite (MC) teacher, writer, and editor, the oldest son of Mahlon T. and Mary Yoder, was born July 30, 1893, at Kalona, Iowa. He attended Hesston College (B.A.), Kansas University, University of Colorado, University of Iowa (M.A.), and University of Pennsylvania (Ph.D.). He taught Latin and Greek at Hesston College (1920-23, 1928-32) and Goshen College (1926-28, 1933-38). He was Dean at Hesston (1929-32) and Dean of Men at Goshen (1935-37). On the editorial staff at Mennonite Publishing House, Scottdale (1938-45), he was general editor of Sunday-school literature, editor of *Advanced Sunday School Quarterly,* editor of peace section of Doctrinal Supplement of the *Gospel Herald,* and librarian of the Mennonite Historical Library. He was coeditor of *Mennonite Historical Bulletin* and an associate editor and frequent contributor to *Mennonite Quarterly Review.* He was the author of *Lessons in Christian Doctrine* (Scottdale, 1939), *Our Mennonite Heritage* (Akron, 1942), *Mennonites of Westmoreland County, Pennsylvania* (Scottdale, 1942), *Must Christians Fight?* (with H. S. Bender and Jesse Hoover, Akron, 1943), *The Christian and Conscription* (with Don. Smucker, Akron, 1945). He became a member of the Mennonite Church (MC) in 1909, and was active in church work. He was secretary of the Curriculum Committee, treasurer of the Historical Committee of Mennonite General Conference, historian of the Southwestern Pennsylvania Conference, superintendent of the Sunday school and secretary of the board of trustees of the Scottdale congregation. On Aug. 4, 1920, he married Estie Miller. They had one son, Virgil Edward. Edward Yoder died March 28, 1945, and is buried in the Scottdale cemetery. He was one of the more able scholars of the Mennonite Church.　　P.E.

Yoder, John K. (1824-1906), was one of the outstanding Amish bishops during the latter half of the 19th century when many midwestern congregations turned away from some of the traditional practices and gradually assumed the name Amish Mennonite (*q.v.*). He was born in Mifflin County (*q.v.*), Pa., where in 1850 he was ordained preacher. In 1855, he with his wife, the former Lydia Zook, moved to Wayne County (*q.v.*), Ohio, where, four years later, he was ordained bishop in the Wayne County Amish congregation (*q.v.*) then numbering 300 members and divided into a north and a south district. When the bishop in the north district and a small following withdrew over the issue of baptizing in a stream, Yoder became the sole bishop of the entire congregation, which in 1862 erected a meetinghouse and later became known as the Oak Grove Amish Mennonite Church (*q.v.*). The same year the first Amish general conference (Allgemeine Dienerversammlung, *q.v.*) was entertained by the congregation. In a few years Yoder's talents and administrative ability gave him a leading role in the conference deliberations. When he was elected moderator in 1864, he secured the adoption of rules of procedure for the conference. A firm advocate of congregational rule he agreed in 1889 to the appointment of a laymen's committee to set up a new discipline allowing departure from certain traditional Amish cultural practices—buttons instead of hooks and eyes on men's clothing, a "barber haircut," and holding evening religious services in the meetinghouse. Although this decision cost him the fellowship of some of his more conservative friends in Pennsylvania, he lived to see the wisdom of his decision vindicated. He was one of the founders of the Ohio Amish Mennonite Conference (q.v.) in 1893 and of the Ohio and Pennsylvania A.M. Conference in 1897, which was later called the Eastern A.M. Conference. J.S.U.

John Umble, "The Oak Grove Amish Mennonite Church . . .," *MQR* XXXI (1957) 163-219, *passim*.

Yoder, Joseph Warren (1872-1956), the son of an Amish preacher, Christian Z. Yoder, and his wife Rosanna McGonegal Yoder, an Irish Catholic orphan reared by an Amish maiden lady. Following his graduation from Brethren Normal School (now Juniata College) in 1895, he served for two years as principal of the Milroy (Pa.) High School. His outstanding personality and his success as an inspiring teacher led to an invitation by John S. Coffman (q.v.) to teach at the Elkhart Institute (q.v.) where he served as an instructor in English, music, and Greek in 1897-1901, interrupted by a period of study at Northwestern University. He returned to Juniata College in 1901 where he secured the B.A. degree in 1904. Following his graduation he taught in Lock Haven (Pa.) Teachers Normal for a number of years. But from 1904 on, one of his major interests was music. He taught music classes for Brethren, Mennonites, Methodists, River Brethren, and Amish Mennonites. He became one of the most widely known "musical directors" at teachers' institutes in Pennsylvania, Indiana, Illinois, and Virginia. His connection with Juniata College as "high school visitor" attracted many young people to that institution. He is widely known for his books: *Rosanna of the Amish* (1940), his mother's story, an intimate, authentic account of Amish family life; *Amische Lieder* (1942), a "first" in the history of musicology—notating the tunes of the hymns sung by the Amish in Mifflin County, Pa.; *Rosanna's Boys* (1949), the sequel to the 1940 volume; and *Amish Traditions* (1950), an effort to show that many divisions arise from unscriptural causes. "J. W." maintained his membership in the Mennonite Church (Maple Grove, at Belleville, Pa.) where he was baptized and where on Nov. 15, 1956, his funeral services were held. He died on Nov. 13, 1956. J.S.U.

Yoder Amish Mennonite Church, Berne, Ind. In 1870 a small schismatic group of Amish Mennonites built a meetinghouse near Berne in Adams County, Ind. The first minister is said to have been a John Richner. In 1886 the congregation bought the Baumgartner meetinghouse. A later minister was Daniel Yoder (1853-1924) of Linn Grove, Ind. In 1892 he attended the fifth annual conference sessions of the Indiana-Michigan A.M. Conference, which met in the Howard-Miami meetinghouse that year. In 1900 the little congregation even served as host to the district conference sessions; they used the Egly Defenseless Mennonite meetinghouse which **was a half-mile west of the Yoder meetinghouse.**

In 1905 there were 12 members in the Yoder congregation. Two years later Yoder moved to Leo, Ind., where his brother Eli was bishop of the Leo A.M. congregation. By 1909 only two aged women remained as members. About that time regular services were discontinued. J.C.W.

Yoder Mennonite Church (MC), located near Yoder, Reno Co., Kan., a member of the South Central Conference, was organized in 1919 with 65 charter members, mostly of Amish background. For a few years persons from the community had united with the West Liberty Mennonite Church near Inman, Kan. Since this church was some 20 miles away, Mennonites at Yoder worshiped in schools or private homes, assisted by interested persons in the Hesston community and the college. In 1919 a church was built. L. O. King moved to the community to be the first pastor of the congregation, continuing as pastor until his death in 1940.

Within a year following April 1942, five young men were ordained as ministers who had grown to manhood in the Yoder church. In 1946 three members went as foreign relief workers, one each to Europe, China, and Ethiopia. The membership in 1957 was 260; the ministers were A. A. Bontrager, Edward Yutzy, and Harry A. Diener, bishop. H.A.D.

York County, Ont. Mennonite interests in York County center about the townships of Markham, Whitchurch, and Vaughan, and the city of Toronto. The Markham settlement, about 20 miles northeast of Toronto, took rise when the Mennonites who came to Waterloo County in 1803 found difficulty with their land titles. In Whitchurch Township the families early met in homes for worship, principally at Huber and Stecklin, named for the pioneering Hoover and Steckley families. Services at Huber and Stecklin ended in 1860, when the church was built at Almira in Markham Township. The Almira congregation has always been small, and not fully organized, but considered a part of the settlement of which the Wideman church is the larger part. Henry Wideman, a minister from Bucks County, Pa., came in 1803. Abraham Grove (Groff), a bishop, came in 1808. The first worship and funeral services were held at Dixon's Hill until about 1817, when a log building was erected on the present site of the Wideman church, about 2 miles north of Markham, which served as church and school. A brick church was built here about 1857, replaced by a larger one in 1928. The membership of the Markham Mennonite (MC) churches has been about 200. Cedar Grove to the southeast began about 1861, when a frame building was erected for funerals. Monthly appointments soon followed. Near it is the Risser (q.v.) Old Order Mennonite Church, the chief place of worship for this body. The Wideman church was shared by Risser and Wideman groups until 1928. The Almira church is still shared.

In Vaughan Township, west of Markham, the Schmitt meetinghouse was the one place of worship until after 1900. Erected in 1824 it is still in fair state of repair and is used for funerals. Peter Musselman, a minister, came here in 1803. The Jacob

Schmitt family came about 1812. Christian Troyer was a minister by 1836, but soon allied himself with the Daniel Hoch (*q.v.*) movement. The M.B.C. and O.O.M. movements both made inroads here 1875-90. (See **Wideman Mennonite Church.**)

The mission in Toronto (*q.v.*) began in 1907 with Samuel Honderich as superintendent. At first it was located in the slums of the city. Since 1914 it has been in the eastern part of the city. The work has grown to include Warden Park, a new Sunday school and worship center 3 miles east of the Danforth Mission and 3 miles south of the Morningside Mission. These fully occupied areas are now served widely by Sunday school, summer Bible school, and preaching services. Four miles northeast was a slum known as Geco, which Mennonite workers from Ellesmere served until 1955, when it was totally dismantled. Ellesmere is 8 miles toward Markham and has grown from a mission in a small settlement to a large suburban housing area with a commodious Mennonite church erected 1952-54. Organizationally these are all combined. In 1958 Emerson McDowell was bishop, Glen Brubacher and John Hess ministers, with a combined membership of 57.   J.C.F.

York County, Pa., was the fifth county carved out (1749) in Eastern Pennsylvania. It has 914 square miles with a population of 202,737. Michael Danner, of the Mellinger Mennonite (MC) congregation in Lancaster County, crossed the Susquehanna River by 1719. The scattered Mennonites at first used private homes for their services; by 1774 Danner, a county commissioner, had obtained a grant from the Penns for 12 acres for church and cemetery purposes. This was the start of the Bair's Hanover congregation, three miles east of the borough of Hanover. In 1798 a request for a lot in York (City) was ordered canceled, but in 1805 such a lot, with similar purposes as at Bair's Hanover, was granted. The meetinghouse at Strickler's, between Wrightsville and Hellam, was built about 1798, the Garber meetinghouse at Menges Mills in 1814. In the Manchester area the Hoover union meetinghouse and private dwellings were used until the substantial stone church was built in 1820. At Witmer's the first meetinghouse was built in 1818, and at Hershey's in 1825. By 1826 a church had been built at Bair's Hanover. Mennonites, scattered well over York County, used at least one other union church. At the turn of the century the leaders were Henry Strickler, Andrew Gerber, and Abraham Flury in the eastern district, Henry Kendig, Joseph Updegraff, and David Witmer at York, John Roth and Abraham Geib at Manchester, John Lethra, Henry Sipe, and Joseph Hershey in the middle district, George Forrey, John F. H. Hershey, and Andrew Boyer at the Gerber church; at least some of these men were ordained. The first known bishop was Abraham Roth (1773-1854), followed by John Hostetter (1791-1866), Frederick Stauffer (1813-84), and Daniel Shank (1832-1906). The churches were then supplied until 1926, when Noah H. Mack (1881-1948) served; Richard Danner was ordained in 1935. The total Mennonite membership, now tak-

ing a new lease on life by colonization, was 375 in 1957, with two missions in York.   I.D.L.

York Mennonite Mission (MC), York, Pa., established in 1954, is located at 451 East Princess Street. In 1957 it had 15 members and was a mission station in the Lancaster Mennonite Conference. M.G.

York (Pa.) Mennonite Church (MC), located on North Hartman Street, is a member of the Lancaster Mennonite Conference. In the 18th century a Mennonite church and cemetery was located on Market Street near Pine Street in York. This meetinghouse, built in or before 1803, was sold in 1917. When it ceased to be used is not known. In 1903 the Fourth United Brethren Church on North Hartman Street was purchased as an outpost for the Stony Brook (then Witmer) congregation. On July 28, 1935, H. Frank Leaman was ordained as pastor-superintendent. On May 11, 1954, he and some of the membership withdrew, and Roy M. Geigley became pastor-superintendent. Lloyd R. Horst was ordained pastor Dec. 26, 1956. The membership in 1957 was 26.
                                                          I.D.L.

York's Corners (N.Y.) Mennonite Church (MC), in Allegany County, in western New York, just north of Genesee, Pa., established in 1952, is a mission station of the Lancaster Mennonite Conference. In 1957 it had 13 members, with J. Ivan Smoker as pastor.   M.G.

Yother, Henry (1810-1900), a pioneer Mennonite (MC) bishop, was born near Mt. Pleasant, Westmoreland Co., Pa., a great-grandson of Hans and Anna Yoder, immigrants from Europe in 1720. In 1845 he was ordained a minister, and in 1857 bishop. He was associated with Bishop John D. Overholt (1797-1878) and minister Martin Loucks (1798-1869), serving at the Pennsville and Stonerville meetinghouses near Scottdale, Pa. He preached in both English and German. On May 27, 1862, at the Oberholtzer meetinghouse in Mahoning County near Columbiana, Ohio, he preached the first English sermon in that congregation at the funeral of Lewis Landis. In 1864 he moved to Cullom in Livingston County, Ill., and in 1871 to Gage County, Neb. In Nebraska he was not officially connected with a Mennonite congregation, but until his death in 1900 he traveled among large and small congregations of Mennonite pioneers of Kansas, Nebraska, western Missouri, and Iowa, conducting baptismal and communion services, and was instrumental in ordaining ministers for smaller congregations. The groups he served were Mennonites (MC), Amish Mennonites, and Russian Mennonites. The Evangelizing Committee of Elkhart, Ind., arranged for him to spend time traveling among the churches and scattered members, serving their spiritual needs. He was instrumental in bringing about the organization of the Kansas-Nebraska Conference. W.D.S.

Edward Yoder, "Henry Yother (1810-1900), Mennonite Preacher and Bishop," *MHB,* June 1944.

Young People's Bible Meeting, the name of the Sunday evening meeting for young people in the Mennonite Church (MC), also called Young People's Meeting, somewhat parallel to the Christian Endeavor which began in 1881. The first YPBM was held in the Prairie Street Mennonite Church at Elkhart, Ind., in 1887, an outgrowth of a children's meeting on Sunday evening before the evening preaching service, initiated in 1884 by John F. Funk with Henry Brenneman and Joseph Summers. The second YPBM was begun in 1889 by C. Z. Yoder at the Oak Grove Mennonite Church near Smithville, Ohio, as the outgrowth of young people's "singings" which had been meeting for several years in other places. The third such meeting was begun at the Waldo Amish Mennonite Church near Flanagan, Ill., in early 1891, and the fourth at the Zion Church near Bluffton, Ohio, in 1892. About the same time young people's meetings sprang up in Ontario following the J. S. Coffman revivals in 1891-92. The movement soon spread over the church, and by 1910 was well established except in the East. By 1906 the church papers, the *Herald of Truth* (in 1908 *Gospel Herald*), published topics and helps for Young People's Meetings, and by 1909 the General Conference appointed a YPBM Topics Committee (in 1931 merged with two other committees into the Commission for Christian Education, *q.v.*), which published program outlines and helps in the *Christian Monitor* and in 1922 began publishing the YPBM Topics Booklet, changed in 1945 to the *Program Builder*. By these means universal common topics were discussed in Sunday evening meetings throughout the Mennonite Church (MC).

Although called Young People's Meetings, usually they became meetings for the entire congregation in which old and young took part, held in the meetinghouse before the evening worship service or as the sole evening service, usually sponsored by a special committee appointed for this purpose, and often with printed programs prepared several months in advance.

In the East, especially in the Lancaster Conference, the meetings were really never held on Sunday evening but were held often on Saturday evening, and then largely only for young people.

About 1940 a movement developed for Junior Bible Meetings, which were held parallel to the adult YPBM on Sunday evening, which have become a fixed feature in most of the well-organized congregations.

The YPBM has made a great contribution to the church in Bible teaching, development of character and conviction, promotion of activity and missions, and increasing denominational loyalty.   H.S.B.

Paul M. Lederach, "History of Religious Education in the Mennonite Church," Chap. VI, "History of the Young People's Bible Meeting" (unpublished doctoral dissertation at Southwestern Baptist Theological Seminary, 1949) pp. 194-222.

Young People's Conference, a youth movement in the Mennonite Church (MC) which flourished for a short time in 1920-23, and led in part to the creation of the Young People's Problems Committee (*q.v.*). It had its origin in a "General Conference of Mennonites in France in Reconstruction Work held at Clermont-en-Argonne, Meuse, France," June 20-22, 1919. (*Report* under the above title printed and available in GCL). This conference was organized

on an intended permanent basis with a constitution whose name was tentatively chosen as "Mennonite Young People's Movement," and which was to meet annually. Its clearly stated purpose was constructive and progressive, and its three annual conference programs represented in effect a Christian Life Conference with accent on the problems of youth, but the movement represented dissatisfaction with the rather slow-moving general church leadership and program, and also a determination to work out a larger and more influential place for the maturer young people in the work and leadership of the church. Since much of the older leadership of the church reacted with skepticism and even suspicion to the new movement, opposition and tension developed. Wiser counsels prevailed in the end and the movement got started in America, its name changed to Young People's Conference. Three annual meetings were held: West Liberty, Ohio, Aug. 28-30, 1920; Sterling, Ill., June 15-18, 1922; Middlebury, Ind. (Forks church), June 14-17, 1923. The general tensions in the church at this time resulting in the closing of Goshen College for the year 1923-24 and division in a number of congregations in Indiana, Ohio, Ontario, and Eastern Pennsylvania led to confusion in the ranks of the leadership of the Young People's Conference, and ultimately to the discontinuance of the annual meetings. The program of the 1923 conference listed the committee in charge elected in 1922 as Harold S. Bender, chairman; Walter E. Yoder, secretary; John L. Yoder, treasurer; Payson Miller, and Vernon Smucker. Part of the energies of the group was channeled into the biweekly periodical, *The Christian Exponent,* established Jan. 4, 1924, and discontinued Sept. 11, 1928, edited by Vernon Smucker.   H.S.B.

Young People's Institute, a retreat of two to four days for young people 16-25 years of age, for worship, instruction, discussion, inspiration, and recreation, held in churches, schools, or retreat grounds, usually during the summer vacation, in the Mennonite Church (MC). The first institute was held on the campus of Goshen College in 1927, sponsored by the Young People's Problems Committee. In 1930 the YPPC sponsored three institutes, one at Scottdale, Pa., one at Goshen, Ind., and one at Kitchener, Ont., then turned the movement over to district conferences and local institutions such as colleges. The movement soon was widely accepted and for years large institutes were held annually at Hesston, Goshen, and Eastern Mennonite College, as well as in other locations east and west. In 1936 the first 12-day institute was held at Arbutus Park, near Johnstown, Pa., which later developed into the Laurelville YPI near Mt. Pleasant, Pa., in 1943. By 1955 the movement had pretty well run its course, but it had been of great value to thousands of young people.   H.S.B.

Young People's Meeting: see Young People's Bible Meeting.

Young People's Paper, an 8-page 10¾ x 14¾ in. illustrated biweekly (changed January 1898 to a 20-page monthly, and in December 1898 to a 24-page monthly) published by the Mennonite Publishing

Co. (MC) at Elkhart, Ind., for the Young People's Paper Association (first appearance in the masthead Oct. 27, 1894) January 1894 to March 1906. Editors were M. S. Steiner to the end of March 1895, C. K. Hostetler to September 1899, S. B. McManus, a non-Mennonite, from then on (in the absence of files of the journal it is impossible to report who had editorial responsibility to the end). Contributing editors during the early period were J. S. Hartzler, Abr. Ebersole, D. H. Bender, Charles McClintic, S. F. Coffman, and Ephraim Weber. The content was general, inspirational, edificatory, educational, some secular but mostly religious, with much reprint material from non-Mennonite sources. In January 1898 a new department was established, "The Young People's Meeting," usually two pages with program outlines and helps. (GCL has a file of 1894-99.)

H.S.B.

Young People's Problems Committee, a standing committee of five of the Mennonite General Conference (MC), appointed in 1924, merged into the Commission for Christian Education and Young People's Work (*q.v.*) in 1937. Its purpose was to assist the church in improving its ministry to its youth, and to help guide the youth organizations springing up in many local churches, especially the literary societies (*q.v.*). It introduced and for a time sponsored the Young People's Institute (*q.v.*) and promoted the holding of Christian Life Conferences. Major leaders in the committee were Noah Oyer (d. 1930) and O. O. Miller. Similar committees were established about the same time in a number of the district conferences (MC) usually called simply "Young People's Committee." H.S.B.

J. B. Shenk, "A History of Organized Youth Work in the Mennonite Church" (unpublished paper in GCL).

Y.P.S. and S.S.U. Notes, the 4-page 5½ x 8½ in. quarterly organ of the Sunday School and Christian Endeavor Unions of the Eastern District Conference (GCM), the forerunner of the present *C. E. Witness.* It was published 1931-40. J.E.F.

Young People's Union (GCM). While a concern for the nurture of its youth was implicit in the General Conference movement from its beginning, the formal establishment of a conference-wide youth organization did not occur until 1941, when a constitution for the Young People's Union of the General Conference Mennonite Church was officially adopted. Prior to this time, however, there had been evident interest in conference youth work as early as 1917, when a Sunday School and Young People's Committee was set up in 1920, a young people's program being presented at General Conference sessions since that year, the first Youth Page appearing in the *Mennonite* on Nov. 22, 1923, and district young people's retreats beginning that same year. By 1935 the movement was clearly under way to organize the young people of the conference into an auxiliary organization of General Conference, though the first draft of a constitution presented in 1938 was rejected.

Since its organization in 1941 the Young People's Union has grown considerably in activity and influence. Counseled under the Board of Education and

Publication, it has its own executive officers, cabinet, annual council of district and institutional representatives, conference-wide retreats, workshops, and its own general assembly meeting in conjunction with the sessions of General Conference. In December 1953 William Gering became its first youth worker, at first on a part-time basis and later full-time. All young people in General Conference churches between the ages 12 and 30 are considered members of the YPU, whose slogan is "A United Mennonite Youth in Christ."

Leading projects carried on by the YPU include editing the Youth Section in the *Mennonite,* preparing program helps for local church use, producing an annual prayer calendar, promoting young people's retreats and voluntary service, sponsoring the missionary education fund to help train foreign students in our schools, and more recently the development of a functional youth program in local churches with a threefold emphasis on (1) Christian faith and life, (2) Christian fellowship, and (3) Christian service. Significant in this last development was the publication of the *Youth Manual* written by Elmer Ediger, to be followed by other manuals on youth work, and the promotion of this "fellowship plan" through retreats, workshops, publications, and church visitation later carried on largely by the youth worker. E.W.

Young People's Union Prayer Calendar has been a publication of the G.C.M. Young People's Union since 1941. At first only a one-page list of prayer reminders for each day of the month, it was developed into a 12-page wall calendar, and in 1955 into a devotional booklet containing suggested Bible readings as well as prayer requests. Recent editors have been: Peter Kehler, Henry Funk, Lois Duerksen Deckert, and John Bertsche. M.SH.

Young People's Union Retreats and Workshops have been sponsored for the inspiration of young people of the General Conference Mennonite Church, usually in connection with the triennial General Conference session. The first one was held at Seven Oaks, Cal., in August 1935. Others have been held at Camp Mack near Milford, Ind., 1947; St. Peter, Minn., 1950; Canon Beach, Ore., 1953; Lake Winnipeg, Man., 1956; and Camp Friedenswald, Mich. The 1950 and 1953 sessions were designated as workshops since attention was given to the development of principles and practices for local youth fellowships. M.SH.

Grace Miller Neufeld, "The Young People's Union," *Menn. Life* VIII (July 1953) 128-30.

Youth Committee of the Mennonite Brethren Conference, consisting of five members, came into being at the 1936 convention of the General Conference. At the 1933 general conference a Young People's Union Committee had been organized which produced several quarterly leaflets of study helps for young people's organizations in the churches in 1934. The Youth Committee began the *Christian Leader* in April 1937, which continued under its jurisdiction until the 1951 general conference sessions, when it became the official English organ of the conference and was placed under the jurisdiction of the Publication Committee. The Youth Committee sponsored Christian Fellowship organizations in the churches, promoted youth camps and other young people's activities. More and more, however, the youth work became a matter of the district conferences because of local conditions; in the revised constitution of the Conference as temporarily adopted in 1954 it became a consultative committee composed of one member at large and representatives from the youth committees of the districts. Since then the youth work has rested almost solely with the districts. O.HA.

Youth Movement in Holland: see **Doopsgezinde Jongerenbond** and **Friese Doopsgezinde Jongeren Bond.**

Youth Office (GCM) was created at 722 Main Street, Newton, Kan., in June 1955, when the first full-time Youth Worker was called to serve the Young People's Union (*q.v.*). This youth office was to help organize and activate local youth fellowships, help Mennonite youth rallies, youth workshops and retreat work, and gather and publish program helps and other necessary youth materials. Youth groups were encouraged to write to the youth office to share their problems and concerns. William Gering served as part-time Youth Worker 1953-55, and full-time 1955- . W.GE.

Youth's Banner, The, was a 4-page, illustrated M.B.C. Sunday-school magazine published apparently from 1897 until at least the latter part of 1907 by H. S. Hallman (*q.v.*) at Berlin, Ont. J. A. Huffman refers to it as a semimonthly, but the few issues available at Goshen College indicate that it was a monthly in 1906-7. It contained inspirational stories, articles, and poems and a discussion of the Sunday-school lesson. N.P.S.

J. A. Huffman, *History of the Mennonite Brethren in Christ Church* (New Carlisle, Ohio, 1920).

Youth's Christian Companion, founded in 1920, was until the end of 1956 an 8-page, 9 x 11½ in. and thereafter a 16-page 5¼ x 8½ in. weekly devoted to the interest of young people, ages 16-24, published and printed by the Mennonite Publishing House, Scottdale, Pa. Until Dec. 31, 1954, Clayton F. Yake was its continuous editor from the beginning of the paper. On Jan. 1, 1955, Urie A. Bender became editor.

The periodical endeavors to serve young people in all areas of Christian life, with Christian fiction, feature articles, poetry, missionary messages, information of church activities, such as MYF, MRSC, I-W, news for youth, schools and colleges, articles on nature and science, vocational guidance, and other inspirational messages for the development of Christian character and the devotional life. The 1958 circulation was about 34,000. C.F.Y.

Youths' Monitor was an 8-page 7½ x 10½ in. illustrated religious magazine published by Daniel Brenneman (*q.v.*) at Goshen, Ind., monthly, 1883-85, "in the interest of the young people and children, adapted especially for the home circle and Sabbath school." It contained articles, stories, and poems,

mostly written by a group of "special contributors" and letters written by the readers and occasionally by the special contributors. For the first seven months the list of special contributors included Mennonites of other groups as well as Evangelical United Mennonites, the group of which Daniel Brenneman was a leader. Later the contributors seem to have been exclusively United Evangelical Mennonites (later a part of the MBC). (GCL has the first volume.) N.P.S.

Ypecolsga, a hamlet in the Dutch province of Friesland, where Leenaert (*q.v.*) Bouwens baptized 20 persons in 1551-54, four in 1554-56, six or seven in 1557-61, and six in 1563-65. Since there was apparently no congregation at Ypecolsga, the converts may have joined the neighboring church of Legemeer (*q.v.*). vDZ.

Yper(en): see **Ieper.**

Ypsilanti (Mich.) **State Hospital** was the location of Civilian Public Service Unit No. 90, which opened in March 1943 and closed in October 1946. Of the 75 men, 25 were in a relief training for foreign relief service. In addition to the men in the unit, an average of 35 women (wives and friends of the men) worked in the hospital. In the summers of 1944-45 Mennonite service units in which 51 young women were enrolled also served the institution. A large, modern, well-equipped, progressive institution, the hospital offered the Mennonite unit a satisfactory service experience. Much of the credit for the outstanding work of the hospital and for the excellent relations between the unit and the hospital was given to its superintendent, Dr. O. R. Yoder, a former Mennonite and graduate of Goshen College. The hospital continued to use conscientious objectors after the war and in 1958 was employing eight Mennonite young men who were doing their alternative (I-W) service here. Unit No. 90 published a yearbook entitled *Ypsi.* M.G.

Melvin Gingerich, *Service for Peace* (Akron, 1949) pp. 231-36.

Ysbrand (Isebrand) **Dircksz Schol** was burned at the stake at Brussels, Belgium, on July 27, 1534, then aged 70. He had been arrested for heresy at Amsterdam as early as 1525, but was released after recanting. In Brussels he had been in prison twice before on a charge of heresy, but was released because of insufficient evidence. It is not clear whether Ysbrand was an Anabaptist; he was probably a Sacramentist (*q.v.*). (Mellink, *Wederdopers,* 344; Verheyden, *Courtrai-Bruxelles,* 61, No. 4.) vDZ.

Ysbrant Scheerjer, an Anabaptist martyr, was burned at the stake at Leeuwarden, Netherlands, on Nov. 16, 1549. He had held religious meetings in his house, and there "read from the Bible and the New Testament." Persisting in his "errors" he was sentenced to death. vDZ.

Sentence Book of the Court of Friesland; J. Reitsma, *Honderd jaren uit de Gesch. der Hervorming . . . in Friesland* (Leeuwarden, 1876) 63.

Ysenbaert, Joost: see **Isenbaert.**

Ysenbeek (IJzenbeek), a former Mennonite family at Harlingen in Friesland, Netherlands, where they were businessmen (e.g., salt works) and pillars of the church from the 17th century. Daniel IJsenbeek (1784-1859), after studying at the Amsterdam seminary, served the congregations of Oost- and West-Graftdijk 1807-9 and Alkmaar 1809-54. Among his publications are a *Leerrede* (Alkmaar, 1834), a sermon to commemorate his 25 years of service at Alkmaar, *Bijbelsch Handwoordenboek van zedelijke Voorbeelden en Onderwerpen ontleend aan de schriften des Ouden en Nieuwen Testaments* . . . (Amsterdam, 1838), and *Bijdragen tot de Geschiedenis der Doopsgezinden en der zelver Volksplantingen in . . . Rusland* (Hoorn, 1848). (*N.N.B.Wb.* I, 1597.)   vDZ.

Ysselstein: see **IJsselstein.**

Ytens (Itens), a hamlet in the Dutch province of Friesland, where there is a Mennonite congregation, formerly called Kromwal (*q.v.*). In 1865 a meetinghouse (still in use) and a parsonage were built at Ytens. The pastor at this time was Gerhard Pol, serving here 1862-83, followed by R. Cuperus 1884-86, P. Zondervan 1889-91, A. Binnerts 1892-97, H. Britzel 1899-1902, E. Engelkes 1902-5, A. de Vries Mzn 1906-14, P. J. Keuning 1914-21, S. I. van der Meulen 1922-29, J. H. van Riemsdijk 1930-d.40, G. M. Kosters 1941-44, T. Hoogslag 1950-56, and M. C. Postema since 1957. The baptized membership numbered 98 in 1861, 122 in 1900, 105 in 1926, 99 in 1958. An organ was acquired in 1900. Church activities include ladies' circles at Ytens and Wieuwerd, a youth group 18-25, a youth club, and Sunday school for children. (*DB* 1890, 139; 1900, 231.)
                                                vDZ.

Yushanlee, a Mennonite estate of the Molotschna settlement in South Russia established by Johann Cornies (*q.v.*), the great organizer. One evening in 1830, while Cornies was driving his flock of sheep on the steppes, he stopped for the night along the Yushanlee River and noticed the next morning that the site was very suitable for a farm. He decided at once to build an advance station of civilization here. Soon a primitive clay hut stood here, which grew into the thriving unique model farm called Yushanlee. The 9,450 acres were leased from the government for an indeterminate period. In 17 years Yushanlee boasted a spacious dwelling, many stables and business buildings, all from the income of a tile factory on the land. In the garden there were 2,000 fruit trees, 1,750 plants of small fruits. A forest was planted with 68,000 trees, and an extensive nursery was kept up. Even though the farm was not Cornies' property, he developed it in exemplary fashion at great expense, and was rewarded by Czar Nicholas I with a gift of 1,350 acres of this land.

In 1879 Yushanlee, against the wishes and without the knowledge of the last surviving Cornies heir, passed into outside possession. The new owner razed the old buildings and put up a small castle with the pertinent buildings. Only the bell tower in the middle of the court remained as a last witness of the gigantic achievement of a great man. After the Revolution the estate was nationalized. D.H.E.

D. H. Epp, *Johann Cornies* (Steinbach, 1946); *ML* II, 448.

Z

Zaandam, a town (pop. *c*46,000 with 1,302 Mennonites in 1955) about 6 miles north of Amsterdam in the Dutch province of North Holland. The Zaan River divides Zaandam into a West Side and an East Side; until the 19th century the East Side was economically the more important part. Some citizens of Zaandam, e.g., Pieter (*q.v.*) Claesz (Pieter de Coster), were executed at Amsterdam in 1535. In 1543 there was an Anabaptist congregation at Zaandam, of which Klaas Noome(n) was the preacher. Meetings were then held in the homes of the members. Leenaert Bouwens baptized 40 persons here in 1564; in the following years Lubbert Gerritsz (*q.v.*) was an elder at Zaandam. Soon after this there were at least three Mennonite congregations at Zaandam: Waterlander, Frisian, and Flemish. Though the history of these groups during the 16th and 17th centuries is in many respects hazy, the following account may serve to clear up the complicated situation.

I. A Waterlander congregation existed at Zaandam from *c*1578. It was represented at a Waterlander conference held at Amsterdam in 1581. In the 16th-early 17th century the Waterlanders living at Koog (*q.v.*) aan de Zaan were members of this congregation until 1646, when they organized an independent congregation. The Zaandam Waterlander congregation, sometimes called "Komejanse Mennonieten" or "Komejannen" (*q.v.*), had a meetinghouse since before 1600, which was replaced in 1656. This meetinghouse was commonly called the North meetinghouse; it was situated on the East Side. The congregation was probably very large in the early 17th century. In 1656 the baptized members numbered 326; they lived on both the East Side and the West Side. About 1655 a second meetinghouse was built on the Dampad on the West Side. In 1675, 137 members lived on the West Side and 254 on the East Side. Soon after the (Ia) East Side, or North congregation, and the (Ib) Dampad congregation on the West Side developed into relatively independent churches, though for some time they had a common fund for the relief of their poor, and other connections as late as 1712.

The West Side Waterlander congregation (Ib) merged in 1687 with the Flemish congregation (IV) to form the United Mennonite Church (VI). This merger came about only after much conflict with the East Side Waterlanders (Ia). The history of this East Side church is continued under VIII.

II. A Frisian Mennonite church of Zaandam, obviously also dating from the 16th century and connected with Frisian groups at Westzaan (*q.v.*), Zaandijk (*q.v.*), and Wormerveer (*q.v.*), had a meetinghouse on the West Side at least from 1613. A new meetinghouse was built in 1628 on the West side, which was usually called the "Oude Huys" (Old house) in the 18th century. On Nov. 13-15, 1628, a general union of several Dutch Flemish and Frisian groups was discussed in this new meetinghouse. The union was, however, not effected because of opposition by the Frisian elder P. J. Twisck (*q.v.*), of Hoorn. After the Frisians at Zaandijk and Wormerveer had founded independent congregations, the Zaandam Frisian Mennonites formed a single congregation with those at Westzaan until *c*1700. Until *c*1670 Westzaan was even the more important part of this congregation, and most of the preachers lived there. But gradually, as many members moved from Westzaan to Zaandam, Zaandam became the center and later on an independent congregation developed there. In 1659 the Westzaan, Zaandam, and Zaandijk congregation numbered 194 baptized members; in 1672 there were 179 Frisian Mennonites at Zaandam and *c*200 in 1700. In the early 17th century this Frisian church was rather conservative, but gradually it became more progressive, in the 18th century even liberal, strongly influenced by Collegiantism (*q.v.*). After the Collegiant meetings had stopped in most churches, they were still held by the Zaandam Oude Huys congregation, led by preachers and laymen; Adrian Rogge (1732-1826), a layman, was still conducting them at the age of 76. At first the preachers and elders were all chosen from the members; they were untrained and unsalaried. Among them were very capable men like Jacob Gerritsz Corver, serving 1608-*c*60, Jan Jansz Muusse 1651-87, Cornelis Ariaensz Loosjes 1693-1720?, Waligh Gerrits Vis 1714-d.67, Jan Lijnsz Rogge 1721-d.59, and Cornelis Gerritsz Meyn Jr. 1727-76. The first salaried minister in this church was Daniel Hovens, who served 1764-70, followed by Anthony de Vries, who was the first minister in this church educated at the Amsterdam Lamist (*q.v.*) seminary, serving 1771-91, T. J. de Hoop 1777-d.1838, Pieter Hollenberg 1793-1801, Matthijs Hesseling 1801-5, Gerbrand Koopmans 1805-14, and Bartel van Geuns 1830-41. During the 18th and 19th centuries the membership dropped from *c*200 to 120 in 1777 and *c*100 in 1801, rising to 150 in 1833. A pipe organ was acquired in 1782. In 1841 the Oude Huys congregation merged with the United Waterlander and Flemish congregation (Nieuwe Huys congregation; see VI). After this merger the old Frisian meetinghouse was sold; it was used as a storehouse until 1932, when it was destroyed by a fire.

III. A congregation commonly called Aris Janszevolk (see **Verwer**), which originated as a schism from the Frisian congregation, existed from 1649 (*c*30 members); it had a meetinghouse on the East Side and had dissolved by 1704. The reason for the schism was their dissatisfaction with the church policy of the Frisian elder Jacob Klaesz, who was on good terms with the Flemish.

IV. A Flemish Mennonite group existed at Zaandam from probably *c*1580. It was a rather small group, though its members were among the wealthiest shipowners and merchants of Zaandam. Concerning its history there is only scarce information.

Until *c*1648 the center of this group was at Koog aan de Zaan rather than Zaandam. In 1649 a Flemish meetinghouse was erected at Zaandam West Side on the Stikkelspad (now Stationsstraat), and the Zaandam part became independent. In 1687 this Flemish congregation merged with the Waterlander Dampad congregation (Ib) into the United Mennonite congregation (VI).

V. At Zaandam there was also a Groningen Old Flemish church, first mentioned in 1673, but probably dating from *c*1632. It had a meetinghouse on the Molenpad on the East Side. It was very conservative, maintaining old practices like footwashing until *c*1760. This church, always very small in membership (*c*40 in 1710), was led by lay preachers. In the 18th century it was commonly called Van Kalkers-volk after its elder Izaak van Kalker, serving 1711-*c*56. They often liberally supported the Prussian brethren. In 1774 the 18 remaining members joined the United Mennonite Church (VI).

VI. When the Dampad Waterlanders (Ib) and the Flemish congregation (IV) merged in 1687, it was resolved to drop the old names and "to forget these signs of former discord." Hence the congregation was called the United Mennonite Church (*Vereenigde Doopsgezinde Gemeente*). The Dampad and the Stikkelspad meetinghouses were abandoned and a new one built on the West Side. This spacious frame building, still in use, was dedicated on Nov. 2, 1687, by Galenus (*q.v.*) Abrahamsz of Amsterdam. For this new meetinghouse the United congregation is unusually called the Nieuwe Huys congregation. The old Dampad Waterlander meetinghouse was sold as a warehouse; the former Flemish church on Stikkelspad was at first for a few years rented to the Zaandam Lutheran congregation and was then used as a warehouse, and in 1712-14 remodeled as an orphanage; its fine rooms with old furniture can still be seen (renovated 1933); it was in use as an orphanage only until 1903; it is now used for church activities.

The Nieuwe Huys congregation developed into a strong congregation; at its founding the baptized membership stood at *c*600, in 1727 it was 763; decreasing to 671 in 1743, 400 in 1777, and only *c*250 in 1827, and again growing to *c*320 in 1840. With 150 members of the Oude Huys congregation (II), which in 1841 merged with the Nieuwe Huys, the membership numbered 461 in this year, 483 in 1847, 531 in 1861, 753 in 1900, 770 in 1926, 779 in 1942, 760 in 1949, when this congregation merged with the Zaandam-Oost congregation (VII).

At first after 1687 the congregation was served by untrained preachers chosen from its members, some of whom, however, received a small remuneration. Among these preachers were representatives of such well-known Zaandam families as Kalff (*q.v.*), Louwe (*q.v.*), three members of the Eyte (*q.v.*, Aytte) family, Middelhoven (*q.v.*), Loosjes (*q.v.*) and Nen (*q.v.*). Jacob Adriaens Ouwejans (*q.v.*) served 1725-41. The first fully salaried minister called from the outside was Gerrit ten Cate Thz, serving here 1755-72, followed by Michiel de Bleyker 1762-81, Jan van Gilse 1774-d.82, Hendrik van Gelder 1781-d.1808, S. Hoekstra Wz 1782-d.86, Pieter Beets Pz 1789-d.1813, Isaac Molenaar 1808-

14, Corn. Leendertz 1813-52, Taco Kuiper 1852-59, Bartel van Geuns, before the merger of 1841 a preacher in the Oude Huys, serving in the Nieuwe Huys 1841-70, Jacob van Gilse 1861-70, Rutger Brouwer 1870-76, Isaac Molenaar 1871-1914, D. Attema 1915-46, H. Wethmar 1946- .

This important Nieuwe Huys congregation was relatively late in calling a minister educated at the Mennonite seminary. The first seminary man to serve here was Isaac Molenaar, called in 1808. In its church government it was also rather conservative: in 1695 it was decided that the ministers were to be chosen by the church board rather than by the brethren of the church. The church board at this time was chosen by the male members, but in the early 18th century the church board became self-perpetuating. This practice continued until 1912. But by this time there was no longer any conservatism; though a proposal of 1913 to make baptism optional or even to abolish baptism was defeated, in 1918 it became possible to join the congregation without baptism.

The meetinghouse of 1687, though remodeled several times and beautifully renovated in 1930, is still in use. But the fine carved oak pulpit, which dated from the old Oude Huys and was placed in Nieuwe Huys in 1687, was removed in 1912. In 1784 a pipe organ was installed.

At the merger of the Frisian congregation (II) with this United Nieuwe Huys congregation in 1841, it was resolved to drop the name of United congregation and to call the congregation henceforth Fries(ch)e Doopsgezinde Gemeente te Zaandam, which was its official name until 1948, when it merged with the Zaandam-Oost (VII) congregation; it was usually called the Zaandam-West congregation.

VII. After 1774 there was only one congregation on the East Side; it was the old Waterlander North congregation (Ia), which since the 18th century is usually called Zaandam-Oost. This congregation, which numbered 254 members in 1675, had 321 baptized members in 1725, 288 in 1750, 268 in 1775, 236 in 1800, and only 195 in 1815, then increasing to 260 in 1846, 355 in 1861, 503 in 1900, 537 in 1926, reaching its peak of 542 members in 1929; from then there was considerable decline: 531 in 1935, 438 in 1942. In the 17th century this congregation for some time sided with the conservative Waterlanders, who conscientiously maintained the Hans de Ries (*q.v.*) confession of faith and opposed Collegiant (*q.v.*) views and practices. Pieter Pietersz (*q.v.*) was its elder 1625-d.51. But by 1688, when Foecke Floris (*q.v.*), who held Collegiant and even Socinian (*q.v.*) views, became a minister, great changes had taken place. In the 18th century the Zaandam-Oost congregation was very progressive. It supported the abortive attempt of the Amsterdam Lamist (*q.v.*) congregation in 1735 to found a Lamist conference, and in 1810 it was one of the three churches—the other two being Amsterdam and Haarlem—to prepare for the founding of the A.D.S.

At first Zaandam-Oost was served by untrained ministers, but as early as 1751 Cornelis Adriaansz Loosjes, a native of Zaandam, who had been educated at the Amsterdam Lamist seminary, was called as (salaried) pastor, serving until 1763. He was followed by Anthony van der Os 1764-95, a former Reformed pastor whose liberal views caused some trouble, not only in the Zaandam congregation, but also in the Rijper (*q.v.*) Sociëteit. Van der Os was followed by Hendrik van Voorst, serving 1779-d.1808, Samuel Muller 1809-14, Gerbrand Koopmans 1814-21, S. E. Wieling 1822-d.35, W. C. Mauve 1836-39, S. Blaupot ten Cate 1848-54, J. Hartog 1854-61, W. Jesse 1862-99, C. B. Hylkema 1899-1908, T. J. van der Ploeg 1908-26, J. G. Frerichs 1927-32, J. J. G. Wuite 1932-34, A. A. Sepp 1934-44, and J. Knot 1944-48.

The old meetinghouse of 1656, a frame building in a dilapidated state, was replaced by a new one dedicated Nov. 24, 1861. In 1867 it was damaged by fire, but was repaired. Formerly this congregation had an orphanage on the Grote Glop, which was used until 1903 and sold in 1919.

On Oct. 14, 1948, the Zaandam-Oost congregation merged with the Frisian West Side congregation (VI); the Zaandam-Oost meetinghouse was used until Sept. 23, 1953, and then sold to a Reformed group.

VIII. The present (United) Mennonite congregation of Zaandam is the result of the merger of 1948. The ministers of this congregation are H. Wethmar since 1948 and H. Luikinga since 1949. The only meetinghouse of the congregation is (since 1953) the former Zaandam-West church. At the merger the membership numbered 1,220, decreased to 950 in 1958. Church activities include three women's circles, a brotherhood, a youth group 18-25, youth group Elfregi (age 6-18), and a Sunday school for children.

The Zaandam congregation, in co-operation with the Dutch Central Committee for the Lodging of the Aged, has established the foundation "Het Mennisten Erf," which is in 1959 to start building a home for the aged with an annex for worship and youth activities.

Since the 16th century Zaandam has been a thriving industrial city (shipping, particularly to Baltic ports), the most important lumber port of the Netherlands. In 1953 it had 28 factories of wood products, many flour mills, and processors of groceries, cocoa, oil, cattle feed, paints, chemicals, and paper. Of the more than 300 picturesque windmills formerly used for these industries, only a few are left. In the 17th-19th centuries most of these businesses were owned by Mennonites, and at present a number of Mennonites are still engaged in manufacturing and trade. Among important 17th-19th century businessmen of Zaandam should be mentioned members of the following Mennonite families: Buys, Cardinaal, Corver, Dekker, Duyn, Eytte, Ghijsen, van der Goot, Honigh, Kalff, Keg, de Lange, Loosjes, Louwe, Mats, Meyn, Middelhoven, Muusse, Noomen, Ouwejans(s), Pondman, Rogge, Schoen, Swager, Taan, Vas, Vis, Visser, Zwaardemaker, later also Verkade. Most of these families now have died out or left Zaandam.

In 1742, 6,421 persons were living at Zaandam-East Side, 858 of whom, over 13 per cent, were Mennonites, and 6,315 persons on the West Side, 1,610 of whom, over 24 per cent, were Mennonites.

Thus in 1742 nearly 20 per cent of the Zaandam population was Mennonite, and in only 10 of the 339 Mennonite families was there a non-Mennonite spouse. In 1889 8.4 per cent of the population was Mennonite, in 1947 3.6 per cent, and in 1955 only 2.8 per cent. vDZ.

(S. Lootsma), *Het Nieuwe Huys, Friesch-Doopsgezinde Gemeente West-Zaandam* (Zaandam, 1937); S. Blaupot ten Cate, *Rede ter Gedachtenis* (Zaandam, 1843); *Inv. Arch. Amst.* I, Nos. 673, 708, 865, 892; II, Nos. 2364-66; II, 2, Nos. 673-76; Blaupot t. C., *Holland* I and II, *passim*; *DJ* 1840, 45; 1850, 26-29, 96; *DB* 1861, 165; 1872, 57, 194; 1873, 195; 1877, 80; 1879, 7; 1883, 72; 1887, 68 f.; 1900, 111; *Naamlijst* 1810, 72-74; *DJ* 1921, 63 ff.; H. Wethmar, "Enkele gegevens over de plaats van de Doopsgezinden in de bevolking en de arbeid van Zaandam," in *Stemmen* VII (1958) No. 1, 1-16; information by J. Aten, H. M. Romijn and G. Honig.

Zaandijk: see **Koog aan de Zaan.**

Zaane (Zaanen, Saanen, Zanen, Zane), **van,** a Dutch Mennonite family, found at Haarlem from the early 17th century. Jacob van Zanen, of Westroen, was trained for the ministry at the Amsterdam Seminary; he served at Oost- and West Graftdijk 1783-1805 and Hoorn 1805-d.13, and also served as secretary of the Rijper (*q.v.*) Sociëteit. (*Naamlijst* 1806, 67; 1815, 87; *DB* 1872, 70-72; *N.N.B.Wb.* V, 1168.)

Zaans(ch)e Fonds: see **Algemeen Pensioen-fonds.**

Zacharias Cornelisz (d. *c*1640) was a Mennonite publisher and printer at Hoorn, Holland, from whose presses appeared a number of Mennonite books beginning not later than 1609, including works by Hendrik Alewijnsz, Dirck Gerrits, and P. J. Twisck. After his death his sons Jan and Pieter continued the printing shop. Pieter Zachariasz (Sacharyesen), who later took the family name of Hartevel(d)t, also published Mennonite books, e.g., the 1644 and 1657 editions of the hymnal *Kleyn Hoorns Liet-boeck*. Of some of these and other editions Zacharias Cornelisz and his sons were not the printers, but only the publishers. Pieter Zachariasz Hartevelt also published the portrait of Menno Simons by J. van de Velde. (*DB* 1887, 90; 1916, 62.) vDZ.

Zacherle, Jörg, and his wife, Anabaptist martyrs of Wels, Austria. Jörg was a furrier of Krems; he and his wife were executed at Wels in 1528. (For particulars, see **Wels** and **Haslinger, Leonhard.**)

Zachte Vriezen: see **Frisian Mennonites.**

Zagradovka, a Mennonite settlement in South Russia, situated on the Ingulez River *c*60 miles slightly northeast of the city of Kherson, consisting of *c*60,000 acres of excellent soil. It was bought of Leo V. Kochubey in 1871 for the landless (*q.v.*) by the Molotschna Mennonite settlement. Eventually 16 villages were settled on this land in 1872-83, with 182 acres for each family.

The villages were Alexanderfeld, Neu-Schönsee, Friedensfeld, Neu-Halbstadt, Nikolaifeld, Orloff, Blumenort, Tiege, Altonau, Rosenort, Münsterberg, Gnadenfeld, Schönau, Steinfeld, Reinfeld, and Alexanderkrone. Nikolaidorf, which was settled in the vicinity but purchased by independent means, considered itself as belonging to the Zagradovka settlement except administratively. About 1908 this village was sold to Russians.

Most of the Zagradovka settlers were poor; the first years were difficult, but by 1900 most of them were moderately well-to-do and had spacious and well-built homes surrounded by lovely trees and gardens, with well-kept fields and green meadows on which cattle and horses of good breed were fed.

During the first years the settlers had to haul their grain by wagon and over very poor roads to Berislav on the Dnieper, a distance of about 50 miles; in 1890 a railway was built to within about 13 miles from the center of the settlement and in 1916 another to within about 6 miles.

By 1914 agriculture was flourishing; industry had been begun: Siemens in Blumenort and Wiebe in Orloff manufactured farm implements; a large and modern flour mill was in operation in Tiege; Alexanderfeld and Neu-Schönsee had smaller mills; several other small factories were in operation. A post office "Tiege," later renamed "Kochubeyevka," and a bank had been opened in the village of Tiege. Each village had its own public school. In 1895 the settlement built a Zentralschule with three classrooms in Neu-Schönsee, which was renovated in 1912, besides three homes for the teachers and one for the caretaker.

The settlement constituted an independent administrative unit, with headquarters in Tiege. In 1877 the volost (q.v.) erected two impressive buildings in Tiege—a drugstore and a medical center.

There were three churches in Zagradovka: (1) a Mennonite church in Nikolaifeld (q.v.), completed in 1891, with a membership of 1,241 in 1922; (2) an M.B. church in Tiege (q.v.), erected in 1888, membership of 427 in 1922; (3) an Evangelical Mennonite church in Orloff, organized in 1907 with 63 members, built in 1914; its membership in 1922 was 214.

Daughter settlements organized by Zagradovka, on rented land each with two villages, were Suvorovka in the Caucasus, 1897; Piessarev, near Berislav, 1903; Trubetskoye, near Berislav, 1904. Hundreds of families left for Siberia, where the government had granted them an area of 605,060 acres.

World War I stopped all progress. The Revolution brought ruin. In 1919 several thousand irregulars under Machno committed fearful atrocities in seven of the villages. A great deal of property was taken or destroyed, and many homes burned to the ground; 206 individuals were murdered and many maimed. In the famine some 329 persons starved to death.

In 1921-41 the Soviets exiled into uninhabited regions or concentration camps 448 individuals. When World War II began the men were deported to the east; most of them were able to return, but 301 have not been heard from. By 1941, 720 families, or 54.1 per cent of all the Mennonite families of the settlement, had been deprived of their head. At the retreat of the German army all the remaining settlers left; about 3,500 were evacuated to the west. Most of them eventually were overtaken by the Russian army and sent to the northern regions, mainly in Asiatic Russia. Zagradovka as a Mennonite settlement had ceased to exist. The last elder of the Mennonite church here, Heinrich Voth, survived the hardships and sufferings and resumed his ministry. He was the chief if not the only active Mennonite elder in Russia in 1953- .   G.L.

G. Lohrenz, Sagradowka (Rosthern, 1947); Dietrich Neufeld, Mennonitentum in der Ukraine; Schicksalsgeschichte Sagradowkas (2d ed., Emden, 1922); Friesen, Brüderschaft, 423-27, 462-65; ML I, 83.

Zahler, Melchior, an Anabaptist deacon in Frutigen in the Swiss canton of Bern, was in 1710 imprisoned for three weeks in Bern on account of his faith. He then betook himself with his youngest children into the Neuenburg region. On the occasion of a visit to his older children in his home town, he fell into the hands of the persecuting authorities and was again put into the prison in Bern. With 60 other Anabaptists he was to have been sent to America on March 18, 1710. In Nijmegen they acquired their freedom. With Benedikt Brechbühl (q.v.) and Hans Bürky (q.v.), Zahler was sent to Amsterdam, to present to the city council a written account of their imprisonment and a confession of faith. Zahler returned to his Swiss home and was seized again and threatened with life imprisonment. (Müller, Berner Täufer, 284 ff.; ML IV.) NEFF.

Zahoriz (Sahorez), a village located five miles southwest of Dubno, Volhynia (q.v.) (Russia). Zahoriz and the neighboring villages of Futtor, Gorrit, Hecker, and others were settled by Swiss-Volhynian Mennonites who organized a congregation soon after 1861, holding services alternately at Zahoriz and Futtor, although neither had a meetinghouse. The time of the arrival of the Mennonites in these villages is unknown, but some apparently settled in Futtor in the early 19th century; by 1829 several families were living there, having come either from Poutchy (q.v.) or Vignanka. Zahoriz was probably settled by people from Poutchy. Before 1861 the Mennonite congregation in these villages was a subsidiary of the congregation at Poutchy; but when that larger settlement moved to the villages of Neumannovka (q.v.) and Kutusovka in eastern Volhynia, a congregation was organized with its center in Zahoriz and Futtor. Elder Johann Schrag of Poutchy moved to Zahoriz in 1861 and shepherded the church. Virtually all of the Mennonites in these villages emigrated to the United States in 1874, settling in Hutchinson and Turner counties, S.D. Ten families of Zahoriz and Futtor left Russia in April 1874 under the leadership of Andreas Schrag and were followed a few weeks later by the inhabitants of Gorrit and Hecker.   M.H.S.

Zaltbommel, a town in the Dutch province of Gelderland, formerly the seat of a Mennonite congregation, usually called Bommel, not to be confused with the Bommel (q.v.) and Ooltgensplaat congregation on the island of Goeree. Of the Zaltbommel congregation there is only scarce information: it had originated by 1595, for in this year the Reformed pastor reported that the Mennonites in his town were increasing and holding public meetings. In the 17th century this congregation belonged to the Flemish branch. It was represented at a Flemish conference at Haarlem in 1649, when its pulpit was vacant. Probably it died out soon after. (*DB* 1910, 10; Blaupot t. C., *Holland* I, 222, 330; II, 45.) vDZ.

Zamersky Filadelphus, a Moravian clergyman, who in 1593 published a large Protestant *Postille* (sermon book) in the Czech language. In it he speaks of the Anabaptists (Hutterites) and involuntarily gives them the testimonial that "through their economic capability and artistic skill in their crafts they distinguish themselves above all others so that herein they offer an almost astonishing spectacle." W.W.

Fr. Hruby, *Die Wiedertäufer in Mähren* (Leipzig, 1935) 36; *ML* IV.

Zandersfelde: see Pastwa.

Zandeweer, a hamlet in the Dutch province of Groningen, where Leenaert (*q.v.*) Bouwens baptized 17 persons in 1563-65, and later two more. Since there was apparently no congregation at Zandeweer the converts may have joined a neighboring congregation like Uithuizen (*q.v.*), Zijldijk (*q.v.*), or Huizinge (*q.v.*). vDZ.

Zandt, Het ('t Zandt), a village in the Dutch province of Groningen, where Anabaptists were found as early as 1534, in the fall of which year Obbe (*q.v.*) Philips preached here. In the course of 1534 it was visited by the Münsterite emissaries Jacob (*q.v.*) Cremer and Antonius (*q.v.*) Kistemaker, and in January 1535 a tumultuous meeting was held on the farm "De Arke" near 't Zandt, where Harm(en) (*q.v.*) Schoe(n)maker was the leader; about a thousand persons were present, over 300 of whom were baptized by Schoenmaker. But soon after this revolutionary Anabaptism a more peaceful Mennonitism arose here. Leenaert (*q.v.*) Bouwens baptized five persons at 't Zandt in 1551-56 and later another three. Concerning the congregation there is not much information; it was small in membership and merged with the Zijldijk (*q.v.*) congregation before 1700. vDZ.

P. G. Bos, "Groninger Wederdooper-woelingen in 1534 en 1535," in *Ned. Archief voor Kerkgeschiedenis* VI (1908) 1-17; *BRN* VII, 136, 362 f., 379; Kühler, *Geschiedenis* I, 144-47; Mellink, *Wederdopers*, 257-61; *DB* 1879, 6, 87; 1905, 91, 97; 1906, 31, 36; 1917, 126.

Zanten (Santen), **Jacobus van** (d. *c*1740), a physician at Haarlem, Holland, and in 1683-*c*1730 an elder of the Den Blok (Flemish) Mennonite congregation, was a conservative Mennonite who stressed the confessions of faith. He was a friend of Herman Schijn (*q.v.*). Besides some medical works van Zanten published a book on Socrates (1710); translations from English: John Milton, *Paradise Lost* under the title *Paradys Verlooren* (Haarlem, 1728), and John Gale *Aanmerkingen op den Kinderdoop* (Leiden, 1741); a theological study on the Apostles' Creed, entitled *De Historie van het Symbolum oft Geloofsformulier der Apostelen* (Haarlem, 1707, repr. Utrecht, 1711); and *Oorzaken van't Verval der Christelyke Godvruchtigheid* (Haarlem, 1717). Being unmarried he willed a considerable part of his property to the Haarlem congregation, which is still administered as the Jacobus-van-Zanten-fonds. vDZ.

N.N.B.Wb. V, 1169; Blaupot t. C., *Holland* II, 30 f., 136; *DB* 1897, 166 f.

Zängerle, Jakob, an Anabaptist martyr, was executed in 1537 at Imbst, Tirol, Austria. (Beck, *Geschichts-Bücher,* 132.)

Zapff, Hauptrecht (1546-1630), a Hutterite Anabaptist, born in Sprendling, Hesse, joined the brotherhood in Moravia as a lad of fourteen. In 1594 he was made Diener des Wortes (minister), and for thirty years he was the secretary-clerk of the bishop. His major contribution was his work on the great chronicle of the Hutterites, the *Geschichtsbuch,* which Kaspar Braitmichel (*q.v.*) had begun to write in the 1570's and completed up to 1542. In the days of the Vorsteher Hänsel Kräl (*q.v.*), 1578-83, Zapff first copied the Braitmichel original (no longer in existence), most likely at the Neumühl (*q.v.*) Bruderhof, and continued it chronologically to 1591. This work was done apparently conjointly with the bishops, first with Hänsel Kräl and then with Claus Braidl (*q.v.*), more or less as Braitmichel had started it. Zapff and the bishops used the large archives at the Neumühl center. The title page of the Chronicle, as it still exists today, bears the name of Kräl and then the initials "H. Z." for the writer. At the end of Braitmichel's "Vorrede an den Leser" Zapff expressly signed also, as "continuer and worker on this book."

Zapff died in 1630 in Slovakia, at the age of 84. Five hymns were written by him, three now in the *Lieder der Hutterischen Brüder,* 846-49, and two in a hymn codex in Bratislava. R.F.

Zapff's share in the Chronicle is told by Zieglschmid, *Chronik,* xxiii-xxiv; Wolkan, *Lieder,* 241; *ML* IV.

Zaporozhe, formerly Alexandrovsk, located on the left bank of the Dnieper River in the Ukraine, 45 miles south of Dnepropetrovsk, below the Dneprostroi Dam, on the main railroad from Moscow to Sevastopol, has today a population of approximately 300,000. It is a significant industrial center with metallurgical plants and chemical works. Mennonites from the Chortitza (*q.v.*) settlement founded the village of Schönwiese (*q.v.*) near this city and soon developed a large-scale milling industry and factories which became the nucleus of its present-day industrial significance.

Among the early Mennonite firms of Schönwiese, now a part of Zaporozhe, were Lepp and Wallmann, A. J. Koop, Hermann Niebuhr, and Hildebrandt and Pries. The strategic location on the Dnieper River and the need for agricultural machinery speeded the rapid growth. The Lepp and Wallmann factory had an annual production of 900,000 rubles and the A. J. Koop factory of 610,000 (1911). The largest milling industry was Niebuhr & Co. After the Revolution the industries were nationalized and developed by the Soviets.

The first combines in Russia were produced by Mennonite engineers in former Mennonite factories of Zaporozhe. Peter Dyck, Gerhard Hamm, Kornelius Pauls, and others, mostly sons of Mennonite industrialists who had studied in Germany, started to build combines in 1925. (Hamm went to the United States to study American industries.) Their success was reported to the industrial headquarters in Moscow. In 1927 after a commission had examined the combines Kalinin himself bestowed the Order of Lenin on the Mennonite engineers and the director of the factory. From now on the "Kummunar" factory received priority till the output reached 10,000 per year. During the wave of exiles in 1933 the Mennonite engineers were sent into exile.

When Hitler's army invaded the Ukraine, the Mennonites who were working in large numbers in these industries were also evacuated. Miraculously some escaped this evacuation and came to North and South America after World War II. It can be assumed that some of the evacuated Mennonites have found their way back to Zaporozhe, although little information is available at this time. (See also **Industry Among the Mennonites in Russia and Ukraine.**)   C.K.

"Mennonite Industry in Russia," *Menn. Life* X (1955) 21; Cornelius Krahn, "Agriculture Among the Mennonites of Russia," *Menn. Life* X (1955); D. H. Epp, "P. H. Lepp," *Bote* (Rosthern, 1928) Nos. 10-13.

Zaug, Hans, an Anabaptist minister of the canton of Zürich, Switzerland, one of "seven of the preachers and principal elders (*Vorsteher*) of the church [who] were apprehended, for whom special prisons were prepared; namely, Uly Bogart, Anthony Hinnelberg, Jegly Schlebach, Hans Zoug, Uly Baumgarten, Christian Christians, and Rhode Peters, in Bern." Van Braght says of the occasion of this persecution: "The little flock of Christ having fled from the confines of Zurich to the regions of Berne, could at this time also there obtain no freedom, inasmuch as those of Berne, following the footsteps of those of Zurich, also undertook to lay hands on them, but especially on the shepherds and leaders of the church, in order that they might by this means, as it seems, cause the more terror among the innocent sheep and lambs of the scattered flock of Christ." They were kept at hard work on poor food, at first told they would be kept in prison for life, but later given a choice of three options: (1) to attend the state church, (2) to be perpetually banished to the galleys, or (3) to be executed. Van Braght reports no further knowledge of their fate, except that they were still in prison in 1659, nor does he know when they were arrested. (*Mart. Mir.* D 826, E 1124.)
H.S.B.

Zaunmacher, Ulrich (Gemmelich), of Ansbach, Württemberg, Germany, defended himself very skillfully in a number of cross-examinations. He said he wanted to live apostolically if he were permitted to do so. One saw well that many good people were killed. He who teaches otherwise than Christ and His apostles have taught is a liar. He did not want to oppose the government. To him communion was a meal of commemoration (in John 16 Christ speaks about His flesh which was committed to the cross and not into His mouth). He would stick to that. He believed that if he ate of this bread in faith, he would not only have Christ's body and blood, he would have the entire Christ and the salvation of his soul. But that Christ's body is essentially here and climbs up and down from heaven, that he would commend to the wise men. He asked whether it would be right or wrong if four or five or six

together were to observe the Lord's Supper in a house as the apostles did.

In a letter to Margrave George in May 1529 he remarked that the clergy had belabored him with all kinds of hair-splitting catch questions; he repeated his views on the Lord's Supper, and commented that the Jews were more mercifully treated than the Anabaptists: they were given more time to sell their property in order to leave the country. He asked the elector not to expel him. Finally he was ordered not to talk to anyone about the sacrament but to stick to his trade, otherwise he would be punished. There is a marginal note: he shall leave in a month. It is probable, but not certain, that Zaunmacher was a full Anabaptist. (*TA Bayern* I 163 f., 167, 181 f., 185, 190, 331; *ML* IV.)   W.W.

Zaunring (*Martyrs' Mirror,* Zaunringerad; Loserth, Zaunried), **Georg** (Jörg or Juriaen) (d.1531 or 1538), an early Tirolean Anabaptist and co-worker with Jakob Hutter. He was born supposedly in Rattenberg (*q.v.*), and seems to have joined the Anabaptists at an early age. In 1528 he was actively working and baptizing both north and south of Bozen (Bolzano), in the center of the Adige (*q.v.*) Valley. In the remote villages of the Ritten Mountains he was fairly successful and became the treasurer (*Säckelmeister*) of the group. It must have been here that he met Hutter, who was likewise working for the Anabaptist cause along the Puster (*q.v.*), Adige, and Eisack valleys (see **Tirol**). Because of severe persecution, Hutter sent a large contingent of these newly converted brethren to Moravia, the "promised land," under the leadership of Zaunring, their preacher (*Diener des Worts*). In 1529 they arrived at Austerlitz (*q.v.*), where they gladly joined the brotherhood shepherded by Jakob Wideman (*q.v.*).

Unfortunately conflicts soon arose (see **Reublin**), and in 1530 the brotherhood split into two groups (*Völklein*): the Southwest Germans remained with Wideman and were henceforth known as the Austerlitz Brethren, while the Tiroleans went to Auspitz (*q.v.*), then an estate of the Abbess of Maria Saal (near Brno), where they began another Bruderhof with a total of 150 baptized persons supervised at first by both Zaunring and Reublin. The establishment of unconditional and full community of goods was, of course, new and by no means an easy affair. In that very first year (1530) it was discovered that Reublin had withheld a sum of money (which he had brought to Moravia) for emergencies (which act occurred more than once later on; see, e.g., **Schützinger**). Thereupon Reublin was expelled from the Auspitz group as a "false Ananias." This act received the approval of Hutter, who had come to Moravia in 1530 to look after the brotherhoods, their discipline, and their pastoral care. From now on Zaunring was the only preacher of the Auspitz group, which was growing steadily by the arrival of newcomers from Tirol.

But the peace was short-lived. The Hutterite chronicle tells the events of 1531 in great detail: Zaunring's wife had committed adultery with a certain brother Thomas Lindl, and of course that involved a delicate situation for the preacher. For a while he practiced "marital avoidance" (*q.v.,* especially *ME* III, 487), but eventually he forgave his wife and took her back. For this reason the brotherhood excommunicated him, thus depriving themselves of their only spiritual leader. At their invitation, Hutter came from Tirol with his new co-worker Sigmund Schützinger (*q.v.*) and restored order and discipline, making Schützinger the new Vorsteher. Soon thereafter Zaunring repented before the entire brotherhood and was accepted back into full membership. But not long afterward the Brethren sent him as a missioner into South Germany, in particular to Franconia. Here, in the bishopric of Bamberg, he was caught by the authorities and soon ·beheaded, becoming a martyr for his faith in 1533. (Wappler, *Stellung* . . . , p. 37, n. 3, 168-72.)

We have from Zaunring's hand two writings: (1) a brief but very fine, typically Anabaptist tract, *Eine kurze Anzeigung des Abendmahles Christi,* also called *Ein Gespräch vom Abendmahl Christi, ein Dialog zwischen der Welt und einem Christen* (published by Lydia Müller, *Glaubenszeugnisse* I, 144-48), and (2) *Eine schöne Epistel an die Heiligen Gottes: "Wem Christus verheissen wird."* This contains Zaunring's motto: "In Gottes Lieb sollst für dich gan/ In Glauben keinen Zweifel han/ In Hoffnung auch nit abelan/ Vor deinem Gott in Demut stan" (Beck, 40 n).   R.F.

Lydia Müller, *Glaubenszeugnisse* I (Leipzig, 1938) 143 ff.; Beck, *Geschichts-Bücher,* 39 ff.; Loserth, *Anabaptismus;* Zieglschmid, *Chronik; Mart. Mir.* D 33, E 440; *ML* IV.

Zealand Flanders (Zeeuws-Vlaanderen), since 1814 a part of the Dutch province of Zeeland (*q.v.*), which borders on Belgium. In the 16th-18th centuries Zealand Flanders, then usually called Staats-Vlaanderen, was governed by the States-General. From about 1567 a large number of refugees from Flanders, both Mennonites and Calvinists, fleeing persecution after the coming of Alva (see **Alba**), came to Zealand Flanders, some of them settling there and others moving northward. The Reformed synod of Walcheren (*q.v.*), which had charge of the Calvinists in Zealand Flanders, as late as 1647 decided to place a guard on the Belgian border to intercept the refugees and to try to win them to the Reformed Church and to prevent their reaching the Mennonite Church. This measure, however, was of little use. About 1630 some Mennonites who had remained in Belgium came secretly to Zealand Flanders, particularly to De Biezen (*q.v.*), near Aardenburg, for worship and to have their marriages performed by a Dutch Mennonite elder. A large number of well-known Mennonite families passed through Zealand Flanders on their way to Vlissingen, Middelburg, and Holland, and some Mennonite refugee families, e.g., Dyserinck and van Eeghen, stayed in this area a few generations, belonging to the Aardenburg (*q.v.*) or the Groede (*q.v.,* Cadzand) congregation. (*DB* 1876, 82 f., 96-108; 1883, 93 f., 108-13; 1884, 114; 1897, 163.)   vDZ.

Zedo, Nikolaus, of Bümplitz near Bern, Switzerland, was, after the execution of Wälti Gerber (*q.v.*), next to Hans Haslibacher the most important preacher of the Bernese Anabaptists. He is described as a man of about 30 years of age with a "pointed black little beard," a crippled hand, and usually dressed in gray trousers. In the *Turmbücher* (*q.v.*) he is often named as an Anabaptist preacher. According to his own statements, he came to the faith through Wälti Gerber. Even in his youth he was active as preacher and pastor. Cathrin Wenger confessed in December 1566 that she had been married in a field near Schorren (near Thun) by Nikli Zedo. Hans Tschanz made the same confession in 1567. Zedo held meetings in the forest near Röthenbach in the Upper Emmental, in Schliern near Köniz, at Seftigen, where Zedo preached and read from the book of Ezra. Zedo's influence extended as far as the canton of Solothurn. He is expressly described as the successor of Wälti Gerber. Almost always he held his meetings during the night for reasons of safety. Under torture Verena Schöni confessed in 1569 that she and her husband had been married two years previously by Nikolaus Zedo "at night time" in a woods along the Aar River near Kresen. He had admonished them out of the Scriptures and had joined their hands "in the name of the Holy Trinity." Near Eggiwil in the Emmental Zedo also "passed out the Lord's Supper" in a forest. Furthermore Zedo confessed later before the court that he had held a meeting and baptized near Steffisburg in Eriz, and also likewise at Seftigen and between Stettlen and Bolligen. Later he had also baptized several persons in the Upper Emmental at the Schallenberg.

Such missionary activity and official acts of an Anabaptist like Zedo, who worked in wide circles and also in the neighborhood of the city of Bern, could not remain concealed from the council. The council finally found and arrested the "stiff-necked disobedient Anabaptist" in the region of Oberdiessbach near Thun *c*1575. Apparently some of the patricians in authority were shocked by this kind of bloody justice; for the Baron of Diessbach was fined 50 pounds for releasing Zedo from imprisonment. The sum of 100 pounds was now set upon the recapture of Zedo. Four men from the region of Steffisburg and Thun earned this money by taking him to Steffisburg; from there the bailiff took him to Bern, accompanied by two men. On Nov. 14, 1580, he was cross-examined on three points: (1) whether he would desist from preaching and baptizing and adapt himself to the Christian church; (2) whether he would be obedient to the Christian divinely ordained and established government; (3) at what places he had held meetings and preached, who had attended, and whom he had baptized.

After Zedo's confession he was declared guilty of disobedience to the Christian regulations and of having shown himself as a mobster and the leader of a seditious party and a false doctrine. He was therefore, on the basis of the Anabaptist mandates, condemned to death by beheading.

But this sentence was not carried out (presumably because of the opposition of some of the members of the council, or perhaps also because of public opinion), as is shown by this entry: on Nov. 29, 1580, his life was granted to him "out of grace and mercy by my gracious lords, councillors, and citizens in the hope of improvement; but he shall give a recantation at those places where he is cited and pay

200 pounds of fine and all the costs." On Dec. 4 Zedo was placed before the congregation in the cathedral at Bern. The court secretary read the record of recantation. Then Zedo was taken to the island, to be taken to Steffisburg on the next day to make his recantation before the congregation there and at other places. In that same night, however, Zedo escaped from the island. Beat Neuenschwander, who helped him escape, was fined 50 pounds. Nothing more is known about Zedo except that he "thereafter still did much harm."   S.G.

S. Geiser, *Die Taufgesinnten-Gemeinden* (Karlsruhe, 1931); *ML* IV.

Zeeland, a Dutch province (1952 pop. 273,690, with *c*650 Mennonites) in the southeastern part of the Netherlands, consists of the territory of Zealand Flanders (*q.v.*), formerly called Staats-Vlaanderen, in 1814 added to Zeeland, and the following islands: Walcheren, South Beveland, North Beveland, Tholen, Sint Philipsland, and Schouwen-Duiveland. Anabaptism was found on Walcheren by 1534 (Middelburg, Veere, Arnemuiden) and at about the same time on Schouwen-Duiveland (Brouwershaven, Zierikzee), and Mennonite congregations developed here *c*1550 or earlier. But this early Anabaptist movement was not strong; the Zeeland congregations were considerably strengthened by the coming of Mennonites from Flanders, Belgium, from *c*1560, and particularly after 1567. Even before this stream of refugees entered Zeeland, there were connections between the Anabaptists-Mennonites of Zeeland and those of Flanders. In the 16th century it was usually not the elders of Holland who baptized in Zeeland, but those of Flanders. The emigrants from Flanders settled in some Zeeland towns, establishing new congregations or strengthening the churches they found there. Most refugees, however, moved on to such places as Rotterdam, Leiden, Haarlem, and Amsterdam, and also to Friesland, to Emden in East Friesland, and to Danzig in Prussia. A number of these Mennonite refugee families lived for two or three generations in Zeeland, and then moved northward, particularly to Haarlem and Amsterdam.

About 1600 the following Mennonite congregations were found in the province of Zeeland: Aardenburg, Groede (or Cadzand), Vlissingen, Middelburg, Veere, Goes, St-Maartensdijk, Zierikzee, and Brouwershaven. Of these congregations only Aardenburg, Vlissingen, Middelburg, and Goes are still in existence. About 1670 the total number of baptized members in Zeeland was perhaps *c*1245. This number was *c*900 in 1730, barely 195 in 1800, 376 in 1900, and 431 in 1958. The large decrease of members from *c*1680 and the dissolution of some congregations was caused partly by the intolerance of the States of Zeeland and of the local magistrates of some towns like Aardenburg, Middelburg, and Zierikzee, but mostly by the fact that the Mennonite refugees from Flanders who had settled as merchants in the Zeeland towns gradually moved to South or North Holland towns where they had better business opportunities.

It was at Middelburg in 1577 and soon after in the whole province of Zeeland that through the benevolence of Prince William I (*q.v.*) of Orange the Dutch Mennonites became officially exempted from the oath and military service.   vDZ.

J. W. te Water, *Reformatie in Zeeland* (1766); K. R. Pekelharing, "Geschiedenis der Hervorming in Zeeland," in *Archief Zeeuwsch Genootschap* VI (1866); Mellink, *Wederdopers*, 316-24; *Inv. Arch. Amst.* I, Nos. 428, 433-41, 1072; II, 2, Nos. 584, 589-91.

Zeeman, Wybe Pietersz (d.1759), a lay preacher in the Mennonite congregation of Heerenveen from 1736, was charged by the Reformed pastors with teaching Socinian (*q.v.*) doctrines, as were his co-preachers Wytze Jeens Brouwer (*q.v.*) and Pieke Tjommes (*q.v.*). Whereas Brouwer and Tjommes were suspended from their office by the governor of Schoterland on June 5, 1739, Zeeman consented to the (Reformed) anti-Socinian formulation and was again permitted to preach.   vDZ.

P. H. Veen, *De Doopsgezinden in Schoterland* (Leeuwarden, 1869) 34 f., 42, 65-71, 163 ff., 167, 169-72.

Zeerijp, a hamlet in the Dutch province of Groningen, the site of the meetinghouse and parsonage of the Leermens (*q.v.*)-Loppersum Mennonite congregation, built in 1835. Hence the Leermens-Loppersum congregation is also called Zeerijp.   vDZ.

Zeeuwsche Sociëteit (Zeeland Conference). In September 1685 an attempt was made to found a Lamist (*q.v.*) Mennonite conference in the Dutch province of Zeeland (*q.v.*) in order to meet the increasing need for capable preachers in the churches. Middelburg took the initiative and invited the congregations of Cadzand, Zierikzee, Brouwershaven, and Aardenburg to support the plan. Vlissingen and Goes, both siding with the Zonists (*q.v.*), were not invited. As far as is known, after a first meeting of the Sociëteit, October 1685, the matter was dropped. (*Inv. Arch. Amst.* II, 2, Nos. 589-91.)   vDZ.

Zeeuws(ch)-Vlaanderen: see Zealand Flanders.

Zegers (Seghersz, Segersz), **Herman** (*c*1576-July 1667), living at Utrecht, Netherlands, owner of a tileworks, was a deacon and in 1639-63 a preacher of the Utrecht Mennonite congregation. In 1632 he signed the Dordrecht (*q.v.*) confession of faith in the name of the Utrecht congregation. In 1660 ff., when a conflict arose in the Utrecht church, Zegers held to conservative views, opposing Willem van Maurik (*q.v.*) and some co-preachers who sided with van Maurik. He was a descendant of the martyr Jeronimus (*q.v.*) Seghersz, and the ancestor of the Hovens (*q.v.*) family. (*DB* 1863, 130; 1916, 152; *Inv. Arch. Amst.* II, No. 2290.)   vDZ.

Zeggelen, van, a Dutch Mennonite family. Wilhemus Josephus van Zeggelen (1811-79), a Roman Catholic, joined the Mennonites in 1848. He was a director of a printing shop at The Hague, Holland, and was known for his humorous poetry. Among his children were Marie Christine van Zeggelen 1870-1953), well-known Dutch novelist and dramatist, and author of children's books, and Constantijn Henri van Zeggelen (1878-1939), a lawyer at Amsterdam, twice a deacon in the congregation, trustee of the A.D.S., in 1914-39 a trustee of the Oranjeappel (*q.v.*) orphanage, and in 1924-39 a trustee of the Christina (*q.v.*) Stichting. vDZ.

Zehender, Stephan, an Anabaptist martyr of Pyrmensdorf, Switzerland, an aged man, was imprisoned in 1539 in the Oethenbach prison of Zürich "in a very damp and unwholesome place, . . . and fed on bread and water" for sixteen weeks, until his death. (*Mart. Mir.* D 815, E 1114 f.; *ML* IV.)

Zehentmayer, Martin (Marthi or Marthan Maler), was a Hutterite martyr, who stemmed from Langenmoosen near Inchenhofen in the Aichach district of Bavaria, Germany. He learned painting probably in the neighboring Augsburg. There he must also have joined the Anabaptists. In 1528 he was expelled from Augsburg and went to Schwäbisch-Gmünd. There he opened the door wide for Anabaptism. He is said to have baptized over 100 persons in chapels and private houses. Then the council became aware of him and in the middle of February they seized him and in succession 40 of his followers, including 19 girls and women. They were given only bread and water and kept in the towers around the city the entire summer and autumn. For 42 weeks Zehentmayer was in arrest. He was also cross-examined on the rack and confessed that he had wanted to have all things held in common. On Dec. 4, 1528, he was tried with several of his fellow believers. The council of Gmünd could risk this, in its confidence in the troops sent by the Swabian League. He was sentenced to execution by the sword. On Dec. 7, 1529 (Wolkan, erroneously 1531), the sentence was carried out outside the city.

Zehentmayer also wrote some songs: "Mit Freuden will ich singen" (*Lieder*, 48 ff.), and another with a companion, "Aus tiefer not schrein wir zu dir" (*Ausbund* with a different text; *Lieder*, 51). In addition these deal with the seven brethren: "Kürzlich hab ich mich besonnen" (according to Beck, 38, written by Peter Riedemann; *Lieder*, 53), "Wer Christo hier will folgen" (*Lieder*, 52), and "Aus herzlichem Muet und euffer kann ich nicht unterlan" (*Lieder*, 55), which was written by Andreas Ehrenpreis. G.Bos.

Beck, *Geschichts-Bücher*, 37 ff.; *Lieder der Hutterischen Brüder* (Scottdale, 1941) 48-59; Wagner, "Die Reichsstadt Gmünd 1526-30," in *Württembergische Vierteljahrshefte*, 1884, 85 ff., 183; Wolkan, *Lieder; idem, Geschicht-Buch; Mart. Mir.* D 32, E 439 f.; *ML* IV.

Zehr is a Mennonite family name found primarily in Illinois and Ontario and in smaller numbers in Iowa, New York, Nebraska, Oregon, and other states. In 1957 eleven Zehrs were serving as Mennonite ministers, six of whom were in the Mennonite Church (MC), three in the Conservative Amish Mennonite, one in the Evangelical Mennonite, and one in a congregation in France. The family is Swiss in origin, but was represented among the Swiss Mennonite refugees in the Palatinate. Members of the Zehr family migrated to America in the 19th century and were prominent in A.M. circles. Peter Zehr (1809-98) came to America in 1838 and served as a minister in the East Zorra (Ont.) A.M. Church near Tavistock. Joseph C. Zehr (1822-1915) was ordained minister in Lewis County, N.Y., 1852, and later served in Ontario. Michael Zehr (1790-

1880) served the A.M. Church in Lewis County, N.Y., as bishop. Peter S. Zehr (1867-1934), a grandson of the above Peter, was a minister in the East Zorra church. David D. Zehr (1864-1924) was born in Illinois and moved to Manson, Iowa, where he was ordained in 1902 and bishop in 1909. Jacob Zehr (1825-98), who settled in Illinois in 1848, served as a bishop in the Goodfield Mennonite Church. He was ordained minister in 1859 and bishop in 1863. Daniel Zehr (1849-1942) was born in Illinois and ordained a Mennonite minister in 1895. Jacob Zehr (1875-1929) was born in Illinois and was ordained minister in the Goodfield Mennonite Church in 1912. Michael S. Zehr (1872-1944) was bishop of the Pigeon River (Mich.) C.A.M. Church. Among the contemporary well-known ministers of this family are Harold Zehr, former minister of the East Bend Mennonite Church, Fisher, Ill.; Howard Zehr, bishop-pastor of the Prairie Street Mennonite Church, Elkhart, Ind.; and John David Zehr, instructor in the Goshen College Biblical Seminary. M.G.

Laura E. Farney and Julius Farney, *Genealogies of Three Large Families (Farney, Virkler, Zehr)* (Watertown, N.Y., 1933).

Zehr, Michael S. (1872-1944), born in Wellesley, Waterloo Co., Ont., the sixth of the seven children of Bishop Christian B. Zehr and Veronica. His great-grandfather, Bishop Michael Zehr, and family immigrated from Alsace to Lewis Co., N.Y., about 1833. On Nov. 29, 1894, he was married to Anna Zehr at Croghan, N.Y. In 1900 they moved to Huron County near Pigeon, Mich., and engaged in farming. Here their only child, Barbara, was born. In 1902 he became Sunday-school superintendent of the new Pigeon River A.M. congregation, was ordained to the ministry on Sept. 22, 1905, and bishop Nov. 30, 1930. He took an active interest in the organization of the Conservative Mennonite Conference, serving two terms as moderator and three as assistant. He served as a member of the Mission Board for 12 consecutive years, and for 11 years prior to his death was a member of the Executive Committee. He was used extensively in evangelistic meetings, Bible conferences, summer and winter Bible schools throughout the church, being deeply interested in missionary efforts. He died at Phoenix, Ariz., where he spent the last seven months of his life. He was buried at Pigeon. J.D.E.

Laura E. Farney and Julius Farney, *Genealogies of Three Large Families (Farney, Virkler, Zehr)* (Watertown, N.Y., 1933).

Zeising (Zeisingk; Czech, *Cizek*), **Johannes.** Hubmaier called him Jan Zeisinger. He was a monk; with two other monks, Michael Weisse and a certain Johannes of Breslau, he came to Leitomischel, having been expelled because of his Lutheran ideas. Zeising translated from Bohemian into German an epistle, which the Bohemian Brethren sent to King Ludwig of Bohemia and Hungary, dated 1525. In 1526 Zeising published Zwingli's book on the communion. Lukas, a well-known leader of the Brethren, thereupon published a reply to this book by Zwingli. It was his idea that the bread is the body of Christ and the wine His blood in a sacramental, spiritual, effective, and actual manner. Thereupon Zeising and Michael Weisse wrote a reply in Latin to Lukas, accusing him of backsliding. They said such doctrines are a denial of faith and a darkening of Christ's intention which He had when He instituted the communion. Zeising thereupon distributed a second book by Zwingli, *Ueber die Schlüssel und die Beichte*.

Zeising was repeatedly warned by leaders of the Bohemian Brethren and threatened by excommunication if he would not yield. With tears he thanked them for their kind and fatherly admonitions and promised to obey, but after only three days he declared that he could not act against his conscience and therefore requested that he be dealt with according to their regulations, that is, be excommunicated, whereby he solemnly promised not to oppose the Brethren all his life. And so he was excommunicated. Zeising soon afterward joined the Swiss Brethren.

Hubmaier dedicated his booklet *Eine Form des Nachmahls Christi* of 1527 to Burion Sobeck, of Kornitz, a former friend of Luther's, and sent it to Sobeck through "his dear brother Jan Zeisinger." As an Anabaptist Zeising suffered death at the stake at Brno on April 10, 1528, together with Thoman Waldhauser (*q.v.*).   W.W.

J. T. Müller, *Geschichte der Böhmischen Brüder* I (Herrnhut, 1922) 426-28 f., 445; Wolkan, *Geschicht-Buch*, 45 note; *ML* IV.

Zeisset, Abraham (d. *c*1786), from 1749 an elder of the Immelhausen (*q.v.*) and Hasselbach (*q.v.*) Mennonite congregations in Baden, Germany. In 1783 (not 1773 as stated *ME* III, 14) he moved to Willenbach (*q.v.*) in Württemberg and served the Willenbach congregation until his death. He played a role in the strife that developed among the South German Mennonites to the left and the right of the Rhine in the 18th century. The occasion for the disputes was the activity of the strongly pietistic Mennonite preacher Peter Weber (*q.v.*) of Hardenberg. Weber's justified interest in awakening new life in the Mennonite congregations which were in many cases congealed in tradition met with opposition to the left of the Rhine under the leadership of Jakob Hirschler of Gerolsheim and a strongly conservative group; on the right of the Rhine from 1766 on, Abraham Zeisset was his most active opponent. Contemporary documents and letters about that quarrel indicate that Zeisset certainly had the honorable intention of preserving the old Anabaptist individuality and of representing it with conviction. On the other hand, it cannot be denied that he was guilty of personal obstinacy and unbrotherly attitudes.

The quarrel began when Zeisset deposed from their office on the strength of his own authority the preachers Georg and Abraham Bechtel, Jost Glück, and Jakob Krehbiel, who were spiritually alive and were friends of Peter Weber. This created great offense in the congregations of these men. They feared a division similar to the one caused by Jakob Ammann (*q.v.*). On Oct. 14 and 15, 1766, a conference took place at Rauhof in which three Swiss Mennonites participated besides the ministers of Baden and the Palatinate. Zeisset himself had invited them. The peace that resulted from this meeting was unfortunately of short duration. The newly awakened disunity was so severe that in 1767 the spring communion was not observed in North Baden.

In 1770 a new effort was made to bring about peace at a conference of elders and preachers on the Himmelhäuserhof (today Immelhäuserhof). Zeisset and other leaders of the dispute were set back from communion "impartially and without respect of person" for Easter of that year, temporarily removed from the office of preaching, and asked to apologize for their previous hostile attitude. But the strife was not yet completely removed. Zeisset even appealed to the civil authorities for help. Not until 1782 was the affair settled.

Abraham Zeisset was also for a time engaged in correspondence between the West Prussian and the South German congregations. But after he had offended other correspondents of the South German congregations and did not succeed in drawing the West Prussians to his side, he dropped out of this circular letter. His relationship with the Swiss Brethren on the whole remained clear, although they were by no means all on his side. In spite of the differing judgments concerning Zeisset, it must be reckoned as a service on his part that he contributed to the closer union between the South German Mennonites of that time and their Swiss brethren.   P.S.

S. Geiser, *Die Taufgesinnten-Gemeinden* (Karlsruhe, 1931) 456 f.; *Gem.-Kal.*, 1930, 139 ff.; 1932, 115; Müller, *Berner Täufer*, 213; D. L. Gratz, *Bernese Anabaptists* (Scottdale, 1953); *ML* IV.

Zeist, a town in the Dutch province of Utrecht, the seat of a Mennonite congregation, which was founded as a Kring (circle) on June 16, 1929, and organized as a congregation on March 23, 1931. From January 1921 until 1929 meetings were held at Zeist more or less regularly. A meetinghouse was built at Zeist in 1931, dedicated on Jan. 10, 1932, by Tj. Kielstra (*q.v.*). The first pastor of the Zeist congregation was C. Nijdam, serving 1933-46, followed by W. Mesdag 1946- .

The baptized membership, numbering *c*100 when the congregation was founded, was 339 in 1958. Church activities include two women's circles and a Sunday school for children. A home for the aged, called Schaerweyde (*q.v.*), was opened at Zeist on Oct. 13, 1951.   vDZ.

Zelis (Zilis, Zielis, Sielis, Zylis), or Zelis Jacobs, a Mennonite elder, a native of Monschau (*q.v.*) in the Eiffel, Germany, was from *c*1554 active in Cologne (*q.v.*) and along the Rhine as far as Strasbourg (*q.v.*). This simple man, a charcoal burner, was a powerful apostle, evangelist, and leader of the church; he also trained ministers. In early 1557, when the Dutch elders Leenaert (*q.v.*) Bouwens, Dirk (*q.v.*) Philips, and Menno (*q.v.*) Simons had begun to practice rigorous banning (see **Ban**), Zelis, Lemken (*q.v.*), and other elders, then usually called High German (*q.v.*) Mennonites, found themselves unable to agree with them. Zelis and Lemken attacked particularly Menno, accusing him in a letter of 1557 (found in *DB* 1894) of leaving his former tolerant views to approve marital avoidance (*q.v.*). Menno answered in *Grontlijcke Onderwys oft Be-*

richt van de Excommunicatie (1558) and, after a second letter of Zelis and Lemken, in *Antwoort . . . op Zylis ende Lemmekens . . .Faemrooven* (1560). In the meantime a large conference of German elders meeting at Strasbourg in 1557 opposed marital avoidance and overly strict banning. In 1559 Dirk Philips and Leenaert Bouwens traveled to South Germany to ban Zelis, Lemken, and the High Germans.

After 1559 there is no information about Zelis; he probably died in 1565. Zelis Jacobs is not identical with Zillis (*q.v.*) Leitgen Kremers, who stayed at Münster (*q.v.*) in 1534. (*ML* IV, 607.) vDZ.

BRN VII, 56, 61, 87, 220, 222, 527; Kühler, *Geschiedenis* I, 318-28; K. Vos, *Menno Simons* (Leiden, 1914) 135 f., 142 f., 191, 253 f.; C. Krahn, *Menno Simons* (Karlsruhe, 1936) 95-97; Rembert, *Wiedertäufer*, 458 f., 501 f.; *DB* 1894, 36 f., 47-53, 58, 60 f.; W. Bax, *Het Protestantisme in het bisdom Luik* I (The Hague, 1937) 302 f., note; *Der Mennonit* IX (1956) No. 1, p. 10.

Zell: see Cellarius.

Zell, Katharina, the wife of Matthäus Zell (*q.v.*), made a true shelter for religious exiles. Schwenckfelders, Waldenses, and Anabaptists were admitted into their house. She paid no attention to names, for as Christians "it is our duty to show love, service, and mercy to everyone; Christ our teacher taught us that." On the evening before his death, her husband urgently asked her to dedicate all her strength to the service of the poor and the persecuted. She was also to tell his assistants and his deacons that they should leave the Anabaptists and all of other faiths in peace, preaching Christ alone and gathering His sheep, not scattering them. Katharina Zell faithfully continued her Christian benevolent activity after her husband's death, although no capital was left at her disposal. Among other things she took into her home the wife of an Anabaptist preacher who had been executed in Liége and then provided a place for her as a worker in an institution for the poor. But when Ludwig Rabus, Zell's successor in office, discovered that an Anabaptist was occupying an important position in a public institution of the city, he insisted that she be removed. Deeply saddened Katharina Zell, an effective writer, on March 14, 1557, wrote "to the young, proud, zealous, who come to the altar too early and before their time" a moving letter defending the Anabaptists. "Now as to the poor Anabaptists, that you are so angry and wrathful about them, and the authorities everywhere chase them as a hunter urges his dogs upon a wild boar or a rabbit. They, after all, confess Christ with us on the main things in which we have parted from the papacy. . . . Shall one then persecute them and Christ in them whom they confess with zeal, and many of them have confessed unto misery, prison, fire, and water? Rather give yourselves the blame that we in our life and teaching are the cause of their separating themselves from us. He who does evil, him shall the government punish, but it shall not compel and govern faith, as you think. It [faith] belongs to the heart and the conscience and not to the external man." Those who were persecuting the Anabaptists, she said, should read the booklet written by Martinus Bellius to Duke Christoph of Württemberg after the death of Servetus in Geneva, in which he had collected the opinions of all the pious and the learned regarding the treatment of erring men called heretics. To be sure, the authorities believed that the Anabaptists would soon begin such a tyranny that the cities and villages would become empty. Strasbourg was not yet an example of mercy, sympathy, and acceptance of the wretched; there was still many a Christian in it whom the authorities would have liked to see driven out. Matthäus Zell had not done this, but had gathered the sheep instead of scattering them. Nor had he consented to such a policy except with a sad heart and great earnestness, since the theologians once complained to the authorities that he had said openly in the pulpit, "I take God, heaven, and earth as my witness on that day that I will be innocent of the cross and the expulsion of these poor people." NEFF, W.W.

T. W. Röhrich, *Mitteilungen aus der Gesch. der Evang. Kirche des Elsasses* III, 165-67 (Paris, 1855); W. Stähelin, *Elsässische Lebensbilder aus dem 16. u. 17. Jahrh.* (1869), 241-42; A. Hulshof, *Geschiedenis van de Doopsgezinden te Straatsburg* (Amsterdam, 1905) 43, note; *ML* IV.

Zell, Matthäus (1471-1541), the founder of the Protestant church in Strasbourg, the most popular preacher in the city, born Sept. 21, 1471, at Kaisersberg, Alsace, studied at the universities of Mainz and Erfurt, lived for a time in Italy, and served in the army of Maximilian I against the Swiss. In 1517 he became the rector of the University of Freiburg, and after the termination of this service became a priest at the cathedral in Strasbourg. He sided vigorously with the Reformation as a follower of Luther, and through his pious deeds and his speaking ability won great respect. He was the first to conduct the Mass in German in Strasbourg and to administer the Lord's Supper in both forms. Therefore he was subject to persecution by the Catholic authorities. In reply to the charge of heresy made against him by the Catholics he published his (originally in Latin) *Christliche Verantwortung Matthes Zell von Kaysersberg . . .* in 1523. He gave faithful support to the Reformers, such as Bucer, Capito, Hedio, and Pollio. In 1524 he married Katharina Schütz, and was therefore excommunicated; nevertheless he was kept in his office by the city magistrate. He was zealous in the care of the church and the school, always retaining a conciliatory mind; thus the Anabaptists, persecuted throughout the world, also found a defender in his wife (see **Katharina Zell**). Although Zell did not agree with the Anabaptists in all points, he opposed the use of violence in combating them. He declared from the pulpit that he was not in agreement with the regulations proposed by Bucer, Capito, and other officials and that he agreed with the principal doctrine of the Anabaptists, i.e., that the government in matters of faith was not justified in using measures of violence. Zell's doctrine of the communion also touched the Anabaptist view. According to Röhrich, he replied to Melanchthon's question on this matter, stating that he did not believe that one received the body and blood of Christ in a communion substantially, essentially, really, and naturally; the devil had brought these words from hell. He said further that

Christ had simply said, This is my body, this is my blood, and he would stick to that and not believe otherwise than Christ his Lord had spoken.

LOSERTH, W.W.

Ludwig Keller, *Ein Apostel der Wiedertäufer* (1885) 167; T. W. Röhrich, *Mitteilungen aus der Gesch. der Evang. Kirche des Elsasses* III, 132 f. (Paris, 1855); W. Stähelin, *Elsässische Lebensbilder aus dem 16. und 17. Jahrh.* (1869) 239; ML IV.

Zeller, Jörg, was very likely won for Anabaptism by Ludwig Haetzer. In his home in Ost-Krautheim, Bavaria, Zeller himself baptized several persons in 1527, one of them being Jörg Dorsch (*q.v.*). Dorsch later confessed that Zeller had said to him that no one could be saved without baptism, for Christ had said to His apostles: "Go ye into all the world and preach the Gospel to every creature. He who believes and is baptized shall be saved." Upon this presentation they had knelt down and Zeller had baptized them and had said: "In the name of the Father, of the Son, and of the Holy Ghost, arise from sins and sin no more; do penance." His brother Andres Dorsch and his wife, as well as Turbe Schnabel, had been baptized by Jörg von Passau (see **Nespitzer**). (*ML IV. TA Bayern I.*)   W.W.

Zellinger, Andreas, an Anabaptist of Halberstadt, Germany, was imprisoned in Rosenheim in 1578. In June of that year he was burned at the stake. His hymn, "Mit Gottes will Trauerns viel hab ich mein Liedlein zu singen," which he composed in prison, in its simplicity breathes religious inspiration and hope for heavenly peace and eternal joy. A poem, *Täufers Sterbelied* (Günther, 24), describes his martyr's death.   W.W.

R. Günther, *Der heilige Garten* (Heilbronn, 1911) 24; *Mennonitische Jugendwarte* V, 146; ML IV.

Zelter, Kunigunde, an Anabaptist, a member of the Baiersdorf (*q.v.*), Bavaria, Anabaptist congregation. With ten fellow believers she lay in the prison in Baiersdorf. Before her judges she said that she had been baptized by Hans Hut; she could not believe that one is reborn through baptism. Baptism is only a sign that they accept a God-fearing life and should desist from sin. She said that Hut had further told them that one should give the government its due. (*ML IV.*)   W.W.

Zemstvos: see Sanitätsdienst.

Zendingsraad, Doopsgezinde (Mennonite Missionary Council). Until 1957 the Dutch Mennonite Mission Association (*q.v.*) acted apart from the A.D.S. (*q.v.*), missions being a concern only of missionary friends. But the annual meeting of the A.D.S. on June 25, 1957, resolved to take over the work administered by the Zendingsraad. This means that the foreign missions of the Dutch Mennonites are now the affair of the entire brotherhood.   W.F.G.

Zeper, a former Dutch Mennonite family (descended from Jan Dircx), from the 16th century at Leeuwarden, Friesland, where they were merchants and soap manufacturers. The Zepers were usually progressive and liberal, in the 18th century adhering to Collegiantism (*q.v.*); Pier Jansz Zeper was baptized by immersion at the Collegiant center at Rijnsburg (*q.v.*) in 1781. At the same time they were loyal

members of the Mennonite church. Jan Dirks Zeper (1736-1801), married to Nieske Tichelaar, like his father operating a soap factory at Leeuwarden, a deacon in his home church, was an ardent Patriot (*q.v.*) and an opponent of the Reformed magistrates. In 1785 he founded a volunteers' corps and in 1787 he was the leader of a revolt against the Frisian government; after the failure of his military expedition Jan Zeper fled to Germany, settling on a large estate at Hahn in Holstein where he engaged in forestry and peat-digging. He was very wealthy. His son Pier Zeper (1761-1845), married first to Neeltje Kool and later to Fenna Hesselink, was the owner of a brewery, a soap factory, and other businesses at Leeuwarden. He too was an ardent Patriot; in 1796 he was banished for his political activity, but soon returned to Leeuwarden where he held high political offices, being a burgomaster of Leeuwarden in 1817. He was a deacon of the Leeuwarden congregation and 1806-36 treasurer of the Conference of Friesland (FDS). His son Dirk Zeper (Leeuwarden, 1803-81), married to Dirkje Bienema, also a manufacturer, was also a deacon at Leeuwarden, from 1837 treasurer of the FDS, and 1835-39 a trustee of the A.D.S. He served as burgomaster of Leeuwarden 1865-71. Other members of this family were Sybrand Allard Waller Zeper (1874-1937), State Archivist at Leeuwarden 1924-35, and Jacobus Waller Zeper, 1903-d.33 a trustee of the Haarlem Mennonite Church.   vdZ.

N.N.B.Wb. IX, 1311 f.; *Encyclopedie van Friesland* (Amsterdam, 1958) 714 f.

Zerotin (Zierotin; in Hutterite spelling, Scherotin), a noble Czech family which flourished in the 16th and early 17th centuries, owning large estates in Moravia and Bohemia. Some of its members admitted the Hutterites to their domains and protected them in times of adversity against royal and imperial oppression.

The ancestral home of the Zerotins lies in northern Moravia, from where they expanded to other parts of the country. They adhered strictly to the teachings of John Hus (d.1415); during the 16th century most of them were members of the Bohemian Brethren (*q.v.*), called Unitas Fratrum, and were among the most ardent supporters of the Brethren, respected by them for their learning, devotion, and generosity.

In the 16th century the family was divided into three main branches: (*a*) Frederick of Zerotin (d. 1598), of the branch residing in Napajedl, Moravia, rose to prominence about the middle of the century, and became the most important personality of the Moravian nobility. He served in various capacities under three Hapsburg rulers: Ferdinand I, Maximilian II, and Rudolphus II. He distinguished himself in the wars against the Turks, and in 1594-98 held the highest office in the provincial government of Moravia, that of governor (*Landeshauptmann*), representing the crown in that province. By his first marriage in 1569 he acquired the manorial estate of Seelowitz (Czech, *Zidlochovice*) in southern Moravia, and in 1574 purchased also the smaller estate of Pausram (Pouzdrany) to round up his possessions. Toward the Anabaptists he was most kindly disposed, and at one time (1589) not less than eight

Bruderhofs existed on his possessions. He died childless in 1598, and his property was divided among his relatives.

(*b*) Bartholomew of Zerotin (d.1569), of another branch of the family, owned land along the Moravian-Hungarian boundary. He purchased the boroughs of Lundenburg (Breclav) with several villages, including Billowitz, *c*1530. After his death the estate passed on to his son John the Younger, and in 1582 to John's son, Ladislav Velen, then still an infant but destined to a leading role in the political life of Moravia. Ladislav Velen received a careful education, studied abroad, and traveled extensively, becoming broad-minded and tolerant. He supported the Hutterites, who always praised him as their great friend. In 1589 there were on his lands not less than ten Bruderhofs. He participated actively in the rebellion of the Protestant nobles against the Hapsburgs and ardently supported the candidacy of the Count Palatine Frederick V to the crown of Bohemia. Under this new king (1619-20) Ladislav Velen headed the provincial administration of Moravia (1619-21). After the collapse of this rebellion he left his homeland to organize campaigns for its reconquest from the Hapsburg rulers. His activities were supported by other Protestant exiles but ended eventually in complete failure. He died somewhere in Poland in 1638.

(*c*) John the Elder, of another branch of the family in southwestern Moravia, attended one of the schools of the Unitas Fratrum, and for some time had the learned bishop of that church, John Blahoslav, as his mentor. John the Elder's loyalty and munificence to the Unitas could hardly be surpassed. Among other things he sponsored the translation of the Old Testament into Czech by a group of scholars. Together with Blahoslav's translation of the New Testament the complete Czech Bible was printed (in 6 volumes) at John's estate of Kralice in 1579-93, and is therefore commonly called the Kralice Bible. In 1562 John purchased the estate of Rossitz (*q.v.*) (Rosice), well known also as one of the earliest Anabaptist settlements.

After John's death his oldest son, Charles (Karl) the Elder (1564-1636), took over a large portion of the family domain, leaving the rest to his younger brother John Divis (sometimes called John Dionysius). Charles resided first at Rossitz and later at Prerau (Prerov). He was considered one of the wealthiest nobles of Moravia. He spent his formative years abroad, partly in Calvinist schools and partly in royal courts, including that of Elizabeth of England, but remained loyal to the Unitas Fratrum. Well known is his correspondence with leading Reformed theologians in Geneva and Basel. He was respected by friends and foes alike for his learning, personal integrity, and tolerant spirit. For many years he held a seat in the highest provincial tribunal, and served as governor of Moravia 1608-15. Unlike his cousin Ladislav Velen, Charles hesitated to join the ranks of the anti-Hapsburg faction, anticipating a collapse of the Protestant revolt of 1618-20. **After the defeat of the Protestant troops at the White Mountain** (1620) he was exempt from trials, confiscations, and fines. Although living in an awkward position, he nevertheless made several interventions

66

on behalf of the Anabaptists who in 1622 were banned from Moravia and hard pressed by the victorious Catholic party (see **Counter Reformation**). In 1627 Charles left his homeland and settled in Silesia, but as his health declined he was granted permission by Ferdinand II to return to his castle in Prerau in 1633. Three years later, in October 1636, he died there.

Charles' brother John Divis had inherited the manorial estate of Seelowitz from his uncle Frederick and held it until his death in 1615. His attitude to the Anabaptists was just as friendly as that of Frederick, so that under his administration their prosperous communities suffered no serious damage in spite of the rising political tensions and the growth of the Catholic Church (see **Moravia**).

O.O.

* * *

The Hutterite Chronicle mentions the different members of the Zerotin family not less than 16 times, testifying always to their kindliness and protection in the face of the encroaching power of the Hapsburgs and the Counter Reformation in Moravia. They are mentioned for the first time in 1545, when a Bruderhof was established at Bartholomew's Lundenburg estate and another at Napajedl. The last record (1624) applies to Karl von Zerotin, who tried unsuccessfully to retain the Brethren in his service in spite of the expulsion order of 1622. During the devastating Turkish Wars Frederick of Zerotin tried in vain to convince the imperial treasury (*Hofkammer*) in Vienna (1596) that the Brethren were not able to pay (or to "loan") the government all the money asked for. No wonder the Anabaptists deeply mourned the death of Frederick in 1598, whom they called "our Fritz."

The Bruderhofs located on the estates of the different branches of the Zerotin family (in 1589 a total of 18 colonies) were as follows: Altenmarkt near Lundenburg 1545, Bisentz 1545, Durdenitz 1559, Gostal (from 1559 a Zerotin possession), Eibis or Meubes (Czech, *Eivany* or *Ivany*), Lundenburg 1545, Napajedl 1545, Neudorf near Lundenburg 1570, Nikolschitz 1570, Nusslau, Pausram 1574, Pillowitz 1545, Pohrlitz 1581, Pribitz, one of the largest Bruderhofs of the Hutterites, 1565, Rampersdorf 1545, Rossitz (from 1562 a Zerotin possession), Wacenowice 1571, Welka-Hulka (or Holka) 1560. (See **Hutterian Brethren,** and maps *ME* II, 858-60.)

R.F.

Peter von Chlumecky, *Carl von Zierotin und seine Zeit, 1564-1615,* 2 vv. (Brno, 1862); Frantisek Hruby, *Ladislav Velen ze Zerotina* (Prague, 1930); Otakar Odlozilik, *Karel starsi ze Zerotina* (Prague, 1936); Beck, *Geschichts-Bücher,* 322; *ML* IV.

Zeugnis der Schrift, a 16-page 6 x 9 inch (several issues of larger format) monthly published by the Herbert (Sask.) Bible School (MB). The first issue, September 1924, contained the catalog of the Bible School. Beginning with November 1925 the journal was published by the Rundschau Publishing House, Winnipeg, Man. William J. Bestvater, the principal of the Bible School, served as editor until publication ceased in December 1929, assisted by A. H. Unruh, principal of the Winkler Bible School, 1925-29. In July 1944 Bestvater resumed the publishing of *Zeugnis der Schrift* as a 12-page mimeographed monthly. He also published an English edition, *Witness of the Word,* a 12-page monthly, with a few exceptions. Both were written and produced by the author at 6908 Park Drive, Bell, Cal., to present a "prophetic" interpretation of the Scriptures. The last German and English issues of the paper found in the BeCL are dated December 1947. **C.K.**

Zeugnisse von Christo, a 4½ x 6¾ inch 36-page monthly, edited and published by Jakob and Abraham Kroeker at Spat, Crimea, Russia, first issue January 1901. Two issues are in GCL (January and February 1901); the further history is unknown. The editors announced the periodical as a "collection of sermons," one to be printed each month, each to be "by a brother and worker in the work of the Lord." The first number contained a full sermon by Jakob Friesen, preacher in Rückenau, on Rom. 1:16, plus an extracted sermon by F. L. Meyer on I Cor. 9:27; the second contained a sermon on Rom. 6:23 by Elder David Dürksen and one by C. H. Spurgeon. The agent for America was J. F. Harms of Medford, Okla. Twenty sermons were collected and published in one volume entitled *Zeugnisse von Christo.*

The BeCL has a volume with nine monthly installments containing two to three sermons each by Jacob Friesen, F. L. Meyer, David Dürksen, Jacob Kröker, Spurgeon, Johann Fast, F. B. Meyer, E. H. Hopkins, Isaak Regehr, Viebahn, Abr. Wall, J. Hudson Taylor, J. G. Kargel, and J. Reimer. **H.S.B.**

Zevenhuizen, a hamlet in the Dutch province of South Holland, formerly the seat of a Flemish Mennonite congregation, which in 1664 sided with the Zonists (*q.v.*). The congregation was small in membership and the pulpit usually vacant. Shortly after 1713 it died out. **vDZ.**

Blaupot t. C., *Holland* I, 330, 341; II, 43; *DB* 1896, 48; 1918, 69.

Ziadowitz (Czech, Zadowice), in the 16th century a manorial estate in Moravia where there was a Hutterian Bruderhof: see **Schädowitz.**

Ziegler (Zeigler, Zigler), a Mennonite family of Swiss origin. The name was formerly prominent in the Franconia Mennonite Conference (MC), and found also among the Mennonites and Amish Mennonites in Lancaster and Butler counties, Pa., and in eastern Ohio. Zieglers have also lived in Fulton County, Ohio, and in Cass County, Mo. Immigrant Michael Ziegler (c1680-c1765) was born in Germany, migrated to America before 1717, settling in Perkiomen Twp., now Montgomery Co., Pa., and was affiliated as a minister with the Skippack congregation (*q.v.*). He was one of the subscribers to the Dordrecht Confession of Faith in 1725. His son Andreas (c1707-c97), a son-in-law of Preacher Dielman Kolb, was ordained preacher in 1746 and bishop in 1762; he also served in the Skippack congregation and preaching circuit. He and Bishop Abraham Swartz deposed Christian Funk from his office of preacher and bishop in 1778 for Funk's favorable attitude toward the American Colonies during their rebellion against the British Crown. Andreas Ziegler

was one of the three signers and possibly chief author of a letter of March 1, 1773, from Skippack to Holland, giving much valuable information on the Pennsylvania Mennonites. (See *MQR* III, 1929, 225-34 for the text of the letter.) The Ziegler family has also played a major role in the life and history of the Church of the Brethren. **J.C.W.**

Ziegler, Dorothea: see Frölichin.

Ziegler, Georg, a tailor of Strasbourg, who associated with the Anabaptists and gave them hiding places and lodging, confessed that he had done it at Capito's request. "He is a suspicious and seditious man. He has composed his doctrines in rhyme and was early an adherent of Hans Denk."

T. W. Röhrich, "Zur Geschichte der strassburgischen Wiedertäufer in den Jahren 1527 bis 1543," *Ztscht für die Hist. Theologie* (1860) 34; *ML* IV.

Zieglschmid, A. J. Friedrich (1903-50), philologist and editor of Hutterite literature. Born in Plauen, Germany, he came to America in 1922; he became professor of Germanic linguistics at Northwestern University, Evanston, Ill., and at the time of his sudden death was professor at the University of Akron, Ohio. In 1938, during a trip to Europe, he discovered Hutterite manuscripts in Slovakia and Hungary, welcomed by him as documents of early New High German. Some of the texts thus collected (epistles) he published later in the *MQR* (1941, 42 and 43) in a letter-perfect edition; in 1940 he published also a lengthy essay on the Hutterites under the title, "Die ungarischen Wiedertäufer bei Grimmelshausen" (*Zeitschrift für Kirchengeschichte* LIX, 1940). Soon thereafter he decided to visit the present-day Hutterites in South Dakota in search of similar linguistic material. To his joy he "discovered" there the original of the Greater Chronicle (and later also the Smaller Chronicle). Since the Wolkan edition of 1923 was exhausted, the Brethren asked him to undertake a new edition, this time—upon his suggestion—in a letter-perfect form. In 1943 *Die älteste Chronik der Hutterischen Brüder* appeared, a volume of 1200 pages, with glossary, bibliography, maps, and ample, valuable footnotes, now an indispensable tool for Anabaptist research, published by the Carl Schurz Foundation in Philadelphia. Four years later, in 1947, the *Klein-Geschichtsbuch der Hutterischen Brüder* followed, a volume of 800 pages, in modernized German, likewise with full scholarly apparatus, issued by the same publisher. Up to the year 1802 Zieglschmid could use Johannes Waldner's (*q.v.*) text, but for the years 1802-1947 he had to find his own way, using an amazing variety of unknown or little-known material of great value, collected in part during many visits at the Bruderhofs of Canada and South Dakota. Next, Zieglschmid set out to produce a new critical edition of *Die Lieder der Hutterischen Brüder* (first edition at Scottdale, 1914), a tremendous undertaking covering more than 4,000 typewritten sheets. His sudden lamentable death cut short his endeavors; the manuscript is still awaiting publication (deposited in GCL).

Starting as a philologist knowing little of the church-historical significance of his subject, Zieglschmid very soon became so intensely interested in the life and fate of the Brethren that all his later work (after 1940) became truly a work of love and dedication. The Hutterites responded warmly to this service and acknowledged it publicly by a letter printed in the *Klein-Geschichtsbuch* (773).

Other publications by Zieglschmid include "The Hutterians on the American Continent," *German-American Review* VIII (1942); and "An Unpublished 'Hausbrief' of Grimmelshausen's Hungarian Anabaptists," *Germanic Review* XV (April 1940).

R.F.

R. Friedmann, "A. J. F. Zieglschmid, an Obituary," *MQR* XXIV (1950) 364 f.

Zielen-weide *der Godvruchtige, of Verzameling van Geestelyke Liederen* (Groningen, 1741), a Dutch hymnal containing a preface by G. T. St., and 271 hymns without notes, on 706 pages.   vDZ.

Zierikzee, a town on the island of Schouwen-Duiveland in the Dutch province of Zeeland (1947 pop. 6,964, with 13 Mennonites), was formerly the seat of a Mennonite congregation. Both Galenus (*q.v.*) Abrahamsz and Pieter Cornelisz Plockhoy (*q.v.*) were natives of Zierikzee. Anabaptism arose here as early as 1534; in 1535 Adriaen (*q.v.*) Aersen suffered martyrdom at Zierikzee, and on Sept. 4, 1536, four Anabaptists were executed here—Adriaen (*q.v.*) Jorisse, Pieter (*q.v.*) Gerritsz, Janneken (*q.v.*) Mels, and Jan (*q.v.*) Jansze; Adriaen (*q.v.*) Cornelisse was executed at Zierikzee in 1537. According to K. Vos all these martyrs were revolutionary Anabaptists. Paulus (*q.v.*) Harrouts died as a martyr at Zierikzee in 1540. None of these victims were natives of Zierikzee; they had come to spread Anabaptist doctrines. The information found in the sentence of Adriaen Cornelisse that he had conversed with many persons in Zierikzee and distributed "many books, full of great errors and heresies" shows that there was also an evangelical Anabaptist movement among the citizens of Zierikzee. Soon after this a small congregation may have arisen; Leenaert (*q.v.*) Bouwens baptized only two persons here. But an influx of Mennonite refugees from Flanders, Belgium, *c*1574 strengthened the Zierikzee congregation. Dirk (*q.v.*) Andries had shortly before been the last martyr to die at Zierikzee. About 1600 the baptized membership stood at *c*100 and the church was active. In 1567, after the Flemish-Frisian quarrels had seriously harassed the Dutch Mennonite brotherhood, the Zierikzee congregation as an exception refused to side with either the Flemish or the Frisians, preferring "to stand still," i.e., to be neutral. They published the booklet *Christelijcke Proeve* (*q.v.*) in 1570 to explain their neutrality, and also to admonish the Flemish and the Frisians to peace and love, insisting on the unity of the church. They were called "Stilstaanders" (*q.v.*) and were banned by both branches. The broad views and real Christian principles of the Zierikzee church may have been strengthened by Valerius (*q.v.*) de Schoolmeester, who for half a year in 1564 had lived at Zierikzee. At first the congregation was disturbed by the Reformed pastors, and on Sept. 4, 6, and 23, 1609, religious disputations were held at Zierikzee

between a Reformed pastor and the Mennonite elders Cornelis de Kuyper (*q.v.*), Jan van der Voort (*q.v.*), and François de Knuyt (*q.v.*). In 1632 Anthonis Cornelisz and Pieter Jansz Timmerman signed the Dordrecht (*q.v.*) confession in the name of the Zierikzee congregation. In 1664 after the *Lammerenkrijgh* (*q.v.*), it wished to recognize both the Lamists (*q.v.*) and the Zonists (*q.v.*) as Christian brethren, though its sympathy was mostly with the Lamists.

Among the membership in the 17th-19th centuries the following family names are found: van der Sluys, Ta(c)k, Kleeuwens, Ammirael, de Blo(c)k, den Boer, van der Kolk, van der Wissel, Hemeryck. Only a few ministers' names have come down: the capable François de Knuyt was its elder in the early 17th century; Anthonis (Tonis) Cornelisz Timmerman, obviously his successor, was still active in 1645. Elder Marinus Kleeuwens is named *c*1700, and the last ministers were Anne Thomassen 1722-d.27, Willem van Gulick 1728-d.61, and Samuel Adriaensz Tack 1765-d.1808. Concerning the membership information is very scarce: in 1750 there were some 50 baptized members, in 1808 only 13. In 1727, 1733, and 1736 the congregation liberally contributed to the relief of the Prussian Mennonites. After the death of Samuel Tack in 1808 no new pastor was called. For a few years the pastors of Middelburg and Goes held occasional services here. By 1820 the congregation had dissolved.   vDZ.

Inv. Arch. Amst. I, Nos. 214, 1164, 1175, 1180, 1996; II, Nos. 1261, 1267, 2367-91; II, 2, Nos. 578 f., 584, 587, 589, 592, 677; Blaupot t. C., *Holland* I, 24, 28 f., 124 f., 192; II, 42, 101, 229, 231; Mellink, *Wederdopers*, 167, 223f., 316 f., 323; H. W. Meihuizen, *Galenus Abrahamsz* (Haarlem, 1954) 5-20; *Naamlijst* 1810, 83 f.; *DB* 1864, 122; 1876, 67; 1897, 106; 1907, 165, 167, 168, 169; 1912, 36, 38; 1917, 172.

Zierikzeeërs: see Stilstaanders.

Ziffersystem (Numerical Musical Notation). Thousands of friends of the chorale and the hymn today still read music from numerical notes, which are used to some extent in Germany, France, and Holland. The most loyal and most numerous adherents of this number system, however, were the Mennonites in Russia. From here the system was carried by the various migrations to the United States and Canada and recently (1922 ff.) to Paraguay, Mexico, and Brazil.

According to *The Story of Notation* by C. Willems, Souhaitty, a Franciscan monk of Paris, suggested in 1677 that the figures 1 to 7 be used instead of *ut, re, me, fa, sol, la, se* and that points be added to locate their position on the staff.

In Rousseau's system and in Raymond's work of 1824 dots above and below the figures were to locate the note in the octave; but this was apparently found inadequate. Then Jacob, a French violinist, advised in 1769 that the staff without a signature should be used and numbers be used instead of notes. Other contributors to the method were Pierre Galin (1786-1821), Aimé Paris (1798-1866), and Emile Chevé. Of all these pioneers Rousseau was perhaps closest to the realization of this idea, a practical, easily learned system. It was developed in

Germany by Bernhard Christian Ludwig Natorp (1772-1836), a theologian, who made it acceptable for singing. In 1813 Natorp used the figures 1 to 7 for the steps of the scale, indicating the location of the note on the staff by placing a single line under, on, or over it, and using a zero as a rest, and indicating length by adding dashes, dots, and commas. His work went through five editions in Germany. Of his works the following can be mentioned: *Ueber den Zweck und die Einrichtungen des Melodienbuches für den Gemeindegesang* (1822) and *Ueber den Gesang in den Kirchen* (1817).

The only Mennonite songbook using numerical notation is the one edited by Heinrich Franz for the Mennonite churches of South Russia, printed at Leipzig, Germany, 1860 and 1880. Five editions were printed in America: two at Elkhart, Ind., 1878 and 1918, and three in Manitoba, the last in Altona in 1953. (*ML* IV.)   J.P.C, E.H.B.

Zijbrandt Claesz, an Anabaptist executed at Amsterdam, Holland, on May 14, 1535. Zijbrandt, a blacksmith of Alkmaar, a follower of Jan (*q.v.*) van Geelen, had participated in the siege of the Amsterdam town hall on May 10-11, 1535. He was put to death in a brutally cruel manner. (Grosheide, *Verhooren,* 63 f.)   vDZ.

Zijldijk, a hamlet in the Dutch province of Groningen, the seat of a Mennonite congregation, formerly belonging to the Groningen Old Flemish branch. The congregation existed from about 1550; Leenaert (*q.v.*) Bouwens baptized eight persons here (possibly only two, the six others having been baptized at 't Zandt, *q.v.*, a village about four miles south of Zijldijk). The Zijldijk meetinghouse, dating from 1791, is a fine specimen of the old barn type. The membership was always small: *c*130 in 1710, 89 in 1733, 33 in 1767, 13 in 1802, 62 in 1861, 83 in 1900, 39 in 1926, 65 in 1958. Most of the members live in the villages surrounding Zijldijk. On Nov. 11, 1686, the congregation was severely struck by a flood, seven adults and fourteen children of members perishing in the waters; much livestock was lost. Among the old family names in this congregation are Dijkema, Eendhuizen, Rengers, Doornbos, Huizinga, Coolman, and Gorter.

Until 1804 the Zijldijk church was served by lay preachers chosen from the members. In that year the first outside minister was called: A. S. Cuperus, serving 1804-d.12, followed by Simon Gorter 1813-56. The first minister educated at the Amsterdam Mennonite seminary to serve here was A. Hermansz ten Cate, serving 1856-66, followed by S. Cramer 1866-70, I. H. Boeke 1870-72, L. T. Goteling Vinnes 1873-73, A. Mulder 1874-88, R. Kuiken 1891-93, D. Haars 1895-1902, A. de Vries Mzn 1903-6, D. Attema 1907-9, S. H. N. Gorter 1910-12, W. J. Hilverda 1913-16, H. Bussemaker 1917-24, N. van der Zijpp 1926-28, W. Mesdag 1929-34, Th. van der Veer 1934-39, Miss M. Knot 1939-46, and M. J. J. Gaaikema 1947- . Church activities are a women's circle, Sunday school, and a young members' group.   vDZ.

Blaupot t. C., *Groningen* I, 52, 87, 127, 140, 142, 197, 238; II, 225; *DJ* 1840, 42; *DB* 1861, 154; 1872, 2; 1879, 6; 1900, 122.

Zijpe, a polder in the northern part of the Dutch province of North Holland, reclaimed in 1553, but afterwards often struck by floods, and practically uninhabitable before 1623. Soon after this there were four Mennonite congregations on this polder: (*a*) Nieuwe-Zijp, or Wieringerwaard; (*b*) Oude-Zijp near Petten, also called Zuid-Zijpe, or de Mennistenbuurt; (*c*) Oudesluis, or Noord-Zijpe, and (*d*) on the Ruigeweg, or Schagerbrug. The (*a*) Nieuwe-Zijp congregation merged with Barsingerhorn (*q.v.*) before 1660. (*b*) Oude-Zijp was a Flemish congregation, which was represented at the Flemish conference at Haarlem in 1649 by Pieter Cornelis and Jochem Gillis. Later it belonged to the Zonist (*q.v.*) conference. This congregation had a meetinghouse at de Mennistenbuurt, which was used until 1869, when a church was built at Burgervlotbrug. In 1840 it numbered 88 baptized members and 78 in 1861. It was served by untrained preachers until 1837, the last of whom was Simon Grin 1785-d.1837. The first minister educated at the Amsterdam seminary to serve here was G. Vissering 1837-42, followed by J. Koning 1844-d.48, Taco Kuiper 1849-50, K. O. Feickens 1850-57, S. J. Andriessen 1857-65, J. P. van der Vegte 1866-68, and J. Bakker 1868-73. After the pulpit had been vacant for five years, it was resolved to merge with the (*c*) Oudesluis congregation.

The (*c*) Oudesluis congregation, as well as the (*d*) Ruigeweg (Schagerbrug) church, which had merged into the Noord-Zijpe congregation before 1647, was Waterlander. It had a meetinghouse at Oudesluis (there was possibly also a meetinghouse on the Ruigeweg near Schagerbrug). The membership of this congregation numbered 77 in 1835 and 99 in 1861. It was served by lay preachers until 1829. The first trained minister of Noord-Zijpe was H. G. Coster, serving 1831-36, followed by J. Bodisco 1837-40, H. C. Dronrijp Uges 1843-47, M. van Geuns 1847-50, A. K. Hovens Greve 1850-51, A. S. Hoitsema 1851-53, and H. U. H. Bouman 1854-78.

The union of (*b*) Oude-Zijp (Mennistenbuurt) and (*c*) Oudesluis (Noordzijpe) came about in 1878; then it was resolved to call the united body the Zijpe congregation, to use the two meetinghouses in Oudesluis and the one in Burgervlotbrug, to abandon the parsonages of Oudesluis and Mennistenbuurt, and to buy a house at Schagerbrug in the center of the congregation to be used as a parsonage. The Oudesluis meetinghouse was remodeled in 1906. Pastors of the Zijpe congregation were: K. Gorter 1879-84, H. van Calcar 1886-1903, C. Vis Jz 1906-9, L. G. Holtz 1909-14, M. Huizinga Jr 1914-18, and B. van der Goot 1919-24. The pulpit being vacant then, an arrangement was made with the neighboring church of Barsingerhorn that the pastor of this congregation should also take charge of Zijpe. Noord- en Zuid-Zijpe together numbered *c*180 baptized members at the merger of 1878, 157 in 1900, 108 in 1926, and only 40 in 1958. There is a ladies' circle.   vDZ.

Inv. Arch. Amst. I, Nos. 510, 896, 1187; II, 2472-74; Blaupot t. C., *Holland* I, 47, 252; II, 203, 205; *DB* 1870, 181; 1879, 141; 1906, 195.

Zijpe, Nieuwe: see **Wieringerwaard.**

Zijpp, van der, a Dutch Mennonite family, originally from Lippenhuizen (*q.v.*) in Friesland, from where Wytse Atses moved to Warns (*q.v.*) about 1745. At Warns this family lived for many generations, all members being farmers until recent times, and often deacons of the church. Wytse Atses was a preacher of the Gorredijk-Lippenhuizen congregation 1726-*c*45 and probably also at Warns, though the years of his serving are unknown. His son Atse Wytses (1725-1808) was a (lay) preacher of the Warns congregation from 1750 until his death. He was a somewhat conservative but capable and assiduous leader, moderator of the Zuiderklasse (*q.v.*). He was nominated curator of the University of Franeker in 1796, when there was question of appointing a Mennonite professor of Theology at this university. He too was a farmer. His children took the family name of van der Zijpp in 1810.

Wietze Sierds van der Zijpp (1831-1915) was a deacon of the congregation at Molkwerum for 42 years. Pieter N. van der Zijpp (1859-1924) was for many years treasurer of the Warns congregation and his brother Jacob N. van der Zijpp (1869-1949) a deacon at Hindeloopen. Nanne (Jacobs) van der Zijpp (b. April 2, 1900, at Warns) was educated for the ministry at the university and Mennonite seminary at Amsterdam and served as pastor at Zijldijk 1926-28, Joure 1928-40, Almelo 1940-46, and Rotterdam 1946- . Since 1946 he has taught Mennonite history in the Amsterdam Mennonite Seminary, since 1954 has been a *lector* (professor) of the Amsterdam University. His chief publication was the *Geschiedenis der Doopsgezinden in Nederland* (Arnhem, 1952); he is assistant editor of the MENNONITE ENCYCLOPEDIA, being responsible for the Dutch part.
vDZ.

N.N.B.Wb. V, 1186 f.; *Naamlijst* 1731, 37; 1743, 31; 1808, 78; Blaupot t. C., *Friesland*, 186, 221, 363; *DB* 1874, 96, 113; 1900, 42 f., 47, 60; 1901, 94-106, 114 f.; *De Zondagsbode* XXII (1908-9) No. 37.

Zilles Leitgen Kremers, an early Anabaptist leader, who was in Münster (*q.v.*) in 1534, sent from there on Dec. 31, 1534, as an emissary to 's Hertogenbosch, Netherlands, but captured at Jülich (*q.v.*), is not identical with the Elder Zelis (*q.v., Zillis, Zylis*). Whether Zilles Leitgen Kremers is the same person as Leitgen(n) (*q.v.*) is doubtful. (Mellink, *Wederdopers,* 314.)
vDZ.

Zillis (Zylis): see **Zelis.**

Zimmerauer: see **Simmerauer.**

Zimmermann, a Mennonite family found in West Prussia and South Germany, and also in the United States. In 1940 there were 33 Zimmermann members of the Mennonite Church in Germany, 19 in West Prussia (Danzig 10, Tiegenhagen 6, Thiensdorf 3), 13 in South Germany (Ueberlingen 5, Ludwigshafen 4, Stuttgart 3, Regensburg one), and Crefeld one. Much information about the West Prussian Zimmermanns is contained in Kurt Kauenhowen, editor, *Mitteilungen des Sippenverbandes der Danziger Mennoniten-Familien Epp-Kauenhowen-Zimmermann* (Göttingen, 1935-43). It is most probable that the West Prussian Zimmermann family was originally called Timmerman (Dutch for

"carpenter") and that Timmermann (*q.v.*) was the form used until the 18th century in the Danzig area. Carl Heinrich Zimmermann (d. 1897) was on the Danzig city council. Louis Edward Zimmermann kept a diary (17 volumes) before the migration to Nebraska and during the pioneer years (BeCL).

There was also a Swiss Mennonite Zimmerman family. Henry Zimmerman came from Wädenswil, Switzerland, to Germantown, Pa., in 1698, but returned to Switzerland. By 1706 he was back in Germantown and by 1710 at Lampeter, Lancaster Co., Pa. His son Emanuel Carpenter, a judge, not a Mennonite, gave the Mennonites important help. The descendants of this branch of the family carried both names, Carpenter and Zimmerman. Hans Timmerman (d.1771) settled in the Cocalico district, Lancaster County, about 1717. Henry and Hans were the ancestors of many Lancaster County Mennonite Zimmermans. Two church cemeteries were named for the family, one at Lichty's and another at Martindale. Among the many ministers of this family name in the Mennonite (MC) and O.O.M. churches were Jacob Zimmerman (1784-1856), bishop at Weaverland 1815-56, "One-Arm John" M. Zimmerman (1829-1903), a preacher at Weaverland, Benjamin F. Zimmerman (1851-1930), bishop in Cumberland County, Pa. (Slate Hill), 1892-1930. Now serving in the Lancaster Conference are Mahlon Zimmerman, a bishop at Ephrata since 1952, and Christian and Norman Zimmerman, ministers at Slate Hill. The O.O.M. in Lancaster County have the ministers Isaac N. Zimmerman, Isaac W. Zimmerman, and Noah Zimmerman.

A Christopher Zimmerman was in Germantown in 1708, and a trustee by the same name was serving the Worcester congregation (MC) in the Franconia Conference in 1739. A Zimmerman family was among the pioneers in the Black Creek Mennonite settlement in Welland County, Ont., near Buffalo at the beginning of the 19th century. John Henry Zimmerman came from Prussia to Beatrice, Neb. Joseph E. Zimmerman (1880-1949) was the bishop of the Milford Amish Mennonite (Neb.) congregation 1916-49. (*ML* IV, 608 f.)   H.S.B., I.D.L.

Zimmermann, Andreas, of St. Georges, Tirol, an Anabaptist martyr, was executed at Michelsburg (*q.v.*) sometime between Sept. 13, 1533, the date of his trial at Michelsburg, and Oct. 15, 1533, when his son Christoph reported his father's death at a court examination. The content of Andreas' testimony is given in Hartmann Ammann, "Die Wiedertäufer in Michelsburg," *XLVI. Programm des K. K. Gymnasiums zu Brixen* (Brixen, 1896) 25 f. (*ML* IV.)

Zimmerman Mennonite Church (MC), now extinct, was a congregation of the Lancaster Conference in Carroll County, Md. The meetinghouse built by John Zimmerman in 1858 is located 2 miles south of the Mason and Dixon Line, and 3½ miles southeast of Linesboro. There had previously been a log meetinghouse across the lane. John K. Zimmerman deeded the tract in 1866 to Abraham Hostetter and Samuel T. Bechtel, trustees of the Hanover congregation. The cemetery near by is mentioned in the farm deed. The congregation was never large, and since the land was not too fertile, the members moved away; by 1921 services were discontinued. It was a part of the York-Adams County Bishop District (q.v.).

Zimmerman was the name of two cemeteries in Lancaster County, one of them associated with the Lichty meetinghouse, although a half mile away, and the other with the Martindale (q.v.) meetinghouse near by. The former is used rarely today, but the O.O.M. use the latter. Both are well kept.

I.D.L.

Zinspenning, Judith: see Sewel, William.

Zinzendorf, Count Nicholas Ludwig von (1700-60), a Silesian Pietist nobleman, renewer of the Moravian brotherhood, b. May 26, 1700, in Dresden, Germany. Although by profession he was a legal adviser at the court of the King of Saxony in Dresden until 1727, his primary interest was the kingdom of God and the saving of men. He was ordained a Lutheran minister at Tübingen in 1734. Banned from Saxony in 1736 because of his "separatistic" activities, he established his headquarters first in western Germany in the Wetterau, then 1751-55 in London, and at last on his own estate in the village of Herrnhut.

The chief interest of Zinzendorf's life, however, was the Moravian Brotherhood (Unitas Fratrum). In 1722 he gave the pitiful remnants of the Bohemian Brethren, fleeing from their homeland, asylum on his family estate of Berthelsdorf. The village which was built for them was named Herrnhut (i.e., The Lord's Protection). In 1727 the Brethren, some 300 in number, were reorganized, with Zinzendorf as their leader, becoming a new church within the general framework of Lutheranism, but with an intense sense of mission to revive the general church and to evangelize the heathen. Zinzendorf was ordained bishop of the Renewed Brotherhood in 1737 and served until 1741, when he resigned. His intense passion for the unity of all true believers, which was a dominant motive throughout his life, made him one of the first "ecumenical" leaders, although in practice no visible results in this direction were attained and he remained throughout his life basically the great leader of a great evangelistic and missionary group, called in America the Moravian Brethren Church.

Zinzendorf spent much of his life from 1737 on in traveling on two continents in the promotion of his missionary and ecumenical vision. His first major trip was to the West Indies in 1739, followed by two (1741-43) years in America (chiefly Pennsylvania). Switzerland, Holland, England, and Livonia were also included. He was directly connected with the establishment of the Moravian settlements in Pennsylvania in 1741, himself giving the name Bethlehem to the new town. Zinzendorf died at Herrnhut, May 6, 1760.

Zinzendorf's direct connection with the Mennonites is limited to two areas, Holland and Pennsylvania. In Holland it was with the Amsterdam Mennonite minister Joannes Deknatel (q.v.; 1695-1759), whom he met during his visit to Amsterdam in February and March 1736. A warm friendship developed between them, and Deknatel, while remaining a Mennonite, actually joined the Moravian Brethren congregation in Amsterdam, organized Nov. 25, 1738. Zinzendorf celebrated communion in Deknatel's home in 1737. The influence of Zinzendorf and the Moravians upon Deknatel, the Dutch Mennonite Pietist, was profound. Later the relationship cooled off, influenced among other things by Zinzendorf's inability to repay a loan from Deknatel.

The second contact with the Mennonites was in Pennsylvania. Zinzendorf attempted to establish a united fellowship of all German-speaking Christians in the colony in 1742, an attempt which failed dismally. For this purpose he called a series of seven synods, to which representatives of all groups were invited, in the hope of forming "The Pennsylvania Congregation of God in the Spirit." These were held as follows: Jan. 1, 1742, at Germantown; Jan. 14, 1742, at the home of the Schwenckfelder George Hiebner; and Feb. 21, 1742, at the home of the Huguenot Jean DeTurck at Oley. Only the first three synods were important, for the movement was obviously a failure, and the remaining four synods accomplished little but to condemn all the sects except the Moravians and the Quakers.

According to the published proceedings Mennonites were present in at least the first three synods, although nothing is known of their identity. On Jan. 12, 1742, Zinzendorf is said to have visited "a venerable but unnamed Mennonite leader" to explain to him the purposes of the synods and the aims of the Unitas Fratrum, and to invite him to attend the Second Synod. "The Mennonite received the count graciously, listened patiently, but declared that the time was too short to send qualified delegates to his meeting" (Stoudt). Apparently the Mennonites in attendance at the synods were not official delegates. One of the last four synods is said to have met in a Mennonite home in the Oley region. No trace of these meetings has been found in any Mennonite records, and there was no observable influence of Zinzendorf's work upon the Mennonites of Pennsylvania.

Augustus Spangenberg, next to Zinzendorf the outstanding leader of the Moravian Brethren, who had come to Pennsylvania as an evangelist and missionary, gave added impetus to a unique interdenominational fellowship established in 1736, called the Associated Brethren of Skippack, of which Henry Antes was the real leader, and which lasted about three years, and may have had some bearing on the Mennonites in this area. Meetings were held monthly at the home of Christoph Wiegner, a Schwenckfelder, on a farm at Skippack. "Some twenty to thirty men from communities as widely separated as Skippack, Fredericktown, Oley, and Germantown comprised the core of the union," whose meetings were for the purpose of "edification and mapping of strategy for evangelizing the Germans." "The Wiegner farm was Spangenberg's home during his first stay of three years in Pennsylvania and his evangelistic labors were greatly facilitated by the co-operation which the group meeting there gave him" (Weinlick). The Associated Brethren was the forerunner of Zinzendorf's ecumenical attempt, and according to Stoudt its membership formed the nucleus of Zinzendorf's synods. It would be surprising if none of the Skippack Mennonites were ever in contact with or attended the meetings of either the Associated Brethren or the synods. (See **Moravian Church, Moravians in the Netherlands, and Pietism.**)　　　　　　　　　H.S.B.

John R. Weinlick, *Count Zinzendorf* (New York, 1956); John J. Stoudt, "Count Zinzendorf and the Pennsylvania Congregation of God in the Spirit, the First American Ecumenical Movement," *Church History* IX (1940) 366-80; *DB* 1885, 71 ff.

Zion Arapahoe (Indian) Mennonite Mission Church (GCM) is located 2 miles south of Canton in Blaine County, Okla. Missionary work among the Arapahoe (*q.v.*) Indians in this district was begun by S. S. Haury at Cantonment 1883-87. Other workers were J. J. Kliewer 1887-89, D. B. Hirschler 1889-90, Paul Mouttet 1890-92, A. S. Voth 1892-93, N. L. Weis 1893-95, and J. A. Funk 1897-1907. In 1907 the church was moved from Cantonment to its present location and continued by J. A. Funk 1907-20, Albert Claassen 1920, G. A. Linscheid 1920-21, H. T. Neufeld 1921-27, H. J. Kliewer 1927-36, G. A. Linscheid 1936-38, Benno Toews 1938-40, Arthur Friesen 1940-47, and Alfred Wiebe 1947- . The total number of Arapahoe baptized has been 236. The present (1952) living members total 111.　　A.Wɪ.

Zion Church of God in Christ Mennonite Church, located near Inman, McPherson Co., Kan., was established when Gerhard Ensz, a minister of a local Mennonite group, and six members withdrew and were baptized on the basis of repentance and the new birth. Worship services were conducted in homes and schools until the meetinghouse was built in 1922. Abraham G. Ensz and Peter A. Friesen, the first resident ministers, were ordained during its history, Ensz serving as pastor until his death in 1936. John A. Ensz and Abe R. Toews were also ordained and are now in charge. The membership in 1954 was 159.　　　　　　　　H.A.E.

Zion Hill Mennonite Church (MC), in the Middle District of the Virginia Conference, is located in the foothills of the North Mountain, 3 miles west of Singers Glen, Va., and 2 miles northeast of Sparkling Springs. In 1925 the first services in this area were held in the home of Charlie Lamb or in the woods near by. The Zion Hill meetinghouse was built in 1927, when L. H. Jones and A. W. Hershberger were serving as ministers. In 1958 Hiram Weaver and Paul S. Good were serving as pastors, with a membership of 49.　　　　　　　H.A.B.

Zion Krimmer Mennonite Brethren Church, located near Dinuba, Tulare Co., Cal., was organized in March 1911 when the meetinghouse was erected, under the leadership of J. Z. Kleinsasser, who served as the first pastor. The principal occupation of its members is grape farming, with cotton and dairy farming next. The following ministers have served: J. Z. Kleinsasser, J. A. Wiens, A. J. Bearg, J. P. Glanzer, J. J. Kleinsasser, D. V. Wiebe, C. F. Plett, and Clarence E. Hofer, who was pastor in 1957. In 1957 the membership was 238.　　　　　C.E.H.

Zion Mennonite Church (MC), Sankra, India: see **Sankra.**

Zion Mennonite Church (GCM), located near Goodland, Jasper Co., Ind., a member of the Central District Conference, organized in 1895 by D. D. Augspurger, the first Central District church in Indiana. In 1898 the present church building was erected. From this congregation came two foreign missionaries, who served under the Congo Inland Mission, two home mission workers, and one minister. The membership in 1957 was 48, with Dale Schertz as minister.　　　　　　　　　　　　D.S.

Zion Mennonite Church (GCM) of Donnellson, Lee Co., Iowa, a member of the Middle District Conference, was organized in the autumn of 1851, and constructed a combined school and church building in 1855, two miles north and one mile west of Donnellson. This building was replaced in 1880 by separate buildings. The present edifice in Donnellson was built in 1909 and the old site is used as a cemetery. The parochial school, begun in 1853, which gradually evolved into a summer German school, was discontinued in 1917.

In 1859 the Zion and West Point congregations invited all Mennonites of North America to a general conference, resulting in the formation in 1860 of the present General Conference Mennonite Church. The Zion congregation co-operated in organizing the Central District Conference (then Western) in 1868. The Iowa churches helped in founding the Wadsworth School (*q.v.*), Ohio, 1868; Christian Schowalter, Zion pastor and teacher, served as its first principal. The membership in 1957 was 208; the pastor was Harold Thiessen.　　　　　　　　　　　　　　V.H.N.

Zion Mennonite Church (GCM), located at Kingman, Kan., was formed when a division occurred in the Bethany Mennonite Church (*q.v.*). In October 1932 the new congregation was accepted into the Western District Conference. Its first leader was Joseph J. Kaufman. The first minister was J. R. Duerksen, followed by J. R. Barkman, Jacob Unruh, J. H. Epp, William Unrau, Ramon H. Jantz. The membership of the group remained near 60 for 25 years; in 1957 it was 56, with B. E. Bonebrake as pastor.　　　　　　　　　　　　J.F.S.

Zion Mennonite Church (GCM), located in Elbing, Butler Co., Kan., a member of the Western District Conference, was organized on June 10, 1883, with 14 charter members, who were a part of the immigrant group which came to Kansas in 1876 from Heubuden and Ladekopp, West Prussia. Originally worshiping with the Emmaus Mennonite Church near Whitewater, they soon found the distance to that church too great and built their own church one-half mile east and one mile north of Elbing. When this first building became too small, a new church was built in Elbing, and dedicated on Oct. 19, 1924, which building is still in use.

The church has shown an active concern for home and foreign missions. It assisted in the founding of Berean Academy (*q.v.*) in Elbing in 1946. Missionaries and ministers coming from the church have been the following: Marie Dyck, later Mrs. Ernst Kuhlman, to China in 1906; Abraham H. Regier, ordained in 1905; Henry J. Dyck, ordained in 1905; Walter H. Dyck, ordained in 1936; Paul Kuhlman, ordained as missionary to China in 1936; Arnold J. Regier, ordained to the ministry in 1940.

Pastors who served the church since its founding have been the following: Peter Dyck (*q.v.*) 1883-85, Cornelius H. Regier 1885-1921, Jacob W. Regier 1892-1919, John P. Andres 1907-32, Henry J. Dyck 1921-51, Cornelius J. Dyck 1951-54, and Waldo W. Kaufman 1954- . The membership in 1957 was 152.

C.J.D.

Zion Mennonite Church (MC), Vestaburg, Mich., is located several miles south of the town. Under the Indiana-Michigan Conference, the congregation was organized in 1914. Erie E. Bontrager was pastor of its 25 members in 1959. M.G.

Zion Mennonite Church (GCM; correct name "Mennonite Zion Church"), located 3½ miles south of Arena, Burleigh Co., N.D., a member of the Northern District Conference, was organized in 1908. The services were held in schoolhouses until 1925 when a school building was bought, removed to the present site and remodeled into a church. In 1956 it was enlarged to seat 80. The first pastor was Sam Preheim in 1910. In 1957 the membership was 38, with Peter B. Loewen as pastor. H.S.B.

Zion Mennonite Church (MC), Archbold, Ohio, is located in the southwest part of the city. Organized in 1955, its meetinghouse was dedicated in 1956. Most of its approximately 250 members formerly were members of the Central Mennonite Church (*q.v.*). In 1959 Philemon L. Frey was its pastor. M.G.

Zion Mennonite Church (MC), now extinct, formerly called Riley Creek, was founded in 1848 about 5 miles west of Bluffton, Allen Co. (*q.v.*), Ohio, by John Thut and a number of his Swiss Mennonite friends. In 1843 Thut had been ordained minister at the Longenecker Mennonite Church (*q.v.*). He and his family were making the wagon-trail journey to Elkhart County (*q.v.*), Ind., when Swiss friends near Bluffton persuaded him to settle in Allen County. But when, at the first communion service, the Swiss did not observe footwashing, Thut's group withdrew and in 1862 erected the Riley Creek church about five miles west of Bluffton. Isaac Steiner, Thut's first helper in the ministry, withdrew when he was criticized for attending his wife's church (the Winebrennerians, *q.v.*). Christian Bare, ordained in 1856, left in 1857 to accept the offer of a farm to preach for the Yellow Creek (*q.v.*) congregation in Elkhart County, Ind. David Geiger, ordained *c*1858, united with the Herrites (Reformed Mennonites, *q.v.*). In 1867 John Thut was ordained bishop, but the same year after a tour of some of the Ohio churches he became ill with typhoid fever and died. Abraham Steiner and Christian P. Steiner, ordained in 1869, the former very conservative and the other progressive, could not agree and were both silenced. Abraham Steiner left to found an Egli (Defenseless) Mennonite Church (now Evangelical

Mennonite Church, *q.v.*), taking with him the deacon. C. P. Steiner was reinstated and worked patiently to rebuild the congregation. Finally with the help of John S. Coffman and Ohio evangelists he built one of the strongest MC congregations in the state. Most of the members were descendants of John Thut or related to the family by marriage. M. S. Steiner (*q.v.*) was a prominent minister. In 1892 the congregation erected a new church building which they named Zion.

During the second decade of the present century the leadership of the Zion congregation passed into the hands of instructors of Bluffton College who had resigned their positions at Goshen College. In the late 1920's, after some difficulties with the Ohio and Eastern A.M. Conference (*q.v.*), the congregation voted to disband and razed the building. The majority of the congregation united with the Bluffton First Mennonite Church (GCM). A small cemetery marks the location of the former Riley Creek meetinghouse. J.S.U.

John S. Umble, "Zion (Bluffton) Congregation" in "Early Mennonite Sunday Schools of Northwestern Ohio," *MQR* V (1931) 179-97.

Zion Mennonite Church (MC), located about 7½ miles northeast of the town of Pryor, Mayes Co., Okla., was organized in May 1911 under the leadership of B. F. Hartzler (minister), who with several other families moved to the community from Cass County, Mo., as a member of the Conservative Amish Conference. In 1912-15 several families from the disintegrating congregation at Stuttgart, Ark., moved in and joined this congregation, comprising about half the membership. In August 1938 the congregation became a member of the South Central Conference.

The first services were held alternately in the Ogreeta schoolhouse and a machine shed. English was always used at the schoolhouse, while the other service was partly German. A church was built sometime later. In 1921 the vacated building at Stuttgart was moved to the present church site and in 1947 a basement was placed under this building. For three periods of one year each the congregation was without a minister, during which the deacon served. The membership in 1957 was 108, with Richard Birky as bishop and John Troyer as pastor to begin official service in May 1959. The membership in 1958 was 104. N.H.

Zion Mennonite Church (MC) is situated on a hill about 4 miles east of Hubbard, Clackamas Co., Ore. Zion formerly belonged to the Western Amish Mennonite Conference, but since the merging of conferences in 1920 it belongs to the Pacific Coast Conference. It had its beginning as a Sunday school in a dwelling house southeast of Hubbard. On June 19, 1893, the congregation was organized in the Rockhill Methodist Church. In 1894 the present site was chosen and the church building built, which was enlarged in 1910. In 1957 the membership was 295; Edward Z. Yoder was the minister, and C. I. Kropf the bishop. In 1958 John Lederach became the pastor. A branch Sunday school conducted by the Zion congregation near Mulino, Ore., became an independent congregation in 1958. E.G.KEN.

Zion Mennonite Church (GCM), located 4 miles from Dallas, Polk Co., Ore., a member of the Pacific District Conference, was organized in 1897 and was discontinued in 1931, when the building was moved to Dallas and the congregation reorganized and renamed the Grace Mennonite Church (*q.v.*). J.M.F.

Zion Mennonite Church (MC), Birdsboro, Pa., is located half way between Reading and Morgantown and a half mile off Route 122. Organized in 1949 as an outpost of the Conestoga (*q.v.*) congregation, it had 98 members in 1958, with Jesse Yoder and Noah K. Mack serving as ministers. It is a member of the Ohio and Eastern Conference. M.G.

Zion Mennonite Church (GCM), now extinct, located in Mann's Choice, Bedford Co., Pa., was begun in 1915 in an abandoned church by Herman Snyder, who served this group together with Napier, 4 miles away, until his death in 1917. The highest membership was 49 in 1926. In 1935 the Eastern District Mission Committee, which had supported the work, closed the church. H.S.B.

Zion Mennonite Church (GCM), located at 203 E. Broad St., Souderton, Montgomery Co., Pa., had its origin in 1887 as a small mission of Mennonite and unaffiliated families led by N. B. Grubb, pastor of the First Mennonite Church of Philadelphia. In 1892, with financial aid from the Eastern District Conference, a church was built 36 x 46 ft. In 1893 the congregation was organized with 19 charter members. The life and growth of the congregation is evident in the record of building renovations and expansion—1908, 1915, 1925, and 1940. In 1954 a 15-acre tract was purchased as a future expansion site, the purpose being to have an integrated church program ministering to the total needs of man—physical, mental, and spiritual. In 1958 the membership, mostly urban, was 655. The following have served as pastors: Allen M. Fretz 1893-1910, J. W. Schantz 1910-16, Reed F. Landis 1916-23, Grover T. Soldner 1923-31, Ernest J. Bohn 1931-44, Ellis Graber 1944-59. E.Gr.

Zion Mennonite Church (MC), York, Pa., located at Canford and East streets, was founded in 1954 under the Ohio and Eastern Conference by a group who withdrew from the Lancaster Conference. In 1957 it had 47 members, with J. Eby Lehman and H. Frank Leaman as ministers. M.G.

Zion Mennonite Church (GCM), Bridgewater, S.D., is a member of the Northern District Conference, but not of the General Conference. With its background in the Hutterian immigration of the 1870's, it was organized in 1940. It is located in Bridgewater. In 1958 Paul Dahlenburg was pastor of its 45 members. P.Da.

Zion Mennonite Church (MC), 3 miles south of Broadway, Rockingham Co., Va., is a member of the Virginia Conference in the Northern District. About 1890 a Sunday school was organized for the summer months, using for its literature the Question Book authorized by the Lancaster Conference and the New Testament. The first meetinghouse, built in 1885, was replaced in 1941 by a new brick building, with a basement and facilities for Sunday school and an audience room for the literary society of the young people. The church yard, which contains five acres of land, has a home for the janitor and a beautiful cemetery adjoining the church. The membership in 1957 was 138; the bishop in charge was J. Ward Shank; the minister was J. Otis Yoder. T.S.

Zion's Call. The first official organ of the Defenseless Mennonite Conference (now Evangelical Mennonite) was a German paper (*Heilsbote*) (*q.v.*) begun in 1898. In the same year an English monthly was begun, edited and printed by D. N. Claudon, and called *Zion's Call*, for many years published in the interests of the Salem Orphanage. In 1913 it was adopted as the official organ. At first it was a 4-page monthly, and for several years, up to about 1918, in pamphlet form of 32 pages. In 1920 authorization was granted to publish *Zion's Call* with *Good Tidings* under the name of *Zion's Tidings*. *Good Tidings* had been a publication of the Mennonite Brethren in Christ Church. In 1953 *Zion's Tidings* and *Gospel Tidings* (a publication of the Evangelical Mennonite Brethren) were merged under the name *The Evangelical Mennonite*, the present name. Others who have served as editor were Ben Rupp, Aaron Sauder, and E. E. Rupp, until 1920. Then Amos Oyer was editor for a few years with G. P. Schultz as assistant, and E. E. Zimmerman as managing editor. About 1924 G. P. Schultz assumed the entire responsibility for printing. Following his resignation H. E. Bertsche assumed the duties. From *c*1942 E. G. Steiner assumed the work as editor. While Bertsche was editor the paper was changed from an 8-page monthly to a 12-page and later to a 16-page. Since the merger in 1953 E. G. Steiner has been editor, C. A. Classen (from the EMB Conference) associate editor, and E. E. Zimmerman executive or general manager (since 1933). At present there are 24 pages. E.E.Z.

Zion's Tidings: see Zion's Call.

Zionsbote, German organ of the Conference of the Mennonite Brethren Church of North America, was first published in the autumn of 1884, as a four-page quarterly at a subscription price of 25¢ per year. It soon (1886) became a semimonthly (enlarged to 8 pages in 1889) in 1904 a weekly of 16 pages, and in 1958 biweekly. It was printed the first two years by the Mennonite Publishing Company at Elkhart, Ind., and thereafter successively at McPherson, Kan.; Hillsboro, Kan.; Medford, Okla.; McPherson again; and since 1913 at Hillsboro.

The purpose of the publication of the *Zionsbote* was to acquaint the churches with the work in the field of evangelism and church polity in order to stimulate the church life. Later it published reports from mission fields, both foreign and home, and also reports from the individual churches. From its beginning subscribers have not been confined to members of the M.B. Church. Until 1914 the *Zionsbote* was widely read in the churches of Russia; nearly 1,000 copies were sent there weekly. The M.B. Publishing House is the publisher. J. F. Harms served as editor 1884-1906 and as assistant editor 1922-34. Other editors have been A. L. Schellenberg, J. D. Fast, and P. H. Berg. The present editor is Orlando Harms, and the subscription stands at 1600-1800.   P.H.B.

Zionspilger, Der (The Pilgrim to Zion), a Swiss Mennonite periodical published by the Emmenthal Mennonite congregation (*q.v.*) at Langnau, canton of Bern, Switzerland, since January 1882, as a 4-page 10 x 14 inch monthly to June 1884, bimonthly July 1884-97, weekly since 1897.

The editor has customarily been the leading elder or pastor of the Emmenthal congregation: Samuel Bähler 1882-d.90, Johann Kipfer 1890-97, 1901-43, Mathias Pohl 1898-1900, Johannes Rüfenacht 1943- . In 1918-40 the journal had a second editor besides Kipfer to represent the Freie Gemeinde, and in 1918-21 the name was changed to *Freie Zeuge (q.v.) vormals Zionspilger*. The *Zionspilger* has been a devotional-type journal with news of the Swiss congregations and in recent years brief items of Swiss and world news. Earlier some correspondence from Germany and America was printed, and in the time of Bähler and Pohl some Anabaptist and Mennonite historical material. A considerable portion of the readership has been non-Mennonite.   H.S.B.

Zirgkendorffer, Bernhard, a victim of the Anabaptist persecutions of the Swabian League (*q.v.*), was captured on April 24, 1528, with Eitelhans Langenmantel (*q.v.*) at Leitheim, Bavaria, and although he recanted Anabaptist teachings in the hope of saving his life for the sake of his family, he was executed at Weissenhorn on May 11, 1528. He was baptized by Burkhard von Ofen at Göppingen, his native town, in the home of the miller in the presence of Conrad Huber and Peter Schleppach of Augsburg and the wife of Peck of Bergen. Of interest is the description of the instruction preceding the baptism. He was active in the care of the poor under the leadership of Nespitzer (*q.v.*). The record of his trial is found in Roth, pp. 12-14 and 24-27. HEGE.

Friedrich Roth, "Zur Geschichte der Wiedertäufer in Oberschwaben; II, Zur Lebensgeschichte Eitelhans Langenmantels von Augsburg," *Ztscht des hist. Vereins für Schwaben und Neuburg* XXVII (1900) 1-132; *ML* IV.

Znaim (Znajmo), Moravia, a city (pop. 19,565) in Czechoslovakia, where Anabaptism found early entry and met with violent persecution in 1528. The Hutterite Chronicle lists seven martyrs at Znaim. That Anabaptism was not wiped out by this persecution is seen from the records of the trials of Anabaptists from Moravia imprisoned in Passau (*q.v.*) in 1535-36 who mention numerous Brethren from Znaim and the vicinity and their leaders. Thus Matthes of Auer confessed that he had been staying for 1½ years in and around Znaim with 50 Brethren. Stoffel Aschenberger, the leader of the group seized at Steinabrunn (1539) and condemned to galley slavery, wrote a letter at Falkenstein, where they were first imprisoned, to the ministers and leaders at Znaim (1540). Although they were from time to time pushed out, they always managed to return. Thus in 1559 they had a religious disputation in Znaim with the emissaries of the Bohemian Unitas, Jan Jelecky and Wenzel Solin. Later the Anabaptists were not beheaded or burned at the stake, but expelled; on Oct. 23, 1571, Balthasar Tischler, Hans Truchel, a woman, and an old glazier met this fate. A similar fate befell the Brethren who had been called by the city council to repair the fountain at the upper square and who had done their work well and cheaply. Among the nobility of the vicinity the Anabaptists had a notable friend in Wenzel Rischan, lord of Rosenstein, who kept them in his mill at Nesslowitz, for which reason he was accused at the imperial court and was consequently compelled to expel the Anabaptists. To avoid carrying out the decree he sold his mill to Adam Kaigel, who was just as benevolent to the Anabaptists as his predecessor. They were considered quiet, industrious, and honest workers and were used by the citizens in their businesses, in spite of objection by the city council and the clergy. According to a note in the archives of the Dominican monastery at Znaim there were Anabaptists also at Zerotitz, Garwitz, Jaispitz, and Durchlass, with a leader who had his seat at the Aumühle near Durchlass, but was expelled with his people by imperial orders in 1613. (Zieglschmid, *Chronik*, 232; *ML* IV.)   LOSERTH.

Zoar Academy and Bible School. At the 1914 annual conference session of the Krimmer Mennonite Brethren, it was agreed to erect a building for a Bible school. The Zoar K.M.B. Church of Inman, Kan., was delegated to take the initiative in planning and building a school at Inman. The following spring a two-story brick building was constructed, with two classrooms on the main floor and an auditorium on the second, on land contributed by Peter Vogt. On Sept. 30, 1915, the building was dedicated, and in a few days the school opened its doors to 29 students for a six months' term. Under the able administration of Frank V. Wiebe the enrollment in a few years increased to 70. After several years the term was increased to eight months and later to nine months. In keeping with the objective of this school, the subjects of the first years were Bible and related subjects. With the nine months' term secular subjects were offered along with the Bible subjects, which remained compulsory. The purpose of this school as stated in its catalog was "To give the student a thorough Bible knowledge, to build and cultivate a strong Christian character, to train for leadership and Christian service."

This school operated for 30 years under the direction and support of the Zoar church and community. It gradually became obvious that better facilities had to be provided. In a united effort with other Mennonite churches in the Hutchinson and Buhler area, an inter-Mennonite corporation was organized, which established the Central Christian High School in Hutchinson, Kan., in 1948, in which the Zoar constituency had an active part.   D.C.P.

Zoar Krimmer Mennonite Brethren Church of Inman, Kan., was organized in 1879. Mr. and Mrs. Gerhard Kornelson, who had been baptized two years earlier, were instrumental in organizing a group of 24 members. Jacob Klassen (d.1918) was their first leader, and later elder. Others who have served as elders or leaders of the church are John Esau, K. K. Willems, D. C. Pauls, and A. L. Friesen. The first meeting place was a sod schoolhouse. In 1883 a church was built 5 miles southwest of Inman. The present building was built in 1901. In 1957 the church had 209 members, with Arnold Ensz as pastor. D.C.P.

Zoar Mennonite Church (GCM), located in Waldheim, Sask., was organized about 1910. A meetinghouse was built in 1912. In 1922 the congregation joined the Canadian and General conferences. Its membership in 1959 was 208, with John A. Block as pastor. J.A.BL.

Zoar Mennonite Church (GCM), near Goltry, Okla., a member of the Western District Conference, was organized in 1909 by settlers coming largely from McPherson County, Kan. The first meetinghouse was built in 1909-10, enlarged in 1939 to a seating capacity of 350. The membership in 1957 was 138, with Victor Graber as pastor. J.BU.

Zoar Mennonite Church (GCM), located in the town of Langham, Sask., a member of the Canadian District Conference, was organized in 1910 and built its meetinghouse in 1911. The membership in 1958 was 180, with Elder Henry A. Wiens as pastor. The church has had one other minister ordained as elder, J. J. Nickel, ordained in 1941. H.A.W.

Zobel, Georg (d.1603), a Hutterite physician in Nikolsburg (*q.v.*), Moravia. Apparently he was a real doctor (not only a barber-surgeon) and the most famous of the numerous Hutterite physicians (see **Medicine, Hutterite**). In 1581/2 he received the special honor of being called to the court of Emperor Rudolph II (*q.v.*) in Prague. The chronicle reports that the emperor "had many famous doctors from Italy, Spain, and other lands," but no one could really help him (he was afflicted with melancholia). As a last resort the doctor of the (generally despised) Anabaptists in Moravia, who was highly esteemed by the nobles, was called. Zobel stayed in Prague for six months, the emperor improved noticeably, and "some of the barons said that the emperor would have died if he had not received our physician." In 1597 (or 1599) Zobel was again called to Prague, this time to advise the government concerning an epidemic then rampant in Bohemia. In 1593 the Hutterites made Zobel a steward (*Diener der Notdurft*). The abbot of the monastery of Klosterbruck near Nikolsburg, who was a violent opponent of the Anabaptists, called Zobel "my dear friend," inviting him for consultation at the monastery (see **Nikolsburg**). When Zobel died in 1603, the chronicle devoted a whole paragraph to his praise. Of his personal life and his relationship to the brotherhood nothing is known. R.F.

John L. Sommer, "Hutterite Medicine and Physicians," *MQR* (1953) 119-21; R. Friedmann, "Hutterite Physicians and Barber-Surgeons," *ibid.*, 128 f.; Zieglschmid, *Klein-Geschichtsbuch; idem, Chronik*, 567, 594; *ML* IV.

Zobelhof, a Hutterite Bruderhof in Hungary: see **Soblahof(f).**

Zoet (Soet), **Jan** (1610-74), a Dutch (non-Mennonite) poet of Amsterdam, and in later years an innkeeper, in whose tavern "De Zoete Rust" (Sweet Rest) some Collegiant (*q.v.*) poets used to meet and discuss religious problems, including the Mennonites Pieter J. van Rixtel (*q.v.*) and Karel Verloove (*q.v.*). Zoet published many volumes of mediocre verse. His poem "Het Groote Vischnet" (The Big Fishnet) criticizes the churches. vDZ.

N.N.B.Wb. I, 1477 f.; G. Kalff, *Geschiedenis van de Nederl. Letterkunde* IV (Groningen, 1909) 460 ff., 516, 547 f.; C. B. Hylkema, *Reformateurs,* 2 vols. (Haarlem, 1900 and 1902) *passim;* K. O. Meinsma, *Spinoza en zijn Kring* (The Hague, 1896) 118-21.

Zoetermeer, a village in the Dutch province of South Holland, in the 17th century the seat of a Flemish Mennonite congregation, usually called Zoetermeer and Zegwaard. Concerning its history very little is known. It was always subsidized by Rotterdam and other Mennonite congregations. About 1695 Jan van Gaveren was its preacher, but its pulpit was mostly vacant. In 1710-11 this very small church contributed 26 guilders to the relief of the Swiss Brethren, but soon after, according to a letter by the church board of Rotterdam of March 13, 1713, it dissolved. vDZ.

Inv. Arch. Amst. II, 2, No. 514; Blaupot t. C., *Holland* II, 43, 131; *DB* 1918, 69.

Zofingen Disputation, an important debate between Swiss Anabaptists and ministers of the Swiss Reformed Church, held in 1532 in the town of Zofingen, almost equidistant from Zürich, Basel, and Bern, some 30 miles west of Zürich. The "Freie Aemter," today's canton of Aargau, an area situated between Zürich, Bern, and Basel, and administered by Bern under the supervision of the other cantons, were the home of an Anabaptist congregation by the fall of 1525. Because of the more complex administrative arrangements it was more difficult for Bern to take action against Anabaptism there, and the preaching of Hans Pfistermeyer (*q.v.*) could continue with few interruptions until he was led to recant in 1531.

In January 1532 the reformers of Bern, assisted by Wolfgang Capito (*q.v.*), laid the foundations of reformed polity in the *Berner Synodus,* which prepared them, for the first time, to act energetically in a sweeping reorganization of the churches, involving also new action against dissenters in the canton and in Bern's subject lands. The success encountered with Pfistermeyer coincided with the need to legitimize a new rigor in repression, making a disputation with the Anabaptists seem doubly desirable, "so that everyone may be satisfied and no one might claim . . . that we attack them without a hearing" (words of the Bern Council). Safe-conduct was promised to all Anabaptists, and Zofingen in the Freie Aemter was chosen as host city rather than Bern so that they might feel freer to come. No outside participants on the Reformed side were invited, in order to forestall the accusation that the preachers in Bern were dependent on Zürich and Strasbourg, but Heinrich Bullinger provided considerable advice by letter.

The proceedings began on July 1, 1532, with 23

Anabaptists present, of whom Martin Weniger (*q.v.*) of Schaffhausen and Hans Hotz were the main speakers. Berchtold Haller and Caspar Megander of Bern and Sebastian Hofmeister of Zofingen led the eight-man Reformed delegation, of which the apostate Pfistermeyer was also a member. Representatives of the four cities of the Aargau presided, the debating etiquette was irreproachable, and the minutes, kept by three secretaries and offered to all parties involved for verification, were printed in Zürich at once and distributed at the expense of the Bern government.

The following questions were debated in sequence: I. That love is the final arbiter of all disagreements; II. Whose "sending" is valid? III. Which is the true church? IV. The ban (and whether it may rightly be administered by the state); V. The magistracy; VI. Should the Christian pay tithes and taxes? VII. The oath; VIII. The calling of preachers by the state; IX. The support of preachers by prebends; X. Whether the Christian should charge interest; XI. Baptism. In spite of superficial agreements under points I, II, IV, and VI, no progress was made and no Anabaptists were persuaded to recant. The debate (and the safe-conduct for the Anabaptists) ended on the evening of July 9, and the irreproachable etiquette gave way again to persecution (since May 16 of that year it was legal to execute Anabaptists without process of law, to get around the complications of administering the subject territories). Both parties claimed to have carried off the victory in the debate.

Zofingen is the most significant of the Swiss Anabaptist disputations, rivaled only by Bern (1538; cf. *ME* I, 289), in which, however, both positions are less succinctly presented. The issue of baptism, which until 1527 had been the only one to be debated at length, is now dealt with last; it is becoming clear that the Reformed party, in declaring "love" (cf. Article I above; "love" is the concern for the unity and peace of Christian society) to be the ultimate exegetical norm, is seriously qualifying its original Biblicism in the interest of church-state harmony. Two views of the church now stand out against one another in bold relief.   J.H.Y.

Handlung oder Acta gehaltner Disputation und Gespräch zu Zofingen inn Bernner Biet mit den Widertöuffern (Zürich, 1532); John Yoder, *Die Gespräche zwischen Täufern und Reformatoren in der Schweiz, 1523-1538* (Basel doctoral dissertation, 1957) (Karlsruhe, 1959) 127 ff.; **J. H. Yoder and Heinold Fast, "How to Deal with Anabaptists, An Unpublished Letter of Heinrich Bullinger,"** *MQR* XXXIII (1959) 83-95; *ML* IV.

Zollikon, a village at the southern edge of Zürich, Switzerland, the seat of the first Anabaptist congregation, which was in existence eight months, from the end of January to August 1525. It was the only Anabaptist congregation ever established in or in the immediate vicinity of the city of Zürich (*q.v.*). The village inhabitants included at this time, as Bruppacher has shown, about 50 large farm owners and 40 small farm owners. Most of the Anabaptists belonged to the latter class, and some 30 of the 40 joined the movement. According to Blanke, from Jan. 22-29, beginning the day after the founding of the Anabaptist brotherhood in the evening meeting in the home of Felix Manz (*q.v.*) in Zürich on Jan.

21, the day on which the Zürich council proscribed Anabaptism, a total of 35 persons are known to have been baptized, 34 men and one woman, 30 of them independent peasants, and four hired hands. They belonged to such old Zollikon families as Breittiner, Bleuler, Hottinger, Kienast, Murer, Rutschmann, and Thomann. The Hottingers were the most numerous in the group. Chief among them, apparently the leader, was Jakob Hottinger (*q.v.*), the only one who persisted in his Anabaptism beyond 1527, and who was put in prison as late as April 1528 because he did not attend the regular church services but arranged special meetings. Other names among the Zollikon members were Unholz, Schuhmucher, and Schad. Three earlier influential members of the Zollikon "Brethren in Christ," as they called themselves (Heini Hottinger, Felix Kienast, and Hans Murer), were among the soldiers in the army of Zürich who died on the field of battle at Cappel in October 1531.

Fritz Blanke's brilliant account of the Zollikon Anabaptists based wholly on the sources as published in the Zürich *Täuferakten* edited by von Muralt and Schmid in 1952 makes it clear (1) that the Zollikon Anabaptist congregation was the result of a genuine religious revival, in which conviction of sin, repentance, and faith in Christ as Saviour were the carrying experience; (2) that the revival in Zollikon followed directly on the great night service of Jan. 21, the birthday of Anabaptism, where Grebel and Blaurock baptized 15 persons; (3) that Johannes Brötli (*q.v.*), a former Catholic priest, who had joined Zwingli's reformatory movement in the summer of 1523 and was living in Zollikon without a church position, was the first one to baptize a Zollikon inhabitant, and thus in a sense the establisher and first leader of the congregation there; (4) that Conrad Grebel (*q.v.*) led the first communion service on Sunday or Monday, Jan. 22 or 23, in Jakob Hottinger's home, but thereafter had no further connection with Zollikon but started his missionary career in another direction (Schaffhausen); (5) that Felix Manz and Georg Blaurock (*q.v.*) were active in Zollikon for a time in the early weeks and performed baptisms; (6) that repeated arrests and harrying of the members of the Zollikon brotherhood finally broke their will to establish an independent free church and prevented the establishment of a full Anabaptist congregation as occurred elsewhere in Switzerland and South Germany.

Johannes Brötli, the first leader, was expelled from the canton of Zürich on Jan. 29, 1525. On the next day, Manz and Blaurock were arrested with 25 local men, the former imprisoned in the Wellenberg prison tower, the latter in the former Augustinian monastery, where they were kept for eight days. Here the three city pastors, Zwingli, Jud, and Megander, after lengthy discussions, succeeded in securing a compromise whereby the Brethren would be allowed to meet in small groups for Bible reading and study, but would leave the preaching and baptism to the regular city preachers. A letter from Brötli (then at Hallau) to the Zollikon group, after he had heard of the compromise, appealing for steadfastness, has been preserved; in fact the Brethren soon regained their footing and abandoned the compromise.

When Blaurock was released from prison at the end of February 1525, he appeared in Zollikon, held several evangelistic services on Feb. 26, and baptized 10 persons, two men and eight women. On March 12 Georg Schad, a peasant, baptized 40 persons in the Zollikon village church. On March 8-15 some 80 more were baptized, 30 by Hans Bichter, seven by Jacob Hottinger, Jr., two by Hans Huiuff, and one each by Hans Oggenfus and Valentes Gredig; others not listed. Three fourths of the baptized were not residents of Zollikon, but were mostly from the neighboring villages of Küssnacht and Höngg. At the Bible meetings preaching was added, and at each service a communion was held. Meetings were held at five different places in homes, and in groups larger than the limit of four imposed by the earlier compromise. Discipline was practiced through the ban. As Blanke says, "Since they had preaching, baptism, communion, and discipline, they had the four marks necessary for a full independent Christian congregation."

The Zürich council now called to account those Zollikoners who had broken their pledge of February. All those who had presumably baptized, 19 men, practically all the leading Anabaptist personalities of Zürich and Zollikon, were imprisoned on March 16, 1525, in the Augustinian monastery for nine days, during which they were questioned and Zwingli endeavored to reconvert them one by one in separate cells. The pressure was too great; all but four of the prisoners yielded to Zwingli and promised "to desist from rebaptizing and not to speak or act against infant baptism." Blanke comments that this was in effect the breaking of the Anabaptist movement among the peasants of Zollikon. Only a few individuals remained steadfast.

An unusual incident occurred in June 1525, when a procession of men, women, and children of Zollikon marched through Zürich's streets and squares shouting that Zwingli was the dragon prophesied in Rev. 12:3, and calling upon the inhabitants of the city to repent, lest a terrible catastrophe befall them. No doubt some of the members of the former Anabaptist group were in the procession, but clearly none of the leaders took part, since no arrests were made, and when later arrests were made no charges or questions about the procession were ever raised. The forcible suppression of Anabaptism no doubt contributed to the explosion. But such action and the corresponding ideas were not at all characteristic of Zürich and Zollikon Anabaptism, Blanke points out, referring to the fact that of the two dozen extant letters from the Anabaptist circle in 1524-25 only two have any eschatological references, and these are letters of Conrad Grebel. The Anabaptist message, he says, was polarized around the themes of sin and forgiveness, not the end of the world; the documents tell of concerns for the preaching of the true Biblical message, the building of the true church, of baptism, of steadfastness under trial, of defense against false accusations.

There is evidence that the suppressed Anabaptists of Zollikon continued to hold their Bible study meetings after March 1525, although they did not baptize anyone, and they probably did not attend the state church services. In July the Zollikon group sent three Bible readers (Rudolf Rutschmann, Rutsch Hottinger, and Felix Kienast) to near-by Nänikon and Wassberg, in response to requests from these villages, to lead Bible study meetings. As a result, in August the Zürich council issued an order to Jacob Hottinger forbidding the Bible meetings which they had earlier authorized in February. Then the Anabaptist group (thirty in number) met in Heini Hottinger's home and decided "to give up baptizing, simply to live together in a Christian way, and to be obedient to the authorities." This meant, says Blanke, the final burial of the plan to establish a permanent free church in Zollikon and the agreement to give up the congregational Bible meetings and to attend the state church services, whatever the private convictions of the individuals may have been.

The last flicker of Anabaptist spirit in Zollikon manifested itself in June 1527 and proved that there still were private convictions under the surface. Five Zollikoners, Jacob, Uli, and Heini Hottinger, Jakob Unholz, and Felix Kienast, visited two Anabaptists held in prison in Grüningen (q.v.)—Jakob Falk (q.v.) and Heini Reimann, who were facing a possible death sentence. The visitors comforted the prospective martyrs and urged them to stand faithful to the truth to the end.

Jakob Hottinger's statement to his inquisitors in August 1525 is characteristic of the position of the Zollikon Anabaptists. "The state has no power over God's word; God's word is free." He appealed to the Zürich council not to compel attendance at the state church services, but to permit the practice of the Christian faith outside the state church apparatus. He demanded freedom of conscience and freedom of church building. This appeal lies at the very heart of the Anabaptist position. Zollikon was the first place in Protestant history where the establishment of a free and voluntary church was attempted. The attempt failed; it was ahead of the time. F.BL., H.S.B.

The above account is drawn from the unusually fine and scholarly portrayal by Fritz Blanke, Professor of Church History in the University of Zürich, in *Brüder in Christo, Die Geschichte der ältesten Täufergemeinde: Zollikon 1525* (Zwingli-Verlag, Zürich, 1955). Part of the same material was given earlier in Blanke's article, "Zollikon, 1525. Die Entstehung der ältesten Täufergemeinde," *Theologische Zeitschrift* VIII (1952) 241-62, which was published in English as "The First Anabaptist Congregation, Zollikon, 1525," *MQR* XXVII (1953) 17-33; *TA Zürich*; A. Nüesch and H. Bruppacher, *Das alte Zollikon* (Zürich, 1899); Heinold Fast and John H. Yoder, "Bullinger's Letter of 1532, 'How to Debate with Anabaptists,'" *MQR* XXXIII (1959); *ML* IV.

Zomerg(h)em, a hamlet near Gent, Belgium, where the Mennonites from near and far used to meet after nearly all the Mennonite congregations in Belgium had died out because of persecution. In 1630 Elder Jacques van Maldeghem (q.v.) was still preaching in the meetinghouse (*preeckhuys*) at Zomergem, but in that year this last center of Flemish Mennonitism was given up. (*DB* 1876, 96, 101-4, 109.) vDZ.

Zon, De, a Mennonite meetinghouse at Amsterdam, Holland, in 1664-1801 the seat of the Zonist (*q.v.*) congregation, which, having separated from the Lamists (*q.v.*) on June 22, 1664, because of the *Lammerenkrijgh* (*q.v.*), held separate meetings, at first worshiping in a warehouse in de Oude Teertuinen. On Sept. 15, 1664, it bought a stately house, a former brewery on the Singel Canal, with the sign of a sun (Dutch *zon*) on the façade, which it adapted as a meetinghouse, and remodeled in 1683. It acquired a pipe organ in 1786 and was used until April 1801, when the Zonist congregation merged with the Lamists. The Zon meetinghouse was sold in 1802 after the organ and the pulpit had been transferred to the Toren (*q.v.*) meetinghouse of Amsterdam.   vDZ.

Naamlijst 1802, 59-68; DB 1898, 1-54, passim; Blaupot t. C., Holland I, 389.

Zon, De kleine, the name of a meetinghouse and congregation, which in 1670 under the leadership of the preachers Pieter Eyssen (*q.v.*) and Isaac van Vreden (*q.v.*) separated from the Amsterdam Zonist (*q.v.*) congregation. The meetinghouse was located in the Prinsenstraat. In 1679 the congregation reunited with the Zonist church. (*DB* 1898, 5; *Inv. Arch. Amst.* II, Nos. 1393, 1404.)   vDZ.

Zondagsbode, De, a Dutch Mennonite weekly, appeared from Nov. 6, 1887, until June 21, 1942, when it was suppressed by the German military forces then occupying the Netherlands. The 1887-94 issues bear the title *De Zondagsbode, weekblad in Doopsgezinde en verwante Christelijke gemeenten;* it was then much read by the Dutch Baptists and contained news from Baptist congregations. From Nov. 7, 1926, it was the official organ of the A.D.S. It was born from an idea launched by S. de Waard at the 1886 yearly meeting of the Zwolsche Vereeniging (*q.v.*). The 1887 meeting of this association appointed a committee to promote a weekly, which was published in the fall of that year with H. Koekebakker Jr, S. Cramer, and L. Hesta as editors. The next issue was edited by Koekebakker alone, who was the editor until his death in October 1890. Thereupon G. ten Cate was the editor (October 1890-October 1894), followed by P. Feenstra Jr (October 1894-April 1916), J. Wuite (May 1916-1930), and W. Koekebakker (1930-1942). Its successor was the *Algemeen Doopsgezind Weekblad* (*q.v.*), started in 1948.   vDZ.

DB 1887, 133; 1888, 137; 1889, 117 f.; 1895, 145; Stemmen uit de Doopsgez. Broederschap I (1952) No. 1, pp. 18-20.

Zondervan, Pieter Sjoerds (Parraga, Dec. 8, 1863-Deventer, Nov. 6, 1937), was trained for the ministry at the university and the Mennonite seminary of Amsterdam, serving as pastor at Ytens 1889-91, Barsingerhorn 1891-92, and Leeuwarden 1892-1924, when he retired. He was a man of great modesty, yet very learned. Besides some sermons he published *Radicale Christusbeschouwingen* (Leeuwarden, 1916) and a paper, *De Beteekenis van een Christologie op kritisch standpunt* (Assen, 1925). (*DJ* 1939, 17-26, with portrait.)   vDZ.

Zonist Conference (*Zonsche Sociëteit*). Soon after the founding of the Amsterdam Zonist congregation (see **Zonists**) Samuel Apostool and other Zonist leaders tried to win over other churches to their views: in 1665, for example, Apostool visited several congregations in the province of Zeeland. As early as Sept. 9, 1664, a meeting of conservative leaders held at Utrecht drew up the outline of the *Verbondt* (*q.v.*) *van Eenigheydt,* which was approved and signed by the delegates of 23 Zonist churches at a second meeting held at Leiden Oct. 1, 2, 1664. In this *Verbondt* they agreed upon certain principles, such as the strict maintenance of the Mennonite confessions of faith and rejection of Collegiantism (*q.v.*). On the basis of the *Verbondt* a conference was founded on July 18, 1674. In the booklet *Grondt-steen* (*q.v.*) *van Vreede en Verdraegsaemheit* other churches were invited to join the Zonist conference, which in 1674 embraced the 23 churches which had signed the *Verbondt* in 1664 and some 25 others. In 1787 the Zonist conference still comprised 39 congregations. Meetings were held annually until 1787, thereafter every two years, from 1684 to 1796 in the Amsterdam Zonist meetinghouse. The purpose of this conference, which was promoted chiefly by the Amsterdam Zonist church, was to maintain the old Mennonite doctrines as formulated in the confessions of faith. Attempts made in 1684 and 1688 to reunite with the Lamists (*q.v.*) failed; likewise a conference between the Zonists and Groningen Old Flemish in 1766 failed to bring about a desired merger. In 1766 the annual Zonist conference approved the project of having a new confession of faith drawn up by Cornelis Ris (*q.v.*); it was introduced by the Hoorn congregation, but was not officially accepted by the conference until 1776, and even then it was used in only a few Zonist churches.

In 1796 the Zonist congregation of Amsterdam withdrew because it no longer wished to stand for the principles of the conference, and because it was preparing a merger with the Amsterdam Lamist congregation. This actually meant the end of the Zonist conference, which did not hold any meetings after May 25, 1796.   vDZ.

Inv. Arch. Amst. I, Nos. 885-944; Blaupot t. C., Holland I, 344; II, 81-90; DJ 1940, 58 f.

Zonists (Dutch, *Zonisten, Zonnisten, Sonnisten*). About 1660 in the Amsterdam Flemish, Frisian, and High German Mennonite congregation, usually called the church "bij't Lam" or Lamist church, a dissension had arisen between a more conservative part, called the Ouderen or Apostoolsen, and a more progressive part, called the Galenisten (see **Lammerenkrijgh**). These quarrels ended in a schism, Samuel Apostool (*q.v.*) with some other preachers and deacons and about 500 of the 2,000 members separating from the main body on June 22, 1664. The Apostoolsen soon met in the Zon (*q.v.*) meetinghouse; hence they were called Zonists. The schism was caused by differences concerning the valuation of the confessions of faith, the Apostoolsen holding that the Mennonite church was the only true Christian church which was denied by the progressives, and the fact that the Galenists (progressive followers of Galenus Abrahamsz) favored Collegiantism, which the conservatives considered a danger to the church. Among the leaders in the Amsterdam Zonist church were, besides Apostool, men like Michiel Fortgens (*q.v.*), Herman Schijn (*q.v.*), and the austere deacon Lambert Bidloo (*q.v.*). Soon after the schism negotiations were held to heal the rupture, but several discussions (1668, 1672, 1684, 1685, 1688, 1722) failed and it was not until 1801 that a merger came about.

The membership of the Amsterdam Zonist church was *c*500 in 1664, *c*550 in 1743, and *c*300 in 1801. Like its Lamist sister church the Amsterdam Zonists started a seminary for the training of ministers; it was led by the pastor Petrus Smidt (*q.v.*) from 1753 until 1781; the number of students was, however, very small, only 18 in all. The Zonist church of Amsterdam also had an orphanage and an old people's home in the Tuinstraat. In the early 18th century Amsterdam Zonist leaders like Herman Schijn corresponded with the Mennonites in Prussia and were very active in their behalf. Soon after the founding of the Zon, a small group, called *De Kleine Zon* (*q.v.*), separated from the Amsterdam Zonist congregation but joined the mother church again by 1679. In 1752 the Old Frisian congregation at Amsterdam merged with the Zonists, and in 1788 the Old Flemish congregation did so.

Ministers of the Amsterdam Zonist church were Samuel Apostool, serving 1664-99, T. T. van Sittert 1664-d.64, Tobias Govertsz van den Wijngaard 1664-69, Isaac van Vreden 1664-70, Gijsbert ter Singel 1664-67, Jan van Dijk 1664-d.78, Pieter Eyssen 1664-70, Samuel van Deyl 1670-87, Pieter Apostool 1672-80, J. Bording 1675-d.82, N. Veen 1675-d.78, P. J. Beets 1682-d.1710, Michiel Fortgens 1682-d.95, Herman Schijn 1690-d.1727, H. Reynskes van Overwijk 1696-1716 and 1717-25, J. Brand 1701-25, D. van Heyst 1701-16, H. Bakker 1723-d.56, G. Maatschoen 1726-50, Petrus Smidt 1728-d.81, A. Westerhuys 1729-d.36, Joh. Couwenhoven 1754-1801, Corn. van Kampen 1755-81, A. H. van Gelder 1780-1801, M. de Bleyker 1781-d.88, J. Chr. Sepp 1788-1801, and Abr. Tieleman 1788-1801. At the merger Couwenhoven, Sepp, and Tieleman retired, whereas van Gelder remained a minister of the united congregation.

The Amsterdam Zonists, at first very strict and conservative, grew rather liberal at the end of the 18th century, even more liberal than the Lamists. A hymnal, the *Groote Bundel* (*q.v.*), introduced in the Amsterdam Zonist congregation in 1796, breathes a very rationalistic spirit, and the confessions of faith then were no longer appreciated.

Not only at Amsterdam, but also in other congregations, dissensions arose in 1660 and shortly after between the conservative members and the progressives, and in a few churches this led to a schism; for example, in the Haarlem "den Blok" (*q.v.*) congregation in 1671. In other places the congregations began to call themselves Zonist or Lamist. Thereupon the familiar old party names like Flemish, High German, etc., were gradually dropped. Among the congregations sympathizing with the Zonists and soon joining the Zonist (*q.v.*) conference, were a number of Waterlander churches in the province of North Holland, and some Waterlander leaders, like E. A. van Dooregeest (*q.v.*) and P. J. Stapper (*q.v.*), became strong Zonist leaders. In Friesland there was little sympathy with the Zonists, nearly all the churches siding with the Lamists. vDZ.

H. W. Meihuizen, *Galenus Abrahamsz* (Haarlem, 1954) 97 f., 101 ff., 114 f., and *passim;* J. Wuite, "De Scheuring tusschen het Lam en de Zon," *DB* 1900, 1-37; *Inv. Arch. Amst.* I, Nos. 875, 907, 912-26, 944; II, Nos. 5a, 49, 253-55, 308 f., 317, 362-78, 593-608, 746-52, 875, 929-31, 1070-77, 1108 f., 1147, 1243-72, 1281-1343, 1406-38; Blaupot t. C., *Holland* I, 341-45; II, 45, 187.

Zonshofje, a Mennonite home for aged women at Amsterdam, Holland, built in 1765 on the site of the former "Arke Noach" Mennonite meetinghouse (1670-79 of the "Kleine Zon," *q.v.*, and 1720-52 of the Frisian congregation). The home was founded by the Amsterdam Zonist (*q.v.*) church for its members. It was enlarged at the end of the 19th century and now has room for 32 unattached women. vDZ.

Zook (Zaug, Zaugg, Zuck, Zug, Zowg), a Mennonite and Amish family from Signau in the Swiss canton of Bern. Caspar Zougck, of Schuselbühl near Sumiswald, was one of the Anabaptist speakers at the Bern (*q.v.*) disputation in 1538. Uli Zougg, a preacher in the canton of Bern, was imprisoned in 1644. Those in America are the descendants of the brothers Christian, Moritz, and Johannes Zug, who were grandsons of Hans Zoug, a Mennonite preacher of Signau, Bern, who with others was imprisoned in Switzerland for his faith 1660-71. The three brothers arrived in Philadelphia in 1742 and settled in Chester County, Pa. The colonial archives of Pennsylvania list seven other Zugs who arrived in Philadelphia 1727-96, but their descendants do not appear in American Amish or Mennonite history. C. Z. Mast in 1942 estimated the total number of living descendants of the three immigrant brothers at 25,000, the largest concentration being in Chester County, Pa. Many are members of the Mennonite, Amish, Brethren, or Quaker churches. Christian Zug's youngest son became an Amish preacher and his congregation, near Malvern, about 1795 built the first A.M. meetinghouse in America. A considerable number of his descendants and also those of Moritz Zug are Quakers. Shem Zook (*q.v.*), Mennonite writer and historian, and C. Z. Yoder (*q.v.*), M.C. leader in Sunday-school and missionary activities at the turn of the 19th century, are descendants of Moritz. The third brother, Johannes, is the progenitor of a large number of Old Order Amish in Chester County. Many of them are members of the John and Daniel Esch families (see **Esch**). Ordained men bearing the name Zook are found in many states from Pennsylvania to Oregon and from Michigan to Florida, but only in those branches originally related to the Amish: Conservative Mennonite, 2 preachers; M.C., 2 bishops, 3 preachers; O.O.A. (in Pennsylvania). 2 bishops, 5 preachers, and (in Tennessee) one preacher. Ellrose D. Zook is executive editor of the Mennonite Publishing House, Scottdale, Pa. J.S.U.

C. Z. Mast and R. E. Simpson, *Annals of the Conestoga Valley* (Churchtown, Pa., 1942) 196-200.

Zook, Shem (1798-1880), the youngest son of John
Zook (1748-1804) and Fannie Yoder, was born Sept.
26, 1798, in Mifflin County, Pa. He was an alert
Amish Mennonite layman, active as a writer, historian, and publisher during the middle of the 19th
century. He married Veronica Yoder (d.1874) and
was the father of ten children. In 1849 he published
a German edition of the *Martyrs' Mirror*, printed on
the press of King and Baird, Philadelphia, Pa. He
contributed articles to several books and periodicals,
including "Omish Mennonites" in I. Daniel Rupp's
History of Religious Denominations (Philadelphia,
1844) 560-61, and "Amish, Omish or Hooker Mennonites," in the *Lewisburg Chronicle* (Nov. 6, 1850).
A letter signed by Shem and David Zook concerning the origin of the Amish sect appears in the
Register of Pennsylvania VII, No. 11 (March 12,
1831) 162. Another short history of the Mennonites
and Amish written by Shem Zook, entitled "Kurzgefasste Geschichte der Deutschen Täufer oder Mennoniten," appeared in *Verhandlungen der Diener
Versammlungen* (Lancaster, 1862) 19-23. A different article "Kurzgefasste Geschichte der Mennoniten," in *Ermahnungen von George Jutzi* (Somerset, 1853) 329-36, was erroneously attributed to Sam.
Zook. Because of his expert German penmanship
Shem Zook was chosen on several occasions to serve
as secretary to the Amish conferences (*Diener-Versammlungen, q.v.*) (1862-78). He served as secretary with his son-in-law J. K. Hartzler (1838-1906)
at the Amish conferences of 1863 and 1864. In 1880
he wrote and published a 31-page pamphlet, *Eine
Wahre Darstellung* (Mattawana), an account of
early Mifflin County Amish church divisions. A
letter of his is published in *Hertzler Genealogy*
(1885), 119. At the time of his death he had in his
possession many documents and records, but unfortunately these were all destroyed at his home near
Mattawana in the flood of 1889. He died on Dec.
17, 1880. He is buried in the A.M. cemetery near
Mattawana.   J.A.H.

Zorgdrager, Kornelius Pietersz: see Sorghdrager.

Zuberhans, an Anabaptist of Heginsberg near Stuttgart, Württemberg, who confessed on March 27,
1528, that he had been baptized on the previous
Christmas Day in Hainbach by Felix [Pfudler], a
shoemaker of Esslingen. He related that Felix had
taken water in his two hands out of a dish and
poured it upon his head as he kneeled, in the name
of the Father, the Son, and the Holy Ghost. He
then gave Felix three kreutzers for the common
treasury. (*TA Württemberg,* 6, 7, 914, 916.) H.S.B.

Zuckenhammer, Hans (d.1598), a Hutterite leader,
born in Genkhofen, Bavaria, also called "Rotbart"
because of his red hair, a smith by trade, very active
as a missioner in Bavaria and Tirol. The Hutterite
Chronicle records with great detail Zuckenhammer's
experience during one of these missionary trips
when he and his companion, Wolf Raufer, were
caught near Salzburg and imprisoned in Tittmoning, Bavaria, for several weeks in 1579. The remarkable fact of this story is that the two brethren
were rather decently treated in spite of their courageous stand for their faith. Finally the Bishop of

Salzburg allowed them to return home. During
their imprisonment they composed three hymns,
now in the *Lieder der Hutterischen Brüder,* 741-52.

In 1585 Zuckenhammer was made a preacher
(*Diener des Wortes*), or at least confirmed as such
(elsewhere the record says that in 1597 he had been
minister for 17 years). One year before his death he
was "tried" on a charge of not maintaining strict
discipline (the Chronicle devotes six pages to this
affair). The "trial" took place at the Bruderhof of
Protzka, Slovakia, and was presided over by Claus
Braidl, bishop. Zuckenhammer admitted that he
did not deserve to serve as preacher because of
slackness and negligence, but the real accusation
does not become too clear. Finally it was decided
to excommunicate him. He asked to be allowed to
remain with the brotherhood, accepting the penalty
and offering to confess in public. Thus he was first
excommunicated, and soon thereafter restored to
full membership. One year later (1598) he died at
Protzka.

Zuckenhammer's name was formerly attached to
an important Hutterite codex, the "Codex Zuckenhammer" (so named by Beck) of 1583, which contains on 325 leaves the well-known *Ein Schön lustig
Büchlein,* which is the great Article Book (*q.v.*),
now at the Library of the Evangelical Church of
Bratislava, Czechoslovakia (sign. 391 kt). Both
Loserth (237) and Wiswedel (140) assumed erroneously that Zuckenhammer was the author simply
because his name was written on the first page, but
this was merely a sign of ownership. Actually this
work goes back to Peter Walpot (*q.v.*), and the
Codex Zuckenhammer is but one of many such
copies, although it is indeed one of the most beautifully written.   R.F.

Loserth, *Communismus,* 237; Wiswedel, *Bilder* II, 140
(Wiswedel devotes an entire chapter to Zuckenhammer);
Beck, *Geschichts-Bücher,* Zieglschmid, *Chronik.*

Zuercher (Zürcher, Zercher, Zurger, Zurcher, Züricher, Zerger), a Mennonite family of Swiss origin
meaning "of Zürich." The family was early found
in the canton of Bern in the villages of Rüderswil,
Langnau, Sumiswald, and Aarburg.

In 1649 Joseph Zürcher was brought before the
Bernese authorities for being an Anabaptist. The
verdict was that he must either leave or be imprisoned. Hans Zürcher, 40, of Frutigen, was deported in 1711 for not recanting. During the early
part of the 18th century members of the family
moved to the Jura. In 1738 André Zürcher of
Sumiswald is listed as living near Moutier with his
family. In 1768 Peter and Joseph Zürcher of Sumiswald were living at Tramelan in the Jura. Members
of the family moved to Montbéliard during the latter part of the 18th century. The Palatinate Mennonite census list of 1738 names Johannes Zerger.
In 1940, eight Zerchers and 31 Zergers were members of Mennonite churches in South Germany. It
is assumed by C. Henry Smith that Michael Zurger,
who arrived in Pennsylvania on the *Charming Polly*
on Oct. 8, 1737, and Ulerich Zercher, who arrived in
Philadelphia on Sept. 23, 1752, were Mennonites.

In 1821 Abraham and David Zürcher left their
Jura homes and settled in the Sonnenberg commu-

nity, Wayne County, Ohio. This name is still a very common one in this Swiss community and is also found in Adams County, Ind., and in the G.C.M. community near Whitewater, Kan. E. E. Zuercher, Hubbard, Ore., and Isaac Zuercher, Orrville, Ohio, were M.C. ministers in 1958, and Dwight Zuercher of Hillsdale, Okla., was a G.C.M. minister. Gerhard Zerger, Moundridge, Kan., for many years served on the Board of Bethel College. D.L.G.

Zuiderhofje, a Mennonite old people's home at Haarlem, Holland, founded in 1640 by Jaques van Damme and his wife Elisabeth van Blenckvliet. It first belonged to the Flemish Den Blok congregation. vpZ.

Zuiderklasse (South group), an association of Mennonite churches in the southwest of the Dutch province of Friesland, founded in 1709 and embracing the congregations of Hindeloopen, Koudum, Warns, Staveren, Bakhuizen, Workum, Makkum, Bolsward, Santfirderrijp, and Molkwerum. It was a kind of independent conference within the Mennonite conference of Friesland (FDS). For some time it did not participate in the activities of the FDS, holding its own Zuiderklasse meetings. In 1772 it resolved to co-operate in conference activities again, though it held exceptional rights as to subsidizing. These exceptions were abolished in 1841 and the Zuiderklasse dissolved. A special aim of the Zuiderklasse was to give mutual aid in cases of a vacant pulpit in one of its members, which soon after its dissolving was taken over by the Ring Bolsward (q.v.). vpZ.

Inv. Arch. Amst. I, No. 958; Blaupot t. C., *Friesland,* 185, 251 f.; *DB* 1895, 16 f.; 1901, 114; 1902, 39; 1905, 47, 55 f.

Zuidholland, a province of the Netherlands: see **South Holland.**

Zuidhollands(ch)-Zeeuws(ch)e Ring, an association of Mennonite congregations, founded at Middelburg in 1862 on the initiative of the Rotterdam congregation. At first this Ring (q.v) included the congregations of Rotterdam, Middelburg, Dordrecht, and Vlissingen, but the next year Dordrecht withdrew, and Leiden and Ouddorp joined the Ring, the newly founded congregation of The Hague joining in 1882. About 1887 this Ring, though not dissolved, ceased activities until 1917. Since then it has held yearly meetings and in case of vacancy in the pulpit in one of the churches of the Ring the other congregations take charge. At present (1959) the following eleven congregations are members of this Ring: Leiden, The Hague, Delft, Rotterdam, Dordrecht, and Ouddorp in South Holland, Goes, Middelburg, Vlissingen, and Aardenburg in Zeeland, and Breda in North Brabant. vpZ.

Inv. Arch. Amst. I, No. 853a; *DB* 1876, 63-77; 1918, 155; *De Zondagsbode* XXX (1916-17) No. 36.

Zuidhollandsche Sociëteit (South Holland Conference), also called Waterlander Conference, or Lamist Conference, was to some extent a continuation of the Waterlander conferences which had been held from time to time from 1568, as for example in 1647 at Amsterdam. In 1674, when the more conservative churches in North and South Holland organized in the Zonist (q.v.) Sociëteit, the more liberal or Lamist churches made an attempt to found a Lamist conference of all the progressive congregations. This conference as such did not come into being, most North Holland congregations feeling that their Rijper (q.v.) Sociëteit was sufficient. Thereupon, on the initiative of the Rotterdam congregation, the delegates of the four leading churches in Haarlem, (then) South Holland (Amsterdam, Leiden, and Rotterdam) held a meeting at Haarlem on Nov. 24, 1675. This can be considered as the founding of the Zuidhollandsche Sociëteit, in whose meetings, at first held annually, several problems were discussed, but especially the decline of many Lamist churches because of a lack of capable ministers. The suggestion of Rotterdam, supported by Leiden, to start a seminary for the education of ministers was rejected, the Haarlem delegates in particular opposing this plan. In the meantime the Amsterdam Lamist congregation had instructed Galenus (q.v.) Abrahamsz on Dec. 5, 1680, to train young men for the ministry, and in 1692, this Amsterdam church officially founded a seminary, which was led by Galenus Abrahamsz until his death in 1706. The proper task of the Zuidhollandsche Sociëteit having been realized, the conference was dissolved in 1694.

Besides its function in the training of ministers it also in its short life took care of catechetical instruction, mutual aid in filling pulpits, and subsidizing poor congregations. Moreover, Jan van Ranst (q.v.) of Rotterdam, as a delegate of the Zuidhollandsche Sociëteit, gave the impulse for the founding of a Mennonite conference in Friesland (FDS), founded in 1695.

Apart from the four congregations listed above, the following churches also joined the South Holland conference: Schiedam, Gouda, Delft, Brielle, Weesp-Overmeer, and Bunschoten. A few other congregations like Wormerveer, Krommenie, Medemblik, Monnikendam, Durgerdam, Alkmaar, and Utrecht also occasionally sent delegates to its meetings. vpZ.

Inv. Arch. Amst. I, Nos. 774-853; Blaupot t. C., *Holland* II, 90-93; *DB* 1872, 60-67; 1918, 49-56.

Zuidhorn: see **Den Horn.**

Zuidland, a hamlet on the island of Putten, Dutch province of South Holland, where there was a small Flemish Mennonite church, which in the 17th century was more or less united with the Geervliet (q.v.) and Spijkenisse congregation. It died out before 1700. It is uncertain when this congregation was founded; it may have existed in the middle of the 16th century. Jan (q.v.) Jansz Brant, of Zuidland, a Mennonite martyr, was executed at Geervliet in 1559. (Blaupot t. C., *Holland* II, 43.) vpZ.

Zuidlaren, a village about 10 miles south of Groningen (q.v.), where there has been a Kring (circle) of Mennonites since Nov. 2, 1950. This group (19 Mennonites and 8 interested non-Mennonites in 1958) is now incorporated in the congregation of Haren-Roden (q.v.), which was founded in 1954. vpZ.

Zuid-Limburg, the official name of the Dutch Mennonite congregation usually called Heerlen, where its meetinghouse and parsonage are located. The history of this church is found in the article **Heerlen.** To this article is to be added: G. Maathuis served as pastor until 1957 and was succeeded by J. Knot. The membership in 1958 was 172.   vDZ.

Zuidveen, a hamlet in the Dutch province of Overijssel, until 1848 the seat of a Mennonite congregation, which in that year was named Steenwijk (*q.v.*). The Zuidveen congregation in the 17th and 18th centuries belonged to the Danzig Old Flemish (*q.v.*) Mennonites, a branch which included a small number of congregations in the Netherlands and which had regular contact with some Mennonite churches in Prussia, including Danzig. Concerning the history of the Zuidveen congregation there is not much information. Leenaert (*q.v*) Bouwens is said to have founded this church *c*1560, but it is more likely that the neighboring Giethoorn-Noord (*q.v.*) congregation was the mother church of Zuidveen, which became independent after a number of Giethoorn members had settled here. Some of the members lived at Steenwijk as early as 1600. About 1600 these Mennonites at Steenwijk and Zuidveen were harassed by the Reformed magistrates of Steenwijk. Though exact figures were not available, it can be assumed that the Zuidveen membership was very small. In 1768 some dissensions arose in this congregation between a conservative and a more progressive part, which led to a schism in 1774. There were then two congregations at Zuidveen: (*a*) Danzig Old Flemish (Oude Huis) and (*b*) Flemish (Nieuwe Huis). In the (*a*) Oude Huis congregation, which held to the old principles and continued to practice footwashing, in 1775 consisting of only three families, Albert Hendriks (Bakker) was the last preacher serving 1761-1806. In 1819 the Giethoorn-Noord congregation took over the property of the Zuidveen Oude Huis and the care of the three remaining members. The meetinghouse was completely washed away by a flood in February 1825.

The separated (*b*) Nieuwe Huis congregation, which was closely connected with that of Giethoorn-Zuid, built a small meetinghouse, to which an old sister of the church, aged over 100, laid the foundation stone in early March 1774. This meetinghouse obtained an organ in 1806 and was enlarged in 1816. Ministers in this Nieuwe Huis were Reinders Pieters (Veen), from 1746 a preacher in the Oude Huis, from 1774 in the Nieuwe Huis, elder from 1796, serving until d.1801, followed by Floris Engel 1802-7, C. Leendertz 1808-14, and K. Hovens Grove 1814-62, during whose ministry the meetinghouse and parsonage at Zuidveen were abandoned in 1848 for a new church and parsonage at Steenwijk. Thereupon the dilapidated meetinghouse of Zuidveen was demolished (last service May 4, 1848). In 1774 the baptized membership of the Nieuwe Huis congregation numbered *c*20, 44 in 1804, and 135 in 1840. For the history after 1848 see **Steenwijk.**   vDZ.

DJ 1850, 39 f.; *DB* 1878, 1-37; 1901, 16, 47; *Inv. Arch.*

Amst. II, 2392-95; Blaupot t. C., *Groningen* I, 102, 104, 218 f., 239; II, 68.

Zuidzijpe: see Zijpe.

Zur Heimath (1875-81), first published as an 8-page 8½ x 11½ monthly by David Goerz at Summerfield, Ill., as the official organ of the Mennonite Board of Guardians (*q.v.*) of which he was the secretary, and distributed free to Mennonite immigrants from Russia by the Board, February to December 1875. When Goerz moved to Halstead, Kan., in late 1875, he organized there the Western Publishing Co., which thenceforth published the journal as an 8-page semimonthly for a subscription price of $1.00, with slightly enlarged page size (1880-81 at 10½ x 15 in.). David Goerz was the editor throughout its history. *Der Nebraska Ansiedler,* a similar periodical published by the Mennonite Publishing Company beginning in June 1878, and transformed into *Die Mennonitische Rundschau* after two years (June 1880), was in a sense a competitor, and with J. F. Harms (*q.v.*), Mennonite Brethren minister, as editor, succeeded in separating a certain segment of the Russian Mennonite constituency in North America from Goerz's paper. The latter became increasingly the servant and organ of the Western District (GCM) Conference (*q.v.*), and finally merged with the *Mennonitischer Friedensbote* (*q.v.*) to form the *Christlicher Bundesbote* (January 1882) as the official German organ of the General Conference Mennonite Church. *Zur Heimath* announced its function in 1876 as being the bearer of reports on immigration and settlement, news out of Russia, and general material from near and far. Later it carried much news of congregational and conference activities as well as doctrinal and historical material. It carried an advertising section, particularly for the steamship and railroad companies interested in immigration.   H.S.B.

Zurflüh, Abraham, was one of the leading Mennonite emigrants from the Bernese Jura to the United States. In early March 1852 Abraham Zurflüh, of Chaluet near Court, started out with a group from Münster. A letter written by him at Bluffton, Ohio, describing the status of the Swiss at that place and of the congregation in Putnam County, was published in 1889 in the *Zionspilger*. Until into the 20th century he corresponded with his brethren and relatives in the Bernese Jura. (*ML* IV.)   S.G.

Zürich, city (1950 pop. 386,485; 1525, 8,000-10,000) and canton in northern Switzerland, the birthplace of the Anabaptist movement. The canton has since 1351 been listed first in the official list of cantons of the Swiss Confederacy. The city has been, through most of its history, the largest city and most important economic center in Switzerland. The city ruled the territory of the canton until 1803, when a democratic republic was established representing the entire cantonal population. Here the Swiss Reformation began with the work of Ulrich Zwingli (*q.v.*), who came to the city as the head pastor in 1519 and led the movement until his death at the Battle of Cappel in 1531. He was followed as leader by Heinrich Bullinger (*q.v.*), who served as head of the Zürich church 1531-d.75. From 1523 to 1798 the church of the canton of Zürich was a pure state church, with a Reformed theology, the Catholic forms of worship having been reformed in May 1525. Since then it is a modified state church.

The Anabaptist movement arose out of the circle of intimate friends and followers of Zwingli in Zürich, who, after failure to persuade Zwingli to establish a free church of believers only, introduced adult baptism on confession of faith on Jan. 21, 1525, in a meeting of some 15 men in the house of Felix Manz's mother on Neustadt Street. The leaders were two young citizens of Zürich, Conrad Grebel (q.v., d.1526 in Maienfeld) and Felix Manz (q.v., executed in Zürich in January 1527), together with Georg Blaurock (q.v., executed in 1529 in Tirol), a former priest of Chur. Grebel and Manz were both sons of prominent Zürich patrician families, both gifted university students, counted by Zwingli among his most devoted and promising followers. The break with Zwingli occurred after the second Zürich religious disputation in October 1523 and came gradually during the ensuing year as the state church policy of Zwingli became clear. For a detailed account of the Anabaptist beginnings see Grebel, Conrad, and Zwingli, Ulrich.

Vigorous suppression of the movement by force, climaxed in 1526 by the institution of the death penalty for teaching or preaching Anabaptism (Felix Manz the first victim), prevented the development of an organized Anabaptist congregation in Zürich at the beginning or later. The first congregation in the neighborhood was that in the adjacent village of Zollikon (q.v.), which existed from February to May 1525, and then was suppressed.

However, Anabaptism did develop into a substantial movement, though never very large, in several of the outlying districts of the canton, especially Grüningen (q.v.) on the east and Horgen (q.v.), Wädenswil, and Knonau on the south, although in the later 16th and early 17th centuries it is clear that all sections of the canton had some Anabaptists, rather thinly spread. It is almost impossible to locate specific and clearly organized congregations at any time, although the records occasionally carry phrases such as "the congregation in Grüningen," or "in Horgerberg," whereby it is not clear whether the total Anabaptist population of a district is meant, with several meeting groups, or a specific congregation with its own local ministers and one meeting (though rotating in location among the homes or barns, or in the forests).

The first center of the movement was apparently in the territory of Grüningen, the southeastern part of the canton, where Grebel, Manz, and Blaurock found a good response among the villagers in the summer and fall of 1525. By 1528, however, the promising growth had been broken here. Later the stronger areas were west of Zürich in the Horgerberg, Wädenswil, and Knonau districts.

The threat of the Anabaptist movement led to important measures of discipline in the Zürich state church whose purpose was to aid in detecting individual Anabaptists and making their key activities illegal. Among these was the introduction of the compulsory baptismal register on May 24, 1526,

compulsory marriage in the church buildings (the Anabaptists married in their own conventicles), and in 1529 compulsory attendance at the state church service. The Anabaptists' justifiable criticism of the low moral state of the clergy as well as the population in general was met by sharp regulations against the most common vices and an elevation of requirements for the clergy. All these measures were combined and intensified in the sharp and comprehensive mandate of March 26, 1530 (Das grosse Sittenmandat), which included in its paragraph #9 a direct attack against the Anabaptists. This paragraph strictly forbade any help or housing for Anabaptists on pain of heavy penalties, for "the council will not tolerate them in any regard," and required all clergy and authorities to report at once every known Anabaptist who would separate himself from the church. The Anabaptists were condemned as leading to the "destruction of all authority." This was a decree by the civil state, designed in part to refute the bitter charges of the Catholic cantons that Zürich was tolerating this "vicious sect," but also designed to meet the threat of a movement which rejected the oath and all military service, although the Anabaptists denied under cross-questioning that they "preached against the state," and there is no direct evidence that they were charged at this time with reducing the military potential of the state in its struggle with the Catholic cantons. In 1531 Bullinger published his first book against them, Von dem unverschampten fraefel. His second book against them, Der Widertöufferen ursprung, appeared in 1560.

The strict mandates led to further executions: Konrad Winkler, a preacher, on Jan. 30, 1530, Heini Karpfis of Grüningen and Hans Herzog of Stadel on March 23, 1532. In 1533, however, a less strict policy was adopted, in line with Bern and other cantons. In June 1535 the council received, on request, from the clergy of the city a declaration of counsel on measures to take regarding the Anabaptists, since the Anabaptists were increasing in number and preaching "in Grüningen, Wädenswil, and all along the lake."

This and other evidence belies the claim of Egli (90 f.) that the movement was dying out after 1530. Continued measures against the Anabaptists throughout the rest of the 16th century indicate that both church and state in Zürich took the movement seriously. Although no more executions took place until 1614, these measures included, besides imprisonment for longer or shorter periods, confiscation of property and expulsion from Zürich territory. Bullinger in particular had great, though misplaced, confidence, in sermons and other instruction to "root out the error," due certainly in part to his extraordinarily high evaluation of preaching as the means whereby God's election operated to reach individuals. Zürich's policy was in fact not so harsh as some of the other cantons, notably Bern, and only four executions took place in the canton, although a number died in prison later on.

One of the consequences of the persecution of the Anabaptists in Zürich as well as in other Swiss cantons was emigration to Moravia, where, except for two brief periods of persecution in 1536 and

1548, toleration by the authorities, as well as a vigorous church life, proved a great attraction. Missioners from the Hutterite colonies there frequently came to Switzerland to solicit immigrants, with considerable success, as the Hutterite *Chronik* repeatedly reports. In 1585, for instance, the *Chronik* says, "So many people came from Switzerland that at several places the doors had to be closed to them because not all could be received, though a good part of them were taken in." The years 1584-88 were a period of unusual emigration. On Aug. 18, 1584, at an eastern Zürich border point, a party of 50 headed for Moravia was apprehended. Not all the emigrants joined the Hutterite colonies, for there were congregations of Swiss Brethren in Moravia until well into the 17th century. Several times Hutterite emissaries were caught in Zürich. For instance, in 1574 three were arrested, questioned, and expelled. In 1584 "seven preachers" were sent to Switzerland, according to the *Chronik*. There is evidence also that at least a few similar emissaries came from the Netherlands, and took some Swiss Brethren back with them. In 1575, for instance, the Zürich archives report an Anabaptist preacher from the Netherlands preaching at various meetings near Bülach, "who had been there before." In 1584 there is specific mention of emigration to the Netherlands. In the mid-17th century there was also a strong emigration to Alsace and the Palatinate (see below).

The Zürich authorities wavered in their attitudes toward the Anabaptist emigration. At times they encouraged it and even expelled members of the group. At other times, as in 1576 (decree of Feb. 11), they forbade it. In all cases they forbade reentry except to those who recanted and returned to the Protestant Church. It is worthy of note that the opposition to the Anabaptists by the state in one of the mandates was based almost exclusively on social and economic (not religious) grounds, such as their rejection of the oath, but especially their emigration with its consequent loss of wealth and manpower to the state and the weakening of the national defense through reduction of soldier material.

An interesting aspect of the relation of Anabaptists to the state church is the recognition by the authorities that the poor behavior of the Zürich clergy, both in morals and in performance of their preaching and pastoral duties, was one cause of the growth of Anabaptism. Repeatedly the failures of the parish clergy in the villages were castigated and measures taken for reform. On Aug. 4, 1585, for instance, the city council sent a message to the Zürich church synod, which was to be read twice yearly at the synod meetings, calling for vigorous reform and improvement of the clergy, since the lack of discipline and poor sense of responsibility of the clergy was the cause for the separation of "many pious, God-fearing people." Their failures, especially moral failures, were to be punished with imprisonment, suspension, or discharge. The conference of the four cantons on July 4, 1585, which had been called primarily to agree upon common measures against the Anabaptists, also decided on a long series of measures calling for a reform of the clergy as well as of the morals of the population in general.

Often the measures against the Anabaptists were of an economic nature. In addition to money fines, withdrawal of permission to participate in the economic life of the village or community was ordered, including denial of acceptance into a village upon attempted transfer from one location to another. Money fines were imposed freely. For instance, the first absence from the state church Sunday preaching service drew a fine of 20 batzen, the second 5 pounds, further absences up to 20 pounds. Attendance at Anabaptist services was fined one pound. Hospitality to an Anabaptist cost 10 pounds. An anonymous communication to the city council in 1560 with the title, "By what means Anabaptists may be resisted, and how the Anabaptists, especially their leaders, may be punished," advocated as the chief measure the imposition of money fines.

The continued repressive measures against the Anabaptists did not succeed in rooting them out of Zürich until after the middle of the 17th century. Neither imprisonment, confiscation, nor emigration brought about a surrender. Evidently the various measures authorized were not always thoroughly and relentlessly applied, even though the clergy were intense in their opposition to the Anabaptists; otherwise the persistence of the movement can scarcely be explained. It is true that no specific congregations can be identified and very few elders and ministers can be named throughout the entire 140-year history of Zürich Anabaptism, and no evidence has emerged of any general meeting or conferences of the entire body in the canton, nor have any records of the group itself survived except petitions or confessions submitted to the authorities. One of the latter is the "Grüningen Petition" (Grüningen Eingabe) of 1528 submitted by Jakob Falk and Heini Reimann, at that time in prison. Another is the petition of April 23, 1589, submitted by Andreas Gut of Affoltern on behalf of the brotherhood. A third petition, of 1589, possibly also drafted by Andreas Gut, entitled "Supplication an den Bürgermeister und Rat der Stadt Zürich von einigen Wiedertäufern," with the further title "Einfältig bekanntnus," treats five main points: the causes for the great division, the value of the Old Testament in comparison to the New, the relation of the fellowship of believers of the New Testament to those of the Old, the attitude toward the state and the holding of public offices, and baptism. The Zürich clergy replied to the "Bekanntnus" with a polemic document of its own, containing ten points of polemic description of the harmful influence of the Anabaptists upon the people, and pointing out their "opposition to the state," including nonswearing of oaths and rejection of military service.

The Anabaptist movement in Zürich experienced a moderate revival in members after 1600. Contributing to this was the serious estrangement between the general peasant population of the villages and the city population and government, which created a great deal of unrest, together with the continuing poor performance of the clergy. The sympathy of the people for the Anabaptists was so strong in some places, such as Grüningen, that it was practically impossible for the police to arrest them or to impose penalties. The magistrate (Vogt) of Wädenswil reported on Oct. 8, 1612, "that they have such a large following that no one wants to lay hands on them." Other reports indicate that the Anabaptists were well enough organized to have a charity fund for the aid of the poor, administered by a "treasurer (deacon?) which received legacies and gifts and even owned a small farm near Sihlbrugg (Hallauergütli)."

In January 1613 a new mandate was issued against the Anabaptists, which was largely a repetition of that of 1585. On the basis of this mandate attempts were first made to win over the Anabaptists peacefully through disputations or conversations. At the first disputation, which took place at Wädenswil (q.v.) on Jan. 26, the Zürich Burgermeister Rahn, aided by J. J. Breitinger, pastor at St. Peter's in Zürich, soon to be the leader of the Zürich church, represented Zürich, while the elders Hans Landis and Rudolph Bachmann and a preacher Galatz represented the Anabaptists. The meeting was fruitless. At the second disputation held at Grüningen on March 3, 1613, sixteen of the forty Anabaptists living in the area appeared, while Stadholder Keller, Vogt Grebel, and J. J. Breitinger represented Zürich. Again the meeting was fruitless. Accordingly the authorities now attempted to carry through the mandate, which was made more difficult by a decree of the council forbidding emigration. At last extreme measures were taken. Six Anabaptist leaders from Wädenswil and Horgen were arrested, among them Hans Landis (q.v.), who finally was executed the following year as the last Anabaptist martyr in Zürich. The Ausbund (from 1655 on) contains a hymn of 47 verses about him. Two of the remaining five emigrated, while three recanted (for the full account see Horgen). The first three had been sentenced to the French galleys but escaped at Solothurn before delivery to the French ambassador.

From 1613 on, J. J. Breitinger, serving as leader of the Zürich church and seeking in every respect to promote her highest welfare, prosperity, and unity, took the lead in measures against the Anabaptists. His chief concern in dealing with the Anabaptists was to maintain unity and prevent any significant loss of members or a schism. He was more moderate than some others in the actual measures undertaken, nevertheless carried through strongly. As a wise statesman he saw that the best way to meet the Anabaptist menace was to undermine the movement by removing some of its supposed causes, hence worked vigorously at a reform of the clergy, improvement of the school system, and better care for the poor. His point of view was dominant in the Aarau meeting of the Protestant cantons on Jan. 18, 1616, which decided to push a vigorous reform of the clergy as the best means of counteracting the Anabaptists. Strong measures, including heavy imprisonment up to lifelong terms, were, however, provided for leaders and for stubborn impenitent members. These measures succeeded in repressing the movement somewhat, and certainly prevented its further growth, but did not completely eradicate it.

After a period of relative quiet the final struggle with the Anabaptists took place in 1633-45. It was inaugurated with a census of the entire population in 1633, which produced a report (from the pastors) of a total of 182 adult (over 20 years of age) Anabaptists, distributed as follows: Affoltern 5, Bärentswil 11, Birmensdorf 11, Bonstetten 2, Cappel 3, Egg 1, Ellikon 8, Grüningen 2, Gryffensee 1, Hinwyl 7, Hirzel 46, Hausen 3, Maschwanden 5, Männedorf 11, Mettmenstetten 6, Ottenbach 3, Pfäffikon 3, Richterswil 12, Stallikon 12, Fischental 8, Wald 4, Wädenswil 8, Wetzikon 2, Wildberg 2, suspects 8. The true numbers were certainly higher than the 182 listed, according to Bergmann (104), who reports that some figures probably represent households, that three of the parishes reported a total of 117 children under 20, and that the Freie Amt had 50 Anabaptists in addition to many suspects. Bergmann believes that there were scarcely any Anabaptists in the city itself. It is interesting to note that the parishes of Birmensdorf and Bärentswil reported their Anabaptists to be very wealthy ("sehr wohlhabend").

On Dec. 28, 1635, four unnamed Anabaptist preachers were arrested and questioned fruitlessly, and after some months released. On Aug. 17, 1635, another disputation was arranged in Knonau, to which all the Anabaptists in the districts of Grüningen, Wädenswil, and Knonau were invited. Many appeared, but not all: 38 of the 58 in Knonau, 36 of the 71 in Wädenswil, 14 of the 61 in Grüningen. Later two disputations were held in the city, on Aug. 22 and Sept. 8, 1635. All discussions were fruitless; so the authorities concluded to try another tack. The individual Anabaptists were asked to reply in writing whether they were ready to recant or to emigrate. Four writings were received in Zürich, all negative, one from Knonau written by Rudolf Egli and bearing 20 signatures, one from Wädenswil written by Peter Bruppacher and bearing 9 signatures ("and many others"), one from Grüningen written by Hans Spori and bearing 9 signatures, one from Gryffensee and Kyburg with 17 signatures, and one from Männedorf with 23 signatures. Certainly the number of Anabaptists in the canton in 1635 must have reached 300 or more. The next step was to arrest most of the Anabaptists and place them in various prisons since the Zürich city prison did not have room. But soon practically all were either released or had escaped. In 1637 again large numbers were arrested. From these prisoners a petition for leave to emigrate was received, which listed a total of 70 men, 100 women, and some 300 children as prisoners. This step was taken with heavy heart, after 20 weeks of imprisonment; but permission was refused. After several months of very severe imprisonment the miserable prisoners escaped in March. Thereupon in the following weeks the police were sent on house searches to arrest the Anabaptists again, and to confiscate their cash and valuable household goods. Bergmann illustrates the suffering of the families by an account of what the family of Rudolph Egli had to go through, until the family finally emigrated to the Palatinate.

A moving account of the sufferings of the Zürich brethren is given in a report prepared for the Dutch Mennonites in 1645, possibly by Hans Müller of Edikon, or Jeremias Mangold. It forms a booklet of 27 pages of small type in small page format, which has been printed in every edition of the Ausbund printed in America, beginning in 1742, under the title *Ein wahrhaftiger Bericht von den Brüdern im Schweitzerland in dem Zürcher gebiet wegen der Trübsalen, welche über sie ergangen sind, um des Evangeliums willen, von dem 1635 sten bis in das 1645 ste Jahr.* Aside from the 4-page summary of the examinations of the prisoners in 1635-36 and the conclusion, it consists of a detailed account of the experiences of individuals in prison (and in part outside), organized under the heads of Klonau (Knonau), Wädenswil and Horgen, and Grüningen. The following persons are treated: Hans Meyli, Hans Müller, Rudolph Hägi, Hans Ringer, Heinrich Frick, Steffen Zänder, Dorothea Grobin, Catharina Müllerin, Heinrich Gut, Otilly Müllerin, Barbara Meylin, Barbara Kolbin, Elisabeth Meylin, Hans Landis, Hans Huber, Conrad Strickler, Hans Rudolph Baumann, Oswald Landis, Feronica Ableny, Jacob Rüsterholz, Felix Landis, Rudolph Sommer, Hans Asper, Werne Pleister, Ulrich Schneider, Gally Schneider, Rudolph Bachmann, Hans Jakob Heess, Hans Müller, Jakob Gochnauer, Jakob Egly, Georg Weber, Jakob Baumgartner, Ulrich Müller, Jakob Müssly (Nissly), Catharina Forrerin, Burckhard Ammen, Elisabeth Hützny, and Heinrich Schnebele. The following are named in the report as ordained ministers (*bestellte Diener*): Hans Landis of Horgerberg and Ulrich Müller of Kyburg; Rudolph Bachmann as elder (*Aeltester*), and Werne Pleister as ordained elder (*bestellter Aeltester*). (It is possible that "bestellter Diener" means elder, and "Aeltester" means deacon.)

The Anabaptist Commission, which had been set up in 1613 and charged with Anabaptist matters, now prepared a detailed account of their dealings with the Anabaptists, entitled *Handlung und Ersprachung mit den Widertöeffern ihrer Irrtums wegen,* which was published as a "Manifest" on Oct. 31, 1639, and distributed among the population of the countryside (probably identical with *Wahrhaffter Bericht Unsers des Burgermeisters des Kleinen und Grossen Rahts . . . der Statt Zürich . . . unsers handlungen gegen den Widertäufferen 1639*). The Anabaptists replied with an "Antimanifest" (so named in the archives) entitled "Christenliche und Kurtze verantwortung der brüderen, dienern, und eltisten im Zürich gebiedt über das büchlein oder manifest so ausgegangen in der Stadt und Landschaft Zürich," probably written in 1640.

In November and December 1639 the final heavy blow was struck. An order went out from the Anabaptist Commission to arrest all Anabaptists, confiscate all goods, and to declare all marriages annulled and all children illegitimate. This was done and the Anabaptists were crowded into the prisons, which had been emptied of criminals, and kept in complete isolation under the harshest conditions. All pleas for mercy were denied. The general population of the countryside, however, was deeply aroused by these measures. Attempts to sell the Anabaptist properties found few buyers, and no one was ready to take over their shops or businesses. In this time of great need the Zürich Anabaptists turned to their brethren in Holland, apparently through a family of Mennonite weavers in Zürich who had come from Holland, Hans Suner. Secret

collections were sent from Holland to the prisoners as early as 1640.

The fruitless intervention of the Dutch Mennonites on behalf of their persecuted Zürich brethren in which they finally called on the Dutch government for help, continued for 20 years for Zürich, and for 50 years longer for Bern. Word regarding the Zürich persecution first reached the Amsterdam Mennonites in 1641, who at once made a connection with the prisoners through a Reformed (or Lutheran) merchant in Amsterdam, Izak Hattavier (*q.v.*). In 1642 a Reformed pastor in Amsterdam, Godefridus Hottonus, wrote to Zürich about the matter and on Aug. 21 received a lengthy letter from Breitinger. A paper war followed in 1643 over the Zürich persecution, between Petrus Bontemps (*q.v.*), a Reformed preacher of Haarlem, Joost Hendriksz (d. 1644), an Amsterdam Mennonite preacher, and A. D. Volbot (*q.v.,* who used the pseudonym Gerard van Vrijburgh). On Feb. 15, 1645, Jeremias Mangold, no doubt a Zürich Anabaptist, sent to Holland a lengthy manuscript report on the Zürich persecution, which, together with a shorter report of February, written by Martin Meyli, was used by Van Braght for a lengthy report in the *Martyrs' Mirror* (1660). The Zürich-Lied, with 49 stanzas, gives an account of the sufferings of the Zürich prisoners, written by one of them, Hans Rycker. It was published in a small songbook called *Ein geistliches Liederbüchlein,* which was published (for the first time?) in 1709 or later. The *Dürsrüttilied* follows it, which likewise gives an account of the Bernese Anabaptist persecution. At the request of the Dutch Mennonites, addressed to the States-General and to the Amsterdam City Magistracy, the States-General on Feb. 19, 1660, addressed a letter to the Zürich government requesting that Zürich permit the Anabaptists to emigrate with their goods. This petition was supported by the cities of Amsterdam and Rotterdam, and by the Knights-Proprietors of Alsace (whose support had no doubt been enlisted by the Mennonites there). To all of these Zürich answered negatively on July 20, 1660.

Much material on the persecution of the Zürich Anabaptists about this time is found in several other sources. The Mangold report of 1645 is apparently the one printed in full in the *Ausbund* (first in the 1742 Germantown edition). An extract of the Zürich Anabaptist archival documents covering Feb. 3, 1639, to Jan. 9, 1643, prepared by Hans Kaspar Suter, probably at the request of the Bernese authorities, appears in two copies in the Bern Staatsarchiv. A similar comprehensive report secured by the Bern Anabaptist Commission in 1659 from the Zürich Anabaptist Commission also appears in the Bern Staatsarchiv. J. H. Ottius, *Annales Anabaptistici,* pp. 204-360, also gives many details in often lengthy items, particularly for 1609-70.

On April 23, 1641, the captives escaped from prison, though many were recaptured. Gradually matters quieted down again and once more the Brethren thought that perhaps an implicit toleration might be their lot, but not so. After the close of the Thirty Years' War in 1648, when immigrants were desired to repopulate southern Germany, most of the Zürich Anabaptists emigrated, along with numerous Reformed families. They settled largely in the Palatinate. A few remained behind as relatives of prisoners with life sentences or for other reasons. In 1654 two brethren named Schmid and Frick underwent examinations and in 1656 Frick finally was freed after 27 months of imprisonment, whereupon he emigrated to the Palatinate. The official records show that a total of 119 Anabaptists left for the Palatinate and Alsace in 1656-57, while some 1,076 Reformed followed the same route. Further records show that among the 4,130 who had emigrated in 1657-61 there were 49 Anabaptists with 70 children.

So the might of the Zürich state after 140 years finally succeeded in exterminating the Anabaptist movement in the land of its beginnings. But Zürich Anabaptism lived on in foreign countries, first in the Palatinate, and finally in Pennsylvania, whither a large number of Palatine Mennonites emigrated in 1707-56. It is probable that 75 per cent of the Mennonites of the Lancaster Mennonite settlement established in 1710-17 consisted of original Zürich families, instead of those of Bernese origin as has been hitherto too easily assumed. Among them are such well-known families as Landis, Brubacher, Snyder, Miller, Weber (Weaver), Hess, Gochnauer, Bauman, Bachmann, Good, Nissley, Snavely, Hege, Huber, Strickler, Kendig, and Graff.

The Zürich Anabaptists have been treated in three literary works, two by major writers, all dealing with the earliest period. Gottfried Keller, an outstanding Swiss novelist, wrote the Novelle *Ursula* (*q.v.*, 1878); Cäsar von Arx, the leading contemporary Swiss dramatist, wrote *Brüder in Christo* (*q.v.*, 1947); and Erich Diebold, a Swiss journalist, wrote the novel *Folge dem Licht* (1945; see **Literature**). Heinrich Bullinger's two major works of 1531 and 1560 against the Anabaptists became standard sources and greatly influenced both official and popular attitudes. Being polemic writings, they contain little purely historical material. They are fully treated under the articles *Von dem unverschampten fräfel* and *Widertoufferen Ursprung.* H.S.B.

TA Zürich; Emil Egli, *Die Züricher Wiedertäufer zur Reformationszeit* (Zürich, 1878); Cornelius Bergmann, *Die Täuferbewegung im Kanton Zürich bis 1660* (Leipzig, 1916); L. von Muralt, *Glaube und Lehre der Schweizerischen Wiedertäufer in der Reformationszeit* (Zürich, 1938); Walther Köhler, "Die Zürcher Täufer," *Gedenkschrift zum 400jährigen Jubiläum der Mennoniten oder Taufgesinnten 1525-1925* (Ludwigshafen, 1925); Max Stiefel, *Die kirchlichen Verhältnisse im Knonaueramt nach der Reformation, 1531-1600* ("Die Wiedertäufer," 152-67) (Affoltern, 1947); Müller, *Berner Täufer; Wahrhaffter Bericht Unsers des Burgermeisters . . . der Statt Zürich. Worinnen grundtlich dargethan wirt, theils Jüngster unsers handlungen gegen den Widertäufferen* (Zürich, 1639, copy in GCL, AML; Dutch editions at Amsterdam 1643 and 1644, both in AML); *Noodigh Ondersoek op den Brieff Geintituleert Waerachtigh Verhael, Van de handelinghen der achtbare Magistraet van Zürich, tegen eenighe weder-doopers* (n.p., 1643, in GCL, AML); J. C. Mörikofer, *J. J. Breitinger und Zürich* (Leipzig, 1874) 149-56; M. H. Brackbill, "On the Origins of the Early Eighteenth Century Pennsylvania Mennonite Immigrants," *MQR* XXVII (1953) 78-82; *Ausbund* (Lancaster County, Pa., 1949), 837-65; *Mart. Mir.* E 1103-5, 1108-24, 1133, 1138, which gives much of the same material as in the *Ausbund* appendix. *ML* IV, 625-40.

Zurich Mennonite Church (MC) located in the village of Zurich, Huron Co., Ont., about 2 miles east of Lake Huron, affiliated with the Ontario Conference, was organized on March 26, 1908, by former members of the Amish congregation near by. Christian Schrag was ordained minister on Feb. 18, 1911. Other ministers with date of ordination were Stephen M. Peachey 1935, Gordon Schrag 1937, Cyril Gingerich 1951, Albert Martin 1949, and Hubert Swartzentruber 1958. Stanley Sauder was licensed to serve as pastor of the Thames Road congregation at Exeter, an outpost of the Zurich congregation. In 1959 the congregation had 148 members, with Albert Martin as bishop-pastor. R.S.K.

Zürich-Lied, a historical hymn of 49 stanzas of 4 lines each, written by Hans Rycher, commemorating the suffering of the Anabaptists imprisoned in the Oetenbach prison in Zürich in 1639-40 ff. Six men are named among the unnamed others: Felix Landsgan (Landis?), Rudolf Sommer, Der Pfister (Pfeister?), Ulrich Schneider, Jakob Erni, and Rudolf Bachmann. Verse 35: "Sie giengen auff der Propheten Weg, da Christus auch ist gangen, sie haben verlassen Haab und Gut, und sind gar lang gefangen." Verse 36: "Das ihren viel gestorben sind, in diesem Ungewitter. O Herre Gott, wir klagens dir, der Streit ist hier gar bitter." Verse 39: "Sie haben mit wainen säyen thun, von nun der Herr wird kommen, Mit Frewden werden sie wieder kon, und bringen ihren Saamen."

The Zürich-Lied appears as the sixth of nine hymns in a small 40-page booklet entitled *Ein Geistliches Lieder-büchlein* (*Gedruckt in diesem Jahr*). The Goshen College Library possesses two editions, one bound in with the 1686 German edition of the Dordrecht Confession (1632), *Christliche Glaubens Bekentnus,* and a collection of prayers and several small song collections, the other bound with the 1691 edition of the same book. The only indication of time is found at the end of the third hymn in the collection, which is signed "B.B.B. 1709," and according to the last verse was written by a prisoner in Bern. The seventh hymn is the *Dürsrüttilied* (*q.v.*), which tells the story of the seizure of a congregation of Anabaptists with their preacher Uli Baumgartner in 1659 in Dursrütti in the Emmenthal in the canton of Bern. The eighth hymn is the noted *Haslibacherlied* (*q.v.*), which tells the story of the martyrdom of Hans Haslibacher at Sumiswald, canton of Bern, in 1571. H.S.B.

Zurkinden, Nikolaus (1506-88), secretary of the council of Bern, Switzerland, in 1534, and magistrate (Landvogt) in Bonmund and Nyon in 1537-44, was one of the outspoken advocates of tolerance in the Reformation period. In a letter to Calvin written on Feb. 10, 1554, he advocated a milder treatment of the Anabaptists.

Albert Ed. Bähler, *Nikolaus Zurkinden von Bern 1506-1588* (Zürich, 1912); Müller, *Berner Täufer*, 76; *ML* IV.

Zusterkring (Sister Circle), a Dutch name for women's organizations. From before 1890 in a few Dutch Mennonite congregations (Amsterdam, Rotterdam, Utrecht, Zwolle) there were women's circles which were active on behalf of missions; at the same time a women's circle of Zaandam-Oost was active in visiting the sick members of the church. Since about 1920 women's circles have been started in nearly all of the Dutch Mennonite congregations; some have two or three. Some of these are sewing circles for relief or in behalf of missions; some are social associations; and some are groups for religious education. Most women's circles now cultivate religious education as well as practical and social activity.

In 1949 nearly all Dutch Mennonite women's circles were organized into the General Federation of Women's Circles (in 1958 c3,500 members). Annual delegate meetings are held at Elspeet (q.v.). A general meeting was held at Amsterdam, Sept. 2-3, 1954, with 2,600 Mennonite women attending. There are also regional associations in Friesland and Groningen.   vDZ.

Zutphen, a town in the Dutch province of Gelderland (pop. 24,000, with 106 Mennonites), the seat of a Mennonite congregation. Concerning the history of Anabaptism-Mennonitism at Zutphen there is little information. Early Anabaptism seems to have had few adherents here in the 1530's, but there was some Anabaptist activity in 1548, when the magistrates discovered that the schoolteacher Claes (q.v.) van Leeuwen had been an Anabaptist; his corpse was exhumed and burned, and his wife Cornelia (q.v.) was executed in 1549. A few others of the small group saved their lives by flight. Not until 1613 is mention made of Mennonites at Zutphen; in that year there were two Mennonite congregations here, one Flemish and one Waterlander, which may have been founded in the 16th century. The Flemish congregation was represented at the Flemish conference at Haarlem in 1649. During the 17th century the Mennonites of Zutphen, as of most other towns, were often disturbed by the local magistrates at the instigation of the Reformed clergy. Not until 1697 did they acquire a meetinghouse, having held their meetings in the homes of members and later in an attic on a back street. In 1697 they bought a warehouse on Molenstraat and remodeled it as a meetinghouse. It is not certain whether this is the same meetinghouse as the church on Apestert, which was later used, remodeled in 1802, enlarged in 1852, and used until 1940. A new church was built on Leeuweriklaan, dedicated on Dec. 10, 1940.

The congregation was always small: c60 baptized members in 1700, c30 in 1740, 12 in 1770, 47 in 1847, 117 in 1900, 160 in 1958. Samuel Muller served here as pastor 1806-11, followed by E. D. van Lennep 1810-11, after eight years of vacancy C. Loosjes Overbeek 1819-38, J. de Liefde 1839-47, A. J. van Pesch (assistant pastor) 1844-48, J. Bodisco 1850-d.72, B. Cuperus 1873-90, S. J. Dekker 1891-1901, S. D. A. Wartena 1902-9, R. Schuursma 1910-29, M. Onnes Msz 1929-46, and J. A. A. Meijer since 1946. This small congregation had the misfortune of being at variance with some of its preachers: Jan Francken was suspended in 1731 because of misconduct; Hendrik Gortinga, who was an Orangist, whereas nearly the whole church sided with the Patriots (q.v.), was bought out in 1795; Jan de Liefde's pietism caused much unpleasantness from 1843 until he retired in 1847. The pastor of Zutphen has since 1956 also served at Winterswijk.

Among the old Mennonite families are the Schimmelpennincks (q.v.), usually wine merchants, and particularly the de Haas family, whose members were for 200 years pillars in the Zutphen congregation. To this family, which died out in the male line in 1878, the congregation owes much, both spiritually and materially; many of its members served as deacons.   vDZ.

Inv. Arch. Amst. I, Nos. 349, 353a, 1152; II, Nos. 1524-26, 2396-2433; II, 2, No. 679; Mellink, *Wederdopers,* 292 f.; Blaupot t. C., *Holland* I, 245 note 1, 330; II, 48 f., 205, 231; *DB* 1861, 148; 1881, 40-63; 1901, 146-63; 1909, 109-14.

Zuttere, de: see **Sutter(e)** (Sitter), **de.**

Zuttere, Pieter de: see **Overd'hage, Petrus.**

Zwaagwesteinde, a village in the Dutch province of Friesland. Mennonites living here in the 17th and 18th centuries belonged to the Kollumerzwaag (q.v.) congregation. As more and more of the members moved to Zwaagwesteinde and because the meetinghouse at Kollumerzwaag was dilapidated, a new meetinghouse was built at Zwaagwesteinde, dedicated on May 5, 1816. The congregation was then generally called Zwaagwesteinde and Kollumerzwaag, or simply Zwaagwesteinde. After the death of the (untrained) preacher A. H. Bosma in 1838 the pulpit remained vacant, and in 1844 the few members who were left joined the neighboring Dantumawoude (q.v.) congregation. In 1897 S. D. A. Wartena, the pastor of Veenwouden (q.v.), started catechetical instruction here, and in 1904 the 47 Mennonites living at Zwaagwesteinde, members of Veenwouden and Dantumawoude, organized a Kring (circle), which built a meetinghouse in the same year. Services were held at Zwaagwesteinde by the pastors of Veenwouden and Dantumawoude and others. In 1949 the Kring Zwaagwesteinde became an independent congregation. The membership in 1958 was 66, served by the pastor of Veenwouden. Church activities include a ladies' circle, a youth group 18-25, Sunday school for children, and a choir. (*DB* 1903, 164-70, 187; 1905, 30, 192 f., 199; *DJ* 1949, 34.)   vDZ.

Zwaardemaker (Swaerdemaker), a Dutch Mennonite family, originally living at Zaandam, where many of its members have served as deacons in the Zaandam-Oost congregation. In the second half of the 17th century Claes Jansz Swaerdemaker was an elder of the Zaandam-Oost Waterlander congregation. He was a well-to-do businessman and an influential leader in the church, who was often called to serve in other congregations. In 1674 he intervened in the Wormerveer (q.v.) Waterlander congregation, when dissensions had arisen there. Dirk Zwaardemaker (1791-1838) and his brother Hendrick (d. 1841) were trustees of the A.D.S., as was Dirk H. Zwaardemaker (d. 1896); all three were manufacturers at Zaandam. K. Zwaardemaker, a lawyer at Bussum, was a trustee of the A.D.S. 1908-d.14. Some Zwaardemakers were deacons at Haarlem and Amsterdam.   vDZ.

Inv. Arch. Amst. I, No. 781b; II, No. 592; Blaupot t. C., *Holland* I, 271; II, 67, 68; *N.N.B.Wb.* I, 1317 f., VI, 1354.·

Zwaardgeesten, a name given to the followers of Jan van Batenburg (*q.v.*).

Zwanzigerweide, a village in the Stuhm (*q.v.*) Lowlands in West Prussia (*q.v.*), Germany. In 1892-1929 the Mennonite congregation in this area was called Zwanzigerweide. Before 1892 and after 1929 it was called Tragheimerweide. For its history see **Tragheimerweide.** vdZ.

Zwarte Kerkje, Het, in the Dutch province of North Holland, was formerly the seat of a Mennonite congregation, of which nothing is known but that it was dissolved before 1700. (Blaupot t. C., *Holland* II, 45.) vdZ.

Zwartewaal, a hamlet in the Dutch province of South Holland. Mennonite activity is mentioned here about 1568, when Hans Busschaert preached. Probably later on there was a congregation, for at least in 1622 Mennonite services were held at Zwartewaal. Among the Mennonites of Zwartewaal were the Arkenbout family. (*Inv. Arch. Amst.* I, No. 415; information by A. A. Arkenbout of Rotterdam.) vdZ.

Zwartsluis, a town in the Dutch province of Overijssel (pop. *c*3,300, with 41 Mennonites), seat of a Mennonite congregation, concerning whose beginning and history little is known. In April 1648 the States of Overijssel discussed whether Mennonite meetings held in Zwartsluis should not be forbidden; but obviously church life went on. Most members were engaged in shipping. The membership was always small: (figures of the 16th-18th centuries not available), 40 in 1840, 47 in 1861, 31 in 1900, 21 in 1958. The present meetinghouse was built in 1842; the organ is of 1881. As early as 1724 the congregation, subsidized by the Lamist church of Amsterdam, was served by a salaried (untrained) minister called from outside. From 1809 the Zwartsluis congregation received financial support from the Dutch government, the first Dutch Mennonite church to which such a contribution was given. Untrained ministers served here until 1860, the last two of whom were Jan Geertsz van Wierum 1788-d.1825 (he died of shock because of a severe flood which destroyed his books) and Harmen Wybes Woudstra 1826-d.60. The first graduate of the Amsterdam seminary to serve here was A. Snellen 1861-67, followed by J. P. Müller 1867-72, C. Leendertz 1873-75, Tj. Kielstra 1876-85, who from 1880 on also served at Meppel (*q.v.*) as did his successor H. Koekebakker Jr., who served at Zwartsluis 1886-d.90. The pulpit then remained vacant until 1896. The agreement with Meppel lasted only until 1892. S. van der Goot served at Zwartsluis 1896-98, followed by A. de Vries Mzn 1898-1903, W. Koekebakker 1904-09, M. Huizinga, Jr. 1910-14, and P. Ens 1915-16. In 1917-41 Zwartsluis was served by the pastors of Meppel and since 1942 by those of Kampen. vdZ.

Inv. Arch. Amst. II, Nos. 2434-55; Blaupot t. C., *Groningen* I, 65; II, 105, 239; *DB* 1861, 174; 1880, 166 f.; 1881, 48; 1882, 118 f.; 1893, 137; 1901, 5.

Zweibrücken, Palatinate, Germany, an industrial city (pop. 25,725) located 20 miles southwest of Kaiserslautern on the edge of the Saar district and only 5 miles from the French (Lorraine) border to the South. It was the capital of the former independent duchy of Pfalz-Zweibrücken (a tiny 400 sq. mi. principality) from 1410 to 1799, when its ruler Maximilian became King of Bavaria. Whereas there were Anabaptists in the district of Bergzabern in the eastern part of the duchy (see **Zweibrücken, Duchy of**), in the immediate area of the city of Zweibrücken there are no evidences of the movement.

In the 17th century, following the close of the Thirty Years' War (1648), Swiss Mennonites from the canton of Bern began to come to the duchy and by 1680 had established a congregation which later became known as Ernstweiler (*q.v.*) because in 1843 it built a meetinghouse in this village very near to the city of Zweibrücken. It was for a time known as "the congregation at Zweibrücken." The *Namensverzeichnis* of 1857 lists the congregation as Zweibrücken (163 baptized members) with Christian Lehmann, Sr. as elder (ord. 1819). An Amish congregation also developed here which came to be known as Ixheim (*q.v.*), because in 1844 a schism resulted in one faction building a meetinghouse in that village, which is now a suburb of Zweibrücken. (The first Amish settlers apparently came from Alsace after Louis XIV had expelled the Mennonites from France in 1712.) It was in existence as a congregation at least by 1759 since it sent two delegates to the Amish Conference at Essingen near Landau in that year, and again to the second Essingen Conference of 1779; both times it is listed in the minutes as the Zweibrücken congregation. It is listed in the Dutch *Naamlijst* of the 18th century usually under the name Hirschberg-Kirschbach (*q.v.*), probably after some of the meeting places used by the congregation. However, the 1888 Mannhardt *Jahrbuch* lists the congregation as Zweibrücken-Ixheim, with 226 baptized members and Joseph Stalter as elder.

The modern Zweibrücken congregation was formed in 1937 by the merger of the Ernstweiler Mennonite and Ixheim Amish congregations. It is a subsidiary to the Kaiserslautern congregation, as Ernstweiler was before 1937, even though it has (1957) 200 baptized members. Services are held in a rented hall in the city, served by Theo Hotel, the Kaiserslautern pastor. Since 1949 the members of the congregation living in the Saar district have been organized as the Saar congregation, with 252 (1957) baptized members. H.S.B.

Zweibrücken Catechism, a name popularly given to the edition of the Elbing catechism of 1778, *Kurze und einfältige unterweisung aus der heiligen Schrift,* which was published at Zweibrücken in the Palatinate, Germany, in 1856 and reprinted there in 1880. The large size, prestige, and age of the Zweibrücken Amish congregation gave additional prestige to the Catechism, which was translated into French and published at Nancy, France, in 1862 and several times thereafter, and became the standard French Mennonite catechism. No original catechism was ever produced or printed at Zweibrücken. H.S.B.

Zwickau Prophets, the name given to three men, Nicholas Storch (q.v.), Thomas Drechsel (q.v.), and Marcus (Thomae) Stübner (q.v.), who came to Wittenberg from Zwickau, Saxony (Germany), about Christmas time in 1521, professing a special message through their study of the Scriptures and through direct revelation from God through the Holy Spirit. They had been influenced by Thomas Müntzer (q.v.), a Lutheran preacher in Zwickau from 1520 to April 1521, recommended by Luther, and had advocated to the textile workers of Zwickau, the proletariat of that industrial city, the establishment of a church of members filled with the Spirit and exercising the ban, equipped with revelation through the "Spirit," while God would destroy the unrighteous. "The laity must become our priests and prelates" was one of his slogans. Annemarie Lohmann, however, holds that it was Storch whose spiritualistic-Taborite ideas influenced Müntzer away from his Lutheran course into radicalism. The Zwickau prophets came with this spirit to Wittenberg and for a time exerted substantial influence even on Melanchthon and Amsdorf. Storch soon left Wittenberg to continue his agitation at other places for several years (e.g., 1524 in Strasbourg and Hof), while Stübner stayed longer and won a number of followers, among them Dr. Gerhard Westerburg (q.v.) and Martin Cellarius (q.v.). Then he too disappeared from the pages of history. Carlstadt (q.v.), the leader at Wittenberg during Luther's absence at the Wartburg (April 1521 to March 1522), agreed on some points with the men from Zwickau but was not of their party.

No church nor movement was established by the Zwickau prophets, but as early as 1530 the theory arose, without any historical foundation to be sure, that Anabaptism was founded by Nicholas Storch in Zwickau. Melanchthon was apparently the first to make this assertion in a letter of February 1530 to Friedrich Myconius, in which he wrote of "Storch and his following, to whom the entire Anabaptist tribe owes its beginning," although he also had the Zwinglians originate in Storch: "Thus from one stork have arisen all those factions of Anabaptists and Zwinglians." Luther in his foreword to Menius' Von dem Geist der Wiedertäufer (1544) even connected the origin of the Anabaptists with Carlstadt and Zwingli.

The earliest writings of Switzerland and South Germany about and against the Anabaptists have nothing to say about a Saxon or Thuringian origin of the Anabaptists in 1521-22. Urbanus Rhegius of Augsburg, one of the very first to write against the Anabaptists (September 1527, Wider den Newen Taufforden), says nothing of the Zwickau origin of Anabaptism. Zwingli knows nothing of such an origin in his writings of 1525-27. In his first book of 1530, Von dem unverschämpten fräfel, Bullinger knows only that Anabaptism is a revival of the ancient heresies of Novatian, Auxentius, and Pelagius; not until his book of 1560, Der Widertöufferen Ursprung, the first chapter of which is titled "Von dem Ursprung des widertoufs, harlangend von Thomas Müntzern und dessen verkehrter ufrürischer leer," does he speak of its origin "down there in Saxony in 1521 and 1522," naming Storch and

Müntzer. Sebastian Franck's Chronica (1531) reports only on South Germany. Nor does Johannes Gast of Basel show any idea of a connection of the Swiss and South German Anabaptists with Saxony and Middle Germany in his De Anabaptismi exordio (Basel, 1544). But all the later historiographers are agreed in their construction of history: the Anabaptist movement began with Storch and Müntzer. Thus Arnold Meshovius says in his Historiae Anabaptisticae (Cologne, 1617): "In my opinion Nikolaus Pelargus (Storch) . . . were some who were leaders (Karlstadt, Melanchthon, Gerhard Westerburg, Markus Stübner, Gabriel Zwilling, Cellarius, Thomas Müntzer)." Of his "Seven Books" the first is devoted exclusively to Wittenburg and Zwickau. It is interesting to note that Meshovius reckons Melanchthon among the Anabaptist leaders, not without some justification if doubts concerning infant baptism are to be considered a mark of Anabaptism. To mention an author of the following century (almost any other would do as well) we cite Ehre-Gott Daniel Colberg, professor at the University of Greifswald, whose book was published in Leipzig in 1710, Das Platonisch-Hermetische Christentum begreifend die historische Erzählung vom Ursprung und vielerlei Sekten der heutigen fanatischen Theologie Unterm Namen der Paracelsisten, Weigelianer, Rosenkreutzer, Quäker, Wiedertäufer, Bourignisten, Labadisten und Quietisten. Chapter IX deals with the Anabaptists, and Section 2 has the heading, "Ursprung der Wiedertäufer. Claus Storch, Thomas Müntzer, Heinrich Pfeiffer." J. C. Füssli in Beiträge zur Erläuterung der Kirchen-Reformation des Schweizerlandes (Vol. I, 1741, p. 109) reflects the position of the historiography of the time in his rejection of the attempt of the Dutch Mennonite historians (especially Schijn) to prove the Waldensian origin of the Anabaptists, saying, "Most historians agree that Anabaptism had its origin from Niclaus Storch and Thomas Müntzer. . . . We will hold with the majority that the Anabaptist sect had its origin from the above restless heads until something else is proved." Füssli knows that Sebastian Franck's Chronica (1531) knew nothing of the Saxon origin of Anabaptism but had it arise during and after the Peasants' War of 1524-25 and in the South; but he rejected this theory, especially because Bullinger in his Reformationsgeschichte had "proved" the opposite.

In the 19th century Johannes Hast is typical, the very title of his book betraying his position: Geschichte der Wiedertäufer von ihrer Entstehung zu Zwickau in Sachsen bis auf ihren Sturz zu Münster in Westfalen (Münster, 1836). Richard Heath called his book Anabaptism from its Rise at Zwickau to its Fall at Münster (London, 1895); but E. B. Bax, with a similar title, Rise and Fall of Anabaptism (N.Y., 1903), specifically rejects the Zwickau origin. Richard Bachmann titled his pamphlet of 1880: Nicholaus Storch, der Anfänger der Zwickauer Wiedertäufer. Examples could be taken at random to illustrate the continued prevalence of this theory in the 19th century and later. Karl Holl (Luther und die Schwärmer, 1923), Karl Heussi (Kompendium der Kirchengeschichte, 10th ed., 1949), and the modern editions of the main encyclopedias (*Calwer Kirchenlexikon*, 1941; *Der grosse Brockhaus*, 1935; *Encyclopedia Britannica*, 1936) continue the theory. C. A. Cornelius with his thorough work, *Geschichte des Münsterischen Aufruhrs*, Vol. II: *Die Wiedertaufe* (Leipzig, 1860), however, finally abolished it and placed the real origin in Zürich. Many important research scholars have followed him.

Under the designation "Anabaptist" the enemies of the Anabaptists of 1525 sought to include all who stood in opposition to the main line of the Reformation on whatever ground, i.e., the entire "left wing." After the Münsterite affair of 1535 the Protestant leaders were convinced that the Anabaptist movement was fanatical-revolutionary in essence, and was accordingly a threat to the existing socio-political order for both state and church. One cannot do justice to their attitude toward the Anabaptists without recognizing this fact. Roland Bainton's latest Luther biography makes this very clear.

In the 16th century the word "Anabaptists" denoted simply the enemies of the truth, opponents of God and His cause, the greatest threat to the existing order, the state, and Christendom. They were considered to be a "devilish sect" of "satanic origin," to be mercilessly eradicated. This was the advice of Luther, Melanchthon, Zwingli, and others to their princes and city councils, and this was the procedure actually followed. (Philip of Hesse was a notable exception.) The representatives of the church and the theologians and historians of later times apparently simply copied these concepts and if possible strengthened them, without considering the sources or the Anabaptists themselves. Nicholas Storch and Thomas Müntzer were the first to attack the Protestant cause from within, and they rejected infant baptism; hence they must have begun the Anabaptist movement. No evidence of factual connections with the later real Anabaptists was needed. H.S.B.

H. S. Bender, "The Zwickau Prophets, Thomas Müntzer, and the Anabaptists," *MQR* XXVII (1953) 2-16; Paul Wappler, *Thomas Müntzer und die Zwickauer Propheten* (Zwickau, 1908); Annemarie Lohmann, *Zur geistigen Entwicklung Thomas Müntzers* (Leipzig, 1931).

Zwicker, Daniel (1612-78), an oculist of Danzig, and for a time a member of the anti-Trinitarian Polish Church (*q.v.*). In 1648 the Hutterite bishop Andreas Ehrenpreis (*q.v.*) had sent missioners to Danzig who contacted members of this Socinian church. Zwicker, a recent member of this church, was profoundly impressed by the Hutterite plea for the primitive Christian form of communal life. A lively correspondence with the Hutterites ensued, of which we have at least three Ehrenpreis letters to Zwicker (of 1649, 1650, and 1654), and one each to Zwicker's friends Hans Martin (1648) and Jobst von Stein (1649), all dealing with the doctrine of the Trinity and defending the principle of community of goods. Zwicker, a rather restless intellectual, decided to visit a Hutterite community. Thus in 1654 (not 1644, as Wilbur has it) he set out with three other men from Danzig to visit Ehrenpreis in Sobotiste (*q.v.*), Slovakia. After a stay of not more than ten days, studying the *Rechenschaft* by Riedemann (*q.v.*) and other doctrinal writings, he decided to

join the brotherhood, in spite of his mental reservations concerning the doctrine of the Trinity. Strangely enough, Ehrenpreis, though well aware of these reservations, was glad to receive Zwicker into the brotherhood, and waived certain affirmations. He was at once made a minister and "missionary to Poland." When he left, Ehrenpreis gave him a handwritten chronicle of the Brethren (Codex "E" in Beck's description, today in Hamburg) that he might be better informed if asked to give account.

Upon his return to Danzig, Zwicker set to work immediately to promote some sort of fusion of the Polish Unitarians and the Slovakian Anabaptists, claiming the moral superiority of the Hutterites. But he was not very successful, for he was ably opposed by two members of the Polish church, Martin Ruarius and Ludwig von Wolzogen. Zwicker concealed the fact that he had accepted membership in the Hutterite brotherhood by affirming the Trinitarian doctrine. He gave the appearance that all he wanted was a loose union of the two groups whereby the Danzig church would have to accept only the communal form of brotherhood living, an ideal once held by his Polish coreligionists. Ruarius convinced his church that Zwicker's proposals were not feasible. Eventually, in 1656, the Danzig Socinian church expelled Zwicker. From 1657 to his death in 1678 he lived in Amsterdam, where he was well received. In the Netherlands Zwicker traveled extensively. He was suspected of Socinianism; he criticized and censured several churches including the Mennonites for their spiritual decay, later even defending the views of Christian Entfelder (*q.v.*) that it was better not to join any church, and disputing particularly in Collegiant (*q.v.*) meetings. Some Collegiant Mennonites like Jacob Jansen Voogd (*q.v.*) opposed Zwicker's views, but others were influenced by Zwicker to leave the church. Zwicker published a number of books, among which were *De noch Staende en Triompherende Sichtbare kerkcke Christi* (Amsterdam, 1660), opposing Galenus (*q.v.*) Abrahamsz, and his most radical work, *Irenicon Irenicorum* (n.p., 1678), translated from Latin into Dutch by his follower Adriaan Swartepaert, under the title *Vredeschrift der Vredeschriften* (1678). Zwicker died in 1678 at Amsterdam. It is not known how the Hutterite chronicle in his possession got to the Hamburg City Library. R.F., vDZ.

Zwicker's life and work has never been thoroughly studied; the best treatment thus far is by Stanislaus Kot, *Socinianism in Poland, the Social and Political Ideas of the Polish Antitrinitarians* (Warsaw, 1932, English translation by E. M. Wilbur, Boston, 1957) 157-63 and 201 (based on extensive original research); E. M. Wilbur, *A History of Unitarianism; Socinianism and Its Antecedents* (Cambridge, Mass., 1946) 573-75, also 510 note; R. Friedmann, "The Encounter of Anabaptists and Mennonites with Anti-Trinitarianism," *MQR* (1948) 161-62; Beck, *Geschichts-Bücher*, 486-92; Chr. Sepp *Polemische en Irenische Theologie* (Leiden, 1882) 131, 134; W. J. Kühler, *Het Socinianisme in Nederland* (Leiden, 1912) 218-21; C. B. Hylkema, *Reformateurs*, 2 vols. (Haarlem, 1900, 1902) *passim*; K. O. Meinsma. *Spinoza en zijn Kring* (The Hague, 1896) 196-99; H. W. Meihuizen, *Galenus Abrahamsz* (Haarlem, 1954) 81. The Ehrenpreis letters are to be published in a future volume of Anabaptist epistles, possibly in 1960.

Zwinger, Hans (Hänsel), a Hutterite preacher, a tanner, therefore called also Gerber, who died in 1568 at Wostitz in Moravia, was the author of the song, "Wollen singen zu dieser Frist," which commemorates the suffering of Hans Arbeiter (*q.v.*) and Heinrich Schuster (*q.v.*).   E.H.B.

Beck, *Geschichts-Bücher*, 253; Wolkan, *Lieder*, 230; Zieglschmid, *Chronik*, 367, 397, 426; *ML* IV.

Zwingli, Huldrych (Ulrich) (1484-1531). Though not the most qualified scholar, the wisest churchman, or the most intelligent theologian in the Swiss-South German Reformation, Huldrych Zwingli was beyond challenge the movement's most significant personality, and merits, if anyone does, the name of father of Reformed Protestantism. As befits a genius, Zwingli shows more vitality than unity in his life and thought; his life is a series of turning points and his doctrinal system shifted with the years. The present article is interested in these movements primarily with respect to their relation to Anabaptism, of which Zwingli is in a certain sense also the father.

From his birth in 1484 in the home of a respectable citizen of Wildhaus (Toggenburg), Swiss canton of St. Gall, through his theological and humanistic studies (Master's degree from the University of Basel, 1506, further study at Vienna) and ten years of priestly service in Glarus (1506-16), Zwingli betrayed nothing of a reformer's character, nor was he even especially religious. By birth and training a patriot, whose first writings argued against the current Swiss practice of sending young men into foreign mercenary service and against Swiss subservience to foreign powers, he nevertheless received a papal pension himself and served as chaplain in foreign wars.

In 1516 Zwingli moved decidedly into the camp of Erasmus. This meant first of all the adoption of a kind of patriotic-humanistic pacifism, further strengthening his antagonism to Swiss involvement in foreign wars. Allegiance to Erasmus meant further a more specifically Christian orientation in his humanism, turning somewhat from the noble and morally noncommittal Greco-Roman antiquities to a rediscovery of the New Testament and the purer, simpler, more demanding faith it portrays. Zwingli himself always referred to 1516 as the major change in his spiritual experience. In this attitude Zwingli preached, still unquestioningly within Roman Catholicism, at the pilgrimage center of Einsiedeln (1516-18) and at the Grossmünster in Zürich, where he began his ministry as the head pastor of Zürich in January 1519. In Zürich he began to preach straight through the Gospel of Matthew and other New Testament books; expository preaching and the development of the city's schools were his program for Christian-humanist renewal.

The second major change in Zwingli's understanding came in 1520. News of Luther's excommunication had come to Zürich. It was becoming evident that the hopes of Erasmus and his friends that through the recovery of the Scriptures all Catholicism could be renewed were to be disappointed. The recovery of the New Testament Gospel and the maintenance of the unity of the church,

the two goals which Erasmus and Luther had hoped to keep together, were suddenly posed as alternatives, thanks to Rome's intransigence. Zwingli had to make a choice which, though its implications were then not clear, made the difference between Erasmus and Luther, humanism and Reformation.

Zwingli's "Pestlied," a poem describing sin and salvation in terms of deadly sickness and recovery, is often interpreted as evidence of a sort of "conversion" during the time of his own serious illness during an epidemic of pestilence in the winter of 1519-20. This is probably incorrect, but the general tone of the song is witness to a deepening in his faith and understanding which was going on during these Erasmian years, brought about as much by his own study of Paul as by Luther's influence. The clearest evidence of Zwingli's deepened insight and commitment is a letter written in late July 1520 to Oswald Myconius, then serving as a teacher in hyper-Catholic Lucerne. Zwingli gathers together all the New Testament references to suffering as the fate of Jesus' disciples. He contemplates seriously the possibility of Luther's being put to death and his own banishment, yet there is no turning back and no opportunistic search for halfway measures. "Born in blood, the church can be restored in no other way but by blood." Though he did not yet draw from this insight all the logically possible consequences, Zwingli's view of the church as a persecuted little flock in a hostile world was new and explosive.

This is the mentality with which Zwingli undertook steps toward Reformation, which were far more than a reorganization of the humanities curriculum. He abandoned his own papal pension and led Zürich to withdraw her alliance with Catholic France and to forbid her sons to serve as mercenaries. In 1522 he blessed with his presence a notorious breach of the lenten fasting regulations, and late in the same year resigned his priesthood and was re-employed by the city council as evangelical pastor, continuing in the same preaching post he had occupied before. During this time he gathered around himself a circle of enthusiastic younger humanists and clergy, several of whom (Grebel, Manz, Reublin, Brötli, Stumpf, *qq.v.*) were later to provide the backbone of the Anabaptist movement.

The Zürich Council obviously needed to justify its unprecedented move of installing a preacher who had just renounced Rome. According to the custom of the times this was done in the form of a disputation, to which all Christian Europe was invited. The disputation was held in January 1523, on the basis of 67 theses submitted by Zwingli. Johannes Faber, vicar of the Bishop of Constance, to whose diocese Zürich belonged, refused to participate in the main portion of the debate since he challenged the competence of a city council either to convoke such an assembly or to rule on its results. Thus a ruling in Zwingli's favor was a foregone conclusion. Yet the council's decision was basically a conservative one: there was no abolition of the Mass, or formal recognition of the Reformation. Zwingli was simply authorized to go on preaching the Gospel. From this point—even though there was no commitment made by the council—dates Zwingli's confidence that the council could be counted on to carry through all of the Reformation, and his consequent willingness to be satisfied with the pace set by the state's refusal (June 1523) to modify tithes legislation; abolition of the Mass deferred from October 1523 to May 1525; evangelical communion celebrated four times yearly instead of daily as Zwingli asked, and changed in form and significance by excluding the congregation from the speaking of the liturgy and by rejecting the connection with the ban.

At the cost of this willingness to compromise Zwingli was able to obtain and to consolidate a pro-Reformation majority in the council. The last pro-Catholic reaction within the city was crushed by the legally irregular execution in October 1526 of the patrician Jakob Grebel (father of Conrad), and from then on until just before his death Zwingli gained constantly in political influence, to the point of practically replacing the democratically elected Great Council by a Secret Council of which he was the dominant member. In this capacity he laid plans to destroy the Swiss Confederacy and set up a new union dominated by Zürich and Bern, as well as an anti-Hapsburg alliance stretching from Venice to Denmark, led by Zürich and Hesse and including the old enemy France. In 1529 Zürich was ready for a war to reshape the Confederacy, and in fact seized most of northeastern Switzerland from the Abbot of St. Gall, but the First War of Cappel ended in a truce without a battle. The second phase of the war found Zürich disunited and ill-prepared when it broke out in 1531. Zwingli accompanied the city's troops to the battlefield of Cappel, where his life, the battle, the war, and all hope of extending the Reformation to more of Switzerland were lost. A few weeks before his death Zwingli had attempted to resign his post in Zürich, because of growing opposition to his political leadership, but had been prevailed on to stay at the helm.

Zwingli and the Anabaptists. During 1523 Zwingli's younger associates became uneasy over their leader's concessions to the conservatism of the political authorities. When in December he finally promised to institute the Lord's Supper with or without state approval and then backed out of his bluff, not to raise the question again for over a year, the impatience could no longer be stemmed by the claim that the concessions he was making were purely tactical, and there began to grow around Conrad Grebel and Felix Manz a circle of dissenters, who in January 1525 were to be driven to found a new church (see **Zürich**).

The first of Zwingli's writings to attack the growing group of dissatisfied disciples within his own camp was his *Who Gives Occasion for Rebellion . . .(Wer Ursach gebe zu Aufruhr)* of December 1524. The main thrust of this tract is its attack on the bishops and princes whose injustice truly provokes revolutions. In addition, however, Zwingli refers to four distinct groups which profess allegiance to the Reformation but misunderstand its intent. One of these—and not the most dangerous

in his judgment—is the circle of those "who are more bloated with the knowledge of the Gospel than they are on fire with love" and who in addition to their narrow-minded spiritual pride reject infant baptism. Already the main lines of Zwingli's defense of infant baptism are visible; arguing that the New Testament does not speak to the issue, he concludes that the identity of baptism with Old Testament circumcision is sufficient proof.

These arguments are repeated in Zwingli's *On Baptism, Rebaptism and Infant Baptism* of May 1525. The impossibility of the Anabaptist appeal to New Testament teaching and usage is assured by declaring that the word "baptism" has numerous distinct meanings in the New Testament, so that it is illegitimate to reason from any one New Testament utterance to another. The most basic distinction is that made between "inner" baptism (subjective faith) and "outer" (water) baptism, which renders illusory any attempt to correlate the two. Since the essential claim of the Anabaptists was precisely that faith and water baptism must be bound together, Zwingli's dualism, building on philosophical postulates which he considered unchallengeable, seemed to be a sufficient answer. Freed from any connection with personal faith, baptism may then be equated with circumcision as the sign of a child's being externally reckoned to belong to God's people.

On the Preaching Office (June 1525) reports that Anabaptists from Zürich were ranging over the whole countryside, demanding rebaptism, and attacking the resident village pastors because they were supported by prebends and did not move about like apostles. Zwingli defends the resident ministry and the traditional means of support on New Testament grounds, and rejects as irrelevant the argument that all Christians should prophesy (I Cor. 14) or that all are priests (I Pet. 2). It is an offense against canon law for the Anabaptists to have taken their objections elsewhere after having been condemned in their home jurisdiction (Zürich). Zwingli reports that the Anabaptists are self-called and claim a private possession of the Holy Spirit mediated neither by Scripture nor by the church; he thus fails to grasp the issue which was truly at stake, namely, where the church was which was empowered to govern and to send. The Anabaptists did not reject the church, as Zwingli's whole argument assumed; they believed rather that their fellowship of committed believers was the church and that the "Milords of Zürich," who thus far had barely begun the Reformation, were not the church.

Zwingli seems to have felt that these two pamphlets had adequately settled the issues involved in Anabaptism, for from this time on, his writings deal with the continuing battle with Catholicism and the beginning debate with Lutheranism about the sacraments. (Zwingli's *Answer to Balthasar Hubmaier's Book on Baptism . . .*, printed in November 1525, was written hastily, at the request of friends, and adds nothing to the debate.) The conflict with Anabaptism now moved to the level of practical politics. Zwingli's personal attitude toward the increasingly repressive police measures taken by the authorities (prison February 1525;

money fines and torture late 1525; death penalty and banishment decreed in 1526 and applied in 1527) has not been adequately studied. On the one hand he seems to have urged moderation and to have intervened personally in favor of some prisoners, yet at the same time he is reported to have preached that repression is the duty of a legitimate government; and in view of his dominant role in Zürich's public life one can hardly conceive of these measures being taken against his will or without his approval.

Zwingli did not return in his writings to Anabaptism until two years later, when two Anabaptist documents came into his hands. One, which he calls a "confutation," is known only because he reproduced it in the process of answering it; it is a direct response to his own arguments and may have been written by Conrad Grebel. The other is the "Brotherly Union" of Schleitheim. Zwingli's *In Catabaptistarum Strophas Elenchus* of August 1527 is his last word on Anabaptism, except for scattered references in his general doctrinal writings. It adds nothing to the argument on baptism but offers numerous historical side lights and represents his only reaction to other aspects of the Anabaptist position (oath, government, ban). Zwingli's interests now clearly lie elsewhere. He has no more personal contacts with Anabaptists, dealing with them only on the basis of writings or of rumor; the *Elenchus* is the epilogue to a chapter already closed.

How Zwingli's relation to Anabaptism should be understood depends largely on one's prior theological commitment. Grebel spoke for all the Anabaptists with the claim that "Zwingli led us into this" and only backed away from his own vision later because of fear. This claim is objectively confirmed in that Zwingli did conceive of the church as a visible, suffering minority between 1520 and 1522, a position which Anabaptism retained while he abandoned it. On the other hand, Zwingli saw an unbroken continuity in his own total work, and applied to the Anabaptists the harsh words of I John, "They went out from among us, but they were not of us." Where between these two claims the truth lies will probably depend on the significance attributed to the "turning point" in mid-December 1523, when Zwingli took a position which he had said a week earlier would make him "guilty of lying before the Word of God." J.H.Y.

Zwitsers (*Zwitsersche Doopsgezinden, Oude Zwitzers, Nieuwe Zwitsers*): see **Swiss Mennonites in the Netherlands.**

Zwolle, capital of the Dutch province of Overijssel (1953 pop. 52,500, with 368 Mennonites), seat of a Mennonite congregation. Anabaptism was found here as early as 1533, then bearing a strongly marked revolutionary character. Jan (*q.v.*) van Geelen was in Zwolle in January 1535. Among the many Anabaptists active here was Harman (*q.v.*) Hoen. Cornelis (*q.v.*) de Vlaminck, a deacon of the early Anabaptist congregation of Amsterdam, was executed at Zwolle in 1535. In 1544 there was still some revolutionary activity here. A Mennonite congregation of Zwolle is first mentioned in 1574, but

Mennonite meetings had been held here at least by 1562. About 1600 there probably were three Mennonite congregations here—Flemish, Waterlander, and High German—but these groups merged before 1649. The united church, sometimes called Flemish and sometimes Waterlander, was represented at the Haarlem Flemish conference in 1649 by Hendrick Theunis, Wynant Jansz, and Thomas Schimmelpenninck. In 1674 the Zwolle congregation joined the Zonist (*q.v.*) Conference. Though there never was an Old Flemish congregation at Zwolle, the Groningen Old Flemish preachers Ubbo Meertens and Lubbert Jansz Kremer (*q.v.*) preached here in 1754 to large audiences. A meetinghouse was probably built in 1638 or shortly after on Wolweversstraat on the site of the present Mennonite church. It was remodeled in 1708, and enlarged in 1846; its organ was secured in 1907. The Zwolle congregation possesses two silver communion cups from 1661, one from 1670, and one from 1851. An old people's home on Koestraat was used until 1781 and then sold. A special hymnal, the *Zwolsche* (*q.v.*) *Bundel,* has been used here since 1808.

Concerning membership little is known; the baptized membership numbered 34 in 1706, 40 in 1796, 170 in 1861, 340 in 1926, 280 in 1958. Members of the old Stroink family are still found here; formerly there was also the Schimmelpenninck (*q.v.*) family, many of whose members were deacons. The small congregation of Zwolle in 1672 contributed 414 Dutch guilders for the Swiss Mennonites and again a considerable gift in 1710, and later also in behalf of the Prussian Mennonites.

Until *c*1695 the congregation was served by untrained and unsalaried ministers chosen from the membership; the first salaried minister was Abraham Blijdenstein, serving from 1700. The conservative leader Jacobus Rijsdijk (*q.v.*) served at Zwolle 1723-28. The first minister educated at the Amsterdam seminary to serve here was Thomas Menalda, 1771-d.94. Assuerus Doyer (*q.v.*), a beloved pastor, served 1795-d.1838. He was followed by L. ten Cate Coster 1833-58, T. Kuiper 1859-62, A. Vis 1862-66, J. Kerbert 1867-84, S. Cramer 1885-90, A. G. van Gilse 1890-1922, W. H. toe Water 1923-38, A. P. van de Water 1939-42, Miss C. Soutendijk 1942-46, and J. Meerburg Snarenberg from 1947. Church activities include two women's circles and a Sunday school for children. vDZ.

S. Elte, "Godsdienstige conflicten in Zwolle . . . 1530-80," in *Verslagen en Mededeelingen Overijsselsch Regt en Geschiedenis* 1936; Mellink, *Wederdopers,* 282-90; *Inv. Arch. Amst.* I, Nos. 84, 134, 267, 886, 1117; II, Nos. 2456-71; Blaupot t. C., *Groningen* I, 18, 96 f., 143 note 1, 150, 215 f., 239; II, 127, 185 f.; *DJ* 1840, 44; 1850, 41 f.; *DB* 1861, 174; 1875, 54 f.; 1882, 108 f.; 1900, 115; 1903, 149; N. van der Zijpp, *Geschiedenis der Doopsgezinden in Nederland* (Arnhem, 1952) 109, 242 note 17; *Algemeen Doopsgez. Weekblad* XI (1956) No. 13.

Zwolsche Bundel (*Zwolsche Liederen*): see **Vervolg van Christelijke Gezangen.**

Zwolsche Fonds (Zwolsche Weduwfonds), a fund for the pensioning of the widows of Mennonite pastors, founded at Zwolle in 1810. In 1897 this fund merged with the *Fonds* (*q.v.*) *ter Ondersteun-*

ing (North Holland Relief Fund for the Pensioning of widows and Orphans of Mennonite Pastors). (*Inv. Arch. Amst.* I, Nos. 985 d-ag.)   vDZ.

Zwolsche Kas: see **Zwols(ch)e Vereeniging.**

Zwols(ch)e Ring, an association of Dutch Mennonite congregations for mutual aid in case of pulpit vacancy, founded shortly after 1860. At present the following congregations belong to the Ring: Zwolle, Kampen, Blokzijl, Zwartsluis, Meppel, and Steenwijk.   vDZ.

Zwols(ch)e Vere(e)niging, a Dutch Mennonite conference, was founded on June 2, 1858, at Zwolle as the "Vereeniging van Doopsgezinde gemeenten in Overyssel, Gelderland, Utrecht en van naburige in het Koninkrijk Pruisen." The purpose of it was to bring more closely together the scattered Mennonites which had not yet been organized into a regional conference. Annual meetings were held to discuss questions pertaining to these churches. By 1861 17 congregations had joined, 15 Dutch and two German—Cleve and Emmerich; by 1871 it had 19 congregations. In the meetings of 1875 and 1876 the question whether to include the congregations of South Holland and Zeeland was discussed. This had no practical result at this time, but in 1879 Rotterdam joined the conference, and in 1883 The Hague, and gradually all the churches of South Holland and Zeeland joined, as well as the newly established congregations of Wageningen, Zuid-Limburg, Eindhoven. At the meeting of 1885 it was decided to call the conference the "Zwolsche Vereeniging." Accounts of the annual meetings of 1870-95 were published in *DB* (except 1878 and 1894).

The Zwolsche Vereeniging took important initiatives: in 1887 it decided to publish a Mennonite weekly (see **Zondagsbode**), and in 1892 Tj. Kielstra, pastor of Middelburg, raised the question of doing something for Mennonites in the Diaspora, which led to a church ministry to them (see **Verstrooiing**). The conference also founded the Zwolsche Kas, a treasury to subsidize poor congregations, which functioned until 1946, when its activity was taken over by the A.D.S.   vDZ.

Inv. Arch. Amst. I, Nos. 966, 1,000g; *DB* 1861, 104 f., 113 ff.; 1876, 118; 1877, 138; 1884, 137 f.; 1888, 137; 1889, 117 f.; *De Zondagsbode* XLVI (1932-33), Nos. 39-41.

Zylis: see **Zelis.**

Zytse Dirckx: see **Sytze Dirks.**

Supplement

Aalst, a town (pop. 43,000) in the Belgian province of East Flanders, was the seat of a Mennonite congregation for a few years about 1539, in which year Rosiane (*q.v.*) 't Kemels was executed here. The congregation was soon extinguished by persecution.
vDZ.

A. L. E. Verheyden, "La Réforme à Alost pendant le XVIe Siècle," in *Revue Belge de Philologie et d' Histoire* XXIX (1951) 1151-62.

Abbotsford (B.C.) Church of God in Christ Mennonite Church was first listed in the Yearbook (CGC) for 1950. In 1958 it had 190 members, served by ministers Frank P. Wiebe, A. W. Baerg, and A. J. Wilson.
M.G.

Abendfrieden home for the aged: see **Pinneberg.**

Aberdeen, Sask., is a district of the Rosenort Mennonite Church. The town of Aberdeen is on the right side of the South Saskatchewan River, and Rosthern, the main part of the Rosenort Mennonite Church, is on the left side of the river. The Rosenort Mennonite Church was organized here in 1907, with C. C. Ens as the first minister. In 1957 the membership was 130, with Frank D. Koop as minister.
J.G.R.

Academy: see **Bible Schools** and **Preparatory Schools.**

Achterhofje, the appendix of several Dutch Mennonite hymnals: see **Lusthof des Gemoets, Rijper Liedt Boecxken,** and **Stapel, Claes.**

Adams Mennonite Brethren Church is a rural church west of Adams, Okla. Organized as the Hooker M.B. Church in 1905, with 30 members, its first leader was H. S. Voth. Its meetinghouse was dedicated in 1906. Several years ago the present name was adopted. The membership in 1957 was 117, with Abe D. Unruh as pastor.
M.G.

Adler, Clemens (d. 1536), a Moravian Anabaptist of Austerlitz belonging to the Stäbler (*q.v.*) party of Jakob Widemann, which later became the Hutterites. On April 12, 1529, he completed the writing of a very important extensive manuscript (apparently never published), which bears the title *Das Urteil von dem Schwert mit unterschidlichem gewalt Dreier Fürstenthum der Welt, Juden, und Christen, mit Anderen Anliegenden sachen.* It exists in only one manuscript copy made c1729, which was found in 1951 by Samuel Geiser (Brügg bei Biel, Switzerland) in the possession of a Mennonite family near Langnau, canton of Bern, which has been transcribed and of which copies are now in BeCL and GCL.

In the preface the author indicates that his purpose is to distinguish the various ages of history and to delineate correctly the difference between the kingdom of God and the kingdom of this world. Christ is the king of peace and the king of righteousness. The church has the power of the keys to discipline its members and to maintain the high standard of the "order of Christ." Adler's writing is a thoroughly nonresistant work, and of high quality. He also treats briefly community of goods and the oath.

It is strange that Adler's name does not appear in the Hutterite Chronicle. It is known from other sources that he died in 1536.
H.S.B.

Samuel Geiser, "An Ancient Anabaptist Witness for Nonresistance," *MQR* (1951) 66-69 and 72.

Adlig Pokraken: see **Pokraken.**

Adriaen Kerstantsz, of Maasland, an Anabaptist martyr, was executed at Leiden, Holland, on July 14. Particulars are lacking. (Mellink, *Wederdopers,* 206.)
vDZ.

Adriaen de Kleermaker (Adriaen Cornelisz Snijer), an Anabaptist martyr of The Hague, was beheaded there on April 10, 1535. Particulars are lacking. (Mellink, *Wederdopers,* 208 f.)
vDZ.

Adriaen Wouters, an Anabaptist martyr, of Schiedam, was beheaded on Oct. 14, 1539, at Veere in the Dutch province of Zeeland. Particulars are lacking except the fact that he was banished from the province of Holland. (Mellink, *Wederdopers,* 225, 324.)
vDZ.

Adrian (Minn.) Amish Mennonite Church, now extinct, in Nobles County, Minn., about 15 miles northwest of Worthington. On Nov. 19, 1893, Jacob Gascho was ordained to the ministry in this congregation, the first members of which came from Canada in 1891. Beginning in March 1893 the congregation held services every two weeks. In early 1894 the community numbered 12 families and 30 members. The *Family Almanac* of 1900 names Joseph Gerber as an O.O.A. bishop, and Jacob Gascho, Joseph Grieser, Joseph Jantzi, John J. Miller, John Rupp, Joseph Schantz, and D. D. Schlabach as Amish ministers. In 1913-16 these ministers were listed as Conservative Amish Mennonite. In 1917 no Amish preachers were listed in Minnesota, nor these men named in any other Amish or Mennonite lists.
M.G.

Adriel School, West Liberty, Ohio, a child welfare school, established in 1957, capacity 37, sponsored by the Mennonite Board of Missions and Charities (MC): see **Orphans' Home.**

Aecht Mathys, the wife of Willem Dirksz Bystervelt, an Anabaptist martyr, was executed with her husband at The Hague, Holland, on March 16, 1535. (*Inv. Arch. Amst.* I, Nos. 744 f.) vDZ.

Aechte Coenen, an Anabaptist martyr, drowned at Leiden, Holland, on July 14, 1544. She was probably a follower of David (*q.v.*) Joris. (Mellink, *Wederdopers,* 206.) vDZ.

Aefke Harmen Thysdochter, captured during the assault of the Oldeklooster (*q.v.*), was drowned at Leeuwarden, Friesland, on April 14, 1535. (Vos, *Menno Simons,* 229.) vDZ.

Aegje Elinxdochter, an Anabaptist martyr, drowned at Alkmaar, Holland, on Feb. 1, 1536. (Mellink, *Wederdopers,* 172.) vDZ.

Aernt (Arent) Gerytsz, a revolutionary Anabaptist who participated in the Poeldijk (*q.v.*) disturbance, was beheaded at The Hague, Holland, March 14, 1536. (Mellink, *Wederdopers,* 219, 221.) vDZ.

Afrika-Missions-Verein (Africa Missionary Society) was organized in 1934, reorganized in 1935, as a private Canadian Mennonite Brethren mission board to operate the Bololo, Congo, Mission. On Jan. 1, 1944, it turned the work over to the Foreign Mission Board of the M.B. Conference. The Bololo Mission had been founded in 1933 as a private faith venture, but when the Conference Mission Board refused to take it over in spite of the appeals of the missionaries, the Society was organized to do so. The Society was managed by a board of directors with the following officers: G. J. Reimer secretary, and H. H. Janzen chairman. Its organ was *Der Kleine Afrika-Bote,* 1935-43. H.S.B.

G. W. Peters, *The Growth of Foreign Missions in the Mennonite Brethren Church* (Hillsboro, 1947) 97-103.

Agape is the organ of the Mennonite Relief and Service Committee (MC), in 1959 a 6-page 9 x 12 in. monthly, first number April 1955. It reports on and promotes interest in Voluntary Service, I-W Service, Relief Work, and related fields of service. H.S.B.

Agape Verlag, with headquarters at Starenstrasse 41, Basel, Switzerland, was established in 1956 as a subsidiary of the Mennonite Publishing House, Scottdale, Pa. Its chief publication to date has been the series of summer Bible school manuals in German and French, which was prepared by a corps of editors originally appointed by the MCC. The manuals are basically translations from the English manuals published at Scottdale. The European Advisory Committee represents the interests of the South German, Swiss, and French Mennonite Conferences. The work was begun c1950, but the name "Agape Verlag" was not adopted until 1956. H.S.B.

Aibonito Mennonite Church, Aibonito, Puerto Rico, was founded in 1958. It had 12 members, with a supply ministry. H.S.B.

Aibonito, Puerto Rico, Mennonite General Hospital (MC), a 32-bed general hospital, is controlled by a local board approved by the Health and Welfare Committee of the Mennonite Board of Missions and Charities, Elkhart, Ind. It was established in 1944 as the La Plata Mennonite Hospital but in March 1957 was moved to the new Aibonito hospital building. Two thirds of the cost ($415,000) of the building was paid by public funds and one third by private monies. In 1958 five doctors and eleven nurses were on its staff, with George D. Troyer, M.D., the chief of staff. John Driver was chairman of the local committee and Mervin Nafziger the administrator. M.G.

Ailsa Craig Boys Farm, located one mile south of Ailsa Craig, Ont., and 24 miles northwest of London, Ont., operated by the Mennonite Central Committee on behalf of the Mennonite Churches of Ontario represented in the Conference of Historic Peace Churches, was established in 1955 as a home for the rehabilitation of delinquent boys. It is supported by contributions from the Ontario Mennonites and funds from the Ontario Provincial government. The CHPC appoints an advisory council and provides the channel for the Mennonite financial support. H.S.B.

Alaska Mennonite Mission (MC) was founded in 1952 by the Mennonite Board of Missions and Charities. In 1958 it had one station at Russian Mission, with one self-supporting missionary couple. H.S.B.

Alberta Community Church (GCM), Portland, Ore., began in 1928 at NE 26th and Alberta streets. The following summer the Alberta Community church building was rented. The work was sponsored by the Pacific District Conference and the Home Mission Board (GCM). On June 29, 1931, the congregation was organized with 11 charter members. In 1938 the Home Mission Board purchased the building in which the congregation had been meeting and remodeled it. The following have served the church: Catharine Niswander, Albert Claassen, Edmond Miller, Arnold Regier, Henry Wiebe, Clyde Dirks, and Harry Albrecht, the minister in 1958, in which year the membership was 74. C.K.

H. D. Burkholder, *The Story of Our Conference and Churches* (n.p., 1951).

Alberta Mennonite Health Society was organized in 1932 as a mutual aid organization to cover medical expenses of its members, who live within 16 miles from Coaldale, Alta., the headquarters. The membership has varied from 100 to the present number of 380. Annual charges have varied from $12.00 to the present $92.00 per family. It serves both the M.B. and the G.C.M. groups. JA.KL.

Alberta Mennonite Home for the Aged, Coaldale, Alta., is owned and operated by the Provincial Conference of the Mennonite Church of Alberta (GCM). The home, dedicated April 11, 1955, has a capacity of 14 guests and accepts them from anywhere in Alberta. Jacob J. Andres has served as superintendent of the home from its beginning. M.G.

Alberta Mennonite Relief Society was organized in 1946 at the instigation of C. F. Klassen to aid Russian Mennonite refugees stranded in Germany, but later devoted itself to aiding the settling of these refugees in Alberta, and to collecting money for relief needs in Paraguay. It serves both the M.B. and G.C.M. groups throughout Alberta.   Ja.Kl.

Alberta Mutual Aid Society is a branch of the Alberta Mennonite Relief Society which provides fire and storm insurance for its members at the rate of 15¢ per $100.00 property value. It serves both the M.B. and G.C.M. groups throughout Alberta.   Ja.Kl.

Alberta-Saskatchewan Mennonite District Mission Board (MC) was authorized in 1920. Among its first active members were Allan Good and Jacob Brenneman. E. S. Hallman served as its president 1920-28, followed by M. D. Stutzman 1928- . It consisted of nine members in 1958 and sponsored five mission stations in Alberta.   M.G.

Alderden, an old and well-known Mennonite family at Aalsmeer, Holland. Maarten Willemsz Alderden was a preacher of the Frisian Mennonite congregation in the early 18th century and Jacob Maartens (probably his son) an elder of the same congregation c1720-60. A number of Alderdens have served as deacons.   vdZ.

Alde(r)werelt, van, a Dutch Mennonite family, whose ancestor Cornelis van Alderwerelt fled from Meenen (q.v.) in Belgium c1580 to Middelburg (q.v.) in the Dutch province of Zeeland, where he was a cloth merchant and probably a deacon of the church. He was married to Cathelijne Pleviers (Plovier), who may have been a daughter of the martyr Lenaert (q.v.) Plovier. Their son Jan van Aldewerelt moved to Amsterdam, where he and his descendants were cloth merchants. Some of them were members of the Flemish congregation, others joined the Waterlanders. Salomon van Alderwerelt (c1624-79) was one of the authors of *Ontdeckte Veinzing* (1655), two pamphlets published anonymously against Galenus (q.v.) Abrahamsz. The van Alderwerelt family left the Mennonite Church in the early 18th century.   vdZ.

Nederl. Patriciaat VII (1916) 8-14, XLII (1956) 23-43; Meihuizen, *Galenus Abrahamsz* (Haarlem, 1954) 201 f.

Alexander (Man.) Mennonite Brethren Church was organized in 1929, although meetings for worship were held in Griswold beginning in 1926. In 1929 a meetinghouse was purchased in Griswold, and until 1954 when a meetinghouse was erected in Alexander it was known as the Griswold M.B. Church. The first leader of the congregation was H. Penner, then A. B. Friesen, and in recent years J. J. Krueger. In 1959 the membership was 81.   H.S.B.

Alexandrabad was a sanatorium on the bank of the Dnepr River in the Ukraine, Russia, near the Chortitza settlement. It was established in 1907 by the Wieler brothers after the pattern of a Dresden sanatorium. Later the industrialist J. Niebuhr purchased and enlarged it. It served the Mennonite constituency and the surrounding population as a health and summer resort.   C.K.

D. A. Hamm, "Das Gesundheitswesen in Chortitza," *Menn. Life* X (1955) 86.

Algeria Mennonite Mission (MC) was founded in 1957 under the Mennonite Board of Missions and Charities, at which time the Miller Stayrooks were appointed missionaries. In 1958 they were residing in Kouba (Alger), Algeria. The Robert Stetters were appointed to this field in 1958.

A small group of Pax men was sent in 1955 to do reconstruction work in the area of the earthquake of 1954, under the administration of the Mennonite Relief and Service Committee. In 1956 the work was concentrated in the village of Flatters, where 30 or more houses were built by 1959 when the work was drawing to a close.   H.S.B.

Allegheny Conference News: see Southwestern Pennsylvania Conference News.

Allegheny Mennonite Conference Mission Board (MC) was organized in 1913 to operate city and rural missions in its territory, among which the Altoona and Johnstown city missions have been prominent.   H.S.B.

Allianz-Bibelschule (1905-18), Berlin, Germany, a Bible institute founded by the Baptist Karl Mascher, the Englishman Broadbent, and others, closely related to the Plymouth Brethren, and attended by numerous Mennonites from Russia 1907-14, among them Abraham Braun, later minister at Ibersheim, Rhenish Hesse. The school was moved to Wiedenest in 1918, where it is still operating.   H.S.B.

All-Russian Union of Towns: see Sanitätsdienst.

All-Russian Union of Zemstvos for Relief of Sick and Wounded Soldiers: see Sanitätsdienst.

Allukrainische Konferenz der Vertreter der Mennonitengemeinden in der USSR convened as a last general conference on a regional scale in Melitopol Oct. 5-9, 1926. The program indicates that the leaders were fully aware of their task and prepared to meet the challenge of the day. A total of 84 representatives met, mostly of the Ukraine, 64 of whom were Mennonites and 19 Mennonite Brethren and Evangelical Mennonite Brethren. Fourteen representatives came from outside the Ukraine: Samara 3, Caucasus 2, Crimea 2, Siberia 3, Orenburg 2, Ufa 1, and Turkestan 1. Two government representatives were present.

The chairmen of the Conference were Jakob Rempel, Johann Töws, Peter Nickel, and Jakob Pätkau. First the KfK gave a report, after which the delegates to the First Mennonite World Conference reported. Local reports from various communities followed. Considerable time was devoted to the constitution of the Conference, a proposed Bible school, the spiritual life of the congregations, work among the young people, proposed publications (songbooks and *Unser Blatt*), and mission work.

Highly interesting and informative are the brief reports given by the representatives from the settlements of Molotschna, Chortitza, Zagradovka, Memrik, etc. The proposed constitution was unanimously accepted. Various significant lectures were presented. The total number of Mennonites of the Ukraine given for 1926 was 46,829. ("Protokoll," *Unser Blatt* II, November 1926, 47-53.)   C.K.

Altmann, a Dutch Mennonite family. Cornelis Sybrand Altmann, b. Feb. 21, 1881, at Rotterdam, who served six times as a deacon of the Rotterdam Mennonite congregation, should be mentioned as treasurer of the Hollandsch (*q.v.*) Doopsgezind Emigranten Bureau, who in 1924 ff. was very active in helping Mennonite refugees from Russia go to Brazil, and promoting the young colonies in this country by financial support. vDZ.

Altonasche Liederen: see **Gezangen, Christelijke.**

Alyt Claesdochter, an Anabaptist martyr, arrested when the Oldeklooster (*q.v.*) was recaptured, drowned at Leeuwarden in Friesland on April 14, 1535. (Vos, *Menno Simons,* 228.) vDZ.

Amazon Valley Indian Mission was established in 1955 at Araguacema, Goias, under an independent Mennonite (MC) board with the same name, whose founder and field director was Howard Hammer (d.1957). In 1958 the work was taken over by the Mennonite Board of Missions and Charities, although the AVIM board has continued to support the work. Since 1955 the *Amazon Valley Indian Mission Newsletter* has been published quarterly. H.S.B.

American Brethren Mission Union: see **Board of Foreign Missions** of the Mennonite Brethren Church.

Amish Mennonite Aid, founded Nov. 10, 1955, is the relief and mission agency of the Beachy Amish Mennonite group. Its work is carried on by an executive committee of three officers: Norman D. Beachy president, Elam L. Kauffman vice-president, and Jacob J. Hershberger secretary-treasurer. It is "dedicated to the rendering of material, moral, and spiritual aid, in the name of Christ, to destitute and needy people." Its only project thus far has been a refugee service center in Berlin, Germany, on behalf of refugees from the East Zone, since 1958 centered in Friedensheim, erected by it in 1958 at Klüberstrasse 26-28, Berlin. In addition to clothing distribution the program includes recreational facilities for children, Bible study classes for young and old, and summer Bible school. A.M.A. also has as one of its purposes the stimulation of interest among the Beachy Amish and Old Order Amish in missions and relief. H.S.B.

Amish Mennonite Storm and Fire Aid Union, Wellesley, Ont., was established about a century ago and serves the Amish Mennonite community in Ontario. In 1953 it had approximately 1,100 members and covered over $13,000,000 worth of property against fire and storm damage. In that year it paid out $6,971.69. M.G.

Amulree Reformed Mennonite Church: see **Northeasthope Reformed.**

Anabaptist Fund (*Täufergut*). In 1670 the cantonal Bern government issued a mandate against the Anabaptists which among other things ordered that the property of Anabaptists expelled from the canton should be confiscated and sold and the proceeds placed in a special fund. The purpose of the decree

was to punish the Anabaptists by sending them out of the country completely stripped of all assets, and also to retain their assets in the canton. These assets were placed in the administration of the state church parishes from which the Anabaptists were expelled, and invested, so that the interest could be applied to church and school purposes. Later the funds were concentrated in the hands of the county authorities (*Aemterweise*) and invested in what was called the Täufergutfonds, and still later a special account was set up in Bern called the Täufer-Urbar (*q.v.*). Anabaptist children returning to the state church could receive their inheritance from this fund, only however in case their parents had had a state church marriage (those of parents with only an Anabaptist marriage being declared illegitimate).

The income (and holdings ultimately) of the Anabaptist fund was used for various purposes. A large part remained until the modern civil structure of the canton was set up and then distributed to the civil authorities of the local units. By these it was usually applied to school and church purposes. Money was used for the repair of church buildings, purchase of pews, bells, and even new church buildings. For instance, in 1692 the parish of Schwarzenegg in the district of Thur received the value of some $4,000 to use on its new church building and for other purposes.

A similar procedure was followed in the canton of Zürich as well as in various places in South Germany, especially in Württemberg where much of the confiscated Anabaptist assets was used for similar purposes, but also for the benefit of the district treasury. H.S.B.

S. Geiser, *Die Taufgesinnten Gemeinden* (Karlsruhe, 1932) 406 f.; E. Teufel, "Die Beschlagnahme und Verwaltung des Täufergutes durch den Fiskus im Herzogtum Württemberg im 16. und 17. Jahrhundert," *Theol. Ztsch* VIII (1932) 296-304.

Andriesz, Johan: see **Aken, J. H. van.**

Angenehme Stunden was a 4-page Sunday-school magazine published monthly by the Mennonite Publishing Company, Elkhart, Ind., beginning April 1887. Appearing concurrently with *Welcome Tidings* (*q.v.*) and having the same format, it was not a translation, but carried completely different text. Occasionally cover pictures for a given issue of the two magazines were the same. Lists of Sunday-school materials appearing in *Herold der Wahrheit* indicate that publication must have ceased between August 1892 and January 1893. N.P.S.

Anna Jacledochter, an Anabaptist martyr, arrested when the Oldeklooster (*q.v.*) was taken, was drowned at Leeuwarden, Friesland, on April 14, 1535. (Vos, *Menno Simons,* 229.) vDZ.

Anne Jansdochter, of Tzum, and **Anne Luytthiedochter,** Anabaptist martyrs, drowned on April 14, 1535, at Leeuwarden, Friesland, after they had been arrested on April 7, when the Oldeklooster (*q.v.*) was recaptured. (Vos, *Menno Simons,* 228.) vDZ.

Anne de Vlaster: see **Anneken Hendriks.** She was the wife of Lambert Jansz Smid and in 1571 was living in Franeker, Friesland.

Anske Lieuwe Hayedochter, an Anabaptist martyr, drowned at Leeuwarden, Friesland, on April 14, 1535, after she had been arrested at the recapture of the Oldeklooster (*q.v.*). (Vos, *Menno Simons,* 228.)
vDZ.

Antrim County (Mich.) Mennonite settlement, now extinct, was begun in 1880 at Mancelona. It was first listed in the 1896 Mennonite Meeting Calendar. Meetings were held every two weeks simultaneously in the Cheatonia and the Wetzell schools, and every two weeks alternately in the Baer and Garber homes. June 15, 1895, the *Herald of Truth* reported communion services at Wetzell's, "where a large congregation was present." The 1899 Calendar no longer listed services for Antrim County. (See also **Mancelona.**)
M.G.

Appelman, Cornelis: see **Cornelis Jan Oliviers.**

Arcade Mennonite Church, Arcade, N.Y., a member of the Ontario Mennonite Conference, had 19 members in 1958, with Leroy Yoder as minister. The church was organized in 1956. In 1958 it purchased a schoolhouse in Yorkshire as a meetinghouse.
M.G.

Arends, a Dutch Mennonite family, at Drachten, Friesland, since the 17th century. Arend Tjeers was a preacher of the Drachten congregation 1772-89, as were his sons Sybolt Arends 1780 (?)-1808 and Tjalling Arends 1789-1805. Some members of this family adopted the family name of Arends and others Frieswijk.
vDZ.

Arentsz, Engel: see **Dooregeest, E. A. van.**

Argentine Chaco Mennonite Mission, South America. In 1958 there were five missionaries with 16 congregations and over 800 adult baptized members and 550 as yet unbaptized adults. The leadership of the congregations is wholly in the hands of the national pastors. Headquarters of the mission were at Saenz Pena, Chaco Province.
H.S.B.

Argentine Mennonite Church (MC), located at 37th and Metropolitan Ave., in Kansas City, Kans., was established in 1946 out of the former Mennonite Gospel Mission (*q.v.*). In 1958 the membership was 74, with Rufus P. Horst and Glen Yoder as ministers. It is a member of the South Central Conference.
H.S.B.

Aris-Jansz-volk: see **Verwer, A. J.**

Arkenbout, a former Mennonite family. Martinus Arkenbout was a preacher of the Flemish congregation at Brielle *c*1689. His son Jan Arkenbout served as preacher at Schiedam 1716-22 and Haarlem (Klein Heiligland congregation) 1722-*c*40, and his grandson Martinus Arkenbout, educated at the Amsterdam Lamist seminary, served at Zwolle 1741-46, Leiden 1746-57, and Haarlem 1757-d.90. In 1782 he dedicated the Mennonite home for the poor on Groot Heiligland, and his sermon *De Zang- en Speelkonst in haar nuttig gebruik . . . ,* preached on July 26, 1771, when the Klein Heiligland Mennonite church acquired its organ, was published at Haarlem in 1771. In the Amsterdam Zonist congregation there were also some Arkenbouts.
vDZ.

Arys Gerritsz, of Limmen, an Anabaptist martyr, was beheaded at The Hague, Holland, on July 28, 1534. He was arrested at Bergklooster (*q.v.*), being among the Anabaptists who had sailed from Amsterdam on their way to Münster (*q.v.*). Arys Gerritsz was the son of Aeffgen (*q.v.*) Lystyncx. (Mellink, *Wederdopers,* 170, 343.)
vDZ.

Ashland County (Ohio) Old Order Amish settlement consisted in 1958 of one congregation located near the city of Ashland, with 65 members and two bishops, Abe D. Troyer and Emanuel E. Schrock.
H.S.B.

Assiniboine Mennonite Mission Camp (GCM), located 15 miles west of Winnipeg near Springstein, Man., was founded in 1949 and owned by a private corporation until it was turned over to the G.C.M. Conference in 1957.
F.C.P.

Associated Mennonite Biblical Seminaries. Beginning with the academic year 1958-59 the Mennonite Biblical Seminary of Elkhart, Ind., and the Goshen College Biblical Seminary of Goshen, Ind., entered a co-operative relationship known under the descriptive name, The Associated Mennonite Biblical Seminaries. By action of the boards of control of the two seminaries, following a Memorandum of Agreement defining and regulating the relationship, a plan of academic co-operation has been set up which provides certain substantial advantages for both schools, while retaining the academic, organizational, and financial independence of each. Provision is made for later adherence of other Mennonite bodies to the Association, and it is hoped that the Association may ultimately become a general center of ministerial and missionary training for the Mennonite brotherhood of North America. The headquarters of the Association are on the Elkhart campus. An Institute for Mennonite Studies, also located on the same campus, has been established as a conjoint operation of the Associated Seminaries.

The following joint committees direct and serve the co-operative program: (*a*) the Joint Co-ordinating Committee representing the boards of control, functioning for the general supervision of the co-operation; (*b*) the Joint Administrative Committee representing the seminaries, composed of the president and dean of each associated seminary, and one representative of each affiliated seminary, to be administratively responsible for the day-to-day functioning of the co-operative program; (*c*) the Joint Library Committee, responsible for the co-ordination of the library program by which the libraries of the two schools function as an operating unit.

In addition to the regular offerings by each seminary of its own required and elective courses, the Associated Seminaries provide a program of joint-course offerings, to be normally given on the Elkhart campus, sufficient to make it possible for a student to take one fourth to one third of his curriculum choices in the conjoint program. In addition, cross-registration by students in the regular offerings of all associated seminaries is permitted by consent of the deans involved.
H.S.B.

Association of Mennonite Aid Societies of the United States and Canada: see **Mennonite Aid Societies, Association of.**

Association of Mennonite Hospitals and Homes: see **Mennonite Hospitals and Homes, Association of.**

Association of Mennonite University Students, a Canadian student organization, was begun in 1951 at the University of Manitoba in Winnipeg. It has since spread to the University of Toronto, and the universities of Saskatchewan (Saskatoon), Alberta (Edmonton), and British Columbia (Vancouver). Activities include usually monthly meetings and an annual banquet, with occasional study conferences, workshops, and special studies. The Manitoba chapter also operates a placement service. A major purpose of the organization is to increase student understanding of and appreciation for the Mennonite heritage and the Mennonite church and its work. A total of over 200 students belong to the several chapters. H.S.B.

Reinhard Vogt, "The Association of Mennonite University Students," *Menn. Life* XII (1957) 39 f.

Atglen (Pa.) **Open Air Singing,** an annual affair held in Kennel's Woods adjacent to the Maple Grove Mennonite Church (*q.v.*), ½ mile north of Atglen, was started in 1933 by Joseph G. Kennel (d. 1949). It meets annually the last Sunday afternoon of July. The program consists of the singing of hymns interspersed with short talks by visiting speakers, and in recent years with special singing by quartets and trios. Maximum attendance was in 1950, with 7,580 persons from 10 states and Ontario. In 1958 the attendance was 3,280. The annual offerings for relief or missions have averaged $1,300 for the last ten years. The organization consists of a chairman (Earl J. Kennel) and a secretary (Vernon Kennel). V.K.

Atse Wytses: see **Zijpp, van der.**

Atte Nanne Sybrandtsdochter, an Anabaptist martyr, drowned at Leeuwarden, Friesland, April 14, 1535. She was arrested when the Oldeklooster (*q.v.*) was recaptured. (Vos, *Menno Simons,* 228.) vDZ.

Attema, a Dutch Mennonite family, originally from Leeuwarden, Friesland. E. Attema (d. 1888), a lawyer at Leeuwarden, was a trustee of the A.D.S. and a curator of its seminary. Jurjen Attema, of Leeuwarden, was preacher of the Nijmegen congregation 1861-81 and also a trustee of the A.D.S. Doede Attema (Leeuwarden, Oct. 2, 1880-Hilversum, Nov. 18, 1954) was pastor of Zijldijk 1907-9, Twisk-Abbekerk 1909-12, IJmuiden 1912-15, and Zaandam-West 1915-46. After retiring he still served as assistant pastor at Oudebildtzijl 1947-49. Doede Attema, who was also for many years a trustee of the A.D.S., was one of the first pastors to promote the Mennonite Youth Movement. For many years he was an advisory member of the board of the Doopsgezinde (*q.v.*) Jongerenbond. He was also secretary of the Zaanse (*q.v.*) Fonds. vDZ.

Atwater M.B. Church: see **Winton M.B. Church.**

Aucke Sieurdtsdochter, an Anabaptist martyr, drowned at Leeuwarden, Friesland, on April 14, 1535, having been arrested at the recapture of the Oldeklooster (*q.v.*). (Vos, *Menno Simons,* 228.) vDZ.

Augsburger Mennonite Church (MC), at Berne, Ind., was formed in 1869, when the families of Preacher Christian Augsburger (1821-1903), George Fox, John Stauffer, and Peter Steiner withdrew from the Berne Mennonite Church (GCM). In the *Herald of Truth* for June 1871 services are listed for the Augsburger Church every three weeks. On April 29 and 30, 1871, John F. Funk (*q.v.*) and Daniel Brenneman visited the Augsburger congregation. Services were conducted in the P. C. Steiner and Christian Augsburger homes, and in a school. On June 11, 1871, Bishop John M. Brenneman of Elida, Ohio, received Augsburger and his group of 11 charter members into the fellowship of the Mennonite Church (MC). Augsburger's death in 1903 marked the end of regular services in the congregation. But as late as 1955 one of Augsburger's daughters was still living, a woman of 82, who still considered herself a member of the M.C. group. J.C.W.

Ayte: see **Eyte.**

Aytta: see **Viglius.**

Bächlingen: see **Vogelstock.**

Baedeker, Friedrich Wilhelm (1823-1906), noted evangelist among the Russians in the early days of the Baptist and Evangelical Christian movement in Russia, who devoted much time to preaching in the Russian prisons, and three times crossed Siberia as far as the island of Sakhalin, was of German origin but lived most of his life in England except when on evangelistic tours. He was a close friend of George Müller of Bristol and Lord Radstock (G. A. W. Waldgrave, 1833-1913), and was originally a member of the Plymouth Brethren (Open Brethren) but later worked as an independent. He worked with Radstock in the first St. Petersburg revival in 1874-76. Both men worked among the nobility at first, using the "drawing-room mission" technique. H.S.B.

Baer, John (1797-1858), an early publisher of Mennonite writings, was born in Upper Leacock, Pa., Jan. 31, 1797, a son of Andrew Baer (d. 1805) and great-grandson of John Henry Baer, the Swiss Mennonite pioneer settler (1727). He grew up in Lancaster. In 1821 he was sole owner of *Der Volksfreund* and in 1834 he also purchased the Lancaster *Beobachter.* These he merged as the *Lancaster Volksfreund und Beobachter,* the only German newspaper in the city. This was continued by his sons. In 1819 he published the first large folio Bible published in America. In 1828 he continued the *Agricultural Almanac* started by William Albright and in 1833 started also the *German Pennsylvania Almanac,* continuing both for years. Later it became *Baer's Almanac,* the 135th issue of which (1960) is soon to be released by Lester Lestz. For years he published many items for the Mennonites, succeeding Ehrenfried (q.v.). Reuben A. and Christian R. Baer continued the firm as John Baer's Sons; grandsons John F. and Charles S. Baer continued the firm until recently.   I.D.L.

Evans and Ellis, History of Lancaster County, 500, 501; Biographical Annals of Lancaster County, 152, 153; and Klein's History of Lancaster County IV, 408.

Bage (Brazil) Mennonite Brethren Church, located at Bage in the state of Rio Grande do Sul, was organized in 1943 when the Bage settlement was established by settlers from the earlier Krauel colony in the state of Santa Catharina. The meetinghouse was built in 1953. In 1957 the membership was 280, with Wilhelm Janzen as leader.   M.A.K.

Bair's Hanover Mennonite Church (MC): see Bair Mennonite Meetinghouse.

Bakels, Pieter Simon (Deventer, 1844-Haarlem, 1921), educated at the Amsterdam Mennonite seminary, was a pastor at Hoorn on the island of Texel 1869-76, Burg on Texel 1876-89, and Koog-Zaandijk 1889-1907, in which year he retired. He was a trustee of the A.D.S. 1889-1908. Herman Bakels (q.v.) was his son. Another son was Reinier Sybrand Bakels (b. den Hoorn, 1873), a well-known painter of portraits and landscapes.   vDZ.

Bakker, a common Dutch family name, meaning Baker. A well-known Mennonite Bakker family, many of whose members served as preachers, stems from the island of Ameland (q.v.), where Sybrand Jans Bakker was an (untrained) minister of the Waterlander congregation 1718-d.61. His great-grandson Jacob Sybrandsz Bakker (Terschelling, 1802-63) was pastor of Woudsend 1828-30 and Terschelling 1830-63. Three of his sons went into the ministry: Rienk Jacob Bakker (1827-61) serving at Warga 1853-57 and Aalsmeer on the Zijdweg 1857-d.61; Jan Fopko Bakker (1843-1911) serving at Zuid-Zijpe 1868-73, Midwolda 1873-75, Middelstum 1875-77, Giethoorn-Zuid 1877-81, and Twisk-Abbekerk 1881-1908; Cornelis Bakker (1842-99) serving at Wolvega 1866-71, Gorredijk-Lippenhuizen 1871-79, and Franeker 1879-d.99. Pastor Gerrit Bakker (q.v.) did not belong to this family. His son Claas Bakker served at Leermens-Loppersum 1836-d.84. Henricus Bakker was 1723-d.56 a preacher of the Amsterdam Zonist church, Hendrik Jacobs Bakker (1752-1848) served at Rasquert 1792-96, Veendam-Wildervank 1796-1804, Heerenveen 1804-9, and Middelie-Azwijk 1809-38. A Jan Michiels Bakker, d. 1849, was a preacher at Oude Niedorp 1813-31 and at Den Ilp 1831-49. (DB 1864, 179 f.; 1889, 17, 22-25.)   vDZ.

Ballincx (Balling, Bailings, Ballinghsz), **Cornelis,** a weaver at Rotterdam, Holland, at first a member of the Waterlander Mennonites, then a member and elder of the High German Mennonites, finally joining the Flemish church of Rotterdam, where he was an elder 1639-44. In 1644 he moved to Haarlem, where he also was an elder, at least until 1648. He was a very quarrelsome man, who was opposed by leaders like Eduard Nabels (q.v.) and Hans de Ries.

During his High German period he was an influential man; he was the first after Jan Cents to sign the Jan Cents confession of 1630.   vDZ.

Inv. Arch. Amst. II, 2203 f.; II, 2, 359-67, 428; K. Vos, Geschiedenis der Doopsgez. Gemeente te Rotterdam (repr. 1907) 4, 13, 42; DB 1907, 169.

Balling, Pieter, a member of the Flemish Mennonite congregation of Amsterdam and an adherent of Galenus (q.v.) Abrahamsz. He published Het Licht op den Kandelaar (Amsterdam, 1662), Verdediging van de Regering der Doopsgezinde Gemeente . . . (Amsterdam, 1663), and Nadere Verdediging van de Regering der Doopsgezinde Gemeente (Amsterdam, 1664), in which he defended Galenus and attacked his opponents. Balling was also a good friend of the Jewish philosopher Baruch de Spinoza. vDZ.

K. O. Meinsma, Spinoza en zijn kring (The Hague, 1896) passim.

Ballot, Johannes Stephanus Simeon, a Dutch Mennonite minister serving at Wolvega 1863-67 and Pieterzijl 1867-d.79, published the paper "Hans de Ries, zijn leven en werken" in DB 1863 and 1864. His brother Anthony Ballot served as pastor at Westzaan-Zuid 1860-64 and Hengelo 1864-d.71.
                    vDZ.

Balthasar Grasbanntner (Tischler) was a Moravian Anabaptist leader who belonged to the Marpeck Brotherhood, and being a joiner or cabinetmaker by trade is generally called Balthasar der Tischler. He probably served as elder of the church at Eibenschitz, for a Moravian chronicler calls him the Anabaptist "Vorsteher." He was a signatory of the important document in the Kunstbuch (q.v.) which constitutes a reply to Marpeck and expresses appreciation for Marpeck's work among the Moravian churches, signed by five men representing seven churches, and dated Sunday, Oct. 7, 1553.

Jarrold Zeman, in his research on the Moravian Brethren and their relation to the Anabaptists, has found that Balthasar Grasbanntner is identical with Balthasar der Tischler who represented the Anabaptists in their second discussion with the Moravian Brethren regarding their differences. The meeting took place at the request of the Anabaptists on April 17, 1559, at Eibenschitz, moving to Znaim the next day. Zeman has shown the importance of this encounter and the relationship between these two groups. In the meeting at Eibenschitz the points presented by the Moravian Brethren were: (1) reception of church members; (2) church discipline and the three steps prescribed by Christ; (3) the Moravian Brethren basis for infant baptism; (4) relation to government and participation in the magistracy. Of the four points the third received most extensive and heated discussion. Then the Anabaptists replied to a few questions: (1) What procedure do you observe in obtaining elders? (2) How many Anabaptist sects are there? (3) How many Anabaptists are there? (4) Where and when did your group originate? Finally Balthasar was asked if he had ever belonged to any other group of Anabaptists, to which he replied that he had not. The reporter comments that after all this talk they departed as they had come; "And so we had worked three whole hours and caught nothing just as those [the disciples] worked a whole night without catching anything."

The background of this discussion is sketched in the article **Hans Uhrmacher** (Supplement) and is on the whole reliably (according to Zeman) given by Müller. Balthasar's desire to communicate with the Moravian Brethren is evidence that the Marpeck Brotherhood existed as a separate body in Moravia as late as 1559, and sought to foster the unity of the church there. The Moravian Brethren had moved so far away from the Anabaptist position on baptism that union with them was out of the question. Furthermore, the Anabaptists did not have the academic equipment (knowledge of church history and exegesis) to counter the arguments of their more learned opponents. Their attempt to compensate by quoting from Erasmus' *Annotations* irritated the Moravian Brethren. Nevertheless Balthasar's desire and initiative in conversing with the Moravian Brethren stands out clearly. Of all the known contacts with the Brethren this seems to have been the most extensive and significant. The date and manner of Balthasar's death are unknown.   W.KL.

J. Th. Müller, "Die Berührungen der alten und neuen Brüderunität mit den Täufern," *Ztscht für Brüdergeschichte* IV (1910) 197-207; Heinold Fast, "Pilgram Marbeck und das oberdeutsche Täufertum," *ARG* XLVII (1956) 233.

Bancroft Mennonite Church (MC), located at 5559 West Bancroft St., Toledo, Ohio, a member of the Ohio and Eastern Conference, began in 1945 as a mission conducted by the Fulton County and Williams County Mennonite congregations. The meetinghouse was dedicated on Dec. 15, 1946. Freeman Aschliman, ordained in 1949, is in charge of this congregation of 38 members.   F.W.A.

Baptism (I, 224-28): Supplement. In the Mennonite Church (MC) and among some of the Amish Mennonites the custom of baptizing by pouring "in the stream," i.e., in a creek or river, arose during the 19th century, and at times has been widely practiced. It is still optional, and is practiced in a number of congregations. The reasons for the introduction of this practice are obscure. Some prefer "living water," i.e., running water; others seek to follow the example of Christ who was baptized in the Jordan River. Baptism "in water with water," as it is sometimes called, has nothing to do with immersion.   H.S.B.

Barbara Diricks, of Wier, and **Barbara Tiardsdochter**, of Sexbierum, Anabaptist martyrs, were arrested on April 7, 1535, during the recapture of the Oldeklooster (*q.v.*) and drowned at Leeuwarden, Friesland, on April 14. (Vos, *Menno Simons,* 229.)   vDZ.

Barbeli, of Sumiswald, living at Studen near Biel, Switzerland, an Anabaptist martyr, was drowned at Bern in late 1537 or early 1538.   vDZ.

D. L. Gratz, *Bernese Anabaptists* (Scottdale, 1953) 22, No. 17.

Barrville Mennonite Church (MC), a member of the Allegheny Conference, located five miles north

of Belleville, Pa., started in 1936 as a mission outpost of the Maple Grove Mennonite Church, was organized in 1956 as a separate congregation. In 1958 it had 35 members, with Elam H. Glick as pastor. A church was purchased in 1953.   H.S.B.

Bart Conservative Mennonite Church, 1½ miles east of Georgetown, Lancaster Co., Pa., was organized in 1950 and its church completed in 1956. It had 49 members in 1959. The ministers were Shem Peachey, M. S. Stoltzfus, and Urbane Peachey.   M.G.

Baucke (Jancke?) **Jorisdochter,** an Anabaptist martyr, drowned at Leeuwarden, Friesland, on April 14, 1535, after she had been arrested at the recapture of the Oldeklooster (*q.v.*). (Vos, *Menno Simons,* 228.)   vDZ.

Baudynken Het, an Anabaptist martyr: see **Dingentgen** (van Hondschooten).

Bavink, a widely ramified Mennonite family, originally living in the district of Twente, Dutch province of Overijssel, later also found at Groningen and Kampen, and in East Friesland, Germany. Some of its members served the church as ministers, e.g., Hendrik Bavink, a merchant and lay preacher in the Waterlander congregation of Kampen in the early 18th century; Pieter Bavink, an untrained preacher of the United Waterlander and Flemish congregation at Groningen 1728-?; Coenraad Bavink, trained at Groningen University and by Pastor P. Beets of Zaandam, served at Groningen as an assistant pastor from 1794, was pastor at Emden 1795-1807 and at Nijmegen 1807-10; Hendrik Bavink served at Norden 1781-84, Veendam 1784-86, and Noordbroek 1786-89; Lodewijk Gerrit Bavink, of Blokzijl, educated at the Amsterdam seminary, was pastor at Wormer-Jisp 1834-36 and Purmerend 1836-73. Many Bavinks served as deacons, particularly at Almelo, Kampen, Emden, and Leer. A side branch of the Bavink family is the Bavink ten Cate family of Almelo.   vDZ.

Beachy Amish Mission Board: see **Amish Mennonite Aid.**

Beacon Bible Camp, Frazer, Mont., established in 1947, is jointly sponsored by the seven Mennonite congregations of Lustre, Wolf Point, and Larslan, Mont. (3 GCM, 3 MB, and 1 EMB), and governed by a camp board appointed by representatives of these churches. The camp is located some 20 miles south of the Lustre community, 5 miles northeast of Frazer.   H.S.B.

Bechterdissen, a Mennonite settlement near Bielefeld, Germany, built by Pax boys, dedicated Oct. 6, 1956. The Mennonites of this settlement form the Mennonite congregation of Bechterdissen, of which Pastor G. Hildebrandt, of Göttingen, is the pastor. (*Der Mennonit* IX, 1956, No. 12, 189 f.)   vDZ.

Beckenknecht, Hans: see **Beck, Hans,** II.

Beckerath, Wolf von (1896-1944), a noted German artist, born at Crefeld, Germany, studied art, history, and philosophy and attended the Crefeld School for

Decorative Art (1921-23). He has been called a representative "Rhenish Painter." Mathias T. Engels calls him an artist "in the true sense of a high tradition . . . of great spiritual tension . . . specifically Rhenish by his express humanity . . . breath and immediacy of life." During World War II Wolf von Beckerath did a series of paintings which are considered his most important work: "Large and complete pictorial creations, mainly of a religious character. Some of these . . . will no doubt one day rank among the best of modern paintings." Engels also gives reproductions of Wolf von Beckerath's "Shepherds' Adoration" and "Wedding of Canaan." He died a victim of a bombing of Crefeld.   E.H.C.

M. T. Engels, *Documents, Revue Mensuelle des Questions Allemandes: German Contemporary Art,* special issue published by the Gesellschaft für übernationale Zusammenarbeit (Offenburg, Germany, 1952) 84-87.

Bedenken (I, 261): Supplement. According to a report by Philipp Kieferndorf in *Menn. Bl.* XL (1893) 108 f., 114 f., 121 f., a copy of the *Prozess* was secured for the Paulus Museum in Worms a.Rh. The full text of the *Prozess* is printed in the report, which is entitled "Eine Streitschrift evangelischer Theologen gegen die 'Wiedertäufer' aus dem 16. Jahrhundert."   H.S.B.

Bedminster Township: see **Bucks County.**

Beechy Mennonite Brethren Church: see **Friedensheim.**

Beek (Beeck), **van,** a widely ramified Dutch Mennonite family, found from the early 17th century at Amsterdam and Haarlem, and also at Utrecht. Most of them were well-to-do merchants. In Amsterdam some belonged to the Lamist (*q.v.*) church, and some to the Zonists. Dirk van Beek, d. Oct. 21, 1762, of Amsterdam, was a Mennonite minister at Schiedam 1722-26 and Rotterdam 1726-53, in which year he retired. As secretary of the Rotterdam church board he was active in supporting the Mennonites who emigrated from the Palatinate, Germany, to America via Rotterdam.   vDZ.

Beerdigungs-Verein zu Leamington (Ont.) was established in 1935 at Leamington and serves Mennonites in the area, covering funeral expenses now averaging $200 per death. From 1935 through 1955 it had paid out $9,129. In 1958 it paid out $1800, covering nine deaths.   M.G.

Bel, a Dutch Mennonite family, formerly living at Amsterdam. Pieter Bel, a merchant at Hoorn and precentor of the Mennonite congregation in his home town, was an ardent Patriot (*q.v.*), who had to flee from the country in 1787 or 1788 with the Mennonite deacon Pieter Houttuyn of Hoorn because of their political activity. They lived at Brussels, Belgium, until about 1795, when they returned. (*Inv. Arch. Amst.* II, 2, No. 178.)   vDZ.

Beldor Mennonite Church (MC), located 4 miles south of Swift Run in Stonewall District, Rockingham Co., Va., was started in 1935 in a former United Brethren Church found vacant by the Y.P.C.A.

of the Eastern Mennonite College. It was purchased by the Mennonites in 1947. In 1958 it had 18 members, with Paul Good as pastor.   H.A.B.

Belgium Mennonite Mission (MC) was founded in 1950 by the Mennonite Board of Missions and Charities. In 1958 there was one missionary couple at work, with two congregations (Brussels and Bourgeois-Rixensart), three outposts, and a total of 24 members. The congregations belong to the Conference of Evangelical Churches of French-Speaking Countries. Mission headquarters are at Ohain (*q.v.*).   H.S.B.

Belleville Mennonite School (MC), until 1952 called K.(ishacoquillas) V.(alley) Christian Day School, located near Belleville, Pa., was founded in 1945 as an elementary school by a group of Mennonites and Amish Mennonites from several congregations in the K.V. who organized a patrons' association which set up a board of directors now called Belleville Mennonite School Board. In 1952 the high-school department was added and in 1958-59 the enrollment was 154 in the elementary school and 83 in the high school. The school was held at Menno (White Hall) the first year, with J. B. Kanagy as teacher, with 28 pupils. In 1946-47 a three-room building was constructed, the next year the high-school building was begun, and in 1958-59 a two-room elementary building was erected. Principals have been: Rhoda Peachey 1946-47, Lester Zook 1947-48, Alphie Zook 1948-56, Laurie Mitton 1956-59, Arthur Byer superintendent 1959- .   H.S.B.

Bellwood Mennonite Church (MC), Milford, Neb., was organized in November 1957 by approximately 13 families of the Milford Mennonite community. The new building, begun in 1958, was dedicated in March 1959. The 1959 membership was 70, with Ivan R. Lind serving as pastor.   M.G.

Ben Israels: see **Ringh, Yemede;** also **Jacobsz, Anthony.**

Benodiging: see **Communion Call.**

Berne Mennonite (MC) Church: see **Augsburger.**

Bethany Bible School, Deverakonda, Andhra Pradesh, India, in the Telugu Mission field of the M.B. Church, was established in 1920 for the training of indigenous workers and has trained nearly all of the 300 ministers, evangelists, teachers, Bible women, and other Christian workers in this field. First located in Nagar-Kurnool, it was transferred to Shamshabad in 1930, and in 1946 to Deverakonda.   H.S.B.

Bethany Christian High School (MC), founded in 1954, is owned and operated by a board of directors appointed by the Indiana-Michigan Mennonite Conference. On a campus of 12 acres located one mile south of Goshen College on Highway 15, it has a new building containing classrooms, library, chapel, and gymnasium, and a remodeled building with classrooms and cafeteria. John S. Steiner has been principal from the beginning. In 1958-59 the enrollment was 235, with a faculty of 12 teachers.   H.S.B.

Bethany Church of God in Christ Mennonite Church, Rich Hill, Mo.: see **Emmanuel** Church.

Bethany Mennonite Brethren Church, Fresno, Cal.: see **Fresno** Mennonite Brethren Church.

Bethany Mennonite Church (MC), Pulguillas, Coamo, Puerto Rico, founded in 1946, had 111 members in 1958. The first meetinghouse, a tabernacle type church, built in 1946, was replaced in 1949. Paul Lauver was the first pastor, followed by Lester Hershey who was still the pastor in 1959. This was the first Mennonite congregation in Puerto Rico. H.S.B.

Gladys Widmer, *We Enter Puerto Rico* (Elkhart, 1952).

Bethany Mennonite Home, at 1910 W. Diamond St., Philadelphia, Pa., was established in 1954 as a Mennonite (MC) home for the aged. In 1958 it had 11 guests. H.S.B.

Bethel Bible Institute (GCM), Abbotsford, B.C., was begun in 1939 by Nick Bahnman in the Coghlan (B.C.) Mennonite Church (GCM), and moved in 1943 to its present site next to the West Abbotsford G.C.M. Church. In 1947 the present academic building was erected, preceded by a girls' dormitory and followed in 1951 by a boys' dormitory. The peak enrollment was 65 in 1952-53; in 1958-59 it was 36. The Institute is an agency of the Conference of United Mennonite Churches of British Columbia (GCM) and is owned and operated by a board of directors consisting of one or two members from each congregation in the province. Since 1954-55 the principal has been Edward Enns, with a staff of one to three additional teachers. The school term is six months in length. Some 400 students have attended the Institute. H.S.B.

Bethel Community Mennonite Church (GCM) is located at 9851 Orr and Day Road, Santa Fe Springs, near Whittier, Cal. The congregation was organized in 1956 and its church built in 1959. The membership was 48 in 1959, with Lyman Hofstetter as pastor. M.G.

Bethel Conservative Mennonite Church, Blountstown, Fla., was first listed in the *Mennonite Yearbook* of 1955 as the Red Oak congregation, with 33 members. In 1958 the Yearbook lists it as Bethel. Raymond Byler has been the pastor of the congregation from its beginning. The membership in 1958 was 54. M.G.

Bethel Conservative Mennonite Church, located 2 miles north and 2½ miles east of Nappanee, Ind., was organized in 1955 and its church built in 1954-55. The 1959 membership was 85, with Homer D. Miller its bishop and Jacob E. Miller its minister. M.G.

Bethel Conservative Mennonite Church, not under conference, located at Millbank, Ont., was organized in 1957 as a schism from the Riverdale Amish Mennonite Church (*q.v.*), in which the bishop, Valentine Nafziger, took a more conservative position on nonconformity in attire and withdrew with a like-minded group. The membership in 1958 was 69, with Nafziger as bishop and Kenneth Brenneman as minister. The Bethel group built its own meetinghouse in 1958. O.G.

Bethel Conservative Mennonite Church (MC) is located 2 miles north of Gladys, Va., and 18 miles south of Lynchburg, Va. The first families moved into the community in 1944, and C. L. Ressler was the minister for the first seven years. The meetinghouse was built in 1953. In 1959 the membership was 22, with Milton A. Hostedler as pastor. H.S.B.

Bethel Deaconess Hospital, Mountain Lake, Minn.: see **Mountain Lake Hospital.**

Bethel Deaconess Hospital School of Nursing is an integral part of the Bethel Deaconess Hospital (*q.v.*). The charter of the Bethel Deaconess Home and Hospital Society of Newton, Kan., issued in 1903, stated: ". . . the purposes for which this corporation is formed are as follows: (*a*) the establishment and maintaining of a training school to educate and train nurses and deaconesses in a hospital to be erected for that purpose in connection with said school."

The Bethel Deaconess Hospital, with its School of Nursing, was dedicated and opened for service June 11, 1908. Sister Frieda Kaufman served as Superintendent and Deaconess Mother. Sister Catherine Voth was director and instructor of student nurses. The first student to enroll was Anna Janz on Sept. 26, 1908. By 1959 approximately 410 students had graduated and are serving as missionaries, ministers' wives, nurses, and homemakers. The alumnae association was organized in 1920. At present the capacity is 60 students in a regular three-year course.

The School of Nursing is accredited and approved by the Board of Nurse Registration and Nursing Education in the State of Kansas. L.M.S.

Bethel Mennonite Church (GCM), Aldergrove, B.C., was organized in 1937. Its first meetinghouse, built in 1937, was replaced by a new one built in 1957, located at 24712 56th Avenue, some 33 miles east of Vancouver. In 1959 the membership was 262, with N. N. Friesen as pastor. H.S.B.

Beth-El Mennonite Church (MC), Colorado Springs, Col., was organized in October 1957 and in 1959 had 43 members with Paul Wittrig as pastor. The congregation is temporarily meeting at the Knob-Hill Community Center; plans are in progress for a new meetinghouse. M.G.

Bethel Mennonite Church (GCM), Dresden, N.D., is located 9 miles west and 1 mile south of Langdon. It was established in 1897 by Elder John D. Bartel. The meetinghouse was erected in 1897. In 1958 it had 49 members, with Clifford E. Koehn as pastor. M.G.

Bethel Mennonite Church (MC), Albuquerque, N. Mex., located at 504 El Paraiso St., N.E., was established in 1950. Joe H. Yoder was the pastor of its 20 members in 1959. M.G.

Bethel Mennonite Church (MC), Apple Creek, Ohio, an unaffiliated congregation, had 49 members in 1958. Lester D. Amstutz was the bishop and Earl J. Amstutz the minister. It was organized in 1955, by members formerly belonging to the Sonnenberg Mennonite Church. Since Jan. 1, 1956, services have been held in the basement of the uncompleted church.   M.G.

Bethel Mennonite Church (GCM), Enid, Okla., at the corner of Nagel Avenue and South 4th Street, originated as a result of Mennonite families moving to Enid from Meno and Taloga, Okla., who originally met for worship in their homes. On March 7, 1938, they decided to organize the Bethel Mennonite Church and in 1940 they erected the present church building. In 1950 the group consisted of 24 members. Heinrich T. Neufeld was the pastor throughout the history of the church. In 1959 the congregation was discontinued and the members joined the Grace Mennonite Church (q.v.) of Enid. H.T.N.

Beth-Haven, 1500 Harrison Hill, Hannibal, Mo., a Mennonite (MC) nursing home, established in 1957 under a local board. In 1958 it had 18 guests.
                                              H.S.B.

Bethesda Mennonite Health Society, Yarrow, B.C., organized c1935, was serving approximately 850 families in the Lower Fraser Valley 20 years later. It covered medical and hospital expenses, paying out approximately $30,000 in 1953.   M.G.

Bethlehem Mennonite Church (GCM), now extinct, Hooker, Okla., organized c1906, was closed c1915. Earlier it had 20 members, 23 in 1911, 7 in 1914. First and last ministers were Henry D. Schroeder and Henry Adrian.   H.S.B.

Bible Fellowship Church is the new name chosen for their denomination by the Mennonite Brethren in Christ (q.v.) of Pennsylvania in their Seventy-fifth Annual Conference on April 11, 1959. The vote for the new name in the congregations was 1,580 for and 507 against the proposition, while in the conference 56 approved it and 6 opposed it.
                                              M.G.

Bierma, a Dutch Mennonite family, living in Friesland. Particularly in the former congregation of Vischbuurt (q.v.) and the present congregations of Holwerd, Ternaard, Hallum, and Oudebildtzijl many members of this family served as deacons.
                                              vDZ.

Biltius, Johannes: see Bilt, Johannes.

Blaauw, a widely ramified Mennonite family in the Netherlands, particularly found in the province of North Holland. Besides Gerrit Blaauw (q.v.), mention should be made of Hendrik J. Blaauw, preacher of the Old Flemish congregation at Norden 1775-76, Heerenveen-Knijpe 1776-82, and Middelie 1782-c1803, and Adriaan Blaauw Kzn (c1855-83), pastor at Wolvega 1881-82 and Wieringen 1882-d.83. A Mennonite Blaauw (Blaeu, Blau, Blauw) family, mostly in business, is found at Amsterdam since the early 17th century. Cornelis Blaauw (Noordeinde van Graft, 1882-Amsterdam, 1957), an accountant at Amsterdam, was active as a deacon of the Amsterdam congregation, a trustee of the A.D.S., and

in many of its activities. (DB 1895, 84-91, 99; DJ 1958, 20 f.; church records of Amsterdam.) vDZ.

Black Mountain Mennonite Mission (MC), Ganado, Ariz., was established in 1953 as a mission among the Navaho Indians by the Mennonite Board of Missions and Charities. In 1958 it had 13 members, with Stanley Weaver as pastor.   H.S.B.

Black Oak Bethel Mennonite Church (MC) is located in southern Fulton County, Pa., with the address of Route 1, Hancock, Md. It was organized in 1953 and is a member of the Ohio and Eastern Conference. In 1959 its membership was 53, with Michael M. Horst as its pastor.   M.G.

Black River Mennonite Church (MC) is located 4½ miles south of Loman, Minn. The congregation was established in 1939 and was known as the Loman Mennonite Church until 1955. It became a fully organized church in 1953. It had 27 members in 1958, with William A. Kurtz as pastor.   M.G.

Black Rock Retreat Association, Inc. (MC), an association of members of the Lancaster Mennonite Conference, was organized in 1954 to own and operate a Mennonite camp. A tract of 50 acres along the Octoraro Creek, 4½ miles southeast of Quarryville, Lancaster Co., Pa., was purchased in 1954, and the Black Rock Camp opened in 1956.   H.S.B.

Blaine Mennonite Church (MC), located 7 miles east of Blaine, Ore., was organized in 1956 and in 1959 had 21 members. Jacob D. Kauffman was its pastor.   M.G.

Bloemcamp: see Oldeklooster.

Bluesky Mennonite Church (MC), at Bluesky in northern Alberta, a member of the Alberta-Saskatchewan Conference, established in 1948, had 16 members in 1958, with Paul Burkholder as pastor.
                                              H.S.B.

Blumenau (Brazil) Mennonite Brethren Church was organized in 1952, the meetinghouse built in 1955. In 1957 the membership was 30, with Hans Kasdorf as leader.   H.S.B.

Blumenau (Santa Catharina, Brazil) Mennonite Brethren Church was organized in 1923 by Elder Jacob Hübert of Witmarsum (Krauel Colony) and continued until 1949 as an affiliate. In that year on petition of the group it was officially accepted by Elder G. H. Rosenfeld of the Waldheim, Witmarsum, congregation as an independent M.B. congregation, connected with Waldheim, and with a membership of fourteen. When the Krauel M.B. group moved to Bage, the Blumenau M.B. congregation transferred its connection to the Curitiba M.B. Church. In 1955 the congregation had 21 members, with Wilhelm Koettker as leader. The congregation was then planning to build a meetinghouse.   H.S.B.
   W. Koettker, "Menn.-Brüder Gemeinde Blumenau, Brasilien," Menn. Rundschau LXXVIII (1955) 81.

Böhem (Behem), David, a minister in the Auspitz (q.v.) congregation in Moravia c1530, who was associated with Jörg Zaunring (q.v.), Burkhard von Ofen (q.v.), and Adam Schlegel (q.v.) in the leadership. He is called "Behemisch David" von der Schweintz (Schweinitz) in the Hutterite Chronicle. In 1531 he was excommunicated, as were Burkhard and Adam. Nothing further is known of him. (Zieglschmid, *Chronik*, 93 f., 99 f., 113, 118.)

H.S.B.

Bolivia. A Mennonite settlement of 37 families was established 1954-57 in the neighborhood of the city of Santa Cruz (pop. 143,600), in the fertile plain east of the Andes Mountains, by emigrants from the Paraguayan Chaco. Twelve families (now 10 families with 70 pop.) came partly (all 5 colonises were represented) from Fernheim Colony, the first six families arriving in 1954 and founding the colony Tres Palmas, 15 mi. n.e. of Santa Cruz. The second group of 25 families, who settled 3 miles beyond Tres Palmas, were conservative families from Menno Colony. The first group came primarily for economic reasons. Nikolai Kröker serves as minister for both groups, although the former adheres to the General Conference Church, and the latter to the Chortitz Church; neither group is organized. The Bolivian government has guaranteed to the Mennonites freedom of religion, exemption from military service, and the privilege of private schools. All such settlers are promised liberal credit from the government. The 1959 total population was 189.

H.S.B.

Bolt, Ulrich, a brother of the Anabaptist Eberli Bolt (*q.v.*), of Lachen in the Swiss canton of Schwyz, first a Catholic priest, then joined the Zwinglian Reformed party by 1524, was made pastor at Fläsch near Maienfeld in Chur, and in the course of 1525-26 apparently joined the Anabaptists. His first appearance in the records as an Anabaptist was in Basel in the spring of 1526, from which he was expelled and went to Grüningen and joined the Brethren there. Arrested by the magistrate of Grüningen, he must have recanted, since he was soon appointed pastor in the parish of Niederhasli in the canton of Zürich, where he remained at least until 1530, although he showed some sympathy for Anabaptism here also.

H.S.B.

Zwingliana I (Zürich, 1897 ff.) 141-43, 178-80; *TA Zürich*, 230, 231, 255.

Bonga, Lykele (Ternaard, Dec. 11, 1892-Leeuwarden, Oct. 16, 1952), at first a teacher, then studied theology at the university and Mennonite seminary at Amsterdam, and served as pastor at Dantumawoude 1921-26, Leiden 1926-34, and Leeuwarden 1934-52. He was also a poet; he wrote the hymn of the Friese (*q.v.*) Doopsgezinde Jongeren Bond and published a volume of poems, *Als glas in lood* (Leeuwarden, 1938). (*DJ* 1953, 11 f.)

vDZ.

Bontreger, Eli J. (1868-1958), a bishop of the Old Order Amish Mennonite Church, who lived in his latter years near Shipshewana, Ind. He was the third child of John E. (Hansi) and Barbara Mishler Bontreger, whose immigrant ancestor, Martin Bornträger of Switzerland, arrived at Philadelphia, Pa., Oct. 5, 1767. Eli was born Jan. 19, 1868, near Shipshewana. He was married Dec. 18, 1890, to Mattie Miller, to whom were born five sons and three daughters. After her death in 1918, he was married

on Dec. 5, 1920, to Amanda Miller. One son was born to them. Eli's first 27 years were spent near Shipshewana, the next 15 in North Dakota, and over 6 years in northern Wisconsin, before he again returned to Shipshewana. He was ordained minister May 13, 1894, at Shipshewana, and bishop near Mylo, N.D., June 18, 1901. In his 64-year ministry Bontreger baptized 437 persons, married 197 couples, preached over 2,600 times, ordained 36 ministers and deacons and 15 bishops, and traveled a total of over 520,000 miles by 1953.

Not only was he instrumental in the organization of the two colonies in North Dakota and Wisconsin, of which he was a part, but he was often asked to assist in the establishment of other colonies. His sincere desire to be impartial in all his dealings both in and out of the church won for him many lasting friendships.

As a writer Bontreger produced many articles for religious and secular papers. He became editor and cofounder of the present *Herold der Wahrheit* in 1912, and in 1923 he finished collecting and compiling material for the *Bontreger History,* which he had published the same year.

During both world wars he gave much valuable assistance to draftees both before and after induction. Also as a member of the Mennonite Central Committee (1942-52) he visited most of the Civilian Public Service camps in the United States as well as units at mental hospitals and men on detached service.

He died Feb. 15, 1958, at Sarasota, Fla., and was buried in the cemetery on his farm near Shipshewana, Ind. His mimeographed autobiography (up to 1955) is available in GCL.

M.E.B.

Boon, a Dutch Mennonite family of Sappemeer (*q.v.*) in the province of Groningen. Hendrick Coops Boon, landowner, farmer, and reclaimer of peat-moors, as were nearly all his descendants, was also elder of the Danzig Flemish Mennonite congregation at Sappemeer from c1680. In 1747 his sister Jantje Coops Boon, married to the preacher Hendrik Wolters, provided that a large room on their farm should be forever at the disposal of the Danzig Old Flemish congregation for religious services. About 1760, however, the Boon family left the Danzig Mennonites to join the Groningen Old Flemish church. (Information by G. N. Schutter, Sappemeer.)

Boothamer, a former Dutch Mennonite family at Workum, Friesland, where Kempe Boothamer (c1700-72), an apothecary, was a deacon. His son Gerrit Boothamer (1725-90) was a pastor at Den Hoorn 1749-51 and Middelburg 1751-d.90. He wrote a history of the Middelburg congregation, which is preserved in manuscript. (*DB* 1873, 145; 1905, 6; *Naamlijst* 1790, 61.)

vDZ.

Bosch, formerly an outstanding Mennonite family at Amsterdam, of brokers, businessmen, bankers, later also physicians; some were deacons in the Lamist congregation. There was a Bosch family, possibly related to the Amsterdam Bosch family, in Alkmaar from the 17th century. Jan Bosch was elder of the Alkmaar Waterlander congregation 1699-1714 and at Haarlem 1714-? His son Gerrit Bosch served the Alkmaar congregation 1721-27. (*DB* 1891, 8; church records of Amsterdam and Alkmaar.) vDZ.

Bosland, a Dutch Mennonite family at Ouddorp. Since the early 17th century many of its members have served as deacons. Paulus Willemsz Bosland (d. 1703) was from 1672 a preacher and from 1686 an elder of the Ouddorp congregation. (*DB* 1907, 153, 155, 162, 165, 166.) vDZ.

Bouman, a former Mennonite family of Emden, East Friesland, Germany. Two of its members went into the ministry. Hermanus Lambertus Bouman (d. 1865) served 1819-24 at? 1824-34 at Makkum, and 1834-64 at Veenwoudsterwal. His son Heyke Uden Heykes Bouman (1828-78) was pastor of Den Ilp-Landsmeer 1853-54 and Noord-Zijpe 1854-78. Both had been educated at the Amsterdam Mennonite seminary. vDZ.

Bouqueirao (Brazil) Mennonite Brethren Church was organized in 1936 at the beginning of the Mennonite settlement made in the Bouqueirao area near the city of Curitiba by settlers moving from the Krauel Colony in Santa Catharina. It was first called the Curitiba M.B. Church. In 1957 it had 260 members, with Peter Hamm as leader. Jacob Huebert was long elder. As it grew, three daughter churches were organized at Guarituba (1957), Villa Guayra (1957), and Saltobach (1955). H.S.B.

Bowman: see Bauman.

Bowman (*Jacob*) Mennonite Church (MC), located near Canal Winchester (*q.v.*), Franklin County, O., southeast of Columbus. Little is known about this church, except that John M. Brenneman, originally living in Fairfield County to the east, lived in Franklin County 1848-55, and was ordained bishop here in 1849, moving in 1855 to Allen County near Elida. H.S.B.

Bragado Mennonite Bible School: see Colegio Biblico.

Brazil Mennonite Mission (MC), under the Mennonite Board of Missions and Charities (*q.v.*), was founded in 1954, and has the following three stations in Sao Paulo State: Bairro Indianopolis (1954), Sertaozinho (1957), and Valinhos (1957). In 1958 the three stations had 7, 7, and 6 baptized members respectively.

In April 1958 the mission board took over the Amazon Valley Indian Mission (*q.v.*) founded in 1955, with its headquarters at Araguacema, Goias State. H.S.B.

Brenz (I, 419b, 1 f.): Supplement. Melanchthon's booklet to which Brenz replied in the title cited by Hege appeared first at Wittenberg in 1528 (probably May); a second edition appeared at Marburg in Oct. 1528, with the Brenz reply attached, which is the title cited by Hege here. The original Wittenberg title was *Underricht Philip. Melanct. wider die Lere der Widerteuffer auss dem latein verdeutscht durch Just. Jonas.* According to Schottenloher's *Bibliographie* (# 44218) the Brenz reply appeared

in 1558 (with an addition to the title) "published by someone friendly to the Anabaptists." H.S.B.

British Honduras: see Honduras.

Brooklyn (N.Y.) **First** Mennonite Church was established in 1958 as a mission church located in the Puerto Rican area of the city. It had 8 members. H.S.B.

Brotherly Aid Liability Plan, Leola, Pa., serves the Lancaster Mennonite Conference (MC). It was established on Jan. 1, 1955, and by June 1959 had 1,788 participants. It covers liability for bodily injury and/or property damage caused by the insured party's motor vehicle, but it does not cover damage to the property or injury to the person or the family of the insured party. In 1957 it paid out over $13,000. M.G.

Buckeye (Ariz.) Mennonite Mission (MC) was established as an outpost mission among the colored migrants of the Phoenix area in 1952 by the Sunnyslope (*q.v.*) Mennonite Church. A meetinghouse was built later and Johnwilliam Boyer was ordained as pastor in 1955. In 1958 Boyer had 12 members under his care. H.S.B.

Buckhorn Mennonite Church (MC), Mathias, W. Va., was organized in 1949 when its meetinghouse was erected. In 1959 it had 30 members, with John F. Shank as pastor. H.S.B.

Buenos Aires (Argentina) Russian Mennonite Church (Evangelische Mennonitische Glaubensgemeinschaft) was begun in 1950, sponsored by the Mennonite Central Committee. Martin Duerksen has served as pastor from the beginning, with support largely from the MCC. Meetings have been held in a rented hall in Villa Bolester, a suburb of Buenos Aires, but a meetinghouse was under construction in 1959. The congregation, which is fully independent although its pastor is a member of the E.M.B. Church (Allianzgemeinde in Paraguay), was officially organized in 1957. The membership in 1958 was 65, with an attendance of *c*100 at the services. There are 700-800 Mennonites of Russian background in Buenos Aires, whom the congregation seeks to serve. H.S.B.

Buffalo (Pa.) Mennonite Church (MC) is located 4½ miles west of Lewisburg on Route 95. A member of the Lancaster Mennonite Conference, it was established in 1948. The members, numbering 85 in 1958, were served by ministers Jacob G. Brubaker and John H. Erb. M.G.

Buhler Preparatory School: see Hoffnungsau Preparatory School.

Buitenleraar: see Buitenmannen.

Bureau of Guardianship of the Foreign Colonists (Russian, *Kantseliaria opekunstva inostrannykh kolonistov*), called Fürsorge-Komitee (*q.v.*) in German, was established in 1818 by Catherine II in connection with the settlement of foreigners in Russia. It was to supervise the activity of the Russian diplomatic representatives in recruiting colonists in foreign countries, to keep a file of lands available for settlement, and to see to it that the foreigners upon their arrival were properly received and aided until they had been settled. This Bureau had the status of a separate ministry and was responsible to the empress, who appointed its chairman. The first chairman was Gregory Orlov, who appointed the other members of the Bureau. It was abolished in 1871. C.K.

David G. Rempel, "The Mennonite Migration to New Russia (1787-1870)," *MQR* IX (1935) 74.

Burgervlotbrug: see **Zijpe.**

Burkhard von Ofen: see **Braun, Burkhard.**

Burkholder, Oscar (1886-1956), a prominent evangelist and Bible teacher (MC), was born at Pickering, Ont., Sept. 24, 1886, the son of Aaron W. and Agnes Wood Burkholder. He received a Biblical training at the Toronto Bible College. He served as pastor of the Cressman Mennonite Church at Breslau, Ont., 1913-54 (ordained bishop 1949). He also served as a teacher in the Ontario Mennonite Bible School 1920-56 and was principal 1948-54. He served on numerous district conference and General Conference committees, was president of the Ontario Mennonite Mission Board for 14 years, and moderator of the Mennonite General Conference 1949-51. He preached over 8,000 sermons, conducted 180 revival meeting series and 89 Bible Conferences. H.S.B.

Burlington (Col.) Mennonite Brethren Church, located on Oak Street, was organized in 1957, its meetinghouse bought and remodeled in 1958. In 1959 it had 36 members, with Eldo Ratzlaff as pastor. H.S.B.

Büro der Molotschnaer Mennonitischer Vereinigung came into being in the Molotschna settlement, Ukraine, Russia, during World War I or the Revolution which followed. Little is known about this organization, which was to give the social, economic, and cultural life of the settlement stability. At the meeting of the Allgemeiner Mennonitischer Kongress (q.v.) in 1917 Johann Willms was the chairman of the Bureau and opened the Kongress in that capacity. The *Protokoll* of the Kongress gives the impression that the Bureau was well established, had 141 delegates, and that it was instrumental in organizing the Kongress. B. H. Unruh followed Willms as chairman of the Bureau, but little else is known about it. The names "Mennozentrum" and "Zeitweiliges Mennonitisches Zentralbüro" were also used to refer to it. C.K.

Burton Mennonite Church (MC), a member of the Ohio and Eastern Conference, located 3 miles northwest of Burton, Ohio, was organized in 1948 by persons largely of Old Order Amish background. A former Methodist church was purchased. In 1959 the membership was 100, with John F. Garber as pastor-bishop. H.S.B.

Bussemaker, a Dutch Mennonite family since the 16th century. Most of its members lived at Borne and Deventer, where some of them served as dea-

cons. B. Barlage Bussemaker served for many years as a treasurer of the Zwolsche Weduwfonds. Hendrik Bussemaker (1881-1925), of Deventer, educated at the Amsterdam university and seminary, served as pastor at Hoorn on the island of Texel 1909-15, Zijldijk 1915-24, and Hindeloopen 1924-25. Paulus Bussemaker (q.v.) was apparently not related to the Borne-Deventer Bussemaker family. He was likely identical with Elder Pauwel (q.v.) at Danzig, who served until d.1612. Having been excommunicated by the Flemish, he joined the Danzig Frisian congregation. (*Inv. Arch. Amst.* II, Nos. 2925 f.; see also II, 2, No. 691; see **Bussemaker, Paulus,** which this article supplements.) vdZ.

Butler Avenue Mennonite Brethren Church, located at 4884 East Butler Ave., Fresno, Cal., was organized in 1956, and built its meetinghouse in 1957. In 1959 the membership was 147, with Elmer A. Martens as pastor. H.S.B.

Buwo, Bernhardus, was a Reformed minister in East Friesland, Germany, during the time of the Reformation. Little was known about him until Walter Hollweg published an article, "Bernhard Buwo, ein ostfriesischer Theologe aus dem Reformationsjahrhundert," in *Jahrbuch der Gesellschaft für bildende Kunst und vaterländische Altertümer zu Emden* (Aurich, 1953). In 1556 Buwo published a book in Low German against the Anabaptists entitled *Een frundtlyke thosamensprekenge van twee personen, von der Döpe der yungen unmundigen Kynderen . . .* (Emden, 1556). The following year a Dutch edition of this book appeared (Emden, 1557), which was followed by a third edition in 1564 and a fourth, revised edition published in Ghent in 1580. In 1563 a German edition followed, translated by Engelbert Faber. Buwo, who (according to Hollweg) was himself influenced by the Anabaptists, used peaceful means in his attempt to win them to the Reformed Church. (See also **Covenant Theology.**) C.K.

Byntgens, Thomas: see **Bintgens.**

Calf(f): see **Kalf.**

Calgary (Alta.) **First** Mennonite Church (GCM): see **Scarboro** Mennonite Mission.

Calvaert (Caluwaert, Kalvaert), a former Mennonite family, found in the 16-17th centuries in the Dutch congregations of Haarlem and Leiden. Adriaen Calvaert, who in the early 17th century was a preacher of the Flemish church at Haarlem, published *Vertooninghe ende Verantwoordinge tot dienst van allen onsen Medegenoten des Geloofs* (Haarlem, 1619). The Calvaerts stemmed from Flanders, Belgium. Here Daniel (q.v.) Calvaerd, of Tielt, died in 1564 as a martyr at Armentières. vdZ.

Calvary Hour, Inc. (MC), a radio program founded in 1936 by Wm. G. Detweiler of Orrville, Ohio, and carried on since his death in 1956 by his sons Bill and Bob Detweiler, with a series of broadcast outlets in the United States and a few foreign countries. It was incorporated in 1946. H.S.B.

Calvary Mennonite Church (MC), La Plata, Puerto Rico, founded in 1946, had 78 members in 1958 with Addona Nissley and Jose A. Santiago as ministers. The church was built in 1946. This is the second Mennonite congregation on the island. Lester Hershey was the first pastor.   H.S.B.

Gladys Widmer, *We Enter Puerto Rico* (Elkhart, 1952).

Calvary Mennonite Mission, Newport News, Va.: see **Madison Avenue** Chapel.

Camp Friedenswald, a church camp located on Shavehead Lake 7 miles north of Union, Mich., owned and operated by the Central District Conference (GCM) through a committee appointed by the conference, was established in 1950; its first operating season was in 1951.   H.S.B.

Camp Hebron (MC), located on Route 2, Halifax, Dauphin Co., Pa., was founded in 1956 and is owned and operated by a board of directors composed of nine members of the Lancaster Mennonite Conference. It provides opportunity for camping for children from the missions of the Lancaster Conference as well as the children of members. The campground is a tract of 315 acres of mostly wooded land on the north slope of Peters Mountain in Powell's Valley *c*15 miles north of Harrisburg and 25 miles southeast of Halifax.   H.S.B.

Camp Luz, located 4 miles south of Orrville, Ohio, was established in 1953 by the Ohio Mennonite Camp Association (MC).   H.S.B.

Camp Rehoboth Association, a private association in the Mennonite Church (MC), founded in 1949, owns and operates Camp Rehoboth, a church camp for colored children, located two miles north of Hopkins Park, Ill., address St. Anne, Ill. H.S.B.

Camps, Mennonite Church, although common in Protestant church life in America, were introduced rather late among Mennonites in North America. The first (1938) was Men-O-Lan, the camp of the Eastern District Conference (GCM), near Finland, Bucks Co., Pa. The second GCM camp was Elim Gospel Beach near Swift Current, Sask., owned and operated by the Mennonite Youth Organization of Saskatchewan (1946). The third and fourth GCM camps were Menoscah (1948) near Murdock, Kan., and Friedenswald, near Union, Mich. (1950). Later GCM camps were Palisades in Idaho, Pike Lake near Saskatoon, Sask., Assiniboine Mission Camp near Springstein, Man., and Swan Lake near Viburg, S.D. In the Mennonite Church (MC) camps started somewhat later, but by 1959 a total of twelve camps had been established: Laurelville near Mt. Pleasant, Pa. (1944), Little Eden at Onekama, Mich. (1945), Chesley Lake near Allenford, Ont. (1947), Rehoboth near Hopkins Park, Ill. (1949), Tel-Hai near Gap, Pa. (1950), Rocky Mountain Camp near Colorado Springs, Col. (1951), Luz near Orrville, Ohio (1953), Sholom near Kearney, Ont. (1954), Hebron near Harrisburg, Pa. (1956), Black Rock near Quarryville, Pa. (1956), Perrin Lakes near Sturgis, Mich. (1958), and Menno-Haven near Tiskilwa, Ill. (1959).

The Mennonite Brethren camp program is operated by the district conferences. The district program began as follows: Southern 1941, Pacific 1946, Central 1952. Camp facilities are leased from other organizations. In California Hartland Camp (*q.v.*) is owned by an M.B.-K.M.B. laymen's organization. The Canadian provincial conferences also have camp programs. In several areas inter-Mennonite camps have been established, especially for children.

Among European Mennonites the Dutch Mennonites alone have developed camps comparable to those in America, and they did so somewhat earlier. Retreat grounds for adults were established by the Gemeentedag (*q.v.*) Movement at Lunteren (1920), Elspeet (1925), and Schoorl (1932), while the Dutch Peace Group established Fredeshiem (1929). Camps have also been established for boys and girls, the first at Oud-Reemst in 1920, later at Elspeet, Giethoorn, etc. These youth camps are under the General Camp Committee, which is a part of the Commissie voor Doopsgezind Broederschapswerk. In recent years some 15 summer camps for catechumens have been held with *c*500 participants.

These church camps operate usually only in the summer months, serving as retreat centers for groups of high-school youth, older young people, and adults with varying interests, usually for periods of a week at a time. They combine living in an outdoor environment where wholesome recreation is available with definite spiritual interests. These interests include (1) training in Bible study, missions, church principles and doctrines, (2) help to youth in solving problems confronting young Christians in a secular world, (3) development of personal devotional life, (4) inspirational addresses, (5) evangelism, (6) cultivation of special interests such as church music.   H.S.B.

Betty van der Smissen, "Mennonite Church Camp Retreats," *Menn. Life* X (1955) 123 f.

Canadian Mennonite, The, is an independent weekly tabloid newspaper, five columns, 11½ in. by 16 in., 8-16 pp., published every Friday at Altona, Man., by D. W. Friesen & Sons, Ltd., founded in October 1953. *The Canadian Mennonite* seeks to serve all Mennonite groups and communities in Canada. It is the first English-language Mennonite newspaper of its kind in Canada. The circulation after six years is *c*3,500. The editor since its founding has been Frank H. Epp. Serving as associate editor is Aaron Klassen.   F.H.E.

Canadian Mennonite Mutual Insurance, Altona, Man., was established in 1923 and incorporated in 1948. Providing protection against fire losses, it covered $2,263,249 worth of property of approximately 300 members in 1959. Most of its clients were Mennonites.   M.G.

Canal Winchester, a town in northeastern Fairfield County, Ohio, near which a Mennonite settlement was started about 1842 by settlers from Franklin County, Pa. Their church, however, and perhaps the settlement, was located across the county line west in Franklin County. The congregation is reported by Daniel Kauffman to have had as many as 60 members, but it had become extinct before the publishing of the Hartzler and Kauffman *Mennonite Church History* in 1905. This was possibly the Bowman (*q.v.*, Supplement) congregation. M.G.

Canton (Okla.) Cheyenne Mennonite Mission Church (GCM) serves the more than 100 Cheyenne Indians living in Custer County between Thomas and Weatherford. This field was turned over to the Mennonites in 1924. On Nov. 11, 1928, a congregation of eleven members was organized and on Feb. 23, 1930, the church, 6½ miles south of Thomas, was dedicated. The following missionaries have served in this field: J. B. Ediger 1924-29 and 1936-47, H. J. Kliewer 1929-36, Arthur Friesen 1947, H. M. Dalke 1947-54, August Schmidt 1954- . The membership in 1955 was 37. A.SCH.

Carel van Gent: see **Karel van Gent.**

Carman (Man.) Mennonite Church (GCM) was founded in 1948 as a mission, organized as a congregation in 1951, and joined the Bergthaler Church in 1956, which supplies the ministers. The meetinghouse was built in 1948. In 1959 the membership was 35. H.S.B.

Carolina: see **North Carolina.**

Cass Lake (Minn.) Mennonite Church (MC) is located 5 miles south and 1 mile east of town. Begun as a mission station in 1948, it was organized as a congregation in 1954. It had 23 members in 1959, with Harry Gascho as pastor. M.G.

Cassel Amish Mennonite Church, located one mile east of the village of Cassel in East Zorra Twp., Oxford Co., Ont., is a branch of the East Zorra A.M. congregation and a member of the Ontario A.M. Conference. In 1935 an unused Evangelical church built in 1900 was first rented for a period of several months to relieve the congested condition at the home church, then bought. The church is a well-built edifice of white brick with a seating capacity of about 200. In 1958 some 200 members worshiped at Cassel, with Joel Schwartzentruber and Vernon Zehr as ministers. Its membership is included in that of the East Zorra congregation.
R.T.B.

Catlett (Va.) Beachy Amish Church, located 2½ miles northwest of Catlett in Fauquier County, was organized in 1950. Its meetinghouse was built in 1951. In 1958 it had 42 members, with Daniel J. Nissley as bishop-pastor. H.S.B.

Cayey-Altura Mennonite Church (MC), a mission in the city of Cayey, Puerto Rico, was begun in 1953. In 1958 it had a membership of 17, with Fidel Santiago in charge. H.S.B.

Cazenovia (Ill.) Mennonite Church (MC) was established in 1949 and had a membership of 21 in 1958. Melvin Hamilton was its pastor. M.G.

Cedar Grove Beachy Amish Mennonite Church was established in 1912 by a conservative schism from

the Mapleview (*q.v.*, Wellesley, Ont.) A.M. congregation, in Wellesley Township, Waterloo Co., led by Bishop Jacob Lichti, and hence is called locally the Lichti group. It built its meetinghouse in 1912 a half mile east of the Poole meetinghouse in Wellesley Township. It is very conservative in spirit though having a meetinghouse. It still uses the German language, and the *Ausbund* in singing. In 1958 it had 200 members, with Samuel Roth as bishop and Samuel Lichti and Noah Gerber as preachers.
H.S.B.

Central Christian High School, 801 Chemical St., Hutchinson, Kan., was incorporated in 1948 as the Central Kansas Bible Academy and opened in 1950 with 5 instructors and an enrollment of 41. Walter O. Ediger served as its principal 1950-59. The name of the school was changed from academy to high school in 1956. The board of directors has representatives from the G.C.M. (4), M.B. (3), K.M.B. (1), and M.C. (1) groups. Its catalogue calls it "inter-Mennonite in control and interdenominational in practice." It offers a four-year accredited high-school course. Its 1958-59 enrollment was 101, representing six Mennonite branches. The school publishes a monthly bulletin, *The Central Lighthouse.*
M.G.

Central District Reporter is the official organ of the Central District of the General Conference Mennonite Church. The merger agreement between the Central Conference of Mennonites and the Middle District of the G.C.M. Church called for the discontinuance of the *Christian Evangel* (*q.v.*), organ of the former, with the June issue of 1957 (the end of volume 47 of the *Evangel*), and the launching of a new publication. Robert W. Hartzler was named editor of the new magazine, which appeared for the first time in July 1957. Although the place of publication has been Goshen, Ind., from the beginning, the issues of 1957 were printed and distributed from Newton, Kan. An 8-page, 9 x 12 in. monthly, it confines itself to reporting activities of the conference and its constituent congregations, institutions, and individual members. N.P.S.

Central Kansas Bible Academy: see **Central Christian High School.**

Centralia (Mo.) Defenseless Mennonite Church (now extinct) was begun in this north-central Missouri area in 1903 ff., reportedly by the Joseph Rediger family. In 1906 J. K. Gerig of Grabill, Ind., held revival meetings in the Centralia settlement. Soon after these meetings a church was organized, and a meetinghouse was constructed in 1907 about 6 miles southeast of Centralia. The highest membership was 55. Ministers serving in the church were Levi Zehr and Sam Ehresman. Because of adverse economic conditions the Mennonites sold their farms and in 1918 their meetinghouse. Most of the families moved to Ohio and Indiana. E.E.Z.

Chappell Mennonite Church (MC), Chappell, Neb., listed in the Mennonite Yearbook up to 1953 as East Fairview (*q.v.*), constructed a new church in Chappell in 1958-59. In 1958 the members living near Julesburg, Col., formed a separate congregation under the Iowa-Nebraska Conference and built a meetinghouse in Julesburg (*q.v.*). The Chappell church, with a membership of 20, then joined the South Central Conference. The community was established in 1886, rather than in 1883 as elsewhere stated.   M.G.

Charity Committee of the Western District of the General Conference Mennonite Church is a committee whose primary responsibility is the aid and support of such destitute persons within the geographical limits of the Western District as are not provided for by individual churches. Its work began in 1893 when David Goerz, chairman of the Western District Conference, appointed a committee whose immediate purpose it should be to provide seed wheat for Mennonite settlers in Hodgeman County, Kan. The committee was also authorized to give other aid as needed. The following year this committee became permanent. Its total receipts in 1958 amounted to $1,507.   J.F.S.

Chelyabinsk district, located east of Southern Urals of Asiatic Soviet Russia, capital city Chelyabinsk, has much agricultural and forested land with large coal deposits. After World War I iron deposits were discovered which have transformed a part of the region into an industrial area. Chief cities are Chelyabinsk, Magnitogorsk, Zlatoust, and Troitsk. During World War II the eastern part of the region was separated and organized as Kurgan (*q.v.*) region. During the period of exile and World War I many of the Mennonites were sent to this region, particularly the industrial areas. Numerous letters have been published in the Canadian papers which give us some information about their life. (See also **Siberia.**)   C.K.

Christian Laymen's Evangelistic Association, Inc., was organized by a group of laymen (MC) largely around Orrville, Ohio, to promote evangelistic tent campaigns and city-wide crusades. Its evangelist at first was Howard Hammer, and after his departure to Brazil as a missionary in 1955 he was succeeded by Myron Augsburger.   H.S.B.

Christian Mennonite Church (GCM), now extinct, located at Meno, Okla., joined the General Conference in 1929 with 21 members but no minister. It was dissolved in 1933.   H.S.B.

Christian Mission Conservative Mennonite Church is located one mile north and one west of Berne, Ind. The congregation was organized in 1956 and in 1959 had 34 members, with William J. Stutzman as its pastor.   M.G.

Christian Service Foundation, Inc., Ft. Wayne, Ind., is a nonprofit organization serving the entire Evangelical Mennonite Church by offering financial help to local churches for building projects, loans and scholarships to students in higher institutions of learning, and also personal loans when funds are available.   M.G.

Christliche Bildungs-Anstalt der Mennoniten Gemeinschaft: see **Wadsworth Mennonite School.**

Christlicher Dienst (Voluntary Service) is an organization among the Mennonite colonies in Paraguay, to provide service for young people outside the colonies on the same basis as Voluntary Service does in North America. Each colony is to have a C.S. Committee, with the Fernheim Colony committee serving as the general co-ordinating committee and Martin Duerksen of Buenos Aires appointed by the MCC to serve as liaison and promoter. The first unit, located at the Paraguayan government mental hospital at Asuncion, began in Feb., 1957, where a team of two workers is maintained. Another unit is at the MCC Leprosy project in East Paraguay. Two additional programs opened in 1958 include a government T.B. sanatorium and a Salvation Army Children's Home. The name Christlicher Dienst emphasizes the Christian character of the service and candidates are carefully chosen from this point of view.   Fr.W.

Christopher Dock Mennonite School, a Mennonite high school named for the noted colonial Mennonite schoolmaster Christopher Dock, founded in 1954, is owned and operated by a board of trustees appointed by the Franconia Mennonite Conference (MC). It is located near Lansdale, Pa., in a former estate building remodeled into an academic building. Its principal from the beginning has been Richard Detweiler. The enrollment in 1958-59 was 198.   H.S.B.

Christus Allein (*Christ Alone*), a monthly 4-page (occasionally 8 pages) German supplement to the French Mennonite monthly *Christ Seul*, first number June 1947, edited to July 1956 by Daniel Wenger of Basel, Switzerland, followed by Ernst Hege. It carried for a time the subtitle "News from the Alsatian Churches."   H.S.B.

Church Bulletins are used in printed or mimeographed form by many congregations of most Mennonite conferences as a guide for the worship service and a source of information on the affairs of the congregation, its members, the minister, Sunday school, conference program, etc. The bulletins consist of two to six pages. As a rule the cover is printed by publishing houses and the contents supplied by the local congregations. The BeCL and GCL collect bulletins from their respective constituencies. These bulletins are a good source of information on current activities of the congregations.   C.K.

Church Letters to certify that a member has been baptized and is a member in good standing in a congregation are used in Mennonite churches, usually for the purpose of transferring membership from one congregation to another. It can be assumed that this practice dates back to the first centuries, particularly among the congregations of Dutch, Prussian, or Russian background. Sometimes the church letters consisted of a printed form filled out by the elder. Numerous letters have been preserved, particularly those of the immigrants of 1874. Some Mennonite groups, notably the Mennonite Church (MC), also issue "conference letters" to ministers who transfer to other conferences. (See also **Church Seals.**)   C.K.

Church of the Bible (EMB): see **Sun Valley.**

Church Penance: see **Horb.**

Churches of God (General Eldership), popularly called Winebrennerians for the founder John Winebrenner, was organized in 1830 at Harrisburg, Pa., where it still has its headquarters. It emerged from the revivalistic preaching (in and around Harrisburg) of Winebrenner (1797-1860), a German Reformed minister of Frederick County, Md., ordained at Hagerstown, Md., in 1820, who severed his connections with his church in 1825. Winebrenner taught a strict nonconformity to the world along with his revivalism, and instituted footwashing as an ordinance, also baptism by immersion. No doubt numbers of Mennonites (MC) in the region adjoining Harrisburg (Lancaster Conference) were won as adherents to the new faith, although no outstanding personalities of such transfers are known. In 1958 the membership was 35,700. H.S.B.

Claassen (Claesen), Jacob, was an elder of the Janjacobsgezinden (*q.v.*), a former branch of the Dutch Mennonites. He was ordained in 1612 and baptized 792 persons. (*Inv. Arch. Amst.* II, 2, No. 9a.) vDZ.

Claes Claesz, an Anabaptist martyr, beheaded at Leiden, Holland, on Dec. 20, 1539. Particulars are lacking. (Mellink, *Wederdopers,* 204.) vDZ.

Claesz, Jan: see **Klaasz, Jan.**

Clarence Center (N.Y.) Mennonite church (GCM), now extinct, was formed in 1875 as a schism from the Clarence Center (MC) congregation when the minister Jacob Krehbiel, Jr., withdrew with about a dozen families. The group affiliated with the GCM body c1880, and the Middle District Conference in 1889. The highest membership was 45 in 1896 but by 1917, when Krehbiel retired, it was only 18. The church was then disbanded. H.S.B.

Classen, David Ivanovitch: see **Claassen, David I.**

Clevelandia (Brazil) Mennonite Brethren Church was organized in 1955. Its meetinghouse was built in 1956. In 1957 its membership was 58, with Jacob Kasdorf as leader. Clevelandia is in the southwest part of the state of Parana, near the Santa Catharina border. H.S.B.

Clinton (Okla.) **First** Mennonite Church (GCM) is located at 19th and Opal streets. It was established in 1951 and had 65 members in 1958, with Walter H. Regier as minister. H.S.B.

Coamo Mennonite Church, Coamo, Puerto Rico, was founded in 1953 as an outpost of the Bethany congregation. In 1958 it had 17 members, with Samuel Rolon as pastor. H.S.B.

Coffman, Samuel Frederic (1872-1954), a leading bishop in the Mennonite (MC) Church in Ontario (Vineland), was born near Dale Enterprise, Rockingham Co., Va., on June 11, 1872, the son of Preacher John S. and Elizabeth J. (Heatwole) Coffman (*q.v.*). On Nov. 20, 1901, he married Ella Mann (d. 1935) of Elkhart, Ind. They had 5 children, all born at Vineland: John, Magdalena, David, Barbara, and Ellen.

Samuel spent most of his school years in Elkhart County, Ind., where his family had moved in 1879. He was graduated from the Elkhart High School in 1890, one of the first Mennonite high-school graduates in the Middle West. He attended the Moody Bible Institute 1894-95 and for six months in 1897-98. In 1890-94 he worked for the Mennonite Publishing Company at Elkhart. He was converted at meetings held in Elkhart by his father and was baptized on May 26, 1888. He was elected superintendent of the Elkhart Mennonite Sunday school on Dec. 28, 1893. In 1894-95 he served in the Mennonite Home Mission at Chicago. Here he was ordained to the ministry on April 21, 1895, by John F. Funk of Elkhart; he was ordained bishop at Vineland, Ont., on Sept. 26, 1903.

Coffman served widely in his denomination beyond the borders of his own congregation and conference. He was moderator of the Ontario Conference in 1931-34, and moderator of the General Conference in 1911 and 1933. He also served as secretary of the General Conference for a time. He was a member of the following General Conference committees: Music Committee from the first (1911) until 1947; Peace Problems Committee 1925-49; Historical Committee from the first (1911) and its chairman 1911-47; General Sunday School Committee from its beginning in 1915 until it was incorporated into the Commission for Christian Education and Young People's Work in 1937. He served for a time on the Missions Committee of the Mennonite Board of Missions and Charities. He served on the Mennonite Board of Education from the first (1905) until about 1944, serving as secretary for about 20 years. He also served on the Publication Board and its Publishing Committee. He was the founder and served as principal of the Ontario Mennonite Bible School at Kitchener, Ont., 1907-47. He was editor of the Bible study department of the *Christian Monitor* from the beginning of its publication in 1909 until 1953. During his service as hymn editor of the Music Committee the following books appeared at Scottdale, Pa.: *Church and Sunday School Hymnal Supplement* (1911); *Life Songs* (1916), of which he was coeditor; *Church Hymnal* (1927); *Songs of Cheer for Children* (1928); and *Life Songs No. 2* (1938), of which he was editor.

He served as pastor of the Moyer congregation at Vineland 1902-d.54, and as bishop of the Niagara District from 1903. He was a charter member of the Nonresistant Relief Organization in Ontario, organized in 1918, and its secretary 1920-54. He was appointed the special correspondent with the Canadian government regarding military service and the immigration of the Russian Mennonites in 1918. He was associated with the Canadian Mennonite Board of Colonization 1922-44 and actively aided the immigration from Russia to Ontario 1922-25. In his earlier ministry he was widely used in Bible conference and evangelistic work. In 1901 on a commission from the Ontario Conference he organized a number of congregations and ordained ministers and deacons in Alberta. He died at Vineland on June 28, 1954. He was one of the outstanding figures of the Mennonite Church (MC) throughout his more than half-century of service in the ministry, and made an extraordinary and lasting contribution to it, always a man of vision, constructive and peace-loving, widely beloved and highly regarded.   R.S.K.

Colegio Biblica Evangelico Menonita (MC), Bragado, Argentina, formerly called Bragado Bible School, was operated in 1935-58 by the Mennonite Board of Missions and Charities with the aid of a local advisory committee elected by the Argentine Mennonite Conference for the purpose of training Argentine Christian workers. In 1958 it was merged with the Mennonite Biblical Seminary (*q.v.*) at Montevideo, Uruguay. Its average enrollment was 12-15 students.   H.S.B.

Collection of Psalms, Hymns, and Spiritual Songs, *Suited to the Various Occasions of Public Worship and Private Devotion of the Church of Christ,* the first English hymnbook of the American Mennonites, was published at Harrisonburg, Va., in 1847 (called, however, *A Selection* instead of *Collection*), reprinted 6 times at Mountain Valley (Singers Glen), Va. (1851, 1855, 1859, 1868, 1872, 1877), by Joseph Funk & Sons (last two editions by Joseph Funk's Sons); also reprinted 4 times by John Baer's Sons at Lancaster (1862, 1864, 1869, 1875) and 3 times by the Mennonite Publishing Company at Elkhart (1880, 1883, 1884, jointly published at Elkhart by John F. Funk 1868, 1872) and was reprinted at Scottdale in 1948, 1953, and 1958. This small hymnal without musical notation, and with 363 hymns (ultimately 402 plus 65 in an appendix) was edited by a committee composed of Joseph Funk, David Hartman, Joseph Wenger. It carried a German appendix of 27 hymns (later 37) from 1857.   H.S.B.

Colorado Springs (Col.) **First** Mennonite Church (MC) is the congregation formerly called Manitou (*q.v.*), which changed its name when it moved to 11 N. 22nd Street, Colorado Springs, on Sept. 19, 1948. In 1958 the membership was 67, with Jacob Weirich as pastor.   H.S.B.

Commemorative Medals (I, 648): Supplement. A medal was issued in 1835 to commemorate the centennial of the Amsterdam seminary and the tricentennial of Menno Simons' leaving the Catholic Church. The medal, engraved by van der Kellen, shows the muse of eloquence standing near a pulpit. There are also many medals of *c*1647, often in silver or gold, issued by Dutch Mennonites to commemorate their silver or gold weddings. These medals are also important for Mennonite history.   vDZ.

Commisaris, name from 1775 given to the elders or "opzieners" of the Groningen Old Flemish conference in the Netherlands. In the Frisian conference of North Holland this name is also found from *c*1724 for what formerly was called "landsdienaar" (traveling elder). (Blaupot t. C., *Groningen* I, 135 f.; *idem, Holland* II, 84.)   vDZ.

Commission for Foreign Needs: see **Fonds voor Buitenlandsche Nooden.**

Community Mennonite Church (GCM), located in Markham, Ill., a suburb of Chicago, was organized in March 1957 with 18 charter members and has been meeting in its new church since Christmas 1958. Ronald Krehbiel was its pastor in 1959. M.G.

Conference Visitor is a monthly multilithed publication produced by the executive secretaries of the General Conference Mennonite Church and its boards for ministers and interested church workers. It was first issued in April 1952, and deals with concerns related to the Conference's mission and service program.   M.SH.

Confessie ende Vredehandelinghe (Haarlem, 1633) is a 48-page booklet (copy in AML) dealing with the unification of the Dutch Flemish Mennonites with the Old Flemish at Dordrecht in 1632. It contains a preface, an introduction, and the Dordrecht (*q.v.*) confession by Adriaan Cornelisz (*q.v.*).   vDZ.

Confession, Public, as a means of discipline was practiced by the Anabaptists, and long after by the Mennonites in all countries. It is still practiced by many of the Mennonite groups in North America. The most common practice is for the guilty member to stand in the meeting, state his transgression (or have it stated for him by the bishop or pastor), and ask forgiveness of the congregation. The minister in charge then takes the vote of the congregation regarding forgiveness and restoration, or if he is empowered to do so, may simply state the forgiveness himself. In some congregations the confession is made to the church council or the board of deacons and dealt with by it. In cases of gross sin it has been the custom in the more conservative congregations to consider the member expelled, even though he is immediately restored; the entire confession and restoration is then made with the transgressor kneeling. This is called "receiving from the knees," and is in a sense the equivalent of renewal of baptism. In some areas of the Mennonite Church (MC) it is required that the one guilty of gross sin remain "banned," i.e., outside the church, for a month, before he can be restored to fellowship as a member. The Anabaptist-Mennonite practice of public confession is similar to that of the first centuries of the Christian church before public confession was discontinued and private confession to the priest was substituted. (See **Discipline, Ban.**)   H.S.B.

Conservative Mennonite Board of Missions and Charities was established in 1919 to serve the Conservative (Amish) Mennonite Conference. Besides home missions in the United States it operates a foreign mission at Espelkamp, Germany, and cooperates with the Eastern Mennonite Board (*q.v.*) in the Luxembourg-France mission.   H.S.B.

Cornelis de Gijselaer: see **Cornelis Cornelisz.**

Costume: see **Dress.**

Cottage City Mennonite Church: see **Cottage City Mennonite Suburban Mission.**

Croghan Conservative Mennonite Church: see **Lowville-Croghan** Conservative Mennonite Church.

Crossroads Bible Church (MC), Mississippi: see **Wayside** Mennonite Church.

Cuba Mennonite Mission (MC), founded in 1954 by the Franconia Mennonite Board of Missions and Charities, had six missionaries and 13 baptized members in 1958. H.S.B.

Daalder, a Dutch Mennonite family on the island of Texel. Many of them served here as deacons; Dirk Reyertsz Daalder was a lay preacher of the Waterlander congregation at Den Hoorn, Texel, 1713-33. Simon Martinus Anton Daalder (b. 1905), educated at the university and seminary at Amsterdam, was pastor of Veendam-Pekela 1933-36, Heerlen-Eindhoven 1936-42, Enschedé 1942-45, and Haarlem 1945. Enno Daalder (b. 1915), also educated at the university and the Amsterdam seminary, was pastor at Oldeboorn 1942-47, Westzaan 1947-51, and Dantumawoude 1951-56. vDZ.

Daily Prayer Guide: see **Prayer Guide.**

Dantuma: see **Roelofs.**

Danzig Werder: see **Marienburg Werder.**

Dauber (Tauber), **Hans,** of Illingen, Württemberg, an Anabaptist, had won a following in Illingen and was arrested, probably in 1581. He was in prison continuously at least until 1617, 1581-82 in Maulbronn, 1582-88 in Hohenurach, 1588-1617 in Hohenwittlingen. In Hohenwittlingen Simon Kress (*q.v.*) was also long in confinement. (*TA Württemberg.*) H.S.B.

D'Auchy, Jacques: see **Jacques D'Auchy.**

Daytonville Mennonite Church (MC), Wellman, Ia., is located in the village of Daytonville, a mile northeast of Wellman. The congregation was established in 1951. The membership was 82 in 1958; Ezra W. Shank was the pastor. M.G.

Deaf, First Mennonite Church for the. The First Mennonite Church for the Deaf in the Lancaster (MC) Conference was begun under authorization of the Lancaster board of bishops in the fall of 1945, with J. Paul Graybill and Aaron H. Weaver in charge. By Dec. 29, 1946, Rossmere meetinghouse in Lancaster city was used for this purpose every second Saturday evening. Soon Reuben Stoltzfus became Aaron Weaver's associate. In 1949 Israel D. Rohrer was ordained as pastor. By 1951 they also used the second floor of the Mellinger meetinghouse. By 1953 Sunday school at the latter place was added. On Aug. 18, 1956, George A. Uhler was ordained to assist. A new meetinghouse for this work, located off the Lincoln Highway East, six miles east of Lancaster, was dedicated on May 12, 1957. With Rohrer and Uhler as pastors and Elmer G. Martin as bishop, the membership in 1958 was 15, with a Sunday school of 34, and a summer Bible school at Roxbury, Franklin County, Pa., of 94. The basement of the meetinghouse east of Lancaster was being used for the Lancaster Mennonite Conference Information Center in 1958-59, a project under the Eastern Board of Missions and Charities. I.D.L.

Deer Park (Wash.) **First** Mennonite Church (GCM), now extinct, was established as a result of a colonization attempt for Russian Mennonite refugees from Harbin, China, 1929-30, sponsored by H. P. Krehbiel. It joined the Pacific District (GCM) Conference in 1939, when it had a membership of *c*25, but it disbanded in 1943 when the members moved away, largely to Newport, some 30 miles north. H.S.B.

Delaplaine Amish Mennonite Church, now extinct, located in Greene County, Mo., was organized by John Hartzler and Levi Miller of Cass County in May 1895. Among the members were C. S. Weaver, J. B. Mischler, and J. B. Schrock, who were appointed on a meetinghouse building committee. The Mennonite meeting calendars of that decade make no reference to the congregation. M.G.

Den Helder: see **Helder.**

Denlinger, Mary (1867-1958), Mennonite mission worker and leader in women's activities, was born Dec. 3, 1867, in Paradise Twp., Lancaster Co., Pa., the third child of Elizabeth Shaub and John B. Denlinger. In 1890 she became a member of the Paradise congregation through the preaching of John S. Coffman. En route to the Elkhart Sunday School Conference in 1894 Abram Metzler recruited her for the new Chicago Mission opened by M. S. Steiner. Here she served for five years. Then she and Amanda Musselman opened the Philadelphia Mission, where she served for the next quarter century. After that she continued her church interest at East Chestnut Street and Paradise congregations in both Sunday-school and sewing circle work. She died Jan. 22, 1958. I.D.L.

Denver Mennonite Church (MC) is located on the northeastern edge of this thriving borough of 1800 in Lancaster County, Pa. Among the early settlers here were the John Bucher, Michael Bear, John Shirk, Jacob Polinger, and Huber families. In 1760 they were worshiping at Hershberger's farm on the west side of Union Station, hence known by his name. It was a part of the Hammer Creek Bishop District and the Indiantown circuit. In 1877 a brick union church was built for the use of German Baptists, German (Old and New) Mennonites, German Lutheran and Reformed in Bucher's of East Cocalico, on a six weeks' schedule, one group meeting each six weeks. The Reformed and the Lutherans built in the borough in 1890 (separating from the others in 1912). On May 8, 1928, the New (Reformed) Mennonites relinquished all rights to the house. The building was thoroughly renovated and Sunday-school rooms added, with an opening on March 13, 1955. An old cemetery adjoins. In 1958 Isaac K. Sensenig was pastor, assisted by the Indiantown ministry, with a membership of 38. I.D.L.

Deutsche Mennonitenhilfe, from May 9, 1922, to its dissolution on Dec. 19, 1926, the name adopted by the Mennonitische Flüchtlingsfürsorge (*q.v.*). H.S.B.

Dewey (Ill.) Mennonite Church (MC) was established in 1941. It had a membership of 36 in 1958, with Ivan L. Birkey as pastor.   M.G.

Dhamtari Christian Hospital, Madhya Pradesh, India, established by the Mennonite Board of Missions and Charities (MC), is now owned and operated by the Mennonite Church in India. This 110-bed general hospital is the outgrowth of the first medical dispensary, begun in 1900, but the first hospital building was erected in 1924.   H.S.B.

Dijk, van, a common Dutch family name, also Mennonite. Besides the Jan van Dijk found in *ME* II, 61, another Jan van Dijk was a preacher of the Danzig Old Flemish church in Amsterdam in 1727-c54, as was his son Pieter van Dijk (d.1803) in 1754-89. There was also a Mennonite van Dijk family at Hamburg, Germany. Sara van Dijk (1714-60) of this family in 1737 married Herman Rahusen (1697-1760).   vᴅZ.

Dirk of Wormer: see **Dirck van Wormer.**

Discipleship. It was the particular genius of 16th-century Anabaptism to interpret the essence of Christianity as discipleship to Christ *(Nachfolge Christi)*. By this the Anabaptists meant something definite in experience, not just a connection with the church, or an espousal of the traditional doctrines of Christianity, or even doing good works. In their understanding the individual responds to the call of Christ, forsakes his life of sin and self, receives a new nature, comes under the lordship of Christ, and takes Christ's life and teachings as normative for himself and for the church, and indeed ultimately for the whole social order. His faith in Christ thus finds expression in "newness of life"; this expression and similar ones such as "a new creature" were common. The uniqueness of Anabaptism lies in its conviction that Christ is more than a divine being to be worshiped, more than a Saviour who brings forgiveness through the cross and deliverance from the penalty and power of sin; He is the Lord to be followed and obeyed, and with whom the Christian enters into a covenant that controls his whole life. Henceforth his life is to be lived so that Christ's life and teachings are to be concretely and realistically expressed by him in principle, in the context of the kingdom of God. This interpretation of Christianity with its attendant concept of the church as a fellowship of obedient disciples, and with its ethic of love, stands in contrast to the Lutheranism of the Reformation whose central emphasis upon man's alienation from God and his restoration (justification) by the grace of God, resulted in the interpretation of Christianity primarily as the experience of forgiveness.

The two Reformation movements, Lutheranism and Anabaptism, with their differing ideological foci, were consciously in opposition to each other. Lutheranism saw in Anabaptist discipleship a works-righteousness and legalism, while Anabaptism saw in Luther's "faith only"—justification a lifeless faith and a compromise with the claims and call of Christ. The two positions, purified of extremes and

misunderstandings, are not in necessary conflict, but should be complementary parts of a full New Testament Christianity.

To describe in detail the meaning of discipleship as the Anabaptists saw it would mean an extensive exposition of their theology and ethics, which is impossible here. Major aspects of the concept include: (1) holy living; (2) suffering in the spirit of Christ, bearing the cross; (3) the practice of love and nonresistance; (4) separation from the world of sin and evil; (5) full brotherhood in the church; (6) obedience to the great commission; (7) a disciplined church; (8) rejection of the use of power by the Christian (e.g., state offices).

In adopting this concept of discipleship the Anabaptists committed themselves existentially to Christ without calculating all the consequences. They did realize that their stand meant a break with the continuity of the past "Christian" social order, the *corpus christianum,* and they consciously took this step. They saw the world as divided into two kingdoms, with the Christian partaking in only one, the kingdom of God, and standing in conflict with the other.

While the Anabaptist vision of discipleship is theoretically clear, its implications have not always been clear to those who have espoused it, Anabaptists, Mennonites, or others. Just how is it to be applied in all respects? For many it has meant withdrawal from the world as we know it in order to share the intimate fellowship and high standards of the Christian brotherhood, not always escaping in the process the temptations of legalism and externalism. Others, having either deliberately or unconsciously moved out into the world, lost much of the essence of the original vision and adopted the common compromises of traditional Christianity with the absolutes of Christ. The current spiritual renascence among Mennonites, particularly in North America, has led to a critical re-examination of the contemporary Mennonite performance in the light of the high discipleship concept, and a search for a fuller and more effective expression of the concept in the context of the modern world.

Where Anabaptist discipleship has been kept from descending into mere ethics or even moralism, it has been by the strong sense of identification with Christ in personal love and dedication, including identification with Him in His sufferings and in His ultimate victory. The Anabaptists had a strong sense of history and of God at work in it, and hence also of eschatology. This sense, combined with their experience of suffering under persecution, produced their "theology of martyrdom," as Ethelbert Stauffer has called it, which was not merely a source of consolation in trial but a real theology of victory.

The Anabaptist concept of discipleship is to be distinguished from another historic concept of following Christ, the one set forth by Thomas à Kempis in his *Imitation of Christ,* written about a century before the Reformation. This book, for all its urging upon the Christian disciple the imitation of the character of his Master by the conquest of the human passions and the vices to which they lead, and its call for the production of the virtues of

Christ, is concerned primarily with the inner world of the soul where the Christian is to cultivate his spiritual life with his eye upon heaven as his goal. Self-renunciation and resignation are the highest virtues; it is mysticism mixed with asceticism. The ideal is withdrawal from society for contemplation; hence the social dimension is almost completely lacking, and there is no criticism of the social or religious order with a view to establishing a full Christian order in the brotherhood and church of the living Christ in the midst of the present world. Thomas à Kempis and the many who follow his concept evade the conflict with the world, and thus escape the cross-bearing experience of true discipleship. Thomas has more kinship with the later Pietists than with the Anabaptists.

The idea of discipleship is not unique with Anabaptism; it has appeared in various forms through the centuries both before and after the Reformation. It was the vision of the earliest Christians, of certain groups through the Middle Ages, of Peter Chelciki of Bohemia (1390-1460), spiritual father of the Bohemian Brethren, of George Fox, of John Wesley, and others, although it did not always take the same form as in Anabaptism. It has been a recurring creative idea throughout Christian history. It was the mission of the Anabaptists to give powerful expression to this vision at a creative moment in history, at the beginning of the "Modern Age," and not only to enunciate the vision but to strive earnestly to put it into practice. But they were ahead of their time. Caught in the crushing grip of a church and state which refused their vision, they were almost destroyed, and largely prevented from becoming a significant factor in the ongoing life of western Christendom. But their vision has survived and continued to challenge the modern church. (See also **Ethics**.)   H.S.B.

H. S. Bender, "The Anabaptist Vision," *The Recovery of the Anabaptist Vision* (Scottdale, 1957) 29-54; idem, "The Anabaptist Theology of Discipleship," *MQR XXIV* (1950) 25-32; J. Lawrence Burkholder, "The Anabaptist Vision of Discipleship," *Recovery*, 135-51; F. H. Littell, *The Anabaptist View of the Church* (Philadelphia, 1952).

Domain (Man.) Mennonite Brethren Church was organized in 1926, and built its meetinghouse in 1952. In 1959 the membership was 50, with Jacob Pauls as pastor. It was formerly called the Osborne (*q.v.*) M.B. Church.   F.C.P.

Don Region, located on the west side of the Don River, Russia, also known as the "Territory of the Don Cossacks," contained a number of small Mennonite settlements. At the mouth of the Don River, west of the city of Rostov, was the Mariupol Mennonite Brethren Church (*q.v.*) which was organized by M.B. evangelists from the Molotschna settlement. The Planerkolonie (*q.v.*), located north of Berdyansk (*q.v.*), consisted primarily of non-Mennonite German settlers, largely Lutheran. Near-by was the Bergthal Mennonite Settlement (*q.v.*), which was dissolved in 1874 when the settlers went to Canada; the five Mennonite villages were incorporated into the Planer settlement. The Planer settlement spread into the eastern part of the Don Basin. Another daughter settlement of Planer originated north of

Berdyansk, consisting of the villages of Neuhoffnung, Neuhoffnungsthal, Rosenfeld, and Neu-Stuttgart. It was here that Eduard Wüst began his evangelistic activities, which spread into the Molotschna Mennonite settlement causing the founding of the Mennonite Brethren. A small Mennonite settlement in the Don Region was the town of Millerovo (*q.v.*), which became an industrial center of the Mennonites. (See **Millerovo** Mennonite Brethren Church.) In addition to Millerovo and Mariupol, the towns of Taganrog and Rostov had some Mennonite population.   C.K.

J. A. Malinowsky, *Die Planerkolonien am Asowschen Meere* (Stuttgart, 1928).

Donnersbergerhof: see **Donnersberg**.

Dörksen, Abraham, leader and elder of the conservative wing of the Bergthal Mennonite Church of the West Reserve of Manitoba, which became known as the Sommerfeld Mennonite Church (*q.v.*). Abraham Dörksen and his followers opposed the progressive educational and religious ideas promoted by the Elder Johann K. Funk (*q.v.*), of the Bergthal Church, and Heinrich H. Ewert (*q.v.*), principal of the Gretna Collegiate Institute (*q.v.*). Dörksen and his group also strongly opposed the public school system which the Canadian government was introducing among the Mennonites, desiring to maintain the old practice brought from Russia of conducting their own school system without interference from the outside. In his conservatism Dörksen was closely related to the leaders of the Chortitz Mennonite Church (*q.v.*) of the East Reserve and the Old Colony Mennonites (*q.v.*) of the West Reserve. Additional information and data about his life and activities are not available, but his active leadership falls approximately in the period 1880-1900.

C.K.

E. K. Francis, *In Search of Utopia* (Altona, 1955); Cornelius Krahn, "Adventure in Conviction. Russia, Canada and Mexico" (manuscript); C. A. Dawson, *Group Settlement. Ethnic Communities in Western Canada* (Toronto, 1936); Paul J. Schaefer, *Heinrich H. Ewert, Lehrer, Erzieher und Prediger der Mennoniten* (Gretna, 1945).

Dos Palos Mennonite Church (GCM) in Merced County, Cal., about 50 miles northwest of Reedley, was in existence 1930-33 with Dan Gerig as pastor. It was discontinued because of failure of promised water for irrigation.   H.S.B.

Dosidorf (Zabara), a Mennonite village in Volhynia: see **Waldheim**.

Doves, a Dutch Mennonite family in the province of North Holland. Jan Dirkssen Doves was an untrained preacher of Oude Zijpe and later until c1755 of the Waterlander Barsingerhorn-Nieuwe Zijp congregation.   vDZ.

Drebbel, Cornelis Jacobsz (Alkmaar, 1572-London, 1633), a noted artist, scientist, engineer, and inventor, among whose inventions was a submarine, was a Dutch Mennonite.   vDZ.

H. A. Naber, *De ster van 1572* (Amsterdam, 1907).

Duerksen (Dürksen, Derksen, Doerksen, Dirks, Derks, and Dirksen, *q.v.*) was a common Mennonite family name originating in the Netherlands from the given name "Dirk." Common in Prussia, Russia, and North and South America, the name appeared in the church records of Danzig, Heubuden, Elbing, Orloff, Schönsee, and other places. A. A. Toews gives biographies of Martin J. Derksen (I, 144) and Johann J. Dürksen (II, 185). Jacob Doerksen was elder of the M.B. church at Kotlyarevo, Memrik, Crimea, 1909-26. In 1958 there were 15 Mennonite ministers listed bearing some form of the name. The M.B. group had 8, all in Canada, two each in British Columbia, Alberta, Manitoba, and Ontario; the G.C.M. had 7, of whom one was in British Columbia, one in Paraguay, and 5 in the United States, only two of whom were active (Neb. and S.D.). Martin Duerksen was pastor of the Buenos Aires (Argentina) congregation, and John P. Duerksen was professor at Hesston College. C.K.

Reimer, *Familiennamen*, 106; A. A. Töws, *Mennonitische Märtyrer* (N. Clearbrook, I 1949, II 1954).

East Africa Mennonite Mission (MC), formerly called Africa Mennonite Mission (*q.v.*), in 1958 had 40 long-term workers, and six short-term workers, with a total African membership of 1,632. It was under the Eastern Mennonite Board of Missions and Charities.   H.S.B.

Merle Eshleman, *Africa Answers* (Scottdale, 1951); Catharine Leatherman, *Ye Are God's Building; The Story of Twenty-Five Years in Tanganyika* (Salunga, Pa., 1959).

East Fairview Mennonite Church (MC), located 7 miles southeast of Lebanon, Ore., developed as an outreach project of the Fairview Mennonite Church (*q.v.*). The meetinghouse was built in 1949, but the congregation was not organized until May 1957. In 1959 the membership was 30, with Ivan Headings as pastor.   H.S.B.

East Pennsylvania Conference of the Mennonite Church (GCM), the name adopted by the J. H. Oberholtzer (*q.v.*) group which was expelled from the Franconia Conference (*q.v.*) in October 1847, which was later changed to Eastern Mennonite Conference and finally to Eastern District Conference (*q.v.*).   H.S.B.

Edmonton (Alberta) **First** Mennonite Church (GCM) began *c*1949 as a mission, and was organized as a congregation April 19, 1959, with 24 charter members. A church building was purchased in 1954. Arthur Dick has been pastor since 1958.
                                            H.S.B.

Educational News Bulletin has been published occasionally since 1950 by the Board of Education and Publication of the General Conference Mennonite Church to promote the cause of Christian education. Its eleven issues (1958) have been circulated among the ministers and church workers.
                                            M.Sh.

Ehrenpreis, Peter, of Illingen, Württemberg, son of the former Schultheiss Wolf Ehrenpreis, was won for Anabaptism *c*1583, went to Moravia when he

was baptized, returned, relapsed for a time, then returned to his faith, and finally moved with his family to Moravia in 1596. His unusually fine life and spirit made a powerful impression upon the community. The Illingen pastor Huttenloch reported in 1596 to the Abbot of Maulbronn that "he is held in higher favor by a large part of the community than all the evangelical preachers." "Like all Anabaptists he leads a quiet, honorable, and blameless life." A certain George Augsburger is reported to have said, "If any man is saved, he will be. And I could wish no better heaven than the one Peter will be in." (*TA Württemberg, passim.*)
                                            H.S.B.

Einlage was a Mennonite village established by Dutch Mennonites during the 17th century on the Nogat River in the Marienburg Werder. The name was also used in Chortitza (Russia), Manitoba, Mexico, and Paraguay.   C.K.

Eirene (Greek word for "Peace"), the name of the service program for European conscientious objectors, similar to Pax (*q.v.*) for United States CO's, which was set up in 1957 by joint action of the Mennonite Central Committee and the Brethren Service Committee. Its first project is a unit located at Oulmes, Morocco, which is to work for local agricultural improvement. The administrative office is handled by the MCC at Kaiserslautern, Germany. The first unit consisted of five men—two French, two Dutch, and one American.   H.S.B.

El Ombu (Uruguay) Mennonite Brethren Church was organized in 1948 in the newly established El Ombu settlement, composed largely of former Polish Mennonite Brethren. Its meetinghouse was built in 1955. In 1957 it had a membership of 84, with Tobias Foth as leader. It has two substations, one in Colonia meeting in a home (Robert Foth, leader) and the Montevideo Mission Home at Calle Pedro F. Berro 1114 (John Wall, missionary, leader).
                                            H.S.B.

Elkhart (Ind.) Mennonite Church (GCM) began holding services in January 1958 and was organized as a congregation with 40 charter members on Aug. 31, 1958. In April 1959 Walter Gering began to serve as pastor. Since its inception the congregation has met in the West Side School but in July 1959 a 4-acre plot with parsonage located at the corner of Hively and Pleasant Plain was purchased on which a meetinghouse will be built.   W.Kl.

Emergency Relief Commission: see **Emergency Relief Board.**

England (II, 220): Supplement. The Mennonite Central Committee, at the urging of Canadian Mennonites, began a modest relief program in England in May 1940, with Theodore Claassen of Newton, Kan., joined by John E. Coffman in Oct., 1940. The various projects, which were developed, were not for emergency relief needs, but planned as a service to needs aggravated by the war, combined with an evangelical peace witness. These projects included: Polish Boys Project in London, aid to Cotswold Bruderhof (Hutterite), Wickhurst Manor (Save the Children Fund), Woodlands (Old People's Home near Birmingham), South Meadows (children's hostel near Liverpool), Taxal Edge (boys home), prisoner of war work, clothing distribution. It was John Coffman who first proposed in 1941 the motto "In the name of Christ," which was adopted by the MCC as a label for all future clothing and food packages. Among the 24 workers who served in England were Peter J. Dyck (July 1941-July 1945) and Mrs. Peter Dyck (1941-45). For the work in London see the article **London: Supplement.** The MCC work in England was closed in 1946, when the opportunity for more urgently needed relief work in Holland opened up, though one worker continued in prisoner of war work until the close of his term in 1947.

In 1952 the Mennonite Church (MC) began mission work in London, and in 1958 had two centers, the one at Free Gospel Hall with 10 members. (See **London.**) (J. D. Unruh, *In the Name of Christ,* Scottdale, 1952.) H.S.B.

England Mennonite Mission (MC), founded by the Mennonite Board of Missions and Charities in 1952, operates the London Mennonite Centre at 14 Shepherd's Hill, and the Free Gospel Hall at 39 Grafton Terrace in London, which had 10 members in 1958. H.S.B.

Englewood Mennonite Church, 832 West 68th Street, Chicago, Ill., is made up of a majority of the congregation formerly known as the Mennonite Home Mission (*q.v.*), established in 1893, and since 1955 called the Union Avenue Mennonite Church. The congregation purchased a church in Englewood where they opened services in October 1957, with a charter membership of 60 which was established in 1958, with Laurence M. Horst as pastor. The main body of the church moved to Englewood, but some of the members remained at the Union Avenue church to help administrate the continuing and growing Sunday school, under the administration of Laurence Horst. H.S.B.

Erie View United Mennonite Church (GCM), located 4 miles west of Port Rowan, Ont., was organized in 1947. The congregation bought an older church and remodeled it in 1957. In 1959 the membership was 37, with Jacob Braun as pastor. H.S.B.

Escola Fritz Kliewer, a new Mennonite high school in Witmarsum, Brazil, was dedicated March 22, 1959. The school has accommodations for 113 students and 7 teachers and is supported by a constituency of 528 persons. G. E. Reimer is principal of the school. M.G.

Ethics. It is impossible to exaggerate the importance of ethics in the life and testimony of the Anabaptist-Mennonites. Throughout their history, Mennonites have sought above all to be holy, pure, and obedient to Christ. Consequently Mennonite preaching, writing, and piety have had a strong ethical emphasis. In fact, the ethical emphasis is so predominant in the writings of Menno Simons and others, that one is sometimes tempted to say that for Mennonites Christianity and ethics are one. At least it is fair to say that Mennonites have given ethics a position of centrality not generally found in Protestantism. Whereas Protestantism has had the tendency to separate faith from conduct in theology and in life as a protection against a religion of works, Anabaptists and Mennonites have held them closely together. It is probably premature to say what are the soteriological implications of the position given ethics by Mennonites. Suffice it to say, the statement of James that "faith without works is dead" represents a concern of Mennonites out of all proportion to a concern for the dangers of a religion of works.

The importance of the ethical life for the Mennonite understanding of Christianity appears in connection with the Anabaptist conception of discipleship. In his "Anabaptist Vision," H. S. Bender declares that for the Anabaptists discipleship was the essence of Christianity. "First and fundamental in the Anabaptist vision was the conception of the essence of Christianity as discipleship." By discipleship the Anabaptists meant the ethical life of radical obedience. "Discipleship" was a concept which meant "the transformation of the entire way of life of the individual believer and of society so that it should be fashioned after the teachings and example of Christ." Further examination of the Anabaptist vision with its almost exclusive preoccupation with ethics, notably nonresistance, nonswearing of oaths, a new concept of the church, and nonconformity to this world, would reinforce the conclusion that discipleship means a conception of Christianity in which "the Christian life is defined most basically in ethical terms."

The full significance of this understanding of Christianity is realized when it is compared with the Protestant Reformation in general. Whereas the Reformation was interested mainly in a reinterpretation of the way of salvation and consequently focused upon the subjective experience of grace and the inner enjoyment of the freedom of the Spirit, Anabaptism concentrated on the objective, concrete, outward manifestations of the Spirit. "The great word of the Anabaptists was not 'faith' as it was with the reformers, but 'following' (*Nachfolge Christi*)" (Bender). Noteworthy is the fact that Anabaptism had little to say about the great questions of faith in relation to divine acceptance. The question of the Anabaptists was, "What does it mean to follow Christ as a disciple?" Hence ethics was central in emphasis and inseparably tied to faith.

In view of the consuming desire of Anabaptists and Mennonites to live ethically it may seem strange that no American has written to date a Mennonite ethic as a theological discipline, although this has been done by the Dutch theologians de Bussy and Hoekstra, although not in the Anabaptist spirit. Numerous tracts, letters, monographs, and articles have been written on specific subjects such as nonresistance, separation, the oath, community, mutual aid, business, marriage, dress, and stewardship. However, no one has attempted to treat ethics systematically as a separate theological discipline. Possibly the principal reasons for this omission are the same as those which account for the paucity of theological literature among the Mennonites in general. Mennonitism has fostered a simple piety and a theological naïvete which has, to be sure, penetrated at times to the heart of the Gospel but which for that very reason is incapable of theological sophistication. More directly, the very simplicity of the Mennonite approach to ethics has tended to obviate a study of the methodology of ethics. In the absence of an explicit Mennonite ethic it is necessary therefore to generalize from numerous writings over a period of four hundred years and draw conclusions from approved Mennonite practice. It should be noted, however, that Guy F. Hershberger's *War, Peace, and Nonresistance* (1944) has served the Mennonite church in recent years virtually as a volume on Christian ethics despite its limited scope. Furthermore his book, *The Way of the Cross in Human Relations* (1958), comes even closer to meeting the need for a Mennonite ethic. Still to come, however, is a volume which seeks to set forth answers to the problems of basic Christian ethics.

Methodologically Mennonite ethics must be understood first and fundamentally as Biblical ethics. The exclusive source of ethical instruction is the Bible—more precisely the New Testament. The Biblicism of the Mennonites comes through most impressively in the settling of ethical questions. Sufficient for a valid imperative is a clearly stated command of Christ to His disciples or a command by one of the apostles. The norms of Mennonite ethics are simply the life and teachings of Christ as contained in the New Testament. Christ's earthly life has been regarded as a pattern to be followed in filial obedience. Generally speaking, Mennonite ethics belongs to the *imitatio Christi* tradition.

Nowhere does the imitation of Christ motif come through more clearly than in the Schleitheim Confession (1527) (see **Brüderliche Vereinigung**). Here the only criterion of valid instruction regarding specific ethical questions is the earthly life of Christ, His teaching, or a testimony to the life of Christ from an apostle. Concerning the sword, for example, the answer is clear and summary: "Christ teaches and commands us to learn of Him, for He is meek and lowly in heart and so shall we find rest to our souls." Concerning whether a Christian should pass sentence in worldly disputes and strife the answer is, "Christ did not wish to decide or pass judgment between brother and brother in the case of the inheritance, but refused to do so. Therefore we should do likewise. They wished to make Christ King, but He fled and did not view it as an arrangement of His Father. Thus shall we do as He did, and follow Him, and so shall we not walk in darkness. For He Himself says: He who wishes to come after me, let him deny himself and take up his cross and follow me."

Of course it must be conceded that all systems of ethics which deserve the name Christian take Christ and His teachings seriously. But the really significant factor which distinguishes one system from the other is *how* the teachings of Christ are used and what is put alongside the example and teachings of Christ within the system. Very seldom do we have a system of ethics which rests on Christ's teachings alone. Even those systems which claim to rely exclusively on the revelation in Christ are very likely to inject historical or philosophical considerations unwittingly. At least it may be said that all ethical systems which take seriously the life of the world and suppose that Christians are responsible for the social and political order inject on the ground floor of ethics certain norms outside the New Testament. The conflict between the perfectionism of Christ's ethic and the ambiguity of the world order makes some concession to a lower ethic necessary. Accordingly, Catholicism has drawn from natural law in Stoicism; Lutheranism has met the problem by the theory of the two realms; Calvinism has lowered the requirement of love to conform to the theocratic ideal of the Old Testament; modern theologians have entered considerations of historical relativism, contextualism, or anti-rationalistic existentialism. The uniqueness of Anabaptist ethics lies in the fact that it accepts the New Testament as the sole norm, assuming that the ethic of discipleship in the New Testament is essentially uniform and that it is a historical necessity and possibility for the church.

It should be remembered, however, that the Mennonite approach to ethics, namely, Biblical command and direct obedience, takes place within the church, the body of Christ, and under the direction of the Holy Spirit. This helps to qualify the legalistic tendencies within Mennonite ethics and to prevent it from becoming nothing more than a detached rationalistic systematization of Jesus' teachings. There is a sense in which the Anabaptists not only imitated Christ but participated in Christ as a living present reality. To be sure, the indwelling Spirit of Christ was not intended to provide an elasticity not permitted by the Biblical injunction. However, it did provide a spiritual context in which the Biblical text came alive in ways not true of later generations of Mennonites, who often succumbed to the spirit of legalism. Also it should be remembered that there has always been a certain childlike naïvete in Mennonite ethical thinking which, having precluded excessive rationalization of Jesus' teachings, has saved them from the despair of Tolstoy and of certain liberals by whom Jesus' teachings were considered a universal possibility.

In this connection it should be pointed out that, according to Mennonite thinking, Christian ethics is expected only of committed Christians. This may seem self-evident. On the contrary, the history of Christendom presents many occasions when Christian ethics have been adapted to the practical possibilities of total populations and were at times for that reason virtually equated with civic morality. But for Mennonites, Christian conduct issues from a vital experience of faith. In fact, it is only on the basis of complete commitment that the radical demands of discipleship are meaningful. Hence Christian ethics are really church ethics when viewed from the standpoint of the ethical agent as well as the context of decision-making.

Basic to the Mennonite ethics is the idea of the church as separated from the world. The dualism of the church and the world provides the comprehensive framework for the Mennonite outlook on duty. The church is defined as the "people of God" (I Peter 2:9) corresponding to the new age, described otherwise in the New Testament as the kingdom of God. Christ lives among the people of God and calls them away from evil in its many forms. The world is defined as the rule of evil. The world takes many social forms and is ever at war with the church. Therefore the church seeks to be nonconformed to the world by living according to the principles of the kingdom of God. According to Schleitheim, "All creatures are in but two classes, good and bad, believing and unbelieving, darkness and light, the world and those who have come out of the world, God's temple and idols, Christ and Belial; and none can have part with the other."

One of the perennial problems of Mennonite ethics is to know where to draw the line between the church and the world. In the realm of theology the line is drawn quite clearly. The reality of God and His work of salvation, including the history of Israel and the true church together with appropriate attitudes and deeds of love, forgiveness, tenderness, and faith, constitute one realm. Satan and his work of opposition, including all evil men, angels, and institutions, constitute the other realm. But in the cultural situation where the church and the world are mixed, it is not always easy to know where to assign certain aspects of cultural life. Hence Mennonites have always been confronted with the task of passing ethical judgment on every major cultural change. Sometimes this has led Mennonites to freeze certain approved cultural patterns and to be suspicious of change in general. On the other hand, sometimes the church has been tempted to discard the task of cultural criticism. The dynamic character of modern change has accentuated the problem of change and consequently certain Mennonites have come to the conviction that the uniqueness of the Mennonite witness in the modern period is at stake.

The central idea of the Christian ethic according to Mennonites is love. Christ not only commanded love (Luke 10:27), but His life and death on the cross gave love concrete meaning. In the cross of Christ the love of God was manifested for the world and the love which is expected of Christians ethically is a re-enactment of the drama of redemption. In other words, the emphasis is on sacrificial love even though Mennonites use the term love to cover relationships of mutuality. Mennonites have clearly perceived that the full meaning of love is known supremely in the cross and the Christian ethic therefore must start with nothing less than complete self-giving.

One of the implications of the love ethic is nonresistance. For over four hundred years Mennonites have accepted nonresistance as the way in which Christians respond to evil. As an absolute principle, nonresistance has had a profound effect on all aspects of Mennonite life, psychological, economic, and political. Belief in nonresistance has expressed itself in conscientious objection to war. Also Mennonites have refused to be drawn into industrial conflict. Furthermore Mennonites have by and large refused active participation in politics. On the personal level, they have interpreted the principle of nonresistance to forbid litigation and, what is more important, they have interpreted it to imply the way of suffering love in cases of personal disputes and misunderstandings. But nonresistance has been regarded not simply as a negative principle. It has been an expression of outgoing redemptive love which looks to healing and reconciliation. For this reason Mennonites have sought to find alternative ways of service during times of war and attempts have been made to find creative alternatives to industrial strife and litigation.

Mennonites have always recognized that nonresistance means suffering and so from the very beginning Christianity and suffering have been linked together. "Living under the cross" has been considered normal Christian experience. Anyone acquainted with Mennonite literature knows that many of the finest and most expressive tracts, hymns, and historical accounts uphold the inevitability of suffering and also the necessity of suffering as a direct implication of true discipleship. As a result of the prolonged intensity of suffering the result has sometimes been a psychology of suffering and frequently suffering has fostered a general attitude of retirement and quietism.

Another implication of the love ethic is brotherhood. This is the form which love takes among those who have been reconciled to God and to one another. Brotherhood love expresses itself in a sense of mutual responsibility for the total welfare of the members of the church. The brotherhood church as the body of Christ is held together by common commitment to meet one another's needs in the spiritual, moral, and material realms. Some of the finest moments of Mennonite life are moments of sharing, especially in times of emergency. Since much of Mennonite history has been a history of persecution, brotherhood mutuality has often constituted the difference between life and death. Sharing has been practiced not only within various congregations but between churches in various countries. During the modern period permanent organizations have taken up the task of mutual aid as the needs have become more numerous and complex.

The principle of brotherhood is also important for ethics in so far as brotherhood has affected the entire community life of Mennonites. Mennonites have traditionally sought to live near to one another, often in semi- or complete isolation from the main centers of population. Accordingly the brotherhood church and the community have frequently been described as one reality. The church, family, farm, school, and business have constituted what may be called "religious community." A deliberate effort has been made within the Mennonite communities to inject the ethic of love into all areas of life. Sometimes the community life of Mennonites has been more instinctive than deliberate. Nevertheless Mennonites have always sought to live together in such a way that the principles of brotherhood may be extended into the social realm.

The form which community life has taken among Mennonites has varied greatly. Its most extreme expression has been Christian communalism. Most notable is Hutterianism with its practice of "full community." Among the Hutterites (*q.v.*) Christian mutuality is understood to mean the abolition of private property. It means also group authority over areas of life normally thought to lie within the province of the individual. Within the Bruderhofs every aspect of life is directed toward brotherhood, including the family and economics. The significance of the Bruderhof lies in the fact that it lifts sharing above an occasional response to specific needs. The Bruderhof involves nothing less than a structure of mutuality. Sharing is a continuous and all-embracing experience.

Among most Anabaptist and Mennonite groups brotherhood has not been organized as systematically as among the Hutterites. In the "open communities" of American Mennonites brotherhood responsibilities have been less pervasive and comprehensive. Most Mennonite groups have made a larger place for self-determination. It is customary for individuals to make their own decisions with respect to marriage, vocation, education, and mobility, subject of course to accepted moral standards, and usually subject to the restriction of no marriage outside the church, and no business and social affiliations which would violate the "unequal yoke" proscription of II Cor. 6.

Having said this, however, it is important to remember that the brotherhood has fostered many traditions and cultural expressions which have had powerful ethical influences. The Mennonite community has been guided to a considerable extent by traditional attitudes and practices, often in the absence of a reasoned and articulate ethic. Ethical decisions have been made by Mennonites largely from the standpoint of what the church has approved in the past. At any rate, Mennonite ethics have been mainly community ethics rising out of a deep sense of belonging to a common life.

A discussion of Mennonite ethics would not be complete without a statement regarding the Mennonite attitude toward the total social order, especially from the standpoint of social justice. With respect to the concern for social justice Mennonites have not entered into this realm except in a few instances, whether as individual participation or as a church. It is true that the early Anabaptists spoke out against religious persecution and the early Pennsylvania Quakers of German Mennonite background (not Mennonites as once thought) were among the first in America to protest against slavery, but as a rule Mennonites have not addressed themselves to the great social and political problems of society. Their reluctance to become involved in the struggle for justice has a number of roots. Certainly one is nonresistance, which when applied to the realm of social change runs counter to the inevitable coercive balances of power and counter to the spirit of the world. The Christian's calling lies primarily in the work of the church and the Christian community rather than in the work of the world. The Christian must be concerned with the realm of redemption with consequent attitudes of minor concern for the world order. The Mennonite concept of "the church leads the Christian to withdraw his major energies from active participation in the general program of world betterment and attempted reconstruction of the entire non-Christian world order and focus them on the building of the Christian community. His hope for the world is the church and the creation of a Christian social order within the fellowship of the church brotherhood" (Bender).

The withdrawal of the Mennonite church from the realms of justice and law does not mean, however, that Mennonites have had no social outreach. The truth is that Mennonites have supported an outstanding program of social service in the form of relief and voluntary service in almost every nation of the world during the past forty years. In fact, Mennonites are among the most active in this area. Undoubtedly the present program of world relief and voluntary service has received much of its stimulus from a search for a moral alternative to military service. However, this is not the only reason. The basic reason is that Mennonites have rediscovered the service motive in discipleship at a time when the world has undergone two major wars and a number of major social revolutions.

One of the consequences of Mennonite involvement in world relief and rehabilitation is a growing interest in the world and its problems from a Christian point of view. This has raised the question of whether Mennonites should not become more active in shaping social and political policy. This is another way of asking whether and in what way Mennonites can witness to government and lesser social powers without forfeiting the position of nonresistance and the primacy of the church in the life of the Christian. Undoubtedly this question has far-reaching consequences for Mennonite ethics.

The problem of social witness and action should also be seen in connection with the rapid assimilation of American Mennonites in the economic and social life of the nation. Especially since World War II, the Mennonite community has lost much of its agrarian isolation, through the forces of urbanization and mass communication. This constitutes nothing less than a crisis in Mennonite ethics, since Mennonite ethical thinking has largely assumed a more or less controlled community. Today the environment of American Mennonitism is secular America. Having lost much of its sociological base, Mennonitism is faced with the question of how to work out a community ethic in a secular environment. Undoubtedly this question calls for a new sense of realism among Mennonites and a critical analysis of such basic ethical concepts as love, justice, and power.

Preoccupation with the categories of social ethics should not lead to forgetting that Mennonites have traditionally held to strict standards of personal morality, such as sexual purity, honesty, Christian attire, and Christian entertainment. Drinking, smoking, and attendance at questionable places of amusement have been discouraged. Instead, Mennonites have been encouraged to live a simple and modest life of godliness. One of the finest treatments of Mennonite ethics, particularly from the standpoint of personal morality, is John C. Wenger's, *Separated unto God*. In this volume, the nonconformed life is described in its manifold relations to the forces of good and evil in society.

In the course of their 400-year history, scattered as they have been by migration from western Europe to Russia, and to North America and South America, and varying in type from urban (in Holland and Northwest Germany) to exclusively rural (Russia, South America, and until recently the United States and Canada), Mennonites have not always maintained a uniform ethical pattern. Particularly in western Europe has there been some deviation from the above outline. This sketch applies most accurately therefore to the Mennonites of the United States and Canada. No attempt has been made to review the history of ethical theory as developed among the Mennonites of Holland by such men as Hoekstra and de Bussy; nor to trace ethical developments in that country. J.L.B.

H. S. Bender, "The Anabaptist Vision," *MQR* XVIII (1944) 78 f.; *ibid.*, John Howard Yoder, "The Anabaptist Dissent," *Concern*, No. 1 (June 1954) 45; Guy F. Hershberger, *War, Peace, and Nonresistance* (Scottdale, 1944); *idem, The Way of the Cross in Human Relations* (Scottdale, 1958); John C. Wenger, "The Schleitheim Confession of Faith," *MQR* XIX (1954) 250-51; H. S. Bender, "The Mennonite Conception of the Church and Its Relation to Community Building," *MQR* XIX (April 1945) 99; H. S. Bender, "Church and State in Mennonite History," *MQR* XIII (1939) 83-103; I. J. L. C. de Bussy, *Ethisch Idealisme* (Amsterdam, 1875); S. Hoekstra, *Zedenleer*, 3 vols. (Amsterdam, 1894); *The Complete Writings of Menno Simons 1496-1561* (Scottdale, 1956); H. S. Bender, *Conrad Grebel 1498-1521, the Founder of the Swiss Brethren Sometimes Called Anabaptists* (Scottdale, 1950); S. Hoekstra, *Beginselen en Leer der Oude Doopsgezinden vergeleken met die van de overige Protestanten* (Amsterdam, 1863); Cornelius Krahn, *Menno Simons (1496-1561). Ein Beitrag zur Geschichte und Theologie der Taufgesinnten* (Karlsruhe, 1936); Robert Kreider, "Anabaptism and Humanism," *MQR* XXI (1952) 129-41; Maynard Shelly, ed., *Studies in Church Discipline* (Newton, 1958); Ulrich Bergfried, *Verantwortung als theologisches Problem im Täufertum des 16. Jahrhunderts* (Wuppertal, 1938); J. Winfield Fretz, "Mennonite Mutual Aid, A Contribution to the Development of Christian Community" (unpublished Ph.D. thesis, University of Chicago, 1941); C. Krahn, J. W. Fretz, and R. S. Kreider, "Altruism in Mennonite Life," in P. Sorokin's *Forms and Techniques of Altruistic and Spiritual Growth* (Boston, 1954); J. W. Nickel, "An Analytical Approach to Mennonite Ethics" (unpublished Th.D. dissertation, Iliff School of Theology at Denver, 1959); A. P. Toews, "The Problem of Mennonite Ethics" (unpublished Th.D. dissertation, Concordia Theological Seminary, St. Louis, Mo.); *ML* I, 612 f.

Ethiopia Mennonite Mission (MC), founded by the Eastern Mennonite Board of Missions and Charities in 1948, had five stations in 1958, at Addis Ababa, Nazareth, Deder, Bedeno, and Dire Dawa, with 35 missionaries and some 150 members. H.S.B.

Eureka Gardens Mennonite Church (MC), 3406 University Ave., Wichita, Kan., is a mission sponsored by the mission board of the South Central Conference, established in 1947. In 1958 it had 19 members, with Leo J. Miller as pastor. H.S.B.

Eureka Mennonite Church (MC), Washington, Iowa, was organized in 1958 with 35 charter members. Vernon Roth is its pastor. The congregation purchased an abandoned church a few miles south of the city for its meetinghouse. M.G.

Euro Pax News, an illustrated four-page quarterly, published by the European Pax Office of Mennonite Central Committee at Frankfurt, Germany, appeared first in September 1954. While it deals primarily with MCC Pax activities in Europe, it includes occasional news about Pax units in the Middle East and North Africa. The editors have been Robert Schrag 1954-56, Arlo Kasper 1956-57, James Eigsti 1958, Gerald Bender 1958- . The page size was changed from 12 x 9 inches to approximately 13½ x 9½ inches with the November 1958 issue. N.P.S.

Evangelical Association, an American denomination founded in 1800 in eastern Pennsylvania by Jacob Albright (hence often called in German "Albrechtsleute"), a Methodist lay preacher, who wished to reach his German brethren with the Methodist message, and because the Methodist church refused to work among the Germans, felt constrained to start a new group. The name Evangelical Association was adopted at the first general conference of the group in 1816. A secession in 1891 led to the formation of the United Evangelical Church, which was reunited in the parent body in 1922 under the name Evangelical Church. In 1946 this body (215,000 members) was merged with the United Brethren Church (*q.v.*) to form the Evangelical United Brethren. In earlier days a number of Mennonites joined the Evangelical Association both in eastern Pennsylvania and elsewhere. The branch of the Evangelical Association established in Germany in 1865 (first mission work in Germany in 1850) is called the Evangelische Gemeinschaft. The Evangelical Synod, which merged with the Reformed Church in 1934 to form the Evangelical and Reformed Church, was a different church, founded in 1840 in St. Louis and is not to be confused with the Evangelical Church (Association). H.S.B.

Evangelische Mennonitische Glaubensgemeinschaft, Buenos Aires, Argentina, is the official name of the Buenos Aires Russian Mennonite Church (*q.v.*). In 1958 it had 65 members, Marten Duerksen pastor.

Eventide Home, Mountain Lake, Minn., was founded in 1921, when a former hospital building was taken over as an inter-Mennonite Home for the Aged. The new building, called Eventide Home, was erected in 1950, with a 54-bed capacity. It is a nursing home as well as a boarding care home. Superintendents have been Margaret Friesen, Margaret Janzen, Katharina Balzer, Susie Ewert, Anna Wall, and Mrs. Anna Isaac, who has been serving since 1950. The home is operated by a board of seven directors elected annually by the shareholders. H.S.B.

Evergreen Church of God in Christ Mennonite Church, Scio, Ore., is located 2½ miles southwest of Stayton. In 1958 it had 19 members. It was listed first in the Yearbook (CGC) for 1958. M.G.

Ewert, Benjamin (1870-1958), minister-at-large of General Conference Mennonite Church, was born Nov. 26, 1870, at Thorn, West Prussia, Germany, the youngest of the twelve children of Wilhelm and Anna Janz Ewert, and a brother to H. H. Ewert (*q.v.*). The family immigrated to America in 1874 and settled on a farm near Hillsboro, Kan. He was educated at the Mennonite Seminary at Halstead, Kan., 1884-90, and the Mennonite Educational Institute, Gretna, Man., 1892-1902. He was baptized in the Halstead Mennonite Church on Jan. 6, 1889, and later joined the Bruderthal Church at Hillsboro.

He farmed 1890-92, then taught a country school near Gretna for 10 years. He also taught one year in the Mennonite Educational Institute at Gretna. He married Emilie A. Ruth of Halstead on Oct. 29, 1895, to whom were born two daughters and two sons. He was ordained to the ministry in the Bergthal Mennonite Church in Manitoba in 1895, serving for 25 years, and then became itinerant minister of the General Conference of the Mennonites of Canada for 17 years until 1938. He had a bookstore and printing plant in Gretna for 15 years, printing *Der Mitarbeiter,* the paper of the Gretna school, pamphlets, etc. He was superintendent of the Bergthal Mennonite Old Folk's Home in Gretna 1919-21. He organized churches in Saskatchewan, officiating with baptismal services, Lord's Supper, election and ordination of ministers, and other services. He opened the Bethel Mennonite Mission (GCM) at Winnipeg in 1938 and supervised it until August 1943, and continued as associate minister until his death. He served as minister-at-large for the Canadian Mennonite Conference, and as statistician for conference committees. He was chairman, vice-chairman, and secretary of the conference as well as a member of numerous committees, and served on the boards of the Bible Society, the Temperance Alliance, and the Board of Education. In 1917, during World War I, he was one of five delegates sent to Ottawa by the Mennonite churches of Western Canada to consult with government officials regarding military service by Mennonite youth. He was president of the Canadian Mennonite *Gesangbuch-Commission.* He died June 22, 1958, at Winnipeg.   J.H.La.

Extinct Mennonite Churches in North America. The limited studies made show that a large number of Mennonite congregations in various conference groups in the United States and Canada have become extinct during the 19th and 20th centuries. Gordon Dyck's study reveals at least 90 such extinct G.C.M. congregations in its hundred years of history, 1847-1959. L. J. Burkholder reports at least 25 for the M.C. group in Ontario. Other M.C. conference histories report like figures (e.g., Wenger's for Franconia, Weber's for Illinois, Wenger's for Indiana-Michigan). It is possible that the M.C. has suffered at least 200 extinct congregations, the G.C.M. 100, the M.B. 50, the remaining groups another 50, making a total of at least 400 organized congregations that have died out.

The reasons for the extinction of these congregations have been varied. Some were poorly conceived colonization attempts on poor land or with few economic possibilities. Some never were large enough to support a healthy economic life or too far from sister congregations to furnish adequate social privileges for the youth, who married "out" and joined other churches. Economic depressions, droughts, crop failures contributed their share of congregational failures. Often poor ministerial leadership was the cause, or factionalism and disunity. Refusal to give up the German language or to adopt new methods of church work, such as the Sunday school, and persistence in traditionalism, closed more than one Mennonite church in the face of aggressive competition from more spiritually alive churches of other denominations. The majority of the extinct churches had a brief life span of not more than a generation, but others died out after 50-100 years of existence. A few were rightfully merged with near-by congregations. H.S.B.

Gordon R. Dyck, "The United States General Conference Extinct Churches (1847-1959)," manuscript in GCL (1959); John Umble, "Extinct Ohio Mennonite Churches," *MQR* XVIII-XX (1944-46); L. J. Burkholder, *History of the Mennonites of Ontario* (Toronto, 1937).

Eyebrow First Mennonite Church (CGM): see **Eyebrow-Tugaske** Mennonite Church.

Fairholme (Sask.) Evangelical Mennonite Brethren Church was established *c*1930 and was organized under the leadership of John Klassen. The church declined in membership when members moved back south to the prairies and others left to join a Holiness group. It had a peak membership of about 50 but with the loss of members the church organization ceased to function. However, mission work is still being carried on in the Fairholme district by the Scripture Mission, a mission of the Evangelical Mennonite Brethren Church, for rural areas. With perhaps only 5 members in the area in 1959, the church no longer holds regular services.   W.J.Pe.

Faith and Life Press is one of the publishing names of the General Conference Mennonite Church. This name was approved by the Executive Committee in 1955 and was first used on *The Youth Hymnary* published in 1956. Other publication names in use are: Mennonite Publication Office, and Board of Education and Publication. Publication work is the responsibility of the Mennonite Publication Office (*q.v.*), an agency of the General Conference's Board of Education and Publication.   M.Sh.

Faith Church of God in Christ Mennonite Church, at Iroquois, S.D., organized in 1950, dedicated its newly erected meetinghouse May 17, 1959. It had 38 members, with Harvey Yost as pastor. The first farm in the community to be purchased by a member of the congregation was bought in 1949. H.S.B.

Farmerstown Mennonite Church (MC), located 4 miles northeast of Baltic, Ohio, a member of the Ohio and Eastern Conference, was organized in 1950, after having been a mission outpost of the Walnut Creek (*q.v.*) congregation since 1936. Its meetinghouse was purchased from the Methodists. In 1958 the membership was 87, with Homer Kandel as pastor.   H.S.B.

Fedde Bindertsdochter, an Anabaptist martyr, arrested at the recapture of the Oldeklooster (*q.v.*), was drowned at Leeuwarden, capital of Friesland, on April 14, 1535. (Vos, *Menno Simons,* 229.)
                                                     vDZ.

Feitema (Feytama), a former Dutch Mennonite family, from the 16th century found at Harlingen in Friesland, where Sibrand Ebes Feitema in the 17th century was the owner of a brickworks and other businesses. From the early 17th century this family was also found at Amsterdam, where they were outstanding businessmen and often deacons of the church. Jacob Yedes Feytama (d.1631) was a wealthy brewer here; his son Yede (Eduard) Feytama in 1616 married Elisabeth Willem-Gysbertsdochter, a sister of the Waterlander elder Reinier Wybrands Wybma (*q.v.*). Sybrand Feytama (Amsterdam, 1694-1758) was in his day a noted poet and playwright. vDZ.

De Vrije Fries XVII (Leeuwarden, 1920) 22-27; church records of Amsterdam; G. Kalff, *Gesch. der Nederl. Letterkunde* V (Groningen, 1910) 450 f., 513, 515, 575; *Algemeen Doopsgez. Weekblad* XI (1956) No. 34.

Felix, Hans: see **Uhrmacher, Hans.**

Fellowship Chapel, an E.M.B. Church, Chilliwack, B.C., was organized in 1957. Its church was built in 1958 when it had 8 members, with Lloyd Pankratz as pastor. H.S.B.

Filadelfia (Paraguay) Mennonite Brethren Church was established in 1930 in the newly located capital of Fernheim Colony, by M.B. refugee settlers from Russia. The meetinghouse was built in the town in 1952, and in 1950 a Bible School and Bible Institute were established in the church to serve the Paraguay M.B. group. The congregation, which had in 1957 a membership of 486, with Gerhard Balzer as leader, includes all of the Fernheim colony villages except the "Harbin corner," which has its own congregation (Orloff, *q.v.*). H.S.B.

Fire Insurance: see **Insurance.**

Flamersheim, in the duchy of Jülich, Germany, was one of the Mennonite congregations which signed the Concept (*q.v.*) of Cologne in 1591. Frans van Rijnbach signed in the name of Flamerse (Flamersheim). Nothing more is known about it. vDZ.

Flemming: see **Vlaming.**

Focke Ublezoon, an Anabaptist martyr, arrested at the recapture of the Oldeklooster (*q.v.*) and beheaded at Leeuwarden, capital of Friesland, on April 10, 1535. (Vos, *Menno Simons,* 228.) vDZ.

Foreign Missions: see **Missions, Mennonite Foreign.**

Fractur (Fraktur): see **Illuminated Manuscripts** among the Pennsylvania Mennonites.

France Mennonite Mission (MC), founded by the Mennonite Board of Missions and Charities in 1953, in 1959 had one station in Paris (Butte Rouge) with four missionaries and nine members. H.S.B.

Frankfurt a. M. (II, 376): Supplement. On Aug. 27, 1527, Dionysius Melander, Evangelical pastor at Frankfurt (1525-35), reported to the city council that Anabaptists were selling books there. In a letter to Capito at Strasbourg in early 1528 Melander confirmed the presence of Anabaptists in the city. Hans Duck, an Anabaptist, was expelled from the

city. On April 14, 1534, the Anabaptist Johann Mettlinger was threatened with expulsion. The Frankfurt book fair was for decades a favorite meeting place of Anabaptists from far and near. In 1544, for example, Endres Nef was sent from Cannstadt "to Frankfurt to the Anabaptists." About 1565 Guido de Brez, the noted Calvinist leader from the Southern Netherlands, claimed to have disputed with the Anabaptists at Frankfurt. (G. Hein, "Anabaptists in Frankfort on the Main," *MQR* XXXIII, 1959, 69-72.) H.S.B.

Frans Metselair, an Anabaptist martyr, arrested at the recapture of the Oldeklooster (*q.v.*) and beheaded at Leeuwarden, capital of Friesland, on April 10, 1535. (Vos, *Menno Simons,* 228.) vDZ.

Fraserview Mennonite Brethren Church, located at 59th Avenue and Culloden, Vancouver, B.C., was established in 1954 from the Vancouver M.B. Church, when its meetinghouse was built. In 1957 it had 449 members, with P. R. Toews as pastor, assisted by David Vogt. H.S.B.

Fredonia (Kan.) **First** Mennonite Church (GCM) is located in the 100 block of North 14th Street. It was established as a fellowship in 1939 and organized as a congregation in 1947. Its membership in 1958 was 28, with Willard A. Schrag as minister. M.G.

Frell, Georg, a Swiss Anabaptist leader and bookseller at Chur, Grisons, in the second half of the 16th century. In the 1560's he was called to account by Reformed clergyman Johannes Fabricius (*q.v.*) for selling Anabaptist books. The affair caused a sharp debate among the authorities on the right of government to compel dissenters to accept doctrine contrary to their conscience. The dispute involved the Reformed leaders Egli, Gantner, and Bullinger. Frell is described as a "quiet, religiously thoughtful" man. Charged with both Anabaptist and Schwenckfeld heresy, he was expelled from Chur in 1570, but returned later and appeared there openly. Nothing is known concerning his later career. (For details on the dispute, see **Chur** and **Grisons.**) E.H.B.

Freyberg, Helene von (II, 397): Supplement. Additional light on this noblewoman is found in the *Kunstbuch* (*q.v.*), No. 28, folios 243-46, where her (undated) confession before the brotherhood in Strasbourg is given. It shows not only the remarkable level of her Christian experience but also the manner in which church discipline was exercised in the second generation Anabaptist congregation at Augsburg under the leadership of Valentine Werner and Pilgram Marpeck. Her transgression is never clearly defined, but apparently involved a business venture. She confessed that at the heart of her sin lay a rebellious attitude which had hitherto refused to accept the admonition and discipline of the brotherhood. She pleaded for the forgiveness of the church and in particular the leaders. A letter discovered by Loserth, written Jan. 6, 1534, by King Ferdinand of Austria at Prague, advises the authorities to compel her to make an open recantation, or at least a private one before the authorities, as an example to the public. (The letter indicates that the nobility were not as a rule forced to recant openly.) If she performed penance and took the sacrament, he would not oppose the return of her property. The above confession may be the one she wrote after her temporary recantation. The few available facts concerning her indicate that her influence was far-reaching. W.KL.

Heinold Fast, "Pilgram Marbeck und das oberdeutsche Täufertum, ein neuer Handschriftenfund," *ARG* XLVII (1956) 212-42; Loserth, *Anabaptismus*, 586.

Friedenshort, the second of the three homes for the aged operated by the German Mennonite organization known as Mennonitische Heime, e.V. (*q.v.*), primarily for the care of aged Mennonite refugees from West Prussia. Founded in 1950 (not 1949 as in *ME* II, 222) through the leasing and renovation of a large building, it has a capacity of some 75. The home is self-supporting through a per capita per diem grant from the government, aided by MCC food contributions. H.S.B.

Friendship Mennonite Church (MC), located at 21881 Libby Road, Bedford Heights (Cleveland), Ohio, was begun in 1949 under the Ohio Mennonite Mission Board. It was organized as an independent congregation in 1957, when the meetinghouse was built. In 1958 the membership was 74, with Dale Nofziger as pastor. H.S.B.

Friesland (Paraguay) Mennonite Brethren Church was organized in 1937 when the group who left Fernheim Colony founded Friesland Colony. It built its meetinghouse in 1952 in Rückenau. It has 194 members, with Johann Goertzen as leader. Kornelius Voth was leader 1937-d. *c*1957. H.S.B.

Froschauer, Simprecht (d. *c*1536), a younger half brother of Christoph (*q.v.*), in whose Zürich print shop he worked, joined the Anabaptists and followed Hubmaier to Nikolsburg, where he became Hubmaier's printer from July 1526 to early 1528. Eighteen Hubmaier prints are known to have come from his press, signed "Simprecht Sorg genant Froschauer." Upon Hubmaier's arrest and execution in 1528 Simprecht fled to Liegnitz in Silesia, where he printed some Schwenckfeld booklets. H.S.B.

P. Leemen, *Die Offizin Froschauer* (Zürich, 1940) 14-16; *ML* II.

Furrow, a furrow plowed in the Kansas prairie in 1873 apparently beginning at the Henry Brunk farm approximately six miles west of Marion Centre (now Marion), Marion Co., Kan., and extending straight west on the present Highway 50 into McPherson County to a point near the home of Daniel Brundage (*q.v.*). This furrow has become legendary in the literature on the Kansas frontier, generally being referred to as the "23-mile furrow" although it was apparently only 14 miles long. Literary accounts credit various individuals for having plowed it, although the records seem to prove that either R. J. Heatwole (*q.v.*) or Daniel Brundage or both participated in this task. Heatwole in 1893 explained that the purpose of the furrow was to enable the scattered Mennonite settlers to "find our course along this furrow back

and forth to worship together without losing the way along which there was nothing to break the monotony of the journey save the flocks of prairie chickens, and the small herds of antelopes cantering from us in the distance." (See also **Kansas**.) M.G.

Melvin Gingerich, "The Twenty-Three Mile Furrow," *Mennonite Historical Bulletin*, October 1949, 3-4; *Menn. Life* IV (July 1949) 6-7.

Futtor, a Mennonite village in Volhynia: see **Zahoriz.**

Garden Park Mennonite Brethren Church, located at 1720 South Alcott Street, Denver, Col., was organized in 1955, its meetinghouse built in 1957. In 1959 the membership was 90, with John J. Gerbrandt as pastor. H.S.B.

Gartental (Uruguay) Mennonite Brethren Church was organized in 1952. It used a remodeled (1956) meeting place. In 1957 the membership was 35, with Kornelius Funk as leader. H.S.B.

Geerdt Nannedochter and **Geert Hansdochter,** two Anabaptist martyrs, arrested at the recapture of the Oldeklooster (*q.v.*). Both women were drowned at Leeuwarden, capital of Friesland, on April 14, 1535. (Vos, *Menno Simons,* 229.) vDZ.

Gemeenschap van Dienende Arbeidsters was an organization of young Dutch Mennonite women, established at Elspeet on June 10, 1934, on the initiative of T. Best, who was the leader of the organization. The aim of the association was to give assistance in households in case of the illness of the housewife. In 1940 the organization was dissolved. (*De G. D. A.,* n.p., n.d.—Borne, 1935.) vDZ.

Gemmelich, Ulrich: see **Zaunmacher, Ulrich.**

General Conference Central Office (GCM) is located in two adjacent buildings, 720 and 722 Main Street, Newton, Kan., sometimes referred to as General Conference Headquarters. Donated by Elva Krehbiel Leisy of Dallas, Tex., in memory of her parents, Henry P. and Matilda Kruse Krehbiel, the 722 building was dedicated as the Krehbiel Building and put into service on July 18, 1943, as the Central Office of the General Conference Mennonite Church. In 1954 Mrs. Leisy made the adjacent building available on an annuity agreement basis. The building was remodeled and enlarged in 1951, 1954, and 1957. In addition to offices for the Boards of the General Conference, the Central Office provides space for the Central Treasury, Young People's Union, Women's Missionary Association, Mennonite Publication Office and Bookstore; and the Western District Conference. The office is supervised by a manager appointed by the Executive Committee of the General Conference Mennonite Church. Persons who have served as managers are P. A. Penner 1943-46, Walter H. Dyck 1946-49, A. Theodore Mueller 1949-50, A. J. Richert 1952-58, William L. Friesen 1959- M.SH.

General Council of the Mennonite General Conference (MC), established in 1951 as the interim representative body for the General Conference, is composed of the officers of the General Conference, and one representative appointed by each district conference, each general board of the church, and each General Conference standing committee, with a total of some 36 members. (See **Mennonite General Conference.**) H.S.B.

General Educational Council (MC) of the Mennonite Board of Education was established in 1949 as a counseling body for all the educational interests of the Mennonite Church (MC) except those purely of the local congregations. It consists of 12 members appointed annually by the Mennonite Board of Education. Under it and responsible to it are the following six councils: Seminary, Collegiate, Seconday School, Elementary School, Winter Bible School, and Nursing Education, whose members are also appointed by the Board. H.S.B.

General Villegas Mennonite Church (MC), Argentina, a member of the Argentine Conference, was established in 1941. In 1958 it had 19 members, with Lawrence Brunk as pastor. H.S.B.

Gesangh-boeck, *Behelzende verscheyde Gesangen, om op alle Feestdagen, en Voor als Na de Predicatie in de Vergaderinge te Singen, Nog Belydenisse des Geloofs, met de Voornaemste Zeden, Korte Wetten, Kerckelyke Ordre en discipline in de Christelycke Gemeynte . . .*, is a Dutch Mennonite hymnal (Haarlem, 1644). A second edition (2 vol., Hamburg, 1684, 1685) has the order of the hymns somewhat changed as well as the tunes. The Hamburg edition was printed on behalf of the Hamburg-Altona Flemish congregation. vDZ.

M. Schagen, *Naamlijst der Doopsgez. schrijveren* (Amsterdam, 1745); Blaupot t. C., *Holland* II, 212 f.

Gezangen ten gebruike in Doopsgezinde Gemeenten: see Leidsche Bundel.

Ghana Mennonite Church and Mission (MC), founded in 1956 by the Mennonite Board of Missions and Charities at Accra, in 1958 had 27 members in Accra and operated five substations with four missionaries. H.S.B.

Gilead Mennonite Church (MC), located 1½ miles northwest of Chesterville, Ohio, is a member of the Ohio and Eastern Conference. The first Mennonite settlers arrived in the community in 1950. Murray Krabill arrived in June 1951 to become the first pastor of the congregation, which was organized in 1952. A basement church was built in 1952; in 1959 the building was enlarged and completed. The congregation had a membership of 35 in 1958. M.Kr.

Glantzer: see Glanzer.

Glendive (Mont.) **First** Mennonite Church (GCM) had 52 members in 1957, with Randall Heinrichs as pastor. First listed as an organized congregation in the 1952 Handbook, its first Sunday morning worship was held on June 13, 1948. Its church was built in 1948-49. M.G.

Glenn (Cal.) Church of God in Christ Mennonite Church is located 10 miles east and 1 mile north of

Willows. In 1958 it had 88 members, served by the ministers Jake H. Loewen and Dick C. Loewen. It was first listed in the Yearbook of 1953. M.G.

Glenwood Springs Mennonite Church (MC) is located in south Glenwood Springs, Col. The congregation was organized in March 1956 and the church built in 1957. The membership numbered 35 in 1959. Samuel Janzen was the pastor. M.G.

"Go Ye" Mission, Inc. (GCM), was started after World War II by S. Mouttet at Choteau, Okla. Since 1945 it has published the bimonthly paper *"Go Ye"* (*q.v.*), to report on its work. The work of the mission includes child evangelism as well as general evangelism. The mission reports unofficially to the Oklahoma Conference (*q.v.*). During the summer children's camps are conducted. The mission bookstore was started in 1948 at Muskogee, Okla. Grace Chapel in the Liberty community, Okla., was completed in 1958. The present leader of "Go Ye" Missions is Homer Mouttet. C.K.

Goethe, Wolfgang von: see article at end of Supplement.

Good Shepherd Mennonite Church, Rabanal, Cidra, Puerto Rico, was founded in 1947 as an outpost of the Calvary (*q.v.*) congregation. The first converts were baptized on March 27, 1949. The meetinghouse was erected on Oct. 3, 1948. In 1958 the congregation had 32 members, with Melquiades Santiago and Addona Nissley as ministers. (Gladys Widmer, *We Enter Puerto Rico*, Elkhart, 1952.) H.S.B.

Goodfield Mennonite Church (MC), a member of the Illinois Conference, now extinct, was an outgrowth of the remnant of the Mackinaw congregation after the Roanoke (*q.v.*) and Rock Creek congregations had been organized from the original settlement established in 1834. The first settlers in the direct Goodfield area arrived c1842, with many others arriving in 1852 and 1853, mostly coming from Ohio and Pennsylvania. Early settlers were families bearing the names Forney, Ropp, Reisser, Zehr, Yoder, Sommer, Ehrismann, Klopfenstein, and Schertz. The town of Goodfield was not created until 1888, but the congregation bearing this name was established c1872, when a group of members began to rent the former Rock Creek meetinghouse for services. A new meetinghouse, 28 x 38 ft., with a council room in the rear, 12 x 14 ft., was erected in 1883 one mile south of Goodfield. Ministers were shared with the Roanoke congregation at first, the early ones being Jacob Zehr and Christian Ropp bishops and Christian Risser preacher. Jacob Zehr served 1895-1929. The last ministers were Daniel Zehr and Harold Oyer. The membership was always small (50-65) and in 1941 the congregation was merged with Morton (*q.v.*). H.S.B.

Goshen College Mennonite Church (MC), Goshen, Ind., was organized Dec. 8, 1903, to meet the need of a congregation for the staff and students of Goshen College (*q.v.*), which opened its doors Sept. 29, 1903, following a transfer of the school from

Elkhart, Ind. Since the members of the congregation came from congregations affiliated with both Indiana-Michigan conferences (MC and AM), the congregation belonged to both conferences and was served by bishops from both conferences until the merger in 1917. The first pastor was J. S. Hartzler, who was succeeded by I. W. Royer 1905-10. Other pastors were P. E. Whitmer, George J. Lapp, I. R. Detweiler, and A. E. Kreider, all serving on the college staff. The charter membership in 1903 was 57; by 1904 it was 129.

Because of the closing of the college in June 1923 and also because of internal friction within the conference, a large part of the congregation withdrew and joined the Eighth Street Mennonite Church (q.v., founded 1913, new meetinghouse built 1920) of the Central Conference (q.v.). I. R. Detweiler joined this church in 1923 and became its pastor. When the college reopened in September 1924, the bishop in charge reorganized the congregation with a new charter membership of 15, which reached 115 by 1925, 201 by 1935, 297 by 1945. Noah Oyer served as pastor 1924-d. 31, followed by C. L. Graber 1931-42, S. C. Yoder 1942-50, and John H. Mosemann 1950- . Bishops have been D. D. Miller 1903-42, S. C. Yoder 1942-56, and John H. Mosemann 1956- . The congregation has had only two deacons—Amos Landis 1906-22 and Levi C. Hartzler 1943- . The membership has grown continuously.

The congregation worshiped in the college chapel from the beginning until 1950, then in the College Union Auditorium until the erection of a joint church-chapel (seats 1,100), dedicated in August 1959, the cost of erection and maintenance being borne equally by the college and the congregation. The church has a circular sanctuary surrounded by rooms for Sunday school and other purposes.

H.S.B.

Goshenhoppen, the name given in colonial times to that part of the Perkiomen valley north of Schwenksville, Pa., also the former name of the present town of Bally, Pa. There is evidence that the Hereford (q.v.) Mennonite Church was sometimes referred to as Goshenhoppen. Also sometime before 1749 J. H. Sprogel, a Lutheran, donated a tract of land in Upper Hanover Township, Montgomery County, Pa., about 5 miles east of Bally, jointly to the Lutheran, Reformed, and Mennonite denominations for church, cemetery, and school purposes. A union meetinghouse was erected on this tract, but the Mennonites never built a meetinghouse of their own here. A number of Mennonites are buried in the cemetery of what is now the new Goshenhoppen Reformed Church, the former union church.

H.S.B.

J. C. Wenger, *History of the Mennonites of the Franconia Conference* (Telford, 1937) 238-40.

Gospel Church of God in Christ Mennonite Church, Barron, Wis., is located 8 miles northwest of Barron. It had 56 members in 1958, with Peter P. Toews as minister. The church was first listed in the Yearbook (CGC) for 1958.

M.G.

Gospel Fellowship Mennonite Church (MC), Shallow Water, Kan., organized in April 1955, meets in a public school but plans to build in Shallow Water. In 1959 it had 28 members, with Eugene Schulz as pastor.

M.G.

Gospel Light Mennonite Brethren Church, 760 McMillan Ave., Winnipeg, Man., was founded as a mission in 1950, received as a full member into the Manitoba M.B. Conference in 1955. In the change to McMillan Avenue in 1959, from 405 Logan Avenue (meetinghouse purchased here in 1950), the name was changed to Fort Rouge M.B. Church. In 1959 the membership was 47, with David Nickel as pastor.

F.C.P.

Gospel Mennonite Church of the Rudnerweide (q.v.) group, at 232 Nassau St., Winnipeg, Man., was organized in 1956. In 1959 the membership was 80, with Ben W. Sawatzky as pastor.

F.C.P.

Grace Bible College: see **Grace Bible Institute.**

Grace Hill Mennonite Church: see **Gnadenberg** Mennonite Church.

Grace Mennonite Church (MC), located at 5700 Nall Ave., Mission, Kan., a suburb of Kansas City, was organized in 1957 by former members of the Argentine Mennonite Church. It is a member of the South Central Conference. In 1959 it had 43 members, with D. Lowell Nissley as pastor. H.S.B.

Gracevale Hutterite Bruderhof of the Schmiedeleut (q.v.) branch, located near Winfred, S.D., was established in 1948 by the Gracevale Bruderhof with ten families from Tschetter Bruderhof. Sam Wipf was chosen to the ministry here in 1950 and ordained in 1957. The Gracevale Bruderhof now (1958) has 104 souls with 30 baptized members.

D.D.

Gramberg, K. P. C. A., a physician, married to Helena Goossen (q.v.), served 1921-46 on Java (q.v.) under the Dutch Mennonite Mission Association. In 1930-43 he was director of the medical mission in this field. In August 1943 he was arrested by the Japanese invaders and interned in a concentration camp. After his release in August 1945 he was for a short time again active in organizing the medical care on the mission field and restoring what had been destroyed or burned down by fanatical Mohammedans. In 1946 he returned to Holland.

vDZ.

Grants Pass (Ore.) Mennonite Church (MC), a member of the Pacific Coast Conference, located 1½ miles south of the junction of highways 99 and 199, was organized in August 1957. In 1959 the membership was 35, with Max G. Yoder as pastor.

M.G.

Griesheim in the Palatinate, Germany, is mentioned in 1732 as a Mennonite congregation, with Hans Burkhalter as preacher. Later on in the 18th century the Griesheim Mennonites belonged to the Oberflörsheim (q.v.) congregation. (*Inv. Arch. Amst.* I, Nos. 1248 f., 1472; Müller, *Berner Täufer,* 211.)

vDZ.

Griswold (Man.) M.B. Church: see **Alexander** M.B. Church.

Groot, Hendrik L. de, composer of the Dutch Mennonite hymnal *Grote Koren Bloem en 't Groen Spruytgen, of toeghift op de Grote Koren-Bloem* (Ter Ghoude, i.e., Gouda, 1622). (Blaupot t. C., *Holland* II, 211.) vDZ.

Grossweide Mennonite Brethren Church, located north of Horndean, Man., was founded in 1896, became a fully recognized M.B. church in 1925, having been organized by former Sommerfeld and Old Colony members. Its present meetinghouse was built in 1954 replacing the former building which burned in 1953. In 1958 the membership was 128, with J. J. Neufeld as pastor. F.C.P.

Gross-Werder: see **Marienburg Werder.**

Guarituba (Brazil) Mennonite Brethren Church was organized in 1957 as a daughter congregation of the Bouqueirao (*q.v.*) M.B. church, although its meetinghouse had been erected in 1952. In 1957 its membership was 56, with Jakob Wiens as leader. H.S.B.

Guavate Mennonite Church (MC), Cayey, Puerto Rico, was founded in 1953. In 1954 a small chapel was erected which was destroyed by a hurricane in 1956. In 1957 a new church was built. In 1958 the membership was 35, with John Driver as pastor. H.S.B.

Gulfhaven Mennonite Church (MC), located 17 miles northwest of Gulfport, Miss., a member of the South Central Conference, was organized Jan. 5, 1922, by Bishop Andrew Shenk of Oronogo, Mo., with 28 charter members. J. B. Brunk was the first pastor, followed later by D. S. Brunk. In 1948 the church was remodeled. The members are largely Mennonites from northern states or their descendants. In 1957 the membership was 62, with Paul Hershey as pastor-bishop. P.H.

Gundy, George (1880-1951), a leader in the Central (Illinois) Conference, was born at Carlock, Ill., son of Jacob Gundy and Lena Kinsinger, and married Clara Strubhar in 1904, with whom he had three sons. He was ordained minister on Oct. 4, 1909, and served two pastorates: Congerville, Ill., 1909-25, and Meadows, Ill., 1925-51. He served as superintendent of the Meadows Old People's Home many years until 1945. He was president of the Central Conference Ministerial Association 1911-26, and member of the conference mission board and of the Congo Inland Mission Board. He died Sept. 16, 1951. H.S.B.

Habecker Mennonite Church (MC), in the Manorland of Lancaster County, Pa., among the settlers of which were Neff, Kauffman, and Baughman families. David Martin was one of the first preachers, followed by Henry Neff. Christian Kauffman was the first native bishop. In 1761 the Penn heirs granted a tract of land to "Henry Neave for the Society of Anna Baptists within and in the neighborhood of said Township (of Manor)." They built a log church, replaced in 1820 by a brick church

35 x 45 ft., in 1898 again by a brick church, 50 x 75 ft. A beautiful cemetery adjoins the church. Sunday school started in 1888. The congregation is a part of the Manor District. In 1959 the membership was 125, and Christian B. Charles and Landis E. Myer were the ministers. I.D.L.

Habermann's Prayerbook, first published in 1567 at Wittenberg, Germany, by Johann Habermann, one of the most widely used Protestant prayerbooks ever published, was popular among the Mennonites of Germany and the eastern United States (first edition in America by Christopher Saur at Germantown, Pa., in 1749). It is still widely used by the Old Order Amish in the form of the smaller edition, *Der Kleine Habermann,* or *Christliche Morgen- und Abend-Gebeter auf alle Tage der Woche.* H.S.B.

Robert Friedmann, *Mennonite Piety Through the Centuries* (Goshen, 1949) 203 f.

Haile Mariam Mammo Memorial Hospital, at Nazareth, Ethiopia, an 80-bed general hospital, was established in 1946 and is operated by the Ethiopia Mennonite Mission under the Eastern Mennonite Board of Missions and Charities. H.S.B.

Handicrafts: see **Ceramics, Crafts, Pottery, Needlework.**

Hannibal (Mo.) **Mennonite Mission:** see **Mennonite Mission Church.**

Hanscke Sascher(s), an Anabaptist martyr, was arrested at the recapture of the Oldeklooster (*q.v.*). On April 7, 1535, he was executed at Leeuwarden, capital of Friesland, by beheading. (Vos, *Menno Simons,* 228.) vDZ.

Hardin County (Ohio) Old Order Amish settlement consisted in 1958 of two districts (congregations), both located south of Kenton, the East with 27 members and Levi M. Beachy as bishop, the West with 22 members and Jonas Mast as minister. H.S.B.

Harmony Corners Beachy Amish Mennonite Church, at Harmony Corners, about 10 miles east of Chestertown, Md., is sometimes known as the Chestertown church. It was organized in 1952, its church built in 1954, and in 1959 had 27 members. The ministers were Rudy Yoder, Sam Beachy, and Arthur Martin Beachy. M.G.

Harmony Mennonite Church (MC), now extinct, located near Harmony, Butler Co., Pa., began in 1814 when Abraham and John Ziegler, Jacob and David Stouffer, Henry Buckle, and John Boyer formed the Harmony Farm Company and bought from the Harmony Society (a Christian communistic group) 9000 acres, including the town of Harmony, and three villages with all their shops, industries, and church. The church was used until 1825 when the present structure was built, which is still in good repair. John Boyer was the bishop and first pastor. Others who followed were Jacob Kolb, Joseph Ziegler, who served the church for 45 years, and possibly Jacob Moyer.

The congregation lived to itself, holding out against English preaching, evangelistic services, and Sunday school until the younger generation had been lost to the church. Services continued until c1900. Memorial services have been held from time to time, the last one July 12, 1950.　J.A.S.

Harrow (Ont.) United Mennonite Church (GCM) was organized in 1953, although the meetinghouse was built in 1950, located 1½ miles north of Harrow in Essex County, Ontario. In 1959 the membership was 63, with Herman R. Lepp as pastor.　H.S.B.

Harshbarger, Emmett Leroy (1901-42), a Mennonite (GCM) teacher and peace worker, was born Sept. 16, 1901, at West Liberty, Ohio, the son of Samuel H. Harshbarger. He graduated from Bluffton College with an A.B. (1925) and received his A.M. (1929) and his Ph.D. (1933) from Ohio State University. He married Eva Grace Geiger Aug. 19, 1925. He taught a number of rural and high schools in Ohio, was instructor of history and speech at Bluffton 1925-30, and professor of history at Bethel College 1933-42. He died July 26, 1942.

Harshbarger was very active in his peace witness, in which capacity he filled various offices in the General Conference and as Dean of the Kansas Institute of International Relations since 1936.
　C.K.

Hartland Christian Association was organized in October, 1945 by members of the M.B. and K.M.B. churches in the Reedley, Cal., area, to own and operate a church camp. In 1946 it purchased 160 acres in Tulare County, Cal., c10 miles east of Badger near the village of Hartland, at an elevation of 4500 ft. Retreats for the youth of the churches had been held since 1940. These were now held at Hartland Camp, and a full range of camp activities for all ages was added. The M.B. Camping Committee provides the programs.　H.S.B.

Harvey Country Mennonite Brethren Church is located 9 miles southwest of Harvey, N.D. It was organized with 10 members in 1898. Christian Reimche was its first pastor, a position he held for about 30 years. After members moved into Harvey, the Harvey City (q.v.) church was built and services were conducted in both places. In 1957 the congregation had 61 members, with Werner Kroeker as its pastor.　M.G.

Hausbreitenbach, a district in western Thuringia (q.v.) jointly administered in Reformation times by Electoral Saxony and Hesse, and hence because of the differences between the two governmental policies toward the Anabaptists and in particular the milder attitude of Philip of Hesse, a territory where Anabaptism could more readily spread. The first traces of Anabaptism here appeared in 1528, coming chiefly from Hersfeld and Sorga in Hesse, with Melchior Rinck (q.v.) as the chief propagator. The first arrests occurred in 1531, the victims divided between Saxony (executed) and Hesse (released). Further arrests were made in 1533, among them Fritz Erbe (q.v.), who was held in prison in Eisen-

ach on the Wartburg until his death in 1548. The remaining prisoners were freed. Until the middle of the century the Anabaptists in Hausbreitenbach continued to maintain themselves vigorously, as is evidenced by the repeated complaints of Justus Menius, superintendent at Eisenach, in whose territory Hausbreitenbach lay. (For a fuller treatment see **Thuringia** and the books by Wappler listed there, especially *Die Stellung Kursachsens.*)
　H.S.B.

Hausmann, Hans: misspelling of Hansmann, Hans, (q.v.).

Hazaribagh, a political district in the Province of Bihar, India, the northern area of which comprises the eastern part of the Bihar Mennonite Mission (MC) (q.v.) field. It contains Kodarma (q.v.), the first place occupied by the missionaries, and Chatra, another important town.　S.J.Ho.

Hebron Mennonite Church (GCM), Mayfair, Sask., was organized in 1928 and its church built in 1929. The membership in 1959 was 38, with Frank Ens as pastor.　M.G.

Hegenwalt, Erhard, once a teacher in the Pfäffers Monastery, Canton of St. Gall, Switzerland, a friend of Conrad Grebel, a student in Wittenberg in 1524-26, wrote a letter to Conrad Grebel from Wittenberg dated Jan. 1, 1525, now preserved in the Stadtbibliothek St. Gallen (Vadiana) ms. 31, 222. The letter is part of a lost correspondence which included at least two letters from Grebel and two from Hegenwalt. Grebel may have met Hegenwalt in January 1523 at the disputation held in Zürich at that time when the latter attended and edited the minutes, which were published soon after. Hegenwalt's letter reports that Luther had received the letter written to him by Grebel and was sending greetings to Grebel from Luther who wanted the group in Zürich to know that he was not "illdisposed" toward them. The Hegenwalt letter is of considerable value because it reports on 13 points mentioned in the Grebel letter to Hegenwalt which Hegenwalt in turn tries to refute. It is possible that the Erhard Hegenwaldt who secured the M.D. degree in Wittenberg, and also a city physician in Frankfurt a.M. by the same name in 1540, were the same as the letter writer.　H.S.B.

For a full discussion of the letter see H. S. Bender, *"Conrad Grebel"* (Goshen, 1950) 119-22; *ADB* XI, 275, "Hegenwald, Erhard," by Bertheau.

Henrick Dacho(s), an Anabaptist martyr, was executed in the Steen prison at Antwerp on Oct. 7, 1558. His wife, Adriana (q.v.) Lambrechts, was executed at the same place on March 19, 1559. (Génard, *Antw. Arch.-Blad.* IX, 17; XIV, 24 f.)
　H.S.B.

Herald Book and Publishing Company: see Herald Publishing Company.

Herald of Truth, a 16-page 9 x 12 in. monthly, printed by the offset process, published at Uniontown, Ohio, by a Publication Board representing two congregations in Ohio which had withdrawn from the

Conservative Mennonite Conference in 1956 and one in Ontario which had withdrawn from the Ontario A.M. Conference in 1956. John J. Overholt has been the editor from the beginning. In Jan., 1959 the Publication Board merged with the Board of Directors of the Pilgrim Mennonite Press to form a new board called Herald of Truth Publications, which announced its intention to publish a youth periodical and Sunday-school lesson helps for all age levels, also tracts on timely topics. The first issue of the periodical was April, 1957.　　　　　　　H.S.B.

Heresy was officially defined in medieval and Reformation times as deviation from the official creeds of the church, e.g., the Nicene Creed (325), the Chalcedonian Creed (451), the Augsburg Confession (1530). It was considered the obligation of the state to uphold and defend the creeds of the church, and to punish heretics, who were thus not only apostates from the church or its faith, but violators of the civil law and punishable as criminals. The Anabaptists were thus in most areas in Reformation times heretics and criminals.　　　　　　　H.S.B.

Hernhut(t)ers: see **Moravians** in the Netherlands.

Herold Book and Publishing Company, the successor to the Western Book and Publishing Company (*q.v.*), was organized Oct. 2, 1909, with the following as directors: H. P. Krehbiel, C. E. Krehbiel, J. W. Krehbiel, D. R. Krehbiel, G. A. Haury, Jacob H. Richert, John C. Goering, J. P. Andres, and J. H. Epp. Officers were: H. P. Krehbiel president, G. A. Haury vice-president, and C. E. Krehbiel secretary-treasurer. H. P. Krehbiel was elected as manager and C. E. Krehbiel as editor. The company maintained the Bee Hive Book Store at 508 Main St., Newton, Kan., and published *Der Herold,* besides doing custom printing.

On Aug. 4, 1914, the Herold store building and stock were destroyed by a fire. The company was then moved to 722 Main St., where a new building was erected. The company was dissolved Dec. 1, 1919, and the store building sold to H. P. and C. E. Krehbiel. Final liquidation of the assets of the company was made in May 1926. Meanwhile, the Herald Publishing Company (*q.v.*) had been organized to carry on the publication and bookstore enterprises of the Herold Book and Publishing Company. ("Minute Book of the Herold Book and Publishing Company.")　　　　　　　J.F.S.

Herrenhagen was a Mennonite village established during the second half of the 17th century by Dutch Mennonites in the Marienburg Werder (*q.v.*) west of the Nogat River.　　　　　　　C.K.

　Horst Penner, *Ansiedlung mennonitischer Niederländer im Weichselmündungsgebiet van der Mitte des 16. Jahrhunderts bis zum Beginn der preussischen Zeit* (Weierhof, 1940) 63.

Hess Mennonite Church (MC), a member of the Lancaster Conference, located northeast of Lititz, Pa., on the farm of Jacob Hess, who acquired his land in 1735. The congregation met in the homes of the members until 1856, when the first meetinghouse

of brick was built. This meetinghouse was replaced by a new one, 54 x 70 ft., in 1891, which was renovated in 1947. The Sunday school opened in 1897. The congregation is a part of the Hammer Creek Bishop District. It was the home of preachers John Hess (1768-1830), a grandson of Jacob, Jonas H. Hess (1841-1919), John S Hess, Richard Hess, and Raymond Bucher. The last three were serving in 1959, with Amos S. Horst and Mahlon Zimmerman as bishops. The membership in 1959 was 274.　　　　　　　I.D.L.

Hesselink (Hesseling) (II, 728 f.): Supplement. There were two branches of this family, one living at Deventer and Groningen, and one at Sneek and Bolsward; the names of both families have various forms: Hesselink, Hesseling, Hesselingh; these branches are probably not related. The ancestor of the Deventer-Groningen branch was (1) Pieter Hesselink (Bocholt 1589-Deventer 1670), who was a manufacturer of bombazine at Deventer. His son (2) Jacob Hesselink (Deventer 1624-Enkhuizen 1712) was an untrained preacher of the Groningen Old Flemish congregation at Enkhuizen. (3) Willem Jacobsz Hesselink (*q.v.,* Enkhuizen 1648-Groningen 1720), a son of (2) Jacob, was an Old Flemish preacher at Groningen, as was his son (4) Jacob Hesselink (d. 1760) from 1725. Three sons of (5) Hendrik Hesselink, of Groningen (a relative of (2) Jacob Hesselink), married to Mayke Wybes Zeeman (daughter of preacher Wybe Pietersz Zeeman, *q.v.,* of Heerenveen), went into the ministry. They were (6) Wybo Hesselink (c1743-78), (7) Gerrit Hesseling (b. 1752, not 1755 as stated *ME* II, 729; d. 1811), and (8) Matthijs Hesselink (Groningen 1755-Hoorn 1839). (Information by C. F. Nanningavan Lessen, of Bussum, Holland.)　　　　　　　vDZ.

Hiebert, Nicholas Nikolai (1874-1957), a Mennonite Brethren teacher and missionary, was born July 29, 1874, in Lichtfelde, Ukraine, South Russia, the oldest of the twelve children of Nikolai C. and Maria Wiens Hiebert. He emigrated with his parents to America in 1875 and settled in Mountain Lake, Minn. He attended McPherson College in 1897-98. On May 28, 1899, he married Susie Wiebe. Among their twelve children were John N. C., Lando, and Waldo Hiebert. He was appointed missionary to India by the M.B. Church in 1898 and sailed in 1899. After selecting and opening a field he returned from India in 1901 because of ill health, and then traveled for the conference in the interest of missions 1901-12 and served as secretary to the Board of Foreign Missions 1903-36. He taught district school five years, served as principal of the Mountain Lake Bible School 1912-27, and was instructor in Bible at Tabor College 1930-32. Residence since retirement: Salem, Ore., 1935-42; Blaine, Wash., 1942-45; Hillsboro, Kan., 1947-d. 57. He published *Missions-Album* (M.B. Publishing House c1914) and *Commentary for Sunday School Quarterly.* He died at Hillsboro, Sept. 11, 1957.　　　　　　　L.Hi.

Hirzel, a town in canton Zürich, Switzerland: see **Horgen.**

Hisse Lambertsdochter, an Anabaptist martyr, arrested at the recapture of the Oldeklooster (*q.v.*). She was drowned at Leeuwarden, capital of Friesland, on April 14, 1535. (Vos, *Menno Simons,* 229.)

vDZ.

Historic Peace Churches is a term widely used for the three denominations which have for centuries held the position that the New Testament forbids Christian participation in war and violence. These three are the Brethren, the Friends, and the Mennonites. The term came into common usage in America between World Wars I and II. In 1922 the Friends initiated the Conference of Pacifist Churches, which met in 1923, 1926, 1927, 1929, and 1931. In the last conference, H. P. Krehbiel, a Mennonite (GCM) leader of Newton, Kan., was appointed a committee of one to arrange the next meeting; but because of the economic depression it was not held until November 1935, when it met in Newton as the "Conference of Historic Peace Churches" (not to be confused with the Conference of Historic Peace Churches—*q.v.*—which was organized in Canada in 1940). Since 1935 the Conference of Historic Peace Churches has met in 1937, 1938, and on numerous other occasions. However, the meetings are not regularly scheduled, and are not always the same in character. They are planned by the Continuation Committee (*q.v.*) set up by the 1935 meeting. Similar conferences have been held in Europe since 1947 by the Continuation Committee of the Historic Peace Churches there. The term "Historic Peace Churches" has become widely accepted beyond the circles of the Christian pacifist churches.   M.G.

Melvin Gingerich, *Service for Peace* (Akron, 1949) 25-38.

Historiography II. Switzerland (II, 757b): Supplement. R. Feller, "Die ersten bernischen Wiedertäufer," *Archiv des historischen Vereins des Kantons Bern,* 1931; "Bernische Reformation und der Staat," in *Berner Universitätsreden* (1928); H. Käser, "Ausserkirchliche christliche Versammlungen im Unter-Emmenthal," in *Brosamen,* 1926, 1-9; "Chorgericht und Landvogt in Behandlung der Täufergeschichte," *Blätter für Bernische Geschichte und Altertumskunde* (1928, No. 2); R. Feller, "Sittengesetze der Bernischen Reformation," in *Festschrift, Fr. E. Welti* (1932) 54-82 (deals with moral criticisms expressed by Anabaptists in the disputations of 1532 and 1538); Leo von Muralt, "Gespräch mit den Wiedertäufern am 22. Januar 1528 zu Bern" (Notizen des Stadtschreibers Peter Cyro), *Ztschr für schweizerische Kirchengeschichte* (1932, No. 4); T. Schiess, "Der Glaubenszwang in der St. Gallischen Kirche des XVII. Jahrhunderts. Der 'Wiedertäufer' Josef Hochreutiner u. Pfarrer Michael Bingg," reprint from *Schriften des Vereins für Geschichte des Bodensees und seiner Umgebung,* No. 51 (n.d.-1925?) 1-23; A. Bucher, *Die Reformation in den Freien Aemtern und in der Stadt Bremgarten (Beilage zum Jahresbericht der Kantonalen Lehranstalt Sarnen),* which is a dissertation at Freiburg (Sw.) 1950, contains a section, "Die Täufer in den Freien Aemtern"; Clyde Smith, *The Amish Man* (Toronto, 1912).   H.S.B.

Hobbe Buwezoon, an Anabaptist martyr, arrested at the recapture of the Oldeklooster (*q.v.*) and beheaded at Leeuwarden, capital of Friesland, on April 12, 1535. (Vos, *Menno Simons,* 228.)

vDZ.

Hoeksteen, the name of two Dutch Mennonite old ladies' homes, one at Amsterdam, of which there is only scarce information, and one at Leiden. The Amsterdam Hoeksteen Hofje (home) was founded before 1647. It then belonged to the Frisian congregation. After the merger of the Frisians with the Zonists (*q.v.*) at Amsterdam in 1752, the "Nieuwe Hofje" was built at the Prinsengracht on the site of the former Arke Noachs (Frisian) meetinghouse. At Lieden the Hoeksteen home on the Levendaal was founded in 1660. Until 1701 it belonged to the Flemish congregation. After the merger of this congregation with the Waterlanders, it was decided to unite the Waterlander Bethlehem home and the Flemish Hoeksteen and give up the Bethlehem home, the Hoeksteen home henceforth to be called Bethlehem. But the planned union did not become effective until 1811, when the old and dilapidated Bethlehem home was sold.   vDZ.

Inv. Arch. Amst. II, 490-520; L. G. le Poole, *Bijdragen tot de Kennis van . . . de Doopsgezinden te Leiden* (Leiden, 1905) 50, 58 ff.

Hof, a German term with various applications used to designate (1) a farm, (2) a farmyard, (3) a court, (4) a courtyard, (5) a country house or manor house, the household of a sovereign. In Anabaptist history it appears in the word Bruderhof to refer to a Hutterite household with its buildings and acreage. In German areas it is used to refer to a farm or large estate which may be occupied by one family (e.g., Althof) or by several with individually owned tracts (e.g., Branchweilerhof). Numerous congregations have been named after such Hofs (e.g., Kohlhof, Weierhof), and in South Germany many congregations began as household (Hof) meetings.   H.S.B.

Gerhard Hein, "The Development of the Mennonite 'Hof' of the Seventeenth Century Palatinate into the Mennonite Church of Pfalz-Rheinland Today," *MQR* XXIX (1955) 188-96.

Hofer Brothers. Joseph and Michael Hofer were two young married brothers of the Hutterian faith in South Dakota, who were drafted in World War I and sent to Camp Lewis in 1918. Because they refused to wear the military uniform and to obey other military orders they were court-martialed and sentenced to 20 years in Alcatraz (California) prison. In November, after suffering terrible mistreatment for four months at Alcatraz, they with two other Hutterites who had endured the same kind of punishment were sent to Ft. Leavenworth. Forced to stand in the cold air for several hours without their outer clothing while waiting for their prison garb, the two men became ill and died a few days later. In the meantime their two friends had to stand for nine hours a day with their hands manacled through the prison bars on a diet of bread and water. Fourteen days of this treatment were alternated with fourteen days of regular diet. Eventually an order from Secretary of War Baker ended this kind of treatment of conscientious objectors. David Hofer was released from prison that winter, but his friend Jacob Wipf was not released until April 13, 1919. "This moving story," wrote C. Henry Smith, "reads more like a page from the martyrology of the European Mennonites in the sixteenth century, than like an actual experience in America in the twentieth." Although this was the most extreme case of mistreatment given conscientious objectors in America during World War I, hundreds of Mennonites and other objectors suffered various forms of indignities and cruelties in camp guardhouses and military prisons during those years, usually, to be sure, at the hands of local camp officials and lower military officers without the full knowledge of the War Department in Washington. Both the President and the Secretary of War showed a sympathetic spirit toward sincere objectors. (See **Conscientious Objectors.**)

M.G.

C. H. Smith, *The Coming of the Russian Mennonites* (Berne, 1927) 276-83; J. S. Hartzler, *Mennonites in the World War* (Scottdale, 1922).

Hoffnungsfeld Mennonite Church (GCM), at Carrot River, Sask., was organized Nov. 24, 1929, its meetinghouse having been built in 1928. In 1958 the membership was 90, with P. G. Epp as pastor.

H.S.B.

Hoffnungsfeld Mennonite Church (GCM) at Rabbit Lake, Sask., was organized at three places in 1928, the three meetinghouses built as follows: Rabbit Lake (1928), membership 23 in 1959; Mayfair (1934), membership 21; Glenbush (1936), membership 55; total membership 99, with Jacob T. Loewen as pastor.

H.S.B.

Hoffnungsfeld-Petaigan (Sask.) Mennonite Church (GCM) was organized in 1937, when it also dedicated its building (begun in 1934). In 1958 it had 29 members, with C. C. Boschmann as elder-pastor.

H.S.B.

Hohburg, Christian: see **Hoburg, Christian.**

Holyrood Mennonite Church (MC), Edmonton, Alberta, was begun in 1956 as a mission. A meetinghouse was built in 1957. Howard Snider has been serving as pastor since 1957. H.S.B.

Home for the Friendless, Hillsboro, Kan., officially the Industrial School and Hygiene Home for Friendless Persons, chartered in 1890, was a co-operative venture for the care of orphan children. Although it was largely controlled by the Krimmer Mennonite Brethren, it was also supported financially by the Brethren in Christ and the Mennonite Church (MC). Financial reports of the Home appeared regularly in the *Herald of Truth* (MC), and for a time Joseph F. Brunk (MC) served as the superintendent of the Home. The project was, therefore, a demonstration of inter-Mennonite co-operation. (See **Industrial School . . . .**) M.G.

Home Missions, a common term among North American Protestants for mission work carried on within the boundaries of the United States and Canada, hence more recently often referred to as "National Missions." The most nearly corresponding German term is "Innere Mission." Home missions are distinguished from foreign missions (*q.v.*). The one exception is the work among the North American Indians carried on by the General Conference Mennonite Church which includes this work under foreign missions because of the native Indian language and culture. Home missions include the following types of missionary outreach, for which the articles appearing in this ENCYCLOPEDIA give detailed reports: **City Missions, Jewish Evangelism, Negro Missions, Rescue Missions,** and **Rural Missions.** See also **Evangelism.** The purpose of all home mission effort is to found churches, except in the case of rescue missions, which seek to "rescue" "down-and-outs" and turn them over to existing churches.

In two of the major North American Mennonite bodies separate boards were organized to carry on home missions, the Home Mission Board of the General Conference Mennonite Church (*q.v.*) and the Home Missions Board of the Mennonite Brethren Church (*q.v.*). In the Mennonite Church (MC) the board which operates the foreign missions has also operated some home missions, usually city only. Every district conference has a mission board; they, with few exceptions, were set up to operate home missions only, and many local congregations operate local mission outposts. Only in the Virginia Conference has a separate home mission board been set up. The total number of home missions, both city and rural, operated by the Mennonite Church under general or district boards and local congregations was over 300 in 1958.

Almost all Mennonite groups in North America engage in home missions in some form, city or rural, and most conferences have a home missions committee or a board for this purpose; in some cases the district conferences have organized committees or boards. Western Gospel Mission (*q.v.*) and Western Children's Mission (*q.v.*) are inter-Mennonite home mission boards in Canada. The Conference of Mennonites in Canada (GCM) has a home mission board, called Pioneer Mission (*q.v.*). (See also **Evangelism.**) H.S.B.

Honduras, a republic of Central America, with a population of 1,700,000 and an area of 43,227 square miles. The country is mountainous, very fertile, though mostly uncultivated, and covered with rich forests. The chief export is bananas, but it also has valuable minerals and extensive cattle raising. The Eastern Mennonite Board of Missions and Charities (MC) established a mission in Honduras in 1950. By 1957 the three stations of Trujillo, Tocoa, and Gualaco had been established. Nine full-time and two short-term workers were on the field, three others were in language school, and two were on furlough. The membership was 30.

North of Honduras is the small colony of British Honduras. In 1958 three Mennonite groups from Mexico were in the process of buying land and settling in British Honduras. These were the Old Colony Mennonites, the Kleine Gemeinde, and the Sommerfelders. Old Colony Mennonites of Durango were negotiating for land in the Republic of Honduras. These Mennonites were leaving Mexico because of their need for more land and because of a feeling that government regulations in Mexico were encroaching too much on the freedom of their settlement life.

In May 1959 a total of over 360 families totaling 1,627 persons (775 children under 14) had settled in three locations in British Honduras, largely in three colonies: Blue Creek settlement in the extreme northwest corner on a 115,000-acre jungle tract; Belize (actually 50 miles west of the city) on an 18,000-acre tract; and Orange Walk (60 miles north of Belize) on scattered individual family farms who expect to settle on a 17,000-acre tract at Shipyard, nine miles south of Orange Walk.   M.G.

Leo Driedger, "From Mexico to British Honduras," *Menn. Life* XIII (October 1958) 160-66.

Hooft, a Dutch Mennonite family of Amsterdam since the 16th century. It was a side branch of the Reformed Hooft family, descending from a West Frisian family of captains of merchant vessels. One of the Reformed descendants was Cornelis Pietersz Hooft (1547-1626), who as a burgomaster of Amsterdam always defended the Mennonites and other nonconformists against the presumption of the Calvinist church, and his son Pieter Cornelisz Hooft (Amsterdam, 1581-The Hague, 1647) was an outstanding Dutch poet.

In the Mennonite branch, whose members were merchants at Amsterdam and in the 17th century also at Haarlem, was Jan Gerritsz Hooft (Amsterdam, 1584-1644). He was director of the Dutch Levantine trade and in 1616-20 a deacon of the Amsterdam Waterlander congregation. In 1625 he sided with Nittert Obbes (*q.v.*) and came into conflict with the church leaders (Yearbook *Amstelodamum* XXV, 1928, 85, 100). Some other members of this family also served the Amsterdam congregation as deacons, e.g., Jan Hooft Hartsen, serving 1777-82 and 1787-92. In Haarlem some Hoofts were deacons and trustees of the Mennonite orphanage. Here Maria Hooft was married to the Haarlem preacher Coenraad van Diepenbroek (*q.v.*).
                    vDZ.

Hoogland, a Mennonite family in the Dutch province of Friesland, mostly farmers and often deacons of the church since the 18th century. They lived in the Bildt region and belonged to the congregations of St. Anna-Parochie and Oudebildtzijl. Sjouke Johannes Hoogland (1866-1939) published a historical paper in *DJ* 1932.   vDZ.

Hooker (Okla.) Mennonite Brethren Church: see **Adams** M.B. Church and **Sharon** M.B. Church.

Hooks and Eyes, German *Haken* (or *Haften*) *und Oesen.* The modern Old Order Amish require the use of hooks and eyes as fasteners on men's and boys' coats and vests (buttons are used on other clothing). These fasteners have become so much a mark of the Amish that they are some-

times called simply the "Hook and Eye People." In South Germany the Amish were known as "Häftler" (*q.v.*) and the Mennonites "Knöpfler" (*q.v.*). The reason for the Amish practice is obscure since no Biblical authority is or can be cited, such as is the case with the beard. The obvious answer is that the Amish have simply perpetuated, out of their basic conservatism and opposition to change, the old type of fastener in use before buttons came into general use. Buttons were at first more expensive and often used primarily for ornamentation; hence their introduction would naturally find opposition as a violation of simplicity and nonconformity.   H.S.B.

Horekill (Hoere Kill, Whorekills), the location of the Plockhoy (*q.v.*) Mennonite colony, which existed in southern Delaware for one year 1662-64. The exact location can no longer be determined. Vissher's map of the New World (*c*1665), of which the relevant section was printed by Harder (p. 64), shows "Hoere Kill" on the west side of the estuary of the Delaware across from Cape May on the eastern shore, which would locate it about 20 miles north of the present town of Lewes. The Vissher map locates "Swanendael" along the west shore some 25 miles north of Hoere Kill. Both names are sometimes used to refer to the Plockhoy colony, but they cannot refer to the same place. The State Archivist of Delaware responded to an inquiry by Harder as follows: "The little colony was clearly in the vicinity of present-day Lewes. The Horekill, or Whorekills, is now called Lewes Creek and serves as a portion of the Lewes and Rehoboth Canal." Plockhoy later had a house and lot in Lewes.

A state highway historical marker at the edge of the town of Lewes erected in 1932 bears the following legend: "Lewes. Under orders from Peter Stuyvesant the Dutch erected a Fort at Hoorn Kil (Lewes Creek) 1659 but were soon dispossessed by the Marylanders. Here was also a communistic settlement established in 1662 by Mennonites from Holland under Peter Cornelis Plockhoy. Sir Robert Carr 1664 'destroyed the Quaking Colony of Plockhoy to a Naile.' "   H.S.B.

Leland Harder, *Plockhoy from Zurik-zee* (Newton, 1952).

Horgen, a town (pop. 10,000) in the canton of Zürich (*q.v.*), Switzerland, some 9 miles south of the city of Zürich on the west bank of the lake of Zürich, a village in Reformation times subject politically and ecclesiastically to the city of Zürich. There are no traces of the Anabaptists in the village and surrounding area in the early 16th century, but the presence of a congregation in the neighborhood (Horgerberg) at the end of the century and the first half of the 17th suggests there must have been some members there earlier. A group of 15 Anabaptists were arrested in Horgen in 1589, four of whom were from Horgen and seven from adjoining Wädenswil. The four from Horgen included two preachers, Hans Landis (*q.v.*) and Heini Landis, also Uli Suter and Hans Summerauer. Hans Landis was the leader of the congregation.

In 1608 the strongest measures were applied to

crush the Anabaptist movement in the region of Horgen, Wädenswil, and Hirzel. The records of the persecution reveal that the authorities estimated the group to consist of 40 men and women, who held their meetings in barns and forests or in the home of the farmer Hans Landis, at that time over 60 years of age. Little is known about the congregation; but it was discovered to have a fund for the aid of the poor administered by Jacob Isler, apparently the deacon. Landis and Isler were arrested in 1608, but both escaped from their prison (the Wellenberg) in Zürich.

On Jan. 6, 1613, a disputation was held in the Wädenswil castle with the 15 Anabaptists who responded to the invitation, at which the Reformed pastors of Wädenswil, Horgen, and Richterswil took part. Among the Anabaptist speakers were Galli Fuchs of Richterswil, who said he had been converted by a missioner from Moravia, and a certain Bachmann. The disputation was fruitless and resulted in the renewed application of severe penalties including confiscation of property, exile, and execution. In the summer of 1613 Landis, Isler, Fuchs, Stephan Zehender, Hans Meili, and Paul Degia (Galatz) were imprisoned. Pressure to recant having failed, vain attempts were made to get them to emigrate voluntarily. The six men were then sentenced to galley slavery, but Isler, Fuchs, and Zehender at last agreed to emigrate. The other three escaped from prison in Solothurn and returned to their homes. The affair awakened great sympathy for them and as a result the Anabaptist congregation grew. After a time the three were again imprisoned. Landis was finally beheaded on Sept. 29, 1614, the last Anabaptist executed in Switzerland, although others later died in prison. Landis' widow was imprisoned for a time.

Upon this execution a number of the Anabaptists emigrated. In 1638 eight Anabaptists were discovered to be living in the environs of Horgen and Hirzel, three of them bearing the name Landis, and one Rudolf Baumann. In 1637 a large number were imprisoned in Zürich, one of them Hans Landis, the son of the martyr. Most of the captives were held in prison until 1640. In this year and the following years the Anabaptist congregation was broken by the confiscation of property, and most of the members apparently emigrated to Alsace and the Palatinate. Among those who suffered confiscation were Hans Landis, Felix Landis, Jakob Rusterholz, Konrad Strickler-Landis, Hans Rudolf Baumann-Landis, Oswald Landis, Uli Furrer, Hans Huber, Hans Asper, Elsbeth Hofstetter, Barbara Bruppach, Verena Bruppach (widow of Michel), and the widow of Heinrich Ritter. The proceeds of the confiscation were applied to the costs of the trials and imprisonment of the Anabaptists, and the remainder offered to the heirs who would return to the state church. This was the end of the Anabaptist congregation in Horgen, Wädenswil, and Hirzel. Numerous descendants of the Landis and Brubacher families are found today in South Germany and in the United States.　　　H.S.B.

Paul Kläui, *Geschichte der Gemeinde Horgen* (Horgen, 1952) 185-93; idem, "Hans Landis of Zürich, the Last Anabaptist Martyr," *MQR* (1948) 203-12.

Horodyszcze (German, *Horodischtz*). A congregation of Swiss-Volhynian Mennonites was located in the Volhynian (western Russia) village of Horodyszcze, 30 miles northeast of Rowno 1837-74. Coming from the Polish villages of Urszulin and Michelsdorf (*q.v.*) in 1837, the group made the move to Horodyszcze because of better farming opportunities. During the same year or soon thereafter twelve families moved from Horodyszcze, beginning the daughter colony at Waldheim. The first baptism at Horodyszcze occurred in 1838. The congregation did not have a church building. Congregational leaders were Jacob Graber, Peter Kaufman, and Joseph Graber. Family names recorded in the church book included Albrecht, Voran, Graber, Kaufman, Flickinger, Prieheim, Gering, Schrag, Stucky, Schwartz, Rysz, Senner, Strausz, and Krehbiel. The congregation at Horodyszcze joined the Waldheim congregation in the emigration to America in 1874. Under the leadership of Elder Peter Kaufman 53 families made the journey to Hutchinson and Turner counties, S.D.　　　M.H.S.

Martin H. Schrag, "European History of the Swiss-Volhynian Mennonite Ancestors of Mennonites now Living in Communities in Kansas and South Dakota" (unpublished master's dissertation, 1956); idem, "The Swiss Volhynian Mennonite Background," *Menn. Life* IX (October 1954) 156-61.

Huber Mennonite Church (MC), New Carlisle, Ohio, was established in 1863. It had 29 members in 1958. It is located approximately 12 miles northeast of Dayton. Paul R. Yoder is pastor.　　　M.G.

Hueff: see Huf.

Huiuff, Hans, one of the first group of Zürich Anabaptists, a member of the Conrad Grebel circle of 1524-25 and cosigner of the letter to Thomas Müntzer of Sept. 5, 1524, a goldsmith, native of Halle a.d. Saale, Germany. Huiuff was evidently the son of the court goldsmith of Cardinal Albrecht of Mainz. His brother brought some of Müntzer's booklets from Saxony to Zürich, which occasioned the negative attitude of the Grebel circle to Müntzer's revolutionary ideas. Huiuff became a full member of the Anabaptist circle in Zürich, apparently a close friend of Heinrich Aberli, and in fellowship with the Zollikon brotherhood. The Zürich *Täuferakten* reports that on Dec. 23, 1525, he was haled before court for a hearing and then released from prison. He must have been imprisoned in November with the other Zürich Anabaptists who were arrested in Grüningen. His testimony suggests that he was weakening in his Anabaptism, since he reports having "gone to church" and makes other qualifying statements.　　　H.S.B.

Karl Simon, "Die Züricher Täufer und der Hofgoldschmied Kardinal Albrechts," *Zwingliana* XI (1934) 50-54; H. S. Bender, *Conrad Grebel* (Goshen, 1950) 257; *TA Zürich.*

Hunsicker Group. In 1851 the bishops Abraham Hunsicker and Israel Beidler and the preachers Henry A. Hunsicker and Abraham H. Grater separated from John H. Oberholtzer's Conference in Eastern Pennsylvania (now GCM). "But having a majority of the members and friends, both in Phoenixville and in Germantown to stand by us, we continued our services at both these places until 1875. After the Meeting Houses in Skippack and Providence were closed against us, we held services at school houses, and in some of the neighboring churches opened to us, until 1854 when we built a church at Freeland, now Collegeville, which was essentially a non-sectarian church, to be open for ministers in good standing in our own and other denominations, who chose to help the church of Christ. Our Church, as well as our school, were both flourishing. We added to the Ministry during these years, Francis Hunsicker, Jarret T. Preston, and Joseph H. Hendricks." (Quotation from Henry A. Hunsicker in the 1907 *Mennonite Year Book and Almanac,* p. 24.)

The church established by the Hunsicker group in 1854 was called the "Trinity Christian Society." In 1888 Hendricks and his church were received into the Reformed Church, which act displeased Henry A. Hunsicker.

The Hunsicker group were for a time known as Reformed Mennonites, at least they were called Reformed Mennonites at Germantown. But this name was already used by a radical sect of Mennonites in Lancaster County, the followers of John Herr, and the "Reformed" Mennonites of Germantown soon became General Conference Mennonites. Indeed the whole Hunsicker group disintegrated. The Collegeville Church became Reformed, the Lutherans acquired the Phoenixville property, and the Germantown Church united with the Eastern District of the General Conference Mennonites. Both Henry A. and Francis R. S. Hunsicker became Presbyterians.   J.C.W.

Abraham Hunsicker, *A Statement of Facts, and Summary of Views on Morals and Religion, as Related with Suspension from the Mennonite Meeting 1851* (Philadelphia, 1851).

Hydro Mennonite Church (GCM), now extinct, located near the now extinct town of Hydro, Mont., near the Canadian border at the mid-point of the state, was organized in 1914 by some 30 persons who came chiefly from Kansas and Oklahoma. In 1926 the congregation disbanded because of crop failures. P. P. Tschetter served as minister here for three years.   H.S.B.

Hymnology (II, 870b, 32): Supplement. In the article **Ochsentreiberin** (IV), note the following additional comment on Anabaptist singing: "At the same time the magistrate was censured because the prisoners were lodged together, so that they 'with much singing, as they are accustomed to sing in their sect, make themselves heard, which is also listened to publicly by the common man, from which nothing good can come.' Furthermore, this merely strengthened and consoled them, for which reason they were to be consoled at once and placed in solitary confinement."

Iglau (Czech, *Jihlava*), a city (pop. 23,413) in Moravia, Czechoslovakia. The Anabaptist movement early gained adherents here, but through the influence of Paul Speratus Lutheranism predominated and Anabaptism was suppressed, with actions in 1529, 1536, and 1537. However, scattered individual Anabaptists continued to be found here and toward the end of the century increased in number. The city council then took special action to suppress them, and among others arrested their leader and preacher Hans Springer (*q.v.*) in 1592, and cruelly executed him.   W.W.

A. Altrichter, "Zur Geschichte der Wiedertäufer in Iglau," *Ztscht des deutschen Vereins für die Geschichte Mährens und Schlesiens* (1928) 157 f.

I.H.V.P.N.: see **Beginsel.**

IJzenbeek: see **Ysenbeek.**

Immanuel Mennonite Church (GCM), Meadow Lake, Sask., organized in 1930 and reorganized in 1948, had 77 members in 1958, with Peter B. Friesen as pastor. Besides Meadow Lake it has four other meeting places—Beaverdale, Daisy Meadow, Compass, and Pierceland.   M.G.

Immeli, Jakob (*c*1495-1543), one of the assistants to Oecolampadius (*q.v.*), the reformer of Basel, in the disputation of August 1525 with the Swiss Brethren. Immeli, who was dean of the arts faculty of the University of Basel in 1522, served as pastor of St. Ulrich's in Basel from May 1523 to February 1525, later at other points near Basel.   H.S.B.

Immersion (III, 15 f.): Supplement. Frank Wray's discovery that Pilgram Marpeck used almost two thirds of Rothmann's (*q.v.*) *Bekenntnisse* as a basis for his *Vermanung* (*q.v.*) throws some further light on the form of baptism used by the Anabaptists in South Germany. Rothmann only once refers to baptism as "waterbesprengung," and prefers terminology which describes baptism as immersion. In contrast Marpeck (with one exception) always adds (at least twelve times) to Rothmann's immersion terminology the phrase "or water poured over him" or similar phrases. Marpeck simply deletes Rothmann's assertion, "Everyone knows well that baptizing means to put under or to thrust into the water." At only one place does Marpeck refer to baptism as immersion (*eindunken*), viz., in the *Verantwortung* where he is defending the description given in the *Vermanung*. The evidence indicates strongly that Marpeck's brotherhood baptized by pouring.

However, Rothmann's writing is not to be interpreted as meaning that the Münsterites used immersion as their mode of baptism. Cornelius Krahn, who examined all the sources carefully, shows that pouring was the mode practiced. Gresbeck, an eyewitness, states that Jan van Leiden said in his trial that they baptized by using "a little water upon the head" (Cornelius).

Wiswedel's article on Silesia (*q.v.*) states that in the town of Habelschwerdt "immersion was apparently practiced" by the Anabaptists, quoting an unnamed source as follows: "For them the whole city was a temple; in private homes of citizens they held their meetings. The Neisse and the Weistritz were the great baptistries, into which adults were immersed and made members of their covenant."

The group at Surhuisterveen, Holland, which practiced immersion, was not Mennonite (see III, 15b) but followers of Alexander Mack, founder of the Church of the Brethren.   W.KL.

Cornelius Krahn, *Menno Simons* (Karlsruhe, 1936) 136-38; C. A. Cornelius, *Berichte der Augenzeugen über das Münsterische Wiedertäuferreich* (Münster, 1853) 370; Kühler, *Geschiedenis*, 83.

Independents, a term used in English church history to refer to the first congregation of English Protestants who withdrew from the Church of England to become independent. They were later called Congregationalists (*q.v.*). They were also called Brownists for a time after Robert Browne, whose congregation in London in 1580 became the first independent congregation. For the relation of the Congregationalists to the Mennonites see **Brownists.**   H.S.B.

Indiana (or Miller) Amish Mennonite Church in Logan and Champaign counties, Ohio, now extinct, developed about 1883 as a result of the refusal of the Walnut Grove and Oak Grove congregations to allow the use of a parlor organ in the home of a member and the use of the English language in Sunday school. Bishop Eli Miller of the Clinton Frame A.M. congregation in Elkhart County, Ind., organized the congregation and ordained Samuel H. Detweiler and John H. Kauffman as bishop and minister, who were accepted as members of the Indiana A.M. Conference. No meetinghouse was ever built; the group used the Oak Grove and Walnut Grove meetinghouses on the alternate Sundays when the regular congregation did not meet. Leading Sunday-school workers at Walnut Grove were D. D. Yoder, Detweiler and Kauffman, and the John Fett family, and at Oak Grove the Hooley brothers, Levi and Jonas. Soon after 1890 the Hooley brothers organized one of the earliest Ohio Young People's Bible Meetings. The congregation never prospered and when the Bethel Mennonite Church was organized at West Liberty in 1895 the remaining active members joined it.   J.S.U.

Indiana-Michigan Mennonite Camp Association, Inc. (MC), founded 1956, owns and operates the Perrin Lakes Camp, established in 1957, located 5 miles north of Sturgis, Mich., near Burr Oak. It is sponsored by the Indiana-Michigan Christian Workers' Conference but controlled by a board of directors appointed by the shareholders.   H.S.B.

Instituto Biblico Menonita (MC), at La Plata, Puerto Rico, was established in 1955 by the Mennonite Board of Missions and Charities as a training school for Christian workers in Puerto Rico.   H.S.B.

Intercollegiate (Mennonite) Peace Fellowship, representing the peace societies or interest groups of the Mennonite and affiliated colleges, was organized in 1948 under the sponsorship of the MCC Peace Section (*q.v.*), with later additional sponsorship by the Council of Mennonite and Affiliated Colleges (*q.v.*). It provides an annual meeting at one of the colleges, occasionally conducts a seminar (e.g., at Washington, D.C., and at the United Nations in New York), and publishes *Peace Notes* as an organ.   H.S.B.

Inthie Claesdochter, of Wier, and **Intte, Jan Eysens'** widow, Anabaptist martyrs, apprehended at the recapture of the Oldeklooster (*q.v.*) and both drowned

at Leeuwarden, capital of Friesland, on April 14, 1535. (Vos, *Menno Simons*, 229.)   vDZ.

Invalid-Funds (Invaliditeitfondsen, i.e., a fund for the pensioning of disabled ministers in the Netherlands). Soon after the ministry in the Netherlands had became a full-time occupation, foundations were established for the pensioning of retired ministers and their widows (see **Algemeen Emeritaatfonds and Pensioenfonds**), and usually also for invalid ministers. Groningen Conference founded a separate Invalid Fund in 1917.   vDZ.

Iowa Experiment of the Stauffer Mennonite Church in Osceola County (1887-1915). Stauffer (*q.v*). Mennonites from Ontario and from Lancaster and Snyder counties, Pa., established a settlement in the frontier country of northwestern Iowa where they could be isolated from the influence of Mennonite churches from which they had separated. Their settlement became extinct because of differences of opinion among the members concerning the introduction of modern conveniences and because of the great economic success of their bishop which led him into compromises disapproved by his members.   M.G.

Iowa Valley Mennonite Church (MC), Lone Tree, Ia., began as a mission in 1949 and was organized as a congregation in 1952. In 1958 the membership numbered 33, with Henry M. Yoder as pastor. The congregation worships in the community-owned Swank Church.   M.G.

Iroquois (S.D.) Church of God in Christ Mennonite Church is located 4 miles north and 1 mile east of Iroquois. It had a membership of 37 in 1959, with Harvey Yost as minister. The congregation was first listed in the Yearbook (CGC) for 1955.   M.G.

Israel Mennonite Mission (MC) was founded in 1953 as a joint work by the Mennonite Board of Missions and Charities, the Eastern M.B. of M. & C., and the Virginia M.B. of M. & C. In 1958 there were four missionaries located at Ramat Gan.   H.S.B.

Jan Quirinsz: see **Quirijn Jansz.**

Janson: see **Janzen.**

Japan Mennonite Mission (MC): see **Japan.**

Jefferson Street Mennonite Church, Lima, Ohio: see **Lima Mission.**

Jewish Evangelism. In his earliest writing, against the "Blasphemy of John of Leiden" (1535), Menno Simons expresses the conviction that "Israel is yet to be converted unto Christ," basing this on Rom. 11:26 and Isa. 59:20 (*Writings*, 38). While neither he nor any other early Anabaptists are known to have made any special effort to win the Jews to Christ, such an interest has developed in this century, particularly among American Mennonites. In the Mennonite Church (MC) the pioneer in Jewish evangelism seems to have been Martin Z. Miller of Elizabethtown, Pa., who after informally witnessing for about 20 years, was appointed (1933) by the Eastern Mennonite Board of Missions and Charities as a worker among Israel. Work of a rather permanent nature has since been undertaken not only by this board in Philadelphia and Washington, D.C., but also (1940) by the Pacific Coast Mission Board in Portland, Ore., and (1951) by the General Mission Board (Elkhart) in New York City. In 1953 Roy and Florence Kreider were sent by a committee representing the Elkhart, Eastern, and Virginia mission boards to open the first Mennonite mission in Israel, now located at Ramat Gan, near Tel Aviv.

In Ontario five Mennonite groups co-operate in sponsoring a Hebrew Mission, located since 1957 in Toronto. An earlier (1920) joint enterprise in Chicago, sponsored by the General Conference Mennonites, Defenseless Mennonites, and Central Conference Mennonites, was given up after three years. Other attempts at Jewish evangelism, e.g., in the Ohio, Virginia, and Franconia conference districts (MC), also failed to develop into a permanent work. It is a difficult field for all denominations. Not only do Jews tend to persist in their historic repudiation of Jesus as Christ, but there are also problems in the integration of peoples who have been so long apart. There are at present a small number of Hebrew Christians in the Mennonite brotherhood. C.Y.F.

Ed. G. Kaufman, *The Development of the Missionary and Philanthropic Interest Among the Mennonites of North America* (Berne, 1931) 127; J. Paul Graybill, *Jewish Evangelism* (Lancaster, 1950) 33, 34.

Joachim de Suickerbacker: see **Joachim Vermeeren.**

Johann von Orvall, an Anabaptist martyr, was drowned in the Rhine on Nov. 29, 1561, at Cologne: see **Orvel.**

Johnson, Elmer Ellsworth Schultz (1872-1959), pastor, educator, historian, was born June 26, 1872, at New Berlinville, Pa., attended Perkiomen Seminary, Pennsburg (1893-95); Princeton University (1895-99); and Hartford Theological Seminary (1899-1902, B.D.; Ph.D., 1911). He was pastor of the Hereford Mennonite Church, Bally, Pa., 1921-47; Professor of Church History, Hartford Theological Seminary, 1922-43; director of the Schwenckfelder Historical Library, Pennsburg, 1919 ff.; and editor of the *Corpus Schwenckfeldianorum* 1904-59.

Johnson was an outstanding scholar whose major contribution besides his monumental work of editing the *Corpus* was the building up of the Schwenckfelder Library, which contains primarily all valuable material pertaining to the Schwenckfelder movement, but also some Anabaptist and Mennonite materials which he collected and purchased abroad and in Pennsylvania. Johnson's ancestry was both Mennonite and Schwenckfelder, and he served both denominations throughout his life, but his membership was in the Schwenckfeld Church at Palm, Pa. He died May 15, 1959. C.K.

Johnsville Conservative Mennonite Church is located in the village of Shauck, Ohio, midway between Mansfield and Mt. Gilead, on U.S. Route 42. The congregation was established in 1951 and had 41 members in 1959, with Ray F. Miller as bishop. M.G.

Joseph II (1741-90), Emperor of the Holy Roman Empire, was a uniquely progressive Hapsburg ruler.

His emphatic reform ideas harmonized with the Enlightenment philosophers, whose (esp. Voltaire's) dedicated student he was (see **Emancipation**). Frederick II of Prussia (*q.v.*) and Czarina Catherine (*q.v.*) of Russia had provided patterns for Joseph's policies designed to induce settlers to come to his lands. Joseph's imperial objectives included attempts to redress long and complicated grievances in law and law court procedures. These efforts, incidentally, brought up the local privileges as regards the Mennonite position on the oath. Refreshingly sound views were aired. (See the discussion by Crous.)

The death of Maria Theresa in 1780 made Joseph the uncontested ruler. Eager to apply reason and enlightenment to the power of state he issued on Oct. 13, 1781, a *Toleranz-Patent* granting freedom to the Greek Orthodox and Protestant confessions. Parallel to Catherine's 1763 Manifesto inviting German farmers to Russia, he issued on Sept. 17, 1781, the "Kolonisten-Patent" opening his eastern provinces to immigrants. This law attracted a number of Palatinate Mennonite families into Galicia (*q.v.*). The decree of acceptance (Annahmedekret) for the Palatine group was handed down on March 29, 1784. Alsatian Amish followed from Montbéliard (*q.v.*). The 1781 events mark a memorable chapter of Joseph's reforms. They reveal him as a just benefactor to Mennonites and other Protestants. His toleration patent brought relief to them and provided an escape avenue far less troublesome than the passage to the New World. E.H.C.

Ernst Crous, "Mennoniten im alten Reich u. Staat," *Die Heimat* (Krefeld, 1939) Part I: "Reichskammergericht und Mennoniteneid," 1-8: "Wie es mit Ablegung des *juramenti calumniae* und sonstiger Eyden in Streitsachen der Mennonisten zu halten seye?" discussed at Wetzlar, July 13, 1768, by the Visitations-Kommission (Imperial Law Revision Commission) relating to commercial cases. With reference to Mennonite immigration into the Austrian dominions see the bibliography under "Galicia"; also Viktor Kauder, *Das Deutschtum in Polen* 2. Teil: *Das Deutschtum in Galizien* (=*Kleinpolen*) 1937. For recent literature see R. Blaas, "Die K. K. Agentie f. Geistl. Angelegenheiten, 1730-1918" *Mitteilungen Oesterr, Staatsarchiv*, 1954, 47-89; Ferdinand Maass, "Maria Theresia u. der Josephinismus" in *Ztscht f. Katholische Theologie*, 1957, 201-13.

Josephus, Flavius (A.D. 37-95), Jewish historian who turned Roman and became a friend of several emperors. His two most renowned works are *The Jewish War* and *Jewish Antiquities*, both favorite readings in Protestant circles. *The Jewish War* contains a detailed description of the War between the Jews and Romans A.D. 66-70 as seen from the Roman camp, in particular the story of the fall of Jerusalem in A.D. 70, of which Josephus had been an eyewitness. The book was translated into German and Dutch rather early in the 16th century and seems to have been widely studied. Bible-oriented Anabaptists naturally were eager to learn all about the prophesied fall of the great city, as well as about the life of the Jews before and after Christ's earthly career. Thus Josephus became as popular as a devotional reader among Anabaptists and Mennonites as Eusebius (*q.v.*).

In a Hutterite codex of 1592 (now Bratislava City Library, Msc. no. 10, formerly Bratislava no. 215, with Beck Cod. XIV) there is a hymn entitled:

"Von der Zerstörung der Stadt Jerusalem, aus Josephus, dem Geschichtsschreiber, reimweis gestellt durch Hans Rogolin." No Rogolin is known, but only a hymnwriter Rogel (*q.v.*), one of whose hymns is found in the *Ausbund*. Most likely it is this Rogel, a schoolteacher of Augsburg, who composed this hymn. How it came into a Hutterite codex is not known.

The other instance of use of Josephus is Schabaelje's (*q.v.*) well-known book *Wandelnde Seele* (1635), a devotional reader composed of three interviews of the wandering soul through the ages. The third and last interview is with a certain Simon Cleophas, an eyewitness of the fall of Jerusalem. Obviously the material for this imagined interview was taken from Josephus. The popularity of this book was instrumental in making Josephus' story widely known among the Dutch and later German Mennonites. Modern Hutterites also read Josephus, as this writer found upon visiting their homes.

R.F.

Julesburg (Col.) Mennonite Church (MC) was established in 1958 by a group who withdrew from the near-by Chappell (Neb.) Mennonite Church, and built a meetinghouse in Julesburg. It had 23 members in 1958, with John Roth as pastor. It is a member of the Iowa-Nebraska Conference.

M.G.

Kalona Mennonite Church (MC), Kalona, Ia., was organized in July 1958. Two years earlier the Baptist church building, then vacated, was rented to the East Union (*q.v.*) Mennonite Church for a year and services were begun as a branch of the mother congregation which was becoming somewhat crowded. It was served by the East Union ministers for several years, but is now an organized congregation in the Iowa-Nebraska Conference. The charter membership was 130, with Eugene Garber as licensed minister.

A.L.S.

Kanker Mennonite Church (MC), Kanker, M.P., India, was organized in 1953. It had 58 members in 1958, with Pyrelal J. Malagar as bishop and Simon Singh as pastor.

M.G.

Kansas City (Mo.) Mennonite Fellowship (MC) was organized in 1957. Its meetinghouse, a remodeled tavern, was dedicated in 1958 at 2500 Holmes Street. The congregation, the outgrowth of a Voluntary Service unit, in 1959 had 58 members, with Roman Stutzman as licensed pastor. H.S.B.

Kansas Volksblatt, Das, was first published by W. J. Krehbiel and David Goerz about 1897. In April 1899, the Newton Kansan Company bought the *Kansas Volksblatt* from W. J. Krehbiel, and D. R. Krehbiel became its editor. It was then sold to the Western Book and Publishing Company (*q.v.*) in April 1901; in the following year it was combined with the *Hillsboro Post* and called *Post und Volksblatt* (*q.v.*).

J.F.S.

Newton Kansan, Fiftieth Anniversary number. "Minute Book, The Western Book and Publishing Company."

Kargel, Johann (*c*1846-1933), a leader of the Russian Baptists and later of the Evangelical Christians, was the son of a German father and an Armenian mother (birthplace unknown), came to Russia from Bulgaria, which was then under Turkish rule, and thus had Turkish citizenship. He worked at first among the Baptists in the Ukraine, later in St. Petersburg among the Evangelical Christians. He was for a time a friend and co-worker with Johann Wieler (*q.v.*) of the Mennonite Brethren, and with him served as chairman of the first Ukrainian Baptist Conference at Novo-Vassilevka in the Molotschna, April 30-May 1, 1884. For many years he was the interpreter for F. W. Baedeker (*q.v.*) on his Russian evangelistic tours.

H.S.B.

W. Gutsche, *Westliche Quellen des russischen Stundismus* (Kassel, 1956) 66 f.

Kasper, a painter: see **Färber, Kaspar, and Kaspar.**

Kelowna (B.C.) **First** Mennonite Church (GCM) organized in July 1947 and built its church in 1951. The membership in 1957 was 45. In 1959 the minister in charge of the congregation was John P. Vogt. He was assisted by Jacob A. Janzen and Jacob H. Enns.

M.G.

Kernstown (Va.) Mennonite Church: see **Winchester** (Va.) Mennonite Church.

Kingview Mennonite Church (MC), in East Scottdale, Pa., a member of the Allegheny Conference, begun as a mission Sunday school in 1906, was organized as a congregation in January 1955. In 1958 it had 59 members, with Edwin Alderfer as pastor. The meetinghouse was built in 1952. H.S.B.

Kiowa County Memorial Hospital, Greensburg, Kan., built by the community in 1950, has been operated by the Mennonite Board of Missions and Charities (MC) since 1954. H.S.B.

Kishacoquillas Valley, Mifflin Co., Pa., is the beautiful valley of the Kishacoquillas Creek extending 26 miles from Mill Creek on the southwest to Reesville on the northeast, between Stone Mountain (west side) and Jacks Mountain (east side), at its widest point some 4 miles across. The chief towns in the valley are Allensville and Belleville. In the *c*160 years since the first Amishmen came to the valley the Amish and their descendants have built solid communities, until in 1959 there were approximately 1500 baptized members, distributed among 12 congregations. (See **Mifflin County.**)

H.S.B.

S. W. Peachey, *Amish of Kishacoquillas Valley* (Scottdale, 1930).

Kissling, Hans: see **Kiessling, Hans.**

Kleinmichel: see **Matschidl, Michael.**

Klein-Werder: see **Marienburg Werder.**

Kliewer, Jakob (1743-1827), elder of the Frisian Mennonite Church of Danzig from 1798, was born Jan. 7, 1743. He continued in this capacity as co-elder with Peter Tiessen (*q.v.*) when the Flemish and Frisian congregations united in 1808. He died Oct. 5, 1827. After his death and the death of Peter

Tiessen, Jacob van der Smissen (*q.v.*) became elder and the change from the lay ministry to the theologically trained ministry was completed.   C.K.

H. G. Mannhardt, *Die Danziger Mennonitengemeinde* (Danzig, 1919) 141, 157.

Knollys Society, Hanserd, named after an English Baptist leader by that name who lived 1599?-1691, was organized in 1845 in London for the reprinting of early Baptist writings and the publication of original records. It dissolved after issuing ten volumes, two of which were an English translation of pp. 1-371 of the second part of the 1685 Dutch edition of van Braght's *Martyrs' Mirror,* edited by Edward Bean Underhill. The issue bore the title, *A Martyrology of the Churches of Christ, Commonly Called Baptist, during the Era of the Reformation* (London, printed for the Society by J. Haddon, 1850, 1853).   H.S.B.

Konferenz: see **Conference.**

Kouts (Ind.) Mennonite Church (GCM), now extinct, was organized in 1918 with 9 members and joined the Central Mennonite Conference (*q.v.*) in that year. Its high point of membership was 42 in 1944. A. D. Egli, the first minister, served 1918-*c*32. The group never had a meetinghouse of its own.   H.S.B.

Kraemer, Gustav (1863-1948), born at Wissen an der Sieg (district Koblenz), Germany, first a Protestant state church pastor, 1887-90, at Düsseldorf-Gerresheim in a metropolitan congregation, and 1892-1901 at Dachwig (district of Erfurt) in a village congregation, then served as Mennonite pastor in Crefeld (*q.v.*) 1903-36 and for several additional years during World War II as substitute for his successor Dirk Cattepoel. His health was never robust. His sermons attracted Mennonites and others, in Crefeld and Neuwied (*q.v.*), in Hanover (*q.v.*) and Berlin (*q.v.*), and in 1942 also in Heubuden (*q.v.*). In 1905-48 he published the *Monatsblätter der (altevangelischen) Mennonitengemeinde(n) Crefeld (und Emden).* He took care of the dying congregations of Cleve (*q.v.*) and Goch (*q.v.*). From 1908 he represented his congregation in the Vereinigung (*q.v.*) and has to his credit particularly the organization of the Prediger-Ruhegehalts-Kasse (Ministers' Pension Foundation).   E.C.

Kroeker, Peter M. (1840-1915), a Mennonite (Kleine Gemeinde) leader, was born June 20, 1840, in Russia, the youngest of the six children of Franz Kroeker (1799-1853). His mother was a Martens, born 1798 in Prussia, and died 1861 in Russia. Peter M. Kroeker's wife was a Braun. Three sons and three daughters were born to them: Margaretha (Mrs. Abram D. Loewen), Anna (Mrs. Cornelius J. Loewen), Peter B. Kroeker, Franz B. Kroeker, and Jakob B. Kroeker. All three of his sons and one of his older brothers became ministers of the church. Peter M. Kroeker was ordained as minister at Borozenko, Nikopol, in 1871. In 1874 the family migrated to Canada and settled in Rosenort, near Morris, Manitoba. In 1878, when P. Toews with the other ministers and part of the church joined the Church

of God in Christ (Mennonite), only Peter Kroeker, his brother Franz Kroeker, and Peter Baerg, near Steinbach, remained as ministers with the Kleine Gemeinde. Peter officiated as elder for approximately 30 years. He died April 15, 1915.   D.P.R.

Kuchenbecker, Hans (Pauli), of Hatzbach near Marburg, Hesse, a leader among the Anabaptists in Hesse in the last quarter of the 16th century. He came to Hatzbach *c*1570, after having earlier lived in Treysa and Homberg, driven from both places because of his Anabaptism. When called before the court at Marburg on Feb. 5, 1577, he freely confessed his faith. In a document of Feb. 17, 1577, he is called "their captain and head, who teaches and preaches for them," although he denied being a preacher and said only that "when they get together they speak together about their faith." Later (examination in June 1578) he admitted preaching at the Anabaptist meetings and justified it. He said at the same time "he and his brethren were Swiss Brethren, they were not agreed with those in Bohemia"; he had been baptized 10 years earlier (1568) by brethren at the Rhine. His testimony on this occasion is very significant material. Nothing further appears in the Hesse records about Kuchenbecker. In 1587 he was still active, however, since *TA Hessen* prints a brief letter from a Moravian elder, Hans Miller of Stignitz, to "Kuchen Hanssn, who is a Swiss minister." (*TA Hessen.*)   H.S.B.

Kulak (Russian word meaning fist), a term introduced during the days of Stalin's rigid collectivization after Lenin's death. Its origin, however, may go back to an earlier date. It refers to the middle class of the peasant society which was blamed for the delay of the collectivization and socialization process within the Soviet system. The kulaks were sent into exile in great numbers as a warning example and to speed up the realization of the Soviet policies. The Mennonites belonging to the middle class were particularly affected by this process. (See also **Concentration Camps, Russia.**)   C.K.

Kurgan district and city are located on the Trans-Siberian Railroad in Asiatic Soviet Russia. This region was established during World War II out of the eastern part of the Chelyabinsk district (*q.v.*), with the city of Kurgan as capital. It is bounded on the east and south by the Kazakh S.S.R. Some Mennonites who were exiled before and during World War II are located in this region. (See **Siberia.**)   C.K.

Kurland, a former Russian province on the eastern shore of the Baltic, now constitutes the Kurzeme and Zemgale provinces of the Latvian S.S.R. According to Friesen, there was a Kurland Mennonite Church before World War I. The members, scattered over various districts, received permission to organize a congregation in 1902. In that year the elder was Johann Wollberg and the congregation consisted of 10 families, 38 members, with a total of 61 persons. The value of the property estimated for the purpose of establishing support due for Mennonite forestry service was 15,000 rubles. It is not known what happened to these Mennonites. **They**

were evidently Prussian Mennonites who had moved into the Baltic area. (Friesen, *Brüderschaft*, 691, 720.) C.K.

La Tena Church of God in Christ Mennonite Church, Chihuahua, Mex., had a membership of 21 in 1959, with Henry B. Koehn as minister. Since 1947 the mission had been listed under Agua Nueva, Saltillo, and La Junta, but since 1957 at La Tena. M.G.

Lake Winnipeg Mission Camp, located on Lake Winnipeg, 70 miles north of the city of Winnipeg, Man., started in 1948, is owned and controlled by a private corporation of members of the M.B. church. F.C.P.

Lambert, George (1853-1928), Mennonite Brethren in Christ minister, was born in Northampton County, Pa., May 11, 1853, the son of David and Catherine Lambert. In 1872 he married Amanda Gehman, daughter of William Gehman of Vera Cruz, Pa. They had eight children, one of whom, Rose, was a missionary at Hadjin, Turkey, for a time. In 1878 he entered the ministry of the M.B.C. Church (ord. 1881), holding pastorates in Kent County, Mich., and in Elkhart County, Ind.—at Southwest, Wakarusa, Bethel, and Jamestown. In 1896 he transferred his membership to the Mennonite Church (MC) at Prairie St., Elkhart, Ind., and in 1898 moved to Elkhart, where he resided until his death on June 30, 1928. He was the agent for the Home and Foreign Relief Commission (*q.v.*) in taking a shipload of wheat to India at the time of the great famine in 1898, which led to the founding of the Mennonite (MC) Mission in India. He wrote *Around the Globe and Through Bible Lands* (Elkhart, 1896) and *India, the Horror-Stricken Empire, Containing a Full Account of the Famine, Plague, and Earthquake of 1896-97. Including a Complete Narration of the Relief Work Through the Home and Foreign Relief Commission* (Berne, 1898). H.S.B.

Lambsheim, a village about 6 miles northwest of Ludwigshafen in the Palatinate, Germany, which Christian Hege assumes to be identical with "Lambesheym," an Anabaptist congregation, whose representatives signed the Concept of Cologne (*q.v.*) of 1591. H.S.B.

Chr. Hege, *Täufer in der Kurpfalz* (Karlsruhe, 1908).

Landsmannschaft der Deutschen aus Russland, with headquarters at Stafflenbergstrasse 66, Stuttgart, Germany, an organization of former residents of Russia of German background, including Mennonites, aims to give legal, cultural, and economic advice to those who are in need of this help. The organization maintains a list and addresses of such residents of Russia. It publishes the monthly paper *Volk auf dem Weg* and the annual *Heimatbuch der Deutschen aus Russland*. The 1959 and earlier volumes contain highly significant articles pertaining to German settlements in Russia, biographical sketches of leaders, many significant maps, and a bibliography of the German element in Russia. Most of this information has significant bearing on Mennonite research. C.K.

Larned (Kan.) Mennonite Church (MC): see **Pleasant View** Mennonite Church, Larned (Supplement).

Lashburn (Sask.) Mennonite Brethren Church is located in town on Highway 5 about 150 miles northwest of Saskatoon. The church was organized with 5 members in 1936. It had 23 members in 1957, with A. H. Dueck as leader. HE.J.W.

Latschar Mennonite Church (MC), located near the small village of Manheim, Waterloo County, Ont., some 6 miles west of Kitchener, was organized *c*1832. The first meetinghouse, of logs, was built in 1839 on land conveyed by Isaac Latschar. A stone structure replaced it in 1853, followed by a brick church in 1908, enlarged in 1923. The first-known minister was Jacob Hallman (1803-78), who came from Montgomery County, Pa., in 1822. He was probably ordained in 1836. An outstanding minister was Moses S. Bowman (1819-98), ordained in 1859, who began a Sunday school in 1874. Manasseh Hallman, a grandson of Jacob, was ordained preacher in 1907 and bishop in 1910. In 1958 the membership was 135, with Osiah Horst as pastor. H.S.B.

Laurel Street Mennonite Church (MC) is located at Laurel and Fremont Streets, Lancaster, Pa. It is the outgrowth of a mission started in 1945 on Groff Avenue, which moved to the present location in 1947. It is now an organized congregation; it had 37 members in 1958, with Ira Nafziger as pastor. I.D.L.

Laurens de Schoenmaker: see **Schu(e)ster, Lorenz.**

Lawrenz Schuster: see **Schu(e)ster, Lorenz.**

Lebanon (Ore.) **Community Hospital,** built by the community in 1948 (1922), has been administered by the Mennonite Board of Missions and Charities (MC) since its construction. H.S.B.

Lebanon (Ore.) Mennonite Church (MC), located at 2100 South Second Street, was organized in 1957 and its new church was dedicated in 1958. George M. Kauffman was the pastor of its 38 members in 1959. M.G.

Leendertz (II, 306): Supplement. Willem Leendertz (b. 1883) was pastor at Nes 1909-22, obtained the Th.D. degree in 1913 with a dissertation on Sören Kierkegaard published at Amsterdam in 1913. From 1946 to 1953 he was professor at the Amsterdam University and at the Mennonite Seminary, where he had been lecturer since 1934. His field was philosophy, ethics, and dogmatics. He wrote numerous scholarly books and articles. His brother Joannes Mathias (b. 1885) was pastor at Wieringen 1910-23, Koog-Zaandijk 1923-27, and Haarlem 1927-50. He served for many years on the executive committee of the Dutch Mennonite Mission Association, was among the founders in 1917 of the Gemeentedag (*q.v.*) movement, and an early and active member of the Dutch Mennonite peace group.

Lelie, De, a few houses on Bloemstraat at Amsterdam, Holland, since the 18th century used as living quarters for aged members of the Amsterdam

Mennonite congregation. There is room for four married couples and four unattached women.

vdZ.

Letter of Intercession: see **William of Orange.**

Leutesdorf, a town on the west side of the Rhine, some 5 miles from Neuwied, location of the Mennonite Home for the Aged, Marienburg, and the grave of C. F. Klassen (*q.v.*, d. 1954) which is located in the cemetery attached to the home.   H.S.B.

Leuven (Louvain), a town in Belgium (1949 pop. 37,220), the seat of a Catholic university, which in the 16th century was a bulwark of Catholic orthodoxy, watching all kinds of heresy. Its theological faculty had eleven books by Erasmus (*q.v.*) put on the Index. A number of Dutch inquisitors fighting the Reformation, some of whom were very active against Anabaptism and Mennonitism, were educated at the Leuven university.

In Leuven there are but scant traces of Anabaptism: Anthoinette van Rosmers, executed at Leuven in 1543, who is said to have been an Anabaptist, was in fact Lutheran. Lemken (*q.v.*) is said to have preached here, but if this is true his results were insignificant. The eight persons burned at the stake at Leuven in January 1526 were apparently Sacramentists (*q.v.*).   vdZ.

W. Bax, *Het Protestantisme in het Bisdom Luik . . . I* (The Hague, 1941) *passim;* L. E. Halkin, *La Reforme en Belgique sous Charles-Quint* (Brussels, n.d., 1957) 44.

Licht und Hoffnung, a 32-page 8 x 10½ in. monthly journal established by J. A. Sprunger (*q.v.*) in 1893 and edited and published by him until his death in 1911, then by his widow until her death in 1934. Vol. IV, No. 2, indicates that it was printed by the Mennonite Publishing Company at Elkhart, Ind., but the place of publication was Chicago, Ill. Sprunger at that time operated a rescue mission at the southwest corner of Harrison Street and May Street. The content of this number indicates that the journal represented a type of piety tinged with what later became known as "holiness" or "pentecostal," and also promoted a deaconess hospital in Cleveland and the support of Armenian orphans. It professed to be nondenominational.   H.S.B.

Liége (III, 341): Supplement. Among the fifteen craftsmen who were banished from Liége in 1533 for heresy and the 36 others who were pardoned, there were undoubtedly some Anabaptists. In the same year (1533) Jean Bomeromenus, a book printer, Lambert van Buren, and Jean Stordeur (*q.v.*), who are indicated as Anabaptists, saved their lives by leaving Liége. Hans Zurelius, a book printer who fled to Strasbourg *c*1538 and later to Ulm, where he collaborated with Sebastian Franck (*q.v.*), was an Anabaptist.

L. E. Halkin, *La Réforme en Belgique sous Charles-Quint* (Brussels, n.d.-1957) 53, 81, 83, 84 f.

Light and Hope, a 16-page 8 x 10 in. monthly nondenominational journal edited and published by J. A. Sprunger (Light and Hope Publishing Co., *q.v.*), first number apparently January 1901. It was published at Cleveland, Ohio, and later at Birmingham,

Ohio. The date of the last number is not known, but the journal was still appearing in April 1909.

H.S.B.

Light and Hope Missionary Society was established by J. A. Sprunger (*q.v.*, 1852-1911) at Berne, Ind., in 1893, as the agency to own and operate the Light and Hope Orphanage (*q.v.*), and a deaconess training school. His Light and Hope Publishing Co. (*q.v.*), established in 1898 at Berne, was a separate though parallel organization.   H.S.B.

Light and Hope Orphanage, founded by J. A. Sprunger and operated by the Light and Hope Missionary Society, was opened April 1, 1893, at Berne, Ind. In 1901 the orphanage was moved to a location 2 miles northeast of the village of Birmingham, Ohio, 10 miles northwest of Oberlin, where some 550 acres were bought and substantial buildings erected. This institution became the headquarters for the Light and Hope Missionary Society with its deaconess training school. Its capacity was 125-50 persons. The school for the institution employed four teachers. The Light and Hope Publishing Company was also located here with its print shop, publishing the two journals, *Licht und Hoffnung* and *Light and Hope,* the promotional journals which raised finances for the whole complex of Light and Hope enterprises, as well as a series of books, some by Sprunger himself. A hospital was also operated in Cleveland. Upon the death of Sprunger in 1911, the Cleveland and Birmingham properties were sold and Mrs. Sprunger moved back to Berne.   H.S.B.

Light and Hope Publishing Company was founded about 1898 by J. A. Sprunger, a Mennonite minister living at Berne, Ind., who had been ordained in Switzerland in 1890, but was a member of the Berne Mennonite (GCM) Church. He was very close to the newly formed Missionary Church Association (*q.v.*) about the same time. The company published the journal *Licht und Hoffnung* (*q.v.*) and the English counterpart *Light and Hope* (*q.v.*). Sprunger, a wealthy millowner, also operated a deaconess training school and an orphanage by the same name, later also a hospital. Among the workers in both print shop and orphanage in Berne were William Egle, H. C. Barthel, and John Horsch. In 1902 Sprunger moved both the orphanage and the publishing company to Cleveland and soon to Birmingham near Cleveland. Here H. J. Dyck joined the group of workers. Numerous workers from "Light and Hope" went as missionaries to China under the H. C. Barthel mission. Sprunger died in 1911. The print shop was then sold to George Lambert, a minister in the M.B.C. church. It later became the Gospel Herald Publishing Company operated by H. B. Musselman, an M.B.C. minister from Eastern Pennsylvania. Mrs. J. A. Sprunger moved back to Berne upon her husband's death, taking the publishing company and the journal with her, which she owned until her death in 1934. At her death the company and the journal were bought by Christian H. Musselman, who had come to Berne in 1913, and founded there in 1925 the Economy Printing Concern. After Musselman took over the Light and

Hope Publishing Company he continued to sell the remaining books of J. A. Sprunger, especially the two-volume work *The Gospel in Types* (English and German editions), also *Outline of Prophecy*. In addition he published other volumes of Bible exposition and sermons, in 1950 a reprint edition of the German *Martyrs' Mirror* and several Mennonite family histories. Musselman was a Mennonite from the Giebelstadt-Würzburg congregation in Germany, who came to Scottdale, Pa., in 1910, and worked in the Mennonite Publishing House until 1913. In 1915 he joined the Missionary Church Association in Berne. He has become in a sense the publisher for the Missionary Church Association.

H.S.B.

Limoges, in France, was the seat of a Mennonite congregation known from correspondence of elders from the Jura with Lorenz Friedenreich in Neuwied in 1783-84 to have been established by four families from the Jura district in Switzerland who settled there. It was, however, dissolved some years later when the families moved to Montbéliard and the southern Sundgau.

vDZ.

D. L. Gratz, *Bernese Anabaptists* (Scottdale, 1953) 86.

Lincoln (Neb.) Mennonite Brethren Church was formed April 5, 1959. Services were temporarily held in another church at 1020 S. 15th Street. J. J. Gerbrandt was the interim pastor.

H.S.B.

Linn County (Oreg.) Amish Mennonite settlement (now extinct) began in 1898, when several Amish families from Arthur, Ill., settled near Hubbard, with Jonas J. Kauffman as the leading bishop. Several families from Iowa joined the group, including minister Jacob Swartzendruber. The congregation was discontinued in 1907 after Bishop Kauffman died. Many families moved to Yamhill County, and others joined the Zion Mennonite Church at Hubbard.

D.E.M.

Logsden Mennonite Church (MC), one mile west of Logsden, Ore., was established as a mission by the Sheridan (*q.v.*) Mennonite Church in 1950. Five years later the Albany church took charge of the Logsden congregation and in July 1956 it was organized as a church, with 19 charter members. Located in a logging community, where there is a large turnover of population, church membership has fluctuated, but in 1959 there were 41 members of whom 18 were no longer living in the community. Eugene Lemons was serving as the licensed pastor of the congregation.

M.G.

London (England) (III, 387 f.): Supplement. A Mennonite center was established in London in 1944 at 68 Shepherd's Hill by the Mennonite Central Committee which had been engaged in a modest program of relief and social service in England since May 1949. Besides serving as headquarters for the "Director of Relief in the European Area" (Glen **Miller, May 1940-Feb., 1945**; Sam Goering 1945, Howard Yoder 1945-46), it was the base for some clothing distribution. In Sept., 1946, the center was turned over to the Brethren Service Committee, and the MCC European headquarters was moved to Amsterdam and then to Basel, Switzerland. John E. Coffman, who had served as an MCC worker in England since 1940, stayed on in London after the closing of the center, serving in a local mission. From 1948 he has served as the London agent of the Menno Travel Service (*q.v.*). In 1952 the Mennonite Board of Missions and Charities (MC) established a Mennonite center for religious work in London, which has been located at 14 Shepherd's Hill since 1954. Quintus Leatherman has been the minister in charge, but no congregation is contemplated. In 1954 the Mission Board opened direct mission work at the Free Gospel Hall, 39 Grafton Terrace, with John E. Coffman as pastor. In 1958 the membership here was 10.

Lost Creek Mennonite Church (MC), Hicksville, Ohio, located 2 miles west of Farmer, on Highway 249, is a member of the Ohio and Eastern Conference. It was organized in 1947 and worships in a former Presbyterian church. The membership in 1959 was 40, with Ralph Yoder as pastor. M.G.

Lost Creek Mennonite Church (MC), in the Lancaster Conference, is located one mile south of Oakland Mills, Juniata County, Pa. Mennonite families named Musser, Sherck, Shellenberger, and Funk moved into this locality in the late 18th century and by 1819 had a log meetinghouse for worship and school. After a few enlargements a new brick structure was built in 1869. A large old cemetery adjoins the church. This was the home congregation of Bishop Jacob Graybill, and preachers Michael Funk, Christian Auker, Henry Shelley, Samuel Gehman Sr. and Jr., Jacob Kurtz, William Graybill, and William Sieber. Sunday school was opened in 1891. The congregation is a part of the Delaware Circuit. The membership in 1958 was 97, with Raymond Lauver as minister. I.D.L.

Lost Creek School, located 1½ miles west of Ophir in Morgan County, Ky., where Mennonites (MC) under the Virginia Mennonite Board of Missions and Charities conducted regular Sunday services and taught the public school 1943-53. There were two baptized members and four resident workers at Lost Creek at the last report. It was last listed in the 1953 *Yearbook and Directory*. L.C.S.

Lostwood (N.D.) Mennonite Church (GCM) in Mountrail County, now extinct, was founded in 1923 by five families with 12 charter members, who had settled here from Mountain Lake, Minn., 1916 ff. The meetinghouse was built two miles west of Lostwood in 1923. In 1929 the membership reached its high point with 60. Because of the drought the congregation dissolved in 1937, the families moving mostly to Warroad, Minn., where they organized the Woodland Mennonite Church. H.S.B.

Louvain: see **Leuven.**

Lower Mennonite Church: see **Maple Hill** Mennonite Church.

Ludenburg: misspelling of Lundenburg (*q.v.*).

Lustgärtlein: see **Geistliches Lustgärtlein.**

Luxembourg-France Mennonite Mission (MC, now called Europe Mennonite Mission), founded in 1951 by the Eastern Mennonite Board of Missions and Charities, in 1958 had two stations in Luxembourg (*q.v.*) at Esch and Dudelange, one in France at Thionville, and one in Germany at Neumühle bei Landsthal (Palatinate) with 10 workers. The mission co-operates with the small local Mennonite church in Luxembourg, which has its meetinghouse at Rosswinkelhof near Consdorf, canton of Echternach. The mission is one of the very few Protestant efforts in Luxembourg. In 1958 it had five members. H.S.B.

Lynside Mennonite Church (MC), Lyndhurst, Va., a member of the Virginia Conference, was organized in 1954 when 24 members and a minister withdrew from the Mountain View (*q.v.*) congregation. The meetinghouse, built in 1954, is located 4 miles south of Waynesboro and 3 miles south of Lyndhurst. In 1958 the membership was 124, with Silas Brydge as pastor. H.S.B.

Lyon Street Mennonite Church, Hannibal, Mo.: see **Mennonite Mission Church**, Hannibal, Mo.

McMahon (Sask.) Mennonite Brethren Church, 25 miles southeast of Swift Current, was organized in the spring of 1927 with 21 members. Jakob Derksen was its first pastor. In 1957 it had 20 members, with H. F. Klassen as pastor. He.J.W.

McMinnville (Tenn.) Evangelical Mennonite Church was established in 1949. It had 12 members in 1957, with Melvin Billings as licensed minister. The founder of this work was Rev. Henry Amstutz, with home missionaries Ellen Hochstetler and Edna Amstutz. R.Sho.

McPherson (Kan.) **First** Mennonite Church (GCM), originally a home mission project of the Western District Conference, was organized as a church on July 29, 1945. The church building was dedicated Oct. 30, 1949. Pastors have been Roland P. Goering and Henry W. Goossen, the pastor in 1958, when the membership was 146. M.G.

Madison Avenue Chapel (MC), Newport News, Va., a Negro mission established by the Warwick River (*q.v.*) congregation in 1952, changed its name to Calvary in 1958, when it had 10 members, with Nelson Burkholder as pastor. H.S.B.

Madrid (Neb.) **First** Mennonite Church (GCM) was organized in 1927 and worships in a meetinghouse purchased from the Methodists in 1928. It had 36 members in 1958 and B. H. Janzen was its pastor. M.G.

Manitoba Mennonite Historical Society was organized April 25, 1958, to promote the study of Manitoba Mennonite history and collect and preserve materials relating to it. H.S.B.

Manson (Iowa) Mennonite Church (GCM) was in existence 1904-7, Peter Schantz having the oversight.

Maple Grove Beachy Amish Mennonite Church, located 4 miles east of Sheakleyville, Pa., was organized in 1929. The church was built in 1942. In 1959

the congregation had 51 members, with Valentine P. Yoder serving as its bishop. M.G.

Maple Grove Conservative Mennonite Church, located 1½ miles south of Hartville, Ohio, was organized in 1922. The meetinghouse is a remodeled schoolhouse which was first used in 1927. In 1958 the membership was 126, with Frank Dutcher as pastor. H.S.B.

Maple Hill Mennonite Church, formerly known as Lower Mennonite Church, 3½ miles southwest of Wadsworth, Ohio, a member of the Wisler (OOM) Mennonite Conference since 1872, before that of the Ohio Mennonite Conference, originated about 1831. It was one of the two meetinghouses of the congregation established in Medina County by settlers largely from Bucks County, but also from Lancaster County, Pa. From 1830 to 1840 the following preachers arrived in the settlement: William Oberholtzer (1830), Jacob Koppes (1832), Abraham Rohrer (1832), Daniel Kreider (1837 from Ontario), and Samuel Koppes (1840). Abraham Rohrer served as bishop 1834-d.78. The meetinghouse may have been built about 1833 although the oldest deed for the property, assigned to the Mennonite minister, is dated June 30, 1837. A new meetinghouse was built in 1881 and remodeled in 1949.

The Wisler (*q.v.*) division of 1872 led to the withdrawal of this congregation from the Ohio Conference, although the deacon Jacob Kreider (d. 1896) and some 25 members remained with the Ohio Conference and used the second (Guilford) meetinghouse of the congregation until 1893 (built 1856), when they built the Bethel meetinghouse and became known as the Bethel congregation (*q.v.*). Later bishops were Isaac L. Good (1841-1917), ordained 1891, and Moses G. Horst (1875-). In the division of 1907 the Maple Hill congregation remained in the Wisler Conference and did not follow the more conservative faction.

In 1959 the membership was 29, with Moses Horst still serving as bishop, and Paul G. Horst and Abram B. Good as ministers. (See **Lower** Mennonite Church, which this article supplements.) H.S.B.

Maple Lawn Beachy Amish Mennonite Church, Nappanee, Ind., is located one mile north and one and one-half miles west of town. The congregation was organized in 1940 and its church built in 1943. Its membership was 95 in 1959, with Steve Yoder as bishop. M.G.

Maria of Monschau: see Montjoie.

Marienburg, the first of the three homes for the aged operated for the care of aged Mennonite refugees from West Prussia by the German Mennonite organization known as Mennonitische Heime e.V. (*q.v.*), established in 1949 at Leutesdorf a. Rh., about 5 miles down the Rhine from Neuwied on the west bank. With a capacity of some 75, it is self-supporting through a government per capita subsidy aided by MCC food. H.S.B.

Marlboro (Ohio) Conservative Mennonite Church was organized in 1955. In 1959 the membership was 102, with Jerry S. Miller as pastor-bishop. A remodeled building located in the village of Marlboro was made the meetinghouse in 1955.   H.S.B.

Marshall Martin Box Gospel Mennonite Brethren Church is a rural church 3½ miles north of Marshall, Ark. In 1957 it had 52 members, with Floyd Born as pastor. It was founded in 1947 and its church was constructed in 1949.   M.G.

Martin Jansen Korendrager: see **Maerten Jansz Corendrager.**

Matthys, Jan: see **Jan Matthijs.**

Mayfair Mennonite Church (GCM), Ave. D and 35th St., Saskatoon, Sask., was organized in 1952, and its meetinghouse built in 1958. In 1959 the membership was 174, with Peter G. Sawatzky as pastor.   H.S.B.

Maysville Conservative Mennonite Church is located one mile east and one and one-half miles south of Apple Creek, Ohio. It was organized in 1949 and the church was built in 1954. There were 142 members in 1959. Tobias Byler was the bishop and David L. Stutzman and Wilfred J. Neuenschwander the ministers.   M.G.

Meadow Mountain Mennonite Church (MC), Swanton, Md., had its beginning in 1938, when Sunday school and preaching services were begun in a school south of Grantsville. A brick church was constructed in 1948 under the Casselman (*q.v.*) church. In 1957 Roy L. Kinsinger was the minister of this congregation of 30 members.   M.G.

Meadville (Pa.) **First** Mennonite Church (MC) was organized in 1953 as an independent congregation, after having existed a number of years as a mission under the Ohio Mission Board. Its meetinghouse, built in 1934 and remodeled in 1954, is located at 339 Wadsworth Avenue in Meadville. In 1959 it had 65 members, with Herman F. Myers as pastor.   H.S.B.

Mecklenburg, former German province lying between Holstein and Pomerania, was the seat of a short-lived Mennonite settlement of refugees from Russia made in 1921 and sponsored by the Mennonitische Flüchtlings-Fürsorge (*q.v.*). The location was Lockwisch-Westerbek near Schönberg, about 10 miles northwest of Neuruppin in the far southeast corner of the province. D. Wiebe, who had come out of Siberia in 1918 and settled here in 1920, was the initiator and leader of the settlement. A letter by him to the Mennonite pastor in Hamburg-Altona, published in *Mennonitische Blätter* for November 1921 (p. 85 f.), reports 37 persons in the settlement (M.F.F. reported 5 families, who were hoping to establish a congregation, to be affiliated with Hamburg-Altona). But the settlement was not a success, and nothing further could be learned about it. (See also **Wismar.**)   H.S.B.

Media Mennonite Chapel (MC) is located on the South 5th Street Road, Oxford, Pa. It is a member of the Ohio and Eastern Mennonite Conference and was organized in 1947. Its membership in 1959 was 82, with Leroy D. Umble and Phares I. Lantz as ministers.   M.G.

71

Menno Mennonite Church (GCM), at Watova (Nowata County, Okla.), now extinct, was organized Aug. 8, 1915. The membership reached *c*50 in 1920 when it bought and remodeled a farmhouse as a meetinghouse. When it discontinued Jan. 1, 1927, it had *c*10 members. It never had a resident minister.   H.S.B.

Menno Simons Mennonite Church (GCM), now extinct, at Boyertown, Pa., was the Oberholtzer faction in Boyertown of the Hereford-Bally congregation in the Oberholtzer schism of 1847. It used the old meetinghouse in Boyertown alternately with the M.C. group until 1883, when having lost a lawsuit for exclusive use of the meetinghouse it was forced to surrender it, and built the Menno Simons meetinghouse on East 4th Street. Christian Clemmer was the minister 1847-83, followed by Abraham Gottshall in 1886. In 1936 the congregation dissolved, most of the members transferring to the Hereford (GCM) church some 5 miles away. The membership never was large, having 25 in 1911, and 10 in 1930.   H.S.B.

Menno Travel Service, Akron, Pa., was established by the Mennonite Central Committee in 1947. Its purpose has been to make travel arrangements for MCC workers, voluntary service personnel, Pax men, foreign missionaries, tour groups, and individuals. Although its primary purpose is to serve its own constituency, it has also served other church groups. It has branch offices in Newton, Kan.; Goshen, Ind.; Amsterdam, Netherlands; Asuncion, Paraguay; London, England; Winnipeg, Man.; and Beirut, Lebanon. Its volume of business in 1958 was approximately $650,000. Arthur Voth was the director of the Service.   M.G.

Menno-Friendly Beneficial Association, Philadelphia, Pa., was organized around 1908 and serves primarily the members of the First Mennonite Church in Philadelphia, offering protection to its members in time of disability and death. Up to Jan. 1, 1944, it had paid $28,500 in benefits.   M.G.

Menno-Haven, a church camp owned and operated by the Illinois Mennonite (MC) Camp Association, located about 5 miles southeast of Tiskilwa, Ill., was established in 1958; its first operating season was in 1959.   H.S.B.

Mennonite Aid, Inc., a subsidiary of Mennonite Mutual Aid, Inc. (*q.v.*), was established in 1949 as a Pennsylvania nonprofit corporation to provide a channel for sharing the financial burdens of sickness, disability, and burial.   H.S.B.

Mennonite Aid, Inc., Goshen, Ind., provides hospital-surgical and burial aid. As of Dec. 31, 1958, the hospital-surgical membership included 29,388 adults and children and the burial aid plan 3,336 adults and children. During that year over $592,000 had been paid for hospital-surgical claims and $3,000 for burial aid claims. For 1958 the hospital-surgical assessment per person was $42.50 and per family was twice this amount, including all children up to the age of 18. Burial aid benefits were $750 per adult and $150 per child. During the last half of 1958, the organization paid 79.7 per cent of its members' total hospital charges and 61.3 per cent of their surgical expenses. Although it serves principally members of the Mennonite Church (MC), all branches of Mennonites in the United States are eligible for membership.   M.G.

Mennonite Automobile Aid, Inc., a subsidiary of Mennonite Mutual Aid, Inc. (*q.v.*), was established in 1954 as a Pennsylvania nonprofit corporation to provide collision and comprehensive insurance on a mutual basis. In April 1959 the vehicle registration was 2,924. The home office is at Goshen, Ind.
                                                          H.S.B.

Mennonite Benevolent Society, North Clearbrook, B.C., operates a boarding home for invalids. In 1959 it had 35 guests and a waiting list, but in March of that year its board decided to build a new home accommodating 35 guests. It serves various groups of Mennonites in the Frazer Valley. Gerhard I. Peters was the chairman of the Society.
                                                          M.G.

Mennonite Benevolent Society, Winnipeg, Man., was organized in 1946 for the purpose of owning and operating Bethania Home for the Aged and Infirm (*q.v.*). It has some 200 members, all from Mennonite groups in Manitoba of Russian Mennonite background, and elects 12 directors who in turn appoint an executive council to operate Bethania.   H.S.B.

Mennonite Biblical Seminary, located at Vilardebo 964, Montevideo, Uruguay, was founded in 1956 as a co-operative effort of the Mennonite Church (MC) and the General Conference Mennonite Church for the training of ministers, missionaries, and church workers for the Mennonite churches of South America. It is sponsored and largely financed by the general mission boards of the two Mennonite conferences named above, but the board of directors also includes members appointed by the co-operative Mennonite groups in South America. The Bragado (Argentina) Mennonite Bible School was merged with it in 1958. It is a bilingual school (Spanish and German) on the secondary level. Nelson Litwiller has been the president from the beginning. The enrollment averages 30-40, including some part-time students.   H.S.B.

Mennonite Bookstore, Newton, Kan., was opened on Oct. 19, 1946, at 710 Main Street by the General Conference Mennonite Board of Publication to serve as its retail outlet for the western United States, having had its beginning as the book department of the Mennonite Publication Office (*q.v.*, Supplement). In 1953 the bookstore management was integrated with the Mennonite Publication Office, whose manager then became manager also of the Bookstore. In 1957 an assistant manager was appointed to care for the store. The store was moved to 720 Main Street in March 1955. Managers of the store have been J. M. Suderman 1946-49, A. F. Tieszen 1949-53, Abe M. Wiebe 1953-56, Walter D. Unrau 1956- , Carlyle D. Groves (assistant manager) 1957- .   M.Sh.

Mennonite Brethren Biblical Seminary, founded in 1955 and located in Fresno, Cal., is the result of the merger of the Bible and Theology Department of Tabor College (*q.v.*) and the graduate work at Pacific Bible Institute (*q.v.*). It is owned and operated by the Board of Education of the Mennonite Brethren Church on behalf of the M.B. Church and the K.M.B. Church. Several members of the faculties of each two schools were chosen to form the new faculty. The first president was B. J. Braun and the first dean G. W. Peters. The B.D. and M.R.E. degrees are offered on the graduate level. By the fall of 1956 the school was located on a six-acre campus at the corner of Chestnut and Buller Streets, adjoining the future campus of the Pacific Bible Institute.   H.S.B.

Mennonite Camp Ground Association (MC), founded in 1944, owns and operates Laurelville Mennonite Camp, located 10 miles northeast of Scottdale, Pa., the oldest M.C. camp.   H.S.B.

Mennonite Central Peace Committee, the forerunner of the MCC Peace Section (*q.v.*), was organized on Sept. 30, 1939, to represent the peace committees of seven Mennonite bodies in the United States in preparing for threatening war. Officers were P. C. Hiebert (MB) chairman, E. L. Harshbarger (GCM) vice-chairman and treasurer, and H. S. Bender (MC) secretary. A preliminary organization had already been formed on March 10, 1939, with the same officers. The MCPC adopted a "Plan of Action for Mennonites in Case of War," which outlined a course of united action which was later followed. It also commissioned the MCC to assume the administration of the Civilian Public Service program (*q.v.*), which it did on Dec. 21, 1940. On Jan. 3, 1942, as a result of an overture by the MCPC, the MCC created the Peace Section to take over the MCPC functions, and on Jan. 13, 1942, the Peace Section was set up, and the MCPC dissolved.
                                                          H.S.B.

J. D. Unruh, *In the Name of Christ* (Scottdale, 1952).

Mennonite Commission for War Sufferers: see Mennonite Relief Commission for War Sufferers.

Mennonite Evangelizing and Benevolent Board (MC), the name from 1896 to 1906 of what became the Mennonite Board of Missions and Charities (*q.v.*).   H.S.B.

Mennonite Executive Aid Committee, of Eastern Pennsylvania, a united committee representing the Mennonite (MC) conferences of Lancaster and Franconia (leader Amos Herr) and the Eastern Pennsylvania Conference (GCM, leader A. B. Shelly) to provide financial and other assistance to needy Mennonite immigrants from Russia, was formed in April 1874. Attempts by the Mennonite Board of Guardians (*q.v.*), organized in the Midwest for the same purpose in 1873, to merge with this committee failed. A similar committee was organized in Ontario about the same time, led by Jacob Y. Shantz (*q.v.*).   H.S.B.

Mennonite Foundation, a subsidiary of Mennonite Mutual Aid, Inc. (*q.v.*), was established in 1954 as an Indiana nonprofit corporation to serve as a depository for tax exempt funds, recognized by the United States Treasury Department. It receives bequests, legacies, and other funds on deposit, subject to distribution by the depositors to religious, charitable, and educational causes.   H.S.B.

Mennonite General Hospital (MC), Aibonito, Puerto Rico, a 32-bed hospital built and operated by the Mennonite Board of Missions and Charities, had its origin in 1944 as an outgrowth of a CPS unit. The present building was erected in 1958.   H.S.B.

Mennonite Gospel Mission, Hannibal, Mo.: see **Mennonite Mission Church.**

Mennonite Home Chapel, 6201 Carpenter St., Chicago, Ill.: see **Chicago Mennonite Gospel Mission.**

Mennonite Hospital Society Concordia, Winnipeg, Man., established in 1928 and incorporated in 1930, operates the Concordia Hospital (*q.v.*) and also carries on the Concordia group hospital insurance plan, which covered over 1500 families in 1954, paying for their hospitalization up to three months per year, including doctor's fee, operating room, and X-rays at actual cost, but not including medicines and drugs. The assessments in 1953 totaled $44,844, while the amount paid out was $69,418. It serves the province of Manitoba.   M.G.

Mennonite Immigration Bureau was organized March 3, 1916, at Newton, Kan., to facilitate the anticipated immigration of Mennonites from Russia as soon as the cessation of hostilities in the European War would permit this. Founders of the Bureau were the ministers G. N. Harms, H. P. Krehbiel, P. H. Richert, Abraham Ratzlaff, and P. H. Unruh. G. N. Harms was president and H. P. Krehbiel was secretary. The Bureau carried on extensive correspondence with state and national officials, transportation companies and land companies to prepare the way for Mennonite settlers from Russia. This migration did not materialize in the early years following the war. When it did become possible to bring Mennonites to North America, the Mennonite Settlers Aid Society (*q.v.*) and the Mennonite Colonization Board (*q.v.*) undertook the implementation of the functions previously outlined by the Mennonite Immigration Bureau (H. P. Krehbiel Collection, in BeCL).   J.F.S.

Mennonite Invalid Home of Manitoba, in Steinbach, Man., owned and operated by the Evangelical Mennonite Church (Kleine Gemeinde), a 38-bed institution, was founded in 1946 by Abram Vogt with the purchase of a private home. A new 40-bed home is to be built in Steinbach to replace the present inadequate building, and a second one at Rosenort near Morris of 20-bed capacity. H.S.B.

Mennonite Medical Messenger is a newsletter published by the Mennonite Medical Association four or five times yearly. Early issues were not dated nor numbered, but publication apparently began in March 1949. The editors have been Carl M. Hostetler 1949-50, Lillie S. Kaufman 1950-51, the executive committee of the association 1951-53, Samuel J. Bucher 1953-58, Samuel J. Bucher and Merle Eshleman 1958- . The place of publication has apparently been the address of the editor, i.e., Goshen, Ind.; East Peoria, Ill.; and Harman, W. Va. The page size is 8½ x 11 inches, and the number of pages varies from issue to issue.   N.P.S.

Mennonite Memorial Home (GCM), Bluffton, Ohio, is sponsored by eight Ohio congregations. Its building, which has 20 guest rooms, several at times occupied by married couples, was dedicated March 20, 1955. Mr. and Mrs. Delvin Kirchhofer served as directors of the Home until July 1956, when they were succeeded by Mr. and Mrs. Abraham Duerksen. The *Mennonite Memorial Home News* has been issued quarterly since April 1949.   D.L.G.

Mennonite Mission and Boarding School (CGC), Ganado, Ariz., is located 3½ miles south of Greasewood Trading Post and serves the Navaho Indians. In 1958 it had a membership of 20 with Vernon Giesbrecht as its minister. It was first listed in the Yearbook (CGC) for 1954.   M.G.

Mennonite Mutual Aid of Ontario, Vineland, Ont., organized in 1944 as the Mennonite Sickness Benefit Society of Ontario, serves Mennonite Brethren and General Conference Mennonites primarily in Ontario but in other provinces also. It is not incorporated. It had approximately 2500 members, including children, in 1955. In that year it paid out approximately $46,000.   M.G.

Mennonite Mutual Burial Aid, Halbstadt, Man., begun in June 1940, was serving over 250 families in 1954 in the vicinity of Halbstadt. In 1953 it had paid claims totaling $675, at the rate of $75 per adult and $40 per child.   M.G.

Mennonite Mutual Fire Aid Plan, Hagerstown, Md., was established in 1912 and provides fire and lightning insurance for approximately 475 members of the Washington County, Md.-Franklin County, Pa., Conference (MC). The assessed valuation of property covered in 1953 was approximately $6,773,000 and the amount paid out that year was $5,421.66. Assessments averaged 75 cents annually on $1,000 of property covered.   M.G.

Mennonite Mutual Fire Insurance Company of Saskatchewan, Ltd., Waldheim, Sask., was established in 1917 and covers fire, lightning, and windstorm. In the 1957-58 fiscal year it paid out approximately $21,500 in losses.   M.G.

Mennonite Mutual Hail Insurance Company for Western Canada, Hepburn, Sask., was established in 1916 and is incorporated. In 1958 it had 2,920 members and in the fiscal year 1958-59 had paid total losses of over $144,000 for crops destroyed by storm.   M.G.

Mennonite Mutual Supporting Society of Arnaud-St. Elizabeth, St. Elizabeth, Man., was organized in 1934. It has approximately 700 members. Upon the death of a member $200 burial aid is paid to the survivors.   M.G.

Mennonite Nurses' Association (MC), founded in 1942, had approximately 525 members in 1958. Its organ, *The Christian Nurse,* a 16-page 6 x 9 in. monthly, was merged in September 1958 with *Mennonite Hospitals and Homes.* It holds its annual meeting in connection with the annual meeting of the Mennonite Board of Missions and Charities.

H.S.B.

Mennonite Printing Union: see **Mennonitischer Druckverein.**

Mennonite Publication Office was organized by the Board of Publication (*q.v.*) of the General Conference Mennonite Church in 1939 to provide an office at Newton, Kan., to have charge of all business affairs connected with the publication of General Conference periodicals and Sunday-school materials, a task which had formerly been invested in the manager of the Mennonite Book Concern (*q.v.*), Berne, Ind. The Publication Office now functions as the publisher for the General Conference. In 1956 it adopted Faith and Life Press as its publishing name. Besides serving as a wholesaler for Conference publications the Publication Office maintains three retail stores: Mennonite Bookstore (*q.v.*), Rosthern, Sask.; Mennonite Book Concern (*q.v.*), Berne, Ind.; and Mennonite Bookstore (*q.v.*), Newton, Kan. As part of its publication and distribution functions it also provides an editorial department, art department, Sunday-school order department, and audio-visual library. Following the merger of the Board of Publication and Board of Education, the manager of the Publication Office also served as the business manager of the Board of Education and Publication. Managers have been: J. M. Suderman 1939-46, Bernhard Bargen 1946-51, Abe M. Wiebe 1951-56, Walter D. Unrau 1956- .

M.SH.

Mennonite Sanitarium (GCM) was located in the foothills near Alta Loma, Cal. It was an institution for tubercular patients, established by the Pacific District Mennonite Conference and dedicated March 1, 1914. It was discontinued later.

M.G.

Mennonite Sunday School Mission of the Lancaster Mennonite Conference (MC) was the successor of the organization known as Mission Advocates (*q.v.*), after Bishop Board objection and after they had decided they had "advocated" long enough and needed action. Their first quarterly meeting was held at the Paradise meetinghouse, Jan. 4, 1896, and most of such meetings were held there alternating with Kinzer, until the Eastern Mennonite Board of Missions and Charities became its successor in early 1917 (although organized in 1914 and chartered in 1915). John H. Mellinger was chairman of the Sunday School Mission throughout. The rest of the first organization was John R. Buckwalter assistant chairman, Amos A. Ressler secretary, and Ira L. Hershey treasurer. Red Well Mission and the Intercourse Sunday School soon blossomed, the former attaining unexpected proportions. The Vine Street Mission soon started, with Philadelphia Mission coming to fruition in 1899 and Columbia Mission in 1907. These were days when Mary Denlinger and A. Hershey Leaman of Paradise made the Chi-

cago Mission a reality, and J. A. Ressler of the same area (then living at Scottdale) went to India, Abram Metzler to Martinsburg in Blair County, Pa., and John M. Kreider and others to Palmyra in northeastern Missouri. These were some of the first fruits of the efforts for carrying out the Great Commission in the Lancaster Mennonite Conference and its outreach.

I.D.L.

Ira D. Landis, *The Missionary Movement Among Lancaster Conference Mennonites* (Scottdale, 1938).

Mennonite Yearbook and Almanac: see **Yearbook** of the General Conference Mennonite Church.

Mennonite Youth Farm of the Saskatchewan Mennonite (GCM) Youth Organization (*q.v.*), located three fourths of a mile south of Rosthern, Sask., is owned by the Conference of Mennonites of Canada, but is operated by a board appointed by the Saskatchewan Mennonite Youth Organization. On the farm, bought in 1943, are located the following institutions (with date of founding and capacity): Rosthern Invalid Home (1944, now 54 beds), Children's Home (1947, 8 beds), Crippled Children's Home (1953, 9 beds), Invalid Home for Women mentally retarded (1953, 12 beds), Invalid Home for Men (1955, 11 beds). In 1951 the Herbert Invalid Home was opened at Herbert, Sask. (25 beds) as a branch of the M.Y. Farm, but operated by a board representing the local community churches in Herbert. The various charitable homes are open to all in need regardless of denomination, and inmates actually come from all of Canada, and from several denominations. Since 1954 the Board appointed by the SMYO has been composed of six members. Henry Friesen has been the long-time chairman.

H.S.B.

Mennonite Youth Village (MC), Route 1, White Pigeon, Mich., established in 1949, is owned by the Mennonite Board of Missions and Charities. A summer camp which serves primarily children of non-Mennonite background from city and rural mission churches, it is operated with a welfare and missionary emphasis. Voluntary service units comprise most of the staff each summer. Mervin Yoder has served as manager and camp director since 1952.

M.G.

Mennonitische Forschungsstelle (Mennonite Research Center), at Weierhof, Germany, was founded by the annual meeting of the Mennonitischer Geschichtsverein on May 23, 1948. It has been directed and built up by the president of the Geschichtsverein, Ernst Crous, in his residence at Calsowstrasse 4. It contains (1) archives of nearly 200 files and boxes comprising written copies, newspaper clippings, photographs, etc., arranged according to subjects, and of more than 100 letter files concerning recent events, as well as over 60 West Russian Mennonite church records; (2) a library of some 1,000 volumes dealing with Anabaptists and Mennonites, Pietism, and other movements inside and outside the church, and general church history, as well as a good number of microfilms and a projector for reading arranged according to subjects, and of Mennonite refugees of 1945 ff. By means of a growing lending library and a large correspondence (in 1958 the letter-books numbered 2,670 entries) requests of many kinds or for assistance in research on Anabaptist-Mennonite history such as for dissertation, genealogical studies, etc., could be serviced. E.C.

The "Rechenschaftsbericht der Mennonitischen Forschungsstelle" for 1947-52 and continuations (mimeographed and distributed gratis by the Forschungsstelle) give full information about the work.

Mennonitische Immigrantenbote, Der, the name used in 1924-26 by *Der Bote* (*q.v.*).

Mennonitisches Altersheim e.V.: see **Mennonitische Heime.**

Mennonitisches Hilfswerk Christenpflicht: see **Christenpflicht.**

Mennonitisch-Russische Bibelgesellschaft von Nord-Amerika, office at Hesston, Kan., was a branch of *Licht dem Osten* (*q.v.*) and published the paper *Auf zum Werk* (*q.v.*). The founder and chairman of the organization, and editor of the paper, was Gustav Enss, a Mennonite (GCM) minister, Moundridge, Kan. Other members of the organization were M. H. Schlichting, P. H. Unruh, P. D. Dirks, and P. Z. Wiebe. Originally it was affiliated with the Russian Bible and Evangelization Society of New York, which had been organized in 1919 by Paul Rader, A. C. Gäbelein, W. Leon Tucker, and others. It is probable that the Mennonite branch under Enss was in existence only during 1921-23 when *Auf zum Werk* appeared. C.K.

Mennozentrum was the executive body and office of the Bureau der Molotschnaer Mennonitischen Vereinigung (*q.v.*) in South Russia organized during the Revolution in 1917. At the meeting of the Allgemeiner Mennonitischer Kongress at Ohrloff in August 1917 the following members were elected to the Mennozentrum, or Zentralbureau, with the highest votes: B. H. Unruh (202), Dr. Peter Dück (192), Heinrich Schröder (182), Heinrich Janz (176), Heinrich Epp (177). This executive body played a significant role in negotiating with the temporary governments such as those of Kerensky and Denikin, the German government, and other organizations including the Verband russischer Bürger deutscher Zunge. The first chairman of this executive body was Johann Willms, who was succeeded by B. H. Unruh. At a regional Molotschna meeting of the Kongress at Rückenau, a Studienkommission (*q.v.*) was appointed to investigate settlement possibilities abroad for the Mennonites of Russia. Those elected were A. A. Friesen, B. H. Unruh, Heinrich Warkentin, and Daniel Enns. The latter declined to serve as did also his alternate Jakob Neufeld. Johann Esau joined the Studienkommission temporarily. Not much is known about the activities of the Mennozentrum after this. C.K.

Protokoll des Allgemeinen Mennonitischen Kongresses (August 1917); "Benjamin H. Unruh," *Bote,* Sept. 26, 1951, p. 2.

Midland (Mich.) Evangelical Mennonite Church was established on April 6, 1952. In 1957 it had 41 members, with Charles L. Rupp as pastor. Its church consisted of a converted store building remodeled in 1952. A new building was being planned in 1959. A parsonage was built in 1957-58. R.Sho.

Midway Mennonite Church (MC), Pekin, Ill., is located between Pekin and South Pekin. It was established in 1950 and had 28 members in 1958. Howard Wittrig was its pastor. M.G.

Milan Valley (Okla.) Mennonite (MC) Church, now extinct, was located near Jet in the northwestern part of the state. Among the first settlers were Troyers and Zimmermans, who were organized as a congregation in 1895 by S. C. Miller. The first minister was Simon Hetrick. Their meetinghouse was built in 1897. By 1913 the membership had reached 55. It is last listed in the 1940 *Mennonite Yearbook* with 11 members and Simon Hershberger as minister. M.G.

Milverton (Ont.) **Nursing Home** (MC) was established in 1955 by the Ontario Amish Mennonite Mission Board, capacity 20 beds. H.S.B.

Minneapolis (Minn.) Mennonite Brethren Church is located at 3900 Tenth Avenue South. The church was organized in December 1955 and in 1959 had 28 members. M.G.

Minot (N.D.) Mennonite Brethren Church was organized May 16, 1955, with 38 charter members. Its meetinghouse was built in 1955 at 4th Avenue and 18th Street. In June 1959 the membership was 77, with Abe D. Unruh as pastor. M.A.K.

Missionary Bulletin, organ of the Conservative Mennonite Board of Missions and Charities, began with the first quarter of 1952. It was published quarterly until 1956 or 1957, when it became a monthly. Raymond Byler has been editor from the beginning. The place of printing is Scottdale, Pa. Each issue consists of 8 pages approximately 11 x 8 inches in size. There are occasional illustrations. N.P.S.

Missionary Challenge, organ of the District Mission Board of the Iowa-Nebraska Mennonite Conference, is an illustrated quarterly published since the last quarter of 1948. The editors have been Fred Gingerich 1948-56, Willard E. Roth 1957-58, Clarence R. Sutter 1959- . The place of publication is apparently the address of the editor. The page size is 9 x 6 inches, and the issues have varied from eight to thirty-two pages. GCL has a complete file. N.P.S.

Missionary Light, official publication of the Virginia Mennonite Board of Missions and Charities, has been published at Scottdale, Pa., since January 1941. At first an 8-page quarterly, it was enlarged to a 16-page bimonthly with the March 1948 issue. The editors have been Byard W. Shank, Linden M. Wenger 1951-53, Laban Peachey 1953- . The page size of the first 18 volumes was 10½ x 7¾ inches. With the first issue of 1959 it was reduced to 9 x 6 inches. It is illustrated. N.P.S.

Missioners: see **Hutterite Missioners.**

Moller (Müller), **Lorenz**, of Görmar, a village near Mühlhausen in Thuringia, an active Anabaptist, associate of Ludwig Spon (*q.v.*) of Ershausen, Hans Rinkleben of Oberdorla, and Klaus Scharf of Mühlhausen, was arrested in May 1533 with six others, then freed, arrested again in January 1535 at Mühlhausen, and again released in mid-1535. He seems to have been unstable, and probably at least twice left and rejoined the Anabaptist group in northern Thuringia. Nothing is known of his further career. (Wappler, *Thüringen*.)   H.S.B.

Molotschna Mutual Fire Insurance: see **Molotschna Fire Insurance.**

Montezuma (Ga.) Beachy Amish Mennonite Church was organized in 1953. During that year a used church in Montezuma was purchased. In 1959 the membership was 112, with Jonas H. Hershberger serving as bishop.   M.G.

Moorepark (Mich.) Mennonite Church (MC) was established as an outpost of the Middlebury, Ind., congregation (MC) in 1947. In 1955 the congregation became independent. The meetinghouse was purchased from a former Reformed congregation. At first the preaching was done by Wilbur Yoder, pastor of the sponsoring congregation, but in 1948 Etril Leinbach was ordained preacher; eight years later he became bishop. In 1958 the membership was 63, with Leinbach serving as pastor.   J.C.W.

Mornington Amish Mennonite Church, a member of the Beachy Amish group, was formed in 1904 by a conservative schism from the Poole (Mornington) A.M. congregation (see **Mapleview**) led by Bishop Nicholas Nafziger, hence locally is often called the Nafziger church. Its meetinghouse was built in 1904 about a mile and a half west of the Poole A.M. meetinghouse in Mornington Township, Perth Co., Ont. In 1958 the membership was 175, with Moses Nafziger as bishop and Samuel Nafziger and Joseph Steckley as ministers.   H.S.B.

Morris Run Mennonite Church (MC) is located near Blossburg, Tioga Co., Pa. The start of the work here was occasioned by a Mennonite hunting camp in Fall Brook. Mennonites often attended the Primitive Baptist Church in this rural town when in the community over Sunday, frequently bringing Mennonite preachers with them. At Wheelerville, near by, Grant Noll and others conducted a prosperous summer Bible school for a decade. Upon invitation the Itinerant Evangelism Committee of the Lancaster Conference started a work in the Primitive Baptist Meetinghouse in Fall Brook in 1954. Melvin L. Kauffman was licensed for the work, finally moving into the area and on Jan. 19, 1958, was ordained as pastor. The present membership is 15.   I.D.L.

Mount Bethel Mennonite Church (GCM), now extinct (see **Mt. Bethel,** MC), located in Bangor, Pa., was from 1847 to 1858 a part of the Oberholtzer Conference. Before 1847 it was a part of the Franconia Conference (MC) and after 1858 a part of the Evangelical Mennonites (*q.v.*), led by Wm. Geh-

man. A brick meetinghouse was built in 1822, which was taken over by the Lutherans in 1865. (See **Rothrock**.)   H.S.B.

Mount Hermon Amish Mennonite Church is an independent congregation in Shelby County, near Shelbyville, Ill. The Amish first moved to the county in 1907 from Elkhart County, Ind., in order to be under the direction of John D. Kauffman (*q.v.*), who preached while in an unconscious state. Kauffman was ordained to the office of bishop in 1911. Joseph Reber, who was ordained minister of the congregation in 1912 and chosen to succeed Bishop Kauffman in 1914, was still serving in 1958. The membership of Mt. Hermon in 1957 was 41, with D. M. Ulrich and Christy Christner as ministers.   M.G.

Mount Joy Mennonite Church (MC) is located approximately 8 miles southeast of Calico Rock, Ark., three fourths of a mile off State Road 5. The congregation was organized in 1949 and the church built in 1953. There were 7 members in 1959, with Manasseh E. Bontreger as pastor.   M.G.

Mount Zion Beachy Amish Mennonite Church is located near Staunton, Va., on State Road 652 between 608 and 651. The congregation was organized in 1954 and the church built in 1955. It had 101 members in 1959, with Adam G. Byler as bishop.   M.G.

Mountain Lake Hospital, Mountain Lake, Minn., owned and operated by the Bethel Hospital Association (*q.v.*), was established in September 1905 as the Mennonite (GCM) Hospital. In 1911 the hospital was affiliated with Bethel Deaconess Hospital of Newton, Kan., and was then incorporated under the new name of Bethel Deaconess Hospital. On June 5, 1921, a new 21-bed hospital was dedicated. Several years later the relationship with the Newton hospital was dissolved and the Mountain Lake hospital was given its present name.

The Bethel Hospital Association now operates also the 55-bed Eventide Home, a home for the aged, which was built in 1950 across the street from the hospital. Both institutions are supported by the eight Mennonite churches of four different branches in the Mountain Lake community.   W.E.J.

Mountain View Mennonite Church (MC), a member of the South Central Conference, was organized in 1947. The meetinghouse, built in 1948, is located in the Buffalo community of Baxter County, Ark. In 1959 the membership was 30, with Fred Meyer as licensed minister.   H.S.B.

Mountain View Nursing Home, Glenwood Springs, Col., sponsored by the Mennonite Board of Missions and Charities (MC), was established in 1956 on a leased basis, capacity 31 beds.   H.S.B.

Mutual Aid Service, Inc. (GCM), was organized in 1958 to replace the former committee on Mutual Aid, a subcommittee of the Board of Christian Service, and is designed to carry on the program of mutual aid and brotherhood sharing services sponsored by this board. This program includes the

Hospital-Surgical Aid Plan, Investment Services, Placement Assistance, and Mutual Aid Assistance Loans. Head offices are in the Conference Headquarters at 722 Main, Newton, Kan.   H.S.B.

Nachbarschaftsheim (Neighborhood Center), a term used by the MCC for its service projects in Germany (e.g., Heilbronn and Berlin) and Austria after World War II, in which a barracks or a purchased or rented house was used as a center for such activities as sewing room, youth meetings, boys' clubs, library and reading room, and some clothing and food distribution. Sometimes Sunday school and other religious services were conducted in them also.   H.S.B.

Nampa (Idaho) Mennonite Church (MC). On Dec. 4, 1899, the congregation now bearing the name Nampa Mennonite Church was organized by George R. Brunk, Sr. The meetinghouse built at about that time, located two miles west of Nampa, was known as the Antioch church. In 1906 the Nampa Home Mission was built and dedicated in the city of Nampa. In 1937 a new building was erected at its present location, 9th Avenue and 6th Street N. The congregation now sponsors a branch Sunday school, a Christian day school (est. 1944), summer Bible schools, and various young people's activities. In 1958 the membership was 150, with E. S. Garber as bishop-pastor, and D. A. Good, Harold Hochstetler, and O. D. Yoder as ministers.   R.E.G.

National Heights Mennonite Church (MC), Richmond, Va., organized in 1951, located in the eastern part of the state capital, is the outgrowth of a survey made by Eastern Mennonite College students. A Bible school and a series of meetings were held in a tent in 1948 and 1949 respectively. After this services were held in private homes, and in a rented building. The Virginia Board of Missions and Charities built a brick church in 1955. In 1958 the membership was 36, with Ralph Ziegler as pastor.   H.A.B.

Nebo Mennonite Church (GCM) at Meade, Kan., was organized c1913 with B. A. Wiens as pastor. It existed until 1923.   H.S.B.

Nebraska Aid Committee was organized in the Mennonite Church (GCM) of Beatrice, Neb., in 1884, to bring at least 20 Mennonite families from Khiva (q.v.), Russia, to the United States. The appeal printed in the *Herald of Truth,* April 15, 1884, suggested that $400 per family would be required to bring them to Kansas or Nebraska. The committee consisted of L. E. Zimmerman, John Penner, J. G. Wiebe, Peter Janzen, and John von Steen. A later announcement by Zimmerman, who was a deacon of the Beatrice church and treasurer of the committee, reported that $3,000 had been received and that additional gifts by *Herald* readers could be sent to John F. Funk, who had agreed to forward gifts to the committee. News items in 1884 indicated that some of these families arrived in America that year. The same appeals were made in the *Bundesbote,* and several reports of the migration appeared there, e.g., June 15, 1884, and Sept. 12, 1884.   M.G.

Needlework. No special Mennonite needlework can be reported except the making of quilts, commonly made in group sewings, often as social occasions and also at women's sewing circles, e.g., in the Mennonite Church (MC) and among the Old Order Amish. The intricate designs often used are borrowed or bought commercially; hence there is little original or creative art expression.

Older generations of Mennonite and Amish women of Pennsylvania Dutch background produced a great deal of needlecraft for household use and as gifts. In this category would come embroidered bedspreads, towels, dresser scarves, and pillowcases, hooked and braided rugs, fancy cushion tops, etc. Many of these items had genuine folk art character, often with typical Pennsylvania Dutch motifs, some of which have found their way into art museums and museums of folk art.   H.S.B.

Neffsville Mennonite Church (MC), a member of the Ohio and Eastern Conference, was organized in 1952 largely by members who had withdrawn from the East Chestnut Street Church of the Lancaster Conference. Its meetinghouse, located at the south edge, of Neffsville, Pa., 3½ miles north of Lancaster, was erected in 1957. In 1958 it had 229 members, with Maurice W. Landis as pastor.   H.S.B.

Nehrung (Binnen-Nehrung), located east of the Vistula River near the Baltic Coast, was occupied by Dutch Mennonites coming from the Danzig Werder. They established Holländerdörfer (q.v.) there during the first decades of the 17th century in accordance with a special agreement with the authorities. Among the villages established were Schönbaum, Nickelswalde, Pasewark, and Prinzlaff. They drained swamps and built dams in a territory which had not previously been under cultivation.   C.K.

Horst Penner, *Ansiedlung mennonitischer Niederländer im Weichselmündungsgebiet von der Mitte des 16. Jahrhunderts bis zum Beginn der preussischen Zeit* (Weierhof, Germany, 1940) 23-33.

Ness City, Kan., Mennonite (MC) settlement, now extinct, consisted of 10 members, as reported by H. P. Krehbiel in 1911. J. Mishler served as the minister in this community, located 8 miles southwest of Ness City.   M.G.

Neufeld, Dietrich (1886-1958), a Russian Mennonite writer, adopted the name Dederich Navall when he became a U.S. citizen. He was born at Orloff, Zagradovka, Russia, on Sept. 2, 1886, the son of Dietrich Neufeld and Anna Berg-Neufeld. In 1907 he completed his secondary training by obtaining a teacher's certificate, after which he taught in Russia until 1919. After this he taught in various schools in Germany and studied at the universities of Basel, Heidelberg, Leipzig, and Jena where he received his Ph.D. in 1922. Meanwhile, he spent some time during the Revolution, 1919-20, in Russia, at the Chortitza and Zagradovka settlements. He married Lotte Ross of Emden, Germany, Dec. 21, 1921. His experiences during the Russian Revolution are related in the books *Mennonitentum in der Ukraine* (Emden, 1922), *Ein Tagebuch aus dem Reiche des Totentanzes* (Emden, 1921), and *Zu Pferd 1000 Km* *durch die Ukraina* (Emden, 1922). Navall was a good writer who greatly appreciated the Russian culture and was influenced by Tolstoi.

In 1923 he came to America and taught at Bluffton College 1923-26, then at Antioch College, University of New Mexico, Pomona College, and George Pepperdine College. In America he wrote the drama *Kanadische Mennoniten* (Winnipeg, 1924), published under the pseudonym Novocampus, and *Russian Dance of Death* (Claremont, Cal., 1930) under the pseudonym Dirk Gora. The latter is a translation of the German *Totentanz*. C.K.

New Friedensberg Mennonite Church (GCM) is located 2½ miles west of Vona, Col. The congregation was organized in 1907 and the church built in 1912. It had 20 members in 1959. In 1957 its pastor was J. W. Bergen. **M.G.**

New Home Mennonite Church (GCM), now extinct, was located 2 miles south of Westbrook, Cottonwood Co., Minn., *c*30 miles from the Immanuel church at Delft. It was organized in 1881 by immigrants from Galicia. The last record of the group is in 1950 when it had 20 members, the highest membership having been reached in 1945 with 46 members. The first minister was Daniel Huber, the last E. E. Hubin. **H.S.B.**

Niagara Mutual Funeral Society, Niagara-on-the-Lake, Ont., was an outgrowth of the Vineland Burial Society, forming a separate organization in 1942. As of March 1956 it had 2,146 members from various Mennonite branches in all areas of Canada. It covered total funeral expenses and in 1953 paid out $1,329.75. **M.G.**

Nigeria (Africa) Mennonite Church (MC) was established in March 1959, when nine congregations of independent Christians in Calabar Province in eastern Nigeria were received into the Mennonite Church by Bishop S. J. Hostetler of the Ghana Mennonite Mission (*q.v.*), upon adoption by each church of a confession of faith of twenty articles. Seventy additional congregations have asked for affiliation. Calabar is one of the most thickly populated areas of West Africa and is full of churches and schools of various denominations. **H.S.B.**

S. J. Hostetler, "Nigeria Churches Join Mennonites," *Gospel Herald*, May 5, 1959, pp. 422 f.

Nikolai, Gerhardus: see Nicolai, Gerhard.

Nonconformists, a term originally meaning those Christians who did not conform to the Act of Uniformity in England issued by Queen Elizabeth in requiring all to conform to the form of worship of the Church of England. It has come to refer to all Protestant bodies in England except the Church of England, not only the Congregationalists and Baptists, who were the first nonconformists. **H.S.B.**

North Battleford (Sask.) Mennonite Church (GCM) had its beginning as a mission in 1951, and was organized as a congregation on Jan. 18, 1959, with 28 charter members and Irvin V. Schmidt as elder-pastor. Its meetinghouse is a remodeled former air force mess hall bought in 1953 and moved to its present location at 1291 109th Street in the summer of 1956. **G.G.E.**

North Central Conference Mission Board (MC) was established in 1921 to operate rural missions in the conference area of North and South Dakota, Montana, and Minnesota. **H.S.B.**

North Clearbrook (B.C.) Mennonite Brethren Church, formerly called North Abbotsford M.B. Church (*q.v.*), in 1957 had 421 members, with A. H. Konrad as leader-pastor, and A. J. Friesen as assistant leader-pastor. **H.S.B.**

North Side Mennonite Church (MC), located at 716 North Locust St., Hagerstown, Md., was established as a mission in 1931. It became an organized congregation in 1956, under the Ohio and Eastern Conference. Its building was purchased in 1949 and remodeled to serve as a church. In 1959 the membership was 34, with Harold A. Lehman as pastor. **M.G.**

Northern Light Gospel Mission (MC) was begun as an independent mission in 1938 by Irwin Schantz and Llewellyn Groff of the Lancaster Mennonite Conference. They established missions in northern Minnesota beginning in 1939. Funds are collected for the mission by a bimonthly newsletter, mostly from Eastern Pennsylvania and the Conservative Mennonite Church. In 1951 the mission churches established in the area either were organized as congregations of the North Central Mennonite District Conference, or were placed under the jurisdiction of an organized congregation, under the North Central Mennonite Mission Board, or, as in the case of Kitichi Pines and Cloverdale, under the sponsorship of Conservative Mennonite churches in Iowa. With the nine stations no longer under his responsibility, Schantz turned his attention to northern Ontario and established a home base at Red Lake, Ont., the northernmost point of the highway. Mission activity is now carried on in the Indian reservations in the Lake of the Woods area. In 1957 the staff of workers numbered about fifteen. **M.G.**

Ohm-Stübchen ("anteroom"), a traditional room next to the entrance to a Mennonite meetinghouse in Prussia, Poland, and Russia, was transplanted to North America. The elder, referred to as Ohm (*q.v.*), and the ministers gathered there to make arrangements for the worship service and to wait for the time to start. This was also the room for business meetings and for interviewing members of the congregation. At the beginning of the worship service the elder led the ministers to the pulpit. Entering the sanctuary, he would at times announce "Peace be with you," as was the practice until after World War I in the Beatrice (Neb.) Mennonite Church (GCM). The modern church structure has eliminated this room by possibly making provision for a minister's study. An almost identical room was used (and is in many places still used) in the same way in the meetinghouses of the Mennonite Church (MC) called in Pennsylvania-German "das Kämmerli." In fact, most Mennonite groups in America formerly had this custom. C.K.

Old Mennonites is not the official name of any Mennonite body, but in North America it is often popularly used to refer to the Mennonite Church (*q.v.*) in contrast to various bodies of "New" Mennonites (*q.v.*) which split off from it.   H.S.B.

Olevian (erroneously Olivian *ME* II, 823), **Caspar** (1536-87), Reformed theologian in Germany active as Calvinist leader, at Heidelberg 1560-76, at Berlenburg 1576-84, and at Herborn 1584-87. He was co-author of the Heidelberg *Catechism* (1563), and active in the introduction of Reformed doctrine, polity, and discipline in the Palatinate and Wittgenstein.   H.S.B.

Olive Branch confession: see **Olijftacxken.**

Olivi, Petrus (1248-98), a leader of the Franciscan Spirituals, an offshoot of the great Franciscan order with strong spiritual and apocalyptic tendencies, which finally led to a break with the papacy and subsequent persecution by the Catholic Church. In 1295-96 Olivi wrote his *Postil on the Apocalypse* (an exposition of the Book of Revelation), which began to circulate after his death and soon became a widely used devotional book. In general it follows the eschatological ideas of Joachim de Floris. The papacy is to Olivi the "antichrist," the woman on the beast, etc. Under Pope John XXII, who resided in Avignon, the grave of Olivi was defaced and his bones burned (1318).

Strangely enough, these facts are mentioned in the early part of the Hutterite Chronicle, apparently because the Hutterites were familiar with this strange *Postil*. Its story is, however, shrouded in darkness. No German translation of the book has become known, but it is assumed that the book had a wide circulation, both in Latin and in German, among medieval sectarians such as the Spirituals and the Waldenses. Since both were severely persecuted, they kept their books secret. Perhaps by way of the Waldenses in Upper Austria (Steyr?) the book reached the Moravian Anabaptists by *c*1530. Caspar Braitmichel (*q.v.*) mentions it expressly in his introduction to the Chronicle. Even though the Brethren were not strongly interested in the Book of Revelation, they were apparently attracted by the *Postil*. The *Postil* has been preserved in at least one old Hutterite codex of 1593 (now in Esztergom, Hungary), called *Auslegung der Offenbarung Johannes in 22 Kapiteln*. When the Brethren came to America they brought a copy with them (now unknown), from which Elias Walter (*q.v.*) made several copies (*c*1900).

The story of this book has some significance in view of the question of continuity of the "old evangelical brotherhoods" (*q.v.*). Here, apparently, a book exists which was handed down from Franciscans to Waldenses and thence to the Anabaptists, thus proving contacts of more than superficial nature; it does not, however, prove full continuity and dependence.   R.F.

R. Friedmann, "A Hutterite Book of Medieval Origin," *MQR* XXX (1956) 65-71; E. Benz, *Ecclesia Spiritualis* (Stuttgart, 1934); Zieglschmid, *Chronik*, 39.

Olyftack Confession: see **Olijftacxken.**

Ostrog, Volhynia (*q.v.*), Russia, a town near which Prussian Mennonite settlers from the Graudenz area settled in 1801-12; they had first settled in 1791 at Michalin, southwest of Kiev. The first village settled was Karolswalde (*q.v.*), four miles south of Ostrog. Ultimately the settlement was composed of 9 villages, most of them south of Ostrog. Virtually the entire group emigrated in 1874 to Canton and Pawnee Rock, Kan., and Avon, S.D. H.S.B.

Ozarks Mission (KMB), located at Compton, Ark., established under the Home Missions Committee, was begun in 1949, when Elizabeth Hofer and Anna Klassen came to Kingston, Ark. In 1959 the work was in charge of the William Ratzlaffs at Ponca and Compton, the J. D. Wiencks at Kingston and Elkhorn, and Elizabeth Hofer at Kingston. It consists of Bible teaching in the school at Kingston, Sunday schools, prayer meetings, young people's work, and preaching services. Some 50 have been baptized, but no K.M.B. congregations are organized; the local members organize themselves.
          H.S.B.

Pacific Mennonite Aid Society, Reedley, Cal., was established in 1941. It serves Mennonites in the United States and Canada and has also on its membership roll many missionaries in foreign countries. It is not incorporated. It has paid 58 death claims since its inception, and has accumulated a surplus of over $51,000.00. It passed the 1,000 mark in membership in 1958.   A.A.S.

Pacifism (IV, 105b). Add to Bibliography: Fred Daniels, "Theories of Conscientious Objectors Toward War in the 16th and 17th Centuries" (unpublished Ph.D. dissertation, Univ. of Minnesota, 1954); Ernst Correll, article **Friedensbewegung** (*ML* I, 706-13); Wm. D. S. Witte, "Quaker Pacifism in the United States 1919-42" (unpublished Ph.D. dissertation at Columbia University, 1954); Sibley Mulford, "Political Theories of Modern Religious Pacifism," *American Political Science Review*, June 1943.

Palm Lake Mennonite Church (GCM), now extinct, located near Lake Charles, La., was started *c*1917 by families largely from Gnadenberg church near Whitewater, Kan. Beginning with 12 members, it reached about 30 in 1923, but about 1925 it disbanded. It never had a resident minister nor a meetinghouse of its own.   H.S.B.

Palo Hincado Mennonite Church, Palo Hincado, Barranquitas, Puerto Rico, was begun in 1948, but the first members were received in 1950. The meetinghouse was built in 1956. In 1958 the membership was 36, with Don Heiser as pastor.   H.S.B.

Gladys Widmer, *We Enter Puerto Rico* (Elkhart, 1953).

Pawnee Rock (Kan.) Mennonite Church: see **Bergthal** Mennonite Church, Pawnee Rock.

Peace and Arbitration Committee, appointed at the Annual Conference of the Mennonite Church of Canada (MC) in 1906 to represent the conference in "advancing the cause of nonresistance in every legitimate way," reported to conference and was re-appointed annually until 1922, when a motion was passed to release it. Those appointed to this committee in 1906 were S. F. Coffman (q.v.), L. J. Burkholder (q.v.), and David Bergey (q.v.). In 1911 the committee was increased to four members. The action calling the committee into existence in 1906 included a recommendation that a Peace and Arbitration Association be organized in each member congregation of the conference. At least one congregation responded, for the Mennonite Historical Library at Goshen College has an undated printed constitution of the Mennonite Peace and Arbitration Association located at the Wideman Church (q.v.), York County, Ont. The stated object of this organization was "the promotion of universal and permanent peace, by means of arbitration and by cultivating the spirit of peace and good will among men." It is not known how extensive its membership and activities were, nor how long it lasted.   N.P.S.

Peasants' War, a social revolution in Germany which, though preceded by a 100-year history of tension and occasional outbreaks, broke out in full bloody revolutionary form in June 1524, and was relatively suppressed by May 1525. Beginning at Stühlingen near Schaffhausen it spread northward and westward via the Black Forest and Alsace, as far as Westphalia, Hesse, and Thuringia, and eastward via the Allgäu and Tirol as far as Hungary. After early success, including considerable destruction of castles and monasteries, it was suppressed in pitched battles (Alsace, May 17, 1525; Württemberg, May 12; Franconia, June 2 and 4; Thuringia-Saxony at Frankenhausen, May 15; around Salzburg as late as 1526). The confusion about the origin and character of the revolution, as well as its relation to Anabaptism and to men like Thomas Müntzer (q.v.), has gradually been cleared. Müntzer joined the movement and was captured in the battle of Frankenhausen, but he was not the originator or even a major leader. Hubmaier (q.v.) has been blamed as the originator, and as the author of the Twelve Articles (Oct., 1524) of the peasants, but both charges have been disproved by sound scholarship. The Anabaptists were nowhere implicated; in fact the origin of Anabaptism in 1525 at Zürich came months after the war began. Some of the disillusioned participants (Melchior Rinck, q.v.) and fellow travelers (Hans Hut, q.v.) later joined the Anabaptists (1526-27), but this proves only that Anabaptist preachers found a hearing in the aftermath. Competent Lutheran historians have asserted that the outcome of the Peasants' War, with total failure of the peasants to win any of their otherwise very reasonable and moderate original demands (12 Articles), and the vicious attacks on the revolutionaries by Luther in which he strongly took the side of the nobles, led to the turning away of the mass of the peasantry from the Reformation. In this disillusioned mass it would be probable that some turned to Anabaptism, which was already critical of Luther and the state church system, and whose offer of the free church with local lay leadership would certainly find sympathy among the peasants, one of whose twelve articles had called for the local election of the pastor by the people and

the administration of the tithe and church finances locally by those who paid them. Franz (p. 479) says flatly, "Many peasants went over (flüchteten) to the Anabaptists. The suppression of the remnants of the Peasants' War and the Anabaptists henceforth went hand in hand." That the Anabaptist concept of Christianity as earnest discipleship under the lordship of Christ, of the church as a free believers' church, and of the ethic of love and sharing had revolutionary implications for traditional European society and Christianity is clear. But nothing is clearer than that the Anabaptist ethic of love and nonresistance made it impossible for Anabaptism to be revolutionary in the sense of the Peasants' War. This does not deny the fact of fringe personalities or fellow travelers here and there who stepped over into radical or revolutionary attitudes, or even into such action as that of the Münsterite kingdom.

H.S.B.

Günther Franz, Der deutsche Bauernkrieg (Munich and Berlin, 1933); H. Böhmer, Urkunden zur Geschichte des Bauernkriegs und der Wiedertäufer (Bonn, 1910, and Berlin, 1933); A. J. Ramaker, "Hubmaier's Participation in the Peasants' Uprising and in the Authorship of the Peasants' Articles of 1525," Rochester Baptist Theological Seminary Bulletin; W. Wiswedel, Dr. Balthasar Hubmaier (Gunzenhausen, 1940); ML I, 137-39.

Penner, Gerhard (1805-78), elder of the Heubuden Mennonite Church, West Prussia, was the leader of the conservative Mennonites who opposed the acceptance of the constitution adopted by the North German Confederation on Oct. 18, 1867, which stipulated that the Mennonites accept noncombatant services. Twenty-three representatives of the West Prussian congregations met in his house at Warnau (Koczelitzky) and a delegation of five was sent to Berlin to interview Roon, the Minister of War. Nevertheless the law pertaining to military service was published, and the delegation was summoned to Berlin once more. When Gerhard Penner, Johann Andreas (q.v.), and others saw that they would be compelled to accept noncombatant service, Penner migrated to Beatrice, Neb., in 1877, with a minority of the large Heubuden congregation. He died there in February 1878. He had served the Heubuden congregation as elder since 1852. In 1877 he resigned because the majority of the members were willing to accept noncombatant service. Gerhard Penner of Irrgang, minister of the Heubuden Church 1861-67, was his nephew. In 1888 Gerhard Penner Jr., son of Elder Gerhard Penner, was ordained as minister and elder of the First Mennonite Church of Beatrice (q.v.) and served until 1920 when he was succeeded by Franz Albrecht. Cornelius Penner, the son of Gerhard Penner, also served the congregation as minister.

C.K.

W. C. Andreas, "High Lights and Side Lights of the Mennonites in Beatrice," Menn. Life I (July 1946) 21 ff.

Perfectionism, the doctrine which teaches both the possibility and actuality of complete freedom from sin in this life for the Christian. Among American Protestants it is more often referred to as entire sanctification of the believer or total eradication of the sinful nature.

John Wesley is held to have advocated perfectionism, though he never claimed it for himself. In any case numbers of his followers, especially in the so-called "holiness" denominations in America, have continued to advocate and claim entire sanctification. Certain other small groups both in Europe and America have arisen at various times to advocate or claim sinlessness. In Emmenthal in the Swiss canton of Bern, Fritz Bergen, a converted drunkard, has led a small movement of perfectionists called "Evangelischer Brüderverein" (Bergerleute).

Extreme advocates of perfectionism usually have either defective ethical standards or an impossible psychology of moral action, or substitute an inner perfection of will and love toward God for outer perfection of character. John Wesley said, "The highest perfection which man can attain . . . does not exclude ignorance, error, and a thousand infirmities."

The Reformers and all the major Protestant denominations reject perfectionism. In so doing they frequently incline toward excusing sin and tend to encourage laxity, emphasizing forgiveness rather than holiness. Dietrich Bonhoeffer has caustically referred to this attitude as "justification in sin" rather than "from sin" and called it the offer of "cheap grace." His sweeping indictment of much of Protestantism is amply justified. Often those Christians and groups of Christians who have honestly and earnestly sought to live a life of high dedication, obedience, and holiness have been not only misunderstood but also frivolously condemned as hypocrites or self-righteous. The attempt to strive toward perfection ("Be ye therefore perfect, even as your heavenly Father is perfect") has often been erroneously labeled perfectionism. The Anabaptists and Mennonites have suffered under this charge from the beginning. It is true that they endeavored to maintain a church "without spot or wrinkle," which is represented in Eph. 5:27 as the goal which Christ has for the church; but this is far from the claim to have reached perfection, as the noting of the insistence upon church discipline by the group quickly shows. However, there is patently on this point a major difference in emphasis between state-church Protestantism with its toleration of almost all degrees of sin in the church, both of omission and commission, and Anabaptism with its insistence on a high level of personal and group performance in character, life, and service.

H.S.B.

R. Newton Flew, *The Idea of Perfection in Christian Theology. An Historical Study of the Christian Ideal for the Present Life* (London, 1934).

Peters, A. B. (1860-1959), an influential Bible teacher and preacher (MB), was born March 26, 1860, in Gnadenheim, South Russia, the son of Bernhard and Agathe Peters. He was a teacher by profession, teaching 11 years at Tiegerweide and 25 years at Tashenak. He was married in 1887 to Katharina Willms (d. 1923); they had 14 children. In 1924 he left Russia with 6 children, settling finally in Winnipeg in 1927. Here he served many years as Bible School teacher, preacher, and pastoral helper. He died May 17, 1959. H.S.B.

Phylloxera Unit, a Mennonite alternative service unit in South Russia, was created in connection with the Forestry Service (*q.v.*). This mobile unit was charged with the responsibility of exterminating plant lice in the vineyards of the Southern Crimea. Since it was a mobile unit operating only during part of the year, its organizational and educational aspects differed from those of the regular forestry camps. (Friesen, *Brüderschaft,* 513, 515, 520, 521.) C.K.

Pilgrim Mennonite Press was organized late in 1958 to be a publishing agency for a group of conservative-minded individuals who had held several interest-meetings at the Pilgrim Mennonite Church (MC), Amelia, Va. On Jan. 18, 1959, before any actual publication was undertaken, it merged with the Herald of Truth (*q.v.*) to form a board of twelve members known as Herald of Truth Publications, Inc., with its principal place of business at Hartville, Ohio. Paul M. Landis of Norfolk, Va., is chairman, as he was of the Pilgrim Press. H.S.B.

Pinneberg, a town (pop. 22,000) 11 miles northwest of the center of Hamburg, Germany, is the seat of a Mennonite home for the aged, opened in 1956 in a house rented for that purpose, and named "Abendfrieden." It is operated by Mennonitische Heime (*q.v.*) and serves mostly aged Mennonite refugees from West Prussia. H.S.B.

Pleasant Hill Mennonite Church (GCM), located at 1305 E. 12th St., Saskatoon, Sask., was begun in 1928 as a mission, and organized as a congregation April 20, 1958, with 20 charter members. In January 1953 a rebuilt recreation hall was dedicated as the meetinghouse. In 1959 the membership was 28, with B. H. Fast as pastor. H.S.B.

Pleasant View Mennonite Church (MC), Larned, Kan., now extinct, was founded by the Kings, Zooks, and others when they met for worship in the Eureka schoolhouse in 1885 and thus was known as the Eureka Mennonite Church. It built a meetinghouse in 1895. Its first minister was David S. King, ordained for this congregation. In the 1908 Yearbook it is listed with 15 members but it does not appear again until the 1916 Yearbook, when it is called the Pleasant View Mennonite Church (membership not given). Others who served the church include Peter Zimmerman, J. B. Brunk, Edward Diener, and Harry Diener. It was last listed in the 1942 Yearbook, with 17 members but without a pastor. M.G.

Plough and **Pflug:** see **Society of Brothers.**

Polish Church: see **Polish Brethren.**

Pottery: see **Ceramics.**

Prairie Mennonite Mutual Fire Insurance Company, Herbert, Sask., was incorporated in 1941, but was in existence earlier. In 1953 it had approximately 600 patrons in southern Saskatchewan. The company covers losses by fire, windstorm, and lightning. In 1953 it paid out about $10,000 on $3 million of insured property. M.G.

Priesthood of All Believers, a major point in Protestant doctrine, was also strongly held by the Anabaptists and is a vital idea in Mennonitism. It means not only that no priest is necessary as a mediator between the human individual and God, so that every man has free access to God by repentance and faith in Christ, but also that all believers have a priestly office to perform for each other in that in Christ each can be a channel of God's grace to his fellow and indeed has a responsibility to be such.

H.S.B.

Privilegium: see **Privileges.**

Prokhanov, Ivan Stepanovitch (1869-1935), founder of the organized church of the Evangelical Christians in Russia, was born in a well-to-do Molokan family in Vladikavkas, North Caucasus, Russia, which later joined the Baptists. He was converted in 1887 and joined the Baptist Church. He graduated in 1893 from the Technological Institute in St. Petersburg as an engineer. Here he joined the leaderless small group of the Evangelical Christians founded in 1876, which Pashkov and Korff had led until their exile in 1884. Driven by a strong sense of call to preach the Gospel to the masses, he soon gave up his career as an engineer. For three years, 1895-98, he studied theology in England (Baptist at Bristol, Congregational at New College in London), in Berlin, Germany, and in Paris. Returning to Russia, he finally settled in St. Petersburg where he found employment in the St. Petersburg branch of the American Westinghouse Brake Company. He now entered upon a remarkable career as preacher, writer, and leader. He reorganized the Evangelical Christians in 1908, of which he served as president until 1928, when he left Russia never to return. He sought, without full success, to unite the Baptists and the Evangelical Christians (the union finally occurred in 1944). In 1913 he began a Bible training program for Christian workers, which he continued until 1928 with the help of Johann Kargel (*q.v.*) and others.

Prokhanov had close connections for a time with the Mennonites of Russia, particularly in connection with the growth of nonresistant convictions in Russia. In 1919 the new Soviet government granted by decree the privilege of alternate service to Mennonites, Baptists, Evangelical Christians, Molokans, Dukhobors, Tolstoyans, and others. Later Prokhanov issued a declaration under severe pressure which stated that the Evangelical Christians should do military service. The Baptists finally did the same in 1923. Prokhanov was for a time president of the *Raduga* (*q.v.*) Publishing House at Halbstadt, co-operating in this project with the Mennonites.

Prokhanov took part in the Baptist World Congress at Stockholm in 1923 when he was chosen a vice-president, and in 1928 at Toronto. Because of dangers in Russia he did not return, but served the emigree Russian evangelical groups in Europe and America. He died in Berlin, Germany, Oct. 6, 1935, and was buried there. H.S.B.

W. Gutsche, *Westliche Quellen des Russischen Stundismus* (Kassel, 1956).

Puerto Rico Mennonite Conference (MC) was organized in 1949 and admitted to membership in the Mennonite General Conference at its 1955 session. In 1958 it had 11 congregations and 3 mission stations, with a total membership of 366. (See **Puerto Rico.**) H.S.B.

Quebec. The Ontario Mennonite Board of Missions and Charities (MC) began mission work in Quebec in 1957. Two missionary couples have been at work, one located in Montreal-Nord, and one in the town of Joliette. H.S.B.

Quiring, Jacob (1876-1942), a Mennonite evangelist and teacher, son of Elder Johann Quiring (*q.v.*) at Köppental, Trakt Mennonite settlement, Russia, was educated in the Realschule at Weierhof (Palatinate, Germany) 1886-92, and the Predigerschule at Basel, Switzerland, 1893-95. Upon his return to Russia he served as conference evangelist in the Mennonite Church 1897-1905. In 1905 he came to America and served as evangelist in General Conference Mennonite churches until 1907. In 1908 he married Dora Haury, daughter of S. S. Haury, Newton, Kan. He was graduated from the Moody Bible Institute in 1909, received the B.A. degree from the University of Chicago in 1912, the B.D. degree from McCormick Theological Seminary in 1913, and the M.A. degree from the University of Chicago that same year. In 1913-15 and 1918-21 he studied in the University of Berlin, where he also served as pastor of the Salem Deaconess Home. In 1921-30 he taught Bible at Bluffton College and Witmarsum Theological Seminary. During the last twelve years of his life he lived in New York City, continuing his Old Testament studies at Columbia University. He died Oct. 27, 1942. In his younger years he was an outstanding Mennonite evangelist, and in his later life an unusual Old Testament scholar. C.K.

The Bluffton College Bulletin (November 1942); Friesen, *Brüderschaft,* 763; *Witmarsum Spirit* (March 1926) 11.

Raber, John A. (b. 1873), Baltic, Ohio, Old Order Amish publisher and bookseller. He has published since 1930 the annual *Der Neue Amerikanische Calender* (*q.v.*), which contains the "Schriften und Lieder" for the Old Order Amish services, and also a complete address list of Amish ordained men with birth and ordination years, plus a list of Old Colony ministers in Mexico and of Hutterite ministers. In 1926 he published a reprint of Menno Simons' *Vollständige Werke.* He compiled and published the *Family Records of Jacob Raber from Germany and His Lineal Descendants.* He is the Amish book supplier for the Middle West and West, especially since L. A. Miller of Arthur, Ill., is no longer active. H.S.B.

Rainham (Ont.) **Reformed** Mennonite Church in Haldimand County near Selkirk was established in 1825. In 1958 it had 5 members. H.S.B.

Red Rock Lake Bible Camp, on Red Rock Lake, Whiteshell Forest Reserve, 120 miles east of the city of Winnipeg, Man., was started in 1946. It is owned and controlled by a private corporation of Mennonites of Steinbach, Man. It receives active support from the E.M.B. Church of Steinbach, the Evangelical Churches of Steinbach and vicinity, and the Emmanuel Mission Church of Steinbach. F.C.P.

Reference and Council, Committee of, of the Mennonite Brethren General Conference, is a standing committee of nine including the General Conference officers (chairman, vice-chairman, and secretary, and six men elected by the conference) to serve as the spiritual adviser and guardian for the church and all its agencies, in a sense the general supervisory body for the entire denomination, therefore of major importance. It was created in 1927 and made a standing committee in 1936. O.H.

Reinländer Mennonite Church was formed in Southern Manitoba in April 1958 by a conservative minority of some 500 members who withdrew from the 3,500 member Sommerfelder Mennonite Church in Manitoba. Twelve of the sixteen ministers of the Sommerfelder group joined the schismatic party, but the elder Johann Friesen did not leave. The new group elected Cornelius Nickel of Blumenthal as their bishop. Elements of the Sommerfelder group in Saskatchewan sympathize with them. The main body of Sommerfelders retained all the meetinghouses. H.S.B.

Religiöser Botschafter, Der (GCM), the first Mennonite church paper in America, was published and edited as an 8-page 10 x 12 inch biweekly by John H. Oberholtzer (*q.v.*) at Milford Square, Pa., from Aug. 23, 1852, to Dec. 31, 1855, when it was renamed *Das Christliche Volksblatt* (*q.v.*) and its publication taken over by the Mennonitischer Druckverein (*q.v.*). Bluffton College Library has a complete file. H.S.B.

Rescue Missions, found in all of the larger urban centers to rescue and rehabilitate "down-and-outers" (alcoholics, vagrants, etc.), have also been operated in a few cases by Mennonite groups. The Mennonite Church (MC) has recently established four such missions, the Hope Rescue Mission (*q.v.*) in South Bend, Ind., the Rock of Ages Rescue Mission (*q.v.*) in Portland, Ore., the Goodwill Rescue Mission at London, Ont., and the Harbour Rescue Mission at Hamilton, Ont. H.S.B.

Resinx: see **Felistis Jans.**

Richmond Mennonite Church (MC), formerly National Heights, Richmond, Va., organized in 1951, located in the eastern part of the state capital, is the outgrowth of a survey made by Eastern Mennonite College students. Two Bible schools and two series of tent meetings were conducted in 1948, followed by services held in private homes, then in a rented building. The Virginia Board of Missions and Charities built a brick church in 1955. In 1958 the membership was 36, with Ralph Ziegler as pastor. H.A.B.

Rittman (Ohio) Home for the Aged (MC) was established in 1901, burned down in 1919, but was rebuilt and dedicated Jan. 1, 1939. It is sponsored by the Mennonite Board of Missions and Charities. In 1958 it had 41 guests. (*Mennonite Community* V, 1951, pp. 7-9.) M.G.

Rock Creek Amish Mennonite Church: see **Yoder** Amish Mennonite Church.

Rock of Ages Rescue Mission (MC), Portland, Ore., was established in 1948 by the mission board of the Pacific Coast Conference. H.S.B.

Rosehill Mennonite Brethren Church: see **Munich,** N.D., Mennonite Brethren Church.

Rosenberg, a village near Sczerzec, Galicia, Austria, was established in 1786. Daniel Bergthold from Harxheim near Heidelberg, Germany, his son Jakob, and Johannes Rupp from Heppenheim, Palatinate, Germany, settled here during the founding year. They had originally planned to settle at Einsiedel (*q.v.*). Some of these families moved to America during the migration of the 1870's. C.K.

Peter Bachmann, *Mennoniten in Klein-Polen* (Lemberg, 1934) 156-58.

Rothrock Mennonite Church (GCM), now extinct, was one of the two meetinghouses of the congregation in Northampton County, Pa., one being Mt. Bethel in Bangor, and the other Rothrock (also called Upper Mt. Bethel) 4 miles east of Bangor. The latter was built sometime before 1794 and before Mt. Bethel. It was a small congregation, the first families having moved into the community c1754, and was supplied by ministers from Bucks and Lehigh counties. The only resident minister was David Henning (1806-81). He was most likely ordained by the Oberholtzer group which divided from the Franconia Conference (MC) in 1847, but withdrew to follow William Gehman and the Evangelical Mennonites (*q.v.*) formed in 1858. It is presumed that the congregation followed him both times in changing conference connection. H.S.B.

Rural Evangel, since January 1948 called **Gospel Evangel,** "Organ of the Indiana-Michigan Mennonite Mission Board," first number Oct. 1, 1920, first appeared as a 4-page quarterly 9¼ x 12½ in. in size, published at Scottdale, Pa., and Elkhart, Ind. (later Elkhart was dropped). Size, format, and issue have changed as follows: July 1930 to date, bimonthly issue; beginning January 1944, 8 pages 8 x 10¾ in.; January 1948 to date, 7¾ x 10½ in.; July 1953 to date, 16 pages. Editors have been J. K. Bixler to July 1925; Allen B. Christophel October 1925 to July 1929; J. S. Hartzler October 1929 to December 1945; Ezra Beachy January 1946 to date. H.S.B.

Rural Missions, mission projects for the extension of the church in rural areas, have been a major concern of the Mennonite Church (MC) since the first decade of the 20th century. City missions in this Mennonite body began in 1893 (Chicago), but the conviction soon developed that the genius of the group lay more in rural than in city work. Consequently city missions remained limited in number and often developed more into churches for Mennonites moving into the city. Rural missions, on the other hand, have been projected into non-Mennonite areas where few Mennonites live or are likely to move. Recently, however, colonization evangelism has been promoted as a form of rural missions, a number of families moving into an area to form the nucleus and working force of a new congregation. The general mission board agreed to leave the rural field to the district conference mission boards and confine itself in the home mission field to city missions.

The first M.C. rural missions program was that of the Virginia Mennonites of the Shenandoah Valley, who began an outreach into neighboring West Virginia (*q.v.*) as early as the time of the Civil War and developed it vigorously after 1900, until by 1957 they had established a total of 21 congregations, missions, and preaching points in this area, with a total of 553 members. In 1958 the Virginia Conference had a total of 51 unorganized congregations, mostly rural. The next vigorous program of rural missions was that inaugurated by the Indian-Michigan Mission Board at its organization in 1911. Its chief work was in Michigan, and ultimately (1958) reached a total of 20 stations, 10 in the Upper Peninsula of Michigan and 4 in Kentucky, while local congregations had established an additional 20 stations, mostly rural. The rural missions had a total of some 500 members, largely of non-Mennonite origin. The conference had a total of 50 unorganized congregations.

Similar programs developed in other conference districts. The Ontario Conference, for example, organized its rural work in 1915 under the Rural Mission Board of Ontario, which was reorganized in 1929 as the Mennonite Mission Board of Ontario to include city work. The Lancaster and Franconia boards have extended their outreach remarkably in rural (and some urban) missions into New York and New England, but also into the South, in Alabama, Georgia, and northern Florida. The total of rural missions operated by all the M.C. district mission boards is over 200, with a membership of over 3,000. This is without doubt the most effective evangelistic effort of this Mennonite body.

The Western Gospel Mission (*q.v.*), organized in 1944 with headquarters at Steinbach, Man., carries on a vigorous program of rural missions in Manitoba, Saskatchewan, and northern Ontario, largely supported by the Evangelical Mennonites (Kleine Gemeinde) and the Rudnerweide group. It has a total of 8 major stations with 15 substations.   H.S.B.

Rurer, Hans (Johann) (d. 1542), returned to Ansbach, Bavaria, Germany, as chaplain in 1528 after a brief service at the Liegnitz academy, one of the pillars of the young church in Brandenburg and Ansbach, a capable church inspector and theological councillor to Margrave George, and highly regarded in the learned circles of the town. In 1542 his son Christoph received a scholarship from the Ansbach *Stift,* both Christoph and his brother having in 1540 received a scholarship of thirty-two guilders—an indication of their father's importance. It was his duty to assist at many Anabaptist examinations. He carried out this role so humanely that the conversion of Anabaptists by pastoral conversation was considered to be his particular gift. Frequently Rurer was sent to other places for this purpose, as for example to Rothenburg on the Tauber (*q.v.*).   E.T.

Hermann Jordan, *Reformation und gelehrte Bildung in der Markgrafschaft Ansbach-Bayreuth* I (Leipzig, 1917); ML III, 572.

Rusburg, Barend (*c*1767-May 9, 1856), a son of Jan Rusburg, of Haarlem, and Maria Tirion, was a Dutch Mennonite minister. At first he was employed in the office of his uncle Tirion, a noted bookseller of Amsterdam. Then he decided to study theology. He was a student in the Amsterdam Mennonite Seminary 1801-4, and thereupon served the congregations of Aalsmeer 1805-7, Hengelo 1807-28, and Kampen 1828-51; in 1851, at the age of eighty-five, he retired. Rusburg published a translation of the prophecies of Micah from the Hebrew (Amsterdam, 1832) and a short biography of two Mennonite industrialists in Hengelo, *Iets over W(olter) and J(ohannes) ten Cate als oprigters der fabrijken* (n.p., n.d.).   vᴅZ.

Ruse, Peter: see **Reusse, Peter.**

Ruseburg, a village in the Löwenhof district in Lorraine(?), listed in the Dutch *Naamlijsts* of 1775 and 1780 as the seat of a Mennonite congregation, of which Nicolaas Koch was an elder and Abraham Esch a preacher.   vᴅZ.

Rüsser: see also **Risser.**

Salem Mennonite Church (GCM), now extinct, located just west of Ruff, Wash. (members living scattered in Grant and Adams counties), was organized in 1910 with 32 members, although services were held in various schoolhouses from the beginning of the settlement in 1903. It built a meetinghouse in 1910. By 1920 it reached its maximum of *c*60 members. This church shared most of its ministers with the Menno Church (*q.v.*) about 18 miles away, to which most of the remaining members transferred when the dwindling membership (24) decided to discontinue in 1937.   H.S.B.

Saltobach (Brazil) Mennonite Brethren Church is a subsidiary congregation to Bouqueirao (*q.v.*), not fully independent. Its meetinghouse was built in 1955. In 1957 its membership was 35, with Franz Heinrichs as leader.   H.S.B.

Salutations. Though salutations are as old as man, nevertheless their peculiar forms express much about the culture within which the greeter lives. The Hebrew greets with the word "Shalom," which is actually a prayer: "May God grant you peace." The Pauline epistles combine the Hebrew greeting with a revised Greek salutation substituting the Christian word "grace" for the Greek word "greetings." Both the Old and the New Testaments agree that when a greeting is extended it is the equivalent of a prayer to God that what it expresses may come into reality in the life of the one saluted. Consequently greetings were withdrawn where they did not find a worthy acceptance (Matt. 10:13), and in the case of false teachers were withheld entirely, for in greeting a false teacher one shared in his wicked work (II John 10, 11).

The Anabaptists took seriously the matter of salutations. In Strasbourg Bucer complained that Marpeck would discuss matters of religion with him in the council chambers, but withheld a civil greeting from him on the street. Furthermore the Anabaptists were noted by their in-group greeting forms. According to Justus Menius they used the Biblical formula: "The peace of the Lord be with you," with the response, "and with your spirit." In Swabia, Thuringia, and Münster this salutation, or one very similar to it, is attested. Spies at times used this greeting to betray members of the group, e.g., Georg Libich.

That this practice was not a mechanical imitation of Biblical practices is clear from Riedemann's (*q.v.*) statement: "He who salutes and he who is saluted must both be children of peace, if God is to add His blessing." Sebastian Franck (*q.v.*) says: "Whoever does not belong to their sect they hardly greet, nor do they offer him the hand," and Schwenckfeld (*q.v.*) concurs by saying, "Indeed they are allowed to greet their brothers, but not the heathen."

Of the Anabaptists of Friesland it was said that they could be recognized by their greeting, "The peace of the Lord be with you!" The response was "Amen," or "May this be true!" with a handshake and a kiss. Or one said, "The peace of God be with you!" and the other replied, "That must be amen." (Vos, *Menno Simons*, 87.)

In later times Anabaptist-Mennonite practice has been commonly dictated by current cultural practices, although in letters one often finds salutations which are more closely in line with the Biblical salutations. It is a frequent practice in some Mennonite groups to use a formalized opening and closing in letters, which are Christian greetings. At the opening such phrases are used as "Greetings in the Name of the Lord Jesus," or "Greetings with [a Scripture verse is quoted]," and at the closing such phrases as "Yours in Christ," or "Yours in His Service." When the kiss is used as a greeting in the Mennonite Church (MC) and related groups, it is accompanied by a handshake and the phrase "God bless you."

W.Kl.

TA Strasbourg I (1959); Sebastian Franck, *Chronica*, folio 444 r.; Fritz Heyer, *Der Kirchenbegriff der Schwärmer* (Leipzig, 1939) 56 f.; *Corpus Schwenckfeldianorum* XII, 107.

Sanitätsdienst (Sanitary or Hospital Service in connection with the army) was a channel of alternative service for the Mennonites of Russia, originating in connection with the Russo-Japanese War (1902) and developing on a large scale during World War I. The original form of alternative service among the Mennonites of Russia was Forestry Service (*q.v.*). The Sanitätsdienst came into being through the work of the All-Russian Union of Towns and the All-Russian Union of Zemstvos which functioned parallel to the Red Cross under government supervision during the Russo-Japanese War. Only very few Mennonites served under the organization during the Russo-Japanese War.

When World War I broke out, the Union of Towns and the Union of Zemstvos took the respon-

sibility for "Circuit Hospitals." In 1916 there were 173,000 Zemstvo beds, 70,000 Union of Towns beds, 48,000 Red Cross beds, and 160,000 beds furnished by the Ministry of War. Most of the Mennonites serving in this form became attached to the Union of Zemstvos, which was a civilian organization. Their work consisted of taking the wounded soldiers from the front to the hospitals in the cities in hospital trains. For this service they had to wear a uniform and had to operate under civilian and military orders but were not inducted into the army, although a few volunteered to do so but were refused. In the beginning of the program in 1915, 3,093 Mennonite young men served in the Sanitätsdienst, and in 1916 there were 6,548 in this service, which constituted more than half the total number of Mennonite young men in service. By 1919, after the Revolution, the Zemstvos were liquidated. Something over 100 Mennonite men lost their lives in the service, including those who died of disease.

The original plan of the Czarist policy of universal military conscription for all Russian males was to admit no exceptions. The protest of the Mennonites to the abrogation of their well-established right of exemption from all military service led to a modification of policy providing for noncombatant service. The Military Service Commission's report of early 1872 read, "Those Mennonites who will be called to military service will only be used behind the front in hospitals, military workshops (not munition factories) or similar establishments, and are to be exempted from the bearing of arms." But the Mennonites insisted they could accept no service under the military department in any form. The ultimate provision clearly set up a wholly nonmilitary forestry service. This was not noncombatant military service. The same was true of the Sanitätsdienst. Although it was direct service to the army, it was not a part of the army. Russian military organization apparently had not yet set up a full army medical corps, but left much of the medical service in the hands of the Red Cross and other civilian organization.

The Mennonites of Switzerland were also permitted by the conscription law of 1870 to do medical corps service, but this was noncombatant service in the army. This was and is also true in the United States and Canada.   C.K.

Frank C. Peters, "Non-Combatant Service Then and Now," *Menn. Life* X (1955) 31-35; Tikhon J. Polner, *Russian Local Government During the War and the Union of Zemstvos* (New Haven, 1930) 53; Cornelius Krahn, "Public Service in Russia," *The Mennonite*, June 22, 1943, p. 2; Jacob Sudermann, "The Origin of Mennonite State Service in Russia, 1870-1880," *MQR* XVII (1943) 23-46.

Sao Paulo (Brazil) Mennonite Church, organized in 1955, meets at the MCC center in Sao Paulo. In 1957 the membership was 20, with Gerhard Rosenfeld as leader.   H.S.B.

Saskatchewan Mennonite Youth Organization: see **Mennonite Youth Organization of Saskatchewan.**

Saxe-Weimar: see article at end of Supplement.

Schädowitz (Schaidowitz), Moravia, today Zadovice, *c*1550 owned by the lord Sigmund von Zastrizil. In 1553 the Hutterites established a Bruderhof here. The *Chronik* reports the death of a number of preachers at this place, including Paul Glock (*q.v.*) 1585, Veit Grünberger (*q.v.*), and Hans Baldauff 1587. During the Bosckay invasion of 1605-6, and again during the early years of the Thirty Years' War the Bruderhof was plundered by hordes of soldiers not less than eleven times. When the Hutterites were summarily expelled from Moravia in 1622, this Bruderhof also had to be abandoned. (Zieglschmid, *Chronik*.)   H.S.B.

Scharpau, located between the Vistula and the Nogat rivers near the Baltic Coast, was settled by Dutch Mennonites from Danzig. By 1590 Mennonites had already located in this area. In 1618 Jacob Jantzen from Emden settled in Beyershorst. Other places settled here at this time were Altebabke, Jankendorf, Kalteherberge, and Tiegenort.   C.K.

> Horst Penner, *Ansiedlung mennonitischer Niederländer im Weichselmündungsgebiet von der Mitte des 16. Jahrhunderts bis zum Beginn der preussischen Zeit* (Weierhof, 1940) 37-43.

Schlettstadt: see **Seléstat.**

Schneeweiss, Sigmund (also called Simon in *TA Bayern* I), Lutheran court preacher at Ansbach, Germany, appears in the archival records repeatedly as a zealous opponent of the Anabaptists 1529-35. He participated frequently in questioning sessions. He was apparently the composer of a theological refutation of the Anabaptists written in 1528, found in the Ansbach Archives (A.R.A. 38, 175-83) but not published by Schornbaum. He was a colleague in these matters of Andreas Althamer (*q.v.*) and Johannes Rurer (*q.v.*). (*TA Bayern* I and II.)   H.S.B.

Schuhmacher (Schoenmaker), **Laurens:** see **Schu(e)-ster, Lorenz.**

Schuster, Heinrich, an Anabaptist, who was imprisoned at Kirweiler (*q.v.*) in the Palatinate together with Hans Arbeiter (*q.v.*) for 29 weeks from July 18, 1568. The two had been sent as missioners to the Palatinate, by the Hutterites in Moravia. The sheriff (*Scherg*) refused to arrest the two men, saying to the magistrate (*Schultheiss*), "I will not submit to the order to arrest these men who are much more pious than I; if I had known of the order to arrest them, I would have warned them." (Zieglschmid, *Chronik,* 427 f.)   H.S.B.

Schwenckfeld, Caspar von (1489-1561), a notable and attractive figure in the German Reformation, though he founded no church, was born in Ossig near Lüben, in the principality of Liegnitz, Silesia, Germany. He came from the ranks of the nobility, and studied at various universities (at Cologne 1505-7), but did not secure a degree, nor was he ever ordained, remaining a layman all his life.

Schwenckfeld's spiritual awakening began in 1518 when the first news of Luther's innovations in Wittenberg reached the court of Brieg, Silesia. Soon thereafter he entered the service of Friedrich II of Liegnitz and in 1522 persuaded the duke to launch the evangelical movement in Silesia. His hearing having become impaired, he left the court and returned to his home in Ossig in 1523, continuing,

however, to serve occasionally as an adviser to the duke. From the beginning he adopted the role of a lay evangelist and remained such throughout his life, winning followers in Silesia and in South Germany.

In December 1525 Schwenckfeld personally presented his spiritual interpretation of the words of institution of the Lord's Supper to Luther in Wittenberg in a fraternal spirit. Three months later Luther wrote him a vehement condemnation, whereupon Schwenckfeld and the Schwenckfelder brotherhood in Liegnitz advocated suspension of the observance of the Supper until a better understanding of it was forthcoming. Schwenckfeld always acknowledged his indebtedness to Luther.

Schwenckfeld prevented his duke from evicting the Anabaptists from his dukedom. The wrath of King Ferdinand of Austria was stirred by the liberal policies of the duke and Schwenckfeld, their appointment of Swiss theologians to the University of Liegnitz, their toleration of Anabaptists, and the publication of two of Schwenckfeld's books by Zwingli and Oecolampadius; the consequence was a mandate by the king demanding that his Silesian subjects return to the old faith. In order to save his duke from further embarrassment, Schwenckfeld voluntarily left Silesia in 1529 and went to Strasbourg. There he was kindly received by Capito and Bucer and remained until 1533, when he set out on a journey to visit friends in Hagenau, Landau, Speyer, Esslingen, and Augsburg, where he lived with Bonifacius Wolfhart for several months, then to Mindelheim, Kempten, Memmingen, and Ulm. In Ulm he was entertained by the city officials. In July 1534 he returned to Strasbourg. The city having adopted a course of suppression of all dissenters, he left the city permanently, and went to Ulm where he resided with the burgomaster, Bernhard Besserer, until 1539. In 1540-47 he lived in the Justingen Castle of the von Freyberg family, and 1547-50 in the Franciscan Monastery at Esslingen. In 1551-61 he was a homeless wanderer, constantly evading his persecutors. In 1561 Agathe Streicher, a daughter of the widow Helena Streicher, invited him to their home in Ulm to receive her medical services. He accepted the invitation and died in the Streicher home three months later, Dec. 10, 1561.

Most of Schwenckfeld's writings are epistles on devotional, religious, and controversial subjects. During his lifetime, with the assistance of friends, he wrote and published 180 books and booklets, a few of which appeared in the year after his death. Four folio volumes of his letters and one of treatises were printed in 1564, 1566, and 1570. Four additional folio volumes of his letters were preserved by faithful friends. A complete edition of his works is in process of publication, the *Corpus Schwenckfeldianorum.* Fifteen volumes of this 18-volume edition appeared in 1907-39. Publication of the three final volumes (1558-61) was resumed in 1958.

"In Schwenckfeld's opinion, spiritual life and experience were of greater importance than creeds, theologies, or any church organization bearing his name. He worked untiringly to the end of his life for one united Christian Church founded on faith and freedom of belief, a fellowship of all who love

God and Jesus Christ, the ecumenical church." "The Christian Church," said he, "is the company of God's people, of all or of many who with heart and soul are believers in Christ, a willing people drawn by the Father. It is the company of those regenerated souls in all lands who worship the Father in spirit and in truth, whether or not they adhere to one doctrine, confession, and order of worship." Schwenckfeld's doctrine of the church and his basically spiritualistic type of Christianity furnished no adequate basis for organizing his followers into a church and he deliberately chose not to establish a church, even though strong groups of his disciples arose in Silesia (Glatz, Goldberg, Jauer, and Wohlau) and Schwenckfelder conventicles met at various places in South Germany. Consequently no Schwenckfelder church was ever organized in Europe. Schwenckfeld used the term "church" only in the generic sense, never to apply to his own followers or to a local congregation. "Questioned in the evening of his life concerning his following or church, Schwenckfeld says he has no church; that his doctrine, being so vehemently spoken against, has comparatively few adherents; these separate themselves from none who love and fear God, but they assemble in conventicles for prayer, for mutual instruction and consultation. It was never Schwenckfeld's aim or desire to found a church or to have a large following, but it was his steadfast purpose to help mankind to a better knowledge of God through a saner interpretation of Scripture" (Schultz, 358).

The details of Schwenckfeld's life and work are given in an excellent full-length biography by Selina Gerhard Schultz, since 1929 Associate and Managing Editor of the *Corpus Schwenckfeldianorum.*

In the late 1520's Schwenckfeld had his first contacts with the Anabaptists, but these were Sabbatarian Anabaptists (*q.v.*), hence Schwenckfeld obtained the erroneous impression that all Anabaptists were legalistic and Judaistic, charges which he repeated in subsequent years. These years were important for the development of his policy of "Stillstand," which meant a temporary halt in the administration of the sacraments. For this practice he gave two reasons: his personal unworthiness to partake, and the lack of an apostolic church in which to partake. Schwenckfeld explicated this policy in his letter about the Lord's Supper drawn up in December 1528. Infant baptism he provisionally rejected because of the abuses connected with it, and not on principle. He certainly would not himself submit to rebaptism, but rather he had come to the conclusion that the outward rites should not overshadow the inner essence. Schwenckfeld's stay in Strasbourg in 1529-33 forced him to take a stand on a number of other issues also, and he there met Martin Bucer (*q.v.*), Capito (*q.v.*), Pilgram Marpeck (*q.v.*), Melchior Hofmann (*q.v.*), and many other Reformation and Anabaptist leaders and writers. His disposition toward the oppressed caused him to intercede for Melchior Hofmann, and in spite of Schwenckfeld's rejection of Hofmann's Christology the positions of the two men on this point are not very different. Schwenckfeld said both Hofmann and Sebastian Franck drew error from his truth as a spider draws poison from

a lovely flower. He met Bernt Rothmann in Strasbourg on one occasion.

Schwenckfeld's Strasbourg Residence. When Schwenckfeld arrived in Strasbourg in early May 1529, he found a city in several respects suited to his search for truth. His views of the Lord's Supper were warmly received by Capito and Bucer; he lived in Capito's home until Capito's wife died in 1531. Here also he formed a close friendship with the Zell family.

Arriving as he did a year after Pilgram Marpeck (*q.v.*), he found the Anabaptist movement in Strasbourg trying to decide among the various approaches of church reform suggested by Hans Bünderlin, Jacob Kautz, and Melchior Hofmann. Marpeck had taken the initiative in attempting to formulate an Anabaptist church order. In a city where Bünderlin's writings were being read in the Anabaptist assemblies this was not an easy task, and caused a major parting of the ways within the Anabaptist movement, with the Bünderlin group on one side, the Hofmann group on the other, and the Reublin-Marpeck group between them. That Schwenckfeld was aware of these tensions appears from his statement about this time that "the Anabaptists call Bünderlin a squabbler (*Zanker*)." Schwenckfeld's awareness of the issues raised by Anabaptism appears also in his writings of this period. For example, he was concerned about the question of authority, and in 1530 wrote a short treatise on the question of the keys. The question of church discipline also occupied him during this period. Being a friend of Capito (as was Marpeck) and Bucer he was caught in the middle in the discussions on infant baptism, and took his stand on the position that it was of little importance. Earlier this had also been Capito's and Bucer's position but through their dealings with Hans Denk, Jacob Kautz, and Clemens Ziegler the Strasbourg Reformers were gradually changing their position. Schwenckfeld decried the fact that the only kind of Christians that the Reformation was able to harvest were "water-Christians," and this is a repeated complaint against the Anabaptists also in later years.

Most clearly Schwenckfeld's position toward the Anabaptists is seen in his *Judicium de Anabaptistis* (ms., 1530), where he takes issue with them on their radical eschatology (Hut, Hofmann?), chides them for being so concerned about events before the beginning of the world and after its end, and expresses the wish that they might spend less time discussing how things are in the presence of God. It is interesting that this same point appeared again in the later controversy between Marpeck and Schwenckfeld when Schwenckfeld chided the Anabaptists for not spending enough time on how matters stand before God. Finally he is critical of the Anabaptists for the haste with which they accept members, and advises them to give new converts catechetical instruction before accepting them. Related to this is his criticism that they appoint a leader so soon after he has become an Anabaptist, without formal instruction. While Schwenckfeld admits that he does not know the Anabaptists too well, and he would wish that they might testify more in the open so that their views could be better known, it is clear that the dividing lines between him and them are already clearly visible at this time. He accuses the Anabaptists of being too much concerned with external baptism and the external letter of the Word, and thus missing its inner and deeper meaning.

Part of Schwenckfeld's criticism of the Anabaptists stems from his program of reform. While in Strasbourg he published two catechisms as a contribution to the Reformation. He also promoted an edition (by Ulhart in 1531) of the *Nachfolge Christi,* and since mention is made of this book in a letter by Scharnschlager (*q.v.*) it is possible that the Anabaptists at Strasbourg used this publication. On the question of his relationship to Anabaptism his letter to John Bader in 1530 is most instructive. Schwenckfeld shows the abuses of infant baptism in the past and therefore rejects it. He does however not take the step to adult baptism, but rejects this approach as forced baptism. Baptism is an external thing, and hence cannot be a requirement for church membership since it is not essential for salvation. In the same letter he refers to a booklet written against him by the Anabaptists, and it is quite possible that this refers to either of the two booklets written by Marpeck in 1531, or perchance to the *Clare verantwurtung* (*q.v.*), which deals with some of his arguments, although its main target was likely Bünderlin.

The clearest evidence of Schwenckfeld's attitude toward Anabaptism is seen in the disruption of his friendship with Wolf Sailer (*q.v.*), who was also a friend of Marpeck and was drawn more and more into the Anabaptist brotherhood. This common friendship with Sailer is notable evidence that Schwenckfeld and Marpeck were close to each other in this period, although after their tensions came out in the open after 1542, Schwenckfeld gives the impression that at first all had gone smoothly between him and Marpeck. Whether this is merely a rhetorical device or was actually the case because of limited knowledge of each other and little common discussion is not clear. It is difficult to see how they could have been close friends. Schwenckfeld follows the Denk-Kautz spiritualistic line which depreciates the sacraments and all external means, while Marpeck follows the active missionary line of Sattler, Hans Hut, and Schiemer, whose major concern was to build the church of Christ here and now. Schwenckfeld's major concern was always to emphasize the spiritual instead of the external, using the method of discussion (oral or written), while Marpeck's was the building of the church through corporate Bible study and mutual exhortation.

Schwenckfeld and Marpeck Literary Debates, 1540-50. The clash between Schwenckfeldian spiritualism and the Marpeck brotherhood became more serious after 1540. In 1560 Schwenckfeld said, "Pilgram was dear to me for many years until he began to warn about me and my teaching." Marpeck appeared surprised at Schwenckfeld's reply to the *Vermanung* (*q.v.*) published by his brotherhood, and considered Schwenckfeld's *Judicium* of 1542 as a malicious attack upon him and the group.

This interchange must be seen in the light of Marpeck's intention to consolidate the Anabaptist movement through the *Vermanung.* A member of his own brotherhood, Helena von Freyberg, handed a copy of the *Vermanung* to Schwenckfeld, requesting his opinion of it. On Aug. 21, 1542, Schwenckfeld indicated in a letter that at the request of certain brothers he had written a refutation of the *Vermanung.* This letter, written to Magdalena Marschalck von Pappenheim (*q.v.*), was Schwenckfeld's reply to her request for instruction. He was deeply disappointed when the reply was written by Marpeck for Magdalena. The letter was addressed to Helena Streicher, but she was close to Schwenckfeld, and the letter contained a number of points directed against Schwenckfeld; so it is clear for whom it was meant. Two factors contributed to the writing of Schwenckfeld's *Judicium:* the request of some, and Schwenckfeld's feeling that the *Vermanung* was directed against him as he explicitly says. In addition to this there were a number of other concerns not mentioned in the *Vermanung,* to which Schwenckfeld addressed himself in the *Judicium.* Through a letter from Valentine Ickelsamer he had found out that Marpeck defended the position that it would have been possible for Christ to sin. Also he had heard that Marpeck believed that Christ suffered in Hades after the crucifixion. He was furthermore concerned about the extent to which the Anabaptists were making an idol of the cross. Finally he was disturbed about the "creaturely" emphasis which their view of Christ contained; he would rather see them stress the exalted Christ a little more. Marpeck's intention to form a church he considered futile, and at numerous places Schwenckfeld ridicules the efforts of the Anabaptists to unite their movement.

The discussion of the differences between the Anabaptists and Schwenckfeld has generally revolved around the idea of infant baptism. A study of the writings of the two men reveals, however, that much more is involved. Torsten Bergsten has not only thoroughly discussed the external features of this discussion such as the dates of the various epistles, but has also laid bare the essential theological differences which stood between them. Although the differences may be put in various ways, such as the place of the rites and ceremonies of the church, the normative place of the Bible, etc., this was actually one of the hardest battles ever waged for the existence of a church. While this controversy never came to public attention, its issues have relevance far beyond the scope of the actual participants in the discussion. Schwenckfeld began with a Christology which is basically Greek (Hilary of Poitiers, Cyril and Athanasius are his favorite church fathers) and stressed the reigning Christ. In his discussions of Christ's life he pushed the glorified Christ so far back into His earthly life that His humanity seems to be somewhat reduced in significance. The corollary to this was that all externals were depreciated, whether in the history of the church or in its practical life today. On church discipline, e.g., he said that he would take a matter to the brotherhood if there were such a brotherhood today as Christ described. To this the Anabaptists replied that even if he had lived in the time of the apostles he would not have been satisfied with the church and would have found some reason for criticizing.

The Anabaptists were disappointed in Schwenckfeld's position on the Old Testament. In the beginning of his writing career, especially in his discussions with Bucer, he held essentially the same position as the Anabaptists, viz., that one should not erase the time line between the Old and New Testaments, but rather make the Incarnation the time point of the division. Later in his discussions with the Marpeck brotherhood he took Bucer's position that the Old and New Covenants are the same in so far as Christ's redemption is retroactive even for the patriarchs. In the second part of the *Verantwortung* the Anabaptists amassed a series of contradictions between the earlier and later Schwenckfeld on the doctrine of the two covenants.

Both Marpeck and Schwenckfeld began with the idea of freedom of religion and the necessity of choice by the individual. Schwenckfeld thought that even the Christian should not be subjected to any kind of restraint (except on a purely individual basis), while for Marpeck the freedom of the Christian was a reality only as he was a part of the body of Christ. Marpeck believed that the church as the body of Christ must continue His sufferings, while Schwenckfeld urged his followers to avoid being persecuted if possible, and it is not by chance that the Schwenckfelders had so few martyrs for their faith. The Anabaptists insisted upon a visible church, whereas Schwenckfeld kept his church invisible.

Schwenckfeld's charge that the Anabaptist movement was legalistic is not entirely justified. He was really showing Marpeck the danger inherent in an approach which takes the Bible seriously, and in so doing he rendered a distinct service not only to Marpeck, but to Anabaptism as a whole. Moreover, Schwenckfeld seems not to have been aware of the danger of his own approach, namely, that so much value will be ascribed to the purely spiritual that the material forms and the historical events to which they point are depreciated and discarded. Certainly for his own group Schwenckfeld rejected the term "church." The reason for this was that he felt that wherever a form comes into being an element of Judaism enters in. This can be illustrated with respect to his view on baptism. After reading the *Vermanung* he wrote that one of the best things about the book was its clear rejection of the identification of John's baptism of repentance with Christian baptism. And yet despite this recognition of the clear distinction between the two baptisms made by the Anabaptists he repeatedly accused them later on of basing their baptism on the baptism of John; indeed, he accused Hans Klöpfer of basing it on the Jewish rite of circumcision. Since Klöpfer's writing is not extant it is impossible to make a historical judgment, but it would have been highly irregular and practically impossible for an Anabaptist to base his argument for adult baptism on circumcision. Instead, it is likely that Schwenckfeld was here reacting against the necessity of baptism as a covenant witness among Anabaptists, and calling this compulsion a form of Judaism.

Schwenckfeld and the Anabaptists, 1550-61. The Marpeck-Schwenckfeld controversy did not die at once. One hears rumblings of it intermittently throughout the rest of Schwenckfeld's life. A host of people were drawn to Schwenckfeld's quiet conventicle type of Christianity as well as to the more aggressive missionary approach of the Anabaptists, which resulted in a continuing church body rather than in an amorphous group of interested persons. Schwenckfeld was interested in discussion, the Anabaptists in commitment within a covenantal community.

One person who clearly shows this is Daniel Graff. Apparently he was at one time a follower of Schwenckfeld. Arriving in Augsburg, Graff met with the group for discussion, and when the Schwenckfelders insisted that the external rites were not necessary, indeed should not be used, Graff disagreed with their interpretation. In an epistolary exchange between him and Schwenckfeld it became clear that Graff was much more a follower of Marpeck's views than of Schwenckfeld's.

Another person who continued the discussion with Schwenckfeld was Hans Klöpfer von Feuerbach, who was an active Anabaptist missionary and won some Schwenckfelders to the Anabaptist cause. Klöpfer wrote to Ursula Heugin urging upon her the necessity of baptism. She turned the letter over to Schwenckfeld so that he might answer it for her. It is surprising to find Schwenckfeld in this correspondence taking in some respects an opposite position to the one which he had taken in the discussions with Marpeck.

Finally there are a number of references in Schwenckfeld's correspondence of these years to "Schweiger," or "silent" Anabaptists. Sibilla Eisler, one of the women with whom Schwenckfeld was in constant correspondence, had an Anabaptist maid who frequently did not speak at all nor greet anyone. She apparently belonged to this small group of Anabaptists in the area of Allgäu. Schwenckfeld was very critical of their habit of not greeting people and not bearing arms. It is not clear whether these are actually the "Schweiger" to whom Sebastian Franck refers, who were apparently a deviant Anabaptist sect, or whether they are merely called that because they greeted only their fellow Anabaptists. These "Schweiger" are mentioned also in Christoph Erhard's and George Eder's lists of the sects of the late 16th century.

There is no notice in the writings of Schwenckfeld of the death of Pilgram Marpeck, although the former must have known about it. About 1550 he knew that Marpeck had been asked to submit the *Testamenterleütterung* (q.v.) to the city council of Augsburg, and was irritated by the fact that Marpeck's services as an engineer had made it possible for him to remain in Augsburg so long. He wrote to Marpeck with sarcastic surprise that he would entangle himself so much in the affairs of this world (alluding to II Tim. 2:4) as to work as an engineer alongside of his work as a leader in the church.

It is apparent that much of the friction between Schwenckfeld and the Anabaptists had a rather slim basis and actually resulted from personality differences and lack of understanding. It would be a mistake, however, to minimize these differences, for at the heart of them lie two entirely different approaches to the problem of the church in the world. Schwenckfeld was a sincere Christian whose piety and integrity were above reproach and who has correctly been termed a Pietist before Pietism. But precisely because he was a Pietist he could not appreciate the Anabaptists and their stress on the visible corporate body of Christ, the church, as taking on a concrete form within a historical context. While he waited for the Spirit to break through with some kind of special revelation, the Anabaptists allowed the Spirit to work through them, using them with their inadequacies and insufficiencies to His own ends. Within this historical context they acknowledged that the Spirit needed to use elements bound by time and space, but they also acknowledged that the Spirit was sovereign, and that no man can force the Spirit to move by going through the motions prescribed in the Scriptures. W.KL.

Corpus Schwenckfeldianorum, ed. C. D. Hartranft and E. E. S. Johnson, Vol. I-XV (Leipzig, 1907-39); Selina Gerhard Schultz, *Caspar Schwenckfeld von Ossig (1489-1561)* (Norristown, 1946); E. Hirsch, "Zum Verständnis Schwenckfelds," *Karl Müller Festgabe* (Tübingen, 1922); H. J. Schoeps, *Vom himmlischen Fleisch Christi* (Tübingen, 1951); Karl Ecke, *Schwenckfeld, Luther und der Gedanke einer apostolischen Reformation* (Berlin, 1911); Torsten Bergsten, "Pilgram Marbeck und seine Auseinandersetzung mit Caspar Schwenckfeld," *Kyrkohistorisk Arsskrift* (Uppsala) 1957 and 1958; Franklin H. Littell, "Spiritualizers, Anabaptists and the Church," *MQR* XXIX (1955) 34-43; J. Wach, "Caspar Schwenckfeld; A Pupil and a Teacher in the School of Christ," in *Types of Religious Experience* (London, 1951), also in *Journal of Religion* XXVI (1946) 1-29; Rufus M. Jones, *Spiritual Reformers of the Sixteenth and Seventeenth Centuries* (London, 1914); F. W. Loetscher, *Schwenckfeld's Participation in the Eucharistic Controversy of the Sixteenth Century* (Philadelphia, 1907); Hans Urner, "Die Taufe bei Caspar Schwenckfeld," *Theologische Literaturzeitung*, 1948, cols. 329-42; Wolfgang Knörrlich, *Kaspar von Schwenckfeld und die Reformation in Schlesien* (Bonn, 1957); *TA Württemberg* contains much material on Schwenckfeld.

Selbstschutz (Self-Defense) was a measure taken in some of the Mennonite settlements of Russia during the Revolution and Civil War in 1918-20. The Bolshevik Revolution in October 1917 gradually spread and reached toward the Mennonite settlements, but the major Mennonite settlements of the Ukraine were occupied by the German army between April and November 1918. When it withdrew, since the new Soviet government had not yet established itself in this area, various temporary forms of government came into being, including the group of followers of Nestor Machno (*q.v.*). They were anarchist in their outlook and set out to destroy any order and to punish those who possessed property. The settlements of Molotschna, Chortitza, Borozenko, and Zagradovka suffered untold hardships from them. The male population of a number of villages was completely annihilated and the food and property were taken. A total of some 600 people were murdered. Old and young women were raped, and consequently venereal diseases spread in the communities. Typhoid fever and other contagious diseases were also brought in. Before the German occupation army withdrew, it had drilled some Selbstschutz units and left weapons and ammunition in some communities. This was prior to the Machno incursions. In some instances the trained young men took up arms to defend their families and their property against the anarchistic bandits when they came, which in turn provoked the bandits to renewed attacks.

The question as to whether it was permissible or even the duty of the young men to defend their families against the bandits caused many discussions and tested the centuries-old principle of nonresistance. Most of the leaders and the majority of the Mennonite population did not support such views. Nevertheless, particularly among the younger generation quite a number felt that in this case it was their duty to take up arms in self-defense.

It is likely that the Molotschna Mennonites were the first to be attacked by the Machno anarchist hordes. Some German officers remained in the Molotschna to lead the Selbstschutz which they had drilled and equipped. One of the significant battles between the Machno group and the Selbstschutz took place twenty miles north of Halbstadt near the Catholic village of Blumental early in March 1919. After a fierce five-day battle, the Selbstschutz unit was overwhelmed by the Machno group which outnumbered them ten to one. Gradually they withdrew to Halbstadt. On March 9 and 10, hundreds of wagons of German refugees (Mennonite, Catholic, and Lutheran) moved toward the Crimea. The regular Red army regiments soon moved in and prevented the Machno bandits from occupying the Mennonite villages, and the Machno followers then subjected themselves to them from March to July 1919. During this time the Mennonites suffered very severely.

A similar fate overtook the Mennonites of the Chortitza (*q.v.*) settlement and the surrounding villages. Between July and September 1919 the White army under Denikin occupied this territory, fighting for the restoration of the old regime. Mennonites who had already experienced the unpredictable situation during the Revolution and had been molested by the Russian peasantry showed their sympathies toward the Denikin army as they had done before with respect to the German occupation army. Some young men were now drafted into the Denikin army. Late in September the Machno bandits moved into the Chortitza settlement, killing hundreds of people and destroying property and burning houses, particularly the families and homes of those where a member had joined the Denikin army. A most vivid description of the tribulations of the Chortitza settlement is given by the report of the eyewitness, Dietrich Neufeld, in *Ein Tagebuch aus dem Reiche des Totentanzes* (in English, *Russian Dance of Death*). According to Karl Stumpp a total of 245 individuals were murdered in the Chortitza settlement in 1919. The Chortitza Selbstschutz was set up at the end of 1918 with Jacob Niebuhr and Jacob Martin Dueck as leaders. It was to include all males 20-35 years of age.

A near-by Chortitza daughter settlement, Nikolaipol (Nikolaifeld) (*q.v.*), also suffered immeasurably. The village Dubovka (Eichenfeld) lost its male population and four women, a total of 85 persons during one night. As in other cases, the population had shown preference to an orderly government. After the occupation by the German and the Denikin armies, some had joined the Selbstschutz. All this, however, does not justify the measures taken by Machno and his bandits, although it may have helped to provoke them. The Machno raids were simply planless anarchistic behavior which expressed itself in these explosive ways under the slogan, "Anarchy is the mother of all order."

One of the settlements which suffered most severely during the Machno period was Zagradovka (q.v.). Here, too, some of the young men had been trained in the use of weapons during the German occupation and the withdrawing Germans left weapons and ammunition with the Mennonites, which was known to the surrounding Russian population. The next government was that of the Petlura bandits and the Bolsheviki, after which the White army of Denikin moved in. Property which had been taken from the Mennonites by the surrounding Russian population was restored during the occupation of the German army and now again by the White army. The fact that some of the Mennonite young men helped in returning the property was later counted against them. On Nov. 29, 1919, the Machno bandits also occupied the Zagradovka settlement. Horrors which the settlers experienced cannot be described. In one village they killed almost the total male population on November 29. Neufeld reports that 214 people were killed here and six villages were destroyed by fire.

In some of the larger Mennonite settlements like Orenburg (q.v.) and Siberia (q.v.) similar Selbstschutz organizations came into being, although they were directed more against the uncontrollable native groups such as the Bashkirs. Examples of complete nonresistance in hours of immeasurable stress and trial were furnished by the Mennonite settlements of Terek (q.v.) and Central Asia (q.v.). The majority of all settlements did not approve of any measure of self-defense although they probably did not always clearly protest against its use. Jacob H. Janzen (later of Waterloo, Ont.) at the request of the Bundeskonferenz served as a chaplain for the Mennonite men serving in the White army. He was vigorously opposed to the Selbstschutz. The total number of the Selbstschutz members given by Ehrt as 2,000 seems rather high. The official leaders and conferences regretted this development and stated publicly that it was a "grave mistake." (See particularly the proceedings of the Allgemeine Mennonitische Kongress in Ohrloff, August 1917 and the records of Allgemeine Mennonitische Bundeskonferenz, Lichtenau, 1918.)

On the whole the Selbstschutz organization was a regrettable deviation from a cherished principle of the Mennonites. It was an illustration of the fact that a peacetime principle tested under unusual conditions will likely not find 100 per cent adherence. On the whole, however, it must not be overlooked that only a small percentage arose in self-defense, which was caused by immeasurable suffering. In view of this fact it is probably more surprising that

not more of the Mennonites participated. Many of those who were in the Selbstschutz remained in Russia. Among those who joined the White army were the "62" who came to the United States via Constantinople.

Much has been written on the subject of "Machno" and the "Selbstschutz" but primarily as an outburst caused by a mortal wound. No scholarly inquiry has been made into the causes of the attack on the Mennonites, the relationship of this attack to the Selbstschutz, and the factors which led to the organization of the Selbstschutz and the opposition to it.   C.K.

Adolf Ehrt, *Das Mennonitentum in Russland* (Berlin, 1932) 113 ff.; *Die Mennoniten-Gemeinden in Russland . . . 1914 bis 1920* (Heilbronn, 1921) 50-101; Heinrich H. Schröder, *Russlanddeutsche Friesen* (Döllstädt, 1936) 52-62; B. H. Unruh, *Die Wehrlosigkeit* (an address delivered at the Allgemeine Mennonitische Konferenz on June 7, 1917); P. Arschinow, *The History of the Machno Movement, 1918-1921* (published by a "group of anarchists in Germany" in the Russian language, Berlin, 1923); Gerhard Lohrenz, *Sagradowka* (Rosthern, 1947); Heinrich Toews, *Eichenfeld-Dubowka* (n.d., Karlsruhe); Johannes Schleuning, *Aus tiefster Not* (Berlin, 1922); H. Görz, *Die Molotschnaer Ansiedlung* (Steinbach, 1950); G. A. Peters, *Menschenlos in schwerer Zeit* (Scottdale); Gerhard Toews (George De Brecht), *Die Heimat in Trümmern* (Steinbach); J. H. Janzen, *Aus meinem Leben* (Rosthern, 1929); Anton Sawatzky, "Bilder von einst und jetzt. Wer das Schwert nimmt," *Mennoblatt* XXIX (May 1, 1958) 5 f.

Silk Industry. The chief center of the silk industry in Germany, and one of the most important in Europe, well able to compete with Lyons, has for a quarter of a millennium been Crefeld (q.v.). The establishment and bringing to flower of this industry was chiefly the achievement of a number of Mennonite families, although in recent decades the Mennonite participation in the industry has been greatly reduced. The chief firm was that of F. and H. von der Leyen, established in 1669. The King of Prussia, eager to promote trade and industry, guaranteed the Mennonites absolute religious freedom because of their initiative, industry, and progressiveness and granted the silk firms special favors of various sorts.

The attempt of Johann Cornies (q.v.) to introduce silk raising in the young Mennonite settlements in the Ukraine in the second quarter of the 19th century through the planting of mulberry trees and the growing of silkworms was discontinued when wheat raising became dominant. An attempt was made in 1874-80 in the Peabody area in Marion County, Kan., by the Mennonite immigrants from Russia to introduce the silk industry.   H.S.B.

G. von Beckerath, "Die wirtschaftliche Bedeutung der Krefelder Mennoniten . . ." (diss. Bonn, 1951); G. Schmoller and O. Hintze, ed., *Die preussische Seidenindustrie* II (Berlin, 1892) (*Acta Borussica*).

Sinclair Church of God in Christ Mennonite Church, Ewart, Man., is located ½ mile west and 3 miles north of Sinclair. In 1959 the membership was 40 and the minister H. H. Barkman. It was first listed in the Yearbook (CGC) for 1954.   M.G.

Sinntal Bruderhof, a community of the Society of Brothers founded in 1955 at Bad Brückenau in northern Bavaria, Germany. In 1959 the population was about 60, most of them having returned **from**

Paraguay. The Sinntal Bruderhof earns its living by toymaking and some market gardening and is particularly active in reaching out to the younger generation in Germany. It publishes *Der Pflug*, the German edition of *The Plough*.   E.C.H.A.

Sipman, Dirck, a well-to-do Mennonite of Crefeld, Germany, one of the three original purchasers of land in Pennsylvania, the others being Jacob Telner and Jan Streypers, each of whom on March 10, 1682 (1683?), bought 5,000 acres of William Penn through Benjamin Furly, Penn's agent in Rotterdam. On Jan. 14, 1686, Sipman bought another 1,000 acres of Govert Remke, who had bought them in 1683. In 1698 he sold his land to Isaac van Bebber. He never went to Pennsylvania.   H.S.B.

W. I. Hull, *William Penn and the Dutch Quaker Migration to Pennsylvania* (Swarthmore, 1935).

Smirna Mennonite Church, Coamo Arriba, Puerto Rico, was founded in 1950 as an outpost of the Bethany congregation. The first converts were baptized Oct. 21, 1951. The meetinghouse was erected in 1953. In 1958 the membership was 19, with Jose M. Ortiz and Lester Hershey as ministers.   H.S.B.

Gladys Widmer, *We Enter Puerto Rico* (Elkhart, 1952).

Smucker, Isaac (1810-93), was the first Amish bishop in northern Indiana. He wrote his name Schmucker in German and Smoker in English, but his son, Jonathan P. Smucker, decided to follow the latter spelling. Isaac Smucker was the great-grandson of Christian Smucker, of Bern, Switzerland, who settled for a time at Montbéliard in France before coming to America. Christian Smucker's son John (1740-1809) married Barbara Stoltzfus of Zweibrücken and settled in Berks County, Pa. John's son Christian (1775-1857) married Elizabeth Stutzman and lived in Lancaster County. On June 10, 1832, Isaac married Sarah Troyer (1811-86) of Holmes County, Ohio. They lived first in Wayne County, Ohio, but in 1838 they settled in Knox County, Ohio, where in the fall of 1838 he was ordained as an Amish preacher. In November 1841 they settled in Elkhart County, Ind., where in 1843 he was ordained bishop, probably by Amish bishops from Ohio. Smucker lived from March 1851 to August 1852 in McLean County, Ill., then settled at the Haw Patch (Topeka) in Lagrange County, Ind., where he lived until his death on Nov. 16, 1893. Personally he retained the dress and appearance of an Amish bishop all his days, but his congregation (now called Maple Grove) gradually became indistinguishable from the Mennonites of northern Indiana. Smucker and Jonas Troyer (from 1854) were the two pioneer bishops in the Elkhart-Lagrange Amish settlement who established the Forks, Clinton (Frame), and Haw Patch (Maple Grove) congregations of Amish Mennonites, which in 1916 merged with the Mennonites of the area.   J.C.W.

Society of Brothers, since 1939 the official name of the new Anabaptists (Hutterites, *q.v.*) founded by Eberhard Arnold (*q.v.*, 1883-1935) in 1922 at Sannerz, Hesse-Nassau, Germany, holding all goods in common like the early Hutterites, though at that time without knowledge of the existence of the con-

tinuing Hutterian brotherhood in North America. The term "Bruderhof," first applied to the group when it established the Rhönbruderhof (*q.v.*) at Neuhof near Fulda, Germany, in 1926, was a conscious imitation of the historic Hutterite term known to Arnold from his study of the 16th-century Hutterites. Contact was established with the North American Hutterites in 1928, and in 1930-31 Arnold visited their Bruderhofs. In December 1930 he was ordained a Hutterite elder at the Stand-Off Colony near Macleod, Alberta, and commissioned to lead the new German Bruderhof group as a part of the ancient Hutterite brotherhood. In 1955 there was a complete break between the old Hutterites and the new Hutterites, now named Society of Brothers, due largely to the differences in cultural practices as well as in general outlook, the "Brothers" being committed to aggressive outreach in the modern world.

The Rhönbruderhof was closed in 1937 by eviction and expulsion from Germany by the National Socialist government who would not tolerate this "communistic" movement. A temporary Bruderhof (Almbruderhof, *q.v.*) was established in the principality of Liechtenstein, at Silum, Post Triesenberg, in 1933-38. The Cotswold Bruderhof (*q.v.*), established in 1936 at Ashton Keynes, Wiltshire, England, became the home of the ongoing movement, which had 250 souls by 1938, when a second Bruderhof was established (1939) at Oaksey near by. The further growth of the brotherhood was interrupted by World War II, and the entire group, except several persons left behind to liquidate the property, migrated to Paraguay with the help of the MCC in 1940-41 under heavy pressure from the British government, who feared they would aid the Germans in a possible invasion. Attempts to secure permission to settle in the United States and Canada near the Hutterite colonies there failed. Meanwhile, the representatives who remained in England were able in 1942 to start a new Bruderhof at Wheathill (*q.v.*) in Shropshire, address Bromdon, Bridgnorth, which in 1959 had a population of 110. A second Bruderhof was founded in Bulstrode, Gerrards Cross, Bucks, in 1958, which had about 100 population in 1959.

In Paraguay meanwhile the Bruderhof settlement called Primavera (*q.v.*), established in 1941, about 80 miles northeast of Asunción, had grown by 1959 to three village communities with a population of over 650, and a "Bruderhof House" in Asunción. The group is incorporated under the name "Sociedad de Hermanos." In 1954 a small Bruderhof was established at El Arado, Montevideo, Uruguay, which had a population of 60 in 1959.

In 1954 a Bruderhof was established at Woodcrest, Rifton, N.Y., about 50 miles north of New York City, which had grown to 230 (70 members, 115 children, rest guests) by 1959. A second American Bruderhof, Oak Lake, was established in 1957 at Farmington, near Uniontown, Pa., which had a population of 150 in 1959 (50 members, 75 children). In 1958 a third American Bruderhof was established at Evergreen, Norfolk, Conn., which had a population of 60 in 1959 (20 members, 30 children). The Forest River Bruderhof, near Fordville,

N.D., which had separated from the old Hutterites to join the Society of Brothers in 1955, was discontinued in 1957. The newest European Bruderhof is Sinntal, established in 1955 at Bad Brückenau, northeast of Frankfurt, near the East Zone border. In 1959 it had a population of some 60. In 1959 the Society had a total population of some 1,500 in all its communities, of whom some 600 were regular or novice members. The name "community" has now supplanted "Bruderhof" everywhere except in Germany. However, all the communities are completely communal in organization and pattern of life.

The publishing agency of the group is the Plough Publishing House at Bromdon, England (Wheathill Bruderhof), established in 1938. The group organ is a quarterly journal, *The Plough,* first number March 1938, discontinued with III, 1 (spring of 1940), resumed in the spring of 1953, with New Series I, 1. It has parallel editions in the German (*Der Pflug*), Spanish (*El Arado*), and Esperanto (*La Pugilo*). Prior to 1938 three Bruderhof Letters were issued (September 1936, Christmas 1936, and August 1937). Pamphlets are also issued annually.

The Society of Brothers is a Christian brotherhood which holds all property in common, regards all work as of equal worth, upholds a radical peace testimony with complete nonparticipation in war and military service, rejects all swearing of oaths, litigation, and office-holding, practices simplicity of life, is governed by unanimous consent of the members in each community, and bases membership on unity of faith in Christ regardless of race, class, or nationality. Candidates for membership are received on probation for a variable period, after which they are received through baptism by vote of the group on profession of adherence to the principles of the brotherhood. All property is surrendered to the group upon reception into membership. The Society reaches out into the world through mission journeys, education, hospital work, youth work camps, and publication. (See **Hutterian Brethren.**) H.S.B., E.C.H.A.

Eberhard Arnold, *The Hutterian Brothers. Four Centuries of Common Life and Work* (Ashton Keynes, 1940); *Living Together* (an illustrated account of the history, life, and work of the Society of Brothers in three continents) (Farmington, 1958); *Ten Years of Community Living. The Wheathill Bruderhof, 1942-52* (Bromdon, 1953); *Eberhard Arnold, From His Life and Writings, A Witness to Community* (Bromdon, 1953); *True Surrender and Christian Community of Goods, From the Great Article Book by Peter Walpot 1577* (Bromdon, 1957), reprint from *MQR XXXI* (1957)

South Danvers Mennonite Church, located 2 miles south of Danvers, was formed by the Hessian Mennonites from Butler County, Ohio, who had begun to have worship in their homes in 1842, then joined the Yoder Amish Church (North Danvers, *q.v.*), when it built its meetinghouse in 1853 about 5 miles northeast of Danvers. But in 1859 the Hessian group withdrew, building its own meetinghouse in 1864, with c100 members. In 1908 it joined the Central Conference (*q.v.*). In 1914 the congregation added a rented church building in the town of Danvers, and in 1919 closed the country building. In 1943, with 34 members left, it merged with North Danvers. Early ministers were Michael Kistler 1842-

55, and Christian Gingerich 1855-1908. John Kinsinger and John Gingerich were the leaders from 1885 to the late 1920's. H.S.B.

South Nampa (Idaho) Mennonite Church (Central Conference), now extinct, located in Nampa, was organized in 1908 by a group of members largely of Central Illinois Conference background but with some who had left the Nampa M.C. congregation and a few of G.C.M. origin. Lee Lantz served as pastor 1908-11 and 1918-c32, when the church closed. Maximum membership was 61 in 1926. The congregation joined the Central Conference in 1910. H.S.B.

South Washington Mennonite Church (Central Conference), now extinct, was organized in 1895 as a schism from the East Washington church when the bishop of the congregation, Michael Kinsinger, withdrew with about 100 members because of the German language question; they built their own meetinghouse about 1½ miles south of the mother church. The maximum membership was about 40 in 1921. In 1937 the congregation of some 75 members reunited with the mother congregation, which had moved into the town of Washington, Ill., in 1925 and renamed itself Calvary Mennonite Church (*q.v.*). John J. Kennel was pastor 1912-32. H.S.B.

Spanish American Mission (CGC), Tucumcari, N.M., had a membership of 27 in 1959, with Dennis Smith as minister. It was first listed in the Yearbook (CGC) for 1950 as the Tucumcari Mission. M.G.

Spiritual Reformers: see Spiritualists.

Spitalmaier, Hans: see Spittelmaier.

Spöhrlin: see Spoerle.

Spörle: see Spoerle.

Starbuck (Man.) **Beerdigungskasse: see Mutual Support Society.**

Streicher, Helena (d. 1549), was the widow of Hans Streicher of Ulm, a shopkeeper by occupation, and the mother of five daughters, Katherina, Helena, Anna, Maria, and Agatha, and a son, Hans Augustin Streicher. Both Agatha and Hans Augustin Streicher were physicians, the latter serving as city physician (*Stadtarzt*) in Ulm in 1561. All members of this family were members of the Schwenckfeld conventicle in Ulm, and Schwenckfeld appears to have spent much time in their home, even sending some letters under the names of members of the family. According to Elmer Johnson and Schwenckfeld's biographer, Mrs. Schultz, there remains little doubt that Schwenckfeld died and was buried in the Streicher home in Ulm. There is no evidence that the Streichers were once Anabaptists as is sometimes claimed.

Apparently Helena Streicher and Magdalena Marschalck von Pappenheim (*q.v.*) were known to each other. The latter became an Anabaptist and represented Marpeck's position to Mrs. Streicher. It is difficult to ascertain how much correspondence moved between these two ladies; most likely all of it reflected the differences between Marpeck and Schwenckfeld. Loserth published Marpeck's letter to Helena (undated), and a reply to her written by Magdalena Marschalck exists in manuscript form in the Zürich Library.

The Streicher family appears to have been outstanding in its piety and is noteworthy for its hospitality and its attitude of mediation between Schwenckfelders and Anabaptists. Much of the strength of the home must have come from this noble widow, Helena Streicher.   W.KL.

Strepers: see Streypers.

Studienkommission, Russlandmennonitische, a committee of three Mennonite leaders of the Ukraine, from the Molotschna settlement, appointed in 1919 after the terrible experiences of the Mennonites of Russia in World War I, the Revolution, and their aftermath, apparently by the Allgemeiner Mennonitischer Kongress (*q.v.*). The primary purpose of the Commission was to report to Western Europe and to America on conditions among the Mennonites in Russia and to study settlement possibilities abroad. The members were A. A. Friesen, chairman, B. H. Unruh, secretary (both teachers in the Kommerzschule in Halbstadt), and C. H. Warkentin, a merchant. Johann Esau, former mayor of Ekaterinoslav, then living in Berlin, Germany, offered to join the group. Friesen and Unruh, together with H. H. Epp of Chortitza, had been sent to Germany in the summer of 1918 as a commission to study the possibilities of repatriation to Germany, where they learned that such a plan was impossible.

The Studienkommission members left Russia Jan. 1, 1920, via Constantinople, and after spending some time in Germany and Holland consulting Mennonite leaders there, reached New York on June 13. Their urging led to the founding of the Mennonite Central Committee at Elkhart, Ind., in July, and the Canadian Central Committee at Rosthern, Sask., on Oct. 18, 1920 (became the Canadian Mennonite Board of Colonization May 17, 1922). As the only preacher in the group, Unruh was sent on a deputation tour of Mennonite churches in the United States and Canada (accompanied for a time by Esau, who soon returned to Berlin, to settle later in California), while Friesen studied settlement possibilities in the western states and provinces and in Mexico. Unruh returned to Europe on Nov. 1, 1920, while Friesen and Warkentin stayed in Canada. Unruh then set up in Karlsruhe a permanent office for Russian Mennonite emigration matters, where he lived until his death in 1959.

The formation in December 1920 of the Dutch Mennonite Algemene Kommissie voor buitenlandsche Nooden at Rotterdam was due in part to a proposal by Unruh. A. A. Friesen was for many years secretary of the CMBC. His files, with much material on the Studienkommission and the immigration of the Russian Mennonites, are now in BeCL. Unruh's files have been lost, but his unpublished manuscript "Fügung und Führung" (copy in CMBC, MCC, and GCL) contains much information on the same area.   H.S.B.

Sumerauer, Leonhard: see Summerauer, Leonhard.

Summer Camps: see Camps, Mennonite Church.

Sunchild Indian Mission (CGC) is located 38 miles northeast of Rocky Mountain House, Alberta. In 1958 it had 13 members, with Dewey Unruh as its superintendent. It was first listed in the Yearbook (CGC) for 1949.   M.G.

Sunday School Conference (Convention), a meeting of Christian workers interested in Sunday-school work, continuing over a day or more, a prominent feature of church life in most North American Mennonite groups in the 20th century. The first known such meeting was the Sunday School Convention in the Eastern District Conference (GCM) on Oct. 2, 1876, sponsored by A. B. Shelly (*q.v.*), and held annually thereafter for many years.

In the Mennonite Church (MC) the first S.S. Conference was held at Kitchener, Ont., in 1891, followed by a general S.S. Conference Oct. 5-8, 1892, held at the Clinton Frame Mennonite Church near Goshen, Ind. This was an epoch-making meeting with unusual influence on missionary development as well as on the growth of the S.S. movement. After a second general conference, held at the Zion Church, Bluffton, Ohio, in 1893, and a third at the Forks Church near Middlebury, Ind., in 1894, the general meetings were replaced by district conferences, organized according to the church conference area: Indiana-Michigan (1895), Ohio (1895), Southwestern Pa. (1895), Kansas-Nebraska (1895), Illinois (1896), etc. Ontario operated its annual conferences apparently without interruption from 1891 on. These annual conventions, usually lasting two days and later often held in a tent purchased or rented for the purpose, and attended by large crowds, became great centers of inspiration, stimulus, and progressive influence. In the 1940's the name of most of these conferences was changed to "Christian Workers' Conference" or "Christian Education Conference." In some areas they have been held attached to the annual church conference or the annual district mission board meeting. Beginning in 1952 (at Goshen) national S.S. conventions have been sponsored by the Commission for Christian Education quadrennially. Some local congregations or groups of congregations established quarterly or semiannual S.S. meetings on a Sunday afternoon and evening. Many of these are still running after 50 years, but some have died out. In the Lancaster Conference since 1934 annual S.S. meetings have been held with different congregations across the conference, recently called Christian Nurture meetings since they are sponsored by the Christian Nurture Committee of the Conference, organized in 1948.

Sunday-school conventions are also popular in the Mennonite Brethren Church, especially in Canada, where district conventions are held annually in each province where there is an organized M.B. Conference. In the General Conference Mennonite Church, Sunday-school conventions have been held particularly in the prairie states and provinces, though not on a permanently organized basis. Other Mennonite groups have also sponsored such conventions, though not always regularly.

Sverdlovsk, district and city (formerly Ekaterinburg), located in Asiatic Soviet Russia, lie on the western slopes of the Ural Mountains. Forest and mineral wealth have transformed it into an industrial region. Chief cities are Sverdlovsk, Nizhni Tagil, and Krasnouralsk. Many Mennonites have found their home in this region since the days of the exile and evacuation before and during World War II. They are primarily located in the industrial areas. (See **Siberia.**) C.K.

Taufers: see **Tauffers.**

Theater, Mennonite Attitude Toward the. The Mennonites of Europe and America originally rejected the theater completely as "a worldly amusement," and most of the Mennonites outside of Europe still do so. The Waterlander group of Dutch Mennonites gave up their opposition to the theater quite early, and Joost van den Vondel (*q.v.*), the noted Dutch poet and dramatist, was a deacon of the Waterlander Church in Amsterdam 1616-20. Jan Theunis (*q.v.*), a member of the same congregation, kept a kind of amusement place, a combination of theater, museum, and wineshop, which was frequented by many Mennonites. By the end of the 18th century the Lamist Mennonites of Holland took full part in the Amsterdam amusements including the theater. In Northwest Germany the opposition to the theater faded out in the 19th century as was the case to some extent in West Prussia and the Palatinate, though not in the congregations in the Badischer Verband (*q.v.*). In Baden, France, Switzerland, and Russia, opposition to the theater has been maintained.

In North America the ban on the public theater has been maintained in most groups. In the General Conference Mennonite group there is no ban in the strict sense although attendance is not widespread and is frowned upon. Exceptions have been made in some groups regarding attendance at the opera, Shakespearean plays, etc. The ban on the theater was usually extended to the commercial motion picture theater when it arose. Although the ban has not always been strictly maintained, attendance at commercial movies is generally frowned upon.

No known case of a Mennonite entering the profession of acting has come to public notice. The Anabaptists who had formerly been participants in the drama guilds in Holland known as the Rederijkers dropped out of such groups when they were converted to Anabaptism (e.g., David Joris).

The performance of dramatics in Mennonite schools and colleges, once banned or frowned upon, has come to be common in most Mennonite colleges, though not in some of the schools of the Mennonite Church (MC). Youth groups in some congregations in some Mennonite bodies, e.g., G.C.M., frequently put on plays with religious or ethical content. It has been quite common to include dialogues and playlets in Christmas programs given by Sunday-school children.

A number of Low German folk plays have been written by Jacob H. Janzen and Arnold Dyck which have been frequently performed in Mennonite schools and communities.

The literary materials written by American Mennonites giving the grounds for the Christian's opposition to the theater, as well as sermons and addresses on the subject, have generally stressed the following points: the low ethical quality of many plays, the association of the commercial theater and its actors with low standards of morality in many places, the insincerity of "acting a part," the temptations to worldliness connected with either the drama or the players, a general opposition to commercialized entertainment and amusements. Very little has actually been published by Mennonites. Among the brief tracts or booklets in this field should be mentioned: Paul Erb, *The Theater* (1928), and C. F. Derstine, *Hell's Playground, Theaters and Movies* (1921).

For a report on the Anabaptist and Mennonite theme in dramatic literature, see **Literature.**

H.S.B.

Thomashof, Bibelheim, located about 3 miles east of Durlach, in Baden, Germany, is an influential Mennonite retreat center and vacation home (*Erholungsheim*), also the mother house of the deaconess work of the *Verband* (*q.v.*). Purchased in March 1924 by a group of Mennonite ministers and laymen from David Horsch, the owner of the adjacent estate of Lamprechtshof, with support from the congregations of the *Verband,* it is managed by a self-perpetuating board of trustees known as the Bruderrat. The original property, consisting of a remodeled wayside inn and a small chapel and about an acre of ground, was augmented in 1955 by a modern 30-bed dormitory. Christian Schnebele has been the housefather from the beginning. Annually a series of short winter Bible "courses" for youth and for ministers are held, in addition to special conferences. The institution is largely self-supporting through paying guests who come for periods of rest and refreshment. H.S.B.

Tiessen, Peter, Jr. and **Sr.,** were ministers and elders of the Danzig Mennonite Church during the time of transition from the lay to the salaried ministry. Peter Tiessen Jr. was elected minister at the age of thirty-six, Aug. 17, 1800, to help his father, Elder Peter Tiessen Sr., who had been elected minister in 1774. It was during their ministry that the Frisian and the Flemish churches were united in 1808. When the father died, March 17, 1825, the son was elected elder. He died Oct. 1, 1826, and was succeeded by Jacob van der Smissen (*q.v.*), the first theologically trained minister of Danzig. C.K.

H. G. Mannhardt, *Die Danziger Mennonitengemeinde* (Danzig, 1919) 134-35, 151-57.

Tilsit, formerly district city in east Prussia, now named Sovetsk, of the Kaliningradsk region of Soviet Russia, is located on the left bank of the Neman River. A "Mennonite Congregation of Lithuania near Tilsit" was listed for decades. The history of this congregation and settlement is found in the articles **Lithuania** and **Gumbinnen.** C.K.

Toews, Johann, was elected minister of a Mennonite church in West Prussia in 1832 and elder in 1853. In that year he joined the Mennonites who migrated

to Russia and established the Trakt Mennonite settlement (*q.v.*) and church, of which Johann Wall (*q.v.*) was the elder. Johann Toews functioned as honorary elder. Little is known about his life. (*Menn. Bl.* 1860, 21; 1862, 15; 1867, 54; 1889, 59.)
C.K.

Tomsk, district and city, are located in Asiatic Russia, on the right bank of the Tom River near its junction with the Ob River. The city is connected with the main line of the Trans-Siberian Railroad, and is an educational center founded in 1602. Formerly the Barnaul (*q.v.*) or Slavgorod (*q.v.*) Mennonite settlement was located in the province of Tomsk. It is now part of the Altai district of the R.S.F.S.R. Since the period of exile and World War II many Mennonites have been transplanted to the Tomsk district and city. Details about their number, location, and occupation are not known. (See also **Siberia.**)
C.K.

Transdanubia, an old name for the westernmost part of the former kingdom of Hungary, roughly the *comitat* of Sopron-Odenburg, today in the main the Austrian province of Burgenland. It has long been known that Anabaptists existed here in the 16th and 17th centuries. Since, however, the Hutterite chronicle mentions this area but slightly, and pertinent research has been carried out exclusively in the Magyar language, Western scholars have much neglected this entire area. The country was settled primarily by German frontiersmen (history speaks of the "Militärgrenze," i.e., a strip of land toward Turkey where every farmhouse was at the same time a small fortress). Because of the Turkish invasion of Balkan countries, many Croatian peasants sought refuge here too. Popularly they were known as Krovoten or Krabaten. Finally, here as elsewhere, the greater part of the land was in the hands of Hungarian manorial lords, and of them it is known that they were rather friendly toward the Anabaptists because of their good craftsmanship and husbandry. Thus it is no small wonder that the archives of these noble families contain many references to Anabaptist craftsmen (mainly potterers; see **Ceramics**) and barber-surgeons (see **Physicians, Hutterite**).

Alexander Payr in his book *Protestant Church History of Oedenburg* (in the Magyar language) claims that city records mention Anabaptist craftsmen on and off from 1547 to 1635. Of course it could be argued that these men were but "loaned out" single brethren from Slovakia who went to work everywhere, without however establishing Anabaptist colonies. But at least in one instance this seems to be contradicted by a passage in the Hutterite Chronicle itself which, for the year 1632, records the death of one brother Lorenz Putz, "Diener des Wortes," at Gissingen, who had served the congregation beyond the Danube in "Krabatenland" for about one year (*Chronik,* 815). Gissingen is to be identified as today's Güssing in Burgenland; a brotherhood settlement must have existed there for some time. Incidentally, the name Putz is well known for the continued craftsmanship of the family in the field of ceramics.

Local research has also proved the existence of Anabaptists in the small town of Güns in the same general area around 1660 (see the article **Güns** by Loserth, who got his information from a local church historian). Noteworthy is also a remark by the late Professor Loesche (1926) that the Lutheran minister of the city of Schlaining, Burgenland, once found in the hands of playing children an old Anabaptist codex of 1612, incomplete and poorly preserved, which contained eleven Anabaptist hymns and several medical recipes. The book is definitely of Hutterite origin and points again to a former presence of these brethren in Transdanubia. A Hungarian scholar informed this writer that at least three places mentioned in the Hutterite Chronicle were erroneously identified by scholars as Moravian or Slovakian, in reality being Transdanubian villages, thus indicating the existence of Bruderhofs in this area. The names are Freischütz, Kreutz, and Gätta; documentation will be given in forthcoming publications. Most important of all, however, the same expert claims that many of the beautiful ceramic tablewares for the nobles (now in museums) were produced in potteries in Transdanubia, as can be gathered from inscriptions on these pieces.

All this seems to indicate that Anabaptists (obviously of the Hutterite variety) were more widely spread in Eastern Europe than was formerly known, mainly in the century 1550-1650. No doubt both pottery and archive records will yield still more information as research in this area proceeds and becomes better known.
R.F.

This article is based in the main on information by the Hungarian scholar Bela Krisztinkovich of Budapest, an expert in the field of ceramics. See also Zieglschmid, *Chronik,* 815; G. Loesche, *Archivalische Beiträge zur Geschichte des Täufertums* (Vienna, 1926) 51-54; Alexander Payr, *A. Sopron ev. egyhazkocsy törtenete,* p. 91.

Tri-State Bible Camp, located on Lake Shetek near Currie, Minn., is operated by a number of Mennonite churches around Mountain Lake, Minn., Luton, Iowa, and Marion, S.D.
H.S.B.

Twenty-Sixth Street Mission, now extinct, located at 26th St. and Halstead St., Chicago, Ill., was founded in 1906 by A. M. Eash under the Mennonite Board of Missions and Charities (MC). A new building was erected in 1910. In 1924 the building was sold to the Central Conference, which took over responsibility for the work. A. M. Eash served continuously as pastor 1900-35, except for some interruptions in 1919 ff. The high point of membership was 72 in 1935, with over 300 in the Sunday school. In 1940 the work was closed and the building sold.
H.S.B.

Tyrol: see Tirol.

Tyumen, district and city, Asiatic Soviet Russia. The city is located 125 miles southwest of Tobolsk and 190 miles east of Sverdlovsk. Established in 1585, it became the first Russian town east of the Ural Mountains. Tyumen district was created in 1945 with Tyumen city as capital. Many Mennonites were sent to this area during the period of exile and evacuation from European Russia. No definite information is available regarding their number nor the areas of concentration. (See **Siberia**.)

C.K.

Uhrmacher, Hans (Felix), of the Marpeck Anabaptist group in Moravia, was the son-in-law of Leupold Scharnschlager (q.v.), having married his daughter Ursula in 1531. They apparently met in Strasbourg where Uhrmacher also became an Anabaptist. In Leupold Scharnschlager's letter to Michel Leubel (q.v.) at Speyer in 1532 he sends greetings from Hans Uhrmacher, who had been to see Leubel at Speyer several times, recently. In 1533 Scharnschlager's wife wrote a letter to her brother stating that the young couple was at present in Moravia. Apart from a few brief visits they appear to have lived in Moravia the rest of their lives and Uhrmacher may well be the "Hans von Strasbourg" referred to in the Hutterian Chronicle who sprang to the defense of Gabriel Ascherham when Jakob Hutter spoke against Gabriel.

A letter from Hans Uhrmacher to his father-in-law dated Oct. 29, 1538, shows that he owed to Scharnschlager his conversion to Anabaptism. It indicates also that a very close spiritual relationship existed between them. The letter was written from Austerlitz (printed by Schiess) and implies the prospect of an imminent visit between the families. A local witness reported that Hans repaired the village clock at Ilanz; this must have happened between 1546 and 1559. In 1538 Hans states that he and his wife had just gone through a siege of illness and unemployment.

Uhrmacher apparently later lived in the town of Znaim (q.v.). On April 18, 1559, at the third discussion (as established by Jarrold Zeman) between the Pilgramites and the Moravian Brethren, the spokesman for the Anabaptists was a brother who had earlier lived in the mountainous country (Müller thinks it was Tirol). He had come across a copy of the apology of the Moravian Brethren and tried to find out more about them by moving to Moravia. Because he was a skilled watchmaker the residents of Znaim retained him when King Ferdinand ordered the expulsion of all Anabaptists from the Moravian cities (probably 1547-54). It is reported by the Moravian recorder that the Anabaptists of Znaim were "a little more peaceable and understanding" in their conversations with the Moravian Brethren than the Anabaptists at Eibenschitz had been.

One problem in identifying this Uhrmacher with Hans Felix is the place of residence. The letter written to Scharnschlager is dated from Austerlitz, while the Moravian Brethren report said that he was living at Znaim, having settled there when he arrived in Moravia. It is possible that this report is not reliable and that Uhrmacher changed his place of residence.

There is other evidence that the Marpeck Brotherhood was most anxious to conduct conversations with the Moravian Brethren, and it thus seems likely that the renowned Uhrmacher so eager to converse with them was indeed Scharnschlager's son-in-law. If this is the case, the Marpeck group did **not** restrict its conversation to fellow Anabaptists, but also sought an interchange of thought with the Moravian Brethren. As in their discussions with the Reformed party, the initiative came from the Anabaptists; they did not give up immediately even though the areas of disagreement were too great by this time to make conversation fruitful.

Uhrmacher's death occurred before that of Scharnschlager (as a letter of the latter's wife indicates) and hence must be placed between 1559 and 1563.

W.KL.

J. Th. Müller, "Die Berührungen der alten und neuen Brüderunität mit den Täufern," *Ztscht für Brüdergeschichte* IV (1910) 197-207; T. Schiess, "Aus dem Leben eines Ilanzer Schulmeisters," *Bündnerisches Monatsblatt* (1916) 73-89; *TA Baden-Pfalz*, 420; Zieglschmid, *Chronik*, 116.

Union Avenue Mennonite Church (MC), the name used for the Mennonite Home Mission (q.v.) from 1955 to 1957 when it moved to Englewood and became the Englewood Mennonite Church (q.v.). The address was 1907 S. Union, Chicago.   M.G.

United Brethren in Christ Church, founded in 1800 by Philip Otterbein, who came to America in 1752 as a missionary of the German Reformed Church, and Martin Boehm, a former bishop of the Mennonite Church in Lancaster County, Pa., who had been excommunicated in 1777 because of teaching Methodistic doctrine. Otterbein and Boehm were elected the first bishops of the church. Boehm took a considerable group of Mennonites with him into the new church, and others joined the church later at various places. Christian Newcomer, an early prominent leader in the U.B. church, was one of the Mennonite ministers to transfer. In 1941, when it had a membership of c381,000, it merged with the Evangelical Church (q.v.) to form the Evangelical United Brethren Church.   H.S.B.

Unruh, Benjamin Heinrich (1881-1959), outstanding Russian Mennonite teacher and later emigration leader, was born at Timir-Bulat (German, Philippstal), Crimea, Russia, on Sept. 17, 1881, the son of Heinrich Benjamin Unruh (q.v., d. 1883) and Elizabeth Wall (an older brother was Abraham H. Unruh). His father was the elder of the Mennonite Church at Karassan, Crimea, but Benjamin was baptized a member of the M.B. Church at Spat at the age of 18. Benjamin attended the Orloff Zentralschule, Molotschna, followed by the pedagogical course at Halbstadt. He passed the teachers' examination at the Russian secondary school at Simferopol, and in 1899 the Russian state examination at Kharkov. His education was crowned by attendance at two higher schools in Basel, Switzerland, followed by the University 1900-7, and the Predigerseminar, parallel in the earlier years. He received the Licentiate in theology, which was equivalent to the doctor's degree, in Church History at Basel, and the honorary Doctor of Theology at the University of Heidelberg in 1937. He also served for a number of years as lecturer in Russian language and literature at the Karlsruhe Technische Hochschule.

Unruh's career in Russia was that of teacher, serving at the Halbstadt Kommerzschule, where he taught German and Religion. He wrote a

Bibelkunde for the Mennonite schools of Russia which caused some controversy in Mennonite circles there. In 1920 he was appointed a member of the Studienkommission (*q.v.*) chosen by the Mennonites of Russia to seek out emigration possibilities in foreign countries. As such he spent most of 1920 in western Europe and North America. After his return to Europe in November 1920 he settled in Karlsruhe, Germany, living most of the time in the suburb of Rüppurr. He died in a hospital in Mannheim on May 12, 1959. His first wife (in 1907) was Frieda Hege (d. 1946), a daughter of Elder Christian Hege of Breitenau; of this marriage eight children were born. His second wife was Paula Hotel, daughter of Elder Johannes Hotel of Batzenhof near Durlach.

From 1920 to the end of his active days, *c*1955, Unruh served the interests of his Russian Mennonite brethren in emigration and resettlement, working in this respect directly as commissioner for the Canadian Mennonite Board of Colonization (*q.v.*) for the emigration to Canada 1921-25 and later, and for the MCC in emigration to Paraguay 1930-33. He long continued a close relationship with the new settlements in both countries by correspondence and the writing of articles in the German Mennonite press. In Germany he was a member of numerous organizations dealing with German refugees from Russia; e.g., Brüder in Not (*q.v.*) 1930 ff., and Landsmannschaft der Deutschen aus Russland (*q.v.*). In his varied service in this field he became widely known and highly regarded and rendered extraordinary service. Although not an ordained minister (he refused ordination unless he could be ordained by all branches of the Mennonites in Russia), and he never transferred his membership to a Mennonite congregation in Germany, he was an able speaker and preacher and was a well-known figure at Mennonite conferences in Germany.

Unruh was the author not only of numerous articles in the German Mennonite press of Germany and Canada but of a major scholarly work, *Die niederländisch - niederdeutschen Hintergründe der mennonitischen Ostwanderungen im 16., 18. und 19. Jahrhundert* (Karlsruhe-Rüppurr, 1955). His "Fügung und Führung im Mennonitischen Welt-Hilfswerk 1920-1933, Streiflichter in persönlicher und dienstlicher Rückschau," published in 1966, has been deposited in manuscript with the Mennonite Central Committee at Akron, Pa., and the Canadian Mennonite Board of Colonization at Saskatoon, Sask.　　　　　　　　　　　　H.S.B.

"Benjamin H. Unruh" (an autobiography), *Der Bote* XXVIII (1951), Sept. 5, 1 f.; Sept. 12, 1-3; Sept. 19, 2 f.; Sept. 26, 2 f.; Horst Quiring, "Benjamin H. Unruh zum 70. Geburtstag," *Gesch.-Bl.* 1952, 27-34; Chr. Schnebele, "Auf Benjamin Unruh's Tätigkeit," *Menn. Jahrbuch,* 1952, 45-47.

Urteil von dem Schwert, Das, an important early Moravian Anabaptist writing of 1529, discovered in manuscript form in Switzerland in 1951, written by Clemens Adler (*q.v.*).　　　　　　　H.S.B.

Valley Mennonite Brethren Church, Pacoima, Cal., was established in 1956 as a Home Missions congregation. It had 23 members in 1959, with James P.

Wiebe as pastor. Plans had been made to break ground for a meetinghouse in 1959.　　　M.G.

Vancouver (B.C.) **Mission** (GCM) was organized March 18, 1956, with 63 charter members. In 1958 it had a membership of 77, with Peter Kehler as pastor.　　　　　　　　　　　　　　M.G.

Vetter, Jakob (1872-1918), a German Pietistic evangelist, at first working in Oberhessen under the Chrischona organization, then after 1902 in the Tent Mission (*Zeltmission*), which he founded. Charles G. Finney was his inspiration and model in evangelization. He rejected the pentecostal movement and universalism, and was in general a well-balanced person. He exerted a strong influence among the Swiss Mennonites, particularly in the Jura where he often held Bible conferences. According to Neff (*ML* I, 616), he was also received among the Mennonites of Württemberg and the Palatinate and exerted considerable influence there.　　　　　　　　　　　　　　　H.S.B.

Hans Bruns, *Jakob Vetter, der Gründer ver Zeltmission* (Giessen and Basel, 1954).

Victoria Avenue Mennonite Church (GCM), 1409 Victoria Ave., Regina, Sask., is not yet organized as a congregation but in 1959 had approximately 50 adult participants. Its church was bought from the Mormons in 1955. Norman D. Bergen was the pastor in 1959.　　　　　　　　M.G.

Villa Guayra (Brazil) Mennonite Brethren Church was organized in 1957 as a daughter congregation of Bouqueirao (*q.v.*). In 1957 it had 58 members, with Johann Froese and Abram Klassen as associate ministers.　　　　　　　　　　　　　H.S.B.

Vine Street Mennonite Church: see **Lancaster Mennonite Mission.**

Vineland Burial Society (Vineland Beerdigungs-Kasse), Vineland, Ont., was established in 1934. Though it serves primarily Mennonites in Ontario, it has members in Manitoba, Saskatchewan, Alberta, British Columbia, and Kansas. In 1953 it had approximately 2,500 members and paid out $1,815 at the rate of $273 per death.　　　　　M.G.

Virgil Plattner: see **Plattner, Vigilg.**

Virginia Mennonite Board of Missions and Charities (MC), organized 1916, incorporated 1919, consists of 21 members elected by the bishop districts and certain congregations of the Virginia Mennonite Conference. In 1959 it operated nine home mission stations (six city missions in Virginia, one city mission in Tennessee, and two rural missions in Kentucky). It also operated foreign missions in Jamaica and Sicily. Its official organ is the *Missionary Light.*　　　　　　　　　　　　　　H.S.B.

Virginia Mennonite Home, Inc., Harrisonburg, Va., a 40-bed home for the aged, was established in 1954 under a local Mennonite (MC) board.　　H.S.B.

Virginia Mennonite Home Mission Board (MC) of the Middle District was organized in 1893 as a committee of six members chosen by and working under the Ministerial Council of the Middle District (*q.v.*) of the Virginia Conference. Its work is largely in the mountains west of Harrisonburg and on into West Virginia.   H.S.B.

Vishenka, a location in the northern Ukraine *c*150 miles northeast of Kiev, where the Hutterites who were fleeing persecution in Walachia first settled in 1770 on the estate of Count Rumjantsev (*q.v.*). Here they lived until 1802 when they moved on to crown land at Radichev (*q.v.*), 10 miles north.   H.S.B.

Volckaimer, Kilian, a furrier of the village of Gross-walbur in Franken, Germany, who was won by Hans Hut (*q.v.*) for Anabaptism in the summer of 1526, and became an active Anabaptist traveling apostle. With Hut and other colleagues including Eukarius Kellerman, Joachim Mertz, and a certain Sebastian, he traveled along the valley of the Main River and its tributary valleys, inviting men and women to the Anabaptist meetings, where Hut was the chief preacher. They won many followers, first in the district of Königsberg in Franken, and then in Thuringia proper. The last recorded trace of Volckaimer is found in the letter of the Nürnberg city council to Margrave Casimir of Brandenburg, dated March 26, 1527. (Wappler, *Thüringen; TA Bayern* I.)   H.S.B.

Volk auf dem Weg is an 8-page monthly, published since 1951 by the Arbeitsgemeinschaft der Ostumsiedler, Stuttgart, and since 1955 by the Landsmannschaft der Deutschen aus Russland. No editor is named. The paper contains numerous contributions dealing with the Mennonites of Russia, including some by B. H. Unruh and Peter Froese (set in BeCL).   C.K.

Walachia, the southern part of Rumania between the Carpathian Mts. and the Danube; its capital is Bucharest; the population is Greek Orthodox. In the 18th century it was a principality under Turkish suzerainty. In Anabaptist history it has significance only for the years 1767-70, when Hutterites fled from Transylvania (*q.v.*) and tried to establish a new Bruderhof in Walachia, hoping for more toleration in Turkish than in Hapsburg lands. In November 1767 they settled first at a place called Choregirle, south of Bucharest, but since much sickness occurred (typhoid fever), they moved in 1768 to Presetchain in a fertile area also near Bucharest. But the great Russo-Turkish War of 1768-74 brought unbelievable hardships upon the brotherhood. Johannes Waldner, the writer of the *Klein-Geschichtbuch,* who was in that group, describes in great detail all the terrible experiences, plundering and brutal treatment by Turks and marauding Rumanian troops. They lost a great part of their possessions, and finally had to flee into near-by woods to save their lives. Thereupon the brotherhood decided to leave this country. The commanding Russian general in Bucharest was kindly disposed to them and recommended that they look for permanent settlements in the Ukraine near Kiev, where religious toleration was granted. Thus they sold what was left of their houses and on April 10, 1770,

began their long trek northward through Moldavia into the Ukraine (see map in *ME* II, 858). In spite of all their hardships the brotherhood remained intact and preserved its communal way of living; also its precious books and sermon notes were saved and taken along into their new settlements in the Ukraine. (See **Vishenka** and **Radichev.**) (Zieglschmid, *Klein-Geschichtbuch,* 303-19.)   R.F.

Waldshut, Baden, Germany, a town of *c*7,000 pop. on the Rhine *c*30 miles east of Basel and *c*25 miles northwest of Zürich, was the seat of an Anabaptist congregation from April to December, 1525. Dr. Balthasar Hubmaier (*q.v.*) came to Waldshut from Regensburg as Catholic pastor in the spring of 1521, where he gradually became a Lutheran (from 1522). Early in 1525 he began to question infant baptism. On Feb. 2, 1525, Hubmaier published his *Oeffentliche Erbietung,* offering to prove in a public debate that infant baptism had no foundation in Scripture, but the request for a disputation was not granted. When Wilhelm Reublin (*q.v.*) appeared in Waldshut from Zürich, he found a ready response in Hubmaier who was baptized on Easter (April 16) with 60 others by Reublin. Hubmaier in turn baptized over 300 others in the days immediately following Easter, using a milk bucket filled with water from the fountain in the town square. He also served the new congregation with the Lord's Supper and washed their feet. Apparently a substantial part of the town's population became Anabaptist.

Strangely nothing further is known about the Waldshut Anabaptists, although the congregation must have continued until the final capture of the city by the forces of the Austrian government, which occurred on Dec. 5, 1525. Hubmaier himself fled, telling the city council at its "surrender" meeting on December 5 that since Catholic worship would be restored by the conquerors he could not stay. (See **Hubmaier, Balthasar,** which does not report on the congregation.)   H.S.B.

Ernst Crous, "Auf Spuren der Täufer am Oberrhein," *Der Mennonit* X (1957) 42 f.

Walraven, Jaques, a Mennonite minister in Amsterdam 1588-1617, concerning whom little is known.   H.S.B.

Wappler, Paul (1868-1915), professor at the Realgymnasium in Zwickau, Saxony, Germany, was born Sept. 18, 1868, at Auerbach (Vogtland), died Jan. 3, 1915, in Zwickau. He was the author of the following books significant for Anabaptist study: *Die Stellung Kursachsens und des Landgrafen Philipp von Hessen zur Täuferbewegung* (Münster, 1910, 254 pp.); *Die Täuferbewegung in Thüringen von 1526 bis 1584* (Jena, 1913, 541 pp.); also *Thomas Münzer in Zwickau und die "Zwickauer Propheten"* (Zwickau, 1908); *Inquisition und Ketzerprozesse in Zwickau zur Reformationszeit dargestellt im Zusammenhang mit der Entwickelung der Ansichten Luthers und Melanchthons über Glaubens- und Gewissensfreiheit* (Leipzig, 1908).

The two volumes on the Anabaptists are thorough and objective, notable also for their extensive publication of sources. The first has 110 pages of sources, largely from the Gesamtarchiv at Weimar; the second has 295 pages containing apparently all the pertinent documents for the study of Anabaptism in Thuringia.   H.S.B.

Wasco (Cal.) Mennonite Brethren Church was organized in October 1958, and built its meeting-house at 2225 South 7th Street in 1959; its member-ship was about 125, with Werner Kroeker as pastor.
                                                H.S.B.

Washington Center Mennonite Church (Central Conference), now extinct, located near Ashley, Mich., some 25 miles north of Lansing, was organ-ized in 1924 by a number of families which had moved into the area from Pekin, Ill., in the early 1920's, together with three families from the Ashley M.C. congregation. The group bought a church in 1924. It never had a minister and never reached more than 27 in membership. In 1933 the group dissolved, some members returning to the M.C. congregation.   H.S.B.

Watauga County, in the extreme northwestern cor-ner of North Carolina, is the seat of a series of K.M.B. congregations around the city of Boone, re-sulting from mission work among the Negroes of this area begun in 1899 at Elk Park by H. V. Wiebe (1899-1907), assisted by J. M. Tschetter (1902-12). P. H. Siemens, who came in 1925, spent over 25 years in the work here. Among the addresses of the ministers of the Negro churches are Darby, Boone, Lenoir, and Laytown. The leading minister is Rondo Horton of Boone. The congregations do not appear in the K.M.B. Yearbook, which reports a total membership of 180 for 1958.   H.S.B.

Wätzenobis (Slovak, *Vacanovice*), a village in Mora-via, lying between Gaya and Bisentz, on land of the Zerotin family, where a Hutterite Bruderhof was located from at least as early as 1571 (first men-tioned in the *Chronik*) to 1622. The Bruderhof was plundered and burned down in 1605 by marauding troops who killed four brethren; later in the same year the manager was killed. At this time Wätzeno-bis was a part of the possessions of General Wallen-stein (*q.v.*), who in 1615 put the manager in prison. On Sept. 21, 1619, the Bruderhof was plundered by Dampierre's troops, Feb. 7, 1620, by Polish troops, and in 1621, after being rebuilt, plundered again by imperial troops. (Zieglschmid, *Chronik*.)   H.S.B.

Weddings, *United States and Canada.* Very little can be found in church records concerning Ameri-can Mennonite wedding practices before the 20th century. An account in *Pennsylvania Dutch and Other Essays,* written by Phebe Earle Gibbons in 1882, describes a Reformed Mennonite wedding in the meetinghouse on a December Sunday morning. The preacher spoke about divorce, the duties of husbands and wives, adultery, and Paul's references to marriage. Having ended his sermon, he called upon the pair desiring to be married to come for-ward. The man rose from the men's side of the church and the woman from the opposite side. They joined in the center aisle and walked forward to the preacher who asked three questions of them. After the questions had been answered, the preacher di-rected them to join hands, pronounced them hus-band and wife, and invoked a blessing upon them. This was followed by a short prayer, after which the wedded pair took their separate seats among the congregation. The audience then knelt in prayer and the service was closed with a hymn. Afterwards a few friends gathered at the bride's home.

Amish weddings follow a pattern today similar to those of the previous century. The "go-between" (Stecklimann), who is the deacon, asks the woman's hand from her parents in behalf of the suitor whom he represents, as well as obtaining the consent of the young woman. This is a mere formality, as the couple had previously made their own arrange-ments. At least two weeks preceding the wedding, the intention of the couple to marry is announced in a Sunday morning worship service. The bride-to-be is customarily absent from this service, but the groom-to-be is expected to attend, although he was privileged to leave before the announcement was made. Autumn is the usual season for Amish weddings, Tuesday or Thursday practically always being chosen and the month of November being preferred. Statistics show that in the late 19th cen-tury December had been the preferred month. The marriage ceremony generally takes place in a neigh-bor's house as the bride's home has been made ready for the wedding meal. In Lancaster County, Pa., the marriage ceremony and the wedding meal are in the same house. At the proper moment in the serv-ice the couple and their attendants appear before the ministers. Following a sermon the bishop asks them the usual questions and then unites them in marriage as he places their clasped hands between his. Following the closing song the bride and groom with their attendants leave for her home, soon to be followed by the wedding guests. Following the sumptuous wedding meal, the afternoon is spent in visiting and singing hymns. Later the young peo-ple play games, and after the evening meal, the guests sing hymns until the hour of departure. Wed-ding days are joyous occasions in the Amish social calendar and the feasting and hilarity often have tended to become objects of criticism by the church leaders. An old Amish church discipline names as undesirable "the imposing weddings with immoder-ate preparations." Bishop Jacob Swartzendruber (*q.v.*) in Civil War days had warned the brother-hood of the inconsistency of feasting when their neighbors were sad because of their losses in the war and many people were without necessary food.

During the previous century Mennonite (MC) weddings had some similarities to Amish weddings, generally taking place in the homes. Marriage no-tices in the *Herald of Truth* during 1870-1900 indi-cate that weddings were nearly always held in the bride's home or in the home of the officiating min-ister. In frontier communities where there were no Mennonite clergy to perform marriage ceremonies, civil instead of church weddings were sometimes used. During the period when in certain Mennon-ite communities it was customary not to receive bap-tism and become members of the church until after marriage the practice of having a civil ceremony was sometimes resorted to since Mennonite bishops were not permitted to marry couples unless both parties were communicant members of the Mennonite church. According to historian Ira D. Landis, from 1729 and into the 1880's Lancaster conference young people were nearly always married by Lutheran and Reformed preachers. In the late 1880's Lancaster Mennonite ministers, both preachers and bishops, again performed marriage ceremonies, but by a decade later this function was reserved exclusively for the bishops. Before church weddings were sanctioned in the Lancaster conference the marriage ceremony was nearly always performed in the bride's home.

Because of the paucity of the records no thorough study has been made on the change from marriages performed in the homes to church weddings. A Virginia Mennonite Conference resolution of 1900 stated that church weddings were not permitted. By 1914, however, the regulation was changed to read that weddings would be permitted in churches only at the time of regular services. Since 1920 in the Mennonite Church (MC) there has been a gradual growth in church weddings held during the week in special services. The *Gospel Herald* reported 421 weddings in the period of January-August 1957. Of these, 329, or 78 per cent, were church weddings. The wedding veil is now used in a few areas of the church as well as the practice of the father giving the bride away in the ceremony. The wedding ring ceremony is not used in the Mennonite (MC) and the more conservative churches. In church weddings traditional wedding music is seldom used but instead appropriate hymns are presented by choral groups. The married couple kneeling for the final prayer, the bride and groom kissing each other immediately after the ceremony, church receptions after the ceremony, lengthy descriptions of the wedding in the local papers, are new practices in Mennonite (MC) circles reflecting the gradual adoption of common Protestant traditions.

Changes such as the above occurred earlier in some General Conference Mennonite and Mennonite Brethren circles where the usual Protestant forms, including the use of the single and double ring ceremony, are being followed. On the other hand, practices within the General Conference churches vary considerably. Rural church weddings among those of Russian background tend to be simpler than among those of a Pennsylvania-German background, including certain sections of the Mennonite Church (MC). In some of their churches it is customary to invite the entire congregation to the wedding, while only those receiving special invitations go to the reception following the ceremony. In South Dakota it is customary to have full wedding dinners for all of the invited guests, who may number several hundred. It is also customary to have a program of music at these wedding feasts. In these church weddings among the Mennonites of Russian background it is customary to have a sermon with the couple seated, either before or after the marriage ceremony. Sometimes a second sermon is given by another minister at the reception. In some of their churches,

the use of wedding rings in the ceremony and the public exchange of kisses by the couple are still disapproved. It is therefore difficult to generalize on wedding practices within the General Conference churches.

In all of the branches there was a tendency for weddings to become more elaborate and costly during the mid-twentieth century, reflecting perhaps America's unprecedented material prosperity. Mennonites, however, were deploring these trends and leaders of the various groups were calling for simplicity and for a renewed emphasis upon the distinctively Christian aspects of the wedding occasion.

A practice common only among Mennonites of the Russian-Prussian background is the holding of religious services in the church at the time of the twenty-fifth and fiftieth wedding anniversary. The observance of "open house" at the home of the couple on these two anniversaries is becoming common in many Mennonite communities. The *Herald of Truth, Gospel Witness, Gospel Herald,* and *Herold der Wahrheit* have printed short notices of marriages from their beginning issues. *The Mennonite* has recently discontinued the practice. *The Christian Witness, Der Bote,* and *Die Mennonitische Rundschau* do not carry marriage news. *The Mennonite Weekly Review* and *The Canadian Mennonite* present more detailed wedding announcements than do other Mennonite papers, thus presenting materials for the study of recent Mennonite wedding practices.

Since the religious ceremony is considered a legal marriage in the United States and Canada, no civil ceremony being necessary, in many states clergymen must have a license to officiate. In all cases the couple wishing to marry must secure a license to do so. In earlier days in many areas before the license was introduced the publishing of the bans in church (usually twice) was required.   M.G.

Russia. Among the Mennonites of Russia weddings contained elements which were transplanted from Prussia. Whether an Umbitter (*q.v.*), as used by the Mennonites of Prussia and their descendants in Nebraska and Kansas to the end of the 19th century, was also used in Russia is not established. The fact that Johann Cornies broke the Hutterite tradition of having parents decide on spouses for their children seems to indicate that traditions along these lines relaxed among the Mennonites of Prussia, possibly before their migrating to Russia. During the beginning of the 20th century a proposal of marriage had become an elaborate occasion. Horses and buggy had to be in prime condition. The suitor possibly even had a coachman take him to the home of the girl of his choice. He would be ushered into the parlor (grosse Stube), visit with the parents, and ask the father whether they would give him their daughter as wife. The Polish artist Chodowiecky, in a series of "Marriage Proposals," features a Mennonite proposal in the presence of the mother. To what extent this was characteristic or perpetuated is not known.

Immediately after the engagement the relatives were invited to the wedding, usually by circulating from neighbor to neighbor a letter containing the invitation and the list of those invited. The wedding took place two or three weeks after the official engagement, usually in the home of the bride; it was possibly held in the barn, which was especially prepared for this occasion. Weddings were rarely solemnized in the churches, probably because guests were entertained with regular meals, and the churches were not equipped for this purpose.

The preparation for the wedding was a significant task. The "hope chest" was a large trunk (still found in museums and some homes of America), into which the bride placed her gradually accumulating household linens and other items. The house and yard had to be spotless. Since the number of invited guests was always large, much baking and cooking had to be done. Immigrants from Russia after World War I brought some of these practices with them. These, like other traditions, are still largely preserved among the Old Colony Mennonites and related groups in Manitoba, Mexico, and Menno, Paraguay. (Arnold Dyck, *Dee Fria*, Steinbach, 1947; Kay Woelk, "Courtship and Marriage of the Russian Mennonites," term paper in BeCL.)
C.K.

Netherlands. At present weddings of Mennonites in Holland do not differ from weddings among non-Mennonites. Until 1795 Mennonite marriages were performed either by the magistrate officials or by the ministers of the congregations, in the latter case with a report to the officials (see **Marriage,** *ME* III, 508). After 1795 marriages were to be performed by the magistrates; if the newly wedded couple wishes it so, the marriage is solemnized afterward (ingezegend, gewijd) in a church meeting. From 1795 until about 1925 such consecration or religious blessing of marriages was rather seldom; at present newly married couples more and more after the performing of the marriage at the town hall come to the church for a religious consecration. The trip to the town hall is customarily made in a hired horse-drawn open coach.   vDZ.

Weickmann, Bernhard, an Anabaptist of Bruchsal, Baden, who with Julius Lober (*q.v.*) and Ulrich Hutscher was examined on April 16, 1531, and recanted. (*TA Bayern* I, 217-19.)   H.S.B.

Welschländer Mennonite Church (Mennonite Church of French-speaking Lorraine), probably called Welsch (French) because this German-speaking group lived in a French environment, existed probably from the early 18th century to c1880. The Dieuze (*q.v.*) congregation was formed out of the families living in the central area of the Welschländer congregation's widely scattered territory, which once extended from near Metz to below Sarrebourg in the southeast. The first Mennonite settlers in the Duchy of Lorraine (*q.v.*) (joined to France in 1766) came as the result of the expulsion order of 1712 issued by the Intendant of Alsace when all "Anabaptists" were ordered to leave. Since Lorraine was then in a sense in the German Empire the Mennonites enjoyed relative toleration here. As early as 1764 the fiscal agent of the Bishop of Metz ordered the cessation of persecution of the Swiss Anabaptists in the bishopric. The Welschländer con-

gregation was represented in the petition of 1808 of the French and Palatine congregations to Napoleon for relief from military service, Christ Engel and Christen Gerber being the signers for the congregation.

On Dec. 25, 1808, the ministers of the congregation wrote to the other congregations calling a meeting at Sarreck near Sarrebourg for Jan. 7, 1809; those signing were Christian Engel, Hannes Hirschi, Joerg Sprunger, Christian Lehman, and Christian Nafziger. Christian Engel was one of the two Mennonite delegates sent to Paris by this meeting to submit a petition to the government. Other names found in the documents relating to this congregation are Joseph Wuerkler, Hans Gingrich, and Christ Roth.

As the families moved gradually further west and south, meeting families moving in from other areas, e.g., Salm, new congregations were formed. Numerous families emigrated to America.   H.S.B.

Pierre Sommer, "Assemblée de la Lorraine Françoise (Welschländer Gemeinde)," *Christ Seul,* April 1931, 5 f.

West Abbotsford and Clearbrook Mennonite Church Funeral Aid, Abbotsford, B.C., was established in 1952. It has 263 members and pays $150 to bereaved families for the burial of an adult and $100 for children under 12.   M.G.

Western District Loan Library functions under the supervision of the Western District Education Committee of the General Conference Mennonite Church. It was begun in 1936 largely through the efforts of Abram Warkentin (*q.v.*), then on the staff of Bethel College. Through gifts and purchase the library was developed until in 1959 it had 3,400 volumes for loan. Since the beginning it has been housed by Bethel College, North Newton, Kans., and is now located in the library.   J.F.S.

Wiens, Johann G. (1874-1951), Mennonite Brethren missionary and Bible school teacher, was born Aug. 3, 1874, at Steinthal, Molotschna, Russia. He received his elementary and secondary education in his home community and attended the Baptist Seminary at Hamburg, Germany, 1899-1903. He married Helene Hildebrand Nov. 12, 1896. They served a term as missionaries in India 1904-10. In 1918-24 he was leader and teacher of the Tchongrav Bible School (*q.v.*) in the Crimea. He migrated to Canada in 1926 where he taught in the Winkler Bible School (*q.v.*). He died in 1951.   C.K.

Friesen, *Brüderschaft,* 567; Abr. Unruh, *Die mennonitische Bibelschule zu Tschongraw, Krim, in Russland* (n.p., n.d.); A. Warkentin, *Who's Who Among the Mennonites* (North Newton, Kans., 1943).

Wigs (Periwigs). When, at the close of the 17th century, it became fashionable in the Netherlands for people of high rank to wear powdered periwigs, some Mennonites began to wear them. Thus difficulties arose in a few congregations, some members considering this fashion too worldly for the plain people of Menno. Claes Jacobsz, the preacher of Den Burg on the island of Texel (*q.v.*), was asked in 1715 to take off his wig; when he refused to do so, he was dismissed. Nevertheless the wearing of wigs was soon tolerated, particularly in larger towns like Amsterdam and Haarlem, and highly esteemed elders like Herman Schijn (*q.v.*) and Pieter Schrijver (*q.v.*) in the early 18th century used to wear periwigs. In the Groningen Old Flemish congregations there was much more opposition. In the Deventer congregation of this branch two brethren were earnestly requested in 1753 to abandon their wigs, at least during the communion service. The very strict "Fijne" (*q.v.*) Mennonites expressly forbade the wearing of "foreign hair" as late as the end of the 18th century. The Lithuanian Mennonites who settled in the Netherlands in 1733 were scandalized to see the delegates of the Dutch Mennonite Committee for Foreign Needs wearing wigs. Also in the Danzig congregation there was a long period of trouble when Mennonites from Holland began to visit the church in 1727 wearing wigs. (See **Periwig Dispute.**) (*Inv. Arch. Amst.* I, No. 2041; II, Nos. 1619-21, 2632 ff.; *DB* 1919, 85 f.)

vDZ.

Wilhelm V, called the Pious, who reigned as Duke of Bavaria 1579-97, a vigorous opponent of the Reformation, and under strong Jesuit influence a bitter persecutor of heretics and also of witches. On Feb. 27, 1587, he issued a mandate ordering the arrest of Wastl Anfang (*q.v.*) and Hans Zuckenhammer (*q.v.*), offering 100 guilders for their capture, but in vain.

H.S.B.

Willem (de Snijder) **Vernon,** an Anabaptist martyr of Hondschote, Belgium, was arrested on May 4, 1570, during a meeting of a congregation held at Tillegem near Brugge, Belgium, with four other brethren, two of whom recanted, but the remaining three were soon burned at the stake. Willem's wife at first escaped but later was caught and executed. The *Martyrs' Mirror* erroneously gives 1568 as the year of these martyrdoms. (*Mart. Mir.* D 369, E 725 f.; Verheyden, *Brugge,* 62, No. 68.)   H.S.B.

Willms, Johann, milling industrialist, Halbstadt, Molotschna, Russia, was a significant leader in economical and cultural life of the Mennonites before and after the Russian Revolution of 1917. He was the chairman of the Bureau der Molotschnaer Mennonitischen Vereinigung (*q.v.*) and cochairman of the Allgemeiner Mennonitische Kongress (*q.v.*) of 1917.

C.K.

Friesen, *Brüderschaft,* p. 694 ff.; "Protokoll des Allgemeinen Mennonitischen Kongresses in Ohrloff, 1917."

Wilmington First Mennonite Church (CAM), Wilmington, Del., had its beginnings in the Wilmington Mission (1948-58) but was organized as a separate congregation in 1958, with a membership of 22. It was associated with the Central Conservative Mennonite Church near Dover and the Laws Conservative Mennonite Church near Harrington, the combined membership of the three in 1959 being 298. Amos Bontrager was the pastor.   M.G.

Witzel, George (1501-73), Lutheran clergyman, formerly pastor in Wenigenlupnitz near Eisenach, Thuringia, and also 1525-31 in Memegk near Bitterfeld, a friend of the Anabaptist leader Melchior Rinck

(*q.v.*), at the time of the latter's imprisonment in Vacha living in the same town, in early 1532 wrote a letter to Rinck seeking to persuade him to renounce Anabaptism and return to the church. A letter of Dec. 24, 1531, by Witzel to M.B.F. reports the alarming growth of Anabaptism in western Thuringia. (To be found in *Wicelii Epistolarum libri quatuor,* Leipzig, 1537.) Witzel was mild in his attitude toward the Anabaptists. In 1533 he returned to the Roman Catholic Church.   H.S.B.

Winebrennerians: see **Churches of God.**

Winschoten, a town in the Dutch province of Groningen. From 1872 regular Mennonite services were held here every three weeks in the Lutheran church. In 1885 a Mennonite Kring (*q.v.*) was organized here as a subdivision of the Midwolda (*q.v.*), Beerta, and de Meeden congregation. In 1893 J. A. Wartena, the pastor of this congregation, moved to Winschoten, which gradually became its center, and since 1900 the old Midwolda congregation is called Winschoten. The pastors after Wartena, who served 1893-1901, were F. Dijkema 1901-5, J. H. van Giessen Jr 1906-21, then after nine years of vacancy Corn. Vis Jzn 1930-38, A. du Croix 1939-44, R. J. Faber 1946-51, and J. H. Rawie 1953- . In 1931 a meetinghouse was built in Winschoten. The membership numbered 120 in 1900 and 97 in 1958. Church activities are ladies' circle, youth group (15-18), and Sunday school for children. (*DB* 1872, 192; 1887, 148; *De Zondagsbode* XXIII, 1909-10, No. 24.)

vDZ.

Wintersdorf: see **Przechovka.**

Wismar, seaport and manufacturing city, Mecklenburg, Germany, was the scene of some Anabaptist activity and conferences. On April 11, 1535, at a conference of evangelical theologians at which action against Anabaptists was taken, Wismar was represented. This does not prove that there were Anabaptists in this city at this early date. When Menno Simons lived at Wismar during the winter of 1553-54 there was a considerable group of Anabaptists there. On Dec. 21, 1553, the refugee congregation led by the Reformed preacher a Lasco arrived there from London. Menno and Martin Micron (*q.v*), the latter representing this refugee congregation, held a debate in Wismar on basic Christian doctrines. On Feb. 6, 1554, another discussion, particularly on the incarnation of Christ, took place, which was continued on February 15. Menno and Micron continued their discussion in several published writings.

Three days after the meeting, Menno was informed by the city council that Anabaptists were not to be tolerated in the city because the discussions had become known. Menno accused Micron of reporting the Anabaptists to the city council. Particularly the Lutheran ministers of Wismar, Smedenstede and Vincentius, aroused the city council against the Anabaptists which decreed that the latter had to leave the city by Nov. 11, 1554. It was probably at this time that Menno left Wismar to find a new shelter at Wüstenfelde (*q.v.*).

A significant meeting of Anabaptist elders in Wismar in 1554 resulted in the Wismar Resolutions (*q.v.*), which played a very significant role in the later development of Anabaptism in the Netherlands and northwest Germany. It is likely that Gillis van Aken (*q.v.*) was received into the fellowship here after having been excommunicated. (Cornelius Krahn, *Menno Simons*, Karlsruhe, 1936, 78-84.)   C.K.

Witmarsum (New) Colony, a Mennonite colony established in 1951 in the state of Parana, Brazil, some 45 miles northwest of Curitiba, by the remainder of the former Krauel (*q.v.*) colony in Santa Catharina, when about half of that group moved to Bagé in Rio Grande do Sul. A tract of *ca.* 20,000 acres was purchased from Senator Robert Glasser by a co-operative composed of the heads of the settler families. By September, 1951, 70 families had purchased farms of 125-250 acres each, but in 1953 only 52 families with a total population of 319 were living there. The occupation is dairy farming and cattle raising. In 1958 three churches had been established in the colony, the Mennonite Church, the Mennonite Brethren Church, and the Free Evangelical Mennonite Church. (J. W. Fretz, *Pilgrims in Paraguay*, Scottdale, 1953, 179-82.)   H.S.B.

Witmarsum Free Evangelical Mennonite Church, Witmarsum Colony, Parana, Brazil, had 50 members in 1958, with Robert Janzen as minister.

Witmarsum Mennonite Church, Witmarsum Colony, Parana, Brazil, founded *c*1951, in 1958 had 102 members, with David Nikkel as elder, and Johann Boldt and Peter Klassen as preachers.

Witmarsum Mennonite Brethren Church, Witmarsum Colony, Parana, Brazil, had 32 members in 1958, with Abram Dueck as minister.

Wohldemfürst, a village of the Kuban Mennonite settlement (*q.v.*), Russia, was established in 1862 and later became known as Velikoknyazheskoye. Another village near by was Alexandrodar, formerly Alexanderfeld. (See **Kuban.**)   C.K.

Wohldemfürst - Alexandrodar Mennonite Church, Kuban Mennonite settlement (*q.v.*), Russia, was established in 1885. At first the worship services were conducted in private homes. In the 1890's a church was erected in Alexandrodar. In 1905 the membership was 124 with a total population of 270. Kornelius Dirks was the first elder and was succeeded by Franz F. Enns (*q.v.*). Jakob Hübert, David Dirks, Johann J. Wiebe, C. C. Peters, and Jakob Braun served as ministers. The church was dissolved under the Soviet regime.   C.K.

Die Kubaner Ansiedlung (Steinbach, 1953) 37; H. Dirks, *Statistik*, 36, 64.

Worcester Reformed Mennonite Church, near Norristown, Pa., erected its meetinghouse in 1890, although members had been living in the area as early as 1864. In 1958 its membership was 15.   H.S.B.

Wouter (Gaultier van der Weyden), an Anabaptist martyr, was burned at the stake at Gent, Belgium, on April 11, 1551. Wouter, who was a native of Lier in the Belgian province of Brabant, had fled with some others to Gent, but they were soon arrested and imprisoned in the Gravensteen castle. Some of this group apostatized, but four of them suffered martyrdom. For particulars, see **Goris Cooman.**   vDZ.

Wünsch, Georg (1887-), professor of ethics and apologetics at the University of Marburg 1927- (1922-27 instructor in Systematic Theology), a theological leader of the Religious Socialists in Germany, a disciple of Ernst Troeltsch. In two of his books he treats Anabaptism briefly. In *Evangelische Ethik des Politischen* (Tübingen, 1936), pp. 202-46, he has a chapter "Anabaptism, Related Groups, and Successors," which treats Müntzer, Hofmann, the Anabaptist congregations (includes Mennonites and Hutterites), English Revolution parties (Independents, Quakers, and Levellers), and Moravians. *Evangelische Wirtschaftsethik* (Tübingen, 1927) also treats the Anabaptists.   H.S.B.

Wymysle: see Deutsch-Wymysle.

Yoder (Rock Creek) Amish Mennonite Church, the mother church of the Central (Illinois) Conference, was organized by the members of the Mackinaw (*q.v.*) congregation living in McLean County. It was called the Yoder church because of its long-time leader, Bishop Jonathan Yoder (1795-1869), who had moved into the community from Juniata County, Pa., in the spring of 1851. In 1853 a meetinghouse was erected at Rock Creek, 4 miles north of Danvers, the first Amish meetinghouse west of Malvern, Pa. The congregation grew rapidly from some 100 to 400 members by 1872. In that year a new meetinghouse was erected two miles south of the old location, later called the North Danvers church. Joseph Stuckey (*q.v.*), the later leader in the founding of the Central Conference, was ordained minister here in 1860 and bishop in 1864, and became the leader of the congregation. In 1871 or 1872 the congregation was renamed North Danvers (*q.v.*).   H.S.B.

Yoder, Jonathan (1795-1869), an outstanding early Amish Mennonite leader in central Illinois, was born in Berks County, Pa., Sept. 2, 1795, the son of Jacob Yoder and Jacobina Esh. He was a carpenter and farmer but also a teacher in the subscription schools of the day. He lived in a number of places in Pennsylvania (Berks, Mifflin, and Juniata counties) and moved to McLean County, Ill., in the spring of 1851. He had been ordained preacher (1825) and bishop in Pennsylvania, and soon became the leader of the Amish Mennonites living in Danvers and Dry Grove townships in McLean County. The congregation he organized here in 1851 became known as the Yoder church, and later as North Danvers was the mother church of the Central (Illinois) Conference (*q.v.*). His successor as bishop here was Joseph Stuckey (*q.v.*). Yoder was also active in the Amish Mennonite General Conference which met annually 1862-78, and served as moderator of the first conference in 1862. He married Magdalena Wagner in 1816; they had 11 children. He died

Jan. 28, 1869, and is buried in the Lantz cemetery southeast of Carlock. H.S.B.

H. F. Weber, *Centennial History of the Mennonites of Illinois 1829-1929* (Goshen, 1931).

Youth Work. Organized work for and among the youth of the church is a relatively modern development among Mennonites. In Europe the South German Mennonite Conference established its Youth Commission (*Jugendkommission*) in 1919, and its youth journal *Mennonitische Jugendwarte* (*q.v.*) in 1920. In Holland, although some youth circles (*Jongerenkring*) were organized a few years earlier, the Doopsgezinde Jongerenbond (*q.v.*) was not organized nationally until 1926, preceded by the Provincial Friese D.J.B. in 1924. The Doopsgezinde Jeugdraad (*q.v., Mennonite Youth Council*) was established by the A.D.S. in 1946 for the purpose of co-ordinating all Dutch Mennonite youth activities. The Swiss Mennonite Conference established its Youth Commission in 1935.

In the United States young people's meetings, usually held on Sunday evenings in connection with the preaching service, were begun in the Mennonite Church (MC) *c*1890 and spread rapidly after 1900. At about the same time in the General Conference Mennonite Church, young people's societies were being organized, usually as Christian Endeavor (*q.v.*) groups, the first in 1886. Organized youth work directed on a national scale came later in both groups. The M.C. national Mennonite Youth Fellowship was organized in 1948, although the Young People's Problems Committee (*q.v.*), set up by the Mennonite General Conference in 1924, had since 1920 promoted earlier forms of youth work such as Young People's Institutes. The G.C.M. Young People's Union (*q.v.*) was set up as a conference-wide youth organization in 1941, a Sunday School and Youth Committee having been set up in 1920. The Youth Committee (*q.v.*) of the M.B. General Conference was set up in 1936.

A significant development in youth work, largely since World War II in North America, has been youth camps (*q.v.*) and retreats, much of the camp work being directed toward youth of high-school age and younger. (See also **Christian Education** and **Young People's Bible Meeting.**) H.S.B.

Zeeuwse Ring, founded *c*1880, an association of the Zeeland congregations of Aardenburg, Vlissingen, Middelburg, and Goes for mutual aid in cases of vacancy of the pulpit in one of these four congregations. This Ring lasted for only a few years, about 1885 the Zeeland churches entering into the *Zuidhollandsche* (*q.v.*) *Ring.* vDZ.

Zemstvos: see **Sanitätsdienst.**

Zentralbureau was the executive body and office of the Bureau der Molotschnaer Mennonitischen Vereinigung (*q.v.*). It was referred to as Mennozentrum (*q.v.*). C.K.

Zernike, Anna, b. 1887 at Amsterdam, studied theology at the university and the Mennonite seminary at Amsterdam and became the first woman minister in the Dutch Mennonite church. She served

1911-15 at Bovenknijpe (*q.v.*) in Friesland. In 1915 she was married to the painter Jan Mankes and retired, but after the death of her husband (1920) she again went into the ministry, serving 1921-48 in the *Protestantenbond* (Dutch union of liberal Protestants) at Rotterdam. In 1921 she obtained her Th.D. degree. She wrote many articles for Dutch periodicals and a few books on art and religion. vDZ.

Zierikzeeërs: see **Stilstaanders.**

Ziffersystem (1028a): The following Mennonite musical publications have been printed with numerical notation: H. Franz, *Choralbuch* (four-part edition, Leipzig, 1860 and 1880) (one-part edition Leipzig, 1865); reprint of the 1865 edition, at Elkhart (1878 and 1918) at Steinbach, Man. (1902, printed at Elkhart), at Altona, Man. (n.d., and 1946); *Choralbuch in vierstimmigem Tonsatz zum Gebrauch in Kirche, Schule und Haus der Mennoniten-Gemeinden, Zusammengestellt im Auftrage der Predigerkonferenz* (n.p., Winnipeg, Man., 1935); Joh. Enss, *Schulchoralbuch* (1886); *Choralbuch* (n.p., 1914); J. H. Janzen, *Choralbuch* (1930 in Canada); A. Sawatzky, *Gesangschule in Noten und Ziffernoten* (n.d., n.p.); G. J. Peters, title unknown (n.p., n.d.); in monthly periodical form, Isaak Born, *Sängerfreund* (1889-90, 18 months) and Is. Born, H. Braun, K. Neufeld, and J. Janzen, *Liederperlen* 1891-1914; songbooks as follows: *Liedersammlung* (von einigen Lehrern 1896); W. N. *Russkije pessni* (1896); W. N. and J. R., *Festgesänge* (Part II, 1897); J. and H. Braun, *Kinder-Harfe* (1902); I. S. Prochanow, *Gussli* (1811); J. Froese, *Sangesblüten* (1914); J. Janzen, *Liederalbum* (Part I, 1914). A mimeographed edition of selections from the four-part edition of 1860 (1680) was published about 1943 in Chortitz, Man. J.P.Kl., H.S.B.

Zim(m)eraw(u)er (Simmerauer), **Hans,** an Anabaptist martyr who was beheaded in 1540 at Schwatz in the Inn Valley in Tirol. He was the author of several hymns (according to the *Chronik*); Wolkan identifies the hymn "In Gotten Namen hebn wir an" (*Ausbund*, No. 121) as one of his. (*Mart. Mir.* D 51, E 455; Zieglschmid, *Chronik,* 223; Wolkan, *Lieder,* 40). NEFF.

Zion Mennonite Church (GCM), now extinct, located in Manns Choice, Bedford Co., Pa., was begun in 1915 in an abandoned church by Herman Snyder, who served this group together with Napier, 4 miles away, until his death in 1917. The highest membership was 49 in 1926. In 1935 the Eastern District Mission Committee, which had supported the work, closed the church. H.S.B.

Zion Mennonite Church (GCM), Lucien, Okla., now extinct, was organized Sept. 25, 1898, with some 10 charter members and John Lichte as minister. It erected a meetinghouse one mile south of Lucien. The highest membership was 17 in 1911. In 1912 it disbanded. H.S.B.

Zion Mennonite Church (MC), Birdsboro, Pa., a member of the Ohio and Eastern Conference, was organized April 24, 1951, with 42 charter members coming largely from the Conestoga congregation with T. K. Hershey as bishop-pastor. The work was started in 1916 as an outpost of Conestoga. Meetings were held in the former Friedens Baptist Church until July 1951, when the former Zion Methodist Church was occupied, which is located 7 miles south of Reading and 8 miles north of Morgantown. Ford Berg served as pastor 1954-57, followed by Jesse Yoder 1957-59 (ord. 1951). In 1958 the membership was 90.   H.S.B.

Zougg (Zaugg, Zowg): see **Zook.**

Zwanzig neue geistliche Lieder, *Das Erste: von einem Drucker Gesellen Thomas von Imbroich genamt, aufs neue Gedruckt Anno 1758,* a Swiss-South German Mennonite hymnal, containing 19 hymns. It contains a supplement printed in 1699, with three long hymns. (See **Hymnology.**) (Wolkan, *Lieder,* 157-60.)   VDZ.

Zweibrücken, Duchy of: see **Pfalz-Zweibrücken.**

Zwolsche Kas: see **Zwols(ch)e Vere(e)niging.**

* * *

Goethe, Wolfgang (1749-1832), and the Mennonites. Known references by Goethe to the Mennonites and contacts with them follow. In 1768, while recovering from a serious illness, Goethe wrote a versified letter to Friederike Oeser, describing himself in a series of similes, including the lines
Bald still, wie ein Hypochondrist,
Und sittig, wie ein Mennonist,
Und folgsam, wei ein gutes Lamm.

On his journey up the Rhine in 1774 with Basedow and Lavater the three stopped at two Mennonite homes at Neuwied near Koblenz principality, the minister, Lorenz Friedenreich, and the noted clockmaker, Peter Kinzing. Lavater's diary makes interesting comment on the personality of the Mennonites. Goethe had some contact with Mennonites during his service as Minister of Economics in the government of Duke Karl August of Saxe-Weimar, when the latter attempted to establish Mennonite farmers on his land to improve agriculture.

The matter of Goethe and the Mennonites needs further inquiry. For further information on the contacts mentioned, see the items below.   E.H.B.

Adolf Bach, ed., *Goethes Rheinreise mit Lavater und Basedow im Sommer 1774* (Zürich, 1923) 119; Ernst Correll, *Das Schweizerische Täufermennonitentum* (Tübingen, 1925) 130 f.; Ernst Crous, "Lavater, Basedow und Goethe bei den Mennoniten in Neuwied," *Menn. Bl.,* 1930, 107.

Saxe-Weimar, a middle German duchy with Weimar as capital (incorporated into Thuringia in 1920), is of interest to Mennonites because of a short-lived settlement of four families c1780 resulting from attempts of Duke Karl August to improve the agriculture of his land by bringing in skilled Mennonite farmers. The four families, probably from Hesse-Darmstadt, were settled as renters on state lands at Wasungen (Kameralgut Zillebach). Goethe, then in the ducal service, commented in a letter on the keen business ability of the Mennonites.   H.S.B.

Ernst Correll, *Das Schweizerische Täufermennonitentum* (Tübingen, 1925) 130 f.

Corrections and Additions

Volume I

xiiib, 31: *for* Rosemary, Man. *read* Rosemary, Alta.

xiiib, 53: *eliminate entire line* R. Foth

xiiib, 54: *for* J.F *read* Jacob H. Franz and J.F.

xiva, 65: *for* L.H. *read* L.Hoo.

xivb, 44: *eliminate entire line* Köhler, Walther

xivb, 55, 56: *eliminate entire lines* Kroeker, Jacob and *Kroeker, Jakob

xivb, 60, 62: correction of duplicate sets of initials: find Kuhn on p. 442, find Kuyf on pp. 511, 552.

Correction of remaining duplicate sets of initials: Braun, J. P. (165) and Bueckert, J. P. (373); Foth, Johannes (179) and Franz, Jacob H. (591); Hein, Gerhard (521, 551, 665) and Hoffman, George (312); Lark, James (311) and Lohrenz, J. H. (214, 506, 542); Mast, J. B. (748) and Miller, Jonas B. (92); Neufeld, Henry (161) and Nussbaumer, Hans (80); Ramseyer, L. L. (370, 636) and Rassi, L. L. (495); Shank, J. W. (156) and Shank, J. Ward (433); Stoll, Henry J. (479) and Stuckey, Harley Jr. (9); Wall, John (630); Weber, Aaron M. (55, 399) and Wiebe, Abe M. (312); Westra, H. (401, 450) and Wiebe, Herman (313).

xvia, 44: *eliminate entire line* Wagler, Joel

1a, 24: *for* July *read* Aug.

3b, 32: *for* Liukinga *read* Luikinga

4a, 35: *for* Broese . . . vacant.) *read* Broese van Gronau 1852-83, J. G. Frerichs 1921-27, F. van der Wissel 1927-32, Abr. Mulder 1932-41, M. J. Nottenius 1941-51, and S. A. Vis 1952- .

11a, 53: *for* Beck *read* Weckh

14a, 44: *Note*: This article confuses two men named Adriaen. One of them, Adriaen Adriaensz, also called Adriaen den Sant, of Hazerswoude, died when the Eewouts house was taken. The other, Adriaen Jorysz van Benschop, was active in Münster and Groningen and probably lost his life in the attack on the Amsterdam city hall on May 10-11, 1535. (Mellink, **Wederdopers.**)

14b, 41: *for* in the same year *read* on July 10, 1565

15b, 35: *for* Gend *read* Gent

23a, 56: *for* Johann *read* Stephan

29b, 25: *for* founded *read* founded in 1837

36a, 33: *for* Dutch *read* (b. 1560), Dutch

43a, 55: *for* Gelle *read* Jelle

43b, 24: *for* 139-266 and 142-44 *read* 139-266

52a, 33, and 53b, 14: *for* Pensionenstichting *read* Pensioenstichting

53b, 47: *for* D. Rahusen *read* G. H. Rahusen

62b, 25: *for* 1926 *read* 1925

96a, 4: *for* Arundel Co. *read* St. Marys Co.

100a, 26: *for* Michelsberg *read* Michelsburg

104a, 39: *for* 1674 *read* 1670

107a, 50: *for* Cosquine *read* Cosquino

133b, 5: *for* Joannis *read* Joannes

133b, 45: *for* 1535 *read* 1534

137a, 34: *for* naeus and Tertullian. Additions were made in the *read* through references made to it by Ire-

145b, 50: *for* Bärber *read* Gärber

158b, 15: *for* Groote Spyker *read* Kleine Spyker

158b, 18: *for* church of the Old Frisians called "De kleine Zon" (Little Sun) *read* "kleine Zon," the church of a splinter group from the Zon located

Arnhem, Ring, 162: Add to bibl.: J. A. A. Meyer, "Hondert jaar Doopsgezind leven in de Ring Akkrum," in *Stemmen* VI (1957) No. 1, 10-19.

162b, 14: *for* I *read* II; *for* II *read* II, 2

171a, 9: *for* 1644 *read* 1694

179a, 26: *for* 1699 *read* 1649

179a, 26: *for* Haarlem and . . . Zonists. *read* Haarlem. In 1664, it joined the Zonists when Cornelis Standertsz, Sybrandt Cornelisz, and Jan Aertsz signed the Verbondt (*q.v.*) van Eenigheydt.

179b, 19: *for* 1946-48 *read* 1946-47

Augsburger, Aaron, 188b: Ord. bishop in 1900; served as president of the Central Conference 1899 and 1906-11, and as conference secretary for many years. Married Emma Schertz Feb. 20, 1889; d. Jan. 8, 1950.

191b, 26: *for* 5, 6, and 7 *read* 5, 6, 7, and 8

191b, 27: *insert* (after by): Georg Blaurock

197b, 12-15: Ambrosius Spittelmayr was not a Schwertler; he is confused here with Hans Spittelmaier who was one.

201a, 41 *for* 1567 *read* 1568

Baer family, 211b: Samuel Bär was preacher in the Immelhausen, Palatinate (*q.v.*), congregation c1766; about the same time Hans Bär served as a preacher in the Bockshaft (*q.v.*) congregation. Henry Baer was ordained minister in 1771 in the Swamp (*q.v.*) congregation in Bucks County, Pa.

215a, 36: *for* Noordhoorn *read* Noordhorn

Balk, 216b: Add to bibl.: Carl F. Brüsewitz, "De Doopsgezinden van Balk," *Stemmen* V (1956) No. 4, 81-95; *idem,* "The Mennonites of Balk, Friesland," *MQR* XXX (1956) No. 1, 19-31; Marie Yoder, "The Balk Dutch Settlement near Goshen, Indiana, 1853-1889," *MQR* XXX (1956) No. 1, 32-43.

215b, 1: *for* became *read* (b. c1645 at Burtscheid, Germany) was one of the delegates sent by the Amsterdam Lamist congregation in 1672 to the Palatine Mennonites to investigate their needs (*Inv. Arch. Amst.* I, Nos. 1410, 1412-16). He became

215b, 28: *for* Mennonites, *read* Mennonites. He was an elder in Flanders, Belgium, and was the author of "Brief tot vereeninge der Vriezen," in de Buyser's (*q.v.*) *Huys-boeck* (1643).

216a, 8: *for* 1854. *read* 1854. It was the last congregation to join the Conference of Friesland (1855).

221a, 25: *for* 193 *read* p. 193

225b, 64: *for* Works II: 201a *read* Writings, 244

226b, 50: *for* at one place *read* at three places (*Writings* 123, 139, 350)

233a, 43: *for* Barber, Jans *read* Barber Jans

265b, 5: (*q.v.*) is to be omitted

269a, 5: *for* preacher *read* elder

269a, 10: *omit Inv. Arch. Amst.* I, Nos. 539, 557, 560-64;

270a, 53: The *Waarachtige Historie* was not written by Corvinus, but is a Dutch translation of *Warhafftige Historie,* attributed by Cornelius (*Berichte der Augenzeugen über das münsterische Wiedertäuferreich*) to joint authorship by Heinrich Dorpius (named in the title) and Dietrich Fabricius von Anholt.

282a, 17: *for* 400 *read* 40

334a, 8: *for* Nicholaes *read* Nicolaes

334a, 36: *for* Peter *read* Pieter

339b, 47: *for* 1646 *read* Aug. 1644

379b, 48: *for* (1881-85) *read* (1881-84), Hindeloopen (1884-85)

341a, 33: *for* DB *read* DJ 1837, 55 ff.; DB 1882, 53;

341a, 33: *for* 64 *read* 64: 1918, 107;

366b, 14: *for* Collegiant . . . Holland *read* Amsterdam

380b, 33: *for* 1936 *read* 1937

380b, 51: *for* 1858 *read* 1868

381a, 1: *for* Willem *read* Willemsz

381a, 43: *for* 517 *read* 499, 517

392b, 20: *for* (from 1716) *read* 1716-37

395a, 52: *for* 1935 *read* 1926

399a, 16: *for* Lancaster *read* Lancaster County

399a, 42: *for* E.M.S. *read* The Old Order group under Bishop Joseph O. Weaver, belonging to the Weaverland Conference, also worships here. E.M.S.

416a, 11: *for* 1740 *read* 1738

424a, 6: *add* author's initials F.E.M.

439b, 29-30: *for* his death . . . 1822 *read* 1822 (d. Apr. 11, 1838)

440a, 6: *for* 1863-67 *read* 1863-68

440a, 13: *for* Joens *read* Jeens

450a, 62: *for* Lamist *read* Bloemstraat Old Frisian

Bruin, 450: There were several other Mennonite preachers with this name.

Bruyn, 455: The C. C. Bruyn mentioned here was Cornelis Claesz Bruyn (Bruin), a preacher in the Amsterdam Old Frisian Bloemstraat congregation, the father of Claas Bruin (*q.v.*). Kornelis Bruyn served at Sneek 1746-57, Aardenburg 1757-63, Sneek 1763-72, and Nijmegen 1772-83. Probably neither belonged to this patrician Amsterdam family.

Buitenpost, 465 f.: The Mennonites of Buitenpost organized on April 20, 1957, as an independent congregation. It now (1959) has 57 baptized members; the pastor of Veenwouden (*q.v.*) is in charge. A meetinghouse, built by a group of Mennonite Voluntary Service workers, was dedicated on Dec. 1, 1957.

466a, 35: *for* 1744). *read* 1744). He was born c1710 at Amsterdam, served at Koog-Zaandijk and Krommenie, and at Alkmaar 1741-d.47.

467b, 11-19: *for* title of first edition, *see* **Widertöufferen Vrsprung**

Bure, Idelette de, 471: Idelette was probably the daughter of Lambert van Buren, who with his daughter, her husband Jean Stordeur, and a few others, was expelled from Liége, Belgium, in 1533, because they were Anabaptists. They moved to Strasbourg (*q.v.*), where Stordeur and his wife were converted by John Calvin (*q.v.*).

475a, 61: *omit* Putnam.

486a, 60: *for* vdZ. *read* J.M. (i.e., J. Maarse)

Calcar, van, 490: The present van Calcar family mostly descends from Peter Lienders (Oberhofen, Switzerland 1677-Sappemeer 1755), who emigrated to Sappemeer (*q.v.*) in 1711. His grandson Pieter Pieters Lienders (Lienderts, Leenerts) took the family name of van Calcar. He lived at Hoogezand near Sappemeer and is the Pieter van Kalker named in this article, serving the church as preacher 1786-1807 (not 1812).

490a, 7: *for* 1755-78 *read* 1755-72

Calvaart family, 494b: see Supplement, p. 1069, for addition

Calvary (495a) Mennonite Church (GCM), Quarryville, Pa.: S. S. Amstutz served as pastor 1919-35. A Baptist minister called in 1957 to serve, led the congregation into "independency"; most of the original Mennonite stock then joined the Bethel (GCM) church in Lancaster.

497a, 52: *for* Psychopanny chia *read* Psychopannychia

499b, 39: *for* 1531 *read* 1532

Cate, ten, 525: Izaak ten Cate, d. 1839 at Noordbroek, was trained for the ministry by pastor A. S. Cuperus (*q.v.*) at Knijpe, and appointed ministerial candidate by the church board of Knijpe. He was the father of Steven Blaupot (*q.v.*) ten Cate and of Herman Izaaksz ten Cate (not Herman J. ten Cate), who also served at Ouddorp 1824-28. A. Hermansz ten Cate (p. 529) was Herman Izaaksz ten Cate's son.

525b, 56: *for* Herman J. ten Cate *read* Herman Izaaksz ten Cate

525b, 56: *for* Pieterzijl *read* Ouddorp 1824-28, Pieterzijl

540b, 13: *for* 1931 *read* 1935

Chelcicki, Peter, 552: Peter Brock's *Political and Social Doctrines of the Unity of Czech Brethren in the 15th and Early 16th Centuries* (The Hague and London, 1957), based on a University of London

Ph.D. diss., is the first comprehensive English treatment of the man.

556b, 64: *for* 1949. *read* 1929, the last issue being Dec. 31, 1950.

584a, 58: *for* 23 *read* 24

585, folio: *for* Gemuetsgespraecht *read* Gemuetsgespraech

586a, 37: *for* Centuries. *read* Centuries; ML II, 66.

589a, 38: *for* Geschiedskundige Naasporingen *read* Geschiedkundige Nasporingen

603a, 14: *for* E.M.S. *read* The Old Order group under Bishop Joseph O. Weaver, belonging to the Weaverland Conference, also worships here. E.M.S.

614a, 58: *for* 1648 *read* 1649

628a, 49: *for* Bevredigte *read* Bevredigde (*q.v.*)

628b, 25: *for* Velderhande *read* Veelderhande

635a, 10: *for* with *read* without; *for* possession *read* use

635b, 14: *for* Revolution *read* Civil War

636a, 34: *for* 12,000 *read* 23,000

655a, 12: *for* 1943 *read* 1743

662a, 37: *add* R. N. C. Hunt, "Communist Experiments of the 16th Century" (*Edinburgh Review*, April 1927)

663a, 32: *for* de Croix *read* du Croix

666a, 37: *for* Arch. f. Ref.-Gesch. *read* Blätter für württ. Kirchengesch. (1937) 64-76

727b, 7: *for* Sarum, Lincon *read* Sarum (i.e., Salisbury), Lincoln

732b, 64: *for* 1490 *read* 1470

744b, 41: *for* necessity. *read* necessity, and partly as a result of stimulation and leadership provided by a small group of G.C.M. Russian Mennonites who settled in Cuauhtemoc town.

745a, 23: *for* its *read* preserving its traditional parochial

747b, 50: *for* in 1947 *read* since 1947

747b, 52: *for* Sunday-school and youth work. *read* Sunday school.

747b, 54: *for* services *read* services and youth work

747b, 59: *for* 1950, 130 baptized members. It *read* 1958, 200 baptized members, with David Koop as minister. By 1950 it

Illustrations, page 24, picture 1: *for* Woman in Church *read* Kuchenfrau

Volume II

xib, 45: change address for Robert Foth to Colonia, Uruguay

Correction of duplicate sets of initials as follows: J. H. Epp (pp. 4, 525, 706, 708); J. D. Hartzler (p. 670) and J. D. Hiebert (p. 538); J.R. and J.I.R. are the same person.

Daele, van, 2: Lambrecht van Dale (Daele) fled from Meenen or Kortrijk, Belgium, to Goch in Germany and from there in 1577 to Haarlem; he was an outstanding linen bleacher and merchant, and greatly stimulated the linen business in Haarlem. He was the ancestor of the Haarlem van Dale family. (S. C. Rechtodoorzee Greup-Roldanus, *Gesch. der Haarlemmer Blekerijen,* The Hague, 1936, 24 f., 27 note 6.)

5b, 48: *for* now called *read* sometimes called

6b, 7: *for* 1767 *read* 1776

11b, 26: *add* Hedwig-Penners-Ellwart, *Die Danziger Bürgerschaft nach Herkunft und Beruf 1536-1709* (Herder Institut, Marburg, 1954) 453 ff.

61b, 29: *for* Leeuwarden *read* Ezumazijl in Groningen

Dirk, Philips, 66a, 50: A previously unknown letter by Dirk Philips was published by J. ten Doornkaat Koolman, "Een onbekende brief van D. P.," in *Nederl. Archief voor Kerkgeschiedenis* XLIII (1959) No. 1, 15-21.

73a, 18: *omit* even Dirk Philips came

79a, 57: *add* author's initials R.F.

99a, 54: *for* Hausmann *read* Hansmann

112b, 35: *for* Oct. 21, 1543 *read* Oct. 23, 1534

Eastern Mennonite College, 134b, 36: Presidents of the college have been J. B. Smith 1917-22, A. D. Wenger 1922-35, J. L. Stauffer 1935-50, J. R. Mumaw 1950- . Deans have been C. K. Lehman 1924-56, Ira Miller 1956- .

135b, 34: *for* 1561 or 1562 *read* 1565 or 1566

138a, 9: *for* 1856 *read* 1855

143b, 6: *for* 1718 *read* 1618

Eiderstedt, 170: Adah B. Roe, *Anna Owena Hoyers, Poetess of the 17th Century* (Ph.D. dissertation at Bryn Mawr College 1915, published as Bryn Mawr College monographs Vol. XIX), treats Anabaptist-Mennonite movements in Eiderstedt (to 1616) and Tönning (to 1642).

175b, 42: *for* J. E. Reimer *read* G. E. Reimer

175b, 43: *for* (1948) *read* (July 1949)

213a, 49: *for* LXIII *read* LXIIII

226a, 17: *for* J. Beets *read* P. Beets

233b, 39: *for* Church *read* E.M.B. church

233b, 42: *for* M.B. *read* E.M.B.

233b, 45: *for* Neb. *read* John F. Epp (b. 1883) was long a minister and elder of the Bethesda G.C.M. Church at Henderson. Aaron J. Epp is pastor of the First G.C.M. Church at Reedley, Cal., and Dan Epp is manager of the Mennonite Press at North Newton, Kan.

236a, 11: *for* D. A. Neufeld *read* A. A. Neufeld

239a, 52: *for* Freiburg, Germany *read* Basel, Switzerland

239b, 5: *for* (1526) *read* (1509)

291a, 50: *for* Unusels *read* Munsels

Fasting, 317: A printed letter (*Brief tot Vreedbereydinge*) was issued by the ministers of the Amsterdam Lamist congregation on Sept. 16, 1627, inviting the Dutch Mennonites who favored the unification of several branches to observe a day of fasting and prayer. (*Handelinghe der Ver-eenigde Vlaemse en Duytse Doops-gesinde Gemeynten . . . ,* Vlissingen, 1666, 36.)

328b, 32: *for* Oct. 2 *read* Oct. 5

330a, 4: *for* lasted . . . reunited. *read* ended in a merger with the de-Hondt-volk. A letter of June 25, 1655 (*Inv. Arch. Amst.* II, 2, No. 64), shows that the group was still in existence in that year, unless the term Lucas-Filipsvolk here means the united body.

332b, 59: *Note* that the illustration referred to is found in Vol. III, p. 13, No. 3

342b, 27: *for* c1700 *read* Sept. 28, 1703

343a, 13: *for* vorbeelden *read* voorbeelden

344b, 27: *for* Netherlands. *read* Netherlands. In 1897 this fund took over the Zwolsche Weduwfonds.

349a, 33: *for* 19 *read* 16

349a, 35: *for* 1874, 12 *read* 1876, 8

349a, 36: *for* 9 *read* 8

350b, 65: *for* whole. *read* whole. Daniel Musser reports in his *Reformed Mennonite Church* (Lancaster, 1873), "The washing of feet, if not rejected, was at least practically omitted for many years" (p. 241).

357b, 19: *for* pages. *read* pages, published in 1626.

358b, 4 and 26: *for* 1562 *read* 1558

394b, 16: *for* J. G. Frerichs, b. 1880 *read* Johan Gerard Frerichs, b. Dec. 8, 1880

407a, 50: *for* 3 per cent). *read* 3 per cent; in 1586, however, one fourth of the population is said to have been Mennonite).

Friesland Sociëteit, 411: Add to bibl.: M. L. Deenik, *De Friesche Doopsgezinde Sociëteit* (Amsterdam, n.d.).

Galicia, 436b: Friedrich Metz, *Die Rheinlande als Auswanderungsgebiet* (1932?), cites Joh. Eimann, *Der deutsche Kolonist oder die deutsche Ansiedelung unter Kaiser Joseph dem Zweiten in den Jahren 1783-1787 im Bacser Comitat* (1820).

471a, 33: *for* E.K.G. *read* E.G.K.

474b, 37: *for* Carel van Gent *read* Karel van Gent

477a, 43: *for* Täuferprozesse *read* Ketzerprozesse

487b, 14: *for* by him *read* by his group, 16 being by Marpeck himself

490a, 7: *for* 1755-78 *read* 1755-72

490a, 11: *for* 1812 *read* 1807

490a, 12: *for* J. D. van Calcar *read* Jan Daniel van Calcar

Gerrets, Vrou, 502: Blaupot ten Cate (*Holland* II, 210) mentions an edition of her *Liedtboecxken* published at Alkmaar in 1619.

502b, 4: *for* composed *read* erroneously considered the author of

Gheestelijck Kruydt-Hofken, 513: The first and second editions were published at De Rijp in 1633 and 1637.

Gherwen, Abraham van, 514: Blaupot ten Cate (*Holland* II, 211) mentions seven editions of van Gherwen's hymnal under differing titles, published at Amsterdam in 1612 and at Gouda in 1617, 1617, 1618, 1620, 1620, and 1818.

519a, 28: *for* grandson *read* great-grandson

520a, 42: *after* 1881 *read* d. Haarlem 1959

530b, 52: *for* Barnaul, *read* Barnaul and Amur,

530b, 53: *for* Man. *read* Man.; Mexico; and Menno, Paraguay.

Goethe, Wolfgang von: see article at end of Supplement.

542, 1: *for* A. G. Marten *read* H. H. Marten

543b, 28: *for* 1948 *read* 1947

543b, 40: *for* Antwerp *read* Gent

544a, 55: *for* The pulpit is now vacant. *read* In 1957 this congregation was combined with Bovenknijpe (*q.v.*); the combined congregation is served (1957) by Pastor H. Anneman, who lives at Gorredijk.

559b, 12: *for* grandson *read* son or grandson

562b, 55: *for* Since . . . vacant. *read* On July 3, 1949, after a vacancy of some years, these congregations made an agreement with the De Rijp (*q.v.*) congregation to be served by its pastor.

Greiner, 577: Add to bibl.: G. Bossert, "Aus der Nebenkirchlichen religiösen Bewegung der Reformationszeit in Württemberg," *Blätter f. Württ. Kirchengesch.* (May 1929) 1-40.

577b, 37: *after* Mennonites *add* in 1814

Grisons, 586b: Add to bibl.: O. Vasella, "Von den Anfängen der bündnerischen Täuferbewegung," *Ztscht für Schweiz. Kirchengesch.,* 1939, 165-84.

601b, 14: *for* 1839 *read* 1829

601b, 59: *for* Zimmerman *read* Nussbaum

603b, 55: *for* Barnaul, *read* Barnaul and Amur,

603b, 56: *for* Kan.; *read* Kan.; East Reserve, Man.;

617b, 19: *for* C.B.H. *read* C.P.H.

617b, 48: *for* 1946 *read* 1948

619b, 56: *for* **Hadewyck** *read* **Hadewych**

Hesse, 727a: Add to bibl.: Allen W. Dirrim, "The Hessian Anabaptists, Background and Development to 1540" (unpublished doctoral dissertation at Indiana University), 1959

Hamburg-Altona, 643: Add to bibl.: Ludwig Brinner, *Die deutsche Grönlandsfahrt (Abhandlungen zur Verkehrs- und Seegeschichte.* Hanseatischer Geschichtsverein) (Berlin, 1913).

Hans Busschaert (648b): This subject is identical with the subject of the article **Busschaert, Hans** (I, 485a)

Haren, 661 f.: The Mennonite circle of Haren developed into a congregation in 1957. This congregation is united with that of Roden (*q.v.*). Miss Offerhaus served as pastor at Haren until 1957. Since 1958 G. de Groot has been the pastor. A Menno-Home was opened on Oct. 17, 1953.

676b, 29: *for* Kreutzinger *read* Kneutzinger

689b, 30: *for* (1957) *read* (1960)

Heilbronn, 692: Add to bibl.: Moritz von Rauch, *Dr. Johann Lachmann, der Reformator Heilbronns* (Heilbronn, 1923).

694a, 57: *for* 337 *read* 227

701a, 21: *for* see **Maren** (Maeren) *read* see **Maeren** (Maren)

703b, 36: *for* deacon *read* preacher 1664-68

703b, 45: *for* articles. *read* articles. He resigned in 1668 because of the continuing strife.

707a, 52: The meetinghouse was sold when there were no longer members living in Heppenheim.

707a, 59: *for* 1935 *read* 1933

707a, 60, 61: *replace* by the following—it was purchased in 1939 by the Mennonite Publishing House and continued under its first name "Graybill Book Store" and under manager Silas Graybill until 1949 when Claude Shisler became manager. In 1951 the name became Herald Book Store.

729a, 1: *for* 1755 *read* 1752

738b, 15: *for* In . . . Sask. *read* In 1955 J. N. Hiebert was the E.M.B. pastor at Dalmeny, Sask. P. G. Hiebert is the C.G.C. pastor at Atmore, Ala., and Franz Hiebert at Swalwell, Alberta.

739a, 41: *for* nephew *read* son

Hindeloopen, 744: Concerning the meetinghouses in Hindeloopen little is known. The present meetinghouse was the former "Kleyne Huys" church, built *c*1680 and remodeled in 1850 and 1931.

752a, 16: *for* by the same author *read* an unknown author (Luther?)

752a, 46: *for* Duck *read* Dick

753a, 17: *for* Gedenkschrift *read* Bericht über die 400 jährige Jubiläumsfeier der Mennoniten

754b, 41: *for* an *read* on

754b, 51: *for* 1949 *read* 1944

756b, 4: *for* Christian Classics, published in 1956 one volume *read* Library of Christian Classics, published in 1957 a volume, *Spiritualist and Anabaptist Writers* as

762b, 61: *for* 1906 *read* 1937

763a, 45: *for* BRN *read* BRN V, 1909

766a, 13: *add* to Rempel book title the following: *Bevölkerung und Wirtschaft, 1825* (Leipzig, 1940) 108pp.

788b, 52: *for* 1857 *read* 1851

Holmes County, 792b, 30: According to W. E. Farver, Jacob Miller, an Amish minister with his sons Henry and Jacob, Jr., in 1808 took up a section of land one mile north of Sugarcreek. In 1809 he brought his family from Pennsylvania, and his wife's nephew, Jonas Stutzman, who settled one-half mile south of Walnut Creek, the first settler in that township. (*Sugarcreek Budget,* June 25, 1959).

Holwerd, 795: The congregation possesses six fine silver communion cups, presented in 1778 by the Reformed church board as a gift because the Reformed congregation had used the Mennonite meetinghouse for nearly two years while its own church was being remodeled.

795b, 7: *for* 1629 *read* 1692, remodeled in 1748

795b, 11: *for* 1850 *read* 1849

812b, 36: *for* 1861, *read* 1860 to replace a former one built in 1735;

823b, 48: *for* Leatherman, Willard *read* Leatherman, Clair Hoffman, Willard

Hubmaier, 834b: Add to bibl.: Leonhard Theobald, "Balthasar Hubmaier," *Ztscht f. bayr. Kirchengesch.* (1941) 153-65.

839b, 41: *for* his death in 1781 *read* 1764. He died in 1781

Hymnology 870a: The article **Anthoenis Courtsen** (I, 129b) points out that much is learned about Anabaptist songs from the 1552 trial of Courtsen. He obtained from a tailor's journeyman a song which he wrote down in a book. He also possessed a *Geestelick Liedtboucksen* which contained many hymns. "From these documents it appears that 'Spiritual songs' were very numerous among the Mennonites, and that many compiled a collection of such hymns for themselves" (vDZ).

Illustrations, page 11, picture 5: *for* Goessel *read* La Junta;

picture 6: *for* La Junta *read* Goessel

Volume III

Ibersheim, 1 f.: The Dutch *Naamlijst* of the 18th century names as ministers at Ibersheim: Daniel Stauffer, elder 1739-*c*68, Jacob Wels (Weiss?) *c*1749-*c*78, Jacob Hiestand 1751-*c*78, Heinrich Seitz *c*1755-*c*70, Heinrich Stauffer, preacher 1758, elder 1768-after 1802, Jacob Müller 1770-*c*78, Jacob Wels 1776-after 1802, Daniel Stauffer 1780-*c*94, Daniel Hirschler 1781-after 1802, and Heinrich Christoph from 1784.

Imbroich, 12: Add to bibl.: Arno Schirokauer, "Der Druckort der Schriften des Thomas von Imbroich," *Modern Language Notes,* 1943, 346-50.

12a, 9: *for* Ilp (Den) *read* Ilp (Den Ilp)

12a, 24: *for* parsonage *read* parsonage of Den Ilp

14a, 52: *for* 1773 *read* 1783

15b, 11-17: The group at Surhuisterveen (*q.v.*) which practiced immersion were not Mennonites but a small group of followers of Alexander Mack, founder of the Church of the Brethren, who lived at Westerveen near Surhuisterveen 1720-29.

23b, 50: *for* 1855-65 *read* 1854

23b, 53: *for* about 1860 *read* 1876

23b, 59: *for* 1874-75 *read* 1874

25a, 38: *for* Reformed Mennonite *read* Apostolic Christian

26a, 2: *for* 1856 *read* 1862

27a, 34: *for* Teegarden in Marshall County *read* Lakeville in St. Joseph County

28a, 28, 35: *for* 1871 *read* 1872

28a, 37: *for* 1874-75 *read* 1875

Industrial School, 31a: In the *Herald of Truth* for July 14, 1904, and Jan. 12, 1905, six months financial reports of the Home for the Friendless were submitted by J. F. Brunk (MC). Already in the issue of Aug. 1, 1894, R. J. Heatwole (*q.v.*) had reported a visit to the Industrial School and Home. (See also **Home for the Friendless.**)

Italy, 55 f.: Add to bibl.: F. C. Church, *Italian Reformers 1534-1564* (N.Y., 1932); Peter Dolbert, "Die

Reformation in den italienischen Talschaften Graubündens nach dem Briefwechsel Bullingers" (unpublished dissertation at Univ. of Zürich, 1948).

87a, 22: *for* year *read* term

91b, 58: *for* Andres *read* Andreas

105a, 22: *for* Flanders, *read* Flanders, in 1562,

116, map: *for* East Union *read* Fairview; *for* Fairview *read* East Union

116a, 9: *for* sheriff *read* constable

122a, 14: *for* 1581 *read* 1851

125b, 34: *for* Flaccius *read* Flacius

131a, 23: *for* 1950 *read* May 1949

Jus Retractus, 132: Add to bibl.: E. H. Correll, *Das Schweizerische Täufermennonitentum* (Tübingen, 1925), full discussion pp. 91-100.

215a, 27: *for* 1785 *read* 1685

Krehbiel, 235: The Peter named in line 27 and the one in line 34 are probably identical. Peter Krehbiel's departure from Switzerland is described in a poem by Daniel Krehbiel, "Peter Krehbiel's Abschied von der Schweiz," *Gem.-Kal.* 1911, 46 f.

235a, 36: *for* 1770 *read* 1784

235a, 37: *for* 15 years later to Russia. *read* in 1796 to Volhynia.

259a, 30: *for* 1957, No. 1 *read* XLVII (1956) 252-59, "Pilgram Marbeck und das oberdeutsche Täufertum. Ein neuer Handschriftenfund."

273, map: Gehman (School) should be north of the turnpike about where the "G" of Gehman is.

276b, 3: *for* Ridenbach *read* Reidenbach

277b, 12: *for* 1835 *read* 1836

284a, 42: *for* p. 12 ff. *read* pp. 26 ff.

336b, 33: *for* frame *read* stone

359b, 32: *for* (1953) *read* (1935)

361a, 35: *for* Wildenbruck's *read* the hero of Wildenbruch's

365b, 33: for *bis in den Tod* read *bis ans Ende*

372a, 38: The fifth edition appeared in 1922.

435a, 51: *for* 1887 *read* 1897

444b, 35: *for* Marpeck, Pilgram *read* Rothenfelder, Jörg

491b, 55: *for* his name *read* his name favorably

493a, 13: *for* October *read* May

493a, 34: *for* held. *read* held. He became a citizen in July 1528.

493a, 35: *for* 1530 *read* 1530 (possibly 1528)

493b, 58: *for* two *read* four

494b, 35: *for* Jan. 31, *read* New Year's Day,

542b, 35: *for* 1533 *read* 1536

567a, 35: *for* 1863 *read* 1852. Mellinger was born at Ruchheim, Palatinate, Germany, became an orphan at 10, landed in America Oct. 16, 1772, was ordained deacon in 1790. He also served the Swiss immigrants who settled near Wooster, Ohio.   W.D.S.

583a, 31: *for* 1537 *read* 1539

583a, 33: *for* 1537 *read* 1538

583a, 62: *for* 1619 *read* 1616

Mennonite Brethren in Christ Church (603b) *of Pennsylvania:* This body changed its name to Bible Fellowship Church April 11, 1959.

629a, 24: *for* Training School for Nurses *read* School of Nursing

629a, 39: *for* tuberculosis *read* tuberculosis (until 1955)

629b, 50: *for* nursing. *read* nursing. The superintendents of the hospital have been Allen H. Erb 1916-51, W. J. Dye 1951-58, and Luke Birky 1958- .

644a, 1: *for* of the *read* of the Association (*Vereinigung*) of

666b, 22: *for* County, *read* County, Ind.,

694a, 61: *for* Kennet *read* Kennel

727a, 48: *for* Müller *read* Muller

791a, 28: *for* pages. *read* pages (copy in GCL).

791a, 37: *for* 1535 *read* 1555

Music, 791b, 65: In 1594 the Anabaptists of the Gladbach area were meeting in Alitgen Cüper's house where their singing could be heard daily, especially in the evening" (see **Rheydt**).

795a, 36: *for* J. G. van der Smissen *read* C. J. van der Smissen

799b, 7: *for* 1663 *read* 1623. About 1725 a mutual fire insurance organization was started at Lunau (Gross-Lunau?) near Culm in Poland.

806a, 56: *for* Darmstadt *read* Hesse-Darmstadt

818b, 50: *for* Neel, Mypeis *read* Neel Mypeis

826b, 52: *for* 1533 *read* 1534

827b, 6: *for* 1544 ff. *read* 1556

828a, 6: *for* baptists." Menno . . . followers. *read* baptists."

828a, 14: *for* Reinier *read* Cornelis

828a, 42: *for* 1567 *read* 1566

828a, 65: *for* to *read* by

828b, 36: *for* In 1598 . . . at *read* In 1589 the stricter ones, soon called Old Frisians, banned Lubbert Gerritsz, who became the leader of the Young Frisians. A special group of the Old Frisians were the Janjacobsgezinden, split off in 1598, named after Jan Jacobsz (*q.v.*), who had a considerable following in Friesland and also at

828b, 52: *for* the Young *read* most of the Young

830a, 19: *for* public *read* Reformed

830b, 1: *for* 50,000 *read* 500,000

831a, 40: *for* they *read* some of them

831b, 1: *for* 1696 *read* 1671

831b, 58: *for* 1829 *read* 1825

832a, 64: *for* acquire *read* give

833b, 64: *for* 1795 *read* 1798

834b, 7: *for* 1624 *read* 1634

834b, 52: *for* Orangist (Monarchist) *read* Orangist

835b, 3: *for* J. J. le Cosquino *read* I. J. le Cosquino

836b, 1: *for* largely *read* partly

837b, 56: *for* adopted *read* compiled

838a, 7: *for* Mankes-Zerneke *read* Zernike

838b, 48: *for* funds *read* fonds

840a, 9: *for* forbidden *read* made impossible

844a, 25: *for* 1742 *read* 1772

850b, 38: *for* brethren *read* Reformed

851a, 47: *for* novel *read* novels

856b, 53: *for* South Russia *read* Russia

856b, 58: *for* farms . . . World War II. *read* farms.

859b, 31: *for* 1614 *read* 1694

860b, 1: *for* in Torney near *read* in the Torney heights in

Note: The Pax men did not build the houses as reported. By special agreement with the MCC, which made some contributions, the German government granted Mennonite refugees from West Prussia the privilege to purchase the houses, which were built by a contractor.

860b, 2: *for* 1950-54 *read* 1950-51

869a, 52: *for* Parmentier. Later . . . Alcmaers *read* Parmentier.

872b, 9: *for* Lutheran *read* Reformed

872b, 20: *for* Johann *read* Jehan

875b, 18: *for* 1860 *read* 1880

878b, 30: *for* Nieuwland *read* the Nieuwland

880b, 7: *for* at Nijmegen on April 9 *read* on April 9

892a, 59: *for* lived *read* mostly lived

904b, 2: *for* Shortly . . . War II *read* By adopting a "conscientious objector law" in 1926

920a, 33: *for* 1569 *read* 1659

Volume IV

5a, 10: *for* 1685 *read* 1585

5a, 13: *omit* (DB 1899, 182)

Oath, 20: After (DB 1875, 93-100) add: In many Dutch towns it became usual that in place of the oath of citizenship the Mennonites declared to have spoken the truth or promised to speak the truth "by mannes waerheyt" (by a man's truth) and eventually by a handclasp ("handtastinger") with the official administering the oath.

8b, 44: *for* 93, 197 ff. *read* 33-41

72a, 6: *for* Fauust *read* Faut

72a, 50: *for* 19— *read* 1930

96b, 48: Add to bibl.: J. Melles, *Joachim Oudaen* (Utrecht, 1958)

99b, 8: *for* a preacher *read* preacher 1649-72

99b, 39: *for* d. about 1666 *read* d. 1682

112b, 56: *after* 2274 *add* II, 2, Nos. 686-90

112b, 71: *after* Naamlijst *add* Paul Schowalter, "Der Kirchenbau in den Mennonitengemeinden von Pfalz-Hessen," *Gem.-Kal.* 1953, 36-44;

133a, 7: *for* Klass *read* Klaas

133a, 29: *for* Sippersz *read* Sippesz

Pennsylvania-German, 142a: Add to bibl.: Otto Springer, "The Study of the Pennsylvania-German Dialect," *Journal of English and Germanic Philology* (Jan., 1943, pp. 1-39).

169a, 36: *for* **Loosevelt** *read* **Loosvelt**

169a, 47: *for* 74 *read* 174

171a, 14: *for* Pieter *read* Peter

173b, 19: *for* 159-61 *read* 160-62

181b, 37: *for* 1827 *read* 1823

Pleasant View (192a) Mennonite Church (MC), Schellsburg, Bedford Co., Pa. Supplement: Settlement was begun in 1872 from the Johnstown district, served by visiting ministers till 1914, meetinghouse built in 1910, organized as a congregation in 1914 when Clayton Graybill was ordained as pastor. Charles Shetler has been pastor since 1939, the congregation is a member of the Allegheny Conference.

196b, 62: *for* see **Pluen** *read* see **Pleun**

216b, 12: *for* **Prette** *read* **Pretle**

219b, 33: *for* Simonatz *read* Simonsz

225b, 3: *for* and Horst *read* Horst, Ausmass, Jamerau, and Dorposch.

225b, 22: *for* 1723 (?) and probably in 1719 *read* in 1723 and once about a decade earlier.

225b, 31-32 (excl. of table): *for* Unruh *read* Unrau; and *for* Foth *read* Voht; and *add* Schmidt, Koehn, Pankratz, Sparling, Frey, and Buller.

225b, 39: *for* Unruh *read* Unrau

226a, 2: *for* Richart *read* Richert

226a, 7: *for* ?—? *read* 1718-?

226a, 8: *for* 1760-80 *read* 1760-1775

226a, 10: *for* Pancratz *read* Pankratz

226a, 11: *add* The first known elder was Berent Ratzlaff, born c1660.

228b, 39: *for* Doopsgezindeperiodeken *read* Doopsgezinde periodeken

229a, 12: *for* Overa *read* Over

235a, 42: *for* Zwartendijke *read* Zwartendijk

252b, 5: *for* 114 *read* 109, 114

256b, 31: *for* vor *read* nach

258a, 47: *for* H.A. *read* H.Ha.

273b, 28: *for* 499 *read* 449

281a, 20: *for* area conferences *read* Area Conference (beginning in 1957)

Reiseprediger, 280-81: Dutch Mennonites have since 1897 had special provision for visiting ministers to serve scattered members. In 1958 ten such "bezoekleerar" were on duty making annual pastoral visits to all diaspora members. (See **Verstrooiing**).

293b, 42: *for* Täfer *read* Täufer

Religious Liberty, 293b: Add to bibl.: Walter Hamel, "Bekenntnisfreiheit," *Ztscht f. d. gesammte Staatswissenschaft* (1953, pp. 54-77), which treats of Anabaptist and Schwenckfelder objections to state-imposed religious formulations advocated by Brenz, Bucer, and Capito.

299b, 47: *for* F.R. *read* Ha.R.

331a, 62: *for* ende *read* en de

331b, 31: *for* Socinians. In Amsterdam . . . Obbesz (*q.v.*). *read* Socinians and even bade him come over for a disputation with their leaders.

334a, 65: *add* author's initials vdZ.

336a, 18: *for* 1884 *read* 1862

336a, 20: *after* Zwolle *add* founded *c*1860

346b : *Note*: Roaring Spring left the S.W. Pa. (MC) conference in April 1912 and joined the Eastern District Conference (GCM) in May 1912. In 1958 the membership was 33. The meetinghouse is in the town.

352a, 31: *for* (*c*1735-1815) *read* (1736-1826), manufacturer and

373a, 54: *for* 1765, *read* 1765 (most of the last two groups were Lutherans),

373b, 13: *for* Nothing *read* Little
Note: The six communion cups and two wine jars were saved.

373b, 29: *for* 31, 1951 *read* 21, 1951

373b, 43:*for* Councillors *read* deacons

376b, 23: *for* (b. 1888) *read* (1888-1958)

379b, 30: *for* 1722 *read* 1772

Russia, 393a: Add to bibl.: Friedrich Matthaei, *Die deutschen Kolonisten in Russland* (Leipzig, 1866, 389 pp.).

Sattler, 427b, 38: Sattler appears in the Zürich court records twice, on March 25 and Nov. 18, 1525, both times as a prisoner, both times required to swear the *Urfehde* and to be expelled from the canton. Both times he was before the court in company with other Anabaptist leaders including Grebel, Manz, and Blaurock. (*TA Zürich*.)

427b, 41: *for* J.J.T. *read* J.J.Th.

446b, 17: *for* 1933 *read* 1938

468a, 35: Herman Schmitt was born June 20, 1899, and Otto Stauffer on Aug. 23, 1904.

472a, 60-61: *Omit* but . . . others.

472a, 63: *for* 15 *read* 16.

472b, 51: *for* Klassen *read* Classen.

473a, 23: *for* Klassen *read* Classen.

Sermons, 503a, 59: *After* Prussian-Russian line *add* as was the practice of the Conservative (fijne) Mennonites in the Netherlands up to the end of the 18th century, and occasionally even until *c*1855.

503b, 42: *After* prolific *add* Van der Zijpp is of the opinion that parts of the first (1539) edition of Menno Simons' *Foundation-Book* go back to sermons preached earlier by Menno.

539b, 60: *add* author's initials C.K.

561a, 65: *Note*: George Fox never used the expression "inner light," but spoke of the "light of Christ," meaning the guidance of the indwelling Christ in the converted individual.

Society of Friends, 565a: Add to bibl.: Anna Corder, "Quakerism in Friedrichstadt 1663-1724," *Journal of the Friends Historical Society* XXXIX (1947), 49-53; H. J. Cadbury, "Quakerism in Friedrichstadt," *ibid.* XLIII (1951) 17-21; Wm. I. Hull, "Quakerism in Danzig," *The Bulletin of the Friends Historical Association* XLI (1952) 81-92; H. J. Calbury, "The First Settlement Meetings in Europe," JFHS XLIV (1952) 11-12. The first established Quaker meetings on the continent of Europe were Amsterdam 1656, Kriegsheim 1657, Rotterdam *c*1658, Hamburg 1659, Alkmaar 1660, Haarlem 1662,

Friedrichstadt 1663, Lippenhuizen and Gorredijk, Lansmeer in Waterland *c*1665, Groningen 1669, Leeuwarden *c*1670, Emden 1674, Crefeld 1679.

582a, 46: *add* author's initials vDZ.

595b, 42: *add* author's initials vDZ.

619a, 45: *for* p. lvii and 274 *read* lviii-lvix and 321-23

633b, 33: *add* author's initials vDZ.

645a, 60: *for* Strawberry *read* Strawberry Hill

663b, 63: *for* Brethren Church *read* Church of the Brethren

Tersteegen, 698: Note in the article **Grombach** the last paragraph reporting the strong interest in the writings of Tersteegen by the Grombach Mennonite preachers, including financial contributions toward publication costs.

Theologia Deutsch, 704: In an epistle in the Kunstbuch (#30) Leupold Scharnschlager refers to *Theologia Deutsch* and *Imitation of Christ* as writing of "Gelassenheit." He is probably the source of the four or five references to *Theologia Deutsch* in the second half of Marpeck's *Verantwortung*.

739b, 47: *for* Griner . . . Townline *read* Griner congregation was established in 1922 as a branch of Townline, and Pleasant Grove in 1948 as a branch of Griner, while Riverview was established in 1952 by former members of both Townline and Griner.

875b, 18: S. B. ten Cate (*Geschiedkundig Onderzock*) was among the last of the Mennonite historians to hold to the Waldensian origin of the Mennonites, although with grave hesitation (vDZ).

883a, 6: *for* 1898 *read* 1897-1905

883a, 61: *for* as did also *read* in 1925.

899b, 31: *for* Three hundred *read* Four hundred *and for* ten congregations, eight *read* seven congregations, five

899b, 36: *for* 289 *read* 403

905a, 23: *for* in 1723 *read* *c*1723. John Weaver was in West Lampeter *c*1717, and in 1721 applied for a grant of land for the three Weaver brothers.

907a, 19: *for* Preussen *read* Preusen

907a, 33: *omit* In Prussia

907a, 49: *for* 79 *read* 76

907b, 19: *for* Cornlius P. Wedel *read* Cornelius P. Wedel and Helena Wiebe

West Prussia. 927b: Add to bibl.: Ernst Wermke, *Bibliographie der Geschichte von Ost- und Westpreussen* (Königsberg, 1933); Hans Jessen, *Gott und der König. Friedrich des Grossen Religion und Religionspolitik* (Berlin, 1936).

945b, 55: *for* Gerhard *read* Bernhard

1000b, 16: *for* J.A.Har. *read* J.A.Ha.

1015b, 43: *Add* author's initials vDZ.

Zürich, 1047a: Add to bibl.: Sinaida Zuber, *Die zürcherische Auswanderung von ihren Anfängen bis gegen Ende des 18. Jahrhunderts* (Zürich Ph.D. dissertation, Turbenthal, 1931); Werner Schnyder, *Bevölkerung der Stadt u. Landschaft Zürich 14. bis 17. Jahrhundert* (Ph.D. dissertation, Univ. of Zürich 1925, publ. in *Schweizer Studien zur Geschichtswissenschaft* XIV, Heft 1).

Biographical Notices of Editors

EDITOR

C. Henry Smith, Ph.D. (1875-1948), was born at Metamora, Ill., June 8, 1875, received his B.A. (1903) and Ph.D. (1907, Phi Beta Kappa) both at the University of Chicago. He was a lifelong teacher of history: Elkhart Institute 1898-1900, Goshen College 1903-5 and 1908-13, and Bluffton College 1913-48, and served as the first dean of Goshen College 1909-13. He was until 1915 a member of the Mennonite Church (MC), thereafter of the General Conference Mennonite Church. He served on the G.C.M. Publication Board 1940-48. For a list of his numerous writings see *ME* IV, 552. He was married to Laura Ioder; they had no children. Residence at Bluffton, Ohio. He died at Bluffton Oct. 18, 1948.

EDITOR

Harold Stauffer Bender, D.Theol., was born at Elkhart, Ind., July 19, 1897, received his B.A. (1918) at Goshen College, B.D. (1922) at Garrett Biblical Institute, M.A. (1923) at Princeton University, Th.M. (1923) at Princeton Theological Seminary, and D.Theol. (1935) at the University of Heidelberg, Germany. He has been a lifelong teacher: Hesston College 1918-20, Goshen College 1924-44 (dean 1931-44), Goshen College Biblical Seminary, professor and dean since 1944, Professor of Church History since 1927. He has been president of the Mennonite Historical Society since its founding in 1925, founder and editor of the *Mennonite Quarterly Review* 1927- , chairman of the Historical Committee of the Mennonite General Conference 1947- (secretary 1935-47), member of the Mennonite Central Committee Executive Committee 1930- , and chairman of the MCC Peace Section 1941- . He has been president of the Mennonite World Conference since 1952. His writings include *Menno Simons, a Quadricentennial Tribute* (1936) and *Conrad Grebel* (1950). He is editor of the series *Studies in Anabaptist and Mennonite History.* He has been a lifelong member of the Mennonite Church (MC). He was married to Elizabeth Horsch in 1923; they have two daughters. Residence at 1901 S. Main St., Goshen, Ind. He died in 1962.

ASSOCIATE EDITOR

Cornelius Krahn, D.Theol., was born Aug. 3, 1902, at Rosenthal near Chortitza, Ukraine, Russia, received his D.Theol. (1936) at the University of Heidelberg, Germany, after study at the seminaries at Wernigerode a.H. and at Neukirchen near Moers 1926-31, and at the universities of Berlin 1932-33, Amsterdam 1933-34, and Heidelberg 1934-36. In 1937 he came to the United States. He took an M.A. in German at the University of Wisconsin in 1939. He has been a teacher of Church History and German since 1939, first at Tabor College 1939-44, then at Bethel College 1944- , where he has also been director of the Bethel College Historical Library and founder and editor of *Mennonite Life.* He has been secretary of the Historical Committee of the G.C.M. Church 1947- . He is the author of *Menno Simons (1496-1561), Ein Beitrag zur Geschichte und Theologie der Taufgesinnten* (1936); revised C. Henry Smith's *Story of the Mennonites* (1950, 1957 ed.); and is editor of the *Mennonite Historical Series.* He is a member of the G.C.M. Church. He was married to Hilda Wiebe in 1940; they have three daughters. Residence at North Newton, Kan.

MANAGING EDITOR

Melvin Gingerich, Ph.D., was born Jan. 29, 1902, at Kalona, Iowa, received his B.A. (1926) at Goshen College, and Ph.D. (1938) in history at the State University of Iowa. He has been a teacher of history at Washington (Iowa) Junior College 1930-41, Bethel College 1941-47, Goshen College part-time 1949- . Since 1947 he has been Research Director of the Mennonite Research Foundation, since 1947 Custodian of the Archives of the Mennonite Church, and since 1937 a member of the Historical Committee of the Mennonite General Conference. His books include *Mennonites in Iowa* (1939), *Service for Peace* (1949), and *Who's Who Among the Mennonites* (1943, Assistant Editor). He has been managing editor of the *Mennonite Quarterly Review* since 1952. He has been a lifelong member of the Mennonite Church (MC). He was married to Verna Roth in 1925; they have one son. Residence at 405 Marilyn Ave., Goshen, Ind.

ASSISTANT EDITOR

(Responsible for Germany)

Ernst Crous, Ph.D., was born March 6, 1882, at Crefeld, Germany. Educated at the universities of Marburg, Munich, Berlin, and Bonn, he received his Ph.D. in 1909 at the University of Bonn. His life career was that of librarian, trained at Hamburg, Jena, and Berlin, active at the Prussian State Library in Berlin 1918-46, where he was director 1920-25 of the project for a complete catalog of incunabula, and also for a time a teacher in the school of library service. Bombed out of Berlin, he moved to Göttingen in 1944; was retired in 1946. He spent the year 1949-50 in the United States as exchange professor at Goshen, Bluffton, and Bethel colleges.

In the German Mennonite Church he served as vice-chairman of the Vereinigung 1932-51, chairman of the Berlin Mennonite Church 1930-46, and chairman of the German Mennonite Relief Committee 1947-51. He organized the Göttingen Mennonite Church in 1946 and served as its elder-pastor to 1953. He has been president of the Mennonitischer Geschichtsverein since 1947, chairman of the Commission for Publication of Anabaptist Documents since 1948, and coeditor of the *Men-*

nonitisches Lexikon 1947-58. He founded the Mennonitische Forschungsstelle (Mennonite Research Center) at Göttingen in 1948 and has been its director continuously. He is the author, in addition to his dissertation, *Die religionsphilosophischen Lehren Lockes (1910),* of numerous writings on the history of printing and type-founding as well as of Anabaptist and Mennonite history. He married Therese (Rose) Genthe in 1918, who was herself a trained librarian on the staff of the Prussian State Library, and who has remained his close associate in all his scholarly enterprises. Their two sons were lost in World War II in 1941. Residence at Calsowstr. 4, Göttingen, Germany. He died in 1967.

ASSISTANT EDITOR
(Responsible for the Netherlands)

Nanne (Jacobs) van der Zijpp was born April 2, 1900, at Warns, Netherlands, and was educated for the ministry at the University of Amsterdam and the Amsterdam Mennonite Seminary 1920-25. He has been a lifelong Mennonite pastor, serving at Zijldijk 1926-28, Joure 1928-40, Almelo 1940-46, and Rotterdam 1946- . Since 1946 he has taught Mennonite history at the Seminary and since 1954 has been Lector at the University of Amsterdam. He has been a trustee of the A.D.S. since 1943 and a member of its executive committee since 1955. He is also a member of two A.D.S. committees, Theology and Spiritual Interests, and a trustee of the Elspeet Association since 1929 and its president since 1946. Chief publications include *Geschiedenis der Doopsgezinden in Nederland* (1952), *De vroegere Doopsgezinden en de Krijgsdienst* (1930), and *De Belijdenisgeschriften der Nederlandse Doopsgezinden* (1954). He has served as editor or coeditor for a number of periodicals, including *Stemmen uit de Doopsgezinde Broederschap* (chairman of the editorial council 1952-58), *Theologie en Practijk* (1948-57), and as contributor to the *Mennonitisches Lexikon* since 1920. He was married to Antje Alberda in 1925; they have three children. Residence at Vredehofweg 36a, Rotterdam, Netherlands. He died in 1965.

ASSISTANT EDITOR
(Responsible for former Austria-Hungary and the Hutterian Brethren)

Robert Friedmann, Ph.D., was born June 9, 1891, in Vienna, Austria, educated as an engineer in the Technical University of Vienna 1908-14, studied history and philosophy at the University of Vienna 1920-24 (Ph.D., 1924). He taught at Gymnasiums in Vienna 1925-38. He began his Anabaptist studies in 1923, when he was commissioned by the Verein für Reformationsgeschichte to edit a volume of Hutterite epistles, which is still to be published, and is to be followed by a volume of Hutterite theological documents (*Glaubenszeugnisse oberdeutscher Taufgesinnter* II) and one of Hutterite bibliography including all the manuscript codices. He left Austria in 1939 and reached the United States the same year, serving as Honorary Fellow at Yale Divinity School in 1940, and as Research Fellow in Anabaptist Studies at Goshen College 1940-43; part of the time he was visiting lecturer at Goshen College. Since 1945 he has been Professor of History and Philosophy at Western Michigan University. His chief publication is *Mennonite Piety Through the Centuries* (1949). He has been a member of the Eighth Street Mennonite Church (GCM) since 1941. He has two sons. Residence at 2109 Glenwood Drive, Kalamazoo, Mich. He died in 1970.

Check List
Of Articles on Anabaptism and Related Themes

The following check list includes persons, places, topics, writers on Anabaptism, and books. Only articles of twenty lines or more are listed. Titles of books appear in italics. Asterisk (*) indicates an author. Two asterisks (**) indicate a martyr. Supplement is indicated by (S). The time period covered is 1520 to 1630.

Aachen
Aalsmeer
Aargau
Aberli, Heinrich
Abraham Picolet**
Acronius, Ruardus
Adam Pastor
Adige (Etsch) Valley
Adler, Clemens (S)
Adriaen Brael**
Adriaen Cornelisz**
Adriaen van 's Graven-
    hage**
Adriaen Jacobs**
Adriaen Lourysz**
Adriaen Pan**
Adriaenken
    Jansdochter**
Aechtken Joris
    Adriaensdochter**
Aeffgen Lystyncx
Aeltjen Baten**
Ahlefeldt
Aichele, Berthold
Ainsworth, Henry
Alba (Alva), Duke of
Alberus, Erasmus
Albrecht of
    Brandenburg
Albrecht V of Bavaria
Albrecht Friedrich
Alcohol
Aldegonde, Philips
Alenson, Hans A.*
Algerius
Alkmaar
Alsace
Althamer, Andreas*
Alzey
Ameland
Amersfoort
Amon, Hans
Amsdorf
Amsterdam
Anabaptist
Anabaptist Fund (S)
Anabaptist Memorial
Anastasius Veluanus
Andreae, Jacob
Anna von Oldenburg
Annales Anabaptistici

Anneken**
Anneken Hendriks**
Anneken vanden
    Hove**
Anneken Jans**
Anshelm, Valerius*
Anthoenis Courtsen**
Anthoenis Elberts**
Anthonis van Cassele**
Anti-Trinitarianism
Antonius von Köln
Antwerp
Anwald, Hermann**
Apocrypha
Apollonia Ottes
Apostolic Succession
Appenzell
Arbeiter, Hans
Armentières
Arnold, Gottfried*
Art
Article Book
Aschelberger, Stoffel**
Ascherham, Gabriel
Augsburg
Augsburg, Peace of
Augsburg Recesses
Ausbund
Auspitz
Austerlitz
Austria
Avoidance
Baden
Bader, Augustin
Bader, Johannes*
Baiersdorf
Baiertal
Balthasar Grasbanntner
    (S)
Bamberg
Ban
Baptism
Barsingerhorn
Bartel de Boeckbinder
Bartholomeus van den
    Berge**
Bartholomeus Panten**
Basel
Bastiaen**
Batenburg, Jan van
Bavaria

Beck, Hans
Beck, Joseph von*
Beckh, Blasius**
Beckum, Mary van**
Beckum, Ursula von**
Bedenken
Beginsel . . .
    Doopsgezinden
Bekentenisse van beiden
    Sacramenten
Bekentenisse, Obbe
    Philipsz
Belgium
Benrath, Karl*
Berbig, Georg*
Bergklooster
Bergmann, Cornelius*
Beringer, Kurt
Berka
Bern
Betz, Hans**
Bible
Bible, Inner and Outer
    Word
Bible Translations
Bibliographies
Bibliotheca Ref. Neerl.
Biel
Biestkens Bible
Binder, Eucharius**
Binder, Matthias
Bisch, Rauff
Blaurer, Ambrosius
Blaurock, Georg**
Blesdijk, Nicholas van
Bocholt
Bogaert, Pieter
Böger, Salomon
Bohemia
Bolsward
Bolt, Eberli**
Bondgenoten
Bosch, Siegmund von**
Bossert, Gustav*
Bosshard, Marx
Both, Hans
Bouterwek, K. W.*
Braght, T. J. van*
Braidl, Klaus
Braitmichel, Kaspar*
Brandenburg-Ansbach

Brandhuber,
    Wolfgang**
Bratislava (Pressburg)
Braun, Burkhard
Braun, Georg**
Breda
Bregenzer Wald
Breitinger, J. J.*
Brenz, Johannes*
Breslau
Brethren
Bretten
Breuning, Franz
Breuning, Hans
Brez, Guy de*
Brielle
Brixen
Brno (Brünn)
Brötli, Johannes**
Brownists
Brubacher, Hans
Bruchsal
Bruck
Bruckmaier, Georg**
Bruderhof
Brüderlich Vereinigung
Brüderliche Vereinigung
Brugge
Brunfels, Otto*
Brussel, Bernhard
Brussels
Bucer, Martin
Büchel, Hans
Bugenhagen, Johann*
Bühel, Konrad van
Bullinger, Heinrich*
Bünderlin, Hans
Bure, Idelette de
Busschaert, Hans
Calvin
Calvinism and
    Mennonitism
Campanus, Johannes
Capito, Wolfgang
Carinthia
Carlstadt, Andreas
Cassander, Georg
Castelberger, Andreas
Castellio, Sebastien
Catabaptist
Cate, S. B. ten*

Goldschmidt, Heinrich**
Goldschmidt, Ottelia**
Goller, Balthasar
Göschl, Martin
Gostal
Gotha
Gouda
Grafeneck, Klaus von
Gran
Graz
Grebel, Conrad
Gredig, Valentin
Greiner, Blasius
Gremser, Hansel
Gresbeck, Heinrich*
Greuwel der . . . Haupt-Ketzeren
Griesbacher, Wilhelm**
Griesinger, Onophrius**
Grisons
Grombach
Groningen
Gross, Jakob
Gross, Veronika
Grossmann, Kaspar
Grouw
Gruber, Lamprecht**
Grumbach, Argula
Grünberger, Veit
Grünfelder, Hans**
Grüningen
Grünwald, Georg**
Gsäl, Waltan
Gufidaun
Güldene Aepffel
Guldin, Nikolaus
Günzlhofen
Gurtzham, Hans**
Haarlem
Haemstede, Adriaen
Haetzer, Ludwig
Haffner, Hans
Hainaut
Halberstadt
Half-Anabaptist
Hall
Hallau
Haller, Berchthold
Hamelmann, Hermann*
Hamster, Hans**
Handbüchlein
Hans Bret**
Hans Dornaert
Hans Knevel**
Hans van Munstdorp**
Hans van Overdamm**
Hans Scheerder
Hans Vermeersch**
Hansmann, Hans**
Hardenberg, Albert
Häring, Christina**
Harlingen
Hartitsch, Dietrich von
Hartz

Hasel
Haslibacher, Hans**
Haslibacher Lied
Haslinger, Leonhard**
Hastenrath, Theunis**
Haug, Jörg
Hauser, Josef
Hazerswoude
Heerenveen
Hege, Christian*
Heilbronn
Hellrigl, Ursula**
Helwys, Thomas
Hendrick Alewijnsz**
Hendrik van Arnhem
Hendrik Maelschap**
Hendrik Naeldeman
Hendrik Terwoort*
Hendrik Verstralen**
Henric Roll
Heppenheim
Herman Timmerman**
Herman van Vlekwijk**
Herrmann, Jerome**
Herrmann, Thomas**
Hersfeld
Hershberger
's Hertogenbosch
Hesse
Hesseling, Pieter
High Germans
Hinwil
Historical Libraries
Historiography
Hochrütiner, Lorenz**
Hoen, Cornelis
Hofmann, Melchior
Hofmeister, Sebastian
Hohenberg
Hohenlohe
Hohenwittlingen
Holstein
Holwerd
Hondschoote
Hoop Scheffer, J. G.*
Hoorn
Horb
Horsch, John*
Hortensius, Lambertus*
Hottinger, Hans
Hottinger, Jakob
Hotz, Hans**
Hoyte, Riencx
Hubmaier, Balthasar**
Huf, Lorenz
Hugwald, Ulrich
Huiskoopers
Humanism
Humstervrede
Hungary
Hut, Hans**
Hutscher, Ulrich
Hutter, Jakob**
Hutterian Brethren
Hutterite Missioners

Hymnology
Ickelsamer, Valentin
Ieper
Illikhoven
Illingen
Imbroich, Thomas van**
Immersion
Immersion (S)
Imperial Recesses
Incarnation
Infant Baptism
Ingolstadt
Inn Valley
Inquisition
Intzinger, Franz
Italy
Jacob van Campen**
Jacob Geldersman**
Jacob van Ossenbrug
Jacob de Rore**
Jacob Scheedemaker
Jacob . . . Weghe**
Jacobs, Jan
Jacobs, Rijk
Jacobsz, Anthoni**
Jacques d'Auchy**
Jan Block**
Jan Claesz**
Jan Everts**
Jan van Geelen
Jan van Genck**
Jan Geertsz**
Jan Jansz Brant**
Jan van Leyden
Jan Matthijsz (Haarlem)
Jan Matthysz (Middelburg)**
Jan van Ophoorn
Jan Poote**
Jan Schut**
Jan Smeitgen**
Jan van Sol
Jan de Swarte**
Jan Trypmaker**
Jan Vervest**
Jan Wagenmaker**
Jan van de Walle**
Jan Willemsz
Jan Woutersz**
Janjacobsgesinden
Janneken van Munstdorp**
Jannetgen Matthijsdochter**
Jannetje Thijsdochter
Jansz, Cornelis
Jater
Jaussling, Ulrich
Jedelshauser, Hans
Jehring, J. C.*
Jena
Jeronimus Segersz**
Jever
Joachim of Floris
Joachim Vermeeren

John Casimir
John III
John Frederick I
John Frederick II
John the Steadfast
Jonas, Justus*
Joos Kint**
Joos de Tollenaere**
Joost Verbeeck**
Joost Verkindert**
Joriaen Ketel**
Joriaen Simonsz**
Joris Leerse**
Joris Wippe**
Judicium
Jülich
Juridical Procedures
Kaiser, Leonhard**
Kalleken Strings**
Käls, Hieronymus**
Kampner, Agatha**
Karel van Gent*
Karg, Georg
Kaspar
Kaufbeuren
Kautz, Jakob
Keller, Ludwig*
Kempten
Keppel, Wilhelm
Kerssenbroick, Hermann*
Kesselsdorf
Ketelbueter**
Ketzer-Historie
Ketzer-Lexikon
Kiessling, Hans
Kirchenordnungen
Kiss
Kitzbühel
Klausen
Kleinhäufler
Klopreis, Johan**
Knipperdolling, Bernhard
Köhler, Walther*
Kolb, Andreas**
Kolb, Franz
Komander, Johann
Königsberg (Franken)
Kortrijk
Kotte, Johann
Kotter, Eustachius**
Krafft, Adam
Krafft, Hans
Kräl, Hans
Krechting, Hinrich
Krems
Kress, Simon
Kreuzenstein
Kreuznach
Kriegsheim
Krohn, B. N.*
Kromau
Kropf, Daniel**
Krufft, Heinrich
Krummhörn

Krüsi, Johannes**
Kufstein
Kühler, W. J.*
Kühn, Johannes*
Künigl, Wolfgang
Kunstbuch
Kuntersweg
Kuonle, Lienhard
Kürnbach
Kürschner, Michael**
Kürschner, Wolf
Kymaeus, Johann*
Landes family
Landis, Hans**
Landshut
Landtsperger, Johannes*
Lang, Laux
Lang, Matthäus
Langenmantel,
    Eitelhans**
Langnau
Lanzenstiel, Leonhard
Lasco, John á
Laurens van der
    Leyen**
Laurens van de Walle**
Leenaert Bouwens
Leeuwarden
Leeuwarden Disputation
Leiden
Lemke
Lenaert Plovier**
Lengbach
Lenz, Paul
Leoben
Leserlin, Georg
Leupold, Hans**
Levina**
Liebich, Jörg
Liechtenstein, John VI
Liechtenstein, Leonhard
Liedeken, Een
Lieder der Hutterischen
Lienz
Lier
Liesveldt, Jacob
Lietboeck
Lietboecxken, Een
Lille
Limburg
Linck, Wenceslaus*
Lind, Esaias
Lindanus, Wilhelmus
Lingg, Martin
Link, Johannes*
Linz
Literature,
    Mennonites in
Lo, Peter
Lober, Julius
Lochmaier, Leonhard**
Lochy
London
Lorch
Lord's Supper
Lörrach

Loserth, Johann*
Louis V
Lourens, Janssen**
Love
Löwenberg
Lower Rhine
Loysen
Lübeck
Lucerne
Luies, Jan
Lundenburg
Lüneburg
Lüsen
Luther, Martin
Lysken Dirks**
Maastricht
McGlothlin, W. J.*
Maerten Jansz C.**
Maeyken Boosers**
Maeyken Christaens**
Maeyken de Corte**
Maeyken Floris**
Maeyken Trams**
Maeyken Wens**
Maeyken Wouters**
Mainz
Mair, Wolf**
Maldegem, Jacques
Maler, Gregor
Malsch
Mandates
Mander, Karel van
Mändl, Hans**
Mändl, Jakob**
Manelfi, Pietro
Manuscripts
Manz, Felix**
Marbach, Johann
Marburg
Margaret of Parma
Marie Baernt G.
Marienburger Werder
Mariken**
Mariken Jansdochter**
Marital Avoidance
Marius, Augustin*
Markirch
Marpeck, Pilgram
Marriage
Marriage, Hutterite
Marschalck, Haug
Martijntgen Aelmeers**
Martin van der
    Straten**
Martyr Books
Martyrdom, Theology
Martyrs
Martyrs, Anonymous
Martyrs' Mirror
Martyrs' Synod
Mary Joris**
März, Joachim**
Maskowitz
Mathesius, Johannes
Mattheus Bernaerts**
Matthias, Emperor

Matthias Servaes**
Matthijs, Hans
Maulbronn
Maurice, Duke
Maurice of Orange
Medicine, Hutterite
Meenen
Meetinghouses
Melanchthon, Philip*
Melander, Dionysius*
Melchiorites
Melk
Memmingen
Memmingen Resolutions
Menius, Justus*
Menno Simons
Meran
Meshovius, Arnold*
Metken**
Meulen, J. P. van der
Meulen, Quiryn van der
Meyer, Christian*
Meyer, Fridolin
Meyer, Sebastian
Michelsburg
Michiel**
Michiel, the Widower**
Micronius, Martinus*
Middelburg
Mierevelt, Michiel
Miertgen**
Ministers, Hutterite
Ministry
Ministry, Call
Missions, Foreign
Mittermaier, Hans**
Mittersill
Mixed Marriage
Moded, Herman
Mödling
Moibanus, Ambrosius
Möller, Georg**
Möller, Heinrich**
Möller, Jobst**
Monnikendam
Moravia
Mühlhausen
Muhr, Hans**
Muiden
Muliers, Pierson de
Müller, Ernst*
Müller, Gallus
Müller, Johannes*
Müller, Johannes
Müller, Karl*
Müllner, Ulrich**
München-Gladbach
Munich
Münster Anabaptists
Müntzer, Thomas
Musa, Antonius
Musculus, Wolfgang*
Music, Church
Mutual Aid
Myconius, Oswald
Nadler, Hans

Names
Nauk, Martin**
Neff, Christian*
Negri, Francesco
Nemschitz
Nespitzer, Georg
Netherlands
Neue Zeytung
Neumühl
Neustadt-Goedens
Newman, A. H.*
Nicasen Aelmeers**
Niclaes, Hendrik
Nicodemus, Gospel of
Nicolai, Gerhard*
Nicolai, Melchior*
Nieu Liedenboeck
Nikolsburg
Nikolsburg Articles
Nikoltschitz
Nippold, Friedrich*
Nonconformity
Nonresistance
Norden
Nördlingen
North Holland
Norwich
Nürnberg
Oath
Obbe Philips
Obbes, Nittert
Oberlehen
Ochino, Bernardino
Ochsenbach
Ochsentreiberin**
Odenbach, Johann
Odenkirchen
Oecolampadius*
Oelbronn
Oetisheim
Oetting
Offer des Heeren
Old Testament
Oldeklooster
Oldenburg
Oldersum
Oldesloe
Olivi, Petrus (S)
Olmütz
Oppelsbohm
Ordinances
Ordnungsbriefe
Original Sin
Ortlep, Christoph**
Osiander, Andreas*
Osiander, Lucas
Ossweil
Ostorodt, Christoph
Otter, Jakob
Ottius, J. H.*
Otto Henry
Outerman, Jacques
Overd'hage, Petrus
Palatinate
Pappenheim
Paracelsus

Paraditz
Pausram
Pellertitz
Penzenauer, Hans**
Pergen
Pestel, Peter**
Peter Bruynen**
Peter van Coelen
Peter van Olmen**
Peter Simons
Peter Witses**
Petersberg
Pfalz-Zweibrücken
Pfeddersheim
Pfersfelder, Elisabeth
Pfersfelder, Georg
Pfistermeyer, Hans
Pforzheim
Philip Mutsemeker
Philippites
Philip of Hesse
Pieter de Guliker**
Pieter de Houtzager
Pieter Pieters**
Pieter Stayaerts**
Pieter Willemsz
Pillowitz
Pistor, Georg
Plattner, Hans**
Platzer, Jacob**
Platzer, Melchior**
Plener, Philipp
Pochtitz
Poor, Care of
Popitz
Portner, Jakob
Prayer
Prele, Paul
Preubler, Andreas
Pribitz
Protzka
Psalms
Pulgram
Punishment
Pürcher, Andreas**
Pürchner, Hans**
Pustertal
Quellen z. Geschichte
Rabe, Ludwig
Rack, Jörg**
Radical Reformation
Raphael van der
 Velde**
Ratheim, Gisbert von
Rattenberg
Reason and Obedience
Rechenschafft
Reformed Authors
Regel, Georg
Regensburg
Regensburger Ordnung
Reimann, Heini**
Reinhardtsbrunn
Religious Liberty
Resch, Ambrosius
Restitution

Reublin, Wilhelm
Reutlingen
Reytse Aysesz**
Rhegius, Urban*
Rheydt
Riedemann, Peter
Ries, Hans de
Rietmaker, Abraham
Rink, Melchior
Ritschl, Albrecht*
Rizzeto, Antonio**
Robbertsz, Robbert*
Roermond
Rooman, Gillis
Roosevelt, Hendrik
 van**
Rossitz
Rostock
Roth, Friedrich*
Roth, Leonhard
Rothenburg
Rothenfelder, Jörg
Rothenfels
Rothmann, Bernhard
Rottenburg
Rotterdam
Rudolph (S)
Ruegger, Hans**
Rüsser, Niklaus
Rutschmann, Rudolph
Sabbatarian
 Anabaptists (S)
Sacrament
Sacramentists
Sailer, Wolfgang
St. Gall
Salminger, Sigmund
Salmuth, Johann
Salutations (S)
Salzburg
Sander Woutersz
Sankt Johann
Sartorius, Johannes
Sattler, Michael
Saxony
Schabaelje, J. P.
Schädowitz (S)
Schaffhausen
Scharnschlager, Leupold
Schenck, George
Schiedam
Schiemer, Leonhard**
Schijn, Herman
Schlaffer, Hans**
Schleitheim
Schmid, Bastl
Schmid, Hans
Schmid, Konrad*
Schmidt, Hans
Schnabel, Georg
Schneider, Michael
Schon...Gesangbüchlein
Schornbaum, Karl*
Schorndorf
Schützenecker, Hans**
Schützinger, Simon

Schwenckfeld, Caspar
 (S)
Schwerdtler
Sega, Francesco della
Seid, Katharina
Sepp, Christian*
Sermons
Sermons, Hutterite
Servetus, Michael
Seu, Johannes*
Sichem, van
Sicke Freerks**
Sigismund III
Signau
Sijntgen van
 Roesselare**
Silesia
Simon Michielsz
Simplicity
Singing, Hutterite
Sleep of the Soul
Slotel, Die
Slovakia
Smalcius, Valentinus
Smyth, John
Sneek
Sobotiste
Social Background
Socinianism
Socinus
Soetken Gerrits
Soetken van den
 Houtte**
Solothurn
Sommelsdijk
Sorga
Spaarndam
Speyer, Diet of
Spiritualism
Spittelmaier, Hans
Spittelmayr,
 Ambrosius**
Stadler, Ulrich
State, Attitude Toward
Steinabrunn
Steinsdorf, Hans**
Steyr
Strasbourg
Strasbourg Conferences
Strasbourg Discipline
Strasser, Gottfried*
Streicher, Helena (S)
Stübner, Markus
Stumpf, Simon
Sturm, Hans**
Styria
Successio Anabaptistica
Summerauer,
 Leonhard**
Swabian League
Swaen Rutgers
Sweet or Bitter Christ
Swiss Brethren
Swiss Brethren in
 Moravia
Switzerland

Tanneken**
Tanneken van der
 Leyen**
Tauber, Caspar
Taxation
Testamenterleütterung
Theologia Deutsch
Theology, Anabaptist
Thessalonica
Theunisz, Jan
Thijs Joriaensz**
Thomas Fransson**
Thum von Neuburg
Thuringia
Tielt
Tirol
Titelman, Pieter
Tiziano
Tjaert Renicx**
Transdanubia (S)
Treyer, Jakob
Trijnken Keuts**
Trijntgen**
Troeltsch, Ernst*
Tryntgen**
Tryon, Pieter
Tunes
Turmbücher
Twente
Twisck, P. J.
Uhrmacher, Hans (S)
Ulm
Ulrich (Württemberg)
Unitarianism
Universalism
Uolimann, Wolfgang**
Utrecht, City
Vadian
Valerius
 Schoolmeester**
Veelderhande Liedekens
Veh, Cornelius
Veldthaler, Michael
Velke Levary
Verantwortung
Verantwortung
Verantwurtung
Verbond
Verbond der vier Steden
Vermanung
Verspeck, Albert
Vienna
Vlissingen
Vogel, Wolfgang
Vondel, Joost van den
Von dem unverschamp-
 ten fräfel
Vorarlberg
Vos, Karel*
Vreden
Wädenswil
Walch, Johannes
Waldhauser, Thomas**
Waldshut (S)
Walpot, Peter
Warendorf

Wassenberger
  Prädikanten
Waterlanders
Wels
Wenger, Geörg
Wernlin, Jörg
Wesel
West Prussia
Westerburg, Gerhard
Westphalia
Weynken Claes**
Wideman, Jakob**
*Widertoufferen
  vrsprung*
Widlingmaier, Anna

Wijnssem, van
Willeboort Cornelisz**
Willem Drooch-
  scheerder**
Willem de Cuyper**
Willem Jansz**
William I of Orange
Wismar (S)
Wismar Resolutions
Witmarsum
Wolkan, Rudolf*
Women, Status of
Workum
Wormer
Worms
Worms Prophets

Worship, Public
Wostitz
Württemberg
Würtzlburger,
  Augustin**
Würzburg
Yetelhauser, Michael
Zaandam
Zapff, Hauptrecht
Zaug, Hans
Zaunmacher, Ulrich
Zaunring, Georg**
Zedo, Nikolaus
Zeeland
Zehentmaier, Martin**
Zeising, Johannes

Zelis
Zell, Katharina
Zell, Mathäus
Zerotin
Zieglschmid, A. J. F.*
Zierikzee
Znaim
Zobel, George
Zofingen Disputation
Zollikon
Zuckenhammer, Hans
Zürich
Zürich-Lied
Zwickau Prophets
Zwingli, Huldrych

Illustrations

Contents

(Continued on page 22)

I. Ordinances

1. Communion with Wine (Netherlands); 2. Communion with Bread (Netherlands).

3

II. Ordinances

1. Footwashing (Netherlands); 2. Baptism (Netherlands).

III. Orphanages

1. Haarlem, Netherlands; 2. Grossweide, Russia; 3. Bad Dürkheim, Germany; 4. Mont des Oiseaux, Weiler, France; 5. Millersville, Pa.; 6. Salem, Flanagan, Ill.

37

FORMULIER

Etlicher Christlichen

Gebäthe.

Welche die versamblete Gläubigen / oder ein Jeder absonderlich nach Gelegenheit der Zeit und der Sachen / nothwendigkeit (für Gott) mit Andacht und gebeugten Knien des Hertzens gebrauchen mögen.

Die
Ernsthaffte
Christenpflicht/
Darinnen
Schöne Geistreiche
Gebäter/
Darmit
Sich fromme Christen = Hertzen zu allen Zeiten und in allen Nöhten trösten können.

Gedruckt im Jahr 1739.
Zu finden in Kayserslautern bey dem Buchbinder.

Neu vermehrtes
Geistliches
Lust-Gärtlein
Frommer Seelen.
Das ist:
Heilsame Anweisung und Reglen eines gottseligen Lebens.

Herborn, gedruckt in der akademischen Buchdruckerey 1787.

Etliche
Christliche
Gebethe/
Welche
Die versammlete Glaubigen/
oder ein jeder absonderlich / nach Gelegenheit der Zeit und der Sachen Nothwendigkeit (für GOtt) mit Andacht und gebeugten Knien des Hertzens gebrauchen mögen.

Gedruckt im Jahr 1702.

IV. Prayerbooks

1. *Formulier Etlicher Christlichen Gebäthe*, 1660; 2. *Ernsthaffte Christenpflicht*, 1739; 3. *Lust-Gärtlein*, 1787; 4. *Etliche Christliche Gebethe*, 1702.

V. Publishing Houses

1. Mennonite Press, North Newton, Kan.; 2. Mennonite Publishing House, Scottdale, Pa.; 3. Mennonite Brethren Publishing House, Hillsboro, Kan.; 4. Christian Press, Winnipeg, Man.

7

VI. Schools: 1. Europe and South America

1. Realanstalt am Donnersburg (Secondary Boys' School), Weierhof, Ger.; 2. Elementary School, Friedensruh, Russia; 3. Marientaubstummenschule (Mary School for the Deaf), Tiege, Russia; 4. Secondary Girls' School, Orloff, Russia; 5. Normal School, Halbstadt, Russia; 6. Secondary School, Filadelfia, Par.; 7. Elementary School, Filadelfia, Par.; 8. Secondary School, Friesland, Par.

VII. High Schools: North America I

1. Lancaster Mennonite, Lancaster, Pa.; 2. Christopher Dock, Lansdale, Pa.; 3. Bethany Christian, Goshen, Ind.; 4. Rockway Mennonite, Kitchener, Ont.; 5. Western Mennonite, Salem, Ore.; 6. Iowa Mennonite, Kalona, Iowa.

9

VIII. High Schools: North America II

1. Central Christian, Hutchinson, Kan.; 2. Oklahoma Bible Academy, Meno, Okla.; 3. Mennonite Educational Institute, North Clearbrook, B.C.; 4. Immanuel Academy, Reedley, Cal.; 5. Mennonite Brethren Collegiate Institute, Winnipeg, Man.; 6. Bethesda Preparatory School (Fortbildungsschule), Henderson, Neb.; 7. United Mennonite Educational Institute, Wheatley, Ont.

IX. Elementary Schools: North America

1. Peter Balzer's School, Goessel, Kan.; 2. Neu-Bergthal School, Altona, Man.; 3. Old Colony Mennonite School, Cuauhtemoc, Mexico; 4. Chortitz School, Chortitz, Man.; 5. Locust Grove, Lancaster, Pa.; 6. Plumstead Christian Day School, Plumsteadville, Pa.; 7. Clinton Christian Day School, Goshen, Ind.; 8. Nampa Mennonite School, Nampa, Idaho.

11

X. Bible Schools: Europe and America

1. European Mennonite Bible School, Basel, Sw.; 2. Mennonite Educational Institute, Wadsworth, Ohio; 3. Mountain Lake Bible School, Mountain Lake, Minn.; 4. Elim Bible School, Altona, Man.; 5. Yarrow Bible School, Yarrow, B.C.; 6. Steinbach Bible Institute, Steinbach, Man.

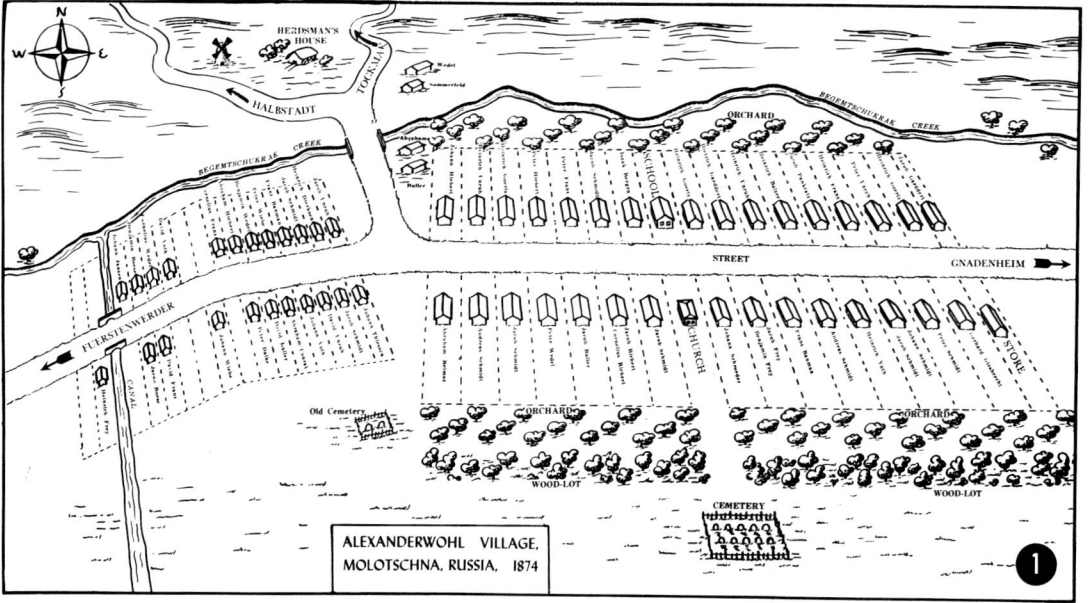

XI. Villages

1. Village Layout, Alexanderwohl, Russia; 2. Village Street, Tiege, Russia.

XII. Portraits: Europe

1. Hans de Ries (1553-1638), Alkmaar, Neth.; 2. J. G. de Hoop Scheffer (1819-93), Amsterdam, Neth.; 3. Menno Simons (1496-1561); 4. Herman Schijn (1662-1727), Amsterdam, Neth.; 5. Pieter Pietersz (1574-1651), Zaandam, Neth.; 6. Hinrich van der Smissen (1851-1928), Hamburg-Altona, Ger.; 7. Gerrit Roosen (1612-1711), Hamburg-Altona, Ger.; 8. Jacob A. Rempel (1883-1941?), Grünfeld, Chortitza, Russia; 9. Benjamin H. Unruh (1881-1959), Karlsruhe-Rüppurr, Ger.

14

XIII. Portraits: Europe and America

1. Pierre Sommer (1874-1952), Grand Charmont, France; 2. Valentin Pelsy (1870-1925), Sarrebourg, France; 3. Samuel F. Sprunger (GCM) (1848-1923), Berne, Ind.; 4. Isaac Peters (EMB) (1826-1911), Henderson, Neb.; 5. Ulrich Steiner (1806-77), Lauperswyl, Sw.; 6. John H. Oberholtzer (GCM) (1809-95), Milford Square, Pa.; 7. Leonhard Sudermann (GCM) (1821-1900), Hillsboro, Kan.; 8. Paul Tschetter (KMB) (1842-1919), Freeman, S.D.; 9. Abraham L. Schellenberg (MB) (1869-1941), Hillsboro, Kan.

XIV. Portraits: North America

1. Emanuel Troyer (Cent. Conf.) (1871-1942), Carlock, Ill.; 2. Jacob Y. Shantz (UMC) (1822-1909), Kitchener, Ont.; 3. Heinrich Voth (MB) (1851-1918), Bingham Lake, Minn.; 4. Aaron Wall (EMB) (1834-1905), Mountain Lake, Minn.; 5. Joseph Stuckey (Cent. Conf.) (1825-1902), Danvers, Ill.; 6. Joseph E. Ramseyer (Miss. Church Assn.) (1869-1944), Ft. Wayne, Ind.; 7. Jacob A. Wiebe (KMB) (1836-1921), Hillsboro, Kan.; 8. Benjamin Rupp (EM) (1862-1928), Flanagan, Ill.; 9. A. B. Yoder (UMC) (1867-1953), Wakarusa, Ind.

XV. Portraits: North America

1. David Toews (GCM) (1870-1947), Rosthern, Sask.; 2. Cornelius H. Wedel (GCM) (1862-1911), Newton, Kan.; 3. C. Henry Smith (GCM) (1876-1948), Bluffton, Ohio; 4. Peter A. Penner (GCM) (1871-1949), Champa, India; 5. Abraham Warkentin (GCM) (1885-1946), Chicago, Ill.; 6. M. S. Steiner (MC) (1866-1911), Columbus Grove, Ohio; 7. J. A. Ressler (MC) (1867-1936), Scottdale, Pa.; 8. Amos D. Wenger (MC) (1867-1935), Fentress, Va.; 9. J. S. Shoemaker (MC) (1854-1936), Freeport, Ill.

17

XVI. Portraits: North America and Europe

1. W. J. Kühler (1874-1946), Amsterdam, Neth.; 2. Heinrich B. Unruh (1845-1927), Halbstadt, Russia; 3. Christian Krehbiel (GCM) (1832-1909), Halstead, Kan.; 4. C. E. Krehbiel (GCM) (1869-1948), Newton, Kan.; 5. A. B. Shelly (GCM) (1834-1913), Quakertown, Pa.; 6. J. W. Kliewer (GCM) (1869-1938), Newton, Kan.: 7. S. E. Allgyer (MC) (1859-1953), West Liberty, Ohio; 8. George J. Lapp (MC) (1879-1951). Goshen, Ind.: 9. J. B. Smith (MC) (1870-1951), Elida, Ohio; 10. Jacob W. Reimer (MB) (1860-1948), Steinbach, Man.; 11. F. C. Thiessen (MB) (1881-1950), Abbotsford, B.C.; 12. George P. Schultz (EMB) (1880-1957), Chicago, Ill.

XVII. Mennonite World Conferences

1. Basel, Switzerland, 1925; 2. Danzig, Germany, 1930; 3. Elspeet, Netherlands, 1936; 4. Newton, Kan., 1948; 5. Basel, Switzerland, 1952 (Editors and Publishers Group); 6. Karlsruhe, Germany, 1957.

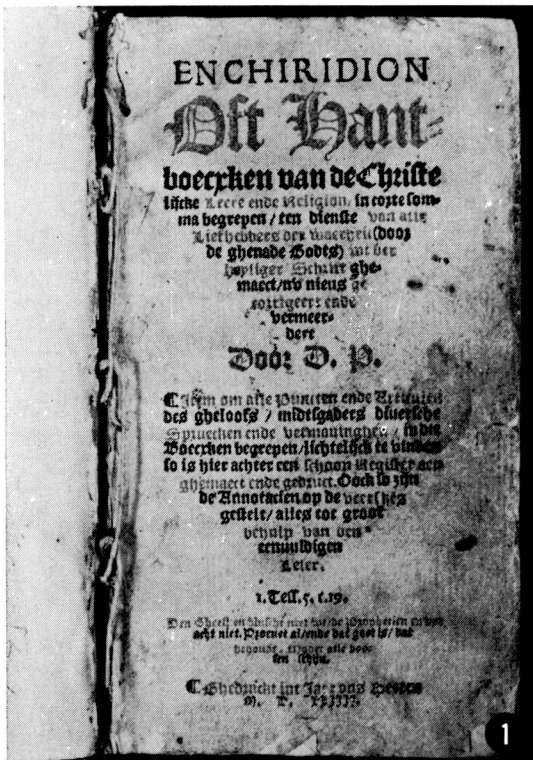

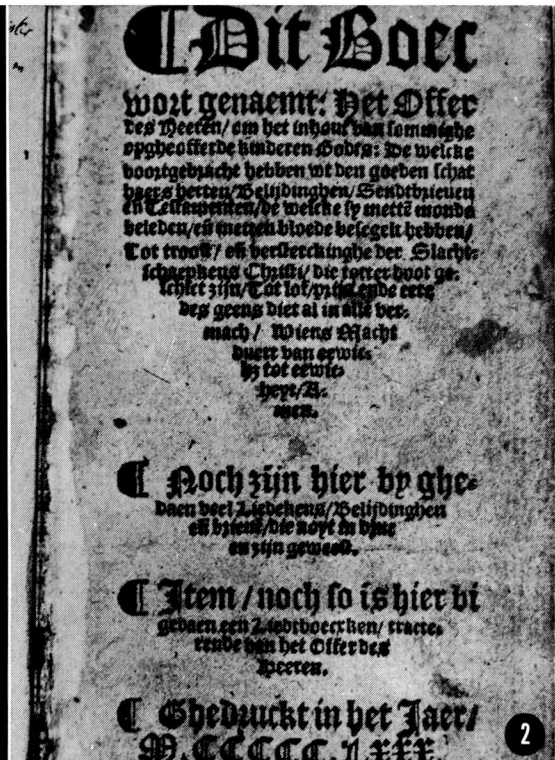

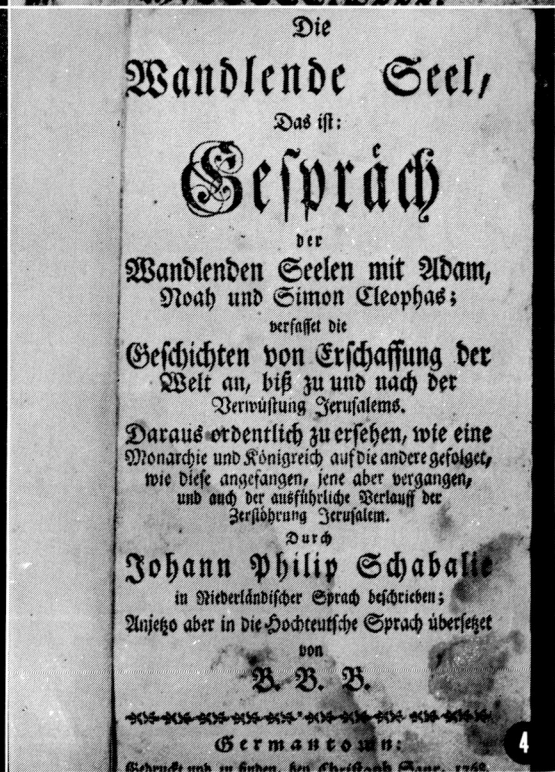

XVIII. Book Title Pages

1. Dirk Philips, *Enchiridion*, 1564; 2. *Het Offer des Heeren*, 1563; 3. J. P. Schabaelje, *Lusthof des Gemoets*, 1638; 4. J. P. Schabaelje, *Wandlende Seel*, 1768.

20

Index of Illustrations

Asterisk (*) indicates a portrait; italics, a book

CONTENTS

(Continued from page 2)

Acknowledgments

Many of the pictures used in the Illustrations for Volume IV came from the picture collections of the Bethel College Historical Library (Cornelius Krahn, Director) or the Mennonite Historical Library of the Goshen College Biblical Seminary (Nelson Springer, Curator), which have again as in previous volumes generously been placed at the disposal of the **Encyclopedia.** The kind assistance of a number of families in making portraits available, as well as of a number of schools and institutions in making building pictures available, is gratefully acknowledged. The book title pages are reproductions of originals in the Goshen Mennonite Historical Library, except the one of the **Lusthof des Gemoets.** The pictures of the secondary and elementary schools in Filadelfia, Paraguay, were furnished by Annemarie Krause. The one of Rockway Mennonite School was furnished by Hunsberger Photos.